C0-ASI-501

MARTINDALE-HUBBELL® LAW DIGEST

—•—

ALABAMA – NEW HAMPSHIRE LAW DIGESTS

MARTINDALE-HUBBELL

A member of the Reed Elsevier plc group

121 Chanlon Road
New Providence, NJ 07974
1-800-526-4902
Email: info@martindale.com
URL: www.martindale.com • www.lawyers.com

Published by Martindale-Hubbell®, a member of the Reed Elsevier plc group

Lou Andreozzi, Chief Operating Officer
Carol D. Cooper, Vice President, Associate Publisher, Martindale-Hubbell
Chuck Doscher, Vice President, Publisher, Martindale-Hubbell Law Digest
Larry D. Thompson, Vice President, Sales
Andrew W. Meyer, Vice President, Administration
Dean Hollister, Vice President, Database Production
John Roney, Vice President, Information Technology
Edward J. Roycroft, Vice President, Ratings

Copyright© 1999 by Reed Elsevier Inc.
All Rights Reserved

———————

Previous Editions
Copyright© 1994, 1995, 1996, 1997, 1998
Reed Elsevier Inc.

———————

Copyright© 1991, 1992, 1993
Reed Publishing (USA) Inc.

———————

Copyright© 1971, 1972, 1973, 1974, 1975, 1976, 1977, 1978, 1979
1980, 1981, 1982, 1983, 1984, 1985, 1986, 1987, 1988, 1989, 1990
Martindale-Hubbell, Inc.

*No part of this publication may be reproduced or transmitted in any form or by any
means, or stored in any information storage and retrieval system,
without prior written permission of Martindale-Hubbell.*

Important Notices

Martindale-Hubbell has used its best efforts in collecting and preparing material for inclusion in the Martindale-Hubbell Law Directory but cannot warrant that the information herein is complete or accurate, and does not assume, and hereby disclaims, any liability to any person for any loss or damage caused by errors or omissions in the Martindale-Hubbell Law Directory whether such errors or omissions result from negligence, accident or any other cause.

The Law Digests are intended for use as general reference sources for lawyers and are not meant to provide legal opinions or advice, and are not a substitute for the advice of counsel. The Law Digests are not to be used as the basis for advice to clients or applied to particular matters. Local counsel in the applicable jurisdiction should be consulted as to the current law applicable to a particular situation.

International Standard Book Number: 1-56160-327-9 (Set)

Printed and Bound in the United States of America
by R.R. Donnelley & Sons Company
Chicago, Illinois, Willard, Ohio and Lancaster, Pennsylvania

MARTINDALE-HUBBELL is a registered trademark of Reed Elsevier Properties Inc., used under license.

ISBN 1 - 56160 - 327 - 9

9 781561 603275

Table of Contents*

UNITED STATES LAW DIGEST

PART I—DIGESTS OF LAWS OF THE STATES, THE DISTRICT OF COLUMBIA, PUERTO RICO, AND THE U.S. VIRGIN ISLANDS, including numerous forms of instruments preferred by local usage

PART II—DIGESTS OF UNITED STATES COPYRIGHT, PATENT AND TRADEMARK LAWS

PART III—APPENDIX OF UNIFORM AND MODEL ACTS

PART IV—AMERICAN BAR ASSOCIATION CODES

INTERNATIONAL LAW DIGEST

PART V—DIGESTS OF LAWS, INTERNATIONAL SECTION

PART VI—INTERNATIONAL CONVENTIONS

*Index and detailed list of contents of each part follows title page of that part

Detailed Table of Contents

UNITED STATES LAW DIGEST

PART I—DIGESTS OF LAWS OF THE STATES, THE DISTRICT OF COLUMBIA, PUERTO RICO, AND THE U.S. VIRGIN ISLANDS:

PART II—DIGESTS OF THE UNITED STATES COPYRIGHT, PATENT AND TRADEMARK LAWS

PART III—UNIFORM AND MODEL ACTS:

* See note at head of respective acts.

† See note at head of Uniform Acknowledgment Act.

†† The Revised Model Business Corporation Act (1984) and the Model Business Corporation Act (1969) were prepared by the Committee on Corporate Law (Section on Corporation, Banking and Business Law) of the American Bar Association. These Model Acts should be distinguished from the Model Business Corporation Act promulgated in 1928 by the Conference of Commissioners on Uniform State Laws as the "Uniform Business Corporation Act." In 1943 the Conference withdrew the Uniform Act and renamed it "Model Business Corporation." In 1957 this latter Act was also withdrawn.

* See note at head of responsive acts.

PART IV—AMERICAN BAR ASSOCIATION CODES:

INTERNATIONAL LAW DIGEST

PART V—DIGESTS OF LAWS, INTERNATIONAL SECTION:

* See note at head of respective acts.

Ontario
Prince Edward Island
Quebec
Saskatchewan
Cayman Islands
Channel Islands (Jersey)
Chile
China, People's Republic of
China, Republic of (See Taiwan,
    Republic of China)
Colombia
Costa Rica
Czech Republic
Denmark
Dominican Republic
Ecuador
Eire (See Ireland)
El Salvador
England
Estonia
European Union
Finland
France
Germany
Gibraltar
Greece
Guatemala
Holland (See Netherlands)
Honduras
Hong Kong
Hungary
India
Indonesia
Ireland (See also Northern Ireland)
Israel
Italy
Japan
Korea, Republic of
Latvia

Lebanon
Liechtenstein
Lithuania
Luxembourg
Malaysia
Malta
Mexico
Mongolia
Netherlands
New Zealand
Nicaragua
Northern Ireland
Norway
Pakistan
Panama
Paraguay
People's Republic of China (See China,
    People's Republic of)
Peru
Philippine Republic
Poland
Portugal
Romania
Russian Federation
Saudi Arabia
Scotland
Singapore
Slovak Republic
South Africa
Spain
Sweden
Switzerland
Taiwan (Republic of China)
Thailand
Turkey
Ukraine
Uruguay
Venezuela
Vietnam

PART VI—INTERNATIONAL CONVENTIONS

FOREWORD

Welcome to the 1999 edition of the **Martindale-Hubbell Law Digest**®.

This invaluable compendium provides summaries of the laws of the United States, Canada and 77 of the world's leading trading nations, as well as the full text of significant Uniform and Model Acts and International Conventions. Four countries are included for the first time – **the Cayman Islands, Estonia, Indonesia and Lithuania.**

The Law Digest is an excellent place to begin legal research. It provides up-to-date and user-friendly summaries of a vast body of statutory law, compiled by preeminent law firms and legal scholars in each jurisdiction. In addition, users will find practical background information, including details on time zones, office hours, holidays, and government and legal practices.

We were pleased by your positive response to last year's reorganization of the **Law Digest**. For the first time, more than 170 legal topics were arranged under 24 broader categories – for example, *Deeds, Landlord and Tenant*, and *Real Property* were organized under *Property* – making it much easier to use. We have continued this arrangement in the 1999 edition, with further refinement of the *Taxation* section.

In addition to this print version, the 1999 **Law Digest** is also available electronically through LEXIS®-NEXIS®. Researchers can find the digests in the "MARHUB" library of the LEXIS® service, and the Uniform and Model Acts in the "MODEL" library.

We wish to extend a very special note of thanks to our Revisers and their knowledgeable staffs, as well as our Law Editors, Professor Michael Zimmer of Seton Hall University, Ms. Maureen Garde, and Dr. John Burke. We also would like to thank our in-house staff, Priscilla Venezia, Law Digest Managing Editor and Padi Sinegra, Law Digest Senior Editor. Without all of their selfless dedication, personal sacrifices, professionalism and attention to detail, no work of this scope and quality could be achieved.

If you have any further ideas or suggestions for future editions of the **Law Digest**, please feel free to contact me.

Thank you for your continued support.

Chuck Doscher
Vice President, Publisher
Martindale-Hubbell Law Digest

Martindale-Hubbell, LEXIS and NEXIS are registered trademarks of Reed Elsevier Properties Inc., used under license.

IMPORTANT NOTICE—Since this Directory is produced under a printing schedule requiring early deadlines, it is possible that changes will occur after printing which can only be reflected in subsequent editions. Accordingly, it is suggested that local counsel should be consulted as to the current law applicable to a particular situation.

Preface

For 130 years, the *Martindale-Hubbell Law Digest* has served as the single most useful legal compendium available in the world. Its scope of coverage, which includes all U.S. states and over 70 countries, is matched only by the quality of the thousands of preeminent lawyers around the world who annually update and revise the information contained in each Digest.

The *Law Digest* summarizes the statutory law in each of the United States, the District of Columbia, Puerto Rico and the Virgin Islands, Canada and its provinces, the European Community and its member countries, as well as major countries involved internationally in business and law. Important Uniform Acts promulgated by the National Conference of Commissioners on Uniform State Laws are printed in their entirety, as are Selected International Conventions to which the United States is a party. The Federal Law Digests summarize United States copyright, patent and trademark laws and the American Bar Association section contains the Model Rules of Professional Conduct and the Code of Judicial Conduct promulgated by the Association, as well as other bar association information.

As always, users should consult local council as to current laws applicable to particular situations.

SCOPE AND USE OF THE DIGESTS
UNITED STATES LAW DIGEST

The Domestic Law Digests*

Part I contains comprehensive digests of the laws of each of the fifty states of the United States, the District of Columbia, Puerto Rico and the Virgin Islands. These fifty-three compilations present under almost a hundred principal subject headings (topics) and numerous subheadings (running to a total of as many as five hundred in some of the digests) that portion of the law of the several jurisdictions which well over a century of experience has shown to be most useful to the legal profession.

The uniform arrangement of the material, supported by the abundant citations (including case citations to the National Reporter System), presents the laws in an organized and quickly accessible form. *To obtain the maximum benefit from the digests the user should become familiar with the Topical Index beginning at page XIII of the prefatory material.*

The digests have been compiled and are revised every year by distinguished lawyers, law professors and law firms who are acknowledged leaders of the bars of their respective jurisdictions. Every effort is made to insure that the digests reflect the most recent enactments of the legislature and changes in the rules of court.

Attention is directed to the numerous forms of instruments preferred by local usage which appear throughout the digests under the appropriate topics, e.g, forms of acknowledgment under the topic "Acknowledgments," subhead "Forms."

---

* The possible impact of Federal law on the laws of the States digested herein must be considered, since that law may override current state legislation in certain areas.

SCOPE AND USE OF THE DIGESTS (Cont.)
The Federal Law Digests

Digests of the Copyright, Patent and Trademark laws of the United States are presented in Part II. The revisers of these three digests are preeminent in their respective fields.

Besides presenting the substantive law controlling the grant of copyright, patent and trademark rights, the digests of these subjects provide information as to the practice to be followed in obtaining, protecting and enforcing such rights, the fee schedules of the respective bureaus, examples of forms in use, and other practical assistance. As in the case of all digests, these are annually revised.

The Uniform Acts

In Part III, the complete texts of many Uniform Acts *including the Uniform Commercial Code and the Uniform Probate Code,* and four Model Acts *including the Revised Model Business Corporation Act* are presented. These Uniform Laws are essential to the legal researcher because they have formed the basis of so much of the statutory law of so many states.

American Bar Association Section

Part IV contains The Model Rules of Professional Conduct of the American Bar Association, The Code of Judicial Conduct and the composition, jurisdiction and rules of procedure of the American Bar Association Standing Committee on Ethics and Professional Responsibility published as a service to the entire Bar of the United States.

INTERNATIONAL LAW DIGEST

The Law Digests — International Section

Digests of the laws of over 70 countries are supplied in Part V, and, in the case of Australia and Canada, digests of the laws of the States and Provinces of these countries are included with the digest of their Federal Laws. Distinguished lawyers and legal scholars of the respective countries have compiled and annually revise these digests. In some instances, the digests are revised by authorities resident in this country with the advice and assistance of local experts.

The aim of these digests is to present the points of law most likely to be of assistance to a lawyer with a matter in hand, some facet of which is controlled by the law of that country. In addition, descriptions of the governmental and legal systems of the countries are given.

Because of its significance to the laws of a number of European countries, a separate, additional digest is included in this portion of the volume, setting forth European Communities Law.

International Conventions

Part VI sets forth the texts of ten international conventions to which the U.S. is a party. Annotations are included.

Suggestions as to how we can make the materials in this volume of still greater use are invited.

MARTINDALE-HUBBELL®/LEXIS®-NEXIS® LEGAL ADVISORY BOARD

The Martindale-Hubbell/LEXIS-NEXIS Legal Advisory Board was formed to ensure that Martindale-Hubbell and LEXIS-NEXIS are responsive to the constantly changing needs of the legal profession. The following lawyers selected from the private, corporate and international sectors of the profession comprise the 1998-1999 Board.

MARTHA W. BARNETT of Holland & Knight, Tallahassee, Florida. Ms. Barnett is the Immediate Past Chair of the House of Delegates of the American Bar Association, the first woman lawyer to be so honored, and has served on the ABA's Board of Governors.

ALLEN E. BRENNECKE of Harrison, Brennecke, Moore, Smaha & McKibben, Marshaltown, Iowa. Mr. Brennecke has served as a Member of the Board of Directors of the National Judicial College, President of the Iowa State Bar Association, a Member of the ABA House of Delegates since 1975 and its Chair, 1984-1986. His prior service to the ABA also includes four years on the Board of Governors and three years as Chair of the IOLTA Commission. He currently serves on the Board of Editors of the American Bar Association Journal and previously served as Chair from 1989 to 1995.

BENJAMIN R. CIVILETTI of Venable, Baetjer, Howard & Civiletti, Baltimore, Maryland. Mr. Civiletti is a former Attorney General of the United States under President Carter, 1979-1981. He has been a Trustee of Johns Hopkins University since 1980. He also serves as Chairman of Venable, Baetjer & Howard. Mr. Civiletti is a Fellow of the American College of Trial Lawyers.

DOUGLAS B. HENDERSON is the Founding and Senior Partner of Finnegan, Henderson, Farabow, Garrett & Dunner, Washington, D.C. Mr. Henderson is a Member of the Board of Advisors of The George Washington University Law School, Member of the Advisory Council of the United States Court of Federal Claims, and a Member of the Board of the Federal Circuit Bar Association. He was formerly Chairman of the Patent Division and Member of Council of the Patent, Trademark and Copyright Law Section of the American Bar Association. He was the Founder of the Federal Circuit Bar Association, a co-founder of the U.S. Court of Federal Claims Bar Association, and a co-founder of the ITC Trial Lawyers Association.

THOMAS G. HEINTZMAN, Q.C., of McCarthy Tétrault, Toronto, Ontario, is a member of the Canadian Bar Association and a Past President (1994-1995). In addition, he is a member of the International Bar Association and serves as the Canadian Delegate to the IBA Council. He is also a member of the Inter-American Bar Association. Mr. Heintzman is a Fellow of the American College of Trial Lawyers and is Chair of its Canadian Judiciary Committee.

THOMAS J. KLITGAARD, formerly Senior Vice President and General Counsel of Sega of America, Inc., is now a partner with Dillingham & Murphy, San Francisco. He is a former Chairman of the California State Bar's Committee on the Maintenance of Professional Competence. Mr. Klitgaard began his legal career as a law clerk to Supreme Court Justice William O. Douglas. From 1963-1985, he was in private practice with the San Francisco law firm of Pillsbury, Madison & Sutro, where he specialized in anti-trust and securities litigation. Since 1979, he has been active in East Asian legal affairs. Fluent in conversational Mandarin Chinese, Mr. Klitgaard is Vice-Chairman of the Shanghai-San Francisco Friendship Committee, and has served as Chairman of the Board of the Chinese Cultural Foundation of San Francisco. He is also a Director of the American Arbitration Association, a Trustee of the University of San Francisco and a member of the Advisory Board for the Southwestern Legal Foundation since 1990.

RALPH I. LANCASTER, JR. of Pierce, Atwood, Portland, Maine. Mr. Lancaster is Past-President of the Maine State Bar Association, and a former member of the House of Delegates of the American Bar Association. He has served as Chairman of the Standing Committee on the Federal Judiciary of the ABA. He is a Fellow of the American College of Trial Lawyers of which he was President, 1989-1990.

JERALYN E. MERRITT, a sole practitioner from Denver, Colorado, is an author and frequent lecturer on criminal defense. She was selected by Chairman Bill McCollum, House Judiciary Committee, Subcommittee on Crime, to present oral and written congressional testimony on federal marijuana sentencing laws on behalf of the National Association of Criminal Defense Lawyers (NACDL) on March 6, 1996, in Washington, D.C. She served as Chair from 1995-1996 while a judicially appointed member of the Standing Committee on the Criminal Justice Act for the United States District Court for the District of Colorado from 1994-1996. Ms. Merritt is currently a member of the Board of Directors and Chair of the Advisory Board for the National Association of Criminal Defense Lawyers, the Director of the Cyberspace Bar Association and a member of the Board of Governors for the American Board of Criminal Lawyers.

HARRIET E. MIERS, President of Locke Purnell Rain Harrell, Dallas, Texas, has previously served as President and Director of the State Bar of Texas as well as President and Chairman of the Board of Directors for the Dallas Bar Association. She is currently Chair of the ABA Journal Board of Editors and a member of the House of Delegates for the American Bar Association. Ms. Miers also serves as Chair of the Texas Lottery Commission and as a member of the Board of Directors of the Attorneys Liability Assurance Society.

WILLIAM G. PAUL of Crowe & Dunlevy, Oklahoma City, Oklahoma. Mr. Paul is the former Senior Vice President & General Counsel, Phillips Petroleum Company, Bartlesville, Oklahoma. He has served as President of the Oklahoma State Bar Association, President of the National Conference of Bar Presidents, a Member of the American Bar Association, House of Delegates 1975-1995 and is a Fellow in the American College of Trial Lawyers. In February 1995, he was nominated to the Board of Governors of the American Bar Association to serve a three-year term, 1995-1998.

FERNANDO POMBO, of Gomez-Acebo & Pombo, Madrid, Spain, has contributed to and authored several publications in the field of international commerce. Currently, he is the International Bar Association Secretary (SGP). Mr. Pombo has been a visiting professor at the Institute on International Legal Studies in Salzburg, Austria since 1985. He is also a former President of LES International and a member of the Spanish Arbitration Court. He is fluent in Spanish, English, French and German.

ROBERTA COOPER RAMO, a shareholder of Modrall, Sperling, Roehl, Harris & Sisk in Albuquerque, NM served as the first woman President of the American Bar Association 1995-1996, and has also been a member of the ABA Board of Governors. She also served on the Board of the American Bar Retirement Association from 1990-1994 and was Chair of the ABA Council of Section Officers from 1984-1986. She is a former President of the Albuquerque Bar Association (1980) and a member (1988-1994) and President (1991-1993) of the University of New Mexico Board of Regents. Currently, she is a member of the State Bar of Texas, the State Bar of New Mexico, the New Mexico Estate Planning Council, and a Fellow of the American College of Trust and Estate Council. She also serves on the University of Chicago Law School Visiting Committee.

WM. REECE SMITH, JR. of Tampa, Florida, is the senior member of Carlton, Fields, Ward, Emmanuel, Smith & Cutler, P.A. A Rhodes Scholar at Oxford University, England, he was later president of The Florida Bar (1972-73), the American Bar Association (1980-81), and the International Bar Association (1988-90). He is a Fellow of the American College of Trial Lawyers and the International Academy of Trial Lawyers and serves on the Council of the American Law Institute. He received the American Bar Association's Gold Medal for "exceptionally distinguished service to the cause of American Jurisprudence."

WALTER H. WHITE, JR. is Managing Director of Steptoe & Johnson International, in Moscow, Russia, and Partner in Steptoe & Johnson L.L.P. in Washington, D.C. Mr. White served as the Wisconsin Commissioner of Securities, 1988-1991. He is a former member of the ABA House of Delegates, and has served on the Board of Milwaukee Foundation and currently is a board member of the Central-Asian-American Enterprise Fund by appointment of President Clinton.

Topical Index

The body of the law suitable for presentation in the Martindale-Hubbell Law Digests of the states of the United States, the District of Columbia, Puerto Rico and the Virgin Islands has been classified under categories and topics, which are uniform in all these Digests. The same classification is followed, as nearly as differing conditions permit, in the Canadian and International Section of the Law Digests.

This Topical Index fulfills, for each Digest, the double object of giving an alphabetical list of the main Digest headings and giving references by which the user may readily ascertain where the particular point which he desires to investigate will be found.

Index headings printed in capitals (**BOLD FACE**, in the actual Digest for each jurisdiction) are the main topics of the Digests, and all references in this Index are to such main topics. References preceded by the words "see also" indicate topics under which may be found matter related to the index heading, but not within it. Each topic is broken down in each of the Digests into appropriate subheads or subtopics (printed in the Digest for each jurisdiction in **Upper and Lower Case, Bold Face**). Where helpful, catchlines (*in italics*) are added under these subheads to further subdivide the law digested.

Forms of many instruments will be found under the appropriate topics, e.g., forms of acknowledgment under category Documents and Records, topic "Acknowledgments", subhead "Forms".

Uniform and Model Acts promulgated by the National Conference of Commissioners on Uniform State Laws (NCCUSL) in effect in the jurisdiction are listed in each Digest under the category Courts and Legislature, topic "Statutes", subhead "Uniform Acts". If the law digested under a specific topic is governed in large part by a Uniform Act, without substantial local deviations, reference to that Act will normally also be made under the specific topic affected, e.g., if the Uniform Commercial Code governs a particular subject, this will be stated, and the reader referred to the category Business Regulation and Commerce, topic Commercial Code.

Texts of Selected Uniform and Model Acts promulgated by the NCCUSL which are within the scope of the Martindale-Hubbell Law Digests are supplied in full in **PART III**.

Abandonment, see category Family, topics Divorce, Husband and Wife.

Abatement, see category Civil Actions and Procedure, topic Actions.

Absconding debtors, see category Debtor and Creditor, topic Attachment.

Absent defendants, see category Civil Actions and Procedure, topic Process.

ABSENTEES.—see also categories Business Organizations, topic Corporations; Civil Actions and Procedure, topics Costs, Limitation of Actions, Process, Venue; Debtor and Creditor, topic Attachment; Estates and Trusts, topics Death, Executors and Administrators; Family, topic Guardian and Ward.

Accidents, see category Transportation, topic Motor Vehicles.

ACCORD AND SATISFACTION.

Accounts, see categories Business Regulation and Commerce, topic Banks and Banking; Estates and Trusts, topic Executors and Administrators; Family, topic Guardian and Ward.

Accounts Receivable, see category Debtor and Creditor, topic Assignments.

Accumulations, see categories Estates and Trusts, topic Trusts; Property, topic Perpetuities.

ACKNOWLEDGMENTS.—See also categories Business Regulation and Commerce, topic Sales; Debtor and Creditor, topic Assignments; Documents and Records, topics Affidavits, Notaries Public; Mortgages, topics Chattel Mortgages, Mortgages of Real Property; Property, topics Deeds, Landlord and Tenant.

ACTIONS.—See also categories Civil Actions and Procedure, topics Appeal and Error, Certiorari, Judgments, Limitation of Actions, Submission of Controversy, Pleading, Practice, Process, Venue; Courts and Legislature, topic Courts; Debtor and Creditor, topics Attachment, Receivers; Employment, topic Labor Relations; Estates and Trusts, topics Death, Executors and Administrators; Family, topics Divorce, Guardian and Ward, Infants, Marriage. For Declaratory Judgments, see category Civil Actions and Procedure, topic Judgments.

Adjudication, see category Civil Actions and Procedure, topic Judgments.

ADMINISTRATION.—See category Estates and Trusts, topic Executors and Administrators.

Administration, when unnecessary, see category Estates and Trusts, topic Executors and Administrators.

Admission, demand for, see category Civil Actions and Procedure, topic Practice.

Admission to bar, see category Legal Profession, topic Attorneys and Counselors.

ADOPTION.

Adultery, see category Family, topic Divorce.

Advancements, see category Estates and Trusts, topic Descent and Distribution.

ADVERSE POSSESSION.—See also category Civil Actions and Procedure, topic Limitation of Actions.

Affidavit of defense, see category Civil Actions and Procedure, topic Pleading.

AFFIDAVITS.—See also categories Civil Actions and Procedure, topics Depositions and Discovery, Evidence, subhead Witnesses, Pleading; Documents and Records, topic Acknowledgments; Estates and Trusts, topic Executors and Administrators.

Affirmation as substitute for acknowledgment, see category Documents and Records, topic Acknowledgments.

Affirmation as substitute for affidavit, see category Documents and Records, topic Affidavits.

Afterborn children, see category Estates and Trusts, topics Descent and Distribution, Wills.

Age, see category Family, topics Adoption, Infants, Marriage.

Agency, see category Property, topic Powers of Attorney. See also categories Business Organizations, topics Corporations, Partnerships; Business Regulation and Commerce, topic Factors; Civil Actions and Procedure, topic Brokers; Employment, topic Labor Relations.

Agent for service of process, see categories Business Organizations, topic Corporations; Civil Actions and Procedure, topic Process; Estates and Trusts, topic Executors and Administrators; Insurance, topic Insurance Companies; Property, topic Absentees; Transportation, topic Motor Vehicles.

Air pollution, see category Environment, topic Environmental Regulation.

Alienation of property, restrictions on, see category Property, topic Perpetuities.

ALIENS.

Alimony, see category Family, topic Divorce. See also category Family, topic Marriage.

Allowances, see category Estates and Trusts, topic Executors and Administrators.

Alternative to acknowledgment, see category Documents and Records, topic Acknowledgments.

Alternative to affidavit, see category Documents and Records, topic Affidavits.

Amendments, see categories Business Organizations, topic Corporations; Civil Actions and Procedure, topic Pleading.

Anatomical gifts, see category Estates and Trusts, topic Wills.

Ancestors, see category Estates and Trusts, topic Descent and Distribution.

Ancillary administration, see category Estates and Trusts, topic Executors and Administrators.

Annulment of marriage, see category Family, topic Marriage. See also category Family, topic Divorce.

Answer, see category Civil Actions and Procedure, topic Pleading.

Antenuptial contracts, see category Family, topic Husband and Wife.

Antitrust, see category Business Regulation and Commerce, topic Monopolies, Restraint of Trade and Competition.

APPEAL AND ERROR.—See also categories Civil Actions and Procedure, topic Certiorari; Courts and Legislature, topic Courts; Taxation, topic Taxes.

Appearance, see category Civil Actions and Procedure, topic Actions, Pleading, Process.

Applicable law, see categories Business Regulation and Commerce, topics Contracts and Sales in certain International Digests.

Apportionment, see category Taxation, topic Taxes.

Appraisal of dissenting shareholder's stock, see category Business Organizations, topic Corporations, subhead Appraisal.

Community property, see category Family, topic Husband and Wife.

Companies, See categories Business Organizations, topics Associations, Corporations, Joint Stock Companies; Business Regulation and Commerce, topic Banks and Banking; Insurance, topics Insurance Companies, Surety and Guaranty Companies.

Comparative negligence, see category Civil Actions and Procedure, topic Damages.

Compelling attendance of witness, see category Civil Actions and Procedure, topic Depositions and Discovery.

Compensation, see categories Employment, topic Relations; Estates and Trusts, topics Executors and Administrators, Trusts; Family, topic Guardian and Ward; Legal Profession, topic Attorneys and Counselors.

Competency, see categories Civil Actions and Procedure, topics Evidence, subhead Witnesses, Limitation of Actions; Estates and Trusts, topics Executors and Administrators, Wills; Family, topics Guardian and Ward, Husband and Wife, Infants, Marriage.

Compilations, see category Courts and Legislature, topic Statutes.

Complaint, see category Civil Actions and Procedure, topic Pleading.

Compromise, see category Civil Actions and Procedure, topic Accord and Satisfaction.

Compromise of death taxes, see category Taxation, topic Taxes, subhead Interstate Co-operation.

Compulsory arbitration, see category Dispute Resolution, topic Arbitration and Award.

Compulsory continuing legal education, see category Legal Profession, topic Attorneys and Counselors.

Conditional sales, see category Business Regulation and Commerce, topic Sales; also category Business Regulation and Commerce, topic Commercial Code.

Condominiums, see category Property, topic Real Property.

Confession of judgment, see category Civil Actions and Procedure, topic Judgments.

Confidential relations, see category Civil Actions and Procedure, topic Evidence, subhead Witnesses.

Conflicts of laws, see category Business Regulation and Commerce, topics Contracts and Sales in certain International Digests.

Consanguinity, see categories Estates and Trusts, topic Descent and Distribution; Family, topic Marriage.

Consent, see category Family, topics Adoption, Marriage.

Consignments, see category Business Regulation and Commerce, topic Factors; also category Business Regulation and Commerce, topic Commercial Code.

Constitutions, see category Introduction, topic Government and Legal System in International Digests only.

CONSUMER CREDIT CODE.—see category Business Regulation and Commerce, topic consumer Credit in states enacting Uniform Consumer Credit Code.

CONSUMER PROTECTION.—See also category Business Regulation and Commerce, topic Sales.

Consumer transactions, see category Business Regulation and Commerce, topic Consumer Protection, also topics Bills and Notes, Interest, Sales.

Contamination, see category Environment, topic Environmental Regulation.

Continuation statement, see categories Business Regulation and Commerce, topic Commercial Code; Mortgages, topic Chattel Mortgages.

Contract provisions as to venue, see category Civil Actions and Procedure, topic Venue.

Contractors' bonds, see category Debtor and Creditor, topic Liens, subhead Mechanics' Liens.

CONTRACTS.—See also categories Business Regulation and Commerce, topic Commercial Code; Documents and Records, topic Seals; Family, topics Husband and Wife, Infants.

Contributions for social security or unemployment compensation, see category Taxation, topic Taxes.

Controversies, see category Civil Actions and Procedure, topic Submission of Controversy. See also categories Civil Actions and Procedure, topic Accord and Satisfaction; Dispute Resolution, topic Arbitration and Award.

Conventions, International, to which U.S. is a party (selected), see Part VI.

Conveyances, see category Property, topic Deeds. See also categories Business Regulation and Commerce, topic Frauds, Statute of; Debtor and Creditor, topic Fraudulent Sales and Conveyances, Mortgages, topic Mortgages of Real Property.

Copartners, see category Business Organizations, topic Partnerships.

Copyright, see United States Copyright Law Digest and category Intellectual Property, topic Copyright in Dominion of Canada and International Digests.

Corporate Seal, see categories Business Organizations, topic Corporations; Documents and Records, topic Seals.

CORPORATIONS.—See also categories Business Organizations, topics Associations, Joint Stock Companies; Business Regulation and Commerce, topics Banks and Banking, Carriers, Commercial Code, Securities; Civil Actions and Procedure, topics Process, Venue; Debtor and Creditor, topic Attachment; Insurance, topics Insurance Companies, Surety and Guaranty Companies; Property, topic Deeds; Taxation, topic Taxes. In International Digests, see also category Citizenship, topic Aliens.

COSTS.

Counselors, see category Legal Profession, topic Attorneys and Counselors.

Counterclaim, see category Civil Actions and Procedure, topic Pleading.

County clerk's certificate, see category Documents and Records, topic Acknowledgments, subhead Authentication.

COURTS.

Coverture, see category Family, topics Husband and Wife, Marriage.

Credit cards, see category Business Regulation and Commerce, topics Consumer Protection, Sales.

Credit, letters of, see category Business Regulation and Commerce, topic Commercial Code.

Credit sales, see category Business Regulation and Commerce, topic Sales; also category Business Regulation and Commerce, topic Consumer Protection.

CREDITORS' SUITS.—See also categories Debtor and Creditor, topics Executions, Fraudulent Sales and Conveyances; Estates and Trusts, topic Executors and Administrators.

CRIMINAL LAW.

Cumulative voting, see category Business Organizations, topic Corporations.

Curators, see category Family, topic Guardian and Ward.

Currency, see category Introduction, topic Currency in International Digests only, also category Foreign Trade and Commerce, topics Foreign Exchange and Foreign Trade Regulations.

CURTESY.—See also categories Estates and Trusts, topics Descent and Distribution, Wills; Property. topic Dower.

Customs, see category Foreign Trade and Commerce, topic Customs Duties in certain International Digests.

DAMAGES.—See also category Estates and Trusts, topic Death.

Days of grace, see category Business Regulation and Commerce, topic Bills and Notes.

Dealerships, see category Business Regulation and Commerce, topic Contracts in International Digests only.

DEATH.—See also categories Documents and Records, topic Records; Employment, topic Labor Relations; Property, topic Absentees.

Death actions, see category Estates and Trusts, topic Death.

Death certificate, see category Documents and Records, topic Records.

Death taxes, see category Taxation, topic Taxes.

Debts of decedents, see category Estates and Trusts, topic Executors and Administrators.

Decedents' estates, see categories Debtor and Creditor, topic Homesteads; Documents and Records, topic Records; Estates and Trusts, topics Descent and Distribution, Executors and Administrators, Wills; Family, topic Husband and Wife; Property, topics Curtesy, Dower.

Deceptive practices, see category Business Regulation and Commerce topics, Consumer Protection, Sales.

Declarations, see category Civil Actions and Procedure, topic Pleading.

Declaratory judgments, see category Civil Actions and Procedure, topics Judgments, Submission of Controversy.

Deed tax, see categories Taxation, topic Taxes subhead Real Estate Conveyance Tax; Property, topic Deeds.

DEEDS.—See also categories Business Regulation and Commerce, topic Frauds, Statute of; Debtor and Creditor, topics Fraudulent Sales and Conveyances, Homesteads; Documents and Records, topics Acknowledgements, Records; Family, topics Husband and Wife, Infants; Mortgages, topic Mortgages of Real Property; Property, topic Real Property.

Deeds of mortgage, see category Mortgages, topic Mortgages of Real Property.

Deeds of trust, see category Mortgages, topic Mortgages of Real Property.

Default, see category Civil Actions and Procedure, topic Judgments.

Defendants, see category Civil Actions and Procedure, topics Actions, Process.

Defense, affidavit of, see category Civil Actions and Procedure, topic Pleading.

Delayed birth certificates, see category Documents and Records, topic Records.

Demurrers, see category Civil Actions and Procedures, topic Pleading.

DEPOSITIONS.—See also categories Civil Actions and Procedure, topic Evidence, subhead Witnesses; Documents and Records, topic Affidavits. Deposits, see category Business Regulation and Commerce, topic Banks and Banking.

DESCENT AND DISTRIBUTION.—See also categories Citizenship, topic Aliens; Debtor and Creditor, topic Homesteads; Estates and Trusts, topics Executors and Administrators, Wills; Family, topics Adoption, Husband and Wife; Property, topics Curtesy, Dower; Taxation, topic Taxes.

Desertion, see category Family, topics Divorce, Husband and Wife.

Devisees, see category Estates and Trusts, topic Wills.

Die, right to, see category Estates and Trusts, topic Wills.

Digests, see category Courts and Legislature, topic Reports.

Direct actions against insurer, see category Transportation, topic Motor Vehicles, subhead Direct Actions.

Directors, see category Business Organizations, topic Corporations.

Disabilities, see categories Citizenship, topic Aliens; Civil Actions and Procedure, topics Evidence, subhead Witnesses, Limitation of Actions; Estates and Trusts. topics Executors and Administrators, Wills; Family, topics Guardian and Ward, Husband and Wife, Infants.

Discovery, see category Civil Actions and Procedure, topics Depositions and Discovery Practice.

Discrimination, see categories Employment, topic Labor Relations; Property, topic Real Property.

Disinheritance, see category Estates and Trusts, topic Wills.

Dismiss, see category Civil Actions and Procedure, topics Judgments, Pleading, Practice.

Dispossession, see category Property, topic Landlord and Tenant.

DISPUTE RESOLUTION.

Disputed domicile in death tax matters, see category Taxation, topic Taxes subhead Interstate Co-operation.

Dissenting shareholder, see category Business Organizations, topic Corporations.

DISSOLUTION OF MARRIAGE.—See also category Family, topics Divorce, Marriage.

Distress, see category Property, topic Landlord and Tenant.

Distribution, see category Estates and Trusts, topics Descent and Distribution, Executors and Administrators.

Distribution if abroad, see category Estates and Trusts, topic Executors and Administrators.

Distributorships, see category Business Regulation and Commerce, topic Contracts in International Digests only.

Division of property of spouses on dissolution of marriage, see category Family, topic Dissolution of Marriage; or topic Divorce.

DIVORCE.—See also categories Family, topics Dissolution of Marriage, Marriage; Property, topics Curtesy, Dower.

Domicile, disputed, see category Taxation, topic Taxes, subhead Interstate Co-operation.

DOWER.—See also categories Debtor and Creditor, topic Homesteads; Documents and Records, topic Acknowledgements; Estates and Trusts, topics Descent and Distribution, Executors and Administrators, Wills; Family, topic Husband and Wife; Property, topics Curtesy, Deeds.

Drafts, see category Business Regulation and Commerce, topics Bills and Notes, Commercial Code.

Durable Power of Attorney, see category Property, topic Powers of Attorney.

Earnings, exemption of, see category Debtor and Creditor, topics Exemptions, Garnishment.

Ecology, see category Environment, topic Environmental Regulation.

Election, see category Estates and Trusts, topic Wills.

Employer and employee, see category Employment, topic Labor Relations.

Employers' Liability, see category Employment, topic Labor Relations.

Energy law, see category Mineral, Water and Fishing Rights, topic Mines and Minerals.

Entirety, tenancy by, in personalty, see category Property, topic Personal Property.

Entirety, tenancy by, in realty, see category Property, topic Real Property.

ENVIRONMENT.

Equity, see categories Civil Action and Procedure, topics Actions, Pleading, Practice; Courts and Legislature, topic Courts.

Equity in redemption, see category Mortgages, topic Mortgages of Real Property. See also category Taxation, topic Taxes.

Error, writ of, see category Civil Actions and Procedure, topic Appeal and Error.

ESCHEAT.—See categories Business Organizations, topic Corporations, subhead Unclaimed Dividends; Business Regulation and Commerce, topic Banks and Banking, subhead Unclaimed Deposits; Estates and Trusts, topics Descent and Distribution, Wills, subhead Unclaimed Legacies; Property, topic Absentees.

Establishing birth records, see category Documents and Records, topic Records.

Estate tax, see category Taxation, topic Taxes.

Estates, see categories Debtor and Creditor, topic Homesteads; Estates and Trusts, topics Descent and Distribution, Executors and Administrators, Trusts, Wills; Property, topics Curtesy, Dower, Real Property.

European Economic Community, see European Union Digest in Part V.

Evasion, see category Taxation, topic Taxes, subhead Penalties.

Evidence, see categories Civil Actions and Procedure, topics Depositions and Discovery, Evidence, subhead Witnesses; Documents and Records, topic Affidavits.

Exchange control, see also categories Foreign Trade and Commerce, topics Foreign Exchange, Foreign Trade Regulation; Introduction, topic Currency in International Digests only.

Excuses for nonperformance, see category Business Regulation and Commerce, topic Contracts in certain International Digests.

EXECUTIONS.—See also categories Civil Actions and Procedure, topics Appeal and Error, Judgments, Sequestration; Debtor and Creditor, topics Attachment, Exemptions, Garnishment.

EXECUTORS AND ADMINISTRATORS.—See also category Estates and Trusts, topics Descent and Distribution, Wills.

EXEMPTIONS.—See also categories Debtor and Creditor, topics Executions, Garnishment, Homesteads; Estates and Trusts, topic Executor and Administrators; Taxation, topic Taxes.

Factorizing, see category Debtor and Creditor, topic Garnishment.

FACTORS.—See also categories Business Regulation and Commerce, topics Agency, Brokers; Debtor and Creditor, topic Pledges.

Family law, see category Family, topics Marriage, Divorce. Husband and Wife. Infants.

Fees, see specified topics, e.g., categories Business Organization, topic Corporations; Business Regulation and Commerce, topic Commercial Code; Mortgages, topic chattel Mortgages, etc.

Fictitious names, see category Intellectual Property, topic Trademarks and Tradenames.

Fiduciaries, see categories Estates and Trusts, topic Executors and Administrators, Trusts; Family, topic Guardian and Ward; Property, topic Powers of Attorney.

Fieri facias, see category Debtor and Creditor, topic Executions.

Filing under Uniform Commercial Code, see categories Business Regulation and Commerce, topic Commercial Code; Documents and Records, topic Records.

Filing fees, see categories Business Organization, topic Corporations; Business Regulation and Commerce, topic Commercial Code; Documents and Records, topic Records; Estates and Trusts, topic Executors and Administrators; Mortgages, topics Chattel Mortgages, Mortgages of Real Property; Property, topic Deeds.

Financial responsibility, see category Transportation, topic Motor Vehicles.

Financing statement, see categories Business Regulation and Commerce, topic Commercial Code; Mortgages, topic Chattel Mortgages.

Forced heirs, see category Estates and Trusts, topic Wills.

Foreclosure, see categories Debtor and Creditor, topic Liens; Mortgages, topics Chattel Mortgages, Mortgages of Real Property.

Foreign automobiles, see category Transportation, topic Motor Vehicles.

Foreign conveyances of incumbrances, see categories Documents and Records. topic Records; Property, topic Real Property.

Foreign corporations, see categories Business Organizations, topic Corporations; Civil Actions and Procedure, topic Process. See also categories Business Regulation and Commerce, topic Banks and Banking; Insurance Companies, Surety and Guaranty Companies. See also category Citizenship, topic Aliens in certain International Digests.

Foreign depositions, see category Civil Actions and Procedure, topic Depositions and Discovery.

Foreign distribution, see category Estates and Trusts, topic Executors and Administrators.

Foreign divorce, see category Family, topic Divorce.

Foreign exchange, see categories Foreign Trade and Commerce, topics Foreign Exchange, Foreign Trade Regulations; Introduction, topic Currency, in International Digests only.

Foreign executors and administrators, see category Estates and Trusts, topic Executors and Administrators.

Foreign guardians, see category Family, topic Guardian and Ward.

Foreign investment, see category Foreign Trade and Commerce, topic Foreign Investment in International Digests.

Foreign judgments, see category Civil Actions and Procedure, topic Judgments.

Foreign marriages, see category Family, topic Marriage.

Foreign operators of motor vehicles, see category Transportation, topic Motor Vehicles.

Foreign trade, see categories Foreign Trade and Commerce, topics Foreign Exchange, Foreign Trade Regulations; Introduction, topic Currency, in International Digests only.

Foreign vehicles, see category Transportation, topic Motor Vehicles.

Foreign wills, see category Estates and Trusts, topic Wills.

Foreigners, see category Citizenship, topic Aliens.

Forms, see categories Civil Actions and Procedure, topics Depositions and Discovery, Judgements; Documents and Records, topics Acknowledgments, Affidavits; Estates and Trusts, topics Executors and Administrators, Wills; Mortgages, topics Chattel Mortgages, Mortgages of Real Property; Property, topic Deeds.

Forthcoming bonds, see category Debtor and Creditor, topics Attachment, Executions, Garnishment.

Franchise taxes, see category Business Organizations, topic Corporations.

FRANCHISES.—See also category Business Regulation and Commerce, topics Securities, Monopolies, Restraint of Trade and Competition, Contracts in International Digests only.

FRAUDS, STATUTE OF.—See also category Business Regulation and Commerce, topic Commercial Code.

FRAUDULENT SALES AND CONVEYANCES.—See also categories Business Regulation and Commerce, topic Commercial Code; Debtor and Creditor, topics Attachment, Creditors' Suits.

Frivolous Claims, see category Civil Actions and Procedure, topic Pleading.

GARNISHMENT.—See also category Debtor and Creditor, topics Attachment, Executions, Exemptions.

Gas, see category Mineral. Water and Fishing Rights, topic Mines and Minerals.

Gasoline tax, see category Taxation, topic Taxes.

Gift tax, see category Taxation, topic Taxes.

Gifts to Minors, see category Family, topic Infants.

ACKNOWLEDGMENTS

The publishers take pleasure in acknowledging their indebtedness to the following lawyers, legal scholars and law firms, whose interest and untiring efforts in the annual revisions of the Law Digests contained in this volume have made possible the presentation to the legal profession of a vast amount of useful information which could not otherwise have been compiled.

PART I

DIGESTS OF LAWS OF THE STATES, THE DISTRICT OF COLUMBIA, PUERTO RICO AND THE VIRGIN ISLANDS

Alabama:—*Revision by* Bradley Arant Rose & White LLP, of Birmingham.

Alaska:—*Revision by* Robertson, Monagle & Eastaugh, A Professional Corporation, of Alaska.

Arizona:—*Revision by* Fennemore Craig, A Professional Corporation, of Phoenix.

Arkansas:—*Revision by* Rose Law Firm, a Professional Association, of Little Rock.

California:—*Revision by* Professor Carol A. Wilson, University of San Francisco School of Law, of San Francisco.

Colorado:—*Revision by* Holme Roberts & Owen, LLP, of Denver.

Connecticut:—*Revision by* Sorokin, Gross & Hyde, P.C., of Hartford.

Delaware:—*Revision by* Richards, Layton & Finger, of Wilmington.

District of Columbia:—*Revision by* Margaret L. Moses, Assistant Professor of Law, Loyola University Chicago School of Law, of Chicago, IL.

Florida:—*Revision by* Professor Jarret C. Oeltjen, College of Law, Florida State University, of Tallahassee.

Georgia:—*Revision by* Alston & Bird, Atlanta.

Hawaii:—*Revision by* Carlsmith Ball, of Honolulu.

Idaho:—*Revision by* Merrill & Merrill, Chartered, of Pocatello.

Illinois:—*Revision by* Celeste M. Hammond, Professor, assisted by Therese Clarke, John Marshall Law School, of Chicago.

Indiana:—*Revision by* Ice Miller Donadio & Ryan, of Indianapolis.

Iowa:—*Revision by* Finley, Alt, Smith, Scharnberg, Craig, Hilmes & Gaffney, P.C., of Des Moines.

Kansas:—*Revision by* Young, Bogle, McCausland, Wells & Blanchard, P.A., of Wichita.

Kentucky:—*Revision by* Stites & Harbison, of Louisville, Frankfort and Lexington.

Louisiana:—*Revision by* Phelps Dunbar, L.L.P., of New Orleans and Baton Rouge.

Maine:—*Revision by* Pierce Atwood, of Portland.

Maryland:—*Revision by* Venable, Baetjer and Howard, LLP, of Baltimore.

Massachusetts:—*Revision by* Professor Richard M. Perlmutter, assisted by David S. Romantz and Herbert N. Ramy, Instructors, Vincent J. Froio, Jr. and Richard Reilly, Suffolk University Law School.

Michigan:—*Revision by* Miller, Canfield, Paddock and Stone, P.L.C., of Detroit, Ann Arbor, Bloomfield Hills, Grand Rapids, Howell, Kalamazoo, Lansing and Monroe, Michigan; Pensacola and St. Petersburg, Florida; Washington, D.C.; and Gdansk and Warsaw, Poland.

Minnesota:—*Revision by* Faegre & Benson LLP, of Minneapolis.

Mississippi:—*Revision by* Watkins & Eager PLLC, of Jackson.

Missouri:—*Revision by* Swanson, Midgley, Gangwere, Kitchin & McLarney, LLC., of Kansas City.

Montana:—*Revision by* Crowley, Haughey, Hanson, Toole & Dietrich P.L.L.P., of Billings.

Nebraska:—*Revision by* Fraser Stryker Vaughn Meusey Olson Boyer & Bloch PC, of Omaha.

Nevada:—*Revision by* Woodburn and Wedge, of Reno and Las Vegas.

New Hampshire:—*Revision by* Wadleigh, Starr & Peters, of Manchester.

New Jersey:—*Revision by* Sills Cummis Zuckerman Radin Tischman Epstein & Gross, P.C., of Newark.

New Mexico:—*Revision by* Rodey, Dickason, Sloan, Akin & Robb, P.A., of Albuquerque and Sante Fe.

ACKNOWLEDGMENTS

New York:—*Revision by* Rogers & Wells, of New York City.

North Carolina:—*Revision by* Womble Carlyle Sandridge & Rice, a Professional Limited Liability Company, of Winston-Salem.

North Dakota:—*Revision by* Nilles, Hansen & Davies, Ltd., of Fargo.

Ohio:—*Revision* by Arter & Hadden, of Cleveland.

Oklahoma:—*Revision by* McAfee & Taft, A Professional Corporation, of Oklahoma City.

Oregon:—*Revision* by Miller, Nash, Wiener, Hager & Carlsen, LLP, of Portland.

Pennsylvania:—*Revision by* Ballard, Spahr, Andrews & Ingersoll, of Philadelphia.

Puerto Rico:—*Revision by* McConnell Valdés, of San Juan.

Rhode Island:—*Revision by* Edwards & Angell, LLP, of Providence.

South Carolina:—*Revision by* Haynsworth, Marion, McKay & Guérard, L.L.P., of Greenville.

South Dakota:—*Revision by* Davenport, Evans, Hurwitz & Smith, L.L.P., of Sioux Falls.

Tennessee:—*Revision by* Armstrong Allen Prewitt Gentry Johnston & Holmes, PLLC, of Memphis.

Texas:—*Revision by* Professor Gilbert A. Holmes, Texas Wesleyan Law School, Fort Worth.

Utah:—*Revision by* Van Cott, Bagley, Cornwall & McCarthy, A Professional Corporation, of Salt Lake City.

Vermont:—*Revision by* Ryan Smith & Carbine, Ltd., of Rutland.

Virgin Islands:—*Revision by* Grunert, Stout & Bruch, of the Virgin Islands Bar.

Virginia:—*Revision by* McGuire Woods Battle & Boothe LLP, of Charlottesville, Richmond, Norfolk and Williamsburg.

Washington:—*Revision by* Perkins Coie LLP, of Seattle.

West Virginia:—*Revision by* Jackson & Kelly, of Charleston.

Wisconsin:—*Revision by* Quarles & Brady LLP, of Milwaukee.

Wyoming:—*Revision by* Brown, Drew & Massey, LLP, of Casper.

PART II

DIGESTS OF UNITED STATES LAWS

Copyright:—*Revision by* Brumbaugh, Graves, Donohue & Raymond, of New York City.

Patent:—*Revision by* Cushman Darby & Cushman, Intellectual Property Group of Pillsbury Madison & Sutro LLP, of Washington, D.C.

Trademark:—*Revision by* Cushman Darby & Cushman, Intellectual Property Group of Pillsbury Madison & Sutro LLP, of Washington, D.C.

PART III

APPENDIX OF UNIFORM AND MODEL ACTS

We are indebted to the National Conference of Commissioners on Uniform State Laws for cooperation in furnishing copies of its Uniform and Model Acts, to the Committee on Corporation Laws of the Section of Corporation, Banking and Business Law of the American Bar Association for the copies of the Model Business Corporation Act and to the National Conference and the American Law Institute for the Uniform Commercial Code, reprints of which appear in this volume.

PART IV

AMERICAN BAR ASSOCIATION CODES

We are indebted to the American Bar Association for furnishing updates for the ABA Model Rules of Professional Conduct and the ABA Model Code of Judicial Conduct, reprints of which appear in this volume.

ACKNOWLEDGMENTS

PART V

DIGESTS OF LAWS, INTERNATIONAL SECTION

Argentina:—*Revision by* Curtis, Mallet-Prevost, Colt & Mosle, of New York City.

Australia:—*Revision by* Arthur Robinson & Hedderwicks, of Melbourne.

Austria:—*Revision by* Zeiner & Zeiner, of Vienna.

Bahamas:—*Revision by* Harry B. Sands & Company, of the Bahamas Bar.

Belgium:—*Revision by* De Bandt, van Hecke & Lagae, of Brussels.

Bermuda:—*Revision by* Appleby, Spurling & Kempe, of Hamilton.

Bolivia:
Brazil: } *Revision by* Curtis, Mallet-Prevost, Colt & Mosle, of New York City

Bulgaria:—*Revision by* Vassil Breskovski, LL.M., in association with Vladimir Petrov, Professor of Law, Sofia University, Bulgaria.

Dominion of Canada:—*Revision by* Borden & Elliot, of Toronto.

  Alberta:—*Revision by* Bennett Jones Verchere, of Calgary.

  British Columbia:—*Revision by* Davis & Company, of Vancouver.

  Manitoba:—*Revision by* Aikins, MacAulay & Thorvaldson, of Winnipeg.

  New Brunswick:—*Revision by* Clark, Drummie & Company, of St. John.

  Newfoundland:—*Revision by* Lewis, Day, of St. John's.

  Nova Scotia:—*Revision by* McInnes Cooper & Robertson, of Halifax.

  Ontario:—*Revision by* Borden & Elliot, of Toronto.

  Prince Edward Island:—*Revision by* Campbell, Lea, Michael, McConnell & Pigot, of Charlottetown.

  Quebec:—*Revision by* McMaster Gervais, of Montreal.

  Saskatchewan:—*Revision by* MacPherson Leslie & Tyerman, of Regina.

Cayman Islands:—*Prepared by* W.S. Walker & Company, of George Town, Grand Cayman.

Channel Islands (Jersey):—*Revision by* Ogier & Le Masurier, of Jersey.

Chile:—*Revision by* Curtis, Mallet-Prevost, Colt & Mosle, of New York City.

China, People's Republic of:—*Revision by* Brand Farrar Buxbaum LLP, of New York City, Los Angeles, Beijing and Ulaanbaatar.

Colombia:—*Revision by* Curtis, Mallet-Prevost, Colt & Mosle, of New York City.

Costa Rica:—*Revision by* Curtis, Mallet-Prevost, Colt & Mosle, of New York City.

Czech Republic:—*Revision by* Zeiner Golan Nir & Partners in co-operation with Professor JUDr. Zdenek Kucera, of Prague.

Denmark:—*Revision by* Garrissen Federspiel Kierkegaard, Law firm, Jan Erlund and Claus Bennetsen, attorneys, of Copenhagen.

Dominican Republic:
Ecuador: } *Revision by* Curtis, Mallet-Prevost, Colt & Mosle, of New York City.
El Salvador:

England:—*Revision by* Faculty of Law, Cambridge University, Cambridge.

Estonia: —*Prepared by* The Law Office of Tark & Co, of Tallinn.

European Union:—*Revision by* De Bandt, van Hecke & Lagae, of Brussels, Belgium.

Finland:—*Revision by* Castrén & Snellman, of Helsinki.

France:—*Revision by* Coudert Brothers, of New York City, and Coudert Frères, of Paris.

Germany:—*Revision by* Boesebeck Droste, of Frankfurt/Main.

Gibraltar:—*Revision by* Marrache & Co., of Gibraltar.

Greece:—*Revision by* Dr. Tryfon J. Koutalidis, of Athens.

Guatemala:
Honduras: } *Revision by* Curtis, Mallet-Prevost, Colt & Mosle, of New York City.

Hong Kong:—*Revision by* Robert W.H. Wang & Co., of Hong Kong.

Hungary:—*Revision by* Nagy és Trócsányi, of Budapest, New York, Basel, Switzerland and Stockholm, Sweden.

India:—*Revision by* Mulla & Mulla & Craigie Blunt & Caroe, of Mumbai.

Indonesia:—*Prepared by* Andrew I. Sriro, Esq., of Jakarta.

Ireland:—*Revision by* Gerrard, Scallan & O'Brien, of Dublin.

ACKNOWLEDGMENTS

Israel:—*Revision by* Yaacov Salomon, Lipschütz & Co., of Haifa and Tel Aviv.

Italy:—*Revision by* Studio Legale Beltramo, of Rome.

Japan:—*Revision by* Blakemore & Mitsuki, of the Tokyo Bar.

Korea:—*Revision by* Kim & Chang, of Seoul.

Latvia:—*Revision by* Klavins, Slaidins & Loze, of the Republic of Latvia, New York, Connecticut and California.

Lebanon:—*Revision by* Khairallah & Chaiban, of Beirut.

Liechtenstein:—*Revision by* Ritter-Wohlwend-Wolff, of Vaduz.

Lithuania:—*Prepared by* Jaunius Gumbis with Lideika, Petrauskas, Valiunas & Partners, of Vilnius.

Luxembourg:—*Revision by* Bonn & Schmitt, of Luxembourg.

Malaysia:—*Revision by* David Chong & Co., of Kuala Lumpur.

Malta:—*Revision by* Rutter Giappone & Associates, of Valletta.

Mexico:—*Revision by* Curtis, Mallet-Prevost, Colt & Mosle, of New York City.

Mongolia:—*Revision by* Brand Farrar Buxbaum LLP, of New York City, Los Angeles, Ulaanbaatar and Beijing.

Netherlands:—*Revision by* De Brauw Blackstone Westbroek, with offices in Amsterdam, The Hague, Rotterdam, Brussels, London, New York, Prague and Warsaw.

New Zealand:—*Revision by* Bell Gully Buddle Weir, of Auckland, Manukau and Wellington.

Nicaragua:—*Revision by* Curtis, Mallet-Prevost, Colt & Mosle, of New York City.

Northern Ireland:—*Revision by* C. & H. Jefferson, of Belfast.

Norway:—*Revision by* Advokatfirmaet STABELL DA, of Oslo.

Pakistan:—*Revision by* Surridge & Beecheno, of Karachi.

Panama:—*Revision by* Icaza, Gonzalez-Ruiz & Aleman, of the Panama Bar.

Paraguay:—*Revision by* Peroni, Sosa, Tellechea, Burt & Narvaja, of Asunción.

Peru:—*Revision by* Curtis, Mallet-Prevost, Colt & Mosle, of New York City.

Philippine Republic:—*Revision by* Ortega, Del Castillo, Bacorro, Odulio, Calma & Carbonell, of Manila.

Poland:—*Revision by* Altheimer & Gray, of Chicago, IL and Warsaw in cooperation with Professor Dr. Hab. A. Calus, Chairman, Department of International Law, Central School of Commerce, Warsaw.

Portugal:—*Revision by* Dr. Nuno Telles Pereira, and Luis Miguel Sasseti Carmona, with M.J.H. Reynolds of Lisbon.

Romania:—*Revision by* Hall Dickler Kent Friedman & Wood, Bucharest, Romania, White Plains, NY and Los Angeles, CA.

Russian Federation:—*Revision by* McDermott, Will & Emery, of Moscow, St. Petersburg, Russia, Boston, Chicago, Los Angeles, Miami, Newport Beach, New York, Silicon Valley, Washington, DC.

Saudi Arabia:—*Revision by* White & Case LLP of New York and Law Office of Hassan Mahassni in Association with White & Case of Jeddah.

Scotland:—*Revision by* Digby Brown, of Glasgow.

Singapore:—*Revision by* David Chong & Co., of Singapore.

Slovak Republic:—*Revision by* Čechová, Rakovský, of Bratislava.

South Africa:—*Revision by* Cliffe Dekker Fuller Moore Inc, of Johannesburg.

Spain:—*Revision by* Garrigues & Andersen, of Madrid.

Sweden:—*Revision by* Baker & McKenzie Advokatbyrå, of Stockholm.

Switzerland:—*Revision by* Pestalozzi Gmuer & Patry, of Zurich.

Taiwan:—*Revision by* Lee and Li, of Taipei.

Thailand:—*Revision by* Tilleke & Gibbins, of Bangkok, and Hanoi and Ho Chi Minh City, Vietnam and Phnom Penh, Cambodia.

Turkey:—*Revision by* Yilmaz Öz, of Ankara.

Ukraine:—*Revision by* Altheimer & Gray, of Chicago, IL and Kyiv, Ukraine.

Uruguay:—*Revision by* Curtis, Mallet-Prevost, Colt & Mosle, of New York City.

Venezuela:—*Revision by* Curtis, Mallet-Prevost, Colt & Mosle, of New York City.

ACKNOWLEDGMENTS

Vietnam:—*Revision by* Tilleke & Gibbins Consultants Limited, of Bangkok, Thailand, and Hanoi and Ho Chi Minh City, Vietnam and Phnom Penh, Cambodia.

PART VI

SELECTED INTERNATIONAL CONVENTIONS

The annotations have been graciously provided by the U.S. Department of State.

Part I

Digests

OF THE LAWS OF

THE STATES, THE DISTRICT OF COLUMBIA, PUERTO RICO AND THE

VIRGIN ISLANDS

(For list of digests see next page)

UNITED STATES DIGESTS

ALABAMA [AL]
ALASKA [AK]
ARIZONA [AZ]
ARKANSAS [AR]
CALIFORNIA [CA]
COLORADO [CO]
CONNECTICUT [CT]
DELAWARE [DE]
DISTRICT OF COLUMBIA [DC]
FLORIDA [FL]
GEORGIA [GA]
HAWAII [HI]
IDAHO [ID]
ILLINOIS [IL]
INDIANA [IN]
IOWA [IA]
KANSAS [KS]
KENTUCKY [KY]
LOUISIANA [LA]
MAINE [ME]
MARYLAND [MD]
MASSACHUSETTS [MA]
MICHIGAN [MI]
MINNESOTA [MN]
MISSISSIPPI [MS]
MISSOURI [MO]
MONTANA [MT]

NEBRASKA [NE]
NEVADA [NV]
NEW HAMPSHIRE [NH]
NEW JERSEY [NJ]
NEW MEXICO [NM]
NEW YORK [NY]
NORTH CAROLINA [NC]
NORTH DAKOTA [ND]
OHIO [OH]
OKLAHOMA [OK]
OREGON [OR]
PENNSYLVANIA [PA]
PUERTO RICO [PR]
RHODE ISLAND [RI]
SOUTH CAROLINA [SC]
SOUTH DAKOTA [SD]
TENNESSEE [TN]
TEXAS [TX]
UTAH [UT]
VERMONT [VT]
VIRGIN ISLANDS [VI]
VIRGINIA [VA]
WASHINGTON [WA]
WEST VIRGINIA [WV]
WISCONSIN [WI]
WYOMING [WY]

Note: Abbreviations for page numbers appear in brackets.

ALABAMA LAW DIGEST REVISER

Bradley Arant Rose & White LLP
Main Office:
2001 Park Place, Suite 1400
Birmingham, Alabama 35203-2736
Telephone: 205-521-8000
Fax: 205-521-8800

Other Birmingham Office: SouthTrust Tower Office, 420 North 20th Street, Suite 2000, 35203-3268.
Telephone: 205-521-8000. Fax: 205-521-8500.

Huntsville Office: 200 Clinton Avenue West, Suite 900, 35801-4900. Telephone: 205-517-5100.
Fax: 205-517-5200.

Reviser Profile

History: Bradley Arant Rose & White LLP was organized in 1904 as Tillman, Grubb, Bradley & Morrow in Birmingham, Alabama; the firm has practiced under its current name since 1963. The firm is the largest in the state, with more than one hundred sixty lawyers, maintaining two offices in Birmingham and one in Huntsville.

Client Base: The firm is general counsel for several enterprises listed on national stock exchanges, for two banks, including the largest bank holding company in Alabama, and serves as regional counsel for a number of national banks, savings banks and other financial institutions. The many individuals, partnerships, corporations, proprietorships, state and local governments and governmental agencies which are clients of the firm engage in a broad variety of businesses and activities, including banking, biotechnology, health care, transportation, energy production and distribution, construction, government contracting, soft drink bottling, timber, pulp and paper, steel, real estate development, publishing, textile and garment trades, manufacturing, materials and aggregate production, coal and mineral mining and distribution, vehicle and equipment leasing, communications, public utilities, and other activities, both domestically and internationally.

Areas of Practice: The largest and most distinct areas of practice of the firm are, alphabetically, as follows:

Antitrust and Trade Practices: The firm represents clients in antitrust and trade practices actions brought under both federal and state antitrust laws, including criminal antitrust prosecution. The firm regularly advises clients on antitrust issues and provides training for antitrust compliance programs.

Banking: The firm offers a full-service banking practice, including acquisition and disposition of financial institutions and branches, regulatory and compliance advice, consumer credit and retail banking, bank holding company matters, commercial lending transactions, and trust services.

Bankruptcy: The firm represents a broad range of creditors and business debtors in insolvency and debt restructuring, negotiations and proceedings, including complex business reorganizations, workouts, corporate restructuring, forbearance agreements, and formal bankruptcy and insolvency proceedings in federal and state courts.

Construction and Government Contracts: The firm's construction law practice is well known regionally, nationally, and internationally for the assistance we provide to clients engaged in domestic and foreign construction projects. The firm's construction practice includes contract negotiation and administration, insurance issues and claims, construction "failure" investigation and claims, safety and other government requirements, federal and state procurement issues, private and government contract claims review, presentation and resolution of both private and government claims before federal and state courts, Boards of Contract Appeals, domestic and international arbitration tribunals, mediators, and other types of alternative dispute resolution. The firm's lawyers also frequently serve as arbitrators or mediators in disputes.

Corporate and Securities: The firm is experienced in all aspects of general business, corporate and securities matters, including equity and debt financings, recapitalizations and other reorganizations, stock and asset purchase and sale transactions, mergers, partnership matters, employee stock ownership plans, venture capital transactions, franchising, licensing matters, syndications and public and private securities offerings.

Employee Benefits: The firm provides services with respect to all tax and nontax aspects of the establishment, operation and termination of welfare benefit plans and deferred compensation plans, represents clients before the Internal Revenue Service, the Department of Labor, and the Pension Benefit Guaranty Corporation, and litigates on behalf of employers, fiduciaries and employee benefit plans.

Environmental and Toxic Tort: The firm routinely advises clients on various environmental issues encountered in the acquisition, ownership, financing, operation and sale of businesses, including permitting matters and compliance with federal, state and local environmental laws. The firm also litigates a wide variety of environmental issues in administrative and civil proceedings.

Health Care: The firm represents numerous health care providers on a variety of health care related issues, including administrative and regulatory matters, the formation of integrated delivery systems and managed care programs, compliance issues, false claims/*qui tam* cases, reimbursement issues, medical staff issues, patient care matters and corporate issues ranging from mergers and acquisitions to licensure and CON matters.

Intellectual Property: The firm's intellectual property practice, which includes three registered patent attorneys, provides expertise in trademark, trade secret, copyright and patent matters. The firm is an active member of the International Trademark Association.

Labor and Employment Law: The firm's practice includes representation of management—public and private—in all areas of labor and employment related law, including litigation before state and federal courts and various administrative agencies, including the EEOC, NLRB, OFCCP, OSHA and the Wage and Hour Division, among others.

Litigation: The firm's practice includes representation of clients before all courts and administrative tribunals in Alabama, trial and appellate courts in a number of other states, in the federal courts, state and federal grand jury proceedings and domestic and international arbitration tribunals. The firm's litigation lawyers are involved in most types of litigation, including defense of product liability and toxic tort cases, class action cases, commercial litigation, including securities regulation, corporate takeovers, antitrust, business torts, consumer torts, construction and government contract disputes, intellectual property matters, employee benefits, environmental matters and First Amendment cases.

Public and Project Finance: The firm has long maintained a leadership position in the region in the public finance field, serving as bond counsel to the State of Alabama and its agencies, as well as to many counties, cities, utility boards, boards of education, hospitals, institutions of higher education and public corporations. The firm also regularly serves as underwriter's counsel with respect to offering of municipal securities. The firm's public finance, real estate, corporate and securities practices also include project finance.

Real Estate: The firm regularly represents clients in major real estate financing projects. In addition, our real estate group has expertise in all issues commonly encountered in the acquisition and development of real estate, including land use and zoning matters.

Tax, Trusts and Estates: The firm's tax practice encompasses a wide variety of federal, state, local and international tax matters. The firm provides a full range of tax-related services for corporations, partnerships, individuals and nonprofit organizations, including ERISA, executive compensation and employee benefit matters. The firm also provides tax and planning services in estate planning, estate and trust administration and estate litigation, including will drafting and planning, settlements of estates and will contests.

Firm Activities: All attorneys are members of the American Bar Association and the Alabama State Bar. One partner is a recent past president of the Alabama State Bar; three are Fellows of the American College of Trial Lawyers; three are Fellows of the American College of Tax Counsel; two are Fellows of the American College of Trust and Estate Counsel; two are Fellows of the American College of Construction Lawyers; one is a Fellow of the American College of Bankruptcy; one is a Fellow of the American College of Bond Lawyers; two are Fellows of the College of Labor and Employment Lawyers; and, one is a Fellow of the American College of Mortgage Attorneys. Three partners are also members of the American Law Institute. Partners also are members of or are affiliated with the National Association of Bond Lawyers, the American Board of Trial Advisors, the International Association of Defense Counsel, the National Association of Railroad Trial Counsel, the American Tax Policy Institute, the Southern Federal Tax Institute, the American Bankruptcy Institute, the Product Liability Advisory Council, the Alabama Law Institute, the American Association of Tax Counsel, and the International Bar Association. Partners also serve as adjunct faculty at the University of Alabama School of Law and the Cumberland School of Law.

ALABAMA LAW DIGEST

(The following is a list of all Categories and Topics, including cross-references, covered in this Digest.)

ALABAMA LAW DIGEST

Revised for 1999 edition by

BRADLEY ARANT ROSE & WHITE LLP of the Birmingham Bar

(Citations, unless otherwise noted, are to Code of 1975. Citations are to title, chapter, and section. Session laws are cited by year, type session if other than regular session, and act number. Alabama Rules of Civil Procedure cited as "ARCP." Alabama Rules of Appellate Procedure cited as "ARAP." Alabama Rules of Juvenile Procedure cited as "ARJP." Alabama Civil Court Mediation Rules cited as "ACCMR." Parallel Citations to the Southern Reporter begin with 81 Ala. and 1 Ala. App. Citations to Ala. end at 295 Ala., and citations to Ala. App. end at 57 Ala. App. All subsequent citations are to So.2d only, beginning with 331 So.2d. Citations to "WL" are to the Westlaw online legal database service. See also category Courts and Legislature, topic Reports.)

NOTE: This Revision covers all Acts of the Alabama Legislature through the 1998 Regular Session.

INTRODUCTION

GOVERNMENT AND LEGAL SYSTEM:

The State of Alabama is a constituent state of the United States of America. For further discussion of the U.S. federal system, see Introduction to the Federal Government of the United States at the beginning of this volume. A great many laws are promulgated by the federal government of the United States and are not reflected in the topics below. See the Introduction to this volume for references to the federal law topics covered.

Like all but one of the United States, Alabama has a common law legal system, with roots in English common law. For information on the courts and legislature of Alabama, see category Courts and Legislature.

HOLIDAYS:

Holidays are: Sundays, Christmas Day, New Year's Day, Martin Luther King, Jr.'s birthday (3d Mon. in Jan.), Robert E. Lee's birthday (3d Mon. in Jan.), George Washington's birthday (3d Mon. in Feb.), Thomas Jefferson's birthday (3d Mon. in Feb.), Confederate Memorial Day (4th Mon. in Apr.), National Memorial Day, Jefferson Davis' birthday (1st Mon. in June), 4th of July, Labor Day, Columbus Day and Fraternal Day (2d Mon. in Oct.), Veteran's Day (11th day of Nov.) and day designated by governor for public Thanksgiving. Mardi Gras is legal holiday in Mobile and Baldwin Counties.

Holiday Falling on Sun.—Observed following Mon.

Holiday Falling on Sat.—Observed preceding Fri.

Legality of Transactions on Sat., Sun. or Holiday.—Bank may do business on any legal holiday except Sun. and may use automated teller machine on any day. (5-5A-30-31). 1975 Code repealed Tit. 9, §21 of 1958 Code which declared void all contracts made on Sun.

OFFICE HOURS AND TIME ZONE:

Alabama is in the Central (GMT −06:00) time zone. Office hours are generally from 9 a.m. to 5 p.m.

BUSINESS ORGANIZATIONS

AGENCY:

Formalities.—Determination of agency based on whether alleged principal has retained right of control over actions of alleged agent. (640 So.2d 940). Relationship of principal and agent created by express or implied contract or operation of law. (676 F. Supp. 1134).

Revocation.—Agency without interest may be revoked orally. Sufficiency or effectiveness of revocation depends on facts of case. Courts consider whether principal gave notice of revocation to agent and parties likely to deal with agent. (988 F.2d 1117).

Common law rules apply.

Authority.—Agent has authority to: (1) do everything necessary, or proper or usual, in ordinary course of business, for effecting purpose of his agency; (2) to make representation respecting any matter of fact, not including terms of his authority, but upon which his right to use his authority depends, and truth of which cannot be determined by use of reasonable diligence on part of person to whom representation is made. (8-2-4).

Agent to Sell.—Entrusted by principal with possession of thing sold, has authority to receive price. (8-2-2). Special agent to sell has authority to receive price on delivery of thing sold, but not afterwards. (8-2-3).

Notice.—As against principal, both principal and agent deemed to have notice of whatever either has notice of, and ought, in good faith and exercise of ordinary care and diligence, to communicate to the other. (8-2-8).

Binding the Principal.—Apparent authority binding when third party in good faith and exercising due care incurs liability or gives value on reliance. (8-2-6).

Set Offs.—Third party may set off, against any claim of principal arising out of same, all claims which he might have set off against agent before notice of agency. (8-2-9).

Negligence.—Unless required by or under authority of law to employ that particular agent, principal is responsible to third parties for negligence of his agent in transaction of business of agency, including wrongful acts committed by such agent in and as part of transaction of such business, and for agent's wilful omission to fulfil obligations of principal. (8-2-7).

Liability.—Corporation liable for slanderous utterance made within line and scope of agent's employment; requirement of prior authorization or subsequent ratification overruled. (385 So.2d 630).

Members of Armed Forces.—No statutory provision.

Warranty.—Person acting as agent thereby warrants, to all who deal with him in that capacity, that he has authority. (8-2-5).

See category Property, topic Powers of Attorney.

ASSOCIATIONS:

Generally, no statutory or common law definition of unincorporated association; common law definition presumptively in effect. Specific forms of unincorporated associations regulated by statute. (10-4-1 to -323). Uniform Unincorporated Nonprofit Association Act adopted with modifications. (10-3B-1, et seq.).

Formation.—No general statutory provisions governing formation of unincorporated associations; common law methods presumptively in effect. Organization of certain specific associations governed by statute. (10-4-1 to -323).

Rights and Powers.—Unincorporated association has power to adopt constitution and enact bylaws, rules and regulations that are not illegal or contrary to public policy. (387 So.2d 140). Constitution, bylaws, rules and regulations constitute contract between members, which is binding upon each member. (387 So.2d 140).

Generally, absent statute unincorporated association without capacity to acquire and hold legal title to real property. (281 Ala. 297, 202 So.2d 83). Statutory provisions expressly authorize certain unincorporated associations to take, hold, convey and defend interest in real property. (10-4-4; 10-4-21; 10-4-41; 10-4-60; 10-4-133; 10-4-192; 10-4-320).

Liabilities.—Unincorporated association may be liable in tort for wrongful acts of members acting collectively in business for which association organized, and responsible for torts of members or employees which association encourages or ratifies. (599 So.2d 9).

Actions.—Actions may be maintained by and in name of unincorporated association and against and in name of any such association for any cause of action upon which members of such organization may be sued. (6-7-80; -81). Property of unincorporated association may be liable for satisfaction of judgment. (6-7-81).

Dissolution.—No specific statutory or common law provision.

Professional Associations.—

Note: Following discussion applies only to professional associations organized prior to Jan. 1, 1984. New professional associations may not be formed in Alabama after that date. (10-10-2[b]). Professional corporations may still be formed. See topic Corporations, subhead Professional Corporations.

Formation by any one or more persons duly licensed to practice profession who desire to associate for purpose of rendering one particular type of professional service. (10-10-4).

Professional association means an unincorporated association as distinguished from partnership; professional service means any type of professional service which requires license from state court or regulatory licensing board or other like agency. (10-10-1).

Articles of association must be executed and recorded in office of probate court in county in which association's principal office located. Recording fee $2.50 plus 15¢ per 100 words. (10-10-5). Within 30 days after organization and within 30 days after Nov. 1 of each year statement must be filed with Secretary of State showing names and addresses of all members or shareholders certifying that all duly licensed to practice in Ala. $50 penalty for failure to file. (10-10-10).

Name for association at discretion of associators but must have suffix "Professional Association" or "P.A." (10-10-5).

Rights and Powers.—Association may render only one specific kind of professional service and cannot engage in any other business. (10-10-6). May own real or personal property appropriate for rendering professional service. (10-10-6). May invest its funds in real estate, mortgages, stocks, bonds, or any other type of investment. (10-10-6). May render services through officers, employees and agents duly licensed within state (10-10-12). May contract in own name, take, hold and sell real and personal property in name and likewise sue and be sued. (10-10-9). Conveyance in name of association executed by president and attested by secretary is conclusive against association, board of governors and members. (10-10-9).

Ownership.—Articles of association may provide for stock-type or nonstock organization. Membership if nonstock, or stock or certificate of membership if stock-type, is freely tranferrable absent limitations in articles of association. Stock purchase or membership limited to persons duly licensed to render same professional services. (10-10-7).

Governing body is board of governors elected by members or shareholders and represented by officers elected by board. Bylaws may be promulgated by members or authority to promulgate may be delegated to board of governors in articles. (10-10-8).

Existence continued as separate entity independent of members or shareholders for period of time provided in articles or until dissolved by two-thirds vote. Partnership dissolution laws not applicable. (10-10-15).

Liabilities.—Members or shareholders not individually liable for debts or claims against association unless such individual personally participated in transaction giving

ASSOCIATIONS . . . *continued*
rise to debt or claim. (10-10-11). Assets of professional association not liable to attachment for individual debt of member or shareholder. (10-10-9).

Laws applicable to relationship between person furnishing professional service and person receiving such service, including liability arising out of such professional service and laws governing confidential relationships, not modified. (10-10-11).

Dissolution.—In stock-type associations, board of governors as trustees apply assets first to payment of debts of association and then to holders of stock as per articles. (10-10-16). In nonstock-type associations, assets distributed or sold and net proceeds applied first to payment of association's debts and remainder distributed to members as per articles. (10-10-16).

See topic Corporations, subhead Professional Corporations.

CORPORATIONS:

For unincorporated associations, see topic Associations.

Alabama Business Corporation Act (10-2B-1.01, et seq.) based on Revised Model Business Corporation Act (1984), which is reprinted in Part III of this publication. Certain material deviations from Revised Model Business Corporation Act set out below.

General Supervision.—Secretary of State, Corporate Division, 11 South Union Street, Montgomery, Alabama 36104.

Purposes.—May be organized under chapter for any lawful purpose or purposes. (10-2B-3.01).

Name.—For any corporation organized after Jan. 1, 1981 or that amends articles after that date to change name, corporate name must contain word "corporation", or "incorporated", or abbreviation of those words, or if banking corporation words "bank", "banking", or "bankers". (10-2B-4.01). Corporate name may not be same as or deceptively similar to: (1) Name of corporation incorporated or authorized to transact business in state; (2) name reserved or registered under §4.02 or 4.03; or (3) fictitious name adopted by foreign corporation authorized to transact business in state because its real name unavailable. (10-2B-4.01).

Term of Corporate Existence.—Unless delayed effective date specified, corporate existence begins when articles of incorporation filed. (10-2B-2.03). Unless articles of incorporation provide otherwise, corporation has perpetual duration. (10-2B-3.02).

Incorporators.—One or more persons may act as incorporator(s). (10-2B-2.01). "Person" means "individual" or "entity." (10-2B-1.40[17]).

Articles of Incorporation.—Names and addresses of initial directors and purposes of corporation must be stated. (10-2B-2.02). In addition to items stated in Model Act, articles of incorporation may state that right to adopt initial bylaws of incorporation is reserved to shareholders. (10-2B-2.02). Unlike Model Act, Act does not permit articles of incorporation to specify that personal liability may be imposed against shareholders for debts of corporation or to eliminate or limit liability of director for breach of director's duty of loyalty to corporation or shareholders. (10-2B-2.02). Two copies of articles of incorporation must be filed. (10-2B-1.25).

Filing of Articles.—Articles of incorporation must be filed with probate judge of county of corporation's initial registered office. (10-2B-2.01).

Incorporation Tax or Fee.—Fees for filing of articles of incorporation: $40 to Alabama Secretary of State; and $35 to probate judge in county of incorporation. (10-2B-1.22).

License to Do Business.—Unless delayed effective date specified, corporate existence begins when articles of incorporation filed. (10-2B-2.03). For authority to transact business for foreign corporations, see subhead Foreign Corporations, infra.

Organization.—Initial directors named in articles of incorporation conduct organizational meeting. (10-2B-2.05).

Paid in Capital Requirements.—No statutory provision.

Amendment of Articles.—Corporation may amend articles of incorporation at any time to add or change provision required or permitted in articles, or to delete provision not required in articles. (10-2B-10.01). Board of directors may amend articles without shareholder action in certain circumstances. (10-2B-10.02). Generally, board of directors submits proposed amendments to shareholders for vote. (10-2B-10.03).

Increase or Decrease of Authorized Capital Stock.—If authorized capital stock to be increased to accommodate stock split and corporation has only that class of outstanding stock, increase in authorized shares may be accomplished by amendment of articles by board of directors. (10-2B-10.02[4]). Other amendments to articles of incorporation regarding stock must be approved by shareholders. (10-2B-10.03).

Bylaws.—Unless right to adopt initial bylaws reserved to shareholders in articles of incorporation, board of directors adopts initial bylaws. (10-2B-2.06). Bylaws may contain any provision regulating affairs of corporation not inconsistent with law or articles of incorporation. (10-2B-2.06).

Stock.—Articles of incorporation must prescribe classes of shares and number of shares in each class corporation is authorized to issue. (10-2B-6.01[a]). If more than one class authorized, articles must prescribe distinguishing designation for each class and preferences, limitations, and relative rights of each class. (10-2B-6.01[a]). Articles must authorize at least one class with unlimited voting rights, and at least one class entitled to receive net assets of corporation upon dissolution. (10-2B-6.01[b]).

Share Certificates.—Unless articles or bylaws provide otherwise, board of directors may authorize issue of some or all of shares of any or all of corporation's classes or series without certificates. (10-2B-6.26[a]). After issue or transfer of shares without certificates, corporation must send shareholder written statement of certain information. (10-2B-6.26[b]).

Issuance of Shares.—Shares may be issued for money, labor done or property actually received. (10-2B-6.21).

Transfer of Stock.—Articles of incorporation, bylaws, agreement among shareholders, or agreement between shareholders and corporation may restrict right to transfer stock. (10-2B-6.27). Restriction must be noted conspicuously on front or back of stock certificate or be contained in information statement required by 10-2B-6.26(b). (10-2B-6.27). Even if not so noted, restriction enforceable against person with actual knowledge of restriction. (10-2B-6.27).

Uniform Simplification of Fiduciary Security Transfers Act repealed eff. Jan. 1, 1997.

Uniform Commercial Code adopted. (7-1-101, et seq.). Uniform Simplification of Fiduciary Security Transfers Act survives and controls if any inconsistency with Uniform Commercial Code. (7-10-104[2]). See category Business Regulation and Commerce, topic Commercial Code.

Stock Transfer Tax.—None.

Shareholders.—§1.42 of Model Act not adopted. Shareholder has preemptive rights except as limited in articles of incorporation. No preemptive rights as to shares issued as, or in connection with, compensation or shares sold for consideration other than money. (10-2B-6.30).

Shareholders' Actions.—§7.40 of Model Act regarding derivative actions not adopted. Common law rules regarding such actions apply. Shareholders may commence judicial proceeding to remove director for fraud, dishonesty, or gross abuse of authority. (10-2B-8.09). Minority shareholders may commence proceeding against majority shareholders and directors for oppression, particularly in close corporation. (621 So.2d 1235). See also subhead Appraisal, infra.

Shareholders' Liabilities.—Shareholders not personally liable for acts or debts of corporation. (10-2B-6.22).

Shareholders' Meetings.—Once holders of at least 10% of votes entitled to be cast at special meeting properly request such meeting, then corporation must, within 21 days of receipt of such demand, cause notice to be given of meeting. (10-2B-7.02). If notice not delivered, or if special meeting not held, holders of at least 10% of votes entitled to be cast may call special meeting. (10-2B-7.02). Court may order meeting if annual meeting not held within earlier of 12 months after end of fiscal year or 15 months after last annual meeting. (10-2B-7.03).

Stock or bonded indebtedness of corporation may not be increased at meeting unless notice of such meeting given under §234 of Constitution of Alabama. (10-2B-7.05).

Corporation may accept authority of revoked proxy, unless notice of such revocation received by corporation before proxy exercised. (10-2B-7.22).

Except as provided in articles, action required or permitted to be taken at shareholders meeting may be taken without meeting if action taken by all shareholders entitled to vote and evidenced by written consent signed by all shareholders entitled to vote. (10-2B-7.04[a]).

Voting Trusts.—One or more shareholders may create voting trust by signing agreement setting out provisions of trust and transferring shares to trustee. (10-2B-7.30).

Directors.—Director must be at least 19 years old. (10-2B-8.02).

Classes.—If articles authorize dividing shares into classes, articles may authorize elections of all or specified number of directors by holders of one or more authorized classes of shares. (10-2B-8.04).

Directors' Meetings.—May be held in or out of state. (10-2B-8.20). Director deemed present in person at meeting if using means of communication whereby he and other persons participating in meeting may simultaneously hear each other during meeting. (10-2B-8.20). Regular meetings of board of directors may be held with or without notice as prescribed by bylaws. (10-2B-8.22). Unless articles of incorporation or bylaws provide otherwise, special meetings require at least two days' notice of date, time, and place of meeting. (10-2B-8.22). Unless articles of incorporation or bylaws require greater number, quorum consists of majority of fixed number of directors if corporation has fixed board size, or majority of fixed number of directors prescribed, or if no number prescribed number in office immediately before meeting begins, if corporation has variable-range size board. (10-2B-8.24). Unless articles of incorporation or bylaws provide otherwise, action required or permitted to be taken at board of directors' meeting may be taken without meeting if taken by all members of board and evidenced by one or more written consents describing action taken and signed by each director. (10-2B-8.21).

Powers and Duties of Directors.—Corporate powers exercised by or under authority of, and business and affairs of corporation managed under direction of, board of directors, subject to articles or agreement authorized under §10-2B-7.32. (10-2B-8.01[b]).

Liabilities of Directors.—§§8.31 and 8.32 not adopted. Fiduciary obligations of directors, officers, employees and controlling shareholders not abrogated or limited by Act. (10-2B-8.31). Director or officer must not act with intent to depreciate stocks or bonds with further intent to buy depreciated stocks or bonds. (10-2B-8.32). Director must discharge duties in good faith, with care ordinarily prudent person in like position would exercise under similar circumstances, and in manner director reasonably believes to be in best interests of corporation. (10-2B-8.30[a]).

Officers.—Corporation has officers described in bylaws or appointed by board of directors; no requirement for specific officers in Act. (10-2B-8.40). Unless bylaws provide otherwise, same person may hold more than one office. (10-2B-8.40[d]).

Liabilities of Officers.—Officer must discharge duties in good faith, with care ordinarily prudent person in like position would exercise under similar circumstances, and in manner officer reasonably believes to be in best interests of corporation. (10-2B-8.42[a]). See also subhead Liabilities of Directors, supra.

Indemnification of Directors and Officers.—In addition to purchasing indemnification insurance on behalf of directors, officers, employees, and agents, corporation may furnish similar protection, including but not limited to trust funds and self-insurance reserves. (10-2B-8.57)

Principal Office.—No statutory provision. Corporation must continuously maintain registered office in state, which may be same as any of its places of business. (10-2B-5.01; 10-2B-15.07).

See note at head of Digest as to 1998 legislation covered.

See Topical Index in front part of this volume.

AL – 2

CORPORATIONS . . . *continued*

Resident Agent.—Corporation must continuously maintain registered agent in state. (10-2B-5.01). If none, or agent cannot with reasonable diligence be served, corporation may be served as provided by ARCP. (10-2B-5.04).

General Powers of Corporations.—Unless articles of incorporation provide otherwise, corporation has same powers as individual to do all things necessary or convenient to conduct business. (10-2B-3.02). Ultra vires defense eliminated by 10-2B-3.04, except for specific instances cited therein. (407 F.Supp. 1270; 479 So.2d 720).

Dividends.—Right to declare dividends limited by articles of incorporation and 10-2B-6.40(c). (10-2B-6.40[a]). Distributions to shareholders prohibited where, following distribution, corporation would be unable to pay debts as due in ordinary course, or corporation's total assets would be less than sum of total liabilities plus amount required to satisfy preferential rights, upon dissolution, of shareholders whose preferential rights superior to those receiving distribution. (10-2B-6.40[c]). Directors can be held personally liable for unlawful declarations of dividends. (10-2B-8.33).

Unclaimed Dividends.—See category Property, topic Absentees, subhead Escheat.

Sale or Transfer of Corporate Assets.—Statutory authority limited by Constitution of Alabama. (10-2B-12.02). Sale or transfer, otherwise than in usual and regular course of business, must be generally recommended by board to shareholders and approved by each voting group entitled to vote, by two-thirds of all votes of such group entitled to be cast. (10-2B-12.02).

Books and Records.—Foreign corporations having principal offices in Alabama subject to same recordkeeping requirements imposed upon domestic corporations. (10-2B-16.01). Any shareholder of domestic corporation or of foreign corporation who has been shareholder of record for 180 days immediately preceding his or her demand or who is holder of record of at least 5% of all outstanding shares (or voting trust certificates) of corporation, upon written demand stating purpose thereof, has right to examine, at any reasonable time or times, for any proper purpose, books and records of account, minutes, and record of shareholders by giving corporation written notice of demand at least five business days before date on which he or she wishes to inspect and copy such records. (10-2B-16.02). If corporation engaged in banking, records of borrowers and depositors who are neither officers, directors or employees nor related to or engaged in business with officers, directors or employees are not subject to examination without court order after in camera inspection; records of bank corporation do not include reports of examination by state or federal supervisory agencies. (10-2B-16.02). Any officer, agent, or corporation refusing to allow examination without reasonable cause liable to shareholder making demand for penalty of amount not to exceed 10% of value of shares owned by shareholder. (10-2B-16.02).

Reports.—Domestic and foreign corporations doing business in Alabama must, between Jan. 1 and Mar. 15 of each year, file with Secretary of State annual report setting forth: (1) Name of corporation and state of incorporation; (2) address of registered office and name of registered agent; (3) address of principal office including, in case of foreign corporation, address of principal office in Alabama or state of incorporation; (4) names and addresses of president and secretary; and (5) brief statement of character of business in Alabama. (10-2B-16.22). Filing of public record information filed with Department of Revenue may serve as annual report, provided $10 fee to State of Alabama accompanies filing. (10-2B-16.22).

Corporate Bonds or Mortgages.—Subject to limitations of Constitution of Alabama of 1901, corporation may mortgage or otherwise encumber any or all of its property, whether or not in usual and regular course of business. (10-2B-12.01).

Merger and Consolidation.—Statutory authority limited by Constitution of Alabama. (10-2B-11.01). Board of directors of each corporation must adopt, and shareholders of each corporation (if required by §10-2B-11.03) must approve, plan of merger. (10-2B-11.01). Transaction must be approved by each voting group entitled to vote by two-thirds of all votes of such group entitled to be cast. (10-2B-11.03). Parent corporation must own at least 80% of outstanding shares of each class of subsidiary corporation to merge subsidiary into parent without approval of shareholders of parent or subsidiary. (10-2B-11.04).

Claims existing against corporation party to merger may be prosecuted as if merger had not taken place, or surviving corporation may be substituted in action for corporation whose existence ceased. (10-2B-11.06).

Share Exchanges or Acquisitions.—Subject to limitations of Constitution of Alabama of 1901, corporation may acquire all outstanding shares of another corporation if board of directors of each corporation adopts plan of exchange and, if required by 10-2B-11.03, shareholders approve plan of exchange. (10-2B-11.02[a]). Plan of exchange must set forth name of corporation whose shares will be acquired, name of acquiring corporation, terms and conditions of exchange, and manner and basis of exchange. (10-2B-11.02[b]).

Tender Offers.—No specific statutory provision, but see subhead Share Exchanges or Acquisitions, supra, and subhead Merger and Consolidation, infra.

Dissolution.—Voluntary dissolution may be effected by: (1) Unanimous written consent of shareholders; or (2) resolution of board of directors followed by recommendation of board to shareholders that corporation be dissolved. (10-2B-14.02). Unless articles of incorporation provide for greater or lesser vote, but in no event less than majority vote, proposal to dissolve must be approved by each voting group entitled to vote by two-thirds of all votes entitled to be cast by that voting group. (10-2B-14.02). If corporation dissolved by written consent of shareholders, must be stated in articles of dissolution and copy of written consents of shareholders must be attached thereto. (10-2B-14.03). Articles of dissolution, and articles of revocation if corporation elects to revoke its dissolution, filed with probate judge of county in which corporation's articles of incorporation filed. (10-2B-14.03). Dissolution does not affect limited liability of shareholders, except with respect to value of assets distributed to shareholders in liquidation of corporation. (10-2B-14.05). Dissolved corporation that publishes notice of dissolution in newspaper of general circulation in county in which principal office located is not subject to unknown claims unless claimant commences proceeding to enforce claim within two years of publication of such notice. (10-2B-14.07). Secretary of State may seek to administratively dissolve corporation if corporation has not filed annual report within six months after due, or upon certain other conditions. (10-2B-14.20; -.21).

Insolvency and Receivers.—Creditor may institute dissolution proceeding against corporation if creditor has obtained judgment against corporation, execution on judgment returned unsatisfied, and corporation insolvent, or if corporation admits in writing creditor's claim owing and corporation insolvent. (10-2B-14.30). Court may appoint receiver to wind up business of and liquidate corporation. (10-2B-14.32). Individual, domestic corporation, foreign corporation authorized to do business in state, or other entity may serve as receiver. (10-2B-14.32). Court may require receiver to post bond. (10-2B-14.32).

Close Corporations.—If formed before Jan. 1, 1995 governed by §10-2A-300 to -313.

Appraisal.—Shareholder entitled to dissent from, and obtain payment of fair value of shares in event of, certain corporate actions set forth in 10-2B-13.02. To assert dissenters' rights, shareholder must deliver to corporation, prior to shareholder vote on proposed action, written notice of intent to demand payment if proposed action is taken, and must not vote shares in favor of proposed action. (10-2B-13.21). Upon receipt of payment demand from dissenter or as soon as proposed action taken, corporation must offer to pay dissenter amount corporation estimates to be fair value of dissenter's shares, plus accrued interest. (10-2B-13.25). If dissenter dissatisfied with corporation's offer of payment, dissenter must notify corporation in writing of dissenter's estimate of fair value of shares and interest due, and demand payment of dissenter's estimate. (10-2B-13.28). Corporation may then petition court to determine fair value of shares and accrued interest. (10-2B-13.30[a]). All dissenters, whether or not residents of state, whose demands remain unsettled are parties to appraisal proceeding and must be served with copy of appraisal petition. (10-2B-13.30[c]). Costs of appraisal proceeding generally assessed against corporation, unless dissenters acted arbitrarily, vexatiously, or not in good faith. (10-2B-13.31).

Foreign Corporation.—May not maintain action without certificate of authority. (10-2B-15.02). All contracts made in state by foreign corporations prior to obtaining certificate of authority void at action of foreign corporation or any person claiming through or under foreign corporation by virtue of contract. (10-2B-15.02[a]). Service of process upon foreign corporation is made upon registered agent of foreign corporation in accordance with ARCP. (10-2B-15.10).

Any corporation or bank of any other state or national bank or corporation organized under laws of U.S. located in another state may act as fiduciary in Alabama without qualification if: (1) Files verified statement with commissioner of revenue and appoints commissioner to receive service of process, (2) it is authorized by laws of own state to act as fiduciary, and (3) laws of own state extend same privileges to Alabama banks on same terms. (10-2B-15.40 to -.45).

Taxation of Corporate Property.—See category Taxation, topics Income Tax, subhead Income-Taxed Corporations; Property (Ad Valorem) Taxes; Unemployment Compensation Tax.

Taxation of Corporate Shares.—Shares subject to ad valorem taxation. (40-14-70-74). See category Taxation, topic Corporate Stock Tax.

Franchise Tax.—Domestic or foreign corporation must make annual report to department of revenue for fixing franchise tax between Jan. 1 and Mar. 15. (40-14-44).

First franchise tax return must be filed and tax due paid thereon by domestic corporation within ten days of organization and by foreign corporation within ten days of qualification. (40-14-53; -54).

Rate of franchise tax: Domestic corporations (except benevolent, educational or religious), $10 per $1,000 of capital stock but never less than total sum of $50 (40-14-40); foreign corporations (except benevolent, educational or religious) $3 per $1,000 of capital employed in Ala., but never less than total sum of $25 (40-14-41). Intangible property belonging to foreign corporation and located elsewhere may be taxable as capital employed in state if corporation carries on principal part of its management functions in Ala. (263 Ala. 533, 83 So.2d 42; 275 Ala. 46, 151 So.2d 778).

Unless foreign corporation dealer in securities, for purpose of determining franchise tax on foreign corporation, exclusion from capital of foreign corporation is allowed equal to amount invested in capital stock of other corporations organized under laws of Ala. or under law of any other state if other corporations also pay franchise tax to state of Ala. (40-14-41[d][1]). In case of foreign corporation (including bank or bank holding company), exclusion from capital of foreign corporation of investment by corporation in capital of any other corporation that does not pay franchise tax to Ala. if foreign corporation owns more than 50% of stock of other corporation, unless other corporation dormant. (40-14-41[d][2]-[3]). For foreign corporations, further deductions from capital employed in Ala. allowed in amounts of: (1) Aggregate amount of loans which have been made by such foreign corporation in Ala. and which are secured by mortgages on real estate in Ala. upon which mortgage recording privilege tax has been paid (see category Taxation, topic Real Estate Conveyance Tax); (2) amount invested by such foreign corporation in bonds or securities of state of Ala. or any political subdivision thereof, and any public corporation organized under laws of state of Ala., unless such foreign corporation dealer in securities; (3) amount invested in pollution control devices; (4) amount invested in certain real and tangible personal property, equipment, facilities and structures, when used by certified or licensed air carrier with "hub operation within this state"; (5) during 20 year period beginning Dec. 1, 1997, amount invested in all new and existing manufacturing facilities in Ala., limited to investment in real and tangible personal property, equipment, facilities, structures, components and inventory, if criteria as to amount invested and number of new employees are met; (6) during 20 year period beginning Jan. 1, 1998, amount invested in purchase of existing manufacturing facility in Ala., limited to investment in all real and tangible personal property, equipment, facilities, structures, components, and inventory on or after Jan. 1, 1998, if certain criteria as to employees and product are met. (40-14-41). If domestic corporation organized, or foreign corporation qualifies, on or after July 1, franchise tax for current year is one-half of annual rate. (40-14-46).

CORPORATIONS . . . *continued*

Payment of Tax.—Domestic and foreign corporations must pay tax for current calendar year by or on Mar. 15. (40-14-47).

Tax must be paid to department of revenue, by check payable to State of Alabama. (40-14-55). Tax due even if corporation in receivership or trusteeship. (40-14-56).

Professional Corporations.—Revised Alabama Professional Corporation Act (10-4-380 to -406) based on Professional Corporation Supplement to Model Business Corporation Act but contains some material variances including provisions with respect to not-for-profit professional corporations. Professional corporations governed by Alabama Business Corporation Act, except when inconsistent with provisions and purposes of Act. (10-4-381).

Purposes.—Professional corporation may be formed only for purpose of rendering a particular professional service; provided, that medical and dental services may be rendered by same professional corporation. (10-4-383).

Applicability.—To corporation whose articles of incorporation include as stated purpose performance of professional services and state that incorporated under Act. (10-4-384).

Name.—Professional corporation governed by rules of regulating board of profession. Name must contain words "professional corporation" or abbreviation "P.C."; must not suggest purpose other than purpose contained in articles; and must not be deceptively similar to reserved name or name of existing corporation. (10-4-387).

Death or Disqualification of Shareholder.—Act contains extensive rules governing transfer of shares by operation of law upon death or disqualification. (10-4-389).

Issuance and Transfer of Stock.—Domestic professional corporation may issue shares of capital stock only to qualified persons (10-4-388) defined as: (1) Individuals authorized to render professional services permitted by professional corporation's articles; (2) general partnerships in which all partners are qualified as above; and (3) professional corporations (domestic or foreign) in which all shareholders are qualified as above (10-4-382). Shareholders may transfer shares only to qualified persons. Any shares issued in violation of this section void. (10-4-388).

Liability.—Employee of domestic professional corporation liable for negligent or wrongful act or omission in which he personally participates as if he rendered such services as sole practitioner. Personal liability of shareholder, employee, director or officer of domestic professional corporation no greater than that of shareholder, employee, director or officer of corporation organized under Alabama Business Corporation Act. Personal liability of shareholder, member, employee, director or officer of foreign professional corporation is determined under law of jurisdiction in which organized. (10-4-390).

Voting Trusts.—Voting trust with respect to shares of domestic professional corporation not valid unless all trustees and beneficiaries thereof are qualified persons, except that voting trust may validly continue for period of 12 months after death of deceased beneficiary or after beneficiary becomes disqualified person. (10-4-392).

Directors.—At least one director of domestic professional corporation and president of domestic professional corporation must be qualified persons; restriction does not apply during 12 month period following death of sole shareholder of domestic professional corporation. (10-4-393).

Amendments to Articles of Incorporation.—Legal representatives of estates of shareholders of domestic professional corporations who hold all outstanding shares of corporation may amend articles by signing written consent to such amendment. Articles of amendment must be executed in duplicate, verified and filed with probate judge of county in which articles filed. Such articles must set forth name of corporation, amendments adopted, date of adoption, and statement that legal representative owns all outstanding shares. (10-4-394).

Merger and Consolidation.—Domestic professional corporation may merge or consolidate with another corporation, or professional corporation, domestic or foreign. Upon such merger or consolidation surviving corporation must comply with Revised Act if it renders professional services. Professional corporation may also merge with unincorporated professional association organized under provisions of 10-10-1-16 provided that surviving corporation is domestic professional corporation. (10-4-395).

See topic Associations.

Deeds.—See category Property, topic Deeds.

Nonprofit Corporations.—Alabama Nonprofit Corporation Act §10-3A-1 to -225 based on 1964 ABA Model Act. Provisions omitted from Model Act: §§81 (Annual Report of Domestic and Foreign Corporations); 82 (Filling of Annual Report of Domestic and Foreign Corporations); 85 (Penalties Imposed Upon Corporation); 87 (Interrogatories by Secretary of State); and 88 (Information Disclosed by Interrogatories). Act provides for authorization and regulation of foreign nonprofit corporations. (10-3A-170 to 186). Labor unions, cooperative organizations, and organizations subject to insurance laws may not be organized under these provisions. (10-3A-4).

Infant Shareholders.—See category Family, topic Infants, subhead Corporations.

Limited Liability Companies.—See topic Limited Liability Companies.

JOINT STOCK COMPANIES:

No statutory provisions. Term "corporation" wherever used in Constitution includes joint stock companies and provisions as to corporations apply thereto. (Const. Art. XII, §241).

Purposes.—See topic Corporations, subhead Purposes.

Formation.—No statutory provision.

Rights, Powers, and Liabilties.—See topic Corporations.

Actions.—No statutory provision.

Dissolution.—See topic Corporations, subhead Dissolution.

Massachusetts Trusts.—No statutory provision.

Professional Associations (or Corporations).—See topics Associations and Corporations.

LIMITED LIABILITY COMPANIES:

Note: Provisions preceded by "*" govern all limited liability companies formed after Jan. 1, 1998, and effective for all Alabama limited liability companies after Dec. 31, 2000. In interim, limited liability companies formed prior to Jan. 1, 1998, may elect whether to be governed by these provisions in articles of organization or operating agreement.

Alabama Limited Liability Company Act adopted. (10-12-1, et seq.).

Purpose.—May be organized for any lawful purpose. (10-12-3).

Name.—Limited liability company name shall contain words "Limited Liability Company" or abbreviation "L.L.C." *or "LLC". Limited liability company name may not contain word or phrase which indicates or implies organization for purpose other than one or more of purposes contained in Articles. (10-12-5).

Formation.—May be formed by two or more persons (*may be formed by one or more persons) by filing Articles with probate judge of county in which initial registered office of limited liability company located. (10-12-9).

Articles of Organization.—Must contain following: (1) Name of limited liability company; (2) period of duration, if not perpetual; (3) purpose(s) for which organized; (4) location and mailing address of initial registered office, and name of initial registered agent at that address; (5) name and mailing addresses of initial (*member or) members (*and, if any, organizer); (6) right, if given, of (*member or) members to admit additional members, and terms and conditions of admission; (7) right, if given, of remaining members to continue business after event of disassociation terminates continued membership of member (*circumstances, if any, under which cessation of membership of one or more members will result in dissolution); (8) if limited liability company to be managed by one or more managers, Articles must so state and must set out names and mailing addresses of manager or managers who are to serve as managers until first annual meeting of managers or until their successors are elected and qualified (*begin serving); and (9) any other provision, not inconsistent with law, which members elect to set forth. (10-12-10).

Property.—May be acquired, held and conveyed. (10-12-23).

Property Interest.—Membership interest is personal property. (10-12-6).

Admission of Additional Members.—Unless otherwise provided in operating agreement, additional members may be admitted upon written consent of all members. Effective time of admission of members is later of date of formation or date provided in operating agreement (or date of admission records if no operating agreement). (10-12-31).

Transferability of Member's Interest.—Membership interest in limited liability company assignable in whole or in part. Assignment entitles assignee only to financial rights of assignor to extent assigned. (10-12-32). Unless otherwise provided in operating agreement, assignee may become member only upon unanimous consent of members. (10-12-33).

Liability to Third Parties.—Unless otherwise provided in Act, member of limited liability company not liable under judgment, decree or order of court, for debt, obligation or liability of limited liability company whether arising in contract, tort or otherwise, or for acts or omissions of any other member, manager, agent, or employee of limited liability company. Member may become liable by reason of member's own acts or conduct. Member may be liable to creditors for written agreement to make contributions to limited liability company. (10-12-20).

Form of Contributions.—Contributions of member may be in cash, property, services previously rendered, or promissory note, or other binding obligation to pay cash, convey property, or to render services. (10-12-26).

Dissolution.—No specific date of dissolution required. Dissolution occurs upon occurrence of first of following events: (1) Events specified in Articles or operating agreement; (2) written consent of all members to dissolve; (3) event of dissociation of member, unless at least two members remain or at least one member remains and new member admitted and legal existence and business of limited liability company continued by written consent of all remaining members within 90 days after occurrence of event of dissociation or as otherwise stated in Articles (*when no remaining member, unless holders of all financial rights agree in writing within 90 days of cessation of membership of last member to continue legal existence and business and appoint one or more new members, and legal existence and business are continued and new member or members appointed in manner stated in articles or operating agreement); (4) when limited liability company not successor in merger or consolidation with one or more limited liability companies or other entities; or (5) upon entry of judicial decree. (10-12-37). Dissociation of member (*cessation of membership) occurs upon occurrence of event specified in §10-12-36.

Management.—Unless otherwise stated in Articles, management of limited liability company vested in members. If Articles vest management in one or more managers, managers have power to manage business or affairs of limited liability company as provided in operating agreement. Unless otherwise provided in operating agreement, manager(s): (1) Must be designated, appointed, elected, removed or replaced by vote, approval, or consent of more than one-half of number of members; (2) need not be members or natural persons; and (3) unless they have been earlier removed or have earlier resigned, hold office until successors elected and qualified. (*Articles of organization may provide for classes or groups of members or managers with certain rights, powers and duties, and may provide for future creation of additional classes or groups having such rights as may be created in manner provided in Articles, including rights, duties and powers senior to existing class or group. Articles may also grant right to vote on certain matters to specified classes or groups based on per capita, number, financial interest, class, group or any other basis. Articles may also specify provisions regarding notice, waiver of notice, action by written consent without meeting, record date, quorum, proxy or any other matter). (10-12-22).

Profits and Losses.—Income, deductions, and credits, and items of income, deduction, and credits of limited liability company allocated among members in manner provided in operating agreement. If operating agreement does not so provide, profits

See note at head of Digest as to 1998 legislation covered.

See Topical Index in front part of this volume.

LIMITED LIABILITY COMPANIES . . . *continued*

and losses, income, deductions, and credits, and items of income, deductions, and credits allocated on basis of pro rata value of contributions made by each member to extent contributions have been made and not returned. (10-12-28).

Filing Fees.—Fees for filing and issuance of certificates collected by judge of probate ("Probate") and secretary of state ("State"): (1) Filing of Articles, $40 to State and $35 to Probate; (2) filing of articles of amendment and issuing certificate of amendment, $10 to Probate; (3) filing restated Articles, $25 to Probate and $10 to State; (4) filing report of name and address of registered agent or statement of change of address of registered agent or change of registered agent or both, $5 to State; (5) filing articles of dissolution, $5 to Probate and $10 to State; (6) filing application for foreign limited liability company for amended certificate of authority to transact business in Ala. and issuing amended certificate of authority, $25 to State; (7) filing certificate of cancellation of foreign limited liability company and issuing certificate, $20 to State; (8) filing copy of articles of merger, $5 plus 50¢ per page in excess of five pages to Probate; (9) filing application for registration as foreign limited liability company and issuing certificate of registration to transact business in Ala., $75 to State; and (10) filing an other statement or report of domestic or foreign limited liability company, $10 to State. When appropriate, two checks must accompany document: one payable to Probate for all charges of Probate and one payable to State of Ala. for all charges of State. Check for State will be forwarded by Probate to State. (10-12-60).

Derivative Action.—Members may sue on behalf of limited liability company if members or managers with authority to do so have refused to bring action or if effort to cause members or managers to bring action unlikely to succeed. If member receives anything as result of action, court may award member reasonable expenses, including reasonable attorney's fees, with remainder of proceeds remitted to limited liability company. (10-12-25).

*Duties of Care and Loyalty.—Only fiduciary duties owed by members and managers are duties of care and loyalty to limited liability companies. (10-12-21).

*Member-Managed.—Members owe duty (1) to account for and hold as trustee property, profit or benefit derived from conduct or winding up of business, or derived from use of limited liability company property, including appropriation of opportunity; (2) to refrain from dealing on behalf of party with interests adverse to limited liability company; (3) to refrain from competition prior to dissolution; (4) to refrain from grossly negligent or reckless conduct, intentional misconduct, or knowing violation of law (duty also owed to other members); and (5) to discharge obligations and exercise rights to limited liability company and other members consistent with obligation of good faith and fair dealing. (10-12-21).

*Manager-Managed.—Member not manager must not disclose or use information from books and records of limited liability company to detriment of limited liability company or other members. Managers and members who, pursuant to operating agreement, exercise some or all managers' rights, to extent member exercises managerial authority, owe duty (1) to account for and to hold as trustee property, profit or benefit derived from conduct or winding up of business, or derived from use of limited liability company property, including appropriation of opportunities; (2) to refrain from dealing on behalf of party with interests adverse to limited liability company; (3) to refrain from competition prior to dissolution; (4) to refrain from grossly negligent or reckless conduct, intentional misconduct, or knowing violation of law; and (5) to discharge obligations and exercise rights consistent with obligation of good faith and fair dealing. (10-12-21).

**Articles or operating agreement may not (1) unreasonably restrict right to information or access to records; (2) eliminate duty of loyalty; (3) unreasonably reduce duty of care; or (4) eliminate obligation of good faith and fair dealing. Articles or operating agreement may (1) modify duties of members; (2) identify types or categories of activities that do not violate duty of loyalty; (3) specify number or percentage of members or disinterested managers that may authorize or ratify, after full disclosure of material facts, specific act or transaction that would otherwise violate duty of loyalty; and (4) determine standards by which performance of obligation of good faith and fair dealing to be measured (provided not materially unreasonable). (10-12-21).

Merger and Consolidation.—Provisions for merger or consolidation contained in §§10-12-54 to -57.

Foreign Limited Liability Companies.—Provisions for admission contained in §§10-12-46 to -53.

Professional Services.—Certain special rules for limited liability companies performing professional services contained in §10-12-45, including provisions governing liability of members rendering professional services.

PARTNERSHIPS:

Alabama Uniform Partnership Act governs effective Jan. 1, 1997. (10-8A-101, et seq.; 10-8A-1104).

Formation.—Association of two or more persons to carry on as co-owners business for profit. (10-8A-101[5]). Association formed under statute other than this Act, predecessor statute, comparable statute of another jurisdiction or any association existing in Ala. prior to Jan. 1, 1972 not partnership. (10-8A-202).

Partnership Property.—Property acquired is property of partnership not individual partners. (10-8A-203). Property is partnership property when (1) Acquired in name of partnership; (2) transferring interest indicates transfer to partnership. Presumed partnership property if purchased with partnership assets. (10-8A-204).

Rights and Liabilities of Partners Inter Se.—Partner credited with amount equal to partner's contributions and profits minus liabilities. Each partner entitled to equal share of profits and chargeable with share of losses in proportion to share of profits. Partnership must reimburse partner for payments made in ordinary course of partnership business. Partner has equal rights to manage partnership business, but may use or possess partnership property only on behalf of partnership. Partner not entitled to payment for services performed for partnership and may only become partner with

consent of all partners. (10-8A-401). Partner has right to access partnership information and records. (10-8A-403).

Rights and Liabilities of Partners as to Third Persons.—Partners agents of partnership for purpose of its business. (10-8A-301[1]). Partnership liable for loss or injury resulting from wrongful act or omission of partner in ordinary course of business or with authority of partnership. (10-8A-305). Partners jointly and severally liable. (10-8A-306).

Dissolution.—Upon occurrence of: (1) Withdrawal, except under dissociation provision §10-8A-601(2) to -(10); (2) end of term; (3) event agreed to in agreement; (4) event making partnership business unlawful; (5) economic purposes of partnership likely to be unreasonably frustrated; (6) upon application for transfer of partner's transferrable interest, judicial determination that equitable to wind up partnership. (10-8A-801-807).

Administration of Partnership Property.—Partnership continues after dissolution only for purpose of winding up business. (10-8A-802; -803).

Liability After Dissolution.—Subject to provisions regarding statement of dissolution partnership bound by partner's acts after dissolution if appropriate for winding up partnership business or if would have bound partnership before dissolution if other party to transaction did not have notice of dissolution. (10-8A-804).

Dissociation.—Upon occurrence of: (1) Partnership notice of will to withdraw; (2) event agreed in partnership agreement to cause dissociation; (3) expulsion under agreement; (4) expulsion on unanimous vote of partnership under specified conditions; (5) expulsion on application by partnership or other parties; (6) becoming debtor in bankruptcy or related actions; (7) death or incapacity of partner; (8) other miscellaneous provision for trusts, estates and other entities not corporations or partnerships. (10-8A-601-705).

Authority of Partners.—Partnership may file statement of partnership authority which must include: (1) Name of partnership; (2) street address of chief executive officer and one official in state (if there is one); (3) names and mailing addresses of all partners or of agent appointed and maintained by partnership; (4) names of partners authorized to execute instrument transferring real property held in partnership name; and (5) may state general authority of partners to enter into other transactions on behalf of partnership. (10-8A-303). Subject to statement of authority in §10-8A-303, partner agent of partnership for purposes of its business. Act of partner apparently carrying on partnership business binds partnership. (10-8A-301).

Out-of-State Partnerships.—No provisions.

Limited Partnership.—Alabama Limited Partnership Act of 1983, repealed Sept. 30, 1998. Alabama Limited Partnership Act adopted Oct. 1, 1998, and unless otherwise noted below all citations are to this Act. (10-9B-101, et seq.).

Limited partnership can be formed for lawful business which a partnership without limited partners may carry on, except insurance and banking. (10-9B-106).

Formation.—Certificate of limited partnership must be filed with judge of probate in county in which registered office maintained. Must include name of limited partnership, registered office address and name and address of registered agent, name and mailing address of each general partner, and date of dissolution. All general partners shall sign. (10-9B-201; -206).

Continuance of partnership beyond time originally fixed for duration thereof and addition of new partners effected by amendment to certificate in similar manner. (10-9B-202).

Name.—Business of limited partnership must be conducted under firm name, followed by word "Limited," or abbreviations "L.P.", "LP" or "Ltd." (10-9B-102[1]). Name may not contain name of limited partner unless also name of general partner or business of limited partnership had been carried on under that name before admission of such limited partner. (10-9B-102[2]). Name may not contain words: "bank," "banking," "banker," "trust," "insurance," "insurer," "corporation," "incorporated," or any abbreviation of such words. (10-9B-102[3]).

Powers.—General partners have all powers of partner in partnership without limited partners. (10-9B-403). Limited partners may not participate in control of partnership for any purpose, or they will be liable as general partners to third parties transacting business with partnership who reasonably believe that limited partner is general partner. (10-9B-303).

Liabilities.—General partners are liable as such. (10-9B-403). Limited partner is not liable to third parties for obligations of limited partnership unless he is also general partner or, in addition to exercise of his rights and powers as limited partner, he takes part in control of business. (10-9B-303).

In bankruptcy or insolvency of partnership no limited partner can claim as creditor until claims of all other creditors are satisfied, except when limited partner has loaned money or transacted other business with partnership his status same as general creditor. (10-9B-805).

Dissolution.—Limited partnership dissolved and affairs to be wound up upon happening of first to occur of following: (1) Event specified in certificate of limited partnership; (2) written consent of all partners; (3) event of withdrawal of general partner (as defined in §10-9B-402), unless at time there is at least one other general partner with authority to carry on business of limited partnership, or within 90 days after withdrawal remaining partners agree in writing to continue business of limited partnerships; or (4) entry of judicial dissolution under §10-9B-802. (10-9B-801).

Foreign limited partnership must register before doing business in state. If there is failure to register, entity may not maintain lawsuit until it registers, but failure to register does not impair validity of prior contracts nor prevent defending lawsuits. Attorney general may sue to enjoin unqualified entities from conducting business in state. (10-9B-901; -908).

Actions.—When partnership sues, complaint must give individual names of partners. (190 Ala. 241, 67 So. 707). Partners may be sued in name of partnership alone, in which case judgment runs against partnership property only. (6-7-70). Any one or more of partners may be sued for damages for obligation of all. (6-7-70).

When suit is brought by or against a partnership, plaintiff not required to prove existence of partnership unless issue raised by specific negative averment. (ARCP 9).

See note at head of Digest as to 1998 legislation covered.

See Topical Index in front part of this volume.

PARTNERSHIPS . . . *continued*

Limited Liability Partnerships.—Alabama Limited Liability Partnership Act, as revised, governs effective Jan. 1, 1997.

Formation.—Registered limited liability partnership must file with judge of probate in county of partnership principal office and with Secretary of State registration stating name of partnership; address of principal office; brief statement of business of partnership. Fee of $35 to judge of probate and $40 to Secretary of State required. Annual fee of $70 to Secretary of State required. Registration effective immediately and partnership is for all purposes same entity existing prior to registration. (10-8A-1001).

Name.—Must contain words "Registered Limited Liability Partnership" or "L.L.P." as last words or letters of name. Failure to disclose status as LLP upon entering contract may subject party to personal liability on contract or undertaking. (10-8A-1003).

Rights and Liabilities of Partners.—Partner not personally liable for debts or liabilities of registered LLP or other partners unless all partners agree otherwise. (10-8A-306).

Cancellation.—Registration cancelled by filing statement with judge of county of registration setting forth name of partnership; date of registration; reason for cancellation; effective date. (10-8A-1005).

Taxation.—Limited liability partnership taxed as partnership in accordance with 40-18-24. (10-8A-1109).

Professional Limited Liability Partnership.—Partners liable for own negligence, act or omission to same extent individual would be liable if sole practitioner. (10-8A-1010).

Foreign Registered Limited Liability Partnership.—Must register with Secretary of State before transacting business in State. (10-8A-1006). Failure to register or appoint and maintain registered agent prevents partnership from maintaining action in courts of State until registered. (10-8A-1008).

REAL ESTATE INVESTMENT TRUSTS:

Alabama Real Estate Investment Trust Act adopted. (10-13-1, et seq.).

Formation.—May be formed by filing declaration of trust with probate judge of county in which initial registered office of real estate investment trust is located. (10-13-6).

Declaration of Trust.—Must contain following: (1) Indicate that trust is real estate investment trust; (2) name of trust; (3) total number of shares of beneficial interest real estate investment trust authorized to issue; (4) annual meeting of shareholders after delivery of annual report; (5) election of trustees at least every three years; (6) number and names of initial trustees; (7) name and address of resident agent; and (8) if shares are divided in classes, description of rights and preferences of each class. Must be signed and acknowledged by each trustee. (10-13-6).

Restrictions.—At least 75% of value of real estate investment trust's assets must be held in real estate assets, mortgages or mortgage related securities, governmental securities, cash and cash equivalents. Real estate investment trust may not use or apply land for farming, agriculture, horticulture or similar purposes. (10-13-10).

Amendment of declaration of trust requires affirmative vote of two-thirds of shares entitled to vote, unless declaration of trust reduces requirement to no less than majority of shares entitled to vote. Board of trustees may act to amend declaration of trust to increase or decrease number of authorized shares or number of shares in class. Declaration of trust may allow trustees to amend by two-thirds vote in order to qualify as real estate investment trust under Internal Revenue Code or under Alabama Real Estate Investment Trust Act. (10-13-14).

Liability of Shareholders.—Shareholders not personally liable for liabilities, duties or obligations of, or claims against, real estate investment trust. (10-13-18).

Liability of Trustees.—Trustees not personally liable for obligations of real estate investment trust. Trustee not relieved of liability to trust or shareholders for acts constituting bad faith, willful malfeasance, gross negligence or reckless disregard of duties. Declaration of trust may not limit liability of trustees to extent: (1) It is proven that trustee actually received improper benefit or profit in money, property or services, or (2) adverse judgment or final adjudication is entered finding trustee's act or failure to act was result of active or deliberate dishonesty and was material to cause of action asserted. (10-13-19).

Share Tax Exemption.—As long as real estate investment trust assets or assets of any "qualified REIT subsidiary" as defined in 26 U.S.C. §856(I) are invested in real estate to extent required by §10-13-10, and qualify as "real estate investment trust" under 26 U.S.C. §856, real estate investment trust exempt from taxation of shares of domestic corporation under §40-14-70. (10-13-22).

Termination.—Real estate investment trust may terminate existence by voluntary dissolution under Alabama Business Corporation Act, §10-2B-14.02. May curtail or cease trust activities by partially or completely distributing trust assets. Attorney General may institute dissolution proceedings for real estate investment trust which has abused, misused or failed to use powers. (10-13-16).

BUSINESS REGULATION AND COMMERCE

BANKS AND BANKING:

"Bank" means any banking corporation or trust company organized under laws of this state under jurisdiction of Superintendent of Banks of this state or organized under laws of U.S. having principal place of business in this state. (5-1A-2, 5-3A-1). Words "Bank," "Banker" or "Banking", or foreign language equivalent, may be used only in name of banking corporations organized under laws of Ala., other states, U.S. or foreign countries. (5-1A-3).

Regulated by.—

Uniform Commercial Code.—Adopted. (7-4-101, et seq.). See topic Commercial Code.

Regional Reciprocal Banking.—Alabama Regional Reciprocal Banking Act repealed. Alabama Regional Reciprocal Savings Institutions Act allows acquisition of savings and loan associations, savings banks and savings and loan holding companies in following states if state has reciprocal law: Ark., Fla., Ga., Ky., La., Md., Miss., N.C., S.C., Tenn., Va., W.Va., and D.C. (5-14A-1-8).

Interstate and International Banking Act.—Alabama Interstate and International Banking Act of 1995 authorizes any bank holding company whose principal place of business in U.S. to acquire banks and bank holding companies located in Ala. under certain conditions. (5-13B-1-65).

Stockholders.—No statutory provision for stockholder liability for assessment. See subhead Taxes, infra.

Deposits.—

In Trust for Another.—Whenever deposit made by person in trust for another, and no further notice given bank concerning legal trust, then, in event of death of trustee, bank may release itself from all liability by paying deposit to person for whom deposit was made. (5-5A-40). Deposits held in trust in savings and loan associations may be similarly treated. (5-16-47). Deposits of trust funds by trust department of bank included in list of deposits for which bank authorized to pledge assets as security therefor. (5-5A-28).

Joint Deposit.—Deposit made in names of two persons payable to either of such persons, upon death of either may be paid by bank to survivor irrespective of whether provision for survivorship made, funds were property of only one depositor, person making deposit evidenced any intent to vest other with present interest in account, only one depositor had right to withdraw such deposit, or there was any delivery of any bank book, account book, savings account book, certificate of deposit or other writing made by person making such deposit to other person. (5-5A-41). Provision applies to savings accounts, checking accounts, certificates of deposit, and to deposits made in names of more than one person where there is express written provision for survivorship in deposit contract. (5-5A-41). §5-5A-41 exempts bank from liability, but title to account determined by intent of parties. (35-4-7; 463 So.2d 129). Deposit made in any savings and loan association in names of two persons, payable to either, or payable to either or survivor, may be paid to either of said persons whether other is living or not and by so paying savings and loan association released from further liability. (5-16-44). Upon death of one of two persons, deposit becomes property of and payable according to its terms to survivor, irrespective of whether funds deposited were property of only one of persons, of whether at time of such deposit there was any intention on part of person making deposit to vest other with present interest, of whether only one of said persons had right to withdraw deposit, and of whether there was any delivery of any account book or savings account book by person making deposit to other person. (5-16-45). Uniform Multiple-Person Accounts Act adopted, effective Mar. 1, 1998. (5-24-1, et seq.).

Fiduciaries.—Uniform Fiduciaries Act in effect. (19-1-1 to -13).

Uniform Commercial Code superseded all special provisions on stop payment orders, forged and altered instruments, delay in presentment, etc. (7-1-101, et seq.).

Unclaimed Deposits.—In case of bank's insolvency, receivership court may make proper provisions for unproven or unclaimed deposits. (5-8A-42). Unclaimed funds in hands of receiver at time of final settlement must be transmitted by him to state treasurer to be held as unclaimed property under Uniform Disposition of Unclaimed Property Act. (35-12-20 to -50). See category Property, topic Absentees, subhead Escheat.

Collections.—Uniform Commercial Code adopted. (7-4-101 to -504). See topic Bills and Notes.

Trust Companies.—Amenable to general banking laws, as applicable. (5-11A-1). Unless prohibited by instrument governing relationship, trust company may purchase securities underwritten or distributed by it. (5-11A-12).

Uniform Common Trust Fund Act.—See category Estates and Trusts, topic Trusts.

Foreign Banks.—See category Business Organizations, topic Corporations, subhead Foreign Corporations.

Securities.—Fiduciary may deposit securities held in fiduciary capacity in clearing corporation. Securities so deposited may be merged and held in bulk in name of nominee of clearing corporation with other securities of same class. Ownership and other interests of said securities may be transferred by entries on books of clearing house without physical transfer of certificates. (19-4-2, -21).

Savings and Loan Associations.—Including associations formerly known as building and loan associations, provided for and regulated by State Banking Department. (5-2A-61).

Small Loans.—Persons, associations, and corporations organized to make loans of $749 or less, other than banks, trust companies, credit unions and savings and loan associations, provided for and regulated by State Banking Department. (5-18-1 to -24). See topic Interest.

Taxes.—On call of Superintendent of Banks, each bank must pay to State Banking Department, assessment fee based on total resources of bank as shown by its last report to State Banking Department. Rate of such assessment fee must be in amount fixed by Superintendent and approved by Banking Board and may be made more frequently than annually. No other assessment or license may be levied against any bank, except ordinary taxes assessed against property in general. (5-2A-20). Failure to make such payments within 30 days after receiving notice from Superintendent of amount of assessment renders bank liable to pay state $100 for each day after such 30 day period. (5-2A-21). Excise tax of 6% of net income levied on financial institutions (including banks, trust companies, loan companies, building and loan associations and other businesses employing moneyed capital in competition with national banks) (40-16-4), returns for preceding taxable year must be filed annually within first 15 days of

See note at head of Digest as to 1998 legislation covered.

See Topical Index in front part of this volume.

AL – 6

BANKS AND BANKING . . . *continued*

Apr., and tax, which may be computed on calendar or fiscal year basis, payable Apr. 15 (40-16-3).

No state tax may be levied upon or made applicable to bank chartered by banking authorities of Ala. unless such tax levied upon and made applicable to all banks and banking institutions, including national banks, doing business in Alabama. (40-1-9).

Credit Cards.—Alabama Credit Card Act authorizes bank holding company to establish credit card bank (5-20-2 to -10). Act provides that lender and debtor may agree to terms and conditions. Credit card bank not considered "bank" for purpose of certain banking laws. (5-20-8).

Loans on or purchases of bank's own stock prohibited. (5-5A-27).

Ownership of stocks of other banks prohibited, with limited exceptions. (5-5A-27).

Exchange.—Banks must remit or pay at par all checks drawn on them and transmitted in cash letter and may not charge exchange on such checks first time presented to them for payment. (5-5A-33).

BILLS AND NOTES:

Uniform Commercial Code adopted. (7-3-101, et seq.). See topic Commercial Code.

Special Requirements.—When extending credit with respect to consumer credit sale, loan or lease other than open-end credit, creditor must furnish duplicate copies of all instruments executed by debtor in connection with transaction. Credit sale contract, loan note or lease must contain following statement in eight point type immediately above space for debtor's signature: "CAUTION—IT IS IMPORTANT THAT YOU THOROUGHLY READ THE CONTRACT BEFORE YOU SIGN IT." (5-19-6).

Judgment Notes.—Provision in note for confession of judgment thereon invalid, but does not invalidate note itself. (8-9-11; 193 Ala. 166, 69 So. 527).

Attorney Fees.—Have been held enforceable if reasonable (205 Ala. 269, 87 So. 552) and not cover for usury (123 Ala. 439, 26 So. 290). Fee is part of plaintiff's total judgment and will not be allowed if defendant succeeds in counterclaim greater than amount of note. If defendant's counterclaim partially successful, fee reduced pro rata. (213 Ala. 551, 106 So. 136). Such clauses in instruments evidencing loan under $750 invalid (5-18-15); for larger amounts fee limited to 15% of unpaid debt after default (5-19-10). See topic Consumer Credit.

Special Defenses.—See topic Consumer Protection; category Debtor and Creditor, topic Consumer Credit.

Promissory Notes Payable Out of Specific Fund.—Contingency for payment out of particular fund must be contained in instrument to prevent payment out of funds from maker's general personal credit. (460 So.2d 861).

Postdated Check.—Bank may change account of drawer for postdated check, even if payment before date, unless drawer gives notice of postdating, and notice received in such time to allow bank reasonable opportunity to act. Bank liable for damages if account charged prior to date specified in notice. (7-4-401).

Writing Required.—Agreement or commitment to lend or forbear repayment of money or modify provisions of existing agreement void unless in writing except consumer loans with principal amount financed less than $25,000. (8-9-2).

Sale of Checks.—No person, as service for fee or other consideration, may engage in business of selling, issuing, or otherwise dispensing checks or receiving money as agent for obligors for purpose of paying such obligors' bills, invoices or accounts without obtaining license. (8-7-3). Violation of §8-7-3 is misdemeanor. (8-7-15). Banks, trust companies, savings and loan associations and U.S. and Ala. governments (and all subdivisions thereof) exempted. (8-7-4).

Bad Checks.—Upon receipt of bad check, lender of money, extender of credit, merchant or assignee who receives check may charge payor bad check charge of not more than greater of $25 or amount equal to actual charge by bank or similar institution. (8-8-15). As of Jan. 1, 1999, maximum amount increases to $26; thereafter maximum charge shall increase by $1 per year through Jan. 1, 2003. (8-8-15). §§13A-9-13.1, 13.2 provide for establishment of prima facie intent to defraud thereby criminal prosecution if drawer does not pay returned check within ten days of statutorily prescribed notice plus service charge not exceeding $20.

Consumer Credit Sale or Consumer Lease.—Seller or lessor may not take negotiable instrument other than check as evidence of obligation. (5-19-5).

BILLS OF LADING:

See topic Carriers.

BILLS OF SALE:

See topic Sales.

BLUE SKY LAW:

See topic Securities.

BROKERS:

Uniform Commercial Code adopted. (7-1-101). See topic Commercial Code.

Licenses.—Certain brokers must be specifically licensed: e.g., real estate brokers by Real Estate Commission (34-27-1 to -11); stock brokers by Securities Commissioner (8-6-3); insurance brokers by Commissioner of Insurance (27-7-4; 27-8-3); and air carrier brokers by Alabama Public Service Commission (37-9-24). In addition, various types of brokers must pay state and county license or privilege tax in varying amounts and may be required to pay municipal license tax. See topic Securities; category Insurance, topic Insurance Companies.

Bond.—Air carrier brokers must furnish bond or other security approved by Alabama Public Service Commission. (37-9-24).

Real Estate Brokers.—Regulated by Alabama Real Estate Commission. (34-27-8). Must be licensed (34-27-30), pass written examination (34-27-33), and meet statutory fitness requirements (34-27-32). Persons who have been convicted of or pleaded guilty or nolo contendere to felony or to crime involving moral turpitude may be rejected by Commission. (34-27-32). All licensed brokers must carry errors and omissions insurance. (34-27-35.1). Obligations and duties of brokers set out in Real Estate Consumer's Agency And Disclosure Act, §§34-27-80 to -88, supersedes any duties of brokers at common law which are inconsistent with duties specified therein. (34-27-87). No agency relationship between broker and consumer without written bilateral agreement establishing terms of relationship. (34-27-82). No specific statutory provision governing real estate commissions.

BULK SALES:

See topic Commercial Code; also category Debtor and Creditor, topic Fraudulent Sales and Conveyances.

CARRIERS:

Carriers by rail and other transportation companies doing business in Ala. and not engaged solely in interstate commerce subject to supervision, regulation and control of Alabama Public Service Commission in all matters relating to performance of their public duties, and their charges therefor. (37-2-1,-3). Such carriers required to pay quarterly fees to Commission for inspection and supervision. (37-2-41).

Uniform Commercial Code adopted. (7-1-101). See topic Commercial Code. Art. 7 on documents of title does not modify or repeal any laws prescribing form of documents of title or services to be provided by carriers; but fact that such laws violated does not affect status of document otherwise complying with definition of document under Uniform Commercial Code. (7-7-103).

Licenses.—Permits and certificates of convenience and necessity required by Commission. (37-2-4 to -7).

Rates.—Commission charged with duty of prescribing and enforcing rates, charges, classifications of freight, storage, demurrage, and car service charges, rules and regulations and of requiring establishment and maintenance of public service, facilities and conveniences. All rates, charges, classifications, rules and regulations adopted or acted upon by any transportation company inconsistent with those prescribed by Commission within scope of its authority, or inconsistent with those prescribed by any statute, unlawful and void. (37-2-3).

Filing of Records.—Each carrier subject to supervision of Public Service Commission must print and file with the Commission and keep open to public inspection tariffs or schedules of rates. (37-2-10). Charges must be in accordance with such tariffs or schedules. (37-2-13).

Discrimination unlawful. (37-2-16).

Limiting Liability.—Every carrier liable to holder of bill of lading for any loss, damage or injury to property covered thereby which was negligently caused by carrier. (37-2-21; 37-2-60 to -62). No contract, stipulation, rule or regulation contained in bill of lading shall exempt carrier from liability. (37-2-21). Damages may be limited by provision that carrier's liability shall not exceed value stated in document if carrier's rates dependent upon value and consignor by carrier's tariff is afforded opportunity to declare higher value or value as lawfully provided in tariff. (7-7-309).

Bills of Lading.—Receipts or bills of lading must be issued according to statutory form. (37-2-21).

Liens.—No statutory provisions other than as contained in Uniform Commercial Code. (7-7-301 to -309).

Unclaimed Freight.—Ordinary freight remaining unclaimed for 40 days, may be sold at public auction on 15 days written notice to consignor or consignee or two weeks publication in newspaper published at point of destination, at any point where best prices may be obtained. (37-2-28). Unclaimed perishable goods may be sold as soon as deemed necessary and notice must be given to consignor and consignee when practicable. (37-2-29).

Claims and Damages.—Measure of damages for loss of, destruction of, injury to, or delay in delivery of or failure to deliver goods prescribed by statute. (37-2-60). Where itemized and verified claim presented to officer or agent of carrier within 60 days after injury or loss, if proper claim, claimant may recover penalty for failure to pay claim within 60 days after presentation. (37-2-61, -62). Suit for such penalty must be brought within one year after presentation of claim. (37-2-62). Failure to make such claim does not forfeit right to recover for loss or injury, but unless timely claim made only actual value of goods or injury may be recovered. (37-2-61).

Storage of Freight.—If destination of freight is city or town having daily mail, carrier not relieved from liability as such by reason of deposit or storage of freight in depot or warehouse, unless within 24 hours after arrival of such freight, notice given to consignee, personally or by mail. (37-2-27).

Where only part of a consignment arrives, carrier may not demand charges on part not received. (37-2-32).

Connecting Carriers.—On intrastate shipments over connecting carriers, both may be sued jointly for injury to goods or failure to deliver. (37-2-34).

Motor Vehicle Carriers.—See category Transportation, topic Motor Vehicles. See also topic Licenses, Business and Professional.

Interstate Commerce.—All the authority, powers and jurisdiction given by law to the Commission over carriers engaged in intrastate commerce also given with respect to carriers engaged in interstate commerce not regulated by federal legislation, extent that exercise by Commission of such authority, powers and jurisdiction over such carriers engaged in interstate commerce is permissible. (37-1-43).

COMMERCIAL CODE:

Uniform Commercial Code adopted. (7-1-101, et seq.). (See Uniform and Model Acts section.)

See note at head of Digest as to 1998 legislation covered.

See Topical Index in front part of this volume.

COMMERCIAL CODE . . . *continued*

Peculiar Local Interpretations.—

Timber and cutting rights with respect thereto treated as chattels. Corresponding amendments made to Arts. 2 and 9. In particular, timber considered goods for Art. 9 purposes. (7-9-105[1][h]). "Timber to be cut" defined in §7-9-105(1)(o). All standing timber and trees, and cutting rights with respect thereto, while owned by or mortgaged to anyone other than owner of land upon which such timber located, considered chattels and not real property when cutting rights limited to ten years from date of conveyance or mortgage. (35-4-363).

*Landlord's Lien.—*Priority of landlord's lien for rent arising by operation of law and security interest in collateral other than crops brought on leased premises determined by whether security interest attaches before or after property brought on premises. (7-9-310). If security interest attaches after property brought onto leased premises, landlord's lien has priority. (7-9-310[2][a]). If security interest attaches before property brought onto leased premises, it has priority over landlord's lien from time security interest is perfected or landlord has notice of it, whichever occurs first, except if secured party files with respect to purchase money security interest before or within 20 days after debtor receives possession of collateral, security interest takes priority over landlord's lien. (7-9-310[2][b]).

*Seller's Warranty.—*Amendments to Art. 2 abolished requirement of privity in personal injury cases for breach of warranty. Any person sustaining personal injury may sue for breach of warranty if reasonable to expect that such person would use, consume or be affected by the defective goods. (7-2-318). Vertical privity requirement eliminated in personal injury actions based on breach of warranty. (336 So.2d 1340). With respect to certain livestock, no implied warranty that such livestock free from disease, provided compliance with all federal and state statutes and regulations concerning inspection, disease prevention and control. (2-15-4).

Deviations.—

§1-201(1) words "recoupment, counterclaim, set-off, suit in equity" replaced with "civil action, counterclaim, cross-claim, third party complaint." (7-1-201[1]).

§1-201(9) word "minehead" replaced with "mine". (7-1-201[9]).

§1-201(37) words "by the court as a matter of law" added before words "by a commercially reasonable rate." First paragraph beginning "Security interest" designated (a), second paragraph beginning "whether a transaction" designated (b), third paragraph beginning "A transaction does not" designated (c) and fourth paragraph beginning "for purposes of this subdivision" is designated (d). Lettered subparagraphs "(a)-(d)" in second paragraph designated "1-4," lettered subparagraphs "(a)-(e)" in third paragraph are designated "1-5" and lettered subparagraphs "(x)-(z)" in fourth paragraph designated "1-3." (7-1-201[37]).

§1-209 not adopted.

§2-107(2) words "or of timber to be cut" omitted following words "described in subsection (1)." (7-2-107[2]).

§2-314 adds subsection (4) which reads: "Procuring, furnishing, donating, processing, distributing, or using human whole blood, plasma, blood products, blood derivatives, and other human tissues such as corneas, bones or organs for the purpose of injecting, transfusing, or transplanting any of them in the human body is declared for all purposes to be the rendition of a service by every person participating therein and whether any remuneration is paid therefor is declared not to be a sale of such whole blood, plasma, blood products, blood derivatives, or other human tissues." (7-2-314[4]).

§2-316 adds subsection (5) which reads: "Nothing in subsection (2) or subsection (3)(a) or in Section 7-2-317 shall be construed so as to limit or exclude the seller's liability for damages for injury to the person in the case of consumer goods." (7-2-316[5]).

§2-318 Alternative B adopted, except first sentence reads: "A seller's warranty, whether express or implied, extends to any natural person if it is reasonable to expect that such person may use, consume or be affected by the goods and who is injured in person by breach of the warranty." Official Comment 3 amended to read "This section is designed for states where the case law has already developed and for those that desire to expand the class of beneficiaries." (7-2-318).

§2-714(2) adds following after "amount": ", and nothing in this section shall be construed so as to limit the seller's liability for damages for injury to the person in the case of consumer goods. Damages in an action for injury to the person include those damages ordinarily allowable in such actions at law." (7-2-714[2]).

§2-719 adds subsection (4) which reads: "Nothing in this section or in Section 7-2-718 shall be construed so as to limit the seller's liability for damages for injury to the person in the case of consumer goods." (7-2-719[4]).

§2-725(2) adds at end of second sentence "; however, a cause of action for damages for injury to the person in the case of consumer goods shall accrue when the injury occurs." (7-2-725[2]).

§2A-101, et seq. Art. 2A adopted with variations as noted below. Gender neutral language adopted. (7-2A-101, et seq.).

§2A-102 Words ", as defined in Section 7-2A-103(1)(j)" added at end. (7-2A-102).

§2A-103(1)(e) Optional language adopted; figure $100,000 inserted. (7-2A-103[1][e]).

§2A-103(1)(g)(iii)(C) Text amended to read "the lease contract or a separate accurate and complete statement delivered to the lessee discloses in writing (a) all express warranties and other rights provided to the lessee by the lessor and the supplier in connection with the lease contract (b) that there are no other express warranties or rights provided to the lessee by the lessor or the supplier in connection with the lease contract, and (c) in a consumer lease, any waiver, disclaimer or other negation of express or implied warranties and any limitation or modification of remedy or liquidation of damages for breach of those warranties or other rights of the lessee in a manner as provided in this article or in Article 2, as applicable; or". (7-2A-103[1][g][iii][C]).

§2A-103(1)(g)(iii)(D) Text amended to read "the lessor, before the lessee signs the lease contract, informs the lessee in writing (a) of the identity of the supplier, unless the lessee has selected the supplier and directed the lessor to purchase the goods from the supplier, (b) that the lessee is entitled under this article to all warranties and other

rights provided to the lessee by the supplier in connection with the lease contract, and (c) to contact the supplier to receive an accurate and complete statement from the supplier of any such express warranties and other rights and any disclaimers or limitations of them or of remedies." (7-2A-103[1][g][iii][D]).

§2A-103(1)(u) Words "the court as a matter of law as" inserted after "the discount is determined by" and before "a commercially reasonable rate". (7-2A-103[1][u]).

§2A-104(1)(a) No specific statutes listed. (7-2A-104[1][a]).

§2A-104(1)(c) Words ", or final consumer protection decision of a court of this state existing on the effective date of this Article" omitted at end. (7-2A-104[1][c]).

§2A-104(2) Words at end read ", and any statute referred to in subsection (1), the provisions of that statute control." (7-2A-104[2]).

§2A-106(1) Text after "other than a jurisdiction in which" amended to read "(a) the lessee resides at the time the lease agreement becomes enforceable or within 30 days thereafter, (b) the goods are to be used, or (c) the lease is executed by the lessee, the choice is not enforceable." (7-2A-106[1]).

§2A-108 Subsections (2) and (4) omitted. Subsection (3) redesignated as subsection (2) with cross-reference to subsection (1) only. (7-2A-108).

§2A-208 Non-Code subsection (3) added. Text reads "The requirements of the statute of frauds section of this article (Section 7-2A-201) must be satisfied if the contract as modified is within its provisions." Code subsections (3) and (4) redesignated as subsections (4) and (5) respectively. (7-2A-208).

§2A-214(2) Text amended to read "Subject to subsection (3): (a) to exclude or modify the implied warranty of 'merchantability,' or any part of it the language must mention merchantability, be by a writing, and be conspicuous. Language to exclude the implied warranty of merchantability is sufficient if it is in writing, is conspicuous and states, for example, 'There is no warranty that the goods will be merchantable.' (b) to exclude or modify any implied warranty of fitness the exclusion must be by a writing and be conspicuous. Language to exclude all implied warranties of fitness is sufficient if it is in writing, is conspicuous and states, for example, 'There is no warranty that the goods will be fit for a particular purpose.' ." (7-2A-214[2]).

§2A-214 Non-Code subsection (5) added to read "Nothing in subsection (2) or subsection (3)(a) or in Section 7-2A-215 shall be construed so as to limit or expand the lessor's liability for damages for injury to the person in the case of consumer goods." (7-2A-214).

§2A-216 Alternative B adopted. Three sentences of section designated (1), (2) and (3). Last words of subsection (3) read "against any person referred to in subsections (1) and (2) of this section". (7-2A-216).

§2A-218(2) Words "the lessor's" inserted after "until" and before "default." (7-2A-218[2]).

§2A-218(3) Second sentence added to read "For this purpose the option to buy shall be deemed to have been exercised by the lessee when the resulting sale is closed, not when the lessee gives notice to the lessor of the lessee's intention to exercise the option." (7-2A-218[3]).

§2A-221(a) Word "avoided" replaced with "voided." (7-2A-221[a]).

§2A-221(b) Word "avoided" replaced with "voided." Words "that is not a consumer lease" after "finance lease" omitted. (7-2A-221[b]).

§2A-303(3) First sentence designated (a) and second sentence designated (b). (7-2A-303[3]).

§2A-308(2) Words "(a) becomes enforceable, not in current course of trade but in satisfaction of or as security for a pre-existing claim for money, security, or the like, and (b)" omitted. (7-2A-308[2]).

§2A-309(4)(a) Number of days changed from "ten" to "twenty". (7-2A-309[4][a]).

§2A-406(b) Words "that is not a consumer lease" after "finance lease" omitted. (7-2A-406[b]).

§2A-503 Non-Code subsection (5) added to read "Nothing in this section or in Secton 7-2A-504 shall be construed so as to limit or expand the lessor's liability for damages for injury to the person in the case of consumer goods." (7-2A-503).

§2A-506(2) First sentence unchanged; rest reads "A cause of action for indemnity accrues (a) in the case of an indemnity against liability, when the act or omission on which the claim for indemnity is based is or should have been discovered by the indemnified party, or when the default occurs, whichever is later, (b) in the case of an indemnity against loss or damage, when the person indemnified makes payment thereof. A cause of action for damages for injury to the person in the case of consumer goods accrues when the injury occurs." (7-2A-506[2]).

§2A-513(1) Words "it is" inserted after "because" and before "nonconforming." (7-2A-513[1]).

§2A-516(2) After "finance lease," and before "if made with," following inserted: "other than a consumer lease in which the supplier assisted in the preparation of the lease contract or participated in negotiating the terms of the lease contract with the lessor,." (7-2A-516[2]).

§2A-516(3)(b) Words at beginning "except in the case of a consumer lease," omitted. (7-2A-516[3][b]).

§2A-516 Non-Code subsection (6) added to read "Subsection (3) shall not apply to a consumer lease." (7-2A-516[6]).

§2A-524(1) Words at beginning "After default by the lessee under the lease contract of the type described in Section 2A-523(1) or Section 2A-523(3)(a) or, if agreed, after one default by the lessee, the lessor may" replaced with "A lessor aggrieved under Section 7-2A-523(1) may:." (7-2A-524[1]).

§2A-529(5) Text reads "After a lessee has wrongfully rejected or revoked acceptance of goods, has failed to pay rent then due, or has repudiated (Section 7-2A-402), a lessor who is held not entitled to rent under this section must nevertheless be awarded damages for nonacceptance under Sections 7-2A-527 and 7-2A-528." (7-2A-529[5]).

Rev. §3-101, et seq. 1990 Revision of Art. 3 adopted with variations as noted below. Old section numbers repealed and reused as needed. (7-3-101, et seq.).

Rev. §3-101(a)(4) Words after "honesty in fact" replaced with words "in the conduct or transaction concerned." (7-3-103[a][4]).

Rev. §3-112(a)(i) Words "until dishonor" inserted after "interest" and before ", and." (7-3-112[a][i]).

See note at head of Digest as to 1998 legislation covered.

See Topical Index in front part of this volume.

COMMERCIAL CODE . . . *continued*

Rev. §3-118 Captions added for each subsection as follows: "(a) Note payable at a definite time.;" "(b) Note payable on demand.;" "(c) Unaccepted draft.;" "(d) Certified check, teller's check, cashier's check and traveler's check.;" "(e) Certificate of Deposit.;" "(f) Accepted draft.;" and "(g) Conversion, breach of warranty and other Article 3 actions." (7-3-118).

Rev. §3-307(b)(2) Subsection (iii) omitted. Word "or" inserted before "(ii)." (7-3-307[b][2]).

Rev. §3-307(b)(4) Subsection (iii) omitted. Word "or" inserted before "(ii)." (7-3-307[b][4]).

Rev. §3-404 Non-Code subsection added at end to read "(e) The adoption of a comparative fault approach in subsection (d) and in Sections 7-3-404 and 7-3-406 is limited to transactions treated under this article and Section 7-4-406 of Article 4 of the Uniform Commercial Code-Bank Deposits and Collections." (7-3-404).

Rev. §3-405(a) Introductory language "(a) In this section:" replaced with "This section applies to fraudulent indorsements of instruments with respect to which an employer has entrusted an employee with responsibility as part of the employee's duties. The following definitions apply to this Section:." (7-3-405[a]).

Rev. §3-415(a) 1993 Amendment adding subsection (e) to list of subsections to which subsection (a) is subject not adopted. (7-3-415[a]).

Rev. §3-420(a) First sentence replaced with "(a) An instrument is converted under circumstances which would constitute conversion under personal property law." (7-3-420[a]).

Rev. §3-603(a) Words "obligation to pay" replaced with "amount due on." Words "and by subsections (b), (c) and (d)" added at end of sentence after "contract." (7-3-603[a]).

Rev. §3-603(b) Words "obligation to pay" replaced with "amount due on." (7-3-603[b]).

Rev. §3-603 Non-Code subsection added at end to read "(d) Acceptance of partial payment by a person entitled to enforce an instrument does not prejudice such person's rights or remedies with respect to the remaining amount due on the instrument or otherwise." (7-3-603).

Rev. §4-101, et seq. 1990 Conforming Amendments to Art. 4 adopted with variations as noted below. (7-4-101, et seq.).

Rev. §4-106 Alternative B adopted. (7-4-106).

Rev. §4-401(b) Words ", except that a bank may charge the amount of the overdraft, interest thereon, and any applicable fee against deposits or other credits to the account, regardless of the source of the deposits or credits." inserted at end. (7-4-401[b]).

Rev. §4-406(a) word "payee" inserted after "described by" and before "item number" in last sentence. (7-4-406[a]).

Rev. §4-406(f) First sentence rewritten and non-Code second sentence added. Both read as follows: "Without regard to care or lack of care of either the customer or the bank, a customer who does not within 180 days after the statement and the items or a legible copy or image of the items are sent to the customer, or within one year after the statement or items are otherwise made available to the customer (subsection (a)) discover and report the customer's unauthorized signature on or any alteration on the item is precluded from asserting against the bank the unauthorized signature or alteration. Without regard to care or lack of care of either the customer or the bank, a customer who does not within one year after the statement or items are sent or made available to the customer, discover and report any alteration on the back of the item or any unauthorized endorsement is precluded from asserting against the bank any such alteration or unauthorized endorsement." Second sentence of Official Text retained as third sentence. (7-4-406[f]).

§4A-101, et seq. Art. 4A adopted. (7-4A-101, et seq.). Part 6, Uniformity, and new section added, reading: "This article shall be applied and construed so as to effectuate its general purpose to make uniform the law with respect to the subject of this article among states enacting it." (7-4A-601).

§5-101, et seq. Repealed effective Jan. 1, 1998. (Act 97-702).

Rev. §5-101, et seq. Revised Art. 5 adopted with variations as noted below. (7-5-101, et seq.).

Rev. §5-103(c) Words "5-106(d)" omitted following words "Sections 7-5-102(a)(9) and (10)." Following text added after phrase "A Term in;" "a letter of credit, confirmation, advice, transfer, amendment, or cancellation" replacing words "an agreement or undertaking." (7-5-103[c]).

Rev. §5-106(d) Omitted.

Rev. §5-108(e). Second and third sentences omitted. (7-5-108[e]).

Rev. §5-111(e) Word "must" following phrase "expenses of litigation" replaced with "may."

§6-101, et seq. Repealed effective May 17, 1996. (Act 96-523). Official repealer of Art. 6 not adopted.

§7-403(1)(b) Optional language omitted. (7-7-403[1][b]).

Rev. §8-101, et seq. Revised Art. 8 (1994 Amendments) adopted with variations as noted below. (7-8-101, et seq.).

Rev. §8-402(c)(2)(ii) Word "considered" replaced with "considers." (7-8-402[c][2][ii]).

Rev. §8-601 Effective date stated as "January 1, 1996" but §7 of enacting legislation was revised to provide that effective date was Jan. 1, 1997. (Act 96-742; §7).

Rev. §9-101, et seq. 1972 Revision of Art. 9 (1994 Conforming Amendments to Revised Art. 8) adopted with variations as noted below. Conforming Amendments (Revised Art. 8) adopted, effective Jan. 1, 1997. 1995 Conforming Amendments (Revised Art. 5) adopted, effective Jan. 1, 1998. (7-9-101, et seq.).

§9-103(1)(d)(i) Words "and before the action is taken" added at end of subdivision. (7-9-103[1][d][i]).

§9-103(5) Word "mine" substituted for "minehead." (7-9-103[5]).

§9-104(b) Subsection reads "To a nonconsensual landlord's lien, except as provided in Section 7-9-310 on priority of such liens; or." (7-9-104[b]).

§9-104(e) Subsection reads "To any security interest created in connection with any of its securities by this state, any municipal corporation, county, public authority, public corporation or other similar public or governmental agency or unit in this state, or any political subdivision of any thereof, or by any educational institution or educational corporation organized under the laws of this state, whether such institution or corporation is public or private; or." (7-9-104[e]).

§9-104(g) Words "or contract for an annuity including a variable annuity" inserted before comma. (7-9-104[g]).

§9-105(1)(g) Subsection reads " 'Encumbrance' includes liens on real estate, other rights that are not ownership interests and real estate mortgages;." (7-9-105[1][g]).

§9-105(1)(h) Conforming change relating to Art. 8 adopted except that last sentence reads " 'Goods' also include the unborn young of animals, growing crops and timber to be cut;." (7-9-105[1][h]).

§9-105(1)(n) Subsection reads " 'Utility' means any person primarily engaged in the railroad, street railway or trolley bus business, the telephone or telegraph business, the transmission of goods by pipeline or the transmission or the production and transmission of electricity, steam, gas or water. The term 'transmission' shall include distribution;." Term "transmitting utility" not used in Alabama Art. 9. (7-9-105[1][n]).

§9-105(1) Subsection added, reading: " 'Timber to be cut' means standing timber and trees, and cutting rights with respect thereto, to the extent, and only to the extent, the same are and are to be considered as chattels and not real property, or any interest therein, as provided by section 35-4-363." (7-9-105[1][o]).

§9-105(2) Cross-references to "Fixture" and "Fixture filing" cite just to "§7-9-313" instead of to "§7-9-313(1)." (7-9-105[2]).

§9-105(3) Words " 'Certificate of deposit.' Section 7-3-104(j)." added after "Sale." (7-9-105[3]).

§9-114(1)(b) Text amended to read "The holder of the security interest, if he has filed a financing statement covering the same type of goods before the date of the filing made by the consignor, receives notification in writing from the consignor before the consignee receives possession of the goods; and". (7-9-114[1][b]).

§9-203(1) Words "or the article on leases" inserted after "sales". (7-9-203[1]).

§9-203(4) Words "any statute of this state governing small loans, retail installment sales, consumer credit or the like" inserted in blank. (7-9-203[4]).

§9-204(2) Phrase "ten days" changed to "20 days." (7-9-204[2]).

§9-301(1) Subsection added, reading: "(e) A landlord's lien entitled to priority under Section 7-9-310." (7-9-301[1][e]).

§9-301(2) "[T]en days" changed to "20 days." (7-9-301[2]).

§9-301(4) Following text added after words "advances made:": "(a) Before he becomes a lien creditor; or (b) Within 45 days after he becomes a lien creditor regardless of the secured party's knowledge of the lien; or (c) More than 45 days after he becomes a lien creditor and prior to receipt by the secured party of written notice of the lien from the lien creditor; or (d) Pursuant to a commitment entered into prior to receipt by the secured party of written notice of the lien from the lien creditor." (7-9-301[4]).

§9-302(1)(b) "[T]en-day" changed to "20-day." (7-9-302[1][b]).

§9-302(3)(b) Words "any certificate of title statute covering automobiles, trailers, mobile homes, boats, farm tractors or the like" inserted in blank. (7-9-302[3][b]).

§9-302 Subsection (5) added, reading: "(5)(a) The filing provisions of this article also do not apply to a security interest in personal property or fixtures of a utility which is created by a mortgage or other security agreement which also covers real property situated in the State of Alabama and which has been filed for record in accordance with the laws of Alabama governing mortgages of real property. Such security interest shall be perfected by such filing, whether such filing shall have been accomplished before or after February 1, 1982; and such security interest shall be and remain effective, both as to the personal property or fixtures covered by the security interest at the time that it is perfected and as to personal property or fixtures which may subsequently be covered by the security interest under any after-acquired property provision of the mortgage or other security agreement creating the security interest, as long as such mortgage or other security agreement shall remain in effect, without the necessity for any refiling under the provisions of this article. (b) Except as otherwise provided in paragraph (a) of this subsection (5), security interests in personal property or fixtures of a utility are subject to sections 7-9-401(5) and 7-9-403(6)." (7-9-302[5]).

§9-306(3) "[T]en days" changed to "20 days" and "ten-day" changed to "20-day." (7-9-306[3]).

§9-306(4)(d)(ii) "[T]en days" changed to "20 days." (7-9-306[4][d][ii]).

§9-307(3) Words "of goods" added after "A buyer." (7-9-307[3]).

§9-307(4) Subsection (4) added as follows: "A secured party may enforce a security interest in farm products against a buyer who, in the ordinary course of business, purchases farm products from, or a commission merchant or selling agent who, in the ordinary course of business, sells farm products for a person engaged in farming operations only where the secured party has signed and filed with the Secretary of State a form containing the following information: (a) the name and address of the borrower; (b) the borrower's signature; (c) the name and address of the secured party; (d) the social security number of the borrower, or in the case of a borrower doing business other than as an individual, the borrower's Internal Revenue Service taxpayer identification number; (e) a description of the farm products subject to the security interest including the amount of such products (where applicable); (f) a reasonable description of the real estate (including county) where the farm products are located; (g) a stockyard buyer or seller is exempt from Sections 7-9-307, 7-9-402, 7-9-403, 7-9-404 and 7-9-407 provided this exemption does not disqualify certification of Sections 7-9-307, 7-9-402, 7-9-403, 7-9-404, and 7-9-407 by the U.S. Department of Agriculture. If this exemption does disqualify Sections 7-9-307, 7-9-402, 7-9-403, 7-9-404 and 7-9-407 for certification by the U.S. Department of Agriculture, this particular subdivision (g) shall be null and void and shall not affect any other parts of this law."(7-9-307[4]).

§9-307(5) Subsection (5) added as follows: "The form described in subsection (4) must be amended in writing within three months, and similarly signed and filed, to reflect material changes. The effectiveness and continuation of the form is to be treated as if it were a financing statement". Filing fee for filing amendatory documents is $5 for first page and $1 for each additional page if statement is in standard form prescribed by Secretary of State and additional $2 for each statement if not in standard

See note at head of Digest as to 1998 legislation covered.

See Topical Index in front part of this volume.

AL – 9

COMMERCIAL CODE . . . *continued*

form. Uniform fee for each name more than one required to be indexed shall be $1. Secured party may at his option show trade name for any person and extra uniform indexing fee of $1 shall be paid with respect thereto. (7-9-307[5]).

§9-307(6) Subsection (6) added as follows: "The uniform fee for filing and indexing and for stamping a copy furnished by the secured party to show the date and place of filing for an original financing statement relating to farm products shall be $10 for the first page and $1 per page for each additional page if the statement is in the standard form prescribed by the Secretary of State and an additional $2 for each statement if not in the standard form. The uniform fee for each name more than one required to be indexed shall be $1. The secured party may at his option show a trade name for any person and an extra uniform indexing fee of $1 shall be paid with respect thereto. The cost of filing the forms described in subsection (4), with the Secretary of State, shall not be charged or assessed to the borrower." (7-9-307[6]).

§9-307(7) Subsection (7) added as follows: "There is hereby created in the State Treasury a fund to be known and designated as the Uniform Commercial Code and Farm Products Central Index System Fund. All funds, fees, charges, costs and collections accruing to or collected by the office of the Secretary of State under the provisions of Sections 7-9-307, 7-9-402, 7-9-403, 7-9-404, 7-9-407, or any fees collected in relation to uniform fees for filing an original financing statement or effective financing statements for farm products shall be deposited into the State Treasury to the credit of the Uniform Commercial Code and Farm Products Central Index System Fund except as provided in subsection (9)." (7-9-307[7]).

§9-307(8) Subsection (8) added as follows: "All funds now or hereafter deposited in the State Treasury to the credit of the Uniform Commercial Code and Farm Products Central Index System Fund shall be expended for the purpose of carrying out the provisions of the law authorizing the collection of such funds and shall be payable from said fund on the requisition of the Secretary of State; provided, however, that no funds shall be withdrawn nor expended for any purpose whatsoever unless the same shall have been allotted and budgeted in accordance with the provisions of Article 4 of Chapter 4 of Title 41, and only in the amounts and for the purposes provided by the legislature in the general appropriation bill." (7-9-307[8]).

§9-307(9) Subsection (9) added as follows: "Funds collected in accordance with the Uniform Commercial Code and Farm Products Central Index System provided in Sections 7-9-307, 7-9-402, 7-9-403, 7-9-404 and 7-9-407, or any other fees collected in direct relation to the Uniform Commercial Code or Farm Products Central Index System during the fiscal year shall be deposited to the credit of the state general fund by the following percentages:

(a) Fiscal Year 1987-88—57.0 percent of total collections for fiscal year 1987-88.
(b) Fiscal Year 1988-89—65.0 percent of total collections for fiscal year 1988-89.
(c) Fiscal Year 1989-90—66.0 percent of total collections for fiscal year 1989-90.
(d) Fiscal Year 1990-91—68.0 percent of total collections for fiscal year 1990-91.
(e) Fiscal Year 1991-92 and each fiscal year thereafter—81.0 percent of total collections for that fiscal year." (7-9-307[9]).

§9-310 Text designated (1) and new (2) added, reading as follows: "Priority conflicts between a landlord's lien for rent arising by operation of law and a security interest in collateral other than crops brought on leased premises shall be determined as follows: (a) If the security interest attaches after the property is brought on the premises the landlord's lien has priority over the security interest; (b) If the security interest attaches before the property is brought on the premises the security interest has priority over the landlord's lien from the time the security interest is perfected or the landlord has notice of the security interest, whichever first occurs; except that if the secured party files with respect to a purchase money security interest before or within 20 days after the debtor receives possession of the collateral, the security interest takes priority over the landlord's lien." (7-9-310).

§9-312(3)(b) Subsection reads as follows: "The holder of the conflicting security interest, if he has filed a financing statement covering the same type of inventory prior to: (i) The date of the filing made by the purchase money secured party, or (ii) The beginning of the 21-day period where the purchase money security interest is temporarily perfected without filing or possession (subsection (5) of section 7-9-304), has received notification in writing of the purchase money security interest before the debtor receives possession of the inventory; and." (7-9-312[3][b]).

§9-312(4) "[T]en days" changed to "20 days." (7-9-312[4]).

§9-313(1)(b) Words "or of a mortgage conforming to the requirements of subsection (6) of Section 7-9-402" added at end. (7-9-313[1][b]).

§9-313(4) "[T]en days" changed to "20 days" in subdivision (a); in both (a) and (b), words "at the time the security interest attaches" inserted preceding "the debtor" and final phrase changed to read "is in possession thereof, or has a present or future possessory interest therein." (7-9-313[4]).

§9-313 Subsection added, reading: "This section does not apply to a landlord's lien arising by operation of law." (7-9-313[9]).

§9-401(1) Second alternative subsection (1) adopted; "judge of probate" fills the two blanks in paragraph (a). Paragraph (b) reads "When the financing statement is filed as a fixture filing (Section 7-9-313) and the the collateral is goods which are or are to become fixtures, then in the office where a mortgage on the real estate would be filed or recorded; and when the collateral is timber to be cut, then in the office of the judge of probate in the county where the land on which the timber is standing is located;". Paragraph (c) reads "In all other cases, in the office of the Secretary of State." (7-9-401[1]).

§9-401(5) Words "Subsections (3) and (4) of section 7-9-302 and subsection (5)(a) of section 7-9-302" inserted after "subsection" and before ", the proper place to file". Phrase "transmitting utility" changed to "utility." Filing is to be made in office of Secretary of State. (7-9-401[5]).

§9-402(1) Third sentence reads "When the financing statement covers the timber to be cut or crops growing or to be grown, or when the financing statement is filed as a fixture filing (Section 7-9-313) and the collateral is goods which are or are to become fixtures, the statement must also comply with subsection (5)." Fourth sentence omitted. In last sentence word "signed" is added before term "security agreement" and before term "financing statement." (7-9-402[1]).

§9-402(3) Subsection reads "(3) A form substantially as follows is sufficient to comply with subsection (1):

Name of debtor (or assignor)..........
Address ....
Name of secured party (or assignee) ....
Address ....

1. This financing statement covers the following types (or items) of property:

(Describe) ....

2. (If collateral is crops) The above-described crops are growing or are to be grown on:

(Describe real estate) ....

(If the debtor does not have an interest of record in the real estate) The name of a record owner of the above-described real estate is:

(Name record owner) ....

This financing statement is to be cross-indexed in the real estate mortgage records.

3. (If collateral is goods which are or are to become fixtures) The above-described goods are or are to become fixtures on:

(Describe real estate) ....
[Same as ¶ 2]

4. (If collateral is timber to be cut) The above-described collateral is standing on:

(Describe real estate) ....
[Same as ¶ 2]

5. (If products of collateral are claimed)
Products of collateral are also covered.

Signature of debtor (or assignor) ....
Signature of secured party (or assignee) ....
(Use whichever is applicable)." (7-9-402[3]).

§9-402(4) Words "which identifies the financing statement by file number" added at end of first sentence. Following words inserted at end of first sentence and before second sentence: "The uniform fee for filing and indexing an amendment shall be $5 for the first page and $1 per page for each additional page if the amendment is in the standard form prescribed by the Secretary of State and an additional $2 if not in the standard form, plus in each case an additional fee of $1 for each name more than one against which the amendment is required to be indexed." (7-9-402[4]).

§9-402(5) First sentence reads "A financing statement covering timber to be cut or covering crops growing or to be grown, or a financing statement filed as a fixture filing (section 7-9-313) where the debtor is not a utility, must show that it covers this type of collateral, must show that it is to be cross-indexed in the real estate mortgage records and must contain a description of the real estate." (7-9-402[5]).

§9-402(7) First sentence replaced by two sentences, reading as follows: "The name of the debtor in the financing statement shall be the individual, partnership or corporate name of the debtor, regardless of trade names or the names of partners. The secured party may at his option add trade names and obtain additional indexing under such names (subsections (4) and (5) of Section 7-9-403)." In last sentence, words "or consents to" are omitted. (7-9-402[7]).

§9-403(2) First sentence reads "Except as provided in subsection (6), a filed financing statement is effective for a period of five years from the date of filing, or, where both (i) the collateral described consists only of consumer goods and (ii) the secured obligation is originally $2,000 or less, then until the 30th day following any maturity date if specified in the financing statement." Following added at end of third sentence: "; but when the effective period expires before the expiration of the 60-day period, the security interest remains continuously perfected beyond the 60-day period only if a continuation statement is filed before expiration of the effective period or a new financing statement is filed between the time of expiration of the effective period and expiration of the 60-day period." Reference to "five-year period" wherever it appears, changed to "effective period." (7-9-403[2]).

§9-403(3) Words "effective" substituted for "five-year" in first sentence; words added to second sentence, reading: "and, may where both (i) the collateral described consists only of consumer goods and (ii) the secured obligation is originally $2,000 or less, specify the maturity date."; in fourth sentence, words "or until the 30th day following any maturity date specified in the continuation statement, whichever is earlier" added following "effective." Sixth sentence ends at "destroy it" and remaining words of sentence deleted. New sentence added after sixth sentence, reading: "Microfilm or other photographic records may be removed and destroyed after five years after the lapse." (7-9-403[3]).

§9-403(4) Reference to §9-403(7) omitted. Phrase "filing officer" is preceded by "The". In second sentence, words "and such trade names as are shown (subsection 7 of section 7-9-402)" inserted following "name of the debtor." Phrase "transmitting utility" replaced by word "utility." (7-9-403[4]).

§9-403(6) Sentence added at end reading: "A financing statement covering a mobile home, other than a mobile home constituting inventory, remains effective, if it so states, until a termination statement is filed." (7-9-403[6]).

§9-403(7) Text reads "When a financing statement covers timber to be cut or crops growing or to be grown, or is filed as a fixture filing, the filing officer shall, in addition to indexing it in the ordinary manner prescribed in subsection (4) of this section, index it in the real estate mortgage records under the names of the debtor and any owner of record shown on the financing statement in the same fashion as if they were the mortgagors in a mortgage of the real estate described and, to the extent that the law of this state provides for indexing the mortgages under the name of the mortgagee, then also under the name of the secured party as if he were the mortgagee thereunder, and where indexing is by description in the same fashion as if the financing statement were a mortgage of the real estate described." (7-9-403[7]).

§9-404(1) First sentence of 1972 Revision of subsection not adopted. "In other cases whenever" in second sentence changed to "Whenever." Subsection otherwise conforms to 1972 Revision. (7-9-404[1]).

See note at head of Digest as to 1998 legislation covered.

See Topical Index in front part of this volume.

COMMERCIAL CODE . . . *continued*

§9-404(2) Words "index it with the financing statement" substituted for "note it in the index" in first sentence. Reference to termination statement inserted following "statement of release" in third sentence. Words "after the financing statement would have lapsed under Section 7-9-403(2)" substituted for last nine words of third sentence. Fourth sentence added, reading: "Microfilm or other photographic records may be removed and destroyed after five years after the financing statement would have lapsed under section 7-9-403(2)." (7-9-404[2]).

§9-405(1) Second sentence refers to subsection (4) and (7) of §9-403. Third sentence omitted. (7-9-405[1]).

§9-405(2) Fourth sentence provides that filing officer shall "index the assignment with the financing statement." Provisions for indexing in real estate records apply only to cases of fixture filings or filings covering timber to be cut or crops growing or to be grown. (7-9-405[2]).

§9-406 In fourth sentence phrase "note the same upon the margin of the index of the filing of" replaced with phrase "index the same with." (7-9-406).

§9-407 Optional section adopted. (7-9-407).

§9-407 New subsection (3) added: "The Secretary of State shall develop and implement a central indexing system containing the information filed with his office pursuant to subsection (4) of Section 7-9-307. Under this sytem the secretary shall record the date and time of filing and compile the information into a master list organized according to farm products. The list shall be organized within each farm product category in alphabetical order according to the last name of the borrower (or, in the case of borrowers doing business other than as individuals, the first word in the name of such borrower), in numerical order according to the social security or tax-payer identification number of the borrower, geographically by county, and by crop year. The master list shall also contain the name and address of the secured party, the name and address of the borrower, a description of the farm products (including amount where applicable) subject to the security interest and a reasonable description of the real estate, including the county, where the farm products are located." (7-9-407[3]).

§9-407 New subsection (4) added: "The Secretary of State shall maintain a list of all buyers of farm products, commission merchants, and selling agents who register with the Secretary of State indicating an interest in receiving the lists described in subsection (5)." (7-9-407[4]).

§9-407 New subsection (5) added: "The Secretary of State shall distribute at regular intervals as determined by him, to each buyer, commission merchant and selling agent registered under subsection (4) a copy in written or printed form of those portions of the master list which the buyer, commission merchant or selling agent has indicated an interest in receiving. The charge for a printed copy of the entire or any portion of master list and any supplements to that list shall be up to a fee of $25 per collateral code requested annually. The charge for receiving a portion of the master list on microfiche shall be $15 per collateral code requested annually." (7-9-407[5]).

§9-407 New subsection (6) added: "Upon request of any person the Secretary of State shall provide, within 24 hours, an oral confirmation of whether there is on file on the date and hour stated, any presently effective financing statement naming a particular debtor to be followed by a written confirmation. The fee for confirming an oral search shall be $5 plus $1 for each financing statement and for each statement of assignment reported therein." (7-9-407[6]).

New section added which reads: "The fees provided in this Part 4 of Article 9 for the performance of certain duties by filing officers shall be in lieu of all other fees otherwise provided by law for the performance of such duties." (7-9-409).

New section added which reads: "The Secretary of State is authorized to promulgate regulations and set reasonable fees which have not been delineated in Sections 7-9-307, 7-9-402, 7-9-403, 7-9-404 and 7-9-407 in order to implement a central filing system which conforms with the requirements of Section 1324 of the Federal Food Security Act of 1985, as now enacted or as hereafter amended. Such regulations and fees shall be adopted in accordance with the Administrative Procedures Act. The Secretary of State also is authorized to conduct user and public training relating to the Uniform Commercial Code and Farm Products Central Index System Program and is entitled to expenses as authorized in the General Appropriations Act." (7-9-410).

§9-504(3) Words "if he has not signed after default a statement renouncing or modifying his right to notification or sale" omitted at end of third sentence. Subsection otherwise conforms to 1972 Revision. (7-9-504[3]).

§9-505(2) Words "if he has not signed after default a statement renouncing or modifying his rights under this subsection" omitted at end of second sentence. Subsection otherwise conforms to 1972 Revision. (7-9-505[2]).

§10-101 Phrase "December 31st following its enactment" replaced with "December 31, 1966." (7-10-101).

§10-102(1) Repeals various Alabama Acts instead of uniform acts listed in Official Text. (7-10-102[1]).

§10-104(2) Subsection added: "This title does not repeal Sections 8-1-81 through 8-1-83, and if in any respect there is any inconsistency between those sections and the article of this title on secured transactions (Article 9), the provisions of said sections shall control." (Act 96-742).

§11-106 Subsections (2) and (3) omitted; (4) redesignated (2). (7-11-106).

Official Options, Alternatives and Amendments.—

§1-209: 1966 Official Optional Amendment not adopted. Section not adopted.

§2-318: Alternative B adopted, with variations.

§2-702: 1996 Official Amendment not adopted.

§2A-101, et seq.: Adopted, with variations. (See subhead Deviations, supra.)

§2A-103(1)(e): Optional language adopted.

§2A-216: Alternative B adopted.

Rev. §3-101, et seq.: Adopted, with variations. (See subhead Deviations, supra.)

Rev. §3-415(a): 1993 Amendment not adopted.

Rev. §4-101, et seq.: 1990 Conforming Amendments adopted, with variations. (See subhead Deviations, supra.)

Rev. §4-106: Alternative B adopted.

§4A-101 et seq.: Adopted, with addition of new §7A-4A-601.

§5-112(1): Optional language adopted.

§5-114(4): Optional language adopted.

§6-101, et seq.: Repealed. Official Repealer of Art. 6 not adopted.

§7-204: Optional subsection (4) not adopted.

§7-209: 1966 Official amendment not adopted.

§7-403(1)(b): Optional language not adopted.

Rev. §8-101, et seq.: Revised Art. 8 (1994 Amendments) adopted, with variations. (See subhead Deviations, supra.)

§9-101, et seq.: 1972 Revision and 1994 Conforming Amendments to Revised Art. 8 adopted with variations. (See subhead Deviations, supra.)

§9-104(e): Optional subparagraph not adopted.

§9-105: Optional subparagraph (f) adopted.

§9-106: Optional phrase not adopted.

§9-401(1): Second alternative subsection (1) adopted, with variations. (See subhead Deviations, supra.)

§9-401(3): Alternative subsection (3) not adopted.

§9-402: Optional language requiring full legal description of real estate not adopted.

Permanent Editorial Board's Recommendations for Optional Amendments.— 1966 Official Optional Amendments to §§1-209, 2-318, 9-105, 9-106 not enacted. As to §2-318, however, see text under subhead Deviations, supra.

1972 Official Amendments adopted, with certain exceptions. (7-11-101).

1973 Official Amendment adopted.

1977 Official Amendments not adopted.

1987 Official Amendments adopted, with certain exceptions. (7-2A-101, et seq.).

1988 Official Amendments not adopted.

1989 Official Amendments adopted.

1990 Official Amendment not adopted.

1994 Official Amendment not adopted.

Filing Fees.—See category Documents and Records, topic Records, subhead Filing Under Commercial Code.

Forms.—See end of this Digest.

See also topics: Banks and Banking, Bills and Notes, Brokers, Carriers, Contracts, Factors, Frauds, Statute of, Sales, Securities, Warehousemen; categories Business Organizations, topic Corporations; Civil Actions and Procedure, topic Limitation of Actions; Debtor and Creditor, topics Assignments, Fraudulent Sales and Conveyances, Liens, Pledges; Documents and Records, topics Records, Seals; Mortgages, topic Chattel Mortgages.

CONDITIONAL SALES:

See topic Sales.

CONSIGNMENTS:

See topic Factors.

CONSUMER CREDIT:

Uniform Consumer Credit Code (UCCC) not adopted. Alabama Consumer Credit Act of 1971 (5-19-1, et seq.), as amended May 20, 1996 (Mini-Code), contains some provisions similar to those in UCCC.

Maximum finance charge for credit transactions (excluding sales made under open-end credit plans) under $2,000 may equal but not exceed total of: $15 per $100 per year for first $750 of original amount financed; and $10 per $100 per year for portion of original amount financed exceeding $750 and less than $2,000. (5-19-3). Maximum finance charge under open-end credit plan 1.75% per month on first $750 or less, and 1.5% per month on unpaid balance in excess of $750. (8-8-14). Debtor and creditor can agree to greater rate of interest, subject to common law limits on unconscionability, if original principal balance not less than $2,000. (8-8-5).

Other Charges.—Creditor permitted to charge fees for pest inspection and flood inspection for loans secured by real property; appraisal fee payable to employee of creditor if employee licensed appraiser. (5-19-4). Creditor permitted to charge debtor, in addition to attorneys' fees for collection, attorneys' fees prior to default in connection with closing or amending credit transaction in excess of $10,000 or secured by real property regardless of amount of credit, provided attorney not salaried employee of creditor. (5-19-10).

Penalties for Excess Finance Charge.—Creditor liable only for debtor's "actual economic damages" resulting from excess finance charge. (5-19-19[a]). If creditor's excess finance charge violation "deliberate" or "reckless," borrower entitled to recover greater of (1) five times actual economic damages or (2) finance charge itself, if not less than $100. (5-19-19[a][2]).

Penalties for Other Mini-Code Violations.—Creditor's violation renders transaction unenforceable only to extent of violation, and debtor's remedies limited to "actual economic damages." (5-19-19[c]). Creditor has no fiduciary duty to debtor. (5-19-19[f]).

Credit Life Insurance.—Amended Mini-Code provides for calculation of credit life, accident and health, and involuntary unemployment insurance premiums. (5-19-20[b]). Credit life coverage limited to declining principal balance plus amount of one scheduled payment. (5-19-20[b]). Accident and health insurance and involuntary unemployment insurance may be calculated based on total of payments. (5-19-20[b]).

Licensing Requirements.—No creditor with place of business or resident employee in Alabama may make consumer loans or take assignments of consumer credit contracts without obtaining license from Ala. superintendent of banks. (5-19-22). Creditor with no Ala. place of business or Ala. resident employee exempt from license requirement. (5-19-22). Merchants engaging in consumer credit sale transactions not required to be licensed. (5-19-22).

CONSUMER CREDIT . . . *continued*

Disclosures.—When extending credit to consumer, other than under open-end credit plan, creditor must provide debtor copy of each instrument executed by debtor. (5-19-6). Note or consumer credit contract must contain following statement in eight point or larger type immediately above space for debtor's signature: "CAUTION—IT IS IM-PORTANT THAT YOU THOROUGHLY READ THE CONTRACT BEFORE YOU SIGN IT." (5-19-6).

Loans not covered include loans to individuals, corporations, trusts, partnerships, or associations of not less than $2,000 (8-8-5), loans involving interest in real property where creditor is approved mortgagee under National Housing Act (5-19-31), and pawnbroking business (5-19-31).

CONSUMER PROTECTION:

Deceptive Trade Practices Act (8-19-1 to -15) similar to Uniform Deceptive Trade Practices Act. In addition to activities proscribed by Uniform Act, Act proscribes following: Falsely representing going out of business; altering motor vehicle odometer with intent to deceive; failing to ship purchased goods within time advertised, or if no time advertised, within 30 days; using chain referral sales plan; selling or offering to sell right to participation in pyramid sales structure; misrepresenting either amount of earnings or extent of market of goods in connection with seller-assisted marketing plan; intentionally misrepresenting warranty rights on certain materially damaged motor vehicles. (8-19-5).

Act does not apply to acts by publisher or employee of newspaper, radio station, television station, or telephone company in dissemination of advertisement that such person did not know to be false or misleading; or to any seller who: (1) disseminates advertisements from manufacturer or other seller without knowledge that false or misleading; (2) provides name and address of such manufacturer or other seller upon request of Attorney General or District Attorney; and (3) on request of Attorney General or District Attorney, agrees in writing to discontinue such dissemination. (8-19-7).

Enforcement.—Restraining orders may be sought to prevent violations. (8-19-8). When consumer monetarily damaged, he may sue under Act to recover actual damages or $100, whichever greater, or in court's discretion up to three times actual damages. (8-19-10). Willful violation of Act Class A misdemeanor (8-19-12).

State of Emergency.—1996 Alabama Unconscionable Pricing Act amended §8-19-5 prohibits charging of unconscionable prices for sale or rental of any commodity or rental facility during periods of declared state of emergency. (8-31-3). Price equal to or in excess of 25% of average price of commodity or facility during last 30 days immediately prior to declared state of emergency prima facie unconscionable. (8-31-4).

Alabama Telemarketing Act.—(8-19A-1, et seq.). Applies to commercial telephone solicitation, defined as unsolicited telephone call for purpose of inducing consumer to purchase or invest in consumer goods or services, or other communication where gift, award or prize offered, consumer invited to call, and salesperson intends to complete sale or enter into purchase agreement in course of telephone call. (8-19A-3). "Other communication" means written or oral notification or advertisement transmitted through any means. (8-19A-3).

Does not apply to isolated transactions, calls for religious, charitable, political, educational or other noncommercial purposes or person soliciting for nonprofit corporation if corporation properly registered with Secretary of State as §501(c)(3) organization under Internal Revenue Code. (8-19A-4). Other specific exemptions listed in statute.

Requires commercial telephone seller to obtain license from Consumer Division of Office of Attorney General. (8-19A-5). Requirements of application for license explicitly set forth in §§8-19A-5 to 8-19A-7. Act requires: (1) commercial telephone seller to identify himself within first 30 seconds of call and to inform purchaser of cancellation rights if sale or agreement to purchase is completed (8-19A-12); (2) seller to submit to Consumer Division of Office of Attorney General statement setting forth each prize and gift discussed along with value, terms and conditions of offer, and odds of receiving item (8-19A-13); and (3) signed written contract for purchase to be final explaining purchaser's rights (8-19A-14).

Provides that person violating Act may be liable for civil penalty of up to $10,000 for each violation. (8-19A-18). In civil action or investigation, Consumer Division recoups reasonable attorneys' fees and costs from non-prevailing party. (8-19A-19). In any civil litigation initiated by Consumer Division, court may award to prevailing party reasonable attorneys' fees and costs if court finds complete absence of justiciable issue or bad faith on part of losing party. (8-19A-19). Soliciting in violation of Act Class C felony punishable under §§13A-5-6 and 13A-5-11. (8-19A-21).

Door to Door Sales.—Consumer right to cancel home solicitation sale until midnight of third business day following execution of agreement or offer to purchase. Seller must obtain buyer's signature to written agreement or offer to purchase, designating as date of transaction date on which buyer actually signs and containing following under conspicious caption:

Form

BUYERS RIGHT TO CANCEL:

If this agreement was solicited at your residence and you do not want the goods or services, you may cancel this agreement by delivering or mailing a notice to the seller. The notice must say that you are cancelling the agreement and must be delivered or mailed before midnight of the third business day after you sign this agreement. The notice must be delivered or mailed to:

. . . .

(insert name and mailing address of seller)

Within ten days of cancellation seller must tender to buyer any payments made or goods traded. Within a reasonable time thereafter buyer, upon demand, must tender at his residence to seller any goods delivered by seller. If seller fails to demand possession within 20 days after receipt of notice of cancellation, goods become property of buyer

without obligation to pay for them. (5-19-12). Seller using FTC forms presumed in compliance.

Lemon Law.—If consumer returns motor vehicle that does not conform to express warranties, and gives notice of nonconforming condition during specified time period, manufacturer must make repairs required to remedy nonconforming condition. (8-20A-2). Manufacturer's obligation ends after earlier of 24 months following delivery or 24,000 miles. (8-20A-2).

Plain Language Law.—No "Plain Language" statute.

CONTRACTS:

Contracts governed by common law except for Tit. 8 of Ala. Code which provides certain interpretative standards and makes particular kinds of contracts invalid or illegal.

Uniform Commercial Code adopted. See topic Commercial Code.

Seal on contract does not foreclose defense based on failure of consideration. (6-5-287). See category Documents and Records, topic Seals.

Franchise Contract.—Wholesaler, manufacturer, or distributor who enters into franchise agreement with retailer of farm, lawn and garden, or light industrial equipment, which agreement requires retailer to maintain inventory, obligated to repurchase inventory when franchise agreement terminated. (8-21A-6). Termination of franchise without good cause renders wholesaler, etc. liable for actual and consequential damages. (8-21A-4; -8). Warranty claims must be approved or disapproved in writing within 60 days after receipt of claim from retailer and paid within 30 days of approval. (8-21A-10). Wholesaler, etc. must compensate retailer for performance of warranty work. (8-21A-10).

Infant's Contracts.—See category Family, topic Infants, subhead Contracts.

Consumer Contracts.—See topic Consumer Credit.

Consumer Protection.—See topic Consumer Protection.

FACTORS:

Uniform Commercial Code adopted (1965). (§7-1-101, et seq.). See topic Commercial Code.

License Requirements.—A commission merchant, as defined in the statute (2-29-1), must obtain annual permit from commissioner of agriculture and industries (fee $10) and supply surety bond in penal sum of $1,000 (2-29-4), or bond equivalent, being either trust fund agreement based on cash, fully negotiable bonds of U.S. Government or of State of Alabama, or irrevocable letter of credit (2-2-71). All forms for issuance of bond or bond equivalent furnished by commissioner of agriculture and industries. (2-2-71). Commission merchant or merchandise broker must also obtain, from judge of probate, state license (fee $25) and county license (fee $12.50). (40-12-40,-81). City license may also be necessary.

Consignment Agreements.—If delivered goods may be returned by buyer even though goods conform to contract, transaction is sale on approval if goods for use, or sale or return if goods for resale. (7-2-326).

Liens.—See topic Commercial Code.

Records.—Commission merchant must keep detailed records subject to inspection by commissioner of agriculture and industries and must mail copy of such record to consignor within 48 hours and remit within seven days or such period as stipulated by written contract. (2-29-7).

Penalties.—Factor, commission merchant or broker punishable upon conviction for overcharging customers or accepting rebates, gratuities, etc. as if he had stolen. (8-11-5).

Reports.—Commission merchants and all persons trading and dealing on commission, assignees and consignees authorized to sell and persons having in their possession goods owned by nonresident must assess such goods for taxation, and must attach last inventory thereof to tax list. (40-7-13). Agent or factor, when legally called on by assessor, is required to list all real and personal property held by him. (40-7-20).

FRANCHISES:

No special legislation, but see The Motor Vehicle Franchise Act. (8-20-1, et seq.). For franchisee suits against franchisor, see 540 So.2d 648.

FRAUDS, STATUTE OF:

Following agreements are void unless agreement or some note or memorandum thereof, expressing consideration, is in writing and signed by party to be charged: (1) Every agreement by its terms not to be performed within one year; (2) every special promise by executor or administrator to answer damages out of his own estate; (3) every special promise to pay for debt, default or miscarriage of another; (4) every agreement, promise or undertaking made on consideration of marriage, except mutual promises to marry; (5) every contract for sale of real estate, except leases for not longer than one year, unless purchase money, or portion thereof paid, and purchaser put in possession by seller; (6) every agreement, contract or promise to make will or to devise or bequeath any real or personal property or right therein; (7) every agreement or commitment, except for consumer loans with principal amount financed less than $25,000; (8) notwithstanding §7-8-113, every agreement for sale or purchase of securities other than through national stock exchange or over-the-counter securities market. (8-9-2). Auctioneer's memorandum made at public auction of real estate (8-9-3), or return or report of officer making judicial, execution or attachment sale (8-9-4; 6-9-141) is sufficient. Representation or assurance concerning character, conduct, ability, trade or dealings not actionable by person to whom made, unless in writing and signed by person sought to be charged. (8-9-5).

Uniform Commercial Code adopted. (7-1-101, et seq.). See topic Commercial Code.

Security agreement governed by §7-9-203.

Contract of sale governed by §7-2-201.

See note at head of Digest as to 1998 legislation covered.

See Topical Index in front part of this volume.

FRAUDS, STATUTE OF . . . *continued*

Part Performance.—Contracts for sale of real estate exempt only if portion of purchase money paid and purchaser put into possession by seller (8-9-2), and Supreme Court has uniformly held that both requisites must be met in order to take contract out of statute (476 So.2d 75). Contract void under statute of frauds cannot be exempted from effect of statute by partial performance so as to permit recovery under contract for any part thereof remaining executory. (18 Ala. App. 350, 92 So. 236).

INTEREST:

Legal rate in absence of written contract fixing rate 6% per annum. (8-8-1).

Maximum Rate.—Interest up to 8% per annum may be contracted for. (8-8-1). Interest that is prima facie usurious under §8-8-1 may be lawful under Consumer Credit Act, §5-19-3. See topic Consumer Credit. Interest up to 6% per annum for entire period of loan may be computed in advance and added to principal even though loan is to be repaid in monthly or other installments. (8-8-2). Lender may charge if provided in contract: (a) Interest surcharge of not more than 6% of part of amount financed, which is not in excess of $2,000; (b) as alternative to other applicable interest limits, prime rate plus 2% ("prime rate" defined as average of prime rate charged by three largest banks in New York City at close of business three days prior to loan); and (c) on open-end credit, 1¾% per month on amounts under $750, and 1½% per month on excess of any unpaid balance. (8-8-14). Any person, corporation, trust, partnership, or association, may agree to pay any rate of interest on loans of $2,000 or more, provided that no law relating to unconscionability in consumer transactions is violated. (8-8-5). State board of education and State institution where education part of program permitted to pay interest not exceeding 15% per annum on loans of $100,000 or more. (8-8-4). Debts under National Housing Act and acts providing veteran's benefits exempt from usury and interest restrictions. (8-8-6). Industrial development boards organized under §§11-54-80, et seq. and medical clinic boards organized under §§11-58-1, et seq. exempt from usury laws and interest regulations. (11-54-97; 11-58-15). Bonds issued by public entity or nonprofit corporation exempt from usury and interest restrictions. (8-8-7). Public housing bonds and state board of education securities may bear interest as determined by issuing authority. (24-1-32; 16-3-28[b]). Bonds, notes, and other securities issued by public hospital corporations exempt from state laws governing usury or limiting interest rates. (22-21-6).

Judgments for payment of money, other than costs, bear interest from day of entry, at rate of 12% per annum; provided, that fees allowed trustee, executor, administrator, or attorney and taxed as part of cost of proceeding bear interest at same rate from day of entry. Judgment based upon contract action bears interest at rate provided in contract. (8-8-10). Prejudgment interest accrues at legal rate of 6% per annum unless statute or written contract otherwise provides. (440 So.2d 321).

Open Accounts.—Do not bear interest until closed, in absence of contract or usage. (220 Ala. 332, 124 So. 884).

Small loans governed by §§5-18-1, et seq. Licensed lender may charge on loans of $75 or less $1 for each $5 advanced if 15 days allowed for repayment of each $5 advanced, and may charge, on loans up to $749, 3% per month on unpaid principal balance up to $200 and 2% per month on unpaid principal balance between $200 and $749, but may not divide loan contracts, and may not contract for or receive any charges, including insurance premiums, other than those specifically authorized. (5-18-15). Licensed lender cannot charge rates in excess of 6% aggregate or 8% simple interest on any part of loan over $749 or any part thereof. (5-18-18). Refunds on prepayment or renewal of loan must be calculated under rule of 78ths. (5-18-15). Bookkeeping and advertising of licensed lender regulated. (5-18-11 to -13). Exaction of usurious interest or failure to comply with statutory requirements that borrower receive clear statement of terms of contract, etc., may result in criminal penalties, revocation of license, and forfeiture of principal and interest. (5-18-5; -16; -18; -21). See topic Consumer Credit. Mini-Code did not repeal Small Loan Act, but should be read in conjunction with Small Loan Act.

Usury results in forfeiture of all interest, and all interest paid is deducted from principal. Cannot be pleaded against holder in due course of negotiable instrument. (8-8-12). Lender violating Small Loan Act forfeits principal and interest. (5-18-16; -21). Creditor charging excessive finance charge forfeits debtor's actual economic damages not to exceed finance charge. If violation deliberate, creditor forfeits greater of entire finance charge imposed or five times debtor's economic damages, but not less than $100. (5-19-19).

Credit Cards.—Alabama Credit Card Act (5-20-1 et seq.) does not limit amount or rate of interest and other financing charges, cash advance charges, charges for extension of credit in excess of preestablished limits, late fees, annual fees, or insurance premiums, which may be provided for in credit card agreement (5-20-5).

Equalization.—Any person or entity may charge interest at maximum rate permitted any other federal or state chartered or licensed lender having principal place of business in Alabama and will be subject to same penalties for excessive interest or finance charges. (8-8-1.1).

Collection of Attorney Fee Clauses.—See topic Bills and Notes.

Savings and Loan Associations.—May charge, on loans secured by savings accounts, rate of interest not exceeding 2% per annum above rate payable on such savings accounts. (8-8-1.2).

Credit unions may charge rates of interest and finance charges as authorized for other financial institutions pursuant to Consumer Credit Act. (5-17-18).

Partial payments applied first to interest due. (8-8-11).

LICENSES, BUSINESS AND PROFESSIONAL:

State license and county license must be procured annually for substantially all businesses and many occupations. (40-12-40, et seq.). In absence of special provision, payment for state and county licenses is due Oct. 1 of each year (delinquent Nov. 1), and licenses are for term of one year ending Sept. 30. (40-12-26). Except as otherwise provided, licenses procured from judge of probate for county in which business to be carried out. (40-12-2).

Municipalities have power to require licenses for any trade, business, occupation, etc., engaged in or carried on in such municipalities or within police jurisdictions, except as prohibited by constitution or laws of state. (11-51-90; 11-51-91). Maximum municipal license tax on public utilities, other than telephone, telegraph, railroad, sleeping car and express companies, is 3% of gross receipts. (11-51-129). State imposes additional 2.2% license tax on gross receipts of public utility companies. (40-21-50).

Utilities furnishing electricity, domestic water or natural gas also subject to following gross receipts tax: Not over $40,000, 4%; $40,001 to $60,000, $1,600 plus 3% of excess over $40,000; over $60,000, $2,200 plus 2% excess over $60,000. (40-21-82). Utilities furnishing telegraph or telephone services are subject to following gross receipts tax: Not over $60,000, 6.7%; over $60,000, $4,020 plus 3.7% of excess over $60,000. (40-21-82).

Commercial Travelers.—Person carrying goods from place to place to sell them. Pays annual license tax of $30 to State and $5 to each county in which he does business. Does not include salespersons soliciting orders. Itinerant peddlers of drugs, ointments, toilet articles, insecticides, and other specified articles subject to special provisions. (40-12-139).

Collection Agencies.—No general provisions regulating same. Collection agency must pay license tax. (40-12-80). Use of unreasonable collection tactics by licensed Small Loan Act lender or his agent is ground for revocation of license (5-18-9); such tactics are defined in part by Regulation No. 18 of Bureau of Loans (promulgated Feb. 15, 1960). Collection agency may be liable to debtor for damages where agency's conduct "exceeds bounds of reasonableness." (272 Ala. 174, 132 So.2d 321). No one save regularly licensed attorney may practice law, and one is said to be practicing law who as vocation enforces, secures, settles, adjusts, or compromises defaulted, controverted or disputed accounts, claims or demands between persons with neither of whom he is in privity or in relation of employer and employee in ordinary sense. (34-3-6; -7). One acting as collection agent may be subject to prosecution for unauthorized practice of law. (34-3-6; -7).

Chain Stores.—Annual license fees exacted at following rates, graduated according to number of stores operated in this state: One store, $1; second to fifth stores, $15 each; sixth to tenth stores, $22.50 each; 11th to 20th stores, $37.50 each; stores in excess of 20, $112.50 each. (40-12-315). Licenses must be obtained from probate judge or license commissioner. Filing fee of 50¢ for each store must accompany application for original issuance or renewal of license. (40-12-312).

"Store" means any store or mercantile establishment owned, operated, maintained, controlled, or for which buying done, by same person, firm, corporation, copartnership or association, either foreign or domestic in which goods, wares or merchandise of any kind sold, at retail or wholesale but excludes places of business at which principal business conducted is sale or distribution of petroleum products, or ice (when less than 4,000 pounds kept in establishment at one time). (40-12-310).

Railroads.—Freight and equipment companies subject to annual license tax of 3½% of 30% value of average number of cars within state for 12-month period preceding Oct. 1. (40-21-52).

Distress Sales and Going-Out-of-Business Sales.—Unlawful to hold distress merchandise sale or going-out-of-business sale without license issued by probate judge. (8-13-2). License must be applied for 30 days in advance of sale, and unless renewed, license authorizes sale of only 30 days duration. (8-13-3 to -12). License requires payment of $10 investigation fee and license fees ranging from $50 to $500, depending on amount of inventory. (8-13-6 to -8). Renewal of license for 30 days or less is $100, issuance fee is $25. (8-13-8). Bond of $2,500 or 5% of amount of inventory, whichever is greater, must be posted to indemnify plaintiffs who suffer loss by misrepresentation. (8-13-4). Bond forfeited to state by noncompliance with licensing act. (8-13-4). Willful violation of act is punishable by fine and imprisonment. (8-13-22).

Auctioneers governed by Auctioneers License Act. (34-4-1, et seq.). Privilege license fees for auctioneers are $50 state license and $25 county license. No license required for apprentice auctioneer. (34-4-27).

Small Loan Act licensees required to pay annual license fee of $400 for each office, branch or place of business to Bureau of Loans of Banking Department. (5-18-5). Fee due Oct. 1 (delinquent Nov. 1). (5-18-5).

Real estate brokers, real estate salespersons, and corporations must be licensed to engage in business of selling, renting or listing real estate. (34-27-30). Applicants for licenses must be U.S. citizens or permanent residents at least 19 years old, must submit to written examination by Commission, and, if nonresident, must: (1) Sign affidavit submitting to jurisdiction; and (2) complete course in real estate approved by Commission. (34-27-32, -33). Conviction of criminal offense involving moral turpitude may disqualify applicant for license as broker or salesperson. Annual license fees are $45 for individual brokers, $35 for individual salesperson, and $35 for corporations or partnerships. (34-27-35). Applicant for original license must also deposit $30 in state real estate recovery fund. (34-27-31). Criminal penalties provided for violation. (34-27-36).

General Contractor.—License fee of $200 originally, $100 renewal. (34-8-2). Failure to secure general contractor's license under §34-8-2 renders construction contract null and void. (417 So.2d 574). Every contractor, whether general or not, must also obtain license. (40-12-84).

Mussel Catchers.—Before taking any type of mollusk from fresh waters of state, must purchase mussel catcher's license. (9-11-372).

Commercial fishing equipment must be affixed with tag stating name, address, and social security or tax identification number of owner. (9-11-22).

Optometrists must be licensed by Alabama Board of Optometry. (34-22-6). License not required for sale of eyeglasses in store on prescription of licensed physician. (34-22-4). $160 license renewal fee. (34-22-22).

See note at head of Digest as to 1998 legislation covered.

See Topical Index in front part of this volume.

AL – 13

LICENSES, BUSINESS AND PROFESSIONAL . . . *continued*

Motor vehicles subject to forfeiture if: (1) Registered in name of driver; and (2) driven by person whose license suspended for driving under influence of alcohol or controlled substance. (32-5A-203).

Alcoholic Beverages.—Alabama Alcoholic Beverage Control Board may not issue license in Class IV municipality for retail sale of alcoholic beverage without approval of municipality. (28-1-7).

Insurance agents must complete at least 12 hours of continuing education. (27-8A-1).

Exemptions.—Certain charitable, religious and civic organizations exempt from licensing requirements. (40-9-9, et seq.).

MONOPOLIES, RESTRAINT OF TRADE AND COMPETITION:

Monopolies or pools or combinations to fix or regulate quantity price or production of commodities prohibited under penalty of $500 to $2,000 fine. (8-10-1 to -3). Person injured by unlawful trust, combination or monopoly may recover actual damages and $500 penalty. (6-5-60). Injunction lies where legal remedy inadequate. (200 Ala. 492, 76 So. 434).

Unfair Trade Practices.—Officer, agent, or servant of railroad, manufacturing, or mining corporation, or factor, commission merchant, broker, attorney, auctioneer, architect, or agent who takes rebates, discounts, drawbacks, return commissions, or gifts or gratuities punishable as if he had stolen amount. (8-11-4,-5).

NEGOTIABLE INSTRUMENTS:

See topic Bills and Notes.

RESTRAINT OF TRADE:

See topic Monopolies, Restraint of Trade and Competition.

SALES:

Sales of personal property governed by Art. 2 of Uniform Commercial Code Jan. 1, 1967. (7-10-101). See topic Commercial Code. Implied warranty of fitness contained in Uniform Commercial Code extended to newly constructed homes. See subhead Conditions or Warranties, infra.

Contracts of Sale.—Formalities and validity in general, see topics Commercial Code; Frauds, Statute of. No statutory requirement as to type size, except as to certain consumer credit sales, loans, leases. See topic Consumer Credit.

Bills of Sale.—Bill of sale not necessary to pass title. (30 Ala. 432; 7-2-401). If seller to deliver document of title, title passes at time when and place where he delivers document. (7-2-401[3][a]). Bill of sale not analogous to chattel mortgage and not required to be recorded. (223 Ala. 677, 138 So. 263). Dealers in livestock for resale or slaughter required to obtain bill of sale from seller of livestock. (2-15-43).

Product Liability.—Modified version of §402A, Restatement 2nd of Torts, applicable both in personal injury and in wrongful death actions, retaining negligence per se concept. (335 So.2d 128; 335 So.2d 134). Defenses available under modified version of §402A include lack of causal relation, product misuse and assumption of risk. (585 So.2d 1336). Uniform Commercial Code abolished defense of privity in suits for personal injury based on breach of either express or implied warranties applicable to sale of goods. (7-2-318; 336 So.2d 1340). No cause of action in tort when commercial product malfunctions or defective and malfunction or defect results in damage only to product itself. (543 So.2d 671). See topic Commercial Code.

Retail Credit Sales.—See topic Consumer Credit.

Consumer Protection.—See topic Consumer Credit.

Bulk Sales.—See topic Commercial Code; category Debtor and Creditor, topic Fraudulent Sales and Conveyances.

Sales of Motor Vehicles.—See category Transportation, topic Motor Vehicles.

International Sales of Goods.—See Part VI this Volume, Selected International Conventions.

Conditions or Warranties.—Governed by Uniform Commercial Code. (7-2-312 to -318). See topic Commercial Code. By analogy to Code, implied warranty of "fitness and habitability" in sales of newly constructed homes (47 Ala. App. 194, 252 So.2d 307, aff'd 287 Ala. 439, 252 So.2d 313), but privity of contract required (477 So.2d 296).

Conditional Sales.—Governed by Uniform Commercial Code. (7-2-401).

SECURITIES:

Ala. Securities Act (8-6-1 et seq.) based upon Uniform Securities Act with material variations.

Uniform Commercial Code adopted. (7-1-101 et seq.). 1990 Revisions of Art. 3 (7-3-101 et seq.) and 1990 Amendments to Art. 4 (7-4-101 et seq.) adopted. See topic Commercial Code.

Supervision.—Director of Securities Commission under direction and supervision of five-man Securities Commission. (8-6-50-60). Address is Suite 570, 770 Washington Street, Montgomery, AL 36130.

Regulatory Powers of Supervising Authority.—May issue order revoking registration of securities if finds such order in public interest, and: (1) Registration statement incomplete, false or misleading as to material facts; (2) parties to issuing of security willfully violated Act; (3) party to issuing of security convicted of felony or misdemeanor involving moral turpitude, security or aspect of securities business; (4) security subject of injunction; (5) issuer's business illegal; (6) offering would constitute fraud on purchasers; (7) offering made on terms unfair, unjust or inequitable; (8) security not eligible for registration in manner attempted; (9) excessive underwriter's and seller's profit; (10) failure to pay registration fee. (8-6-9).

Registration of Dealers, Salesmen and Investment Advisors.—Registration is effected by filing application together with consent to service of process and payment of fee. Initial registration fee, and annual renewal registration fee, $200 for dealer and $50 for agent, $200 for investment advisor and $50 for investment advisor representative. Commissioner must require that: (1) All applicants (and, in case of corporation or partnership, officers, or partners) pass written examination as evidence of knowledge of securities business or accept in lieu of any such examination either examination given by National Association of Securities Dealers (NASD) or Securities and Exchange Commission Examination (SECO Exam); and (2) dealer have minimum net worth as set by Commissioner. Commission will require by rule or order all or any applicants to post bonds, of not less than $50,000, and will determine conditions. (8-6-3). Regulation of investment advisors and investment advisor representatives. (8-6-2[18], [19]).

Securities to Which Act Applicable.—Definition of "securities" includes annuity contract (unless issued by insurance company), bankers' shares, trustees' shares, investment participating bonds, investment trust debentures, units, shares, bonds, and certificates in, for, respecting or based upon any form of securities or collateral, subscriptions and contracts covering or pertaining to sale or purchase on installment plan of any security as therein defined; or subscriptions or contracts covering or pertaining to sale or purchase of beneficial interest in title to property, profits or earnings; or any right to subscribe to any of foregoing. (8-6-2).

Exempt securities include securities: (1) Issued or guaranteed by U.S., any state, or political subdivision thereof; (2) issued or guaranteed by Canada, Canadian province, or political subdivision thereof, or any other government with which U.S. maintains diplomatic relations; (3) issued by and representing interest in or debt of, or guaranteed by, any bank organized under laws of U.S. or any bank, savings institution or trust company organized and supervised under laws of Ala.; (4) issued by and representing interest debt of or guaranteed by any federal savings and loan association or similar association organized under laws of Ala.; (5) issued or guaranteed by any federal credit union or any credit union, industrial loan association, or similar association organized and supervised under laws of Ala.; (6) issued or guaranteed by any railroad, other common carrier, public utility or holding company; (7) national market system security under §11A of Securities Exchange Act of 1934; (8) issued by nonprofit person exclusively for religious, educational, or charitable purpose after notice to commission specifying terms of offer; (9) commercial paper which evidences obligation to pay cash within nine months of date of issuance; (10) investment contract issued in connection with employee's stock purchase, pension, profit sharing, or similar benefit plan; (11) issued by issuer registered as open-end management investment company or investment trust under §8 of Investment Company Act of 1940. (8-6-10).

Exempt transactions include: (1) Isolated non-issuer transaction, whether effected through dealer or not; (2) non-issuer transaction in outstanding security by registered dealer subject to reporting requirements or life of issuer prior to transaction; (3) non-issuer transaction affected by or through registered dealer pursuant to unsolicited order or offer to buy; (4) transaction between issuer and underwriter or among underwriters; (5) transaction in bond or other evidence of indebtedness secured by mortgage or deed of trust if offered and sold as unit; (6) offering at judicial, executors, administrators, guardian, or conservators sale, or at any sale by receiver or trustee in insolvency or bankruptcy; (7) transaction executed by bona fide pledge without purpose of evading Blue Sky law; (8) offer or sale to financial institution or institutional buyer or to dealer, whether purchaser is acting for itself or in some fiduciary capacity; (9) ULOE transaction not part of issue with no more than ten purchasers in 12 months when issuer reasonably believes all buyers are purchasing for investment and not with view to distribution; (10) offer to existing security holders of issuer if no commission paid and after five days notice to Commission; (11) offer, but not sale of security for which registration statements have been filed; (12) issuance of dividend; (13) transaction incident to reclassification, recapitalization, reorganization, stock split, merger, consolidation, or sale of assets; or (14) "small offering" exemption limited to $500,000 in 12 months with maximum purchase per investor of $15,000 unless accredited, purchased for investment, without Commission, issuer and proceeds must be of "intra-state" character, and after five business days notice to Commission. (8-6-11). Filing fee of $250 for application submitted with application. (8-6-11[c]).

Registration of Securities.—Filing fee of $40, plus registration fee of 1/10 of 1% of aggregate offering price of securities offered in Ala., but not to exceed $1,000, must be paid to Commission. (8-6-8).

Securities held by corporate fiduciary may be registered in name of nominee, without mention of fiduciary relationship in instrument evidencing such securities, or on corporate books, provided that fiduciary retains instrument in its exclusive possession and records clearly show capacity in which it holds securities, beneficial owners thereof, and other pertinent facts of ownership. Registration does not relieve fiduciary of liability it may otherwise incur. (19-3-7,-8).

Registration by notification permissible if: (1) Issuer and any predecessors have been in continuous operation for at least five years without default and with average net earnings of 5% of amount of securities in preceding three fiscal years; (2) registered for non-issuer distribution and any security of same class has ever been registered or issued pursuant to exemption; and (3) national market system security under §11A of Securities Exchange Act of 1934. (8-6-5).

Registration by coordination permissible when registration statement in connection with same offering has been filed under Securities Act of 1933. (8-6-6).

Registration by qualification for all securities; less extensive information required in registration statement than Uniform Act, but issuers must file verified quarterly reports of financial condition. (8-6-7).

Issuer desiring to be discharged from further supervision must file notice with Commissioner. (8-6-8).

Consent to Service.—Every applicant for registration as dealer or salesman, and every issuer proposing to issue securities in Ala. through person acting on agency basis in common-law sense (other than issuers whose securities registered by coordination) must file irrevocable consent appointing Secretary of State as agent for receipt of service of process in any noncriminal action. (8-6-12).

See note at head of Digest as to 1998 legislation covered.

See Topical Index in front part of this volume.

SECURITIES ... *continued*

Bonds.—Dealers must maintain net capital of not less than $50,000, investment advisors must maintain net capital of not less than $10,000, and both must post $50,000 surety bond in addition to net capital, unless ordered otherwise by Commission. (8-6-3[e]).

Advertisements and all sales literature used in connection with offering must be authorized in writing by Commission before use, unless within requirements of NASD. (Sec. Reg. 830-X-2-.06).

Liabilities.—

Criminal.—Willful violation of statute is Class C felony with five year limitation period. Willful violation of any rule or order of Commission is Class A misdemeanor.

Civil.—Purchaser may bring action to recover consideration paid, together with 6% interest, and attorneys' fees, less any income received. If purchaser no longer owns security, damages equal amount that would be recoverable upon tender less value of security when buyer disposed of, plus interest from date of disposition. Damages for fraud or deceit against person who receives direct or indirect consideration for advice as to value of securities are recovery of consideration paid for such advice and any loss due to such advice with 6% interest and reasonable attorneys' fees less amount of any income received from such advice. Every person who directly or indirectly controls liable person or materially aids and conduct giving rise to liability is jointly and severally liable. (8-6-19).

Simplification of Fiduciary Security Transfer Act has been adopted. (8-6-70-80). Any inconsistency between Art. 8 of Uniform Commercial Code and Uniform Act for Simplification of Fiduciary Security Transfers is controlled by latter. (7-10-104).

Uniform Securities Ownership by Minors Act adopted with significant modifications. (8-6-90-95).

Uniform TOD (Transfer on Death) Security Registration Act adopted. (Act 97-703).

TRUST RECEIPT SECURITY:

See category Debtor and Creditor, topic Pledges.

WAREHOUSEMEN:

Warehouses regulated as to standards by inspection and investigation of complaints, and by licensing requirements. (8-15-1; -18). Commissioner of Agriculture and Industries enforces provisions of Act (8-15-1; 8-15-11), and may take over operation of any warehouse, if he finds operated in violation of law or in jeopardy of public interest (8-15-14).

Uniform Commercial Code adopted.

See topic Commercial Code.

Bonds.—Bond of no more than $5,000 is required to operate warehouse (8-15-7); amount determined by Commissioner (8-15-7). Bond must be filed and recorded in probate office of county where warehouse located. (8-15-8[a]).

Licenses.—Warehousemen, before engaging in business, must procure permit from Commissioner, and no probate judge may issue license to person not having such permit. (8-15-3). Person operating public warehouse without license subject to penalty not over $1,000. (8-15-10[a]).

Warehouse Receipts.—Warehousemen must give receipts or bills of lading for goods actually delivered to them. (8-15-15). By retaining receipt depositor does not necessarily agree to all its terms. (292 Ala. 147, 290 So.2d 636).

Lien.—Governed by Uniform Commercial Code. (7-7-209; -210).

CITIZENSHIP

ALIENS:

Property.—Resident or nonresident alien may take, hold, dispose of and transmit real and personal property to same extent as native citizen. (Const., Art. I, §34; 35-1-1).

CIVIL ACTIONS AND PROCEDURE

ACCORD AND SATISFACTION:

Accord is agreement to accept, in extinction of obligation, something different from or less than that which person agreeing to accept is claiming or entitled to. (8-1-20). Satisfaction is acceptance of consideration of accord and extinguishes obligation. (8-1-22). Seal, or new consideration, not necessary to validate written composition or release of existing obligation. (12-21-31; 8-1-23). Until fully executed, accord does not extinguish existing obligation. (8-1-21). Receipt or release in writing given such effect as parties intended. (12-21-109).

Compromise.—Following are sufficient legal consideration to support agreement to settle: bona fide claim based on colorable right, such as conflicting or indeterminate testimony from which inferences can be drawn; result of proceeding on claim is doubtful; some reasonable ground for controversy exists. Existence of mere controversy will not suffice to support agreement to settle. (263 Ala. 557, 83 So.2d 201).

Pleading.—Accord and satisfaction must be set forth as affirmative defense. (ARCP 8[c]).

See category Business Regulation and Commerce, topic Commercial Code.

ACTIONS:

See topic Practice.

Pursuant to rule-making authority given it by legislature (Const. Amd. 328, §6.11), Supreme Court of Alabama has adopted and promulgated Alabama Rules of Civil Procedure (cited ARCP) governing procedure in civil actions in circuit courts, in courts of full, like jurisdiction, in district courts as provided in subparagraph "(dc)" of each

rule, in small claims courts as provided in Rule N of Small Claims Rules, and in all other courts where appeals lie directly to Supreme Court or Court of Civil Appeals except probate courts not exercising statutory equitable jurisdiction and proceedings enumerated in ARCP 81. (ARCP 1). These rules in general conform to Federal Rules of Civil Procedure (cited FRCP) but contain modifications required for adaptation to state practice and existing state court system.

Equity.—ARCP 2 provides for merger of law and equity. (436 So. 2d 873). Office of clerk and office of register in chancery preserved for administrative purposes only. (ARCP 81[d]). Cases filed with clerk or register as prior to adoption of ARCP, unless court orders otherwise. (ARCP 79[f]).

Form of Action.—Only one form of action known as "civil action." (ARCP 2).

Conditions Precedent.—Action must not be commenced against county until claim has been presented to county commission, disallowed or reduced by commission, and reduction refused by claimant. (6-5-20[a]). Claimant can recover punitive damages in action for libel on account of publication only if, five days or more before commencement of action, claimant makes written demand on defendant for public retraction of charge or matter published. (6-5-186). In pleading performance or occurrence of conditions precedent, sufficient to aver generally all conditions precedent have been performed or have occurred. Denial of performance or occurrence shall be made specifically and with particularity. (ARCP 9[c]).

Commencement.—See topics Process, Pleading.

Parties.—

Capacity.—FRCP 17(a) effective except for deletions of matters not relevant to state practice and special provision for subrogation. (ARCP 17[a]). Alabama law determinative of capacity of party to sue or be sued. (ARCP 17[b]). Party whose name unknown may be fictitiously designated in original complaint and true name may be later substituted, provided that substitution not used to change parties where plaintiff originally sued wrong party. (ARCP 9[h], 15[c]). See topic Pleading; category Family, topic Infants, subhead Actions.

Joinder of Parties.—FRCP 19 and 20 effective except for deletions of matters not relevant to state practice. (ARCP 19, 20). FRCP 21 effective. (ARCP 21). Necessary party plaintiff who refuses to join can be joined as involuntary plaintiff if active plaintiffs provide bond to protect him from costs and judgment. (6-7-50). Requirement that bond be filed with clerk of court not jurisdictional and may be waived. (377 So.2d 1082).

Class Actions.—FRCP 23 effective. (ARCP 23). In connection with shareholder's derivative actions, see ARCP 23.1. In connection with actions relating to unincorporated associations, see ARCP 23.2. Uniform Class Actions Act has not been adopted.

Intervention.—FRCP 24 effective except for deletions of matters not relevant to state practice. (ARCP 24).

Interpleader.—FRCP 22(1) effective. (ARCP 22[a]). Party seeking interpleader may deposit with court amount of property claimed and court may thereupon order such party discharged from liability. (ARCP 22[b]). Court may allow attorneys' fees to one or more parties if claimed in complaint or answer. (ARCP 22[c]).

Third Party Practice.—FRCP 14 effective except for deletions of matters not relevant to state practice. (ARCP 14). Plaintiff may assert claims against third-party defendant arising out of subject matter of original suit (ARCP 14[a]); failure to assert such claims estops plaintiff from asserting said claims in subsequent proceeding (359 So.2d 414). Severance of third-party claims for trial is authorized. (ARCP 14[a]).

Joinder of Causes of Action.—FRCP 18 effective except for deletion of matters not relevant to state practice. (ARCP 18). Jury trial of liability insurance coverage question jointly with trial of related damage question against insured not permitted. (ARCP 18[c]).

Splitting of Causes of Action.—Where contract is entire, only one action maintainable for breach. If severable or breaches occur at successive periods in entire contract (as money to be paid in installments), action lies for each breach. All breaches up to time of action must be included therein. (6-5-280).

Consolidation of Actions.—FRCP 42 effective except preservation of right to trial by jury referenced solely to Art. 1, §11, Alabama Constitution of 1901. (ARCP 42[b]).

Severance of Actions.—FRCP followed.

Stay of Proceedings.—FRCP 62 effective except for deletions of matters not relevant to state practice and except for certain clarifications of FRCP 62. (ARCP 62).

Abatement and Revival.—Action by or against unmarried woman not abated by her marriage, but continues under her married name after suggestion of marriage made on record. Judgment can be satisfied out of her estate. (6-5-460).

In proceedings not of equitable nature, claims upon which action has been filed, claims upon which no action has been filed on contract, and personal claims upon which action has been filed except for injury to reputation, survive in favor of and against personal representative; personal claim upon which no action has been filed survives against personal representative of deceased tortfeasor. (6-5-462). Equitable claims survive in favor of and against heir, successor or personal representative regardless of whether action filed. (6-5-464). Tort causes of action do not survive death of injured party when no action is pending at time of death (437 So.2d 1230); where death is caused by tortfeasor, claim actionable under wrongful death statute (6-5-410; 497 So.2d 120). Real property claims with respect to which actions have been filed survive in favor of heirs, devisees or personal representatives and against heirs, devisees, tenants, or personal representatives according to their respective rights; court must direct record and judgment to be framed to secure their rights and declare their respective interests. (6-5-463).

If claim survives, civil action based thereon does not abate by death of party but may be revived by motion to substitute by any party or by successors or representatives of deceased party not later than six months after death is suggested upon record by service of statement of fact of death. (ARCP 25[a][1]; see also 6-5-465 which directs that final judgment against personal representative may not be entered over his objection until six months after grant of letters testamentary or of administration). If claim survives only to

See note at head of Digest as to 1998 legislation covered.

See Topical Index in front part of this volume.

ACTIONS . . . *continued*
surviving plaintiffs or only against surviving defendants, action does not abate by death of one or more plaintiffs or defendants and action shall proceed in favor of or against surviving parties. (ARCP 25[a][2]). In any such pending action, failure of any party to present claim within six months after grant of letters testamentary or of administration or five months from date of first publication of notice, whichever is later (43-2-350), does not bar claim against estate to extent estate is entitled to assert any right under any contract providing for payment of judgment in said action (ARCP 25[a][3]). See also category Estates and Trusts, topic Executors and Administrators.

Statutory abatement under §6-5-440 applies to competing individual actions; common-law abatement to competing class actions; and "myriad" equitable factors to hybrid situations. (1997 WL 772923).

Limitation of.—See topic Limitation of Actions.

Small Claims.—See category Courts and Legislature, topic Courts.

Termination of Actions.—Actions, counterclaims, cross claims or third party claims may be dismissed voluntarily or by order of court upon defendant's motion for failure to prosecute or failure to comply with Rules or court order. Involuntary dismissal operates as adjudication upon merits unless court specifies otherwise, except that dismissals for lack of jurisdiction, improper venue or failure to join party under ARCP 19 are deemed without prejudice. (ARCP 41).

Prohibited Actions.—§§6-5-330 to 6-5-337 exempt certain classes of persons from liability under certain circumstances.

Administration.—See category Estates and Trusts, topic Executors and Administrators.

Direct Actions Against Insurer.—See category Transportation, topic Motor Vehicles, subhead Direct Actions.

Counterclaims and Cross-Claims.—FRCP 13(b, e-i) effective. (ARCP 13[b, e-i]). FRCP 13(a) effective; in addition, compulsory counterclaim not required if opposing party's claim for damage covered by liability insurance policy under which insurer has right or obligation to conduct defense. (ARCP 13[a][3]). If otherwise compulsory claim not asserted in reliance upon ARCP 13(a) exceptions, relitigation of claim may be barred by res judicata or collateral estoppel by judgment. (ARCP 13[a]). Compulsory counterclaim is action for purposes of §6-5-440, which bars plaintiff from prosecuting two actions in courts of Alabama at same time for same cause and against same party. (628 So.2d 598). FRCP 13(c) effective except that counterclaims maturing or acquired after pleading do not relate back to time original plaintiff's claim arose. (ARCP 13[c]). Right to assert counterclaims or claim credits against State of Alabama or officer or agency thereof governed by Alabama Constitution of 1901. (ARCP 13[d]; see also 259 Ala. 177, 66 So.2d 141).

Appealed Actions.—Where action commenced in court from which appeal lies to circuit court for trial de novo, ARCP 13(a) compulsory counterclaim must be stated as amendment to pleadings within 30 days after appeal perfected or within such further time as court allows. (ARCP 13[j]). When plaintiff appeals lower court decision to circuit court, he is limited to jurisdictional amount of lower court except when defendant asserts counterclaim in excess of said jurisdictional amount; when defendant appeals lower court decision to circuit court, plaintiff can claim full amount of his claim without regard to jurisdictional limit of lower court. (ARCP 13[j]).

APPEAL AND ERROR:

Appellate jurisdiction in Supreme Court, Court of Civil Appeals and Court of Criminal Appeals. (Const. Amend. 328). Review by Supreme Court of decisions of Courts of Appeal by certiorari. (See topic Certiorari.) Supreme Court authorized to make rules governing administration of and procedure in all courts. (Const. Amend. 328; 12-2-7). ARCP and Alabama Rules of Appellate Procedure (cited ARAP) in effect.

Appeal Bond.—Unless appellant exempted by law or rule, or has filed supersedeas bond or other undertaking that includes security for payment of costs on appeal, security for costs on appeal must be filed by appellant with notice of appeal in trial court. Security for costs must be approved by clerk of trial court. (ARAP 7).

Stay of Proceedings.—Appellant in civil case not entitled to stay of execution of judgment pending appeal (except as provided in ARCP 62[e]) unless he executes supersedeas bond, approved by trial court, payable to appellee. (ARAP 8). Execution of judgment in criminal cases stayed pending appeal. (12-22-170; 12-22-171; 12-22-172; 12-22-173).

Extent of Review.—

Circuit Court.—Law and facts decided de novo on appeal of final district court judgments. (12-11-30[3]; 12-12-71).

Court of Civil Appeals.—Ordinarily limited to questions of law. Where evidence presented ore tenus, judgment of trial court on evidence presumed correct and not to be reversed on appeal unless plainly and palpably wrong. (659 So.2d 675). Where facts undisputed, ore tenus rule inapplicable and inquiry is whether relevant law has been correctly applied. (587 So.2d 349). Review of entry of summary judgment de novo. (631 So.2d 1023).

Court of Criminal Appeals.—Questions of law and fact may be reviewed. (12-12-72; 12-22-240; 12-22-241).

Character of Hearing.—

Circuit Court.—Trial is de novo in civil and criminal appeals. (12-11-30[3]; 12-12-71; 12-22-113). In civil cases, appellant not entitled to jury trial unless demanded in notice of appeal. Appellee not entitled to jury trial unless written demand filed in circuit court within 14 days of appellant's notice of appeal. (12-12-71).

Court of Civil Appeals.—Court reviews proceeding of lower court. (12-12-70[a]; 12-12-72).

Court of Criminal Appeals.—Court reviews proceeding of lower court. (12-12-70[b]; 12-12-72; 12-22-131; 12-22-240; 12-22-241; ARAP 45[A][B]).

Supreme Court.—Court reviews proceedings of lower court. (12-12-72; ARAP 39[k]).

To Court of Civil Appeals.—Court of Civil Appeals has exclusive appellate jurisdiction of all civil cases where amount involved, exclusive of interest and costs, does not exceed $50,000, all appeals from administrative agencies other than Alabama Public Service Commission, all appeals in workers' compensation cases, domestic relations cases, and all extraordinary writs arising from appeals in said cases. When recovery in court below of any amount other than costs, amount of such recovery deemed to be amount involved; otherwise amount claimed is deemed to be amount involved. In actions of detinue, alternate value of property found by court or jury deemed to be amount involved. (12-3-10).

To Supreme Court.—Appeal to Supreme Court as a matter of right available only where not reserved to Courts of Appeal. (12-2-7; 12-22-2; 12-1-4). In general, review of decisions of courts of appeals by writ of certiorari. (ARAP 39). Supreme Court may deflect appealed civil cases to Court of Civil Appeals except where case (1) presents substantial question of federal or state constitutional law; (2) involves novel legal question; (3) is utility rate case appealed directly to Supreme Court under §37-1-40; (4) is bond validation proceeding appealed to Supreme Court under §37-1-140; or (5) is bar disciplinary proceeding. (12-2-7).

To Court of Criminal Appeals.—Court of Criminal Appeals has exclusive appellate jurisdiction of all misdemeanors, including violation of town and city ordinances, habeas corpus, all felonies, and all post-conviction writs in criminal cases. (12-3-9). Automatic appeals from cases in which death penalty imposed. (12-22-150).

To Circuit Court.—Circuit courts have appellate jurisdiction of all civil, criminal and juvenile cases before district courts and prosecutions for ordinance violations in municipal courts, except in cases in which direct appeal to courts of civil or criminal appeals is provided by law or rule. (12-11-30[3]).

Administrative Rulings.—Under provisions of Ala. Administrative Procedure Act, persons aggrieved by rulings of most administrative agencies may seek judicial review in Circuit Court of Montgomery County, in circuit court of county in which agency maintains headquarters or in county where party resides. Corporation may seek review in county of registered office or principal place of business within state. (41-22-20).

Supreme Court.—Ordinarily limited to questions of law. Where evidence presented ore tenus to trial court, presumption of correctness exists as to conclusions on issues of fact and determination will not be disturbed unless clearly erroneous, without supporting evidence, manifestly unjust, or against great weight of evidence. (608 So.2d 391). Where facts undisputed, ore tenus rule inapplicable and inquiry is whether relevant law has been correctly applied. (568 So.2d 752). No weight given to decision of trial judge upon facts when evidence not taken orally before judge, but in such cases Court will weigh evidence and give judgment as it deems just. (12-2-7[1]). Review of entry of summary judgment de novo. (665 So.2d 190). In reviewing decisions of courts of appeals, scope is that generally employed by certiorari and ordinarily limited to review of facts stated in opinion of appellate court. Application of law to stated facts included in scope of review. (ARAP 39[k]).

Judgment or Order on Appeal.—

Circuit Court.—Law and facts decided de novo on appeal of final district court judgments. (12-11-30[3]; 12-12-71).

Supreme Court and Court of Civil Appeals.—Upon reversal of judgment or decree, appellate court may remand for further proceedings or may enter such judgment or decree as lower court should have rendered, when record enables it to do so. (12-22-70). When appellate court is of opinion that case should be reversed solely on basis of excessive lower court judgment, appellate court will require appellee to file remittitur of excessive amount. Failure to file such remittitur will result in reversal and remand of case. If appellee files such remittitur appellate court will affirm case and enter judgment for reduced amount. (12-22-71). When appeal is dismissed or judgment affirmed, execution may issue and other proceedings be had thereon in all respects as if no appeal had been prosecuted. (12-22-75).

Court of Criminal Appeals.—Upon reversal, appellate court may order new trial or that defendant be discharged or that he be held in custody until discharged by due course of law or make such other order as case may require. (12-22-242; 12-22-245). Upon affirmation of judgment carrying death penalty, appellate court must direct sentence to be executed. If day appointed for execution of sentence has passed, appellate court must specify new date. (12-22-243).

Time for Taking Appeal.—Appeals permitted by law as of right to Supreme Court or Courts of Appeal must be taken within 42 days of entry date of judgment or order appealed from, except time of appeal is 14 days from interlocutory order on injunction, interlocutory order appointing or refusing to appoint receiver, interlocutory order determining right to public office or any judgment in action for validation of public obligation. (ARAP 4[a][1]). Post-trial motion suspends running of time for appeal; 42 days run from grant or denial of motion. (ARAP 4[a][3]). Post-trial motion pending more than 90 days without disposal deemed denied. (ARCP 59.1). Filing of notice of appeal by facsimile not accepted. (622 So.2d 929).

In civil and criminal cases, appeals from district to circuit court must be taken within 14 days of judgment or denial of post-trial motion. (12-12-70).

Time of appeal from judgments or decrees of probate court to circuit court varies from seven days to 42 days, according to subject matter. (12-22-21).

Mode of Taking Appeal.—Appeals in civil cases taken by: (a) Filing notice of appeal with clerk of trial court specifying party taking appeal, judgment, order or part thereof appealed from, and court to which appeal is taken (ARAP 3); (b) paying $100 docket fee (ARAP 12, 35A); (c) giving security for costs of appeal to be approved by clerk or register (ARAP 7), or giving supersedeas bond approved by court (ARAP 8).

Notice of Appeal.—Appeal must be dismissed if notice of appeal not timely filed. (ARAP 2). Clerk or register of trial court serves notice of appeal on appellee. (ARAP 3).

Interlocutory Decrees.—Appeals of interlocutory orders permissive and limited to civil cases within original appellate jurisdiction of Supreme Court involving controlling question of law. (ARAP 5).

BONDS:

Bonds in legal proceedings generally payable to the party entitled to benefit thereof, and generally approved by the court, board or officer before whom taken. Statute requiring bond indicates to whom bond should be payable, amount of same, etc. See 39-1-1 regarding bond requirements for public works.

Additional bonds may be required from personal representatives (43-2-292), conservators (26-3-7), and certain officials (36-5-40).

Sureties.—See categories Business Regulation and Commerce, topic Commercial Code; Insurance, topic Surety and Guaranty Companies.

Enforcement.—For breach of official bond or undertaking of state officer, executor, administrator, or guardian, or of bond or undertaking given in official capacity to state or any officer thereof, person aggrieved may sue in his own name, assigning appropriate breach. (6-5-30). In other cases, where bond returned forfeited by sheriff, constable, or deputy, execution issues thereon without further proceedings.

New Bond.—Upon application of surety, new bond may be required, effect of which is to discharge surety on old bond as to breaches subsequent to execution and approval of new bond. Execution of additional bond does not affect liability on old bond. (36-5-60-68).

CERTIORARI:

Jurisdiction.—Supreme Court may grant writs of certiorari to all inferior courts as at common law. (Const., Amend. No. 328, 6.02; 12-2-2). Judges of Courts of Appeals may issue writs of certiorari and supersedeas to all inferior courts. (12-22-6; 12-3-8). Circuit court judges may grant writs of certiorari as permitted by common law (12-17-26), and to grant such writs directed to judges of district and municipal courts in all cases in which appeals lie from such courts to circuit court (12-17-28).

Grounds.—Writ of certiorari, when directed to courts other than Supreme Court, available only when relief cannot be had by appeal or writ of error; it is, however, sole method of obtaining Supreme Court review of decisions of Courts of Appeals. (Const., Amend. No. 328, 6.02; ARAP 39; 12-2-2; 243 Ala. 130, 8 So.2d 824). Certiorari to Supreme Court in criminal cases in which death penalty imposed considered as matter of right. (ARAP 39). In all other cases, civil or criminal, petitions for writs of certiorari to Supreme Court granted only from: (1) Decisions initially holding valid or invalid city ordinance, state statute or federal statute or treaty, or initially construing controlling provision of Alabama or Federal Constitution; (2) decisions that affect class of constitutional, state or county officers; (3) decisions where material question requiring decision is one of first impression in Alabama; (4) decisions in conflict with prior decisions of Supreme Court or Courts of Appeals; and (5) where petitioner seeks to have controlling Supreme Court cases overruled which were followed in decision of Court of Appeals. (ARAP 39; 285 Ala. 72, 229 So.2d 27).

Proceedings.—Application commenced by petition verified by affidavit. Defendant may plead or answer as to all matters necessary for defense. (6-6-640; see also ARCP 81[a][19]). Application must be made to Supreme Court for writ of certiorari to Courts of Appeals within 14 days after petition for rehearing in such court has been made and denied. (ARAP 39[b]).

Review.—Limited to review of questions of law and does not extend to review of weight and preponderance of evidence. (642 So.2d 437).

CHARITABLE IMMUNITY:

See topic Damages.

COMMISSIONS TO TAKE TESTIMONY:

See topic Depositions and Discovery.

COSTS:

Costs allowed as matter of course to prevailing party unless court otherwise directs or unless expressly provided otherwise in statute. (ARCP 54[d]). FRCP 41(d) effective as to costs of previously dismissed action when subsequent action based upon or including same claim against same defendant. (ARCP 41[d]). FRCP 68 effective as to costs incurred after making offer of judgment. (ARCP 68). Costs and attorneys' fees imposed against any attorney or party who brings civil action, asserts claim, or interposes defense that court determines to be without substantial justification. (12-19-272).

Security for Costs.—Probate judge must take and approve security for costs in suits within jurisdiction of his court commenced by or for use of nonresident. (12-19-48). Security required for temporary restraining order. (ARCP 65[c]).

Liability of Attorney.—Attorney may be liable for filing action or asserting claim that is groundless in law or without substantial justification. (12-9-272; 614 So.2d 409).

DAMAGES:

Common law generally prevails as to compensatory damages. Procedure for determining future damages in §6-11-3 held to violate Alabama Constitution of 1901. (589 So.2d 184). Recovery of damages against governmental entity limited to $100,000 for bodily injury or death per person, to $300,000 aggregate on account of bodily injury or death arising out of any single occurrence, and to $100,000 for damage to property arising out of any single occurrence. (11-93-2). But, $100,000 cap does not apply to amount of damages recoverable in lawsuit filed to recover damages for wrongful termination. (613 So.2d 318). Compensatory and punitive damages for indivisible injury may not be apportioned among joint tortfeasors. (523 So.2d 1042). $250,000 limit on punitive damages in §6-11-21 held to violate Alabama Constitution of 1901. (627 So.2d 878). Statute providing no presumption of correctness on appeal of punitive damages award held unconstitutional. (581 So.2d 414). Where jury verdict challenged as excessive, trial court will review damage award and determine whether evidence warrants remittitur based on several factors. If punitive damage award appealed, appellate court will conduct its own review. (701 So.2d 524). Punitive damages may not be recovered in libel actions unless publication was made with knowledge of falsity or with reckless disregard as to falsity and written demand for retraction made at least five days before bringing suit. (6-5-186). Punitive damages allowed by statute in some ejectment actions. (6-6-296). Profits of unestablished business recoverable if proved with reasonable certainty. (506 So.2d 317).

Comparative Negligence Rule.—Not adopted.

Charitable Immunity.—Charity liable for torts of servants. (226 Ala. 109, 145 So. 443; 191 Ala. 572, 68 So. 4).

Sovereign Immunity.—Not abrogated by statute. However, Board of Adjustment has power to hear and determine claims for injuries to person or property or for death occasioned by State of Alabama or any of its agencies, commissions, boards, institutions or departments where in law, justice or good morals same should be paid. (41-9-60,-62). Mayor and City Council, in their individual capacities, entitled to absolute immunity from personal liability in performance of their legislative duties. (418 So.2d 102).

No-Fault Insurance.—See category Transportation, topic Motor Vehicles, subhead No-Fault Insurance.

Uniform Contribution Among Tortfeasors Act (Revised).—Not adopted.

See also categories Business Regulation and Commerce, topic Sales, subhead Product Liability; Estates and Trusts, topic Death, subhead Actions for Death.

DECLARATORY JUDGMENTS:

Uniform Act adopted. (6-6-220, et seq.). See also ARCP 57.

DEPOSITIONS AND DISCOVERY:

Taking and use of depositions are regulated by ARCP, based on FRCP (except recently enacted mandatory disclosures) with modifications to conform to state court practice. (See topic Practice.) In certain proceedings not governed by ARCP manner of taking and use of depositions specially provided for by statute: Proceedings before arbitrators (6-6-7); election contests (17-15-24,-25,-29,-55 to 62); proceedings before Public Service Commission (37-1-92); proceedings for contest of will (43-8-194) and proving will (43-8-168); proceedings for sale of land belonging to estate (43-2-452); proceedings for settlement of account of executor or administrator (43-2-513); proceedings before Board of Dental Examiners (34-9-47); proceedings before Board of Hearing Instrument Dealers (34-14-9); proceedings before Board of Medical Examiners to revoke certification to practice medicine or osteopathy (34-24-365); criminal proceedings (15-7-2; 12-21-260, -263).

Parties may obtain discovery of any matter not privileged and relevant to subject matter involved in pending action, by one or more of following: Deposition upon oral examination or written questions; written interrogatories; production of documents or things or permission to enter upon land or other property, for inspection and other purposes; physical and mental examinations; and requests for admission. (ARCP 26). See subhead Insurance Agreements, infra.

Uniform Foreign Depositions Act not adopted.

Within State for Use Within State.—See subhead Before Whom Taken, infra.

Within State for Use Elsewhere.—Person desiring to take depositions may produce to judge of circuit court where witness resides commission authorizing taking of such depositions or proof of notice duly served, whereupon judge must issue necessary subpoenas. (ARCP 28[c]).

Outside of State for Use within State.—See subhead Before Whom Taken, infra. Party, upon notice to other parties and persons affected, may apply for order compelling party to submit to discovery in court in which action pending or to any court having general civil jurisdiction in place where deposition taken. Application for such order against nonparty shall be made to court having general civil jurisdiction in place where deposition taken. Failure to comply with such order may be considered contempt of court. (ARCP 37). State circuit judge may not grant order authorizing party to take deposition before federal magistrate in another state. (460 So.2d 855).

De Bene Esse.—See subhead Perpetuating Testimony, infra.

Perpetuating Testimony.—FRCP 27 substantially adopted, with appropriate changes in wording applicable to state practice. Production of documents and things and entry upon land for inspection and other purposes (ARCP 34) and physical and mental examination of persons (ARCP 35) may be obtained before action or pending appeal. Notice must be served at least 30 days before date of hearing on application to perpetuate testimony before action, as opposed to 20 days under FRCP 27(a)(2). (ARCP 27[a][2]).

Before Whom Taken.—Based generally on FRCP 28. Depositions must be taken before officer authorized to administer oaths by laws of U.S., or of State of Ala., or of state or other place where examination held, or before person appointed by court in which action pending. Depositions must not be taken before relative or employee or attorney or counsel of any party, or relative or employee of such attorney or counsel, or person financially interested in action. (ARCP 28). Unless court orders otherwise, parties may by written stipulation provide that depositions may be taken before any person. (ARCP 29).

Commissions.—See subhead Before Whom Taken, supra. Additional provisions: Governor may appoint commissioners in other states and territories of U.S. to take and certify depositions in actions pending in courts of Alabama; commissioners so appointed hold office for four years. (36-1-1).

Compelling Attendance of Witness.—Attendance of witnesses may be compelled by subpoena in accordance with ARCP 45. (ARCP 30[a]). Resident may be required to attend examination only in county in which he resides or is employed or transacts business in person, or at such other convenient place as fixed by order of court. Nonresident subpoenaed within state may be required to attend only in county in which served, or at place within state not more than 40 miles from place of service, or at such other convenient place fixed by order of court. (ARCP 45[d]). Failure without adequate excuse to obey subpoena served may be deemed contempt of court. (ARCP 45[f]).

Examination of Witnesses.—See subhead Discovery, infra.

See note at head of Digest as to 1998 legislation covered.

See Topical Index in front part of this volume.

AL – 17

DEPOSITIONS AND DISCOVERY .... *continued*

Interrogatories.—Answerable within 30 days after service of interrogatories or, if responding party is defendant, within 45 days of service of summons and complaint. Limit of 40 interrogatories to any other party without leave of court. (ARCP 33[a]).

Discovery.—Parties may obtain discovery of any matter not privileged and relevant to subject matter involved in pending action. Similar to FRCP 26, except that limits of insurance not discoverable and limitation on frequency of use of discovery methods not express. (ARCP 26). See subhead Insurance Agreements, infra.

Demand for Admission of Facts.—Party may serve upon another party written request for admission of truth of discoverable matters, including genuineness of documents. Matter admitted unless response by later of 30 days after service of request, or, if responding party defendant, 45 days after service of summons and complaint. (ARCP 36[a]). If party fails to admit matter under ARCP 35 and requesting party thereafter proves genuineness of matter, requesting party may apply for reasonable expenses, including attorneys' fees, necessary to prove matter. (ARCP 37[c]).

Return.—FRCP 30(f); 31(b), (c) apply. (ARCP 30[f]; 31[b], [c]).

Form.—Deposition may be in substantially following form:

Forms

IN THE CIRCUIT COURT OF THE . . . .
JUDICIAL CIRCUIT IN AND FOR . . . .
COUNTY, ALABAMA

A. B., plaintiff
    vs.   Case No.
C. D., defendant   . . . . . .

         [city]
         [date]

BEFORE: [name], Commissioner
APPEARANCES:
    [name], for Plaintiff.
    [name], for Defendant.

I, [name], a Court Reporter of [city and state], acting as Commissioner, certify that on this date, as provided by Rule 30 of the Alabama Rules of Civil Procedure, there came before me at [address], [city and state], beginning at [time], [witness' name], witness in the above cause, for oral examination, whereupon the following proceedings were had: [witness' name]
being first duly sworn, was examined and testified as follows:
EXAMINATION BY [attorney's name]:
Q:
A:
    . . .
FURTHER DEPONENT SAITH NOT

Certificate of Commissioner should be in substantially the following form:
STATE OF . . . .
. . . . COUNTY

I hereby certify that the above and foregoing deposition was taken down by me in stenotype, and the questions and answers thereto were reduced to typewriting under my supervision, and that the foregoing represents a true and correct transcript of the deposition given by said witness upon said hearing.

I further certify that I am neither of counsel nor of kin to the parties to the action, nor am I in any wise interested in the result of said cause.

                 . . . .
                              COMMISSIONER

Note.—Above form should be modified by insertion in preamble or by attachment of appropriate stipulations of counsel as permitted under ARCP 29. Should such stipulations include a waiver of any of matters covered in commissioner's certificate, certificate should be modified only to that extent.

When Depositions May Be Taken.—FRCP 30(a) applies. (ARCP 30[a]).

Notice of Examination; Time and Place.—FRCP 30(b) and 31(a) apply in substantial part. Under ARCP 30(b)(5), notice to party deponent may be accompanied by request that he produce books and other tangible things needed as basis for examining party. Party deponent may, within five days after service of notice, serve upon deposing party written objection to inspection or copying of any or all of designated materials. (ARCP 30[b][5]). Thereafter, deposing party may not inspect materials except pursuant to order compelling discovery under ARCP 37(a). (ARCP 30[b][5]). ARCP 34, rather than ARCP 30, must be used where primary purpose is inspection of documents rather than examination of witnesses. ARCP 31(a) differs from FRCP 31 in that party receiving notice of deposition on written questions, after making demand upon deposing party of time and place of taking of testimony, may attend deposition in person and cross-examine witness orally. (ARCP 31[a]). In such case, deposing party also has right to attend deposition in person and examine witness orally in rebuttal. (ARCP 31[a]). ARCP 31(a) further differs from FRCP 31 in that cross questions must be served within 15 days after notice and written questions are served, and recross questions must be served within five days after service of redirect questions. (ARCP 31[a]).

Use in Court Proceedings.—FRCP 32 applies, and in addition to those witnesses whose deposition may be used for any purpose, ARCP adds witness who is out of state or licensed physician or dentist. (ARCP 32).

Requests for Production.—Requests for production of documents and things and entry upon land for inspection and other purposes may be served on parties and, in contrast to Federal practice, on nonparties. (ARCP 34). Nonparty must be personally served with production subpoena in accordance with ARCP 45 and copy of subpoena must be served on each party in accordance with ARCP 5 at least 15 days prior to service on nonparty. (ARCP 34). Party upon whom request served must serve written response within 30 days, except that defendant may serve response within 45 days after service of summons and complaint. (ARCP 34).

Insurance Agreements.—Amount of coverage under insurance agreement under which person carrying on insurance business may be liable to satisfy part or all of judgment which may be entered in action or to indemnify or reimburse for payments made to satisfy judgment not discoverable, but existence of coverage under insurance agreements or, when relevant and not privileged, contents of insurance agreement (other than limits of coverage) are discoverable. (ARCP 26[b][2]).

EQUITY:

See topic Actions.

EVIDENCE:

See topic Depositions and Discovery.

Witnesses.—Idiots, lunatics during lunacy and children who do not understand nature of oath incompetent. (12-21-165[a]).

See also topic Depositions and Discovery.

Privileged Communications.—Privileges recognized: (1) Attorney and client (ARE Rule 502); (2) priest and penitent (ARE 505); (3) counselor and client (ARE 503A); (4) husband and wife (ARE 504); (5) psychiatrist and patient (ARE 503); and (6) therapist and client. (1997 H.B. 208).

Husband and wife may, in civil proceeding, testify for or against each other, unless matter disclosed would interefere with confidential relation of husband and wife, or came to knowledge of witness only by reason of such relation. (486 So.2d 504). Similar rule prevails in criminal prosecution, except that neither spouse may be compelled to testify against other. (12-21-227). Wife's testimony from first criminal trial may be used in retrial if they were not married during first trial. (52 Ala. App. 702, 296 So.2d 796).

Communications or Transactions with Persons Since Deceased or Incompetent.—No person interested in action may testify as to transaction with or statement by deceased person whose estate interested in result or who acted in representative or fiduciary relation to person against whom testimony is offered. (12-21-163).

Self-Incrimination.—Criminal defendant cannot be compelled to give evidence against himself. (Const. Art. I, §6).

Compelling Attendance.—See topic Depositions and Discovery.

Interest.—No person is incompetent by reason of interest in subject matter of suit. (12-21-163).

Conviction of Crime.—Conviction of perjury or subornation of perjury disqualifies witness; conviction of other crime involving moral turpitude merely affects credibility. (12-21-162). Prosecution witness's juvenile records have been held admissible to impeach in criminal case. (477 So.2d 1385).

Attorney.—No attorney or his clerk is competent to testify for or against client to any matter, knowledge of which acquired from client by virtue of relations as attorney, or by reason of anticipated employment as attorney, unless called to testify by client. (12-21-161).

Clergyman or person whom he counsels in confessional, spiritual, or marital matter may refuse to disclose and may prevent other party from disclosing in legal or quasi-legal proceeding anything said by either party during such counselling session. (12-21-166).

Psychologists' and psychiatrists' communications with clients treated same way as those between attorney and client. (34-26-2).

Collateral Source Rule abolished, but obligation to repay expenses also admissible. (12-21-45).

INJUNCTIONS:

Injunctions generally issued if plaintiff's injury is immediate, irreparable, and no adequate remedy at law exists. (503 So.2d 1211).

Federal Rules of Civil Procedure (FRCP) substantially adopted. See topic Practice.

Jurisdiction.—Supreme Court (Const., §140, 12-2-2), Circuit Court (Const., §144; 12-2-2), Court of Civil Appeals (6-6-500) or Court of Criminal Appeals (6-6-500) may grant injunction (6-6-500).

Prerequisites.—No application made to justice of Supreme Court or judge of Court of Civil Appeals for temporary restraining order or other equitable process which may be granted by any other judge or officer unless same made to such other judge or officer and refused. (12-22-8; ARCP 65).

Procedure.—FRCP 65 substantially adopted. (ARCP 65).

Bond.—FRCP 65 substantially adopted. No security need be provided by State of Alabama or officer or agency thereof or, in discretion of court, in domestic relations cases. (ARCP 65).

Temporary Injunction.—FRCP 65 substantially adopted. (ARCP 65). If application made to circuit court judge for temporary restraining order and refused, no other circuit judge can act on application. Application may be made to judge of Court of Civil Appeals or Supreme Court, and if refused by judge of Court of Civil Appeals, may be renewed to judge of Supreme Court, but no other officer. If refused by judge of Supreme Court, cannot be renewed. Application to appellate judge must be made and acted upon in accordance with ARCP 65. (12-22-7).

Appeal.—Losing party may appeal to Supreme Court within 14 days; such appeal may be given preferred standing on docket in that court. (ARAP 4[a][1][A], ARAP 2[b]).

Dissolution.—FRCP 65 substantially adopted. Motion to dissolve will lie to granting of preliminary injunction only for matters subsequently occurring. (6-6-501).

JUDGMENTS:

Judgments may be interlocutory or final.

ARCP based on FRCP. "Judgment" used in procedural rules includes decree and any order from which appeal lies. (ARCP 54). See topic Practice.

Judgment of court of record of this state, or of U.S. court held in this state, when properly authenticated, may be registered in office of judge of probate of any county in this state. (6-9-210).

See note at head of Digest as to 1998 legislation covered.

See Topical Index in front part of this volume.

JUDGMENTS . . . *continued*

Judgments by Confession.—In law constitute release of errors. (12-22-1). No surety, when sued, may confess judgment if principal debtor willing to defend at own cost, and gives security to surety, to be approved by court. (8-3-12).

Judgments by Consent.—Recital in judgment or decree rendered by court of competent jurisdiction that parties interested are sui juris and consented or agreed to entry is, in absence of vitiating fraud in premises, conclusive of facts recited and imports absolute verity. (277 Ala. 471, 172 So.2d 35).

Judgments on Pleadings.—FRCP 12(c) applies. (ARCP 12[c]).

Summary Judgments.—FRCP 56 adopted with requirement of 30 day waiting period before moving for summary judgment. (ARCP 56).

Declaratory Judgments.—Uniform Act adopted; §§14-17 omitted. (6-6-220, et seq.). See also ARCP 57.

Default Judgments.—FRCP 55 substantially adopted. Court may set aside entry of default any time before judgment. Default judgment may be set aside by court's own motion or on motion by party within 30 days of entry. (ARCP 55[c]). In ejectment, judgment by default is admission of title in plaintiff, but to recover costs plaintiff must prove defendant's possession of premises at commencement of suit. (6-6-290). Default judgment against trade name is judgment against individual doing business under trade name if individual served with complaint. (601 So.2d 465).

Offer of Judgment.—FRCP 68 substantially adopted with requirement that offer of judgment be made at least 15 days before trial. (ARCP 68).

Docketing.—Judgments entered upon minutes of court are parts of record of causes to which they pertain, and need not be copied into final record. (12-20-21). Minute entry showing judgment constitutes final record of judgment. (16 Ala. App. 51, 74 So. 864). See also ARCP 58.

Vacation or Modification.—FRCP 59 and 60 substantially adopted. (ARCP 59, 60). On motion within 30 days of entry of judgment, judgment may be set aside and new trial granted. (ARCP 59[b]). In criminal trials, judgment may be set aside and new trial ordered in accordance with §15-17-5. Statute cumulative with common law power of court to set aside judgment and grant new trial. (251 Ala. 163, 36 So.2d 513). Within 30 days of entry of judgment, court of its own initiative may order new trial for any reason it might have granted new trial on motion of party. (ARCP 59[d]). Unlike practice under FRCP, if case is tried before jury, new trial must be granted as to all issues or denied as to all. (ARCP 59[a]). Motion to alter, amend, or vacate judgment must be served not later than 30 days after entry of judgment. (ARCP 59[e]). Court may require remittitur as condition to overruling of motion for new trial, but plaintiff's acceptance of such remittitur does not prejudice right to have verdict reinstated in full amount upon appeal by defendant. (ARCP 59[f]). Unless time limit extended by consent of parties or by appellate court to which appeal from judgment would lie, failure of trial court to rule on motion under ARCP 59 within 90 days deemed denial of motion. (ARCP 59.1). When judgment invalid on face of record because of lack of jurisdiction, court must, upon application of interested party, vacate such judgment without regard to time limits. (270 Ala. 715, 121 So.2d 885; 151 Ala. 242, 44 So. 184). Same principle applies where judgment based upon complaint which fails completely to state substantial claim. (274 Ala. 273, 147 So.2d 803; 244 Ala. 667, 15 So.2d 462).

Lien.—Judgment is not lien (89 Ala. 538, 7 So. 637) but registration of judgment of court of record creates lien on all property of defendant in county where registered, which continues for ten years. (6-9-211). For judgment creditor to have priority over prior executed deed, judgment creditor must show that its rights accrued before prior executed deed recorded, and it did not, at time of judgment, have notice of deed. (477 So.2d 328).

Revival.—No execution shall issue on judgment or decree of district or circuit court on which execution has not been sued out within ten years of its entry, until same has been reviewed by appropriate motion or action under ARCP. (6-9-192). Assignee of judgment or decree, if assignment written, may have same revived in assignee's name by appropriate motion or action under ARCP (6-9-196[d]). Judgment or decree cannot be revived after 20 years from entry. (6-9-190).

Assignment.—If assignment endorsed on execution docket or margin of record of judgment and attested by clerk, register or judge of probate, assignee may have execution thereon in name of plaintiff for use of assignee (6-9-196[b]), and may maintain any action thereon in own name (6-9-196[c]).

Satisfaction.—No statutory form of satisfaction; marginal notation on judgment record "Received payment in full.", signed by judgment creditor, sufficient.

Actions.—Independent action may be maintained on judgment. (234 Ala. 654, 176 So. 363). Conversely, action can be maintained to subject property to lien of judgment despite availability of statutory means of enforcement. (226 Ala. 313, 146 So. 807). See also category Debtor and Creditor, topic Fraudulent Sales and Conveyances, subhead Remedies.

Foreign Judgments.—Foreign judgment is not enforceable unless final and not subject to modification of any liability thereunder. (275 Ala. 305, 154 So.2d 661). Proper form of action to enforce foreign judgment is action of debt or statutory equivalent. (36 Ala. App. 360, 58 So.2d 129). To enforce foreign judgment, certified, exemplified, or otherwise properly authenticated copy of judgment must be before Ala. court as part of trial record. (477 So.2d 396).

Revised Uniform Enforcement of Foreign Judgments Act adopted. (6-9-230, et seq.).

Nonsuit.—FRCP 41(b) applies. (ARCP 41[b]).

Amendment.—FRCP 60 substantially adopted. (ARCP 60). Motion for relief from final judgment, order, or proceedings should be made not more than four months after judgment, order, or proceeding entered or taken. (ARCP 60[b]).

LIMITATION OF ACTIONS:

Actions must be brought within following periods after respective causes of action accrue:

Twenty Years.—Actions on judgments of courts of record. (6-2-32).

Ten Years.—Actions on sealed instruments; for recovery of lands; brought on behalf of state against public officers for nonfeasance, misfeasance or malfeasance in office. (6-2-33).

Seven Years.—All claims, whether in tort or contract, against all persons who performed or furnished design, planning, supervision or construction of improvements on real property (6-5-218), held unconstitutional (435 So.2d 725).

Six Years.—Actions for trespass to persons or to personal or real property; for conversion; on unsealed instruments; for recovery of money on loan on stated or liquidated account; for recovery of rent due upon parol demise (oral rental); for use and occupation of land; motions and actions against sureties of public officers and personal representatives; against attorneys at law for failure to pay over money to clients, or for neglect of duty (but see category Legal Profession, topic Attorneys and Counselors, subhead Legal Services Liability, concerning two year limitation on actions under Alabama Legal Services Liability Act); for recovery upon simple contract not otherwise enumerated. (6-2-34).

Five Years.—Actions founded on equities of redemption; by state or any subdivision thereof for taxes and licenses. (6-2-35).

Four Years.—Actions or motions against surety on bond executed in cause in any of federal courts or of any other state or country. (6-2-36). Breach of contracts of sale under Uniform Commercial Code. (7-2-725).

Three Years.—Actions to recover money due on open or unliquidated account; proceedings to disbar attorneys. (6-2-37).

Two Years.—Actions by representatives to recover damages for wrongful act, omission, or negligence causing death of decedent. (6-2-38[a]). Certain civil actions under Securities Act of Ala. (8-6-19[f]).

Actions for malpractice against physicians, surgeons, dentists, medical institutions, or other health care providers, whether based on tort or contract, except that if cause was not and could not have reasonably been discovered, then six months after it was or should have been discovered, but in no event more than four years, except minor under four years old shall have until his eighth birthday. (6-5-482).

Actions by and against common carrier to recover charges or overcharges. (6-2-38[b]-[f]). Actions to charge real estate with debts and obligations of decedents. (6-2-41).

Actions for malicious prosecution; seduction; penalty prescribed by statute; libel or slander; any tort not specifically provided for; actions seeking to hold master liable for actions of agent; actions for injury to property of decedent; actions for recovery of wages. (6-2-38[h]-[o]).

Action based on intentional blasting proximately causing damage by concussion is action of trespass on case, not of trespass, and is governed by one-year limitations period of §6-2-39 (now two years—see 6-2-38) rather than six-year period of §6-2-34. (472 So.2d 1044).

Actions arising under 42 U.S.C. §1983. (576 So.2d 210).

Actions against architects, engineers, and certain licensed general contractors, whether written express warranty, contract, or indemnity regarding construction of real property; all actions occurring more than 13 years after substantial completion of construction are barred. (6-5-227).

One Year.—Actions against creditor for charging excessive finance charges in violation of Consumer Credit Act. (5-19-19). Product liability actions against original seller. (6-5-502).

Six Months.—Actions under bulk sales provisions of Uniform Commercial Code. (7-6-111). Actions to test validity of bond elections or issuance of bonds or levying of taxes pursuant to such elections must be commenced within six months from declaration of election results. (6-2-40).

Actions Not Specifically Provided For.—All actions for injury to person or rights of another not arising from contract and not otherwise provided for must be brought within two years of accrual. (6-2-38[1]).

New Actions.—On arrest or reversal of judgment for plaintiff, suit may be brought again within one year. (6-2-38[p]).

Foreign Cause of Action.—When statute of limitations of another state or foreign country bars action upon contract made or act done in such state or country, bar effective in this state against any action brought thereon in same manner.

Disabilities of Plaintiff.—Infants and insane persons have three years or such lesser applicable statutory period after removal of disabilities to bring action; provided that disabilities shall not extend for more than 20 years from time cause of action accrued. Imprisoned persons have right to commence action and to make any proper appearances on their behalf in such actions. (6-2-8[a]). Rule operates only in favor of disabled and not to one succeeding to disabled person's rights. (416 So.2d 743). Disability not existing when cause of action accrued does not suspend statute. (6-2-8[c]). When two or more disabilities coexist at time cause of action accrued, limitation does not attach until all removed. (6-2-8[b]). Savings provision applies even though guardian appointed for infant, insane person. (404 So. 2d 576).

Absence or Concealment of Defendant.—Time does not run during absence of defendant from state (6-2-10), but special statutory methods for service of process on nonresidents create presence within state sufficient to prevent this section from tolling statute of limitations. (299 F.2d 173).

Interruption of Statutory Period.—Statute does not run while action stayed by injunction or statutory prohibition. (6-2-12).

Public Rights.—No time limitation within which state may bring action for recovery of lands of state and of state educational and governmental institutions, nor within which counties or municipal corporations may bring actions for recovery of lands. (6-2-31).

See note at head of Digest as to 1998 legislation covered.

See Topical Index in front part of this volume.

LIMITATION OF ACTIONS . . . continued

Revival of Barred Claims.—Partial payment, or interest payment (230 Ala. 513, 161 So. 486), by party sought to be charged, made before bar in effect, sets new date from which full period must run. After bar in effect, debt or obligation cannot be revived except by unconditional promise in writing signed by party to be charged. (6-2-16).

Contractual Limitations.—Except as otherwise provided by Uniform Commercial Code, agreement limiting time for bringing action to less than that prescribed by law is void. (6-2-15).

Pleading.—Limitation must be specially pleaded. (ARCP 8[c]).

Uniform Commercial Code adopted. (7-10-101). See category Business Regulation and Commerce, topic Commercial Code.

Computation of Time.—In motions or actions against sureties for public officers and representatives for misfeasance or nonfeasance, time computed from act done or omitted by principal, which fixes liability of surety. (6-2-34[7]). In actions to recover money due by open or unliquidated account time computed from date of last item of account, or from time when by contract or usage account due. (6-2-37[1]).

When right of entry on lands accrues, entry must be considered as having been made and cause of action as having then accrued. (6-2-4). When there are mutual accounts between persons who are not merchants, time computed from date of last item, unless account liquidated, and balance struck. (6-2-11). When right exists, but demand necessary to entitle party to action against any officer, agent, or attorney, limitation commences from commission or omission of act giving right of action, and not from date of demand. (6-2-7). In actions seeking relief on ground of fraud, including actions otherwise barred by statute, aggrieved party has two years after discovery of facts constituting fraud within which to prosecute. (6-2-3; see also 43-8-5 with respect to intestate succession and wills).

Civil action for injury resulting from exposure to asbestos accrues on first date injured party should have reason to discover injury giving rise to such action. (6-5-502).

Time for limitation of action by principal against deputy or agent for latter's act or omission does not commence until liability of the principal ascertained by suit against him. (6-2-6).

When either party to a contract is subject or citizen of country with which U.S. is at war, time of continuance of war not included. (6-2-13).

Federal Employers' Liability Act cause of action against state-owned railroad tolled while pending in federal court. (620 So.2d 637).

Time between death and grant of letters testamentary or of administration, not exceeding six months, not part of time limit for actions by or against estate. (6-2-14).

Contest of Wills.—See category Estates and Trusts, topic Wills, subhead Contest.

PARTITION:

Jurisdiction and Venue.—Jurisdiction proper in circuit (35-6-20) or probate (35-6-40) court of county where property located. Original jurisdiction of circuit court unaffected by jurisdiction statutorily conferred on probate court. (74 Ala. 198).

Proceedings.—

Circuit Court Proceeding.—If proceeding is in circuit court, ARCP apply (ARCP 1; see also 35-6-20) and all questions pertaining to controverted title or equity of party may be disposed of in action (35-6-23). Concerning nonresident, unknown, or absent parties, see category Property, topic Absentees, subhead Partition.

Probate Court Proceeding.—In probate court proceeding one or more of joint owners or tenants in common must make petition to court, stating names of all parties and names of guardians of infant parties; their residence if known and whether they are over or under 19 years old and description of property; number of shares into which it is to be divided; and interest of various parties therein. (35-6-40; -42). There must be hearing. (35-6-43). Commissioners must be appointed; property divided or sold; and papers filed and registered as conveyances. (35-6-45; -49). Concerning nonresident, unknown, or absent parties, see category Property, topic Absentees, subhead Partition.

Partition in Kind or Sale.—Any property, real, personal or mixed, held by joint owners or tenants in common, may be divided among them, or sold for division, on written application of one or more of them to circuit (35-6-20) or probate (35-6-40) court of county in which property situated. Such application to probate court may be made by executor or administrator of deceased person in interest, or by guardian of minor or person of unsound mind. (35-6-40).

Partnership Property.—Whenever partner retires or dies, and if business continues without settlement of accounts between him or estate and partnership, he or his legal representative may have value of interest at date of dissolution ascertained and shall receive, as ordinary creditor, value of partnership interest or plus profits attributable to partnership interest since dissolution. (10-8-103).

PLEADING:

Governed by ARCP, derived in large part from FRCP. See topic Practice.

Pleadings Permitted.—FRCP 7 effective except motions subject to obligations of ARCP 11. (ARCP 7).

Complaint.—FRCP 8(a, e, f) effective except jurisdiction need not be pleaded. While there are not many technical requirements of pleadings, intent and effect of pleading rules is to permit claim to be stated in general terms, and thus ARCP 8 envisages statement of circumstances, occurrences, and events in support of claim presented. (ARCP 8).

Answer.—FRCP 8(b, c, d, e, f) effective except parties allowed 30 days for responsive pleading. (ARCP 12[a]). Parties allowed 14 days for responsive pleading in district court. (ARCP 12[dc]).

Counterclaim or Set-Off.—Substantially same as FRCP 13 except compulsory counterclaims not mandatory if claim of defendant whose defense will be managed by liability insurer, or claim exceeding jurisdictional amount of inferior court having direct appeal to Supreme Court or Court of Civil Appeals. (ARCP 13). See category Civil Actions and Procedure, topic Actions, subhead Counterclaims and Cross-Claims.

Reply.—FRCP 7(a) effective. (ARCP 7[a]).

Demurrer.—Not permitted (ARCP 7[c]), but use of word "demurrer" shall be understood to mean "motion to dismiss for failure to state a claim" or "motion to strike an insufficient defense" as set out in ARCP 12 (ARCP 81[e]).

Amended or Supplemental Pleadings.—FRCP 15 effective with modifications. Party can amend pleading without leave of court any time within 42 days before first trial setting. Thereafter, party can only amend pleading for good cause and upon court approval. Party can respond to amended pleading within time remaining to respond to original pleading or within ten days after service of amended pleading, whichever is longer. (ARCP 15[a]). Also, amendment shall not be refused under ARCP 15(a) or (b) solely because it adds claim or defense, changes claim or defense, or works complete change in parties. (ARCP 15[b]). When party ignorant of name of opposite party and uses fictitious name in pleadings, and subsequently learns real name of opposing party, amendment substituting real name not amendment changing party against whom claim is asserted. (ARCP 9[h] and 15[c]).

Affidavits of Merits.—FRCP 56(e) applies to affidavits supporting motion for summary judgment. (ARCP 56[e]).

Affidavits of Defense.—FRCP 56(e) applies to affidavits opposing motion for summary judgment. (ARCP 56[e]).

Bills of Particulars.—No provisions.

Verification.—FRCP 11 effective. (ARCP 11).

Service.—FRCP 5(a,b,c) effective. (ARCP 5).

Filing.—FRCP 5(d,e) effective, except if court determines discovery papers need not be filed, and filing by electronic means not allowed. (ARCP 5).

Time.—Answer, answer to cross-complaint, and reply, if ordered by court, must be served within 30 days after service. If motion permitted under ARCP 12 is made, period of time for answer, answer to cross-complaint or reply, shall be ten days after notice of court's denial or postponement of motion or after service of more definite statement if court grants a motion for more definite statement. (ARCP 12[a]). All counterclaims other than those maturing or acquired after pleading shall relate back to time original plaintiff's claim arose. (ARCP 13[c]). Time computed and may be extended as under FRCP 6. (ARCP 6).

Frivolous Claims.—Court may award attorney's fees and costs against attorney or party who has brought civil action or asserted claim or defense that court determines to be without substantial justification. (12-19-272[a]). Court may assess attorney's fees and costs against any attorney or party if court finds that claim or defense interposed for abuse of discovery, delay, or harassment. (12-19-272[c]).

Proof of Claims.—Handling of accounts may be facilitated by forwarding itemized statement of account verified by affidavit of competent witness. Following form of affidavit, supporting such accounts, is suggested:

Form

State of . . . .
County of . . . .
Before me, ..., a Notary Public, in and for said County in said State, personally appeared . . . . . ., who, being by me first duly sworn, deposes and says, that he is . . . . . . for the firm of . . . . . . (or as the case may be); that the annexed statement of the account of said . . . . . against . . . . . ., of . . . . . ., is just, true and correct; that there is now due on said account the sum of $. . . ., after deducting all credits, set-offs or counterclaims.

. . . .

Sworn to and subscribed before me this . . . . day of . . . . . ., 19. . . . Witness my hand and official seal.

. . . .
(Notary Public)

Small Claims.—See category Courts and Legislature, topic Courts. See also topic Practice.

PRACTICE:

Pursuant to rule making authority given it by legislature (12-1-1), Supreme Court has adopted and promulgated Alabama Rules of Civil Procedure (ARCP) governing procedure in civil actions in circuit courts, in courts of full, like jurisdiction, and in all other courts where appeals lie directly to Supreme Court or Court of Civil Appeals, except probate courts and proceedings enumerated in ARCP 81. ARCP conform to FRCP but contain modifications required for adaptation to state practice and existing state court system.

Small Claims.—See category Courts and Legislature, topic Courts.

Discovery.—Except for mandatory initial disclosure of core information required under recent amendments to FRCP 26(a), ARCP 26-37 are substantially same as Federal Rules, providing for following methods of discovery: depositions upon oral examinations or written questions; written interrogatories, limited to 40 interrogatories (ARCP 33[a]), including subparts; production of documents or things or permission to enter upon land or other property for inspection or other purposes; physical and mental examinations; and requests for admission (ARCP 26[a]). See topic Depositions and Discovery, subhead Insurance Agreements.

Demand for Admission of Facts.—FRCP 36 effective, with minor modifications. (ARCP 36).

Direct actions against insurer not allowed.

Dismissal.—FRCP 41 effective with minor modifications. (ARCP 41).

Pre-Trial Conference.—With exception of allowing any party to request pre-trial conference, ARCP 16 providing for pre-trial conferences is similar to FRCP 16. Under ARCP 16, however, trial court is not instructed to enter scheduling order.

Setting of Cases.—Trial of actions shall be set by entry on trial docket at least 60 days before date set for trial unless shorter period of time is agreed by all parties,

---

See note at head of Digest as to 1998 legislation covered.

See Topical Index in front part of this volume.

PRACTICE . . . *continued*

interests of justice so require, or case involves default, injunction, domestic relations, habeas corpus, or action appealed to circuit court for de novo review. (ARCP 40[a]). Clerk must notify all out-of-county attorneys of record by personal service or mail within three days of placing case on trial docket. (ARCP 40[b]).

Trial.—Civil cases are tried without jury unless demand for jury trial is made by any party not later than 30 days after service of last pleading directed to issue for which jury trial is sought. (ARCP 38, 39). Trial of all issues so demanded shall be by jury unless right of jury trial is found not to exist under State Constitution or statutes, or unless parties or their attorneys subsequently file written stipulation or make oral stipulation with court, consenting to trial by court sitting without jury. (ARCP 39). Notwithstanding failure of party to demand jury trial in action in which such demand might have been made as matter of right, court in its discretion upon motion may order trial by jury of any or all issues. (ARCP 39[b]).

See also topics Actions, Appeal and Error, Depositions and Discovery, Injunctions, Judgments, Pleading, Process; category Debtor and Creditor, topics Attachment, Executions, Garnishment.

PROCESS:

Civil action commenced by filing complaint with court. (ARCP 3[a]). Service of process, unless otherwise provided by law, shall be made as provided in ARCP. (6-4-20).

FRCP form basis of ARCP. See topic Practice.

General Requisites.—Complaint and summons follow pattern of FRCP. (ARCP 3, 7).

By Whom Issued.—Upon filing of complaint, clerk of court shall issue summons or other process for service on each defendant. Clerk of court can issue additional summons upon request. (ARCP 4[a][1]).

Who May Serve.—Summons and complaint served together with complaint by sheriff or other officer of county in which party to be served resides or may be found, or by someone, not less than 18 years old, especially appointed by court, or by certified mail. (ARCP 4.1, 4.2).

Multiple Defendants.—In case involving multiple defendants, clerk must issue separate summons directed to each defendant. (ARCP 4[a][2]).

Limits of Effective Service.—All process may be served anywhere within territorial limits of State and, when authorized by law or ARCP, may be served outside State. (ARCP 4[b]).

Execution and Return of Service.—Summons must be executed promptly; when person serving process unable to serve copy of process within 30 days, he must endorse that fact and reason therefor on process and return process and copies to clerk who must make appropriate entry on docket sheet of action. Failure to make service within 30 day period and failure to make proof of service do not affect validity of service. (ARCP 4.1[b][4]). However, failure of plaintiff to attempt to obtain service within reasonable time may amount to failure to prosecute warranting dismissal of case. (474 So.2d 642).

Execution and Return of Service in Proceedings Not Governed by ARCP.—All original and mesne process and notices must be immediately executed and returned by officer executing same, unless otherwise provided by law; all executions and venditioni exponas must be made returnable 90 days after issue. (6-4-1).

All executions and other process issuing from court of probate, or issued by judge thereof, may be made returnable, if no other day provided by law, not less than three nor more than six months after such issue. (12-13-6).

In actions for forcible entry and unlawful detainer notice must be served on defendant at least six days before return day of process, and may be served on him anywhere within state. If service cannot be made personally, service may be had by giving notice to any person residing on premises. If no one residing on premises, service may be had by posting notice on premises and mailing complaint to mailing address of premises.

In attachment proceedings, when defendant nonresident of state, notice must be advertised once a week for three successive weeks in newspaper of general circulation in county in which property found, and copy mailed to defendant. (6-6-81). When defendant resident of county notice may be given in writing, in person, or by leaving writing at defendant's residence. If defendant resident of state but not of county, notice must be posted at courthouse door and copy mailed to defendant. (6-6-82).

Detinue begun as other actions and writ of seizure issued pending action if plaintiff executes affidavit and bond; but defendant may retain property upon giving bond with surety in double value of property. (6-6-250, et seq.). See topic Replevin.

Garnishment may issue on summons, pending writ, when affidavit and bond given. (6-6-390 to -393).

When garnishment issued on judgment in which appearance has not been entered for defendant, notice of garnishment must be served on him contemporaneously with service of process of garnishment on garnishee. Notice must be accompanied by statement of rights of exemption, as set forth in ARCP 64A. See category Debtor and Creditor, topic Garnishment.

In actions against foreign or domestic receivers holding, owning, claiming or operating property in state, service may be had by delivery of copy of summons and complaint to receiver if he is found within state, or, if outside state, by leaving copy of summons and complaint with receiver's agent (6-6-627).

Service on Absentee.—See subheads Service by Publication and Long Arm Statute, infra.

Personal Service on Individual.—By serving individual or by leaving copy of summons and complaint at individual's dwelling house or usual place of abode with person of suitable age and discretion residing therein or by delivering copy of summons and complaint to agent authorized by law to receive service. (ARCP 4[c][1]).

Personal Service on Partnership.—Service on partnership may be made by delivering summons and complaint to partner, limited partner, manager, or member, or by serving entity by certified mail at any of its usual places of business. (ARCP 4[c][7]).

Personal Service on Unincorporated Association or Organization.—By serving it in its entity name by certified mail at any of its usual places of business or by serving officer or agent of any such organization or association. (ARCP 4[c][8]).

Personal Service on Domestic Corporation.—Upon corporation, by serving agent authorized by appointment or by law to receive service of process or by serving corporation by certified mail at any of its usual places of business or by serving officer or agent. (ARCP 4[c][6]).

Personal Service on Professional Association, Professional Corporation or Limited Liability Company.—By serving it in its entity name by certified mail at place where offices maintained or by serving shareholder, or by serving agent authorized by appointment or by law to receive service. (ARCP 4[c][9]).

Personal Service on Infant.—By serving any one of following: father, mother, guardian, or individual having care of such person or with whom he lives, or spouse, if infant is married and, if infant is more than 12 years old, by also serving infant personally. (ARCP 4[c][2]).

Personal Service on Joint Stock Company.—No statutory provision.

Personal Service on Foreign Corporation.—Same as domestic corporation. (ARCP 4[c][6]).

Personal Service on Incompetent Person.—Upon incompetent person not confined, by serving incompetent and his guardian but, if no guardian has been appointed, by serving incompetent and person with whom he lives or person who cares for him. (ARCP 4[c][3]).

Upon incompetent person not having guardian and confined in any institution for mentally ill or mentally deficient, by serving superintendent of institution or similar official or person having responsibility for custody of incompetent person. (ARCP 4[c][4]).

Personal Service on Incarcerated Person.—By serving individual, except when individual infant. (ARCP 4[c][5]).

Personal Service on Public Bodies.—

(1) State: Upon this state or any one of its departments, offices and institutions by serving officer responsible for administration of department, office or institution, and by serving attorney general of this state. (ARCP 4[c][10]).

(2) County: Upon county or upon any of its offices, agencies, districts, departments, institutions or administrative units, by serving chairman or presiding officer or member of governing body of such county. (ARCP 4[c][11]).

(3) Municipal Corporation: Upon municipal corporation or upon any of its offices, departments, agencies, authorities, institutions or administrative units by serving mayor or presiding officer or councilman, commissioner or other member of municipal corporation. (ARCP 4[c][12]).

(4) Other Governmental Entity: Upon any governmental entity not mentioned above by serving person, officer, group or body responsible for administration of that entity or by serving appropriate legal officer, if any, representing entity. Service upon any person who is member of "group" or "body" having responsibility for administration of entity shall be sufficient. (ARCP 4[c][13]).

Service by Publication.—Service by publication available for claims historically equitable involving property under control of court or marital status where identity or residence of defendant unknown or where resident defendant has been absent from his residence for more than 30 days since filing of complaint and method of service by publication in such instances not specifically provided by statute and for claims against defendant who avoids service of process. (ARCP 4.3[a]). Affidavit is required reciting reason for need to serve by publication. (ARCP 4.3[d][1]). Publication must be made once a week for four consecutive weeks in newspaper published in county where action is pending, if any, or, if none, in newspaper published in adjoining county. (ARCP 4.3[d][2], [d][3]). When name of defendant unknown and cannot be ascertained, upon presentation of complaint to clerk with affidavit stating that plaintiff does not know defendant's name after diligent inquiry, and that he believes defendant's residence not in state, clerk must make publication. (ARCP 4.3). Appropriate basis exists for service of process outside state when person nonresident or resident or resident absent from state with sufficient contacts with state as set forth in ARCP 4.2(a)(2) so that prosecution of action not inconsistent with constitution of this State or U.S. method of out-of-state service by certified mail, or upon written request to clerk, by delivery by process server, except when service by publication available. (ARCP 4.2).

Service By Mail.—Service may be made by certified mail when plaintiff files written request with clerk requesting such service. (ARCP 4.1[c]; ARCP 4.2[b][1]).

Personal Service Outside State.—Plaintiffs may file request with clerk for order designating service by nonparty process server not less than 18 years old. (ARCP 4.2[b][2]).

Long Arm Statute.—Jurisdiction extends to limits of due process. (ARCP 4.2[a][2][I]).

Nonresident Motorist.—See category Transportation, topic Motor Vehicles, subhead Action Against Nonresident or Absent or Concealed Resident.

Proof of Service.—When personal service is made by delivery, person serving process shall endorse that fact on process and return it to clerk who must make appropriate entry on docket sheet of action. (ARCP 4.1[b][3]; ARCP 4.2[b][2][B]). When service made by certified mail, return receipt requested, clerk must enter fact of mailing and receipt of return receipt on docket sheet of action. (ARCP 4.1[c][2]; ARCP 4.2[b][1][A]).

Substitute Service.—For various transactions provided by statute in addition to above provisions. Service may be had by certified mail, or in certain cases by publication, on nonresident or resident. (ARCP 4.1[c], 4.2[b][1], 4.3). When defendant in any action involving real or personal property or effects situated in this state secrets himself, on affidavit being filed, service may be had by publication. (ARCP 4.3). Unknown heirs or defendants may also be served by publication after affidavit filed. (ARCP 4.3[d][1]). Service may be had by publication on domestic or foreign corporation whenever shown by affidavit that corporation has failed to elect officers or appoint agents or that officers

---

See note at head of Digest as to 1998 legislation covered.

See Topical Index in front part of this volume.

PROCESS . . . *continued*

or agents have been absent from state for 30 days since complaint filed. (ARCP 4.3[c]). Service on nonresident executors and administrators may be made by filing copy of summons in probate court granting letters and by mailing copy thereof to such nonresident executor or administrator and serving copy thereof upon resident surety if any. (43-2-198). No post office address of nonresident executor given and no resident surety, service may be made by publication in newspaper published in county where proceeding is pending for two consecutive weeks, or, if none, by posting on door of courthouse for 15 days. (43-2-199).

Acknowledgment or Waiver.—Resident or nonresident defendant or his attorney may make acknowledgment or waiver of service by writing signed by defendant in presence of credible witness, who must subscribe name. (ARCP 4[h]).

See topic Practice.

REPLEVIN:

Statutory detinue used instead of replevin. (6-6-250, et seq.). Detinue statute held facially unconstitutional to extent it permits attachment without prior notice and hearing. (362 F.Supp. 520; 60 F.R.D. 104). Rules of practice, effective subsequent to decision, require notice and hearing before issuance of writ of seizure prior to judgment, unless plaintiff shows that defendant about to remove, conceal or dispose of personalty sought. (ARCP 64).

Proceedings.—After action commenced for recovery, plaintiff, his agent, or his attorneys makes, affidavit that property belongs to plaintiff and submits bond in amount approved by clerk. Sheriff required to take possession unless defendant gives bond double value of property. If defendant neglects to post bond, sheriff delivers property to plaintiff, and plaintiff must post bond double value of property within five days. (6-6-250).

Repossession.—Successful party may obtain writ of attachment or execution when practicable, if losing party does not deliver property. (6-6-263). Repossession prior to judgment requires defendant to serve written request for hearing on plaintiff within five days from seizure date. (ARCP 64).

Claims of Third Persons.—Any person not party claiming interest may intervene by order of court as of right. Within five days of order, third person may submit affidavit that entitled to possession of property and give bond double value of property in favor of party otherwise entitled to possess to obtain possession, unless party in possession gives similar bond to retain possession. (6-6-252).

Judgment or Order.—Against either party must be for property sued for, or its value, with damages for detention to time of trial. (6-6-256).

SEQUESTRATION:

Where there is judgment directing party to do any specific act and party fails to comply, court may direct act to be done at disobedient party's expense; includes land conveyance, document delivery, or any specific act. (ARCP 70).

SERVICE:

See topic Process.

STAY OF EXECUTION:

See topic Appeal and Error; category Debtor and Creditor, topic Executions.

SUBMISSION OF CONTROVERSY:

No statutory provisions.

VENUE:

Legal Actions Against Individuals.—(1) Recovery of, possession of, and trespass to land in county in which land (or material part of) located; (2) contracts, in county in which any permanent Alabama defendant resides; (3) other personal actions (if there is any permanent Alabama resident defendant), in county in which defendant resides or in county in which act or omission may have been done or occurred. (6-3-2).

Equitable Actions Against Individuals.—(1) Real estate subject of matter, in county in which land (or material part of) located; (2) to enjoin proceedings on judgments in other courts, in county in which proceedings pending or judgment entered; (3) (with some exceptions) must be commenced in county in which defendant or material defendant resides; (4) where nonresident, in county subject of (or portion of) action was when claim arose or act on which action founded was to be performed. (6-3-2).

Executors or administrators, in county where letters granted. (43-2-130).

Actions for work and labor done or breaches of contracts or covenants as to easements or rights-of-way, in county in which work done or land situated (as to which easement or right-of-way granted). (6-3-3).

Unincorporated organizations or associations that issue policies or certificates of insurance to members, in county where they do business or where they issue such policies or certificates. (6-3-4).

Person, firm or corporation that issues policies or certificates of insurance subject to civil action in county where policy- or certificate-holder resides, except that against foreign insurance corporation, only in county where it does business. Acts effected by mail or otherwise constitute doing business in county: (1) Making, issuance, delivery of insurance contracts to county residents; (2) solicitation of applications for such contracts; (3) collection of premiums, membership fees, assessments or other considerations for such contracts; or (4) any other transaction of insurance business. (6-3-5).

Actions against unincorporated organization or association, in county where it does business or has branch or local organization. (6-3-6).

Civil actions for damages for personal injury, death, or property damage against county or municipality, in county or in county in which municipality is located or in county where act or omission complained of occurred. (6-3-11).

Foreign corporation, in county it does business by agent. (6-3-7).

Domestic corporation in county it does business by agent or was doing business when cause of action arose, provided that personal injury actions must be in county injury occurred or plaintiff resides if corporation does business by agent in county of plaintiff's residence. (6-3-7).

Other specific venue rules apply to breach of official bonds (6-3-8) and action involving prison system (6-3-9).

Actions Arising in Other States.—Whenever, either at common law or under statutes of another state, a cause of action, either upon contract or in tort, has arisen in such other state against any person or corporation, such cause of action enforceable in courts of this state, in any county in which jurisdiction of defendant may legally be obtained, in same manner in which jurisdiction could have been obtained if cause of action had arisen in this state. Forum non conveniens applies, but dismissal subject to defendant's consent to other jurisdiction. (6-5-430).

If venue improperly laid, court shall on timely motion transfer action to court in which action might have been properly filed and case must proceed as though originally filed therein. If venue might have been proper in more than one court, defendant shall have right to select court to which case shall be transferred. (6-3-21; ARCP 82[d]). Ruling on transfer of venue may be raised either on appeal from judgment or by petition for writ of mandamus. (540 So.2d 720).

Change of Venue.—Venue may be changed if either party, by affidavit, shows that he cannot have fair trial in county where suit pending (6-3-20), or for convenience of parties and witnesses (6-3-21.1).

Contract provisions changing or altering venue void. (6-3-1).

See also category Insurance, topic Surety and Guaranty Companies.

WITNESSES:

See topic Evidence, subhead Witnesses.

COURTS AND LEGISLATURE

COURTS:

United States District Courts.—

Northern District.—Clerk's office: 140 Hugo L. Black U.S. Courthouse, 1729 Fifth Ave. N., Birmingham 35203, or Clerk's Office, 101 Holmes Avenue, N.E., Huntsville, 35801.

Clerk's fee, to be paid when suit is filed, is $150.

Northeastern Division.—Counties of Cullman, Jackson, Lawrence, Limestone, Madison and Morgan.

Court sits at Huntsville and Decatur.

Eastern Division.—Counties of Calhoun, Clay, Cleburne and Talladega.

Court sits at Anniston.

Southern Division.—Counties of Blount, Jefferson and Shelby.

Court sits at Birmingham.

Western Division.—Counties of Bibb, Greene, Pickens, Sumter and Tuscaloosa.

Court sits at Tuscaloosa.

Northwestern Division.—Counties of Colbert, Franklin and Lauderdale.

Court sits at Florence.

Middle Division.—Counties of Cherokee, DeKalb, Etowah, Marshall and St. Clair.

Court sits at Gadsden.

Jasper Division.—Counties of Fayette, Lamar, Marion, Walker and Winston.

Court sits at Jasper.

Southern District.—Clerk's office: 113 St. Joseph St., Mobile 36602.

Deposit.—Payment of $150 clerk's filing fee required when suit is filed.

Northern Division.—Counties of Dallas, Hale, Marengo, Perry and Wilcox.

Court sits in Selma for Northern Division and in Mobile for Southern Division as condition of docket requires.

Southern Division.—Counties of Baldwin, Choctaw, Clarke, Conecuh, Escambia, Mobile, Monroe and Washington.

Middle District.—Clerk's office: 15 Lee St., Montgomery 36104.

Deposit required when suit is filed, clerk's fee of $150.

Northern Division.—Counties of Autauga, Barbour, Bullock, Butler, Chilton, Coosa, Covington, Crenshaw, Elmore, Lowndes, Montgomery and Pike.

Court sits at Montgomery.

Eastern Division.—Counties of Chambers, Lee, Macon, Randolph, Russell and Tallapoosa.

Court sits at Opelika.

Southern Division.—Counties of Coffee, Dale, Geneva, Henry and Houston.

Court sits at Dothan.

Supreme Court.—

Jurisdiction.—Supreme Court has original jurisdiction of all cases and controversies as provided by constitution, to issue such remedial writs or orders as may be necessary to give it general supervision and control of courts of inferior jurisdiction, and to answer questions of state law certified by court of U.S. (Const. Amend. 328, §6.02; 12-2-7); to issue writ of quo warranto and mandamus in matter where no other court has jurisdiction (12-2-7).

Supreme Court has appellate jurisdiction coextensive with state, under restrictions and regulations prescribed by law. (12-2-7).

If case was in Court of Appeals, in order to have it reviewed by Supreme Court, party must apply for rehearing in Court of Appeals. If denied, petition for certiorari supported by brief must be made within 14 days after application for rehearing by Court of Appeals denied. (ARAP 39).

Transfer.—Supreme Court may transfer to Court of Civil Appeals, for determination, any civil case appealed to Supreme Court and within appellate jurisdiction of Supreme Court, except following: (1) Case that Supreme Court determines presents substantial question of federal or state constitutional law; (2) case that Supreme Court determines

COURTS . . . *continued*
involves novel legal question, resolution of which will have significant statewide impact; (3) utility rate case appealed directly to Supreme Court under provisions of §37-1-140; (4) bond validation proceeding appealed to Supreme Court under provisions of §6-6-754; or (5) bar disciplinary proceeding.

Place Where Court Sits.—Supreme Court sits in Montgomery.

Clerk's Office.—445 Dexter Avenue, P.O. Box 157, Montgomery, Alabama 36101.

Courts of Appeal have no original jurisdiction except to issue all writs necessary or appropriate in aid of appellate jurisdiction of courts of appeal. (Const. Amend. 328 §6.03).

Court of Criminal Appeals.—Court of Criminal Appeals has exclusive appellate jurisdiction of all misdemeanors, including violation of town and city ordinances, habeas corpus and all felonies, including all post conviction writs in criminal cases. (12-3-9).

Court of Civil Appeals.—Court of Civil Appeals has exclusive appellate jurisdiction of all civil cases where amount involved, exclusive of interest and costs, does not exceed $50,000, all appeals from administrative agencies other than Alabama Public Service Commission, all appeals in workmen's compensation cases, all appeals in domestic relations cases, including annulment, divorce, adoption and child custody cases, and all extraordinary writs arising from appeals in said cases. When there is recovery in court below of any amount other than costs, amount of such recovery shall be deemed to be amount involved, otherwise amount claimed shall be deemed to be amount involved, except that in actions of detinue alternate value of property as found by court or jury shall be deemed to be amount involved. (12-3-10). Each court of appeals has original jurisdiction in issuance and determination of writs of quo warranto and mandamus in relation to matters in which it has appellate jurisdiction. Each court has authority to issue writs of injunction, habeas corpus and such other remedial and original writs as necessary to give it general superintendence and control of jurisdictions inferior to it and in matters over which it has exclusive appellate jurisdiction and to punish for contempts. (12-3-11).

When case is improperly submitted to Supreme Court or court of appeals, it will be transferred to proper court. (12-1-4).

Circuit Courts.—

Jurisdiction.—General jurisdiction. (Const. Amend. 328 §6.04). Circuit courts have exclusive original jurisdiction of all civil actions in which matter in controversy exceeds $10,000 and concurrent jurisdiction with district courts in all civil actions in which matter in controversy exceeds $3,000 exclusive of interest and costs. (12-11-30[1]).

Circuit courts have exclusive original jurisdiction of all criminal prosecutions for felonies and misdemeanor or ordinance violations which are lesser included offenses or which arise from same incident as felony charge, except district courts have concurrent jurisdiction with circuit courts to receive pleas of guilty in non-capital felony cases. (12-11-30[2]).

Circuit courts have appellate jurisdiction of civil, criminal and juvenile cases in district court and prosecutions for ordinance violations in municipal courts except in cases in which direct appeal to courts of civil or criminal appeal is provided by law or rule. Appeals to circuit courts are tried de novo with or without jury as provided by law. (12-11-30[3]).

Circuit courts have original jurisdiction over matters in equity. (12-11-31).

Involuntary commitment proceedings of adults may be transferred from probate court to circuit court upon motion of party to proceeding. (12-11-10).

Cases within exclusive jurisdiction of circuit courts filed in district courts, and cases within exclusive jurisdiction of district courts filed in circuit courts, will be transferred to appropriate court by judge or clerk. (12-11-9).

Venue.—See ARCP 82. (See also category Civil Actions and Procedure, topic Venue.)

Rules of Practice.—ARCP apply. (See also topic Practice.)

Appeals.—See ARAP. (See also category Civil Actions and Procedure, topic Appeal and Error.)

There are 40 circuits. (12-11-2).

Place Where Court Sits.—Statute requires circuit courts of the several counties to be open at all times for transaction of any and all business or judicial proceedings of every kind. (12-11-4).

Ala. counties, circuit to which each county belongs, and places where each circuit court sits are as follows:

(Place named is county seat; where two places are named, first is county seat.)

Autauga County: Nineteenth Circuit; court sits at Prattville.
Baldwin County: Twenty-eighth Circuit; court sits at Bay Minette.
Barbour County: Third Circuit; court sits at Clayton and Eufaula.
Bibb County: Fourth Circuit; court sits at Centreville.
Blount County: Thirtieth Circuit; court sits at Oneonta.
Bullock County: Third Circuit; court sits at Union Springs.
Butler County: Second Circuit; court sits at Greenville.
Calhoun County: Seventh Circuit; court sits at Anniston.
Chambers County: Fifth Circuit; court sits at La Fayette.
Cherokee County: Ninth Circuit; court sits at Centre.
Chilton County: Nineteenth Circuit; court sits at Clanton.
Choctaw County: First Circuit; court sits at Butler.
Clarke County: First Circuit; court sits at Grove Hill.
Clay County: Fortieth Circuit; court sits at Ashland.
Cleburne County: Seventh Circuit; court sits at Heflin.
Coffee County: Twelfth Circuit; court sits at Elba and Enterprise.
Colbert County: Thirty-first Circuit; court sits at Tuscumbia.
Conecuh County: Thirty-fifth Circuit; court sits at Evergreen.
Coosa County: Fortieth Circuit; court sits at Rockford.
Covington County: Twenty-second Circuit; court sits at Andalusia.
Crenshaw County: Second Circuit; court sits at Luverne.
Cullman County: Thirty-second Circuit; court sits at Cullman.
Dale County: Thirty-third Circuit; court sits at Ozark.
Dallas County: Fourth Circuit; court sits at Selma.
De Kalb County: Ninth Circuit; court sits at Fort Payne.
Elmore County: Nineteenth Circuit; court sits at Wetumpka.
Escambia County: Twenty-first Circuit; court sits at Brewton.
Etowah County: Sixteenth Circuit; court sits at Gadsden.
Fayette County: Twenty-fourth Circuit; court sits at Fayette.
Franklin County: Thirty-fourth Circuit; court sits at Russellville.
Geneva County: Thirty-third Circuit; court sits at Geneva.
Greene County: Seventeenth Circuit; court sits at Eutaw.
Hale County: Fourth Circuit; court sits at Greensboro.
Henry County: Twentieth Circuit; court sits at Abbeville.
Houston County. Twentieth Circuit; court sits at Dothan.
Jackson County: Thirty-eighth Circuit; court sits at Scottsboro.
Jefferson County: Tenth Circuit; court sits at Birmingham and Bessemer.
Lamar County: Twenty-fourth Circuit; court sits at Vernon.
Lauderdale County: Eleventh Circuit; court sits at Florence.
Lawrence County: Thirty-sixth Circuit; court sits at Moulton.
Lee County: Thirty-seventh Circuit; court sits at Opelika.
Limestone County: Thirty-ninth Circuit; court sits at Athens.
Lowndes County: Second Circuit; court sits at Hayneville.
Macon County: Fifth Circuit; court sits at Tuskegee.
Madison County: Twenty-third Circuit; court sits at Huntsville.
Marengo County: Seventeenth Circuit; court sits at Linden.
Marion County: Twenty-fifth Circuit; court sits at Hamilton.
Marshall County: Twenty-seventh Circuit; court sits at Guntersville and Albertville.
Mobile County: Thirteenth Circuit; court sits at Mobile.
Monroe County: Thirty-fifth Circuit; court sits at Monroeville.
Montgomery County: Fifteenth Circuit; court sits at Montgomery.
Morgan County: Eighth Circuit; court sits at Decatur.
Perry County: Fourth Circuit; court sits at Marion.
Pickens County: Twenty-fourth Circuit; court sits at Carrollton.
Pike County: Twelfth Circuit; court sits at Troy.
Randolph County: Fifth Circuit; court sits at Wedowee.
Russell County: Twenty-sixth Circuit; court sits at Phenix City.
Shelby County: Eighteenth Circuit; court sits at Columbiana.
St. Clair County: Thirtieth Circuit; court sits at Ashville and Pell City.
Sumter County: Seventeenth Circuit; court sits at Livingston.
Talladega County: Twenty-ninth Circuit; court sits at Talladega.
Tallapoosa County: Fifth Circuit; court sits at Dadeville and Alexander City.
Tuscaloosa County: Sixth Circuit; court sits at Tuscaloosa.
Walker County: Fourteenth Circuit; court sits at Jasper.
Washington County: First Circuit; court sits at Chatom.
Wilcox County: Fourth Circuit; court sits at Camden.
Winston County: Twenty-fifth Circuit; court sits at Double Springs.

District Courts.—

Jurisdiction.—District courts are courts of limited jurisdiction. (12-12-1).

Original civil jurisdiction of district courts is concurrent with circuit courts, except as noted below, and includes all civil actions in which matter in controversy does not exceed $10,000, and civil actions based on unlawful detainer. (12-12-30). District courts have exclusive jurisdiction over civil actions in which matter in controversy, exclusive of interest and costs, does not exceed $3,000. (12-12-31[a]; 533 So.2d 617). District courts do not have jurisdiction over: (a) Actions seeking equitable relief other than equitable questions in juvenile cases within jurisdiction of district courts, and equitable defenses asserted or compulsory counterclaims filed by party in action within jurisdiction of district courts; (b) actions enumerated in ARCP 81 other than actions based in negligence against municipalities, actions seeking substitution of lost or destroyed records or instruments, summary motion proceedings, or relieving disabilities of nonage; (c) actions seeking declaratory judgments; and (d) appeals from probate or municipal courts. (12-12-30).

Concurrent juvenile jurisdiction with circuit courts. (12-12-34).

Adoption proceedings may be transferred from probate court to district court upon motion of party to proceeding. (12-12-35).

Exclusive original trial jurisdiction over prosecutions of all misdemeanors except: (a) Prosecutions by municipalities having municipal courts, (b) any prosecution which also involves felony which is within exclusive jurisdiction of circuit courts, and (c) any misdemeanor for which indictment has been returned by grand jury. However, district courts may exercise original jurisdiction concurrent with circuit courts to receive pleas of guilty in prosecutions of felonies not punishable by death. (12-12-32).

Exclusive original jurisdiction of misdemeanor prosecutions for traffic infractions, except ordinance infractions prosecuted in municipal courts. (12-12-51).

May exercise jurisdiction over proceedings relating to demands for extradition made by another jurisdiction pursuant to Alabama laws governing extradition. (12-12-33).

May issue all writs necessary to preserve and enforce their jurisdiction and authority. (12-12-7).

Exercise exclusive jurisdiction to hold preliminary hearings in prosecutions for felonies. Finding by district court of no probable cause is not res judicata as to that issue and state is not barred from proceeding further (15-11-2).

Place Where Court Sits.—In each county seat, in each municipality containing population of 1,000 or more where no municipal court exists, to be restricted to municipal cases, and at other locations within counties where geographical venue lies in more than one place. (Const. Amend. 328 §6.05; 12-12-1[b]).

Venue lies in county where venue would lie for civil or criminal actions brought in circuit court except: (a) In counties where venue for inferior court has lain in area of lesser geographic extent than county, venue lies in such lesser geographic area; (b) venue of prosecutions for violations of municipal ordinances lies in district court sitting in municipality, or if none, district court within county and nearest to municipality. If action filed where venue does not lie, any party may move to transfer action to location where venue proper. (12-12-36).

Rules of Procedure and Trials.—ARCP apply to all civil actions brought in district courts except as otherwise provided by law or rule. (12-12-11). ARCP specifies special

See note at head of Digest as to 1998 legislation covered.

See Topical Index in front part of this volume.

AL – 23

COURTS . . . *continued*
rules for district courts, identified under specific rule as (dc). All issues of law and fact tried by judges of district courts. (12-12-3). Where district court sits as municipal court it takes judicial notice of ordinance of municipality for which it sits. (12-14-7; see also category Civil Actions and Procedure, topic Practice).

Appeals.—Any party may appeal from final judgment of district court in civil case by notice filed in district court within 14 days from later of date of judgment or date of denial of post-trial motion, together with security for costs required by law or rule. Defendant may appeal from final judgment in criminal case by filing notice, together with any bond required by law or rule, within 14 days from later of date of judgment or date of denial of post-trial motion. If appeal in civil or criminal case to appellate court, time governed by ARAP. State or municipality may appeal only from judgment holding statute or ordinance invalid. (12-12-70). Appeals to circuit court for trial de novo (12-12-71), except that appeals in both civil and criminal cases may be direct to appropriate appellate court: (a) If adequate record or stipulation of facts is available and right to trial by jury is waived by all parties entitled thereto; or (b) if parties stipulate that only questions of law are involved and district court certifies question. (12-12-72). Supersedeas bond in twice amount of judgment required by appellant in civil appeals to circuit court. (12-12-73).

Juvenile Courts.—

Jurisdiction.—Circuit court and district court exercise original concurrent jurisdiction sitting as juvenile court. (12-15-2[a]). Judge of district court serves as juvenile court judge in those districts having only one district judge; in districts having more than one district judge, presiding judge of circuit court designates from time to time district judge or circuit judge to hear juvenile cases. (12-15-3). Juvenile court has exclusive original jurisdiction in proceedings in which child alleged to be delinquent, dependent, or in need of supervision; proceedings to determine custody or to appoint legal custodian or guardian of person of child when child is otherwise before court; removal of disabilities of nonage; proceedings under Interstate Compact on Juveniles; proceedings for commitment of mentally ill or mentally retarded child; proceedings for adoption of child when such proceedings have been removed from probate court on motion of any party to proceeding; and termination of parental rights. (12-15-30). Juvenile court has exclusive original jurisdiction: (a) To try any minor or adult charged with: aiding, encouraging, or causing any child to become or remain delinquent, in need of supervision or dependent; disregarding or failing to obey any lawful order made by judge of juvenile court or interfering with custody of any child under jurisdiction of juvenile court; interfering with custody of, or removal or attempting to remove any dependent or delinquent child, or one in need of supervision, or one so alleged to be, or any child whose custody subject of controversy in court, or in custody of court, or of probation officer or any other officer or person designated by court as special officer, or any such child who has been by court committed to any person, persons, institutions, associations, corporation, agency, department of youth services or department of pensions and security; knowingly interfering with, opposing, or otherwise obstructing any probation officer or representative of department of human resources in performance of duties; (b) in proceedings to establish paternity of child born out of wedlock; (c) to try any minor or adult charged with desertion and nonsupport in violation of law; (d) in proceedings for commitment of mentally ill or mentally retarded minor; or (e) to make parents or guardians of child parties to all juvenile court actions. (12-15-31).

Juvenile court may, upon motion by prosecution, transfer for criminal prosecution minor of 14 or more years of age if charges would constitute crime if committed by adult. Conviction following such transfer of minor shall terminate juvenile court's jurisdiction with respect to pending and future allegations of delinquency and to pending and future criminal charges. (12-15-34).

Transfer.—Criminal or quasi criminal cases involving child must be transferred to juvenile court unless case involves child who has been previously transferred for criminal prosecution and convicted or adjudicated youthful offender on criminal charge or child 16 years or older charged with traffic offense other than driving under influence of alcohol or controlled substances. (12-15-33).

Venue.—If delinquency or need of supervision alleged, venue lies in district where acts constituting allegation occurred. If dependency alleged, venue lies in district where child resides or in district where child is present when proceedings commenced. (12-15-35).

Appeals.—Appeals from final orders arising out of jurisdiction of juvenile court over minors and adults taken directly to appropriate appellate court if adequate record or stipulation of facts available and right to jury trial granted or waived, or if parties stipulate that only questions of law are involved. In all cases involving minors and adults, appeals to circuit court which tries case de novo. (Rule 28, ARJP). In cases arising out of jurisdiction of court over child, appeals to: (1) Court of Criminal Appeals in proceedings in which child is adjudicated delinquent and proceedings in which motion seeking order to transfer child to adult court for criminal prosecution is either granted or denied; (2) to Court of Civil Appeals in any other case. (Rule 28, ARJP).

Municipal Courts.—All prosecutions for breach of ordinances of municipality within its police jurisdiction. Concurrent jurisdiction with district court of all acts constituting violations of state law committed within police jurisdiction of municipality which may be prosecuted as breaches of municipal ordinances. (12-14-1). Cases tried by judge without jury. (12-14-6). All appeals from judgments of municipal court to circuit court of circuit in which violation occurred for trial de novo. Municipality may appeal within 60 days without bond from judgment holding ordinance invalid. Defendant may appeal in any case within 14 days from entry of judgment by filing notice of appeal and giving bond conditioned upon defendant's appearance in circuit court (unless bond waived due to indigency). (12-14-70).

Probate Courts.—

Jurisdiction.—General jurisdiction of orphan's business, and of adoptions, and has power to grant letters testamentary, and of administration, and of guardianship, and such further jurisdiction as provided by law, provided that whenever circuit court has taken jurisdiction of settlement of estate, it has power to do all things necessary for settlement of such estate, including appointment of administrators, executors, guardians and trustees. (Const. Amend. 364). Original and general jurisdiction as to probate of wills, granting and revoking of letters testamentary and of administration, controversies in relation to right of executorship, or of administration, settlement of accounts of executors and administrators, sale and disposition of real and personal property belonging to and distribution of intestate's estate, business of minors and persons of unsound mind, allotment of dower, partition of lands within their counties, change of name and in such other cases as jurisdiction may be given by law. (12-13-1). Involuntary commitment proceedings may be transferred to circuit court on motion of any party to proceeding. (12-11-10). Proceedings for adoption of child may be removed to district court on motion of any party to proceeding. (12-12-35).

Place and Terms of Court.—Probate courts open at all times except Sat., Sun., holiday. (12-13-3).

Probate court sits at county seat. In following counties court sits also at places named: Barbour County, at Eufaula; Coffee County, at Enterprise; Jefferson County, at Bessemer; St. Clair County, at Pell City.

LEGISLATURE:

Legislature must convene on second Tues. in Jan. next succeeding its election in organizational session and must remain in session for not longer than ten consecutive calendar days. Commencing in year 1999, annual sessions of Alabama legislature must commence on first Tues. in Mar. of first year of term of office of legislators, on first Tues. of Feb. of second and third years of term and on second Tues. in Jan. of fourth year of term. Regular sessions limited to 30 legislative days and 105 calendar days. (29-1-4).

Special or Extraordinary Sessions.—Governor may call special sessions (Const. Art. V, §122), which must be limited to 12 legislative days and 30 calendar days (29-1-5).

Initiative and Referendum.—No statutory provision.

Lobbyists.—Registration of lobbyists required by Jan. 31 each year or within ten days after first undertaking. (36-25-18). $100 registration fee. (36-25-18).

State Ethics Commission composed of five members created in Oct. 1995. (36-25-3).

Statement of economic interests must be filed with Commission no later than Apr. 30 each year by all: (1) Elected public officials; (2) appointed public officials whose base pay is $50,000 or more annually; (3) candidates; (4) members of Alabama Ethics Commission; (5) all full-time non-merit employees; (6) chief clerks and chief managers; (7) chief county clerks and chief county managers; (8) chief administrators; (9) chief county administrators; (10) public officials or employees whose primary duty is to invest public funds; (11) chief administrative officers of political subdivision; (12) chief and assistant county building inspectors; (13) county or municipal administrators with power to grant or deny land development permits; (14) chief municipal clerks; (15) chiefs of police; (16) fire chiefs; (17) city and county school superintendents and school board members; (18) city and county school principals or administrators; (19) purchasing or procurement agents; (20) directors and assistant directors of state agencies; (21) chief financial and accounting directors; (22) chief grant coordinators; (23) employees of Legislature or agencies; (24) employees of judicial branch. (36-25-14). Statements must contain: (1) Names and addresses of family and business; (2) occupations; (3) total combined household income; (4) if party has engaged in business providing certain services, number of clients and income; (5) if retainers exist for certain client categories, list of categories and anticipated income; (6) list of real estate held for investment; (7) list of indebtedness to businesses operating in Ala. (36-25-14).

Penalties.—Intentional violation of 36-25-1, et seq. class B felony. (36-25-27).

Administrative Procedure Act.—Promulgation of rules and regulations by administrative agencies governed by Administrative Procedure Act (41-22-1, et seq.), which provides for public notice of adopted agency rules, for declaratory ruling by agency on petition of persons substantially affected by rule, for notice and hearing in contested cases, and for judicial review of contested cases.

REPORTS:

Official Reports.—Minor Reports, one volume; Stewart's Reports, 3 volumes; Stewart & Porter's Reports, 5 volumes; Porter's Reports, 9 volumes; Alabama Reports, 295 volumes; Court of Appeals Reports, 57 volumes; Alabama Edition of Southern Reporter, current series, beginning with 331-333 So. 2d.

Unofficial Reports.—Opinions of Supreme Court and Court of Appeals reported unofficially in Southern Reporter, 1887 to 1941, and Southern Reporter, Second Series, 1941 to date.

Digests.—Philip's, Minor to 13 Alabama; Brickell's, Minor to 76 Alabama; Clark's (Criminal), 44 to 63 Alabama; Lomax's (Criminal), 64 to 100 Alabama; Mayfield's, Minor to 180 Alabama; Michie's, complete; Alabama and Southern Reporter Digest (West Publishing Company); Alabama Digest (West Publishing Company); Alabama Digest (2d) (West Publishing Company).

STATUTES:

Contained in Code of 1975. ARCP contained in "Alabama Rules of Court" (West Publishing Company) and in Code of 1975.

Uniform Acts of National Conference of Commissioners on Uniform State Laws adopted are: Anatomical Gift (1969); Appointment of Commissioners (1951); Act to Secure Attendance of Witnesses From Without a State in Criminal Proceedings (1977); †Brain Death (1979); †Business Corporation (1959, am'd 1980); †Certification of Questions of Law (A.R.A.P. Rule 18) (1975); Child Custody Jurisdiction (1980); Commercial Code (1965, am'd 1982); †Common Trust Fund (1943, am'd 1949, 1967); Condominium (effective Jan. 1, 1991); Conservation Easement (1997); Controlled Substances (1971); Criminal Extradition (1931); †Cy-Pres (1940); Declaratory Judgments (1935, am'd 1947); †Desertion and Nonsupport (1915, am'd 1919); †Disclaimer of Property Interests (1981); Disposition of Unclaimed Property (1971, am'd 1973); †Division of Income for Tax Purposes (1967); Durable Power of Attorney (1981); Eminent Domain

See note at head of Digest as to 1998 legislation covered.

See Topical Index in front part of this volume.

AL – 24

STATUTES . . . *continued*

Code (Model) (1985); Enforcement of Foreign Judgments (1986); Federal Lien Registration (1989); Fiduciaries (1943, am'd 1961); Fraudulent Transfer (1989); Gifts to Minors, Revised (1957, am'd 1965, am'd 1967) (repealed 1986 and replaced by Transfers To Minors Act); Guardianship and Protective Proceedings (1987); Insurers Liquidation (1943); Interstate Family Support (1997); †Revised Limited Partnership (1983); Mandatory Disposition of Detainers (1978); Motor Vehicle Certificate of Title and Anti-Theft (1973); Multiple-Person Accounts (1997); †Non-Profit Corporation (1955); †Parentage (1984); †Partnership (1996); †Photographic Copies of Business and Public Records as Evidence (1951); †Principal and Income (1939); Reciprocal Enforcement of Support (as am'd) (1953); †Securities (1959); †Securities Ownership by Minors (1961); Simplification of Fiduciary Security Transfers (1961); Simultaneous Death (1949); †State Administrative Procedure (1961) (Model) (1981); †Testamentary Additions to Trusts (1961); TOD (Transfer on Death) Security Registration (1997); Transfers To Minors (1986); Unincorporated Nonprofit Association (1995); Veterans' Guardianship (1931, am'd 1936).

Uniform Division of Income for Tax Purposes Act adopted by approval and adoption of Multistate Tax Compact through Alabama Income Tax Conformity Act of 1997. (40-27-1 to -6).

Uniform Probate Code used as guide for Alabama Law of Intestate Succession and Wills, but many material differences exist between Uniform Probate Code and Alabama law.

Uniform Commercial Code adopted Jan. 1, 1967. 1972 Official Amendments adopted Feb. 1, 1982, with some Alabama differences. Adopted 1990 Revision of Art. 3 and 1990 Amendments to Art. 4 effective Jan. 1, 1996. Repealed Art. 6 "Bulk Transfers" (Act No. 96-523) effective May 17, 1996. See category Business Regulation and Commerce, topic Commercial Code.

†Adopted with significant modifications.

For text of Uniform Acts falling within the scope of the Martindale-Hubbell Law Digests see Uniform and Model Acts section.

Other Uniform Acts adopted are: Commercial Driver License; Motor Vehicle Safety Responsibility (1951, am'd 1965).

UNIFORM LAWS:

For list of Uniform Acts in force in this state see topic Statutes. For text of Uniform Acts within the scope of the Martindale-Hubbell Law Digests see Uniform and Model Acts section.

CRIMINAL LAW

BAIL:

See topic Criminal Law.

CRIMINAL LAW:

Criminal Code and Code of Criminal Procedure contained in Tit. 13A and Tit. 15. Alabama Rules of Criminal Procedure effective Jan. 1, 1991.

Indictment or Information.—All felonies and all misdemeanors originally prosecuted in district court or circuit court are indictable offenses. (15-8-2). Indictable offenses must be prosecuted by indictment, unless otherwise provided by Constitution or Legislature. (Const. Art. I, §8). In certain other cases warrant based on affidavit is sufficient. (15-7-1; -22). Indictments presented by grand jury. (15-8-70).

Bail.—All offenses bailable as of right except in capital offenses where court of opinion that defendant guilty of offense. (15-13-2; -3). Capital offenses bailable as matter of right where continuance had twice by state, without consent of accused, for testimony of absent witnesses. (15-13-3).

Interstate Compact for Supervision of Parolees and Probationers in effect. (15-22-l).

Uniform Criminal Extradition Act in effect. (15-9-20; -30 to -49; -60 to -65).

DEBTOR AND CREDITOR

ASSIGNMENTS:

All bonds, contracts, and writings for payment of money, or other things, or performance of any act assignable by endorsement. (8-5-20). Personal service contracts generally not assignable. (286 Ala. 72, 237 So.2d 463). Verbal assignment of chose in action effective in equity. (218 Ala. 221, 118 So. 404). Claims against railroad companies for injuries to property may be assigned in writing. (8-5-23).

Uniform Commercial Code adopted. (7-9-101, et seq.). See category Business Regulation and Commerce, topic Commercial Code.

Instrument Transferring Title.—No special requirements.

Filing.—See category Business Regulation and Commerce, topic Commercial Code.

Recording.—See categories Business Regulation and Commerce, topic Commercial Code; Documents and Records, topic Records.

Notice.—See category Business Regulation and Commerce, topic Commercial Code.

Effect.—Assignment by endorsement authorizes action thereon by each successive endorsee. (8-5-20).

Credits Against Assigned Claims.—All contracts and writings, except those governed by Uniform Commercial Code and paper issued to circulate as money, subject to all payments, setoffs, and discounts had or possessed against same, prior to notice of assignment or transfer. (8-5-25).

Actions on Assigned Claims.—On all contracts assigned by writing not governed by Uniform Commercial Code, in order to charge endorser or assignor, suit must be

brought against maker within 30 days after suit can properly be brought, and if judgment obtained, execution must be issued as authorized by law, and inability of maker to pay such judgment proved by return of "no property." (8-5-26). Time for bringing suit against maker may be extended or waived by consent of indorser or assignor in writing (8-5-27), and holder is excused from bringing suit, obtaining judgment and issuing execution under certain specified circumstances (8-5-28). Costs in suit against maker on such assigned or indorsed contract recoverable in suit against assignor or indorser. (8-5-30).

Assignment of wages void. (8-5-21).

Assignment of Life Insurance Policies.—See category Insurance, topic Insurance Companies.

ATTACHMENT:

Actions in Which Allowed.—May issue in actions founded on contract or tort. (58 Ala. 139).

Courts Which May Issue Writ.—Attachment to enforce collection of debt or liquidated money demand may be issued by judge or clerk of circuit court, returnable to any county, or by judge of probate or district judge within their respective counties. Attachment to recover unliquidated damages for breach of contract or on claim sounding in damages merely can be issued only by judge of circuit court or judge of probate, returnable to any county. (6-6-43).

In Whose Favor Writ May Issue.—No limitation imposed on issuance of writ on account of residence or citizenship of plaintiff, whether natural person or corporation. (6-6-30; 6-6-48; 6-6-49). Executors and administrators may commence suit by attachment in their representative characters. (6-6-47).

Against Whom Writ May Issue.—No limitation on imposition of writ on account of residence or citizenship of defendant, whether natural person or corporation. (6-6-30; 6-6-48; 6-6-51). Executors and administrators subject to writ; no judgments may be rendered against executors and administrators on answer in attachment until six months after grant of letters testamentary or of administration. (6-6-144).

Claims on Which Writ May Issue.—May issue in following kinds of actions: (1) To enforce collection of debt, whether due or not; (2) for liquidated money demand; (3) to recover unliquidated damages for breach of contract; and (4) when action sounds in damages only. (6-6-41). Attachment may issue in action by state for recovery from public officer of public money (6-5-4); on arbitration awards, whether for delivery of property or particular act or omission (6-6-13); and on judgments in detinue for recovery of specific property (6-6-263).

Grounds.—May issue in cases where defendant: (1) Resides outside state; (2) absconds; (3) secretes himself to avoid service of process; (4) about to leave state; (5) about to remove his property from state; (6) about to fraudulently dispose of his property; (7) fraudulently disposed of his property; or (8) has money, property or effects liable to satisfaction of debts which he fraudulently withholds. (6-6-42). When summons to defendant resident of county returned "not found", plaintiff may sue out attachment on making affidavit that defendant evaded service of process. (6-6-121). Plaintiff may also sue out attachment in aid of pending suit under same conditions as if in original attachment proceeding. (6-6-120). Similar rules prevail in respect to attachments to enforce certain specific liens (35-9-34; -37; -60 to -65; 35-11-5; -431), and in suits to collect municipal taxes (11-51-26).

Proceedings to Obtain.—Complaint must be filed within 15 days after suing out attachment if demand was then due; otherwise within 15 days after claim or demand becomes due. (6-6-140). Summons must issue on complaint so filed, but has no effect on levy, lien or enforcement of attachment. (6-6-141). If defendant appears and pleads, case proceeds as in actions commenced by complaint; if defendant fails to appear or to plead within time required by law, plaintiff may take judgment by default and if necessary, court may determine amount of damages pursuant to ARCP. (6-6-141; see also ARCP 55).

Action for recovery of or possession of specific personal property under detinue statutes (6-6-250 to -264) or other provision whereby owner of security interest in personal property seeks possession prior to judgment must follow procedure set forth in ARCP 64.

Notice of attachment must be given nonresident defendant by publication and by mail if residence can be ascertained. (6-6-81). Personal notice or notice left at his residence must be given defendant who is resident of county; notice by posting at court house door and by mail must be given defendant who is resident of some other county. (6-6-82).

Notice necessary for attachment for enforcement of arbitration award (6-6-13) and where hereinabove expressly stated; see also ARCP 70.

Affidavit.—In order to obtain attachment to enforce collection of debt or liquidated money demand, plaintiff, his agent or attorney must make written oath of amount of debt, that debt or demand is justly due or to become due, that one of grounds for attachment exists, and that attachment not sued out to harass defendant. (6-6-44).

Special Affidavits.—In order to obtain attachment to recover unliquidated damages for breach of contract or to enforce a claim sounding in damages merely, plaintiff, his agent or attorney must, in addition, make affidavit as to special facts and circumstances enabling judge to determine amount for which levy must be made. (6-6-46). Nonresident seeking attachment against another nonresident, in addition to other requirements, must make affidavit that defendant has not sufficient property within state of his residence wherefrom to satisfy debt and must also give bond with surety resident in this state. (6-6-48).

Attachment Bond.—Except where attachment sued out on ground that defendant is nonresident, plaintiff must supply bond in double amount claimed with sufficient surety. (6-6-45). Defendant may bring action on attachment bond within three years for actual damages if attachment wrongfully sued out and may recover vindictive damages if attachment was sued out maliciously. (6-6-148).

ATTACHMENT . . . *continued*

Alias writ of attachment may be issued without renewal of bond or affidavit required in original proceeding in cases where insufficient property has been found or, pending action, plaintiff wishes to garnish other persons. (6-6-75).

Levy.—Attachment may be levied on real estate, personalty (whether or not in possession of defendant) or choses in action (6-6-70), and also on joint and separate estate of joint obligors, promisors or partners. (6-6-72).

Levy on Investment Securities.—No attachment or levy upon outstanding security valid until security actually seized by officer making levy, but security surrendered to issuer may be levied on at source. Creditor whose debtor owns security, whether certificated, uncertificated, or security entitlement, entitled to injunctive relief in reaching security. Interest of debtor in uncertificated security reached by legal process on issuer or on secured party if registered in name of secured party. Interest in security entitlement reached by legal process on securities intermediary where securities account maintained. (7-8-112).

Levy on Goods Covered by Negotiable Document.—Except where document was issued upon unauthorized bailment, there can be no valid attachment of goods in possession of bailee for which negotiable document is outstanding unless document be surrendered to bailee or its negotiation enjoined. (7-7-602).

Where Levy Made.—Attachment may be executed by sheriff of county in which property located. (6-6-73; -74).

Indemnity.—Sheriff may demand indemnity when doubt exists as to defendant's title to personal property on which levy required. (6-6-80). Such demand may be made either before or after levy. (98 Ala. 503, 12 So. 789).

Lien.—Levy or service of garnishment creates lien in favor of plaintiff. (6-6-76).

Priorities.—Liens of attaching creditors given priority according to dates of levies. (99 Ala. 292, 13 So. 305).

Release of Property.—Defendant or, in his absence, stranger, may on execution of approved bond in amount double value of property, replevy attached property. Value determined by levying officer. (6-6-100 to -102).

Third Party Claims.—Third party claiming title, legal or equitable, or lien paramount to right, title or interest in property of defendant in writ, may try right to such property before sale thereof upon making affidavit by himself, his agent, or attorney, that he holds title to, or such lien upon, property claimed and by executing bond, with sufficient sureties, payable to plaintiff in amount double value of property levied on and claimed, with condition that property will be forthcoming for satisfaction of judgment or claim of plaintiff if it shall be found liable therefor and also for payment of costs and damages as may be recovered for interposing claim for delay. (6-6-160). Entry of judgment against defendant in writ suspended pending determination of third party claim. (6-6-145).

Vacation or Modification.—Attachment issued without required affidavit and bond may be dismissed on motion of defendant filed within 30 days after service of complaint (6-6-142), but plaintiff allowed liberal right to cure defects in affidavit or bond and to supply bond after such plea made (6-6-143).

Witnesses.—Attachment may issue against subpoenaed witness absent from civil trial. (556 So.2d 390).

Sale.—Plaintiff, after judgment, may obtain sale of property levied on. Court, on motion of either party, must before judgment order sale of property if perishable or if expense of keeping great; sheriff retains proceeds to await final disposition of cause. (6-6-77). Sheriff must sell at public auction goods so perishable that they will deteriorate greatly in value before meeting of court, and if charge of keeping very great; proceeds of such sales must be paid into court. (6-6-77).

Proceeds of Sale.—Plaintiff, on notice to defendant and execution of proper bond, in absence of adverse third person's claim and of sworn denial by defendant of plaintiff's claim, may before judgment obtain proceeds of sale. (6-6-78).

Judgment.—Where contest arises concerning title to or right in attached property, no judgment can be entered against defendant in attachment until trial of such collateral issues. (6-6-145). When plaintiff fails to obtain judgment against defendant in attachment because claim for trial of right to property has been interposed, attached property must be restored to claimant at cost of plaintiff. (6-6-146). If judgment for plaintiff not satisfied by property attached, execution may issue thereon against any property of defendant (6-6-147), but this does not apply to nonresident who fails to appear (109 Ala. 270, 19 So. 814).

Forms of attachment and other proceedings provided in Code. (6-6-40; ARCP 64).

CREDITORS' SUITS:

Creditors in certain cases may file complaints to compel discovery and to subject property of debtors to payment of debts except where it is held in trust. (6-6-180 to -187). Code authorizes complaints of discovery as to collusive judgments and attachments (6-6-181), and also authorizes creditor, without judgment or lien, to file such complaint. (6-6-182). Two or more creditors may join in such suit. (6-6-184). Judgment creditors of corporation, where execution is returned "no property found," may file complaint to subject unpaid subscriptions of one or more stockholders in such corporation to Execution. (6-6-187). (See also topics Executions, subhead Supplementary Proceedings; Fraudulent Sales and Conveyances; category Estates and Trusts, topic Executors and Administrators.)

EXECUTIONS:

Kinds of Execution.—In general, execution may issue on judgment or decree, whether for payment of money or return of specific property or land. (6-9-1). Execution cannot issue for amount of negotiable instrument lost or destroyed by theft or otherwise before maturity until judgment creditor executes bond to indemnify judgment debtor. (6-5-284). Execution may also issue in following special cases: On judgment in action of detinue, for specific property involved or for value thereof (6-6-259; -261 to -263); for costs against parties obtaining division in suit for partition of real estate (35-6-54; cf. 35-7-4); on judgment establishing materialman's or mechanic's lien (35-11-226); for certain taxes, assessments and penalties (28-3-14; 11-51-7. See also 40-1-15).

Forms of Writ of Execution provided in Code. (6-9-1).

Issuance in Favor of Representatives.—Provision made for issuance of execution in favor of personal representative of deceased judgment creditor or in favor of successor executor, administrator, guardian or trustee, without revival (6-9-193), and for revival of judgment in favor of personal representative of judgment creditor (6-9-194).

Exemptions.—See topic Exemptions.

Time for Issuance.—Execution must issue within 90 days from entry of judgment or decree unless otherwise directed by trial judge or by written direction of judgment creditor. (6-9-21). Execution may issue after expiration of 30 days but may be issued before expiration of 30 day period on showing of sufficient cause supported by affidavit of judgment creditor (6-9-22; ARCP App. III), and must be issued before such expiration on affidavit that judgment debtor is about fraudulently to dispose of or to remove his property (6-9-23).

Revival.—No execution may issue on judgment or decree of district or circuit court on which execution has not been sued out within ten years of its entry, until same revived by appropriate motion or action under ARCP. (6-9-192; cf. ARCP App. III). Judgment or decree cannot be revived after lapse of 20 years from its entry. (6-9-190).

Writ of execution issued and received by sheriff during life of judgment debtor may be levied after latter's death, or alias writ may be issued and levied within ten years from date of judgment if at time of judgment debtor's death certificate of judgment filed for record in county in which property is located. (6-9-62). Revival may be had in any case after six months from grant of letters testamentary or of administration, and revival unnecessary if judgment for recovery of real or personal property. (6-9-63).

Stay.—Except as otherwise provided by ARCP 62, statute or order of court for good cause shown, no execution can issue upon judgment nor may proceedings be taken for its enforcement until expiration of 30 days after entry. (ARCP 62).

Lien.—Execution is lien only: On lands of judgment debtor within county in which it is received by officer authorized to execute writ from time of receipt, provided judgment properly filed and recorded (6-9-60; 35-4-132); on personal property subject to levy and sale, from time of levy thereon, whether or not judgment has been registered (6-9-60).

Destruction of Lien.—Lien destroyed by execution of supersedeas bond or by issuance of injunction or restraining order against enforcement of judgment. (6-9-61). Notice of claim by filing lis pendens nullified before judgment entered enforcing lien by executing bond in double amount of fair market value of land described in lis pendens. (35-4-137).

Levy.—Executions may be levied on: Real property to which debtor has legal title, perfect equity or vested legal interest in possession, reversion or remainder; personal property (except choses in action); equity of redemption in either land or personal property. (6-9-40). Undivided interest of debtor in any property may be levied on and sold without taking property into actual possession. (6-9-85).

Growing crops exempt from levy. (6-9-41). Right of redemption is not subject to levy and sale under execution, attachment, or alienation; but if right or privilege perfected by redemption, subject to levy, sale, alienation or other disposition. (6-5-250).

Except when negotiable document issued upon unauthorized bailment, no lien attaches by virtue of any judicial process to goods in possession of bailee for which negotiable document outstanding unless document first surrendered to bailee or negotiation enjoined, and bailee must not be compelled to deliver goods pursuant to process until document surrendered to him or impounded by court. (7-7-602).

Indemnity Bond.—Sheriff may require indemnity bond from judgment creditor when reasonable doubt exists as to ownership of personal property, or as to whether property subject to levy and sale. (6-9-81; cf. 6-6-80). If party having prior lien refuses to give such bond, party having next lien in order may give it and have property sold for his benefit. (6-9-81).

Surety may, on application supported by affidavit, secure levy first on property of principal. (6-9-83).

Return.—All executions must be made returnable within 90 days after issuance thereof. (6-4-1; 6-9-80).

Claims of Third Persons.—A third person claiming paramount interest in personal property levied on may, on giving affidavit respecting title and execution of approved bond with sureties, obtain possession of such property and trial of title thereto. (6-6-160-166). Such contest does not prevent judgment creditor from levying on other property of judgment debtor. (6-6-167). Third party claimant, on other hand, by proceeding under these sections, releases any claim against sheriff for seizing property levied upon. (6-6-168).

Satisfaction presumed ten years after rendition of judgment or decree on which no execution has been issued or ten years after date of last execution issued (6-9-191), and presumption conclusive after lapse of 20 years (6-9-190).

Marshaling of Debtor's Assets.—Marshaling of judgment debtor's assets for benefit of vendees required when debtor sells part of property subject to lien. (6-9-84).

Judgment Creditor's Death Prior to Sale.—Duty of officer making levy to proceed to sale not affected by death of judgment creditor or judgment debtor after issuance or levy of execution. (6-9-94).

Sale of Perishables.—Officer levying on perishable goods must sell them at such time, on such notice and at such place as sound discretion may warrant. (6-9-88; 6-6-77).

Substitution of Property to be Sold.—Judgment debtor has right, on day of sale to substitute equally valuable property in lieu of that levied upon (6-9-91) and may at time of levy point out to officer property to levy upon and sell first (6-9-90).

Notice of Collection.—Officer making sale must notify judgment creditor of collection. (6-9-92).

See note at head of Digest as to 1998 legislation covered.

See Topical Index in front part of this volume.

AL – 26

EXECUTIONS . . . *continued*

Repossession.—Judgment debtor may repossess personal property on execution of forthcoming bond except in cases of executions based upon judgments against officers of court for failure to pay over money collected in official capacities. (6-9-160).

Execution of Deeds.—Officer making sale, on tender of purchase price plus all fees due, must, within five days after sale, execute deed to real estate or interest therein sold (6-9-149); and purchaser at such sale of any stock, share, interest, judgment or decree of judgment debtor becomes owner thereof as if it had been regularly assigned to him by judgment debtor (6-9-144). Similarly, any sale made under judicial process conveys title as effectually as if made by person against whom process issued. (6-9-140).

Sale Under Void Process.—Judgment debtor bound by sale held under void process if proceeds thereof applied to valid liens against him and if present at sale and did not object. (6-9-148).

Warranties.—Purchaser of lands at sale under execution takes covenants of warranty running with land incorporated in previous title deeds (6-9-145), but covenant of warranty contained in sheriff's deed binds officer only if made with that intention and for valuable consideration and in writing. (6-9-142).

Redemption.—Certain enumerated persons may redeem real estate or any interest therein sold under execution, or by virtue of any judgment in court of competent jurisdiction, or under any deed of trust or power of sale in mortgage, from purchaser or his vendee, within one year after sale. (6-5-248, -249). Statutory enumeration of persons entitled to redeem exclusive (206 Ala. 310, 89 So. 719; 259 Ala. 553, 67 So.2d 834), and statutory right of redemption is personal and not property right (6-5-250).

Provision made respecting priority of right of various persons enumerated to redeem. (6-5-248).

Failure of debtor, or anyone holding under him, to deliver possession within ten days after purchaser makes written demand therefor forfeits right to redeem. (6-5-251). Conversely, person entitled to redeem may in writing demand from purchaser or his vendee written statement of debt and of all lawful charges; failure to furnish such statement within ten days forfeits right to compensation for improvements. (6-5-252).

Tender of amount of purchase money, with interest at 12% and all other lawful charges, necessary to redeem. (6-5-253). Permanent improvements constitute lawful charge which must be valued, in event of disagreement, by referees appointed by parties. (6-5-254). If purchaser or his vendee fails or refuses to reconvey on proper tender of purchase price plus all lawful charges, one entitled to redeem who made such tender may file complaint to force redemption in circuit court. (6-5-255; -256).

Supplementary Proceedings.—In aid of judgment or execution, judgment creditor, or his successor in interest when that appears of record, may obtain discovery from any person, including judgment debtor, in accordance with ARCP. (ARCP 69[g]). Judgment creditor may file complaint for discovery and subjection of legal and equitable assets against judgment debtor where execution for money issued and not satisfied. (6-6-180; -183 to -184). Similar complaint may be filed by judgment creditor of corporation when execution returned "no property found" against shareholders for unpaid stock subscriptions. (6-6-187). Complaint for discovery may also be filed against defendant charged with having confessed and paid wholly or in part judgment with intent to hinder, delay or defraud creditors. (6-6-181). Where execution has been returned "no property found," judgment creditor may file complaint for discovery, to which judgment debtor must answer under oath listing all property in which he has any legal or equitable interest, including choses in action; provision made for examination of debtor and court must make such orders or decrees, including appointment of receiver, as necessary and proper to reach assets so disclosed. (6-6-183 to -186. Compare 6-6-620 to -628 which provide for appointment of receiver in aid of pending suit).

Judgment creditor, where execution returned "no property found", may alternatively, on written request to clerk or register, require judgment debtor to file in court within 30 days sworn statement of all his assets, whether legal or equitable, including choses in action. (6-6-200; cf. ARCP App. II). If necessary, and on affidavit filed by such judgment creditor, oral examination of judgment debtor may be had in such proceedings. (6-6-200-204; cf. ARCP App. II).

Priorities.—When any judgment creditor redeems, all recorded judgments, recorded mortgages and recorded liens with existing higher priority revived against redeemed real estate and redeeming party. (6-5-248). When any debtor, mortgagor, or transferees of such, redeem, all existing recorded judgments, recorded mortgages and recorded liens revived and further redemption by other parties precluded. (6-5-248).

Body Execution.—None.

Assignees.—Assignment of judgment or decree endorsed and properly attested on execution docket or on margin of record of judgment or decree, gives assignee substantially all rights and remedies of original judgment creditor. (6-9-196). Similarly, surety paying judgment or decree against principal entitled to rights and remedies of judgment creditor. (8-3-41).

Death of one or more of several judgment creditors does not prevent the issuance of an execution in favor of survivors. (6-9-195).

EXEMPTIONS:

In addition to homestead following exempt to resident: Burial place and church pew (6-10-3 to -9); personal property, except for wages, salaries or other compensation, to $3,000, selected by resident, all necessary wearing apparel, family portraits or pictures, and all books used in family (6-10-6); wages, salaries and other compensation for personal services exempt from levy under writs of garnishment or other process for collection of debts or judgments rendered in tort in amount equal to 75% of such wages, salaries, or other compensation (6-10-7; 5-19-15); worker compensation benefits (25-5-86[2]); partner's right in partnership property (10-8-72[b][3]) (repealed eff. Jan. 1, 2001); and certain personal property (6-10-126).

See also 15 U.S.C. §1673(a).

Exemptions granted by 11 U.S.C. §522(d) not available.

Growing or Ungathered Crops.—Exempt from levy and sale except for enforcing liens for rent, advances or labor. (6-9-41).

Proceeds of Insurance.—See category Insurance, topic Insurance Companies.

Wages and Salaries.—See introductory paragraph.

Debts Against Which Exemptions Not Allowed.—Except as otherwise specifically stated above, exemption may not be claimed against judgment for tort (158 Ala. 65, 48 So. 341) or execution for costs taxed in actions ex delicto (201 Ala. 344, 78 So. 200). No partnership property exempt against co-partners or partnership creditors. (6-10-9).

Waiver of Exemption.—May waive his right to exemption by instrument in writing (Const. Art. I, §210; 6-10-120); as to personal property, waiver may be made by separate instrument in writing or by stipulation incorporated in any bond, bill or note (6-10-121), but such waiver may not be implied (25 Ala. App. 117, 141 So. 723); as to homestead, waiver must be by separate instrument in writing and attested by one witness (6-10-122). Waiver of exemption ineffectual as to certain cooking utensils, furniture and other items described in statute. (6-10-126). Rights of surviving spouse to homestead allowance, exempt property and family allowance may be waived in writing before or after marriage or in complete property settlement entered into after, or in anticipation of, separation or divorce. (43-8-72).

Necessity of Claiming Exemption.—Claims of exemption filed in office of judge of probate of county in which property lies if homestead, or, if personal property, in which judgment debtor resides. (6-10-20). After claim filed, exempt property not subject to levy unless waiver endorsed on process or claim contested. (6-10-24). Defendant may claim exemption after levy and prior to sale with officer making levy. (6-10-26).

Contest of Claim.—Plaintiff, on giving bond with sureties, may contest claim filed in office of judge of probate and secure levy of execution (6-10-25); or, in event claim filed with officer making levy, may contest without execution of bond (6-10-26). If defendant gives bond within five days after notice of contest, may take property; if he does not give bond, plaintiff, within five days thereafter, may give bond and take property; if no bond given within ten days after notice of contest, property delivered to defendant without bond. (6-10-27).

Earnings.—See topic Garnishment.

FORECLOSURE:

See topic Liens; category Mortgages, topics Chattel Mortgages, Mortgages of Real Property.

FRAUDULENT SALES AND CONVEYANCES:

Transfer of all or substantially all debtor's property subject to execution by which preference on priority of payment to one or more creditors is given over remaining creditors to pay for prior debt will inure to benefit all creditors. (8-9-8). Grantor of realty may invalidate transfer where material part of consideration is grantee's agreement to support grantor. (8-9-12). Defrauding secured creditors misdemeanor. (13A-9-46).

Uniform Fraudulent Transfer Act adopted. (8-9A-1, et seq.). Language in uniform act dealing with obligations omitted.

Uniform Fraudulent Conveyance Act not adopted. See supra subhead Uniform Fraudulent Transfer Act.

Remedies.—When execution has been returned unsatisfied (6-6-180) or defendant has confessed or suffered judgment (6-6-181) or property has been, or attempted to be, fraudulently transferred or conveyed (6-6-182), creditor may file complaint against debtor or others (6-6-183) to compel discovery of debtor's assets. Court must enter orders and may appoint receiver to allow creditor to recover discovered property. (6-6-185).

Bulk Sales.—Former Uniform Commercial Code sections (7-6-101, et seq.) repealed (Acts 96-523), May 17, 1996.

GARNISHMENT:

Plaintiff in pending action for recovery of money or owner of judgment may reach and subject to attachment money or property of defendant in possession of third person or debts or liabilities owed to defendant. (6-6-370). No garnishment can issue prior to final judgment absent extraordinary circumstances. (6-6-390). Prior to entry of judgment, creditor may not attach unpaid earnings of debtor by garnishment; after judgment, with respect to consumer loans, sales or leases, amount of earnings subject to garnishment limited. (5-19-15). Executor or administrator may obtain process of garnishment and may be garnished for debts of decedent. (6-6-411).

Caveat.—See 395 U.S. 337 (1969).

Property Which May Be Reached.—Debts due defendant from testator or intestate held by executors and administrators (6-6-411), money in hands of attorney, sheriff or other officer of court (6-6-412), corporate stockholders who have not fully paid subscriptions (6-6-414), trustees (6-6-413) and salaries of state, county or city officials (6-6-481; -483) may be garnished.

Jurisdiction.—Court where action pending or where judgment entered. (6-6-391).

Proceedings to Obtain.—Plaintiff or attorney, to obtain garnishment writ, must file with clerk of court affidavit stating amount due from defendant, and that process of garnishment believed to be necessary. (6-6-391). Bond required where garnishment issued in pending action. (6-6-392).

Answer of Garnishee.—Garnishee must answer under oath within 30 days under penalty of judgment. (6-6-393; -450 to -457).

Garnishee may suggest adverse claimant. (6-6-463).

Practice.—Officer issuing garnishment must issue notice to defendant. Defendant may post bond in amount approved by judge or clerk payable to plaintiff and money or property held by garnishee will be discharged from garnishment, and if garnishee liable to defendant for money or property, judgment will be entered against defendant and sureties on bond. (6-6-430). If garnishee admits possession of money belonging to defendant, he must pay money in amount of plaintiff's claim into court. (6-6-452). If

See note at head of Digest as to 1998 legislation covered.

See Topical Index in front part of this volume.

AL – 27

GARNISHMENT . . . *continued*
garnishee admits indebtedness to defendant, judgment thereon must be entered for amount admitted. Execution suspended until debt's maturity. (6-6-454).

Adverse Claims.—Garnishee must allege adverse claimants in answer. Claimant must appear and propound claim in writing to clerk of court. (6-6-463).

Judgment.—Entered against garnishee for indebtedness to defendant (6-6-454) or for delivery for personal property (6-6-455) or for effects of defendant (6-6-456). Conditional judgment entered against garnishee if fails to answer. (6-6-457).

Earnings.—See topic Exemptions.

Claims on Which Writ May Issue.—Garnishment may be issued on unpaid ad valorem assessments (11-51-8; 40-5-20) or use tax assessments (40-25-44). Creditors of losing party in gambling transaction may garnish winner. (8-1-151).

Exemptions.—Seventy-five percent of wages exempt from garnishment (6-10-7), except that exemption does not apply to withholding orders for child support, which are governed by separate statutory provisions (30-3-60-71). Employee cannot waive exemption. (143 Ala. 243, 39 So. 368). With respect to consumer debts, see topic Consumer Credit.

Code.—See also 15 U.S.C. §1673(a).

Examination of Garnishee.—Garnishee may, if required by plaintiff, be examined orally in presence of court. (6-6-450).

Lien.—Service of garnishment creates lien in favor of plaintiff. (6-6-76).

Delivery of Property.—Where garnishee liable to debtor for delivery of personal property, court must ascertain value thereof, and order garnishee to deliver said property to sheriff by stipulated day, or be liable for such value. (6-6-455).

Rights of Defendant Giving Bond.—Defendant may give bond and collect from garnishee; or may give bond in double amount of plaintiff's claim and dissolve garnishment. (6-6-430,-431).

HOMESTEADS:

Homestead of resident of state exempt from levy and sale under execution or other process for collection of debts during life and occupancy of such resident. (6-10-2).

Interest of Owner.—Homestead right attaches irrespective of whether resident owns fee simple interest or lesser estate in land and whether held in common or severalty. (6-10-2).

Limitation of Value.—Of exempt homestead, with improvements and appurtenances to owner, is $5,000. (6-10-2). See subhead Rights of Surviving Spouse and Family, infra.

Limitation of Area.—That may be held exempt is 160 acres; such area may not be enlarged by reason of any encumbrance on property or character of estate or interest owned therein. (6-10-2).

Debts or Liabilities against Which Exemption Not Available.—Liens of laborer, merchant or materialman for work, labor, or materials furnished; or any vendor for unpaid purchase money; or validity of any deed, mortgage or lien relating to homestead, which has been lawfully executed or created. (6-10-4). Homestead not exempt from judgment for tort. (103 Ala. 539, 15 So. 852).

Designation of Homestead.—Resident of state entitled to claim homestead may, at any time, file in office of probate judge of county where such property located sworn declaration describing property claimed as homestead. (6-10-20). After declaration filed, homestead property exempt from levy, unless fact of waiver of exemption endorsed on process under which levy attempted. (6-10-24).

Claim of Exemption.—Right of homestead not lost by failure, before levy of process, to file declaration claiming homestead. (6-10-26). Any time after levy and prior to sale, defendant may file with officer making levy claim in writing. Plaintiff must then contest claim in manner provided for claims which have been filed prior to levy (6-10-25), except that no bond required. Levy discharged if plaintiff does not institute contest within ten days after notice of claim. (6-10-26).

Waiver of Exemption.—Must be by separate written instrument subscribed by party making same and attested by one witness and if such party is married man, waiver not valid without voluntary signature and assent of wife and acknowledgment by her. (6-10-122). See category Documents and Records, topic Acknowledgments, subhead Married Persons. If owner is married woman, waiver generally must be joined by husband. (6-10-122).

Loss of Exemption.—Homestead exemption may be lost by failure to file proper claim before actual sale of property. (6-10-26). Right of homestead forfeited through abandonment without intent to return. (6-10-41; 231 Ala. 493, 165 So. 593).

Alienation or Encumbrance.—No mortgage, deed or other conveyance of homestead by married person valid unless made with voluntary signature and assent of husband or wife evidenced by his or her general acknowledgment. (6-10-3). See category Documents and Records, topic Acknowledgments, subhead Married Persons.

Proceeds of Sale.—Proceeds of voluntary sale of properties exempt from levy under homestead right are not exempt. (65 Ala. 439).

Rights of Surviving Spouse and Family. —Surviving spouse of decedent who was domiciled in state entitled to homestead allowance of $6,000 from property of estate, other than property specifically devised, selected by surviving spouse, but value of any constitutional right of homestead in family home charged against homestead allowance. If no surviving spouse, each minor and each dependent child of decedent has same right to homestead allowance of $6,000, divided by number of such children. (43-8-110). Homestead allowance in addition to any share passing to surviving spouse or minor or dependent children by intestate succession. (43-8-110). Homestead allowance has priority over payment of family allowance. (43-8-112). See category Estates and Trusts, topic Executors and Administrators, subhead Allowances.

Proceeds of insurance on homestead exempt. (194 Ala. 477, 69 So. 916).

JUDGMENT NOTES:

See category Business Regulation and Commerce, topic Bills and Notes.

LEVY:

See topics Attachment, Executions.

LIENS:

Common Law Liens.—Common law lien is right to retain possession of personal property until debt due on or secured by property paid. (94 So. 354, 208 Ala. 334). Continuous possession essential to creation and preservation of common law lien. (Id).

Statutory liens as follows: Cleaners, pressing establishments, launderers and menders of household linens and articles of wearing apparel, including hats and shoes (35-11-170); jewelers, watchmakers or silversmiths, for repairs or work done to personal property (35-11-150); materialmen, laborers, etc., on watercraft for furnishings, repairs, wages (including master), etc. (35-11-60); owner of self-service storage facility on personal property located therein for rent labor and other charges (8-15-33); rentors and lessors of equipment for use in construction or improvements to land or in clearing or improving land (35-11-430); riparian owners, on vessels for use of booms and bulkheads, and piles (35-11-310); tenants in common of crops, on such crops, for services and supplies (35-11-350); railroad laborers and employees, except officers, for work and labor done (35-11-90); agricultural laborers and superintendents on crops, subordinate to landlord's lien for rent and advances and to any other lien for supplies furnished (35-11-91); livery stable keepers and agisters, on stock (35-11-70; 35-11-190); owners of bulls, stallions, jacks, rams, he-goats or boars, on the young and on the female (35-11-330); sawmill laborers and employees, for wages (35-11-270); owners of land, on timber sold therefrom for stumpage (35-11-20); owner of cotton gin, peanut machine or picker, hay baling machine or press, or plant for drying or processing planting seeds, on commodity processed thereby (35-11-290); sawmill owners or operators, for lumber sawed (35-11-250); hotel, inn, boardinghouse and restaurant keepers, on personal baggage and goods of guests and boarders (35-11-130); hospitals, on judgments from any causes of action which patients may have arising out of cause of hospitalization (35-11-370); duly licensed veterinarians, on animal treated (35-11-390); persons furnishing by contract with landowner labor or materials for improvements in or on public streets, or abutting land for work and labor done (35-11-410).

Uniform Commercial Code adopted. (7-10-101). See category Business Regulation and Commerce, topic Commercial Code.

Vendor's Lien.—No implied vendor's lien exists for purchase money on property, except realty when delivered to purchaser under contract. (231 Ala. 27, 163 So. 334).

Waiver, Loss, or Extinguishment.—Unless otherwise provided, proceedings to enforce statutory liens must be commenced within six months after demand becomes due; or lien lost. (35-11-6).

Enforcement.—In most instances statutory liens are enforceable by writ of attachment. (35-11-1). Plaintiff must execute affidavit and bond payable to defendant, with sufficient sureties, to protect defendant in event of wrongful attachment. (35-11-5). In addition to method of enforcement based on attachment, Code provides for sales in satisfaction of liens in certain instances. Notices and other requirements vary with statutory liens involved. (See generally c. 11, Tit. 35.) Statutory methods for enforcement by attachment, etc., cumulative and not exclusive, and enforcement may be had by any other common law or equitable remedy available. (35-11-1). Person regularly engaged in performing services upon articles left in custody for that purpose may dispose of articles in any manner, subject to statutory waiting periods and notice to owner. (35-12-6).

Mechanics' and Materialmen's Liens.—Every mechanic or other person, firm or corporation, that performs any work, labor or furnishes any materials, fixtures, engines, boilers, waste disposal services and equipment, or machinery for building or improvement on land, or repair, alteration or beautification thereto, under or by virtue of contract with owner or proprietor, or owner's agent, architect, trustee, contractor or subcontractor, has lien therefor on building, improvements and land for such work and improvements. (35-11-210). Foreign corporation not qualified to do business generally prohibited from filing mechanic's lien statement. Mechanic's lien subordinate to any security interest under Uniform Commercial Code which was perfected prior to time work was done, unless secured party authorized work. (35-11-110).

Subcontractor's lien extends only to amount of unpaid balance due from owner to original contractor, unless before material furnished subcontractor gives owner statutory notice that he will claim lien for all such work and materials. (35-11-210). Laborers and materialmen under contract with prime contractor and subcontractors also have lien on buildings and improvements, but only (unless statutory notice given) to extent of unpaid balance due prime contractor by owner. (35-11-210; 257 Ala. 332, 58 So.2d 614).

Notice of Lien Claim.—Every person, except original contractor, claiming lien, must, before filing statement in probate office, give written notice of such claim to owner or proprietor unless owner notified in advance. (35-11-218; 529 So.2d 201).

Lien Statement.—Verified statement by mechanic or contractor, claiming benefit of this law, setting out demand, description of property and name of owner, must be filed in court of probate, within six months by original contractor, within 30 days if by journeymen or day laborers, and by every other person within four months after last item of work or labor performed, or material furnished. (35-11-213; 35-11-215).

Building or Improvement on Leased Property.—When building or improvement erected on leased land at tenant's behest, and improvement not in violation of lease, lien attaches to building or improvement and to unexpired term of lease, and lienor or purchaser at foreclosure sale may avoid forfeiture of lease by fulfilling obligations of lease, and may remove improvement from such leased property within reasonable time after expiration of term of lease. (35-11-212[a]). But lessor may prevent removal of such improvement by discharging lien prior to sale of property. (35-11-212[b]).

List of Employees of Contractor.—Original contractor must, when required, furnish list of employees, laborers, and materialmen to owner or proprietor or forfeit lien. (35-11-219).

See note at head of Digest as to 1998 legislation covered.

See Topical Index in front part of this volume.

AL – 28

LIENS ... *continued*

Priorities.—All liens, except in favor of original contractor, entitled to equal priority. (35-11-228).

Lien as to land and buildings or improvements thereon, has priority over all other liens, mortgages or incumbrances created subsequent to commencement of work. As to liens, mortgages or incumbrances created prior to commencement of work, lien for such work has priority only against product of such work which is an entirety, separable from land, building or improvement subject to prior lien, and which can be removed therefrom without impairing value or security of any prior lien, and persons entitled to such lien may have it enforced by sale of building or improvement and purchaser may, within reasonable time thereafter, remove same. (35-11-211).

Assignment.—Mechanic's and materialmen's liens may be assigned or transferred to other security. (35-11-233).

Satisfaction of liens must be acknowledged on the margin of record in probate office. (35-11-231).

Enforcement.—When amount involved exceeds $50, actions may be brought in circuit court in county where property is situated. In all other cases, district courts have jurisdiction. (35-11-220). Action for enforcement of mechanics' or materialmen's lien must be commenced within six months after maturity of entire indebtedness. (35-11-221). No special pleadings, other than allegation of lien and entitlement to enforce needed to invoke equity jurisdiction. (35-11-222).

If suit by employee or materialman of contractor, contractor is necessary defendant. (35-11-227).

Public Works.—Person contracting with state, county or municipal corporation for construction of public work or building must furnish bond with surety, conditioned to pay mechanics and materialmen. (39-1-1).

Attachment Lien.—See topic Attachment.

Attorney's Lien.—See category Legal Profession, topic Attorneys and Counselors.

Collateral Security.—See topic Pledges.

Execution Lien.—See topic Executions.

Judgment Lien.—See category Civil Actions and Procedure, topic Judgments.

Landlord's Lien.—See category Property, topic Landlord and Tenant.

Liens on Exempt Property.—See topic Exemptions.

Liens on Homestead.—See topic Homesteads.

Real Estate Mortgage Lien.—See category Mortgages, topic Mortgages of Real Property.

Tax Lien.—See category Taxation, topic Property (Ad Valorem) Taxes, subhead Lien.

MECHANICS' LIENS:

See topic Liens.

PLEDGES:

Pledges are governed generally by the rules of common law, except where supplanted or supplemented by Uniform Commercial Code. (Tit. 7). Essential elements of pledge are that possession of pledged property pass from debtor to creditor, that legal title remain in debtor, and that creditor have lien for payment of debt due him by debtor or some other party. (8 Ala. App. 487, 62 So. 537; 7-9-305).

Remedies of Pledgee.—Governed by Uniform Commercial Code. (7-9-504).

Rights and Duties When Pledge is in Pledgee's Hands.—Governed by Uniform Commercial Code. (7-9-207).

Receipt for Collateral.—All persons engaged in making discounts, lending money, or taking collateral must, if demanded, give receipt in writing, designating and describing collateral, stating character of debt, time of maturity and amount. Where collateral consists of negotiable bonds, series numbers, if any, must be given. (8-1-3).

RECEIVERS:

Appointed at discretion of court only when suit is pending, except in cases affecting infants and mental incompetents. (227 Ala. 173, 149 So. 216).

Jurisdiction.—May be appointed by circuit judge, or by register or clerk in absence of circuit judge, on application in writing. (6-6-620).

Proceedings.—Applicant must post bond in amount prescribed by judge, register, or clerk when appointment in advance of final hearing on merits. (6-6-622[b], 271 Ala. 249, 123 So.2d 109). Reasonable notice of application for appointment of receiver must be given to necessary or interested parties unless notice would jeopardize property or party would sustain irrevocable injury. (291 Ala. 39, 277 So.2d 343). Order appointing receiver may be appealed to circuit judge and must be suspended upon appellant entering sufficient bond prescribed by register or clerk. (6-6-621). Any person damaged by appointment may bring action on applicant's bond after vacation or discharge. (6-6-622).

Eligibility and Competency.—Subject to judicial discretion. (6-6-622).

Qualification.—Must obtain state and county license. (40-12-40).

Powers and Duties.—Receiver stands in place of and has no greater power than party whose property is being subjected to receivership. (220 Ala. 529, 126 So. 102). Duty to act as arm of court to care for and preserve property pending litigation. (159 Ala. 510, 48 So. 870).

Compensation.—Amount within sound discretion of court after consideration of responsibility, business experience, time spent, but not necessarily what receiver would have earned in some other business. (202 Ala. 609, 81 So. 551).

Discharge.—Shall not be dismissed except by order of court. (ARCP 66).

Attachments and Levies.—Commencement of proceedings for appointment of receiver of partnership or corporation dissolves all attachments and levies of execution

not completed, made within 60 days next preceding, but attachments and executions revive if property taken from receiver so as no longer to be subject to order of court or on termination of receivership pending settlement. (6-6-624).

Suability.—Receiver or manager of property may be sued with respect to any act or transaction of his in carrying on business connected with such property in state, without previous leave of appointing court. (6-6-626).

REDEMPTION:

See topic Executions; categories Mortgages, topics Chattel Mortgages, Mortgages of Real Property; Taxation, topic Real Estate Conveyance Tax.

SUPPLEMENTARY PROCEEDINGS:

See topic Executions.

TRUSTEE PROCESS:

See topic Garnishment.

USURY:

See category Business Regulation and Commerce, topic Interest.

DISPUTE RESOLUTION

ALTERNATIVE DISPUTE RESOLUTION:

Mandatory Dispute Resolution.—
Arbitration.—United States Supreme Court rejected "contemplation of substantial interstate activity" test used by Alabama Supreme Court, holding that relevant inquiry is whether contract in fact involved interstate commerce, not whether parties contemplated such commerce. (115 S.Ct. 834).

Voluntary Dispute Resolution.—
Mediation.—Participation strictly voluntary. (ARCP 16[c][7]). Circuit Court may on its own motion or at request of parties direct parties to appear before it and consider possibility of mediation pursuant to Alabama Civil Court Mediation Rules (ACCMR). Upon entry of order for mediation, court proceedings stayed. (ACCMR 2). Mediator does not have authority to impose settlement upon parties. (ACCMR 9). Any party can terminate mediation process at any time. (ACCMR 13).

See also topic Arbitration and Award.

ARBITRATION AND AWARD:

Uniform Arbitration Act not adopted. Arbitration agreements enforceable under both common law and statutory rules. (6-6-1; 6-6-2; 6-6-16). Courts under duty to encourage arbitration of pending actions. (6-6-1).

Form and Requisites of Submission.—At common law, agreement of submission may be oral and terms general. (135 Ala. 522, 33 So. 179). By statute, parties must concisely state in signed writing matter in dispute and desire to leave determination with arbitrator. Such signed writing must be delivered to arbitrator together with list of witnesses either party may desire to examine. (6-6-3). Written submission not required when arbitration ordered in pending action. (90 Ala. 493, 7 So. 840).

Common law arbitration is also recognized. (6-6-16).

Contract to Arbitrate Future Disputes.—General provision in contract for arbitration of any dispute that may arise thereunder not ordinarily enforceable (8-1-41), and does not displace jurisdiction of courts (202 Ala. 384, 80 So. 466). Arbitration clauses in contracts within scope of Federal Arbitration Act, 9 U.S.C. §§1-14, apparently enforceable. (452 So.2d 860). Contract within scope of Federal Arbitration Act if parties contemplated substantial interstate activity. (115 S.Ct. 834). See also topic Alternative Dispute Resolution.

Rescission.—Arbitration itself is matter of contract, not of law, and parties can be required to arbitrate only if they have agreed to do so. (655 F.2d 607). Arbitration agreements designed to defeat jurisdiction of courts as to subject matter void as against public policy. (202 Ala. 384, 80 So. 466).

Powers of Arbitrators.—May administer oaths, subpoena witnesses at request of either party and, on application of either party, issue commission to take depositions of witnesses residing outside of county. (6-6-7). Power of arbitrator ceases when award made. (108 Ala. 118, 19 So. 367).

Award and Enforcement Thereof.—Award must be made in writing, signed and dated by arbitrator and delivered to parties or their agents or attorneys. (6-6-4). Award conclusive and final between parties under statute and at common law unless arbitrator is guilty of fraud, partiality or corruption in making award. (6-6-14; 208 Ala. 595, 94 So. 745). If award not performed within ten days after notice and delivery thereof, successful party may, if action pending, cause submission and award to be returned to court in which action pending. If no action pending, submission and award may be returned to clerk of circuit court of county in which award was made. Such award has force and effect of judgment, upon which execution may issue as in other cases. (6-6-12). Either party may appeal award to appropriate court within ten days after notice of award. (6-6-15). Award may be pleaded in bar to subsequent suit on same claim or demand. (229 Ala. 39, 155 So. 533).

Mandatory Arbitration.—No specific statutory provisions. See topic Alternative Dispute Resolution.

Services.—In disputes arising out of rendering or failure to render services, parties may enter into written agreement, signed by both parties, to settle such disputes by arbitration. (6-5-485 [medical liability actions]; 6-5-575 [legal services liability actions]).

See note at head of Digest as to 1998 legislation covered.

See Topical Index in front part of this volume.

DOCUMENTS AND RECORDS

ACKNOWLEDGMENTS:

Uniform Law on Notarial Acts, Uniform Acknowledgment Act, and Uniform Recognition of Acknowledgments Act have not been adopted.

Acknowledgment may be taken on any day, including Sunday (230 Ala. 423, 161 So. 806) by following officers:

Within State.—Judge of Supreme Court, Court of Civil Appeals, Court of Criminal Appeals, circuit court, district court; clerk of any of above courts; register of circuit court; judge of probate court; notary public. (35-4-24).

Outside State but within United States.—Judge or clerk of federal court or state court of record; notary public; commissioner appointed by Governor of Alabama; commissioner of deeds in state wherein taken. (35-4-26).

Outside United States.—Judge of court of record; mayor or chief magistrate of city, town, borough or county; notary public; diplomatic, consular or commercial agent of U.S. (35-4-26).

Persons in or with U.S. Armed Forces may take acknowledgment anywhere outside this state, signature of such officer being prima facie proof of authority without seal. (35-4-26).

General Requirements as to Taking.—Notary public must ascertain identity of person whose signature is attested. (380 So.2d 301).

General Requirements of Certificate.—Seal of officer (except of U.S. Armed Forces, see subhead Persons in or with U.S. Armed Forces, supra) taking acknowledgment outside state must be affixed (106 Ala. 663, 18 So. 74), and purpose of notary to affix official seal should appear in certificate (203 Ala. 446, 83 So. 338). This appearing, court will presume officer's commission had not then expired. (212 Ala. 280, 102 So. 221).

Married Persons.—Voluntary signature and assent of husband or wife to alienation of homestead must be shown by certificate of officer authorized to take acknowledgment of deeds. (6-10-3). Single certificate may include acknowledgments of both husband and wife in conveyance of homestead or in waiver of homestead exemption. (212 Ala. 481, 103 So. 452).

Attorneys in Fact.—Powers of attorney or other instruments conferring authority to convey property or to enter satisfaction of mortgages or other liens may be proved by two witnesses or acknowledged and recorded in same manner and must be received as evidence to same extent as conveyances. (35-4-28).

Corporations.—Any deed, mortgage, or other conveyance of property which purports on its face to have been executed in name of corporation by person as its president, vice-president, or secretary, when attested by one or more witnesses or acknowledged by such person before any officer authorized to take and certify acknowledgments, prima facie evidence that conveyance was executed in name of corporation by person as officer and that person was officer of corporation and duly authorized by corporation to execute conveyance. (35-4-67[a]). Once such deed, mortgage, or other conveyance is recorded, it will be received in evidence in any court of Alabama without further proof. (35-4-67[b]).

Foreign Acknowledgments.—See subhead Outside United States, supra.

Effect of Acknowledgment.—Conveyance of real or personal property which has been acknowledged as required by law or proven by two attesting witnesses and recorded, may be received in evidence without further proof, and transcript of record, duly certified, may be received in evidence on proof that original has been lost, destroyed, or is beyond control of party proffering same. (35-4-65).

All instruments of conveyance, affidavits or contracts purporting to be acknowledged, proved or verified as prescribed by law, and which are recorded in office of probate judge of proper county, and all transcripts of such documents taken from record, are prima facie evidence that seal of officer acknowledging or attesting such instrument was his official seal and was affixed in his official capacity, whether he be officer of Alabama or any other state, territory or district of U.S. (35-4-27).

Proof by Subscribing Witness.—All conveyances (other than those properly acknowledged [156 Ala. 432, 47 So. 205]) admitted to record on proof must be attested by two witnesses. (35-4-68).

Authentication.—Conveyances of property, real or personal, or any interest therein, whether absolute or on condition, which are acknowledged or proved according to law and recorded may be received into evidence in any court without further proof. If court determines that original conveyance lost or destroyed or party offering transcript does not have custody or control thereof, court must receive transcript, duly certified, in place of original, unless reputed maker is in bona fide possession of property and makes and files affidavit that conveyance is forgery. (35-4-65).

Forms

Acknowledgment for individual must be substantially in following statutory form:

The State of . . . . . ., ... County. I, ... (name and style of officer) hereby certify that . . . . . . whose name is signed to the foregoing conveyance, and who is known to me, acknowledged before me on this day that, being informed of the contents of the conveyance, he executed the same voluntarily on the day the same bears date. Given under my hand this . . . . . . day of . . . . . ., A. D. 19. . . (signature and title of officer). (35-4-29).

Homestead Acknowledgment. (See category Debtor and Creditor, topic Homesteads.) No form prescribed by statute. Form in general use recites separate examination of wife, although such is not required, as follows:

The State of . . . . . ., ... County. I, ... (name and style of officer), hereby certify that on the . . . . . . day of . . . . 19. . . ., came before me the within named . . . . . ., known to me to be the wife of the within named . . . . . ., who, being examined separate and apart from the husband touching her signature to the within named . . . . . ., acknowledged that she signed the same of her own free will and accord, and without fear, constraints, or threats on the part of the husband. Given, etc. (as in form above).

Probate of conveyance, or proof by subscribing witness, must be in following form:

The State of . . . . . ., ... County. I, ... (name and style of officer), hereby certify that . . . . . ., a subscribing witness to the foregoing conveyance, known to me, appeared before me on this day, and being sworn, stated that . . . . . ., the grantor, voluntarily executed the same in his presence, and in the presence of the other subscribing witness, on the day the same bears date; that he attested the same in the presence of the grantor, and of the other witness, and that such other witness subscribed his name as a witness in his presence. Given, etc. (as in form above). (35-4-30).

Form for official or other person in representative capacity must be substantially as follows:

The State of . . . . . ., ... County. I, ..., a . . . . . ., in and for said County in said State, hereby certify that . . . . . ., whose name as . . . . . . (here state representative capacity) is signed to the foregoing conveyance and who is known to me, acknowledged before me on this day that, being informed of the contents of the conveyance, he, in his capacity as such . . . . . ., executed the same voluntarily on the day the same bears date. Given, etc. (as in form of acknowledgment above). (35-4-29).

Form for corporation must be substantially as follows:

The State of . . . . . ., ... County. I, ..., a . . . . . . in and for said County in said State, hereby certify that . . . . . . whose name as . . . . . . of . . . . . ., a corporation, is signed to the foregoing conveyance and who is known to me, acknowledged before me on this day that, being informed of the contents of the conveyance, he, as such officer and with full authority, executed the same voluntarily for and as the act of said corporation. Given, etc. (as in form above). (35-4-29).

Form for corporation in representative capacity must be substantially as follows:

The State of . . . . . ., ... County. I, ..., a . . . . . . in and for said County in said State, hereby certify that . . . . . . whose name as . . . . of . . . . . ., a corporation as . . . . of the estate of . . . . . . (or as the case may be) is signed to the foregoing . . . . . ., and who is known to me, acknowledged before me on this day, that being informed of the contents of said . . . ., he, as such officer, and with full authority, executed the same voluntarily for and as the act of said corporation, acting in its capacity as . . . . . . as aforesaid. Given, etc. (as in form above). (35-4-29).

No form specified for acknowledgment by attorney or for authentication of officer's certificates.

Validating Acts.—When validly executed instrument, not properly acknowledged and recorded, has for ten years been of record in office of judge of probate, original or duly certified transcript shall have same force and effect as evidence as original or transcript would have had if instrument had been duly acknowledged and recorded. (35-4-72).

Alternative to Acknowledgment or Proof.—No statutory provision.

AFFIDAVITS:

By Whom Taken.—

Within state affidavits may be taken by judges of supreme court, court of civil appeals, court of criminal appeals, or circuit courts, and district courts and clerks of such courts, registers of circuit courts, judges of probate and notaries public. (35-4-24). Notaries may charge fee of 50¢ for acknowledging affidavit. (36-20-6).

Outside state but within United States they may be taken by judges or clerks of any federal court or any state court of record, notaries public, commissioners appointed by Governor of Ala., commissioner of deeds for state wherein acknowledgment taken or commissioned officers of U.S. Armed Forces. (35-4-26).

Outside of United States they may be taken by judge of any court of record, mayor or chief magistrate of any city, town, borough or county, notary public or any diplomatic, consular or commercial agent of the United States or commissioned officers of U.S. Armed Forces. (35-4-26).

Limitation.—Foregoing provisions appear in connection with provision relating to acknowledgments and proofs of conveyances under general heading of conveyances and are perhaps limited to affidavits relating to conveyances.

In Judicial Proceedings.—Affidavits required in commencement or progress of suit or judicial proceeding may be taken outside Ala. before any commissioner appointed by Governor of Ala., any judge or clerk of federal court or any court of record, or notary public, who must certify under his hand and seal of office, if any. (12-21-4).

Authentication.—Extrinsic evidence of authenticity as condition precedent to admissibility not required with respect to documents accompanied by certificate of acknowledgment executed in manner provided by law by notary public or other officer authorized by law to take acknowledgments. (Alabama Rule of Evidence 902[8]).

General Requirements as to Administration.—Duty is imposed on notary public to ascertain identity of person whose signature is attested. (380 So.2d 301).

General Requirements of Jurat.—Seal of officer (except of U.S. Armed Forces, see topic Acknowledgments) taking acknowledgment outside state must be affixed (106 Ala. 663, 18 So. 74), and purpose of notary to affix official seal should appear in certificate (203 Ala. 446, 83 So. 338). This appearing, court will presume officer's commission had not then expired. (212 Ala. 280, 102 So. 221).

Use of Affidavit.—Ex parte affidavits not generally received as evidence. (259 Ala. 306, 66 So.2d 836). However, ex parte affidavits may be received in certain proceedings. (ARCP 65[b]). Affidavits to show relationship of parties to real estate conveyances as well as certain other information relative thereto may be recorded (35-4-69) and when recorded are admissible in evidence under specified circumstances (35-4-70). Affidavits of jurors inadmissible to impeach verdicts, but admissible to sustain them. (285 Ala. 477, 233 So.2d 484; 590 So.2d 893).

See note at head of Digest as to 1998 legislation covered.

See Topical Index in front part of this volume.

AL – 30

AFFIDAVITS . . . *continued*

Form

No statutory form, following sufficient:

The State of . . . . . ., County of . . . . . . Before me (name and style of officer) personally appeared . . . . ., who is known to me and who being duly sworn, deposes and says . . . . . . (Signature of affiant). Subscribed and sworn to before me this . . . . . day of . . . . . ., 19. . . ., as witness my hand and seal of office. (Signature and title of officer). (Official seal). My commission expires . . . . . .

Alternative to Affidavit.—No statutory provision.

NOTARIES PUBLIC:

Notaries are appointed by judges of probate for counties (36-20-1) ("county notaries") and for state at large (36-20-30) ("state notaries"), and commissions are for four years (36-20-1).

Qualification.—Must give bond with sureties in amount of $10,000, approved by judge of probate of county for which appointed. (36-20-3; 36-20-31).

Authentication.—See topic Acknowledgments, subhead Authentication.

Seal.—For county notaries for authentication of official acts, notary must provide seal, which states name, office, state and county for which appointed. (36-20-4). For state notaries for authentication of official acts, notary must provide seal, which must state name, office and state for which appointed. (36-20-32).

Powers and Duties.—(1) To administer oaths in all matters incident to exercise of office; (2) to take acknowledgment or proof of instruments relating to commerce or navigation; (3) to demand acceptance and payment of bills of exchange, promissory notes and all other writings governed by commercial law as to days of grace, demand and notice of nonpayment; to protest same for nonacceptance or nonpayment and to give notice thereof as required by law; and (4) to exercise such other powers as, according to commercial usage or the laws of Ala., belong to notaries. (36-20-5).

Territorial Extent of Powers.—For state notaries, jurisdiction extends to any county of state. (36-20-30). For county notaries, jurisdiction unclear but may be limited to county in which appointed. (36-20-1).

Expiration of Commission.—Statement on certificate of date of expiration of commission not required, but often included where certificate to be used in another state.

Fees.—Entitled to following fees: $1.50 plus necessary postage for services rendered in connection with protest of bill of exchange for acceptance, or of any bill of exchange, promissory note, check, or other writing for payment; 50¢ for oath, certificate and seal taken; 20¢ for each 100 words for giving copies from register; 25¢ for certificate and seal to copy; 50¢ for giving other certificate and affixing seal of office. (36-20-6).

Commissioners of Deeds.—None.

Officers of U.S. Armed Forces.—No specific provision.

RECORDS:

Probate judge in county where property located has charge of records, except when Uniform Commercial Code has designated office of Secretary of State as place of filing. Uniform Commercial Code adopted. (7-1-101, et seq.). 1990 Revision of Art. 3 (7-3-101, et seq.) and 1990 Amendments to Art. 4 (7-4-101, et seq.) adopted.

Recordable Instruments.—

Recording Necessary for Full Effect.—Except as otherwise provided for by Uniform Commercial Code (See subhead Filing Under Commercial Code, infra), all deeds, mortgages, deeds of trust, bills of sale, contracts or other documents conveying any right, or interest in any real estate or personal property, and all assignments and extensions thereto, recordable in office of probate judge of any county. (35-4-51). All conveyances or mortgages of real property void as to purchasers for valuable consideration, mortgagees, and judgment creditors without notice, unless recorded before accrual of right of such purchasers, mortgagees, and judgment creditors. (35-4-90[a]). Also required to be recorded for full effect are following: Deeds of assignment for benefit of creditors (35-4-57); final condemnation orders or applications therefor (476 So.2d 1224); defeasance of absolute conveyances of realty (35-4-90[b]); remainders after estate for life in realty (35-4-91); all loans in writing, wills, or conveyances creating estates in personal property, on condition, in reversion or remainder or in which use separated from right and under which possession remains for three years with party entitled to estate or use but excluding any lease, or any security interest under Uniform Commercial Code (35-4-94); conveyances of personal property to minors when parents have control and possession (35-4-96); conveyances of personal property in consideration of marriage when possession remains with husband solely or with husband and wife jointly (35-4-93); remainder estates in personal property created in another state when personal property brought by life tenant into state but excluding any leases (35-4-54); transfers of standing timber, trees, and cutting rights therein (35-4-92).

Memorandum summarizing lease, rather than lease itself, may be recorded if certain information contained in memorandum. (35-4-51.1).

Permissive Recording.—Following instruments may be recorded and recording thereof constitutes legal notice of contents of such instruments: Petition in bankruptcy (35-4-52); bond for title or other written contracts for sale of land (35-4-53); federal or state patents to land in Ala. (35-4-56); affidavits showing relationship of parties to conveyances (35-4-69).

Place of Recording.—Conveyances of real property must be recorded in office of probate judge in county where such property located. (35-4-50). Record offices are maintained at various county seats. *For list of Counties and County Seats, see first page for this state in volume containing Practice Profiles Section.* In following counties, record offices maintained at places named and instruments must be recorded in office in division where properties located: Coffee County, at Elba and Enterprise; Jefferson County, at Birmingham and Bessemer; St. Clair County, at Ashville and Pell City; Barbour County, at Clayton and Eufaula.

Recording in Several Counties.—After deed, mortgage, map, or other paper affecting title to property filed in any probate office in Ala. certified copy of same may be filed in any other probate office in Ala. with same effect as filing of original. (35-4-66).

Requisites for Recording.—Probate judge may refuse to indorse "filed" on any instrument, or to record same, until registration fees paid and unless instrument witnessed, probated, or acknowledged as required by Code. (35-4-58). Attestation or acknowledgment not required to admit instrument to record. (39 Ala. App. 72, 96 So.2d 432). Instrument must: Show name and address of individual who prepared it (35-4-110); marital status of grantor or vendor (35-4-73); and have plat attached to instrument if land described by reference to plat (35-4-74).

Recording Fees.—

Documents Filed For Record (12-19-90[22])	$2.50/page
Oil, gas, mineral and/or coal leases (12-19-90[23])	$7.50/page
Certificate of Incorporation for Profit (12-19-90[28])	$35
Certificate of Incorporation Non-Profit (12-19-90[29])	$15
Satisfaction of a Mortgage (12-19-90[31])	$ 1
Certificate of Judgment (12-19-90[35])	$2.50
Plats (per map) (12-19-90[46])	$.50 for each lot, but not less than $10 nor more than $200

Original or Continuation Financing Statement (UCC-1) (7-9-403) $10 first page, $1 each additional page, $1 for each additional name to be indexed, plus $2 if not in standard form prescribed by Secretary of State.

Amendment Statement (UCC-3) (7-9-402[4]) $5 first page, $1 for each additional page, plus $2 if not in standard form prescribed by Secretary of State.

Assignment of Record (UCC-3) (7-9-405) $5 first page, $1 for each additional page, plus $1 if timber or crops, plus $2 if not in standard form prescribed by Secretary of State.

Statement of Release (UCC-3) (7-9-406) $5 first page, $1 for each additional page, plus $2 if not in standard form prescribed by Secretary of State.

Recording Taxes.—See category Taxation, topic Real Estate Conveyance Tax.

Foreign Conveyances or Encumbrances.—No statute authorizing recording of instrument executed and acknowledged in conformity with law of state where executed but not in conformity with law of this state. If effective under laws of this state to pass equitable interest, can be recorded even though not acknowledged, attested or proven in accordance with laws of this state. See subhead Requisites for Recording, supra.

Effect of Record.—Recording in proper office of any instrument which may be legally admitted to record operates as notice of contents even if not acknowledged or proved. (35-4-63). Instrument considered recorded from day of delivery to probate judge. (35-4-59). Instruments acknowledged or proved according to law and recorded may be received in evidence without further proof, and certified transcript of record may be received in evidence when original lost or destroyed, unless reputed maker in bona fide possession of property and makes and files affidavit that instrument is forged. (35-4-65). See topic Acknowledgments. Proof for record requires instrument be attested by two witnesses. (35-4-68).

Torrens Act.—Not adopted.

Transfer of Decedent's Title to real estate to devisees is shown by recordation of will, duly probated, in office of probate judge of county in which real estate lies. In case of intestacy, record of administration proceedings will usually show that title has passed to heirs, but if not shown, or if no administration, affidavits of heirship must be recorded in office of probate judge.

Filing Under Commercial Code.—

Place of Filing.—When reference to probate judge made in following list, reference to probate judge of county of debtor's residence, or if debtor not resident of state, then to probate judge of county where collateral kept. When collateral is crops growing or to be grown, such reference is to probate judge of county where land located. When collateral is timber to be cut, reference to probate judge of county where land on which timber standing located. Where collateral goods which are or are to become fixtures, filing in office where mortgage on real estate would be filed or recorded. (7-9-401). For collateral, including fixtures, of utility, see 7-9-401(5). Reference to Secretary of State means filing with Office of Secretary of State, 11 South Union Street, Montgomery, Alabama 36130.

Type of Collateral	Place of Filing
Accounts Receivable (General)	Secretary of State
Accounts Receivable (Farm)	Judge of Probate
Automobiles (Consumer Goods)	Judge of Probate
Automobiles (Business)	Secretary of State
Perfected by delivery of certificate of title with name and address of lienholder and date of security interest to Department of Revenue.	
Chattel Paper	Secretary of State
Consumer Goods	Judge of Probate
Contract Rights (General)	Secretary of State
Contract Rights (Farm)	Judge of Probate
Crops	Judge of Probate (Both for county where debtor resides and where crops are growing)
Central filing system established in accordance with Food Securities Act of 1985.	
Documents of Title	Secretary of State (plus possession)
Equipment (General)	Secretary of State
Equipment (Farm)	Judge of Probate
Farm Products	Judge of Probate
Fixtures (includes "to become Fixtures")	Judge of Probate

See note at head of Digest as to 1998 legislation covered.

See Topical Index in front part of this volume.

RECORDS . . . *continued*

Intangibles (General)	Secretary of State
Intangibles (Farm)	Judge of Probate
Inventory	Secretary of State
Proceeds (if perfected in original collateral)	Unnecessary
Timber	Judge of Probate

Filing requirements for accounts, contract rights, general intangibles, and equipment relating to another jurisdiction and also filing requirements for goods coming into state already subject to security interest set forth in 7-9-103. See category Business Regulation and Commerce, topic Commercial Code.

Filing Fees.—Alabama Uniform Commercial Code provides for uniform filing fees as follows: Original or continuation financing statement (7-9-403)—$10 for first page, $1 for each additional page, plus $2 if not in standard form prescribed by Secretary of State; and for financing statements, additional $1 for each additional name, including trade names, to be indexed, amendment statement (7-9-402[4]), separate assignment of record (7-9-405), and statement of release (7-9-406)—$5 for first page, $1 for each additional page, plus $2 if not in standard form prescribed by Secretary of State. See subhead Recording Fees, supra.

Vital Statistics.—Births, deaths and marriages registered with Office of Vital Statistics, Ala. Dept. of Public Health, RSA Tower, 201 Monroe St., Montgomery, AL 36111. (22-9A-1, et seq.). See also category Family, topic Marriage.

Establishing Birth Record.—Statute requires certificate to be filed within five days after birth. (22-9A-7).

Delayed registration may be filed for child under one year old on regular form in manner set forth in §22-9A-7. For persons aged one to five years old and must be signed by attending physician or parent if no physician available. (22-9A-9[2]). If person is 18 years old and competent, may be sworn to by individual whose birth being registered. Otherwise, must be sworn to by parent, guardian, next of kin, or other person having knowledge of birth. All certificates for persons more than five years old must be accompanied by at least three pieces of supporting documentary evidence. (22-9A-9[3]).

Court procedure for establishing birth provided for persons unable to meet aforesaid requirements. (22-9A-10).

Lis Pendens.—In suit in any court to enforce lien upon, right to, or interest in or to recover land or where application made to county probate judge for order of condemnation, or any interest therein, notice containing names of all parties to suit or persons named in application for condemnation order, description of real estate and statement of nature of lien, writ, application or suit must be filed in office of probate judge of county where land is situated. Unless notice of suit or application recorded, such suit or application shall not affect rights of bona fide purchaser, lessee, mortgagee or other lienee. (35-4-130, et seq.).

Fees.—Specified in 22-9A-23:

Search and one certified copy, if found	$12.00
Additional fee for same day expedited service	$10.00
Each additional copy	$4.00
Authenticated copy	$20.00
Amendment to original record and one certified copy	$15.00
New birth certificate after adoption and one certified copy	$20.00
Delayed certificate and one certified copy	$20.00

SEALS:

Not necessary for conveyance of land (35-4-21) or execution of bonds (1-3-2). Writings which import on face under seal deemed sealed instruments. (35-4-22). Word "seal" alone insufficient. (378 So.2d 721). Affixing seal to writing evidencing contract for sale or offer to buy or sell goods does not constitute writing sealed instrument. (7-2-203). Consideration of sealed instruments may be inquired into by plea. (6-5-287). Notary public taking acknowledgment outside state should affix seal. (106 Ala. 663, 18 So. 74).

Uniform Commercial Code adopted. (7-1-101, et seq.). See category Business Regulation and Commerce, topic Commercial Code.

Personal Seal.—Scroll or letters L. S. sufficient, but purpose to seal must be declared in body of instrument. (123 Ala. 222, 26 So. 203).

Corporate Seal.—Deed, mortgage or other conveyance of property can be validly executed without using corporate seal. (Implied by 35-4-67.) Presence of corporate seal establishes prima facie that instrument to which affixed act of corporation, and dispenses with necessity of proof executed by proper officers, or that they have authority to execute or that all proceedings to legalize execution were had unless corporation rebuts such presumption. (232 Ala. 471, 168 So. 693). Instrument must declare in body that corporate seal affixed to make seal effectual; when such declaration made use of word "seal" sufficient. (250 Ala. 229, 33 So.2d 904).

Effect of Seal.—All deeds, powers of attorney, instruments of conveyance, affidavits or contracts purporting to be verified by law recorded in probate judge's office and transcripts thereof are prima facie evidence that seal acknowledging such instrument is official seal affixed in official capacity. All such instruments and certified copies thereof must be received in court without further proof of due execution or seal. (35-4-27). See also category Civil Actions and Procedure, topics Limitation of Actions, subhead Ten Years, Accord and Satisfaction.

VITAL STATISTICS:

See topic Records, subhead Vital Statistics.

EMPLOYMENT

EMPLOYER AND EMPLOYEE:

See topic Labor Relations.

LABOR RELATIONS:

State Department of Labor has jurisdiction over labor matters.

Hours of Labor.—No statutory provision, with exception of child labor (see subhead Child Labor, infra).

Wages.—No statutory provision regarding minimum wage. Child Support withholding order takes priority over other writs of garnishment, irrespective of when withholding order served on employer. (30-3-67). Wages may be ordered withheld by court to pay criminal restitution. (15-18-140, et seq.).

Assignment of Wages.—See category Debtor and Creditor, topic Assignments.

Child Labor.—Employment of minors regulated in detail, and under general supervision of Department of Industrial Relations. (25-8-32, et seq.).

Child under 16 years old may not be employed, except in agricultural services or otherwise provided in chapter. (25-8-33). Children 14 or 15 may work outside school hours and during school vacation, except in certain occupations. (25-8-33). Work hours for children under 18 are expressly limited. (25-8-36). Certain specified occupations and places of work prohibited for children under 16. (25-8-35). Employment of child under 18 in or about certain specified occupations, positions or places prohibited. (25-8-43). Special regulations governing employment of minors in or about places where alcoholic beverages sold. (25-8-44). Employment of child in violation of child labor act is negligence per se, and employer liable for injury which is proximate result of such violation. (204 Ala. 649, 87 So. 168).

Permits must be obtained by minors or their employers in certain cases. (25-8-45, et seq.).

Penalties.—Violation of any provision of child labor act or of any lawful order issued thereunder punishable by fine of $100 to $500 for first offense and $500 to $1,000 for subsequent offenses. (25-8-59).

Female Labor.—Employers of women in stores or shops as clerk or saleswoman must provide accommodations for sitting or resting when not actively at work and separate sanitary facilities. (25-1-2).

Penalties.—Violation punishable by fine of $50 to $500. (25-1-2).

Discrimination in employment against employee 40 years and over on basis of age prohibited under Ala. law as of Aug. 1, 1997. (25-1-20, et seq.). No statutory provision regarding discrimination on basis of disability, race, color, religion, sex, or national origin.

Labor Unions.—Must file copies of constitution, by-laws and amendments thereto with State Department of Labor and make annual financial reports to Department. (25-7-5).

Labor Disputes.—Prohibited: (1) Interference by force, coercion, or intimidation with person's freedom to join or refrain from joining labor organization (25-7-6); (2) use of force or threats of violence to prevent any person from doing or contracting to do work or furnish materials (25-7-9); (3) seeking by force or threat of force to secure or prevent attendance at any meeting or place where strike vote taken (25-7-11); (4) collection or demand of money for privilege of working (25-7-12); (5) membership by professional, executive, administrative or supervisory employees in union which permits membership by others than such employees. (25-7-13).

Workers' Compensation Law.—(25-5-1, et seq.).

When employer subject to Workers' Compensation Act, compensation according to schedules therein contained must be paid for injury to or death of employee caused by accident arising out of and in course of his employment without regard to negligence except under specified circumstances. (25-5-51). Employee may not waive benefits provided by Act. (475 So.2d 872). Injury which occurs subsequent to original compensable injury is itself compensable if direct and natural result of original injury. (474 So.2d 1125).

All other rights and remedies of employee against employer and officer, director, agent, servant, employee and workers' compensation carrier of such employer and officer, director, agent, servant or employee of such workers' compensation carrier, and also against any labor union or any official or representative thereof, making safety inspection for benefit of employer or employees limited to willful conduct. Employer immunity does not extend to third party suits by tortfeasor to enforce contractual indemnity for claim arising out of injury to employee of same employer. (629 So.2d 633). Prohibits discharge in retaliation for filing workers' compensation claim or for filing notice of safety rule violations. (25-5-11.1).

Presumption as to Applicability of Act.—Every employer and employee presumed to have accepted and will be subject to provisions relating to payment and acceptance of compensation. (25-5-54).

Exception of Certain Employments.—Act does not apply to domestic employees, farm laborers, persons whose employment at time of injury is casual and not in usual course of business, or to any employer who regularly employs less than five employees in any one business, to any municipality of less than 2,000 persons according to most recent federal decennial census, unless such employer or such municipality or school district accepts provisions thereof by filing written notice with Department of Industrial Relations and by posting copies of such notice in employer's place of business. Withdrawal may be accomplished by giving like notice. (25-5-50).

Written notice of accident must be given to employer within five days unless prevented by physical or mental incapacity (other than infancy), fraud, deceit or other good reason (25-5-78, 656 So.2d 897). In any event notice must be given within 90 days after accident or death. (25-5-78). No notice required if actual knowledge of employer dispenses with notice. (213 Ala. 399, 104 So. 756).

To Whom Compensation Payable.—Compensation payable only to employee or certain dependents. (25-5-60,-66). Partner not employee of partnership. (292 Ala. 718, 298 So.2d 34).

Amount of Compensation.—Minimum and maximum weekly compensation is 27½% and 100%, respectively, of average weekly wage of state as determined by Director of Industrial Relations pursuant to statutory formula. (25-5-68; 25-5-57). No compensation allowed for first three days of disability unless disability lasts 21 days (25-5-59), but

See note at head of Digest as to 1998 legislation covered.

See Topical Index in front part of this volume.

AL – 32

LABOR RELATIONS . . . *continued*
medical, surgical and hospital expenses allowed from date of injury less benefits otherwise payable for such expenses without loss of benefit to employee (25-5-77). Normally, employer not liable for costs of medical or surgical treatment obtained by employee without justification or notice to employer. (355 So.2d 1133).

Rehabilitation.—Refusal of employee to accept rehabilitation at employer's request and expense results in loss of compensation for each week of period of refusal. (25-5-77[c]-[d]). (Note: As to standards for determining whether employee has right to vocational rehabilitation at employer expense, see 25-5-77[c]; 477 So.2d 408.)

In case of injury to a minor who, at the time thereof, is employed in violation of child labor law compensation is double what it would have been had employment been legal. (25-5-34).

Lump Sum Settlements.—With circuit court approval, parties may make lump sum settlements on basis of present value of payments to be made calculated on a 6% basis. (25-5-83). All matters of compensation may be settled by parties between themselves, but settlement must be in amount same as benefits stipulated by Act unless circuit court approves settlement for lesser amount. Settlement may be vacated within six months for fraud, undue influence or coercion. (25-5-56). After any settlement not approved by circuit court, employer must, within ten days, make report to Department of Industrial Relations. (25-5-5).

Recovery is barred when: (1) Injury caused by employee's willful misconduct; (2) employee intended to injure himself or another employee; (3) injury due to employee's willful failure to use safety appliances provided by employer; (4) accident due to injured employee being intoxicated from use of alcohol or being impaired by illegal drugs (positive drug test creates conclusive presumption of impairment from use of illegal drugs); (5) employee refused to cooperate in blood or urine test after accident after being warned in writing that such refusal would forfeit right to recovery; (6) employee knowingly and falsely misrepresented in writing physical or mental condition and condition aggravated by work-related accident. Burden of proof on employer. (25-5-51).

Limitations Period.—Claims barred two years after accident or death. Time extended in case of incapacity of claimant other than infancy. Partial payments toll limitations. (25-5-80). Statute may be tolled by fraud or estoppel. (504 So.2d 1217).

Actions.—In case of dispute, either party may file verified complaint in circuit court, of county which would have jurisdiction over tort action. Case tried summarily by court unless jury demanded to try issue of employee's willful misconduct. Party aggrieved by decree may obtain review in Court of Civil Appeals. (25-5-81; -88).

Subrogation.—If employee or dependents elect to receive compensation from employer, employer (or employer's insurer) subrogated to all rights of employee or dependents against third persons for injury or death of employee. (25-5-11).

Self-Insurers.—Employer can be authorized to self insure upon satisfactory proof to Director of Industrial Relations of employer's ability to pay compensation. (25-5-8). Director of Industrial Relations also empowered to issue regulations under which two or more employers can agree to pool liabilities for purpose of qualifying as self-insurers (25-5-9) or for purpose of providing excess coverage above self-insured retention levels maintained by individual employee groups (25-5-9).

False Statement.—Felony offense to make false statement for purpose of obtaining compensation under Act. (13A-11-124).

Jones Act (48 USC §688 [1982]) not exclusive remedy for seaman seeking to recover worker's compensation under Alabama law; Jones Act is fault-based system for recovery; double recovery precluded. (668 So.2d 775).

Occupational Diseases.—Disablement or death of employee caused by contraction of occupational disease arising out of and in course of employment and resulting from nature of employment, treated as injury by accident and employee or dependents (in case of death) entitled to compensation as provided in Workers' Compensation Act. (25-5-111).

Employers' Liability Act abrogates fellow servant rule and defenses of assumption of risk and contributory negligence in certain specified cases. (25-6-1). Damages recovered by employee not subject to payment of debts or legal liabilities, except judgments in favor of dependents. (25-6-2). Personal representative may sue when employee's injury results in death. (25-6-3). Insurance benefit or contract of employment no bar to recovery. (25-6-4). Superseded by Workers' Compensation Act, but still applicable in cases which cannot be brought under Workers' Compensation Act. (See 237 Ala. 387, 187 So. 468.)

Unemployment Compensation.—Unemployed individual may receive benefits if director finds employee: (1) Has made claim; (2) has registered for work and reported to employment office; (3) is capable of doing work and available for work; (4) has been totally or partially unemployed in such week; (5) has made reasonable and active effort to secure work which he is qualified to perform; and (6) has during base period been paid wages for insured work equal to or exceeding $1^1/_2$ times total of wages for insured work paid to him in that quarter of such base period in which such total wages were highest; provided, however, that no otherwise eligible individual who shall have received benefits in preceding benefit year shall be eligible to receive benefits in succeeding benefit year unless and until such otherwise eligible individual, subsequent to beginning date of preceding benefit year, worked in insured employment for which work he earned wages equal to at least eight times weekly benefit amount established for such individual in preceding benefit year. (*Note*: individual may also be required to participate in reemployment services in certain circumstances.) (25-4-77).

Right to Work.—Right of person to work may not be denied or abridged on account of membership or nonmembership in any labor union or labor organization. Agreements requiring membership in labor union or organization as condition of employment or continuation of employment prohibited. No employer may require employee to pay union dues as condition or continuation of employment. Any person denied employment or deprived of continuation of employment in violation of statute may recover damages. (25-7-30 to -36).

Individuals Disqualified for Benefits.—(1) For any week in which his unemployment is directly due to labor dispute in active progress in establishment in which he is or was last employed; (2) if he has left his employment voluntarily without good cause connected with such work (with possible exceptions connected to sickness or disability); (3) if he was discharged for dishonest or criminal act committed in connection with his work, for sabotage, act endangering safety of others, or use of illegal drugs or refusal to submit to drug test after previous warning; (4) for any week of unemployment because of revocation or suspension of required license, certificate, bond, or surety; (5) if he fails without good cause either to apply for or to accept available suitable work; (6) for any week with respect to which he is receiving or has received remuneration in form of wages in lieu of notice, dismissal or separation allowance or back pay; (7) for any week with respect to which he has received or is seeking unemployment benefits under law of another state or U.S.; (8) for any week with respect to which he has received, or has been determined eligible to receive, any pension, annuity or similar periodic payment based on previous work; (9) for any week with respect to which he has received or is seeking compensation for temporary disability under any workmen's compensation law; (10) for any week that individual is employed in federal or state public works or work relief; (11) for any week he is self-employed; (12) for any week with respect to which he has applied for or received training allowance; (13) for any week which commences between sports seasons to any individual for which benefits claimed are on basis of participation in sports events; (14) for any week for which benefits claimed on basis of services of alien, unless alien lawfully admitted to U.S. and lawfully present for such services, residing under color of law, or admitted for temporary residence. (25-4-78).

WORKER'S COMPENSATION LAW:

See topic Labor Relations.

ENVIRONMENT

ENVIRONMENTAL REGULATION:

General Supervision.—Air, water and hazardous waste pollution control monitored by Department of Environmental Management. (22-22A-1, et seq.). Coal surface mining and reclamation monitored by Surface Mining Commission by Surface Mining Control and Reclamation Act of 1981. (9-16-70, et seq.). Soil and water resources monitored by Alabama Agricultural and Conservation Development Commission. (9-8A-1, et seq.). Underground storage tanks and protection of wellhead areas of public water supply systems monitored by Department of Environmental Management. (22-36-1, et seq.). Public wastewater collection systems monitored by Department of Environmental Management (ADEM). (22-25-1, et seq.).

Prohibited Acts of Pollution.—Air pollution standards governed by Air Pollution Control Act. (22-28-1, et seq.). Water pollution standards governed by Water Pollution Control Act. (22-22-1, et seq.). Hazardous waste standards governed by Hazardous Wastes Management and Minimization Act. (22-30-1, et seq.). No specific acts prohibited by above Acts; however, broad powers are conferred on ADEM to adopt regulations for control, abatement, prevention of air and water pollution, on Mining Commission to control and regulate reclamation of surface mined lands, and on Agricultural Commission to provide funds for encouragement of soil conservation, water quality improvement and improved forestry practices.

Enforcement.—ADEM may conduct hearings; subpoena witnesses; require owner or operator of any air contaminant source to establish and maintain equipment and records for monitoring and reporting. ADEM empowered by emergency procedures to order persons causing or contributing to air pollution to reduce or immediately discontinue emission of air contaminants and hold hearing within 24 hours. (22-28-21).

ADEM also empowered to order to cease violations of water pollution statutes, regulation, order or permit and may require violator to file full report outlining steps implemented to control discharge. (22-22-9). ADEM, Attorney General, or any district attorney may file civil action for violation of water pollution act. Actions for pollution of air also authorized. (22-22-9,-14; 22-28-22).

Surface Mining Commission, enforces Alabama Surface Mining Control and Reclamation Act of 1981 and may promulgate rules and regulations, hold hearings, subpoena witnesses, issue orders to cease violations, issue and revoke permits and initiate civil or criminal actions. (9-16-70, et seq.). Private citizens may bring actions requiring Commission to perform enforcement duties. (9-16-95, et seq.).

Penalties.—Knowingly violating, failing or refusing to obey or comply with act or knowingly submitting false information may lead to maxium $10,000 fine and additional maximum $10,000 penalty for each day of continuing violation and sentence of hard labor for maximum of one year. (22-28-22).

Willful or grossly negligent violations punishable by fines of $2,500 to $25,000 per day and/or imprisonment for maximum of one year, with harsher penalties for subsequent convictions. Knowingly falsifying any information reportable or required maintained under Act is punishable by maximum fine of $10,000 and/or maximum of six months imprisonment. (22-22-14).

Surface Mining Commission may impose maximum civil penalty of $5,000 per violation at administrative hearing on violation of Act. (9-16-94). Commission may also cite violations and issue cessation orders. (9-16-93). For failure to correct violation, minimum penalty of $750 for each day violation continues for maximum of 30 days, may be imposed. Willful misrepresentation of any fact, willful violation of any permit or order issued by Commission or willful interference with Commission punishable by maximum fine of $10,000, and/or by maximum imprisonment of one year. (9-16-94).

Statute provides for penalties and recovery costs related to clean up of hazardous wastes. (22-30A-1, et seq.).

Exemptions.—None; however, ADEM may grant individual variances beyond limitations prescribed by Air Act, if it finds that compliance imposes serious hardship without equal or greater benefits to public, and emissions occurring or proposed to occur do not endanger human health or safety, comfort, and asethetic values. In granting variance, ADEM may impose certain conditions and policies, but variance period cannot exceed one year. (22-28-13).

See note at head of Digest as to 1998 legislation covered.

See Topical Index in front part of this volume.

AL – 33

ENVIRONMENTAL REGULATION ... *continued*

Fees For Waste Disposal.—Base fee of $41.60 per ton on all hazardous waste identified or listed under §3001 of Resource Conservation and Recovery Act of 1976 and on PCB wastes required to be disposed in chemical waste landfill approved under Federal Toxic Substance Control Act; and additional fee of $62 per ton on certain waste listed in 40 C.F.R. 261.33(e), or additional fee of $25 per ton on certain waste listed in 40 C.F.R. 261.33(f), or fee of $11.60 per ton on all other waste. (22-30B-2).

Hazardous Materials.—Pipelines and other facilities used in state for transporting hazardous liquids required to be constructed and maintained in accordance with specific safety standards. Alabama Public Service Commission empowered to regulate such activities, conduct inspections and otherwise enforce safety standards. (37-4-90, et seq.).

Permits required for construction, installation, modification or use of equipment or other device causing or contributing to air pollution. ADEM may require that applications for permits be accompanied by plans, specifications and other information. (22-28-16,-17). Permits required for discharge of sewage, industrial waste, or other waste into waters of state. ADEM examines all applications and grants permits, stipulating conditions under which such discharge may be permitted. (22-22-9).

License must be obtained from Surface Mining Commission before coal surface mining or exploration; permit for particular location of mining is required. (9-16-81, et seq.).

No license to collect, haul and/or dispose of solid waste may be issued by county commission or municipality without first obtaining permit and posting performance bond. (22-27-5).

ESTATES AND TRUSTS

ADMINISTRATION:

See topic Executors and Administrators.

ADVANCEMENTS:

See topic Descent and Distribution.

ALLOWANCES:

See topic Executors and Administrators.

CLAIMS:

See topic Executors and Administrators; category Civil Actions and Procedure, topic Pleading.

DEATH:

Person absent and unheard from for five years presumed dead and estate may be administered as decedent's estate. (43-2-231).

Survivorship.—Uniform Simultaneous Death Act adopted. (43-7-1, et seq.).

Actions for Death.—When death of minor child caused by wrongful act, omission or negligence, father or mother may, in certain cases named in statute, recover such damages as jury may assess. (6-5-391). If suit not brought within six months from death of minor, personal representative of such minor may, within two years, bring suit. (6-2-38; 6-5-391). Cause of action for death to fetus caused by tort to mother. (293 Ala. 95, 300 So.2d 354). No cause of action for wrongful death of nonviable fetus, meaning fetus not capable of living outside uterus. (613 So.2d 1241). Cause of action for wrongful birth. (624 So.2d 1022).

Personal representative may sue in Ala., and not elsewhere, and recover such damages as jury may assess, for wrongful act, omission or negligence causing death of decedent, if decedent could have sued had not death resulted from such act, omission or negligence. Such action must be brought within two years after death, and amount recovered is not subject to decedent's debts or liabilities. (6-5-410). Alabama Wrongful Death Act provides only for punitive damages, not for compensatory or actual damages. (444 So.2d 373). No statutory limitation of amount recoverable.

Death Certificate.—See category Documents and Records, topic Records, subhead Vital Statistics.

Uniform Anatomical Gift Act adopted. (22-19-40, et seq). See also topic Wills.

Living Wills.—See topic Wills.

DECEDENTS' ESTATES:

See topics Executors and Administrators, Descent and Distribution, and Wills.

DESCENT AND DISTRIBUTION:

Alabama Probate Code (43-8-1, et seq.) based on Uniform Probate Code 1974 edit., with many and material variances from Uniform Probate Code.

Distinction between real and personal property abolished. (43-8-1[25]).

Estate of decedent not effectively disposed of by will in excess of share of surviving spouse, or all such property if no surviving spouse, passes as follows, each class of which member is living taking to exclusion of subsequent classes: (1) Issue of decedent in equal shares if all issue of same degree of kinship to decedent, but by representation (see infra) if of unequal degree; (2) parent or parents equally; (3) issue of parents or either of them by representation; (4) in equal shares to more remote paternal and maternal kindred in following manner: (a) grandparent or grandparents equally, (b) issue of grandparents in equal shares if all issue of same degree of kinship to decedent, but by representation if of unequal degree; (5) if no paternal or maternal kindred on one side, entire estate to relatives on other side; (6) to state. (43-8-42 to -44). Except where estate could pass to state, heir must survive decedent five days. (43-8-43). Issue of person means all lineal descendants of all generations. (43-8-1[15]).

For representation, estate divided into as many shares as surviving heirs in nearest degree of kinship and deceased persons in same degree who left issue surviving decedent, each surviving heir in nearest degree receiving one share and share of each

deceased person in same degree being divided among issue of such deceased heir in same manner. (43-8-45).

Surviving Spouse.—Takes intestate share as follows: All if no surviving issue or parent of decedent; first $100,000 plus one-half of balance if decedent survived by parent or parents and no surviving issue; first $50,000 plus one-half of balance if decedent survived by issue all of whom are also issue of surviving spouse; one-half if decedent survived by issue one or more of whom are not issue of surviving spouse. If estate located in two or more states, surviving spouse's share may not exceed in aggregate amounts allowable under Ala. law. (43-8-41). Person divorced from decedent or whose marriage has been annulled not surviving spouse. (43-8-252). Surviving spouse who feloniously and intentionally kills decedent not entitled to any intestate share. (43-8-253).

Half Blood.—Relatives of half blood inherit same share as if they were of whole blood; no distinction between ancestral and general estate property. (43-8-46).

Posthumous Children or Other Issue.—Relatives of decedent conceived before decedent's death and born thereafter inherit as if born in lifetime of decedent. (43-8-47).

Illegitimates.—Heir of mother, and mother and kindred of illegitimate child on part of mother may inherit estate of such child. Illegitimate child is also heir of his father if: (1) Natural parents participated in marriage ceremony before or after birth of such child, even though marriage void, or (2) paternity established. Established paternity ineffective to entitle father or his kindred to inherit from or through child unless father openly treated child as his and has not refused to support child. (43-8-48). See also category Family, topic Infants, subhead Legitimation.

Adopted Children.—See category Family, topic Adoption.

Determination of Heirship.—No statutory proceedings.

Advancements.—If person dies intestate as to all his estate, property he gave in lifetime to heir is advancement against heir's share of estate only if declared in contemporaneous writing by decedent or acknowledged in writing by heir to be advancement. If recipient predeceases decedent, advancement not charged against intestate share of recipient's issue unless declaration or acknowledgment provides otherwise. Property valued at time heir came into possession or enjoyment of property or death of decedent, whichever first occurs. (43-8-49). Debt owed decedent not charged against intestate share of any person except debtor, and if debtor predeceases decedent, debt not charged against intestate share of debtor's issue. (43-8-55).

Election.—Surviving spouse has right to elective share equal to lesser of all of estate of deceased reduced by value of surviving spouse's separate estate or one-third of estate of deceased. (43-8-70).

See also topic Executors and Administrators.

Renunciation.—Person, or representative of deceased, incapacitated person, protected person, incompetent or ward, who is heir may disclaim in whole or in part right of succession to any property by delivering or filing written disclaimer (43-8-291) in probate court where administration of decedent's estate is, or could be, administered, or in case of real property in office of probate judge of county in which property located. Filing must be within nine months after death of decedent; qualified disclaimer of transfer of interest must be delivered not later than nine months after later of date of transfer or day on which disclaimant attains age 21. Copy of disclaimer must be delivered or mailed by registered or certified mail to personal representative of decedent. (43-8-292). Disclaimed property devolves as if disclaimant had predeceased decedent. (43-8-294). Uniform Disclaimer of Property Interests Act adopted with significant modifications. (43-8-290, et seq.).

Escheat.—Upon failure of heirs, decedent's intestate estate passes to state. (43-8-44).

ELECTION:

See category Wills.

ESTATES:

See category Property, topic Real Property.

EXECUTORS AND ADMINISTRATORS:

Jurisdiction.—Probate court has jurisdiction over probate of wills and administration of estates. (12-13-1).

Before final settlement, heir, devisee, legatee, distributee, executor or administrator may have administration of estate removed from probate court to circuit court without assigning any special equity. (12-11-41).

Venue.—Probate court of any county may grant letters of administration on estate of intestate: (1) Where intestate was inhabitant of county at time of death; (2) where intestate, though not inhabitant of state, left assets in said county, or assets were subsequently brought therein; (3) where property left in said county and intestate, though inhabitant of state, left no assets in county of residence and no letters of administration granted in said county of residence within three months after death. (43-2-40).

Preferences in Right to Administer.—Letters of administration granted to competent and willing persons in following order: (1) Husband or widow; (2) next of kin entitled to share in distribution of estate; (3) resident creditor with largest claim; (4) in counties having population of 400,000 or more, county or general administrator; in other counties, such other person as judge of probate appoints; (5) in counties having population of 400,000 or more, such other person as judge of probate appoints. (43-2-42). Whole blood preferred to half blood, and when several persons equally entitled, court may grant letters to one or more. Letters to which married woman entitled may be granted to husband in her right. (43-2-44). Preference may be relinquished, and lost unless letters applied for within 40 days after death known. (43-2-43).

No regular letters granted until five days have elasped after death of intestate known. (43-2-45).

Eligibility and Competency.—No person under 19 years of age or convicted of infamous crime or deemed unfit by court, may serve as administrator. Nonresident

EXECUTORS AND ADMINISTRATORS . . . . *continued*

cannot be appointed administrator except when duly qualified and acting executor or administrator of same estate under appointment of some other state or territory. (43-2-22).

Letters may be issued to married woman without consent of husband, and husband not responsible for her acts. (43-2-23).

Minor named as executor may join in administration with persons previously appointed when his disabilities removed. (43-2-24).

Nonresident may be granted letters testamentary under will of resident or nonresident decedent. (43-2-191). When probated in foreign state or territory, nonresident executor must file in office of judge of probate copy of will, together with certificate of judge of court in which will probated, stating that will regularly proved, established and admitted to probate, and that letters testamentary were issued thereon, before local letters testamentary will be issued. (43-2-192). Nonresident may be appointed administrator of deceased nonresident leaving assets in state if no application made by resident relative or creditor, in preference to any other person, on production and recordation of duly certified copy of letters issued by state of decedent's domicile. (43-2-193). Nonresidents seeking issuance of letters testamentary, or appointment as administrator, subject to same terms, conditions and requirements as residents, all subject to approval of judge of probate. (43-2-190 to -198).

Corporations with requisite corporate authority may act as executors or administrators. See category Business Organizations, topic Corporations, subhead Foreign Corporations.

Qualification.—Personal Representative or Special Administrator must post bond in amount equal to value of estate (exclusive of real estate) plus one year's income, unless court otherwise directs. (43-2-851).

Exemption from Bond.—Testator may by will exempt personal representative from giving bond, except where person interested in estate makes affidavit, showing affiant's interest and alleging that interest will be endangered by lack of security or where, in opinion of court, estate likely to be wasted to prejudice of any interested person. Personal representative may overcome exceptions by showing cause against application to give bond. (43-2-851).

Issuance of Letters.—See subhead Eligibility and Competency, supra.

Removal.—Administrator may be removed from office on account of his removal from state (43-2-290), but executor's removal from state not necessarily cause for removal from office (43-2-275). Either administrator or executor may be removed for: (1) Imbecility, intemperance, continued sickness rendering him incapable to discharge duties, or when reason to believe he is not suitable person to have control of estate; (2) failure to make and return inventories or accounts of sales, failure to make settlements as required by law or failure to do any act as such executor or administrator, when lawfully required by judge of probate; (3) waste, embezzlement or other maladministration; (4) using funds of estate for own benefit; (5) sentence of imprisonment or for hard labor for county for 12 months or more. (43-2-290).

Special Kinds of Administration.—

Administrator ad colligendum may be appointed wherever necessary. Authority of such administrator ceases upon grant of letters testamentary or of administration, and he must render account of his proceeding, under oath, to probate court. (43-2-47).

Administrators D. B. N. and C. T. A.—If sole executor, or all executors or administrators die, resign, or are removed, probate court must grant letters of administration, with will annexed, or of goods and chattels, rights and credits, unadministered, to person entitled thereto, as in cases of intestacy. (43-2-272).

Administrator ad litem without bond may be appointed where estate of deceased person must be represented in probate or circuit court and when no executor or administrator of such estate, or such executor or administrator is adversely interested. (43-2-250).

Ancillary Administration.—See subhead Foreign Executors or Administrators, infra.

Public Administrators.—Judge of probate must appoint general administrator for county, to take charge of cases when no one else will take charge, and none other appointed by court. (43-2-170).

Inventory and Appraisal.—Within two months after appointment, personal representative must file inventory of property owned by decedent at time of death, indicating fair market value of each item at time of death. Testator may exempt personal representative from filing inventory through express provision in will, but court may still require inventory if in its absence estate likely to be wasted to detriment of interested person. (43-2-311 to -314; 43-2-835).

General Powers and Duties.—Personal representative has broad powers to handle assets of estate without prior court approval if acting prudently for benefit of interested persons. (43-2-843). Court approval required for some actions, most notably selling or purchasing assets and mortgaging or leasing real or personal property. (43-2-844). Any fiduciary may deposit securities held in fiduciary capacity in clearing corporation. Securities so deposited may be merged and held in bulk in name of nominee of clearing corporation with other securities of same class. Ownership and other interests of said securities may be transferred by entries on books of clearing house without physical transfer of certificates. (19-4-1, et seq.).

Notice of Appointment.—Personal representative must give actual notice as soon as practicable to known creditors and must give publication notice within 30 days from grant of letters. (43-2-60).

Notice to Creditors.—Personal representatives must give notice of appointment to creditors. Actual notice must be given as soon as practicable after creditor's identification known, to all creditors known or reasonably ascertainable within six months from grant of letters. Publication notice when required must be given within 30 days from grant of letters. Actual notice when required must be given by first-class mail addressed to creditor's last known address or by other mechanism reasonably calculated to provide actual notice. Publication notice must be given by publishing notice once a week for three consecutive weeks in newspaper published in county in which letters granted, or if none published there, in one published nearest to courthouse thereof or in adjoining county. (43-2-60; -61).

Presentation of Claims.—Made by filing verified claim or verified statement in office of judge of probate by whom letters granted, and must be docketed with note of date of presentation; and, if required, statement must be given by judge, showing date of presentation. (43-2-352).

All claims not presented as above provided, within six months after grant of letters, or within five months from date of first publication of notice, whichever later to occur, barred and payment prohibited, provided that creditor entitled to actual notice pursuant to 43-2-61 must be allowed 30 days after notice within which to present claim. (43-2-350 to -352).

Minors and persons of unsound mind, who have no legal guardian at time of grant of letters testamentary or of administration, allowed six months after appointment of guardian or, if none appointed, six months after removal of respective disabilities, in which to present claims. (43-2-351).

Unmatured claims must be presented in same manner as matured claims. (43-2-350 to -375).

Contingent claims, including future rentals, excepted. (282 Ala. 492, 213 So.2d 225).

Debts secured by mortgage or other security can be enforced without filing claims to extent of security, but claims must be filed in order to charge general estate. (1 Ala. 708; 226 Ala. 52, 145 So. 318).

Revival of an action pending against any person at time of death, which by law survives against personal representative, by notice served on executor or administrator, within six months after grant of letters, considered as presentation of claim on which action founded. (43-2-353).

Claims of personal representative of decedent or by assignee, or transferee, or in which he has an interest, whether due or to become due, must be presented within six months after grant of letters, or within five months from date of first publication of notice, whichever later to occur, provided however, that creditor entitled to actual notice as prescribed in §43-2-61 must be allowed 30 days after notice to present claim, by filing claims, or statement thereof verified by affidavit, in office of judge of probate. Such claims not so presented and filed barred, and payment or allowance thereof prohibited. Does not apply to claim for compensation or to sums properly disbursed in course of administration. (43-2-350).

Claims for waste and conversion against decedent as executor or administrator of any other estate enforceable against his personal representative. (43-2-112).

Proof of Claims.—Every claim or statement presented must be verified by oath of claimant or some person having knowledge of correctness thereof, that amount claimed justly due or to become due, after allowing all proper credits. Defect or insufficiency in affidavit may be supplied by amendment at any time. (43-2-352).

Form.—Following is suggested:

Form

In the Probate Court of . . . . . . County.
In the matter of
the Estate of
. . . .
No. . . . .
To the Honorable . . . .
Judge of Probate in Said County.

Statement of Claim
. . . .
Signature.

State of . . . . }
. . . . County }

Before me . . . . . ., a Notary Public in and for said County in said State, personally appeared . . . . . ., who is known to me and who, being by me first duly sworn, deposes and says that he is . . . . . . of . . . . . ., the claimant, and that he has full and complete knowledge of the correctness of the above claim against the Estate of . . . . . ., deceased, and that the amount claimed is justly due (or to become due) after allowance of all proper credits.

. . . .
Affiant.

Sworn to and subscribed before me,
this . . . . . . day of . . . . . ., 19 . . . . . . As
witness my hand and official seal.

. . . .
Notary Public, ... County,
State of . . . .

Approval or Rejection of Claims.—Claims filed after six months of grant of letters or after five months of first notice publication barred and payment or allowance thereof prohibited. (43-2-350). Can only pay claims against estate which are barred by statute of limitations at decedent's death if testator expressly directs in will. (43-2-373). Any claim not presented by filing verified claim or verified statement in office of judge of probate within six months after grant of letters, or within five months from date of first publication of notice, whichever later to occur, barred and payment prohibited, provided that creditor entitled to actual notice pursuant to §43-2-61 must be allowed 30 days after notice within which to present claim. (43-2-350 to -352). Executor or administrator must render sworn list of claims six months after appointment and when thereafter required by court or by person interested in estate. (43-2-318).

Personal Representative to Give Claimant Written Notice that Claim Disputed.—Judge of court having jurisdiction of administration of estate must, on written application by either party, hear and pass on validity of claim, first giving ten days notice to interested parties; either party may appeal to circuit court for trial de novo. (43-2-354).

See note at head of Digest as to 1998 legislation covered.

See Topical Index in front part of this volume.

EXECUTORS AND ADMINISTRATORS . . . *continued*

Presentation of claim suspends running of limitations until written notice from representative, heir or devisee disputing validity. (6-2-9).

Payment of Claims.—Claims may be paid after six months from grant of letters. (43-2-374).

Unmatured claims may be paid at any time after six months from grant of letters, provided creditor accepts, in discharge of debt, such amount as, with interest to date of maturity, equals amount of debt. (43-2-375).

Priorities.—Debts of solvent (43-2-371) and insolvent (43-2-700) estates are paid in following order: (1) Funeral expenses; (2) expenses of administration; (3) expenses during last sickness; (4) taxes prior to death; (5) debts due employees during year of decedent's death; (6) other debts. (43-2-371). No preference as to debts in same class. (43-2-372). In insolvent estates, claims of creditors of same class paid ratably. (43-2-700).

Sales.—All property of decedent, except as otherwise provided, charged with payment of his debts, and, if necessary, may be sold for that purpose. (43-2-370).

Executor or administrator must petition court and be granted authority, before selling: property to pay debts; or he may be permitted to sell real estate to pay debts or for distribution among heirs but may not petition for permission to sell for division absent written consent of one of heirs. Lands may also be ordered sold by court for payment of pecuniary legacies when they are made charge on such lands and will does not authorize sale. (43-2-441 to -444; 43-2-480; 43-2-844).

Personal property of decedent may be sold only by order of court, on written and verified application of executor or administrator, unless power to sell conferred by will, in following cases: (1) For payment of debts; (2) to make distribution among distributees or legatees; (3) to prevent waste or destruction of property liable to waste or perish. Notice of application to sell and notice of sale must be given. (43-2-410; -417). Crops, farm products and stocks of goods may be sold at public or private sale. (43-2-418; -419; 43-2-421). Return of accounts of sale must be made on oath within 30 days and must be recorded. (43-2-422).

Actions by Representative.—Civil actions commenced by special administrator not abated by appointment of executor or administrator. (43-2-132). Succeeding executor or administrator may prosecute any civil action commenced by personal representative. (43-2-133).

Actions against Representative.—No suit can be commenced against executor or administrator until six months after grant of letters unless executor or administrator has given notice of disallowance of claim. (43-2-131). Presentation of claim is condition precedent to action thereon. (24 Ala. App. 344, 135 So. 412).

Time between death and grant of letters testamentary or of administration, not exceeding six months, not to be taken as part of time limited for commencement of actions by or against executors or administrators. (6-2-14).

Civil actions commenced by special administrator do not abate by appointment of administrator or executor, but may be prosecuted by latter. (43-2-132).

Allowances.—Surviving spouse and minor and dependent children entitled to reasonable family allowance for maintenance during administration. Allowance may not continue for more than one year if estate inadequate to discharge allowed claims. Allowance payable as follows: To surviving spouse, if living, for use of surviving spouse and minor children living with surviving spouse; otherwise, to children or persons having their care and custody; partially to spouse and partially to children or their guardians or persons having their care if child living apart from surviving spouse. Family allowance not chargeable against intestate share of surviving spouse or minor and dependent children. (43-8-112). Personal representative may determine allowance not to exceed $6,000 for one year, but personal representative or any interested person may petition court for larger or smaller allowance. (43-8-113). Homestead allowance (see category Debtor and Creditor, topic Homesteads) has priority over family allowance. (43-8-112). In addition to homestead following exempt to surviving spouse, or if no surviving spouse to decedent's children jointly, personal property to $3,500 (43-8-11); following exempt to resident: burial place and church pew (6-10-5); wages, salaries and other compensation for personal services exempt from levy under writs of garnishment or other process for collection of debts or judgments rendered in tort in amount equal to 75% of such wages, salaries, or other compensation (6-10-7; 5-19-15); worker compensation benefits (25-5-86[2]); partner's right in partnership property (10-8-72[b]) (repealed eff. Jan. 1, 2001); and certain personal property (6-10-126). See also 15 U.S.C. §1673(a). Exemptions granted by 11 U.S.C. §522(d) not available.

Widow's Quarantine.—Surviving spouse may retain possession of dwelling house where surviving spouse resided with decedent, with offices and buildings appurtenant thereto and plantation connected therewith. Decedent's estate retains obligation to pay any rent due. (43-8-114).

Intermediate Accountings.—Executor or administrator must make annual settlement of administration, and may be required to make settlement at any time. (43-2-500). When executor or administrator dies, resigns, or is removed, accounting must be made within one month; when moves from state, sureties must make accounting within six months after grant of letters. (43-2-550).

Final Accounting and Settlement.—May be made at any time after six months from grant of letters if debts paid and condition of estate permits (43-2-501), on notice by publication and notice by mail to resident distributees (43-2-505). In case of intestacy, order of distribution may be made, on application of any distributee, after six months from grant of letters. (43-2-641). Representative may be compelled to settle by citation and attachment from court having jurisdiction of estate. (43-2-530).

In making settlement, executor or administrator must file sworn statement of account, together with all affidavits or other legal evidence relied upon to sustain credit side of account. (43-2-502). After notice and on day appointed, court must audit account, hear contestants and render decree. (43-2-507, 43-2-511; 43-2-516). When estate free from debt, and court deems best, settlement may be referred to arbitration if parties consent thereto. (43-2-600).

If administration of estate completely inactive for 20 years, excluding six months after issuance of letters testamentary or of administration, and all bequests and legacies have been payable or demandable for such time, conclusive presumption arises that final settlement made and decree to that effect may be obtained. (43-2-660 to -664).

Consent Settlement.—If all debts of estate paid and all distributees and legatees (or, in case of intestacy, all heirs and next of kin) are of age (or, if not, represented by guardian not adversely interested to ward), order of final settlement can be entered without notice or publication upon filing of verified petition of executor or administrator consented to by such distributees and legatees, or heirs and next of kin. (43-2-506).

Distribution.—Executor or administrator may, if satisfied estate solvent, make distribution, with or without order, after six months of grant of letters. (43-2-640). When under terms of will or trust indenture fiduciary to satisfy pecuniary gift by distribution of properties from corpus or estate, absent contrary instructions in governing document, fiduciary must select properties which fairly reflect net appreciation or depreciation of said corpus or estate in satisfaction of such gift. (19-3-9).

Distribution If Abroad.—Whenever upon settlement of an estate it is shown that any persons entitled to share in estate are residents and subjects of foreign country, and not represented by counsel of own employment, custodian of funds must pay over such person's share to accredited consular officer of foreign country, in whose jurisdiction court situated. (6-8-20).

Liabilities.—Except where executor or administrator fails to give notice of his appointment to creditors in order that they may present their claims, not liable beyond amount of assets which have come to his hands or which have been lost by his negligence. (43-2-62 to -110). Personal representative and sureties liable to parties in interest for distribution of damages recovered on account of death of decedent. (43-2-111). If exercise of power concerning estate is improper, personal representative liable to interested persons for damage or loss resulting from breach of personal representative's fiduciary duty to same extent as trustee of express trust. (43-2-840).

Compensation of Representatives.—Personal representative entitled to reasonable compensation as may appear to court to be fair, not to exceed 2½% of receipts and 2½% of disbursements. Court may consider ten enumerated factors. (43-2-848). Representative entitled to expenses and attorneys' fees for any proceeding defended or prosecuted in good faith regardless of outcome. (43-2-849). Compensation paid to attorneys, accountants, investment advisors and other agents will be reviewed by court upon petition by interested person. (43-2-850). Unless expressly authorized in will, personal representative must have prior court approval before paying compensation to personal representative. (43-2-844).

When Administration Unnecessary.—Where estate consists of personal property only, value which does not exceed $3,000, surviving spouse or, if none, distributees, may initiate proceeding for summary distribution of estate provided certain conditions met. (43-2-690 to -696).

Small Estates.—See subhead When Administration Unnecessary, infra.

Foreign Executors or Administrators.—When nonresident dies, leaving assets in state, letters of administration granted to representative appointed by foreign court on written application with exemplified copy of will and foreign letters attached. (43-2-192; -193).

Foreign and Ancillary Administration.—After 60 days from date of death, personal representative appointed by foreign court may collect and execute release for indebtedness or bank deposit owing to deceased in Alabama, first filing in probate office exemplified copy of letters. No collection may be made, however, if grant of letters in Ala. made or pending. (43-2-195).

Foreign executor or administrator of decedent not inhabitant of this state at time of death, and who has not taken out letters in this state in accordance with above, may maintain suits and recover or receive property in this state by recording, before judgment or receipt of property, duly authenticated copy of his letters in probate office of county where suit brought or property received or by giving bond. (43-2-211). Grant of letters in this state does not bar suit by foreign administrators, but local administrator or executor may intervene. (43-2-212). See also topic Wills, subhead Foreign Probated Wills.

Uniform Fiduciaries Act adopted with modifications. (19-1-1, et seq.).

Revised Uniform Principal and Income Act adopted with modifications. See topic Trusts. (19-3-270 to -282).

Uniform Simplification of Fiduciary Security Transfers Act adopted. Act survives and controls if inconsistency with Uniform Commercial Code. (7-10-104[2]).

Uniform Anatomical Gift Act adopted. (22-19-40, et seq.). See topic Wills.

Beneficiaries.—Legatees and distributees, if more than sufficient assets to pay debts, after six months may apply for payment of legacies and for distribution. Legatee or distributee must give refunding bond, on which liable also for interest, before receiving payment. (43-2-580 to -586).

Insolvent Estates.—When executor or administrator satisfied that estate insolvent, must file with probate judge report to that effect, together with statements listing property, claims, heirs, legatees and distributees, which must be verified by affidavit. (43-2-701; -703). After notice, hearing, and decree of insolvency, executor or administrator must make final settlement. Creditors, according to amount of claims, nominate administrator. Verified claims must be filed within six months after declaration of insolvency or after accrual thereof and settlement must be made from six to 12 months from declaration of insolvency. (43-2-740). If no opposition made to claim within six months after declaration of insolvency, it must be allowed without further proof. When, prior to declaration of insolvency, claim filed in office of judge of probate, such claim considered as filed under insolvency provision. Objection to any claim within six months after declaration of insolvency. (43-2-704 to -720; 43-2-740 to -747; 43-2-770).

As to priorities among claims against insolvent estates, see supra, subhead Priorities.

Substitution.—No statutory provision.

See note at head of Digest as to 1998 legislation covered.

See Topical Index in front part of this volume.

FIDUCIARIES:

See topics Executors and Administrators, Trusts; category Family, topic Guardian and Ward.

INTESTACY:

See topic Descent and Distribution.

PROOF OF CLAIMS:

See topic Executors and Administrators; category Civil Actions and Procedure, topic Pleading.

TRUSTS:

Kinds.—Trusts may be created for benefit of grantor, family or third persons, or for any other lawful purpose, including specific charities. (35-4-251).

Creation may be express, resulting or constructive. Trust in real property must be in writing. (257 Ala. 614, 60 So.2d 346). Trust in personalty need not be established in writing. (270 Ala. 311, 119 So.2d 23).

Appointment of Trustee.—Trust will not fail for lack of trustee. (454 So.2d 1350). When trust exists without appointed trustee, or where all trustees renounce, die, or are discharged, circuit court must appoint another trustee. (19-3-251). Trustee has no authority to appoint successor unless such authority expressly conferred. (142 Ala. 163, 37 So. 929).

Eligbility and Competency.—Nonresident permitted to act as trustee of Alabama trust. (263 Ala. 106, 81 So.2d 610).

Qualification.—In absence of express provision in will, testamentary trustee not required to furnish bond. (228 Ala. 170, 153 So. 238). Testator's directions respecting bond may be disregarded to protect substantive property rights created by will. (241 Ala. 591, 4 So.2d 140). When express trust created for payment or security of debts, and terms do not require trustee's bond, any interested creditor may apply to circuit court for order requiring trustee to give bond. (64 So. 960).

Removal of Trustee.—Upon filing of complaint by interested party, including settlor, circuit court may remove trustee who: has or threatened to violate trust; is insolvent or likely to become so; has removed from state; has any pecuniary interest which may be adverse to interests of trust; or court may require bonds to protect interests of parties. (19-3-211). Statute not limitation on power of court; sufficient ground for removal generally within court's discretion. (264 Ala. 145, 85 So.2d 395).

General Powers and Duties of Trustees.—Determined by instrument; court will not permit trustee to exercise absolute or unbridled powers. (474 So.2d 53). If not determined in instrument, powers of trustee defined by statute; in exercising powers, trustee must act as prudent person, in light of trust purposes. (19-3-322). If trustee also beneficiary, unless trust expressly refers to §19-3-324 and provides to contrary, trustee not entitled to certain powers. (19-3-324[a]). If multiple trustees, unless trust provides to contrary, and except in certain circumstances, concurrence of all trustees required on acts connected with administration of trust. (19-3-325). In investing, trustee must act with care, skill, prudence and diligence under circumstances then prevailing that prudent person acting in like capacity and familiar with such matters, would use. (19-3-120.2). Trustee must consider role that investment plays within account's overall portfolio of assets and may consider general economic conditions, anticipated tax consequences of investment, attributes of account portfolio, general economy, and needs and objectives of beneficiaries as they existed at time of investment decision. (19-3-120.2).

Sales.—When trustee conveys legal title to stranger without court order or authority given by settlor, beneficiary may assert right of constructive trust against stranger, except purchaser for value and without notice. (35-4-256; 238 Ala. 531, 192 So. 258). Circuit court may direct sale of trust property and reinvestment, though not authorized by settlor, if conditions such that it is in interest of trust estate. (204 Ala. 541, 86 So. 376). Court may authorize sale to highest bidder of doubtful debts or choses in action belonging to trust estate. (19-3-39). Notice to creditors must be given before sale of real property belonging to trust estate. (19-3-40).

Investments by fiduciaries regulated by Const., §74, as am'd by Amend. 40, §§19-3-120 to -132, and §§19-4A-1 to -7. Prudent person standard for trustee investment and management. (19-3-120.2). Trust instrument may exempt trustee from constitutional and statutory restrictions on investment of trust funds. (274 Ala. 659, 151 So.2d 225).

Securities in Name of Nominee.—Corporate fiduciary may hold securities in name of nominee subject to certain conditions. (19-3-7). Any fiduciary may deposit securities held in fiduciary capacity in clearing corporation. (19-4-2[a]). Securities so deposited may be merged and held in bulk in name of nominee of clearing corporation with other securities of same class. (19-4-2[b]). Ownership and other interests of said securities may be transferred by entries on books of clearing house without physical transfer of certificates. (19-4-2[c]).

Bequests and Devises to Inter Vivos Trusts.—See topic Wills, subhead Testamentary Additions to Trusts.

Accounting.—Trustee under duty to furnish beneficiary complete and accurate information as to nature and amount of trust property. (450 So.2d 798).

Compensation.—Trustee entitled to repayment, out of trust property, of all expenses properly incurred in performance of trust, and for unlawful expenditures made in good faith, if productive of actual benefit to trust estate. (19-3-4). Trustee may render estate liable for payment for necessary services rendered to him, or for necessary repairs in estate, or for necessaries furnished him, if he is or becomes insolvent without having paid for same, and if he has not charged estate with, and received credit for, such services, repairs or necessaries. (19-3-100). If trustee defends or prosecutes proceeding in good faith, whether successful or not, trustee may be entitled to receive from trust estate reasonable expenses and disbursements, including attorneys' fees incurred. (19-3-326).

Discharge.—Circuit court may remove trustee who (1) violates or threatens to violate trust; (2) is insolvent or will be; (3) has removed from state; or (4) is otherwise unsuitable to execute trust. (19-3-211). Circuit court may also remove trustee who has pecuniary interest which may be adverse to interests of trust. (19-3-211).

Uniform Common Trust Fund Act adopted with modifications. (5-12A-1 to -15).

Revised Uniform Principal and Income Act adopted with modifications. (19-3-270-282). Act applies (1) to all transactions relating to trusts created after Sept. 19, 1939; and (2) to all transactions Sept. 19, 1939-May 31, 1941, relating to trusts created before Sept. 19, 1939, to extent that such application is not unconstitutional. See 259 Ala. 346, 67 So.2d 8; 254 Ala. 5, 47 So.2d 203; 249 Ala. 631, 32 So.2d 368; 241 Ala. 606, 4 So.2d 170. Act not applicable when enacted after death of testator. (381 So.2d 8).

Gifts to Minors.—See category Family, topic Infants.

Uniform Fiduciaries Act adopted with modifications. (19-1-1 to -13).

Accumulations.—See category Property, topic Perpetuities.

Perpetuities.—See category Property, topic Perpetuities, subhead Accumulation.

Pour Over Trusts.—See topic Wills, subhead Bequests and Devises to Inter Vivos Trusts.

Renunciation.—No statutory provision.

Trust with spendthrift provisions providing for payment of profits or income, and, at grantor's election, as much of principal as trustee deems required for support and maintenance of relative by blood or marriage valid. (19-3-1[a]). Certain qualified trusts concerning retirement benefits under Internal Revenue Code now protected. (19-3-1[b]).

Business trusts provided for in §§19-3-60 to -67. See category Business Organizations, topic Joint Stock Companies.

Cy Pres.—Many decisions of Supreme Court of Alabama prior to 1940 rejected doctrine of cy pres. However, these decisions did not distinguish between judicial and prerogative cy pres, and it is difficult to determine whether court rejected both judicial and prerogative cy pres or only prerogative cy pres. Even though cy pres by name was not applicable to save charitable trust, Supreme Court decisions historically authorized courts of equity to apply equitable doctrine of approximation under which details of administration could be varied to preserve trust and carry out general purpose of trust donor. (215 Ala. 271, 110 So. 381). Opinion expressed by Supreme Court that judicial cy pres and Alabama doctrine of equitable approximation merely different names for same doctrine (258 Ala. 238, 61 So.2d 817), but decisions indicate that judicial cy pres goes beyond power to modify details of administration, permitting court to carry out general charitable purpose of trust donor, even when particular beneficiaries identified by donor no longer in existence (19 Ala. 814; 215 Ala. 271, 110 So. 381; 249 Ala. 597, 32 So.2d 526). §35-4-251 provides that "if a trust for charity is impracticable, or too indefinite to admit enforcement, or ceases to admit of practicable enforcement, a court on application of the trustee or of any person charged alone or with others with the administration of the charity may order an approximate or cy pres carrying out of the trust." (35-4-251). This statute explicitly adopts doctrine of judicial cy pres. (258 Ala. 238, 61 So.2d 817). By empowering circuit court to use alternatively equitable approximation or cy pres, statute evinces intention not only to confirm already established power to vary administrative details of charitable trust but also to innovate cy pres power to alter purpose of charitable trust that otherwise would have failed because intended beneficiaries did not exist or identified purpose indefinite or impossible. (6 Ala. Lawyer 17).

When land held under trust created by deed and, because of change in circumstances, it becomes impossible to carry out purpose of trust in exact accordance with terms of deed, circuit court may order sale of such land and direct proceeds of such sale to be used to secure original object of trust, as near as may be, according to intent of grantor. (19-3-171).

Uniform Cy Pres Act adopted in modified form. (35-4-251).

Trust Instruments.—All trusts concerning lands, unless implied or constructive, must be created by instrument in writing signed by creator or authorized agent or attorney (provided authorization written). (35-4-255).

Recordation.—Such trust instrument, when recorded in county in which lands lie, equivalent to actual notice to all persons claiming under subsequently created lien or subsequent conveyance. (35-4-257). Neither express nor implied trusts defeat title of creditor or purchaser for value without notice. (35-4-256).

Remedial trusts in nature of constructive and resulting trusts recognized under appropriate circumstances.

Legal title vested in beneficiary of dry or passive trust by operation of law. (35-4-250).

Extinguishment by operation of law when object of trust entirely fulfilled or becomes impossible or unlawful. (19-3-2). When market value of trust less than $25,000 and, relative to cost of administration of trust, continuance of trust will defeat or substantially impair trust process, trustee may terminate trust and distribute trust property. (19-3-323).

Estate of Trustee.—Whenever trust estate created, legal estate in trustee sufficient for purpose of trust will be implied, if possible; but trustee takes no greater estate than necessary for complete execution of trust. (19-3-3).

Misapplication of Funds.—Persons making payments to trustees not responsible for application of such moneys in absence of collusion with trustee or knowledge of intended misapplication. (35-4-254). But persons assisting trustee and having knowledge of trustee's misapplication of trust assets liable to injured beneficiaries. (19-3-105).

WILLS:

Law of Intestate Succession and Wills (43-8-1 to -298), effective Jan. 1, 1983, repealed in large part prior law of wills found in tit. 43, c. 1 of Code of Alabama 1975 as amended. Uniform Probate Code 1974 edit., was used as guide for new law, but there are many material variances from Uniform Probate Code.

Person 18 years old or more who is of sound mind may make will. (43-8-130).

See note at head of Digest as to 1998 legislation covered.

See Topical Index in front part of this volume.

AL – 37

WILLS . . . *continued*

Testamentary Disposition.—No limitations as to amount or recipient of testamentary dispositions.

Execution.—Will must be in writing signed by testator or in testator's name by some other person in testator's presence and by his direction, and must be signed by at least two persons each of whom witnessed either signing or testator's acknowledgment of signature or of will. (43-8-131). Person generally competent to be witness may witness will. (43-8-134[a]). Witness's subsequent incompetency will not prevent probate of such will, if otherwise satisfactorily proved. (43-8-163).

Attestation Clause.—No prescribed form.

Following form complies with statutory execution requirements:

Form

The foregoing instrument was signed by . . . . (or signed in the name of . . . . in the testator's presence and at his direction) as and for his last will and we, having witnessed the signing (or the testator's acknowledgment of the signature) (or the testator's acknowledgment of the will), have by our signatures hereunto subscribed our names and addresses as attesting witnesses on the date last above written.

Signed (name) . . . . (address) . . . .
Signed (name) . . . . (address) . . . .

Holographic Wills not recognized because of statutory requirement that every will must be witnessed and attested by at least two persons. (474 So.2d 696). Will written in handwriting of testator and attested by at least two witnesses is not holographic will. See also subhead Foreign Executed Wills, infra.

Nuncupative Wills not recognized.

Revocation by subsequent will which revokes prior will or part expressly or by inconsistency. Entire will revoked by being burned, torn, canceled, obliterated or destroyed, with intent and for purpose of revoking same by testator or by another person in his presence by his consent and direction, and if physical act by someone other than testator, consent and direction of testator must be proved by at least two witnesses. (43-8-136). Divorce or annulment after execution of will revokes any disposition or appointment of property made by will to former spouse, any provision conferring general or special power of appointment on former spouse and any nomination of former spouse as executor, trustee or guardian, unless will expressly provides otherwise; property so devised to former spouse passes, and other provisions conferring power or office on former spouse are interpreted, as if spouse failed to survive decedent. (43-8-137).

Revival.—If second will which, had it remained effective at death, would have revoked first will in whole or in part, is thereafter revoked by being burned, torn, canceled, obliterated or destroyed, first will is revoked in whole or in part unless evident from circumstances of revocation of second will or from testator's contemporary or subsequent declarations in writing that testator intended first will to take effect as executed. If second will which, had it remained effective at death, would have revoked first will in whole or in part, is thereafter revoked by third will, first will is revoked in whole or in part, except to extent it appears from terms of third will that testator intended first will to take effect. (43-8-138). Provisions revoked by divorce or annulment revived by testator's remarriage to former spouse. (43-8-137).

Testamentary Gifts to Subscribing Witnesses.—Will or any provision thereof not invalid because signed by interested witness. (43-8-134[b]).

Bequests and Devises to Inter Vivos Trusts.—Pour-over trusts valid if trust identified in will, terms of trust written (other than in will) and executed before or concurrently with execution of testator's will or in last valid will of person who predeceased testator. (43-8-140). Trust may be amended subsequent to date of testator's will. (43-8-140).

Testamentary Guardians.—See category Family, topic Guardian and Ward, subhead Appointment of Guardian.

Probate.—

Jurisdiction.—Probate court has jurisdiction to probate wills. (12-13-1[b]).

Venue.—Wills must be proved in probate court of county of which testator was inhabitant at time of death (43-8-162[1]) or in county designated by testator in will if testator owns property therein at time of death (43-8-162[5]). When testator not inhabitant of state, will must be proved in probate court of county in which testator died leaving assets therein (43-8-162[2]), in county in which testator left assets even though testator died in another place (43-8-162[3]), or in county into which assets of testator are brought (43-8-162[4]).

Time for Probate.—Will must be filed for probate within five years after testator's death. If testator not inhabitant of state at time of death, will may be admitted to probate in this state provided will admitted to probate in state, territory or country where testator resided within five years after testator's death, however, probate in this state not effective against persons purchasing from heirs of nonresident testator if purchase made more than five years after testator's death and prior to Feb. 24, 1959. (43-8-161).

Any will not propounded for probate within 12 months after testator's death inoperative and void as to bona fide purchasers and mortgagees, provided acquisition occurs prior to propounding of will for probate and provided purchaser lacked actual notice of will. (43-8-172).

"File for probate" language of §43-8-161 (formerly 43-1-37) denotes action beyond turning will over to clerk for recordation and involves further action evidencing intent to probate. (387 So.2d 156).

Statute of Limitations.—Statute imposing time limit for probating will considered statute of limitations; must be affirmatively pleaded. (459 So.2d 868).

Who May Apply for Probate.—Any executor, devisee or legatee named in will, or any person interested in estate, or who has custody of will may have will proved before probate court. (43-8-160). Upon request of interested person, any person having custody of will must deliver it to person able to secure probate of same or, if none known, to appropriate court. (43-8-270).

Notice.—Surviving spouse and next of kin residents of state must be given ten days notice before application for probate heard (43-8-164), and if nonresidents or outside state, must be notified by publication or posting of application (43-8-166) or as provided in ARCP (by registered mail). Minor served by giving notice in manner required by ARCP and guardian ad litem must be appointed to represent minor in proof and probate of will. (43-8-165; ARCP 4[c]). See category Civil Actions and Procedure, topic Process.

Proof.—One or more subscribing witnesses must prove will or, if satisfactorily shown all are dead, insane or absent from state or have become incompetent since attestation, proof of handwriting of testator and at least one witness may be received. Testimony of one witness sufficient if no contest filed. (43-8-167).

Self-proved Wills.—Any will may be simultaneously executed, attested and made self-proved by acknowledgment by testator and affidavits of witnesses before authorized officer in substantially following form (43-8-132[a]):

Form

I, ..., the testator, sign my name to this instrument this . . . . day of . . . ., 19. . . ., and being first duly sworn, do hereby declare to the undersigned authority that I sign and execute this instrument as my last will and that I sign it willingly (or willingly direct another to sign for me), that I execute it as my free and voluntary act for the purposes therein expressed, and that I am 18 years of age or older, of sound mind, and under no constraint or undue influence.

. . . .
Testator

We, ... and . . . ., the witnesses, sign our names to this instrument, being first duly sworn, and do hereby declare to the undersigned authority that the testator signs and executes this instrument as his last will and that he signs it willingly (or willingly directs another to sign for him), and that each of us, in the presence and hearing of the testator, hereby signs this will as witness to the testator's signing, and that to the best of our knowledge the testator is 18 years of age or older, of sound mind and under no constraint or undue influence.

. . . .
Witness

. . . .
Witness

State of . . . .
County of . . . .

Subscribed, sworn to and acknowledged before me by . . . ., the testator, and subscribed and sworn to before me by . . . . and . . . ., witnesses, this . . . . day of . . . ., 19. . . . . .

[SEAL] (Signed) . . . .

. . . .
(Official Capacity of Officer)

Attested will may at any time subsequent to its execution be made self-proved by acknowledgment by testator and affidavits of witnesses before authorized officer in substantially following form (43-8-132[b]):

Form

State of . . . .
County of . . . .

We, ..., ... and . . . ., the testator and the witnesses, respectively, whose names are signed to the attached or foregoing instrument, being first duly sworn, do hereby declare to the undersigned authority that the testator signed and executed the instrument as his last will and that he had signed willingly (or willingly directed another to sign for him), and that he executed it as his free and voluntary act for the purposes therein expressed, and that each of the witnesses, in the presence and hearing of the testator, signed the will as witness and that to the best of his knowledge the testator was at that time 18 years of age or older, of sound mind and under no constraint or undue influence.

. . . .
Testator

. . . .
Witness

. . . .
Witness

Subscribed, sworn to and acknowledged before me by . . . ., the testator, and subscribed and sworn to before me by . . . . and . . . ., witnesses, this . . . . . day of . . . ., 19. . . . .

[SEAL] (Signed) . . . .

. . . .
(Official Capacity of Officer)

If will self-proved, must be admitted to probate without further proof of compliance with requirements for execution, unless proof of fraud or forgery affecting acknowledgment or affidavit. (43-8-132[c]).

Living Wills.—Governed by Alabama Natural Death Act. (22-8A-1; -10).

Contest.—Before probate, will may be contested by interested person, or by person who would have been heir or distributee of testator if testator had died intestate, by filing written allegations that will not duly executed, testator of unsound mind or other valid objections, and such issue must be tried by jury on demand of either party. (43-8-190). Contest must be transferred to circuit court on written demand of either party made at time of filing initial pleading; appeal may be taken to supreme court within 42 days after entry of judgment in circuit court. (43-8-198). After final determination of contest, transcript and papers must be returned to probate court to be recorded. (43-8-198).

Within six months after admission of will to probate, person who has not contested will as outlined above may contest same by filing complaint in circuit court. (43-8-199). Under limited conditions, infants and persons of unsound mind granted additional time

See note at head of Digest as to 1998 legislation covered.

See Topical Index in front part of this volume.

AL – 38

WILLS . . . *continued*

to contest will, but in no case to exceed 20 years after admission of will to probate. (43-8-201).

Legacies.—If assets of estate sufficient to pay debts of decedent, legatee may compel payment of legacy six months after grant of letters. (43-2-580 to -586). Absent express order of abatement in will, shares of distributees abate, without preference as between real and personal property, as follows: (1) Property not disposed of by will; (2) residuary devises; (3) general devises; (4) specific devises. (43-8-76[a]).

Surviving spouse may elect to take elective share six months after later of death of decedent or probate of decedent's will. (43-8-73). Values of property included in estate which pass, have passed or would have passed to surviving spouse but renounced first applied to satisfy elective share, and liability for balance of elective share equitably apportioned ratably among recipients of estate. (43-8-75). See subhead Election, infra.

Unclaimed Legacies.—Uniform Disposition of Unclaimed Property Act adopted. (35-12-20-48).

Lapse.—Any person who fails to survive decedent five days deemed to have predeceased decedent for purposes of homestead allowance, exempt property and intestate succession. (43-8-43). Devisee who fails to survive testator five days treated as if predeceased decedent, unless will contains language dealing explicitly with simultaneous deaths, deaths in common disaster or requirement that devisee survive testator or survive for stated period. (43-8-220).

If devisee grandparent or lineal descendant of grandparent of testator is dead at time of execution of will, fails to survive testator or is treated as if predeceased testator, issue of deceased devisee who survive testator five days take in place of deceased devisee; such issue take in equal shares if of same degree of kinship to devisee, but by representation if of unequal degree. One who would have been devisee under class gift had he survived testator treated as devisee whether he died before or after execution of will. (43-8-224).

Except as provided in §43-8-224, if devise, other than residuary devise, fails, it becomes part of residue. (43-8-225[a]). Except as provided in §43-8-224, if residue devised to two or more persons and share of one residuary devisee fails, his share passes to other residuary devisees ratably. (43-8-225[b]).

Children.—Any surviving child not provided for in will born or adopted after execution of will, takes intestate share unless: (1) Omission intentional; (2) estate devised substantially to other parent of omitted child and at time will executed testator had other children; or (3) testator provided for omitted child outside will with intent transfer be in lieu of testamentary provision. Living child omitted because believed dead takes intestate share. (43-8-91).

Election.—Surviving spouse of resident decedent has right to take elective share which is lesser of: (1) All of decedent's estate reduced by value of separate estate of surviving spouse; or (2) one-third of decedent's estate. (43-8-70). "Separate estate" of surviving spouse defined to include all property owned by spouse after death of decedent, all legal and equitable interests spouse acquired by surviving decedent and all income and beneficial interests under trust, proceeds of insurance and under any employee pension, stock bonus, etc. plans. (43-8-70). Election must be filed within later of six months after decedent's death or probate of decedent's will. (43-8-73[a]). Election personal to surviving spouse, but guardian, custodian, curator or conservator appointed for surviving spouse may exercise such election upon order of court if exercise is necessary to provide adequate support for spouse during probable life expectancy. (43-8-71).

Surviving spouse entitled to homestead allowance, exempt property and family allowance, whether or not right of election exercised. (43-8-74). Spouse may waive right of election and rights to homestead allowance, exempt property and family allowance. (43-8-72).

Contribution.—Share of pretermitted child satisfied in same order as shares of distributees abate (43-8-91[c]), and share of omitted spouse satisfied in same manner (43-8-90[b]). Liability for any balance of elective share not satisfied by values of property otherwise passing to spouse, as determined under 43-8-75(a), equitably apportioned ratably among recipients of estate. (43-8-75[b]). See subhead Legacies, supra.

Renunciation.—Renunciation of succession must comply with Ala. Uniform Disclaimer of Property Interests Act (43-8-290 to -298) or as otherwise provided by law (43-8-251).

Foreign Executed Wills.—Written will valid if executed in compliance with Ala. law, with law at time of execution of place where will executed, with law of place where at time of execution or at time of death testator is domiciled, has place of abode or is national. (43-8-135). Not condition precedent to probate of will of nonresident that such will first be probated in state of testator's domicile. (43-8-162; 198 Ala. 137, 73 So. 442).

Foreign Probated Wills.—If testator nonresident but inhabitant of another state or territory, district or country subject to jurisdiction of U.S. and will duly proved in such other jurisdiction, it may be admitted to probate in proper court of Ala. upon presentation of exemplified copy of will and probate thereof to probate judge. If will admitted to probate elsewhere than in such jurisdiction and undertakes to dispose of real or personal property situated in Ala., such will must be probated in same manner as will of resident and is subject to contest. (43-8-175). Letters testamentary must be issued to nonresident executor of will probated in another state or territory if there is to be administration of assets in Ala. (43-2-192). See also topic Executors and Administrators, subhead Foreign and Ancillary Administration.

Simultaneous Death.—See topic Death, subhead Survivorship.

Testamentary Trusts.—See topic Trusts.

Uniform Anatomical Gift Act adopted. (22-19-40 to -47). Such gift may be made by filing affidavit and so indicating specific gift on drivers' license. (22-19-60).

Incorporation by Reference and Events of Independent Significance.—Testator may incorporate by reference any writing in existence when will executed if writing identified and intent manifested in language of will. (43-8-139). Will may dispose of property by reference to acts and events which have significance apart from effect upon dispositions made by will, whether they occur before or after execution of will or testator's death. (43-8-141).

Testamentary Additions to Trusts.—§1 of Uniform Testamentary Additions to Trusts Act adopted. (43-8-140).

Record.—If it appears on proof taken that will was duly executed, testimony of witnesses must be reduced to writing, signed by witnesses and recorded with will. (43-8-169). Every will so proved must have certificate endorsed thereon, and every will so proved or endorsed, or copy thereof transcribed from record and certified by probate judge, may be read in evidence in any court of state without further proof. (43-8-170; -171).

Omitted Spouse.—Surviving spouse not provided for in will who married testator after execution of will, takes intestate share unless: (1) Omission intentional; or (2) testator provided for omitted spouse outside will with intent transfer be in lieu of testamentary provision. (43-8-90). See also subhead Election, infra.

Contracts Concerning Succession.—Contract to make will or devise, not to revoke will or devise or to die intestate, executed after Jan. 1, 1983, effective only if: (1) Will sets forth material provisions of contract; (2) express reference in will to contract and extrinsic evidence proving terms of contract; or (3) writing signed by decedent evidences such contract. Execution of joint or mutual wills does not create presumption of contract not to revoke will. (43-8-250).

Construction.—Will construed to pass all property testator owns at death including property acquired after execution of will. (43-8-223). Specific devise of securities, rather than equivalent value, entitles specific devisee to: (1) As much of devised securities as is part of estate at death; (2) additional securities of same entity derived from specifically devised securities owned by testator through action initiated by entity; (3) securities of another entity derived from specifically devised securities owned by testator as result of merger, consolidation, etc.; and (4) additional securities of entity owned by testator as result of plan of reinvestment of regulated investment company as defined in §851 of Internal Revenue Code of 1954, as amended. (43-8-226). Specific devise passes subject to mortgage interest, regardless of general directive in will to pay debts. (43-8-228). Property which testator gave in lifetime to person is treated as satisfaction of devise, only if: (1) Will provides for such deduction; (2) testator declares in contemporaneous writing that gift to be deducted; or (3) devisee acknowledges in writing that gift in satisfaction. (43-8-231). All of foregoing applies unless contrary intent of testator indicated in will. (43-8-222). Four separate, but consistent, wills held to be valid. (598 So.2d 892).

FAMILY

ADOPTION:

Any adult person or husband and wife jointly who are adults may petition to adopt. (26-10A-5). Any minor may be adopted. (26-10A-6). New legislation also provides for adoption of adult who is disabled or mentally retarded. (Act 98-101). No uniform act adopted.

Consent Required.—Following persons must consent to adoption or relinquishment for adoption: (a) Adoptee if 14 or older, except where court finds adoptee lacks mental capacity to give consent; (b) adoptee's mother; (c) adoptee's presumed father, regardless of paternity if certain conditions are met; (d) agency to which adoptee has been relinquished or which holds permanent custody, unless court finds adoption is in best interest of child and agency has unreasonably withheld consent; (e) putative father if made known by mother or otherwise, provided he responds within 30 days of notice. (26-10A-7). Consent may be implied by actions. (26-10A-9). Minor parent cannot consent unless guardian ad litem appointed. (26-10A-8). Consent not required of person whose parental rights have been terminated by Alabama Child Protection Act. (26-10A-10; 26-18-1 to -10). Consent not required from parent adjudged incompetent, parent who has relinquished minor child to department of human resources or licensed child placing agency, parent presumed deceased, alleged father who has signed written statement denying paternity, natural father when natural mother indicates natural father is unknown, unless he is otherwise known to court. (26-10A-10). Statute specifies form to be used for consent or relinquishment of minor for adoption. (26-10A-11; -12). Consents must be filed with court in which petition for adoption pending before final decree of adoption entered. (26-10A-13). Consent may be withdrawn for any reason within five days after latter of filing or birth of child. (26-10A-13). Consent may be withdrawn if reasonable and in best interest of child, within 14 days after latter of filing or birth of child (26-10A-13), or any time before final decree if consent obtained by fraud, duress, mistake, or undue influence (26-10A-14). Consent not challengeable on any ground after one year from final decree, except in cases of kidnapping. (26-10A-14; -25[d]). Statute specifies form to be used for withdrawal of consent. (26-10A-14).

Conditions Precedent.—Except as specifically provided by statute, court may not grant final decree of adoption unless it finds by clear and convincing evidence: (a) Adoptee has been in actual physical custody of petitioners for 60 days; (b) all necessary consents, relinquishments, terminations have been obtained; (c) service has been made or dispensed with as to all persons entitled to notice under 26-10A-17; (d) petitioners have prevailed in all contests brought under 26-10A-24; (e) petitioners would make suitable parents; (f) adoption in best interests of adoptee; (g) statute complied with in all respects. (26-10A-25[b]).

Jurisdiction.—Probate court has original jurisdiction over proceedings brought under statute. (26-10A-3). If party whose consent required does not consent, case should be transferred to juvenile court for limited purpose of termination of parental rights. (26-10A-3). Statute provides for appeals. (26-10A-26).

Venue.—Petitions may be filed in probate court of county in which minor resides, petitioner resides or guardian is located. (26-10A-4).

Petition.—Must be filed within 30 days after minor placed with prospective adoptive parents unless minor in custody of Department of Human Resources or licensed child

---

ADOPTION... *continued*
placing agency, unless good cause shown. (26-10A-16). Petition must be signed and verified by each petitioner and must state: (1) Full name, age, and place of residence of each petitioner, and place and date of marriage; (2) date and birth place of adoptee; (3) birth name and adoptee's proposed new name; (4) place of residence of adoptee now and after adoption; (5) statement of petitioner's fitness to adopt; (6) disclosure of prior court orders which affect custody, visitation, or access to adoptee; (7) relationship of each petitioner to adoptee; (8) name and address of placing agency; (9) name and address of all persons who are required to give consent. (26-10A-16).

Preplacement investigation of petitioners must occur before adoption decreed. (26-10A-19).

Proceedings.—Upon filing of motion contesting adoption, hearing must be held. (26-10A-24).

Decree.—Final decree of adoption may not be attacked collaterally, except in cases of fraud or where adoptee has been kidnapped, after expiration of one year from entry of final decree and after all appeals. (26-10A-25[d]).

Name.—Petitioner designates adoptee's name. (26-10A-29[a]). Court's final decree of adoption shall include new name of adoptee and shall not include any other name by which adoptee has been known or names of natural or presumed parents. (26-10A-25[c]). Petitioner shall receive new birth certificate in new name with names of adopting parents. (26-10A-32). After issuance of new birth certificate, original certificate not subject to inspection except for good cause shown. (26-10A-31; -32).

Effect of Adoption.—Person related to decedent through two lines of relationship entitled to only single share based on relationship entitling him to larger share. (43-8-58). Decree of adoption must be final for adopted person to have same rights as natural child inter sese under descent and distribution statutes. (283 Ala. 257, 215 So.2d 585).

Setting Aside Adoption.—Action to set aside final decree of adoption must be commenced within five years from date of final order. (590 So.2d 279).

Effect of Decree.—Upon final decree of adoption, natural parents, except for natural parent who is spouse of adopting parent, are relieved of all parental duties. (26-10A-29[b]). After adoption, adoptee treated as natural child of adopting parents and has all rights of, and subject to all duties, arising from that relationship, including right of inheritance. (26-10A-29; 43-8-48).

Confidentiality of Records.—Upon entry of final decree, records are sealed and open to inspection only upon order of court for good cause shown. (26-10A-31). Natural parents or adoptee 19 or older may obtain nonidentifying information. (26-10A-31[g], [i]). Adoptee 19 or older may petition for identifying information. (26-10A-31[j]).

Putative Father Registry.—Department of Human Resources must establish putative father registry which must record information of certain persons under certain conditions. (26-10C-1[a]). If clerk of court determines man to be father of child born out of wedlock, clerk must immediately notify Department of Human Resources. (26-10C-1[b]). Statute specifies what must be contained in notice of intent or acknowledgment of paternity. (26-10C-1[c]; 26-10C-1[g]). Person may revoke his notice of intent to claim paternity. (26-10C-1[e]). Department of Human Resources must provide registry information to any court that requests such information. No other person may receive information unless court orders it for good cause. Under certain circumstances, Department of Human Resources shall forward notice of intent to claim paternity to courts in which adoption proceedings pending. Court in which proceeding pending must then notify putative father of such proceeding and biological mother of putative father's registry. (26-10C-1[f]). Other than those exceptions, registry shall be kept confidential. (26-10C-1[h]). If person claiming to be natural father of child fails to file notice of intent to claim paternity prior to within 30 days of birth of child born out of wedlock, he is deemed to have given irrevocable implied consent in any adoption proceeding. (26-10C-1[i]). Knowingly or intentionally registering false information is Class A misdemeanor. Knowingly or intentionally releasing confidential information in violation of Section Class A misdemeanor unless Department of Human Resources acting in good faith with reasonable diligence. (26-10C-1[j]). This chapter is effective Jan. 1, 1997. (26-10C-2).

Adoption by Relatives.—Statute provides for adoption by relative or stepparent in certain circumstances. (26-10A-27; -28). In case of adoption by relative or stepparent, natural grandparents may obtain visitation. (26-10A-30).

Fees and Charges.—No person or legal entity may accept any fee whatsoever for bringing adopting parent or parents together with adoptee or natural parents. (26-10A-23[a]). Violation punishable under §26-10A-33. Court will approve all reasonable expense incurred by petitioners or persons acting in their behalf. (26-10A-23[b]). Request for reimbursement must be in writing and filed with court. (26-10A-23[b]). In addition, petitioners must file statement that is full accounting of all disbursements paid in adoption. (26-10A-23[d]). Paying or offering money or anything of value to natural parents in violation of 26-10A-34 prohibited; violation is Class A Misdemeanor. (26-10A-36[3]).

Advertisement for offering adoption and placement services prohibited. Violation is Class A Misdemeanor. (26-10A-36).

ALIMONY:

See topic Divorce.

COMMUNITY PROPERTY:

System does not obtain in Alabama.

DESERTION:

See topics Divorce, Husband and Wife.

DISSOLUTION OF MARRIAGE:

See topic Divorce.

DIVORCE:

This subject is governed by 30-2-1 to 12, -30, -31, -50, -51, -52, -54, -55; 30-3-1.

Grounds for Absolute Divorce.—For either party, incapacity at time of marriage, adultery, physical violence, abandonment for one year, imprisonment in penitentiary for two years under sentence of seven years or more, crime against nature before or after marriage, for becoming addicted after marriage to habitual drunkenness or to habitual use of certain drugs, five successive years in mental hospital after marriage, spouse so confined being hopelessly and incurably insane when bill filed, irretrievable breakdown of marriage so that further attempts at reconciliation impractical or futile and not in best interest of parties or family, or final decree of divorce from bed and board or final decree of separate maintenance in effect for more than two years, or complete incompatability of temperament of such nature that parties can no longer live together. (30-2-1,-2). Husband may obtain divorce on ground of wife's pregnancy at time of marriage without his knowledge or agency. (30-2-1). Wife may obtain divorce for nonsupport for two years. (30-2-1).

Grounds for Legal Separation.—May be decreed for cruelty or for any cause justifying divorce if plaintiff desires separation only. (30-2-30). *Note:* In 1999, §§30-2-30 and 30-2-31 will be replaced with legislation containing following: Legal separation may be decreed if certain conditions met, including jurisdictional requirements, finding that marriage irretrievably broken or complete incompatibility of temperament exists or one or both parties desires to live separate, and child custody taken into consideration. (Act 98-105).

Residence Requirements.—Alabama courts do not have jurisdiction to grant divorce if neither party domiciled in Alabama; personal appearance by both parties does not confer jurisdiction to grant divorce. (251 Ala. 73, 36 So.2d 236; 252 Ala. 103, 39 So.2d 406). Domicile defined as usual. (258 Ala. 423, 63 So.2d 364). Plaintiff must have resided in state at least six months if defendant is nonresident. (30-2-5). Jurisdiction over marriage res is conferred upon court by proof of domicile of plaintiff where defendant is nonresident (256 Ala. 629, 56 So.2d 344) or by proof of domicile of defendant where plaintiff is nonresident (252 Ala. 103, 39 So.2d 406). Wife seeking divorce on ground of nonsupport must have resided in state for two years and husband and wife must have been separated during such time. (30-2-1).

Complaint must allege that necessary residence existed immediately prior to filing of complaint and such allegation must be proved, failing in which court without jurisdiction and decree of divorce void even on collateral attack. (173 Ala. 106, 55 So. 632; 191 Ala. 305, 68 So. 143). Court can sua sponte declare divorce invalid on ground it was obtained by fraud on court, if complaint falsely alleged necessary residence. (272 Ala. 67, 128 So.2d 725; noted 75 Har. L. Rev. 568). Where nonresident procured divorce by fraud and later sought bill of review to set aside divorce, bill was not subject to demurrer on grounds of laches, "clean hands" or estoppel. (276 Ala. 303, 161 So.2d 588).

Jurisdiction.—Circuit court has jurisdiction of divorce actions. (30-2-1).

Venue.—County of defendant's residence; county where parties resided at time of separation; or county of plaintiff's residence if nonresident defendant. (30-2-4). Venue for all proceedings to modify child custody, visitation rights or child support will lie in: (1) Original circuit court; or (2) county wherein custodial parent and child or children have resided for three consecutive years prior to institution of action to modify prior circuit court decree. Current custodial parent shall choose venue regardless of who commences action. (30-3-5).

Process.—Personal service required, but service by publication may be had on resident defendant who avoids service. (30-2-8; ARCP 4-4.4).

Pleading.—Cause for which divorce sought must be alleged in complaint. (30-2-8).

Practice.—As in other actions formerly cognizable in equity, but answer of defendant cannot be considered as evidence. (30-2-7).

Judgment or Decree.—Court shall not enter final judgment of divorce until after expiration of 30 days from date of filing of summons and complaint. (30-2-8.1).

Temporary Alimony.—Pending action for divorce, court may make allowance for support of either spouse, suitable to spouse's estate and condition in life of parties, for period of time not longer than necessary for prosecution of complaint for divorce. (30-2-50).

Allowance for Prosecution of Suit.—Pending suit for divorce, court may make allowance for support of either spouse from estate of other spouse, suitable to spouse's estate and condition in life of parties, for not longer than necessary for prosecution of suit. (30-2-50).

Permanent Alimony.—If either spouse has no separate estate, or if it be insufficient for maintenance, upon granting divorce, court may, at its discretion, decree either spouse allowance out of estate of other spouse. (30-2-31; -51). Property acquired before marriage or by gift or inheritance may not be considered, unless such property or income therefrom has been used regularly for common benefit of both parties during marriage. (30-2-51). Present value of any future or current retirement benefits may be considered at court's discretion and under certain circumstances. (30-2-51[b]). If retirement benefits are distributed as alimony, amount is not payable until covered spouse begins to receive benefits. (30-2-51[b]). Alimony may be terminated upon proof that spouse receiving alimony has remarried or is living openly or cohabiting with member of opposite sex. (30-2-55; Const. Amend. 390). Factors considered in determining amount of alimony (and in making equitable division of property) include earning ability of parties, future prospects, age, health, duration of marriage, accustomed standard of living, source, value and type of property, and conduct of parties as related to marriage. (473 So.2d 1091).

If divorce granted at suit of either spouse for misconduct of other court may, in its discretion, enter order for allowance to either spouse from estate of other spouse, and such misconduct may be considered in determining amount. In such cases, any property acquired prior to marriage or by gift or inheritance may not be considered in determining amount. (30-2-52).

See note at head of Digest as to 1998 legislation covered.

See Topical Index in front part of this volume.

AL – 40

DIVORCE . . . *continued*

Foregoing rules apply only when suit for divorce a vinculo (214 Ala. 219, 106 So. 866), but similar results reached on equity principles in suits for divorce a mensa (115 Ala. 474, 22 So. 448; 214 Ala. 219, 106 So. 866).

Wife may sue for alimony without divorce. (190 Ala. 527, 67 So. 400).

Alimony must be allowed, if at all, at time of or before final decree. (98 Ala. 373, 13 So. 412). Spouse failing to pay alimony in accordance with decree guilty of contempt, and may be committed to jail. (ARCP 70).

Division of Property of Spouses.—In court's discretion, separate property of one spouse may be ordered paid for support of other spouse provided that such separate property not acquired prior to marriage or by inheritance or gift. (30-2-51). Divorce decree silent on property held jointly with right of survivorship does not automatically destroy existing survivorship provisions. (472 So.2d 630). Any property used regularly for common benefit of parties during marriage may be awarded in property settlement. (30-2-51; 377 So.2d 141).

Change of Wife's Name.—Court may in its discretion, enjoin divorced wife from use of given name or initials of divorced husband. (30-2-11).

Custody of Children.—Court may, in its discretion, award custody of children to either parent. (30-3-1). Court may also award joint custody if it is in best interests of child. (30-3-150; -157). In case of abandonment of husband by wife, husband, if suitable, entitled to custody of children after they reach seven years of age. (30-3-1). Spouse may be awarded custody of children even though neither natural nor adoptive parent. (52 Ala. App. 539, 295 So.2d 260). Decree awarding custody of children may be modified at any time. (176 Ala. 299, 58 So. 195).

Rebuttable presumption that child should not be in custody of parent who perpetrates domestic violence. (30-3-131; -133). Visitation by parent committing domestic violence only if adequate provision for safety of child or parent-victim. (30-3-135).

In custody case, court may in its discretion, award visitation rights to grandparents of such children. (30-3-4).

Uniform Child Custody Jurisdiction Act adopted. (30-3-20, et seq.).

Child of parties to divorce case may testify. (461 So.2d 1332). Such testimony may be disallowed under Ala. R. Evid. 601 where child lacks sufficient competency and maturity. (699 So.2d 220).

Allowance for Support of Children.—Court may make orders respecting support of children upon granting divorce and pending action. (30-3-1). Child support decrees modifiable. (30-3-5). In determining child support, court shall apply Rule 32 of Alabama Rules of Judicial Administration. (30-3-155).

Remarriage.—Neither party may remarry (except each other) within 60 days after decree or pending appeal. (30-2-10). Then, either party may remarry unless decree expressly disallows right of guilty party, in which case guilty party may not remarry without permission of court. (30-2-8,-10).

Separation Agreements.—Enforced when sufficient consideration, fairness, and absence of coercion. (435 So.2d 1292).

Annulment of Marriage.—See topic Marriage.

Antenuptial Contracts.—Enforced in divorce proceeding when sufficient evidence to establish adequate consideration and entire transaction fair, just and equitable from point of view of party seeking to avoid operation. (519 So.2d 1347). See topic Husband and Wife.

Uniform Interstate Family Support Act adopted.

Defenses.—Recrimination, condonation, or husband's knowledge or connivance is a defense in bar, when divorce is sought on ground of adultery. (30-2-3).

Appeal from decree of divorce must be taken within 42 days (ARAP 4[a]) and decree is suspended pending appeal.

GUARDIAN AND WARD:

Uniform Guardianship and Protective Proceedings Act adopted. (26-2A-1 et seq.). Probate court has jurisdiction over guardianship and conservatorship proceedings (26-2A-31; 26-2A-20[3]), but administration may be removed to circuit court (26-2-2). Venue lies where minor or incapacitated person resides or is present at time proceedings commence (26-2A-74), and for incapacitated person where person resides or is present or institutionalized at time proceedings commence (26-2A-101).

Selection of Guardian.—If two or more appointments for guardianship of minor, last in time has priority. (26-2A-71). Court appointing guardian for minor 14 years or older must choose minor's nominee unless court finds appointment contrary to child's best interest. (26-2A-76). For incapacitated person, court must appoint person designated in most recent durable power of attorney unless good cause dictates otherwise. (26-2A-104). If no durable power of attorney, court follows statutory priorities, where spouse has highest priority. (Id.)

Eligibility and Competency.—Court has discretion to appoint suitable person, such as spouse, adult child, parent, relative with whom incapacitated person resided six months prior to petition or person nominated by one caring for incapacitated person. (26-2A-104).

Appointment of Guardian.—Guardian may be appointed by parent in will or by other acknowledged or witnessed writing, by court. (26-2A-71, -73). Minor 14 years or older may block parental appointment. (26-2A-72). Guardian for incompetent person may be appointed by parents, spouse or court. (26-2A-100).

Qualification.—Court must appoint as guardian person it determines in best interest of child. (26-2A-76). Conservator of estate must post bond in amount of value of estate plus one year's expected income. (26-2A-139). Parent may nominate conservator in will and waive bond. (Id.).

Inventory.—Conservator must file inventory of entire estate subject to control within 90 days following appointment. (26-2A-146).

Powers and Duties.—Guardian generally has powers and responsibilities of parent regarding health, support, education and maintenance. (26-2A-78).

Investments.—Conservator held to standard of care applicable to trustees (i.e., standards observed by prudent person dealing with property of another). (26-2A-145).

Securities in Name of Nominee.—See category Estates and Trusts, topic Trusts, subheads Securities in Name of Nominee, and Securities.

Real Estate.—With prior court approval, conservator may dispose of real property for cash or credit at private or public sale and manage, develop, improve, partition or change character of estate real property. (26-2A-152[d]).

Liabilities of Guardian.—Not liable to third parties for acts of ward. (26-2A-78[a], -108).

Accounts.—Conservator must give accounting to court at least once every three years and upon termination. (26-2A-147).

Termination of Guardianships.—Upon minor's death, adoption, marriage, or attainment of majority by ward, or by resignation or by removal of guardian. (26-2A-79, -81). Resignation not effective until approved by court. (26-2A-79).

Insane Persons.—Guardian ad litem may be appointed to defend person alleged to be of unsound mind. (26-2-46).

Foreign Guardians.—Upon proof of appointment and delivery of affidavit, fiduciary appointed by state of residence of protected person may receive debts, property, stock or chose in action belonging to protected person if no proceeding pending in this state. (26-2A-159). Foreign conservator may file copies of letters of appointment and bond in county where property of protected person located and thereafter exercise powers of conservator appointed. (26-2A-160).

Gifts to Minors.—See topic Infants.

Uniform Fiduciaries Act adopted. (19-1-1, et seq.).

Uniform Simplification of Fiduciary Security Transfers Act adopted. (8-6-70 to -80). Controls if any inconsistency with Uniform Commercial Code. (7-10-104[2]).

Foreign Conservators.—Must file letters of appointment and bond and has same powers as domestic conservator. (26-2A-160).

Removal of Property.—If property of nonresident minor to be removed from state, application for removal must be: (1) In writing; (2) signed by person having legal custody; (3) verified by affidavit; and (4) accompanied by transcript, duly certified, of appointment of guardian by court of competent jurisdiction in state of person having legal custody, and of bond of such guardian with sureties approved by such court. (26-8-41). If such guardian corporate fiduciary, not required by laws of state wherein appointed to give bond, certificate from appointing authority may be filed in lieu of bond. (26-8-41; -52).

Veterans' Guardianship.—Uniform Act adopted. (26-9-1, et seq.).

Developmentally Disabled Persons.—Subject to certain specified limitations, probate court has authority and duty to appoint suitable person or agency as guardian for person whose general intellectual functioning or adaptive behavior impaired and expected to continue to be impaired indefinitely by reason of mental retardation, cerebral palsy, epilepsy, autism, or any similar condition, where condition constitutes substantial burden to impaired person's ability to perform normally in society. (12-13-21). Petition for appointment of such guardian may be filed by any interested person. (12-13-21).

Curators.—§§26-7A-1-17 repealed 1995, Acts 95-751.

HUSBAND AND WIFE:

Husband not liable for his wife's torts, debts or contracts, whether antenuptial or postnuptial. (30-4-6,-7). Doctrine of necessaries held unconstitutional when applied to husband as gender-based classification. (596 So.2d 578).

Disabilities of Married Women.—No disabilities of married women in disposition of property, except as set forth in subheads Contracts and Conveyance or Encumbrance of Property, infra.

Separate Property.—Property acquired by wife before or after marriage (Const., §209; 30-4-1), earnings received by her from third persons (30-4-2), and damages which she may recover for injuries to person or reputation (30-4-4) are wife's separate property and not subject to husband's debts.

Distinction between equitable and statutory separate estates, except in case of active trusts for benefit of wife, abolished. (30-4-5; 84 Ala. 585, 4 So. 421).

Contracts.—Wife has full legal power to contract, except as otherwise provided by law. (30-4-8). Husband and wife may contract with each other, but all such contracts subject to rules of law as to contracts between persons standing in confidential relations. (30-4-9).

Antenuptial Contracts.—Valid but scrutinized for informed consent and equity to spouse. (386 So.2d 749; 550 So.2d 999). Agreement must be signed by parties. (8-9-2). Spouse must waive statutory right to share of spouse's estate to allow assets of first marriage to go to first marriage's children. (43-8-72).

Wife as Surety for Husband.—Prior to June 21, 1957, statute governing contracts between husband and wife (30-4-9) contained provision that "the wife shall not, directly or indirectly, become the surety for the husband," and holdings prohibiting wife from being surety of her husband explicitly based on such statutory provision (203 Ala. 97, 82 So. 111). Effective June 21, 1957, provision deleted. Deletion noted by Supreme Court in manner indicating recognition of legislative intent to change prior rule, but no decision has yet affimatively declared right of wife to act as surety for her husband's debts. (See 279 Ala. 303, 184 So.2d 815; 267 Ala. 491, 102 So.2d 904.)

Actions.—Wife must sue or be sued alone, whether action concerns her separate property, her contracts or torts committed by or against her. (30-4-11). Husband and wife may join in one action as plaintiffs if they assert any right to relief jointly, severally or in alternative and such right arises out of same transaction or occurrence and question of law or fact common to all parties; they may be joined as defendants if any such joint right to relief asserted against them. (ARCP 20[a]). Either spouse may sue other. (201 Ala. 41, 77 So. 335). Action by or against woman not abated by her marriage. (6-5-460). Wife may sue or defend any action in her husband's name where

See note at head of Digest as to 1998 legislation covered.

See Topical Index in front part of this volume.

AL – 41

HUSBAND AND WIFE . . . *continued*

he deserted family, confined in insane asylum or imprisoned for term of two years or more. (6-7-1).

Agency.—No statutory provision.

Conveyances or Encumbrance of Property.—Statutory requirement that husband join in wife's conveyances of her lands or any interest therein held unconstitutional. (345 So.2d 631; 6-10-3). See also categories Property, topic Deeds, subhead Covenants; Documents and Records, topic Acknowledgments, subhead Forms, catchline Homestead Acknowledgment. Except as stated below, conveyance by husband of his lands does not affect homestead rights of wife unless she joins in deed or otherwise releases said rights. (6-10-3). See category Debtor and Creditor, topic Homesteads. Husband may convey his land (except homestead) without joinder of wife, where she has been judicially declared insane, or confined in Alabama state hospital for insane, and superintendent thereof certifies in writing to probate judge of county of husband's residence that wife's insanity is permanent. Certificate must be recorded in office of probate judge, and copy of judgment or certificate, as case may be, must be attached to husband's deed, which itself must recite that husband married and wife insane. (30-4-30,-31). Spouse of insane person, by proceedings of equitable nature in circuit court, may obtain decree conferring authority on him or her to make conveyance as if single. (30-4-32 to -37).

Desertion and Nonsupport.—Intentionally failing to provide support when able and legally obligated constitutes misdemeanor crime of nonsupport. (13A-13-4). Desertion of child with intent to wholly abandon constitutes misdemeanor crime of abandonment. (13A-13-5).

Revised Uniform Reciprocal Enforcement of Support Act.—Earlier version adopted. (30-4-80 to -98). Repealed effective Jan. 1, 2000.

Community Property.—System does not exist.

Protection from Abuse.—Protection from Abuse Act adopted. (30-5-1, et seq.). Family Violence Protection Order Enforcement Act adopted. (30-5A-1, et seq.).

INFANTS:

Infants attain majority at age 19. All laws in conflict herewith are repealed with exception of §§15-19-1; -7. (26-1-1). Minimum age for purchase of alcoholic beverages 21. (28-1-5).

Emancipation.—Juvenile court, on proper proceedings, may relieve minor over 18 years old of disabilities. (26-13-1). Duly certified copy of decree of court of competent jurisdiction in another state relieving minor nonresident of this state of disabilities may be recorded in any county in which such minor owns property and when so recorded decree has same force in this state as in state where rendered. (26-13-8).

Disabilities.—Infants incompetent to become parties to express contract. (See 215 Ala. 31; 109 So. 574.) Person under 14 years of age incapable of contracting for marriage. (30-1-4). See Child Labor Laws. (25-8-1; -12). Written consent of parent or legal guardian necessary before unemancipated woman has abortion, except under special circumstances. (26-21-3).

Ratification of Contracts.—Infant liable for reasonable price of necessaries, but otherwise contract voidable and may be either affirmed or avoided after coming of age. (16 Ala. 186; 75 Ala. 555; 101 Ala. 658, 14 So. 399). Minor of 15 years old or more at nearest birthday may contract for life, health and accident insurance, endowment and annuity contracts on himself or on another, except that minor not bound by unperformed agreement to pay premium thereon. With respect to policy or annuity for which contracted, minor may give discharge for payments received. Policy or annuity procured by or for minor as above to be made payable either to minor or his estate or to person having insurable interest in life of minor. (27-14-5).

Actions.—Infant representative, such as general guardian or like fiduciary, may sue in name of infant. If no representative, he may sue by next friend. Court must appoint guardian ad litem for infant defendant not otherwise represented in action, and such guardian must be qualified to represent infant in capacity of attorney and must not be related to plaintiff or attorney or clerk or judge of court. Infant 14 years old has 30 days after perfection of service to nominate choice of guardian ad litem. If failure to nominate within 30 days or before first hearing in action, whichever is first, court must appoint guardian ad litem. (ARCP 17).

Support of Minor.—Man or woman commits crime of nonsupport if he or she intentionally fails to provide support to dependent child less than 19 years old. Nonsupport is misdemeanor. (13A-13-4).

Parental Responsibility.—Parents of unemancipated minor under age of 19 years old liable in civil action for minor's theft of property. (6-5-271). Parents of minor under 18 with whom minor living and who have custody of minor liable for minor's intentional, willful or malicious destruction of property up to $500.

Adoption.—See topic Adoption.

Uniform Transfers to Minors Act.—Adopted. (35-5A-1 to -24). Age of majority under new act is 21. (35-5A-2[1]).

Legitimation.—Marriage of mother and reputed father of illegitimate child renders it legitimate, if recognized by father as his child. (26-11-1). Father of illegitimate child may seek to legitimate it and render it capable of inheriting his estate by filing notice of declaration of legitimation attested by two witnesses, stating name, sex, and supposed age of child, name of child's mother and stating that he recognizes child as his, capable of inheriting his estate as if born in wedlock. Declaration must be acknowledged and filed in office of judge of probate of father's residence or child's residence. Upon notice to child's mother and to child, probate judge must conduct informal hearing to determine whether legitimation in best interest of child. Order granting or denying legitimation issued by probate judge of father's or child's residence. (26-11-2). Legitimization by father cannot be repudiated. (48 Ala. App. 276, 264 So.2d 198). Statutory scheme declared unconstitutional in part insofar as it precluded children who did not have opportunity to be legitimized during life of father from later achieving such status. (697 F.2d 999).

Termination of Parental Rights.—If court finds on clear and convincing evidence that parents unable or unwilling to discharge parental duties. (26-18-7). Department of Human Resources must file termination of parental rights petitions in cases in which child has been in foster care for 15 of most recent 22 months, in cases in which child has been abandoned, or in cases in which court has determined that parent of child has assaulted child or assaulted or killed another child of parent or has aided in such action. (Act 98-370 amending 26-18-5 and 26-18-7). Petition may be filed by state, licensed child-placing agency, parent or any interested party. (26-18-5; 474 So.2d 715). Complaint must set forth, and petitioner must prove, petitioner's ability and willingness to assume custody of child. (26-18-4). Proceedings are governed by statutory juvenile court procedure (12-15-1 to -156), and court's order terminates all parental rights absolutely (26-18-7). It is required that foster parents, pre-adoptive parents, and relatives providing care to child be given notice and opportunity to be heard at any hearing on any child in care in their home. (Act 98-372 amending 12-15-62 and 12-15-65).

Medical Treatment.—Provides that Department of Human Resources may pursue any legal remedy and discovery to provide medical care to prevent serious harm to child or to prevent withholding of medically indicated treatment to disabled infants with life-threatening conditions; discloses records; provides public disclosure of child fatality or near fatality; prohibits disclosure of non-indicated reports for purposes of employment or other background checks; provides good faith immunity for disclosure. (Act 98-371 amending 26-14-7.2; 26-14-8, and 26-14-9).

Veterans.—Disabilities of minor veterans and minor wives of veterans removed with respect to contracts made under servicemen's readjustment or rehabilitation acts. (31-1-2).

Oversight Committee of Children in State Care.—Establishes Permanent Joint Legislative Oversight Committee of Children in State Care; creates Interdepartmental Council of Children in State Care; establishes State case registry; provides for confidentiality of information; provides penalties. (Act 98-612).

Corporations may treat infant holders of securities as adults and infants may not disaffirm actions with respect to such securities, provided corporation has no written notice of infancy. (10-6-1,-2). Infant shareholder may also receive dividends from such securities, such receipt discharging corporation for dividends, whether or not corporation has actual or written notice of infancy. (10-6-3). Rules also apply to banks, brokers, issuers (as defined), third parties or transfer agents. (8-6-90 to -95).

Uniform Securities Ownership by Minors Act adopted with significant modifications. (8-6-90-95).

Uniform Child Custody Jurisdiction Act adopted. (30-3-20 to -44).

MARRIAGE:

Age of consent is 14. (30-1-4).

Consent Required.—Personal or proved written consent of parents and bond for $200 required where person under 18, unless minor has previously been married. (30-1-5). Marriage not invalid because license issued without parents' consent. (205 Ala. 502, 88 So. 577). Section addresses solemnized marriages, not common law marriages. (559 So.2d 1084). See subhead Common Law Marriages, infra.

Medical Examination.—None.

License.—No marriage may be solemnized without license, issued by judge of probate. Any license issued invalid if marriage for which issued has not been solemnized within 30 days from date of issuance, and every license must so state. (30-1-9). License must be issued by judge or his duly qualified clerk; authority cannot be otherwise delegated. (109 Ala. 48, 19 So. 917). Penalty imposed on person solemnizing marriage for which license not issued. (30-1-11).

Waiting Period.—60 days following divorce. No marriage during pendency of appeal. (30-2-10).

Ceremonial Marriage.—Marriage may be solemnized by licensed minister of gospel in regular communion with Christian church or society of which he is member, or by judge or retired judge of supreme, appellate, circuit or district court anywhere within state, or by judge or retired judge of probate within his county. (30-1-7[a]).

May be solemnized by pastor of religious society according to rules ordained or custom established by such society. (30-1-7[b]). Mennonites, or Quakers, or any other Christian society having similar rules or regulations, may solemnize marriages according to their forms by consent of parties, published and declared before congregation assembled for public worship. (30-1-7[c]).

Judge or licensed minister of gospel celebrating rites of matrimony is entitled to $2. (30-1-8).

Reports of Marriages.—Judge of probate must keep register of licenses issued by him. (30-1-12).

Clerk or keeper of minutes of each religious society must keep register, and enter thereon particular account of all marriages solemnized by society; which register, or sworn copy thereof, is presumptive evidence. (30-1-7[b]).

Persons or religious societies solemnizing marriage must notify judge of probate, which certificate must be recorded in book kept for registry of licenses. (30-1-13).

Record.—See category Documents and Records, topic Records, subhead Vital Statistics.

Common Law Marriages.—Recognized. (194 Ala. 613, 69 So. 885). Capacity to marry, present agreement or consent, public recognition of marriage, and consummation must exist. (567 So.2d 869). Mere cohabitation insufficient to establish common law marriage; must also have mutual intent to be married. (465 So.2d 378). Common law marriage cannot exist if spouse previously married and has not obtained valid divorce. (477 So.2d 316).

Proxy Marriages.—Not authorized.

Marriages by Written Contract.—Not authorized.

Prohibited Marriages.—Marriage during life of former consort is crime, unless former consort absent for last five years preceding second marriage, and not known that

MARRIAGE . . . *continued*
he or she was living, or unless valid divorce from former consort obtained prior to second marriage and said divorce did not prohibit person from marrying again. (13A-13-1; 30-2-9). Same sex marriages invalid and void. (1998 H.B. 152).

Issue of incestuous marriage, before annulment, not illegitimate. (30-1-3).

Foreign Marriages.—Valid except when marriage from other states contrary to positive statute or pronounced public policy. (235 Ala. 564, 180 So. 577). Generally, validity of marriage determined by law of place where contracted. (223 Ala. 155, 134 So. 651).

Annulment.—Annulment not statutory remedy, but within general equity powers of courts with respect to contracts. (249 Ala. 419, 31 So.2d 579). Grounds for annulment include insanity of one party at time of marriage (28 Ala. 565), fraudulent intent not to perform marriage vows, (241 Ala. 223, 2 So.2d 443), bigamy (245 Ala. 145, 16 So.2d 401), and incest (235 Ala. 564, 180 So. 577). Bona fide domicile of one party sufficient to confer jurisdiction on Alabama court. (242 Ala. 70, 4 So.2d 901). Where person under age of consent, marriage voidable while under that age. (201 Ala. 531, 78 So. 885). Certified copies of marriage certificate may be obtained by persons having proper interest from state registrar of vital statistics, upon payment of statutory fees. (22-9A-22, -23).

Antenuptial Contracts.—See topic Husband and Wife.

MARRIED WOMEN:

See topics Husband and Wife, Marriage; categories Civil Actions and Procedure, topic Evidence, subhead Witnesses; Debtor and Creditor, topic Homesteads; Documents and Records, topic Acknowledgments; Estates and Trusts, topics Executors and Administrators, Wills; Property, topic Dower.

INSURANCE

INSURANCE COMPANIES:

Regulated by §§27-1-1 et seq.

Supervision by Commissioner of Insurance, 201 Monroe St., Suite 1700, Montgomery, Ala. 36104.

Department of Insurance charged with administration of all laws relating to insurance, insurance companies and associations, and agents and representatives. Commissioner of Insurance is chief officer of Department of Insurance with power to perform all duties required by law in relation to supervision, regulation and control of insurance companies and title insurance companies. (27-2-1 et seq.). Title must be complied with to transact business of insurance in Alabama. (27-1-5).

Rates.—§§27-13-1, et seq.

Annual statements must be filed with Commissioner on or before Mar. 1 (Commissioner may grant 30 day extension for good cause shown), verified statement of financial condition, transactions, and affairs during preceding calendar year (27-3-26); verified statement showing total amount of premiums and annuity considerations received during preceding calendar year must be filed on or before such date. (27-4-3). Every property or casualty insurer required to file annual statement with commissioner must include statement by qualified independent loss reserve specialist. (27-3-26.1). Filing fee $500. Annual continuation or renewal fee $500. Other fees as set forth in §27-4-2. (27-4-2).

Policies.—Express entire contract between parties when life insurance or annuities (27-15-5), industrial life insurance (27-16-5), or disability insurance (27-19-4) involved; hence application, or summary of application, if to be considered part of policy, must be endorsed thereon or attached to policy when issued. In event of discrepancies between original application and summary of application, contents of original govern. When summary of application attached to policy, insurer must keep and maintain original application for insurance or copy for three years after date policy issued. (27-15-5). Each policy must specify on face its character, names of parties to contract, risks insured against, subject of insurance, period during which policy in effect, premium, and conditions pertaining to insurance. (27-14-11). Policy must be mailed or delivered to insured within reasonable period of time after issuance, except where condition required by insurer has not been met by insured, and insurer may be estopped from asserting coverage conditions or otherwise valid exclusions for failure to do so. (27-14-19). Section does not apply to surety contracts or to group insurance policies.

Insurers providing health, accident, or dental coverage must provide written description of terms and conditions. (27-1-20).

Discrimination.—Prohibition against discrimination between insured of same class. (27-12-11).

Rebates.—Prohibited unless expressly provided for in insurance contract. (27-12-12).

Liens.—No statutory provision.

Agents and Brokers.—§27-4-2 outlines license fees and other charges. Insurance company must procure license for each agent. (27-7-4; -8; 27-8-3). Partnership or corporation may be licensed agent or broker. (27-7-6). Provision made for examination and control of all agents by Commissioner. (27-7-1 to -38; 27-8-1 to -28). No insurer may accept applications for insurance, issue any policy or assume direct liability as to subject of insurance resident, located or to be performed in state unless through licensed agents, solicitors, or brokers. Section does not apply to title insurance or insurance of rolling stock, vessels or aircraft of common carriers in interstate commerce, life or disability insurance not delivered or issued for delivery in Ala., and lawfully solicited outside Ala. Property, casualty, and surety insurers doing business in Ala. must have duly licensed resident agents execute or countersign all their contracts of insurance; solicitors, managing general agents, service representatives, or employees of such companies cannot execute or countersign property, casualty, or surety policies. (27-3-28).

Process Agent.—Insurer must appoint Commissioner. (27-3-24).

Investments.—§§27-1-8; -9 and 27-41-1 to -41.

Foreign Insurance Companies.—Foreign insurer may become domestic insurer. (27-3-30). Foreign company may obtain certificate authorizing it to do business in this state by filing with Commissioner certified copy of charter, articles of incorporation, or other charter documents with all amendments thereto, sworn statement of financial condition in "convention" form as of next preceding Dec. 31, or certified copy of report of last examination, appointment of Commissioner as agent for service of process, certificate of public official supervising insurance in its state showing that it is legally organized and authorized to transact kinds of insurance proposed to be transacted in this state, and showing of required deposit (see subhead Deposit Requirements, infra). (27-3-17 to -24). Commissioner must be satisfied that such insurance company meets requirements before issuing certificate of authority specifying kinds of insurance authorized to transact in this state. (27-3-18).

Retaliatory Laws.—If any other state imposes taxes, penalties, or other obligations or penalties on insurance companies of this state doing business in such other state in excess of those imposed by this state upon insurance companies of such other states, like taxes, penalties, or other obligations or prohibitions will be imposed on all similar insurance companies of such state doing business in this state. (27-3-29).

Premium Tax.—Every insurer (27-1-2) must pay Commissioner premium tax as established by §27-4A-3 for premiums received by insurer for business done in Ala. whether same was actually received by insurer in Ala. or elsewhere. Premium tax exclusive and in lieu of all other taxes and licenses of state or any county imposed on or measured by premiums received by insurer for business done in Ala. (27-4A-5). Every insurer failing to pay this tax subject to penalty of between $1,000 and $10,000. Upon any violation, Commissioner may suspend or revoke insurer's certificate of authority. (27-4A-4). Insurers paying premium tax pursuant to §27-4A-3 exempt from income taxes under Title 40, c. 18 or similar laws. (27-4A-6).

Privilege Tax.—None.

Uniform Insurers Liquidation Act adopted. (27-32-1-41).

No-Fault Insurance.—See category Transportation, topic Motor Vehicles, subhead No-Fault Insurance.

Plain Language.—See category Business Regulation and Commerce, topic Consumer Protection.

Capital Requirements for Companies Authorized to Do Business.—All insurance companies applying for original certificate of authority to transact insurance in Ala. must possess and maintain unimpaired paid-in-capital stock (if stock insurer) or unimpaired surplus (if foreign mutual or foreign reciprocal insurer) in amount not less than applicable for particular kind of insurance required by §27-3-7, plus, in either case, insurers must possess additional funds as special surplus, at time of application, in amount required by §27-3-8. Insurance company previously authorized to transact business in state may continue as before enactment of capital requirements, but no such insurer can be authorized to transact any other or additional kinds of insurance until capital requirements met. (27-3-7[b]). Certain mutual aid associations, subject to limits on size and type of risk, may insure in manner like that authorized under Title 27, c. 3 for domestic life and disability insurers. (27-30-34).

Credit Insurance.—Insurance written in connection with credit transaction under Small Loan Act subject to same restrictions and regulations as creditor under Alabama Consumer Credit Act, set out at §5-19-1, et seq. Insurance may not exceed amount and terms of credit. (5-18-17).

Beneficiaries.—Insured may effect policy on own life for any beneficiary; but insurable interest necessary where beneficiary procures policy on life of insured. (27-14-3).

Assignment of Life Insurance Policies.—Life insurance policy taken out by insured or by person having insurable interest in life of insured, in good faith, may be lawfully assigned without regard to whether assignee has insurable interest, unless policy provides otherwise. (27-14-21).

Loans.—Maximum interest that can be charged on policy loans provided by statutory formula. (27-15-8.1).

Reinstatement.—With some exceptions, at any time within three years after date of premium default, lapsed life insurance policies may be reinstated by application of insured. Application must include evidence of insurability, payment of overdue premiums, and payment of other debts to insurer, including interest at rate not to exceed policy loan rate. (27-15-11).

Defenses Available to Company.—Misrepresentation in application by insured will not prevent recovery under policy or contract unless fraudulent, or material to acceptance of risk or to hazard assumed by insurer, or insurer, in good faith, either would not have issued policy or would not have issued policy at premium rate applied for if true facts had been known by insurer. Plea of misrepresentation in connection with life insurance policy or annuity contract must be accompanied by payment into court of all premiums paid on policy. (27-14-7). Validity of life insurance policy incontestable, except for nonpayment of premiums, after in force for two years during lifetime of insured from date of issue. (27-15-4). Insurer's assertion of required age or sex adjustment clause not contest of policy and any amount payable under policy will be such as premium would have purchased at correct age or sex. (27-15-6). Alabama has adopted Standard Nonforfeiture Law for life insurance policies. (27-15-28).

Proceeds.—If effected by any person on his own life or on another life in favor of person other than himself or assigned to any such person (except in cases of transfer with intent to defraud creditors) other than insured, exempt from liability for insured's (or person effecting such insurance) debts or engagements. If person effecting such insurance, or assignee of such insurance, is wife of insured, proceeds exempt from liability for wife's debts or engagements. (27-14-29). If contract so provides, proceeds of annuity contract or life insurance policy retained by issuing company for purpose of making installment payment to beneficiaries cannot be reached by judicial process for payment of debts, contracts, or engagements of such beneficiaries. (27-14-30; -32).

Surplus Line Brokers.—See generally §§27-10-20; -38. Provision made for examination of officers and records of surplus line brokers (27-2-21), and annual taxation of

See note at head of Digest as to 1998 legislation covered.

See Topical Index in front part of this volume.

AL – 43

INSURANCE COMPANIES . . . *continued*
such brokers (27-10-31). Duty of determining financial soundness of surplus line insurance carrier on surplus line broker. (475 So.2d 545).

Claims on health and accident policies are payable within 45 days of receipt of proof of loss. If claim not denied for proper reason by end of 45 day period, insurer must pay insured 1½% interest per month on amount of claim until finally settled or adjudicated. (27-1-17). Tort of bad faith refusal to pay insurance proceeds is recognized. (405 So.2d 1; 461 So.2d 1320). To establish claim plaintiff must show entitlement to directed verdict on insurance contract claims. (419 So.2d 1357; but see 507 So.2d 396).

Deposit Requirements.—All insurers (other than alien insurers) must deposit and maintain deposited in trust with treasurer of this state cash or securities eligible under §27-6-3 of minimum value of $100,000 as continuing prerequisite for certificate of authority. (27-3-11). Special additional deposits required of surety and title insurers. (27-3-12; -13). Deposit requirements for alien insurers governed by §27-3-14; -15. Statute effective Jan. 1, 1998 provides for annual valuation of reserves for life insurance policies and annuity and endowment contracts. (27-36-7).

Examinations.—Commissioner may examine affairs of authorized insurer, domestic or foreign, including attorney-in-fact of reciprocal insurer insofar as insurer transactions involved, as often as he deems advisable and at least every three years for each domestic insurer; all examinations made at expense of company. (27-2-21; -25). Commissioner has discretion to accept as true and correct certified full report of last recent examination of foreign or alien insurer made by insurance supervisory official of another state. (27-2-21[c]).

Sale of Stock.—Stock and mutual insurers which desire to sell stock in this state must obtain solicitation permit from Commissioner. (27-27-4; -14).

Lloyd's Plan Associations.—Associations formed on "Lloyd's" plan may do business in this state other than life or title insurance but, if foreign or alien insurer, it must have successfully been in business in domiciliary state for ten years and if domestic insurer must be comprised of at least 30 underwriters with no individual underwriter retaining risk as to any one subject of insurance in amount exceeding 2% of his total net worth. "Lloyd's" plan insurers subject to deposit requirements (see subhead Deposit Requirements, supra). (27-3-16).

Ownership and sale of insurance securities by insiders are governed by statute similar to §16 of Securities Exchange Act. (27-27-52; -60). See category Business Regulation and Commerce, topic Securities.

Fees.—See §27-4-2.

SURETY AND GUARANTY COMPANIES:

Subject to regulation by Commissioner of Insurance as "insurers" under Insurance Code, Tit. 27, Code of Alabama of 1975. (27-1-1). See topic Insurance Companies. Surety Insurance Contracts are governed specifically by 27-24-1 to -8.

Venue.—Any official bond or undertaking executed by such a company may be sued on in county of residence of principal, or in which he resided at time of execution of bond or undertaking; suit by state must be brought in Montgomery County. (27-24-6).

Insurer Estopped.—No such company having signed any official bond or undertaking may deny its corporate or other power to execute such instrument or to incur liability in any proceeding to enforce liability of such company thereunder. (27-24-7).

Rights of Insurer.—Such a company as surety on an official bond, undertaking, or obligation entitled to all rights and remedies of other sureties on such instruments. (27-24-8).

INTELLECTUAL PROPERTY

TRADEMARKS AND TRADENAMES:

Trademark may be acquired by anyone who produces or deals in particular thing or conducts particular business. (8-12-1).

What May Be Used.—Any form, symbol or name which has not been appropriated by another may be used as trademark to designate origin or ownership. May not use designation which relates only to name, quality, or description of thing or business, or place where thing produced, or business carried on. (8-12-1).

Registration.—Secretary of State has since about 1927, maintained trademark register and kept trademark applications filed in office and other documents, such as assignments and surrenders, filed in this connection.

Tradenames, trademarks and service marks, may be registered by filing application with Secretary of State on form furnished by Secretary, setting forth following: (1) Name and business address of person applying for registration and, if corporation, state of incorporation; (2) description of goods, services or business with which mark is used and mode or manner in which mark is used, and class (as statutorily defined) in which such goods, services or business fall; (3) date when mark first used anywhere and date when first used in state by applicant or his predecessor in business; and (4) statement that applicant is owner of mark and that no other person has right to use such mark in state either in identical form or in such near resemblance as might be calculated to deceive or be mistaken therefor. Application must be signed and verified by applicant or by member of firm or officer of corporation or association applying for it. Every application must be accompanied by specimen or facsimile of mark in triplicate. Every application must be accompanied by filing fee of $30, payable to Secretary of State. (8-12-8).

Registration effective for ten years and may be renewed for successive periods of ten years in like manner, during six-month period prior to expiration. Renewal fee is $30. (8-12-10).

Assignment.—Trademarks and attendant registrations assignable with good will of business with which connected. Assignment must be in writing, duly executed, and may be recorded with Secretary of State, for fee of $30. Assignment void against subsequent purchaser for value without notice, unless recorded within three months after date of purchase or prior to subsequent purchase. (8-12-11).

Protection Afforded.—Ownership of marks flows from use, not from registration, so registration will not presumptively prove ownership. (8-12-7; 8-12-9, see Comment in both sections). Registration will make assignment of mark easier as common law did not provide for assignment. (8-12-11).

Infringement.—Anyone using trademark without consent of registrant subject to civil equitable and monetary penalties. (8-12-16; 8-12-18).

Tradenames included in definition of mark and registrable under Alabama Trademark Act. (8-12-6, et seq.; see subhead Registration, supra).

Containers.—Marks or devices for bottles, boxes, kegs, etc., may be registered (8-12-20), and it is a crime for anyone to refill, deal in, or remove marks upon same, without owner's consent (8-12-21).

TRADE SECRETS:

Alabama Trade Secrets Act contains definitions of trade secrets (8-27-2), describes elements of tort of trade secret misappropriations (8-27-3), sets out remedies (8-27-4) and prescribes statute of limitations (8-27-5).

LEGAL PROFESSION

ATTORNEYS AND COUNSELORS:

Integrated bar; admission to practice automatically results in membership in State Bar Association.

Jurisdiction over Admissions.—Vested in Supreme Court.

Eligibility.—Applicants must be at least 19 years old. No citizenship or residency requirements. All applicants must be approved by State Bar Association's Committee on Character and Fitness. Applicant not approved by this Committee may appeal to Board of Commissioners of State Bar.

Registration as Law Student.—Students entering law school with intention of applying for admission to Alabama Bar must register with Secretary of Board of Commissioners of State Bar within 60 days following commencement of study. If registration not filed within 390 days, must submit affidavit to Committee on Character and Fitness showing reasonable cause for having failed to file timely registration.

Educational Requirements.—

Prelegal.—Applicant who did not graduate from law school on approved list of American Bar Association or American Association of Law Schools at time of applicant's graduation must give proof that applicant has received baccalaureate degree from college or university which, at time of applicant's graduation, appeared on approved list of any standard accrediting agency or association in various states, or accepted by accrediting agency as meeting substantially same standards required for appearing on approved list of agency and that degree received before entering law school. Proof must be had by filing certified copy of diploma or certificate with Secretary of Board of Commissioners of Alabama State Bar. Proof of prelegal education by applicants who did graduate from law school on approved list of American Bar Association or American Association of Law Schools at time of applicant's graduation may be required by Committee on Character and Fitness.

Legal.—Applicant must file proof of completion of legal study with Secretary of Board of Commissioners of Alabama State Bar.

Graduation after course of law study of at least three years of at least 30 weeks each from law school which, at time of graduation, has been approved by American Bar Association or Association of American Law Schools, or graduation after course of study of four years of at least 30 weeks each from Birmingham School of Law, Jones School of Law, Miles College of Law, or Faulkner University. (34-3-2.1).

Petition for Admission.—Admission governed by Rules Governing Admission To The Alabama State Bar, as adopted by Board of Commissioners of Alabama State Bar and approved by Supreme Court. Admitted attorneys must take prescribed oath or affirmation prior to commencing practice. (34-3-15).

Examination.—Except as hereinafter stated, all applicants for admission must stand written examinations held at Montgomery on Mon., Tues., and Wed. of week in July and Feb. when Multi-State Bar Examination administered. Board of Commissioners of State Bar may prescribe subjects upon which candidates examined, conduct of examinations, time and place of examinations, and certification of persons found qualified. (34-3-2). Multi-State Bar Examination used, including legal ethics and professional responsibility. Other subjects tested: Wills, trusts and estates; pleading and practice; taxation (state and federal); business organizations (including partnerships and other forms of business associations); UCC; equity. Multi-State Bar Examination score from another jurisdiction accepted for transfer within 20 months from time taken provided MBE scaled score of 140 or above. Examination fee set by board of commissioners but may not exceed $500 for applicants not required to take examination and not to exceed $400 for residents required to take examination; nonresidents required to be examined must pay additional sum set by Board of Commissioners not to exceed $500. (34-3-3).

Clerkship.—No requirement prior to admission.

Admission Without Examination.—Certain teachers who have taught full-time for three years at accredited Alabama law schools and who have been admitted to bar of another state may apply for admission to bar without taking examination. Foreign attorneys no longer admitted to Alabama Bar without examination.

Admission Pro Hac Vice.—Attorney licensed to practice in other jurisdictions permitted to appear in particular case before any court or administrative agency in Alabama, provided such attorney associates himself with Alabama attorney.

Licenses.—$250 per year. (40-12-49). In addition, municipality may levy license tax.

Privileges.—No specific provisions.

Disabilities.—When client's ability to make adequately considered decisions in connection with representation impaired, attorney must maintain normal attorney-client

See note at head of Digest as to 1998 legislation covered.

See Topical Index in front part of this volume.

AL – 44

ATTORNEYS AND COUNSELORS . . . *continued*
relationship with client. Attorney may seek appointment of guardian or take other protective action with respect to client only when attorney reasonably believes client cannot adequately act in own interest. (Rule 1.14, Ala. Rules of Pro. Conduct).

Liabilities.—See category Civil Actions and Procedure, topic Costs.

Compensation.—Governed by §§34-3-60 to -62 and Rule 1.5, Ala. Rules of Pro. Conduct. Contingent fee agreements permitted. No requirement regarding filing of contingent fee agreements. No specific limitations on contingent fee amounts. See subhead Lien, infra.

Lien.—Attorney shall have lien for fees for services rendered: (1) On all papers and money of their clients in their possession; (2) on actions and judgments for money; and (3) on actions for real or personal property, on judgment therefor, and property recovered by action. (34-3-61).

Disbarment or Suspension.—Certain enumerated causes grounds for disbarment, suspension, public censure, private reprimand, or private informal admonition pursuant to Rules of Disciplinary Procedure (Interim) promulgated by Supreme Court and administered by Disciplinary Board of Ala. State Bar. §§34-3-80 to -89 sets forth procedural rules for disciplinary proceedings.

Unauthorized Practice.—Attorney must not practice law in jurisdiction where doing so violates regulation of legal profession or assist person not member of bar in unauthorized practice of law. (Rule 5.5, Ala. Rules of Pro. Conduct). Unlicensed person or those whose licenses expired who acts or holds himself out to public as attorney, guilty of misdemeanor and can be fined up to $500 or imprisoned for up to six months or both. (34-3-1). Any person, firm or corporation who is not regularly licensed and who engages in unauthorized practice of law guilty of misdemeanor. Any person, firm or corporation who conspires with, aids and abets in unauthorized practice of law guilty of misdemeanor. (34-3-7). Restrictions on practice of law by specific categories of individuals set by statute. (34-3-8 to -14).

Mandatory Continuing Legal Education.—Governed by Alabama State Bar Mandatory Continuing Legal Education Rules and Regulations.

Specialty Certification Requirements.—Governed by Alabama State Bar Rules of Specialization.

Professional Association.—See category Business Organizations, topic Associations, subhead Professional Associations.

Attorney Ethics.—American Bar Association Rules of Professional Conduct adopted with modifications.

Powers.—Attorney may bind client in action or proceeding by agreement in writing relating thereto or entry made on minutes of court. (34-3-21). Attorney may guarantee emergency financial aid if client ultimately liable. (Rule 1.8[e][3], Ala. Rules of Pro. Conduct.

Legal Services Liability.—Anyone licensed to practice law by State of Alabama or engaged in practice of law in State of Alabama subject to provisions of "The Alabama Legal Services Liability Act" (6-5-570, et seq.), which provides that legal service providers must exercise reasonable care, skill and diligence as other similarly situated providers in same general line of practice and locality, or, if certified specialist, reasonable care, skill and diligence as other providers practicing as specialist in same area of law (6-5-572; -580). Action must be commenced within two years after act or omission giving rise to claim, provided that action may be commenced within six months from date act or omission was discovered but not more than four years after act or omission occurred. (6-5-574). Parties to action may agree to settle dispute by arbitration. (6-5-575). Plaintiff has burden of proving that legal service provider breached applicable standard of care. (6-5-580).

MINERAL, WATER AND FISHING RIGHTS

MINES AND MINERALS:

Director of Department of Industrial Relations must appoint sufficient number of mining inspectors and employees, including at least one mining engineer. (25-9-3).

Operation of Mines.—Alabama Coal Mine Safety Law (25-9-1, et seq.), purpose to provide laws to promote safety and health of those engaged in coal mining and protection and preservation of property. Alabama Service Mining Act (9-16-1, et seq.), objective to provide for safe and reasonable reclamation of lands on which surface mining has occurred, to preserve natural resources within state and to protect and promote health and safety of people of state.

Safeguarding of Employees.—Special provisions regarding gases, machines, cages, working places, openings, ventilation, props, pipes, doors, lamps, explosives, etc., and methods of work; penalties provided. (25-9-40 to -284). Some statutory confusion, but it would appear that operators of other underground mines and of all surface mines subject to safety regulation by Department of Industrial Relations. (25-9-270; 9-16-106).

Inspection of Mines.—Mine inspector, who must be qualified elector, possess mine foreman certificate of competency of State, have eight or more years practical experience, and be at least 28 years old, vested with power to examine mines as to safety, health, etc., and to see that mining laws complied with. (25-9-6; -7). Inspector may order suspension of activities if violations imminently hazardous to workmen. (25-9-365). Coal mines inspected every 45 days. (25-9-20). Representative of miners at mines may accompany inspector. (25-9-7). Inspector's decisions take effect as specified in written notice to superintendent of mine and not subject to review, unless within ten days after giving such notice owner or operator appeals to chief for review, who must render decision within ten days of notice of appeal. (25-9-366). Board of examiners issues certificates of competency to mine foremen and fire bosses (25-9-9; -10), who have duties under Coal Mine Safety Act (25-9-16; -19).

Oil and Gas.—Drilling and production of oil and gas regulated by State Oil and Gas Board, which has broad powers, including limiting and prorating production, requiring pooling of separately owned tracts, and making regulations and orders for purpose of efficient operation, prevention of waste, etc. (9-17-6). Validity of such regulations and orders may be tested in circuit court. (9-17-15). Administrative fine limit of Oil and Gas Board for violations of this chapter $10,000 per day per act. (9-17-32).

Upon termination of any recorded lease, tenant who fails after 30 days written notice to cancel lease on record or furnish landlord with cancellation instrument, liable for damages and attorney's fee. (9-17-50).

Taxes.—On oil and gas, 8% of gross value at point of production. (40-20-2[a][1]). Incremental oil or gas production produced during year resulting from qualified enhanced recovery project taxed at 4% of gross value at point of production, as approved by State Oil and Gas Board. (40-20-2[a][2]). All wells producing 25 barrels or less of oil per day or 200,000 cubic feet or less of gas per day taxed at 4% of gross value of oil or gas at point of production. (40-20-2[a][3]). Oil and gas produced from on-shore discovery wells, oil and gas produced from on-shore development oils on which drilling commenced within four years of completion date of discovery of well and producing from depth of 6,000 feet or greater, and oil and gas produced from on-shore development wells on which drilling commenced within two years of completion date of discovering of well and producing depth less than 6,000 feet taxed at 6% of gross value of oil and gas at point of production for five years from date production begins from discovery in development wells; certain qualifications to such tax rates exist. (40-20-[a][4]). Oil or gas produced by offshore production greater than 18,000 feet below sea level taxed at 6% of gross value at point of production. (40-20-2[a][5]). For any well for which initial permit issued by State Oil and Gas Board dated on or after July 1, 1988, except for replacement well for which initial permit issued dated before July 1, 1988, rates provided in 40-20-2(a)(1) and (5) reduced by 2%. (40-20-2[a][7]). Applicable rate reduced by 50% for well permitted between July 1, 1996 and June 30, 1999, or replacement well permitted before July 1, 1996 (in addition to tax pursuant to §40-20-2[a][7]; -[8]). Tax levied upon basis of entire production in State. (40-20-2[b]). Under certain circumstances, department of Revenue determines "value" of gas (40-20-1[3]), which may be challenged by taxpayer if other than actual sale price (638 So.2d 886). Tax on iron ore, 3¢ per ton, but Department of Revenue, with approval of Governor, may fix lower rates. (40-12-128). On coal or lignite, 20¢ per ton. (40-13-31).

Production Tax and Permit Fee.—In addition to severance tax, tax of 2% of gross value, at point of production, of all oil and gas produced imposed for defraying expenses of Oil and Gas Board, and permit fee of $300 per well required prior to drilling. (9-17-24; -25).

Transfer Tax.—Tax on recording of instruments involving severed interests and non-producing oil, gas or minerals. (40-20-31 to -32).

Tax credits allowed based upon annual tonnage of coal mined. (40-18-220).

Surface Mining.—Operators engaged in surface mining must obtain license and permit for each location mined from Surface Mining Commission by filing application with Commission, together with license fee of $1,000. (9-16-81). See also category Environment, topic Environmental Regulation.

See also category Business Organizations, topic Partnerships.

MORTGAGES

CHATTEL MORTGAGES:

Uniform Commercial Code adopted. (7-1-101; -108). See category Business Regulation and Commerce, topic Commercial Code.

Filing.—Uniform Commercial Code governs. Official text—1990 adopted with some variations. See category Business Regulation and Commerce, topic Commercial Code for specific variations from official texts. Except as provided in Uniform Commercial Code, general recording statute still applies. See category Documents and Records, topic Records, subhead Recordable Instruments.

Place of Filing.—Uniform Commercial Code governs. (7-9-401). See category Documents and Records, topic Records, subhead Filing Under Commercial Code for details of place of filing.

Filing Fees.—Uniform Commercial Code governs. (7-9-402[4], 7-9-403[5]). See category Documents and Records, topic Records, subhead Filing Under Commercial Code for specific fee details.

Taxation.—See category Taxation, topic Real Estate Conveyance Tax.

Forms.—No forms prescribed by statute. Secretary of State has approved following standard forms: (a) UCC-1 financing statement; (b) UCC-3 statements of continuation, partial release, assignment, etc. (also used for termination, amendment and both full and partial assignment); (c) UCC-1F farm products financing statement; (d) UCC-3F farm products financing statement—continuation, termination, assignment and amendment; (e) UCC-E additional page; and (f) UCC-11 request for information or copies.

Alabama standard forms printed by various printers will be accepted by Secretary of State. List of approved printers can be obtained from Secretary of State.

UCC-1 and UCC-3 forms at end of this Digest have been approved by Secretary of State. Additional filing fee of $2 imposed when nonstandard form (i.e. not prescribed by Alabama Secretary of State) used. Secretary of State strongly urges that standard prescribed forms be used, that information recorded thereon be typed, not handwritten, and, if nonstandard form used, unsigned but otherwise completed standard form also be submitted to assist with indexing filing.

Security Agreement.—No prescribed, official or approved forms of security agreement.

COLLATERAL SECURITY:

See category Debtor and Creditor, topic Pledges.

MORTGAGES OF PERSONAL PROPERTY:

See topic Chattel Mortgages.

See note at head of Digest as to 1998 legislation covered.

See Topical Index in front part of this volume.

AL – 45

MORTGAGES OF REAL PROPERTY:

Mortgages must be executed and acknowledged or witnessed in same manner as deeds. (35-4-57). In law, mortgages treated as defeasible conveyances; in equity, as security for debt. Trust deeds are in general use, but more frequent practice is to use defeasible conveyance containing power of sale.

Execution.—Mortgages must be executed and acknowledged or witnessed as deeds. (35-4-57).

Recording.—Except as otherwise provided by Uniform Commercial Code, all deeds, mortgages, deeds of trust or other documents conveying any right, title, or interest in real property to be recorded in office of probate judge of county where property situated. (35-4-51; -62). Recording operates as notice. (35-4-63). All deeds, mortgages, deeds of trust or other conveyances void as to purchasers, mortgagees and judgment creditors without notice, unless such instruments are recorded before accrual of right of such third parties. (35-4-90).

Recording Fees.—See category Documents and Records, topic Records.

Taxes.—See category Taxation, topic Real Estate Conveyance Tax.

Trust Deeds.—Recognized. (35-4-51; -90; 142 Ala. 422, 38 So. 244). Also, when deed absolute on its face given to secure debt, treated in equity as mortgage. (256 Ala. 73, 53 So.2d 613).

Future Advances.—Mortgage not satisfied until all agreements for future advances satisfied. (35-10-26).

Priorities.—Mortgage void as to other bona fide purchasers without notice unless mortgage recorded before accrual of right. (35-4-90).

Subordination Agreements.—No statutory provisions. Generally considered valid.

Assignment.—Transfer of mortgage by mere delivery is equitable assignment, but passes no rights at law. (59 Ala. 183). Transfer by mere delivery of note secured by mortgage, if for valuable consideration, operates as equitable assignment of mortgage to transferee. (190 Ala. 530, 67 So. 426). Power to sell lands, given in mortgage, is part of security, and may be executed by person or personal representative who by assignment or otherwise becomes entitled to money secured; and conveyance to purchaser of lands sold under such power of sale executed by mortgagee, any assignee or other person entitled to money secured, his agent or attorney, or auctioneer making sale, vests legal title in purchaser. (35-10-1). Purchaser of property against which there are recorded mortgages or liens protected in assuming that record owner of such liens is owner of indebtedness secured thereby (35-4-64), since all assignments should be recorded at once.

Release.—Mortgagee may release any part of property from lien of mortgage by appropriate instrument duly recorded, or by entry on margin of record of mortgage. (35-10-27).

Satisfaction.—Mortgagee, at written request of mortgagor, must enter on margin of record of mortgage date and amount of full or partial payments (35-10-21 to -23) or file separate written instrument so stating (35-10-24). If after 30 days request not complied with, mortgagor may recover $200 from mortgagee. (35-10-30). Judge of Probate or clerk must attest full satisfaction, or full satisfaction may be made by attorney in fact authorized by instrument executed and acknowleged as conveyance, and filed for record. (35-10-27; -28).

Properly attested satisfaction in full by any one of several joint mortgagees which is noted on margin of record, or properly notarized and recorded release by any one of several joint mortgagees acknowledging full satisfaction of any mortgage in names of joint mortgagees, sufficient to extinguish lien of mortgage. (35-10-28).

Duly appointed executor or administrator of deceased mortgagee may enter satisfaction on margin of record of mortgage paid during lifetime of decedent. (35-10-25).

Discharge.—See subheads Satisfaction and Release, supra.

Foreclosure.—

For Mortgages Executed On or Before Dec. 31, 1988.—If deed of trust or mortgage, with power of sale, silent as to place or terms of sale, or as to notice, sale may be made at courthouse door of county where land situated for cash to highest bidder, after 30 days' notice of time, place and terms of sale by notice once a week for four consecutive weeks in newspaper published in county where property situated. (35-10-2). If no power of sale in mortgage or deed of trust, grantee may foreclose in court having jurisdiction of subject matter, or by selling for cash at courthouse door of county where property situated, to highest bidder, after notice of time, place, terms, purpose of sale given by four consecutive weekly insertions of notice in newspaper published in county where lands situated. (35-10-3). Where lands situated in two or more counties and no provision made in mortgage for sale, then lands may be sold at courthouse door of county wherein any portion of lands situated, after 30 days' notice of time, place, terms and purpose of such sale, by publishing notice once a week for four consecutive weeks in newspaper in each county in which said lands or portion thereof situated. (35-10-4). In foreclosure under §35-10-2 to -4, foreclosure deed executed by mortgagee conveys legal title. (35-10-5). Sale of part of property conveyed by mortgage operates as foreclosure of mortgage only as to property sold, other property continues as security for mortgage debt. (35-10-6). All sales of real estate under powers of sale contained in mortgages and deeds of trust must be held in county where all or part of said real estate situated. (35-10-7). Notice of sale must be given in manner provided in mortgage or deed of trust or in county where mortgagor resides and land, or part thereof, located; but if mortgagor does not reside in county where land or part thereof located, then notice must be published in county where land, or part thereof is located; but notice of sale under powers of sale contained in mortgages and deeds of trust executed after July 1, 1936, where amount secured $500 or more, must be given by publication once a week for three successive weeks in newspaper published in county in which land or portion thereof situated, and notice must give time, place and terms of sale, with description of property. (35-10-8). Sales under powers contained in mortgages or deeds of trust contrary to provisions of article void, notwithstanding agreement to contrary. (35-10-9).

For Mortgages Executed After Dec. 31, 1988.—Notice of sale must be given in county where land located. (35-10-13). Notice must be given by publication once a week for three successive weeks in newspaper published in county or counties in which land located. If land in more than one county publication to be made in all counties where land located. Notice must give time, place and terms of sale, together with description of property. (35-10-13). Power to sell must be exercised at front or main door to courthouse of county where land or material part located. Sale must be held between 11:00 A.M. and 4:00 P.M. on day designated. (35-10-14). Sale of part of property conveyed by mortgage or similar instrument operates as foreclosure only as to property sold, if debt not satisfied in full, other property in mortgage continues as security. (35-10-15).

Sales.—See subhead Foreclosure, supra.

Deficiency Judgments.—Mortgagee may sue on mortgage indebtedness without first foreclosing mortgage, or may foreclose mortgage and sue for deficiency judgment on any resulting deficiency. (228 Ala. 281, 153 So. 412).

Moratorium.—None.

Redemption.—See category Debtor and Creditor, topic Executions, subhead Redemption.

Form.—No prescribed form. Following is in general use:

Form

The State of Alabama . . . County. Know all men by these presents: That whereas, the undersigned . . . (hereinafter "Mortgagor") has become justly indebted to . . . (hereinafter "Mortgagee") in the sum of . . . Dollars due by promissory note and whereas, the said Mortgagee is desirous of securing the prompt payment of said note when the same shall fall due, now, therefore, in consideration of said indebtedness, and to secure the prompt payment of the same at maturity, the Mortgagor has bargained and sold, and does hereby grant, bargain, sell and convey unto the Mortgagee the following described real estate situated in . . . County and State of Alabama, to-wit: (description) warranted free from all encumbrances and against any adverse claims.

To have and to hold the above granted premises unto the Mortgagee, its heirs, executors, successors and assigns forever, and for the purpose of further securing the payment of said promissory note, Mortgagor does hereby agree to pay all taxes and assessments when imposed legally upon said premises, and should Mortgagor make default in the payment of same, the said Mortgagee may, at Mortgagee's option, pay off the same; and to further secure said indebtedness Mortgagor agrees to keep said property insured for at least . . . Dollars, loss, if any, payable to said Mortgagee as interest may appear, and if Mortgagor shall fail to keep said property insured as above specified, then the said Mortgagee may, at Mortgagee's option, insure said property for said sum for Mortgagee's own benefit, the policy, if collected, to be credited on said indebtedness, less cost of collecting same; all amounts so expended by said Mortgagee shall become a debt to said Mortgagee additional to the indebtedness hereby specifically secured, and shall be covered by this Mortgage and bear interest from date of payment by said Mortgagee and be due and payable at the maturity of any of the principal or any interest thereon.

Upon condition, however, that if the Mortgagor shall pay said note and reimburse said Mortgagee for any amounts Mortgagee may have expended as taxes, assessments or other charges and insurance and interest thereon, then this conveyance to be null and void; but should default be made in the payment of any sum so expended by the said Mortgagee, or should said note or any part thereof, or interest thereon, remain unpaid at maturity, or should the interest of said Mortgagee or of its heirs, executors, successors and assigns in said property become endangered by reason of the enforcement of any prior lien or encumbrance thereon, so as to endanger the debt hereby secured, then in any one of said events the whole of the said indebtedness shall at once become due and payable, and this mortgage shall be subject to foreclosure as now provided by law in case of past due mortgages, and the said Mortgagee and its agents, heirs, executors, successors and assigns, shall be authorized to take possession of the premises hereby conveyed, and after notice by publication once a week for three consecutive weeks of the time, place and terms of sale, together with a description of the premises by publication in some newspaper published in the county in which the premises are located, to sell the same, as a whole or in parcels, in front of the main or front courthouse door, of said last named county, at public outcry, to the highest bidder for cash, and apply the proceeds of said sale: first, to the expense of advertising, selling and conveying, including a reasonable attorney's fee; and, second, to the payment of any amounts that may have been expended or that may then be necessary to expend, in paying insurance, taxes, assessments, or other encumbrances, with interest thereon; and, third, to the payment of said note in full, whether the same shall or shall not have fully matured at the date of said sale; but no interest shall be collected beyond the day of sale; and, fourth, the balance, if any, to be turned over to the Mortgagor; and Mortgagor further agrees that said Mortgagee, its agents, heirs, executors, successors and assigns, may bid at said sale, and purchase said property, if the highest bidder therefor; and Mortgagor further agrees to pay a reasonable attorney's fee to Mortgagee or its assigns, for the foreclosure of this mortgage. Should the same be foreclosed, said fee to be a part of the debt hereby secured.

Witness the undersigned's hand and seal this . . . day of . . . ., 19 . . .

WITNESSES:

. . . .

. . . .

. . . . (Seal)

. . . . (Seal)

(Acknowledgments)

Title passing by mortgage will not divest until all secured obligations paid and there is no commitment or agreement by mortgagee to make advances, incur obligations or otherwise give value under any agreement. (35-10-26).

Presumption of Payment.—As to third persons without notice or knowledge, the indebtedness secured by recorded mortgage or reservation of vendor's lien covering real estate is, on becoming 20 years past due, conclusively presumed paid, unless recorded record of such mortgage or lien shows credit by owner of debt of one or more payments on such indebtedness within last 20 years. (35-10-20).

See note at head of Digest as to 1998 legislation covered.

See Topical Index in front part of this volume.

PROPERTY

ABSENTEES:

Care of Property.—In sale of lands of decedent for payment of debts or for division, nonresident heirs or devisees may be brought into court by publication. (43-2-446). Unknown heirs and devisees may likewise be proceeded against by publication on proper averments. (43-2-447). Funds to which such parties are entitled are paid into court and there retained until ascertainment of persons entitled thereto. (43-2-447).

Process Agent.—See category Transportation, topic Motor Vehicles.

Escheat.—Uniform Disposition of Unclaimed Property Act adopted. (35-12-20 to -50).

Partition.—In probate court, nonresident can be made defendant in partition proceedings through publication carried out in same manner as when property in hands of executor is distributed. (35-6-43). Partition proceedings against unknown defendant without naming him are authorized upon averment that diligent inquiry has not disclosed his identity and after proper publication of character in which he is being sued and with reference to his title or interest in property. (35-6-44). When known party cannot be located, or when it cannot be ascertained whether he is alive, he can be made defendant in his name by publication, provided that petitioner specifically alleges facts showing diligence of his search for absent defendant. (35-6-44). Court shall appoint guardian ad litem to represent interest of absent defendant. (35-6-44).

In circuit court, nonresident in partition proceedings (35-6-20 to -25) can be made defendant through proper publication (ARCP 4.3). Unknown party can be made defendant without naming him upon averment of diligent inquiry concerning his identity and after proper publication. (ARCP 4.3). Known party who cannot be located, or about whom it cannot be ascertained whether he is alive, can be made defendant in his own name through publication, provided specific facts are alleged by petitioner showing diligence of search for absent defendant's whereabouts. (35-6-25). Court must appoint guardian ad litem for absent defendant and decree is binding on both him and his heirs. (35-6-25).

Nonresident parent or guardian having legal custody of minor may, by proper application showing that said parent or guardian has legal custody in state of residence, obtain order from court having jurisdiction of estate of such minor authorizing removal of property of minor from state to conservator and authorizing such conservator to receive it. (26-8-40 to -43). Property belonging to nonresident ward, either minor or ward, may on petition by nonresident guardian to judge of probate of county in which property is situated be removed to state of residence of minor or ward. (26-8-44 to -52; 235 Ala. 314, 179 So. 215).

ADVERSE POSSESSION:

Adverse possession, to bar entry on, or recovery of, real estate must be open, actual, exclusive, notorious, hostile and continuous. (255 Ala. 569, 52 So.2d 207).

Character of Possession.—Adverse possession cannot confer or defeat title to land unless: (1) Deed or other color of title has been recorded in office of judge of probate of county in which lands lie, for at least ten years before action has been commenced; (2) claimant or predecessor in title has annually listed land for taxation for ten years prior to action; or (3) claimant has acquired title by descent cast or devise from predecessor in title who was in possession. (6-5-200[a]). To complete time required under color of title, time of any predecessor in title may be added. Accident, oversight or misdescription will not defeat claim based on listing for taxation. (6-5-200[b]). Coterminous owner may acquire title by adverse possession for ten years without any of above three alternative requirements. (6-5-200[c]; 294 Ala. 189, 314 So.2d 65).

In cases where none of above requirements are met, common law prescriptive period of 20 years applies. (6-2-8; 230 Ala. 197, 160 So. 336; 264 Ala. 492, 88 So.2d 868).

Action for recovery of land, or possession thereof, must be commenced within ten years, except as otherwise provided by law. (6-2-8; 6-2-33). See category Civil Actions and Procedure, topic Limitation of Actions, subhead Ten Years.

No statute of limitations exists on actions for recovery of lands belonging to State of Alabama or any of its public, educational, or governmental institutions, counties or municipal corporations (6-2-31, 6-6-281), except for "sixteenth section lands" held under color of title and which had been in possession for more than 20 years prior to May 1, 1908 (16-20-6).

Duration of Possession.—Where purchaser to whom land was sold for payment of taxes in actual adverse possession under claim of right, action to recover land must be brought within three years from date purchaser became entitled to demand deed therefor, but if owner was at time of sale minor or insane, he, his heirs or legal representatives must be allowed one year after disability removed to bring suit; otherwise suit is barred. Rule does not apply to any action brought by State, nor to cases in which owner of land sold had paid taxes prior to sale, nor to cases in which land sold was not at time of assessment or sale subject to taxation. (40-10-82).

Easements.—Established by use and enjoyment for 20 years adverse to owner of servient estate, under claim of right, exclusive, continuous, and uninterrupted, with actual or presumptive knowledge of owner. (252 Ala. 296, 40 So.2d 873).

Disabilities.—Person entitled to make entry on land or enter defense founded on title to land who is, at time such right accrues, less than 19 years old, insane, or imprisoned for term less than life, has three years after termination of such disability (or shorter period if provided by law) to commence action or enter defense to action. Period may not extend beyond 20 years. (6-2-8[a]). When two or more disabilities coexist at time claim accrues, limitation does not attach until all disabilities removed. (6-2-8[b]). Disability not existing at time claim accrues does not suspend operation of limitation. (6-2-8[c]).

Allowance for Improvements.—Adverse possession for three years will entitle defendant in ejectment to allowance of value of any permanent improvements made by him, and if value in excess of value of use and occupation he is entitled to judgment for such excess. (6-6-286). If such judgment not paid within one year and if defendant pays

to plaintiff or clerk of court in which issue has been tried the value of land and of use and occupation as assessed by jury, plaintiff barred from writ of possession. (6-6-286).

Damages When Land Held Under Color of Title.—Person holding possession under color of title, in good faith, not responsible for damages or rent for more than one year before commencement of action. (6-6-289).

CONDOMINIUMS:

See topic Real Property.

CONVEYANCES:

See topic Deeds.

CURTESY:

Estate of curtesy abolished. (43-8-57).

DEEDS:

Person of legal capacity may alienate any present, future or contingent interest in land by will or by executing and delivering deed. (35-4-1). See topic Real Property for types of estates.

Execution.—Valid deed must be signed at foot by grantor, or duly authorized agent, and must be duly acknowledged by grantor, or its execution must be attested by subscribing witness. (35-4-20). If grantor signs by making mark or through amanuensis, instrument must be duly acknowledged or attested by two witnesses in writing. (35-4-20).

For circumstances in which spouse must join, see categories Debtor and Creditor, topic Homesteads, subhead Alienation or Encumbrance; Documents and Records, topic Acknowledgments; Family, topic Husband and Wife, subhead Conveyance or Encumbrance of Property.

Consideration or recitation therein not necessary for validity or effectiveness of deed or other conveyance creating or transferring any interest in land, except for option to purchase land. (35-4-34; 445 So.2d 902).

Seal not necessary to convey legal title (35-4-21), and writing importing on face to be under seal has same effect as if seal of parties were affixed thereto (35-4-22).

While seal not essential to validity of deed of corporation (35-4-67), general practice to affix corporate seal, which constitutes prima facie evidence that deed was duly executed by proper officer acting with full authority (232 Ala. 471, 168 So. 693; 285 Ala. 371, 232 So.2d 616).

Recording.—Recordation in office of judge of probate in county in which property situated necessary to constitute notice to subsequent purchasers, mortgagees, etc., who do not have actual notice of deed. (35-4-50; -62; -63). See also category Documents and Records, topic Records.

Recording Fees.—See category Documents and Records, topic Records.

Operation and Effect.—Recorded deed, properly acknowledged or probated, is self-proving in court, unless reputed maker has bona fide possession and files affidavit of forgery. (35-4-65).

Taxes.—Deed tax imposed at rate of 50¢ for first $500 or less of value, and 50¢ for each $500 or fraction thereof of excess. Tax applies only to value in excess of any mortgage or vendor's lien on property on which mortgage tax (see category Taxation, topic Real Estate Conveyance Tax) paid. (40-22-1).

Form.—No prescribed form of warranty deed. Following is effective:

Form

Know All Men By These Presents, That we (Tom Brown) and (Sarah Brown), his wife, for and in consideration of the sum of (one thousand dollars) to us in hand paid by (John Doe) the receipt whereof we hereby acknowledge, do grant, bargain, sell and convey unto the said (John Doe), the following described real estate, all situated in (Jefferson County, State of Alabama) to-wit: (Description).

To Have and to Hold the aforegranted premises to the said (John Doe), his heirs and assigns, forever.

And we, for ourselves and our heirs and assigns, do hereby covenant with the said (John Doe), his heirs and assigns, that we are lawfully seized in fee of the aforegranted premises; that they are free from all incumbrances; that we have good right to sell and convey the same, and that we will warrant and defend the said premises to the said (John Doe), his heirs and assigns, forever against the lawful claims and demands of all persons.

In Witness Whereof, we (Tom Brown) and (Sarah Brown), his wife, have hereunto set our hands and seals this . . . day of . . . ., 19. . . . .
Witnesses:

. . . .

. . . .   Tom Brown   (L. S.)

                       Sarah Brown   (L. S.)

   (Acknowledgment.)

Quitclaim deed may be in like form, except "do hereby remise, release, quitclaim and convey" should be substituted for "do grant, bargain, sell and convey" and paragraph containing covenants should be omitted.

Construction.—Fees tail have been abolished (35-4-3), and every deed conveying estate in lands is taken as in fee simple, even though no words of inheritance appear, unless intention to convey lesser estate clearly appears (35-4-2).

Covenants.—In all conveyances of estates in fee statutory warranty words "grant," "bargain," and "sell," unless it clearly appears otherwise from conveyance, must be construed as (1) express covenant to the grantee, heirs and assigns, that grantor seized of estate in fee, free from encumbrances done by grantor, except rents and services that may be reserved; (2) express covenant for quiet enjoyment against grantor, heirs and assigns unless limited by express words of conveyance. (35-4-271).

Conveyance by Attorney.—See topic Powers of Attorney.

DEEDS OF TRUST:

See category Mortgages, topic Mortgages of Real Property.

DOWER:

Estate of dower has been abolished. (43-8-57).

ESCHEAT:

See topic Absentees, subhead Escheat; categories Business Regulation and Commerce, topic Banks and Banking, subhead Unclaimed Deposits; Estates and Trusts, topic Descent and Distribution, subhead Escheat, and Wills, subhead Unclaimed Legacies.

LANDLORD AND TENANT:

Uniform Commercial Code Art. 2A adopted. (7-2A-1 to -532).

Kinds of Tenancy.—Tenancy for life, years, month to month, at will, and at sufferance recognized.

Leases for over one year must be in writing. (8-9-2). Leasehold estate cannot be created for longer term than 99 years. Leases for more than 20 years void for excess unless acknowledged as conveyances and recorded within one year in county in which leased property situated. (35-4-6).

Security Deposits.—No statutory provision.

Recording.—See subhead Leases, supra.

Rent.—When one party furnishes land and other party labor with stipulation to divide crop, relationship of landlord and tenant exists and portion of crop to which party furnishing land is entitled is rent thereof. (35-9-37). Reasonable satisfaction may be recovered for use and occupation of land: (1) When demise by deed or parol and no specific sum agreed on as rent; (2) when defendant in possession under sale not consummated; (3) when tenant remains on land by sufferance; (4) when tenant obtains possession of land unlawfully; (5) when defendant estopped from disputing plaintiff's title. (35-9-100).

Rent accruing after judgment may be recovered on motion. (6-6-293). In ejectment proceedings tenant in possession under license or lease from another liable only for rent in arrears as long as possession continues. (6-6-288).

Lien.—Common law methods of distress for rent abolished and replaced by giving lien on tenant's goods enforceable by attachment in certain cases. (35-9-34). Landlord has lien on crops for rent for current year and for advances. (35-9-30). Unless otherwise agreed, such rent due Nov. 1 of year in which crop grown. (35-9-31). Lien continues and attaches to crops of succeeding year. (35-9-32). Landlord may assign rights and remedies for rents and advances. (35-9-33).

Landlords of storehouses and dwelling houses or other buildings have lien for rent on goods, furniture, and effects of tenants. (35-9-60). Such lien has precedence over all other liens, except those for taxes and perfected security interest in collateral that attaches before collateral brought on leased premises. (7-9-310[2]). May be enforced by attachment on basis of: (1) fraudulent disposal; (2) near fraudulent disposal of tenant's goods; (3) assignment for benefit of creditors; (4) or transfer of substantially all of his goods without payment of rent. (35-9-61). Assignee of rent has all rights and remedies of assignor. (35-9-655).

Landlord has lien on livestock raised or grazed upon land rented from him for rent of said land for current year. (35-11-72).

Termination of Tenancy.—Where no time is specified for termination of tenancy, the law construes it to be from Dec. 1 to Dec. 1, but if expressly tenancy at will, then either party may terminate it at will, by ten days notice in writing. (35-9-3). Hiring of lodging or dwelling house for unspecified term presumed to have been made for such term as parties adopt for estimation of rent. In absence of agreement respecting term or rent, hiring presumed to be monthly. (35-9-4).

Holding Over.—When tenant by month or for any term less than one year holds over without special agreement, tenancy may be terminated by giving tenant ten days notice in writing. (35-9-5).

Uniform Residential Landlord and Tenant Act not adopted.

Distress.—See subhead Lien, supra.

Dispossession.—Two statutory methods for removing holdover tenants. One method (6-6-310; -353) requires service of complaint no sooner than ten days after written demand for possession of premises (6-6-310; -330). Trial may not be postponed longer than 15 days after defendant answers complaint. (6-6-335). District Court of county in which unlawful detainer occurs has exclusive jurisdiction over action. (6-6-330). Tenancies for terms of less than one year may be terminated by giving tenant ten days notice in writing. (35-9-5). If tenancy is to be terminated for breach of lease, termination may be accomplished by giving ten days notice in writing of such termination. (35-9-6).

Second method of obtaining possession from holdover tenants is by writ of restitution issued on strength of landlord's affidavit. (35-9-80 to -88).

Default.—When default made in any term of lease, ten days notice to quit may be written and served. (35-9-6).

Remedies.—Landlord's grantee, assignee or respective heirs or personal representatives have same remedies by entry, action or otherwise against lessee as landlord would have. (35-9-9). Tenant's assigns or personal representatives have same remedies by action or otherwise against landlord's grantees, assignees or representatives for breach of any agreement in tenant lease as would have against landlord, except for actions based on covenants against encumbrances or relating to title or possession of demised premises. (35-9-10). In all cases where demised premises are sublet or assigned, landlord has same right to enforce lien against subtenant or assignee as against tenant to whom premises demised. (35-9-11).

Mitigation.—Generally, landlord has no duty to mitigate damages. (338 So.2d 413).

Arbitration.—Tenant objecting to rent claimed by landlord or amount of compensation for sale or transfer of improvements by landlord may demand arbitration of dispute if landlord is corporation organized under §10-4-190. (10-4-194).

Attachment.—Landlord may enforce lien by attachment after demand or after removal by tenant. Additionally, landlord may enforce lien by attachment: (1) When good cause to believe tenant about to remove from premises or otherwise dispose of any part of crop without paying rent or advances and without consent of landlord; (2) when tenant has removed from premises or otherwise disposed of any part of crop without paying rent or advances and without consent of landlord; (3) when tenant has disposed of, or there is good cause to believe he is about to dispose of, any articles advanced or obtained by purchase with money advanced or by barter in exchange for any article advanced, in fraud of rights of landlord. (35-9-34). Plaintiff must make affidavit and bond. (35-9-35). Attachment may be levied on crop or proceeds and on articles advanced or on property obtained by advances. (35-9-36). When attachment sued out by superior landlord, crop of tenant in chief must be exhausted before that of subtenant is levied on. (35-9-39). Subtenant may require attachment against tenant in chief when sufficient cause exists, and on landlord's failure so to attach he loses right against subtenant. (35-9-41).

Failure to Plant Crops.—When tenant of farm lands fails or refuses without just cause to plant crops on substantial portion thereof prior to Mar. 20, landlord may recover possession by action of unlawful detainer. (35-9-38).

Emblements.—Tenant at will is entitled to his emblements, if crop is sowed before notice to quit by landlord, or before tenancy otherwise suddenly terminated, as by sale of estate by landlord, or by judicial sale, or death of landlord or tenant. (35-9-2).

When tenant abandons or removes from premises landlord may seize and harvest crops and apply proceeds toward expenses and labor of harvesting such crops and toward rent and advances due landlord. Tenant may redeem before sale by tendering rent and compensation. (35-9-12).

LEASES:

See topic Landlord and Tenant.

PARTITION:

See category Civil Actions and Procedure, topic Partition.

PERPETUITIES:

Common law rules are applicable to both real and personal property (35-4-4), but do not apply to pensions, profit sharing and stock bonus trusts created by employers for benefit of their employees or trusts consisting solely of policies of life, health, accident or disability insurance, or proceeds thereof (35-4-259; -260). Rule against perpetuities does not apply to business trusts. (19-3-65); see category Business Organizations, topic Joint Stock Companies, subhead Business Trust.

Accumulations.—No trust for purposes of accumulation only may extend for term longer than ten years, or until infant beneficiary, in being at time of creation of inter vivos trust or at death of creator of testamentary trust, becomes of age. (35-4-252). Court may direct application of suitable sum for benefit of destitute minor who is beneficiary of such trust, notwithstanding accumulation provision. (35-4-253). See category Estates and Trusts, topic Trusts.

Alienation of Proceeds of Annuities, etc., Retained by Insurance Company.—Where, under annuity contract or life insurance policy (or agreement in writing supplemental to either) issued by any life insurance company, proceeds are to be retained by company at maturity, no person entitled to such proceeds may alienate, anticipate, or encumber any part of interest or principal due therefrom, if such contract, policy or supplemental agreement expressly withholds such permission. (27-14-30).

PERSONAL PROPERTY:

Tenancy by the entirety not recognized. (212 Ala. 45, 101 So. 663). Attempt to create tenancy by entirety may indicate sufficient intent to create survivorship estate under §35-4-7 and may result in tenancy with right of survivorship. (447 So.2d 185).

POWERS OF ATTORNEY:

Attorneys In Fact.—Power of attorney to execute deed disposing of real estate must be in writing executed by grantor with formalities of deed. (35-4-294). Must be recorded to preserve unbroken chain of title.

Formalities.—Same as requirements for passing any other real estate interest. (35-2-294; 35-2-28).

Revocation.—Reservation of absolute power of revocation returns power to grantor. (35-4-290).

Uniform Durable Power of Attorney Act adopted, with modifications. (26-1-2).

Members of Armed Forces.—No special provision.

REAL PROPERTY:

Common law estates generally recognized. No leasehold estate for term longer than 99 years may be created. Leases for more than 20 years void for excess over said period unless lease or memorandum thereof acknowledged or approved as required by law for conveyances of real estate and recorded within one year from date of execution in office of judge of probate in county in which property is located. (35-4-6).

See also topic Deeds.

Rule in Shelley's Case abolished. (35-4-230).

Condominiums created on or after Jan. 1, 1991 governed by Alabama Uniform Condominium Act of 1991 ("1991 Act"). (35-8A-101 et seq.). Condominiums created prior to Jan. 1, 1991 governed by Condominium Ownership Act (35-8-1 et seq.), provided, however, that certain sections of 1991 Act apply to all condominiums created prior to Jan. 1, 1991.

REAL PROPERTY . . . *continued*

Foreign Conveyances or Encumbrances.—Ala. law governs manner of execution of and competency of parties to conveyance of land situated in Ala. (243 Ala. 651, 11 So.2d 374). See category Documents and Records, topic Records, subhead Foreign Conveyances or Encumbrances.

Presumption of Tenancy in Common.—Real property held jointly presumed held in equivalent of tenancy in common, unless instrument creating tenancy shows intent to create joint tenancy with use of words "right of survivorship" or similar words to that effect. (35-4-7).

Forfeitures.—No estate or interest can be defeated, discontinued or extinguished by act of any third party having possessory or ulterior interest, except in cases specially provided for by statute. (35-4-170). Conveyance by tenant for life or years, purporting to convey greater interest than he possesses or can lawfully convey, passes to grantee all estate which tenant could lawfully convey, rather than forfeit estate. (35-4-232).

Survivorship, as incident of joint tenancy, abolished, except when instrument creating joint tenancy states that there shall be survivorship. (35-4-7). Tenancy by entirety not recognized. (212 Ala. 45, 101 So. 663).

Absolute Powers.—When absolute power of disposition, not accompanied by any trust, given to owner of particular estate for life or years, it is absolute fee as to creditors or purchasers, but subject to future estates if power not executed or lands sold for satisfaction of debts during continuance of such estate. (35-4-292).

Livery of seisin and attornment of tenant not recognized. (35-4-31,-32).

Groundwater.—Reasonable use rule applicable where conflict involves proprietary competition over water itself. (553 So.2d 89). But, laws of nuisance apply, as opposed to reasonable use rule, where one party's use interfered with by second party's diversion incidental to some use of second party's land. (388 So.2d 900).

See also topics Curtesy, Deeds, Dower, Landlord and Tenant; categories Civil Actions and Procedure, topic Partition; Debtor and Creditor, topic Homesteads; Family, topic Husband and Wife; Mortgages, topic Mortgages of Real Property.

TRUST DEEDS:

See category Mortgages, topic Mortgages of Real Property.

TAXATION

ADMINISTRATION:

Alabama Department of Revenue supervises administration of tax laws. Commissioner of Revenue is Chief Executive Officer of Department of Revenue and all powers, authority, and duties vested in Department of Revenue exercised by Commissioner. (40-2-11).

State Taxes.—Alabama Department of Revenue exercises general supervision and control of valuation, equalization, and assessment of property, privilege, or franchise taxes and collection of property, privilege, license, excise, intangible, franchise, or other taxes for state and counties. (40-2-11). Information, forms, and waivers, etc., may be obtained by contacting Alabama Department of Revenue, 50 N. Ripley St., Montgomery, AL 36130, (334) 242-1170.

County, School and Municipal Taxes.—County Revenue Commissioner supervises assessment and collection of taxes. (1998 AL H.B. 213, signed into law 3/3/98). County Commissioner has authority to levy tax for general county purposes or special purposes. (11-3-11). Municipal corporations may levy tax to purchase school property or land to erect school buildings thereon. (11-47-13). Governing body of incorporated towns and cities authorized to levy property tax (11-51-1), sales tax (11-51-200), and excise tax (11-51-202).

Assessment of Taxes.—State, county and municipal ad valorem taxes are assessed as of Oct. 1 of tax year, and from that date are lien on all property of taxpayer, which may be enforced by sale. (40-7-2; 40-1-2). Each taxpayer or his agent must make return to tax assessor before Jan. 1 under penalty. (40-7-4). Assessor must assess all property not claimed on tax return by owner for which varying service fee and 10% penalty added to tax. (40-7-22 to -25). Notice of assessment of property not assessed within preceding five years must be given owner or his agent by registered or certified mail. (40-7-23). Nonresident taxpayer, resident taxpayer subject to disabling infirmity or woman taxpayer may send in duly sworn list, or such list may be rendered by agent having knowledge of his or her taxable property. (40-7-7). Final assessment of ad valorem tax may be appealed to circuit court by taxpayer (40-7-45), and by state; conditions precedent to exercise of right and procedure to be followed depend on official or body making assessment (40-7-45; 40-3-25). Assessment on common areas must take into account value of all encumbrances on common areas. (659 So.2d 607). Initial assessment has no preclusive effect in future tax years. (668 So.2d 768).

Special rules govern and special procedure obtains in reference to assessment of taxes on tangible and intangible property of public utilities. (40-21-1, et seq.).

Protest of Taxes Assessed by Revenue Department.—If taxpayer does not agree with preliminary assessment, he may appeal and request conference with operating division. (40-3-24). Taxpayer may appeal final assessment of ad valorem taxes on real or personal property by filing notice in writing with officer, board or commission of intent to appeal and bond of $100 (40-7-46) and by appealing to appropriate Circuit Court (40-7-45). Assessments for all other taxes may be appealed by requesting hearing with administrative law division, final order from which may be applied for rehearing or appealed to Circuit Court. (40-2A-9).

Exemptions.—

Generally.—Specifically identified exemptions set forth as §40-9-1. Certain organizations exempt from all state, county and municipal taxes, licenses and fees. (40-9-9, et seq.).

Ad Valorem Taxes.—Exemptions from ad valorem taxation granted with respect to public property, property of religious, educational, charitable, etc., institutions used for such purposes and certain property of residents of state, frequently limited as to value.

Lease for profit to entity using land for religious, educational, or charitable purposes does not entitle owner to ad valorem tax exemption. (601 So.2d 474).

Homestead of resident of state, to extent of $4,000 in assessed value and 160 acres in area for owner not over age 65, and without limit for owner over age 65, retired due to total and permanent disability without regard to age or blind without regard to age or whether such person is retired, is exempt from state ad valorem taxation. For tax years beginning on and after Oct. 1, 1981, homestead of resident of state, to extent of $2,000 or 160 acres for owner not over age of 65, exempt from county ad valorem taxes, except countywide and school district ad valorem taxes levied for school purposes, and homesteads of resident, to extent of $5,000 if owner over age 65 with annual adjusted gross income less than $12,000 in previous year, or retired due to total and permanent disability or blind without regard to age or whether person is retired, in assessed value and 160 acres in area, exempt from county ad valorem taxation (40-9-19), provided claim for exemption is filed with tax assessor. Such claim needs to be made only once and may be verified each year thereafter by mail on form affidavit provided by tax assessor. (40-9-21.1).

Principal residence and 160 acres adjacent thereto, if single-family residence owned and occupied by individuals totally disabled, or age 65 or older having net taxable income of $7,500 or less as shown on latest U.S. income tax return of individual and spouse, exempt from ad valorem taxation. (40-9-21.1). Once made, claim verified yearly by mail under 40-9-21.1.

Factories manufacturing calcium cyanamide (lime nitrogen), aluminum or aluminum products exempt from state, county and municipal taxation, except taxes on land, for ten years after beginning construction. (40-9-5).

Penalties.—

Income Tax.—Failure to file return on time is misdemeanor punishable by fine up to $1,000. (40-18-50). Failure to timely file return carries penalty of 10% of any additional tax required to be paid with such return or $50, whichever greater. (40-2A-11). In addition to other penalties, willful failure to pay tax, file return or supply information misdemeanor punishable by fine of not more than $25,000, or $100,000 for corporation, or imprisonment for not more than one year, or both, plus costs of prosecution. (40-29-112). If any underpayment due to negligence, penalty of 5% of tax attributable to negligence assessed. (40-2A-11). If underpayment due to fraud, penalty of 50% of underpayment attributable to fraud assessed. (40-2A-11). If fraud penalty asserted, no other penalty may be asserted. (40-2A-11).

Sales Tax.—Penalty for failure to keep records or make reports is fine of $25 to $500 (40-23-11), or $50 to $500 and/or up to six months imprisonment for willful refusal to keep records or make reports (40-23-12). In addition to other penalties, willful failure to pay tax, file return or supply information is misdemeanor punishable by fine of not more than $25,000, or $100,000 for corporation, or imprisonment for not more than one year, or both, plus costs of prosecution. (40-29-112).

Contractors Tax.—Penalty for failure to file returns and make payments same as those applicable to state sales tax. (40-23-50).

Use Tax.—Penalty up to $500 for failure to make payment, and fine of $300 to $5,000 and/or imprisonment up to one year for fraudulent evasion. (40-23-88).

Hotel and Motel Tax.—Fine from $25 to $500 for failure to make reports and keep records (40-26-8), and $50 to $500 fine and/or imprisonment for up to six months for willful refusal to make reports or permit examination of records. (40-26-9).

Securities Tax.—Penalty of 10% of taxes assessed for failure to file report. (40-14-72).

Interstate Cooperation.—Multistate Tax Compact adopted. (40-27-1).

Taxpayer Bill of Rights.—Alabama Taxpayers' Bill of Rights and Uniform Revenue Procedures Act adopted. (40-2A-1, et seq.).

ALCOHOLIC BEVERAGE TAXES:

Alcoholic beverage taxes governed by §§28-3-183, et seq.; and §§28-7-16; 28-7A-1 to -6.

CIGARETTE TAXES:

Sales tax, use tax and excise tax governed by §§40-25-1, et seq.

COAL SEVERANCE TAX:

Covered generally in §40-13-1, et seq. Every producer who severs coal within state subject to tax of 13^1/$_2$¢ per ton of coal severed. (40-13-2). "Producer" defined as person who ultimately owns right to extract coal. (464 So.2d 95). Additional tax levied by Department of Revenue on persons severing coal or lignite within state of 20¢ per ton of coal or lignite severed. (40-13-31). Certain counties also impose additional coal severance tax.

CORPORATE STOCK TAX:

Financial Institutions State Franchise Tax.—See category Business Regulation and Commerce, topic Banks and Banking.

Tax on Corporate Stock.—Tax assessed at 20% of value of shares to person in whose name such shares stand on books of corporation. (40-14-70[a]). Calculation of tax and procedures for payment more fully described in §§40-14-70; -72.

CORPORATION LICENSE TAX:

Taxation of foreign corporations governed by §§40-14-1 to -4; 40-14-20; -23, and domestic corporations by §§40-14-22; -23; 40-14-40 to -58.

ESTATE AND INHERITANCE TAX:

Taxable Property.—There is imposed upon all net estates passing by will, devise or under intestate laws of State of Alabama, or otherwise, which are lawfully subject to imposition of estate tax by State of Alabama, tax equal to full amount of state tax permissible when levied by and paid to State of Alabama as credit or deduction in computing any federal estate tax payable by such estate according to act of Congress in

See note at head of Digest as to 1998 legislation covered.

See Topical Index in front part of this volume.

ESTATE AND INHERITANCE TAX . . . *continued*

effect, on date of death of decedent, taxing such estate with respect to items subject to taxation in Alabama. (40-15-2).

Rates of Tax and Exemptions.—Estate and inheritance tax is equivalent to full credit or deduction permissible in computing Federal estate tax under Federal Act in effect at date of decedent's death on account of any estate or inheritance tax payable to state. (Const., 23rd Amendment, 40-15-2).

Exempt Transfers.—Money, credits, securities and other intangibles within state but not employed in any business within state exempt from tax, if owned by nonresident domiciled in another state which imposes tax (40-15-8) and which grants similar exemption to Alabama resident (40-15-9).

Administration and Enforcement.—Not applicable.

Deductions.—Use applicable federal statutes. (40-15-2).

Valuation Date.—Use applicable federal statutes. (40-15-2). Because state estate tax is calculated with reference to federal estate tax, no express provision concerning alternate valuation date. However, use of alternate valuation date allowed under federal law might be reflected in state tax.

Valuation of Particular Transfers.—Not applicable.

When Due; Interest.—Interest charged at legal rate from original due date. (40-15-4).

Returns and Reports.—Executor must file with State Department of Revenue, duplicates of all returns required to be filed with federal authorities. (40-15-3).

Tax due must be paid to Department of Revenue and return required by §40-15-3 must be filed within nine months after death. Extension of time may be granted in cases of hardship, with such extension not to exceed ten years. (40-15-4). Taxes not paid before delinquent date bear interest at same rate established by Secretary of Treasury pursuant to 26 U.S.C. §6621 until paid. (40-1-44).

Foreign Representatives.—See category Estates and Trusts, topics Executors and Administrators, Wills and Trusts.

Taxable Transfers.—Not applicable.

Reciprocal Agreements.—Reciprocity is effective only as to property of residents of states which grant to property of residents of Ala. similar exemption from death taxation. (40-15-9).

Waivers.—Not applicable.

Access to Safety Deposit Boxes.—See category Estates and Trusts, topics Executors and Administrators, Wills and Trusts.

GASOLINE AND SPECIAL FUELS TAXES:

Gasoline tax imposed on selling, distributing, storing or withdrawing from storage in this state for any use at following rates: Gasoline 16¢ per gallon levied expressly on consumer (40-17-31; 40-17-220), with refund of 11¢ per gallon used on farm for agricultural purposes (40-17-102); diesel fuels 17¢ per gallon (40-17-2; 40-17-220); lubricating oil 6¢ per gallon (40-17-171; 40-17-220); aviation fuel 2.7¢ per gallon for fuel to power reciprocating engines and 9¢ per gallon for fuel to power jet or turbine engines, both rates subject to changes according to fixed schedule based upon total revenues derived from tax on aviation fuel and according to exceptions for "hub" operations (40-17-31). Cities and towns may not levy any new or additional tax, exise, or license on sale, distribution, storage, consumption, or use of aviation fuel. (40-17-50). Wholesale dealers in illuminating, lubricating or fuel oils pay additional ½ of 1% of gross sales. (40-17-174). All motor carriers must pay excise tax on motor fuels used in their operations within this state at same rate imposed on fuels sold within state (40-17-141, et seq.), except liquefied petroleum gas used as fuel (40-17-160). Requirements as to licensing of distributors of motor fuels (40-12-190, et seq.) and reports required of carriers and warehousemen handling motor fuels (40-17-200—203). Privilege taxes are imposed on producers of oil and gas (40-20-1; 40-20-2). International Fuel Tax Agreement applies. (40-17-270, et seq.).

Liquefied Petroleum Gas Tax.—In lieu of excise tax on liquefied petroleum gas used to propel motor vehicles, annual fee levied on following using liquefied petroleum gas as fuel: (1) Passenger automobiles, pickup trucks under one ton, $75; (2) recreational vehicles and vans and trucks one ton or over but with rear axle carrying capacity less than 14,000 pounds, $85; (3) bobtail trucks, $150; (4) tractor/trailer units, $175. (40-17-160).

Motor Carriers Fuel Tax.—Motor carriers subject to tax in effect for fuels (40-17-141), allowing for setoff of fuel tax paid (40-17-142).

Special Fuels Tax.—Not applicable.

GENERATION SKIPPING TAX:

Tax on transfer of intangible personal property of transferor domiciled in state and tangible personal and real property which is located in state. Tax equal to full amount of state tax permissible as credit in computing federal generation skipping tax. (40-15A-1, et seq.).

GIFT TAX:

None.

INCOME TAX:

Income tax imposed on net income, in excess of exemptions, of: (a) Every individual resident of state, (b) every nonresident individual receiving taxable income from property located or business transacted in state, (c) every corporation, association or joint stock company domiciled in Alabama or licensed or qualified to transact business in Alabama, (d) every corporation, association or joint stock company doing business in Alabama or deriving income from sources located within Alabama, and (e) resident fiduciaries, estates and trusts (40-18-2). Natural persons domiciled, maintaining permanent abode within state, or spending more than seven months of tax year within state

presumed to be residents. (40-18-2). Certain organizations exempt, e.g., labor, agricultural or horticultural organizations, fraternal benefit societies, civic organizations, federal income taxation (40-18-32), certain charitable trusts, and trusts under pension or profit sharing plans for benefit of employees, etc. (40-18-25).

Interest on, or other income from, obligations of U.S. or its agencies or instrumentalities or of corporations organized under U.S. laws (40-18-4) and income of officers or agents of U.S. or its agencies or instrumentalities or its contractees (40-18-3) included in gross income for income tax purposes insofar as state may lawfully tax such income.

Returns.—Individuals (40-18-72) and fiduciaries must file returns Apr. 15 if on calendar year basis, or on 15th day of fourth month following close of fiscal year (40-18-29). Corporations must file returns Mar. 15 if on calendar year basis, or on 15th day of third month following close of fiscal year. (40-18-39). Any taxpayer's time to pay tax may be extended by department for no more than three months. (40-18-42). State returns may be inspected by federal or foreign state agents. (40-18-53).

Taxes Are Payable.—Individual's tax must be paid in full on filing return. (40-18-42). Debts to specified state agencies may be set off against refunds due. (40-18-102).

Individuals in Military and Public Health Services of U.S.—Income of officers or agents of U.S. or its agencies from U.S. or its agencies is subject to income tax levied by state as other income is taxed, except that compensation for act of service in combat zone is not subject to state taxation. (40-18-3).

Income Taxed—Individuals.—For individuals, net income defined (40-18-12) as gross income (40-18-14) less allowable deductions (40-18-15). Deductions for individuals include all taxes imposed by U.S. (40-18-15[a][3][a]), state, local and foreign occupational license taxes, state and local personal property taxes, and generation-skipping transfer taxes (40-18-15[a][3][b], [c], [d], [e]). Deductibility of certain taxes limited to extent to which taxes deductible for federal income tax purposes. (40-18-15[a][3][f]). Right of individual to deduct from gross income amount of federal income tax protected by state constitution. (Const. 225th Amendment). In lieu of itemized deductions allowed, individual taxpayer may deduct lessor of $2,000 or 20% of adjusted gross income plus amount of federal income tax and married persons filing jointly may deduct lesser of $4,000 or 20% of adjusted gross income plus amount of federal income tax. (40-18-15[b][1]). Consumer interest limitations and limitations on travel, entertainment and business meal expenses of Tax Reform Act of 1986 incorporated by reference. (40-18-15[a][2]). (See also Ala. Admin. Code, Revenue §810-3-1.1-.01, et seq. conforming Alabama's income tax regulations to Tax Reform Act of 1986 without corresponding statutory amendments.)

Rate.—Rates for single individuals, and heads of family and married persons filing separate returns, on net income in excess of exemptions, are 2% on first $500 or part thereof, 4% on next $2,500 or part thereof (excess over $500 up to $3,000), 5% on all excess over $3,000. (40-18-5. See also Const., 25th Amendment.) Rates for married persons filing joint return, on net income in excess of exemptions, are: 2% on first $1,000 or part thereof, 4% on next $5,000 or part thereof (excess over $1,000 up to $6,000), 5% on all excess over $6,000. (40-18-5; see also Const., 25th Amendment.)

Exemptions allowed are: Single individual or married person not living with spouse, $1,500; head of family, $3,000; husband and wife living together have single exemption of $3,000 which may be taken by either or divided between them; for each dependent other than spouse, receiving over half of support from taxpayer, $300. (40-18-19[a]). Dependent defined as person within certain degrees of kinship or affinity. (40-18-19[a]). By statute (40-18-19) validity of which has not been tested (Const., 25th Amendment) nonresident is only allowed such proportion of above exemptions as adjusted gross income from sources within state bears to entire adjusted gross income. Retirement allowances, pension, and annuities or optional allowances approved by Board of Control of Teachers' Retirement System of Alabama or Employees' Retirement System of Alabama; effective Jan. 1, 1991, all amounts paid to former police officers by police retirement system, and to firefighters by any firefighting agency and annuities from U.S. Government civil service retirement and disability fund exempt. (40-18-19). Compensation for active service as member of Armed Forces of U.S. in combat zone so designated by Executive Order of President exempt (40-18-3); effective Jan. 1, 1989, all payments made under any military retirement program (40-18-20[d]).

Tax Credits.—(1) Credit for Taxes Paid to Other States: Individual resident taxpayers, including corporations, allowed credit for taxes paid to other states, which cannot exceed amount due at Alabama rate on income with respect to which tax was levied by such other state (40-18-21); (2) Credit for Certain Development Projects: Credits allowed for certain development projects of predominately industrial, warehousing or research business activity (40-18-190, et seq.); (3) Credit for Coal Production: Credits allowed based upon annual tonnage of coal production (40-18-220); (4) Credit for Rural Physicians: Credits allowed for certain physicians recruited to practice and actually practicing in small or rural community (40-18-132).

Optional Tax Table.—Not applicable.

Nonresidents.—Every nonresident individual is taxed on income from property owned or business transacted in state. (40-18-2[6]).

Income Taxed—Corporations.—For corporations net income defined (40-18-33) as gross income (40-18-33) less allowable deductions (40-18-35). Deductions for corporations include all taxes imposed by U.S., except income taxes; and all taxes imposed by any state or territory or any taxing subdivision of any state or territory, except income taxes and taxes assessed for local benefits of kind tending to increase value of property assessed. (40-18-35). (See also Ala. Admin. Code, §810-3-1.1-.01, et seq. conforming Alabama's income tax regulations to Tax Reform Act of 1986 without corresponding statutory amendments.)

Withholding and Declarations.—Comprehensive withholding statute requires employers to withhold income tax on employees' wages (40-18-71), to remit such tax to state (40-18-74), and to furnish withholding statements to employees (40-18-75). Declarations of estimated tax, together with prescribed payments to complement any tax withheld from wages, must be made (i) by any single person, or married person filing separate return, whose net income from sources other than wages reasonably expected to exceed $1,500; and (ii) by any married couple filing jointly whose net income from sources other than wages reasonably expected to exceed $3,000. (40-18-82, 40-18-83). Declarations and payments of estimated tax must be made by corporations whose

See note at head of Digest as to 1998 legislation covered.

See Topical Index in front part of this volume.

INCOME TAX . . . *continued*
Alabama income tax liability reasonably expected to exceed $5,000. (40-18-82; 40-18-83.1).

Rate.—Domestic corporations, associations and joint stock companies pay 5% on entire net income. (40-18-31). Foreign corporations, associations and joint stock companies pay 5% on net income derived from property situated within or business transacted within this state. (40-18-31). Certain deductions allowed. (40-18-35).

MARIJUANA AND CONTROLLED SUBSTANCES TAX:

No dealer allowed to possess, distribute, sell, transport, import, transfer or otherwise use any marijuana or controlled substance upon which tax imposed unless tax paid as evidenced by stamp or other official indicia. (40-17A-4). Nothing in §40-17A-1, et seq., provides immunity for dealer from criminal prosecution. (40-17A-5). Tax imposed at following rates: (1) $3.50 on each gram or portion of gram of marijuana; and (2) $200 on each gram or portion of gram of controlled substance; or (3) $2,000 on each 50 dosage units of controlled substance not sold by weight, or portion thereof. (40-17A-5).

Penalty of 100% of tax in addition to amount of tax. In addition to penalty, dealer who fails to affix appropriate stamp, labels, or other indicia guilty of Class C felony. (40-17A-9).

MOTOR CARRIER FUEL TAX:

See topic Gasoline and Special Fuel Taxes.

MOTOR VEHICLE USAGE TAXES:

Excise tax imposed on storage, use or other consumption in this state of automotive vehicle or truck trailer, semitrailer, and mobile home set-up materials and supplies, purchased at retail on or after Oct. 1, 1965, for storage, use or other consumption in this state at rate of 2% of sales price or amount of tax collected by seller, whichever greater. (40-23-61[c]). Excise or use tax upon every person, firm or corporation purchasing outside state, other than at wholesale, any automotive vehicle, motor boat, truck trailer, trailer, semitrailer or travel trailer, required to be registered or licensed with judge of probate of any county in this state for use, storage, or other consumption within this state tax equal to 2% of purchase price. (40-23-102[a]).

POLLUTION ABATEMENT AUTHORITY TAX:

Excise tax of 4% of sales price per month on storage, use, or other consumption of electricity, domestic water, and natural gas. (40-21-102[a]). For total sales price of utility services of $40,000 or more, different rates are applied under §40-21-102.

PROPERTY (AD VALOREM) TAXES:

All real estate, with improvements thereon, and all personal property taxable to party last assessing same or to owner of record. (40-7-1).

Taxable Situs.—(1) Every piece, parcel, tract, or lot of land in this state, including therein all things pertaining to such land; (2) all steamboats, barges, vessels, and watercraft, however propelled, plying waters of this state in county wherein owner thereof resides; and if such vessel is owned by corporation then in county where principal office located; or if owner individual not residing in this state or being corporation with no prinicipal office in this state, then in county or counties where used; and all such steamboats, barges, vessels, or watercraft which have acquired permanent situs in this state; (3) all money hoarded, whether in custody of owner in this state or in another state or in any safety deposit box, safe vault or elsewhere, except money on deposit in banks; (4) all property including heavy duty equipment used for construction purposes brought into this state after Oct. 1 of any year shall be subject to taxation same as if it had been held or owned in this state on Oct. 1. If heavy duty equipment brought into this state after Oct. 1 it will be subject to taxation as if it had been held or owned in this state on Oct. 1; except that such tax shall be prorated with respect to number of months remaining in year. (40-11-1).

Exemptions from ad valorem taxation granted with respect to public property, property of religious, educational, charitable, etc., institutions used for such purposes and certain property of residents of state, frequently limited as to value. Lease for profit to entity using land for religious, educational, or charitable purposes does not entitle owner to ad valorem tax exemption. (601 So.2d 474). Following exemptions should be noted: U.S., Alabama, and Alabama county and municipal bonds; all cemeteries, school and religious property; mortgages on property within state on which recording tax has been paid; all security agreements and security interests under Commercial Code; money on deposit in any banking institution and other solvent credits (40-9-1[1]); raw materials, including coke produced during calendar year when stocked at any plant for manufacturing purposes in Alabama (40-9-1[13]); all manufactured articles, including pig iron, in hands of producer or manufacturer for 12 months after production or manufacture (40-9-1[14]); cotton, livestock, or agricultural products raised or grown in Alabama in hands of producer, his landlord or cooperative association (exempt for all time) or in hands of purchaser or manufacturer (exempt for one year) (40-9-1[9]); cotton, wherever grown, stored in any licensed warehouse in Alabama for period not exceeding 12 months (40-9-1[10]); warrants issued by city and county board of education for school purposes (40-9-1[1]); property owned by certain veterans organizations (40-9-1[4]); property of deaf mutes and insane persons ($3,000) and blind persons ($12,000) (40-9-1[7]); religious books kept for sale by ministers and colporteurs (40-9-1[6]); pollution control devices (40-9-1[20]); tobacco leaf stored in hogsheads (40-9-1[21]); various items of personal property owned by individuals usually kept in home (40-9-1[18]); aircraft and parts, components, ground support equipment used by air carrier operating hub within state (40-9-1[24]); all vessels and equipment thereon, used predominantly in business of commercial shrimping by owners thereof (40-9-1[26]); personal property in transit through state or in storage in public or private warehouse or other storage facility for shipment outside state (40-9-6); personal property manufactured, compounded or processed remaining property of manufacturer, compounder or processor and held by licensed public warehouse for distribution (40-9-7); property used exclusively in hospitals providing specific amounts of charitable treatment, or stock in corporation owning such hospital, but not to exceed $75,000 in either case (40-9-1[2], [3]); all property described in 12 U.S.C. 1701 (Q) (40-9-1[25]); property or literary and scientific institutions and societies (40-9-1[5]); family portraits (40-9-1[8]); farming provisions and supplies (40-9-1[11]); revenue from athletic stadiums owned by schools (40-9-1[12]); property owned by National Guard (40-9-1[15]); all poultry (40-9-1[16]); property of incompetent veterans ($3,000) (40-9-1[17]). Home of any veteran acquired pursuant to provisions of P.L. 702, 80th Congress, as am'd, exempt if owned and occupied by veteran or his unremarried widow. (40-9-20).

Homestead of resident of state, to extent of $4,000 in assessed value and 160 acres in area for owner not over age 65, and without limit for owner over age 65, retired due to total and permanent disability, without regard to age, or who are blind without regard to age or whether such person retired, is exempt from state ad valorem taxation. For tax years beginning on and after Oct. 1, 1981, homestead of resident of state, to extent of $2,000 or 160 acres for owner not over age of 65, exempt from county ad valorem taxes, except countywide and school district ad valorem taxes levied for school purposes, and homesteads of resident, to extent of $5,000 if owner over age 65 with annual adjusted gross income less than $12,000 in previous year, or retired due to total and permanent disability or blind without regard to age or whether person retired, in assessed value and 160 acres in area, exempt from county ad valorem taxation (40-9-19), provided claim for exemption is filed with tax assessor. Such claim need be made only once and may be verified each year thereafter by mail on form affidavit to be provided by tax assessor. (40-9-21.1).

Principal residence, and 160 acres adjacent thereto, if single-family residence owned and occupied by individuals totally disabled, or age 65 or older having net taxable income of $7,500 or less as shown on latest U.S. income tax return of individual and spouse, exempt from ad valorem taxation. (40-9-21). Once made, claim verified yearly by mail under 40-9-21.1.

Factories manufacturing calcium cyanamide (lime nitrogen), aluminum or aluminum products exempt from state, county and municipal taxation, except taxes on land, for ten years after beginning construction. (40-9-5).

Certain organizations exempt from all state, county and municipal taxes, licenses and fees. (40-9-9, et seq.).

State Tax Rates.—Property assessed for purpose of taxation according to following classifications: (1) Agricultural, forest, residential property, and historic buildings, 10%; (2) utilities, 30%; (3) private automobiles and motor trucks ("pickups") not used for hire, 15%; and (4) all other property, 20%. (Const., §217; 373d Amendment; 40-8-1[a]). Maximum rates of taxation on assessed value of taxable property are: For state 65/100 of 1% all of which is currently levied. (Const., §214; 40-8-2). Property and activities of U.S. and its agencies taxable as other property and activities to extent of state's constitutional power. (40-11-2).

Local Tax Rates.—Maximum rates of taxation on assessed value of taxable property for counties 75/100 of 1% plus special levy for school purposes of 9/10 of 1%, if voted, all of which, totaling 1.65%, currently levied by every county. (Const., §215, 3d, 111th and 202d Amendments). Certain counties given power to levy additional taxes for specified purposes. (See Const., e.g., 30th, 34th and 36th Amendments.) Municipalities may levy ad valorem tax of 1/2 of 1%, proceeds to be used for any purpose (Const., §216), and, if voted, additional ad valorem tax of 3/10 of 1% for school purposes (Const., 3d Amendment). Other constitutional provisions empower specified municipalities to levy other taxes for various purposes at rates varying up to additional 1%, so that in some municipalities, e.g., Birmingham, total rate for state, county and city taxes is 3.6%.

Assessment.—State, county and municipal ad valorem taxes are assessed as of Oct. 1 of tax year. (40-7-2). Each taxpayer or his agent must make return to tax assessor before Jan. 1 under penalty. (40-7-2). Assessor must assess all property not claimed on tax return by owner for which varying service fee and 10% penalty added to tax. (40-7-22, -25).

Omitted Property.—Notice of assessment of property not assessed within preceding five years must be given owner or his agent by registered or certified mail. (40-7-23).

Nonresident taxpayer, resident taxpayer subject to disabling infirmity or woman taxpayer may send in duly sworn list, or such list may be rendered by agent having knowledge of his or her taxable property. (40-7-7). Final assessment of ad valorem tax may be appealed to circuit court by taxpayer (40-7-45), and by state; conditions precedent to exercise of right and procedure to be followed depend on official or body making assessment (40-7-45; 40-3-25). Assessment on common areas must take into account value of all encumbrances on common areas. (659 So.2d 607). Initial assessment has no preclusive effect in future tax years. (668 So.2d 768).

Special rules govern and special procedure obtains in reference to assessment of taxes on tangible and intangible property of public utilities. (40-21-1, et seq.).

Municipal ad valorem taxes become due on Dec. 1 and delinquent on Jan. 1, but by ordinance municipal corporation may provide that such taxes become due Oct. 1 and delinquent Jan. 1. In either case they bear legal rate of interest after delinquency. (11-51-2).

Review of Assessment.—If taxpayer does not agree with preliminary assessment, he may appeal and request conference with operating division. (40-3-24).

Real Property and Personal Property.—Taxpayer may appeal final assessment of ad valorem taxes on real or personal property by filing notice in writing with officer, board or commission of intent to appeal and bond of $100 (40-7-46) and by appealing to appropriate Circuit Court (40-7-45).

Payment.—All taxes due must be remitted to Department of Revenue, with any checks made payable to Treasurer. (40-1-5). Payment deemed made as of date of U.S. Postmark if delivered by U.S. Mail. (40-1-45). Commissioner may enter into written agreements with taxpayers for installment payments. (40-2A-4).

Collection.—Collected by tax collector and authorized deputies. (40-5-2). State and county taxes are due and payable Oct. 1 of each year and become delinquent on Jan. 1 following (40-11-4) except that taxes become due and payable at once when taxpayer about to move from county or to dispose of all assets (40-11-4, 40-7-43, 40-5-17, 40-5-31, 40-5-32). All delinquent taxes bear interest at same rate established by U.S. Treasury pursuant to 26 U.S.C. §6621 (40-1-44), except ad valorem taxes, which bear

See note at head of Digest as to 1998 legislation covered.

See Topical Index in front part of this volume.

AL – 51

PROPERTY (AD VALOREM) TAXES . . . *continued*
interest at 12% per annum (40-5-9), and delinquent taxpayer must, in addition, pay certain demand fees (40-5-6).

Lien.—Arises in favor of state if any person liable to pay any tax, other than ad valorem taxes, neglects or refuses to pay tax. (40-1-2). Lien arises when property becomes assessable and continues until taxes paid. (40-1-3).

Sale.—No property exempt from levy and sale for payment of taxes, fees and charges lawfully incurred in making assessment and collection against owner thereof. (40-5-18). Tax collector must give ten days notice of time and place of sale by placing same at three or more public places. Sale made at public outcry to highest bidder for cash. Collector allowed $5 fee. (40-5-14).

Tax collector required to sell personalty (40-5-14), including corporate shares (40-5-16), and may garnish choses in action (40-5-20; -22), before selling delinquent taxpayer's realty (40-5-19).

Probate court of each county may order sale of lands therein for default in payment of taxes. (40-10-1).

Tax collector must enter, in book provided for that purpose, each parcel of real estate, or interest therein, assessed to any person against whom taxes have been assessed which are not paid; and all real estate or interest therein which has been assessed against unknown owner. (40-10-2). Book must be delivered to judge of probate by Mar. 1 (40-10-3), and he must issue notice to each person against whom unpaid taxes are assessed; notice may be given by publication in certain instances (40-10-4; 40-10-5). Hearing thereupon held in which said tax book is prima facie evidence of amount of taxes and fees due. (40-10-9). Court, after such hearing, may proceed to decree sale of land in satisfaction of taxes due. (40-10-8; 40-10-11, et seq.). Tax collector, on 30 days notice by publication, must proceed to sell real estate ordered to be sold immediately at end of term of court in which such decree was rendered. (40-10-12).

Redemption.—Real estate sold for taxes or purchased by state may be redeemed at any time before title passes from state, or if purchased by any other purchaser, may be redeemed at any time within three years from date of sale by owner, his heirs, or personal representatives, or by any mortgagee or purchaser of such lands, or any part thereof, or by any person having interest therein, or in any part thereof, legal or equitable, in severalty or as tenant in common, including judgment creditor, or other creditor having lien thereon, or on any part thereof. Infant or insane person entitled to redeem at any time before expiration of three years from sale, may redeem at any time within one year after removal of disability. (40-10-120). One who seeks to redeem under mortgage or other instrument creating lien which was duly recorded at time of tax sale may redeem at any time within one year from date of written notice from purchaser of his purchase of said land at tax sale served on either original mortgagee or lien holder or his transferee of record or his heirs, personal representatives or assigns. (40-10-73, 40-10-74). To redeem land sold to state, redemptioner must deposit with judge of probate of county in which land situated amount for which land was sold with interest at 12% per annum, together with amount of all taxes due on such land from date of sale, including any municipal taxes not assessed during period of state ownership, with interest thereon at 12% per annum and all costs and fees due to officers. (40-10-121). To redeem land sold to one other than state, redemptioner must deposit with probate judge of county where land lies amount for which land was sold, together with amount of taxes theretofore paid upon such land by purchaser with interest at rate of 12% per annum from date of sale on all such amounts, plus taxes then due on property and all costs and fees due to officers because of sale and redemption. (40-10-122).

When distinct parcels of land have been included in one assessment and sold for taxes under one decree, any person, including owner, whose interest in one or more of such parcels is such as to entitle him to redeem, may redeem parcels of land in which he has such interest without redeeming remainder; owner must, however, first pay all personal property assessments together with court costs and advertising fees. (40-10-123; cf. 40-10-120).

Public Service Corporation Property Tax.—Department of Revenue has duty to assess for taxation property of all public service or public utilities corporations and owner, president, general manager, agent, trustee, receiver or other person or persons having control of company's affairs in this state must make returns of all property of company located in state with Department of Revenue. (40-21-1).

Valuation and Assessment.—No specific statutory provision.

Review of Assessment (by Revenue Cabinet).—No specific statutory provision.

Reports.—No specific statutory provision.

Local Taxes.—No specific statutory provision.

PROVIDER TAX:

Privilege tax imposed on business activities of every provider of pharmaceutical services to Alabama citizens, except for pharmacy serving hospital in-patient or owned and operated by State of Alabama, at rate of 10¢ for each prescription with retail price of $3 or more. (40-26B-2). Tax due on or before 20th day of following month after tax accrues. (40-26B-3). Every pharmaceutical provider should also file statement showing total number of prescriptions filled at retail price of $3 or more by provider for previous month and taxes due along with payment of tax. (40-26B-4[a]). When tax due does not exceed $10 for any month, quarterly return and remittance allowed. (40-26B-4[a]). Penalty for nonpayment 10% of amount of tax due, together with interest in addition to tax amount. (40-26B-4[b]).

Privilege or license tax levied against every provider of cellular radio telecommunication services doing business in State of Alabama. (40-21-121[a]). Rate is 4% against gross sales or receipts from monthly charges for cellular services, or at rate set forth in §40-21-82(b). Tax added to charge for services and collected from purchaser. (40-21-121[b]). Following excluded from gross sales or receipts of cellular provider: (1) Furnishing of cellular services which State of Alabama prohibited from taxing; (2) furnishing of cellular services which are otherwise taxed under §§40-23-1 through 40-23-36; and (3) wholesale sales. (40-21-122).

RACE TRACKS:

Privilege tax of 1% of pari-mutuel pool on all pari-mutuel races imposed upon all dog race track operators in Alabama. (40-26A-2[a]). In addition, privilege tax of 1% of pari-mutuel pool on all pari-mutuel races requiring selection of three or more racers imposed on every dog race track operator. (40-26A-2[b]). Statement showing pari-mutuel pool gross receipts of race track operation for next preceding month, must be submitted, in addition to amount of taxes due, to Department of Revenue on or before 20th of each month. (40-26A-3). Any person who fails to make any report shall be guilty of Class B misdemeanor. (40-26A-5).

REAL ESTATE CONVEYANCE TAX:

Deed tax imposed at rate of 50¢ for first $500 or less of value, and 50¢ for each $500 or fraction thereof of excess. Tax applies only to value in excess of any mortgage or vendor's lien on property on which mortgage tax paid. (40-22-1).

All deeds, bills of sale and like instruments conveying title subject to recording tax of 50¢ for $500 or less of property conveyed and 50¢ for every additional $500 of property or fraction thereof. That part of value of property covered by mortgage or other security interest and upon which mortgage recording tax paid exempt from tax. (40-22-1). All mortgages, deeds of trust, contracts of conditional sale and like instruments to secure payment of debt, including security agreements and financing statements under Uniform Commercial Code, if required to be filed with judge of probate, subject to recording tax of 15¢ for first $100 or less of indebtedness and 15¢ for each additional $100 or fraction thereof. Tax does not apply to security agreements or financing statements relating solely to accounts, contract rights or general intangibles, as defined in Uniform Commercial Code. Tax imposed only on initial indebtedness at time of filing, and no tax imposed upon subsequent advances against collateral covered by financing statement provided secured indebtedness remains unchanged in amount and time of maturity. Alternatively, instruments securing open end or revolving indebtedness with any interest in residential property may be taxed based upon maximum principal indebtedness as stated in instrument or any amendment thereto, irrespective of cumulative amount advanced from time to time. With respect to real property, tax at time of filing payable only on amount of initial indebtedness, but owner of instrument must execute bond to secure payment to state of tax which may become due upon indebtedness to be incurred thereafter. If any part of property described in mortgage or like instrument located outside Ala., indebtedness upon which tax must be paid is that proportion of indebtedness secured by instrument which value of property located in this state bears to whole property. (40-22-2).

Corporations and associations created under Federal Farm Loan Act as amended by Farm Credit Act of 1933, corporations or associations engaged exclusively in making farm or crop loans not subject to tax with respect to instrument to secure loan to one of its stockholders or members for agricultural purposes. (40-22-5). Conveyances for purpose of division or merger of religious organizations exempt from recording taxes. (40-22-5).

SALES AND USE TAXES:

Sales Tax.—In addition to all other taxes and licenses, imposed as follows: (1) 4% of gross proceeds of all sales, leases and rentals made by any person, firm or corporation in business of selling, leasing or renting at retail any tangible personal property, except stocks and bonds, and sales of materials for painting, repairing or reconditioning water-going crafts of over five tons load displacement. (40-23-2[1]). Municipal privilege license flat tax passed on to consumer excluded from gross proceeds. (40-23-3). When both retail and wholesale business conducted, tax must be paid at retail rate on all gross proceeds unless segregated accounts of each type of transaction are kept. (40-23-2). (2) 4% of gross receipts received by any person, firm or corporation in business of conducting any amusement places, billiard and pool rooms, bowling alleys, amusement and musical devices, theaters, opera houses, moving picture shows, vaudevilles, amusement parks, athletic contests, including wrestling and prize fights, boxing and wrestling exhibitions, football and baseball games, skating rinks, race tracks, golf courses, public bathing, and public dancing halls. (40-23-2[2]). (3) 1½% of gross proceeds of all sales of machines used in mining, quarrying, compounding, processing and manufacturing of tangible personal property and attachments, parts and replacements therefor necessary to operation of such machines and customarily so used, upon every person, firm or corporation engaged in business of selling at retail such machines and attachments, parts and replacements therefor. (40-23-2[3]). (4) 2% of gross proceeds of all sales of automotive vehicles, truck trailers, semitrailers, or house trailers, or mobile home set-up materials and supplies, upon every person, firm or corporation in state engaged in business of selling at retail such vehicles. Where used vehicles taken in trade as part payment on sale of new or used vehicles, tax paid on net difference. (40-23-2[4]). 2% of purchase price of sale of any automotive vehicles, motorboats, truck trailers, semitrailers, and travel trailers required to be registered or licensed with judge of probate of any county and purchased other than at wholesale from any person, firm, or corporation not licensed dealer engaged in selling same. (40-23-101[a]). (5) 1½% of gross proceeds of all sales of agricultural machines or equipment and parts and attachments necessary to operation of such equipment, upon every person, firm or corporation engaged in business of selling at retail such equipment. When any used agricultural equipment taken in trade as part payment on sale of new or used equipment, tax paid only on net difference. (40-23-37). (6) 3% of gross proceeds of all sales through coin operated dispensing machines of food and food products for human consumption, not including beverages other than coffee, milk, milk products and substitutes therefor. (40-23-2[5]).

4% tax added to sales price as follows: 4¢ for each whole dollar or sales price, and on that part of sales price which is fractional part of dollar, in addition to whole dollar, and on sales of less than dollar no tax collected on 1¢ to and including 10¢; 1¢ on sales from 11¢ to and including 30¢; 2¢ on sales from 31¢ to and including 54¢; 3¢ on sales from 55¢ to and including 73¢; and 4¢ on sales from 74¢ to and including 99¢. Taxes levied at rate of less than 4% are added to sale price in amount equal to prescribed percentage of such sales price. (40-23-26).

Use Tax.—Imposes excise tax, at same rates provided in sales tax act. Generally, Alabama use tax levied on personal property purchased outside state and later brought

See note at head of Digest as to 1998 legislation covered.

See Topical Index in front part of this volume.

SALES AND USE TAXES . . . *continued*
into state for storage, use, or consumption. (40-23-61). Credit on use tax allowed for sales and use taxes paid to other states on property brought into Alabama, provided credit allowed by other states for taxes paid on similar property in Alabama. (40-23-65).

Utilities Gross Receipts.—Privilege or license tax levied against every utility furnishing electricity, domestic water or natural gas in State of Alabama. (40-21-82[a]). Amount of tax based upon application of rates against amount of monthly gross sales or receipts from furnishing of such services. (40-21-82[a]). Separate tax rate structure applies to every utility furnishing telegraph or telephone services in state. (40-21-82[b]). Certain entities exempt from tax (40-21-82.1); and also certain revenues excluded from gross receipts or sales of utility (40-21-83).

Exemptions from Sales and Use Taxes.—Certain specified transactions, businesses, and organizations exempt from sales tax. (40-23-4, 40-23-4.1, 40-23-4.2, 40-23-5). Storage, use or consumption of certain tangible personal property exempt from use tax. (40-23-62; see also 40-23-5).

Returns.—Taxes levied payable on 20th of each month succeeding month in which accrued (40-23-7), but taxes payable on account of credit sales may be deferred until collections made (40-23-8). Taxpayer whose average monthly sales tax liability was $1,000 or greater must make estimated tax payments on 20th day of month in which liability incurred, equal to lesser of 66⅔% of tax payable for same month in prior year or 66⅔% of current month's estimated liability. When total tax does not exceed $10 per month, quarterly return and payment may be made. Returns must be made, and tax paid, to Department of Revenue. (40-23-7). Tax must be collected before vehicle can be registered or licensed. (40-23-104). For use tax, returns must be made, and tax paid, quarterly to Department of Revenue on 20th day of each month succeeding quarter for which tax accrues. (40-23-68).

Penalty for failure to keep records or make reports fine of $25 to $500 (40-23-11), or $50 to $500 and/or up to six months imprisonment for willful refusal to keep records or make reports (40-23-12). In addition to other penalties, willful failure to pay tax, file return or supply information is misdemeanor punishable by fine of not more than $25,000, or $100,000 for corporation, or imprisonment for not more than one year, or both, plus costs of prosecution. (40-29-112). For use tax, fine up to $500 for failure to make payment, and fine of $300 to $5,000 and/or imprisonment up to one year for fraudulent evasion. (40-23-88).

SPECIAL FUELS TAX:

See topic Gasoline and Special Fuels Tax.

STAMP TAX:

None except for stamps on tobacco. (40-25-3; -6).

UNEMPLOYMENT COMPENSATION TAX:

For purposes of providing unemployment benefits, there is imposed on all employers (except those engaged in certain specified employments) who employ one or more persons in 20 or more weeks in year, tax of 2.7% of total wages payable or paid, not in excess of $8,000 per annum to any individual. Actual rate determined according to experience rating. For years beginning on or after Jan. 1, 1991, maximum contribution rate based on experience rating ranges from 5.4% to 6.8% depending on financial condition of unemployment trust fund. (25-4-8, 25-4-16, 25-4-50, 25-4-54).

Delinquent payments bear 1% interest per month (25-4-132), plus penalty of 10% of tax due, or if failure to pay due to fraud, additional penalty of 15% charged (24-4-133).

UNIFORM FEDERAL LIEN REGISTRATION ACT AMENDED:

Not adopted. Adopted Alabama Uniform Federal Lien Registration Act at §§35-11-42 through 35-11-48.

USE TAX:

See topic Sales and Use Taxes.

TRANSPORTATION

MOTOR VEHICLES:

Director of Department of Public Safety, Montgomery, Ala. 36104 responsible for administering and enforcing all laws relating to operation or movement of vehicles on public highways. (32-2-1-5). Uniform Motor Vehicle Safety-Responsibility Act adopted. (32-7-1 et seq.). Uniform Motor Vehicle Certificate of Title and Anti-Theft Act adopted. (32-8-1 et seq.).

Vehicle license required annually (40-12-240-271); not issued until ad valorem taxes on vehicle paid (40-12-253). Ten-day grace period may be granted. (40-12-264). License tags must be displayed on rear. (32-6-51). Where vehicle stored in state and not used or operated between Oct. 1st and Mar. 31st following, one-half license fee plus $1 due. (40-12-258). Person registering commercial vehicle must state under oath name, address and whether vehicle owned by resident or nonresident. (40-12-263). Commercial drivers subject to Alabama Uniform Commercial Driver License Act. (32-6-49.1 et seq.). Passenger vehicles owned and operated by active members of Ala. national guard, active members of state guard when organized in lieu of national guard, service-connected disabled veterans, and officer, warrant officer, or enlisted person serving as active member of U.S. armed forces reserve organization or service-connected disabled veteran who were residents of Alabama at time of entering service and still Alabama residents, or owned by civil air patrol exempt from license tax and registration fee. (31-2-12; 40-12-244).

Any person whose driver's license issued in this or another state or whose driving privilege as nonresident has been canceled, denied, suspended or revoked as provided in this article and who drives any motor vehicle upon highways of this state while his or her license or privilege is canceled, denied, suspended or revoked shall be guilty of misdemeanor. Penalties will be imposed. (32-6-19).

Operator's license required every four years (32-6-1); not issued to person under 16 years old or any person whose driving privilege suspended or revoked or to habitual drunkard or addicted to use of narcotic drugs or person considered physically or mentally unable to exercise reasonable and ordinary control over motor vehicle. (32-6-7). Also not issued to person under 19 not in school, not graduated from high school who does not present acceptable documentation for not being in school. (16-28-40). Issued by Director of Public Safety after application to judge of probate. (32-6-4).

No special provisions exempting members of Armed Forces from operator's license requirements. However, members thereof will generally be covered by one of following exemptions: employee of federal government exempt while driving official government vehicle on official business; nonresident at least 16 years old and has on his person valid driver's license issued in his home state or county. (32-6-2).

Titles.—Owner of motor vehicle designated 1975 year model or later or mobile home or travel trailer designated 1990 year model or later required to be registered under motor vehicle laws and for which no certificate of title has been issued by Department of Revenue must make application to judge of probate, Commissioner of Licenses, Director of Revenue or other county official authorized and required by law to issue motor vehicle license tages for certificate of title. (32-8-30). If mobile home affixed to parcel of real property and ownership of mobile home and property identical, owner may obtain cancellation of title. (32-8-30[c]). Dealer of vehicles required to be titled who does not comply with requirements guilty of misdemeanor and, upon conviction, fined sum not exceeding $500. (32-8-30[e]). No certificate of title required for: Vehicle owned by agency thereof; vehicle owned by manufacturer or dealer and held for sale; vehicle owned by nonresident and not required by law to be registered; vehicle regularly engaged in interstate transportation for which currrently effective certificate of title issued in another state; vehicle moved solely by animal power; implement of husbandry; special mobile equipment; pole trailer; mobile homes; travel trailers; and mobile trailers designated 1989 year models and prior year models. (32-8-31).

Sales.—Dealer in used motor vehicles who is nonresident, or who does not have permanent place of business in state, and person who brings used motor vehicle into state for purposes of sale or resale, except as trade-in, must, within ten days from date of bringing used motor vehicle into state, register motor vehicle with probate judge of county in which used motor vehicle is brought, and must execute bond payable to probate judge for use or benefit of purchaser for losses due to fraud. Bond must be in full amount of sales price of used vehicle, not to exceed $1,000. (32-16-2). Motor vehicle manufacturers, distributors, dealers, and their representatives, and dealings between manufacturers and distributors and wholesalers and dealers, extensively regulated. (8-20-1 et seq.).

Handicapped drivers may have distinctive placards, license plates, or tags. (32-6-231, 40-12-300).

Liens.—Security interest in vehicle perfected by delivery to Department of Revenue of existing certificate of title, if any, application for certificate of title containing name and address of lienholder and date of security agreement and required fee. Perfected as of time of creation if delivery completed within 20 days thereafter, otherwise, as of time of delivery. (32-8-61).

If owner creates security interest in vehicle, owner must immediately execute application in space provided on certificate of title, or on separate form prescribed by Department of Revenue to named lienholder on certificate showing name and address of lienholder and date of security agreement, and cause certificate, application and required fee to be delivered to lienholder. Lienholder must immediately cause certificate, application and required fee to be mailed or delivered to Department of Revenue. (32-8-62).

Above procedures for security interests do not apply to or affect: Lien given by statute or rule of law to supplier of services or materials for vehicle; lien given by statute to U.S., state or political subdivision of state; security interests in vehicle traded by manufacturer or dealer who holds vehicle for sale, but buyer in ordinary course of trade from manufacturer or dealer takes title free of security interest. (32-8-60).

Person acquiring vehicle under legal proceedings or repossession under authority of conditional sales contract, security agreement, mortgage, or other lien, must file, within ten days, with probate judge or other official authorized by law to issue vehicle license tags in county of owner's residence, if owner is individual, or in county of vehicle's use, if owner is firm, corporation, or association, copy of court order or memorandum of sale, signed by auctioneer or other person selling vehicle, along with report of change in ownership, on forms provided by State Department of Revenue and order or memorandum shall be properly noted on duplicate license and retained in office of probate judge or other officer. (40-12-260[d]). Filing fee, $1. (40-12-261). Transferee who fails to report change of ownership within ten days of change penalized $1.50. (40-12-260[e]).

Operation prohibited by person under influence of alcohol or controlled substances (32-5A-191), or by person without license (32-6-1).

Size and Weight Limits.—Regulated by 32-9-20.

Permits for Overweight and Oversize Vehicles.—Director of Highway Department may, at his discretion, upon application and for good cause being shown therefore, issue special permits for operation and movement of overweight or oversize vehicle or combination of no more than two vehicles over public highways. (32-9-29[a]). Director of Department of Transportation may issue annual permit to operate vehicle which exceeds maximum limits otherwise provided for in article for rubber-tired equipment used solely in scope and operation of mining refractory grade bauxite. (32-9-29[b]).

Equipment Required.—Regulated by 32-5-210, et seq. Seat belts must be worn by each front seat occupant of passenger car. (32-5B-4).

Lights Required.—Regulated by 32-5-240. Permissible other lighting is specified (32-5-241), and Highway Director may set up standard specifications, approve lighting and prohibit sale of substandard lighting apparatus (32-5-252).

Abandoned vehicles are governed by 32-13-1, et seq. Person who has abandoned motor vehicle on his or her property, under certain conditions, must provide notice to persons with lawful interest in abandoned motor vehicle. (32-13-3).

Accidents.—Driver must stop, make himself known, render assistance to any person injured, and report injury or death to local police. (32-10-1-12).

See note at head of Digest as to 1998 legislation covered.

See Topical Index in front part of this volume.

AL – 53

MOTOR VEHICLES . . . *continued*

Liability of Owner.—Generally not liable for negligence of bailee or borrower while operating car, unless owner knew or should have known of incompetence. (220 Ala. 101, 123 So. 897; 470 So.2d 1141).

Guests.—Owner or operator not liable for injury to or death of gratuitous guest unless guilty of willful or wanton misconduct. (32-1-2).

Proof of Financial Responsibility.—Uniform Motor Vehicle Safety-Responsibility Act adopted. (32-7-1-42).

Insurance not required. Liability insurance issued must provide for payment to insured of damages which he may be legally entitled to recover from owner or operator of uninsured motor vehicle. Insured can reject such coverage. (32-7-23). Coverage for uninsured motorist must be rejected in writing by named insured personally. (292 Ala. 103, 289 So.2d 606).

Clauses reducing insured's recovery where other uninsured motorist coverage available to cover portion of damages void. (286 Ala. 606, 243 So.2d 736). Insurer not permitted to setoff workmen's compensation payments against recovery on uninsured motorist coverage so long as total recovery of insured does not exceed his damages. (287 Ala. 462, 252 So.2d 619).

No-Fault Insurance not adopted.

Foreign Vehicles.—Private car of nonresident, duly registered in home state and displaying license plates required by law of home state, may operate without license or registration for 30 days from date of entering state. Department of Revenue may make reciprocal agreements with other states for exchange of rights and privileges. (40-12-262).

Vehicles registered under International Registration Plan governed by §§40-12-262(b)-(g).

Nonresident Operators.—Nonresident at least 16 years old, who has immediate possession of driver's license issued in home state or country is exempt from license requirements; nonresident of like age whose home state or country does not require driver's license exempt for not more than 90 days in calendar year, if vehicle duly registered in home state or country. (32-6-2).

Actions Against Nonresidents.—Action against nonresident, except foreign corporation licensed to do business in state having designated agent residing in state to receive process, arising out of operation of vehicle in state or against resident driver or resident owner of motor vehicle involved in highway accident, who is absent from state at time process issues (ARCP 4.2[a]), may be commenced by having clerk place copy of process and complaint or document to be served in envelope addressed to person to be served at last known address with instructions to forward. Envelope to be sent by certified mail with return receipt requested. (ARCP 4.2[b][1][A]). If return receipt shows failure of delivery, service is complete when serving party files affidavit with clerk setting forth facts indicating reasonable diligence utilized to ascertain whereabouts of party to be served (ARCP 4.2[b][1][C]) and service made by publication (ARCP 4.3).

Direct Actions.—Action by injured person against insurer not allowed. Judgment creditor who recovers from insured in personal injury action, however, may proceed against insurance company to recover judgment. (27-23-2).

Motor Vehicle Carriers.—Intrastate operation of common and contract carriers by motor vehicles is regulated in detail by Alabama Motor Carrier Act of 1939 (37-3-1, et seq.), and by Alabama Air Commerce Act of 1945 (37-9-1, et seq.) and under general supervision and control of Alabama Public Service Commission (37-9-2-7). Common carriers must obtain certificates of convenience and necessity, and contract carriers must obtain permits. (37-9-16; 37-3-10-13).

No person may operate commercial motor vehicle in this state, or fail to maintain required records or reports, in violation of Federal Motor Carrier Safety Regulations as prescribed by U.S. Department of Transportation. Foregoing act specifically repealed §22-30-15.1 of Code of Alabama in 1975, but did not repeal or supersede any other laws relating to operation of motor vehicles. Penalties will be imposed for violation of foregoing act.

Mileage tax levied on every motor vehicle transporting passengers within state. (40-19-1 et seq.).

Rates vary according to rated carrying capacity as follows: 9 to 16 passengers, $1/4$¢ per mile; 17 to 21 passengers, $1/2$¢ per mile; 22 to 25 passengers, $3/4$¢ per mile; over 25 passengers, 1¢ per mile. (40-19-3). Tax increased by 50% for carriers not paying Alabama annual license tax. (40-19-3).

Every motor carrier must file sworn returns with Department of Revenue by 15th day of each month, and payment of tax must accompany return. (40-19-4).

Fee on Vehicles Using Liquefied Petroleum Gas as Fuel.—In lieu of excise tax on liquefied petroleum gas used to propel motor vehicles, annual fee levied on following using liquefied petroleum gas as fuel: (1) Passenger automobiles, pickup trucks under one ton, $75; (2) recreational vehicles and vans and trucks one ton or over but with rear axle carrying capacity less than 14,000 pounds, $85; (3) bobtail trucks, $150; (4) tractor/trailer units, $175. (40-17-160).

Privilege License Tax on Vehicles for Hire Transporting Property.—Based on "gross vehicle weight," which means empty weight of truck or truck-tractor, plus heaviest load to be carried, and, in case of combinations, empty weight of heaviest trailer with which power unit can be placed in combination plus heaviest load to be carried. Rates vary according to "base amount" and "additional amount" weight schedules. (40-12-248). Trucks operated to transport farm products, to transport forest products from point of severance to sawmill, papermill, or concentration yard, or operated exclusively within state and also within 15 miles of corporate limits of municipality where customarily domiciled, taxed at special rates. (40-12-248).

Gasoline Tax.—See category Taxation, topic Gasoline and Special Fuels Taxes.

Odometer alteration prohibited.

Inspection.—None of personal vehicles.

Traffic Regulations.—Set out in 32-5A-1 et seq.

Lemon Law.—See category Business Regulation and Commerce, topic Consumer Protection.

RAILROADS:

See category Business Regulation and Commerce, topic Carriers.

COMMERCIAL CODE FORMS

See also categories Business Regulation and Commerce, topic Commercial Code; Mortgages, topic Chattel Mortgages.

Financing Statement.—Preferred format is printed Form UCC-1 sized 8" × 10" with original and four carbons. Typewritten facsimiles will be accepted.

Three copies are sent to filing officer, who returns one copy as an acknowledgment.

Form

STATE OF ALABAMA—UNIFORM COMMERCIAL CODE—FINANCING STATEMENT

FORM UCC-1 ALA.

__Important: Read Instructions on Back Before Filling out Form.__

☐ The Debtor is a transmitting utility as defined in ALA Code 7-9-105(n)	No. of Additional Sheets Presented:	This FINANCING STATEMENT is presented to a Filing Officer for filing pursuant to the Uniform Commercial Code.

1. Return copy or recorded original to:

THIS SPACE FOR USE OF FILING OFFICER
Date, Time, Number & Filing Office

Pre-paid Acct. # _____

2. Name and Address of Debtor   (Last Name First if a Person)

Social Security/Tax ID # _____

2A. Name and Address of Debtor   (IF ANY)   (Last Name First if a Person)

Social Security/Tax ID # _____

☐ Additional debtors on attached UCC-E

FILED WITH:

3. NAME AND ADDRESS OF SECURED PARTY (Last Name First if a Person)

4. ASSIGNEE OF SECURED PARTY   (IF ANY)   (Last Name First if a Person)

Social Security/Tax ID # _____

☐ Additional secured parties on attached UCC-E

5. The Financing Statement Covers the Following Types (or items) of Property:

5A. Enter Code(s) From Back of Form That Best Describes The Collateral Covered By This Filing:

___ ___   ___ ___
___ ___   ___ ___
___ ___   ___ ___
___ ___   ___ ___
___ ___   ___ ___
___ ___   ___ ___

Check X if covered: ☐ Products of Collateral are also covered.

6. This statement is filed without the debtor's signature to perfect a security interest in collateral (check X, if so)

☐ already subject to a security interest in another jurisdiction when it was brought into this state.

☐ already subject to a security interest in another jurisdiction when debtor's location changed to this state.

☐ which is proceeds of the original collateral described above in which a security interest is prefected.

☐ acquired after a change of name, identity or corporate structure of debtor.

☐ as to which the filing has lapsed.

7. Complete only when filing with the Judge of Probate:
The initial indebtedness secured by this financing statement is $_____

Mortgage tax due (15¢ per $100.00 or fraction thereof) $_____

8. ☐ This financing statement covers timber to be cut, crops, or fixtures and is to be cross indexed in the real estate mortgage records (Describe real estate and if debtor does not have an interest of record, give name of record owner in Box 5)

Signature(s) of Secured Party(ies)
(Required only if filed without debtor's Signature—see Box 6)

Signature(s) of Debtor(s)

Signature(s) of Secured Party(ies) or Assignee

Signature(s) of Debtor(s)

Signature(s) of Secured Party(ies) or Assignee

Type Name of Individual or Business

Type Name of Individual or Business

(1) FILING OFFICER COPY—ALPHABETICAL   (3) FILING OFFICER COPY—ACKNOWLEDGEMENT
(2) FILING OFFICER COPY—NUMERICAL   (4) FILE COPY—SECURED PARTY(IES)   (5) FILE COPY DEBTOR(S)

STANDARD FORM—UNIFORM COMMERCIAL CODE—FORM UCC-1
Approved by The Secretary of State of Alabama

See note at head of Digest as to 1998 legislation covered.

See Topical Index in front part of this volume.

INSTRUCTIONS—UCC-1

1. Please type this form in black. Do not write in Filing Office space.
2. If the space provided for any item(s) on this form is inadequate, the item(s) should be continued on an additional sheet(s), preferably the UCC-E EXTENSION FORM, but you may use any 5" × 8" or 8" × 10" sheet. Three copies of such additional sheets should be presented to the filing officer with a set of at least three copies of the UCC-1 financing form.
3. Each debtor box should contain only one name and address. The UCC-E should be used for any additional debtors or debtor addresses.
4. The filing fee for the UCC-1 form is $10.00 with one debtor and one debtor address and $1.00 for each additional debtor or debtor address. If the UCC-E form is used for additional sheets, there is no charge for the sheet itself but there is a $1.00 per page charge for any other additional sheets. Please state at top of form the number of additional sheets presented.
5. If the debtor is a UTILITY as defined in ALA CODE 7-9-105(n), check box 1.
6. If this is an original filing for a security interest that has been assigned, you may type the name and address of the assignee in box 4 at no additional charge.
7. The financing statement must be signed by the debtor unless one of the reasons in block 6 applies. The secured party must sign if you check one of the boxes in block 6.
8. If collateral is timber to be cut, crops, or fixtures and is to be cross indexed in the real estate mortgage records, check box 8 and describe real estate and if debtor does not have an interest of record, give name of record owner in box 5.
9. Please choose the collateral code(s) below that best describe(s) the collateral set out in block 5 and enter one or more in block 5A.

000—ACCOUNTS
    001—ACCOUNTS RECEIVABLE
100—CHATTEL PAPER
    101—INSTRUMENTS
    102—LEASES
    103—SECURITY AGREEMENTS
200—CONTRACT RIGHTS
300—EQUIPMENT
    301—FARM
    302—FURNITURE
    303—HEAVY
400—FARM PRODUCTS
    401—CROPS
    402—LIVESTOCK

500—FIXTURED
600—GOODS
    601—AUTOMOBILES
    602—MOBILE HOMES
700—INTANGIBLES
800—INVENTORY
    801—APPLIANCES
    802—AUTOMOBILES
    803—FURNITURE
    804—MOBILE HOMES
900—SECURITIES
    901—BONDS
    902—STOCKS

THESE CODES ARE NOT TO BE USED AS LEGAL DESCRIPTION. They are only for sorting purposes and you may use the first code under each section that is applicable or define it further by using a code under that section that more closely describes the collateral.

Example: If inventory is the collateral you may use "800" or if this inventory is mobile homes you may choose to use "804" instead.

See note at head of Digest as to 1998 legislation covered.

See Topical Index in front part of this volume.

Statements of Continuation, Release, Assignment, or Termination.—Preferred format is printed Form UCC-3 sized 8" × 10" with original and four carbons. Typewritten facsimiles will be accepted. Three copies are sent to filing officer, who returns one copy as an acknowledgement.

STATE OF ALABAMA
UNIFORM COMMERCIAL CODE
STATEMENTS OF CONTINUATION, PARTIAL RELEASE, ASSIGNMENT, ETC.—FORM UCC-3

Important: Read Instructions on Back Before Filling out Form.

☐ The Debtor is a transmitting utility as defined in ALA Code 7-9-105(n)	No. of Additional Sheets Presented:	This FINANCING STATEMENT is presented to a Filing Officer for filing pursuant to the Uniform Commercial Code.

1. Return copy or recorded original to	THIS SPACE FOR USE OF FILING OFFICER Date, Time, Number & Filing Office
Pre-paid Acct. # _____	
2. Name and Address of Debtor (Last Name First if a Person)	
Social Security/Tax ID # _____	
2A. Name and Address of Debtor (IF ANY) (Last Name First if a Person)	
Social Security/Tax ID # _____	
☐ Additional debtors on attached UCC-E	FILED WITH:

3. NAME AND ADDRESS OF SECURED PARTY (Last Name First if a Person)	4. ASSIGNEE OF SECURED PARTY (IF ANY) (Last Name First if a Person)
Social Security/Tax ID # _____	
☐ Additional secured parties on attached UCC-E	
5. ☐ This statement refers to original Financing Statement bearing File No. _____	
Filed with _____	Date Filed _____, 19__

6. ☐ Continuation.   The original financing statement between the foregoing Debtor and Secured Party, bearing file number shown above, is still effective.

7. ☐ Termination.   Secured Party no longer claims a security interest under the financing statement bearing the file number shown above.

8. ☐ Partial or   The Secured Party's right under the financing statement bearing file number shown above to the property described in item 11 or to all of the
   ☐ Full   property listed on this file, is assigned to the assignee whose name and address appears in item 4.
   Assignment.

9. ☐ Amendment.   Financing statement bearing file number shown above is amended as set forth in item 11.

10. ☐ Partial Release.   Secured Party releases the collateral described in item 11 from the financing statement bearing the file number shown above.

11.

11A. Enter Code(s) From Back of Form That Best Describes The Collateral Covered By This Filing:

— — —   — — —
— — —   — — —
— — —   — — —
— — —   — — —
— — —   — — —

Check X if covered: ☐ Products of Collateral are also covered.

Signature(s) of Debtor(s)	Signature(s) of Secured Party(ies)
Signature(s) of Debtor(s) (necessary only if item 9 is applicable)	Signature(s) of Secured Party(ies)
Type Name of Individual or Business	Type Name of Individual or Business

(1) FILING OFFICER COPY—ALPHABETICAL   (3) FILING OFFICER COPY—ACKNOWLEDGEMENT   STANDARD FORM—UNIFORM COMMERCIAL CODE—FORM UCC-3
(2) FILING OFFICER COPY—NUMERICAL   (4) FILE COPY—SECURED PARTY(IES)   Approved by The Secretary of State of
    (5) FILE COPY DEBTOR(S)   Alabama

See note at head of Digest as to 1998 legislation covered.

See Topical Index in front part of this volume.

INSTRUCTIONS—UCC-3

1. Please type this form in black. Do not write in Filing Office space.
2. If the space provided for any item(s) on this form is inadequate, the item(s) should be continued on an additional sheet(s), preferably the UCC-E EXTENSION FORM, but you may use any 5" × 8" or 8" × 10" sheet. Three copies of such additional sheets should be presented to the filing officer with a set of at least three copies of the UCC-3 form.
3. The debtor box should contain only one name and address. The UCC-E should be used for any additional debtors or debtor addresses.
4. The filing fee for the UCC-3 form is $10.00 for continuations and $5.00 for all other filings with one debtor and one debtor address and $1.00 for each additional debtor or debtor address. If the UCC-E form is used for additional sheets, there is no charge for the sheet itself but there is a $1.00 per page charge for any other additional sheets. Please state at top of form the number of additional sheets presented.
5. If the debtor is a UTILITY as defined in ALA CODE 7-9-105(n), check box at top of form.
6. This form should be used for continuation, assignment, partial release, amendment, and/or termination. Select and check the appropriate purpose(s) on the form, boxes 6-10.
7. This form must be signed by the secured party of record at the time of filing and also by the debtor, if item 9 is applicable.
8. Please choose the collateral code(s) below that best describe(s) the collateral set out in block 11 and enter one or more in block 11A.

000—ACCOUNTS	500—FIXTURES
001—ACCOUNTS RECEIVABLE	600—GOODS
100—CHATTEL PAPER	601—AUTOMOBILES
101—INSTRUMENTS	602—MOBILE HOMES
102—LEASES	700—INTANGIBLES
103—SECURITY AGREEMENTS	800—INVENTORY
200—CONTRACT RIGHTS	801—APPLIANCES
300—EQUIPMENT	802—AUTOMOBILES
301—FARM	803—FURNITURE
302—FURNITURE	804—MOBILE HOMES
303—HEAVY	900—SECURITIES
400—FARM PRODUCTS	901—BONDS
401—CROPS	902—STOCKS
402—LIVESTOCK	

THESE CODES ARE NOT TO BE USED AS LEGAL DESCRIPTION. They are only for sorting purposes and you may use the first code under each section that is applicable or define it further by using a code under that section that more closely describes the collateral.

Example: If inventory is the collateral you may use "800" or if this inventory is mobile homes you may choose to use "804" instead.

ALASKA LAW DIGEST REVISER

Robertson, Monagle & Eastaugh, P.C.
1400 West Benson Boulevard, Suite 315
Anchorage, Alaska 99503
Telephone: 907-277-6693
Fax: 907-279-1959

Juneau, Alaska Office: Goldbelt Place Office Building, 801 West 10th Street, Suite 300, Juneau, Alaska 99801. Telephone: 907-586-3340. Fax: 907-586-6818.

Reviser Profile

A History of the Firm: This is the oldest continuously practicing law firm in the state, having been founded in 1909 by Royal Arch Gunnison in Juneau. Mr. Gunnison was joined in 1912 by R.E. "Bob" Robertson. The firm from its earliest days had a statewide practice, and was deeply involved in almost all important economic activities in the region and throughout the state. The firm represented about half of the early salmon canners. It represented miners of gold and many other minerals. Its clients included airlines which pioneered air service to the state, shippers, and other early businessmen. The firm incorporated a major pulp processing company and has represented many interests in the timber industry since its very early days. It was involved in the formation of early insurance companies, and more recently formed the first reciprocal insurer in the state. It has represented municipalities for several decades.

The firm has, in the natural course of its life, been deeply involved in the communities in which it practiced, as well as the affairs of the state. Bob Robertson was a delegate to the State Constitutional Convention. Fred Eastaugh served as City Attorney for Juneau, Wrangell and Skagway, as member of local, state and federal planning commissions, in the State Legislature, as a municipal judge, and in many other public and eleemosynary roles. Four members of the firm have been governors of the state bar association, including its first President, Mike Monagle; two have been Commissioners of Uniform State Laws; four have been or are Fellows of the American Bar Foundation. Others have served on a municipal assembly, state and federal bar committees, and a wide range of civic groups.

The firm takes great pride in the history of accomplishments of its members, and strength from the tradition of leadership.

The Firm Today: Robertson, Monagle & Eastaugh has offices in Juneau and in Anchorage, as well as in Washington, D.C. It engages in a wide practice, but limits its work to what its members and staff are most experienced and accomplished at doing.

A significant proportion of the work of the firm is in civil litigation. We represent air carriers and their insurers; manufacturers and distributors of products; those accused of professional negligence, including design professionals, attorneys, stockbrokers and real estate brokers; and a wide range of commercial litigants. The firm also does a significant amount of condemnation and workers compensation litigation.

Another large part of the work of the firm is devoted to commercial practice, including advising developers. Tax and estate planning and representation before the IRS and other agencies, and representation of both debtors and creditors in commercial bankruptcies are also important.

We continue to be very much involved in the natural resources and environmental issues of our state, representing important segments of the timber industry, as well as many of Alaska's largest mining concerns. This representation includes business advice, regulatory representation, environmental litigation, and legislative and regulatory lobbying.

We have particular expertise in insurance, including experience in liability defense, coverage issues, bad Faith claims, ERISA issues, regulatory representation, and lobbying for the major casualty property insurer trade association and major life companies.

Our Washington, D.C. and Virginia offices facilitate and strengthen our representation of natural resources companies, regulated industries, and others before the Congress and federal agencies, and litigate in the state and Federal courts.

The firm continues to build carefully on past accomplishments, and looks forward to serving the people of Alaska and those doing business here for decades to come.

ALASKA LAW DIGEST

(The following is a list of all Categories and Topics, including cross-references, covered in this Digest.)

ALASKA LAW DIGEST

Revised for 1999 edition by

ROBERTSON, MONAGLE & EASTAUGH, A Professional Corporation, of the Alaska Bar.

(Citations unless otherwise noted are to Alaska Statutes [AS], with 1997 revisions. Rules of Civil Procedure are cited: Civ. R.P., Rule of Criminal Procedure: Crim. R.P.)

Note: This revision covers 1998 Session Laws through June 1998.

Uniform Probate Code and 1975 Official Amendments adopted. See category Estates and Trusts, topic Wills.

INTRODUCTION

GOVERNMENT AND LEGAL SYSTEM:

The State of Alaska is a constituent state of the United States of America. For further discussion of the U.S. federal system, see Introduction to the Federal Government of the United States at the beginning of this volume. A great many laws are promulgated by the federal government of the United States and are not reflected in the topics below. See the Introduction to this volume for references to the federal law topics covered.

Like all but one of the United States, Alaska has a common law legal system, with roots in English common law. For information on the courts and legislature of Alaska, see category Courts and Legislature.

HOLIDAYS:

Legal holidays, in addition to Sundays, are: Jan. 1; 3d Mon. in Jan. (Martin Luther King, Jr. Day); 3d Mon. in Feb. (Presidents' Day); last Mon. in Mar. (Seward's Day); last Mon. in May (Memorial Day); July 4; 1st Mon. in Sept. (Labor Day); Oct. 18 (Alaska Day); Nov. 11 (Veteran's Day); 4th Thurs. in Nov. (Thanksgiving Day); Dec. 25; every Sun.; any day designated by President or Governor as legal holiday. (44.12.010). When holiday falls on Sat., preceding Fri. is also holiday. (44.12.025). When holiday falls on Sun., following Mon. is also holiday. (44.12.020).

OFFICE HOURS AND TIME ZONE:

Alaska is in the Alaska (GMT −09:00) time zone. Office hours are generally from 8 a.m. to 5 p.m.

BUSINESS ORGANIZATIONS

AGENCY:

No statute. Common law rules apply.

Husband and Wife.—A husband or wife may appoint either his or her attorney in fact, to control or dispose of his or her property, and may revoke same to same extent and manner as other persons. (25.15.040).

ASSOCIATIONS:

Cooperatives may be organized as corporations. See topic Corporations.

Cemetery association authorized. (10.30.010-.155). Association may be formed by not less than five persons. Record of organizational meeting to be filed with recorder and clerk of superior court. Not less than three trustees to be elected to have perpetual succession and power to contract and prosecute and defend actions. Cemetery not exceeding 80 acres exempt from execution and appropriation to public purposes. Exempt from taxation if nonprofit.

Professional Corporations.—See topic Corporations, subhead Professional Corporations.

CORPORATIONS:

Alaska Corporations Code effective July 1, 1989. (10.06).

Purposes.—Corporations may be organized for any lawful purpose except insurance. (10.06.005).

Name.—Must contain word "corporation", "company", "incorporated", or "limited" or abbreviation of above. Must not be deceptively similar to another corporation name. Must not contain word "city", "borough" or "village" or otherwise imply it is municipality. (10.06.105). Corporate name may be reserved for 120 days by filing application with commissioner if it is available. (10.06.110-115). Reserved name can be transferred by filing notice of transfer with commissioner, signed by holder of name and specifying name and address of transferee. (10.06.120).

Terms of Existence.—Perpetual unless limited by Articles of Incorporation. (10.06.010).

Incorporators.—One or more natural persons at least 18 years of age. (10.06.205).

Articles of Incorporation.—Shall set out: (1) name of corporation; (2) purpose(s); (3) address of initial registered office and name of initial registered agent; (4) name and address of each alien affiliate or statement that there are not alien affiliates; (5) if authorized to issue only one class of shares; (6) if corporation authorized to issue more than one class of shares, or if class of shares is to have two or more series, (a) total number of shares of each class authorized to issue, and total number of shares of each series that corporation is authorized to issue or of which board is authorized to fix number of shares, (b) designation of each class or series or board may determine designation of any series, (c) privileges, rights, preferences and restrictions imposed on respective classes or series, (d) if board authorized to fix number of shares of series, whether board may increase or decrease those shares. (10.06.208). May set out: (1) power to levy assessments upon shares or class of shares, (2) removing shareholders preemptive rights to subscribe to any or all issues of shares or securities; (3) special

qualifications of shareholders; (4) limit on duration of corporations existence to specified date; (5) restriction or elimination of power to adopt, amend, or repeal provisions of bylaws; (6) requirement of larger percentage of vote; (7) limit or restrict business of corporations or powers of corporation; (8) to allow holder of evidence of indebtedness right to vote; (9) right of shareholders to determine consideration for which shares shall be issued; (10) requirements of approval of shareholders of outstanding shares for corporate action; (11) that one or more classes or series are redeemable; (12) confer or impose powers of directors upon delegates; (13) elimination or limitation of personal liability of director for breach of fiduciary duty, but not (a) breach of loyalty, (b) acts not in good faith or intentional misconduct or knowing violation, (c) wilful or negligent conduct in payment of dividends or repurchase of stock, (d) transaction resulting in improper personal benefit; (14) reasonable restrictions on transfer; (15) names and addresses of persons appointed to act as initial directors; (16) any other provision not in conflict for management of business and conduct of its affairs (10.06.210).

Filing of Articles.—Original and exact copy of articles of incorporation shall be delivered to commissioner. (10.06.213). Also include separate statement of codes under 10.06.870 which most closely describe activities in which corporation will initially engage. (10.06.215).

Incorporation and Filing Fee.—Filing fee is fixed by regulation without reference to amount of authorized shares. (10.06.828).

License to do Business.—Corporate existence begins on issuance of certificate of incorporation. Certificate is conclusive evidence that corporation has been incorporated. Doctrines of de jure compliance, de facto corporations and corporations by estoppel are abolished. (10.06.218).

Organizational Meeting.—After issuance of certificate, either incorporators or board shall meet at call of majority of incorporators or directors for purpose of electing directors, officers and/or other business with 20 days notice by mail to each incorporator or director. (10.06.223). If directors are not named in articles, then incorporators may do whatever necessary to perfect organization. (10.06.225).

Paid in Capital Requirements.—None.

Amendment of Articles.—Permitted amendments: Corporation may amend provisions that would be lawful to file originally including, but not limited to (1) change its corporate name; (2) duration; (3) change limitation upon its corporate purpose; (4) increase or decrease number of shares it is authorized to issue; (5) exchange, classify, reclassify or cancel all or part of its shares whether issued or not; (6) change designation; preferences, limitations, and relative rights of shares; (7) create new classes or shares; (8) otherwise change shares and shares' rights. Corporation may not amend its articles of incorporation to change original names and addresses of first directors or initial agent. (10.06.502).

Procedure to Amend Articles.—(1) If shares have not been issued, board shall adopt resolution or board and shareholders shall approve amendment if shares have been issued. Board may delete names and addresses of initial directors and/or registered agent, enlarge whole shares of only class outstanding, without approval by shares. (10.06.504).

Bylaws.—Unless in Articles, bylaws shall state number of directors. Number of directors cannot be amended or changed to less than five if more than 16⅔% of outstanding shares vote against it. (10.06.230). Bylaws may contain any lawful provision for management not in conflict with Articles including but not limited to: (1) provision referred to in 10.06. 210(2), (3), or (4); (2) proxies; (3) qualifications, duties, compensation, election of directors and requirements of quorum; (4) appointment, duties, compensation, tenure of officers; (5) appointment, duties, compensation of committees of board. (10.06.230). Bylaws required to be available for inspection by shareholders at principal executive office in this state. (10.06.233).

Stock.—If authorized by Articles, corporation may issue one or more classes or series of stock or both (10.06.305), preferred or special classes of stock (10.06.308), shares in series (10.16.310).

Stock Certificates.—Shall state corporation is organized under laws of state, name of person to whom issued, number and class of shares, designation of series that certificate represents. If corporation authorized to issue shares of more than one class, then shall state that upon request and without charge corporation will furnish statement of designations, preferences, limitations and relative rights of each class and series, if applicable. (10.06.350). Shares may be issued without certificate if information required on certificates sent to shareholder in writing. (10.06.349).

Issuance of Stock.—Board shall set dollar price for shares unless Articles reserve that right to shareholders. (10.06.335). Share may not be issued until fully paid. (10.06.353). Payment may be made in money, property, tangible or intangible, or in labor or services actually performed by corporation. Promissory note or future service does not constitute payment. (10.06.338).

Transfer of Stock.—To fix records for determining shareholders entitled to notice or vote at meeting of shareholders or adjournment of meetings or shareholders entitled to receive dividend or any other proper purpose, transfer books closed for no more than 70 days. If books closed to determine shareholders entitled to notice of or vote at

See note at head of Digest as to 1998 legislation covered.

See Topical Index in front part of this volume.

AK – 1

CORPORATIONS . . . *continued*

meeting of shareholders, closed for at least 20 days immediately preceding meeting. Bylaws or board may fix date as record date no more than 60 days, and in case of meeting of shareholders, not less than 20 days before date. (10.06.408).

Uniform Simplification of Fiduciary Security Transfers Act.—Not adopted.

Uniform Commercial Code.—Adopted. (45.01.101-45.09.507).

Stockholders.—Unless provided otherwise in Articles, majority of shares entitled to vote constitutes quorum; however, quorum may never be less than one-third of shares entitled to vote. Once quorum established business may be transacted even if thereafter quorum not present. (10.06.415).

Stockholders Actions.—Shareholder may bring action in right of corporation. Costs may be awarded if plaintiff successful. (10.06.435).

Liability of Shareholders.—No liability other than payment of full consideration for shares. (10.06.438).

Shareholders' Meetings.—Written notice stating place, day and hour of meeting (if special meeting, purpose must be given) shall be delivered not less than 20 or more than 60 days before meeting to each record shareholder. (10.06.410). Proxies allowed but expires after 11 months unless irrevocable proxy. Proxy revoked by writing delivered to corporation, by subsequent proxy, or by attending and voting in person. Dates contained on proxy forms determinative of order of execution. Proxy not revoked by death or incapacity unless written notice received by corporation prior to count of votes. Proxy that states irrevocable is irrevocable for time specified if certain conditions met. (10.06.418). Cumulative voting allowed. (10.06.420). Action may be taken without meeting upon written consent of all shareholders entitled to vote unless prohibited by articles or bylaws. (10.06.423).

Voting Trusts.—Allowed by entering into written agreement specifying terms and agreements, depositing copy of agreement at corporation's registered office and transferring shares to trustee(s). Cannot exceed ten years. (10.06.425).

Directors.—Board shall consist of more than one person. If number of directors not set, number is three. (10.06.453). If board consists of three or more members, articles may provide that directors be elected as two or three classes with terms staggered. (10.06.455). Vacancies filled by majority of directors unless otherwise provided. (10.06.465). Need not be resident of state or shareholder. (10.06.450).

Director's Meetings.—Chairman, president, vice-president, secretary or director may call meeting inside or outside of state. No notice needed for regular meeting set in bylaws, special meeting required notice is ten days for written notice, 72 hours for person to person communication and disclosure of business and purpose. Director waives notice by signing waiver before or after meeting or attends meeting without protesting before meeting or at its commencement. (10.06.470). Majority of directors fixed by corporation is quorum unless larger number fixed. (10.06.473). Meeting may be conducted by conference telephones or similar communications. No meeting necessary upon identical written consents by all directors. (10.06.475).

Powers and Duties of Directors.—Set forth in 10.06.450.

Liabilities of Directors.—Set forth in 10.06.480.

Indemnification of Directors and Officers.—May be indemnified by corporation if acted in good faith and in manner person reasonably believed to be in or not opposed to best interests of corporation and with criminal proceeding, had no reasonable cause to believe conduct unlawful. (10.06.490).

Officers.—Shall have president, secretary, treasurer chosen by board and who serve at pleasure of board. Any two or more offices may be held by same person except offices of president and secretary. (10.06.483).

Resident Agent.—Corporation shall continuously maintain in this state registered agent and registered office. Registered agent may either be individual resident of state or domestic or foreign corporation authorized to transact business in state who has as their business office same as registered office. (10.06.150). To change registered office or agent corporation must file verified statement. Explained in detail in 10.06.165.

General Powers of Corporations.—10.06.015 discards defense of ultra virus with certain exceptions.

Dividend.—Distribution of dividends to corporation shareholders is not allowed if as result of distribution corporation would be likely to be unable to meet its liabilities as they mature. (10.06.360). See generally 10.06.360-10.06.385.

Unclaimed Dividends.—See category Property, topic Absentees, subhead Escheat.

Sale or Transfer of Corporate Assets.—In order to sell financially all of property and assets of corporation sale shall be recommended to shareholders by resolution approved by board and submitted to vote of shareholders. (10.06.568).

Books and Records.—Corporation organized under this chapter shall keep correct and complete books and records of account, minutes of proceedings of its shareholders, board and committees of board, and record of its shareholders, containing names and addresses of all shareholders and number and class of shares held by each. These books and records shall be written or capable of being converted into written form within reasonable time. (10.06.430). These records shall be reasonably available for inspection and copying at registered office or principal place of business in state by shareholder of corporation. Shareholder inspection shall be upon written demand, stating with reasonable particularity purpose of inspection. (10.06.430).

Reports.—Domestic corporation and foreign corporation authorized to transact business in state shall file biennial report. (10.06.805). Biennial report is due by Jan. 2 of filing year. (10.06.811). Contents of biennial report are set out in 10.06.808. In event of change in officer, director or alien affiliate of corporation during first year of biennial reporting period or change in a 5% of shareholder before Sept. 30th of first year of biennial reporting period, corporation shall file notice of change amending biennial report of corporation before following Jan. 2nd. (10.06.813). Penalty for failure to file biennial report is penalty of 10% of amount of corporation tax assessed against it for period beginning Jan. 1st of year for which report should have been filed. (10.06.815).

Merger and Consolidation.—Two or more domestic corporations may merge into one of such corporations under plan of merger approved in manner provided in 10.06.530—10.06.582. Resolution of board of each corporation shall be proposed setting out names of corporations and name of surviving corporation into which they propose to merge; terms and conditions of proposed merger; manner and basis of converting shares of each merging corporation into shares or other securities or obligations of surviving corporation; statement of changes in articles of incorporation of surviving corporation caused by merger; and other provisions of merger considered necessary or desirable. (10.06.532). Same procedure should be carried out for consolidation of corporations. (10.06.534 and 10.06.536). Plan is approved if it receives affirmative vote of at least two-thirds of outstanding shares of each corporation. Each outstanding share of each corporation may vote on proposed plan whether or not share has voting rights under articles of corporation. (10.06.146). 10.06.574 to 10.06.582 set out rights and procedures for dissenting shareholders. Two or more cooperatives may merge or consolidate pursuant to plan of merger or consolidation adopted in manner provided in 10.15.405 to 10.15.415. These four filing articles of incorporation, application for certificate of authority, amendatory articles, or other application with department are set forth in regulations.

Share Exchanges or Acquisitions.—All of issued or outstanding shares of one or more classes of domestic corporation may be acquired through exchange of all of issued or outstanding shares of class or classes by another domestic or foreign corporation under plan of exchange approved in manner provided in 10.06.530 to 10.06.582. (10.06.538).

Dissolution.—See 10.06.605 through 10.06.678. Dissolution may be voluntary or involuntary. If corporation has been completely wound up without court proceedings majority of directors in office shall sign and verify articles of dissolution as set out in 10.06.620. Original and exact copy of articles of dissolution shall be delivered to commissioner and for issuance of certificate of dissolution. (10.06.623). Upon issuance of certificate of dissolution existence of corporation ceases. (10.06.625). Grounds for involuntary dissolution by commissioner are set out in 10.06.633. After all of known debts and liabilities of corporation has been paid or adequately provided for, board shall distribute all remaining corporate assets among shareholders according to their respective rights and preferences and, if there are no shareholders, to persons entitled to assets. (10.06.665). 10.06.673 provides for plan of distribution.

Foreign Corporations.—To transact business in state foreign corporation must be issued certificate of authority by commissioner. Foreign corporation that transacts business in state without certificate of authority is liable to state for years or portions of years during which it transacts business in state without certificate of authority and in amount equal to all fees and corporation taxes that would have been imposed if it had received certificate of authority. Additionally, all penalties imposed by this chapter for failing to pay fees and corporation taxes plus penalty of up to $10,000 per calendar year would also be imposed. (10.06.710). Foreign corporation transacting business in this state without certificate of authority may not maintain action suit or proceeding in court of this state until it obtains certificate of authority. (10.06.713). However, failure of foreign corporation to obtain certificate of authority to transact business in this state does not impair validity of contract or act of corporation and does not prevent corporation from defending action suit or proceeding in court of this state. (10.06.715). 10.06.718 sets forth activities not constituting transacting business in this state. Application for certificate of authority must set out name of corporation and assumed name if any, and state or country under whose laws it is incorporated; date of incorporation and period of duration of corporation; address of principal office of corporation in state or country under whose laws it is incorporated; address of proposed registered office of corporation in this state and name of its proposed registered agent in this state at that address; purpose corporation proposes to pursue and transaction of business in this state; names and addresses of directors and officers of corporation; statement of aggregate number of shares that corporation may issue, itemized by classes, par value of shares, shares without par value, and series, if any, within class; statement of aggregate number of issued shares itemized by classes, par value of shares, shares without par value, and series, if any, within class; statement expressed in dollars of amount of stated capital of corporation; estimate expressed in dollars of (a) value of all property to be owned by corporation for following year; (b) value of property of corporation to be located in state during following year; (c) gross amount of all business that will be transacted by corporation during following year; (d) gross amount of business that will be transacted by corporation at or from places of business in state during following year; additional information necessary or appropriate to enable commissioner to determine whether corporation is entitled to certificate of authority and to determine and assess fees and taxes that are payable; names and address of each alien affiliate, percentage of outstanding shares controlled by each alien affiliate and specific description of nature of relationship between foreign corporation and its alien affiliate. Or statement that there are no alien affiliates; name and address of each person owning at least 5% of shares or 5% of any class of shares and percentage of shares or class of shares owned by that person. (10.06.730). 10.06.740 provides that foreign corporation that has received certificate of authority enjoys same but no greater rights and privileges as domestic corporation organized for purposes set out in application under which security of authority is issued and is subject to duties, restrictions, penalties and liabilities now or hereafter imposed up domestic corporation of like character.

Taxation of Corporate Property.—See category Taxation, topic Corporate Property Tax.

Professional Corporations.—10.45.240 provides that professional corporations enjoy powers and privileges and are subject to duties, restrictions and liabilities of other corporations. Professional corporation means corporation organized under this chapter to render professional service. Professional person means person licensed to render professional service. Professional service means type of highly skilled, technical and specialized personal service rendered to public by persons licensed by state. (10.45.500). 10.45 is Alaska Professional Corporation Act.

Deeds.—See category Property, topic Deeds.

See note at head of Digest as to 1998 legislation covered.

See Topical Index in front part of this volume.

CORPORATIONS . . . *continued*

Model Nonprofit Corporation Act.—Alaska has not adopted. Alaska Nonprofit Corporation Act is contained in 10.20.

JOINT STOCK COMPANIES:

No statute. See topics Associations, Corporations.

LIMITED LIABILITY COMPANIES:

Purpose.—Limited liability companies may be organized for any lawful purpose. (10.50.010).

Name.—Must contain words "limited liability company" or abbreviation "LLC," or "L.L.C." Must not contain "city", "borough", or "village" or otherwise imply that company is municipality. (10.50.020).

Articles of Organization.—Shall set out: (1) name of company; (2) purpose; (3) mailing address of registered office and registered agent; (4) terms of existence; and (5) if applicable, whether company will be managed by manager. (10.50.075).

Filing of Articles.—Signed articles must be delivered to Department for filing. (10.50.070).

Registered Office and Registered Agent.—Company shall continuously maintain registered agent and office in this state. Registered agent may either be individual resident of state or domestic or foreign corporation authorized to transact business in state who has as their business office same as registered office. (10.50.055).

Management.—Company may be managed by its members or manager. If managed by manager, manager has exclusive power to manage to extent of operating agreement. (10.50.110).

Dissolution.—Company dissolved if (1) event occurs which operating agreement identifies as causing dissolution; (2) written consent of all members; and (3) court enters decree for judicial dissolution. (10.50.400).

PARTNERSHIPS:

Uniform Partnership (32.05.430-380) and Limited Partnership (32.10.280) acts adopted.

BUSINESS REGULATION AND COMMERCE

BANKS AND BANKING:

Regulated by Department of Commerce. Title 6. Alaska Statutes.

Banking Code (06.05.005) and subsequent amendments covers definitions, effect on existing banks, establishment and duties of Department of Commerce and Economic Development, banking practices, trust business, reserves, loans, investments, etc., bank collections, organization and corporate functions of banks, liquidation, dissolution and reorganization, prohibited practices, sanctions. Alaska Savings Association Act repealed. (06.30.915). Mutual Savings Bank Act. (06.15.010-.370).

Liability of Directors and Officers.—Issuing officer, director, executive or managing officer of state bank who knowingly or with gross negligence permits loans or overdrafts in unsound manner or in violation of law or policies is personally liable for all such loans or overdrafts. (06.05.215).

Uniform Commercial Code enacted. (45.01.101). Uniform Commercial Code—Bank Deposits and Collections 45.04.101; collections 45.04.301—.303.

Deposits.—Deposits made on behalf of minor or person with disability when paid to such minor on check or order, such payment is valid in all respects. (06.05.100). Joint deposits and deposits in trust allowed. (13.31.020). Express right of survivorship cannot be changed by will. (13.31.020[e]). Sums on deposit at death of party to joint account belong to surviving party. (13.33.212).

Foreign Banks.—Model Foreign Banks Loan Act adopted. (06.10).

Unclaimed Deposits.—See category Property, topic Absentees, subhead Escheat.

Uniform Common Trust Fund Act adopted. (06.35).

BILLS AND NOTES:

Uniform Commercial Code in effect. (45.01.101). Criminal and civil penalties are provided for issuing insufficient funds checks. (11.46.280 and 09.65.115).

See topic Commercial Code.

Judgment Notes.—Not in use.

Attorney Fees.—Reasonable provisions for costs of collection and attorney fee clauses enforceable, otherwise determined by court under Rules of Civil Procedure.

Negotiable Instruments.—Uniform Commercial Code 45.03.101-805.

See also topic Consumer Protection.

BILLS OF LADING:

See topic Carriers.

BILLS OF SALE:

See topic Sales.

BLUE SKY LAW:

See topic Securities.

BROKERS:

Uniform Commercial Code adopted. (45.01.101).

Money, bill, note and stock brokers must have annual Alaska Business License, initial fee $25. (43.70.030). Insurance agents and brokers must have annual license.

See also topics Securities, Commercial Code; category Insurance, topic Insurance Companies.

Real Estate Brokers.—Licenses granted by examining board. (08.88.071). Licensing requirements: 08.88.171.

BULK SALES:

See topic Commercial Code; category Debtor and Creditor, topic Fraudulent Sales and Conveyances.

CARRIERS:

Liens allowed upon personal property for just and reasonable charges. (34.35.220). May sell property to cover charges three months after performance. (34.35.225).

Pipelines regulated by Alaska Pipeline Commission. (42.06).

Uniform Commercial Code adopted. (45.01.101).

See topics Licenses, Business and Professional, Commercial Code; category Debtor and Creditor, topic Liens.

COMMERCIAL CODE:

Uniform Commercial Code 1958 Official Text adopted, effective midnight, Dec. 31, 1962. (45.01.101). Recommended amendments included in 1962 Official Text not adopted. Local variations from 1962 Official Text, in addition to those noted above are found in §§2-106—section added relating to door-to-door sales (09.02.106[e]), 2-201(1)—sales of boats and vessels included, 2-316—section added excluding sale of human blood, blood plasma, or other human tissue from implied warranties of merchantability and fitness, 2-318—alternative A adopted, 2-326—art works on exhibit or consignment sale not subject to claims of art dealer's creditors, 2-329—additional section relating to door-to-door sales (45.05.125), 3-121—alternative A adopted, 4-106—optional language not adopted, 4-109—not adopted, 4-202—optional language adopted, 4-212—optional subsection adopted, 5-112—optional language adopted, 5-114—optional subsections adopted, 6-104—list and schedule to be filed in office of recorder in which any part of goods is located, 6-106—optional section adopted, optional subsection (4) not adopted, 6-107—optional subsection (2)(e) adopted, 6-108—optional subsection (3)(c) adopted, 6-109—optional subsection (2) adopted, 7-204—subsection (4) omitted, 7-210—subsection (2)(f), "three conspicuous places" substituted for "six conspicuous places", 7-403—subsection (1)(b) optional language omitted, 8-320—completely reworded (45.08.320), 9-102—deletes "Section 9-103 on multiple state transactions" and substitutes "apply", 9-104—in paragraph (a), inserts "such as Ship Mortgage Act, 1920" following "any statute of the United States." Adds final paragraph "to loans by pawnbrokers which do not exceed $200." (45.09.104[13]), 9-105—reference to "account" in subsection (2) is to 45.09.204 (Alaska statutory equivalent of Section 9-204), 9-203—subsection (4) reads: "A transaction, although subject to AS 45.09.101-45.09.507, may also be subject to other statutes dealing with loans and retail installment sales, and in the case of conflict between AS 45.09.101-45.09.507, and other statutes, the provisions of the other statutes control. Failure to comply with an applicable statute has only the effect which is specified in it." 9-302—subsection (3)(b) statutory reference is to AS 28.10, 9-306—omits flush language from subsection (3), 9-401—second alternative enacted; blank filled in paragraph (a) by "recorder;" bracketed material reads "Department of Natural Resources." In subsection (1)(a), substitute "recording district" for "county." In subsection (5), substitute "Department of Natural Resources" for "Secretary of State.", 9-402—in subsection (3), item 3 in the form reads: "If the collateral is goods which are to become fixtures, timber to be cut, or minerals or the like (including oil and gas) or accounts to be financed at the wellhead or minehead of the well or mine: (Describe real estate) . . . . and this financing statement is to be filed for record in the real estate records. (If the debtor does not have an interest of record) The name of a record owner is . . . ." Subsection (4) reads: "A financing statement may be amended by filing a writing signed by both the debtor and the secured party. An amendment does not extend the period of effectiveness of a financing statement. The term 'financing statement' as used in 45.09.101-45.09.507 means the original financing statement and amendments, but if an amendment adds collateral, it is effective as to the added collateral only from the filing date of the amendment." In subsection (6)(d), omits "duly." 9-403—sub-section (5) reads: "The uniform fee for filing and indexing and for stamping a copy furnished by the secured party to show the date and place of filing for an original financing statement or for a continuation statement is as prescribed by the Department of Natural Resources. In addition, the Department of Natural Resources may establish extra uniform fees for (1) statements not in the standard form prescribed by the department; (2) statements subject to the provisions of 45.09.402(f); (3) each name more than one required to be indexed; and (4) the exercise of a secured party's option to show a trade name for any person." 9-404—blank in subsection (1) reads "July 1, 1983." Second sentence of subsection (1) substitutes "a termination statement that" for "a termination statement to the effect that"; last sentence reads: "If the affected secured party fails to file the termination statement within 10 days after proper demand for it, the secured party is liable to the debtor for $100 and in addition, for any loss caused to the debtor by this failure." Subsection (3) reads: "The uniform fee for filing and indexing a termination statement is as prescribed by the Department of Natural Resources. In addition, the Department of Natural Resources may establish extra uniform fees for (1) termination statement not in the standard form prescribed by the department; and (2) each name more than one against which the termination statement is required to be indexed." 9-405—in subsection (1), following is substituted for sentence relating to fees: The uniform fee for filing, indexing, and furnishing filing data for a financing statement so indicating an assignment is as prescribed by the Department of Natural Resources. In addition, the Department of Natural Resources may establish extra uniform fees for (1) financing statements not in the standard form prescribed by the department; and (2) each name more than one against which the financing statement is required to be indexed. In subsection (2), following is substituted for sentence relating to fees: "The uniform fee for filing, indexing, and furnishing filing data about the separate statement of assignment is as prescribed by the Department of Natural Resources. In addition,

See note at head of Digest as to 1998 legislation covered.

See Topical Index in front part of this volume.

COMMERCIAL CODE... *continued*

the Department of Natural Resources may establish extra uniform fees for (1) separate statements not in the form prescribed by the department; and (2) each name more than one against which the statement of assignment is required to be indexed." 9-406—last sentence reads: "The uniform fee for filing and noting the statement of release is as prescribed by the Department of Natural Resources. In addition, the Department of Natural Resources may establish extra uniform fees for (1) statements of release not in the standard form prescribed by the department; and (2) each name more than one against which the statement of release is required to be indexed." 9-407—optional section adopted. Last two sentences of subsection (2) read: "The uniform fee for the certificate is as prescribed by the Department of Natural Resources for each financing statement and for each statement of assignment reported in the financing statement; the Department of Natural Resources may establish an extra uniform fee for requests for certificates which are not in the standard form prescribed by the department. Upon request, the filing officer shall furnish a copy of a filed financing statement or statement of assignment for a uniform fee as prescribed by the Department of Natural Resources." 9-504—subsection (2) still refers to "contract rights" after "sale of accounts." All other sections of Alaska UCC have deleted reference to contract rights in conformance with 1972 Official Amendments. All business filings under Art. 9, other than relating to consumer goods, farming operations and fixtures, to be in office of Uniform Commercial Code Filing, Department of Natural Resources, 3601 C St., Suite 820, Anchorage, Ak 99503. (U.C.C. §9-401, 45.09.401).

Permanent Editorial Board's Recommendations for Amendments.— 1966 Official Amendments to §§2-702, 3-501 and 7-209 not enacted.

Permanent Editorial Board's Recommendations for Optional Amendments.— 1966 Official Optional Amendments to §§1-209, 2-318, 9-105 and 9-106 not enacted.

1972 Official Amendments.—Not adopted.

1973 Official Amendment adopted.

1977 Official Amendments.—Not adopted.

See also topics: Banks and Banking, Bills and Notes, Carriers, Factors, Frauds, Statute of, Sales, Securities, Warehousemen; categories Business Organizations, topic Corporations; Civil Actions and Procedure, topic Limitation of Actions; Debtor and Creditor, topics Assignments, Fraudulent Sales and Conveyances, Liens, Pledges; Documents and Records, topics Records, Seals; Mortgages, topic Chattel Mortgages.

CONDITIONAL SALES:

See topic Sales.

CONSIGNMENTS:

See topic Factors.

CONSUMER PROTECTION:

Uniform Deceptive Trade Practices Act not adopted.

Unfair competition and deceptive conduct of trade or commerce are unlawful. Included are: fraudulent conveyance of goods or services, false representation of origin, nature, standard etc. of goods or services; false or misleading advertising of goods or services or their price; falsely representing frozen meat, fish or poultry as fresh; failure to deliver written contract for installment sales; using chain referral sales plan, etc. (45.50.471). Contact Alaska Department of Law, Pouch K, Juneau, 99811 for information.

Damages.—Private and class actions allowed. (45.50.531). Person may recover greater of $200 or actual damages. (45.50.531). Person may not commence action more than two years after discovery of loss from act or practice declared unlawful under 45.50.471.

"Unsolicited goods" statute adopted. (45.45.105).

Consumer paper nonnegotiable. (45.50.541).

Plain Language.—No plain language statute adopted.

CONTRACTS:

Uniform Commercial Code adopted. (45.01.101).

FACTORS:

Uniform Commercial Code adopted. (45.05).

FRANCHISES:

Uniform Franchise and Business Opportunities Act not adopted. See topics Monopolies, Restraint of Trade and Competition, Securities.

FRAUDS, STATUTE OF:

Uniform Commercial Code adopted. (45.01.101).

a. In the following cases and under the following conditions an agreement, promise, or undertaking is unenforceable unless it or some note or memorandum of it is in writing and subscribed by the party charged or by his agent:

(1) an agreement that by its terms is not to be performed within a year from the making of it;

(2) an agreement the performance of which is not to be completed by the end of a lifetime. This provision includes a contract to bequeath property or make a testamentary disposition of any kind, a contract to assign or an assignment, with or without consideration to the promisor, of a life or health or accident insurance policy, or a promise, with or without consideration to promisor, to name a beneficiary of that type of policy. But this provision does not include an insurer's promise to issue a policy of insurance, or any promise or assignment with respect to a policy of industrial life or health or accident insurance;

(3) a special promise to answer for the debt of another;

(4) an agreement by an executor or administrator to pay the debts of his testator or intestate out of his own estate;

(5) an agreement made upon consideration of marriage other than mutual promises to marry;

(6) an agreement for leasing for a longer period than one year, or for sale of real property, or of any interest in real property, or to charge or encumber real property;

(7) an agreement concerning real property made by an agent of the party sought to be charged unless authority of the agent is in writing;

(8) an agreement authorizing or employing an agent or broker to sell or purchase real estate for compensation or commission; however, if the note or memorandum of the agreement is in writing, subscribed by party to be charged or by his lawfully authorized agent, contains a description of the property sufficient for identification, authorizes or employs the agent or broker named in it to sell the property, and expresses with reasonable certainty amount of commission or compensation to be paid the agent or broker, the agreement of authorization or employment is not unenforceable for failure to state a consideration;

(9) an agreement to establish a trust;

(10) a subsequent or new promise to pay a debt discharged in bankruptcy;

(11) a conveyance or assignment of a trust in personal property;

(12) an agreement to pay compensation for services rendered in negotiating a loan, effecting procurement of a business opportunity, or purchase and sale of a business, its good will, inventory, fixtures, or an interest in it, including a majority of the voting stock interest in a corporation and including the creating of a partnership interest, other than an agreement to pay compensation to an auctioneer or an attorney at law.

(13) Agreement to lend more than $50,000 or to grant or extend credit of more than $50,000, if loan or grant or extension of credit is not primarily for personal, family, or household purposes and if person who agrees to loan or grant or extend credit is engaged in business of lending or arranging for lending of money or granting or extension of credit and this paragraph alone secured solely by residential property consisting of one to four dwelling units is considered to be loan primarily for personal, family, or household purposes.

b. No estate or interest in real property, other than a lease for a term not exceeding one year, nor any trust or power concerning the property may be created, transferred, or declared, otherwise than by operation of law, or by a conveyance or other instrument in writing subscribed by party creating, transferring, or declaring it or by his agent under written authority and executed with the formalities that are required by law. If interest is created, transferred or declared to, or for benefit of, nonresident alien, instrument shall so state and shall contain alien's name and address. This does not affect power of testator in disposition of his real property by will, nor prevent trust's arising or being extinguished by implication or operation of law, nor affect power of court to compel specific performance of agreement in relation to property. (09.25.010).

Exceptions to Statute of Frauds.—A contract, promise, or agreement which is subject to §09.25.010, which does not satisfy requirements of that section, but which is otherwise valid is enforceable if either

(1) There has been full performance on one side accepted by the other in accordance with the contract; or

(2) there is a memorandum which would satisfy requirements except for error or omission in recital of past events; or

(3) there is a memorandum which would satisfy the requirements except for error or omission which could be corrected by reformation if it occurred in formal contract; or

(4) party against whom enforcement is sought admits, voluntarily or involuntarily, in his pleadings or at any other stage of this or any other action or proceeding the making of an agreement; or

(5) it is a contract of employment for a period not exceeding one year from the commencement of work under its terms. (09.25.020).

Part performance also can remove bar of statute. (519 P.2d 814).

Representations as to Credit, Skill, or Character of a Third Person.—No evidence is admissible to charge a person upon a representation as to the credit, skill, or character of a third person unless representation or some memorandum of it is in writing, and either subscribed by or in the handwriting of party to be charged. (09.25.030).

Sale of Goods.—Except as otherwise provided a contract for sale of goods, including sale or transfer of a boat or vessel, for price of $500 or more is not enforceable by way of action or defense unless there is some writing sufficient to indicate that a contract for sale has been made between the parties and signed by party against whom enforcement is sought or by his authorized agent or broker. A writing is not insufficient because it omits or incorrectly states a term agreed upon but the contract is not enforceable under this paragraph beyond the quantity of goods shown in such writing. (45.02.201).

Between merchants if within a reasonable time a writing in confirmation of the contract and sufficient against sender is received and party receiving it has reason to know its contents, it satisfies the requirements unless written notice of objection to its contents is given within ten days after it is received. (45.02.201).

Exceptions: Sale of Goods.—A contract which does not satisfy requirements of the statute but which is valid in other respects is enforceable

(a) if the goods are to be specially manufactured for buyer and are not suitable for sale to others in ordinary course of seller's business and seller, before notice of repudiation is received and under circumstances which reasonably indicate that the goods are for buyer, has made either a substantial beginning of their manufacture or commitments for their procurement; or

(b) if party against whom enforcement is sought admits in his pleading, testimony, or otherwise in court that a contract for sale was made, but the contract is not enforceable under this provision beyond the quantity of goods admitted; or

(c) with respect to goods for which payment has been made and accepted or which have been received and accepted. (45.02.201).

INTEREST:

Legal rate in absence of contract fixing rate, 10.5%, interest charged by express agreement in contract or loan commitment dated after June 4, 1976 may not exceed 5% above annual rate which is charged member banks for advances by 12th Federal Reserve District on day which contract or loan commitment is made; but commitment exceeding $100,000 in principal amount is exempt. Statute does not require that contract for more than 6% interest shall be in writing. (45.45.010).

Judgment.—Interest rate on judgments, including prejudgment interest, is three percentage points above 12th Federal Reserve discount rate in effect on Jan. 2 of year in which judgment is entered unless based on written contract providing for specified rate, in which case judgment bears interest at contract rate provided such rate is set forth in judgment. (09.30.070). Prejudgment interest accrues from day process is served on defendant or day defendant receives written notification that injury has occurred and that claim may be brought against that defendant, whichever is earlier. Prejudgment interest may not be awarded for future economic damages, future noneconomic damages, or punitive damages. (09.30.070).

On money due on settlement of matured accounts, interest runs from the day when the balance is ascertained. (45.45.010).

Small Loans.—Rates applicable to unpaid balance equal to or less than indicated amount. Loan maximum $25,000. $850 or less, 3% per month; $850 to $10,000, 2% per month; $10,000 to $25,000, 1% per month. (06.20.230). Option available for open-ended small loans or contracted loans between $10,000 to $25,000: Three percent per month on that part of unpaid principal of loan not exceeding $850, 2% on unpaid principal between $850 and $10,000, and at rate agreed by contract for remaining unpaid principal less than $25,000. (06.20.230).

Usury results in forfeiture of all interest (45.45.040) and person paying usurious interest may recover double amount thereof by action brought within two years (45.45.030). Interest on loans under $10,000, payable in installments in seven years or less may be collected in advance. (45.45.080).

See also topic Sales, subhead Retail Credit Sales.

LICENSES, BUSINESS AND PROFESSIONAL:

Alaska General Business License levied upon all businesses, 43.70.020-120, but numerous businesses and professions are covered by special acts. See category, Taxation, topic Taxes, subhead Business License Tax. Unless exempted, license fee for all Alaska businesses is $25. (43.70.030).

Engaging in business without proper state license is a misdemeanor punishable by fine up to $2,000, up to six months imprisonment or both. (43.05.290[A]).

A centralized occupational and professional licensing section is established in Department of Commerce and Economic Development. (08.01).

Collection Agencies.—License required from and biennial fee set by Department of Commerce. (08.01.065). License not required of attorneys, banks, fiduciaries, financing institutions, common carriers, title insurers doing escrow business, real estate brokers, substation payment offices of public utilities. (08.24.090-08.24.100).

MONOPOLIES, RESTRAINT OF TRADE AND COMPETITION:

All statutory provisions found in c. 50 of Title 45.

Prohibited Restraints of Trade and Competition.—Every contract, combination and monopoly in restraint of trade or which lessens competition is unlawful. (45.50.562-.566). Contracts restraining trade are voidable. (45.50.574). Acquisitions and mergers of stock, share capital or assets of corporation which substantially lessen competition are unlawful and court may order divestiture. (45.50.568). Interlocking directorates and relationships between competitive business entities which substantially lessen competition likewise unlawful and court may terminate interlocking relationship. (45.50.570). Violations constitute misdemeanor other violations may result in imposition of (45.50.578), civil penalty, treble damages, reasonable attorney's fees and costs to any person injured (45.50.576).

Act does not apply to labor, agricultural or horticultural groups created for self-help; fishing industry; public utilities certified for public convenience; carriers; banks and financial institutions; and arrangements under Alaska Native Claims Settlement Act. (45.50.572).

NEGOTIABLE INSTRUMENTS:

See topic Bills and Notes.

RESTRAINT OF TRADE:

See topic Monopolies, Restraint of Trade and Competition.

SALES:

Uniform Commercial Code adopted. (45.01.101).

Contracts of Sale.—See Uniform Commercial Code, §2-106. (45.02.106). See topics Frauds, Statute of; Consumer Protection.

Bills of Sale.—No statutory requirements.

Conditions or Warranties.—See Uniform Commercial Code, §§2-313-2-317. (45.02.313-.315).

Consumer Protection.—See topic Consumer Protection.

Product Liability.—See Uniform Commercial Code, §§2-313-2-317. (45.02.313-.317). Privity not required of family household or guest in home, U.C.C. §2-318. (45.02.318).

Transfer of Title.—See Uniform Commercial Code, Art. 2, §2-401. (45.02.401).

Delivery.—See Uniform Commercial Code.

Stoppage in Transitu.—See Uniform Commercial Code.

Remedies of Seller.—See Uniform Commercial Code.

Remedies of Buyer.—See Uniform Commercial Code.

Conditional Sales.—See Uniform Commercial Code.

Retail Credit Sales.—Alaska Retail Installment Sales Act (45.10.010-230) provides comprehensive statutory provisions regulating installment sales and covering documents, prepayment, charges of all kinds, insurance, actions by Attorney General, penalties, etc.

Service charge included in retail installment contract, retail charge or revolving account must be agreed to by seller and buyer.

Bulk Sales.—See Uniform Commercial Code.

Sales of Vehicles.—See category Transportation, topic Motor Vehicles.

SECURITIES:

Uniform Securities Act adopted with some changes (c. 198, SLA 1959; c. 105, SLA 1961 and c. 55, c. 86, SLA 1972) as Alaska Securities Act of 1959 (45.55). Substantial deviations from Uniform Act set forth:

§202, Registration Procedure.—Last sentence of Subsection (a), relating to automatic registration of agents who are partners, etc., deleted. In Subsection (f), bonds required to provide that suits must be brought within three years after sale or other act on which suit is based. (45.55.040).

§303, Registration by Coordination.—Subsection (a) reads: "A security for which a registration statement has been filed under the Securities Act of 1933 or any security for which filing has been made under regulations A, E, and F pursuant to (b) of §3 of the Securities Act of 1933 in connection with the same offering may be registered by coordination." (45.55.090).

§401, Definitions.—Subsection (g)(2) deleted. Last clause of Subsection (12) reads: "Security' does not include an insurance or endowment policy or annuity contract under which an insurance company promises to pay a fixed or variable sum of money either in a lump sum or periodically for life or for some other specified period." (45.55.990).

Following two sections are added to part IV of Act:
"Application to Alaska Native Claims Settlement Act Corporations. The initial issue of stock of a corporation organized under Alaska law pursuant to the Alaska Native Claims Settlement Act (P.L. 92-203; 85 Stat. 688; 43 USC 1601 et seq.) is not a sale of a security under AS 45.55.070 and AS 45.55.130 (10) (§§301 and 401[10] of the Uniform Act)." (45.55.138).

"Reports of Corporations. A copy of all annual reports, proxies, consents or authorizations, proxy statements and other materials relating to proxy solicitations distributed, published or made available by any person to at least 30 Alaska resident shareholders of a corporation which has total assets exceeding $1,000,000 and a class of equity security held of record by 500 or more persons and which is exempted from the registration requirements of AS 45.55.070 by AS 45.55.138, shall be filed with the administrator concurrently with its distribution to shareholders." (45.55.139).

§402, Exemptions.—Paragraph (a)(3) reads: "A security issued by and representing an interest in or a debt of, or guaranteed by, a bank organized under the laws of the United States, or a bank, savings institution, savings and loan association, building and loan association, or trust company organized and supervised under the laws of a state or of the United States." (45.55.900[a][3]).

Paragraph (a)(5) reads: "A security issued by and representing an interest in or a debt of, or guaranteed by, an insurance company organized under the laws of a state and authorized to do business in this state; but this exemption does not apply to an annuity contract, investment contract, or similar security under which the promised payments are not fixed in dollars but are substantially dependant upon the investment results of a segregated fund or account invested in securities; except that policies or annuity contracts of insurance companies admitted to do business in the state are not subject to this chapter." (45.55.900[a][7]).

Paragraph (a)(10) adds at end following clause: "If the commercial paper is of the type eligible for discount by a federal reserve bank" (45.55.900[a][4]).

Paragraph (b)(9) reads: "sales by an issuer (A) to no more than 10 persons in this state other than those designated in [§401(b)(8)]during a period of 12 consecutive months whether or not the seller or any of the buyers is then present in this state, if (i) no commission or other renumeration is paid or given directly or indirectly for soliciting a prospective buyer in this state; (ii) the total dollar amount invested during a period of 12 consecutive months does not exceed $100,000; (iii) a legend is placed on the certificate or other document evidencing ownership of the security, stating that the security is not registered under this chapter and cannot be resold without registration under this chapter or exemption from it; (iv) offers are made without public solicitation or advertisements; and (v) the issuer files with the administrator a notice specifying the issuer, the security to be sold and the terms of the offer at least two days before any sales are made; (B) to no more than 25 persons in the state other than those designated in (4) of this section during a period of 12 consecutive months whether or not the seller or any of the buyers is present in this state, if (i) the sales are made solely in the state; (ii) before any sale, each prospective buyer is furnished access to the information that would be provided to a prospective buyer in a registration under AS 45.55.100 [§304] (which information shall be furnished to the administrator upon his request); (iii) the total dollar amount invested during a period of 12 consecutive months does not exceed $500,000; (iv) commissions or other remuneration meet the requirements of this chapter and are only made to persons registered under AS 45.55.040 [§202]; (v) a legend is placed on the certificate or other document evidencing ownership of the security, stating that the security is not registered under this chapter and cannot be resold without registration under this chapter or exemption from it; (vi) the issuer obtains a signed agreement from the buyer acknowledging that he is buying for investment purposes and that the securities will not be resold without registration under this chapter; (vii) offers are made without public solicitation or advertisement; and (viii) the issuer files with the administrator a notice specifying the issuer, the security to be sold, and the terms of the offer at least two days before any sales are made." (45.55.900[b][1]-[5]).

See note at head of Digest as to 1998 legislation covered.

See Topical Index in front part of this volume.

SECURITIES ... *continued*

Following sections are added to Alaska version of §402(b):

"(13) a transaction incident to a right of conversion or a statutory or judicially approved reclassification, recapitalization, reorganization, quasi-reorganization, stock split, reverse stock split, merger, consolidation or sale of assets, if (A) no commission or other remuneration, other than a standby commission is paid or given directly or indirectly for soliciting a security holder in this state; and (B) the issuer files a notice in the form specified by the administrator not less than 30 days before making the offer;

"(14) a stock dividend, whether the corporation distributing the dividend is the issuer of the stock or not, if nothing of value is given by stockholders for the dividend other than the surrender of a right to a cash or property dividend when each stockholder may elect to take the dividend in cash or property or in stock;

"(15) an act incident to a class vote by stockholders, under the certificate of incorporation or the applicable corporation statute, on a merger, consolidation, reclassification of securities or sale of securities of another corporation;

"(16) the offer or sale by a registered broker-dealer, acting either as principal or agent, of securities previously sold and distributed to the public if (A) the securities are sold at prices reasonably related to the current market price at the time of sale, and if broker-dealer is acting as agent, the commission collected by the broker-dealer on account of the sale is not in excess of usual and customary commissions collected with respect to securities and transactions having comparable characteristics; (B) the securities do not constitute the whole or a part of an unsold allotment to or subscription or participation by the broker-dealer as an underwriter of the securities or as a participant in the distribution of the securities by the issuer, by an underwriter or by a person or group of persons in substantial control of the issuer or of the outstanding securities of the class being distributed; and (C) the securities have been lawfully sold and distributed in this state under this chapter;

"(17) offers or sales of certificates of interest or participation in oil, gas, or mining rights, titles or leases, or in payments out of production under such rights, titles or leases, if the purchasers (A) are or have been during the preceding two years engaged primarily in the business of exploring for, mining, producing, or refining oil, gas, or minerals; or (B) have been found by the administrator upon written application to be substantially engaged in the business of exploring for, mining, producing, or refining oil, gas, or minerals so as not to require the protection provided by AS 45.55.070 [§301]." (45.55.140 [b][13]-[17]).

§403, Filing of Sales and Advertising Literature—delete "unless the security or transaction is exempted by §402" (45.55.150).

A section is inserted following §407 which reads:

"*Reimbursement of expenses incident to examination.*(a) An issuer, broker-dealer, agent, or investment adviser shall reimburse the administrator for actual travel expenses and per diem incurred in connection with an examination incident to a registration under this chapter. (b) The administrator may by rule or order adopt a schedule of charges for annual examination fees of issuers, broker-dealers, agents and investment advisers. (c) If an issuer, broker-dealer, agent or investment adviser fails to pay the fees and expenses provided for in the section, the fees and expenses shall be paid out of the funds of the administrator in the same manner as other disbursements made by the administrator. The amounts paid from the funds of the administrator are a lien upon all of the assets and property in this state of the issuer, broker-dealer, agent or investment adviser and the amount may be recovered by the attorney general on behalf of the state. (d) Failure of the issuer, broker-dealer, agent or investment adviser to pay fees and expenses under this section is a willful violation of this chapter and the violation falls within the provisions of AS 45.55.060, 45.55.120, 45.55.920 and 45.55.925. [§§204, 306, 408, 409]." (45.55.915).

§408 After "he may" delete "in his discretion" and insert "if he considers it in the public interest or for the protection of investors, issue an order (A) directing the person to cease and desist from continuing the act or practice, (B) directing the person, for a period not to exceed three years, to file the annual reports, proxies, consents or authorizations, proxy statements, or other materials relating to proxy solicitations required under AS 45.55.139 with the administrator for examination and review 10 working days before a distribution to shareholders, and (C) voiding any proxies obtained by a person required to file under AS 45.55.139, including their future exercise or actions resulting from their past exercise, if the proxies were solicited by means of an untrue or misleading statement prohibited under AS 45.55.160; or" (45.55.200 [a] [1]). After "post a bond", insert "Before issuing an order under (a) (1) of this section the administrator shall give reasonable notice of and an opportunity for a hearing. However, the administrator may issue a temporary order pending the hearing which order shall remain in effect until 110 days after the hearing is held and which shall become final if the person to whom notice is addressed does not request a hearing within 15 days after the receipt of notice." (45.55.920[b]).

§409 (a) delete "or imprisoned not more than three years, or both;" and insert "or by imprisonment for not less than one year nor more than five years, or both. Upon conviction of an individual for a felony under this chapter, imprisonment for not less than one year is mandatory." (45.55.925[a]).

§410 (a) reads:

"A person is liable to the person buying the security from him for the consideration paid for the security, together with interest at 6% a year from the date of payment, costs, and reasonable attorneys' fees, less the amount of income received on the security, upon the tender of the security, or for damages if he no longer owns the security, if he (1) Offers or sells a security in violation of AS 45.55.030(a), AS 45.55.070, or AS 45.55.170(b) or of a rule or order under AS 45.55.150 which requires the filing of sales literature before it is used, or of a condition imposed under AS 45.55.100(d) or AS 45.55.110(g) or (h), or (2) Offers or sells a security by means of an untrue statement of a material fact, or omits to state a material fact, the omission of which makes a statement misleading." (45.55.930[a]).

A section is added after §410(a) which reads:

"(B) Damages are the amount that would be recoverable upon a tender less the value of the security when the buyer disposed of it and interest at 6% a year from the date of disposition." (45.55.930[b]).

In paragraph (e) substitute "three" for "two" (45.55.930[f]).

§411—Review is to superior court. Delete last part of subparagraph (a) beginning with "the findings of the administrator as to the facts." (45.55.940[a]) "The Administrative Procedure Act (AS 44.62) applies to all regulations issued or authorized under this chapter." (45.55.960).

Delete §§415, 417, 418 and 419.

Uniform Commercial Code enacted. (45.02). See topic Commercial Code.

Supervision.—By Department of Commerce and Economic Development, Pouch D, Juneau, Alaska 99811. (45.55.180).

Fees.—Broker-dealer filing fees, initial $200, annual renewal $200. Agent and investment advisor fees, initial $75, annual renewal $75. Registration of successor fee $75. (45.55.040). Filing fee for security registration is 1/10 of 1% of maximum offering price with $50 minimum and $1,500 maximum. (45.55.110).

Minimum Capital Required.—Administrator must require minimum capital and bond for broker-dealers and investment advisors, and may require bond up to $10,000 for broker-dealers, agents and investment advisors. (45.55.040).

Takeover Bid Disclosure Act may subject violators to fine of $5,000 or imprisonment for three years or both, and civil liability. (45.57.070-.080).

Uniform Simplification of Fiduciary Security Transfers Act not adopted.

Uniform Securities Ownership by Minors Act not adopted.

STATUTE OF FRAUDS:

See topic Frauds, Statute of.

TRUST RECEIPT SECURITY:

See category Debtor and Creditor, topic Pledges.

WAREHOUSEMEN:

Uniform Commercial Code adopted. (45.05.002).

CITIZENSHIP

ALIENS:

Native born citizens of Canada are accorded the same mining rights and privileges as are accorded to citizens of the United States in British Columbia, and the Northwest Territory, under dominion or provincial laws, but no greater rights are thus accorded than citizens of the United States, or those who have declared intention of becoming such may enjoy. (formerly codified in 48 U.S.C.A. §392). Aliens not lawfully admitted to U.S. prohibited from commercial fishing activities or taking marine mammals in waters of state. (16.05.905). Alien convicted of violation of AS 16.05.905 is guilty of misdemeanor. Aliens are not disqualified from intestate succession. (13.11.06).

CIVIL ACTIONS AND PROCEDURE

ACCORD AND SATISFACTION:

In absence of statute, common law applies. (01.10.010). See category Business Regulation and Commerce, topic Commercial Code.

Pleading.—Assert affirmative defense. (Rule 8[c] Civ. R.P.).

By Use of Instruments.—If good faith tender of instrument in full payment of unliquidated disputed claim with conspicuous statements offered in full satisfaction is accepted, claim discharged. (45.03.311).

ACTIONS:

Rules of Civil Procedure (Civ. R.P.) based upon Federal Rules, control in Superior and district courts. See topic Practice.

Civil actions against state authorized. (09.50.250).

Equity.—Distinction between actions at law and suits in equity is abolished. There is but one form of action, which is denominated civil action. (Rule 1 Civ. R.P.).

Forms of Action.—There is but one form of action, which is denominated civil action. (Rule 1 Civ. R.P.).

Commencement.—By filing a complaint with court. (Rule 3 Civ. R.P.).

Parties.—Every action must be prosecuted in the name of the real party in interest, except that an administrator, guardian, executor, trustee of express trust, or person expressly authorized by statute, may sue without joining with him person for whose benefit action is prosecuted. (Rule 17[a] Civ. R.P.).

Heirs of decedent, whose names and addresses are unknown, may be proceeded against as "the unknown heirs of" such decedent in any action or suit relating to real property in Alaska. (09.45.900).

Class Actions.—One or more members of class may sue or be sued as representative parties on behalf of all only if (1) class is so numerous that joinder is impracticable; (2) common questions of law and fact; (3) claims are typical of class; (4) representative class will fairly and adequately protect class. (Rule 23 Civ. R.P.).

Intervention.—As a matter of right or by permission depending whether applicant is so situated that disposition would impede ability to protect interest, unless interest is adequately protected by parties. (Rule 24 Civ. R.P.).

Interpleader.—Persons having claims against plaintiff may be joined as defendants and required to interplead when their claims expose plaintiff to double or multiple liability. (Rule 22 Civ. R.P.).

See note at head of Digest as to 1998 legislation covered.

See Topical Index in front part of this volume.

ACTIONS . . . *continued*

Third Party Practice.—Defendant as third party plaintiff may serve complaint on person not a party who may be liable to defendant on plaintiff's claim. (Rule 14 Civ. R.P.). Defendant may serve complaint on person not party who may be at fault for purposes of apportioning fault. (09.17.080; Rule 14[c] Civ. R.P.; Rule 82[e] Civ. R.P.).

Joinder of Causes of Action.—Pleadings may include either independent or alternate claims legal and equitable as may be against opposing party. (Rule 18 Civ. R.P.).

Splitting Causes of Action.—Common law rules govern.

Consolidation of Actions.—Actions involving common issues of law or fact, court may join any matters in issue. (Rule 42 Civ. R.P.).

Severance of Actions.—Any claim against a party may be severed and proceeded with separately. (Rule 21 Civ. R.P.).

Abatement.—No action abates by reason of death or disability of a party or transfer of interest, if cause of action survives, but in case of death or disability of a party the court may, at any time within two years thereafter, on notice, allow action to be continued by or against personal representative or successor in interest of such party. (09.15.040).

Upon Death.—Uniform Probate Code adopted with no substantial variations. (13.16.460, 13.16.640, 13.16.645).

Limitation of.—See topic Limitation of Actions.

Small Claims.—See category Courts and Legislature, topic Courts.

Prohibited Actions.—Certain claims against state authorized but many forms of tort claims prohibited including discretionary acts of state employees. (09.50.250). Actions may be brought against municipalities subject to exceptions. (09.65.070).

Direct Actions Against Insurer.—See category Transportation, topic Motor Vehicles, subhead Direct Actions.

Limitation on Damages.—Recovery of certain noneconomic damages limited to $400,000 or injured person's life expectancy multiplied by $8,000, whichever is greater, except in cases of disfigurement or severe physical impairment wherein recovery limited to $1,000,000 or injured person's life expectancy multiplied by $25,000, whichever is greater by 09.17.010-09.17.900. (See topic Damages.)

APPEAL AND ERROR:

Federal Rules of Civil Procedure form basis for rules of procedure in all courts. Time allowed for taking appeal is 30 days after entry of judgment. (204[a][1], Appellate Rules). Time allowed for taking appeal is 15 days after clerk's distribution in child custody cases. (218[d], Appellate Rules).

From Municipal Magistrates.—No specific provision, but appeal lies to superior court from subordinate court. (22.10.020).

From Administrative Agency.—Appeal lies to superior court. (22.10.020). Appeal to be heard without jury. Court may admit new evidence. (44.62.570; 609b).

From District Courts.—Appeal lies to superior court in civil action and to court of appeals in most criminal matters (see category Courts and Legislature, topic Courts). No appeal after plea of guilty in criminal case except for excessive sentence. State has no right of appeal in criminal actions except to test sufficiency of information. (22.10.020). Notice of Appeal to Court of Appeals must be filed within 15 days after date shown in clerk's certificate of distribution on judgment being appealed. (217, Appellate Rules).

From Superior Court.—Appeal lies to supreme court for most civil matters and to court of appeals for most criminal matters (see category Courts and Legislature, topic Courts). State may not appeal in criminal case except to test sufficiency of indictment or information, or that sentence is too lenient. (22.05.010).

Appeal Bonds.—Cost bond on appeal required. (204[c] Appellate Rules). Indigents and municipalities are exempt from bond provisions on appeal. (09.65.040).

Stay of Proceedings.—Giving of supersedeas bond may result in a stay of proceedings. (Rule 62, Civ. R.P.).

Time.—Generally, Notice of Appeal must be filed within 30 days from date shown in clerk's certificate of distribution on judgment being appealed. (204, Appellate Rules). Within 15 days in child custody cases. (218, Appellate Rules).

See topic Practice.

BONDS:

Surety must be resident within state; attorney or counselor at law, marshal, deputy marshal, magistrate, clerk or other officer of any court may not become bail in any action. (Rule 80[b] Civ. R.P.).

A corporation which has complied with laws of United States and of Alaska relative to surety companies, may be surety upon any bail, recognizance, stipulation, bond or undertaking. (Rule 80[b] Civ. R.P.).

New surety may be substituted on application of principal, surety or obligee and presentation of bond of new qualified surety conditioned as in former bond and accepting all liability theretofore or thereafter accruing under either former bond or new bond. (45.70.010).

Official Bonds.—Official undertaking or other security of a public officer to any city, town or other municipal or public corporation of like character is deemed security to the state or to such city, town, etc., and also to all persons severally. (09.55.470). Any person injured by official misconduct or neglect of officer or entitled to benefit of his security may maintain action in his own name against the officer and his sureties (09.55.470). Judgment may not be rendered against surety for more than excess of penalty of undertaking over any judgments previously recovered against him otherwise than by confession. (09.55.490).

Official bond must be joint and several, be payable to the State and cover faithful discharge of all duties required by any law in force at time of execution or subsequently enacted. Surety may be released from further liability by filing written application with Commissioner of Administration, serving it on principal and publishing notice for 30 days in newspaper published in Juneau. (39.15.010-100).

Performance and payment bonds required on any contract exceeding $100,000 for construction, alteration or repair of any State or political subdivision public building or work, and procedure established for suit on such bonds. (36.25.010). Municipality may exempt contractors from bond under listed circumstances. (36.25.025).

CERTIORARI:

Appeal from final judgment of Superior Court is matter of right, except State in criminal case may appeal only to test sufficiency of indictment or leniency of sentence. (Rule 202, App. R.). Party may petition for review of other orders or decisions. (Rule 402, App. R.).

Jurisdiction.—Supreme Court may issue writ of certiorari and all other writs necessary or proper to complete exercise of its jurisdiction. (22.05.010).

CHARITABLE IMMUNITY:

See topic Damages.

COMMISSIONS TO TAKE TESTIMONY:

See topic Depositions and Discovery.

COSTS:

The prevailing party is entitled to costs. (09.60.010, Rule 54[d] Civ. R.P.).

Attorney's Fees.—In all courts reasonable sum as attorney's fee is included in costs. Fees set by rule unless modified by Court. (Rule 82, Civ. R.P.; 09.60.015). For costs covered see Rule 79, Civ. R. P.

Offer of Judgment as Affecting Costs.—If defendant offers in writing to allow entry of judgment for a specific sum, or for specific property, together with costs and disbursements to date of offer, plaintiff is not entitled to costs, if he recovers no more than the sum or property offered, but defendant is entitled to costs accruing after offer. (Rule 68 Civ. R.P.).

At any time more than ten days before trial begins, either party may make offer of judgment. If not accepted in ten days, offer is deemed withdrawn. If judgment is not more favorable to offeree: (1) Interest rate on judgment will be reduced by 5% if offeree is party making claim; or (2) interest rate on judgment will be increased by 5% if offeree is defending against claim. (09.30.065).

For all actions accruing on or after Aug. 7, 1997, if judgment is at least 5% less favorable to offeree than offer, or if multiple defendants, at least 10% less favorable to offeree than offer, offeree shall pay costs and attorney fees incurred by offeror as follows: (1) if offer is made 60 days or less after C.R. 26 disclosures, offeree shall pay 75% of offeror's attorney fees; or (2) if offer made more than 60 days after disclosures but more than 90 days before trial, offeree shall pay 50% of offeror's attorney fees; or (3) if offer made 90 days or less but more than ten days before trial begins, offeree shall pay 30% of offeror's attorney fees. (09.30.065).

DAMAGES:

Common law generally prevails as to compensatory damages. Damages are awarded on basis of several liability only for causes of action accruing after Mar. 5, 1989. (09.17.080[d]). Statutory limitation of $400,000 or injured's life expectancy multiplied by $8,000, whichever is greater, except in cases of disfigurement or severe physical impairment wherein statutory limitation is $1,000,000 or injured person's life expectancy multiplied by $25,000, whichever is greater. (09.17.010).

Comparative negligence rule pure form adopted. (540 P.2d 1037). Uniform Comparative Fault Act not adopted. Several liability established for causes of action accruing after Mar. 5, 1989. After Mar. 5, 1989, fault allocated to all parties to action and only to parties to action. (09.17.080; Benner v. Wichman, 874 P.2d 949 (Alaska 1994). After Aug. 7, 1997, fault may be allocated to nonparty depending upon whether person is protected by statute of repose, is not precluded from joinder by law or court rules, is within court's jurisdiction, and is reasonably locatable. (09.17.080). Contribution abolished; joint liability abolished. Defendant may use third-party defendant procedures to bring in others for purposes of establishing proportion of fault. (Id., Rules 14[c], 82[e], 79[e] Civ. R.P.).

Charitable immunity doctrine not recognized. (14 Alaska 546, 118 F. Supp. 399).

Torts of Minors.—Parents or legal guardian liable for malicious or willful destruction of real or personal property by minors under 18 up to $10,000 for each tort. (34.50.020).

Sovereign Immunity.—Claims against State may be pursued in state court pursuant to 09.50.250 et seq., which is patterned after Federal Tort Claims Act.

Statutory Provisions.—Various statutes provided for penalties and recovery of compensatory, double or treble damage in civil actions based on trespass to trees and shrubs (09.45.730), waste by guardian or tenant (09.45.740), allowing fire to escape (41.15.170), failing to discharge satisfied lien, mortgage or deed of trust (34.35.215, 34.35.485).

Uniform Contribution Among Tortfeasors Act (Revised) adopted. (09.16.010). Repealed for causes of action accruing after Mar. 5, 1989.

See category Estates and Trusts, topic Death, subhead Action for Wrongful Death.

DEPOSITIONS AND DISCOVERY:

Governed by Civ. R.P. based on Federal Rules of Civil Procedure.

Uniform Foreign Depositions Act not adopted. State rules similar to federal rules. (Civ. R.P. 1-98).

See note at head of Digest as to 1998 legislation covered.

See Topical Index in front part of this volume.

DEPOSITIONS AND DISCOVERY . . . continued

Within the State.—Depositions may be taken in state before officer authorized to administer oaths in any action at any time after jurisdiction of defendant acquired, and in any special proceeding after question of fact has arisen, if the witness is a party adverse or an officer of a corporation which is a party adverse to the party seeking the deposition, resides or is about to remove more than one hundred miles from place of trial, or is too infirm to attend trial; or if testimony is to be used on motion or other proceeding where oral examination not required. (Rule 28 [a] Civ. R.P.).

Outside of the State.—Depositions may be taken outside of the state, but within United States, before an officer authorized to administer oaths by laws of U.S. or state where taken. (Rule 28 [b], Civ. R.P.).

Commissions to take deposition out of the state may be issued when necessary or convenient on such terms as are just and appropriate.

The commission must authorize the person taking the deposition, to administer oaths to witnesses and take testimony.

Compelling Attendance of Witnesses.—Attendance of witnesses may be compelled by use of subpoena as provided in Rule 45, Civ. R.P. Superior court clerk shall issue subpoena upon proof of service of notice to take deposition (Civ. R.P. 45[d]), and may direct production of designated books, records, papers, documents, or tangible things constituting or containing evidence, subject to Civ. R.P. 30. Resident of judicial district in which deposition is to be taken may be required to attend an examination at any place within district; nonresident of judicial district in which deposition is to be taken, and nonresident of state subpoenaed in state, may be required to attend at any place within district wherein he is served with subpoena, unless otherwise ordered by court. (Civ. R.P. 45[d] [2]). Failure to obey without adequate excuse may be deemed contempt. (Civ. R.P. 45[f]). If party willfully fails to appear before officer who is to take his deposition, court on motion and notice may strike all or any part of any pleading of that party, or dismiss action or proceeding or any part thereof, or enter a judgment by default against that party. (Civ. R.P. 37[d]).

Return.—Officer taking deposition must certify it, enclose it in sealed envelope indorsed with title of action and send it to party requesting deposition. Notice of filing must be given by party taking deposition to other parties. (Rule 30 [f], Civ. R.P.).

EQUITY:

See topic Actions.

EVIDENCE:

See topic Depositions and Discovery.

Witnesses.—Questions regarding the competence, creditability or privileges of witnesses are governed by Supreme Court rule. (Crim. R.P., Civ. R.P.).

Competency and Creditability.—A person is disqualified to be a witness if court finds that he is incapable of expressing himself concerning the matter so as to be understood by court and jury either directly or through interpretation by one who can understand him or if he is incapable of understanding duty of a witness to tell the truth. Parties or other persons who have an interest in the action, persons who have been convicted of crime and persons on account of their opinions on matters of religious belief are not disqualified to be witnesses.

Privileges.—The following privileges are found in the rules: husband-wife; attorney-client; confessor-confessant; physician-patient; and against self-incrimination.

INJUNCTIONS:

Jurisdiction.—Supreme and superior courts have jurisdiction of injunctions. (22.05.010; 22.10.020). Injunction may be allowed by court or judge at any time after commencement of action and before judgment.

Bond.—No injunction shall issue except upon giving of security by applicant in such sum as court deems proper. (Civ. R.P. Rule 65[c]).

Prerequisites.—Injunction may issue when it appears by complaint that plaintiff entitled to relief demanded, and such relief consists in restraining commission or continuance of some act commission or continuance of which during litigation would produce injury to plaintiff; or when it appears by affidavit that defendant is doing, or threatens, or is about to do, or is procuring or suffering to be done, some act in violation of plaintiff's rights concerning subject of action, and tending to render judgment ineffectual; or when it appears by affidavit that defendant threatens or is about to remove or dispose of his property, with intent to delay or defraud his creditors. (09.40.230).

An injunction is only allowed as a provisional remedy, and when a judgment is given enjoining a defendant, it is effectual and binding on him without other proceeding or process, and may be enforced, if necessary, by punishing disobedience or neglect thereof as for contempt.

JUDGMENTS:

Federal Rules of Civil Procedure form basis of statutory and civil rule provisions. (AS Title 9; Rules 54-63, Civ. R.P.). See topic Practice.

Offer of Judgment.—See topic Costs, subhead Offer of Judgment as Affecting Costs.

Judgment as Lien.—A certified copy of judgment or decree of a court of this state or a court of record of the United States upon which execution may issue, enforcement of which has not been stayed, may be recorded with recorder of a recording district. From the recording, the judgment or decree becomes lien upon real property of defendant which is in the recording district, which is not exempt from execution, and which is owned by him at the time or acquired by him afterward but before lien expires. Lien continues during time execution may issue on the judgment or decree but for not more than ten years from date of entry of the judgment or decree. After expiration of lien, court may grant leave for issuance of execution upon the judgment or decree. From date of recording the judgment or decree, together with order allowing issuance of execution, the judgment or decree becomes a lien as above. (09.30.010).

A **conveyance of real property** or interest in real property is void against a judgment lien that is recorded before conveyance is recorded. (09.30.020).

Declaratory judgments may be obtained in case of an actual controversy. (22.10.020[g]).

Foreign Judgments.—Uniform Enforcement of Foreign Judgments Act (09.30.200) and Uniform Foreign Money Judgments Recognition Act (09.30.100) adopted. See also subhead Judgment as Lien, supra.

Judgments for Custody.—See category Family, topic Guardian and Ward.

LIMITATION OF ACTIONS:

Uniform Commercial Code adopted. (45.01.101).

Actions must be brought within following periods after respective causes of action accrue:

Ten years: actions for recovery of real property, or for recovery of possession thereof (09.10.030); upon judgment or decree of any court of U.S., or of any state or territory within U.S.; upon sealed instrument. (09.10-040). Ten-year period governs with respect to any action not otherwise provided for. (09.10.100).

Six years: action for waste or trespass on real property. (09.10.050).

Four years: an action for breach of any contract for sale must be commenced within four years after cause of action has accrued. By original agreement parties may reduce period of limitation to not less than one year but may not extend it. (45.02.725, U.C.C. §2-725). Also action for restraint of trade, and action by Attorney General suspends running of statute against private parties. (45.50.588).

Three years: action upon contract or liability except as provided by law or waived by contract (09.10.053); action upon statute for penalty or forfeiture, where action is given to party aggrieved, or to such party and U.S., except where statute prescribes different limitation (09.10.060); on mutual, open, and current account, but if more than one year has elapsed between any of series of items, they are deemed not to constitute such account (09.10.110).

Two years: action for libel, slander, assault, battery, seduction, false imprisonment, or for any injury to person or rights of another not arising on contract and not herein especially enumerated, or for taking, detaining, or injuring personal property and for recovery thereof; upon statute for forfeiture or penalty to State of Alaska, upon statutory liability, other than penalty or forfeiture. (09.10.070). See also category Estates and Trusts, topic Death, subhead Action for Wrongful Death.

One year: action against a peace officer for the escape of a person arrested or imprisoned on civil process (09.10.080); statute for penalty given in whole or part to person prosecuting for same, unless not commenced within such time by private party, when same may be commenced within two years by State (09.10.090).

Six months: no action may be brought under Art. VI of Uniform Commercial Code (45.05.002) relating to Bulk Transfers more than six months after date on which transferee took possession of goods unless transfer has been concealed, in which case actions may be brought within six months of discovery.

Upon Death.—Uniform Probate Code adopted with no substantial variations. (13.16.460, 13.16.640, 13.16.645).

Absence or Concealment.—Time does not run during period person against whom cause of action exists, is out of district or concealed therein. (09.10.130).

Disabilities.—Minors, persons incompetent by reason of mental illness, and persons imprisoned on criminal charge or in execution under sentence for term less than life, at time cause of action accrues, may commence action within two years after such disability ceases; for personal injury action to person under eight years of age, period before person's eighth birthday is not included within time limit for commencing civil action. (09.10.140).

Acknowledgment or promise is not sufficient evidence of a new or continuing contract, whereby to take the case out of the operation of the statute, unless same is contained in some writing, signed by the party to be charged and, as to instruments affecting real estate, acknowledged and recorded in the office of the recorder wherein the original contract shall have been filed or recorded; but this does not alter the effect of any payment of principal or interest. (09.10.200).

Payment on Account.—When a past due payment of principal or interest is made upon any evidence of indebtedness, running of time within which an action may be commenced starts from time last payment was made. (09.10.210).

Part Payment.—Where an indebtedness is secured by lien on real estate, no payment thereon can extend the lien beyond its original or extended period, as against subsequent purchasers, optionees, mortgagees, creditors or persons acquiring a lien upon the real estate, unless prior to expiration of the statutory time for bringing action upon the contract and extensions as exhibited by terms of the recorded instrument, a memorandum of such payment, signed and acknowledged by the owner of the contract of indebtedness, or someone for him, is recorded in office of recorder of the district wherein the real estate is situated. Unless period of instrument disclosed therein, maturity date deemed ten years from date thereof. As to existing recorded lien instruments not disclosing period of instrument, an instrument extending period may be recorded prior to Jan. 1, 1956. (34.20.140-150).

Foreign Causes of Action.—No action may be maintained in Alaska on a cause of action arising in any state, territory, or country between nonresidents of this district, which by the laws of such state, territory, or country cannot be maintained by reason of lapse of time. (09.10.220).

Limited Liability Act adopted. (10.50).

PARTITION:

Tenants in common may maintain an action against each other for a partition of their property. (09.45.260).

Plaintiff must make lien creditors defendants. (09.45.280).

See note at head of Digest as to 1998 legislation covered.

See Topical Index in front part of this volume.

PLEADING:

Rules of Civil Procedure are in effect, based on Federal Rules. See also topic Practice.

Amended or Supplemental Pleadings.—Additional subsection to Rule 15, as follows:

"*(e) Form.*—Unless otherwise permitted by the court, every pleading to which an amendment is permitted as a matter of right or has been allowed by order of the court, must be retyped or reprinted and filed so that it will be complete in itself, including the exhibits, without reference to the superseded pleading. No pleading will be deemed to be amended until this subdivision of this rule has been complied with. All amended pleadings shall contain copies of all exhibits referred to in such amended pleadings. Permission may be obtained from the court, if desired, for the removal of any exhibit or exhibits attached to prior pleadings, in order that the same may be attached to the amended pleading." (Rule 15[e], Civ. R.P.).

Filing.—As in federal rule, except that following papers, unless ordered by court on motion of party or its own motion, may not be filed with court unless or until they are actually used in proceedings: (a) Notices of taking depositions, (b) interrogatories and request for admissions and answers thereto, (c) request for production and responses thereto, (d) subpoenas, including subpoenas duces tecum, (e) offers of judgment, (f) proof of service of any of above, (g) copies of correspondence between counsel, and (h) exhibits. (Rule 5[d][2] Civ. R.P.).

Claims for Collection.—If a claim sent to this state for collection is on an open account, the account should be itemized in detail and sworn to be correct by the creditor or an officer of the creditor company. If the claim is on a written instrument or a negotiable instrument, the original instrument should be forwarded. The letter forwarding the claim should give a full, complete and comprehensive statement of the facts upon which the claim is founded. It should also give the full name and address of each party. If a partnership is claimant, the full names and residences of the individuals composing it should be given. If a corporation is to be a party or is claimant the exact corporate name and state of incorporation should be given. If the claimant operates under a tradename, the name of claimant and his or their tradename should be given. If the action is contested, the claim must be proven by witnesses or deposition or both.

An assignment in blank of the account should be forwarded with the account, as action on an assigned account can be brought in the name of the assignee.

Proof of Claims.—In forwarding claims from another state sufficient information should be given to enable local attorneys to prepare complaint. If defendant contests, proof of issues must be made by deposition if witnesses cannot appear to testify in court.

See also topic Practice.

Small Claims.—See category Courts and Legislature, topic Courts.

Frivolous Claims.—Alaska Rule of Civil Procedure 11 parallels FRCP 11, except that it does not contain any language regarding sanctions for violation of rule.

PRACTICE:

Rules of Civil Procedure govern civil procedures in all courts. Rules are adapted from Federal Rules, without current Federal amendments. Probate and certain statutory matters are excepted.

Demand for Admission of Facts.—If facts in request not denied within 30 days of service, they are deemed admitted, except that defendant need not answer until 45 days after service of complaint. Court may shorten time. (36 Civ. R.P.).

Discovery.—Local rules based on Federal Rules. Interrogatories limited to 30 questions. (26[a] Civ. R.P.).

Direct actions against insurer not allowed.

Liability in tort actions is several for causes of action accruing after Mar. 5, 1989. (09.17.080).

Small Claims.—See category Courts and Legislature, topic Courts.

See also topics Actions, Appeal and Error, Depositions and Discovery, Injunctions, Judgments, Pleading, Process; category Debtor and Creditor, topics Attachment, Executions, Garnishment.

PROCESS:

Generally, as provided in Federal Rule 4, with deviations as noted below. Summons is issued by the court or its clerk and is served together with complaint by peace officer, by person specially appointed by Commissioner of Public Safety for that purpose or, where rule so provides by registered or certified mail. (Rule 4, Civ. R.P.). Subpoena may be served by peace officer, or by any person not less than age 18 who is not party to action.

Copies of summons and complaint served must be certified by plaintiff, his agent or attorney, or by clerk of court. (Rule 4 Civ. R.P.).

Who May Serve.—See introductory paragraph, supra.

Personal Service on Infant.—By personally delivering copy of summons and complaint to infant, and also to infant's father, mother or guardian, or if no parent or guardian within state, then to any person having care or control of infant, or with whom infant resides, or in whose service infant is employed, or if service cannot be made on any of them, then as provided by order of court. (Rule 4, Civ. R.P.).

Personal Service on Incompetent Persons.—By personally delivering copy of summons and complaint to guardian of person or competent adult member of his family with whom he resides, or if he is living in institution, then to director or chief executive officer of institution, or if service cannot be made upon any of them, then as provided by order of court; and unless court otherwise orders also to incompetent. (Rule 4, Civ. R.P.).

Personal Service on Corporation.—Upon domestic or foreign corporation, by delivering copy of summons and complaint to officer, managing or general agent, or to any other agent authorized by appointment or by law to receive service of process. (Rule 4, Civ. R.P.).

Personal Service on Partnership.—By delivering copy of summons and complaint personally to member of such partnership, or to managing or general agent of partnership, or to any other agent authorized by appointment or by law to receive service of process, or to person having control of business of partnership; or if service cannot be made upon any of them, then as provided by order of court. (Rule 4, Civ. R.P.).

Personal Service on Unincorporated Associations.—By delivering copy of summons and complaint personally to officer, managing or general agent, or to any other person authorized by appointment or by law to receive service of process, or if service cannot be made upon any of them, then as provided by order of court. (Rule 4, Civ. R.P.).

Personal Service on State of Alaska.—By delivering copy of summons and complaint personally to Attorney General and to person in judicial district designated by him in writing filed with clerk of court, and when service is made upon such person so designated by also sending copy of summons and of complaint by registered or certified mail to attorney general of Alaska at Juneau, Alaska. (Rule 4, Civ. R.P.).

Personal Service on Officer or Agency of State.—By serving State of Alaska as provided in preceding paragraph, and by delivering copy of summons and complaint to such officer or agency. If agency is corporation copies shall be delivered as provided in rule for personal service on corporation. (Rule 4, Civ. R.P.).

Personal Service on Public Corporation.—Upon borough or incorporated city, town, school district, public utility district, or other public corporation in state, by delivering copy of summons and complaint to chief executive officer or chief clerk or secretary thereof. (Rule 4, Civ. R.P.).

Personal Service Outside State.—By procedure provided for under subhead Service by Mail, infra. (Rule 4, Civ. R.P.).

Service by Mail.—Process may be served within state or U.S. or any of its possessions by registered or certified mail upon individual other than infant or incompetent person and upon corporation, partnership, and unincorporated association. Process shall be mailed by clerk for restricted delivery only to party to whom summons or other process is directed or to person authorized under federal regulation to receive his restricted delivery mail. All receipts shall be so addressed that they are returned to party requesting summons or process or his attorney. Proof of service shall be made by affidavit forthwith. (Rule 4, Civ. R.P.).

Substituted Service.—When it appears by affidavit by person having knowledge of facts filed with clerk that after diligent inquiry party cannot be personally served, service may be made by publication or as otherwise directed by court. Court, in its discretion may allow service in any manner reasonably calculated to give absent party actual notice of proceedings and opportunity to be heard, so long as order permitting such service is entered before service of process is made. (Rule 4, Civ. R.P.).

Service by Publication.—Absent defendants may be served with summons by publication if affidavit filed with clerk stating that diligent inquiry, as defined in Civil Rule 4, made and service within state not possible. (Rule 4 Civ. R.P.).

Notice shall be published once a week for four consecutive calendar weeks in newspaper published in district in which action is pending. If no newspaper is published in district, then in newspaper published in state which circulates in that district. Prior to last publication copy of notice and complaint or pleading shall be sent by registered mail, postage prepaid, to absent parties' residence or place where party receives mail addressed in care of party, unless it appears by affidavit that absent parties' residence or place is unknown and cannot be ascertained after inquiry. Notice shall be in form of summons, stating briefly nature of action, relief demanded, and why party named in notice has been made party. If action involves real property, notice shall include property's legal description. Notice shall state time within which party is to appear or answer or plead, and effect of failure to do so. In case of published notice, absent parties shall respond not more than 30 days after last date of publication, and court may proceed after that time as if absent party had been served. Proof of publication made by affidavit of newspaper's publisher, printer, manager, foreman, or principal clerk, or by attorney for party at whose instance service was made. Affidavits shall be accompanied by copy of printed notice marked with name of newspaper and dates published. (Rule 4, Civ. R.P.).

Long Arm Statute in Effect.—State court having jurisdiction over subject matter has jurisdiction over a person served in an action according to rules of civil procedure when: (1) Defendant is present in state, domiciled, domestic corporation or engaged in substantial activity; (2) statute specifically confers personal jurisdiction; (3) in action claiming injury arising out of act or omission in this state; (4) where injury in state was caused by act or omission outside state if solicitation was carried on in state or products used in this state; (5) in contract situations where activity is centered in this state; (6) actions involving real property and tangible property in state; (7) in action for annulment, divorce or separate maintenance when personal claim asserted and parties in state six consecutive months during preceding six years, plaintiff still in state and defendant receives notice; (8) in various other areas of deficiency judgment, domestic corporation, its officers and directors, taxes, insurance, actions against personal representatives on claim against deceased person; (9) action for collection of taxes; (10) action which arose out of promise which occurred in this state or promisee was resident; (11) action against personal representative to enforce claim against deceased if grounds in (2)-(10) would have conferred jurisdiction. (09.05.015).

Proof of Service.—Made by affidavit, if not made by peace officer; must be in writing, stating manner, place, date and papers served. Proof of mailing and publication by affidavit, with copy of notice and dates attached. (Rule 4, Civ. R.P.).

Miscellaneous.—Process may be served on Commissioner of Commerce if foreign corporation fails to appoint registered agent or whenever registered agent cannot with reasonable diligence be found or whenever certificate of authority of foreign corporation is suspended or revoked. (10.06.765).

See note at head of Digest as to 1998 legislation covered.

See Topical Index in front part of this volume.

AK – 9

PROCESS . . . *continued*

Process may be served on Commissioner of Commerce if electric or telephone cooperative fails to appoint registered agent or whenever registered agent cannot with reasonable diligence be found. (10.25.500).

Every applicant for registration under Blue Sky Law (see category Business Regulation and Commerce, topic Securities) and every issuer which proposes to offer a security in state through person acting on agency basis in common-law sense must file irrevocable consent with Commissioner of Commerce appointing Commissioner to be attorney to receive process in any noncriminal action. When any person, including nonresident, engages in conduct prohibited by act, and he has not filed consent to service of process, such conduct is considered equivalent to appointment of Commissioner as attorney to receive process. (45.55.990[g]).

Domestic or foreign insurance companies must file with Director of Insurance resolution of board of directors consenting that service of process on Director of Insurance in suits or actions against it in Alaska is valid service on company, which consent is irrevocable so long as any policy remains in force in the state or any loss remains unpaid thereon. (21.09.180).

Licensed nonresident insurance agent, broker or adjuster must appoint Director of Insurance as attorney to receive process. (21.27.280).

Service may be made on Lieutenant Governor for unauthorized doing of insurance business. (21.33.025).

Nonresident Motorist.—See category Transportation, topic Motor Vehicles.
See also topic Practice.

REPLEVIN:

In pending action for recovery of possession of personal property, plaintiff, at any time, may claim immediate delivery thereof, by filing an affidavit required by the court with an undertaking executed by sufficient sureties to effect that they are bound in double value of the property for prosecution of the action and return of the property to defendant.

Defendant may except to sufficiency of sureties or he may require return of the property by giving an undertaking approved by Clerk of Court and executed by sufficient sureties to effect that they are bound in double value of the property for delivery of the property to plaintiff if so adjudged.

Peace Officer taking the property into custody is responsible for it until it is delivered to party entitled to it.

If third person makes an affidavit claiming ownership or right to possess property, property may be released to him unless plaintiff indemnifies Peace Officer against the third party claim by an undertaking approved by Clerk of Court. (09.40.260-310).

SEQUESTRATION:

No statute.

Provisional remedy available. (Rule 64, Civ. R.P.).

Writ available. (Rule 70, Civ. R.P.).

SERVICE:

See topic Process.

STAY OF EXECUTION:

See category Debtor and Creditor, topic Executions.

SUBMISSION OF CONTROVERSY:

Unnecessary under Civil Rules of Procedure.

VENUE:

Venue for all actions shall be set under rules established by supreme court. (22.10.030, Rule 3 Civ. R.P.).

COURTS AND LEGISLATURE

COURTS:

United States District Court.—Clerk's office: Anchorage 99501.

Court headquarters are located at Anchorage. As need arises, court also sits in cities of Nome, Fairbanks, Juneau, and Ketchikan.

Filing Fees.—Plaintiff, $150; defendant, none. For filing fees in bankruptcy cases, see 28 U.S.C. §1930.

Supreme Court.—Supreme Court is composed of a Chief Justice and four Associate Justices.

Jurisdiction.—Supreme Court has appellate jurisdiction in all matters. Court may issue injunctions and other writs. Any Justice may issue writ of habeas corpus. Chief Justice is administrative head of all State courts, and Supreme Court promulgates all rules of procedure for all courts. (22.05.010).

Court of Appeals.—Court of Appeals is composed of three judges.

Jurisdiction.—Court of Appeals has appellate jurisdiction in all criminal matters involving criminal prosecution and sentencing (including matters involving criminal law violations by minors), post-conviction relief, extradition, habeas corpus, probation and parole, bail, and children's court matters. (22.07.020).

Superior Court.—

Jurisdiction.—Superior Court has statewide jurisdiction. Original jurisdiction in all civil and criminal matters, exclusive jurisdiction of probate, guardianship, adoption, juveniles and title to real property. Court has appellate jurisdiction from subordinate courts and administrative agencies. (22.10.020). When jurisdiction concurrent between superior and district courts, action may not be filed in superior court, except for

petitions for injunctive relief in cases involving domestic violence or except as provided by supreme court rules.

Filing Fees.—Plaintiff, $100.

Districts.—

First Judicial District: Southeastern Alaska Court sits at Ketchikan, Juneau, and Sitka.

Second Judicial District: Barrow, Kotzebue and Nome.

Third Judicial District: Anchorage, Kenai, Kodiak, Palmer and Valdez.

Fourth Judicial District: Fairbanks and Bethel.

District and Magistrate Courts.—District courts have statewide civil and criminal jurisdiction. They have original civil jurisdiction in matters when amount claimed exclusive of costs, interest and attorney fees does not exceed $50,000. District court's civil jurisdiction does not extend to actions involving questions of title to real property nor to actions for false imprisonment, libel, slander, malicious prosecution, equitable actions nor actions in which state is defendant.

Filing Fees.—Plaintiff, $60.

Magistrates' jurisdiction is same as that of District Judges except that in civil actions jurisdiction is limited to $5,000.

First Judicial District: Court sits at Juneau and Ketchikan. Magistrates located in following towns: Angoon, Craig, Haines, Hoonah, Juneau, Kake, Ketchikan, Pelican, Petersburg, Sitka, Skagway, Wrangell and Yakutat.

Second Judicial District: Court sits at Nome. Magistrates located in Barrow, Gambell, Kiana, Kotzebue, Nome, Noorvik, Point Hope, Savoonga, Selawik, Shungnak, and Unalakleet.

Third Judicial District: Court sits in Anchorage, Palmer and Homer. Magistrates in Anchorage, Cold Bay, Cordova, Dillingham, Glennallen, Homer, Kenai, King Salmon (Naknek Court), Kodiak, Palmer, St. Paul Island, Sand Point, Seldovia, Seward, Unalaska, Valdez and Whittier.

Fourth Judicial District: Court sits in Fairbanks. Magistrates in Delta Junction, Fairbanks, Ft. Yukon, Galena, Healy, Nenana, Tanana, and Tok.

Bethel Area: Magistrates in Aniak, Bethel, Emmonak, Hooper Bay, Medoryuk, Mt. Village, Quinhagak, St. Marys and Tununak.

Small Claims Courts.—See subhead District and Magistrate Courts, supra. Matters involving amounts of $5,000 or less exclusive of interest and costs are handled as small claims; procedure is same basically as set forth in Civil Rules for all other cases except formal pleadings are not required and potential litigants are required to be advised that mediation, conciliation, and arbitration services are available as alternatives to litigation. (22.15.040). Satisfaction of judgment obtained by same procedure as all other judgments. No jurisdiction over actions for specific relief, declaratory judgments, injunctions. (District Court Civil Rule 1).

Filing Fees.—Plaintiff, $25-$50.

LEGISLATURE:

Convenes annually in Jan. (24.05.090).

Special Sessions.—Governor may call special session, at locations throughout state, and legislature may call itself into session if two-thirds of membership responds in affirmative to poll conducted by presiding officers of respective houses. (24.05.100).

Initiative and Referendum.—May be exercised by people of every political subdivision of state (29.26.100-.190), and by people of state (Constitution, Art XI).

Ethics.—Conflict of interest standards for state legislators and legislative employees. (24.60.010-24.60.120).

Lobbyists.—Provisions administered by Alaska Public Offices Commission. (24.45).

REPORTS:

Decisions of supreme court are reported in Pacific Reporter (West. Pub. Co.). (1960—). Territorial cases reported in Alaska Reports.

Digests.—Alaska Digest (West Pub. Co.) covers all Alaska Supreme Court and Alaska Federal District Court cases.

STATUTES:

Alaska Statutes (AS), officially adopted 1963 (1.05.006), is only official compilation. As supplemented with replacement pages after each legislative session. There are also session laws containing legislation of each session of legislature.

Uniform Acts adopted are: Air Licensing (1929); Alcoholism and Intoxication Treatment (1972); Anatomical Gift (1970); Arbitration (1968); Attendance of Witnesses From Without the State in Criminal Proceedings (1962); Child Custody Jurisdiction (1977); Commercial Code (1962); Common Interest Ownership Act (1986); Common Trust Fund (1964); Criminal Extradition (1962); Disposition of Community Property Rights at Death (1984); Enforcement of Foreign Judgments (1972); Estate Tax Apportionment (1958 Act) (1973); Extradition of Persons of Unsound Mind (1923); Federal Tax Lien Registration (1933); Foreign Acknowledgments (1915); Foreign Bank Loan (1960); Foreign Money-Judgments Recognition (1972); Gifts to Minors, Revised (1967); Insurers Liquidation (1966); Interstate Compact on Juveniles (1960); Interstate Family Support Act (1995); Land Sales Practices (1968); Limited Partnership (1917); Multi-State Tax Compact (1970); Narcotic Drug (1943); Partnership (1917); ‡Probate Code (1972); Reciprocal Transfer Tax (1933); Recognition of Acknowledgments (1981); Residential Landlord and Tenant (1974); ‡Securities (1959); Simultaneous Death (1987); Testamentary Additions to Trusts (1967); Trade Secrets (1988).

‡Adopted with significant variations or modifications. See appropriate topics as to Acts within scope of Digests volume.

For text of Uniform Acts falling within the scope of the Martindale-Hubbell Law Digests see Uniform and Model Acts section.

See note at head of Digest as to 1998 legislation covered.

See Topical Index in front part of this volume.

CRIMINAL LAW

BAIL:

See topic Criminal Law.

CRIMINAL LAW:

Crimes are defined by AS Title 11. Criminal procedure is regulated by Rules of Criminal Procedure (Crim. R.P.) based on Federal Rules of Criminal Procedure and by Code of Criminal Procedure. (AS Title 12).

No person can be held to answer for an infamous crime unless on presentment or indictment of a grand jury, except in cases arising in armed forces in time of war or public danger. Indictment may be waived, however, in which case prosecution may be by information. (12.80.020; Crim. R.P. Rule 7).

Death penalty abolished.

Victims Rights.—Victim impact statement is part of presentence and sentencing reports of each felony offender. (12.55.022 and 12.55.025). Victims rights include: To be informed of dates of trial and sentencing, to be informed of victim compensation procedures, to obtain immediate medical assistance (12.61.010), to comment on parole of prisoner (33.16.087), and to receive protection from harm arising out of cooperation with police (12.61.010).

Failure to ensure these rights does not give rise to separate cause of action. (12.61.010).

Bail.—Defendant is entitled to be admitted to bail before conviction as a matter of right if alleged victim can be reasonably protected through imposition of bail and conditions of release. (12.30.010).

Computers.—Criminal use of is class C felony. (11.46.740 and 11.46.990).

Sentencing Procedures.—12.55.025.

Interstate Compact for Supervision of Parolees and Probationers.—Adopted. (33.36.110).

Uniform Criminal Extradition Act.—Adopted at 12.70. This is old act and not new amended one.

DEBTOR AND CREDITOR

ASSIGNMENTS:

Uniform Commercial Code adopted. (45.01.101—45.09.507).

Common law rules apply. Assignee of chose in action may sue in his own name.

Any assignment, pledge or other transaction, irrespective of form, intended to create a security interest in personal property, including goods, documents, instruments, chattel paper, accounts receivable or contract rights, is governed by Uniform Commercial Code, Art. 9, effective Jan. 1, 1963. (45.01.101).

Recording.—Assignments of choses in action relating to real property should be recorded in office of the recorder for the district in which the real property is situated. See also category Business Regulation and Commerce, topic Commercial Code.

Assignment of Wages.—To Department of Labor for prosecution up to $5,000 allowed. (23.05.220-260).

ATTACHMENT:

Actions in Which Allowed—Grounds.—At any time after complaint is filed, writ of attachment may be secured by plaintiff: (1) In any action on contract, for payment of money which is not secured by a lien on property, or if so secured, when security is insufficient to satisfy a judgment for amount justly due plaintiff; (2) in any action on contract against a defendant not residing in state; (3) in any action for collection of any state tax or license fee. (09.40.010).

Courts Which May Issue Writ.—Superior, district and magistrate courts.

In Whose Favor Writ May Issue.—No distinctions made between residents and nonresidents as to right to secure attachment.

Property Subject.—All property not exempt from execution is liable to attachment. (09.40.010).

Proceedings to Obtain.—File affidavit showing grounds for attachment, amount of debt with allowance for setoff and counterclaim, no intent to hinder action or defraud creditors, and that defendant not in bankruptcy proceedings or that debt not extinguished by such proceedings. Notice and hearing within three to seven days required unless: (1) Defendant nonresident and ex parte writ needed for jurisdiction or (2) plaintiff establishes probable validity of claim and fact that defendant about to flee, dispose or conceal himself or possessions. (Rule 89, Civ. R.P.). Generally, hearing required before seizure. (502 P.2d 146).

Undertaking.—Before the writ issues, an undertaking with one or more sureties, for not less than $100, and at least equal to the amount for which judgment is claimed, must be filed by the plaintiff. With the undertaking must also be filed affidavits showing that the sureties are qualified and that, taken together, they are worth penalty of undertaking. (09.40.020).

Provisional Levy.—Property may be attached and held during pendency of motion for issuance of execution reviving judgment and until final ruling.

Release of Property.—Upon giving redelivery bond. (09.40.110).

It is a good defense to an action on a redelivery bond that the property did not, at the time of the execution of the writ of attachment, belong to the defendant against whom it was issued.

Discharge of Attachment.—Provided where perishable goods have been sold. (Rule 89, Civ. R.P.).

Lien on Real Estate.—Certificate shall be made by peace officer containing title of cause, names of parties, description of property attached, date of attachment, statement

that writ issued, date of issuance, and within ten days deliver certificate to recorder of recording district in which real property is situated. (A.S. 09.40.050).

Third Party Liability.—All persons having in their possession personal property belonging to defendant or owing debt to defendant at time of service upon them of writ and notice shall deliver, transfer or pay property or debts to peace officer or be liable to plaintiff until plaintiff satisfied. (09.40.040).

Levy on Mortgaged Personalty.—See category Mortgages, topic Chattel Mortgages.

Third Party Claims.—See topic Executions.

CREDITORS' SUITS:

Creditors may file bill to set aside conveyances or assignments, in writing or otherwise, made with intent to hinder, delay, or defraud creditors. See topics Executions, Fraudulent Sales and Conveyances.

EXECUTIONS:

Time for Issuance.—Ten days must elapse after entry of judgment except default, consent, or confession. (Civ. R.P. 62[a]).

Writ and Return.—The writ is issued by the clerk and directed to the officer serving writ. It contains the name of the court, the names of the parties to the action, and the title thereof, and such other matters as are required by law, depending upon the kind of execution, including in all cases a substantial description of the judgment. It is returnable within 60 days, if issued from the superior court; within 30, if issued from a district magistrate's court. Until levy, property is unaffected by execution. (9.35.010).

Exemptions.—See topic Exemptions.

Stay of Execution.—Stay may be granted upon cause shown. (Rule 62 Civ. R.P.).

Third Party Claims.—If a third party by affidavit claims title to and states value of property levied on under execution or attachment, officer may release levy if plaintiff, on demand, indemnifies officer by bond of two sureties qualifying in double amount of value of property. (9.35.130).

Levy on Mortgaged Personalty.—See category Mortgages, topic Chattel Mortgages.

Sales.—All auction sales in the state, when made by order of court, must be held between the hours of 9 A.M. and 4 P.M. (09.35.150).

Notice must be given (1) in case of personal property, by posting written or printed notice of time and place of sale in three public places within five miles of place where sale is to take place, not less than ten days prior to sale, one of such notices to be posted at the post-office nearest place of sale (9.35.140). (2) in case of real property, by posting similar notice particularly describing property for 30 days prior to sale in three public places as above provided, and publishing copy thereof once a week for four weeks in newspaper published nearest place of sale.

Officer holding the execution or his deputy cannot be a purchaser. Personalty, capable of manual delivery and not in possession of a third person, must be within view of persons attending sale, unless otherwise ordered by court. Property must be sold in such parcels as are likely to bring highest price. Realty, when consisting of several known parcels, may be lumped or sold separately whichever is likely to bring highest price; and, when portion of realty is claimed by a third person, it must be sold separately if he so requires. (9.35.150).

Redemption.—Judgment-debtor or his successor in interest may, prior to confirmation of sale redeem real property sold under execution, and the judgment-debtor within 12 months from such order of confirmation, may redeem by paying amount of purchase money, with interest at 8% per annum from date of sale, together with any taxes and authorized expenses paid by purchaser after purchase. (9.35.250).

Lien-creditor may redeem like property within 60 days from date or order confirming sale, by paying purchase money, interest, and amount of taxes and authorized expenses as aforesaid, together with amount of prior lien, if any. (9.35.230).

In case of unpatented mining claims, taxes include annual assessment work required by law to be performed. (9.35.230).

Leasehold with less than two years unexpired term not subject to redemption. (9.35.210).

Form.—Notice to debtor shall include instructions substantially as follows:

Form
NOTICE

The . . . . Court of the State of Alaska, ... Judicial District, has issued a judgment that you must pay to . . . . the sum of $ . . . . . A writ of execution has been issued against you, a copy of which is attached to this form. This writ is an order of the court by which your property can be taken from you and sold to pay the judgment and any court costs which have been assessed against you.

The following property, believed to be yours, has been seized and is now being held by the court:

	Person in Possession	
Description	at Time of Levy	Date of Levy

Both federal and state law provide that certain types of property (up to specified dollar evaluations) and certain percentages and types of wages are exempt from execution. Details of legal exemptions to which you may be entitled are available to you at . . . . [name and address of court issuing judgment], or you may contact any attorney of your choice, or other available legal service, for an explanation of your rights.

After having determined whether or not you are entitled to an exemption on the property described above, please complete and sign the following form and deliver or mail it to the court WITHIN 15 DAYS of the receipt of this notice:*
TO BE COMPLETED BY DEBTOR:
I have investigated my rights as to exemption from execution on the property described above, now in possession of the court, and find that (1) I AM . . . . (2) AM NOT . . . . entitled to an exemption. (Complete the following ONLY

See note at head of Digest as to 1998 legislation covered.

See Topical Index in front part of this volume.

EXECUTIONS . . . continued

if you have checked block #1, indicating that you claim an exemption.) Therefore, I claim an exemption up to the amount (or evaluation) of $ . . . . . . on property or money presently in custody of the court.

Signature of Debtor . . . .

* IF YOU HAVE CLAIMED NO EXEMPTIONS, OR IF YOU FAIL TO RETURN THE ABOVE FORM TO THE COURT WITHIN 15 DAYS OF THE RECEIPT OF THIS NOTICE, THE PROPERTY DESCRIBED ABOVE WILL BE SOLD TO SATISFY THE JUDGMENT AGAINST YOU IN THIS CASE. Any money in possession of the court which was seized to satisfy this judgment will be turned over to the judgment creditor. If you claim an exemption, and that exemption is disputed by the judgment creditor, a hearing on your claim will be held within three days after the claim for exemption is filed or as soon thereafter as practicable.

Please retain one copy of this form for your records and submit the other to the court as requested above.

Supplementary Proceedings.—Court may order a peace officer to arrest judgment debtor and bring him before the court upon satisfactory proof that he is leaving state with intent to defraud his creditors or absconding. Upon being brought before court, he may be ordered to enter into an undertaking with one or more sufficient sureties that he will appear before court when directed, and that he will not, during pendency of proceedings, dispose of any portion of his property not exempt from execution. In default of entering into undertaking, he may be committed to jail. (9.35.320).

EXEMPTIONS:

Judgment debtor is entitled to exemptions in property not to exceed aggregate value of $3,000 from following categories of property: (1) Household goods and wearing apparel. (2) Books and musical instruments reasonably held for debtor or dependent. (3) Family portraits and heirlooms. Exemption of jewelry up to $1,000. Judgment debtor is entitled to exemption up to $2,800 for professional books and tools of trade. Judgment debtor is entitled to exemption of pets up to $1,000. Individual is entitled to exemption of one motor vehicle to extent that value not exceed $3,000, if full value of motor vehicle does not exceed $20,000. (09.38.020).

Life Insurance Policies.—Policies and their reserves or present value to value of $10,000 thereof are exempt from claims of creditors. (09.38.025).

Waiver of exemption is not prohibited by statute.

Claim of Exemption.—Property to be held exempt must be selected and reserved by the judgment debtor or his agent at time of levy, or as soon thereafter, and before sale, as levy is known to him. (09.35.030).

Earnings.—Judgment debtor is entitled to exemption of his weekly net earnings not to exceed $350. If judgment debtor does not receive weekly earnings then maximum of that exemption is $1,400 per month. Creditor may levy upon these earnings if money is held outside correctional facility and claim is for court-ordered restitution resulting from crime conviction or adjudication of delinquency. (09.38.030).

Child Support Payments.—Amount ordered paid to court trustee as child support payments under Rule 67 Civ. R.P. is exempt from execution. (09.35.065).

Claims Enforceable Against Exempt Property.—(1) Child support, (2) state and local taxes, (3) one month's personal service income, (4) purchase price of property or loan for purchase price, (5) labor or materials for property, (6) special assessment for public improvement to property. (09.38.065).

Homestead Exemption.—See topic Homesteads.

See also topic Executions.

FORECLOSURE:

See topic Liens; category Mortgages, topics Chattel Mortgages, Mortgages of Real Property.

FRAUDULENT SALES AND CONVEYANCES:

Uniform Commercial Code adopted. (45.01.101).

Intent to Defraud.—Every conveyance of interest in lands, or the rents or profits thereof, and every charge upon lands or upon the rents and profits thereof, made or created with the intent to defraud prior or subsequent purchasers, for a valuable consideration, of the same lands, rents or profits is void, as against such purchasers. (34.40.020).

Except as provided in AS 34.40.110, every conveyance or assignment, in writing or otherwise, of any estate or interest in lands, or in goods, or things in action, or of any rents or profits issuing therefrom, and every charge upon lands, goods, or things in action, or upon rents or profits thereof, made with intent to hinder, delay, or defraud creditors or other persons of their lawful suits, damages, forfeitures, debts, or demands, and every bond or other evidence of debt given, action commenced, decree or judgment suffered, with like intent, as against persons so hindered, delayed, or defrauded, is void. (34.40.010).

Trusts.—Person who in writing transfers property in trust may provide that beneficiary's interest in trust may not be voluntarily or involuntarily transferred before payment or delivery of interest to beneficiary. If trust contains restriction, creditors and others prevented from satisfying claim out of interest unless certain conditions are met. (AS 34.40.110).

Bulk Sales.—Uniform Commercial Code adopted. (45.01.101).

Uniform Fraudulent Conveyance Act not adopted.

GARNISHMENT:

Garnishment is used as an aid to attachment.

Property Subject to Garnishment.—All property not exempt is subject to attachment. (09.40.030).

Duties of Garnishee.—Upon service of writ of attachment on a garnishee, he must furnish within reasonable time and within 24 hours a certificate of property of defendant which is in his possession. If he refuses to do so, or certificate is unsatisfactory to plaintiff, garnishee may be required by order to appear for examination on oath concerning same, and disobedience to such order may be punished as contempt. (09.40.060).

Order for Appearance.—An order requiring a person to appear for examination as garnishee must state the time and place for appearance. (Rule 89[1] Civ. R.P.).

Interlocutory Remedies Against Garnishee.—A garnishee may be restrained from disposing of defendant's property at time of making order for appearance and before judgment against him. (Rule 89[f] Civ. R.P.). He may be proceeded against for refusal to make or making unsatisfactory certificate to service of the writ of execution the same as when served with writ of attachment. (Rule 98[1]).

Discovery.—Plaintiff may utilize rules of discovery under supervision of court with respect to all matters relating to property of defendant believed to be in possession of garnishee. Refusal or failure to make discovery is governed by Civ. R.P. 89(1)(3).

Reply to Garnishee's Answer.—The plaintiff may reply to the garnishee's answer, and issues are tried as ordinary issues of fact between plaintiff and defendant. (Rule 89[1] Civ. R.P.).

Witnesses may be required to appear and testify in garnishee proceedings. (Rule 89[1] Civ. R.P.).

Judgment Against Garnishee.—If answer or trial disclose that garnishee had any property of the defendant liable to attachment at the time of service upon him of a copy of the writ of attachment, judgment may be given for the value thereof in money. Garnishee may discharge himself at any time before judgment by delivering, paying or transferring property of the debtor held by him to the officer. (Rule 89[1][5] Civ. R.P.).

Execution may issue upon judgment against garnishee as upon ordinary judgment between plaintiff and defendant, and costs and disbursements allowable and recoverable in same manner. (Rule 89[1] Civ. R.P.).

HOMESTEADS:

For acquiring land in Alaska see subhead Homestead Entry, infra.

Limitations of Value, Area.—A homestead is exempt, but it must be principal residence and cannot in any instance exceed $54,000 in value. (9.38.010). Homestead exemption may be claimed by owner or owner's spouse, dependent, agent or attorney. (09.38.090). No discrimination against alien residents. Exemption extends to proceeds of sale of homestead.

Conveyance or Incumbrance.—Husband and wife must join in any deed, conveyance or mortgage of family homestead owned by either. (34.15.010). Required joinder in execution of conveyance does not create proprietary right not otherwise vested in such joining spouse. Failure of joinder does not affect validity of conveyance unless such nonjoining spouse appears on title; but such conveyance shall be sufficient to convey legal title; provided such conveyance otherwise sufficient and no suit filed in court of record in judicial division, wherein real property situated, within one year from date recording such conveyance, by nonjoining spouse to set aside, alter, change, or reform such conveyance, or nonjoining spouse does not file notice of interest in property within one year with recorder in whose precinct property is situated. (34.15.010).

Death of Owner.—Homestead is exempt from sale or judicial process after death of person entitled thereto, for the collection of any debts for which same could not have been sold during his lifetime. (9.35.060).

Homestead Allowance.—See category Family, topic Husband and Wife.

Homestead entry on Federal lands in Alaska is to be abolished on tenth anniversary of enactment of P.L. 94-579, Tit. VII, §702(a), Oct. 21, 1976. Any land formerly available under homestead laws has already been removed by Public Land Order 5418, published in Federal Register Mar. 28, 1974.

State of Alaska under Statehood Act, 72 U. S. St. L. 339, is allowed to select within 25 years after date of admission to Union 400,000 acres of vacant and unappropriated national forest land, and 400,000 acres from other vacant, unappropriated and unreserved public land, all of which must be adjacent to established communities or suitable for prospective community centers and recreational areas. In addition Alaska may select within 25 years after date of admission to Union 102,550,000 acres of public land, vacant, unappropriated and unreserved at time of selection. Any lease, permit, license or contract issued under the Mineral Leasing Act of Feb. 25, 1920 (41 Stat. 437; 30 U.S.C., §181 et seq., as amended), or under the Alaska Coal Leasing Act of Oct. 20, 1914 (38 Stat. 741; 30 U.S.C., §432 et seq., as amended), has the effect of withdrawing the lands subject thereto from selection by the state unless application to select such land is filed with Secretary of Interior within period of five years from date of admission of Alaska into Union. (Alaska Statehood Act, 72 Stat. 339, as amended by H.R. 5849, which was signed by the President Aug. 18, 1959).

Homestead entry on state lands classified as agricultural or grazing lands may be authorized by Director of Division of Lands of Department of Natural Resources with approval of Commissioner of Natural Resources. (39.09.-010). Director's office located at Anchorage.

State is directed to classify, survey and plat 25,000 acres of State land for purpose of erecting residential dwellings. Six year residents of state may apply for permit to build upon such land and may acquire patent to land upon satisfaction of certain requirements. (39.04).

Reserved to the State out of every grant of land are oils, gases, coal, ores, minerals, fissionable materials, and fossils of every name, kind or description, and the right to explore for such minerals, and the right to enter for purpose of opening, developing and working mines and taking out and removing such minerals, and the right to erect, construct, maintain and use all buildings, machinery, pipelines, powerlines, and railroads, remove soil and to remain on the land for the foregoing purposes and to occupy so much of the land as may be necessary or convenient for such purposes. (38.05.125).

LEVY:

See topics Attachment, Executions.

LIENS:

Uniform Commercial Code adopted. (45.01.101).

Artisans.—Any person who makes, alters, repairs, or bestows labor on any article of personal property at request of owner or lawful possessor thereof, has a lien thereon for just, reasonable charges for labor performed and/or material furnished for that purpose, and may hold and retain possession of the personalty until those charges are paid; but no such lien continues, after delivery of the chattel to its owner, as against rights of third persons, who, prior to filing of lien notice, may have acquired title to such chattel in good faith, for value and without knowledge of lien. Before delivery to owner, in order to preserve lien, a "chattel lien notice" must be filed, in office of recorder of recording district in which chattel is kept, stating name of claimant, name of owner, description of chattel, amount for which lien is claimed, date upon which expenditure of labor or material thereon was completed, and signed by claimant or someone in his behalf. Possessor of chattel, under agreement for purchase thereof, whether title is in him or his vendor, is deemed owner. Lien is preferred to any lien, mortgage or other encumbrance which may attach subsequently to time of commencement of performance of labor or furnishing of materials, and is also preferred to any lien, mortgage or other encumbrance which may have attached previously but which was not filed or recorded so as to create constructive notice prior to that time and of which lien, mortgage or other encumbrance claimant has no notice. If claim is not paid within three months, and claimant has not parted with possession of chattel, he may summarily foreclose lien by three weeks notice published in newspaper or, if no newspaper, posted. If lien notice has been filed, may foreclose by suit in equity brought within six months after filing of lien. (34.35.175 to 34.35.215).

Carriage, Storage, Pasturage, etc.—Any person who is a common carrier, or who shall, at the request of the owner or lawful possessor of any personal property, carry, convey, or transport the same from one place to another; and any person who shall safely keep or store any grain, wares, merchandise, and personal property at the request of the owner or lawful possessor thereof; and any person who shall pasture or feed any horses, cattle, hogs, sheep, or other live stock, or bestow any labor, care, or attention upon the same at request of owner or lawful possessor thereof, has a lien upon such property for his just and reasonable charges, and may retain possession of such property until such charges are paid. And if not paid within three months after the care, attention, and labor have been performed or bestowed, or the materials or food furnished, lienor may sell the property at public auction, after three weeks published notice of sale. (34.35.220-225).

Employee Benefit Fund Lien.—When an employer has agreed with an employee or group of employees to make payment to a medical, health, hospital, welfare, or pension fund or such other fund for benefit of employees, or has entered into a collective bargaining agreement providing for payments but fails to make the payments when due, a lien is created in favor of each affected employee on earnings of his employer and on all property of his employer used in operation of his employer's business to extent of the money, plus any penalties due to be paid on employee's behalf to qualify him for participation in the fund and for any expenses incurred by him for which he would have been entitled to reimbursement under the fund if required payments had been made. (23.10.047).

Logging.—Laborers and loggers have a lien for labor on or in assisting to obtain saw-logs, spars, piles, cordwood, fuelwood, shingle bolts, or other timber. (34.35.235).

Oil Wells, etc.—Laborers, material men and contractors have a lien for work, labor and materials for the construction, altering, digging, drilling, boring, operating, completing or repairing of gas wells, oil wells, or other wells, gas pipe lines or oil pipe lines. (34.35.125).

Fish or Aquatic Animals.—Laborers and material men have a lien for labor or materials furnished that contributes to the preparation of fish or aquatic animals for food, fish meal, fertilizer, oil or other article of commerce. (34.35.320).

Mines, Mining Machinery, etc.—Laborers and miners have a lien for labor and work in, on and about mines and mining property. (34.35.125).

Work or labor performed on a mine, mining claim, oil, gas or other well, dredge, steam shovel, derrick, mill or machine by person having right of possession thereof or having possession thereof with owner's knowledge is deemed done at instance of owner, mortgagee or lien claimant of the property and interest of such owner, mortgagee or lien claimant is subject to lien for such work or labor unless such owner, mortgagee or lien claimant, within ten days after obtaining knowledge of such work or labor being performed, posts nonliability notices in three conspicuous places on such mine or claim, near such well or on such dredge, steam shovel, derrick, mill or machine. Notice by mortgagee or other lien claimant must state nature of lien and amount due thereon and refer to volume and page of record of lien. (34.35.150). Notice need not be posted on any drag line, electric shovel, tractor, scraper, hoist, truck or mobile equipment or machinery, or personal property which is readily moveable or is required to be moved from place to place in course of mining operations. (34.35.150).

Codification.—The laws relating to liens of laborers in and about mines, liens for work on or repair of chattels, liens of carriers and warehousemen, liens for labor on logs, piles and other timber products, and liens of cannery and saltery workers, fishermen and watchmen have been codified and all conflicting laws repealed.

Mechanics' Liens.—Person has lien for contract price if he performs labor on, furnishes materials or equipment used for construction, alteration or repair of building or improvement at request of owner or his agent. General contractors, employee benefit trusts of laborers with direct contract with agent or owner, and those preparing plans, surveys, architectural or engineering plans for owner or agent, whether or not used, also have lien. (34.35.050). Every contractor, sub-contractor, architect, builder, or other person in charge of such work or part thereof, is deemed agent of the owner in establishing such lien. (34.35.115).

Mechanic's lien extends to the land on which the structure was constructed, to a sufficient extent for convenient use or occupation, or to the mine developed, provided at the time the materials were begun to be furnished, or labor to be performed, the person causing the same to be done was owner thereof, but only to the extent of his estate therein. The extent of land necessary for use or occupation may be determined by the court, in its discretion.

Stop payment notice may be given to construction lendor. (34.35.062).

Original construction lien preferred to prior encumbrance, but other liens not prior to encumbrances recorded before claim of lien or notice of right to lien recorded. (34.35.060).

Materials furnished for such an improvement are not subject to legal process against the purchaser, except it be for the purchase price thereof, if in good faith they have been or are about to be used in the improvement. (34.35.105).

Notice of Nonresponsibility.—Owner of, or person claiming interest in land on which improvement is made, if he had knowledge thereof, is deemed to have caused improvement to be made, and be liable, unless within three days after obtaining knowledge thereof, he posts written and signed notice that he will not be responsible, at conspicuous place where work is being done. Posting is attested to by witness and posting is recorded. (34.35.065).

Notice of completion may be made by recording notice and giving notice at least five days before recording to all claimants who have given notice of right to lien or stop-payment notice to owner and lender prior to ten days before recording notice of completion. (34.35.071).

Claim of lien must be filed within ten days after notice of completion is filed. (34.35.071). Certain claimants have up to 15 days after notice of completion is recorded. (34.35.068). If notice of completion not recorded by owner, lien claim must be recorded within 90 days after contract completed, or person ceases to furnish labor, material, services or equipment. (34.35.068). Claim must contain true statement of demand after deducting all just credits or offsets, name of owner or reputed owner if known, name of person by whom claimant was employed or to whom he furnished material and description of property to be charged. Claim must be verified by oath of claimant or some other person having knowledge of facts. (34.35.070).

Bond.—If claim of lien is in dispute, owner or contractor or subcontractor may free property from effects of a claim of lien by posting bond in penal sum of 1½ times lien claim, guaranteeing sum lien claimant may claim, together with lien claimant's reasonable cost of suit if he recovers on lien claim. (34.35.072).

Public Works.—See category Civil Actions and Procedure, topic Bonds.

Attachment Lien.—See topic Attachment.

Attorney's Lien.—See category Legal Profession, topic Attorneys and Counselors.

Collateral Security.—See topic Pledges.

Execution Lien.—See topic Executions.

Judgment Lien.—See category Civil Actions and Procedure, topic Judgments.

Landlord's Lien.—See category Property, topic Landlord and Tenant.

Liens on Exempt Property.—See topic Exemptions.

Liens on Homestead.—See topic Homesteads.

Real Estate Mortgage Lien.—See category Mortgages, topic Mortgages of Real Property.

Tax Lien.—See category Taxation, topic Property (Ad Valorem) Tax, subhead Lien.

Foreclosure.—Action to enforce the lien must be commenced within six months after filing the lien claim, or if credit be extended, within six months after expiration of term of credit, or if supplemental notice is filed, within six months of filing, but in any event, within one year. (34.35.080).

The procedure in foreclosure is similar to foreclosure of a mortgage on real property. Such actions have a preference on the calendar of the court. Costs may be recovered, including expenses of filing claim and recoverable attorney's fees.

Redemption.—There is no specific statute as to redemption from foreclosure sale. But see topic Executions, subhead Redemption.

Priorities.—See subhead Mechanics' Liens, supra. Among lien holders, priority where proceeds of sale insufficient as follows: laborers, employment benefit trusts, materialmen, subcontractors and prime contractors, and general contractor. (34.35.112).

Anticipated Payments.—Payments made by the owner to a contractor or subcontractor, before 90 days after completion of improvement, are invalid as against all other lienholders, except in so far as moneys so paid were applied to payment of such persons. (34.35.090).

Watchmen of real or personal property have lien for services as such, coordinate with any lien for labor or material. (34.35.395).

MECHANICS' LIENS:

See topic Liens.

PLEDGES:

Uniform Commercial Code adopted. (45.01.101).

RECEIVERS:

A receiver may be appointed in any civil action or proceeding, other than an action for the recovery of specific personal property:

(1) Provisionally, before judgment, on either party's application, when party's right to property which is subject of action and which is in adverse party's possession, is probable, and the property or its rents or profits are in danger of being lost or materially injured or impaired; (2) after judgment, to carry the same into effect; (3) to dispose of the property according to the judgment, or to preserve it during the pendency of an appeal, or when an execution has been returned, unsatisfied and the debtor refuses to apply his property in satisfaction of the judgment; (4) in cases provided in the code, or by other statute when a corporation has been dissolved, or is in solvent or in imminent

RECEIVERS . . . *continued*
danger of insolvency, or has forfeited its corporate rights; (5) in case when a debtor has been declared insolvent. (09.40.240).

REDEMPTION:

See topics Executions, Liens; categories Mortgages, topic Mortgages of Real Property; Taxation, topic Property (Ad Valorem) Tax, subhead Redemption.

SUPPLEMENTARY PROCEEDINGS:

See topic Executions.

TRUSTEE PROCESS:

See topic Garnishment.

USURY:

See category Business Regulation and Commerce, topic Interest.

DISPUTE RESOLUTION

ALTERNATIVE DISPUTE RESOLUTION:

Mandatory Dispute Resolution.—
Alaska Railroad Corporation Employees.—If impasse develops when attempting to resolve disputes, dispute shall go to mediation. (42.40.840). 42.40.840 details mediation procedure. If mediation ends with no resolution, employees may strike unless corporation enjoins strike. If deadlock still exists after injunction issued, it shall be submitted to binding arbitration. (42.40.850). See 42.40.850 for details.
Public Employees.—Before employees of municipal school district, regional educational attendance area, or state boarding school can strike, they must first submit to advisory arbitration. (23.40.200).
Small Claims.—All small claim litigants shall be informed if mediation, conciliation, and arbitration services are available as alternative to litigation. (22.15.040).

Voluntary Dispute Resolution.—Court may order mediation upon motion by any party or upon its own motion whenever it determines that mediation may result in equitable settlement. (Civ. R.P. 100). For details see Civ. R.P. 100.
Dental and Medical Malpractice.—Patient and healthcare provider may execute agreement to submit dispute arising out of treatment to arbitration. Such agreement must state on its face and in bold print that agreement to arbitrate is not and cannot be condition of treatment or agreement is void. Attorney General must first approve form. Patient has 30 days to revoke agreement. (09.55.535). For additional details see 09.55.535.
Divorce.—Within 30 days of filing complaint or cross-complaint in action for divorce, party may request settlement mediation. Court may require settlement mediation sua sponte. (25.24.060).
Landlord and tenant may agree to mediate or arbitrate disputes arising out of rental agreement. (34.04.345). Such mediation or arbitration agreement shall be included within rental agreement, referenced in rental agreement, or attached to rental agreement. (34.03.345).
Motor Vehicles.—Under certain circumstances, owner of motor vehicle may be required to submit to nonbinding alternate dispute resolution before pursuing other remedies. (45.45.355). For details see 45.45.355.
Partners.—Before partnership claim or liability can be submitted to arbitration, all partners must authorize. (32.05.040[c][5]).
Public employees may agree in writing with employer to submit dispute arising from interpretation or application of collective bargaining agreement. (23.40.200[e]). Parties to collective bargaining agreement may provide in agreement contract for arbitration to be conducted solely according to Uniform Arbitration Act. (23.40.200[f]). For details see 23.40.200.

ARBITRATION AND AWARD:

Uniform Arbitration Act adopted (09.43) but does not apply to labor-management contracts unless incorporated by reference or provided for by statute. Compulsory arbitration of claims of $3,000 or less may be required by Supreme Court rule. (09.43.190).

Voluntary arbitration procedures specifically established for malpractice claims. (09.55.535). In absence of arbitration agreement, court may appoint expert advisory panel in malpractice cases. (09.55.536).

Award and Enforcement Thereof.—Majority of arbitrators shall make award on writing and each arbitrator joining shall sign award. Copy shall be delivered personally to each party or sent by registered mail. (09.43.040—.080).

Judgment on Award.—Upon granting of order confirming, modifying or correcting award judgment or decree shall be entered in conformity with award and be enforced as any other judgment or decree. Court may award costs. (09.43.140).

Contracts to Arbitrate Future Disputes.—Valid, enforceable and irrevocable. (09.43.010).

DOCUMENTS AND RECORDS

ACKNOWLEDGMENTS:

Uniform Acknowledgment Act not adopted.

Uniform Recognition of Acknowledgment Act.—Adopted. (09.63.050-09.63.100).

Within State.—Acknowledgments may be made within State of Alaska before any justice, judge, magistrate, clerk or deputy clerk of court, notary public, postmaster municipal clerk carrying out clerk's duties, or other authorized officer. (09.63.010). Fee is not regulated by statute.

Outside State.—Notarial acts, including acknowledgments, performed outside state will be recognized if performed by authorized notary public, justice, judge, magistrate, clerk or deputy clerk of court of record in place in which notarial act is performed, officer of foreign service of U.S., consular agency, or person authorized by regulation of Department of State, or other persons authorized to perform notarial acts in place in which act is performed. (09.63.050).

Persons in or with U.S. Armed Forces.—Commissioned officer in active service with armed forces or person authorized by regulation of armed forces to perform notarial acts may take acknowledgments for merchant seamen of U.S., member of armed forces of U.S., person serving with or accompanying armed forces of U.S. or his dependants. (09.63.010).

Real Estate Conveyances, Within State.—Acknowledgments may be made within state of Alaska before any clerk of court, notary public, postmaster, or commissioner by subscribing witness or handwriting. Officer must endorse on instrument certificate of acknowledgment and date it was taken under his hand. (34.15.150).

Real Estate Conveyances, Outside State, But Within U.S.—Acknowledgments may be made within any state, territory, or district of U.S. outside of Alaska, before any judge of court of record, justice of peace, notary public, or other officer authorized to take acknowledgments by law of jurisdiction in which taken. (34.15.160).

Real Estate Conveyances, Outside U.S.—Conveyance executed in foreign country in accordance with that country's laws may be acknowledged under laws of Alaska. (34.15.180).

General Requirements as to Taking.—Officer taking acknowledgment must certify that person acknowledging appeared before him and acknowledged execution of instrument and that person acknowledging was known to person taking acknowledgment or person taking acknowledgment must have satisfactory evidence that person acknowledging was person described in and who executed instrument. (09.63.030; 09.63.080).

General Requirements of Certificates.—Certificate must conform to laws and regulations of state or other place in which acknowledgment is taken or certificate must contain words "acknowledged before me" or their substantial equivalent. (09.63.080). For real estate, endorsement by officer taking acknowledgment of certificate of acknowledgment and date of making acknowledgment. (34.15.150).

Attorneys in Fact.—Uniform Durable Power of Attorney Act not adopted. Uniform Probate Code applies. (13.26.325-13.26.330).

Corporations.—No special provisions.

Foreign Acknowledgments.—Conveyance may be executed according to laws of foreign country and execution of it acknowledged under 09.63.050-09.63.130.

Effect of Acknowledgment.—Entitles conveyance to be read in evidence without further proof or recorded and filing is constructive notice of conveyance's contents to subsequent purchasers or mortgagees. (40.17.090).

Proof by Subscribing Witness or Handwriting.—Proof of execution of an instrument may be made before any officer authorized to take an acknowledgment thereof by a subscribing witness thereto, who must state his own residence, and that he knew the person described in, and who executed the instrument. Officer must either personally know witness or have satisfactory proof of his identity. (34.15.210). Conveyance may be proved before superior court by proving handwriting of grantor and a subscribing witness. (34.15.220).

Authentication.—Certificates of acknowledgment shall be recognized if certificate is in form prescribed by laws and regulations of state or other place in which acknowledgment is taken or certificate contains words "acknowledged before me" or their substantial equivalent. (09.63.080).

Form.—No form is specifically required by statute. Statute includes five forms from Uniform Recognition of Acknowledgments Act for various types of acknowledgments. (09.63.100).

Alternative to Acknowledgment or Proof.—Matter required or authorized to be supported, evidenced, established or proven by sworn statement, declaration, verification, certificate, oath or affidavit, in writing of person making it (other than deposition, acknowledgment, oath of office, or oath required to be taken before specified official other than notary public) may be supported, evidenced, established or proven by person certifying in writing under penalty of perjury that matter is true. Certification shall state date and place of execution, fact that notary public or other official empowered to administer oath is unavailable and following: "I certify under penalty of perjury that the foregoing is true." (09.63.020).

Validation.—Defective acknowledgments of deeds, contracts, leases, powers of attorney, mortgages and other instruments pertaining to real property validated, provided no suit to change, set aside or reform instrument filed in court of record in judicial district wherein property located within ten years from date of instrument or of acknowledgment; judicial sales deeds, executors' and administrators' sales and deeds, and defective tax deeds also validated. (34.25.010).

Married Women.—No special requirements.

AFFIDAVITS:

Every justice, judge, magistrate, clerk of court, notary public, U.S. postmaster, municipal clerk and commissioned officer under 09.63.050(4) may administer oaths or affirmations. (09.63.010).

General Requirements.—No prescribed form of jurat, except in claims for game bounties. (16.35.150).

Use of Affidavit.—Extensively permitted in administration of specific statutory provisions and court proceedings. They may be entitled to recordation. (27.10.170, 34.20.080).

Alternative to Affidavit—Matter required to be supported, evidenced, established, or proven by affidavit in writing may be supported, evidenced, established, or proven by person certifying in writing under penalty of perjury that matter is true. Certification

See note at head of Digest as to 1998 legislation covered.

See Topical Index in front part of this volume.

AFFIDAVITS . . . *continued*
shall state date and place of execution, fact that notary public or other official empowered to administer oath is unavailable, and following: "I certify under penalty of perjury that the foregoing is true." (09.63.020).

NOTARIES PUBLIC:

Oath that person is resident of Alaska, and $1,000 bond required. (44.50.120-.150). Have usual powers. Authority extends throughout state. Seal required for all notarial acts. (28.50.080). Must state date of expiration of commission in all certificates. False certificate of acknowledgment is misdemeanor. (44.50.010). Fee for notary public services: Certifying and taking affidavit and affixing court seal or taking acknowledgment of any instrument in writing is $3.

See also topic Acknowledgments.

RECORDS:

Uniform Commercial Code adopted. (45.01.101).

Recordable Instruments.—Conveyances acknowledged, proved or certified may be recorded in recording district where land located. (40.17).

Instruments entitled to record are recorded in the offices of the recorders of the various recording districts.

A certified copy of a public record is admissible in evidence. (Rule 902 evidence). Similar to Uniform Photographic Copies of Business and Public Records as Evidence Act. (Rule 44 Civ. R.P.).

Recording Districts.—Districts are defined by supreme court. Information may be obtained by writing the Administrator of Courts, 303 K Street, Anchorage, AK 99501.

Requisites for Recording.—Real property conveyances must be acknowledged. (40.17). See topic Acknowledgments. Financing statement should contain name, address and signature of debtor or assignor, secured party or assignee, description of secured property, description of real estate if crops or fixtures to be security and statement that proceeds covered if applicable. (45.05.770).

Recording fees for all documents: $15 for first page and $3 for each additional page; no charge for releases of tax liens; $2 for indexing each name or location over six; and for filing plats: $20 for first sheet and $5 for each additional sheet.

Inspection.—Public records are subject to inspection by Commissioner of Revenue; but particulars of taxpayer's business or affairs are confidential except for official investigation or court proceeding.

Torrens system has not been adopted.

Filing Under Commercial Code.—If collateral is consumer goods or farm related products or intangibles, then proper place for filing is office of recorder in recording district of debtor's residence or where property is located if debtor is not resident. If collateral is fixtures then in office where mortgage on real estate would be filed. In all other cases in Department of Natural Resources. (45.09.401).

Vital Statistics.—Vital Statistics Bureau, Rm. 115, Alaska Office Bldg., Pouch H-03 Juneau, Ak 99811. Department Health and Social Services is Registrar. Uniform Vital Statistics Act adopted. (18.50.370). Fee for certificates (marriage, birth, death), $5.

SEALS:

Private seals and scrolls as a substitute therefor are abolished and are not required to any instrument, but when used, do not alter effect of instrument. (09.25.090).

TORRENS ACT:

Not adopted.

VITAL STATISTICS:

See topic Records.

EMPLOYMENT

LABOR RELATIONS:

Hours of Labor.—Employment over 40 hours a week and eight hours in one day prohibited unless compensation at $1^1/_2$ times regular rate paid, with statutory exceptions and exemptions. (23.10.055, 23.10.060). Overtime provision does not apply to person exempt under §13(a), (b) and (c) of U.S. Fair Labor Standards Act, 39 U.S.C.A. §§201-219, as am'd; person working on mining job where not more than 12 persons employed, where work time is not in excess of 12 hours per day or 56 hours per week during period of not more than 14 work-weeks during mining season. (23.10.060).

Exception to provisions of act is individual employed in farming; catching fish or shellfish; hand picking shrimp; domestic service in private home; government, U.S., state or political subdivision thereof; work in nonprofit organization if services rendered voluntarily; delivery of newspapers; watchman in plant not in productive use for four months or more; executive, administrative or professional work, outside selling or selling on straight commission basis; search for minerals; part time work of not more than 30 hours per week if employee under 18 years of age; certain employment at nonprofit educational or childcare facility; driving taxicabs; guiding for first 60 days; nonprofit organization where services are rendered under work activity requirement at Alaska temporary assistant program; emergency medical activities or full-time fire department on voluntary basis. (23.10.060).

Wages.—Not less than 50¢ an hour greater than prevailing Federal Minimum Wage Law or $2.60 an hour, whichever is greater (23.10.065), except for individuals impaired by physical or mental deficiency, apprentices or learners, upon issuance of certificate by Commissioner of Labor (23.10.070). Employer may not apply fringe benefits as credit toward payment of minimum wage. (23.10.065). Wages must be paid in lawful money of U.S. or by negotiable checks, drafts or orders payable, without discount, on presentation, by some bank or depository in Alaska. (23.10.040). Employer must establish monthly pay days or semimonthly if employee elects, unless annual initial contract provides for monthly, and on such day payment must be made for all labor performed. On termination of employment, wages must be paid within three working days after termination. (23.05.140). Employee may collect as liquidated damages amount equal to sum owed him by employer for unpaid minimum wages or unpaid overtime compensation when employer violates act unless employer shows good faith and reasonable grounds for not believing violation of law by clear and convincing evidence. (23.10.110).

Child Labor.—Children under 14 may be employed outside school hours in domestic employment, baby sitting and handiwork about private homes, newspaper deliveries or sales, or supervised work casing cans in cannery warehouse (23.10.335) and work by children under direct supervision of parent in business owned and operated by parent or work of child on boat owned or operated by parent is not prohibited (23.10.330). Children under 16 may be employed between 6 A.M. and 7 P.M. but for not more than total of nine hours school attendance and employment in any one day, nor for more than 23 hours of work in any one week, domestic work and baby sitting excepted. (23.10.340). No minor under 18 years of age may work: (1) More than six days a week; (2) in hazardous excavation or underground in mines; or (3) in occupation dangerous to life or limb or injurious to his health. But commissioner may exempt in writing minor 16-18 years of age. (23.10.350). No person under 21 may be employed to sell or serve intoxicating liquors or work in any room or place where intoxicating liquors are sold for consumption on premises (23.10.355), except person 16-18 years of age may enter and remain upon these premises in course of his employment if employment does not require serving or mixing of alcoholic beverages and person has written consent of parent and exemption from Dept. of Labor (04.16.049; 23.10.355). Also, no child under 17 may work without written permit from Labor Commissioner except pursuant to Labor Dept. Regulations or for parent-owned business or boat. (23.10.332).

Female Labor.—See subheads Discrimination, infra and Child Labor, supra.

Discrimination because of race, religion, color, national origin, age, physical handicap, sex, marital status, changes in marital status, pregnancy or parenthood prohibited where reasonable demands of position do not require distinction (18.80.220); and unequal payment of wages as between sexes for work of comparable character or work in same operations, business, or type of work in same locality is prohibited.

Superior Court has jurisdiction to remedy violations by declaratory or injunctive relief, or award of damages. (22.10.120, 549 P.2d 1349).

Labor Unions.—Statutory provisions regulating employment agencies do not apply to bona fide labor organizations. (23.15.330). Public employees may organize for collective bargaining. State and its political subdivisions required to enter into labor organization contracts, unless political subdivisions reject Public Employment Relations Act. (23.40.070-23.40.260).

Labor Disputes.—Commissioner of Labor authorized to act as mediator in labor disputes. (23.05.060). Striking employee, or one subject to lockout, shall receive earned compensation on or before next regular pay day. (23.05.170). No "right to work" law.

Employer's Liability.—A person, association or corporation engaged in manufacturing, mining, constructing, building, or other business, or occupation, carried on by means of machinery, or mechanical appliances, is liable to employees for damages resulting from negligence of any of employer's officers, agents or employees, or by reason of any defect, or insufficiency, due to their negligence, in the machinery, appliances and works. Contributory negligence is not a bar to recovery where employee's contributory negligence was slight and employer's negligence gross in comparison, but damages shall be diminished proratably to negligence attributable to employee. All questions of negligence and contributory negligence are left to the jury. Recovery cannot be barred by contract of employment, insurance, relief benefit, or indemnity for injury or death. (23.25.010-040). Survivors may also collect. Action must be brought in two years. (23.25.040).

Workers' Compensation.—Act covers employee of any person or persons, partnership, joint stock company, association or corporation and employee of State or any of its political subdivisions. Includes high school students (treating them as state employees) while performing work under work-study courses. Includes executive officer of corporation other than municipal corporation or charitable, religious, educational or other nonprofit corporation. Sole proprietor or member of partnership may elect coverage as employee by making written application to insurer. Part-time babysitters, cleaning persons, harvest help and similar part-time or transient help, persons who officiate on contractual basis at sporting events where players are not compensated, entertainers employed on contractual basis, and commercial fishermen, certain taxicab drivers, and participants in Alaska temporary assistance program excluded from coverage. (23.30.230-265).

Notice of injury or death must be given within 30 days of such injury or death to Alaska Workmen's Compensation Board and to employer. Notice must contain name and address of employee and statement as to time, place, nature and cause of injury or death. (23.30.100).

Period of limitations in which claim to compensation for disability must be filed is two years from time employee has knowledge of nature of disability and its relation to employment. Claim for death benefit must be filed within one year after death, except if payment of compensation has been made without award on account of such injury or death, claim may be filed within two years of last payment. Maximum time for filing a claim in any event other than arising out of an occupational disease is four years from date of the injury. However, where latent defects cause compensable disability, Board may make an award without regard to any time limitation. (23.30.105).

Hearings on claim held before Alaska Workmen's Compensation Board, established within Department of Labor. (23.30.005).

Compensation calculated under 23.30.175. For temporary partial disability see 23.30.200. For permanent partial disability see 23.30.190. For temporary total disability see 23.30.185. For permanent total disability see 23.30.180.

Death benefit includes reasonable funeral expenses up to $2,500. Payment of 80% of average wages of deceased is made to surviving spouse with no children: with one child, 40% to surviving spouse, 40% to child: with two or more children, 25% for surviving spouse and 55% to be divided equally among children; 80% to one child

See note at head of Digest as to 1998 legislation covered.

See Topical Index in front part of this volume.

AK – 15

LABOR RELATIONS . . . *continued*

where no surviving spouse; 80% to be divided equally among two or more children where no surviving spouse. If surviving spouse remarries, spouse is entitled to amount that would otherwise have been due had surviving spouse not remarried in two years following date of remarriage. If no surviving wife or dependent husband or children, then for support of father, mother, grandchildren, brothers and sisters, dependent upon deceased at time of injury, 35% of average weekly wage, share and share alike, not exceeding $20,000. Except where surviving spouse is either permanently or totally disabled or has attained age of 52 years, death benefit shall be reduced to 66²/₃% of benefit then being paid after five years, further reduced to 50% after eight years, and terminated after ten years. Where benefits are payable to surviving children of deceased by former marriage, benefits shall equal amount payable under decree of child support, any remainder to be distributed pro rata to those entitled. (23.30.215).

Second Injury Fund.—Contributions on sliding scale of 0-6% based on status of fund reserve for temporary total disability, temporary partial disability, permanent partial disability or permanent total disability. If employee suffers death, is unmarried and leaves no dependents, $10,000 shall be paid to fund (Commercial Fisherman's Fund). (23.30.040).

Occupational diseases covered by Act. (23-35.-010-.150). Applies to disabled fishermen only.

Lien.—Every employee and every beneficiary entitled to compensation under Act shall have lien, including costs and disbursements and attorney's fees, upon all of property in connection with construction, preservation, maintenance or operation of which work of such injured or deceased employee was being performed at time of injury or death of such employee. (23.30.165).

Rehabilitation program supervised by WCB includes: Vocational, academic or on job training for new job or special training or worksite modification for same or similar job. (23.15.010-.210).

Unemployment Compensation.—Benefits are payable to individual who has earned wages in his base period not less than $1,000, paid in at least two of calendar quarters of his base period. Basic weekly benefits run $38—$188 plus allowance increments for each dependent of $24 with $72 as limit on individual allowance for dependants. (23.20.350). Extension of benefits possible. (23.20.406). See category Taxation, topic Unemployment Compensation Tax.

WORKERS' COMPENSATION LAW:

See topic Labor Relations.

ENVIRONMENT

ENVIRONMENTAL REGULATION:

General Supervision.—Department of Environmental Conservation duties include coordination and development of programs related to environment of state; responsibility for promulgation and enforcement of regulations setting standards for prevention and abatement of water, land, subsurface land and air pollution; and promote programs for protection and control of environment. Department of Natural Resources regulates forests, private and public. (41.17.030). Alaska Coastal Policy Council administers Alaska coastal management program. (44.19.155-162 and 46.40).

Prohibited Acts of Pollution.—Pollution of air, land, subsurface land or water is prohibited. Plans for sewage systems or treatment works must be approved by Department before installed or operated. DDT or other pesticides which may cause damage to health or property and discharge of petroleum or coal products on water or land is prohibited. Ballast water discharge from vessel is regulated. (43.03.720-.850).

Enforcement.—Department may issue compliance orders when person is violating or about to violate pollution regulations. Department may hold hearings and rescind, modify or affirm compliance order. State employee authorized by Department or state police officer may enforce pollution regulations. (46.03.850).

Penalties.—Various criminal penalties provided for in 46.03.790.

Violation of Petroleum or Oil Products Pollution.—State may bring civil action for penalty of $1 to $10 per gallon, or $500,000, whichever is less if spill over 18,000 gallons. Penalty increased by five times for gross negligence, intentional spill, or failure to take reasonable measures to contain. (46.03.758-.759). Civil damages from $500 to $100,000 for initial violation, plus up to $5,000 per day for continuing violations of permits. (46.03.760).

Permits.—Inquiries regarding any permits that are required prior to conducting activities that may affect environment can be made to Department of Environmental Conservation, Pouch O, Juneau, AK 99811, or any regional office of department. Application for required permits issued by various state agencies may be made on one master application to department. Department will coordinate issuance of permits required by other agencies and conduct required hearings. (46.35.010-210).

Smoking.—Prohibited in certain vehicles and indoor places (18.35.300) with exemptions for designated smoking sections (18.35.320).

ESTATES AND TRUSTS

ADMINISTRATION:

See topic Executors and Administrators.

ADVANCEMENTS:

See topic Descent and Distribution.

ALLOWANCES:

See topic Executors and Administrators.

CLAIMS:

See topic Executors and Administrators; category Civil Actions and Procedure, topic Pleading.

DEATH:

Definition.—Irreversible cessation of circulatory and respiratory functions, or irreversible cessation of all functions of entire brain, including brain stem. Death may be pronounced before artificial means of maintaining respiratory and cardiac function are terminated. (09.68.120).

Person missing continuously for five years is presumed dead. (13.06.035[3]).

Survivorship.—Person failing to survive decedent by 120 hours is presumed to have predeceased decedent and decedent's heirs determined accordingly. This presumption not applied if state takes intestate estate. (13.12.104).

Action for Wrongful Death.—Personal representative of decedent may bring action against one whose wrongful act or omission caused decedent's death. Such action must be brought within two years after decedent's death. Damages for loss of statutory beneficiaries and recovery, less expenses of action, inures to exclusive benefit of widow, surviving husband and dependents of children of decedent. If no statutory beneficiaries survive, damages are recovered for loss of estate and amount recovered will be administered as other personal property of decedent. (09.55.580). Damages for decedent's pain and suffering not recoverable under this statute. Parents and guardians may also maintain action for death of minor. (09.15.010).

Survivorship Actions.—Personal representative may bring or defend any action decedent could have. (09.55.570). Decedent's pain and suffering recoverable under this statute.

Certificates of Death.—See category Documents and Records, topic Records, subhead Vital Statistics.

Inquiry by jury of six before magistrate may establish presumption of missing person's death, and furnish basis for "Presumptive Death Certificate"; issuance six months thereafter. (9.55.020).

Uniform Anatomical Gift Act.—13.50.010-.090. See topic Wills.

Uniform Simultaneous Death Act.—See 13.13.792 for similar law.

DECEDENTS' ESTATES:

See topics Descent and Distribution, Executors and Administrators, Wills.

DESCENT AND DISTRIBUTION:

Uniform Probate Code, including 1975 Official Amendments, adopted. (13.06.005-13.36.100). See topic Wills.

Surviving spouse has right of election of one-third of augmented estate. (13.12.202).

Half Blood.—Inherit same as if whole blood. (13.02.107).

Posthumous Children or Other Issue.—Posthumous child receives as if born in lifetime of decedent. (13.02.108).

Illegitimate.—Is child of mother. Is child of father if natural parents participate in marriage ceremony before or after birth of child or paternity is established by adjudication before death of father or established thereafter by clear and convincing proof. Unless father has openly treated child as his and has not refused to support child father cannot inherit from or through child. (13.12.114).

Adopted Children.—Adopted person is child of adopting parent and not natural parents. (13.12.114[b]).

Advancements.—Property given in person's lifetime to heir is treated as advancement only if declared in contemporaneous writing by decedent or acknowledged in writing by heir to be advancement. (13.12.109).

Escheat.—If decedent is survived by no spouse, issue, parent, issue of parent, grandparent or issue of grandparent, then intestate estate passes to state. (13.12.105).

ESTATES:

See category Property, topic Real Property.

EXECUTORS AND ADMINISTRATORS:

Uniform Probate Code, including 1975 Official Amendments, adopted. (13.06.005-13.36.100). See topic Wills.

Uniform Fiduciaries Act not adopted.

Uniform Principal and Income Act not adopted.

Uniform Simplification of Fiduciary Security Transfers Act not adopted.

Preferences in Right to Administer.—Order of priority for appointment as personal representative: (1) person nominated in will; (2) surviving spouse of decedent who is also devisee; (3) other devisees; (4) surviving spouse; (5) other heirs; (6) 45 days after death of decedent, any creditor. (13.16.065).

Eligibility and Competency.—Must be 19 years old or older; no residence requirement. (13.16.065).

Qualification.—Bond required unless waived in will, beneficiaries waive requirement; personal representative is qualified corporate fiduciary. Must file statement of acceptance which consents to personal jurisdiction. (13.16.245-.250).

Removal.—Appointment terminates one year after closing statement filed; upon order closing estate; or upon resignation with 15 days' written notice to interested persons, resignation effective upon delivery of assets to appointed and qualified successor representative. (13.16.290). May be removed for cause by petition of interested person on following grounds: (1) best interests of estate, (2) intentional misrepresentation of material facts in appointment proceedings, (3) disregard of court order, (4) incapability of discharging duties; (5) mismanagement of estate; (6) failure to perform any duty of office. (13.16.295).

EXECUTORS AND ADMINISTRATORS . . . *continued*

Inventory and Appraisal.—Inventory must be filed within three months after appointment (13.16.365). Copy must be sent to interested persons who requested it. (13.16.365). Supplemental inventory required. (13.16.375). Qualified and disinterested appraisers may be employed. (13.16.370).

General Powers and Duties.—Personal representative shall take control of decedent's property. (13.16.380). Same power as absolute owner except in trust for benefit of creditors and interested persons. (13.16.390). Transactions authorized, unless restricted or otherwise provided for in will, listed in 13.16.410.

Notice of Appointment.—Within 30 days' of appointment personal representative must give information of appointment to heirs and devisees. (13.16.360).

Notice to Creditors.—Personal representative shall publish notice once a week for three consecutive weeks in newspaper of general circulation. Claims barred if not presented within four months of date of first publication. (13.16.450).

Presentation of Claims.—Written statement of claim indicating basis, name and address of claimant, and amount may be delivered or mailed to personal representative or statement of claim may be filed with clerk of court. (13.16.465). Must be presented within four months from date notice first published. (13.16.450).

Approval or Rejection of Claims.—Personal representative approves or rejects claim. (13.16.475). Claimant has 60 days from rejection to file allowance in court or commence proceeding against personal representative or claim barred. (13.16.475). Failure of personal representative to mail claimant notice of action on claim for 60 days after time for original presentation of claim has expired has effect of notice of allowance. (13.16.475).

Payment of Claims.—Personal representative will pay allowed claims four months from date of first publication of notice to creditors. (13.16.480).

Priorities.—If estate insufficient to pay all claims, paid in following order: (1) costs and expenses of administration; (2) reasonable funeral expenses; (3) debts and taxes with preference under federal law, past due child support payments; (4) reasonable and necessary medical and hospital expenses of last illness of decedent; (5) debts and taxes with preference under state law; (6) all other claims. (13.16.470).

Sales.—Personal representative may acquire or dispose of asset, including land, for cash or credit, at private or public sale. (13.16.410).

Actions by Representative.—Personal representative of decedent domiciled in this state at death has same standing to sue and be sued as decedent had immediately before death. (13.16.350).

Allowances.—See 13.12.401-13.12.405.

Widow's Quarantine.—None.

Final Accounting and Settlement.—Final accounting must include accounting of all cash and property transactions. (AK Probate Rule 12). Petition for settlement must state (a) estate fully administered, (b) all claims presented disposed of, (c) taxes and expenses of administration paid or provided for, (d) amount of compensation paid to personal representative and agents employed by her, (e) date of hearing on formal closing and any objections will be presented prior to hearing and (f) plan of distribution. (AK Probate Rule 12). (See also 13.16.620, 13.16.625, 13.16.630, 13.16.695.)

Liabilities.—Individually liable only if personally at fault. (13.16.485).

Compensation of Representative.—Personal representative entitled to reasonable compensation. (13.16.430). Customary fee $10-$20/hr. (Gudschinsky v. Hartill, 815 P.2d 851 [Alaska 1991]).

Small Estates.—When value of entire estate less liens and encumbrances does not exceed allowances, costs of administration, and reasonable and necessary medical and hospital expenses of last illness, personal representative, without giving notice to creditors, may immediately disburse and distribute estate to persons entitled to it and file closing statement. (13.16.690). To close small estate must file verified statement that (1) to best knowledge of personal representative, estate meets above requirements, (2) estate fully disbursed and distributed to those entitled, (3) copy of closing statement sent to all distributees and unpaid or non-barred creditors, and (4) full account in writing given to distributees. (13.16.695). Appointment of personal representative terminates one year after filing closing statement if no action pending. (A.S. 113.16.695).

Foreign executors or administrators may file authenticated copies of appointment and official bond if no local administration. (13.21.030). Upon filing copies, foreign personal representative may exercise as to assets in this state all powers of local personal representative and may maintain actions subject to conditions imposed on nonresident parties generally. (13.21.035). Application for local administration of estate terminates powers of foreign personal representative. (13.21.040). Foreign personal representative may be allowed by court to act to preserve estate. (13.21.040). By filing copies or acting as personal representative in this state subjects her to personal jurisdiction of Alaska Courts. (13.21.055).

Uniform Anatomical Gift Act adopted. (13.50.010-.090).

FIDUCIARIES:

See topics Executors and Administrators, and Trusts; also category Family, topic Guardian and Ward.

INTESTACY:

See topic Descent and Distribution.

LIVING WILLS:

See topic Wills.

PROOF OF CLAIMS:

See topic Executors and Administrators; category Civil Actions and Procedure, topic Pleading.

TRUSTS:

Uniform Common Trust Fund Act adopted, c. 14, SLA 1964. (06.35.010-050)

Uniform Probate Code, including 1975 Official Amendments adopted. See topic Wills.

Kinds.—Testamentary trusts providing for settlement of estates of decedents without administration recognized with limitations. (13.36.005-100, 13.16.595). Trust powers of banks organized under Alaska Banking Code (06.05) and trust companies organized under state law (06.25) include those of fiscal and transfer agents, trustee under certain mortgages, deeds of trust and bonds, accept municipal and corporate trusts, married women's separate property, by court appointment as trustee for minors, insane, idiots, spendthrifts, drunkards, receivers in insolvency proceedings, executor or administrator of estates of decedents, and any legal trust regarding real and personal property, trusts and powers conferred by any body politic or domestic or foreign corporation; and trust companies may engage in certain limited banking privileges, deal in real estate, deal in and invest in securities, and other lawful trusts.

Creation.—By oral contract or course of conduct regarding personal property and by written contract or court order. Trustee of trust with principal place of administration in state under duty to register trust with court. (13.36.005). Registration outlined. (13.36.005—.025).

Appointment of Trustees.—By trustor, by contract or by court order upon application.

Eligibility and Competency.—No statutory restrictions as to foreign and corporate trustees.

Qualification.—Bond not needed unless required by trust, beneficiaries or court. (13.36.085).

Removal.—Subject to removal by court for unfitness or violation of terms of trust.

General Powers and Duties.—To accept trusts mentioned in subhead Kinds, supra, and act as trustee subject to limitations of law and as to banks and trust companies under regulations of Department of Commerce and Economic Development. (06.05.180). Additionally trust companies have powers conveyed by general corporation laws of state. (06.25.080).

Sales of real property by trust company required within three years. (06.25.240). Generally requires court order, public auction, publication of notice, and confirmation where court has jurisdiction of trust. Sales of property conveyed by deeds of trust require public auction and 30 days public notice. (34.20.070-110).

Income and Principal.—Duties of trustees as to receipts, expenditures, apportionment of income and what constitutes principal. (13.38.010-13.38.130).

Investments in name of nominee allowed. (06.25.215). Investments by fiduciaries regulated. (06.25.080-220).

Securities in name of nominee allowed by statute. (06.05.197).

Accounting.—Uniform Trustee's Accounting Act not adopted.

Uniform Common Trust Fund Act adopted. (06.35.010-050).

Uniform Principal and Income Act not adopted.

Gifts to Minors.—See category Family, topic Infants.

Uniform Fiduciaries Act not adopted.

Uniform Simplification of Fiduciary Security Transfers Act not adopted.

Accumulations.—No statutory provisions.

Perpetuities.—See category Property, topic Real Property.

Pour Over Trusts.—See topic Wills.

WILLS:

Uniform Probate Code and 1975 Official Amendments adopted with no significant modifications. (13.06.005-13.36.100).

Execution.—Must be over 18 years old. (13.12.501). Must be in writing signed by testator or at testator's direction and witnessed by two people. (13.12.502). Interested witnesses allowed. (13.12.525).

Holographic Wills.—Recognized as valid, whether or not witnessed, if signature and material provisions are in handwriting of testator. (13.12.502; 504).

Revocation.—By subsequent will; by being burned, torn, canceled, obliterated or destroyed with intent and for purpose of revoking it. (13.12.507). Divorce or annulment after execution revokes any disposition to former spouse. (13.12.802).

Revival.—Upon revocation of second will which revoked first will, first will only revives if testator's contemporary or subsequent declarations so indicate. (13.12.509).

Simultaneous Death.—See topic Death, subhead Survivorship.

Testamentary Trusts.—See topic Trusts.

Unclaimed Legacies.—See category Property, topic Absentees.

Uniform Anatomical Gift Act.—Adopted. (13.50.010-.090).

FAMILY

ADOPTION:

Any person may be adopted. (25.23.010).

Adoption may be by husband and wife together; unmarried adult, including father or mother of person to be adopted; married person without other spouse joining if person to be adopted is not his spouse and if: (1) Other spouse is parent of person to be adopted and consents, or (2) need for consent is excused by court for reason of unexplained absence, etc., or (3) spouses are legally separated. (25.23.020).

Consent Required.—Written consent to adoption must be executed by: mother of minor; father of minor if married to mother at or after conception, or if minor is already adopted or otherwise legitimated by him under Alaska law; anyone entitled to custody

ADOPTION ... *continued*

or empowered to consent; court having custody jurisdiction if no other legal guardian is empowered to consent; minor over ten unless court dispenses with minor's consent; spouse of minor to be adopted; any adult to be adopted and his spouse or guardian, if adult is incapacitated. (25.23.040).

Evidence of Consent.—Consent shall be executed in presence of court or person authorized to take acknowledgments. Consent must state person has right to withdraw consent as provided in A.S. 25.23.070 and person consenting must acknowledge receipt of copy of consent form. Consent operates as power of attorney and is effective upon delivery of child to adoptive parent. (25.23.060).

Consent and Notice Not Required.—(1) From parent who has abandoned child without providing means of child's identification, or for period of six months under 47.10.080(c) (B); (2) from parent of child which has been in another's custody for a year and who has failed unjustifiably, as by indigency, to communicate with or provide care and support for child as required by law or judicial decree; (3) from father of minor unless married to mother at or after conception or if minor is his adopted or otherwise legitimated child under Alaska law; (4) from parent who has relinquished right to consent or had it terminated by court order; (5) from parent judicially declared mentally incompetent and court dispenses with consent; (6) from parent of child over 19 years of age and court dispenses with consent; (7) from any guardian failing to respond in writing within 60 days to request or who unreasonably withholds consent; spouse of person to be adopted if consent requirement waived by court. (25.23.050).

Conditions Precedent.—Before final decree of adoption, other than for stepchild, minor must have lived in adoptive home and qualified person designated by court have had opportunity to investigate adoptive home. (25.23.110).

Jurisdiction and Venue.—In superior court in district where, at time of filing or granting petition, petitioner resides or is in military service or where agency with custody of child is located, or the person to be adopted resides. (25.23.030).

Petition.—Must be signed and verified by petitioner, filed with clerk of court and contain personal data about petitioner and person to be adopted. Should also include birth certificate, required consents, relinquishments and termination orders. (A.S. 25.23.080).

Proceedings.—Commenced by filing petition and financial report of petitioner showing expenses incurred in connection with adoption. Prior to hearing date notice must be given to people whose consent required, and affidavit evidencing reasonable investigation has been made by petitioner or Department of Health and Social Services to notify necessary people. Investigation of adoptive home and conditions and antecedents of minor must be made by person designated by court, and report of investigation with recommendation as to adoption must be filed prior to hearing. Investigation and report may be waived by court for cause. Presence of petitioner and person to be adopted not required at hearing. (25.23.120).

Name.—New birth certificate in adopted name may be requested within 30 days after final adoption decree. (25.23.170).

Effect of Adoption.—Except with respect to a spouse of petitioner and relatives of spouse, adoption relieves natural parents of parental rights and responsibilities and terminates all legal relationships between adopted person and his relatives, including inheritance rights unless otherwise provided. Creates parent-child relationship between petitioner and adopted person for all purposes including inheritance and applicability of documents etc., unless expressly otherwise provided. (25.23.130).

Setting Aside Adoption.—Parent-child relationship may be terminated and right to receive notice of adoption hearings relinquished by writing signed by parent with a copy given to parent, in presence of agency taking custody of child. Parent has right of withdrawal within ten days of signing or of birth of child, otherwise relationship may be terminated: (1) Where petitioner has had custody for two years and parent has received notice of adoption proceeding and court finds granting of adoption in best interest of child; (2) by court order under 47.10 proceeding for abandonment or if parents unreasonably withhold consent. Petition for termination of parent-child relationship may be made by either parent if termination is sought with respect to other parent or by petitioner for adoption by an agency, or by any other person with legitimate interest. Notice of petition hearing must be given. (25.23.180).

ALIMONY:

See topic Divorce.

COMMUNITY PROPERTY:

Alaska enacted Alaska Community Property Act which became effective May 22, 1998. (34.75.010-34.75.995).

Uniform Disposition of Community Property Rights at Death Act.—Adopted. (13.41.005—13.41.055).

DESERTION:

See topics Divorce, Husband and Wife.

DISSOLUTION OF MARRIAGE:

See topic Divorce.

DIVORCE:

Uniform Marriage and Divorce Act not adopted. Divorce is governed by 24.24.

Jurisdiction of divorce actions is in the superior court.

Grounds for divorce are: (1) Failure to consummate at time of marriage and continuing at commencement of action; (2) adultery; (3) conviction of felony; (4) wilful desertion for one year; (5) cruelty impairing health or endangering life or personal indignities rendering life burdensome; (6) incompatibility of temperament; (7) drunkenness, habitual and gross, contracted after marriage, and continuing for one year after

commencement of action; (8) incurable mental illness when spouse confined to institution for at least 18 months preceding commencement of action; (9) addiction after marriage to habitual use of drugs. (25.24.050). Husband and wife may together petition court to dissolution of marriage on ground of incompatibility if they have agreed on custody, support and property rights. Either spouse may petition separately on ground of incompatibility if other spouse's whereabouts are unknown and spouse cannot be served personally within or without state. (25.24.200).

Legal Separation.—Available under common law, though not provided for by statute. No grounds necessary. Also, in action for divorce, spouse may acquire separate residence or domicile without reference to misconduct or consent of other spouse. (25.24.110).

Residence Requirements.—When a marriage has been solemnized in state and plaintiff is a resident of state, an action to declare marriage void may be brought at any time. If marriage has not been solemnized in state, action may be maintained if one spouse resident. Residence is defined as physically present 30 days with intent to remain indefinitely. (01.10.055).

Final decree is entered immediately on determination of issue. Time for hearing governed by Rule 40 Civ. R.P.

Child support is set by formula in Alaska Civil Rule 90.3.

Child Custody.—Uniform Child Custody Jurisdiction Act adopted. (25.30.010 to 25.30.910).

Community Property.—Alaska Community Property Act became effective May 22, 1998, wherein husband and wife domiciled in Alaska may elect to classify any or all of their property as community property. (34.75.010-34.75.995). Uniform Disposition of Community Property Rights at Death Act adopted. (13.41.005 to 13.41.055).

Support and Maintenance.—Uniform Interstate Family Support Act adopted. (25.25.101-25.25.903). Uniform Reciprocal Enforcement of Support Act repealed.

Alimony, Maintenance and Custody of Children.—Pending action, court may make order: For one spouse to pay other spouse money to prosecute or defend action; for care, custody, and maintenance of minor children; for freedom of one spouse from other spouse's control during pendency of action; restraining either party or both parties from disposing of property pending action. (9.55.200). If marriage is declared void or dissolved, court may further decree: For payment by either or both parties of such amount of money, in gross or installments, as may be just and proper for parties to contribute for support and maintenance of children; for recovery by one party from other, without regard to which party is at fault, amount of money, in gross or installments, as may be just and proper for such party to contribute to maintenance of other; for delivery to either of their personal property in other's possession or control at time of giving judgment; to change name of one of parties when he is not party in fault; and for division between parties of joint property of parties, or separate property of each, in such manner as may be just. (25.24.160).

Division of Property of Spouses.—Essentially marital property state in which property obtained during marriage divided by court. Court may for equity divide property obtained by either spouse prior to marriage. (25.24.160). However, Alaska enacted Alaska Community Property Act, effective May 22, 1998, which allows husband and wife domiciled in Alaska to classify any or all of their property as community property. (34.75.010-34.75.995).

Change of name allowed. (25.24.165; 09.55.010; Rule 84 Civ. R.P.).

Custody of Children.—Court may award shared custody of child if in best interest of child. (25.20.060). Court should consider best interest of child including emotional needs of child, child's preference, capability of parent, and other factors. (25.24.150). Court may appoint guardian ad litem to protect interest of child. (13.26.195).

Foreign Divorce.—Uniform Divorce Recognition Act not adopted.

Remarriage.—No restrictions. (25.24.180).

Uniform Child Custody Jurisdiction Act adopted. (25.30).

GUARDIAN AND WARD:

Uniform Probate Code, including 1975 Official Amendments, adopted. See topic Wills.

Jurisdiction and Venue.—For minor child, in Superior Court pursuant to Uniform Probate Code. For persons under disability in Superior Court at or near place of residence. (13.26.100). When required for unmarried minor child, if all parental rights of custody have been terminated or suspended by circumstances or prior court order. (13.26.045). For person under disability, only when necessary to promote and protect well-being of person, and only to extent necessitated by person's actual mental and physical limitation. (13.26.090).

Selection of Guardian.—For minor child, pursuant to Uniform Probate Code. (13.26.030.070). For persons under disability, pursuant to filing petition and subsequent investigation and hearing. (13.26.105, .116).

Appointment of Guardian.—For minor child, by Judge of Superior Court, pursuant to Uniform Probate Code. (13.26.030.065). For person under disability, by Superior Court order, specifying basis for order and specific authority and duties of guardian-ward relationship. (13.26.116).

Status of Ward.—For minor child, ward has parent-child relationship with guardian. (13.26.070). For person under disability, ward retains all civil and legal rights except those limited by court or granted to guardian by court.

Powers and Duties.—For minor child: (1) Take reasonable care of ward's personal effects, (2) exercise due care over ward's finances, (3) provide for ward's education and medical requirements, and (4) report on condition of ward and ward's estate as required by court. (13.26.070). For person under disability, general duty to encourage ward's participation in his own affairs to extent possible. Partial guardian has only duties granted by court. Full guardian has relationship of parent to minor child except for liability for care and maintenance of ward and liability based solely on guardianship for

GUARDIAN AND WARD . . . *continued*

harm caused by ward. Also series of specific limitations concerning civil rights. (13.26.150).

Securities in Name of Nominee.—No specific provision. See category Estates and Trusts, topic Trusts, subhead Securities in Name of Nominee.

Termination of Guardianship.—For minor child, termination upon death, resignation, removal of guardian or upon minor's death, adoption, marriage, or attainment of majority. Resignation must be approved by court. (13.26.075). For person under disability, by death of guardian or ward, determination of incapacity of guardian, removal of guardian by court, resignation of guardian, by term or period specified by court order establishing guardianship. (13.26.125).

Special Provisions.—For minor child, court shall appoint person nominated by minor unless not in minor's best interest. (13.26.055). For person under disability, nonbinding priority given to nominee of ward, spouse, child, or other relatives or friends of ward, private association with guardianship program, or public guardian. (13.26.145).

Public Guardian.—Public administrator serves as public guardian. Court may order public guardian to act as guardian for specific ward if no private guardian is available. Public guardian has duty to find private guardian if possible. (13.26.380).

Foreign Guardians.—See subhead Selection of Guardian, supra.

Gifts to Minors.—Statutory provisions for gifts of securities to minors providing for custodian, registration, compensation of custodian, liability of custodian, and appointment of successor by court not exclusive method. (45.60.010-45.60.120). See topic Infants.

Testamentary Guardians.—Father, or mother if divorced and awarded custody, may by last will in writing appoint guardian for his child, including after born child, for its minority or a lesser time. Same powers, duties and qualifications as for other guardians except no residence or ownership requirement. (13.26.035, 13.26.075). For person under disability, parent or spouse may appoint guardian by will and grant all rights held by grantor. (13.26.095).

Uniform Fiduciaries Act not adopted.

Uniform Simplification of Fiduciary Security Transfers Act not adopted.

HUSBAND AND WIFE:

No civil disabilities are recognized as to a married person which are not recognized as to other spouse. (25.15.110).

Separate Property.—Each married person may manage, sell, convey or devise that person's property and pecuniary rights, and these rights acquired by gift, devise or inheritance not subject to debts or contracts of other spouse. (25.15.060).

Homestead Allowance.—(09.38.010).

Contracts.—A married person may make contracts, which may be enforced by or against person as if unmarried. (25.15.100).

Liability for Debts of Spouse.—Neither spouse has such interest in the property of the other as to make his or her property liable in any way for contracts or liabilities of the other. (25.15.010).

Antenuptial Debts.—Neither a husband nor wife is liable for debts of the other which were incurred before marriage. (25.15.050).

Agency.—Either spouse may appoint other as attorney in fact. (25.15.040).

Conveyances, etc.—Either spouse may convey his real property, by separate deed, as though unmarried. (25.15.060).

Either spouse may convey, transfer, or execute liens to or in favor of the other, to the same extent as they may to third persons. (25.15.030).

Tenancy by the Entirety.—Husband and wife who acquire real property hold as tenants by entirety unless expressly declared otherwise. (34.15.110 and 34.15.150).

Community Property.—Effective May 22, 1998, Alaska enacted Alaska Community Property Act. (34.75.010-34.75.995). Upon death of married person, who held real or personal property that was acquired as or became, and remained, community property under laws of this or another jurisdiction, or was acquired with rents, issues, or income of, proceeds from or in exchange for that community property, one-half of this property goes to surviving spouse while other half is property of decedent subject to testamentary disposition. (13.41.005-13.41.015).

Desertion.—Parent, guardian or other person legally charged with care of child under ten years of age commits class C felony, endangering welfare of minor, by intentionally deserting child under circumstances creating substantial risk of physical injury to child. (11.51.100).

Displaced Homemakers Program.—Person who worked as homemaker for at least three years, faces significant reduction in income or support and has difficulty in finding employment is eligible for assistance. (47.90.010-.070).

Domestic Violence.—Person subjected to domestic violence may petition superior or district court for injunctive relief. (25.35.200).

Uniform Interstate Family Support Act adopted. (25.25.101-25.25.903).

Uniform Reciprocal Enforcement of Support Act repealed.

Uniform Child Custody Jurisdiction Act adopted. (25.30).

INFANTS:

Age of majority 18 both sexes. (25.20.010). Person emancipated by lawful marriage or upon reaching marriageable age of consent. (25.20.020). Person under 21 years may not knowingly consume, possess or control alcoholic beverages except those furnished off licensed premises by parent to child, guardian to ward or spouse to legal spouse. (04.16.051).

Disabilities.—May be removed by 16 year old living separate and apart from parents or guardian if capable of self-support and financial management upon consent of parent through petition of court. (09.55.590).

Parental Responsibility.—Liable for malicious or willful destruction of property by unemancipated minor under age of 18 not to exceed $10,000 and court costs. (34.50.020).

Infants may commence and prosecute actions either by guardian, guardian ad litem or next friend. (Rule 17[c] Civ. R.P.). Child support, visitation rights and custody are covered in 09.55, 11.51, 25.25 and 47.23.

Infants who have reached age 16 are considered competent to receive and give full acquittance and discharge for insurance payments not exceeding $3,000. (21.42.290).

Support of Minor.—Class A misdemeanor of criminal nonsupport when person in legal charge of child under 18 years fails to support child. (11.51.120).

Adoption.—See topic Adoption.

Gifts of Securities to Minors Act (Asso. of Stock Exchange Firms form) adopted. (45.60.010).

Revised Uniform Gifts to Minors Act adopted. (45.60). Age of majority under Act is 18.

Uniform Securities Ownership by Minors Act not adopted.

Torts of Minors.—See category Civil Actions and Procedure, topic Damages.

MARRIAGE:

Civil contract, persons aged 18 or older. (25.05.011).

Consent Required.—Persons between 16 and 18 require written, verified consent of parents or guardians or of parent having actual care, custody and control of minor, before license issued. Persons between 14 and 18 may receive court approval if court finds that marriage is in best interest of minor and parents have consented or parental nonconsent unreasonable. (25.05.171).

License Required.—Before issuance each contracting party shall, under oath, state that contemplated marriage meets requirements of law, giving name, relationship if any, residence, occupation, and age of each party; naming guardians of any party under legal age for marriage; and describing any prior marriage of either party, and manner of its dissolution. Application for license must be filed three days before issuance thereof. (25.05.091). In case where three-day waiting period would result in undue hardship, magistrate or marriage commissioner may waive three-day requirement. (25.05.161).

Ceremonial Marriage.—No waiting period required between issuance of license and solemnization of marriage. Marriages may be solemnized by minister or priest of any church in state anywhere in state; by marriage officer appointed by presiding judge of superior court; by any judicial officer of state in his jurisdiction; or officer of Salvation Army commissioned in state. (25.05.261[a]). Marriage solemnized before person professing to be minister, priest or judicial officer is not void, nor is validity affected if persons married or either of them believes they have been lawfully married (25.05.281), and licensed marriage solemnized before religious organization according to established ritual is valid (25.05.261[b]).

Reports of Marriages.—Reports of licenses issued and marriage ceremonies performed recorded with local registrar of vital statistics within seven days. (25.05.321; 18.50.270).

Common Law Marriages.—Not recognized, if attempted in Alaska since 1917. (364 P.2d 60; 555 F.2d 737).

Proxy Marriages.—Not authorized.

Marriages by Written Contract.—Not authorized.

Prohibited marriages are: (1) When either party thereto has a husband or wife living at the time of marriage; (2) when the parties thereto are related to each other within and not including the fourth degree of consanguinity, whether of the whole or half blood, computed according to rules of the civil law. Such marriages are void. (25.05.021).

When either party to a marriage is incapable of consenting for want of legal age or sufficient understanding, or when consent of either party is obtained by force or fraud, or failure to consummate, marriage is voidable, but only at suit of party laboring under disability or upon whom force of fraud is imposed. Such marriages are voidable. (25.05.031).

Illegitimate children are legitimized by subsequent marriage of parents, written acknowledgment of paternity, or court decree of paternity. (25.20.050).

Foreign Marriages.—No statutory provisions.

Residence Requirements.—When marriage solemnized and plaintiff is resident of state, action to declare marriage void may be brought any time. If marriage not solemnized in state, residence of other spouse inures to plaintiff and action can be instituted if other spouse is, at its commencement, qualified as to residence to institute similar action. (25.24.080-.090).

MARRIED WOMEN:

See topics Husband and Wife, Marriage; categories Civil Actions and Procedure, topic Evidence, subhead Witnesses; Debtor and Creditor, topic Homesteads; Documents and Records, topic Acknowledgments; Estates and Trusts, topics Executors and Administrators, Wills; Property, topic Dower.

HEALTH

SMOKING:

See category Environment, topic Environmental Regulation.

See note at head of Digest as to 1998 legislation covered.

See Topical Index in front part of this volume.

INSURANCE

INSURANCE COMPANIES:

Regulated by AS, Title 21.

Supervision by Director of Insurance, Pouch D, Juneau, Alaska 99811.

Rates regulated by director under provisions of AS 21.39.

Annual statements must be filed with director. (21.09.200).

Policies.—Forms to be filed and approved. (21.42.120). Standard provisions required (21.42.140) for particular kinds of insurance: Life (21.45.020); loans of cash value (21.45.080); group life (21.48.010); disability (21.51.020); group and blanket disability (21.54.010); credit life and disability (21.57.030).

Discrimination.—Unfair discrimination defined and prohibited (21.36.090) and exceptions stated (21.36.110).

Rebates.—Prohibited to property, casualty and surety insurers. (21.36.120).

Liens.—During pendency of delinquency proceeding liens obtained within four months of commencement are void. (21.78.190).

Agents and Brokers.—Agents, brokers, solicitors, and adjusters must be licensed. (21.27.010). Issuance and renewal of licenses controlled to prevent untrustworthy and incompetent licensees. (21.27.020).

Process Agent.—Appointment of director required (21.09.180) and name and address of person to whom process served on director is to be forwarded (21.09.180[c]).

Investments of domestic insurers are regulated (21.21); those of foreign insureres shall be as permitted by laws of domicile provided quality substantially as high as required of domestic insurers (21.21.330).

Foreign Insurers.—Certificate of authority required to transact insurance (21.09.010) with stated exceptions relating to liquidation, contracts without jurisdiction, surplus lines and reinsurance (21.09.020). Requirements provided as to name (21.09.050), general eligibility (21.09.040), capital funds (21.09.070, am'd effective 6/28/85), deposit of $300,000 (21.09.090, 21.24.030), and submissions for certificate of authority (21.09.110).

Retaliatory Laws.—If laws of another state or foreign country impose taxes, licenses, fees, fines, penalties, deposit requirements, prohibitions, or restrictions upon Alaska insureres in excess of those imposed on similar insurers, director shall impose them on insurers of that state or country doing or seeking to do business in this state. (21.09.270).

Premium Tax.—Imposed at rates of 2.7% for domestic and foreign insurers except hospital and medical service corporations; 6% of gross premiums less claims paid for hospital and medical service corporations. (21.09.210).

Privilege Tax.—Premium tax is in lieu of all other franchise or privilege taxes or fees measured by income of insurer. (21.09.210).

Direct Actions Against Insurer.—See category Transportation, topic Motor Vehicles, subhead Direct Actions.

Uniform Insurers Liquidation Act adopted. (21.78.200).

Uniform Unauthorized Insurers Process Act not adopted.

Unauthorized Insurers.—21.33.011-21.33.075 subjects certain insurers to jurisdiction of director on proceedings before director and courts in suits by state, insureds or beneficiaries on insurance contracts.

Medical Indemnity Corp.—Recently created public corp. to provide health care providers with adequate insurance against liability for negligence associated with medical or dental care. (21.88).

SURETY AND GUARANTY COMPANIES:

Accepted as sureties on bonds and undertakings if they have complied with federal and state statutes.

INTELLECTUAL PROPERTY

TRADEMARKS AND TRADENAMES:

Person who adopts and uses trademark in state may file for registration with Alaska Department of Commerce and Economic Development. Filing fee is $50. Certificate of registration is issued for ten years and may be renewed for five year periods at $25 or assigned at $2. (45.50.020-200). Seal for handicrafts also allowed. (45.65.010).

What May Be Used.—Trademark is any word, name, symbol, or device but may not consist of immoral or deceptive or scandalous matter, flags of U.S. states or foreign countries, living persons (unless consent by such person), or similar trademark registered to another or mark merely descriptive or deceptively misdescriptive of applicant's goods or primarily surname or primarily geographically descriptive or deceptively misdescriptive. (45.50.010).

Registration.—Anyone who adopts and uses a trademark in state may file with Department of Commerce and Economic Development on form supplied together with facsimile or specimen of trademark in triplicate. Fee $50. (45.50.030).

Assignment.—Must be in writing and recorded with Department of Commerce upon payment of $25 fee. (45.50.120).

Infringement.—See subhead Protection Afforded, infra.

Protection Afforded.—In addition to enforcement of common law rights, registrant may sue to enjoin infringement and may in certain cases recover damages or profits derived from misuse of trademark. (45.50.170-.190).

Resale Price Agreements.—No statutory provision.

Tradenames.—No statutory material.

Logs.—Brands may be registered with Department of Natural Resources at prescribed fee, subject to five-year term renewals. (45.50.210-.325).

TRADE SECRETS:

Uniform Trade Secrets Act adopted. (45.50.910-.945).

LEGAL PROFESSION

ATTORNEYS AND COUNSELORS:

Alaska Bar Association created by Alaska Integrated Bar Act. (08.08.250). Only active members of Alaska Bar may engage in private practice of law.

Admission on Examination.—Bar examinations shall be held in months of Feb. and July of every calendar year in principal cities in state under supervision of Board of Governors.

Applicant for admission on examination: (a) Must be graduate of law school approved or accredited by Council of Legal Education of ABA or Association of American Law Schools when applicant entered or graduated or be person who has not graduated from accredited law school but who has been licensed to practice law in one or more U.S. jurisdictions for five years since his admission; (b) has attained age of 18 years; (c) is of good moral character; (d) must have passed Alaska Bar Examination, and date for examination shall be at least 120 days after application for admission is made. (Rules 2, 3, Alaska Bar Rules). Examination is two and one half days, includes Multi-State Bar Examination (recent scores from other jurisdictions not transferable) and essay exam on Alaska law and Alaska practicum. Attendance at Ethics CLE also required. Multistate Professional Responsibility Exam administered separately also required. Contact Alaska Bar Association, P.O. Box 100279, Anchorage, AK 99510.

Law Clerks.—One may register as law clerk to qualify as general law applicant without completing law school by presenting proof of bachelor's degree and completion of first year of law school. Law clerk must obtain regular and full-time employment with Alaska judge or attorney, have tutor and meet other specified study requirements. (08.08.207).

Admission Pro Hac Vice.—Member of bar in good standing in other jurisdictions may be entitled to appear in courts of Alaska under rules prescribed by court rule; requires resident associate. (Rule 81, Civ. R.P.).

Liabilities.—See category Civil Actions and Procedure, topic Costs.

Compensation and Lien Therefor.—Attorney has lien for his compensation. (34.35.430). As to attorneys' fees allowed by court, see Rule 82, Civ. R.P.

Discipline.—Attorney may be disbarred or suspended for any violation of standards of Code of Ethics of American Bar Association, or for any other reasons enumerated by Rules of Board of Governors. Upon conviction of serious crime attorney suspended by court until final disposition of disciplinary proceedings. (Rule 26, Alaska Bar Rules).

Licenses.—Annual license fee fixed by Board of Governors.

Unauthorized Practice.—Any person not active member of Alaska Bar who engages in or represents himself as entitled to engage in private practice of law in Alaska, except as authorized by Bar Act, is guilty of misdemeanor and upon conviction shall be punished by fine of not more than $5,000 or imprisonment for not more than one year, or by both fine and imprisonment. (08.08.230).

Professional Corporation.—See category Business Organizations, topic Corporations, subhead Professional Corporations.

Attorney Ethics.—American Bar Association Model Rules of Professional Conduct not adopted. See, Alaska Code of Professional Responsibility, Code of Judicial Conduct.

MINERAL, WATER AND FISHING RIGHTS

MINES AND MINERALS:

Department of Natural Resources, Division of Mines, in charge of all matters affecting exploration, development and mining of mineral resources of State, collection and dissemination of mining information and administration of laws respecting mining. (27.05.010).

Department may inspect all mines, and machinery and appliances used therein, with view to health and safety of miners. (27.20.021).

For supplement to United States laws relating to location and holding of mining claims, see 27.10.010; 38.05.200.

See also category Property, topic Powers of Attorney, subhead Adverse Claims to Mining Lands.

Grub stake agreements must be in writing subscribed by parties, and recorded in recording district wherein locations are made. Parties and duration must be stated. (27.10.020).

Mining Tax.—See category Taxation, topic Mining Tax.

Incentive Clause.—All new mining operations exempted from mining tax for $3^1/_2$ years from date production begins. (43.65.010).

See also category Business Organizations, topic Agency.

Oil and Gas Leases.—Type of competitive bidding chosen by Commissioner. Essentially bids will be cash bonus with fixed royalty of at least $12^1/_2$% or share of net profit, or both. (38.05.180). Gas Pipeline Financing Authority created. (44.55). If oil or gas is extracted from well by person without right but who asserts claim of right in good faith or who acts under honest belief, damages are value of oil and gas at time of extraction, without interest. (31.30.010). Lease of rights-of-way over state land for transportation of oil and gas granted noncompetitively by commissioner. (38.35.010-330). Production license required prior to commencing production. (35.05.207). Prospecting permits limited to 100,000 acres in aggregate. (35.05.250).

See note at head of Digest as to 1998 legislation covered.

See Topical Index in front part of this volume.

MINES AND MINERALS... *continued*

Surface Mining of Coal.—State program enacted to regulate coal surface mining under standards of federal law. (27.21.230).

MORTGAGES

CHATTEL MORTGAGES:

Uniform Commercial Code adopted. (45.05).

What May Be Mortgaged.—See U.C.C., Article 9; accounts etc. (45.09.106); consumer goods (45.09.109); contract rights (45.09.106); equipment (45.09.109); farm products (45.09.109); general intangibles (45.09.106); inventory (45.05.109); proceeds (45.09.306).

After-acquired Property.—See U.C.C. (45.09.108 & .204).

Floating Stock.—See U.C.C. (45.09.103).

Future Advances.—See U.C.C. (45.09.204).

Requisites of Instrument.—See U.C.C. (45.09.402).

Execution of Instrument.—Name of debtor and secured party; debtor signature; address for debtor and secured party; description of collateral. (45.09.402).

Filing.—Central filing in Uniform Commercial Code Filing, Department of Natural Resources, 3601 C Street, Suite 1132, Anchorage, Alaska 99503.

Recording.—If collateral is consumer goods, farm equipment etc., in office of recorder of debtor's residence, or if debtor not a resident of state, in office of recorder where goods are kept. If collateral is goods which are or are to become fixtures, in office of recorder where realty concerned is situated. All other cases, central filed in Department of Natural Resources. (45.09.401).

Refiling or Extension.—Continuation statements may be filed or recorded. (45.09.403).

Removal of Property by Mortgagor (Debtor).—If removal is default see U.C.C. default procedures. (45.09.501).

Sale of Property by Mortgagor (Debtor).—If sale is default see U.C.C. default procedures. (45.09.501).

Concealment or Destruction of Property by Mortgagor (Debtor).—See U.C.C. default procedures. (45.09.501).

Release.—See U.C.C. release provisions. (45.09.406).

Satisfaction or Discharge.—See U.C.C. termination statement provisions. (45.09.404).

Foreclosure by Court Proceedings.—See U.C.C. provisions. (45.09.501).

Sale by Mortgagee (Secured Party).—See U.C.C. collection rights (45.09.502), right to take possession (45.09.503), and right to dispose of collateral (45.09.504).

Redemption.—See U.C.C. provision limited to time prior to disposition or contract to dispose. (45.09.506).

Foreign Mortgages.—See U.C.C. provisions as to law which prevails. (45.09.103). Generally, law of jurisdiction where collateral is located when last event necessary to perfect security interest occurs, prevails. (45.09.103[a][1]). For exceptions see 45.09.103.

Taxation.—No statutory provisions.

Forms.—All filings and/or file search requests must be on approved forms; fee of $1 is charged if non-approved forms are used. For forms and fees, contact Uniform Commercial Code Filing, Department of Natural Resources, 3601 C St., Suite 1132, Anchorage, Ak 99503 (phone: 907-561-2020). Checks must be made payable to "Alaska Department of Revenue."

See also category Transportation, topic Motor Vehicles.

COLLATERAL SECURITY:

Uniform Commercial Code adopted. (45.01.101).

MORTGAGES OF PERSONAL PROPERTY:

See topic Chattel Mortgages.

MORTGAGES OF REAL PROPERTY:

Execution and Recording.—The same rules as to execution, acknowledgments and recording as apply to other conveyances, apply to mortgages. They must be recorded in the office of the recorder of the district in which the land lies. Recording fees are the same as for deeds. See category Property, topic Deeds.

Extensions of the liens may be made by recording in office of recorder wherein real estate is situated, prior to expiration of statutory time for bringing action upon original contract, a memorandum of payment on indebtedness, which memorandum must be signed and acknowledged by the owner of the contract of indebtedness. Unless period of instrument disclosed therein, maturity date deemed ten years from date thereof. As to existing recorded lien instruments not disclosing period of instrument, an instrument extending period may be recorded prior to Jan. 1, 1956. (34.30.140-150).

A mortgage may be assigned and the assignment recorded, but in the absence of actual notice, the mortgagor is protected as to payments made to the mortgagee. (34.20.010).

Remedies of Mortgagor.—Mortgagee who neglects or refuses to discharge mortgage or execute and acknowledge certificate of discharge or release for ten days after being requested in writing, mortgage debt being paid, is liable to mortgagor for $300 damages plus all damages occasioned by such neglect or refusal. (34.20.050).

Remedies of Mortgagee.—A mortgage is not construed as implying a covenant for payment of the money secured, and if there is no express covenant for such payment, or bond, or other instrument to secure it, the remedies of the mortgagee are confined to the

land mortgaged. (34.15.090). In other cases a deficiency judgment may be entered against the mortgagor.

Foreclosure.—A mortgage of real property is not deemed a conveyance so as to enable the owner of the mortgage to recover possession of the real property without a foreclosure and sale according to law, and a judgment thereon. (09.45.170-220).

Foreclosure may be had in superior court, in accordance with rules of equity. There is no moratorium on mortgage foreclosures.

Redemption.—Property sold under foreclosure may be redeemed according to rules governing redemption of real property sold under execution (09.45.190). See category Debtor and Creditor, topic Executions.

Deeds of Trust.—Where deed of trust has been executed conveying real property to trustee as security for payment of indebtedness providing that in case of default or noncompliance with terms of trust trustee may sell property, trustee may sell property on conditions and in manner set forth in trust deed, without securing court decree of foreclosure and order of sale if not less than 30 days after default and not less than three months before sale trustee records details of deed and default and, within ten days thereafter gives notice to grantor, his successors, lienholders and those in possession of land. Default may be cured before sale if amount of default, plus attorney fees and costs actually incurred by trustee due to default, are paid. Trustee may elect to refuse payment and proceed with sale if notice of default has been recorded twice or more previously under same trust deed. (34.20.070). Sale shall be at public auction after notice. (34.20.080). No deficiency judgment on sale pursuant to deed. (34.20.100).

Chattel Mortgages.—See Chattel Mortgages.

PROPERTY

ABSENTEES:

Care of Property.—If owner of property disappears and cannot be found after reasonable inquiry, on application of any person who would be an heir if such absentee were dead, a guardian for the estate may be appointed. (13.26.165). See category Estates and Trusts, topics Death, Descent and Distribution.

Process Agent.—No statutory provision.

Escheat.—Property held by consignees or bailees not claimed within one year may be sold. (34.35.030). Intangible property unclaimed for five years presumed abandoned and is subject to custody of state if last known address in state and other conditions. (34.45.110—34.45.120). Specific types of personal property provided for in 34.45.140—34.45.260. Uniform Unclaimed Property Act. (34.45 et seq.). See category Estates and Trusts, topic Death.

Uniform Unclaimed Property Act.—(34.45.110—34.45.780).

ADVERSE POSSESSION:

Uninterrupted, adverse, notorious, possession of real property under color and claim of title for seven years or more is conclusively presumed to give title thereto, except as against U.S. or State of Alaska. (09.45.052). Without color of title, ten-year period required. (09.10.030).

See category Civil Actions and Procedure, topic Limitation of Actions.

CONVEYANCES:

See topic Deeds.

CURTESY:

Uniform Probate Code adopted. (13.06-13.16).

DEEDS:

Any estate or interest in real property may be conveyed by deed, executed by a grantor of full age, or by a duly authorized agent or attorney. (34.15.010).

Execution.—Deeds executed outside of the state may be executed in accordance with the laws of the state in which executed and execution of conveyance may be acknowledged under 09.63.050-09.63.130. (34.15.160).

For circumstances when spouse must join, see category Debtor and Creditor, topic Homesteads.

Acknowledgment and Recording.—All deeds must be recorded in recording district in which land affected by conveyance is located. (40.17.020). For deed to be recorded it must be legible, capable of being copied, accompanied by proper fee, accompanied by or including mailing addresses of all persons named in document who grant or acquire interest under document if it is conveyance, name and address of person to whom document is to be returned after recording. Signature acknowledgment seal or witness is required for document to be eligible for recording only when required for this specific document. (40.17.030). If not recorded, deed is void as against innocent purchasers in good faith for value whose conveyances are first duly recorded. (40.17.080).

Married Persons.—Husband and wife shall join in deed or conveyance of family home or homestead. (34.15.010).

Recording fees are as follows: $15 for first page or fraction thereof, $3 each additional page plus $2 for indexing each name over six.

Covenants are not required, nor are they implied, whether or not the deed contains express covenants. (34.15.080).

Construction.—The word heirs, or other words of inheritance, are unnecessary for the creation of an estate in fee simple. (34.15.060; 13.05.220). Any deed of real property passes the entire estate of the grantor, unless a contrary intent appears in express terms, or by necessary implication. (34.15.070; 13.05.220).

Deed of quitclaim and release, of a form of common use, is sufficient to pass all the real estate which the grantor could lawfully convey by deed of bargain and sale. (34.15.050).

See note at head of Digest as to 1998 legislation covered.

See Topical Index in front part of this volume.

DEEDS . . . *continued*

Forms.—Statutory Warranty and Quitclaim Deeds. (34.15.030-.040).

Form
WARRANTY DEED

The grantor [insert name and place of residence] for and in consideration of [insert consideration] in hand paid, conveys and warrants [insert grantees name and residence] the following described real estate [insert legal description of property], located in the State of Alaska.

Dated this ___ day of _____, 19__.

Validation.—May be validated through acknowledgment (34.15.150), through subscribing witness (34.15.210), or through proving handwriting (34.15.220). See also category Documents and Records, topic Acknowledgments, subhead Validation.

DEEDS OF TRUST:

See category Mortgages, topic Mortgages of Real Property.

DOWER:

Dower has been abolished.

ESCHEAT:

See topic Absentees, subhead Escheat; categories Business Regulation and Commerce, topic Banks and Banking, subhead Unclaimed Deposits; Estates and Trusts, topics Descent and Distribution, subhead Escheat, Wills, subhead Unclaimed Legacies.

LANDLORD AND TENANT:

Kinds of Tenancy.—Tenancies recognized are: Tenancy in common (34.15.110), tenancy by entirety (34.15.140), common law tenancy from year to year and month to month. Joint tenancy abolished. (34.15.130).

Recording.—Lease, other than for less than one year, void as against subsequent innocent purchaser or mortgagee for value whose conveyance is first duly recorded. (40.17).

Exactly conformed copy of a lease may be recorded in district where property located and may be read in evidence in any court in state with same effect as original. (34.15.340). Defective acknowledgment of lease made in good faith is valid if no suit is filed in judicial district where property located within ten years from date of instrument. (34.25.010).

Action or Forcible Entry or Unlawful Detainer.—No person may enter upon a tenement except where entry right given by law; entry only by peaceable manner. (09.45.060). When forcible entry is made upon any premises, or when an entry is made in peaceable manner and possession is held by force, person entitled to premises may maintain an action to recover possession. (09.45.070).

Lease of public lands must stipulate that annual rental is subject to adjustment at five year intervals. Waiver of adjustment possible if single-family residence best use and actually occurs. (38.05.105).

Uniform Residential Landlord and Tenant Act (34.03.010-380).—Major variations from ULTA: expands applicability of law under definition of "dwelling unit"; tenant may not sublet premises without landlord's consent unless otherwise agreed in writing; consent may be withheld only on reasonable ground of insufficient credit, number of persons in household, etc. (34.03.060); security deposit or prepaid rent not to exceed two months periodic rent unless monthly rent exceeds $2,000, and must be paid promptly into special trust account (34.03.070), omits provisions for lessee self help for minor defects (§4.103 ULTA); omits landlord's remedies for failure to maintain (§4.202 ULTA); provides for disposition of abandoned property (34.03.260); expands landlord's actions for possession (34.03.220-230); allows increased rent if substantial expenditures for capital improvements or increase in property tax or market rental price, etc. (34.03.310); provides for service of process on nonresident landlords (34.03.340).

LEASES:

See topic Landlord and Tenant.

PERPETUITIES:

See topic Real Property.

PERSONAL PROPERTY:

Joint tenancy as to interests in personalty not abolished. (34.15.130).

POWERS OF ATTORNEY:

Uniform Durable Power of Attorney Act not adopted.

Formalities.—Must be signed by principal and notarized. (13.26.332).

Revocation.—Agent's notice of principal's disability or death revokes power of attorney unless it specifically states disability will not affect agent's powers. (13.26.332, 13.26.356). Execution of new power of attorney revokes old one. (13.26.332). Principal can revoke at any time. (13.26.332).

Recorded Powers as Evidence.—For all issues related to recording see 40.17.

Recording Revocation.—No letter of attorney, or other instrument so recorded, shall be deemed to be revoked by any act of the party by whom it was executed unless the instrument containing such revocation be also recorded in the same office in which instrument containing the power was recorded. (34.15.330).

Adverse Claims to Mining Lands.—During patent proceedings to mining lands the adverse claim allowed (30 U. S. C. 30) may be verified by oath of any duly authorized agent or attorney (30 U. S. C. 31).

Members of Armed Forces.—No statute.

Statutory Form Power of Attorney (13.26.338-13.26.353) is as follows:

GENERAL POWER OF ATTORNEY

THE POWERS GRANTED FROM THE PRINCIPAL TO THE AGENT OR AGENTS IN THE FOLLOWING DOCUMENT ARE VERY BROAD. THEY MAY INCLUDE THE POWER TO DISPOSE, SELL, CONVEY, AND ENCUMBER YOUR REAL AND PERSONAL PROPERTY, AND THE POWER TO MAKE YOUR HEALTH CARE DECISIONS. ACCORDINGLY, THE FOLLOWING DOCUMENT SHOULD ONLY BE USED AFTER CAREFUL CONSIDERATION. IF YOU HAVE ANY QUESTIONS ABOUT THIS DOCUMENT, YOU SHOULD SEEK COMPETENT ADVICE.

YOU MAY REVOKE THIS POWER OF ATTORNEY AT ANY TIME.

Pursuant to AS 13.26.338-13.26.353, I, <>, of <>, do hereby appoint <>, my attorney(s)-in-fact to act as I have checked below in my name, place, and stead in any way which I myself could do, if I were personally present, with respect to the following matters, as each of them is defined in AS 13.26.344, to the full extent that I am permitted by law to act through an agent:

THE AGENT OR AGENTS YOU HAVE APPOINTED WILL HAVE ALL THE POWERS LISTED BELOW UNLESS YOU DRAW A LINE THROUGH A CATEGORY; AND INITIAL THE BOX OPPOSITE THE CATEGORY.

- Real Estate Transactions [ ]
- Transactions Involving Tangible Personal Property, Chattels, and Goods [ ]
- Bonds, Shares, and Commodities Transactions [ ]
- Banking Transactions [ ]
- Business Operating Transactions [ ]
- Insurance Transactions [ ]
- Estate Transactions [ ]
- Gift Transactions [ ]
- Claims and Litigation [ ]
- Personal Relationships and Affairs [ ]
- Benefits from Government Programs and Military Service [ ]
- Health Care Services [ ]
- Records, Reports, and Statements [ ]
- Delegation [ ]
- All Other Matters, Including Those Specified as follows: [ ]
  <Fill In> [ ]

IF YOU HAVE APPOINTED MORE THAN ONE AGENT, CHECK ONE OF THE FOLLOWING:

[ ] Each agent may exercise the powers conferred separately, without the consent of any other agent.

[ ] All agents shall exercise the powers conferred jointly, with the consent of all other agents.

TO INDICATE WHEN THIS DOCUMENT SHALL BECOME EFFECTIVE, CHECK ONE OF THE FOLLOWING:

[ ] This document shall become effective upon the date of my signature.

[ ] This document shall become effective upon the date of my disability and shall not otherwise be affected by my disability.

IF YOU HAVE INDICATED THAT THIS DOCUMENT SHALL BECOME EFFECTIVE ON THE DATE OF YOUR SIGNATURE, CHECK ONE OF THE FOLLOWING:

[ ] This document shall not be affected by my subsequent disability.

[ ] This document shall be revoked by my subsequent disability.

IF YOU HAVE INDICATED THAT THIS DOCUMENT SHALL BECOME EFFECTIVE UPON THE DATE OF YOUR SIGNATURE AND WANT TO LIMIT THE TERM OF THIS DOCUMENT, COMPLETE THE FOLLOWING:

This document shall only continue in effect for <date> years from the date of my signature.

NOTICE OF REVOCATION OF THE POWERS GRANTED IN THIS DOCUMENT.

You may revoke one or more of the powers granted in this document. Unless otherwise provided in this document, you may revoke a specific power granted in this power of attorney by completing a special power of attorney that includes the specific power in this document that you want to revoke. Unless otherwise provided in this document, you may revoke all the powers granted in this power of attorney by completing a subsequent power of attorney.

NOTICE TO THIRD PARTIES

A third party who relies on the reasonable representations of an attorney-in-fact as to a matter relating to a power granted by a properly executed statutory power of attorney does not incur any liability to the principal or to the principal's heirs, assigns, or estate as a result of permitting the attorney-in-fact to exercise the authority granted by the power of attorney. A third party who fails to honor a properly executed statutory form power of attorney may be liable for the principal, the attorney-in-fact, the principal's heirs, assigns, or estate for a civil penalty, plus damages, costs, and fees associated with the failure to comply with the statutory form power of attorney. If the power of attorney is one which becomes effective upon the disability of the principal, the disability of the principal is established by an affidavit, as required by law.

IN WITNESS WHEREOF, I have hereunto signed my name this <date>.

. . . .

<name>

SUBSCRIBED AND SWORN to or affirmed before me at <city & state> on <date>.

. . . .

NOTARY PUBLIC FOR ALASKA

My Commission Expires: . . . .

REAL PROPERTY:

For homesteading of land in Alaska, see category Debtor and Creditor, topic Homesteads.

Joint tenancy is abolished, except interests in personalty and tenancy by entirety, and all persons having undivided interests in realty are tenants in common. A tenant in

See note at head of Digest as to 1998 legislation covered.

See Topical Index in front part of this volume.

REAL PROPERTY . . . *continued*

common may sue cotenant for latter's receiving more than his just proportion of rents and profits. (34.15.120-140).

Tenancy by the entirety is recognized and may be created by husband and wife between themselves. Estates, other than homesteads, by the entirety are liable for debts of either or both tenants. (34.15.010).

Subdivisions and dedications authorized according to prescribed procedures. (40.15.010).

Rule in Shelley's Case abolished by statute. (34.27.020).

Rule against perpetuities modified by statute. Perpetuities period measured by actual events. Interests violating rule reformed to approximate intention of creator of interest. Perpetuities period measured by life whose continuance has causal relationship to vesting or failure of interest. (34.27.050).

Destructibility of contingent remainders abolished by statute. Remainder effective on occurrence of contingency as springing or shifting executory interest. (34.27.030).

Condominiums.—Horizontal Property Regimes Act enacted 1964. (34.07.010-.460). Does not apply to common interest community created after 1/1/86. Uniform Common Interest Ownership Act adopted, effective 9/1/86. (34.08.010).

Uniform Land Sales Practices Act enacted. (34.55).

Uniform Probate Code enacted (13.06.005-13.36.300) with some additions and modifications.

Solar easement must be in writing and is subject to recording requirements for other conveyances of real property. (34.15.195).

See topics Curtesy, Deeds, Dower, Landlord and Tenant; categories Civil Actions and Procedure, topic Partition; Debtor and Creditor, topic Homesteads; Documents and Records, topic Records; Family, topic Husband and Wife; Mortgages, topic Mortgages of Real Property.

TRUST DEEDS:

See category Mortgages, topic Mortgages of Real Property.

TAXATION

ADMINISTRATION:

State and Local Taxes.—Alaska Department of Revenue has general supervision of state tax laws. Taxes imposed by cities and boroughs are administered by officials of these political subdivisions.

Review of Assessment.—By city council or borough assembly. (29.45.110).

Exemptions.—Nonprofit, religious, charitable, cemetery or educational property exempt. (Art. IX §4). Otherwise exemptions provided by general law. No exemption for members of Armed Forces, veterans, etc. Property of organizations whose membership is wholly veterans of war of U.S. or auxiliaries, is exempt. Real property, permanent abode of resident 65 years old or older or disabled veteran or surviving spouse of either who is 60 years old or older is exempt. (29.45.030; 29.45.040). Municipalities may, by ordinance, exempt certain land, property (real and personal) from taxation as provided for in statute. (29.45.050).

Penalties.—

Generally.—See 43.05.220 for civil penalty, 43.05.225 for interest, and 43.10.035 for lien resulting from failure to file or pay.

Civil penalties of 5% added to tax for each 30 day period or fraction of period during which taxpayer fails to timely file return or fully paid tax due. Penalty not to exceed 25% in aggregate. (43.05.220). Additional penalties for civil fraud up to 50% of tax due or $500, whichever is greater. (43.05.220).

Unpaid municipal real property taxes subject property to lien, foreclosure, penalty of 20% of all unpaid taxes, interest at 15%, publication and court costs. Judgment of foreclosure and sale for delinquent taxes operates as conveyance to municipality subject to redemption for one year after which clerk conveys unredeemed property to municipality. (29.45.250). Notice must be provided 30 days prior to end of redemption period. Property may be sold provided it is not required for public purpose. Record owner may repurchase personal property not designated for public purpose prior to sale of property. Unpaid municipal personal property taxes subjects owner to personal liability, penalty 20% and interest 8% as provided by ordinance (29.45.250), and costs of action or distraint sale (29.45.310).

Unlawful acts against laws or regulations providing for administration of state revenue laws, including failing to file return of tax, or making false or fraudulent return, or concealing property or evidence, constitute misdemeanors punishable by fine of not more than $1,000 for each offense. (45.05.010-.130).

Enforcement and collection of taxes by Attorney General in civil and criminal actions. (43.10.010). Distraint on property applicable to all revenue statutes for collection of taxes or license fees. (43.10.030). Provision for permanent file and index in each recording district of state tax liens. (43.10.040).

Nonresident businesses required to file statement and tax bond not less than $1,000 with Department of Revenue. (43.10.160).

Civil and Criminal Penalties.—All civil and criminal penalties for all violations of Alaska tax statutes governed by 43.05.220 and 43.05.290.

Nonresident Business Tax.—To insure collection of state taxes and license fees, all nonresident businesses, operating as individual, partnership, or corporation, must file with Commissioner of Commerce and Economic Development on or before June 1st each year sworn statement giving name and address of taxpayer, names and addresses of all officers of corporation, estimated gross business receipts for current year, total estimated Alaskan payroll for current year, total estimated taxes and license fees that will be due state for current year, description and fair market value of all realty in Alaska on which such taxes may become first lien. If value of realty is not equal to twice amount of estimated taxes, bond in amount of twice estimated taxes but not less

than $1,000 must also be filed with Commissioner, unless showing is made that filing such bond would be undue hardship, in which event Attorney General may waive bond requirement. In addition, there must be filed with Commissioner of Commerce and Economic Development appointment naming Commissioner of Administration agent for service of process in any action for recovery of state taxes or license fees. Failure to comply may result in penalty of $1,000 or one year imprisonment, or both. (43.160-.170).

Utility Cooperatives.—Telephone cooperatives taxed percentage of gross revenue. Electric cooperatives taxed on number of kilowatt hours sold at retail.

ALCOHOLIC BEVERAGE TAX:

Imposed by 43.60.010-.040.

Brewers, distillers, etc. are primarily liable for tax and must give surety bond for $25,000 payable to Commissioner of Revenue; retailers and buyers are secondarily liable for tax and State has lien therefor on liquors in their possession. (43.60.040).

CIGARETTE TAX:

Imposed by 43.50.080; 43.50.090; 43.50.190.

COIN OPERATED DEVICES AND PUNCHBOARDS:

Coin operated devices are classified into three classes, each subject to annual tax of $48, $120, and $240. (43.35.010). Punchboards are classified and taxed annually at $2 or $4 for each board. (43.35.100).

CORPORATE PROPERTY TAX:

Domestic corporation must pay $100 before Jan. 2nd of each filing year. Foreign corporations must pay $200 before Jan. 2nd of each filing year. Corporation that fails to pay biennial corporation tax before Feb. 1 of filing year, must pay to commissioner penalty of $25 for each year or part of year of delinquency. (10.06.845). Income tax on corporations is set out in 43.20.011. There is imposed for each taxable year upon entire taxable income of every corporation derived from sources within state tax computed as follows:

If taxable income is:	Then tax is:
Less than $10,000	1% of taxable income
$10,000 but less than $20,000	$100 plus 2% of taxable income over $10,000
$20,000 but less than $30,000	$300 plus 3% of taxable income over $20,000
$30,000 but less than $40,000	$600 plus 4% of taxable income over $30,000
$40,000 but less than $50,000	$1,000 plus 5% of taxable income over $40,000
$50,000 but less than $60,000	$1,500 plus 6% of taxable income over $50,000
$60,000 but less than $70,000	$2,100 plus 7% of taxable income over $60,000
$70,000 but less than $80,000	$2,800 plus 8% of taxable income over $70,000
$80,000 but less than $90,000	$3,600 plus 9% of taxable income over $80,000
$90,000 or more	$4,500 plus 9.4% of taxable income over $90,000

Corporation that fails to pay tax or make report is precluded from commencing suit action or proceeding in court in this state. (10.06.848).

ESTATE TAX:

Estate tax is imposed upon transfer of estate of person who was resident at time of his death, computed as follows: (1) Determine amount of credit allowable under applicable federal revenue act for estate, inheritance, legacy and succession taxes actually paid to several states; (2) determine for each of other states amount of all constitutionally valid estate, inheritance, legacy and succession taxes, actually paid to each of other states in respect to property owned by decedent or subject to these taxes as part of or in connection with his estate; (3) determine for each other state in which property is located, owned by decedent, or subject to estate, inheritance, legacy or succession taxes as part of or in connection with his estate proportion of amount of credit allowable under applicable federal revenue act for estate, inheritance, legacy and succession taxes actually paid to several states, as value of property taxable in that state bears to value of entire gross estate wherever situated.

Amount of tax is amount of allowable credit as determined in (1) less sum of smaller figures of (2) or (3) for each of other states in which decedent's property is situated. (43.31.011).

In case of nonresident decedent who was resident of U.S., all realty situated and tangible personal property having actual situs in this state, and intangible personal property having business situs in Alaska including stocks, bonds, debentures, notes and other securities or obligations of corporations organized under laws of this state, is taxed in sum equal to such proportion of amount of credit allowable under applicable federal revenue act for estate, inheritance, legacy and succession taxes actually paid to several states as value of property taxable in this state bears to value of estate taxable by U.S. wherever situated. (43.31.021).

In case of nonresident of U.S., all realty situated in and tangible personalty having actual situs in, and tangible personalty physically present in this state is taxed sum equal to such proportion of credit allowable under applicable federal revenue act for estate, inheritance, legacy and succession taxes actually paid to several states as value of property taxable in this state bears to value of estate taxable by U.S. wherever situated. (43.31.031).

Situs of Property.—As to property of alien, stock of corporation organized under laws of Alaska is deemed physically within state. Amount receivable, as insurance upon

ESTATE TAX ... *continued*
life of alien decedent, and monies deposited in bank by or for alien decedent not engaged in business in U.S. at time of death are not deemed physically present in this state. (43.31.031[b]).

Returns.—Executor within two months after decedent's death, or after qualifying as such, must give written notice thereof to Department of Revenue on form provided by department designated "Preliminary Notice and Report". If Federal Estate Tax return required, copy of "Federal Preliminary Notice" may be filed in lieu of state form. Return must be made in all cases where executor is required by U.S. laws to file Federal Estate Tax return and when gross estate of decedent who at time of death was not domiciled in U.S. includes realty situated and tangible personalty having actual situs in this state and intangible personalty physically present in state. Department must allow extension of time for filing upon filing of federal extension. On failure to make return, or on making of false return, department must make up return from its own knowledge and information, which will be prima facie good and sufficient for all legal purposes. (43.31.111-.131).

Payment or Collection.—Tax is due and payable 15 months after decedent's death. Department may extend time, no extension to be more than one year and aggregate of amount of tax at least 11%. (43.31.141). If deficiency is willful, made with intent to defraud, penalty is 50% of tax. (43.31.171). Lien arises when assessment made. (43.05.225). If tax paid was in excess of amount properly due, it will be refunded by department, but no refund can be recovered after two years from payment of tax or determination of federal tax unless notice of such determination is filed with department within 60 days from final determination. (43.31.280). Executor is personally liable if distribution is made without having paid or secured tax due, to full extent of full value of property belonging to person or estate which may come into his hands, custody or control. (43.31.221). Department shall hear questions of tax or deficiency if notice given within 60 days after receipt of notice from department. (43.05.240). If tax is not paid within 90 days from date due, and time of payment has not been extended, commissioner may levy on and sell real and personal property of estate. (43.31.191). Tax is payable from whole estate and if one interested person pays all or part of tax, he is entitled to reimbursement from undistributed portion of estate or contribution from other interested persons. (43.31.201). Executor may sell real property of estate in order to pay tax. (43.31.230).

Department may sue to recover any tax, penalty or interest. (43.31.240). Department may make agreement as to amount of taxes due and payment in accordance with such agreement is discharge of tax debt. (43.31.260). Tax receipt must be given on any payment of tax, and on executor filing completed return and making application for determination of tax and discharge from personal liability therefor, department must notify executor of amount of tax due within one year, and on payment thereof executor is discharged from personal liability for additional tax thereafter found due and entitled to receive from department written discharge. Such discharge does not release gross estate while it remains in hands of executor, heirs, devisees, or distributees; but does release estate after it has passed to bona fide purchaser for value. (43.41.181). No final account of executor of nonresident estate or estate of resident with value exceeding $60,000 may be allowed by court unless such account shows that all taxes have been paid. (43.21.250).

Property of estate is deemed acquitted and discharged of all liability for estate or inheritance taxes under this act after lapse of ten years from date notice of debt is filed with department, or after lapse of ten years from date of filing estate tax return with department, whichever occurs first, unless department records notice of lien in recording district where part of estate is situated. No lien for estate and inheritance taxes continues for more than 20 years from death of decedent. (43.31.290).

Penalties.—Failure to produce records is penalty of not more than $1,000. (43.31.350). Criminal penalties outlined in 43.05.290.

For purposes of topic Estate Tax, "executor" means executor, administrator or curator or if none then any person who is in actual or constructive possession of property included in gross estate of decedent. (43.31.420).

FISHERIES TAX:

Persons engaging in fisheries business required to obtain annual license and pay license based on value of fisheries resources processed, as follows (43.75.015[a]): Salmon canned at shore-based cannery: 4½%; salmon otherwise processed by shore-based fisheries business: 3%; all other fisheries resources processed by shore-based fisheries business: 3%; fisheries resources processed by floating fisheries business: 5%.

Special rates for persons engaged in fisheries business which includes processing developing commercial fish species. (43.75.015[b]). Developing commercial fish species processed by shore-based fisheries business: 1%; developing commercial fish species processed by floating fisheries business: 3%.

Tax computation to be based on total fisheries resources processed, including those processed for other fisheries businesses. (43.75.015[c]).

Security for collection of taxes required from license application. (43.75.055).

GASOLINE AND SPECIAL FUELS TAX:

See topic Motor Fuels Tax.

GIFT TAX:

None, but estate tax applies to gifts in contemplation of death or intended to take effect at or after death.

INCOME TAX:

Income Tax—Individuals.—Personal income tax repealed.

Income Tax—Corporations.—Corporate income derived from sources within Alaska taxable as follows: 1% of first $10,000; plus 2% of second $10,000; plus 3% of third $10,000; plus 4% of fourth $10,000; plus 5% of fifth $10,000; plus 6% of sixth $10,000; plus 7% of seventh $10,000; plus 8% of eighth $10,000; plus 9% of ninth $10,000; plus 9.4% of income over $90,000. (43.20.011).

INHERITANCE TAX:

Repealed. See topic Estate Tax.

INVESTMENT TAX CREDITS:

Taxpayer may apply as credit against eligible taxes following percentage of investment credit allowed as to federal taxes under 26 U.S.C. 38 (Internal Revenue Code) on only first $250,000,000 of qualified investment in state for each taxable year after Dec. 31, 1984, for gas processing project, for exploration, drilling of wells, development, or mining of minerals and other natural deposits listed in 26 U.S.C. 613(b) other than sand or gravel unless mining of sand or gravel is ancillary to mining development involving qualified natural deposit other than sand or gravel: (1) 100% on first $50,000,000 of qualified investment; (2) 80% on qualified investment over $50,000,000 but not exceeding $100,000,000; (3) 70% on qualified investment over $100,000,000 but not exceeding $150,000,000; (4) 60% on qualified investment over $150,000,000 but not exceeding $200,000,000; and (5) 40% on qualified investment over $200,000,000 but not exceeding $250,000,000. Credit may not be allowed under this subsection for investment credit that is allowed as to federal taxes for leased property by reason of 26 U.S.C. 168(f).

Taxpayer may not claim investment tax credit unless gas processing project or mining project began operation and production after Dec. 31, 1984. Taxpayer may not claim additional investment tax credit under 43.20.036(b) for investment for which special industrial incentive investment tax credit is claimed. If taxpayer is member of group of affiliated corporations filing consolidated return, amount of investment tax credit is limited to amount taxpayer would have been eligible to claim had consolidated return not been filed. Investment tax credit per taxable year may not exceed 60% of eligible tax liability. Any unused portion of investment tax credit shall be subject to carry forward provisions in 26 U.S.C. 46(b)(3) except that unused credit may not be carried forward to tax years beginning after Dec. 31, 1999. (43.20.042).

MINING TAX:

Mining tax is imposed on extraction, mining or taking from earth, by any operation, of valuable metals, ores, minerals, asbestos, gypsum, coal, marketable earth or stone, or any of them, but not including extraction or production of oil and gas, based upon net income from Alaska property (computed with allowable depletion) plus royalty on Alaska mining property, viz., over $40,000 but not over $50,000, 3%; over $50,000 but not over $100,000, $1,500 plus 5% of excess over $50,000; over $100,000, $4,000 plus 7% of excess over $100,000. Depletion allowances: coal, 10%; metals, fluorspar, flake graphite, vermiculite, beryl, feldspar, mica, talc, lepidolite, spodumene, varite, ball and sagger clay, rock, asphalt, potash, 15%; sulphur, 23%; of gross income from property during taxable year, excluding from gross income rents or royalties for property; but, not to exceed 50% of net income (computed without depletion allowance, but allowable depletion shall not be less than reasonable cost). Gross income defined, also "ordinary treatment processes", also net income. (43.65.110-.060).

MOTOR FUELS TAX:

Imposed by 43.40.010-.110.

MOTOR VEHICLE TAX:

Annual registration tax imposed; schedule set forth at 28.10.431.

OIL AND GAS PRODUCTION TAX:

This is levied on wellhead value of oil and gas based upon amount produced less any amount exempt from taxation. Tax on oil is maximum of 12.25% of wellhead value based upon sliding scale that is keyed to economic efficiency of producing well. Tax rises to 15% after June 30, 1981, except that new commercial production is taxed at 12.25% for first five years of production. Should 12.25% of wellhead value be less than 60¢ per barrel, higher figure will be used. Gas is taxed at either 10% of wellhead value or $.064 per 1,000 cubic feet of gas, whichever is higher. Provisions are made for "old" oil and "new" oil. (43.55.011; 43.55.016). Surcharge of 3¢ per barrel on certain oil produced from lease or property in state. (43.55.300). Producers of oil must pay 2¢ per barrel surcharge on oil produced from each lease or property in state in addition to tax. (43.55.201).

PROPERTY (AD VALOREM) TAX:

State and Local Tax Rules.—Home rule and first class cities inside boroughs, and boroughs of all classes may levy general property tax not to exceed 3%. Second class cities may by referendum levy general property tax as first class city not to exceed ½ of 1%. (29.45.010; 29.45.090; 29.44.560; 29.45.590).

Assessment.—By city and borough officials under ordinance. (29.45.110).

Review of Assessment.—By city council or borough assembly. (29.45.110).

Payment.—As provided by city or borough ordinances.

Collection.—By city officials except when cities are located within borough. Borough is exclusive agency for assessment and collection for all property within borough. Taxes collected by borough that were levied by city within borough are returned in full to levying city. (29.35.170). See subhead Assessment, supra.

Lien.—All unpaid real property taxes are liens upon property taxed; liens are superior to all other liens and encumbrances against property assessed. (29.45.300). Cities and boroughs have right of distraint and sale for unpaid personal property taxes. (29.45.310).

Sale.—Foreclosure authorized by city or borough levying tax. (29.45.320). See topic Administration, subhead Penalties.

Redemption.—Allowed within one year of decree foreclosing lien of unpaid real property taxes. (29.45.400).

See note at head of Digest as to 1998 legislation covered.

See Topical Index in front part of this volume.

SALES AND USE TAXES:

Sales Tax.—Boroughs and cities of all classes, if approved by referendum, may levy sales tax. (29.45.650-29.45.710).

Use Tax.—No general use tax. Boroughs and cities of all classes levying sales tax may by ordinance levy use tax equal to sales tax. (29.45.650[b], 29.45.700, 29.53.450).

STAMP TAX:

No documentary stamp tax.

UNEMPLOYMENT COMPENSATION TAX:

Unemployment compensation tax in form of contribution to Alaska Unemployment Compensation Fund. Employer is any employing unit which for some portion of day within calendar year has or had in employment one or more individuals, except service in farming or domestic service in private home. Wages include all remuneration for service, including commissions and bonuses and cash value of remuneration in any medium other than cash, but no tax payable on wages in excess of $10,000 paid to any employee during year. Rate of contribution according to formula. Benefit payments according to formula. Dependency allowances established. (23.20). See category Employment, topic Labor Relations.

TRANSPORTATION

MOTOR VEHICLES:

Motor vehicle titles, licensing, and registration, and operator licensing regulated by Department of Administration, Motor Vehicle Division, 3300 Fairbanks St., Anchorage, Alaska 99503; highway safety and financial responsibility regulated by Department of Administration. See subhead Size and Weight Limits, infra.

Vehicle Registration.—Application for (28.10.021), suspension of (28.10.051), registration procedures (28.10.108), front and rear registration plates required on each vehicle (28.10.161 and 28.10.171). Emission testing, if required by municipal ordinance. (28.10.041). Exemption from registration fee and tax for citizens over 65 available upon written application. (28.10.411).

Operator's License.—Person must have license to drive vehicle. Issued by Department of Public Safety. License expires on date of birth in fifth year following issuance of license. Age limit, 16. Instruction permit may be issued to person at least 14 years of age. (28.15.010-.151). Driver License Compact enacted. (28.37.010-.190).

Titles.—Application for. (28.10.211).

Sales.—New owner within 30 days after transfer must apply for new certificate of title and registration. (28.10.321).

Identification Marks.—Altering, forging, or counterfeiting certificate of title or registration, registration plate, tab, decal or sticker punishable as felony. (28.10.491).

Operation prohibited to persons under age 16, to persons who fail to appear in court when required to do so for adjudication of vehicle, driver or traffic offense, to persons who are habitual users of alcohol or drugs to degree that person is incapable of safe vehicle operation, persons adjudged mentally ill or disabled and not legally restored to competency, persons medically unable to safely operate vehicle, persons unable to understand traffic control devices and laws, persons who knowingly make false statements in application for driver's license, persons required by AS 28.20 to furnish proof of financial responsibility and who have not done so. (28.15.030). See also 28.15.161-28.15.211 for grounds for revocation, suspension or cancellation of license.

Size and weight limits regulated by Commissioner of Public Safety. (28.05.011).

Equipment Required.—Regulated by Commissioner of Public Safety. (28.05.011).

Lights Required.—Regulated by Commissioner of Public Safety. (28.05.011).

Liens.—Instrument creating lien or encumbrance filed with Department of Public Safety together with certificate of title last issued. (28.10.381).

Accidents.—Operator of vehicle involved in accident resulting in injury or death has duty to stop, give information, and render assistance to injured persons. Failure to comply punishable by fine or imprisonment. (28.35.060). Whenever accident involves injury or death or property damage in excess of $2,000 driver must immediately, by quickest means possible, inform Dept. of Public Safety or local police department if accident occurs within municipality. (28.35.080). Persons making repairs must report to police if damage appears to be caused by collision. (28.35.070).

Guests.—No limitation of liability of owner or operator for injury to guest.

Child Safety Devices.—Driver must provide devices for and secure children under 16 years as specified in this section. (28.05.095-28.05.099).

Proof of Financial Responsibility.—Motor Vehicle Responsibility Act. Deposit of security must be made by driver or owner to Department of Public Safety when involved in accident resulting in injury or death to other person or property damage in excess of $500 to any one person. If security is not given, license suspended. Security not necessary when driver or owner adjudicated not liable, released from liability by injured party, or when agreement made to pay for injury, or when payment made upon judgment. Security not to be less than $50,000 for injury to one person, $100,000 for injury to two or more, and $25,000 for property damage. (28.20.010-640).

Insurance.—Alaska Mandatory Automobile Insurance Act. Motor vehicle liability insurance required. Both owner and operator of motor vehicle are required to maintain coverage under motor vehicle liability policy or through certificate of self-insurance. Proof of compliance required when accident or charge of traffic law violation. (28.22.200-28.22.210).

No Fault Insurance.—Not adopted.

Foreign Vehicles.—Vehicles owned by nonresident exempt from registration for 60 days. Nonresident who becomes employed or takes other action evidencing intent to become resident must register within ten days of date of employment or of taking action to become resident. Nonresident owner of vehicle must register vehicle if it is leased or rented to person having established place of business, residence, or employment within state. Full time post-secondary students not required to register foreign vehicle unless student establishes residence or accepts full time employment within state. Exemption only applies to extent state in which vehicle registered allows similar exemption to Alaskan vehicle. (28.10.121).

Nonresidents.—Nonresident at least 16 years of age who has valid operator's license exempt from state license requirements for 60 days after entry into state except that one must register within ten days after starting employment or otherwise taking action indicating intent to become resident. (28.10.121).

Actions Against Nonresidents.—Service of process may be made upon Commissioner of Administration. (09.05.020).

Traffic.—Municipalities of first class by ordinance may regulate traffic, sell abandoned vehicles, fix fares, designate one-way streets. (29.10.111-171). State may sell abandoned vehicles. (28.30.010).

Offenses.—It is unlawful to drive vehicle without owner's consent. (11.46.484). Reckless driving, driving while under influence of intoxicating liquor and driving by persons addicted to excessive use of intoxicating liquors or narcotic drugs prohibited. (28.35.030). Unlawful to use cancelled, revoked or suspended license, or to lend operator's license to someone else, or to use someone else's license, or to permit any unlawful use of license. (28.15.281 and .291). State may sell abandoned vehicles after notice to owner and lienholders. (28.11.070).

Implied Consent.—Operation of vehicle gives implied consent to chemical test for determining alcoholic content of blood if lawfully arrested. Refusal to submit to test will result in suspension, denial or revocation of license. (28.35.031-.032).

Direct actions not allowed against insurer.

Motor Vehicle Taxes.—See category Taxation, topic Motor Vehicle Tax.

Gasoline Tax.—See category Taxation, topic Gasoline and Special Fuels Tax.

Warranties.—(45.45.300-45.45.360).

See note at head of Digest as to 1998 legislation covered.

See Topical Index in front part of this volume.

ARIZONA LAW DIGEST REVISER

Fennemore Craig, P.C.
3003 North Central Avenue
Suite 2600
Phoenix, AZ 85012-2913
Telephone: (602) 916-5000
Fax: (602) 916-5999
Email: fc@fclaw.com

Reviser Profile

OVERVIEW

Fennemore Craig, P.C. is the oldest and one of the largest law firms in Arizona. Founded in 1885, the firm has over 110 attorneys with offices in Phoenix and Tucson.

For more than one hundred years, the firm has evolved and expanded in response to the changing needs of our clients. Today, Fennemore Craig continues to provide the knowledge and resources necessary to solve the complex challenges faced by businesses and individuals. Over a century of experience has granted us the foresight to anticipate change and prepare our clients for the demands of tomorrow.

We address our clients' needs by focusing the skills and experience of individual attorneys within practice groups that concentrate on specific areas of the law. In addition, the firm provides multi-disciplined teams of attorneys that combine the broad range of talent necessary to confront issues that exceed the bounds of traditional practice areas.

COMMERCIAL SECTION

Corporate and Securities: Fennemore Craig attorneys have substantial experience in a wide variety of corporate, commercial and securities related transactions, including public offerings, private placements, corporate reorganizations, mergers and acquisitions, leveraged lease financing, leveraged buyouts, syndications and venture capital financing. The firm's attorneys also represent clients before federal and state administrative agencies regulating securities transactions and the securities industry.

Trusts and Estates: Fennemore Craig attorneys have extensive experience in all aspects of estate planning, trust and estate administration, all aspects of the probate process, probate litigation, post-mortem planning, elder law, and estate, gift and generation-skipping taxation and in the income taxation of trusts, estates, and their beneficiaries. In addition to representing a broad range of individual clients, the firm represents some of the leading trust companies in Arizona and has served as counsel to banks' trust departments.

Banking and Lending: The firm counsels banks, savings and loan associations, savings banks, credit unions, mortgage lenders, and others in various aspects of federal and state financial institution regulation. We advise clients on compliance with federal and Arizona banking laws, the formation, acquisition and licensing of financial institutions, and the expanding powers of financial institutions in areas such as the sale of securities and insurance products. We structure, negotiate and document a variety of financing transactions, such as loan and security agreements, project financing, interest rate exchange and Eurodollar credit agreements, loan workouts, letters of credit, and acquisition financing. The firm handles the drafting, lobbying and monitoring of legislative proposals for interested clients. We also counsel clients on the environmental consequences of making or foreclosing on loans secured by real property. We have experience in representing clients before the Arizona State Banking Department. The firm also represents clients before the federal agencies regulating financial institutions.

International: Fennemore Craig attorneys offer clients the experience in international commercial transactions necessary for business survival in today's competitive world markets. The firm's experience covers a broad range of international legal issues, from transactions and joint ventures through ongoing representation of businesses with substantial overseas presence to developing and drafting foreign commercial law. Our attorneys are also familiar with the General Agreement on Tariffs and Trade and international tax treaties that play a crucial role in structuring commercial agreements.

Labor and Employment: The firm represents employers in all aspects of labor and employment relations, including pension and benefit matters, wage and hour disputes, and litigation before administrative bodies and in federal and state courts alleging employment discrimination and wrongful discharge. We handle National Labor Relations Board proceedings, contract negotiations, labor disputes, grievance arbitrations and litigation. We appear on behalf of employers before the Arizona Industrial Commission in worker's compensation proceedings, and counsel our clients on employment practices, including personnel manuals, supervisor training, and employee discipline.

Legislation and Lobbying: Our services include researching and drafting legislative proposals, lobbying, testifying before legislative committees, and tracking pending legislation. Our attorneys have been instrumental in formulating Arizona's Groundwater Code, the Arizona "anti-takeover" statute, and Arizona's tax code relating to business entities. The firm has also been involved in legislative proposals in the mining, water, environmental, unemployment compensation and worker's compensation fields.

Natural Resources and Environmental: The firm's natural resources and environmental practice includes environmental, water, mining, timber, oil and gas, energy, Indian and public land law. The firm consults with and represents clients on all aspects of permitting, planning and compliance as well as in transactions and due diligence investigations. The firm regularly practices before federal, state and local administrative agencies. Fennemore Craig is very active in environmental and natural resources legislation and regulatory development and has participated in the negotiation and drafting of nearly every major water, environmental and natural resources measure passed by the state legislature. Our clients include major mines, forest products companies, railroads, banks, manufacturers, land developers, utilities, oil companies as well as small family-held entrepreneurial concerns.

Real Estate: The section has several members who are certified by the State Bar of Arizona as real property specialists. The firm handles a wide variety of real property matters including financing, purchase, sale, and lease of improved and unimproved real property (including oil and gas, geothermal, and mineral leases), land use planning and zoning, secured transactions, partnership issues, landlord and tenant subjects, title concerns, and construction and development contracts.

Taxation: The firm handles tax planning for individuals, partnerships, and corporations, and represents clients before the Internal Revenue Service and the courts. The firm's work relates to the tax consequences of mergers and acquisitions, pension, profit sharing and other employee benefit plans, tax-exempt organizations, and real estate transactions. We have a significant practice involving Arizona income taxation, and state and local excise and property taxation.

Utilities Regulation: Fennemore Craig represents several utilities, including US WEST Communications, Inc., Tucson Electric Power Company, and Arizona Water Company. We appear before the Arizona Corporation Commission in rate-making, certification, rule-making, and financing proceedings. We also represent utilities in federal and state court actions challenging regulatory decisions.

High Technology: The firm regularly counsels high technology clients on a broad range of matters such as negotiation and drafting of agreements, the formation of business entities, and shareholder rights and employment issues. Fennemore Craig's experience specifically includes negotiating and drafting software and hardware acquisition agreements, software development and distribution agreements, and licenses for software products. The firm also advises clients regarding intellectual property issues, including securing copyright, trademark, and common law protection.

Employee Benefits: Fennemore Craig has an extensive practice counseling employers on all aspects of the design, implementation, and operation of executive compensation, qualified retirement, and profit sharing plans, including employee stock ownership plans and Section 401(k) savings plans. We routinely represent employers on qualified plan matters before the Internal Revenue Service, the Department of Labor, and the Pension Benefit Guaranty Corporation. We regularly advise clients concerning fiduciary and prohibited transaction issues. We also advise employers regarding the implications and liabilities involved with participation in multi-employer union pension plans. The firm regularly advises clients on the tax implications and laws governing the provision of medical benefits, disability coverage, and life insurance, including employers' liability for health continuation coverage under COBRA.

LITIGATION SECTION

Fennemore Craig's litigation practice encompasses virtually all areas of state and federal civil litigation and appellate work, as well as adversarial proceedings before federal and state administrative agencies.

Antitrust Law and Trade Regulations: Fennemore Craig represents business entities in litigation alleging unlawful restraints of trade, price-fixing conspiracies, and a variety of other federal and state antitrust law violations. The firm recently participated in major antitrust actions involving the cable television, consumer electronics and petrochemical industries. We assist many clients in connection with mergers and acquisitions covered by the Hart-Scott-Rodino Antitrust Improvements Act of 1976.

Appeals: Fennemore Craig handles appellate matters in federal and state courts as well as before federal and state administrative agencies. The scope of our appellate practice covers almost all areas of civil, administrative and regulatory law.

Bankruptcy and Creditors' Rights: Fennemore Craig has a prominent and active bankruptcy practice in Arizona. Our attorneys represent a diverse group of clients including secured creditors, unsecured creditors, financial institutions, debtors, and trustees and purchasers of financially distressed businesses, in Chapter 11 cases, debt restructuring, liquidation cases, out-of-court workouts, and other insolvency proceedings. The practice focuses extensively on creditor representation, and together with attorneys from other disciplines in the firm, the group is active in planning and negotiating complex workouts and restructures.

Our bankruptcy attorneys are highly visible in various local, state and national bankruptcy groups, have written numerous articles on bankruptcy topics for both state and national publications, and have participated and spoken at numerous local, state and national seminars. They also have established meaningful relationships with the Arizona federal courts and court personnel.

Commercial Litigation: Fennemore Craig represents large and small business entities and individuals in all types of commercial disputes, including cases involving lender liability allegations, securities, corporate control, contracts, First Amendment, the Uniform Commercial Code and eminent domain, real property and title disputes. We maintain and defend suits for patent and trademark infringement and other aspects of intellectual property law. The firm also handles engineering, construction and public contract disputes.

Labor and Employment: Fennemore Craig has broad experience in litigation alleging breach of employment contract, wrongful termination, employment discrimination and related claims. In addition, our attorneys frequently represent clients before federal and state administrative agencies, including the Arizona Civil Rights Division, the Equal Employment Opportunity Commission, the Department of Economic Security, and the National Labor Relations Board. Fennemore Craig also counsels employers about personnel manuals and procedures, drug and alcohol testing policies, and compliance with specific state and federal statutes and regulations.

Natural Resources and Environmental Litigation: The firm's natural resources and environmental practice group handles all forms of litigation in the area. Recent litigation in which the firm has been active includes environmental and toxic torts, environmental policy suits, regulatory challenges, cost recovery actions, property devaluation and natural resource torts, complex water cases, general adjudication of water rights, mining title disputes, flood cases, and environmental compliance actions. Members of the firm have served as special counsel to the state in Arizona v. California and other water law cases of statewide interest.

Tort and Insurance Litigation: Fennemore Craig represents litigants in a wide variety of personal injury and business tort actions ranging from individual negligence actions to complex multi-party litigation. Asbestos, railroad liability, product liability, insurance bad faith and subrogation, and toxic torts and professional liability encompass a significant part of our tort litigation practice.

Unemployment Compensation: Fennemore Craig's unemployment compensation practice includes the full range of services relating to unemployment insurance, taxes and benefits. The firm defends against benefit claims in the Appeal Tribunal, Appeals Board and appellate courts. We also represent employers in proceedings against the Department of Economic Security. The firm has participated extensively in legislative revisions to the unemployment insurance statutes and in Department of Economic Security rule-making proceedings.

Workers' Compensation: Fennemore Craig counsels many major corporations in the area of workers' compensation. The firm represents employers in litigation before the Industrial Commission of Arizona and Arizona's appellate courts. It also advises clients on the various legal and administrative issues that arise in connection with workers' compensation claims outside the litigation arena.

High Technology: Fennemore Craig has been involved in significant litigation involving intellectual property, including patent and copyright infringement, trade secrecy, software licenses, nondisclosure agreements, and covenants not to compete. The firm represented an industrial software client in a successful action in Federal District Court and the Ninth Circuit Court of Appeals that resulted in the first Ninth Circuit pronouncement on the scope of copyright protection for the structure, sequence and organization of software.

Construction and Government Contacts: Fennemore Craig represents developers, owners, architects, engineers and contractors in the preparation of contract documents and litigation. The firm has considerable experience in federal and state actions, as well as administrative proceedings before the Arizona Registrar of Contractors and the Arizona Department of Real Estate.

The firm also has broad experience in federal and state procurement law and government contract disputes. We have litigated bid protests before the Comptroller General of the General Accounting Office and various state agencies. The firm also has represented government contractors against city, county, state and federal governments. The firm has prosecuted claims against numerous federal agencies before the various Boards of Contract Appeals and the Claims Court.

Counsel For: ADFlex Solutions, Inc.; Arizona Water Co.; ASARCO Incorporated; Bridgestone/Firestone, Inc.; Burlington Northern Santa Fe Corp.; Cable Systems International, Inc.; Carefree Partners, L.L.C.; Catellus Development Corporation; Citicorp, Real Estate, Inc.; Cyprus Amax Minerals Company; Desert Highlands Development Company, Inc.; Desert Mountain Properties; DMB Associates, Inc.; GIANT Industries, Inc.; The FINOVA Group, Inc.; FINOVA Capital Corporation; Hensley & Company; Kennecott Corporation; Mayo Clinic Scottsdale; Merrill Lynch, Pierce, Fenner & Smith Inc.; Norwest Bank Arizona, N.A.; Orbital Sciences Corp.; Pep Boys; PETsMART, Inc; Phelps Dodge Corporation; Phoenix Suns Limited Partnership; Pima Community College; Robson Communities; Southern Pacific Transportation Company; Southwest Airlines Co.; St. Joseph's Hospital and Medical Center; State Savings Bank, FSB; Sturm, Ruger & Co.; Sunbelt Holdings, Inc.; Tessenderlo Kerley, Inc.; The B.F. Goodrich Company; The Goodyear Tire & Rubber Company; Tosco Marketing Co.; Trejo Oil Company, Inc.; UDC Homes; US WEST Communications, Inc.; U.S. WEST Marketing Resources Group, Inc.; Viad Corp.

ARIZONA LAW DIGEST

(The following is a list of all Categories and Topics, including cross-references, covered in this Digest.)

ARIZONA LAW DIGEST

Revised for 1999 edition by

FENNEMORE CRAIG, P.C.

(References, unless otherwise indicated, are to Arizona Revised Statutes, 1956 [cited by section number, i.e., 21-406], Arizona Rules of Civil Procedure, 1956 [cited by rule number, i.e., Civ. 5(a)] and Arizona Rules of Civil Appellate Procedure, 1978 [cited by rule number, i.e., App. 7]. Parallel citations begin with 1 Arizona and 25 Pacific Reporter [1866]).

Uniform Probate Code, but not 1977 or later amendments, adopted and in effect. (14-1101 et seq.).

NOTE: *This revision covers all Acts adopted by Legislature in its 1998 regular session and approved by Governor, Chapters 1 to 300.*

INTRODUCTION

GOVERNMENT AND LEGAL SYSTEM:

The State of Arizona is a constituent state of the United States of America. For further discussion of the U.S. federal system, see Introduction to the Federal Government of the United States at the beginning of this volume. A great many laws are promulgated by the federal government of the United States and are not reflected in the topics below. See the Introduction to this volume for references to the federal law topics covered.

Like all but one of the United States, Arizona has a common law legal system, with roots in English common law. For information on the courts and legislature of Arizona, see category Courts and Legislature.

HOLIDAYS:

Legal Holidays.—Sundays, and Jan. 1, 3d Mon. in Jan., 3d Mon. in Feb., 2d Sun. in May, last Mon. in May, 3d Sun. in June, July 4, 1st Sun. in Aug., 1st Mon. in Sept., Sept. 17 or Sun. preceding, 2d Mon. in Oct., Nov. 11, 4th Thurs. in Nov. and Dec. 25. (1-301[A]).

Holidays Falling on Sat. or Sun.—When any holiday falls on Sat., preceding Fri. is observed as holiday. When any holiday, other than holiday designed to fall on Sun., falls on Sun., following Mon. is observed as holiday. (1-301[B] to [C]).

Legality of Transactions on Holidays.—Public offices and courts of justice may not be opened on holidays, and no judicial business may be transacted, except for following purposes: To give instructions to deliberating jury on its request, to receive verdict or discharge jury, and for exercise of powers of magistrates in criminal proceedings. Injunctions, attachments, claim and delivery and writs of prohibition may be issued and served on any day. (1-302).

OFFICE HOURS AND TIME ZONE:

Arizona is in the Mountain (GMT −07:00) time zone. Office hours are generally from 9 a.m. to 5 p.m.

BUSINESS ORGANIZATIONS

AGENCY:

Rules of common law apply in absence of statutory provisions.

ASSOCIATIONS:

Caveat: For disclosure requirements in conveyances of real property made or taken in representative capacity, see category Property, topic Deeds.

Business Trusts.—Permitted as a recognized form of association. (10-1871 et seq.). Subject to applicable provisions of general corporate law. (10-1879).

Associations Not for Profit.—Cooperative marketing associations and electric cooperative nonprofit membership corporations are governed by 10-2001 et seq. and 2051 et seq., respectively. Nonprofit electric cooperatives are subject to 10-2121 et seq. Names for electric cooperatives are governed by 10-2054. Solicitation of funds for charitable purposes is governed by 44-6551 et seq.

Fraternal Societies.—Regulated by 10-2101 et seq. May elect not less than three nor more than nine of their members as trustees to care for property and transact related business of society. (10-2101). Such trustees may have seal, and for all purposes for which they are authorized to act are deemed corporations; may possess, manage, control, purchase, lease, receive, recover, hold, sell, convey, mortgage and improve all property of such societies; and may sue and be sued. (10-2102). Trustees must be elected annually. (10-2104). Classification of trustees permitted. Any two may call meeting, and majority may transact business. (10-2104).

Professional Corporations.—Governed by 10-2201 et seq. See topic Corporations.

Actions.—Pleading capacity to sue or be sued is as provided by Civ. 9(a); actions by or against governed by Civ. 23.2.

CORPORATIONS:

General Supervision.—Exercised by Arizona Corporation Commission. Administration Division: 1200 W. Washington St., Phoenix, Arizona 85007. Telephone: (602) 542-4140. General Information: (602) 542-3076. Corporations Division: 1300 W. Washington St., Phoenix, Arizona 85007. Telephone: (602) 542-3026 or (800) 345-5819.

Arizona Business Corporation Act became effective Jan. 1, 1996. (10-001 et seq.). Act is based on Model Business Corporation Act (1984), with substantial variations as noted below. Note that new Act applies to all existing corporations as of Jan. 1, 1996. (10-1701). Corporations formed prior to Arizona's statehood may take steps to retain previously valid article provisions. (10-1701).

Material variations from Official Text, as set forth in Uniform and Model Acts section, are:

§1.20 (10-120).—Filing requirements differ. Delivery may be made by facsimile. See 10-122 for schedule of fees.

§1.24 (10-124).—Filing requirements differ.

§1.25 (10-125).—Documents are not "filed" until Commission has reviewed them for statutory compliance. (10-123). If in compliance, documents will be considered "filed" as of date of delivery to Commission. If not in compliance, documents will be returned unfiled. (10-123).

§1.26 (10-126).—Omitted.

§1.27 (10-127).—Stamp affixed to copy of document bearing signature of executive secretary of Commission (which may be by facsimile) and seal of Commission is conclusive evidence that original is on file with Commission.

§1. 28 (10-128).—Requirements differ for certificate of good standing.

§1.29 (10-129).—Omitted as duplicative of A.R.S. Title 13, c. 27 and 10-1631. Officers, directors or agents who knowingly or wrongfully authorize, sign or make false reports, certificates, other statements or public notices, or authorize or make wrongful alterations to books, records or accounts of corporation are jointly and severally personally liable to creditor or shareholder of corporation who relied on false material representations or alterations. Limitation on actions is two years after discovery of false representation or alteration, and six years after certificate, report, public notice or other statement or alteration was made. (10-1631). Commission must direct detailed interrogatories to any person listed in certificate of disclosure who has been involved two or more times in corporate bankruptcy, receivership, revocation, administrative dissolution or judicial dissolution in any state. (10-1623). Interrogatories must be answered within 30 days after mailing, and failure to comply is Class 1 Misdemeanor. (10-1623). False statements constitute Class 5 Felony. (10-1623). Commission must not file articles of incorporation or application for authority to transact business by foreign corporation until all outstanding interrogatories are answered to its satisfaction. (10-1623). Upon filing petition for bankruptcy or appointment of receiver, corporation must deliver statement to Commission disclosing information regarding all officers, directors, trustees and holders of greater than 20% interests in corporation within one year. If holder of more than 20% of stock is corporation, statement must list similar information for corporate stockholders. (10-1623). Failure to comply is Class 1 Misdemeanor, and giving false information is Class 5 Felony. (10-1623). See 10-1631 et seq. for further requirements of interrogatories and additional criminal penalties. Commission may propound to any domestic or foreign corporation any interrogatories it deems reasonably necessary and proper to ascertain compliance with law by corporation, and interrogatories must be answered in writing and under oath within 30 days after mailing. (10-1633).

§1.41 (10-141).—Oral notice not permitted if written notice is specifically required.

§2.01 (10-201).—Incorporators must deliver certificate of disclosure to Commission along with articles of incorporation.

§2.02 (10-202).—Substantially revised. Articles may set forth any matters which are not inconsistent with other laws, including limitation or elimination of director liability. Certificate of disclosure must set forth information regarding each officer, director, trustee, incorporator, and 10% or greater shareholder, and must be supplemented for any person attaining such position after filing articles of incorporation.

§2.03 (10-203).—Corporate existence begins at time of delivery, not "filing," of articles of incorporation and certificate of disclosure. If articles and certificate are later rejected by Commission as not in compliance with law, corporate existence terminates at time of rejection, and is not retroactively terminated. Articles must be published within 60 days after "filing" with Commission, and affidavit of publication must be filed within 90 days after filing of articles. Foreign corporations may be domesticated in Arizona (10-220), and Arizona corporations may transfer their domicile to another jurisdiction (10-226).

§2.04 (10-204).—Imposes joint and several liability for preincorporation and post-termination transactions on persons who act with actual knowledge that no corporation exists.

§2.05 (10-205).—Requires board of directors to complete organization of corporation after incorporation.

§2.06 (10-206).—Board of directors must adopt initial bylaws.

§3.02 (10-302).—Corporate bonds may be signed by facsimile signature, and may be authenticated by trustee.

§3.04 (10-304).—Attorney General may enjoin corporation from transacting unauthorized business.

§4.01 (10-401).—"Association" or "bank" may be used to denote corporate form; use of words "bank," "deposit," "trust" and "trust company" is restricted.

§5.01 (10-501).—Corporations must maintain "known place of business" and "statutory agent," which are not required to have same address. (10-502).

§5.03 (10-503).—Statutory agent must give corporation written notice of resignation.

§5.04 (10-504).—Service may be made pursuant to Arizona Rules of Civil Procedure.

See note at head of Digest as to 1998 legislation covered.

See Topical Index in front part of this volume.

CORPORATIONS . . . *continued*

§6.01 (10-601).—Cumulative voting for election of directors is limited by Const., Art. XIV, §10 and 10-728.

§6.02 (10-602).—Prior to issuing shares of class or series, corporation must file "statement pursuant to §10-602" with Commission, which constitutes amendment to articles of incorporation. (10-602[D]).

§6.20 (10-620).—Certain provisions not limited to preincorporation subscriptions. Board of directors may release, compromise or settle any subscription or any claim, dispute or action arising out of subscription. Subscription agreement not enforceable unless in writing and signed by party to be charged or his agent. Remedies of rescission or forfeiture available only when defaulting subscriber fails to cure default after notice.

§6.21 (10-621).—Stock may not be issued in exchange for promissory notes or future services. Shares issued by banking and insurance corporations may require par value. (Const., Art. XIV, §11).

§6.24 (10-624).—Issuance of rights, options and warrants must be subject to any pre-existing conditions in articles of incorporation. Provisions adjusting terms upon specified occurrences may be included in rights, options or warrants. "Poison pill" and similar provisions are permitted. (10-629).

§6.25 (10-625).—No certificates may be issued unless shares fully paid.

§6.26 (10-626).—Corporation must provide shareholder with certificate upon request.

§6.27 (10-627).—Allows restrictions on transfer or registration if not manifestly unreasonable.

§6.31 (10-631).—Board of directors may file "statement pursuant to §10-631" with Commission, which constitutes amendment to articles without shareholder action.

§7.01 (10-701).—Contains special rules for water users' associations.

§7.02 (10-702).—Provision allowing certain percentage of shareholders to call special meetings must be included in articles or bylaws to be effective.

§7.03 (10-703).—Shareholder petitions may be made when three months have passed since annual meeting date specified in bylaws or 15 months since last annual meeting.

§7.04 (10-704).—Delivery of consent to corporation is not condition of effectiveness. If not specified in consent, effective date is date last shareholder signs, unless ten days' written notice is required to nonvoting shareholders. Shareholders may revoke consent by delivering signed revocation to president or secretary before date last shareholder signs.

§7.05 (10-705).—Unless otherwise set by 10-703 or 707, record date is day before effective date of first notice to shareholders.

§7.21 (10-721).—Water users' associations may further limit voting rights in articles or bylaws.

§7.22 (10-722).—Appointment of proxy may be for less than 11 months. Proxies whose appointments are coupled with interest include persons with purchase options, any other right to acquire shares, and creditors who continue credit to corporation. Water users' associations may limit or eliminate right to vote by proxy in articles of incorporation.

§7.25 (10-725).—Articles or bylaws may provide that shares present at meeting may be withdrawn for quorum purposes.

§7.26 (10-726).—Voting by individual voting groups need not be simultaneous.

§7.28 (10-728).—Cumulative voting is mandatory.

§7.30 (10-730).—Voting trust agreements may contain any lawful provision consistent with purposes of trust.

§7.31 (10-731).—Voting agreements may specify that voting agreement is not specifically enforceable.

§7.32 (10-732).—Board of directors may not be eliminated. Shareholder agreements must be filed with corporation. Procedures in 10-732 are not exclusive methods of agreement among shareholders.

§7.40 (10-740).—"Independent person" is defined as having "no personal interest in the transaction and no personal or other relationship which influences the person."

§7.42 (10-742).—Derivative proceedings may be commenced sooner than 90 days after demand if statute of limitations will expire within 90-day period.

§7.44 (10-744).—Requirements differ. Court may dismiss proceedings on motion of corporation "on any legal grounds."

§8.01 (10-801).—Corporations must be governed by board of directors.

§8.03 (10-803).—Restrictions on board of directors materially changing size of board without shareholder approval have been omitted.

§8.04 (10-804).—Voting groups may be comprised of specified series of stock within class.

§8.06 (10-806).—Requirements differ. Staggered boards generally permitted without regard to total number of directors and without limiting number of classes. See also 82 Ariz. 299, 313 P.2d 379, which may otherwise limit number of classes.

§8.07 (10-807).—Notice of resignation may specify event upon which resignation is effective.

§8.08 (10-808).—If less than entire board is to be removed, director shall not be removed if number of votes sufficient to elect him by cumulative voting is voted against his removal.

§8.09 (10-809).—Standard for removal is limited to fraudulent or intentional criminal conduct. Time period for which court may remove director is no longer than five years.

§8.10 (10-810).—Any officer or shareholder may call special meeting of shareholders to fill director vacancies when no directors remain in office.

§8.20 (10-820).—Shareholders may use modern communications technology for shareholder meetings, as permitted by sole discretion of board of directors. (10-708).

§8.21 (10-821).—Directors may revoke consents by delivering signed revocation to president or secretary before date last director signs.

§8.24 (10-824).—Directors have until 5:00 p.m. on next business day to dissent or abstain from action taken at board meeting.

§8.25 (10-825).—Committees may consist of one or more members. Committees may not set director or committee compensation. Board may designate alternate committee members to replace absent members.

§8.30 (10-830).—Directors retain all legal defenses and presumptions ordinarily available to directors. Directors are presumed to have acted in accordance with law, and burden is on challenging party to rebut presumption by clear and convincing evidence.

§8.33 (10-833).—Directors must properly dissent to unlawful distributions or will be presumed to have assented if present at meeting. (10-833[B]). Limitation on actions against directors is four years.

§8.42 (10-842).—Officers may rely on directors. Officers retain all legal defenses and presumptions ordinarily available. Officers are presumed to have acted in accordance with law, and burden is on challenging party to rebut presumption by clear and convincing evidence.

§8.43 (10-843).—Officer resignations may be effective upon specified date or event.

§8.50 (10-850).—Certain definitions have been expanded or added. "Liability" includes expenses which have not yet been paid or incurred by person to be indemnified. "Outside director" is director who is not also officer, employee or holder of more than 5% of any class of stock.

§8.52 (10-852).—Outside directors have presumptive right to mandatory indemnification and advancement of expenses, unless articles provide otherwise or court finds that outside director failed to meet standard of conduct.

§8.53 (10-853).—Procedures differ. Advances to outside directors are governed by 10-852.

§8.61 (10-861).—Burden is on challenging party to prove by clear and convincing evidence that requirements of subsection (B) were not met by director.

§10.02 (10-1002).—In event of stock split, all shares must be treated identically.

§10.03 (10-1003).—Shareholders may initiate amendments, if permitted in articles of incorporation.

§10.06 (10-1006).—Articles of amendment must be published within 60 days after filing with Commission, and affidavit of publication must be filed within 90 days after filing of articles of amendment.

§10.07 (10-1007).—Articles of restatement must be published within 60 days after filing with Commission, and affidavit of publication must be filed within 90 days after filing of articles of restatement.

§10.08 (10-1008).—Articles of amendment must be published within 60 days after filing with Commission, and affidavit of publication must be filed within 90 days after filing of articles of amendment.

§11.03 (10-1103).—Articles of incorporation may provide for separate voting by voting groups. Abandonment of plan is permitted at any time prior to filing of articles of merger or share exchange.

§11.05 (10-1105).—Plan of merger or share exchange is filed as separate document with Commission. See subsection (A)(2) for requirements of articles of merger or share exchange. Merger or share exchange takes effect as provided in 10-123. If articles of merger or share exchange include amendments to articles of incorporation of surviving corporation, document must be titled "articles of amendment and merger." Articles of merger or share exchange must be published within 60 days after filing with Commission, and affidavit evidencing publication must be filed within 90 days after filing of articles of merger or share exchange.

§11.07 (10-1107).—Domestic and foreign limited liability companies, limited partnerships and registered limited liability partnerships may merge or exchange shares with domestic corporations pursuant to 10-1108.

§13.02 (10-1302).—Does not apply if shares of class or series are redeemable securities issued by registered investment company. Unless articles provide otherwise, does not apply to shares registered on national securities exchange, listed on NASDAQ or held by at least 2,000 shareholders on relevant record date.

§13.30 (10-1330).—Right to jury trial is eliminated. Court may appoint master in proceeding, rather than appraiser.

§13.31 (10-1331).—Court is not precluded from assessing costs and awarding fees on other grounds, such as giving effect to offer of judgment.

§14.03 (10-1403).—Additional requirements apply, including tax clearance from Department of Revenue, payment of all fees owed to Commission, and submission of affidavit of publication of articles of dissolution.

§14.06 (10-1406).—Contingent claims which become known claims after effective date of dissolution may be disposed of pursuant to this section.

§14.07 (10-1407).—Enforceable claims also include contingent claims or claims based on events occurring after effective date of dissolution.

§14.20 (10-1420).—Grounds for administrative dissolution include failure to make publications and file affidavits as required by law, and failure to update certificate of disclosure for new officers, directors, trustees or shareholders in accordance with 10-202(F).

§14.21 (10-1421).—If corporation has not applied for reinstatement within six months after effective date of dissolution, Commission must release corporate name for use by others.

§14.22 (10-1422).—Corporations have three years to apply for reinstatement. Applications for reinstatement need only recite corporation name, effective date of administrative dissolution, and nonexistence or elimination of grounds for dissolution. If another corporation or person has adopted corporate name as name of entity or trade name, application for reinstatement shall include articles of amendment adopting new name. (10-401 et seq.).

§14.23 (10-1423).—Omitted. Commission has established administrative procedures for appeal. See Arizona Administrative Code R14-3-101 and 112.

§14.31 (10-1431).—Venue for attorney general proceedings lies in county of corporation's known place of business. Subsection (d) regarding shareholder notices has been omitted.

§14.32 (10-1432).—Receiver is appointed both to liquidate and manage property and business affairs of corporation.

§14.40 (10-1440).—Payments may be made to legal representative of creditor, claimant or shareholder who is not competent to receive them. Distributions are

---

See note at head of Digest as to 1998 legislation covered.

See Topical Index in front part of this volume.

CORPORATIONS . . . *continued*
processed through Unclaimed Property Division of Department of Revenue, rather than state treasurer.

§15.01 (10-1501).—Being limited partner or member of limited liability company without more does not constitute "transacting business" requiring authority from Commission. This section does not apply to insurance corporations or corporations only lending money to religious, social or benevolent associations in Arizona.

§15.02 (10-1502).—Penalties for failure to obtain authority differ. Attorney general or any other person may bring action to enjoin foreign corporation from transacting business without authority.

§15.03 (10-1503).—Application requirements differ. Certificate of disclosure is required. Commission must review application for compliance with law. Application must be published within 60 days after filing of application, and affidavit of publication must be filed within 90 days after filing of application. Foreign corporations authorized to transact business are subject to 10-1623 regarding involvement of persons in corporate bankruptcies, receiverships, revocations, and administrative or judicial dissolutions. (10-1623). No certificates are issued; date of filing is date on which Commission grants authority to transact business.

§15.04 (10-1504).—New authority from Commission must be obtained if foreign corporation changes either its actual name or name under which it was granted authority to transact business. Filing requirements differ. If foreign corporation amends or restates its articles of incorporation for any reason, certified copy must be delivered to Commission within 60 days.

§15.06 (10-1506).—Words "association" and "bank" may be used to denote corporateness; "limited" may not be used. Use of "bank," "deposit," "trust," and "trust company" is restricted. Certain other requirements differ. If foreign corporation amends or restates its articles of incorporation for any reason, certified copy must be delivered to Commission within 60 days.

§15.07 (10-1507).—Addresses of known place of business and statutory agent need not be identical.

§15.08 (10-1508).—Requirements differ. Addresses of known place of business and statutory agent need not be identical.

§15.09 (10-1509).—Procedures differ.

§15.10 (10-1510).—Requirements differ. Service may be made on statutory agent or pursuant to Arizona Rules of Civil Procedure.

§15.20 (10-1520).—Requirements differ. Application for withdrawal is not complete without state tax clearance, payment of all fees owed to Commission, and filing of affidavit that application for withdrawal has been published. Commission must review application for conformance with law.

§15.30 (10-1530).—Grounds for revocation include failure to make any publication or file affidavit of publication required by law, and failure to update certificate of disclosure.

§15.32 (10-1532).—Omitted. Commission has established procedures for appeal to Commissioners. See Arizona Administrative Code R14-3-101 and 102.

§16.01 (10-1601).—Corporations must keep copies of any shareholder agreements under 10-732 at its principal office, known place of business or office of statutory agent.

§16.02 (10-1602).—Shareholder must be holder of record for at least six months immediately preceding demand, or holder of record of at least 5% of all outstanding shares, before right to inspect arises, unless shareholder obtains court order compelling inspection.

§16.20 (10-1620).—Any shareholder may obtain corporation's most recent annual financial statements upon written request at any time.

§16.21 (10-1621).—Reporting on indemnification or advancement of expenses is not limited to derivative proceedings. Reporting requirement is tied to delivery of annual financial statements, rather than notice of next shareholders' meeting.

§16.22 (10-1622).—Requirements differ. Annual reports must include certificate of disclosure, names of shareholders holding more than 20% of any class of shares, statement regarding filing of state income tax returns, and statement of financial condition. Filing deadline assigned by Commission. Commission may stagger annual report filing date for all corporations and adjust annual registration fee on pro rata basis.

§17.01 (10-1701).—All provisions of Act are fully applicable to all existing business corporations and to all new business corporations formed after effective date (Jan. 1, 1996). Corporations organized under laws of territory of Arizona (prior to Arizona's statehood) may amend or restate articles of incorporation and retain any previously valid provisions of their articles, which shall continue to be applicable to corporation and all persons dealing with it. Act does not apply to statutes governing close corporations (10-1801 et seq.), business trusts (10-1871 et seq.), or professional corporations (10-2201 et seq.), except as specifically provided in respective statutes.

§17.03 (10-1703).—Omitted. Arizona courts have held that substantive legal rights (as distinguished from procedural expectations) may not be impaired once vested. (173 Ariz. 19, 839 P.2d 439).

§17.04 (10-1704).—Omitted. Arizona has recognized severability. (139 Ariz. 525, 679 P.2d 548).

§17.05 (10-1705).—Omitted. New Act is complete substitute for prior Arizona corporation law.

§17.06 (10-1706).—Omitted. Effective date is Jan. 1, 1996.

Takeovers.—Regulated by 10-2701 et seq.

Deeds.—See category Property, topic Deeds.

Name.—Regulated by 10-401 et seq.

Franchise or License Taxes.—None.

Filing Fees.—Regulated by 10-2601 (nonprofit corporations).

Income Tax on Corporations.—See category Taxation, topic Income Tax, subhead Rates for Corporations.

Sales Tax.—See category Taxation, topic Sales and Use Taxes, subhead Transaction Privilege Taxes.

Stock Transfer.—Uniform Commercial Code adopted. (47-1101 et seq.). See category Business Regulation and Commerce, topic Commercial Code. Uniform Simplification of Fiduciary Security Transfers Act repealed by 1995, c. 153, §6. See 47-8101 et seq. for same subject matter.

Unclaimed Dividends.—See category Property, topic Absentees, subhead Escheat.

Close Corporations.—Such corporations are subject to provisions of Model Business Corporation Act as adopted in Arizona unless 10-1801 modifies or differs from those provisions, in which case close corporations act prevails. (10-1801 et seq.).

Articles of incorporation must contain name of corporation, names and addresses of managers and original investors (which may not exceed ten), initial contributions of each, aggregate initial contributions to corporation, and name and address of statutory agent. (10-1803). See 10-1804 et seq. for additional provisions regarding close corporations.

Limited Liability Companies.—See topic Limited Liability Companies.

Nonprofit Corporations.—Arizona Nonprofit Corporation Act becomes effective Dec. 31, 1998. (10-3101 et seq.). Act replaces corporation code chapter on nonprofit corporations (10-2301 et seq.) and adds section regulating sale and merger of nonprofit hospitals (10-31251 et seq.). Note new Act applies to all existing corporations as of Jan. 1, 1999. (10-31701). Corporations formed prior to Arizona's statehood may elect to retain previously valid article provisions. Filing fees governed by 10-2601. Solicitation of funds for charitable purposes governed by 44-6551 et seq.

Immunity.—Directors immune from civil liability from third-party lawsuits for good faith actions in their official capacity. (10-3830). Articles of incorporation may limit liability of directors to corporation or members for breach of fiduciary duty. (10-3202).

Professional Corporations.—Such corporations are subject to provisions of Model Business Corporations Act as adopted in Arizona, unless 10-2201 et seq. modifies or differs from those provisions, in which case Professional Corporations Act prevails. Name must include "professional corporation," "professional association," "service corporation," "limited," "chartered," or abbreviation thereof. (10-2215). Professional can use any other corporate form not prohibited by licensing authority. (10-2213). Business corporations can amend articles to become professional corporations. (10-2210). Professional corporations can amend articles to become business corporations. (10-2241). Foreign professional corporation must obtain grant of authority to transact business if it maintains or intends to maintain office in Arizona. (10-2244 to 2246). Professional corporations may engage in two or more categories of professional service and any other business purpose, unless prohibited by licensing law or authorities (10-2211); broad range of other activities permitted (10-2211 to 2214). At least 51% of voting shares must be owned by licensed professionals, which may include partnerships, other professional corporations, professional limited liability companies or similar entities in certain circumstances. (10-2220). Up to 49% of voting shares may be owned by other persons. (10-2220). Shares held by professionals may be transferred only to professionals; shares held by other persons may be transferred to any qualified person. (10-2222). At least one-half of directors and president, if any, must be licensed professionals. (10-2230). Professional corporation may merge with any other entity. (10-2240).

Uniform Gifts to Minors Act.—Repealed by 1988, c. 81, §3.

Uniform Securities Ownership by Minors Act not adopted.

Uniform Simplification of Fiduciary Security Transfers Act repealed by 1995, c. 153, §6. See 47-8101 et seq. for same subject matter.

JOINT STOCK COMPANIES:

Subject to same statutory regulations as corporations.

Professional Corporations.—See topic Corporations.

LIMITED LIABILITY COMPANIES:

One or more persons may form limited liability company by filing articles of organization with Corporation Commission. (29-631 et seq.). Unless articles of organization state otherwise, management of limited liability company is vested in its members. (29-681). Members of limited liability company may adopt operating agreement which relates to business of limited liability company, conduct of its affairs, its rights or powers and rights or powers of its members, managers, officers, employees or agents. (29-682).

Interest in limited liability company may be issued in exchange for capital contribution and/or enforceable promise in writing to make capital contribution in future. (29-701). Limited liability company cannot make distribution to member if after making that distribution, liabilities of limited liability company would exceed fair value of assets of limited liability company (29-706). Member may bring derivative action to recover judgment in favor of limited liability company (29-831).

Professional limited liability companies are governed by 29-841 to 847. Professional limited liability companies may render professional services only through members, managers, officers, agents and employees who are licensed persons qualified in Arizona to perform those professional services. (29-844).

LIMITED PARTNERSHIP:

Revised Uniform Limited Partnership Act (1976) with 1985 amendments adopted (29-301 et seq.) with material variations and additions, including: (1) Secretary of State is default agent for service of process, notice or demand, if agent not appointed or resigns (29-304); (2) banking and insurance are prohibited activities (29-306); (3) distributions to limited partners upon withdrawal from limited partnership formed or resulting from merger after Oct. 31, 1996 are governed by 29-334(B), unless otherwise provided in written partnership agreement; (4) judicial dissolution may be requested by assignees or successors-in-interest (29-345); (5) define certain activities by foreign corporations as not transacting business without registration (29-354[E]); (6) application to limited partnership existing on July 24, 1982 (29-364); (7) effect of enactment on accrued rights (29-365); and (8) fees (29-366).

See note at head of Digest as to 1998 legislation covered.

See Topical Index in front part of this volume.

AZ – 3

PARTNERSHIPS:

Uniform Partnership Act (1994) adopted with significant variations and additions. (29-1001 et seq.). Delayed repeal of existing Uniform Partnership Act (29-201 et seq.) until Jan. 1, 2000 (1996, c. 226, §46). Before Jan. 1, 2000, new Uniform Partnership Act only governs: (1) partnerships formed after July 20, 1996, unless partnership is continuing business of dissolved partnership and (2) existing partnerships that elect to be governed by new Act. (1996, c. 226, §48[A]). Beginning on Jan. 1, 2000, new Act governs all partnerships, including all general and limited partnerships that have filed statement of qualification or application for registration as limited liability partnership under prior law. (1996, c. 226, §48[B]). Effect of enactment on accrued rights. (29-1111). Liability to third parties of partners in partnerships and limited liability partnerships that elect to be governed by new Act. (1996, c. 226, §48[C]).

Revised Uniform Limited Partnership Act (1976) with 1985 amendments adopted with material variations and additions. (29-301 et seq.). See topic Limited Partnership.

Fictitious Names.—Every partnership transacting business under ficticious name or designation must record with county recorder of county in which place of business is located certificate signed and acknowledged by each partner, stating full names of partners and their residence addresses. New certificate must be recorded upon any change in partnership membership. (29-102).

Persons doing business contrary to this provision cannot maintain any action based on any contract made or transactions had in their partnership name until they have first recorded required certificate. (29-102). This provision does not apply to commercial or banking partnerships established and transacting business outside Arizona nor to law firms, public accounting firms, domestic limited partnerships which have filed or recorded certificates of limited partnership, foreign limited partnership which has registered under 29-349, domestic limited liability partnership that is registered pursuant to 29-244 or 1101, or foreign limited liability partnership that is registered pursuant to 29-248 or 1106. (29-103).

Undisclosed Use.—If a person transacts business as a merchant or trader with the addition of the word "agent," "factor," "company" or "co." or other words of like significance and fails to disclose the name of any other person interested in such business by a sign in letters easy to read, at the place where the business is transacted, or transacts business in his own name without such addition, all property, stock, money and choses in action used or acquired in such business, except property exempt from execution, are liable for his debts and are to be treated in all respects as his property in favor of his creditors. (29-101).

Caveat: For disclosure requirements in conveyances of real property made or taken in representative capacity, see category Property, topic Deeds.

Conversion.—Of one type of partnership to another governed by 29-368 et seq.

Merger.—Governed by 29-372 et seq.

BUSINESS REGULATION AND COMMERCE

BANKS AND BANKING:

Uniform Commercial Code adopted. See topic Commercial Code.

Regulation.—Banking department, under management of superintendent of banks, has charge of execution of laws in relation to banks and banking. (6-110 et seq.). Superintendent may assess civil penalty against any person, or anyone participating in his affairs, for any knowing violations of laws or rules. (6-132). Classifications of criminal penalties for violations of laws and rules. (6-133 to 134). To halt violations, superintendent may issue cease and desist order which remains effective until modified or terminated by superintendent or reviewing court. Superintendent may apply to Maricopa County Superior Court for temporary restraining order, preliminary injunction, or permanent injunction. (6-137). Reporting requirements imposed if credit card revolving loan accounts are issued. (6-140). Acquisition of 15% or more of voting securities or power to elect majority of directors of bank, trust company, savings and loan association or controlling entity thereof requires approval of superintendent, except as provided in 6-143. (6-141 et seq.). In certain situations, superintendent may remove or suspend from office or financial duties any financial director, officer, or financial institution member. If removal order is final, financial institution must receive prior written approval of superintendent to employ removed person. (6-161). Banking permit required unless national banking association with home office in Arizona or bank authorized to do business in Arizona. (6-201). Merger or consolidation with or acquisition of in-state bank by out-of-state bank requires approval of superintendent. (6-321 to 322). Out-of-state financial institution may establish bank, savings and loan association or holding company through de novo entry. (6-324).

Deposits.—Bank deposits may be made in name of two or more persons, including minors, payable to either or any of them or to any or sole survivor. (6-235).

In Trust.—Deposits may be made by one or more persons as trustees for one or more beneficiaries. Upon death of last surviving trustee, remaining balance shall be paid to or on order of any living designated beneficiary. Receipt order or acquittance of such beneficiary is sufficient release and discharge of bank. (6-236).

Unclaimed Deposits.—See category Property, topic Absentees, subhead Escheat.

Stock Assessment.—May be imposed to extent of par value of stock held in addition to amount invested. (Const., Art. XIV, §11).

Limitation of Loans.—Bank may lend to single borrower amount not more than 15% of its capital plus additional 10% of its capital if additional amounts are fully secured by readily marketable collateral with value at least equal to loan. (6-352). No bank may make any loan to its officers, directors, or employees, which loan causes outstanding loans to such person to exceed 1% of bank's capital account, unless loan is expressly authorized by board of directors, with interested director being disqualified to vote. (6-353). Balloon payments prohibited on loans of $10,000 or less for term of up to three years if loan is secured by lien (other than first lien) on owner-occupied

dwellings, excepting transactions involving sale of real property and excepting all federal or state chartered financial institutions. (6-114).

Pledge of Assets.—Bank may pledge assets to secure deposits or borrowings from one business day to next or from Federal Reserve Bank or any federal agency, but may only pledge assets to secure obligations other than deposits when value of assets so encumbered does not exceed capital account unless superintendent of banks approves otherwise. (6-245).

Savings Banks.—Regulated by 6-401 et seq. Investment of funds and interest payments are restricted. (6-442, 446).

Advance Fee Loan Brokers.—Regulated by 6-1301 et seq. Prohibited acts and registration requirement. (6-1305, 1309).

Transmitters of Money.—Regulated by 6-1201 et seq. License required. (6-1202). Bond required. (6-1205).

Escrow Agents.—Regulated by 6-801 et seq. License requirement and surety bond requirement. (6-813 to 814). Regulation of escrow rates. (6-846). Contributions to escrow guaranty fund. (6-847.02).

Premium Finance Companies.—Regulated by 6-1401 et seq.

Trust Companies.—Persons engaged in trust business are certified, regulated and may be removed by superintendent of banks. (6-859). Banks and savings and loans are exempt from certification and other trust company requirements (except trust account administration requirements) if members of F.D.I.C. or F.S.L.I.C. and otherwise authorized to engage in trust business under federal or state laws. (6-853). Certified public accountant must audit corporate records and trust business of each trust company at least annually, with report filed with state banking superintendent. (6-859). Any bank, savings and loan or trust company qualified to act as fiduciary may establish and administer common trust funds. (6-871).

Holding Companies.—Regulated by 6-1101 et seq. Superintendent's approval required for person to acquire, directly or indirectly, control of financial institution or controlling person. (6-1102). Exceptions contained in 6-1103.

Debt Management Companies.—Regulated by 6-701 et seq.

Uniform Common Trust Fund Act adopted. (6-871 et seq.).

Uniform Fiduciaries Act adopted, except that words "actual knowledge" are changed to "actual constructive knowledge" throughout Arizona act. (14-7501 et seq.).

Foreign Banks.—See category Estates and Trusts, topic Executors and Administrators.

Building and Loan Association.—Regulated by 6-401 et seq.

Savings and Loan Associations.—Regulated by 6-401 et seq. Withdrawal of funds from savings and loan by negotiable order is authorized by 6-423(B)(1) and 429(C). Superintendent of banks can be appointed receiver to liquidate (6-482[A]).

Uniform Unclaimed Property Act adopted. (44-301 et seq.).

Credit Unions.—Organization and operation regulated by 6-501 et seq.

Investment in Government Obligations.—Regulated by 6-386.

Permitted Investments.—Bank or trust company acting as fiduciary may invest in securities of open-end or closed-end investment company or investment trust registered under Investment Company Act of 1940, if it discloses to all persons whose funds are invested that bank provides services for and receives fees from investment company or investment trust. (6-246).

Sale of Securities.—Financial institutions may only sell or offer to sell equity securities or debt instruments with superintendent's prior written approval and if they disclose to purchaser that equity security or debt instrument is not federally insured. (6-116).

BILLS AND NOTES:

Uniform Commercial Code adopted. (47-1101 et seq.). See topic Commercial Code.

Attorneys' Fees.—Clause for collection is valid. (77 Ariz. 107, 267 P.2d 740).

Judgment Notes.—See category Civil Actions and Procedure, topic Judgments, subhead Judgment by Confession.

BILLS OF LADING:

See topic Commercial Code.

BILLS OF SALE:

See topic Sales.

BLUE SKY LAW:

See topic Securities.

BROKERS:

Uniform Commercial Code adopted with revisions. See topic Commercial Code.

Real Estate Brokers.—Licensed and regulated by State Real Estate Commissioner. (32-2121 et seq.). Real estate broker also may be licensed as cemetery broker and membership camping broker. (32-2122). Application, experience, completion of training course and examination required. (32-2123 to 2124). Corporation, limited liability company, and partnership also may be licensed as real estate broker. (32-2125). Attorney need not be licensed as broker when performing duties of attorney. (32-2121). Continuing education requirements for license renewal. (32-2130). Administrative penalties no more than $1,000 for each infraction of statutes, for violating rules or orders issued by Commissioner or for unlawful practices. (32-2160.01).

Licensed real estate broker or real estate salesperson, when acting for parties or one of parties to sale, exchange, or trade, or renting and leasing of property, has right to

BROKERS . . . *continued*

draft or fill out, without charge, instruments incident thereto including, but not limited to, preliminary purchase agreements and earnest money receipts, deeds, mortgages, leases, assignments, releases, contracts for sale of realty and bills of sale. (Const., Art. XXVI, §1).

Mortgage Brokers.—Licensed and regulated by superintendent of banks. Pertains only to persons engaged in business of making or negotiating real property mortgage loans not regulated under another law. Excludes, e.g., banks, savings and loans, trust companies, credit unions, insurance companies, consumer loan companies, mortgage bankers and attorneys. (6-901 et seq.).

Bond.—For mortgage bankers, $10,000 bond required for licensees with only institutional investors, and $15,000 bond required for licensees whose investors include any noninstitutional investors. (6-903[H]). One year statute of limitation against bond from date of alleged act, except for fraud and mistake claims. (6-903[G]).

Land Sale Regulation.—See category Property, topic Real Property.

BULK SALES:

Uniform Commercial Code, Article 6 adopted. (47-6101 et seq.).
See topics Commercial Code and Sales.

CARRIERS:

All railroad, electric, transmission, telegraph, telephone or pipeline corporations, for transportation of persons or or electricity, messages, water, oil or other property for profit, other than municipal corporations, are common carriers subject to regulation by Corporation Commission. (Const., Art. XV, §§2, 3, 10). Commission prescribes rates, charges, rules and regulations for common carriers. (Const., Art. XV, §3).

Rates, rules and regulations must not be unjust or unreasonable and must not discriminate. (Const., Art. XV, §12).

Uniform Commercial Code adopted. See topic Commercial Code.

Bills of Lading.—Governed by Commercial Code. (47-7101 et seq.). See topic Commercial Code.

Gross Receipts Tax.—See category Taxation, topic Gasoline Tax as to certain carriers.

Motor Vehicle Carriers.—See category Transportation, topic Motor Vehicles.

COMMERCIAL CODE:

Uniform Commercial Code adopted Feb. 20, 1967 and effective Jan. 1, 1968. Article 4A, Funds Transfers, adopted Apr. 30, 1991. Article 2A, Leases, adopted June 15, 1992. Article 6, Bulk Sales, adopted Apr. 30, 1992. Article 3 and Revised Article 4, Negotiable Instruments, adopted Apr. 15, 1993. Revised Article 8, Investment Securities, adopted Mar. 26, 1990. Arizona Revised Statutes, Title 47, §§1101 to 11107. Cite as A.R.S. §47-1101, etc.

With exception of Chapters 10 and 11, section numbers of Arizona U.C.C. follow U.C.C. section numbers. Section numbers of Arizona U.C.C. Chapters 10 and 11 and corresponding Official U.C.C. sections (See Uniform and Model Acts section for 1962 Official Text of U.C.C.) follow:

A.R.S	U.C.C.
47-10101	10—102
47-10102	10—104
47-11101	11—102
47-11102	11—103
47-11103	11—104
47-11104	11—105
47-11105	11—106
47-11106	11—107
47-11107	11—108

Material Variations.—Material variations from 1990 Official Text and 1990 Official Amendments (see Uniform and Model Acts section) are:

§2A-219.—New subsection added permitting parties to lease to determine risk of loss by written agreement. (47-2A219[C]).

§4-107.—Contains additional material: Service on bank as garnishee shall be made pursuant to 12-1577. Knowledge of or receipt of notice by one bank branch or separate office is not actual or constructive notice to other branches or offices, and does not impair latter's holder in due course rights. (47-4107).

§4-404.—Omitted.

§6-103[3][1][i].—Increases from ten to fifty thousand dollars value of sale of assets excluded from Article. (47-6103[12][a]).

§8-101.—This chapter may be cited as Uniform Commercial Code—Investment Securities. (47-8101 et seq.).

§8-102.—Definition of "security" is obligation of issuer or share, participation or other interest in issuer or property or enterprise of issuer, except as otherwise provided in §47-8103. (47-8102[A][15]).

§8-108.—Person who transfers certificated security to purchaser for value warrants to purchaser, indorser and to any subsequent purchaser that certificate is genuine and has not been materially altered and that there is no adverse claim to security. (47-8108[A]).

§8-110.—Local law of issuer's jurisdiction, as specified in subsection (D), governs validity of security. (47-8110).

§8-201.—With respect to obligation on or defense to security, "Issuer" includes, generally, person that places or authorizes placing of its name on security certificate, other than as authenticating trustee, registrar or transfer agent, to evidence share. (47-8201[A][1]).

§8-401.—If certificated security in registered form is presented to issuer with request to register, transfer or similar request is made to transfer uncertificated security, issuer shall register transfer as required if seven criteria are met. (47-8401[A]).

§9-105.—Removes "certificated security" from definition of "instrument." (47-9105[A][11]).

§9-105(1).—Omits last clause of first sentence of subparagraph (b). New definition of "legal description" as designation by reference to recorded plat, metes and bounds, course and distance survey, or governmental survey system. (47-9105[A][12]).

§9-206(1).—44-144 remains applicable to buyers or lessees of consumer goods; otherwise, section is same. (47-9206).

§9-208.—New subsection added making special provision for organizations maintaining branches or branch offices. (47-9208[D]).

§9-301(2).—Increases from ten to 20 days time for perfecting purchase money security interest. (47-9301[B]).

§9-302.—Omits reference to trust in subparagraph (1)(c). (47-9302[A]). Removes securities from interests where filing not necessary for perfection. (47-9302[A][6]). New subsections added relating to financing statement for utility security agreements. (47-9302[E] to [F]).

§9-311.—Collateral subject to security interest required to be shown on certificate of title may not be transferred without secured party's written consent. (47-9311).

§9-312.—Subsection changed to remove future advances made under 47-8321 on "securities" as having same priority for purposes of subsection (D). (47-9312[F]).

§9-312(2).—Omitted. (47-9312).

§9-313(4).—Word "equipment" used in place of "factory or office machines" in subparagraph (c). (47-9313[D][3]). New subparagraph (5) added. Gives priority to fixture purchase money security interest in certain multiple section mobile homes. (47-9313[D][5]).

§9-401(5).—Omitted. (47-9401).

§9-402.—Words "a carbon, photographic or other reproduction of a security agreement or a financing statement is sufficient as a financing statement if the security agreement so provides or if the original has been filed in this state" omitted. (47-9402[A]).

§9-402(3).—Revised substantially and reads: "If collateral is goods which are or are to become fixtures, timber to be cut, or minerals or the like (including oil and gas) or accounts to be financed at the wellhead or minehead of the well or mine . . . and this financing statement is to be filed in the office where a mortgage on the real estate would be recorded. (If the debtor does not have an interest of record) the name of a record owner is . . . " (47-9402[C][3]).

§9-402(5).—Words "where the debtor is not a transmitting utility" omitted. Material in brackets omitted. (47-9402[E]).

§9-403(6).—First sentence omitted. (47-9403[F]). New subsection (G) added. Provides for effectiveness of filed financing statement covering multiple section mobile homes. No continuation statement required at any time. (47-9403[G]).

§9-404.—Subsection added to read: "On presentation to the county recorder of such a termination statement, he shall record the termination statement and note it in the index or indices. When so recorded the county recorder shall deliver the termination statement to the debtor." (47-9404[A]).

§9-404(1).—Omits phrase "within one month or" from first sentence. Provides additionally that termination statement must identify financing statement by file number, or, in case of filing with county recorder, by docket and page number. (47-9404[A]). Also contains subsection on organizations maintaining branches or branch offices. (47-9404[B]).

§9-404(3).—Omitted. (47-9404).

§§9-405 and 9-406.—Additional material added dealing with recording of financing statements with county recorder. Provisions on fees omitted. (47-9405 to 9406).

§9-407.—Sentence added at end of paragraph. "If the person filing the statement or notice requests the filing officer to mail the statement or notice, the person shall provide the filing officer with an appropriately sized, addressed and stamped envelope." (47-9407[A]).

§9-504(3).—Provides that secured party proposing to dispose of or retain collateral may sign and file notice of proposed disposition of collateral specifying names and addresses of debtor and secured party and identifying collateral, which notice shall be effective for six months. (47-9409).

Second to last sentence of §9-504(3) revised to read: "In other cases notification shall be sent to any person who (at the time of the filing of a notice of proposed disposition of collateral by the secured party under 47-9409) either was in possession of the collateral or was the person from whom the secured party obtained possession of the collateral or had duly filed a financing statement indexed in the name of the debtor in this state." (47-9504[C]).

§9-505(2).—Fourth sentence revised to read: "In other cases notice shall be sent to any person who (at the time of the filing of a notice of proposed disposition of collateral by the secured party under 47-9409) either had duly filed a financing statement indexed in the name of the debtor in this state or was the person from whom the secured party obtained possession of the collateral." (47-9505[B]).

§11-101.—Omitted.

Optional Provisions.—Options and alternatives have been treated as follows:

§2-318.—Alternative A adopted. (47-2318).

§4-106.—Alternative A adopted. (47-4106[B]).

§5-112.—Optional language not adopted. (47-5112).

§5-114.—Optional subsections 4 and 5 not adopted. (47-5114).

§6-102.—Alternative A adopted. (47-6102[5][C]).

§7-403(1)(b).—Optional language adopted. (47-7403[A][2]).

§9-401(1).—Second alternative subsection adopted. (47-9401).

§9-401(3).—Original subsection 3 adopted. (47-9401).

§9-407.—Section enacted without provision for fees. (47-9407). Also, secured party proposing to dispose of collateral (47-9504) or to retain collateral (47-9505) in satisfaction of obligation may file notice of proposed disposition of collateral. (47-9409).

Permanent Editorial Board's Recommendations for Amendments.—

1966 Official Amendments to 2-702, 3-501 and 7-209 not enacted.

1972 Official Amendments, including Art. XI, adopted except for material variations outlined above.

Forms.—See end of this Digest.

See note at head of Digest as to 1998 legislation covered.

See Topical Index in front part of this volume.

COMMERCIAL CODE... *continued*

See also topics Banks and Banking, Bills and Notes, Brokers, Carriers, Contracts, Factors, Frauds, Statute of, Sales, Securities, Warehousemen; categories Business Organizations, topic Corporations; Civil Actions and Procedure, topic Limitation of Actions; Debtor and Creditor, topics Assignments, Fraudulent Sales and Conveyances, Liens, Pledges; Documents and Records, topics Records, Seals; Mortgages, topic Chattel Mortgages.

CONDITIONAL SALES:

See topic Sales.

CONSIGNMENTS:

See topic Factors.

CONSUMER PROTECTION:

Consumer Fraud.—Use or employment by any person of any deceptive act or practice, fraud, or misrepresentation of any material fact in connection with sale or advertisement of merchandise is unlawful, irrespective of whether anyone has in fact been misled or damaged. (44-1522). Attorney General is empowered to investigate fraud, serve subpoenas and seek injunctions or other remedies. (44-1524 et seq.). Person found to have wilfully violated 44-1522 is subject to $10,000 civil penalty. (44-1531). Person who violates any injunction issued pursuant to 44-1521 et seq. is subject to $25,000 civil penalty. (44-1532). Consumer has private cause of action. (110 Ariz. 573, 521 P.2d 1119).

Motor Vehicles.—Tampering with motor vehicle odometer is fraudulent practice and misdemeanor. (44-1223). Retail installment contracts for sale of motor vehicles regulated by 44-281 et seq. Service companies and contracts regulated by 20-1095 et seq. Motor vehicle warranty repairs and refunds regulated by 44-1261 et seq. See category Transportation, topic Motor Vehicles, subhead Motor Vehicle Warranties.

Fictitious Names.—Any person other than partnership conducting business under fictitious name must record actual name with county recorder. (44-1236). See also category Business Organizations, topic Partnerships.

Labeling of Drugs.—All drugs, devices, poisons and hazardous substances must be labeled and provided in accordance with applicable federal acts and regulations. Labels of prescription-only drugs in final dosage form must identify manufacturer (and, if different, packer or distributor), and quantity information. (32-1967[16]). Legend drug product in finished solid oral dosage form must be clearly marked with code imprint identifying product and manufacturer. (32-1975).

Consumer Reporting Agencies.—Permissible uses of consumer reports are limited; consumer is guaranteed access to reporting agency file; agency has 30 days to admit or deny mistake once written notice of inaccuracy is received; liability of agency to consumer is limited to refusal to correct inaccuracy, gross negligence and willful and malicious conduct. (44-1691 et seq.). See topic Sales.

Home Solicitation and Referral Sales Act adopted. (44-5001 et seq.).

Precious Items.—Dealers of precious items must keep records of sale for six months. (44-1601 et seq.).

Equipment dealers and suppliers regulated by 44-6701 et seq.

Pawnbrokers regulated by 44-1621 et seq.

Health spa contracts regulated by 44-1791 et seq.

Public power entities shall address: deceptive abuses of business practices including deposit requirements, reconnection fees, and ontime advertising practices.

Discount buying services regulated by 44-1797 et seq.

Bulk Food Sales.—Detailed regulation provided for sales of bulk food. (36-971 et seq.).

Charitable solicitation governed by 44-6551 et seq.

Telephone solicitation governed by 44-1271 et seq.; requires registration of sales information with Secretary of State.

Securities Fraud.—See topic Securities.

Pyramid Promotional Schemes.—Person may not establish, operate, advertise or promote pyramid promotional scheme. (44-1735). Purchaser may declare such sale or contract void and bring action to recover consideration paid to participate in scheme plus costs and attorneys' fees. (44-1733).

Sales Representative Contracts regulated. (44-1798 et seq.).

Unsolicited Merchandise.—No duty to return to sender. If addressed to recipient, deemed gift and may be used without obligation, except for goods received by mistake. (44-1222).

Uniform Fraudulent Transfer Act adopted. (44-1001 et seq.).

Uniform Deceptive Trade Practices Act not adopted.

Uniform State Antitrust Act adopted. (44-1401 et seq.).

Plain language statutes not enacted.

CONTRACTS:

Uniform Commercial Code adopted. (47-1101 et seq.). See topic Commercial Code. See also categories Documents and Records, topic Seals; Family, topic Infants.

Third Party Beneficiaries.—Contract must reveal parties' intention to benefit third party directly.

Attorneys' Fees.—In any contested action arising out of contract, court (not jury) may award reasonable attorneys' fees to successful party. Fees awarded are intended to mitigate burden of litigation and need not equal or relate to fees actually contracted or paid, but may not exceed amount paid or agreed to be paid. (12-341.01).

Indemnification.—Indemnity agreements in construction contracts and architect-engineer professional service contracts void. (32-1159).

FACTORS:

Except as stated below, there are no statutory regulations as to factors or commission merchants.

Uniform Commercial Code adopted with certain material variations. (47-1101 et seq.). See topic Commercial Code.

Fraud.—Factor who knowingly and with intent to defraud makes to his principal or consignor false statement concerning price obtained for, or quantity or quality of, any property consigned or entrusted to him, is guilty of Class 2 Misdemeanor. (44-1212).

Theft.—Person who knowingly converts for unauthorized term or use services or property entrusted to him or placed in his possession for limited authorized term or use commits theft. (13-1802[A][2]).

Farm and Citrus Products.—Commission merchants dealing in citrus products must be licensed by state, give bond in amount of $10,000 and keep records of receipt, packing, loading, shipments and sales. (3-448 to 449). Hay brokers must be licensed and give bond in amount not less than $10,000 nor more than $100,000. (3-2712, 2714).

Consignment Agreements.—Sales of fine art by dealers regulated. (44-1771 et seq.).

FRANCHISES:

No general regulatory legislation.

Grant of franchise by municipal corporation governed by 9-501 et seq. Corporation cannot lease or alienate any franchise to relieve franchise from liabilities incurred during operation or use of franchise. (Const., Art. XIV, §7).

FRAUDS, STATUTE OF:

Actions Barred.—No action may be brought in any of following cases, unless promise or agreement or some memorandum thereof is in writing and signed by party to be charged or by some person by him duly authorized (44-101):

Charging an Executor or Administrator.—On any promise to answer for debt or damages due from his testator or intestate out of his own estate.

Assuming Another's Debt, Etc.—On a promise to answer for the debt, default or miscarriage of another.

Marriage as Consideration.—On an agreement made on consideration of marriage, except a mutual promise to marry.

Delayed Performance.—On an agreement not to be performed within one year from the making thereof, or an agreement not to be performed in lifetime of promisor, or agreement to make any provision for any person by will.

Agency.—On an agreement authorizing or employing an agent or broker to purchase or sell real property or mines for a compensation or commission.

Sales of Personalty.—On contract to sell for sale of goods or choses in action of $500 value or more, unless buyer accepts part of goods or choses in action and receives same, or gives something in earnest to bind bargain or in part payment; but, when sale is at auction, entry by auctioneer in his sale book of kind of property sold, terms of sale, price and names of parties, is sufficient.

Sales of Realty.—On agreement or sale of real property or interest therein. Authority of any agent to make such contract must be in writing.

Leases.—On agreement for leasing of real property for period of longer than one year.

Loans or Credit.—On agreement to loan money or extend credit, or modify loan or extension of credit, involving amount exceeding $250,000 and not made primarily for personal purposes.

Uniform Commercial Code adopted with certain material variations. (47-1101 et seq.). Following situations are covered by Code:

Sale of Goods.—Sale of goods $500 or more. See U.C.C. provisions. (47-2201).

Lease Contract.—See U.C.C. provisions. (47-2A201).

Guaranty on Commercial Paper.—See U.C.C. provisions. (47-3416).

Sale of Securities.—See U.C.C. provisions. (47-8319).

Sales of Personal Property Not Otherwise Covered.—See U.C.C. provisions. (47-1206).

INTEREST:

Legal rate is 10% per annum unless different rate is contracted for in writing in which case any rate may be agreed to. Interest on judgment in condemnation proceeding shall be payable at rate prescribed by 28-7101. Judgment on agreement bearing higher rate not in excess of maximum permitted by law shall bear rate provided in agreement. (44-1201).

Judgments.—See introductory paragraph, supra.

Small Loans.—On loans not exceeding $1,000, licensed money lenders may charge rate not exceeding 3% per month. On loans exceeding $1,000, licensed money lenders may charge rate not exceeding 3% per month of unpaid principal balance not exceeding $500, and 2% per month of unpaid principal balance exceeding $500 and not exceeding $10,000. Prepaid finance charges (points) prohibited on loans not exceeding $10,000. (6-652). Disclosure of charges required by 6-651.

Installment Loans.—Generally, see 44-1205.

Usury.—Any person receiving greater value for loan or forbearance of money or goods than maximum permitted by law shall forfeit all interest. (44-1202). Where rate of interest is greater than maximum permitted by law, all payments shall be deemed made on account of principal. (44-1203). If such payments exceed principal, judgment may be given in favor of debtor with interest thereon at rate of 10% per annum. (44-1204). Lender may add to principal and charge interest on any lawful charge, fee, cost or expense paid by or due to lender on behalf of borrower with consent. (44-1207).

LICENSES, BUSINESS AND PROFESSIONAL:

Automobile and Driver's License.—See category Transportation, topic Motor Vehicles.

Liquor Licenses.—License required for manufacture, sale, or dealing in spirituous liquors by individual, corporation, partnership, club, restaurant, or motel-hotel. (4-101 et seq.). Domestic farm winery or microbrewery license required. (4-205.04). Person who assigns, transfers or sells business which has liquor license must notify superintendent. (4-203). Special event licenses and interim or temporary permits may be issued. (4-203.01 et seq., 3-1013). Applicant bears burden of proving license should be issued. (4-201). Board may apply to superior court to enjoin selling of liquor without license. (4-212). Retailers required to post conspicuously warning of effects of liquor on pregnant women. (4-261).

Music Licenses.—Practices relating to licensing of music are governed by 44-6901 et seq.

Professions and Occupations.—Licenses required for acupuncturists (32-3921), adult care home managers (36-448 et seq.), agricultural pest control advisors (3-361 et seq.), adjusters (20-281 et seq.), ambulance services (36-2201 et seq.), architects (32-101 et seq.), assayers (32-101 et seq.), attorneys-at-law (Sup. Ct. R. 31-73), bail bond agents (20-282.01 et seq.), barbers (32-301 et seq.), bingo (5-401 et seq.), cemetery brokers and salespersons (32-2101 et seq., 2194 et seq.), certified public accountants (32-701 et seq.), chauffeurs (28-401 et seq.), children's camp operators (8-551 et seq.), child welfare agencies (8-505, 36-591), chiropractors (32-901 et seq.), cigarette, cigar, tobacco and controlled substance distributors and sellers (42-1203), citrus fruit dealers, brokers, packers, shippers, commission merchants (3-441 et seq.), clinical laboratories (36-451 et seq.), collection agencies (32-1001 et seq.), contractors (32-1101 et seq.), cosmetologists, aestheticians and nail technicians (32-501 et seq.), counselors (32-3301), credit unions (6-501 et seq.), cremationists and crematory operators (32-1393), dairy product processors and distributors (3-601 et seq.), day care centers (36-881 et seq.), debt management companies (6-701 et seq.), dentists, denturists and dental hygienists (32-1201 et seq.), dispensing opticians (32-1671 et seq.), driver training schools and instructors (32-2351 et seq.), emergency medical services (36-2201 et seq.), employment agencies (23-521 et seq.), engineers (32-101 et seq.), escrow agents (6-801 et seq.), foster homes (8-501 et seq.), funeral directors and embalmers (32-1321 et seq.), geologists (32-101 et seq.), hearing aid dispensers (36-1901 et seq.), homeopathic physicians (32-2901 et seq.), horse and dog racing (5-101 et seq.), hospitals and health care centers (36-401 et seq.), insurance agents, brokers and solicitors (20-281 et seq.), jewelry auctioneers (44-1671 et seq.), livestock officers, owner and sellers (3-1201 et seq.), manufacturers, salespeople, installers and subassemblers of factory built homes, mobile homes and recreational vehicles (41-2175 et seq.), emergency medical services (36-2201 et seq.), medical physicians (32-1422) and physician assistants (32-2501 et seq.), mammographic technologists (32-2841 et seq.), midwives (36-751 et seq.), mortgage bankers (6-811 et seq., 971 et seq.), mortgage brokers (6-901 et seq.), naturopaths (32-1501 et seq.), nurses (32-1601 et seq.), nursing care institution administrators (36-446), occupational therapists (32-3401 et seq.), optometrists (32-1701 et seq.), osteopaths (32-1801 et seq.), pawnbrokers (44-1621 et seq.), pesticide users and sellers (3-363), pharmacists (32-1901 et seq.), physical therapists (32-2001 et seq.), podiatrists (32-801 et seq.), private investigators (32-2401 et seq.), private vocational programs (32-3021 et seq.), psychologists (32-2061 et seq.), public weighmasters and commercial measuring device servicemen (41-2091 et seq.), radiologic technologists (32-2801 et seq.), real estate appraisers (32-3601 et seq.), real estate brokers and salespersons (including corporations) (32-2101 et seq.), real estate certificate schools (32-2135), recovery care centers (36-448.51 et seq.), practice of respiratory care (32-3501 et seq.), schoolteachers (15-531 et seq.), security guards and guard agencies (32-2601 et seq.), sellers of meat (3-2081), slaughterers of animals (3-2001 et seq.), solar contractors (32-1170 et seq.), structural pest control companies (32-2301 et seq.), surveyors (32-101 et seq.), taxidermists (17-363), technical and business school operators and grantors of degrees (32-3021 et seq.), timeshare or membership camping brokers and salespersons (32-2101 et seq.), title insurance agents (20-1579 et seq.), title insurers (20-1561 et seq.), transmitters of money (6-1201 et seq.), and veterinarians (32-2201 et seq.).

Standards of Competency.—Industrial Commission may establish standards for individuals involved in inspecting, constructing, relocating, altering, dismantling, maintaining or repairing elevators, dumbwaiters, escalators, moving walks, boilers and pressure vessels. (23-431).

Collection Agencies.—Persons conducting collection agency must apply to state banking superintendent for license and pay required fees. (32-1021, 1028). Financial statement and bond to be computed on basis of gross annual income of licensee must accompany application for each proposed office in state. (32-1021 to 1022). License must be renewed annually not later than Jan. 1 of each year. (32-1025). Licensed collection agent from another state may be licensed if specified conditions met. (32-1024). Failure to obtain license is Class 1 Misdemeanor (32-1056), and license subject to suspension or revocation for violation of law (32-1055) or state banking superintendent regulations (32-1053).

Debt Management Companies.—Persons engaged in receiving money as agent of debtor for distribution to debtor's creditors must apply to state banking superintendent for license and pay required fees unless specifically exempted from licensing requirement. (6-702 to 703, 706, 715). Initial application must be accompanied by not less than $5,000 cash, property or surety bond, and blank copy of contract to be used between licensee and debtor. (6-704). Branch agencies may be licensed upon separate application to state banking superintendent. (6-705). All licenses must be renewed annually on or before June 15. (6-707). Licenses are subject to statutory requirements and prohibitions. (6-709 to 710, 715).

Contractors.—Primarily governed by 32-1101 et seq.

License required for all contractors, subject to limited exemptions. (32-1101, 1121, 1151). Enumerated qualifications must be fulfilled for issuance of license. (32-1122). Acceptable surety bond is required for benefit of persons damaged by contractor. (32-1152). Alternatives to surety bond are cash deposit, bank certificate of deposit, or savings and loan investment certificates or share accounts. (32-1152.01). Residential contractors also are required to either contribute to Residential Contractors' Recovery Fund or furnish additional surety bond or cash deposit. (32-1152). Proof of license is prerequisite for contractor to maintain civil suit for collection of compensation. (32-1153). License may be suspended or revoked for commission of enumerated acts or omissions (32-1154) and fine imposed (32-1164). Provision for filing complaint seeking suspension or revocation (32-1155) and hearing (32-1156). Renewal after suspension possible. (32-1161). Licensed contractor also must be licensed solar contractor to install or repair solar devices. (32-1170.01).

Registrar of contractors has both rulemaking powers (32-1104 to 1105) and enforcement powers (32-1106).

Work on public buildings and structures requires notice to contractors of intention to receive bids and enter contract. (34-201). Prior to contract, successful bidder required to post bonds. (34-222). Provision is made for preference among contractors, subcontractors, and materials. (34-241 et seq.).

Construction of factory built buildings, manufactured homes, mobile homes, recreational vehicles and accessory structures regulated by Office of Manufactured Housing. (41-2151 et seq.).

Residential Contractors' Recovery Fund.—Person receiving judgment against licensed residential contractor for injury caused by contractor's act, representation, transaction, or conduct in violation of statute or regulation may recover up to $20,000 from Contractors' Recovery Fund. (32-1131 et seq.). Recovery limited to actual damages. Attorneys' fees and costs will not be awarded except in cases appealed to superior court. (32-1132). Two year statute of limitations. (32-1136). Fund liability limit of $100,000 for acts of any one contractor. Contractor's license suspended if fund pays any amount. No renewal without repayment to fund by contractor, with interest. (32-1139).

MONOPOLIES, RESTRAINT OF TRADE AND COMPETITION:

Uniform State Antitrust Act adopted. (44-1401 et seq.).

Antitrust Generally.—Contracts, combinations and agreements to fix prices, limit production or regulate transportation of any product are forbidden. (Const., Art. XIV, §15). Contracts, combinations or conspiracies in restraint of or to monopolize trade are unlawful. (44-1402).

Establishment, maintenance or use of monopoly or attempt to establish monopoly for purposes of excluding competition or controlling, fixing or maintaining prices is unlawful. (44-1403).

State or county may bring action for injunction and civil penalties, including taxable cost, reasonable attorneys' fees and other reasonable fees and expenses, for violation. Civil penalty assessed not to exceed $150,000 for each violation. (44-1407). State or subdivision may bring action for injunction and damages, costs and attorneys' fees; persons threatened with injury or injured may bring action for injunction and damages, costs and attorneys' fees, damages to be increased as much as three times if violation flagrant. (44-1408).

Civil action barred after four years or after one year after conclusion of action by state. (44-1410).

Courts may use constructions of federal antitrust statutes as guide to interpreting state antitrust statute. (44-1412).

Unfair Competition in Public Contracts.—Contract, conspiracy or act prohibited by Uniform State Antitrust Act (44-1401-13) regarding contract between governmental agency and person or between subcontractor and contractor for governmental agency for purchase of equipment or construction or repair of highways, buildings, or structures which is in restraint of trade is Class 4 Felony. (34-252). Contract, conspiracy or act prohibited by Uniform State Antitrust Act (44-1402) per se unlawful and Class 4 Felony if it involves contract or subcontract with governmental agency for purchase of equipment, services, labor, goods, materials and commodities of any kind. (44-1416). Governmental agency entering into contract that is subject of contract, conspiracy or act prohibited by Uniform State Antitrust Act (44-1401-13) may recover actual damages trebled or 10% of contract price trebled and taxable costs, attorneys' fees and expenses. (34-254). Person convicted of violating 34-252 is not eligible, directly or indirectly, to contract with governmental agency for period up to three years from date of conviction. (34-255). Person convicted of entering into contract or conspiracy in restraint of trade may be suspended from bidding with governmental agency for up to three years. (34-257). Provisions of this article may be enforced by state or by counties. (34-258).

Fair Trade Act repealed.

NEGOTIABLE INSTRUMENTS:

See topic Bills and Notes.

RESTRAINT OF TRADE:

See topic Monopolies, Restraint of Trade and Competition; category Intellectual Property, topic Trademarks and Tradenames.

SALES:

Uniform Commercial Code adopted. (47-1101 et seq.). See topic Commercial Code.

Definitions, Etc.—See U.C.C. §2-103 et seq. (47-2103 et seq.).

Bills of Sale.—Power of real estate broker or salesperson to draft. (Const., Art. XXVI, §1).

Contracts of Sale.—See U.C.C. §2-201 et seq. (47-2201 et seq.).

Obligations and Warranties.—See U.C.C. §2-301 et seq. (47-2301 et seq.).

Product Liability.—See U.C.C. §§2-313 to 317. (47-2313 to 2317). Privity not required of family household or guest in home. See U.C.C. §2-318. (47-2318).

Title.—See U.C.C. §2-401 et seq. (47-2401 et seq.).

Performance.—See U.C.C. §2-501 et seq. (47-2501 et seq.).

Breach, Repudiation and Excuse.—See U.C.C. §2-601 et seq. (47-2601 et seq.).

Remedies.—See U.C.C. §2-701 et seq. (47-2701 et seq.).

SALES . . . *continued*

Rental-Purchase Agreements.—Special provisions regarding rental-purchase agreements. (44-6801 et seq.).

Leases.—See U.C.C. §2A-101 et seq. (47-2A101 et seq.).

Bulk Sales.—See U.C.C. §6-101 et seq. (47-6101 et seq.).

Retail Credit Sales.—Special provisions governing retail installment sales practices. Maximum legal finance charge established by contract. If no interest rate specified, legal rate is 10% (A.P.R.). (44-1201). Person contracting for, receiving or reserving any greater value than legal rate forfeits all interest. (44-1202, 6001 et seq.).

Consumer Protection.—Consumer Fraud Act is 44-1521 et seq.; Consumer Reporting Agencies Act is 44-1691 et seq. See topic Consumer Protection.

Motor Vehicle Time Sales Disclosure Act adopted. (44-281 et seq.).

Fair Trade Act repealed.

Unfair Trade Act repealed.

SECURITIES:

Uniform Commercial Code adopted. See topic Commercial Code.
Blue Sky Law known as "Securities Act of Arizona" in effect. (44-1801 et seq.).

Supervision.—Administration of Securities Act is vested in Director of Securities appointed by Corporation Commission. (44-1811).

Regulatory Powers of Supervising Authority.—Broad regulatory powers are provided over dealers, salesmen and applicants, as well as over registration. (44-1801 et seq.). Registration fees. (44-1861). When securities registered by description are recorded in register of securities by Director of Securities, they may be sold by registered dealers or registered salesmen of registered dealers. (44-1873). Issuer of securities registered by qualification will be notified by mail that securities may be sold. (44-1898).

Commission, Director of Securities or designated agent may make any investigation necessary to determine whether rules have been or will be violated (44-1822) and may require testimony and production of records (44-1823).

Prerequisites to Sales or Offerings.—No securities, except exempt securities, those sold in exempt transactions or those registered by description or qualification or those sold by open-end companies after filing required notices with Corporation Commission, may be sold or offered for sale. (44-1841). Violation is Class 4 Felony. (44-1841).

Securities to Which Act Applicable.—Security is any note, stock, treasury stock, bond, commodity investment contract, commodity option, debenture, evidence of indebtedness, certificate of interest or participation in any profit-sharing agreement, collateral-trust certificate, preorganization certificate or subscription, transferable share, investment contract, voting-trust certificate, certificate of deposit for security, fractional undivided interest in oil, gas or other mineral rights, real property investment contract, or, in general, any interest or instrument commonly known as "security" or any certificate of interest or participation in, temporary or interim certificate for, receipt for, guarantee of, or warrant or right to subscribe to or purchase, any of foregoing. (44-1801).

Exempt Securities.—(1) Securities issued or guaranteed by U.S., any state, territory, or insular possession or by their political subdivisions, by District of Columbia or any agency or instrumentality of foregoing; (2) securities issued by banks, credit or savings and loan associations, insurance companies, railroads and public utilities which are subject to supervision by U.S., or state or territory; (3) securities of bona fide nonprofit corporations; (4) securities listed on New York Stock Exchange, American Stock Exchange, Mid-West Stock Exchange or any other national securities exchange designated by Commission and securities designated on national market system of national securities association requested under Exchange Act; (5) commercial paper which arises out of current transactions or proceeds of which are to be used for current transactions evidencing obligation to pay cash within nine months of date of issuance or sale; (6) securities issued or guaranteed by any foreign government with which U.S. maintains diplomatic relations, if registered under federal securities act; (7) notes or bonds secured by mortgage, deed of trust on, or contract or agreement for sale of, real estate or chattels, if sold or offered for sale as unit, except for real property investment contracts; and (8) mortgage related securities as defined by §3(a)(41) of Exchange Act. (44-1843). Certain industrial development bonds, bond anticipation notes, out-of-state bonds secured by special assessment, improvement district bonds, and public subdivision securities not exempted unless certain conditions met. (44-1843.01).

Exempt Transactions.—(1) Transactions by issuer not involving any public offering; (2) sale by executor, administrator, guardian or conservator, bank as trustee, receiver or trustee in insolvency or bankruptcy, or pledgee; (3) sales by owner other than issuer or underwriter in isolated transaction and not made in repeated or successive transactions of similar character and not made for direct or indirect benefit of issuer or underwriter; (4) stock dividends or distributions out of retained earnings by corporation to stock or other security holders; (5) transactions pursuant to statutory or judicially approved reorganization, merger, triangular merger, consolidation or sale of assets incident to vote by security holders; (6) exchange by issuer with existing security holders; (7) sale to bank, savings institution, insurance company, dealer, or agency of U.S. or of state or to person principal part of whose business consists of buying securities; (8) conversion of securities; (9) issuance to original incorporators, not exceeding ten, where not resold to third parties within 24 months unless incorporator experiences bona fide change in financial circumstances; (10) certain sales by dealers; (11) sale of commodity investment contracts traded on commodities exchange recognized by Commission; (12) sale or issuance of securities in connection with employee benefit plans which qualify under Internal Revenue Code; (13) transactions within exclusive jurisdiction of Commodity Futures Trading Commission granted by Commodity Exchange Act; (14) certain transactions involving purchase of precious metals; (15) commodity investment contract transactions between producers, processors, commercial users, or merchants of such

commodity or any by-product; (16) certain nonissuer transactions in outstanding securities; (17) certain sales of securities to nonresidents not present in state which are not blind pool offerings; and (18) transactions involving offers or sales of promissory notes secured by first lien on single parcel of real estate with structure and participation interest exempt under §4 of Exchange Act. (44-1844).

Arizona Corporation Commission.—Has authority to promulgate general orders exempting securities and transactions other than those enumerated above. (44-1845 et seq.). Has authority to investigate, license, and regulate investment companies and investment advisors. (44-3131 et seq.). Securities Regulation and Enforcement Fund and Investment Management Regulatory and Enforcement Fund administered by Commission. (44-2039, 3298). To enlarge capital markets available to Arizona, Commission is empowered to negotiate formal or informal agreements with other states to lessen burden of registering public securities offerings in multiple states, Mexico and Canada. (44-2056).

Registration of Offerors or Issuers.—Must be made by verified application to Commission. (44-1941 et seq.).

Registration of Securities.—Must be registered with Commission, either by description or by qualification. Registration by description requires verified registration statement showing name and address of person filing statement and of issuer; title and amount of securities; price per unit and in aggregate, amount of underwriting discounts or commissions or other selling expenses and net amount to be received by issuer; amount of securities to be offered in state, offering price and amount of registration fee; copy of prospectus filed with S.E.C. (if registered under federal Act); statement of facts and financial statements; and consent to service if nonresident or if not registered dealer. (44-1872). Commission may register certain securities by uniform limited offering registration. (44-1902).

Registration by qualification requires application to Commission stating name and address of issuer; title, amount, unit and aggregate price of securities to be offered; date registered under federal act (if so registered); eligibility in other states; charter and bylaws of issuer; any underwriting agreement; specimens of securities; opinion of counsel as to validity of issuance; statement of corporate structure; amount of securities outstanding; financial statements (44-1893); copy of prospectus on file with S.E.C. (44-1901). Offering must be made through firm commitment underwriting by members of registered national securities association, registered in state, not affiliated with issuer. If right to purchase shares, offering price and exercise price must be at least $5. Total amount sold must exceed $3,000,000. Certain undertakings must be avoided for four years after registration. Audit report must not express reservations about viability as going concern or show negative shareholder equity or working capital. For limited partnership interests, investment must not exceed 10% of purchaser's net worth; purchaser must meet income, net worth requirements; and general partners' net worth must exceed $1,000,000. (44-1901). Generally, registration effective 20 business days after filing and date registration is effective under Securities Act. (44-1901).

Registration of Dealers.—It is felony for any dealer to sell or offer for sale or, under certain circumstances, to purchase securities without being registered with Commission. (44-1842). This provision also applies to salesmen and investment advisors. (44-1842, 3241). For registration fees, see 44-1861, 3181 and 3324. For denial, revocation or suspension of dealer's registration, see 44-1961; for salesmen, see 44-1962; for investment advisors, see 44-3201 to 3231.

Except where specifically exempted, all investment companies and their representatives must be licensed by Commission. (44-3151 to 3152). They must comply with all Commission regulations and reporting and auditing requirements in order to do business in state. (44-3101 et seq.).

Advertisements.—Advertising of registered securities is governed and methods and practices in connection therewith are prescribed by Commission. (Regulation R14-4-103).

Litigation.—State securities law conforms to federal Private Securities Act of 1995. (44-1991 et seq.).

Liabilities.—Sale of unregistered security is felony. (44-1841). Sale of registered security by unregistered dealer or salesman is felony. (44-1842). Engaging in fraudulent practices as defined by 44-1991 et seq. is felony. (44-1995). Violation of rule, regulation or order of Commission for which penalty not provided is misdemeanor. (44-2040). Violators of Securities Act or any rule, regulation or order of Commission may be ordered to stop violation and make restitution. (44-2032). Penalty of up to $5,000 for each violation of Securities Act or any rule or order of Commission. (44-2036 et seq.). Penalty of up to $20,000 for each violation of court order or injunction. (44-2037). Sales of unregistered securities are voidable at option of purchaser. (44-2001).

Subdivision Offerings.—See subhead Registration of Dealers, supra.

Uniform Simplification of Fiduciary Security Transfers Act repealed July 13, 1995.

Uniform Gifts to Minors Act repealed.

Uniform Securities Ownership by Minors Act not adopted.

Pyramid Sales.—See topic Consumer Protection.

STATUTE OF FRAUDS:

See topic Frauds, Statute of.

TRUST RECEIPT SECURITY:

See category Debtor and Creditor, topic Pledges.

WAREHOUSEMEN:

Uniform Commercial Code adopted. (47-1101 et seq.). See topic Commercial Code.

See note at head of Digest as to 1998 legislation covered.

See Topical Index in front part of this volume.

CITIZENSHIP

ALIENS:

Constitutional restriction against employment on public works (Const., Art. XVIII, §10) declared null and void (351 F.Supp. 735).

Corporations and associations not qualified to transact business in Arizona may not buy, lease or sublease state lands. (37-240).

Practice of immigration and nationality law by nonlawyers is prohibited. (12-2701 et seq.).

CIVIL ACTIONS AND PROCEDURE

ACCORD AND SATISFACTION:

In absence of statute, common law rules control accord and satisfaction as well as compromise and settlement. Answer must plead these defenses affirmatively. (Civ. 8[c]). See category Business Regulation and Commerce, topic Commercial Code.

ACTIONS:

Arizona Rules of Civil Procedure are based on Federal Rules of Civil Procedure. (Civ. 1-86).

Equity.—Distinction between law and equity abolished. (Civ. 1).

Forms of Action.—Form known as "civil action" is used. (Civ. 2).

Commencement.—Civil action is commenced by filing complaint with court. (Civ. 3). See topics Process, Pleading; category Transportation, topic Motor Vehicles, subhead Action against Nonresident.

Parties.—Every action must be prosecuted in name of real party in interest, except that executor, administrator, guardian, bailee, trustee of express trust, party with whom or in whose name contract has been made for benefit of another or party authorized by statute may sue without joining with him person for whose benefit action is brought; and when statute so provides, action for use or benefit of another must be brought in name of state. (Civ. 17[a]).

Executor, administrator or guardian appointed in Arizona may commence action in same manner as testator or intestate. Judgment is conclusive except for fraud or collusion. (Civ. 17[a]).

Third-party defendants may be brought in within ten days from date of filing answer without leave of court or subsequently by court order. (Civ. 14[a]).

All parties jointly interested must be joined as plaintiffs or defendants, but, if consent of one who should have been joined as plaintiff cannot be obtained, he may be made defendant or in proper cases involuntary plaintiff. Court must order such additional parties brought in when complete determination of controversy cannot otherwise be had. (Civ. 19[a]).

Unknown heirs may be made defendants in action involving title to realty. (Civ. 4.1[o]). See topic Process.

Class Actions.—Representative(s) of class may sue or be sued on behalf of class only if class is so numerous that joinder is impracticable, common questions of law or fact exist, claims or defenses of representative(s) are typical of those of class, representative(s) will fairly and adequately protect interests of class and at least one of additional prerequisites enumerated by Civ. 23(b) is met. (Civ. 23[a]). Class action cannot be compromised or dismissed without court approval. (Civ. 23[e]). For shareholder derivative actions, see Civ. 23.1.

Intervention.—Any person having statutory right or interest liable to be adversely affected must, on motion, be permitted to intervene. Any person whose claim or defense has question of law or fact in common with main action may, on motion, be permitted to intervene. (Civ. 24).

Interpleader.—Persons having claims against plaintiff may be joined as defendants and required to interplead when their claims may expose plaintiff to double or multiple liability. Such joinder may be invoked though claims do not have common origin or are not identical, and though it is alleged that interpleaded party is not liable in whole or in part to any or all of claimants. (Civ. 22[a]).

Joinder.—Party may join as many claims, legal or equitable, as he has against opposing party, as either independent or alternate claims. (Civ. 18[a]).

Splitting Causes of Action.—See subhead Severance of Actions, infra.

Consolidation of Actions.—Court may consolidate pending actions involving common question of law or fact or may order joint hearing or trial of any issue. (Civ. 42[a]).

Severance of Actions.—To further avoidance of prejudice, convenience, expedition and economy, court may order separate trial of any claim, crossclaim, counterclaim, third-party claim or separate issue, or of any number thereof, preserving right of jury trial. (Civ. 42[b]).

Stay of Proceedings.—If party or officer, director or managing agent of party designated to testify on behalf of such party fails to obey court order to permit discovery, to appear before officer who is to take his deposition, to serve answers or objections to interrogatories, or to serve written response to request for inspection, court may stay proceedings. (Civ. 37).

Court may stay proceedings in action until plaintiff pays costs, if any, arising from previously dismissed action. (Civ. 41[d]). No postponement of trial except for sufficient cause, supported by affidavit, or by consent of parties, or by operation of law. (Civ. 42[c]).

Writs of injunction granted to stay proceedings are returnable only to court where action is pending. (Civ. 65[i]).

Abatement.—Action does not abate by death of party if cause of action survives. Motion for substitution must be made not later than 90 days after death is suggested on record. (Civ. 25[a]). Action for personal injury or death does not abate on death of defendant. (Civ. 25[a]-[b]).

Survival of Causes of Action.—Every cause of action, except for damages for breach of promise to marry, seduction, libel, slander, separate maintenance, alimony, loss of consortium or invasion of privacy, survives death of person entitled thereto or liable therefor, and may be asserted by or against personal representative of such person, except that, on death of person injured, damages for pain and suffering of such injured person are no longer allowed. (14-3110).

Limitations.—See topic Limitation of Actions.

Small Claims.—See category Courts and Legislature, topic Courts.

Termination of Actions.—Default or final judgment terminates action. (Civ. 54 et seq.).

Direct Actions Against Insurer.—See category Transportation, topic Motor Vehicles, subhead Direct Actions.

APPEAL AND ERROR:

Arizona Rules of Civil Appellate Procedure effective for appeals filed after Jan. 1, 1978. (App. 1-31). Arizona Rules of Civil Procedure are based on Federal Rules of Civil Procedure. (Civ. 1-86). See topic Practice.

To Superior Court.—Appeal may be taken from judgment of justice of the peace to superior court of same county where amount involved exceeds $20, exclusive of costs, or where validity of toll, tax assessment or state statute is involved. (22-261).

Notice of appeal and cost bond must be filed with trial court within five days of judgment. (12-1179).

Hearing on appeal to superior court is trial de novo. (Super. Ct. R. Civ. App. 11[2]).

To Court of Appeals.—Court of appeals has appellate jurisdiction in all actions and proceedings originating in or permitted by law to be appealed from superior court except criminal actions involving crimes for which sentence of death has been imposed. (12-120.21). Judgments and orders which may be appealed are specified in 12-2101.

Notice of Appeal and Bond.—Appeal from superior court is taken by notice filed with superior court within 30 days from entry of judgment or order appealed from unless different time is provided by law, and by filing within such time bond for costs on appeal. Bond is $500 unless court fixes different amount or unless appellant deems supersedeas bond necessary to prevent execution on his property, in which case bond must be conditioned for satisfaction of judgment together with costs, interest and damages for delay. (12-120.22; Super. Ct. R. Civ. App. P. 7-10).

To Supreme Court.—Appeal may be taken only to supreme court in any criminal matter where sentence of death has actually been imposed. (13-4031). In addition, supreme court may review decision rendered by court of appeals if such further review is requested after adverse decision or following denial of motion for rehearing by court of appeals. (12-120.24).

BONDS:

Bond required by law for faithful performance of duty or obligation, or in judicial proceeding must be executed by: (1) Authorized corporate surety; or (2) principal and two sureties, provided each surety is resident and freeholder or householder of Arizona and of county in which bond was given and each surety justifies by affidavit that his worth equals amount of bond over and above all just debts and liabilities, exclusive of property exempt from execution. (7-101, 103). Party may deposit money in lieu of bond. (7-106).

In state court action, adverse party may object to sufficiency of bond within three days after receiving notice that bond was given. (7-107). In proceeding for injunction, attachment or garnishment, defendant may object to irresponsible surety. (7-121).

CERTIORARI:

Relief previously obtained by writ of certiorari (12-2001 et seq.) must now be obtained by special action order. See topic Practice, subhead Special Actions.

CHARITABLE IMMUNITY:

See topic Damages, subhead Charitable Immunity.

COMMISSIONS TO TAKE TESTIMONY:

See topic Depositions and Discovery.

COSTS:

Successful party to civil action may recover all costs from adverse party unless otherwise provided by law. (12-341). Costs defined in 12-331 et seq. Although state, county and political subdivisions usually exempt from court costs (12-345), in certain circumstances, expenses may be recovered against state or city, town or county (12-348). Provision is made for filing of statement of costs and objections thereto. (12-346). In contested action arising out of express or implied contract, court may award successful party reasonable attorneys' fees. (12-341.01). Attorneys' and reasonable experts' fees may be awarded prevailing party (other than state) in civil actions brought by state against party. (12-348). Reasonable attorneys' fees may be assessed in civil actions against party bringing unjustified claims, suing to harass, unreasonably delaying proceedings, or abusing discovery. (12-349). Reasonable costs incurred in civil action by nonparty witness complying with subpoena are assessed against requesting party. (12-351).

Security for Costs.—Nonresident or resident plaintiff without property in state out of which costs can be obtained by execution is required to give security for costs if defendant brings motion supported by affidavit. Suit will be dismissed without notice if fixed security is not given. (Civ. 67[d]). If plaintiff within five days of order requiring security makes strict proof of inability to give security, order for security shall be vacated. (Civ. 67[e]). Intervenor or counterclaiming defendant is required to give such security as is required of plaintiff. (Civ. 67[f][3]). State, county, and executors, administrators and guardians appointed under laws of state are exempt from giving security for costs. (Civ. 67[f][1]).

See note at head of Digest as to 1998 legislation covered.

See Topical Index in front part of this volume.

COSTS . . . *continued*

Liability of Attorney.—No provisions for assessment of costs. However, in civil actions, court can assess reasonable attorney fees against attorney or party bringing unjustified claims, bringing claims to harass, unreasonably delaying proceeding, or abusing discovery. (12-349).

DAMAGES:

Common law generally prevails as to compensatory damages. To obtain punitive damages, plaintiff must prove that defendant was guided by evil mind, which may be shown by either: (1) Evil actions; (2) spiteful motives; or (3) outrageous, oppressive or intolerable conduct that creates substantial risk of tremendous harm to others. Future damages arising from medical malpractice action payable in periodic installments or discounted to present value. (12-581 et seq.).

Charitable Immunity.—Doctrine of charitable immunity not recognized.

Comparative Negligence Rule.—Adopted. (12-2505). Defendant not liable where plaintiff was under influence of alcohol or drugs and was at least 50% responsible for harm, where plaintiff was harmed while committing felony, or where plaintiff was harmed by defendant's negligence or gross negligence while attempting to commit or committing misdemeanor criminal act on defendant or defendant's property. (12-711 to 712). For statute governing comparative fault in Employer's Liability Law, see 23-806.

Death.—See category Estates and Trusts, topic Death, subhead Action for Death.

Defamation.—Defamation retraction governed by 12-653.01 et seq.

Employer Subsidized Day Care Immunity.—Employer that subsidizes child care given qualified immunity for damages caused by independent licensed day care center. (36-883.03).

Governing Body Immunity.—Person on governing body of district not liable for good faith acts within scope of official capacity. (48-187).

Health Care Utilization Committee Immunity.—Person on health care utilization committee not liable for decisions absent malice. Absence of malice presumed. (36-441).

Interspousal Immunity.—Judicially abrogated. (132 Ariz. 447, 646 P.2d 878).

Manufacturer or Seller of Drugs.—No liability for punitive damages where manufacturer or seller complied with FDA license or where drug is generally recognized as safe and effective. (12-701).

Mental Health Providers Immunity.—No liability except as provided by 36-517.02.

Public Employees' Immunity.—Public employees not personally liable for acts done in official capacity in good faith reliance on written opinion of government lawyer. (38-446).

No-Fault Insurance.—Not adopted.

Products Liability.—Affirmative defenses, rights between seller and manufacturer, and evidence of defect governed by 12-681 et seq. For statute of limitations on strict liability claims, see topic Limitation of Actions.

Racketeering.—Person who sustains reasonably foreseeable injury due to pattern of racketeering may recover up to treble damages plus costs. Punitive or emotional damages available in event of bodily injury. (13-2314.04).

Sovereign Immunity.—Common law doctrine retained as modified by statute. (12-820 et seq.). Absolute and qualified immunities apply to certain conduct (12-820.01 and 12-820.02) and affirmative defenses exist (12-820.03). Punitive and exemplary damages may not be assessed against public entity or public employee within scope of employment. (12-820.04). For other immunities see 12-820.05.

Torts of Minors.—Parents or legal guardian liable for malicious or willful misconduct up to $10,000 for each tort. (12-661).

Uniform Contribution Among Tortfeasors Act (Revised).—Adopted. (12-2501 et seq.).

DECLARATORY JUDGMENTS:

See topic Judgments.

DEPOSITIONS AND DISCOVERY:

Federal Rules of Civil Procedure followed with some important modifications to require disclosure. (Civ. 1-86). See topic Practice.

Administrative Hearings.—Prehearing depositions and subpoenas for production of documents may be ordered by officer presiding at hearing. (41-1062[A][4]).

Before Whom Taken.—Federal Rules of Civil Procedure adopted with no material variation, except that deposition can be taken before officer authorized by State of Arizona. (Civ. 28).

Limitations.—Right to depose upon oral examination presumptively limited to testimony of parties, any expert witnesses expected to be called, and document custodians to secure production of documents and to establish evidentiary foundation. (Civ. 30[a]). Depositions must be of reasonable length, and oral depositions must not exceed presumptive limit of four hours. (Civ. 30[d]). Objections to form of question or responsiveness of answer during taking of deposition must be concise and not suggest answers to witness, and continuous and unwarranted off the record attorney-deponent conferences during deposition are prohibited. (Civ. 32[d][3][D]-[E]).

Compelling Attendance of Witnesses.—Parties need not be subpoenaed, only noticed (Civ. 30[b]); all others may be subpoenaed to avoid imposition of costs on deposing party if deponent fails to appear (Civ. 30[g]). If party or officer, director or managing agent of party fails to appear for duly noticed deposition without applying for protective order, court shall require party failing to appear or attorney advising that party to pay reasonable expenses and attorneys' fees caused by failure unless failure is substantially justified. (Civ. 37[f]). Superior court clerk must issue subpoena upon proof of service of notice to take deposition. (Civ. 45[a]). Subpoena to produce documents, if objected to, may be modified or quashed by court. (Civ. 45[c]). Resident of county in which deposition is to be taken may be required to attend only in county where he resides, is employed or transacts business in person, or at such place as court may order. Nonresident must attend only in county in which he is served with subpoena or within 40 miles of place of service, or at such place as court may order. (Civ. 45[c]). Person to whom subpoena is directed may, within 14 days after service of subpoena or before time specified for compliance if time is less than 14 days after service, serve upon attorney designated in subpoena written objections to inspection or copying designated material. If objection is made, party serving subpoena shall not be entitled to inspect material except pursuant to court order. (Civ. 45[c]). Failure to obey subpoena without adequate excuse is contempt of court. (Civ. 45[e]).

Perpetuating Testimony.—Deposition to perpetuate testimony may be used in any action involving same subject matter subsequently brought between same parties and as permitted by Arizona Rules of Evidence. (Civ. 32[a]). Federal Rules of Civil Procedure adopted with no material variations. (Civ. 27[b]).

Within State for Use Within State.—Federal Rules of Civil Procedure adopted with no material variations, except that leave of court must be obtained prior to taking deposition of nonparties (except expert witnesses). (Civ. 30-32).

Within State for Use Outside State.—Party wishing to take deposition must file application under oath, captioned as is foreign action, which contains: (1) Caption of case, court in which pending and names of all parties and their attorneys; (2) reference to law of foreign jurisdiction authorizing taking of deposition in another state and facts necessary under foreign law to entitle party to take deposition and have subpoena issued; (3) certified copies of notice of taking deposition, court order authorizing deposition, commission or letters rogatory or such other pleadings as, under foreign jurisdiction's law, are necessary in order to take deposition; and (4) description of both notice given to other parties and its service of application to be made on other parties to action. Upon filing application, clerk of superior court of county in which deposition is to be taken will issue subpoena or subpoena duces tecum. Affidavit of service of application on all other parties to action must be filed with clerk. Any party or witness may subsequently make such motions under Arizona Rules of Civil Procedure as may be appropriate. (Civ. 30[h]).

Form.—No particular form prescribed or required.

Outside of State for Use Within State.—Taking of depositions outside state for use in Arizona is governed by Civ. 28.

Uniform Foreign Depositions Act repealed.

Written Interrogatories.—Federal Rules of Civil Procedure adopted with no material variations except answers or objections required within 40 days of service, but defendant has 60 days after service of summons and complaint. Parties presumptively limited to serving no more than 40 interrogatories (uniform or nonuniform) upon any other party. (Civ. 33-33.1).

EQUITY:

See topic Actions.

EVIDENCE:

Witnesses.—Religious opinions or want of religious belief do not disqualify. (12-2201).

No person is incompetent because he is party to suit or proceeding or interested in issue tried, or because he has been indicted, accused or convicted of crime. (12-2201).

Persons of unsound mind at time they are called to testify and children under age of ten who appear incapable of receiving just impressions are incompetent. (12-2202). Children under age of ten may testify concerning sexual offense or physical abuse on or witnessed by minor, if conditions of statute are satisfied. (13-1416).

See also topic Depositions and Discovery.

Privileged Communications.—Information imparted by reason of confidential relationship may not be disclosed by attorney, physician, surgeon, clergyman, or priest without consent of person from whom obtained. (12-2231 et seq.). Persons engaged in newspaper, radio, television or reportorial work not compelled to testify as to source of information procured for publication in newspaper or broadcasting media. (12-2237).

Husband and Wife.—One spouse cannot testify against other without consent of other, nor can either testify, during marriage or afterwards, as to communications during marriage, without consent of other, except in action for dissolution or civil action between spouses, action for alienation of affections, action for damages against another for adultery committed by spouse or in criminal proceeding in manner provided for in criminal code. (12-2231 to 2232).

Communications or Transactions with Persons Since Deceased or Incompetent.—In action by or against executors, administrators or guardians, neither party is allowed to testify as to transactions with or statements by testator, intestate or ward unless called to testify thereto by opposite party or required to do so by court. This provision also extends to all actions by or against heirs, devisees and legatees or legal representatives of decedent arising out of any transaction with decedent. (12-2251).

INJUNCTIONS:

Arizona Rules of Civil Procedure are based on Federal Rules of Civil Procedure. (Civ. 1-86). See topic Practice.

Jurisdiction and Prerequisites.—Judges of superior court may grant writs of injunction: (1) When it appears that applicant for writ is entitled to relief demanded, and such relief or part thereof requires restraint of some act prejudicial to applicant; (2) when, pending litigation, it appears that party is doing, threatens, is about to do or is procuring or suffering to be done, some act respecting subject of litigation and in violation of applicant's rights which would tend to render judgment ineffectual; and (3) in all other cases where applicant shows himself entitled to writ under principles of equity. (12-1801).

Procedure.—Injunction may be granted at time of commencing action on verified complaint or at any time before judgment on affidavit. (12-1803). If injunction is

See note at head of Digest as to 1998 legislation covered.

See Topical Index in front part of this volume.

INJUNCTIONS . . . *continued*
granted on verified complaint or affidavit, copy of complaint or affidavit shall be served with injunction. (12-1803[C]). Before hearing on injunction is held, notice of hearing, together with copy of complaint or affidavits upon which application for injunction is based, shall be served on parties sought to be enjoined. (12-1804).

Bond.—Judge to whom application for writ of injunction is made fixes amount of bond to be given by applicant as prerequisite to issuance of writ. Bond requirement does not apply to State or officers and agencies thereof. (Civ. 65[e]).

Answer.—Motions to dissolve or modify preliminary injunction without determining merits of action may be heard after answer is filed and notice is provided to opposite party.

Restrictions.—No injunction may be granted: To stop a judicial proceeding pending at the commencement of the action unless such restraint is necessary to prevent a multiplicity of proceedings; to stay proceedings in a United States court; to stay proceedings in another state upon a judgment of a court of that state; to prevent enforcement of a public statute by officers of the law for the public benefit; to prevent the breach of a contract which would not be specifically enforced; to prevent the exercise of public or private office in lawful manner by person in possession; or to prevent legislative act by municipal corporation. (12-1802). Injunctions to stay execution of judgment must be made within one year of date of judgment, except in cases of fraud, by party recovering judgment, made at time of or after judgment, or because of equitable matters arising after date of judgment, or within two years if applicant for injunction was absent from state when judgment was rendered. (12-1806).

Temporary Restraining Order.—Valid for not more than ten days, as set by court, unless extended. May be granted without notice to adverse party when it clearly appears necessary and when applicant's attorney provides court written certification of efforts made to give notice or reasons for not giving notice. (Civ. 65[d]).

JUDGMENTS:

Arizona Rules of Civil Procedure are based on Federal Rules of Civil Procedure. (Civ. 1-86). See topic Practice.

Judgment is decree or order from which appeal lies. (Civ. 54[a]). Judgment may be given as to one or more parties and one or more claims for relief, but fewer than all, only on determination that no just reason for delay exists. (Civ. 54[b]). Judgment may pass title to property without any act to be done by party against whom judgment runs. (33-456; Civ. 70). Judgment may be entered after death of party on verdict or decision upon issue of fact rendered in party's lifetime. (Civ. 54[e]).

Judgment by Confession.—May not be entered under power of attorney on written instrument for payment of money unless power of attorney was executed and acknowledged subsequent to due date of instrument. (44-143).

Judgment on Pleadings.—After pleadings are closed but before trial, any party may move for judgment on pleadings. If matters outside pleadings are presented and not excluded by court, motion will be treated as one for summary judgment. (Civ. 12[c]).

Summary Judgment.—Either party may move, with or without affidavits, for summary judgment. If made with affidavit, adverse party must set forth specific facts showing genuine issues for trial. Party opposing motion must file response within 15 days after service of motion. Moving party has five days thereafter to serve reply. Summary judgment will be given only if no genuine issues of material fact exist and moving party is entitled to judgment as matter of law. Interlocutory judgment may be given on issue of liability alone. (Civ. 56[a]-[e]).

Judgment by Default.—When party against whom judgment for affirmative relief is sought has failed to plead or otherwise defend as provided by Rules and that fact is shown by affidavit or otherwise, clerk must enter his default on written application by party seeking default. Notice must be given to party in default if whereabouts known and to his attorney if known to be represented by attorney. Default entered by clerk is effective ten days after filing application for entry of default. Court may then enter judgment on motion, where claim is for sum which can by computation be made certain, or on hearing, in all other cases. Court may set aside entry of default for good cause, and may set aside judgment pursuant to Rule 60(c) (see subhead Review, Vacation or Modification of Judgment, infra). (Civ. 55[a]-[c]).

Offer of Judgment.—Any party may serve offer of judgment on adverse party at anytime more than 30 days before trial. If offer is not accepted within 30 days, it is deemed withdrawn, except that offer made within 60 days after service of complaint remains effective for 60 days. If judgment obtained is equal to, or more favorable to offeror, offeree must pay reasonable expert witness fees, double costs offeror incurred after making offer and prejudgment interest on unliquidated claims from date of offer. (Civ. 68).

Review, Vacation or Modification of Judgment.—Judgment may be reviewed by motion for new trial or judgment notwithstanding verdict. (Civ. 50[b], 59[c]). If court's judgment is rendered upon judgment of another state or foreign country and foreign judgment is subsequently reversed, then court shall set aside, vacate, and annul its judgment. (Civ. 60[d]). Clerical mistakes and errors arising from oversight or omission may be corrected by court at any time. (Civ. 60[a]-[b]). Party may be relieved from judgment within six months due to his mistake, inadvertence, surprise, excusable neglect or newly discovered evidence, fraud or other misconduct by adverse party. (Civ. 60[c]). If judgment is rendered on service by publication, defendant who did not appear may apply for new trial within one year and new trial may be granted for good cause shown. (Civ. 59[j]). Court will not modify or vacate judgment because of error in proceedings unless failure to do so would be inconsistent with substantial justice. (Civ. 61).

Docketing.—Copy of judgment, certified by clerk, is lien on real property of judgment debtor if filed and recorded in office of county recorder in each county in which property is situated. (33-961). In case of reversal or remittitur, clerk must enter on docket and judgment creditor must correct recording. (33-965). Judgment creditor must file satisfaction of judgment with county recorder when judgment is paid. (33-964).

Lien of Judgment.—If properly recorded, extends to all of debtor's real property in county, except exempt property, and continues for five years from date of rendition of judgment. (33-964). Judgment lien in mortgage foreclosure on $2^1/_2$ acre or smaller parcel used for one or two family residence is not extended to other property. (33-729). Judgment against railroad company for injury to any person or property is lien in county where recovered superior to lien of any mortgage or trust deed. (33-966).

Revivor or Renewal.—Judgment may be revived by action thereon within five years after date of judgment. (12-1611). Judgment may be renewed by affidavit of judgment creditor, his agent or attorney, and continued as lien for five years from date of filing affidavit, which must contain matters prescribed by statute and be made within 90 days next preceding expiration of five year period from date of entry of judgment. Additional renewal affidavits may be filed within 90 days preceding expiration of five year period from date of filing prior renewal affidavit. (12-1612 to 1613).

Foreign Judgments.—Foreign judgment is any judgment, decree or order of court of U.S. or any other court entitled to full faith and credit in Arizona. (12-1701). Action on foreign judgment must be brought within four years after determination on appeal or passage of time for appeal in other jurisdiction. (12-544[3]). Such action is barred in Arizona if, by laws of state or country in which judgment is rendered, such action would be barred and judgment thereupon incapable of being otherwise enforced there. (12-549). Filing fee for foreign judgment is governed by 12-284.

Revised Uniform Enforcement of Foreign Judgments Act adopted. (12-1701 et seq.).

Uniform Declaratory Judgments Act adopted. (12-1831 et seq.).

LIMITATION OF ACTIONS:

Actions are barred unless commenced within following periods after particular causes of action accrue (12-501 et seq.):

Ten years: To recover any lands, tenements or hereditaments from one having peaceable and adverse possession, cultivating, using and enjoying same. (12-526).

Eight years: For action or arbitration based in contract against person who develops real property or who designs, engineers or contracts improvements. No effect on actions for personal injury or death and periods in express written warranties. (12-552).

Six years: For debt on any written instrument executed in Arizona. (12-548).

Five years: To recover real estate as against adverse possessor paying taxes on same and claiming under recorded deed not forged (12-525); city lot, same (12-524); against sheriff and his sureties for not returning execution (12-547).

Four years: On written instrument executed outside of state; on foreign judgment; for penalty or damages on bond to convey real estate; for partnership accounting; on mutual and current accounts concerning trade between merchants (12-544); on bond of executor or guardian (12-545); for specific performance of contract to convey real property (12-546); on contracts of sale under Commercial Code (47-2725); on any action not otherwise provided for by law (12-550).

Three years: To recover real estate as against person in peaceable and adverse possession under title or color of title. (12-523). For debt not evidenced by writing; on stated or open account other than mutual and current accounts concerning trade between merchants; for relief on ground of fraud or mistake. (12-543).

Two years: To recover possession of real estate as against person who claims real property by right of possession only. (12-522). For injury to real or personal property; for wrongful taking or detention of personal property; for trespass or conversion; for forcible entry and detainer; for personal injury; for medical malpractice; for wrongful death. (12-542); on bulk transfers if concealed (47-6110).

One year: For libel, slander, malicious prosecution, false imprisonment, breach of promise to marry or seduction, and on liability created by statute other than penalty or forfeiture (12-541); for sale of unregistered securities or fraudulent sale of securities (44-2004); on bulk transfers unless concealed (47-6110); for all actions against public entity (12-821).

Six months: To foreclose mechanics' or materialmen's lien. (33-998).

Time From Which Statute Runs.—For personal injury generally, from date of injury; for injury when death ensues, at death; for fraud or mistake, on discovery thereof or from time when exercise of reasonable care would have led to discovery; on mutual and current accounts between merchants, on cessation of dealings; on other stated or open accounts, from date of last item; for partnership accounting, on cessation of dealings; on bond of executor or administrator, from time of his death or removal; for forcible entry or detainer, at commencement of entry or detainer; for improvements on real property, not until substantial completion of improvement.

Saving of Timely Commenced Action.—If action terminated other than by abatement, voluntary dismissal, dismissal for lack of prosecution or final judgment on merits, new action for same cause can be brought within six months of termination. If action terminated for exceptions cited above, court has discretion to provide extension period not exceeding six months. Applies to judgments on appeal. (12-504).

Disabilities.—Limitation period for cause of action in favor of or against person who dies ceases to run for 12 months, unless representative qualifies sooner, but automatic four-month tolling. (14-3109, 3802). As to tolling during marriage of cause of action barred by interspousal immunity, see 116 Ariz. 512, 570 P.2d 199. Limitations do not run against person of unsound mind until disability is removed. (12-502). Limitations do not run against prisoner until person imprisoned discovers or should have discovered right to bring action. (12-502, 528). Limitations do not run against person under 18 years of age. (12-502).

Absence.—Limitations do not run in favor of absentee (not amenable to service of process) defendant. (12-501).

Acknowledgment of justness of claim made after it becomes due, to affect limitations, must be in writing and signed by party to be charged. (12-508).

Person Moving Into State.—Action against person moving into Arizona is not barred by limitations until he has lived within state for one year. But if, prior to his

LIMITATION OF ACTIONS . . . *continued*
moving into Arizona, his cause of action was barred by law in state of his former domicile, it may not be sued upon in Arizona. (12-506 to 507). Same for foreign judgments. (12-549).

Pleading.—Statute of limitations is affirmative defense which must be pleaded in order to be available. (Civ. 8[c]).

Uniform Commercial Code adopted. (47-1101 et seq.). See category Business Regulation and Commerce, topic Commercial Code.

PARTITION:

Real Property.—Owner of interest in real estate may compel partition between himself and other owners by filing action for such partition in superior court. (12-1211). Upon hearing cause, court must adjudge interest of each party to real estate and settle any matters of title that may be in issue. (12-1213). If it appears to court that fair partition of property cannot be made without depreciating value thereof, or that sale is more beneficial to any of parties, court shall enter judgment that property be sold and proceeds divided (12-1218); otherwise, court will appoint three commissioners to partition property (12-1215). If commissioners find property cannot be equitably divided and court concurs it must order property sold and proceeds divided among parties entitled. (12-1218).

Personal Property.—Partitioned in proceedings similar to those for partition of real estate. (12-1222).

Estates.—Prior to formal or informal closing of estate, when two or more heirs are entitled to undivided interest in any property, one or more of them may petition court to make partition. After notice to interested parties, court parti-tions property in manner prescribed for partition actions. If court cannot equitably partition property, personal representative must sell property. (14-3911).

PLEADING:

Arizona Rules of Civil Procedure are based on Federal Rules of Civil Procedure and govern in all civil suits whether cognizable as cases at law or in equity. (Civ. 1). Each county has particular uniform and local rules.

Pleadings Permitted.—Complaint; answer; reply, if answer contains counterclaim; answer to cross-claim, if answer contains cross-claim; third-party complaint, if person who was not original party is summoned as third-party; answer to third-party complaint. No other pleading is allowed, except court may order reply to answer or third-party answer. (Civ. 7[a]).

Form of Pleadings.—Every pleading must contain caption setting forth name of court, title of action, file number and designation as to nature of pleading filed. In complaint, title of action must include names of all parties; in other pleadings, it is sufficient to state name of first party with appropriate indication of other parties. All averments of claim or defense must be made in numbered paragraphs. (Civ. 10). All pleadings must be on $8^1/2$ by 11 inch paper. (Civ. 10[d]).

Every pleading of party represented by attorney must be signed by at least one attorney of record in his individual name, with address stated; unrepresented parties must sign pleading and state their address. (Civ. 11[a]). Signature of attorney or party certifies pleading is well grounded in fact after reasonable inquiry, supported by existing law or good faith argument for extension or reversal of existing law, and not interposed for improper purpose; sanctions available for violation. (Civ. 11[a]).

Complaint.—Action commenced when complaint filed. (Civ. 3). No technical forms of pleadings required. To state claim for relief, pleading must contain short and plain statement of basis for jurisdiction, statement of claim showing that pleader is entitled to relief, plus demand for relief to which he deems himself entitled. Demand for relief in alternative or of different types permitted. (Civ. 8).

Frivolous Claims.—Sanctions for frivolous pleadings, motions and other papers filed with superior court similar to Rule 11 of Federal Rules of Civil Procedure. (Civ. 11). Sanctions for frivolous appeals or appellate motions. (12-2106).

Answer.—Responsive pleading must state in short and plain terms pleader's defenses to each claim asserted and must admit or deny averments in complaint. If pleader intends in good faith to deny all averments in complaint, he may do so by general denial. (Civ. 8[b]).

Affirmative Defenses.—Following defenses must be set forth in responsive pleading: Accord and satisfaction; arbitration and award; assumption of risk; contributory negligence; discharge in bankruptcy; duress; estoppel; failure of consideration; fraud; illegality; laches; license; payment; release; res judicata; statute of frauds; statute of limitations; waiver; and any other matter in avoidance or affirmative defense. (Civ. 8[d]).

Counterclaim.—Pleading may state as counterclaim any claim against opposing party and must state as counterclaim any claim which arises out of same transaction or occurrence as is subject of opposing party's claim. (Civ. 13[a]-[b]).

Reply.—Reply is mandatory only when answer contains counterclaim denominated as such. Court may in its discretion order reply to answer of defendant or third party. (Civ. 7).

Amended or Supplemental Pleadings.—Party may amend his pleading once as matter of course at any time before responsive pleading is served, or, if pleading is one to which no responsive pleading is permitted, at any time within 20 days after service. Otherwise, leave of court or written consent of adverse party is necessary. (Civ. 15).

Bills of Particulars.—If pleading is so vague or ambiguous that party cannot reasonably be required to frame responsive pleading, he may move for more definite statement. (Civ. 12[e]).

Verification.—Except when otherwise specifically required by rule or statute, pleadings need not be verified. (Civ. 11[a]). Responsive pleading setting up any of following matters must be verified by affidavit; (1) Plaintiff has no legal capacity to sue; (2) plaintiff is not entitled to recover in capacity in which he sues; (3) another action is pending in Arizona between same parties for same claims; (4) defect of parties exists; (5) denial of party's partnership or incorporation; (6) denial of execution by defendant or by his authority of any instrument in writing on which any pleading is based and alleged to have been executed by him or by his authority; (7) denial of genuineness of written instrument's endorsement or assignment; (8) written instrument on which pleading is based lacks consideration or consideration has failed in whole or in part; or (9) account which is basis of plaintiff's action is not just. (Civ. 9[i]).

When equitable relief is demanded and party demanding such relief makes oath that allegations of pleading are true, responsive pleading of opposite party must be under oath, unless waived, and each material allegation not denied under oath is taken as admitted. (Civ. 11[c]).

Verified complaint or affidavit is required in order for temporary restraining order to be granted without notice to adverse party. (Civ. 65[d]).

Service.—Complaint must be personally served on defendant in accordance with Civ. 4. Every pleading subsequent to original complaint must be served on each party, unless court orders otherwise because of numerous defendants. (Civ. 5[a]). Where party represented by attorney, service must be on attorney. (Civ. 5[c]).

Filing.—Except for offers of judgment under Civ. 68, all papers after complaint required to be served on party or to be filed with court within specified time must be both filed and served within that specified time. (Civ. 5[g]). Service of summons and complaint must occur within 120 days of filing of complaint. (Civ. 4[i]).

Time to Answer or Otherwise Plead.—20 days if served within state and 30 days if served outside state. (Civ. 12[a], 4.2[l]).

Claims Against Estates.—See category Estates and Trusts, topic Executors and Administrators, subhead Proof of Claims.

Accounts.—A pleading need not set forth items of account therein alleged but on a written demand an itemized account must be furnished to the defendant within ten days from the time of the demand. (Civ. 12[f]).

Small Claims.—See category Courts and Legislature, topic Courts.

PRACTICE:

Regulated by Rules of Civil Procedure based on Federal Rules of Civil Procedure with some important modifications to require disclosure (Civ. 1-86) and rules made by supreme court (12-109). In addition, certain special proceedings are governed by statute.

Discovery.—Federal Rules of Civil Procedure followed with some important modifications to require disclosure. (Civ. 26-37). Discovery ends either 60 days after certificate of readiness for trial is filed, or ten days before trial, or when certificate of readiness is filed, depending upon which section of Uniform Rule V is adopted by particular superior court. (Super. Ct. Uni. R. Prac. V). Generally, subpoena duces tecum for doctor's records must be served ten days before production date. (12-2282). Answers or objections to written interrogatories and requests for production of documents and things or admissions required within 40 days after service, except defendant has 60 days after service of summons and complaint. (Civ. 33[a], 34[b], 36[a]).

Major Limitations on Discovery/Trial Preparation.—Each side is presumptively entitled to one independent expert on an issue. (Civ. 26[b][4][D]). Parties presumptively limited to serving no more than 40 interrogatories (uniform or nonuniform) upon any other party. (Civ. 33.1[a]). After commencement of action, parties are presumptively limited to one request for production of documents and things, which presumptively must not provide for more than ten distinct items or specific categories of items. (Civ. 34[b]). Each party presumptively limited to 25 requests for admissions and each request is limited to one factual matter or request for genuiness of all documents or categories of documents. (Civ. 36[b]). Opinion evidence on same issue presumptively limited to one independent witness per side. (Civ. 43[g]). See also topic Depositions and Discovery, subhead Limitations.

Disclosure Statements.—Parties must disclose as fully as possible within 40 days of filing responsive pleading: factual basis of claim or defense; legal theory of claim or defense; names, addresses and telephone numbers of witnesses or others with relevant information, including expert witnesses and those who have given statements; computation and measure of damages alleged; existence and location of tangible evidence; and list of relevant documents. Disclosure duty is continuing, each party must make additional or amended disclosures whenever new or different information discovered. (Civ. 26.1).

Setting of Civil Cases for Trial.—In every civil case, counsel for plaintiff must, or counsel for any other party may, file and serve on all other parties motion to set and certificate of readiness pursuant to Rule V, Uniform Rules of Practice of Superior Court. In some counties, local rules require listing of witnesses and exhibits by both parties before motion to set and certificate of readiness are filed. Failure to list witnesses and exhibits in timely manner may preclude their use at trial.

Pretrial Statements.—Before each civil case, counsel shall file written statement stipulating contested and uncontested material facts, contested material issues of fact and law, trial exhibits, witness list and summary of depositions to be offered at trial. (Super. Ct. Uni. R. Prac. VI[a]).

Pretrial Conferences.—Upon written request of any party or upon its own motion, court shall schedule comprehensive pretrial conference to determine and narrow issues for trial. (Civ. 16[b]-[c]).

Mandatory Settlement Conferences.—Except upon good cause shown, settlement conferences required upon request of any party for most cases in which motion to set and certificate of readiness is filed. Each party must furnish court with detailed settlement memorandum. Upon motion of party or on its own motion, court may schedule comprehensive pretrial conference pursuant to Rule 16. (Super. Ct. Uni. R. Prac. VI[e]).

Special Actions.—

Nature of Special Action.—Relief previously obtained by writs of certiorari (12-2001 et seq.), mandamus (12-2021 et seq.) and prohibition (common law) must now be obtained by special action order.

Generally, special action not available where person has equally plain, speedy and adequate remedy by appeal. Rules of Procedure for Special Actions do not alter scope

See note at head of Digest as to 1998 legislation covered.

See Topical Index in front part of this volume.

PRACTICE . . . *continued*
of writs but merely establish uniform procedure for obtaining their remedies. Interpretation of said Rules subsumes decisions under writ law as it stood prior to adoption of Rules. (Spec. Act. R. 1).

Parties.—Persons who previously could institute application for writ of certiorari, mandamus or prohibition now may institute proceeding for special action order. Complaint must join officer, body or person against whom relief is sought as defendant. Where public entity named as defendant, real party in interest must also be joined. Court may allow other persons to intervene, or may order their joinder as parties, or may allow their participation as amicus curiae. Court may direct that notice of action be given to any person. (Spec. Act. R. 2).

Questions Raised.—Only following questions may be raised in special action: (1) Whether defendant has failed to exercise discretion which he has duty to exercise or to perform legal duty as to which he has no discretion; (2) whether defendant has proceeded or is threatening to proceed without or in excess of his jurisdiction or legal authority; or (3) whether determination by defendant was arbitrary and capricious or abuse of discretion. (Spec. Act. R. 3).

Procedure.—

Jurisdiction.—Special action may be brought in superior court in any county, court of appeals or supreme court. (Spec. Act. R. 4[a]).

Selection of Court.—Action in superior court is brought in county in which officer or body has or should have determined matter to be reviewed, or, in case of state officer or body, either in Maricopa County or in county of plaintiff's residence; in case of any public officer or body, or private corporation, in county of same's principal place of business; or, where private corporation defendant has no principal place of business in Arizona, in Maricopa County or county of plaintiff's residence, at his option. Action in court of appeals is brought before whichever division has territorial jurisdiction over county in which action may have been brought if in superior court. (Spec. Act. R. 4[b]). Any action may also be brought originally in supreme court. (Spec. Act. R. 4[a]). Whenever plaintiff brings action in appellate court which might lawfully have been initiated in lower court, he must set forth circumstances rendering review by particular appellate court appropriate. (Spec. Act. R. 7[b]).

Time for Service of Complaint and Answer.—Special action may be instituted with or without application for order to show cause why requested relief should not be granted. Service of summons, complaint and order to show cause, if any, are subject to Civ. 4, unless court otherwise specifies manner and time within which service must be made. (Spec. Act. R. 4[c]).

Pleadings.—Complaint by plaintiff, and answer or such other responsive pleading as may be appropriate by defendant or real party-in-interest. In appellate courts, complaint is called petition and answer is response; plaintiff is called petitioner and defendant is respondent. (Spec. Act. R. 4[d], 7).

Stay of Proceedings Below.—Filing of special action complaint and setting of matter for hearing does not stay proceedings before court or tribunal as to which relief is sought, unless court hearing special action specifically orders stay. Such interlocutory orders are subject to Civ. 65. See topic Injunctions. (Spec. Act. R. 5).

Judgment.—In special action brought in superior court, judgment is in form used for civil actions generally, with no special requirements formerly peculiar to writs. Judgment may grant part or all of relief requested, or may dismiss action either on merits or without prejudice. (Spec. Act. R. 6).

Special Appellate Court Provisions.—Petition and all papers must be served forthwith by petitioner, time and manner of service to be specified by Chief Judge of court of appeals or chief justice of supreme court, according to court where filed. Objections to such relief, in whatever form, must be in writing, and filed and served within seven days after service of petition upon respondent, or such lesser time as court may order. If special action relief is granted, form of order granting relief is as court directs but must be in writing and grounds therefor stated. If relief denied, no written opinion required. (Spec. Act. R. 7).

Appeal and Rehearing.—See Spec. Act. R. 8-9.

Provisional Remedies.—In response to constitutional attacks on Arizona's law of prejudgment remedies, state legislature in 1976 enacted 12-2401 et seq., "Provisional Remedies," consolidating and substantially amending prior law as to attachment, prejudgment garnishment and replevin. (Garnishment of wages is not provisional remedy.) Following entry deals with provisions of 12-2401 et seq. applicable to all three remedies. See also category Debtor and Creditor, topics Attachment, Garnishment and Replevin for provisions specifically applicable to each.

Who May Issue Remedy.—Judges of superior court and justices of peace. (12-2402).

Issuance Without Notice.—Provisional remedy may be issued by any superior court judge or justice of peace before judgment and without prior notice to defendant in any of following cases:

(1) When defendant is about to remove permanently from state and has refused to secure debt, or has secreted, disposed of or is about to dispose of property with intent to defraud creditors.

(2) When plaintiff is lawfully entitled to possession of property claimed, has satisfied affidavit and bond requirements (12-1301, 1303), and is seeking provisional remedy in nature of replevin (except that such remedy cannot be used to enforce security interest in consumer goods other than purchase money security interest).

(3) When provisional remedy is required to obtain jurisdiction.

(4) When plaintiff has received bulk sales notice (47-6105) concerning property and such bulk sale will not provide plaintiff full payment (12-2402[A]).

Affidavit.—Before remedy may issue, plaintiff must establish by affidavit to court's satisfaction that facts supporting his claim are sufficient for issuance, that one of 12-2402(A) requirements has been met and that plaintiff will file such other pleadings and affidavits as may be required by law. (12-2402[B]).

See also affidavit requirements under specific provisional remedies.

Motion to Quash.—Upon issue of remedy, defendant may immediately move to quash. Motion must be heard within five days of filing, exclusive of weekends and holidays. Issues at hearing are limited to probable validity of plaintiff's claim(s), defenses and claims of personal property exemptions of defendant, existence of statutory requirements for issuance of specific remedy and existence of 12-2402(A) requirements. (12-2402[C]).

Subsequent Notice.—Within three days of actual attachment, garnishment or seizure, plaintiff must exercise reasonable diligence to notify defendant of action ordered by court and of defendant's right to immediate hearing contesting same. (12-2402[D]). Upon filing of provisional remedy application, court must issue notice to defendant in prescribed form. (12-2402[E]).

Issuance With Notice.—Except as provided in 12-2402, supra, provisional remedy may not issue until plaintiff has complied with statutory requirements for specific remedy sought, filed application for issuance of remedy and notice thereof with court and served copies of both on defendant, and until defendant has been afforded hearing or opportunity to request hearing. (12-2403). Plaintiff may apply for provisional remedy at any time after filing civil action. Application must set forth factual and legal basis for each remedy sought. (12-2404). Court then issues notice to defendant in prescribed form. (12-2405).

Service of Notice and Application.—Copies of notices prescribed in 12-2402 and 2405, and of application for issuance of remedy, must be served on defendant by sheriff, constable or private process server in same manner as summons and complaint. (12-2406).

Hearing Request.—Defendant must file written request for hearing date with clerk of court within ten days after service of notice. Clerk must mail copy of request to plaintiff's attorney. (12-2407).

Default.—If defendant makes no hearing request, plaintiff may file affidavit of default stating that service was made, that no hearing request was filed and that defendant was in default. Plaintiff must also file proposed form of written order described in subhead Judicial Review of Default Application, infra. Party in default loses right to hearing. (12-2408).

Judicial Review of Default Application.—Within five days, exclusive of weekends and holidays, after entry of default, court must review pleadings, affidavits and other documents on file to determine that: (1) Affidavit has been filed by person who served application and notice, (2) affidavit of default has been filed and default entered, (3) plaintiff's claim(s) are based on sufficient facts in supporting affidavit to make claim(s) valid, (4) any statutory requirement for issuance of specific remedy has been met and (5) any other pleadings or affidavits required as prerequisites for remedy have been filed. (12-2409[A]). If these requirements are met, provisional remedy is issued by written order including findings that 12-2409(A) requirements have been met. (12-2409[B] to [C]).

Hearing.—Hearing must be conducted by judge or justice of peace within five days exclusive of weekends and holidays after filing of hearing request, or at later time with consent of all parties. Issues at hearing are limited to probable validity of plaintiff's claim(s), defenses and claims of personal property exemptions of defendant and existence of statutory requirements for issuance of specific remedy. If after hearing court finds probable cause to believe plaintiff's claim is valid and statutory requirements for specific remedy have been met, such remedy is issued. (12-2410).

Attorney's Fees.—If hearing is held and original remedy order is quashed or no provisional remedy is ordered, court may award reasonable attorney's fees to defendant. (12-2411).

Waiver of Right to Hearing.—Void and unenforceable. (12-2412).

Compulsory Arbitration.—See category Dispute Resolution, topic Arbitration and Award.

Direct Actions Against Insurer.—See category Transportation, topic Motor Vehicles, subhead Direct Actions.

Small Claims.—See category Courts and Legislature, topic Courts.

See also topics Actions, Appeal and Error, Depositions and Discovery, Injunctions, Judgments, Pleading, Process; category Debtor and Creditor, topics Attachment, Executions, Garnishment.

PROCESS:

Federal Rules of Civil Procedure followed with some important modifications to require disclosure. (Civ. 1-86). See topic Practice.

Who May Serve.—On filing of complaint, clerk issues summons which may be served only by sheriff, his deputy, person not attorney or party appointed by court or person not less than 21 years of age registered with clerk as private process server. Fees for service set by statute. (Civ. 4[d], 11-445). Summons and pleading must be served together within 120 days of filing. (Civ. 4[i], 4.1[b]).

Personal Service.—Summons and pleading must be served personally or by leaving copies at defendant's dwelling or place of abode with person of suitable age or discretion residing there or upon agent authorized by appointment or law to receive service. Service on minor for whom guardian of estate has been appointed must be on both guardian and ward. Service on minor under 16 made by serving minor and parent, guardian or person in loco parentis; on incompetent, by serving incompetent and either guardian or person designated by court. (Civ. 4.1). After appearance by counsel, service must be made on attorney unless service on party is ordered by court. (Civ. 5[c]). Service by mail complete on date acknowledgment of receipt is executed. (171 Ariz. 449, 831 P.2d 448).

Service by Mail within Arizona.—Upon certain persons or entities, service may be effected by first-class mail within Arizona by mailing summons and complaint along with two copies of notice and acknowledgment of receipt to defendant. Absent good cause, defendant must return notice and acknowledgment within 30 days or pay costs of personal service. (Civ. 4.1[c]).

Summons in action against state must be served upon attorney general. Service of county, municipal corporation or other governmental subdivision must be made by delivering copy of summons and pleading to chief executive officer, secretary, clerk or recording officer thereof. (Civ. 4.1[h]-[i]).

Summons in action against domestic or foreign corporation or upon partnership or other unincorporated association subject to suit in common name must be served

See note at head of Digest as to 1998 legislation covered.

See Topical Index in front part of this volume.

PROCESS . . . *continued*

upon officer, partner, managing or general agent or any other agent authorized by appointment or law to receive service and if statute authorizing agent to receive service so requires, by also mailing copy to defendant. (Civ. 4.1[k]).

Summons in action against partnership may be served on one partner and such service authorizes judgment against partnership and against partner actually served. (29-104[A]). Service on limited liability partnership's statutory agent is lawful personal service. (29-104[B]).

Summons in action against domestic corporations that have no agents within state upon whom service can be made may be served by delivering two copies of summons and complaint to Corporation Commission. (Civ. 4.1[l]).

Agent resident in Arizona must be appointed for each domestic and foreign corporation upon whom service of process against corporation may be made. (10-501, 10-1507).

Service on Nonresident Motorists.—See category Transportation, topic Motor Vehicles.

Service on Unknown Heirs.—By publication. (Civ. 4.1[o], 4.2[f]).

Service on Insurance Company.—Service on authorized foreign insurer, agent or broker shall be made on Director of Insurance. (20-221, 304). Service on resident insurer shall be made in manner applying to corporations generally or upon insurer's attorney-in-fact if reciprocal insurer. (20-221[B]). If resident insurer fails to maintain statutory agent, service shall be on Director of Insurance. (20-221[D]). Service on unauthorized insurer may be made on Secretary of State in action by Director (20-401.03), or on Director in action by any other person (20-403).

Summons, Alternative Methods of Service.—

(a) By Registered Mail.—Service when whereabouts of party outside state is known, may be made by mailing copy of summons and complaint in post office by any form of mail requiring signed and returned receipt, and by subsequently filing affidavit showing circumstances warranting service by mail, that copy of summons and complaint was dispatched to defendant, that it was received as evidenced by attached receipt, that receipt is genuine, and on what date receipt was returned to sender. Affidavit is prima facie evidence of personal service. Service is deemed complete on date of receipt by party being served. (Civ. 4.2[c]). Whenever party has right or is required to do act or initiate proceeding within prescribed period after service on him of notice or other paper (except notice of entry of judgment) and such papers are served by mail, five days are added to prescribed period. (Civ. 6[e]).

Service by mail may be made upon party within state by mailing copy of summons and complaint to party, together with two copies of notice and acknowledgment of receipt of summons and complaint and return envelope, postage prepaid, addressed to sender. Service is complete on date on which acknowledgment of receipt is executed. (Civ. 4.1[c]; 171 Ariz. 449, 831 P.2d 448).

(b) Direct Service.—Service out of state may also be made in same manner as provided in Civ. 4.1(b) by person authorized to serve process under law of state where such service is made. Service is complete when made. (Civ. 4.2[b]). Before default, must file affidavit of process showing why Civ. 4.2 service used, plus process server's affidavit. (Civ. 4.2[b]).

Service by Publication.—Where by law personal service is not required, and person is subject to service under Civ. 4.1 (see supra), such service may be made by either of methods set forth in Civ. 4.2 (see supra) or by publication. Service by publication is made by publication of summons in newspaper published in county where action is pending, and in newspaper published in county of last known address of person to be served, and if no newspaper is published in such county, then in newspaper published in adjoining county, at least once a week for four successive weeks. (Civ. 4.1[n]). Service is complete 30 days after first publication. (Civ. 4.1[n]). When residence of defendant is known, party must on or before date of first publication mail copy of summons and complaint, postage prepaid, directed to defendant at his place of abode. Plaintiff must file affidavit showing publication and mailing and circumstances warranting utilization of procedure under Civ. 4.1 which is prima facie evidence of compliance. If residence is unknown, affidavit must so state. (Civ. 4.1[n]).

When defendant's present address is unknown, but last known address was out of state, service may be had by publication of summons at least once a week for four successive weeks in newspaper published in county where action is pending. If no newspaper is published in such county, publications shall be made in newspaper published in adjoining county. Service is complete 30 days after first publication. (Civ. 4.2[f]).

Summons, Time Limit.—Court must dismiss without prejudice actions filed but not served within 120 days, unless plaintiff demonstrates good cause why service not made. (Civ. 4[i]).

Long-Arm Statute.—See subhead Summons, Alternative Methods of Service, supra, for Civ. 4.2(a).

Mandamus.—Relief previously obtained by writ of mandamus (12-2021 et seq.) must now be obtained by special action order. See topic Practice, subhead Special Actions.

PROHIBITION:

Relief previously obtained by writ of prohibition (common law) must now be obtained by special action order. See topic Practice, subhead Special Actions.

REPLEVIN:

Caveat: In response to constitutional attacks on Arizona's law of prejudgment remedies, state legislature in 1976 enacted 12-2401 et seq., "Provisional Remedies," consolidating and substantially amending prior law as to attachment, prejudgment garnishment and replevin. (Garnishment of wages is not provisional remedy.) See topic Practice, subhead Provisional Remedies before proceeding. Remainder of this entry deals only with provisions specifically applicable to replevin.

Affidavit.—If plaintiff claims possession of specific personal property in his complaint, he may at any time after compliance with provisional remedy requirements (12-2401 et seq.) and before judgment file affidavit showing: (1) That he is owner of property claimed (sufficiently describing it) or is entitled to possess it; (2) that it is wrongfully detained by defendant; (3) its actual value; and (4) that property has not been seized under any process, execution or attachment, or, if so seized, that it is exempt from such seizure (12-1301).

Order for Seizure.—After compliance with provisional remedy requirements (12-2401 et seq.) and upon filing of foregoing affidavit, judge or justice of peace must order sheriff or constable to take property specified and deliver it to plaintiff (12-1302).

Bond.—Officer to whom order is directed must not take property until plaintiff executes and delivers to him bond payable to defendant in amount not less than double value of property as alleged in affidavit, conditioned that plaintiff will prosecute his action to effect and without delay, that he will return property to defendant if such return is adjudged, and that in default of such return he will pay assessed value of property, all damages for taking and detaining it, and costs in action including reasonable attorneys' fees. (12-1303).

Seizure and Delivery of Property.—Officer must take property and deliver it to plaintiff, unless defendant within two days after seizure gives bond for same amount and containing same conditions as required of plaintiff. In such case, defendant remains in possession. (12-1304).

Claims of Third Persons.—Third-party claims to personal property are made by presenting written claim under oath to levying officer and posting bond equal to double value of property (12-1331), conditioned on claimant's return of property in good condition or payment of its value plus damages and costs if he fails to establish his claim (12-1332). Property must then be returned to claimant (12-1333), and claim and bond returned to proper court and docketed there for hearing on question of ownership (12-1335 et seq.).

Judgment.—If court finds that defendant is owner of property and is entitled to its possession, it must then find value of property together with any damage defendant may have suffered by wrongful seizure. In such case, where judgment must be made both for return of property and also against plaintiff and sureties on replevin bond for value of property, plus damages for its detention, costs of action and reasonable attorneys' fees, defendant must elect whether he will take return of property or money judgment. (12-1308). If judgment is for defendant and plaintiff is not in possession of property, judgment is limited to value of property, damages, costs and reasonable attorneys' fees. (12-1309).

If judgment is against defendant and he is in possession of property by reason of redelivery bond, judgment must be made both for return of property to plaintiff and also against defendant and sureties on his bond for value of property, damages for its detention and costs of action. Plaintiff must elect between return of property or money judgment. (12-1310).

SEQUESTRATION:

No statutory provision, but see topic Practice, subhead Provisional Remedies.

SERVICE:

See topic Process and category Transportation, topic Motor Vehicles, subheads Dealers, and Action against Nonresident.

STAY OF EXECUTION:

See topic Appeal and Error; category Debtor and Creditor, topic Executions.

SUBMISSION OF CONTROVERSY:

Uniform Certification of Questions of Law Act adopted. (12-1861 et seq.). Under Act, Arizona Supreme Court may answer questions of state law certified by U.S. Supreme Court, Circuit Courts of Appeal, and Federal District Court if it appears that questions of state law are determinative of cause and it appears to certifying court that there is no controlling Arizona precedent.

Material variations from Official Text are:

§1 (12-1861).—Alternative permitting certification by courts of another state not adopted.

§2 (12-1862).—Language expressly authorizing invocation of Act by motion of any party is omitted.

§§8-13.—Omitted.

VENUE:

Superior Court.—General rule is that venue in civil case is in county in which defendant resides, but numerous special rules apply as follows (12-401):

Action Against Nonresident.—In county in which plaintiff resides.

Action Against Married Person.—In county in which such person's spouse resides, or, if defendant and spouse are living separate and apart, in county in which defendant resides.

Action Against Transient Person.—In county where defendant is found.

Action for Debt.—In county where debt was contracted or where defendant resides; if debt was contracted outside state, wherever defendant is found.

Action on Written Contract to Perform Obligation in One County.—In such county or where defendant resides.

Action Against Several Defendants.—In county in which one or more of defendants reside.

Action Against Estate of Decedent.—In county of administration.

Action Against Public Officer.—In action for fraud, in county where fraud was committed or defendant resides or may be found; in all other cases, in county where defendant or any of defendants hold office.

Action for Damages for Trespass.—In county where trespass was committed or where defendant resides or may be found.

VENUE . . . *continued*

Action Concerning Personal Property.—In county where such property is located or wherever defendant may be found.

Action Concerning Real Property.—In county where any part of such property is situated.

Action Against Corporation.—In county where cause of action arose, where defendant has agent or representative, or where defendant has property or conducts business.

Action for Dissolution of Marriage or Legal Separation.—In county in which petitioner or petitioners reside at time petition is filed.

Action to Enjoin Court Proceedings.—In county where proceedings are pending or where judgment was rendered.

Action Against County.—In defendant's county or, if there are several defendants, in any defendant's county.

Action Against or on Behalf of State.—In county where seat of government located.

Surety Insurers.—Suable in any county where bond, etc., was made, or where insurer has its principal office. (20-1532).

Change of Venue.—Court may order on consent of parties or on usual grounds. (12-405). Where change in venue results from improper filing of original complaint, plaintiff must pay transmittal fee set forth in 12-284 within 20 days of transmittal order, and filing fee required by court to which action is transferred within 30 days, or face dismissal without prejudice. In all other cases, party requesting change of venue must pay transmittal fee set forth in 12-284 within 20 days after transmittal order. (12-407).

Justice Courts.—Rules governing venue in superior court apply also in justice courts, except: Word "precinct" must be substituted for word "county"; actions against estate are brought in precinct in which county seat is located; actions against persons who contract debts in one precinct and thereafter move to another precinct are brought in any precinct of county in which such person is found, at option of plaintiff; actions for collection of account or enforcement of contract are brought in precinct where account or contract was made or entered into, or where defendant lives, at option of plaintiff; and actions involving civil traffic violation are brought in any precinct in which violation is alleged to have occurred. (22-202).

Venue may be changed if suit is in wrong precinct. (22-204).

COURTS AND LEGISLATURE

COURTS:

United States District Court.—Clerk's office: 230 North First Avenue, Phoenix, Arizona 85025. Deputy clerk's office: 55 E. Broadway, Tucson, Arizona 85702. Entire state constitutes only one district, but court sits at Globe, Phoenix, Prescott and Tucson as cases are set in those communities. Causes may be transferred to any of above places at Court's discretion. Interlocutory orders may be made at any of above places.

Deposits and Fees.—$120 deposit on filing original action or on filing removal. Fees are payable in cash, check or post office money order only at time of rendering service.

Supreme Court.—Court consists of five justices. (12-101).

Jurisdiction.—Supreme court has original jurisdiction of writs and extraordinary orders, such as habeas corpus, quo warranto, injunction and mandamus (see category Civil Actions and Procedure, topic Practice, subhead Special Actions), directed to state officers; original and exclusive jurisdiction of causes arising between counties concerning boundaries or claims of one against another; appellate jurisdiction in all actions and proceedings except civil and criminal actions originating in courts not of record, unless validity of tax, impost, assessment, toll, statute or municipal ordinance is involved; power to issue writs and extraordinary orders, such as habeas corpus, injunction, review, certiorari, mandamus and prohibition (see category Civil Actions and Procedure, topic Practice, subhead Special Actions) necessary and proper to complete exercise of its appellate and revisory jurisdiction. Each justice of supreme court has power to issue writs of habeas corpus. (Const., Art. VI, §5). Court must make rules of pleading, practice and procedure for all state courts (12-109); procedure in civil matters is governed by rules which, with some exceptions, are same as Federal Rules of Civil Procedure. Court may answer questions of law certified to it by certain federal courts or tribal courts. (12-1861 et seq.).

Sittings.—At Phoenix.

Court of Appeals.—Court of appeals is divided into two divisions designated as Division 1 and Division 2. Division 1 consists of Maricopa, Yuma, La Paz, Mohave, Coconino, Yavapai, Navajo and Apache Counties and its 16 judges sit three each in Departments A, B, C, D and E and chief judge serves as their administrative supervisor. Division 2 consists of Pima, Pinal, Cochise, Santa Cruz, Greenlee, Graham and Gila Counties and its six judges sit three each in Departments A and B. Sessions may be held at places other than Phoenix or Tucson when in opinion of majority of judges of division or department justice so requires. (12-120 to 120.04).

Jurisdiction.—Court of appeals has appellate jurisdiction in all actions and proceedings originating in or permitted by law to be appealed from superior court, except criminal actions involving crimes for which sentence of death has been imposed; jurisdiction to issue writs of certiorari to review lawfulness of awards of Industrial Commission and to enter judgment affirming or setting aside awards; jurisdiction to issue writs and extraordinary orders, such as injunction, review, certiorari, mandamus and prohibition (see category Civil Actions and Procedure, topic Practice, subhead Special Actions) necessary and proper to complete exercise of its appellate jurisdiction. (12-120.21).

Sittings.—Division 1: at Phoenix. Division 2: at Tucson.

Superior Court.—Only one superior court for whole state, divided into county divisions. Superior court is nisi prius court.

Jurisdiction.—Superior court has original jurisdiction in all cases of equity and of cases at law which involve title to or possession of real property or legality of tax, impost, assessment, toll or municipal ordinance; in all other cases where demand or value of property in controversy amounts to $1,000 or more, exclusive of interest and costs; in actions of forcible entry and detainer; in proceedings in insolvency; of all matters probate; of divorce; in all cases of felonies; in all cases of misdemeanor not otherwise provided for by law; and in all other cases in which jurisdiction is not exclusively vested in other courts. Court has power to issue writs and extraordinary orders, such as habeas corpus, injunction, quo warranto, review, certiorari, mandamus and prohibition (see category Civil Actions and Procedure, topic Practice, subhead Special Actions). Court also has exclusive jurisdiction of juvenile matters, and appellate jurisdiction of appeals from justice courts in criminal cases and in civil cases. (Const., Art. VI, §§14-18).

Sittings.—

Apache County: at St. Johns.
Cochise County: at Bisbee.
Coconino County: at Flagstaff.
Gila County: at Globe.
Graham County: at Safford.
Greenlee County: at Clifton.
La Paz County: at Parker.
Maricopa County: at Phoenix.
Mohave County: at Kingman.
Navajo County: at Holbrook.
Pima County: at Tucson.
Pinal County: at Florence.
Santa Cruz County: at Nogales.
Yavapai County: at Prescott.
Yuma County: at Yuma.

Superior court ordinarily meets at county seat, but sessions may be held at places other than county seat when authorized by county supervisors or when in judge's opinion public interest so requires. (12-130). Trial jury must be drawn in each court in Jan. and July. (21-311).

Superior court may, by rule, provide that all claims in which amount in controversy does not exceed $50,000 must be submitted to arbitration. Court may waive arbitration requirement if good cause shown and parties stipulate in writing. Claims may also be referred to arbitration by agreement of reference signed by parties. (12-133).

Upon request of presiding judge of superior court in any county, chief justice of supreme court may appoint judge pro tempore of superior court of such county, subject to approval of board of supervisors. (12-141).

Arbitration and Mediation.—Court may use mediation and other alternative dispute resolution procedures to help resolve actions filed in court. (12-134, 2238).

Court Commissioners.—Court commissioners may be appointed in counties having three or more judges, with powers as prescribed by supreme court or statute. (12-213). Commissioners presently appointed in Maricopa and Pima Counties.

Court of Conciliation.—Courts of conciliation may be created by superior court for purpose of preserving, promoting and protecting family life, institution of matrimony and rights of children, and to provide means for reconciliation of spouses and amicable settlement of domestic and family controversies. (25-381.01).

Probate Courts.—Probate jurisdiction is exercised by superior court. (Const. Art. VI, §14).

Tax Court jurisdiction is exercised by superior court (12-161) over cases involving legality, imposition, assessment, or collection of tax (12-163). Principal office in Maricopa County, but hearings may be held in any county seat. (12-162). With few exceptions, Rules of Civil Procedure in superior court govern tax court proceedings. (12-166). Appeals must be filed within 30 days of judgment. (12-170). Decisions of public interest other than decisions relating to ad valorem property tax must be published and distributed in same manner as decisions by supreme court. (12-171). Taxpayer may sometimes elect to use small claims procedures. (12-172). Judgment in small claims case is conclusive. (12-174).

Justice Courts.—Counties are divided into justice precincts. Each precinct has justice of peace. Generally, justice courts have original jurisdiction of civil cases when amount involved, exclusive of interest, costs and attorneys' fees is $5,000 or less, and over certain misdemeanors. They do not have jurisdiction over causes in which title to or ownership of real property is in issue but can try right to possession of real property. Justice of peace may require arbitration or other dispute resolution methods. (22-201). Rules governing procedure and practice in superior court when applicable and when no other is specially prescribed govern procedure and practice in justice courts. (22-211).

Small Claims Courts.—Small claims division of justice court has jurisdiction concurrent with justice court, with certain exceptions, of civil matters less than $2,500, exclusive of interest and costs, and certain equitable remedies. (22-503). Fees are statutorily set. (22-281). Clerk sets hearing date within 60 days after filing of answer. (22-515). Hearing is before hearing officer without attorneys unless stipulated by both parties. No appeals allowed, findings of hearing officer are final and binding. (22-511 et seq.). See also subhead Justice Courts, supra.

Municipal Courts.—Every incorporated city or town must have municipal court. Municipal courts have jurisdiction of all cases arising under ordinances of city or town and concurrent jurisdiction with justices of peace in precincts where city or town is established over all limits of city or town. (22-402).

Military Courts.—In general, 26-1001 et seq. Jurisdiction over members of National Guard. (26-1002). Concurrent jurisdiction with other courts if other courts generally may try person or offense. (26-1021). Three types of courts-martial: General, special, summary. General consists of military judge and at least five members (or only one military judge if requested by accused). Powers include fine (not more than $200); forfeiture of pay and allowances; reprimand; dismissal or dishonorable discharge; demotion of noncommissioned officer. Pretrial procedure in 26-1030 et seq. Trial procedure in 26-1036 et seq. Punishable offense listed in 26-1077 et seq. Special consists of at least three members (or only one military judge if requested by accused); cannot impose fine above $100 or try commissioned officers. Summary consists of one commissioned officer; cannot impose fine above $25 or try officers and candidates. (26-1016 et seq.).

See note at head of Digest as to 1998 legislation covered.

See Topical Index in front part of this volume.

LEGISLATURE:

Annual Sessions.—Begin on second Mon. in Jan. Governor may call special session whenever advisable in his judgment. (Const., Art. IV, pt. 2, §3).

Initiative and Referendum.—Guaranteed by Const., Art. IV, pt. 1, §1.

Lobbyists.—Any person employed, retained or representing another person, with or without compensation, for purpose of attempting to influence passage or defeat of any legislation by communication or attempted communication with any legislator or for purpose of attempting by communication or attempted communication influencing of official actions of state officer or member of state agency, board, commission or council must be registered by principal with Secretary of State. (41-1232.01). Principal must periodically report certain lobbying expenditures. (41-1232.02). Lobbyists must disclose to legislators that they are lobbying. (41-1233.01).

REPORTS:

Cases.—Decisions of supreme court reported from 1866 to date in Arizona Reports. Decisions of court of appeals reported from 1965 to 1976 in Arizona Appeals Reports (Volumes 1-27). Beginning with Volume 114, Arizona Reports, decisions of supreme court and court of appeals combined in Arizona Reports. Decisions of both courts reported from 1866 to date in Pacific Reporter.

Digests.—Digest by Peter V. Ross covers Volumes 1-16 of Arizona Reports. Arizona Digest (West Publishing Company and Bancroft Whitney Company), with pocket supplements, covers all reports from 1866 to date.

STATUTES:

Arizona Revised Statutes (1956), cited A. R. S., contain all statutes in force through 1956 legislative session. This recodification replaces Arizona Code Annotated, 1939. Citations throughout this digest are to section numbers of A. R. S. or to rule numbers of Rules of Civil or Appellate Procedure, which are contained in separate volume. A. R. S. and Rules may be obtained from Arizona Secretary of State or from West Publishing Company.

Uniform Acts adopted are: Acknowledgments (1971) (33-511 et seq.); Anatomical Gift (1970) (36-841 et seq.); Arbitration (1962) (12-1501 et seq.; repealed eff. Jan. 1, 1996); †Certification of Questions of Law (1984) (12-1861 et seq.); Child Custody Jurisdiction (1978) (8-401 et seq.); †Commercial Code (1968) (47-1101 et seq.); Common Trust Fund (1971) (6-871 et seq.); †Condominium (1985) (33-1201 et seq.); †Conservation Easement (1985) (33-271 et seq.); †Contribution Among Tortfeasors (Revised) (1984) (12-2501 et seq.); Controlled Substances (1981) (36-2501 et seq.); Criminal Extradition (1978) (13-3841 et seq.); Declaratory Judgments (1927) (12-1831 et seq.); †Disclaimer of Property Interests (1994) (14-2801); Division of Income for Tax Purposes (1983) (43-1131 et seq.); †Durable Power of Attorney (1974) (14-5501 et seq.); Revised Enforcement of Foreign Judgments (1971) (12-1701 et seq.); †Evidence, Rules of (1977) (17A A.R.S.); Federal Lien Registration, (1990) (33-1031); Fiduciaries (1974) (14-7501 et seq.); Fraudulent Transfer (1990) (44-1001); †Guardianship and Protective Proceedings (1974) (14-5201 et seq.); Insurers Liquidation (1954) (20-611 et seq.); Interstate Family Support (1993) (25-621 et seq.); Limited Partnership, Revised (1982) (29-301 et seq.); Mandatory Disposition of Detainers (1973) (R. Crim. P. R. 8.3[b]); Marriage and Divorce (1973) (25-311 et seq.); Minor Student Capacity to Borrow (1971) (44-140 to 140.01); Motor Vehicle Safety Responsibility (1951) (28-1101 et seq.); †Nonprofit Corp. (1979) (10-2301 et seq.); ††Partnership (1954 and 1994) (29-201 et seq.); Premarital Agreement Act (1991) (25-201 et seq.); Revised Principal and Income Act (1984) (14-7401 et seq.); Probate Code (1973) (14-1102 et seq.); Recognition of Acknowledgments (1971) (33-501 et seq.); Residential Landlord and Tenant (1973) (33-1301 et seq.); Simultaneous Death (1993) (14-2702); Single Publication (1953) (12-651 et seq.); †State Administrative Procedure (1971) (41-1001 et seq.); State Antitrust (1974) (44-1401 et seq.); Statutory Rule Against Perpetuities (1994) (14-2901 et seq.); Testamentary Additions to Trust (1991) (14-2511); To Secure Attendance of Witnesses from Without a State in Criminal Proceedings (1937) (13-4091 et seq.); Trade Secrets (1990) (44-401 et seq.); Transfers to Minors (1988) (14-7651 et seq.); Trustees' Powers (1984) (14-7231 et seq.); Unclaimed Property Act (1983) (44-301 et seq.).

† Adopted with significant variations or modifications. See appropriate topics.

†† 1994 Act enacted with delayed repeal of 1954 Act. See category Business Organizations, topic Partnerships.

For text of Uniform Acts falling within the scope of the Martindale-Hubbell Law Digest, see Uniform and Model Acts section.

UNIFORM LAWS:

For list of Uniform Acts in force in Arizona, see topic Statutes. For text of Uniform Acts within scope of Martindale-Hubbell Law Digests, see Uniform and Model Acts section.

CRIMINAL LAW

BAIL:

See topic Criminal Law.

CRIMINAL LAW:

Crimes and affirmative defenses are statutory only. (13-103). Criminal offenses primarily governed by 13-101 et seq. Criminal procedure governed by Rules of Criminal Procedure (17 A.R.S.) and by 13-3841 to 4315.

Indictment or Information.—See Rules of Criminal Procedure, 17 A.R.S. State grand jury created by 21-421.

Bail.—Crimes punishable by death not bailable where proof of guilt is evident or presumption thereof is great. (13-3961[A]). Convicted felon, sentenced to imprisonment, cannot be bailed unless court determines that continued confinement would endanger his life. (13-3961.01). Felonies are not bailable where there is clear and convincing evidence that person charged poses substantial danger to another person or community. (13-3961[B]). Defendant charged with offenses bailable as matter of right must be released on recognizance before conviction unless otherwise determined, in which case least onerous conditions to reasonably insure appearance may be imposed. (R. Crim. P. 7.2[a]). Bail after conviction limited (R. Crim. P. 7.2[b]) and burden of proof on defendant (R. Crim. P. 7.2[c]).

Exclusionary Rule.—Trial court shall not suppress evidence which is otherwise admissible in criminal proceeding if court determines that evidence was seized by peace officer as result of good faith mistake or technical violation. This rule does not apply to unlawful electronic eavesdropping or wiretapping. (13-3925).

Guilty Except Insane Defense.—Defendant must prove his insanity by clear and convincing evidence. (13-502[B]).

Rules of Criminal Procedure.—Contain provisions covering preliminary proceedings (R. Crim. P. 2-5); rights of parties (R. Crim. P. 6-11); pretrial procedures (R. Crim. P. 12-16); pleas of guilty and no contest (R. Crim. P. 17); trial (R. Crim. P. 18-23); post-verdict proceedings (R. Crim. P. 24-29); appeal and other post-conviction relief (R. Crim. P. 30-32); powers of court (R. Crim. P. 33-38).

Interstate Compact for Supervision of Parolees and Probationers adopted. (31-461 et seq.).

Uniform Criminal Extradition Act 1926 version, adopted. (13-3841 et seq.). Individuals arrested in Arizona for crime committed in another state can waive extradition proceedings. (13-3865.01[A]). Governor's warrant not required if prisoner previously waived extradition as term of prior release and proper identification of prisoner has been made. (13-3865.01[C]).

Uniform Controlled Substances Act adopted. (36-2501 et seq.).

Uniform Act to Secure the Attendance of Witnesses From Without a State in Criminal Proceedings adopted. (13-4091 et seq.).

Victims' Rights Implementation Act adopted. (13-4401 et seq.). Registered neighborhood association may invoke victim's rights. (13-4401.01). Victim has right to conference with prosecuting attorney. (13-4419). Court shall minimize contact between victim and defendant and victim and defendant's family through appropriate safeguards. (13-4431). Victim has right to withhold his phone number, address, and other locating information from defendant and public unless compelling need for information exists. (13-4434).

DEBTOR AND CREDITOR

ASSIGNMENTS:

In general, rights, debts and choses in action are assignable in accordance with common law rules.

Maintenance of Action.—Action may be maintained in name of assignee (Civ. 17[a]; 103 Ariz. 435, 443 P.2d 690), but assignment of chose in action cannot prejudice right to setoff or defense, except as to holder in due course (44-144). Holder or assignee of negotiable instrument other than check or draft evidencing consumer obligations may be subject to defenses and setoffs arising from sale or lease if written notice given to seller or lessor by certified mail within 90 days. (44-145).

Creation of Security Interest.—Any assignment, pledge or other transaction, irrespective of form, intended to create security interest in personal property or fixtures including goods, documents, instruments, general intangibles, chattel paper or accounts is governed by Art. 9 of Commercial Code. (47-9101 et seq.). See category Business Regulation and Commerce, topic Commercial Code.

Assignment of Wages.—If person obligated to pay child support or spousal maintenance is in arrears, for amount equal to at least one month's payment, court shall order assignment of portion of person's earnings. Order shall direct holder of monies to withhold and pay to person or agency entitled to receive monies. (25-323, 25-504).

Assignment of Mortgages.—Must be recorded to protect holder of assignment against subsequent purchasers and mortgagees without notice. (11-461 to 462, 33-411; 45 Ariz. 1, 40 P.2d 81).

Uniform Commercial Code adopted. See category Business Regulation and Commerce, topic Commercial Code.

ATTACHMENT:

Caveat: In response to constitutional attacks on Arizona's law of prejudgment remedies, State Legislature in 1976 adopted 12-2401 et seq., "Provisional Remedies," consolidating and substantially amending prior law as to attachment, prejudgment garnishment and replevin. (Garnishment of wages is not provisional remedy.) See category Civil Actions and Procedure, topic Practice, subhead Provisional Remedies before proceeding. Remainder of this entry deals only with provisions specifically applicable to attachment.

When Writ May Issue.—Plaintiff, after compliance with provisional remedy requirements (12-2401 et seq.), may attach defendant's property, unless defendant gives security to pay judgment, in following cases: (1) In action on contract, express or implied, for payment of money when payment is not fully secured by real or personal property, or, if originally so secured, when value of such security has, without any act of plaintiff or person to whom security was given, substantially diminished below balance owed; (2) when suit is pending for damages and defendant is about to dispose of or remove his property beyond jurisdiction of court in which action is pending; (3) in action for damages or on contract, express or implied, against nonresident defendant or foreign corporation doing business in state; (4) in action on judgment of any state; (5) when plaintiff has received bulk sale notice dealing with defendant's property and such bulk sale does not provide for full payment of plaintiff's debt. (12-1521).

See also subhead Debt Not Due, infra.

ATTACHMENT . . . *continued*

After compliance with provisional remedy requirements, clerk of Superior Court or justice of peace must issue writ of attachment upon receiving from plaintiff affidavit showing that one or more of requirements for writ set forth in 12-1521 have been met. (12-1522).

Debt Not Due.—After entry of order pursuant to provisional remedy requirements, attachment may issue on debt or demand not yet due (although final judgment may not be entered until such debt or demand becomes due) on filing of plaintiff's affidavit showing: (1) That defendant is indebted to plaintiff on contract, express or implied, for direct payment of money, stating amount and that debt is not due; (2) that such contract was made or is payable in Arizona; (3) that payment has not been secured by mortgage, pledge or lien; (4) character of debt; (5) that there are no legal set offs or counterclaims against debt; (6) that defendant is about to remove permanently from Arizona and has refused to secure debt, or that defendant has secreted property for purpose of defrauding creditors, or that defendant is about to remove property from state without leaving sufficient property to pay debts, or that defendant has disposed of property wholly or in part with intent to defraud creditors, or that defendant is about to dispose of property with intent to defraud creditors, (7) that plaintiff has received from defendant bulk sale notice dealing with defendant's property and that such bulk sale does not provide for full payment of plaintiff's debt; and (8) that attachment is not for purpose of injuring or harassing defendant and that plaintiff will probably lose debt unless attachment is issued. (12-1523).

Facts set forth in foregoing affidavit may be denied by defendant, and issue so formed must be tried as are other questions of fact. (12-1523[D]).

If judgment is for defendant, court must include in judgment reasonable attorney's fees and enter judgment for such fees against sureties on attachment bond. (12-1523[E]).

Bond.—Plaintiff must give bond in not less than amount of debt sued for, conditioned that he will prosecute his writ to effect and will pay all damages and costs adjudged against him for wrongfully seeking such attachment. (12-1524).

Number of Writs.—One or more writs may issue at same time and to different counties. (12-1528).

Quashing Writ.—Attachment issued without affidavit and bond must be quashed on motion of defendant, but affidavit and bond are not void for want of form if they contain all essential matters. (12-1525).

Indemnity.—Officer levies at own risk but may require indemnity bond. (12-1529).

Levy is made in same manner as writ of execution. Levy on real property is made by filing copy of writ with description of property with county recorder in whose county real property is situated and serving defendant or, failing that, posting property. Levy on personal property is made by seizure when practical. (12-1530).

Lien.—Attachment constitutes lien on property from date of levy. (12-1532).

Return.—Writs are returnable at any time within 30 days after levy. (12-1531).

Sale.—Perishable personal property may be sold prior to final judgment on order of court issuing writ. (12-1533).

Release of Property.—At any time before judgment, defendant may replevy attached property by giving bond in double amount of plaintiff's debt or, at defendant's option, for value of property, conditioned that defendant will satisfy any judgment which may be rendered in action or will pay value of property. (12-1536).

Claims of Third Persons.—Third-party claim to personal property is made by presenting written claim under oath to levying officer and posting bond equal to double value of property (12-1331), conditioned on claimant's return of property in good condition or its value plus damages and costs if he fails to establish his claim (12-1332). Property must then be returned to claimant (12-1333), and claim and bond returned to proper court and docketed there for hearing of question of ownership (12-1335 et seq.).

CREDITORS' SUITS:

No statutory provision.

EXECUTIONS:

Arizona Rules of Civil Procedure are based on Federal Rules of Civil Procedure. See category Civil Actions and Procedure, topic Practice.

Executions are either general or special. (12-1552 et seq.).

Exemptions.—See topic Exemptions.

Time for Issuance.—Writs of execution may be issued at any time within five years after entry or renewal of judgment, and are executed by sheriff or constable. No execution shall issue after death of judgment debtor unless it is for recovery of real or personal property or enforcement of lien thereon. This limitation does not apply to judgments and orders for support of minor or for those children whose support is extended beyond age of emancipation pursuant to 25-501(A) or 25-320(B). (12-1551).

Time for Return.—Executions are returnable in not less than ten nor more than 90 days in superior court (12-1555) and in 60 days in justice courts (22-244).

Stay of Execution.—Court may stay execution pending disposition of motion for new trial or to amend judgment, for relief from judgment or order, for judgment in accordance with motion for directed verdict, for amendment of findings or for additional findings. (Civ. 62[b]). No injunction to stay execution may be granted after one year from rendition of judgment unless application was delayed by fraud or false promises of prevailing party at time or after rendition, except for equitable matter or defense arising after rendition. Injunction may be granted within two years of judgment if applicant was absent from state when judgment was rendered. (12-1806).

Levy.—To levy on real estate, officer must endorse levy on writ and record copy of same with county recorder. On livestock running at large that cannot be herded or penned without great inconvenience, levy is made by designating number and describing marks and brands in presence of two witnesses, serving notice on owner or agent and recording copy of writ; on outstanding corporate shares of stock, by seizing stock as provided in 47-8112; on partnership interest, by notice to one or more partners or to clerk of partnership; on personalty, by taking possession or by giving notice to person entitled to possession if other than defendant; on personalty not removable due to bulk or other cause, by recordation of certified copy of execution and return of levy with county recorder in county where located within three days after levy. (12-1559).

Sale of Personalty.—Notice of sale under execution of perishable personal property must be given by posting written notices of time and place of sale in three public places, two in precinct and one at door of courthouse of county in which sale is to take place, for reasonable period of time. In case of other personal property, similar notice of place and time of sale must be posted for not less than ten days successively before sale day. (12-1621.) Sale must be by public auction. (12-1622).

Claims of Third Persons.—Third-party claim to personal property is made by presenting written claim under oath to levying officer and posting bond equal to double value of property (12-1331), conditioned on claimant's return of property in good condition or its value plus damages and costs if he fails to establish his claim (12-1332). Property must then be returned to claimant (12-1333) and claim and bond returned to proper court and docketed there for trial on question of ownership (12-1335 et seq.).

Sale of Realty.—Notice of sale must be posted for 15 days successively before sale day in three public places in county, including courthouse door, and copy thereof published in newspaper published within county, for three weeks before day of sale. Real property must be sold at courthouse door of county in which property is situated. (12-1621). Sale must be made at public auction to highest bidder, between 10 a.m. and 4 p.m. (12-1622).

Redemption.—Real property may be redeemed by judgment debtor from execution or judicial sale, including foreclosure of mortgage, or other lien where estate is greater than leasehold for two years (12-1626), within six months from time of sale, except when property was adjudged to be both abandoned and not used primarily for agricultural or grazing purposes, in which case it may be redeemed within 30 days after date of sale. If no such redemption is made by judgment debtor, senior creditor having lien upon premises subsequent to judgment under which sale was made may redeem within five days after expiration of applicable redemption period for judgment debtor, and each subsequent lienholder, in succession, according to priority of liens, may redeem within five days after time allowed to prior lienholder (12-1282); provided, however, that to entitle subsequent lienholder to redeem he must, within applicable redemption period, file with county recorder and serve on sheriff of county where sale is made written statement of his intention to redeem (12-1284). Deeds are issued at time of expiration of period for redemption. (12-1286).

Supplementary Proceedings.—After judgment has been entered and docketed, judgment creditor may conduct examination concerning judgment debtor's property by hearing or deposition. After execution has issued, the creditor, on affidavit that judgment debtor is withholding property from satisfaction of the judgment, may have the debtor brought into court, or any person indebted to or having property of the debtor in excess of $50, and upon hearing the court may order any property of the debtor, not exempt by law, to be applied to satisfaction of the judgment; and if any person denies a debt due to the debtor or claims interest in property adverse to debtor, court may order suit instituted against him. (12-1631 et seq.). Property of debtor in possession of third party cannot be seized without notice to debtor. (636 F.Supp. 168).

EXEMPTIONS:

Statute enumerates large number of articles of personal property, in some instances limited as to value, which may be held exempt from attachment, execution, garnishment, replevin, sale or any final process issued by court. (33-1121 et seq.). If married, each spouse entitled to exemptions. Such exemptions may be combined with that of other spouse in same property or taken in different exempt property. (33-1121.01). Note that property enumerated is not exempt from process utilized to enforce security interest in or pledge of such property, or to obtain possession of leased property. (33-1122). Arizona residents not entitled to federal exemptions provided by federal Bankruptcy Code. (33-1133).

Specified household furniture, furnishings and appliances personally used by debtor, up to aggregate fair market value of $4,000, are exempt. (33-1123).

Food, fuel and provisions actually provided for debtor's individual or family use for six months are exempt. (33-1124).

Personal items (wearing apparel, etc.) used primarily for personal, family or household purposes are exempt up to specified amounts. (33-1125).

Money benefits or proceeds defined and exempted by statute include: Money received by or payable to surviving spouse or child upon life of deceased spouse, parent or legal guardian, not exceeding $20,000; earnings of minor child of debtor, except as against liability created for special benefit of that child; money received by or payable to person entitled to receive child support or spousal maintenance pursuant to court order; proceeds from health, accident or disability insurance policy, except for premiums payable for debt of insured secured by pledge or collection of obligation for which insured or beneficiary has been paid under plan or policy and except for payment of amounts ordered for support of person from proceeds and benefits furnished in lieu of earnings which would have been subject to such order and subject to any exemption applicable to earnings so replaced; money arising from claim of damage to exempt property; cash surrender value of insurance policies on specified persons, not to exceed $25,000 in aggregate; claims for damages arising from wrongful taking or detention of exempt property; $150 in single account in any one financial institution; and assets payable from or any interest in retirement plan qualified under Internal Revenue Code, except for amounts contributed within 120 days before bankruptcy filing. Arizona resident age 18 or over who does not claim homestead exemption may claim prepaid rent, including security deposits, for claimant's residence, not exceeding lesser of $1,000 or $1^1/_2$ months' rent, as personal property homestead exempt from all process. (33-1126).

Tools, equipment, instruments and books of debtor or debtor's spouse primarily used in, and necessary to carry on, commercial activity, trade, business or profession of

EXEMPTIONS . . . *continued*
debtor or debtor's spouse, not in excess of $2,500 are exempt. Machinery, utensils, feed, seed, grain and animals not in excess of $2,500 belonging to debtor whose primary income is derived from farming are exempt. (33-1130).

Disposable earnings of debtor (wages, salary or compensation minus withholding) are not subject to process beyond lesser of 25% of disposable earnings for each week or amount by which disposable earnings for that week exceed 30 times federal minimum hourly wage. Where court has ordered support of any person by debtor, only 50% of debtor's disposable earnings for any pay period are exempt. Such exemptions do not apply in case of order of bankruptcy court under c. 13 or debt due for any state or federal tax. (33-1131).

Waiver of exemption rights is void and unenforceable except as provided in 33-1122 (process utilized to enforce security interest or to obtain possession of leased property) and when done with notice. (33-1132).

Estates at will or by sufferance are chattel interests not liable as such to sale on execution. (33-202).

Homestead exemptions are discussed in topic Homesteads.

FORECLOSURE:

See category Mortgages, topic Mortgages of Real Property.

FRAUDULENT SALES AND CONVEYANCES:

Uniform Fraudulent Transfer Act adopted with minor variations. (44-1001 et seq.).

Goods or Chattels.—Sale or assignment of goods or chattels in transferor's possession not accompanied by immediate change of possession is prima facie evidence of fraud. (44-1061).

Bulk Sales.—Uniform Commercial Code adopted with certain material variations. (47-6101 et seq.). See category Business Regulation and Commerce, topic Commercial Code.

Securities.—See category Business Regulation and Commerce, topic Securities.

See also category Business Regulation and Commerce, topic Consumer Protection.

GARNISHMENT:

Caveat: See category Civil Actions and Procedure, topic Practice, subhead Provisional Remedies, regarding prejudgment garnishment. (Garnishment of wages is not provisional remedy.)

In response to constitutional attack on Arizona's post-judgment garnishment proceedings (606 F. Supp. 1453), state legislature in 1986 substantially amended prior law as to garnishment (12-1570 et seq.). Garnishment of monies or property governed by 12-1570 et seq. Garnishment of earnings governed by 12-1598 et seq.

Property Which May Be Reached.—(1) Indebtedness owed to judgment debtor by garnishee for monies which are earnings. (Earnings become monies other than earnings on their disbursement by employer to or for account of employee, except disbursements into pension or retirement fund.) (12-1598.01); (2) indebtedness owed to judgment debtor by garnishee for monies which are not earnings; (3) monies held by garnishee on behalf of judgment debtor; (4) judgment debtor's personal property that is in garnishee's possession; and (5) judgment debtor's shares and securities of garnishee corporation (12-1570.01).

Jurisdiction.—Writs of garnishment issued by justice court or superior court. (12-1571, 1598.02).

Proceedings to Obtain.—Judgment creditor must file application (and bond in case of monies that are not earnings if no judgment has been entered) to obtain writ of garnishment and summons. (12-1572 et seq., 1598.03 et seq.).

Answer of Garnishee.—

Monies or Property.—Answer of garnishee to writ of garnishment must be under oath, signed, and state: (1) Whether garnishee was indebted to or otherwise in possession of monies of judgment debtor when writ served and amount of any such indebtedness or monies; (2) amount of indebtedness or monies withheld and not withheld by garnishee pursuant to writ, and reason for not withholding; (3) whether garnishee held judgment debtor's personal property when writ was served and description of any such property; (4) list of personal property withheld by garnishee pursuant to writ; (5) what other person or entity garnishee knows to be indebted to judgment debtor or in possession of judgment debtor's personal property; (6) if garnishee is corporation in which judgment debtor owns stock or other interest, description of such stock or interest; (7) name, address and telephone number of garnishee; and (8) date and manner of delivery of copy of writ, notice and answer to judgment debtor and copy of answer to judgment creditor. (12-1579).

Earnings.—Answer of garnishee to writ of garnishment must be under oath, signed, and state: (1) Whether judgment debtor was employed by garnishee when writ was served; (2) whether garnishee anticipates owing earnings within 60 days after service; (3) if garnishee is unable to determine judgment debtor's identity after good faith effort, statement of effort made and reasons for such inability; (4) dates of next two paydays after service; (5) judgment debtor's pay period (weekly, etc.); (6) amount of judgment due and owing as stated in writ; (7) whether judgment debtor is subject to existing wage assignment, garnishment or levy, and if so, name, address, and telephone number of that judgment creditor; (8) name, address and telephone number of garnishee; and (9) date and manner of delivery of copy of notice and request for hearing form and answer to judgment debtor and copy of answer to judgment creditor. (12-1598.08).

Practice.—

Monies or Property.—Judgment creditor must serve on garnishee two copies of summons and writ of garnishment, one copy of judgment, four copies of answer form, two copies of notice to judgment debtor and request for hearing form and one copy of instructions. Within three days, excluding weekends and holidays, garnishee must deliver to judgment debtor copy of summons, writ of garnishment, judgment, notice to judgment debtor and request for hearing form. (12-1574).

Special procedure must be followed where writ is to be served upon branch of financial institution (banking corporation or association, savings bank, savings and loan association, credit union, trust company or title insurance company). (12-1577).

Garnishee must answer writ within ten days. (12-1578.01). Judgment creditor and debtor have ten days after receipt of answer to file objection to writ or answer. Hearing on objection must be held within five days of request, excluding weekends and holidays. (12-1580).

Garnishee is discharged if his answer shows that he did not owe nonexempt monies to judgment debtor or possess any of judgment debtor's nonexempt personal property when writ was served on him and no written objection to his answer has been timely filed. (12-1581).

Earnings.—Judgment creditor must serve on garnishee two copies of summons and writ of garnishment, one copy of judgment, four copies of answer form, two copies of notice to judgment debtor and request for hearing form and instructions, and four copies of nonexempt earnings statement. (12-1598.04).

Writ of garnishment is lien on earnings until: (1) Order of continuing lien is entered; (2) no order is entered for 45 days after answer filed; or (3) writ is quashed, released or becomes ineffective. (12-1598.05).

Garnishee must answer writ within ten days. (12-1598.06). Objection to writ, answer or nonexempt earnings statement must be filed within ten days after receipt of answer or nonexempt earnings statement. Hearing on objection must be held within ten days of request. (12-1598.07).

Garnishee is discharged if his answer shows that he did not employ judgment debtor when writ was served, would not owe earnings to judgment debtor within 60 days after service of writ, or was unable after good faith effort to determine identity of judgment debtor. (12-1598.09).

Judgment.—

Monies or Property.—If no objection to writ or answer is timely filed, on application by judgment creditor, court must enter judgment against garnishee for nonexempt monies of judgment debtor owed or held at time of service of writ or court must enter order against garnishee to hold nonexempt personal property of judgment debtor held at time of service of writ pending writ of special execution. If objection is filed, court must hold hearing before entering judgment or order. (12-1584 to 1585). Order expires if no writ of special execution is served on garnishee within 90 days after entry of order. (12-1585).

If no judgment or order is entered against garnishee within 90 days after filing of answer, garnishee is discharged on writ unless objection filed. Discharge does not apply to monies or property held for trustee in bankruptcy or under provisional remedies. (12-1587).

Earnings.—If no objection to writ or answer is timely filed, on application by judgment creditor, court must order that nonexempt earnings withheld by garnishee after service of writ be transferred to judgment creditor and court must order continuing lien against nonexempt earnings. If objection is filed, court must hold hearing before entering orders. (12-1598.10). If court determines that: (1) Writ is valid against judgment debtor, and (2) debt was not, at time of service of writ, subject to effective agreement between judgment debtor and qualified consumer credit counseling service, and (3) garnishee employed judgment debtor when writ was served or garnishee owned or would owe earnings to judgment debtor within 60 days after service of writ, then court shall order transfer of nonexempt earnings withheld by garnishee to judgment creditor and continuing lien against nonexempt earnings of judgment debtor; otherwise, court shall order garnishee discharged from writ. (12-1598.10[B] to [C]). While order of continuing lien is in effect, garnishee must withhold judgment debtor's nonexempt earnings (12-1598.11) and judgment creditor must follow reporting requirements (12-1598.12). Court, sitting without jury, may reduce amount of nonexempt earnings in order to avoid economic hardship by judgment debtor. (12-1584, 12-1598.10[F]).

Exemptions.—See topic Exemptions.

Forms.—Justice court and superior court provide forms at no charge. (12-1596, 1598.16).

Sanctions.—If party willfully or with gross negligence fails to comply with certain duties imposed by garnishment law, court must award injured party his actual losses, attorney fees, costs and an additional amount. (12-1593, 1598.13).

See also topic Homesteads.

HOMESTEADS:

Any person age 18 or over who resides in Arizona may hold as homestead exempt from attachment, execution and forced sale any one of following not exceeding $100,000 in value: (1) interest in real property in one compact body upon which exists dwelling in which claimant resides; (2) interest in one condominium or cooperative in which claimant resides; (3) mobile home in which claimant resides; and (4) mobile home in which claimant resides plus land upon which mobile home is located at time of filing. Only one homestead may be claimed by married couple or single person. (33-1101).

Debts or Liabilities Against Which Exemption Not Available.—Consensual lien, including mortgage, deed of trust or contract of conveyance; lien for labor or materials claimed pursuant to 33-981. (33-1103[A]).

Claim and Designation of Homestead.—Person entitled homestead exemption holds exemption by operation of law and no written claim or recording required. If person has more than one property interest to which homestead exemption applies, creditor may require person to designate which property is protected by homestead exemption. (33-1102). Homestead is exempt from process and from sale under judgment or lien. (33-1103[A]).

Loss of Exemption.—Abandonment of homestead occurs only by declaration or waiver, by grant thereof, or by permanent removal of claimant from residence or Arizona. Claimant may remove from homestead for two years without abandonment or waiver. Declaration of abandonment, waiver or grant shall be executed by claimant and acknowledged. Such declaration is effective only from time of recording in county where homestead is located. (33-1104).

See note at head of Digest as to 1998 legislation covered.

See Topical Index in front part of this volume.

HOMESTEADS . . . *continued*

Proceeds of Sale.—Judgment creditor, other than mortgagee or beneficiary under trust deed, may elect judicial sale of property in which debtor claims homestead under 33-1101(A), if its interest in property exceeds sum of judgment debtor's homestead plus amount of any consensual liens on property sharing priority to judgment. Officer in charge of sale may not accept bid which does not exceed amount of homestead exemption plus consensual liens on property plus costs of sale. Proceeds are distributed as follows: (1) Debtor in amount of homestead; (2) priority holders of consensual liens; (3) costs of sale; and (4) judgment creditor in satisfaction of lien. (33-1105). If homestead recorded before date of voluntary or involuntary sale of property, homestead exemption not exceeding $100,000 automatically attaches to claimant's interest in identifiable cash proceeds from sale. Such exemption continues for 18 months after date of sale or until claimant files new claim of homestead, whichever period is shorter. (33-1101[C]).

Uniform Probate Code (but not 1977 or later amendments) adopted and was substantially amended in 1994. (14-1101 et seq.).

JUDGMENT NOTES:

See category Civil Actions and Procedure, topic Judgments, subhead Judgment by Confession.

LEVY:

See topics Attachment, Executions.

LIENS:

Uniform Commercial Code adopted (with minor changes). (47-1101 et seq.). See category Business Regulation and Commerce, topic Commercial Code.

Personal Property Liens.—Carpenter, mechanic, artisan or other workman has lien for labor or materials on articles, implements, utensils, or vehicles (except motor vehicles) and may retain same until fully paid. (33-1021). Drycleaner or launderer has lien for labor on garment, wearing apparel or other article and may retain same until fully paid or may foreclose on same after 90 days if certain notice conditions are met. (33-1021.01). Persons who fabricate products from equipment or material furnished by customer have lien on equipment and material in their possession until fully paid. (33-1022.01). Proprietors of garages and repair and service stations have liens on motor vehicles and aircraft and parts and accessories thereon for agreed amount of charges for labor, materials, supplies and storage, but lien may not impair other liens or conditional sale contracts of record. (33-1022). Except as provided in 33-1021.01, property held for 20 days pursuant to above liens may be sold at auction after notice specified in 33-1023. Hotel, inn, boarding house, lodging house, apartment house and auto camp keepers have lien on guests' baggage and other property for accommodation and things furnished at request of guests, and property so liened may be advertised for sale after charges have remained unpaid for four months and sold after four weeks from time of first advertisement. (33-951 to 952). Self-service storage facility has lien, for rent due and unpaid, on all stored personal property. (33-1703).

Farm Services Liens.—Person who labors, or who furnishes labor, machinery or equipment related to planting crops has lien on crops. (33-901 et seq.). Person who furnishes pasture or feed on his premises has lien on stock. (3-1295).

Health Care Lien.—Health care provider has lien, for care and treatment or transportation rendered, on claims for damages accruing to person treated. (33-931 et seq.). Release of claims on which lien is based is invalid unless lienholder joins therein. (33-934). Lien must be recorded in county of injury within 30 days after patient has received services relating to injury, except that hospital may record within 30 days of patient's discharge. (33-932). Lienholder may enforce lien against party liable for damages where there has been judgment or settlement with such person. (33-934).

Mechanics' and Materialmen's Liens.—

Who May Acquire.—Person who labors or furnishes professional services, materials, machinery, fixtures or tools to be used in construction, alteration, or repair of any building or improvement has lien on such building or improvement whether same was done or articles furnished at instance of owner or his agent. Person required to be licensed as contractor who does not hold valid license or person furnishing professional services without valid certificate of registration does not have lien rights. Person furnishing professional services can enforce lien only if he has agreement with owner of property or with architect, engineer or contractor who has agreement with owner. Contractor, subcontractor, architect, builder, or other person having charge or control of work, either fully or in part, is agent of owner, and owner is liable for reasonable value of labor, materials or professional services furnished at instance of such agent. (33-981). Owner may avoid lien provisions pertaining to agents by requiring person with whom he contracts to furnish payment bond equal to full amount of contract between them. Bond and contract containing legal description of land on which work is to be done must be recorded in office of county recorder. (33-1003[A]). Liens also arise when labor or materials are furnished to factories or mills (33-984), to domestic vessels (33-985), to cut or load wood, logs or ties (33-986), to railroads (33-988), in construction or repair of waterways, highways or excavations or improvement of private lands (33-987) or for improvements to city lots (33-983). Miners and others who furnish labor or materials for use in mines or on mining claims under contract with owners, lessees, purchasers or optionees have priority lien on same for unpaid amounts. (33-989). If mine is operated by lessee, owner may avoid lien by posting and recording "no lien" notice. (33-990).

Preliminary 20-Day Notice.—Except for person laboring for wages, every person wishing to preserve right to claim lien must file notice with owner, original contractor and construction lender within 20 days of first furnishing labor, materials or professional services. (33-992.01). *Caveat:* Licensed subcontractors whose contracts require that they furnish labor or professional services on site and incidental materials and equipment need not give preliminary 20-day notice. (141 Ariz. 381, 687 P.2d 389). Notice must describe what was furnished, contain names of person contracting for and person furnishing labor, materials or professional services, description of jobsite sufficient for identification, and advise owner of procedure to protect against filing of lien. (33-992.01[C]). Within ten days after receipt of written request from person intending to file notice, owner must provide such person with description of job site, name and address of owner, name and address of original contractor, and name and address of construction lender. (33-992.01[I]). If information in notice is inaccurate, claimant must serve amended notice within 30 days. (33-992.01[J]). Additional notices related to same building, structure, or improvement not required unless different contract is involved or actual price exceeds estimated price by 20% or more. (33-992.01[G]). Notice may be served by first class, registered or certified mail. (33-992.01[F]). Proof of service required. (33-992.02).

Extent of Lien.—Lien extends to lot or lots on which building is situated; if situated outside of town, city, subdivision or townsite, to not more than ten acres of land; and if on mining claims, to entire group. (33-991). Person who furnishes professional services or material or labors on lot in incorporated city or town or any parcel of land not exceeding 160 acres in aggregate, or fills in or otherwise improves lot or such parcel of land, or street, alley or proposed street or alley, within, in front of or adjoining lot or parcel of land, at instance of owner of lot or parcel of land, has lien on lot or parcel of contiguous land not exceeding 160 acres in aggregate and buildings, structures and improvements on lot for professional services or materials furnished and labor performed. (33-983).

Owner-Occupant Dwelling.—No lien is allowed against dwelling of owner-occupant except by person having executed contract directly with owner-occupant. (33-1002).

Preference.—Liens generally preferred over subsequent encumbrances and are on equal footing with each other. Lien for professional services does not attach for priority purposes until labor has begun or materials have been furnished. (33-992, 1000 to 1001).

Notice and Claim of Lien.—Notice must contain: Legal description of land and improvements; names of owners or reputed owners of property; name of person by whom lienor was employed or to whom he furnished materials; terms of contract, if oral, and copy of contract, if in writing; lienor's demand after deducting credits and offsets; date of completion of work; and date of service of preliminary 20-day notice and copy and proof of service thereof. Notice must be under oath. (33-993[A]).

Perfection of Lien.—Person securing lien, within 20 days after completion, alteration or repair of building, structure or improvement, or if notice of completion has been recorded, within 60 days must make duplicate copies of notice and claim of lien, record one copy with county recorder and, within reasonable time thereafter, serve remaining copy on owner, if found in county. (33-993[A]).

Limitation of Lien.—Suit to enforce lien must be brought within six months from time lien is recorded in recorder's office. In action to enforce lien, court may award successful party attorney fees. (33-998). Must file notice of pendency of action pursuant to 12-1191 in county where property is located.

Release of Lien.—Within 20 days of satisfaction or of request by owner-occupant where lien prohibited, lienholder must issue release to person against whom lien was claimed. Failure to grant release subjects lienholder to statutory penalty. (33-1006).

Tax Liens.—Uniform Federal Lien Registration Act adopted. (33-1031 et seq.).

Restitution Lien.—State has lien for amount of restitution, fine and other costs owed by convicted criminal. (13-804[J]). Lien covers real, personal, and other property. Lien must be filed to be perfected. (13-806).

Condominiums.—Condominium association has lien on unit for any assessments or monetary penalties levied against that unit. (33-1256). Lien extinguished unless proceedings to enforce lien are instituted within three years from date assessment becomes due. (33-1256[F]). Judgment creditor of association holds lien against all units at time judgment entered, not against common elements. (33-1257[A]).

Other Liens.—Attachment liens, see topic Attachment. Collateral security, see topic Pledges. Judgment liens, see category Civil Actions and Procedure, topic Judgments. Landlord's liens, see category Property, topic Landlord and Tenant. Lien on homestead, see topic Homesteads. Real estate mortgage liens and liens on mobile homes, see category Mortgages, topic Mortgages of Real Property.

MECHANICS' LIENS:

See topic Liens.

PLEDGES:

See category Business Regulation and Commerce, topic Commercial Code.

Remedies of Pledgee.—Uniform Commercial Code remedies adopted. (47-9207, 9501 to 9505).

Trust Receipts.—Uniform Commercial Code adopted. (47-1101 et seq.). See category Business Regulation and Commerce, topic Commercial Code.

Pawnbrokers.—Regulated. See 44-1621 et seq.

RECEIVERS:

Superior court judges may appoint receivers even if action includes no other claim for relief. (12-1241). Trustee or beneficiary involved in sale of trust may file action with superior court for appointment of receiver. (33-807[B]). Powers of receivers are set forth in Civ. 66(c).

Application for Receiver.—Application must be verified. (Civ. 66[a]).

Notice.—Adverse party must be notified except where affidavit shows that reasonable efforts to notify have been made and have failed or where there is substantial cause for appointing receiver before service can be made. (Civ. 66[a]).

Eligibility.—Party to suit or person interested in suit cannot be appointed receiver in that action, except upon adequate notice when property has been abandoned or duties of receiver will consist chiefly of preserving property. Before commencing duties, receiver must file bond and take oath to discharge duties and obey court orders. (Civ. 66[b]).

Bond.—Applicant must file bond set by court where no actual notice to adverse party. (Civ. 66[a]).

Hearing.—May be ordered on application in less than ten days. (Civ. 66[a]).

Removal.—Receiver may be discharged on motion or by court. (Civ. 66[c]).

See note at head of Digest as to 1998 legislation covered.

See Topical Index in front part of this volume.

AZ – 19

REDEMPTION:

See topic Executions; category Mortgages, topics Chattel Mortgages, Mortgages of Real Property.

SUPPLEMENTARY PROCEEDINGS:

See topic Executions.

TRUSTEE PROCESS:

See topic Garnishment.

USURY:

See category Business Regulation and Commerce, topic Interest.

DISPUTE RESOLUTION

ALTERNATIVE DISPUTE RESOLUTION:

Mandatory Dispute Resolution.—All civil actions where amount in controversy does not exceed $50,000 or lesser amount set by superior court rules are subject to mandatory arbitration. (12-133). Compulsory arbitration clauses in contracts are valid and binding. (12-1501). See topic Arbitration and Award.

Upon motion of either party, or upon its own initiative after consultation with parties, court may direct parties in any action that is not subject to compulsory arbitration to submit dispute to alternative dispute resolution program. (Civ. 16[g]).

Voluntary Dispute Resolution.—

Arbitration.—Any case, regardless of whether or not suit has been filed, may be referred to arbitration by agreement of reference signed by parties or counsel for both sides. (12-133[d]). Parties to contract may provide that dispute arising under contract will be submitted to arbitration. (12-1501 et seq.). See topic Arbitration and Award.

Other Alternative Dispute Resolution Programs.—Court may use mediation and other alternative dispute resolution procedures to help resolve cases filed in court. (12-134). Mediation process is confidential. With narrow exceptions, communications made, materials created for or used and acts occurring during mediation are not subject to disclosure. (12-134, 2238).

ARBITRATION AND AWARD:

Compulsory Arbitration.—Superior court must require arbitration of claims where amount in controversy does not exceed $50,000 or lesser amount set by superior court, except court may waive arbitration requirement upon showing of good cause if parties file written stipulation waiving it. (12-133). Arizona Uniform Rules of Procedure for Arbitration apply. Any party to arbitration proceeding may appeal arbitration award by filing demand for trial de novo with court. (12-133).

Uniform Arbitration Act adopted (12-1501 to 1518) but does not apply to arbitration agreements between employers and employees or their representatives (12-1517). Under Uniform Arbitration Act, written agreement to submit controversy to arbitration is binding. Unlike court-ordered compulsory arbitration under 12-133 (see subhead Compulsory Arbitration, supra), arbitration awards pursuant to arbitration clause may be set aside only in narrowly defined circumstances such as fraud, corruption or other prejudicial misconduct. (12-1512).

Any state agency, board, commission or political subdivision of state is permitted to use services of American Arbitration Association or other similar body. State agencies, boards and commissions must include agreements to arbitrate in public works contracts where amount in controversy is less than $100,000, and in contracts subject to compulsory arbitration. (12-1518).

See also category Courts and Legislature, topic Courts.

DOCUMENTS AND RECORDS

ACKNOWLEDGMENTS:

What Persons May Take.—Governed by 33-501 et seq.:

Within State.—Clerk or deputy clerk of court having seal; notary public; county recorder; justice of peace; judge of court of record; recorder of deeds. (33-511).

Outside State But Within United States.—Judge, clerk or deputy clerk of court of record; notary public; any other person authorized by laws of other jurisdiction to take acknowledgments. (33-501).

Outside United States.—U.S. foreign service officer; consular agent; other person authorized by Department of State; foreign notary public with proof of authority. (33-501 to 502).

Acknowledgment of Military Personnel or Merchant Seamen.—Commissioned officers or other persons authorized by Armed Forces regulation. (33-501).

Corporations.—Authorized officer or agent. (33-505).

Fees.—Authorized fees for taking acknowledgments, set forth. (41-314).

General Requirements of Certificate.—Certificate accepted if in form recognized in Arizona or in place where acknowledgment taken or if words "acknowledged before me" or their substantial equivalent appear. (33-504).

Uniform Recognition of Acknowledgments Act adopted. (33-501 et seq.).

Uniform Acknowledgment Act adopted. (33-511 et seq.).

Attorneys-in-Fact and Married Women.—No special requirements in taking acknowledgments of married women, attorneys-in-fact, or corporations.

Authentication.—Required as provided in §2 of Uniform Recognition of Acknowledgments Act. Clerk of superior court may authenticate certificate of acknowledgment for use outside Arizona. Fee, $10. (12-284[E], 33-502).

Foreign Acknowledgment.—Instrument affecting real property in Arizona is valid and may be recorded if executed, acknowledged and certified in another state or territory according to local law. (33-411). Provisions of Uniform Act also apply.

Effect of Acknowledgment.—No instrument is deemed lawfully recorded unless acknowledged according to law. (33-411). Any written instrument, except promissory notes, bills of exchange and wills, may be acknowledged, and proper certificate of acknowledgment entitles instrument to be received in evidence without proof of execution. (12-2261).

Letters from U.S.—Letters patent from U.S. or grant from government may be recorded without further acknowledgment. (33-411[E]).

Proof by Witnesses.—No statutory provision.

Form.—Certificate must be substantially as follows (33-506):

Form

State of . . . . . ., County of . . . . . ., ss.: The foregoing instrument was acknowledged before me this . . . . . . day of . . . . . ., 19. . . ., by (if by natural person, here insert name or names; if by person acting in representative or official capacity, or as attorney in fact, then insert name of person and capacity; if by officer of corporation, then insert name of officer and his title, and name of corporation, and state where incorporated; if by partner or agent of partnership, then insert name of acknowledging partner or agent and name of partnership).

(Notarial Seal)

. . . .
Notary Public

My commission expires
. . . .

See Uniform Recognition of Acknowledgments Act (33-501 et seq.) for other forms.

Alternative to Acknowledgment or Proof.—No statutory provision.

AFFIDAVITS:

See topic Acknowledgments (same rules). As to fees, see topic Notaries Public.

Form.—No particular form is required.

Alternative to Affidavit.—No statutory provision.

NOTARIES PUBLIC:

Bond.—Notary must give bond in sum of $5,000. (41-312[B]). Fee for recording bond with secretary of state is no more than $25. (41-126).

Residence.—Notary must reside in county from which appointed. (41-312[A]).

Seal.—Notary must have seal with his name, name of county in which commissioned and words "notary public" engraved thereon. Official acts must be under seal. (41-321).

Powers and Duties.—Notary has authority to administer oaths, perform jurat, and affirmations, and to take acknowledgments of instruments in writing and give certificate thereof. (41-312 to 313).

Territorial Extent of Powers.—Acknowledgments may be taken and oaths administered by notary in any county of state. (41-312[A]).

Records.—Notary must keep, maintain and protect as public record journal of all official acts performed. (41-313). Upon resignation, revocation or death, journal must be delivered by certified mail to county recorder in notary's county of residence. (41-317).

Official Character of Notary.—Certified by superior court clerk. Fee $10. (12-284).

Fees.—Notaries may receive no more than $2 per signature for acknowledgments, for jurat, and for oaths and affirmations without signature. For certified copies, fee may be no more than $2 per page certified. (41-316).

RECORDS:

County records are kept by county recorder. (11-461). *For list of counties and county seats, see first page for this state in Volume containing Practice Profiles Section.* State records are kept by Department of Library, Archives and Public Records, State Capitol Building, Phoenix, Arizona 85030. (41-1331 et seq.).

Any person may examine or be furnished copies of public records. (39-121.01). When copies are sought for commercial purpose, certified statement must describe such purpose and fee will be charged accordingly. Penalties prescribed for commercial use of copies obtained without indication thereof in statement. Commercial purpose defined as any use (including resale or solicitation) from which purchaser can reasonably anticipate monetary gain. (39-121.03).

Uniform Commercial Code adopted. (47-1101 et seq.).

Filing and Recording Under Commercial Code.—See categories Business Regulation and Commerce, topic Commercial Code; Mortgages, topic Chattel Mortgages and end of this Digest for addresses and fees for filing and recording.

Necessity for Recording.—Instruments affecting real property, marriage settlements, deeds of trust and mortgages of either real or personal property are void as against creditors and subsequent bona fide purchasers unless recorded. (33-412).

See also category Property, topic Deeds, subhead Recording.

Fees for Recording.—Papers required or authorized by law to be recorded with county recorder are $5 for first five pages, plus $1 for each additional page, total not to exceed $250. Fee for recording termination statement under 47-9404, release of collateral under 47-9406 or instrument of satisfaction under 47-10101, $3. For issuing certificate under 47-9407, $10, plus $1 for each financing statement or statement of assignment reported in certificate. Certified copies are $3, plus $1 per page. If mailing is required, each of these fees is increased by $1. For additional details, see statute. (11-475). Fee for recording oversized maps and plats, $20. (11-481).

Additional fee of $2 must be paid prior to recording any deed or contract relating to sale or transfer of real property. (42-1611). Each deed must have appended to it affidavit declaring value of and other information concerning real property transferred and

RECORDS . . . *continued*
personal property involved in sale. (42-1612). Additional fee of $5 must be paid prior to recording any affidavit of performance. (27-208).

County may charge extra recording fee of up to $4 per document. (11-475.01).

Fees for Filing.—Copy of document in file, 10¢ per page; filing and recording official bond and transmitting commission for notary public, $25; filing application for registration or renewal of trademark or recording assignment of trademark, $15; filing application for registration or renewal of tradename or recording assignment of tradename, $10; issuing certificate of registration of tradename or trademark, $3; filing financing statement or amendment thereto, $3; filing assignment, $3; filing continuation statement, $3; filing statement of release, $2; filing termination statement, $2; issuing certificate as provided in 44-3146, $6, plus 50¢ per page for documents accompanying certificate; filing, recording or certifying any other document not specified, $3. (41-126).

Recordable Instruments.—Any instrument may be recorded with county recorder if instrument: (1) Has caption briefly stating its nature, e.g., warranty deed; (2) is original or copy sufficiently legible for recorder to make certified copies; and (3) contains original signatures or carbon copies of same. (11-480). Each instrument dated and executed on or after Jan. 1, 1991 must (1) be no larger than 8½ inches by 14 inches, (2) have print size no smaller than ten point type, and (3) comply with margin requirements. (11-480).

Effect of Recordation.—Any instrument duly recorded in proper county is notice to all persons. (33-415 to 416).

Torrens Act.—Not adopted.

Transfer of Decedent's Title.—Sufficiently shown by probate records. No provision for further record. In case of nonresident decedent, ancillary administration is necessary.

Uniform Federal Lien Registration Act adopted. (33-1031 et seq.). Filing fee, $3 for each notice.

Vital Statistics.—Records of births and deaths kept by, and certified copies of certificates obtainable from, Department of Health Services, Vital Records Section, P.O. Box 3887, 1740 W. Adams St., Phoenix, Arizona 85030. Fee per copy for birth and death certificates established by director of Department of Health Services. (36-342). All birth certificates 75 years or older available on microfiche for access by anyone through State Department of Library, Archives and Public Records. (36-322). Same true for all death certificates 50 years or older. (36-327). Marriage license records kept by clerk of superior court of county where marriage performed. (25-123). Fee per certified copy, $10. (12-284).

Establishing Birth Records.—Births within state are filed with registrar designated by statute. (36-322). When a person has not been previously registered, a certificate of delayed birth registration may be filed under rules of board of health which prescribe evidentiary requirements. (36-324). For infants of unknown parentage, person assuming custody must report certain information to registrar within seven days. (36-323). New certificate may be issued following adoption, legitimation, paternity determination and sex change. (36-326). As to certain foreign-born adoptees and "putative father registry", see category Family, topic Adoption.

SEALS:

Uniform Commercial Code adopted. (47-1101 et seq.). See category Business Regulation and Commerce, topic Commercial Code.

No private or corporate seal or scroll is necessary to the validity of a contract, bond or conveyance or other instrument affecting either real or personal property, and addition of such seal or scroll does not affect instrument. (1-202). Every contract in writing imports consideration. (44-121).

TORRENS ACT:

Not adopted.

VITAL STATISTICS:

See topic Records.

EMPLOYMENT

EMPLOYER AND EMPLOYEE:

See topic Labor Relations.

LABOR RELATIONS:

Industrial Commission (five members) charged with administration and enforcement of all laws for protection of employees where duty not specifically delegated to another board or officer, and assist where duty is so delegated, and authorized and required to promote voluntary arbitration and mediation of labor disputes, regulate processing of workmen's compensation claims, license and supervise private employment agencies, investigate alleged unsafe or injurious employments or places of employment, and publish statistics. (23-107). Review of Commission workmen's compensation decisions and child labor cease and desist orders is by writ of certiorari to court of appeals. (23-951). Review of all other Commission orders is by superior court. (23-946).

Hours of Labor.—Maximum of eight hours per day for employees in laundries (23-284) and employees of State or subdivisions (Const., Art. XVIII, §1). Employees and hoisting engineers at underground mines may work maximum of eight hours per day unless employer has adopted policy of longer periods of employment based upon collective bargaining agreement, in which case affected employees may work up to maximum of 12 hours in 24 hour period. (23-282). Truck and bus operators may not be on duty more than ten consecutive hours or ten aggregate hours per day without at least eight hours rest. (23-286). Railroad employees may not work more than 16 consecutive hours without at least nine hours rest. (23-287).

Wages.—Pay days must not be more than 16 days apart, and all wages up to date of pay day must be paid, except that overtime and exception pay and wages for up to five days prior thereto may be withheld when employee continues in employment, and wages for school employees may be prorated. Overtime and exception pay must be paid no later than 15 days after wages are earned. Employer may personally deliver wages to employee or deposit wages within U.S. mail within required timelines. Employers whose principal places of business and payrolls are located outside Arizona may designate one fixed pay day per month for certain professional, administrative, executive and sales employees. (23-351). When employee is discharged, wages must be paid by earlier of three working days or end of next regular pay period, whichever is sooner; when employee quits, wages must be paid by regular pay day for period during which quit occurred. (23-353). If employer fails to pay wages due, employee may file civil action to recover treble amount of unpaid wages or, if amount does not exceed $2,500, may obtain determination from Industrial Commission's Labor Department. (23-355 et seq.). Department or employee may obtain judgment, garnishment, attachment or other available remedies for collection. (23-356).

Equal Wages.—Variation in rates of pay based upon sex of employee is prohibited. (23-341).

Priority of Wage Claims.—Wages of salesmen, clerks or laborers earned within 60 days preceding assignment for benefit of creditors or insolvency proceedings, up to $200, are preferred claims. Where employer dies, such wages have priority over all claims except funeral and last illness expenses, estate administration costs and family allowance. (23-354).

Wages of Minors.—To extent not pre-empted by federal law, Industrial Commission has duty to investigate wages of minors and, upon recommendation of wage boards appointed for that purpose, establish minimum fair wage rates. Employer must post orders establishing such rates. Minor paid less than minimum wage may recover in civil action treble minimum wage plus attorneys' fees and costs, less amount actually paid as wages. (23-311 et seq.).

Assignment of Wages.—See category Debtor and Creditor, topic Assignments.

Exemption of Wages.—See category Debtor and Creditor, topic Exemptions.

Child Labor.—Certain employments prohibited for children under 18. (23-231). Additional employments prohibited for children under 16. (23-232). Hours, night work, solicitation sales and door-to-door deliveries are restricted for children under 16 except children delivering newspapers. (23-233). Exemptions from child labor restrictions for employment by parents or other specified relative in certain occupations, entertainment performance, career or vocational training, and apprenticeship programs if married or have high school diploma or equivalent. (23-235). Employers who violate child labor laws are fined $1,000 and are required to desist from violation. (23-236).

Discrimination.—Unlawful for employer, employment agency or labor organization to discriminate on account of age over age of 40, race, color, religion, sex, handicap, or national origin. (41-1461 et seq.).

Discharge.—Employer may be liable in civil damages for discharging employee in violation of public policy. Legislature, and not courts, create public policy of state. Employment relationship is contractual in nature, but absent written contract, either party may sever relationship at any time. Employee has wrongful discharge claim if (1) employer terminates employee in breach of written contract, (2) employer terminates employee in violation of state statute, (3) employer terminates employee in retaliation for certain acts of employee, or (4) employee has constitutional, statutory, or other public right to continued employment. (23-1501). Constructive discharge limited to specific conditions. (23-1502).

Agricultural Labor.—Agricultural Employment Relations Board regulates agricultural employers, employees and labor organizations. Board hears disputes and has power to prevent unfair labor practices. (23-1381 et seq.).

Labor Unions.—No person may be denied the opportunity to obtain or retain employment because of nonmembership in a labor organization. (Const., Art. XXV).

Black List.—Prohibited. (Const., Art. XVIII, §9; 23-1361). Certain communications between former and prospective employers are allowed and privileged. (23-1361).

Occupational Safety and Health.—Industrial Commission's Division of Occupational Safety and Health and occupational safety and health review boards responsible for promulgating and enforcing standards and regulations. (23-401 et seq.).

Workers' Compensation Act.—Administered by Industrial Commission. (23-107). Act applies to every employer (including state and municipal corporations) (23-902) of any employees (sole proprietor may be deemed employee [23-901]), which may include volunteer workers of state and local governments (23-901.06), except employers of domestic servants (23-902), businesses that entered into written agreement with independent contractor (23-902), certain real estate licensees (23-910), and certain motion picture employers (23-909). Exempted employers may come under Act voluntarily. (23-902). Act applicable to employment in both intrastate and interstate commerce governed by federal compensation or liability system only where intrastate work is separate and distinct. (23-903). Employers may secure compensation by insuring with either state compensation fund or authorized insurance carrier; or by furnishing satisfactory proof of financial self-insurance ability to Industrial Commission. (23-961), or by joining self-insurance pools with similar employers, subject to approval of Industrial Commission (23-961.01). Provisions are compulsory on both employer and employee and remedies provided against both employer and insurance carrier are exclusive except that employees may reject Act and retain right to sue by filing written notice with employer prior to injury. (23-906, 1022). Every employee who is killed or injured within scope of employment, unless injury was self-inflicted or employee was under influence of alcohol or unlawful drugs and use of such substance(s) caused injury or death, is entitled to compensation for losses. (23-1021). Person entitled to workers' compensation, injured or killed by negligence or wrong of another not in same employ, may pursue remedy against such person but, if does not so pursue within one year after cause of action accrues, claim shall be deemed assigned to insurance carrier. (23-1023). Compensation is percentage of wages dependent on nature and extent of injury or number of dependents in case of death. Maximum award two-thirds of average monthly wage for life. (23-1044 to 1046). Maximum average monthly wage set by statute. (23-1041). Commission may supplement award with payments from special fund for employees who suffer additional impairment of preexisting physical impairment. (23-1065). Commission may

See note at head of Digest as to 1998 legislation covered.

See Topical Index in front part of this volume.

LABOR RELATIONS... *continued*
grant lump sum commutation not to exceed $50,000. (23-1067). Claim must be filed within one year after injury occurs or becomes manifest or when claimant knows or in exercise of reasonable diligence should know he sustained compensable injury. (23-1061). Request for hearing may be filed on any issue connected with claim within 90 days after disputed action. (23-947). Hearings held before administrative law judges of Commission. (23-941 et seq.). Review of workers' compensation awards is by court of appeals under writ of certiorari. (23-951).

Occupational Diseases.—Law is administered by Industrial Commission. Certain occupational diseases are included in definition of "personal injury by accident arising out of the employment," and thus, are included within general provisions related to workmen's compensation with some special rules applying. (23-901.01 et seq.).

Employer's Liability Law.—Any employer liable for injuries of any employee engaged in hazardous occupation. (23-801 et seq.). Comparative negligence may diminish damages. (23-806).

Unemployment Compensation.—Administered by Department of Economic Security. (41-1953, 1966, 23-601 et seq.). Unless not employee (23-613.01) or exempt (23-617), any unemployed resident of state, or individual residing in state which has entered into reciprocal agreement (23-644), or under certain conditions individual who is working outside state but is directed or controlled by employer in state, is eligible to file claim for benefits (23-771 to 772). Maximum benefits $195 weekly (23-779) for 26 weeks not to exceed one-third yearly base pay (23-780). Department shall deduct all child support obligations from unemployment compensation. (23-789). Individual is entitled to receive shared work unemployment compensation if employer has elected to participate in such program. (23-762 to 763). Unemployment compensation is subject to federal and state tax, and individual may elect to have federal and state tax withheld. (23-792). Seasonal employment is employment with single employer who experiences substantial slowdown during season or seasons each year, notifies employees of seasonal status in writing, is not delinquent in unemployment insurance tax, and has experience rating account chargeable with 12 consecutive months of benefits. (23-793).

Working Conditions.—Statutory duty to furnish workplace free from recognized hazards. Common condition or practice within industry is not recognized hazard unless standard regarding condition has been developed pursuant to statutes. (23-403).

Drug Testing.—Employers are authorized to reliably test their employees and prospective employees for presence of drugs and alcohol impairment. (23-493 et seq.).

WORKERS' COMPENSATION LAW:

See topic Labor Relations.

ENVIRONMENT

ENVIRONMENTAL REGULATION:

General Supervision.—

Air Pollution Control.—Primarily responsibility of Department of Environmental Quality. (49-401 et seq.). Director must maintain state implementation plan as required by federal Clean Air Act. (49-404). Director may take any action necessary to abate environmental nuisances. (49-141). Governor may designate status and classification of areas of state pursuant to attainment of national ambient air quality standards. (49-405). County boards of supervisors adopt rules and regulations to control localized air pollution. (49-479). County regulations enforced by county health departments or county air pollution control districts and county air pollution control hearing boards or by multi-county air quality control region and joint region hearing board. (49-402, 473 to 478). In vehicle emissions control area, designated agency must develop transportation-related air quality measures. (49-402[E]). Governor must certify metropolitan planning organization to conduct transportation planning process in non-attainment areas for ozone, carbon monoxide or particulates and if no such agency exists, Department is so certified. (49-406). Motor vehicles in certain counties subject to annual emissions, tampering inspection, and random on-road testing program. (49-541 et seq.). Motor vehicles in certain counties subject to voluntary no-drive program. (49-506). Travel Reduction Task Force established to review and approve Travel Reduction Programs. (49-581 et seq.). Certain gasoline dispensing sites are required to install gasoline vapor control system during 1993 and 1994. Gasoline for use in certain areas regulated. (41-2124 to 2124.01). Counties with population in excess of 500,000 must establish voluntary lawn mower emissions reduction program. (49-474.02). Some cities must develop clean burning fireplace ordinance. (9-500.16, 11-875).

Hazardous Waste.—Primarily responsibility of Director of Department of Environmental Quality, who promulgates rules and regulations on management, construction and operation of hazardous waste disposal facilities (49-905) and on characteristics, identification, listing, generation, transportation, treatment, storage and disposal of hazardous wastes equivalent to and consistent with federal program (49-922). Owners or operators of underground storage tanks with petroleum or hazardous substances must maintain leak or release detection system, must notify Department of Environmental Quality in event of leak, and must meet other regulatory requirements. (49-1001 et seq.). Party performing corrective action may informally appeal Department determinations. (49-1091). Person who acquires ownership or control of property where underground storage tank is located is not owner of underground storage tank if satisfies certain requirements. (49-1001.01). State Fire Marshall is required to maintain library of all state and local rules and applicable federal regulations relating to hazardous materials control. (41-2163). Fund created for cleanup of hazardous substance sites for which no private party will take responsibility. (49-282). Transportation, use and disposal of used oil regulated. (49-801 et seq.). Contaminated soil remediation standards created. (49-151 et seq.). Party may appeal agency decision if it takes action that is arbitrary, capricious, or not in accordance with law. (41-1092.12, 1091).

Nonhazardous Solid Waste.—Primarily responsibility of Department of Environmental Quality. (49-761). Department of Environmental Quality must adopt rules on storage, processing, treatment and disposal of solid waste. (49-761). Certain facilities must prepare and obtain approval of solid waste facility plan. (49-762). Other facilities must comply with self-certification procedures. (49-762.01). Procedures are established for variances. (49-763.01). All disposal of solid waste at landfills is regulated. (49-761). Sale and disposal of waste tires (44-1301 et seq.) and lead acid batteries (44-1321 et seq.) regulated. Department must establish medical sharp labeling rules. (44-1341).

Radioactive Materials.—Primarily responsibility of Radiation Regulatory Agency and Radiation Regulatory Hearing Board. Regulatory Agency promulgates radiation protection standards and rules and regulations for licensing, registration, transport, and disposal of sources of radioactive materials and radioactive material processing operations. Regulatory Hearing Board conducts hearings, reviews orders, and makes recommendations on regulations. (30-651 et seq.).

Water Pollution Standards, Permits, Rules and Regulations.—Promulgated and administered by Department of Environmental Quality. (49-201 et seq.). Unless otherwise exempted, acquifer protection permits required for all facilities which add pollutants to land or water. (49-241 et seq.). Wastewater Management Authority provides financing for public wastewater treatment facilities. (49-371 et seq.). By Jan. 1, 1999, Department shall establish monitoring assistance program to aid public water systems in complying with federal law. (49-360). City, town, county, or sanitary district may adopt any ordinances necessary for implementing and enforcing pretreatment requirements under Federal Water Pollution Control Act amendments of 1972. Fines not exceeding $25,000 per day may be imposed for violation of such ordinances. (49-391). Director of Water Resources in consultation with Director of Department of Environmental Quality may inspect wells for gross contamination and take appropriate remedial actions. (45-605[A], 49-282.04[A]).

Pesticide Control.—Responsibility of Director of Department of Agriculture, which promulgates and enforces rules and orders (3-102 et seq.), including publishing list of highly toxic and odoriferous pesticides (3-362), adopting rules to regulate pesticides and charging fees and issuing licenses, permits and certificates for pesticide use (3-363). Any money collected pursuant to these sections shall be deposited in State General Fund. (3-283). Pesticide management areas to be designated by Director. (3-366). Integrated pest management program established to reduce use of chemical pesticides. (3-381). Pesticide registrants must submit information related to hazards of groundwater contamination to Department of Environmental Quality. (49-301 et seq.). Restrictions on ability of Department of Environmental Quality to distribute consumer product information and to recommend substance as pesticide. (49-969).

Enforcement.—

Air Pollution.—State Department of Environmental Quality has original jurisdiction over sources, permits and violations for certain defined major sources, smelting of metal ore, petroleum refineries, coal fired electrical generating stations, portland cement plants, portable sources, mobile sources for emissions inspections, and in counties after Nov. 15, 1993 without permit program. (49-402[A]). Counties or multi-county air quality control regions have jurisdiction for other sources. (49-402[B]). Jurisdiction not granted as to air pollution solely within commercial or industrial plants or shops. (49-448[1]). Unitary (installation/operating) permit required for certain sources of hazardous air pollutants and for persons beginning actual construction or operating any building, structure, facility or installation that may cause or contribute to air pollution or use of which may eliminate, reduce or control omission of air pollution. (49-426[A]). Certain sources exempted from permit requirement. (49-426[B]). Public notice of permit required, and public comment and hearing provided for. (49-426[D]). Special conditions required for permits allowing burning of used oil or hazardous waste or fuel derived thereof in any machine, incinerator or device. (49-426[G]). General permits allowed if certain conditions are met. (49-426[H]). Changes allowed without permit revision. (49-426.01). Department must adopt rules to administer and enforce federal and state hazardous air pollutant programs. (49-426.03, 426.06). Department may by rule designate state list of hazardous air pollutants (49-426.04) and categories of sources subject to state program (49-426.05). Permit or permit revision applications must be denied if source will violate emissions statute or rules. (49-427). Appeals to hearing board of Department permit, permit revision or conditional order decisions allowed for applicants and any person who filed written comments, and appeals to superior court allowed under certain conditions. (49-428, 443). Transfer of permits allowed under certain conditions. (49-429). Department may grant conditional orders allowing applicant to vary from certain rules. (49-437 to 441). Public disclosure required of nonconfidential Department records. (49-432[C]). Department may request in writing production of documents if reasonable cause of violation appears. (49-460). Department may issue order of abatement (49-461), seek injunctive relief (49-462) and civil penalties of not more than $10,000 per day, per violation (49-463). After Oct. 31, 1994, violators subject to felony and misdemeanor criminal penalties. (49-464). Citizen suits to enforce statutes permitted. (49-407). Governor may declare air pollution emergencies and restrict, prohibit or condition certain activities. (49-465). County air pollution control follows similar enforcement procedure as state. (49-471 et seq.). Department and counties required to establish small business stationary source technical and compliance assistance program. (49-456, 507). Certain businesses must stagger work hours to reduce air pollution. (49-454). Some major employers must comply with regional travel reduction programs by providing employees with information on alternative transportation. (49-588). Alternative fuel vehicles requesting tax credits must meet certain requirements. (41-1516, 43-1086.01, 1174, 1174.01). All gasoline sold in county of 1,200,000 or more persons must comply with certain standards. (41-2123). Governor shall appoint agricultural best management committee to determine best management practices. (49-457). County with more than 400,000 persons shall establish voluntary vehicle repair and retrofit program. (49-474.03). Director must submit report to Governor and Legislature concerning number of fleet vehicles and their use of alternative fuels. (41-803). Civil penalties of up to $100 for violation of burning restrictions on some residential fireplaces. (11-871).

Hazardous Waste.—Violation of motor vehicle regulation while transporting hazardous material, substance or waste that Corporation Commission requires to be placarded is Class 2 Misdemeanor, unless specified as Class 1 Misdemeanor or Felony. (28-1033). Director of Department of Environmental Quality is authorized to regulate and set criteria standards for characteristics, identification, listing, generation, transportation,

See note at head of Digest as to 1998 legislation covered.

See Topical Index in front part of this volume.

AZ – 22

ENVIRONMENTAL REGULATION . . . *continued*
treatment, storage, continuing release and disposal of hazardous waste. (49-922). Director may order compliance or seek court injunction. (49-923). Person who violates any permit, rule, regulation or order is subject to civil penalty not exceeding $25,000 for each day of violation. (49-924). Intentional, reckless, or knowing transportation of hazardous waste to unauthorized facility, generation of hazardous waste and causing or allowing transportation of waste to unauthorized facility, or treatment, storage, or disposal of waste without authority is felony. (49-925). Any agency required to select possible hazardous waste disposal site shall first send notice to property owners within specified proximity to proposed site. (49-941). Parties responsible for release or threatened release of hazardous substance are considered owners, operators, disposers, and transporters. (49-283[A]). Limitations on lender and fiduciary liability defined. (49-283[I]). In limited circumstances, owner, operator, disposer, or transporter may avoid cleanup liability. (49-283[B] to [D]). Provider or user of remediated water not liable for damages caused by use or distribution of remediated water, except on showing of willful, malicious or grossly negligent conduct. (49-283.01[A]). Owner or operator of facility must notify Director in event of release of reportable quantity of hazardous substance. (49-284). Responsible parties may be held strictly, jointly, and severally liable for remedial action costs for releases of hazardous substances. (49-285). Any person may apply to undertake voluntary remedial action. (49-282.05). Remedial action order recipient is entitled to expedited discovery and trial priority if there is threat of imminent and substantial danger to public health or environment. (49-287[E]). Based on information of possible release of hazardous substance, Director may conduct preliminary investigation. (49-287.01). If Director determines remedial investigation of site necessary and cost recovery may be appropriate, Department must investigate for liable parties. (49-287.02). After evaluating site, Director must develop proposed remedial action plan. (49-287.04). Additional investigations, proceedings and hearings may be held. (49-287.05 et seq.). Remedial actions may be financed by Water Quality Assurance Revolving Fund, if remedial action plan meets certain requirements. (49-289). Remedial costs borne by state create lien against contaminated property. (49-295).

Nonhazardous Solid Waste.—Department of Environmental Quality must adopt rules on storage, processing, treatment and disposal of solid waste. (49-761). Certain substances are exempt from definition of solid waste. (49-701.02). Certain facilities must prepare and obtain approval of solid waste facility plan. (49-762). Other facilities must comply with self-certification procedures. (49-762.01). Beginning July 1, 1998, Director may, in limited circumstances, require corrective actions for solid waste management. (49-762.08). Procedures are established for variances. (49-763.01). All new facilities must submit plans meeting financial assurance requirements (49-770), and all new landfill facilities must also submit plans meeting restrictive covenant (49-771) and location restriction requirements (49-772). Public notice and hearing requirements for facilities. (49-767). Solid waste facilities with certain zoning approval exempt. Department may issue agency compliance orders (49-781), suspend, amend, withdraw, condition or revoke approval to operate (49-782), and seek injunctive relief (49-783) for violation of solid waste statute, rule or facility plan condition. Fire Code Authority may require installation of backflow prevent equipment on certain fire protection systems. (49-746[E]). Violators subject to maximum $1,000 per day civil penalty not to exceed $15,000 per violation. (49-783[B]). Violation of solid waste statute, rule or facility plan condition punishable as misdemeanor. (49-791[B]). Improper sale or disposal of waste tires or lead acid batteries punishable by civil penalty not to exceed $500 per tire or battery. (44-1307, 1324).

Radioactive Materials.—Any person receiving, using, possessing, transferring, installing or servicing any source of radiation must be licensed or exempted by Radiation Regulatory Agency. (30-673). Radiation sources shall be registered, licensed or exempt at discretion of Radiation Regulatory Agency and shall be available for inspection. (30-671[B]). Sites used for concentration, storage, or disposal of radioactive waste material are regulated by Agency in name of state. (30-692). Any person building or operating commercial nuclear generator assessed annual amount set by legislature for development of plan for off-site response to accident at plant. (26-306.01). Southwestern Low-Level Radioactive Waste Disposal Compact adopted. (30-721). Disposal of low-level radioactive waste governed by Southwestern Low-Level Radioactive Waste Disposal Compact. (30-721).

Water Pollution.—Unlawful to discharge wastes, agricultural, irrigation or drainage waters into waters of state (surface or groundwater) in violation of established standards, or to discharge pollutants into waters of state without such permit as may be required by rules and regulations. (49-241). Director of Department of Environmental Quality is authorized to administer permit program. (49-203). Department of Environmental Quality may adopt water quality standards and procedures for enforcement. (49-203). Complaint ordering corrective action may be served on violator of law, regulation or order of Department, with right to request hearing. Orders of Director are appealable to court. (49-321). Denials of permits are appealable to Water Quality Appeals Board and then to superior court. (49-323). Department may inspect property and examine records relating to waste discharges. (49-203). Department may seek injunctive relief where necessary to protect public health in event any statutory provision, regulation or permit condition is violated. (49-262). Violators subject to civil penalties up to $25,000 per day per violation or guilty of misdemeanor, Class 6 Felony for criminally negligent violations, Class 5 Felony for knowing violations and Class 2 Felony where violation manifests extreme indifference for human life. (49-262 to 263). Citizen suits available against violators, with potential award of attorneys' fees. (49-264). Affirmative defense available to civil liability for causing or contributing to violation of water quality standards. (49-262[F]). Department of Environmental Quality is designated as responsible agency to take all necessary and appropriate action to insure proper quality of all potable water sold or distributed through public and some semipublic water systems. Department may allocate only $500,000 per year to bioremediation or other alternative technologies. (49-282). (49-351 et seq.). Wastewater collection and treatment regulated by 49-361 et seq.

Pesticide Control.—Certain pesticides cannot be applied in buffer zones around schools, day care centers, health care institutions and neighborhoods of at least 25 residences adjoining fields to be sprayed. (3-365). Private right of action provided in superior court. (3-367). Director of Department of Agriculture responsible for enforcement and receives all complaints. (3-368). Director determines type of violation that has occurred. If de minimis, citation is issued and record kept for three years. If nonserious or serious, citation is issued and hearing set. (3-368). Decision of hearing officer appealable to Director within 20 days. (3-369). Penalty for nonserious and serious violations is probation or suspension, revocation, nonrenewal or denial of permit, license or certification. Penalty may include civil fine not to exceed $500 for nonserious violations and $10,000 for serious violations. Nonserious violators guilty of Class 1 Misdemeanor. Serious violators guilty of Class 6 Felony. (3-370). Director or Director of Department of Health Services may issue cease and desist orders to terminate application of pesticides prior to hearing. (3-371). Violators may apply for emergency relief from suspension. (3-372).

All pesticides distributed, sold or offered for sale within state, delivered for transportation, transported in intrastate commerce or between points within state through any point outside state must be registered annually with Chemicals Division of Department. (3-351[A]). If deemed necessary, submission of complete formula of any pesticide or confidential statement of formula may be required.

Light Pollution.—Regulated by 49-1101 et seq.

Hazardous Materials.—Department of Health Services must adopt standards, rules, and remedies regarding lead-based paint. (36-1677).

Disclosure of Soil Abatement.—See category Property, topic Real Property, subhead Land Sale Regulation.

Penalties.—See subhead Enforcement, supra.

Permits.—See subhead Enforcement, supra.

See category Mineral, Water and Fishing Rights, topic Mines and Minerals.

See also category Business Regulation and Commerce, topic Licenses, Business and Professional, subhead Contractors.

ESTATES AND TRUSTS

ADMINISTRATION:

See topic Executors and Administrators.

ADVANCEMENTS:

See topic Descent and Distribution.

ALLOWANCES:

See topic Executors and Administrators.

CLAIMS:

See topic Executors and Administrators; category Civil Actions and Procedure, topic Pleading; and category Dispute Resolution, topic Arbitration and Award.

DEATH:

Person absent from last domicile for five successive years is presumed to have died at end of those five years. (14-1107). If estate is acquired on such presumption, it may be subsequently restored to party presumed dead by action in which it is shown that absentee is living. In such case, rents, profits and interest may also be recovered. (12-509). See also category Property, topic Absentees.

Simultaneous Death.—Uniform Simultaneous Death Act adopted, and, on adoption of Uniform Probate Code, renumbered to become part of Code. (14-2702).

Action for Death.—Whenever death is caused by such wrongful act as would have entitled injured person to maintain suit if death had not ensued, person causing such death is liable in action brought by personal representative of deceased. Either parent may sue for death of child; guardian may sue for death of ward. (12-611 et seq.).

Time to sue is within two years after death. (12-542).

Amount recoverable may not be limited by statute. (Const., Art. II, §31).

Death Certificate.—See category Documents and Records, topic Records, subhead Vital Statistics.

Uniform Anatomical Gift Act adopted. (36-841 et seq.).

Living Wills.—See topic Wills, subhead Living Wills and Health Care Directives.

DECEDENTS' ESTATES:

See topics Descent and Distribution, Executors and Administrators, Wills; category Debtor and Creditor, topic Homesteads.

DESCENT AND DISTRIBUTION:

Uniform Probate Code (but not 1977 or later amendments) adopted (14-1101 et seq.) with following exceptions:

Surviving spouse takes as follows: (1) If intestate left issue, one or more of whom are not issue of surviving spouse also, one-half of intestate separate property and no interest in decedent's one-half of community property; (2) if no surviving issue or issue all of whom are issue of surviving spouse also, entire intestate estate. (14-2102).

Election.—Surviving spouse has no right to take elective share.

Governing Instruments.—Definition significantly expanded. (14-1201).

Distribution.—"Representation" defined as per capita at each generational level. "Per stirpes" defined by statute. (14-2709). "Worthier title" doctrine abolished. (14-2710).

Disqualification.—Right to disclaim may not be restricted, although disclaimer does not effect interests of disclaimant's heirs. (14-2801). Person who divorces is not surviving spouse, subject to exceptions. (14-2802). Person who feloniously and intentionally kills decedent forfeits all rights to estate, and share passes as if it were disclaimed. (14-2803).

See note at head of Digest as to 1998 legislation covered.

See Topical Index in front part of this volume.

DESCENT AND DISTRIBUTION . . . *continued*

Right of Exclusion.—Testator may limit or exclude right of succession to property that passes by intestacy. That person's or class' share passes as if excluded disclaimed share. (14-2101).

Survival.—120-hour survival requirement for all instruments, including joint bank accounts.

Community Property.—See category Family, topic Husband and Wife.

Administrators.—See topic Executors and Administrators.

Escheat.—If no taker by will or intestacy laws, intestate estate passes to state. (14-2105).

Securities and security accounts may be registered in order to accomplish nonprobate transfer upon death of owner. Such accounts function like joint tenancy accounts. (14-6301 et seq.).

ELECTION:

See topic Wills.

ESTATES:

See category Property, topic Real Property.

EXECUTORS AND ADMINISTRATORS:

Uniform Probate Code (but not 1977 or later amendments) adopted. (14-1101 et seq.). Executor and administrator are included in term "personal representative". (14-1201).

Superior court has jurisdiction of probate and administration. Registrar administers informal probate procedure unless contested. Venue is in county of decedent's domicile at death, or, if no Arizona domicile, any county where decedent's property was located at time of death. (14-3201).

Eligibility and Competency.—Following cannot serve as personal representative: (1) Minor; (2) person found unsuitable by court; and (3) foreign corporation. (14-3203[F]).

Preferences in Right to Administer.—In appointment, preference is given to: (1) Person named in probated will; (2) surviving spouse who is devisee; (3) other devisees; (4) surviving spouse; (5) other heirs; (6) Arizona Veterans Service Commission; (7) 45 days after decedent's death, any creditor; and (8) public fiduciary. (14-3203).

Qualification.—Personal representative must file bond, if required, and statement of acceptance of duties of office. (14-3601). If required, bond must be in amount not less than personal representative's sworn best estimate of decedent's personal estate, real estate, less encumbrances thereon, and income from personal and real estate during next year. Bond may be reduced by amount of real estate, less encumbrances thereon, if letters restrict sales of realty as in supervised administration. (14-3604[A]).

Exemption from Bond.—Personal representative must give bond unless: (1) Will expressly waives bond; (2) all heirs or devisees waive bond in writing; (3) personal representative is bank or savings and loan or title insurance company authorized to do business in state, trust company holding certificate to engage in trust activities or public fiduciary; or (4) value of estate permits summary proceedings and surviving spouse or nominee is personal representative. (14-3603).

Issuance of Letters.—Five days after death of resident or 30 days after death of nonresident, and after application for informal appointment submitted under oath, registrar may appoint personal representative. (14-3307). Superior court can make formal determination of who is entitled to appointment. (14-3414).

Prior to issuance of letters, personal representative must file bond, if required, and written acceptance. (14-3601).

Removal.—Any interested person may petition for removal of personal representative at any time for: (1) Best interests of estate; (2) intentional misrepresentation of material facts by personal representative during appointment proceedings; (3) disregard of court order; (4) incapability; (5) mismanagement; (6) failure to perform any duty; or (7) disregard of decedent's written wishes for disposition of remains. (14-3611).

Special Kinds of Administration.—In addition, supervised administration is authorized by 14-3501, whereby personal representative must not make any distribution without prior order of court. Sale of property requires confirmation by court. (14-3504).

Public Administrators.—Office of public fiduciary established and governed by 14-5601 et seq.

Arizona Veterans Service Commission may act as guardian or conservator for incapacitated veteran or such veteran's incapacitated spouse. (41-603, 605). Before letters testamentary or of administration are issued, public fiduciary may, upon court order, with regard to person who dies intestate or testate without personal representative, take possession of property including real property, make funeral arrangements, and sell perishable property. Pending such court order, law enforcement agency shall protect all properties of deceased person. (14-5602, 5606).

Inventory and Appraisal.—Personal representative must file or send copy as provided by 14-3706 within three months of appointment of inventory of property owned by decedent at time of death, showing fair market value, community or separate nature, and type and amount of existing encumbrances. (14-3706).

General Powers and Duties.—Representative has all powers specified in Uniform Probate Code, including power to mortgage or lease estate assets. (14-3715). Personal representative bound by standard of care and duty of accounting applicable to trustees. (14-3703). Person on whom duty of burial is imposed must comply with decedent's reasonable, written wishes. (36-831.01).

Notice of Appointment.—Within ten days of appointment, representative must give notice of his appointment by mail or delivery to heirs and devisees. Failure is breach of duty but does not invalidate appointment. (14-3705).

Notice to Creditors.—Upon appointment, representative must publish notice once a week for three successive weeks in newspaper of general circulation in county. Representative must give notice to all known creditors, notifying them of personal representative's appointment. (14-3801). Claims barred forever if not presented within earlier of either: (1) two years after decedent's death plus time remaining in period commenced by notice pursuant to §14-3801; or (2) time prescribed by §14-3801(A) or (B). (14-3803).

Presentation of Claims.—All claims which arose before decedent's death must be presented within four months of first publication or mailed notice. Claims barred if nonclaim statute in decedent's domicile. Claims described in §14-3803 and barred by nonclaim statute of decedent's domicile before giving of notice to creditors in this state are barred. All claims arising at or after death must be presented as follows: (1) Claim based on contract with representative, within four months after performance by representative is due; and (2) any other claim, within four months after it arises. Excepted are enforcement of mortgages, pledges or other liens, and actions to establish decedent's or representative's liability covered by liability insurance. All claims not presented within these limits are barred. (14-3803).

Proof of Claims.—No particular form of proof of claim is prescribed. Written statement by claimant mailed or delivered to representative is sufficient. Statement must include basis and amount of claim, name and address of claimant, description of contingent or unliquidated nature of claim and any security held for claim. (14-3804).

Approval or Rejection of Claims.—Claims approved or rejected by representative. No action by representative within 60 days after expiration of time for original presentation has effect of notice of allowance. Disallowed claims are barred unless claimant files petition for allowance or commences proceeding within 60 days of mailing of notice of disallowance. (14-3806).

Payment of Claims.—Representative may pay claims beginning four months from first publication of notice to creditors, after making provision for statutory allowances, claims already presented and unbarred claims which may yet be presented, and costs and expenses. (14-3807).

Priorities.—(1) Costs of administration; (2) reasonable funeral expenses; (3) debts and taxes preferred under federal law; (4) expenses of last illness; (5) debts and taxes due under Arizona law; and (6) all other claims. (14-3805). All payments except (1) above subject to statutory allowances. See subhead Allowances, infra.

Sales.—See subhead General Powers and Duties, supra.

Actions by Representative.—Representative may prosecute and defend claims for protection of estate and representative in his duties. (14-3715[22]). For claims by decedent not barred by statute of limitations at his death, limitation of action ceases to run until appointment of representative or 12 months after death, whichever occurs first, but in no case sooner than four months after death. (14-3109).

Actions Against Representative.—Death of defendant abates actions for breach of promise to marry, seduction, libel, slander, separate maintenance, alimony, loss of consortium and invasion of privacy. All other actions may be continued against personal representative, but pain and suffering damages are not allowed. (14-3110).

Any statute of limitations not measured from death or advertisement of claims against decedent is suspended during four months following death. (14-3802). Claim in writing must be delivered or mailed to representative, or action must be commenced in any court having jurisdiction over representative. (14-3804). See subhead Presentation of Claims, supra.

Allowances.—If decedent was domiciled in Arizona, following are available: (1) Allowance in lieu of homestead of $18,000 to surviving spouse and dependent children. If no surviving spouse, $18,000 is divided among dependent children. If dependent children reside with surviving spouse or there are no dependent children, allowance is payable to surviving spouse. If dependent child is not living with surviving spouse, allowance may be made partially to child or his guardian and partially to surviving spouse. Allowance in lieu of homestead is exempt from and prior to all claims against estate except administration expenses. (14-2402). (2) Exempt personal property with value not in excess of $7,000 to surviving spouse and dependent children. If dependent child is not living with spouse, allowance may be made partially to child or his guardian and partially to surviving spouse. If no surviving spouse, minor or dependent children are entitled jointly to allowance. If assets are encumbered or insufficient, exempt property allowance has priority over all claims against estate except administration expenses, allowance in lieu of homestead and family allowance. (14-2403). (3) Family allowance to surviving spouse and dependent children. If dependent child is not living with surviving spouse, allowance may be made partially to child or his guardian and partially to surviving spouse. Allowance may be in periodic installments or lump sum. Representative may determine up to $12,000 lump sum or $1,000 per month for one year. Family allowance is exempt from and prior to all claims except administration expenses and allowance in lieu of homestead. (14-2404 to 2405). All statutory allowances are chargeable against any share passing by decedent's will, unless will provides otherwise. Property specifically devised is not used to satisfy allowance if estate otherwise sufficient. Portion of statutory allowances payable to surviving spouse are chargeable first to decedent's share of community property. Portion of allowances payable to dependent children are chargeable first to decedent's separate property. (14-2405).

Widow's Quarantine.—None.

Final Accounting and Settlement.—Estate may be settled by: (1) Petition for order of complete settlement (14-3931); (2) petition under informally probated will (14-3932); (3) except when under court prohibition or supervision, verified statement of representative that he has published notice to creditors as provided in 14-3801, first publication occurring more than four months prior to statement, and that he has fully administered estate and made complete accounting thereof to all distributees (14-3933).

Consent Settlement.—Representative may compromise claims against estate. (14-3813).

See note at head of Digest as to 1998 legislation covered.

See Topical Index in front part of this volume.

AZ – 24

EXECUTORS AND ADMINISTRATORS... *continued*

Distribution.—Personal representative may settle and distribute estate without court order unless he presents questions to court. If administration is supervised, representative may not distribute without court order. (14-3504).

Distribution If Abroad.—No statutory provisions.

Liabilities.—Representative is not liable on contract unless he fails to reveal representative capacity, but representative is liable for obligations and torts during administration if personally at fault. (14-3808).

Compensation of Representatives.—Representative is entitled to reasonable compensation for services. He may renounce compensation set forth in will and be entitled to reasonable compensation unless compensation is set by contract with decedent. (14-3719).

Foreign Executors and Administrators.—As to assets in Arizona, such representatives exercise all powers of local personal representative and may maintain actions subject to any conditions imposed on nonresidents generally (14-4205), but only if no administration or petition for administration is pending in Arizona. Petition for Arizona administration terminates power of foreign personal representative. (14-4206).

Summary Administration.—See subhead Small Estates, infra.

When Administration Unnecessary.—Decedent's successor may collect personal property owed decedent at death by affidavit stating that: (1) Value of all personal property in decedent's estate, wherever located, less liens and encumbrances, does not exceed $50,000; (2) 30 days have elapsed since death; (3) proceeding to appoint personal representative is not pending or if granted, representative has been discharged or more than one year elapsed since closing statement was filed; and (4) successor is entitled to payment or delivery of property. Successor may acquire decedent's interest in real property, including any debt secured by lien on real property, by filing with court in county in which decedent was domiciled at time of death or in county where real property is located if decedent was not domiciled in Arizona, affidavit describing real property and decedent's interest therein and stating that: (1) Net value of real property located in Arizona does not exceed $30,000; (2) six months have elapsed since death as shown in certified copy of decedent's death certificate attached to affidavit; (3) no proceedings for appointment of personal representative are pending or if granted, representative has been discharged or more than one year elapsed since closing statement was filed; (4) funeral expenses, expenses of last illness and all unsecured debts have been paid; (5) affiant is entitled to property by reason of allowance in lieu of homestead and exempt property, intestate succession as sole heir or heirs, or by devise under valid last will, copy of which is attached to affidavit or has been probated; (6) no other person has right to property; (7) no federal or Arizona estate tax is due on decedent's estate; and (8) affiant affirms that all statements are true. (14-3971). Payment releases payor. (14-3972).

Small Estates.—If estate inventory value is less than allowance in lieu of homestead, exempt property allowance, family allowance, administration costs, funeral expenses and expenses of last illness, representative may make immediate distribution and close estate by filing verified statement that: (1) Estate did not exceed items above; (2) representative has distributed estate to those entitled thereto; and (3) representative has sent copy of closing statement to all distributees and to all creditors, and has furnished full written accounting of administration to distributees affected thereby. If no proceedings involving representative are pending in court one year after filing of closing statement, representative's appointment is terminated. (14-3973 to 3974).

Uniform Fiduciaries Act adopted. (14-7501 et seq.).

Revised Uniform Principal and Income Act adopted. (14-7401 et seq.).

Uniform Simplification of Fiduciary Security Transfers Act repealed July 13, 1995.

Uniform Anatomical Gift Act adopted. (36-841 et seq.).

Caveat.—For disclosure requirements in conveyances of real property made or taken in representative capacity, see category Property, topic Deeds.

FIDUCIARIES:

See topics Executors and Administrators, Trusts; category Family, topic Guardian and Ward.

Uniform Unclaimed Property Act adopted. (44-301 et seq.).

Foreign corporation cannot be appointed personal representative but may be appointed testamentary trustee. (14-3203). See also topic Trusts.

Uniform Fiduciaries Act adopted with minor changes. (14-7501 et seq.). See category Business Regulation and Commerce, topic Banks and Banking.

Uniform Simplification of Fiduciary Security Transfers Act repealed by 1995, c. 153, §6. See 47-8101 et seq. for same subject matter.

INTESTACY:

See topic Descent and Distribution.

PROOF OF CLAIMS:

See topic Executors and Administrators; category Civil Actions and Procedure, topic Pleading.

TRUSTS:

Caveat: For disclosure requirements in conveyance of real property made or taken in representative capacity, see category Property, topic Deeds.

Testamentary Trusts.—Uniform Probate Code (but not 1977 or later amendments) adopted. (14-1101 et seq.). No significant variations or modifications.

Uniform Common Trust Fund Act adopted. (6-871 et seq.).

Uniform Fiduciaries Act adopted with minor changes. (14-7501 et seq.). See category Business Regulation and Commerce, topic Banks and Banking.

Revised Uniform Principal and Income Act adopted with minor changes. (14-7401 et seq.).

General Powers and Duties of Trustees.—Uniform Trustees' Powers Act adopted with minor changes. (14-7231 et seq.).

Transfers to Minors.—See category Family, topic Infants.

Uniform Simplification of Fiduciary Security Transfers Act repealed July 13, 1995.

Accumulations.—See category Property, topic Perpetuities.

Perpetuities.—See category Property, topic Perpetuities.

Pour Over Trusts.—See topic Wills.

WILLS:

Uniform Probate Code (but not 1977 or later amendments) adopted. (14-1101 et seq.).

Testamentary Disposition.—Any person 18 years or over and of sound mind may make will. (14-2501). Spouse's power of testamentary disposition of community property limited to one-half. (14-3101). Testator may dispose of his property in any manner he wishes, subject, however, to right of surviving spouse and dependent children to statutory allowances. (14-2401 et seq.). Testator may devise or bequeath property to existing written trust, and terms of such trust instrument govern property even though trust may be amended or revoked after execution of will or after death of testator. (14-2511). Heir must survive decedent by 120 hours. (14-2104).

Execution.—Will must be in writing, signed by testator or by someone in his presence and at his direction. Will must be signed by at least two persons, within reasonable time after witnessed either signing or acknowledgment of signature or will by testator. Intent to make will may be shown by extrinsic evidence. (14-2502). Testator may incorporate existing document into will if will's language manifests this intent and sufficiently describes document. (14-2510).

Holographic Will.—Will which does not comply with 14-2502 is valid as holographic will, whether or not witnessed, if signature and material provisions are in handwriting of testator. (14-2503).

Nuncupative Will.—Not recognized.

Self-Proved Will.—Any will may be simultaneously executed, attested and made self-proved by acknowledgment thereof by testator and affidavits of witnesses, each made before officer authorized to administer oaths under laws of state where execution occurs and evidenced by officer's certificate, under official seal, in form and content substantially as follows (14-2504):

Form

I, ..., the testator, sign my name to this instrument this .... day of ..... ., 19....., and being first duly sworn, do declare to the undersigned authority that I sign and execute this instrument as my will and that I sign it willingly or willingly direct another to sign for me, that I execute it as my free and voluntary act for the purposes expressed in that document, and that I am eighteen years of age or older, of sound mind, and under no constraint or undue influence.

....
Testator

We, ...,..........., the witnesses, sign our names to this instrument, being first duly sworn and do declare to the undersigned authority that the testator signs and executes this instrument as his/her will and that he/she signs it willingly, or willingly directs another to sign for him/her, and that each of us, in the presence and hearing of the testator, signs this will as witness to the testator's signing, and that to the best of our knowledge the testator is eighteen years of age or older, of sound mind, and under no constraint or undue influence.

....
Witness

....
Witness

STATE OF ....
County of .... } ss.

Subscribed, sworn to and acknowledged before me by ...., the testator, and subscribed and sworn to before me by .... and ...., witnesses, this .... day of ....

....
(Signed)

(SEAL)

....
(Official capacity of officer)

Attested will may at any time subsequent to its execution be made self-proved by acknowledgment thereof by testator and affidavits of witnesses, each made before officer authorized to administer oaths under laws of state where acknowledgment occurs and evidenced by officer's certificate, under official seal, attached or annexed to will in form and content substantially as follows:

Form

STATE OF ....
County of .... } ss.

We, ...,...... and ......, the testator and the witnesses, respectively, whose names are signed to the attached or foregoing instrument being first duly sworn do declare to the undersigned authority that the testator signed and executed the instrument as the testator's will and that he/she signed willingly, or willingly directed another to sign for him/her, and that he/she executed it as his/her free and voluntary act for the purposes expressed in that document, and that each of the witnesses, in the presence and hearing of the testator, signed the will as witness and that to the best of his/her knowledge the testator was at that time eighteen years of age or older, of sound mind and under no constraint or undue influence.

See note at head of Digest as to 1998 legislation covered.

See Topical Index in front part of this volume.

WILLS . . . *continued*

. . . .
Testator

. . . .
Witness

. . . .
Witness

Subscribed, sworn to and acknowledged before me by . . . . . . , the testator, and subscribed and sworn to before me by . . . . . . and . . . . . . , witnesses, this . . day of . . . .
(SEAL)

. . . .
(Signed)

. . . .
(Official capacity of officer)

Revocation.—Will or any part thereof is revoked by subsequent will which revokes prior will or part of such will expressly or by inconsistency or by its being burned, torn, canceled, obliterated or destroyed, with intent and for purpose of revoking it, whether or not the burn, tear or cancellation touched any of words of will, by testator or by another person in his presence and by his direction. (14-2507). In case of subsequent annulment, divorce or dissolution of marriage, all provisions in will, including provisions conferring some power or office, in favor of former spouse or any issue of former spouse not also issue of testator, are revoked unless will expressly provides otherwise. Decree of legal separation not terminating marital status is not considered divorce or dissolution. Property prevented from passing to former spouse because of revocation passes as if former spouse failed to survive decedent, and other provisions conferring some power or office on former spouse are interpreted as if spouse failed to survive decedent. If provisions are revoked solely by application of this provision, they are revived by testator's remarriage to former spouse. No other change of circumstances revokes will or any part thereof. (14-2508).

Revival.—If second will which, had it remained effective at death, would have revoked first will in whole or in part, is thereafter revoked by acts under 14-2507, first will is revoked unless it is evident from circumstances of revocation of second will or from testator's contemporary or subsequent declarations that he intended first will to take effect as executed. If second will is thereafter revoked by third will, first will is revoked in whole or in part except to extent it appears from terms of third will that testator intended first will to take effect. (14-2509).

Testamentary Gifts to Subscribing Witnesses.—Will or any provision thereof is not invalid because will is signed by interested witness. (14-2505).

Probate.—Jurisdiction over probate matters is vested in superior court. Venue for first informal or formal testacy or appointment proceedings after decedent's death is in county where decedent had his domicile at time of his death, or, if decedent was not domiciled in Arizona, in any county where property of decedent was located at time of his death. (14-3201). Art. 3 of Uniform Probate Code gives interested persons right to choose either formal or informal procedures in probate of estate. See topic Executors and Administrators for material variations from Official Text of Code.

Abatement.—Unless will expresses order of abatement, express or implied purpose of devise would be defeated by order of abatement provided by statute, shares of distributees abate in following order: (1) Property not disposed of by will; (2) residuary devises; (3) general devises; and (4) specific devises. For purposes of abatement, general devise charged on any specific property or fund is specific devise to extent of value of property on which it is charged. Abatement within each classification is in proportion to amounts of property beneficiaries would have received if full distribution of property had been made in accordance with terms of will. (14-3902).

Unclaimed Legacies.—See topic Descent and Distribution, subhead Escheat.

Pretermitted Children.—Intestate share is given to any child born or adopted after execution of will, and not provided for therein, unless: (1) Will shows omission was intentional; (2) testator had one or more children when will was executed and devised substantially all his estate to parent of omitted child; (3) testator provided for child by transfer outside will and statements of testator, amount of transfer or other evidence show that such transfer was intended to be in lieu of testamentary provision; (4) testator devised all or substantially all of estate to other parent of omitted child. If will fails to provide for living children solely because testator believes, at time of execution, that child is dead, child receives intestate share. Where pretermitted child takes share of estate, devises made by will abate as provided in 14-3902. (14-2302).

Lapse.—If devisee who is grandparent or lineal descendant of grandparent of testator is dead at time of execution of will, fails to survive testator or is treated as if he predeceased testator, issue of deceased devisee who survive testator by 120 hours take in place of deceased devisee. If all are of same degree of kinship to devisee, they take equally, but, if of unequal degree, those of more remote degree take by representation. This anti-lapse rule also applies to one who would have been devisee under class gift if he had survived testator. (14-2603). Except as provided in 14-2605, if devise other than residuary devise fails for any reason, it becomes part of residue, or, if residue is devised to two or more persons and share of one of residuary devisees fails for any reason, his share passes to other residuary devisee or to other residuary devisees in proportion to their interests in residue. (14-2604).

Contribution.—No statutory provision except for share of pretermitted child. See subhead Pretermitted Children, supra.

Exoneration.—Specific devise passes subject to any mortgage existing at date of death, without right of exoneration regardless of any general directive in will to pay debts. (14-2607).

Foreign Executed Wills.—Written will is valid if its execution complies with law at time of execution of place where will is executed, or with law of place where, at time of execution or at time of death, testator is domiciled, has place of abode or is national. (14-2506).

Foreign Probate Wills.—Art. 4 of Uniform Probate Code adopted without material variations. See topic Executors and Administrators.

Simultaneous Death.—Uniform Simultaneous Death Act adopted. (14-2702).

Small Estates.—See topic Executors and Administrators, subhead Small Estates.

Living Wills and Health Care Directives.—Person may execute health care power of attorney (36-3221), pre-hospital medical care directive (36-3251), and living will (36-3261). Optional forms in statute. Out-of-state health care directives are valid in Arizona if valid in place where and at time when it was adopted, and if it does not conflict with Arizona criminal laws. (36-3208). Health care decisions for adult incapacitated persons made by statutorily-determined surrogate, except for decision to stop artificial administration of food or fluid. (36-3231). Interested persons may challenge directive or surrogate in superior court. (36-3206).

Person may execute pre-hospital medical care directive banning medical personnel from performing specified emergency procedures. (36-3251). Form not prepared by Department of Health Services may be used if it meets requirements of this section. (36-3251[J]).

FAMILY

ADOPTION:

Child, or foreign born person 21 or under who is not illegal alien, and who is present within state at time petition for adoption is filed, may be adopted. (8-102). Child is person under 18 years of age. (8-101). Department of Economic Security regulates adoption agencies (8-126) and subsidizes parents adopting child otherwise unadoptable because of physical, mental, emotional conditions; age, race, sibling relationship or nationality. (8-141, 144). Department of Economic Security can enter into compact with other states to provide for reciprocal enforcement of adoption assistance agreements. (8-171 et seq.).

Adoptive parents or guardian of adoptee who is at least 18, adoptee who is at least 21, any progeny of deceased adoptee who is at least 21, spouse of deceased adoptee, birth parents of adoptee, and parents of deceased birth parent may use services of confidential intermediary to arrange contacts and to obtain information relating to adoption. (8-134[A]). State-licensed adoption agency, Department of Economic Security or individual who meets certain requirements may serve as confidential intermediary. (8-134[B], [F] to [G])).

Consent Required.—Child if age 12 or over; both birth parents unless they are incompetent, their parental rights have been judicially terminated or they previously consented to agency placement; court appointed guardian which has been given authority to consent; and agency or division which has been given authority to consent by parents or through legal proceedings. (8-106). Consent is irrevocable unless obtained by fraud, duress or undue influence. Court may waive consent requirement after hearing, if in best interest of child. (8-106). Consents must be in writing, signed by person giving consent and witnessed or acknowledged. Consent given within 72 hours of birth of child is invalid. (8-107).

Before mother consents to adoption, affidavit signed by mother listing all potential fathers must be filed with court. Notice under civil service of process must be served on all potential fathers. Notice must inform potential fathers of planned adoption and of possible right to grant or withhold consent. (8-106). Persons claiming paternity may file notice of willingness and intent to support child in "putative father registry" with Department of Health Services. Court shall determine whether claimant is father, and no final decree of adoption may be filed without diligent search of registry. (8-106.01). Failure to file paternity action within 30 days of notice bars potential fathers from bringing action to assert interest in child. (8-106 to 106.01).

Condition Precedent.—Certification by court of fitness to adopt. Not required for spouse of natural parent or for uncle, aunt or grandparent of whole or half blood or by marriage if child resided with person for 24 months prior to death of natural relative and is not ward of court. (8-105).

Jurisdiction and Venue.—Jurisdiction of adoption cases is vested in superior court (8-102.01) and venue is in county in which petitioner resides (8-104).

Petition and Proceedings.—Any adult person may adopt another adult person who is stepchild, niece, nephew, cousin or grandchild of adopting person, by agreement approved by adoption court. Foster parent may adopt adult if adoptee was juvenile when placed in foster parent's care and continuous five year familial relationship exists. Agreement shall be in writing and contain consent of both parties. (8-132[B]). Married person, not legally separated, cannot adopt adult person without consent of adopting person's spouse. (8-132[C]). Necessary elements of petition for adoption set forth in 8-132(F). Husband and wife may jointly adopt children. (8-103). Commenced by verified petition. (8-109). Limited payments available to parents of child placed for adoption, including living expenses, with court order; these payments, however, do not obligate birth mother to place child for adoption and valid consent to adoption can only be given after child's birth. (8-114[A] to [B]). Limited payments available to attorney assisting in adoption. (8-114[D]). Investigation and written report required. (8-105). Accounting of adoption-related expenditures required. (8-114 to 114.01). Date for removal hearing not sooner than six months after petition but expedited hearing available in certain circumstances. Removal from adoptive home only by juvenile court order or voluntary return to placing agency. Petitioners have right of physical custody, capacity to give medical, social and athletic consent, and support responsibility during probationary period. (8-113). Attorney assisting in direct-placement adoption must file affidavit confirming compliance with adoption laws. (8-130). Filing fee, $20, plus surcharge of $30. Person contesting adoption proceedings must pay $10 to clerk of court. (12-284). Court may charge reasonable fee for costs of pre-adoption investigation of prospective parents. (8-133[B]).

State Reimbursement.—State must be reimbursed for delivery and prenatal costs paid by Arizona Health Care Cost Containment System (AHCCCS). (8-548.07). AHCCCS may receive confidential adoption information in order to recover delivery and prenatal costs. (36-2903.01[S]).

See note at head of Digest as to 1998 legislation covered.

See Topical Index in front part of this volume.

AZ – 26

ADOPTION . . . *continued*

Decree.—No interlocutory decree. Court order is final. (8-116).

Name.—Petition gives name of child and change of name, if desired. (8-109).

Prohibition of Racial Preferences.—Adoption placement must not be denied based on race or national origin of adoptive parents or child. (8-105.01).

Foster Parents.—Child must not be removed from foster parents solely because foster parents began adoption proceedings. (8-105.02).

Effect of Adoption.—Upon entry of decree, child receives all rights natural child of adopting parents would have. All rights, duties, etc., between natural parents and child are severed except that, when adoptive parent is spouse of natural parent, relationship to that parent is unchanged. (8-117). State registrar must establish new certificate of birth for certain foreign-born adoptees. (36-326.01).

Criminal Penalties.—Knowing violation of adoption laws is punishable as felony. (8-128).

ALIMONY:

See topic Dissolution of Marriage.

COMMUNITY PROPERTY:

See topic Husband and Wife.

DESERTION:

See topic Dissolution of Marriage.

DISSOLUTION OF MARRIAGE:

Governed by 25-311 et seq.

Grounds for Absolute Dissolution.—Court will enter decree of dissolution of marriage if residency requirements (one party domiciled for 90 days prior to filing) are met, conciliation provisions of 25-381.09 either do not apply or have been met, marriage is irretrievably broken, and, to extent it has jurisdiction, court has considered and provided for child custody and support, spousal maintenance, and property disposition. (25-312).

Grounds for Legal Separation.—Court will enter decree of legal separation if requirements for dissolution of marriage have been met (except, as to marriage being irretrievably broken, enough if one or both parties desire to live separately), and if other party does not object to decree. If other party objects to decree, court will direct that pleadings be amended to seek dissolution once 90-day domicile requirement is met. Decree of separation ends community property rights and liabilities unless parties agree otherwise. (25-313).

Annulment.—See topic Marriage.

Residence Requirements.—Prior to issuance of decree dissolving marriage, one of parties, at time action is commenced, must be domiciled in state, or stationed in state while member of armed services, for 90 days. (25-312). For issuance of decree of legal separation, one of parties, at time action is commenced, must be domiciled in state or stationed in state while member of armed services. (25-313).

Jurisdiction.—Superior court vested with original jurisdiction to hear and decide matters relating to dissolution of a marriage. (25-311).

Fees.—See 25-311.01 and 12-284.

Pleading.—Verified petition must set forth vital statistics of parties if duty to support exists pursuant to §25-501, date and place of marriage, vital statistics of children, whether wife is pregnant, details of agreements between parties relating to support, custody and visitation of children and maintenance of spouse, and relief sought. Only defense to petition of dissolution or separation is that marriage is not irretrievably broken. (25-314).

Proceedings.—Trial or hearing on dissolution or separation cannot commence until 60 days after service or acceptance of process. (25-329).

Maintenance.—Court may grant a maintenance order for either spouse after considering all relevant factors. (25-319). In any proceeding in which court orders person to pay spousal maintenance, court may order that person to assign earnings to person or agency entitled to receive maintenance. (25-504). Person obligated to pay or person receiving support may file request for ex parte order. (25-504). Without hearing, superior court clerk must order assignment of person's income sufficient to pay amount requested. (25-504). Obligor has 14 days to contest assignment before employer deducts amount. (25-504). Employer or payor who does not comply with terms of assignment may be liable for amounts not paid and subject to contempt. (25-504). Court may order assignment although person owed support has not requested it. (25-504). Assignment has priority over all other attachments, executions, garnishments or assignments. (25-504). Out-of-state support orders may produce ex parte assignment of earnings. (25-323.02). Clerk of court may provide consumer reporting agencies with copies of court orders obligating person to pay child support or spousal maintenance. (12-283).

Division of Property of Spouses.—See subhead Disposition of Property, infra.

Disposition of Property.—Community property system of distribution. Court assigns each spouse's sole and separate property and divides community, joint tenancy, and other property held in common equitably, though not necessarily in kind, without regard to marital misconduct. Property acquired outside state is deemed community property regardless of date of acquisition if such property would have been community property if acquired in Arizona. Community, joint tenancy or other common property not disposed of by court is held by parties as tenants in common. (25-318).

Change of Wife's Name.—Court will order restoration of former name of any party upon request at any time prior to court signature of decree of dissolution or annulment. (25-325).

Custody of Children.—Superior court vested with jurisdiction to decide child custody matters pursuant to statutory directives. (25-401). Parent will not be preferred as custodian because of that parent's sex. (25-403). No motion to modify custody determination can be made for one year unless child's physical, mental, moral or emotional health is seriously endangered. (25-403). Court may issue order for joint custody, if both parents submit written joint custody agreement to court and court finds it in child's best interests. (25-403). Custody should not be awarded to persons with drug convictions or history of committing domestic violence. (25-403).

Grandparents' and Great-Grandparents' Visitation Rights.—Superior court may grant grandparents and great-grandparents visitation rights, which automatically terminate if minor child has been adopted or placed for adoption, unless spouse of natural parent that remarries adopts child. (25-409).

Allowance for Support of Children.—Court shall order either or both parents owing duty of support to child to pay support after considering all relevant factors. (25-809). Support may be ordered past age of majority for mentally or physically disabled child. (25-809). Parent of minor child who knowingly fails to furnish reasonable support for child commits felony. (25-511). If payment is not received within ten days of due date, person receiving support may use any available civil remedy to enforce order. (25-503). Child support at least two months in arrears may result in hearing to suspend obligor's driver's license. (25-517, 320.01, 28-413). When child support has not been awarded but court deems it appropriate, court may order payment of past child support. (25-320). Court shall assign responsibility for providing medical insurance for child. (25-320). Court must order assignment of earnings of parent who is obligated to pay child support. Employee benefits also subject to attachment and garnishment. (9-931, 968). See topic Garnishment. Employer or payor who does not comply with terms of assignment may be liable for amounts not paid and subject to contempt. Assignment has priority over all other attachments, executions, garnishments or assignments. (25-323, 504). On death of supporting parent, future support may be modified, revoked or commuted to lump sum payment and has priority in estate equal to right for family allowance. (25-327). Clerk of court may provide consumer reporting agencies with copies of court orders obligating person to pay child support or spousal maintenance. (12-283). Relocation of child requires 60 days' prior written notice unless previous order provides otherwise. (25-408).

Remarriage.—Parties may remarry immediately after final judgment. Appeal from decree of dissolution which does not challenge that marriage was irretrievably broken does not prevent a party from remarrying. (25-325).

Temporary Restraining Order or Permanent Injunction.—Upon filing for separation or dissolution, court clerk will order preliminary injunction to prevent parties from independently selling community property, harassing or disturbing each other or parties' children, or removing any of children from state without consent of court or other party. Certified copy of preliminary injunction may be filed by either party with sheriff in jurisdiction where party resides; moving party must show proof of service on spouse. Orders effective until final decree of dissolution or legal separation filed, or action dismissed. (25-315).

Court of Conciliation.—A court of conciliation may be created by superior court for purpose of preserving, promoting and protecting family life, institution of matrimony, rights of children and to provide means for reconciliation of spouses and amicable settlement of domestic controversies. Court has jurisdiction whenever controversy exists between spouses which may result in dissolution or annulment of marriage and there is minor child of either of spouses whose welfare might be affected thereby. (25-381.01 et seq.). Court's jurisdiction may be invoked by filing of petition for conciliation which prohibits filing of action for divorce, annulment, separate maintenance, or separation from bed and board for period of 60 days and transfers any such action then pending to court of conciliation (25-381.09, 381.18), which can require attendance of parties at one or more conferences as condition to further proceedings (25-381.23).

Revised Uniform Reciprocal Enforcement of Support Act (as am'd) adopted. (25-591, 621, 661). See subhead Uniform Interstate Family Support Act (UIFSA), infra.

Uniform Child Custody Jurisdiction Act adopted. (25-431 et seq.).

Uniform Interstate Family Support Act (UIFSA).—Adopted, effective June 30, 1995. If Arizona handles case arising subsequent to June 30, 1995, from state that has not enacted UIFSA, then Revised Uniform Reciprocal Enforcement of Support Act applies. (25-651 et seq.).

Separation Agreements.—Terms of agreement, except those pertaining to children, will be binding on court and incorporated into final decree if court finds that they are fair. (25-317).

Uniform Marriage and Divorce Act adopted. (25-311 et seq.).

DIVORCE:

See topic Dissolution of Marriage.

GUARDIAN AND WARD:

Uniform Probate Code (but not 1977 or later amendments) adopted. (14-1101 et seq.). Permanent and/or temporary guardian may be appointed for minor. (8-525 et seq., 14-5201 et seq.). Permanent and/or temporary guardian may be appointed for incapacitated person. (14-5301 et seq.). Permanent and/or temporary conservator may be appointed for protection of property of minor or person under other disability. (14-5401 et seq.). Court may appoint public fiduciary where no person or corporation is qualified and willing to act as guardian or conservator. (14-5601 et seq.). Person may for fee serve as court appointed guardian, provided he or she is registered as private fiduciary with supreme court. (14-5651).

Jurisdiction and Venue.—Superior court has jurisdiction over both guardianship and protective proceedings, and such proceedings involving same person may be consolidated. (14-5102). Venue for guardianship of minor is place where minor resides or is present. (14-5205). Venue for guardianship of incapacitated person is county where person resides or is present, or county where court sits which has ordered person admitted to institution. (14-5302). For subsequent proceedings, court where minor ward resides has concurrent jurisdiction with court that appointed guardian or in which acceptance of appointment was filed (14-5211); for other guardianships, court where

See note at head of Digest as to 1998 legislation covered.

See Topical Index in front part of this volume.

AZ – 27

GUARDIAN AND WARD . . . *continued*

ward resides has concurrent jurisdiction with court in which acceptance of appointment was filed (14-5313).

Court in which petition seeking appointment of conservator is filed has: Exclusive jurisdiction to determine need for conservator or to grant other protective order until proceedings are terminated; exclusive jurisdiction to determine how estate of protected person will be managed, expended or distributed; and concurrent jurisdiction to determine validity of claims against person, estate or title of protected person. (14-5402). Venue is in county where person to be protected resides, regardless of appointment of guardian elsewhere, or, if person to be protected is nonresident, county in which he has property. (14-5403).

Selection of Guardian.—Guardian of unmarried minor may be appointed by parent's will if minor under 14 years and if minor 14 years or older does not object, or by court if all parental rights of custody have been terminated or suspended. (14-5202 to 5204). Any person whose appointment would be in best interests of minor may be guardian, and court may appoint nominee of minor 14 years or older. (14-5206). Proposed temporary or permanent guardian or conservator, must provide court, under oath, information requested in 14-5106. Guardian unrelated to minor may be appointed only after check of fingerprint and criminal history records. (14-5206). Permanent guardian may be appointed if minor has been in custody of prospective guardian for at least nine months, and reunification with parents is not practical or in minor's best interests. Any competent person may be guardian of incapacitated person. Court shall appoint qualified investigator to inquire into proposed guardian's background and suitability, as well as to condition of alleged incapacitated person. (14-5308). Priority of selection is guardian or conservator, individual or corporation nominated by incapacitated person, person nominated in incapacitated person's most recent durable power of attorney, spouse, relative with which incapacitated person has resided for more than six months, nominee of person caring for incapacitated person or paying benefits to him, private fiduciary, professional guardian, conservator or Arizona Veteran's Service Commission. (14-5311). Conservator may be individual or corporation, with general power to serve as trustee. Priority of consideration is conservator or other fiduciary appointed by court where protected person resides, nominee of protected person if latter is 14 years and has sufficient mental capacity, person nominated in protected person's most recent durable power of attorney, spouse, adult child, parent or person nominated by will of deceased parent, relative with whom protected person resided more than six months and nominee of person caring for or paying benefits to protected person. (14-5410).

Qualification.—Guardian, conservator, or private fiduciary, unless national banking association, holder of state banking permit, savings and loan authorized to conduct trust business in state, title insurance company qualified to do business in state, trust company holding certificate to engage in trust business from superintendent of banks, or public fiduciary, may be required to furnish bond. (14-5105, 5411 to 5412, 5651).

Powers and Duties.—Guardian of minor ward has powers and responsibilities of custodial parent regarding ward's support, care and education, except not personally liable for ward's expenses and not liable to others, solely by reason of guardianship, for acts of ward. Other powers and duties are enumerated. (14-5209). Permanent guardian acquires legal custody of minor, but does not terminate parent's rights or child's inheritance rights. Other powers and duties are enumerated. (8-525 to 525.01). Guardian of incapacitated person has powers, rights and duties of parent, except not liable to others, solely by reason of guardianship, for acts of ward. Where conservator also appointed, guardian controls custody and care of ward and is entitled to reasonable compensation for services rendered. (14-5312). Guardian shall submit written report to court on each anniversary date of qualification as guardian, on resignation or removal, and on termination of ward's disability. (14-5315). Conservator has general duty to act as fiduciary, observing standard of care prescribed by statute for trustees. Other powers and duties include inventory, record keeping, accounting, holding title to all of protected person's property and enumerated statutory powers of administration, distribution, estate planning and claims payment. (14-5417 to 5420, 5424 to 5428).

Real Estate.—Conservator has power, without court authorization, to collect, hold and retain assets, including land in another state, until he judges disposition should be made; to acquire and dispose of assets, including land in another state, for cash or on credit, at public or private sales; to repair, alter, improve or demolish buildings and other structures; to subdivide, develop or dedicate land; to enter into leases; to grant and take options; and has other enumerated powers. (14-5424).

Caveat.—For disclosure requirements in conveyance of real property made or taken in representative capacity, see category Property, topic Deeds.

Liabilities.—Conservator may be sued in his fiduciary capacity for claims based on contracts entered into in that capacity, on obligations arising from ownership or control of estate, or on torts committed in course of administration of estate, regardless of individual liability therefor. (14-5429).

Accounts.—Conservator must file accounting at least annually, unless for good cause shown filing requirement is relieved by court. (14-5419).

Termination of Guardianship.—Guardianship of minor ward terminates on death, resignation or removal of guardian, on minor's death, adoption, marriage or attainment of majority, or on formal denial of probate where testamentary appointment under informally probated will, but guardianship cannot be terminated by resignation until approved by court. (14-5210). Permanent guardianship terminates if there is significant change of circumstances. Party petitioning for revocation must prove changed circumstances by clear and convincing evidence and show that revocation is in child's best interests. (8-525.02). Guardianship of incapacitated person terminates on death of guardian or ward, on determination of incapacity of guardian, on removal or resignation of guardian or on formal denial of probate where testamentary appointment under informally probated will. (14-5306). Conservatorship is terminated on death, resignation or removal of conservator for good cause, or on determination that minority or disability of protected person has ceased. (14-5415, 5430).

Insane Persons.—Persons impaired because of mental illness, mental deficiency or mental disorder are included in definition of incapacitated persons. (14-5101).

Foreign Guardians.—If no local conservator appointed and no petition in protective proceeding pending, domiciliary foreign conservator may, on filing certified copy of appointment and bond with court in county where protected person has property, exercise as to assets in state all powers of local conservator and maintain action subject to general conditions imposed on nonresident parties. (14-5432).

Transfers to Minors.—See topic Infants.

Uniform Fiduciaries Act adopted. (14-7501 et seq.).

Uniform Simplification of Fiduciary Security Transfers Act repealed by 1995, c. 158, §6. See 47-8101 et seq. for same subject matter.

HUSBAND AND WIFE:

Separate Property.—All property, real or personal, owned by either spouse before marriage or thereafter acquired by gift, devise or descent, and increase, rents, issues and profits thereof, is separate property of such spouse. (25-213). Each spouse has sole management, control and disposition rights of his or her separate property. (25-214). Separate property of spouse is not liable for separate debts or obligations of other spouse, absent agreement of property owner to contrary. (25-215). Separate property of married person 18 years or older may be conveyed without spouse joining in conveyance. (33-451).

Community Property.—All property acquired other than by gift, devise, descent by either husband or wife during marriage (if spouses are living in Arizona at time they acquire property or reside in state which has community property law similar to Arizona's except property defined above as separate property) or that acquired after service of petition that results in dissolution of marriage, legal separation or annulment. (25-211).

Upon person's death, his separate property and his share of community property pass by testamentary disposition or by intestate succession, subject to allowances, creditors' claims and administration costs. (14-3101). By intestacy, surviving spouse receives decedent's share of community property and all his separate property when expressly declared in grant, transfer or devise to be estate in community property with right of survivorship, and if no surviving issue or if surviving issue also are issue of surviving spouse. If surviving issue are not issue of surviving spouse, decedent's share of community property and one-half of decedent's separate property passes to issue. (14-2102 to 2103).

Joint tenancy in husband and wife may be created, provided it clearly appears that spouses agreed that property would be accepted in such status. Agreement may be shown by extrinsic evidence. (11 Ariz. App. 395, 464 P.2d 982).

Either spouse separately may acquire, manage, control or dispose of community property, or bind community (25-214); but any transaction of guaranty, indemnity, or suretyship and any conveyance or encumbrance of community realty requires joinder of spouse (25-214[c], 33-452).

Community property is liable, in part, for premarital separate debts of spouse incurred after Sept. 1, 1973, and for spouse's debts incurred outside Arizona during marriage if such debts would have been community debts if incurred in Arizona. (25-215).

Marital rights in property which is acquired in state during marriage by persons married outside of Arizona who then move into state are controlled by Arizona law. (25-217).

See also topic Dissolution of Marriage, subhead Disposition of Property.

Matrimonial Agreements.—See topic Marriage, subhead Matrimonial Agreements.

Contracts.—Except with regard to real property and guarantyship, indemnity or suretyship, either spouse may contract debt and otherwise act for benefit of community. In action on such debt, spouses must be sued jointly and debt satisfied, first from community property, and second from separate property of spouse contracting debt. (25-215).

Domestic Violence.—Counties can establish deferred prosecution programs for certain individuals accused of domestic violence to complete diversion program and avoid prosecution. (11-361). If domestic violence involved pregnant woman—increased sentencing allowed. (11-3601). Aggravated domestic violence deferred. (13-3601.02).

Agency.—Either spouse may act as attorney in fact for the other with respect to either separate property or community property if so authorized by other spouse and authorization is properly executed and acknowledged. (33-454).

Conveyances, Encumbrances, Etc.—Spouses have equal management, control and disposition rights over their community property and have equal power to bind community. (25-214).

Court of Conciliation.—See topic Dissolution of Marriage.

Interference With Marital Relations.—Common law action for alienation of affections abolished. (25-341).

Desertion and Nonsupport.—See topic Dissolution of Marriage, subheads Revised Uniform Reciprocal Enforcement of Support Act and Uniform Interstate Family Support Act (UIFSA).

INFANTS:

Age of Majority.—18 for both sexes. (1-215). Exception is minimum age (21) for consumption of alcoholic beverages.

Action by or against Minor.—May be brought or defended in name of minor by guardian, guardian ad litem or next friend. (14-1403; Civ. 17[g]).

Support of Minor.—See subheads Parental Responsibility, Revised Uniform Reciprocal Enforcement of Support Act, and Uniform Interstate Family Support Act (UIFSA), infra.

Juvenile Court.—See category Courts and Legislature, topic Courts.

Parental Responsibility.—Parents liable for wilful torts of minor. See category Civil Actions and Procedure, topic Damages. Parents or legal guardians civilly liable for shoplifting thefts of minor. (12-691 et seq.). Parents liable for support of child until age

INFANTS . . . *continued*
18 or completion of high school or equivalency program, if child becomes 18 while in high school. (12-2451 et seq.). Department of Economic Security may act as payee for benefits where it has care, custody or control of child or where it is paying cost of care (41-1954[B]), and may seek support order if public assistance payments are being made (46-401 et seq.). Court must order assignment of earnings of parent who is obligated to pay child support and may impose lien on property if parent is delinquent at least one month. (12-2454, 2463). Notice and failure to appear in court result in child support arrest warrant, with fee necessary before release. (12-2491). Liability for child support payments must be disclosed when filing for unemployment compensation. Department of Economic Security shall deduct all child support obligations from unemployment compensation for direct payment to guardian. (23-789). Department of Economic Security shall encourage employers to ask employees if they are obligated to pay child support. Employer is encouraged to report this and other employee information to facilitate child support enforcement and prevent benefit fraud in assistance programs, but employer cannot be penalized for noncompliance. (23-722.01 to 722.02).

Termination of Parental Rights.—Parent-child relationship may be terminated due to abandonment, neglect, wilful abuse, mental illness, mental deficiency, chronic drug or alcohol abuse, certain felony convictions, relinquishment, potential father's failure to timely file paternity action or where, pursuant to court order: (1) Child has been in out-of-home placement for cumulative period of nine months and parent has not remedied circumstances which caused child to be placed out-of-home; (2) child has been out-of-home for cumulative period of 18 months, parent has been unable to remedy circumstances which caused child to be placed out-of-home, and there is substantial likelihood that parent cannot exercise proper and effective parental care and control in near future; (3) identity of parent unknown following three months of diligent effort to identify and locate parent; (4) parent had parental rights to another child terminated within preceding two years for same cause and is currently unable to discharge parental responsibilities due to same cause; or (5) child cared for in out-of-home placement, responsible agency made diligent efforts to reunify and (a) child, pursuant to court order, returned to legal custody of parent from whom child removed, (b) within 18 months thereafter, child removed from that parent's legal custody for same cause, is being cared for in out-of-home placement, and parent currently unable to discharge parental responsibilities. (8-533).

Disabilities.—Capacity to contract and transfer property governed by common law. (47-1103). Infants may be required to pay reasonable price for necessaries. (53 Ariz. 336, 89 P.2d 496). Minor students 16 years or older can contract for educational loans if enrolled. (44-140 et seq.). Minors can contract for medical care for diagnosis and treatment of venereal disease. Minors who are emancipated, married, or homeless can contract for hospital, medical, and surgical care. (44-132 to 132.01). Minors 12 years or older are deemed to have consented to medical care if under influence of dangerous drug. (44-133.01). Parental consent generally required for abortion performed on unmarried minor. (36-2152).

Emancipation.—Veteran entitled to benefits under provisions of Servicemen's Readjustment Act of 1944, or spouse of any such veteran, is under no legal disability by reason of minority to make any contract, nor is any contract made by any such veteran, or spouse, invalid or voidable by reason of minority. (44-131).

Injuries and Death.—Either parent may maintain action for death or injury of child, and guardian for injury or death of ward. (12-612, 641). Child abuse punishable as criminal offense. (13-3623). Infant less than one year of age shall not be deprived of nourishment with intent to cause or allow its death. Infant shall not be deprived of necessary lifesaving medical treatment or surgical care, except where risk to infant's life or health outweighs potential benefit of treatment or care. (36-2281). Health care institutions must report suspected incidents of denial of medically necessary treatment or nourishment with intent to allow death of infant. (36-2282).

Child Abuse.—Punishable as criminal offense. (13-3623). Behavioral health services providers must have employees fingerprinted and certify whether they are awaiting trial or have been convicted of or committed certain crimes against children. (36-425.03, 46-141). Subject of investigation of child abuse, alleged victim, and alleged victim's siblings, have right to privacy, with listed exceptions. (8-807).

Legitimacy.—Every child is legitimate child of its natural parents and entitled to support and education as if born in lawful wedlock. (8-601).

Maternity and Paternity Proceedings.—Regulated by 8.106 et seq., 12.841 et seq., and 36-322 et seq.

Surrogate parentage contracts illegal. Surrogate is legal mother of child and entitled to custody. (25-218). Rebuttable presumption that husband of surrogate is legal father of child. (25-218).

Adoption.—See topic Adoption.

Firearms.—Minors in Maricopa or Pima County may not knowingly carry on his/her person or in means of transportation firearm in any place open to public, subject to few exceptions. (13-3111).

Restricted Occupations.—Employment of children is regulated as to age, education, character of occupation and hours. Employment of children of specified age in prohibited occupations is misdemeanor. (23-230 et seq.)

Revised Uniform Reciprocal Enforcement of Support Act (as am'd) adopted. (12-1651 et seq.). See subhead Uniform Interstate Family Support Act (UIFSA), infra.

Uniform Child Custody Jurisdiction Act adopted. (8-401 et seq.).

Uniform Interstate Family Support Act (UIFSA).—Adopted, effective June 30, 1995. If Arizona handles case arising subsequent to June 30, 1995, from state that has not enacted UIFSA, then Revised Uniform Reciprocal Enforcement of Support Act applies. (12-1751 et seq.).

Revised Uniform Gifts to Minors Act repealed.

Uniform Transfers to Minors Act adopted with minor changes. (14-7651 et seq.).

Uniform Securities Ownership by Minors Act not adopted.

Interstate Compact on Juveniles adopted. (8-361 et seq.).

Uniform Minor Student Capacity to Borrow Act adopted. (44-140 to 140.01).

MARRIAGE:

Consent Required.—Persons under 18 must have parental consent to marry. Persons under 16 must also have approval of superior court judge. (25-102). Consent of one parent (if parents living apart, parent with custody of minor) or guardian is sufficient. (25-122).

License.—Persons desirous of marrying must procure license from superior court clerk, authorized city or town clerk, or designated justice of peace, and both parties must make oath to age, name, residence, and relationship between parties. (25-121, 126). Superior court clerk will charge and collect fee of $20 for each marriage license. (12-284[C]).

Reports of Marriage.—Clerk of superior court must keep record of all licenses issued and acts of solemnization performed. Person solemnizing marriage shall endorse solemnization on license and return to clerk within 30 days. (25-123).

Record.—See category Documents and Records, topic Records, subhead Vital Statistics.

Blood Test.—Requirement of premarital syphilis tests abolished.

Ceremony.—No waiting period required between issuance of license and solemnization of marriage although solemnization must occur before 12-month marriage license application expires.

All regularly licensed or ordained clergymen, judges of courts of record, municipal court judges, justices of peace, justices of U.S. Supreme Court, judges of courts of appeals, district courts and courts that are created by act of Congress, bankruptcy court and tax court judges, U.S. magistrate judges, and judges of Arizona Court of Military Appeals may solemnize marriages between persons authorized to marry. (25-124).

Contract of Marriage.—Marriage contract must be licensed and solemnized by person authorized by law or by someone purporting to act in such capacity and believed to be such, in good faith, by at least one of parties. (25-111).

Covenant Marriage.—Couples sign "declaration of intent", agree to special premarital counseling, and agree to seek counseling if problems. Dissolved only because of adultery, felony with prison or death sentence, living apart one year, "ill-treatment", abuse, drug or alcohol abuse, or both parties agree. Court may order child support and spousal maintenance. (25-901 et seq.).

Common Law Marriages.—Common law marriages may not be contracted in Arizona. Common law marriages valid where contracted are recognized in Arizona. See subhead Foreign Marriages, infra.

Contract or Proxy Marriages.—Not authorized. (25-111, 125).

Prohibited Marriages.—All marriages between parents and children, grandparents and grandchildren of every degree; between brothers and sisters of half as well as whole blood; between uncles and nieces, aunts and nephews, and first cousins (except if both cousins are over 65 years old or if one of them is unable to reproduce), and between persons of same gender are void. (25-101, 125).

Foreign Marriages.—Marriage valid by laws of place where contracted is valid in Arizona, except prohibited marriages. Marriage contracted by Arizona residents in another state to evade Arizona law is void. (25-112).

Matrimonial Agreements.—Uniform Premarital Agreement Act adopted. (25-201 et seq.).

Annulment.—Marriage may be annulled by superior court because of existence of impediment rendering marriage void. (25-301). Void includes voidable. (54 Ariz. 1, 91 P.2d 700).

No statute or case setting forth time within which suit for annulment on ground of nonage must be brought. Common law rule applies.

Jurisdictional and procedural requirements are same as for dissolution of marriage. Court shall divide property and establish rights concerning any children of marriage. (25-302).

Fees.—At commencement of each action for annulment, petitioner must pay $60 and respondent must pay $30. (12-284, 25-303[A]). In county with conciliation court, add $50 for each party on appearance. (25-303[B]).

MARRIED WOMEN:

See topics Husband and Wife, Marriage; categories Civil Actions and Procedure, topics Actions, Evidence, subhead Witnesses; Debtor and Creditor, topic Homesteads; Documents and Records, topic Acknowledgments; Estates and Trusts, topics Executors and Administrators, Wills; Property, topics Deeds, Dower.

INSURANCE

INSURANCE COMPANIES:

Regulation.—Statutory regulation of insurance and insurance business, including agents, brokers, solicitors, adjusters, etc., is set out at length in 20-101 et seq. No person (or company, society, etc.) may transact business of insurance in Arizona, or business involving insurance to be performed in Arizona, without complying with applicable provisions of above statutes. (20-401.01). Aggravated or multiple violations of insurance code, including transaction of insurance business after revocation of license, is felony. (13-3714). Service companies and service contracts are regulated by 20-1095 et seq.; mechanical reimbursement reinsurers are regulated by 20-1096 et seq. Prepaid legal insurance corporations and prepaid legal insurance contracts are regulated by 20-1097 et seq. Bail bond agents are regulated by 20-319 et seq. Risk retention groups are regulated by 20-2401 et seq. Agents reviewing inpatient medical services and outpatient surgery services are regulated by 20-2501 et seq. Domestic insurers filing risk-based capital reports is governed by 20-488 et seq. Foreign insurers filing risk-based capital reports is governed by 20-488.09. Standard valuation law established at 20-510.

See note at head of Digest as to 1998 legislation covered.

See Topical Index in front part of this volume.

AZ – 29

INSURANCE COMPANIES . . . *continued*

Administration and Enforcement.—Director of Insurance, appointed by Governor, administers Department of Insurance. Director may make reasonable rules and regulations necessary for effectuating any provision of insurance law. (20-143). Copies of rules available on request to Director of Insurance, 1601 W. Jefferson St., Phoenix, Arizona 85030. Director has mandatory and discretionary revocation and suspension powers. (20-219 to 220). Director can impose civil penalties based on unfair practices (20-456, 2117) and for violation of any law relating to insurance or regulation promulgated by director (20-220), and may establish grounds for suspension or revocation (20-220).

Contracts of Insurance.—Act of 1954 did not invalidate or modify contracts legally in force prior to Jan. 1, 1955. (20-110). With certain exceptions, policies must be countersigned by resident agents if state of residence of nonresident agent requires countersignature. Exceptions include insurance on life, disability, title and transportation, insurance issued by salaried agents, reinsurance and bid bonds issued by surety in connection with public or private contracts. (20-229). Insurers are required to provide ten-day free-look period for annuity contracts. (20-1233). Director can disapprove contract made with health service corporation when benefits unreasonable in relation to premium. (20-826).

Statutory provisions governing insurance contracts in general are found in 20-1101 et seq. Director shall make rules and regulations governing form and readability of policies. (20-1110.01). Insurer is estopped from enforcing boilerplate limitation on coverage that conflicts with insured's reasonable expectation of coverage if certain tests are met. (140 Ariz. 383, 394, 401, 682 P.2d 388, 399, 406).

Investigation.—Director shall examine affairs, transactions, accounts, records and assets of each authorized insurer, as often as he deems advisable. Each insurer applying for initial certificate of authority to do business in state is examined in like manner. In lieu of making own examination, Director may accept full report of last recent examination of foreign or alien insurer, certified by insurance supervisory official of another state. (20-156). Expense of examination paid by Insurance Examiners' Revolving Fund. (20-156, 159).

Fees.—See 20-167.

Authority.—No person may act as insurer and no insurer may transact business in Arizona except as authorized by subsisting authority granted to it by Director, except as otherwise provided in Act. (20-206).

Qualifications.—Generally, see 20-207.

Kinds of Insurance Insurer May Transact.—See 20-209, 251 et seq., 1661 et seq., 1801 et seq., and 2301 et seq.

Insurance Administrators.—Requirements and limitations regulated by 20-485.

Types of Insurers.—See 20-701 et seq.

Title Insurers.—Regulated by 20-375 to 379.

Funds and Deposit Required and Financial Requirements.—See 20-210 to 214 and 288.

Financial Provisions and Procedures.—See 20-501 et seq.

Investments.—Regulated by 20-531 et seq. and 20-562.

Administration of Insolvency.—See 20-169 et seq. and 661 et seq.

Premium Tax.—Domestic and foreign or alien insurers each pay tax of 2.0% of net premiums, except that tax on fire insurance premiums is 2.2%. (20-224). In addition, all insurers pay tax of .4312% of net premiums received for all insurance carried for or on vehicles. (20-224.01).

Insurer that paid premium tax of $2,000 or more on net premiums received during preceding calendar year pursuant to 20-224(B), 224.01, 837, 1010, 1060 and 1097.07 must pay on or before 15th day of each month from Mar. through Aug. 15% of amount paid during preceding year pursuant to 20-224(B), 224.01, 837, 1010, 1060 and 1097.07. (20-224[E]). Overpayments refunded within three months after due date. (20-224.02). Insurer who fails to pay tax prescribed by 20-224, 224.01, 837, 1010, 1060 and 1097.07 subject to civil penalty equal to greater of $25 or 5% of amount due plus interest at rate of 1% per month from date tax was due. (20-225). Certificate must be revoked if tax not paid within 30 days of due date. (20-225).

Agents and Brokers.—Examination is given to applicant for license as agent, broker or solicitor. (20-292). Some exceptions are provided, including waiver of examination in case of one already licensed in another state if reciprocal arrangements have been made. (20-293, 303). Firm or corporation may be licensed only as agent or broker, not as bail bond agent, unless each owner or stockholder is licensed bail bond agent. (20-295). Bond is required of applicant for broker's license. (20-299). Agent is deemed agent of insurer if within authority or apparent authority or if insurer authorizes or ratifies agent's actions; includes bail bond agents. (20-282).

Temporary license may be granted in certain cases. (20-307).

Foreign agent or broker cannot act as or hold himself out as adjuster unless licensed, except for adjuster licensed in his state of domicile who is sent on behalf of insurer to adjust particular loss or series of losses resulting from common disaster. (20-312). Foreign agent or broker is subject to continuing education requirements pursuant to 20-2901 et seq.

Rental Car Agent License.—May be issued to rental companies for automobile insurance offered in connection with rental agreements. (20-295.01).

Unauthorized Insurers.—Unauthorized insurer who knowingly transacts any unauthorized act is guilty of Class 5 Felony. (20-401.06). Injunctive relief provided. Contract of insurance effectuated by unauthorized insurer is valid and such insurer may defend actions, but insurer without certificate of authority may not maintain action. (20-402). Premium receipts tax of 3% of gross premiums, less premiums returned due to cancellation or reduction of premium, imposed on industrial insureds obtaining contracts from unauthorized insurers. (20-401.07).

Disclosure.—Insured can have access to and request correction of personal information. (20-2108 to 2109). Specific reason for adverse underwriting decision must be provided to applicant and mere fact of previous adverse underwriting decision shall not affect future applications. (20-2110 to 2112). Insurer must not, subject to certain exceptions, disclose personal or privileged information unless consented to by insured. (20-2113). Disclosure violations may result in imposition of civil penalties. (20-2117). Private remedy exists for disclosure violations. (20-2118 to 2119). For specific regulations on disclosure of HIV information, see 20-448.01. See generally 20-2101 et seq.

Exemptions.—Annual certificate of exemption available to charitable, nonprofit life, disability and annuity insurers. Fee, $65. (20-401.05).

Charitable Gifts.—Charitable organization that enters into agreement for qualified charitable gift annuity must provide written notice to donor in annuity agreement that states charitable gift annuity not insurance under laws of this state. (20-103, 119).

Health Insurance Portability and Accountability Act.—Arizona law conforms to this federal act. (20-2301 et seq.).

Process.—Each authorized foreign or alien insurer, each licensed foreign agent and broker, and each domestic insurer without statutory agent must irrevocably appoint Director of Insurance as attorney to receive service of legal process. (20-221, 304). Service on unauthorized insurer may be made on Secretary of State in action by Director (20-401.03), or on Director in action by any other person (20-403).

Direct Actions Against Insurer.—See category Transportation, topic Motor Vehicles, subhead Direct Actions.

Rates and Rating Organizations.—Regulated by 20-341 et seq. and 381 et seq.

Insurance Holding Companies.—Authorized and regulated by Director of Insurance. Registration required. (20-481 et seq.).

Health Care Service Organizations.—Regulated by 20-1051 et seq. and 2501 et seq.

Accountable Health Plans.—Regulated by 20-2301 et seq. Child medical support regulated by 25-531 et seq.

Medical Malpractice Insurance.—State joint underwriting plan offers primary and excess coverage for physicians, registered nurses, hospitals and other health care providers under certain conditions. Malpractice claim reports and investigations required. (12-570, 20-1742, 32-3201 et seq.).

Unfair Practices and Frauds.—See 20-118, 441 et seq. and 461.

Plain Language.—See category Business Regulation and Commerce, topic Consumer Protection.

Motor Vehicle Insurance.—See category Transportation, topic Motor Vehicles, subhead Insurance.

Reinsurance.—Regulated by 20-261 et seq. and 486.01 et seq.

Producer Controlled Property and Casualty Insurance.—Regulated by 20-487 et seq.

SURETY AND GUARANTY COMPANIES:

Surety and guaranty companies are regulated per Insurance Act, 20-101 et seq.; surety insurance defined, 20-257; specific provision, 20-1531 et seq.; surety bonds, 7-101 et seq.; premium tax, 20-224 et seq.

Inspection of Records.—Records, books and files of sureties are at all times liable and subject to visitorial and inquisitorial powers of state. (Const., Art. XIV, §16).

Action by Creditor.—Any person bound as surety upon contract for payment of money or performance of act, when right of action has accrued, may, by notice in writing, require creditor or obligee forthwith to bring action upon contract. If creditor or obligee, not being under legal disability, fails to bring action within 60 days after receiving notice, and prosecute it to judgment and execution, surety giving notice is discharged from all liability thereon. (12-1641).

Subrogation.—Where surety compelled to pay judgment or part thereof, judgment remains in force and right to enforce is subrogated. (12-1643).

Licensing.—Surety company authorized to transact business in state, which undertakes to complete contract on which it issued performance or completion bond, is not required to be licensed as contractor, provided all construction work is performed by licensed contractors. (32-1121).

Security Under Procedural Rules.—Where Rules of Civil Procedure require or permit giving of security and security involves undertaking with surety, surety submits to jurisdiction, appoints clerk of superior court as agent for service and may be held liable without necessity of independent action. (Civ. 65.1).

INTELLECTUAL PROPERTY

TRADEMARKS AND TRADENAMES:

Subject to certain prescribed limitations, any person who adopts and uses trademark or service mark in Arizona may file application for registration with Secretary of State on form supplied by him. Upon determination that application complies with this section, Secretary will issue Certificate of Registration which is admissible in evidence as proof of such registration in any judicial proceeding. Fee, $15. (41-126, 44-1443 to 1444).

Registration is effective for ten years, renewable for successive like terms upon application filed three months prior to expiration of term. Fee, $15. Issuance of Certificate of Registration, $3. (41-126, 44-1445).

Mark and its registration are assignable with good will of business. Assignment must be written and may be recorded with Secretary of State. Fee, $15. Assignment void as to subsequent bona fide purchasers unless recorded within three months of assignment or prior to each subsequent purchase. (41-126, 44-1446).

Owner of registered mark has cause of action against anyone who uses mark or similar mark in connection with any goods or services in confusing or deceptive manner. Relief may be granted by way of injunction, damages, accounting for profits,

TRADEMARKS AND TRADENAMES . . . *continued*

costs, attorney fees, confiscation of computer software, or cancellation of registration. This article does not affect rights in marks acquired in good faith at any time at common law. (44-1451 to 1452).

Willful reproduction, copying, forging or counterfeiting of any mark usually affixed by any person to his goods is Class 3 Misdemeanor, if acting with intent to pass off goods to which such mark is, or is intended to be, affixed, is Class 2 Misdemeanor. (44-1453 to 1454). Sale of goods to which counterfeit mark is affixed with knowledge that mark is counterfeit is Class 2 Misdemeanor. (44-1455). Commercial use of unauthorized copy of computer software that in any way displays registered mark is Class 5 Felony. (44-1455).

Similar provisions for registration of tradenames. (44-1460 et seq.). Fee, $10. (41-126). Secretary of State cannot file application for registration of any trade name, if same as, deceptively similar to, or if not readily distinguishable from existing or reserved corporate name. (44-1460.01.). Period of registration is five years, renewable for like period upon application filed within six months of end of term. Fee, $10. (41-126, 44-1460.02). Trade name may be assigned and recorded. Fee, $10. (41-126, 44-1460.03). Issuance of Certificate of Registration, $3. (41-126, 44-1460.03). Exclusive right to use trade name available if registered prior to reservation of corporate name or filing of articles of incorporation, subject to right acquired in good faith at common law. (44-1460.05).

Fair Trade Act repealed.

Tradenames.—See category Business Organizations, topic Partnerships.

TRADE SECRETS:

Uniform Trade Secrets Act adopted. (44-401 et seq.).

LEGAL PROFESSION

ATTORNEYS AND COUNSELORS:

All lawyers must belong to public corporation called "State Bar of Arizona." (Sup. Ct. R. 31[a]).

Jurisdiction Over Admission.—Vested in supreme court. (Sup. Ct. R. 31).

Eligibility.—Applicant must be over 21 at time of examination, of good moral character, mentally and physically able to practice law, and in good standing in every other state in which he is admitted to practice. (Sup. Ct. R. 34).

Educational Requirements.—Unless he has actively practiced law in another state in five of seven years preceding application, applicant for admission must be graduate of law school fully or provisionally approved by American Bar Association at time of graduation. (Sup. Ct. R. 34). Active State Bar member must complete minimum 15 hours of continuing legal education including three hours of professional responsibility. (Sup. Ct. R. 45).

Residence Requirements.—None.

Registration as Law Student.—Not required.

Application for Admission.—Application and supporting documents, plus examination fee of $200 and filing fee of $100, must be filed not later than first day of Sept. if application is for following Feb. examination, and not later than first day of Feb. if application is for following July examination. (Sup. Ct. R. 34).

Requests for information should be addressed to State Bar of Arizona, 111 West Monroe, Suite 1800, Phoenix, Arizona 85003-1742.

Investigation.—Formal or informal hearings may be held. (Sup. Ct. R. 36[b]-[c]).

Written Examination.—Admission without examination is not permitted. All applicants for admission must meet examination requirements. Portion of examination consists of Multistate Bar Examination and Multistate Professional Responsibility Examination. Written examinations held in Feb. and July. Transfer of Multistate Professional Responsibility score from another jurisdiction accepted if examination was taken within three years prior to Arizona examination date. (Sup. Ct. R. 35).

Admission Pro Hac Vice.—Attorney practicing in another state may be permitted, on motion, to associate with local counsel in trial of any particular action.

Fees.—Active member of bar must pay annual fee, as required by supreme court. (Sup. Ct. R. 31). Member failing to pay fee after two months notice of delinquency will be suspended from practice, but may be reinstated. (Sup. Ct. R. 31).

Disabilities.—No attorney of record of either party to an action or proceeding may be a surety. (7-109).

Suspension or Disbarment.—Disciplinary Commission of Supreme Court of Arizona (seven lawyers, two non-lawyers [Sup. Ct. R. 47]), proceeding initially through local hearing committees or hearing officers that have authority to prepare findings of fact and conclusions of law, issue orders and impose discipline. (Sup. Ct. R. 48). Respondent may appear before committee, hearing officer and commission and if objects to results may appeal to supreme court. (Sup. Ct. R. 53).

Professional Corporations.—See category Business Organizations, topic Corporations.

Attorney Ethics.—Model Rules of Professional Conduct of ABA adopted as amended by Arizona Supreme Court. (Sup. Ct. R. 42).

Unlawful Practice.—It is misdemeanor to practice law unless active member of State Bar in good standing, except that officer of corporation who is not active State Bar member may represent corporation in justice or police court (Sup. Ct. R. 31); parties may be represented by non-lawyer before Industrial Commission (23-674) and for small claims procedures in Arizona Tax Court (Sup. Ct. R. 31); parties may be represented by lawyer not member of State Bar in informal proceedings before Civil Rights Division (41-1471). Representing taxpayers before Department of Revenue is not practicing law. (42-145). Limited practice by clinical law professors and law students allowed. (Sup. Ct. R. 38).

Real Estate Transactions.—See category Business Regulation and Commerce, topic Brokers.

MINERAL, WATER AND FISHING RIGHTS

MINES AND MINERALS:

Governed by 27-101 et seq.

Requirements for location of lode or placer claims on U. S. public domain (27-201) and on state land are substantially same.

Department of Mines and Mineral Resources.—Duties include promotion and development of mineral resources and cooperation with agencies responsible for regulation of state lands, mining securities and mineral technology. (27-102).

State Mine Inspector.—Responsible for inspection of mine operations, conditions, safety, machinery, equipment, sanitation and ventilation, mined land reclamation and prevention of hazardous dust conditions. (27-124, 128 to 129, 901 et seq.).

Arizona Geological Survey.—Duties include investigating and interpreting geological setting of state and its mineral resources and providing information on geological research. (27-152.01).

Mining Rights and Claims.—Lode, placer or millsite claims upon public domain of U.S. may be located and secured to discoverer by: (1) Erecting, on surface on centerline within boundaries of claim, monument of stones not less than three feet high or post not less than four feet high and posting signed notice containing name of claim, name and address of locator, date of location, width and length of claim and distance from monument to each end, general course of claim and locality with reference to natural object or permanent monument and section, township and range, if known (27-202); and (2) recording within 90 days after location copy of location notice, in office of county recorder where claim is located, attaching plat, map, or sketch of claim (27-203). Boundaries of claim must be monumented with monument marked to indicate corner or end of center of claim. (27-204 to 205). State lands also may be explored under mineral exploration permit prior to seeking mineral lease. (27-251 et seq.).

Improvements and Labor.—Before Dec. 31 of any year in which performance of annual labor or making improvements is required, affidavit may be recorded in office of county recorder where claim is located and constitutes prima facie evidence of performance of labor or improvements. (27-208). When mineral lease is obtained on state land, rental is at least average rental assessed per acre by States of Colorado, New Mexico and Utah and royalty is at least 2% of gross value of all minerals produced and sold from mineral leases. (27-234). Leases may be offered at public auction. (27-235). State Land Commissioner may inspect lands held under mineral lease. (27-239).

Operation of Mines.—Statutory provisions govern inspection, safety, reporting, waste dumps, abandoned shafts, use of explosives, hoists, mine structure and maintenance, hazardous dust and gas conditions, open pit mines, and sand and gravel operations. (27-301 et seq.).

Oil, Gas and Geothermal Resources.—Oil and Gas Conservation Commission administers provisions on production and conservation of oil, gas and geothermal resources. (27-501 et seq., 651 et seq.). Corporation Commission regulates transportation of gas and hazardous liquids and gas and hazardous liquids pipeline facilities. (40-441 et seq.). Land Department leases state lands for exploration and development, with exploratory unitization allowed. (27-551 et seq.). State lands within known producing structures may be leased only through sealed bids, and leases are subject to annual rental of $1 per acre and minimum royalty of 12½%. (27-556). State lands not in known producing structures may be leased noncompetitively with annual rental of $1 per acre and royalty of 12½%. State Land Commissioner may require permittee or lessee of state land to post surety bond which can be used for performance or restoration purposes. (37-132). Such leases are renewable after five years if no production has occurred, with double annual rental. If lease produces, it continues during production in paying quantities, and lease may be extended for two years where there are diligent drilling, completion or reworking operations. (27-555). Lease shall not contain any provisions for assessment other than those required by statute. Royalties paid to state may be in cash or in kind at option of Land Department. (27-563). Arizona refinery business may purchase royalty oil which State Land Department received from lessee. (27-565 et seq.). Land Department may exchange unleased or unclaimed subsurface rights and interests and leased oil and gas rights for subsurface rights and interests owned by others subject to certain requirements. (37-604.01). Oil, gas, helium or geothermal wells may not be subject to water laws. (45-591.01). Geothermal resources not subject to water laws unless commingled or causing impairment to groundwater supply. Wells drilled to obtain groundwater are subject to water laws. (27-667). Geothermal leases on state land require minimum wellhead royalty of 12½% and minimum annual rental of $1 per acre. (27-671).

Radioactive Materials.—See category Environment, topic Environmental Regulation.

Taxes.—Severance tax imposed upon mining activities. (42-1461 et seq.).

Water.—See category Property, topic Real Property.

MORTGAGES

CHATTEL MORTGAGES:

Uniform Commercial Code, Article 9 (1972 Official Text), adopted with revisions. (47-9101 et seq.).

What May Be Mortgaged.—See U.C.C., Art. 9; accounts, etc. (47-9102); consumer goods (47-9109[1]); equipment (47-9109[2]); farm products (47-9109[3]); general intangibles (47-9102); inventory (47-9109[4]); proceeds (47-9306).

After-acquired Property.—See U.C.C. (47-9204).

Future Advances.—See U.C.C. (47-9204).

See note at head of Digest as to 1998 legislation covered.

See Topical Index in front part of this volume.

CHATTEL MORTGAGES . . . continued

Requisites of Instrument.—See U.C.C. (47-9203, 9402).

Execution of Instrument.—Signature of debtor generally required. (47-9203, 9402).

Filing.—If collateral is consumer goods, farm equipment, farm products, etc., in office of county recorder of debtor's residence, or if debtor not resident of state, in office of county recorder in county where goods are kept. If collateral is growing crops, in office of county recorder in county where land is located. If collateral is fixtures, timber to be cut, or minerals, in office where mortgage on real property would be recorded. In all other cases, in Office of Secretary of State, State Capitol Building, Phoenix, Arizona 85007. (47-9401).

Refiling or Extension.—Original filing valid for six years. Continuation statements may be filed or recorded. (47-9403).

Removal of Property by Mortgagor (Debtor).—If removal is default, see default procedures. (47-9501 et seq.).

Sale of Property By Mortgagor (Debtor).—If sale is default, see default procedures (47-9501 et seq.).

Concealment or Destruction of Property by Mortgagor (Debtor).—See default procedures. (47-9501 et seq.).

Release.—See release provisions. (47-9406).

Satisfaction or Discharge.—See termination statement provisions. (47-9404).

Foreclosure by Court Proceedings.—See U.C.C. (47-9501).

Sale by Mortgagee (Secured Party).—See collection rights (47-9502), right to take possession (47-9503), and right to dispose of collateral (47-9504).

Redemption.—Limited to time prior to disposition or contract to dispose. (47-9506).

Foreign Mortgages.—To determine which law applies, see U.C.C. (47-9103).

Taxation.—No provision.

Forms.—UCC-1, UCC-2, UCC-3 and UCC-4 forms modified and approved by Secretary of State. See end of this Digest.

COLLATERAL SECURITY:

Uniform Commercial Code adopted. (47-9101 et seq.). See category Business Regulation and Commerce, topic Commercial Code.

MORTGAGES OF REAL PROPERTY:

Lien theory prevails. Mortgages are regulated by 33-701 et seq. Any interest in real property capable of being transferred may be mortgaged. (33-701). Every transfer of realty other than in trust, made only as security for performance of another act, is deemed mortgage. (33-702). Mortgagor entitled to possession. (33-703). Liens on multiple section mobile homes affixed to real property perfected according to laws on liens on real property or laws on security interests in fixtures. (28-325[k]).

Execution.—Mortgage can be created, renewed or extended only by writing executed with formalities required of deed, including acknowledgment. (33-701). Mortgage may provide for assignment to mortgagee of mortgagor's interest in leases, rents, issues, income or profits from covered property. (33-702[B]).

Recording.—Unrecorded mortgage valid as between parties but void as to all creditors and subsequent purchasers for valuable consideration without actual notice. (33-412). Assignment of mortgage may be recorded, which constitutes notice to person subsequently deriving title to mortgage from assignor. (33-706). Recording of false lien creates liability in favor of owner or beneficial title holder of at least $5,000 or treble actual damages, whichever is greater. (33-420[A]).

Fee.—$5 for recording first five pages and $1 for each additional page, total not to exceed $250. (11-475).

Trust Deeds.—Performance of contract also may be secured through transfer of real property by trust deed. Provisions for foreclosure and sale, deficiency judgment and recordation similar to those for mortgages. (33-801 et seq.).

Caveat: For disclosure requirements in conveyances of real property made or taken in representative capacity, see category Property, topic Deeds.

Priority of Purchase Money Mortgage.—Mortgage or deed of trust given as security for loan to purchase property secured has priority over all other liens and encumbrances incurred against purchaser prior to acquiring title to property.

Contracts for Conveyance.—Contracts requiring conveyance of full title upon payment of amounts due are subject to rules mitigating against forfeiture of purchaser's equitable title. Acceleration of amount due limits seller's remedy to foreclosure as mortgage. (33-748). Absent acceleration, purchaser's interest can be forfeited only after expiration of fixed period of time determined by percentage of total consideration already paid. (33-742[D]). Notice of election to forfeit must be recorded and served after applicable period has expired. (33-743). Statutory form of notice provided. (33-743[B]). Upon receipt of notice, purchaser must be allowed at least 20 additional days to pay amount due. (33-743[D]). Seller must file statutory notice of reinstatement upon payment of amount due by date specified in notice. (33-743[F]). If no payment is timely made, seller can complete forfeiture by quiet title action (33-744) or, where account servicing agent has been appointed, recordation of statutory affidavit of completion of forfeiture (33-745[A]). Rights of all persons having lien or encumbrance on property subordinate to seller's priority are also lost. (33-744, 745[B]).

Due On Sale Clauses.—Not enforceable in mortgages made between July 8, 1971 and Oct. 15, 1982 and transferred prior to Oct. 14, 1987 which are secured by residential property containing one to four family units situated on 2½ acres or less. Lender is limited to ½% increase in interest rate when such property is transferred subject to mortgage. (33-1571, 806.01[D]).

Satisfaction and Release.—Mortgagee, trustee or person entitled to payment, on receiving full satisfaction of mortgage or deed of trust, must acknowledge satisfaction by delivering to person making satisfaction or by recording sufficient release or satisfaction of mortgage or deed of release and reconveyance of deed of trust. (33-707[A]).

Same duty imposed upon executor or administrator of mortgagee's or trustee's estate where indebtedness is satisfied before decedent's death. (33-709). Failure in this respect, after 30 days, creates liability of $100 and for all actual damages suffered by mortgagor. Executor or administrator may be personally liable. (33-709, 712[A]). Foreign executor, administrator, conservator or guardian, attorney in fact, or heir or legatee, may release mortgage. Foreign executor, administrator, conservator or guardian must first file and record authenticated copy of appointment in recorder's office in county where mortgage is recorded. (33-708, 710 to 711).

Foreclosure.—Mortgage or trust deed securing property located in Arizona and in one or more other states may be foreclosed only by action at law, notwithstanding any provisions therein. (33-721). In contrast, exercise of power of sale does not require court action. (33-807). If separate actions are brought on debt and to foreclose mortgage securing it, plaintiff must elect one and other will be dismissed. (33-722). In foreclosure action, junior lienholder is entitled to assignment of mortgage holder's interest by paying him amount secured, with interest and costs, together with amount of other superior liens of same holder. (33-723). State may be made party to foreclosure action. (33-724). Sale of real property shall be credit on judgment in amount of either fair market value or sales price of property, whichever greater. (12-1566[B]).

Deficiency Judgment.—Court must render judgment for entire amount determined due under mortgage and direct sale of mortgaged property. (33-725[A]). If mortgaged property does not on foreclosure sale bring sufficient price to satisfy judgment, court may issue execution for balance of judgment against mortgagor where there has been personal service on him or he has appeared in foreclosure action. (33-725[B], 727[A]). Sale of real property shall be credit on judgment in amount of either fair market value or sales price of property, whichever greater. (12-1566[B]). Exceptions made for purchase money mortgages on parcel of 2½ acres or less used for single one-family or single two-family dwelling, where deficiency is not due to debtor's voluntary waste, and for situations in which both mortgage or deed of trust and security agreement are given to secure payment of purchase price of real property and consumer goods or services, when there would be no deficiency under mortgage or deed of trust alone. (33-729 to 730).

Redemption.—Payment to officer directed to sell mortgaged property before sale operates to redeem property and has same effect as satisfaction. (33-726). Property sold on foreclosure of mortgage or trust deed may be redeemed under rules applicable to executions. See 12-1281 et seq., 33-726 and category Debtor and Creditor, topic Executions.

Form.—Mortgage is created by instrument in form of ordinary deed (see category Property, topic Deeds) with defeasance clause added as follows: "to be void upon condition that I pay . . . . . ." (33-402).

PROPERTY

ABSENTEES:

Care of Property.—No statutory provisions, but see subhead Uniform Unclaimed Property Act, infra.

Process Agent.—No statutory provisions.

Escheat.—Where death presumed from five year successive absence (see category Estates and Trusts, topic Death) and intestate absentee has no heirs, all property escheats to state. Such property is sold and proceeds paid into state treasury. (12-881 et seq.). Person entitled to such proceeds may recover same by filing claim form with Department of Revenue within seven years from time of sale of escheated property. (12-886). Agreement to recover escheated property charging fee exceeding 30% is unenforceable. (12-890). Persons entitled to unclaimed shares or dividends may file claim with Department of Administration, Division of Finance. (10-401).

Unclaimed Dispositions.—See category Estates and Trusts, topic Executors and Administrators.

Uniform Unclaimed Property Act adopted. (44-301 et seq.).

Uniform Probate Code (but not 1977 or later amendments) adopted. (14-1102 et seq.).

ADVERSE POSSESSION:

Possession of real property for two years by one who claims only by right of possession is sufficient to establish that right as against suit to recover by person who shows no better right. (12-522).

Character of Possession.—Possession must be uninterrupted and visible appropriation of land, inconsistent with and hostile to claim of another, by persons in privity of estate (i.e., tacking permitted). (12-521).

Duration of Possession.—Action to recover real property must be commenced within stated periods after cause of action accrues: (1) Three years, if possessor claims land under title or color of title; (2) five years, if land is city lot or being cultivated or otherwise used and possessor claims under duly recorded deed and has paid taxes on land for five years; (3) ten years for land which possessor has cultivated, used and enjoyed, up to 160 acres or lesser area actually enclosed, or land described in written and duly recorded memorandum of title other than deed. (12-523 et seq.).

Prescriptive Easements.—Established by continuous hostile use for ten years. (12-526).

Disabilities.—Persons of unsound mind or who are under 18 have same time to bring action after removal of such disability as is allowed to others. Period of disability for imprisoned person exists only until person knew or reasonably should have known of right to bring action. (12-528).

CONVEYANCES:

See topic Deeds.

See note at head of Digest as to 1998 legislation covered.

See Topical Index in front part of this volume.

CURTESY:

Abolished. (1-201).

DEEDS:

See topic Real Property for types of estates.

Acknowledgment.—Every deed must be signed by grantor and properly acknowledged before authorized officer. (33-401[B]). Despite defects in certificate of acknowledgment, deed recorded for longer than ten years is deemed to be duly acknowledged on or after date of recording. (33-401[C]). For purposes of proving notice to subsequent purchasers or lien holders, deed containing any defect, omission, or informality in certificate of acknowledgment recorded for longer than one year is deemed to have been lawfully recorded. (33-411[C]).

Uniform Recognition of Acknowledgments Act adopted. (33-501 et seq).

Execution.—No witness is required for deed or other instrument, but all deeds must be acknowledged. (33-401). See categories Debtor and Creditor, topic Homesteads; Family, topic Husband and Wife.

Married person who is 18 or older may convey separate property without being joined by spouse in such conveyance, but conveyance or incumbrance of community real property is not valid unless executed and acknowledged by both husband and wife. (33-451 to 452). Husband and wife must join in and acknowledge conveyance of family homestead. (33-453).

Caveat: Every deed or conveyance of real property located within state, or interest therein, executed after June 22, 1976, in which grantor or grantee is described or acts as trustee, must give names and addresses of beneficiaries for whom grantor or grantee holds title and identify trust or other agreement under which grantor or grantee is acting or refer to document number or docket and page of instrument of public record in county in which land conveyed is located. Grantee who holds title as trustee must record notice of any change in beneficiary within 30 days after receiving actual knowledge of such change. Noncompliance renders conveyance voidable by other party to conveyance. Any action to void conveyance must be commenced within two years of recordation. If any interest in or lien on real property is acquired for value, such interest or lien is not impaired by failure of any person to comply with disclosure requirements. (33-404).

"Grant" or "Convey".—By statute, use of such words in conveyance implies warranty that, at time of execution of instrument, grantor had not conveyed same estate or any right, title or interest therein to other than grantee, and that such estate was free from encumbrances, including taxes, assessments and all liens. Action will lie to enforce such convenants as though expressly stated. (33-435).

Grant of Fee.—Presumed, unless estate conveyed is limited by deed. (33-432).

Joint Tenancy and Tenancy in Common.—See topic Real Property; category Family, topic Husband and Wife.

Defective Conveyance.—When instrument intended as conveyance of real property fails, wholly or in part, it is nevertheless valid as contract, and may be enforced as permitted by law. (33-437).

Lien or Encumbrance.—Sale of property subject to lien or encumbrance or where seller's interest is held under option, contract of purchase, or in trust is voidable by buyer unless instrument evidencing lien or encumbrance or option, contract of purchase, or trust agreement expressly states that buyer will receive title free of lien or encumbrance or option, contract of purchase, or trust agreement upon buyer's completion of all required payments and performances, or unless buyer actually receives clear title. Action to void sale must be commenced within two years after discovery or completion of buyer's performance, whichever comes first. Lien or encumbrance does not include taxes, assessments, reservations in patents, easements, rights-of-way, reservations of mineral rights, covenants, conditions or restrictions. (33-438).

Recording.—Deed must be acknowledged and recorded in office of county recorder in county where land is situated in order to be valid as against creditors and subsequent purchasers for value without notice. (33-412[A]). Document evidencing sale or other transfer of any legal or equitable interest in real estate (excluding leases) must be recorded by transferor within 60 days, or else transferor must indemnify transferee in any action contesting latter's interest in real estate. (33-411.01). Only documents that are lawfully recorded are deemed to give constructive notice to subsequent purchasers or lien holders. (33-411[A]). See category Documents and Records, topic Records, subhead Fees for Recording.

Affidavit.—Affidavit declaring value of property, name and address of seller and purchaser, legal description, transaction conditions, date of sale, price paid, amount of cash downpayment, type of financing, amount of personal property, tax code number, use and description of property transferred must be appended to deed evidencing transfer of title or to contract relating to sale of property at time of recording. (42-1612). Form available from Department of Revenue.

Exemptions.—See 42-1614.

Taxes.—None.

Forms

Quit Claim.—For the consideration of . . . . . I hereby quit claim to . . . . . all my interest in the following real property (description).

Grant and Convey.—For the consideration of . . . . . . I hereby convey to . . . . . . the following real property (description).

Warranty.—Add to last form "and I warrant the title against all persons whomsoever."

DEEDS OF TRUST:

See category Mortgages, topic Mortgages of Real Property.

DOWER:

Abolished. (1-201).

ESCHEAT:

See topic Absentees, subhead Escheat; category Estates and Trusts, topic Descent and Distribution, subhead Escheat.

LANDLORD AND TENANT:

Following principles apply to all landlord-tenant relationships arising out of rental of dwelling units which are not governed by Uniform Residential Landlord and Tenant Act (33-1301 et seq.) and Mobile Home Parks Residential Landlord and Tenant Act (33-1401 et seq.):

Lease need not be in writing, unless for longer than one year. (44-101). As to recording, see category Documents and Records, topic Records.

Tenant-in-possession is estopped to deny his landlord's title. Person in possession of land out of which rent is due is liable for proportion of rent due from lands in his possession. (33-323 to 324).

Damage to Building.—Destruction or injury so as to make it unfit for occupancy without fault or neglect of lessee terminates liability for rent unless otherwise provided in lease. (33-343).

Tenant's Obligation.—Tenant must exercise diligence to keep premises in as good condition as when tenant took possession, ordinary wear and tear excepted. Removal or alteration of any part of buildings or furnishings or defacement of or injury to buildings, furnishings, garages or fences is misdemeanor. (33-321 to 322).

Termination of Tenancy.—Tenancy from year-to-year terminates at end of year unless written permission is given to remain longer time; tenancy from month-to-month may be terminated by either party by ten days' notice. In cases of nonpayment of rent, no notice is required. Tenant on semi-monthly basis may terminate by five days' notice. (33-341). Tenancy of holdover lessee is from month-to-month. (33-342).

Recovery of Rent.—Owner of any lands, or his assignee or their executors or administrators, may sue and recover rent therefor, or fair and reasonable satisfaction for use and occupation thereof, in any court of competent jurisdiction, in any of following cases:

(1) When rent is due and in arrears on a lease.

(2) When lands are held and occupied without any special agreement for rent or when tenant remains in possession after termination of his right of possession.

(3) When possession is obtained under agreement, written or verbal, for purchase of premises, and before deed is given such right to possession is terminated by forfeiture or in compliance with agreement, and possession is wrongfully refused or neglected to be given on demand made by party entitled to it.

(4) When land is sold upon judgment and deed is issued, and parties to such judgment or persons claiming under them wrongfully refuse or neglect to surrender possession after demand by person entitled to possession. (12-1271).

Reentry.—If tenant neglects or refuses to pay his rent when due and it remains unpaid for five days, or whenever tenant violates any provision of his lease, landlord or person to whom rent is due, or his agent, has right to reenter and take possession, or may, without any formal demand of reentry, commence action for recovery of possession of premises in justice or superior court, which must then be tried in not more than 30 days thereafter, and in case of appeal by tenant he must execute bond in amount set by court, and pending appeal he must pay all damages, costs and rent adjudged against him. (33-361). Forcible entry and detainer governed by 12-1171 et seq.

Lien.—Landlord has lien upon all property of tenant not exempt by law, placed upon or used in leased premises until his rent is paid. (33-362[A]). If tenant neglects or refuses to pay rent, landlord may seize personal effects of tenant found on premises, unless exempt by law, hold same as security or sell same after 60 days to satisfy claim for rent. (33-361[D]).

Distress.—Landlord may seize for rent any personal property of tenant found on premises rented and not exempted by law. (33-361[D]).

Uniform Residential Landlord and Tenant Act adopted with some modifications and additions. (33-1301 et seq.).

Mobile Home Parks Residential Landlord and Tenant Act adopted. (33-1401 et seq.).

LEASES:

See topic Landlord and Tenant.

PERPETUITIES:

Uniform Statutory Rule Against Perpetuities adopted prospectively with its two-step "wait and see" approach. (14-2901 et seq.). Supercedes common law rule, and courts are authorized to reform instruments created before Dec. 31, 1994, which violate old law. (14-2905 to 2906). Exclusions to rule in 14-2904.

PERSONAL PROPERTY:

All property acquired during marriage, except by gift, devise or descent, is community property of husband and wife. (25-111 et seq.).

POWERS OF ATTORNEY:

Attorneys in Fact.—Attorney in fact or agent with power of attorney governed generally by Arizona Probate Code. Authority may continue beyond disability, incapacity or uncertainty as to whether principal is dead or alive, if so provided in writing (14-5501), or if attorney in fact or agent acts in good faith without actual knowledge of death or disability of principal (14-5502). Real estate or any interest therein may be conveyed by agent acting pursuant to written authority. (33-401).

Caveat: For disclosure requirements in conveyance of real property made or taken in representative capacity, see topic Deeds, subhead Execution.

REAL PROPERTY:

Estates in land are divided into estates of inheritance, for life, for years, at will and by sufferance. (33-201). Estate of inheritance and for life are freeholds. Estates for years are chattels real. Estates at will or by sufferance are chattel interests. Estate pur autre vie is freehold during life of grantee and after death is chattel real. (33-202).

Fee Tail.—Abolished. Conveyance of fee tail deemed conveyance in fee simple. (33-201, 224).

Rule in Shelley's Case.—Abolished. (33-231).

Expectant Estate.—Cannot be defeated or barred unless so provided in creation of estate. (33-225 to 226).

Estate for Life and Remainder.—May be created in term of years. (33-233).

Alternative Future Estates.—Permitted. (33-221 to 222, 227, 233). See also topic Perpetuities.

Estates Created.—Grant or devise to two or more persons creates tenancy in common, except those to trustees, executors or administrators, in which cases joint tenancy is created. Joint tenancy with right of survivorship may be created by express words in grant. (33-431). Grant to husband and wife presumed to establish community tenancy, but joint tenancy between husband and wife may be created if deed contains language expressly creating such estate and deed is expressly accepted and signed by grantees showing knowledge of that provision. (50 Ariz. 265, 71 P.2d 791). Grant to husband and wife may create estate of community property with right of survivorship. (33-431[C]). No livery of seisin. (22 Ariz. 461, 198 Pac. 712).

Condominiums.—Permitted and regulated by 33-1201 et seq.

Land Sale Regulation.—Sale or lease of certain subdivided and unsubdivided land requires notice by subdivider to real estate commissioner of intent to subdivide or offer for sale or lease and issuance by commissioner of public report authorizing such sale or lease. (32-2181[A], 2195[A]). Initial fee, $500. Before issuance of public report, prospective buyer may give reservation deposit, not to exceed $5,000 per single lot. Seller must provide prospective buyer with copy of public report within 15 calendar days after it is issued by commissioner. Upon receiving copy of public report, prospective buyer and prospective seller have seven business days to enter contract for purchase of lot, or else reservation automatically terminates and deposit refunded. (32-2181.03). Types of holders of ownership interest, such as corporations, partnerships or trusts, must be identified, and interest of each principal in such entities must be listed in public report. (32-2181[A][1], 2195[B][1]). Land divided for sale or lease into five or fewer lots that does not result in subdivision pursuant to 32-2101.50 must result in lots which comply with minimum applicable county zoning requirements and have legal access. Access or zoning deficiencies must be noticed in deed. (11-809). Plan for sale or lease of unsubdivided lands cannot be materially changed without notifying commissioner. (32-2195.10). Advertising and other promotional matters are regulated. (32-2183.01, 2195.05[B]). Conveyances of subdivided lands must be accomplished by one of three methods specified in 32-2185.01(A). Conveyances of unsubdivided lands must be accomplished by one of three methods specified in 32-2195.04(A). Purchaser of subdivided or unsubdivided lands may rescind purchase agreement within seven days of execution. (32-2185.04[D], 2195.04[D]). Neither instruments transferring interest in subdivided land nor covenants or restrictions affecting real property may contain provisions limiting right of party to appear or testify regarding zoning changes, building permits, or other official acts affecting any real property. (32-2181[I], 2195[I]). Owners with actual knowledge of soil remediation must disclose prior to transfer. (33-434.01). Knowing violation of land sale statute or regulation or knowing omission or misstatement of material fact contained in statement of record or property report filed or issued pursuant to 32-2181 et seq. or 2195 et seq. subjects violator to criminal penalties. (32-2195.08). Civil penalties apply for violations of statutes, rules or regulations or for unlawful practices. (32-2185.09). All land sold must have provisions made for permanent access by motor vehicles. (32-2185.02, 2195[E]).

Protected Development Rights.—Established and regulated by 9-1201 et seq. and 11-1201 et seq. Right to undertake and complete development and use of property under terms and conditions of plan submitted by landowner and approved by city or town, without compliance with subsequent changes in zoning regulations and development standards, except as provided by 9-1204 and 11-1204. City or town may adopt moratorium on land construction or development in certain situations. (9-463.06 et seq.). Development rights may be transferable. (9-462.01).

Planned Communities.—Regulated by 33-1801 et seq.

Soil Remediation Standards.—See category Environment, topic Environmental Regulation, subhead General Supervision.

Time Shares.—Real Estate Department regulation of real estate time shares. (32-2197 et seq.).

Water.—Rights for owners of stream beds established. (37-1101 et seq.). Ombudsman represents interest of private property owner in proceedings involving government. (41-1311 et seq.). Surface water and water flowing in definite underground channels are administrated by Department of Water Resources under doctrine of prior appropriation. (45-101 et seq.). Judicial decisions established that percolating groundwater is subject to doctrine of reasonable use, i.e., owner of land has right to pump amounts of waters needed for reasonable and beneficial use on his land. (45 Ariz. 221, 42 P.2d 403). Under new groundwater code, however, groundwater may not be used and wells may not be drilled in statutorily designated active management areas except pursuant to previously established water rights or permit. (45-132 to 133, 512). Permit for underground storage facility required. (45-811.01). Water stored pursuant to water storage permit may be used or exchanged only in manner and location in which it was permissible to use or exchange water before it was stored. (45-832.01). Stored water is recoverable on annual basis pursuant to certain conditions. (45-851.01). "In lieu" water delivered pursuant to groundwater storage facility permit is deemed to be groundwater for all purposes of Title 45, c. 2 as if recipient of "in lieu" water had withdrawn it from well. (45-873.01). In active management areas, subdivision lots and subdivided land may not be sold without certificate from Department of Water Resources that sufficient water supply available. (45-576, 11-806.01). Subdivider also may obtain written commitment of water service for subdivision from city, town, or private water company designated as having assured water supply by Director of Water Resources. (9-463.01[I]). Outside active management areas subdivided lots may be sold subject to disclosure of adequacy or inadequacy of water supply. (32-2181[F], 2183, 2195[H], 45-108). Active Management Area Water Augmentation Authority established. (45-1901 et seq.). County Water Authority may be established in any county with population more than 90,000 persons and less than 120,000 persons. (45-2201 et seq.). Water deemed reasonably safe and fit for use if it complies with contaminant levels established in 49-351 to 354 or Safe Drinking Water Act. (12-820.08).

Caveat: For disclosure requirements in conveyance of real property made or taken in representative capacity, see topic Deeds.

See also topics Curtesy, Deeds, Dower, Landlord and Tenant; categories Civil Actions and Procedure, topic Partition; Debtor and Creditor, topic Homesteads; Family, topic Husband and Wife; Mortgages, topic Mortgages of Real Property.

TRUST DEEDS:

See category Mortgages, topic Mortgages of Real Property.

TAXATION

Note: Statutes have been renumbered effective Jan. 1999 and are shown as follows: "(42-1002 et seq.)" is now "(42-102 et seq., formerly 42-1002 et seq.)".

ADMINISTRATION:

Department of Revenue has general supervision of most matters relating to generation of revenue. (42-102 et seq., formerly 42-1002 et seq.). Department, with approval of attorney general, may abate any uncollectible balance or balance where amount owed by taxpayer exceeds administration and collection costs, and release any related liens. (42-104, formerly 42-1004). Department may require taxpayer to file bond to secure payment. (42-112, formerly 42-1102). In certain circumstances, delinquent taxpayer may be enjoined from engaging or continuing in business. (42-112.01, formerly 42-1103). Joint legislative committee has authority to set state property tax rates and analyze state tax structure. (41-1322).

Exemptions.—Exemptions from property tax are set forth in 42-271 to 271.01, 274.01, and 278 to 279. These exemptions are repealed effective Jan. 1999. Except for inventory, livestock and property used for religious worship, taxpayer claiming exemption must appear before county assessor, make affidavit or furnish evidence as to eligibility, or all of foregoing. (42-274 to 275). Failure to do so will constitute waiver. (42-275).

Penalties and Interest.—

Income, Estate, Use and Transaction Privilege Taxes.—See generally 42-134 formerly 42-1123 to 1127. For failure to file return on notice and demand by Department, penalty is 25% of tax. For failure to furnish information requested by Department, penalty of 25% of deficiency tax is assessed. For failure to file return, 4.5% of tax will be added for each month or fraction of month elapsing between due date of return and date filed, total not to exceed 25% of tax. For failure to pay tax, penalty of .5% for each month or fraction of month during which failure continues, not to exceed 10%. Total of failure to file and failure to pay penalties cannot exceed 25%. Waiver of tax penalty, with certain exceptions, if taxpayer voluntarily files return and pays additional tax. (42-136 formerly 42-1125). $25 fee for bad checks. (42-136.01 formerly 42-1126). Taxpayer liable for costs of collecting delinquent taxes, interest and penalties. (42-137.01 formerly 42-1128). Interest upon unpaid amount or deficiency at rate established pursuant to I.R.C. §6621 will be added. Interest outstanding on Jan. 1 is added to principal and accrues interest. (42-134 formerly 42-1123).

Property Tax.—Any person who knowingly fails to file report of taxable property or renders false or fraudulent information is guilty of Class 2 Misdemeanor, and is liable for amount of taxes due plus penalty equal to taxes due on concealed property for year in which discovery was made. (42-252). Penalty for failure to report property when requested by assessor is 10% of value. (42-223). Interest on delinquent amounts due at rate of 16% simple interest. (42-608).

CIGARETTE TAX:

Cigarette tax imposed by 42-1231.

COMPANIES:

Commercial Airline Companies.—Flight property of such companies is assessed and taxed as unsecured personal property by Department of Revenue. Property value is determined as of first Mon. in June of valuation year, as defined in 42-201. Portion of value apportioned to this state depends on time on ground and total mileage scheduled within state during previous calendar year. (42-704). Small flight property operated within state valued at 30% of original cost less depreciation and additional allowed obsolescence. (42-704). Tax rate is average imposed for all purposes in several taxing districts of state for current year. (42-705).

Annual report must be filed by each company with Department of Revenue by Apr. 1 of each year containing information to be considered in making its valuation. (42-703).

Private Car Companies.—Companies which operate, furnish or lease cars operating over railroad lines not owned, leased or operated by them are subject to tax on full cash value of such cars. (42-741 to 745). Full cash value is determined as of Jan. 1 of valuation year, as defined in 42-201. (42-745). Tax must be imposed at rate equal to average rate for all purposes in several taxing districts of state for current year, and is in lieu of all other taxes upon companies' properties except license tax and registration fee. Tax for each prior calendar year is collected by Department of Revenue between Oct. 1 of following year and Nov. 1 of following year. (42-746).

Annual statement must be filed by each company on or before Apr. 1. (42-743).

See note at head of Digest as to 1998 legislation covered.

See Topical Index in front part of this volume.

COMPANIES . . . *continued*

Railroad Companies.—Department of Revenue appraises and assesses all taxable property of railroad companies except real estate owned by such companies not used in the continuous operation of railroads (county assessor values such property). Railroad property valued as of Jan. 1 of valuation year, as defined in 42-201. (42-762).

Annual statement must be filed with Department of Revenue on or before Apr. 1. (42-761).

Telecommunications Companies.—As of Jan. 1 of valuation year, as defined in 42-201, Department of Revenue must assess value of all property of telecommunications companies operating in state and providing local telecommunications service at full cash value as provided by 42-793.01; and value of property of other telecommunications companies operating in state at full cash value. (42-793).

Annual statement must be filed with Department of Revenue on or before Apr. 1. (42-792).

Foreign Insurance Company Tax.—See category Insurance, topic Insurance Companies.

Surety Company Tax.—See category Insurance, topic Surety and Guaranty Companies.

ENTERPRISE ZONES:

Tax incentives governed by 41-1525, 43-1074 and 1161 (repealed effective July 1, 2001).

ENVIRONMENTAL TECHNOLOGY MANUFACTURING INCENTIVES:

Tax incentives governed by 42-162, 227, 1310.01, 1310.03, 1310.11, 1310.12, 1310.16, 1409, 43-1076, 1080 et seq., 1164 and 1169 et seq.

ESTATE TAX:

Estate tax is imposed by 42-1501 formerly 42-4001 et seq.

Gross estate means gross estate as defined in I.R.C. §2031 as amended and in effect as of Jan. 1, 1997, but excluding all changes to Code after Jan. 1, 1997. (42-101 formerly 42-1001[4], 4001[4]).

Tax on Resident's Estate.—Tax imposed is equal to federal estate tax credit reduced by lesser of: (1) Death taxes paid in other states credited against federal estate tax, or (2) portion of federal estate tax credit based on ratio of value of property in other states subject to foreign death tax to value of decedent's gross estate. (42-1521 formerly 42-4051).

Tax on Nonresident's Estate.—Tax imposed is equal to portion of federal estate tax credit based on ratio of value of real property and tangible personal property with Arizona situs to value of decedent's gross estate. (42-1522 formerly 42-4052).

Generation Skipping Tax.—Percentage of maximum amount of credit allowed under federal tax law for state taxes is due, based on ratio between value of real property and tangible personal property with Arizona situs and intangible personal property owned by trust administered in Arizona at time of generation skipping transfer to value of all property included in generation skipping transfer. (42-1531, 1532 formerly 42-4101 to 4102).

Return.—Personal representative required to file federal estate tax return must file state return and copy of federal return on or before date that federal return must be filed. (42-1502 formerly 42-4002). Department of Revenue accepts federal extensions for filing federal estate tax return. (42-116 formerly 42-1107).

Payment.—Unless time is extended by Department of Revenue, payment must accompany return. Department may abate small tax balances if administration costs exceed amount of tax due. If federal estate tax is paid in installments under I.R.C. §6166 and tax due exceeds $50,000, tax may be paid at same time and in same manner as federal tax. (42-4004).

Administration.—Tax is administered by Department of Revenue. (42-1517).

Determination of Tax and Appeals.—Department examines returns and determines estate tax due. (42-1515). Personal representative may appeal determination to Department. After exhausting administrative appeals, personal representative may bring suit in superior court to review determination of state board of equalization within 30 days. (42-122, 124).

Safe Deposit Boxes.—Unlawful to open after death without consent of Department of Revenue. (42-1513).

Transfer of Stock.—Except as otherwise provided by statute, domestic corporation and foreign corporation authorized to conduct business in state may not transfer on its books stock belonging to decedent who was resident of Arizona, or to resident decedent and others jointly, without written consent of Department of Revenue. (42-1514).

Transfer of Property.—Except as otherwise provided by statute, no person or corporation having possession or control of property of decedent, or of decedent and others jointly, may transfer such property to anyone without obtaining written consent of Department of Revenue. $10,000 in each bank deposit is exempt from this provision. (42-1514).

Lien.—Tax is lien on all property of decedent until paid. (42-1511). Sheriff of county where property subject to tax lien is located may by levy and sale collect tax not paid after five years from date due. (42-1507).

Estate Tax Due and Unpaid.—Personal representative is personally liable for tax to extent of value of that portion of estate that is or has come into his possession. (42-1510).

Interstate Cooperation.—No procedure available for compromise of death taxes where decedent's domicile is disputed.

Gift Tax.—None, but estate tax applies to gifts in contemplation of death or to take effect at or after death of donor.

GASOLINE TAX:

Imposed by 28-5601 et seq.

Motor Carriers Tax.—Unlicensed carriers required to obtain single trip fuel tax permit. Rate is $49 for over 50 miles traveled on state highways and $12 for 50 or less miles traveled on state highways. Permit valid for 96 hours, fee $1. (28-1559). Tax based on vehicle weight and miles traveled on state highways imposed against each motor vehicle of licensed motor carrier. This tax is in addition to all other taxes and fees (28-1599.05); however, no other transaction privilege tax or tax on gross receipts derived from operation of motor vehicle on public highway may be imposed (28-1599.05[J]). Periodic reports are required on forms provided by Director of Department of Transportation together with payment of motor carrier taxes, interest and penalties due. (28-1599.06). Validity of tax may be tested within one year after payment. (28-1599.11). *Note:* Beginning Jan. 1, 1994, there may be reduction of motor carriers tax based upon fuel purchased and used within state. (28-1599.14). This tax does not apply to school buses or to motor vehicles used in production of motion pictures. (28-1599.05).

INCOME TAX:

Tax is imposed on natural persons, corporations, trusts and estates. Tax is based upon adjusted gross income for individuals and taxable income for other entities, as computed under federal Internal Revenue Code as in effect on Jan. 1, 1997, including those provisions that became effective during 1990 with specific adoption of their retroactive effective dates but excluding all changes to such Code enacted after Jan. 1, 1997, subject to certain adjustments listed below. (42-102, 104, formerly 42-1002, 1004, 1501[6]). For Arizona additions to adjusted gross income see 43-1021 as to individuals and 43-1121 as to corporations. For amounts specifically included or excluded from nonresident's income see 43-1091 et seq. For procedure governing illegally obtained income see 43-207.

Rates for Individuals and Fiduciaries.—For single persons or married persons filing separately: for first $10,000, 2.9% of taxable income; for $10,001-$25,000, $290 plus 3.3% of excess over $10,000; for $25,001-$50,000, $785 plus 3.9% of excess over $25,000; for $50,001-$150,000, $1,760 plus 4.8% of excess over $50,000; for over $150,000, $6,560 plus 5.17% of excess over $150,000. For married couple filing jointly or single head of household: for first $20,000, 2.9% of taxable income; for $20,001-$50,000, $580 plus 3.3% of excess over $20,000; for $50,001-$100,000, $1,570 plus 3.9% of excess over $50,000; for $100,001-$300,000, $3,250 plus 4.8% of excess over $100,000; for over $300,000, $13,120 plus 5.17% of excess over $300,000. (43-1011).

Rates for Corporations.—Every corporation is taxed at 9% of net income or $50, whichever amount is greater. (43-1111). Special capital gain rate repealed for years after Jan. 1, 1988. (43-1111). Foreign corporations pay tax on net income derived in state. (43-1133 et seq.). All corporations doing business in state must file return, whether taxable or not. (43-307).

Exemptions and Deductions.—Certain additions and subtractions are required in computing adjusted gross income. Deduction allowed for federal income tax paid or accrued. See generally 43-1021 et seq. as to individuals; 43-1121 et seq. as to corporations; and 43-1201 et seq. as to other organizations. Exemption amounts are $2,100 for individual ($4,200 for husband and wife) (43-1043), $2,300 per dependent (43-1023) and persons over 65 supported by taxpayer (43-1023), $1,500 if blind, $2,150 for taxpayers 65 or older filing separate or joint return and spouses 65 or older filing joint return. (43-1023). Optional standard deduction for single person or married person filing separately is $3,600, for married couple filing jointly or single head of household, $7,200. (43-1041). Tax credit given to residents for: (a) Income taxes paid to other states (43-1071); (b) property taxes if residents 65 or older; (c) contributions to school tuition organization, but not exceeding $500 in any taxable year (43-1089); (d) contributions to public school for support of extra curricular activities, but not exceeding $200 in any taxable year (43-1089.01). Corporate tax credits governed by 43-1161 to 1168. Calculation of taxable income, exemptions, and deductions for nonresidents governed by 43-1091 to 1099. Calculation of taxable income, exemptions and deductions for corporations governed by 43-1101 to 1163. Calculation of taxable income, exemptions and deductions for estates and trusts governed by 43-1301 to 1346. Small business corporations may elect tax status (Subchapter S). (43-1126). Nondeductible items listed in 43-961.

Withholding shall be 10%, 17%, 20%, 22%, 28%, or 32% of federal income tax withheld if employee's annual wage is less than $15,000, and 17%, 20%, 22%, 28%, or 32% of federal income tax withheld if wage exceeds $15,000. (43-401). Certain types of employment excluded from withholding requirement. (43-403). Military pensions, payments under U.S. Civil Service Retirement System and annuity payments treated as wages if requested by taxpayer. (43-404). Winnings from legalized gambling (43-405) and early withdrawal by public employees from certain public pension funds (43-406) are subject to withholding. If withheld amount did not exceed average of $1,500 in each of four preceding quarters, withholding must be paid to Department by Apr. 30, July 31, Oct. 31 and Jan. 31 for preceding calendar quarter. If withholding exceeded $1,500 in each of preceding four calendar quarters, withheld amount must be remitted to Department at same time employer is required to make deposits of federal tax pursuant to I.R.C. §6302. (43-401).

Partnership.—Individual carrying on business in partnership shall be liable for tax only in his individual capacity (43-1411), and shall include, in computing taxable income, whether distributed or not, his distributive share of partnership's gains, losses, dividends, debts, depreciation, etc. as described in 43-1412.

Religious, Charitable and other Nonprofit Corporations.—Exempt from tax on income related to their religious, charitable or other purposes which make exemption available. (43-1201 to 1217, 42-1310.09 formerly 42-5069).

Returns and Payment.—Following taxpayers are required to file returns: Individual, if he has for taxable year, Arizona adjusted gross income of $5,500 if single or married filing separate return; or $11,000 if married filing jointly, or gross income of $15,000 or more, regardless of amount of taxable income; (43-301); agent or guardian of taxpayer

See note at head of Digest as to 1998 legislation covered.

See Topical Index in front part of this volume.

AZ – 35

INCOME TAX . . . *continued*
unable to make own return (43-303); fiduciary acting for individual, estate, trust, or decedent, as required by 43-304 to 305; every partnership and corporation (43-306 to 307). Returns must be filed if above criteria met regardless whether taxpayer filed federal return or whether taxpayer had taxable income for federal tax purposes. "Gross income" means gross income as defined in Internal Revenue Code minus income included in gross income but excluded from taxation under this title. Husband and wife may file joint return or separate returns. (43-301, 309 to 311).

Information returns are required to be filed by following: Trust companies operating common trust funds (43-341); exempt organizations (43-342); trusts claiming charitable, religious, scientific, literary or educational deductions (43-343); persons subject to subtitle F, c. 61, subchap. A, Part III, subpart B of Internal Revenue Code (43-344).

Returns are due at Department of Revenue on Apr. 15th following close of calendar year or on 15th day of fourth month after close of fiscal year. (43-325). Individual must pay tax on 15th day of Apr. following close of calendar year or, if return is made on basis of fiscal year, on 15th day of fourth month following close of fiscal year. (43-501). S-corporations must pay tax on 15th day of third month following close of taxable year, and unrelated business income tax of tax exempt organization is due on 15th day of fifth month following close of taxable year. (43-501, 1241). Any taxpayer may elect to pay tax in advance. (43-504). Any individual may make payments of estimated tax during tax year as set forth in 43-581. Corporation subject to tax must make estimated tax payments if tax liability exceeds $1,000 per annum. Penalties and interest assessed for failure to file timely return. (42-134, 136, 43-582).

Refunds paid within 60 days of last day for filing or 60 days from actual filing do not include interest. Interest at rate determined under I.R.C. §6621 begins to accrue on 61st day. (42-134 formerly 42-1123).

INHERITANCE TAX:

None. As to estate tax, see topic Estate Tax.

MOTION PICTURE PRODUCTION:

Refunds for in-state motion picture production activity governed by 42-1322.01 formerly 42-5015.

MOTOR CARRIERS TAX:

See topic Gasoline Tax.

MOTOR VEHICLE TAX:

See category Transportation, topic Motor Vehicles.

PROPERTY TAXES:

Property Tax Generally.—Levy on unsecured personal property occurs during month following its first inclusion on tax roll. (42-605, 607 repealed effective Jan. 1999).

Assessment.—All property subject to taxation in each county is assessed by county assessor, who is required to ascertain names of all persons owning, claiming or having possession or control thereof, and to determine full cash value of all such property. (42-221, 227). Department of Revenue may direct county assessor to adjust value of any property that has not been appraised within three years. (42-221). Upon notice by assessor, owner must return list of property on or before May 1. (42-223). Listing is required within 45 days for property valued under 42-601 to 601.01. (42-223). Owner notified of valuation after Mar. 1. (42-221). Valuation for property tax purposes is governed by 42-227. There are special rules for valuation and assessment of oil, gas, and geothermal interests (42-143); gas, water, and electric utilities and pipelines (42-144 et seq.); shopping centers (42-147), golf courses (42-146), feeder livestock (42-147.01); property purchased by Game and Fish Commission (17-272); school districts (42-227, 15012); and, class III personal property (42-235.02).

Unsecured Personal Property.—When county assessor assesses personal property of persons owning real estate within county of value of less than $200, he must enter assessment on tax roll provided for that purpose and known as "Unsecured Personal Property Tax Roll," disclosing name and residence of person owning personal property or having it in his possession and returning such property for taxation, if person is known, description of property sufficient to identify it, location of property and rate of taxation levied against it. If name of owner of property is not known, property must nevertheless be listed, assessed and entered upon tax roll to "unknown owner." (42-601). Tax may be declared uncollectible if property and owner are not located. Such property will be removed from records but may be reinstated if either property or owner is located. (42-616). Tax roll must provide proper columns for extension of tax levied upon property. (42-601). Mobile homes which are permanently affixed to real property are included in unsecured property tax roll until after affidavit of affixture is filed. Such homes will then appear on next real property tax roll. (42-641.01, 642).

Possessory interests in property tax repealed. Legislative study committee currently considering taxation of possessory interests, and will make recommendations for taxation that will be retroactive beginning with 1995 tax year.

Review of Assessment.—Person whose property has been assessed by county assessor must be notified of valuation before Mar. 1 of each year and may appeal assessment to county assessor within 60 days after date assessor mailed notice. Assessor must rule on taxpayer's petition by Aug. 15 of each year. (42-221). Procedures for valuation and review in case of new construction, additions, deletions and changes in use are established (42-221.01). Within 25 days from date of assessor's decision, appeal may be made to county board of equalization if established or to state board of equalization if county board of equalization does not exist. (42-221, 241.01). Board of supervisors of each county convenes as board of equalization as often as is necessary in order to hear petitions filed pursuant to 42-241.01. County board must complete all hearings and issue all decisions on or before Dec. 15 of each year. (42-246). Fees and other expenses shall be awarded to party successfully challenging state assessment or collection of tax. (12-348). Taxpayer claims for refunds of overpayments, erroneous assessments or duplicate payments must be filed within three years of payment. (11-505 to 506, 42-149).

Board of supervisors convenes as board of equalization of unsecured personal property on day designated by board as its regular meeting day pursuant to 11-214. Any person may present objections to his assessment at that time, and if unsatisfied with action of board, may appeal to superior court before taxes become delinquent or may petition state board of equalization within 15 days from date of board's decision. (42-245). Taxpayer aggrieved by decision of state tax appeals board may bring action in tax court. If amount in dispute is less than $5,000, Department may not bring action in tax court unless issue is of substantial significance to State. (42-124).

Payment and Collection.—One half of tax on real property and personal property secured by real property is due and payable Oct. 1 and becomes delinquent Nov. 1. Remaining half is due and payable on Mar. 1 and becomes delinquent May 1, unless either first half of taxes paid before delinquent or full year paid by Dec. 31. (42-342, 381, 384). If amount of tax is $25 or less, full amount is due Oct. 1 and becomes delinquent Nov. 1. (42-342).

Unsecured personal property taxes for each month become due and payable on second Mon. of each month and become delinquent 30 days thereafter. (42-608). Interest at rate of 16% is charged on delinquent taxes. (42-608). County treasurer is charged with collecting tax. (42-310, 608). Taxes may be prorated on certain rented or leased personal property and on property new to tax rolls. (42-601.01 to 601.02).

Lien.—Personal property is liable for taxes levied on real property, and real property is liable for taxes levied on personal property. (42-312). Tax levied against unsecured personal property is lien against it, prior and superior to all other liens. (42-609). Where ownership of mineral rights in land is separate from ownership in other interests of land, taxes assessed against one may not be lien against another. (42-255). Department may accept voluntary liens on real or personal property as security for taxes not paid when due. (42-1825).

Sale.—Real property upon which taxes, including personal property taxes secured thereby, are unpaid and delinquent, is subject to tax lien sale. (42-381 et seq.). County treasurer sells tax liens on real property in Feb. of each year. Property tax liens that cannot be sold are conveyed to state in consideration of taxes, interest, penalties and charges. Neither sale nor foreclosure of redemption extinguishes easements on or appurtenant to parcel. (42-390). Notice of sale is mailed to owner and published in newspaper two to three weeks before sale. (42-387 to 388). Tax lien must be sold for cash at time of sale to person who pays taxes, interest, penalties and charges, and who offers to accept lowest rate of interest upon that amount, not to exceed 16% per year simple, until redeemed. (42-393). State as assignee will charge interest at rate of 16% per year simple, for redemption. (42-393).

A purchaser at tax sale has been held to have a lien only and therefore may get title by adverse possession. (85 Ariz. 56, 331 P.2d 257).

Unsecured personal property is sold by county sheriff on order of county treasurer given within five days after delinquency. Sheriff seizes property within six months of order and advertises it for sale at auction for cash. He is empowered to enter any real property to make seizure. Five-day notice of time, place and terms of sale must be given by posting two notices in public places within county and one where property is located. (42-611, 613). Only so much of personal property is sold as is necessary to pay taxes, interest and costs of sale. If no bid is sufficient to pay that amount, property is sold to county which in turn sells it at public auction or private sale for best price obtainable. (42-614).

Redemption.—
Real property may be redeemed within three years or thereafter at any time before delivery of treasurer's deed to purchaser by any person having legal or equitable claim by payment of amount for which real property tax lien was sold with interest thereon, amount of all taxes accruing on property and paid by purchaser with interest thereon and certain statutory fees. (42-421). If not redeemed within three years, purchaser or state as assignee may by action foreclose right to redeem and obtain deed. (42-451 to 452). If not redeemed within five years, purchaser may have treasurer publish notice of application for deed once in each of two consecutive weeks, conduct title search and give 90 days notice to owner by registered mail. If property is not then redeemed purchaser may receive deed. (42-461 to 462).

Unsecured personal property may be redeemed by owner at any time prior to actual sale by paying taxes, interest and costs to sheriff. (42-614).

REAL ESTATE CONVEYANCE TAX:

None, but deed evidencing transfer of title or contract relating to sale of real property must at time of recording have affidavit of value appended. (42-1612). See category Property, topic Deeds.

Exemptions.—See 42-1614.

RESEARCH AND DEVELOPMENT EXPENSES:

Credit allowed. (43-1168).

SALES AND USE TAXES:

Sales Tax.—See subhead Transaction Privilege Taxes, infra.

Use tax (42-1401 formerly 42-5151 et seq.) is imposed on storage, use, mail-order solicitation or consumption within state of tangible personal property purchased from retailer. Rate is determined by reference to combined rates of transaction privilege and other taxes imposed on same type of business activity. (42-1408 formerly 42-5155). Tax does not apply to use, mail-order solicitation, storage or consumption of properties listed in 42-1409 formerly 42-5159.

Transaction Privilege Taxes.—Instead of sales tax, transaction privilege tax is imposed on gross proceeds of sale or gross income of certain trades or businesses carried on in addition to all other licenses and taxes levied by law. (42-1301 formerly 42-5001 et seq.). Gross income, gross receipts and gross proceeds do not include amount collected as tax by taxpayer from his customers. Direct freight costs charged by retailer

See note at head of Digest as to 1998 legislation covered.

See Topical Index in front part of this volume.

AZ – 36

SALES AND USE TAXES . . . *continued*

are excluded from gross income, receipts, or proceeds of sale. (42-1302 formerly 42-5002). Establishing entitlement to deduction governed by 42-1316 formerly 42-5009.

Note: Arizona transaction privilege tax code was recodified in 1988, effective July 1, 1989. Following references are to code provisions as renumbered.

Rates.—Tax is imposed at following rates:

(1) 3¹/₈% on mining, quarrying or producing for sale or commercial use oil, natural gas, limestone, sand, gravel or nonmetalliferous minerals or combinations thereof. (42-1310.12, 42-1317[A][3] formerly 42-5010[A][3], 5072).

(2) 0% on business of leasing use or occupancy of real property for consideration, except property: (a) Classified as transient lodging; (b) related to Arizona Coliseum and Exposition Center Board or County Fair Commission; (c) leased to lessee who subleases, if lessee is member of commercial lease class; (d) leased before Dec. 1, 1967, generally; (e) leased by corporation to affiliated corporation; (f) leased for sublease if tenant is subject to rental occupancy tax; (g) used for residential or agricultural purposes; (h) used for boarding horses; (i) leased by nonprofit organization associated with major league baseball teams or national touring professional golfing association; (j) leased to nonprofit organization sponsoring rodeo featuring primarily farm and ranch animals (42-1317[A][4], 42-1310.09 formerly 42-5010[A][4], 5069); and (k) leased to private entity of transportation facility (28-3075). Suspended through Mar. 31, 1993 for lessor of single property to U.S. if property is listed on national register of historic places or used as postal facility. (1990, c. 251).

(3) 5¹/₂% on business of operating, for occupancy by transients, hotel, motel, inn, tourist home, dude ranch, resort, campground, studio, bachelor hotel, lodging house, rooming house, apartment house, dormitory, public or private club, mobile home or house trailer at fixed location or other similar structure, including space, lot or slab which is occupied or intended or designed for occupancy by transients in mobile home or house trailer furnished by them for such occupancy. (42-1317[A][2], 42-1310.10 formerly 42-5010[A][2], 5070). "Transient" is defined as any person who obtains lodging space or use of lodging space on daily or weekly basis or any other basis for less than 30 consecutive days. (42-1310.10 formerly 42-5070).

(4) 5% on business of transporting for hire persons, freight or property by motor vehicle, railroads or aircraft intrastate, except: (a) Transport by motor carriers or lightweight motor vehicles subject to other tax; (b) transport by aircraft preempted by federal law; (c) ambulance services; (d) public transportation program services for Dial-A-Ride programs and special needs transportation services; and (e) transport by railroad operating exclusively in Arizona of freight or property for hire if part of single shipment involving more than one railroad and crossing state line. (42-1317[A][1][a], 42-1310.02 formerly 42-5010[A][1][a], 5062).

(5) 5% on business of producing or furnishing to consumers electricity, natural or artificial gas and water, except sale of electricity, gas or water for resale. (42-1317[A][1][b], 42-1310.03 formerly 42-5010[A][1][b], 5063).

(6) 5% on business of providing intrastate telecommunications services, except sale by cable television system. (42-1317[A][1][c], 42-1310.04 formerly 42-5010[A][1][c], 5064).

(7) 5% on business of operating pipelines for intrastate transportation of oil or natural or artificial gas through pipes or conduits. (42-1317[A][1][d] formerly 42-5010[A][1][d], 5067).

(8) 5% on business of operating private car lines intrastate. (42-1317[A][1][e], 42-1310.08 formerly 42-5010[A][1][e], 5068).

(9) 5% on business of publishing newspapers, magazines or other periodicals and publications if published in state, except: (a) Manufacturing or publishing books; (b) sales of magazines or other periodicals or other publications by state to encourage tourist travel. (42-1317[A][1][f], 42-1310.05 formerly 42-5010[A][1][f], 5065).

(10) 5% on business of job printing, engraving, embossing and copying. (42-1317[A][1][g], 42-1310.06 formerly 42-5010[A][1][g], 5066).

(11) 5% on business of prime contracting and dealership of manufactured buildings, except sale of used manufactured buildings. Exemption for installation, repair, etc. of machinery and equipment used as production equipment if not attached to structure. (42-1317[A][1][h], 42-1310.16 formerly 42-5010[A][1][h], 5075).

(12) 5% on improvements of real property sold by owner/builder before 24 months after improvement is substantially completed. (42-1317[A][1][i], 42-1310.17 formerly 42-5010[A][1][i], 5076).

(13) 5% on business of operating or conducting theaters, movies, operas, shows of any type or nature, exhibitions, concerts, carnivals, circuses, amusement parks, menageries, fairs, races, contests, games, billiard or pool parlors, bowling alleys, public dances, dance halls, boxing and wrestling matches, skating rinks, tennis courts, video games, pinball machines, sports events, hayrides and other animal-drawn amusement rides or any other business charging admission or user fees for exhibition, amusement, entertainment or instruction, except: (1) Activity or projects of bona fide religious or educational institutions; (2) private or group instruction activities including, but not limited to, performing arts, martial arts, gymnastics and aerobics; (3) Events by Arizona Coliseum and Exposition Center Board or County Fair Commission; (4) musical, dramatic or dance group or botanical garden, museum or zoo qualified as charitable organization under I.R.C. §501(c)(3); (5) exhibit events sponsored by nonprofit, tax-exempt organization under I.R.C. §§501(c)(3), (4) or (6), associated with major league baseball teams or national touring professional golfing association; and (6) rodeos featuring primarily farm and ranch animals sponsored by nonprofit, tax-exempt organization under I.R.C. §§501(c)(3), (4), (6), (7) or (8). (42-1317[A][1][j], 42-1310.13 formerly 42-5010[A][1][j], 5073).

(14) 5% on business of operating restaurants, dining cars, dining rooms, lunch rooms, lunch stands, soda fountains, catering services or similar establishments where articles of food or drink are sold for consumption on or off premises. (42-1317[A][1][k], 42-1310.14 formerly 42-5010[A][1][k], 5074).

(15) 5% on business of leasing or renting tangible personal property for consideration, except: (a) Leasing or renting films, tapes, or slides by those under amusement classification or used by television or radio stations; (b) activities by Arizona Coliseum and Exposition Center Board or County Fair Commission; (c) leasing or renting by

parent corporation to subsidiary; and (d) operating laundromats. (42-1317[A][1][l], 42-1310.11 formerly 42-5010[A][1][l], 5071).

(16) 5% on business of selling tangible personal property at retail, with numerous exceptions. (42-1317[A][1][m], 42-1310.01 formerly 42-5010[A][1][m], 5061).

Licenses.—Every person or corporation engaged in any activity upon which transaction privilege tax is imposed must procure license which is effective indefinitely and is not transferable. Fee $12. Violation of statute or rules may result in revocation of license. (42-1305 formerly 42-5005). Certain contractors and manufacturers of manufactured housing must post bond to assure payment of tax. (42-1305.02 formerly 42-5007).

Returns and Payment.—Verified return must be made and tax paid by 20th day of month following that for which tax accrued. Tax is delinquent if not postmarked by 25th day of that month or paid by mail or in person on business day before last business day of month. Transient taxpayer may be required to make return and pay tax on daily, weekly or transaction-by-transaction basis. (42-1322, 42-1412 formerly 42-5014, 5162).

Records.—Every person engaging in any business in Arizona on which state law imposes tax must keep appropriate records of gross income, gross receipts and gross proceeds of sales of business, and any other books or accounts necessary to determine his tax liability, plus such person must keep for two years all invoices of luxuries purchased for resale. Such records must be kept available for examination at any reasonable time by Department of Revenue. (42-114 formerly 42-1105, 1214).

Exemptions.—Gross revenues realized from many transactions are exempt from tax. Exemptions are set out in provision applicable to each business category.

Education Excise Tax.—Repealed retroactive to July 1, 1985.

Penalties.—Failure to obtain privilege license is misdemeanor. (42-1305 formerly 42-5005). Failure to allow examination of records is misdemeanor. (42-1332 formerly 42-5025).

Intermunicipal Taxes.—Municipal transaction privilege tax on taxable transaction is payable only once; method of allocating taxpayer liability between municipalities is prescribed. (42-5302 formerly 42-1302). Virtually all Arizona cities and towns have adopted Model City Tax Code. Modifications or amendments to Model City Tax Code require hearing after 15 day notice and not effective until 30 days after hearing (42-1554 formerly 42-5304).

Note: Credit is allowed against taxes imposed by Transaction Privilege Tax Section for expenses incurred in accounting and reporting taxes due. (42-1322.04 formerly 42-5017).

Government Property Lease Excise Tax.—Government leases property, levies and collects annual excise tax. Rates based on square footage and usage. Exemptions available. (15-1636, 42-1901 to 1905, 1931 to 1932, 1961 to 1962).

County hotel excise tax imposed by 42-1496.

Telecommunication services excise tax imposed by 42-1471 formerly 42-5251 et seq.

Rental Vehicle Tax.—5% surcharge on rental vehicle contracts for 180 days or less. (28-1591.05).

SEVERENCE TAX:

Tax imposed upon severer engaged in business of timbering and mining. (42-1461 formerly 42-5201 et seq.).

STAMP TAX:

Luxury Privilege Tax.—Stamp taxes, payable by affixing to containers, etc., stamps obtainable from Department of Revenue, are imposed on spirituous liquor, cider, malt liquor, cigarettes, tobacco, cigars, cannabis and controlled substances, by 42-1201 et seq.

SUCCESSOR LIABILITY:

Successor liability imposed by 42-1110.

TRAILER-MOBILE HOME TAX:

See category Transportation, topic Motor Vehicles.

UNEMPLOYMENT COMPENSATION TAX:

Imposed, in form of "contributions," on every employer who, in each of 20 different weeks (not necessarily consecutive) in current or preceding calendar year, has or had in employment at least one individual, for some portion of a day, not necessarily simultaneously, or who pays $1,500 or more in wages or meets certain service criteria. (23-613). Base rate is 5.4% of payroll, subject to reduction or increase based on experience classification. (23-728 et seq.). Contributions are based on entire payroll, and due and payable according to regulations prescribed by Department of Economic Security. (23-726 et seq.). Contributions for each month must be paid on or before last day of succeeding month.

Exempted employments are, among others: Certain agricultural labor; certain domestic service in private home; crews on non-U.S. vessels or aircraft; service in employ of son, daughter or spouse, or service by child under age of 21 in employ of father or mother; service in employ of other state or political subdivisions or U.S. Government; service with organization in which unemployment compensation is provided by Act of Congress generally; service performed in any calendar quarter in employ of any organization exempted from income tax under I.R.C. §501; service performed in any calendar quarter in employ of any school, college or university if such service is performed by student who is enrolled and is regularly attending classes at any school, college or university; service performed as intern or student nurse in employ of hospital; service performed by individual for employing unit, as insurance agent or solicitor, real estate broker or salesman, or licensed cemetery broker or salesman, if all such service performed by such individual for such employing unit is performed for remuneration solely by way of commissions; service performed by certain individuals in delivery, distribution, or sale of newspapers; service performed in employ of foreign government or of

UNEMPLOYMENT COMPENSATION TAX . . . *continued*
instrumentality wholly owned by foreign government; and casual labor not in course of employer's trade or business. (23-617).

UNIFORM LAWS:

Revised Uniform Federal Tax Lien Registration Act repealed. (1990, c. 158, §1).

Uniform Federal Lien Registration Act adopted. (33-1031 et seq.).

Uniform Division of Income for Tax Purposes Act adopted effective Jan. 1, 1984. (43-1131 et seq.).

TRANSPORTATION

MOTOR VEHICLES:

Traffic and Vehicle Regulation.—(28-601 et seq.). Vehicle insurance and financial responsibility. (28-4001 et seq.). Vehicle Equipment Safety Compact adopted. (28-1801 et seq.). Multistate Highway Transportation Agreement adopted. (28-1821 et seq.). Nonresident Violator Compact adopted. (28-1871 et seq.).

General supervision is responsibility of Director of Department of Transportation, 1801 W. Jefferson St., Phoenix, Arizona 85007.

Dealers, including brokers, are regulated by Director and are required to have license, pay filing fee of $15 and annual fee of $100. (28-4301 et seq.). Sellers of mobile medical clinics are required to have license. (28-4335). Director may enforce license regulation through suspension of license, issuance of cease and desist order, and imposition of civil penalties. (28-4491 et seq.). Director also may bring and maintain action in superior court on behalf of state to restrain violation. (28-4497). Director deposits dealer licensing fees and civil penalties in state highway fund. (28-4304).

Motor vehicle subleasing regulated by 12-631 et seq.

Vehicle license by residents required annually. (28-2153). Definition of "residents" includes persons who remain in state for aggregate of seven months or more per calendar year, who are employed within state in other than seasonal agricultural work, who declare residency to obtain residential rates for state license or tuition at public educational institution, or who place children in public schools without payment of nonresident tuition, as well as any individual, partnership, company, firm, corporation or association which operates motor vehicles within state for other than seasonal agricultural work or which maintains main or branch offices or warehouse facilities and bases and operates motor vehicles within state. (28-2001). Exceptions exist. (28-2001). Registration of vehicle used by nonresident daily commuter. (28-2291 et seq.). Foreign vehicle registration by nonresidents. (28-2321). Temporary general use registration. (28-2156). Special licenses required for horseless carriages, classic cars and historic vehicles. (28-2481 et seq.). Special title and license plate provisions apply to off-road vehicles. (28-2512). Certain specialty plates are permitted. (28-2412 to 2418). Penalty for delinquency. (28-2161 to 2162). License plates must be displayed on rear of motor vehicle, trailer, or semitrailer, either on rear or on front and rear of vehicles for which two plates are issued. (28-2354). Director may authorize third parties to perform licensing and registration functions. (28-5101 et seq.). Registration fee exempts official vehicles. (28-2511).

Operators' license required. (28-3001 et seq.). Driver License Compact adopted. (28-1851 et seq.). Members of armed services exempt from license requirement while operating motor vehicles for military purposes. (28-3152). Licenses expire on 60th birthday, and thereafter on birthday five years after issuance. (28-3171[A]). License can be renewed by mail in certain cases. (28-3171[E]). Extension up to six months is available by mail for residents who are out-of-state at time license expires and will be out-of-state at least 30 days thereafter. (28-3172[E]). Veterans not required to renew license for six months after discharge. (28-3171[D]). Family members living out-of-state with military personnel may renew license by mail. (28-3172[A]). Licensee required to update photo and pass vision test every 12 years. (28-3173). Medical information may be put on licenses. (28-3167). Information on license application, other than medical records, is generally available to public unless driver prohibits disclosure. (28-452). Information on license application, other than driver histories, is available for commercial purposes (28-452[B]) for $600 per million records searched with minimum of $30 per thousand records provided (28-452[D]).

Titles, Sales and Liens.—Application for certificate of title must be made within 30 days of purchase or transfer and must be accompanied by odometer disclosure statement if vehicle was previously registered. (28-2051). Certificate of title must contain odometer disclosure statement, and owner of registered vehicle must deliver statement to transferee upon transfer or assignment. (28-2055, 2058). No vehicle shall be operated upon highways until registered. (28-2153). Exceptions exist. (28-2153[D]).

Security agreement, conditional sale or other contract of reservation of title (other than lien dependent on possession), and contract for conveyance, deed of trust or mortgage securing lien on both mobile home and real property, is invalid against creditors or subsequent purchasers without notice, unless application for title or registration shows lien or encumbrance on vehicle. (28-2131). No new certificate of title issued when outstanding certificate of title shows lien or encumbrance, unless such has been satisfied or its holder has consented in writing to transfer of title (28-2132[D]), owner furnishes proof of payment of underlying debt and affidavit that lienholder cannot be found (28-2134[B]), or certificate of title issued within one year by jurisdiction where liens must be recorded does not show lien (28-2134[C]). Salvage vehicles restored or rebuilt cannot be transferred until restored salvage certificate of title issued. (28-2095).

Identification Marks.—Intentional removal, defacement, alteration, or destruction of manufacturer's serial or identification number is class five felony. (28-2531[A]).

Fuel.—Department of Weights and Measures regulates dispensing machines (41-2051 et seq.) and tests machines at random (41-2065). Department regulates sale of fuel (41-2082 et seq.), oxygenation requirement (41-2122 et seq.). Definition of alternate fuel. (1-215[3]). Interstate transportation of fuel requires report. (28-5624 et seq.).

Size and Weight Limits.—Regulated by 28-1091 et seq. Special permits for excess weight and size may be obtained. (28-1103). Envelope permits may be obtained for fee. (28-1141 et seq.).

Driver License Classes and Endorsements.—Regulated by 28-3101 et seq.

Passenger Restraint System.—Person shall not operate motor vehicle on highways when transporting child under five years of age unless secured in child passenger restraint system. (28-907). Each front seat occupant of motor vehicle built in or after 1972 and designed for ten or fewer passengers, must wear lap and shoulder belt or lap belt. (28-909[A]). Driver is responsible for ensuring that front seat passengers under age 16 are properly utilizing passenger restraint system. (28-909[B]).

State Highway Speed Limits.—(28-702 et seq.).

Safety.—Driver liable for expenses of emergency response if driver enters street or highway covered by water and barricaded. (28-910).

Vehicle Emissions Inspection.—Required by 49-541 et seq.

Modular Motor Homes.—Definitions and disclosure requirements. (28-2097).

Person who signs application for instruction permit, driver's license or motorcycle permit on behalf of minor is liable for negligence or willful conduct of minor, unless proof of financial responsibility is shown on behalf of minor. (28-3160). Owner allowing operation by unlicensed minor under age 18 is liable for negligence or willful conduct of such minor. (28-3163). Owner of car kept for family use is liable for negligence of any family member. (81 Ariz. 325, 305 P.2d 463).

Guests.—No guest statute.

Proof of financial responsibility generally required by 28-4001 et seq. Exemptions exist. Operators of motor vehicles required to have evidence of current financial responsibility within vehicle. (28-4133[B]). Applicant for registration of motor vehicle must consent to comply with state financial responsibility requirements and cooperate with verification efforts. (28-4142[A]). Civil penalties for violations, including minimum fine of $250, driver's license suspension, and registration and license plate suspension. (28-4135). Compliance with financial responsibility requirements mandatory for reinstatement of suspended license. (28-4147).

Operators of commercial vehicles with gross weight exceeding 20,000 pounds, vehicles transporting hazardous substances, and passenger carrying vehicles for hire, except carpool operators, are subject to financial responsibility requirements. (28-4032 to 4033).

Insurance.—Mandatory motor vehicle insurance. (28-4131 et seq.). Insurance company, at request of insured, must provide insured with uninsured/underinsured motorist coverage. (20-259.01). Insured must corroborate any claim when uninsured/underinsured coverage if cause of accident is unidentified motor vehicle. (20-259.01[M]). Limitations imposed on right of auto insurers to cancel or renew insurance (20-1631 et seq.) and to increase premiums (20-263). Statutory presumptions govern primary and excess coverage when two or more policies cover same loss. (28-4010). Automobile rental agency's insurance is primary coverage for rental vehicle, but rental agency is not insurer of renter and has no obligation to defend driver beyond limits of coverage provided. (28-2166).

No-Fault Insurance.—Not adopted.

Foreign Vehicle.—Unlawful to operate foreign vehicle owned by nonresident on state highways, unless there is displayed on vehicle current registration number plates issued by owner's state or country of residence. (28-2322). Foreign vehicles used in commerce must be registered and licensed in Arizona. (28-2321[A]). There are special provisions for temporary registration and for registration of vehicles owned by residents of adjoining states. (28-2323 to 2324). Nonresident purchaser of unregistered vehicle within state for removal to purchaser's state of residence may secure special 30 day nonresident registration. (28-2154[A]). Vehicle owned by foreign government, Indian tribal government, or nonprofit organization need not pay registration fees, but must register and display official plates. (28-2511[A]). Licensing, registration, and insurance requirements apply to operators of foreign vehicles if foreign country does not grant reciprocal privileges to Arizona operators. (28-3152[B], 2322, 4037[A]).

Action against nonresident, including minor, insane or incompetent person, arising out of operation of motor vehicle in this state may be commenced by service of process on Director. (28-2326[B]). Notice of such service and copy of summons and complaint must be sent to defendant by registered mail or served on him by officer qualified to serve process in state where defendant is found. (28-2327[A]). Long-arm jurisdiction exists under Civ. 4.2.

Consent.—Operators of motor vehicles within state, if arrested or in accident involving serious injury or death, impliedly consent to tests of blood, breath, or urine to determine alcohol or drug content. (28-1321 et seq.).

Direct actions against insurer not permitted.

Motor vehicle carriers regulated in accordance with Multistate Highway Transportation Agreement adopted in 28-1821 et seq. Every motor carrier and transporter of hazardous materials must maintain books and records within state, which are available for inspection. (28-5231). Director may suspend registration or license if operation of vehicle endangers public safety. (28-5232). Penalties for violation governed by 28-5232 et seq. Commercial vehicles between 20,000 and 26,000 pounds must carry liability insurance of $300,000. (28-4033[A][1][b]). Larger vehicles, certain passenger-carrying commercial vehicles and vehicles carrying hazardous substances must have more insurance. (28-4033[A]). Motor Vehicle Division may require certificate of compliance. (28-4034). Motor vehicle fee reduced for agricultural carriers (28-5857) or limited mileage (28-5867).

Hours of Labor.—No common, contract or private carrier may allow drivers or helpers to remain on duty more than ten consecutive hours, after which they must have at least eight consecutive hours off duty, and any such person on duty ten hours in aggregate in any 24-hour period must have eight consecutive hours off duty, except in case of casualty, unavoidable accident or act of God. (23-286).

Taxation of Motor Vehicle Carriers.—See category Taxation, topics Sales and Use Taxes, subhead Transaction Privilege Taxes; Gasoline Tax, subhead Motor Carriers Tax.

See note at head of Digest as to 1998 legislation covered.

See Topical Index in front part of this volume.

AZ – 38

MOTOR VEHICLES . . . *continued*

Motor Vehicle Tax.—Tax rate is $4 on each $100 of value. Value for first 12 months is 60% of manufacturer's base retail price. (28-5801[B]). Value diminished by 15% each 12-month period thereafter. (28-5801[B]). Certain veterans (28-5802) and disabled individuals exempted (28-5803).

Motor Vehicle Warranties.—Regulated by 44-1261 et seq. If new motor vehicle does not conform to express warranty and if consumer reports nonconformity within two years or 24,000 miles following delivery or within term of express warranty, whichever is earlier, repairs must be made. (44-1262). If defect substantially impairs use and value of motor vehicle and if, after reasonable number of attempts, repairs cannot conform vehicle to express warranties, manufacturer must replace motor vehicle or refund full purchase price less reasonable allowance for use. (44-1263[A]). For manufacturer with prior direct written notification of defect (44-1264[C]), it is presumed that reasonable number of attempts have been made if either: (1) Same defect has been subject to repair four or more times within two years or 24,000-mile warranty term, whichever is earlier, or (2) motor vehicle is out of service by reason of repair for cumulative total of 30 or more days during term or two-year period or 24,000 miles, whichever is earlier. (44-1264[A]). Manufacturer's informal dispute settlement procedures must be resorted to prior to refund or replacement under 44-1263. (44-1265[A]). Statute of limitations for action under this article is six months following expiration of express warranty or two years or 24,000 miles following date of original delivery of motor vehicle, whichever is earlier. (44-1265[B]). Consumer entitled to reasonable costs and attorneys' fees. (44-1265[B]).

Trailer—Mobile Home Tax.—Mobile homes permanently affixed to real property subject to tax as real property. (42-640). Other mobile homes subject to ad valorem personal property tax (42-642), and, if customarily kept in state, must be titled with Department of Transportation (42-643). Unlawful to move or sell mobile home before paying any delinquent taxes. (42-610). Department of Transportation issues annual listing of delinquent, unsecured personal property taxes on mobile homes. (28-304.02). †(28-2062).

Aircraft operation and registration. (28-8201 et seq.).

Construction of mobile homes and recreational vehicles regulated by Department of Building and Fire Safety, Office of Manufactured Housing. (41-2141 et seq.). Movement of mobile homes on state highways regulated by 28-1104(E).

Fee Surety Bond.—See category Civil Actions and Procedure, topic Bonds.

Gasoline Tax.—Imposed. (28-5606 et seq.).

Petroleum Products Franchises.—Full-service gasoline station must provide attendant for physically disabled persons at self-service portion during full-service hours. (44-1562).

Use Fuel Tax and Surcharge.—Established by 28-5701 et seq.

Construction of Highways.—Transportation Board may make loans to cities or towns to fund local highway projects. (9-500.17, 28-7673). Highway expansion or extension loan program advisory committee created to form guidelines and make requests for financial assistance for highway projects. (28-7672 et seq.).

RAILROADS:

See category Business Regulation and Commerce, topic Carriers.

See note at head of Digest as to 1998 legislation covered.

See Topical Index in front part of this volume.

COMMERCIAL CODE FORMS

See also categories Business Regulation and Commerce, topic Commercial Code; and Mortgages, topic Chattel Mortgages.

Financing Statement.—UCC-1.

Return copy or recorded original to:	**ARIZONA UNIFORM COMMERCIAL CODE FINANCING STATEMENT—Form UCC—1** This FINANCING STATEMENT is presented for filing (recording) pursuant to the Arizona Uniform Commercial Code.
1. Debtor(s) (last name first and address):	2. Secured Party(ies) and address:
3. Name and Address of Assignee of Secured Party(ies):	4. ☐ If checked, products of collateral are also covered.
	5. This Financing Statement covers the following types (or items) of property:
6. If the collateral is crops, the crops are growing or to be grown on the following described real estate:	

7. If the collateral is (a) goods which are or are to become fixtures; (b) timber to be cut; or (c) minerals or the like (including oil and gas), or accounts resulting from the sale thereof at the wellhead or minehead to which the security interest attaches upon extraction, the legal description of the real estate concerned is:

And, this Financing Statement is to be recorded in the office where a mortgage on such real estate would be recorded. If the Debtor does not have an interest or record, the name of a record owner is:

8. This Financing Statement is signed by the Secured Party instead of the debtor to perfect or continue perfection of a security interest in:

☐ collateral already subject to a security interest in jurisdiction when it was brought into this state.

☐ collateral as to which the filing has lapsed or will lapse.

☐ proceeds of collateral because of a change in type or use.

☐ collateral acquired after a change of name, identity, or corporate structure of the Debtor.

_____

_____

_____

SIGNATURE(S) OF DEBTOR(S) OR ASSIGNOR

(USE WHICHEVER IS APPLICABLE)

FILING COPY

Dated: _____

_____

_____

SIGNATURE OF SECURED PARTY OR ASSIGNEE

Fees may be paid by check payable to the filing or recording office with the amount in blank, but with the notation "not to exceed $_____."

To file the form with the Secretary of State of Arizona, mail or deliver the form, together with the applicable fees, to:

Secretary of State of Arizona
1700 West Washington, 7th Floor
Phoenix, Arizona 85007
(Telephone: (602) 542-4285)

To record the form with a County Recorder, mail or deliver the form, together with the applicable fees to:

COUNTY RECORDERS

Apache County Recorder
P.O. Box 425
St. Johns, AZ 85936
(520) 337-4364

Cochise County Recorder
P.O. Box 184
Bisbee, AZ 85603
(520) 432-9270

Coconino County Recorder
Courthouse
Flagstaff, AZ 86001
(520) 779-6585

Gila County Recorder
1400 East Ash Street
Globe, AZ 85501
(520) 425-3231, ext. 230/232

Graham County Recorder
Courthouse
Safford, AZ 85546
(520) 428-3560

Greenlee County Recorder
P.O. Box 1625
Clifton, AZ 85533
(520) 865-2632

La Paz County Recorder
P.O. Box 940
Parker, AZ 85344
(520) 669-6136

Maricopa County Recorder
111 South Third Avenue
Phoenix, AZ 85003
(602) 506-3535

Mohave County Recorder
P.O. Box 70
Kingman, AZ 86402
(520) 753-0701

Navajo County Recorder
P.O. Box 668
Holbrook, AZ 86025
(520) 524-4190

Pima County Recorder
115 North Church
Tucson, AZ 85701
(520) 740-8151

Pinal County Recorder
P.O. Box 848
Florence, AZ 85232
(520) 868-7100

Santa Cruz County Recorder
2150 N. Congress Dr.
Nogales, AZ 85621
(520) 761-7800

Yavapai County Recorder
255 East Gurley Street
Prescott, AZ 86301
(520) 771-3244

Yuma County Recorder
198 South Main Street
Yuma, AZ 85364
(520) 329-2061

See note at head of Digest as to 1998 legislation covered.

See Topical Index in front part of this volume.

Financing Statement Change—UCC-2.

Return copy or recorded original to:	**ARIZONA UNIFORM COMMERCIAL CODE** **FINANCING STATEMENT CHANGE—Form UCC—2** This Statement is presented for filing (recording) pursuant to the Arizona Uniform Commercial Code.

1. Debtor(s) (last name first and address):	2. Secured Party(ies) and address:

3. This Statement refers to original Financing Statement File No. _____ Docket _____Page _____

Filed (recorded) with _____ Date filed (recorded) _____, 19 _____

4. ☐ CONTINUATION. The Financing Statement described above is continued.

☐ TERMINATION STATEMENT. The Financing Statement described above is terminated.

☐ ASSIGNMENT. The interest of the Secured Party under the Financing Statement described above has been assigned to the Assignee whose name and address appear below.

☐ AMENDMENT. The Financing Statement described above is amended as set forth below.

☐ PARTIAL RELEASE. The Secured Party releases the collateral described below from the Financing Statement described above.

5.

_____   Dated: _____

_____   _____

SIGNATURE(S) OF DEBTOR(S)   Signature of Secured Party or Assignee of Record
(Required only on Amendments)

Fees may be paid by check payable to the filing or recording office with the amount in blank, but with the notation "not to exceed $_____."

To file the form with the Secretary of State of Arizona, mail or deliver the form, together with the applicable fees, to:

> Secretary of State of Arizona
> 1700 West Washington, 7th Floor
> Phoenix, Arizona 85007
> (Telephone: (602) 542-4285)

To record the form with a County Recorder, mail or deliver the form, together with the applicable fees to:

COUNTY RECORDERS

Apache County Recorder
P.O. Box 425
St. Johns, AZ 85936
(520) 337-4364

Cochise County Recorder
P.O. Box 184
Bisbee, AZ 85603
(520) 432-9270

Coconino County Recorder
Courthouse
Flagstaff, AZ 86001
(520) 779-6585

Gila County Recorder
1400 East Ash Street
Globe, AZ 85501
(520) 425-3231, ext. 230/232

Graham County Recorder
Courthouse
Safford, AZ 85546
(520) 428-3560

Greenlee County Recorder
P.O. Box 1625
Clifton, AZ 85533
(520) 865-2632

La Paz County Recorder
P.O. Box 940
Parker, AZ 85344
(520) 669-6136

Maricopa County Recorder
111 South Third Avenue
Phoenix, AZ 85003
(602) 506-3535

Mohave County Recorder
P.O. Box 70
Kingman, AZ 86402
(520) 753-0701

Navajo County Recorder
P.O. Box 668
Holbrook, AZ 86025
(520) 524-4190

Pima County Recorder
115 North Church
Tucson, AZ 85701
(520) 740-8151

Pinal County Recorder
P.O. Box 848
Florence, AZ 85232
(520) 868-7100

Santa Cruz County Recorder
2150 N. Congress Dr.
Nogales, AZ 85621
(520) 761-7800

Yavapai County Recorder
255 East Gurley Street
Prescott, AZ 86301
(520) 771-3244

Yuma County Recorder
198 South Main Street
Yuma, AZ 85364
(520) 329-2061

Request for Information or Copies.—UCC-3.

ARIZONA UNIFORM COMMERCIAL CODE
REQUEST FOR INFORMATION OR COPIES—Form UCC—3
REQUEST FOR INFORMATION OR COPIES—Present in duplicate to filing (recording) officer.

1. Debtor(s) (last name first and address):	2. Party requesting information or copies (name and address):

☐ List below any presently effective Financing Statements naming the above named Debtor(s) and any statements of assignment thereof.

☐ Furnish exact copies of each page of Financing Statements and statements of assignment listed below.

FILE NUMBER OR DOCKET REF.	DATE AND HOUR OF FILING (RECORDING)	NAMES AND ADDRESSES OF SECURED PARTIES AND ASSIGNEES

CERTIFICATE: The undersigned officer hereby certifies that:

☐ The above list is a record of all presently effective Financing Statements and statements of assignment which name the above Debtor(s) and which are filed (recorded) in this office as of _____, 19__ at _____. M.

☐ The attached _____ pages are true and exact copies of all available Financing Statements or statements of assignment listed in the above request.

Dated: _____

_____
Secretary of State/County Recorder

By _____

Standard Form UCC-3 Approved By The Secretary of State of Arizona

See reverse side for instructions

FILING COPY

Fees may be paid by check payable to the filing or recording office with the amount in blank, but with the notation "not to exceed $_____."

To file the form with the Secretary of State of Arizona, mail or deliver the form, together with the applicable fees, to:

Secretary of State of Arizona
1700 West Washington, 7th Floor
Phoenix, Arizona 85007
(Telephone: (602) 542-4285)

To record the form with a County Recorder, mail or deliver the form, together with the applicable fees to:

COUNTY RECORDERS

Apache County Recorder
P.O. Box 425
St. Johns, AZ 85936
(520) 337-4364

Cochise County Recorder
P.O. Box 184
Bisbee, AZ 85603
(520) 432-9270

Coconino County Recorder
Courthouse
Flagstaff, AZ 86001
(520) 779-6585

Gila County Recorder
1400 East Ash Street
Globe, AZ 85501
(520) 425-3231, ext. 230/232

Graham County Recorder
Courthouse
Safford, AZ 85546
(520) 428-3560

Greenlee County Recorder
P.O. Box 1625
Clifton, AZ 85533
(520) 865-2632

La Paz County Recorder
P.O. Box 940
Parker, AZ 85344
(520) 669-6136

Maricopa County Recorder
111 South Third Avenue
Phoenix, AZ 85003
(602) 506-3535

Mohave County Recorder
P.O. Box 70
Kingman, AZ 86402
(520) 753-0701

Navajo County Recorder
P.O. Box 668
Holbrook, AZ 86025
(520) 524-4190

Pima County Recorder
115 North Church
Tucson, AZ 85701
(520) 740-8151

Pinal County Recorder
P.O. Box 848
Florence, AZ 85232
(520) 868-7100

Santa Cruz County Recorder
2150 N. Congress Dr.
Nogales, AZ 85621
(520) 761-7800

Yavapai County Recorder
255 East Gurley Street
Prescott, AZ 86301
(520) 771-3244

Yuma County Recorder
198 South Main Street
Yuma, AZ 85364
(520) 329-2061

Notice of Proposed Disposition of Collateral.—UCC-4.

<table>
<tr>
<td colspan="2">Return copy or recorded original to:</td>
<td colspan="2">

ARIZONA UNIFORM COMMERCIAL CODE
NOTICE OF PROPOSED DISPOSITION OF
COLLATERAL—FORM UCC—4
This NOTICE OF PROPOSED DISPOSITION OF
COLLATERAL is presented for filing (recording)
pursuant to the Arizona Uniform Commercial Code.

</td>
</tr>
<tr>
<td colspan="2">1. Debtor(s) (last name first and address):</td>
<td colspan="2">2. Secured Party(ies) or Assignee and address:</td>
</tr>
<tr>
<td colspan="4">3. Information concerning the security interest may be obtained from the address given in item 3 or:</td>
</tr>
<tr>
<td colspan="4">4. Notice is hereby given that the Secured Party(ies) or Assignee, because the Debtor is in default, proposes to dispose of the following collateral:</td>
</tr>
<tr>
<td colspan="4">

5. This Notice refers to original Financing Statement File No. _____

Docket _____ Page _____ filed (recorded) with _____

_____ Dated filed (recorded) _____, 19____

</td>
</tr>
<tr>
<td colspan="4">

Dated: _____

_____

_____
SIGNATURE OF SECURED PARTY OR ASSIGNEE
(Not Valid until Signed)

Standard Form UCC-4 Approved By The Secretary of State of Arizona

FILING COPY

</td>
</tr>
</table>

Fees may be paid by check payable to the filing or recording office with the amount in blank, but with the notation "not to exceed $_____."

To file the form with the Secretary of State of Arizona, mail or deliver the form, together with the applicable fees, to:

Secretary of State of Arizona
1700 West Washington, 7th Floor
Phoenix, Arizona 85007
(Telephone: (602) 542-4285)

To record the form with a County Recorder, mail or deliver the form, together with the applicable fees to:

COUNTY RECORDERS

Apache County Recorder
P.O. Box 425
St. Johns, AZ 85936
(520) 337-4364

Cochise County Recorder
P.O. Box 184
Bisbee, AZ 85603
(520) 432-9270

Coconino County Recorder
Courthouse
Flagstaff, AZ 86001
(520) 779-6585

Gila County Recorder
1400 East Ash Street
Globe, AZ 85501
(520) 425-3231, ext. 230/232

Graham County Recorder
Courthouse
Safford, AZ 85546
(520) 428-3560

Greenlee County Recorder
P.O. Box 1625
Clifton, AZ 85533
(520) 865-2632

La Paz County Recorder
P.O. Box 940
Parker, AZ 85344
(520) 669-6136

Maricopa County Recorder
111 South Third Avenue
Phoenix, AZ 85003
(602) 506-3535

Mohave County Recorder
P.O. Box 70
Kingman, AZ 86402
(520) 753-0701

Navajo County Recorder
P.O. Box 668
Holbrook, AZ 86025
(520) 524-4190

Pima County Recorder
115 North Church
Tucson, AZ 85701
(520) 740-8151

Pinal County Recorder
P.O. Box 848
Florence, AZ 85232
(520) 868-7100

Santa Cruz County Recorder
2150 N. Congress Dr.
Nogales, AZ 85621
(520) 761-7800

Yavapai County Recorder
255 East Gurley Street
Prescott, AZ 86301
(520) 771-3244

Yuma County Recorder
198 South Main Street
Yuma, AZ 85364
(520) 329-2061

See note at head of Digest as to 1998 legislation covered.

See Topical Index in front part of this volume.

Fees are to be paid by direct payable to the filing or reporting office when submitted in blank, but with the Abstract thereto, etc., etc.

to the Secretary of State of Arizona, until it delivered for filing then with the applicable fee, to:

Secretary of State of Arizona
1700 West Washington, 7th Floor
Phoenix, Arizona 85007
(Telephone: (602) 542-4285)

To record the Financing Statement, mail or deliver the form, together with the applicable fees, to:

COUNTY RECORDERS

Apache County Recorder
P.O. Box 425
St. Johns, AZ 85936
(520) 337-4364

Cochise County Recorder
P.O. Box 184
Bisbee, AZ 85603
(520) 432-8350

Coconino County Recorder
Coconino
Flagstaff, AZ 86001
(520) 779-6585

Gila County Recorder
1400 East Ash Street
Globe, AZ 85501
(520) 425-3231, ext. 5022

Graham County Recorder
and more
Safford, AZ 85546
(520) 428-3560

Greenlee County Recorder
P.O. Box 1625
Clifton, AZ 85533
(520) 865-9679

La Paz County Recorder
P.O. Box 900
Parker, AZ 85344
(520) 669-6136

Maricopa County Recorder
111 South Third Avenue
Phoenix, AZ 85003
(602) 506-3535

Mohave County Recorder
P.O. Box 70
Kingman, AZ 86402
(520) 753-0701

Navajo County Recorder
P.O. Box 668
Holbrook, AZ 86025
(520) 524-4190

Pima County Recorder
115 North Church
Tucson, AZ 85701
(520) 740-4351

Pinal County Recorder
P.O. Box 848
Florence, AZ 85232
(520) 868-6700

Santa Cruz County Recorder
2150 N. Congress Dr.
Nogales, AZ 85621
(520) 761-7800, ext. 2

Yavapai County Recorder
255 East Gurley Street
Prescott, AZ 86301
(520) 771-3244

Yuma County Recorder
190 South Main Street
Yuma, AZ 85364
(520) 329-2001

See note at head of Discharge heading legislation covered

See Topical Index in front and of this volume.

ARKANSAS LAW DIGEST REVISER

Rose Law Firm,
A Professional Association
120 East Fourth Street
Little Rock, Arkansas 72201-2893
Telephone: 501-375-9131
Fax: 501-375-1309

Reviser Profile

History: Rose Law Firm, a Professional Association, traces its organization from November 1, 1820, when Robert Crittenden (1797-1834), the first Territorial Secretary of Arkansas, and Chester A. Ashley (1791-1848) formed a partnership. Following the death of Mr. Crittenden, George C. Watkins (1815-1872) became a partner with Mr. Ashley in 1837, with the firm name of Ashley and Watkins. Judge U. M. Rose (1834-1913) formed a partnership with Judge Watkins in 1865. The name Rose has continued in the Firm since that time, as later George B. Rose became a partner with his father. The present Firm, a professional association, is a successor to several preceding partnerships.

Areas of Emphasis and Growth: The Firm engages in a general practice of law with particular specialization in areas of Taxation, Corporation, Corporate and Municipal Finance, Commercial Litigation, Labor Relations, Healthcare, Bankruptcy and Banking Law. The Firm presently is staffed with 33 lawyers.

Client Base: Clients represented by the Firm include national manufacturing and industrial firms, as well as leading insurers and financial institutions. Corporate clients include those engaged in retailing, distribution, insurance, poultry products, electronic technology, health care, investment banking, and environmental technology.

Firm Activities: Members of the Firm are active in professional organizations and are frequent lecturers in continuing legal education programs. Members also serve on numerous public boards and commissions, as well as civic bodies. All members and attorneys associated with the Firm are members at least of the American Bar Association, the Arkansas Bar Association, and the Pulaski County Bar Association. In addition, some members of the Firm are members of professional associations relating to accounting and engineering. Several members of the Firm have served as president of the Arkansas Bar Association. The Firm is a member of the State Capital Law Firm Group and Lex Mundi. Members of the Firm weekly digest significant Eighth Circuit decisions for publication in the regional legal newspaper.

Management: As a professional corporation, management of the Firm is vested in a board of directors composed of all members of the Firm. A three-member executive committee of the board of directors deals with administrative matters, professional development of attorneys, employment and formation of Firm policies. Various committees are created of members and associations for functional responsibilities and planning. There are presently 23 members of the Firm.

Significant Distinctions: Members of the Firm, since its founding, have been active in civic and professional affairs. Chester A. Ashley was United States Senator from Arkansas and chairman of the Senate Judiciary Committee. U. M. Rose was president of the American Bar Association (1900-1901), and ambassador to the Second Hague Peace Conference (1902) by appointment of President Theodore Roosevelt. Members of the Firm and its predecessors serving in judicial positions include Arkansas Supreme Court Chief Justice George C. Watkins, and Associate Justices Wilson E. Hemingway and George Rose Smith. Three members have served as members of the National Conference of Commissioners on Uniform State Laws; Philip Carroll served as president of the Conference (1985-1987); M. Jane Dickey served as President of the National Association of Bond Lawyers (1992-1993).

ARKANSAS LAW DIGEST REVISER

Rose Law Firm
A Professional Association
120 East Fourth Street
Little Rock, Arkansas 72201-2893
Telephone: 501-375-9131
Fax: 501-375-1309

Reviser Profile

History. Rose Law Firm, a Professional Association, traces its organization from November 1, 1820, when Robert Crittenden (1797-1834), the first Territorial Secretary of Arkansas, and Chester A. Ashley (1791-1848) formed a partnership. Following the death of Mr. Crittenden, George C. Watkins (1815-1872) became a partner with Mr. Ashley in 1837, with the firm name of Ashley and Watkins. Judge U.M. Rose (1834-1913) formed a partnership with Judge Watkins in 1865. The name Rose has continued in the Firm since that time, when George B. Rose became a partner with his father. The present Firm, a professional association, is a successor to several predecessor partnerships.

Areas of Emphasis and Growth. The Firm engages in a general practice of law with particular specialization in areas of Taxation, Corporation/Corporate and Municipal Finance, Commercial Litigation, Labor Relations, Healthcare, Bankruptcy and Banking Law. The Firm presently is staffed with 53 lawyers.

Client Base. Clients represented by the firm include national manufacturing and industrial firms, as well as leading national and international manufacturers. Corporate clients include those engaged in retailing, distribution, insurance, poultry products, electronics, technology, health care, investment banking, and environmental technology.

Firm Activities. Members of the Firm are active in professional organizations and are frequent lecturers in continuing legal education programs. Members also serve on numerous public boards and commissions, as well as civic bodies. All members and attorneys are associated with the Firm are members of the American Bar Association, the Arkansas Bar Association, and the Pulaski County Bar Association. In addition, some members of the Firm are members of professional associations relating to accounting and engineering. Several members of the Firm have served as president of the Arkansas Bar Association. The Firm is a member of the State Capital Law Firm Group and Lex Mundi. Members of the Firm weekly digest significant Eighth Circuit decisions for publication in the regional legal newspaper.

Management. As a professional corporation, management of the Firm is vested in a board of directors composed of all members of the Firm. A three-member executive committee of the board of directors deals with administrative matters, professional development of attorneys, employment and formation of Firm policies. Various committees are created of members and associates for functional responsibilities, and planning. There are presently 23 members of the Firm.

Significant Dedications. Members of the Firm, since its founding, have been active in civic and professional affairs. Chester A. Ashley was a United States Senator from Arkansas and chairman of the Senate Judiciary Committee. U.M. Rose was president of the American Bar Association (1901-1902) and ambassador to the Second Hague Peace Conference (1907) by appointment of President Theodore Roosevelt. Members of the Firm and its predecessors serving in judicial positions include Arkansas Supreme Court Chief Justice George C. Watkins and Associate Justices William B. Hemingway and George Rose Smith. Three members have served as members of the National Conference of Commissioners on Uniform State Laws. Philip Carroll served as president of the Conference (1965-1971), M. Jane Dickey served as President of the National Association of Bond Lawyers (1993-1994).

ARKANSAS LAW DIGEST

(The following is a list of all Categories and Topics, including cross-references, covered in this Digest.)

ARKANSAS LAW DIGEST

Revised for 1999 edition by
ROSE LAW FIRM, a Professional Association, of the Little Rock Bar.

(Citations, unless otherwise indicated, refer to chapters or sections of Arkansas Code 1987, Official Edition. Subsequent statutes are cited by year and act number. Effective July 1, 1979, Arkansas Supreme Court established certain procedural rules superseding many statutory provisions. These rules are Rules of Civil Procedure (RCP), Rules of Appellate Procedure (RAP), and Rules for Inferior Courts (RIC) which are cited by abbreviations indicated in parentheses. Parallel citations to South Western Reporter begin with 47 Ark.)

(Note: 1997 legislation includes session laws through May 1997.)

INTRODUCTION

GOVERNMENT AND LEGAL SYSTEM:

The State of Arkansas is a constituent state of the United States of America. For further discussion of the U.S. federal system, see Introduction to the Federal Government of the United States at the beginning of this volume. A great many laws are promulgated by the federal government of the United States and are not reflected in the topics below. See the Introduction to this volume for references to the federal law topics covered.

Like all but one of the United States, Arkansas has a common law legal system, with roots in English common law. For information on the courts and legislature of Arkansas, see category Courts and Legislature.

HOLIDAYS:

Legal holidays are Jan. 1, 3d Mon. in Jan., 3d Mon. in Feb., last Mon. in May, July 4, 1st Mon. in Sept., Nov. 11, 4th Thurs. in Nov., Dec. 24, Dec. 25. (1-5-101), Following days are not legal holidays but are memorial days to be commemorated by appropriate proclamation by Governor: Jan. 26; Feb. 12; 1st Tues. in Mar.; 3d Mon. in Mar.; Fri. preceding Easter; Apr. 19; Apr. 26; June 3; Oct. 12. (1-5-106).

If legal holiday falls on Sun., the following Mon. is legal holiday. Legal holidays falling on Sat. will be observed on preceding Fri. (1-5-101).

Commercial Paper Payable on Holiday.—Bills of exchange, drafts or promissory notes payable on a legal holiday are payable on the next succeeding day. (1-5-105).

Transactions on legal holidays are valid, except that contract made on Sunday is void unless ratified on a subsequent weekday. (177 Ark. 183; 173 Ark. 60).

OFFICE HOURS AND TIME ZONE:

Arkansas is in the Central (GMT −06:00) time zone. Office hours are generally from 9 a.m. to 5 p.m.

BUSINESS ORGANIZATIONS

AGENCY:

Agent is person who, by agreement with another called principal, acts for principal and is subject to his control. (Ark. Model Jury Instr. 701; 326 Ark. 1040).

ASSOCIATIONS:

Subject to common law rules. An unincorporated association has no legal entity and cannot be sued by its society or company name, but all the members must be made parties (150 Ark. 398, 234 S.W. 464) and may be liable as partners (171 Ark. 399, 284 S.W. 755).

Unincorporated association cannot take title to real property. (259 Ark. 784, 536 S.W.2d 709; 235 Ark. 124, 685 S.W.2d 153).

Benevolent associations may be incorporated under special provision. (4-28-201-224). Model Non-Profit Corporation Act adopted, with revisions, effective Jan. 1, 1994. (4-33-101 et seq.).

Professional Associations.—See topic Corporations, subhead Professional Corporations.

CORPORATIONS:

See also topic Limited Liability Companies.

Act 958 of 1987 (codified at Ark. Code Ann. Title 4, c. 27) adopted modified version of official text of Revised Model Business Corporation Act (1984) ("Model Act"). Act applies to all domestic corporations incorporated on or after Jan. 1, 1988, and to all foreign corporations desiring to transact business in Arkansas on or after Jan. 1, 1988. Foreign corporations qualified to do business in Arkansas on Dec. 31, 1987 are governed by Act but need not obtain new certificate of authority.

All domestic corporations incorporated before Jan. 1, 1988 may irrevocably elect to be governed by Act by amending articles of incorporation. Any domestic corporation incorporated before Jan. 1, 1988 not electing to be governed by Act will continue to be governed by Arkansas Business Corporation Act (codified at Ark. Code Ann. Title 4, c. 26).

Act is based on Model Act with following significant variations:

(1) Articles of Incorporation must set forth (in addition to Model Act provisions): (i) Number of shares corporation is authorized to issue, classes (if any), par value (if any); (ii) purposes for which corporation is organized (4-27-202[a][2], [5]);

(2) Articles of Incorporation may set forth (in addition to Model Act provisions) provision eliminating or limiting director's personal liability to corporation or shareholders for monetary damages for breach of fiduciary duty as director, provided that such provision may not eliminate or limit liability of director for breach of duty of loyalty, for acts or omissions not in good faith or intentional misconduct or knowing violation of law, for unlawful distributions under 4-27-833, for transactions where director derived improper personal benefit or for any act or omission creating third-party liability to anyone other than corporation or stockholder (4-27-202[B][3]);

(3) Act controls use of fictitious names. (4-27-404-405). See fictitious name provisions of Arkansas Business Corporation Act summarized below for similar provisions;

(4) Guarantees right of all shareholders to vote on proposal to increase capital stock or bond indebtedness (4-27-601[C][1], Ark. Const., art. XII, §8); board of directors of investment company (defined at 4-27-140[27]) may increase or decrease authorized stock, unless such act is prohibited by articles of incorporation (4-27-601[E]);

(5) Corporation issuing shares pursuant to subscription agreement entered into before incorporation must comply with Act (4-27-620);

(6) Consideration for issuance of shares may be money paid, labor done or property actually received; neither promissory notes nor promise of future services constitute valid consideration for issuance of shares (4-27-621[B]);

(7) Shares having par value may not be issued for consideration less than par value (4-27-621[C]);

(8) Shares may not be issued until full consideration has been paid (4-27-621[F]);

(9) Face of share certificate must state par value of shares (if any) (4-27-625[B][4]), and must bear corporate seal (4-27-625[D][2]);

(10) If allowed by articles or bylaws, board of directors of investment company (defined at 4-27-140[27]) may delegate to committee or officers of corporation authority to determine amount of, declare and distribute dividends (4-27-640[G]);

(11) If articles or bylaws so provide, investment company (defined at 4-27-140[27]) not required to hold annual meeting where no action taken that requires shareholders vote, unless such meeting is called by majority of shareholders or directors (4-27-701[D]);

(12) Action on proposals to increase capital stock or bond indebtedness of corporation may be taken without meeting of shareholders if written consents are signed by all shareholders. Any other action requiring shareholder approval may be taken without meeting of shareholders if written consents are signed by holders of outstanding shares having not less than minimum number of votes necessary to take such action at meeting where shares were present and voted (4-27-704[A]);

(13) Corporation shall notify shareholders of date, time and place of each annual and special shareholder's meeting no fewer than 60 nor more than 75 days before meeting if proposal to increase authorized capital stock or bond indebtedness is to be submitted; in all other cases notice shall be given no fewer than ten nor more than 60 days (4-27-705[A]); annual meeting at which proposal to increase authorized capital stock or bond indebtedness is to be submitted, deemed special meeting (4-27-705[C]);

(14) Director's indirect interest in transaction with corporation should be considered by board of directors (4-27-831[B]);

(15) Corporation may indemnify any person who was or is party or is threatened to be made party to any threatened, pending or completed action, suit or proceeding, whether civil or criminal, administrative or investigative (other than action by or in right of corporation), by reason of fact he is or was director, officer, employee or agent of corporation or serving another corporation at request of corporation, against expenses (including attorneys' fees), judgments, fines, and amounts paid in settlement, actually and reasonably incurred by him if he acted in good faith and in manner he reasonably believed to be in or not opposed to best interest of corporation and, with respect to criminal action or proceeding, had no reasonable cause to believe his conduct unlawful. Lack of good faith not presumed from settlement or nolo contendere plea. Indemnification of expenses (including attorney's fees) allowed in defense or settlement of derivative actions except no indemnification in respect to any claim, issue or matter as to which any such person has been adjudged to be liable unless court decides indemnification is proper. To extent any such person succeeds on merits or otherwise, he shall be indemnified against expenses (including attorney's fees). Determination that person to be indemnified met applicable standard of conduct is made by board of directors by majority vote of quorum consisting of directors not party to such action, suit or proceeding or, if quorum not obtainable or disinterested quorum so directs, by independent legal counsel or by shareholders. Expenses may be paid in advance upon receipt of undertaking to repay unless it shall ultimately be determined that he is not entitled to be indemnified by corporation. Corporation may purchase indemnity insurance. Right of indemnification continues as to person who has ceased to be director, officer or agent unless otherwise provided in authorization granting or ratifying indemnification or advancement of expenses (4-27-850);

(16) Foreign corporation liable for civil penalty between $100 and $5,000 if it transacts business in Arkansas without certificate of authority. Secretary of State to promulgate resolutions for determining penalty, taking into account size and assets of corporation, amount business transacted by corporation in Arkansas (4-27-1502[D]);

(17) Foreign corporation's application for certificate of authority must contain statement of par value (if any) of corporation's capital stock owned by Arkansas residents (4-27-1503[A][6]);

(18) Foreign corporation may use fictitious name only where real name unavailable (4-27-1506[A][2]).

See 4-27-1622 and 26-54-101 et seq. for requirements of Annual Franchise Tax Report.

See note at head of Digest as to 1998 legislation covered.

See Topical Index in front part of this volume.

CORPORATIONS . . . *continued*

Arkansas Business Corporation Act, codified at Ark. Code Ann. Title 4, c. 26, applies to all domestic corporations incorporated before Jan. 1, 1988 unless corporation elects to be governed by Ark. Code Ann. Title 4, c. 27. See supra. (For unincorporated organizations see topic Associations.)

General Supervision.—Secretary of State, 256 State Capitol Bldg., Little Rock, AR 72201; telephone: (501) 682-1010; telecopy: (501) 682-3510.

Purposes.—Corporation may be organized for any lawful purpose unless required to be organized under other statute. Corporation organized under any other statute continues subject to provisions of Business Corporation Act to extent Business Corporation Act is not inconsistent with other statute. (4-26-103).

Corporations may be formed for transaction of any lawful business outside of state. (4-26-204).

Name of corporation must indicate its corporate character and must not be same as, or confusingly similar to, name of any domestic corporation existing under laws of this state or any foreign corporation authorized to transact business in this state. (4-26-401).

Name may be reserved for six months by filing written application with Secretary of State and right to exclusive use thereof may be transferred by filing in office of Secretary of State a notice of such transfer, specifying name and address of transferee. Reservation is not renewable. (4-26-402). Fee for formal reservation of name is $25. (4-27-1705). Secretary of State will advise on availability of name only upon filing of notification form.

Fictitious name may be used only where corporation first files with Secretary of State and, in case of domestic corporation, with county clerk of county where corporation's registered office is located (unless it is located in Pulaski County), form supplied or approved by Secretary of State giving full information as required by corporation act. (4-26-405).

Term of corporate existence is unlimited unless limited in articles of incorporation. (4-26-204).

Incorporators.—One or more natural persons of age of 21 years or more may act as incorporators. (4-26-201).

Articles of Incorporation.—Incorporators must sign duplicate original articles setting forth name of corporation which must indicate its corporate character; period of duration, which may be perpetual; purpose for which organized; aggregate number of shares, and with reference to each class, par value or a statement that such shares are without par value; if shares are divided into classes, a statement of preferences, limitations and relative rights of each class; if preferred or special class in series, designation of each series and statement of variations in relative rights and preferences insofar as same are to be fixed in articles and statement of any authority to be vested in directors to establish series and determine variations in relative rights and preferences; that corporation will not commence business until consideration of at least $300 has been received for issuance of shares; any provisions limiting or enlarging preemptive rights; any provisions not inconsistent with law for regulation of affairs of corporation; address of initial registered office and name of initial registered agent at such address; number of directors constituting initial board of directors, and if either one or two, then statement specifying number to be elected at annual meeting (or special meeting called for that purpose) of shareholders next following time when shares become owned by more than one or two, and name and address of each incorporator. It is unnecessary to set forth powers enumerated in corporation act. (4-26-202).

Fees chargeable under Model Act, Act 958 of 1987 (codified at Ark. Code Ann. Title 4, c. 27): Articles of incorporation, $50; application for use of indistinguishable name, no fee; application for reserved name, $25; notice of transfer of reserved name, $25; application for registered name, $50; application for renewal of registered name, $25; corporation's statement of change of registered agent or registered office or both, $25; agent's statement of change of registered office for each affected corporation not to exceed total of $125; agent's statement of resignation, no fee; amendment of articles of incorporation, $50; restatement of articles of incorporation with amendment of articles, $100; articles of merger or share exchange, $100; articles of dissolution, $50; articles of revocation of dissolution, $150; certificate of administrative dissolution, no fee; application for reinstatement following administrative dissolution, $50; certificate of reinstatement, no fee; certificate of judicial dissolution, no fee; application for certificate of authority, $300; application for amended certificate of authority, $300; application for certificate of withdrawal, $300; certificate of revocation of authority to transact business, no fee; articles of correction, $30; application for certificate of existence or authorization, $15; or any other document required or permitted to be filed, $25; service of process on Secretary of State, $25 (subject to recovery); copies, 50¢ per page; certificates, $5. (4-27-122).

Fees chargeable for corporations operating under Arkansas Business Corporation Act, Act 576 of 1965 (codified at Ark. Code Ann. Title 4, c. 26) are: Articles of incorporation, $50; amendment to articles of incorporation, $50; articles of merger or consolidation, $100; corporation's statement of registered agent or officer, both $25; agent's statement of change of registered office or agent for each affected corporation, not to exceed $200; application for fictitious name, $25; application for reserved name, $25; for another filing under this act with annexed certificate, $25; for other certificates, $25; copies, 50¢ per page; certificates, $5; receiving service for corporation, $25; receiving service for individual, $10. (4-27-1705).

Fees of the county clerk are: For filing articles or other document $25; for recording any document $1 per page for first three pages of manuscript filed for record and 50¢ for each additional page or partial page, and certificate of Secretary of State is one page; for every certificate 50¢; for indexing each record 10¢; for any other service, fee is governed by then applicable scale fixed by law for clerk's office. (4-26-1203).

License to do Business.—None.

Organization.—Organization meeting of shareholders for purpose of electing directors and transacting such other business as may come before meeting must be called by notice signed by majority of incorporators, setting a place either within or without state and stating purpose of meeting. Notice must be given at least three days before meeting but may be waived by incorporators entitled to receive notice. (4-26-203).

Paid in Capital Requirement.—Amount of capital with which a corporation will begin business may not be less than $300. (4-26-206).

If corporation begins business before amount of capital required has been paid in, its directors become liable for any deficiency. (4-26-811).

Amendment of Articles.—Corporation may at any time amend its articles in any respect which would be permissible in original articles and which is proposed by vote of directors and approved by at least two-thirds of shares entitled to vote thereon. Amendments must be voted upon according to class of shareholders. (4-26-301/303).

Executed duplicate articles verified by a least one signing officer must set forth: Name of corporation; copy of amendment so adopted; date of adoption by shareholders; number of shares outstanding, number of shares entitled to vote including shares of any class entitled to vote; number of shares voted for and against amendment, including shares of any class entitled to vote; manner of effecting any exchange, reclassification or cancellation of issued shares; manner of effecting any change in amount of stated capital and statement expressed in dollars of stated amount as changed. (4-26-304).

Articles may be amended to give effect to any plan of reorganization order confirmed by any court of competent jurisdiction pursuant to any applicable statutes of U.S. so long as articles remain consistent with provisions of corporation act. (4-26-307).

Amended articles are filed in duplicate with Secretary of State in same manner as original articles. (4-26-305).

Increase of Stock or Indebtedness.—All fictitious increases of stock or indebtedness are void; and stock or bonded indebtedness of private corporation may not be increased except in pursuance of general laws nor until consent of persons holding larger amount in value of stock is obtained at meeting held after notice given for not less than 60 days. (Const. art. XII, §8). The 60 days may be waived by accepting stock or bonds. (104 Ark. 517, 149 S.W. 336).

Reduction of capital may be effected by redeeming or purchasing redeemable shares and filing with Secretary of State statement of cancellation. Redeemed shares are restored to status of authorized but unissued shares unless articles prohibit reissuance. In this event statement of cancellation amends articles to reduce number of shares of the class which corporation may issue by number of shares cancelled. (4-26-614).

Statement of cancellation, executed in duplicate and verified by one of signing officers, must set forth: Name of corporation; number of redeemable shares cancelled itemized by class and series; aggregate number of issued shares itemized by class and series after giving effect to such cancellation; amount in dollars of stated capital of corporation after giving effect to cancellation; if articles provide cancelled share may not be reissued, then number of shares which corporation may issue itemized by class and series after giving effect to cancellation. (4-26-614).

Corporation may not redeem its shares if at time or as result thereof there is reasonable ground for believing that corporation would be unable to meet its obligations as they become due in ordinary course of business; or its remaining assets would be less than 1¼ times amount of its liabilities to creditors; or if by such redemption net assets would be reduced below aggregate amount payable to holders of shares to remain outstanding which have prior or equal rights to its assets upon dissolution; or if there exist any unpaid accrued preferential dividends with respect to any shares having priority as to dividends over shares to be redeemed. (4-26-613).

Corporation may cancel its treasury stock by filing similar statement of cancellation. (4-26-612).

If all or part of stated capital is represented by shares without par value, stated capital may be reduced by directors with approval of shareholders and filing of appropriate statement in duplicate with Secretary of State. (4-26-615).

By-laws, not inconsistent with law or articles, may be adopted for management of affairs of corporation, and, if adopted, must be adopted initially by directors, and thereafter amended, repealed, or new by-laws adopted by directors except to extent such power may be reserved by articles to shareholders. (4-26-809).

Emergency by-laws may be adopted by directors, subject to repeal or change by shareholders, for managing affairs of corporation during any emergency and until its termination. (4-26-810).

Stock.—Business corporation has right to issue shares of different classes, with or without par value, with different voting rights and with such other designations, preferences, limitations and relative rights as stated in articles. (4-26-601).

Corporation may purchase its own shares of stock only as authorized by statute and not prohibited by its articles. (4-26-611).

Stock options may be granted to purchase shares not subject to preemptive rights, but options may be issued to directors, officers, or employees of issuer or subsidiary only with approval of majority of shares entitled to vote; but shareholder approval not required of some corporations reporting to United States Securities and Exchange Commission. (4-26-712).

Stock Certificates.—Each certificate must state that corporation is organized under laws of this state; name of person to whom issued; number and class of shares and designation of series, if any, which such certificate represents; relative rights, preferences and limitations of shares of each class or that corporation will furnish such information upon request, where corporation is authorized to issue shares of more than one class; par value of each share represented by certificate or statement that shares are without par value, must be signed by president or vice-president and secretary or assistant secretary and may be sealed if corporation has adopted a seal. Signatures of officers may be facsimiles if certificate is countersigned by transfer agent or registered by registrar. Certificates may be issued despite death or resignation of officer signing them. Consideration for certificate must be fully paid before it is issued. (4-26-608).

Corporations may issue certificates for fractional shares and scrip, subject to limited rights, exchangeable in aggregate for full share. (4-26-609).

CORPORATIONS . . . *continued*

Issuance of Stock.—Private corporation may not issue stock except for money or property actually received or labor done. (Const. art. XII, §8). Notes for stock and stock certificates issued thereon are void except in hands of innocent holder. (177 Ark. 190, 5 S.W. 2d 937).

Shares with or without par value may be issued for such consideration as is fixed by directors or by person or persons designated by board of directors unless articles reserve to stockholders right to fix consideration. (4-26-604).

Subscriptions for shares must be in writing signed and delivered by subscriber. Valid preincorporation subscriptions are irrevocable for six months unless otherwise provided, and if accepted by corporation become enforceable. Acceptance by corporation of subscription shall be evidenced by resolution of directors. (4-26-603).

Board of directors may designate relative rights and preferences of series of preferred stock. (4-26-602).

Transfers of stock are covered by Uniform Commercial Code. (4-8-101-408).

Restrictions may be imposed on transfer, hypothecation, or other disposition of shares, if authorized by articles or by-laws and if conspicuously noted on certificates subject to restriction. (4-26-610). "Unreasonable restraint on alienation" has no effect on validity or enforceability of some such written agreements on or after Mar. 21, 1973. (4-26-610).

Directors may close stock transfer books or fix record date not to exceed 65 days to determine shareholders entitled to notice of meeting, to receive dividends, or for any proper purpose and to be not less than ten days if purpose is to determine shareholders entitled to notice or to vote. (4-26-702).

Uniform Securities Ownership by Minors Act adopted. (9-26-301-305).

Uniform Simplification of Fiduciary Security Transfers Act not adopted.

Stock Transfer Tax.—None.

Books and Records.—Each corporation must maintain correct and complete books and records of accounts and minutes of proceedings of shareholders and directors and must keep at its registered office or principal place of business or at office of its transfer agent or registrar a record of shareholders with names, addresses, number and class of shares held by each. (4-26-715).

Any holder of record for at least six months may at any reasonable time and for proper purpose examine and copy records, and if refused may sue to compel such examination in circuit court of county wherein is located principal place of business or registered office of corporation. (4-26-715).

Upon shareholder's written request corporation must mail most recent financial statements showing, in reasonable detail, assets, liabilities, and results of operation. (4-26-715).

Shareholders.—For failure to pay subscription, corporation may proceed to collect amount due in same manner as any debt due corporation or, after 20 days demand, may declare subscription and all previous payments forfeited. (4-26-603).

Preemptive Rights.—Unless articles provide otherwise, shareholders may subscribe for their proportionate share of: Stock issued of same class; any stock with voting or dividend rights which would adversely affect their voting or dividend rights; or securities convertible into either of foregoing. Unless articles provide otherwise, such preemptive rights do not extend to shares authorized in original articles and issued within two years from filing of articles, or issued for consideration other than money, or to satisfy conversion or option rights theretofore granted. (4-26-711).

Shareholder may not sue in right of domestic corporation unless he was holder of shares at time of transaction of which he complains or his shares devolved upon him by operation of law from one who was a holder at such time. (4-26-714).

Tender Offers.—See category Business Regulation and Commerce, topic Securities, subhead Tender Offers.

Stockholders Actions.—Security for costs, including attorney's fees, may be required in derivative actions by holders of less than 5% of class of shares, unless such shares valued in excess of $25,000, upon motion by corporation or any defendant stating limited grounds. (4-26-714).

Stockholders Liabilities.—None beyond payment for shares. (4-26-716).

Stockholders meetings may be held within or without state as may be provided in by-laws and in absence of such provision must be held at registered office. Annual meetings must be held as provided in by-laws but failure to hold meetings will not work dissolution of corporation. Special meetings may be called by president, directors, holders of not less than 1/10 of all shares entitled to vote, or by such other officer or person authorized in articles or by-laws (4-26-701) upon written notice of place and purpose given not less than 60 nor more than 75 days before date of meeting if to consider proposal to increase authorized capital stock or bonded indebtedness and in all other cases not less than ten nor more than 50 days (4-26-703). If mailed, notice is deemed delivered when deposited in mail addressed to shareholder as it appears on books of corporation, postage prepaid. (4-26-703).

Informal Action.—Any action required to be taken at meeting of shareholders may be taken without such meeting if written consent setting forth action is signed by all shareholders entitled to vote on subject matter. (4-26-710).

Officer or agent in charge of stock transfer books prepares ten days prior to meeting of shareholders a list of shareholders entitled to vote. Failure to keep such list does not affect validity of action taken at meeting but makes officer or agent liable to any stockholder suffering damages on account of such failure. (4-26-704).

Unless limited or denied by articles, each share outstanding is entitled to one vote upon each proposal presented. Shareholders may vote by written proxy which is valid for 11 months unless provided otherwise in proxy. (4-26-708).

Where actions require affirmative vote of a certain percentage of holders of all shares of each class, for corporations having 500 or more shareholders, each class is bound by affirmative vote of at least two-thirds of members of such class present in person or by proxy, provided due notice of meeting has been given to all members of class and at least 50% of shares in such class are present in person or by proxy. (4-26-707).

Cumulative voting by shareholders is permitted at all elections for directors. (4-26-708).

Voting trusts are limited in duration to ten years. Counterpart of agreement must be deposited with corporation and shares must be transferred to trustee. (4-26-706).

Directors.—Business of corporation must be managed by directors who need not be residents of state or shareholders unless required by articles or by-laws. (4-26-801). There must be not less than three directors unless all shares are owned of record by either one or two shareholders, in which event number may be one or two but not less than number of shareholders. Articles must state number of directors to constitute initial board who hold office until first annual meeting of shareholders and until their successors are elected and qualified. Thereafter number of directors may be increased or decreased by provision in by-laws. (4-26-802).

Vacancies may be filled by remaining directors unless otherwise provided in articles or by-laws and if there are no directors in office any shareholder or executor or administrator of estate of any shareholder may call a special meeting of shareholders. (4-26-803).

Directors may be removed at shareholders' meeting called expressly for that purpose. (4-26-804).

Directors Meetings.—Majority of number of directors constitutes quorum for transactions of business unless provided otherwise in articles or by-laws. (4-26-806).

Directors may not vote by proxy. (4-26-801).

Where permitted by articles or by-laws, majority of directors may act without meeting by all directors signing and filing for inclusion in corporate minute book written memorandum consenting to informal action and showing nature of action taken. (4-26-807).

Executive committee of not less than three directors to act with limited powers may be provided in articles or by-laws. (4-26-808).

Meetings of directors may be held within or without state. As provided in by-laws, regular meetings may be held, with or without notice, and special meetings with notice, which notice may be waived by written waiver before or after meeting. Notice of regular or special meetings need not state purpose unless required by by-laws. (4-26-805).

See also subhead Officers, infra.

Powers and Duties of Directors.—Business and affairs shall be managed by directors. (4-26-801). Duty to exercise diligence and good faith. (130 Ark. 551, 197 S.W. 1163; 179 Ark. 1087, 20 S.W.2d 186).

Liabilities of Directors.—Unless acting in good faith in reliance on financial statements presented by financial officer or independent accountants, directors voting for or assenting to declaration of dividends or purchase or redemption of corporation's own shares, contrary to Business Corporation Act; distribution of assets in liquidation without making adequate provision for payment of debts; making of loans secured by shares of corporation; or commencing business without receipt of $300; held jointly and severally liable to corporation in particular amount. Any director held liable entitled to contribution from shareholders who receive dividend with knowledge of violation and from other directors who voted for or assented to action on which claim is based. (4-26-811).

Officers and agents are elected by directors for such terms and have such powers as by-laws or directors may provide. Any two or more offices may be held by same person except offices of president and secretary, but any two or more offices may be held by same person if all of voting stock is owned by one stockholder. (4-26-812).

Liabilities of Officers.—Liable for fraud against corporation and for dealings in bad faith. (182 Ark. 779, 32 S.W.2d 618).

Indemnification of Directors and Officers.—Corporation may and, in some cases must, indemnify directors, officers and agents acting in good faith on behalf of corporation against expenses of litigation, judgment, fines, and amounts paid in settlement. (4-26-814). Corporation may purchase and maintain insurance against liabilities for indemnification. (4-26-814).

Principal Office.—Need not be within state nor same as registered office. (4-26-501).

Registered Office and Agent.—Every corporation must maintain registered office and registered agent which may be individual resident of state or corporation having business office identical with registered office. (4-26-501). Corporation may change its office or agent or both, by filing with Secretary of State duplicate originals of statement setting forth name of corporation, address of its then office, address of office to be changed, name of its then agent, name of successor resident agent, and that address of registered office is identical with address of business office of agent. (4-26-502).

Registered agent may resign by filing with Secretary of State duplicate written resignation. (4-26-502).

Where registered office is outside Pulaski County, changes of registered office and changes or resignations of registered agent (bearing Secretary of State's file marks) must be filed with County Clerk in county of registered office. (4-26-502).

Service of process on corporation may be made on registered agent, or, if none maintained or found at registered office, then on Secretary of State. (4-26-503).

General Powers of Corporations.—Every corporation may: have perpetual succession; sue and be sued; have seal; elect or appoint officers and agents and define their duties; adopt by-laws; subject to restrictions in its articles, make gifts to governmental units or grantees organized and operated exclusively for religious, charitable, literary, scientific, or educational purposes or for prevention of cruelty to children or animals, no part of net earnings of which inures to benefit of any private stockholder or individual; in time of war transact any lawful business in aid of U.S.; subject to restriction in its articles, invest its funds in other corporations; surrender its corporate franchise. (4-26-204).

Unless limited by its articles, it may: acquire, own, hold, improve, use and otherwise deal in and with real and personal property; sell, convey, lease, exchange, transfer and otherwise dispose of all or any part of its property; enter into contracts of guaranty or suretyship or make other financial arrangements, including undertakings of

See note at head of Digest as to 1998 legislation covered.

See Topical Index in front part of this volume.

AR – 3

CORPORATIONS . . . continued

such character for benefit of any of its employees, not to include any person holding as much as 10% of shares entitled to vote for election of directors; procure for its benefit insurance on life of any employee or officer whose death might cause financial loss to corporation; acquire, own, hold, vote, sell, mortgage, lend, pledge, or otherwise dispose of, or otherwise use and deal in shares or obligations of, other domestic or foreign corporation or obligations of any associations, partnerships, or individuals, or any direct or indirect obligations of U.S. or any government, state, territory, governmental district on municipality or any instrumentality thereof; with shareholder approval or express authority in articles, enter into general partnership agreements with another corporation or corporations, and/or with any individual, individuals or partnerships, and may become a limited partner, or enter into joint adventure arrangement with any corporation or corporations and/or any individual, individuals or partnership, for joint prosecution of single undertaking, or prosecution of successive joint undertakings or business activities over period not exceeding five years; contract and incur liabilities, borrow money, issue its notes, debentures, bonds and other obligations, and secure any of its obligations by mortgage, pledge, security interest or other form of encumbrance upon all or any of its property (including after-acquired property), franchises and income; lend money for its corporate purposes; pay pensions and establish pension, profit-sharing or other incentive plans; conduct its business anywhere in world; and have and exercise all additional powers necessary or convenient to effect any or all purposes for which organized. (4-26-204).

Dividends may be paid in cash, property or shares. Dividends other than shares must be paid only out of unreserved and unrestricted earned surplus, or out of certain capital surplus, or current net earnings and only if there are reasonable grounds for believing that upon payment thereof liabilities of corporation will not exceed assets, or corporation will be unable to pay its obligations to creditors as they become due in ordinary course of business, or highest liquidation preferences of shares entitled to such preferences over shares receiving dividends will exceed corporation's net assets, and payment must not be contrary to articles. (4-26-617-619).

Corporation exploiting wasting assets such as timber or oil may compute earned surplus or net profits without deduction for depreciation of such assets or lapse of time. (4-26-619).

Where 95% of capital stock is owned by one or more other corporations, dividends may be paid out of assets in excess of its liabilities provided remaining assets equal 1¼ times corporation's liabilities and provided such dividends will not impair its ability to pay its debts as they mature. (4-26-619).

Share dividends may be paid subject to numerous restrictions. (4-26-618).

Dividends in partial liquidation may be made subject to numerous restrictions. (4-26-620).

Corporation may by loan agreement restrict payment of dividends or distribution in partial liquidation. (4-26-621).

Unclaimed Dividends.—See category Property, topic Absentees, subhead Escheat.

Sale or Transfer of Corporate Assets.—Directors may sell, lease, or exchange all, or substantially all, property and assets of corporation when done in usual course of business. (4-26-902). When not done in usual course of business, directors must recommend such transfer and it must be approved by vote of holders of at least ⅔ of outstanding shares, whether or not shares are otherwise entitled to vote, in meeting held upon written notice stating purpose thereof. (4-26-903).

Dissenting shareholder is entitled to payment of fair value for his shares upon his filing written objection to proposed transaction prior to or at shareholders' meeting and by making written demand therefor within ten days after shareholders' meeting. If fair value is agreed upon and paid, dissenting shareholder ceases to have any interest in corporation, but if not agreed upon within 30 days after transfer he may within 60 days after expiration of 30 day period petition circuit court wherein is located registered office of corporation for determination of fair value. Upon payment of judgment, he ceases to have any interest in corporation. If dissenting shareholder does not timely make demand or file petition, he is bound by transfer. (4-26-904).

Reports.—Each corporation must file franchise tax report with Director of Finance and Administration on or before June 1 of reporting year, sworn by president, vice president, secretary, treasurer or controller along with forms and other information required by Director. Any newly formed corporation is not required to file report until year immediately following year of incorporation. Reports must show corporation's condition and status as of Dec. 31 last preceding or as of last day of fiscal year of corporation for tax purposes. (26-54-105). On failure to file timely, corporation may be assessed lump tax equal to tax previously paid plus $100 in addition to any penalty. Some corporations (to which lump tax inapplicable) may be assessed tax at lesser of maximum rate based on entire outstanding capital stock (whether or not employed in Arkansas) or double last previous year's tax but in no event less than $25 plus applicable penalties. (26-54-106).

Corporate Bonds or Mortgages.—Private corporation may not issue bonds except for money or property actually received or labor done. (Const. art. XII, §8).

Merger and Consolidation.—Two or more domestic corporations may merge into "surviving" corporation (4-26-1001) or consolidate into "new" corporation (4-26-1002). Directors of each corporation must approve plan of merger or consolidation which must be submitted to shareholders of each corporation upon at least 20 days written notice stating purpose of meeting and with copy of plan included in notice. Each outstanding share is entitled to one vote whether or not otherwise entitled to vote in articles. Plan must be approved by at least ⅔ vote of each corporation. (4-26-1003).

After approval, duplicate executed articles of merger or consolidation verified by signing officer must be filed with Secretary of State setting forth: plan of merger or consolidation, effective date, and as to each corporation numbers of shares outstanding by class and those voting for and against plan by class. (4-26-1004).

Merger or consolidation is effective upon filing of articles or in such time not more than 60 days after filing as may be specified in articles. (4-26-1005).

The several corporations become single corporation and all corporations except surviving or new corporation cease to exist. Surviving or new corporation is subject to corporation act and has all rights and liabilities of several corporations. (4-26-1005).

One or more foreign and one or more domestic corporations may merge or consolidate and if to be governed by laws of another state must qualify to transact business in this state. (4-26-1006).

Dissenting shareholder may file written objection to plan prior to or at shareholders' meeting and he must within ten days after vote make written demand on surviving or new corporation, domestic or foreign, for payment of fair market value of his shares. If fair market value is agreed upon and paid, dissenting stockholder ceases to have any interest in corporation. If fair market value is not agreed upon within 30 days after merger or consolidation, dissenting stockholder may within 60 days after expiration of 30 day period petition circuit court of county wherein registered office of surviving domestic corporation is located or in Pulaski County circuit court if surviving corporation is foreign corporation for determination of fair market value of his shares. Upon payment of any judgment, dissenting shareholder ceases to have any interest in corporation. (4-26-1007).

Unless dissenting shareholder timely makes demand or files petition, he is bound by terms of merger or consolidation. (4-26-1007).

After merger or consolidation, each constituent corporation continues to exist indefinitely for limited purpose of enabling it to execute formal instruments evidencing transfer of its property from such constituent to surviving or new corporation. Such transfer takes effect through operation of law but such power is given for exercise in respect to properties in foreign jurisdictions which may not recognize transmittal of title by such operation of law and in other situations where directors of surviving or new corporation consider such execution of instruments desirable. (4-26-1008).

This state gives effect to transfers of title to real property located in this state effected by operation of law through merger or consolidation under laws of another state where copy of agreement or certificate of merger certified by Secretary of State wherein surviving or consolidated corporation is domiciled is filed with Secretary of State of this state. (4-26-1008).

Corporation owning at least 95% of outstanding shares of each class of another corporation may merge such other corporation into itself without approving vote of shareholders of either corporation. (4-26-1009).

Dissolution may be authorized at meeting of shareholders held after notice to all shareholders whether or not entitled to vote by vote of holders of ⅔ of all outstanding shares entitled to vote and of ⅔ of outstanding shares of class entitled to vote as class. (4-26-1101). Duplicate certificate of dissolution executed by president or vice-president and attested by secretary or assistant secretary showing: Name of corporation, names and addresses of officers, copy of resolution of dissolution, and number of shares of each class outstanding and how voting must be filed with Secretary of State. (4-26-1102-1103).

Dissolution is effective on filing certificate of dissolution but corporation continues for purpose of winding up its affairs. (4-26-1102-1103).

Creditors may be given notice to present their claims in writing and in detail at specified place and manner within 120 days of first publication of notice published once a week for three successive weeks in newspaper of general circulation in county wherein place of business of corporation is located on date of dissolution. (4-26-1105).

On or before first date of publication, corporation must mail copy of notice, postage prepaid, to last known address of each person believed to be creditor, which notice does not constitute recognition of validity of claim or waive any defenses of corporation thereto. Disputed claims may be submitted for determination to court supervising liquidation, and if none, then to any court of competent jurisdiction. Claims not timely filed or disallowed are forever barred. (4-26-1105).

Laborers' wages are preferred claims and entitled to payment before other claims out of assets in excess of valid prior claims. (4-26-1105).

Circuit or chancery court upon petition of corporation or upon petition of interested person and finding that corporate assets are being, or are about to be, wasted and that creditors and shareholders are threatened with irreparable damage may supervise generally liquidation of corporation. (4-26-1106).

Attorney General may proceed in name of state by action in circuit court of county wherein is located principal place of business of corporation or if none then in county wherein its registered office is situated to dissolve corporation for procuring its articles through fraud, for continuing to exceed or abuse its corporate authority, or failing to maintain registered agent or registered office, or misrepresentation of any material matter in any document submitted pursuant to corporation act. (4-26-1107).

Circuit or chancery court may liquidate corporation in proper action by shareholder in case of deadlock or for mismanagement of affairs of corporation, by creditor whose claim has been admitted in writing or has been reduced to judgment and execution thereon returned unsatisfied and it is established that corporation is insolvent, or by Attorney General. (4-26-1108).

Assets distributable to creditor or shareholder who is unknown or cannot be found or who is under disability and there is no person legally competent to receive them must be reduced to cash and deposited with state treasurer and paid to person satisfactorily shown to be entitled thereto. (4-26-1109).

Insolvency and Receivers.—See category Debtor and Creditor, topic Receivers.

Close Corporations.—One or more natural persons of age of 21 years or more may act as incorporators. (4-26-201). Tax treatment similar to Federal "subchapter S" treatment may be elected by corporations eligible for like Federal election. (26-51-409). See also subheads Stockholders Meetings, and Directors, supra.

Appraisal.—See subheads Sale or Transfer of Corporate Assets, and Merger and Consolidation, supra.

Foreign Corporations.—See generally Model Act, Act 958 of 1987. (4-27-1501, et seq.).

Franchise Tax.—Corporations, domestic and foreign, active and inactive, organized or qualified in Arkansas including any person or group of persons, any association, joint stock company, business trust, or other organizations constituting separate legal

See note at head of Digest as to 1998 legislation covered.

See Topical Index in front part of this volume.

CORPORATIONS . . . *continued*
entity with purpose of obtaining some corporate privilege or franchise which is not allowed to them as individuals or attempting to exercise corporate type acts are subject to franchise tax (not applicable to nonprofit corporations or corporations exempt from federal income tax). (26-54-102). Effective with tax reports due on and after Jan. 1, 1988, rates are: Insurance companies having capital stock of less than $500,000, tax is $100; insurance companies having outstanding capital stock of $500,000, or more, tax is $200; legal reserve mutual insurance corporations having assets of less than $100,000,000, tax is $100; legal reserve mutual insurance corporations having assets of $100,000,000 or more, tax is $200; mutual assessment insurance corporation, tax is $100; mortgage loan corporations, tax is 0.27% of that proportion of par value of capital stock that its aggregate outstanding loans in Arkansas bears to its total outstanding loans, minimum tax $100; other corporations without authorized capital stock tax is $100; and other corporations, tax is 0.27% of that proportion of par value of its outstanding capital stock that value of real and personal property in Arkansas bears to total real and personal property of corporation, minimum $50. (26-54-104). No par value stock is computed at $25 a share for determining tax. (26-54-105; 1991 Act 1140). Tax due June 1 of reporting year. (26-54-105; 1991 Act 1140). See subhead Reports, supra. Taxes and penalties are first lien on all property of corporation. (26-54-108).

Income Tax.—See category Taxation, topic Income Tax. See also subhead Close Corporations, supra.

Taxation of Corporate Stock or Securities.—Corporate stock, bonds and securities are assessed and taxed as personal property. (26-3-201).

Professional Corporations.—Physicians (4-29-301-311), dentists (4-29-401-411), and others licensed to perform professional services such as certified public accountants, architects, engineers, and attorneys at law, and including physicians and dentists (4-29-201-213), permitted to form professional corporations under specified conditions. No person is personally liable for any obligation or liability of any shareholder, director, officer, agent or employee of such professional corporation or professional corporation, itself, solely because such person is shareholder, director, officer, agent, or employee of such professional corporation. (4-29-101).

Deeds.—See category Property, topic Deeds.

Model Non-Profit Corporation Act adopted, with revisions, effective Jan. 1, 1994, Act 1147 of 1993. (4-28-101, et seq.).

Non-profit Corporations.—See topic Associations, subhead Benevolent Associations.

JOINT STOCK COMPANIES:

No statutory provision.

Validity of Massachusetts trusts is recognized. (159 Ark. 621, 252 S.W. 602).

Professional Corporations.—See topic Corporations, subhead Professional Corporations.

LIMITED LIABILITY COMPANIES:

Small Business Entity Tax Pass Through Act, Act 1003 of 1993, applies to all Limited Liability Companies ("LLC's") organized or doing business in Arkansas on or after Apr. 12, 1993. (4-32-101, et seq.).

Name of each Limited Liability Company ("LLC") must contain words "Limited Liability Company" or "Limited Company" or abbreviations of "L.L.C.", "L.C.", "LLC", or "LC". LLC name may not be same or deceptively similar to name of any LLC, Limited Partnership or Corporation existing under laws of this state, or name reserved under 4-32-104, except in two narrow exceptions in statute. (4-32-103[c]).

Name of LLC which performs Professional Services shall contain words "Professional Limited Liability Company" or "Professional Limited Company" or abbreviations "P.L.L.C", "P.L.C.", "PLLC", "PLC". (4-32-103[d]).

Exclusive right to use name may be reserved by filing with Secretary of State application to reserve specified name. (4-32-104).

Purposes.—LLC may be organized under this Act for any lawful purpose including performance of Professional Services and related activities. (4-32-106).

Registered Office and Agent.—Every LLC must maintain registered office and registered agent that is individual resident of state, LLC or corporation of state, or foreign LLC or corporation authorized to transact business in state. Copy of LLC's operating agreement must be at registered office at all times. (4-32-105[a]).

Registered agent must sign document making appointment or deliver statement to Secretary of State accepting appointment. (4-32-105[b]).

LLC may change its office or agent, or both, by filing with Secretary of State statement setting forth name of LLC, address of its current office, address to which office is to be changed, name and address of current registered agent, and name and address of successor agent. (4-32-105[c]). Registered agent may resign by filing with Secretary of State duplicate written resignation. (4-32-105[e]).

Service of Process.—Service of legal process to be served upon any LLC shall be made on registered agent of LLC in State of Arkansas. In cases where legal process cannot by due diligence be served on registered agent, it shall be lawful to serve process against LLC upon Secretary of State for fee of $25. (4-32-107).

Formation.—One or more persons may form LLC by signing or causing to be signed Articles of Organization and delivering same Articles to Secretary of State for filing. (4-32-201). LLC is formed when Articles of Organization are delivered to Secretary of State for filing. (4-32-206).

Articles of Organization shall set forth: name; address of registered office and address of registered agent; latest date upon which LLC is to dissolve; and if management of LLC is vested in manager or managers, statement to that effect. (4-32-202).

Amendment of Articles of Organization.—Articles of LLC may be amended by filing Articles of Amendment with Secretary of State. (4-32-203).

Agency Power of Members and Managers.—If Articles of Organization do not provide that management of LLC is vested in manager, every member is agent of LLC for purpose of its business and act of any member binds LLC, unless member has no authority to act for LLC and person with whom member is dealing has knowledge of lack of authority. If Articles provide that management of LLC is vested in manager, no member solely by reason of being member is agent of LLC and every manager is agent of LLC for purpose of its business and manager's act binds LLC, unless manager has no authority to act for LLC in particular matter and person with whom manager is dealing has knowledge of this lack of authority. (4-32-301-303).

Liability of Members.—Except for personal liability of person providing Professional Service (4-32-308), member, manager, agent or employee of LLC is not liable for debt or obligation of LLC, or for acts or omissions of any other member, manager, agent, or employee of LLC (4-32-304).

Professional Services.—Individual rendering Professional Service may be personally liable for any results of that individual's acts or omissions. No member, manager, or employee of LLC shall be personally liable for acts or omissions of any other member, manager or employee of LLC. (4-32-308).

Management.—Unless Articles of Organization or Operating Agreement indicate that management of LLC is vested in manager, management of business shall be vested in members. (4-32-401).

Duties of Managers and Members.—Unless provided in Operating Agreement, manager or member generally will not be liable for any actions taken or failure to act on behalf of LLC unless act or omission constitutes gross negligence or willful misconduct. Also, unless otherwise provided in Articles or Operating Agreement, members and managers must account to LLC for any profit or benefit received without informed consent of more than one-half by number of disinterested managers or members. (4-32-402).

Voting.—Unless otherwise provided in Operating Agreement or this Act, affirmative vote of either members or managers, depending on management structure of LLC, shall be required to decide any matter connected with business of LLC. Unless otherwise provided in Operating Agreement, affirmative vote of all members shall be required to amend written Operating Agreement or authorize manager or member to do any act that contravenes written Operating Agreement. (4-32-403).

Limitation of Liability and Indemnification.—Operating Agreement may limit liability of members or managers and provide for indemnification of members and managers. (4-32-404).

Records and Information.—Certain information is to be kept at LLC's principal place of business. Members, at member's own expense, have right to inspect and copy LLC's books and records during ordinary business hours. (4-32-405).

Contributions.—Member may contribute property, services, cash, promissory note or other obligation to contribute cash, property, or to perform services to LLC in exchange for LLC interest. Member's obligations to make any agreed contribution may only be compromised as provided for in Operating Agreement or upon unanimous consent of other members. Creditors may enforce member's obligation to make contribution if credit was extended upon reliance of obligation to contribute. (4-32-501-502).

Profits and Losses.—Members may, in Operating Agreement, allocate LLC's profits among themselves. Unless otherwise provided, they are to share equally in profits. (4-32-503).

Distributions.—In absence of provision to contrary in Operating Agreement, profits, losses and distributions of LLC are allocated or distributed to members in proportion to number of members after all liabilities are satisfied. (4-32-601, 602, and 905).

Ownership of Property.—Property transferred to or otherwise acquired by LLC is property of LLC and not of members. (4-32-701).

Transfer of Real Property.—If articles of organization vest management in manager(s), property of LLC can be transferred by instrument executed by any manager in name of LLC. If articles of organization do not vest management in manager(s), property of LLC can be transferred by instrument by any member in name of LLC. (4-32-702).

Transfers of Interests.—Member's interest in LLC may, unless otherwise provided in Operating Agreement, be assigned in whole or in part, and such assignment will not dissolve LLC. However, unlike sale of stock, assignment of member's interest does not automatically entitle assignee to all of rights and privileges held by assignor. Generally, assignment of member's interest only transfers assignor's right to share of LLC's distributions. Assignor of LLC interest continues to be member and to generally have power to exercise any rights of member until assignee of LLC's interest becomes member. (4-32-704). Assignee of membership interest may become member of LLC only upon unanimous approval of all members, or as may be provided in Operating Agreement. (4-32-706).

Admission and withdrawal of members is governed by numerous restrictions. (4-32-801-802).

Rights of Judgment Creditor of Member.—Judgment creditor of member of LLC can apply to court of competent jurisdiction and court can charge member's LLC interest with unsatisfied judgment with interest; once so charged, judgment creditor has only rights of assignee of member's LLC interest, supra. (4-32-705).

Right to Sue.—Unless otherwise provided in Operating Agreement, suit on behalf of LLC may generally only be brought in name of LLC by one or more members or managers of LLC who are authorized to do so. (4-32-1101-1103).

Merger or Consolidation.—Arkansas LLC may merge with another LLC, or any other business entity. (4-32-1201). Unless otherwise provided in writing in Operating Agreement, merger or consolidation must be approved by more than one-half of members. (4-32-1202). Merger or consolidation is effective upon later of effective date of filing of Articles of Merger or Consolidation or date set forth in Articles of Merger or Consolidation. (4-32-1203).

See note at head of Digest as to 1998 legislation covered.

See Topical Index in front part of this volume.

AR – 5

LIMITED LIABILITY COMPANIES...*continued*

Dissolution.—LLC is dissolved and shall be wound up upon happening of first of following to occur: expiration of time period stated in Articles or Operating Agreement; unanimous consent of all members; "event of disassociation" of member unless (1) LLC is continued by unanimous consent of remaining members on or before 90th day following occurrence of any such event or (2) otherwise provided in Operating Agreement; or, upon application of member if Chancery Court determines that it is not reasonably practicable for LLC to operate in conformity with its Operating Agreement. (4-32-901-902).

Winding Up.—Generally, members or managers that have authority to manage LLC prior to dissolution or members or managers who have not wrongfully dissolved LLC may wind up affairs of LLC. (4-32-903-904).

Distribution of Assets Upon Dissolution.—Upon winding up of LLC, order of distribution of assets is set by statute. (4-32-905).

Articles of Dissolution.—After completion of winding up, members or managers must file Articles of Dissolution with Secretary of State. (4-32-906).

Claims Upon Dissolution.—LLC may dispose of known claims against it by filing Articles of Dissolution and then providing notice to its known claimants of dissolution. (4-32-907). As to its unknown claimants, LLC may publish statutory notice of its dissolution requesting that persons with claims against it present them in accordance with notice. (4-32-908).

Foreign LLC.—Foreign LLC's internal affairs are governed by laws of its state of organization. (4-32-1001). In order to "transact business" in Arkansas foreign LLC must register with Secretary of State. To register, foreign LLC must pay requisite fee, provide evidence of its organization under another state's laws, and submit duplicate Application for Registration setting forth following: (a) Foreign LLC's name and, if different, name under which it will transact business; (b) its state of organization and date of formation; (c) name and address of its registered agent; (d) statement that Secretary of State is appointed to accept service of process if it fails to appoint registered agent; (e) address of its principal office; and (f) statement evidencing that foreign LLC is "Foreign Limited Liability Company". (4-32-1002). Name of foreign LLC must satisfy same requirements as name of Arkansas LLC. (4-32-1004). Foreign LLC that is registered in Arkansas may withdraw from State by submitting Application for Cancellation seeking Certificate of Withdrawal from Secretary of State. (4-32-1006). Application for registration of Foreign LLC can be amended by filing articles of amendment with Secretary of State. (4-32-1005). Foreign LLC transacting business in Arkansas may not maintain action in Arkansas court until it has registered in Arkansas. (4-32-1007).

Fees.—Secretary of State shall collect following fees: Articles of Organization—$50; Application for Name—$25; Application for Reserved Name—$25; Transfer of Reserved Name—$25; Change of Registered Office—$25; Agent's Statement of Resignation—$25; Amendment of Articles of Organization—$25; Articles of Merger or Share Exchange—$50; Articles of Dissolution—$50; Certificate of Authority by Foreign Limited Liability Company—$300; Amended Certificate of Authority by Foreign LLC—$300; Articles of Correction—$30; and Certificate of Existence or Authorization by Domestic LLC—$15. (4-32-1301).

Tax Status.—Every LLC having two or more members shall make return for each taxable year as required for every partnership pursuant to Arkansas law. Income and expenses of every LLC having only one member shall be reported on member's income tax return. (4-32-1313).

PARTNERSHIPS:

Uniform Partnership Act has been adopted (4-42-101-702) with modifications in definition of dissolution (4-42-601) and causes of dissolution (4-42-603). Revised Limited Partnership Act has been adopted (4-43-101-1108) with modifications of liabilities of general partner (4-43-403), variations in voting rights (4-43-302) and provision for persons who erroneously but in good faith believe they are limited partners (4-43-304). Uniform Limited Partnership Act and Foreign Limited Partnership Act were repealed by 1991 Act 1175. Repealed material is encompassed by Revised Limited Partnership Act.

BUSINESS REGULATION AND COMMERCE

BANKS AND BANKING:

Uniform Commercial Code adopted. See topic Commercial Code.

Supervision is by Bank Commissioner subject to regulation by State Bank Department. (23-46-201).

Deposits.—Money deposited in checking and savings accounts and in certificates of deposit in names of two or more persons is held as joint tenants with right of survivorship, and may be drawn out by either one or will go to, or on order of, any one of survivors of joint tenants after death of any one or more of them, unless contrary written designation is given to bank. (23-47-204). Deposits by two as husband and wife, whether or not they are, are held by entirety and may be paid to or on order of either depositor during their lifetime, or to or on order of survivor after death of one. (23-47-204). Deposits in names of two or more designated as tenants in common may be paid to any one in lifetime of parties unless contrary written designation is given to bank, but after death of one pro rata share must be paid to decedent's estate. (23-47-204).

Unclaimed deposits subject to Uniform Disposition of Unclaimed Property Act with modification providing that within seven years of mail communications by bank, if unreturned by postal system, considered abandoned. (18-28-201-214; 216-227; 229-230; 301-303).

Trust Powers.—Commissioner may grant to state bank applying therefor right to operate trust department. (23-47-701-709). Bank may also authorize affiliate to any trust or estate for which bank acts as trustee or fiduciary, provided certain requirements are met, without approval, consent or specific authorization in trust instrument. (23-47-710, 28-71-105). Bank holding company may create, form and establish subsidiary trust companies. (23-47-801-807).

Trust companies, other than national trust companies and subsidiary trust companies, in existence on May 30, 1997, must cease operations as trust companies, and instead will automatically become business corporations subject to Arkansas Business Corporation Act of 1987, 4-27-101, et seq. (23-48-102).

Foreign banks and investor companies authorized to acquire or participate in loans secured by mortgages on real property in state, to sue and be sued in connection with such loans, and to deal generally with such loans and lands acquired by foreclosure or by deeds in lieu of foreclosure without qualifying to do business in state. (23-32-1501, 1503, 4-27-302).

Fiduciaries.—Foreign banks and trust companies authorized to act as fiduciaries within state if state where they are organized have their principal office grants reciprocal authority to Arkansas banks and trust companies. (4-31-301-303).

Uniform Common Trust Fund Act adopted. (28-69-201-202).

Industrial loan institutions, are subject to supervision by Bank Commissioner. (23-36-101-116).

Bank holding companies regulated. Bank Holding Company Act of 1983 allows bank holding company, as defined, to own more than one bank subsidiary (except limited to one subsidiary with its main office in state if such bank has de novo charter) subject to overall limitation on ownership of 25% of deposits held by all banks having main offices in Arkansas. (23-48-405-406). Provides for ownership by in-state banks of shares of banker's bank. (23-48-325). Emergency acquisitions permitted upon application to State Bank Department. (23-48-511). There are criminal penalties for willful violation. (23-48-403). State Bank Department shall administer and issue regulations. Effective Sept. 30, 1983. (23-48-403-404). Bank holding company securities are exempt from registration provisions of Arkansas Securities Act. (23-42-503). See topic Securities. Bank holding companies may create and establish separate trust company subsidiaries which may assume fiduciary accounts of affiliate banks. (23-47-801-807).

Confidentiality of bank department records and submissions. (23-46-101).

Bank Directors' Standard of Care.—(23-48-322).

Bank Reorganization; Plan of Exchange.—State bank may reorganize by plan of exchange, adopted by board, approved by majority of bank shareholders and fairness of which is approved by State Bank Commissioner. (23-48-601-602). Pursuant to plan, bank holding company acquires all shares of bank, subject to dissenting bank shareholders' appraisal rights. Bank existence continues. (23-48-603-605).

Reserves.—State bank not member of Federal Reserve Board must maintain reserve fund as required by Federal Reserve Board, unless otherwise required by State Bank Department. (28-48-202).

Branch Banking.—No banking institution shall engage in core banking activities in this state other than at main banking office or full service bank branch unless otherwise permitted by law. If approved by its supervisory banking authority, any Arkansas bank may establish full service branch and customer-bank communication terminals as follows: (i) located within same or contiguous county as bank's principal banking office; (ii) if use as banking facility is uninterrupted, relocating bank may continue to use its former office location as full service branch. After Dec. 31, 1998, bank with its main office located within State of Arkansas or registered out-of-state bank may locate one or more full service branches anywhere in state. Without regard to above exceptions, bank may purchase business and assets or assume liabilities of, Arkansas bank located within any incorporated city or town in this state and operate it as full service branch, provided that full service banks shall not be established if one or more of banks is Arkansas bank which has de novo charter. (23-48-702).

Customer-Bank Communication Terminals.—Bank, individually or jointly with one or more other banks in state, may establish, maintain and use one or more customer-bank communication terminals anywhere in state, and in any one or more other states if permitted by applicable law of such other state. (23-48-802). Any out-of-state bank may establish customer-bank communications terminal anywhere in state. (23-48-804).

Savings and Loan and Building and Loan Associations regulated. (23-37-101-706, 23-38-101-404).

Credit Unions regulated. (23-35-101-805).

Application Fee.—Any applicant to acquire Arkansas bank or BHC shall pay fee of not less than $5,000 and not more than $15,000 as determined by rule or order of commissioner. (23-32-1803[c]).

Acquisition or Control by Bank Holding Company.—Bank holding company domiciled in State of Arkansas may acquire ownership or control of banks domiciled outside State of Arkansas if applicable federal or state law permits. Except as authorized by federal law or as specifically authorized by Arkansas Banking Code of 1997, no bank holding company domiciled outside state may acquire direct or indirect control of bank domiciled within state. (23-48-406).

Compliance.—Any regional BHC, not organized under laws of Arkansas, that has Arkansas subsidiary must: (1) Qualify to do business in Arkansas; (2) advise commissioner of name and location of its initial registered agent at its registered office in Arkansas; (3) agree to be bound by Regional Reciprocal Banking Act of 1988 ("Act"); and (4) promptly advise commissioner of any changes in its registered office and registered agent. (23-32-1803[d]).

Violations.—Any individual willfully participating in violation of Act or any regulation or order thereof, must, upon conviction, be fined between $1,000 and $5,000 or imprisoned not more than one year, or both. (23-48-403).

BANKS AND BANKING... *continued*

Application.—Regional BHC seeking to acquire Arkansas bank or BHC must file application with commissioner containing information specified. (23-32-1804).

Reports.—State Banks and trust companies must submit to reports by Commissioner at least two times each year. In addition, Commissioner has power to call for reports from state banks and subsidiary trust companies whenever deemed necessary. (23-46-501).

Examinations.—Thorough examination into affairs of each state bank or subsidiary trust will be made by Commissioner at least once every 24 month period. (23-46-503-506).

Interstate Bank Mergers and Branching.—With prior approval of Banking Board and Commissioner, state bank may establish one or more branches in other states pursuant to interstate merger transaction in which state bank is resulting bank. State bank must file application with responsible federal bank supervisory agency and Commissioner. Arkansas bank, provided it does not have de novo charter, may enter into interstate merger transaction with out-of-state bank in which out-of-state bank is resulting bank, and out-of-state bank may thereafter maintain and operate branches in Arkansas of any Arkansas bank that was party to merger. (23-48-902-903).

De Novo Interstate Branches.—No state bank may establish or maintain de novo interstate branch or acquire an interstate branch. No out-of-state bank may establish or maintain de novo interstate branch in Arkansas or acquire interstate branch in Arkansas. (23-48-904).

BILLS AND NOTES:

Uniform Commercial Code applies. (4-3-101-805). Arkansas Law of Comparative Fault. (16-64-122). Standard of failure to exercise ordinary care applies in cases of alteration or unauthorized signatures. (4-3-406 and 4-406). See topic Commercial Code.

Attorneys fees may be awarded to successful party by court. (16-22-308).

Insurance Premiums.—Note for insurance premiums must state for what purpose given and is not negotiable until delivery of policy, unless policy issued in form and at rate applied for and coverage is effective prior to issuance or approval. (23-79-122).

Minor's note given to bank for expenses of higher education or necessaries is valid as if minor were of age. (23-32-912).

Prepayment.—Waivable noncumulative privilege to prepay 20% unpaid principal annually subject to payment of premium declining from 5% to 1% per year. After five years no premium can be charged. Applies only to obligations secured by lien on real estate used primarily for agriculture or livestock purposes. Attempt to apply more restrictive prepayment requirements is misdemeanor and causes forfeiture of principal and interest and obligation for debtor's attorney's fees. (23-32-908).

Student Loans.—Minority is no defense on loan guaranteed by Arkansas Student Loan Authority. (6-81-125).

BILLS OF LADING:

See topic Carriers.

BILLS OF SALE:

See topic Sales.

BLUE SKY LAW:

See topic Securities.

BROKERS:

The rules of common law apply to brokers (207 Ark. 1, 179 S.W.2d 156) and they may be licensed and taxed by municipalities (14-54-103[10]).

Real estate brokers and salesmen are licensed by state. (17-42-101-603). Only individuals may be licensed as brokers, but licensed broker may do business as professional corporation. (17-42-103).

Uniform Commercial Code applies to brokerage of investment securities. (4-8-1026[14]; 108-109; 115-116). See topic Commercial Code.

BULK SALES:

Uniform Commercial Code Bulk Transfers Act repealed for transactions after effective date of repeal of July 15, 1991; Bulk Transfers Act applies to transaction before July 15, 1991. (4-6-101-111, 4-9-111).

See category Debtor and Creditor, topic Fraudulent Sales and Conveyances.

CARRIERS:

Arkansas State Highway and Transportation Department and Arkansas State Highway Commission have power to supervise, regulate and control common carriers. (23-2-209, 23-2-302). Arkansas Public Service Commission has exclusive regulation of pipeline companies which are common carriers. (23-2-209). Uniform Commercial Code has been adopted. See topic Commercial Code.

Limiting Liability.—A railroad may not contract for the purpose of abridging its common law or statutory duties. (23-10-408).

Bills of Lading.—Uniform Commercial Code applies. (4-7-101-105, 4-7-301-603).

Liens.—Uniform Commercial Code applies. (4-7-307-308).

Discrimination.—Railroads may not vary rates or give preferences, or discriminate against any person, firm, corporation or company. (23-10-104-106, 23-4-710).

Motor Vehicle Carriers.—See category Transportation, topic Motor Vehicles.

COMMERCIAL CODE:

Uniform Commercial Code was adopted by Act approved Mar. 7, 1961 and became effective midnight Dec. 31, 1961.

1962 Amendments adopted except as noted below.

1972 Official Amendments adopted with effective date of Jan. 1, 1974.

1977 Official Amendments adopted with effective date of June 28, 1985.

1987 Official Amendments (Article 2A), as revised in 1990, adopted with effective date of Aug. 13, 1993.

1988 Official Amendments (Repeal of Article 6) adopted with effective date of July 15, 1991.

1989 Official Amendments (Article 4A) adopted with effective date of July 15, 1991.

1990 Revised Article 3 (With Conforming and Miscellaneous Amendments to Articles 1 and 4) adopted, except revised 4-312, with effective date of July 15, 1991.

1994 Revised Article 8 with conforming and miscellaneous amendments to Articles 1, 4, 5, 9, and 10 adopted with effective date of July 27, 1995.

Intentional variations from 1962 Official Text in Arkansas Code are the following:

§1.102(6) added as follows "any notice required or authorized by this Act to be given by registered mail may be given by certified mail."

§1.209 1966 Official Optional Amendment enacted.

§2.316(3)(d). Implied warranties of merchantability and fitness not applicable to contract for sale of blood and other human tissue. Implied warranty that livestock offered for sale is free from disease does not exist unless owner knowingly sells diseased animals. (4-2-316[3][d]).

§2.318 1966 Optional Amendment Alternative A adopted. Extensive changes to Official Text of 2.318 have been enacted through two additional sections to its Uniform Commercial Code. Lack of privity between plaintiff and defendant shall be no defense in any action brought against manufacturer or seller of goods to recover damages for breach of warranty, express or implied, or for negligence, although plaintiff did not purchase goods from defendant, if plaintiff was person who manufacturer or seller might reasonably have expected to use, consume or be affected by goods. (4-2-318). Liability extends to suppliers as well as sellers. (4-2-318).

§2.326 does not apply to placement of works of fine art on consignment. (4-2-326[5]).

§2.702 words "or lien creditor" omitted. (4-2-702).

§2A.103(1)(e) Optional language adopted ($25,000). (4-2A-103[1][e]).

§2A.104(1) Adds sections (d) and (e) to 4-2A-104(1) which reads as follows:

"(d) statute of this state creating conditions of the effectiveness and enforceability of the lease contract, including, but not limited to §§6-62-601-613; 12-8-301-310; 14-16-108-110; 14-94-110; 14-138-111; 14-169-1003; 14-169-1011; 14-184-119; 14-29-101; 14-362-126; 19-1-213; 22-2-114; 22-2-115; 22-3-1101; 22-4-105; 22-4-501; 23-11-314; 23-12-404; 27-65-114; 28-51-203; 28-51-303; and 28-72-204; or

(e) statute of this state dealing with a person's capacity or authority to enter into a lease or contract."

§2A.109(2) Words "lack of" are inserted before words "good faith under subsection (1)."

§2A.216 Alternative C adopted.

§2A.218(3) Words "If a lessee has an insurable interest" are used in place of "Notwithstanding a lessee's insurable interest."

§2A.304(2) Words "of that lessor" are omitted.

§2A.309(9) Words "including the lessor's residual interest" are inserted after phrase "of a lessor of fixtures."

Revised §4.106(b) Alternative B adopted.

§4.406 provides for modified comparative fault. For unauthorized signature or alteration by same wrongdoer, customer has reasonable time period, not exceeding 30 days to examine item or statement and notify bank.(4-4-406[d][2]).

§5.112(1) Optional language omitted.

§5.114(4), (5) Optional subsections omitted.

Effective July 15, 1991, Chapter 6 (Bulk Sales) was repealed by enacting Alternative A of 1989 Official Amendment. 1989 Official Amendment for revised Article 6 has not been adopted. For transactions prior to its effective date of repeal, (July 15, 1991), §6.104(1)(c) omits "or files the list and schedule in (a public office to be here identified)." (1991 Act 344).

For transactions prior to its effective date of repeal, (July 15, 1991), §6.104(2) Last sentence omitted. (1991 Act 344).

For transactions prior to its effective date of repeal, (July 15, 1991), §6.106 Optional section omitted. (1991 Act 344).

For transactions prior to its effective date of repeal, (July 15, 1991), §6.111 is omitted. (1991 Act 344).

§7.204(4) Subsection omitted.

§7.205 Comma and words "except the grains listed below," inserted following "fungible goods" and second sentence added, reading "This section shall not apply to rice, soybeans, wheat, corn, rye, oats, barley, flaxseed, sorghum, mixed grain, nor other food grains or oilseeds." (4-7-205).

§7.209 1966 Official Amendment enacted.

§7.210(2)(b) 1962 Amendment not adopted. (4-7-210[2][b]).

§7.403(1)(b) optional language adopted; "provided" substituted for "but".

§9.105(1)(h) adds "commodity contracts" after words "investment property."

§9.109(3) new second sentence added, reading: " 'Farm products' shall also include fish grown for sale on any farm." (4-9-109[3]).

§9.111 Although Act 1991, No. 344 apparently was intended to repeal this section as well as Chapter C (Bulk Transfers) of this title, repeal of this section was not given effect by that act.

§9.204(2), §9.301(2), §9.302(1)(b), §9.306, (3) and (4), §9.312(4); 10 day period in each of these sections changed to 21 days.

§9.303(1) omits reference to §9-115.

See note at head of Digest as to 1998 legislation covered.

See Topical Index in front part of this volume.

COMMERCIAL CODE . . . *continued*

§9.306(2) Second sentence added reading as follows: "A security interest in farm products shall not be considered waived nor shall authority to sell, exchange, or otherwise dispose of farm products be implied or otherwise result from any course of dealing between the parties or by any trade usage." (4-9-306[2]).

§9.312(2) Subsection amended by Act 560 of 1987 to read as follows, effective Apr. 2, 1987:

"(2)(a) A production money security interest takes priority over a conflicting security interest in the collateral, and also in the proceeds and products of the collateral, to the extent that (i) a financing statement covering the collateral is filed before, or within 20 days after, the debtor receives property or services the value of which is secured by the production money security interest, and (ii) before the debtor receives such property or services, the production money secured party (A) sends a notification in writing by certified mail addressee only to the holder of the conflicting security interest if, before the date of the filing made by the production money secured party, the holder had filed a financing statement covering the same types of farm products, and (B) the notification states that the person giving the notice has or expects to acquire a production money security interest in farm products of the debtor, identifies the debtor, describes such farm products and, in the case of crops, describes the year or years in which the crops will be grown and the land where the crops are growing or to be grown, and (iii) the holder of a conflicting security interest in the collateral who has received the notice prescribed in paragraph (ii) has not notified the production money security interest holder within five days after the receipt of the notice that the holder of the conflicting security interest will provide substantially all of the new value the debtor will require to enable production of the collateral.

"Subsection (5) governs priority between conflicting production money security interests, and also priority between conflicting production and purchase money security interests; except that in the case of crops, where a production money secured party provided substantially all of the new value the debtor received to enable production of the collateral, the secured party's priority under this subsection extends to other value the secured party provided the debtor that is secured by the collateral and that was given at any time in connection with the debtor's farming activities.

"(b) A production money security interest is a security interest in farm products for new value given to enable the debtor to produce or raise the collateral by (i) paying necessary farm operating expenses, incurred while producing or raising the farm products, except that operating expenses do not include obligations owed with respect to land; or, (ii) acquiring goods or services to be used in producing or raising the farm products, except that a security interest in farm products taken or retained by the seller, lessor, or any other supplier or financier of equipment to secure a debt owed with respect to the equipment is not a production money security interest.

"Producing or raising the farm products includes any activity related to the production, raising, or marketing of the collateral.

"(c) Unless otherwise agreed a security interest in farm products continues in products of the collateral; and the security interest in products is a continuously perfected security interest if the interest in the original collateral was perfected.

"(d) Creating or perfecting a production money security interest shall not operate under any circumstances as a default on, an accelerating event under, or otherwise as a breach of: any note or other instrument or agreement of any kind or nature to pay debt; any loan or credit agreement; or any security arrangement of any kind or nature whether the collateral is real or personal property.

"(e) [Repealed, effective Mar. 17, 1989]

"(f) The provisions of paragraphs (a) through (d) of this subsection shall not be applicable to institutions chartered under the 'Farm Credit Act of 1971,' Public Law 92-181, national banks or state banks holding a conflicting security interest securing an obligation which originated at the bank. The following is applicable to institutions chartered under the 'Farm Credit Act of 1971,' Public Law 92-181, national banks and state banks holding a conflicting security interest securing an obligation which originated in that bank; a perfected security interest in crops for new value given to enable the debtor to produce the crops during the production season and given not more than three (3) months before the crops become growing crops by planting or otherwise takes priority over an earlier perfected security interest to the extent that such earlier interest secures obligations due more than six (6) months before the crops become growing crops by planting or otherwise, even though the person giving new value had knowledge of the earlier security interest."

§2 of Act 560 provides as follows:

"SECTION 2. The following Commentary is hereby adopted and shall be used for the interpretation of this Act:

"Arkansas Statute 85-9-312(2) is an instance of the preference which the Uniform Commercial Code gives a new-value secured party. The principle of this provision is that a person who extends credit that enables a debtor to produce new crops or raise livestock, and secures this credit with a security interest in the farm products, gets first claim to the collateral, outranking the interest of another secured party who claims the collateral merely as after-acquired property to secure a debt not directly related to the production of the farm products. So Arkansas Statute 85-9-312(2) creates an exception to the first-to-file-or-perfect rule of Arkansas Statute 85-9-312(5), as do subsections (3) and (4) of that Statute. The purposes behind all these exceptions are the same: to enable free-market forces to operate with respect to a debtor's acquisition of new property and to prevent unjust enrichment. Arkansas Statute 85-9-312(2) has the effect of putting farming on a par with any other business with respect to secured financing.

"The notification requirement is to protect an earlier secured party who may periodically extend credit with respect to the same farm products, such as a bank lending farm operating expenses to the debtor. See Arkansas Statute 85-9-312(3)(b). The filing requirement serves subsequent creditors by providing a means whereby they can learn of existing or expected interests in the collateral.

"The holder of a production money security interest may extend value more than once with respect to the same farm products. The holder need not give the notice or make a filing each time value is extended. Rather, a single notice and filing, properly accomplished, protects the holder as to all value the holder contemporaneously and subsequently extends with respect to farm products covered by the notice and filing.

"Priority under Arkansas Statute 85-9-312(2) is not conditioned on the production money secured party being without notice or knowledge of the conflicting security interest: the production money secured party takes priority although he actually or constructively knows of it. In this respect, Arkansas Statute 85-9-312(2) is no different from Arkansas Statute 85-9-312(3) and (4).

"The usual rule for determining priority between conflicting new-value interests in any kind of collateral is first-to-perfect. Accordingly, priority among production money security interests in the same farm products is usually covered by Arkansas Statute 85-9-312(5), which also governs when a purchase money security interest in livestock conflicts with a production money security interest in the animals. There is a limited exception, however, in the very last clause of Arkansas Statute 85-9-312(2)(a), which is designed to encourage a creditor with whom the debtor may have enjoyed a long relationship to continue to finance the debtor's production of crops. This exception broadens the priority of a production money secured party who substantially finances this year's crop so that his priority extends not only to the value he contributed to the current crop that is the collateral, but extends also to any other farm related debts secured by the collateral, including debts for producing crops grown in previous years.

"The value that will support a production money security interest includes a loan of money by a lender or other financier or by extension of credit by a seller or other supplier of goods or services. See Arkansas Statute 85-1-204(44). A production money security interest is created for new value given in the good faith belief that the value will be used to enable the debtor to produce or raise the collateral even though the value is not in fact so used by the debtor. Conditioning the priority of a production money security interest on proof that the value was actually used in producing or raising the collateral would impose on farm lenders and suppliers unreasonable burdens of accounting and tracing.

"Producing or raising farm products entails a wide range of many activities, each of which is useful or necessary to the process. Security interests based on value extended for all of these activities must qualify for the priority of this subsection so that the debtor can freely shop for enabling credit at every step of production. Thus, Arkansas Statute 85-9-312(2) deliberately defines 'producing or raising farm products' broadly: any causally related activity, including activities associated with marketing the collateral.

"Producing crops thus includes preparing the land for planting, cultivating or otherwise tending crops, harvesting, preparing crops for sale or storage prior to sale, storing crops prior to sale, transporting to sale, selling, or engaging in any other activity that proximately relates to the growing and marketing of crops or products of crops. Similarly, raising livestock includes feeding or grazing, fencing, providing health care, breeding, slaughtering, preparing for sale, transporting to sale, selling, or engaging in any other activity that proximately relates to the care and marketing of livestock or products of livestock.

"Advances to cover current operating expenses, and to sustain the farmer and his family, are as important to producing farm products as credit extended to buy seed for the new crop or feed for the livestock. Operating expenses are the costs of doing business, i.e., the usual and necessary costs of maintaining the farming operation that produces the collateral, excluding obligations owed with respect to the farmland such as rent, mortgage principal or interest. The land itself always serves as collateral for a mortgagee or vendor of the real estate. Statutory liens on the crops commonly protect cash rent due landlords.

"The financer of farm machinery or other farm equipment in a sense enables the production of crops or raising of livestock. Yet, this person has the security of a first claim to the equipment itself and as to farm products should rank below suppliers of goods, services, and money that is consumed in the production process.

"The priority granted by Arkansas Statute 85-9-312(2) extends to proceeds of farm products, see Arkansas Statute 85-9-306, and also to products of the collateral including milk and eggs. Products are expressly, separately covered in the subsection, without limitation, to make clear that the production money interest itself (Arkansas Statute 85-9-312(2)(c)), and the priority of the interest (Arkansas Statute 85-9-312(2)(a)), continue in products of the collateral free from the requirements that must be satisfied under Arkansas Statute 85-9-109(3) for products of crops and livestock to be classified as farm products. Thus, under Arkansas Statute 85-9-312(2)(c) a production money security interest in crops, livestock or other farm products extends automatically to products of the collateral, even though the debtor is no longer in possession of them (compare Arkansas Statute 85-9-306(2)); and, under Arkansas Statute 85-9-312(2)(a), this continuing interest in products enjoys the same absolute priority as the production money security interest in the original collateral that is the source of the products so long as the products are identifiable as such. If products are confused with other goods and can no longer be identified, that is, their identity is lost in the mass, the security interest is not lost. Rather, the interest continues, and priority is determined, pursuant to Arkansas Statute 85-9-315. Because Arkansas Statute 85-9-315(1) provides for the survival only of perfected security interests in goods that are confused or commingled, Arkansas Statute 85-9-312(2) provides that a security interest in products is continuously perfected if the interest in the original collateral was perfected. *The continuity of perfection as to both original collateral and products thereof is, however, subject to the provisions of Act 16 of the Second Extraordinary Session of 1986, compiled as Arkansas Statute 85-9-307(4) through (6), which is not repealed or otherwise affected by this Act.*"

[Ed. Note: §9-307(4) through (6), referred to above, was repealed, effective July 1, 1989.]

"The purposes behind Arkansas Statute 85-9-312(2) could be frustrated by typically unbargained-for, boilerplate language in loan agreements that could be construed to prohibit a debtor from creating production money security interests. So this sort of language is neutered. A creditor should not be allowed through contract to accomplish a result that contravenes the policy of positive law." (4-9-312[2]).

§9-312(4) Ten-day period changed to 21 days, effective Mar. 21, 1983. (4-9-312[4]).

§9-401(1) Third alternative subsection (1) adopted Reference to "clerk of the circuit court and ex-officio recorder" inserted in (1)(a). References to Secretary of State and clerk of circuit court inserted in (1)(c). (4-9-401[1]).

COMMERCIAL CODE... *continued*

§9-401(5) Reference to Secretary of State inserted. (4-9-401[5]).

§9-402(6) Sentence added, effective Aug. 13, 1993, reading: "All recording, satisfaction, and termination fees shall be collected by the Circuit Clerk and the Secretary of State at the time of the initial filing". (4-9-402[6]).

§9.404(3) Subsection amended by Act 104 of 1995 to read as follows: "(3) The uniform fee for filing and indexing a termination statement, including sending or delivering the financial statement, shall not exceed $6. However, this fee shall be collected by the filing officer at the time of the initial filing and indexing of the original financing statement." (4-9-403[3]).

§9.406 Last sentence added which reads as follows: "There shall be a fee for filing and noting such a statement of release not to exceed $6." (4-9-406).

Section added reading as follows:

"Destruction of old records.—Unless the filing officer has notice of an action pending relative thereto, he may remove from the files and destroy (a) a lapsed financing statement, a lapsed continuation statement, a statement of assignment or release relating to either, and any index of any of them, one year or more after lapse; and (b) a termination statement and the index on which it is noted, one year or more after the filing of the termination statement." (4-9-409).

10-101 Second sentence omitted; section not codified in Arkansas Statutes.

10-104 See §85-7-106. Optional subsection (2) not adopted.

§11-101 to §11-108 Article 11 not adopted.

Code appears as Title 4 of Ark. Code Ann. (1991). Section Numbers of Arkansas Code with the prefix "4" correspond to those of 1962 Official Text, except with respect to Articles 3 and 4 which coincide to Section Numbers in 1990 Revised Article 3 (With Conforming and Miscellaneous Amendments to Articles 3 and 4) effective July 15, 1991. (1991 Act 572).

Following options and alternatives in 1962 Official Text have been exercised: §3.121, Alternative B adopted (prior to repeal and adoption of revised Article 3); §4.106, optional phrase adopted (prior to repeal and adoption of revised Article 4); §4.202(1)(b), optional phrase adopted; §4.212, optional sub-section (2) adopted (prior to repeal and adoption of revised Article 4); §5.112(1), optional phrase omitted; §5.114, optional sub-sections (4) and (5) omitted; §6.106, optional section omitted (prior to effective date of repeal); §6.107(2) optional paragraph (e) is omitted (prior to effective date of repeal); §6.108(3) optional paragraph (c) omitted (prior to effective date of repeal); §6.109 optional sub-section (2) omitted (prior to effective date of repeal); §7.204, option to refer to local statutes not exercised and optional sub-section (4) omitted; §9.203(2), option to refer to local statutes not exercised and optional subsection (2) omitted; §9.302(3)(b), Alternative A adopted; §9.401(1), optional paragraphs (a) and (c) adopted; §9.401, alternative sub-section (3) not adopted; §9.407, optional section adopted.

Forms.—See end of this Digest.

Filing Fees.—For offices for filing and fees under Art. 9, see category Documents and Records, topic Records, subhead Filing Under Commercial Code.—Place; Fees.

See also topics Banks and Banking, Bills and Notes, Brokers, Carriers, Contracts, Factors, Frauds, Statute of, Sales, Securities, Warehousemen; categories Business Organizations, topic Corporations; Civil Actions and Procedure, topic Limitation of Actions; Debtor and Creditor, topics Assignments, Fraudulent Sales and Conveyances, Liens, Pledges; Documents and Records, topics Records, Seals; Mortgages, topic Chattel Mortgages.

CONDITIONAL SALES:

See topic Sales.

CONSIGNMENTS:

See topic Factors.

CONSUMER PROTECTION:

Following are unlawful practices: Concealment, suppression, or omission of material facts with intent that others rely on it (4-88-108); pyramiding devices (4-88-109); knowingly making false representations concerning goods or services; disparaging goods, services or business of another by false or misleading representation of facts; advertising goods or services with intent not to sell as advertised; knowingly taking advantage of consumer unable to protect his or her interest; making false representation that contributions solicited for charitable purposes will be spent in specified manner or for specified purposes; refusal to deliver with goods any electronic or mechanical apparatus warranty provided by manufacturer; employment of "bait and switch" advertising; knowingly failing to identify goods damaged by water, fire or accident or any other unconscionable or deceptive practices (4-88-107); solicitation for charitable organizations without disclosing income to charity and identity of and income to private firm conducting solicitation (4-88-110).

Conviction for unlawful practice is punishable as Class A misdemeanor. (4-88-103).

Civil enforcement is by petition of consumer protection division of office of Attorney General to Circuit or Chancery Court of Pulaski County or county where respondent resides or transacts business. (4-88-111-113). Elderly or disabled persons have express cause of action under Act and may recover actual and punitive damages and reasonable attorney's fees. Enhanced civil penalties apply when victim is disabled. Elder and Disabled Victims Fund created by Act to investigate and prosecute deceptive acts against disabled and elderly. (4-88-201-207).

Attorney General enforces Act by injunction and court may return to purchaser money or property acquired by any unlawful practice and may award damages and assess costs and fees, suspend corporate charter or other permit to do business of any person in willful violation of Act, and may assess penalties of $10,000 per violation of Act. (4-88-113).

Following are exceptions: practices subject to and in compliance with any rule of Federal Trade Commission; dissemination of information by broadcasters, printers and publishers without knowledge of deceptive nature of practice; actions or transactions of public utility acting under authority of certain regulatory bodies; and actions subject to State and Federal regulatory bodies. (4-88-101). Any civil action brought under this chapter is subject to five year statute of limitations. (4-88-115).

Unsolicited Merchandise.—When delivered to person for whom it is intended, said person may refuse to accept delivery of unsolicited merchandise or may deem it to be a gift and use it or dispose of it at will without obligation to sender. (4-86-103).

Equal Consumer Credit.—It is unlawful for any creditor or credit card issuer to discriminate on basis of sex or marital status. Consumer may recover $100 to $500 and costs and attorney's fees. (4-87-101-105).

Mail and Phone Solicitation.—Arkansas Mail and Telephone Consumer Product Promotion Fair Practices Act regulates offering of gifts or prizes by mail or phone intended to induce purchase of consumer product and pay-per-call services. Contracts of purchase must be in writing to be enforceable. Violations of Act are punishable as Class B misdemeanor; if amount solicited exceeds $200, violations are Class D felonies. All remedies available to Attorney General under Deceptive Trade Practices Act are available under Act. (4-95-101-108).

Regulation of Telephonic Sellers.—Act regulates telephonic sellers who solicit sales and imply that prospective purchaser will receive prize or gift or additional items for making purchase or that price offered is below regular price of item and also regulates solicitation made by telephone in response to inquiries generated by notifications sent by sellers indicating or implying that recipient is specially selected or will receive gift. Certain solicitations are exempted from regulation. Prospective purchasers must be supplied with certain information at time of solicitation and prior to sale. Telephonic sellers must obtain bond for $50,000 in favor of State and must register with Consumer Protection Division ten days before doing business in state. Registration is $100 to be paid and renewed annually. Telephonic sellers who fail to register are guilty of Class A misdemeanor. Willful violations of Act are punishable as Class D felony. Attorney General may enforce Act in same manner as Deceptive Trade Practices Act. (4-99-101-112).

Prize Promotion Act.—Requires that Arkansas consumers be provided with all relevant information necessary to make informative decision concerning sweepstakes, contests, and prize promotions. Act prohibits misleading and deceptive prize promotions. Defines "prize" as gift, award, or other item or service that is offered or awarded to participant in real or purported contest, etc. (4-102-101-102). Requires prize sponsor to provide written prize notice describing, inter alia, identity of sponsor; retail value of prize, odds of receiving such prize; requirements for payment of shipping or handling fees, etc.; any restrictions on receipt; limitations on eligibility; maximum number of persons in group or purported group with enhanced likelihood of receiving prize; etc. Act describes specific form of notice. (4-102-106).

Act substantially limits representations that plan sponsor can make, directly or by implication, regarding prizes or probability of receipt of prize. Sponsors are prohibited from requesting any individual to disclose phone numbers, ages, birth dates, credit card ownership, or financial data in connection with prize promotion which is not in compliance with Act. (4-102-105).

Exemptions include: advertising media; free prize promotions; promotions in connection with sale or purchase of books, recordings, video cassettes, periodicals, and similar goods through membership group, continuity plan, or subscription arrangement; and sales by catalog seller. Pari-mutuel wagering on horse racing and greyhound racing permitted and regulated by Arkansas law is also exempt. (4-102-104).

Violation of Act is also violation of Arkansas Deceptive Trade Practices Act, and subject to those enforcement provisions. (Ark. Code Ann. §4-88-101 et seq.). In addition, person suffering pecuniary loss because of intentional violation of Act may bring action in court of competent jurisdiction. Recovery includes costs, reasonable attorney's fees, and greater of (1) $500, or (2) twice amount of pecuniary loss. (4-102-103).

Pay-Per-Call.—Arkansas Pay Per Call Consumer Protection Act regulates pay per call services. Act requires services to provide delay time in which consumer can disconnect without being charged and disclosure message for services of interest to children under 18. Advertising of pay-per-call services must include specified information. Consumers may recover damages, treble damages, costs, and attorney's fees for violation of Act. Attorney General may enforce in same manner as Deceptive Trade Practices Act. (4-98-101-105).

Home Solicitation Sale.—Act regulates sale of certain goods and services in an amount exceeding $25 where solicitation takes place away from premises where seller normally carries on business or where goods are normally offered for sale or by telephone. (4-89-102). Seller is required to give statutory notice of right of cancellation to buyer when sales agreement is signed by furnishing completed form captioned "Notice of Cancellation". (4-89-108). There is three day cooling-off period in which buyer may cancel sales agreement. (4-89-107). By mailing or delivering to seller written notice of cancellation buyer has absolute right to cancel home solicitation contract until midnight of third day, excluding Sundays and holidays, after day on which he signs agreement. (4-89-107). Within ten days after cancellation, seller must tender any payment or trade-in and note or other evidence of debt received from buyer. (4-89-109). Within 20 days after cancellation buyer must tender goods to seller upon demand but if within this time seller fails to demand possession of goods, goods become property of buyer without obligation to pay for them. (4-89-110).

Certain transactions and contracts are excepted from regulation. (4-89-103). Violation of Act is misdemeanor punishable up to $250 fine and/or imprisonment up to one year. (4-89-104). Consumer may recover actual damages plus greater of $100 or 10% of transaction total. (4-89-105).

Plain Language.—The Life and Disability Insurance Policy Language Simplification Act sets minimum standards to make easier to read policies, contracts and certificates of life insurance and annuities, disability insurance, and credit life insurance delivered in Arkansas. (23-80-201-208). The Property and Casualty Insurance Policy Simplification Act sets minimum language and format standards to make property and casualty insurance policies easier to read. (23-80-301-308).

Rental Purchase Agreements.—Treated as true leases and not as credit sales or retail installment contracts or as creating security interest. Consumer has right to

CONSUMER PROTECTION ... *continued*

reinstate agreement upon failure to make timely rental payment by paying all rents and charges due or returning merchandise to lessor within specified time. Agreement must disclose: whether merchandise is new or used; amount, timing and number of rental payments; total amount to be paid to acquire ownership; amount and purpose of other charges; that consumer does not acquire ownership rights until ownership terms of agreement are satisfied; and whether consumer liable for loss or damage to merchandise, and consumer's reinstatement rights. Consumer may recover from lessor: actual damages, 25% of amount equal to total amount of payments required for ownership, and reasonable attorney's fees up to 15% of allowable recovery and court costs for violations under Act. Attorney General may enforce Act in same manner as Deceptive Trade Practices Act. (4-92-101-107).

Also covered are: Credit services organizations (4-91-101-109), automobiles (4-90-201-305), credit reporting disclosures (4-93-101-104), health spas (4-94-101-109), farm machinery (4-96-201-202), retail pet stores (4-97-101-103), going out of business sales (4-74-101-111), and motor vehicle transfers (4-100-101-103).

Fracture-Filled or Clarity-Enhanced Diamonds.—Persons engaged in business of selling fracture-filled or clarity-enhanced diamonds or jewelry containing fracture-filled diamonds shall disclose to customer that diamond has been treated. Business required to post notice at conspicuous place at entrance of business. Violation is Class B misdemeanor. (4-101-201).

Odometer Fraud.—Act prevents sale or transfer of motor vehicles without statement of actual mileage of vehicle accompanying sale. Transferor of motor vehicle must give transferee written disclosure of cumulative mileage registered on odometer, or that mileage is not actual if transferor knows that odometer is incorrect. Violators subject to Attorney General enforcement under Deceptive Trade Practices Act and private action by aggrieved party. Violators also subject to maximum criminal penalties of up to three years in prison and $50,000 fine. (4-90-201-207).

Uniform Deceptive Trade Practices Act has not been adopted.
See also topics Interest and Sales.

CONTRACTS:

Commercial Code applies. See topic Commercial Code.

Contracts of Infants.—See category Family, topic Infants.

FACTORS:

Liens covered by Uniform Commercial Code. See topic Commercial Code.

Consignment agreements intended as security, covered by Uniform Commercial Code. (4-9-101-507). Consignments that are not intended as security interests are covered by Uniform Commercial Code. (4-9-114, 4-2-326).

FRANCHISES:

Arkansas Franchise Practices Act defines "franchise," in general, as any agreement providing for grant of license to use trade name, trademark or service mark within area or to sell or distribute goods or services within area. (4-72-202[1]). Franchisor may not terminate, cancel or fail to renew franchise without good cause, as defined in Act. (4-72-204). With limited exceptions, franchisors must give advance written notice of intent to terminate, cancel or fail to renew franchise. In some instances franchisees may remedy deficiencies so as to void notice. (4-72-204). Franchisees must provide franchisors written notice of proposed transfers of franchise and franchisors must, within 60 days, either approve of transfer or notify franchisee of material reason relating to character, financial ability or business experience of transferee why transfer will not be permitted. (4-72-205). If franchisor terminates franchise without good cause, at franchisee's option, franchisor must repurchase franchisee's inventory, supplies, and equipment. (4-72-209).

Certain practices by franchisors are illegal, including: (i) requiring franchisees to waive rights under Act; (ii) interference with free association among franchisees; (iii) unreasonable prohibitions against change in management of franchisees; (iv) restricting issuance of equity or debt securities by franchisees to extent such action does not harm financial condition of franchisee or constitute sale of franchise; (v) refusal to deal with franchisees in commercially reasonable manner; (vi) collection from franchisee of advertising fees not used to advertise business of franchisee. (4-72-206). Franchisees' remedies include injunctive relief and/or actual civil damages and right to recover attorneys' fees and costs. (4-72-209).

Act prohibits fraud, making fraudulent misrepresentations or omitting to state material fact in connection with offer and sale of franchise. Violations of anti-fraud provisions constitute Class B felony (4-72-207) and, if committed by franchisor, will entitle franchisee to recover treble damages. (4-72-208). Attorney General may bring injunctive proceedings to remedy violations of Act. (4-72-208).

Act applies only to franchises entered into, renewed or transferred after Mar. 4, 1977 and certain provisions do not apply to franchises subject to FTC regulations. (4-72-203).

Franchises of farm equipment retailers, petroleum products suppliers, dealers, and distributors and restaurants are governed by additional statutory provisions. (4-72-301-310; 4-72-401-403; 4-72-501-503; 4-72-601-603).

FRAUDS, STATUTE OF:

A memorandum signed by the person to be charged, or some one properly authorized, is necessary to bind person for debt of another; to declare or create trust of any land; or promise to pay debt incurred in infancy or to convey land, or lease for longer term than one year; or on promise not to be performed within one year; or on promise by executor or administrator to pay any debt out of estate; or on promise in consideration of marriage; or to extend credit, or modify or renew existing credit, in amount greater than $10,000. (4-59-101-103).

Contracts of Sale.—Covered by Uniform Commercial Code. (4-1-206; 4-2-201; 4-2-209; 4-2-326).

Promissory estoppel, will estop assertion of statute of frauds where injustice can be avoided only by enforcement of promise. (271 Ark. 840, 611 S.W.2d 201).

Bankrupt's Debts.—Promise to pay debt discharged in bankruptcy must be in writing. (4-59-101[b]).

Contract for Lease of Goods.—Covered by Uniform Commercial Code. (4-2A-201).

Campaign Services Contract.—No action shall be brought to charge any candidate upon any contract, promise, or agreement for service rendered to candidate unless there is memorandum signed by party to be charged. (7-6-101).

Part Performance.—Substantial part performance, so that the party having performed cannot be put in status quo without injury, takes case out of the statute. (1 Ark. 391).

INTEREST:

Non-consumer maximum rate is 5% per annum above Federal Reserve Discount Rate at time of contract. (Const., art. 19, §13). Contracts calling for more than lawful rate are void as to unpaid interest and debtor may recover twice amount of interest paid. (Const., art. 19, §13).

Consumer credit maximum rate is 5% per annum above Federal Reserve Discount Rate at time of contract, with absolute cap of 17% per annum. (Const., art. 19, §13; 280 Ark. 106, 655 S.W.2d 426). Consumer contracts calling for more than 17% per annum are void as to principal and interest, and buyer retains goods. (Const., art. 19, §13; 225 Ark. 96, 279 S.W.2d 556).

Default rate is 6% per annum for contracts in which no rate of interest is specified. (Const., art. 19, §13).

Judgments on contracts bear interest at rate provided in contract or 10% per annum, whichever is greater, but in no event more than that allowed by Art. 19, §13 of Arkansas Constitution. (16-65-114).

Other judgments bear interest at 10% per annum, but in no event more than that allowed by Art. 19, §13 of Arkansas Constitution. (16-65-114).

Interest on negotiable instruments is governed by Uniform Commercial Code. (4-3-112). Open accounts bear interest after maturity. (275 Ark. 235, 628 S.W.2d 869).

LICENSES, BUSINESS AND PROFESSIONAL:

Licenses are required for a large number of occupations, etc., enumerated and provided for in various statutes.

Commercial Travelers.—No state license is required, but cities and towns may require licenses and fix fee. (14-54-103).

Collection agencies are regulated by 17-24-101-404.

State Board of Collection Agencies authorized to charge annual license fee of $125 for each agency and $15 for each employee. (17-24-305).

Collection agencies which fail to remit collections to client within calendar month following month of collection are not entitled to collection fee. (17-24-104).

MONOPOLIES, RESTRAINT OF TRADE AND COMPETITION:

Monopolies.—Corporation, association, partnership or individual becoming party to any trust or combination (within or without state) to regulate (within or without state) price of any article or price or premium to be paid for insuring property or maintain said price, or being party to any pool or combination in state to fix or limit in state the amount or quality of any article is guilty of conspiracy. Penalty fine of from $200 to $5,000 for each day's offense, in addition to which corporation forfeits all franchises and all corporate rights. (4-75-301-314).

Unfair Practices.—Corporation, association, partnership or individual engaging in trade practice with intent to destroy competition through price discrimination, predatory pricing, or secret payments within industry is guilty of unfair practices. (4-75-201-211). Penalties for violations range from $100 to $1,000 for each offense, up to six months' imprisonment, or both. (4-75-204). After three violations, corporation's charter, franchises, and other rights may be revoked. (4-75-205). Civil remedies include injunctions, damages, and treble damages. (4-75-211). Trade secrets are protected. (4-75-601-607).

Sales of cigarettes, automobiles, milk and other dairy products, and motion pictures are governed by additional provisions. (4-75-701-713; 4-75-401-412; 4-75-801-809; 4-75-901-906).

Resale Price Agreements.—See category Intellectual Property, topic Trademarks and Tradenames.

Franchising.—See topic Franchises.

NEGOTIABLE INSTRUMENTS:

See topic Bills and Notes.

RESTRAINT OF TRADE:

See topic Monopolies, Restraint of Trade and Competition.

SALES:

Uniform Commercial Code applies to sale of goods. (4-2-101-725).

Products Liability.—Actions for injuries based on breach of warranty are governed by Uniform Commercial Code (4-2-313-318) but for actions based on breach of warranty or on negligence, privity is not required if plaintiff is person whom manufacturer or seller might reasonably have expected to use, consume, or be affected by goods (4-86-101). See topic Commercial Code.

Person engaged in business of manufacturing, assembling, leasing or otherwise distributing products is liable in damages for harm caused by it if supplied in a defective condition which rendered it unnecessarily dangerous and condition was proximate cause. (4-86-102).

See note at head of Digest as to 1998 legislation covered.

See Topical Index in front part of this volume.

SALES . . . *continued*

Implied warranty that livestock offered for sale is free from disease does not exist unless owner knowingly sells diseased animal. (4-2-316[3][d][ii]).

Home Solicitation Sales.—Buyer has absolute right to cancel contract until midnight of third day after signing, excluding Suns. and holidays. (4-89-107). Home solicitation sales contract must contain statutory Notice of Cancellation. Three day period does not begin until notice given. (4-89-108). Violations of home solicitation sale statute constitute violations of Deceptive Trade Practices Act punishable by Attorney General and prosecuting attorneys of various districts and counties of state. (4-89-106; 4-88-101-113). Sales contracts initiated by seller through mail or by telephone by offering gift and failing to fully describe sales terms must be in writing, signed by buyer. (4-95-105-106).

Conditional Sales.—Uniform Commercial Code applies. (4-9-101-507). 1972 Official Amendments adopted.

There are no statutory requirements as to type size in printed contracts.

Retail Credit Sales.—No special restrictions.

Bulk Sales.—Uniform Commercial Code chapter on Bulk Transfers not adopted. See topic Commercial Code; see also category Debtor and Creditor, topic Fraudulent Sales and Conveyances.

See also category Transportation, topic Motor Vehicles, subhead Liens and Encumbrances.

Contracts of Sale.—There are no statutory requirements as to type size in printed contracts.

Revised Uniform Deceptive Trade Practices Act not adopted.

Consumer Protection.—See topic Consumer Protection.

SECURITIES:

(Title 23, c. 42). See also Uniform Commercial Code. (4-8-101-603).

The Arkansas Securities Act is based on the Uniform Securities Act, promulgated by the National Conference of Commissioners on Uniform State Laws, but contains numerous variations from that act. Accordingly, the Arkansas statute is summarized below. For text of the Uniform Act, see Uniform and Model Acts section.

Supervision is by State Securities Commissioner, to whom all requests for information or forms should be addressed. Address: 201 East Markham, Little Rock, AR 72201, (501) 324-9260.

Regulatory Powers of Supervisory Authority.—All broker-dealers, agents, and investment advisers must register annually either with Arkansas Securities Department or Securities and Exchange Commission (23-42-301[c]) and pay any prescribed fees (23-42-304). Commissioner has supervision over broker-dealers, agents, and investment advisers (23-42-301) and over all records of applicants, registered issuers, registered broker-dealers, and registered investment advisers (23-42-306). Commissioner may deny, suspend, or revoke registration if he finds it in public interest and applicant or registrant has committed any of specified acts. (23-42-308).

Prerequisites to Sales or Offerings.—It is unlawful for any person to offer or sell any security unless registered, security is exempt or security is covered security. (23-42-501). Criminal penalties (23-42-104-105) and civil liabilities (23-42-106) are provided.

Securities to Which Act is Applicable.—Act applies to any instrument commonly known as a security, including any note; stock; treasury stock; bond; debenture; evidence of indebtedness; certificate of interest or participation in any profit-sharing agreement; collateral-trust certificate; preorganization certificate or subscription; transferable share; investment contract; variable annuity contract; voting trust certificate; certificate of deposit for a security; certificate of interest or participation in an oil, gas, or mining title or lease, or in payments out of production therefrom. Act does not apply to any insurance or endowment policy or annuity or variable annuity contract issued by insurance company. (23-42-102[15]). Sale of unit in general partnership held to be sale of security within meaning of Arkansas Securities Act. (292 Ark. 602, 732 S.W.2d 836).

Covered Securities.—(23-42-509).

Exempt securities are: securities issued or guaranteed by State of Arkansas or any political subdivision or agency thereof or any certificate of deposit for such securities; any security issued or guaranteed by any foreign government with which U.S. currently maintains diplomatic relations recognized as valid obligations by issuer or guarantor; any security of national or state bank or federally insured savings bank; any security issued by any state or federal savings and loan association; any securities issued by bank holding company regulated under Federal Bank Holding Company Act of 1956, as amended; securities issued by public utility or holding company which is subject to federal regulation; any security issued by nonprofit corporation operated exclusively for charitable, educational, religious or trade purposes; any investment contract issued in connection with employee's stock purchase, savings, pension, profit-sharing or similar benefit plan. Plans not meeting qualification requirements under U.S. Internal Revenue Code, must file prior to any offer or sale, notice specifying terms of plan, which Commissioner may disallow within ten days. Also included are: Any other class of securities added by Commissioner by rule, where aggregate amount of issue does not exceed $1,000,000; enumerated securities of domestic and certain foreign agricultural cooperative associations; any securities which Commissioner by rule or order exempts from registration as not being necessary or appropriate in public interest or for protection of investors. (23-42-503).

Proof of exemption must be first filed as to certain exempted securities and Commissioner must not have disallowed exemption within next five full business days, before issuance. Filing fee on graduated scale from $100 to $500 required. (23-42-503[d]).

Exempt transactions are: isolated non-issuer transactions; any nonissuer transaction by registered agent of registered broker-dealer, and any resale transaction by sponsor of unit investment trust registered under Investment Company Act of 1940, in security of class that has been outstanding in hands of public for at least 90 days provided, at time of transaction: (1) issuer of security is actually engaged in business and is not blank check, blind pool or shell company whose primary plan of business is to engage in merger or combination of business with, or acquisition of, unidentified person or persons, (2) security is sold at price reasonably related to current market price of security, (3) security does not constitute whole or part of unsold allotment to, or subscription or participation by, broker-dealer as underwriter of security, (4) nationally recognized securities manual designated by rule or order of Commissioner or document filed with Securities and Exchange Commission that is publicly available through Securities and Exchange Commission's Electronic Data Gathering and Retrieval System (EDGAR) and contains specific information regarding issuer, and (5) issuer of security has class of equity securities listed on national securities exchange registered under Securities Exchange Act of 1934, or designated for trading on National Association of Securities Dealers Automated Quotation System, with certain exceptions; any transaction between issuer and underwriter or among underwriters; issuance of bond or other evidence of indebtedness secured by mortgage on tangible property where entire mortgage and bonds are sold as unit; transactions by executor, administrator, sheriff, marshal, receiver, trustee in bankruptcy, guardian, or conservator; transactions of bona fide pledgees; any offer or sale to bank, savings institution, trust company, insurance company, investment company, pension or profit-sharing trust, any other financial institution or institutional buyer, and broker-dealers; transactions pursuant to offer and sale to not more than 35 persons in this state, other than nonprofit corporations, within any period of 12 consecutive months if seller reasonably believes that buyers are purchasing for investment and no commission is paid directly or indirectly for soliciting any prospective buyer unless person receiving such commission is registered broker-dealer or agent in this state; sales to holders of certain existing securities if no commissions are paid; any offer of security for which registration statements have been filed under this Act and Securities Act of 1933 and no stop order is in effect. (23-42-504). Commissioner by Rule 504.01(a)(14) has adopted Uniform Limited Offering Exemption set forth in Rule 506 of Regulation D under Securities Act of 1933, subject to foregoing conditions; any other transaction which Commissioner by rule or order exempts as not being necessary or appropriate in public interest or for protection of investors. (23-42-104-109, 202, 205, 302-305, 404, 503-506).

Proof of exempt transaction must first be filed as to certain exempted transactions and Commissioner must not have disallowed exemption within next five full business days. Filing fee on graduated scale from $25 to $500 required. (23-42-504[b]).

Registration of Securities by Notification.—The following securities, whether or not also eligible for registration by coordination, may be registered by notification upon filing required forms and information with Commissioner: (1) any security whose issuer has been in continuous operation for at least five years without default in current fiscal year or within three preceding fiscal years in payment of principal, interest or dividends and has had specified earnings during past three fiscal years; (2) any security (other than certificate of interest or participation in oil, gas, or mining title or lease, or in payments out of production therefrom) registered for non-issuer distribution if any security of same class has ever been registered or if originally exempt. If no stop order is in effect or under hearing, registration by notification is effective at three o'clock, P.M., Central Standard Time, of second full business day after filing registration statement, or at such earlier time as Commissioner may determine. (23-42-401).

Registration by coordination may be had for any security for which registration statement has been filed under Securities Act of 1933 and upon filing with Commissioner detailed information and exhibits. Registration statement becomes effective at moment federal registration becomes effective if no stop order is in effect or under hearing, registration has been on file with Commissioner for at least ten days, and statement of maximum and minimum proposed offering prices and maximum underwriting discounts and commissions have been on file two full business days. (23-42-402).

Registration by qualification may be had for any security. Detailed information and specified documents must be submitted to Commissioner. (23-42-403).

Every applicant for registration, every person making notice filing, and every issuer for whom registration or exemption from registration or notice filing is required to appoint commissioner as its agent for service of process for any noncriminal action arising under Act. This provision does not apply to applicants, persons making notice filings and issuers who have place of business in Arkansas, have qualified to do business in Arkansas with Secretary of State, and have either agent for service or have executed consent appointing Secretary of State agent for service. (23-42-107).

Registration statement may be filed by issuer, any other person on whose behalf offering is made, or registered broker-dealer. (23-42-404[a]).

Fee for filing registration statement is 1/10th of 1% of amount for which securities are to be offered in this state, with a minimum fee of $150 and maximum of $2,000. If registration statement is withdrawn before effective date, or if pre-effective stop order is entered, Commissioner retains $150 of fee. (23-42-404[b]).

Registration statement must set forth in detail information as to securities. (23-42-404[c]).

Registration statement is effective for one year from effective date and, upon renewal, for any longer period during which security is being offered or distributed in nonexempted transaction except during time stop order is in effect. Renewal registration for subsequent 12 month periods requires written application and payment of additional filing fees. So long as registration statement is effective, Commissioner may require filing of reports to keep reasonably current information contained in statement and to disclose progress of offering. (23-42-404).

Commissioner may require any security issued within past three years or to be issued to a promoter for a consideration substantially different from public offering price, or offered for a consideration other than cash, to be deposited in escrow and proceeds from sale impounded until issuer receives a specified amount. (23-42-404[g]).

Stop order may be issued by Commissioner denying, suspending, or revoking effectiveness of registration statement in public interest and if statement is incomplete, false, or misleading, or otherwise in violation of Act. (23-42-405).

See note at head of Digest as to 1998 legislation covered.

See Topical Index in front part of this volume.

AR – 11

SECURITIES . . . *continued*

Registration and Licensing of Dealers.—Broker-dealer, agent, investment adviser, or representative transacting business in state must register annually and may obtain initial or renewal registration by filing with Commissioner or Commissioner's designee application and fee together with consent to service of process. (23-42-302). Every applicant for initial registration and every person making notice filing shall pay filing fee of $300 in case of broker-dealer, $75 in case of agent, $300 in case of investment advisor, and $75 in case of representative. (23-42-304[a]). If application has been processed, in whole or in part, any filing fee shall be nonrefundable. (23-42-304[c]). Minimum capital requirement for broker-dealer is set by Commissioner and for registered investment adviser $12,500. (23-42-303[a]). Minimum net capital requirement shall not apply to any registered investment advisers which maintain their principal place of business in state other than Arkansas, that are registered or licensed as such in that state and are in compliance with applicable net capital requirements of that state. (23-42-303[b]). Commissioner may deny, suspend, or revoke any registration in public interest or for numerous enumerated causes, which action becomes final after 15 days notice and opportunity for hearing. (23-42-308).

Tender offers are governed by Investor Protection Take-Over Act. (23-43-101-117). It is unlawful to make takeover offer involving "target company" (issuer (i) organized under Arkansas law or with its principal offices in Arkansas, or (ii) majority in interest of whose equity security holders reside in Arkansas) unless offer is effective under Take-Over Act or is exempted. (23-43-102[6], -111[a]). Applies to all equity interests. Offers made to Arkansas must be substantially identical to those made in other states. (23-43-112[a]). Solicitation materials must be filed with Commissioner. (23-43-111[b]). Offeree has right to withdraw tendered securities. (23-43-112[b]).

Ownership information must be filed within ten days after directly or indirectly acquiring more than 5% of any class of equity security. Statement must contain material information regarding identity of offeror, source of funds to be used in tender offer, and ownership of other equity securities of offeror. (23-43-110).

Exemptions from Act are available for: transactions effected by or through broker-dealer in ordinary course of business; exchange offers of securities exempted from registration; offers made to not more than 35 persons in state during any 12 consecutive months; offers made to all equity shareholders of target company, if total number of equity holders does not exceed 100; offers involving 2% or less of target's securities of that class; and offer by target company for its own equity securities. (23-43-102[5]).

Bond to Protect Purchasers.—Subject to certain exceptions, registered broker-dealers must maintain bonds in amounts as Commissioner may prescribe. Subject to certain exceptions registered investment must maintain bonds in amount of $50,000. (23-42-305).

Records and Financial Reports.—Subject to certain exceptions, every registered broker-dealer and investment adviser must prepare, maintain and make available such records and financial reports as Commissioner may require. (23-42-306).

Advertising.—Commissioner may require filing of prospectus, advertisement, or other sales literature intended for distribution as part of registered or exempt offering. (23-42-502).

Information Public.—All information contained in or filed with any registration statement, notice filing, application or report, is available to public and photostatic or other copies of any document of public record will be furnished upon such charge as Commissioner may prescribe. (23-42-206-207).

Opinions.—Commissioner in his discretion may honor requests from interested persons for interpretive opinions under Act. (23-42-206[e]).

Appeal from any final order by Commissioner may be taken to any court of competent jurisdiction within 60 days after entry of order. (23-42-210).

Liabilities.—Any person who offers or sells a security in violation of act, or by means of misrepresentation, is liable to purchaser for consideration paid for security, together with interest at 6%, costs and attorneys' fees, less any income received from security, upon tender of security and any income received on it, or for damages if purchaser no longer owns security. Every controlling person, partner, officer, or director of seller or broker dealer or agent of seller who materially aids in sale is also liable unless he proves he did not, or reasonably could not, know of facts constituting grounds for liability. Cause of action survives. Limitations on such action are five years after sale. (23-42-106). Waiver of liability by purchaser is void. (23-42-109). However, cause of action terminates as to purchasers who failed to accept rescission offers by seller which comply with certain requirements of Act. (23-42-106[f]). Right of action is in addition to all other remedies at law or in equity. (23-42-108).

Money Order and Check Issuers.—Any person other than incorporated telegraph company, governmental department, or bank, credit union, or savings and loan association organized under Federal or Arkansas law which is (i) federally insured and (ii) authorized to do business in state, engaged in business of selling or issuing its check, draft, money order or other written instrument for transmission or payment of money or credit as service or for fee or other consideration must first qualify with State Securities Commissioner and thereafter comply with detailed statutory provisions. (23-41-101-122).

Franchising, Pyramid Sales, Etc.—Governed by Arkansas Franchise Practices Act (4-72-201-210); Consumer Protection Act (4-88-101-112, 4-89-101-110). See topic Franchises.

Uniform Simplification of Fiduciary Security Transfers Act not adopted.

Uniform Securities Ownership by Minors Act adopted. (9-26-301-307).

STATUTE OF FRAUDS:

See topic Frauds, Statute of.

TRUST RECEIPT SECURITY:

Uniform Commercial Code applies. 1972 Official Amendments adopted. (Act 116, 1973). See topic Commercial Code; category Debtor and Creditor, topic Pledges.

WAREHOUSEMEN:

A system of bonded warehouses and cooperative marketing of farm, orchard and ranch products is provided by 2-17-201-416.

Public grain warehouses are supervised by Director of State Plant Board, No. 1 Natural Resources Drive, Little Rock, Arkansas 72205.

Title to grain in possession of public grain warehouseman does not pass unless owner signs such title over to warehouseman. (2-17-303).

Bonds.—Licensed warehouse must execute bond with corporate surety to state. Bond must be in amount of 20¢ per bushel for first 1,000,000 bushels, 15¢ per bushel between 1,000,000 and 2,000,000 bushels, and 10¢ per bushel for over 2,000,000 bushel capacity, with $20,000 minimum; may self insure with permission of Director. (2-17-209, 210).

Assets.—Licensed warehouse must maintain net assets equal to at least 10¢ per bushel licensed to handle with minimum of $10,000. (2-17-217).

License is issued by Director upon compliance with bonding and net assets requirement. (2-17-211). Director may revoke license if insolvent or violates Act. (2-17-215, 236).

Supervision.—Certified warehousemen must be in charge of warehouse and are under supervision of State Plant Board, which may regulate charges, refuse permit to do business if there are sufficient facilities in vicinity and close any warehouse and liquidate it for cause. (2-17-206, 236).

Lien.—See Uniform Commercial Code 4-7-602 and 4-9-312.

Penalties.—Issuing receipts without license is Class D felony. (2-17-204).

See also category Debtor and Creditor, topic Fraudulent Sales and Conveyances, subhead Bulk Sales.

Warehouse Receipts.—Uniform Commercial Code applies. (4-7-101-210, 401-603).

Receipts must be issued for not more than one year and be on form prescribed by Director, and be consecutively numbered. (2-17-221-223, 4-7-202).

Buyer in ordinary course of business of fungible goods, except grains listed below, sold and delivered by warehouseman also in business of buying and selling such goods takes free of any claim under warehouse receipt even though it has been duly negotiated. Inapplicable to rice, soybeans, wheat, corn, rye, oats, barley, flaxseed, sorghum, mixed grain, or other grains or oilseed. (4-7-205).

Self-Service Storage.—Operating rules, establishment of operator's liens and sale of stored property allowed under 18-16-401-409.

CITIZENSHIP

ALIENS:

Aliens may acquire any estate in land by deed, inheritance or will, and may hold, alienate and devise or bequeath real or personal property same as citizens. (18-11-101 and 28-9-211). Alien spouse takes dower or curtesy. (28-11-202). Acquisition of title to agricultural land, or leasing same for ten or more years, requires registration with Circuit Clerk within 60 days. (2-3-103). Nonresident aliens compensated same as residents under workers compensation laws with certain exceptions. (11-9-111). Certain aliens not eligible for employment security benefits. (11-10-511).

CIVIL ACTIONS AND PROCEDURE

ACCORD AND SATISFACTION:

Common law rules govern.

Pleading.—Defense of accord and satisfaction must be affirmatively pleaded. (RCP 8[c]).

Uniform Commercial Code adopted. See category Business Regulation and Commerce, topic Commercial Code.

ACTIONS:

All former forms of actions or suits are abolished, and there is but one form of civil action. Actions in equity shall be brought in chancery court and actions at law shall be brought in circuit court. (RCP 2).

Commencement.—See topics Pleading, Process.

Parties.—An action must be prosecuted in name of real party in interest. (RCP 17[a]). Court may order necessary parties who are subject to service of process to be joined. (RCP 19[a]). If necessary party cannot be joined, court shall determine whether action should proceed among parties before it, or should be dismissed. (RCP 19[b]).

Class actions may be brought where (1) class is so numerous that joinder is impracticable, (2) there are common questions of law or fact, (3) claims or defenses are typical of class, and (4) representative parties will fairly and adequately protect interests of class. (RCP 23). Uniform Class Actions Act not adopted.

Intervention.—One claiming interest in property or transaction involved whose ability to protect interest may be impaired by disposition of action may intervene as matter of right. Permissive intervention is authorized when applicant's claim or defense has question of fact or law in common with main action. (RCP 24[a] and [b]).

Interpleader.—Persons with claims against plaintiff exposing plaintiff to multiple liability may be joined and required to interplead. Defendant exposed to similar liability may interplead by cross-claim, third party complaint or counterclaim. Plaintiff who disclaims any interest in money or property that is subject of interpleader action

See note at head of Digest as to 1998 legislation covered.

See Topical Index in front part of this volume.

ACTIONS ... *continued*

shall, upon depositing money or property in registry of court, be discharged from all liability. (RCP 22).

Third Party Practice.—Rules substantially same as Rule 14 of Federal Rules of Civil Procedure on actions by third party plaintiff are adopted, except that section (c) of Federal Rule is omitted in its entirety. (RCP 14).

Joinder of Causes of Action.—Joinder of all claims is permitted. (RCP 18).

Consolidation of Actions.—Actions involving common question of law or fact may be consolidated by court in its discretion. Court may make such orders concerning procedures therein as may tend to avoid unnecessary costs or delay in administration of justice. (RCP 42[a]).

Severance of actions or claims may be ordered by court in its discretion for convenience or to avoid prejudice. (RCP 42[b]).

Revivor.—If action survives, on death of party court may order substitution upon motion. If motion for substitution is not made within 90 days after death is suggested on record, action may be dismissed as to deceased party. If there is no administrator, special administrator may be appointed for action. (RCP 25).

See also category Estates and Trusts, topic Executors and Administrators.

Limitation of.—See topic Limitation of Actions.

Administration.—See category Estates and Trusts, topic Executors and Administrators.

Lis Pendens.—Action affecting title to, or lien on, real or personal property must be accompanied by lis pendens notice filed with recorder of deeds setting forth title and object of cause, description of property, name of parties, and style of court. (16-59-101 and 102).

Direct Action Against Insurer.—On casualty insurance contract if judgment remains unsatisfied after 30 days from service of notice of entry of judgment upon attorney for insured or upon insured or upon insurer or after execution is returned unsatisfied on account of insolvency or bankruptcy of insured, injured person or his personal representative may sue insurer directly for amount of judgment not exceeding amount of policy (23-89-101 and 102).

Insurer of any cooperative nonprofit organization or state or political subdivision or any other person not subject to suit for tort may be sued directly by any person injured by such person so exempt to extent of insurance carried. (23-79-210).

Person having claim for personal injury or property damage arising out of use of motor vehicle in foreign country by another who at time of injury or damage was covered by policy with insurer subject to jurisdiction of court of this state may sue insurer directly in county where injured person was resident at time of injury or damage. (23-79-201).

Small Claims.—See category Courts and Legislature, topic Courts, subheads Justices' Courts, Municipal Courts, Small Claims Courts.

APPEAL AND ERROR:

Constitutional Amendment 58 authorized Court of Appeals. 16-12-101 created Court of Appeals, and jurisdiction of Court of Appeals is set by Supreme Court by rule.

Court of Appeals is comprised of 12 members. (16-12-101).

Supreme Court Rule 1-2 provides all appeals shall be to Court of Appeals except following shall be filed in Supreme Court: interpretation or construction of state Constitution; criminal cases in which death penalty or life imprisonment imposed; extraordinary writs (e.g., mandamus, prohibition) directed to courts or government officials; election cases; discipline of attorneys at law and judges; cases previously appealed to Supreme Court; appeals required by law.

From Court of Appeals.—Supreme Court will exercise its discretion to review appeal decided by Court of Appeals only on application by party to appeal, upon certification of Court of Appeals, or if Supreme Court decides should have originally been assigned to Supreme Court. Court of Appeals may certify matters to Supreme Court if matter should properly be heard by Supreme Court under Rule 1-2 or if it involves matters of significant public interest or legal principle of major importance.

From Circuit, Chancery and Probate Courts.—Appeal of final judgments and certain interlocutory orders may be taken from Circuit, Chancery and Probate Courts to Supreme Court or Court of Appeals. Appeals shall be taken by filing notice of appeal with clerk of court from which appeal is taken. Notice shall specify party taking appeal, designate judgment, decree, order or part thereof appealed from, designate contents of record on appeal, and certify transcript has been ordered and required financial arrangements for court reporter have been made pursuant to Ark. Code Ann. §16-13-510(c). Notice shall also state whether appeal is to Court of Appeals or Supreme Court and basis for Supreme Court jurisdiction. (RAP 3). Generally notice must be filed within 30 days from entry of judgment, decree or order appealed from, and notice of cross-appeal must be filed within ten days after receipt of notice of appeal. (RAP 4). Record, prepared by trial court reporter, shall be filed by appellant with clerk of Supreme Court within 90 days from filing of first notice of appeal, except trial court may extend such time up to seven months from date of entry of judgment, decree or order appealed from. (RAP 5). Record of appeals from certain interlocutory orders must be filed in 30 days.

Stay of Proceedings.—Except where appeal is by State (RCP 62[e]) or where notice of lis pendens was filed by appellant claiming interest in realty (241 Ark. 629, 408 S.W.2d 871) appeal does not stay proceedings on judgment or order unless supersedeas order is issued. Supersedeas order issued by trial court clerk unless record has been lodged with appellate court in which event appellate court clerk issues. (RAP 8). Supersedeas order may not be issued until filing of surety bond conditioned upon satisfaction of that part of judgment stayed, costs, interest and damages for delay. (RAP 8).

Extent of Review.—Fact issues in cases tried to jury will be affirmed if findings are supported by any substantial evidence. (313 Ark. 229, 853 S.W.2d 278). In equity

cases cause is heard de novo on appeal, and Appellate Court passes on facts as well as law (28 Ark. App. 295, 773 S.W.2d 853), but Court does not revise decree in equity cases unless findings are clearly against preponderance of evidence (6 Ark. App. 37, 638 S.W.2d 263).

From County Courts.—Appeals to circuit court are granted as a matter of right. Appeals may be taken from judgments related to bond issues within 30 days and from all other judgments within six months after rendition by filing affidavit and prayer for appeal with clerk of circuit court. Trial in circuit court is de novo. (16-67-201, 207).

From Probate Courts.—Appeals may be taken as matter of right to Court of Appeals, in same manner and time as appeals from chancery courts. (Rule 1-2).

From Municipal and Justice of the Peace Courts.—Appeal to circuit court may be taken from any judgment rendered by a municipal court or justice of the peace by filing record of proceeding with circuit clerk within 30 days of entry of judgment. (RIC 9). Trial on appeal is de novo. (16-17-703). Either party may appeal without bond, but such appeal does not operate as suspension of judgment. (RIC 9).

From Transportation Commission.—Appeal from Transportation Commission lies to Pulaski Circuit Court within 30 days after entry of any order, and is begun by filing written motion with any member of Commission or with secretary thereof praying for appeal. Thereupon appeal is granted as matter of right and secretary of Commission is required to prepare and file transcript of all proceedings before Commission. (23-2-425).

From Public Service Commission.—Party aggrieved by order must apply to commission for rehearing within 30 days after service of order. Application for rehearing is deemed denied unless acted on by commission within 30 days. Judicial review is obtained by filing notice of appeal with Court of Appeals identifying order complained of and reasons why order is unlawful and praying that order be remanded, modified or set aside. Notice of appeal must be filed within 30 days after commission order on rehearing or within 30 days after application for rehearing is deemed denied. (23-2-421-424).

From Workmen's Compensation Commission.—Appeal from decision of administrative law judge must be filed with Commission within 30 days from receipt of order or award. Appeal from decision of Commission lies with Court of Appeals and is taken by filing notice of appeal within 30 days of receipt of order or award. (11-9-711).

In Injunction or Receivership Cases.—Appeals shall be taken in same manner as appeals from Circuit or Chancery Court. Trial Court may suspend, modify, restore or grant injunction during pendency of appeal, as it considers proper for security of rights of adverse party. (RCP 62).

BONDS:

Bonds required in judicial proceedings may not be held insufficient for want of form if intention of bond can be deduced from its face. (16-68-204).

If a bond required in judicial procedures is adjudged defective, new bond may be required with same effect as though given when first was. (16-68-205).

Sureties may be required to justify qualifications by affidavit before officer taking bond. When justification so made shows surety sufficient, officer taking is protected. (16-68-203). Individual sureties must be Arkansas residents with net worth double sum to be secured. (16-68-203).

Surety bonds required for public work projects must be made with surety companies which are authorized to do business in Arkansas. (22-9-402).

Certificates of Deposit issued by Arkansas savings and loans or banks, or any direct, general obligation security issued by state, its agencies or instrumentalities or U.S. may be substituted for required corporate surety or security bonds. (4-25-102).

Enforcement.—Every bond taken on sale of property under order or decree in chancery or on sale under execution, and every stay bond or forthcoming bond, has force and effect of judgment on which execution may issue. (16-66-117). Upon affirmance by Supreme Court of superseded judgment, court shall award execution against securities or supersedeas bond. (16-67-325).

CERTIORARI:

Supreme Court may issue writs of certiorari in aid of its appellate and supervisory jurisdiction. (Const., art. 7, §4).

Circuit Court may issue writs of certiorari to inferior tribunals, officers, town councils or boards to correct erroneous or void proceedings; temporary restraining orders may be entered; affidavits and evidence outside record may be introduced. Record of inferior tribunal conclusive but acts of officer or board only prima facie evidence of regularity and legality. Court may enforce its judgment by mandamus, prohibition or other appropriate writ. (16-13-205).

CHARITABLE IMMUNITY:

See topic Damages, subhead Charitable Immunity.

COMMISSIONS TO TAKE TESTIMONY:

See topic Depositions and Discovery.

COSTS:

Costs are recoverable by prevailing party if court so directs or if statute or rule makes such award mandatory. (RCP 54).

Security for Costs.—Nonresident plaintiff, intervenor, or corporation other than domestic bank, when commencing action, must file bond to be approved by clerk for costs or cash deposit that may accrue in any court to which case may be taken (16-68-301), in default of which action may be dismissed upon motion of defendant (16-68-301). For minority shareholders bringing derivative action, see category Business Organizations, topic Corporations, subhead Stockholders Actions.

See note at head of Digest as to 1998 legislation covered.

See Topical Index in front part of this volume.

COSTS . . . *continued*

Liability of Attorney.—Where a plaintiff who is required to furnish security for costs (see subhead Security for Costs, supra) fails to do so, plaintiff's attorney is liable as surety for costs. (16-68-306).

Dismissal of Action.—Costs of action previously dismissed may be recovered from plaintiff who has once dismissed or who has suffered involuntary dismissal of action based upon same claim against same defendant in any state or federal court which is then reinstituted in any state or federal court. (RCP 41).

Attorney Fees.—In civil action to recover account or note relating to purchase or sale of goods or services, or breach of contract, prevailing party may recover reasonable attorney fee unless otherwise provided by law or contract which is subject of action. (16-22-308).

Recovery of Attorney Fees for Non-Justiciable Issues.—Where court finds action or defense to be lacking justiciable issue of law or fact and was commenced in bad faith solely to harass or maliciously injure another or to delay adjudication or party or party's attorney knew or should have known of lack of justiciable issue, court shall award attorney fees to prevailing party in amount not exceeding lesser of $5,000 or 10% of amount in controversy. (16-22-309).

Offer of Judgment.—If judgment (exclusive of interest from date of offer of judgment) finally obtained by offeree is not more favorable than offer, offeree must pay costs incurred after making of offer. (RCP 68).

DAMAGES:

Compensatory Damages.—Common law generally prevails.

Punitive Damages.—Common law generally prevails. Arkansas' "shocks the conscience" standard of review for awards of punitive damages is constitutional. (14 F.3d 373).

Statutory penalties may be assessed as follows:

Treble damages for violation of Unfair Trade Practices Act (4-75-211); twofold damages for injuries resulting from agreement between manufacturer or wholesale distributor and retail distributor of motor vehicles to finance sale of vehicles only with or through a designated person (4-75-412); not less than $1,000 nor more than $5,000 for each day of discrimination in rates or service by person engaged in furnishing news for publication (4-75-503); double damages for killing or wounding stock by railroad upon failure of railroad to pay damages fixed by arbitration within 30 days (23-12-912); double charge made by employer engaged in trade or business for goods sold to employees in payment of wages for prices higher than reasonable or current market value thereof in cash (11-4-404); double value of timber, or lumber, staves or shingles made therefrom, knowingly cut, purchased or received from state's or another's land (15-32-301); triple damages for knowingly injuring, destroying, or carrying away property of another (18-60-102); three times monthly rental value for period of unlawful detainer of property entirely or partly commercial (18-60-309); and triple damages for removing improvements from land forfeited for taxes after confirmation of title in state (5-40-103).

Modified Comparative Fault Rule adopted under which plaintiff's fault must be less than defendant's fault in order for plaintiff to recover. (16-64-122). Damages are reduced by degree of plaintiff's fault.

No-Fault Insurance.—See category Transportation, topic Motor Vehicles, subhead No-Fault Insurance.

Charitable immunity prevails (246 Ark. 1231, 442 S.W.2d 243) but see topic Actions, subhead Direct Action Against Insurer. For immunity of governmental entities and nonprofit, tax-exempt corporations, see 16-120-101-104. For volunteer immunity, see 16-6-101-105.

Sovereign immunity prevails but political subdivision of state required to maintain liability insurance on or self insure motor vehicles. (Ark. Const. Art. 5, §20, 21-9-301-303).

See also topic Death, subhead Action for Death.

DECLARATORY JUDGMENTS:

See topic Judgments.

DEPOSITIONS AND DISCOVERY:

Arkansas Rules of Civil Procedure became effective July 1, 1979 and have been amended several times. They generally follow Federal Rules of Civil Procedure.

Any party may take the deposition of any person, including a party, regarding any matter not privileged, upon oral examination or by written interrogatory for discovery or use as evidence or for both purposes. (RCP 30-32).

Uniform Foreign Depositions Act not adopted.

When Taken.—Deposition may be taken without leave of court except when plaintiff seeks to take deposition prior to expiration of 30 days after service of summons and complaint or when witness is confined in prison. (RCP 30).

Compelling Attendance of Witnesses.—Upon filing of notice pursuant to RCP 30(b), clerk of court where action pending may issue subpoena, to be served by sheriff, or other authorized person. (RCP 45). Disobedience is punishable as court deems just, and party may be liable in damages to injured party for failing to appear. (RCP 37).

Use of Depositions.—In any trial or hearing, any part or all of deposition may be used as follows: (1) by any party to impeach deponent as witness or for any purpose permitted by Arkansas Rules of Evidence; (2) by adverse party for any purpose if deponent is party or anyone who, at time of taking deposition was officer, director or managing agent of corporation, partnership, association or governmental agency which is party; (3) by any party for any purpose if court finds (a) that witness is dead, or (b) that witness is more than 100 miles distant or out of state unless absence was procured by party offering deposition, or (c) that witness is unable to attend because of age, illness, infirmity, or imprisonment, or (d) that party offering deposition has been unable to procure attendance of witness by subpoena, or (e) upon application and notice, use would be in interest of justice. If only part of deposition is offered, adverse party may require introduction of all parts that in fairness ought to be considered with part introduced. Use is not affected by substitution of parties, and depositions taken in action dismissed may be used in subsequent action involving same subject matter and parties or their representatives or successors in interest and as otherwise permitted by Rules of Evidence. (RCP 32). Once one party has used part of deposition at trial, opposing party may introduce any other parts, regardless of declarant's availability subject to rules of evidence. (318 Ark. 750, 887 S.W.2d 526). Discovery depositions may be taken in aid of judgment or of execution thereon. (RCP 69). Court may order, upon showing of good cause, videotape depositions which may be presented at trial in lieu of testimony of alleged sexual offense victim under age of 17. (16-44-203).

Perpetuating Testimony.—Before action, depositions to perpetuate testimony may be taken on order of circuit court on verified petition filed in county of residence of any expected adverse party. Petition must show that petitioner expects to be party to action which he is presently unable to bring, subject matter and his interest therein, facts to be established and his reasons to perpetuate testimony, parties expected to be adverse and their addresses if known, names and addresses of persons to be examined, and substance of testimony expected to be elicited. Petitioner must serve 20 days notice and copy of petition on all persons expected to be adverse parties, but if such service cannot be made with due diligence, court may order service by publication and appoint attorney to represent adverse parties. Pending appeal, depositions may be taken on order of trial court upon motion. (RCP 27).

Before Whom Taken.—Depositions within U.S. must be taken before officer authorized to administer oaths or before person authorized by court in which action is pending. Depositions in foreign country may be taken on notice before person authorized to administer oaths either by law of that place or of U.S. or before person commissioned by court or pursuant to any applicable treaty or convention or pursuant to letter of request. Depositions may not be taken before relative, employee, or attorney of any of parties, or relative or employee of such attorney, or person financially interested in action. (RCP 28). Unless court orders otherwise, by written stipulation of parties, depositions may be taken before any person at any time or place on any notice and in any manner. (RCP 29).

Within State for Use in Foreign Country.—Judge of circuit, chancery or probate court in county where witness resides, upon presentation of commission or letter rogatory authorizing taking of deposition upon notice duly served, issues subpoena requiring witness to attend at specified time and place for examination. (RCP 28).

Within State for Use in Other State.—Upon filing certified copy of notice of deposition in compliance with Rule 30(b) with circuit clerk of county where deposition will be taken, circuit clerk shall issue subpoena in accordance with notice. Objections shall be heard by circuit or chancery judge of same county. (RCP 45).

Depositions upon oral examination may be taken by party after reasonable notice in writing given to every other party. Witness must be sworn and his testimony taken by officer personally or by someone under his direction and in his presence recorded stenographically or by sound or sound-and-visual means. Evidence objected to is taken subject to objections noted by officer on deposition. On motion and showing that examination is conducted in bad faith or in such manner as unreasonably to annoy, embarrass, or oppress deponent or party, court in which action is pending or court in district where deposition is being taken may by order terminate deposition or limit scope and manner of its taking. If taking is terminated, it may be resumed only upon order of the court in which action is pending. (RCP 30).

If requested by deponent or party, deponent shall have 30 days after notice that transcript or recording is available to review it, and if there are changes in form or substance, to sign statement reciting such changes and reasons for making them.

Officer must certify that witness was sworn and that deposition is true record of his testimony. Upon payment of reasonable charges therefor, officer must furnish a copy to any party or to deponent. Party taking deposition must furnish one copy for opposing parties and give prompt notice of filing to all parties. (RCP 30).

If party giving the notice to take depositions fails to attend and proceed therewith or fails to serve witness with a subpoena and witness because of such failure does not attend, court may order him to pay the reasonable expenses, including reasonable attorney's fees, of any other party attending in person or by attorney. (RCP 30).

Deposition upon written interrogatories may be taken by service of interrogatories upon every other party with a notice stating name and address of witness and name and address of officer before whom the deposition is to be taken. Cross interrogatories may be served within 14 days; re-direct within seven days; re-cross within seven days. Copy of notice and of all interrogatories must be delivered to officer by party taking deposition. Officer must proceed as in case of depositions upon oral interrogatories to take testimony and prepare, certify, file or mail deposition, with copy of notice and interrogatories attached thereto. When deposition is filed, party taking it must notify all other parties. (RCP 31).

Objections to admissibility may be made at trial or hearing to receive in evidence any deposition or part thereof for any reason which would require exclusion of evidence if witness were present and testifying. (RCP 32). Objection to taking deposition because of disqualification of officer before whom deposition is taken are waived unless made before taking begins or as soon thereafter as disqualification becomes known or could be discovered with reasonable diligence, and errors occurring in oral examination in manner of taking, in form of questions or answers, in oath, or in conduct of parties, and errors which might be obviated if promptly presented, are waived unless objected to at time. (RCP 32). Objections to competency of witness or to competency, relevancy, or materiality of testimony are not waived by failure to make them unless ground of objection might have been obviated at time. Objections to written interrogatories are waived unless timely served in writing upon party propounding them. Objections to manner in which testimony is transcribed or deposition is dealt with by officer are waived unless motion to suppress is promptly made. (RCP 32).

Refusal to Make Discovery.—For refusing to answer questions on oral or written examination, the court in county where deposition is being taken may require the

DEPOSITIONS AND DISCOVERY . . . *continued*

refusing party and the attorney advising the refusal or either of them to pay the examining party reasonable expenses, including reasonable attorney's fees, for obtaining from the court an order compelling an answer. Refusal to answer after being directed to do so may be considered a contempt of court. Court in which action is pending may make such other orders as are just, including an order that the matters shall be taken to be established in accordance with claim of party who obtained order; an order refusing to allow disobedient party to support or oppose designated claims or defenses; an order striking pleadings or parts thereof, or staying further proceedings until the order is obeyed, or dismissing the action or proceedings or any part thereof, or rendering judgment by default against disobedient party. (RCP 37).

Depositions in Criminal Cases.—If prospective witness unable to attend or prevented from attending trial or hearing, if testimony is material, and if taking of deposition is necessary to prevent failure of justice, court may, after filing of indictment or information, upon motion of either party and with adequate notice, order taking of deposition. At trial or hearing, deposition may be used if it appears witness is out of state, dead, or unable to attend because of sickness or infirmity. Deposition will be taken in same manner as in civil actions, by written interrogatories or orally, upon notice. (16-44-201-202; 269 Ark. 44, 598 S.W.2d 96; 227 Ark. 889, 302 S.W.2d 796).

Form

(Caption). The deposition of . ., taken between the hours of . . A.M. and . . P.M., on the . . day of . ., 19. . ., at the . ., in the . . of . . state of . ., to be read as evidence in an action between . ., plaintiff, . . and . ., defendant . ., pending in the . . court, on the part of the . . .

(Certificate).—State of . ., county of . ., I, . ., a qualified . . in and for said county, do hereby certify that the foregoing deposition . . of . . w. . taken before me and w. . read to and subscribed by . . in my presence, at the time and place and in the action mentioned in the caption, the said witness . . having been first sworn by me that the evidence, . . should give in the action should be the truth, the whole truth and nothing but the truth; and . . statements reduced to writing by me in . . presence (or by . . in my presence), the plaintiff . . alone (or the defendant . ., or both plaintiff . . and defendant . ., or either party, in person or by attorney, according to the facts) being present at the examination. Witness my hand and seal this . . day of . ., 19. . .

EQUITY:

See topic Actions.

EVIDENCE: See topic Depositions and Discovery.

Witnesses—Uniform Rules of Evidence adopted with some changes and with omission of Rules 303(c) and 411 and with addition of Rule 803(25) concerning hearsay statements by children under ten in sex offense cases (16-41-101).

INJUNCTIONS:

Injunctions may issue in cases where authorized by the principles of equity or by special statute. The collection of any illegal tax or assessment may be enjoined. (Const., art. 16, §13).

Jurisdiction is ordinarily in chancery court. Circuit court, or county court in absence of circuit judge, may issue injunction as a provisional remedy. (16-55-112; 16-113-301).

Procedure.—Preliminary injunction or temporary restraining order may be granted without notice where by affidavit or verified complaint it is shown that irreparable harm will or might result. In all other cases, reasonable notice and hearing is required. Injunction to stop construction, ordinary business operations, or nuisance requires notice and bond. If injunction or temporary restraining order is granted without notice, hearing shall be held by issuing court as quickly as possible. (RCP 65).

Bond.—May be required at court's discretion, and is required on injunctions halting construction, nuisance, or ordinary business operations. (RCP 65).

Duration.—Preliminary injunction or temporary restraining order remains in effect until dissolved or until final order, and may, upon good cause shown, be made permanent. (RCP 65).

JUDGMENTS:

Governed in general by Rules of Civil Procedure adopted by Supreme Court effective July 1, 1979, which are similar to Federal Rules of Civil Procedure.

All judgments rendered in open court by court of record are effective from date rendered and not from date of entry of record. (16-65-121).

Judgment by confession may be entered with consent of plaintiff against defendant personally appearing in court and confessing judgment. It is enforceable as other judgments, and confession operates as a release of errors. (16-65-301-304).

Judgments by consent are not appealable. (79 Ark. 95, 94 S.W. 932).

Summary judgment may be obtained on motion by surety against principal or cosurety, by client against attorney, and by litigant against sheriff, constable or other officer for money or property collected for litigant. (16-65-201). Ten days notice of hearing on motion is required. (16-65-201).

For Plaintiff.—After 20 days from commencement of action or after service of motion for summary judgment by adverse party, plaintiff may move, with or without supporting affidavits, for summary judgment for all or any part of relief sought. (RCP 56).

For Defendant.—Defendant may at any time move, with or without supporting affidavits, for summary judgment in his favor as to all or any part thereof. (RCP 56).

Procedure.—Motion for summary judgment must be served at least ten days before time fixed for hearing. Adverse party may serve opposing affidavits prior to day of hearing. Judgment must be rendered forthwith if pleadings, depositions, and admissions on file, together with affidavits, if any, show there is no genuine issue as to any material

fact and that moving party is entitled to judgment as matter of law. Summary judgment interlocutory in nature may be rendered on issue of liability alone although there is genuine issue as to damages. (RCP 56).

Form of Affidavits.—Affidavits must be made on personal knowledge, set forth facts admissible in evidence, and show affirmatively that affiant is competent to testify. Sworn or certified copies of all papers referred to in affidavit must be attached thereto or served therewith. Court may permit affidavit to be supplemented or opposed by deposition or further affidavit. If it appears that any such affidavit is presented in bad faith or solely for purpose of delay, court may order party employing it to pay other party amount of reasonable expenses incurred, including reasonable attorneys fees, and any offending party or attorney may be adjudged guilty of contempt. (RCP 56).

Declaratory Judgment.—Uniform act adopted with variations. (16-111-101-111). Procedure is in accordance with RCP 57.

Default judgments may be entered only by court. Court has power to conduct hearing or require trial by jury on damages or to establish any other issue. Court may set aside previously entered default. Complaint against defendant who is constructively summoned and does not appear must be proved unless plaintiff files affidavit that allegations are true, and cannot be proved, except by defendant's answer. (RCP 55; 16-63-216).

Offer of judgment by defendant, which is refused imposes liability for subsequent costs on plaintiff unless recovery exceeds amount offered. Claimant has ten days to respond. (RCP 68).

Vacation or Modification.—Ninety days after judgment is filed with clerk, court may vacate or modify judgment (except default judgment) by granting new trial because of newly discovered evidence; for misprision of clerk; fraud of successful party; erroneous proceedings against infant or insane person where neither disability nor error appears on record; death of party before judgment; or for errors shown by infant within one year after reaching majority. Party seeking relief must show valid defense. Default judgment against defendant constructively summoned, except for divorce, may be reopened on motion within two years after entry, but plaintiff may reduce period to one year by service of certified copy of judgment on defendant. (RCP 60).

Lien.—Judgments and decrees of circuit, chancery and supreme court of this state and U.S. district or bankruptcy courts are liens on real estate of defendant within county in which rendered. Such judgments may be made liens on land in other counties by filing certified copies in office of circuit clerks therein. (16-65-117). Lien on realty expires at end of ten years, but may be extended for successive ten year periods by scire facias. (16-65-117; 501). Judgments of justice of peace courts become lien on real estate by filing transcript with clerk of circuit court. (RIC 8). Judgment debtor is required to file schedule of exempt property within 45 days of entry of judgment. Final judgment order shall require such filing but failure to do so will not invalidate judgment. (16-66-221).

Revival.—All judgments and decrees are barred after ten years, but they may be revived within that period by suing out scire facias and serving it on defendant or his legal representatives. (16-65-501).

Assignment of judgment or cause of action must be acknowledged like deed and filed in the action. (16-65-120).

Satisfaction must be entered upon the judgment record by the party, his attorney or agent duly appointed in writing, within 60 days after receipt of payment. (16-65-602).

Usual form of satisfaction: The within judgment is satisfied in full. (Date and signature.)

Judgment notes are not permitted.

Bonds Having Effect of Judgments.—See topic Bonds.

Foreign Judgments.—Uniform Enforcement of Foreign Judgments Act has been adopted. (16-66-601-608).

LIMITATION OF ACTIONS:

Uniform Commercial Code prescribes time when an action accrues on contract for sale of goods (4-2-725) and imposes limitation of four years for actions brought for breach of contract (4-2-725) and prescribes time when action accrues on commercial paper (4-3-118) and imposes following limitations:

One year.—Limitation period for reporting to bank unauthorized endorsement. (4-4-406).

Thirty Days.—Limitation period for reporting to bank unauthorized signature or altered instrument. (4-4-406).

Actions must be commenced within following periods after respective causes of action accrue. (16-56-101-127; 18-11-102-104; 18-61-101-105).

Ten Years.—Actions on judgments. (16-56-114).

Eight Years.—Actions on bonds of executors or administrators. (16-56-113).

Seven Years.—Actions for recovery of real property. (18-61-101).

Five Years.—Actions to enforce written obligations, duties, or rights (16-56-111); actions for deficiency in design, planning, supervision or observation of construction (16-56-112); all actions not otherwise provided for (16-56-115). For will contest, see category Estates and Trusts, topic Wills, subhead Contest.

Four Years.—Actions on official bonds (but not on bonds of executors or administrators) (16-56-110).

Three Years.—Actions on open accounts, on express or implied contracts not in writing, for trespass on lands, for taking or injuring goods or chattels, to recover possession of personal property, for personal injury or libel. (16-56-105). Wrongful death. (16-62-102).

Two Years.—Actions for medical malpractice. (16-114-203).

One Year.—Actions for assault and battery, false imprisonment or slander. (16-56-104).

LIMITATION OF ACTIONS . . . continued

New action may be brought after time, if brought within one year after judgment of nonsuit or reversal, or of arrest of judgment in action brought in time. (16-56-126). Wrongful death action may be refiled within one year of nonsuit. (16-62-102).

Deficient Design or Construction.—Actions on contracts for damages resulting from deficiency in design, planning, or supervision of construction or construction of improvements on real property must be brought within five years after substantial completion of construction; for personal injury or wrongful death resulting from such deficiency within four years after substantial completion; for personal injury occurring during third year after substantial completion not later than five years after substantial completion; provided no action may lie against person furnishing design if design not used within three years from date furnished. (16-56-112).

Foreign Debtors.—If debtor fraudulently absconds from any other state, territory or district to Arkansas without knowledge of his creditor, such creditor may commence suit against such debtor within time prescribed for particular action, period running from time when creditor becomes apprised of residence of absconding debtor. (16-56-121).

Disabilities of Plaintiff.—Where person in whose favor cause of action accrues is, at time of such accrual, an infant, insane or imprisoned outside of the state, action may be commenced within three years after disability is removed. (16-56-116).

Person in U. S. armed services while U. S. is engaged in war has one year after the end of such war and six months thereafter in which to sue to collect debt or to recover property, provided action was not barred prior to his entry into the armed services. (16-56-118). Statutes of limitation are suspended during time of war so far as they affect claim or cause of action of person in armed forces and for six months thereafter. (16-56-118).

Death of Plaintiff.—If a person entitled to sue dies before expiration of limitation his representative has one year after death to bring action, though limitation expires before end of year. (16-56-117).

Barred debts may be revived by part payment or written acknowledgment.

Vendor's or mortgagee's lien expires when the debt is barred, and is not extended by payments unless entered on the margin of the record of the deed and dated and attested by the circuit clerk. (18-49-101).

Contractual limitations are permitted. (52 Ark. 11, 11 S.W. 1016; 101 Ark. 310, 142 S.W. 176; 258 Ark. 1009, 531 S.W.2d 8).

Statute as to unknown tortfeasor may be tolled by filing complaint in appropriate court along with affidavit stating that identity of tortfeasor is unknown. (16-56-125). See also category Business Regulation and Commerce, topic Securities.

PARTITION:

Real estate owned in common may be partitioned by proceedings in either circuit or chancery court (18-60-401) and, if it is shown to be incapable of division in kind without great prejudice to owners, may be sold and proceeds divided according to interests of parties (18-60-420). When undivided interest in parcel of land containing at least ten acres is purchased after June 28, 1985, by stranger to title, purchaser shall not have cause of action to partition land until expiration of three years. However any persons or entities which individually or in combination own 50% or more of parcel may institute partition proceedings at any time. (18-60-404).

PLEADING:

Rules of procedure adopted by Arkansas Supreme Court on July 1, 1979 are similar to Federal Rules of Civil Procedure.

Pleadings Permitted.—Only pleadings allowed are complaint, answer, counterclaim, reply to counterclaim denominated as such, answer to crossclaim, third party complaint, and third party answer. (RCP 7).

Complaint must contain statement supporting jurisdiction and venue, statement of facts showing pleader is entitled to relief, and demand for relief to which pleader considers himself entitled. (RCP 8). Averments of fraud, mistake, duress or undue influence must be stated with particularity. (RCP 9).

Demurrers are abolished. (RCP 7).

Answer must state defenses to each claim asserted and must admit or deny averments upon which opponent relies. General denials are allowed where pleader intends in good faith to controvert all averments. Avoidances and affirmative defenses must be set forth affirmatively. Items not denied are admitted. (RCP 8).

Counterclaim may be unconnected with transaction or occurrence that is subject matter of opposing party's claim. Counterclaims arising from same transaction or occurrence which is subject matter of opposing party's claim must be raised. (RCP 13).

Amendments of complaint may be made without leave of court at any time. Upon motion, court may strike amendments or grant continuances if prejudice results or if amendment would cause undue delay. Amendments must be answered within time remaining for response to original pleading or within 20 days after service. (RCP 15).

Verification is generally not required. (RCP 11).

Service of pleadings subsequent to complaint is made by delivering copy to party if required or to his attorney, by mailing to him at his last known address, or by leaving it with clerk of court if no address is known. (RCP 5[b]). See also topic Process.

Filing.—Pleadings must be filed with clerk of court either before service or within reasonable time after service. (RCP 5).

Time allowed for answer is 20 days after service of summons in state, whether service is personal or on designated or statutory agent, 30 days for nonresident defendants and 30 days after date of first publication of warning order in case of constructive service. Time for reply to counterclaim is 20 days after service. (RCP 12).

Where accounts are sued on, affidavit of plaintiff or agent, filed with complaint, that same are just and correct is taken as prima facie true, unless controverted under oath as

to whole or part by defendant, then other evidence is necessary to prove that part disputed. (16-45-104).

Frivolous claims are subject to sanctions under RCP 11 which is substantially similar to FRCP 11.

In inferior court written complaint is required. (RIC 4).

Small Claims.—See category Courts and Legislature, topic Courts, subheads Justices' Courts, Municipal Courts, Small Claims Courts.

PRACTICE:

Governed by Rules of Civil Procedure which are based on Federal Rules with modifications. (Tit. 16, Rules 1-86).

Discovery procedure is generally based on Rules 26-37 of Federal Rules of Civil Procedure with some modifications. Generally, time for answering interrogatories is 30 days. (RCP 33).

Demand for Admission of Facts.—Any party has right to written request for admission of truth of any discoverable matter. Generally, matter is admitted unless objection is made within 30 days. (RCP 36).

See also topics Actions, Appeal and Error, Depositions and Discovery, Injunctions, Judgments, Pleading, Process; category Debtor and Creditor, topics Executions, Garnishment.

Direct Actions Against Insurer.—See topic Actions, subhead Direct Action Against Insurer.

Small Claims.—See category Courts and Legislature, topic Courts, subheads Justices' Courts, Municipal Courts.

See also topics Actions, Appeal and Error, Depositions and Discovery, Injunctions, Judgments, Pleading, Process; category Debtor and Creditor, topics Attachment, Executions, Garnishment.

PROCESS:

Summons is issued by clerk upon filing of complaint. (RCP 4).

Who May Serve.—Summons is served by sheriff or person appointed by court for that purpose or by plaintiff or his attorney by mail as allowed by rules. Service upon defendant, other than unknown tortfeasor, whose identity or whereabouts is unknown may be by warning order. (RCP 4).

Personal Service Inside State.—By delivery of copy of summons and complaint to defendant, or if he refuses it, by offering copy, or by leaving copy at his usual place of abode with some person residing there at least 14 years of age, or by delivering copy to authorized agent. (RCP 4[d]). Service may also be by any form of mail return receipt requested and delivery restricted to addressee or his agent, but such service shall not support default judgment unless record shows signed return receipt or evidence of refusal. (RCP 4[d][8]).

Service Outside State.—May be by personal delivery or by any form of mail with return receipt requested and delivery restricted to addressee. (RCP 4[e]).

Upon Defendant Whose Identity or Whereabouts is Unknown.—Service must be by warning order issued by clerk and published weekly two consecutive weeks in newspaper of general circulation in county where action filed and by mailing copy of complaint and warning order to defendant at last known address by any form of mail delivery restricted to addressee. This procedure does not apply to unknown tortfeasors. (RCP 4[f]).

On Infant.—Where defendant is under 14 years, service must be upon parent or guardian or other person having care and control of infant and with whom infant lives. Where infant is at least 14 years, service shall be upon him. (RCP 4[d] [2]).

On Incompetent Person.—Service must be upon individual and his appointed guardian; if confined to institution for mentally ill, upon superintendent of institution and upon guardian. (RCP 4[d] [3]).

On Defendant Confined in State or Federal Penitentiary or Correctional Facility.—Service must be upon keeper or superintendent of institution who shall deliver copy of summons and complaint to defendant. Copy of summons and complaint shall also be delivered to spouse of defendant, if any, unless court excuses. (RCP 4[d] [4]).

Upon Domestic or Foreign Corporation, Partnership, Limited Liability Company or Unincorporated Association.—Service is by delivering copy of summons and complaint to officer, partner other than limited partner, managing or general agent, or to any agent authorized by appointment or by law to receive service. (RCP 4[d][5]).

In Suit Against Insurer.—Domestic insurer is served by serving president, chairman of board, or agent. Service on foreign insurers may be had upon Commissioner of Insurance who shall mail by registered mail copy of such process to defendant at its principal place of business. (23-79-205, 23-63-301-302).

On Owner or Operator of Motor Buses or Trucks.—Service may be upon any clerk or agent selling tickets or transacting any business for owner or operator, or upon any driver or chauffeur of any bus, coach, or truck being or driven by servant, agent, or employee. (16-58-122).

On Issuer of or Dealer in Securities.—In action arising out of sale of securities, service may be upon Securities Commissioner. Plaintiff must send copy to defendant and file affidavit of compliance before return day. (23-42-107).

In Action for Personal Injury or Wrongful Death.—Service may be had in addition to other methods by serving any agent who is regular employee of party to be served and on duty at time of service. (16-58-118).

Service on Secretary of State.—Any resident or nonresident who commits acts in state sufficient to give individual cause of action against person committing act deemed to have appointed Secretary of State as agent for service of process. Service on Secretary of State sufficient if person has subsequently absented himself from state or upon executor, administrator, or personal representative of estate if notice sent by certified

PROCESS . . . *continued*

mail to defendant at last known address and return receipt attached to summons and filed with court. (16-58-120).

Long Arm Jurisdiction.—Court may exercise personal jurisdiction over all persons, and all causes of action or claims for relief, to maximum extent permitted by due process of law clause of Fourteenth Amendment of U.S. Constitution. (16-4-101).

When exercise of personal jurisdiction is authorized by this section, service may be made either within or outside state. (16-4-101).

Uniform Interstate and International Procedure Act adopted with omission of §§3.01 and 3.02. (16-4-101-108).

Nonresident Motorist.—See category Transportation, topic Motor Vehicles.

REPLEVIN:

Action in replevin may be brought for the recovery of specific personal property.

Affidavit.—Plaintiff must file with complaint an affidavit describing the property, stating its value and any damages for detention, showing plaintiff's ownership or right to possession, asserting the cause for wrongful detention, stating that property has not been taken for a tax or fine or by judicial process and that cause of action accrued within three years. (18-60-810).

If plaintiff files additional affidavit that property has been concealed, removed or disposed of with intent to defeat plaintiff's action, court may order sheriff, if property cannot be had, to arrest defendant. (18-60-811).

Opportunity for hearing upon notice required before order to deliver property obtained. (18-60-805). If defendant served notice with summons and complaint order may be entered after five business days notice. (18-60-808). Plaintiff may obtain possession upon court order by giving bond to defendant that plaintiff will duly prosecute action, perform judgment of court, return property if adjudged, and pay any sum adjudged against him, not to exceed double value of property and costs. (18-60-812).

Hearing Before Notice.—Order impounding property prior to hearing may be issued if genuine danger shown that property will be removed, damaged or concealed. (18-60-807).

Redelivery may be obtained by defendant by filing with sheriff, within two days after taking of property by sheriff, bond similar to that required of plaintiff. (18-60-816).

Claim of third persons may be asserted by filing with sheriff an affidavit showing right to possession of property. Sheriff is not then required to keep property or deliver it to plaintiff unless plaintiff, within two days after receiving copy of affidavit, gives sheriff a bond in double the value of the property, indemnifying him against such claim. (18-60-818).

Judgment for plaintiff is for delivery of the property or its value in case delivery cannot be had, and for damages for detention. Judgment for defendant is for return of property, or its value, and damages for taking. (18-60-820).

Replevin procedure in 18-60-809-822 may be unconstitutional to extent defendant denied use of property without notice and opportunity for hearing. (407 U.S. 67).

SEQUESTRATION:

See topic Replevin.

SERVICE:

See topic Process.

STAY OF EXECUTION:

See topic Appeal and Error; category Debtor and Creditor, topic Executions.

SUBMISSION OF CONTROVERSY:

A question may be submitted on agreed case of a civil nature to a court in which it might be litigated, without action, if it appears by affidavit that the controversy is real and submitted in good faith, to determine the rights of the parties. The court may render judgment, enforceable and subject to reversal as in other cases, unless otherwise agreed in the submission. (16-118-101).

VENUE:

Pleading.—Complaint must include facts showing that court has jurisdiction and that venue is proper. (RCP 8[a]).

Real Actions.—Actions for recovery or partition of real property, for foreclosure of incumbrance thereon or injury thereto, must be brought in the county where the land or some part thereof is located. (16-60-101).

Personal actions, in general, may be brought in county in which any defendant resides or is summoned. (16-60-116).

Where action is local rather than transitory, summons may be served on defendant in any county in which he may be found. (16-60-117).

Action for personal injury or death occurring inside state must be brought in county where accident occurred or in county where injured/deceased person resided at time of injury. (16-60-112). Action for personal injury or death occurring outside state must be brought in county where person injured or killed resided at time of injury or in any other county where any defendant resides or is summoned. (16-60-112).

All actions against, or brought by, state, state boards, state commissions, or state officers on account of their official acts must be brought in Pulaski County. (16-60-103).

Action for wrongful or negligent damage to personal property, whether arising from contract, tort or conversion, may be brought in county where damage occurred, or in county where property was converted, or in county of residence of owner of property when cause of action arose. (16-60-113).

Contract action by resident subcontractor, supplier or materialman against nonresident prime or subcontractor may be brought in county where plaintiff resided when cause arose. (16-60-114).

Action against domestic corporation may be brought in the county in which it is situated or has a principal office, or in which its chief officer resides, but if it is a bank or insurance company, action may be brought in any county where it has a branch office, if the cause arose from transaction of branch. (16-60-104).

Action for divorce is brought in county of plaintiff's residence or county of defendant's residence if plaintiff is nonresident (9-12-303), but may be transferred to county of either party's residence upon agreement of parties and both courts (16-60-207). When spouse initiates action for absolute divorce, divorce from bed and board, or separate maintenance, venue for initial action shall be venue for any of these named actions filed by other spouse regardless of residency of other spouse. (9-12-303). If both parties establish residency in another district six months after issuance of final decree, proceedings may be brought in county of residence of custodial parent or where final decree is rendered. (9-12-320).

Action against a railroad for injury to person or property may be brought in any county through which it passes. (16-60-106; 161 Ark. 552, 256 S.W. 862).

Action on contractor's performance bond may be brought in county where loss occurred, county of insured's residence at time of loss, or county of beneficiary's residence at time of loss. (16-60-115).

Action to recover a fine, penalty or forfeiture, or against a public officer, or upon official bond of public officer must be brought in county where cause of action, or some part, arose. (16-60-102).

Probate and administration of will shall be in county where decedent resided at time of death or, if nonresident, where property is located, where decedent died, or where personal representative can maintain cause of action. (28-40-102).

Action to annul marriage may be brought in county where plaintiff resides. (9-12-202).

Action against insurance company must be brought in county where loss occurred, or insured died, or county of insured's residence at time of loss or death. (23-79-204). Actions brought against insurer when insured is legally immune may be brought in county where damage occurred or where one of plaintiffs resided at time of damage. (23-79-204). Venue of other action against insurers are governed by 16-60-104. (23-79-204).

Action against nonresidents or non-qualified foreign corporations may be brought in any county in which they may have property or debts due them. (16-60-108; 260 Ark. 874; 545 S.W.2d 612). However, venue cannot constitutionally be had against foreign corporations in any county where suit would not be proper against domestic corporation. (289 Ark. 27, 709 S.W.2d 74).

Action for fraud may be brought in county where any plaintiff resides or any defendant is located, in county where any act of inducement, perpetuation, or concealment performed, or in county where any part of fraudulent scheme was originated or was communicated from or into by any means. (16-60-113).

Actions on debt, account or note may be brought in county in which defendant resided at time cause of action arose (16-60-111).

Contract actions against nonresidents or foreign corporations may be brought in county in which plaintiff resided at time cause of action arose. (16-60-109). However, this section is unconstitutional when foreign corporation is one that has qualified to do business in state. (326 Ark. 100, 928 S.W.2d 796).

Change of Venue.—Civil actions in jury cases may be changed upon verified motion stating that the party verily believes fair trial cannot be obtained in that county on account of undue prejudice in county or adversary's undue influence. (16-60-201). Venue shall not be changed unless court finds that change is necessary to obtain fair and impartial trial of cause. (16-60-202). Domestic relations cases may be transferred to county of either party's residence upon agreement of parties and court. (16-60-207).

COURTS AND LEGISLATURE

COURTS:

United States District Courts.—

Eastern District.—Clerk's office: Little Rock 72203.

Eastern Division is composed of following counties: Cross, Lee, Monroe, Phillips, St. Francis and Woodruff. Sessions are held at Helena.

Northern Division is composed of following counties: Cleburne, Fulton, Independence, Izard, Jackson, Sharp and Stone. Sessions are held at Batesville.

Jonesboro Division is composed of following counties: Clay, Craighead, Crittenden, Greene, Lawrence, Mississippi, Poinsett and Randolph, Sessions are held at Jonesboro.

Western Division is composed of following counties: Conway, Faulkner, Lonoke, Perry, Pope, Prairie, Pulaski, Saline, Van Buren, White and Yell. Sessions are held at Little Rock.

Pine Bluff Division is composed of following counties: Arkansas, Chicot, Cleveland, Dallas, Desha, Drew, Grant, Jefferson and Lincoln. Sessions are held at Pine Bluff.

Fees.—A fee of $150 must be deposited with clerk on commencement of an action. In addition, marshal's fees for service of process must be paid.

Western District.—Clerk's office: Fort Smith 72902.

Texarkana Division is composed of following counties: Hempstead, Howard, Lafayette, Little River, Miller, Nevada and Sevier. Sessions are held at Texarkana.

Fort Smith Division is composed of following counties: Crawford, Franklin, Johnson, Logan, Polk, Scott and Sebastian. Sessions are held at Fort Smith.

Harrison Division is composed of following counties: Baxter, Boone, Carroll, Marion, Newton and Searcy. Sessions are held at Harrison.

El Dorado Division is composed of following counties: Ashley, Bradley, Calhoun, Columbia, Ouachita and Union. Sessions are held at El Dorado.

COURTS . . . *continued*

Hot Springs Division is composed of following counties: Clark, Garland, Hot Spring, Montgomery and Pike. Sessions are held at Hot Springs.

Fayetteville Division is composed of following counties: Benton, Madison and Washington. Sessions are held at Fayetteville.

Fees.—A fee of $150 must be deposited with clerk on commencement of an action. In addition, marshal's fees for service of process must be paid.

Out of State counsel must associate with local counsel.

Supreme Court.—Supreme Court has appellate jurisdiction of all cases in circuit and chancery courts, and general superintending control over all inferior courts of law and equity. Initial appellate jurisdiction for all cases in circuit and chancery courts lies in Court of Appeals except for following: cases involving Arkansas Constitution; criminal cases in which death penalty, life imprisonment, or sentence of more than 30 years is imposed; cases in which state statute, municipal ordinance or agency relation is challenged; appeals from Highway Commission or Pollution Control and Ecology Commission; post-conviction petition under A.R.Crim.P.37; cases of quo warranto, prohibition, injunction, or mandamus directed to state, county, or municipal officials or to circuit, chancery or probate courts; cases pertaining to elections; discipline of attorneys or judges; motions for rule on clerk; where earlier appeal in same case was heard by Supreme Court; interlocutory appeal permitted by statute or rule; usury cases; product liability cases; oil, gas or mineral rights cases; tort cases; and cases involving construction of deeds or wills. (Rules of Supreme Court 1-2[a]). In aid of its appellate and supervisory jurisdiction, it has power to grant an appeal, issue writs of error, supersedeas, certiorari, habeas corpus, prohibition, mandamus, quo warranto, and other remedial writs. It has original jurisdiction to issue quo warranto to circuit judges and chancellors and to officers of political corporations when legal existence of such corporations is questioned.

$100 fee for costs must be paid to Clerk of Supreme Court by appellant or petitioner, in advance, in all civil actions and misdemeanors filed in Supreme Court or Court of Appeals. $25 must be paid, in advance, to Clerk of Supreme Court, by petitioner for each petition for review of decision of Court of Appeals. (21-6-401).

Court sits at Little Rock.

Court of Appeals.—Created July 1, 1979; jurisdiction established by Supreme Court rule as initial appellate level for civil and criminal appeals. Appeals filed through Clerk of Supreme Court. Court sits at Little Rock and may sit in divisions. (16-12-101-114).

Circuit Courts.—Have appellate and supervisory control over county courts, courts of common pleas, corporation courts and justices' courts: have original jurisdiction over all cases where amount in controversy exceeds $100 exclusive of interest; have original jurisdiction in criminal matters. $5 may be collected from each defendant as costs upon conviction and upon each guilty plea in felony and misdemeanor cases. (16-92-110).

Chancery Courts.—Chancery courts have jurisdiction of all cases in equity, and of divorce and paternity. (16-13-304). Juvenile divisions of chancery courts have jurisdiction over juvenile delinquency and violations of criminal laws committed by juveniles, previously vested in juvenile division of circuit court and over "juveniles in need of supervision" and "dependent-neglected juveniles", previously vested in juvenile division of probate court. (16-13-601-07).

Circuit and Chancery Courts sit as follows:

Arkansas County: Eleventh District-East; court sits at DeWitt. Northern District, court sits at Stuttgart.
Ashley County: Tenth District; court sits at Hamburg.
Baxter County: Fourteenth District; court sits at Mountain Home.
Benton County: Nineteenth District; court sits at Bentonville.
Boone County: Fourteenth District; court sits at Harrison.
Bradley County: Tenth District; court sits at Warren.
Calhoun County: Thirteenth District; court sits at Hampton.
Carroll County: Nineteenth District; Western District, court sits at Eureka Springs. Eastern District, court sits at Berryville.
Chicot County: Tenth District; court sits at Lake Village.
Clark County: Ninth District-East; court sits at Arkadelphia.
Clay County: Second District; Eastern District, court sits at Piggott. Western District, court sits at Corning.
Cleburne County: Sixteenth District; court sits at Heber Springs.
Cleveland County: Eleventh District-West; court sits at Rison.
Columbia County: Thirteenth District; court sits at Magnolia.
Conway County: Fifteenth District; court sits at Morrilton.
Craighead County: Second District; Jonesboro District, court sits at Jonesboro. Lake City District, court sits at Lake City.
Crawford County: Twelfth District; court sits at Van Buren.
Crittenden County: Second District; court sits at Marion.
Cross County: First District; court sits at Wynne.
Dallas County: Thirteenth District; court sits at Fordyce.
Desha County: Tenth District; court sits at Arkansas City and at McGehee.
Drew County: Tenth District; court sits at Monticello.
Faulkner County: Twentieth District; court sits at Conway.
Franklin County: Fifth District; Ozark District, court sits at Ozark; Charleston District, court sits at Charleston.
Fulton County: Sixteenth District; court sits at Salem.
Garland County: Eighteenth District-East; court sits at Hot Springs.
Grant County: Seventh District; court sits at Sheridan.
Greene County: Second District; court sits at Paragould.
Hempstead County: Eighth District; court sits at Hope.
Hot Spring County: Seventh District; court sits at Malvern.
Howard County: Ninth District-West; court sits at Nashville.
Independence County: Sixteenth District; court sits at Batesville.
Izard County: Sixteenth District; court sits at Melbourne.
Jackson County: Third District; court sits at Newport.
Jefferson County: Eleventh District-West; court sits at Pine Bluff.
Johnson County: Fifth District; court sits at Clarksville.
Lafayette County: Eighth District; court sits at Lewisville.
Lawrence County: Third District; Western District, court sits at Powhatan. Eastern District, court sits at Walnut Ridge.
Lee County: First District; court sits at Marianna.
Lincoln County: Eleventh District-West; court sits at Star City.
Little River County: Ninth District-West; court sits at Ashdown.
Logan County: Fifteenth District; Northern District, court sits at Paris. Southern District, court sits at Booneville.
Lonoke County: Seventeenth District-West; court sits at Lonoke.
Madison County: Fourth District; court sits at Huntsville.
Marion County: Fourteenth District; court sits at Yellville.
Miller County: Eighth District; court sits at Texarkana.
Mississippi County: Second District; Osceola District, court sits at Osceola. Chickasawba District, court sits at Blytheville.
Monroe County: First District; court sits at Clarendon.
Montgomery County: Eighteenth District-West; court sits at Mt. Ida.
Nevada County: Eighth District; court sits at Prescott.
Newton County: Fourteenth District; court sits at Jasper.
Ouachita County: Thirteenth District; court sits at Camden.
Perry County: Sixth District; court sits at Perryville.
Phillips County: First District; court sits at Helena.
Pike County: Ninth District-East; court sits at Murfreesboro.
Poinsett County: Second District; court sits at Harrisburg.
Polk County: Eighteenth District-West; court sits at Mena.
Pope County: Fifth District; court sits at Russellville.
Prairie County: Seventeenth District-East; Northern District, court sits at Des Arc. Southern District, court sits at Devalls Bluff.
Pulaski County: Sixth District; court sits at Little Rock.
Randolph County: Third District; court sits at Pocahontas.
Saline County: Seventh District; court sits at Benton.
Scott County: Fifteenth District; court sits at Waldron.
Searcy County: Twentieth District; court sits at Marshall.
Sebastian County: Twelfth District; court sits at Greenwood. Court also sits at Fort Smith.
Sevier County: Ninth District-West; court sits at De Queen.
Sharp County: Third District; Southern District, court sits at Evening Shade. Northern District, court sits at Hardy. Jurisdiction at either place co-extensive with county.
St. Francis County: First District; court sits at Forrest City.
Stone County: Sixteenth District; court sits at Mountain View.
Union County: Thirteenth District; court sits at El Dorado.
Van Buren County: Twentieth District; court sits at Clinton.
Washington County: Fourth District; courts sits at Fayetteville.
White County: Seventeenth District-East; court sits at Searcy.
Woodruff County: First District; court sits at Augusta.
Yell County: Fifteenth District; Danville District, court sits at Danville; Dardanelle District, court sits at Dardanelle.

Probate Courts.—Probate courts have exclusive jurisdiction in matters pertaining to probate of wills, administration of estates of decedents, and guardianship of minors and insane persons.

For most purposes probate courts have been consolidated with chancery courts. (Const. Amendment 24). Judge of chancery court is judge of probate courts for all counties within his chancery district. Circuit clerk is clerk of probate courts in all counties having less than 15,000 population according to last census; in more populous counties, county clerk is clerk of probate court.

Chancellor may appoint Referee in Probate to handle all business of Probate Court (except in commitment process of mentally ill persons) (16-14-201-205), but order of Referee is not final and must be approved by Chancellor (214 Ark. 755, 217 S.W.2d 849).

County Courts.—County courts have exclusive original jurisdiction in matters relating to county taxes, roads, erection of bridges and county buildings, paupers, bastardy, apprenticeship, elections, property of county, and settlement of demands against county and disbursement of money for county purposes (14-14-1105) and over petitions by landowners outside city or town to vacate public utility easements over land (18-60-901).

Common Pleas Courts.—Common pleas courts are established in certain counties by special legislation and presided over by county and probate judges. Their jurisdiction is limited to amounts of $1,000 and less in contract and civil matters not affecting title to or liens upon realty, and is concurrent with circuit and justices' courts. (16-16-201-1115).

Justices' Courts.—Justices of peace have jurisdiction concurrent with municipal courts and exclusive of circuit court of actions on contracts involving not more than $100, exclusive of interest, concurrent with municipal courts and circuit court of actions on contracts involving no more than $300, exclusive of interest, of actions of replevin of property not exceeding $300 in value, and of actions for damages to personal property not involving over $100. (16-19-401).

Their territorial jurisdiction includes their counties, in cases of replevin, attachment, or garnishment, but in other cases is limited to their townships. (16-19-402).

Municipal Courts.—May be established in cities of 2,400 population or over or in county-seat towns of less than 2,400 by city ordinance. (16-17-204). These courts have exclusive jurisdiction over violations of ordinances passed by city council or quorum court of county where municipal court situated, exclusive of justices of peace and concurrent with circuit court's jurisdiction over misdemeanors committed in county and issuance of search warrants, concurrent with justices of peace and exclusive of circuit court's jurisdiction over matters of contract not to exceed $100, exclusive police powers, concurrent jurisdiction with circuit courts in actions not to exceed $5,000 for matters of contract, recovery or for damages to personal property and for personal injuries. (16-17-704). Municipal police or city courts may collect from defendant $5 as

See note at head of Digest as to 1998 legislation covered.

See Topical Index in front part of this volume.

AR – 18

COURTS . . . continued

costs on each felony, misdemeanor and traffic violation offense. (16-17-111). Municipal judges may appoint maximum of two magistrates. (16-17-107). Governing body of city which has created municipal court may prescribe by ordinance method of election of judge of that court. (16-17-120).

Small Claims Courts.—Each municipal court shall establish "small claims division" with jurisdiction in matters of contract, recovery of personal property, and damage to personal property not exceeding $5,000. (16-17-602 and 16-17-704). Action commenced by complaint in substantially form prescribed by 16-17-607. (16-17-607). No prejudgment attachment or garnishment. (16-17-613). Execution on judgments same as for other courts. (16-17-613). Judgment may include order of delivery for recovery of property subject to plaintiff's security interest. (16-17-613). No discovery allowed except in aid of execution. (16-17-612). Corporations organized under laws of state and with no more than three shareholders and corporations in which 85% or more of voting stock is held by persons related within third degree of consanguinity and "closely held corporations" by unanimous vote of shareholders may sue and be sued in small claims division. (16-17-605). Collection agencies, assignees and others engaged primarily or secondarily in business of lending money at interest are prohibited from suing in small claims division. (16-17-604).

See also subheads Justices' Courts and Municipal Courts, supra.

City Courts.—May be established in any city of first class with population of 5,000 or less. City court is in lieu of municipal court. Jurisdiction is concurrent with Justices of the Peace, except that jurisdiction is exclusive for prosecutions for violations of city ordinances. (16-18-111-112).

Juvenile Division of Chancery Court.—In determining whether case involving juvenile should be transferred to another court, Court should consider: (1) seriousness of offense and whether violence was used, (2) whether offense is part of repetitive pattern, (3) prior history, character traits, mental ability and other factors reflecting juvenile's prospects for rehabilitation. (9-27-318).

Statements made by juveniles during intake process not useable or admissible against juvenile. (9-27-321).

Juvenile court may expunge records of juvenile and shall expunge (i.e., destroy) all records of juvenile upon his 21st birthday in delinquency, dependency-neglect, or Families in Need of Services cases. (9-27-309).

Where there is probable cause to believe juvenile is dependent/neglected and that immediate removal of juvenile from custody of his/her parent(s), guardian, or custodian is necessary to protect health or physical well-being of juvenile from immediate danger or prevent juvenile's removal from state, court shall issue emergency ex parte order for juvenile's removal from custody of parent(s), guardian, or custodian. (9-27-314).

Juveniles taken into custody on allegation of delinquency and not released shall be given hearing before Court as soon as possible, but in no event later than 72 hours (excluding weekends and holidays) of time juvenile was first taken into custody. (9-27-313).

Court Reporters.—Official court reporters in this State are state employees. (16-13-501). Court reporters are not liable, criminally or civilly, for unintentional loss, damage or destruction of their official records more than five years old. (16-13-507). Transcript fees are set by statute. (16-13-506). Judicial Department Executive Secretary of State must establish program to make available use of interpreters (transliterators) in cases involving hearing-impaired and bilingual proceedings. (16-10-127).

Appointment of Temporary Judge.—Litigants in any court, except in criminal causes, may stipulate to appointment of temporary judge licensed in Arkansas to practice law. (16-10-115).

Filing By Facsimile.—Pleadings may be filed by facsimile if pleading is transferred onto bond-type paper that can be preserved for at least ten years, or nonbond paper if original is to be substituted for facsimile within ten days of transmission and required number of copies transmitted. (16-20-109). Facsimile copy of court pleading shall be deemed received and filed by court clerk when it is transmitted and received on court clerk's fax machine, regardless of the hours of operation of the clerk's office. (16-20-109).

LEGISLATURE:

Meets biennially starting second Mon. of Jan. in odd years. (10-2-101).

Special sessions may be called by Governor. (Const., art. 6, §19).

Initiative and referendum are provided. (Const., amendment 7).

Lobbyists.—Registration and other filings with Secretary of State required within five days after beginning lobbying. (21-8-601-607). Lobbyists must file quarterly reports within 15 days after each quarter and monthly reports within ten days after end of each month in which General Assembly is in session. (21-8-603).

Extended Session.—In Wells v. Reviere (269 Ark. 156, 599 S.W.2d 375), Arkansas Supreme Court cast doubt on validity of legislative actions taken in extended session (as distinct from extraordinary sessions pursuant to call from governor).

REPORTS:

Decisions of Supreme Court are reported in Arkansas Reports, beginning with vol. 1. Decisions of Court of Appeals are reported in Arkansas Reports beginning with vol. 272 and in Arkansas Appellate Reports beginning with Vol. 1. Arkansas decisions after Vol. 46 Arkansas Reports are also reported in Southwestern Reporter.

Digests are Crawford's Arkansas Digest, six volumes covering vols. 1-181 of reports, with 1938 supplement covering vols. 182-192; and West Pub. Co.'s Arkansas Digest, covering all cases and kept to date with pocket supplements.

STATUTES:

Official compilation prepared by Michie Company under direction of Arkansas Statute Revision Commission dated 1987, with pocket supplement, is currently in use.

Uniform Acts which have been adopted are: Acknowledgment (1943); †Administrative Procedure (1967); †Adoption, Revised (1977); 1987 Anatomical Gift (1989); †Arbitration (1955); Attendance of Witnesses from Without the State in Criminal Cases (1935); Bus. Corp., Revised (1987); Child Custody Jurisdiction (1979); Commercial Code (1961), 1972 Official Amendments (1973); Common Trust Fund (1947); Conflict of Laws-Limitations (1985); †Conservation Easement (1983); Controlled Substances (1970); Contribution Among Tortfeasors (1941); Criminal Extradition (1935); Custodial Trust Act (1991); Declaratory Judgments (1953); Determination of Death (1985); Disposition of Community Property Rights at Death (1981); Disposition of Unclaimed Property, Revised (1979); Division of Income for Tax Purposes (1961); †Durable Power of Attorney (1981); Enforcement of Foreign Judgments (1949); Escheat of Postal Savings System Accounts (1971); Evidence, Rules of (1975) (*Caveat*: Passed in extended session. See topic Legislature; adopted by Arkansas Supreme Court, 290 Ark. 100, 717 S.W. 2d 488); Facsimile Signature of Public Officials (1959); Federal Lien Registration (1989); Fraudulent Transfer (1987); Insurers Liquidation (1959); Interstate and International Procedure Act (1963); Interstate Fresh Pursuant (1959); Revised Limited Partnership Act of 1991 (1979); Machine Gun (1935); Military Justice, Code of (1969); Motor Vehicle Driver's License (1937); Motor Vehicle Safety Responsibility (1953); *Narcotic Drug (1937); *Amendment to Narcotic Drug Act (1959); Partnership (1941); Photographic Copies of Business and Public Records Act (1953); Premarital Agreement (1987); Revised Principal and Income (1971); Revised Reciprocal Enforcement of Support (1969); Regulating Traffic on Highways (1937); Rendition of Prisoners as Witnesses in Criminal Proceedings (1959); Rights of the Terminally Ill (1987); Securities Act (1959); Securities Ownership by Minors Act (1963); Simultaneous Death (1941); Special Power of Attorney for Small Property Interests (1965); Testamentary Additions to Trusts Act (1963); Trade Secrets (1979); Transfers to Minors (1985); Unauthorized Insurers (1939); Veteran's Guardianship (1929).

†Adopted with significant variations or modifications. See appropriate topics.
*Uniform Controlled Substances Act largely supersedes these Acts.

Other Uniform Acts adopted are: Motor Vehicle Administration Certificate of Title and Antitheft (1949).

Uniform Commercial Code adopted, effective Jan. 1, 1962. See category Business Regulation and Commerce, topic Commercial Code.

For text of Uniform Acts falling within the scope of the Martindale-Hubbell Law Digests see Uniform and Model Acts section.

UNIFORM LAWS:

For list of Uniform Acts in force in this state see topic Statutes. For text of Uniform Acts within the scope of the Martindale-Hubbell Law Digests see Uniform and Model Acts section.

CRIMINAL LAW

BAIL:

See topic Criminal Law.

CRIMINAL LAW:

Crimes are defined in Title 5, cc. 1-77 and procedure in Title 16, cc. 80-97 and Arkansas Rules of Criminal Procedure, 1-38, adopted by Supreme Court rule, effective Jan. 1, 1976.

Indictment or Information.—All public offenses are indictable by grand jury or information, except those of public officers when different procedure is prescribed, those exclusively in jurisdiction of justices of peace or of police or city courts, and those of military origin. (Const. Amend. 21; 16-80-101). Public offenses punishable by fine only may be prosecuted by suit for penalty. (16-80-101).

Bail.—All cases are bailable except capital cases where proof is evident or presumption great. (Const., Art. 2, §8).

Sentence.—Length of sentence according to classification of offense is found in 5-4-401.

Fines.—Amounts are laid out according to classification of offense in 5-4-201.

Drug Paraphernalia.—It is illegal to knowingly finance, manage, supervise, or direct, all or part of business that deals in drug devices. (5-64-802).

Uniform Act for Out-of-State Parolee Supervision adopted. (16-93-901-903).

Uniform Act to Secure the Attendance of Witnesses from Without the State in Criminal Cases adopted. (16-43-401-409).

Uniform Criminal Extradition Act adopted. (16-94-201-231).

Uniform Controlled Substances Act in effect. (5-64-101-1203).

Uniform Rendition of Prisoners as Witnesses in Criminal Proceedings Act adopted. (16-43-301-311).

DEBTOR AND CREDITOR

ASSIGNMENTS:

Uniform Commercial Code applies. (4-2-210; 3-408; 5-116; 8-308; 9-102; 9-104; 9-206; 9-301; 9-302; 9-311; 9-318; 9-405). See category Business Regulation and Commerce, topic Commercial Code.

All bonds, bills, notes and agreements in writing for the payment of money or property are assignable, but are subject to defenses in law or equity which would have been available against assignor. (4-58-102, 105). Assignments of rent are subject to rules of real property conveyancing. (87 B.R. 565).

Open Accounts.—Written assignments of accounts receivable or of money due on open accounts or contracts are valid, and when completed no interest in the account superior to that of assignee may thereafter be acquired from assignor. Payments by

ASSIGNMENTS...*continued*

debtor without notice of assignment to one acquiring an interest in the account after assignment acquits debtor to extent thereof and recipient of payments is liable as trustee to prior assignee. (4-58-105).

Instrument Transferring Title.—Assignments of written instruments must be correctly dated. (4-58-104). Blank assignments are taken as of date most favorable to defendant. (4-58-104).

Judgments or causes of action after suit must be assigned by acknowledged instrument filed with court. (16-65-120).

Leases.—Uniform Commercial Code applies. (4-2A-101 et seq.).

Mortgages, deeds of trust and vendors liens may be assigned by written instrument, which, when acknowledged, may be recorded. (18-40-109).

Assignment of wages to secure loan of less than $200 is not valid against employer until accepted by him in writing and filed, with the acceptance, with recorder of county of assignor's residence and assignment of wages by married man is invalid without wife's written consent. (11-4-101).

Liability on Assigned Instrument.—Assignors or endorsers of written instruments for the payment of money are equally liable with the maker, and may be sued jointly or severally, provided they are given notice of nonpayment or of protest. (4-58-104). *Consideration* for assignment need not be set forth on assigned paper. (4-58-103). Assignments for benefit of creditors, to extent not superseded by Bankruptcy Code, controlled by 16-117-401-407. (184 Ark. 312, 42 S.W.2d 214).

ATTACHMENT:

Statutory provisions relating to prejudgment attachment in Arkansas (16-110-101 through 16-110-309) have been declared unconstitutional (296 Ark. 231, 755 S.W.2d 566). Until provisions are amended to comply with due-process standard articulated by U.S. Supreme Court (424 U.S. 319), prejudgment attachment is not allowed in Arkansas.

CREDITORS' SUITS:

See topics Fraudulent Sales and Conveyances, Executions.

EXECUTIONS:

Execution may be issued on any final money judgment of a court of record (16-66-101), and upon judgment of justice of peace court (16-19-1002).

Exemptions.—See topic Exemptions.

Time for Issuance.—Execution may issue after ten days from entry of judgment, and at any time until collection is barred by statute of limitations. (RCP 62; 16-66-103).

Stay.—On giving of bond with good security for amount of judgment, execution may be stayed for six months from date of judgment (16-66-303), except judgment against collecting officer or attorney for failure to pay over moneys collected, or against principal by his surety, or judgment for specific property, or for enforcement of lien in favor of vendor or mortgagee, or for injuries resulting in death caused by neglect of another. (16-66-302).

Stay on Appeal.—Upon giving of supersedeas bond, appellant may obtain stay while appeal is taken. (RCP 62[d]).

Lien.—An execution is a lien on property to which judgment extends from time of delivery of writ to officer in proper county to be executed. (16-66-112).

Levy.—Any property, real or personal, not exempt, is liable to seizure under execution (16-66-201). Property subject to prior lien is subject to execution and sale by making prior lienor party to process and satisfying prior lien out of proceeds of sale. (16-66-203).

Indemnity.—If the officer doubts whether the personal property upon which he makes a levy is subject to execution, he may require of the plaintiff an indemnifying bond before proceeding to subject property to execution. (16-66-405). If security was good when taken, officer is protected against action by claimant or purchaser of property. (16-66-405).

Return on execution from court of record must be made in 60 days; on execution from justice court in 30 days. (16-66-416; 16-19-1001).

Claims of Third Persons.—Claimants of personal property levied on may suspend sale by giving bond in double value of property, and have right tried. (16-66-304).

Quashing.—Judge of court out of which execution issues may quash same on good cause therefor being shown. (16-66-301).

Sale.—All property taken under execution may be disposed of by sale on the day advertised, between 9 o'clock A. M. and 3 o'clock P. M. at public auction to the highest bidder on a credit of three months. Credit may be waived by the purchaser. (16-66-409; 413). Notice must be advertised for at least 20 days of time, place and terms of sale. (16-66-408). Except where defendant requests that sale be made on premises, it must be at court house door. (16-66-409). If sale fails for want of bidder, officer may hold new sale at court house door or on the premises. (16-66-409).

Redemption.—Any debtor, or his representative or his judgment creditor, may redeem real estate sold under execution within 12 months after date of sale by paying purchase price with 15% interest. (16-66-502-504).

Supplementary proceedings for discovery in equity may be had after return of no property found. (16-66-418). Discovery in aid of judgment or execution is also available in accordance with Rules of Civil Procedure. (RCP 69).

EXEMPTIONS:

Personal property, to be selected by debtor, not exceeding $500 for a resident of the state married or the head of a family, and $200 for an unmarried resident, and the wearing apparel of the debtor and his family, are exempt from process for collection of a debt founded on contract. (Const., art. 9, §§1-2).

Debts Against Which Exemptions Not Allowed.—No article is exempt as against claim for the purchase price thereof while title and possession are held by the vendee. (Const., art. 9, §1; 48 Ark. 213, 2 S.W. 785).

Waiver of Exemptions.—Except in case of homestead (16-66-212), failure to claim exemption or file schedule prior to execution sale is waiver of exemption. (202 Ark. 495, 151 S.W.2d 656).

Necessity of Claiming Exemption.—Debtor must file petition to claim any of exemptions provided by law (except homestead) specifying particular property claimed to be exempt within 20 days of receiving any writ of execution and statutory notice to defendant. Court to hold prompt hearing to determine validity of claimed exemptions. (16-66-104). Within 45 days of entry of final judgment debtor shall prepare schedule, verified by affidavit, of all his property, both real and personal, including monies, bank accounts, rights, credits and choses in action held by himself or others for him, and specify particular property which he claims as exempt under provisions of law. (16-66-221).

Wages of laborer for 60 days exempt if amount thereof plus personal property owned does not exceed constitutional exemption. (Const., art. 9, §§1-2; 16-66-208). First $25 per week of net wages of laborer is absolutely exempt without necessity of filing claim for exemption. (16-66-208). See also topic Garnishment.

Insurance Proceeds.—Former statute (16-66-209) allowing exemptions for insurance proceeds was declared unconstitutional as applied to bankruptcy. (92 B.R. 827, 93 B.R. 181). (Applicability outside of bankruptcy is questionable.)

Homestead Exemption.—See topic Homesteads.

FORECLOSURE:

See topic Liens; category Mortgages, topic Mortgages of Real Property.

FRAUDULENT SALES AND CONVEYANCES:

Transfer made or obligation incurred by debtor is fraudulent as to creditor if debtor made transfer or incurred obligation with actual intent to hinder, delay, or defraud creditor or without receiving reasonably equivalent value in exchange for transfer or obligation. (4-59-204). Defenses of transferee are found in 4-59-208.

Uniform Commercial Code adopted. (4-3-202-203; 4-2-402-403; 4-2-702; 4-2-721).

Uniform Fraudulent Transfer Act adopted. (4-59-201-213).

Remedies.—Avoidance of transfer to extent necessary to satisfy creditor's claim, attachment or other provisional remedy against asset transferred or other property of transferee, injunction, appointment of receiver, or other relief circumstances may require. (4-59-207).

Bulk Sales.—Uniform Commercial Code bulk sales provisions repealed. (1991 Act 344).

GARNISHMENT:

May issue against person indebted to or having possession of property of defendant, either in aid of attachment (16-110-102) or after judgment in aid of execution (16-66-418). Wage garnishments may continue until judgment and costs are paid and satisfied. (16-110-415).

Salaries of employees of state and its subdivisions and institutions are subject to garnishment after judgment. (16-110-413).

Wages of railroad employees cannot be garnished before judgment in an action for less than $200. (16-110-414).

Earnings.—See also topic Exemptions.

Bond.—Plaintiff seeking garnishment in aid of attachment must give bond to indemnify garnishee. (16-110-102).

Issuance of Writ.—Writ of garnishment may issue from circuit court of one county to any other county. (16-110-412). Circuit court shall attach to writ notice of defendant's right to keep certain money and wages despite garnishment. (16-110-402).

A judgment rendered in the justice of the peace courts may be filed in the office of the justice of the peace in the township in which the debtor resides and then has the force and effect of a judgment in the latter court upon which garnishment or execution may issue. (16-110-412).

Proceedings.—When the writ is issued the plaintiff must file interrogatories with the clerk of the court, directed to the garnishee, concerning any goods, chattels, moneys, credits or effects which he may have belonging to the defendant. (16-110-404). If garnishee is employer, plaintiff must also serve garnishee with notice referring to exemptions under federal law, and priority of child support awards. (16-110-416). Payor may withhold $2.50 in administrative costs from each paycheck for court-ordered withholdings. Garnishee must on return date file answer under oath. If garnishee neglects or refuses to answer interrogatories on or before 20 days after service of writ, court, upon motion of plaintiff, may issue notice to garnishee, requiring him to appear personally at hearing. After hearing and reviewing evidence and testimony of both parties, court may render judgment against garnishee in such amount, if any, as court finds garnishee held at time of service of writ, together with costs. (16-110-407).

HOMESTEADS:

A resident of the state, who is married or the head of a family, is entitled to an exemption of a homestead. Homestead must be owned and occupied as residence. (Const., art. 9, §3, 16-66-210).

Limitation of Value.—The homestead may not exceed $2,500 in value, including improvements, except that in a city, town or village, at least one-quarter acre, and elsewhere at least 80 acres, may be held exempt regardless of value. (Const., art. 9, §§4-5, 16-66-210; 218).

Limitation of Area.—The homestead may not exceed, in area, one acre in city, town or village or 160 acres elsewhere. (Const., art. 9, §§4-5, 16-66-210). If homestead outside city, town or village is annexed or made part of city, town or village, may retain

HOMESTEADS . . . *continued*

exemption as long as land remaining rural in nature and has significant agricultural use. (16-66-210). Corporate city, town or village limits do not control determination of whether property is urban or rural. Use of property and attributes of location are important considerations. (260 Ark. 735, 543 S.W.2d 920; 128 B.R. 224).

The exemption is not available against purchase money, taxes, vendors', mechanics' or other specific liens or judgment for trust funds. (Const., art. 9, §3, 16-66-210).

Loss of Exemption.—A husband does not lose his homestead rights because of death of his wife and his children attaining the age of majority. (43 Ark. 429).

Alienation or Incumbrance.—A conveyance, mortgage or other instrument executed by spouse and affecting homestead, except purchase money mortgage, or other specified lien, is void unless other spouse joins therein, or conveys by separate document, and acknowledges it. (18-12-403).

See category Property, topic Deeds, subhead Execution.

Proceeds of Sale.—Proceeds of voluntary sale of homestead are not exempt pending investment in another homestead, but surplus from forced sale to satisfy lien is exempt as long as intention to invest it in another homestead exists. (252 Ark. 701, 480 S.W.2d 567).

Rights of Surviving Spouse and Family.—If decedent and surviving spouse were continuously married to each other for over one year and surviving spouse has no separate homestead, he or she and children during minority succeed to rights of decedent, whether they reside on property or not. If surviving spouse dies, children retain right while minors. If children die, or when they become of age, surviving spouse has entire right. (Const., art. 9, §6, 28-39-201).

JUDGMENT NOTES:

Not permitted.

LEVY:

See topics Attachment, Executions.

LIENS:

The following common law or statutory liens are recognized:

Agent paying taxes on principal's lands has lien for reimbursement. (26-35-402).

Attachment Lien.—See topic Attachment.

Attorney's Lien.—See category Legal Profession, topic Attorneys and Counselors.

Automobile repairmen have a lien upon vehicle for labor and materials. Enforceable, if possession retained, by sale after 30 days from completion of work. Demand by lienholder by registered letter and public notice are required. Notice and bond are required to be filed with justice of peace. If possession surrendered, repairman may file account with circuit clerk within 120 days after completion of work and bring suit within 18 months after filing (18-45-207). Claimant may have specific attachment of property upon which lien is claimed by praying for it in complaint and providing bond as required by law for attachment. (18-45-201-207).

Lien upon automobile for storage charges may be enforced, if possession of automobile is retained, by sale in the manner provided for liens of automobile repairmen. (18-48-401-404).

Blacksmiths, horseshoers, wheelwrights and airplane repairmen, machine shops, farm implement repairmen, and automotive storagemen have lien enforceable in same manner as automobile repairmen's lien, supra. (18-45-201-207).

Chattel Mortgage Lien.—Uniform Commercial Code applies. (art. 9).

Cleaners, dyers, laundries, tailors, hat renovators and shoe repairers have lien for labor and material, enforceable in similar manner as automobile repairmen's lien, except that property cannot be sold until 90 days after completion of work. (18-45-401-405).

Collateral Security.—See topic Pledges.

Cotton ginners have lien for charges on cotton and seed, enforceable by private sale after 30 days, or if possession has been surrendered, by suit within six months. (18-48-505-506). Processors of other farm products have similar lien enforceable by private sale. (18-48-501-504).

Doctors, dentists, nurses and hospitals have lien on patient's cause of action for injury. Verified notice must be served on tortfeasor and copy filed with circuit clerk of county where services were or are being rendered. Lien expires in 180 days unless renewal notice is served and filed. When patient files suit lienholder may file claim in action and thereafter no renewal notices are required. Tortfeasor settling patient's claim without paying lienholder is liable for amount of lien or up to amount of settlement if less than lien. (18-46-101-117).

Electrical equipment repairman has lien for labor and material, enforceable by sale after 90 days. If possession has been surrendered, lienholder may file itemized account with circuit clerk within 90 days after work or labor is performed and bring suit within 90 days after filing. Lien has priority over mortgage if, before commencing work, repairman gives notice to mortgagee by registered mail and no objection to work is made in ten days. (18-45-301-305).

Engineers, architects, surveyors, appraisers, abstractors and title insurance agents performing work on land or building under contract with owner or agent have lien on property to extent of agreed or reasonable price for services. Lien does not attach until filed with Circuit Clerk of county in which property is located and is enforceable in same manner as mechanic's lien. (18-44-105, 133).

Merchandise Liens.—Uniform Commercial Code applies. (4-9-101, et seq.).

Execution Lien.—See topic Executions.

Factor's Lien.—See category Business Regulation and Commerce, topic Factors.

Innkeeper's Lien.—The keeper of an inn, hotel, rooming house or boarding house has a lien on the baggage of his guests for his charges and for advancements up to $200. Baggage may be detained until debt is paid. (20-26-305). Baggage can be sold after 90 days. Public notice is required. Notice must be mailed to guest.

Judgment Lien.—See category Civil Actions and Procedure, topic Judgments.

Laborers' Lien.—Laborers have a lien upon the product of their labor, effective from the time it is performed. Enforceable by suit within eight months. Laborer must make sworn statement before justice of peace or circuit clerk, determined by jurisdictional amount. Notice must be given to defendant. Sheriff or constable takes possession of product of labor at commencement of suit, and court may order its sale. Where labor was done on building, not exceeding two acres of surrounding land may be sold with building. (18-43-101-117). Agricultural laborers, including cropdusters, also have laborer's lien. Agricultural laborer's liens must be filed in manner prescribed for materialmen's liens. (18-43-118).

Laborer performing work on improvements upon land also has mechanic's lien; see subhead Mechanics' and Materialmen's Liens, infra.

Laborer performing work on oil or gas well, pipe line, quarry or mine has lien, enforceable in same way as mechanic's lien. (18-44-201-211, 301-305).

Landlord's Lien.—See category Property, topic Landlord and Tenant.

Liens on Homestead.—See topic Homesteads.

Liens on Exempt Property.—See topic Exemptions.

Livery stable keeper has lien for his charges on stock left in his care, enforceable by public sale after 30 days notice to owner and publishing notice. (18-48-101-102).

Mechanics' and Materialmen's Liens.—Every contractor, subcontractor, or material supplier who supplies labor, services, material, fixtures, engine, boiler, or machinery in construction or repair of improvement to real estate, or any boat or vessel of any kind, by virtue of contract with owner, proprietor, contractor or subcontractor, has lien upon improvement and up to one acre of land upon which improvement is situated, or to extent to any number of acres of land upon which work has been done or improvements erected or repaired. (18-44-101). Lien applies only to interest or title of owner in said land, improvement, etc. (18-44-102). Lien attaches to building or improvement in preference to any prior lien or mortgage upon land before said building or improvement was begun, unless prior lien or mortgage was given for purpose of raising funds for improvements. (18-44-110). Persons other than original contractor, desiring to avail themselves of act, must give ten days' notice of amount of labor performed or material furnished. Service of notice may be by certified mail, return receipt requested, or by person or officer authorized by law to serve process of civil actions. (18-44-114). For residential real estate containing four or fewer units, suppliers of materials or subcontractors acquire no lien pursuant to foregoing provisions unless, prior to furnishing of materials or labor, owner or his authorized agent receives by personal delivery or certified mail, following notice:

IMPORTANT NOTICE TO OWNER

I UNDERSTAND THAT EACH PERSON SUPPLYING MATERIAL OR FIXTURES IS ENTITLED TO A LIEN AGAINST PROPERTY IF NOT PAID IN FULL FOR MATERIALS USED TO IMPROVE THE PROPERTY EVEN THOUGH THE FULL CONTRACT PRICE MAY HAVE BEEN PAID TO THE CONTRACTOR. I REALIZE THAT THIS LIEN CAN BE ENFORCED BY THE SALE OF THE PROPERTY IF NECESSARY. I AM ALSO AWARE THAT PAYMENT MAY BE WITHHELD TO THE CONTRACTOR IN THE AMOUNT OF THE COST OF ANY MATERIALS OR LABOR NOT PAID FOR. I KNOW THAT IT IS ADVISABLE TO, AND I MAY, REQUIRE THE CONTRACTOR TO FURNISH TO ME A TRUE AND CORRECT FULL LIST OF ALL SUPPLIERS UNDER THE CONTRACT, AND I MAY CHECK WITH THEM TO DETERMINE IF ALL MATERIALS FURNISHED FOR THE PROPERTY HAVE BEEN PAID FOR. I MAY ALSO REQUIRE THE CONTRACTOR TO PRESENT LIEN WAIVERS BY ALL SUPPLIERS, STATING THAT THEY HAVE BEEN PAID IN FULL FOR SUPPLIES PROVIDED UNDER THE CONTRACT, BEFORE I PAY THE CONTRACTOR IN FULL. IF A SUPPLIER HAS NOT BEEN PAID, I MAY PAY THE SUPPLIER AND CONTRACTOR WITH A CHECK MADE PAYABLE TO THEM JOINTLY.

SIGNED:

ADDRESS OF PROPERTY

DATE:

I HEREBY CERTIFY THAT THE SIGNATURE ABOVE IS THAT OF THE OWNER OR AGENT OF THE OWNER OF THE PROPERTY AT THE ADDRESS SET OUT ABOVE.

CONTRACTOR

(18-44-115).

Notice must be given exactly as stated, in all capital letters. Notice may be incorporated into contract, or affixed thereto, and shall be conspicuous. Principal contractor has duty to give notice but other lien claimant may do so. Contractors who fail to give required notice shall be guilty of misdemeanor and shall be punished by fine not exceeding $1,000. (18-44-115). Notice warns owner of lien possibility and method of protection. Notice not required if bond supplied or if transaction is direct sale to property owner. (18-44-115). Newly enacted statute provides that advance notice requirement is condition precedent to imposition of material supplier's lien only for construction of or improvement to residential real estate containing four or fewer units. (New statutory provision constitutionally suspect in light of Arkansas Supreme Court Opinion rendered in Urrey Ceramic Tile Co. v. Mosely, 304 Ark. 711, 805 S.W.2d 54 [1991]). For commercial real estate, no material supplier or laborer shall be entitled to lien unless material supplier or laborer notifies owner of commercial real estate being improved, in writing, that such material supplier or laborer is currently entitled to payment but has not been paid. Such notice shall be sent to owner and to contractor by registered mail, return receipt requested, before 75 days have elapsed from time that labor was supplied or materials furnished. Such notice shall contain general description of labor, service, or material furnished and amount due and unpaid, name and address of person furnishing labor, service, or materials, name of person who contracted for

See note at head of Digest as to 1998 legislation covered.

See Topical Index in front part of this volume.

LIENS . . . *continued*

purchase of labor, service, or materials, description of job site sufficient for identification and following statement set out in bold face type:

NOTICE TO PROPERTY OWNER

IF BILLS FOR LABOR, SERVICES, OR MATERIALS USED TO CONSTRUCT AN IMPROVEMENT TO REAL ESTATE ARE NOT PAID IN FULL, A CONSTRUCTION LIEN MAY BE PLACED AGAINST THE PROPERTY. THIS COULD RESULT IN THE LOSS, THROUGH FORECLOSURE PROCEEDINGS, OF ALL OR PART OF YOUR REAL ESTATE BEING IMPROVED. THIS MAY OCCUR EVEN THOUGH YOU HAVE PAID YOUR CONTRACTOR IN FULL. YOU MAY WISH TO PROTECT YOURSELF AGAINST THIS CONSEQUENCE BY PAYING THE ABOVE NAMED PROVIDER OF LABOR, SERVICES, OR MATERIALS DIRECTLY, OR MAKING YOUR CHECK PAYABLE TO THE ABOVE NAMED PROVIDER AND CONTRACTOR JOINTLY.

(18-44-115).

Parties desiring to avail themselves of act must file itemized and verified statements with Circuit Clerk of labor performed or material furnished, within 120 days of time said labor is performed or material furnished after giving ten days notice to owner. Action to enforce such liens must be commenced in 15 months after filing lien. (18-44-117).

Contractor has duty to defend at own expense all actions liens filed by persons other than himself. (18-44-124). Contractor who knowingly or willfully with purpose to defraud fails to apply payment to discharge of lienable indebtedness within ten days of final receipt of payment under contract subject to fine and imprisonment. (18-44-132).

Redemption.—Real estate sold may be redeemed within a year by paying purchase price with 15% interest. (16-66-502, 503).

Churches and Charitable Institutions.—Action on bond for labor or materials supplied must be brought within six months of completion of improvement. If no bond is filed, lien attaches to property. Contractor must first furnish church or charitable organization bond equal to sum of contract if contract is greater than $1,000. (18-44-504).

Public Works.—Highway construction and public building contractors must furnish bonds such as will protect subcontractors, laborers and material men if contract exceeds $20,000. Actions for claims on bond must be brought within 12 months from date final payment was approved on contract. (18-44-503).

Criminal Penalty.—Exists for knowingly or willfully failing to pay supplier or subcontractor within 30 days of final receipt of payment. (5-37-525).

Marina Operators.—Operator of marina facility has lien on property stored in leased space for rent, labor, or other related charges. (18-48-702).

Miners have lien on output, machinery and tools for amounts due for work, enforceable in same manner as laborer's lien on production of his work. (18-43-103).

Railroad Property.—Mechanics, contractors, sub-contractors, builders, artisans, workmen, laborers, supply men, and materialmen, who have helped toward the construction, equipment or operation of railroad, whether under contract with company, or with contractor or sub-contractor, and all persons who shall sustain loss or damage to person or property from a railroad, shall have a lien on said railroad superior, whether prior in time or not, to that of all persons interested as managers, lessees, mortgagees, trustees and beneficiaries under trusts or owners. Limitation on this lien is one year. (18-44-401-403).

Real Estate Mortgage Lien.—See category Mortgages, topic Mortgages of Real Property.

Self-Service Storage.—See category Business Regulation and Commerce, topic Warehousemen.

Tax Lien.—Uniform Federal Lien Registration Act adopted. (18-47-201-207). Also see category Taxation, topic Uniform Federal Lien Registration Act.

Redemption.—There is no right of redemption after sale under any of above liens, except mechanic's lien.

MECHANICS' LIENS:

See topic Liens.

PLEDGES:

Covered by Uniform Commercial Code. (4-8-306, 4-8-320 and 4-9-101-507). 1972 Official Amendments adopted.

Delivery and retention of possession are essential to a pledge, unless pledge creates security interest in instrument (other than certificated security) pursuant to new value given under written security agreement, then perfected for 21 days from time security interest attached. (4-9-304). Otherwise, if possession is surrendered or lost lien is extinguished. Pledgee is required to exercise only ordinary care with reference to pledged property, and if pledged property is instrument or chattel paper, such care includes preserving rights against prior parties. (4-9-207).

Foreclosure.—Pledged property may be foreclosed by sale or acceptance of collateral in discharge, but must be in accordance with any agreement and Uniform Commercial Code. (4-9-501). Unless collateral is perishable, threatens to decline speedily in value or is of type customarily sold on recognized market, must give notice to debtor (4-9-504) or deficiency judgment barred (291 Ark. 37, 722 S.W.2d 555). Must conduct sale in commercially reasonable manner (4-9-504) or deficiency judgment barred (35 Ark. App. 168, 815 S.W.2d 392).

Trust Receipts.—Covered by Uniform Commercial Code. (4-9-101-507).

RECEIVERS:

Courts of equity have usual equity powers to appoint receivers for any lawful purpose whenever necessary and proper. Court determined bond required. Reports required every six months or as required by court. Others may be employed by receiver on court approval. Good cause required for receiver removal. Court order required to dismiss action where receiver appointed. (RCP 66). Receiver pendente lite may be appointed. (16-117-207).

REDEMPTION:

See topics Executions, Liens; categories Mortgages, topic Mortgages of Real Property; Taxation, topic Property Taxes, subhead Redemption.

SUPPLEMENTARY PROCEEDINGS:

See topic Executions.

TRUSTEE PROCESS:

See topic Garnishment.

USURY:

See category Business Regulation and Commerce, topic Interest.

DISPUTE RESOLUTION

ALTERNATIVE DISPUTE RESOLUTION:

Mandatory Dispute Resolution.—Buyer of agricultural seed damaged by failure of seed to produce or perform as represented by label attached to seed must initiate arbitration proceeding against dealer within ten days after alleged defect or violation becomes apparent as prerequisite to maintaining legal action. (2-23-101-110). Report of arbitration shall be binding upon parties to extent they have agreed in contract of sale. (2-23-107). In absence of agreement to be bound by arbitration, buyer may commence legal proceedings against seller or assert such claim as defense in action brought by seller at any time after receipt of report of arbitration. (2-23-107).

Under Arkansas Farm Mediation Act, creditor with secured indebtedness of $20,000 or more may not commence proceeding against farmer to foreclose mortgage on agricultural property, to terminate contract for deed to purchase agricultural property, to repossess or foreclose security interest in agricultural property, to set off or seize account, moneys, or other asset which is agricultural property, or to enforce any judgment against agricultural property, without first obtaining release under Act. (2-7-302). Prior to commencing such proceeding, creditor must serve notice on farmer that farmer may request mandatory mediation of farm indebtedness. (2-7-303). Creditor may then obtain release from mediation upon request under Act if creditor has paid any required fees and (1) creditor has attended initial mediation meeting with farmer; (2) creditor has served mediation notice on farmer and farmer has not requested mediation within time allowed; (3) farmer has waived mediation; (4) agricultural property has been abandoned by farmer; (5) in discretion of Director of Division of Agricultural Development if default is other than monetary; (6) when court finds that mediation would be unduly burdensome and extreme hardship on creditor; or (7) upon failure of farmer to appear at scheduled mediation meeting. (2-7-310).

Voluntary Dispute Resolution.—See also topic Arbitration and Award. Act 673 of 1995 (16-7-101-104) established Arkansas Alternative Dispute Resolution Commission to promote use of alternative dispute resolution (ADR). Commission has authority and responsibility to establish standards and regulations for certification, professional conduct, discipline, and training of persons serving as neutral parties in ADR; to develop recommended guidelines; to assist local courts and governmental agencies with development and implementation of ADR programs; to develop standardized forms for use in state and local courts for reference of cases to ADR; and to establish fees to be levied by courts, governmental and other agencies and paid by parties utilizing ADR processes. (16-7-104).

ARBITRATION AND AWARD:

Uniform Arbitration Act adopted with modifications. (16-108-201-224). Act specifically excludes applicability to personal injury or tort matters, employer-employee disputes, and insured or beneficiary under insurance policy or annuity contract. (16-108-201[b]). Exclusion does not apply to written agreement to submit existing controversy to arbitration. (16-108-201[a]).

Arkansas Alternative Dispute Resolution Commission.—Commission established to promote and create uniform regulations for alternative dispute resolution. (16-7-102).

Prior Laws.—As Act is optional and limited in scope and does not supersede nonconflicting prior laws nor apply retroactively, following material is still of interest:

Parties may submit all controversies, which might be the subject of a suit, for arbitration by rule of court having jurisdiction of the subject matter, or by consent in vacation. (16-108-102).

Arbitrators.—Controversies may be submitted to one or more arbitrators or to two arbitrators and their umpire. (16-108-102).

Requisites of Submission.—Where no suit is pending, a written agreement stating the matter submitted must be filed and noted on the court record. (16-108-102).

Proceedings and Award.—Rule of court must state the time in which the award shall be made, but this time may be enlarged. (16-108-102). Arbitrators meet on notice and hear evidence adduced by either party, and make their award in writing, stating therein time it was made, and sign same. One copy is delivered to each contending party and original returned to court, entered of record and made judgment or decree of court, unless on exceptions filed, award is set aside. (16-108-107). Every reasonable presumption is in favor of award. (76 Ark. 153, 88 S.W. 915).

Unless the illegality of the decision of the arbitrators appears upon the face of the award, the court will not set it aside on the ground that they mistook the law or decided contrary to the rules of established practice. (44 Ark. 166).

Matters within jurisdiction of a justice of the peace may be submitted to arbitrators by order, rule or agreement entered on his record book but either party may appeal to the circuit court from judgment of justice on award as in other cases. (16-108-106).

Ark. Code Ann. §§16-7-201-205 require courts, state and local officers and agencies, and governments to encourage use of dispute resolution processes as alternatives to litigation and recommends that attorneys do likewise. Ark. Code Ann. §16-7-206 also makes confidential communications by participants in dispute resolution process. Ark. Code Ann. §16-7-207 relieves impartial third parties administering or participating in

ARBITRATION AND AWARD . . . *continued*
ADR process from liability for civil damages in absence of willful or wanton misconduct.

DOCUMENTS AND RECORDS
ACKNOWLEDGMENTS:

Uniform Acknowledgment Act (not Acknowledgments Act) has been adopted. (16-47-201-210, 213-216). §2 amended to add "any former judge of a court of record who served at least four or more years." (16-47-202). §9 amended to delete requirement of authentication if acknowledgment by officer authorized by §3. (16-47-209). Section is added concerning validation of unauthenticated writings affecting title to property recorded or executed prior to July 19, 1971. (16-47-211). Uniform Acknowledgment Act is optional and prior statutes provide alternative means of valid acknowledgments. (16-47-201 and 212). Uniform Law on Notarial Acts not in effect. (21-14-101-110).

Within State.—See 16-47-103 and 202 for officers who may take acknowledgments. Entitlement to fee for taking acknowledgment in certain employment contracts set forth in 18-42-101.

Outside State but Within U.S.—See 16-47-103 and 203 for officers who may take acknowledgments.

Outside U.S.—See 16-47-103 and 204 for officers who may take acknowledgments.

Persons in or with U.S. Armed Forces.—See 16-47-109 validating all acknowledgments of Armed Forces personnel prior to Mar. 20, 1945, and also 16-47-213 which is §11 of Uniform Acknowledgment Act.

General Requirements as to Taking.—No special requirements. Officer taking acknowledgment shall know or have satisfactory evidence that person making acknowledgment is person described in and who executed instrument. (16-47-106 and 205).

General Requirements of Certificate.—Certificate of acknowledging officer shall be completed by signature, official seal if applicable, title of office and date commission expires if officer is Notary Public. (16-47-208). Failure of Notary Public to state date commission expires does not invalidate acknowledgment. (21-14-108).

Married Persons.—No special requirements. Acknowledgment of married person may be made in same form as if he or she were sole, without any examination separate and apart from spouse and without necessity for specific reference to interest conveyed or relinquished. (16-47-102).

Corporations.—No special requirements. Statute contains form for acknowledgment by corporation of instruments affecting or purporting to affect title to real estate situated in this state. (16-47-107).

Foreign Acknowledgments.—Acknowledgment which is valid where taken in state, territory or possession of U.S. or in District of Columbia, or Philippine Islands is valid in Arkansas. (16-47-210).

Effect of Acknowledgment.—Instruments affecting real estate must be proven or acknowledged to be filed of record and when recorded may be read in evidence without further proof. (16-47-101 and 110; 18-12-201 and 209). But defective acknowledgment does not affect validity of mortgage as between makers. (304 Ark. 143, 801 S.W.2d 36).

Proof by Subscribing Witness.—Writings affecting real estate may be proved by affidavit of one or more of subscribing witnesses to court or officer stating that witness saw grantor sign instrument or heard grantor acknowledge instrument and stating that witness subscribed instrument at grantor's request. (16-47-106 and 18-12-206). If witnesses are dead or cannot be had, handwriting of grantor and of at least one subscribing witness may be proved by two or more disinterested persons swearing to each signature. (16-47-106 and 18-12-206).

Authentication.—See §9 of Uniform Acknowledgment Act. (16-47-209).

Forms.—See §7 of Uniform Acknowledgment Act. (16-47-207).

Any form of acknowledgment is sufficient which shows state and county or other place where it was taken, sets out name of person acknowledging and, if he or she acknowledges otherwise than in his or her own right name of entity for whom or which he or she acknowledges and shows that he or she acknowledged execution of instrument. (16-47-102).

Certificate of proof by subscribing witnesses may be in the following form or like effect (16-47-106):

State of . ., County of . . Be it remembered that on this day came before me, a notary public in and for said county and state, . . one of the subscribing witnesses to the foregoing deed, to me personally well known, who being by me first duly sworn, stated that he saw . . the grantor in said deed, subscribe the same on the day of its date (or that he acknowledged in his presence on the . . day of . ., 19. ., that he had executed said deed for the consideration and purposes therein contained) and that he and . . the other subscribing witness subscribed said deed as attesting witnesses at the request of said grantor. In testimony whereof, I have hereunto set my hand and seal of office on this . . day of . ., 19. . .

　　　　　　　　　　　　　　　　　　　　　　　(Signature and Title)

Proof of handwriting of grantor and subscribing witness may be in the following form or like effect. (16-47-106):

State of . ., County of . . Be it remembered that on this . . day of . ., 19. ., came before me, a notary public in and for said county and state, . . and . . and upon their oaths stated that the signatures of . . the grantor in the foregoing deed, and of . . a witness thereto, are genuine, and are in the handwriting of said . . and . . respectively.

In testimony whereof I have hereunto set my hand and seal of office, on this . . day of . ., 19. . .

　　　　　　　　　　　　　　　　　　　　　　　(Signature and title).

Validating Acts.—Acknowledgments made subsequent to enactment of 16-47-203, 209 and 217 in accordance with Uniform Acknowledgment Act are validated. (16-47-217 and 218). Instruments recorded or executed prior to July 19, 1971 which are defective due to lack of authentication required by 16-47-209 and 210 are validated. (16-47-211). Acknowledgments taken before Mar. 20, 1945 by officers of U.S. Armed Forces acknowledging signature of soldiers are validated in every respect. (16-47-109).

Alternative to Acknowledgment or Proof.—No statutory provision.

AFFIDAVITS:

Within the State.—May be made within state before judge of a court, justice of the peace, notary public, clerk of a court, or mayor of a city or incorporated town. (16-45-102).

Outside of the State.—May be made before a commissioner appointed by the Governor of Arkansas to take depositions, judge of a court, mayor of a city, notary public or justice of the peace, whose certificate is proof of the time and manner of its being made. (16-45-102).

Persons in armed services of the U. S. may make oath to any affidavit before any commissioned officer of any branch of the services, who must show rank, branch of service, outfit and place where made, if permissible, in certificate. (16-2-104).

Requisites.—Every affidavit must be subscribed by affiant, and certificate of officer before whom it is made must follow the signature of affiant. (16-45-103).

Use of Affidavit.—May be read into evidence to verify pleadings; to prove service of process; to obtain provisional remedy, stay of proceedings, or warning order; and to establish account. (16-45-101, 104).

May be made by agent or attorney to verify pleading, obtain warning order, provisional remedy or other order. (16-63-203).

Alternative to Affidavit.—No statutory authority.

Form
Usual form of jurat: Subscribed and sworn to before me this . . day of . ., 19. . .

NOTARIES PUBLIC:

Qualification.—Notary must file $4,000 surety bond or contract in office of circuit clerk of county of his residence or county where employed in case of resident of adjoining state. (21-14-101).

Authentication.—See topic Acknowledgments, subhead Authentication.

Seal.—Notary must provide a seal. (21-14-107). Facsimile signature and seal of notary public is allowed on commercial documents if notary makes filing with Secretary of State. (21-14-201-205).

Powers include administration of oaths, taking of acknowledgments and making declarations and protests. (21-14-105-106). It is unlawful for notary to acknowledge instrument executed by or to bank or other corporation of which he is stockholder, director, officer, or employee, if notary is party to instrument, individually or as representative of corporation, or to protest negotiable instrument owned or held for collection by such corporation if notary is individually party to instrument. (21-14-109).

Territorial Extent of Powers.—Authority to administer oaths and take affidavits and acknowledgments is coextensive with state (21-14-104), but office is vacated and powers terminate if notary ceases to be resident of county for which appointed (156 Ark. 216, 245 S.W. 498).

Expiration of Commission.—Date on which commission expires should be stated in certificate, but its omission does not invalidate action of notary. (21-14-108).

Fees.—For protest, $5; for notice of protest, $5; for any other certificate, $5. Notary Public who knowingly charges, demands or receives any greater fees is guilty of misdemeanor and can be fined not less than $100 for each offense. (21-6-309).

Uniform Acknowledgment Act, as amended by the Conference in 1942, by adding §11 providing for acknowledgments by persons in the U. S. Armed Forces, has been adopted. (16-47-201-216). See also topic Acknowledgments.

RECORDS:

Circuit clerk of each county is ex-officio recorder. (Ark. Const., Art. 7, §19).

Necessity for Recording.—Any conveyance affecting the title to real estate must be acknowledged and filed for record in the circuit clerk's office of county in which real estate is situated, in order to constitute notice to third persons. (14-15-404). *For list of Counties and County Seats see first page for this state in Volume containing Practice Profiles Section. Note:* Some counties have two county seats with separate jurisdictions.

Each instrument affecting title to real estate must be accompanied by transfer tax affidavit, must have proper amount of revenue stamps affixed (26-60-107) and must bear notation substantially as follows: "This instrument was prepared by . . . . (name) . . . . (address)" (14-15-403). See also category Taxation, topic Stamp Tax.

Recording of instrument without notation is notice, but one paying recording fees may recover them from Recorder within six months from filing. (14-15-403).

Recording Fees.—Instruments to be recorded should be forwarded to circuit clerk of proper county with check in amount of recording costs or request to remit bill for proper amount. Recorder may insist upon payment of recording costs before filing instrument. Fees for most recorded instruments are $6 for first page (one side only) and $2 for each additional page. Costs should be confirmed with county clerk prior to recording. (21-6-306).

See also categories Mortgages, topic Mortgages of Real Property; Property, topic Deeds.

Filing Under Commercial Code.—Place; Fees.—Proper place of filing in order to perfect security interest under Art. 9 of Commercial Code (1972 Official Amendments) is as follows: (a) When collateral is equipment used in farming operations, farm products, or accounts or general intangibles arising from or relating to sale of farm products by farmer, or consumer goods, then in office of circuit clerk in county of debtor's residence; or, if debtor is nonresident, then in office of circuit clerk in county where goods are kept, and in addition when collateral is crops growing or to be grown, then in office of circuit clerk in county where land is located; (b) when collateral is

RECORDS . . . *continued*

timber to be cut or minerals or the like or goods, which at time security interest attaches are or are to become fixtures, then in office where mortgage on real estate concerned would be filed or recorded and including acknowledgment on attached page (18-12-201) (mortgage meeting requirements of 4-9-402(6) is effective as financing statement); and (c) in all other cases, in office of Secretary of State, and in addition if debtor has place of business in only one county, also in office of circuit clerk of such county, or, if debtor has no place of business in state but resides in state, also in office of circuit clerk in county in which he resides. (4-9-401). Fees for certificates of filings may be fixed by filing officer not to exceed $6, but fee for furnishing copy of instruments is $6 for first page and $2 for each additional page or exhibit up to maximum fee of $100. (4-9-407). Fee for filing and indexing termination statement (including sending or delivering financing statement) and for filing, indexing and furnishing filing data about statement of assignment shall not exceed $6 for first page and $2 for each page or exhibit thereafter not to exceed maximum fee of $100. (4-9-404-405). Fee for filing and noting Statement of Release shall not exceed $6 for the first page and $2 for each page or exhibit thereafter not to exceed maximum fee of $100. (4-9-406). All fees for recording, satisfaction and termination of mortgages as fixture filings may be collected at time of filing. (4-9-402).

Filing of statement pertaining to security interest of entity primarily engaged in railroad or street railway business, furnishing telephone or telegraph service, transmission of oil, gas or petroleum products by pipeline, or production transmission or distribution of electricity, steam, gas, or water, in personal property or fixture is in office of Secretary of State and no real estate description is required if goods are to become fixtures, or for security interest in rolling stock, perfection may be as prescribed in §20(c) of Interstate Commerce Act or under Commercial Code with Secretary of State, and remains effective until terminated without filing continuation statement. (4-19-102-104, 4-9-403). Mailing address of Secretary of State is Secretary of State, State Capitol, Room 25, Attention: UCC, Little Rock, Arkansas 72201.

Admissibility in Evidence.—Certified copy of duly acknowledged or proved recorded instrument is admissible on showing that original is lost or not within control of party offering copy. (16-47-110, 18-12-209).

Transfer of Decedent's Title.—Arkansas has no system for determining ownership of real property transferred by death of former owner. Ordinarily it is established by affidavit, though of course there is occasional litigation which settles matter.

Torrens Act has not been adopted.

Vital Statistics.—Certificates of birth, deaths, fetal deaths, induced terminations of pregnancy, marriage, annulment and divorce must be registered by State Registrar of Vital Records, Arkansas Department of Health, 4815 West Markham, Little Rock, AR. 72205. (20-18-201-604).

Establishing Birth Records.—Birth records of Bureau of Vital Statistics begin Feb. 1, 1914.

Record of birth, one year or more after date of birth, may be established by filing certificate in accordance with regulation of State Board of Health (20-18-402) and if rejected petition to establish date of birth may be filed with court of competent jurisdiction. If court finds petitioner was born in state it must issue order, which order must be registered by State Registrar and constitutes birth certificate. (20-18-403).

Fee is $4 for death certificate ($1 for each additional copy) and $5 for all other searches and certificates. (20-7-123). No charge made to veterans or their dependents when certified copies are required by Veterans Administration. (20-18-306).

SEALS:

Certain state officers are required to have a seal of office. (1-4-108). Use of private seals has been abolished and they are not necessary on any instrument. (Const., Schedule §1; 32 Ark. 410).

Corporate Seals.—Seals may be used by corporation. (4-26-204).

Effect of Seal.—Uniform Commercial Code applies. (4-2-203).

TORRENS ACT:

Not adopted.

VITAL STATISTICS:

See topic Records.

EMPLOYMENT

EMPLOYER AND EMPLOYEE:

See topic Labor Relations.

LABOR RELATIONS:

Department of Labor's purpose is to promote welfare of wage earners of state, improve their working conditions, and advance their opportunities for profitable employment. (11-2-101).

Board of Health shall issue regulations controlling health hazards. (11-5-205).

Amusement Rides.—Labor Department must inspect amusement rides. (20-27-101).

Hours of Labor.—In saw mill work ten hours is a legal day's work. (11-4-102).

It is unlawful for railroads to permit telegraph or telephone operators engaged in handling of trains to remain on duty more than eight hours in any 24 consecutive hours. (23-12-510).

See also infra, subheads Child Labor, Female Labor.

Wages must be paid in money and not in goods, penalties being provided for noncompliance. (11-4-403-404). Employer may not discriminate in payment of wages as between sexes for comparable work. (11-4-610). Employer who discriminates on basis of sex guilty of misdemeanor. (11-4-601). Corporations must pay wages at least

semi-monthly, unless narrow exception is satisfied, penalties being provided for non-compliance. (11-4-401).

Minimum wage $5.15. (11-4-210). Students working not to exceed 20 hours per week in school year, and 40 hours per week when school is not in session may receive 85% of applicable rate. (11-4-210). For employees receiving gratuities allowance is made for up to 50% of minimum wage, provided employee actually received that amount in gratuities. (11-4-212). Where furnished, additional allowance of 30¢ per hour may be made for reasonable value of board, lodging or apparel. (11-4-213). Special regulations may be made for handicapped workers and for learners, apprentices and full-time students. (11-4-208, 214-215). Employer must maintain records, post notice of law, and is subject to penalties for violation. (11-4-206, 216-217).

Not less than minimum prevailing rate of wages for work of similar character in county in which work is performed must be paid in construction of public works. (22-9-301).

Workweek longer than 40 hours prohibited unless employee paid one and one-half times regular rate of pay. Agricultural workers exempt from overtime provisions. (11-4-211).

As to assignment of wages, see category Debtor and Creditor, topic Assignments.

Child Labor.—Children under 14 may not be employed in remunerative occupations except during school vacations and then only by parents or guardians or in occupations controlled by them. (11-6-104). Children under 16 may in no event be employed in occupations dangerous to life or injurious to health or morals, nor in any place where alcohol of any kind is sold or dispensed (11-6-105), nor upon stage of any theater in connection with theatrical performance, exhibition or show, except when child and parent or guardian perform together; nor may any such child be employed who has not passed four yearly grades in public school or equivalent thereof (11-6-106). No child under 16 may be employed in following occupations: (1) Adjusting any belt to machinery; (2) sewing or lacing machine belts in any workshop; (3) oiling or cleaning machinery; (4) operating circular or band saws, wood shapers, wood jointers, planers, sandpaper or other kindred employments; (5) in proximity to any hazardous or unguarded belt, machinery, or gearing; (6) upon any railroad. (11-6-107). No child under 16 may be permitted to work more than six days a week nor more than 48 hours a week, nor more than eight hours a day; nor earlier than 6 A.M. nor later than 7 P.M., except on nights preceding nonschool days to 9 P.M. (11-6-108). No child under 18 may be permitted to work more than six days a week, more than 54 hours a week, nor more than ten hours in any one day, nor before 6 A.M. nor after 11 p.m., except on nights preceding nonschool days. (11-6-110). Not applicable to person who is graduate of high school, vocational or technical school, or is married or is parent. (11-6-102). Except for provisions relating to hours of employment, Act does not apply to employee employed in agriculture outside of school hours of school district where such employee is living while employed, if such employee is at least 14 years of age. (11-6-114). Act generally does not apply to any child employed for domestic labor, or any occasional, irregular, or incidental work related to or around private residences, including babysitting, pet sitting, similar household chores and manual yard work. (11-6-115). Act also does not apply to child care services in connection with church services or functions. (11-6-115). See also category Mineral, Water and Fishing Rights, topic Mines and Minerals.

Civil penalty per violation: Not less than $50 and not more than $1,000. (11-6-103).

Female Labor.—Arkansas Civil Rights Act prohibits discrimination based on gender. (16-123-101-108).

See also category Mineral, Water and Fishing Rights, topic Mines and Minerals.

Hospital Facilities.—Railroad must provide hospital facilities within the state where hospital dues are collected. (23-12-508).

Jury Duty.—Employer may not penalize employee serving on grand or petit jury. (16-31-106).

Blacklisting is prohibited. (11-3-202).

Labor Unions.—No person may be denied employment because of membership in or failure or refusal to join a labor union, nor be compelled to pay union dues as a condition to continued employment. (11-3-303).

Foreign labor agent, before entering state to take any labor out of state, must obtain license from Director of Department of Labor. (11-11-101).

Employer's Liability.—The fellow servant rule is abolished as to all corporations (11-8-103), all railroad companies operating in the state whether or not incorporated (23-12-503) and all companies engaged in mining of coal whether or not incorporated (11-8-109), but not as to partnerships (143 Ark. 390, 220 S.W. 479).

The doctrines of assumption of risk and of contributory negligence do not apply in case of violation by a corporation or a common carrier of law enacted for safety of employees. (23-12-505-506; 11-8-104-105).

In an action against a corporation for injury to or death of an employee, contributory negligence is not a bar but may reduce damages. (11-8-104).

Note: Above provisions superseded by Arkansas Workers Compensation Law for employees coming within that Act.

Mediation.—Arkansas Mediation and Conciliation Service Nondisclosure Act guarantees confidentiality of information disclosed to Arkansas Mediation and Conciliation Service of State Department of Labor. (11-2-204).

Workers' Compensation Law (11-9-101-1001) is administered by Workers' Compensation Commission, Justice Building, Little Rock, AR 72201. Act 796 of 1993 effected significant changes to workers' compensation statutes.

Act applies to all employers employing three or more persons, except domestic service, gardening, maintenance, repair, remodeling or similar work in or about private home of employer, agricultural farm labor, state and its subdivisions (with limited exceptions), person for whom rule of liability for injury or death in course of employment is provided by federal law, charities, persons selling or distributing newspapers, magazines, or periodicals and person who is both licensee under 17-42-103(10) and qualified real estate agent under 3508(b)(1) of Internal Revenue Code of 1986 as amended. Act also applies to building contractors employing two or more persons, subcontractors employing one or more employees, and contractors who subcontract

LABOR RELATIONS . . . *continued*
having one or more employees. Sole proprietors, partners of partnership or members of limited liability company engaged full time may elect not to be covered by filing for and receiving "Certificate of Non-Coverage Under the Workers' Compensation Act" from Commission. (11-9-102).

Insurance.—Employers subject to Act must carry insurance. (11-9-404). If application for insurance is rejected Insurance Commissioner shall designate insurance carrier who must issue policy. (23-67-304, 305). Employer may become self-insurer with consent of Commission. (11-9-404). Two or more employers may pool liabilities to qualify as self-insurers and for other purposes. (11-9-404). License fee of $100 is required for qualification as self-insurer, and employer must pay tax annually to Commission not to exceed 3% of amount which would otherwise have been required for insurance premiums. (11-9-302, 304).

License fee of $500 is required for qualification as insurance carrier, and annual tax to be fixed by Commission at not over 3% of all premiums received must be paid to Commission by Apr. 1 of following year. (11-9-302, 303, 306).

Compensation is provided for various injuries and for total and partial disability, including disability resulting from occupational diseases, as defined with qualifications. (11-9-601-602). Weekly payments not to exceed 66⅔% of employee's average weekly wage, with $20 per week minimum and subject to following maximums: (A) For death or disability occurring July 1, 1987 through Dec. 31, 1988, maximum is $189; (B) for death or disability occurring during 1989, maximum shall be 66⅔% of state average weekly wage; (C) for death or disability occurring on or after Jan. 1, 1990 maximum shall be 70% of state average weekly wage (11-9-501); (D) for death or disability occurring on or after Jan. 1, 1996, maximum shall be 85% of state average weekly rate, if certain conditions are met; (E) after Jan. 1, 1994 weekly benefit rate shall be rounded to nearest whole dollar (11-9-501). Benefits may be paid for up to 450 weeks. (11-9-502). Maximum limitations of time and total compensation do not apply to cases of permanent total disability or death. (11-9-502). Benefits are not assignable or subject to attachment except for child support. (11-9-110). Death benefits are payable to dependents. (11-9-527). First $75,000 of weekly benefits for death or permanent total disability paid by employer or insurer. All benefits in excess of $75,000 payable from Death and Permanent Total Disability Trust Fund. (11-9-502). Reimbursement for medical and hospital expenses is required (11-9-508-517), and funeral expenses not exceeding $6,000 if death occurred on or after July 1, 1993 (11-9-527). Death benefits are payable according to schedule of persons wholly and actually dependent upon deceased. (11-9-527). Act authorizes and directs Commission, on or before July 1, 1994, to establish rules and regulations to implement system of managed health care. (11-9-508).

Notice of injury or death must be given to employer in form prescribed or approved by Commission, but Commission may excuse noncompliance. (11-9-701).

Claim for compensation for other than occupational disease or occupational infection must be filed within two years after compensable injury or death, or within one year after discovery of fraud which prevented filing within usual limitation period. (11-9-702). Claim for compensation for disability due to occupational disease or infection must be filed within two years of date of last injurious exposure to hazards of disease or infection. (11-9-702). Claims are heard before Commission, with right of appeal to Court of Appeals. (11-9-711). This remedy is exclusive, except that employee who fails to recover because of employer's noncompliance with Act may sue in courts and in such case common law defenses are denied to employer. (11-9-105).

Unemployment Compensation.—Arkansas has compulsory unemployment compensation program. (11-10-102). "Employers" (units employing one or more for some portion of ten days within current or preceding calendar year or successor of such units [11-10-209]) pay contributions to State based on experience to be held as unemployment compensation fund (11-10-704, 706, 801). Benefits are payable upon involuntary unemployment of individual in amount equal to 1/26th of total wages paid during one quarter of base period in which wages were highest; provided no weekly benefits shall be less than 12% of state average weekly wage for insured employment for preceding calendar year nor more than 66⅔% of state average weekly wage for insured employment for previous calendar year. (11-10-502). Employee is eligible only if employee files proper claim, has registered for work, is physically and mentally able to work and is available, has been unemployed for waiting period of one week, has earned wages of at least 27 times his weekly benefit amount and has earned wages for insured work in at least two quarters of base period (first four of last five completed calendar quarters immediately preceding first day of benefit year [11-10-201]) (11-10-507), and his unemployment is not result of labor dispute (11-10-508). "Benefit year" is 12 consecutive month period beginning first day of calendar quarter in which valid claim for benefits is filed. (11-10-203). Late contributions bear interest at 1½% per month until paid. (11-10-716). Act excludes certain domestic employment, certain agricultural labor, and enumerated other occupations (11-10-210), but noncovered employing units may elect coverage (11-10-403).

Employees engaged in approved shared work program may be eligible for unemployment compensation benefits. (11-10-609).

WORKERS' COMPENSATION LAW:

See topic Labor Relations.

ENVIRONMENT

ENVIRONMENTAL REGULATION:

Arkansas Environmental Quality Act of 1973 adopted in 1973 to protect environment. (15-20-301-319). Arkansas Water and Air Pollution Control Act adopted to prevent pollution. (8-4-101-107, 8-4-201-231, 8-4-301-315). Arkansas Solid Waste Management Act adopted in 1971 to regulate collection and disposal of solid wastes. (8-6-201-222). Arkansas Hazardous Waste Management Act of 1979 regulates hazardous waste disposal. (8-7-201-226). Arkansas Resource Reclamation Act of 1979 further regulates hazardous waste disposal and transportation. (8-7-301-309). Arkansas Surface Coal Mining and Reclamation Act of 1979 regulates surface coal mining. (15-58-101-510). Joint County and Municipal Solid Waste Disposal Act adopted for formation of sanitation authority. (14-233-101-122).

General supervision over environment preservation is by Arkansas Natural Heritage Commission, 1500 Tower Building, 323 Center Street, Little Rock, AR 72201. (15-20-304-309). General supervision over pollution, and handling and disposal of hazardous waste, is by Arkansas Pollution Control and Ecology Commission, 8001 National Drive, Little Rock, AR 72209. (8-4-201-230; 8-6-207).

Nuclear planning and response program administered by State Department of Health, 4815 W. Markham, Little Rock, AR 72201 to monitor nuclear generating facilities and to formulate emergency evacuation plans. (20-21-401-405). Counties to formulate and administer plan. (20-21-501-505). Ionizing radiation regulated. (20-21-201-222). Radiation from electronic products regulated. (20-21-301-312).

Prohibited acts of pollution include discharge into waters of State any sewage, industrial and other wastes to create nuisance or to render them injurious to public health, safety, and welfare, and to domestic, commercial, industrial, agricultural, recreational or beneficial use or to animal life; to construct or operate any system for doing so without authority of Department; to sell detergents for laundry or dishwashing that contain phosphorus (8-4-217, 8-4-102); emitting into air any substance which may cause it to become materially injurious to human, plant, or animal life or to property; to construct or operate any facility which does so without authority of Department (8-4-310, 8-4-303); operation without permit from Department of any facility for processing or disposing of refuse in solid or semi-solid form, other than disposing of waste from household activities under circumstances not creating nuisance or health hazard (8-6-205); disposition of solid wastes on land of another without owner's consent or upon public property (8-6-205); handling or disposal of hazardous wastes without license or permit (8-7-205). Wastewater treatment plants are regulated by and operators are licensed by Commission. (8-5-201-209). Arkansas Privatization Act (8-5-601-612) provides for private ownership and operation of public waste treatment facilities. Laboratories may be certified by Commission. (8-2-201-209).

Open cut and surface mining is under supervision of Arkansas Pollution Control and Ecology Commission and is closely regulated. (15-57-201-320, 15-58-101-510). See category Mineral, Water and Fishing Rights, topic Mines and Minerals.

Exemptions.—Air pollution does not include agricultural operations and equipment in growing crops and raising fowl and animals; use of barbecue equipment or outdoor fireplaces for residential use; land clearing operations or land grading; road construction operations; incinerators and heating equipment in residences used exclusively for dwellings for not more than four families; fires authorized by governmental authority, or open fires used at construction site for purposes of warming persons on site during cold weather unless prohibited by municipal or county ordinance and provided fire meets certain statutory specifications. (8-4-305). Commission may grant specific variances upon application and based on equitable principles. (8-4-313).

Enforcement is by proceedings before Commission upon ten days notice of alleged violation with appeal to Circuit Court of county in which business, industry, municipality, or thing involved is situated. (8-4-212-214, 8-4-218-229). Private right of action exists for violation of Arkansas Solid Waste Management Act. (8-6-206).

Penalties.—Pollution of State's waters and air is misdemeanor. (8-4-103). Punishable by imprisonment for not more than one year or fine of not more than $25,000. (8-4-103). For purpose of fines only, each day's continuance of such violation constitutes separate offense. (8-4-103). It constitutes felony to purposely, knowingly or recklessly pollute waters or air of State not otherwise permitted by law or to do so and then leave State. (8-4-103). Unlawful processing or disposing of solid wastes is misdemeanor and conviction carries imprisonment not to exceed one year or fines not to exceed $25,000, or both, each day's continuance of such violation constitutes separate offense for purpose of fines only. (8-6-204). It is felony to unlawfully process or dispose of solid wastes and then leave State. (8-6-204). Unlawful hazardous waste disposal constitutes misdemeanor and is punishable by imprisonment for not more than one year or fine of not more than $25,000, or subject to both fine and imprisonment. (8-7-204). For purposes of fines only, each day of violation constitutes separate offense. (8-7-204). One who purposely, knowingly or recklessly releases hazardous wastes into environment or creates substantial likelihood of endangering human or animal health or property, shall be guilty of felony, punishable by imprisonment for not more than ten years or fine of not more than $100,000, or subject to both fine and imprisonment. (8-7-204). Violation of permits and orders issued under Arkansas Surface Coal Mining and Reclamation Act is misdemeanor punishable by maximum one year imprisonment and $10,000 fine. (15-58-304). Each day's violation constitutes separate offense. (15-58-304). Interference with Director in performance of duties pursuant to Arkansas Surface Coal Mining and Reclamation Act is misdemeanor punishable by maximum one year imprisonment or $5,000 fine or subject to both fine and imprisonment. (15-58-305). Engaging in open-cut mining without permit is punishable by civil penalty not to exceed $5,000 per violation. (15-57-305).

Permits.—Commission may issue, modify, and revoke permits for operation of facilities to discharge sewage, industrial and other wastes into waters of State and into air (8-4-203-205) and facilities for processing and disposing of solid wastes (8-6-207). Permits for hazardous waste disposal issued by Commission. (8-7-215-222).

Operators of waste water plants must be licensed by Department. (8-5-207).

Unless applicant is publicly-held company required to file periodic reports under Securities and Exchange Act of 1934, or wholly-owned subsidiary of publicly-held company, all applicants for issuance or transfer of any permit, license or operational authority issued by Department of Pollution Control and Ecology shall file disclosure statement with their applications pursuant to requirements herein. (8-1-106).

Operators of commercial medical waste incineration facilities must obtain permit from Department. (8-6-1305-1306). Transporters of commercial medical waste must obtain operating license from Arkansas Department of Health. (20-32-107).

See note at head of Digest as to 1998 legislation covered.

See Topical Index in front part of this volume.

AR – 25

ESTATES AND TRUSTS

ADMINISTRATION:

See topic Executors and Administrators.

ADVANCEMENTS:

See topic Descent and Distribution.

ALLOWANCES:

See topic Executors and Administrators.

CLAIMS:

See topic Executors and Administrators; category Civil Actions and Procedure, topic Pleading.

DEATH:

In the absence of proof to the contrary, a resident of the state absent for five successive years is presumed dead in any case in which his death may come into question. (16-40-105).

Definition.—Person is legally dead when there is irreversible cessation of circulatory and respiratory functions or irreversible cessation of all brain and brain stem functions. (20-17-101).

Survivorship.—Uniform Simultaneous Death Act is in force. (28-10-101-111).

Action for death may be maintained by the personal representative, or if none by the heirs for the benefit of the widow and next of kin. Suit must be filed within three years. (16-62-102). If nonsuit taken, action must be recommenced within one year of nonsuit. (16-62-102).

Except as provided under Workers Compensation Act, damages for death may not be limited. (Const., art. 5, §32). Punitive damages may be allowed in wrongful death action. Amount recovered is distributed as in case of intestacy of person killed (16-62-102), but where action is for death of employee not within coverage of Workmen's Compensation Act against railroad or corporation (except while engaged in interstate commerce), amount recovered is distributed according to pecuniary injury suffered by each claimant (23-12-503, 11-8-103; 186 Ark. 1082, 57 S.W.2d 818).

Death Certificate.—See category Documents and Records, topic Records, subhead Vital Statistics.

Rights of the Terminally Ill or Permanently Unconscious Act.—See topic Wills, subhead Living Wills.

Uniform Anatomical Gift Act.—See topic Wills, subhead Living Wills.

DECEDENTS' ESTATES:

See topics Descent and Distribution, Executors and Administrators, Wills; category Debtor and Creditor, topic Homesteads.

DESCENT AND DISTRIBUTION:

Regulated by 28-9-201-220.

"*Heritable estate*" is intestate's real and personal property after provision for dower, curtesy, homestead rights, statutory rights and allowance of surviving spouse and minor children, refund on joint federal income tax returns, and administration of estate, if any. (28-9-206). "Heritable estate" passes as follows (each class with living members taking to exclusion of subsequent classes) to intestate's: (1) Surviving children and descendants of deceased children; (2) surviving spouse, but if married to intestate less than three years at death, surviving spouse takes only 50%, other 50% passing as if spouse had not survived intestate; (3) surviving parents, sharing equally, or to sole surviving parent if only one living; (4) if survived by no descendant but survived by spouse of less than three years, that portion of estate which does not pass to spouse under subdivision(s) passes to surviving parents; (5) brothers and sisters and descendants of deceased brothers and sisters; (6) surviving grandparents, uncles, and aunts and descendants of deceased uncles and aunts; (7) surviving great-grandparents, great uncles and great aunts, and by representation descendants of deceased great uncles and great aunts; (8) surviving spouse, even if married to intestate less than three years; (9) heirs of deceased spouse if marriage not ended by divorce; and (10) county wherein deceased resided at death. (28-9-214-215).

Where persons entitled to take are all of same degree of kindred to decedent they take per capita; otherwise they take per stirpes. (28-9-204).

Surviving Spouse.—Where intestate leaves no descendants and has been continuously married not less than three years before death, surviving spouse takes all and if continuously married less than three years before death, then only 50%. (28-9-214).

Half Blood.—Relatives of half and whole blood share alike. (28-9-213).

Posthumous lineal descendants of intestate inherit as if born in lifetime of intestate. (28-9-210).

Illegitimate children may inherit from mother and her blood kindred. An illegitimate child whose father marries his mother after birth and recognizes child as his is deemed legitimate. Illegitimate child may inherit from father and his blood kindred if action is commenced against father's estate within 180 days of father's death and statutory conditions evidencing paternity are satisfied. (28-9-209).

Adopted Children.—See category Family, topic Adoption.

Determination of Heirship.—Any person claiming interest as heir or distributee in property of deceased or personal representative of deceased may petition probate court for determination of heirs of deceased. Notice thereof required by publication and personal notice or by registered or certified mail, return receipt requested, where addresses are known. (28-53-101; 28-1-117).

Advancements.—If a person dies intestate as to all his estate, property given in his lifetime to an heir is treated as an advancement against heir's share of estate if declared in writing by decedent or acknowledged in writing by heir to be an advancement. Value of advancement is that as of time when heir came into possession or enjoyment of property or as of time of decedent's death, whichever first occurs. If recipient of property fails to survive decedent, property is not computed in share of recipient's descendants. (28-9-216).

Community Property.—Half of all personal property, wherever situated, which was acquired as or became and remained community property under laws of another jurisdiction or proportionate part of that property acquired with rents, issues or income of, or proceeds from, or in exchange for, that community property, or traceable to that community property, and half of all or proportionate part of any real property situated in this state which was acquired with rents, issues, or income of, proceeds from, or in exchange for, property acquired as or which become and remained community property under laws of another jurisdiction or property traceable to that community property is property of surviving spouse and is not subject to testamentary disposition by decedent or distribution under Arkansas law of intestate distribution. Remaining half of property is property of decedent and is subject to testamentary disposition or intestate distribution under Arkansas Laws. Half of property which is property of decedent is not subject to surviving spouse's right to elect against will, and no estate of dower or curtesy exists in such property. (28-12-101; 103).

Disclaimers.—See category Taxation, topic Estate Tax, subhead Disclaimers.

Election.—See category Taxation, topic Estate Tax, subhead Disclaimers.

Escheat.—Where decedent left no issue, kindred or surviving spouse, and where spouse left no heirs, estate escheats to county of decedent's residence at date of death. (28-9-215).

ESTATES:

See category Property, topic Real Property.

EXECUTORS AND ADMINISTRATORS:

Governed by Title 28, cc. 38-53.

The person named executor in the will may, before probate of will and granting of letters testamentary, take reasonably necessary action in management and preservation of property rights of decedent, and, subject to prior rights of members of decedent's immediate family, arrange for his burial. If court refuses to probate will, or if such person does not qualify, he is not liable for acts done in good faith and for which he would not have been liable had he been the lawful executor, but he must promptly account to personal representative when appointed. (28-40-106).

Venue for probate of will and for administration is county where decedent resided; or if he did not reside in state, then county wherein is located greater part in value of his property or if decedent had no residence or property within state but died in state, then of county in which he died; or if decedent had no residence or property within state and died outside of state, then of any county in which his personal representative may maintain cause of action. (28-40-102).

Any interested person may petition proper court for appointment of executor if one is nominated in will or for appointment of administrator if no executor is nominated or if the person so named is disqualified or unsuitable or refuses to serve or if there is no will. He may at the same time petition for probate of will. (28-40-107). If no demand for notice is filed, court may, in its discretion, hear petition forthwith. (28-40-109).

Any interested person desiring to be notified before will is admitted to probate or before personal representative is appointed may file with clerk demand for notice, and thereafter no will may be admitted to probate and no personal representative, other than special representative may be appointed until notice has been given. (28-40-108).

Application for letters of administration subject to few exceptions must be within five years after decedent's death. (28-40-103).

Preference in Right to Administer.—Domiciliary letters are granted in following order of priority: Executor nominated in will, surviving spouse or nominee upon petition filed within 30 days after decedent's death, one or more distributees or nominee upon application within 40 days after decedent's death where there is surviving spouse and within 30 days where there is no surviving spouse, any other qualified person. (28-48-101).

Eligibility and Competency.—Married or unmarried woman may serve as executrix or administratrix. (9-11-502, 28-48-101). Letters will not be issued to minor (unless emancipated [9-26-104]); person of unsound mind; convicted and unpardoned felon; corporation not authorized to act as fiduciary in this state; person whom court finds unsuitable; nonresident of state unless he appoints agent to accept service. (28-48-101).

Letters are issued when bond (if required) is approved and personal representative files with clerk his written acceptance of appointment. (28-48-102).

Ancillary Administrator.—Foreign personal representative, filing authenticated copy of domiciliary letter and bond, and appointing agent for service may be issued letters in Arkansas. (28-42-102-104). Corporate foreign personal representative need not qualify to do business in Arkansas to serve as ancillary administrator. (28-42-102). Foreign personal representative is preferred for ancillary administration. (28-42-102). Prior to final distribution of ancillary estate, court may order transfer of all or part of assets to domiciliary jurisdiction for administration and distribution. (28-42-106).

Any time after 60 days from death of nonresident, any person indebted to estate of decedent or having control of personal property belonging to estate of such decedent may pay debt or deliver personal property to domiciliary foreign personal representative of decedent upon being presented with proof of his appointment and affidavit made by or on behalf of representative stating: (1) Decedent's date of death; (2) that no local administration or application therefor is pending in this state; and (3) that domiciliary foreign personal representative is entitled to payment or delivery. (28-42-110).

Removal.—Court may remove personal representative for incompetency, for mismanagement of estate, for failure to perform any duty, or when he becomes nonresident without appointing agent for service, but removal after issuance of letters does not invalidate his official acts performed prior to removal. (28-48-105). Representative of estate of deceased or incompetent personal representative has duty to protect estate

EXECUTORS AND ADMINISTRATORS . . . *continued*
being administered by deceased or incompetent until successor or special representative is appointed. (28-48-106).

Bond is required, with two or more sufficient sureties, who are residents of state, in not less than double estimated value of property which may reasonably be expected to pass through hands of personal representative, except that if bond is executed by corporate surety authorized to do business in state, amount may not be less than estimated value of such property. (28-48-201).

Except for nonresident administrator, court may dispense with or reduce amount of bond when testator so directed, when personal representative is member bank of Federal Reserve System whose deposits are insured by F. D. I. C., or when all distributees are competent, have filed written waivers of bond, and there are no unsecured claims. (28-48-206).

Unless authorized by special order of court, no sheriff, clerk, or deputy of either, judge, or attorney may be surety. (28-48-203).

Bond must be examined and approved by court or by clerk subject to confirmation by court with approval endorsed thereon. (28-48-205).

If personal representative fails to give bond or, if no bond is required, fails to file written acceptance of appointment within time fixed by court, another person is appointed in his stead and letters, if issued, are revoked. (28-48-202).

Special Kinds of Administration.—Upon death, removal or resignation of personal representative, court may appoint a successor. (28-48-107). Such successor or administrator with the will annexed has all powers of executor nominated in will except those personal to him. (28-48-107). Court may appoint special administrator before or after appointment of executor or general administrator for specified time, to perform duties respecting specified property, or to perform particular acts. Order is not appealable. (28-48-103).

Public Administrator.—Sheriff acts as public administrator if person dies in county without known spouse or next of kin and no one petitions for letters, if person dies elsewhere leaving in the county property not in possession of some responsible person, and when court directs him to do so. (28-48-301). He must prepare inventory (28-48-302), and court may require bond (28-48-303). If general personal representative is appointed, public administrator must account to him. (28-48-304).

Inventory and Appraisal.—Within two months after his qualification or as court may direct, personal representative must file complete inventory of decedent's property, describing each item and giving his appraisal of the fair market value thereof, with affidavit that inventory is complete to best of his knowledge and belief and that he was not indebted to decedent at the time of his death except as stated in inventory. (28-49-110). Filing of inventory may be waived by written waiver of all competent distributees and guardians of estate of all incompetent distributees unless court finds need for inventory or any claimant makes written demand for it. (28-49-110). Errors or omissions must be corrected by supplemental inventory or with next accounting or as court may direct. (28-49-110).

General Powers and Duties.—Personal representative must take possession of all personal property subject to the rights of dower and statutory allowances to widow or minor children. (28-49-101).

Real property is an asset in personal representative's hands when so directed by will or when court finds such property must be sold, mortgaged, leased, or exchanged for payment of claims or legacies, or for protection, distribution, or best interests of estate. (28-49-101). Personal representative may recover property fraudulently transferred by decedent (28-49-109), abandon valueless property and property that is of no benefit to estate (28-49-106), and may compromise claims due estate (28-49-104).

If decedent purchased real or personal property without completing payment therefor or mortgaged real or personal property and neither devised the property nor by will provided for payment or redemption, court may order personal representative to pay balance of purchase price or redeem out of assets of estate. (28-49-107-108).

Personal representative may compel discovery of assets (28-49-103), may borrow money, execute notes and mortgage property of estate (28-49-113), may invest funds of estate (28-49-115), and except as otherwise directed in will, may join with decedent's spouse in making joint income tax return and may consent, for gift tax purposes, to gifts made by decedent's spouse so that such gifts may be treated for gift tax purposes as if made one-half by decedent and one-half by spouse (28-49-117). He must perform decedent's contracts of sale of real and personal property when decedent himself could have been compelled to perform and must, when required by contract, give warranties which are binding on estate. (28-49-114). Personal representative may lease or mortgage personal and real property under same general provisions relating to sales. Except in cases of oil, gas and other minerals, leases of real property may not exceed three years. (28-51-303).

By specific reference to statute in will, broad powers specified in statute may be granted to executor or testamentary trustee as fiduciary. (28-69-301-304).

Continuing Decedent's Business.—Unless decedent's will directs otherwise, executor or administrator may continue decedent's business for time period not exceeding one month following date of grant of letters without an order of court and if the business be that of farming it may continue for three months or until the end of the calendar year in which the decedent's death occurred, whichever is longer. Thereafter, the court may order further continuance of the business for additional period not exceeding three months and for additional period not exceeding one year if farming operation. Estate, but not representative, is liable for damages resulting from torts or other acts committed by agents and employees of estate. (28-49-112).

Notice to Creditors.—Promptly after letters are granted, the personal representative must publish, once a week for two consecutive weeks in a newspaper published and of general circulation in county of probate, or of general circulation in county if none is published in county, notice of his appointment, stating date thereof, and requiring all persons having claims against estate to exhibit them, properly verified, to him within three months from date of first publication (six months in case of tort claims) or be precluded from any benefits of estate. Personal representative must serve copy of notice on each known or reasonably ascertainable heir, devisee, and unpaid creditor within one month after publication. (28-40-111). If value of estate does not exceed $1,000, publication may be by posting notice in courthouse. In addition, court may require notice by ordinary mail to all persons named in petition.

Disclaimer.—(28-2-101-109). See category Taxation, topic Estate Tax, subhead Disclaimers.

Presentation of Claims.—All claims are barred unless presented to personal representative or filed with the court within three months (six months for claims for injury or death caused by negligence of decedent) after date of first publication of notice to creditors (28-40-111 and 28-50-101) and in any event are barred at end of five years after date of decedent's death unless within said period letters have been issued and notice to creditors published (28-50-101). Some tort claims involving liability insurance or uninsured motorist coverage may be brought within limitation period otherwise provided. (28-50-101).

Revival of action pending against decedent at time of his death and commencement of action against personal representative after decedent's death have effect as claims duly filed from the time of such revivor or commencement if plaintiff files with probate court a copy of petition for revivor or of the complaint. (28-50-102).

Unmatured claims must be presented. (28-50-108).

Contingent claims must be presented. (28-50-110).

Secured claims must be presented. (28-50-109).

Proof of Claims.—Claim must be in writing, describing the nature and amount, and if presented upon a written instrument, the original or a copy with all endorsements must be attached. Original instrument must be exhibited upon demand unless lost or destroyed in which case its loss or destruction must be stated in claim. (28-50-103).

Verification.—Claim must be verified by affidavit stating that the amount is justly due, or if not yet due, when it will or may become due, that no payments have been made thereon which are not credited, that there are no offsets to same, and the nature of any contingent claim, to the knowledge of affiant except as stated therein. A claim assigned after testator's death must be verified by or for person owning claim at date of decedent's death and by or for his assignee. (28-50-103). Affidavit can be made out of state before commissioner for Arkansas, judge of court or other authorized officer. (16-45-102).

Form

Form of affidavit to claims:

By individual claimant:

I, ..., do solemnly swear that the attached claim against the estate of . . . . ., deceased, is correct, that nothing has been paid or delivered toward the satisfaction thereof except what is credited thereon, that there are no offsets to the same, to the knowledge of this affiant, except as therein stated and that the sum of . . . . . . Dollars ($. . . .) is now justly due (or will or may become due as stated therein). I further state that if this claim is based upon a written instrument, the copy thereof, including all endorsements, which is attached hereto, is true and complete.

. . . .

State of . . . ., County of . . . .

Subscribed and sworn to before me, this . . . . day of . . . ., 19 . . .

. . . .

(Official Title)

If the affidavit is made by anyone other than an individual in his own behalf, the representative capacity of the affiant must be clearly stated.

Allowance or Rejection of Claim.—Any claim approved by personal representative in writing and duly filed may be allowed by court at any time without formal hearing. A claim disapproved or not acted upon by personal representative must be set for hearing. Court must allow claim in whole or in part and classify it or disallow it. Order allowing claim has effect of a judgment and bears legal interest unless claim provided a different rate. (28-50-105).

Small Claims.—Notwithstanding requirements on filing claim with verification, personal representative may pay claims amounting in the aggregate to $3,000 or less none of which may exceed the sum of $300, and take credit therefor in his settlement. (28-50-105).

Payment of Claims.—Six months after first publication of notice to creditors and final adjudication of all claims filed, personal representative must pay claims allowed against estate. Prior to expiration of six months' period, court may order payment of claims and require bond from creditor. (28-50-113).

Unmatured Claim.—Allowed at present value and paid as an absolute claim, except creditor must agree where obligation upon which such claim was founded was entered into before effective date of Code; otherwise court may order personal representative to retain sufficient funds to satisfy claim upon maturity; or if distributee gives sufficient bond, court may order such bond to be given in satisfaction of the claim and close estate. (28-50-108).

Secured Claim.—If creditor surrenders security, payment is made upon basis of full amount as an unsecured claim. If creditor liquidates and applies to payment of claim the proceeds of all or part of security and surrenders any part not so liquidated, payment is upon basis of balance of claim remaining unpaid as an unsecured claim. Creditor may waive claim against estate and rely only on his security. (28-50-109).

Contingent claim is paid as an absolute claim if it becomes absolute before distribution of estate; otherwise court may order personal representative to distribute estate but to retain sufficient funds to pay claim if and when it become absolute, but for this purpose estate is not kept open longer than two years after remainder of estate is distributed. (28-50-110).

Priorities.—Claims are classified and paid in the following order: (1) costs and expenses of administration; (2) reasonable funeral, medical, and other expenses incidental to last illness, and wages of decedent's employees; and (3) all other allowed claims. No preference is given in payment of any claim over another of the same class. (28-50-106). If assets are sufficient to pay part but not all claims of single class, assets applicable thereto must be apportioned between them. (28-50-113).

See note at head of Digest as to 1998 legislation covered.

See Topical Index in front part of this volume.

AR – 27

EXECUTORS AND ADMINISTRATORS . . . *continued*

Sales.—Real and personal property may be sold only by order of court except where power of sale was given to personal representative in will. Sale may be on credit not to exceed 90% of purchase price and to be paid within ten years from date of sale. (28-51-102, 103, 105). Personal property may be sold at public or private sale, and court may require confirmation. (28-51-201). Personal representative may sell perishable personal property without order of court but is responsible for actual value unless he promptly files report and obtains court's approval. (28-51-202). Sale of real property, absent power of sale in will, must be on personal representative's petition for hearing upon notice given, except court may waive notice if value of property is not more than $1,500. (28-51-301). Certified appraisement must be filed with clerk before rendition of order of sale. (28-51-302). Order must describe property to be sold, require adequate bond of personal representative, provide for private or public auction and, if latter, place of sale. Sale at public auction must be for not less than three-fourths of appraised value and at private sale for not less than full appraised value. (28-51-303).

If sale is at public auction, personal representative must publish once a week for three consecutive weeks in a newspaper published or having a general circulation in the county in which the real property is located notice describing property and stating time, place and terms of sale, except if value of property is less than $500, in lieu of newspaper publication, personal representative may post notices in courthouse, on each tract of land to be sold, and in three additional places in county where property is located. (28-51-304).

Personal representative must file a verified report of sale within ten days after date of sale, and the court may affirm or reject the sale. (28-51-305).

Actions.—There is no suspension of the right to sue on a claim against a decedent's estate and action on a claim may be commenced within the time allowed for presentation thereof, without other presentation. Action pending against decedent at time of death may be continued against representative if cause of action survives. (28-50-102).

Allowances.—In addition to their homestead, dower and curtesy rights, surviving spouse and minor children of decedent or either in absence of other may select personal property of value of $2,000 as against distributees and $1,000 as against creditors. In addition and without regard to distributees or creditors, surviving spouse, if living with decedent at time of his or her death, may have furniture reasonably necessary for occupation of his or her dwelling and during period of two months after decedent's death, surviving spouse and minor children or either in absence of other may receive from estate amount not to exceed $500 for sustenance. (28-39-101).

Accounting and Settlement.—Personal representative must file verified account of administration upon filing petition for final settlement, upon revocation of his letters, upon his application to resign and before his resignation is accepted, annually during the period of administration unless court directs otherwise, and at any time when directed by the court on its own motion or on application of an interested person (28-52-103). In absence of written demand for accounting and where all distributees are competent and have filed written waivers, formal accounting need not be filed if personal representative files verified statement that notice to creditors has been published as required and time for filing claims has expired, that there are no unpaid claims, that all state and federal estate taxes have been paid, copy of federal estate tax return has been made available to distributees bearing portion of tax, and that full distribution has been made to distributees. (28-52-104).

Compensation of Representatives.—Compensation is allowable when and as earned but not to exceed 10% of first $1,000, 5% of next $4,000, and 3% of balance of value of personal property (28-48-108), but when personal representative has performed substantial duties with respect to real property, court may allow additional compensation to be borne as provided in will or by distributees benefited by such service (28-48-108).

Compensation for legal services, unless otherwise contracted with personal representative or heirs, is allowable on basis of total market value of real and personal property as follows: 5% of first $5,000; 4% of next $20,000; 3% of next $75,000; 2 3/4% of next $300,000; 2 1/2% of next $600,000; and 2% of balance of value of all other property and may be increased or decreased if necessary under circumstances to provide fee commensurate with value of services rendered. (28-48-108).

Distribution.—After the time for filing claims but before final settlement, court may order partial distribution and require security. (28-53-102). Final distribution is made upon approval of representative's final account and after hearing on at least 60 days notice but court may approve final account immediately on filing when competent parties and guardians of incompetents waive notice and hearing. (28-53-103).

Income During Administration.—Unless will indicates contrary intent: (i) General legacies of solvent estates bear interest at legal rate, commencing 15 months after administration begins; (ii) specific devises include income or increment during administration; and (iii) income during administration on items devised to trust goes to income beneficiary of trust. (28-53-112).

Improper Distributions to Beneficiaries.—Distributee of property improperly distributed or paid is liable for return of property, income thereon, and, interest at 6% per annum on money improperly paid. Distribution without deduction of, or payment for, apportioned death taxes is deemed improper distribution. (28-53-110).

Distribution Where Distributee Unavailable.—If distributee cannot be found, or if for any reason personal representative is unable to deliver to distributee his share of estate and take a receipt therefor, court may order personal representative to sell nonliquid assets distributable to such distributee and deposit proceeds in registry of court, and clerk's receipt therefor constitutes an acquittance to personal representative. Court may authorize clerk to deposit fund in a designated bank, the deposits of which are insured by FDIC, or to invest fund in bonds of United States or State of Arkansas until ultimate distribution. (28-53-116).

Distribution If Abroad.—No special provision.

When Administration Unnecessary.—Distributees of an estate are entitled thereto without administration when no petition for appointment of personal representative is pending or has been granted; 45 days have elapsed since decedent's death; the value, less encumbrances, homestead and statutory allowances to widow or minor children, does not exceed $50,000, and when a distributee files with clerk an affidavit that there are no unpaid claims and that Department of Human Services furnished no federal or state benefits to decedent or, if it did furnish such benefits, that it has been reimbursed in accordance with state and federal law, and giving itemized description and valuation of decedent's property, including legal description of any real property, names and addresses of persons having possession of or residing on property, and names, addresses and relationship to decedent of persons entitled to and who will receive property, certified copy of which affidavit must be furnished to every person owing any money, having custody of any property, or acting as registrar or transfer agent of any evidence of interest, indebtedness, property or right of estate. In order to allow claims against estate to be presented, distributee of estate containing real property may cause notice of death and filing of affidavit to be published. Notice shall contain decedent's name, address, date of death, statement that affidavit was filed, legal description of real property, statement requiring all persons to exhibit claims within six months of first publication of notice or they shall be forever barred, name and address of distributee or their attorney, and date of first publication. Publication of notice does not affect or prevent any action or proceeding to enforce any mortgage, pledge or other lien upon property of estate. Publication of notice is as provided for Notice to Creditors in normal estate administration, discussed above. (28-41-101).

Any person making payment, transfer, or delivery pursuant to such affidavit is released to same extent as if making payment to personal representative, and any person refusing payment or transfer may be compelled by appropriate action to pay. After publication of notice to creditors, distributee of real property is authorized to issue to himself deed of distribution for real property of decedent as if made by personal representative of decedent. (28-41-102).

Either with or without administration, if court determines that testator's personal property does not exceed statutory dower and allowances to widow or minor children, it may by order specifically describing the property vest the entire estate in them. (28-41-103). Court may set such order aside within one year. (28-41-104).

Small Estates.—See subhead When Administration Unnecessary, supra.

Foreign executor or administrator may, upon execution of same bond required of other nonresidents, sue in Arkansas. (16-61-110). See also topic Wills, subhead Foreign Probated Wills.

Uniform Fiduciaries Act not adopted.

Revised Uniform Principal and Income Act adopted. (28-70-101-119).

Uniform Simplification of Fiduciary Security Transfers Act not adopted.

Uniform Anatomical Gift Act.—See topic Wills.

Uniform Transfers to Minors Act adopted (9-26-201-227); Uniform Gifts to Minors Act repealed (9-26-227).

FIDUCIARIES:

See topics Executors and Administrators, Trusts; category Family, topic Guardian and Ward.

INTESTACY:

See topic Descent and Distribution.

PROOF OF CLAIMS:

See topic Executors and Administrators; category Civil Actions and Procedure, topic Pleading.

TRUSTS:

The rules of common law and equity apply generally to trusts, and courts of equity have jurisdiction to enforce them. (101 Ark. 451, 142 S.W. 848). All declarations of trusts of lands must be in writing (4-59-103), but this is required only of express trusts and not implied or resulting trusts. (136 Ark. 481, 207 S.W. 22). Express trustee may sue without joining beneficiary. (RCP 17). Word "Trustee" or "Agent" after name of grantee in deed is no notice to any person dealing with land that trust or agency exists and such words are ineffective. (18-12-604). Broad fiduciary powers may be granted by reference in instrument to 28-69-304. 4-88-107 includes, as deceptive trade practice, offering for sale or drafting of any trust document by nonlawyer, except by bank trust department or trust company. Act 940 of 1997 is Arkansas Trust Institutions Act.

Uniform Trustees' Accounting Act not adopted.

Revised Uniform Principal and Income Act adopted. (28-70-101-118).

Eligibility and Competency.—Trustees of testamentary and inter vivos trusts are defined to include corporation without distinction as to domestic or foreign (28-69-301) but no other specific statutory provisions. Foreign corporations acting in fiduciary capacity must strictly comply with provisions of statute. (4-27-201-205, 301-305).

Uniform Testamentary Additions to Trusts Act adopted. (28-27-101-106).

Investments by fiduciaries are regulated by 28-71-101-107.

Securities in Name of Nominee.—No statutory provision.

Bequests and Devises to Inter Vivos Trusts.—See topic Wills.

Uniform Custodial Trust Act adopted. (28-72-401-422).

Accounting.—No statutory provision.

Accumulations.—No statutory provision.

Perpetuities.—See category Property, topic Perpetuities.

Disclaimer.—See category Taxation, topic Estate Tax, subhead Disclaimers.

Divisions of trust into two or more separate trusts authorized if trustee determines that division is in interest of beneficiaries or could result in federal tax savings. (Act 585 of 1997).

Uniform Common Trust Fund Act adopted. (28-69-201-202).

Transfers to Minors.—See category Family, topic Infants.

See note at head of Digest as to 1998 legislation covered.

See Topical Index in front part of this volume.

TRUSTS . . . *continued*

Uniform Fiduciaries Act not adopted.

Uniform Simplification of Fiduciary Security Transfers Act not adopted.

Private Foundations.—Governing instrument requirements are supplied for trusts by 28-72-302, unless avoided by affirmative actions specified in statute.

Pour Over Trusts.—See topic Wills, subhead Bequests and Devises to Inter Vivos Trusts.

WILLS:

Governed by Title 28, cc. 24-27.

Any person of sound mind 18 years of age or older may make a will. (28-25-101).

Testamentary Disposition.—There are no limitations upon testator's power to dispose of property, nor any restrictions upon gifts to religious or charitable institutions.

Execution of will (other than holographic) must be by signature of testator and of at least two witnesses. The testator must declare to the attesting witnesses that the instrument is his will and either himself sign, or acknowledge his signature already made; or sign by mark, his name being written near it and witnessed by a person who writes his own name as a witness to the signature, or at his discretion and in his presence have someone else sign his name for him (the person so signing must write his own name and state that he signed the testator's name at the request of the testator), and the signature must be done in the presence of two or more attesting witnesses who must sign at testator's request and in his presence. (28-25-103).

Form

The ordinary form of attestation clause is as follows:

"We hereby bear witness that the testator signed the foregoing will in the presence of each of us (or acknowledged to each of us that he had subscribed the foregoing will); that the testator at the time of making (or acknowledging) the subscription declared the instrument subscribed to be his will and testament and requested us to sign our names as bar witnesses."

In case the subscription was by a person other than the testator, at the testator's request, the foregoing form should, of course, be changed to show that fact.

Deposit of will may be made by testator with probate court of the county of his residence with directions to whom it should be delivered after testator's death. During testator's lifetime will may be delivered only to him or to one authorized by him. (28-25-108).

Holographic Wills.—When the entire body of the will and the signature are in handwriting of the testator, it may be established by the evidence of at least three disinterested witnesses to the handwriting and signature of the testator, without subscribing witnesses. (28-25-104).

If a typewritten will is not attested, it becomes good when the testator adds a codicil referring to it, written entirely in his own hand and signed. (176 Ark. 287, 3 S.W.2d 26).

Joint wills to take effect at death of survivor are invalid. (35 Ark. 17).

Revocation.—A will, or any part thereof, can be revoked only by subsequent will; or by being burned, torn, canceled, obliterated or destroyed with intent to revoke, by testator or another person in his presence and at his direction. Where there is partial revocation, reattestation of remainder of will is not required. (28-25-109). Subsequent divorce revokes all provisions of will in favor of testator's spouse so divorced. (28-25-109). Testator's subsequent agreement to convey property devised in will does not revoke devise, but property passes subject to same remedies on agreement against devisee as might have been enforced against decedent if he had survived, but contract to devise property must be proven according to statutory standards. (28-24-101). Subsequent charge or encumbrance does not revoke previous will but devisee takes subject thereto. (28-26-105).

Revival.—Will revoked or which becomes invalid can be revised only by re-execution or by execution of another will in which revoked or invalid will or part thereof is incorporated by reference. (28-25-110).

Testamentary gift to subscribing witness does not invalidate will, but, unless will is attested by two qualified disinterested witnesses, interested witness forfeits so much of provision made for him as in aggregate exceeds in value as of date of testator's death what witness would have received had testator died intestate. (28-25-102).

Bequests and Devises to Inter Vivos Trusts.—Pour over trusts are in common practice. Uniform Testamentary Additions to Trusts Act adopted. (28-27-101-106).

Testamentary Guardian.—See category Family, topic Guardian and Ward, subhead Eligibility.

Probate.—Venue for probate of will is the county where decedent resided at time of death; if he had no residence in Arkansas, the county wherein is located the greater part in value of his property; if he had no residence or property in Arkansas, the county where he died; if he had no residence or property in Arkansas and died outside the state, the county in which a cause of action may be maintained by a personal representative. (28-40-102).

Any interested person may petition proper court for admission of will to probate, although it may not be in his possession, or may be lost, destroyed, or without the state, and at same time may petition for appointment of executor or administrator. (28-40-107). If no demand for notice is filed, court may hear petition forthwith. (28-40-109).

Any interested person desiring to be notified before a will is admitted to probate may file with the clerk a request for notice, and thereafter no will may be probated until notice has been given. (28-40-108).

Application to probate will must be within five years after decedent's death. (28-40-103).

Testator may bring declaratory judgment action prior to death to establish validity of will. (28-40-201-203).

Self-proved Wills.—If probate of will is uncontested, will may be proved by affidavits of attesting witnesses acknowledged before notary public. Affidavit may be made at time of execution of will or after testator's death and shall be written on will, if practicable, or attached to will or true copy. (28-25-106, 28-40-118).

Form

Ordinary form of affidavit is as follows:

Proof of Will

We, . . . and . . ., on oath state:

We are the subscribing witnesses to the attached written instrument, dated . . . day of . . ., 19. ., which purports to be the last will of . . ., deceased. On the execution date of the instrument the testator, in our presence, signed the instrument at the end thereof, or acknowledged his signature thereto, declared the instrument to be his will, and requested that we attest his execution thereof; whereupon, in the presence of the testator each of us signed our respective names as attesting witnesses. At the time of execution of the instrument the testator appeared to be eighteen years of age or older, of sound mind, and acting without undue influence, fraud or restraint.

Dated this . . . day of . . ., 19. .

. . . . .
. . . . .
(Acknowledgment)

Contest.—Probate of a will or any part thereof may be contested before final distribution of estate is ordered or approved and within five years from decedent's death for newly discovered will; and if contest is on any other ground, then before hearing on petition for probate where notice has been given pursuant to demand for notice; within three months after date of first publication of notice of probate or within 45 days after service of notice of probate on him or his predecessor in interest where contestant has been given notice and is not otherwise barred. (28-40-113). Objections to foreign will probated in this state must be filed within same time as against resident's will or thereafter within 45 days after will is set aside in state of decedent's domicile. (28-40-113).

Executor or Administrator with will annexed or other interested person defending will, whether or not successful, is allowed reasonable attorney's fees and necessary expenses out of estate. (28-48-109).

Record.—Wills admitted to probate are recorded in probate clerk's office. The will, or the record thereof, or the transcript of the record, duly certified, is admissible in evidence without further proof. (28-40-122). Personal representative must record, at expense of estate, certified copy of will in recorder's office in each county other than county of probate in which real property of decedent is located. (28-40-123).

Children.—Child born or adopted subsequent to execution of will takes as though testator had died intestate unless mentioned or provided for therein specifically or as member of class. Failure to mention then-living child in will at time of execution, specifically or as member of class, creates intestacy as to him. (28-39-407).

Legacies.—See topic Executors and Administrators, subhead Distribution.

Unclaimed legacies subject to escheat. (18-28-207). See also topic Executors and Administrators, subhead Distribution Where Distributee Unavailable.

Lapse.—Unless contrary intent is indicated, legacy or devise to child or descendant of testator does not lapse on death of beneficiary before testator if beneficiary leaves child or descendant surviving testator, who then takes. (28-26-104).

Election.—When married person dies testate as to any part of estate surviving spouse if married to decedent more than one year may elect between will and such part of property as would have been taken on intestacy including dower or curtesy and homestead and statutory allowances. If there is residue of property undisposed of by will after assignment of dower or curtesy, payment of all statutory allowances, taxes, and debts, and satisfaction of all bequests and devises, surviving spouse takes residue by intestacy in absence of surviving children, natural or adopted, parent, brother, sister, grandparent, uncle, aunt, great-grandparent, great-uncle, or great-aunt, or lineal descendants of any of them. (28-39-401). Election must be made within one month after expiration of time limited for filing claims; provided that if at expiration of such period pending litigation might affect amount to be received by surviving spouse, election may be made within one month after date of final order adjudicating litigation. (28-39-403).

Election to take against the will must be in writing, signed and acknowledged, and filed in the office of the probate clerk. (28-39-404).

A duplicate original or certified copy of election must be filed with recorder of each county in which testator owned at time of his death estate of inheritance in real property. (28-39-404).

Right of election is personal, non-transferable, and does not survive surviving spouse. (28-39-405).

An election to take against the will may not be revoked except within the time for filing an election and before any distribution made on the basis of such election, or thereafter for such causes as justify rescission of a deed. (28-39-406).

Form

Form for election shall be substantially as follows:

I, A. B., surviving wife (or husband) of C. D., Deceased, hereby renounce and disclaim any and all benefits under the will of C. D., and elect to take from the estate of C. D. only the property and benefits which (because of this election) will accrue to me under Section 33 of Act No. 140, approved February 23, 1949, as amended.

Dated: . . . .   Signed . . . .
Acknowledgment. (28-39-404).

Lost Wills.—Wills lost or destroyed by accident or design are proved in the chancery court in the same way as lost deeds (28-40-301), or in probate court by evidence competent and sufficient to establish lost will in equity. Existence of will at testator's death or its fraudulent destruction in his lifetime must be proved, and its provisions

WILLS . . . *continued*

must be proved by two witnesses, correct copy being equivalent to one witness. (28-40-302).

Foreign Executed Wills.—Will executed outside Arkansas in manner prescribed by Arkansas Code or by law of place where executed or by law of testator's domicile at time of execution has same effect in State as if executed in Arkansas in compliance with Code. (28-25-105).

Foreign Probated Wills.—Will of nonresident probated elsewhere may be probated in Arkansas by filing authenticated copy thereof with an authenticated copy of order admitting it to probate elsewhere. (28-40-120). See also Executors and Administrators, subhead Ancillary Administrator.

Renunciation.—See category Taxation, topic Estate Tax, subhead Disclaimers.

Simultaneous Death.—See topic Death, subhead Survivorship.

Testamentary Trusts.—See topic Trusts.

Uniform Anatomical Gift Act (1987) adopted. (20-17-601-617).

Living Wills.—Individual may execute declaration governing withholding or withdrawal of life-sustaining treatment. Such declaration may direct withholding or withdrawal of such treatment or designate Health Care Proxy to make these decisions for individual. Forms of declaration provided in 20-17-202. Immunities and penalties established by 20-17-208, 209. Out of state declarations executed in compliance with law of state of execution are recognized. (20-17-212).

FAMILY

ADOPTION:

Revised Uniform Adoption Act (1977, with 1979, 1983, 1995 and 1997 amendments) adopted (9-9-201-224) with modifications in notice of petition, investigation and hearing requirements (§12), and application for new birth records (§19). It is felony for any parent, agency or guardian of minor to receive consideration (other than reasonable reimbursement for costs incurred) in exchange for relinquishment of minor for adoption. (9-9-206). Enacted putative father registry for man who is not legally presumed or adjudicated to be biological father of child but who claims or is alleged to be father of child with amended notice procedures for cases involving child born to unmarried mother at time of child's birth. (20-18-701-705). Statutory procedure exists for establishing and operation of mutual consent voluntary adoption registry to permit adoptees upon obtaining majority and natural parents to indicate their willingness to have their identity and whereabouts disclosed to each other. (9-9-501-508). Any person disclosing confidential information except in accordance with statute or court order is guilty of misdemeanor. (9-9-502).

Interstate Compacts on Placement of Children (9-29-201-208) and Adoption and Medical Assistance (9-29-301) adopted. Public funds are available to parents who adopt children with special problems. (9-9-401-412).

ALIMONY:

See topic Divorce.

COMMUNITY PROPERTY:

System does not apply in Arkansas.

DESERTION:

See topics Divorce, Husband and Wife.

DISSOLUTION OF MARRIAGE:

See topic Divorce.

DIVORCE:

This subject is governed by Tit. 9, c. 12.

Grounds for absolute divorce are adultery; impotency at time of marriage continuing to time of bringing action for divorce; conviction of felony or infamous crime; habitual drunkenness for one year; cruel and barbarous treatment endangering life of innocent party; indignities to person of innocent party rendering his or her condition intolerable; that parties have lived apart for eighteen months without cohabitation, whether voluntary or by mutual consent; willful nonsupport. (9-12-301).

Where living apart was due to incurable insanity of defendant, insane spouse must have been continuously confined in institution for at least three years and have been adjudicated to be of unsound mind.(9-12-301).

Even though the cause of divorce occurred out of the state, the laws of Arkansas as to causes of divorce govern exclusively. (9-12-307).

Citizenship Requirements.—None.

Residence Requirements.—Plaintiff or defendant must have resided in the state for at least 60 days before commencement of action and for at least three months before final judgment of divorce. (9-12-307). Where defendant does not enter appearance or personal service cannot be had, proof of actual residence in state for three months before final judgment of divorce is required. (9-12-307). See 229 Ark. 842, 318 S.W.2d 793 concerning full faith and credit of Arkansas divorce decree.

Jurisdiction of divorce actions is in the chancery courts. (9-12-302).

Venue of divorce action is county of plaintiff's residence or county of defendant's residence if plaintiff is nonresident (9-12-303), but process may be directed to any county in state. (9-12-303). When spouse initiates action for divorce or separate maintenance, venue for initial action shall be venue for subsequent action filed by other spouse regardless of that spouse's residency. (9-12-303). When six months have passed since final decree and both parties have established residence in county of another chancery district, further action upon case may be brought in county of residence of custodial parent or where final decree was rendered. (9-12-320).

Pleading and Proof.—Plaintiff must prove, but need not allege, that cause of divorce existed or occurred in state, or, if out of state, that it was legal cause of divorce in state; that cause of divorce occurred or existed within five years before commencement of suit. (9-12-307).

In contested suits residence, grounds for divorce and proof of separation and continuity of separation with cohabitation must be corroborated, but corroboration of injured party's grounds may be waived in writing by other spouse. (9-12-306).

In uncontested suits corroboration is required for residence but not for ground other than ground of continuous separation without cohabitation which may be corroborated by oral testimony or verified affidavit of non-parties. (9-12-306). Complaint is not taken as true for failure of defendant to answer or because of his or her admission. (9-12-305).

Independent action for alimony or separate maintenance without asking for divorce may be brought. (See 21 Ark. App. 287.)

Practice.—Court has discretion to hear divorce and related actions in privacy with only parties and counsel present. (16-13-318).

Allowance and reasonable attorney's fee may be allowed either party during pendency of action of divorce, separate maintenance, or alimony. Court may reduce award to judgment and allow execution upon all marital property except homestead to pay allowance. (9-12-309). Court may allow additional fees for enforcement. (9-12-309).

Judgment or Decree.—Final decree not rendered until at least 30 days after filing complaint, except when defendant is constructively summoned by publication of warning order, one year noncohabitation, and bigamy. (9-12-310).

Alimony and Children.—Court may decree alimony and care of children and may require bond for compliance with decree as to care of children (9-12-312), income withholding for noncustodial parent delinquent in support payments in amount equal to total court-ordered support payable for 30 days (9-10-112), and may enforce decree for alimony or maintenance by sequestration of defendant's property or that of his or her sureties (9-12-313).

Alimony may be awarded as reasonable based upon circumstances of parties and nature of case to either party in fixed installments for specific period of time, subject to remarriage of receiving party, or such other contingencies as are set forth in award, so that such payments qualify as "periodic payments" under Internal Revenue Code. (9-12-312). Alimony will automatically cease unless otherwise ordered by court or agreed by parties upon remarriage of recipient if court orders another person to pay child support to recipient or if recipient is ordered by court to provide support of another individual. (9-12-312).

Additional attorneys' fees may be allowed for enforcement of alimony and maintenance. (9-12-309).

Alimony and maintenance may be modified by court as may be proper. (9-12-314).

Support of Insane Spouse.—Where divorce was due to incurable insanity of defendant, spouse suing for divorce on that ground must provide for care and maintenance of insane spouse during spouse's lifetime. (9-12-301).

Division of Property of Spouses.—On entry of final decree each party is restored to undisposed property which she or he brought into marriage. (9-12-315).

All marital property shall be distributed one-half to each party unless court finds such division inequitable. (9-12-315). When Court divides marital property other than one-half to each party, it must state in its order basis for unequal division. (9-12-315). Court may take into account federal income tax consequences of division of marital property. (9-12-315).

When stocks, bonds or securities of corporation or government entity are marital property, court in final order shall designate specific securities each party is entitled to or determine securities' fair market value and distribute securities to one party on condition other party receives one half of fair market value. (9-12-315). If real estate cannot be divided, Court shall order sale and divide proceeds. (9-12-315).

Estate by entirety is dissolved by divorce decree unless otherwise specifically provided by decree. (9-12-317). Court may award estate in entirety to one spouse when other spouse has been convicted of felony. (9-12-317). Decree of divorce shall be bar to all claims of dower and curtesy. (See 206 Ark. 623, 177 S.W.2d 32.) Court is not required to address division of property at time divorce decree is entered if either party is involved in bankruptcy proceedings. (9-12-315).

Marital property means all property acquired by either spouse after marriage except: Property acquired by gift, bequest, devise or descent; property acquired in exchange for that acquired before marriage or in exchange for that acquired by gift, bequest, devise or descent; property acquired after decree of divorce from bed and board; property excluded by valid agreement of parties; increase in value of property acquired before marriage or by gift, devise or descent, or in exchange therefor; benefits received or to be received from workers' compensation claim, personal injury claim, or social security claim when those benefits are for any degree of permanent disability or future medical expenses; and income from property acquired prior to marriage, or by gift, devise or descent, or in exchange therefor. (9-12-315).

Change of Wife's Name.—Court may restore previous name to wife. (9-12-318).

Remarriage.—No statutory restrictions on remarriage after divorce.

Separation agreements in contemplation of separation or divorce may be enforced by equitable remedies, including sequestration, garnishment and contempt proceedings. (9-12-313).

Annulment of Marriage.—See topic Marriage.

GUARDIAN AND WARD:

Governed by 28-65-101-603 which is cumulative to Uniform Veterans' Guardianship Act (28-66-101-124) and in case of conflict governs except as to assets derived through Veterans Administration (28-65-102).

Venue for appointment of guardian is county of ward's domicile, or if ward is not domiciled but resides in state, then county of his residence, or if ward is neither domiciled nor resides in state, then county in which greatest part of ward's property by value is situated. (28-65-202).

See note at head of Digest as to 1998 legislation covered.

See Topical Index in front part of this volume.

GUARDIAN AND WARD . . . *continued*

Guardian of person or estate or both may be appointed for unmarried minors, those detained by foreign power, persons who have disappeared, or those who are incapacitated as that term is defined by statute. (28-65-104, 28-65-201).

Not more than one guardian of person may be appointed unless they be husband and wife. One or two guardians of estate may be appointed. (28-65-214).

Eligibility.—Natural persons who are residents of state, 18 years of age, of sound mind and not convicted and unpardoned felon may be appointed guardian of person and estate; State Human Services Department or other charitable domestic corporation may be appointed guardian of person and estate of minor primarily supported by it or when parents of minor have abandoned him or are incompetent for duties of guardianship or if there is no other suitable person; parent under 18 may be appointed guardian of person of his children; corporation authorized to do business in state and having proper corporate power may be guardian of estate of ward; bank or similar institution with trust powers may be appointed guardian of estate; nonresident natural person otherwise qualified who has appointed agent to accept service may be appointed guardian. No person found unfit, and no sheriff, probate judge or clerk unless related to ward within third degree of consanguinity may be appointed guardian of person or estate of ward. Except as provided above, no public agency or employee of public agency acting in his official capacity may be appointed guardian of person and can be appointed as temporary guardian only if related to incapacitated person within third degree of consanguinity and court determines any potential conflict of interest is insubstantial and appointment is in best interests of ward. (28-65-203).

Temporary guardian may be appointed for specific period not to exceed 90 days if court finds imminent danger to life or health of ward or of loss, damage or waste of ward's property and that such danger requires immediate appointment. Appointment may be to perform duties respecting specific property or to perform particular acts. Immediate notice as specified by statute must be given. Special notice provisions apply where ward is over age 14. Full hearing on merits is required within three working days of entry of temporary guardianship order.(28-65-218).

Power of Attorney for Infirm.—See category Property, topic Powers of Attorney.

Preference in appointment is to parents of unmarried minor or either of them, if qualified. Otherwise court shall consider request by parent or legal custodian in written instrument, request by minor 14 years of age or older, request by spouse of ward, and relationship by blood or marriage to ward. (28-65-204).

Qualification.—Letters of guardianship shall be issued upon court approval of posted bond or upon written acceptance of appointment if no bond is required. (28-65-216).

Inventory must be filed by guardian in same manner and subject to same requirements for inventory of decedent's estate. (28-65-321).

Powers.—Guardian of person is entitled to custody of ward but cannot bind ward or his property. (28-65-301). Guardian of estate has general custody and control of ward's real and personal property, but title remains in ward. (28-65-304). All third party actions seeking to charge or benefit estate of ward shall be brought against or by guardian of estate. (28-65-305). Ward retains all legal and civil rights except those expressly limited by court order or specifically granted to guardian by court order. (28-65-106).

See also category Property, topic Absentees.

Duties.—Guardian of person, out of ward's estate, must care for and maintain ward, and, if he is minor, educate him. (28-65-301). Guardian of estate must exercise care to protect and preserve it; invest it; perform all other duties required by law; at termination of guardianship deliver it to person entitled to it (28-65-301); pay all claims allowed or approved by court whether incurred before or after guardianship and whether arising in contract, tort, or otherwise (28-65-317); and may with approval of court sell, mortgage, lease or exchange ward's real or personal property (28-65-314). Specific statutory procedure for court approval of transactions dealing with oil, gas or other mineral interests must be followed, or transaction may be nullity and guardian may be guilty of misdemeanor. (28-65-315).

Order of appointment shall specify amount of bond to be posted, whether guardianship is limited or general, and if limited, specific powers, authorities and duties of guardian. (28-65-214).

Bond of guardian of person only must not exceed $1,000 and may be dispensed with entirely; otherwise controlled by provisions relative to bonds of personal representatives of estates of decedents except that value of realty shall not be considered in computing amount of bond and if estate is all cash bond may be dispensed with if deposited in insured account and applicable insurance limits are not exceeded. (28-65-215).

Annual accounting by guardian is required. (28-65-320).

Investments by guardians are regulated by Code. (28-65-311-312).

Securities in Name of Nominee.—See category Estates and Trusts, topic Trusts, subhead Securities in Name of Nominee.

Compensation.—Reasonable compensation is allowed to guardian; compensation shall be fixed for attorneys and others and allowed as administration expense. (28-65-108, 28-65-319).

Termination of guardianship without court order occurs when ward dies or upon adjudication of competency of ward if ward is not minor; as to person but not estate when ward marries if guardianship is solely because of minority. Guardianship is terminated by court order when minor obtains majority or has disabilities removed, when ward becomes nonresident of state, or if guardianship for any reason is no longer necessary. (28-65-401). Upon death of ward, guardian of estate may administer estate of deceased ward after further letters are issued to him upon hearing pursuant to petition for letters, testamentary or of administration, filed not later than 40 days after date of death, unless upon hearing court grants petition to someone else for letters testamentary or of administration filed not later than 40 days after date of death. (28-65-323).

When Guardianship Unnecessary.—Parents, or one of them, if otherwise qualified, are natural guardians of person of each unmarried minor child without judicial appointment, and have care and management of minor's estate derived by gift from parents. Where ward's estate does not exceed $5,000, court may authorize delivery to ward or to someone else for his use. (28-65-501-502).

Person under duty to pay money or deliver property not exceeding $5,000 yearly to minor may pay or deliver to: (1) person having custody of minor, with whom minor resides; (2) minor, if 18 or married; (3) minor's guardian of person; (4) financial institution, if federally insured savings account in minor's sole name, with notice to minor. If amount so treated exceeds $1,000 yearly, approval must be obtained from probate court in county of minor's residence. Procedure not available if payor knows that guardian of estate has been appointed or proceeding for appointment of same have been instituted. Persons receiving money (other than minor or financial institution) are obligated to apply money for minor's support and education, but may not pay themselves except to reimburse for out-of-pocket expenses for goods and services necessary for minor's support. Persons paying or delivering under procedure are not responsible for proper application of funds. (9-26-102).

Procedure for Appointment.—Any person may petition for appointment of qualified person, including himself, as guardian of incapacitated persons. Contents of petition are specified by statute. (28-65-205). Notice as specified by statute must be given prior to hearing for appointment. (28-65-207). Except when appointment is being made because of minority, disappearance, detention, or confinement by foreign power, or pursuant to §28-65-218, evaluation must be conducted prior to petition hearing by professional or professionals with expertise appropriate for respondent's alleged incapacity. Evaluations shall include recommendation on specific area for which assistance is needed and least restrictive alternatives available. (28-65-212). Petitioner has burden of proving incapacity by clear and convincing evidence. (28-65-213). Petitioner must bear cost of proceeding but is entitled to reimbursement from ward's estate if guardian is appointed. (28-65-211).

Insane Persons.—Person charged with being of unsound mind may be examined and committed by probate court. (20-47-101-105).

Foreign guardians may be authorized to remove ward's property from this state to domiciliary state of guardian and his ward, to sell, mortgage, lease or exchange property located in Arkansas and remove proceeds to domicile of guardian and ward, and to sue in this state in behalf of his ward. If foreign guardian is corporation, it need not qualify to do business in this state to entitle it to administer ward's property situated in this state. (28-65-601-603).

Conservators act with powers and duties of guardian of estate but may be appointed for one who, by reason of advanced age or physical disability (rather than incapacity), is unable to manage his property and consents to conservatorship. (28-67-101-111).

Transfers to Minors.—See topic Infants.

Uniform Fiduciaries Act not adopted.

Uniform Simplification of Fiduciary Security Transfers Act not adopted.

HUSBAND AND WIFE:

All disabilities of married women are removed, except as hereinafter stated.

Separate Property.—A married woman may acquire and hold property of any kind and do business, as femme sole. Property acquired before or after marriage not liable for husband's debts. (Const., art. 9, §7).

Surviving spouse is entitled to refund of federal income tax paid on joint income tax return. (28-38-101).

Control or Use of Spouse's Property.—That married person permits spouse to have control, custody and management of separate property raises presumption, prima facie only, that spouse is acting as agent or trustee and is not by itself evidence that married person has relinquished title. But if wife allows her husband to use her separate property as his own, contracting debts on faith of his apparent ownership, she is estopped to claim it as against husband's creditors. (9-11-513; 215 Ark. 2, 219 S.W.2d 420).

Conveyances.—Married person may convey or release homestead, dower, or curtesy to spouse's grantee, lessee or mortgagee through duly appointed attorney in fact. (18-12-503).

Husband and wife may convey to each other by deed. (18-12-401). Deed by husband to himself and wife creates entirety. (219 Ark. 676, 244 S.W.2d 625).

See category Property, topic Deeds, subhead Execution; also category Debtor and Creditor, topic Homesteads, subhead Alienation or Incumbrance.

Antenuptial Contracts.—Man and woman may enter antenuptial contracts. Form, content, effect and enforceability controlled by 9-11-301-305, 401-413.

Desertion and Nonsupport.—Person is guilty of Class A misdemeanor if without just cause he fails to support physically or mentally infirm or financially dependant spouse, legitimate or illegitimate child less than 18, or dependent child who is physically or mentally infirm. If prior conviction for nonsupport or if remains without state to avoid prosecution, then enhanced to Class D felony. (5-26-401). Nonsupport is Class B felony if person owes more than $25,000 in past-due child support.

Jurisdiction for prosecution lies in county where violation occurred or where defendant may be apprehended or where injured person resides at time of filing indictment or information. (5-26-410).

Court may order temporary support for wife or child, pendente lite, and punish for violation as for contempt. (5-26-413).

Court may direct payment of fine in whole or in part to wife or to guardian or custodian of child. (5-26-412).

Court may, before trial with consent of defendant, at trial on plea of guilty, or after conviction, in lieu of penalty, order defendant to make periodic payments for period not to exceed one year to spouse or guardian of child and release defendant on own recognizance or with sureties on condition that he appear in court on day certain. Failure to appear is punishable by imprisonment of not less than ten or more than 90 days. (5-26-414-415).

Marriage and parenthood are proved with same evidence as is required in civil actions. (5-26-411).

HUSBAND AND WIFE ... *continued*

Business Dealings.—Husband and wife may transact business with each other. (95 Ark. 523, 130 S.W. 515).

Agency.—Either spouse may act as attorney in fact for the other.

Liability of Spouses.—Neither spouse is liable for antenuptial debts of other (9-11-506) nor for debts contracted by other in trade or business as to separate property (9-11-508).

Actions.—If husband and wife are sued together, wife may defend for her own right and, if husband neglects to defend, for his also. (16-61-102). Husband and wife may sue each other. (183 Ark. 626, 37 S.W.2d 696).

Community property system does not apply.

INFANTS:

Age of majority is 18, except for matters involving sale or purchase of alcoholic beverages. (9-25-101).

Uniform Transfers to Minors Act with many changes in effect. (9-26-201-227). Age of majority under Act is 21.

Uniform Securities Ownership by Minors Act adopted. (9-26-301-307).

Child Welfare Agency Licensing Act adopted. (9-28-401-409).

Emancipation.—Circuit or chancery court may remove disabilities of resident who has reached his or her 16th birthday (9-26-104) for general purposes and of nonresident infant of such age in order to enable infant to convey real property in county in which court sits (9-26-104).

Powers.—Infants may deposit in, and withdraw from, bank accounts (23-32-1002) and may invest in, and withdraw from, savings and loan accounts unless parent or guardian restricts authority (23-37-501).

Parental Responsibility.—Recovery up to $5,000 from parents of any minor living with parents who maliciously or willfully destroys property of person or entity bringing action. (9-25-102).

Deserting Parents.—Finance and Administration Department is authorized to disclose to Office of Child Support Enforcement of Human Services Department address of any deserting parent from whom support is charged to Enforcement Office. (26-51-813).

Support.—Person under duty to pay money, or deliver personal property, to minor may perform, in amounts not exceeding $5,000 per annum, by payment or delivery to: (1) Minor, if 18 years or married, (2) any person having care or custody of minor with whom he resides, (3) guardian of person of minor, or (4) financial institution for deposit in federally insured savings account in sole name of minor and giving notice of deposit to minor; provided, any amount in excess of $1,000 must be approved by Probate Court in county in which minor, or person delivering property resides or is domiciled. These provisions are inapplicable if person making delivery has actual knowledge of appointment of guardian of estate or that proceedings for appointment of guardian for estate of minor are pending. (9-26-102).

Paternity—Rights of Putative Father.—Man alleging to be father of illegitimate child is authorized to petition county court for determination of paternity. (9-10-104).

Illegitimate Children—Custody.—Father who has established paternity or mother of illegitimate child may petition county court of county in which child resides for custody. (9-10-113). Father of illegitimate child responsible for minimum level of support until child attains age 18. (9-10-110-111; 115).

Infants—Testing.—All newborn infants must be tested for hypothyroidism, galactosemia and phenylketonuria, and all non-Caucasian newborns must be tested for sickle cell anemia. (20-15-302).

Actions of infant must be brought by next friend or guardian. Defense by guardian, regular or ad litem. (16-61-103-104; 108).

Rescission of contract by infant 18 years old or older is permitted only upon full restitution by infant of property or money received by infant. (9-26-101).

Ratification of Infant's Contract.—Promise made after majority to pay debt contracted during infancy must be in writing. (4-59-101).

Adoption.—See topic Adoption.

MARRIAGE:

Age of consent, males 17, females 16. (9-11-102). If either party is under 18, marriage is voidable by parents or guardian if consent is not obtained, except that if female is pregnant judge of probate court in county in which application for license is made may, upon filing certificate as to pregnancy by licensed physician, birth certificates of both parties and parental consent of each party under age, authorize county clerk to issue marriage license; but if female has given birth to child, no physician's certificate as to pregnancy is required. (9-11-102-105).

Consent Required.—Satisfactory evidence of consent of parent or guardian is required where person is under 18. (9-11-102).

License is required; issued by county clerk of any county, but may not be issued when either party is visibly under influence of intoxicating drinks or drugs. (9-11-201-203, 207). Clerk is required to record social security numbers of persons obtaining license on license application or coupon for marriage license. (9-11-201). County clerks usually require both parties to appear in person when applying for license.

Notice of Intention to Marry.—No marriage license may be issued until after notice of intention to marry, signed by both parties, is filed with county clerk and age of applicants is verified. (9-11-205). Failure to comply does not make marriage void, but fine of $100 to $500 is provided for noncompliance. (9-11-205).

Medical Examination.—No longer required.

Same Sex Marriage.—Void. (9-11-109).

Members of Armed Forces.—County court upon petition and after hearing may waive bond, and consent of parents, and authorize issuance of license to resident of state on active duty with Armed Forces or to resident marrying person on such active duty. (9-11-211).

Ceremonial Marriage.—Marriage may be solemnized by Governor, judge of court of record, former justice of Arkansas Supreme Court, justice of the peace of county where ceremony is performed, regularly ordained and registered minister or priest of any religious sect or denomination, mayor of city or town, any official appointed for that purpose by Quorum Court of county where marriage is performed or elected municipal court judges. (9-11-213).

Record.—See category Documents and Records, topic Records, subhead Vital Statistics.

Common law marriages are not recognized (97 Ark. 272, 133 S.W. 1037), except a common law marriage contracted in another state and valid there is valid in Arkansas (82 Ark. 76, 100 S.W. 747).

Proxy marriages are not authorized by any statute.

Prohibited Marriages.—Between: Parent and child; grandparent and grandchild; brother and sister (half blood included); uncle and niece; nephew and aunt; first cousins. (9-11-106).

Foreign Marriages.—A marriage valid in state where contracted is valid in Arkansas if parties resided in other state at time of marriage and marriage would be valid under laws of that state. (9-11-107). This section does not apply to marriage between persons of same sex. (9-11-107).

Antenuptial agreements establishing rights and obligations concerning property of either or both parties, whenever and wherever acquired or located, right to buy, sell, encumber, etc. any property, disposition of property upon separation, marital dissolution, death or other event, modification or elimination of spousal support, execution of wills, trusts or other arrangements to carry out agreement, ownership rights in and disposition of death benefit from life insurance policies, choice of law and any other matter including personal rights and obligations, except in violation of public policy or criminal statute, shall be enforceable. Agreement adversely affecting child support not enforceable. Agreement is not enforceable if party did not execute agreement voluntarily or agreement was unconscionable when executed and before execution that party: (1) Was not provided fair and reasonable disclosure of property and financial obligations of other party, (2) did not voluntarily and expressly waive in writing after consulting with legal counsel any right to disclosure beyond that provided and (3) did not have or reasonably could not have had adequate knowledge of property or financial obligations. If premarital agreement modifies or eliminates spousal support and this causes one party to be eligible for public assistance at separation or marital dissolution, court may require support to avoid eligibility. (9-11-401-413). If marriage is determined to be void, agreement that would otherwise have been premarital agreement is enforceable only to extent necessary to avoid inequitable result. (9-11-407).

Annulment.—Where either party to a marriage was incapable of consent from lack of age or understanding or was incapable from any physical cause, or where consent was obtained by force or fraud, the marriage may be declared void by the chancery court. (9-12-201).

Action to annul a marriage must be brought in county where plaintiff resides. (9-12-202). Action to annul on ground of nonage may be brought before legal age is attained. (180 Ark. 1152, 24 S.W.2d 867).

Abandonment.—Where one party to a marriage abandons the other and resides beyond the limits of the state, and the abandoned spouse is, for five years, without knowledge whether the other spouse is living, a presumption arises that such other spouse is dead, and a remarriage of the abandoned spouse is valid. (9-11-108).

Separate Property.—Property which married person owns at time of marriage, or which comes to him or her by gift, bequest, descent or transfer from any person; or which he or she has acquired by trade, business, labor or services carried on or performed on his or her sole or separate account, and income and proceeds from all such property shall, notwithstanding marriage, be and remain his or her sole and separate property and may be used or invested in his or her own name and may be sold or transferred without interference of his or her spouse. See topic Divorce for use of "marital property" idea in division of property. No contract made by married person with respect to his or her separate property shall be binding upon his or her spouse. Separate property of married person shall not be liable for his or her spouse's debts, except as may have been contracted for support of spouse or support of children of marriage. (9-11-503-508, 515).

See also topic Husband and Wife.

MARRIED WOMEN:

See topics Divorce, Husband and Wife, Marriage; categories Civil Actions and Procedure, topic Evidence, subhead Witnesses; Debtor and Creditor, topic Homesteads; Documents and Records, topic Acknowledgments; Estates and Trusts, topics Executors and Administrators, Wills; Property, topic Dower.

INSURANCE

INSURANCE COMPANIES:

Regulated by Tit. 23.

Supervision by Department of Insurance, under Insurance Commissioner, 1200 West 3rd Street, Little Rock, AR 72201, who administers laws regulating all insurance companies and conducts such examinations and investigations of insurance matters as he may deem proper to determine violation of Arkansas's insurance laws. (23-61-103). Commissioner may investigate suspected fraudulent acts and persons engaged in business of insurance. (23-66-504).

Fees payable to Insurance Commissioner are: For reviewing all documents for issuance of original certificates of authority $500; for reviewing annual certificate of authority $100; filing annual statement $50; amendment to articles of incorporation $25; annual license for each property, casualty, surety agent $15; each continuance and

INSURANCE COMPANIES . . . *continued*
license for other agent $10; original and renewal license for broker $30; copies of documents $1 per page; certificate authenticating any document $5. (23-61-401).

Rates are regulated in manner to promote competition or to regulate price in absence of competition. (23-67-201). Insurance Commissioner determines if noncompetitive market exists. (23-67-207).

Rating organizations must be licensed by Insurance Commissioner. (23-67-214).

Cancellation.—No policy covering damage to property can be cancelled solely as result of claims arising from natural causes. (23-63-109).

Discrimination.—Life companies are prohibited from discriminating among policy holders by allowing a discount on premium under pretense of making policy holder an agent of company. (23-66-311).

Rebates by property, casualty, and surety companies are prohibited. (23-66-308).

Unfair methods of competition are prohibited as follows: Misrepresentation of terms of policy contract; publishing false information with respect to the business of insurance or with respect to any person in the conduct of such person's insurance business; defamation with respect to the financial condition of an insurer; boycott, coercion, and intimidation resulting in unreasonable restraint of business of insurance; filing false financial statements and keeping false records by insurer; issuing or delivering agency company or other stock as an inducement to insure; unfair discrimination between individuals of the same class and equal expectancy of life with respect to contracts of life insurance or between individuals of the same hazard with respect to contracts of accident or health benefits; rebates of premiums on any contract of life insurance, life annuity, or accident and health insurance, except as expressly provided by law; unfair claim settlement practices; failure to maintain complaint handling procedures; cancellation of policy in force over 60 days, except for nonpayment of premium, fraud, material change in risk, violation of applicable regulations or ordinances substantially increasing risk, nonpayment of dues, or any material violation of material provision of policy; refusing to issue or limiting amount of coverage on property or casualty risk based upon knowledge of insurer's nonrenewal of previous policy; refusing to insure solely because of race, color, creed or sex; churning of business and failing to maintain conflict of interest procedures. (23-66-206). Specific disclosure requirements apply to lending institution's insurance activities. (23-66-606).

Mandatory Reporting of Fraudulent Acts.—Person engaged in business of insurance that has reasonable belief that fraudulent insurance act is being, will be or has been committed shall provide notice thereof to Commissioner. (23-66-505).

Agents and Brokers.—Detailed licensing and examination requirements for agents and brokers established by 23-64-201-229. Licensing requirements for viatical settlement providers established by 23-81-503.

Policies.—Life, health, certain group insurance and accident policies must be approved by Commissioner as to form before issuance. (23-79-109).

Life and disability policies must be approved by Commissioner as to language simplicity. (23-80-201-208).

Policies insuring against damage to person or property of another must contain a clause subrogating injured person or his representative to insured's rights against insurer. (23-89-101). Provisions regulate insurance purchased by creditor providing coverage to collateralized property of debtor. (23-101-101-114).

Limitations of right of action provided in policies as to time are void. (23-79-202). Provisions depriving insured or beneficiary of right to jury trial are void. (23-79-203).

Policy Language.—See category Business Regulation and Commerce, topic Consumer Protection, subhead Plain Language.

Policy Loans, Interest.—Guidelines are set for life insurers to include in policies provision for periodic adjustment of loan interest rates. (23-81-109).

Health and Accident Insurance.—Contracts must include dental services performed by dentist if service would be covered if performed by physician. (23-79-114). Health policies which cover insured and members of insured's family must include coverage for newborn children. (23-79-129). Disability insurance policies must provide identical outpatient coverage for certain inpatient services, unless policyholder rejects it in writing. (23-85-133). Exclusions for preexisting conditions are regulated. (23-86-304). Provisions guarantee renewability and availability for employers in group market. (23-86-311-312).

Group life insurance is authorized for a restricted class of policyholders and with limited coverages. Form of policy must be approved by Commissioner. (23-83-101-122).

Group disability policies providing hospital, surgical or major medical coverage must contain provision allowing member to continue coverage for up to 120 days after membership would ordinarily end due to termination of employment, membership or change of marital status. (23-86-114).

Valued Policies.—Fire policies on real estate, in case of total loss, are liquidated demands for full amount of policy, or full amount upon which premium is charged. (23-88-101).

Proof of substantial compliance with terms of fire policy on personal property supports recovery. (23-79-207).

Fire Insurance.—Applicants for fire insurance must submit anti-arson application disclosing information required by Commissioner. (23-88-207). Insurer providing arson information to law enforcement agency must notify insured within 90 days of report. (12-13-303).

Life Insurance.—A wife may insure the life of her husband for the benefit of herself and children. In case of his death, his creditors can claim only such sums as he paid for premiums with intent to defraud, and the insurance company is justified in paying the wife at any time before it is notified in writing of the claims of creditors. (23-79-128).

Viatical Settlement Contracts.—Consent and disclosure requirements apply to agreements to pay less than death benefit in return for policyholder's assignment of policy. (23-81-501-512).

Group Annuities—Life Insurance.—Model National Association of Insurance Commissioner's legislation defining group annuities and group life insurance is adopted. (23-83-101-127).

Gift Annuities.—Effective Jan. 1, 1994, charities issuing gift annuities must comply with Commissioner's regulations. (23-63-201).

Standard Valuation Law for Life Insurance and Annuities.—Revised standard valuation law for life insurance and annuities and standard nonforfeiture law for life insurance are adopted. (23-84-101-112; 23-81-201-213).

Standard Nonforfeiture for Individual Deferred Annuities Act adopted. (23-81-301-312).

Title Insurance.—There are separate minimum capital and surplus requirements for title insurance companies. (23-63-205).

Penalty of 12% and attorney's fees are recoverable as to cargo, fire, marine, casualty, fidelity, surety, cyclone, tornado, life, health, accident, hospital, medical or surgical insurance for failure to pay in time specified in policy. (23-79-208). Not assessable if amount recovered is less than 80% of amount demanded. (23-79-208). Claim shall be paid by check or draft; if insurer unreasonably delays processing of check or draft for more than three days, penalty may be collected. (23-63-106-107).

Tort of bad faith for refusal to pay claims may be established if affirmative acts of misconduct which are dishonest, malicious, or oppressive are shown on part of insurer. (281 Ark. 128, 664 S.W.2d 463).

Coverages not procurable from authorized insurers may be procured from unauthorized insurers subject to specific conditions. (23-65-305-306).

Attorney's fee allowed in insurer's suit to cancel policy or insured's suit for reinstatement, if judgment is against insurer. (23-79-209). Attorney's fees allowed on loss claims, if judgment is against insurer. (23-79-208).

Investments of domestic companies are regulated by 23-63-801-840.

Foreign insurance companies must file with Commissioner copy of its articles of incorporation, copy of its by-laws if mutual company, certified by secretary or other officer having custody thereof, submit financial statement as of next preceding Dec. 31, copy of report of last examination certified by supervisory official, appointment of Commissioner as its agent for service, certificate of supervising official showing authority to transact proposed business, any required bond or deposit, specimen policies, and detailed digest of company history detailing successful operation. (23-63-209). Foreign and alien surplus lines insurers must annually file verified statement of financial condition, transactions and affairs. (23-65-310). Uniform Unauthorized Insurers Process Act has been adopted. (23-65-201-205). See also subhead Fees, supra.

Foreign corporation must furnish evidence it has been organized and actively engaged in business in state of its incorporation for three years prior to date of applying for admission and must maintain certain reserves. (23-63-202).

Mutual assessment life or disability company may not transact business in state unless authorized to do so on Jan. 1, 1960 and after Jan. 1, 1968 must maintain reserves in accordance with 23-84-101-112 and 23-63-607, must insert in life insurance policies and annuity and endowment contracts issued after Jan. 1, 1968 nonforfeiture provision in accordance with 23-81-201-213, and must have at least 2,000 members regularly paying their assessments and at least $10,000 of surplus funds. (23-72-104).

Insurance holding companies regulated. (23-63-501-530).

Retaliatory Law.—Whenever laws of any other state require of Arkansas insurers taxes, licenses and other fees, and any fines, penalties, deposits requirement, or material obligations greater than those required of similar insurer of such state, same must be imposed upon insurers of such other state seeking to do business in Arkansas (23-63-102), except provision not applicable to foreign insurance company if more than 15% of its capital stock is owned by Arkansas corporation (23-63-101).

Franchise Tax.—See category Business Organizations, topic Corporations, subhead Franchise Tax.

Premium Tax.—All foreign companies are subject to an additional tax, payable to state treasurer on or before Mar. 1 of each year, based on total premium receipts from business within state during preceding year less dividends, and reduction in or refund of premiums and premium refunds or returns at following rates: 2½% as to all kinds except ¾ of 1% on gross underwriting profit of wet marine and foreign trade insurance. (23-60-102, 24-11-809, 26-57-601-607).

Premium tax applies to domestic as well as foreign or alien insurance. (23-60-102, 26-57-601-605). Two-thirds of premium tax revenue on motor vehicles insurance from foreign insurance companies must be paid to qualified Police Officers' Pension and Relief Fund. (24-11-301).

Workmen's Compensation Tax.—See category Employment, topic Labor Relations.

Uniform Insurers Liquidation Act adopted. (23-68-101-120).

Direct Actions Against Insurer.—See category Civil Actions and Procedure, topic Actions, subhead Direct Action Against Insurer.

No-Fault Insurance.—See category Transportation, topic Motor Vehicles, subhead No-Fault Insurance.

Competitive Bidding for Municipal Insurance Contracts.—Cities of first class must abide by provisions of competitive bidding (14-58-303) for purchase of all types of insurance (14-58-304).

Plain Language.—See category Business Regulation and Commerce, topic Consumer Protection, subhead Plain Language.

See category Family, topic Infants, subhead Infants—Testing.

SURETY AND GUARANTY COMPANIES:

State Insurance Commissioner has general supervision.

Capital And Deposit Requirements.—Certain minimum capital requirements apply (23-63-205) and securities of market value of not less than $100,000 must be deposited

See note at head of Digest as to 1998 legislation covered.

See Topical Index in front part of this volume.

AR – 33

SURETY AND GUARANTY COMPANIES . . . *continued*
through Insurance Commissioner (23-63-206). Securities for deposit must qualify (23-63-903) and be made through office of Commissioner (23-63-910-912).

Powers.—Such companies may become surety upon judicial, official, administrators, receivers, fiduciary, and other like bonds (23-63-1001) and may be sole surety on bonds of State, county or municipal officers (23-63-1002).

Agent must file with Commissioner an application for certificate of authority accompanied by applicable fees, certified copy of corporate charter, certified by-laws if a mutual company, power of attorney and members' agreement if a foreign reciprocal insurer or declaration if a domestic reciprocal insurer, copy of financial statement as of Dec. 31 next preceding sworn to by at least two executive officers or certified by supervisory official of insurer's domicile which statement may be in form currently approved by National Association of Insurance Commissioners, copy of report of last examination certified by supervisory official, appointment of Commissioner as agent for process, if foreign insurer certificate of supervisory official showing authority to transact in state of domicile insurance proposed to be transacted in this State, if alien insurer copy of appointment and authority of U.S. manager certified by its officer having custody of its records, required bond or deposit, specimen copies of policies proposed to be issued, and detailed digest of company's history. (23-63-209).

Process Agent.—Foreign insurer and domestic reciprocal insurer must file with Commissioner its appointment of Commissioner as agent on whom process may be served. (23-63-301). Service on domestic insurer must be as provided for service on corporate defendant. (23-79-205). (See also category Civil Actions and Procedure, topic Process.)

INTELLECTUAL PROPERTY

TRADEMARKS AND TRADENAMES:

Any individual, firm, partnership, corporation, association or union, adopting and using in this state, any word, name, symbol, or device, or any combination thereof to identify and distinguish goods or services made or sold by person may register such trademark or service mark. (4-71-201, 4-71-203).

What May Be Used.—Following cannot be registered: Immoral, deceptive or scandalous matter; anything which may disparage or falsely suggest a connection with persons, living or dead, institutions, beliefs, or national symbols, or bring them into contempt or disrepute; flag or coat of arms or other insignia of U.S. or of any state or municipality or foreign nation; name, signature or portrait of any living individual without his written consent; mark which is merely descriptive or deceptively misdescriptive, geographically descriptive or deceptively misdescriptive or surname; mark which so resembles a mark registered or used in this state and not abandoned or registered in U.S. Patent Office and not abandoned as to cause confusion or mistake or to deceive. (4-71-202).

Registration is obtained by filing with Secretary of State an application stating name and business address of applicant, and if applicant is a corporation, state of incorporation, or if partnership, state in which partnership is organized and names of general partners; goods or services in connection with which mark is used, class of goods as classified in act, and manner in which mark is used; date when mark was first used anywhere and date when it was first used in this State; that applicant is owner and that no other person has right to use it in this State either in its identical form or in such near resemblance as to deceive. Application must be signed and verified by applicant or by a member of firm or by an officer of corporation. Application must be accompanied by a specimen or facsimile of mark in triplicate. Fee for registration is $50. (4-71-203).

Assignment.—See subhead Protection Afforded, infra.

Protection Afforded.—Registration is effective for term of five years, and upon application filed within six months prior to expiration on form furnished by Secretary of State may be renewed for like term. In like manner, registration may be renewed for successive periods of five years. Fee for each renewal is $50. (4-71-206).

Assignment of mark may be made with transfer of goodwill of business in which mark is used by written instrument recorded with Secretary of State. Assignment, without such recordation within three months after date of assignment or before subsequent purchase, is void as against subsequent purchaser for valuable consideration without notice. Fee for registering assignment is $20. (4-71-207).

Infringement may be enjoined and for willful infringement registrant may recover all profits derived and/or all damages suffered therefrom. (4-71-212, 4-71-214).

Fraudulent Registration.—Any person who procures registration of mark by knowingly making any false or fraudulent representation is liable to pay damages to injured party. (4-71-211).

Cancellation.—Marks are subject to cancellation which are not renewed; for which holder requests cancellation; which court has found to be abandoned, not owned by holder, to have been improperly granted or fraudulently obtained, mark has become generic name of goods or services for which it was registered, or so similar to mark registered by another person in U.S. Patent Office prior to date of filing for registration as likely to cause confusion or to deceive, or which court cancels on any other grounds. (4-71-209).

Classification.—Specific goods and services for which marks may be registered are numerously classified for convenience of Secretary of State but mark may include any and all goods and services for which used. (4-71-210).

Common law rights in trademark are not affected by statutory provisions. (4-71-216).

Resale Price Agreements.—Arkansas Fair Trade Act repealed, 1975.

Tradenames.—Person conducting a business under any name other than his real name must file in office of county clerk of each county in which he conducts such business an acknowledged certificate setting forth name under which such business is conducted and true full name and post office address of each person conducting same. Filing fee, $1. On disposing of his interest therein, or withdrawing therefrom, each person must likewise file a certificate setting forth that fact. Each day of violation is a separate offense punishable by a fine not less than $25 nor more than $100. Domestic and foreign corporations and domestic and foreign limited partnerships and limited liability companies lawfully doing business in state are exempt. (4-70-201-206).

Franchising.—Governed pursuant to Arkansas Franchise Practices Act. (4-72-201-210). See category Business Regulation and Commerce, topic Franchises.

TRADE SECRETS:

Uniform Trade Secrets Act (1979) adopted. (4-75-601-607).

LEGAL PROFESSION

ATTORNEYS AND COUNSELORS:

The state bar is not integrated.

Eligibility.—Every citizen or alien lawfully residing in U.S. of good moral character and possessing requisite qualifications may be admitted to practice. (16-22-201). See subhead Educational Requirements, infra.

Courts of state, not any single justice or judge, shall have power to license applicants. (16-22-204). All applicants must be admitted to practice by state Supreme Court. (16-22-206).

Residency requirements eliminated by Per Curiam Order of Supreme Court dated July 1, 1985.

Registration as law students not required.

Prerequisite to General Examination.—Applicant must score 75% or better on Multistate Professional Responsibility Examination. MPRE may be taken before graduation. It must be taken within one year of general examination. There is no limit to number of times applicant may take MPRE. (Rules Governing Admission to the Bar IX B).

Examination.—Administered by Board of Examiners appointed by Supreme Court. Address: Justice Building, 625 Marshal Street, Little Rock, AR 72201. Examinations for admission conducted Feb./Mar. and July/Aug., in Little Rock. (Rules Governing Adm. to Bar II). Until July 1999 filing period, application to be made 60 days prior to examination. *Note:* Effective for July 1999 filing period and thereafter, application must be made by Nov. 15 for Feb. exam and by Apr. 1 for July exam. (Rules Governing Adm. to Bar X).

Applicants must make combined average grade of 75% on all subjects. Subjects covered by exam include: Business organizations; commercial transactions; wills, estates and trusts; practice and procedure; equity and domestic relations; constitutional law; contracts; criminal law and procedure; evidence; property; and torts. Applicant may elect to retain either average essay score or Multi-State Bar Examination scale score for use in any succeeding bar examination if such examination is given within three years or six consecutive examination sessions after either score is obtained. (Rules Governing Adm. to Bar IX). Applicant is not limited in number of times he or she may take Arkansas Bar Examination. (Rules Governing Admission to Bar XII).

Educational Requirements.—To be eligible to take examination, candidate must have graduated from school of law approved by American Bar Association. (Rules Governing Adm. to Bar XII).

Clerkship.—None required.

Admission Without Examination.—Admission under Reciprocity Rule eliminated by Per Curiam Order of Supreme Court dated July 1, 1985.

Admission Pro Hac Vice.—Nonresident attorneys who meet comity standards may practice before all state courts; rules of local court may require association of local counsel. (Rules Governing Adm. to Bar XIV).

Licenses.—Annual license fee of $100 is levied on attorneys who have been licensed for three or more years. Annual fee for new enrollees licensed less than three years is $75. (Rules Governing Adm. to Bar VII).

Disabilities.—A lawyer may not become surety or bail in any case. (16-68-203 but see, 16-68-306).

Liabilities.—Attorneys are liable for neglect resulting in dismissal (16-22-306) and unreasonable increase of costs (16-22-305), and summarily liable for retaining client's money (16-22-307). Attorneys not liable to persons not in privity of contract except in cases of fraud or intentional misrepresentation or where primary intent of client was to benefit third parties, but liability to third parties may be limited where attorney identifies in writing to client those persons who may rely on services and sends copy of writing to those persons identified. (16-22-310). See also category Civil Actions and Procedure, topic Costs.

Compensation is governed by agreement, express or implied, which is not restrained by law (16-22-302), except in workmen's compensation claims (11-9-715). Contingent fee agreement shall be in writing. (Model Rules of Professional Conduct 1.5).

Lien.—Attorney has a lien on client's cause of action, claim, or counterclaim, commencing with service by certified mail, return receipt as proof, upon adverse party of notice specifically enumerating cause(s) of action, signed by client and attorney, that attorney shall have such lien. Lien attaches to any settlement, verdict, or other resolution in client's favor, and proceeds thereof, and cannot be defeated by any subsequent compromise by parties. Same lien attaches where notice is not served, as of commencement of action or special proceeding, or service of answer containing counterclaim on behalf of attorney who signs pleading when attorney had been employed to represent client as to that action or counterclaim. (16-22-304). If compromise or settlement is made after service of notice, or suit filed, without consent of attorney, judgment for reasonable fee (not necessarily limited to amount of settlement) may, on motion, be entered against all parties to compromise or settlement. Judgment for fee may also be entered against agent through whom settlement was effected, or against opposing attorney if settlement was with attorney's knowledge or on attorney's advice. (16-22-

ATTORNEYS AND COUNSELORS . . . *continued*

303). Lien enforceable in Chancery Court or in whichever court action was instituted or is pending (16-22-304). Lien shall apply to proceedings before Workers' Compensation Commission. (16-22-304[c]).

Disbarment or Suspension.—Lawyers may be suspended or disbarred for malpractice, conviction of felony, habitual drunkenness, improperly retaining client's money, deceit, or misdemeanor in professional capacity or any ungentlemanly conduct in practice of the profession. (16-22-401).

Attorney Ethics.—Supreme Court has been authorized to make rules governing practice of law and conduct of attorneys (Const. Amendment 28), and has adopted Model Rules of Professional Conduct of American Bar Association, with minor changes, and appointed committee to investigate and prosecute breaches of professional conduct. Trial is before circuit judge or chancellor of county in which accused resides or in which alleged offense was committed (16-22-402), with appeal to Supreme Court for trial de novo on record made below (16-22-413).

Unauthorized Practice.—Practicing law without authority is contempt of court and punishable as such. (16-22-209).

Mandatory Continuing Legal Education.—Members of Arkansas Bar who are residents of Arkansas must complete 12 hours of CLE annually, at least one hour of which is ethics. Nonresident members must comply with minimum CLE requirements of their resident state, and file annual certification of such compliance. Attorneys on inactive status are exempt from CLE. Twelve excess CLE credits may be carried forward for succeeding reporting period only, which may include one hour of ethics. By Aug. 31 of each year, each affected attorney shall file with Arkansas Continuing Legal Education Board affidavit confirming compliance.

Specialty Certification Requirements.—Arkansas Supreme Court in 1982 generally approved plan of specialization to be drafted, implemented and enforced by Board of Legal Specialization. (276 Ark. 600, 637 S.W.2d 589). Board of Specialization recognizes specialty in tax law. (Per Curiam order of Supreme Court dated Jan. 21, 1985, 284 Ark. 585).

Professional Corporation.—See category Business Organizations, topic Corporations, subhead Professional Corporations.

MINERAL, WATER AND FISHING RIGHTS

MINES AND MINERALS:

(Title 15, c. 56).

Open-cut mining means mining of clay, bauxite, sand, gravel or other minerals by removing overburden lying above natural deposits and mining directly for natural deposits exposed. (15-57-303).

Where land containing minerals still belongs to United States the recording of mining claim notices may be done with the county clerk of the county in which the land is located. County Recorder must keep plat of each mining claim located for free use of miners. (15-56-201, 205).

Mining companies are organized under general incorporation law. See category Business Organizations, topic Corporations.

Inspection of Mines.—Mining inspector, and assistant who must be practical miners, are appointed by Governor.

Their duties are to inspect all mines and see that the provisions of the act are carried out. Violations of act must be reported to circuit judge, who must restrain operation of mine until law has been complied with. (11-7-204-210).

Operation of Mines.—Operation of open cut mining is under supervision of Department of Pollution Control & Ecology. Operator must have permit issued by Commission and file bond or securities or post cash. (15-57-310). Fees for permits are graduated from minimum of $50 covering up to two acres, $250 covering two up to ten acres, and $10 per acre with minimum of $500 for ten acres or more. (15-57-311). Requirements for operation are numerous and detailed in Arkansas Open-Cut Land Reclamation Act. (15-57-301, et seq.). Violation can result in assessment of amount not to exceed $5,000 per day per violation. (15-57-305). See category Environment, topic Environmental Regulation.

Employees.—State certification required for designation as fire boss, hoisting engineer, foreman or coal miner. (11-7-403-407). Noncertified apprentices are allowed. (11-7-413).

Safeguarding of Employees.—Escapeways of specified construction and ventilation must be provided; mines must be examined for fire damp; bore holes must be provided 20 feet in advance of working place; not more than eight persons may descend or ascend in cage; suitable means of signaling, cages of specified construction, gates and bonnets and specified safety appliances for engines and gangways must be provided. Water must be used on cutting machines to prevent dust. Washroom facilities and lockers must be provided for all employees. Report of all accidents must be made to state mine inspector. Medical and emergency supplies must be kept at each mine. (11-7-304-318).

Weighman at a mine must, before entering on his duties, take an oath to weigh the output carefully and honestly. The miners have the right to select a check-weigher. Strict regulations are provided so that miners may have the benefit of their exact output. This legislation applies specially to coal mines. (15-59-106-114).

It is unlawful to transport coal from mine on public roads before it has been weighed by official coal weigher. (15-59-105).

Forms must be filed annually with Arkansas State Police on July 1 of each year giving true account of coal mined each month for preceding year. (15-59-115). Failure is misdemeanor and subject to fine of between $25-$100 per day. (15-59-115).

When employed, fire boss must inspect all working places in mine at least once a day. (11-7-315).

In mines with more than three employees, bond for semimonthly payment of wages must be filed with chancery court in county where labor is to be performed. (11-7-319). Noncompliance is misdemeanor subject to fine of between $1,000-$5,000 per violation.

Map of entire workings of mine must be deposited with clerk of county court between Jan. 1 and June 1 each year. When mine is worked out or abandoned it must be reported to State Mine Inspector. (11-7-303).

Oil and Gas.—Drilling for oil and gas is under regulation of Oil and Gas Commission, from which permit must be obtained. Proof of financial responsibility must be filed before permit can be issued. Productive sands must be cased off, gas conserved, abandoned wells plugged, logs of drilling kept and recorded. Provisions for inspection and supervision are comprehensive. (15-72-101-218). Manufacture of carbon black from natural gas prohibited. (5-69-102). Permit must be obtained from Oil and Gas Commission to perform field seismic operations. Application must have $50,000 to $250,000 bond, to be prescribed by Commission. Noncompliance is unlawful and subject to fine of $1,000 per each day of violation. (15-71-114).

Continuing production from lands in section, or pooling unit, will extend lease term but will not extend term on other lands under same lease. (15-73-201).

Proceeds from sale of production must be paid to lessor within six months of initial sale and thereafter within 60 days from end of calendar month in which sale was made. (15-74-601).

Before entering upon site for exploration, notice by certified mail must be given to surface owner, containing proposed location and approximate date of drilling. (15-72-203).

Surface owner has lien upon fixtures and equipment of operator to secure payment of all damages recoverable under oil and gas lease or under laws of State of Arkansas. (15-72-213).

Severance taxes are imposed. See category Taxation, topic Severance Taxes.

MORTGAGES

CHATTEL MORTGAGES:

Covered by Uniform Commercial Code. (4-9-102-507).
1972 Official Amendments adopted.

Filing.—See category Documents and Records, topic Records, subhead Filing Under Commercial Code.—Place; Fees.

Forms.—See end of this Digest.

COLLATERAL SECURITY:

See category Debtor and Creditor, topic Pledges.

MORTGAGES OF PERSONAL PROPERTY:

See topic Chattel Mortgages.

MORTGAGES OF REAL PROPERTY:

Mortgages of real estate are executed and acknowledged in same manner as deed. (18-40-101). Arkansas follows lien theory of mortgages. (166 Ark. 455, 266 S.W. 65).

Recording.—In order to become a lien as against third persons, a mortgage must be filed for record in office of circuit clerk of county where land lies. (18-40-101-103).

Recording Fees.—$6 first page (one side only) and $2 for each additional page. (21-6-306). Instrument sent for recording should be accompanied by check for amount of fee.

See also category Documents and Records, topic Records, subhead Necessity for Recording.

Future advances may be covered. (252 Ark. 79, 477 S.W.2d 446; 16 Ark. App. 116, 697 S.W.2d 940). However, when advances are optional, prior mortgagee cannot, after notice that subsequent lien has attached, deplete value of equity to disparagement of its lienors by advances, which if refused, would not have been in force. (Id.).

Priority between mortgages is determined by time of recording unless one mortgage contains recitals recognizing priority of another. (158 Ark. 21, 249 S.W. 354).

Assignment.—Mortgage may be assigned by instrument duly acknowledged and recorded. Circuit clerk must note fact of assignment and reference to record thereof on margin of original record. Clerks in counties which do not use paper recording systems shall not allow assignment by marginal notation after Dec. 31, 1995. (18-40-109).

Extension or Renewal.—Requires filing acknowledged written agreement between parties. (18-40-103).

Lien of a mortgage or deed of trust does not extend beyond life of the debt secured thereby, and is not extended against third persons by payments unless entered on the margin of the record and attested and dated by the clerk. (18-49-101).

Prepayment.—See category Business Regulation and Commerce, topic Bills and Notes, subhead Prepayment.

Satisfaction of a mortgage must be entered on the margin of the record; provided, effective Jan. 1, 1996, marginal notations of satisfaction do not apply to counties which use other than paper recording systems—separate release instruments must be filed. (18-40-107). Failure to enter satisfaction of mortgage which has been paid, within 60 days after request, subjects mortgagee or his assignee to civil action for damages. (18-40-104). Satisfaction on record must be signed by party acknowledging same and attested and dated by circuit clerk. (18-40-106). Satisfaction may also be by separate release deed or instrument duly acknowledged and recorded. (18-40-107).

Satisfaction of deed of trust may be made by the trustee or the beneficiary. (18-40-106).

Foreclosure.—Mortgages on real property held by bank, savings and loan or mortgage company may be foreclosed under power of sale subject to statutory cure provisions. This does not apply to real property used primarily for agricultural purposes. (18-50-116).

MORTGAGES OF REAL PROPERTY . . . *continued*

In power of sale foreclosure, mortgage must be properly filed of record, mortgagor must be in default, mortgagee must file of record notice of default and intention to sell, notice must be served on mortgagor and others, no action to recover debt secured by mortgage can be pending, 60 days must have elapsed since recording of notice of default, notice must be published in newspaper of general circulation once a week for four consecutive weeks with final publication appearing no more than ten days prior to sale, and affidavit of mailing and publication of notice of default must be recorded prior to sale of mortgaged property. Accepted bid may not be less than two-thirds of entire indebtedness due on date of sale. (18-50-103-107).

In judicial foreclosure, the court renders a decree fixing the amount of the indebtedness and allowing the defendant ten days within which to pay. Upon defendant's failure to pay, clerk of court, as commissioner, advertises property for sale. Property is sold on credit of not less than three, nor more than six, months, lien on land being retained and purchaser giving bond with surety, which has force and effect of judgment. Mortgagee may bid at sale, and may credit upon his bid amount awarded to him by decree. If property is sold for less than amount of decree, difference may be recovered by execution against mortgagor. (18-49-103-105). Mortgagee, trustee, or vendor shall publish notice of sale in newspaper published and having general circulation in county in which property is situated or, if this is not available, then in newspaper of general statewide daily publication one time. Publication shall be at least ten days prior to sale. (18-49-104). Mortgagor and all persons who acquired interests in property after effective date of mortgage must be made parties to action. (95 Ark. 97, 128 S.W. 570).

Redemption.—Where property is sold under foreclosure by power of sale, right of redemption is terminated. (18-50-108). In judicial foreclosure, mortgagor may redeem property within 12 months of sale by paying purchase price plus interest. Right of redemption is waivable. (18-49-106).

Form

No particular form of mortgage is necessary; any instrument showing upon its face an intent that land referred to therein shall secure a debt, undertaking or obligation will be construed as a mortgage. A form in general use is as follows: Know all Men by These Presents:

That . . for and in consideration of the sum of One Dollar ($1.00) to . . in hand paid, and the premises hereinafter set forth, do hereby grant, bargain and sell unto . . and unto . . heirs and assigns forever, the following property:

(Here describe property)

. . hereby covenant with the said . . that . . will forever warrant and defend the title to the said property against all lawful claims. And . . wife of the said . . for the consideration aforesaid do hereby release unto the said . . all . . right of dower and homestead in and to the said lands.

The sale is on the condition that whereas . . justly indebted unto said . . in the sum of . . Dollars, ($. .) evidenced by . . .

(Here describe notes)

Now, if . . shall pay said moneys, at the times and in the manner aforesaid, then the above conveyance shall be null and void. And in case of nonpayment, the said grantee . . or assignee . . shall have power to sell said property at public sale, to the highest bidder, for cash, at . . in the . . of . . County of . . and state of Arkansas, 60 days following the recording of a notice of default and intention to sell and publication of notice in a newspaper of general circulation in said county for thirty days, once a week for four consecutive weeks prior to the date of sale with the final publication no more than seven days prior to the sale, at which sale the said grantee or . . assignee may bid and purchase as any third person might do . . hereby authorize the said grantee . . or assignee . . to convey said property to anyone purchasing at said sale, and to convey an absolute title thereto, and the recitals of his deed of conveyance shall be taken as prima facie true, and the proceeds of said sale shall be applied; first, to the payment of all costs and expenses attending said sale; second, to the payment of said debt and interest; third, to all inferior recorded lienholders as their interests may appear in order of priority; and the remainder, if any, shall be paid to said grantor. We hereby waive any and all rights of appraisement or redemption under the laws of the State of Arkansas, and especially of redemption under the Act of the General Assembly of the State of Arkansas, approved May 8, 1899.

Witness . . hand and seal on this . . day of . ., 19. .

. . . . (Seal)
. . . . (Seal)

(Acknowledgment).

Chattel Mortgages.—See topic Chattel Mortgages.

PROPERTY

ABSENTEES:

Escheat.—Uniform Disposition of Unclaimed Property Act (Revised 1966) adopted with one requirement for abandonment presumption. §15 of Uniform Act is eliminated and generally there is seven year waiting period. (18-28-201-230).

See categories Business Regulation and Commerce, topic Banks and Banking, subhead Unclaimed Deposits; Estates and Trusts, topic Descent and Distribution, subhead Escheat, also topic Wills, subhead Unclaimed Legacies.

Nonresident Wards.—Foreign guardian may, with probate court approval, sell, mortgage, or lease ward's property and remove proceeds or property to domicile of guardian and ward or take other action authorized for local guardian. (28-65-601-603).

ADVERSE POSSESSION:

Character of Possession.—In order for adverse possession to ripen into ownership, possession must be actual, open, notorious, continuous, hostile, exclusive and accompanied with intent to hold against true owner. (278 Ark. 498, 647 S.W.2d 438). Possessor must also have either (1) color of title for seven years which may be established by payment of ad valorem taxes for seven years on unimproved and unenclosed land or 15 years on wild and unimproved land or (2) color of title to contiguous property and have paid ad valorem taxes on contiguous property for seven years. (18-11-106).

Duration of Possession.—Seven years for real property. (18-61-101). Three years for personal property. (16-56-105, 320 Ark. 1). Unimproved and unenclosed lands are in constructive possession of one who pays taxes under color of title for at least seven years in succession. (18-11-102). Payment of taxes for 15 consecutive years on wild and unimproved land creates presumption of color of title. (18-11-103). Two years' possession is sufficient by one holding tax deed, but such possession is not valid against improvement districts. (18-60-212).

Easements.—Open, continuous and adverse use by public for more than seven years establishes easement by prescription and easement so acquired is lost by nonuse for seven years. (269 Ark. 126, 598 S.W.2d 752). Use of way over unenclosed and unimproved land is presumed to be permissive rather than adverse. (268 Ark. 901, 597 S.W.2d 828).

Disabilities.—Infants and insane persons have three years after removal of disability in which to bring action, and tacking of disabilities is not permitted. (18-61-101).

Publicly Owned Land.—Title to publicly owned land cannot be defeated by adverse possession. (22-1-204).

Cemeteries.—Cemetery located on private land that has been open to public use for at least 50 years shall be deemed public property unless certain conditions are met. (18-15-1408).

Tenancy in Common.—Because possession by cotenant is not ordinarily adverse to other cotenants, cotenant must give actual notice to other cotenants that his possession is adverse to their interests or commit sufficient acts of hostility so that their knowledge of his adverse claim may be presumed. (51 Ark. App. 47, 908 S.W.2d 96).

CONVEYANCES:

See topic Deeds.

CURTESY:

Common law curtesy is abolished. In its place a statutory allowance, called curtesy, is provided. Allowance is same as widow's dower (see topic Dower). (28-11-301). No conveyance by spouse without assent of other spouse passes title free of curtesy or dower. (28-11-201). Also see category Estates and Trusts, topic Descent and Distribution.

DEEDS:

Anyone claiming title to real property may sell and convey his interest as if he were in actual possession of real estate, notwithstanding another may be in adverse possession at the time. (18-12-602).

Execution.—Seals are unnecessary. (Const., sched. 1). There should be two disinterested subscribing witnesses, unless deed is acknowledged, in which case none is required. (18-12-104; 16-47-103; 18-12-203; 5 Ark. 693).

When the grantor's spouse joins, special mention should be made in deed that he or she releases dower or curtesy and homestead rights. See also topics Dower, subhead Bar, and Real Property; categories Debtor and Creditor, topic Homesteads, subhead Alienation or Incumbrance; Documents and Records, topic Records, subhead Necessity for Recording; Family, topic Husband and Wife, subhead Conveyances.

Recording.—In order to be effective as against third persons without notice, a deed must be recorded in the office of the circuit clerk of the county where the land is situated. (16-47-110; 18-12-209; 14-15-404). Person recording deed must supply name of grantee and address to which future tax statement should be mailed. (26-26-709). Name and address of preparer must appear on face of first page of deed. (14-15-403).

It is unlawful to knowingly record instruments lacking authenticity affecting title to real property with intent of adversely affecting title to real property. Person violating this section is guilty of Class A misdemeanor. Owner, lessee, or assignee of real property located in Arkansas who suffers loss or damages as result of such conduct and must bring civil action to remove any clouds from their title or interest in real property is entitled to treble actual damages, punitive damages, attorneys fees and costs. This provision does not apply to bona fide filings of lis pendens, materialmen's liens, laborer's liens and other legitimate notice and protective filings as provided by law. (5-37-226).

Recording fees are $6 for first page (one side only) and $2 for each additional page. (21-6-306). Instrument sent for recording should be accompanied by check in amount of fee. See also category Documents and Records, topic Records.

Taxes.—For amount of tax and required affidavit, see category Taxation, topic Stamp Tax.

Operation and Effect.—All deeds are construed to convey fee simple title unless expressly limited by appropriate words. (18-12-105). Words, "grant, bargain and sell" are construed as express covenant of warranty, unless limited by express words in deed. (18-12-102).

The word "trustee" or "agent" appearing after the name of a grantee, without a statement of the trust, is not sufficient notice, and does not put any person dealing with the land on inquiry, that a trust or agency exists. (18-12-604).

The word "heirs" is not necessary to convey estate of inheritance. (18-12-105). Deed purporting to convey in fee simple passes after acquired title (18-12-601); alter in case of quitclaim deed. (201 Ark. 1011, 148 S.W.2d 318).

See topic Real Property for types of estates.

Form

Know all Men by These Presents: That we . . and . ., husband and wife, for and in consideration of the sum of . . dollars, do hereby grant, bargain, sell and convey unto . . and unto . . heirs and assigns forever, the following lands lying in the county of . . and state of Arkansas, to wit: (describe lands) To have and to hold the same unto the said . . and unto . . heirs and assigns forever, with all appurtenances thereunto belonging. And . . hereby covenant . . with said . . that . . will forever warrant and defend the

See note at head of Digest as to 1998 legislation covered.

See Topical Index in front part of this volume.

AR – 36

DEEDS . . . *continued*

title to the said lands against all claims whatever, and that the same is free from all liens and incumbrances. And we, . . for and in consideration of the said sum of money, do hereby release and relinquish unto the said . . all rights of dower, curtesy and/or homestead in and to the said lands. Witness our hands and seals on this . . day of . . 19. .

(Acknowledgment)

. . . . .L. S.

. . . . .L. S.

If for a single person or one spouse deeding lands, same form may be used with appropriate modifications.

For quitclaim deed, use same form but change granting clause to "grant, sell and quitclaim" and omit warranty.

DEEDS OF TRUST:

See category Mortgages, topic Mortgages of Real Property.

DOWER:

If person dies intestate leaving surviving spouse and child or children, surviving spouse is vested of life interest in one-third of all real property of which his or her spouse was seized of estate of inheritance during marriage, unless released by surviving spouse in legal form (28-11-301), and fee title in one-third of personal property of which decedent died seized (28-11-305). When decedent leaves surviving spouse but no children, surviving spouse is entitled to one-half of both real and personal property absolutely as against collateral heirs and one-third as against creditors, except that if real estate be ancestral, dower or curtesy right is life estate in one-half real estate as against collateral heirs and one-third as against creditors. (28-11-307). Also see category Estates and Trusts, topic Descent and Distribution.

Timber, Oil, Gas and Mineral Property.—If person dies, leaving surviving spouse and child or children, surviving spouse is entitled absolutely to one-third of all money received from sale of timber, oil, gas or other mineral leases, royalties or mineral sales from lands in which surviving spouse has dower, curtesy or homestead interest, unless surviving spouse has released same in legal form. (28-11-304).

Release.—Married person may release dower or curtesy in real estate by joining in spouse's deed, or by separate deed to spouse's grantee or assigns, duly acknowledged. (18-12-402). By duly acknowledged and recorded power of attorney, person may authorize another to release dower or curtesy to his or her spouse's grantee, lessee or mortgagee. (18-12-503).

Bar.—Inchoate dower or curtesy in particular land is barred where spouse's rights have become barred by seven years adverse possession (see topic Adverse Possession) or where spouse's deed conveying land has been of record for seven years. (28-11-203).

Election between dower or curtesy and testamentary provision see category Estates and Trusts, topic Wills. See also category Taxation, topic Estate Tax, subhead Disclaimers.

ESCHEAT:

See topic Absentees, subhead Escheat; categories Business Regulation and Commerce, topic Banks and Banking, subhead Unclaimed Deposits; and Estates and Trusts, topics Descent and Distribution, Wills, subhead Unclaimed Legacies.

LANDLORD AND TENANT:

Common law rules govern as to rights and liabilities of landlord and tenant and as to kinds of tenancy permitted.

Leases for a term longer than one year must be in writing. (4-59-101). Acknowledgment is required for recording. (14-15-404).

Security Deposit.—Landlord owning more than five units may receive sum equal to no more than two months rent as security deposit. Landlord must give tenant written notice within 30 days after termination of all or part of deposit to unpaid rent or damages suffered by landlord for noncompliance with rental agreement, or return full deposit. Tenant has cause of action for deposit plus double that amount plus attorneys fees for deposit wrongfully withheld unless landlord can show good faith dispute. (18-16-303-306).

Recording in office of circuit clerk of county where lands are situated is necessary to give constructive notice of lease. (14-15-404). Acknowledgment is required for recording. (14-15-404). Tenant's possession is notice of unrecorded lease. (173 Ark. 633, 293 S.W. 36).

Lien.—Farm landlord has lien on crop for rent and advances to make and gather crop. (18-41-101, 103). Landlord has lien on personalty placed on premises by tenant to secure all sums due under lease. (18-16-108). Purchase money security interest has priority over landlord's conflicting lien. (315 Ark. 218, 866 S.W.2d 390). Priority of landlord's lien is dependent upon time of attachment. (315 Ark. 218, 866 S.W.2d 390).

Termination of Tenancy.—Common law rules govern as to notice required. Lessor of farmlands leased under oral agreement is required to give written notice by certified registered mail to lessee by June 30 to terminate lease for following year. (18-16-105).

Holding Over.—Tenant who holds over after having given landlord written notice of intention to quit is liable for double the rent. (18-16-107). Tenant for life or years, or one holding under such tenant, is liable for double rent if he holds over after termination of term and 30 days notice to surrender possession. (18-16-106). When rent is unpaid, holding over premises after ten days notice to vacate is misdemeanor. (18-16-101).

Dispossession.—Tenant in default may be dispossessed by unlawful detainer proceedings after three days written notice to vacate. (18-60-304). Landlord must give tenant in default statutory notice served by sheriff. (18-60-307). To obtain immediate possession, if such right is disputed, plaintiff must give bond in amount set by court,

and defendant may retain possession by providing cross-bond in amount set by court. (18-60-307).

Plaintiff is entitled to rental value of residential property for period of its unlawful detention and triple rental value of commercial property. (18-60-309).

Uniform Residential Landlord and Tenant Act not adopted.

Self-Storage Rentals.—Governed by 18-16-401-409.

LEASES:

See topic Landlord and Tenant.

PERPETUITIES:

Unless an estate vests during the lifetime of a person or persons in being and 21 years thereafter it is violative of the rule against perpetuities and is void. (Const. art 2, §19). Thus, Arkansas follows common law rule. (283 Ark. 496, 677 S.W.2d 851; 295 Ark. 318, 748 S.W.2d 344). However, trusts may be created for perpetual care of cemetery lots. (20-17-904). Rule has no application to reversionary interests, which remain in transferor and heirs. (304 Ark. 37, 800 S.W.2d 418).

Accumulations.—Common law rules govern. See also category Estates and Trusts, topic Trusts.

PERSONAL PROPERTY:

Tenancies by entirety exist in personal property (281 Ark. 167, 662 S.W.2d 815; 306 Ark. 646, 816 S.W.2d 878), in bank accounts and certificates of deposit (23-47-301), and in savings accounts (23-37-502). Simultaneous death results in distribution of one-half property to each spouse's estate as if each survived. (28-10-103) All survivorships in personalty are proscribed (28-8-101); however, statute does not abolish survivorship in choses of action (19 Ark. 267) or where joint tenancy authorized by statute (205 Ark. 523, 169 S.W.2d 643). Bank accounts and certificates of deposit may be held by two or more persons as joint tenants or tenants in common. (23-47-204). Savings accounts may be held by two or more persons as joint tenants or tenants in common. (23-37-502). As to property subject to bulk transfer issues, Act 344 of 1991 repealed Bulk Transfer Act of Arkansas Uniform Commercial Code.

See categories Business Regulation and Commerce, topic Warehousemen; Taxation, topic Estate Tax.

POWERS OF ATTORNEY:

Attorneys in Fact.—Conveyance or mortgage of real estate may be executed by attorney in fact, but power of attorney must be acknowledged and recorded in order that record of deed or mortgage constitute notice to third person. (18-12-501; 39 Ark. 182).

Durable power of attorney, executed as required by statute, survives principal's subsequent incapacity. (28-68-101, 201-203). Follows Uniform Durable Power of Attorney Act, except portion of UDPAA entitled "Proof of Continuance of Durable Powers of Attorney by Affidavit" omitted.

Owner of limited property ($20,000) and income ($6,000) with approval of probate judge of county of his domicile may appoint attorney to manage his person or property or both in lieu of having guardian appointed. (28-68-301-313).

REAL PROPERTY:

Estate in fee simple is presumed unless expressly stated otherwise. (18-12-105). An estate in lands that would by common law be a fee tail, becomes an estate for life and remainder in fee simple absolute to the person to whom the estate tail would first pass according to the common law. (18-12-301). Grant or devise to two or more creates tenancy in common unless joint tenancy is specified. (18-12-603). Joint ownership of husband and wife creates estate by entirety. (18-12-401). No relationship restrictions on holding property as joint tenants with right of survivorship. (18-12-106). Except in specified instances, all instruments affecting homestead of married person must be joined by spouse or conveyed by separate documents, and acknowledged. (18-12-403).

See also topic Deeds, and category Debtor and Creditor, topic Homesteads.

Rule in Shelley's Case applies (58 Ark. 303, 24 S.W. 490), except as to estates tail (18-12-301; 140 Ark. 109, 215 S.W. 693).

Tenancy by Entirety.—Conveyance to husband and wife creates estate of entirety with right of survivorship. (29 Ark. 202).

Condominiums authorized and must be recorded with clerk of subject county. (18-13-101-120).

Time-Share Interests.—The Arkansas Time-Share Act regulates registration, operation, sale and development of time-share interests. (18-14-101-703).

See also topics Curtesy, Deeds, Dower, Landlord and Tenant; categories Civil Actions and Procedure, topic Partition; Debtor and Creditor, topic Homesteads; Family, topic Husband and Wife; Mortgages, topic Mortgages of Real Property.

TRUST DEEDS:

See category Mortgages, topic Mortgages of Real Property.

TAXATION

ADMINISTRATION:

Ad valorem taxes on real and tangible personal property are assessed by all counties. Each county has tax assessor and tax collector who are responsible for assessment and collection of taxes.

Director of Department of Finance and Administration has general supervision over other state-wide taxes.

Assessment.—

Utilities and Carriers.—Arkansas Public Service Commission has supervision over all tax matters and assessing unit properties of utilities (except carriers) and fixes annually the percentum of value for assessment of all property. Such persons as are

ADMINISTRATION . . . *continued*

assessed by this Commission report on a prescribed form to the Commission on or before Mar. 1 (Mar. 31 for motor carriers) full information for all property owned Jan. 1 preceding. (26-26-1602). Hearings may be had on the assessment, which is completed and certified to county assessors on or before July 15, and taxes are extended and collected as are other taxes (26-26-1609, 1612). Notice of assessment is given to owner, and petition for review may be filed within ten days after date of notice which is heard on or before 1st day of Nov. after assessment notice, except hearings on petitions of motor carriers, bus lines, airlines, water transportation companies and private car companies are heard on or before last day of Dec. (26-26-1610).

Carriers other than those operating entirely within a city's limits are under jurisdiction of Arkansas Transportation Commission. (23-2-209, 302, 303).

Railroads are under jurisdiction of Arkansas Transportation Commission. (23-2-209, 302, 303).

All other property is assessed by county assessors as of Jan. 1 preceding, except stocks of goods, which are assessed at average value during preceding year. (26-26-1201). Real property is assessed by assessor annually between first Mon. in Jan. and first day of July. (26-26-1101). Property owners must list for assessment all property before May 31, after which penalty of 10% of taxes accrues. (26-26-201, 1408). Assessment of personal property by mail and telephone allowed. (26-26-1114). Review of assessor's valuation may be had before county equalization board by 3d Mon. in Aug. Equalization board is in session from 3d Mon. in Aug. to 3d Mon. in Sept. and review of assessor's findings is had before board by 1st Sat. before 3d Mon. in Sept. Appeal to county court from equalization board may be had by 2d Mon. in Oct. and disposed of by 1st Mon. in Nov. (26-27-317, 318).

Overall increases in assessed valuation as result of countywide reappraisal or reassessment of property are generally limited to produce tax revenues no greater than 10% above revenues of base year, which is year in which taxing unit completes reassessment and equalization of taxable real and personal property as part of statewide reappraisal program. (26-26-402). Limitation on increase is adjusted for newly discovered real property and new construction and improvements to realty.

Reassessment, after assessment and payment of any property, privilege or excise tax, may not be had except for actual fraud of taxpayer; but failure to assess is prima facie evidence of fraud. (26-34-107).

Computerized Assessment.—County utilizing unit tax ledger system may initiate computerized tax assessment and collection process.

Interstate Cooperation.—No statutory provisions.

Penalties.—Penalty for delinquency is 10%. (26-35-501). As to real and personal property taxes, see also subhead Sales, supra. See topics detailing particular taxes.

ALCOHOLIC BEVERAGE TAXES:

Annual license taxes or fees are levied, as follows: on wine and beer (3-5-101-1310); distilling spirituous liquors and/or manufacturing malt liquors (3-4-601-605). In addition, cities, towns and counties may license manufacture and sale of spirituous and malt liquors and vinous liquors, except wine, license fee not to exceed one-half of state fee. (3-4-201, 202, 208).

Direct taxes on all liquor sold or offered for sale in state imposed by 3-7-104. These taxes are paid by stamps affixed by wholesaler. Stamps and records for spirituous liquors are subject to special regulations. (3-7-112).

Beer containing more than 5% alcohol by weight subject to tax by 3-5-205, 206, 209, 214; 3-7-104.

Special tax on liquor, cordials, liqueurs, specialties, sparkling and still wines imposed by 3-7-201, 205.

COIN OPERATED AMUSEMENT DEVICES:

Coin operated amusement devices subject to tax by 26-57-301-421.

ESTATE TAX:

(26-59-101-122).

Director of Department of Finance and Administration has supervision of collection of estate taxes. (26-59-105).

Taxable Transfers.—A transfer tax is imposed on any present or future interest in property, in possession or enjoyment, passing by descent, devise, bequest or gift in contemplation of death. (26-59-102, 106).

Exemptions.—Property passing to or for use of State, municipal corporations or other political subdivisions thereof, for exclusively public purposes, or to public institutions of learning or any public hospital not for profit, within state, or without if other state reciprocates, is exempt. (26-59-108).

Disclaimers.—By compliance with detailed statute, person may disclaim broad class of property interests, whether otherwise passing by will, intestate succession, operation of law as in insurance policy, or with reference to power of appointment. (28-2-101).

Amount of Tax.—In the case of a resident of the state the tax is a sum equal to Federal credit allowable under Federal Estate Tax laws, 26 U.S.C. §§2001 et seq. in effect on Jan., 1983. If property of estate is located in another state participating in Federal credit allowable, tax is proportionate part of credit allowable as Arkansas property bears to entire estate, except that if other state has reciprocal provision for nontaxability of property of nonresidents, all of Federal credit allowable is paid to this state. (26-59-106).

In the case of a nonresident of the state all real, tangible and intangible personal property located in Arkansas is taxed in the amount which shall be a sum equal to the proportion of the Federal credit allowable provided for under Federal Estate Tax laws, 26 U.S.C. §§2001 et seq. in effect on Jan., 1983 for estate, inheritance, legacy and succession taxes that Arkansas property of such deceased person bears to property of entire estate wherever located; provided, term "Arkansas property" shall be construed to include following intangible personal property: (a) Debts (including bank deposits) owed to decedent by any individual resident of Arkansas, or by any bank or other

corporation organized under laws of Arkansas, or by any national bank doing business in Arkansas (without regard to physical location of any written evidences of indebtedness); and (b) shares of capital stock of any Arkansas corporation (without regard to physical location of stock certificates); but, provided, however, that if decedent at time of death was resident of state or territory of U.S. which, at time of his death, provides exemption to residents of Arkansas from transfer or death taxes, then said nonresident of other state or territory is exempt from payment of estate or inheritance tax in Arkansas. (26-59-107).

Return.—Representative of estate must, within two months after his qualification, give notice thereof to Department of Finance and Administration. (26-59-119). Tax return must be filed with Department of Finance and Administration at the same time federal estate tax return is filed. Return may be made on blanks furnished by Department of Finance and Administration or a copy of the federal return may be filed. (Dept. Reg.). Return must be made in all cases where resident of state or U.S. left gross estate in excess of $600,000, any part of which might be taxable, and in all cases where nonresident of U.S. who is not citizen of U.S. left gross estate in U.S. of $600,000, part of which is located in Arkansas. (26-59-109). Extension may be obtained by timely filing federal application for extension with Director and attaching copy of document granting federal extension. (26-59-111). If representative fails to file return, Director may prepare return from such information as he can obtain, and his return is prima facie correct. (26-59-112).

Payment.—When federal government determines value of estate and computes federal basic tax, representative of estate must then furnish this computation in writing to Department of Finance and Administration, with remittance for amount of tax. (Dept. Reg.). Tax is payable nine months after date of death. (26-59-113). Where timely payment would impose hardship, Department of Finance and Administration may grant successive extensions of not more than 18 months each, not to exceed five years in all. (26-59-113). Interest from due date of tax is charged at 10%. (26-18-508). Provisions of 26 U.S.C. §6166 in effect on Jan. 1, 1989 permitting representative of estate to elect to pay federal estate tax due on certain qualifying assets in installments for period of up to 15 years at 4% interest rate has been adopted as state estate tax law. Four percent interest rate only applies to "4-percent portion" of estate as that term is defined in 26 U.S.C. §6601(1)(2). (26-59-113; 26-18-508). Any timely filed election to pay federal estate taxes in installments serves as election to pay state estate taxes in installments for same period specified in federal election. (26-59-113).

Refund.—See topic Income Tax, subhead Refunds.

Limitations.—See topic Income Tax, subhead Limitations.

Deficiencies.—See topic Income Tax, subhead Deficiencies.

Lien and Enforcement.—See topic Income Tax, subhead Enforcement.

Liability of Representative.—Representative who distributes property without making payment of tax or obtaining release of lien is personally liable to extent of value of property coming into his hands. (26-59-117).

Release of Property From State Estate Tax Lien.—Upon personal representative's filing a complete return and making written request for determination of amount of tax and discharge from personal liability, within one year of such application Department determines tax. Upon payment of amount so determined, personal representative is discharged from personal liability. After such discharge, lien for any additional tax on property in gross estate is not released until title has passed to bona fide purchaser for value. (26-59-114).

Sale by Representative.—Representative may sell property of estate for payment of tax in same manner as for payment of other debts. (26-59-118).

Certificate of Nonliability.—Where showing of nonliability is made, Department may issue certificate of nonliability to representative, for which no fee is charged. (Dept. Reg.).

Transfer of Corporate Stock.—A waiver of the estate tax is not required as a condition to the transfer of corporate stock owned by the decedent.

Reciprocity.—See supra, subhead Amount of Tax.

Assets from Which Tax Payable.—Except as otherwise directed by will, the burden of the tax must be spread among the distributees, so that each will bear his proportionate part. (26-59-115). No apportionment is applied against property received by surviving spouse when its value is deductible for federal estate tax purposes. Donees of gifts in contemplation of death under federal law also bear proportionate part of tax. (248 Ark. 500, 446 S.W.2d 202). Donee of charitable bequest must also bear proportionate part of tax. (256 Ark. 1028, 511 S.W.2d 640).

Reimbursement of Beneficiary.—If tax is paid or collected out of part of estate passing to any person other than representative of estate, he is entitled to reimbursement from undistributed part of estate, and to contribution from other distributees, in such manner that burden of the tax will be borne in same proportions as if it had been paid prior to any distribution. (26-59-116).

Corporate representative of estate of nonresident must file notices and returns and may bring actions with reference to the tax in like manner as an individual, even though it may be prohibited from acting as representative within the state. (26-59-121).

Penalty.—See topic Income Tax, subhead Penalty.

Applications for forms should be made to Department of Finance and Administration, Little Rock.

Residence in Arkansas.—Provision is made for proceedings in court to establish change of domicile to Arkansas. (9-3-101-120).

Actions.—See topic Income Tax, subhead Limitations.

Life of Act.—Act will remain in force so long as federal government continues to impose an estate tax. (26-59-103). Rules of interpretation and construction applicable to federal estate tax laws are to be followed in interpretation of state tax. (26-59-104).

Valuation date for purpose of estate tax is same as Federal estate tax. (26-59-102, 104).

See note at head of Digest as to 1998 legislation covered.

See Topical Index in front part of this volume.

FRANCHISE TAXES:

See categories Business Organizations, topic Corporations; Insurance, topic Insurance Companies.

GASOLINE AND SPECIAL FUELS TAX:

Gasoline tax imposed by 26-55-201-511 and 26-55-1002. Certain "gasohol" fuels are excepted. (26-55-205, 207).

Special fuel tax imposed on distillate special fuels (26-56-101-221) and on liquefied gas special fuels (26-56-301-315 and 26-56-502).

GIFT TAX:

None; but estate tax applies to gifts in contemplation of death.

INCOME TAX:

Imposed on net income of every resident individual, trust or estate, and on net income derived from business done or property owned within this state of every nonresident individual, trust or estate and of every domestic or foreign corporation. (26-51-201-205). "Gross income" defined. (26-51-404). "Net income" defined. (26-51-403).

Exemptions for single individual whose gross income does not exceed $7,700 for any income year; for married couple filing joint return $15,500; for unmarried head of household, $12,000; reduced tax tables provided for low income individuals. (26-51-301).

Certain enumerated corporations, trusts, and other entities are entirely exempt. (26-51-303-304).

Certain provisions of Internal Revenue Code of 1986 as in effect on Jan. 1, 1987, are adopted and incorporated by reference: cafeteria plans under I.R.C. §125 (26-51-404[b][12]), alimony and separate maintenance under I.R.C. §§71, 215 (26-51-417), and at-risk limitations under I.R.C. §465 (26-51-436[1]). Miscellaneous itemized deductions are subject to 2% floor. (26-51-437).

Certain provisions of Internal Revenue Code of 1986 as in effect on Jan. 1, 1989, are adopted and incorporated by reference: group term life insurance under I.R.C. §79 (26-51-404[b][14]), disability and health payments under I.R.C. §§104-106 (26-51-404[b][15]), dependent care assistance programs under I.R.C. §129 (26-51-404[b][13]), capitalization of certain expenses under I.R.C. §263A[a]-[h] (26-51-439), corporate liquidations under I.R.C. §§332, 334, 336, 337, and 338 (26-51-413), and U.S. citizens living abroad under I.R.C. §§911-912 (26-51-310).

Certain provisions of Internal Revenue Code of 1986 as in effect on Jan. 1, 1991, are adopted and incorporated by reference: ITC and depreciation for luxury autos under I.R.C. §280F(a)-(d) (26-51-436[3]), depletion under I.R.C. §§611-613, 613A, 614, 616 and 617 (26-51-429), and subchapter S under I.R.C. §§1361-1379 (26-51-409).

Certain provisions of Internal Revenue Code of 1986 as in effect on Jan. 1, 1993, are adopted and incorporated by reference: expenses and interest relating to tax-exempt income under I.R.C. §265(a) (26-51-431[b]), allocation of unstated interest under I.R.C. §483 (26-51-443[a]), sale of property to comply with conflict-of-interest requirements under I.R.C. §1043 (26-51-442), taxation of foregone interest on "below-market" loan under I.R.C. §7872 (26-51-443[b]) and charitable remainder trust provisions under I.R.C. §664 (26-51-309).

Certain provisions of Internal Revenue Code of 1986 as in effect on Jan. 1, 1995, are adopted and incorporated by reference: business expenses under I.R.C. §162 except subsection (n) (26-51-423[a]), charitable deductions under I.R.C. §170 (26-51-419), moving expenses under I.R.C. §217 (26-51-423[a][4], travel and entertainment expenses under I.R.C. §274 (26-51-423[b]), passive activity loss limitations under I.R.C. §469 (26-51-436[2]), itemized deductions limitations under I.R.C. §68 (26-51-436[4]), annuities under I.R.C. §72 (26-51-414), interest deductions under I.R.C. §163 (26-51-415), depreciation under I.R.C. §§167-168 and expensing of property under I.R.C. §179 (26-51-428), medical and dental expense deductions under I.R.C. §213 (26-51-423[a][2]), individual retirement accounts under I.R.C. §219 (26-51-414), employee benefit plans under I.R.C. §§401-404, 406-416 and deferred compensation plans of state and local governments and tax-exempt organizations under I.R.C. §457 (26-51-414), amortization of goodwill and other intangibles under I.R.C. §197 (26-51-428[c]), income from discharge of indebtedness under I.R.C. §§108 and 1017 (26-51-404[b][11]), exclusion from gain on small business stock under I.R.C. §1202 (26-51-815[c]), inclusion in income of reimbursed moving expenses under I.R.C. §82 (26-51-404[b][16]), exclusion from gross income of meals or lodging under I.R.C. §119 (26-51-404[b][17]), exclusion from gross income of cost-sharing payments under I.R.C. §126 (26-51-404[b][18]), exclusion from gross income of foster care payments under I.R.C. §131 (26-51-404[b][19]), exclusion from gross income of fringe benefits under I.R.C. §132 (26-51-404[b][20]), installment method of accounting under I.R.C. §§453, 453A and 453B (26-51-411[e]), exclusion of agricultural cost-sharing program payments and deductions of soil and water conservation payments under I.R.C. §§126 and 175 (26-51-404[b][21]).

Certain provisions of Internal Revenue Code of 1986 as in effect on Jan. 1, 1997, are adopted and incorporated by reference: tuition savings program in accordance with I.R.C. §529 (Act 1309 of 1997); income tax credit equal to 30% of federal low-income housing tax credit in accordance with I.R.C. §42 (Act 1332 of 1997).

Subchapter M of Internal Revenue Code of 1986, as in effect on Jan. 1, 1995, relating to regulated investment companies and real estate investment trusts is adopted. (26-51-440).

Members of U.S. armed services, including auxiliaries, are exempt from income tax on first $6,000 of service income. (26-51-306). §§112 and 692 of Internal Revenue Code as in effect on Jan. 1, 1991, relating to combat pay of members of armed forces and income taxes of members of armed forces on death, are adopted. (26-51-306[a][4]).

Exempt income includes certain reinvested gains from involuntary conversions; gains from sale of principal residence when reinvested in another principal residence within two years before or after sale or exchange of residence; life insurance policy proceeds; gifts, bequests, devises or inheritances; interest on obligation of U.S. or its possession or obligations of this state or its political subdivisions; receipts through accident or health insurance, workmen's compensation or damages as compensation for sickness or injuries; Social Security and Railroad Retirement benefits; dividends received by corporation doing business in this state from 80% owned subsidiary; income from domestic corporations when earned from places of manufacture, production, or merchandising outside state; rental value of home furnished to or rental allowance paid to minister; other items listed above that exempt by adoption I.R.C. sections. (26-51-404). First $6,000 of benefits received from public or private employment-related retirement systems, regardless of method of funding, is exempt from state income tax. (26-51-307).

Rates for all taxpayers apply to income as follows: for individuals, trusts, or estates, on net income 1% on first $2,999 or part thereof; 2.5% on next $3,000 or part thereof; 3.5% on next $3,000 or part thereof; 4.5% on next $6,000 or part thereof; 6% on next $10,000 or part thereof; 7% on $25,000 and above; for corporations, on net income 1% on first $3,000; 2% on next $3,000; 3% on next $5,000; 5% on next $14,000; 6% on next $75,000; on net income exceeding $100,000, flat rate of 6½%. (26-51-201, 205).

Capital Gains.—Maximum capital gains tax rate of 6% for individuals and S corporations. (26-51-815). Taxpayer over age of 55 may elect one-time exclusion of gain from sale of principal residence up to $125,000, $62,500 for married persons filing separate return. (26-51-305[b][1]).

Credits.—After tax has been computed, following credits allowed: for single individual, $20; for head of household, surviving spouse or married individual living with husband or wife, $40; husband and wife living together get only one personal tax credit of $40 whether they file jointly or separately; an additional $20 for each single or married taxpayer who is age 65 or older; additional $20 for taxpayer who is deaf or blind; additional $40 for taxpayer who is deaf and blind; for each dependent with gross income less than $3,000 other than spouse, $20; for each resident fiduciary, $20, but varies where fiduciary died or became insolvent; for nonresident taxpayer, proportion of tax credited that gross income within state bears to entire gross income wherever derived (26-51-501; 26-51-504); for resident taxpayer deriving income outside of state, amount of income tax paid to any other state or territory on account of such income, not exceeding tax at Arkansas rates (26-51-504); for each taxpayer maintaining mentally retarded child in his home, $500. (26-51-503). Credit for qualified taxpayers who incur child care expenses at approved child care facilities. (26-51-502). Credit available for individual is also available to fiduciary and partnership residing or domiciled in Arkansas (26-51-504). Business qualifying for gross receipts tax exemption under §26-52-401(29) (business operating child care facilities for exclusive purpose of providing child care services to its employees) is allowed income tax credit of 3.9% of annual salaries of employees employed exclusively in providing child care services. Credit is available in year following year in which salaries were paid, and credit is available only if revenue to child care facility does not exceed direct operating cost of facility. (26-51-502). Business qualifying under Arkansas Enterprise Zone Act is entitled to income tax credit equal to 100 times average hourly wage paid with maximum of $2,000 per net new permanent employee of business. (15-4-1701-1708). Resident taxpayer 62 or older with household income less than $15,000 may be entitled to credit or rebate for ad valorem tax paid on personal residence (26-51-601-608); credit is allowed for establishment or expansion of manufacturing enterprise creating new jobs in state (26-51-505); for donation of new machinery and equipment to qualified educational institution or sale below cost and for expenditures for qualified research program, 33% up to 50% of tax liability of corporate or individual taxpayer (26-51-1102-1103); credit is allowed for waste reduction, reuse or recycling equipment by taxpayer engaged in business of reducing, reusing or recycling solid waste for commercial purposes (26-51-506); qualified aircraft business allowed $2,000 credit per net new employee if business employs at least 50 net new employees within 60 months of receiving certification (15-4-807).

Returns and Payment.—Income tax returns must be made to Department of Finance and Administration on or before May 15, or within four and one-half months after close of fiscal year. Every Subchapter C corporation, as defined in 26 U.S.C. 1361(a), must attach completed copy of its federal income tax return including all attachments, to its state return. Automatic extension of time to file for same period received on Federal extension if federal application for extension is attached to State form. Tax is payable on date when return is filed and bears interest at 10% from due date. (26-51-806, 807). Affiliated corporate group may elect to file consolidated return. (26-51-805).

Electronic Funds Transfer.—Commissioner of Revenues is authorized to require that tax payments be made by electronic funds transfer for following: when taxpayer's monthly withholding under gross receipts tax, compensating tax, privilege tax, special alcoholic beverage excise tax, alcoholic beverage supplemental taxes, and any taxes supplemental thereto exceeds $50,000 or monthly liability exceeds $20,000; when taxpayer's monthly tax liability on tobacco products or spirituous liquors, wines, and beer exceeds $20,000 for calendar year 1994 or any calendar year thereafter; when corporation's quarterly state income tax liability equals or exceeds $20,000. (26-19-101-108).

Limitations.—Department may assess deficiency within three years after filing of return, or at any time in case of fraudulent return or failure to file return or within eight years after filing of return if net income changed by I.R.S. or, if assessment by I.R.S. is appealed by taxpayer, three years from later of date of final I.R.S. assessment or payment of federal assessment by taxpayer, or within six years if gross income is understated by 25% or more, or if tax is underpaid by 25% or more in cases other than income tax. Any assessment of tax within limitation period may be collected by levy or proceeding in court within ten years after assessment. Amended return or verified claim for refund must be filed within three years from time return was filed or two years from time tax was paid, whichever is later. (26-18-306).

Deficiencies.—Director of Department of Finance and Administration assesses all state taxes. (26-18-401). When he determines that deficiency exists, he proposes assessment of additional tax plus penalties and must give notice of this to taxpayer. (26-18-403). Taxpayer may file written protest with Director and/or may request hearing before hearing officer whose findings shall be final unless revised by Director. (26-18-404-405). Taxpayer may appeal Director's decision by paying deficiency under protest and filing suit to recover such amount within one year of payment or by posting bond in

INCOME TAX . . . *continued*
double amount of tax deficiency and filing suit within 30 days after filing bond and diligently prosecuting suit to final determination. (26-18-406).

Refunds.—Within six months after amended return or verified claim for refund is filed, Director must make written determination and give notice to taxpayer whether or not refund is due. Taxpayer may appeal decision by filing in Pulaski County Chancery Court or Chancery Court where taxpayer resides within 90 days after issuance of Director's decision. (26-18-507). Portion of any tax refund may be contributed to U.S. Olympic Committee Program. (26-51-441).

Enforcement.—After final assessment, Director may enforce by issuing Certificate of Indebtedness to appropriate circuit clerk who enters same as judgment against taxpayer. Entry of judgment is lien upon title of any real and personal property of taxpayer located in county. Director may further direct clerk to issue unit of execution directed to Director or sheriff authorizing levy upon taxpayer's property. (26-18-701). Transferee liability is imposed on transferee of taxpayer's property. (26-18-502). Taxpayers are given certain rights in connection with assessment and collection process. (26-18-801-812).

Penalty for failure to file any return is 5% of tax shown on return for each month or part thereof not to exceed 35%; for failure to pay tax, penalty is 5% (1% for individuals) for each month or part thereof not to exceed 35%; for any deficiency due to negligence or intentional disregard of rules, penalty is 10% of deficiency; for any deficiency due to fraud, penalty is 50% of deficiency. (26-18-208). Criminal penalties provided by 26-18-201-207.

Withholding by employer from wages of employee based on tables to be promulgated by Department of Finance and Administration and reported and paid annually if withheld amount is less than $200 per year or monthly if withheld amount is $200 or more per year. (26-51-905, 908). Severe penalties imposed for failure of employer to make timely report or payment. (26-18-501).

Estimated tax declarations and first payments are due 15th day of fifth month of income year, from all taxpayers who may reasonably expect estimated tax to exceed $250. Remaining payments are due on 15th days of 6th and 9th months of income year and 15th day of first month after close of year. Individuals whose farming income equals at least two-thirds of total gross income may declare or pay estimated tax on 15th day of second month after income year or file return and pay tax for year on or before 15th day of third month after income year. Joint declarations may be filed by husband and wife. (26-51-911-913). Penalty for failure to pay estimates at least 90% of actual liability, on quarterly basis, is 10% of amount of understatement. No penalty where estimate equals or exceeds liability shown on return for preceding 12 month year or if tax shown on return for such year is $250 or less. (26-18-208[6]).

Multistate Tax Compact (26-5-101) as enacted lets taxpayer elect its apportionment provisions or those otherwise effective (26-51-701-722).

Refunds on federal income tax, see category Family, topic Husband and Wife.

INHERITANCE TAX:

None. As to estate tax, see topic Estate Tax.

PREMIUM TAX:

Premium tax on: Insurance companies, see category Insurance, topic Insurance Companies; insurers under Workmen's Compensation Act, see category Employment, topic Labor Relations.

PRIVILEGE TAX UPON MOTOR VEHICLES:

See category Transportation, topic Motor Vehicles.

PROPERTY TAXES:

Real and Personal Property Taxable.—All property is subject to tax (26-3-201), except as specified by exemptions (26-3-301; Const., art. 16, §5).

Exemptions.—Public property, (including waterworks systems owned by nonprofit property owners association), churches, cemeteries, school buildings and apparatus, libraries and grounds, and public charity property, are exempt. (Const., art. 16, §5; 26-3-301). Homesteads of residents are exempt from state property taxation to extent of $1,000 of assessed value. (Const. Amendment 22). Homestead and personal property of disabled veteran and of surviving spouse and minor children of disabled veteran are exempt. (26-3-306). See category Courts and Legislature, topic Legislature.

Owner of new manufacturing or processing establishment to be located within state, or owner making addition to existing establishment, may contract with the state for exemption from state property taxes upon such establishment or addition for not more than ten years. (Const. Amendment 27).

Textile mills are exempt from property tax for period of seven years after locating in state. (26-3-304).

Tangible personal property in transit through State or manufactured, processed or refined in State and stored for shipment outside of State is exempt. (26-26-1102).

Items of household furniture and furnishings, clothing, appliances, and other personal property within home, if not held for sale, rental, or other commercial or professional use, are exempt from all ad valorem taxes levied by any city, county, school district, or other taxing unit in this state. (Const. Amend. 71).

No exemption for members of the armed forces.

Intangible personal property is exempt from ad valorem taxation. (26-3-302). See category Courts and Legislature, topic Legislature.

Payment.—Real estate and personal property taxes are due and payable from first business day in Mar. to Oct. 10. (26-36-201). Taxes to and including tenth day of Oct. of year succeeding that in which levy was made may be paid in installments as follows: One-fourth from third Mon. in Feb. to and including third Mon. in Apr.; one-fourth from third Mon. in Apr. to and including third Mon. in July; one-half from third Mon. in July to and including tenth day of Oct. Penalty for delinquency is 10%. (26-35-501).

Proof of payment of personal property taxes is required to obtain motor vehicle license. (26-26-1401).

Tax credits on ad valorem property taxes on home. See topic Income Tax, subhead Credits.

Sales.—Sale of real property for delinquent taxes must comply with statutory procedure. (26-37-201-213).

Lien for taxes attaches 1st Mon. in Jan. of year of assessment and is superior to all other incumbrances. As between grantor and grantee lien attaches on last day fixed by law (now 3rd Mon. in Feb. of year in which tax is payable) for county clerk to deliver tax books to collector in each year after tax lien attaches. (26-34-101).

Redemption.—Tax delinquent lands may be redeemed by owner within two years of state's receipt of land. Land will be sold at auction if not redeemed within two years. (26-37-301). Insane persons, minors, or persons in confinement may redeem land within two years after disability ceases. (26-37-305). Exception for insane persons, minors, or persons in confinement is not applicable to improvement district forfeitures. (14-86-1503).

Apportionment.—Person who acquires ownership of portion of parcel of real property may require county assessor to apportion current assessment between remaining portion of parcel and that acquired by person making request within 30 days of request. (26-26-1115).

Local improvement districts organized under general and special laws assess taxes, which are liens, and all titles are subject thereto and to sale and forfeiture. These districts are numerous and unlimited in number and amount of separate tax. All nonresident owners should acquaint themselves with local situation of their land in this respect.

Technical College Districts.—Formation reconstitution of technical college districts are authorized, and voters of such districts may levy ad valorem taxes to support districts. (6-53-601-605).

Limitation on suits to collect overdue taxes owing because of under-assessment on tangible property is five years; on intangible property seven years. (26-34-105-106).

REAL ESTATE CONVEYANCE TAX:

See topic Stamp Tax.

SALES AND USE TAXES:

Sales Tax.—Superseded by gross receipts tax, as to which see subhead Gross Receipts Tax, infra.

Gross Receipts Tax.—(26-52-101-1006).

Subject to exemptions hereinafter mentioned, tax of $4^{1}/_{2}$% is levied on gross receipts from all sales or exchanges of tangible personal property, sales of gas, electricity, water, ice, steam, telephone use, telegrams, cable television and other utility services except transportation services, sewer services and sanitation or garbage collection services; services of furnishing rooms on less than month to month basis; services in repair of motors and numerous specified items of personal property; sales of printing and photography; and sales of admission to athletic, entertainment and recreational events (26-52-301-302); special provisions apply to short term rental of tangible personal property (26-52-310); gross receipts from certain coin-operated pinball and music machines or other devices (26-52-308); gross receipts from machinery and equipment used to produce or repair replacement dies, molds, or other repair parts (26-52-402); gross receipts on service of collecting debt or account receivable (26-52-301[3][E]); gross receipts of florists delivering by telegraph or telephone (26-52-507); sales of computer software and services on computer hardware (26-52-304). Deduction from gross receipts allowed for bad debts. (26-52-309). "Sale" includes transfers of either title or possession, except in case of leases or rentals, for valuable consideration, regardless of manner by which transfer is accomplished and includes exchange, barter, lease or rental of tangible personal property. Term includes sale, giving away, exchanging or other disposition of admissions, dues or fees to clubs, places of amusement, recreational or athletic events, or for privilege of having access to or use of amusement, athletic or entertainment facilities. (26-52-103). If adjoining cities are divided by state line and city in adjoining state is of greater population than Arkansas city, rate in Arkansas city is same as in adjoining city, but not to exceed 5%. (26-52-303). Tax not applicable to out-of-state telephones sent to state for repairs. (26-52-418). Additional 2% gross receipts tax applicable to certain items related to tourism. (26-52-1001-1006).

Additional excise tax of $^{1}/_{8}$ of 1% is levied on all taxable sales of property and services subject to tax levied on Arkansas Gross Receipts pursuant to 26-52-101 et seq. (Const. Amendment 75).

Exemptions.—Gross receipts from following sales are exempt: Sales for resale to persons regularly engaged, within or without state, in reselling the articles purchased, if purchaser has a sales permit (26-52-401[12][A]); sales of property to be used in manufacturing, processing or assembling, provided property retains its identity as recognizable integral part of finished product (but all sales to building contractors are taxable) (26-52-401[12][B]); new custom manufactured homes constructed from materials on which gross receipts or use tax paid (26-52-803); sale of manufactured home under $10,000 (26-52-504); sale of mobile home or house trailer under $2,500 (26-52-504); sale of motor vehicle, trailer or semi-trailer under $2,000 (26-52-510); sales, for human use, of prescription drugs and oxygen (26-52-406); isolated sales not made by established business (26-52-401[17]); resale of tangible personal property which was accepted as part of purchase price of other tangible property on which tax was paid (26-52-401[22]); sales taxation of which is prohibited by state or federal constitution (26-52-401[16]); sales of newspapers, gasoline, unprocessed crude oil (26-52-401[4], -401[11], -401[23]); machinery and equipment purchased for and used directly in processing commercial articles manufactured or processed in Arkansas plants (26-52-402[a][1]); advertising space in newspapers, periodicals and bill boards (26-52-401[13]); gate admission fees for fairs and for nonprofit rodeos (26-52-401[15]); sales of natural gas and electricity to qualified manufacturers of steel (26-52-901-903); sales of certain farm, dairy and agricultural products when sold by farmer (26-52-401[18]); sales by charitable organizations, except when engaged in business for profit (26-52-

See note at head of Digest as to 1998 legislation covered.

See Topical Index in front part of this volume.

AR – 40

SALES AND USE TAXES . . . *continued*
401[2]); sales to federal government (26-52-401[5]); sales of motor vehicles and adaptive equipment to disabled veterans purchasing with financial assistance of Veterans Administration under 38 U.S.C. §§1901-1905; (26-52-401[6]) sales of new cars to veterans blinded by Service-connected injuries (26-52-415); sales of new motor vehicles to nonprofit corporations for performance of contracts with DHS or purchased with Urban Mass Transit funds, provided purchased in lots of ten vehicles or more for use in DHS (26-52-420) programs; sales to governmental agencies for free distribution to poor or to inmates of institutions (26-52-401[19]); sales to charitable hospitals or sanatoriums (26-52-401[21]); sales to orphans' or children's homes not operated for profit (26-52-413); sales of cotton, cotton seed, lint cotton, baled cotton, bagging and tie materials sold to and used by cotton gins, and seed sold for use in production of agricultural products (26-52-401[18][A]); sale of baby chickens (26-52-401[18][F]); machinery and equipment used in feed manufacturing, poultry hatching and poultry, egg and livestock processing (26-52-402); sales of personal property and services to Boy and Girl Scouts (26-52-401[8]); sales of some pollution control devices (26-52-402); sales of foods in cafeterias of public schools and colleges operated primarily for teachers and students and not for profit (26-52-401[3]); sales of coin-operated car washes (26-52-301[3][C][ii]); sales of motor vehicles to municipalities and counties (26-52-410); sales of agriculture fertilizer, limestone, chemicals and medical preparations used in treating livestock and poultry and chemicals, nutrients and other ingredients used in commercial production of yeast (26-52-405; 26-53-119); sales of insulin and test strips for testing human blood sugar levels; sales of tickets for athletic events and scholastic activities at public and private elementary and secondary schools and colleges and universities (26-52-419, 26-52-412); sales of electricity used in manufacturing aluminum metal by electrolytic reduction process (26-52-401[24]); sales to specified charitable or social organizations (26-52-401[2]); sales of following public utilities service: transportation, sewer, sanitation and garbage collection (26-52-301[2]); sales or construction of and repairs to vessels, barges and towboats of at least 50 tons load displacement (26-52-407); new and used farm machinery used exclusively and directly for agricultural production of food or fiber as business (26-52-403); photoprocessing incidental to printing and processing of scrap metal for steel production (26-52-402[b]); sale of first 500 kilowatt hours of electricity per month to households with less than $12,000 annual income (26-52-416); rental or lease of specialized equipment used in filming of motion picture qualifying for tax incentives under 26-4-201 (26-52-402[c][3]); repair and remanufacture of certain industrial metal rollers (26-52-301[3][C][v]); proceeds for transfer of fill material by business engaged in transporting or delivering fill material when such material is obtained by delivery service free of charge and charge to consumer is only for delivery (26-52-401[31]); sales of natural gas used as fuel in process of manufacturing glass (26-52-423); gross receipts derived from sale of foodstuffs to nonprofit agencies organized under Arkansas Non-Profit Corporation Act for free distribution to poor and needy (26-52-421); sales of publications sold through regular subscription, regardless of type or content of publication or place printed or published (26-52-401[14]); sale of any tangible personal property specifically exempted from taxation by Arkansas Compensating Tax Act, §26-53-101 et seq. (26-52-401[29]); sales to Fort Smith Clearinghouse (26-52-424); sale of substitute fuel in producing, manufacturing, fabricating, assembling, processing, finishing, or packaging of articles of commerce at manufacturing or processing plants or facilities in state (26-52-425); sales of forms constructed of plaster, cardboard, fiberglass, natural fibers, synthetic fibers, or composites thereof which determine physical characteristics of item of tangible personal property and which are destroyed or consumed during manufacture of item for which form was built (26-52-422). Sales of prescription drugs to physicians (26-52-406); sales of residential lawn care service (Act 1252 of 1997); sales of school buses for use in Arkansas school district (Act 1303 of 1997).

Rental Vehicle Tax.—Rental vehicle tax, levied on gross receipts derived from rentals of licensed motor vehicles leased for period of less than 30 days (other than vehicles rented or leased for residential moving), is collected in lieu of collecting gross receipts tax on sale of vehicle. (26-52-311).

Sales Permits.—It is unlawful to transact within the state any business subject to the tax without obtaining sales permit from Department of Finance and Administration, criminal penalties being provided. $50 deposit required for sales tax permit. Separate permit must be displayed at each place of business. If seller has no established place of business in state, cash deposit must be made, or bond given, to obtain permit. Permit may be revoked for noncompliance with tax statute, after notice and a hearing from which appeal may be taken to chancery court within 30 days. (26-52-201-208). Nonrefundable fee of $50 is required with submission of each new application for gross receipts tax permit (26-52-203).

Records, Returns and Payment.—Persons subject to tax and persons making sales for resale must keep records of sales. (26-52-501). Returns for each month must be made to Department of Finance and Administration by 20th day of succeeding month, but returns may be made quarterly if tax does not exceed $100 in any month. (26-52-501). Payment must be made when return is filed, and 2% discount may be taken if payment is made on or before due date of return, with discount being limited to $1,000 per month. (26-52-503). Retailers having average net sales exceeding $200,000 per month must make installments of 40% of tax due on monthly average net sales by 12th and 24th of each month with balance payable by 20th day of following month (2-52-512). 2% discount may be taken on each installment, if timely postmarked. Department of Finance and Administration may permit purchaser to remit tax directly to Revenue Division instead of paying tax to seller. (26-52-509-510).

Penalty.—See topic Income Tax, subhead Penalty.

Criminal penalty for doing business without first obtaining permit from Department of Finance and Administration is fine of not more than $1,000 or by imprisonment for not more than one year or both, and each day of violation is separate offense. (26-52-201). Willful failure to file return or pay tax is Class D felony. (26-18-202).

Wholesalers must furnish Department of Finance and Administration on its request with names of retailers to whom sales have been made and the amount of such sales for any given period. (26-50-102).

Tax on automobiles is collected when license is issued, instead of by dealer. (26-52-510)

Limitations period for assessment of deficiency, interest or penalty is three years from date set for filing of monthly return provided that return was filed and it was not fraudulent. (26-18-306).

Multistate Tax Compact adopted. (26-5-101).

Aircraft sellers are specially regulated. (26-52-505). Manufacturer's investment sales and use tax credit is available for investments of $5 million. (26-52-701-706). Exemption available for service of repairing, modifying, converting or maintaining commercial jet aircraft and for tangible personal property which becomes part of commercial jet aircraft. (26-52-301[3][C]; 26-52-401[28]).

Arkansas Enterprise Zone Act.—When specific qualifications are met, Department of Finance & Administration shall authorize refund of sales and use tax imposed by state and municipality or county, if municipality or county authorized refund of its local tax, on purchases of material used in construction of building or buildings, or any addition or improvement thereon, for housing any legitimate business enterprise, and machinery and equipment to be located in or in connection with such building. (15-4-1704).

Cities of first class, second class or incorporated town may levy tax not in excess of 3% on gross receipts of hotels, motels, restaurants, cafes, and cafeterias. (26-75-602).

Regulations governing tax and forms may be obtained from Department of Finance and Administration.

Compensating Tax.—(26-53-101-303).

Subject to exemptions hereinafter mentioned, tax of 4½% of sales price is levied against each person for privilege of storing, using, distributing, or consuming within state any tangible personal property (26-53-106-107) including computer software, machinery, equipment, repair or replacement parts, materials and supplies used, stored, distributed, or consumed by contractor but no tax due on such property upon which an equal or greater tax has been paid in another state provided it grants credit for tax paid on such property in this state (26-53-203). Every vendor selling tangible personal property for storage, use or consumption in state including those selling by mail order, newspaper, catalog, radio or television, must register with Department of Finance and Administration. (26-53-121).

Tax levied against gross purchase price of tangible personal property of motor carriers, railroads, public pipeline carriers, air line carriers, telephone and telegraph companies, gas, water and power utilities is 4½%. (26-53-107-108).

Exemptions.—Following property is exempt: Property, storage, use, distribution or consumption of which state is prohibited from taxing under federal Constitution or laws or state Constitution; property, sales of which are not subject to or specifically exempted from Gross Receipts Tax (26-53-112); sales of natural gas and electricity to qualified manufacturers of steel; sales of natural gas used as fuel in process of manufacturing glass (26-53-134); unprocessed crude oil; food stuffs used for free distribution by governmental agency to poor or to public penal and eleemosynary institutions; machinery and equipment used directly in producing article of commerce at manufacturing plant in Arkansas, or machinery purchased to replace such existing machinery in its entirety; some pollution control devices (26-53-112-114, 127); some aircraft, aircraft equipment, railroad parts, cars, and equipment and some tangible personalty owned by aircraft, airmotive, or railroad companies (26-53-106 and 115); sales and construction of and repairs to vessels, barges and towboats of 50 tons load displacement (26-53-116); custom manufactured homes on which gross receipts tax paid (26-53-118); agricultural fertilizer, limestone, chemicals and feedstuffs used in livestock and poultry production (26-53-119-120); carbonaceous materials used in electrolytic reduction process and prescription drugs purchased, sold or used by licensed pharmacists, hospitals or dispensing physicians licensed under 17-93-102 (26-52-406). Property stored for sale or use outside state is not subject to compensating tax. (26-53-201).

Payment and Returns.—Vendor must collect tax from purchaser and remit to Department of Finance and Administration monthly on or before 20th day of month and must file with Department on or before 20th day of each month return for preceding monthly period. (26-53-124-125).

Every person subject to the tax and who has not paid the vendor must file with Department on or before the 20th day of each month a return for the preceding monthly period accompanied by a remittance of the tax due. (26-53-125). Department may extend for not more than 90 days time for making return and by general order may extend time for making returns for any taxpayer. (26-18-505).

Penalties and limitations same as in subhead Income Tax, supra.

Multistate Tax Compact adopted. (26-5-101).

Contractors and subcontractors are specially regulated. (26-53-201-206).

Tax on new and used cars is collected when license is issued instead of by dealer. (26-52-510).

Regulations governing tax and forms may be obtained from Department of Finance and Administration.

Public utilities engaged in distribution of gas, electricity, water or steam for heating purposes are taxed ⅖ of 1% on gross earnings from properties within state. (23-3-110).

Service vending machines, except coin box telephones and postage stamp vending machines, are subject to tax by 26-57-308.

SEVERANCE TAXES:

Severance taxes, at varying rates, are imposed on natural resources (oil, gas, minerals, timber) taken from the soil. (26-58-101-303).

STAMP TAX:

Stamp tax on conveyances of realty for consideration in excess of $100 is $3.30 for each $1,000 or fractional part thereof, of which one half is paid by seller and one half is paid by purchaser. Exclusions are provided for transfers to U.S., Arkansas, or any of their instrumentalities, agencies or political subdivisions, instruments solely to secure debt or to correct or replace instrument previously recorded and on which tax had been paid, conveyances of leasehold interest, deeds for timber to be removed within 24 months, instruments for land sold for delinquent taxes, instruments transferring property in judicial action to enforce security interest or instruments for transfers in lieu of or to avoid judicial action to enforce security interest, property settlement transfers pursuant

See note at head of Digest as to 1998 legislation covered.

See Topical Index in front part of this volume.

AR – 41

STAMP TAX . . . *continued*

to divorce whether by agreement or court order, instruments conveying new home financed by Federal Housing Administration or Veterans Administration if sales price of house is $50,000 or less and seller files sworn statement by buyer that neither buyer nor buyer's spouse has owned any home within three years of closing and stating sales price and instruments conveying land between corporations or between corporation and its shareholders incident to reorganization, merger, consolidation or liquidation. (26-60-105, 102). This tax is in addition to other recording fees mentioned under topics Deeds, Mortgages of Real Property, and Records.

Willful violation of Act subject to $500 fine or 1% of transaction, whichever greater and other penalties. (26-60-111).

Recordation is forbidden unless stamps, when required, are affixed. (26-60-110).

Form.—Instrument must contain statement that "I certify under penalty of false swearing that legally correct amount of documentary stamps have been placed on this instrument" which is signed by grantee or his agent and contains grantee's address, or following affidavit must be attached in triplicate. (26-60-107, 110). Exempt transfers need not have either of above if clearly exempt, but certification or affidavit may be required. (26-60-107).

ARKANSAS
REAL PROPERTY TRANSFER TAX AFFIDAVIT

STATE OF ARKANSAS
COUNTY OF

Before the undersigned, Notary Public, duly qualified and acting in and for said county and state, appeared the undersigned, to me well known or satisfactorily proven to be the Affiant herein, who stated under oath that:

1. He/She/They is/are the Grantee(s) in the attached Deed or the Agent of the Grantee(s)
2. That the names and addresses of all parties to the attached real estate transfer transaction are as follows:
   A) Grantee (buyer)_____
   Name
   _____
   Address

   B) Grantee's Agent: (To be completed only if this Affidavit is being signed by Agent rather than Grantee. If the Agent is a corporation the person signing the Affidavit must show authority to sign for the corporation.)

   _____
   Name
   _____
   Address
   C) Grantor (Seller)_____
   Name
   _____
   Address
3. The property was transferred on: _____
   Date
4. The property is located in: _____   _____
   County   District
5. The full value of the consideration given for the property was_____
   ($_____).
   (NOTE: This amount should include down payment, the amount of any mortgage given or assumed as well as the value of any property given in trade.)
   OR
   The transfer of property reflected on the attached instrument is not subject to the Real Property Transfer Tax because: _____
   NOTE: All transfers of real property for which Grantor (Seller) receives something of value in exchange for the property are subject to the tax except those specifically exempted at Ark. Code Ann. 26-60-102.
6. Real Property Tax Stamps Affixed to Deed:

Stamp Denominations:	Stamp Serial Numbers:	Stamp Values:
_____	_____	_____
_____	_____	_____
	Total Stamp Values	$ _____

7. He/She/They understand that a false statement on this Affidavit may constitute perjury; further it is understood that any person signing a deed for record who knowingly, willfully and fraudulently files the same in violation of the Real Property Transfer Tax Act may be subject to a fine of $500.00 or 1% of the transaction; whichever is greater.

_____
GRANTEE/BUYER/AFFIANT OR AGENT

Subscribed and sworn to before me this __ day of ____, 19__.

_____
Notary Public

My Commission Expires:
_____

_____

TAXATION OF CORPORATE STOCK OR SECURITIES:

See category Business Organizations, topic Corporations.

TOBACCO TAX:

Tobacco products are taxed under 26-57-201-254.

UNEMPLOYMENT COMPENSATION TAX:

Unemployment compensation tax is imposed by 11-10-101-226, 401-405 on every "employer," which means any individual or employing unit which, for some portion of each of ten different days (whether or not consecutive) in current or preceding calendar year, has or had in employment one or more individuals, and meaning of "employer" is extended to include certain combinations of employing units, etc. (11-10-209).

Employment within the Act does not include certain enumerated activities. (11-10-210[f]).

Rate of tax (termed "contributions") is 2.9% of payroll, except that after employer has paid tax for three years his rate is adjusted annually according to his benefit experience. Employer also required to pay stabilization tax and advance interest tax based upon variable scale. Maximum wages of employee on which tax is payable is governed by federal unemployment tax act. (11-10-701-715).

Returns must be made and tax paid to Commissioner of Labor, Unemployment Compensation Department, quarterly on the last day of month following close of each quarter. Penalty for failure to file return $10 or 5% of tax, whichever greater, if filed within 20 days after due date; $20 or 10% of tax, whichever greater, if filed more than 20 days after due date. Interest at 1 1/2% per month is charged for nonpayment of tax when due. (11-10-716-722).

Employees are not taxed. (11-10-701).

State has adopted comprehensive Multistate Tax Compact authorizing state to participate with other states in forming a Commission for adopting uniform regulations covering income, capital stock, gross receipts, sales, and use taxes. (26-5-101-108).

UNIFORM FEDERAL LIEN REGISTRATION ACT:

Uniform Federal Lien Registration Act adopted. (18-47-201-207). Revised Uniform Tax Lien Registration Act not adopted.

TRANSPORTATION

MOTOR VEHICLES:

General supervision is by Department of Finance and Administration, P.O. Box 1272, Room 106, Revenue Building, Little Rock, AR. 72203.

Statutes applicable are: Title 27, cc. 1-8.

The Uniform Act Regulating Traffic on Highways has been adopted with many variations, (27-49-101). Uniform Motor Vehicle Administration, Certificate of Title and Antitheft Act has been adopted. (27-14-101-2212). Uniform Motor Vehicle Safety Responsibility Act has been adopted with variations. (27-19-101-721).

Abandoned or Scrap Vehicles.—Procedures are given for disposition of abandoned vehicles (27-50-1101), those having only scrap value (27-14-913), and for salvage operators to obtain title by bill of sale if no certificate of title is available (27-14-913).

Vehicle license required annually. Number plate must be displayed in rear. (27-14-716). Registration of semitrailers under reciprocal agreements was repealed by Act 809 of 1997. Some small or medium size trailers may be permanently registered as may three or more wheeled all-terrain cycles. (27-14-1201-1207, and 27-20-207). Trucks with gross loaded weight between 68,001 and 73,280 pounds may be licensed for quarter-year. (27-14-601).

Disabled American veterans issued an automobile under any public law are issued free licenses (27-15-502) nontransferable to person not so entitled (27-15-504), but issuable to surviving spouse upon payment of $1 (27-15-407, Act 1327 of 1997). Members of U.S. Military Reserve may have special license tags. (27-15-1102). Certain former prisoners of war entitled to one permanent license. (27-15-1001-1003). Persons receiving Purple Heart medal while serving in U.S. armed forces or unmarried surviving spouse of any such Purple Heart medal recipient entitled to register one vehicle and receive one free permanent license plate. (27-15-901-903, Act 269 of 1997). Persons receiving Congressional Medal of Honor, and their surviving spouses, entitled to receive free special license plate. (23-15-801-807). Retired members of U.S. armed forces and surviving spouses of disabled American veterans may receive special license tags. (27-15-1201-1204; 27-15-407). No other exception for members of armed forces.

Operator's License.—Uniform Motor Vehicle Driver's License Act adopted, (27-16-101). Person under 16 years old may not be licensed as operator except that person at least 14 years old may be granted restricted license (27-16-604), nor person under 18 as commercial driver (27-16-604). Nonresident not required to have commercial driver's license before employed by Arkansas resident if he has in his immediate possession valid commercial driver's license issued by his home state or country. (27-16-603). New resident may obtain Arkansas driver's license by simply surrendering current valid out-of-state license, paying transfer fee and passing eye exam (but not written driver exam). (27-16-807). Before securing current license, operator must exhibit receipt showing payment of currently due personal property tax (27-14-706) or former certificate of registration with endorsement showing payment of all personal property taxes and current assessments for future taxes (27-14-706) and must submit proof of filing assessment for personal property (27-14-1015). Effective Jan. 1, 1998, before securing current license, owner of every vehicle subject to registration in Arkansas must assess vehicle with county tax assessor in county where required by law and within time required by law. In addition to registration fees, owner must pay $2.50 for each annual license plate validation decal. On or before Jan. 1, 1999, Director of Department of Finance and Administration will institute system whereby county assessor and collector will electronically notify Director that vehicle has been assessed and that owner owes no delinquent personal property taxes. Prior to instituting system, proof of assessment and proof of payment of personal property taxes will continue to be required. (Act 974, 1997). State Revenue Commissioner may issue "drive out tag" good for 14 days for $2

See note at head of Digest as to 1998 legislation covered.

See Topical Index in front part of this volume.

MOTOR VEHICLES . . . *continued*
fee. (27-14-2103, 2104). Municipalities may regulate use of mopeds, three wheeled vehicles and similar vehicles. (27-49-106).

Any person while operating motor vehicles in service of U.S. armed forces is exempt from requirements for operator's licenses. (27-16-603).

Officer issuing citation for offense which authorizes possession and retention of license is required to give cited person option of surrendering his driver's license or posting bond to assure his appearance in court, unless such person is charged with driving while intoxicated. (27-50-609).

Liens and Encumbrances.—Lien, other than by possession, perfected by filing true copy of evidence of lien with Title Department of Motor Vehicle Division, Department of Finance and Administration, and having lien shown on certificate of title. (27-14-801-804). Fee is $1 for filing each instrument. (27-14-806). Lien holder on motor vehicle may perfect lien by filing copy with Revenue Division of Department of Finance. (27-14-805-807).

Identification Marks.—Misdemeanor to alter or remove serial numbers or other identification marks of maker, or knowingly to deal with or possess car so altered. (27-14-2211).

Operation Prohibited.—Driving when under the influence of intoxicating liquor or drug is punishable by fine and/or imprisonment and revocation of operator's license. (5-65-103-104). Completion of Alcohol Education Program may be required prior to reinstatement of driving privileges for any person whose license is administratively suspended or revoked. (5-65-104).

Size and Weight Limits.—Highway Department may issue permit for operation of vehicles in excess of limits. (27-35-201-212). Rules and regulations apply to movement of houses on highways. (27-35-309).

Forestry machinery is exempt from width and height limitations, other than on federal interstate highway system. (27-35-209). Overweight fees. (27-35-202). General gross vehicle weight is established as 80,000 pounds. (27-35-203). Federal bridge formula applies with some exceptions. (27-35-203).

Equipment Required.—Regulated by 27-37-202-206, 301-306, 501-503, 601. Specific limitations on window tinting. (27-37-306).

Lights Required.—Regulated by 27-36-201-220.

Inspection.—Effective Jan. 1, 1998, only certain vehicles will be required to be inspected annually, but all vehicles must be in safe mechanical condition or operator may be subject to citation and fines. (Act 974 of 1997).

Traffic Regulations.—Right turn on red signal permitted after stop unless otherwise prohibited by sign, and left turn on red into one-way street permitted from one-way street. (27-52-107[a][3][A][i], [ii]).

Mandatory seat belt use required for driver and front seat passengers. Penalty of $25 for noncompliance. (27-37-701-706). Evidence of failure to wear properly fastened seat belt is not admissible into evidence in civil action subject to limited exception for certain product liability claims. (27-37-703).

Accidents.—Driver must stop, give assistance if necessary, give name and address of owner and driver and license numbers if demanded, and report accidents to State Police Department. (27-53-103-105; 201-208). Leaving scene of auto accident involving death or personal injury is felony. (27-53-101). Subsequent to accident involving only property damage, driver shall, if possible, remove his vehicle from roadway. (27-53-102).

Liability of Owner.—Owner is liable for negligence of others only when car operated by his servant or agent within scope of authority and duty. Owner of car kept for family use not liable for negligence of member of family unless acting in capacity of agent or servant, or owner has knowledge that driver is careless and reckless. (187 Ark. 1107, 63 S.W. 2d 971). Driver of vehicle colliding with vehicle stopped illegally on travelled portion of road is not liable for damages. (27-51-1303[a][2][B]). Officer is required to notify landowner of vehicle accident damaging his property (fence or other attachment). When motor vehicle damages fence or gate of another and damage allows livestock to escape, immunity is given to owner of escaped livestock from damages until actual notice received and opportunity given to repair fence or gate. (2-39-109).

Child Passengers.—Children under five years of age must be secured in child passenger safety seat system meeting federal motor vehicle standards although safety belt is sufficient for children at least four years of age or at least 40 pounds in weight. (27-34-104). Violation punishable by fine of $25-$100. (27-34-103). Violation carries no presumption of negligence. (27-34-106).

Guests.—Owner or operator is liable for injury to or death of guest resulting from owner's or operator's negligence. (Act 13 of 1983, repealing Arkansas Guest Statute; Act 13 since repealed, but Guest Statute not included in 1987 Code).

Proof of Financial Responsibility.—Proof of financial responsibility means proof of ability to pay damages resulting from operation of motor vehicle in any one accident of $25,000 for bodily injury to or death of one person, $50,000 for bodily injury to or death of two or more persons, and $15,000 for damage to property (27-19-701) and may be made by depositing with Commissioner of Revenues certificate of insurance showing issuance and maintenance of appropriate policies of insurance, or appropriate surety bond, or receipt of Treasurer of State showing deposit with him of approved securities in appropriate amounts (27-19-711) or by certificate from Commissioner that person has deposited $65,000 in cash or securities with him (27-19-717).

Commissioner must suspend license and all registration plates of any person convicted of manslaughter arising out of the operation of a motor vehicle unless such person gives and thereafter maintains proof of financial responsibility (27-19-703; 27-50-307) and of any person who fails, for period of 30 days, to satisfy any qualifying final judgment, payment of amounts specified being satisfaction of judgment for purposes of act (27-19-706-707).

Discharge of judgment by bankruptcy relieves debtor from requirements of act. (27-19-708). Act applies to nonresidents. (27-19-705).

Upon failure, without meritorious defense, to pay within 60 days after notice any claim for property damage for $1,000 or less resulting from motor vehicle collision, defendant is liable for double damages, court costs, and attorneys fee of not less than $250. (27-53-402).

Insurance.—Mandatory motor vehicle liability insurance required. Satisfactory proof of insurance required prior to issuance of vehicle license. (27-13-102; 27-22-101-104). Beginning Jan. 1, 1998, check of Vehicle Insurance Database maintained by Revenue Division of Department of Finance and Administration will verify compliance with motor vehicle liability insurance laws (27-14-414), and proof of liability insurance need not be shown at registration (Act 974 of 1997).

No-Fault Insurance.—Effective July 1, 1974, every automobile insurance policy covering private passenger motor vehicles must provide minimum medical and hospital benefits, income disability and accidental death benefits for named insured, members of his family residing in same household, passengers injured while occupying insured vehicle, and to persons other than those occupying another vehicle stuck by insured vehicle, without regard to fault. Medical and hospital benefits cover all reasonable and necessary expense incurred within 24 months after accident not to exceed $5,000 per person. Income disability covers 70% loss of income from work during a period commencing eight days after accident, not to exceed 52 weeks and not to exceed $140 a week. For non-income earners, benefits cover expenses not to exceed $70 a week reasonably incurred for essential services in lieu of those injured person would have performed without income during a period commencing eight days after accident not to exceed 52 weeks. Accidental death benefits are $5,000 if death results from accident within one year. Named insured may reject in writing one or more of coverages, and such rejection continues until insured withdraws it. Insurer may exclude benefits to insured when injury is intentionally self-inflicted or when received in commission of felony or in seeking to elude lawful arrest by officer. Tort liability is retained. Insurer is entitled to reimbursement less costs of collection from recipient out of any settlement or judgment recovered for injury. (23-89-202-208).

Foreign Vehicles.—Privately owned passenger vehicles, duly registered in home state or country and displaying license plates required by laws of home state or country may be operated by visitors or tourists without license for 90 days. Following foreign cars may operate without charge: Vehicles used only for marketing farm products raised by operator or those associated with him; cars owned by nonresidents not operated for hire but used to and from place of regular employment or making trips to purchase goods; vehicles operated by member of U.S. armed forces during any period of emergency. Vehicles used to make occasional trips, not for hire, may get gratuitous permits. (27-14-704).

All terrain vehicles of three, four or six wheel variety may not be operated on public streets or highways. (27-21-101-109).

Action against nonresident owner or operator of automobile, or against resident owner or operator who becomes nonresident, arising out of accident in state, may be commenced by serving three copies of process on Secretary of State and paying Secretary of State sum of $25. (16-58-120). Such service is good and will warrant personal judgment if notice of service and copy of process are forthwith sent by plaintiff or his attorney, by registered mail, to defendant at his last known address and defendant's return receipt or affidavit of compliance are appended to writ and filed with clerk of court. Same rules apply to action against personal representative of owner or operator. (16-58-121).

Direct Actions.—See category Civil Actions and Procedure, topic Actions, subhead Direct Action Against Insurer.

Motor vehicle carriers are regulated by Transportation Commission. (23-13-208). Must have special license and when operated over fixed route must have certificate of public convenience and necessity. (23-13-218, 219). Common carriers must file tariffs showing rates for all services (23-13-244) and contract carriers must file schedule of minimum rates for all services (23-13-245-250). Bond, or insurance policy, including uninsured motorist coverage, to indemnify passengers and others injured by operation must be filed. (23-13-227).

Taxicab operators must carry liability insurance. (27-14-1501). Muncipalities may impose additional insurance requirements. (Act 1223 of 1997).

Motorcycles on highways and licensing of operators regulated by 27-20-101-117. Motorcycles and motorized bicycles must be registered each year. (27-20-105). Persons riding bicycles or animals on highway have same rights and duties as drivers of vehicles. (27-49-111).

Gasoline Tax.—See category Taxation, topic Gasoline and Special Fuels Tax.

Privilege tax may be levied by county and/or municipality (26-78-102) each not to exceed $5 annually on each motor vehicle operated upon public roads of county and/or municipality (26-78-104).

Manufactured home units are any trailer unit constructed for use as dwelling, office or classroom exceeding eight feet in width or 60 feet in length, and may be moved on highways, roads, and streets in state by procurement of special permit. Trailers eight feet or less in width and 60 feet or less in length may be moved on highways of state without obtaining permit. (27-35-301-310).

Special permit for moving manufactured home units on highway obtained from any weight station. (27-35-304).

Mobile homes are subject to motor vehicle registration (27-14-703) and are required to display sticker showing assessment for ad valorem taxes (26-26-1106).

Motor clubs and similar organizations must provide deposit and surety bonds. (23-77-101, 105-109).

RAILROADS:

See category Business Regulation and Commerce, topic Carriers.

See note at head of Digest as to 1998 legislation covered.

See Topical Index in front part of this volume.

AR – 43

COMMERCIAL CODE FORMS
See also categories Business Regulation and Commerce, topic Commercial Code; Mortgages, topic Chattel Mortgages.
Following are standard forms currently in use.
Forms

Financing Statement.—UCC-1

This FINANCING STATEMENT is presented to a Filing Officer for filing pursuant to the Uniform Commercial Code	Date:	3. Maturity date (if any):
1. Debtor(s) Name (Last Name First)	2. Debtor(s) Address	This space for use of Filing Officer. Number
4. Secured Party(ies)	5. Secured Party(ies) Address	
6. Assigned Party(ies)	7. Assigned Party(ies) Address	

8. This financing statement covers the following types (or items) of property:

This Instrument Prepared By . . . .

Description of Real Estate. (Use this only if applicable)

Check (X) if covered: ( ) Proceeds of Collateral are also covered ( ) Products of Collateral are also covered. No. of additional sheets presented: ( )

Filed with Circuit Court Clerk of . . . . County. ( ) Secretary of State.

. . . .

By: . . . . By: . . . .
            Signature(s) of Debtor(s)   Signature(s) of Secured Party(ies)
FILING OFFICER COPY

Statement of Termination—Attached to page 2 of Form UCC-1.

TERMINATION STATEMENT
This statement of termination of financing is presented to a Filing Officer for filing pursuant to the Uniform Commercial Code. The Second Party certifies that the Secured Party no longer claims a security interest under the financing statement bearing the file number above.

. . . .

Dated: . . . . 19 . .

By: . . . .
(Signature of Secured Party or Assignee of Record—Not Valid until signed)
FILING OFFICER COPY ACKNOWLEDGMENT—Filing Officer is requested to note file number, date and hour of filing on this copy and return it to the person filing, as an acknowledgment.

Statement of Continuation, Partial Release or Assignment, etc.—Form UCC-3.

This FINANCING STATEMENT is presented to a Filing Officer for filing pursuant to the Uniform Commercial Code		3. Maturity date (if any):
1. Debtor(s) Name (Last Name First) and Addresses	2. Secured Party(ies) and Addresses	This space for use of Filing Officer (Date, time and Filing Office.)

This statement refers to original Financing Statement No. . . . . Dated . . . . 19 . . . . . .

A. Continuation . . . . ( ) The original financing statement between the foregoing Debtor and Secured Party, bearing the file number shown above, is still effective.	B. Partial Release . . . . ( ) From the collateral described in the financing statement bearing the file number shown above, the Secured Party releases the following:	C. Assignment . . . . ( ) The Secured Party certifies that the Secured Party has assigned to the Assignee whose name and address is shown below, Secured Party's rights under the financing statement bearing the file number shown above in the following property:	D. Termination Statement ( ) This statement of termination of financing is presented to a Filing Officer for filing pursuant to the Uniform Commercial Code. The Secured Party certifies that the Secured Party no longer claims a security interest under the financing statement bearing the file number shown above.	E. Other ( )

Dated: . . . . 19 . . . . . . By: . . . .

(Signature of Secured Party or Assignee of Record).
Not Valid unless signed.

FILING OFFICER COPY—

CALIFORNIA LAW DIGEST REVISER

Carol A. Wilson
Director of Academic Support
University of San Francisco
School of Law
2130 Fulton Street
San Francisco, California 94117
Telephone: 415-422-2985
Fax: 415-422-6433
Email: WilsonC@usfca.edu

Assisted By:
Professor Sharon A. Meadows
University of San Francisco
School of Law

Reviser Profile

Carol A. Wilson has taught at the University of San Francisco School of Law since 1990. She is director of the Academic Support Program and teaches courses in Legal Drafting, Legal Research and Writing, and Legal Analysis and exam writing. She received her B.A. from the University of Oregon, her M.A. from the School for International Training, and her J.D. from the University of San Francisco School of Law. Prior to joining the teaching staff at the University of San Francisco School of Law she was in a private litigation practice in San Francisco which specialized in Attorney Malpractice Defense and Insurance Defense. She was admitted to the California Bar in 1988.

Sharon A. Meadows has been a Professor of Law at the University of San Francisco School of Law since 1990, supervising the criminal law and juvenile law components of the USF Law Clinic. She received her B.A. and M.A. from Cornell University and her J.D. from the University of Michigan. She has worked in both the Public Defender's Office and the Federal Public Defender's Office. She was Chief Counsel of the Community Defender Project in the Bayview-Hunter's Point neighborhood in San Francisco from 1980-1983. She was appointed by Chief Judge Robert Peckham of the United States District Court for the Northern District of California to monitor an affirmative action consent decree in the construction industry. In 1994, she assisted in the establishment of a Criminal/Juvenile Law Clinic at the University of the West Cape in South Africa. Professor Meadows was admitted to the California Bar in 1975.

The University of San Francisco was established in 1855 by the Jesuit Fathers as San Francisco's first institution of higher learning. The School of Law was established in 1912. Nearly 700 students are enrolled in the School of Law and approximately 200 students receive the Juris Doctor degree from USF each year. Since the Law School's inception, its graduates have distinguished themselves in private practice and as attorneys in city, county, state and federal offices. Graduates have become members of both the state and federal judiciaries, including Justices of the California Supreme Court, as well as prominent members of local, state and federal legislative bodies. The School of Law offers full-time and part-time programs leading to the Juris Doctor degree, as well as a concurrent degree program leading to Juris Doctor and Master of Business Administration degrees. In addition, the School of Law offers a Master of Laws (LL.M.) for foreign lawyers who have first degrees in law from a non-American university. The school has 28 resident full time faculty members and seven Legal Research and Writing Instructors in addition to a large adjunct faculty of practicing lawyers and judges. The University of San Francisco School of Law is fully accredited by the American Bar Association and the Association of American Law Schools.

CALIFORNIA LAW DIGEST REVISER

CALIFORNIA LAW DIGEST REVISER

Carol A. Wilson
Director of Academic Support
University of San Francisco
School of Law
2130 Fulton Street
San Francisco, California 94117
Telephone: 415-422-2085
Fax: 415-422-6433
Email: Wilson@usfca.edu

Assisted By:

Professor Sharon A. Meadows
University of San Francisco
School of Law

Reviser Profile

Carol A. Wilson has taught at the University of San Francisco School of Law since 1990. She is Director of the Academic Support Program and teaches courses in Legal Drafting, Legal Research and Writing, and Legal Analysis and exam writing. She received her B.A. from the University of Oregon, her M.A. from the School for International Training, and her J.D. from the University of San Francisco School of Law. Prior to joining the teaching staff at the University of San Francisco School of Law, she was employed by the litigation practice of Susman Godfrey, which specialized in Antitrust, Intellectual Defense and Insurance Defense issues as administration of California, Inland, 1986.

Sharon A. Meadows has been a Professor of Law at the University of San Francisco School of Law since 1976. She currently teaches criminal law and juvenile law components of the USF Law Clinic. She received her B.A., and M.A. from California State University, and her J.D. from the University of Michigan. She has worked in both the public, defender office, and the federal public defender's office, as the Chief Counsel of the Community Defense Project at the Bay View Hunter's Point neighborhood Visitor Program in both 1980-1983. She was appointed by Chief Judge Robert Peckham of the United States District Court for the Northern District of California to monitor an administrative action concerning Antitrust continuing activity. In 1994, she traveled to the establishment of a Criminal Juvenile Law Clinic at the University of the Western Cape in South Africa. Professor Meadows was admitted to the California Bar in 1975.

The University of San Francisco was established in 1855 by the Jesuit fathers as the first institution of higher learning in San Francisco. The School of Law was established in 1912. Nearly 700 students are enrolled in the School of Law and approximately 700 students receive the Juris Doctor degree from USF each year. Since the Law School's inception, its graduates have distinguished themselves in every area because they are supervisors in city, state, and federal offices. Graduates have become members of both the state and federal judiciaries, including justices on the California Supreme Court, as well as prominent members of local, state, and federal legislatures. In addition to the School of Law's three-year part-time program leading to the first Juris Doctor degree, as well as a concurrent degree program leading to a Juris Doctor and Master of Business Administration degrees. In addition, the School of Law offers a Master of Law (LL.M.) for foreign lawyers who have their degrees in law from a non-American university who the School has determined has studied an overall need. The School of Law is accredited in addition to a long tradition of preparing lawyers and judges. The University of San Francisco School of Law is accredited by the American Bar Association and the Association of American Law Schools.

CALIFORNIA LAW DIGEST REVISER

CALIFORNIA LAW DIGEST

(The following is a list of all Categories and Topics, including cross-references, covered in this Digest.)

CALIFORNIA LAW DIGEST

Revised for 1999 edition by

PROFESSOR CAROL WILSON, University of San Francisco School of Law, San Francisco, CA.

(For explanations of abbreviations used in citations herein see the topic "Statutes". Parallel citations to the Pacific Reporter begin with 64 C.—1 C. A. "C.C.R." refers to California Code of Regulations. For explanations of other abbreviations used in citations herein see category Courts and Legislature, topic "Statutes".)

Note: Legislature in recess at time of going to press. This Revision incorporates the Statutes of 1998 passed by the Legislature and approved by the Governor through July 3, 1998.

Note: Unification of Municipal and Superior Courts approved by voters June 2, 1998. Enabling legislation in process at time of going to press. See Senate Bill 2139.

INTRODUCTION

GOVERNMENT AND LEGAL SYSTEM:

The State of California is a constituent state of the United States of America. For further discussion of the U.S. federal system, see Introduction to the Federal Government of the United States at the beginning of this volume. A great many laws are promulgated by the federal government of the United States and are not reflected in the topics below. See the Introduction to this volume for references to the federal law topics covered.

Like all but one of the United States, California has a common law legal system, with roots in English common law. For information on the courts and legislature of California, see category Courts and Legislature.

HOLIDAYS:

Legal holidays are Suns., Jan. 1, 3d Mon. in Jan., Feb. 12, 3d Mon. in Feb., Mar. 31, last Mon. in May, July 4, 1st Mon. in Sept., Sept. 9, 2d Mon. in Oct., Nov. 11, Dec. 25, Good Friday from noon until 3 p. m., any day appointed by President or Governor for public fast, thanksgiving or holiday. Except for Thanksgiving Day these holidays shall not apply to city, county or district unless made applicable by such governing body. (Govt. C. 6700).

Holiday Falling on Sunday.—When Jan. 1, Feb. 12, Mar. 31, July 4, Sept. 9, Nov. 11 or Dec. 25 falls on Sun., following Mon. is holiday. (Govt. C. 6701).

Holiday Falling on Saturday.—When Nov. 11 falls on Sat., preceding Fri. is holiday. (Govt. C. 6701).

Legality of Transactions on Saturday, Sunday or Holiday.—If any legal holiday falls on Sat., board of supervisors of any county may provide that alternate day shall be holiday for employees of county and superior, municipal, and justice courts in county except court clerks or attachés. (Govt. C. 6701). Sat. from noon until midnight is holiday as regards transaction of business in public offices of state, and also in political divisions thereof where laws, ordinances or charters provide that public offices shall be closed on holidays; provided, this shall not be construed to prevent or invalidate issuance, filing, service, execution or recording of any legal process or written instrument during said 12 hours. (Govt. C. 6702). However, county clerk need not keep his office open on Sat. mornings unless required to do so by judges of superior court of county. (28 Ops. Atty. Gen. 92). But county courts should remain open on statewide election day where county ordinance requires that county offices be open on such day. (48 Ops. Atty. Gen. 99). Special or holidays of limited effect may be appointed by President or Governor. (Govt. C. 6705). Sat. is holiday for acts performed at or by bank, and if July 4, Sept. 9, or Dec. 25 falls on Sat., preceding Fri. is bank holiday. (C.C. 7.1, 9). If Jan. 1, Feb. 12, July 4, Sept. 9, Nov. 11, or Dec. 25 falls on Sun. following Mon. is bank holiday. When secular act shall be performed, or last day for performance of any act falls on holiday, it may be performed on next business day. (Govt. C. 6706; C.C. 11; C.C.P. 13). "Holiday" includes Sats. for last day for performance of act. (C.C.P. 12a). Except as otherwise provided, all elections shall be held on a Tues. No election shall be held on day before or day after state holiday. (Elec. C. 2520).

If any city, county, state or other public office (other than branch) is closed for whole of any day, as to its business day shall be considered as holiday in computing time when act is legally required to be performed within specified period. (C. C. P. 12b).

When date of maturity of commercial paper falls on Sat., Sun., or holiday, instrument is payable on next business day not Sat. Specified days are designated optional bank holidays, on which holder of negotiable instrument payable at bank may present it (if bank is open thereon), with option of presentation on next business day not Sat. (Com'l. C. 3123).

OFFICE HOURS AND TIME ZONE:

California is in the Pacific (GMT −08:00) time zone. Office hours are generally from 9 a.m. to 5 p.m.

BUSINESS ORGANIZATIONS

AGENCY:

In general, any person having capacity to contract may appoint agent, and any person may be agent. (C. C. 2296). Agent may be authorized to do any acts which his principal might do, except those to which latter is bound to give his personal attention. (C. C. 2304).

ASSOCIATIONS:

Unincorporated association is legal entity. (17 C.A. 3d 824, 95 C. Rptr. 259).

Property.—Any unincorporated association, labor organization, and certain medical associations may, without incorporation, purchase, receive, own, hold, lease, mortgage, pledge, or encumber, by deed of trust or otherwise, manage and sell all such real estate and other property as may be necessary for any legal business purpose of unincorporated association; and may receive all property not so necessary, and hold it for period of up to ten years. (Corp. C. 20001-20003, 21200).

Interest of member of unincorporated association is personal property. (Corp. C. 20000). Association may file its name or insignia with Secretary of State and such name or insignia will be entitled to protection from unauthorized use. (Corp. C. 21300-21310).

Membership.—Applicant for membership in professional organization is entitled to due process in consideration of his application and in event his application is rejected, he is entitled to showing of just cause therefor and opportunity to defend himself. (12 C.3d 541, 116 C. Rptr. 245, 526 P.2d 253).

Rights and Duties of Members.—Articles of association, or constitution, or by-laws, of association constitute contract between association, as a whole, and its members, and rights and duties of members as between themselves and their relation to association in all matters affecting its internal government and management of its affairs are measured by their terms. Membership in association is personal right of which member can, generally, only be divested in manner provided in articles of association or by-laws. (130 C. 116, 62 P. 486).

Member of association is entitled to full and fair hearing on charge leading to expulsion, hearing must be in accordance with rules of association and law of land, member is entitled to adequate notice, adequate opportunity to defend himself, properly constituted tribunal and decision based upon evidence presented. (262 C.A.2d 211, 68 C. Rptr. 653). Internal administrative remedies, if provided, must be exhausted before suit for reinstatement or damages. (17 C.3d 465, 131 C. Rptr. 90, 551 P.2d 410).

Member of association has no general authority to bind his associates. (35 C. 365; 91 Adv. Dec. 107).

Liabilities of Members.—Only property of unincorporated association may be resorted to to satisfy money judgment against association, unless judgment is also against member who is party defendant. As between themselves, each member liable to pay only his numerical proportion of indebtedness of association. (32 C. A. 264, 162 P. 654; Corp. C. 24002).

Members of nonprofit association are not personally liable for debts incurred by association in acquiring lands or buildings for purposes of association, except by written contract. (Corp. C. 21100-101). Members of unincorporated association that is organized medical society are not individually liable for debts incurred to acquire buildings or for other nonprofit purposes of organization. (Corp. C. 21200).

Actions.—Persons associated in business under common name may sue and be sued by such common name. Member of association may be joined as party in action against association, if service of process is made on such member, and judgment may be obtained against him based on personal liability, whether liability is joint, joint and several, or several. (C.C.P. 369.5).

Member of unincorporated association may bring derivative action similar to shareholder's derivative action. (Corp. C. 800). Corp. C. 24003-24007 provide for filing of statement for service of process and govern means of service on association, including, where no agent has been designated or can be found, service on one or more members constitutes service on association.

Dissolution.—Unless otherwise provided for in its articles of association, charter or by-laws, association cannot be voluntarily dissolved except by unanimous consent of all its members. If such consent cannot be had, application must be made to court to declare dissolution. (250 C.A. 2d 925, 59 C. Rptr. 180).

Joint Stock Associations.—See topic Joint Stock Companies.

Professional Associations.—See topic Corporations, subhead Professional Corporations.

Real Estate Investment Trusts.—Defined by statute. (Corp. C. 23000). No shareholder of real estate investment trust shall be personally liable for any liabilities, debts, obligations or claims against real estate investment trust. (Corp. C. 23001). Real estate investment trust shall not issue any security redeemable at option of holder. (Corp. C. 23003). Real estate investment trust treated as corporation for purposes of reorganization and bankruptcy provisions. (Corp. C. 1400, 1402, 23005).

CORPORATIONS:

(For unincorporated associations, see topic Associations.)

General Corporation Law effective Jan. 1, 1977, governs corporations for profit including foreign corporations qualified to do business in California. Law applies to all corporations organized under it or to any business or private corporation organized under predecessor laws. Law contains provision for orderly application to corporations existing on, and to actions taken by directors and shareholders of such corporations before or after, effective date. Law does not affect Corporate Securities Law (see

CORPORATIONS . . . *continued*
category Business Regulation and Commerce, topic Securities), unincorporated associations (see topic Associations), partnerships (see topic Partnerships), and certain others. Law is contained within Corporations Code, §100 et seq.

Model Business Corporation Act has not been adopted.

General Supervision.—Secretary of State, 1230 J Street, Sacramento, CA 95814.

Purposes.—Corporation may be formed for any lawful purpose. (Corp. C. 202).

Name.—Any name may be used which is not likely to mislead public, and not already in use unless consent is obtained from current user. Use of words "bank", "trust", "trustee", or words related thereto is restricted. For insurers, Secretary of State will not file articles unless certificate approving name is attached to articles. Close corporation name must contain "corporation", "incorporated", or "limited", or abbreviation thereof. Permissible name may be reserved with Secretary of State for $10 fee for 60-day period which is not consecutively renewable. (Corp. C. 201, 202; Govt. C. 12199). Availability of name may be determined by writing Secretary of State at above address, Attention: Name Availability Unit.

Term of Corporate Existence.—Perpetual, unless expressly limited by law or in articles. (Corp. C. 200).

Incorporators.—One or more natural persons, partnerships, associations or corporations, domestic or foreign, may form corporation. (Corp. C. 200). No statutory restrictions as to citizenship or residence. Existing business association organized as trust may incorporate.

Articles of Incorporation.—Must state: (a) Name; (b) one of four specific statements regarding purpose, depending on whether corporation is "general", will engage in specific profession permitted to be incorporated, or is professional bank or trust company or insurance company; (c) name and address in California of corporation's initial agent for service of process; (d) if only one class authorized, total number of authorized shares; (e) if more than one class of shares or if any class to have two or more series, (1) total number of authorized shares of each class or of each series or that board is authorized to determine number of shares in any series, (2) designation of each class, and designation of each series or that board may determine designation of each series, (3) rights, preferences, privileges and restrictions as to each class or series, or that board of directors may determine or alter rights, preferences, privileges and restrictions upon any wholly unissued class or series. For any series whose number to be fixed by board, articles may authorize board to increase or decrease (but not below number of shares outstanding) number of shares of series after issue of shares or series. (Corp. C. 202). If articles authorize class of shares to be issuable in series, articles must include designation and number of shares for at least one series within class or authorize common shares. If articles authorize, and if articles state number of shares in class, articles may be amended by approval of board alone to increase or decrease (but not below number of shares outstanding) number of shares of series. (Corp. C. 203.5). Articles may contain: (a) Assessment rights, preemptive rights, qualifications concerning shareholders, "super-majority" vote of either shares or directors, limitation on existence, voting rights of debt holders, shareholders' rights as to determination of consideration for shares, requirement of shareholder or share approval for any corporate action, restrictions on corporation's business and powers and provisions limiting director liability for certain monetary damages and providing for indemnification of agent; (b) reasonable restrictions upon right of transfer of unissued shares; (c) names and addresses of initial directors; (d) other lawful provisions. With respect to close corporations, foregoing optional provisions may be contained in shareholders' agreement. (Corp. C. 204). Certain provisions of articles may be made dependent on facts ascertainable outside of articles. (Corp. C. 109.5). Each of initial directors named in articles signs and acknowledges; if initial directors are not named in articles, articles shall be signed by incorporators. (Corp. C. 200).

Filing of Articles.—Original executed articles must be filed with Secretary of State whereupon corporate existence begins. (Corp. C. 200).

Filing Fee.—On filing articles fee of $100 payable to Secretary of State. (Govt. C. 12201). Minimum annual corporation franchise tax of $800 for income years beginning after Dec. 31, 1989 must be paid when articles filed. (See infra, subhead Taxation.)

Organization.—If initial directors not named in articles, incorporator, until directors are elected, may do whatever necessary and proper to perfect organization, including adoption and amendment of by-laws and election of directors and officers. (Corp. C. 210).

Paid-in Capital Requirements.—No statutory requirement as to amount of paid-in capital which corporation must have before commencing business.

Amendment of Articles.—Corporation may amend its articles in any way so long as amended articles contain only such provisions as would be lawful in original articles filed at time of amendment. (Corp. C. 900). Amendment adopted: (1) Before any shares issued, by majority of incorporators or if directors were named in articles or subsequently elected, by majority of directors; (Corp. C. 901), and (2) after shares issued, by board and majority of outstanding shares, except that board alone may adopt amendment for stock split where one class of shares outstanding and to delete first directors or initial agent for process (Corp. C. 902). Amendment must be approved by outstanding shares of class, whether or not entitled to vote thereon, if amendment would: (a) Change aggregate number of authorized shares of class (except for stock split or exercise of option or conversion rights), (b) effect exchange, reclassification or cancellation of shares of class (except for stock split, but including reverse stock split), (c) effect exchange of share of another class into shares of such class, (d) change rights, preferences, privileges or restrictions of shares of class, (e) create new class or increase rights, preferences or privileges or number of authorized shares of any class having rights, preferences or privileges prior to shares of such class, (f) divide class of preferred shares into series having different rights, preferences, privileges or restrictions or authorize board to do so, or (g) cancel or otherwise affect accrued, but unpaid, dividends on shares of class. (Corp. C. 903). Amendment making shares assessable or subjecting fully paid shares to action for collection of assessment must be approved by all outstanding shares affected unless corporation is mutual water company within meaning of §2705 of Public Utilities Code, which in some instances, requires approval by only two-thirds of shareholders affected. (Corp. C. 911[e], 904[b].

In case of amendments adopted after issuance of shares, officers' certificate of amendment must be filed with Secretary of State, stating: (1) Wording of amendment, (2) that amendment has been approved by board, (3) if approval of outstanding shares is required, that amendment was approved by required vote; total number of outstanding shares of each class entitled to vote; and that number of shares of each class voting in favor of amendment equaled or exceeded vote required, specifying percentage vote required of each class and (4) if board approval alone is required, statement of facts pertaining thereto. If amendment is pursuant to merger, filing of certificate under such procedure is in lieu of filing of this statement. (Corp. C. 905). In case of amendment adopted by incorporators or board prior to issuance of shares, certificate of amendment signed and verified by majority of incorporators or board must be filed stating that signers constitute at least majority of incorporators or board, that corporation has issued no shares and that they adopt amendment therein set forth and, if amendments are adopted by incorporators, that directors were not named in original articles and have not been elected. (Corp. C. 906). Certificate of amendment must establish wording of amendment or amended articles by: (a) Stating that articles amended to read as therein set forth in full, (b) stating that identified provisions of articles must be stricken from articles or amended to read as set forth in certificate, or (c) stating that provision set forth therein must be added to articles. If purpose is to effect stock split or to reclassify, cancel, exchange or otherwise change outstanding shares, amended articles must state effect on outstanding shares. (Corp. C. 907). Amended articles are effective upon filing of certificate of amendment. (Corp. C. 908).

Corporation formed for limited term may at any time subsequent to expiration of its term amend articles to remove limit and provide for perpetual existence as long as it has continuously acted as corporation and has done business as such. (Corp. C. 909).

Corporation may restate in single certificate entire text of its articles as amended by filing officers' certificate, or where incorporators or board may amend articles pursuant to Corp. C. 901 and 906, certificate signed and verified by majority of incorporators or board, entitled "Restated Articles of Incorporation of . . . ." setting forth articles as amended to date of filing. Subject to compliance with provisions for amendment, such certificate may itself alter or amend articles; if certificate alters or amends articles, it is subject to amendment requirements summarized herein. Restated articles of incorporation supersede original articles and all amendments filed prior thereto. (Corp. C. 910).

Bylaws may be adopted, amended or repealed either by approval of majority of outstanding shares or by board of directors, except that after issuance of shares, bylaw changing number of directors may only be adopted by approval of outstanding shares. Bylaws must set forth number of directors or maximum and minimum number, with exact number to be fixed by board or shareholder approval, unless articles require larger proportion of vote. Bylaws may contain any provision consistent with law and articles for management of business and conduct of affairs of corporation. Original or copy of bylaws as amended to date must be kept at principal executive or business office of corporation in California for inspection by shareholders or if no such office in state, corporation must furnish, upon request, to shareholders. (Corp. C. 211-213).

Stock.—Corporation may issue one or more classes or series of shares or both with full, limited or no voting rights and with such other rights, preferences, privileges and restrictions as stated or authorized in articles. Must always have at least one class of stock with full voting rights. Must always have at least one class or series entitled to unlimited dividend and liquidation rights. (Corp. C. 400). Solely for purpose of statute or regulation imposing tax or fee based on capitalization of California corporation, each share deemed to have $1 par value. (Corp. C. 205).

Before corporation issues any shares whose rights, preferences, privileges, restrictions, or number or designation of series, are not set forth in articles, corporation must execute and file officers' certificate setting forth copy of board resolution, number of shares of class or series and stating that none of such shares issued. (Corp. C. 401).

Provisions of filed certificate of determination may be amended by board resolution and filing of officers' certificate setting forth resolution as long as no shares of class or series covered issued yet; if shares issued, certificate may be amended only by adoption and approval of amendment in accordance with provisions regarding amendment of articles summarized above, and filing of certificate of amendment.

Corporation may provide in its articles for redemption at option of corporation at price, time or happening of events as are stated in articles and also, for preferred shares, at option of holder or upon vote of majority of shares to be redeemed, but no mandatory redemption rights may be issued except as to open-end investment company. Method of selecting shares for partial redemption must be set forth in articles. (Corp. C. 402).

Rights, preferences, privileges and restrictions for preferred shares may provide that vote of specified proportion of outstanding shares that is less than majority will approve corporate action, except where majority or greater proportion required by Corp. Code. May also provide that in addition to vote of shares representing 50% of voting power, specified percentage (not to exceed $66^2/_3\%$) of preferred class or series needed for corporation to voluntarily wind up and dissolve. (Corp. C. 402.5).

If provided in articles, corporation may issue convertible shares; unless otherwise provided in articles, corporation may also issue convertible debt securities. (Corp. C. 403). Corporation may grant options to purchase shares either in connection with issue of securities or independently thereof. (Corp. C. 404). If, because of exercise of conversion or option rights, which were previously approved by shareholders, insufficient number of shares remain authorized to satisfy such rights exercised, board may without further shareholder approval amend articles to increase authorized shares to such number as will be sufficient to satisfy such exercise. (Corp. C. 405). Unless articles provide otherwise, board may issue securities having conversion or option rights without first offering them to shareholders of any class. (Corp. C. 406). Corporation may issue fractional shares originally or upon transfer. (Corp. C. 407). Corporation may adopt and carry out employee stock purchase plan or employee stock option plan. (Corp. C. 408).

See note at head of Digest as to 1998 legislation covered.

See Topical Index in front part of this volume.

CA – 2

CORPORATIONS . . . *continued*

Stock Certificates.—Each shareholder entitled to have stock certificate certifying number of shares and class or series of shares, signed by chairman or vice-chairman of board or president or vice-president and by chief financial officer or assistant treasurer or secretary or assistant secretary. Signatures may be facsimile. However, if certain conditions are satisfied, corporation may provide for system of uncertificated securities. (Corp. C. 416). If shares are classified or if any class has two or more series, special legend must appear on certificate setting forth rights, preferences, privileges and restrictions or summary thereof and reference to full provisions or statement setting forth location for finding same. (Corp. C. 417). If shares are subject to transfer restrictions, assessable or not fully paid, certificate must conspicuously state such or summary thereof. If shares are subject to voting agreement, irrevocable proxy or other voting restrictions, or redeemable or convertible, certificate must state such. All certificates representing shares of close corporation must contain specific conspicuous legend; and, any attempted voluntary inter vivos transfer of shares of close corporation resulting in number of holders exceeding maximum number specified in its articles is void if certificate contains such legend. (Corp. C. 418).

Issuance of Stock.—Unless exempt, no corporation may offer or sell stock or other securities unless qualified under California Corporate Securities Law of 1968 (see category Business Regulation and Commerce, topic Securities).

Shares may be issued as dividend or upon stock split or for such consideration as is determined by board or by shareholders if articles so provide, consisting of: money paid, labor done, services actually rendered to or for benefit of corporation or in its formation or reorganization, debts or securities cancelled, or property actually received; but promissory notes of purchaser (unless adequately collateralized by property other than shares being issued) or future services can not constitute payment for shares. Corporation may issue shares as partly paid subject to call for remainder of consideration to be paid therefor, if certificate states total amount of consideration to be paid therefor and amount paid. Board by resolution must state its determination of fair value to corporation in monetary terms of any consideration other than money for which shares are issued. (Corp. C. 409).

Each subscriber to and original issuee of shares is liable to corporation for full consideration agreed to be paid, which shall be paid prior to or concurrently with issuance of shares, unless they are issued as partly paid shares. (Corp. C. 410).

Transfer of Stock.—Uniform Commercial Code governs. (Com'l. C. 8301 et seq.). See category Business Regulation and Commerce, topic Commercial Code. Good faith transferee of partly paid shares, without knowledge, is liable to corporation only for amount stated on certificate as unpaid. (Corp. C. 411).

Uniform Simplification of Fiduciary Security Transfers Act.—Repealed by Uniform Commercial Code. (Com'l. C. 8402-8404, 8318). See category Business Regulation and Commerce, topic Commercial Code.

Stockholders.—See following subheads: Stockholders' Liabilities; Stockholders' Meetings; Voting Rights, infra.

Shareholder Actions.—See subhead Shareholders' Derivative Actions, infra.

Stockholders' Liabilities.—Unless shares are assessable, shareholders liable only to extent of full consideration agreed to be paid for shares. Shares are assessable only if articles confer authority upon corporation or board or if otherwise provided by statute, and if assessable board may levy and collect assessments in conformity with Corp. C. 423.

Stockholders' Meetings.—Shareholders' meetings may be held within or out of California as provided in by-laws, and if no place is stated, then at principal executive office of corporation. Annual meeting of shareholders for election of directors shall be held at date and time provided in accordance with bylaws. Court may order annual meeting if no meeting set or held for specific period. Shareholders' special meetings may be called by board, chairman thereof, president, 10% of voting shares or additional persons as provided in articles or bylaws. Notices of meetings must be given not less than ten days or if at least 500 shareholders, 30 days if by third class mail, nor more than 60 days before date of meeting. Notice must specify certain matters. Notice need not be given of adjourned meeting if time and place thereof are announced at meeting at which adjournment is taken, provided that if adjournment is for more than 45 days or new record date fixed, notice must be given. (Corp. C. 600-601).

Unless otherwise provided in articles, majority of voting shares, in person or proxy, constitute quorum, but in no event can quorum consist of less than one-third of voting shares or, except in case of close corporation, of more than majority of voting shares. If quorum present, majority vote of shares at meeting carries unless articles or law require supermajority. Withdrawal of shareholders from meeting ending quorum does not disqualify action approved by at least majority of shares required to constitute quorum thereafter taken. In absence of quorum shareholders' meeting may be adjourned by majority vote of shares present. (Corp. C. 602).

Unless otherwise provided in articles, action may be taken without meeting and without prior notice if written consent specifying action taken is signed by shareholders having voting power sufficient to take action at meeting. Notice of shareholders approval by less than unanimous written consent must be given at least ten days before consummation of action authorized, and must be sent to shareholders who have not consented. (Corp. C. 603).

Voting Rights.—Except as otherwise provided in articles and cumulative voting for directors each outstanding share entitled to one vote on matters submitted to vote of shareholders. (Corp. C. 700). Form of proxy distributed to ten or more shareholders of corporation with 100 or more shareholders must provide opportunity to approve or disapprove each matter other than elections to office and that proxy will be voted accordingly. Proxy marked by shareholder "withhold" in case of election of directors must not be voted for election of director. (Corp. C. 604).

Board may fix record date for voting in advance, not more than 60 nor less than ten days prior to date of meeting. If no record date is fixed, record date for voting is day preceding day notice is sent or, if notice is waived, day preceding meeting. (Corp. C. 701). Voting of shares by fiduciaries, corporations and otherwise governed by Corp. C. 702 through 704.

No proxy is valid after expiration of 11 months from its date unless otherwise provided in proxy. Proxy continues in effect until revoked by written revocation delivered to corporation, by subsequent proxy executed by person executing previous proxy and presented at meeting, or by attendance at meeting and voting in person by person executing proxy. Proxy not revoked by death or incapacity of maker unless, before vote is counted, written notice of such is received by corporation. Proxy is irrevocable for period specified therein when held by pledgee, purchaser of shares or holder of option to purchase shares, creditor, employee, beneficiary of trust, or person designated in close corporation agreement. Notwithstanding period of irrevocability specified, proxy becomes revocable when events giving rise to irrevocability terminate. Transferee without knowledge of provision that proxy is irrevocable may revoke proxy unless irrevocability appears in legend on certificate. (Corp. C. 705).

Agreement among shareholders of corporation may provide for exercising voting rights as to shares held by them as provided in agreement or in accordance with procedure agreed upon by shareholders. Agreement may provide that transferee is bound. Such agreement is specifically enforceable notwithstanding availability of remedy at law. (Corp. C. 706).

Shares may be transferred to trustee under voting trust agreement for up to ten years, subject to renewal for additional maximum ten-year period. Duplicate of voting trust agreement must be filed with secretary of corporation, open to shareholder or voting trust certificate holder inspection. (Corp. C. 706).

Shareholder may cumulate votes for director whose name has been placed in nomination prior to vote at election of directors, provided that shareholder has given notice at meeting prior to voting of intent to cumulate votes. If any shareholder gives notice, all shareholders may cumulate votes. (Corp. C. 708).

Shareholders' Derivative Actions.—Plaintiff in such action generally must have been record or beneficial shareholder, or holder of voting trust certificates, at time of alleged wrongdoing, or thereafter became owner by operation of law from holder who was holder at such time. Plaintiff must attempt to obtain desired action from board or state why such attempt was not made. Procedure for such action set forth in Corp. C. 800. Plaintiff may be required to furnish security for expenses, including attorney's fees. For discussion of security for expenses, see category Civil Actions and Procedure, topic Costs.

Directors and Management.—Subject to law and any limitations in articles as to shareholder action, all corporate powers are exercised by or under direction of board of directors. Close corporation shareholders' agreement permits close corporation to operate without corporate formalities. (Corp. C. 300). Members of board need not be shareholders. No statutory requirement as to citizenship or residence of directors. Except where directors are divided into classes, directors are elected at each annual shareholders' meeting to hold office until next annual meeting and hold office until election and qualification of successors. Articles may provide for election of directors to represent shares of any class or series voting as such. (Corp. C. 301). Directors of "listed" corporations, i.e., corporations listed on NYSE, AMEX, or corporations listed on NASDAQ with 800 or more equity securities holders, may serve up to three years depending on number of classes involved. (Corp. C. 301.5). Board may declare vacant office of director of unsound mind or convicted of felony. (Corp. C. 302). Directors may be removed without cause prior to expiration of term by approval of outstanding shares; however, no director may be removed (unless entire board removed) when votes against removal would be sufficient to elect director if voted cumulatively at election at which same total number of votes cast and all directors authorized at time of director's most recent election were then being elected. Similarly, no director of classified board may be removed if votes cast against removal were voted cumulatively at election at which same total number of votes cast and either number of directors elected at most recent annual meeting or, if greater, number of directors whose removal sought, were being elected. (Corp. C. 303). Court may at suit of 10% of outstanding shares remove director in case of fraud, dishonesty or gross abuse of authority. (Corp. C. 304). Unless otherwise provided in articles or by-laws and except for vacancy created by removal, vacancies may be filled by majority of directors then in office or, if number of remaining directors is less than quorum, by unanimous consent of directors then in office, vote of majority of remaining directors at duly held meeting, or by sole remaining director. Unless articles or bylaws otherwise provide, only majority of shareholders may fill vacancies created by removal. Majority of outstanding shares may elect director to fill vacancy not filled by directors. If filling of vacancy by directors results in elected directors constituting less than majority, special meeting of shareholders may be called. Resignation of director effective upon giving notice unless notice specifies later time. (Corp. C. 305). If corporation has not issued shares and no directors in office, court may appoint directors upon application by any party in interest. (Corp. C. 306).

As provided in articles or by-laws, number of directors may be specific or may be not less than stated minimum nor more than stated maximum (not greater than twice stated minimum minus one), with exact number to be fixed by board or shareholders. Minimum number not less than three except that: (1) Before shares issued, number may be one or two, (2) corporation with one shareholder, number may be one or two, (3) corporation with only two shareholders, number may be two. (Corp. C. 212).

Directors' Meetings.—May be called by chair of board or president or any vice-president or secretary or any two directors, unless otherwise provided in articles or bylaws. Regular meetings may be held without notice if time and place fixed by bylaws or board. Special meetings held upon four days' notice by mail or 48 hours' notice delivered personally or by telephone, including voice messaging system or other technology designed to record and communicate messages, facsimile, electronic mail or other electronic means. Notice may be waived by director. Majority of directors present at meeting may adjourn meeting, and if adjourned for more than 24 hours, notice must be given to directors not present. Transactions at meeting validated by directors' waiver of notice, consent to holding of meeting and approval of minutes. Any action required at meeting may be taken without meeting if all members consent in writing. Meetings may be held at place within or without State that has been designated in notice. Meetings may be held by use of conference telephone, electronic video screen communication, or similar communications equipment, so long as all

CORPORATIONS . . . *continued*
members participating can communicate with all others and each member provided with means of participating in all matters, including proposals and objections, and corporation implements means of verifying that person communicating by electronic means is director and that all statements, questions and votes are made by that director and not another person. Majority of authorized number of directors constitutes quorum. Articles or by-laws may not provide that quorum be less than one-third or less than two, whichever is larger, unless authorized number of directors is one. If quorum exists initially, withdrawal of director does not affect validity of meeting if action taken is approved by majority of required quorum. (Corp. C. 307).

If even-numbered board deadlocked to detriment of corporation, court may appoint impartial provisional director upon action brought by any director or holder of at least one-third of voting power. (Corp. C. 308).

Liabilities of Directors.—Directors' standard of care is to serve, in good faith, in best interests of corporation and its shareholders and with such care, including reasonable inquiry, as ordinarily prudent person in like position would use under similar circumstances. Director may rely on information and other documents prepared by reliable or competent officers or employees, counsel, accountants, or board committees, so long as director acts in good faith after reasonable inquiry as indicated by circumstances. (Corp. C. 309). Interests of director in transaction with corporation do not invalidate contract if full disclosure and shareholder or disinterested board approval or person asserting its validity sustains burden of proving contract just and reasonable. (Corp. C. 310).

Board may delegate board authority to committees except as to: (a) Designated shareholder approval matters, (b) filling of vacancies, (c) fixing of compensation of directors, (d) change of by-laws, (e) change of any board resolution, (f) certain distribution to shareholders, and (g) appointment of other committees or their members. (Corp. C. 311). Corporation must have chairman of board or president or both, secretary, and chief financial officer. May have such other officers as stated in by-laws or determined by board. Unless articles or by-laws provide otherwise, any number of offices may be held by same person. Except as otherwise provided, officers are chosen by board and serve at its pleasure. (Corp. C. 312).

Any corporate instrument when executed by chairman, president or any vice president and secretary, chief financial officer, assistant secretary or assistant treasurer is not invalidated as to corporation by any lack of authority by signing officers if other person is without actual knowledge that signing officers had no authority to execute instrument. (Corp. C. 313). If majority of shareholders entitled to act approve, corporation may make loan or guarantee obligations of any person upon security of its shares or of its parent. Without shareholder approval, loans or guarantees to officers or other persons may be made only under certain circumstances. (Corp. C. 315).

Directors who approve following corporate actions are jointly and severally liable to corporation, for benefit of entitled creditors or shareholders: (1) Making of distribution to shareholders to extent contrary to Corp. C. 500 through 503, (2) distribution of assets to shareholders after institution of dissolution without paying or adequately providing for known liabilities, and (3) making of loan or guarantee contrary to Corp. C. 315. Director who is present at meeting of board at which such action is taken shall be considered to have approved action if he abstains from voting. (Corp. C. 316).

Corporation may indemnify its agents in proceedings if agents acted in good faith, believed to be in best interests of corporation (and, for [b], its shareholders), as follows: (a) In third party action, for expenses, including attorney's fees, and any amounts paid; and (b) in derivative action, for expenses and amounts paid upon court approval (which is not necessary if agents successful in proceeding). Indemnification requires: (a) Majority vote of quorum of disinterested directors (if such quorum not attainable, opinion of independent legal counsel), (b) approval of disinterested shareholders, or (c) court approval. Corporation may advance corporate funds pending final disposition of proceeding, on agent's undertaking to repay. Indemnification authorized by Corp. C. 317 not exclusive of any additional rights to indemnification for breach of duty if such rights provided in articles and if not involving breach of duty, not exclusive of rights provided by bylaws, agreements, vote of shareholders or disinterested directors. But no indemnification to be made under this section if inconsistent with articles, bylaws, shareholder resolution, agreement, or court-imposed condition to settlement. Corporation may acquire insurance covering agents' liability notwithstanding corporation's power to indemnify. (Corp. C. 317).

Resident Agent.—All corporations must designate, as agent for purpose of service of process, natural person residing in California or corporation which has complied with Corp. C. 1505 and whose capacity to act as such agent has not terminated. (Corp. C. 1502).

General Powers of Corporation.—Subject to any limitations in articles and compliance with laws, corporation has all powers of natural person in carrying out its business activities, including power to: (a) Use corporate seal, but failure to affix seal does not affect validity of any instrument; (b) adopt, amend and repeal by laws; (c) qualify to do business in other jurisdictions; (d) deal in and with its own shares and other securities; (e) make donations for public welfare or community fund, hospital, charitable, educational, scientific, civic or similar purposes; (f) pay pensions and employee benefit plans; (g) assume obligations, enter contracts, incur liabilities, borrow and lend money, and secure any of its obligations; and (h) participate in partnership, joint venture or other arrangement. (Corp. C. 207).

Dividends and Other Distributions.—Corporation may make distribution to its shareholders (transfer of cash or property without consideration by way of dividend other than stock dividend, purchase or redemption of shares, or otherwise) either: (1) Out of retained earnings, or (2) if, after giving effect to distribution, assets of corporation (exclusive of certain intangibles) are at least equal to one and one-quarter times its liabilities (excluding certain deferred items) and its current assets are at least equal to its current liabilities or certain other tests are satisfied. In determining amount of assets, profits from exchange of assets not included unless assets received are currently realizable in cash, and corporation can include certain receivables. Amount of distribution payable in property determined on basis of value at which property is carried on corporation's financial statements in accordance with generally accepted accounting principles. With respect to distributions incurred by corporation in connection with purchase of shares: (1) There shall be deducted from liabilities any amount added at time obligation to purchase is incurred, but not in excess of principal unpaid after distribution, and (2) there shall be added to retained earnings any amount deducted therefrom at time obligation was incurred, but not in excess of principal which is unpaid prior to distribution. (Corp. C. 500). Above provisions do not apply to broker-dealers as long as corporation after distribution in compliance with certain net capital rules. Notwithstanding above, no distribution may be made if, or as result thereof, corporation likely to be unable to meet its liabilities as they mature. (Corp. C. 501). Further restrictions on distributions to shareholders having junior liquidation or dividend preferences. Articles or by-laws may also impose additional restrictions upon declaration of dividends or purchase or redemption of shares. (Corp. C. 502-505). Above distribution restrictions inapplicable to redemption of deceased or disabled shareholder's shares from life insurance proceeds on such shareholder's life in excess of total amount of all premiums paid by corporation, in order to carry out agreement between corporation and such shareholder. (Corp. C. 503.1-503.2).

Any shareholder knowingly receiving illegal distribution is liable to corporation for benefit of creditors and shareholders for amount received plus legal interest, up to the then amount of liabilities. Any shareholder sued may implead other liable shareholders. (Corp. C. 506). If distribution other than one chargeable to retained earnings, source of distribution to be identified in notice to shareholders. (Corp. C. 507). Under Corp. C. 509, procedure for redemption of shares set forth. When corporation reacquires its own shares, those shares are restored to status of authorized but unissued shares, unless articles prohibit such reissuance. (Corp. C. 510). Corp. C. 510(b)-(f) contain provisions governing reacquisition of authorized shares of class or series where articles prohibit reissuance of those shares, or reacquisition of authorized shares of series of shares where articles only prohibit reissuance of those shares as shares of same series.

Unclaimed Dividends.—See category Property, topic Absentees, subhead Escheat.

Corporate Mortgages.—Board may authorize mortgage, deed of trust, pledge or other hypothecation of corporation's property to secure payment or performance of contract or obligation, without approval of shares unless articles otherwise provide. (Corp. C. 1000).

Sale or Transfer of Corporate Assets.—Corporation may sell, lease or otherwise dispose of all or substantially all of its property in transaction not in usual and regular course of corporation's business if principal terms thereof are approved by board and majority of outstanding shares. Transaction involving reorganization is excluded from rule. Notwithstanding prior shareholder approval, board may abandon proposed transaction without further shareholder action, subject to any contractual right of third parties. (Corp. C. 1001).

Merger.—Any two or more corporations may be merged into one by agreement stating terms and conditions of merger, any amendments to articles of surviving corporation, name and place of incorporation of constituent corporations, name of surviving corporation, which may be same as any constituent corporation, manner of converting shares of constituent corporations into shares of surviving corporation, and other desired provisions. Equal treatment required of all holders of same class of shares of any constituent corporation unless unanimous consent of class obtained. (Corp. C. 1100 and 1101).

Consolidation Eliminated Under General Corporation Law.—Triangular mergers treated as direct mergers with parent corporation issuing securities. Issuance of securities must be qualified under Corporate Securities Law. Any amendment of articles must comply with amendment procedures.

Merger agreement signed by chairman of board, president or vice-president and secretary or assistant-secretary of each constituent corporation. (Corp. C. 1102). Mergers must be approved by board and, if required by Corp. C. 1200 et seq., by majority of outstanding shares of each class of each constituent corporation. After approvals above and after filing Franchise Tax Board certificate of satisfaction, surviving corporation must file copy of agreement of merger with officers' certificate attached, whereupon merger is effective. (Corp. C. 1103). Agreement of merger may be amended in same manner as original agreement. (Corp. C. 1104). Board may abandon merger notwithstanding shareholders' approval, subject to third party's contractual rights. (Corp. C. 1105). Upon effectiveness of merger, separate existence of disappearing corporations ceases and surviving corporation succeeds to all rights and property thereof and subject to all liabilities thereof. (Corp. C. 1107). Merger of domestic and foreign corporations permitted pursuant to Corp. C. 1108. Prescribed certificate or certified copy of merger agreement filed in county where real property of disappearing corporation is located will evidence record ownership in surviving corporation. (Corp. C. 1109).

Short form merger under Corp. C. 1110 allowed where parent corporation owns all or not less than 90% of outstanding shares of each class of subsidiary corporations. Merger effected by board resolutions and filing of certificate of ownership setting forth matters specified in section, which certificate is filed after filing of Franchise Tax Board certificate of satisfaction. Merger effective upon filing of certificate of ownership. If parent corporation is not owner of all outstanding shares of subsidiary, surviving corporation must give 20 days' notice to other shareholders who are given same right to dissent and receive in cash fair market value of their shares, as in other cases (see below). (Corp. C. 1110).

If disappearing corporation in merger is close corporation and surviving corporation is not, merger must be approved by holders of two-thirds of outstanding shares of disappearing corporation, unless articles or shareholders' agreement provide for lesser vote, but not less than majority. (Corp. C. 1111).

If parent corporation is merged into one of its subsidiaries, merger plan shall provide for pro rata conversion of outstanding shares of parent corporation into shares of surviving corporation and may require shareholder approval. (Corp. C. 1110[c]).

Reorganizations.—Under Corp. C. 181 reorganization defined to encompass three basic methods of combination: (a) Merger other than short-form merger ("merger reorganization"), (b) exchange of shares by corporation for securities of another ("exchange reorganization"), and (c) exchange of securities by corporation for assets

See note at head of Digest as to 1998 legislation covered.

See Topical Index in front part of this volume.

CORPORATIONS . . . *continued*

of another ("sale of assets reorganization"). If buyer in control or under common control with seller in sale of assets reorganization must be approved by at least 90% of voting power unless: (a) Sale in consideration of nonredeemable common shares of purchasing corporation or its parent, or (b) terms and conditions of sale previously approved by Corporation's Commissioner, Commissioner of Financial Institutions, Insurance Commissioner, or Public Utilities Commission. (Corp. C. 1001). Board approval required of each constituent corporation in merger reorganization, acquiring corporation in exchange reorganization, both corporations in sale of assets reorganization, and "parent party" where applicable. (Corp. C. 1200). Majority of all outstanding shares of each class regardless of voting rights must approve, except that if rights of surviving, acquiring or parent corporation's preferred shares remain unchanged, vote of such preferred shares is not required. No shareholder approval is required of corporation if it or its shareholders, after reorganization, own more than 5/6ths of surviving corporation's voting equity securities. However, shareholder approval is required in merger reorganization if articles amended, in merger or sale of assets reorganization if shareholders to receive shares with different rights or if in close corporation, its shareholders are to receive shares of corporation which is not close corporation. (Corp. C. 1201).

Board approval also required for share exchange offer (§183.5) pursuant to Corp. C. 1200. Principal terms of share exchange tender offer as defined in Corp. C. 183.5 require approval of outstanding shares of each class involved, except that no approval of preferred shares of either corporation necessary if rights, preferences, privileges and restrictions of class unchanged. No shareholder approval required if corporation or its shareholders, after share exchange, own more than 5/6ths of voting equity securities of either corporation making tender offer or corporation whose shares used in tender offer. (Corp. C. 1201.5).

Principal terms of merger reorganization require unanimous shareholder approval if all shares of corporation to be cancelled without consideration; principal terms of merger or sale of assets reorganization require approval by sufficient percentage of class of preferred shares to amend articles, if holders of such class to receive less than amount required by articles; and if parent party is foreign corporation not subject to Corp. C. 2115, necessity of shareholder approval determined by law of jurisdiction of incorporation. (Corp. C. 1202).

Corp. C. 1203 specifies content and procedure for required fairness opinion if tender offer, including share exchange tender offer, or written proposal for approval of reorganization or sale of assets made to shareholders by interested party.

Dissenters' Rights.—Each holder of dissenting shares whose approval is required under reorganization, and those in short form merger, may require issuing corporation to purchase such shares for cash at fair market value, which is determined as of day before first announcement of terms of reorganization or short form merger (excluding any appreciation or depreciation resulting from proposed transaction, and adjusted for any stock split, reverse stock split or share dividend becoming effective thereafter). Dissenting shares defined to exclude listed securities and to constitute shares not voted in favor of reorganization, which holder has demanded that corporation purchase at fair market value, and which holder has submitted to corporation for endorsement. (Corp. C. 1300). Procedure includes: (a) Corporation mailing copy of dissenters' statutes and notice of approval of reorganization setting forth price determined by corporation to represent fair market value and brief description of procedure to be followed, and (b) demand by shareholder setting forth number of class of shares held and statement of shareholder's claim of fair market value, and presentation of share certificates to corporation for endorsement. (Corp. C. 1301 and 1302). If shareholder and corporation fail to agree upon fair market value of shares, court may determine whether shares are dissenting shares and fair market value thereof and may appoint appraiser to make determination. (Corp. C. 1304-1305). If corporation is prohibited from purchasing its own shares (see subhead Dividends and Other Distributions, supra), holders of dissenting shares become creditors of corporation until payment is permissible, subordinate to other creditors in liquidation proceeding. (Corp. C. 1306). Sole remedy of dissenting shareholders is appraisal right. (Corp. C. 1312).

Books and Records.—Corporation must keep books, records of account, minutes of meetings, and record of shareholders. (Corp. C. 1500). Shareholders and directors have rights of inspection as to shareholder records (Corp. C. 1600 and 1602) and accounting books and records and minutes (Corp. C. 1601), which rights of inspection are subject to enforcement by court action.

Reports.—Corporation must send to shareholders annual report within 120 days after close of fiscal year, unless in case of corporation with less than 100 shareholders, such requirement is waived in by-laws. Shareholder of any corporation has right to receive upon written request copy of certain financial statements. Even where such requirement not so waived, reports for corporations with less than 100 shareholders need not conform to generally accepted accounting principles if reasonably set forth assets, liabilities, income and expenses of such corporation and accounting basis used. (Corp. C. 1501). Annual report must contain balance sheet, income statement, statement of changes of financial position, report of independent accountant or officer's certificate if no such report, and where corporation has 100 or more shareholders, no registered securities, must describe briefly various interested transactions, indemnifications or indemnification advances. (Corp. C. 1501).

Corporation annually must file with Secretary of State statement containing: (1) Vacancies on board, (2) names and addresses of incumbent directors, (3) names and addresses of chief executive officer, secretary and chief financial officer, (4) address of principal executive and business office, (5) statement of general type of business, and (6) agent of corporation for service of process. If there has been no change in information of last filed statement, corporation may file on form prescribed by Secretary of State that no changes have occurred. (Corp. C. 1502).

Dissolution.—Involuntary dissolution may be initiated by: (a) One-half or more of directors, (b) shareholders owning at least one-third of outstanding shares or any shareholder of close corporation, (c) any shareholder if corporate period has terminated without extension, or (d) any person expressly authorized to do so in articles, on grounds of (1) corporation abandonment of business for more than one year, (2) even

number of directors equally divided and unable to agree, (3) internal dissension with shareholders deadlocked on conducting business to shareholders' advantage or, for two consecutive annual meetings, on election of directors, (4) fraud, mismanagement or abuse of authority by those in control, (5) if 35 or less shareholders, where liquidation is reasonably necessary for protection of rights of complaining shareholders, or (6) corporate period has terminated without extension. (Corp. C. 1800). Attorney General may also bring action for dissolution upon certain grounds. (Corp. C. 1801). Court has authority to appoint provisional director or receiver in certain instances and may make such orders as required. (Corp. C. 1802-1804). Proceedings in involuntary dissolution, jurisdiction of court, and otherwise, under Corp. C. 1805-1809.

Voluntary dissolution may be had by majority shareholder vote or by board alone where corporation: (a) Has begun business and issued no shares, (b) is bankrupt, or (c) has disposed of all assets and not done business for five years. (Corp. C. 1900). Upon commencement of voluntary dissolution, certificate of election to dissolve must be filed with Secretary of State (Corp. C. 1901), unless vote is by all outstanding shares and statement to that effect added to certificate (Corp. C. 1901). When dissolution completed, certificate of dissolution similarly filed, but only after Franchise Tax Board certificate of satisfaction filed unless dissolution vote is by all outstanding shares, in accordance with Corp. C. 1901. (Corp. C. 1905).

In both involuntary and voluntary dissolution proceedings, corporation or, if it does not elect to purchase, noninitiating shareholders of 50% or more of shares, may avoid dissolution by purchasing shares for cash of initiating shareholders at fair value. Determination of fair value not limited to liquidation value of assets of business, but taken into account is possibility of sale of entire business as going concern. If fair value unable to be agreed upon, court may appoint appraisers for such determination. (Corp. C. 2000).

During dissolution proceedings directors and officers have certain powers and duties. (Corp. C. 2001). After determining that all known debts and liabilities have been paid or adequately provided for, remaining corporate assets distributed among shareholders according to their rights and preferences. (Corp. C. 2004). Distribution may be made in money or property and installments or lump sum. (Corp. C. 2006). Plan of distribution may be adopted by board and shareholders approval. (Corp. C. 2007).

Close Corporations.—Corp. C. 158 defines close corporation and establishes procedures for creation and termination of close corporation status. Corporation may achieve close corporation status by including in its articles provision that all of corporation's issued shares of all classes must be held of record by not more than specified number of persons, not exceeding 35, and statement that "This corporation is a close corporation." Corporation may elect close corporation status after issuance of shares only upon unanimous approval of shareholders. Close corporation may voluntarily terminate its status by amending articles but two-thirds vote of each class of outstanding shares is required unless articles provide for lesser vote but not less than majority. Close corporation status also terminates if corporation has more than maximum number of holders of record of shares stated in its articles as result of valid transfers of shares. When close corporation status terminates corporation must execute and file amendment to its articles deleting close corporation provisions. Shareholders may provide in agreement among them to vote for termination of close corporation status upon lapse of specified period of time or upon occurrence of certain event or condition or otherwise.

Following sections of Corp. C. contain specific reference to close corporations, as indicated: 186 (shareholders' agreement), 202(a) (name of corporation), 204 (shareholders' agreement, optional articles provisions), 300 (provisions in shareholders' agreement regarding management and effect of failure to observe corporate formalities), 418 (legend on share certificate and restrictions on transfer), 421 (consent to restrictions on transfer), 706 (voting trust agreements) 1111 (merger), 1201 (shareholder approval in reorganizations with non-close corporations), 1800 (involuntary dissolution by any shareholder) and 1904 (voluntary dissolution). Note rules of Cal. Commissioner of Corporations pertaining to securities of small corporations. See category Business Regulation and Commerce, topic Securities.

Appraisal.—See subheads Reorganizations, Dissenters' Rights, and Dissolution, supra.

Foreign Corporations.—No foreign corporation may transact intrastate business in California without first having obtained from Secretary of State certificate of qualification. (Corp. C. 2105). Transacting intrastate business is defined as entering into repeated and successive transactions of business in California, other than interstate or foreign commerce. (Corp. C. 191, which also provides for specific exclusions). Foreign corporation not transacting intrastate business may register its corporate name, if name would be available to new California corporation. Such registration may be renewed annually. (Corp. C. 2101). To obtain certificate of qualification, foreign corporation must file on prescribed form statement and designation signed by corporate officer stating name, state or place of incorporation or organization, address of principal executive office, address of principal office in California, name of agent for service of process, and irrevocable consent to service. Good standing certificate from place of incorporation must accompany statement. (Corp. C. 2105). Fee for filing certificate of qualification is $100. (Govt. C. 12204). For income years beginning after Dec. 31, 1979, prepayment of franchise tax must also be made. (Rev. & Tax C. 23153 and 23221).

Qualified foreign corporations shall file on prescribed form annual statement with Secretary of State containing: (1) Names and addresses of chief executive officer, secretary, and chief financial officer, (2) address of principal executive office, (3) address of principal office in California, if any, (4) statement of general type of business, and (5) corporation's agent for service of process. (Corp. C. 2117).

Foreign corporation which has qualified may surrender such right by filing officers' certificate of surrender with Secretary of State. (Corp. C. 2112)[a]). Tax clearance certificate issued by Franchise Tax Board pursuant to §23334 of Revenue and Taxation Code shall be filed with certificate of surrender. (Corp. C. 2112[b]).

No statutory restrictions on holding real property by foreign corporation in California.

See note at head of Digest as to 1998 legislation covered.

See Topical Index in front part of this volume.

CORPORATIONS . . . *continued*

Foreign corporation which transacts intrastate business and which has wilfully not qualified may be subject to $20 per day penalty, is deemed to consent to jurisdiction of California, may not maintain any action or proceeding on intrastate business until it has complied and paid $250 penalty, and may be guilty of misdemeanor, punishable by fine of from $500 to $1,000. (Corp. C. 2203 and 2258).

Directors of foreign corporation transacting intrastate business are liable to corporation, its shareholders, creditors, receiver, liquidator or trustee in bankruptcy for making of unauthorized dividends, purchase of shares or distribution of assets or false certificates, reports or public notices or other violations of official duty, whether done in California or elsewhere, which liability may be enforced in California courts. (Corp. C. 2116).

Taxation of foreign corporation, see subhead Taxation, infra.

Under Corp. C. 2115 "pseudo-foreign corporation" is required to comply with certain sections of California law, for protection of California creditors and shareholders, to exclusion of law of jurisdiction in which it is incorporated. Section applies to any foreign corporation (including foreign parent corporation which does not itself transact intrastate business, but excluding foreign association or foreign nonprofit corporation) if more than one-half of its business is conducted in California and more than one-half of its outstanding voting securities are held of record by persons residing in California (subject to certain rules for securities held in names of broker-dealers). Determination of extent of foreign corporation's business conducted in California based on average of corporation's property factor, payroll factor and sales factor, defined in Rev. & Tax Code 25129, 25132 and 25134, for purposes of computing portion of corporation's income allocable to this State in its franchise tax return. Determination of such factors with respect to any parent corporation must be made on consolidated basis. Provisions of law applicable to pseudo-foreign corporation include annual election of directors, removal of directors without cause, removal of directors by court proceedings, filling of director vacancies where less than majority in office elected by shareholders, directors' standard of care, liability of directors for unlawful distributions, indemnification of directors, officers and others, limitations on corporate distributions in cash or property, liability of shareholder who receives unlawful distribution, requirement for annual shareholders' meeting and remedy if same not timely held, shareholders' right to cumulate votes at any election of directors, supermajority vote requirement, limitations on mergers or sales of assets, reorganizations, dissenters' rights, records and reports, actions by Attorney General, and rights of inspection. Pseudo-foreign corporation provisions not applicable to any foreign corporation with outstanding securities listed on NYSE or AMEX or if securities are qualified for trading as national market security on NASDAQ if such corporation has at least 800 holders of its equity securities or if all of its voting shares owned directly or indirectly by corporation(s) not subject to pseudo-foreign corporation provisions.

Taxation of Corporate Property.—Rules largely same as for taxation of property of individual. See category Taxation, topic Property Taxes. Corporate income and franchise taxes are in lieu of personal property tax and license fees (other than those related to motor vehicles) for certain banks and financial corporations. (Rev. & Tax C. 23182).

Taxation.—Bank and Corporation Franchise Tax Law imposes following taxes:

Franchise tax is imposed on all corporations doing intrastate business in California for privilege of exercising corporate franchise. (Rev. & Tax C. 23151, 23181). Franchise Tax Board can determine corporation not doing business within state if only corporate activities are: (a) Purchase of personal property or services for its (including affiliates) own use outside state if (i) it has 100 or fewer employees in state with limited duties, (ii) it has 200 or fewer employees in state with limited duties and the personal property or services purchased are used for the construction or modification of a physical plant or facility out of state, and (iii) the combined number of employees in state pursuant to (i) and (ii) is 200 or fewer; and/or (b) presence of its employees for purpose of attending school (Rev. & Tax C. 23101.5). It is annual tax based upon net income from business done in California for preceding year. Rate for corporations other than financial and banks is 8.84% of such net income with minimum annual tax of $800 with respect to corporations other than credit unions ($25 in case of certain mining companies). (Rev. & Tax C. 23151, 23153).

Financial corporations, including national banking associations and other banks, are taxed on their net income allocable to state at rate determined by Franchise Tax Board. For income years ending Dec. 31, 1995 tax rate on banks and financial institutions shall be rate specified in Rev. & Tax C. 23151 plus 2%. (Rev. & Tax C. 23186).

For tax years beginning on or after Jan. 1, 1992, estates and trusts must pay estimated taxes similar to Federal provisions. (Rev. & Tax C. 18682).

Conformity to Federal Tax Reform.—Areas of taxation which now generally conform to federal law include: REMIC's and Financial Asset Securitization Investment Trusts (except as to prohibited transactions) (Rev. & Tax C. 24870-72); alternative minimum tax, with some modifications (Rev. & Tax C. 23400-23459); research and development, low-income housing, and drug testing credits based on IRC 28, 41 & 42 (Rev. & Tax C. 23609, 23609.5, 23610.4, 23610.5); business and entertainment expense deductions (Rev. & Tax C. 24343, 24343.2, 24443); uniform capitalization rules, as per IRC 263A (Rev. & Tax C. 24422.3); passive activity losses and credits as per IRC 469, with some modifications (Rev. & Tax C. 24692); corporate liquidations and reorganizations are as per IRC Subchapter C (Rev. & Tax C. 24451); S Corporation treatment (with some modifications) when federal election is made, but corporation still pays 1.5% tax or minimum $800 franchise tax (Rev. & Tax C. 23800-23811); net operating loss deduction, except that NOL carrybacks are not permitted, amount of loss eligible for carryforward by taxpayers other than new and small businesses is reduced by 50%, and number of years to which NOL may be carried over is reduced (Rev. & Tax C. 24416-24416.3). References to Internal Revenue Code mean Internal Revenue Code as in effect on specified date (Jan. 1, 1997 for income years beginning in 1997) for respective income years.

Corporation income tax is imposed only on corporations not subject to franchise tax, such as foreign corporations engaged exclusively in interstate or foreign commerce in California, domestic holding companies, foreign holding companies which have acquired "commercial domicile" here and business corporations not doing business in California but deriving income from California sources. Banks and financial corporations are not subject to such tax. It is annual tax imposed at rate of 8.84% of net income derived from sources within California. For years after Dec. 31, 1999, rate of tax is rate specified for those years in Rev. & Tax C. 23151. (Rev. & Tax C. 23501). There is no minimum corporate tax.

Alternative minimum tax is imposed on corporations (excluding S corporations) at 7% rate. California follows IRC 55-6 with modifications. (Rev. & Tax C. 23400-23459).

Allocation of Income.—Uniform Division of Income for Tax Purposes Act adopted for years beginning after Dec. 31, 1966. "Combined Report" of incomes of commonly controlled corporations may be required where corporations engage in "unitary business". (Rev. & Tax C. 25104). Certain qualified taxpayers may elect to determine their California income pursuant to water's-edge election that excludes most foreign corporations from group. (Rev. & Tax C. 25110-25112).

Payment.—Franchise and corporation income taxes are payable to Franchise Tax Board. (Rev. & Tax C. 25555). Returns generally are due within two months and 15 days after close of income (calendar or fiscal) year. (Rev. & Tax C. 25401). Board may grant extensions not exceeding seven months for filing return. (Rev. & Tax C. 25402). Taxes are due and payable in full by general corporations on normal due date of return without regard to extensions. (Rev. & Tax C. 25551). Financial corporations and banks pay greater of franchise tax based on total rate for preceding year and minimum tax, on or before 15th day of third month following close of preceding year. Balance, if any, payable on or before 15th day following mailing of notice of Board's determination of current rate. Refund allowed if applicable. (Rev. & Tax C. 25553, 25553.5). Effective Dec. 31, 1991, interest on "large" (over $100,000) corporate tax underpayments is increased by additional 2% per annum. (Rev. & Tax C. 19269).

Estimated Tax.—Every corporation subject to franchise tax and corporate income tax must make estimated tax payments during its income year. (Rev. & Tax C. 25561-25563). If estimated tax is less than minimum tax, entire amount is payable on or before 15th day of fourth month of income year; otherwise payable: as follows: If minimum tax exceeded by first day of fourth month, greater of 25% or minimum tax on or before 15th day of fourth month of income year, and 25% before 15th day of each of sixth, ninth and 12th months; if minimum tax exceeded after last day of third month and before first day of sixth month, 33 1/3% before 15th day of each of sixth, ninth and 12th months; if minimum tax exceeded after last day of fifth month and before first day of ninth month, 50% on 15th day of each of ninth and 12th months; if minimum tax exceeded after last day of eighth month and before first day of 12th month, 100% on 15th day of 12th month. (Rev. & Tax C. 25563).

Exempt Corporations.—Religious, charitable, etc., corporations and labor unions are not subject to either franchise tax or income tax (Rev. & Tax C. 23701 et seq.) except as to certain "unrelated business income" (Rev. & Tax C. 23731 et seq.). Insurance companies are exempt from Bank and Corporation Tax Law but are taxed under other statutes on basis of premiums or underwriting income. (See category Insurance, topic Insurance Companies, subhead Premium Tax.)

Penalties.—Penalty of 5% of tax for each month or fraction thereof that tax is delinquent, up to 25% maximum, for inexcusable failure to file return, and of 25% of unpaid tax for refusal to furnish information or file return after written demand by Franchise Tax Board; if failure to file is fraudulent, penalty is 15% of tax that is delinquent, up to 75% maximum. (Rev. & Tax C. 25931, 25933). Rights and privileges of domestic and foreign corporations may be suspended or forfeited if taxes due are not paid within period set by statute. (Rev. & Tax C. 23301 et seq.). Any person attempting to exercise privileges of corporation whose rights have been so suspended is subject to fine and/or imprisonment. (Rev. & Tax C. 19719). Fine and/or imprisonment, together with costs of investigation and prosecution, may result from wilful failure to file return or filing of false return. (Rev. & Tax C. 19701, 19705, 19706).

Penalty of up to 25% of total unpaid tax for failure to pay tax when due or upon notice. (Rev. & Tax C. 25934.2). Penalties in conformity with corresponding federal penalties in effect on Jan. 1, 1997 are also imposed for filing of frivolous returns, substantial understatement of tax liability, negligence or disregard of rules, substantial valuation misstatements, promoting abusive tax shelters, aiding and abetting substantial understatement of tax liability and fraud. (Rev. & Tax C. 25935, 25957.1, 25957.2, 17024.5).

Addition to tax is made for underpayment of estimated tax. (Rev. & Tax C. 25951 et seq.).

Business and Industrial Development Corporations.—See category Business Regulation and Commerce, topic Banks and Banking, subhead Other Related Businesses Regulated by Financial Code.

Professional corporations are regulated by Moscone-Knox Professional Corporation Act (Corp. C. 13400-13410), and where not inconsistent with foregoing, General Corporation Law also applies. (Corp. C. 13403). Corporation may be formed under General Corporation Law for purpose of qualifying as professional corporation and rendering professional services. (Corp. C. 13404). Certificate of registration must be obtained from governmental agency regulating particular profession. (Corp. C. 13404). All shareholders must be licensed professionals. (Corp. C. 13405). Foreign professional corporation may qualify as foreign corporation to transact intrastate business. (Corp. C. 13404.5). Bus. & Prof. C. regulates particular professional corporations. Following professional corporations are authorized: Law corporations (Bus. & Prof. C. 6160-6172); medical corporations, podiatry corporations and osteopathic corporations (§§2406-2454, 2285); nursing corporations (§§2775 et seq.); chiropractic corporations (§§1050-1058); acupuncture corporations (§§4975 et seq.); dental corporations (§§1800-1808, 1658-1658.7); pharmacy corporations (§§4120 et seq.); physical therapy corporations (§2690 et seq.); psychological corporations (§§2995 et seq); optometric corporations (§§3160-3167); accountancy corporations (§§5150-5157); shorthand reporting corporations (§§8040-8047); clinical social workers' corporations (§4998); marriage, family and child counseling corporations (§4987.5); speech, language, pathology and audiology corporations (§2536); physician's assistants corporations (§3540); professional architectural corporations (§5610).

See note at head of Digest as to 1998 legislation covered.

See Topical Index in front part of this volume.

CA-6

CORPORATIONS . . . *continued*

No professional corporation may be formed to cause any violations of laws, rules or regulations relating to fee splitting, kickbacks, etc., by physicians and surgeons or psychologists. (Corp. C. 13408.5).

Deeds.—See category Property, topic Deeds.

Model Non-Profit Corporation Act has not been adopted. Nonprofit mutual benefit corporations (Corp. C. 5059), nonprofit public benefit corporations (Corp. C. 5060), and nonprofit religious corporations (Corp. C. 5061) are governed by Non-Profit Mutual Benefit Corporation Law (Corp. C. 7110-8910), Non-Profit Public Benefit Law (Corp. C. 5110-6910), and Non-Profit Religious Corporation Law (Corp. C. 9110-9690), respectively. Nonprofit public benefit corporations may be formed for any public or charitable purpose (Corp. C. 5111), including practice of law (Corp. C. 13406). Nonprofit mutual benefit corporation may be formed for any lawful purpose; however, it may not be corporation all of assets of which are irrevocably dedicated to charitable, religious, or public purposes and which, as matter of law or as required by articles or bylaws, upon dissolution, must distribute assets to persons carrying on charitable, religious or public purpose. (Corp. C. 7111). Nonprofit religious corporations may be formed primarily or exclusively for any religious purposes. (Corp. C. 9111). These statutes provide for: (1) Purposes, powers and formation of such corporations; (2) their articles of incorporation; (3) directors and management; (4) members; (5) distributions; (6) meetings; (7) voting of memberships; (8) amendment of articles; (9) sales of assets; (10) mergers; (11) records, reports and inspection rights; and (12) voluntary and involuntary dissolution. Provisions pertaining to corporation sole are contained in Corp. C. 10000 to 10015.

See also category Business Regulation and Commerce, topic Monopolies, Restraint of Trade and Competition.

JOINT STOCK COMPANIES:

No statutory provisions except for prohibitions against unauthorized use of another's name in advertisement of any joint stock association, existing or intended to be formed, in order to mislead, and against fraud by officers, directors, agents and promoters. (Corp. C. 22000-22003). Director of joint stock association deemed to have sufficient knowledge of affairs of his association to determine if any act of association violates statutory prohibitions. (Corp. C. 22003).

Joint stock companies are hybrid entities having some features of corporation and some of partnership. They are generally regarded as forming distinct class of association of individuals. (35 C. 365). As unincorporated associations, joint stock companies may sue and be sued in common name (C.C.P. 388) and in area of liability, usually are treated as partnerships: members are liable as general partners unless agreement with creditor provides otherwise (81 C.A. 502, 253 P. 971).

Issuance of securities is within Corporate Securities Law. (Corp. C. 25000). See category Business Regulation and Commerce, topic Securities.

LIMITED LIABILITY COMPANIES:

Beverley-Killea Limited Liability Company Act adopted effective Sept. 30, 1994. (Corp. C. 17000-17705).

Formation of Limited Liability Companies.—Limited liability company must have two or more members. Articles of organization must be filed with Secretary of State, but need not be executed and filed by member of limited liability company. Members must enter into operating agreement. (Corp. C. 17050). Requirements for contents of articles of organization set forth in Corp. C. 17051. Within 90 days of filing original articles and thereafter annually, limited liability company must file statement containing (1) name of company and Secretary of State's file number, (2) name and street address of agent for service of process, (3) street address of principal executive office, (4) name and complete business or residence address of manager or manager and chief executive officer, or if no manager appointed then address of each member, and (5) general type of business constituting limited liability company's principal business activity. (Corp. C. 17060).

Name of Limited Liability Company.—Shall contain either "limited liability company" or abbreviation "LLC" or "L.L.C." as last words in name. Abbreviations "Ltd." and "Co." may be used. Name may contain name of one or more members. Name may not mislead public or be same as or resemble so closely as to deceive, (1) name of any limited liability company that has filed articles of organization under Corp. C. 17050, or (2) name of any foreign limited liability company registered under Corp. C. 17451, or (3) any name reserved for another limited liability company under Corp. C. 17053, except upon consent of that limited liability company and finding by Secretary of State that public not likely to be misled. Name may not contain following words: bank, insurance, insurer, insurance company or words suggesting issuance of insurance policies, trust, trustee, incorporated, inc., corporation, or corp. (Corp. C. 17052).

Amendment of Limited Liability Company Articles.—Amendment of articles of organization allowed at any time where amendments would have been lawful to insert in original articles. Articles amended by filing certificate of amendment with Secretary of State executed by at least one manager (except where greater number is provided in articles of organization) containing name and Secretary of State's file number of limited liability company, and text of amendment. (Corp. C. 17054).

Liability of Members.—Except as provided in Corp. C. 17254, no member is personally liable for any debt, obligation, or liability of limited liability company solely by virtue of membership in company. Member is personally liable for any debt, obligation, or liability of limited liability company under same or similar circumstances and to same extent that shareholder of corporation is personally liable for debt, obligation or liability of corporation. Member may agree to be personally liable for debts, obligations and liabilities under certain statutory guidelines. (Corp. C. 17101[e]). (Corp. C. 17101).

Management.—Unless articles provide that limited liability company will be managed by one or more managers, every member is agent of limited liability company for purpose of conducting its business or affairs and has ability to bind limited liability

company, unless member in fact has no authority to act in particular matter and person with whom member is dealing has actual knowledge of fact that member has no authority. (Corp. C. 17157[a]). However, if articles provide for limited liability company to be managed by one or more managers, no member may act on behalf of company in his or her capacity as member. (Corp. C. 17157[b]). Manager owes members same fiduciary duties that partner owes to partnership and to partners of partnership. (Corp. C. 17153). Managers and officers are not liable for limited liability company obligations solely by reason of being manager or officer. (Corp. C. 17158). Manager may agree to be personally obligated under certain statutory guidelines. (Corp. C. 17158[b]).

Dissolution of Limited Liability Company.—Limited liability company is dissolved and its affairs wound up on happening of whichever occurs first: (a) time specified in articles of organization, (b) happening of events specified in articles of organization or written operating agreement, (c) vote of majority interest of members or greater percentage of voting interests of members as specified in articles or operating agreement, (d) except as otherwise provided in articles of organization or operating agreement, upon death, withdrawal, resignation, expulsion, bankruptcy or dissolution of member who is manager (unless business of company is continued by vote of majority interest of remaining members within 90 days of that event) or (e) entry of decree of judicial dissolution under Corp. C. 17351. (Corp. C. 17350).

Class Actions and Derivative Actions.—Any member of limited liability company may bring class action to enforce claim common to all or class of members. Such actions governed by law governing class actions generally. (Corp. C. 17500).

Mergers.—Limited liability companies permitted to merge with one or more California or out of state limited liability companies, corporations, limited partnerships, general partnerships, business trusts, real estate investment trusts or unincorporated associations, except nonprofit association, if merger would also be allowed in statutes governing merger partner. (Corp. C. 17550[a]). More than 50% but less than 90% owner of California limited liability company cannot force out minority without obtaining fairness determination from California Department of Corporations. (Corp. C. 17551[b]).

Winding Up of Limited Liability Company.—In event of dissolution, winding up of limited liability company may be effected by managers or members upon written notice of commencement of winding up by mail to all known creditors and claimants whose addresses appear on records of limited liability company. (Corp. C. 17352). Managers must file certificate of dissolution of company with Secretary of State which sets forth: (a) name of limited liability company and file number, (b) event causing dissolution and date of dissolution, (c) effective date of certificate of dissolution if it is not effective upon filing, (d) statement that person, limited liability company or other business entity assumes any tax liability of dissolving company, and (e) any other information managers or members determine necessary. (Corp. C. 17356). Under specified circumstances court of competent jurisdiction may decree dissolution. (Corp. C. 17351).

Foreign Limited Liability Companies.—Laws of state or foreign country under which foreign limited liability company organized govern its organization and internal affairs and liability and authority of managers and members. (Corp. C. 17450).

Registration.—Foreign limited liability company must file application with Secretary of State setting forth (1) name of foreign limited liability company and, if different, name under which it proposes to transact business in California, (2) state and date of organization and statement that company is authorized to exercise its powers and privileges in that state, (3) name and address of agent for service of process as specified in Corp. C. 17061 (unless corporate agent is designated, in which case only name of agent required), (4) statement that Secretary of State is appointed agent of company for service of process if agent has resigned and not been replaced, or if agent cannot be found or served with reasonable diligence, and (5) address of principal executive office and principal office in California, if any. (Corp. C. 17451).

Taxes and Fees on Limited Liability Companies.—Governed generally by Rev. & Tax. C. 23091 et seq.

Classification of Limited Liability Companies for Federal Tax Purposes.—Limited liability companies can be classified as partnerships for federal tax purposes. (See e.g. Rev. Rul. 88-76, 1988-2 C.B. 360.)

PARTNERSHIPS:

General Partnerships.—Uniform Partnership Act has been adopted with certain modifications. (Corp. C. 15001-15046).

Limited Partnerships.—Uniform Limited Partnership Act was repealed effective July 1, 1984. (1983 Statutes, c. 1223). California Revised Limited Partnership Act. (Corp. C. 15611-15723), effective July 1, 1984, governs limited partnerships organized after July 1, 1984. Limited partnerships organized before July 1, 1984 continue to be governed by prior law unless all partners, or such lesser number as partnership agreement provides, make written election to be governed by new law, and partnership files with Secretary of State certificate (see subhead Formation of Limited Partnership, infra), including date of original filing under prior law. (Corp. C. 15711, 15712). No action may be maintained by limited partnership in any California court until certificate has been filed. (Corp. C. 15712[b][4]). Following subheads summarize provisions of California Revised Limited Partnership Act, which are applicable to limited partnerships organized after July 1, 1984 and preexisting limited partnerships which elect to be governed by new law. If counsel is advising California limited partnership organized prior to July 1, 1984, provisions of Uniform Limited Partnership Act may still be applicable.

Formation of Limited Partnership.—All partners must sign partnership agreement, general partners must sign, acknowledge, and file with Secretary of State certificate of limited partnership, on prescribed form, stating: (1) Name, (2) street address of principal executive office, (3) names and addresses of general partners, (4) name of agent for service of process and, if not corporate agent, address, (5) other matters

PARTNERSHIPS . . . *continued*

general partners determine to include. (Corp. C. 15621[a]). Limited partnership is formed at time of filing of certificate. (Corp. C. 15621[b]).

Name of Limited Partnership.—Shall contain words "limited partnership" or abbreviation "L.P." at end of name. Shall not contain: (a) Words "bank", "insurance", "trust", "trustee", "incorporated", "inc.", "corporation", or "corp."; (b) name which Secretary of State determines is likely to mislead public or name confusingly similar to existing California limited partnership or registered foreign limited partnership, (see subhead Out-of-State Limited Partnership, infra), or reserved name, unless existing partnership (with similar name) consents to such use and Secretary of State determines that public is not likely to be misled. (Corp. C. 15612). Name may be reserved with Secretary of State for 60-day period, not consecutively renewable. (Corp. C. 15613). In case of limited partnership which has filed certificate pursuant to Corp. C. 15621, any name other than name on file will be fictitious business name. (Bus. & Prof. C. 17900[4]).

Amendment of Limited Partnership Certificate.—Amendment of certificate of limited partnership, on prescribed form, must be signed, acknowledged, and filed with Secretary of State by all general partners (unless lesser number is provided in certificate of limited partnership) and by each general partner designated in certificate of amendment as new partner (see exception; Corp. C. 15625) within 30 days after: (1) Change in name, (2) change in address of principal executive office, (3) change in address of general partner or agent for service (if not corporation) or appointment of new agent, (4) admission of general partner or cessation of general partner to be general partner, (5) discovery of false or erroneous material statement in certificate or any amendment. (Corp. C. 15622). Certificate may also be amended at any other time in any other respect that general partners determine.

Rights and liabilities of general partner with respect to partnership and other partners may be limited by partnership agreement. (Corp. C. 15643). General partner may hold limited partnership interest that is separately designated in partnership agreement. (Corp. C. 15644).

Admission of and Cessation as General Partner.—Unless otherwise provided by agreement, after filing of partnership certificate, general partner may be admitted only: (1) By written consent of each general partner and vote of majority in interest of limited partners (in cases in which there is no remaining or surviving general partner, greater vote may be required—see Corp. C. 15636); or (2) in case of general partner ceasing to be general partner for reasons other than removal and at least one general partner remaining, all partners agree to admit additional general partners(s). (Corp. C. 15641). Person ceases to be general partner upon happening of any of following: (1) Withdrawal from partnership; (2) removal; (3) certain bankruptcy or related proceedings; (4) in case of general partner who is individual: (a) death, or (b) order adjudicating partner incompetent; (5) and certain other circumstances when general partner is trustee, partnership, corporation, limited liability company or estate. (Corp. C. 15642). Person ceasing to be general partner deemed to be acting as general partner with respect to third party doing business with partnership until amended certificate filed. (Corp. C. 15642).

Rights and Liabilities of Limited Partners.—Limited partner who participates in control of business is liable only to persons who transact business with partnership with actual knowledge of that partner's participation in control and who reasonably believe that partner to be general partner at time of transaction. Limited partner who knowingly permits use of his name in partnership name (other than where business of limited partnership had been carried on under name in which his name appeared before his admission) is liable for partnership obligations to persons who reasonably believed that limited partner was general partner at time of transaction. Limited partner does not participate in control of business solely by doing one or more of following: (a) Being contractor for or agent or employee of limited partnership or of general partner, or officer, director or shareholder of corporate general partner; (b) consulting with and advising general partner with respect to business of limited partnership; (c) acting as surety for limited partnership or general partner or guaranteeing one or more specific debts of limited partnership; (d) approving or disapproving amendment to partnership agreement; (e) winding up partnership; (f) serving on audit committee or committee performing functions of audit committee; (g) executing certificate of limited partnership or certificate of amendment (upon failure of general partner to do so in reasonable time after demand), certificate of dissolution, or certificate of cancellation; (h) exercising any right or power permitted to limited partners under Revised Limited Partnership Act and not specifically enumerated in list in Corp. C. 15632(b); (i) voting on or calling partners' meeting for one or more of following matters: (1) Dissolution and winding up of limited partnership, (2) sale, exchange, lease, mortgage, pledge, or other transfer of all or substantial part of assets of limited partnership other than in ordinary course of business, (3) incurrence of indebtedness by limited partnership other than in ordinary course of business, (4) change in nature of business, (5) transactions in which general partners have actual or potential conflict of interest with limited partners or limited partnership, (6) removal of general partner, (7) election to continue business other than under circumstances described in clauses (9) or (10), (8) admission of general partner other than under circumstances described in clauses (9) or (10), (9) admission of general partner or election to continue business after general partner ceases to be general partner where there is no remaining or surviving general partner, (10) admission of general partner or election to continue business of limited partnership after removal of general partner where there is no remaining or surviving general partner, (11) matters related to business of partnership which partnership agreement states may be subject to approval or disapproval of limited partners. (Corp. C. 15632, 15636). Limited partners have dissenting rights to sell their interest in partnership for fair market value in case of merger, acquisition or reorganization. (Corp. C. 15679.1 et seq.).

Records and Reports.—At an office in California, limited partnership shall keep: (a) Current alphabetical list of names, addresses, contribution, and share in profit and loss of each partner, (b) copies of partnership agreement and amendments and certificate of limited partnership and amendments, with executed copies of powers of attorney under which certificates or amendments were executed, (c) copies of tax or information returns for last six taxable years, financial statements for last six fiscal years, and partnership books and records as they relate to internal affairs of partnership for current and last three fiscal years. (Corp. C. 15615). All of foregoing can be inspected and copied by limited partner during normal business hours on reasonable request, and limited partner can require delivery to him at partnership expense of copies of name list, agreement, certificate, and amendments. Limited partners may obtain from general partners copies of partnership income tax and information returns for each year as soon as they become available. All partners must be sent tax information within 90 days after end of taxable year, and in case of limited partnerships with 35 or fewer limited partners, copy of partnership's federal, state and local income tax or information returns for year must accompany such information. Partners of limited partnership with over 35 limited partners must be sent annual report containing balance sheet, income statement, and statement of changes in financial position within 120 days after end of fiscal year. These and other specified rights of access to and delivery of copies of records are enforceable by court action, with reimbursement of attorney's fees if court finds failure to comply was without justification. (Corp. C. 15634). Attorney General may also under certain circumstances bring suit to enforce such rights. (Corp. C. 15635).

Mergers of limited partnerships are regulated by Corp. C. 15678.1 et seq. which provides, in part, for filing certificate of merger with Secretary of State (Corp. C. 15678.4), creditors' rights (Corp. C. 15678.6) and merger of domestic and foreign limited partnerships (Corp. C. 15678.7). Mergers of limited partnerships with domestic corporations are regulated by Corp. C. 1109, 1113.

Dissolution of Limited Partnership.—Limited partnership is dissolved and its affairs shall be wound up upon happening of first to occur of following: (a) At time or upon happening of events specified in partnership agreement; (b) except as otherwise provided in partnership agreement, written consent of all general partners and majority in interest of limited partners; (c) general partner ceases to be general partner (other than by removal), unless: (1) there is at least one other general partner and partnership agreement permits business of limited partnership to be carried on by remaining general partner and such partner does so, or (2) at time there is no remaining general partner, majority in interest of limited partners or greater interest provided in partnership agreement agree in writing to continue business and to admission of new general partner(s); (d) entry of decree of judicial dissolution. (Corp. C. 15681).

Winding Up of Limited Partnership.—In event of dissolution, winding up of limited partnership may be effected: (a) Except as otherwise provided in partnership agreement (and unless dissolution is by entry of judicial decree), by general partners who have not wrongfully dissolved limited partnership or, if none, limited partners, or (b) by decree of court of competent jurisdiction upon petition of limited partners representing 5% or more of interests of limited partners, or three or more creditors, if winding up appears necessary for protection of any parties in interest. (Corp. C. 15683).

Out-of-State Limited Partnership.—

Registration.—Before transacting intrastate business, foreign limited partnership shall file application for registration with Secretary of State setting forth following: (a) Name of foreign limited partnership and, if different, name under which proposes to register and transact business in California; (b) state or country and date of formation and statement that foreign limited partnership is authorized to exercise its powers and privileges in such state or country; (c) name and address of California agent for service of process; (d) statement that Secretary of State is appointed agent of foreign limited partnership for service of process if agent has resigned and has not been replaced or if agent cannot be found or served with exercise of reasonable diligence; (e) address of principal executive office of foreign limited partnership and of its principal office in California, if any; (f) names and business or residence addresses of general partners. (Corp. C. 15692).

Penalty for Failure to Register.—Foreign limited partnership transacting intrastate business in California suffers following penalties until it registers in California: (a) Inability to maintain any action in any California court; (b) $20 penalty for each day up to maximum of $10,000. Failure of foreign limited partnership to register in California does not impair validity of any of its contracts or acts or prevent it from defending any action in any California court. By law, Secretary of State is appointed agent for service of process on foreign limited partnership transacting intrastate business in California without registration, with respect to actions arising out of such transactions. (Corp. C. 15697).

Out-of-State General and Limited Partnership Designation of Agent for Service of Process.—Every partnership, other than foreign limited partnership subject to c. 3 (commencing with §15691) of Tit. 2 of Corp. Code or commercial or banking partnership established and transacting business outside U.S., which is domiciled outside California and has no regular place of business within California, shall, within 40 days of commencing business in California, file statement with Secretary of State designating agent for service of process. By law, service may be made on Secretary of State, Assistant Secretary of State, or Deputy Secretary of State, if agent has not been designated, or if agent designated cannot be found with due diligence, or if agent designated is no longer authorized to act. (Corp. C. 15800).

Classification of Limited Partnerships for Federal Tax Purposes.—In Rev. Rul. 89-123, 1989-2 C.B. 261, Internal Revenue Service determined that California Revised Limited Partnership Act (Corp. C. 15611-15723) corresponds to Uniform Limited Partnership Act for purposes of §301.7701-2 of Treasury's Procedure and Administration Regulations.

Mining Partnership.—See category Mineral, Water and Fishing Rights, topic Mines and Minerals.

See note at head of Digest as to 1998 legislation covered.

See Topical Index in front part of this volume.

BUSINESS REGULATION AND COMMERCE

BANKS AND BANKING:

Regulated by.—Banking business in California is primarily regulated by Financial Code (1951, c. 364), Uniform Commercial Code (1963, c. 819), and laws, rules and regulations of Federal Deposit Insurance Corporation (12 U.S.C. 1811 et seq.). Statutory scheme divides banks into commercial banks and trust companies, although banks may carry out trust operations in separate department of bank. (Finan. C. 103; 1500.1). Since only corporations may do banking business (Finan. C. 102), banks are also subject to California corporate laws to extent not inconsistent with Financial Code (Finan. C. 101). Corporation cannot engage in commercial banking or trust business without certificate of authority. (Finan. C. 403).

Banks are subject to supervision of Department of Financial Institutions, chief officer of which is Commissioner of Financial Institutions. (Finan. C. 200; 210). State regulatory scheme calls for extensive examinations and reports concerning banks' condition no less than once every two years. (Finan. C. 1900-1916, 1930-1939, 1583-1585).

Shares.—Common shares of every banking corporation are subject to assessment to restore impairments of contributed capital. (Finan. C. 662). Par value may be determined by banks' boards. (Finan. C. 620). Distributions to shareholders may not be made (with some exceptions requiring prior approval by commissioner) in amount which exceeds lesser of retained earnings or net income for last three fiscal years less distributions made during such time. (Finan. C. 640-646).

Deposits and Withdrawals.—Bank accounts by or in name of married person or minors must be held for exclusive right and benefit of such persons, whose receipt is valid release and discharge to bank. (Finan. C. 850-851). Deposits in joint accounts may be made to one or more parties whether or not mention of right to survivorship. (Finan. C. 852; Prob. C. 5130). Bank account agreements can be made providing for payment on death to designated person. Such "pay-on-death" provisions shall not be deemed to effect testamentary disposition of property. (Prob. C. 5100-5407). Totten Trust (defined in Prob. C. 80) may be paid to any trustee. If deceased trustee survived other trustees and beneficiaries, payment to his representative or heirs, unless beneficiary had vested interest. If beneficiary survived all trustees, payment to beneficiary or his heirs. (Prob. C. 5404). Statements of account conclusively presumed correct if no objection within four years from rendition. (Finan. C. 861). Bank under no obligation to customer to pay noncertified check presented more than six months after its date, but bank may charge customer's account for payment made thereafter in good faith. (Com'l. C. 4404). Bank has right of set off against deposits if it has matured claim against depositor. (See gen. C.C. 3054.) Set off right limited if depositor is natural person and matured claim relates to personal, family or household debt. (Finan. C. 864; 6660). Any bank certifying check must immediately charge account of drawer. (Finan. C. 970). Checks drawn by authorized agent of depositor in authorized manner may be assumed by bank to be drawn for authorized purpose and within scope of agent's authority, even though drawn to personal order of agent. (Finan. C. 953). Bank must notify holders of time deposits, in writing of maturity date, within ten (but no sooner than 60) days prior to such date. (Finan. C. 855). Bank cannot charge penalty for failure to deposit or late deposit into savings account where depositor has agreed to make installment deposits. (Finan. C. 863).

Bank deposits and collections are also governed generally by Com'l. C. 4101-4504. See Com'l. C. 3101-3605; 4201-4403 for significant provisions governing checks. See topic Commercial Code, subhead Material Variations from 1990 Official Text.

Financial institutions (term that includes, inter alia, banks, savings and loan associations and credit unions) must pay no less than 2% simple annual interest on money prepaid into impound accounts established to protect value of mortgagee's security interest by providing for payment of property taxes, insurance premiums and other property related costs. (C. C. 2954.8).

Account Disclosures.—Banks must make disclosures as to charges and interest rates to their depositors, including persons identified in bank's records as having interest in account with bank. (Finan. C. 865.4[b]). If more than one depositor has interest in account, notice need only be given to one depositor. (Finan. C. 865.4[d]). Banks must maintain and display, or maintain and publicly display means of obtaining, in each office or branch written schedule of amount or method of determining charges on accounts (Finan. C. 865.2[l]; 865[c]) and written schedule concerning interest rates paid (Finan. C. 865.2). Required disclosure not limited to truth-in-lending and Regulation Z disclosures. (Finan. C. 865.2). Provision is also made for notifying new depositors of charges (Finan. C. 865.4[a]), for notifying all depositors of changes in type or amount of charges and interest rates (Finan. C. 865.4[b]), and notifying all customers and potential customers of bank's policy as to when customer may withdraw funds deposited by check in customer's account (Finan. C. 866 et seq.). Sanctions potentially imposed on bank for failure to comply. (Finan. C. 866.4). There are varying maximum holding periods after which depository institution must permit depositor to draw upon deposited amount. (Finan. C. 867).

Unclaimed Deposits.—Modified version of Uniform Disposition of Unclaimed Property Act adopted. (C.C.P. 1500-1527). Under this Act, and provisions of C.C.P. 1300, et seq. pertaining to unclaimed property, deposits held or owing by banking organizations are presumed abandoned if owner has not, within three years, caused activity in or with respect to them. (C.C.P. 1513).

Lien.—Banker, or savings and loan association, has general lien, dependent on possession, upon all property in his hands belonging to customer for balance due from customer in course of business. (C.C. 3054). Banker's exercise of this lien with respect to deposit accounts is subject to limitations and procedures set forth in Finan. C. 864. Lien on depositors' accounts is more accurately termed right of set-off, based on general principles of equity. (Bank's exercise of right of set-off not state action and need not conform to standards of procedural due process. [11 C.3d 352, 113 C. Rptr. 449, 521 P.2d 441]). Exercise of right of set off in connection with debt secured by real property constitutes one form of action which precludes foreclosure on real property. (152 C.A.3d 767, 199 C. Rptr. 557). See category Mortgages, topic Mortgages of Real Property.

Subsidiary Activities.—State banks and their subsidiaries may engage in real property investment, including partnerships and joint ventures, for purpose of purchasing, subdividing and developing real property. (Finan. C. 751.3). Subsidiaries may engage in other nonbanking activities, subject to regulations of commissioner. (Finan. C. 772[a]). Subsidiary may not act as insurance company, insurance agent or insurance broker. (Finan. C. 772[b]).

Sale, Merger and Conversion; Change of Control.—Cross-industry sales, mergers and conversions by and among state banks, national banks, state savings and loan associations and federal savings and loan associations are permitted with approval of appropriate regulator. (Finan. C. 4800 et seq.). Acquisition of control (other than by sale, merger or conversion) requires approval of Department of Financial Institutions. (Finan. C. 700 et seq.).

Foreign banks (other nation and other state) may not maintain office or agency unless licensed. (Finan. C. 1700 et seq.). Other state banks may not transact banking business in state; other nation banks may do so when so licensed. (Finan. C. 1750). Foreign banks when carrying on activities listed in Corp. C. 191(d) shall not be deemed transacting business. (Finan. C. 1750[b][2]). Commercial banking activities and trust business of other nation banks are limited. (Finan. C. 1755; 1503).

Savings and Loan Associations.—S&L's are independently regulated by Department of Savings and Loan. (Finan. C. 5000-10050). Statutory framework as to deposits and withdrawals, unclaimed deposits and liens is substantially similar to banks and follows federal deposit disclosure laws. (Finan. C. 6660 et seq.). Significant differences exist in certain areas. Three year, staggered terms for directors are mandated for S&L's. (Finan. C. 6153). Investment powers and permissible service corporation activities more liberal than those of banks requires prior written consent of Savings and Loan Commissioner. (Finan. C. 6500-6530; 7200-7704). Limits on loans to single borrower substantially greater than banks. (Finan. C. 7451; 1221). Shareholder derivative action may only be brought upon notice to Commissioner of Savings and Loan and finding by Commissioner that suit is proposed in good faith and that there is reasonable probability that prosecution of suit will benefit S&L and its shareholders. (Finan. C. 6052).

Other Related Businesses Regulated by Financial Code.—Check sellers and cashers (12000-12403); credit unions (14000-16154); escrow agents (17000-17654); industrial loan companies (including mortgage bankers) (18000-18643); finance lenders (22000-22780); trust companies (1500-1591); business and industrial development corporations (31000-31953); sellers of payment instruments (33000-34301).

Franchise tax on banks, see category Business Organizations, topic Corporations, subhead Taxation.

BILLS AND NOTES:

Uniform Commercial Code has been adopted. (1963, c. 819; see Com'l. C. 3101 to 3805). See topic Commercial Code.

Days of grace have been abolished and paper matures according to its terms (Com'l. C. 3123), but if day of maturity falls on Sun., Sat. or holiday (including closing of bank pursuant to statute due to emergency), instrument is payable on next succeeding business day which is not Sat. (Com'l. C. 3123). See also category Introduction, topic Holidays. Acceleration clauses are permitted. (Com'l. C. 3109).

Community property is liable for debt incurred by either spouse before or during marriage, regardless of which spouse has management and control of property or whether one or both spouses are parties to debt or to judgment for debt. (Fam. C. 910, 911). Earnings of non-debtor spouse during marriage are not liable for debtor spouse's prenuptial debts so long as earnings are held in separate account and not commingled with community property. (Fam. C. 910, 911). Debtor's separate property is liable for his debts incurred before or during marriage. (Fam. C. 913). Separate property of non-debtor spouse is not liable for debts of other spouse incurred before or during marriage unless debt was incurred for necessaries while spouses were living together or common necessaries while spouses were separated. (Fam. C. 913, 914). Joinder or consent of one spouse to encumbrance of community property to secure payment of other spouse's debt does not subject non-debtor spouse's separate property to liability for debt unless non-debtor spouse also incurred debt. (Fam. C. 913).

Secured Notes and Bonds.—California abides by "one form of action rule", which permits only one form of action on debt secured by real estate mortgage or deed of trust. (C.C.P. 726). Deficiency judgments are barred on purchase money mortgages or mortgages of dwelling for not more than four families, occupied by purchaser. (C.C.P. 580b). Deficiency judgments are also barred when mortgagee has elected to foreclose by power of sale rather than through judicial foreclosure. (C.C.P. 580d). Creditor proceeding against both real and personal property security must do so according to laws relating to real property and Commercial Code. See category Mortgages, topic Mortgages of Real Property, subheads Foreclosure and Deficiency Judgment. See also topic Commercial Code.

Negotiable instrument may provide for costs of collection or attorney's fee or both. (Com'l. C. 3106). Such provisions are enforceable. (84 C.A. 430, 258 P. 407).

Judgment Notes.—See category Civil Actions and Procedure, topic Judgments, subhead Judgment by Confession.

BILLS OF LADING:

See topic Carriers.

BILLS OF SALE:

See topic Sales.

BLUE SKY LAW:

See topic Securities.

See note at head of Digest as to 1998 legislation covered.

See Topical Index in front part of this volume.

CA – 9

BROKERS:

Real Estate Brokers.—Employment of real estate broker must be in writing. (C.C. 1624[d]). Authority to sell real estate includes authority to give usual covenants of warranty. (C.C. 2324).

Real estate brokers and salesmen are required to obtain license from State Real Estate Commissioner, and manner of conducting business is carefully regulated. (Bus. & Prof. C. 10000 et seq.). Statutory definition of "real estate broker" is broad, and includes one who, for compensation and for another, makes certain solicitations or conducts certain negotiations in respect of "business opportunity," or loans secured by real property. (Bus. & Prof. C. 10131; cf. 10131.1, 10133.1).

Real Property Securities Dealers.—Only real estate broker whose license has been specially endorsed as Real Property Securities Dealer may sell real property securities to public, accept funds for continual reinvestment in real property securities, or otherwise act as real property securities dealer. (Bus. & Prof. C. 10237.3, 10237, 10237.1). Information which brokers must disclose to prospective purchasers of such securities (Bus. & Prof. C. 10232.5, 10237.4, et seq.) and to prospective borrowers of loans secured by real property (Bus. & Prof. C. 10240, et seq.; Calif. Adm. Code, Title 10, c. 6), as well as other features of real estate brokerage transactions, are extensively regulated.

Other brokers regulated by legislation and required to be licensed are, inter alia, insurance brokers (Ins. C. 1631, et seq.), mineral, oil and gas brokers (Bus. & Prof. C. 10500, et seq.), motor transportation brokers (Pub. Utils. C. 4801, et seq.), pawnbrokers (Finan. C. 21300 et seq.) and personal property brokers (persons making loans secured by certain contracts for personal property or liens on wages, etc.) (Finan. C. 22000-22780), yacht and ship brokers (Harb. & Nav. Code 700 et seq.). Travel promoters are also regulated by statute. (Bus. & Prof. C. 17540 et seq.). Uniform Commercial Code has been adopted. See topic Commercial Code.

BULK SALES:

See category Debtor and Creditor, topic Fraudulent Sales and Conveyances.

CARRIERS:

Common carriers are under jurisdiction, control and regulation of Public Utilities Commission which has power to regulate and supervise carriers and to do any and all necessary acts to exercise its power and jurisdiction. (Pub. Utils. C. 216, 701-02).

Rates.—Freight and passenger rates are established by Public Utilities Commission. (Pub. Utils. C. 201 et seq.). After ejecting passenger, carrier has no right to require payment of any part of fare. (C.C. 2190).

Discrimination.—No discrimination in charges or facilities may be made for same class of freight or passengers. (Pub. Utils. C. 494, 556).

Bills of Lading.—Uniform Commercial Code has been adopted. (1963, c. 819). See topic Commercial Code, subhead Material Variations from 1990 Official Text. Carrier has lien on goods covered by bill of lading for charges subsequent to date of its receipts of goods for storage or transportation and for expenses necessary for preservation of goods incident to transportation or reasonably incurred in their sale pursuant to law. Carrier loses any such lien on goods voluntarily delivered or goods whose delivery is unjustifiably refused. (Com'l. C. 7307). Enforcement of carriers' liens governed by Uniform Commercial Code and Commercial Code §7308.

Liens.—Carrier has lien for freightage, for services rendered, for money advanced to discharge prior liens and for fines and expenses due to owner's provision of false or erroneous certifications of gross cargo weight. (C.C. 2144). Common carrier has lien upon luggage of passenger for payment of such fare as he is entitled to from him. (C.C. 2191).

Limited Liability.—Common carrier may limit its liability except for gross negligence, fraud or willful wrong. (C.C. 2175). Common carrier may limit its liability with respect to personal property, when value of such property is not named and also to loss or injury to live animals by stating these limitations of liability on ticket, bill of lading or written contract for carriage accepted by passenger, consignor or consignee. Other modifications of carrier's liability require passenger's signature. (C.C. 2176). Railroad's liability on following items is limited as follows, unless it has consented in writing to assume greater liability: trunk and contents, $100; valise or suit case and contents, $50; box or package and contents, $10. (C.C. 2178). Carriers liable for delay only when caused by want of ordinary care. (C.C. 2196). Under C.C. 2197, 2197.5, party delivering or taking freight who causes delay, liable for specified charges to motor carrier. Carrier must exercise that duty of care with respect to goods which reasonably careful man in like circumstances would exercise. (Com'l. C. 7309).

Elevators.—Owner of any elevator, except those under jurisdiction of U. S. Government and certain residential elevators, must have permit conspicuously posted in elevator car to operate same issued by Division of Occupational Safety and Health of Department of Industrial Relations. (Lab. C. 7301, 7317). Permits issued for one year period, and all elevators must be inspected at least once a year. (Lab. C. 7304).

Motor Vehicle Carriers.—See category Transportation, topic Motor Vehicles.

COMMERCIAL CODE:

Uniform Commercial Code has been adopted (1963, c. 819) effective Jan. 1, 1965. California refers to Articles as "Divisions", Parts as "Chapters" and section numbers without hyphenation. California revisions (1974, c. 997) effective Jan. 1, 1976 bring California's version somewhat in line with 1972 official text, but significant deviations exist. Art. 2A Leases of Official Text governing personal property leases adopted (1988, c. 1359) as Division 10 effective Jan. 1, 1990 with some variations from Official Text. See 10101 et seq. 1995 Revised Art. 5 adopted (1996, c. 176) with no material variations effective July 1, 1996. Adopted Revised Art. 6 with deviations and additional sections. 1994 Revised Art. 8 relating to Investment Securities adopted (1997, c. 497) as Division 8 effective Jan. 1, 1997 with some variations.

Material Variations from 1990 Official Text.—

1102: (5)(b) reads: "Words of the masculine or feminine gender include the masculine, the feminine, and the neuter, and when the sense so indicates words of the neuter gender may refer to any gender."

1109: Omitted.

1201: Adopted 1977 version of subsections (5), (14), and (20); and 1972 version of subsection (9). (3) substitutes "and" for "or" after "trade" in first sentence. (6) adds, "that by its terms evidences the intention of the issuer that the person entitled under the document (Sec. 7403[4]) has the right to receive, hold and dispose of the document and the goods it covers. Designation of a document by the issuer as a 'bill of lading' is conclusive evidence of that intention. 'Bill of lading' includes an air bill" after "forwarding goods, and" in first sentence. (15) substitutes "gin ticket or compress receipt" for "or order for the delivery of goods" and "entitled under the document (Section 7403[4]) has the right" for "in possession of it is entitled" in first sentence. Substitutes "shall" for "must" and omits "or addressed to" after "to be issued by" in second sentence. (20) "Holder" with respect to negotiable instrument, means person in possession if instrument is payable to bearer, or, in case of instrument payable to identified person, if identified person is in possession. "Holder" with respect to document of title, means person in possession if goods are deliverable to bearer or to order of person in possession. (26) Substitutes "those" for "such" and "that" for "as" in first sentence; and "any of the following occurs" for "when" at end of second sentence. Substitutes "these" for "such" in subsection (b). (31) omitted; subsequent subsections renumbered in sequence. (38) adds after second sentence: "When a writing or notice is required to be sent by registered or certified mail, proof of mailing is sufficient, and proof of receipt by the addressee is not required unless the words 'with return receipt requested' are also used." (45) reworded: " 'Warehouse receipt' means a document evidencing the receipt of goods for storage issued by a warehouseman (Section 7102), and which, by its terms, evidences the intention of the issuer that the person entitled under the document (Section 7403[4]) has the right to receive, hold and dispose of the document and the goods it covers. Designation of a document by the issuer as a 'warehouse receipt' is conclusive evidence of such intention." (37) third paragraph, adds section on motor vehicle and trailer leases.

1202: Reworded: "(1) A bill of lading, policy or certificate of insurance, official weigher's or inspector's certificate, consular invoice, or any other document authorized or required by the contract to be issued by a third party is admissible as evidence of the facts stated in the document by the third party in any action arising out of the contract which authorized or required the document. (2) In any action arising out of the contract which authorized or required the document referred to in subdivision (1): (a) A document in due form purporting to be the document referred to in subdivision (1) is presumed to be authentic and genuine. This presumption is a presumption affecting the burden of producing evidence. (b) If the document is found to be authentic and genuine, the facts stated in the document by the third party are presumed to be true. This presumption is a presumption affecting the burden of proof."

1206: Adds section on qualified financial contracts.

1209: Optional section adopted.

1210: New section added: "Except as otherwise provided in Section 1202, the presumptions established by this code are presumptions affecting the burden of producing evidence."

2107: (3) adds "in the same manner" after "recorded."

2201: Adds section on qualified financial contracts.

2203: Omitted.

2205: Added subdivision: "(b) Notwithstanding subdivision (a), when a merchant renders an offer, oral or written, to supply goods to a contractor licensed pursuant to the provisions of Chapter 9 (commencing with Section 7000) of Division 3 of the Business and Professions Code or a similar contractor's licensing law of another state, and the merchant has actual or imputed knowledge that the contractor is so licensed, and that the offer will be relied upon by the contractor in the submission of its bid for a construction contract with a third party, the offer relied upon shall be irrevocable, notwithstanding lack of consideration, for 10 days after the awarding of the contract to the prime contractor, but in no event for more than 90 days after the date the bid or offer was rendered by the merchant; except that an oral bid or offer, when for a price of two thousand five hundred dollars ($2,500) or more, shall be confirmed in writing by the contractor or his or her agent within 48 hours after it is rendered. Failure by the contractor to confirm such offer in writing shall release the merchant from his or her offer. Nothing in this subdivision shall prevent a merchant from providing that the bid or offer will be held open for less than the time provided for herein."

2302: Omitted.

2313: Same as 1972 Official Text; additional consumer protection granted in Title 1.7 of Civil Code. See topic Consumer Protection, subhead Consumer Warranties.

2318: Omitted.

2326: (3)(a) omitted. Added to (3): "(d): Delivers goods which the person making delivery used or bought for use for personal, family, or household purposes." Also added "(5) If a person delivers or consigns for sale goods which the person used or bought for use for personal, family, or household purposes, these goods do not become the property of the deliveree or consignee unless the deliveree or consignee purchases and fully pays for the goods. Nothing in this subdivision shall prevent the deliveree or consignee from acting as the deliverer's agent to transfer title to these goods to a buyer who pays the full purchase price. Any payment received by the deliveree or consignee from a buyer of these goods, less any amount which the deliverer expressly agreed could be deducted from the payment for commissions, fees, or expenses, is the property of the deliverer and shall not be subject to the claims of the deliveree's or consignee's creditors."

2402: (2) adds "or void" after each "fraudulent".

2403: (3) adds: "for the purpose of sale, obtaining offers to purchase, locating a buyer, or the like" after "retention or possession."

2501: (1)(c) reworded: "if the contract is for the sale of unborn young or future crops, when the crops are planted or otherwise become growing crops or the young are conceived."

See note at head of Digest as to 1998 legislation covered.

See Topical Index in front part of this volume.

CA – 10

COMMERCIAL CODE . . . *continued*

2512: (1)(b) new section reads: "despite tender of required documents, the circumstances would justify injunction against honor under this code (sub. [b] of Sec. 5109)."

2702: In (3) "or lien creditor" deleted following "good faith purchaser".

2718: (1) reads: "(1) Damages for breach by either party may be liquidated in the agreement subject to and in compliance with Section 1671 of the Civil Code. If the agreement provides for liquidation of damages, and such provision does not comply with Section 1671 of the Civil Code, remedy may be had as provided in this division."

2719: (3) second sentence reads: "Limitation of consequential damages for injury to the person in the case of consumer goods is invalid unless it is proved that the limitation is not unconscionable." Adds third sentence: "Limitation of consequential damages where the loss is commercial is valid unless it is proved that the limitation is not unconscionable."

2725: Secured party's action to recover deficiency from buyer is barred by this section if more than four years elapse since breach of security agreement, despite fact that date of repossession and resale is within four year period. (62 C.A.3d 1024).

Chapter 8, Retail Sales, §§2800 and 2801 were added to Division 2. (1970, c. 972).

2800: "As used in this chapter 'goods' means goods used or bought for use primarily for personal, family or household purposes."

2801: "In any retail sale of goods, if the manufacturer or seller of the goods issues a written warranty or guarantee as to the condition or quality of all or part of the goods which requires the buyer to complete and return any form to the manufacturer or seller as proof of the purchase of the goods, such warranty or guarantee shall not be unenforceable solely because the buyer fails to complete or return the form. This section does not relieve the buyer from proving the fact of purchase and the date thereof in any case in which such a fact is in issue.

The buyer must agree in writing to any waiver of this section for the waiver to be valid. Any waiver by the buyer of the provisions of this section which is not in writing is contrary to public policy and shall be unenforceable and void."

California enactment of Official Text Article 2A described infra in Section 10102 et seq.

Adopted Revised Art. 3, and Amendments conforming other sections of Code to Revised Art. 3.

3302: (a), introductory text, inserts "both of the following apply" at end.

3303: (a), introductory text, inserts "any of the following apply" at end.

3305: (a), introductory text, inserts "all of" following "subject to".

3312: Added to UCC in 1991: (b), introductory text, inserts following third sentence: "The warranty is made to the obligated bank and any person entitled to enforce the check." (c), inserts "after the claim became enforceable," following "subsection (b)(4) and".

3404: (d), omits "substantially".

3416: (a), introductory text, inserts "all of the following" preceding "to the transferee"; (a)(6) added: "(6) If the instrument is a demand draft, creation of the instrument according to the terms on its face was authorized by the person identified as drawer." Section (e) added: "If the warranty in paragraph (6) of subdivision (a) is not given by a transferor under applicable conflict of law rules, then the warranty is not given to that transferor when that transferor is a transferee."

3417: (a), introductory text, inserts "all of the following" following "warrant"; Subsection (a)(4) added: "(4) If the draft is a demand draft according to the terms on its face was authorized by the person identified as drawer"; Section (g) added: "(g) A demand draft is a check, as provided in subdivision (f) of Section 3104"; Section (h) added: "(h) If the warranty in paragraph (4) of subdivision (a) is not given by a transferor under applicable conflict of law rules, then the warranty is not given to that transferor when that transferor is a transferee".

4106: Adopted Alternative B of subsection (b).

4202: (a), introductory text, adds "all of the following" at end.

4207: (a), introductory text, inserts "all of the following are applicable" at end.

4208: (a), introductory text, inserts "all of the following apply" at end.

4210: (a), introductory text, inserts "all of following are applicable" at end.

4406: (4) (b), adds following sentence at end: "A bank shall provide, upon request and without charge to the customer, at least two items or a legible copy thereof with respect to each statement of account sent to the customer." (d), introductory text, inserts "any of the following" preceding "against the bank". (e) omits "substantially". (g) reads: "(g) This section shall remain in effect only until Jan. 1, 2001, and as of that date is repealed, unless a later enacted statute, which is enacted before Jan. 1, 2001, deletes or extends that date."

1995 Revised Art. 5 with no material variations, adopted 1996, c. 176, effective July 1, 1996.

5114: omitted.

5115: elects "cause of action" in each bracketed portion of section.

5116: (d) Omits "4A".

Adopted Revised Art. 6 (Alternative B) and amendment to Art. 1 of Code conforming to Revised Art. 6 (Alternative B) by L.1990, c. 1191.

6101: Reworded: Bulk Sales. §§6101–6111 vary substantially from Uniform Commercial Code Official Text. Revised Art. 6 with additional §§6106.2 and 6106.4.

6102: (a)(1), inserts "and equipment" following "inventory" in both instances. (3) reads: "(3) 'Bulk sale' means either of the following: (i) In the case of a sale by auction or a sale or series of sales conducted by a liquidator on the seller's behalf, a sale or series of sales not in the ordinary course of the seller's business of more than half of the seller's inventory and equipment, as measured by a value on the date of the bulk-sale agreement. (ii) In all other cases, a sale not in the ordinary course of the seller's business of more than half the seller's inventory and equipment as measured by value on the date of the bulk-sale agreement." (a)(5)(iii) selects Alternative B.

6103: (a)(1) reads: "The seller's principal business is the sale of inventory from stock, including those who manufacture what they sell, or that of a restaurant owner." (c)(7), inserts "debtor in possession," following "bankruptcy." (c)(9)(iv), (c)(10)(iii), and (c)(11)(iii) read: "Records and publishes notice of the assumption not later than 30 days after the date of the bulk sale in the manner provided in Section 6105." (c)(12)(ii), substitutes "five million dollars ($5,000,000)" for "$25,000,000". Adds (c)(14) which reads: "A transfer of personal property, if the personal property is leased back to the transferor immediately following the transfer and either there has been compliance with subdivision (h) of Section 3440.1 of the Civil Code." Adds (c)(15) which reads: "A transfer which is subject to and complies with Article 5 (commencing with Section 24070) of Chapter 6 of Division 9 of the Business and Professional Code, if the transferee records and publishes notice of the transfer at least 12 business days before the transfer is to be consummated in the manner provided in Section 6105 and the notice contains the information set forth in paragraphs (1) to (4) inclusive of subdivision (a) of 6105." Adds (c)(16) which reads: "A transfer of goods in a warehouse where a warehouse receipt has been issued therefor by a warehouseman (Section 7102) and a copy of the receipt is kept at the principal place of business of the warehouseman and at the warehouse in which the goods are stored."

6104: Section reads: "In a bulk sale defined in subparagraph (ii) of paragraph (3) of subdivision (a) of Section 6102 the buyer shall do each of the following: (a) Obtain from the seller a list of all business names and addresses used by the seller within three years before the date the list is sent or delivered to the buyer. (b) Give notice of the bulk sale in accordance with Section 6105. (c) Comply with Section 6106.2 if the bulk sale is within the scope of that section."

6105: (b)(3) reads: "(3) Delivered or sent by registered or certified mail to the county tax collector in the county or counties in this state in which the tangible assets are located. If delivered during the period from March 1 to the last Friday in May, inclusive, the notice shall be accompanied by a completed business property statement with respect to property involved in the bulk sale pursuant to Section 441 of the Revenue and Taxation Code."

6106: Omitted.

6106.2: (a) This section applies only to bulk sale where consideration is $2,000,000 or less and is substantially all cash or obligation of buyer to pay cash in future to seller or combination thereof. (b) Upon every bulk sale subject to this section except one made by sale at auction or sale or series of sales conducted by liquidator on seller's behalf, it is duty of buyer or, if transaction is handled through escrow, escrow agent to apply cash consideration in accordance with this section so far as necessary to pay those debts of seller for which claims are due and payable on or before date of bulk sale and are received in writing on or prior to date specified as last date to file claims with person designated in notice to receive claims. This duty of buyer or escrow agent runs to each claimant timely filing claim. (c) If seller disputes whether claim is due and payable on date of bulk sale or amount of any claim, buyer or escrow agent shall withhold from distribution amount equal to (1) 125% of first $7,500 of claim, and (2) amount equal to that portion of claim in excess of first $7,500, or pro rata amount under subdivision (b) of §6106.4, if applicable, and shall send written notice to claimant filing claim on or before two business days after distribution that amount will be paid to seller, or to other claimants in accordance with subdivision (b) of §6106.4, as case may be, unless attached within 25 days from mailing of notice. Any portion of amount withheld which is not attached by claimant within that time shall be paid by buyer or escrow agent to seller, or to other claimants in accordance with subdivision (b) of §6106.4 if they have not been paid in full. Attachment of any amount so withheld shall be limited in its effect to amount withheld for attaching claimant and shall give attaching claimant no greater priority or rights with respect to its claim than claimant would have had if claim had not been disputed. For purposes of this subdivision, claimant may obtain issuance of attachment for claim which is less than $500 and which otherwise meets requirements of §483.010 of Code of Civil Procedure or which is secured claim or lien of type described in §483.010 of Code of Civil Procedure. Remedy in this subdivision shall be in addition to any other remedies claimant may have, including any right to attach property intended to be transferred or any other property. (d) If cash consideration payable is not sufficient to pay all of claims received in full, where no escrow has been established pursuant to §6106.4, buyer shall follow procedures specified in subdivisions (a) to (c), inclusive, of §6106.4, and immunity established by paragraph (3) of subdivision (a) of that section shall apply to buyer. (e) Buyer or escrow agent shall, within 45 days after buyer takes legal title to any of goods, either pay to extent of cash consideration claims filed and not disputed, or applicable portion thereof to extent of cash consideration under subdivision (b) of §6106.4, or institute action in interpleader pursuant to subdivision (b) of §386 of Code of Civil Procedure and deposit consideration with clerk of court pursuant to subdivision (c) of that section. Action shall be brought in appropriate court in county where seller had its principal place of business in this state. §§386.1 and 386.6 of Code of Civil Procedure shall apply in action. (f) Notice shall state, in addition to matters required by §6105, name and address of person with whom claims may be filed and last date for filing claims, which shall be business day before date stated in notice pursuant to paragraph (4) of subdivision (a) of §6105: Claims shall be deemed timely filed only if actually received by person designated in notice to receive claims before close of business on day specified in notice as last date for filing claims. (g) This section shall not be construed to release any security interest or other lien on property which is subject of bulk sale except upon voluntary release by secured party or lienholder.

6106.4: In any case where notice of bulk sale subject to §6106.2 states that claims may be filed with escrow agent, intended buyer shall deposit with escrow agent full amount of purchase price or consideration. If, at time bulk sale is otherwise ready to be consummated, amount of cash deposited or agreed to be deposited at or prior to consummation in escrow is insufficient to pay in full all of claims filed with escrow agent, escrow agent shall do each of following: (a)(1) Delay distribution of consideration and passing of legal title for period of not less than 25 days nor more than 30 days from date notice required in paragraph (2) is mailed. (2) Within five business days after time bulk sale would otherwise have been consummated, send written notice to each claimant who has filed claim stating total consideration deposited or agreed to be deposited in escrow, name of each claimant who filed claim against escrow and amount of each claim, amount proposed to be paid to each claimant, new date scheduled for passing of legal title pursuant to paragraph (1) and date on or before which distribution will be made to claimants which shall not be more than five days after new date specified for passing of legal title. (3) If no written objection to

See note at head of Digest as to 1998 legislation covered.

See Topical Index in front part of this volume.

COMMERCIAL CODE . . . *continued*

distribution described in notice required by paragraph (2) is received by escrow agent prior to new date specified in notice for passing of legal title, escrow agent shall not be liable to any person to whom notice required by paragraph (2) was sent for any good faith error that may have been committed in allocating and distributing consideration as stated in notice. (b) Distribute consideration in following order of priorities: (1) All obligations owing to U.S., to extent given priority by federal law. (2) Secured claims, including statutory and judicial liens, to extent of consideration fairly attributable to value of properties securing claims and in accordance with priorities provided by law. Secured creditor shall participate in distribution pursuant to this subdivision only if release of lien is deposited by secured creditor conditioned only upon receiving amount equal to distribution. (3) Escrow and professional charges and brokers' fees attributable directly to sale. (4) Wage claims given priority by §1205 of Code of Civil Procedure. (5) All other tax claims. (6) All other unsecured claims pro rata, including any deficiency claims of partially secured creditors. (c) To extent that obligation of buyer to pay cash in future is part of consideration and cash consideration is not sufficient to pay all claims filed in full, apply all principal and interest received on obligation to payment of claims in accordance with subdivision (b) until they are paid in full before making any payment to seller. In that case, notice sent pursuant to subdivision (a) shall state amount, terms, and due dates of obligation and portion of claims expected to be paid thereby. No funds may be drawn from escrow, prior to actual closing and completion of escrow, for payment, in whole or in part, of any commission, fee, or other consideration as compensation for service that is contingent upon performance of any act, condition, or instruction set forth in escrow.

6107: (c) reads: "A buyer who made a good faith and commercially reasonable effort to comply with the requirements of Section 6104 or to exclude the sale from the application of this division under subdivision (c) of section 6103 is not liable to creditors for failure to comply with the requirements of Section 6104. The buyer has the burden of establishing the good faith and commercial reasonableness of the effort." (d)(1) adds "except to the extent that the payment or application is applied to a debt which is secured by the assets and which has been taken into consideration in determining the net contract price." after "seller or a creditor". (d)(2) adds "except to the extent that the payment or application is applied to a debt which is secured by the assets and which has been taken into consideration in determining the net contract price." after "which is allocable". Omitted subsection (11).

6109: Omitted.

6110: Section (3) omitted.

6111: (a) Except to extent provided in subdivision (b), this division shall apply to bulk sale if date of bulk sale is on or after Jan. 1, 1991. (b) If date of bulk sale is on or after Jan. 1, 1991, and date of bulk-sale agreement is before Jan. 1, 1991, all of following shall apply: (1) Paragraph (2) of subdivision (a) of §6103 and subdivision (b) of §6103 shall not apply and this division shall apply only if goods are located in this state. (2) Subdivision (a) of §6104 shall not apply. (3) Buyer is required under subdivision (b) of §6104 to give notice in accordance with §6107, as in effect on Dec. 31, 1990, rather than §6105. (4) Buyer is required under subdivision (c) of §6104 to comply with §6106, as in effect on Dec. 31, 1990, if bulk sale is within scope of that section, rather than §6106.2. (5) §6105 shall not apply, and §6107, as in effect on Dec. 31, 1990, shall apply. (6) §§6106.2 and 6106.4 shall not apply, and §§6106 and 6106.1, as in effect on Dec. 31, 1990, shall apply. (7) No action may be brought under this division as in effect either before or on or after Jan. 1, 1991, if provisions of this division, as in effect on Dec. 31, 1990, have been complied with.

7102: Omits (1)(d) in its entirety. In (1)(g) omits "except that in relation to an unaccepted delivery order it means the person who orders the possessor of goods to deliver" at end of first sentence.

7104: New subdivision (3) added: "(3) A nonnegotiable warehouse receipt and a nonnegotiable bill of lading must be conspicuously (Section 1201) marked 'nonnegotiable.' In case of the bailee's failure to do so, a holder of the document who purchased it for value supposing it to be negotiable may, at his option, treat such document as imposing upon the bailee the same liabilities he would have incurred had the document been negotiable."

7202: (2) (e) adds "and except that where goods are stored in a public utility warehouse having a lawful tariff on file with the Public Utilities Commission, a statement that the rate of storage and handling charges are as provided in such tariff is sufficient" at end of sentence.

7204: (2) adds "nor permit recovery in excess of the actual value of the goods" at end of first sentence. (4) adds "Section 1630 of the Civil Code nor any of the provisions of the Public Utilities Code or the Agricultural Code or any lawful regulations issued thereunder" at end.

7206: (4) adds "and payment of any amount necessary to satisfy the warehouseman's lien and reasonable expenses incurred under this section" at end.

7209: In (1), substitutes "deposited" for "covered by a warehouse receipt" and adds "processing incidental to storage," after "charges for storage," in the first sentence; omits "and it is stated . . . to other goods" before "the warehouseman also has a lien" in second sentence; and omits "in an amount or at a rate" before "specified on the receipt" in third sentence. First sentence of (2) reworded to read: "The warehouseman may also reserve a security interest against the bailor for charges other than those specified in subdivision (1), such as for money advanced and interest, but if a receipt is issued for the goods such a security interest is not valid as against third persons without notice unless the maximum amount thereof is conspicuously specified (Section 1201) on the receipt."

7210: In (2)(f) adds "published in the judicial district" after "circulation" in first and fourth sentences.

7403: In (1)(b) substitutes "case of damage or destruction by fire" for "such cases".

7501: In (4) omits "unless it is established that the negotiation is not in the regular course of business or financing or involves receiving the document in settlement or payment of a money obligation" at end.

7502: In (1)(d) omits "In the case of a delivery order the bailee's obligation accrues only upon acceptance and the obligation acquired by the holder is that the issuer and any indorser will procure the acceptance of the bailee."

7503: Renumbers (3) as (2) and omits (2) in its entirety.

7601: Substitutes "an undertaking" for "security" and "such security" in second and third sentences of (1) and second sentence of (2).

7603: Adds "or warehouseman" after "bailee".

NOTE: Division 8, enacted in 1984, was repealed in 1996, c. 497. New Division 8, reflecting revised 1994 text of Art. 8 of Uniform Commercial Code, was simultaneously enacted.

8102: (a)(5) adds "any of the following" after "means". (6) adds "either" after "to". (13) adds "both of the following apply" after "which". (15) adds "that is all of the following" after "issuer." (17) adds "(commencing with Section 8501)" after "Chapter 5". (18)(c) adds "(commencing with Section 1101" after "Division 1".

8107: (a)(4) adds: "or the beneficiary of a security as defined in subdivision (d) of Section 5501 of the Probate Code, registered in beneficiary form, as defined in subdivision (a) of Section 5501 of the Probate Code, if the beneficiary has survived the death of the registered owner or all registered owners".

8108: (b)(4) adds "all of the following will be applicable" after "purchaser".

8115: (a) adds "did one or more of the following" after "bailee".

8208: (a) adds "all of the following" after "warrants".

8306: (a) adds "all of the following were true" after "signing". (b) adds "all of the following were true" after "signing".

8401: (a) adds "the following conditions are met" after "if".

8404: (a) adds " in any of the following circumstances" after "registered".

8408: Repealed, 1996, c. 497.

8503: (c) adds "inclusive" after "8508".

8601: Reads: "This division becomes operative Jan. 1, 1997".

8603: (b) adds "and that financial statement shall contain a statement that it is being filed pursuant to this section" after "perfect" in last sentence.

9102: (2) substitutes "inventory lien" for "factor's lien". Adds subdivisions (4) through (9): "(4) Notwithstanding anything to the contrary contained in this division, but subject to subdivisions (5), (6), and (7), no nonpossessory security interest, other than a purchase money security interest, may be given or taken in or to the inventory of a retail merchant held for sale consisting of beer, wine, or liquor. The phrase 'purchase money security interest' as used in this subdivision does not extend to any after- acquired property other than the initial property sold by a secured party or taken by a lender as security as provided in Section 9107.

(5) Except as provided in this subdivision, any nonpossessory security interest in the inventory, other than beer, wine, or liquor, of a retail merchant shall be effective with respect to goods in which the debtor acquires rights before, on, or after July 1, 1985, provided the requirements of subdivision (1) of Section 9203 are met before, on, or after July 1, 1985. Any nonpossessory security interest in the inventory, other than beer, wine, or liquor, of a retail merchant whose sales of goods for personal, family, or household purposes exceeded 75 percent in dollar volume of his or her total sales of all goods during the 12 months preceding the filing of the financing statement perfecting the security interest shall not be valid unless:

(a) The security interest is a purchase money security interest as defined in Section 9107; or

(b) The security interest secures a debt as to which the secured party has made no restrictions as to use of funds, other than those which are commercially reasonable and made in good faith.

(6) Subdivisions (4) and (5) do not apply to the following:

(a) Inventory consisting of durable goods having a unit retail value of at least five hundred dollars ($500) or motor vehicles, housetrailers, trailers, semitrailers, farm machinery, construction machinery, or aircraft, or repair parts of any of the foregoing.

(b) Inventory of a debtor which is a cooperative association organized pursuant to Chapter 1 (commencing with Section 54001) of Division 20 of the Food and Agricultural Code (agricultural cooperative associations) or Part 3 (commencing with Section 13200) of Division 3 of Title 1 of the Corporations Code (Fish Marketing Act).

(7) For purposes of this section, a 'retail merchant' is a merchant whose sales for resale did not exceed 75 percent in dollar volume of his or her total sales of all goods during the 12 months preceding the filing of the financing statement perfecting the security interest; and for the purpose of this subdivision, a sale of goods to a contractor, who is required to be licensed, for the purpose of incorporating such goods at any time into improvements or repairs to real property, is a sale for resale.

(8) A financing statement or a continuation statement filed on or before July 1, 1985, if otherwise sufficient in accordance with this division (other than Section 9102), shall be effective with respect to a security interest which first becomes permissible under Section 9102 on or after July 1, 1985.

(9) This section shall become effective on July 1, 1985."

9103: (1)(a) adds "rights to proceeds of written letters of credit" after "instruments". Subsection (1)(e) added: "(e) If goods are or become fixtures (§9313[1][a]) in relation to real estate located in this state, the conflicting interest of an encumbrancer or owner of the real estate is governed by §9313." (2)(a) adds "whether such certificate is designated a 'certificate of title,' 'certificate of ownership,' or otherwise." at end of sentence. Subsection (6) omitted and replaced by "(6)(a) This subdivision applies to investment property. (b) Except as otherwise provided in paragraph (f), during the time that a security certificate is located in a jurisdiction, perfection of a security interest, the effect of perfection or nonperfection, and the priority of a security interest in the certificated security represented thereby are governed by the local law of that jurisdiction. (c) Except as otherwise provided in paragraph (f), perfection of a security interest, the effect of perfection or nonperfection, and the priority of a security interest in an uncertificated security are governed by the local law of the issuer's jurisdiction as specified in subdivision (d) of Section 8110. (d) Except as otherwise provided in paragraph (f), perfection of a security interest, the effect of perfection or nonperfection, and the priority of a security interest in a security entitlement or securities account are governed by the local law of the securities intermediary's jurisdiction as specified in subdivision (e) of Section 8110. (e) Except as otherwise

See note at head of Digest as to 1998 legislation covered.

See Topical Index in front part of this volume.

CA – 12

COMMERCIAL CODE . . . *continued*
provided in paragraph (f), perfection of a security interest, the effect of perfection or nonperfection, and the priority of a security interest in a commodity contract or commodity account are governed by the local law of the commodity intermediary's jurisdiction. The following rules determine a "commodity intermediary's jurisdiction" for purposes of this paragraph: (i) If an agreement between the commodity intermediary and commodity customer specifies that it is governed by the law of a particular jurisdiction, that jurisdiction is the commodity intermediary's jurisdiction. (ii) If an agreement between the commodity intermediary and the commodity customer does not specify the governing law as provided in subparagraph (i), but expressly specifies that the commodity account is maintained at an office in a particular jurisdiction, that jurisdiction is the commodity intermediary's jurisdiction. (iii) If an agreement between the commodity intermediary and commodity customer does not specify a jurisdiction as provided in subparagraphs (i) or (ii), the commodity intermediary's jurisdiction is the jurisdiction in which is located the office identified in an account statement as the office serving the commodity customer's account. (iv) If an agreement between the commodity intermediary and commodity customer does not specify a jurisdiction as provided in subparagraphs (i) or (ii) and an account statement does not identify an office serving the commodity customer's account as provided in subparagraph (iii), the commodity intermediary's jurisdiction is the jurisdiction in which is located the chief executive office of the commodity's intermediary. (f) Perfection of a security interest by filing, automatic perfection of a security interest in investment property granted by a broker or securities intermediary, and automatic perfection of a security interest in a commodity contract or commodity account granted by a commodity intermediary are governed by the local law of the jurisdiction in which the debtor is located. The rules in paragraphs (c) (d) and (e) of subdivision (3) apply to security interests to which this paragraph applies."

9104: (b) omitted. (e) adds "including creation of a security interest," after "to a transfer." Subsection (g) reworded to read "to any loan made by an insurance company pursuant to the provisions of a policy or contract issued by it and upon the sole security of the policy or contract; or" (j) adds: "and to any interest of a lessor and lessee in any such lease or rents" after "thereunder" (l) omitted and replaced by: "(l) to any security interest created by the assignment of the benefits of any public construction contract under the Improvement Act of 1911 (Division 7 (commencing with Section 5000), Streets and Highways Code)"; Subsection (m) omitted and replaced by: "(m) To transition property, as defined in Section 840 of the Public Utilities Code, except to the extent that the provisions of this division are referenced in Article 5.5 (commencing with section 840) of Chapter 4 of Part 1 of Division 1 of the Public Utilities Code".

9105: In (e) adds word "negotiable" before "certificate of deposit," (h) adds "investment property" before "accounts," (i) omitted and replaced by: "(i) 'Instrument' means a negotiable instrument (defined in Section 3104) or any other writing which evidences a right to the payment of money and is not itself a security agreement or lease and is of a type which is in ordinary course of business transferred by delivery with any necessary endorsement or assignment. The term does not include investment property". In (m), last sentence omitted and replaced by: "If a security interest is in favor of a trustee, indenture trustee, agent, collateral agent, or other representative, the representative is the secured party." In (2) the following definitions and sections where the definitions appear are added: "Commodity contract. Section 9115; Commodity Customer. Section 9115; Commodity intermediary. Section 9115; Control. Section 9115; Investment Property. Section 9115; Broker. Section 8102; Certificated security. Section 8102; Clearing corporation. Section 8102; Control. Section 8106; Delivery. Section 8301; Entitlement holder. Section 8102; Financial asset. Section 8102; Letter of credit. Section 5102; Securities intermediary. Section 8102; Security. Section 8102; Security certificate. Section 8102; Security certificate. Section 8102; Security entitlement. Section 8102; Uncertificated security. Section 8102".

9109: In (4) inserts words "leased or" before words "so furnished."

9110: Replaces second sentence with "Personal property may be referred to by general kind or class if the property can be reasonably identified as falling within such kind or class or if it can be so identified when it is acquired by the debtor."

9111: Omits Section 9111.

9203: (1) revised to read: "Subject to the provisions of Section 4210 on the security interest of a collecting bank, Sections 9115 and 9116 on security interests in investment property, and Section 9113 on a security interest arising under the divisions on sales and leases, a security interest is not enforceable against the debtor or third parties with respect to the collateral and does not attach unless all of the following are applicable:", (a) adds "The collateral is investment property and the secured party has control pursuant to agreement" before "or the debtor". Specifies state laws to which transaction also subject.

9208: Adds subsection (4): "(4) If the secured party is an organization maintaining branches or branch offices the requests herein provided for shall be sent to the branch or branch office at which the security transaction was entered into or at which the debtor is to make payment of his obligation, and the secured party's statement, unless otherwise specified, shall be deemed to apply only to indebtedness entered into at or payable to such branch or branch office and to any collateral taken by such branch or branch office."

9301: In (1)(c), deletes reference to buyer of farm products in ordinary course of business; (d) adds "and investment property" after "intangibles"; adds to (3) following: "'Lien creditor' does not include a creditor who by filing a notice with the Secretary of State has acquired only an attachment or judgment lien on personal property, or both."

9302: In (1)(b), adds "certificated securities" after "instruments". Adds "or boat" after "vehicle" in (1)(d); Exemption from filing in (1)(e) omitted. Renumbers 1(f), (g) as 1(e), (f) and adds "(g) A security interest in a deposit account. Such a security interest is perfected:

(i) As to a deposit account maintained with the secured party, when the security agreement is executed.

(ii) As to a deposit account not described in subparagraph (i), when notice thereof is given in writing to the organization with whom the deposit account is maintained.

Subsection (h) added: "A security interest in investment property that is perfected without filing under Section 9115 or 9116".

(i) A security interest in or claim in or under any policy of insurance including unearned premiums. Such interest shall be perfected when notice thereof is given in writing to the insurer."

Rewords "(3) The filing of a financing statement otherwise required by this division is not necessary or effective to perfect a security interest in property subject to any of the following:

(a) A statute or treaty of the United States which provides for a national or international registration or a national or international certificate of title or which specifies a place of filing different from that specified in this division for filing of the security interest.

(b) The provisions of the Vehicle Code which require registration of a vehicle or boat, or provisions of the Health and Safety Code which require registration of a mobile home or commercial coach; but during any period in which collateral is inventory, the filing provisions of this division (Chapter 4 (commencing with Section 9401)) apply to a security interest in that collateral.

(c) A certificate of title statute of another jurisdiction under the law of which indication of a security interest on the certificate is required as a condition of perfection (subdivision [2] of Section 9103).

(d) Provisions of the Health and Safety Code which require registration of all interests in approved air contaminant emission reductions (Section 40709 to 40713, inclusive, of the Health and Safety Code)."

9304: (1) adds after first sentence: "A security interest in the rights to proceeds of a written letter of credit can be perfected only by the secured party's taking possession of the letter of credit"; omits "certified securities" after "other than" in parenthesis; in (5)(b) adds "or certificated security" after "instrument".

9305: Omits "letters of credit and advices of credit (subsection (2)(a) of Section 5116)" and "(other than certificated securities)" from first sentence; adds second sentence: "A security interest in the right to proceeds of a written letter of credit may be perfected by the secured party's taking possession of the letter of credit".

9306: (1) adds: "Any payments or distributions made with respect to investment property collateral are proceeds"; (2) substitutes "Except where this division or subdivision (4) of Section 8321" for "Except where this Article"; (3)(c) renumbered (3)(d) and new subsection (c) added: "The original collateral was investment property and the proceeds are identifiable cash proceeds"; (3)(d) adds "or Division 8 (commencing with Section 8101) after "this division".

9307: In (1) deletes exclusion and thus affords protection to person buying farm products from person engaged in farming operations. Omits (2). (3) omits "or more than 45 days after the purchase, whichever first occurs," after "knowledge of the purchase," and omits "and before the expiration of the 45 day period" at end. See also federal legislation protecting purchasers of farm products, 99 Stat. 1354, Section 1324.

9308: cross-reference regarding bona fide purchaser of security is to Section 8302 rather than 8-301.

9309: substitutes "Section 8303" for "8302".

9311: After words "any transfer", substitutes: "but a provision in the security agreement making the transfer constitute a default is valid."

9312: (1) adds: "Section 9115 on security interests in investment property" after "consignments"; omits (2); (4) substitutes "20 days" for "ten days"; (7) omits "Section 8321" and adds "Section 9115 or 9116 on investment property" after "or under".

9313: (1)(b) omits "filed or" preceding "recorded". (4)(a) and (b) replace "the security interest is perfected by a fixture filing" with "a fixture filing covering the fixtures is filed." (4)(c) omits "and before the goods become fixtures the security interest is perfected by any method permitted in this article" at end. (4)(d) omits words following "consumer goods."

9318: (2) substitutes "acquired" for "acquires" before "corresponding rights". (4) Operative Jan. 1, 1990, add "a security interest in chattel paper" after "creation of".

9401: "(1) The proper place to file in order to perfect a security interest is as follows: (a) When the collateral is consumer goods, then in the office of the county recorder in the county of the debtor's residence or if the debtor is not a resident of this state, then in the office of the county recorder of the county in which the goods are kept; (b) When the collateral is crops growing or to be grown, timber to be cut or is minerals or the like (including oil and gas) or accounts subject to subdivision (5) of Section 9103, then in the office where a mortgage on the real estate would be recorded. (c) In all other cases, in the office of the Secretary of State." Adopts first alternative subsection (3). (5) substitutes "notwithstanding subdivision (1)," for "notwithstanding the preceding sentence." Adds subsection (7): "(7) The proper place to file a financing statement filed as a fixture filing is in the office where a mortgage on the real estate would be recorded."

9402: (1) Substitutes "A certified copy of a financing statement or security agreement is sufficient as a financing statement if the original thereof was filed in this state." for official last sentence. (2) adds: "or as a fixture filing covering:" at end of first paragraph. (3) includes line on form for debtor's trade name or style, if any, deletes item [5] of the form and adds "(Describe Real Estate)" to end of item [3] of form. (4) adds ", or by the secured party alone in the case of an amendment pursuant to subdivision (7)" at the end of first sentence. (5) First sentence provides for recording in real estate records. Optional language adopted at end of first sentence. Third sentence added "A financing statement filed as a fixture filing (Section 9313) where the debtor is not a transmitting utility must also recite either that to be filed as a fixture filing or that it covers goods which are or are to become fixtures." (7) substitutes "or an appropriate amendment to the filed financing statement is filed before the acquisition of the collateral by the debtor" for "is filed before the expiration of that time" at the end of the second sentence. (8) adds "A financing statement filed as a fixture filing (Section 9313) where the debtor is not a transmitting utility is not effective if it does not recite that it is to be recorded in the real estate records and either that it is filed as a fixture filing or that it covers goods which are or are to become fixtures." Adds subsections (9) and (10): "(9) A financing statement substantially complying with the requirements of this section creates a security interest only to the extent of the interest

COMMERCIAL CODE . . . *continued*
of the debtor. (10) No person or entity acting for or on behalf of the parties to a financing statement shall incur any liability for the consequences of recording a financing statement in the real estate records, and no action may be brought or maintained against any such person or entity as a result of the recordation."

9403: (1) substitutes "and" for "or" following "fee." In (2) substitutes last three sentences of official text with following three sentences: "Upon such lapse the security interest becomes unperfected unless it is perfected without filing. If the security interest becomes unperfected upon lapse, it is deemed to have been unperfected as against a person who became a purchaser or lien creditor before lapse. Upon lapse of a fixture filing, it is deemed to have been ineffective as against a person who became a purchaser or lien creditor before lapse." (3) substitutes "continued" for "still effective" in second sentence. (3) omits third sentence and substitutes "A continuation statement filed to continue the effectiveness of a financing statement filed as a fixture filing (Section 9313) is not effective unless the following requirements are met: (a) If the debtor did not have an interest of record in the real estate as of the date of the filing of the original statement, the continuation statement shall contain the name of a record owner of the real estate as of the date of the filing of the original statement. (b) The continuation statement shall contain substantially the following statement: 'This continuation statement is filed to continue the effectiveness of a financing statement filed as a fixture filing'; provided, that such statement shall clearly indicate the intent to continue the effectiveness of a financing statement as a fixture filing." In sixth sentence, omits "Unless a statute on disposition of public records provides otherwise," before "the filing officer." Adds new last sentence: "The filing officer shall not destroy a financing statement and related filings as to which he or she has received written notice that there is an action pending relative thereto." (4) substitutes "time" for "hour" in first sentence; adds new last sentence: "The filing officer shall mark each continuation statement with the date and time of filing and shall index the same under the file number of the original financing statement" at the end. (5) reworded: "The uniform fee for filing, indexing and furnishing filing data (subdivision [1] of Section 9407) for an original financing statement, an amendment or a continuation statement shall be twenty dollars ($20) if the statement is in the standard form prescribed by the Secretary of State and otherwise shall be thirty dollars ($30)." (7) reworded "A financing or continuation statement covering collateral described in paragraph (b) of subdivision (1) of Section 9401 or filed as a fixture filing shall be recorded and indexed by the filing officer in the real property index of grantors under the name of the debtor and any owner of record shown on the financing statement. A financing or continuation statement so recorded and indexed and containing a description of real property affected thereby shall constitute constructive notice from the time of its acceptance for recording to any purchaser or encumbrancer of the real property of the security interest in such collateral." Subdivision (8) added, provides that amendments to subdivision (3) shall become operative June 1, 1998. Subdivision (9) added; provides that Section in effect until Jan. 1, 2000.

9403.1: New section: "The county recorder may destroy any index of financing statements, including any amendments, releases, continuations, terminations, assignments, any other document related to an original financing statement, if the last entry in the index is six or more years old."

9403.5: New: "For purposes of Section 9403:

(1) A financing statement becomes effective on the date when filed, other than that portion of the day preceding the time of filing.

(2) The final day of effectiveness of a financing statement or continuation statement is, except as provided in subdivision (3), the same day of the year as the filing of the financing statement, in five-year increments specified in Section 9403. The financing statement or continuation statement is in effect for the entirety of its final day of effectiveness.

(3) If, under subdivision (2), the final day of effectiveness of a financing statement or continuation statement would occur on a Saturday, Sunday, or legal holiday, the effectiveness thereof is extended until the next day that is not a Saturday, Sunday, or legal holiday. If, under subdivision (2), the last day of effectiveness would occur on February 29 in any calendar year that does not include February 29, the final day of effectiveness is February 28.

(4) A continuation statement may be filed at any time on the final day of effectiveness of the financing statement or prior continuation statement.

(5) This section clarifies the meaning of Section 9403. As this section affects lapse and continuation, it shall be applied to all financing and continuation statements, whether filed before or on or after January 1, 1986, so long as the effectiveness of the financing statement has not lapsed prior to that date."

9404: Reworded: "(1) Whenever there is no outstanding secured obligation and no commitment to make advances, incur obligations or otherwise give value, the secured party of record must on written demand by the debtor send the debtor a statement that he or she no longer claims a security interest under the financing statement, which shall be identified by date, names of parties thereto and file number. If the affected secured party of record fails to send such a termination statement within 10 days after proper demand therefor he or she shall be liable to the debtor for all actual damages suffered by the debtor by reason of such failure, and if the failure is in bad faith for a penalty of One Hundred Dollars ($100.00). (2) The filing officer shall mark each such termination statement with the date and time of filing and shall index the same under the name of the debtor and under the file number of the original financing statement. If the filing officer has a microfilm or other photographic record of the financing statement and related filings, the filing officer may remove the originals from the files at any time after receipt of the termination statement and destroy them, or if he or she has no such record, he or she may remove them from his or her files at any time after one year after receipt of the termination statement and destroy them. (3) The uniform fee for filing, indexing and furnishing filing data (subdivision (1) of section 9407) for a termination statement shall be twenty dollars ($20) if the statement is in the standard form prescribed by the Secretary of State and otherwise shall be thirty dollars ($30)." (4) provides that section in effect until Jan. 1, 2000.

9405: Addresses release of security interests rather than assignments of security interests and provides: "(1) A secured party of record may by a writing release his or her security interest in all or a part of the collateral covered by a filed financing statement. A statement of release is sufficient if it is signed by the secured party of record, contains a statement describing the collateral being released, the name and address of the debtor, and the file number of the original financing statement. (2) The filing officer shall mark each such statement with the date and time of filing and index the same under the name of the debtor and under the file number of the original financing statement. (3) The uniform fee for filing, indexing and furnishing filing data (subdivision [1] of section 9407) for a statement of release on a form conforming to standards prescribed by the Secretary of State shall be twenty dollars ($20) or, if such a statement otherwise conforms to the requirements of this section, thirty dollars ($30)." (4) provides that section in effect until Jan. 1, 2000.

9406: Addresses assignments of security interests (covered in Official Text in 9–405) and provides: "(1) If a secured party assigns or transfers his or her security interest in any collateral as to which a financing statement has been filed, a statement of such assignment may be filed. Such statement shall be signed by the secured party, describe the collateral as to which the security interest has been assigned, give the name and mailing address of the assignee or transferee, the name and address of the debtor and the file number of the original financing statement. (2) The filing officer shall mark each such statement of assignment or transfer with the date and time of filing and shall index the same under the name of the debtor and under the file number of the original financing statement. (3) A statement of assignment may be filed at the time of the filing of the financing statement, in which event the filing officer shall first file the financing statement and index the assignment under the name of the debtor and under the file number given the financing statement. An assignment endorsed on the financing statement before it is filed with the filing officer need not be indexed by the filing officer. (4) The uniform fee for filing, indexing and furnishing filing data (subdivision [1] of Section 9407) for a separate statement of assignment on a form conforming to standards prescribed by the Secretary of State shall be twenty dollars ($20) or, if such a statement otherwise conforms to the requirements of this section, thirty dollars ($30). (5) Whenever a continuation statement, an amendment to a financing statement, a termination statement, a statement of release or a statement of assignment signed by one other than the secured party of record is presented for filing it must be acccompanied by a statement of assignment signed by the secured party of record covering the collateral to which such continuation statement, amendment, termination statement, release, or assignment applies. (6) Wherever in this code reference is made to the secured party of record it means the secured party named in the original financing statement or, if a statement of assignment has been filed, or an assignee has been named in the financing statement before it is filed, the assignee or transferee of the security interest in the collateral affected. Any continuation statement, amendment to a financing statement, termination statement, statement of release or statement of assignment signed by one other than the secured party of record as to the collateral affected thereby shall be ineffective for any purpose except as between the parties thereto." (7) provides that section in effect until Jan. 1, 2000.

9407: Text is similar to but not identical to optional Official Text and provides: "(1) If the person filing any financing statement, amendment, termination statement, statement of assignment, continuation statement, or statement of release, furnishes the filing officer a copy thereof, the filing officer shall upon request note upon the copy of a financing statement the file number and upon the copy of any of such statements the date and time of the filing of the original and deliver or send the copy to such person. (2) Upon request of any person, the filing officer shall issue his or her certificate showing whether there is on file on the date and time stated therein, any presently effective financing statement naming a particular debtor and any statement of assignment thereof and if there is, giving the date and time of filing of each such statement and the names and addresses of each secured party therein. Upon request, the filing officer shall furnish a copy of any filed financing statement or related filings. If the filing officer is a county recorder, the fee for a certificate for each name searched shall be set by the filing officer in an amount that covers actual costs, but that, in no event, exceeds fifteen dollars ($15), and the fee for copies shall be in accordance with Section 27366 of the Government Code. If the filing officer is the Secretary of State, the certificate shall be issued as part of a combined certificate pursuant to Section 9409 of the Commercial Code, and the fee for the certificate and copies shall be in accordance with that section. (3) Fees to be charged by the Secretary of State for daily or less frequent summaries or compilations of filings, which he or she may furnish, shall be sufficient to pay at least the actual cost of such service. Fees shall be determined by the Secretary of State with the approval of the Department of Finance. Such summaries or compilations may be in the form of microfilm copies or such other form as may be provided for the required information." (4) provides that amendments to subdivision (2) become operative June 1, 1998.

9407.1: New section: Relates to recordation in lieu of filing and use of microphotography by filing officer and provides: "In lieu of filing all financing statements, termination statements, partial releases, assignments, or other related papers falling under this code, the filing officer may record those papers. The filing officer may employ a system of microphotography, optical disk, or reproduction by other techniques which do not permit additions, deletions, or changes to the original document. All film used in the microphotography process shall comply with minimum standards of quality approved by the United States Bureau of Standards and the American National Standards Institute. A true copy of the microfilm, optical disk, or other storage medium shall be kept in a safe and separate place for security purposes. A reproduction of any document filed, recorded, stored, or retained on microfile, optical disk, or by other technology pursuant to this section shall be admissible in any court as the original itself."

9407.2: New section: Provides: "Should the filing officer choose to record rather than file all financing statements and related papers, he shall mark each financing statement with a consecutive file number. All other related papers affecting such financing statement shall thereafter bear the same file number. He shall index the same under the name of the debtor (or assignor or seller) in a separate index or in his general index, and under the file number of the original statement."

See note at head of Digest as to 1998 legislation covered.

See Topical Index in front part of this volume.

CA – 14

COMMERCIAL CODE . . . *continued*

9407.3 New section: Provides: "Upon recording the financing statement or other related papers, the originals or copy of the same shall be returned to the parties entitled thereto."

9409: New section: "(a) Upon request of any person, Secretary of State shall issue a combined certificate showing information as to financing statements as specified in Section 9407 of this code, information as to state tax liens as specified in Section 7226 of Government Code, information as to attachment liens as specified in Section 488.375 and 488.405 of Code of Civil Procedure, information as to judgment liens as specified in Section 697.580 of Code of Civil Procedure, and information as to federal liens as specified in Section 2103 of Code of Civil Procedure. (b) Fee for such a combined certificate is twelve dollars ($12). (c) Copies of financing statements and lien notices listed in certificate and copies of any related filings must be provided by Secretary of State together with certificate at no additional fee. (d) Copies of financing statements, lien notices, and related filings requested separately from certificate must be provided by Secretary of State at a fee established by Secretary of State not in excess of fee that could have been charged for certificate and copies together if the latter had been or could have been requested. (e) Fees established by subdivisions (b), (c) and (d) become operational only after Uniform Commercial Code Program Optical Disk System has been installed and is functioning. Until then, fee for certificate must be eleven dollars ($11), and fee for copies must be one dollar ($1) for the first page and fifty cents ($0.50) for each page thereafter.

9501: Adds after "collateral" in (3) (a) "and deal with the debtors liability for any deficiency"; substitutes for (4) following:

"(4) If an obligation secured by a security interest in personal property or fixtures (Section 9313[1][a]) is also secured by an interest in real property or an estate therein:

(a) The secured party may do any of the following:

(i) Proceed, in any sequence, (1) in accordance with the secured party's rights and remedies in respect of real property as to the real property security, and (2) in accordance with this chapter as to the personal property or fixtures.

(ii) Proceed, in any sequence, as to both some or all of the real property and some or all of the personal property or fixtures in accordance with the secured party's rights and remedies in respect of the real property, by including the portion of the personal property or fixtures selected by the secured party in the judicial or nonjudicial foreclosure of the real property in accordance with the procedures applicable to real property. In proceeding under this subparagraph, (A) no provision of this chapter other than this subparagraph, subparagraph (iii) of paragraph (d), and paragraphs (g) and (h) shall apply to any aspect of the foreclosure; (B) a power of sale under the deed of trust or mortgage shall be exercisable with respect to both the real property and the personal property or fixtures being sold, and the sale may be conducted by the mortgagee under the mortgage or by the trustee under the deed of trust. The secured party shall not be deemed to have elected irrevocably to proceed as to both real property and personal property or fixtures as provided in this subparagraph with respect to any particular property, unless and until that particular property has been actually disposed of pursuant to a unified sale (judicial or nonjudicial) conducted in accordance with the procedures applicable to real property, and then only as to the property so sold.

(iii) Proceed, in any sequence, as to part of the personal property or fixtures as provided in subparagraph (i), and as to other of the personal property or fixtures as provided in subparagraph (ii).

(b) (i) Except as otherwise provided in paragraph (c), provisions and limitations of any law respecting real property and obligations secured by an interest in real property or an estate therein, including, but not limited to, Section 726 of the Code of Civil Procedure, provisions regarding acceleration or reinstatement of obligations secured by an interest in real property, or an estate therein, prohibitions against deficiency judgments, limitations on deficiency judgments based on the value of the collateral, limitations on the right to proceed as to collateral, and requirements that creditor resort either first or at all to its security do not in any way apply to either (1) any personal property or fixtures other than personal property or fixtures as to which the secured party has proceeded or is proceeding under subparagraph (ii) of paragraph (a), or (2) the obligation.

(ii) Pursuant to, but without limiting subparagraph (i), in the event that an obligation secured by personal property or fixtures would otherwise become unenforceable by reason of Section 726 of the Code of Civil Procedure or any requirement that a creditor resort first to its security, then, notwithstanding that section or any similar requirement, the obligation shall nevertheless remain enforceable to the full extent necessary to permit a secured party to proceed against personal property or fixtures securing the obligation in accordance with the secured party's rights and remedies as permitted under this chapter.

(c) (i) Paragraph (b) does not limit the application of Section 580b of the Code of Civil Procedure.

(ii) If the secured party commences an action, as defined in Section 22 of the Code of Civil Procedure, and the action seeks a monetary judgment on the debt paragraph (b) does not prevent the debtor's assertion of any right to require the inclusion in the action of any interest in real property or an estate therein securing the debt. If a monetary judgment on the debt is entered in the action, paragraph (b) does not prevent the debtor's assertion of the subsequent unenforceability of the encumbrance on any interest in real property or an estate therein securing the debt and not included in the action.

(iii) Nothing in paragraph (b) shall be construed to excuse compliance with Section 2924c of the Civil Code as a prerequisite to the nonjudicial sale of real property, but that section has no application to the right of a secured party to proceed as to personal property or fixtures except, and then only to the extent that, the secured party is proceeding as to personal property or fixtures in a unified sale as provided in subparagraph (ii) of paragraph (a).

(iv) Paragraph (b) does not deprive the debtor of the protection of Section 580d of the Code of Civil Procedure against a deficiency judgment following the sale of the real property collateral pursuant to a power of sale in a deed of trust or mortgage.

(v) Paragraph (b) shall not affect, nor shall it determine the applicability or inapplicability of, any law respecting real property or obligations secured in whole or in part by real property with respect to a loan or a credit sale made to any individual primarily for personal, family, or household purposes.

(vi) Paragraph (b) does not deprive the debtor of the protection of Section 580a of the Code of Civil Procedure following a sale of real property collateral.

(vii) If the secured party violates any statute or rule of law that requires a creditor who holds an obligation secured by an interest in real property or an estate therein to resort first to its security before resorting to any property of the debtor that does not secure the obligation, paragraph (b) does not prevent the debtor's assertion of any right to require correction of the violation, any right of the secured party to correct the violation, or the debtor's assertion of the subsequent unenforceability of the encumbrance on any interest in real property or an estate therein securing the obligation, or the debtor's assertion of the subsequent unenforceability of the obligation except to the extent that the obligation is preserved by subparagraph (ii) of paragraph (b).

(d) If the secured party realizes proceeds from the disposition of collateral that is personal property or fixtures, the following provisions shall apply:

(i) The disposition of the collateral, the realization of the proceeds, the application of the proceeds, or any one or more of the foregoing shall not operate to cure any nonmonetary default.

(ii) The disposition of the collateral, the realization of the proceeds, the application of the proceeds, or any one or more of the foregoing shall not operate to cure any monetary default (although the application of the proceeds shall, to the extent of those proceeds, satisfy the secured obligation) so as to affect in any way the secured party's rights and remedies under this chapter with respect to any remaining personal property or fixtures collateral.

(iii) All proceeds so realized shall be applied by the secured party to the secured obligation in accordance with the agreement of the parties and applicable law.

(e) An action by the secured party utilizing any available judicial procedure, as provided in subdivision (1), shall in no way be affected by omission of a prayer for a monetary judgment on the debt. Notwithstanding Section 726 of the Code of Civil Procedure, any prohibition against splitting causes of action or any other statute or rule of law, a judicial action which neither seeks nor results in a monetary judgment on the debt shall not preclude a subsequent action seeking a monetary judgment on the debt or any other relief.

(f) As used in this subdivision, 'monetary judgment on the debt' means a judgment for the recovery from the debtor of all or part of the principal amount of the secured obligation, including, for purposes of this subdivision, contractual interest thereon. 'Monetary judgment on the debt' does not include a judgment which provides only for other relief (whether or not that other relief is secured by the collateral), such as one or more forms of nonmonetary relief, and monetary relief ancillary to any of the foregoing, such as attorneys' fees and costs incurred in seeking the relief.

(g) If a secured party fails to comply with the procedures applicable to real property in proceeding as to both real and personal property under subparagraph (ii) of paragraph (a) a purchaser for value of any interest in the real property at judicial or nonjudicial foreclosure proceedings conducted pursuant to subparagraph (ii) of paragraph (a) takes that interest free from any claim or interest of another person, or any defect in title, based upon that noncompliance, unless:

(i) The purchaser is the secured party and the failure to comply with this chapter occurred other than in good faith; or

(ii) The purchaser is other than the secured party and at the time of sale of the real property at that foreclosure the purchaser had actual knowledge of the failure to comply with this chapter and that the noncompliance occurred other than in good faith.

Even if the purchaser at the foreclosure sale does not take his or her interest free of claims, interests, or title defects based upon that noncompliance with this chapter, a subsequent purchaser for value who acquires an interest in that real property from the purchaser at that foreclosure takes that interest free from any claim or interest of another person, or any defect in title, based upon that noncompliance, unless at the time of acquiring the interest the subsequent purchaser has knowledge of the failure to comply with this chapter and that the noncompliance occurred other than in good faith.

(h) If a secured party proceeds by way of a unified sale under subparagraph (ii) of paragraph (a), then, for purposes of applying Section 580a of subdivision (b) of Section 726 of the Code of Civil Procedure to any such unified sale, the personal property or fixtures included in the unified sale shall be deemed to be included in the 'real property or other interest sold,' as that term is used in Section 580a or subdivision (b) of Section 726 of the Code of Civil Procedure.

(5) When a secured party has reduced his or her claim to judgment the lien of any levy which may be made upon his or her collateral by virtue of any execution based upon the judgment shall relate back to the date of the perfection of the security interest in the collateral. A judicial sale, pursuant to that execution, is a foreclosure of the security interest by judicial procedure within the meaning of this section, and the secured party may purchase at the sale and thereafter hold the collateral free of any other requirements of this division."

Adds new subsection: "(6) this section shall be repealed on Jan. 1, 1996."

9502: (2) divided into subsections; first sentence of (2) designated (a). Remainder of subsection reads as follows: "(b) if the security agreement secures an indebtedness, the secured party must account to the debtor for any surplus.

(c) If the security agreement secures an indebtedness, the debtor is liable for any deficiency unless otherwise agreed, but only (i) if the secured party in collection pursuant to this section has proceeded in a commercially reasonable manner, or (ii) as provided in paragraph (d).

(d) If the secured party in collecting pursuant to this section has provided proper notice pursuant to subdivision (3) of Section 9504, but has not proceeded in a commercially reasonable manner, the debtor is liable, subject to paragraph (e), for any deficiency only if the balance of the indebtedness immediately before the collection exceeds the amount which the secured party establishes would have been realized had

COMMERCIAL CODE . . . *continued*
the secured party in collecting pursuant to this section proceeded in a commercially reasonable manner, and the liability is limited to the excess.

(e) Notwithstanding paragraph (d), if the secured party in collecting pursuant to this section has not proceeded in a commercially reasonable manner, and if the transaction was entered into by the debtor primarily for personal, family, or household purposes or if the amount of the indebtedness immediately before the collection was one hundred thousand dollars ($100,000) or less, then the debtor is not liable for any deficiency.

(f) Upon entry of a final judgment that the debtor is not liable for a deficiency by reason or either paragraph (d) or paragraph (e), the secured party may neither obtain a deficiency judgment not retain a security interest in any other collateral of the debtor that secured the indebtedness for which the debtor is no longer liable.

(g) To the extent, subsequent to a collection which does not satisfy the condition set forth in clause (i) of paragraph (c), or subsequent to a disposition which does not satisfy any one or more of the conditions set forth in clause (i) of paragraph (b) of subdivision (2) of Section 9504, the secured party collects pursuant to this section on other collateral securing the same indebtedness, the debtor may, to the extent that he is no longer liable for a deficiency judgment by reason of paragraph (d) or paragraph (e), or by reason of paragraph (c) or paragraph (d) of subdivision (2) of Section 9504, recover the proceeds realized from those subsequent collections, as well as any damages to which the debtor may be entitled if the subsequent collection is itself noncomplying or otherwise wrongful. Except for secured transactions entered by the debtor primarily for personal, family, or household purposes, neither the subsequent collections nor the exercise of any other remedy by the secured party subsequent to a noncomplying collection or disposition shall be deemed tortious or otherwise wrongful based, in whole or part, on the fact that it occurred subsequent to a noncomplying collection or disposition.

(h) If the underlying transaction was a sale of accounts or chattel paper, the debtor is entitled to any surplus or is liable for any deficiency only if the security agreement so provides. The provisions of subdivision (b) of Section 701.040 of the Code of Civil Procedure relating to the payment of proceeds apply only if the security agreement provides that the debtor is entitled to any surplus.

(i) Nothing herein shall deprive the debtor of any right to recover damages from the secured party under subdivision (1) of Section 9507 or to offset any such damages against any claim by the secured party for a deficiency, or by any right or remedy to which the debtor may be entitled under any other law. However, except in the case of any secured party which has willfully failed to proceed in a commercially reasonable manner in collection pursuant to this section, or in the case of a debtor who entered the secured transaction primarily for personal, family, or household purposes, any damages recoverable by the debtor shall be reduced by the amount of any deficiency that would have resulted had the secured party in collecting pursuant to this section proceeded in conformity with the condition set forth in clause (i) of paragraph (c) regardless whether or not the debtor is liable for the deficiency under paragraph (c) or (d)."

Subsection (3) added, reading "(3) This section shall be repealed on January 1, 1996".

9504: (1)(c) adds to end of first sentence: "and to the satisfaction of any subordinate attachment lien or execution lien pursuant to subdivision (b) of Section 701.040 of the Code of Civil Procedure if notice of the levy of attachment or execution is received before distribution of the proceeds is completed." (2) deviates from Official Text substantially, reads

(2)(a) If the security interest secures an indebtedness, the secured party must account to the debtor for any surplus except as provided in Section 701.040 of the Code of Civil Procedure.

(b) If the security interest secures an indebtedness, the debtor is liable for any deficiency unless otherwise agreed or otherwise provided in the Retail Installment Sales Act, and in particular Section 1812.5 of the Civil Code or any other statute, but only (i) if the debtor was given notice, if and as required by subdivision (3), or the disposition of the collateral in accordance with subdivision (3), and the disposition of the collateral by the secured party pursuant to this section was conducted in good faith and in a commercially reasonable manner, or (ii) except for secured transactions entered by a debtor primarily for personal, family, or household purposes, as provided in paragraph (c).

(c) If the secured party has provided notice to the debtor pursuant to subdivision (3), if so required, but has not proceeded in a commercially reasonable manner in the disposition of the collateral, the debtor is liable, subject to paragraphs (b) and (d), for any deficiency only if the balance of the indebtedness immediately before the disposition exceeds the amount that the secured party establishes would have been realized had the disposition of the collateral by the secured party pursuant to this section been conducted in conformity with the conditions set forth in clause (i) of paragraph (b), and the liability is limited to the excess. This paragraph does not apply to secured transactions entered by a debtor primarily for personal, family, or household purposes.

(d) Notwithstanding paragraph (c), if any one or more of the conditions set forth in clause (i) of paragraph (b) are not proved by the secured party to be satisfied with respect to the disposition, then the debtor is not liable for any deficiency if either:

(i) All of the collateral immediately before the disposition was consumer goods and the amount of the indebtedness immediately before the disposition was one hundred thousand dollars ($100,000) or less.

(ii) The amount of the indebtedness immediately before the disposition was fifty thousand dollars ($50,000) or less.

(e) Upon entry of a final judgment that the debtor is not liable for a deficiency by reason of either paragraph (c) or paragraph (d), the secured party may neither obtain a deficiency judgment nor retain a security interest in any other collateral of the debtor that secured the indebtedness for which the debtor is no longer liable.

(f) To the extent, subsequent to a disposition that does not satisfy any one or more of the conditions set forth in clause (i) of paragraph (b), or subsequent to a collection that does not satisfy the condition set forth in clause (i) of paragraph (c) of subdivision (2) of Section 9502, the secured party disposes pursuant to this section of other collateral securing the same indebtedness, the debtor may, to the extent he or she is no longer liable for a deficiency judgment by reason of paragraph (c) or paragraph (d), or by reason of paragraph (d) or paragraph (e) of subdivision (2) of Section 9502, recover the proceeds realized from the subsequent dispositions, as well as any damages to which the debtor may be entitled if the subsequent disposition is itself noncomplying or otherwise wrongful. Except for secured transactions entered into by debtor primarily for personal, family, or household purposes, neither the subsequent dispositions nor the exercise of any other remedy by the secured party subsequent to a noncomplying disposition or collection shall be deemed tortious or otherwise wrongful based, in whole or in part, on the fact that it occurred subsequent to a noncomplying disposition or collection.

(g) If the underlying transaction was a sale of accounts or chattel paper, the debtor is entitled to any surplus or is liable for any deficiency only if the security agreement so provides. The provisions of subdivision (b) of Section 701.040 of the Code of Civil Procedure relating to the payment of proceeds and the liability of the secured party apply only if the security agreement provides that the debtor is entitled to any surplus.

(h) Nothing herein shall deprive the debtor of any right to recover damages from the secured party under subdivision (1) of Section 9507 or to offset any such damages against any claim by the secured party for a deficiency, or of any right or remedy to which the debtor may be entitled under any other law; provided, however, that, except in the case of any secured party that has willfully failed to conduct the disposition of collateral in good faith and in a commercially reasonable manner or in the case of a debtor who entered the secured transaction primarily for personal, family, or household purposes, any damages recoverable by the debtor shall be reduced by the amount of any deficiency that would have resulted had the disposition of the collateral by the secured party been conducted in conformity with the conditions set forth in clause (i) of paragraph (b) regardless whether or not the debtor is liable for the deficiency under paragraph (b) or (c)."

Subsection (3) substantially deviates from Official Text with respect to requirements for realization upon collateral. Provides "(3) A sale or lease of collateral may be as a unit or in parcels, at wholesale or retail and at any time and place and on any terms, provided the secured party acts in good faith and in a commercially reasonable manner. Unless collateral is perishable or threatens to decline speedily in value or is of a type customarily sold on a recognized market, the secured party must give to the debtor, if he or she has not signed after default a statement renouncing or modifying his or her rights to notification of sale, and to any other person who has a security interest in the collateral and who has filed with the secured party a written request for notice giving his or her address (before that secured party sends his or her notification to the debtor or before debtor's renunciation of his or her rights), a notice in writing of the time and place of any public sale or of the time on or after which any private sale or other intended disposition is to be made. Such notice must be delivered personally or be deposited in the United States mail, postage prepaid, addressed to the debtor at his or her address as set forth in the financing statement or as set forth in the security agreement or at such other address as may have been furnished to the secured party in writing for this purpose, or, if no address has been so set forth or furnished, at his or her last known address, and to any other secured party at the address set forth in his or her request for notice, at least five days before the date fixed for any public sale or before the day on or after which any private sale or other disposition is to be made. Notice of the time and place of a public sale shall also be given at least five days before the date of sale by publication once in a newspaper of general circulation published in the county in which the sale is to be held or in case no newspaper of general circulation is published in the county in which the sale is to be held, in a newspaper of general circulation published in the county in this state that (1) is contiguous to the county in which the sale is to be held and (2) has, by comparison with all similarly contiguous counties, the highest population based upon total county population as determined by the most recent federal decennial census published by the Bureau of the Census. Any public sale shall be held in the county or place specified in the security agreement, or if no county or place is specific in the security agreement, in the county in which the collateral or any part thereof is located or in the county in which the debtor has his or her residence or chief place of business, or in the county in which the secured party has his or her residence or a place of business if the debtor does not have a residence or chief place of business within this state. If the collateral is located outside of the state or has been removed from the state, a public sale may be held in the locality in which the collateral is located. Any public sale may be postponed from time to time by public announcement at the time and place last scheduled for the sale. The secured party may buy at any public sale and if the collateral is customarily sold in a recognized market or is the subject of widely or regularly distributed standard price quotations he or she may buy at private sale. Any sale of which notice is delivered or mailed and published as herein provided and that is held as herein provided is a public sale."

Subsection (b) added, reading "(b) This section shall be repealed on January 1, 1999."

9505: (1) inserts "or within a reasonable time after such 90-day period" after "takes possession".

9507: (1) Last sentence providing for specified minimum penalty omitted if collateral is consumer goods.

9508: New section which reads as follows: "No renunciation or modification by the debtor of any of his rights under this chapter as to consumer goods shall be valid or enforceable unless the renunciation or modification is in consideration of a waiver by the secured party of any right to deficiency on the debt."

Former Division 10 (Effective Date and Repealer), corresponding to Article 10 of Official Text, redesignated Division 13 as of Jan. 1, 1990. California enactment of Official Text Article 2A (Personal Property Leases) designated as Division 10.

Material Variations from Article 2A of 1990 Official Text are listed below (references are to California Division 10 numbers where subsections are designated [a], [b], etc. and subdivisions [1], [2], etc.):

10103: (a)(5) omits "if the total payments to be made under the lease contract, excluding payments for options to renew or buy, do not exceed $_____". (a)(7)(C)(iii) omits "or" at end. (a)(7)(C)(iv) omits "if the lease is not a consumer lease" at beginning.

See note at head of Digest as to 1998 legislation covered.

See Topical Index in front part of this volume.

CA – 16

COMMERCIAL CODE . . . *continued*

10104: (a)(1) reads: "(1) Certificate of title statute of this state, including the provisions of the Vehicle Code that required registration of a vehicle or boat and provisions of the Health and Safety Code that require registration of a mobilehome or commercial coach." (a)(3) reworded: "(3) Consumer law of this state, both decisional and statutory, including, to the extent that they apply to a consumer lease transaction, Chapter 5 (commencing with Section 17200) of Part 2 of Division 7 of the Business and Professions Code, Chapter 1 (commencing with Section 17500) of Part 3 of Division 7 of the Business and Professions Code, and Part 4 (commencing with Section 1725) of Division 3 of the Civil Code." (b) reads "(b) In case of conflict between this division, other than Section 10105, subdivision (c) of Section 10304, and subdivision (c) of Section 10305, and a law referred to in subdivision (a), that law controls."

10106: (b) omits second "or" adding "," after "thereafter"; adds "or in which the lease is executed by the lessee," after "to be used". (b) substitutes "a forum that would not otherwise have jurisdiction over the lessee "with" in a county other than the county in which the lessee in fact signed the lease, the county in which the lessee resides at the commencement of the action, the county in which the lessee resided at the time the lease contract became enforceable, or the county in which the goods are permanently stored".

10108: Official Text section on unconscionability omitted.

10109: Official Text section on option to accelerate at will omitted.

10201: (a)(1) adds "In a lease contract that is not a consumer lease," at beginning.

10203: Official Text section providing that seals inoperative omitted.

10216: Official Text section on third party beneficiaries of express and implied warranties omitted.

10221: (2) omits "that is not a consumer lease" after "finance lease".

10307: (d) omits "or more than 45 days after the lease contract becomes enforceable, whichever first occurs," and "and before the expiration of the 45-day period."

10308: (a) adds "or void" after "fraudulent" both places. (b) omits (b) "becomes enforceable, not in current course of trade but in satisfaction of or as security for a preexisting claim for money, security, or the like, and".

10309: (a)(2) omits "filed or". (4)(a) and (b), and (5)(a)-(c) of Official Text combined in California Code into (d)(1)-(6). (d) reads "The interest of a lessor of fixtures has priority over a conflicting interest of an encumbrancer or owner of the real estate if:". (d)(1) substitutes "a fixture filing covering the fixtures is filed before the goods become fixtures or within 20 days thereafter" for "the interest of the lessor is perfected by a fixture filing before the goods become fixtures or within ten days thereafter" and omits last "or". (d)(2) substitutes "A fixture filing covering the fixtures is filed" for "the interest of the lessor is perfected by a fixture filing". (d)(3) omits "and before the goods become fixtures the lease contract is enforceable; or". (d)(4) omits "or". (9) of Official Text omitted.

10402: (a) adds ", other than a consumer lease," before "with respect to". Subsection (b) added: "(b) The rights and remedies of the parties to a consumer lease in connection with a repudiation of that lease shall be determined under other laws, and this section shall not affect the applicability or interpretation of those laws."

10406: (a)(2) omits "that is not a consumer lease".

10504: (a) substitutes "subject to and in compliance with Section 1671 of the Civil Code" for "but only at an amount or by a formula that is reasonable in light of the anticipated harm caused by the default or other act or omission." (b) omits "or such provision is an exclusive or limited remedy that circumstances cause to fail of its essential purpose".

10506: (a) adds "In a lease contract that is not a consumer lease" at beginning of second sentence.

10516: (b) adds "other than a consumer lease in which the supplier assisted in the preparation of the lease contract or participated in negotiating the terms of the lease contract with the lessor," after "finance lease" in second sentence. (c)(2) omits "except in the case of a consumer lease,". Adds subdivision (f): "(f) Subdivision (c) shall not apply to a consumer lease."

10517: (b) omits "Except in the case of a finance lease that is not a consumer lease," at beginning.

10529: (a)(1) omits "within a commercially reasonable time". (a)(2) adds "where the lessor has never delivered the goods or has taken possession of them or the lessee has tendered them to the lessor" after "contract".

10600: Transition provision for Division 10 added: "This division shall apply to all lease contracts that are first made or that first become effective between the parties on or after January 1, 1990. This division shall not apply to any lease contract first made or that first became effective between the parties prior to January 1, 1990, or to any extension, amendment, modification, renewal, or supplement of or to the lease contract, unless the parties thereto specifically agree in writing that the lease contract, as extended, amended, modified, renewed, or supplemented, shall be governed by this division."

New Division 11 governing funds transfers (wholesale wire transfers) which is equivalent of new Article 4A of 1989 Official Text added; applies to fund transfers in which originator's payment order is transmitted on or after Jan. 1, 1991.

Material deviations from Official Text as follows (references are to California Division 11 numbers):

11103(a)(1): Adds "all of the following apply" after "if" at end of opening sentence.

Forms.—See end of this Digest.

See also topics: Banks and Banking, Bills and Notes, Brokers, Carriers, Consumer Protection, subhead Consumer Warranties, Contracts, Factors, Frauds, Statute of, Sales, Securities, Warehousemen; categories Business Organizations, topic Corporations; Civil Actions and Procedure, topic Limitation of Actions; Debtor and Creditor, topics Assignments, Fraudulent Sales and Conveyances, Liens, Pledges; Documents and Records, topics Records, Seals; Mortgages, topic Chattel Mortgages.

CONDITIONAL SALES:

See topic Sales.

CONSIGNMENTS:

See topic Factors.

CONSUMER PROTECTION:

Consumer Affairs Act (Bus. & Prof. C. 300 et seq.) created Department of Consumer Affairs. Basic purpose of Act is to promote and protect interests of consumer. Department includes Consumer Advisory Council, Licensing Boards and Division of Consumer Services. Director has power and duty to receive complaints from consumers concerning: (a) Unfair methods of competition and unfair or deceptive acts or practices in conduct of trade or commerce, (b) production, distribution, sale and lease of goods and services which may endanger public health, (c) violations of code relating to licensed businesses and professions. Director has authority to: (a) Propose legislation, (b) undertake research, (c) intervene in proceedings to represent consumer interests, (d) hold public hearings, (e) create and develop consumer education programs and other similar functions. Licensing functions of Department cover wide range of professions and vocations.

Financial Privacy.—California Right to Financial Privacy Act (Govt. C. 7460 et seq.) provides that no officer, employee or agent of state or local agency as defined, or any department thereof may request or obtain from financial institution, as defined, copies of financial records or information from such records on any customer except in specified circumstances and by specified procedures and limits use of financial records authorized to be received. Violation is misdemeanor and injunctive relief may be sought. Specified persons, corporations and licensees are required to authorize certain state agencies to examine their financial records as condition of doing business, obtaining license, or exercising privileges of business or profession.

Personal Information.—Information Practices Act of 1977 (C. C. 1798 et seq.) declares that all individuals have right to privacy in connection with information pertaining to them and that this right is being threatened by indiscriminate maintenance, collection and dissemination of personal information and by increased use of computers and other technology. Act establishes Office of Information Practices; requires each state agency maintaining system of records containing personal information to file with Office of Information Practices notice concerning records maintained by agency; requires state agencies to maintain personal information only if necessary to accomplish constitutional or statutory or federally mandated purpose and to collect information directly from individual who is subject thereof if practicable; prohibits disclosure of personal information except where consistent with several specified conditions; provides for individual inquiries and access to records and for individual's right to request amendment in personal information contained in such records and provides for individual's right to bring civil action against agency under certain conditions; specifies penalties for willful violations and prevents agencies from changing or destroying information to avoid compliance with Act.

Confidentiality of Medical Information.—Confidentiality of Medical Information Act (C. C. 56 et seq.) provides specific requirements, exemptions and sanctions concerning dissemination of individual's medical records to outside sources to prevent widespread release of sensitive information in field of health care.

Promotional Techniques, Deceptive Practices.—Unfair competition is defined in Bus. & Prof. C. 17200. It has been held that it includes not only deceptive and fraudulent conduct, but any unlawful act or practice. (Bus. & Prof. C. 17200; 38 C.3d 913, 216 C.Rptr. 345, 702 P.2d 503). Injunctive relief and civil penalties for unfair competition may be sought by Attorney General, district attorneys and other designated prosecuting attorneys. (Bus. & Prof. C. 17201 et seq.). Any person in interest may bring action for injunctive relief or restitution under Bus. & Prof. C. 17203.

Under Veh. C. 28050 et seq. tampering with odometer on motor vehicle is unlawful.

Bus. & Prof. C. 17500 et seq. deals broadly with prohibition of false and misleading advertising and contains several detailed provisions relating to particular abuses. Injunctive relief and civil penalties for violation of these provisions may be sought by Attorney General and District Attorney, or other designated prosecuting attorneys. Any person may seek injunctive relief or restitution under Bus. & Prof. C. 17535. Violations of these provisions are included in definition of unfair competition under Bus. & Prof. C. 17200. Label may be advertisement for purposes of this legislation. (58 Ops. Atty. Gen. 297).

Consumer Legal Remedies Act (C. C. 1750 et seq.) was enacted to secure protection to consumer for acts designated in C. C. 1770 as illegal when undertaken in transactions intended to result or which do result in sale or lease of goods or services to consumer. Act provides for recovery of damages as well as injunctive relief and punitive damages; provision is also made for class actions. Act contains specific notice provisions which must be complied with prior to actions for damages.

Discount buying industry is regulated under C. C. 1812.100 et seq. Statute is designed to provide protection to consumer from fraudulent discount buying operations. Discount buying organizations as defined in statute must maintain minimum bonds, make certain disclosures prior to entering into contracts, satisfy certain requirements with respect to form and content of contracts, make goods available within specified period of time and grant to buyer cancelation rights. Remedies include treble damages and reasonable attorney's fees against discount organization.

Lay-away practices governed by C. C. 1749 through 1749.4. Gift certificates governed by C. C. 1749.5.

"Bait and switch" techniques are unlawful under Bus. & Prof. C. §12024.6, providing that it is unlawful to advertise, solicit or represent product for sale or purchase if solicitation is intended to entice consumer into transaction different from transaction originally represented.

Solicitation by invoice prohibited unless document contains specified statement that it is solicitation not bill. Violation constitutes misdemeanor. Violator is liable for civil penalties and person damaged can recover three times sum solicited. (C. C. 1716).

See note at head of Digest as to 1998 legislation covered.

See Topical Index in front part of this volume.

CA – 17

CONSUMER PROTECTION . . . *continued*

Unconscionable Contract.—Language of Commercial Code §2302, 1962 Official Text has been enacted as C. C. 1670.5.

Reassignments of retail installment contracts secured by mortgage prohibited by specified financial institutions when such right is reserved to financial institution as assignee upon default of party to contract. (Bus. & Prof. C. 17350-17351).

Transactions Off Trade Premises.—Persons conducting mail order or catalog business in California, including by catalog, telephone, radio, television or other telecommunication device, involving sale of consumer goods are regulated by provisions of Bus. & Prof. C. 17538 et seq.

Home solicitation contracts and offers are regulated by provisions of C. C. 1689.5 et seq., Bus. & Prof. C. 17500.3, and by Contractors State License Law (Bus. & Prof. C. 7000 et seq.) to extent that sales or installations of home improvement goods or services as defined in Bus. & Prof. C. §7151 are involved.

Specific Regulations Particular Industries.—Legislative standards have been enacted regulating activities of swimming pool contractors (Bus. & Prof. C. 7165 et seq.), sale of fine prints (C. C. 1740 et seq.), contracts for commercial dance studio lessons (C. C. 1812.50 et seq.), dating and weight loss services (C. C. 1694 et seq.), electronic shopping services (C. C. 1789 et seq.), activities of travel promoters (Bus. & Prof. C. 17540-17540.16), charitable solicitations (Bus. & Prof. C. 17510 et seq.), telephonic sellers (Bus. & Prof. C. 17511 et seq.), electronic and appliance repair dealers (Bus. & Prof. C. 9800 et seq.) and conduct of automotive repair dealers (Bus. & Prof. C. 9880 et seq.) which latter Act establishes in Department of Consumer Affairs, Bureau of Automotive Repair.

Retail Installment Sales Act (C. C. 1801 et seq.), cited as the "Unruh Act", applies to credit sales of consumer goods and services by retail seller to retail buyer. Finance charge limitations are imposed. Revolving, or open-end, agreements as well as closed end contracts are covered. Form and content of retail installment contract or account are prescribed and specific disclosure requirements are imposed, subject to Federal Truth-in-Lending Act and Regulation Z. Also contains provisions regarding disclosure and finance charge limitations with respect to add-on sales. On default, holder of contract or account may retake goods or recover judgment for balance due. Deficiency judgments are specifically prohibited. Violation of statute is misdemeanor. Holder of contract or account barred from recovery of finance or similar charges if statute not complied with and holder has knowledge, unless violation is non-willful and is rectified in accordance with C. C. 1812.8. Treble damages recoverable for violation of add-on sales provisions. Specific provision is made for application of Act to transactions involving California and another state where specified contacts exist or occur in California. (C. C. 1802.19).

Areias-Robbins Retail Installment Account Full Disclosure Act of 1986 (C. C. 1810.20 et seq.) requires certain disclosures in any application form or preapproved written solicitation for credit card issued in connection with retail installment account which is mailed on or after Oct. 1, 1987.

Consumer Credit Contracts Act (C. C. 1799.90 et seq.) requires notice in English and Spanish regarding guarantee obligations under consumer credit contracts to be delivered to and acknowledged by debtors who do not receive money, property or services covered by contract, where signature of more than one person is required on such contract (unless persons are married).

Automobile Sales Finance Act (C. C. 2981 et seq.) governs sale of any motor vehicle which is bought for personal or family use pursuant to conditional sales contract. Form and content of any contract are prescribed, required disclosures as to sale and credit terms are set forth, including disclosures required by Regulation Z. Limitations on finance charges provided. Buyer is given certain rights and remedies for failure of seller to comply with statute. Provides for holder's remedies upon buyer's default.

Motor Vehicle Leasing Act (C. C. 2985.7 et seq.) contains detailed provisions relating to lease of motor vehicles for personal or family purposes. Prescribes form and content of lease contract and disclosure requirements including notice that there is no "cooling off" period. (C. C. 2985.8). Provides for civil actions and enforcement by Department of Motor Vehicles. Lessor-retailers (as defined in Veh. C. 373) who make retail sales of vehicles must be licensed by Department of Motor Vehicles. (Veh. C. 11600 et seq.).

The Credit Services Act of 1984 (C. C. 1789.10 et seq.) regulates persons who, with respect to extension of credit by others, sell, provide, or perform, or represent that they can, for consideration, improve or assist with improving buyer's credit record, history or rating, or obtain, or assist with obtaining, extension of credit for buyer. Requires provision of information statement, containing specified disclosures, to customer prior to execution of contract. Prescribes form and content of contract between credit services organization and customer and provides five-day cancellation right to customer. Requires specified disclosures to customers. Provides for recovery by customer of actual and punitive damages, plus attorney's fees and costs. Attorney General, district attorneys and city attorneys may prosecute misdemeanor actions and institute equity procedures for violations.

Consumer Credit Reporting Agencies Act (C. C. 1785.1 et seq.) is designed to give consumer access to files kept by Consumer Credit Reporting Agencies, to limit information which may be disclosed in consumer credit report, to limit persons to whom consumer credit reports can be provided, to require such agencies to expunge certain types of information contained in files after specified periods of time, to provide consumer opportunity to dispute credit information contained in files and to provide remedies for violations of statute.

Investigative Consumer Reporting Agencies, which gather noncredit personal information regarding consumers for provision to third parties to be used for employment or insurance purposes, receive similar regulation. (C. C. 1786 et seq.).

Holden Credit Denial Disclosure Act of 1976 (C. C. 1787.1 et seq.) requires that creditor inform consumer of creditor's decision whether or not to extend credit within 30 days after receipt of application, and, if credit is denied, creditor must provide statement of reasons for denial or inform consumer of his right to request statement of reasons from creditor and of address from which statement may be obtained. Statement must include both credit and non-credit information that provides basis for denial.

Credit card issuers are regulated by Song-Beverly Credit Card Act of 1971. (C. C. 1747 et seq.). Statute defines standards with respect to issuance and use of credit cards and rights and liabilities which may arise between issuer and card holder. C.C. 1747.8 prohibits requiring identification information on credit card transaction form. C.C. 1748.1 prohibits surcharge for use of credit card in lieu of other means of payment, but permits discount for non-credit card payment. Issuer of credit card must give card holder 30 days written notice of intention to cancel credit card with specified exceptions. (C. C. 1747.85). Areias-Robbins Credit Card Full Disclosure Act of 1986 requires certain disclosures to be included in any application form or preapproved written solicitation for open-end credit card account to be used for consumer purposes which is mailed on or after Oct. 1, 1987. (C. C. 1748.10 et seq.). Issuer of credit card must give notice to cardholder that cardholder can prohibit release of defined marketing information regarding cardholder. (C. C. 1748.12). Issuers of charge cards (as defined in C. C. 1748.21) are subject to similar disclosure requirements with respect to any charge card application form or preapproved written solicitation for charge card mailed on or after Oct. 1, 1987, pursuant to Areias-Robbins Charge Card Full Disclosure Act of 1986. (C. C. 1748.20 et seq.).

Several provisions of Financial Code require that banks, savings and loan associations and credit unions make disclosures as to charges, interest rates and dividends to depositors, including persons having interest in any account at any such institution. See also topic Banks and Banking.

Consumer Warranties.—Song-Beverly Consumer Warranty Act (C. C. 1790 et seq.) goes considerably beyond protection set forth in warranty sections of Uniform Commercial Code in placing upon manufacturers and retailers special duties and obligations with respect to fulfillment of warranty obligations and also creates special implied warranties of merchantability and of fitness in favor of purchaser of consumer goods, their duration generally coextensive with express warranty accompanying goods. Contains some provisions governing form of express warranties. There are special provisions on motor vehicle warranties. (C. C. 1795.90 et seq.). Persons installing, servicing or repairing new or used consumer goods must do so in workmanlike manner. (C. C. 1796 et seq.).

Grey Market Goods.—New act requires specific disclosures regarding warranties on grey market goods. (C. C. 1797.8 et seq.).

Consumer Debt Collection.—The Robbins-Rosenthal Fair Debt Collection Practices Act (C. C. 1788 et seq.) prohibits persons who regularly collect consumer debts, on behalf of themselves or others, from engaging in unfair or deceptive acts or practices, including use of threats, misrepresentations, harassment and obscene language. Prohibits communication by debt collector with debtor's employer, family and others except under certain circumstances. (C. C. 1788.12). Act also prohibits debtors from applying for credit without intention to pay or supplying false information (C. C. 1788.20), and using account after termination (C. C. 1788.22). Debtor is required to notify creditor of change of name, address or employment (C. C. 1788.21), and loss of credit card or similar instrument if creditor has disclosed these requirements to debtor in writing. (C. C. 1788.22). Act allows recovery by debtor for violations of actual damages, penalty not less than $100 or greater than $1,000, and attorney's fees and costs (C. C. 1788.30).

Cemetery Authorities.—Various provisions in Business and Professions and Health and Safety Codes prescribe form of contracts of cemetery authorities to provide plot, niche or vault or merchandise or service. Cemetery authorities must file report of endowment care funds annually to Cemetery Board, which regulates cemeteries, and such reports are available for public inspection. (Bus. & Prof. C. 9600 et seq.).

Labels and Branding.—The Sherman Food, Drug, and Cosmetic Law regulates labeling and branding of food, drugs, devices and cosmetics to protect purchasers from deception and misrepresentation. (H. & S.C. 109875 et seq.). Bus. & Prof. C. 12001 et seq. contain variety of provisions relating to labeling of weights and measures. Fair Packaging and Labeling Act (Bus. & Prof. C. 12601 et seq.) is designed to require disclosure of quantity, contents and source of consumer commodities and protect against deceptively designed containers. Marketing of poisons and hazardous substances is also regulated under California Hazardous Substances Act. (H. & S.C. 108100 et seq.).

Credit Transactions—Marital Status.—No person, regardless of marital status, may be denied credit or offered less favorable terms if such person's earnings and property over which he or she has management and control are such that person of opposite sex with same earnings and property would receive credit. Discrimination based on marital status alone prohibited. Requires credit information concerning spouses and former spouses having joint accounts to be separately maintained by credit agencies. Provides for recovery of actual and punitive damages, injunctive relief, attorney's fees and costs. (C. C. 1812.30-1812.35).

Automatic Dialing—Announcing Devices.—Telephone corporations must approve connection of such devices to telephone lines. Called party must consent to listen to prerecorded message. (Pub. Utils. C. 2871-2876).

Seller Assisted Marketing Plans.—Sellers must make specified disclosures to purchasers, file disclosure statement with Secretary of State, include specified provisions in contracts, refrain from misleading practices, grant to purchasers three day cancellation right. Violations subject to criminal and civil penalties. Provides for recovery of actual and punitive damages. (C. C. 1812.200-1812.221). See also topic Sales.

Organic Foods Act of 1990.—H. & S.C. 26569.20-26569.50 specifies standards for sale of food as organic, establishes record keeping certification and inspection provisions, and makes violations of provisions subject to injunctive relief, and civil penalties.

See note at head of Digest as to 1998 legislation covered.

See Topical Index in front part of this volume.

CONSUMER PROTECTION . . . *continued*

Aircraft Repair.—Bus. & Prof. C. 9793 provides that person having repairs or service on noncommercial aircraft has right on request to written estimate or maximum charge which may not be exceeded without his consent.

Plain Language.—No "Plain Language" statute.

Mobile Homes.—The Mobile Homes-Manufactured Housing Act of 1980 (H. & S.C. 18000 et seq.) governs construction, sale, registration and titling of mobile homes. Mobile home warranties covered by C. C. 1797 et seq. Permit required for dwelling use. (H. & S.C. 18613). Mobile home park construction and operation subject to permit requirements of H. & S.C. 18200 et seq. Tenants' rights are protected by statute. (C. C. 798 et seq.).

Membership Camping Contracts.—C. C. 1812.300 regulates for profit membership camping operators, terms of contracts, required disclosures.

Creditor Remedies: Disability Insurance.—Creditors who directly arrange sale or receive compensation for sale of credit disability insurance may not invoke creditors' remedies because of debtor's nonpayment of sums due during disability until reasonable time has passed for disability insurance claim to be filed, verified and processed. Specified disclosures by creditor required when insurance is sold and by insurer when claim forms sent. (C. C. 1812.400 et seq.).

Athletic Facilities.—Contracts for health studio services are regulated by C. C. 1812.80 et. seq. New C. C. 1812.97 requires warning regarding sale, use or exchange of anabolic steroids, testosterone and human growth hormone be included in contracts by health facilities and be posted after June 1, 1990.

CONTRACTS:

Contracts governed by common law as modified and interpreted by C.C. 1549-1701. Uniform Commercial Code has been adopted. (1963, c. 819). See topic Commercial Code, subhead Material Variations from 1990 Official Text.

Breach of implied covenant of good faith and fair dealing may give rise to action in tort as well as contract in insurance contracts (50 C.2d 654, 328 P.2d 198), and under certain circumstances, in other commercial contracts (36 C.3d 752, 686 P.2d 1158, 206 C. Rptr. 354). Covenant of good faith and fair dealing applies to employment contracts, but breach of covenant does not give rise to tort damages. (47 C.3d 654, 765 P.2d 373, 254 C. Rptr. 211). There is covenant of good faith and fair dealing implied by law in every contract governed by California law. (34 C.2d 559, 212 P.2d 878).

Seal does not replace consideration required for contract. (C.C. 1629).

See also topics Consumer Protection, Frauds, Statute of; categories Civil Actions and Procedure, topic Accord and Satisfaction; Documents and Records, topic Seals; Family, topic Infants.

FACTORS:

Uniform Commercial Code has been adopted. (1963, c. 819). See topic Commercial Code.

Factor Defined.—Factor is agent employed, as independent calling, by another to sell property over which he is given possession and control or is authorized to receive payment therefor. (C. C. 2026).

Authority of Factor.—Factor has ostensible authority to deal with property of his principal as his own in transactions with persons not having notice of actual ownership. (C. C. 2369).

In addition to authority of agents in general factor has actual authority from his principal, unless specially restricted: (1) To insure property consigned to him uninsured; (2) to sell on credit anything entrusted to him for sale, except such things as it is contrary to usage to sell on credit; but not to pledge, mortgage, or barter same; and (3) to delegate his authority to his partner or servant, but not to any person in independent employment. (C. C. 2368). Factor must obey instructions from his principal although, if principal forbids sales at market price, factor, upon notice to principal stating time and place of sale, may, for his reimbursement, proceed as pledgee to make such sales. (C. C. 2027).

Lien.—Factor has general lien, dependent on possession, for all that is due him as such, upon all articles entrusted to him by same principal. (C. C. 3053). No requirement that notice of lien be filed or recorded. But see category Debtor and Creditor, topic Liens, subhead Lien on Merchandise.

Consignment Agreements.—Except to extent that Com'l. C. §2326 applicable, no provision for filing or recording consignment agreement in order to protect rights of consignor.

Sales on Credit.—Factor may sell consigned property on such credit as usual but may not extend agreed terms of credit. (C. C. 2028).

Guaranty Commissions.—If factor charges principal with guaranty commission upon sale, he assumes absolutely to pay price when it falls due, as if it was his own debt. He does not thereby assume further responsibility for safe remittance of proceeds. (C. C. 2029). Such liability on guaranty of sales or remittance of proceeds cannot be avoided by factor without consent of principal. (C. C. 2030).

FRANCHISES:

Franchise as defined in Corp. C. 31005 is (a) contract or agreement, either express or implied, whether oral or written, between two or more persons by which: (1) franchisee is granted right to engage in business of offering, selling or distributing goods or services under marketing plan or system prescribed in substantial part by franchisor; and (2) operation of franchisee's business pursuant to such plan or system is substantially associated with franchisor's trademark, service mark, trade name, logotype, advertising or other commercial symbol designating franchisor or its affiliate; and (3) franchisee is required to pay, directly or indirectly, franchise fee. (b) Franchise is also following: (1) any contractual agreement between petroleum corporation or distributor and gasoline dealer, or between petroleum corporation and distributor, under which petroleum distributor or gasoline dealer is granted right to use trademark, trade name, service mark, or other identifying symbol or name owned by other party to agreement, or any agreement between petroleum corporation or distributor and gasoline dealer, or between petroleum corporation and distributor, under which petroleum distributor or gasoline dealer is granted right to occupy premises owned, leased, or controlled by other party to agreement, for purposes of engaging in retail sale of petroleum and other products of other party to agreement; (2) any contract between refiner and petroleum distributor, between refiner and petroleum retailer, between petroleum distributor and another petroleum distributor, or between petroleum distributor and petroleum retailer, under which refiner or petroleum distributor authorizes or permits petroleum retailer or petroleum distributor to use, in connection with sale, consignment, or distribution of gasoline, diesel, gasohol, or aviation fuel, trademark which is owned or controlled by such refiner or by refiner which supplies fuel to petroleum distributor which authorizes or permits such use. (c) Franchise does not include nonprofit organization operated as cooperative by and for independent retailers which wholesale goods and services primarily to its members. However, such organizations must satisfy additional statutory criteria to be awarded exemption.

Regulation of Offers and Sales of Franchises.—(Corp. C. 31000-31157). California law mandates registration and pre-sale disclosure of franchises, as described below:

Registration of Offers and Sales of Franchises.—It is unlawful to offer or sell franchise in California unless franchise proposed to be offered is registered with Commissioner of Corporations or offer and sale is exempted by statute or regulation of Commissioner. (Corp. C. 31110, 31100—31105). Registration application must be in form of Uniform Franchise Registration Application. (10 C.C.R. 310.111, 310.114.1). Included in application must be prospectus, known as "Uniform Franchise Offering Circular" or "UFOC", referred to below.

Pre-sale Disclosure.—It is unlawful to sell any franchise in California which is subject to registration without first providing to prospective franchisee, at least ten business days prior to execution by prospective franchisee of any binding franchise or other agreement, or at least ten business days prior to receipt of any consideration, whichever occurs first, copy of offering circular, together with copy of all proposed agreements relating to sale of franchise. (Corp. C. 31119). Offering Circular, or "UFOC", must contain information required by Uniform Franchise Registration Application, as amended by North American Securities Administrators Association, Inc., on Nov. 21, 1986. (Corp. C. 31114; 10 C.C.R. 310.114.1). UFOC prescribes information concerning franchisor, controlling persons, franchises being offered, and relevant historical information. Franchisor's audited financial statements, prepared in accordance with generally accepted accounting principles, must be included in UFOC. (Corp. C. 31111). These financial statements must refer to balance sheet as of date within 90 days prior to date of application, and profit and loss statements for each of three fiscal years preceding date of balance sheet and for period, if any, between close of last fiscal year and date of balance sheet. Balance sheet as of date within 90 days prior to date of application need not be audited. However, if it is not audited, audited balance sheet as of end of franchisor's most recent fiscal year must be filed in addition. In extraordinary cases Commissioner may temporarily waive requirement for audited statements if statements have been prepared by independent certified public accountant or public accountant. (10 C.C.R. 310.111.2).

Modification of Franchise.—It is unlawful to solicit agreement of franchisee to proposed material modification of existing franchise without first delivering to franchisee written disclosure, which has been previously registered with Commissioner of Corporations, in form prescribed by Commissioner, either five business days prior to execution of any binding agreement by franchisee to such modification or containing statement that franchisee may, by written notice mailed or delivered to franchisor or specified agent within not less than five business days following execution of such agreement, rescind such agreement to material modification. (Corp. C. 31125). Exemption from requirements in Corp. C. 31110 et seq. if: (1) modification connected to resolution of bona fide dispute between franchisee and franchisor or resolution of franchisee default and (2) franchisee receives written modification at least five business days prior to execution of agreement provided agreement not executed within 12 months after date of franchise agreement and modification does not waive any right of franchisee under Bus. & Prof. C. 20000 et seq., but modification may include general release of all claims by party to modification and (3) modification is not applied on franchise systemwide basis at time it becomes binding. (Corp. C. 31125[c][1]-[3]). Application for registration of material modification must conform to model in 10 C.C.R. 310.125.

Exemptions.—Exemption from both registration and disclosure requirements of California law is available by statute under following circumstances: (1) transaction relating to bank credit card plans (Corp. C. 31103); and (2) offer and sale of franchise by petroleum corporation or distributor which meets certain experience criteria and other conditions (Corp. C. 31104).

Exemption from registration and disclosure requirements in Corp. C 31110 et seq. also available for offer and sale of franchise by franchisor which satisfies certain minimum net worth and business activity standards and which files with Commissioner notice of exemption and pays prescribed fee prior to offer or sale of franchise during any calendar year in which one or more franchises is sold. (Corp. C. 31101). This exemption, however, does require limited disclosure. (Corp. C. 31101[c]).

Exemption from registration, but not from disclosure, is available by statute for offer or sale of franchise by franchisee for his own account if sale not effected by or through franchisor. (Corp. C. 31102).

Transactions designated by Commissioner or not comprehended within purposes of franchise law may be made exempt from any and all statutory registration and disclosure requirements. By rule of Commissioner following are exempt from both registration and disclosure: (1) offer or sale of franchise subject to registration solely because franchise required to pay fee of $100 or less each year (10 C.C.R. 310.011); and (2) offer or sale of franchise subject to registration solely because franchise purchases or rents business equipment (10 C.C.R. 310.011.1). Commission rules exempt three types of franchise transactions from registration only: (1) offer or sale of subsidiary of company which satisfies minimum net worth requirements of Corp. C. 31101 (10

See note at head of Digest as to 1998 legislation covered.

See Topical Index in front part of this volume.

CA – 19

FRANCHISES ... *continued*

C.C.R. 310.100); (2) negotiated sales meeting specified criteria (10 C.C.R. 310.100.2); and (3) offer or sale of franchise to resident of foreign state, territory, or country who is neither domiciled in California to knowledge of seller nor actually present in California, and if sale of such franchise is not in violation of any law of foreign state, territory or country concerned or of law of U.S. (10 C.C.R. 310.100.1).

Changes, Renewal.—Franchisor must promptly notify Commissioner in writing by application to amend registration, of any material change in information contained in original registration. (Corp. C. 31123). In addition, registration is normally valid for period of one year (unless Commissioner specifies different period) (Corp. C. 31120) and may be renewed for additional one year periods by submitting registration renewal statement no later than 15 business days prior to expiration of registration period (Corp. C. 31121).

Advertising.—No franchise advertising may be published in California offering franchise subject to registration requirements of California law unless copy of advertisement has been filed with Commissioner of Corporations at least three business days prior to first publication, or unless advertisement exempted by rule of Commissioner. (Corp. C. 31156).

Regulation of Relationship Between Franchisors and Franchisees.—California statutes (Bus. & Prof. C. 20000-20043 and Corp. C. 31220) regulate certain substantive aspects of relationship between franchisor and its franchisees, as described below:

Termination of Franchises.—No franchisor may terminate franchise prior to expiration of its term, except for good cause. "Good cause" includes, but is not limited to, failure of franchisee to comply with any lawful requirement of franchise agreement after being given notice thereof and reasonable opportunity, which in no event need be more than 30 days, to cure failure. (Bus. & Prof. C. 20020). Statute also enumerates 11 circumstances, occurrence of which justifies immediate notice of termination of franchise without opportunity to cure. (Bus. & Prof. C. 20021). Grounds for immediate termination without opportunity to cure include: Bankruptcy, abandonment of franchise, mutual written agreement, material misrepresentations by franchisee in connection with purchase of franchise, failure to correct compliance with laws applicable to operation of franchise, repeated contract noncompliance, seizure of franchised business by government official, or foreclosure by creditor, conviction of felony or other criminal misconduct by franchisee relevant to operation of franchise, failure to cure payment default within five days after written notice, and reasonable determination by franchisor that continued operation of franchise by franchisee will result in imminent danger to public health or safety.

Nonrenewal (Bus. & Prof. C. 20025).—No franchisor may fail to renew franchise unless such franchisor provides franchisee at least 180 days prior written notice of its intention not to renew and either (1) gives franchisee opportunity during 180 days prior to expiration to sell his business to purchaser meeting franchisor's then current requirements for granting new franchises, or if it is not then granting new franchises, then current requirement for granting renewal franchises; or (2) refusal to renew is not for purpose of converting franchisee's business premises to company-owned operation and franchisors agree not to seek to enforce any noncompetition covenant or franchise; or (3) termination of franchise would be permitted under prohibitions described in preceding paragraph; or (4) parties agree in writing not to renew; or (5) franchisor withdraws from geographic market served by franchisee and certain other standards are met.

Succession (Bus. & Prof. C. 20027).—No franchisor may deny surviving spouse, heirs, or estate of deceased franchisee or majority shareholder of franchisee opportunity to participate in ownership of franchise under valid franchise agreement for reasonable time after death of franchisee or majority shareholder of corporate franchisee. During that time survivor must either satisfy then current qualifications for purchase of franchisee or sell, transfer or assign franchise to person who does so. Franchisor may exercise right of first refusal. Section does not apply to certain agreements made before 1984.

Notice of Termination (Bus. & Prof. C. 20030).—All notices of termination or nonrenewal required by statute must be in writing, sent by registered, certified or other receipted mail, delivered by telegram or personally delivered to franchisee; and contain statement of intent to terminate or not renew franchise with reasons and effective date of termination or nonrenewal or expiration.

Franchisee Associations (Corp. C. 31220).—It is unlawful (but not crime) for any franchisor, directly or indirectly, to restrict or inhibit right of franchisees to join trade associations or to prohibit right of free association among franchisees.

Uniform Franchise and Business Opportunities Act, promulgated in Aug., 1987 by National Conference of Commissioners on Uniform State Laws (NCCUSL) has not been adopted in California.

FRAUDS, STATUTE OF:

Uniform Commercial Code has been adopted (1963, c. 819), effective Jan. 1, 1965. See topic Commercial Code.

Estate in real property, other than estate at will or for term not exceeding one year, can be transferred only by operation of law, or by instrument in writing, subscribed by party disposing of same, or by party's agent thereunto authorized by writing. (C. C. 1091). (See also C.C.P. 1971.)

No evidence is admissible to charge person upon representation as to another's credit, unless such representation or memorandum thereof be in writing, and either subscribed by or in handwriting of party to be charged. (C.C.P. 1974).

Contracts.—Following are invalid, unless same or some note or memorandum thereof be in writing and subscribed by party to be charged, or by his agent: (1) agreement that by its terms is not to be performed within a year from making thereof; (2) special promise to answer for debt, default or miscarriage of another; except in cases specified by C.C. 2794; (3) agreement for leasing for longer period than one year, or for sale of real property, or of interest therein; (4) agreement authorizing or employing agent, broker or any other person to purchase or sell real estate or to lease real estate for longer than one year, or to procure, introduce or find purchaser or seller

of real estate or lessee or lessor of real estate where such lease is for longer period than one year, for compensation or commission; (5) agreement which by its terms is not to be performed during lifetime of promisor; (6) agreement by purchaser of real property to pay indebtedness secured by mortgage or deed of trust on property purchased unless assumption is specifically provided for in conveyance of property; (7) contract, promise, undertaking or commitment by person engaged in business of lending money or extending credit for loan or extension of credit exceeding $100,000 and not primarily for personal, family, or household purposes (C.C. 1624); however, C.C. 1624 does not apply to Division 10 (Personal Property Leases) of Com'l Code; (8) personal representative's special promise to answer in damages or pay decedent's debts out of own estate (Prob. C. 9604); (9) oral contract modifying written contract if contract as modified falls into category of C.C. 1624 (C.C. 1698).

Contracts of Sale of Personal Property, Goods, Securities.—Uniform Commercial Code governs. (Com'l. C. 1206, 2201, 2209, 2326). See topic Commercial Code, subhead Material Variations from 1990 Official Text.

Oral Contracts, Enforcement of If Fraud Involved.—Contract required by law to be in writing but if not set in writing due to fraud of party, enforceable against fraudulent party. (C.C. 1623).

Part performance may remove agreement from statute. (163 C.A.2d 384, 329 P.2d 599).

Agent's authority to enter into contract required to be in writing must itself be in writing. (C.C. 2309).

Debts.—Revival of debt barred by statute of limitations must be in writing and signed by person charged. (C.C.P. 360).

INTEREST:

See also topic Banks and Banking.

Maximum Rate.—For loans made primarily for personal, family or household purposes rate shall not exceed 10% per annum. For loans not intended primarily for above purposes, which by definition do not include loans primarily for purchase, construction or improvement of real property, maximum allowable interest rate is higher of: (a) 10% or (b) 5% plus discount rate charged by Federal Reserve Bank of San Francisco on 25th day of month preceding earlier of: (i) date of execution of loan agreement or promissory note, or (ii) date loan is actually made. (Const. Art. XV, §1). Foregoing restrictions do not apply to loans made by building and loan associations, industrial loan companies, credit unions, pawnbrokers or personal property brokers, banks, agricultural cooperatives, incorporated insurer, or to any loan made or arranged by licensed real estate broker. As to these classes, legislature may prescribe maximum rates of interest which can be charged.

Following are also exempt from constitutional interest rate limitations by specific legislation: Incorporated insurer (Ins. C. 1100.1), licensed broker-dealers (Corp. C. 25211.5), indebtedness issued pursuant to Corporate Securities Law (Corp. C. 25116), licensed Business and Industrial Development Corp. (Finan. C. 31410), California state bank, or other state bank that maintains branch office in California, acting in fiduciary capacity as trustee (Finan. C. 1504), foreign (other nation) banks (with some special qualifications) (Finan. C. 1716), bank holding companies and their nonbank subsidiaries (Finan. C. 3707), state and federal savings and loan associations, savings and loan holding companies, and their respective service corporation subsidiaries (Finan. C. 7675).

Because of broad class of lenders exempt from California usury law, federal preemption of state usury ceilings in certain loan transactions (pursuant to Federal Depository Institutions Deregulation and Monetary Control Act of 1980) has minimal impact in California.

Rate of interest on judgments if set by legislature not more than 10%. (Const. Art. XV, §1).

Small Loans.—Under Finance Lenders Law (Finan. C. 22000-22780), persons licensed thereunder may charge no more on unpaid balances than 2¹/₂% per month on first $225; 2% per month on next $675; 1¹/₂% per month on next $750; and 1% per month on remaining balance in excess of $1,650; or, alternatively, greater of: (i) 1.6% per month on unpaid principal balance, or (ii) rate determined by formula adjusted by rate on Federal Reserve Bank of San Francisco advances to member banks (Finan. C. 22303, 22304). Administrative fee of lesser of $50 or 5% of loan of not more than $2,500 or of up to $75 on loan in excess of $2,500 also permitted. (Finan. C. 22305).

Credit union interest rate on loans shall be determined by board of directors from time to time. Interest rate on existing loans may be decreased but not increased by board. (Finan. C. 15000). Industrial loan companies may charge, on unpaid principal balances, up to 2% per month on unpaid balance up to and including $1,000, and 1% on unpaid balance over $1,000, or rate not exceeding 1.6% per month on unpaid principal balance; or alternatively, at rate not exceeding ⁵/₆ of 1% per month plus percentage per month equal to ¹/₁₂ of annual rate prevailing on 25th day of second month of calendar quarter immediately preceding calendar quarter during which loan is made. Charges calculated on unpaid balance of any loan. (Finan. C. 18212; 18212.1). No pawnbroker may charge more on unpaid principal balance than 2¹/₂% per month on first $225, 2% per month on next $675, 1¹/₂% per month on next $750, and 1% on unpaid balance over $1,650 (Finan. C. 21200). However, different schedule pertains to loans of less than $2,500 for not more than 90 days. (Finan. C. 21200.5).

Usury results in forfeiture of all interest, and three times amount of usurious interest paid may be recovered; may also be felony if willful. (1919, p. lxxxiii; G. L. Act 3757; 52 C.2d 834, 345 P.2d 457). Agreement for usurious interest is separable from promise to pay principal sum and does not render latter illegal. (29 C. 267). No cause of action for usury exists for any loan made before Nov. 6, 1979, if loan would not have been usurious under amended usury law found in Const., Art. XV, §1. (109 C. A. 3d 141, 167 C.Rptr. 62).

Retail installment sales contracts governed by special provisions. (C. C. 1801-1812.20).

See note at head of Digest as to 1998 legislation covered.

See Topical Index in front part of this volume.

LICENSES, BUSINESS AND PROFESSIONAL:

Licenses are required to conduct large number of business and professional activities in state. Department of Commerce is required to compile comprehensive listing of all state licenses, permits and registrations required of any person desiring to operate business enterprise in state (Govt. C. 15367), except for permits pertaining to "development projects" (Govt. C. 65925-65963.1). Department of Commerce publishes handbook available to public which sets forth this comprehensive listing.

Following is abbreviated list of some of more common business and professional activities that are licensed: Life insurance agents (Ins. C. 1622, 1631) and insurance brokers (Ins. C. 1623, 1631); dealers of agricultural produce (Fd. & Agric. C. 56181-56196); sellers of alcoholic beverages (Bus. & Prof. C. 23300-23455); clinical laboratories (Bus. & Prof. C. 1260-75); contractors (Bus. & Prof. C. 7065-7077); health care facilities (H. & S.C. 1250-1300); mobile home dealers (H. & S.C. 18024-18024.6); outdoor advertising (Bus. & Prof. C. 5301); pest control (Fd. & Agric. C. 11701); real estate brokers (Bus. & Prof. C. 10150) or salesmen (Bus. & Prof. C. 10151); and yacht and ship brokers (Harb. & Nav. C. 719).

Following is partial list of those professions and businesses licensed under Business and Professions Code: Chiropractors, dentistry, medical doctors, midwifery, physical therapy, nursing, pharmacy, accounting, architecture, attorneys, professional engineers, geologists, land surveyors and automobile repair.

There may also be separate business licensing requirements imposed by local municipality in which business transacts business. (Govt. C. 37101).

Collection agencies must be licensed by Chief of Collection and Investigative Services and employees must be registered. (Bus. & Prof. C. 6870). Chief of Agency may refuse to issue licenses under certain circumstances (Bus. & Prof. C. 6906), and licenses may be revoked under certain circumstances and procedures (Bus. & Prof. C. 6925, et seq.).

See topic Consumer Protection.

MONOPOLIES, RESTRAINT OF TRADE AND COMPETITION:

All statutory provisions are found in Part 2, Division 7, of Business and Professions Code.

Contracts in Restraint of Trade.—Every contract whereby one is restrained from exercising lawful profession, trade or business is, to that extent, void (Bus. & Prof. C. 16600), except that seller of goodwill of business, or shareholder of corporation disposing of all his shares, or shareholder of corporation which sells (a) substantially all its operating assets and goodwill of corporation, (b) substantially all operating assets and goodwill of division or subsidiary, or (c) all shares of subsidiary, may agree with buyer to refrain from carrying on similar business within specified counties or cities, or parts thereof, in which business sold has been carried on, so long as buyer, or person deriving title to goodwill or shares from him carries on like business therein (Bus. & Prof. C. 16601), and on dissolution of partnership or limited liability company members may agree not to carry on similar business in specified counties or cities so long as any member or person deriving title or goodwill therefrom carries on like business therein (Bus. & Prof. C. 16602, 16602.5).

Prohibited Restraints of Competition.—Combination of capital, skill or acts of two or more persons, partnerships, corporations or associations to restrict trade or commerce, limit or reduce production or increase price, prevent competition or fix prices is an illegal trust. (Bus. & Prof. C. 16720). Contracts prohibiting use of or dealing in competing goods are likewise unlawful. (Bus. & Prof. C. 16727). Such combination subjects domestic corporations and associations to forfeiture of charter rights, franchises and privileges (Bus. & Prof. C. 16752), and foreign corporations or associations to revocation of license to do business in state (Bus. & Prof. C. 16753). There is also liability to fine and imprisonment (Bus. & Prof. C. 16755), civil penalty, treble damages, injunctive relief, reasonable attorney's fees, and costs to any person injured regardless whether injured person dealt directly or indirectly with defendant (Bus. & Prof. C. 16750). Mandatory injunction may issue to preserve competition. (Bus. & Prof. C. 16754.5).

Act does not apply to combinations of laborers or agreements setting price of labor (Bus. & Prof. C. 16703) or forbid agreements or combinations designed to promote, encourage or increase competition or which are in furtherance of trade (Bus. & Prof. C. 16725).

Unfair Practices Act (Bus. & Prof. C., 17000 et seq.) prohibits creation of locality price discriminations not based on differences in cost of manufacture, sale, delivery or transportation and sales at less than cost with intent to destroy competition. There is liability to fine and imprisonment as well as civil damages and injunctions.

Express Discrimination Policy of Third Party.—Exclusion of any person from business transaction on basis of express written discrimination policy imposed by third party prohibited. (Bus. & Prof. C. 16721). Unlawful to grant or accept any letter of credit (or similar document) or enter into any contract for exchange of goods or services when document contains any provision which requires any person to discriminate against or to certify that such person has not dealt with any other person on basis of sex, race, color, religion, ancestry or national origin or on basis of person's lawful business association or refuse to grant or accept any letter of credit (or similar document) or refuse to enter into any contract for exchange of goods or services because it does not contain discrimination provision. (Bus. & Prof. C. 16721.5). Adjudication of violation of discrimination policy provisions referred to, may result in substantial fines and potential prison terms, and may result in revocation of corporate license to do business in California for foreign corporation. (Bus. & Prof. C. 16753, 16755[a]). Express discrimination policy is to be interpreted so as not to conflict with federal law or regulations with respect to foreign or interstate commerce not preempted by Export Administration Act of 1969. (Bus. & Prof. C. 16721.6).

Enforcement.—In addition to private persons, Attorney General and district attorney of county are authorized to prosecute actions for restraint of trade on behalf of state, public agency or political subdivision; district attorneys expenses may be paid from proceeds of action or in amount equal to 10% of such proceeds, whichever is greater. (Bus. & Prof. C. 16750, 16753, 16754, 16755 & 16760). Any action for restraint of trade must be commenced within four years after cause of action accrued. (Bus. & Prof. C. 16750.1).

Resale Price Agreements.—See category Intellectual Property, topic Trademarks and Tradenames. Fair Trade Act repealed. (1975, cc. 402, 429).

Federal Authority Applies.—Federal decisions under Sherman Act are authoritative in cases under California law. (20 C. 3d 367, 143 C. Rptr. 1, 572 P.2d 1142; 212 C.A.2d 618, 28 C. Rptr. 190).

NEGOTIABLE INSTRUMENTS:

See topic Bills and Notes.

RESTRAINT OF TRADE:

See topic Monopolies, Restraint of Trade and Competition.

SALES:

Uniform Commercial Code has been adopted. (1963, c. 819, Com'l. C. 2101-2801). See topic Commercial Code, subhead Material Variations from 1990 Official Text. Division 2 of Commercial Code applies to transactions in goods. (Com'l. C. 2102). Code does not apply to real estate transactions or to insurance or construction contracts. While generally applicable to consumer transactions, Com'l C. provides that in transactions subject also to Retail Installment Sales Act (C. C. 1801 et seq.), Automobile Sale Finance Act (C. C. 2981 et seq.), Industrial Loan Law (Finan. C. 18000 et seq.), Pawn Broker Law (Finan. C. 21000 et seq.), Personal Property Brokers Law, (Finan. C. 22000 et seq.), provisions of such statutes control in case of conflict.

Bills of Sale.—Transfer may be made without writing in every case in which a writing is not expressly required by statute. (C. C. 1052). Sale is defined as passing of title from seller to buyer for price. (Com'l. C. 2106). Subject to Division 2 on sales and Division 9 on secured transactions of Com'l. Code, title to goods passes from seller to buyer in any manner and on any conditions explicitly agreed upon by parties. (Com'l. C. 2401[1]). "Present sale" is defined as sale which is accomplished by making of contract. (Com'l. C. 2106[1]). Thus, except as specifically provided by statute, written bill of sale of personal property is not required. Parties to sale transaction frequently agree to and require use of bill of sale. Interest in ship can be transferred only by operation of law or by written instrument subscribed by party making transfer or by his agent. (C. C. 1135). Transfers of title to nonnegotiable instruments and to accounts receivable and chattel paper transferred as part of sale of business are deemed perfected against third persons when such property rights have been endorsed or assigned in writing and, in case of such instruments or chattel paper, delivered to transferee. (C.C. 955). Similarly, transfer of general intangible consisting of any right to payment and transfer of any accounts or chattel paper excluded from coverage of Division 9 of Commercial Code is deemed perfected against third persons upon execution and delivery to transferee of assignment in writing. (C.C. 955.1).

Products Liability.—

Strict Liability in Tort.—Manufacturers, retailers, and distributors strictly liable in tort for marketing defective article, knowing it will be used without inspection, which causes injury. (59 C.2d 57, 377 P.2d 897, 27 C.Rptr. 697; 61 C.2d 256, 391 P.2d 168, 37 C.Rptr. 896). Occasional sellers exempted. (265 C.A.2d 228, 71 C.Rptr. 306). Second-hand dealers held not strictly liable. (101 C.A.3d 268, 161 C.Rptr. 789). Lessors, bailors, licensors and franchisors may also be liable (2 C.3d 245, 466 P.2d 722, 85 C.Rptr. 178; 3 C.A.3d 319, 82 C.Rptr. 420). Developers of residential homes and buildings may also be held strictly liable in tort for manufacturing and design defects. (See, e.g. 123 C.A.3d 898, 176 C.Rptr. 886.) Employees' exclusive remedy for job site injuries is through workers' compensation unless employers operate in "dual capacity" (39 C.2d 781, 249 P.2d 8), although "dual capacity" concept has been severely limited by Lab. C. 3602. Proper plaintiffs may include ultimate users, innocent third-party bystanders, family members, employees, passengers or licensees. (See, e.g. 70 C.2d 578, 451 P.2d 84, 75 C.Rptr. 652; 38 C.2d 399, 240 P.2d 575; 3 C.A.3d 319, 82 C.Rptr. 420.) Commercial entity generally may not assert strict tort liability claim against another manufacturer or distributor. (55 C.A.3d 737, 127 C.Rptr. 838). Claims may be based on defect in manufacture (e.g., 59 C.2d 57, 377 P.2d 897, 27 C.Rptr. 697), defect in design (e.g., 20 C.3d 413, 573 P.2d 443, 143 C.Rptr. 225), failure to warn of danger or inadequate use instructions (e.g., 95 C.A.3d 338, 157 C.Rptr. 142). Product has been held to be defective in design if it fails to perform as safely as ordinary consumer would expect when used in intended or reasonably foreseeable manner or if there is risk of danger inherent in design which outweighs benefits of that design. (20 C.3d 413, 143 C.Rptr. 225, 573 P.2d 443). Liability may be imposed under certain circumstances based upon manufacturer's market share. (26 C.3d 588, 163 C.Rptr. 132, 607 P.2d 924).

Negligence.—Negligent manufacturers, retailers, distributors, lessors, bailors, and endorsers may be held liable for foreseeable harm done by product to foreseeable plaintiff. Claims against parties in chain of distribution may be based on manufacturing defects, negligent design (e.g., 2 C.3d 465, 85 C.Rptr. 629, 467 P.2d 229), failure to test (e.g., 20 C.2d 410, 126 P.2d 345) or negligent failure to warn (e.g., 218 C.A.2d 855, 32 C.Rptr. 754). Claims against parties not in chain of distribution may be based on negligent misrepresentation. (276 C.A.2d 680, 81 C.Rptr. 519). With respect to manufacturing defects, California courts have adopted Restatement of Torts Section 395. (185 C.A.3d 135, 229 C.Rptr. 605).

Breach of Warranty.—California recognizes six specific statutory warranties (Com'l. C. 2313, 2314, 2315, C.C. 1791.1[a], and 1791.1[b], 1791.2), as well as concept of common law warranty, on which breach of warranty claim may be based. Plaintiff must show that warranty existed, that defendant breached warranty, and that defendant's breach proximately caused injury to plaintiff. (146 C.A.3d 194, 194 C.Rptr. 77). Although California courts generally require privity of contract for maintenance of breach of warranty claim, many exceptions exist; e.g., privity is not required where food and drugs are involved (14 C.2d 272, 93 P.2d 799; 182 C.A.2d 602, 6 C.Rptr. 320) or where plaintiff is family member (14 C.3d 104, 120 C.Rptr. 681, 534 P.2d 377) or employee (54 C.2d 339, 5 C.Rptr. 863, 353 P.2d 575) of

See note at head of Digest as to 1998 legislation covered.

See Topical Index in front part of this volume.

CA–21

SALES . . . *continued*

purchaser. Buyer of defective product may receive consequential damages, including injury to person on property, proximately resulting from seller's breach of warranty. (Com'l. C. 2715[2]).

Bulk Sales.—See topic Commercial Code. Division 6 of Commercial Code applies to bulk transfers.

Retail Credit Sales.—See topic Consumer Protection.

Sales of Motor Vehicles.—See topic Consumer Protection.

Motor Vehicle Leasing.—See topic Consumer Protection.

Consumer Protection.—See topic Consumer Protection.

SECURITIES:

Uniform Commercial Code has been adopted with certain modifications. (1963, c. 819).

California Corporate Securities Law of 1968 has been adopted, effective Jan. 2, 1969. (Corp. C. Title 4, Div. 1). Law governs offers and issues of securities.

Supervision.—Law is administered by California Department of Corporations, chief officer of which is Commissioner of Corporations, 3700 Wilshire Boulevard, Los Angeles, CA 90010-3001.

Regulatory Powers of Supervisory Authority.—See subheads Necessity for Qualification and Civil Liability for Violations of Corporate Securities Law, infra.

Prerequisites to Sales or Offerings.—Unless security or transaction is exempt or not subject to qualification under Corp. C. 25100-25105 (see subhead Exempt Securities, infra), no security may be offered or sold without first qualifying with Commissioner. (Corp. C. 25110 requiring qualification in issuer transactions; 25120 requiring qualification of changes in rights, exchanges and mergers; and 25130 requiring qualification in nonissuer transactions). Qualification may be by coordination as to security for which registration statement has been filed under Securities Act of 1933 in connection with same offering (Corp. C. 25111), by notification as to security registered under §12 of Securities Exchange Act of 1934 or issued by investment company registered under Investment Company Act of 1940 (Corp. C. 25112), or all securities may be qualified by permit (Corp. C. 25113).

Securities to Which Act Applicable.—Any note; stock; treasury stock; membership in an incorporated or unincorporated association; bond; debenture; evidence of indebtedness; certificate of interest or participation in any profit-sharing agreement; collateral trust certificate; preorganization certificate or subscription; transferable share; investment contract; voting trust certificate; certificate of deposit for security; interest in limited liability company and any class or series of such interests (including fractional or other interest in such interest) except membership interest in limited liability company in which person claiming this exception can prove that all members are actively engaged in management of limited liability company; certificate of interest or participation in oil, gas or mining title or lease or in payments out of production under such title or lease; put, call, straddle, option, or privilege on any security, certificate of deposit, or group or index of securities (including any interest therein or based on value thereof); or any put, call, straddle, option, or privilege entered into on national securities exchange relating to foreign currency; any beneficial interest or other security issued in connection with funded employees' pension, profit sharing, stock bonus, or similar benefit plan; or, in general, any interest or instrument commonly known as "security;" or any certificate of interest or participation in, temporary or interim certificate for, receipt for guarantee of, or warrant or right to subscribe to or purchase, any of foregoing. (Corp. C. 25019).

Franchise Investments.—Unless exempt as large franchisor under Corp. C. 31101, offer or sale of franchise must be registered. (Corp. C. 31000-31516). Exemption based upon net worth of franchisor, experience of franchisor, conduct of franchise business, and written disclosure to prospective franchisee. (Corp. C. 31101). California Franchise Relations Act contains provisions pertaining to termination, nonrenewal and transfer of franchises. (Bus. & Prof. C. 20000 et seq.). See topic Franchises.

Tender Offers.—See category Business Organizations, topic Corporations.

Exempt Securities.—Under Corp. C. 25100, following are among securities exempt from qualification: Those issued or guaranteed by U.S., state, city, county or other governmental entity, Canada, its political subdivisions, or any foreign government with which U.S. currently maintains relations, national or California bank, federal or California savings and loan association, federal land bank, savings associations, joint land bank or national farm loan association; securities whose issuance is subject to Insurance Commissioner, Public Utilities Commissioner or Real Estate Commissioner; interests in real property which are subdivision land; mutual capital certificates or savings accounts issued by authorized savings association; securities issued or guaranteed by federal credit unions or credit unions organized and supervised, or regulated, under Credit Union Law; subject to certain conditions, securities of or guaranteed by railroad, other common carrier, public utility, or public utility holding company; subject to certain conditions, securities of nonprofit organizations; subject to certain conditions, notes, drafts, bills of exchange, or banker's acceptances; securities of California agricultural cooperatives; beneficial interests in qualified pension, profit-sharing, stock bonus or similar benefit plans; securities listed or approved for listing on national securities exchange certified by Commissioner of Corporations; promissory notes (but not part of series) secured by lien on real property; medical malpractice trust funds; subject to certain conditions, securities of certain consumer cooperatives; and, subject to certain conditions, certain pooled mortgage loans and securities issued as open-end management company or unit investment trust under Investment Company Act of 1940. Additionally, Corp. C. 25101 exempts from non-issuer qualification requirements of Corp. C. 25130, securities issued by person which is issuer of securities listed on national securities exchange certified by Commissioner, or, if national securities exchange is not certified by Commissioner, issuer meets certain other conditions, however, exemption does not apply to securities offered pursuant to registration under Securities Act of 1933 if exceeds $50,000.

Exempt Transactions.—Under Corp. C. 25102, following are among transactions exempt from issuer transaction requirements: Offers but not sales in nonpublic offering where agreement contains certain legend, no consideration paid or received and no securities issued until sale qualified; subject to certain conditions, offers but not sales of securities for which registration statement has been filed under Securities Act of 1933 but not yet effective, or for which offering statement under Regulation A has been filed but has not yet been qualified; offers but not sales pursuant to negotiating permit issued by Commissioner of Corporations; transactions between issuer and underwriter or among underwriters if sale is qualified prior to distribution in California or exempt; offers or sales of debt instruments in nonpublic offerings; subject to certain conditions, offers or sales (other than to pension or profit-sharing trust of issuer) to 35 or fewer persons who meet certain criteria for sophisticated investors, and without publication of any advertisement; offers or sales in nonpublic transaction of conditional sale agreement, equipment trust certificate or certificates of interest or participation therein, covering railroad equipment, motor vehicles, or aircraft; subject to certain conditions, offers or sales of voting common stock of any corporation if, immediately after sale and issuance, only one class of stock outstanding owned beneficially by no more than 35 persons, with legend on certificates, no advertisement of offer or sale, no selling expenses paid, consideration for stock only of certain types, no promotional consideration paid, and notice filed with Commissioner of Corporations (see Rules of Cal. Corporations Commissioner pertaining to application of this transactional exemption to small corporations); subject to certain conditions, offers or sales to banks, savings and loan associations, trust companies, insurance companies, registered investment companies, pension or profit sharing trusts, or certain others, or to corporations with outstanding securities registered under §12 of Securities Exchange Act of 1934; subject to certain conditions, offers or sales of certificates in oil or gas title or lease; offers or sales under bankruptcy plan of reorganization or arrangement; offers or sales of options, warrants, puts, calls or straddles, or guarantees of such securities in certain cases by non-issuers; offers or sales of stock to pension, profit-sharing, stock bonus or employee stock ownership plan, subject to certain conditions; any offer or sale of security in transaction, other than offer or sale of security in rollup transaction, that meets certain criteria; any offer or sale of security issued pursuant to stock purchase plan or agreement or issued pursuant to stock option plan or agreement, where security is exempt from registration under Securities Act of 1933. (Corp. C. 25102).

Following transactions exempt from qualification requirements for issuer transactions, recapitalization and reorganization: Negotiations or agreements prior to solicitation of shareholders' approval, and subject to such approval, of changes in rights, preferences, privileges, or restrictions on outstanding securities or merger, consolidation or sale of corporate assets in consideration of issuance of securities; changes in rights, preferences, privileges or restrictions of outstanding securities unless 25% of outstanding shareholders affected adversely are California residents; exchanges incident to merger, consolidation or sale of assets in consideration of issuance of securities of another corporation unless 25% of outstanding shares whose holders are to receive securities are California residents; changes, other than stock split or reverse stock split, in rights, preferences, privileges, or restrictions on outstanding shares except certain changes if they substantially and adversely affect any class of shareholders; stock splits or reverse stock splits except in certain instances; changes in rights of outstanding debt securities except in certain instances if substantially and adversely affect any class of securities; exchanges incident to merger, consolidation, or sale of assets, other than roll up transaction in consideration of issuance of equity securities of another entity, if exchange meets certain conditions. (Corp. C. 25103).

Following transactions exempt from non-issuer requirements: Offers or sales by bona fide owner for own account if unaccompanied by advertisement and not effected through broker-dealer in public offering; offers or sales effected by licensed broker-dealer pursuant to unsolicited order or offer to buy; offers or sales to bank, savings and loan association, and others under certain conditions; transactions between person on whose behalf offering is made and underwriter if sale is exempt from qualification at time of or qualified prior to distribution; offers or sales for bona fide secured party selling security in ordinary course of business to liquidate bona fide debt; transactions by executor, administrator, sheriff, marshall, receiver, trustee in bankruptcy, guardian or conservator; offers but not sales of securities for which registration statement filed under Securities Act of 1933 but not yet effective, or for which offering statement under Regulation A has been filed but has not yet been qualified; under certain conditions, offers or sales if qualification of securities of same class was effective within 18 months prior thereto (or longer subject to commissioner order), as to issuer transactions or 12 months as to non-issuer transactions or reorganizations or recapitalizations. (Corp. C. 25104).

Exemption by Commissioner's Rule: Commissioner of Corporations may by rule exempt other transactions. (Corp. C. 25105).

Necessity for Qualification.—Commissioner of Corporations has authority to issue stop order, suspend or revoke qualification or permit previously issued, may refuse to issue permit unless he finds proposed plan of business or of recapitalization or reorganization, or proposed issuance, to be fair, just and equitable; Commissioner may impose as condition of qualification deposit of securities in escrow, imposition of legend condition restricting transferability, impounding of proceeds from sale, limiting expense in connection with sale, restrictions on promotional shares, and otherwise; Commissioner may hold hearings where securities are proposed to be issued in exchange. (Corp. C. 25140-25143).

Consent to Service of Process on Commissioner.—All applicants for qualification or notice under Corp. C.§§25100.1, 25102.2 and 25230.1 or for exemption from qualification (other than California corporations, California licensed broker-dealers, and those with consents already on file) shall file consent appointing Commissioner to receive service of process. (Corp. C. 25165).

Civil liability for violations of Corporate Securities Law include rescission and recovery of damages. (Corp. C. 25500-25510). Professionals who pursuant to rule of Commissioner consent to use of their statement as part of offering are jointly and severally liable with any other person liable for untrue statement or omission in connection with sale or purchase of security. (Corp. C. 25504.2). Securities actions for

SECURITIES . . . *continued*

fraud, price or trading manipulation, misrepresentation or insider trading must be brought: (1) Within four years of act or transaction constituting violation, or (2) within one year of discovery by plaintiff of facts constituting violation, whichever is earlier. (Corp. C. 25506). Securities actions against professionals for untrue statements or omissions must be brought within one year after discovery of facts constituting violation, or after such discovery should have been made by exercise of reasonable diligence, but in no event after three years of violation. (Corp. C. 25506.1). Securities actions for failure to qualify securities or failure to comply with condition of qualification shall be brought before expiration of: (1) Two years after violation, or (2) one year after discovery by plaintiff of facts constituting such violation, whichever comes first. (Corp. C. 25507). No buyer may rescind or obtain damages for failure to qualify or failure to comply with qualification condition if before lawsuit is instituted, commissioner-approved rescission letter is delivered to buyer, and buyer fails to accept offer. (Corp. C. 25507). Willful violations may constitute crimes. (Corp. C. 25540-25542). Commissioner of Corporations has power to institute actions for injunction, receivership, etc.; bring class action on behalf of persons injured; make investigations, take possession of records, subpoena, and otherwise; Commissioner may issue desist and refrain orders. (Corp. C. 25530-25534).

Broker-Dealers.—Broker-dealer may not effect transactions in, or induce purchases or sales of, securities unless Commissioner of Corporations has issued certificate authorizing broker-dealer to act (Corp. C. 25210). Broker-dealers registered under Securities Exchange Act of 1934 who have no previously denied or revoked certificates and who have no place of business in California and direct offers to sell or buy only to specified customers are exempt from broker-dealer certificate requirements. (Corp. C. 25200). Real estate broker licensed by Real Estate Commissioner is exempt from broker-dealer certificate requirement when engaged in transactions in any interest in any general or limited partnership, joint venture, unincorporated association, or similar organization (but not corporation) owned by no more than 100 persons and formed solely for purposes of investing in real property. (Corp. C. 25206). Requirements of certificate application are set forth in Corp. C. 25211.

Investment Advisers.—Investment adviser may not conduct business unless Commissioner has issued certificate authorizing him to act. (Corp. C. 25230). Investment advisers registered under Investment Advisers Act of 1940 who have no place of business in California and: (1) Whose only clients fall into specified categories; or (2) during any period of 12 consecutive months has had fewer than six client residents of state and complies with Corp. C. 25230.1, are exempt from investment adviser certificate requirements. (Corp. C. 25202). Requirements of certificate applications are set forth in Corp. C. 25231.

Commodities.—Commissioner of Corporations regulates offer and sale of commodities and commodity contracts, as defined in Corp. C 29500 et seq.

Commissioner of Corporation has authority to censure, suspend, deny and revoke certificate, may establish standards with respect to training, experience, and other qualifications, may require licensed broker-dealer and investment adviser to post surety bond up to $10,000, and fidelity bond. (Corp. C. 25212, 25216, 25217, 25232, 25236, 25237). See Rules of Cal. Corporations Commissioner for extensive regulation of broker-dealers and investment advisers. (10 C.C.R. 250.9 et seq.).

Insider Trading.—See Corp. C. 25402, 25502, 25502.2, 25506 (statute of limitations), 25540(b).

Advertisements.—Unless exempted, no advertisement concerning securities sold or offered may be made unless true copy thereof first filed in Commissioner's office at least three business days prior to publication. (Corp. C. 25300). No publication may be made after Commissioner's adverse finding and notification to person involved. (Corp. C. 25302).

Uniform Simplification of Fiduciary Security Transfers Act repealed by Uniform Commercial Code. (Com'l. C. 8402-8407). See topic Commercial Code.

STATUTE OF FRAUDS:

See topic Frauds, Statute of.

TRUST RECEIPT SECURITY:

See category Debtor and Creditor, topic Pledges.

WAREHOUSEMEN:

Warehousemen are no longer regulated by State Public Utilities Commission. (1980, c. 1063).

Uniform Commercial Code has been adopted. (1963, c. 819, Com'l. C. 7201-7210). See topic Commercial Code. Civil Code Division III, Part 4, Tit. III deals with deposits of goods. C. C. §§1851-1857 address deposits for hire. Depositary for hire has lien upon property stored for storage charges, advances and certain insurance and other expenses. (C. C. 1856). C. C. §§1880-1881.2 deal with private bulk storage of grain.

CITIZENSHIP

ALIENS:

Resident aliens eligible for citizenship have same rights as citizens, with exception of voting rights. Any alien may take, hold, and dispose of property, real or personal. (C. C. 671).

Sections of Labor Code providing that aliens may not hold public office or be employed by state, county or city governments, were repealed in 1970.

Property Rights.—Sections of Civil Code preventing aliens, not residing in U. S., from taking real or personal property by succession or testamentary disposition were repealed in 1974. Any alien may take, hold and dispose of property, real or personal. (C. C. 671).

CIVIL ACTIONS AND PROCEDURE

ACCORD AND SATISFACTION:

Accord and satisfaction governed by Civil Code and common law.

An accord is an agreement to accept, in extinction of an obligation, something different from or less than person agreeing to accept is entitled. (C.C. 1521).

Though parties to accord are bound to execute it, it does not extinguish obligation until fully executed. (C.C. 1522).

Acceptance, by creditor, of consideration of accord extinguishes obligation, and is called satisfaction. (C.C. 1523).

Part performance of obligation, either before or after breach thereof, when expressly accepted by creditor in writing, in satisfaction, or rendered in pursuance of agreement in writing for that purpose, though without any new consideration, extinguishes obligation. (C.C. 1524).

Part Payment of Disputed Sum.—In case of dispute over total money due on contract, if conceded by parties that part of money is due, debtor may pay, without condition, amount conceded to be due, leaving to other party all remedies to which he might otherwise be entitled as to any balance claimed. (C.C. 1525).

If any conditions attached to payment, this section not deemed to have limited remedies available to other party under other provisions of law on original amount claimed. (C.C. 1525).

Pleading.—Accord and satisfaction must be specially pleaded. (220 C. 402, 31 P.2d 359).

Uniform Commercial Code has been adopted with certain modifications. See category Business Regulation and Commerce, topic Commercial Code.

Novation is substitution of new obligation for existing one. (C.C. 1530).

Novation is made by substitution of new obligation between same parties with intent to extinguish old obligation; by substitution of new debtor in place of old one with intent to release latter; or by substitution of new creditor in place of old one with intent to transfer rights of latter to former. (C.C. 1531).

Novation is made by contract and is subject to general rules of contract. (C.C. 1532).

Compromise.—Common law rules govern.

ACTIONS:

There is only one form of action (C.C.P. 307), which is commenced when complaint is filed (C.C.P. 350). See also topic Submission of Controversy.

Equity.—Substantive distinctions between legal and equitable rights and remedies are preserved. Both may be set up in same action, formal distinction of pleadings being abolished. (4 C. 6). Legal or equitable nature of cause of action determined by relief sought. (10 C.3d 665, 517 P.2d 1157).

Commencement.—See topic Process.

Parties.—Actions must be prosecuted by real party in interest (C.C.P. 367), except that executor or administrator, or trustee of express trust or other person authorized by statute may sue without joining beneficiary (C.C.P. 369), and homeowners association may sue for enforcement of governing documents and for damages to: (1) Common areas or (2) separate interests which it is obligated to maintain or repair without joining individual owners (C.C.P. 383).

Persons may join as plaintiffs in a single action if they assert any right to relief jointly, severally or in the alternative, concerning same transaction, occurrence or series of transactions or occurrences and if any question of law or fact common to all will arise in the action. Persons also may join as plaintiffs in a single action if they have a claim, right or interest adverse to defendant in property or controversy which is subject of action. (C.C.P. 378[a]). It is not necessary that each plaintiff be interested as to every cause of action or as to all relief prayed for. (C.C.P. 378[b]).

All persons may be joined in one action as defendants if there is asserted against them: (1) Any right to relief jointly, severally, or in alternative which arises from same transaction, occurrence or series of transactions or occurrences and if any question of law or fact common to all these persons will arise in action, or (2) claim, right, or interest adverse to them in property or controversy which is subject of action. (C.C.P. 379[a]). It is not necessary that each defendant be interested as to every cause of action or as to all relief prayed for. (C.C.P. 379[b]). If plaintiff is in doubt as to person from whom he is entitled to redress, he may join two or more defendants, with intent that question as to which, if any, of defendants is liable may be determined between parties. (C.C.P. 379[c]).

Any number of lien holders may join in action to foreclose their liens. (C.C. 3149).

Person who is subject to service of process and whose joinder will not deprive court of jurisdiction shall be joined if complete relief cannot be afforded in his absence or if he claims interest in subject of action and is so situated that disposition of action in his absence may impair his ability to protect that interest or expose persons already parties to risk of double, multiple, or inconsistent liability. (C.C.P. 389[a]). If such person cannot be joined, court must determine whether action should proceed. In making decision, court should consider extent of possible prejudice to all concerned, possibility of lessening prejudice by protective provisions, adequacy of possible judgment, and alternate remedies available to claimant if action dismissed. (C.C.P. 389[b]).

Class Actions.—Requirements generally follow FRCP 23. (12 C.3d 447). But, more lenient regarding notice. See C.C. 1781; 184 C.A.3d 1491. Dismissal of part or entire class action only on court approval.

Intervention.—Upon timely application, any person having interest in matter in litigation or in success of either party may intervene. Intervention takes place by joining plaintiff, by uniting with defendant or by asserting demand adverse to both parties, and is made by complaint filed by leave of court and served upon other parties. (C.C.P. 387[a]). Separate provisions found in C.C.P. 389.5 (to recover property or to determine conflicting claims thereto), C.C.P. 1250.230 (eminent domain) and 1421 (escheat).

See note at head of Digest as to 1998 legislation covered.

See Topical Index in front part of this volume.

ACTIONS . . . *continued*

Interpleader.—Defendant in an action upon contract or for specific personal property may, prior to answering, apply upon affidavit and notice for court order to discharge him from liability and to substitute another party in his place, upon depositing in court amount of contract claim or property or its value. Alternatively, defendant may file verified cross complaint in interpleader, applying upon notice for order directing another party to deliver amount or value in question to specific person. (C.C.P. 386[a]).

Whenever conflicting claims which would give rise to double or multiple liability are or may be made against person, he may bring action to compel them to interplead and litigate their claims. (C.C.P. 386[a]). Action of interpleader may be maintained even though claims have no common origin, are not identical but are adverse to and independent of one another. (C.C.P. 386[a]). Separate provisions relating to particular claims found in Com'l. C. 7603 (consigned goods); C.C. 3214 (public improvements); Rev. & Tax C. 4988 (conflicting property assessments).

Joinder of Causes of Action.—Plaintiff who alleges cause of action against one or more defendants may unite with such cause any other causes which he has alone or with any co-plaintiffs against any such defendants. (C.C.P. 427.10).

Person filing cross-complaint may unite with cause of action asserted in cross-complaint any other causes he has against any of cross-defendants (other than plaintiff in eminent domain proceeding) whether or not such cross-defendant already is a party to action. (C.C.P. 428.30). Must file cross-complaint for indemnity to pursue right under case law adoption of concepts of comparative indemnity. (20 C.3d 578; 578 P.2d 899).

Consolidation or Severance.—Court may consolidate actions involving common question of law or fact and, to further convenience, expedition and economy or avoid prejudice, may order a separate trial of any cause of action or issue, preserving right of jury trial. (C.C.P. 1048).

Survival.—No cause of action is lost by reason of death of any person, but may be maintained by or against his executor or administrator, except exemplary damages may not be awarded against deceased. When person having cause of action dies before judgment, damages recoverable by his personal representatives are limited to damages sustained by decedent before death, including exemplary damages, but excluding damages for pain, suffering or disfigurement. (C.C.P. 377.20 et seq.).

Small Claims.—See category Courts and Legislature, topic Courts.

Prohibited Actions.—No cause of action arises for criminal conversation, seduction of a person over the age of consent, alienation of affections or breach of promise to marry. (C.C. 43.5).

Fraudulent promise to marry or to cohabit after marriage does not give rise to cause of action for damages. (C.C. 43.4).

Certificate of Meritorious Malpractice Action.—In most malpractice actions against architects, professional engineers or land surveyors, condition precedent to filing of action is filing of certificate under oath by plaintiff's attorney that he has reviewed case, has consulted with and received opinion from knowledgeable member of profession involved that defendant or cross-defendant was or was not negligent, and has concluded that there is reasonable and meritorious cause for filing of action. (C.C.P. 411.35). Failure to file is ground for demurrer (C.C.P. 430.10) or motion to strike (C.C.P. 435).

Limitation of.—See topic Limitation of Actions.

Administration.—See category Estates and Trusts, topic Executors and Administrators.

Direct Actions Against Insurer.—See category Transportation, topic Motor Vehicles, subhead Direct Actions.

APPEAL AND ERROR:

From Justice and Municipal Courts.—There is appellate department of superior court in every county, which determines most appeals from municipal courts and justice courts in county. (C. C. P. 77, 904.2). Appeals from small claims court of municipal or justice court result in trial de novo, and are also heard by superior court, but not in its appellate department. (C. C. P. 77, 904.2, 116.770). Upon appeal of small claims court judgment to superior court no party has right to trial by jury. (C.C.P. 116.770[b]).

Appeal may be taken by aggrieved party from final judgment, except judgment of contempt which is final and conclusive. (C. C. P. 902, 904.2, 1222). Appeal ordinarily may not be taken from interlocutory judgment. (C. C. P. 904.2). In addition to judicial qualifications on "one final judgment" principle, statute specifically authorizes appeal from: Order made after appealable judgment; order changing or refusing to change place of trial; order granting motion to quash service of summons; order granting motion to stay or dismiss on ground of inconvenient forum; order granting new trial or denying motion for judgment notwithstanding verdict; order discharging or refusing to discharge attachment; order granting right to attach; order granting or dissolving injunction, or refusing to grant or dissolve injunction; order appointing receiver; and judgment of small claims court. (C. C. P. 904.2).

Appeal is taken, except in appeals from small claims court, by filing notice of appeal with clerk of trial court within 30 days after date of mailing notice of entry of judgment by clerk, or 30 days after date of service of written notice of entry by any party, or 90 days after entry of judgment, whichever is earliest. (Rule 122[a], California Rules of Court). Timely filing of notice of appeal is jurisdictional. Special rules regulate time where certain post-trial motions or cross-appeal involved. (Rule 123, California Rules of Court). Special rule requires liberal construction of notice on appeal from small claims court in favor of its sufficiency. (Rule 152, California Rules of Court). Underlying statute may mandate additional rules. (Rule 122[a], California Rules of Court).

Plaintiff in Small Claims Court May Not Appeal.—Plaintiff electing to assert claim in small claims court is bound by result; defendant with respect to plaintiff's claim, or plaintiff with respect to claim of defendant, may appeal and secure trial de novo in superior court of county where matter heard. (C.C.P. 116.710, 116.770). Defendant's insurer may appeal where judgment exceeds $2,500 and insurer stipulates to coverage. (C.C.P. 116.710[c]).

Transfer of Appeals from Justice or Municipal Court.—Appeal in case within original jurisdiction of justice or municipal court may be transferred from appellate department of superior court to court of appeal when transfer appears necessary to secure uniformity of decisions or settle important questions of law. (C.C.P. 911).

From Superior Court.—Appeal may be taken by aggrieved party from final judgment, except judgment of contempt which is final and conclusive (C.C.P. 1222, but see topic Certiorari, C.C.P. 1067) and judgment of superior court or its appellate department on appeal from municipal or justice court (C.C.P. 904.1, 902). Appeal ordinarily may not be taken from interlocutory judgment. (C.C.P. 904.1). Appeal may not be taken from judgment granting or denying petition for issuance of writ of mandamus or prohibition directed to municipal or justice court or judge(s) thereof which relates to matter pending in municipal or justice court except upon petition for extraordinary writ. (C.C.P. 904.1[a]). In addition to judicial qualifications on "one final judgment" principle, statute specifically authorizes appeal from: Some interlocutory judgments and certain orders made after appealable judgment; order granting motion to quash service of summons; order granting motion to stay or dismiss on ground of inconvenient forum; order granting new trial; order denying motion for judgment notwithstanding verdict; order discharging or refusing to discharge attachment; order granting right to attach; order granting or dissolving injunction, or refusing to grant or dissolve injunction; order appointing receiver; appropriate interlocutory judgment or order made in action to redeem real or personal property from mortgage or lien; appropriate interlocutory judgment in action for partition; orders and decrees in probate actions or proceedings made appealable by Probate Code or Family Law Act; and superior court judgment directing payment of monetary sanctions exceeding $5,000. (C.C.P. 904.1). Lesser sanction judgments may be reviewed on appeal after entry of final judgment in main action or, at discretion of court of appeal, upon petition for extraordinary writ. (C.C.P. 904.1[k]).

Appeal is taken by filing notice of appeal, and simultaneous delivery of filing fee and any required deposit to clerk of superior court within 60 days after date of mailing notice of entry of judgment by clerk, or 60 days after date of service of written notice by any party, or 180 days after entry of judgment, whichever is earliest. (Rules 1, 2, California Rules of Court). As to appealable orders, time runs from date of entry in court minutes or date formal order filed (see Rule 2[b], California Rules of Court). Special statutes or rules regulate time for filing where certain post-trial motions, cross-appeals, or special circumstances are involved. (Rules 2, 3, California Rules of Court). Timely filing of notice of appeal is jurisdictional. Failure to simultaneously deliver fee may result in appeal dismissal. (Rules 1[c], 10[a], California Rules of Court).

Stay of Proceedings.—Appeal from trial court stays proceedings in court below on judgment or order appealed from (C.C.P. 916) except where appeal is from judgment for money (unless bond posted) (C.C.P. 917.1), judgment or order to take remedial actions in response to release or threatened release of hazardous substances (C.C.P. 917.15), judgment or order directing assignment or delivery of personal property or foreclosure sale (C.C.P. 917.2), judgment or order directing execution of instrument (C.C.P. 917.3), judgment or order directing sale or delivery of real property (C.C.P. 917.4), judgment appointing receiver (C.C.P. 917.5), judgment of right to attach order (C.C.P. 917.65), judgment containing provisions dealing with child custody (C.C.P. 917.7), judgment that building or place is nuisance, judgment or order directing corporation to permit inspection of books, and judgment that party usurped public office (C.C.P. 917.8). Where trial court orders parties to post bond but parties fail to do so, judgment or order not stayed by appeal. (C.C.P. 917.9). Generally see C.C.P. 917.1-917.9 for details and exceptions as to operation of above mentioned exceptions.

Appeal does not continue attachment in force unless additional bond given by appellant. (C.C.P. 921).

Stay of Execution.—See category Debtor and Creditor, topic Executions.

Record on Appeal.—Appeal may be supported by clerk's transcript and original papers (judgment roll); by clerk's transcript (or appendix or joint appendix) and reporter's transcript; by Superior Court file; by agreed statement; or by settled statement. (Rules 4, 5, 5.1, 5.2, 6 and 7 [Superior Court] and 124, 125, 126, 127 [Municipal Court], California Rules of Court). Appeal from small claims court involves limited record and trial de novo. (Rules 153, 155, California Rules of Court, C.C.P. 116.770).

Statutory Writ to Review Certain Interlocutory Orders.—Statutes specifically provide for review by writ of some orders that may not be appealed. See C.C.P. 400 (location of trial); 418.10 (motion to quash service, motion to stay or dismiss action).

BONDS:

"Admitted surety insurer" means corporate insurer or reciprocal or interinsurance exchange to which Insurance Commissioner has issued certificate of authority to transact surety insurance in California, as defined in §105 of Insurance Code. (C.C.P. 995.120). Unless statute providing for bond requires execution by admitted surety insurer, bond shall be executed by two or more sufficient personal sureties or by one sufficient admitted surety insurer or by combination of sufficient personal sureties and admitted surety insurers. (C.C.P. 995.310). If statute provides for bond with any number of sureties, one sufficient admitted surety insurer may become sole surety on bond. (C.C.P. 995.610).

Neither state, nor any political subdivision thereof, nor any federal agency is required to give bond when it is party in any civil action or proceeding. (C.C.P. 995.220).

Justification.—When undertaking or bond is authorized or required, bond executed by personal sureties shall be accompanied by affidavit of qualification including name, occupation, residence and business address and that they are each residents and either owners of real property or householders, within state, and are each worth sum specified in undertaking or bond, over and above all their just debts and liabilities, exclusive of property exempt from execution; if undertaking or bond exceeds $5,000,

See note at head of Digest as to 1998 legislation covered.

See Topical Index in front part of this volume.

CA – 24

BONDS . . . *continued*
affidavit must describe property, nature of affiant's interest, estimate of cash value, amount of outstanding liens and any other known cloud on title; but when amount specified in undertaking or bond exceeds $10,000, and there are more than two sureties thereon, they may state in their affidavits that surety is worth less than amount of bond and bond may stipulate that liability of surety is limited to worth of surety stated in affidavit, so long as aggregate worth of all sureties executing bond is twice amount of bond. (C.C.P. 995.520).

CERTIORARI:

Writ of certiorari may be denominated writ of review. (C.C.P. 1067).

Jurisdiction to Grant.—Writ of review may be granted by any court, except municipal or justice court, when there is no appeal nor, in judgment of court, any plain, speedy and adequate remedy for inferior tribunal, board or officer exercising judicial functions in excess of jurisdiction. (C. C. P. 1068).

Procedure.—Application is made by verified petition of party beneficially interested, and court may require notice of application to adverse parties, or may grant order to show cause why writ should not be allowed, or may grant writ without notice. (C. C. P. 1069). Demurrer proceedings upon return available as response as well as verified answer, or both. (C. C. P. 1069.1, 1089; Judicial Council Rules).

Writ must command party to whom directed to certify fully to court issuing writ, at time and place specified by court (in writ or order), transcript of record and proceedings for review and to desist from further proceedings in matter to be reviewed. (C. C. P. 1071). However, inclusion of stay of proceedings being reviewed in writ lies in discretion of issuing court. (C. C. P. 1072).

Writ must be served in same manner as summons in civil action, except where otherwise expressly directed by court. (C. C. P. 1073). See C. C. P. 413.10-417.40.

Review extends only to determination whether inferior tribunal, board, or officer has regularly pursued its or his authority. (C. C. P. 1074).

Use.—Used frequently to review convictions of contempt. Not available to review decisions of administrative agencies (11 C.3d 28); administrative mandamus is appropriate remedy (C.C.P. 1094.5). Certiorari not substitute for appeal or remedy to review error in nonappealable orders. (148 C.A.3d 891).

CHARITABLE IMMUNITY:

See topic Damages.

COMMISSIONS TO TAKE TESTIMONY:

See topic Depositions and Discovery.

COSTS:

In general, costs are allowed, as of course, to prevailing party. (C.C.P. 1032). Costs are generally within court's discretion when prevailing party recovers judgment that could have been rendered in court of lesser jurisdiction. (C.C.P. 1033). When party recovers in municipal or justice court amount less than small claims limit, but suit could not have been brought in small claims court, costs limited to filing fee, service, and if specifically allowed by law, reasonable attorney fees. (C.C.P. 1033[b]). Prevailing party in civil action entitled among his costs to expenses of jury, and cost of depositions unless same were unnecessary. (C. C. P. 1033.5).

Security for Costs.—On defendant's motion, nonresidents and foreign corporations, as plaintiffs, may be required to give bond for costs. (C. C. P. 1030).

In shareholder's derivative action, plaintiff may be required to furnish security for costs and attorney's fees, of such nature and amount not exceeding $50,000 as court may direct, upon motion of corporation or of defendant who is officer or director of corporation. Security may be ordered for corporation or for individual defendant if movant shows that there is no reasonable probability that action against it will benefit corporation or its security holders. Security may also be ordered as to individual defendant if he shows that he did not participate in transaction in any capacity. (Corp. C. 800).

In action against licensed architect, engineer, building designer or land surveyor upon motion and supported by affidavit showing claim is frivolous, plaintiff may be required to furnish undertaking of not to exceed $500 as security for costs except for actions for injury, death or small claims court actions. (C. C. P. 1029.5).

In personal injury action against physician, surgeon, other medical and dental professionals for professional negligence, plaintiff may be required to furnish security for costs in sum not to exceed $500 for each defendant. (C. C. P. 1029.6).

DAMAGES:

Common law generally prevails, various statutes provide for imposition of exemplary damages and penal damages. (C.C. 3294-95, 3345-48).

Exemplary Damages.—May be awarded in actions for breach of noncontractual obligations if proven by clear and convincing evidence that defendant guilty of oppression, fraud or malice. (C.C. 3294[a]). Employer not liable for employee's acts except in specified circumstances. (C.C. 3294[b]).

Penal Damages.—Provided for, or may be awarded, in cases involving: Unfair or deceptive practices against senior citizens or disable persons or injuries to timber. (C.C. 3345, 3346).

Comparative Fault.—"Pure" form adopted. Liability for personal or property damage assigned in proportion to fault of persons whose negligence caused damage. (13 C.3d 804, 532 P.2d 1226, 119 C. Rptr. 858). Comparative fault applies to government tort liability. (68 C.A. 3d 481, 137 C. Rptr. 512). Regarding apportionment of damages among joint tortfeasors, and setoff principles, see 148 C.A. 3d 963, 196 C. Rptr. 417 and 26 C. 3d 131, 604 P.2d 208, 161 C. Rptr. 87, respectively.

Principles of comparative fault apply to strict product liability cases. Defendant tortfeasor has equitable cause of action for partial indemnity against other tortfeasors to enforce contribution from them in proportion to their contributing fault. (20 C. 3d 578, 578 P.2d 899, 146 C. Rptr. 182). Equitable principle of apportionment of fault among joint tortfeasors applies between negligent defendant and strictly liable defendant. (21 C. 3d 322, 579 P.2d 441, 146 C. Rptr. 550). However, for causes of action arising after 1986, liability of each defendant for noneconomic damages is several, not joint. (9 C.A. 4th 70, 11 C. Rptr.2d 454).

In actions for personal injury, property damage, or wrongful death, each tortfeasor's liability for noneconomic damages is several only and not joint. "Economic damages" means objectively verifiable monetary losses. (C.C. 1431.2).

Loss of Consortium.—Each spouse has action for loss of consortium caused by negligent or intentional injury to other by third party. (12 C.3d 382, 525 P.2d 669, 115 C. Rptr. 765). Children have no action for loss of parental consortium caused by third party's negligence. (19 C.3d 441, 563 P.2d 858, 138 C. Rptr. 302).

Doctrine of charitable immunity does not apply. (37 C.2d 356, 232 P.2d 241).

Guests.—Negligent defendant driver is not protected by "guest statutes". (8 C.3d 855, 506 P.2d 212, 106 C. Rptr. 388).

Liquidated Damages.—Except as set forth below, provision in contract liquidating damages for breach of contract is valid unless party seeking to invalidate provision establishes that provision was unreasonable under circumstances at time of contract. (C.C. 1671[b]). Provision in contract liquidating damages for breach of contract is void under following circumstances unless parties agree upon amount and it would be impracticable or extremely difficult to fix actual damage: (1) Where liquidated damages are sought to be recovered from party to contract for retail purchase, or rental of personal property or services, primarily for personal uses; or (2) where liquidated damages are sought by party leasing dwelling. (C.C. 1671[c]).

Uniform Contribution Among Tortfeasors Act.—Not adopted.

Sovereign Immunity.—Abrogated by "California Tort Claims Act of 1963". (Govt. C. 814-818.9).

See also category Estates and Trusts, topic Death, subhead Action for Wrongful Death.

DECLARATORY JUDGMENTS:

See topic Judgments, subhead Declaratory Judgments.

DEPOSITIONS AND DISCOVERY:

Within State.—Testimony by deposition may be taken in action after service of summons and in special proceeding after service of petition or appearance of defendant or respondent. Leave of court required if plaintiff notices deposition within 20 days of service of summons or appearance of defendant. (C. C. P. 2025[b][2]). Depositions before action or pending appeal allowed with leave of court to perpetuate testimony. (C. C. P. 2035, 2036).

Outside of State for Use Within State.—Proceedings for depositions outside state for use within state ordinarily same as those for depositions to be taken within state. Where necessary or convenient, court issues commission, letters rogatory, or letter of request. (C.C.P. 2026, 2027). In foreign state or country depositions may be taken on notice before any person authorized to administer oaths, any person or officer appointed by commission or under letters rogatory, or anyone agreed to by parties. (C.C.P. 2027[c]). Person before whom deposition is to be taken may be designated in notices or commissions either by name or descriptive title and letters rogatory or letters of request may be addressed: "To the Appropriate Judicial Authority in [name of foreign nation]". (C.C.P. 2027[c]). Within U.S., or its territories or possessions, depositions may be taken before any person authorized to administer oaths or before person appointed by court. (C.C.P. 2026[c]).

Within State for Use Outside State.—Where by mandate, writ, letters rogatory, letters of request, commission, or by notice or agreement deposition of witness within state for use in action outside state is required, deposition may be taken and attendance compelled in same manner as in actions within state. (C.C.P. 2029).

Proceedings upon Oral Examination.—Party may take oral deposition of any person in this state on serving upon every other party previous written notice of date, time and place of examination and name, address and telephone number of each person to be examined if known, otherwise general description sufficient to identify person, class, or group to which person belongs. If documents are sought, materials or categories must be described with reasonable particularity. If deposition to be video or audio taped, notice must so state. (C. C. P. 2025[c],[d]). Except for unlawful detainer actions, such notice must be given before deposition by at least ten days, plus five days if notice is given by mail to address located within state of California, or ten days if address is outside state of California but within U.S., or 20 days if address is located outside U.S. (C. C. P. 1013, 2025[f]). In unlawful detainer actions, notice must be given before deposition by at least five days but not later than five days before trial. (C.C.P. 2025[f]). For good cause shown, court may extend or shorten time. (C.C.P. 2025[f]). No order for taking of deposition is necessary.

Compelling Attendance of Witnesses.—Subpoena must be served upon nonparty witness to compel his attendance, and must be issued by clerk of superior court of county wherein attendance is pending or by attorney of record for party. (C.C.P. 1986, 2020, 2025[h][2]). Except as otherwise ordered, deposition of natural person, whether or not party, shall be taken either within 75 miles of deponent's residence, or within county where action is pending and within 150 miles of deponent's residence, at option of party giving notice. (C.C.P. 2025[e]). Deposition of organization that is party shall be taken either within 75 miles of organization's principal executive business office in California or within county where action is pending and within 150 miles of that office, at option of party giving notice. Deposition of nonparty organization shall be taken within 75 miles of organization's principal executive business office in California. If no executive offices in California, within 75 miles of any business office in California or within county where action is pending. (C.C.P. 2025[e]).

Examination of Witnesses.—Examination and cross-examination of deponents may proceed as permitted at trial. (C.C.P. 2025[l][1]). Deponent may be examined on any matter not privileged, which is relevant to subject matter of action or pending motion,

See note at head of Digest as to 1998 legislation covered.

See Topical Index in front part of this volume.

CA – 25

DEPOSITIONS AND DISCOVERY . . . *continued*
if matter is admissible or appears reasonably calculated to lead to discovery of admissible evidence. (C.C.P. 2017[a], 2025[a]).

If witness refuses to answer any question or produce any document specified in notice, party seeking discovery may apply for order compelling answer or production of documents if motion made within 60 days after completion of record of deposition, and accompanied by declaration stating facts showing reasonable and good faith attempt at informal resolution of each issue presented by motion. (C.C.P. 2025[o]).

Videotaping of depositions is permitted if notice states that proceedings will be videotaped, or if parties agree. Stenographic transcript made simultaneously is official record, and court may permit use of videotape at trial. (C.C.P. 2025[c], [l], [p], [u]).

Fees.—Any person subpoenaed and required to give deposition is entitled to witness fees and mileage, as if subpoenaed and required to testify before court. (C.C.P. 1986.5, 2020[f]). Court may set fees of expert witnesses in accordance with prescribed guidelines. (C.C.P. 2034; Govt. C. 68092.5).

Deposing Organizations.—Partnership, association, governmental agency, or public or private corporation may be named as deponent, in which case subpoena or notice shall specify subject of deposition. Organization is then required to designate and produce officers or employees most qualified to testify on its behalf on specified subject matter. Subpoena shall advise nonparty organization of duty to make such designation and shall describe with particularity matters on which examination is requested. (C.C.P. 2025[d][6]).

Return.—Deposition, when completed, is made available to witness for 30 days for reviewing, correcting and signing, unless parties agree to different period. (C.C.P. 2025[q]). For good cause shown, court may shorten time. Original transcript is retained by attorney for party who noticed deposition. If deponent fails or refuses to sign, deposition shall have same force and effect as though signed. It is not filed in court unless contents become relevant to trial. Rough draft of transcript may not be certified or cited at any time to rebut certified transcript of deposition. (C. C. P. 2025[q]-[s]).

To Perpetuate Testimony.—Applicant may file vertified petition in superior court of county of residence of any expected adverse party or if no expected adverse party is California resident, in superior court of county where action may be filed. Petition must show that applicant expects to be party to action cognizable in courts of this state but is presently unable to cause it to be brought, name and address of witnesses to be examined and expected adverse parties, facts to be established and reasons to perpetuate, names and addresses of expected adverse parties subject matter of expected action, and interest therein. Notice to expected adverse parties required. (C.C.P. 2035).

If deposition is taken to perpetuate testimony, it may be used against any party named in petition as expected adverse party in any subsequent action involving same subject matter. (C.C.P. 2035[g]).

Use of Deposition.—At trial or other hearing, any part or all of deposition, so far as admissible under rules of evidence, may be used against any party who was present or represented at taking of deposition or who had due notice thereof, as follows: (1) Deposition may be used to contradict or impeach deponent who testifies as witness; (2) deposition of party, of officer or agent of party, or of person for whose immediate benefit action is brought, may be used by adverse party for any purpose; and (3) deposition of witness may be used for any purpose if witness is unavailable, where exceptional circumstances exist, or when witness resides more than 150 miles from place of trial. If party introduces only part of deposition, any other party may introduce any other parts. (C.C.P. 2025[u]).

Substitution of parties does not affect right to use depositions previously taken; and, when action in any court of U.S. or of any state has been dismissed and another action involving same subject matter is afterward brought between same parties or their representatives or successors in interest, all depositions lawfully taken and duly filed in former action may be used in latter as if originally taken therefor. (C. C. P. 2025[u][7]).

For depositions taken after Jan. 1, 1998, copy of transcript or other recording of testimony shall be made available to any person requesting copy upon payment of reasonable fee unless protective order issued by court. Notice to deponent required if transcript not part of court record. (C.C.P. 2025.5).

EQUITY:

See topic Actions.

EVIDENCE:

See topic Depositions and Discovery.

Witnesses.—Except as otherwise provided by statute, every person, irrespective of age, is qualified to be witness except person incapable of expressing himself or herself concerning matter so as to be understood directly or through interpretation, or person incapable of understanding duty of witness to tell truth. In any proceeding held outside presence of jury, court may reserve challenges to competency of witness until conclusion of direct examination of that witness. (Evid. C. 700-01).

See also topic Depositions and Discovery.

Privileged Communications.—Attorney cannot, without consent of client, be examined as to any confidential communication made by client to attorney, or attorney's advice given thereon, in course of professional employment. (Evid. C. 950-55). Attorney-client privilege does not apply when: (1) Services of lawyer sought or obtained to aid crime or fraud (Evid. C. 956); (2) communication relevant to an issue between parties all of whom claim through deceased client (Evid. C. 957); (3) communication relevant to issue of breach of duty arising out of lawyer-client relationship (Evid. C. 958); (4) communication relevant to issue of intention or competence of client executing an attested document of which lawyer is an attesting witness, or concerning execution or attestation of document (Evid. C. 959); (5) communication relevant to issue concerning intention of deceased client with respect to deed, will or other writing executed by client purporting to affect interest in property (Evid. C. 960); (6) communication relevant to validity of deed, will or other writing executed by deceased client purporting to affect interest in property (Evid. C. 961); (7) communication relevant in civil proceeding between former joint clients (Evid. C. 962); (8) communication relevant to client act likely to result in death or substantial bodily harm (Evid. C. 956.5). This and other privileges may be waived. (Evid. C. 912).

Penitent may refuse to disclose communication made in confidence to priest, minister or religious practitioner who under religious order is authorized to hear communication and has duty not to disclose it. (Evid. C. 1030-34).

Physician cannot, without consent of patient, disclose information obtained during examination and diagnosis. (Evid. C. 990-992). This privilege does not apply in proceeding to recover damages on account of conduct of patient if communication is relevant to issue concerning condition of patient and good cause is shown for disclosure. (Evid. C. 999). This privilege also does not apply in other situations, including will contests or any actions after death of patient involving validity of any instruments executed by patient conveying or transferring real or personal property, as to matters bearing on physical or mental condition of patient when placed in issue in litigation. (Evid. C. 990-1007, 1010-1026).

Psychotherapist, including some counselors and social workers, also cannot disclose information without patient consent. (Evid. C. 1010 et seq.). No psychotherapist has privilege when patient is child under 16 and psychotherapist has reasonable cause to believe that patient has been victim of crime and that disclosure is in best interests of child. (Evid. C. 1027).

Public officer cannot be examined as to communications made to him or her in official confidence when public interest would suffer by disclosure. (Evid. C. 1040). Privilege for identity of informer is granted if disclosure is against public interest. (Evid. C. 1041). When party in criminal proceeding demands disclosure of informer's identity, hearing may be had outside presence of jury to determine whether nondisclosure will deprive defendant of fair trial. (Evid. C. 1042).

Person connected with or employed on newspaper, magazine, or other periodical publication, press association, wire service, radio or television station cannot be adjudged in contempt for refusing to disclose source of any information procured for and used for news or news commentary purposes, or for failing to disclose any unpublished information obtained or prepared in gathering, receiving or processing such information. (Evid. C. 1070). Evid. Code 1070 does not preclude court from holding newspaper reporter in contempt for failure to disclose names of attorneys and court attaches who gave him information in violation of pre-trial publicity order. (22 C.A.3d 60, 99 C.Rptr. 342).

Person has privilege to refuse to disclose tenor of vote at public election where voting by secret ballot unless he voted illegally or previously made unprivileged disclosure. (Evid. C. 1050).

If owner of trade secret or agent or employee claims privilege, owner can refuse to disclose secret, and prevent another from disclosing it, if will not tend to conceal fraud or work injustice. (Evid. C. 1060). Owner of trade secret may seek protective order in criminal proceeding. (Evid. C. 1061[b], 1062).

Husband and Wife.—Married person has privilege not to testify against spouse in any proceeding, and not to be called as a witness in any proceedings in which spouse is a party. Witness spouse holds privilege. (Evid. C. 970-973). Both spouses hold privilege during and after marriage to refuse to disclose, and to prevent another from disclosing, confidential communication made during marriage. (Evid. C. 980). Witness privilege and communication privilege do not apply in: (1) Proceeding brought by one spouse against another; (2) spouse's commitment or competency proceedings; (3) certain juvenile court proceedings; (4) proceedings in which spouse charged with crime against other spouse or child, parent, relative, or cohabitant of either or with crime against third person committed in course of crime against spouse; (5) bigamy; (6) proceeding in which spouse is charged with willfully omitting to provide minor child with necessary food, clothing, shelter or medical attendance, abandonment of minor child, or failing to provide support for spouse; (7) child, family, or spousal support proceedings. (Evid. C. 972, 982-986). Marital communication privilege does not apply: (1) When communication was made to aid crime or fraud (Evid. C. 981); (2) in proceeding between surviving spouse and person who claims through deceased spouse (Evid. C. 984[b]); (3) in criminal proceeding in which communication is offered in evidence by spouse defendant. (Evid. C. 987). For exception in case of enforcement of support obligation, see Fam. C. 4930.

Communications or Transactions with Persons Since Deceased.—Dead Man's Statute abolished. Evidence of statement by deceased is not made inadmissible by hearsay rule if offered against plaintiff in action for wrongful death. (Evid. C. 1227).

Evidence of statement is not made inadmissible by hearsay rule when offered in action upon claim or demand against estate of declarant if statement was made upon personal knowledge of declarant at time when matter had been recently perceived by him and while his recollection was clear. (Evid. C. 1261[a]).

Evidence of statement is inadmissible under this section if statement was made under circumstances such as to indicate its lack of trustworthiness. (Evid. C. 1261[b]).

Self-Incrimination.—Privilege against to extent granted by state (Cal. Const., Art. 1, §15, cl. 6) or federal constitution (Evid. C. 940). Witnesses in felony case may be compelled to testify upon grant of immunity. (P. C. 1324).

Compelling Attendance.—See topic Depositions and Discovery.

Adverse Witnesses.—Adverse party or person with adverse interest may be called by party to action and examined as if under cross-examination. (Evid. C. 776).

INJUNCTIONS:

Injunctions are governed by Code of Civil Procedure and Rules of Court.

Injunction may issue to protect rights in accordance with generally established principles of equity which have been substantially incorporated into statute and also may be granted in accordance with various statutory provisions. (C. C. 3420 et seq., C. C. P. 525 et seq.).

Jurisdiction.—Temporary restraining orders and preliminary and final injunctions may be granted by superior court. (Const., Art. VI, §10). Municipal courts may issue temporary restraining orders and preliminary injunctions to take accounts, and to appoint receivers where necessary to preserve property rights of any party to action of

INJUNCTIONS . . . *continued*
which court has jurisdiction; and to appoint receiver and to make any order or perform any act pursuant to California Enforcement of Judgments Law. (C.C.P. 86[a][8]).

Prerequisites.—Injunctions may be provisional or final. (C.C. 3420).

Injunction may be granted when it is shown that applicant is entitled to relief restraining commission or continuance of act; when commission or continuance of some act during litigation would produce waste, or great or irreparable injury, to party; when party is doing, or threatens, or is about to do some act in violation of rights of another party respecting subject of action tending to render judgment ineffectual; when pecuniary compensation would not afford adequate relief or would be extremely difficult to ascertain; where necessary to prevent multiplicity of judicial proceedings; where obligation arises from trust (C.C.P. 526); to prevent harrassment (C.C.P. 527.6) or to enjoin concerted acts of violence (C.C.P. 527.7).

Injunctions may also be granted in number of specific instances provided for by statute, e.g., breach of collective bargaining agreements (Lab. C. 1126); labor disputes (C.C.P. 527.3 and Lab. C. 1116); nuisance (C.C.P. 731); unfair competition (Bus. & Prof. C. 17203); to protect trademarks, tradenames and business reputation (Bus. & Prof. C. 14330, 14340, 14402, 14493).

Final injunction may be granted where pecuniary compensation is inadequate or difficult to ascertain, to avoid multiplicity of suits or where obligation arises from trust. (C. C. 3422; C. C. P. 526).

Injunctive relief may not be granted: To stay judicial proceedings in federal court, or state court except to prevent multiplicity of such proceedings; to stay proceedings in another state upon judgment of court of that state; to prevent breach of contract (other than certain written contracts involving unique personal services and over $50,000/ year) which could not be specifically enforced; to prevent exercise of public or private office; to prevent legislative act by municipal corporation (C. C. 3423; C. C. P. 526) or to enforce penalty or forfeiture except in case of nuisance or unfair competition (C. C. 3369; Bus. & Prof. C. 17202). It may not be granted to prevent execution of public statute, unless statute unconstitutional. (11 C.3d 842, 523 P.2d 682).

Procedure.—Preliminary injunctions and temporary restraining orders may be granted upon verified complaint or affidavit if they show sufficient grounds. (C. C. P. 527[a]). Preliminary injunction may not be obtained without notice to opposite party. Temporary restraining order ordinarily requires notice to other party but may be granted without notice upon showing by affidavit or verified complaint that great or irreparable injury would result prior to hearing on notice and good faith effort made to inform opposition, or other specific good reason. (C.C.P. 527[c]). (Court rules in some counties require that notice be given to opposing counsel before issuance of temporary restraining order in all cases.) If temporary restraining order granted without notice, matter must be made returnable on notice or order to show cause within 15 days or, if good cause, 22 days from date of order. (C.C.P. 527[a]). Injunction granted without notice may be dissolved or modified on application by party enjoined. (C. C. P. 532, 533).

Labor Disputes.—Granting of temporary restraining orders and injunctions in labor disputes is limited by statute. (C. C. P. 527.3).

Bond.—On granting preliminary injunction, except when granted upon application of state, county or municipal corporation, or to either spouse in action against other for dissolution or separate maintenance, court must require written undertaking on part of applicant with sufficient sureties, to effect that he will pay to party enjoined such damages as such party may sustain by reason of injunction if court finally decides that applicant was not entitled thereto. (C. C. P. 529). Regarding construction projects, see C. C. P. 529.1. Undertaking on temporary restraining order is not required by C. C. P. 529 (36 C.A.3d 321, 111 C. Rptr. 658) but may in discretion of court be required.

JUDGMENTS:

See also category Debtor and Creditor, topics Executions and Exemptions.

Judgment by Default.—If defendant in action upon contract or judgment for recovery of money or damages only, fails to plead or move within specified time from date of service, judgment by default may be entered by clerk or judge upon written application including interest and costs and in certain cases, attorney's fees. (C.C.P. 585[a]). In other classes of actions, after entry of default, application supported by evidence must be made to court for relief sought in complaint. (C.C.P. 585[b]). Where service is by publication, application for judgment must in all cases be made to court and proof of allegations in complaint is required. If defendant is not California resident, plaintiff shall be examined respecting payments made to plaintiff. Where service is by publication and affects title to or possession of real property, no judgment shall be rendered only upon mere occupancy, unless said occupancy shall have continued for time necessary to confer title by prescription. Where plaintiff bases his claim upon paper title, court shall require evidence establishing plaintiff's equitable right to judgment. (C.C.P. 585[c]). Entry of default judgment may be obtained on cross-complaint if judgment properly awardable on cross-complaint and separate judgment on cross-complaint would not substantially delay final disposition. (C.C.P. 585[e]). Court may permit use of affidavits in lieu of personal testimony as to all proof required. (C.C.P. 585[d]). For further information on default judgments, see C.C.P. 585-587.5.

Judgment by confession without action may be entered in following manner in any court having jurisdiction for amount due (C.C.P. 1132): statement in writing must be made, signed and verified by defendant, to following effect: (1) It must authorize entry of judgment for specified sum; (2) if it be for money due or to become due it must state concisely facts out of which indebtedness arose and show that sum confessed therefor is justly due or to become due; (3) if it be for purpose of securing plaintiff against contingent liability it must state concisely facts constituting liability and show that sum confessed does not exceed same (C.C.P. 1133). Judgment will be entered by clerk of court upon filing of such statement with endorsement upon it and payment of fees by plaintiff. (C.C.P. 1134).

Judgment by confession shall be entered only if attorney independently representing defendant signs certificate that he has examined proposed judgment and has advised defendant with respect to waiver of rights and defenses under confession procedure and has advised defendant to utilize such procedure. Certificate must be filed with statement required to be filed that authorizes entry of judgment by confession. (C.C. P. 1132).

See also infra, subhead Foreign Judgments.

Judgments on Pleadings.—Party may move for, or court on own motion may grant, judgment on pleadings. Grounds are failure to state cause of action or sufficient defense or lack of subject matter jurisdiction. (C.C.P. 438).

Declaratory Judgments.—In case of actual controversy relating to legal rights and duties of parties relating to written instrument excluding will or trust, or under contract, or who desire declaration of rights or duties with respect to one another, judgment giving declaratory relief may be had whether or not there has been any breach of obligation. Original action may be filed in superior court or cross-complaint filed in pending action in superior, municipal or justice court. In granting such relief court can determine any question of construction or validity arising under instrument or contract which is basis for action. Such declaration has force of final judgment. (C.C.P. 1060).

Summary judgment may be ordered, in whole or in part, by superior or municipal court in all proceedings where plaintiff claims there is no defense or defendant claims action has no merit and there is no triable issue as to any material fact. (C.C.P. 437c[a]). Summary judgment should be granted if there is no triable issue as to any material fact and moving party is entitled to judgment as matter of law. (C.C.P. 437c[c]). Court will consider all evidence submitted unless timely objection is made. (C.C.P. 437c).

Motion may be made 60 days after opposing party's general appearance, or at earlier time upon court order, but must be heard no later than 30 days before trial, except for good cause. Minimum of 28 days notice is required. Additional five days notice required if notice is served by mail within California. Extra ten days is added if mailing is outside California but within U.S., 20 days is added if place of address is outside U.S. and two court days are added if notice is by facsimile transmission or overnight delivery. (C.C.P. 437c[a]).

Motion shall be supported by affidavits, declarations, depositions, admissions, and answers to interrogatories. Supporting papers must set forth a separate statement of material facts that are contended to be undisputed and followed by reference to supporting evidence. Opposing papers must respond to moving party's contentions and must separately set forth material facts contended to be in dispute. Any opposition to motion shall be served and filed not less than 14 days and reply not less than five days preceding hearing date unless court for good cause orders otherwise. Motion shall be granted if no triable issue of material fact and movant entitled to judgment. (C.C.P. 437c).

Consent judgment may be entered on stipulation of parties. (13 C. 191).

Offer of Judgment.—Any party may serve written offer upon any other party to allow judgment to be taken against offering party in accordance with terms and conditions stated in offer. Offer must take place not less than ten days before trial or arbitration pursuant to C.C.P. 1281 or 1295. If offer is accepted, offer with proof of acceptance shall be filed and judgment shall be entered or proof of acceptance filed with arbitrator. If offer is not accepted before trial or within 30 days of its making, whichever occurs first, offer is deemed withdrawn and cannot be introduced in evidence. If defendant's offer is not accepted and plaintiff's judgment or award is not more favorable than defendant's offer, plaintiff may not recover postoffer costs and must pay defendant's costs from time of offer and court or arbitrator in its discretion may order plaintiff to pay defendant's costs from date of complaint and for experts. If plaintiff's offer is not accepted and defendant does not obtain judgment or award more favorable than offer, court or arbitrator in its discretion may order defendant to pay for plaintiff's experts in addition to plaintiff's costs. If offer made by defendant is not accepted and plaintiff fails to obtain more favorable judgment or award, defendant's costs from time of offer are deducted from plaintiff's award. If costs exceed amount of plaintiff's judgment or award, net difference awarded to defendant and judgment or award entered accordingly. Offer of judgment or award does not apply to plaintiffs in eminent domain actions or labor arbitrations under Gov't. C. 3512. (C.C.P. 998).

Entry.—Judgment must be entered by clerk within 24 hours after verdict if trial by jury regardless of whether judgment notwithstanding verdict is pending. Judgment is entered immediately after bench trial. Judgment is ineffectual for any purpose until entered. (C. C. P. 664).

Vacation or Modification.—Party may move court to vacate or modify judgment on ground that it was entered on erroneous legal basis, is not supported by facts or by special verdict, or it was taken through mistake, inadvertance, surprise or excusable neglect of party or counsel. (C.C.P. 663, 663a, 473).

Lien.—Entry of judgment in court by which rendered does not create any lien, but abstract of judgment or decree of any court of record of state or of United States, certified by clerk of court, may be recorded with recorder of any county and from such recording judgment or decree becomes lien on all nonexempt real property of judgment debtor in county, then owned by him or acquired before lien expires. (C.C.P. 697.310-697.410). Certified copies of judgments may be acceptable in specified cases. See C.C.P. 697.320 (support payments); 697.320(a), 667.7 (judgment against health care provider); and 697.320(a), 697.330 (worker's compensation awards). Judgment lien on certain types of business personal property also available. (C.C.P. 697.510-697.740). Abstract of judgment or decree of court being recorded must contain all of following: (a) Title of court where judgment or decree is entered and cause and number of action; (b) date of entry of judgment or decree and of any renewals of judgment or decree and where entered in records of court; (c) name and last known address of judgment debtor and address at which summons was either personally served or mailed to judgment debtor or his attorney of record; (d) name and address of judgment creditor; (e) amount of judgment or decree as entered or last renewed; (f) social security and drawer's license number of judgment debtor if known and if not known that fact shall be indicated; (g) whether stay of enforcement has been ordered by court and, if so, date stay ends; (h) date of issuance of abstract. Form for liens

JUDGMENTS . . . *continued*

prescribed by Judicial Council. Judgment debtor receives automatic exemption from lien on real property for debtor's real property dwelling. (C.C.P. 704.710-704.850). If judgment debtor has recorded declaration of homestead he receives additional exemptions. Judgment debtor must own interest in property and reside there to be eligible for declared homestead status. (C.C.P. 704.910-704.995). Judgment exceptions do not apply, if judgment to be entered is for foreclosure of mortgage, deed of trust, or other lien or encumbrance on property. (C.C.P. 703.010, 688.030). Lien continues for ten years unless enforcement of judgment stayed on appeal or by execution of sufficient undertaking. (C.C.P. 697.310[b], 697.320[b]).

Where property has been attached, lien of judgment, abstract of which is properly recorded, relates back to date of attachment. (C.C.P. 697.020).

Exempt Property from Satisfaction of Judgment: (a) Motor vehicles—equity of $1,900 or less (C.C.P. 704.010[a]); (b) household furnishings, appliances, and personal effects (C.C.P. 704.020); (c) material applied to residence repair or improvement not to exceed $2,000 (C.C.P. 704.030); (d) jewelry, heirlooms, and works of art not to exceed $5,000 (C.C.P. 704.040); (e) health aids (C.C.P. 704.050); (f) tools, specified personal property used in business, up to $5,000 if only used by one spouse, $10,000 if used by both (C.C.P. 704.060); (g) paid earnings as follows: (1) all of paid earnings are exempt if prior to payment they were subject to earnings withholding order or wage assignment for support; (2) 75% of paid earnings that are levied upon or otherwise sought to be subjected to enforcement of money judgment are exempt if prior to payment they were not subject to earnings withholding order or wage assignment for support (C.C.P. 704.070) (See also C.C.P. 706.050-.052 for restrictions on earnings withholding.); (h) deposit accounts—exemption is from $2,000 to $3,000 (C.C.P. 704.080); (i) funds of incarcerated judgment debtor at $1,000 per spouse (C.C.P. 704.090); (j) life insurance policies (C.C.P. 704.100); (k) retirement benefits (C.C.P. 704.110 and 704.115); (l) state employee vacation credits (C.C.P. 704.113); (m) unemployment benefits (C.C.P. 704.120); (n) disability or health insurance benefits (C.C.P. 704.130); (o) personal injury settlement or award (C.C.P. 704.140); (p) wrongful death settlement or award (C.C.P. 704.150); (q) worker's compensation claim and award (C.C.P. 704.160); (r) social services aid (C.C.P. 704.170); (s) relocation benefits (C.C.P. 704.180); (t) financial aid while attending school (C.C.P. 704.190); (u) family and cemetery plots (C.C.P. 704.200).

Revival.—Judgment which has not been enforced within ten years may be revived and enforced by filing application for renewal with court within ten year period of enforceability. (C. C. P. 683.130). Notice of renewal shall be sent to judgment debtor. (C. C. P. 683.160). Application for renewal shall include: (a) Title of court where judgment is entered and number of action; (b) date of entry of judgment and of any renewals of judgment and where entered in records of court; (c) name and address of judgment creditor and name and address of judgment debtor; (d) in case of money judgment, information necessary to compute amount of judgment as renewed. In case of judgment for possession or sale of property, description of performance remaining due. (C.C.P. 683.140). Compliance renews judgment for ten years from date application to renew was filed. (C.C.P. 683.120[b]). Rules differ where judgment has already been renewed, (C.C.P. 683.110[b]), or where judgment is in installments (C.C.P. 683.130[b][1]). Judgment for child or spousal support, including all lawful interest and penalties computed thereon, is exempt from requirements for renewal and is enforceable until paid in full. (C.C.P. 683.130[c]). Renewal application may not be filed if judgment has been discharged in bankruptcy. (11 U.S.C. 362).

Assignment of Judgment.—Judgments are assignable, but assignee may not enforce judgment under Enforcement of Judgments Law (C.C.P. 681.010 et seq.) unless acknowledgment of assignment of judgment to that assignee has been filed under C.C.P. 673 or assignee has otherwise become assignee of record (C.C.P. 681.020).

Satisfaction of money judgment may be entered on superior or municipal court register of actions or justice court docket upon execution returned satisfied or on acknowledgment of satisfaction filed with clerk or judge, or by court order. (C. C. P. 724.020).

Form for acknowledgment of satisfaction of judgment is prescribed by Judicial Council. Acknowledgment of partial satisfaction of judgment may now be required. (C. C. P. 724.110, 724.120).

Actions on Judgments.—Nothing in Enforcement of Judgments Law (C.C.P. 681.010 et seq.) limits judgment creditor's right to bring action on judgment (C.C.P. 683.050). Such action must be brought within ten years. (C.C.P. 337.5).

Foreign Judgments.—Effect of judicial record of sister state is same in this state as in state where it was made, except that it can only be enforced here by action or special proceeding, and except, also, that authority of guardian, conservator, or committee, or of personal representative, does not extend beyond jurisdiction of government under which he was invested with his authority. (C. C. P. 1913).

Effect of judicial record of court of admiralty of foreign country is same as if it were record of court of admiralty of U. S. (C. C. P. 1914).

Judgment obtained by confession in another state, pursuant to terms of promissory note, is enforceable in California. (114 C. A. 272, 299 P. 738).

Uniform Enforcement of Foreign Judgments Act has not been adopted.

Uniform Foreign Money-Judgments Recognition Act enacted. (C. C. P. 1713 et seq.).

Enforcement of Sister State Money Judgments.—Expands scope of Foreign Money Judgments Recognition Act providing streamlined process whereby enforcement of sister state money judgments can be obtained by registering new cause of action and judgment based on sister state judgment. Specifically excludes foreign support orders. (C.C.P. 1710.10 et seq.).

Requires that application for entry of judgment be executed under oath and include a statement that an action in California on sister state judgment is not barred by applicable statute of limitations; a statement based on applicant's information and belief that no stay of enforcement of sister state judgment is currently in effect in sister state; a statement of amount remaining unpaid, including accrued interest computed at rate of interest applicable to judgment under law of sister state; statement that no action based on sister state judgment is currently pending in this state and has not been previously entered in California; statement of name and last known address of judgment debtor if individual; if corporation, statement of name, place of incorporation, and whether corporation is qualified to do business in California; statement of name and address of judgment creditor and properly authenticated copy of sister state judgment must be attached to application. (C. C. P. 1710.15). Application must be filed in office of clerk of municipal, justice, or superior court, depending on judgment amount, for county in which judgment debtor resides or if judgment debtor not resident, in any county of state. (C. C. P. 1710.20). On filing of application, clerk shall enter judgment for unpaid amount of sister state judgment plus interest and cost of filing. From time of entry, interest shall accrue at rate of interest applicable to judgment under law of sister state. (C.C.P. 1710.25). Judgment shall not be enforced by any means until at least 30 days after judgment creditor serves notice of entry of judgment and proof filed in accordance with C.C.P. 417.10. (C.C.P. 1710.45). Judgment may be vacated on any ground which would be defense to action in California on sister state judgment including ground that amount of interest is incorrect. (C.C.P. 1710.40[a]).

Entry of judgment prohibited where a stay of enforcement is in effect in sister state; where an action based on sister state judgment is pending in any California court; where judgment based on sister state judgment has previously been entered in California proceeding. (C.C.P. 1710.55).

Revised Uniform Interstate Family Support Act adopted. (Fam. C. 4900 et seq.).

LIMITATION OF ACTIONS:

No limitation on actions to recover money or property deposited with bank, banker, trust company, building and loan association or savings and loan society, or evidenced by certificate issued by industrial loan company or credit union, unless such organization has become insolvent, in which case statute commences to run from beginning of liquidation (C.C.P. 348), or prosecutions for offense punishable by death or by imprisonment in state prison for life or for life without possibility of parole, or for embezzlement of public money including case where defendant is minor at time of commission of offense and prosecutor could have petitioned court for fitness hearing under Welf. & Inst. C. 707. (P. C. 799).

Uniform Commercial Code governs limitation of actions on bulk transfers (Com'l. C. 6110); breach of contract for sale (Com'l. C. 2725); and unauthorized signature on item charged against bank account (Com'l. C. 4406).

See also category Business Regulation and Commerce, topic Commercial Code.

Other actions commonly brought must be commenced within following time periods after accrual of cause of action.

Ten years: On bonds or coupons issued by State of California; on general obligation bonds or coupons, not secured by lien on real property, issued by political subdivision of State of California; and on judgment or decree of courts of U.S. or any state (C.C.P. 337.5); real property actions by state (C.C.P. 315); action based on latent defects or deficiency in development or improvement of real property, including action against construction surety or action for indemnity but excluding actions based on willful misconduct or concealment (C.C.P. 337.15). By Attorney General to enforce or impose charitable trust or to recover property or proceeds thereof. (Govt. C. 12596). After determination of liability or during period lien is in force due to recorded abstract or state tax lien, Franchise Tax Board can bring action for taxes, penalties, and interest. (Rev. & Tax C. 19371).

Eight years: Civil action for sexual molestation of minor by family or household member shall be brought within eight years of child reaching majority or within three years of discovery of cause of action after majority, whichever is later. (C.C.P. 340.1).

Seven years: Contract to render personal service, other than contract of apprenticeship, may not be enforced against employee beyond seven years from commencement of service under it unless employee is party to contract to render personal service in production of phonorecords. (Lab. C. 2855).

Six years: Except for bonds or other evidences of indebtedness of public district or corporation, on any bonds, notes or debentures issued by any corporation or pursuant to permit of Commissioner of Corporations, or on any coupons issued with such bonds, notes or debentures (if such bonds, notes or debentures have been issued to or held by public); on any mortgage, trust deed or other agreement pursuant to which such bonds, notes or debentures were issued (C.C.P. 336a); against notary public on his or her bond or in his or her official capacity, except that action based on malfeasance or misfeasance must be commenced within three years of notarial act or within one year of plaintiff's discovery of facts giving rise to cause of action, whichever is later (C.C.P. 338[f]); injury to unborn child (C.C. 29); or for prosecution of offense punishable by imprisonment in state prison for eight years or more (P. C. 800).

Five years: Action for mesne profits of real property (C.C.P. 336) or for recovery of real property or possession thereof (C.C.P. 318). Action to redeem mortgage of real property. (C.C.P. 346).

Four years: On any contract, obligation or liability founded upon instrument in writing, except as noted above in case of bonds, notes or debentures, provided that action to collect balance due after sale of realty pursuant to foreclosure under deed of trust or mortgage must be brought within three months after time of sale (C.C.P. 337[1], 580a); upon book account whether consisting of one or more entries; upon account stated based upon account in writing, but acknowledgment need not be in writing; upon balance due upon mutual, open and current account items of which are in writing, except that time begins to run from date of last item (C.C.P. 337[2], 344, 345); upon rescission of contract in writing, action accruing on date facts entitling rescission occurred. In cases of fraud or mistake time runs from discovery of facts constituting fraud or mistake. In case of misrepresentation under Ins. Code 359, time runs from when representation becomes false (C. C. P. 337[3]); upon written lease of real property (C. C. P. 337.2).

Action for damages for patent deficiency (such as is apparent by reasonable inspection) in design, supervision, survey, or construction of improvement to real property,

---

See note at head of Digest as to 1998 legislation covered.

See Topical Index in front part of this volume.

LIMITATION OF ACTIONS . . . *continued*
or injury to person or property resulting therefrom, within four years after substantial completion of improvement, except that if injury to person or property occurs during fourth year, action may be commenced within one year after date of injury but not more than five years after substantial completion of improvement. (C. C. P. 337.1).

Deceptive stock practices four years from date of transaction, or one year from discovery, whichever is later (Corp. C. 25506); and actions not otherwise provided for (C. C. P. 343).

Action against sureties on guardian's or conservator's bond may be commenced within four years of guardian's or conservator's removal or discharge subject to tolling if person entitled to bring action was under legal disability. (Prob. C. 2333).

Under Commercial Code §2725: Secured party's action to recover deficiency from buyer is barred by this section if more than four years elapse since breach of security agreement, despite fact that date of repossession and resale is within four year period. (62 C.A. 3d 1024, 133 C. Rptr. 497).

See also category Business Regulation and Commerce, topic Monopolies, Restraint of Trade and Competition, subhead Enforcement.

Three years: On liability created by statute, other than penalty or forfeiture (C.C.P. 338[a]); for trespass upon or injury to real property (C.C.P. 338[b]); for taking, detaining or injuring goods or chattels including actions for specific recovery of personal property except that cause of action on theft of any art or artifact is not deemed to accrue until discovery of whereabouts by aggrieved party, his or her agent, or law enforcement agency which originally investigated theft (C.C.P. 338[c]); for relief on ground of fraud or mistake, cause of action not deemed to have accrued until discovery of facts by aggrieved party (C.C.P. 338[d]); on bond of public official, cause of action based on fraud or embezzlement not deemed to have accrued until discovery of facts (C.C.P. 338[e]); against notary public on his or her bond or in his or her official capacity, except that action for misfeasance or malfeasance must be brought within one year of discovery thereof or within three years of notarial act giving rise to action, whichever is later, but in any case within six years (C.C.P. 338[f]); for slander of title to real property (C.C.P. 338[g]); or for prosecution of offense punishable by imprisonment in state prison (P. C. 801). Action under §17536 of Business and Professions Code, cause not deemed to have accrued until discovery by aggrieved party, Attorney General, district attorney, county counsel, city prosecutor, or city attorney of facts constituting grounds for commencement of action (C.C.P. 338[h]); action under Porter-Cologne Water Quality Control Act (Water C. 13000 et seq.) of California law relating to hazardous waste control (H. & S.C. 25100 et seq.), cause not deemed to accrue until discovery by State Department of Health Services, State Water Resources Control Board, or regional water quality control board of facts constituting grounds for commencing action (C. C. P. 338[i]); action to recover damages to property under theory of eminent domain (C.C.P. 338[j]). Action commenced under Division 26 of Health & Safety Code (H. & S.C. 39000 et seq.) is not deemed to accrue until discovery by State Air Resources Board or regional district board of facts constituting grounds for commencing action under its jurisdiction. (C.C.P. 338[k]). Action commenced under Fish & G. C. 1603.1 or 5650.1 not deemed to accrue until discovery by agency bringing action of facts constituting grounds for commencing action. (C.C.P. 338[l]).

Civil action for sexual molestation of minor by family or household member, three years after discovery, or should have discovered, injury or illness after age of majority or within eight years of child reaching majority, whichever is later. (C.C.P. 340.1).

Action against health care provider for professional negligence, within three years after date of injury or one year after plaintiff discovers, or by reasonable diligence should have discovered, injury, whichever is less unless tolled by fraud, intentional concealment, or presence of non-therapeutic, non-diagnostic foreign body in person of plaintiff. Actions by minor under age six years must commence within three years or prior to age eight, whichever is longer, unless tolled by fraud or collusion of parent or guardian and defendant's insurer or health care provider in failure to bring action for minor injured as result of professional negligence. (C. C. P. 340.5).

Complaints against contractor licensees for acts or omissions must be filed with registrar of contractors within three years; accusations and citations must be filed within four years after act or omission or within 18 months from complaint filing, whichever is later, except that accusation of misrepresentation in obtaining license may be filed within two years after discovery of facts constituting fraud or misrepresentations. Accusations of breach of express, written warranty for period greater than three years must be filed within duration of warranty. (Bus. & Prof. C. 7091).

Action for false claim against state funds under Govt. Code 12652 must be filed within three years after date of discovery by state or political subdivision official and within ten years after violation committed. (Govt. C. 12654).

For payments into or out of Public Employees' Retirement Fund for adjustment of error or omissions. (Govt. C. 20164).

See also category Transportation, topic Motor Vehicles, subhead Insurance.

Two years: On contract, obligation or liability (other than accounts governed by C. C. P. 337[2]) not founded upon instrument of writing; upon certificate or abstract or guaranty of title of real property or policy of title insurance, cause being deemed to have accrued upon discovery of loss or damage suffered (C.C.P. 339[1]); against sheriff, coroner, or constable upon liability arising from his acts or omissions in official capacity including nonpayment of money collected in enforcement of judgment (C.C.P. 339[2]); or upon rescission of contract not in writing, action accruing on date facts entitling rescission occurred except in cases of fraud and mistake where time runs from discovery of facts (C. C. P. 339[3]); upon lease of real property not in writing, time to run from breach of lease and abandonment of property, or from termination of right to possession, whichever is earlier (C. C. P. 339.5). Action to foreclose street improvement lien must be brought within two years after maturity of last installment of assessment (C. C. P. 329); against public entity or employees of entity (Govt. C. 950.2) if written notice of rejection of claim not given (Govt. C. 945.6[a][2]). Sex discrimination action for wages, except that cause of action arising out of wilful violation may be commenced within three years after it occurs. (Lab. C. 1197.5[h]).

Action for violation of pest control regulations by director, attorney general, district attorney, city prosecutor or attorney must be within two years of violation or within one year of submission of investigation to director. (Fd. & Agric. C. 11895). Action for violation of agricultural chemicals, livestock remedies, and commercial feeds regulations by director, attorney general, district attorney, city prosecutor or attorney must be within two years of violation or within one year of submission of investigation to director. (Fd. & Agric. C. 13000).

One year: For libel, slander, assault, battery, false imprisonment, seduction of one below age of consent, wrongful death or injury (C.C.P. 340[3]) (unless action is for injury or illness based on exposure to asbestos [C. C. P. 340.2], or against health care provider [C. C. P. 340.5]); upon statute for penalty or forfeiture when action is given to individual or to individual and state unless statute prescribes different limitation (C.C.P. 340[1], [2]); by depositor against bank for payment of raised or forged check or check bearing forged or unauthorized endorsement (C.C.P. 340[3]); against any person who boards or feeds animals or who practices veterinary medicine for such person's neglect resulting in injury or death to said animal (C.C.P. 340[3]); against officer to recover damages for seizure of any property for statutory forfeiture to state, or for detention or injury of property so seized or for damages done to any person in making such seizure (C.C.P. 340[4]); or for damages against defendant from date of judgment based on commission of felony unless longer period is proscribed for specific action (C.C.P. 340.3); by good faith improver of land of another, action accruing on date true ownership of property discovered (C. C. P. 340[5]); prosecution for offense not punishable by death or imprisonment in state prison except that prosecution for misdemeanor sex offenses committed with or upon minor under age 14 must be commenced within two years (P.C. 802). Claims must be presented to public board for all claims against public entities other than for death or injury to person, personal property, or growing crops unless settlement procedure for specific claim involved is otherwise provided for by special statute (Govt. C. 911.2) and failure to present such claim within such time bars action against employees of entity as well as entity (Govt. C. 950.2). Uninsured motorist provision (Ins. C. 11580.2[i]); mechanics lien provision (C. C. 3144).

Actions against attorney for wrongful act or omission, other than fraud, arising in performance of professional services, must be commenced within one year after plaintiff discovers, or through use of reasonable diligence should have discovered, facts constituting wrongful act or omission, or four years from date of wrongful act or omission, whichever occurs first. (C.C.P. 340.6).

Request of State Personnel Board to file charges against employee for discipline must be filed within one year of event(s). (Govt. C. 19583.5).

Notice of motion to modify order awarding spousal support must not be filed until one year after entry of previous order unless request for modification is based on significant decrease in income of moving party. (C. C. 4801.9).

Six months: Against public entity or employees of entity (Govt. C. 950.2) if written notice of claim rejection given, time runs from date notice is personally delivered or deposited in mail but is tolled during plaintiff's imprisonment (Govt. C. 945.6). Against officer, or officer de facto to recover certain personal property or value thereof, or damages for making seizures in his official capacity as tax collector (C.C.P. 341[1]); to recover stock of corporation sold for delinquent assessment (C.C.P. 341[2]); and to set aside or invalidate any action taken or performed by majority of trustees of any corporation heretofore or hereafter dissolved by operation of law, including revivor of any such corporation (C. C. P. 341[3]). Actions contesting validity of acts or proceedings for authorization, sale, or issuance of bonds under color of law by certain public bodies must be brought within six months from date of authorization, sale or issuance of said bonds. (C. C. P. 349.2). Actions contesting proceedings for formation, dissolution or change of organization or boundaries of certain public entities (C. C. P. 349.1); tax refunds if notice of action on claim not mailed (Rev. & Tax C. 19085). Claim must be presented to public board for all claims against public entities for death or injury to person, personal property or growing crops (Govt. C. 911.2), and failure to present such claim within such time bars action against employees of entity as well as against entity (Govt. C. 950.2). When such claim is presented late, written notice must be given within 45 days that claim was not filed timely (Govt. C. 911.3) and written application may be made to public entity for leave to present such claims within reasonable time not to exceed one year after accrual of cause of action (Govt. C. 911.4).

Three months: To collect balance due after sale pursuant to foreclosure under deed of trust or mortgage (C. C. P. 580a); actions contesting validity of proceedings for incorporation, annexation of territory or consolidation of municipal corporation (C. C. P. 349½).

One hundred and eighty days: To enjoin, abate, or for damages on account of, underground trespass, use or occupancy, by means of well drilled for oil or gas or both from surface location or for conversion or taking or removing of oil, gas or other liquid, or fluids by means of any such well. (C. C. P. 349¾).

One hundred and twenty days: Actions challenging local government decisions must be commenced within 90 days after legislative body's decision unless action is in support of development of housing projects for low and moderate income in which case one year after accrual of cause of action is allowed. (Govt. C. 65009[c], [d]).

One hundred days: Service of response requesting correction or vacation of arbitration award. (C. C. P. 1288.2).

Ninety days: For recovery or conversion of personal property from hotel and other named establishments must be brought within 90 days from departure of owner from said establishment (C. C. P. 341a); tax refunds (Rev. & Tax. C. 6933, 19083, 26103); action to foreclose mechanics lien must be commenced within 90 days after lien recorded (C. C. 3144); action to enforce stop notice against private (C. C. 3172) and public (C. C. 3184, 3210) works of improvement.

Sixty days: Mechanics lien of original contractor must be recorded within 60 days of recording notice of completion/cessation of work, or if no such notice has been recorded, within 90 days of completion. (C. C. 3115).

See note at head of Digest as to 1998 legislation covered.

See Topical Index in front part of this volume.

CA – 29

LIMITATION OF ACTIONS . . . *continued*

Thirty days: Any action to contest assessment levied by legislative body of any municipality under terms of Local Improvement Act of 1901, must be commenced within 30 days after entry upon minutes of such legislative body of resolution provided for in §8 of said Act. (C. C. P. 349). Any action to contest assessment by chartered city against real property for public improvements must be commenced within 30 days of levy of assessment. Any appeal from final judgment in such action must be perfected within 30 days after entry of judgment (C. C. P. 329.5); action against State after relief from late filing (Govt. C. 946.6[f]).

Mechanics lien of subcontractor must be recorded within 30 days of recordation of notice of completion/cessation of work, or if no such notice has been recorded, within 90 days of completion. (C. C. 3116).

Action to determine existence or nonexistence of father and child relationship, brought by man not presumed father for purpose of declaring he is natural father of child having presumed father if mother consents to adoption of child, must be brought within 30 days after he received notice under C.C. 7017 that he could be father, or birth of child, whichever is later. (C.C. 7006).

Fifteen days: Contest of civil penalties for payment of wages less than minimum wage must be commenced within 15 business days after issuance of citation. (Lab. C. 1197.1).

Actions Not Specifically Provided For.—Any cause of action not otherwise provided for must be commenced within four years after it accrues. (C. C. P. 343).

Absence of Defendant.—Time of absence of defendant from state is not part of time limited for commencement of action (C. C. P. 351), provided, however, that statute of limitations is not tolled in cause of action arising out of ownership or operation of motor vehicle (wherein summons may be served upon defendant outside state) commenced since Sept. 7, 1956, except when defendant cannot be located through exercise of reasonable diligence (Veh. C. 17463).

Disabilities of Plaintiff.—Certain disabilities (infancy, insanity, imprisonment) prevent statute running during continuance of disability, except in case of action for damages relating to conditions of confinement, action against public entity or employee on cause of action for which claim is required under Govt. C. (C. C. P. 352) or in case of claim under uninsured motorist clause of automobile policy (248 C.A.2d 517, 56 C. Rptr. 609).

Where person is under disability to commence action because of existence of state of war, time during which such disability continues is not part of time limited for commencing such action. (C. C. P. 354).

Death of Either Party.—Where person entitled to bring action dies before expiration of time limited for commencement thereof, and cause of action survives, action may be brought by representatives after expiration of that time and within six months from death. If person against whom action may be brought dies before expiration of time limited for commencement thereof, and cause of action survives, action may be commenced within one year after date of death and time otherwise limited for commencement of action does not apply. Claim based on action against decedent must be filed within four months after date letters issued unless court grants relief. (C. C. P. 366.2; Prob. C. 9100, 9103).

Acknowledgment, New Promise or Part Payment.—No acknowledgment or promise is sufficient evidence of new or continuing contract by which to take case out of operation of statute of limitations unless same is contained in some writing signed by party to be charged thereby, but payment on account of principal or interest on promissory note is sufficient acknowledgment to stop, from time to time as any such payment is made, running of statute of limitations and to start running of new period, but no such payment of itself revives cause of action once barred. (C. C. P. 360). No waiver bars defense of statute of limitations in any action unless it be in writing and signed by person obligated; and no such writing shall be effective more than four years from expiration of time limited for commencement of action involved, except that waivers executed after expiration of time limited for action involved shall be effective for not more than four years from date thereof. Waiver may be renewed for further four-year period and waivers may be made successively. (C. C. P. 360.5).

Foreign Causes of Action.—When cause of action has arisen in another state, or in foreign country, and by laws thereof, action thereon cannot be maintained against person by reason of lapse of time, action thereon shall not be maintained against him in this state, except in favor of one who has been citizen of this state and who has held cause of action from time it accrued. (C. C. P. 361).

Contractual limitations are permitted if term is not so unreasonable as to show undue advantage. (183 C. 618, 192 P. 292).

Pleading.—It is sufficient to state that cause of action is barred by section of Code of Civil Procedure relied upon. If such allegation be controverted, party pleading must establish facts showing bar. (C. C. P. 458).

PARTITION:

Partition action may be brought by owner of real or personal property held concurrently with other persons or in successive estates. (C. C. P. 872.210). Real and personal property may be partitioned in one action. (C. C. P. 872.240).

Venue.—See topic Venue.

Sale.—If court determines that sale of property would be more equitable than division, or if parties have agreed to sale, court may order entire property sold (C. C. P. 872.820) or part sold (C. C. P. 872.830). Sale may be by public auction or private sale as determined by court to be more beneficial to parties. (C. C. P. 873.520). Sale may be made on terms agreed to in writing by parties or deemed proper by court. (C. C. P. 873.600, 873.610, 873.630).

PLEADING:

Code pleading state, but with significant modifications of traditional code pleading. California has not adopted use of Federal Rules of Civil Procedure.

Pleadings Permitted.—Pleadings allowed in civil actions are complaints, demurrers, answers and cross-complaints. (C.C.P. 422.10). For pleading procedure for Municipal and Justice Courts, see discussion of economic litigation in subhead Economic Litigation in Municipal and Justice Courts, infra.

Complaint or cross-complaint must contain statement of facts constituting cause of action in ordinary and concise language and demand for relief. (C.C.P. 425.10). Amount claimed shall be stated unless action is in Superior Court for personal injury or wrongful death, in which event amount shall not be stated in complaint or cross-complaint but must be provided to opposing party at least 60 days prior to trial or upon request, or if no request, in statement of damages required before default may be taken. (C.C.P. 425.10, 425.11). See also topic Actions. Plaintiff may include fictitious ("Doe") defendants if ignorant of name of defendant. (C.C.P. 474).

Answer to complaint or cross-complaint must contain: (1) General or specific denial of material allegations controverted; (2) statement of any new matter, separately stated, constituting defense. (C.C.P. 431.30[b]). Material allegations in complaint or cross-complaint not controverted by answer assumed to be true. (C.C.P. 431.20[a]). Statement of new matter in answer, in avoidance or constituting defense, deemed automatically controverted. (C.C.P. 431.20). Defenses shall be separately stated. (C.C.P. 431.30[g]). Affirmative relief may not be sought in answer. (C.C.P. 431.30[c]).

Usual time to respond after service of summons and complaint is 30 days; but time to be specified in summons varies for certain cases. (C.C.P. 412.20; cf., C.C.P. 1167.3—unlawful detainer). Time for response is extended if service is by mail five days if within California, ten days if served outside California but within U.S., and 20 days if outside U.S. (C.C.P. 1013[a]).

Filing answer is general appearance. (C.C.P. 1014; and see, C.C.P. 410.50).

Counterclaim.—Counterclaims are abolished, and any cause of action formerly asserted by counterclaim shall be asserted by cross-complaint. (C.C.P. 428.80).

Cross-complaint is filed as of right when filed with answer. (C.C.P. 428.50). Filing after answer requires leave of court. (C.C.P. 428.50, 426.50). Joinder of parties governed by usual rules. (C.C.P. 428.20). Third-party defendant in indemnification action may file "special answer" to assert additional defenses to answer to original complaint. (C.C.P. 428.70).

Subject to certain exceptions, related causes of action against complainant must be asserted in cross-complaint. (C.C.P. 426.10, 426.30, 426.40). Permissively asserted claims include: (1) Any cause of action cross-complainant has against parties who asserted complaint or cross-complaint against him; (2) any cause of action which arises out of same transaction, occurrence, or series of transactions or occurrences as same brought against him, or which asserts claim, right, or interest in property or controversy which is subject of cause brought against him. (C.C.P. 428.10; see also, C.C.P. 428.70).

Reply as such not used in California. Cross-complaint responded to as if complaint. (C.C.P. 432.10).

Standard Pleading Forms.—Judicial council has adopted standard forms that may be used in actions for personal injury, property damage, wrongful death, unlawful detainer, breach of contract and fraud, but use is not mandatory. (C.C.P. 425.12; Rule 982.1, California Court Rules).

Demurrer is appropriate to raise following objections where appearing on face of complaint or cross-complaint or from matter judicially noticeable: (1) Court has no jurisdiction of subject of action; (2) person who filed pleading lacks capacity to sue; (3) there is another action pending between same parties for same cause; (4) there is defect or misjoinder of parties; (5) pleading does not state facts sufficient to constitute cause of action; (6) pleading is uncertain (ambiguous or unintelligible); (7) in action on contract, pleading does not disclose whether contract is written, oral or implied by conduct; (8) in most malpractice actions, failure to file certificate of merit as required by C.C.P. 411.35; (9) in certain construction negligence actions, failure to file certificate of merit as required by C.C.P. 411.36. (C.C.P. 430.10, 430.30). Demurrer may also be interposed to answer on grounds (5), (6) and (7) above. (C.C.P. 430.20). Demurrer to complaint or cross-complaint must be filed within 30 days after service of complaint or cross-complaint. Demurrer to answer must be filed within ten days after service of answer. (C.C.P. 430.40). Demurrers in Municipal and Justice Courts limited to grounds (1) and (5) above. (C.C.P. 92). Demurrers not available in family law cases. (California Court Rules 1215). Demurrer is general appearance. (C.C.P. 1014).

Amendment.—Any pleading may be amended once by party of course, and without costs, at any time before answer or demurrer filed, or after demurrer and before hearing thereon. (C.C.P. 472). Court may, in its discretion, after notice to adverse party, allow amendment to any pleading or proceeding and postponement of trial. (C.C.P. 473, 576).

Supplemental Pleadings.—Either party may be allowed, on motion, to file supplemental complaint or answer, alleging facts material to case occurring after former complaint or answer. (C.C.P. 464).

Affidavits of merits not used in California except in professional malpractice actions. (C.C.P. 411.35). Court order required for claim against officer or director of nonprofit corporation serving without compensation. (C.C.P. 425.15).

Affidavits of defense not used in California.

Bill of Particulars.—Not necessary to set forth in pleadings items of account therein alleged, but upon demand copy of account must be delivered to adverse party within ten days. (C.C.P. 454).

Subscription and Verification.—Complaint need not be verified unless special statute applies. (C.C.P. 446; cf., C.C.P. 527, 1166). If complaint verified, general denial precluded, and answer must, with some exceptions, be verified. (C.C.P. 431.30, 431.40, 446). When plaintiff public agency or officer, answer must with some exceptions be verified. (C.C.P. 446).

Verification must be by party unless absent from county where party's attorney has office, in which event attorney or person having knowledge may verify. (C.C.P. 446).

See note at head of Digest as to 1998 legislation covered.

See Topical Index in front part of this volume.

CA – 30

PLEADING . . . *continued*

Verification may be affidavit or declaration under penalty of perjury. (C.C.P. 446, 2015.5). Verification by corporation may be by any officer. (C.C.P. 446).

Filing and Service.—Filing complaint with clerk commences action and tolls statute of limitations. (C.C.P. 411.10). Summons issued on filing and payment of fees. (C.C.P. 411.20, 412.10) No summons required on cross-complaint against party who has appeared. (C.C.P. 428.60). Where party has attorney in action or proceeding, service of demurrer, answer or cross-complaint can be made on attorney, with alternative methods prescribed by statute. (C.C.P. 1015; 1011 et seq.).

Time.—Complaints must be served within three years of filing date. (C.C.P. 583.210[a]). Return of service must be filed within three years and 60 days of filing date. (C.C.P. 583.210[b]). Answers and/or demurrers are to be filed within 30 days of date of service of complaint or cross-complaint, with extensions for alternate forms of service, (see subhead Answer, supra).

Pretrial conference order, if there is one, supersedes pleadings; but is also subject to amendment. (Rule 212, California Court Rules; C.C.P. 576).

Economic Litigation in Municipal and Justice Courts.—(C.C.P. 90-100). Applies to every Municipal and Justice court action where amount in controversy (defined) does not exceed $25,000. (C.C.P. 91). Pleadings are limited to complaints, cross-complaints, answers, answers to cross-complaints, and general demurrers. Special demurrers are not allowed and motions to strike are limited. (C.C.P. 92). Discovery is limited to any combination of 35 of following: Interrogatories, demands to produce, and requests for admission, and one deposition unless stipulated otherwise or upon good cause showing court grants additional discovery. (C.C.P. 94, 95). Plaintiff may serve case questionnaire with complaint and require defendant to serve completed questionnaire with answer. (C.C.P. 96). No more than 45 days nor less than 30 days before trial any party may serve request for witnesses and evidence. Responding party must serve response within 20 days and no additional, amended, or late response can be served except by stipulation or noticed motion. (C.C.P. 96). Serving party may bar witnesses and evidence not disclosed by opposing party, except for impeachment, or unless party calls himself or adverse party, or unless court finds good faith effort to comply and failure due to mistake, surprise, inadvertence or excusable neglect. (C.C.P. 97). Testimony by affidavit is permitted under limited circumstances. (C.C.P. 98). Collateral estoppel effect of judgment is limited. (C.C.P. 99).

Frivolous Claims.—Court has discretion to award or deny costs (C.C.P. 1033, 1033.5) and may award defense costs in certain tort cases brought in bad faith (C.C.P. 1038). Court may add just damages to costs of frivolous appeal. (C.C.P. 907).

Special Pleading Requirements.—In certain types of cases special information is required to be pleaded. See, e.g., C.C.P. 429.10 (marriage dissolution petitions), C.C.P. 429.30 (complaints charging infringement of literary, artistic, or intellectual productions) and C.C.P. 1250.310, 1250.320 (eminent domain actions).

Small Claims.—See category Courts and Legislature, topic Courts.

PRACTICE:

Practice governed by Code of Civil Procedure and Rules of Court.

Discovery.—Depositions of parties and nonparties may be taken by oral examination (C.C.P. 2019, 2020, and 2025-2029) or by written questions (C.C.P. 2028). (See topic Depositions and Discovery.) In addition, written interrogatories may be served on any adverse party, before or after deposition (but at least ten days after service of summons and complaint unless leave of court is obtained). (C. C. P. 2030). Discovery and production of documents and things for inspection, copying, or photographing are provided by statute (C. C. P. 2031) as are physical, mental or blood examinations (C. C. P. 2032). Sanctions are provided for abuses of discovery process and for failure or refusal to respond to discovery. (C.C.P. 2023).

Demand for Admission of Facts.—After service of summons or appearance, any party may request from any other party admissions with respect to genuineness of any relevant document or to truth of any relevant matters of fact. If not responded to in timely manner, after noticed motion for order that matters be deemed admitted, such requests may be deemed admitted. (C.C.P. 2033[k]). Following specified written notice, severe limitations are provided on relief from requests deemed admitted. (C.C.P. 2033[m]). After denial of genuineness or truth, demanding party who proves genuineness or truth entitled to ask for expenses therefor including reasonable attorney's fees. (C.C.P. 2033[o]).

Discovery of Expert Witnesses, Reports.—Specific procedures provided. (C. C. P. 2034).

Direct Action Against Insurer.—See category Transportation, topic Motor Vehicles, subhead Direct Actions.

Small Claims.—See category Courts and Legislature, topic Courts.

See also topics Actions, Appeal and Error, Certiorari, Depositions and Discovery, Injunctions, Judgments, Pleading, Process; category Debtor and Creditor, topics Attachment, Executions, Garnishment.

PROCESS:

Actions are commenced by filing complaint with clerk of court. (C. C. P. 411.10). See also topic Pleading.

See topic Actions, subhead Certificate of Meritorious Malpractice Action.

By Whom Issued.—On filing complaint and paying fees, plaintiff may have summons issued by clerk. (C. C. P. 412.10).

Content of Summons.—Summons must be signed by clerk, under seal of court, and must contain following: Title of court; names of parties; notice that written answer required within 30 days or default may be entered, which could result in garnishment of wages or taking money or property; introductory legend at top of summons, in boldface type, in English and Spanish, stating "Notice] You have been sued. The Court may decide against you without your being heard unless you respond within thirty days. Read information below"; a statement, in boldface type, which reads "You

may seek the advice of an attorney in any manner connected with the complaint or this summons. Such attorney should be consulted promptly so that your pleading may be filed or entered within the time required by this summons." Summons in form approved by Judicial Council is deemed satisfactory. (C. C. P. 412.20).

Notice in Spanish.—Warnings regarding default on civil summons forms must be printed in both English and Spanish. Any county may, by ordinance, require that warning appear in any other language. (C. C. P. 412.20).

Who May Serve.—Summons may be served by any person at least 18 years of age, not party to action. (C. C. P. 414.10).

General Rule as to Service.—Summons may be served by personal delivery of copy of summons and complaint (C.C.P. 415.10, 416.90); if personal service cannot be accomplished after exercising reasonable diligence, by leaving copy of summons and complaint with person in charge of party's office or competent member of party's household, at least 18, and thereafter mailing copy of summons and complaint to party (C.C.P. 415.20); or by mailing same to person along with notice and acknowledgment specified in C.C.P. 415.30. Summons may be served by first-class mail postage prepaid, requiring return receipt, on persons outside state. (C.C.P. 415.40).

If service is against corporation, dissolved corporation, joint stock company, unincorporated association or public entity, service may be accomplished by leaving copy of summons and complaint at its office during usual office hours with person apparently in charge and thereafter mailing copy of summons and complaint to party. (C. C. P. 416.10-.50).

When service is against corporation (C.C.P. 416.10) or against associates conducting business under common name (C.C.P. 388), summons must state that person served is served on behalf of corporation or unincorporated association as person upon whom copy of summons and of complaint may be delivered to effect service. If notice does not appear, no default may be taken. (C. C. P. 412.30).

Process against minor under 18 years of age if at least 12 years old must be served on parent, guardian or other person in care or control of minor and minor if he or she is at least 12 years of age. (C. C. P. 416.60).

Process against incompetent person must be served on incompetent and on his guardian or his conservator but for good cause court may dispense with delivery to incompetent. (C. C. P. 416.70).

Process Against Domestic Partnership.—Governed by C.C.P. 416.40 and Corp. C. 24003. May be served by delivery of copy to general partner, or general manager of partnership, or person designated as agent. (C.C.P. 416.40; Corp. C. 24003). If no agent for service is designated and service cannot be effected by alternate means, summons may be served pursuant to court order by delivering copy to member of partnership and mailing copy to partnership's last known address. (C.C.P. 416.40; Corp. C. 24007).

Process against domestic corporation may be served by delivery to president or other head of corporation, vice-president, secretary, assistant secretary, general manager, or person designated for service or authorized to receive service. Process against bank may be served by delivery to any of aforementioned officers or agents or to cashier or assistant cashier. (C.C.P. 416.10; Corp. C. 1701). If such corporate officer or agent cannot be found or no such designation has been made, by delivery to Secretary of State pursuant to court order, and Secretary of State must forward process by registered mail to corporation with request for return receipt. (C.C.P. 416.10; Corp. C. 1702).

Personal Service on Association.—Associates may be sued in name of association, and summons served on one or more of associates. (C.C.P. 412.30). Service may also be made upon agent for service of process or president or other officers of association. (C.C.P. 416.40; Corp. C. 24007).

Process Against Joint Stock Company.—See subhead Process Against Domestic Corporation, supra. (C.C.P. 416.30).

Process Against Foreign Corporation.—In suit against foreign corporation, or nonresident joint stock company or association, doing business in state, process may be served on president, vice-president, secretary, assistant secretary, or general manager in this state, or if corporation is bank, on cashier or assistant cashier or on any natural person designated by it as agent for service of process; or if corporation has designated corporate agent on any person named in certificate of such corporate agent; or if no such person can be found after diligent search, on Secretary of State pursuant to court order, who must forward copy of process and court order to specified corporate offices by registered air mail, return receipt requested. (C.C.P. 416.10; Corp. C. 2110, 2110.1, 2111 and 2114).

Service on Foreign Partnership.—Service may be effected on agent for service of process or general partner. (C.C.P. 416.40). General partnership must designate agent for service of process. If none designated, or if designated agent cannot be found with due diligence, service made on Secretary of State, by personal delivery of process, with statement of last-known address, and $50 service fee. Secretary must forward process to defendant by registered mail. (Corp. C. 15800). If no agent for service is designated for general or limited partnership and service cannot be effected by alternate means, summons may be served pursuant to court order by delivering copy to member of partnership, and mailing copy to partnership's last known address. (Corp. C. 24007).

Service by Publication.—Summons may be served by publication if upon affidavit it appears to satisfaction of court where action pending that party to be served cannot with reasonable diligence be served in another manner and that cause of action exists against party, or he is necessary or proper party to action, or party has or claims interest in real or personal property in this state which is subject to jurisdiction of court, or relief demanded in action consists wholly or in part in excluding party from any interest in such property. (C.C.P. 415.50). Copy of summons and complaint must be mailed to person to be served if his address is ascertained before expiration of time prescribed for publication. Publication must be at least once a week for four successive weeks. (C.C.P. 415.50; Govt. C. 6064).

PROCESS . . . *continued*

Personal Service Outside State.—Summons may be served by any manner provided in article or by sending copy of summons and complaint to person to be served by first class mail, postage prepaid; service by this form of mail complete on tenth day after mailing. (C.C.P. 415.40).

Delay in Issuance or Service of Summons.—Unless summons is served within three years after commencement of action, action shall be dismissed. (C.C.P. 583.210, 583.250). Trial Court Delay Reduction Act (Govt. C. 68605), if applicable, may shorten time, consult local rules. Time during which defendant was not amenable to process shall not be counted. (C.C.P. 583.240).

Long Arm Statute.—California courts may exercise jurisdiction on any basis not inconsistent with California or U.S. Constitutions. (C.C.P. 410.10).

Proof of Service.—Made by return of summons with certificate of service; if summons lost after service but before return, affidavit showing facts of service may be returned in lieu of summons. (C.C.P. 417.30). Return must be made within 60 days after deadline for service of summons. (C.C.P. 583.210). Certificate of personal service (C.C.P. 415.10), service on corporation or association (C.C.P. 415.20), substituted service at person's home or usual place of business (C.C.P. 415.20) or service by notice and acknowledgment (C.C.P.415.30) must contain affidavit showing time and place of service; manner of service; facts showing service properly accomplished; and name and title of person to whom delivery was made (C.C.P. 417.10). If service was by notice and acknowledgment, affidavit must include written acknowledgment. Certificate of service by publication must contain affidavit of publisher or printer or certain of their employees and affidavit showing time and place summons and complaint were mailed. (C.C.P. 417.10). Certificate of service by posting (C.C.P. 415.45) must contain affidavit showing time and place of posting and time and place summons and complaint were mailed (C.C.P. 417.10). Proof of service may also be made by written admission of person served. (C.C.P. 417.10). Proof of personal service must be made on form approved by Judicial Council (C.C.P. 417.10). Return of registered process server upon process or notice establishes presumption, affecting burden of producing evidence, of facts stated in return. (Evid. C. 647).

Nonresident Motorist.—See category Transportation, topic Motor Vehicles.

REPLEVIN:

Statutory remedy of claim and delivery supplants common law replevin. (C. C. P. 511.010-516.050).

Proceedings.—Upon filing complaint or thereafter, person claiming property in possession of another may seek writ of possession. (C.C.P. 512.010).

Affidavit.—To gain property during litigation plaintiff or cross-complainant may apply for writ of possession by written application under oath which must show: (1) Basis of plaintiff's claim and right to possession, together with any writing which is basis of claim; (2) wrongful detention of property by defendant; (3) manner in which defendant came into possession; (4) plaintiff's best information and belief as to reason for detention; (5) description of property with statement of value; (6) plaintiff's best knowledge, information and belief as to location of property and if in private place showing of probable cause to believe property located there; and (7) property not taken for tax, assessment or fine, or seized under execution. (C.C.P. 512.010).

Bond.—Court shall not issue temporary restraining order or writ of possession until plaintiff has filed undertaking. Bond must be in amount not less than twice value of defendant's interest in property. (C.C.P. 515.010).

Issuance.—No writ of possession issues except after hearing on noticed motion, but writ may issue ex parte if probable cause appears that: (1) Defendant gained possession by felonious taking except where defendant fraudulently appropriated property, or obtained it by fraud, false pretense or embezzlement; (2) property is credit card; or (3) defendant acquired in ordinary course of business for commercial purposes and (i) property not necessary for support of defendant or his family and (ii) existence of immediate danger property will become unavailable to levy due to concealment, removal or substantial impairment in value and (iii) ex parte issuance is necessary to protect property. (C.C.P. 512.020).

Repossession.—Defendant whose property has been seized pursuant to ex parte order may apply for order quashing writ of possession and releasing property by filing noticed motion. Upon defendant's application, court may stay delivery of property pending outcome of hearing. If court determines that plaintiff not entitled to writ of possession, court shall award to defendant damages caused by levy of writ and loss of possession. (C.C.P. 512.020).

Upon issuance of writ, defendant may prevent plaintiff from taking possession or may regain possession if, no later than ten days after levy: (1) Defendant objects to plaintiff's undertaking and court finds plaintiff's undertaking insufficient (C.C.P. 515.030); or (2) defendant files undertaking in amount equal to plaintiff's undertaking and providing for payment of all costs and judgment damages sustained by plaintiff because of loss of possession, up to amount of undertaking, if plaintiff recovers judgment (C.C.P. 515.020). Plaintiff may object to defendant's undertaking within ten days after it is filed. (C.C.P. 515.030). If plaintiff's objection fails, court will grant defendant possession and plaintiff may not gain possession of property prior to judgment for possession after trial. If third party claims property, rules applicable in cases of third-party claims after levy under execution apply. (C.C.P. 514.050).

Temporary Restraining Order.—Upon application for writ plaintiff may apply for temporary restraining order which may be issued ex parte under certain conditions. (C.C.P. 513.010, 515.010).

Forms.—Judicial Council shall prescribe forms. (C.C.P. 516.020).

SEQUESTRATION:

No statutory provision.

SERVICE:

See topic Process.

STAY OF EXECUTION:

See category Debtor and Creditor, topic Executions.

SUBMISSION OF CONTROVERSY:

Parties to question in difference, which might be subject of civil action, may, without action, agree upon case containing facts upon which controversy depends, and present submission of same to any court which would have jurisdiction if action had been brought; but it must appear by affidavit that controversy is real and proceedings in good faith. Court must thereupon hear and determine case, and render judgment thereon, as if action were pending. (C. C. P. 1138).

Judgment must be entered as in other cases but without costs (C. C. P. 1139), and may be enforced in same manner as if it had been rendered in action, and is in same manner subject to appeal (C. C. P. 1140).

VENUE:

Subject to power of court to change place of trial (C. C. P. 397), following actions must be tried in county in which all or part of real property is situated: (1) Actions for recovery of real property or of estate or interest therein or for determination of such right or interest, and for injuries to real property; (2) for foreclosure of liens or mortgages on real property (C. C. P. 392).

In partition action proper county for trial is: (1) Where subject of action is real property or real and personal property, county in which all or part of real property is situated; (2) where subject of action is personal property, county in which personal property is principally located or in which any defendant resides at commencement of action. (C. C. P. 872.110[b]).

Following actions must be tried in county where cause arose, subject to power of court to change place of trial: (1) For recovery of penalty or forfeiture imposed by statute; (2) against public officer for act done by him by virtue of his office. (C. C. P. 393).

Action against executor, administrator, guardian, conservator, or trustee in his representative capacity on claim for money or for recovery of personal property must be tried in county which has jurisdiction of estate. (C. C. P. 395.1).

Proceeding for dissolution of marriage must be heard in county of petitioner's residence for three months. (C. C. P. 395[a]). In proceeding to enforce obligation of support under Family Code §3900, county in which child resides is proper county for trial of action. (C. C. P. 395[a]).

Proper county for trial in all other cases is county in which defendants or some of them reside at commencement of action, except that action for injury to person or personal property or for death from wrongful act or negligence may be tried in county where injury occurred or where defendants or some of them reside at commencement of action, and action on contract may be tried in county where contract was made or is to be performed, or where any defendant resides. (C. C. P. 395[a]).

Corporation or association may be sued in county where contract is made, is to be performed, where obligation or liability arises, breach occurs, or in county where it has its principal place of business. (C. C. P. 395.5). Unincorporated association may be sued in any county where plaintiff can sue a member of association (C. C. P. 395; 37 C.2d 760, 235 P.2d 607; 43 C.A.3d 219, 117 C.Rptr. 588), however, if association files statement with Secretary of State listing its principal place of business then principal place of business is only in such county for venue purposes (C. C. P. 395.2[a]).

If no defendant resides in state or county of residence is unknown, proper county is any county designated in complaint. (C. C. P. 395[a]).

If defendant about to depart from state, action may be tried in any county where either of parties resides or where service is made. (C. C. P. 395 [a]).

Place of trial may be changed in following cases: (1) When court designated in complaint is not proper court; (2) when there is reason to believe that impartial trial cannot be had therein; (3) when convenience of witnesses and ends of justice would be promoted by change; (4) when from any cause there is no judge of court qualified to act; (5) when proceeding for dissolution of marriage has been filed in county in which petitioner has resided for three months and respondent is resident of state, to respondent's residence when ends of justice would be promoted by change. (C. C. P. 397).

COURTS AND LEGISLATURE

COURTS:

United States District Courts.—

Fees required are governed by Title 28, U. S. Code §§1914-1917, 1921. Filing fee for civil action is $120.

Northern District.—Clerk's office: U.S. Courthouse, Federal Building, 450 Golden Gate Avenue, San Francisco 94102.

Northern District is composed of following counties: Alameda, Contra Costa, Del Norte, Humboldt, Lake, Marin, Mendocino, Monterey, Napa, San Benito, Santa Clara, Santa Cruz, San Francisco, San Mateo and Sonoma.

Court sits at San Francisco, San Jose, Oakland and Eureka. (28 U.S.C. 84).

Eastern District.—Clerk's office: U.S. Courthouse, 650 Capitol Mall, Sacramento 95814.

Eastern District is composed of following counties: Alpine, Amador, Butte, Calaveras, Colusa, El Dorado, Fresno, Glenn, Inyo, Kern, Kings, Lassen, Madera, Mariposa, Merced, Modoc, Mono, Nevada, Placer, Plumas, Sacramento, San Joaquin, Shasta, Sierra, Siskiyou, Solano, Stanislaus, Sutter, Tehama, Trinity, Tulare, Tuolumne, Yolo and Yuba.

Court sits at Sacramento, Fresno, and Redding. (28 U. S. C. 84).

Central District.—Clerk's office: U.S. Courthouse, 312 N. Spring St., Los Angeles 90012.

See note at head of Digest as to 1998 legislation covered.

See Topical Index in front part of this volume.

COURTS . . . *continued*

Central District is composed of following counties: Los Angeles, Orange, Riverside, San Bernardino, San Luis Obispo, Santa Barbara and Ventura.

Court sits at Los Angeles and Santa Ana. (28 U. S. C. 84).

Southern District.—Clerk's office: U.S. Courthouse, 940 Front Street, San Diego 92101.

Southern District is composed of following counties: Imperial and San Diego.

Court sits at San Diego. (28 U. S. C. 84).

Supreme Court.—Supreme Court is court of last resort in California.

Original Jurisdiction.—Extraordinary relief such as mandamus, certiorari, prohibition and habeas corpus. (Const., Art. VI, §10).

Appellate Jurisdiction.—Has appellate jurisdiction when judgment of death has been pronounced. (Const., Art. VI, §11). May transfer to itself cause in court of appeal before decision in that court becomes final. (Const., Art. VI, §12). Petition for hearing after decision in Court of Appeal regulated by court rules. (Rules 28, 29, California Rules of Court).

Court sits at 303 Second St., San Francisco; 303 So. Spring St., Los Angeles; and 100 Library and Courts Building, Sacramento.

Courts of Appeal.—These courts are intermediate appellate courts. Number of districts is prescribed by legislature, which may also provide for divisions consisting of presiding justice and two or more associate justices. (Const., Art. VI, §3). There are six districts, of which three are divided into divisions. (Govt. C. §§69100 et seq.). Court which sits in divisions will in rare cases sit en banc.

Jurisdiction.—Original: Extraordinary relief such as mandamus, certiorari, prohibition and habeas corpus. (Const., Art. VI, §10).

Appellate: Has appellate jurisdiction when superior courts have original jurisdiction and in other causes prescribed by statute. (Const., Art. VI, §11). Court of Appeal has discretion to transfer appeals pending in appellate departments of Superior Court to itself where necessary to secure uniformity of decision or settle important questions of law. (C. C. P. 911).

First District.—Sits at 300 Second St., San Francisco. Has five divisions. Comprises counties of Alameda, Contra Costa, Del Norte, Humboldt, Lake, Marin, Mendocino, Napa, San Francisco, San Mateo, and Sonoma.

Second District.—Sits at 303 So. Spring St., Los Angeles. Has seven divisions. Comprises counties of Los Angeles, Santa Barbara, Ventura, and San Luis Obispo.

Third District.—Sits at 300 Library and Courts Building, 914 Capitol Mall, Sacramento. Has one division. Comprises counties of Alpine, Amador, Butte, Calaveras, Colusa, El Dorado, Glenn, Lassen, Modoc, Mono, Nevada, Placer, Plumas, Sacramento, San Joaquin, Shasta, Sierra, Siskiyou, Sutter, Tehama, Trinity, Yolo and Yuba.

Fourth District.—Has three divisions. Division One sits at San Diego. Division Two sits at San Bernardino. Division three sits at Santa Ana. Comprises counties of Imperial, Inyo, Orange, Riverside, San Bernardino and San Diego.

Fifth District.—Sits at 2525 Capitol St., Fresno. Has one division. Comprises counties of Fresno, Kern, Kings, Madera, Mariposa, Merced, Stanislaus, Tulare and Tuolumne.

Sixth District.—Sits at 333 W. Santa Clara St., San Jose. Has one division. Comprises counties of Monterey, San Benito, Santa Clara, and Santa Cruz.

Superior Courts.—Each county has superior court which sits at respective county seats and elsewhere in county as prescribed by statute.

Venue.—Rules as to venue are found, in most cases, in C.C.P. 392 et seq.

Original Jurisdiction.—Superior courts have original jurisdiction in all causes except those given by statute in other trial courts. (Const., Art. VI, §10).

Probate Court.—Probate jurisdiction is exercised by superior courts, in designated departments, which sit as courts of probate. (Prob. C. 7050).

Family Conciliation Court.—Superior court sitting as family conciliation court has jurisdiction over controversies between spouses or unmarried parents that may result in dissolution of marriage or affect household to detriment of minor child, or where controversy involves domestic violence, regardless of minor children. (Fam. C. 1810, 1830). Either spouse or parent may invoke jurisdiction of family conciliation court by filing timely petition, or court may transfer dissolution proceeding to family conciliation court. (Fam. C. 1800 et seq.). Under certain circumstances court may accept case not involving welfare of minor child. (Fam. C. 1842, 1830).

Juvenile Court.—Superior court sitting as juvenile court has specially delegated jurisdiction in certain cases involving persons under 18 years of age. (Welf. and Inst. C. §§200-945).

Municipal Courts.—Legislature specifies organization and jurisdiction of municipal courts, and has delegated to county boards of supervisors authority to define districts. (Const., Art. VI, §5; Govt. C. §71040). Except in San Diego County, no city may have more than one district. (Const., Art. VI, §5). District names closely identify cities included if more than one. (Govt. C. §§71042, 71045).

Venue.—Rules as to venue are found, in most cases, in C.C.P. 392 et seq.

Jurisdiction.—Jurisdiction of municipal courts is detailed in C.C.P. 86 for civil cases, P.C. §1462 for criminal. In civil cases: Where amount in controversy is test, jurisdiction is generally limited to cases where demand does not exceed $25,000. Equitable jurisdiction of courts is specifically defined by statue. (C.C.P. 86). In criminal cases: Extends to all misdemeanor cases involving offenses committed in county of court's location excepting those coming before juvenile court and those of which other courts are given exclusive jurisdiction. Each municipal court shall have exclusive jurisdiction in all cases involving violation of ordinances of cities or towns situated within court's district. (P.C. 1462).

Mandatory Arbitration.—In each superior court with ten or more judges, and in such other superior and municipal courts as so provided by local rule, cases in which amount in controversy is less than $50,000 must be submitted to arbitration. (C.C.P. 1141.10 et seq.). Amount in controversy limitation for mandatory arbitration does not limit amount arbitrator may award. (C.C.P. 1141.26). Following cases are, however, excluded: Actions for equitable relief (C.C.P. 1141.13); consumer class actions (C.C.P. 1141.11[c]; C.C. 1781); actions in small claims court (C.C.P. 116.2; 1141.11[c]); unlawful detainer actions (C.C.P. 1141.11[c]; 1161); actions excepted by

Judicial Council (C.C.P. 1141.15); and actions in which all parties stipulate that amount in controversy exceeds $50,000 (C.C.P. 1141.16[a]). After arbitration losing party can require trial de novo in court but must pay specified costs if better result is not obtained. (C.C.P. 1141.20 and 1141.21).

Small Claims Court.—Municipal court judges and, in judicial districts where there is no municipal court, justice court judges exercise jurisdiction sitting as small claims courts. Jurisdiction of court is confined to cases for recovery of money only, where amount does not exceed $5,000; to actions to enforce payment of unsecured property taxes where amount claimed does not exceed $5,000 and legality of tax is not contested; and to confirm, correct or vacate binding fee arbitration award not exceeding $5,000 between attorney and client or to conduct hearing de novo between attorney and client after nonbinding arbitration of fee dispute involving no more than $5,000. Court has jurisdiction over defendant guarantor only where demand does not exceed $2,500. (C.C.P. 116.220). Party may not file more than two actions for more than $2,500 in same calendar year except as provided in C.C.P. 116.232. (C.C.P. 116.231). Court may also award equitable relief in form of rescission, restitution, specific performance, or reformation in lieu of, or in addition to money damages and shall retain jurisdiction until full payment and performance of any judgment or order. (C.C.P. 116.220).

Venue is same as for civil actions filed in justice or municipal courts. Court shall determine whether venue is proper. If not, court shall dismiss without prejudice unless all defendants are present and agree that action be heard. Defendant may challenge venue by writing to court in lieu of appearance. (C.C.P. 116.370).

Actions are commenced upon filing of claim. (C.C.P. 116.320).

No claim may be filed or prosecuted in small claims court by assignee of such claim for purpose of collection (C.C.P. 116.420) and normally no attorney-at-law or person other than plaintiff and defendant may take any part in filing or prosecution or defense of litigation in court (C.C.P. 116.530). Corporation or any other entity may appear in small claims court only through employee or elected officer or director who has duties other than exclusive representation of entity in small claims court. (C.C.P. 116.540[b]–[c]). Representative of insurer may advise litigant, except at hearing. (C.C.P. 116.531). Parties may present evidence by witnesses (C.C.P. 116.520). No formal pleadings other than claim and notice are necessary (C.C.P. 116.310). Defendant may himself file claim in proceeding and must deliver copy of his claim to plaintiff in person at least five days prior to time set for hearing. (C.C.P. 116.360). No attachment may issue from court, but enforcement of judgment may be had pursuant to C.C.P. 680.010–724.260, C.C.P. 674 and C.C.P. 1174 (C.C.P. 116.820), but enforcement is automatically stayed without bond until time for appeal runs (C.C.P. 116.810). If appeal is taken, judgment is stayed until outcome of appeal is determined. (C.C.P. 116.810).

Plaintiff has no right to appeal claims asserted. Defendant has no right to appeal judgment on defendant's claims for affirmative relief. Otherwise, defendant, with respect to plaintiff's claims, or plaintiff with respect to defendant's claims, may appeal and case shall be tried de novo in superior court. (C.C.P. 116.710 and 116.770). No jury trial on appeal. (C.C.P. 116.770). Defendant's insurer may appeal where judgment exceeds $2,500 and insurer stipulates to coverage. (C.C.P. 116.710). Judgment on trial de novo shall be final and non-appealable (C.C.P. 116.780). Court may award attorney fees up to $1,000 if appeal not based in good faith. (C.C.P. 116.790).

In Municipal Courts with four or more judges, at least one Sat. or night session per month is required. (C.C.P. 116.250).

Legal advisors are generally made available to litigants on request at no charge. (C.C.P. 116.260 and 116.940).

With consent of parties, court may order case to be heard by temporary judge. (C.C.P. 116.240).

LEGISLATURE:

Regular sessions convene at noon on first Mon. in Dec. of each even-numbered year and adjourn on Nov. 30 of following even-numbered year. (Const., Art. IV, §3[a]; Govt. C. 9020). Governor may convene legislature in special session on extraordinary occasions. (Const., Art. IV, §3[b]). Powers of initiative and referendum have been reserved to people. (Const., Art. IV, §1). Lobbyists required to register with Secretary of State. Lobbyists' activities regulated; periodic reports required. (Govt. C. 86100-86300). See also topic Statutes.

REPORTS:

California Reports contain Supreme Court decisions; California Appellate Reports contain decision of courts of appeal and, beginning with Volume 106, of appellate departments of superior court. First series of California Reports (1-220) covers period 1850-1934; second series (1-71) covers period 1934-1969; third series (1-54) covers period 1969-1991; and fourth series started with 1 C. 4th in 1991. First series of California Appellate Reports (1-140) covers period 1905-1934; second series (1-276) covers period 1934-1969; third series (1-235) covers period 1969-1991; and fourth series started with 1 C.A. 4th in 1991. West's California Reporter, started in 1960, covers decisions of Supreme Court, Courts of Appeal, and appellate departments of superior court, beginning with cases reported in 53 C.2d—176 C.A.2d; first series (1-286) covers period 1959-1991, and second series started with 1 C. Rptr.2d in 1991. California Unreported Cases, series of seven volumes containing opinions of Supreme Court and courts of appeal not officially reported, covers period from 1855 to 1883. Other reporters are Labatt's District Court Reports (1857-8), Myrick's Probate Reports (1872-79), Coffey's Probate Decisions (1883-1915), Ragland, Superior Court Decisions (1921-1926) and California Decisions (1890-1940).

Decisions of California Supreme Court and Courts of Appeal are also reported in Pacific Reporter beginning with cases reported in 64 C.—1 C.A. Coverage of cases reported in C.A.2d ends with those reported in 175 C.A.2d. Later decisions of Courts of Appeal are reported in West's California Reporter (C.Rptr.). Beginning with 347 P.2d Pacific Reporter reports only California Supreme Court decisions (1959).

No opinion superseded by granting of review, hearing, rehearing or other judicial action shall be published in Official Reports. (California Rules of Court 976[d]).

REPORTS . . . *continued*

Digests.—California decisions are digested in McKinney's New California Digest, McKinney's California Digest of Official Reports 3d Series, West's Pacific Digest, West's California Digest, and West's California Digest, 2d ed. Cyclopedic treatise on California law entitled California Jurisprudence 3d Series, having pocket parts, is also available. Witkin's Summary of California Law, 9th ed., Witkin's California Procedure, 3d ed., Witkin's California Crimes, Witkin's California Criminal Procedure, and Witkin's California Evidence 3d ed. are briefer treatises on California law, each with supplemental volumes or pocket parts.

STATUTES:

California has following codes, cited herein as shown in parentheses:

(Bus. & Prof. C.)	Business & Professions
(C.C.)	Civil
(C.C.P.)	Code of Civil Procedure
(Com'l. C.)	Commercial
(Corp. C.)	Corporations
(Educ. C.)	Education
(Elec. C.)	Elections
(Evid. C.)	Evidence
(Fam. C.)	Family
(Finan. C.)	Financial
(Fish & G. C.)	Fish & Game
(Fd. & Agric. C.)	Food and Agricultural
(Govt. C.)	Government
(Harb. & Nav. C.)	Harbors & Navigation
(H. & S.C.)	Health & Safety
(Ins. C.)	Insurance
(Lab. C.)	Labor
(Mil. & Vet. C.)	Military and Veterans
(P. C.)	Penal
(Prob. C.)	Probate
(Pub. Cont. C.)	Public Contract
(Pub. Res. C.)	Public Resources
(Pub. Utils. C.)	Public Utilities
(Rev. & Tax. C.)	Revenue & Taxation
(Str. & H. C.)	Streets & Highways
(Un. Ins. C.)	Unemployment Insurance
(Veh. C.)	Vehicle
(Water C.)	Water
(Water C. App.)	Water Code Appendix
(Welf. & Inst. C.)	Welfare and Institutions

Former Banking, School and Political Codes have been repealed, their provisions incorporated in other codes.

Official compilation is series of volumes entitled "Statutes and Amendments to the Codes," published by California State Printer. There are two unofficial annotated compilations, each with many volumes of differing dates, for which pocket supplements are printed. One, known as "Deering's California Codes," is published by Bancroft-Whitney Company, San Francisco. Some uncodified statutes are published in one volume of this set known as "Uncodified Initiative Measures and Statutes." Other set, known as "West's Annotated California Codes," is published by West Publishing Co., St. Paul.

Uniform Acts which have been wholly or substantially adopted: Aircraft Financial Responsibility (1968); Anatomical Gift (1970); Child Custody Jurisdiction and Enforcement (1998); †Civil Liability for Support (1955); †Commercial Code (1963, effective Jan. 1, 1965); Common Trust Fund (1947); Controlled Substances Act (1972); Criminal Extradition (1937); †Criminal Statistics (1955); Determination of Death (1982); †Disposition of Unclaimed Property (1959); †Division of Income for Tax Purposes (1966); Divorce Recognition (1970); Durable Power of Attorney (1981); Facsimile Signatures of Public Officials (1959); Federal Lien Registration (1979); Foreign Money-Judgments Recognition (1967); Fraudulent Transfer (1986); International Wills (1979); Interstate Arbitration of Death Taxes (1949); Interstate Compromise of Death Taxes (1949); Interstate Family Support (1997); †Limited Partnership Act, Revised (1984); Management of Institutional Funds (1973); Parentage (1975); Partnership (1949); Paternity (1992); Photographic Copies of Business and Public Records as Evidence (1951); Premarital Agreement (1985); †Principal and Income, Revised (1967); Simultaneous Death (1931); Single Publication (1955); Supervision of Trustees for Charitable Purposes (1959); Testamentary Additions to Trusts (1965); To Secure Attendance of Witnesses from Without a State in Criminal Proceedings (1937); Trade Secrets (1984); Transfers to Minors (1984); Vendor and Purchaser Risk (1947).

†Adopted with significant variations or modifications. See appropriate topics, for those acts within scope of Digest.

For text of Uniform Acts falling within scope of Martindale-Hubbell Law Digests, see Uniform and Model Acts section.

UNIFORM LAWS:

For list of Uniform Acts in force in this state see topic Statutes. For text of Uniform Acts within the scope of the Martindale-Hubbell Law Digests see Uniform and Model Acts section.

CRIMINAL LAW

BAIL:

See topic Criminal Law.

CRIMINAL LAW:

Crimes and criminal procedure are defined in Penal Code.

Indictment and Information.—Defendant may be brought to trial by information of district attorney after preliminary examination (P.C. 739), or may be indicted by grand jury (P.C. 917). Defendant no longer entitled to post-indictment hearing. (Const. Art. 1, §14.1).

Bail.—Defendant is entitled to bail before conviction as matter of right except for offenses punishable by death. (P.C. 1270.5, 1271; 9 C.3d 345, 107 C.Rptr. 401, 508 P.2d 721).

Upon appeal, defendant convicted of offense not punishable by death may be released on bail if demonstrates not likely to flee, no danger to community (considering especially whether conviction is for violent felony), and appeal raises substantial legal question. (P.C. 1272.1). Defendant must notify prosecuting attorney five court days in advance of bail hearing. (P.C. 1272). Defendant entitled to bail as matter of right pending appeal of misdemeanor. (P.C. 1272).

Uniform Act for Out-of-State Parolee Supervision in effect. (P.C. 11175-11179).

Uniform Criminal Extradition Act in effect. (P.C. 1547-1558).

Interstate Corrections Compact in effect. (P.C. 11189-11197).

Uniform Act on Fresh Pursuit in effect. (P.C. 852-852.4).

Uniform Act to Secure the Attendance of Witnesses From Without a State in Criminal Proceedings in effect. (P.C. 1334-1334.6).

Uniform Controlled Substances Act in effect. (H. & S.C. 11000-11651).

Western Interstate Corrections Compact in effect. (P.C. 11190).

Colorado River Crime Enforcement Compact in effect. (P.C. 853.1-853.2).

DEBTOR AND CREDITOR

ASSIGNMENTS:

Note: Uniform Commercial Code has been adopted. (1963, c. 819). See category Business Regulation and Commerce, topic Commercial Code, subhead Material Variations from 1990 Official Text.

Generally, property of any kind may be transferred by assignment. (C. C. 1044). May be oral except where writing expressly required by statute. (C.C. 1052). No particular form is required, but must indicate intent to effect transfer without further action. Consideration generally not required as to completed assignment (C. C. 1040) with principal exceptions of executory transfers and those not enforceable at common law. Despite statutory provision prohibiting assignment of mere possibility not coupled with interest (C. C. 1045), assignment of contingent expectancy enforced by courts (36 C.A.3d 350, 111 C.Rptr. 468). Choses in action are assignable when arising out of obligation or violation of property right, but not when arising out of purely personal contract or personal tort. (C. C. 954; 206 C. 461, 274 P. 959). Statutory procedure relating to assignment for benefit of creditors has been repealed (1980, c. 135); assignment for benefit of creditors pursuant to common law is available. (51 C.2d 294, 333 P.2d 23).

Subject to compliance with any applicable statute requiring recording or filing and except for transfers intended to create security interest, transfer of certain contracts and instruments may be perfected against third persons by endorsement or written assignment and delivery; transfer of certain other rights to payment can be perfected as to third persons by delivery of written assignment, and bona fide assignee can secure priority by written notice to obligor. (C. C. 955-955.1). See category Business Regulation and Commerce, topic Commercial Code. Assignment in bulk of stock in trade and of fixtures or equipment of certain businesses requires special procedures. See topic Fraudulent Sales and Conveyances and category Business Regulation and Commerce, topic Commercial Code.

Assignment of wages not valid unless: (1) Contained in separate written instrument; (2) consented to by husband or wife of assignor or by parent or guardian of minor assignor or contains statement by assignor that he or she is unmarried and an adult; (3) no other assignment, or earnings withholding order is in force. Assignment must be authenticated by notary and filed with employer. Unearned wages cannot be assigned except for, and to person furnishing, necessities of life and then only for amount needed to furnish such necessities. Such restrictions do not apply to certain deductions and withholdings made by employers. (Lab. C. 300). Upon filing of claim, Labor Commissioner will take assignments of claims relating to wages and work. (Lab. C. 96-97). (Com'l. C. 9104[d] specifically exempts "wages" from application of Division 9 of Code.) See generally Wage Garnishment Law (C.C.P. 706.011-706.154) for procedures for withholding of wages by employers.

Assignment of accounts receivable is governed by Uniform Commercial Code. (Com'l. C. 9101-9508). See category Business Regulation and Commerce, topic Commercial Code, subhead Material Variations from 1990 Official Text.

See also category Civil Actions and Procedure, topic Judgments.

ATTACHMENT:

Actions in Which Allowed.—Action must be based upon contract, express or implied. (C.C.P. 483.010[a]). Special rules apply for attaching property of nonresident defendants. (C.C.P. 492.010 et seq.).

Courts Which May Issue Writ.—Attachment may issue from any trial court, except small claims court. (C.C.P. 116.220, 483.010).

In Whose Favor Writ May Issue.—Statute places no restriction on types of plaintiff that may obtain attachment.

Against Whom Writ May Issue.—Attachment may issue against any corporation, partnership, or unincorporated association; attachment against natural person allowed only if claim arose out of individual's conduct of trade, business, or profession. (C.C.P. 483.010[c]).

Claims On Which Writ May Issue.—Attachment may issue only on claims for money in which total sum claimed is fixed or readily ascertainable and not less than $500. (C.C.P. 483.010[a]). Attachment is not available if claim is otherwise secured by

See note at head of Digest as to 1998 legislation covered.

See Topical Index in front part of this volume.

ATTACHMENT . . . *continued*
any interest in real property unless security has become valueless. (C.C.P. 483.010[b]). Attachment is unavailable against defendant who is natural person on claim based on sale or lease or license of property, furnishing of services, or loan of money if such property sold, licensed or leased, services furnished, or money loaned was used primarily for personal, family or household purposes. (C.C.P. 483.010[c]).

Grounds.—See subheads Claims on Which Writ May Issue, supra, and Proceedings to Obtain, infra.

Property Subject to Attachment.—In case of corporate or partnership defendants, all corporate or partnership property for which method of levy is provided (see subhead Levy, infra) is subject to attachment. (C.C.P. 487.010[a], [b]). If defendant is natural person, types of property subject to attachment include most business assets as well as other specified assets. (C.C.P. 487.010[c]).

Property Exempt from Attachment.—Property exempt from attachment includes: Property exempt from execution (see topic Executions); property necessary for support of individual defendant and members of household; all compensation payable by employer to employee for personal services, however denominated. (C.C.P. 487.020).

Proceedings to Obtain.—Attachment may be obtained on noticed hearing. (C.C.P. 484.010 et seq.). At time of filing complaint or any time thereafter, plaintiff may apply for right to attach order and writ of attachment. (C.C.P. 484.010). Required papers include application (C.C.P. 484.020), notice of application (C.C.P. 484.050), and supporting affidavits (C.C.P. 484.030). Required papers must be served on defendant within time prescribed in C.C.P. 1005(b). (C.C.P. 484.040). Defendant wishing to oppose attachment must file notice of opposition and supporting affidavits at least five court days prior to hearing. (C.C.P. 484.060[a], 484.070). In notice of opposition, defendant must claim exemption of property described in plaintiff's application. (C.C.P. 484.070[a]) and may claim exemption of property not described in such application (C.C.P. 484.070[b]). Plaintiff wishing to oppose claim of exemption must file and serve notice of opposition to exemption at least two days prior to hearing. (C.C.P. 484.070[f]). At hearing, court shall consider pleadings and other papers of record and, upon good cause shown, court may receive additional evidence, additional points and authorities or even continue hearing for production of such additional evidence or points and authorities. (C.C.P. 484.090[d]). Court shall issue right to attach order if it finds claim is one upon which attachment may be issued, plaintiff has established probable validity of claim, attachment is not sought for purpose other than recovery on such claim, and amount to be secured is greater than zero. (C.C.P. 484.090[a]). In addition, if court finds defendant has failed to prove property is exempt, and plaintiff has provided undertaking (see subhead Attachment Bond, infra), court shall issue writ of attachment. (C.C.P. 484.090[b]).

At time of application for right to attach order, plaintiff may seek temporary protective order to prevent defendant from transferring attachable assets prior to hearing. (C.C.P. 486.010). At ex parte hearing, court shall issue temporary protective order, upon plaintiff's filing sufficient undertaking, if it finds: claim is one upon which attachment may be issued; plaintiff has established probable validity of claim; such order is not sought for purpose other than recovery upon claim; and plaintiff will suffer great or irreparable injury if order is not issued. (C.C.P. 486.020).

Right to attach order and writ of attachment may issue upon ex parte proceeding if, in addition to requirements for granting upon noticed motion, plaintiff shows great or irreparable injury would result if issuance of order is delayed until noticed hearing and amount to be secured is greater than zero. (C.C.P. 485.010[a], 485.220[a]). Great or irreparable injury is defined. (C.C.P. 485.010[b]). Contents of application and affidavits are specified. (C.C.P. 485.210). If writ of attachment issued ex parte, defendant may, upon noticed motion, set aside right to attach order, quash writ of attachment, and release any property upon which writ has been levied. (C.C.P. 485.240). If plaintiff applies ex parte for right to attach order and writ of attachment, court has discretion to grant only temporary protective order and treat application as upon noticed motion. (C.C.P. 486.030).

Attachment Bond.—Before court will issue writ of attachment or temporary protective order, plaintiff must file undertaking. (C.C.P. 489.210). Amount of bond is $2,500 in justice or municipal court and $7,500 in superior court (C.C.P. 489.220[a]); if defendant objects and court determines probable recovery for wrongful attachment exceeds these amounts, court shall order amount of undertaking increased to such amount (C.C.P. 489.220[b]).

Levy.—Statute prescribes contents of writ of attachment, contents of notice of attachment and general instructions to levying officers. (C.C.P. 488.010 et seq.).

Statute provides many different methods of levy dependent upon type of property to be attached. (C.C.P. 488.300-488.485).

Indemnity.—Levying officer has no right to require indemnity, though he may require deposit for taking and keeping property. (C. C. P. 488.050). See subhead Attachment Bond, supra.

Lien.—Levy of writ of attachment creates lien on property valid against subsequent transferees. (C.C.P. 488.500). Unless sooner released, no attachment shall have effect at expiration of three years from date of issuance of writ of attachment. (C.C.P. 488.510[a]). Lien may be extended one year on noticed motion (C.C.P. 488.510[b]), but maximum period of attachment, including extensions, shall not exceed eight years (C.C.P. 488.510[d]). Death of debtor whose property is attached does not terminate attachment. (C.C.P. 488.510[e]).

Service of temporary protective order creates lien upon property described in order; lien is not valid as against bonafide purchaser or transferee in ordinary course of business. (C.C.P. 486.110[a], 697.740[a]). Lien of temporary protective order is perfected upon levy of writ of attachment or terminates upon date of expiration specified in order. (C.C.P. 486.110[b]).

Attachment lien merges into subsequent lien created by levy of execution (see topic Executions); lien of attachment on real property merges into lien of judgment (see category Civil Actions and Procedure, topic Judgments). (133 C.A.2d 283, 284 P.2d 185). Attachment lien on real property is defeated by subsequent declaration of homestead (see topic Homesteads). (214 C. 753, 7 P.2d 1027). Lien of attachment or of temporary protective order is terminated upon making of general assignment for benefit of creditors and upon filing petition commencing voluntary or involuntary bankruptcy proceeding, if lien was created within 90 days prior to making of general assignment or filing of petition. (C.C.P. 493.010-493.060).

Priorities.—Attachment liens on same property have priority based upon date of creation. (C.C. 2897).

Release of Property.—Post-levy exemption claiming procedures are provided. (C.C.P. 482.100).

Court may allow defendant, upon noticed motion, to substitute undertaking in order to release property from attachment or temporary protective order. (C.C.P. 489.310, 489.320).

Levying officer shall release attachment when he receives written directive from plaintiff's attorney or when he receives certified copy of court order for release, or when otherwise required to release property. (C.C.P. 488.730[a]).

Sale.—Court may order sale of property subject to attachment prior to judgment if such property is perishable or will greatly deteriorate or greatly depreciate in value or if interests of parties will be best served by sale. (C.C.P. 488.700[a]). If levying officer determines property is extremely perishable or will greatly deteriorate or greatly depreciate in value before court order could be obtained, he may take any action necessary to preserve value of property or may sell property. (C.C.P. 488.700[b]).

Third Party Claims.—Third party claims treated in same manner as in executions. (See topic Executions.) (C.C.P. 488.110).

Vacation or Modification.—Defendant may move to modify or vacate ex parte right to attach order or temporary protective order. (C.C.P. 485.240, 486.100).

Wrongful Attachment.—Statute defines acts of wrongful attachment and establishes liability therefor. (C.C.P. 490.010 et seq.). Statute does not limit right to recover for damages caused by attachment or protective order on any common law theory of recovery. (C.C.P. 490.060).

Garnishment.—See topic Garnishment.

Forms.—Mandatory forms have been promulgated by California Judicial Council to implement attachment statute pursuant to authority granted in C.C.P. 482.030.

CREDITORS' SUITS:

Judgment creditor may bring action against third party who has possession or control of property in which judgment debtor has interest. (C.C.P. 708.210). Judgment creditor may obtain restraining order preventing third party from transferring property. (C.C.P. 708.240). Creditors' suits for claims against property held by third party in which defendant has interest or third party who is indebted to defendant, when property or debt has been attached by lien governed by C.C.P. 491.310-491.370. Statutory summary processes for creditors' suits are attachment (C.C.P. 481.010-488.740), claim and delivery of personalty (C.C.P. 511.010-516.050), third party claims of ownership or possession (C.C.P. 720.110-720.170), third party claims of security interest or lien (C.C.P. 720.210-720.290) and foreclosure of trust deeds or mortgages (C.C.P. 725a-730.5).

EXECUTIONS:

Judgments are enforceable according to provisions of Enforcement of Judgments Law. (C.C.P. 680.010 et seq.). Comprehensive statutes provide for enforcement of money judgments (C.C.P. 695.010), judgments for possession of personal property (C.C.P. 714.010 et seq.), judgments for possession of real property (C.C.P. 715.010), judgments for sale of real or personal property (C.C.P. 716.010), and other judgments (C.C.P. 717.010).

Exemptions.—See topic Exemptions.

Time for Issuance.—Judgment is generally enforceable upon entry (C.C.P. 683.010) and may be enforced for ten years thereafter (C.C.P. 683.020). Judgment creditor may obtain multiple renewals of ten year period by filing application with court in which judgment was entered. (C.C.P. 683.110 et. seq.).

Stay of Execution.—Trial court may stay enforcement of any judgment or order regardless of status of appeal, except that if enforcement would be stayed on appeal only by giving of undertaking, stay cannot extend for more than ten days beyond last day to file notice of appeal without consent of adverse party. (C.C.P. 918). C.C.P. 918.5 guides court's discretion when judgment debtor has pending claim against judgment creditor. See category Civil Actions and Procedure, topic Appeal and Error, subhead Stay of Proceedings.

Lien.—Judgment creditor may create judgment lien on real property by recording abstract of judgment with County Recorder (C.C.P. 697.310 et. seq.) and on certain personal property by filing notice of judgment lien in office of Secretary of State (C.C.P. 697.510 et. seq.). Levy on property under writ of execution creates execution lien on property from time of levy for two-year period unless sooner satisfied. (C.C.P. 697.710).

Levy.—Except as otherwise provided by statute, all property of judgment debtor is subject to enforcement of money judgment. (C.C.P. 695.010, 695.030). After entry of money judgment, judgment creditor upon application may obtain writ of execution. (C.C.P. 699.510[a]). Writ must require levying officer to enforce money judgment. (C.C.P. 699.520). Detailed statutes provide for methods of levy for various types of property. (C.C.P. 700.010-700.200).

Return.—Levying officer shall return writ to court with report of levying officer's actions and accounting within specified periods not to exceed two years. (C.C.P. 699.560).

Priorities.—Lien of execution has priority based upon date of levy. (C.C. 2897, C.C.P. 697.710).

Claims of Third Persons.—Third person claiming ownership, right to possession, security interest, or lien in property levied upon may file claim with levying officer. (C.C.P. 720.110, 720.210[a]). Property must be released unless judgment creditor files

EXECUTIONS . . . *continued*

undertaking or deposits with levying officer amount claimed by secured party or lienholder. (C.C.P. 720.140, 720.240). Creditor or third party may petition court to determine validity of claim and disposition of property. (C.C.P. 720.310).

Satisfaction.—Money judgment may be satisfied by payment in full or by acceptance of lesser sum in full satisfaction of judgment. (C.C.P. 724.010). Upon payment of part or all of judgment and demand by judgment debtor, judgment creditor shall execute acknowledgment of payments. (C.C.P. 724.030 et seq.).

Sale.—Written notice of sale must be given stating date, time, and place of sale, and must describe property to be sold. (C.C.P. 701.530, 701.540). Statutes provide for distribution of proceeds of sale. (C.C.P. 701.810 et seq.). Sale must be by auction to highest bidder. (C.C.P. 701.570[b]).

Redemption.—Execution sale is absolute and may not be set aside, unless sale was improper, judgment creditor was purchaser at sale, and judgment debtor brings action within 90 days to set aside sale. (C.C.P. 701.680).

Supplementary Proceedings.—Judgment creditor may propound written interrogatories to judgment debtor requesting information to aid in enforcement of judgment. (C.C.P. 708.020). Judgment creditor may obtain ex parte order requiring judgment debtor to appear before court to furnish information to aid in enforcement of judgment. (C.C.P. 708.110 et seq.). Court may appoint receiver to enforce judgment. (C.C.P. 708.620).

Body Execution.—Judgment creditor may obtain ex parte order requiring judgment debtor to appear before court to furnish information to aid in enforcement of judgment. (C.C.P. 708.110 et seq.). If judgment debtor fails to appear, court may issue warrants to bring him before court and may punish him for contempt. (C.C.P. 708.170).

EXEMPTIONS:

There are numerous exemptions from attachment or execution of personal property, in many cases limited as to amount. (C. C. P. 703.010 et seq.). For list of exemptions, see also category Civil Actions and Procedure, topic Judgments, subhead Exempt Property from Satisfaction of Judgment.

Substitution.—Debtor who does not own articles specifically exempted may not hold other articles or money exempt in lieu thereof. (2 C.2d 63, 38 P.2d 784).

Waiver of Exemption.—Contractual or other prior waiver of exemptions, other than by failure to claim exemptions, is void. (C.C.P. 703.040).

Necessity of Claiming Exemptions.—Certain property is exempt without making claim. (C.C.P. 704.210). Otherwise, claimant must make claim of exemption (C.C.P. 703.510 et. seq.).

Homestead Exemption.—See topic Homesteads.

FORECLOSURE:

See topic Liens; category Mortgages, topics Chattel Mortgages, Mortgages of Real Property.

FRAUDULENT SALES AND CONVEYANCES:

Uniform Commercial Code has been adopted (1963, c. 819), effective Jan. 1, 1965. See also topic Assignments, subhead Assignment of Accounts Receivable.

Uniform Fraudulent Transfer Act adopted (1986, c. 383) to replace Uniform Fraudulent Conveyance Act (C. C. 3439 et seq.); applies to transfers made on or after Jan. 1, 1987.

Transfer of Personal Property.—Every transfer of personal property made by person in possession or having control of property and not accompanied by immediate delivery and followed by actual and continued change of possession, is void against secured or unsecured creditors of transferor while he remains in possession and against good faith buyers from tranferor subsequent to transfer. Several exceptions apply. (C.C. 3440, 3440.1). Subdivision (2) of §2402 and subdivision (1) of §10308 of Commercial Code are not restricted by provisions of this section.

Bulk Sales.—Uniform Commercial Code governs. See category Business Regulation and Commerce, topic Commercial Code, subhead Material Variations from 1990 Official Text. See also C. C. 3440.1.

GARNISHMENT:

Garnishment is form of attachment or execution and is means by which plaintiff may levy upon property of defendant which is in possession of third party. See topics Attachment and Executions.

Property Which May Be Reached.—For prejudgment garnishment, all property subject to attachment. Contingent and uncertain obligations are not subject to garnishment. (70 C.A.3d 367, 138 C. Rptr. 807). (See topic Attachment, subhead Property Subject to Attachment.) For post-judgment garnishment, all property subject to execution. (See topic Executions, subhead Levy.)

Jurisdiction.—See topic Attachment, subhead Courts Which May Issue Writ.

Proceedings to Obtain.—See topic Attachment, subhead Proceedings to Obtain. See topic Executions, subhead Time for Issuance.

Practice.—Any person owing debts to defendant in excess of $250 or having possession or control of personal property of defendant may be required to appear before court for purpose of examination on oath regarding such property. (C. C. P. 491.110[a]). If person so examined admits debt, or if he denies debt or claims interest adverse to defendant, but court determines existence of debt or interest in property pursuant to C.C.P. 491.170, court may order such debt or property to be attached. (C. C. P. 491.190). In such proceeding, witnesses, including nonresident, may be required to appear and testify as to matters relating to examination of third person. (C. C. P. 491.120).

Judgment.—If judgment is for defendant, all property in hands of levying officer shall be delivered to person from whom it was collected. (C. C. P. 488.740).

Adverse Claims.—See topic Attachment, subhead Third Party Claims. See also topic Executions, subhead Claims of Third Persons.

Earnings.—See topics Attachment, subhead Property Subject to Attachment; Executions, subhead Levy; Exemptions.

HOMESTEADS:

Civil Code §§1237 through 1304 relating to declared homestead are superseded by Code of Civil Procedure §§704.710-704.850 (claimed homestead exemption) and 704.910-704.995 (declared homesteads). As restraint on ability to convey, encumber, or partition property (former §§1240 and 1242), declared homestead is superseded by more general provisions governing conveyance, encumbrance, and partition of community and separate property and imposing obligations on spouses for mutual support and to provide dwelling; ability of one spouse to affect separate property of other spouse is not continued except as provided in §§752-754, 2035(c), 2036.5 of Family Code. See Family Code §§770 (wife may convey separate property without husband's consent; husband may convey separate property without wife's consent), 1100 (spouse may not convey or encumber community personal property used as dwelling without written consent of other spouse), 1102 (both spouses must join in conveyance or encumbrance of community real property), 720 (spouses' obligation of mutual support), 752; 754; 2035(c) (right to occupy dwelling of spouse and restraining on alienation of dwelling); Code Civ. Proc. §872.210(b) (no partition of community property).

Homestead Exemption.—

Value Exempt.—$125,000 if judgment debtor or spouse is 65 years or over or is unable to engage in substantial gainful employment due to disability or is 55 years or over with gross annual income of not more than $15,000, or, if married, joint gross annual income of not more than $20,000, and sale is involuntary. $75,000 if judgment debtor or spouse is member of family unit and there is at least one member of family unit who owns no interest in homestead or whose only interest in homestead is community property interest with judgment debtor, $50,000 for all other persons. In any event, aggregate exemptions of both spouses on same judgment may not exceed $75,000 or $125,000 as applicable. (C.C.P. 704.730).

Property Exempt.—Dwelling where person resides continuously from date judgment lien attaches until date court determines dwelling is homestead. Dwelling includes, without limitation: (1) House together with outbuildings and land upon which they are situated; (2) mobile home together with outbuildings and land upon which they are situated; (3) boat; (4) condominium; (5) planned development; (6) stock cooperative; (7) community apartment project. (C.C.P. 704.710).

Enforcement Sale.—Dwelling may be sold to enforce money judgment only upon court order, unless dwelling is personal property or leasehold estate with unexpired term less than two years. (C.C.P. 704.740). If no bid is received at court-ordered sale that exceeds amount of homestead exemption plus any additional amount necessary to satisfy all liens and encumbrances, dwelling shall not be sold, and same judgment creditor may not make application for sale for period of one year. Sale must be for 90% or more of fair-market-value of dwelling except upon permission of court to accept highest bid. (C.C.P. 704.800). Sale does not trigger "due-on-sale" clause or prepayment penalty under lien or encumbrance. (C.C.P. 704.810). If judgment debtor is co-owner or owns less than fee, only judgment debtor's interest shall be sold, and judgment debtor is entitled to apply his or her exemption to such interest. (C.C.P. 704.820). Judgment creditor entitled to receive costs incurred in enforcement sale, unless no bid exceeds aggregate of exemption and all liens and encumbrances. (C.C.P. 704.840).

Proceeds.—If homestead sold by enforcement sale or damaged or destroyed, or is acquired for public use, proceeds of sale, insurance or condemnation award are exempt to extent of applicable value of exemption for six months after receipt, unless homestead exemption is applied to other property of judgment debtor or spouse during that period. (C.C.P. 704.720).

Declared Homestead.—

Value Exempt.—Same as for statutory homestead exemption above. (C.C.P. 704.950). If homestead declaration is recorded and thereafter exemption is increased, applicable exemption is in effect on date creditor obtains lien. (C.C.P. 704.965).

Property Exempt.—Limited to any interest in real property that is "dwelling" as defined in C.C.P. 704.710, but does not include leasehold with unexpired term less than two years or interest of beneficiary of trust. (C.C.P. 704.910).

Declaration of Homestead.—Homestead may be formally declared by filing declaration of homestead. (C.C.P. 704.920). Declaration must contain: (1) Name of declared homestead owner; (2) description of declared homestead; (3) statement that declared homestead is principal dwelling of declared homestead owner or spouse and that owner or spouse reside there on date of recordation; and (4) statement that facts stated in declaration are known to be true as of personal knowledge of person executing and acknowledging declaration. Declaration must be executed and acknowledged as though conveyance of real property, and may be executed by guardian, conservator or authorized agent of homestead owner or spouse. (C.C.P. 704.930). Declaration must be recorded in county where dwelling is located. (C.C.P. 704.920).

Enforcement Sale.—Same as statutory homestead exemption above. (C.C.P. 704.970).

Proceeds.—Same as statutory homestead exemption above. (C.C.P. 704.960).

Voluntary Sale.—Proceeds exempt for six months after sale. If reinvested in new dwelling within six months, new homestead may be recorded with effect as though recorded at time prior homestead was recorded. (C.C.P. 704.960).

Abandonment.—Declared homestead may be abandoned by recordation of declaration of abandonment (C.C.P. 704.980) or automatically upon recordation of homestead declaration for different property (C.C.P. 704.990).

Probate Homestead.—Surviving spouse and minor children entitled to remain in possession of family dwelling, and dwelling exempt from enforcement of money judgment, until 60 days after filing probate inventory or as ordered by court. (Prob. C. 6500). Upon application, court may set apart for limited period for use of surviving spouse and/or minor children, one homestead from community, quasi-community,

HOMESTEADS . . . *continued*
commonly owned property of decedent and spouse or separate property of decedent. (Prob. C. 6520-6528).

Bankruptcy Homestead.—Exemption available in bankruptcy regardless of existing money judgment or money judgment enforced by execution. (C.C.P. 703.140).

JUDGMENT NOTES:

See category Civil Actions and Procedure, topic Judgments, subhead Judgment by Confession.

LEVY:

See topics Attachment, Executions.

LIENS:

No attempt is here made to discuss at length ordinary common-law or equitable liens.

Uniform Commercial Code was adopted effective in 1965. See category Business Regulation and Commerce, topic Commercial Code.

California has great number of statutory liens which are non-consensual and which can arise in unexpected situations. Care must be taken when dealing with certain businesses or undertaking certain transactions to ensure that unanticipated statutory liens do not arise to impair party's position. Statutory lien legislation is not located in one particular place in California statutes. Rather, this legislation is dispersed throughout numerous Code divisions. Majority of statutory liens are found in following Codes: Food & Agricultural Code; Civil Code; Commercial Code; Financial Code; Government Code; Harbor and Navigation Code; Health and Safety Code; Public Utilities Code; and Revenue and Taxation Code.

Discussion of selected liens and matters regarding them follows:

Jewelers have lien dependent upon possession, for any account due for work and materials. (C. C. 3052a).

Repairmen and keepers of garages for automobiles have lien, dependent on possession, for their labor, services and materials in caring for and safe keeping such automobiles and trailers. (C. C. 3051, 3068).

Lien on Merchandise.—Uniform Commercial Code governs. (Division 9 of Commercial Code). See category Business Regulation and Commerce, topic Commercial Code.

Vendors and Vendees of Real Property.—Vendors of real property have lien independent of possession for unpaid and unsecured portions of purchase price. (C. C. 3046). Vendee of real property has lien, independent of possession, for such part of amount paid as he may be entitled to recover back in case of failure of consideration. (C. C. 3050).

Lien for Services Rendered.—Persons who make, alter or repair items of personal property at request of owner thereof, has special lien, dependent upon possession, for compensation due for his services in amount of reasonable charges and cost of materials. (C. C. 3051). Lien subject to limitations discussed below.

Other Liens.—There are also agricultural laboror's liens, shipmaster's liens, seamen's liens, warehousemen's liens, liens of keepers of apartments, of persons who cut logs and lumber, liens of workers on, and suppliers for, aircraft, and liens of persons who furnish labor, material or services to an oil or gas leasehold. Banker's "lien," properly "right of set-off," not state action and not subject to Constitution. (11 C.3d 352, 521 P.2d 441, 113 C.Rptr. 449).

See also topics Attachment, Pledges; categories Business Regulation and Commerce, topics Carriers, Factors; Civil Actions and Procedure, topic Judgments; Mortgages, topics Chattel Mortgages, Mortgages of Real Property; Taxation, topic Administration, subhead County and Municipal Taxes, catchline Lien; Transportation, topic Motor Vehicles.

Waiver, Loss or Extinguishment.—Liens under C. C. 3051 are valid in varying amounts depending upon type of lien and whether notice to and consent of owner of property is first obtained. (C. C. 3051a and 3068). Lien is accessory to act performance of which it secures and is extinguishable in like manner with any other accessory obligation. (C. C. 2909). Sale of any property on which there is lien, in satisfaction of claim secured thereby, or in case of personal property, its wrongful conversion by person holding lien, extinguishes lien thereon. (C. C. 2910). Lien is extinguished by lapse of time as provided by statutes of limitation for principal obligation. Special rules exist for extinguishment of liens on real property to secure payment of public improvement assessments. (C.C. 2911). Partial performance of act secured by lien does not extinguish lien. (C.C. 2912). Voluntary restoration of property to owner by lienholder extinguishes lien dependent upon possession as to owners in absence of agreement to contrary, and extinguishes it as to creditors and subsequent bona fide purchasers notwithstanding such agreement. (C.C. 2913). Foregoing rules do not apply to transactions or security interests governed by Uniform Commercial Code. (C.C. 2914).

Enforcement.—Statutes provide in detail for sale of goods on which there is lien to satisfy principal obligation which is due and unpaid. Goods may be sold at public auction by giving prescribed notice to owner, advertising sale, etc. (C.C. 3052, 3052a, 3066, 3071-3074).

Mechanics' Liens.—Mechanics, materialmen, contractors, subcontractors, lessors of equipment, artisans, architects, machinists, builders, teamsters and draymen, registered engineers, licensed land surveyors and all persons and laborers of every class performing labor upon or bestowing skill or other necessary services on, or furnishing materials or leasing equipment to be used or consumed in, or furnishing appliances, teams, or power contributing to a work of improvement shall have lien upon property upon which they have bestowed labor or furnished materials or appliances or leased equipment for value of such labor done or materials furnished and for value of use of such appliances, teams, or power, whether done or furnished at instance of owner or of any person acting by his authority or under him, as contractor or otherwise. (C.C. 3110). See C.C. 3060 for lien for work or materials relating to mine. With respect to mechanics' liens every contractor, subcontractor, architect, builder, or other person having charge of construction, alteration, addition to, or repair, in whole or in part, of any building or other work of improvement shall be held to be agent of owner. (C.C. 3106, 3110).

Preliminary 20-Day Notice.—Unless he is laborer for wages or under direct contract with owner, or an express trust fund as provided under C.C. 3111, lien claimant must give specified notice to owner, original contractor or reputed contractor and construction lender, not later than 20 days after claimant has first furnished labor, services, equipment, or materials to jobsite. (C.C. 3097, 3114).

Claim of Lien.—Each claimant, in order to enforce lien, must record his claim of lien within 90 days after completion of work of improvement if no notice of completion or cessation was recorded, or within 60 days after filing of such notice in case of original contractor, and within 30 days after such date in case of other claimants. (C. C. 3115, 3116). Where improvement is made under two or more original contracts, owner may, within ten days after completion of any such contract, record notice of completion containing specified data. (C. C. 3093, 3117). Upon such filing, original contractor under contract covered by notice must, within 60 days after filing, and other claimant must, within 30 days after filing, record his claim of lien. (C. C. 3117).

Release Bond.—Owner of, or in certain cases contractor or subcontractor upon, property sought to be charged with claim of lien may free property from such claim by recording bond in penal sum one and one-half times amount of claim. (C. C. 3143).

Amount of Lien.—Mechanics' liens are direct liens, and shall be for reasonable value of labor, services, equipment, or materials furnished or for price agreed upon by claimant and person with whom he contracts, whichever is less. Such lien is not limited in amount by price stated in contract, except where original contract and a bond are filed. (C.C. 3123, 3235, 3236).

Land Affected.—Land upon which any improvement is situated together with convenient space about same, or so much as may be required for convenient use and occupation thereof, if at commencement of work, or of furnishing of material for same, land belonged to person who caused such improvement to be constructed, but if such person owned less than fee simple estate in such land, then only his interest therein is subject to such lien, except as provided in C.C. 3129. (C.C. 3128).

Duration and Enforcement of Lien.—No lien binds any property longer than 90 days after its recording unless proceedings be commenced in proper court within that time to enforce such lien, or unless credit is given and notice of fact and terms of such credit is recorded prior to expiration of 90-day period; and if enforcement proceedings are not prosecuted to trial within two years after commencement, they may be dismissed at court's discretion. (C.C. 3144, 3147). Unless notice of pendency of proceedings filed, no subsequent purchaser has constructive notice. (C.C. 3146).

Priority.—Mechanic's lien is preferred to any other lien which may attach subsequent to commencement of work of improvement and to any other lien of which lien claimant had no notice and which was unrecorded at time work of improvement was commenced (C.C. 3134) except if holder of lien procures and records specified payment bond, then lien shall be preferred to liens for labor, services, equipment, or materials furnished after such recordings (C.C. 3096, 3138). Mechanics' liens with respect to site improvements (defined in C.C. 3102) are also preferred to any mortgage, deed of trust, or other encumbrance recorded before commencement of site improvement work which was given for sole or primary purpose of financing such site improvements, unless loan proceeds are placed in control of lender under binding agreement with borrower containing specified restrictions on disposition of proceeds, or unless owner of land or holder of lien procures and records specified payment bond before completion of work of improvement. (C.C. 3096, 3137, 3139).

Stop Notices for Private Works of Improvement.—Any person entitled to mechanic's lien, other than original contractor: (a) May give stop notice (defined in C.C. 3103) to owner, and (b) unless payment bond recorded in accordance with C.C. 3235, may give stop notice or bonded stop notice (defined in C.C. 3083) to construction lender. (C.C. 3158, 3159). Any person who fails to serve stop notice on owner after written demand from owner therefor, shall forfeit right to mechanic's lien. (C.C. 3158). Service of stop notice or bonded stop notice effective only if made prior to expiration of period within which claim of lien must be recorded under C.C. 3115, 3116 or 3117, and preliminary 20-day notice given in accordance with C.C. 3097. (C.C. 3160). Upon receipt of stop notice, owner shall and construction lender may, and upon receipt of bonded stop notice construction lender shall, withhold sufficient money to answer claim, unless payment bond recorded in accordance with C.C. 3235. (C.C. 3161, 3162). Upon filing of specified bond in penal sum equal to 1¼ times amount stated in stop notice, funds withheld in response to stop notice or bonded stop notice shall be released. (C.C. 3171). Action to enforce claim stated in stop notice or bonded stop notice must be commenced not later than 90 days following expiration of period within which claims of lien must be recorded. (C.C. 3172). Action not brought to trial within two years after commencement thereof may be dismissed in court's discretion. (C.C. 3173).

Stop Notice for Public Work.—Except for original contractor, any person entitled to mechanic's lien, trust fund lien, site improvement lien, contracting for wastework or furnishing provisions, provender or other supplies to public work (defined in C.C. 3099, 3100) may serve stop notice upon public entity responsible for such public work. (C.C. 3181). To enforce stop notice, claimant must have given preliminary 20-day notice (public work) in accordance with C.C. 3098, and must have served stop notice before expiration of: (a) 30 days after recording of notice of completion or notice of cessation (defined in C.C. 3092), or (b) if neither is recorded, 90 days after completion or cessation. (C.C. 3183, 3184). Upon receipt of stop notice, public entity so notified must withhold money or bonds sufficient to answer claim stated in such stop notice and to provide for reasonable cost of any litigation thereunder. Public entity may satisfy duty by refusing to release money held in escrow pursuant to Pub. Cont. C. 10263 or 22300. (C.C. 3186). Public entity may, in its discretion, permit original contractor to file specified bond in amount equal to 125% of claim stated, and public entity shall not withhold moneys or bonds upon filing of such bond. (C.C.

See note at head of Digest as to 1998 legislation covered.

See Topical Index in front part of this volume.

CA – 37

LIENS . . . *continued*

3196). Original contractor who disputes claim may have question determined in summary proceedings pursuant to C.C. 3198-3205. (C.C. 3197). Action to enforce claim stated in stop notice must be commenced at any time after ten days from date of service of stop notice and not later than 90 days following expiration of period within which stop notice must be filed. (C.C. 3210). Action not brought to trial within two years after commencement thereof may be dismissed in court's discretion. (C.C. 3212).

Effect on Arbitration Rights.—Recording and enforcing mechanic's lien does not thereby waive any right to arbitration that otherwise exists, if, at time of filing action to enforce lien, claimant presents to court application that such action be stayed pending arbitration of any relevant issues. Failure of defendant to file C.C.P. 1281.2 petition waives right to compel arbitration. (C.C.P. 1281.5).

Constitutionality.—Mechanic's lien and stop notice procedures held constitutional. (17 C.3d 803, 132 C.Rptr. 477; 553 P.2d 637).

Revised Uniform Federal Lien Registration Act enacted. (C.C.P. 2100 et seq.).

MECHANICS' LIENS:

See topic Liens.

PLEDGES:

Uniform Commercial Code has been adopted. (1963, c. 819). See category Business Regulation and Commerce, topic Commercial Code.

Remedies of Pledgee.—Uniform Commercial Code governs. (Com'l. C. Div. 9). See category Business Regulation and Commerce, topic Commercial Code, subhead Material Variations from 1990 Official Text.

RECEIVERS:

When Appointment Proper.—Receiver may be appointed by court in which action is pending:

(1) In action by vendor to vacate fraudulent purchase of property, or by creditor to subject any property or fund to his claim, or between partners or others jointly owning or interested in any property or fund, on application of plaintiff, or of any party whose right to or interest in property or fund, or proceeds thereof, is probable, and where it is shown that property or fund is in danger of being lost, removed or materially injured. (2) In action by secured lender for foreclosure of his deed of trust or mortgage and sale of property upon which there is lien under deed of trust or mortgage where it appears that property is in danger of being lost, removed or materially injured, or that condition of deed of trust or mortgage has not been performed, and property is probably insufficient to discharge deed of trust or mortgage debt. (3) After judgment, to carry judgment into effect. (4) After judgment, to dispose of property according to judgment, or to preserve it during pendency of appeal, or pursuant to Tit. 9 commencing with C.C.P. 680.010 (enforcement of judgments), or after sale of real property or pursuant to decree of foreclosure, during redemption period, to collect, expend, and disburse rents as may be directed by court or otherwise provided by law. (5) In cases when corporation has been dissolved, or is insolvent, or in imminent danger of insolvency, or has forfeited its corporate rights. (6) In action of unlawful detainer. (7) At request of Public Utilities Commission pursuant to §855 of Public Utilities Code. (8) In all other cases where receivers have heretofore been appointed by usages of courts of equity. (9) At request of Office of Statewide Health Planning and Development, or Attorney General. (10) In action by secured lender for specific performance of assignment of rents provision in deed of trust, mortgage, or separate assignment document. (11) In case brought by assignee under assignment of leases, rents, issues, or profits under C.C. 2938(g). (C. C. P. 564).

Eligibility.—No party, or attorney, or person interested in action, or related to any judge of court by consanguinity or affinity within third degree, can be appointed receiver therein without written consent of parties, filed with clerk. (C. C. P. 566).

Bond in Case of Ex Parte Appointment.—If receiver be appointed upon ex parte application, court, before making order, must require from applicant undertaking in amount to be fixed by court, to effect that applicant will pay to defendant all damages he may sustain by reason of appointment of receiver and entry by receiver upon duties, in case applicant shall have procured such appointment, wrongfully, maliciously or without sufficient cause; and court may, in its discretion, at any time, require additional undertaking. (C. C. P. 566).

Powers.—Receiver has, under control of court, power to: Bring and defend actions in his own name, as receiver; take and keep possession of property; receive rents; collect debts, to compound for and compromise same; to make transfers; and do such other acts as court may authorize. (C. C. P. 568).

REDEMPTION:

See topics Executions, Liens; categories Mortgages, topic Mortgages of Real Property; Taxation, topic Property Taxes, subhead Redemption.

SUPPLEMENTARY PROCEEDINGS:

See topic Executions.

TRUSTEE PROCESS:

See topic Garnishment.

USURY:

See category Business Regulation and Commerce, topic Interest.

DISPUTE RESOLUTION

ALTERNATIVE DISPUTE RESOLUTION:

Legislature has declared that courts should encourage greater use of alternative dispute resolution techniques when administration of justice will be improved and counties should consider increasing use of alternative dispute resolution in their operations as plans for court reform are developed and implemented. (Bus. & Prof. 465[d][e]).

Mandatory Dispute Resolution.—Various statutes require alternative dispute resolution (ADR) in specific types of cases.

Superior Court Cases Up to $50,000.—Civil case in superior court with ten or more judges where amount in controversy is $50,000 or less must be referred to nonbinding arbitration. (C.C.P. 1141.10 et seq.).

Uninsured Motorist Coverage Claims.—Auto insurance policies must provide for binding arbitration of disputes between insurer and insured under uninsured or underinsured motorist coverage. (Ins. C. 11580.2[f]).

Public Works Claims Against Local Agency.—Lawsuits for $375,000 or less by public works contractor against local agency must be referred to mediation within 60 days after responsive pleadings filed unless parties stipulate otherwise. (Pub. Cont. C. 20104.4).

Contract Claims Against State.—Arbitration is only remedy available for resolution of contract claim against state. (Pub. Cont. C. 10240).

Child custody and visitation matters must be mediated prior to any contested hearing. (Fam. C. 3160 et seq.).

Attorney-Client Fee Disputes.—If client requests, any suit for attorney fees must be arbitrated by approved local bar association program, or by State Bar if no local program. Attorney must advise client of this option when lawsuit filed. Award binding unless any of parties seeks trial de novo within 30 days after notice of arbitration award. (Bus. & Prof. C. 6200 et seq.).

Cumis Counsel/Insurer Fee Disputes.—Fee disputes between counsel hired by insurer to represent insured because of conflict of interest, if not settled by other means specified in insurance policy, must be resolved by final and binding arbitration using single, neutral arbitrator selected by parties. (C.C. 2860[c]).

Warranty Claims Against Motor Vehicle Manufacturers.—Such disputes must be submitted to qualified third party dispute resolution process, if one has been adopted by manufacturer, before buyer may utilize certain statutory presumption. (C.C. 1793.2, Bus. & Prof. C. 472-472.5).

Complaints Against Contractors.—Complaint against contractor arising from home improvement contract, or alleging violation of contractors' state license law, must be referred to arbitration if contract price or damages alleged is less than $5,000. (Bus. & Prof. C. 7085).

Cost of Maintaining Easement.—In suit by easement owner against co-owners for contribution to cost of maintenance, court will appoint private arbitrator to apportion cost according to use. If arbitrator's award not accepted by all owners, court may enter judgment determining proportionate liability. (C.C. 845).

Workers' Compensation Proceedings.—Various issues subject to binding arbitration if claimant is represented by counsel including: (1) existence of insurance coverage, (2) rights of contribution where medical benefits have been provided from several sources; and (3) in some cases, issue of permanent disability. (Lab. C. 5275).

Enforcement of Common Interest Development Governing Documents.—Where dispute exists between condo owners' association and one of owners as to enforcement of governing documents, parties must endeavor to resolve dispute by some ADR method. (C.C. 1354).

Statutes Requiring Mediation.—Various statutes require mediation of disputes including: Labor disputes (Lab. C. 65-66; 18 Ops. Atty. Gen. 216), disputes between schools and parents of handicapped child (Educ. C. 56500.3, 56501[b][2]), habitual truants (Welf. & Inst. C. 601.1-601.3), disputes between public entities and their employee organizations (Govt. C. 3502.2, 3507.1, 3518, 3589, 3590, 3548, Pub. Utils. C. 125524), disputes between public transit operators and local agencies (Pub. Utils. C. 120477), and disputes between labelers and any persons concerning label statements required by California Seed Law (choice between conciliation, mediation or arbitration) (Fd. & Agric. C. 52332[g]).

Statutes Requiring Arbitration.—Various statutes require arbitration of disputes including: Disputes between community college and employee (Educ. C. 87674), apportionment of liability for hazardous substance clean-up (H. & S.C. 25356.2, 25356.3), insurance policies issued to self-employed persons (Lab. C. 5308), garment industry disputes (Lab. C. 2685-2692), value of oil or gas tract (Pub. Res. C. 3647), protection of fish and game (Fish & G. C. 1601-1603, 15512, 7710.1), and tax liability to more than one state (Rev. & Tax. C. 38006). Rules governing arbitration found in C.C.P. 1141.10-1141.31.

Voluntary Dispute Resolution.—Some statutes authorize use of ADR but do not mandate it. Examples include: Land use disputes (Govt. C. 60030 et seq.), penalties against nursing home facility (H. & S.C. 1428[j]), certification determinations for escrow agents and employees (Finan. C. 17331.3), and disputes between guide dog schools and users (Bus. & Prof. C. 7215.5).

See also topic Arbitration and Award.

ARBITRATION AND AWARD:

Written agreement to submit existing or future controversy to arbitration is valid, enforceable and irrevocable, save upon grounds existing for revocation of any contract, waiver of right, or if party to arbitration agreement is also party to pending court action arising out of same transaction and there is possibility of conflicting rulings on common questions. In latter circumstances court, on petition, may order arbitration to proceed, to be stayed or to proceed only as to those persons not party to court proceeding. Separate arbitration proceedings may, on certain conditions, be ordered consolidated. (C.C.P. 1281.2). Right to arbitration pursuant to agreement may be

ARBITRATION AND AWARD . . . *continued*

waived. (C.C.P. 1281.2[a]). Private arbitration agreements must provide dispute resolution procedures with minimum levels of integrity. Parties can agree to less than totally neutral arbitrator. See 28 C.3d 807; cf. 99 C. A.3d 501, 160 C. Rptr. 303. Significant or substantial business relationships between party and neutral arbitrator must be disclosed. See 108 C. A.3d 772, 166 C. Rptr. 774. Arbitrator must disqualify self upon demand of party where judicial disqualification grounds exist except in arbitration proceedings conducted under collective agreement between employers and employees or between their respective representatives. (C.C.P. 1281.9).

Uniform Arbitration Act has not been adopted.

Powers of arbitrators are to set time and place, adjourn or postpone, rule on all questions of procedure and evidence at hearing (C.C.P. 1282.2); issue signed but otherwise blank subpoenas to party requesting them (C.C.P. 1282.6); administer oaths (C.C.P. 1282.8); and order depositions for discovery (C.C.P. 1283, 1283.05) or for use as evidence. Arbitrator may enforce discovery rights, remedies and procedures just as are available in like circumstances in civil action except lacks power to order arrest or imprisonment of person. (C.C.P. 1283.05).

Award and Enforcement.—Award must be in writing and include determination of all necessary questions. (C.C.P. 1283.4). Confirmed award may be entered as judgment and enforced like civil judgment. (C.C.P. 1287.4).

Judgment on Award.—Within four years after award made, any party may petition court to confirm award. (C.C.P. 1285, 1288). If award confirmed, judgment must be entered in conformity therewith. (C.C.P. 1287.4). Within 100 days after service of award, any party may petition court to correct or vacate award (C.C.P. 1288) on grounds specified in C.C.P. 1286.2 and 1286.6 after satisfying prerequisites of C.C.P. 1286.8. Corrected award must be confirmed by court. (C.C.P. 1286.6).

Labor Disputes.—California has adopted policy that favors arbitration of disputes arising under collective bargaining agreements. (12 C.3d 608; 56 C.2d 169, 363 P.2d 313). See also 24 C.3d 442, 595 P.2d 129. Labor dispute over injury is subject to arbitration if it involves insurance coverage, right of contribution, or permanent disability of 20% standard or less. (Lab. C. 5275).

Medical Malpractice Disputes.—Any contract for medical services may contain provision for arbitration of any dispute as to professional negligence of health care provider if it contains express language required by C.C.P. 1295.

Judicial Arbitration.—In counties with ten or more superior court judges all actions in which, in opinion of court, less than $50,000 per plaintiff is in controversy, arbitration is mandatory. In counties with less than ten superior court judges, court may provide by local rule for mandatory arbitration consistent with statute. (C.C.P. 1141.11). Absent court assignment to arbitration, parties may stipulate to arbitration regardless of amount in controversy or plaintiff may elect arbitration if he agrees award shall not exceed amount in controversy limit applicable where case filed. (C.C.P. 1141.12). Any court determination or stipulation of amount in controversy is without prejudice to any finding of value by arbitrator or trial de novo. (C.C.P. 1141.16). Powers of arbitrator and procedural rules are set forth in California Rules of Court 1600-1618. See also category Courts and Legislature, topic Courts, subhead Mandatory Arbitration.

Public Construction Contracts.—Such contracts may contain specified provisions relating to judicial review of such arbitration. (C.C.P. 1296). Claims on state construction contracts must be arbitrated. (Pub. Cont. C. 10240). Local entities are authorized to use arbitration with public construction contracts. (Pub. Cont. C. 22200, 22201).

DOCUMENTS AND RECORDS

ACKNOWLEDGMENTS:

No Uniform Acts adopted.

Within State.—May be made, at any place within state, before justice, retired justice or clerk of Supreme Court or any court of appeal, or judge or retired judge of superior court (C.C. 1180); or, at any place within state before notary public, or within county or city and county for which officer was elected or appointed, before clerk of superior, municipal or justice court, or judge or retired judge of municipal or justice court, county clerk, court commissioner, district attorney, clerk of board of supervisors or city clerk, county counsel or city attorney (C.C. 1181). Various officials have power to take acknowledgments specifically given by individual code sections.

Without State but within United States.—May be made, within jurisdiction of officer, before justice, judge or clerk of any court of record of United States or any state; notary public; or any other officer of state where made, authorized by its laws to take such proof or acknowledgment. (C.C. 1182). Commissioners no longer appointed. All authority to appoint commissioners (former Govt. C. 8300-8308) has been repealed.

Without United States.—May be made before minister, commissioner or chargé d'affaires of United States, resident and accredited in country where made; consul, vice-consul or consular agent of United States resident in country where made; a judge of court of record of country where made; commissioners appointed by Governor or Secretary of State for that purpose; or notary public. If before notary public, notary public's signature shall be proved or acknowledged: (1) Before judge of court of record of country where proof or acknowledgment is made, or (2) by any American diplomatic officer, consul general, consul, vice consul or consular agent, or (3) by apostille (certification) affixed to instrument pursuant to terms of Hague Convention Abolishing the Requirement of Legalisation for Foreign Public Documents. (C.C. 1183). Commissioners no longer appointed. All authority to appoint commissioners (former Govt. C. 8300-8308) has been repealed.

Deputies.—When any of above mentioned officers authorized by law to appoint deputy, acknowledgment or proof may be taken by such deputy in name of his principal. (C.C. 1184).

Acknowledgments of Persons in U.S. Armed Forces.—As to notarial powers of officers in Armed Forces, see topic Notaries Public. See infra subhead Forms.

General Requirements as to Taking.—Officer taking acknowledgment shall "personally know" or have "satisfactory evidence" (oath or affirmation of "credible witness" or reliance upon certain specified documentary evidence) that person making acknowledgment is individual described in and who executed instrument. (C.C. 1185).

General Requirements of Certificate.—Officer must affix seal of office if required to have such seal by laws of state or country where acknowledgment taken or by whose authority officer is acting. (C.C. 1193).

Attorneys in Fact.—See infra, subhead Forms.

Corporations.—See infra, subhead Forms.

Signature by Mark.—Where instrument is signed by mark, two witnesses to such signature are necessary before acknowledgment. (C.C. 14; C.C.P. 17).

Proof of instrument, as alternative to acknowledgment, may be made by party executing instrument, by subscribing witness or by other witnesses under C.C. 1198 (C.C. 1195) personally known to officer taking proof to be person whose name is subscribed to instrument as witness, or proved to be such by oath of credible witness (C.C. 1196), or by proof of handwriting of party and of subscribing witness, if there is one, when all parties and all subscribing witnesses dead; or, when parties and all subscribing witnesses nonresidents of state; or when place of their residence unknown and cannot be ascertained by exercise of due diligence; or when subscribing witness conceals himself or refuses to testify for space of one hour, after his appearance (C.C. 1198).

Fees.—Fee of notary public for taking acknowledgment or proof, including seal and writing certificate, is $10 for each signature. (Govt. C. 8211). Fee of county recorder for taking acknowledgment is 75¢. (Govt. C. 27375).

Authentication.—Authentication not required of acknowledgment taken within state. (Evid. C. 1451).

If proof or acknowledgment is made before notary public without U.S., signature must be authenticated before certain designated officials. (C.C. 1183). Acknowledgment taken without state is good if sufficient under laws where made. (C.C. 1189). On documents to be filed without state or in another U.S. jurisdiction, California notary public may complete any acknowledgment form as required provided form does not require notary to determine or certify that signer holds particular representative capacity or to make other determinations and certifications not allowed by California law. (C.C. 1189).

Fee for each certificate to official capacity of any public official is $2.25. (Govt. C. 26852). Fee for each certificate to official capacity of any public official is $6. California notary public must take and subscribe oath of office in office of County Clerk or before another notary public in that county. When oath and bond filed, County Clerk transmits certificate to Secretary of State setting forth fact of filing and containing copy of official oath. County Clerk also delivers bond to County Recorder for recording. (Govt. C. 8207, 8213).

Effect of Acknowledgment or Proof.—Private writings, except wills, when acknowledged or proved and certified, are prima facie evidence of facts recited in certificate and genuineness of signature of each person by whom writing purports to have been signed if certificate is valid under applicable law. (Evid. C. 1451). Certain documents, including letters patent (U. S.), mineral leases in which U.S. is lessor, copies of interdepartmental letters relative to such leases, may be recorded without normal requirement of acknowledgment or further proof. (Govt. C. 27285 et seq.).

Married Women.—No special requirements.

Foreign Acknowledgments.—See supra subhead Without United States.

Validating Acts.—Most significant curative statute provides that instrument affecting title to real property, one year after copy into record book, imparts notice to subsequent purchaser and encumbrancer, notwithstanding any defect or omission in acknowledgment, or absence of such certificate. (C.C. 1207).

Forms

General Form For Within State: State of California, County of . . . . —ss.: On . . . . before me, (name and title of officer), personally appeared. . . . . ., personally known to me (or proved to me on the basis of satisfactory evidence) to be the person whose name is subscribed to the within instrument and acknowledged to me that he executed the same in his authorized capacity, and that by his signature on the instrument the person, or the entity upon behalf of which the person acted, executed the instrument. Witness my hand and official seal.
Signature. . . . . . (Seal). (C.C. 1189).

Note: The following five forms (Individual, Corporation, Public Corporation, Partnership, and Attorney in Fact) were repealed in 1990 but remain valid for acknowledgments provided prior to Jan. 1, 1993.

Individual: State of . . . . , County of . . . —ss.: On this . . . . day of . . . . in the year 19 . . . . before me, ... , a Notary Public of said State, duly commissioned and sworn, personally appeared . . . . personally known to me (or proved to me on the basis of satisfactory evidence) to be the person whose name is subscribed to the within instrument, and acknowledged that he executed the same.
In Witness Whereof, I have hereunto set my hand and affixed my official seal the day and year in this certificate first above written.
. . . .
Notary Public in and for said State. (C.C. 1189).

Corporation: State of . . . . , County of . . . . —ss.: On this . . . . day of . . . . in the year 19 . . . . before me, ... , a Notary Public of said State, duly commissioned and sworn, personally appeared . . . . . ., personally known to me (or proved to me on the basis of satisfactory evidence . . . . .) to be the person who executed the within instrument as president (or secretary) or on behalf of the corporation therein and acknowledged to me that such corporation executed the same.
In Witness Whereof, etc. (as in form for individual). (C.C. 1190).

ACKNOWLEDGMENTS ... *continued*

(This alternative ending may be used with specified evidentiary effect C.C. 1190.1: "and acknowledged to me that such corporation executed the within instrument pursuant to its bylaws or a resolution of its board of directors.")

Public Corporation, Agency or Political Subdivision.—State of . . . . County of . . . . ss: On this . . . . . day of . . . . . in the year . . . . . before me . . . . a Notary Public of said State, duly commissioned and sworn, personally appeared . . . . personally known to me (or proved to me on the basis of satisfactory evidence . . . .) to be the person who executed this instrument as (title of officer) of (name of public corporation, agency or political subdivision) and acknowledged to me that such (public corporation, agency or political subdivision) executed the same.

In Witness Whereof, etc. (as in form for individual). (C.C. 1191).

Person in U.S. Armed Forces: On this the . . . . day of . . . ., 19 . . . ., before me, ..., the undersigned officer, personally appeared . . . . known to me (or satisfactorily proven) to be (a) serving in or with the Armed forces of the United States (b) spouse of a member of the Armed Forces of the United States (c) a person serving with, employed by, or accompanying the armed forces of the United States outside the United States and outside the Canal Zone, Puerto Rico, Guam and the Virgin Islands, and to be the person whose name is subscribed to the within instrument and acknowledged that . . . . he or she . . . . executed the same. And the undersigned does further certify that he or she is at the date of this certificate a commissioned officer in the active service of the Armed Forces of the United States having the general powers of a notary public under the provisions of Section 936 or 1044a of Title 10 of the United States Code (Public Law 90-632 and 101-510).

Signature of officer, rank, branch of service and capacity in which signed. (C.C. 1183.5).

To any affidavit subscribed and sworn to before such officer there should be attached a jurat in substantially the following form: Subscribed and sworn to before me on this . . . . day of . . . ., 19 . . . . Signature, etc., of officer as above.

Proof by Witness.—No particular form required but following form may be used: State of . . . ., County of . . . .—ss: On this . . . . day of . . . . 19 . . . . before me, ..., a Notary Public of said State, duly commissioned and sworn, personally appeared . . . . known to me to be the person whose name is subscribed to the within Instrument, as a witness thereto, who being by me duly sworn, deposes and says: That he resides in . . . . and that he was present and saw . . . . personally known to h . . . . to be the same person whose name . . . . subscribed to the within and annexed Instrument, execute and deliver the same, and he acknowledged to said affiant that he executed the same; and that said affiant subscribed h . . . . name thereto as a Witness.

In Witness Whereof, I have hereunto set my hand and affixed my official seal the day and year in this certificate first above written.

. . . . (Signature and title of officer).

Authentication of Officer's Certificate.—No particular form required but following may be used:

State of . . . . County of . . . . ss: I, ... (name of clerk of court), the undersigned , certify: I am the clerk of the . . . . (name of court); that court is a court of record of . . . . (name of county or district) which is the . . . . (either county or district) where the acknowledgment of the instrument to which this certification is affixed was taken.

The officer certifying the acknowledgment is . . . . (name), who is authorized by the law of . . . . (specify jurisdiction) to certify acknowledgments within this . . . . . . (either county or district). The signature of . . . . (name of certifying officer) to the attached certificate of acknowledgment is his true and genuine signature, and the acknowledgment was taken in accordance with the laws of . . . . (specify jurisdiction).

Dated: . . . . Signature of Clerk of Court

Alternative to Acknowledgment or Proof.—Not available for documents signed outside of California. See also topic Affidavits, subhead Alternative to Affidavit.

AFFIDAVITS:

Within the state, affidavits may be taken before any officer or person authorized to take testimony in any action or proceeding. (C. C. P. 2012, 2093). Fee of notary public for administering oath or affirmation to one person and executing jurat is $10. (Govt. C. 8211). Fee for taking affidavit, except criminal case, adoption proceedings, juvenile proceedings, or for any service to state is $6. (Govt. C. 26853.1 and 26857).

Without the state but within the United States, affidavits may be taken before commissioner appointed by Governor of this state, notaries public in another state, or any judge or clerk of court of record having seal. (C. C. P. 2013).

Without the United States, affidavits may be taken before ambassador, minister, consul, vice-consul, or consular agent of U. S., or judge of court of record having seal. (C. C. P. 2014).

Affidavits of Persons in U. S. Armed Forces.—See topics Acknowledgments, Notaries Public.

General Requirement as to Administration.—Although no restriction upon taking affidavit by notary public who also is affiant's attorney, such practice not recommended. (56 C. 588).

General Requirement of Jurat.—Absence of seal is not fatal to affidavit's validity. (160 C. 695, 117 P. 905). Notary public seal must show expiration date of commission; if commissioned on or after Jan. 1, 1992, sequential identification number must also appear. (Govt. C. 8207, 8207.1).

Authentication.—Authentication required, in case of affidavits taken before judge or court outside state, by certificate of clerk of court under seal thereof, verifying genuineness of signature of judge, existence of court and fact that such judge was at the time member thereof. (C. C. P. 2015).

Authentication of signatures, when instruments are to be used without the state, is made by county clerk whose fee is $2.25. (Govt. C. 26852).

Use.—Affidavit may be used to verify pleading or paper in special proceeding; to prove service of summons, notice, or other paper in action or special proceeding; to obtain provisional remedy, examination of witness, or stay of proceedings; in uncontested proceedings to establish record of birth; or upon motion, and in any other case expressly permitted by statute. (C. C. P. 2009).

Publication of document or notice in newspaper may be proved by affidavit of printer, his foreman or principal clerk. (C. C. P. 2010).

Form

No particular form required, the following is usual: State of . . . ., County of . . . .—ss.: . . . ., being first duly sworn, deposes and says: (Here state fully and clearly, but in ordinary language, matters necessary to be shown).

. . . .

Subscribed and sworn to before me this . . . . day of . . . . .
(Signature and full official designation of officer)

Alternative to Affidavit.—Whenever, under any law of this state, or rule, regulation, order or requirement made pursuant to law of this state, any matter is required or permitted to be supported, evidenced, established, or proved by affidavit, such matter may with like force and effect be supported, evidenced, established or proved by unsworn statement in writing of person, stating date and place of execution, and subscribed by him and certified or declared to be true "under penalty of perjury." Certification or declaration may be as follows: "I certify (or declare) under penalty of perjury under the laws of the State of California that the foregoing is true and correct." (C. C. P. 2015.5).

NOTARIES PUBLIC:

For authentication of authority, see topic Acknowledgments, subhead Authentication.

Qualification.—To be notary public, person must be 18 years or older, legal resident of California (or citizen of U.S., if appointed for service on military or naval reservation), and must pass test given by Secretary of State. (Govt. C. 8201). Notary appointed for military or naval reservation must be federal civil service employee at that reservation. (Govt. C. 8203.3). Within 30 days after beginning of notary's term of office, or transfer of notary's principal place of business to another country, bond for $15,000 and oath of office must be filed with clerk of county of notary's principal place of business. (Govt. C. 8212, 8213).

Bond.—See subhead Qualification, supra. On application, court may release surety from responsibility for future acts of notary and cite notary to give other security. (Govt. C. 8216).

Seal of notary must bear name of notary, state seal, words "Notary Public", county where bond and oath of office are filed and expiration date of notary public commission. Notary must authenticate all official acts with seal. Seal of every notary public commissioned on or after Jan. 1, 1992 shall contain sequential identification number assigned to notary and to manufacturer or vendor. (Govt. C. 8207).

Powers and Duties.—Notaries must, upon request, demand acceptance and payment of foreign and inland bills of exchange and promissory notes; protest such instruments for nonacceptance and nonpayment; with regard to nonacceptance or nonpayment of bills and notes, exercise such other powers or duties as may be performed by notaries under law of nations and according to commercial usages, or by laws of any other state, government, or country; take acknowledgments or proofs of powers of attorney, mortgages, deeds, grants, transfers, and other executed instruments; give certificates of proof or acknowledgments, endorsed on or attached to instrument and signed in notary's own handwriting; take depositions and affidavits and administer oaths and affirmations, signed in notary's own handwriting; certify copies of powers of attorney, signed in notary's own handwriting; furnish Secretary of State certified copies of notary's journal; respond, within 30 days to written requests by Secretary of State for information relating to official acts performed; notary may not accept incomplete acknowledgment or incomplete proof of instrument (Govt. C. 8205); in locked and secured area keep sequential journal of all official acts (which shall include date, time and type of each official act, character of instrument acknowledged or proved, signature of person whose signature is notarized, statement of notary's personal knowledge of identity of person signing or signature of witnesses affirming identity of signer or details of document establishing identity, and fee charged). If document notarized is deed, quitclaim deed, or deed of trust affecting real property, notary shall require signing party to place thumbprint or any available fingerprint if thumbprints unavailable in notary's journal, or explanation of physical condition preventing signing party from giving thumbprint. When requested, and upon payment of no more than 30¢ per page, notary must provide any person copy of any specified line item from journal. Notary must provide journal for examination and copying in his/her presence upon receipt of subpoena duces tecum or court order. (Govt. C. 8206). If notary resigns, is disqualified, is removed, or allows appointment to expire without obtaining reappointment within 30 days, notarial records and papers must be delivered to clerk of county in which notary's current official oath of office is on file. Willful failure or refusal to deliver within 30 days is misdemeanor and creates personal liability for damages to any person injured. Upon death of notary public, deceased's personal representative shall promptly notify Secretary of State and deliver all notarial records to clerk of county in which notary public's official oath of office is on file. (Govt. C. 8209). Notary, who has direct financial or beneficial interest in transaction, may not act as notary with respect to such transaction. This does not include notary who is agent, employee, insurer, attorney, escrow, or lender of person with direct interest in such transaction. (Govt. C. 8224). Notary may not acknowledge or prove instruments signed by him or take his own deposition or affidavit. (Govt. C. 8224.1).

Territorial Extent of Powers.—Notary may act in any part of California. (Govt. C. 8200). Notary for military or naval reservation may act only within boundaries of that

NOTARIES PUBLIC . . . *continued*
reservation. (Govt. C. 8203.2). Name of reservation must appear in notary's jurat. (Govt. C. 8203.5).

Fees.—No fee for notarial service need be charged, except fees required to be remitted to State or any other public agency. (Govt. C. 6100). If charged, fees cannot exceed: Acknowledgment or proof of deed, $10 for each signature; administering oath or affirmation to one person and executing jurat, $10; for all services rendered in connection with deposition, $20 plus $5 for administering oath to witness and $5 for certificate to such deposition; protest for nonpayment of promissory note or nonacceptance for nonpayment of bill of exchange, order, draft or check, $10; for serving every notice of nonpayment of promissory note or of nonpayment or nonacceptance of bill of exchange, order, draft, or check, $5; for certifying copy of power of attorney, $10. (Govt. C. 8211).

Authentication.—See topic Acknowledgments.

Court Commissioner.—Subject to supervision of court, every court commissioner may take acknowledgments and proof of deeds, mortgages, and other instruments requiring proof or acknowledgment for any purpose under laws of California or any other state or country. (C. C. P. 259).

Officers of U.S. Armed Forces.—Any officer on active duty or performing inactive duty training in U.S. armed forces having general powers of notary public under 10 U.S.C. 936 or 1044a may perform all notarial acts, in or out of U.S., for any person, or spouse of any person, in armed forces, and for any person employed by or accompanying armed forces. Place of execution or acknowledgment need not be stated and seal or authentication of officer's certificate of acknowledgment or of any jurat is not required, but officer must endorse on or attach to any acknowledgment signed certificate, and to any affidavit signed jurat, substantially in form authorized by California law (see topic Acknowledgments). (C. C. 1183.5).

RECORDS:

County recorder has charge of records relating to property.

Uniform Commercial Code has been adopted. See category Business Regulation and Commerce, topic Commercial Code.

Recordable Instruments.—Any instrument or judgment affecting title to or possession of real property may be recorded (Govt. C. 27280), including fictitious oil and gas leases (C. C. 1219) and fictitious mortgages and deeds of trust (C. C. 2952). (For effect see subhead, Necessity for Recording, infra.)

Instrument in foreign language may be recorded only if accompanied by court certified translation, unless provisions in foreign language are translations of English provisions and translations thereof are specifically set forth in state or federal law. (Govt. C. 27293). Keeping of photographed or microfilm copies of instruments is provided for. (Govt. C. 27322, 27322.2-27322.4, 27323).

Place of Recording.—Instruments entitled to be recorded must be recorded by county recorder of county in which real property located. (C. C. 1169). *For list of Counties and County Seats, see first page for this state in Volume containing Practice Profiles Section.*

Requisites for Recording.—In general, before instrument can be recorded it must be properly acknowledged by person executing it or proved by subscribing witness (Govt. C. 27287) or, in specified cases, by proof of handwriting (C. C. 1198, 1199). Certain instruments (Govt. C. 27282-27286; C. C. 1202, 1203, 1219, 2952, 3084, 3093) are exempted from requirements of acknowledgment or further proof to be recordable (Govt. C. 27287). First page of each document shall include $2^1/_2$ inch blank space at top (for recording information) and $3^1/_2$ inch space on left-hand margin (to show name of person requesting recording and name and address to which document to be returned after recording). All items for recordation shall be on paper and print that will reproduce legibly by photo or microphotographic process as set forth in Govt. C. 26205.5 and 27322.2 now required. (Govt. C. 27361.6). Uniform Simplification of Land Transfers Act has not been adopted.

Filing Under Uniform Commercial Code.—See categories Business Regulation and Commerce, topic Commercial Code; Mortgages, topic Chattel Mortgages.

Fees of recorder are fixed by Govt. C. 27360-83, 27387, 27387.1. Among fees so fixed are: for recording and indexing instrument, paper or notice required or permitted by law to be recorded, $4 for recording first page and $3 for each additional page (for forms printed with more than nine lines per vertical inch or more than 22 characters and spaces per inch measured horizontally for not less than three inches in one sentence, there is additional charge of $1 for each page on which such printing appears, unless printing is directive or explanatory or on vital statistics form); $3 fee is charged for filing any document not required by law to be recorded. Additional fees are charged if document refers to more than one other recorded instrument (Govt. C. 27361.2) or if additional indexing is required by law (Govt. C. 27361.8). Each county may charge additional fee of $1 for each document recorded. (Govt. C. 27361.4).

Necessity for Recording.—Every conveyance of real property or estate for years, other than lease for term not exceeding one year, is void as against any subsequent purchaser or mortgagee of same property or any part thereof in good faith and for valuable consideration, whose conveyance is first duly recorded, and as against any judgment affecting title unless such conveyance shall have been duly recorded prior to record of notice of action. (C. C. 1214).

In addition to instruments affecting title to or possession of real property following must be recorded to be valid against all persons: assignments for benefit of creditors, marriage certificates (see infra, subhead Vital Statistics).

Foreign Conveyances and Encumbrances.—Conveyance or encumbrance acknowledged in conformity with law of state where acknowledged may be recorded. (C. C. 1189). See topic Acknowledgments, subhead Authentication, for further discussion.

Effect of recording is to charge subsequent purchasers and mortgagees with constructive notice of contents of instrument. (C. C. 1213).

Torrens Act.—System of land registration based on Torrens system, formerly in effect, has been abolished, all registers of title and all documents and records pertaining thereto having become part of records of respective county recorders. (1955, c. 332).

Transfer of decedent's title to real estate to his heirs or devisees is evidenced by recordation in office of recorder of county in which such real estate situated of certified copy of order of distribution. (Prob. C. 7263). Administration in California courts required, even though decedent was nondomiciliary. (Prob. C. 7052).

Vital Statistics.—Reports of births (H. & S.C. 102400), fetal deaths (20 weeks or more gestational age) (H. & S.C. 102950) and deaths (H. & S.C. 10200) must be filed in office of local registrar of births and deaths within ten days for births, eight days for deaths; reports of marriages with local registrar of marriages for county in which marriage license was issued within 30 days after ceremony (Fam. C. 359, 423); reports of dissolution of marriage, annulment or legal separation with state registrar (H. & S.C. 103200).

Fee for each certified copy of fetal death or death record is $3; birth record, $7; marriage or marriage dissolution record, $6 (H. & S.C. 103625); for file search where no copy is made, fee is same as fee charged for certified copies under H. & S. C. 103625. (H. & S.C. 10606).

Establishing Birth, Death and Marriage Records.—If local birth, death or marriage records are unavailable, facts may be established by order of superior court after hearing on prescribed form of verified petition. (H. & S.C. 103450-103490).

SEALS:

All distinctions between sealed and unsealed private writings have been abolished. (C.C. 1629; C.C.P. 1932). Scroll or other sign indicating seal affixed by proper party is deemed private seal. (C.C.P. 1931). Corporation may adopt and use corporate seal, but failure to affix seal does not affect validity of instrument. (Corp. C. 207[a]).

Uniform Commercial Code has been adopted. (1963, c. 819). See category Business Regulation and Commerce, topic Commercial Code.

TORRENS ACT:

See topic Records.

VITAL STATISTICS:

See topic Records.

EMPLOYMENT

EMPLOYER AND EMPLOYEE:

See topic Labor Relations.

LABOR RELATIONS:

Statutory regulation of labor relations primarily covers following areas: wages, hours and working conditions of adults and minors; mode and manner of wage payment; hours of work; nondiscrimination in employment; industrial homework; apprenticeship standards; workers' compensation; industrial safety and health care. Statutes are administered by Department of Industrial Relations.

Industrial Welfare Commission has authority to establish minimum wages, maximum work hours and standard working conditions for employees and has done so in wage orders applicable to various industries. (Lab. C. 1182). These orders are enforced by Division of Industrial Welfare. (Lab. C. 1193.5). Civil sanctions are imposed for violation of orders. (Lab. C. 1193.6, et seq.).

Child Labor.—Minimum age for most employments is 16 years. (Lab. C. 1290, 1394). Specific provisions regulate employment of minors, including requirements for work permits and registration. (Educ. C. 1802, 48230, Lab. C. 1285-1312, 1390-1399).

Hours of Labor.—Maximum hours in most occupations for minors are eight hours per day and 40 hours per week. (Lab. C. 1391), subject to certain exemptions. Hours of labor for minors are also regulated by wage orders appliable to their particular industry.

With certain specified exceptions (including employees covered by collective bargaining agreement and employment of less than 30 hours per week and six hours per day), no employer shall cause employees to work more than six days in seven. (Lab. C. 552-556). Special provisions relate to hours of labor for employees in railroads (Lab. C. 600, et seq.), smelters and underground workings (Lab. C. 750, et seq.), lumber (Lab. C. 800, et seq.), pharmacies (Lab. C. 850, et seq.), ski industry (Lab. C. 1182.2), commercial fishing industry (Lab. C. 1182.3), camps (Lab. C. 1182.4) and employers in manufacturing operating 24 hours per day (Lab. C. 1182.6).

Wages.—Minimum wage is $4.25/hr. for all employees without exception. (Lab. C. 1182, 1197, 1197.1, IWC Order No. MW-88). Two-tiered minimum wage unlawful. See 46 C.3d 1262, 252 C. Rptr. 278. Minimum wages for minors are established in wage orders covering particular industries.

Mode and manner of payment of wages to employees is regulated. (Lab. C. 200-227.3). Wages must be paid at least twice a month on regular pay days, excepting wages of executive, administrative, and professional employees, which may be paid once a month on or before the 26th. (Lab. C. 204, 207). With certain exceptions, all earned wages must be paid immediately to employees terminated by employer and within 72 hours to employees who quit without notice. (Lab. C. 201, 202). Statutory penalties are provided for failure to pay wages. (Lab. C. 203, 210, 225.5, 256). In action for nonpayment of wages, fringe benefits, or pension funds, court must award reasonable attorney's fees and costs to prevailing party if requested upon initiation of action. (Lab. C. 218.5). Itemized statement showing all deductions must be furnished with each payment of wages. (Lab. C. 226). If payment is by check, it must be payable in cash within California. (Lab. C. 212).

With certain limitations wage claims have preferred status against claims of other creditors. However, wage claims have lower status against other claims in probate

See note at head of Digest as to 1998 legislation covered.

See Topical Index in front part of this volume.

CA – 41

LABOR RELATIONS . . . *continued*

proceedings. (C.C.P. 1204-1206; Prob. C. 11402, 11420-11421). As to assignment of wages, see Lab. C. 300 and category Debtor and Creditor, topic Assignments.

Equal Pay.—Female employees must receive same wage rate as male in same establishment for same quantity and quality of same classification of work. Violators may be liable for additional wages and liquidated damages. (Lab. C. 1197.5). Minors under 18 years who have graduated high school or its equivalent must be paid same rate as adult for performing same job. (Lab. C. 1391.2).

Labor Unions.—No statutory provisions, such as in National Labor Relations Act, require employers to recognize or bargain with labor unions. (53 C.2d 455, 349 P.2d 76).

"Yellow Dog" contracts in which employees promise to join or not to join labor unions are against public policy and unenforceable. (Lab. C. 921-922).

Collective bargaining agreements are enforceable at law or in equity, and violations may be restrained by injunctive relief. (Lab. C. 1126; 49 C.2d 45, 315 P.2d 322; 398 U.S. 235, 247 [1970]).

Mediation services are available to parties involved in labor dispute. (Lab. C. 65). No "right to work" statutory provisions.

Labor Disputes.—Employees hired during labor dispute, strike or lockout must be informed of existence of disturbance and false representations to prospective employees are unlawful. (Lab. C. 970-974). Advertisement for such employees must contain notice of labor dispute. (Lab. C. 973). Employers are prohibited from knowingly hiring persons who have worked as strike replacements in preceding five-year period on three or more occasions for two or more employers involved in labor dispute. (Lab. C. 1133, 1134, 1134.2).

Jurisdictional strike is against public policy of state and is unlawful (Lab. C. 1115) and is subject to injunctive relief and damages (Lab. C. 1116).

As to arbitration of labor disputes, see category Dispute Resolution, topic Arbitration and Award. As to issuance of injunctions in labor disputes, see category Civil Actions and Procedure, topic Injunctions.

Political Activities.—Employers are prohibited from influencing and controlling political activities of their employees. (Lab. C. 1101-1105).

Voting Time.—Under certain circumstances employees must be permitted time off to vote in general and primary elections. (Elec. C. 14350).

Other Employment Regulations.—Right of employer to require bond or photograph of employee or applicant for employment is limited. (Lab. C. 400, et seq.). Employer may not require applicant or employee to submit to polygraph test as condition of employment unless employer is federal, state or local government or any agency or subdivision thereof. (Lab. C. 432.2).

Employer who has agreed through collective bargaining or otherwise to make payments to welfare or pension fund or other plan for benefit of employee must upon written request furnish employee with annual statement of payments. (Lab. C. 227.5).

Employment establishments must meet certain health and sanitation requirements. (Lab. C. 2260-2441).

Mutual obligations of employer and employee and termination of employment are regulated. (Lab. C. 2750-2929). Causes of action permitted against employer for breach of implied contract (116 C.A.3d 311, 171 C.Rptr. 917), breach of implied covenant of good faith and fair dealing (111 C.A.3d 443, 168 C.Rptr. 722), and wrongful termination in breach of public policy (27 C.3d 167, 164 C.Rptr. 839). Erosion of at-will employment as provided by statute. (Lab. C. 2922). Foley v. Interactive Data Corp. (47 C.3d 654, 254 C.Rptr. 211) limits wrongful termination damages to foreseeable contract damages, specifically eliminating tort damages, including punitives for breach of implied covenant of good faith and fair dealing claims.

No discrimination allowed against workers injured in course and scope of employment. (Lab. C. 132a).

Industrial Homework—Industrial homework is regulated (Lab. C. 2650, et seq.) and manufacture of certain specified articles by industrial homework is prohibited (Lab. C. 2651).

Apprenticeship.—Apprentice Labor Standards Act creates apprenticeship council to establish standards for minimum wages, maximum hours and working conditions for apprenticeship agreements. (Lab. C. 3070, et seq.). Certain required provisions for apprenticeship agreements are specified. (Lab. C. 3078).

Employment and Counseling Agencies.—All employment agencies, counseling and job listing services are regulated and must provide customers with written contracts with terms and notices specified in statute. (C. C. 1812.500, et seq.). Chapter does not apply to employment agencies which charge fees only to employee or nonprofit organizations meeting certain requirements. (Civ. C. 1812.502). Athlete agencies and talent agencies regulated. (Lab. C. 1500, et seq., 1700.5 et seq.).

Public Works.—Employees on public works must be paid prevailing wage (Lab. C. 1771), and may not work more than eight hours per calendar day and 40 hours during calendar week unless compensated at one-and-one-half times basic rate of pay for each hour in excess of eight in any day (Lab. C. 1811-1815).

Worker's Compensation Law (Lab. C. Div. 4 & 4.5) is administered and enforced by Division of Workers Compensation (Lab. C. 60). It provides comprehensive worker's compensation and insurance plan constituting exclusive remedy (with minor exceptions noted, infra) before Worker's Compensation Appeals Board applicable to all employees not engaged in interstate commerce (with exceptions). (Lab. C. 3203, 3351-52). Occupational diseases are covered. (183 C. 273, 191 P. 26).

Dispute is subject to arbitration if it involves insurance coverage, right of contribution, or permanent disability of 20% standard or less. (Lab. C. 5275).

Rates of compensation vary according to weekly earnings and degree and duration of disability. Death benefit of up to $115,000 maximum for two total dependents; minimum of $95,000 with one total dependent with additional amounts available up to $115,000 maximum with partial dependents. Maximum and minimum benefits are $135,000 and $115,000 respectively for injuries occurring after July 1, 1994. (Lab. C. 4702). Death benefits allocated between dependents. Every employer is required to

carry insurance either by private insurers or by State Compensation Insurance Fund or with consent of Division by self insurance, either as individual employer or in group of employers. (Lab. C. 3700). If employer fails to carry insurance, employees may, as alternative to their remedies before Appeals Board, bring action in court, in which action it is presumed that employer was negligent and in which contributory negligence, assumption of risk and fellow servant rule are no defenses. (Lab. C. 3706, 3708).

Safeguarding of Employees.—Safety in employment is rigorously regulated by administrative safety orders of Division of Occupational Safety and Health. (Lab. C. 6500).

Unemployment Insurance Code adopted. Under this code weekly benefits are granted to persons unable to work because of nonindustrial disability resulting from illness or injury (Unemployment Compensation Disability—UCD), as well as benefits received during periods of unemployment (Unemployment Compensation—UC). Supplemental unemployment benefit plans are approved by statute and are not construed as wages. (Un. Ins. C. 1265).

See also category Taxation, topic Unemployment Compensation and Disability Tax.

Fair Employment Practices.—Employer may not discriminate in employment or in selection for training program or harass employees on basis of race, religious creed, color, national origin, ancestry, physical disability, mental disability, medical condition, marital status, sex, or sexual orientation. (Govt. C. 12940). Physical handicap includes contagious illness (480 U.S. 273), and AIDS (Fair Employment and Housing Commission, No. 83-84, 1987). Sex includes pregnancy, childbirth and related medical conditions. (Govt. C. 12926). Certain restrictions also apply to age discrimination. (Govt. C. 12941). Discrimination based on sexual orientation may be prohibited by local ordinance and may give rise to action for interference with employee's political activity. (Lab. C. 1101, 1102; 24 C.3d 458, 156 C. Rptr. 14, 595 P.2d 592).

Employer must provide leave and reinstatement to employees disabled by pregnancy. (Govt. C. 12945[b][2]; 479 U.S. 272). Employer with more than 50 employees subject to family care and medical leave requirements. (Govt. C. 12945.2).

Employer may not discriminate on basis of medical condition which includes genetic characteristics or any health impairment related to or associated with diagnosis of cancer for which person has been rehabilitated or cured, based on competent medical evidence. Genetic characteristics means any scientifically or medically identifiable gene or chromosome that is (1) known to cause disease in person or his or her offspring, or (2) is determined to be associated with statistically increased risk of development of disease or disorder, or (3) or inherited characteristics that may derive from individual or family member, not presently associated with any symptoms of any disease or disorder. (Govt. C. 12926[h]). Fair Employment & Housing Department has been established to enforce this policy in accordance with procedures prescribed by statute. (Govt. C. 12930).

Employers of 25 or more must reasonably accommodate employee wishing to voluntarily enter alcoholic or drug rehabilitation program. (Lab. C. 1025, et seq.).

Agricultural Labor Relations.—Act creates Agricultural Labor Relations Board. (Lab. C. 1141). Act adopted to provide collective-bargaining rights for agricultural employees. (Lab. C. 1140.2). Board is accorded broad investigatory powers. (Lab. C. 1151 et seq.).

Employees Rights.—Agricultural employees are furnished certain rights with which employers may not interfere. Such rights include right to self-organize, assist labor organizations and bargain collectively through representatives of their choice. (Lab. C. 1152, 1153). Restrictions are also placed on activities of labor organizations. (Lab. C. 1154).

Elections.—Specific provisions have been enacted to govern election of labor representatives. (Lab. C. 1156 et seq.).

Prevention of Unfair Practices and Judicial Enforcement.—Board shall have power to issue complaint and to hold hearings thereon. (Lab. C. 1160.2, 1160.3). Decisions of board may be appealed to appropriate court of appeal. (Lab. C. 1160.8). Suits involving agricultural labor contracts shall be brought in Superior Court. (Lab. C. 1165).

WORKERS' COMPENSATION LAW:

See topic Labor Relations.

ENVIRONMENT

ENVIRONMENTAL REGULATION:

Environment Reports.—California Environmental Quality Act (Pub. Res. C. 21000 et seq.) requires that public agencies prepare, with input from other agencies and general public, environmental impact report for any project proposed or approved by public agency which may have significant impact on environment, subject to specified exemptions (Pub. Res. C. 21100); if project involves more than one agency, lead agency (Pub. Res. C. 21067) shall prepare Environmental Impact Report (Pub. Res. C. 21100). If lead agency determines proposed project does not have significant effect on environment, it shall adopt negative declaration to that effect. (Pub. Res. C. 21064, 21080). Environmental impact report for military base or reservation reuse may be made in context of physical conditions present at time of closure of base or reservation. (Pub. Res. C. 21083.8, 21083.8.1). Public agency shall not approve or carry out any project for which Environmental Impact Report shows any significant environmental effects without making one or more of following specified findings: changes have been required in project which mitigate or avoid identified significant environmental effects thereof; changes are within responsibility of another public agency and have been adopted by such other agency or can and should be adopted by it; or specific, economic or social or other considerations make identified mitigation measures or project alternatives infeasible. (Pub. Res. C. 21081). Subsequent or supplemental environmental impact report may be required. (Pub. Res. C. 21166). Act expressly allows actions to review, set aside, void or annul acts or decisions of public agency for noncompliance with Act. (Pub. Res. C. 21167). Subject to specified exceptions, lead agency shall set time limits, not to exceed one year, to certify and complete

See note at head of Digest as to 1998 legislation covered.

See Topical Index in front part of this volume.

ENVIRONMENTAL REGULATION . . . *continued*
Environmental Impact Reports on projects and, not to exceed 180 days to complete and adopt negative declaration, measured from date project's approval application is received and accepted as complete by lead agency. (Pub. Res. C. 21100.2).

Development Projects.—Development projects, as broadly defined (Govt. C. 65927 & 65928), must be approved or disapproved by lead agency within 180 days from date of lead agency's certification of environmental impact report; if negative declaration is completed and adopted or project is exempt from regulation, project shall be approved or disapproved within 60 days from lead agency's adoption of negative declaration or exemption determination. Project applicant and public agency may mutually agree in writing to extension of such time limits. (Govt. C. 65950 et seq.). Other responsible public agencies must act on project within 180 days of either date of approval of project by lead agency or within 180 days of date application to such other responsible agency is received and accepted as complete, whichever is longer. At time decision by lead agency to disapprove development project becomes final, applications for that project filed with responsible agencies shall be deemed withdrawn. (Govt. C. 65952). For reasonable fee, public agencies must determine in writing completeness of application within 30 days of receipt and, if incomplete, specify what is required to complete, but can require no new or additional information from applicant thereafter. (Govt. C. 65943 & 65944). Failure of applicant to submit complete or adequate information may be grounds for disapproving project. If lead agency fails to disapprove or approve project within prescribed time limits, this failure to act either may be appealed or, if requisite public notice has been given, will be deemed project approval. (Govt. C. 65956, 65956.5). Lead agency alone determines whether Negative Declaration or EIR is required for project and, for private applicant projects, must do so within 45 days of acceptance of application as complete. (Pub. Res. C. 21080.1 & 21080.2).

Air Resources.—Law was recodified in 1975. (H. & S.C. §39000 et seq.).

State Air Resources Board has general responsibility for controlling motor vehicle emissions. (H. & S.C. 39500). Board is control agency for all purposes set forth in federal law and administers and coordinates all air pollution research funded by state. (H. & S.C. 39602, 39703).

Local and regional authorities have primary responsibility for controlling air pollution from non-vehicle sources. (H. & S.C. 40000 et seq.). State divided into air pollution districts, each of which appoints air pollution control officer. (H. & S.C. 40750 et seq.). Each district has hearing boards who may issue abatement orders, permits and variances. Boards have subpoena power and are governed by specified notice to hearing standards. (H. & S.C. 40800 et seq.).

Non-Vehicular Control.—Except as expressly provided, no person shall discharge air contaminants sufficient to cause injury, detriment, etc. to any considerable number of persons. (H. & S.C. 41700 et seq.). Use of open outdoor fires for non-agriculture purposes is restricted. (H. & S.C. 41800 et seq). Agricultural burning is allowed by permit and according to board standards. (H. & S.C. 41850 et seq.). State Air Resources Board adopts standards and certification procedures for testing of vapor control systems in gasoline marketing operations. Applies to cargo tanks on vehicles as well as stationary tanks. Operation of uncertified tank vehicle prohibited after July 1, 1977. (H. & S.C. 41954, et seq.).

Violation of provisions of section is misdemeanor, punishable by fine of up to $1,000 and up to six months in jail. Each day violation occurs is separate offense. (H. & S.C. 42400). Violation of section also subjects violator to civil penalty of $1,000 for each day violation occurs. (H. & S.C. 42402). No liability in excess of $1,000 under H. & S.C. 42402 unless conduct was intentional or negligent. (H. & S.C. 42402). Any person who negligently or intentionally violates any order of abatement is liable for civil penalty of up to $25,000 for each day. (H. & S.C. 42401). Each day person negligently emits air contaminant or owns or operates any source of air contaminant in violation of specified sections of H. & S.C. is guilty of misdemeanor and subject to $15,000 fine, nine months imprisonment or both. (H. & S.C. 42400.1). Any such person who knew of emissions and failed to take corrective action within reasonable time under circumstances or who intentionally falsifies document required to be kept by this provision or who owns or operates source of air contaminant which causes actual injury to health or safety of public and who knew of emissions and failed to take corrective action is guilty of misdemeanor and is subject to fine of $25,000, one year's imprisonment, or both (H. & S.C. 42400.2) and to civil penalties up to $25,000 (H. & S.C. 42402.2).

Use of monitoring devices to detect pollution is encouraged. (H. & S.C. 42700 et seq.).

General Authority.—State board has authority to prescribe emission standards applicable to motor vehicles and to evaluate pollution control devices. Special provisions apply to racing vehicles and motorcycles. (H. & S.C. 43000 et seq.).

New Vehicles.—New vehicles which violate emission standards or test procedures shall not be sold or registered in this state. (H. & S.C. 43105).

Manufacturers and dealers responsible for giving notice of applicable emission standards and manufacturers and distributors who fail to comply with appropriate standards and test procedures subject to civil penalty of $50 for each such vehicle sold in state. (H. & S.C. 43212). Enforcement is by state board and may also be by California Highway Patrol, Department of Motor Vehicles, and the bureau of automotive repairs in Department of Consumer Affairs. (H. & S.C. 43213).

Used Vehicles.—State board adopts emission standards for used vehicles but installation of devices on used vehicles must be mandated by statute. Exhaust devices certified for used cars limited by price and maintenance costs. (H. & S.C. 43604). Board sets standards and certifies devices and may also revoke, suspend or restrict certification. (H. & S.C. 43600 et seq.).

Financing.—Authority for public financing of pollution control governed by Calif. Pollution Control Financing Authority Act. (H. & S.C. 44500 et seq.).

Water Pollution.—

General Supervision.—State Water Quality Control Board designated as state water pollution control agency and coordinates state activities with regard to water pollution by sewerage, oil and other wastes. Statewide and regional protection and abatement of water pollution outlined in Porter-Cologne Water Control Act. (Water C. 13200 et seq.). State divided into nine regional control boards which coincide with nine major drainage basins of state. (Water C. 13200). State authorized to implement Federal Water Pollution Control Act. (Water C. 13370, et seq.).

Prohibited Acts of Pollution.—Unlawful to discharge sewage or other waste, or effluent of treated sewage or other waste, in any manner which will result in contamination, pollution or nuisance. (H. & S.C. 5411).

Unlawful to permit certain listed pollutants to pass into state waters or place them where they can pass into state waters. (Fish & G.C. 5650, et seq.).

With exception of certain public entities (Water C. 13270), any person discharging waste or proposing to discharge waste within any region that could affect quality of waters of state, other than into community sewer system, any person who is citizen, domiciliary, or political agency or entity of this state discharging waste, or proposing to discharge waste outside boundaries of state in manner that could affect quality of waters of state within any region, or any person operating or proposing to construct injection well, shall file with regional board report of discharge containing such information as may be required by board. Exceptions for persons supplied with recycled water if suppliers of water meet prescribed requirements. (Water C. 13260).

Any person failing to file such report, or pay fee, when so requested by regional board or discharging hazardous waste, furnishing false report, wilfully failing to report or wilfully withholding material information is guilty of misdemeanor and substantial civil penalties up to $1,000 a day, each day being separate offense, may be assessed. If action before Superior Court, up to $5,000 a day civil penalty. (Water C. 13261).

Regional board, after any necessary hearing, shall prescribe requirements as to nature of any proposed discharge, existing discharge, or material change in existing discharge, with relation to condition existing in disposal area or receiving waters upon or into which discharge is made or proposed. (Water C. 13263).

No person shall initiate any new discharge of waste or make any material change in any discharge or initiate discharge to, make any material changes in discharge to, or construct injection well, prior to filing required report with control board and prior to whichever occurs first: issuance of waste discharge requirements by that board or expiration of 120 days after compliance with §13260 if certain criteria apply. (Water C. 13264).

Any person discharging waste in violation of discharge restrictions, after such violation has been called to his attention in writing by regional board, is guilty of a misdemeanor and liable to substantial civil penalties administratively imposed by regional board up to $1,000 a day. (Water C. 13265). If action before Superior Court, up to $5,000 a day civil penalty. (Water C. 13265). Civil penalties may be administratively imposed by up to $5,000 a day for release of hazardous waste. (Water C. 13265). If action before Superior Court, up to $25,000 a day civil penalty.

Enforcement board may issue order to cease and desist and direct persons not complying with requirements or discharge prohibitions to (a) comply forthwith, (b) comply in accordance with time schedule set by board, or (c) in event of threatened violation, take appropriate remedial or preventive action. (Water C. 13301).

Any person who discharges waste into waters of state in violation of waste discharge requirement or other order issued by regional board or state board, or who intentionally or negligently threatens to cause, causes or permits any waste to be discharged or deposited where it is, or probably will be, discharged into waters of state and creates or threatens to create a condition of pollution or nuisance, shall upon order of regional board clean up such waste or abate effects thereof or in case of threatened pollution or nuisance, take other necessary remedial action. Owner liable for all costs of abatement, and if agency expends such costs, amount constitutes a lien. (Water C. 13304).

Attorney General, at request of board, when necessary, shall petition Superior Court for issuance of cleanup or abatement order. (Water C. 13304). Civil penalty for violation of order or requirement not to exceed $15,000 for each day of violation. (Water C. 13350.) Violations under state authorized federal control act punishable by maximum $25,000 per day of violation. Sums paid to State Water Pollution Cleanup and Abatement Account. (Water C. 13385). Negligent or wilful violations punishable by maximum $25,000 per day, or one year imprisonment for first violation, and by $50,000 or two years imprisonment for violations after previous conviction. (Water C. 13387). For entities other than natural persons maximum penalties $1,000,000 for first criminal conviction, $2,000,000 for subsequent convictions. (Water C. 13387).

Transfers of Oil and Hazardous Substances.—Installation of monitoring devices is required to warn against imminent overflow of oil or other "hazardous substances" into waters of this state during transfer of such substances between vessel and either shore or another vessel. (Harb. & Nav. C. 135[a]). See subhead Hazardous Substances—Clean-Up, Control and Disclosure, infra.

Coast Line Preservation.—California Coastal Zone Act of 1976 (Pub. Res. C. 30000, et seq.) places California Coastal Commission and six Regional Coastal Commissions within California Resources Agency. California Coastal Commission controls all coastline development within its jurisdiction over permit area from 1,000 yards inland from mean high tide line to seaward limit of State's jurisdiction, with extensive and detailed planning and control functions. (Pub. Res. C. 30103). Persons with vested rights obtained prior to effective date of Act or who have obtained permit pursuant to California Coastal Act of 1972 not required to secure additional permit if no substantial change and construction is pursued within three years of granting of permit. (Pub. Res. C. 30608).

Enforcement.—Any person may sue to enjoin violation or enforce duties imposed by Act or Commission or any governmental agency, and to recover civil penalties. (Pub. Res. C. 30803-30805). Maximum civil fine $30,000 in addition to $1,000 to $15,000 per day for each day of intentional violation, plus exemplary damages, for intentional violators. (Pub. Res. C. 30820-30822).

Litter Control, Recycling, and Resource Recovery.—See subhead Hazardous Substances—Clean-Up, Control and Disclosure, infra.

Hazardous Substances—Clean-Up, Control and Disclosure.—The Carpenter-Presley-Tanner Hazardous Substances Control Act is state superfund statute paralleling federal superfund act. Act provides money to clean up hazardous waste disposal sites, for emergency response and to compensate victims of hazardous wastes. Law

See note at head of Digest as to 1998 legislation covered.

See Topical Index in front part of this volume.

CA – 43

ENVIRONMENTAL REGULATION . . . *continued*

authorizes injunctive relief and imposes strict liability standards for clean-up costs. (H. & S.C. 25300 et seq.). Hazardous waste control statutes regulate generators, including resource recovery facilities such as recyclers, disposal sites and waste haulers and contain permit, manifest and reporting requirements. (H. & S.C. 25100 et seq.). Extensive regulations are contained in Title 26 of California Code of Regulations. Substantial civil and criminal penalties for violations. (H. & S.C. 25189 et seq.). Law also extends to regulating local land use to extent property is contaminated by hazardous waste. (H. & S.C. 25149.3, 25202.5, 25220-25241).

Businesses which handle hazardous materials are required to prepare and file emergency response plan with various agencies. (H. & S.C. 25503.5). Employers are required to implement written hazard communication program for workplace, which includes proper labeling and employee education. (8 C.C.R. 5194). Acutely hazardous materials are subject to additional reporting requirements. (H. & S.C. 25533-25534). Chemicals which cause cancer or reproductive toxicity may not be released if they might pass into any source of drinking water. (H. & S.C. 25249.5). Businesses may not expose any individual to chemicals which cause cancer or reproductive toxicity without giving clear and reasonable warning. (H. & S.C. 25249.6). State maintains list of such chemicals, which is updated annually. (H. & S.C. 25249.8). Sellers of nonresidential property must notify buyers of releases of hazardous substances on property and lessees must notify lessors in writing of any release of hazardous substances on property. Substantial fines for failures to notify, and lessors may terminate lease. (H. & S.C. 25359.7).

Underground Tank Regulation.—Underground tanks are also subject to extensive regulatory and monitoring requirements pertaining to maintenance and/or removal of such tanks. (H. & S.C. 25280 et seq.). County or city governments are authorized to enforce these statutes and rules promulgated thereunder. Violations may result in fines of $500 to $5,000 per day. (H. & S.C. 25299). Hazardous substances are defined in Lab. C. 6382 or H. & S.C. 25316.

ESTATES AND TRUSTS

ADMINISTRATION:

See topic Executors and Administrators.

ADVANCEMENTS:

See topic Descent and Distribution.

ALLOWANCES:

See topic Executors and Administrators.

CLAIMS:

See topic Executors and Administrators.

DEATH:

Determination of Death.—There is disputable presumption of death if person is not heard from in five years. (Evid. C. 667).

Uniform Determination of Death Act adopted. (H. & S.C. 7180). Person who has sustained either irreversible cessation of circulatory and respiratory function or irreversible cessation of all functions of entire brain is dead. (H. & S.C. 7180). Determination of death requires independent confirmation of another physician. (H. & S.C. 7181).

Death Certificate.—See category Documents and Records, topic Records, subhead Vital Statistics, catchline Fee.

Survivorship.—Uniform Simultaneous Death Act has been adopted with some variance. (Prob. C. 103; 220-226; 230-234; 6403).

Action for wrongful death may be brought by personal representative or heirs of any deceased adult or of certain designated minor decedents. (C. C. P. 377.60). Action must be commenced within one year of date of death (C. C. P. 340) but if action is against health care provider limitation period is generally three years (C. C. P. 340.5). Such damages are awarded as are deemed just under circumstances, measured by pecuniary loss sustained by heirs by reason of decedent's death. (122 C.A.2d 466, 265 P.2d 183). See also 19 C.3d 59, 67-68, 137 C. Rptr. 863, 562 P.2d 1022.

Survival of Actions.—No cause of action is lost by reason of death of any person. (C.C.P. 377.20). Exemplary or punitive damages that would have been recoverable against decedent not recoverable against his executor or administration in action brought pursuant to this section; nor are damages for pain, suffering or disfigurement of decedent recoverable in action brought by executor or administrator pursuant to this section. For procedure in action for injury to unmarried minor child, see C.C.P. 376. In action brought by decedent's executor or administrator (C. C. P. 377.34) punitive damages are recoverable; damages for pain, suffering or disfigurement are not.

Natural Death Act.—Allows adult persons to execute directive in form set forth in Code (H. & S. C. 7188) good for five years, and revocable at any time, to withhold or withdraw life-sustaining procedures in case of terminal condition. Directive must be witnessed by two persons unrelated to declarant who are not his physician and who will not share in his estate. Act relieves physicians from civil liability or criminal prosecution for following such directive. Such act shall not constitute suicide nor impair life insurance. (H. & S. C. 7185-7194.5).

Uniform Anatomical Gift Act.—See topic Wills.

DECEDENTS' ESTATES:

See topics Descent and Distribution, Executors and Administrators, Wills; categories Debtor and Creditor, topic Homesteads; Family, topic Husband and Wife.

DESCENT AND DISTRIBUTION:

All separate property, both real and personal, of decedent which is not disposed of by will, or if there is excess of such property over share of surviving spouse (as to which see infra, subhead Surviving Spouse) or entire estate if there is no surviving spouse, descends and is distributed as follows, any class of which member is living taking to exclusion of subsequent classes (Prob. C. 6402): (1) Issue of decedent, equally if all of same degree, otherwise pursuant to Prob. C. 240; (2) parents or surviving parent; (3) issue of parents or either of them, equally if same degree of kinship or, if unequal pursuant to Prob. C. 240; (4) grandparents or issue of grandparents, equally if same degree of kinship or if unequal pursuant to Prob. C. 240; (5) issue of predeceased spouse equally if of same degree, or if unequal pursuant to Prob. C. 240; (6) next of kin of equal degree, except that those claiming through nearest ancestor take to exclusion of those of equal degree claiming through more remote ancestor; (7) parents of predeceased spouse or issue of each parent, equally if same degree or if unequal pursuant to Prob. C. 240.

If decedent left no spouse or issue, and predeceased spouse died not more than 15 years before decedent, portion of decedent's estate attributable to decedent's predeceased spouse, as defined, shall pass in equal shares to issue of predeceased spouse by right of representation, if any, otherwise to parents of predeceased spouse, or survivor, if any, otherwise to parents or issue of deceased parents of predeceased spouse and their descendants by right of representation. (Prob. C. 6402.5). Portion of decedent's estate attributable to predeceased spouse includes one-half of community property in existence at death of predeceased spouse which such spouse transferred to surviving spouse or which vested in decedent upon death of predeceased spouse. Such portion includes all separate property of predeceased spouse (Prob. C. 6402.5[f][4]). Remaining portion of decedent's estate shall be distributed according to intestate rules stated above. If portion of decedent's estate attributable to predeceased spouse would escheat to state because there is no kin of decedent to take, that portion then passes to next of kin of predeceased spouse. (Prob. C. 6402.5[a][5]).

Statutory scheme provides for distribution among heirs or beneficiaries, for both intestacy and where will or trust. (Prob. C. 240-247).

Surviving Spouse.—Share of surviving spouse in separate property of deceased spouse is: (1) One-third if decedent left more than one child, one child and issue of one or more deceased children or issue of two or more deceased children; (2) one-half if decedent left only one child or only issue of one deceased child or no issue but parent or parents or issue of deceased parent or parents; (3) all if decedent left none of aforementioned relatives. (Prob. C. 6401).

As to rights of surviving spouse in community property and certain property which is treated as community, see category Family, topic Husband and Wife.

Kindred of the half blood inherit same share they would inherit if they were of whole blood. (Prob. C. 6406).

Afterborn Heirs.—Relatives of decedent conceived before decedent's death but born thereafter inherit as if born in lifetime of decedent. (Prob. C. 6407).

Illegitimates.—Uniform Parentage Act adopted providing procedures to establish parent-child relationship without regard to marital status of natural parents. (C. C. 7000 et seq.). Rights of succession by natural or adopted child, and by issue through deceased child, are dependent upon existence of parent-child relationship between decedent and child, as defined by C. C. 7000 et seq.; succession to estate of deceased child, by and through parent, also depends upon existence of such relationship. When child has no presumed father or presumed father is deceased, parent-child relationship may not be established for intestate succession unless court order of paternity was entered during father's lifetime or paternity established by evidence of open and notorious holding out of child as father's own. (Prob. C. 6408).

Foster or Stepchild.—Parent and child relationship exists if relationship commenced during minority of child, continued during joint lives and clear and convincing evidence established that adoption would have been accomplished except for legal barrier to adoption. (Prob. C. 6454).

Adopted Children.—See category Family, topic Adoption.

Determination of Heirship.—Any time after first letters are issued to representative and before order for final distribution, representative or any person claiming to be beneficiary or entitled to distribution, may petition for court determination of who is entitled to distribution. As provided in Prob. C. 1220, notice must be mailed to all interested persons. Any person may appear and file written statement of interest he claims. (Prob. C. 11700-11702).

Right of Representation.—Defined as division at nearest generation with living members into equal shares with issue of predeceased members of generation receiving equal share. (Prob. C. 240).

Aliens.—As to right to inherit, see category Citizenship, topic Aliens.

Advancements.—Gift before death by decedent to heir is not considered advancement unless that intention is expressed by decedent in contemporaneous writing or acknowledged by donee in writing. (Prob. C. 6409). Gift is not taken into account if donee predeceases decedent in determining intestate share of donee's issue unless otherwise provided. (Prob. C. 6409[d]).

Election.—Surviving spouse may be required to elect whether to take community share or under will. See topic Wills, subhead Election.

Escheat.—If decedent leaves no one to take his estate, it escheats to state as of date of death of decedent with certain exceptions. (Prob. C. 6404, 6800 et seq.).

Community Property.—As to rights of surviving spouse therein see category Family, topic Husband and Wife.

See also topic Executors and Administrators.

Disqualification for Homicide.—Person who feloniously and intentionally kills decedent shall not inherit various described property and rights. (Prob. C. 250-257).

Release or Assignment of Expectancy.—Heir may assign his inheritance. (Prob. C. 11604). Heir may release his expectancy. (104 C. 570, 38 P. 414).

See note at head of Digest as to 1998 legislation covered.

See Topical Index in front part of this volume.

DESCENT AND DISTRIBUTION . . . *continued*

Disclaimer of Inheritance.—Heir or next of kin may refuse any interest in various kinds of property and rights to which he would be entitled. Writing is required and disclaimer must occur within reasonable time after heir or next of kin acquires knowledge of interest. Nine months is conclusively presumed to be timely in many cases. Disclaimer relates back to date of creation of interest, and disclaimed interest is distributed as if person disclaiming had predeceased person creating interest. Right to disclaimer exists regardless of spendthrift provision or other limitation on interest. (Prob. C. 260-295). Court approval is required for minors, conservatees, and sometimes for decedents. (Prob. C. 277).

ELECTION:

See topic Wills.

ESTATES:

See category Property, topic Real Property.

EXECUTORS AND ADMINISTRATORS:

Title to both real and personal property of decedent vests in his heirs, devisees and legatees at time of his death, but both types of property are subject to administration in superior court. (Prob. C. 7000, 7001, 7050).

Wills must be proved, and estates administered in Superior Court (1) of county where decedent was domiciled; (2) in case of nondomiciliary of this state, if property is in same county, in county where he died; or (3) otherwise, in any county where he left estate. (Prob. C. 7050-52).

In connection with ongoing revision of Prob. C., extensive recodification of provisions regarding administration of decedent's estates became effective on July 1, 1988 and July 1, 1989. New sections define "personal representative" (hereafter referred to as "representative") as executor, administrator, administrator with will annexed, special administrator, or person performing similar functions. "General personal representative" excludes special administrators. (Prob. C. 58).

Executors.—Except for payment of funeral charges and necessary measures for preservation of estate, no person has any powers as executor until appointed representative. (Prob. C. 8400). In absence of objection, person named as executor in decedent's will has right to appointment as representative unless not competent or waives right. (Prob. C. 8420, 8402). If person named executor is minor and another person named, latter may be appointed and may administer estate until majority of minor, who may then be appointed coexecutor. If no other person named, another person may be appointed, but appointment may be revoked when minor reaches majority and is appointed executor. (Prob. C. 8424). Nonresident may serve as representative, subject to certain requirements. (Prob. C. 8570-77). Acceptance by nonresident as representative or removal from state of representative constitutes automatic appointment of Secretary of State as attorney for service of process and notice of motion in any action against such executor relating to estate. (Prob. C. 8572).

Preferences in Right to Administer.—Following persons are entitled to administer intestate estate in this order: Surviving spouse (except if party to separation, maintenance, annulment or dissolution action and living apart from decedent at his death, when has priority after brothers and sisters under Prob. C. 8463), children, grandchildren, other issue, parents, brothers and sisters, issue of brothers and sisters, grandparents, issue of grandparents, children of predeceased spouse, other issue of predeceased spouse, other kin, parents of predeceased spouse, issue of parents of predeceased spouse, conservator or guardian of estate who has filed first account and is not acting as conservator or guardian for any other person, public administrator, creditors, any other person. (Prob. C. 8461). Relatives of decedent have priority only when entitled to succeed to all or part of estate or either takes under will of, or are entitled to succeed to all or part of estate of, another deceased person who is entitled to succeed to estate. (Prob. C. 8462).

Court may appoint competent person as administrator at written request, filed in court, of person, guardian, or conservator entitled to appointment. If person making request is surviving spouse, child, grandchild, other issue, parent, brother or sister, or grandparent of decedent, nominee has priority next after those in class of person making request; otherwise court, in its discretion, may appoint either such nominee or person of class subsequent in rank to that of person making request; but other members of class of person making request shall have priority over such nominee. (Prob. C. 8465).

Administrator with will annexed granted in same order of priority as administrators, except that one taking under will has priority over one not so taking and need not be entitled to succeed to estate or some portion thereof under laws of succession. (Prob. C. 8441[b]). Person who takes more than 50% of value of estate under will may request that court appoint as administrator person not otherwise entitled to be appointed as matter of priority. (Prob. C. 8441).

Eligibility and Competency.—Person not competent to act as representative if minor, subject to conservatorship, or subject to Prob. C. 8502 grounds for removal (mismanagement, fraud etc.). Also cannot be nonresident of U.S. or objected-to surviving partner of decedent unless named as executor in will. (Prob. C. 8402).

Foreign corporation may not act as executor or administrator in California unless licensed to do so. (Finan. C. 1750, 106).

Bond required unless will waives such requirement or where waived by all beneficiaries (Prob. C. 8480-8481) or executor or administrator is corporation (Prob. C. 301). Court can require bond even though will or beneficiaries have waived bond. (Prob. C. 8481). Court may fix amount of bond but maximum amount cannot exceed sum of (1) estimated value of property; (2) probable annual gross income of estate; (3) if independent administration granted as to real property, estimated value of decedent's interest therein. If bond given by personal sureties, twice above amount. If bond given by admitted surety insurer, court may establish fixed minimum amount based on minimum premium required by insurer. (Prob. C. 8482). Additional bond required before confirming sale of real property. (Prob. C. 8482). Representative allowed reasonable cost of bond. (Prob. C. 8486). Court may order reduction of bond if funds deposited in bank or savings associations subject to withdrawal only on court order. (Prob. C. 8483).

Oath that representative will perform according to law is necessary before letters issue. (Prob. C. 8403). Representative, other than trust company, must file acknowledgment of receipt of statement of duties and liabilities of office. (Prob. C. 8404).

Removal.—In response to petition or whenever court has reason to believe that representative has wasted, embezzled, mismanaged, wrongfully neglected or defrauded estate, or is about to do any such things, or is incapable of executing duties, court must cite representative to show cause why letters should not be revoked. (Prob. C. 8500, 8502).

Special Kinds of Administration.—Court may appoint special administrator when needed for immediate preservation of estate. (Prob. C. 8540). Powers are limited to those listed in Prob. C. 8544 but may be made general when necessary. (Prob. C. 8545).

Public Administration.—In each county there is public administrator, who must take immediate charge of property within his county of persons who have died when no representative has been appointed and consequently property is being wasted, uncared for or lost, and of all estates ordered into his hands by court. (Prob. C. 7601). He must petition for appointment as representative if no person having higher priority has petitioned and for any other estate public administrator determines proper. (Prob. C. 7620). Public administrator may have summary administration of estates which do not appear to exceed $100,000. If value of estate appears to be $20,000 or less, public administrator may dispose of property without application to court. (Prob. C. 7660, 13100).

Independent Administration of Estates Act creates optional procedure for administration of decedent's estate with minimum court supervision. (Prob. C. 10400 et seq.).

Inventory and appraisement must be filed within four months after appointment of representative, unless court extends time, and shall be in form prescribed by statute. (Prob. C. 8800, 8802). Concurrent with filing inventory and appraisement, representative must file certification that Rev. & Tax C. 480 requirements satisfied or inapplicable. (Prob. C. 8800). Appraisement is made by representative, expert, or probate referee as set forth by statute. (Prob. C. 8900). Court may waive appointment of probate referee, for good cause. (Prob. C. 8903). Any person interested in estate may challenge values. (Prob. C. 11001).

General Powers and Duties.—Whenever it shall appear to be to advantage of estate, court may authorize representative to execute notes and mortgages (Prob. C. 9800) or leases (Prob. C. 9941, 9942), or to sell property (Prob. C. 10000), or exchange it for other property (Prob. C. 9920), or give options to purchase real property (Prob. C. 9960), or continue decedent's business (Prob. C. 9760).

Representative must take possession of all real and personal property and collect all debts due. (Prob. C. 9650).

Court may authorize representative to compromise debt (Prob. C. 9830) or claim for wrongful death or injury to decedent (Prob. C. 9835).

Notice to Creditors.—Petitioner must publish notice of death and of petition to administer estate, at least three times in local newspaper with first publication at least 15 days before hearing. (Prob. C. 8121). Additional notice must be provided directly to known or reasonably ascertainable creditors within four months after letters first issued; notice must be given within four months from date letters first issued or 30 days after personal representative first has knowledge of creditor, whichever is later. (Prob. C. 9050-9052).

Presentation of Claims.—Claims on contract, funeral expenses, specified taxes and claims for damages for injury to person or property or for death, are barred unless presented to representative and clerk of court from which letters issued before expiration of later of: Four months after date letters are first issued; or 60 days after date notice of administration given to creditor if notice is at least 60 days prior to expiration of time provided in C.C.P. 366.2. (Prob. C. 9100). Upon petition by creditor or personal representative, court may allow claim to be filed after expiration of time for filing claim in Prob. C. 9100 if (1) personal representative failed to send proper and timely notice to creditor and petition is filed within 60 days after creditor has actual knowledge of administration of estate or; (2) creditor has no knowledge of facts reasonably giving rise to existence of claim more than 30 days prior to time for filing claim and petition is filed 60 days after creditor has actual knowledge of facts reasonably giving rise to existence of claim and of administration of estate. (Prob. C. 9100, 9103). Court shall not allow claim to be filed after earlier of order for final distribution, and one year after date letters are first issued and court may condition claim on just terms. (Prob. C. 9103). Unmatured claims and claims on which actions were pending when decedent died must be presented like other claims. (Prob. C. 9000). No filing is required where decedent had liability insurance in amount greater than claim or excess is waived. (Prob. C. 554, 9390).

Secured claim may be enforced without presentation as to property subject to lien, but must be presented in order to participate in general assets. (Prob. C. 9391).

Proof of Claims.—Claims filed must be verified, and must show all particulars, and originals or copies of documents, but reference to record is sufficient in case of mortgages. (Prob. C. 9151, 9152). Claims barred by limitation may not be allowed. (Prob. C. 9253). For form for proof of claim, see end of Digest, after UCC forms.

Approval or Rejection of Claims.—Claims should be acted on within 30 days after their presentation; and failure to act on claim within such time may, at claimant's option, be deemed equivalent to rejection on 30th day. (Prob. C. 9256).

Unmatured or Contingent Claims.—Where claim is unmatured or contingent, amount sufficient for payment must be paid into court, there to remain until claim matures or becomes absolute, but if holder of unmatured claim appears and assents to deduction of legal interest until maturity, claim, as thus reduced, may be paid at same time as other claims. (Prob. C. 11462, 11463).

See note at head of Digest as to 1998 legislation covered.

See Topical Index in front part of this volume.

CA – 45

EXECUTORS AND ADMINISTRATORS . . . *continued*

Disputed claim against estate may be contested by interested person any time prior to settlement of account reporting claim even though allowed and approved (Prob. C. 11001, 1043), and may be compromised by representative and claimant after time for filing creditor's claims expires (Prob. C. 9830, 9831).

Priorities, in case estate insufficient to pay all claims in full, are: (1) Administration expenses (with respect to obligations secured by mortgage, deed of trust, or other lien, including, but not limited to, judgment lien, only those expenses of administration incurred that reasonably relate to administration of property by which obligations are secured shall be given priority over these obligations); (2) obligations secured by mortgage, deed of trust or lien (excess of secured claim over security prorates with general demands); (3) funeral expenses; (4) expenses of last illness; (5) family allowance; (6) wage claims; and (7) general debts. (Prob. C. 11420).

Sales of estate property are regulated in detail. Some sales may be made without prior court order, especially where representative is granted power of sale by will. Except when acting under independent authority (Prob. C. 10503), sales must be confirmed by court or approved by it (Prob. C. 10308). With some exceptions, no executor or administrator may purchase any property of estate, directly or indirectly. (Prob. C. 9880).

Actions.—Representative may sue or be sued on causes of action surviving decedent. (C.C.P. 377.20). See category Civil Actions and Procedure, topic Actions.

Actions Against Representative.—Presentation of claim is condition precedent to right to sue thereon, except to enforce lien on specific property (Prob. C. 9391), and right to sue is suspended until claim is rejected. (Prob. C. 9370). Rejection may be by written notice to claimant, but failure to act on claim within 30 days after its presentation may, at claimant's option, be deemed equivalent to rejection. Action on claim is barred unless commenced within three months after service on claimant of written notice of rejection or, if claim is unmatured, within three months after maturity. (Prob. C. 9256, 9353).

Representative may be substituted as party to action pending against decedent when he died, if cause of action survives (C.C.P. 368.5), but no recovery may be had in absence of proof that claim was presented in manner provided by Prob. C. 9370.

Allowances.—Surviving spouse, minor children, incapacitated dependent adult children, and in court's discretion other dependent adult children and dependent parent are entitled to reasonable allowance for maintenance, which may be granted by court before or after inventory filed. (Prob. C. 6540 et seq.).

Accounts are to be rendered as ordered by court; final account when estate is in condition to be closed. (Prob. C. 10950-51, 10902).

Distribution.—Preliminary distribution of all or portion of estate to beneficiaries may be had at any time after lapse of two months from issuance of letters to general representative when it can be made without loss to creditors or injury to estate or parties. (Prob. C. 11620, 11621). If distribution before four months have elapsed, bond required. If after four months, bond only if court requires. (Prob. C. 11622).

Final distribution, however, can only be made when all debts have been paid or provided for, or if estate insolvent and in condition to be closed. (Prob. C. 11640). When order settling final account and distribution entered, representative may immediately distribute property. (Prob. C. 11641).

Uniform Simplification of Fiduciary Security Transfers Act repealed by Uniform Commercial Code. (Com'l. C. 8402-8404, 8115). See category Business Regulation and Commerce, topic Commercial Code.

Liabilities.—Outgoing representative liable until estate delivered to new representative. (Prob. C. 8525). Representative liable for any damage caused as result of his neglect or misconduct in relation to any sale. (Prob. C. 10380). Representative not liable for acts of corepresentative in absence of collusion, negligence, knowledge, or impropriety. (Prob. C. 2105.5). He must make no profit by increase, nor suffer loss by decrease or destruction without his fault, of any part of estate. (Prob. C. 9657).

Distribution if Abroad.—No special provision for distributees residing abroad, unless whereabouts unknown. Provision made for disposition of personal property payable to distributee to whom it is not possible to distribute property for some reason such as minority or incompetency. (Prob. C. 11850-51). See category Property, topic Absentees.

When Administration Unnecessary.—When total value of decedent's property in California, over and above certain wages for services, certain kinds of property in which decedent had joint ownership and any motor vehicle or vessel of which decedent is owner or legal owner, does not exceed $100,000, successors of decedent, or conservator of estate of such person, or guardian of estate of any minor, insane or incompetent successor, or trustee of any trust created during decedent's lifetime, may, 40 days after decedent's death without procuring letters of administration, collect and receive such money and property owing or due from any person or entity having custody of such property upon furnishing affidavit reciting above facts. (Prob. C. 13100, 13101). Similar affidavit procedure available for summary transfer of real property where gross value of all decedent's real property in California does not exceed $20,000. (Prob. C. 13200). Summary petition and court order procedure may be used to transfer real property where total gross value of decedent's real and personal property does not exceed $100,000. (Prob. C. 13151). Net estates (over and above all liens and encumbrances at decedent's death, and value of homestead property set apart) under $20,000, under certain circumstances, go to surviving spouse or if none, to minor children subject only to liens, as of time of decedent's death, and expenses of last illness, funeral, and administration, by order of court on verified petition after return of inventory. (Prob. C. 6600 et seq.). If nondomiciliary decedent's property satisfies Prob. C. 13100 requirements, sister state representative may use affidavit procedure to collect personal property of decedent. (Prob. C. 12570-72).

Small Estates.—See subhead When Administration Unnecessary, supra.

Foreign executors or administrators ordinarily have no power over decedent's estate in California. (C. C. P. 1913). California courts may order delivery of property in state to foreign representative and if necessary direct a sale of real property and a like delivery of proceeds. (Prob. C. 12540-41).

Foreign and Ancillary Administration.—No procedural distinction between domiciliary and ancillary probate or administration. (Prob. C. 12510-13). See topic Wills, subhead Foreign Probated Wills.

Uniform Fiduciaries Act has not been adopted.

Revised Uniform Principal and Income Act has been adopted with variations. (Prob. C. 16300-15).

Uniform Anatomical Gift Act.—See topic Wills.

FIDUCIARIES:

See topics Executors and Administrators, Trusts; category Family, topic Guardian and Ward.

INTESTACY:

See topic Descent and Distribution.

PROOF OF CLAIMS:

See topic Executors and Administrators; category Civil Actions and Procedure, topic Pleading.

TRUSTS:

(Prob. C.—Division 9; §§15000-18200). Trust of real or personal property or both may be created, subject to rules as to alienation, vesting, etc. (see category Property, topic Perpetuities), and subject to Statute of Frauds (Prob. C. 15206), for any purpose that is not illegal or against public policy (Prob. C. 15203). Common law of trusts, as modified by statute, is law governing trusts. (Prob. C. 15002).

Kinds.—Express trusts recognized by statute. (Prob. C. 15200). New Trust Law does not affect prior law relating to constructive or resulting trusts. (Prob. C. 15003). Resulting trust on failure of express trust is also recognized. (1 C.2d 724, 37 P.2d 76; 28 C.2d 154, 168 P.2d 946). Tentative or "Totten" trust doctrine, applicable to bank or savings deposits, has been recognized. (Prob. C. 80).

Jurisdiction over Trusts.—Superior court, as court of general equitable powers, has jurisdiction over inter vivos trusts. (Prob. C. 17000). Court in which will creating trust was probated retains jurisdiction over such trust for most purposes, except for trusts created by will after July 1, 1977 unless trustor provides otherwise. (Prob. C. 17300-01). Procedures are established to remove testamentary trust from continuing court jurisdiction. (Prob. C. 17350-54). Procedures are established to allow acceptance of trusts transferred from outside California (Prob. C. 17450-57), and to transfer trust to jurisdiction outside California (Prob. C. 17400-05).

Creation.—Trusts may be created inter vivos or by will. Inter vivos trusts may be created by specific methods. (Prob. C. 15200). Oral trusts are valid as to personalty. (Prob. C. 15207). To be enforceable, trusts of realty must be evidenced by writing unless created by operation of law. (Prob. C. 15206).

Appointment of Trustee.—Whenever there is vacancy and trust fails to provide practical method of appointment, vacancy can be filled by trust company if all adult beneficiaries agree. If beneficiary has conservator, conservator may agree to successor trustee on beneficiary's behalf without court approval. If beneficiary has designated attorney in fact who has power to agree to successor trustee, attorney in fact may do so. If vacancy not filled in any of these methods, court can appoint trustee giving consideration to nominee of beneficiaries over age of 14. (Prob. C. 15660). Public guardian shall not be appointed unless court finds no other qualified person willing to act as trustee. (Prob. C. 15660.5).

Eligibility and Competency.—Trustee may be individual, or bank or trust company qualified to conduct trust business in California. (Finan. C. 1500-02).

Foreign corporation cannot act as trustee except to limited extent provided in Finan. C. 1503 which permits such corporation to act as trustee for delivery, payment, registration, exchange, cancellation and the like of bonds, or as trustee under indenture securing bonds of railroad operating in California and extending into another state; but it cannot maintain office or agency in California unless complying with applicable provisions of Financial Code.

Qualification.—Trustees of inter vivos trusts and named trustees of testamentary trusts need not furnish bond unless trust instrument so requires or court finds necessary. Unnamed trustees appointed to fill vacancies in trusts must furnish bond. (Prob. C. 15602). No oath is required of trustees.

Removal of Trustee.—Superior Court may remove any trustee who has breached, or is unfit to execute trust. (Prob. C. 15642). Where hostility or continued lack of cooperation among co-trustees impairs administration of trust, where trustee fails or declines to act, where trustee's compensation is excessive, where sole trustee is disqualified person under Prob. C. 21350, or for other good cause, court may remove one or more trustees. (Prob. C. 15642).

General Powers and Duties of Trustees.—Trustee is general agent and may bind trust property within scope of authority conferred by trust instrument and by law. (Prob. C. 16200). Trustee may give proxies to vote any shares held in trust. (Prob. C. 16234, Corp. C. 702-05).

Where there are several co-trustees all must unite in any act to bind trust estate unless trust instrument otherwise provides (Prob. C. 15620), except in emergencies (Prob. C. 15622) or if vacancy in co-trusteeship occurs (Prob. C. 15621).

Sales and Leases.—Sales of trust property may be made in accordance with trust provisions. (Prob. C. 16226). Trustee has power to lease trust property, including options, for term beyond term of trust. (Prob. C. 16231-32).

Investments.—Governed by Prob. C. 16040, adopting standard of "prudent persons" managing their own affairs, except as otherwise provided by terms of particular trusts.

See note at head of Digest as to 1998 legislation covered.

See Topical Index in front part of this volume.

CA – 46

TRUSTS . . . *continued*

Uniform Common Trust Fund Act in substance adopted, with additional provisions that such fund is separate entity owned by trustee, and that administration of participating relationship requires no allocation or apportionment between capital and income different from that for such fund. (Finan. C. 1564; and see Corp. C. 10250).

Securities in Name of Nominee.—Fiduciary permitted to hold securities in name of nominee without disclosure of trust so that title to security may pass by delivery. (Prob. C. 16238). Trustee may also deposit securities in securities depositary. (Prob. C. 16239).

Bequests and Devises to Inter Vivos Trusts.—See topic Wills, subhead Bequests and Devises to Inter Vivos Trusts.

Uniform Simplification of Fiduciary Security Transfers Act repealed by Uniform Commercial Code. (Com'l. C. 8402-8404, 8115). See category Business Regulation and Commerce, topic Commercial Code.

Accounting.—Uniform Trustees Accounting Act has not been adopted. Trustees of revocable living trust established before July 1, 1987 are not required to account annually. (Prob. C. 16062[b]). Annual accountings required of all trustees (Prob. C. 16062), unless requirement waived in trust instrument or by beneficiary in writing (Prob. C. 16064).

Court Supervision.—Any trustee or beneficiary may petition superior court to determine among other things, construction of trust, to whom property passes, settle account, instructions, compel accounting, grant powers, fix compensation, appoint or remove trustee, accept resignation of trustee, allow removal to another jurisdiction, amend trust to qualify as charitable trust, divide into two or more separate trusts. (Prob. C. 17200).

Compensation.—Trustee entitled to compensation as provided in trust instrument. Court has authority to raise or lower such compensation as equity demands. If instrument does not provide for compensation, reasonable compensation as determined by court is allowed. (Prob. C. 15680). If several trustees, compensation must be apportioned according to services rendered by each, unless trust instrument or trustee agreement provides otherwise. (Prob. C. 15683).

Modification or Termination.—Upon petition of trustee or beneficiary, court may modify or terminate trust if value of trust principal is so low in relation to costs of administration that continuance will defeat purposes of trust. (Prob. C. 15408). Trustee may terminate trust worth less than $20,000 without court approval. (Prob. C. 15408[b]). All beneficiaries may consent to terminate trust if continuation of trust not necessary to carry out material purpose of trust or unless court finds material purpose outweighed by circumstances. (Prob. C. 15403). Settler and all beneficiaries may modify or terminate trust. (Prob. C. 15404). Modifications and termination of trust permitted upon showing of changed circumstances. (Prob. C. 15409).

Discharge.—Trustee may resign only by one of following methods: As provided in trust; with court approval; for revocable trust, with consent of person holding power to revoke; for nonrevocable trust, with consent of all beneficiaries or pursuant to court order obtained by trustee under Prob. C. 17200. (Prob. C. 15640). Trustee's resignation does not release him from liability for his actions. (Prob. C. 15641).

Spendthrift Trusts.—Principal and income restrictions valid (Prob. C. 15300-01), subject to certain exceptions for support trusts (Prob. C. 15302), discretionary trusts (Prob. C. 15303), claims for child or spousal support (Prob. C. 15305), public support claims (Prob. C. 15306), and self-settled trusts (Prob. C. 15304). In addition, surplus of income beyond that needed for education and support of beneficiary is liable to creditor's claims, when no valid directions for accumulation given. (Prob. C. 15307).

Revised Uniform Principal and Income Act adopted with significant modifications. (Prob. C. 16300-16315).

Gifts to Minors.—See category Family, topic Infants.

Uniform Fiduciaries Act not adopted.

Uniform Supervision of Trustees for Charitable Purposes Actadopted. (Govt. C. 12580-99).

Trust deeds to secure debts, see category Mortgages, topic Mortgages of Real Property.

Accumulations.—Accumulation of income permitted but may not extend beyond time permitted for vesting of future interests. (C. C. 724). Express direction to accumulate required. (See C. C. 733; 38 C.2d 289, 239 P.2d 617.)

Perpetuities.—See category Property, topic Perpetuities.

Pour Over Trusts.—See topic Wills, subhead Bequests and Devises to Inter Vivos Trusts.

Disclaimer.—All or portion of interest in trust may be disclaimed under certain circumstances by following procedures within reasonable time after person able to disclaim acquires knowledge of interest. (Prob. C. 260-295).

WILLS:

Every person of sound mind, 18 or older, may make will. (Prob. C. 6100). As to limitations on testamentary power of married persons, see category Family, topic Husband and Wife, subhead Community Property System. No limitations on gifts to religious, charitable, etc. institutions. Limitations on transfers to drafters. (Prob. C. 21350 et seq.).

Contract to make or not revoke will or to die intestate, if made after Dec. 31, 1984, can be established only by will stating material contract provisions; express reference in will to contract and extrinsic evidence proving contract terms; or writing signed by decedent evidencing contract. Execution of joint or mutual wills does not create presumption of contract not to revoke. (Prob. C. 150). Conditional wills must be granted or denied probate, or denied effect after probate, in conformity with condition. (Prob. C. 6105).

Execution.—Wills must be in writing, and, other than holographic, must be signed either by testator, or by some one for him, in his presence and by his direction or by conservator pursuant to court order to make will under Prob. C. 2580. Will must be witnessed by being signed by at least two persons each of whom: (1) Being present at same time, witnessed either signing of will or testator's acknowledgment of signature of will and (2) understand that instrument they sign is testator's will. (Prob. C. 6110). Any person generally competent to be witness may witness will. (Prob. C. 6112).

Attestation Clause.—

Form

The foregoing instrument was on the date thereof, by John Doe, subscribed and declared to be his Will, in the presence of us, who at his request, and in his presence, and in the presence of each other, do sign the same as witnesses thereto.

Andrew Black, residing at . . . .

George Red, residing at . . . .

Holographic Wills.—Will not complying with Prob. C. 6110 is valid as holographic will, whether or not witnessed, if signature and material provisions are in testator's handwriting. If holographic will does not state date of its execution and: (1) Omission results in doubt as to whether its provisions or inconsistent provisions of another will control, holographic will is invalid to extent of inconsistency unless time of execution is established as after date of other will's execution; (2) testator lacked capacity when will might have been executed, will is invalid unless established that it was executed when testator had capacity. (Prob. C. 6111).

Statutory Wills.—Specific form of printed statutory will or statutory will with trust with limited choice of dispositive clauses is valid. (Prob. C. 6200-6243).

Revocation.—Marriage after making will revokes will as to surviving spouse, unless spouse is provided for by marriage contract or outside of will in manner indicating intention that transfer be in lieu of testamentary provision, or is mentioned in will in such way as to show intention to make no provision. (Prob. C. 21610, 21611). In case of child of such marriage, will is revoked as to child, with similar exceptions, or, if more than one child, substantially all of estate is devised to other parent of omitted child. (Prob. C. 21620, 21671).

Divorce or annulment revokes will as to former spouse for most part. (Prob. C. 6122).

Except as aforesaid, will may be revoked or altered only by subsequent will revoking prior will expressly or by inconsistency or by being burnt, canceled, obliterated or destroyed with intent and for purpose of revoking it, by testator or another person in his presence and at his direction. (Prob. C. 6120).

Revival.—Antecedent will not ipso facto revived by revocation of subsequent will. It must appear by terms of such revocation that it was intention to revive first will. (Prob. C. 6123).

Disclaimer.—Beneficiaries and other recipients may disclaim interests in whole or in part. (Prob. C. 260, et seq.).

Testamentary Gift to Subscribing Witnesses.—Will or any of its provisions is not invalid because interested witness signed it. (Prob. C. 6112[b]). Unless at least two disinterested witnesses signed will, devise to subscribing witness creates presumption that witness procured devise by duress, menace, fraud or undue influence. (Prob. C. 6112[c]). If devise fails because presumption applies and witness fails to rebut it, interested witness takes such proportion of devise as does not exceed share of estate which would be distributed to him if will were not established. (Prob. C. 6112[d]).

Testamentary Guardian.—See category Family, topic Guardian and Ward, subhead Eligibility.

Probate.—Any interested person, may at any time after death of testator petition Superior Court having jurisdiction to have will proved. (Prob. C. 8000). Petition for probate of will must state: (1) Date and place of death; (2) address of decedent's residence; (3) name, age, address, relation of heirs and devisees; (4) character and estimated value of property; (5) name of proposed representative; (6) copy of will; (7) whether named executor consents to or waives appointment. (Prob. C. 8002). If no one contests probate, will may be proved on evidence of one of subscribing witnesses such as affidavit to which photographic copy of will is attached or affidavit in original will incorporating attestation clause. If no subscribing witness resides in county, deposition of witness can be elsewhere upon court direction. (Prob. C. 8220). If no evidence of subscribing witness can be procured, will may be proved by handwriting of testator and either handwriting of subscribing witness, writing in will with signatures of all subscribing witnesses or affidavit of person with personal knowledge of execution of will. (Prob. C. 8221).

Self-proved Wills.—Uncontested wills may be admitted on affidavit of subscribing witness to which photographic copy of will attached or which is contained in will and includes attestation clause. (Prob. C. 8220).

Contest.—Any person interested may contest will by filing written grounds of opposition to probate thereof any time before hearing of petition for probate. (Prob. C. 1043). Within 120 days after will is admitted to probate as recorded in clerk's minutes, any interested party, not party to or with knowledge of prior contest, may contest will. (Prob. C. 8225, 8270).

Bequests and Devises to Inter Vivos Trusts.—Uniform Testamentary Additions to Trusts Act adopted. (Prob. C. 6300 et seq.).

Life Insurance and Similar Trusts.—Under certain circumstances, benefits payable on death pursuant to life insurance contracts and employee benefit plans may pass to trustee named in will without becoming subject to administration. (Prob. C. 6321, 6323).

Legacies and Devises.—General pecuniary legacies unpaid one year from testator's death bear interest at rate of interest one percentage point greater than minimum rate of EE U.S. Savings Bond, and if no such minimum rate, three percentage points less than legal rate on court judgment. (Prob. C. 21135).

Gift before death constitutes satisfaction of devise in whole or part only if will so provides; or testator so declares in contemporaneous writing; or devisee so acknowledges in writing. (Prob. C. 6174).

See note at head of Digest as to 1998 legislation covered.

See Topical Index in front part of this volume.

CA – 47

WILLS . . . *continued*

Unclaimed Legacies.—Disposition of unclaimed property from estates of deceased persons governed by C. C. P. 1440-1449. Escheat of estates controlled by Prob. C. 6800 et seq. and C. C. P. 1300 et seq. See also topic Executors and Administrators, subhead Distribution if Abroad; and category Property, topic Absentees.

Child Not Provided for.—When testator omits to provide in his will for living child solely because he believes child to be dead or is unaware of child's birth, such child receives share in estate equal in value to that which child would receive if testator died intestate. (Prob. C. 21622). When testator fails to provide in will for child born or adopted after execution of will, child receives similar share in estate, unless failure to provide appears from will to be intentional, or child is otherwise provided for. (Prob. C. 21620, 21671).

Contribution.—Share of omitted child must first be taken from estate not disposed of by will, balance as necessary from all devisees and legatees proportionately unless will indicates contrary intention. (Prob. C. 21623).

Election.—Surviving spouse has no right of election between testamentary provision, if any, and share of separate property of decedent as in case of intestacy, except in certain cases of nonresidents. (Prob. C. 120). See categories Family, topic Husband and Wife, subhead Community Property System; Property, topics Curtesy, Dower.

Community Property.—If one spouse attempts testamentary disposition of more than half of community property, surviving spouse must elect whether to take under will or to take his or her half of community property. (29 C. 337). Unless terms of will show contrary intent, surviving spouse can take community share as well as property given under will. (166 C. 450, 137 P. 37). Election may be made any time prior to distribution unless will provides contrary or spouse estopped. (147 C. 95, 81 P. 315; 15 C.3d 907, 126 C.Rptr. 820, 544 P.2d 956). Where wife dies before making election and before distribution of husband's estate, executrix may file election on widow's behalf. (15 C.3d 907, 126 C.Rptr. 820, 544 P.2d 956).

When either husband or wife dies intestate, or dies testate leaving all or part of estate passing or belonging to surviving spouse, such property passes to surviving spouse without probate or administration; however, surviving spouse may elect that interest of deceased spouse in community property, or interests of both spouses, be probated or administered. (Prob. C. 13500-13502). Unless interests of both spouses are probated or administered, surviving spouse is personally liable for debts of deceased spouse chargeable against community property and quasi-community property; such liability is limited to value of community property and quasi-community property which did not pass through probate or administration. (Prob. C. 13550-13554). For these purposes, procedures exist for determining community property and apportioning debts. (Prob. C. 13650, 11440-46).

Lapse.—If devisee or legatee, who is kindred of testator or is kindred of surviving, deceased or former spouse, is dead when will is executed or dies before testator, leaving lineal descendants who survive testator, such descendants take under will as devisee or legatee would have taken had he survived testator, unless will expresses statutory intention or substitute disposition. In other cases, death of devisee or legatee before death of testator causes lapse unless will provides otherwise. (Prob. C. 21110, 21111).

Foreign Wills.—Will made outside of state is valid in state if executed as required by laws of this state, executed according to laws of place where executed or executed according to laws of place where at time of execution or time of testator's death testator is domiciled, has place of abode, or is national. (Prob. C. 6113). Uniform International Wills Act adopted. (Prob. C. 6380 et seq.).

Foreign probated wills or foreign proved or established wills may be probated in appropriate superior court. (Prob. C. 12510, 7050). (See topic Executors and Administrators.) Authenticated copy of will and of order or decree admitting it to probate or other evidence of its proof or establishment must be filed with petition for letters. Such order, decree or other evidence must satisfy certain Evidence Code requirements. (Prob. C. 12520-23).

Simultaneous Death.—See topic Death, subhead Survivorship.

Testamentary Trusts.—See topic Trusts.

Uniform Anatomical Gift Act adopted. (H. & S. C. 7150-7156.5).

FAMILY

ADOPTION:

Any adult may adopt any unmarried minor child if former is at least ten years older, and if in best interest of both, court may approve adoption by stepparent or certain classes of relatives without regard to relative ages. (Fam. C. 8600-01, 8714.5). Any adult may adopt any younger adult person, except adopter's spouse. (Fam. C. 9300-07, 9320-28, 9340, 200, 212). Relatives of child freed for adoption have placement preference over other applicants if in best interest of child. (Fam. C. 8710). Foster parent considered equally with all other applicants. (Fam. C. 8704, 8710). Foster parent or relative caretaker of child declared dependent of juvenile court has adoption preference over others if substantial ties to child. (Welf. & Inst. C. 366.25[g]). Placement preferences for racial background or ethnic identification. (Fam. C. 8708-10).

Consents Required.—Of child's parents, including presumed father (Fam. C. 7611), if living; in certain cases, consent of single parent having sole custody, after other spouse has been given notice in manner provided for service of summons in civil action. Parent's consent is unnecessary where parent is judicially deprived of child's custody by court, or has deserted child without provision for its identification, or has signed and acknowledged statement relinquishing child for adoption. (Fam. C 8604-8606). Consent to adoption, once given, can be withdrawn by natural parent, in case of independent adoption only within 90 days of signature (Fam. C. 8814.5, 8815) and in case of stepparent adoption only if court approves (Fam. C. 9005, 200). Consent of child necessary if it is over 12 (Fam. C. 8602), as is consent of spouse of adult or married minor adoptee (Fam. C. 200, 212, 9301, 9302, 9307, 9320-28, 9340). Where not lawfully separated from spouse, married person cannot (a) adopt another adult without consent of adopter's spouse or (b) be adopted without consent of adoptee's spouse. (Fam. C. 8603, 200, 212, 9301, 9302, 9307, 9320-28, 9340). Regarding independent, stepparent, intercountry, and participation by Dept. of Health or licensed agency, see Fam. C. 200, 8800-9007.

Illegitimates.—Uniform Parentage Act adopted, providing procedures to establish parent-child relationship without regard to distinctions based on legitimacy. (Fam. C. 7600 et seq.). Such relationship can exist between child and natural or adoptive parents. (Fam. C. 7601, 7610).

Venue.—Petition to be filed in superior court of county in which petitioner resides. (Fam. C. 8714, 8802).

Proceedings.—Delineated by Fam. C. 8700 et seq., 8800 et seq. and 9000 et seq. for agency, direct and stepparent adoptions and by Fam. C. 9300-07, 9320-28, 9340, 200, 212 for adult and married minor adoptions.

Name.—Adoptee may take family name of adopter. (Fam. C. 8616, 8618, 9304-05).

Effect of Adoption.—Adopter and adoptee sustain legal relation of parent and child with all its rights and duties. (Fam. C. 8616, 8618, 9304-05). Natural parents of adoptee are relieved of all parental duties and responsibilities and have no rights. (Fam. C. 8617; 9306). Adoptee deemed descendant of adopter as though natural child, for all purposes of succession. Adopted child normally does not succeed to estate of natural parent or relative, and neither natural parent nor relative normally inherits from child adopted by another. (Prob. C. 6451). Under certain circumstances, adopted person in stepparent adoption may succeed to estate of natural parent and relatives and natural parent or relative can inherit from child adopted by another. (Prob. C. 6454).

Setting Aside Adoption.—Within five years from decree of adoption, adopting parents may petition to set aside adoption of minor child because of mental deficiency or mental illness of which adopting parents had no notice. (Fam. C. 200, 9100, 9101).

Information on Parentage.—Procedure available for disclosure of names and addresses of adoptees who have reached age of 21 if adult adoptee consents in writing. Disclosure of names and addresses of birth parents contained in records permitted if birth parents consent in writing. Release of information to adoptees under age of 21 authorized if medical necessity or other extraordinary circumstance justifies disclosure. Licensed adoption agencies are mandated to respond to such requests. (Fam. C. 9203).

Information on Siblings.—Procedure available to adoptee 21 or older for disclosure of name and address of biological sibling 21 or older who has also requested contact. (Fam. C. 9205).

ALIMONY:

See topic Dissolution of Marriage.

ANNULMENT:

See topic Marriage.

COMMUNITY PROPERTY:

See topic Husband and Wife, subhead Community Property System.

DESERTION:

See topic Husband and Wife, subhead Desertion and Nonsupport.

DISSOLUTION OF MARRIAGE:

Subject is covered by Fam. C. 310 et seq. (effective Jan. 1, 1994).

Rules.—Family law matters are governed in large part by California Rules of Court which prescribe specific procedures, such as use of judicial forms. Rules should always be consulted. (Cal. R. Ct. 1201 et seq.).

Grounds.—Court may decree a dissolution of marriage or legal separation on either of following grounds, which shall be pleaded generally: (1) Irreconcilable differences, which have caused irremediable breakdown of marriage; (2) incurable insanity. (Fam. C. 2310). Irreconcilable differences are grounds determined by court to be substantial reasons for not continuing marriage and which make it appear that marriage should be dissolved. (Fam. C. 2311). Dissolution of marriage on grounds of incurable insanity requires proof on competent medical or psychiatric testimony, that insane spouse was at time petition was filed, and remains, incurably insane. (Fam. C. 2312, 2313, 2332).

Residence Requirements.—Petitioner or respondent must have been resident of state for six months, and of county for three months, next preceding commencement of action. (Fam. C. 2320, 2321).

In proceedings for legal separation in which neither party, at time such proceeding was commenced, has complied with residence requirements of Fam. C. 2320, 2321, either party may upon so complying, amend his pleading to request that judgment decreeing dissolution of marriage be entered and date of filing of such amended pleading shall be deemed to be date of commencement of proceeding for dissolution of marriage for purposes of residence requirement only. (Fam. C. 2320, 2321).

Jurisdiction.—Court has jurisdiction to inquire into and render any judgment and make orders that are appropriate concerning status of marriage, custody and support of minor children of marriage, including children born after initial petition or final decree of dissolution, and children for whom support is authorized under Fam. C. 3910, 4400-01, support of either party, settlement of property rights and awarding attorney's fees and costs. (Fam. C. 200, 2010, 2060). If either party has minor child whose welfare might be affected, or if controversy involves domestic violence whether either party has minor child, case may be transferred to conciliation court presided over by superior court judge, who will endeavor to effect reconciliation Fam. C. 1830 et seq.). See category Courts and Legislature, topic Courts, subhead Superior Courts, catchline Family Conciliation Court.

See note at head of Digest as to 1998 legislation covered.

See Topical Index in front part of this volume.

DISSOLUTION OF MARRIAGE . . . *continued*

Process.—Dissolution of marriage action commenced by personal service of summons and petition as in other cases. Service may be made by publication in proper cases. See category Civil Actions and Procedure, topic Process.

Petition must contain certain factual data, including date and place of marriage, date of separation, years from marriage to separation, number of children of marriage, age and birthdate of each minor child and social security numbers of both spouses if available. (Fam. C. 2330).

Practice.—No decree of dissolution or of legal separation can be granted upon default of one of parties or upon finding of referee. Court must in addition to any finding by referee require proof of alleged grounds by testimony or affidavit. In all cases involving minor children each affidavit or offer of proof shall include estimate of monthly income of each party. If no knowledge of estimated income, declarant or affiant shall state why he or she has no knowledge. In cases where there is community estate, each affidavit or offer of proof shall include estimate of value of assets and debts of declarant or affiant proposed be distributed to each party. (Fam. C. 2336).

In any proceeding for legal separation or dissolution of marriage, evidence of misconduct is inadmissible except as otherwise provided by statute. (Fam. C. 2335).

Final Judgment.—If court determines that dissolution ought to be granted, judgment shall be entered declaring that parties are entitled to have their marriage dissolved. (Fam. C. 2338). Where judgment of dissolution or nullity of marriage or legal separation of parties is to be granted upon default, signature of defaulting spouse shall be notarized and clerk shall give notice of entry of judgment to each party. No judgment shall be final until six months have expired from date of service of copy of summons and petition or date of appearance of respondent, whichever occurs first. However, court may extend six-month period for good cause shown. Decree declaring marriage dissolved shall specify date on which decree becomes finally effective for purpose of terminating marriage relationship of parties. If appeal is taken from judgment or motion for new trial is made, dissolution of marriage shall not become final until such motion or appeal has been finally disposed of. Filing of appeal or motion for new trial shall not stay effect of judgment insofar as it relates to dissolution of marriage status unless appealing party in notice of appeal or motion for new trial specifies objection to termination of marriage status. (Fam. C. 2339-44).

Summary Procedure.—Available to couples filing joint petition and attesting certain conditions have been met. (Fam. C. 2400-05).

Remarriage.—No restrictions on remarriage of either party after final judgment.

Support of Insane Spouse.—Dissolution of marriage on ground of incurable insanity does not relieve spouse obtaining such dissolution of any obligation imposed by law for support of incurably insane spouse and court may make such order for support or require a bond therefor as circumstances require. (Fam. C. 2312-13, 2332).

Change of Wife's Name.—Whether or not so requested in petition, except in action for legal separation, court must upon request of wife, restore her birth name or former name; fraud is only basis for denial. (C. C. P. 1279.6; Fam. C. 2080-82).

Legal Separation.—Either spouse may maintain an action for legal separation and a court may render a judgment decreeing legal separation with consent of both parties or where one party has not made a general appearance. (Fam. C. 2333-34, 2345, 2347). Court has jurisdiction to inquire into and render such judgments and make such orders as are appropriate concerning status of marriage, custody and support of minor children of marriage, including children born after initial petition or final decree of dissolution, and support of children for whom support may be ordered, support of either party, settlement of property rights and awarding of attorneys' fees and costs. (Fam. C. 200, 2010).

Grounds for legal separation are same as for dissolution of marriage (see subhead Grounds, supra).

Support of Children.—Both parents have equal statutory duty to support and educate minor children. (Fam. C. 3900). This support obligation extends to earlier of age 19 or completion of 12th grade if unmarried child is not self-supporting and goes to school full time. (Fam. C. 3901). If support of minor child is at issue, court may order either or both parents to pay any amount necessary for support, maintenance and education of child. (Fam. C. 3028, 3651-53, 4001, 4007, 4009, 4011-13). State must inform mother of right to retroactive child support. (H. & S.C. 10125.6). Comprehensive statutory scheme establishes mandatory minimum child support level and procedures for determining parents' contribution. (Fam. C. 4050 et seq.). Support payments have priority over debts to creditors. Parties required to provide such support may for good cause be required to give reasonable security therefor. Any order for child support may be modified or revoked as court may deem necessary, except as to amounts accrued prior to filing motion to amend. (Fam. C. 3028, 3653, 4001, 4007, 4009, 4011-13). In any order issued on or after July 1, 1990 which establishes or modifies support, court shall order obligor to assign to obligee that portion of earnings due or to be due in future as will be sufficient to pay support order and shall include amount to be paid toward liquidation of arrearage or past due support amount. Obligee alleging arrearages must specify amount. (Fam. C. 5208, 5230-31, 5260). Court may stay such assignment only upon finding of good cause. (Fam. C. 5208, 5230-31, 5260). Where support order issued or modified before July 1, 1990 does not include wage assignment, obligee may seek order by application, notice of motion or order to show cause, or pursuant to Fam. C. 5208, 5230-31, 5260. (Fam. C. 5208, 5250, 5253). Order for wage assignment is binding on any existing or future employers of obligor who have been served with copy of such order. (Fam. C. 5231, 5281, 5282). Such assignment made pursuant to court order has priority over any attachment, execution, or other assignment, as specified in C.C.P. 706.031. (Fam. C. 5238, 5234).

Court may require record of employment search from parent who attributes default on support order to unemployment. (Fam. C. 4505). State professional licensing agencies, including Dept. of Motor Vehicles, precluded from issuing or renewing license of parent in violation of child support orders. (Welf. & Inst. C. 11350.6).

Custody of Children.—Uniform Child Custody Jurisdiction and Enforcement Act adopted. (Fam. C. 3, 3401). During pendency of actions for dissolution or nullity of marriage, legal separation or custody or visitation, or at any time thereafter, court may issue orders for custody of minor child of marriage, as may seem necessary or proper. Court has wide discretion to award custody according to best interests of child. Parents have fundamental right to custody of their children, and nonparent will not be awarded custody in preference to parent without dual findings that award of custody to parent would be detrimental to child and that particular custody award required to serve best interests of child. (Fam. C. 3020-22, 3040, 3043). Such order may be modified or revoked thereafter as natural rights of parties and best interests of child require. (Fam. C. 3120).

Upon application of either parent joint custody may be ordered in discretion of court. "Joint custody" means joint physical custody and joint legal custody, but court may specify sole physical custody or sole legal custody as well. (Fam. C. 3002-04, 3006-07, 3024-25, 3080-89). Court must grant reasonable visitation rights to parents unless detrimental to child and may grant such rights to stepparents and in some circumstances to other family members. Where visitation ordered in case involving domestic violence and where protective or restraining order issued, visitation order must specify time, day, place and manner of child's transfer so as to limit child's exposure to domestic conflict or violence. (Fam. C. 3100-03). Court may not award physical or legal custody or unsupervised visitation to person required to be registered as sex offender where victim was minor unless no risk to child. Court may not award custody or visitation to person convicted of rape under Pen. C. 261 if child was conceived as result of the rape. (Fam. C. 3030). Custodial parent has right to change child's residence but may be ordered to notify other parent of plan to move child. (Fam. C. 3024, 7501).

Court may appoint private counsel to represent interests of minor child, determine counsel's compensation and order it paid by parents in proportions deemed just. (Fam. C. 3150-53).

Temporary Spousal and Child Support.—During pendency of any proceeding for legal separation or dissolution of marriage, court may order either spouse to pay any amounts necessary for support and maintenance of other spouse and for support, maintenance and education of children. (Fam. C. 200, 3600-04). Order may be modified or revoked prospectively. (Fam. C. 3680 et seq.).

Permanent Support of Spouse.—In any judgment decreeing dissolution of marriage or legal separation, court may order either party to pay for support of other party any amount and for such period of time as court may deem just and reasonable based on standard of living established during marriage having regard for circumstances of respective parties, including duration of marriage, ability to pay, tax consequences, ability of supported spouse to engage in gainful employment without interfering with interests of children of parties in custody of such spouse, balance of hardships to each party, and goal that supported party shall be self-supporting within reasonable period of time. (Fam. C. 3651, 3653-54, 4320, 4330-37, 4339). Except as otherwise agreed by parties in writing, there shall be rebuttable presumption, affecting burden of proof, of decreased need for support if supported party is cohabiting with person of opposite sex. Upon finding circumstances have changed, court may modify payment of support. (Fam. C. 4323). Order for support may be modified prospectively from date notice of motion is filed, or date of order to show cause. (Fam. C. 3651, 3653-54, 4320, 4330-37, 4339). Except as otherwise agreed by parties in writing, obligation of any party under order or judgment for support and maintenance of other party terminates upon death of either party or upon remarriage of obligee. (Fam. C. 3651, 3653-54, 4320, 4330-37, 4339). Court ordered support payments terminate upon happening of specified contingencies. Failure of supported party to notify other party of happening of contingency renders supported party liable to refund any and all monies received prior to happening of contingency. (Fam. C. 3651, 3653-54, 4320, 4330-47, 4339). Court ordered support payments terminate at end of specified period and cannot be extended unless jurisdiction is retained in original order. (Fam. C. 3651, 3653-54, 4320, 4330-37, 4339). Order for support may include necessary costs and expenses of retraining or education. (Fam. C. 3651, 3653-54, 4320, 4330-37, 4339). Jurisdiction to extend support is retained if support order permits modification. (171 C.A.3d 907, 217 C. Rptr. 589).

In enforcement of its decree, judgment, or order of support, court must first resort to earnings, income, or accumulations of either spouse, while living separate and apart from other spouse, which would have been community property if spouse had not been living separate and apart; then community property; then quasi-community property; and finally separate property of spouse ordered to make support payments. (Fam. C. 4338).

Revocation of Spousal Support.—Except as otherwise agreed to by parties in writing, there shall be rebuttable presumption of decreased need for support if supported spouse is cohabiting with person of opposite sex. If court finds changed circumstance, it may modify support payment. (Fam. C. 4323).

Division of Property of Spouses.—Community property jurisdiction. Parties to dissolution and separation proceedings must make complete preliminary and final written disclosure of all assets and liabilities unless parties stipulate to waiver of such disclosure. (Fam. C. 2100, 2104-07). Except upon written agreement by parties or stipulation in open court, court must, in its judgment decreeing dissolution, or upon judgment decreeing legal separation, or at later time if jurisdiction is expressly reserved, divide equally, community and quasi-community property, but court not precluded from awarding particular asset to one party as court deems proper to effect substantially equal division of property, or by way of additional award or offset against existing property where one spouse deliberately misappropriated community or quasi-community property of other spouse. Community property personal injury damages shall be assigned to party suffering injuries unless otherwise indicated by economic condition and needs of each party, time elapsed since recovery of damages, and other facts. (Fam. C. 780, 2550-53, 2600-04, 2620-27). Property rights determined in final judgment may in certain circumstances be reconsidered upon such terms as may be just. (C.C.P. 473). Voluntary written agreement regarding property or support should be incorporated into judgment, or court ordered enforcement may be unavailable.

See note at head of Digest as to 1998 legislation covered.

See Topical Index in front part of this volume.

CA – 49

DISSOLUTION OF MARRIAGE . . . *continued*

All real property situated in California, and personal property wherever situated, acquired during marriage which is not separate property, is community property. (Fam. C. 700, 760, 803). Upon dissolution or legal separation, property acquired in joint form, including tenancy in common, joint tenancy and tenancy by entirety is presumed to be community property. Presumption may be rebutted by certain written evidence that it is separate property. (Fam. C. 2581).

Presumption that property acquired during marriage is community property is inapplicable to property, legal and equitable, which is held by person at time of his death, if marriage of party was dissolved more than four years prior to such death. (Fam. C. 802).

Transmutation.—Married persons may agree to transmute separate or community property with or without consideration, so long as it is in writing and expressly declares consent of spouse whose interest is adversely affected. Third parties are not affected by transmutation of real property without notice unless recorded. Gifts of tangible personal property are excepted unless of substantial value. Requirement of writing only applies to transmutations after Jan. 1, 1985. (Fam. C. 850, 852).

Attorneys' Fees and Costs.—Court may order any nongovernmental party to pay attorneys' fees and costs of maintaining or defending proceeding. (Fam. C. 2030). Either party may encumber his or her interest in community property to pay reasonable attorneys' fees and costs (Fam. C. 2033), and court may order such fees and costs paid directly to attorney entitled thereto (Fam. C. 272).

Legal separation agreements in writing are valid and may divide property and make provision for support of either party and/or children during separation or upon dissolution of marriage. (Fam. C. 1620, 3580).

Annulment of Marriage.—See topic Marriage.

Foreign Divorces.—California has adopted Uniform Divorce Recognition Act. (Fam. C. 3, 2090-93). Dissolution of marriage obtained in another jurisdiction is of no force and effect if both parties to marriage were domiciled in California at time proceeding was commenced. (Fam. C. 2091). Prima facie evidence that party was domiciled in California includes proof that party was domiciled in California within 12 months prior to commencement of dissolution proceeding and within 18 months after departure, or that such person maintained residence in California. (Fam. C. 3).

DIVORCE:

See topic Dissolution of Marriage.

GUARDIAN AND WARD:

Guardianships available for minors, conservatorship utilized for adults. Comprehensive statute scheme covers both. (Prob. C. 1400 et seq.). Limited conservatorship for developmentally disabled adults also available. (Prob. C. 1801[d]).

Jurisdiction and Venue.—Superior court of county in which minor or conservatee resides or such other county as may be in best interests of proposed ward or conservatee may appoint guardian or conservator of person and/or estate. (Prob. C. 2201). If proceedings for guardianship or conservatorship are instituted in more than one county, guardianship or conservatorship first granted shall govern and all other proceedings shall be dismissed. (Prob. C. 2203).

Selection of Guardian.—Parent may nominate guardian of person or estate by will or otherwise if other parent consents in writing, is dead, lacks legal capacity to consent, or consent would not be required for adoption. (Prob. C. 1500). Court shall appoint person nominated unless court determines nominee is unsuitable. (Prob. C. 1514). Petition for appointment of guardian may be filed by relative of minor or minor if 12 years of age or older. (Prob. C. 1510). Investigation made by court investigator; report filed with court. (Prob. C. 1513).

Selection of Conservator.—Proposed conservatee may nominate conservator if of sufficient capacity to form intelligent preference. Court shall appoint nominee absent finding that nominee not in best interests of conservatee. (Prob. C. 1810). Court guided by best interests of proposed conservatee. (Prob. C. 1812). Preference to be given as follows: (1) Spouse or nominee of spouse, (2) adult child or child's nominee, (3) parent or nominee of parent, (4) brother or sister or nominee of same, and (5) any other person or entity eligible. Nominees of persons with preference subordinate to other persons in same class. (Prob. C. 1812). Appointment of successor conservator by court after noticed hearing. Conservatee entitled to appear personally or present report by court investigator of conservatee's objections. (Prob. C. 2680 et seq.).

Eligibility.—Any competent person, including nonresident, may be appointed guardian or conservator of estate or person (Prob. C. 2100 et seq.); nonprofit charitable California corporation authorized by articles to act as guardian or conservator in California which has been providing care to proposed ward, under certain circumstances may be appointed guardian or conservator of estate. (Prob. C. 2104). When two joint conservators, both must concur in exercise of power, when more than two, majority must concur. (Prob. C. 2105).

Appointment of Guardian or Conservator.—Temporary guardianships and conservatorships available in expedited proceedings upon showing of good cause for such appointment. (Prob. C. 2250). Legal counsel may be appointed by court for ward, proposed ward, conservatee, or proposed conservatee if person not otherwise represented and appointment would be helpful. (Prob. C. 1470).

Qualifications.—Guardian or conservator must take oath to perform duties of office and, with certain exceptions, give bond for performance as fixed by court. (Prob. C. 2300, 2320). Additional bond normally required on sale or mortgage of real property. (Prob. C. 2330). Applications can be made for reduction of bond or for furnishing of new security. (Prob. C. 2329, 2330).

Inventory and Accounts.—Guardian and conservator must return to court verified inventory of estate of ward within 90 days after appointment (Prob. C. 2610) and render verified account one year after appointment and thereafter as directed by court but at least biennially (Prob. C. 2620). With smaller estates, guardian or conservator may, upon meeting certain conditions, file affidavit that all income, if not retained, was spent for benefit of ward or conservatee in lieu of regular accounting. (Prob. C. 2628). Court authorized to require spouse of conservatee to apply community property to support and maintenance of conservatee. (Prob. C. 3080 et seq.).

Powers and duties of guardians and conservators as to person of ward and conservatee include care, custody, control and education. (Prob. C. 2350 et seq.). Guardians or conservators of estate must pay all debts of their wards or conservatees, collect all claims, represent in all actions and otherwise manage estate of their ward or conservatee. (Prob. C. 2400 et seq.). Income from estate used for support, maintenance, and education of ward or conservatee. (Prob. C. 2420). Court authorized to permit transfers of property as gifts, releases of conservatee's power of appointment, right to revoke revocable trust, and other such transfers in same manner as if conservatee or ward had capacity to act. Procedure outlined to permit exercise of "substituted judgment" in Prob. C. 2580 et seq. Action can be initiated by conservator or other interested person. Court also has authority to grant certain delineated extraordinary powers to guardian or conservator if in best interests of ward or conservatee. (Prob. C. 2590, 2570-74).

Investments governed by Prob. C. 2570.

Securities in Name of Nominee.—See category Estates and Trusts, topic Trusts, subhead Securities in Name of Nominee.

Gifts to Minors.—See topic Infants.

Real property may be sold, encumbered, or leased when in best interests of estate, but only after authorization by court. (Prob. C. 2540 et seq.).

Liabilities.—Relationship of guardian and ward and conservator and conservatee is fiduciary relationship, and is governed by law of trusts. (Prob. C. 2101). Guardian or conservator who breaches fiduciary duty is chargeable with various liabilities depending on circumstances. (Prob. C. 2401.3, 2401.5). Guardian can be removed for mismanagement, failure to perform duties, felony conviction, adverse interest and other causes. (Prob. C. 2650). Settlement of guardian's current account is not final as between guardian and ward. (3 C.2d 225, 44 P.2d 562). Action against sureties on bond must be commenced within four years of removal, discharge or surcharging of guardian or conservator and in no event later than six years after date of judgment or order on which action is based. (Prob. C. 2333). Upon reaching majority, ward may settle accounts with guardian and give valid release if obtained fairly; otherwise guardian is not entitled to discharge until one year after ward reaches majority. (Prob. C. 2627).

Termination.—Guardianship of person or estate terminates when ward attains majority or dies. Guardianship of person terminates on adoption or emancipation of ward under Fam. C. 7002. (Prob. C. 1600). Upon petition, court may terminate guardianship if no longer necessary or in best interests of ward. (Prob. C. 1601). Conservatorship terminated only by death of conservatee or by order of court. (Prob. C. 1860).

Legal Capacity.—Appointment of conservator of estate is adjudication that conservatee lacks legal capacity to enter transactions that obligate conservatorship estate. (Prob. C. 1872). Court may order that conservatee is authorized to enter into certain transactions. (Prob. C. 1873). Person who enters transaction which affects real property of conservatorship estate acting in good faith and for valuable consideration and without knowledge of conservatorship, is not affected by conservatorship unless notice of same recorded in county where real property located prior to transaction. (Prob. C. 1875). Unless adjudged to lack capacity to give informed consent for medical treatment, conservatee may consent to receive medical treatment. If court concludes conservatee lacks capacity to give informed consent, conservator's consent is sufficient except in certain exceptional situations. (Cf. Prob. C. 2354-2357). Conservatorship does not affect capacity of conservatee to marry, although court may by order determine to contrary. (Prob. C. 1900, 1901). Ward's capacity, see topic Infants.

Unless otherwise ordered by court, wages and salaries earned by ward and conservatee during continuance of guardianship or conservatorship are to be paid to ward or conservatee and are not part of estate. (Prob. C. 2601).

Conservatee of limited conservatorship retains all legal and civil rights not removed by court. (Prob. C. 2351, 2351.5).

Rights and Restrictions.—No ward or conservatee can be placed in mental health treatment facility against his or her will without compliance with provisions of Lanterman-Petris-Short Act. (Welf. & Inst. C. 5000 et seq.). No experimental drugs may be given or convulsive treatment performed on ward or conservatee under authority of provisions of this division. No minor can be sterilized under authority of this division. (Prob. C. 2356).

Other Protective Proceedings.—Up to $5,000, or property not exceeding that value, may be paid to parent of minor entitled to custody, to be held until majority, without requiring appointment of guardian if parent verifies in writing that total estate of minor excluding "custodial property" does not exceed $5,000. (Prob. C. 3400 et seq.).

When minor has disputed claim for damages, money or other property and does not have guardian, parent with custody has right to compromise or settle minor's claim with approval of superior court. If parents live together, then either one may compromise or settle such claims with court's approval. (Prob. C. 3500).

Foreign Guardians or Conservators.—Nonresident with duly appointed guardian, conservator, or comparable fiduciary in place of residence may petition to have property of nonresident removed from this state to place of residence, when no petition for guardianship or conservatorship is pending or contemplated in this state. If court determines removal of property will not impair rights of creditors or nonresident, it shall grant leave to remove, absent showing of good cause to contrary. (Prob. C. 3800 et seq.).

Uniform Fiduciaries Act has not been adopted.

Uniform Simplification of Fiduciary Security Transfers Act repealed by Uniform Commercial Code. (Com'l. C. 8402-8404, 8115). See category Business Regulation and Commerce, topic Commercial Code.

See note at head of Digest as to 1998 legislation covered.

See Topical Index in front part of this volume.

CA – 50

HUSBAND AND WIFE:

Husband and wife may hold property as joint tenants, tenants in common, or as community property. (Fam. C. 750).

Separate Property.—Neither husband nor wife has any interest in separate property of other (Fam. C. 752), but neither can be excluded from other's dwelling (Fam. C. 753), except, in divorce, annulment or separate maintenance proceedings, upon court order (Fam. C. 754).

As to what constitutes separate property as distinguished from community property, see infra subhead Community Property System.

Contracts.—Either spouse may enter into any engagement or transaction with other, or with any other person, respecting property, which either might if unmarried. (Fam. C. 721). But husband and wife cannot, by any contract, alter their legal relations, except as to property (Fam. C. 1620), and except that they may agree, in writing, to immediate separation, and make provision for support of either of them and of their children during such separation (Fam. C. 3580).

Married woman may become bound as surety for any person, including her husband. (26 C.A. 589, 147 P. 607).

Uniform Premarital Agreement Act adopted. (Fam. C. 1600-1617).

Liability for Debts of Spouses.—Separate property of spouse is liable for that spouse's debts contracted before or during marriage. (Fam. C. 913). However, separate property of either spouse is liable for debts contracted by either spouse for necessaries of life. (Fam. C. 914).

Neither separate property nor earnings after marriage of spouse is liable for debts of other spouse contracted before marriage. (Fam. C. 910, 911, 913).

Joinder or consent of spouse to encumbrance of community property does not subject separate property to liability unless spouse also incurred debt. (Fam. C. 913[b][2]).

Liability for Torts.—Married person not liable for tort of other spouse except where liable if marriage did not exist. If liability of married person arises from activity performed for benefit of community, liability is first satisfied from community estate and second from married person's separate property. Otherwise, liability is first satisfied from married person's separate property and second from community estate. (Fam. C. 1000).

Actions.—Married person may sue or be sued without his or her spouse being joined as party. (C. C. P. 370). If husband and wife are sued together, each may defend his or her own right, and if other spouse neglects to defend, may defend other's right also. (C. C. P. 371). Either spouse may sue other for personal torts, intentional or negligent, and may sue other to recover separate property appropriated by other. (58 C.2d 683, 26 C. Rptr. 97, 376 P.2d 65; 58 C.2d 692, 26 C. Rptr. 102, 376 P.2d 70).

Agency.—Either spouse may act as attorney in fact for other.

Desertion and Nonsupport.—Spouse is not liable for other spouse's support when other spouse by agreement lives separately, unless such support is stipulated in agreement. (Fam. C. 4302). Spouse must support other spouse while they are living together out of spouse's separate property when there is no community or quasi-community property. (Fam. C. 4301).

Uniform Interstate Family Support Act provides civil and criminal procedure for enforcement of duties of support where more than one state is concerned. (Fam. C. 4900-4976). Court jurisdiction is vested in superior court. (Fam. C. 200). Uniform Civil Liability for Support Act is in effect. However, sections under that title have been recast in Family Code with only definitions from former Civil Code §241 (definitions of state, obligor, obligee, child and parent) omitted. (See Fam. C. 200, 3550, 3551, 3554, 3651, 4000, 4002, 4005, 4300, 4303, 4320, 4400, 4402, 4404, 4405.)

Separation.—Earnings and accumulations of each spouse after separation are separate property of that spouse. (Fam. C. 771). Debts incurred after separation and unrelated to community are also separate. (74 C.A.3d 591, 600, 141 C. Rptr. 597).

Community Property System.—All property owned by either spouse before marriage, and that acquired afterwards by gift, bequest, devise or descent, with rents, issues and profits thereof, is separate property and may be conveyed without consent of other spouse. (Fam. C. 770). Personal injury damages is separate property, in certain cases. (Fam. C. 781). All other real property situated in this state and all other personal property wherever situated acquired during marriage by married person while domiciled in this state and property held in trust pursuant to §761 is community property. All other real property situated in this state and all other personal property wherever situated acquired during marriage by married person while domiciled in this state is community property. (Fam. C. 760). Unless trust instrument or instrument of transfer expressly provides otherwise, community property that is transferred in trust remains community property during marriage if trust provides that it is revocable as to that property during marriage. This section applies to transfers made before, on, or after July 1, 1987. (Fam. C. 761). Exceptions to this rule are that earnings of wife which husband has given or relinquished to her (100 C. 276, 34 P. 775) and earnings of spouse and of children living with or in custody of that spouse while living separate from other spouse are separate property of that spouse (Fam. C. 771). After judgment decreeing legal separation, earnings and accumulations of each party are separate property of acquiring party. (Fam. C. 772).

Quasi-Community Property.—All real and personal property wherever situated heretofore or hereafter acquired (1) by either spouse while domiciled elsewhere which would have been community property if acquiring spouse had been domiciled in state, or (2) in exchange for real or personal property wherever situated, which would have been community property if acquiring spouse had been domiciled in state, is quasi-community property. (Fam. C. 125).

Joint Tenancy.—Property taken in names of husband and wife as joint tenants is not ordinarily community property (214 C. 767, 7 P.2d 1003), but may be shown to be such in accordance with intention of parties (6 C.A.3d 248, 85 C. Rptr. 742). Joint tenancy in dissolution proceeding is presumed to be community property (Fam. C. 2581), but separate property contributions are reimbursed under certain circumstances (Fam. C. 2640).

Transmutation.—Beginning Jan. 1, 1985, transfers from separate to community and community to separate must be in writing. (Fam. C. 850).

Respective interests of husband and wife in community property during continuance of marriage relations are present, existing and equal interests. (Fam. C. 751).

Presumptions as to Character of Property.—There is prima facie presumption that property owned by husband or wife is community property, but whenever any property is acquired prior to Jan. 1, 1975, by married woman by instrument in writing presumption is that same is her separate property, and if so acquired by such married woman and any other person presumption is that she takes part acquired by her as tenant in common, unless different intention is expressed in instrument; except that when any of such property is acquired by husband and wife by instrument in which they are described as husband and wife, presumption is that such property is community property, unless different intention is expressed in instrument. These presumptions are conclusive in favor of purchaser or encumbrancer in good faith and for valuable consideration. (Fam. C. 760, 803). Property owned at death by person whose marriage was dissolved more than four years prior thereto is not presumed to be community property. (Fam. C. 802).

Management, Control and Disposition of Community Personalty.—Either spouse has management and control of community personal property, with like power of disposition, other than testamentary, as spouse has of his or her separate estate; however, a spouse cannot give away such property or sell, convey, or encumber furniture, furnishings, or fittings of home, or clothing or wearing apparel of other spouse or minor children that is community, without written consent of other spouse. Spouse operating or managing business or interest in business which is community property has primary management and control of said business or interest. Managing spouse may act alone in all transactions but must give prior written notice to other spouse of transaction involving substantially all personal property used in business, unless notice is otherwise prohibited by law. (Fam. C. 1100).

Management, Control and Disposition of Community Realty.—Either spouse has management and control of community real property, but both spouses must join in executing any instrument by which such community real property or any interest therein is leased for longer period than one year; or is sold, conveyed, or encumbered; provided, however, that sole lease, contract, mortgage or deed of husband, holding record title to community real property, to lessee, purchaser or encumbrancer, in good faith without knowledge of marriage relation shall be presumed to be valid if executed before Jan. 1, 1975, and that sole lease, contract, mortgage, or deed of either spouse, holding record title to community real property to a lessee, purchaser, or encumbrancer, in good faith without knowledge of marriage relation, shall be presumed to be valid if executed on or after Jan. 1, 1975. No action to avoid such instrument shall be commenced after expiration of one year from filing for record of such instrument in recorder's office in county in which land is situated. (Fam. C. 1102).

On death of either husband or wife one half of community property and quasi-community property belongs to surviving spouse and other half is subject to testamentary disposition of decedent, and in absence of such disposition goes to surviving spouse. (Prob. C. 100, 101, 6101, 6401[a]and [b]).

On or after Jan. 1, 1985, when either husband or wife dies intestate, or dies testate leaving all or part of property to surviving spouse, such property passes to surviving spouse without probate or administration; however, surviving spouse may elect that interest of deceased spouse, or interests of both spouses, be probated or administered. (Prob. C. 13500, 13502). If probate is not elected, procedures exist for confirmation of spouse's ownership of property passing from deceased spouse. (Prob. C. 13650). Unless interests of both spouses are probated or administered, surviving spouse may be personally liable for debts of deceased spouse chargeable against community property; such liability is limited to value of community property which did not pass through probate or administration. (Prob. C. 13550-52). For these purposes, procedures exist for determining community property and apportioning debts. (Prob. C. 13650, 11440-42).

See also category Civil Actions and Procedure, topic Damages, subhead Loss of Consortium.

INFANTS:

Age of majority is 18. (Fam. C. 6502).

Emancipation.—Under Emancipation of Minors Act (Fam. C. 7000-7110), emancipated minor now defined as any person under age of 18 who: (1) Has entered valid marriage, whether or not marriage subsequently terminated by dissolution; or (2) is on active duty with any of Armed Forces; or (3) received declaration of emancipation pursuant to Fam. C. 7122. (Fam. C. 7002). Minor may petition Superior Court of county of residence or where temporarily domiciled for declaration of emancipation by setting forth in verified petition facts showing qualification for emancipation. (Fam. C. 7120). Court is required to sustain petition when it finds that minor is or has been married or in Armed Forces. (Fam. C. 7002). Where petition based solely upon minor living apart from parents or legal guardian and minor is at least 14 years of age and otherwise qualified under Fam. C. 7120, court must sustain petition unless emancipation contrary to interest of minor. (Fam. C. 7122[a]). Rescission of declaration available in some instances. (Fam. C. 7130, 7132).

Emancipated minor treated as adult for purposes of consent to medical treatment, right to contract, right to sue or be sued, right to earnings, right to buy, sell and transfer real and personal property interests, right to make gifts, wills, and trusts, and other delineated rights. (Fam. C. 7050).

Disabilities.—Minor cannot give delegation of power or make contract relating to real property or any interest therein, or relating to any personal property not in his immediate possession or control (Fam. C. 6701), but minor may make any other contract in same manner as adult, subject to his power of disaffirmance and subject to statutes relating to marriage and master and servant (Fam. C. 6700).

Disaffirmance of Contracts.—Minor cannot disaffirm otherwise valid contract to render artistic or creative services in entertainment field, or to render services as

INFANTS... *continued*
participant in professional sports, or contracts under which minor agrees to purchase, secure, sell, lease, license, or dispose of literary, dramatic, or musical property, where such contract has been approved by superior court in county where minor resides or is employed or in county in which any party to contract maintains its principal office in state. (Fam. C. 6750, 6751).

Minor cannot disaffirm otherwise valid contract to pay reasonable value of things necessary for his or his family's support, entered into by him when not under care of parent or guardian able to provide for him or them, if such things have actually been furnished to him or his family (Fam. C. 6712); nor can minor disaffirm obligation, otherwise valid, entered into by him under express authority or direction of statute (Fam. C. 6711).

Medical care to unemancipated woman for prevention or treatment of pregnancy (Fam. C. 6925) or for treatment or care of minor of age 12 or older for any infectious, contagious or communicable disease is not subject to disaffirmance (Fam. C. 6926). Consent of parent or court order required for abortion. (Fam. C. 6925).

Otherwise, general rule governs that minor may disaffirm either before his majority or within reasonable time thereafter or in case of his death, within that period, by his heirs or personal representatives. (Fam. C. 6710).

If, before minor has disaffirmed, goods he has sold have been transferred to innocent purchaser for value, minor cannot recover them from such innocent purchaser. (Fam. C. 6713).

Torts.—Minor civilly liable for wrong done by him but not liable for exemplary damages unless at time of act he was capable of knowing it was wrongful. (Fam. C. 6600). Parents and guardians are civilly liable for death, personal injury, property damage or defacement of property of another with paint or similar substance caused by willful misconduct of minor in their custody and control; such liability not to exceed $10,000 for each tort of minor. (C. C. 1714.1; see also, Educ. C. 48904; Govt. C. 53069.5).

Uniform Gifts to Minors Act has been repealed. Uniform Transfers to Minors Act adopted. Provides detailed method for lifetime gifts and gifts at death to custodian. Latest specified age for lifetime gifts is 21; latest specified age for gifts at death is 25; otherwise custodianship terminates at age 18. (Prob. C. 3900-3925).

Uniform Securities Ownership by Minors Act has not been adopted.

Actions.—Minor may enforce his rights by civil action or other legal proceeding in same manner as person of full age except that guardian must conduct same. (Fam. C. 6601).

Uniform Parentage Act, adopted with some omissions, abolishes incidents of illegitimacy and establishes legal equality of children without regard to marital status of parents. (Fam. C. 7600 et seq.).

Custody.—Mother and father (under presumptions of Fam. C. 7611) of unemancipated minor child are equally entitled to its custody, services and earnings. If either father or mother dead, or unable or refuse to take custody, or has abandoned his or her family, other is entitled to its custody, services and earnings. (Fam. C. 3010, 7500). No preference permitted to either parent because of parent's sex. (Fam. C. 3040). Joint physical and legal custody is preferred and presumed in best interest of child if parents agree. (Fam. C. 3080).

Authority of parent ceases: (1) On appointment, by court, of guardian of person of child; (2) on marriage of child; or (3) on its attaining majority. (Fam. C. 7505).

Action to have minor declared free from parental custody and control may be brought when minor abandoned by parent(s), when minor subjected to cruel treatment or neglect, and in certain cases of parental depravity, habitual use of alcohol or certain drugs, felony conviction, nonsupport of minor, mental illness or two-year foster home residence of minor. (Fam. C. 7820 et seq.). Mother of child may bring proceeding to declare father unfit to have custody or control of child if child was conceived as result of rape in violation of Pen. C. 261. (Fam. C. 7825).

If parent neglects to provide articles necessary for his child under his charge, according to his circumstances, third person may in good faith supply such necessaries, and recover reasonable value thereof from parent. (Fam. C. 207).

Parents have equal responsibility to support child in manner suitable to child's circumstances. (Fam. C. 3900). Parents of minor child criminally liable for its nonsupport. (P.C. 270).

Adoption.—See topic Adoption.

Child Restraint Systems.—See category Transportation, topic Motor Vehicles.

MARRIAGE:

Statutes fix no age under which persons may not lawfully marry. (Fam. C. 301-303).

Consent Required.—Properly verified written consent of parent or guardian, along with Superior Court order granting permission, must be filed with clerk issuing license where applicant is under 18. (Fam. C. 302). Court may also order premarital counseling where applicant is under 18. (Fam. C. 304).

License must be secured from county clerk (Fam. C. 350), and shall not be granted when either party lacks capacity to enter into valid marriage, or is under influence of intoxicating liquor or narcotic drugs at time of making application for license. (Fam. C. 352). License expires 90 days after its issuance. (Fam. C. 356).

When unmarried man and unmarried woman, not minors, have been living together as man and wife they may, without health certificate, be married upon issuance of appropriate authorization. (Fam. C. 500, 501). Person solemnizing marriage must authenticate marriage certificate for parties and file it with county clerk within 30 days of ceremony. (Fam. C. 506). No other record is necessary; certificate remains confidential and date of marriage will not be disclosed except upon order of court issued upon showing of good cause. (Fam. C. 511).

Solemnization and consent are necessary to constitute marriage. (Fam. C. 300). Marriage may be solemnized by any judge, retired judge, judge who has resigned from office, commissioner or assistant commissioner of court of record or justice court, commissioners or retired commissioners of civil marriages, federal judge or magistrate, or by any priest, minister or rabbi of any denomination of age of 18 years or older (Fam. C. 400, 401).

Reports of Marriages.—Person solemnizing marriage must file license and certificate showing date, place, witnesses, and official position with county recorder within 30 days after marriage, and on request give either party marriage certificate. (Fam. C. 422-424). Also certificate of registry setting forth certain information in nature of vital statistics, such as age, former marriages, etc., obtained from county clerk and presented to person performing ceremony, must be filed by him with county recorder within 30 days after ceremony. (Fam. C. 359).

Record.—See category Documents and Records, topic Records, subhead Vital Statistics.

Common law marriage cannot be contracted within California. (Fam. C. 300). Out of state common law marriage recognized if valid in state where contracted. (Fam. C. 308; 136 C.A.3d 487, 186 C. Rptr. 321; 28 C. 2d 276, 169 P.2d 633).

Proxy marriages are not authorized.

Marriages by written contract are not authorized. (Fam. C. 300).

Prohibited Marriages.—Between: Parent and child; ancestor and descendant of every degree; brother and sister, including half-blood; uncle and niece or aunt and nephew whether relationship legitimate or illegitimate. All such marriages are incestuous and are void. (Fam. C. 2200). Bigamous marriages are void. (Fam. C. 2201).

Annulment.—Marriage is voidable and may be adjudged nullity on several grounds. (Fam. C. 2210).

Action to obtain decree of nullity of marriage, for causes mentioned in Fam. C. 2210 must be commenced within certain period and by certain parties as per Fam. C. 2211. Attorney's fees and costs may be granted to innocent party. (Fam. C. 2255).

Children.—Uniform Parentage Act adopted, providing procedures to establish parent-child relationship without regard to distinctions based on legitimacy. (Fam. C. 7600 et seq.). Court may provide for custody, care, education, maintenance and support of minor children as may seem necessary and proper. (Fam. C. 2253, 3020 et seq.).

Foreign Marriages.—Marriages contracted outside of state and valid under laws of jurisdiction where contracted are valid in California. (Fam. C. 308).

MARRIED WOMEN:

See topics Husband and Wife, Marriage; categories Business Organizations, topic Corporations, subhead Transfer of Stock; Civil Actions and Procedure, topic Evidence, subhead Witnesses; Debtor and Creditor, topic Homesteads; Documents and Records, topic Acknowledgments; Estates and Trusts, topics Executors and Administrators, Wills; Property, topic Deeds.

INSURANCE

INSURANCE COMPANIES:

Pursuant to provisions of Insurance Code, insurance divided into following classes: Life, fire, marine, title, surety, disability, plate glass, liability, workmen's compensation, common carrier liability, boiler and machinery, burglary, credit, sprinkler, team and vehicle, automobile, mortgage, aircraft, mortgage guaranty, insolvency, legal insurance, miscellaneous. (Ins. C. 100). Code extensively defines and regulates business of each class.

Insurers subject to provisions of general corporation law (see category Business Regulation and Commerce, topic Corporations), except as otherwise provided in Insurance Code. (Ins. C. 1140).

Supervision.—Laws with respect to insurance companies and business of insurance are enforced by Insurance Commissioner, who has general power to require from every insurer full compliance with all provisions of Code. (Ins. C. 12921, 12926). Commissioner may procure injunction or issue stop orders against unfair or deceptive practices (Ins. C. 790-790.10) and may issue orders reasonably necessary to eliminate practices liable to render insurer insolvent (Ins. C. 1065.1). Commissioner may also take action against unauthorized insurers sending false advertising into California. (Ins. C. 1620.1-1620.7). Automobile liability insurer may not discriminate against applicant on basis of race, color, religion, national origin, ancestry, location within geographic area, occupation or inability to speak, read, write or comprehend English language except occupation may be considered condition or risk in determining rate or scope of coverage. (Ins. C. 11628[a]).

Commencing Nov. 8, 1989, and subject to exception for life insurance, title insurance, mortgage insurance and certain classes described in Ins. C. 1851, insurance rates must be approved by Insurance Commissioner prior to use (Ins. C. 1861.01[c]), and every insurer which desires to change its rates must file a complete rate application (Ins. C. 1861.05[b]). Rates may not be excessive, inadequate or unfairly discriminatory. (Ins. C. 1861.05[a]).

Certificate of Authority.—Insurer must obtain certificate of authority from Commissioner (Ins. C. 700), which certificate is for indefinite term, but may be revoked if insurer is in arrears for fees, licenses, taxes, assessments, fines, or penalties to state or to any county or city in state, or is otherwise in default for failure to comply with any laws of state regarding governmental control (Ins. C. 701). Unlawful transaction of business is punishable by fine, imprisonment, or both. (Ins. C. 700). Commissioner may suspend certificate of authority of insurer who conducts business fraudulently, does not carry out its contracts in good faith, or habitually compels claimants under policy, or liability judgment creditors of insured, to accept less than amount due or to resort to litigation to secure payment of amount due (Ins. C. 704) or if holder of more than 10% of insurer's shares or director or officer of insurer has been convicted of or pleaded guilty or nolo contendere to certain felonies (Ins. C. 704.5). Commissioner may, for cause, amend, alter, or revoke permit. (Ins. C. 843). Fee for initial application for certificate is $1,770 (Ins. C. 705.1); annual fee thereafter is $177 (Ins. C. 705).

See note at head of Digest as to 1998 legislation covered.

See Topical Index in front part of this volume.

CA – 52

INSURANCE COMPANIES ... *continued*

Certificate of authority will not be issued to insurer owned, operated or controlled by foreign governmental subdivision or agency unless insurer fulfills stated criteria (Ins. C. 699.5) nor, with specified exceptions, to unincorporated insurer (Ins. C. 699).

See also subhead Foreign Insurance Company, *infra*.

Reports.—Every insurer must file, on or before Mar. 1 of each year, statement exhibiting its condition and affairs for year ending preceding Dec. 31 (Ins. C. 900) and, on or before June 30, audited financial report covering same period (Ins. C. 900.2[a]). Filing fee is $118. (Ins. C. 900.5). Willful failure to file statement subjects insurer to penalty of $336 and additional penalty of $404 for each month thereafter that such insurer continues to transact business until statement is filed. (Ins. C. 924).

Policies.—Policy must specify parties between whom contract is made; property or life insured; interest of insured in property insured, if he is not absolute owner thereof; risks insured against, period during which insurance continues and either statement of premium or if exact premium then undeterminable, rates and basis on which final premium to be determined. (Ins. C. 381). Standard forms of policies for various kinds of insurance are prescribed by Insurance Code: fire, 2070-2083; county mutual fire, 6010-6021; long-term care, 10230-10235. Insurance Code also prescribes policy provisions for other kinds of insurance: life, 10127.10-10127.13, 10150-10176.3; group life, 10201-10225; funeral, 10244, 10248; group disability, 10270.6; family expense disability, 10270.8; disability, 10329-10369.12; fraternal benefit societies, 11060-11068; liability, 11580-11580.2; workers' compensation, 11651-11663; home protection, 12740-12743.

See also category Transportation, topic Motor Vehicles, subhead Insurance.

Cancellation.—Ins. C. 660-670, 673, 674-679.5 set forth specific requirements and procedure for cancellation or failure to renew automobile insurance policy, financed insurance policy and property insurance policy, respectively. Group health care service providers must notify subscribers in writing of policy cancellation. (H. & S.C. 1367.23; Ins. C. 10199.44, 10199.46). Cancellation of insurance other than workmen's compensation or automobile based on marital status, sex, race, color, religion, national origin or ancestry is forbidden. (Ins. C. 679.70-.73).

Payment of Proceeds.—Life insurance proceeds unpaid within 30 days after death of insured bears interest at rate not less than current rate on death proceeds left on deposit with insurer computed from date of death. (Ins. C. 10172.5).

Agents and Brokers.—With certain exceptions, no person may act as insurance agent, broker, solicitor or analyst until license secured from Commissioner. (Ins. C. 1631). Various license fees are provided. (Ins. C. 1750-1751.6, 1755, 1811, 1842).

Referrals.—It is unlawful for any insurance broker or agent to receive any benefit or consideration for referring insured to auto repair facility. (Ins. C. 753).

Stock.—Shares of stock of insurer must have specified par value. (Ins. C. 690).

Sale of Securities.—No insurer may sell any security of its own issue without permit from Commissioner, which, on proper application, is granted if Commissioner finds that (a) Proposed plan of business of applicant is not unfair, unjust or inequitable, (b) applicant intends to transact its business fairly and honestly and (c) securities applicant proposes to issue and methods to be used by it will not work fraud on purchaser thereof or upon its stockholders or policy holders. (Ins. C. 827, 839).

Any person who is officer or director of domestic insurer or owns more than 10% of stock must file statement of stock holdings with Commissioner, along with additional statements, whenever there is change in his stock holdings. (Ins. C. 1104.2). Short-swing profits by insiders are also governed by Insurance Code. (Ins. C. 1104.2-1105).

As to sale of securities generally, see category Business Regulation and Commerce, topic Securities.

Investments are governed by provisions of Insurance Code. (Ins. C. 1100-1254).

Foreign insurance company, before obtaining certificate of authority from Commissioner, must file certified copy of its last annual statement or verified financial statement (Ins. C. 706); certified copy of its articles of incorporation or, if no articles of incorporation, certified copy of law, charter or deed of settlement under which insurer is organized; certificate of officer having supervision of insurance in jurisdiction of its organization, stating that insurer is properly organized and has amount of capital stock or assets required by California Insurance Code (Ins. C. 708); certificate verified by chief officer, secretary, agent, or manager, setting forth (a) nature and character of business, (b) location of its principal office, (c) if not incorporated, names of ten persons who own largest interest or, if incorporated, names of all officers and persons by whom business is managed, (d) amount of actual capital to be employed therein (Ins. C. 709); and copy of written articles of agreement or association (Ins. C. 710). Admitted foreign insurer may become domestic insurer by designating its principal place of business in California. (Ins. C. 709.5).

Foreign insurers may be subject to retaliation because of laws of home jurisdiction. (Ins. C. 685-685.4). If so, they must file annual retaliatory tax information return by Apr. 1st of each year. (Rev. & Tax C. 12281).

Alien insurer must deposit securities in amount equal to minimum amount of paid-in capital required by this Code to transact class of business which insurer is transacting, which deposit must be of securities authorized for investment of assets of domestic incorporated insurers. (Ins. C. 1581-1583).

Process Agent.—Foreign corporations must: (a) designate agent for service of process (Ins. C. 1600); and (b) file agreement that, if at any time it leaves this state, ceases to transact business in this state, or is without agent for service of process in this state, service may be made on Insurance Commissioner and shall have same effect as if made on insurer (Ins. C. 1604).

Service of process may be made on nonadmitted foreign insurers, who have not appointed agent for service, by delivering copies thereof to Commissioner. (Ins. C. 1610-1611).

Premium Tax.—Insurance companies are subject to tax based on gross premiums received from business done in California, less returned premiums, at rate of 2.35% per annum, except rate applied to basis in respect to years 1982 to 1985 is 2.33% per annum. Special rates apply to premiums upon policies issued in connection with certain pension or profit-sharing plans. (Const., Art. XIII, §28; Rev. & Tax C. 12202, 12221). This tax is in lieu of all taxes except taxes on real estate, retaliatory exactions, ocean marine insurance or motor vehicle or vehicle registration license fees imposed by state. (Rev. & Tax C. 12204). Special provisions apply to surplus line brokers and in cases where title or marine insurance business is done. Person insuring own property with non-admitted insurer must pay tax of 3% per annum on premiums. (Rev. & Tax C. 13201 et seq.).

Rev. & Tax C. 12202.1, enacted in 1988, requires Board of Equalization to adjust gross premiums tax rate paid by any insurers for any premiums collected between Nov. 8, 1988 and Jan. 1, 1991 in order to compensate for changes in gross premiums tax revenues that might otherwise result from newly enacted Ins. C. 1861.01 et seq., providing for reduction and control of insurance rates.

Unemployment Insurance Code adopted.

Direct Action against Insurer.—See category Transportation, topic Motor Vehicles, subhead Direct Actions.

SURETY AND GUARANTY COMPANIES:

Such companies organized under general corporation laws but subject to regulation by Insurance Commissioner. Surety insurers (Ins. C. 105), both domestic and foreign (Ins. C. 707, 708, 709), must procure certificate of authority from such Commissioner (Ins. C. 105, 700). Willful failure to obtain such certificate is punishable by imprisonment not exceeding one year and/or fine not exceeding $100,000. (Ins. C. 700). Minimum capital requirement for such companies set forth in Ins. C. 700.01. Such companies must maintain specified financial condition to do business in state. (Ins. C. 12091, 12092). Surety companies possessing certificate of authority from Commissioner authorizing them to write surety insurance may act as sole surety in any case where undertaking or bond required by law (C.C.P. 995.310), and special provisions are made for their justification (C.C.P. 995.640, 995.660).

INTELLECTUAL PROPERTY

TRADEMARKS AND TRADENAMES:

Trademark is any word, name, symbol or device or any combination thereof adopted and used to identify goods made or sold to distinguish them from goods made or sold by others. (Bus. & Prof. C. 14207).

Service mark means a mark used in sale or advertising of services to identify services of one person and distinguish them from services of others. (Bus. & Prof. C. 14206).

Registration.—With certain categorical exclusions (Bus. & Prof. C. 14220), mark may be registered by one who adopts and uses mark by filing verified application on form furnished by Secretary of State accompanied by $70 filing fee and specimen of facsimile of mark in triplicate (Bus. & Prof. C. 14230-14233). Translation must accompany mark with any part not in English. (Bus. & Prof. C. 14234).

Protection Afforded.—Certificates of registration remain in force for ten years. Certificates are subject to renewal for a like period by filing renewal application with Secretary of State accompanied by $30 fee. (Bus. & Prof. C. 14250).

Grounds for Relief.—Court will look to whether infringement likely to injure business reputation or dilute distinctive quality of registered mark. (Bus. & Prof. C. 14330).

Comparative advertising not prohibited. (Bus. & Prof. C. 14335).

Relief Available.—Court may grant injunctive relief and order compensation of up to three times profits plus three times damages sustained by registered trademark owner. (Bus. & Prof. C. 14340).

Marks acquired in good faith at any time at common law are valid and enforceable. (Bus. & Prof. C. 14210).

Assignment.—Right to use any mark may be assigned with good will of business by written instrument, duly executed and acknowledged, and recorded with Secretary of State for fee of $30. (Bus. & Prof. C. 14260).

Resale Price Agreements.—California Fair Trade Contracts Law repealed. (1975, cc. 402, 429). Resale price agreement is unlawful restraint of trade. See category Business Regulation and Commerce, topic Monopolies, Restraint of Trade and Competition. Retail price maintenance provisions of Bus. & Prof. C. 24756, et seq. (relating to alcoholic beverages) were found invalid as violation of Sherman Antitrust Act. (21 C.3d 431, 146 C.Rptr. 585, 579 P.2d 476).

Trade Names (Fictitious Business Names).—Person doing business in state under fictitious name, or partnership doing business under fictitious name or designation not showing names of all partners, other than limited partnership which has filed certificate of limited partnership, or registered limited liability partnership or foreign limited liability partnership that has filed registration under Corporations Code, or corporation doing business under name other than corporate name stated in articles of incorporation or in case of individual, name that does not include surname or which suggests existence of additional owners, or in case of limited partnership that has filed certificate of limited partnership with Secretary of State and in case of foreign limited partnership that has filed for registration with Secretary of State, any name other than name of limited partnership as on file with Secretary of State, or in case of limited liability company, any name other than name stated in articles of incorporation and in case of foreign limited liability company that has filed for registration with Secretary of State, any name other than name of limited liability company on file with state, or name that suggests existence of additional owners. (Bus. & Prof. C. 17900), must file Fictitious Business Name Statement with county clerk where principal place of business located or, with Sacramento County Clerk if there is no place of business in state (Bus. & Prof. C. 17913, 17915). Statement must be published and affidavit of publications filed. (Bus. & Prof. C. 17917). Except as provided in Bus. & Prof. C. 17920(b) and (c), statement expires five years from date it was filed with county clerk. (Bus. &

TRADEMARKS AND TRADENAMES . . . *continued*

Prof. C. 17920). No person or other entity required to file statement or assignee may maintain action on account of contract made or transaction had under fictitious business name, until statement filed and published. (Bus. & Prof. C. 17918). Nonprofit corporations and certain real estate investment trusts do not have to file statement. (Bus. & Prof. C. 17911, 17912).

Filing of Fictitious Business Name Statement establishes rebuttable presumption or exclusive right to use as trade name, fictitious business name. (Bus. & Prof. C. 14411). Filing articles of incorporation in case of domestic corporation or obtaining certificate of qualification in case of foreign corporation establishes rebuttable presumption of exclusive right to use as trade name, name of corporation. (Bus. & Prof. C. 14415). Filing Articles of Incorporation pursuant to §200 of Corporations Code, shall not authorize use in this state of corporate name in violation of rights of another under Federal Trademark Act, Trademark Act, Fictitious Business Names Act, or common law. (Bus. & Prof. C. 14417).

For protection of names other than trade names, i.e., names of noncommercial organizations and associations, see Bus. & Prof. C. 14492-14495.

TRADE SECRETS:

Uniform Trade Secrets Act adopted (1984, c. 1724, §1) with minor revisions, enacted as C.C. 3426 et seq., applies to misappropriations occurring on or after Jan. 1, 1985. California statute does not include Official 1985 Amendments.

Significant Deviations from Uniform Trade Secrets Act (as amended by 1985 Amendments).—(All references to section numbers of California Statute).

3426.1: Subdivision (d)(1) substitutes "from not being generally known to the public or to" for ", and not being readily ascertainable by proper means by,".

3426.2: Subdivision (a) omits "reasonable" before "period of time." Subdivision (b) reworded: "If the court determines that it would be unreasonable to prohibit future use, an injunction may condition future use upon payment of a reasonable royalty for no longer than the period of time the use could have been prohibited."

3426.3: Section on damages reworded:

"(a) A complainant may recover damages for the actual loss caused by misappropriation. A complainant also may recover for the unjust enrichment caused by misappropriation that is not taken into account in computing damages for actual loss.

(b) If neither damages nor unjust enrichment caused by misappropriation are provable, the court may order payment of a reasonable royalty for no longer than the period of time the use could have been prohibited.

(c) If willful and malicious misappropriation exists, the court may award exemplary damages in an amount not exceeding twice any award made under subdivision (a) or (b)."

3426.7: Subdivision (a) reworded "Except as otherwise expressly provided, this title does not supersede any statute relating to misappropriation of a trade secret, or any statute otherwise regulating trade secrets."

New Subdivision (c) added:

"(c) This title does not affect the disclosure of a record by a state or local agency under the California Public Records Act (Chapter 3.5 (commencing with Section 6250) of Division 7 of Title 1 of the Government Code). Any determination as to whether the disclosure of a record under the California Public Records Act constitutes a misappropriation of a trade secret and the rights and remedies with respect thereto shall be made pursuant to the law in effect before the operative date of this title."

3426.10: Section on effective date states: "This title does not apply to misappropriation occurring prior to January 1, 1985. If a continuing misappropriation otherwise covered by this title began before January 1, 1985, this title does not apply to the part of the misappropriation occurring before that date. This title does apply to the part of the misappropriation occurring on or after that date unless the appropriation was not a misappropriation under the law in effect before the operative date of this title."

Tort Liability.—Voluntary, intentional and unauthorized disclosure of trade secrets to competitor in any legislative, judicial or other official proceeding is not privileged publication for purposes of tort liability as defined in C.C. 43 et seq. (C.C. 3426.11).

Evidentiary Rules to Protect Trade Secrets.—Owner of trade secret or agent or employee may claim privilege to refuse to disclose trade secret, and to prevent other from disclosing it, if allowance of privilege will not conceal fraud or work injustice. (Evid. C. 1060). Court may issue protective order protecting trade secret information when owner of trade secret asserts privilege during criminal proceeding and certain criteria met. (Evid. C. 1061). Court may close portions of criminal proceeding to public, pursuant to specified procedures, if necessary to prevent disclosure of trade secrets. (Evid. C. 1062).

LEGAL PROFESSION

ATTORNEYS AND COUNSELORS:

The bar is integrated as "The State Bar of California". (Bus. & Prof. C. 6001). Members of State Bar are all persons admitted and licensed to practice law, except justices and judges of courts of record during their continuance in office. (Bus. & Prof. C. 6002).

Practice of law is regulated by Business and Professions Code, §6000 et seq.

Jurisdiction over Admissions.—Supreme Court is vested with power to admit to bar as attorney at law any applicant certified by examining committee as having fulfilled requirements. (Bus. & Prof. C. 6064).

Eligibility.—Any person, of age of at least 18 years, of good moral character, who possesses necessary qualifications of study and ability, and who has passed uniform examination, is entitled to admission to State Bar and thereupon to practice law in California. (Bus. & Prof. C. 6060-62).

No person who advocates overthrow of government of U. S. or of this state by force, violence, or other unconstitutional means, may be admitted to bar. (Bus. & Prof. C. 6064.1).

Educational Requirements.—Before commencing study of law applicants for examination must have completed two years of college work, or have attained in apparent intellectual ability equivalent of at least two years of college work. (Bus. & Prof. C. 6060 [c][1]-[2]). Legal education must have resulted in graduation from law school accredited by examining committee or approved by American Bar Association requiring substantially full time of its students for three years, or graduation from part-time law school after attendance for four years (Bus. & Prof. C. 6060[e][1]-[2]), or proof that applicant has otherwise diligently and in good faith studied law for at least four years as follows: (1) in law school approved to confer professional degrees which requires 270 classroom hours a year (Bus. & Prof. C. 6060[e][3][i]); (2) under supervision of State Bar member who has practiced at least five years (Bus. & Prof. C. 6060[e][3][ii]); (3) under supervision of state judge (Bus. & Prof. C. 6060[e][3][iii]); (4) from authorized correspondence law school (Bus. & Prof. C. 6060[e][3][D]); or any combination thereof (Bus. & Prof. C. 6060[e][3][iv]).

Persons who received legal education in foreign country where common law of England not in effect must demonstrate to examining committee qualification to take bar exam. (Bus. & Prof. C. 6060[e][3][i]).

Law Student Registration and Examination.—Applicant must register with examining committee within three months after beginning study of law; committee may for good cause permit later registration. (Bus. & Prof. C. 6060[d]).

Student in law school which is not accredited by Committee of Bar Examiners must take preliminary bar examination at end of first year of law study. (Bus. & Prof. C. 6060).

Final bar examinations are held in Feb. and July of each year by examining committee at Los Angeles, Sacramento, San Diego and San Francisco. Application for Feb. bar examination must be filed by preceding Nov. 1, and application for July bar examination must usually be filed by preceding Apr. 1. Examinations use Multi-State Bar Examination. Committee of Bar Examiners of State Bar of California, P.O. Box 7908, 555 Franklin Street, San Francisco, California 94102 and 1149 South Hill Street, Los Angeles, California 90015 is responsible for preparation, administration and evaluation of state bar examination.

Admission of Out of State Attorneys.—In order to be certified to Supreme Court for admission and license to practice law person who has been admitted to practice law outside of state must: (1) be at least 18 years old, (2) be of good moral character, (3) have passed general bar exam given by examining committee. If person has been active member in good standing of bar of admitting sister state or U.S. jurisdiction, possession or territory for at least four years immediately preceding application to take general bar examination, he or she may elect to take Attorney's exam rather than general bar exam. Attorneys admitted less than four years and attorneys admitted four years or more in another jurisdiction but who are not active members in good standing of their admitting jurisdiction must take general bar exam, (4) have passed professional responsibility or legal ethics exam. (Bus. & Prof. C. 6062).

Admission of Foreign Attorneys.—In order to be certified to Supreme Court for admission and license to practice law person who has been admitted to practice law outside U.S. or U.S. jurisdiction, possession or territory must: (1) be at least 18 years old, (2) be of good moral character, (3) have passed general bar exam given by examining committee, and (4) have passed professional responsibility or legal ethics exam. (Bus. & Prof. C. 6062).

Admission Pro Hac Vice.—Out of state attorney, not admitted and not engaged in regular business or professional activities in California, may be permitted upon written application to appear as counsel pro hac vice, provided that active member of California Bar is attorney of record. (Rules of Court 983).

Professional Responsibility Examination.—Additional examination covering professional responsibility of attorney must also be successfully taken; examination held three times per year (Mar., Aug. and Nov.). Applications must usually be received by first day of month preceding month of examination.

Licenses.—Annual active membership fee in State Bar ranges from $192 to $291 per year depending on number of years member has been active plus any increases authorized by statute and is payable on or before Feb. 1 of each year. (Bus. & Prof. C. 6140-6140.9). Additional fee of $110 for improved discipline systems, and limited discretionary annual increases for bar programs. (Bus. & Prof. C. 6140.3-6140.9). Inactive membership fee is $40. Inactive members who attain age of 70 shall not be required to pay annual fee. Failure to pay results in suspension from membership. (Bus. & Prof. C. 6141, 6143).

Powers.—Attorney may bind client at any stage of action or proceeding by his agreement filed with clerk, or entered upon minutes of court, and not otherwise. Also has power to receive money claimed by client in action or proceeding, during pendency thereof, or after judgment, unless a revocation of his authority is filed, and upon payment thereof, and not otherwise, to discharge claim or acknowledge satisfaction of judgment. (C. C. P. 283).

Change of Attorneys.—Cannot be changed in action or proceeding, except upon consent of both client and attorney, filed with clerk, or entered upon minutes, or by order of court upon application of either client or attorney, after notice from one to other. (C. C. P. 284).

Liabilities.—May be held strictly to a fiduciary and trust character. (206 C. 689, 275 P. 941). Attorney-client relationship is one of special confidence and trust demanding that member of profession be held to strictest account in matters affecting relationship of attorney and client. Attorney is guilty of misdemeanor punishable by imprisonment, fine or both if party to deceit or collusion, willfully delays suit with view to own gain, or misappropriates money or other property of client. (Bus. & Prof. C. 6128).

Compensation.—Stipulations in security instruments as to payment of attorney's fee, after default are legal, but compensation shall be such as court finds reasonable, not exceeding amount named in instrument. (Com'l. C. 9504). Compensation is left to agreement of parties, except where fixed by statute. (C. C. P. 1021). For proceedings commenced after July 1, 1991, fees in probate cases are fixed on same basis as public

See note at head of Digest as to 1998 legislation covered.

See Topical Index in front part of this volume.

ATTORNEYS AND COUNSELORS . . . *continued*

administration or personal representative, with exception of additional compensation defined by statute. (Prob. C. 7666, 10800, 7623). Attorney's fees generally left to private agreement in bringing petition for court order determining ownership of property by surviving spouse. (Prob. C. 13660). Contingency fee contracts generally must be in writing and governed by Bus. & Prof. C. 6146-6147.5. Other fees must be in writing where it is reasonably foreseeable that total expense to client will exceed $1,000. (Bus. & Prof. C. 6148). System for arbitration or mediation of disputes involving attorneys' fees. (Bus. & Prof. C. 6200 et seq.).

Disbarment or Suspension.—Supreme Court may disbar or suspend attorneys. (Bus. & Prof. C. 6100). Member may be disbarred or suspended for conviction of crime involving moral turpitude; record of conviction is conclusive evidence. (Bus. & Prof. C. 6101, 6102). It shall constitute cause for disbarment or suspension to engage in insurance fraud. (Ins. C. 1871.1, 1871.4; Bus. & Prof. C. 6106.5). It shall constitute cause for discipline to violate any provision of Miller-Ayala Athlete Agents Act or to violate any provision of c. 1 of Part 6 of Division 2 of Labor Code or to violate any provision of law of any other state regulating athlete agents. (Bus. & Prof. C. 6106.7). Board of Governors of State Bar, after hearing, has power to make disbarment or suspension recommendations to court or to take lesser disciplinary actions. (Bus. & Prof. C. 6078). Although Board's findings are not binding on court, petitioner has burden of showing wherein decision of Board is erroneous or unlawful. (50 C.2d 202, 323 P.2d 1003; 62 C.2d 17, 41 C. Rptr. 1, 396 P.2d 33). Attorney may be subject to involuntary inactive enrollment in discretion of Board for: (i) Failure to comply with §6002.1 (maintenance of informational records with State Bar), (ii) conducting himself in manner which poses as substantial threat of harm to his clients or public, or (iii) violation of terms of any probation imposed by State Bar. (Bus. & Prof. C. 6007).

Attorney-Client Privilege.—Governed by Evidence Code §950 et seq.

Unauthorized Practice.—No one except active members of State Bar may practice law in California. (Bus. & Prof. C. 6125).

Attorney Ethics.—ABA Model Rules of Professional Conduct not adopted. Governed by Rules of Professional Conduct of the State Bar of California (May, 1989) and Bus. & Prof. C. 6000 et seq. Attorney advertising regulated by Bus. & Prof. C. 6157 et seq.

Professional Association or Corporation.—See category Business Organizations, topic Corporations, subhead Professional Corporations.

MINERAL, WATER AND FISHING RIGHTS

MINES AND MINERALS:

Extensive 1988 recodification of mining statutes. Pub. Res. C. 2301-26 replaced by 3900-24; 2351-61 by 3940-50; 2551-59 by 3960-68; and 2601-06 by 3980-85. No substantive changes.

General supervision of mines and mining is vested in state geologist who is chief of Division of Mines and Geology, Department of Conservation.

State laws provide for location and development of mining claims. (Pub. Res. C. 3900-24).

Surface Mining and Reclamation Act of 1975 (Pub. Res. C. 2710 et seq.) regulates and requires permits for specified surface mining operations where operations entailing removal of 1,000 cubic yards of overburden or more are undertaken on location of more than one acre.

Corporations for this purpose are organized under general laws. Shareholder may examine any of corporation's mines with his expert on application to president of corporation. $1,000 liquidated damages plus costs by statute for refusal. (Pub. Res. C. 3984).

Mining partnership exists when two or more persons who own or acquire mining claim actually engage in working claim. (Pub. Res. C. 3940). Express agreement to become partners or share profits and losses is not necessary. (Pub. Res. C. 3941).

Member of mining partnership shares in profits and losses thereof in proportion which his interest or share in mine bears to whole partnership capital or number of shares. (Pub. Res. C. 3942).

Each partner has lien on partnership property for debts due creditors thereof, and for money advanced by him for its use. Lien exists, notwithstanding agreement among partners that it shall not. (Pub. Res. C. 3943).

Mining ground, owned and worked by partners in mining, whether purchased with partnership funds or not, is partnership property. (Pub. Res. C. 3944).

One of partners in mining partnership may convey his interest in mine and business without dissolving partnership. Purchaser becomes member of partnership. (Pub. Res. C. 3945).

Purchaser of interest in mining ground of mining partnership takes subject to liens existing in favor of partners for debts due all creditors thereof, or advances made for benefit of partnership, unless he purchased in good faith, for valuable consideration, without notice of such lien. (Pub. Res. C. 3946).

Purchaser of interest of partner in mine when partnership is engaged in working it takes with notice of all liens resulting from relation of partners to each other and to creditors. (Pub. Res. C. 3947).

No member of mining partnership or other agent or manager thereof can, by contract in writing, bind partnership, except by express authority derived from members. (Pub. Res. C. 3948).

Decision of members owning majority of shares or interests in mining partnership binds it in conduct of its business. (Pub. Res. C. 3949).

Upon failure of any co-owner of mine or mining claim to contribute his proportionate share of taxes which have been levied and assessed upon mine or claim for five years, any co-owner who has paid said taxes may serve notice for contribution. (C. C. P. 850).

Safeguarding of Employees.—See category Employment, topic Labor Relations.

Oil and Gas.—General supervision of oil and gas is vested in State Oil and Gas Supervisor who is chief of Division of Oil and Gas, Department of Conservation. Supervisor has duty of supervising drilling, operation, maintenance and abandonment of wells and facilities attendant to oil and gas production to prevent damage to life, health, property, natural resources, oil and gas deposits, loss of oil and gas and damage to underground and surface waters. (Pub. Res. C. 3106). "Well" broadly defined to include drilling to inject fluids or gas into earth or utilize underground storage. (Pub. Res. C. 3008). Either blanket or individual well indemnity bonds required from any entity engaging in drilling, redrilling, deepening, or permanently altering casing of any well. (Pub. Res. C. 3204 et seq.). Unreasonable (Pub. Res. C. 3300-14) and willful (Pub. Res. C. 3500-03) waste of gas is prohibited. Where subsidence has occurred, as in Wilmington oil field, supervisor may compel unitization if necessary to repressuring program to ameliorate subsidence and exercise surveillance over all repressuring operations. (Pub. Res. C. 3315-3347). Spacing and location of oil and gas wells is regulated by statute, and improper spacing or location of well may make it nuisance. (Pub. Res. C. 3600-09).

State Owned Land.—Administered by State Lands Commission. Authority for, form and contents of mining prospecting permits and leases (Pub. Res. C. 6890-6996) and oil and gas leases, including those on tide and submerged lands (Pub. Res. C. 6871-79), are prescribed.

See category Business Regulation and Commerce, topic Securities, as to jurisdiction of Commissioner of Corporations over certain mineral and oil and gas interests.

Claims.—Method of filing claims covered by Pub. Res. C. 3900, 3924.

Brokers.—State laws provide comprehensive licensing system for mineral, oil, and gas brokers. It is unlawful for person to act as mineral, oil, or gas broker for compensation, or in expectation of compensation, without license. (Bus. & Prof. C. 10500, et seq.).

Servitudes Upon Land.—Right of taking minerals, or other things, may be attached to other land as easement (C. C. 801) or may be granted and held, even though not attached to land (C. C. 802).

Termination of Dormant Mineral Right.—Mineral right may be terminated if, for period of 20 years preceding commencement of action, there is no production of minerals and no exploration, drilling, mining, development, or other operations that affect minerals, no separate tax assessment is made or paid on minerals, and no instrument creating, reserving, transferring, or otherwise evidencing mineral right is recorded. (C. C. 883.110, et seq.).

MORTGAGES

CHATTEL MORTGAGES:

See category Debtor and Creditor, topic Fraudulent Sales and Conveyances, subhead Bulk Sales, as to mortgage of fixture or store equipment of baker, cafe, restaurant or garage owner, machinist, dyer, cleaner or wholesale or retail merchant; see also categories Business Regulation and Commerce, topic Consumer Protection; Debtor and Creditor, topic Liens.

Uniform Commercial Code has been adopted. (1963, c. 819). See category Business Regulation and Commerce, topic Commercial Code, subhead Material Variations from 1990 Official Text.

What May Be Mortgaged.—Uniform Commercial Code governs. (Com'l. C. 9102, Div. 9 esp.).

After-Acquired Property.—Uniform Commercial Code governs. (Com'l. C. 9204).

Future Advances.—Uniform Commercial Code governs. (Com'l. C. 9204).

Requisites of Instrument.—Uniform Commercial Code governs. (Div. 9 esp., 9203, 9303, 9402).

Filing and Refiling.—Uniform Commercial Code governs. (Div. 9 esp., Ch. 4, 9302, 9403).

Documents Filed.—Uniform Commercial Code financing statement (Com'l. C. 9402), continuation statement (Com'l. C. 9403), termination statement (Com'l. C. 9404), statement of release (Com'l. C. 9405) and statement of assignment (Com'l. C. 9406). See category Business Regulation and Commerce, topic Commercial Code, subhead Material Variations from 1990 Official Text.

Place of Filing.—Secretary of State's office, Sacramento or Los Angeles, California, except as to: Consumer goods (county recorder's office in county of debtor's residence, or if nonresident, where goods are kept); crops or timber to be cut (county recorder's office of county where located). Organization's residence is county of its principal place of business. (Com'l. C. 9401).

Fees.—$20 per statement filed if form conforms to standards set by filing officer, otherwise $30. (Com'l. C. 9403[5]). For certification of existing filings, if filing officer is county recorder, fee to cover all costs, but not more than $15 per statement and copies per Govt. C. 27366; if Secretary of State, fee per Com'l C. 9409. (Com'l. C. 9407).

Removal of Property by Mortgagor.—Uniform Commercial Code governs. (Com'l. C. Div. 9 esp., 9401).

Mortgages of Motor Vehicles.—See category Transportation, topic Motor Vehicles, subhead Liability of Owner.

Foreign Mortgages.—Uniform Commercial Code governs. (Com'l. C. 9103).

Stipulation for Attorney's Fees.—See category Legal Profession, topic Attorneys and Counselors.

Acts of Mortgagor Constituting Theft.—It is theft where with intent to defraud and during existence of mortgage, mortgagor sells, transfers, destroys, or further encumbers mortgaged property (with certain exceptions), or removes mortgaged property from its location at time of mortgage, unless mortgagor informs purchaser of existence of mortgage, and obtains written consent of prior mortgagee. (P. C. 538).

See note at head of Digest as to 1998 legislation covered.

See Topical Index in front part of this volume.

CHATTEL MORTGAGES . . . *continued*

Judgment Liens.—Subject to judgment lien on personal property. (C.C.P. 697.530, Com'l. C. 9301). See category Civil Actions and Procedure, topic Judgments.

Assignment of debt secured by mortgage carries security. (C. C. 2936).

Redemption.—Uniform Commercial Code governs. (Com'l. C. 9506).

Taxation.—Mortgages exempt from taxation. (Rev. & Tax C. 212).

Foreclosure.—Uniform Commercial Code governs. (Com'l. C. Div. 9, Ch. 5). See category Business Regulation and Commerce, topic Commercial Code, subhead Material Variations from 1990 Official Text.

Forms.—No single form for security agreement approved by Secretary of State or in common use. Secretary of State has approved forms at end of this Digest.

COLLATERAL SECURITY:

See category Debtor and Creditor, topic Pledges.

MORTGAGES OF PERSONAL PROPERTY:

See topic Chattel Mortgages.

MORTGAGES OF REAL PROPERTY:

Any interest in real property which is capable of being transferred may be mortgaged. (C. C. 2947).

Characteristics of Real Property Security Devices.—Deed of trust is most common real property security device in California, with mortgage very seldom used. Mortgage with power of sale is similar in legal effect and economic function to deed of trust. Both are governed by same procedures and limitations with respect to foreclosure whether judicial or nonjudicial and both are subject to same redemption provisions and same antideficiency limitations. Title to property subject to mortgage remains in mortgagor subject to lien of mortgagee. While legal title is said to have passed to trustee in case of deed of trust, courts regard deeds of trust as practically and substantially mortgages with power of sale. (217 C. 644, 20 P.2d 940). One distinction between two devices is application of statute of limitations. In deed of trust title is treated as having passed to trustee and statute does not run against exercise of power of sale even though enforcement of obligation secured has been barred. Statute of limitations runs against mortgage and lien is extinguished when action is barred on principal obligation. (C. C. 2911). Power of sale may be conferred by mortgage. (C.C. 2932). Installment land sale contract is occasionally used as security device and it frequently includes power of sale. Such devices have not received statutory and judicial recognition that has occurred with respect to mortgage and deed of trust. Vendor of real property has lien thereon independent of possession for unpaid balance of purchase price when unsecured otherwise than by personal obligation of buyer. (C. C. 3046). Form and legal effect of deed of trust have never received legislative delineation as compared with mortgage. (C. C. 2920-2955.5). Deed of trust has, however, been treated by analogy to mortgages subject to general features of California real property law and to formalities of conveyancing.

Execution.—Mortgage can be created, renewed or extended only by writing executed with formalities required in case of grant of real property. (C. C. 2922). Same rule applies to deed of trust. Acknowledgment and recordation are not essential to validity of mortgage or deed of trust, but acknowledgment is usual method of proving execution and is prerequisite to recording. Recording in office of county recorder of county in which land is situated is necessary to establish priority over other liens and bona fide purchasers. (C. C. 2898). If property is community property both husband and wife must execute instrument. (Fam. C. 1102).

Recording.—Notice-race statute. (C. C. 1214). Also see subhead Execution, supra.

Recording Fees.—See category Documents and Records, topic Records, subhead Fees.

Trust Deeds.—See subhead Characteristics of Real Property Security Devices, supra.

Taxes.—No transfer taxes are required when mortgage or deed of trust is created (Const., Art XIII, §3; Rev. & Tax C. 212), but upon foreclosure sale transfer taxes may be imposed by local ordinance (Rev. & Tax C. 11926).

Obligations Secured.—Mortgage or deed of trust can secure any debt or obligation. (C. C. 2920). Obligation may be that of someone other than mortgagor or trustor and need not carry personal liability of anyone, but existence of underlying and enforceable debt or obligation is essential to validity of lien of mortgage or deed of trust. If obligation secured is not measurable in monetary terms, enforcement of lien may not be possible.

Future Advances.—Mortgage or deed of trust will secure future advances provided instrument so states. (C. C. 2884).

Property Encumbered.—Any interest in real property which is transferable may serve as security for deed of trust. (C. C. 2947). Trust deed must identify and describe security with sufficient clarity. Instrument may include personal property but is not enforceable against third parties unless executed and perfected in accordance with formalities required for personal property security interest. (Com'l. C. 9101 et seq.). Fixtures are included under lien of deed of trust, but lien is lost if fixtures are severed and removed from property. Complicated priority problems may arise with respect to claims by third parties, and "fixture filing" may be required in some circumstances. (Com'l. C. 9313).

Assignment.—Assignment of obligation transfers security. (C. C. 2936). In addition to endorsing note to assignee, there should be instrument assigning beneficial interest under deed of trust or mortgage executed, acknowledged and recorded. Borrower is entitled to notice of transfer and is not liable to assignee for payments made to assign or prior to receiving written notice. (C.C. 2937).

Priorities.—Obligatory advances have priority as of date of recording deed of trust. Optional advances will retain priority over intervening lien if lender making advance does not have actual knowledge of intervening lien. Constructive notice resulting from recordation of intervening lien is not equivalent of actual knowledge. Good practice, however, dictates that lender obtain title search and protection of title insurance before making optional advance. As mechanic's liens attach as of date work of improvement was commenced (C. C. 3134) they may gain priority over deed of trust or mortgage recorded after commencement of work. Mortgage or deed of trust given for price of real property at time of its conveyance has priority over all other liens created against purchaser subject to operation of recording laws. (C. C. 2898). Lender will thus take priority over outstanding judgment liens that immediately attach to any asset purchaser acquires but purchase money lien does not take priority over liens that already encumber property conveyed such as existing mechanic's lien or existing mortgage or deed of trust. (195 C.A.2d 355, 15 C. Rptr. 710; 87 C. 619, 25 P. 919). Lien of deed of trust or mortgage is terminated by foreclosure and sale under prior deed of trust or mortgage property conducted. General rule, however, as stated in C. C. 2897 is "[o]ther things being equal, different liens upon the same property have priority according to the time of their creation, . . .". This priority is subject to operation of recording laws.

Subordination.—C. C. 2934 provides that any instrument by which mortgage or deed of trust is subordinated in priority may be recorded and from date of recordation instrument acts as constructive notice to all persons. C. C. 2953.1-2953.4 contain statutory requirements for subordination agreements but subordination agreements exceeding $25,000 or those executed in connection with loan exceeding $25,000 are specifically exempted. (C. C. 2953.5). Protection afforded vendor by these provisions is requirement that security instrument or agreement which effects subordination to another security instrument must contain statement in boldface type at top of instrument to this effect. At bottom of instrument, statute requires specific notice that security interest may or will become subject to another or later security instrument. Despite exemption for transactions in excess of $25,000, title insurance companies in California generally require insertion of those provisions on subordinated deeds of trust and subordination agreements which are to be recorded. Several California cases have held that unless subordination clause specifies in considerable detail terms of loan to which seller's security interest will be subordinated to that clause, contract providing for such clause is too indefinite and uncertain to be specifically enforced. (253 C.A.2d 383, 61 C. Rptr. 377). Under "just and reasonable" test announced in Handy v. Gordon (65 C.2d 578, 55 C.Rptr. 769, 422 P.2d 329), unless contract contains terms sufficiently defining and minimizing risk to seller, clause will not be specifically enforceable. Court suggests that such terms might include limits on use of proceeds, maximum amounts of loan not to exceed specified percentage of construction cost or value of property and other similar limits designed to protect security. Court's demands for explicitness concerning enforcement of subordination clauses has been somewhat weakened by recent cases. (See, e.g., 131 C.A.3d 291, 182 C. Rptr. 287; 128 C.A.3d 361, 180 C. Rptr. 253.)

Substitution of Trustee.—There are several methods of substituting trustee in deed of trust: (1) By mutual agreement between beneficiary and trustor; (2) pursuant to express provisions of deed of trust; and (3) pursuant to C. C. 2934(a). In practice standard printed forms provided by title insurance companies contain specific language authorizing unilateral substitution by beneficiary by execution of simple document.

Release and Reconveyance.—Within 30 days after mortgage has been satisfied, mortgagee or assignee must execute and record certificate of discharge of mortgage or request to trustee of deed of trust for full reconveyance and failure to do so renders mortgagee or beneficiary liable for all damages sustained together with penalty of $300. (C. C. 2941). Any person willfully violating §2941 is also guilty of misdemeanor. (C. C. 2941.5). Partial release clauses are encountered in transactions involving incremental development of property such as subdivision of parcel into several small parcels for sale as lots or for construction of improvements and subsequent sale of lot with improvements. It is unlawful for subdivider under Bus. & Prof. C. 11013.2 to sell or lease lots or parcels in subdivision that is subject to blanket encumbrance unless there is release clause allowing purchaser or lessee to obtain legal title free and clear of such blanket encumbrance. Just and reasonable test applied in Handy v. Gordon, supra, also applies to release clauses requiring that they be free from ambiguity and uncertainty. Similar weakening of explicit requirement has occurred with respect to release clauses. (See, e.g., 101 C.A.3d 626, 162 C. Rptr. 52.)

Satisfaction.—See subhead Release and Reconveyance, supra.

Discharge.—See subhead Release and Reconveyance, supra.

Maturity of the Obligation.—Normally instrument evidencing obligation such as promissory note will have standard acceleration clause entitling holder to accelerate in event of default in payment of any installment or performance of any provision or condition contained in deed of trust. Absent such provision in note or in deed of trust, or both, foreclosure may be limited to delinquent installments. Acceleration clause is valid accessory to secured note. (Com'l. C. 3109). There is no requirement that beneficiary give notice of his election to accelerate or demand that trustor perform except when beneficiary of deed of trust or mortgage with power of sale elects to sell nonjudicially in which event he must elect and notify by notice of default and notice of sale. (C. C. 2924 et seq.). Security instruments frequently contain "due-on-sale" clause providing that if security or any interest therein is sold or further encumbered secured obligations may at option of holder become immediately due and payable. For specified residential properties, C. C. 2924.5 requires this clause be set forth in its entirety both in body of trust deed or mortgage and on promissory note or other document evidencing secured obligation. C. C. 2949 provides that no mortgage or trust deed may be declared in default nor accelerated solely by reason of owner further encumbering real property where it contains only single family owner occupied dwelling. Financial institutions often limit right of prepayment to specified amounts annually and charge penalty in form of additional interest where prepayment privilege is exercised. C. C. 2954.9, while not eliminating right of lender to make prepayment charge, substantially restricts amount of charge and right of lender to prevent prepayment until loan matures for specified residential properties. Late charges on loans secured by certain residential mortgages or deeds of trust after Jan. 1, 1976, may be added no earlier than ten days after payment has become due and late payment charge

See note at head of Digest as to 1998 legislation covered.

See Topical Index in front part of this volume.

MORTGAGES OF REAL PROPERTY . . . *continued*
may not exceed 6% of installment or $5, whichever is greater. (C. C. 2954.4). §2954.5(a), applicable to most lenders, requires that borrower be given at least ten days from mailing of default notice before assessing late payment charge. C. C. 1916.5 restricts changes in interest rates on certain variable interest loans encumbering residential property. C. C. 1921 requires that certain lenders offering variable interest residential loans provide prospective borrowers copy of most recent available publication of Federal Reserve Board so that public has descriptive information regarding adjustable rate mortgages.

Foreclosure.—Two methods by which mortgage or deed of trust may be foreclosed, providing they contain power of sale, are by court proceedings or by trustee's or mortgagee's sale under power. If mortgage does not contain power of sale, only method of foreclosure is by court proceedings. Most security instruments used in California expressly provide for power of sale and thus remedies of court foreclosure or foreclosure under power of sale can be exercised alternatively or concurrently. Beneficiary can elect either option at any time prior to sale. "One action" rule set forth in C. C. P. 726 requires secured creditor to resort to security until it is exhausted or valueless. Mortgagee or beneficiary cannot circumvent this requirement by waiving security and suing borrower directly on debt. Restriction may, however, be waived by borrower for separate and independent consideration at later time or by failure to raise matter as affirmative defense to action by beneficiary seeking to impose personal liability without foreclosing real property security. While beneficiary must foreclose security even though it was valueless as security at time security instrument was executed, where security was adequate at time transaction was entered into but thereafter became valueless either through destruction or foreclosure of senior encumbrance beneficiary, under certain circumstances, may bring direct action against trustor. While one action rule requires resort to security whether security interest is in form of mortgage or deed of trust, it does not mean that beneficiary of deed of trust may not conduct separate trustee sales on separate items of securities whether they be all real property or combined real and personal property for single debt. Beneficiary is prevented from recovering deficiency judgment by foreclosing nonjudicially (C. C. P. 580d), but he is not prevented by one action rule from holding series of nonjudicial sales. With respect to combined real and personal property, Com'l. C. 9501(4) gives to creditor several alternatives as to sequence of actions creditor may take to realize upon creditor's security. Creditor must be cautious in selection of its remedy where mixed collateral is involved. Judicial foreclosure is most frequently used where there are questions as to validity of security instrument, complicated priority problems involving number of parties, or where there are problems involving title. Trustee sale under power of sale is most frequently used method of realizing upon security as it is comparatively fast and efficient and terminates debtor's right of redemption effectively and inexpensively. Sale is conducted under provisions of C. C. 2924 et seq. Typically title insurance company is named as trustee and sale is conducted by title company's foreclosure department. Upon recordation and mailing of notice of default trustor, when obligation is one which may be reinstated, has until five business days prior to date set for sale of property within which to pay delinquent installments, costs and expenses incurred, and thereby cure default. (C. C. 2924c). Where default is nonreinstatable such as in event of outright sale by trustor where security is subject to due-on-sale clause it is still required that beneficiary record notice of default in form prescribed in Civil Code, await three month period and thereafter publish notice of sale under C. C. 2924f. Right to reinstate delinquent note is retained by trustor or mortgagor during reinstatement period despite fact that beneficiary has accelerated entire obligation under terms of note itself. Once reinstatement period has elapsed, however, and notice of sale under power of sale has been published before date of sale, then trustee has conducted sale in manner prescribed under C. C. 2924g and h, neither trustor nor any other person having interest in property has any further right of redemption. Statutory right of redemption after judicial sale exists for three months after sale if proceeds of sale are sufficient to satisfy indebtedness with interest and costs of action and sale, and one year after sale if proceeds of sale are not sufficient to satisfy such indebtedness, interest and costs. (C. C. P. 729.030).

Deficiency Judgment.—Where foreclosure sale produces net proceeds less than amount of debt and expenses mortgagee or beneficiary may pursue deficiency subject to statutory limitations contained in C. C. P. 580a through d. There can be no deficiency after foreclosure under power of sale in deed of trust or mortgage. (C. C. P. 580d). Beneficiary may, however, without seeking personal liability against trustor, realize on other security that he may have by foreclosing under power of sale. After exhausting all of security by means of foreclosure under power of sale, beneficiary cannot then seek personal deficiency judgment against debtor. After judicial foreclosure, mortgagee or beneficiary may seek deficiency judgment provided that obligation is not within deficiency prohibitions set forth in C. C. P. 580b. This statute prohibits deficiency judgment against buyer under deed of trust, mortgage or contract given to secure any part of purchase price of real property, provided property purchased, purchaser and creditor fall within statutory requirements.

Sales.—See subhead Foreclosure, supra.

Moratorium.—None.

Redemption.—See subhead Foreclosure, supra.

Form.—Code form for real property mortgage is set forth in C. C. 2948. Both mortgage and deed of trust must be in writing but no particular form is required. There are no statutory provisions setting forth form of deed of trust but form has become highly standardized and is printed by institutional lenders and title companies.

Form of Deed of Trust (which is usually used) is as follows (some parts being omitted):

This Deed of Trust, made this . . . day of . . ., TRUSTOR, whose address is . . ., . . ., TRUSTEE, and . . ., BENEFICIARY,

WITNESSETH:

That Trustor irrevocably grants, transfers and assigns to Trustee in trust, with power of sale, that property in . . . County, California, described as: . . . together with the rents, issues and profits thereof, subject, however, to the right, power and authority given in and conferred upon Beneficiary herein to collect and apply such rents, issues and profits.

For the purpose of securing performance of each agreement of Trustor contained herein and payment of the indebtedness evidenced by one promissory note of even date herewith in the principal sum of $. . . executed by Trustor in favor of Beneficiary, and to protect the security of this Deed of Trust, Trustor agrees:

(Here are usually incorporated detailed provisions relating to protection of security.)

Chattel Mortgages.—See topic Chattel Mortgages.

PROPERTY

ABSENTEES:

Distribution made to named absentee or any known assignee. If absentee is minor or incompetent, distribution made to his fiduciary. If without fiduciary, absentee's whereabouts unknown, or absentee refuses to give receipt for property, distribution may be deposited with county treasurer in absentee's name and can be claimed pursuant to Prob. C. 11854. (Prob. C. 11850-52). Special provisions relating to absentee distribution repealed July 1, 1989.

Care of Property.—Conservator can be appointed for any person who is missing and whose whereabouts are unknown. (Prob. C. 1804). Court must find that missing person owns or is entitled to possession of real or personal property in California, that such estate requires attention and that such person is missing. (Prob. C. 1849). Provisions of conservatorship law apply except those dependent upon knowledge of whereabouts of missing person. (Prob. C. 1848).

Administration and Distribution of Estate.—After five years unexplained absence, California property of absentee may be administered. (Prob. C. 12401-02). Estates may be administered as generally provided for administration of estates of deceased persons. (Prob. C. 12402). Procedure is specified for recovery of property if missing person appears within five years after initial petition. (Prob. C. 12408).

Process Agent.—Nonresidents or residents leaving California for over year, who incur any tax liability to State, must designate natural person as agent for service of process with respect to such liability. (C.C.P. 1018).

Escheat.—Specific provisions covering disposition of unclaimed property contained in C.C.P. 1300, et seq. Modified version of Uniform Disposition of Unclaimed Property Act adopted. (C.C.P. 1500 et seq.).

See also categories Business Regulation and Commerce, topic Banks and Banking, subhead Unclaimed Deposits; Citizenship, topic Aliens; Estates and Trusts, topic Wills, subhead Unclaimed Legacies.

ADVERSE POSSESSION:

Character of Possession.—When occupant claims under judgment or written instrument possession deemed adverse when continuous occupation for five years and possession of part of single plot or piece deemed possession of whole except where tract divided into lots. (C. C. P. 322-23). Occupation defined as usually cultivated or improved, protected by substantial inclosure, or used for supply of fuel, fencing-timber, pasturage, or ordinary use of occupant. (C.C.P. 323). Where there is no judgment or written instrument land must have been protected by substantial inclosure, usually cultivated or improved. (C. C. P. 325). Occupant claiming adverse possession must pay all taxes during such five-year period. (C. C. P. 325).

Duration of Possession.—Land must be continuously occupied and claimed for period of five years. (C. C. P. 321).

Easements may be acquired by prescriptive user for five years. (C.C. 1007; 1 C.3d 679, 686, 83 C.Rptr. 359, 463 P.2d 711). Necessary elements same as for title except need to pay taxes arises only if easement has been separately assessed. (1 C.3d 679, 686, 463 P.2d 711).

Disabilities.—If person against whom adverse title is asserted is either under age of majority, insane or imprisoned for term less than life at time he acquires title, time during which such disability continues, not to exceed 20 years, may not be included in five-year period required for acquiring title by adverse possession. (C. C. P. 328). No adverse possession possible of state or public entity land or land dedicated to public use by public utility. (C. C. 1007).

CONVEYANCES:

See topic Deeds, subhead Operation and Effect.

CURTESY:

No estate by curtesy. (Prob. C. 6412). Surviving spouse of nonresident decedent has same rights to take noncommunity real property against decedent's will as though such property were situated in decedent's domicile. (Prob. C. 120).

See also categories Estates and Trusts, topic Descent and Distribution; Family, topic Husband and Wife, subhead Community Property System.

DEEDS:

Execution.—Deeds of real property must be in writing, signed and delivered. (C. C. 1054, 1091). Acknowledgment or proof of execution (see category Documents and Records, topic Acknowledgments) not necessary to validity of deed between parties but necessary to entitle it to be recorded. (Govt. C. 27287-8). Seals and witnesses unnecessary, except that witnesses required if signature is made by mark. (C. C. 14). Practice is to use quitclaim deed if grantor in doubt regarding his title. See also categories Debtor and Creditor, topic Homesteads; Family, topic Husband and Wife, subhead Community Property System, catchline Management, Control and Disposition of Community Realty.

Recording not necessary to validity of deed as between parties or as to persons not bona fide purchasers (C. C. 1217); but deed must be recorded in office of recorder of

See note at head of Digest as to 1998 legislation covered.

See Topical Index in front part of this volume.

CA – 57

DEEDS . . . *continued*

county in which land is situated in order to constitute constructive notice to subsequent bona fide purchasers or encumbrancers (C. C. 1169, 1214). See also category Documents and Records, topic Records.

Fees are: For recording and indexing, $4 for first page (8½ by 14 inches) and $3 per additional page or fraction of page. Additional $1 charged for each page on which there is printing, other than of words which are directive or explanatory in nature or on vital statistics forms, spaced more than nine lines per vertical inch or more than 22 characters and spaces per inch measured horizontally for not less than three inches in one sentence. (Govt. C. 27361 and 27361.5). Each county may charge additional fee of $1 for each document recorded. (Govt. C. 27361.4). See also category Documents and Records, topic Records.

Operation and Effect.—If word grant is used in deed conveying title in fee simple or estate of inheritance, it implies, unless restrained by express terms in same conveyance, these covenants only: That grantor has not previously conveyed such estate or any interest therein to any other person; and that at time of conveyance such property is free from any encumbrances done, made or suffered by grantor or any person claiming under him. (C. C. 1113). Unless it appears from conveyance that lesser estate was intended, it is presumed that grant is intended to convey fee simple title. (C. C. 1105).

Conveyance to more than one person presumed to be as tenants in common, unless acquired by partnership, or unless instrument provides specifically for joint tenancy or property acquired as community property. (C. C. 686).

Form.—Short form of grant contained in C. C. 1092. Following form will serve most purposes:

Form

A. B., a single man, for value received, hereby grants to C. D., a single man, all that real property situated in the County of Los Angeles, State of California, described as follows: Block Y of Ball's Tract, as per map recorded in Book 12, page 24, of Maps, Records of said county. Subject to existing taxes and assessments, easements and rights of way and any and all restrictions of record.

Dated . . . ., 19 . . . . . A.B. (Add acknowledgement.)

It is not customary to use covenants in deed, custom being to rely on covenants against grantor implied by statute and examination or insurance of title.

Foregoing form may be used for quitclaim deed by substituting "quitclaims" in place of "grants".

DEEDS OF TRUST:

See category Mortgages, topic Mortgages of Real Property.

DOWER:

No dower and curtesy rights. (Prob. C. 6412). Surviving spouse of nonresident decedent has same rights to take non-community real property against decedent's will as though such property were situated in decedent's domicile. (Prob. C. 120).

See also categories Estates and Trusts, topic Descent and Distribution; Family, topic Husband and Wife, subhead Community Property System.

ESCHEAT:

See topic Absentees, subhead Escheat; categories Business Regulation and Commerce, topic Banks and Banking, subhead Unclaimed Deposits; Citizenship, topic Aliens; Estates and Trusts, topics Descent and Distribution, subhead Escheat, Wills, subhead Unclaimed Legacies.

LANDLORD AND TENANT:

Leases.—Agreement for leasing for period longer than year must be in writing and subscribed by party to be charged to be valid. (C. C. 1624). Lease must be acknowledged to be recorded. (Govt. C. 27287). To create tenancy in mobile home park lease must be in writing and must contain specified provisions. (C. C. 798.15). Mobile home park tenant's term of tenancy must be not less than 12 months unless otherwise requested by tenant. (C. C. 798.18).

Recording.—Unrecorded lease is valid between parties and those who have notice thereof (C. C. 1217), but, except as to lease for one year or less, is void as against any subsequent purchaser or mortgagee in good faith and for valuable consideration, whose conveyance is first recorded and as against any judgment affecting title. (C. C. 1214).

Term.—Hiring of real property other than lodgings and dwelling houses in places where there is no custom or usage on subject is presumed to be month to month tenancy unless otherwise designated in writing. (C. C. 1943).

Hiring of lodgings or dwelling house for unspecified term is presumed to have been made for such length of time as parties adopt for estimation of rent. In absence of any agreement respecting length of time or rent hiring is presumed to be monthly, but hiring of property for agricultural or grazing use is presumed to be for one year unless otherwise expressed. (C. C. 1943, 1944).

No lease or grant of any town or city lot for longer period than 99 years, in which shall be reserved any rent or service of any kind, is valid. (C. C. 718). No lease or grant of land for agricultural or horticultural purposes for longer period than 51 years, in which is reserved any rent or service of any kind, is valid. (C. C. 717).

Holding Over.—Any automatic renewal or extension provision in residential lease is voidable by party who did not prepare lease if lease is printed and provision not printed in at least eight-point boldface type in lease and recited in same type above place where lessee signs. (C. C. 1945.5). If lessee remains in possession after expiration of hiring, and lessor accepts rent from him, parties are presumed to have renewed hiring on same terms and for same time, not exceeding one month when rent is payable monthly, nor in any case one year. (C. C. 1945). On agricultural lands, if lessee holds over for 60 days without demand of possession or notice to quit by

landlord, lessee entitled to hold over under same terms for additional year. (C. C. P. 1161).

Renewal.—Hiring of real property for term not specified by parties is deemed to be renewed as stated above, at end of term implied by law, unless one of parties gives written notice to other of his intention to terminate same, at least as long before expiration thereof as term of hiring itself, not exceeding 30 days, except that tenancies from month to month may be terminated by 30 days notice at any time; and parties may agree at time such tenancy is created that notice may be given at any time not less than seven days before expiration of term. (C. C. 1946).

Tenancy at will may be terminated by 30 days written notice (C. C. 789), except tenants in mobile home park, who must be given 60 days notice (C. C. 798.55), upon specified grounds (C. C. 798.56).

Rent.—When there is no usage or contract to contrary, rents are payable at termination of holding, when it does not exceed one year. If holding is by day, week, month, quarter, or year, rent is payable at termination of respective period, as it successively becomes due. (C. C. 1947). Permissible required amount and use of security deposit by landlord is limited. (C. C. 1950.5, 1950.7). Landlord or landlord's agent may charge applicant screening fee to cover costs of obtaining information about applicant. Fee is limited to actual out-of-pocket costs of gathering information, up to $30. (C. C. 1950.6).

Repairs.—Lessor of building intended for occupation of human beings must, in absence of agreement to contrary, put it into condition fit for such occupation, and repair all subsequent dilapidations thereof which render it untenantable, except those occasioned by want of ordinary care by tenant. (C. C. 1941). Untenantable dwelling defined as lacking water proofing, weather protection, gas facilities, plumbing, water, heat, electricity, cleanliness, or garbage receptacles or floors, stairways, and railings maintained in good repair. (C. C. 1941.1). Tenants have affirmative obligations and landlord incurs no duty to repair where tenant's substantial violation of affirmative obligations interferes substantially with landlord's obligation to repair or contributes substantially to existence of dilapidation. (C. C. 1941.2). Failure of landlord within reasonable time after notice to repair dilapidations rendering premises untenantable entitles tenant to repair and deduct cost up to one month's rent, or to vacate and be discharged from lease obligations. This remedy available not more than twice in 12-month period. (C. C. 1942). Retaliation against tenant for exercising available remedies or complaining about tenantability of dwelling is penalized. (C. C. 1942.5). Landlord's breach of implied warranty of habitability bars eviction of residential tenant, provided tenant pays reduced rent determined by court. (10 C.3d 616, 111 C.Rptr. 704, 517 P.2d 1168).

Dispossession.—Landlord may recover possession by summary proceeding known as unlawful detainer action when tenant continues in possession after term or after default in payment of rent and three days notice in writing requiring its payment (stating amount which is due) or possession of property, has been served upon him, or when he continues in possession after failure to perform other conditions or covenants of lease including any covenant not to assign or sublet, and three days notice in writing requiring performance of such conditions or covenants has been served upon him, if conditions or covenants can be performed, or gives notice of intention to terminate hiring or makes offer to surrender possession which is accepted in writing and then fails to deliver possession at time specified. (C. C. P. 1161). If landlord declares forfeiture of lease in notice to quit, lease may remain in effect if tenant performs within three days or if landlord waives breach. (C.C.P. 1161.5). When proceeding is for unlawful detainer after default in payment of rent, execution may not issue for five days after entry of judgment provided: (1) Lease term has not expired and (2) landlord's three-day notice did not forfeit lease, and tenant shall be restored to his estate by payment within such time. (C. C. P. 1174). If judgment declares forfeiture of lease, landlord still may pursue remedies set forth in C. C. 1951.2. (C.C.P. 1174.5).

Plaintiff may have immediate possession on motion to court and filing undertaking where it appears to satisfaction of court, after hearing, that defendant is outside state or cannot be found. (C. C. P. 1166a).

Distress.—There is no distress for rent in this state.

Access to Dwelling.—Landlord may enter dwelling unit only in case of emergency, to make necessary repairs, alterations or improvements, to supply necessary or agreed services, to show unit to actual or prospective purchasers, mortgagees, tenants, workmen or contractors, when tenant has abandoned or surrendered premises, or pursuant to court order. (C. C. 1954).

Modification or Waiver.—Provision of lease or rental agreement for dwelling unit is void as contrary to public policy if it requires lessee to modify or waive his right to certain statutory remedies, to assert cause of action which may arise in future, to notice or hearing as required by law, to procedural rights in litigation, or to have landlord exercise duty of care to prevent personal injury or property damage. (C. C. 1953).

LEASES:

See topic Landlord and Tenant.

PERPETUITIES:

Lease to commence at certain time or upon happening of future event becomes invalid if its term does not actually commence in possession within 30 years after its execution. (C.C. 715).

Conditions restraining alienation, when repugnant to interest created, are void. (C.C. 711).

Uniform Statutory Rule Against Perpetuities.—"American common-law" rule against perpetuities in former C.C. 715.2 superseded by Uniform Statutory Rule Against Perpetuities in Prob. C. 21205-21208. Exception to rule against perpetuities in first clause of former C.C. 715.3 superseded by Prob. C. 21225(f) (excludes from coverage of Uniform Statutory Rule Against Perpetuities nonvested property interests

PERPETUITIES . . . *continued*
including pensions, profit-sharing, stock bonus, health, disability, death benefits, and income deferral). Exception from prohibition on accumulations in second clause of former C.C. 715.3 continued in C.C. 724(b) (exception from prohibition on accumulations with regard to income arising from real or personal property held in trust [1] forming part of profit-sharing plan for benefit of employees or [2] forming part of retirement plan). Former C.C. 715.4 restated without substantive change in Prob. C. 21225(h) (excludes from coverage of Uniform Statutory Rule Against Perpetuities trusts that provide beneficiaries with hospital service contracts, group life insurance, group disability insurance, group annuities, or any combination of such insurance). Former C.C. 715.5 superseded by Prob. C. 21220 (reformation under Uniform Statutory Rule Against Perpetuities). Former C.C. 715.6 superseded by Uniform Statutory Rule Against Perpetuities, in particular, Prob. C. 21205-21207.

Accumulations.—Directions for accumulations are void as respects time beyond above limits. (C.C. 725).

PERSONAL PROPERTY:

Personal property governed by common law as modified and interpreted by C.C. 654-1422. Tenancy by entirety in personal property is not recognized. (C.C. 683, 702; 156 C. 195, 103 P. 931; 142 C. A. 2d 252, 298 P.2d 551). Joint tenancies in safe-deposit boxes are prohibited. (C.C. 683.1).

See also categories Business Regulation and Commerce, topic Commercial Code; Debtor and Creditor, topic Assignments; Mortgages, topic Chattel Mortgages.

POWERS OF ATTORNEY:

Uniform Durable Power of Attorney Act has been adopted. (Prob. C. 4124-4127, 4206, 4304, 4305). Incapacity of principal to contract will not terminate agency if instrument creating agency so provides (Durable Power of Attorney). (Prob. C. 4124). Requirements and legally sufficient form for durable power of attorney for health care decisions adopted. (Prob. C. 4121, 4401, 4606, 4612, 4700, 4701).

Form of Authorization.—Oral authorization is sufficient for any purpose, except that authority to enter into contract required by law to be in writing (see category Business Regulation and Commerce, topic Frauds, Statute of) can only be given by instrument in writing. (C. C. 2309). Where original authority must be in writing, ratification must also be in writing. (C. C. 2310).

Power of attorney to execute mortgage must be in writing, subscribed, acknowledged, or proved, certified, and recorded in order that transaction may be valid as against third persons. (C. C. 2933).

Termination of Agency.—Power not coupled with interest is terminated by revocation by principal, death of principal or incapacity of principal to contract; however, any bona fide transaction entered into without actual knowledge of such revocation, death, or incapacity shall be binding upon principal, his or her heirs and other successors in interest. (C. C. 2356). Revocation may render principal liable in damages (5 C.2d 687, 56 P.2d 226). Where power to execute instruments effecting real property is recorded, revocation must be recorded in same office where originally recorded. (C. C. 1216).

Usable special power of attorney form is as follows:

Form

SPECIAL POWER OF ATTORNEY

I, (name of principal), of (address, city, county and state), do hereby appoint (name of attorney in fact) of (address, city, county and state), my true and lawful attorney in fact, for me and in my name, place, and stead, and for my use and benefit, to (specify powers granted as completely as necessary to confer powers intended).

I further give and grant unto my said attorney in fact full power and authority to do and perform every act necessary and proper to be done in the exercise of any of the foregoing powers as fully as I might or could do if personally present, with full power of substitution and revocation, hereby ratifying and confirming all that my said attorney shall lawfully do or cause to be done by virtue hereof.

(Optional time limitation provision) All power and authority hereinabove granted shall in any event terminate on (specify date).

EXECUTED this . . . . . . day of . . . ., 19 . . . . . ., at (city and state).

(Signature)
(Typed Name)

(If power is to be recorded, it must be acknowledged).

Members of Armed Forces.—If absentee (member of uniformed service determined to be in missing status) executed power of attorney that expires during period of absentee status, power of attorney continues until 30 days after absentee status is terminated. (Prob. C. 3720). Although divorce or legal separation will generally terminate power of attorney as between spouses (as principal and attorney in fact), power of attorney made by person who becomes absentee will not be terminated by divorce or legal separation, if it so provides. (Prob. C. 3722, 4154).

REAL PROPERTY:

Estates in real property, in respect to duration, are either estates of inheritance or perpetual estates, estates for life, estates for years or estates at will. (C.C. 761). Estates tail are abolished. (C.C. 763). Joint tenancy and tenancy in common are recognized and defined (C.C. 682-83, 685), but joint tenancy is created only when expressly declared in transfer to be such (C.C. 683). No tenancy by entirety is recognized. (156 C. 195, 103 P. 931; 142 C.A.2d 252, 299 P.2d 281). C.C. 1073 abolishes doctrine of worthier title.

Condominium is recognized as estate consisting of undivided interest in common in portion of parcel of real property together with separate interest in space called unit, with boundaries sufficiently described on recorded final map, parcel map or condominium plan, and filled with air, earth, or water, or any combination thereof. (C.C. 783, 1351[f]).

Rule in Shelley's Case has been abolished. (C.C. 779).

See also topics Curtesy, Deeds, Dower, Landlord and Tenant; categories Civil Actions and Procedure, topic Partition; Debtor and Creditor, topic Homesteads; Documents and Records, topic Records; Family, topic Husband and Wife; Mortgages, topic Mortgages of Real Property.

TRUST DEEDS:

See category Mortgages, topic Mortgages of Real Property.

TAXATION

ADMINISTRATION:

No single officer or board has general supervision of administration of tax laws. Information and forms relating to indicated taxes may be obtained at these offices in Sacramento: State Controller (Estate Tax and Generation-Skipping Tax); Franchise Tax Board (Income); State Board of Equalization (Sales and Use). County (or city) assessor administers most property taxes.

State Taxes.—California property taxes are generally not administered, assessed or collected by state.

County and Municipal Taxes.—Local property taxes consist of ad valorem property taxes upon all property, real and personal, as defined above.

County taxes levied and collected in accordance with following outline.

Most cities levy and collect property taxes in accordance with county scheme. Many cities assess property and collect taxes through county officers, thus making for uniformity and eliminating confusion.

Exemptions.—See topic Property Taxes, subhead Exemptions.

Standing timber is exempt from local property taxation, but taxable under state legislation according to value of timber at time of harvest. (Rev. & Tax C. 38101, et seq.).

Liability of Corporations.—Banks and insurance companies subject to county and municipal taxes on any real estate they possess (but on real estate only). (Const. Art. XIII, §§27, 28[f][1]). Other corporations subject to all local taxes.

Valuation of Property.—All property subject to general property taxation assessed at full value. (Rev. & Tax C. 401). Certain open-space properties are subject to special valuation treatment. (Rev. & Tax C. 421-430.5). Maximum amount of any ad valorem tax on real property is limited to 1% of "full cash value". (Const. Art. XIIIA, §1). Full cash value is defined as fair market value as of lien date for 1975 or, for property which is purchased, newly constructed or changes ownership after 1975 lien date, date of purchase or change of ownership or on which new construction is completed (or, if uncompleted, on lien date). (Rev. & Tax C. 110.1). Adjustments thereafter to full cash value may reflect from year to year change in California Consumer Price Index not to exceed 2% for any given year or comparable data for area under taxing jurisdiction, or may be reduced to reflect substantial damage, destruction or other factors causing decline in value. (Const., Art. XIII A, §2; Rev. & Tax C. 51). Relief from reassessment is provided for certain transfers including intrafamily transfers (Rev. & Tax C. 62[m], 62[n], 63, 63.1), certain transfers by senior citizens (Rev. & Tax C. 69.5) and disaster victims (Rev. & Tax C. 69). "Purchased" defined. (Rev. & Tax C. 67). "Change in ownership" defined. (Rev. & Tax C. 60-66, 68). "Newly constructed" defined. (Const., Art. XIII A, §2; Rev. & Tax C. 70, 73-74).

Assessment.—All property (except state-assessed property) within state is assessed by county or city assessors on first day of Jan. preceding fiscal year for which taxes are levied. (Rev. & Tax C. 405, 2192). Property changing ownership or newly constructed is subject to supplemental assessments, based upon reappraisals of full cash value on date change of ownership occurs or new construction is completed. (Rev. & Tax C. 75-75.80). New construction does not include alterations done to make structure accessible to disabled persons. (Rev. & Tax C. 74.6).

All persons owning, claiming, possessing, controlling or managing taxable personal property having aggregate cost of $100,000 or more for any assessment year and any other owners of such property, must file annual signed property statement with assessor. (Rev. & Tax C. 441, 442). Assessor will estimate value of property based upon his own information in absence of compliance with written request therefor. (Rev. & Tax C. 501). Penalty for failure to file annual statement (subject to possible abatement for reasonable cause) is 10% of value of unreported taxable tangible property placed on current roll. (Rev. & Tax C. 463). If any person conceals tangible personal property to evade taxation, penalty imposed is 25% of additional assessed value. If any person obtains reduced assessment of tangible property through fraud, penalty imposed is 75% of additional assessed value. (Rev. & Tax C. 502-04). Interest at rate of 0.75% per month is added to tax. (Rev. & Tax C. 506). Upon change of ownership of real property transferee must file change of ownership statement in county where property located. (Rev. & Tax C. 90, 480). Penalty of greater of $100 or 10% of current year's taxes on property for noncompliance (with maximum of $2,500 if noncompliance was not willful and with possibility of abatement if reasonable cause exists). (Rev. & Tax C. 482, 483). Changes in control of corporation, partnership, limited liability company or other legal entity are subject to similar requirements. (Rev. & Tax C. 480.1, 480.2, 482).

Property which escapes assessment shall be assessed within four years after July 1 of assessment year in which it escaped assessment or was underassessed. In event of willful concealment of tangible personal property or fraud, assessment shall be made six years after July 1 of assessment year in which it escaped assessment. (Rev. & Tax C. 532).

Assessor prepares and delivers to auditor two assessment rolls listing all property in county on or before July 1 of year (unless State Board of Equalization ["SBE"] grants extension of deadline). (Rev. & Tax C. 601, 155, 616, 617). (For procedure regarding supplemental rolls, see Rev. & Tax C. 75.10-75.55.) State assessed property and real and personal property, taxes on which are lien on real property sufficient to secure payment of taxes, are placed on secured roll. All other property is placed on unsecured roll. (Rev. & Tax C. 109). Changes in assessments are easiest to obtain from county

See note at head of Digest as to 1998 legislation covered.

See Topical Index in front part of this volume.

CA – 59

ADMINISTRATION . . . *continued*

assessor before completion and delivery of assessment rolls. (See Rev. & Tax C. 616, 1613-1614). For later correction of defects not involving exercise of judgment as to value, see Rev. & Tax C. 4831 et seq.

Notice of increases (other than increase due to annual inflation adjustments or to changes in assessment ratio) is given to each assessee of real property on secured roll. (Rev. & Tax C. 619). Persons affected by regular assessment may apply to county board of equalization or assessment appeals board for reduction between July 2 and Sept. 15. (Rev. & Tax C. 1603[b]). Applications for reduction of supplemental assessments must be made 60 days from date of special notice. (Rev. & Tax C. 75.31[c]). Filing period is 12 months following date of notice if assessor and assessee stipulate in writing to error in assessment resulting from assessor's value determination. (Rev. & Tax C. 1603[c]). Application must be in writing (on form prescribed by SBE) and verified, show facts claimed to require reduction, and state applicant's opinion as to full value of property. (Rev. & Tax C. 1603[a]).

Board may announce its decision on application for reduction at conclusion of hearing or may take case under submission after first finding full value of property. (See Rev. & Tax C. 1610.8.) Subject to certain exceptions, applicant's opinion of market value will prevail if assessment appeals board fails to make final determination on application within two years of its filing, unless taxpayer and board agree in writing to extension. (Rev. & Tax C. 1604[c]).

Claim for refund may be filed with board of supervisors. (Rev. & Tax C. 5097). Grounds for recovery are in Rev. & Tax C. 5096. Claim for refund must be filed within later of four years after making tax payment or one year after later of date tax collector mails notice of overpayment under Rev. & Tax C. 2635 or period agreed to pursuant to Rev. & Tax C. 532.1. (Rev. & Tax C. 5097[a][2]). Claim for refund of escape assessment must be filed within 60 days after final determination by assessment appeals board. (Rev. & Tax C. 5097[c]). Application for reduction of assessment may be sufficient refund claim. (Rev. & Tax C. 5097[b]).

Time for Payment.—Taxes upon property on unsecured roll are due and payable on Mar. 1 lien date. (Rev. & Tax C. 2192, 2901). Taxes on unsecured roll as of July 31 if unpaid are delinquent Aug. 31 and thereafter 10% (or possibly greater) penalty payable. Taxes added to unsecured roll after July 31, if unpaid are delinquent and subject to 10% penalty (with possibility of further increases) on last day of month succeeding month of enrollment. (Rev. & Tax C. 2922). Taxes upon all personal property on secured roll, and one-half of taxes upon real property are due and payable on Nov. 1 (Rev. & Tax C. 2605), become delinquent Dec. 10 next thereafter at 5 P.M. and, unless paid prior thereto, are subject to 10% penalty (Rev. & Tax C. 2617). Remaining half of taxes on real property payable Feb. 1 (Rev. & Tax C. 2606), delinquent Apr. 10 at 5 P.M. and unless paid, subject to 10% penalty (Rev. & Tax C. 2618). If Dec. 10 or Apr. 10 is Sat., Sun. or holiday, taxes delinquent at 5 P.M. on next business day. (Rev. & Tax C. 2619). Taxes due on supplemental assessments are due on mailing date of bill and are delinquent on Dec. 10 (first installment) and Apr. 10 (second installment) if assessment is mailed within months of July through Oct. or, otherwise, on last day of month following month in which bill is mailed (first installment) and last day of fourth month following date first installment is delinquent (second installment). (Rev. & Tax C. 75.52). Payment by electronic fund transfer may be required under some circumstances. (Rev. & Tax C. 2503.2).

Lien.—Taxes on real property are lien on property assessed. (Rev. & Tax C. 2187). Exception, in some instances, for real property which has escaped assessment and which has been subsequently transferred. (Rev. & Tax C. 531.2). Under certain circumstances personal property taxes may be lien on any real property of owner. (Rev. & Tax C. 2189). Lien attaches on first day in Mar. preceding fiscal year for which taxes are levied and continues until tax paid. (Rev. & Tax C. 2192).

Sale and Deeding for Delinquent Taxes.—On or before June 8, tax collector publishes notice of impending default for failure to pay taxes on real property. (Rev. & Tax C. 3351). On July 1 unpaid taxes are, by operation of law declared in default. (Rev. & Tax C. 3436). Annually, on or before Sept. 8, tax collector publishes affidavit that real property is in default together with list of all such real property and notice that property may be redeemed. (Rev. & Tax C. 3371-3372). Annually, on or before June 8, tax collector publishes notice of intent to sell all property which will be tax defaulted five years or more. (Rev. & Tax C. 3361). Notice of such intent also mailed to last known address of last assessee not less than 21 nor more than 35 days before date power to sell for nonpayment of taxes arises. (Rev. & Tax C. 3365). Five years or more after property becomes tax-defaulted, tax collector may sell and shall attempt to sell all or portion of property which has not been redeemed. (Rev. & Tax C. 3691). Property must be offered for sale for not less than total amount necessary to redeem, plus costs. (Rev. & Tax C. 3698.5).

Penalties.—See under this subhead, catchlines Assessment, Time for Payment, Sale and Deeding for Delinquent Taxes, supra.

Process Agent for Tax Actions.—Every foreign corporation or nonresident individual incurring any tax liability to state or being guardian, receiver or fiduciary of any individual, estate, trust or corporation, or member of partnership, incurring such tax liability must file with Secretary of State designation of agent to receive service of process in any action relating to such tax. (C.C.P. 1018).

ALCOHOLIC BEVERAGES TAX:

Various taxes are levied on beverage alcohol. (Rev. & Tax C. 32001 et seq.).

CIGARETTE TAX:

Imposed by Rev. & Tax C. 30001 et seq.

CORPORATE TAXES:

See category Business Organizations, topic Corporations, subhead Taxation.

ENVIRONMENTAL TAXES AND FEES:

See Energy Resources Surcharge Law (Rev. & Tax C. 40016 et seq.), Hazardous Substances Tax Law (Rev. & Tax C. 43001 et seq.), Solid Waste Disposal Site Cleanup and Maintenance Fee Law (Rev. & Tax C. 45001 et seq.), Oil Spill Response, Prevention, and Administration Fees (Govt. C. 8670.48; Rev. & Tax C. 46001 et seq.), and Underground Storage Tank Maintenance Fee Law (Rev. & Tax C. 50101 et seq.).

FRANCHISE TAX:

See category Business Organizations, topic Corporations.

GASOLINE AND SPECIAL FUEL TAXES:

Fuel Tax.—Imposed by Rev. & Tax C. 7301 et seq.

Gasoline Tax.—See subhead Fuel Tax, supra.

GIFT TAX:

See topic Inheritance Tax and Gift Tax.

INCOME TAX:

Personal income tax is imposed by Personal Income Tax Law. (Rev. & Tax C. 17001-19442).

On Whom Imposed.—Individuals, fiduciaries, estates, trusts and common trust funds are subject to annual tax on their entire taxable income. Residents are taxed on their worldwide income. Nonresidents are taxed on income derived from California sources. (Rev. & Tax C. 17041). If decedent was resident at time of death, all estate income is taxable by California. Entire trust income is taxable by California if either fiduciary or beneficiary is resident. (Rev. & Tax C. 17742).

Deductions include many of those provided by Internal Revenue Code. Standard deductions for 1992 are $2,343 (single or married filing separate return) and $4,686 (married filing joint return, unmarried head of household, or qualifying widow[er]). (Rev. & Tax C. 17073.5).

Credits for Personal Exemptions.—For taxable year beginning on or after Jan. 1, 1988: Single person, married filing separate return, or unmarried head of household $52; married filing joint return or surviving spouse $104; subject to certain exceptions, $52 for each dependent, additional $52 for married filing separate return if spouse blind, has no gross income and not dependent of another taxpayer; $52 if taxpayer blind; if age 65 or over, additional $52. (Rev. & Tax C. 17054). Above credits are indexed for inflation. (Rev. & Tax C. 17054, 17054.5). Beginning in 1991, personal exemption credits are phased out where federal adjusted gross income exceeds indexed threshold amounts ($207,200 [joint return or surviving spouse], $155,400 [head of household], or $103,600 [single or married filing separate]). (Rev. & Tax C. 17054.1). Credit not to exceed $250 is allowed for 30% of net tax otherwise payable by qualified joint custody head of household or other qualified individuals. (Rev. & Tax C. 17054.5). Credit is allowed for 2% of taxable income of qualified senior head of household. (Rev. & Tax C. 17054.7).

Estates and trusts are allowed credits of $10 and $1 respectively against tax. (Rev. & Tax C. 17733).

Nonresidents and part-year residents must prorate credits. (Rev. & Tax C. 17055). Compensation of certain employees of foreign country is exempt. (Rev. & Tax C. 17146).

Credits allowed for 10% of cost of certain solar energy systems installed during taxable years beginning on or after Jan. 1, 1990 and before Jan. 1, 1994 (Rev. & Tax C. 17052.5); for certain employment related expenses incurred for care of children and dependents until Dec. 1, 1993 (Rev. & Tax C. 17052.6); for specified research and development activities (Rev. & Tax C. 17052.12); for 40% of cost of certain recycling equipment (Rev. & Tax C. 17052.14); for establishing, constructing, or contributing to certain child care programs or facilities for primarily taxpayer's employees or employees of taxpayer's tenants (Rev. & Tax C. 17052.17, 17052.18); for employer-provided transportation and vanpools (Rev. & Tax C. 17053); for 40% of vanpool costs incurred or paid in California by employee in nonemployer-sponsored vanpool program (Rev. & Tax C. 17053.1); to certain qualified renters (Rev. & Tax C. 17053.5); for 10% of certain wages paid to prisoners (Rev. & Tax C. 17053.6); for 10% of wages paid to persons registered in state employment and training program (Rev. & Tax C. 17053.7); for a percent of qualified wages paid to disadvantaged individuals in enterprise zones (Rev. & Tax C. 17053.8); for a percent of wages paid to persons for construction work in Los Angeles Revitalization Zone (Rev. & Tax C. 17053.10); and for excess contributions for state disability insurance (Rev. & Tax C. 17061).

Rates.—Personal income tax computed in accordance with following tables, subject to adjustment for inflation for 1992 and later taxable years (Rev. & Tax C. 17041):

For resident other than head of household, if taxable income is—

over—	but not over—	computed tax is—	of excess over—
$ 0	$ 3,650	$ 1.0%	$ 0
3,650	8,650	36.50 + 2.0%	3,650
8,650	13,650	136.50 + 4.0%	8,650
13,650	18,950	336.50 + 6.0%	13,650
18,950	23,950	654.50 + 8.0%	18,950
23,950	100,000	1,054.50 + 9.3%	23,950
100,000	200,000	8,127.15 + 10.0%	100,000
200,000	—	18,127.15 + 11.0%	200,000

See note at head of Digest as to 1998 legislation covered.

See Topical Index in front part of this volume.

INCOME TAX . . . *continued*

For resident head of household, if taxable income is—

over—	but not over—	computed tax is—	of excess over—
$ 0	$ 7,300	$ 1.0%	$ 0
7,300	17,300	73.00 + 2.0%	7,300
17,300	22,300	273.00 + 4.0%	17,300
22,300	27,600	473.00 + 6.0%	22,300
27,600	32,600	791.00 + 8.0%	27,600
32,600	136,115	1,191.00 + 9.3%	32,600
136,115	272,230	10,817.90 + 10.0%	136,115
272,230	—	24,429.40 + 11.0%	272,230

Alternative minimum tax is imposed primarily in accordance with IRC 55-59, at rate of 8.5% for any taxable year beginning on or after Jan. 1, 1991, and before Jan. 1, 1996. For any taxable year beginning on or after Jan. 1, 1996 rate is 7%; credit primarily as per IRC 53. (Rev. & Tax C. 17062-17063).

Returns and Payment.—Return must be filed with Franchise Tax Board on or before 15th day of fourth month following close of calendar or fiscal year. (Rev. & Tax C. 18566). Franchise Tax Board may grant up to six month extensions of time to file returns (but not to pay tax) with respect to individual, fiduciary, and partnership returns due on or after Apr. 15, 1992. (Rev. & Tax C. 18567).

Tax is payable at time fixed for filing return, without regard to any extension of time for filing return. (Rev. & Tax C. 18551). Each taxpayer who owes California tax not covered by withholding at source must make estimated tax payments. Amount determined under I.R.C. §6654 as modified by Rev. & Tax C. 19136 is added to regular tax due for any underpayment of estimated tax. (Rev. & Tax C. 19136). No amount is added if: (a) Regular tax (after credits) for current year is less than $100 ($50 for married filing separately); (b) 80% or more of regular tax for preceding taxable year (after credits other than tax withheld on wages) was paid by withholding of tax on wages; (c) 80% or more of estimated tax for year will be paid by withholding; or (d) 80% or more of adjusted gross income for year consists of items subject to withholding. (Rev. & Tax C. 19136).

Persons in military service serving beyond limits of U.S. and their spouses are granted automatic extension of time for filing returns and paying tax, except on income withheld at source. (Rev. & Tax C. 18570). Franchise Tax Board may grant reasonable extensions for filings including for taxpayers residing or traveling abroad. (Rev. & Tax C. 18567).

Tax Conformity.—California's Personal Income Tax law now incorporates by reference much of Internal Revenue Code as in effect on Jan. 1, 1993. (Rev. & Tax C. 17024.5[a]). Areas of taxation which now generally conform to federal law include following: Alternative minimum tax as per IRC 55-59 at rate of 8.5% for any taxable year beginning on or after Jan. 1, 1991, and before Jan. 1, 1996. For any taxable year beginning on or after Jan. 1, 1996, rate is 7%, credit in accordance with IRC 53 (Rev. & Tax C. 17062-63); items specifically included in or excluded from gross income (Rev. & Tax C. 17081, 17131); annuities as per IRC 72, with some modifications (Rev. & Tax C. 17085); business and entertainment expense deductions (Rev. & Tax C. 17270-17271); nondeductibility of sales tax (Rev. & Tax C. 17201); accounting periods and methods, subject to certain exceptions (Rev. & Tax C. 17551); limit on interest deductions as per IRC 163 (Rev. & Tax C. 17201); modified ACRS depreciation for assets placed in service on or after Jan. 1, 1987 (Rev. & Tax C. 17250); pass-through of S corporation income to shareholders (Rev. & Tax C. 17087.5); net operating loss deductions, except that no deduction is permitted for income years beginning before Jan. 1, 1987, NOL carrybacks are not permitted, amount of loss eligible for carryforward by taxpayers other than new and small businesses is reduced by 50%, and number of years to which NOL may be carried over is reduced (Rev. & Tax C. 17276-17276.3).

Penalties.—Inexcusable failure to timely file return, 5% of tax for each month or fraction thereof, not to exceed 25% of tax; if failure to file is fraudulent, penalty is 15% of tax for each month or fraction thereof, not to exceed 75% of tax; if return is 60 days late, minimum penalty is lesser of $100 or 100% of tax (Rev. & Tax C. 18681); lesser of 5% plus 0.5% per month (not to exceed 40 months), and 25% of total unpaid tax, for inexcusable failure to pay tax required to be shown on return within 15 days of demand (Rev. & Tax C. 19132); accuracy-related and fraud penalties imposed as provided in I.R.C. 6662-3 (Rev. & Tax C. 19164). Penalties are also imposed for failure to timely file information returns (Rev. & Tax. C. 18681.9, 19136, 19172-19175, 19181-19184), for underpayments of estimated tax (Rev. & Tax C. 18682) and failure to meet disclosure requirements with respect to quid quo pro contributions (Rev. & Tax C. 19182.5). Interest at adjusted annual rate established pursuant to Rev. & Tax C. 19521 on deficiencies and on penalties. (Rev. & Tax C. 19104-19106). Criminal penalties and fines are also provided for evasion of tax, false returns, and willful failure to remit withheld tax. (Rev. & Tax C. 19701-19714). Collection cost recovery fees also imposed. (Rev. & Tax C. 19254).

As to taxes on corporations, based on income, see category Business Organizations, topic Corporations, subhead Taxation; also category Insurance, topic Insurance Companies.

INHERITANCE TAX AND GIFT TAX:

Inheritance Tax and Gift Tax (former Rev. & Tax C. 13301-14902 and 15101-16652) repealed effective June 9, 1982. Maximum allowable credit under federal estate tax law for state death taxes is attributable to property located in California imposed as California estate tax. (Rev. & Tax C. 13302).

Procedures respecting administration and collection of such tax enacted effective June 30, 1982, in Rev. & Tax C. 13530 et seq. Personal representative shall file copies of federal estate tax return with state controller. (Rev. & Tax C. 13501). Tax is payable at decedent's death and is delinquent nine months thereafter. (Rev. & Tax C. 13531-13532).

Tax is also imposed on all generation skipping transfers as defined by federal law taxing such transfers, where original transferor is resident of California at date of original transfer, or where property transferred is in California. (Rev. & Tax C. 16702, 16710). Provisions respecting administration and collection of tax in Rev. & Tax C. 16830 et seq. Returns reporting generation skipping transfers must be filed on prescribed form stating amount of tax due with State Controller on or before last day for filing comparable federal return. (Rev. & Tax C. 16720-16721). Tax becomes delinquent from and after last day for filing return. (Rev. & Tax C. 16752).

PROPERTY TAXES:

Exemptions.—Property (real or personal) exempt from taxation includes property owned by state or, subject to certain exceptions, by local government (Rev. & Tax C. 202), property of nonprofit and public corporations leased to and used exclusively by government (Rev. & Tax C. 231), property used for free public libraries and museums or for public schools, community and state colleges and state universities (Rev. & Tax C. 202), property used exclusively for religious worship (Rev. & Tax C. 207), certain property used for religious, hospital, scientific or charitable purposes (including property used for housing and related facilities for certain elderly or handicapped families or emergency or temporary shelter for homeless persons, or portion of rental property serving lower income households), or school purposes of less than collegiate grade, or nursery school or noncommercial educational FM broadcast station or educational television station, and owned and operated (or leased to exempt governmental or certain educational entities) by certain nonprofit organizations (Rev. & Tax C. 214, 214.6), property leased for 35 years or more used exclusively for low income housing and operated by charitable organizations (Rev. & Tax C. 236), all personal and certain real property used for qualifying purposes by certain nonprofit veterans organizations (Rev. & Tax C. 215, 215.1), personalty of nonprofit zoological society and possessory interests in publicly owned land used by zoological society (Rev. & Tax C. 222, 222.5), property of nonprofit cemeteries (Rev. & Tax C. 204), seed potatoes (Rev. & Tax C. 234), growing crops (Rev. & Tax C. 202), immature fruit and nut trees and vines and certain immature forest trees (Rev. & Tax C. 211), oceanic cargo-containers (Rev. & Tax C. 232), large vessels in state and engaged in transportation of freight or passengers (Rev. & Tax C. 209), large vessels while under construction (Rev. & Tax C. 209.5), certain vessels with market value of $400 or less (Rev. & Tax C. 228), aircraft in state solely for repairs (Rev. & Tax C. 220), aircraft of historical significance under certain conditions (Rev. & Tax C. 220.5), computer equipment of San Diego Supercomputer Center (Rev. & Tax C. 226), business inventories (Rev. & Tax C. 219), notes, debentures, bonds, deeds of trust, mortgages, solvent credits, shares, and cash on hand in ordinary course of business and intangible assets and rights of taxable property (Rev. & Tax C. 212), personal property brought into state exclusively for exhibition (Rev. & Tax C. 213), miscellaneous articles displayed in publicly owned art gallery or museum for at least 90 days during preceding year, including certain aircraft displayed in aerospace museums (Rev. & Tax C. 217, 217.1), personal effects, household furnishings and pets (Rev. & Tax C. 224), and many motor vehicles subject to vehicle licensing fees (Rev. & Tax C. 10758). Partial exemptions are available for $20,000 of full value of owner-occupied principal residence (Rev. & Tax C. 218), $40,000-$150,000 for principle residence of blind or disabled veterans or their widows effective until 2001 (Rev. & Tax C. 205.5), $4,000 of property of certain veterans or, if deceased, of certain of their parents or unmarried spouses (Rev. & Tax C. 205, 205.1), and $1,500 of stock in trade of vending stand operated by licensed blind person (Rev. & Tax C. 216). Exemption claim procedure. (Rev. & Tax C. 251-279.5).

Property Taxable.—All property not exempt under laws of California or U.S. is taxable in proportion to its full value (which may be fair market value or other value as specified by California Constitution or state statute). (Const. Art XIII, §1). Property includes all matters and things, real, personal and mixed, capable of private ownership. (Rev. & Tax C. 103).

Redemption.—Tax-defaulted property may be redeemed until right of redemption is terminated. (Rev. & Tax C. 4101). Absolute right to redeem anytime within five years of date of declaration of default. (46 C.A. 363, 189 P. 314). Application to redeem made to tax collector who estimates amount necessary to redeem. (Rev. & Tax C. 4105, 4105.1). Upon request of redemptioner, tax collector issues certificate of redemption when tax-defaulted property is redeemed. (Rev. & Tax C. 4105.2). Partial redemption permitted under specified circumstances. (Rev. & Tax C. 4131-4159). Redemption in installments permitted. (Rev. & Tax C. 4216-4226).

Penalties.—See topic Administration, subhead County and Municipal Taxes, catchlines Assessment, Time for Payment, Sale and Deeding for Delinquent Taxes. See topics Income Tax, subhead Personal Income Tax, Sales and Use Taxes, subheads State Sales Tax, and State Use Tax, catchline Penalties.

REAL ESTATE CONVEYANCE TAX:

See topic Stamp Tax.

SALES AND USE TAXES:

State sales tax at rate of 6% of gross receipts is imposed on sales of tangible personal property by retailers. (Rev. & Tax C. 6051, 6051.2, 6051.3). Exemptions include, among others: gross receipts from sale of aircraft sold to (or for leasing to) common carriers, foreign governments, and nonresidents (Rev. & Tax C. 6366, 6366.1), vessels of more than 1,000 tons burden (Rev. & Tax C. 6356), food products under certain circumstances (Rev. & Tax C. 6359), prescription medicines (Rev. & Tax C. 6369), certain mailing lists (Rev. & Tax C. 6379.8), master tapes or master records (Rev. & Tax C. 6362.5), certain motor vehicle fuel used in propelling aircraft (Rev. & Tax C. 6357), aircraft fuel and petroleum products sold to air common carrier, if first destination is foreign (only until federal exemption is repealed) (Rev. & Tax C. 6357.5), sales, furnishing or service of gas, electricity and water, including steam and geothermal steam, when delivered to consumers through mains, lines or pipes (Rev. & Tax C. 6353), sales to U.S., its agencies, instrumentalities, and wholly owned corporations (Rev. & Tax C. 6381), occasional sales (Rev. & Tax C. 6006.5, 6367), and

See note at head of Digest as to 1998 legislation covered.

See Topical Index in front part of this volume.

CA – 61

SALES AND USE TAXES . . . *continued*

certain sales to common carriers or foreign air carriers, for use outside state (Rev. & Tax C. 6385).

Tax also imposed on certain leases of personal property. (Rev. & Tax C. 6006[g]). Sales or use tax on rentals payable under lease of tangible personal property is payable only during time personal property is situated in California. (Rev. & Tax C. 6006.1, 6010.1, 6390).

Unless State Board of Equalization ("SBE") requires different period, payments and returns are quarterly, to be made to SBE before end of month following quarter. (Rev. & Tax C. 6451-6452, 6455). SBE may require posting of security to insure payment (Rev. & Tax C. 6701), and if estimated measure of sales and use tax liability averages $20,000 or more monthly, as determined by SBE, may require prepayments according to specified schedule. (Rev. & Tax C. 6471-6472). If estimated tax liability averages $20,000 or more monthly, payment by electronic funds transfer required except where person collects use tax on voluntary basis. (Rev. & Tax C. 6479.3). Prepayment may also be required for certain distributions of motor vehicle fuel. (Rev. & Tax C. 6480-6480.8).

Penalties are payable of: 10% of any deficiency assessed upon failure to make return or on late returns and payments (Rev. & Tax C. 6511, 6591); additional 25% upon failure to file due to fraud (Rev. & Tax C. 6514). Interest is payable on deficiencies at IRC 6621 rate plus three percentage points. (Rev. & Tax C. 6513, 6591, 6591.5, 6592.5, 19521). Relief from interest imposed if noncompliance due to disaster. (Rev. & Tax C. 6593). In addition, 50% penalty is imposed for certain knowing failures to obtain valid seller's permit (Rev. & Tax C. 7155), illegal registration of vehicle, vessel or aircraft outside state (Rev. & Tax C. 6485.1, 6514.1), etc. Filing of false or fraudulent return with intent to evade tax is misdemeanor. (Rev. & Tax C. 7152).

Local Sales Tax.—City and county sales and use taxes are authorized and differ by locality.

Bradley-Burns Uniform Local Sales and Use Tax Law, effective Apr. 1, 1956 (Rev. & Tax C. 7200-7212), permits adoption of sales and use taxes by city, county, city and county or city redevelopment agency. Any such sales and use tax ordinance must be substantially similar to state sales and use tax law. (See Rev. & Tax C. 7202.) SBE acts as collection agency. Combined state and local return is filed with SBE. County rate is 1¼%, city rate is 1% or less. (Rev. & Tax C. 7202[a][1], 7202[a][8][A]). Sales and use taxes of any conforming city within county are credited against county tax so that combined city and county tax rate does not exceed 1¼%. (Rev. & Tax C. 7202[a][8]). Act is in force in all counties.

Additional Transactions and Use Taxes may be imposed by cities, counties, and special taxing districts. (Rev. & Tax C. 7251-7262, 7275-7279.6).

State use tax at rate of 6% of sales price of tangible personal property is imposed on storage, use or other consumption in state of tangible personal property purchased from retailer. (Rev. & Tax C. 6201, 6201.2, 6201.3). Exemptions include storage, use or consumption of property, gross receipts from sale of which are subject to the sales tax (Rev. & Tax C. 6401), aircraft sold to common carriers, foreign governments, and nonresidents (Rev. & Tax C. 6366, 6366.1), certain food products sold under certain conditions (Rev. & Tax C. 6359), prescription medicines (Rev. & Tax C. 6369), master tapes or records (Rev. & Tax C. 6362.5), certain motor vehicle fuel used in propelling aircraft (Rev. & Tax C. 6357), aircraft fuel and petroleum products sold to air common carrier, if first destination is foreign (until Jan. 1, 1994) (Rev. & Tax C. 6357.5), sales, furnishing or service of gas, electricity and water, including steam and geothermal steam, when delivered to consumers through mains, lines or pipes (Rev. & Tax C. 6353), certain property purchased from unincorporated agency or instrumentality of U.S. (Rev. & Tax C. 6402), qualified property used in space flight (Rev. & Tax C. 6380), certain tangible personal property purchased by new business for use in manufacturing or research and development (Rev. & Tax C. 6377) and tangible personal property, transfer of which is occasional sale (Rev. & Tax C. 6006.5, 6367).

Taxation of certain rentals of personal property is achieved primarily through imposition of use tax on such rentals. (Rev. & Tax C. 6009, 6010.1, 6390).

Retailer must make returns and payments same as in case of sales tax. Every retailer doing business in state must collect use tax on sales subject thereto. (Rev. & Tax C. 6203). Use tax on sales of certain vehicles or undocumented vessels collected by Department of Motor Vehicles. (Rev. & Tax C. 6292-6294).

Penalties basically same as for sales tax (see subhead State Sales Tax, supra).

STAMP TAX:

No stamp tax imposed on corporate stock or other instruments.

Documentary transfer on deeds or instruments by which real property valued in excess of $100 (exclusive of existing liens and encumbrances) is transferred, if adopted by city and county. (Rev. & Tax C. 11901 et seq.). County rate is $1.10 per $1,000 of value of interest or property conveyed, and city rate is ½ county rate (with credit against county tax) for conforming ordinances. (Rev. & Tax C. 11911). Both seller and buyer are responsible for tax. (Rev. & Tax C. 11912). Chartered cities may adopt transfer tax ordinances that do not conform to state legislation at higher rates. (Const. Art. XI, §5).

TIMBER YIELD TAX:

Imposed by Rev. & Tax C. 38101 et seq.

UNEMPLOYMENT COMPENSATION AND DISABILITY TAX:

Unemployment compensation and disability tax, in form of "contributions" is imposed by Unemployment Insurance Code.

Contributions are required from subject employers to provide for unemployment compensation benefits and from subject employees to provide for disability benefits.

Contributions are required from every employer having in his employ which for some portion of day within current or preceding calendar year employed one or more employees and paid in wages in excess of $100 during any calendar quarter (Un. Ins. C. 675) and from each of his employees (Un. Ins. C. 2901).

Exemptions.—Applicable to both employer and employee contributions include among others, certain domestic service; service on non-American vessel; employment of parents, spouse or minor children of employer; federal government employment except as provided otherwise by federal or state legislation; services for certain non-profit organizations; services covered by unemployment compensation law enacted by Congress (Un. Ins. C. 629-656).

Rates of contribution are: Employers' rates based on contributions and benefit experience varying from 0.1% to 5.4%. (Un. Ins. C. 977-982). Schedules of rates used vary according to balance in State unemployment fund. Employee's rate is not more than 1.3%. (Un. Ins. C. 984). No contributions are required on wages from employers after first $7,000 and from employees after first $31,767 of wages for calendar year 1993. (Un. Ins. C. 930, 985).

Withholding.—Contributions of employees must be withheld from wages by employer. (Un. Ins. C. 986).

Payment.—Employer contributions to state unemployment fund are due and payable on first day of calendar month following close of each calendar quarter. (Un. Ins. C. 1110). Depending upon timing and amounts collected, employee contributions collected during month may be remitted in conformity with IRC 6302, on or before 15th day of month subsequent to collection, or on or before last day of month following close of calendar quarter. Certain large employers are required to remit following end of eighth-monthly periods. Payment by electronic funds transfer required under some conditions. (Un. Ins. C. 13021). If contributions not paid before becoming delinquent, penalty of 10% plus interest at rate determined semiannually by Franchise Tax Board. (Un. Ins. C. 1110-13, 13021). Additional penalties are imposed for failure to make required returns. (Un. Ins. C. 1112.5, 1126).

Voluntary Plan.—Employer may make provision for payment of disability benefits under approved voluntary plan of insurance or self insurance (Un. Ins. C. 3251-3272) and in such case no employee contributions are required (Un. Ins. C. 3252) but employer is authorized to deduct amount not exceeding employee contributions authorized in Un. Ins. C. 984 and 985. (Un. Ins. C. 3260).

See also category Employment, topic Labor Relations, subhead Unemployment Insurance Code.

UNIFORM FEDERAL LIEN REGISTRATION ACT:

Enacted. (C.C.P. 2100 et seq.).

TRANSPORTATION

MOTOR VEHICLES:

Regulated by State Department of Motor Vehicles, 2415 First Ave., Sacramento, CA 95818. No Uniform Laws adopted.

Vehicle License.—Registration required annually. (Veh. C. 4601, 1651.5). When only one plate issued, must be displayed rear. (Veh. C. 5200). Specified vehicles exempt from registration fees. (Veh. C. 4002, 4003). Nonresident members of Armed Forces on active duty within state exempt if vehicle registered in member's state of residence. Resident and nonresident members of Armed Forces exempt if vehicle registered in state where member was regularly assigned and stationed at time of registration. If member of Armed Forces is owner or driver of motor vehicle, must comply with Veh. C. 16021. (Veh. C. 6701). For registration and license fees, see Veh. C. 9250 et seq.

Operator's license required (Veh. C. 12500); original license valid until fifth birthday following date of application (Veh. C. 12816); renewal license valid until fifth year birthday following expiration of renewed license (Veh. C. 12816); but licenses of servicemen absent from state continue during service (Veh. C. 12817). Persons under 16 may not be licensed, except in special cases (Veh. C. 12513), and may not be employed to drive on highways (Veh. C. 12515, et seq.). Applicants must submit satisfactory proof that presence in U.S. is authorized under federal law. (Veh. C. 12801.5). For members of Armed Forces, see subhead Nonresident Operator, infra.

Titles must be registered with Department of Motor Vehicles, which issues certificates of registration and of ownership. (Veh. C. 4000, 4450). Registration of off-road vehicles, as defined (Veh. C. 38006), required (Veh. C. 38010).

Sales.—On sale, certificate of ownership must be endorsed and dated by seller (Veh. C. 5600, 5750-53), and purchaser must file same with Department within ten days (Veh. C. 5902). Upon any sale or transfer previous owner must within five days notify Department, giving date of transfer, names and addresses of parties and actual mileage as indicated by odometer. (Veh. C. 5900). Dealer must give notice of transfer of vehicle and mileage indicated on odometer within five days after transfer, except when he transfers new unregistered vehicle to another dealer. (Veh. C. 5901). On sale of new car bill of sale must be issued and filed with Department. Conditional sales contracts for automobiles regulated by Rees Levering Act. (C. C. 2981, et seq.).

Liens.—No security interest in registered vehicle, whether or not registered before creation of interest, is perfected until secured party or his successor or assignee has deposited either physically or by electronic transmission, with Department certificate of legal ownership or application for registration as legal owner. (Veh. C. 6300). Deposit with Department of certificate of ownership showing secured party as legal owner perfects security interest, and rights of all persons in vehicle are subject to Uniform Commercial Code (Veh. C. 6301) but vehicle is subject to certain liens for repairs, storage, etc. (C. C. 3068 et seq., 3051a). Fee for filing application for transfer of registration to secured party is $3. (Veh. C. 9256). Special provisions relate to new security interests created within ten days after discharge of prior security interest (Veh. C. 5905) and security interests in vehicles constituting inventory (Veh. C. 5907).

Identification Marks.—Misdemeanor knowingly to buy, sell, receive, dispose of, offer for sale, or have possession of vehicle or component part thereof from which manufacturer's serial or identification number has been removed, defaced, altered or

See note at head of Digest as to 1998 legislation covered.

See Topical Index in front part of this volume.

MOTOR VEHICLES . . . *continued*

destroyed for purpose of concealment or misrepresenting identity or weight rating. (Veh. C. 10751, 40000.9).

Operation Prohibited.—By intoxicated person (0.08% or more blood alcohol) (Veh. C. 23152), or without license (Veh. C. 12500).

Size and Weight Limits.—Regulated by Veh. C. 35000, et seq.

Equipment Required.—Regulated by Veh. C. 24000, et seq. Specific requirements for off-road vehicles. (Veh. C. 38335, 38355, 38365 and 38390).

Lights Required.—Regulated by Veh. C. 24250 et seq.

Inspection.—Upon initial registration, transfer of ownership or registration of previously out-of-state vehicle must have pollution control compliance certificate for most vehicles. (Veh. C. 4000.1, 4000.2). Mechanical condition and equipment inspections by California Highway Patrol provided for. (Veh. C. 2814). Other various inspections are provided for. (Veh. C. 2802, et seq.).

Traffic Regulations.—Regulated by Veh. C. 21000-23336.

Accidents.—Driver involved in accident must stop (Veh. C. 20001, 20002); if property damage only must advise of his and owner's name, address and registration number of vehicle he is driving and exhibit driver's license and evidence of financial responsibility upon request (Veh. C. 20002). If bodily injury or death, driver must give above information and give assistance, and, upon death, report same without delay to authorities if none present at scene, and in all injury or death accidents must file written report within 24 hours with police or highway patrol for accidents in cities and highway patrol for accidents outside cities. (Veh. C. 20003-04, 20008). Other reports required to be filed within ten days where property damage exceeds $500 or bodily injury or death involved. (Veh. C. 16000, et seq.; see subhead Financial Responsibility Act of 1975, infra).

Drunk Driving.—Person with 0.08% blood alcohol level (0.01% if under age 21) prohibited from driving motor vehicle. (Veh. C. 23136, 23152).

Liability of Owner.—Owner of motor vehicle is liable for negligence of any person operating same with his consent, express or implied. (Veh. C. 17150). No limitation on liability of owner for his own negligence or that of his agent or servant; but in other cases liability imputed under statute is limited to following amounts in any one accident: $15,000 for death of or injury to one person; $30,000 for death of or injury to two or more persons in same accident; $5,000 for damage to property (Veh. C. 17151); and payment by such owner or bailee of owner, personal representative of decedent owner, or bailee in settlement of bona fide claims, whether reduced to judgment or not, aggregating $30,000 to two or more persons injured or killed in one accident extinguishes liability (Veh. C. 17155). Owner who is held liable under above provision is subrogated to claim against operator. (Veh. C. 17153). Vendor under conditional sale contract or mortgagee not in possession is not owner within meaning of above provision. (Veh. C. 17156).

Guests.—Owner or operator is liable for injury to or death of guest in vehicle through accident in course of operation thereof where such accident was caused by negligence, or willful misconduct of operator. (8 C.3d 855, 106 C.Rptr. 388, 506 P.2d 212. When owner is passenger see Veh. C. 17158).

Financial Responsibility Act of 1975 requires all California licensed drivers to meet certain financial responsibility limits. (Veh. C. 16020 et seq.). Department of Motor Vehicles must suspend driving privilege of any person willfully failing, refusing, or neglecting to make an accident report as required. (Veh. C. 16004). Every driver and owner of a motor vehicle must maintain some form of financial responsibility consisting of either self-insurance; maintenance of a liability insurance policy which covers driver of vehicle involved in accident, bond or cash deposit; or by showing vehicle is owned or operated by U.S., State of California or municipality. (Veh. C. 16020, 16021). Minimum limits of policy or bond are set at $15,000 for bodily injury or death to one person or $30,000 for injury or death of more than one person, and minimum of $5,000 for property damage. (Veh. C. 16056). Driving privileges will be suspended for those failing to comply with financial responsibility requirements. (Veh. C. 16070). §§16070-16078 establish procedural details regarding suspensions, burden of proof, and revision of records. Operator's license and registration of vehicles of owner of involved vehicle will be suspended upon showing of failure for 30 days to pay judgment against him. (Veh. C. 16370). Hearing is required prior to suspension to determine whether or not requisite injury or property damage had occurred, and whether driver did or did not have necessary form of financial responsibility. (Veh. C. 16075). Driver whose privilege is suspended may apply for restricted license to drive to work. (Veh. C. 16076).

Insurance.—Must comply with financial responsibility requirements set forth in Veh. C. 16021. (See subhead Financial Responsibility Act of 1975, supra.) There are detailed statutory provisions regarding contents of automobile liability policies. (Ins. C. 11580.05 et seq.).

Uninsured Motorist Insurance, Required Policy Provisions.—Every automobile bodily injury liability insurance policy issued or delivered by any insurer licensed in state upon any vehicle then principally garaged or used in state must contain a provision with coverage limits at least equal to financial responsibility requirements insuring insured for damages he is legally entitled to recover from owner or operator of an uninsured motor vehicle and entitling him to recover them from his own insurer. Policy must provide that determination as to whether insured is legally entitled to recover damages, and if so entitled, amount thereof, shall be made by agreement or by arbitration. Insurer paying such a claim is subrogated to rights of insured against any person causing injury to extent payment was made. (Ins. C. 11580.2).

No-Fault Insurance.—None.

Foreign Vehicles.—Nonresident owner, including member of armed services on duty in state, of foreign vehicle may operate such vehicle in California without registering or paying fees if vehicle is duly registered in place of residence of owner or, in case of serviceman, in place where he was required to be by military orders when plates were issued. (Veh. C. 6700-01). Nonresident with valid license plates from another state may operate motor vehicle in California until gainful employment is accepted in California or until residency is established in California, whichever occurs first. Application to register vehicle must be made within 20 days thereafter. (Veh. C. 6700). Every nonresident with established place of business in California must register vehicle upon entry into state. (Veh. C. 6702). Vehicles used to transport persons for hire or property must register immediately, subject to exception where vehicle is registered as private passenger-carrying vehicle in another state, and subject also to such privileges and exemptions as are reciprocally granted by such state to California vehicles. (Veh. C. 6850, 8000). Nonresident vehicles leased to resident or business resident must be registered if used in state except if exempt under reciprocity provisions of §8000, et seq. (Veh. C. 6853).

Nonresident operator over 18, including nonresident servicemen over 18, licensed in home state, or by Office of Foreign Missions of U.S. State Department, may operate vehicle without obtaining California license. If home state does not require license, operator driving his own vehicle may drive for 30 days without California license. Where nonresident operator is under 18 he may operate for only ten days without California license, except minor serviceman has 60 days. Upon establishing residence, former nonresident has ten days to obtain California license. (Veh. C. 12502-05 and 12518).

Actions against nonresident growing out of accidents occurring within California may be commenced by service of process (binding upon executor or administrator if so served when nonresident is deceased) upon Director of Department of Motor Vehicles, provided plaintiff forthwith sends notice of such service and copy of summons and complaint to defendant, or his estate's representative, by registered mail and secures return receipt from defendant. (Veh. C. 17450 et seq.). Special rule for tolling of statute of limitations prevails. (Veh. C. 17459-17463).

Direct Actions.—Direct action against insurer by injured person normally not allowed. Garnishment of obligations of insurer of nonappearing nonresident for purposes of quasi in rem jurisdiction not permitted. (17 C.3d 629).

Motor vehicle carriers are regulated by Public Utilities Commission. (Pub. Util. C. 3901, 3902).

Motor Vehicle Taxes.—Vehicle License Fee Law (Rev. & Tax C. 10701 et seq.) imposes annual license fee ("in lieu tax") for privilege of operating motor vehicle. Although it is excise/privilege tax, not property tax, it is measured by vehicle value currently 2% of market value. (Rev. & Tax C. 10752). Exemptions. (Rev. & Tax C. 10781-10789).

Gasoline Tax.—See category Taxation, topic Gasoline and Special Fuel Taxes.

Child Restraint System.—Parents must transport child under four years or 40 pounds in approved child passenger restraint system on highways. (Veh. C. 27360-27364). Others must also transport such children in approved child passenger restraint system. (Veh. C. 27360[b]). Exception where child passenger restraint system would be impractical because of child's physical unfitness, medical condition, or size. (Veh. C. 27363).

RAILROADS:

See category Business Regulation and Commerce, topic Carriers.

COMMERCIAL CODE FORMS

See also categories Business Regulation and Commerce, topic Commercial Code; Mortgages, topic Chattel Mortgages.

NATIONAL FINANCING STATEMENT (FORM UCC1) (TRANS) (REV. 12/18/95)

IMPORTANT—READ INSTRUCTIONS ON BACK BEFORE FILLING OUT FORM—DO NOT DETACH STUB

THIS SPACE FOR USE OF FILING OFFICER

FINANCING STATEMENT — FOLLOW INSTRUCTIONS CAREFULLY

This Financing Statement is presented for filing pursuant to the Uniform Commercial Code and will remain effective, with certain exceptions, for 5 years from date of filing.

A. NAME & TEL. # OF CONTACT AT FILER (optional)	B. FILING OFFICE ACCT. # (optional)

C. RETURN COPY TO: (Name and Mailing Address)

D. OPTIONAL DESIGNATION [if applicable]: ☐ LESSOR/LESSEE ☐ CONSIGNOR/CONSIGNEE ☐ NON-UCC FILING

1. DEBTOR'S EXACT FULL LEGAL NAME - insert only one debtor name (1a or 1b)

1a. ENTITY'S NAME

OR

1b. INDIVIDUAL'S LAST NAME	FIRST NAME	MIDDLE NAME	SUFFIX

1c. MAILING ADDRESS	CITY	STATE	COUNTRY	POSTAL CODE

1d. S.S. OR TAX I.D.#	OPTIONAL ADD'NL INFO RE ENTITY DEBTOR	1e. TYPE OF ENTITY	1f. ENTITY'S STATE OR COUNTRY OF ORGANIZATION	1g. ENTITY'S ORGANIZATIONAL I.D.#, if any ☐ NONE

2. ADDITIONAL DEBTOR'S EXACT FULL LEGAL NAME - insert only one debtor name (2a or 2b)

2a. ENTITY'S NAME

OR

2b. INDIVIDUAL'S LAST NAME	FIRST NAME	MIDDLE NAME	SUFFIX

2c. MAILING ADDRESS	CITY	STATE	COUNTRY	POSTAL CODE

2d. S.S. OR TAX I.D.#	OPTIONAL ADD'NL INFO RE ENTITY DEBTOR	2e. TYPE OF ENTITY	2f. ENTITY'S STATE OR COUNTRY OF ORGANIZATION	2g. ENTITY'S ORGANIZATIONAL I.D.#, if any ☐ NONE

3. SECURED PARTY'S (ORIGINAL S/P or ITS TOTAL ASSIGNEE) EXACT FULL LEGAL NAME - insert only one secured party name (3a or 3b)

3a. ENTITY'S NAME

OR

3b. INDIVIDUAL'S LAST NAME	FIRST NAME	MIDDLE NAME	SUFFIX

3c. MAILING ADDRESS	CITY	STATE	COUNTRY	POSTAL CODE

4. This FINANCING STATEMENT covers the following types or items of property:

5. CHECK BOX [if applicable]	This FINANCING STATEMENT is signed by the Secured Party instead of the Debtor to perfect a security interest (a) in collateral already subject to a security interest in another jurisdiction when it was brought into this state, or when the debtor's location was changed to this state, or (b) in accordance with other statutory provisions [additional data may be required]	7. If filed in Florida (check one) ☐ Documentary stamp tax paid ☐ Documentary stamp tax not applicable

6. REQUIRED SIGNATURE(S)	8. ☐ This FINANCING STATEMENT is to be filed [for record] (or recorded) in the REAL ESTATE RECORDS Attach Addendum [if applicable]
	9. Check to REQUEST SEARCH CERTIFICATE(S) on Debtor(s) [ADDITIONAL FEE] (optional) ☐ All Debtors ☐ Debtor 1 ☐ Debtor 2

(1) FILING OFFICER COPY — NATIONAL FINANCING STATEMENT (FORM UCC1) (TRANS) (REV. 12/18/95)

See note at head of Digest as to 1998 legislation covered.

See Topical Index in front part of this volume.

General Instructions for National Financing Statement (Form UCC1) (Trans)

Please type or laser-print this form. Be sure it is completely legible. Read all Instructions.

Fill in form very carefully; mistakes may have important legal consequences. Follow Instructions completely. If you have questions, consult your attorney. Filing officer cannot give legal advice.

Do not insert anything in the open space in the upper portion of this form; it is reserved for filing officer use.

When properly completed, send Filing Officer Copy, with required fee, to filing officer. If you want an acknowledgment, also send Acknowledgment Copy, otherwise detach. If you want to make a search request, complete item 9 and send Search Request Copy, otherwise detach. Always detach Debtor and Secured Party Copies.

If you need to use attachments, use 8-1/2 × 11 inch sheets and put at the top of each additional sheet the name of the first Debtor, formatted exactly as it appears in item 1 of this form, you are encouraged to use Addendum (Form UCC1Ad).

Item Instructions

1. **Debtor name:** Enter only one Debtor name in item 1, an entity's name (1a) or an individual's name (1b). Enter Debtor's exact full legal name. Don't abbreviate.

1a. Entity Debtor. "Entity" means an organization having a legal identity separate from its owner. A partnership is an entity; a sole proprietorship is not an entity, even if it does business under a trade name. If Debtor is a partnership, enter exact full legal name of partnership; you need not enter names of partners as additional Debtors. If Debtor is a registered entity (e.g., corporation, limited partnership, limited liability company), it is advisable to examine Debtor's current filed charter documents to determine correct name, entity type, and state of organization.

1b. Individual Debtor. "Individual" means a natural person and a sole proprietorship, whether or not operating under a trade name. Don't use prefixes (Mr., Mrs., Ms.). Use suffix box only for titles of lineage (Jr., Sr., III) and not for other suffixes or titles (e.g., M.D.). Use married woman's personal name (Mary Smith, not Mrs. John Smith). Enter individual Debtor's family name (surname) in Last Name box, first given name in First Name box, and all additional given names in Middle Name box.

For both entity and individual Debtors: Don't use Debtor's trade name, D/B/A, A/K/A, F/K/A, etc. in place of Debtor's legal name, you may add such other names as additional Debtors if you wish.

1c. An address is always required for the Debtor named in 1a or 1b.

1d. Debtor's social security or tax identification number is required in some states. Enter social security number of a sole proprietor, not tax identification number of the sole proprietorship.

1e,f,g. "Additional information re entity Debtor" is optional. It helps searchers to distinguish this Debtor from others with the same or a similar name. Type of entity and state of organization can be determined from Debtor's current filed charter documents. Organizational I.D. number, if any, is assigned by the agency where the charter document was filed; this is different from taxpayer I.D. number; this should be entered preceded by the 2-character U.S. Postal identification of state of organization (e.g., CA12345, for a California corporation whose organizational I.D. number is 12345).

Note: If Debtor is a transmitting utility as defined in applicable Commercial Code, attach Addendum (Form UCC1Ad) and check box Ad8.

2. If an additional Debtor is included, complete item 2, determined and formatted per Instruction 1. To include further additional Debtors, or one or more additional Secured Parties, attach either Addendum (Form UCC1Ad) or other additional page(s), using correct name format. Follow Instruction 1 for determining and formatting additional names.

3. Enter information, determined and formatted per Instruction 1. If there is more than one Secured Party, see Instruction 2. If there has been a total assignment of the Secured Party's interest prior to filing this form, you may provide either assignor Secured Party's or assignee's name and address in item 3.

4. Use item 4 to indicate the types or describe the items of collateral. If space in item 4 is insufficient, put the entire collateral description or continuation of the collateral description on either Addendum (Form UCC1Ad) or other attached additional page(s).

5, 6. All Debtors must sign. Under certain circumstances, Secured Party may sign instead of Debtor; if applicable, check box in item 5 and provide Secured Party's signature in item 6, and under certain circumstances, in some states, you must also provide additional data; use Addendum (Form UCC1Ad) or attachment to provide such additional data.

7. If filing in the state of Florida you must check one of the two boxes in item 7 to comply with documentary stamp tax requirements.

8. If the collateral consists of or includes fixtures, timber, minerals, and/or mineral-related accounts, check the box in item 8 and complete the required information on Addendum (Form UCC1Ad). If the collateral consists of or includes crops, consult applicable law of state where this Financing Statement is to be filed and complete Ad3b, and Ad4 if required, on Addendum (Form UCC1Ad) and, if required, check box in item 8.

9. Check box 9 to request Search Certificate(s) on all or some of the Debtors named in this Financing Statement. The Certificate will list all Financing Statements on file against the designated Debtor currently effective on the date of the Certificate, including this Financing Statement. There is an additional fee for each Certificate. This item is optional. If you have checked box 9, file copy 3 (Search Request Copy) of this form together with copies 1 and 2. Not all states will honor a search request made via this form; some states require a separate request form.

Instructions re Optional Items A-D

A. To assist filing officers who might wish to communicate with filer, filer may provide information in item A. This item is optional.

B. If filer has an account with filing officer or is authorized to pay fees by means of a card (credit or debit) and wishes to use such means of payment, check the appropriate box and enter filer's account number in item B, or, in the alternative, filer may present this information by a cover letter.

C. Complete item C if you want acknowledgment copy returned and you have presented simultaneously a carbon or other copy of this form for use as an acknowledgment copy.

D. If filer desires to use titles of lessee and lessor, or consignee and consignor, instead of Debtor and Secured Party, check the appropriate box in item D. This item is optional. If this is not a UCC security interest filing (e.g., a tax lien, judgment lien, etc.), check the appropriate box in item D, complete items 1-9 as applicable and attach any other items required under other law.

Statement of Continuation, Termination, Etc.—

This **STATEMENT** is presented for filing pursuant to the California Uniform Commercial Code

1. FILE NO. OF ORIG. FINANCING STATEMENT	1A. DATE OF FILING OF ORIG. FINANCING STATEMENT	1B. DATE OF ORIG. FINANCING STATEMENT	1C. PLACE OF FILING ORIG. FINANCING STATEMENT

2. DEBTOR (LAST NAME FIRST)		2A. SOCIAL SECURITY NO., FEDERAL TAX NO.	
2B. MAILING ADDRESS	2C. CITY, STATE		2D. ZIP CODE

3. ADDITIONAL DEBTOR (IF ANY) (LAST NAME FIRST)		3A. SOCIAL SECURITY OR FEDERAL TAX NO.	
3B. MAILING ADDRESS	3C. CITY, STATE		3D. ZIP CODE

4. SECURED PARTY	4A. SOCIAL SECURITY NO., FEDERAL TAX NO. OR BANK TRANSIT AND A.B.A. NO.
NAME MAILING ADDRESS CITY STATE ZIP CODE	

5. ASSIGNEE OF SECURED PARTY (IF ANY)	5A. SOCIAL SECURITY NO., FEDERAL TAX NO. OR BANK TRANSIT AND A.B.A. NO.
NAME MAILING ADDRESS CITY STATE ZIP CODE	

6.

A ☐ CONTINUATION—The original Financing Statement between the foregoing Debtor and Secured Party bearing the file number and date shown above is continued. If collateral is crops or timber, check here ☐ and insert description of real property on which growing or to be grown in Item 7 below.

B ☐ RELEASE—From the collateral described in the Financing Statement bearing the file number shown above, the Secured Party releases the collateral described in Item 7 below.

C ☐ ASSIGNMENT—The Secured Party certifies that the Secured Party has assigned to the Assignee above named, all the Secured Party's rights under the financing statement bearing the file number shown above in the collateral described in Item 7 below.

D ☐ TERMINATION—The Secured Party certifies that the Secured Party no longer claims a security interest under the Financing Statement bearing the file number shown above.

E ☐ AMENDMENT—The Financing Statement bearing the file number shown above is amended as set forth in Item 7 below. (Signature of Debtor required on all amendments.)

F ☐ OTHER

7.

8.			C O D E	9. This Space for Use of Filing Officer (Date, Time, Filing Office)
(Date) _____ 19 ____				
By: _____ SIGNATURE(S) OF DEBTOR(S) (TITLE)			1 2	
By: _____ SIGNATURE(S) OF SECURED PARTY(IES) (TITLE)			3 4	

10.

Return Copy to:

NAME
ADDRESS
CITY AND
STATE

```
C
O
D
E
1
2
3
4
5
6
7
8
9
```

(1) FILING OFFICER COPY   UNIFORM COMMERCIAL CODE—FORM UCC-2
Approved by the Secretary of State

See note at head of Digest as to 1998 legislation covered.

See Topical Index in front part of this volume.

INSTRUCTIONS (Rev. 1/90)

1. PLEASE TYPE THIS FORM USING BLACK TYPEWRITER RIBBON.

2. IF THE SPACE PROVIDED FOR ANY ITEM IS INADEQUATE.

    a. Note "contd." in the appropriate space(s).

    b. Continue the item(s) preceded by the Item No. on an additional 8½" × 11" sheet.

    c. Head each additional sheet with the Debtor's name (Last Name First) appearing in Item No. 2 of this form. Be sure to attach a copy of the additional sheet to each copy of the form.

3. NUMERICAL IDENTIFICATION: Social Security, Federal Tax, Transit/ABA Numbers and ZIP Codes are to be included if possible, so that Statements may be more readily indexed and information rapidly retrieved through the use of electronic data processing equipment in the Secretary of State's Office.

    a. If the Debtor, Secured Party or Assignee is an individual, include Social Security Number in the appropriate space.

    b. If the Debtor, Secured Party or Assignee is other than an individual or a bank, show Federal Taxpayer Number in the appropriate space.

    c. If the Secured Party or Assignee is a bank, show Transit and ABA Number in the appropriate space.

4. Be sure to indicate type of Statement being filed by checking the appropriate box in Item No. 6.

5. Remove Secured Party and Debtor copies.

Send the *ORIGINAL AND FIRST COPY* with interleaved carbon paper to the Filing Officer with the correct filing fee. The original will be retained by the Filing Officer. The copy will be returned with the filing date and time stamped thereon. *Indicate the name and mailing address of the person or firm to whom the copy is to be returned in Item No. 10.*

6. FILING FEE: Enclose filing fee*   payable to the appropriate Filing Officer.

7. SIGNATURES: Before mailing be sure that the Statement has been properly signed. Continuation, Release, Assignment, or Termination Statements require only the signature of the Secured Party of Record. An Amendment requires the signatures of both the Debtor and Secured Party of Record.

* For current fee to the Secretary of State Call (916) 445-8061

State of California
Uniform Commercial Code - Request For Information Or Copies - Form UCC-3
IMPORTANT-Read instructions on back before completing form
REQUEST FOR INFORMATION OR COPIES. (Present in Duplicate to Filing Officer)

1. ☐ **INFORMATION REQUEST.** Filing Officer, please furnish certificate showing whether there is on file any presently effective financing statement naming the Debtor listed below and any statement of assignment thereof, and if there is, giving the date and hour of filing of each such statement and the names and addresses of each Secured Party named therein.

1A. _____ 1B. _____

DEBTOR (Last Name, First)   Social Security or Federal Tax No.

1C. _____ 1D. _____ 1E. _____

Mailing Address   City, State   Zip Code

1F. _____ 19 _____   _____

Date   (Signature of Requesting Party)

2. **CERTIFICATE:**

File Number	Date and Hour of Filing	Name(s) and Address(es) of Secured Party(ies) and Assignee(s), if any

The undersigned Filing Officer hereby certifies that the above listing is a record of all presently effective financing statements and statements of assignment which name the above Debtor and which are on file in my office as of _____ 19_____ at _____ ____ M.

_____ 19 _____   _____

(Date)   (Filing Officer)

By: _____

3. ☐ **COPY REQUEST.** Filing Officer, please furnish _____ copy(ies) of each page of the following statements concerning the Debtors listed below: ☐ Financing Statement ☐ Amendments ☐ Statements of Assignment ☐ Continuation Statements ☐ Statement of Release ☐ Termination Statement ☐ All Statements on File.

File Number	Date of Filing	Name(s) and Address(es) of Secured Party(ies) and Assignee(s) (if any)	Debtor's Soc. Sec. or Fed Tax No.

_____ 19 _____   _____

(Date)   (Filing Officer)

4. **CERTIFICATE:**

The undersigned filing officer hereby certifies that the attached copies are true and exact copies of all statements requested above.

_____ 19 _____   _____

(Date)   (Filing Officer)

By: _____

5.   **Mail Information or Copies to**

NAME
ADDRESS
CITY AND
STATE

UNIFORM COMMERCIAL CODE—REQUEST FOR INFORMATION OR COPIES—FORM UCC-3 (4/91)

See note at head of Digest as to 1998 legislation covered.

See Topical Index in front part of this volume.

INSTRUCTIONS

1. PLEASE TYPE THIS FORM USING BLACK TYPEWRITER RIBBON.

2. IF THE SPACE PROVIDED FOR ANY ITEM IS INADEQUATE:
   a. Note "contd." in the appropriate space(s).
   b. Continue the item(s) preceded by the Item No. on an additional 8½" × 11" sheet.
   c. Head each additional sheet with the Debtor's name (Last Name, First) appearing in Item No. 2 of this form Be sure to attach a copy of the additional sheet to each copy of the form.

3. NUMERICAL IDENTIFICATION: Social Security, Federal Tax, Transit/A.B.A. Numbers and ZIP Codes are to be included, if possible, so that Statements may be more easily indexed and information rapidly retrieved through the use of electronic data processing equipment in the Secretary of State's Office.
   a. If the Debtor, Secured Party, or Assignee is an individual, include Social Security Number in the appropriate space.
   b. If the Debtor, Secured Party, or Assignee is other than an individual or a bank, show Federal Taxpayer Number in the appropriate space.
   c. If the Secured Party or Assignee is a bank, show Transit and A.B.A. Number in the appropriate space.

4. Be sure to indicate type of Statement being filed by checking the appropriate boxes in #1 or #3.
   a. Information Requests Only: Check #1 and complete all items. (1A through 1F; item 1B is optional). May contain only one Debtor Name and Address. If more than one address is required for a specific Debtor, show "Any Address" in item 1C.
   b. Copies Requests Only: Check #3 and indicate desired documents by checking appropriate box. List File Number(s), Debtor Name(s) and Address(es) or "Any Address". Requesting party MUST sign for copies. If Signature, Debtor Name or File Number is not shown, UCC-3 will be rejected.

5. If you do not know the File Number, you can submit an Information Request and check for $11.00 to the UCC Division and receive a certificate showing the file number(s), or you can check both the Information and Copy Requests boxes, #1 and #3, and submit along with a check that reads: "Not to Exceed $35.00", exact amount to be completed by the Secretary of State.

6. Remove requesting party copy. Send WHITE and CANARY COPIES to the Filing Officer with the correct filing fee. Requestor MUST complete Mail Information portion of form; the Canary copy will be returned to the address in section 5.

7. Filing Fees: (payable to the appropriate Filing Officer)
   a. Information Request only: $11.00
   b. Copies Request Only: $1.00 per document and $.50 per attachment.

8. Signatures: Before mailing, be sure that the Request For Information has been properly signed. Information Requests and Copy Requests, #1 and #3, must be signed by the Requesting Party.

   Mail Requests to: Secretary of State
                       UCC Division
                       P.O. Box 1738
                       Sacramento, CA 95808

This document is only a general form which may be proper for use in simple transactions and in no way acts, or is intended to act, as a substitute for the advice of an attorney. The printer does not make any warranty, either express or implied, as to the legal validity of any provision or the suitability of these forms in any specific transaction.

UNIFORM COMMERCIAL CODE—REQUEST FOR INFORMATION OR COPIES—FORM UCC-3 (4/91)

See note at head of Digest as to 1998 legislation covered.

See Topical Index in front part of this volume.

STATE OF CALIFORNIA
SECRETARY OF STATE
UNIFORM COMMERCIAL CODE DIVISION
REQUEST FOR INFORMATION - FORM UCC3

SoS 10-24-94

Filing Officer please provide the following type(s) of information concerning the debtor named below:
(For personal name, show LAST NAME, FIRST NAME)

DEBTOR NAME:
SSN/FTN: *(optional)*

ADDRESS:
CITY: **STATE:**   **ZIP:**   **COUNTRY:**

** PLEASE CHECK AT LEAST ONE REQUEST TYPE BELOW **

_____ **CERTIFICATE**   A list of active filings containing the information stated above.

_____ **COPIES**   If copies are requested **at the same time** as a CERTIFICATE, copies of all filings appearing on the CERTIFICATE will be provided, unless otherwise noted.

If only copies are requested, up to 10 file numbers may be listed below. **Copies are not certified unless requested. An additional fee is required in that case.**

Special Instructions: _____

(This section applies if only COPIES are requested)

FILE NUMBER	TYPE OF DOCUMENT	FILE DATE	QUANTITY/INSTRUCTIONS

SIGNATURE OF REQUESTOR: _____ Date: _____

This Space Reserved for Use
by the Filing Office

RETURN INFORMATION TO

NAME:

ADDRESS:
CITY:
                              STATE: **ZIP:**
COUNTRY:

See note at head of Digest as to 1998 legislation covered.

See Topical Index in front part of this volume.

Form

8-23

| ATTORNEY OR CREDITOR WITHOUT ATTORNEY (Name and Address): | TELEPHONE NO.: | *FOR COURT USE ONLY* |

ATTORNEY FOR (Name):

SUPERIOR COURT OF CALIFORNIA, COUNTY OF SAN DIEGO
STREET ADDRESS:
MAILING ADDRESS:
CITY AND ZIP CODE:
BRANCH NAME:

ESTATE OF (NAME):

DECEDENT

CASE NUMBER:

CREDITOR'S CLAIM*

(for estate administration proceedings filed after June 30, 1988)

> You must file this claim with the court clerk at the court address above before the LATER of (a) four months after the date letters (authority to act for the estate) were first issued to the personal representative, or (b) thirty days after the date Notice of Administration was given to the creditor, if notice was given as provided in Probate Code section 9051. Mail or deliver a copy of this claim to the personal representative. A proof of service is on the reverse.

1. Total amount of the claim is: $

2. Claimant (name):

   a. ☐ an individual.

   b. ☐ an individual or entity doing business under the fictitious name of (specify):

   c. ☐ a partnership. The person signing has authority to sign on behalf of the partnership.

   d. ☐ a corporation. The person signing has authority to sign on behalf of the corporation.

   e. ☐ other (specify):

3. Address of claimant (specify):

4. Claimant is ☐ the creditor ☐ a person acting on behalf of creditor (state reason):

5. ☐ Claimant is ☐ the personal representative ☐ the attorney for the personal representative.
   (Claims against the estate by the personal representative and the attorney for the personal representative must be filed within the claim period allowed in Probate Code section 9100. See the notice box above.)

6. I am authorized to make this claim which is justly due or may become due. All payments on or offsets to the claim have been credited. Facts supporting the claim are ☐ on reverse ☐ attached.

I declare under penalty of perjury under the laws of the State of California that this creditor's claim is true and correct.

Date:

▶

....
(TYPE OR PRINT NAME AND TITLE)

_____
(SIGNATURE OF CLAIMANT)

INSTRUCTIONS TO CLAIMANT

A. On the reverse, itemize the claim and show the date the service was rendered or the debt incurred. Describe the item or service in detail, and indicate the amount claimed for each item. Do not include debts incurred after the date of death, except funeral claims.

B. If the claim is not due or contingent, or the amount is not yet ascertainable, state the facts supporting the claim.

C. If the claim is secured by a note or other written instrument, the original or a copy must be attached (state why original is unavailable). If secured by mortgage, deed of trust, or other lien on property that is of record, it is sufficient to describe the security and refer to the date or volume and page, and county where recorded. (See Probate Code section 9152.)

D. Mail or take this original claim to the court clerk's office for filing. If mailed, use certified mail, with return receipt requested.

E. Mail or deliver a copy to the personal representative. Complete the Proof of Mailing or Personal Delivery on the reverse.

F. The personal representative will notify you when your claim is allowed or rejected.

(Continued on reverse)

* See instructions before completing. Use Creditor's Claim form No. DE-170 for estates filed before July 1, 1988.

Form Approved by the
Judicial Council of California
DE-172 [New July 1, 1988]
PR-53
LP7 '88

CREDITOR'S CLAIM
(Probate)

Probate Code, §§ 9000 et seq., 9153

See note at head of Digest as to 1998 legislation covered.

See Topical Index in front part of this volume.

ESTATE OF (NAME):		CASE NUMBER:
	DECEDENT	

FACTS SUPPORTING THE CREDITOR'S CLAIM
☐ **See attachment** *(if space is insufficient)*

Date of Item	Item and Supporting Facts	Amount Claimed
	TOTAL	$

PROOF OF ☐ MAILING ☐ PERSONAL DELIVERY   TO PERSONAL REPRESENTATIVE
(Be sure to mail or take the original to the court clerk's office for filing)

1. I am the creditor or a person acting on behalf of the creditor. At the time of mailing or delivery I was at least 18 years of age.

2. My residence or business address is *(specify)*:

3. I mailed or delivered a copy of this Creditor's Claim to the personal representative as follows *(check either a or b below)*:

a. ☐ **First-class mail.** I deposited a copy of the claim with the United States Postal Service, in a sealed envelope with postage fully prepaid. I used first-class mail. I am a resident of or employed in the county where the mailing occurred. The envelope was addressed and mailed as follows:

    (1) Name of personal representative served:

    (2) Address on envelope:

    (3) Date of mailing:

    (4) Place of mailing *(city and state)*:

b. ☐ **Personal delivery.** I personally delivered a copy of the claim to the personal representative as follows:

    (1) Name of personal representative served:

    (2) Address where delivered:

    (3) Date delivered:

    (4) Time delivered:

I declare under penalty of perjury under the laws of the State of California that the foregoing is true and correct.

Date:

▶

....
(TYPE OR PRINT NAME OF CLAIMANT)

_____
(SIGNATURE OF CLAIMANT)

DE 172 [New July 1, 1988]   **CREDITOR'S CLAIM** *(Probate)*   Page two

See note at head of Digest as to 1998 legislation covered.

See Topical Index in front part of this volume.

COLORADO LAW DIGEST REVISER

Holme Roberts & Owen LLP
Suite 1400, 1700 Lincoln
Denver, Colorado 80203
Telephone: 303-861-7000
Fax: 303-866-0200
Email: hro@hro.com
Webpage: http://www.hro.com

Reviser Profile

Overview: Holme Roberts & Owen LLP was founded in 1898, only 40 years after Denver's birth, by two experienced litigators whose primary clients were railroad and mining companies. Today the firm still represents such interests, among them the Southern Pacific Railroad and Newmont Gold Company, but now its lawyers number 180 or more and its clients also include local and national leaders in such industries as telecommunications, banking, corporate finance, health care, electronics and oil and gas.

The firm is one of the oldest and largest in the Rocky Mountain region, with Colorado offices in Denver, Boulder and Colorado Springs, a Utah office in Salt Lake City and a London office established in 1991 to serve our clients' interests abroad.

Practice: To best serve our diverse clientele, the firm's lawyers work in teams called "practice groups" that mirror aspects of our clients' individual and multiple ever-changing needs. This often results in the creation of new practice groups; for example, our environmental team, formed five years ago, is now one of our largest groups. This also often results in lawyers from more than one practice group working together on a single client project. Paraprofessionals support each practice group.

Our clients include many small concerns and those in genesis. Small businesses have long been a major part of our practice, and we recognize their continuing role in our growth.

Other: The firm's five locations function as a single law office and are interconnected by state-of-the-art word processing, data retrieval and facsimile transmission equipment. All of this is a reflection of our continued commitment to cost-effective delivery of services through efficient staffing, timeliness and, above all, sensitivity to client needs.

COLORADO LAW DIGEST

(The following is a list of all Categories and Topics, including cross-references, covered in this Digest.)

COLORADO LAW DIGEST

Revised for 1999 edition by

HOLME ROBERTS & OWEN, LLP, of the Denver, Boulder and Colorado Springs Bars.

(Citations, unless otherwise noted, are to titles, articles and sections of Colorado Revised Statutes. "Rule" indicates Rules of Civil Procedure and "App. Rule" indicates Appellate Rules. Parallel citations to Pacific Reporter begin with 7 Colo. and 1 Colo. App. and official reports end with 199 Colo. and 43 Colo. App., 1980. HB and SB refer to those House Bills or Senate Bills that have been enacted into law.)

Note: This revision covers all enactments of the Sixty-first General Assembly, Second Regular Session, 1998.

INTRODUCTION

GOVERNMENT AND LEGAL SYSTEM:

The State of Colorado is a constituent state of the United States of America. For further discussion of the U.S. federal system, see Introduction to the Federal Government of the United States at the beginning of this volume. A great many laws are promulgated by the federal government of the United States and are not reflected in the topics below. See the Introduction to this volume for references to the federal law topics covered.

Like all but one of the United States, Colorado has a common law legal system, with roots in English common law. For information on the courts and legislature of Colorado, see category Courts and Legislature.

HOLIDAYS:

Legal holidays are: Jan. 1; 3d Mon. in Jan.; 3d Mon. in Feb.; last Mon. in May; July 4; 1st Mon. in Sept.; 2d Mon. in Oct.; Nov. 11; 4th Thurs. in Nov.; Dec. 25; and any day appointed by governor or president as day of fasting, prayer or thanksgiving. (24-11-101[1]). Legal holidays treated as Sun. for holding of court and all purposes regarding payment, acceptance, protesting or giving notice of dishonor of negotiable instruments. (24-11-101[1]). If legal holiday falls on Sun., following Mon. shall be considered holiday and shall be treated as Sun. (24-11-101[2]). Any return or adjournment date in any suit, matter or hearing before court on any day above mentioned is continued to next succeeding day, unless Sun., then next succeeding secular or business day. (24-11-101[2]).

When public offices are closed on holidays, Sats., or otherwise, official acts or duties, appearances or filings required then to be performed are continued until next full business day. (24-11-110).

Agencies in executive branch of state government may do business on any legal holiday. Employees under jurisdiction of state personnel system who are required to work on any legal holiday are granted alternate day off in same fiscal year or are paid in accordance with state personnel system or state fiscal rules in effect on Apr. 30, 1979. (24-11-101[3]).

Banking institutions may close on Sats. in which event Sat. is equivalent of legal holiday with respect to bank. (11-6-103). However, fact that bank remains open for business on all, or less than all, Sats. shall not make that day, or any part thereof, banking day for purposes of 4-4-104(A)(3), C.R.S. of Uniform Commercial Code. Sats., Suns. and holidays are excluded from code definition of banking day. (4-4-104[A][3]).

OFFICE HOURS AND TIME ZONE:

Colorado is in the Mountain (GMT −07:00) time zone. Office hours are generally from 9 a.m. to 5 p.m.

BUSINESS ORGANIZATIONS

AGENCY:

The common law governs the relation of principal and agent except as affected by the Uniform Fiduciaries Law. (15-1-101 to 113).

ASSOCIATIONS:

Nonprofit associations generally may be incorporated under Colorado Revised Nonprofit Corporation Act (7-121-101 to 7-137-108) or may operate as unincorporated nonprofit associations (7-30-101 to 7-30-119). Cooperative associations may be incorporated, with or without stock, for mutual benefit of members for cooperative transaction of any lawful business. (7-55-101 to 7-55-121; or may elect to be governed by 7-56-101 to 7-56-901).

Fraternal benefit society may be formed as unincorporated society, order or lodge, without capital stock, and operated on lodge system, having representative government and providing death, endowment, annuity, disability, medical, monument or tombstone benefits or other benefits authorized for life insurers. (10-14-101 to 10-14-705). Certain officials of churches and religious societies may incorporate their offices as corporations sole for purpose of holding title to property, contracting, suing and being sued on behalf of churches or religious societies. (7-52-101 to 7-52-106). Labor unions and associations are declared not to be unlawful. (8-2-101).

Uniform Unincorporated Nonprofit Association Act adopted, without material variations, effective July 1, 1994. (7-30-101 to 7-30-119).

Actions.—Unincorporated association may sue or be sued in its common name. (13-50-105; CRCP Rule 17[b]). Judgment binds only joint property of association and separate property of named parties personally served or who have entered appearance. (13-50-105; CRCP Rule 54[e]). Action brought by or against members of unincorporated association as class by naming certain representative members may be maintained only if representative members will fairly and adequately protect interests of association and its members. (CRCP Rule 23.2).

Professional Associations.—Medical practice by use of professional service corporations is permitted provided, however, their sole purpose is to conduct medical practice through persons licensed by Colorado, and all shareholders are licensed practitioners and actively engaged in practice of medicine in offices of corporation. Shareholders are jointly and severally liable unless liability insurance carried by shareholders or corporation meets certain standards. (12-36-134). Dental practice by use of professional service corporations is permitted on same terms as medical practice. (12-35-112). Professional service corporations for practice of podiatry (12-32-109.5), chiropractic (12-33-124), optometry (12-40-125), physical therapy (12-41-124), and psychology (12-43-211) are authorized. Professional service corporations also authorized for accountants (12-2-117), architects (12-4-110), engineers (12-25-104) and surveyors (12-25-204). Attorneys are permitted to form professional service corporations by Supreme Court Rule. See category Legal Profession, topic Attorneys and Counselors.

CORPORATIONS:

NOTE: Colorado Business Corporation Act adopted effective July 1, 1994, based on Model Business Corporation Act (1984), prepared by Committee on Corporate Laws (Section of Corporation, Banking and Business Law) of American Bar Association. For text of Model Business Corporation Act (1984), see Uniform and Model Acts section. Law as digested below relates only to variances of Colorado Business Corporation Act from Model Business Corporation Act (1984), contained in Uniform and Model Acts section.

General Supervision.—Secretary of State, 1560 Broadway, #200, Denver, Colorado 80202, telephone (303) 894-2251; telecopy (303) 894-2242.

Fees.—§1.22 of Model Act not adopted. Secretary of State charges and collects fees as provided in 24-21-104(3) and 7-101-203.

Reservation of Name (and Transfer or Renewal)		$5.00
Articles of Incorporation, Certificate of Limited Partnership		$50.00
Articles of Amendment		$25.00
Restated Articles of Incorporation		$60.00
Certificate of Correction		$5.00
Statement of Change of Registered Office or Agent		$5.00
Statement Establishing Series of Shares		$25.00
Articles/Certificate of Merger		$60.00
(a) If Restated Articles included, add		$60.00
Articles of Dissolution or Certificate of Cancellation of Limited Partnership (and Statement of Intent and Revocation)		$10.00
Application for Certificate of Authority for Foreign Corporation or Limited Liability Company & L.P.		$75.00
Report (biennial) of Colorado Corporation, LLC, LLP, LLLP (does not apply to L.P.)		$25.00
Report (biennial) of Foreign Corporation, LLC, LLP, LLLP (does not apply to L.P.)		$100.00
Certificate of Assumed or Trade Name		$10.00
Trademark/Service Mark		$50.00
Furnishing written information on each Corporation, Limited Partnership, Limited Liability Company	(per name)	$5.00
Copy of document	(per page)	1st page is free. $.50 per page thereafter.
(a) Certification of above copy		$2.00
Expedited Service (in addition to the above fees)		$15.00
Copy orders returned by Fax		$2.50 per page
Service of process upon Secretary of State as resident agent	(per defendant)	$50.00
Resignation of Registered Agent and/or officers—directors		$5.00 ea.
Late filing of Report (Does not apply to L.P.)		$20.00
Reinstatement (Does not apply to L.P.)		$25.00
Certificate of Good Standing		$5.00

Uniform Transfers to Minors Act.—11-50-101.

Uniform Simplification of Fiduciary Security Transfers Act adopted. (15-1-601 to 611). See category Business Regulation and Commerce, topic Securities.

Uniform Commercial Code adopted. (4-1-101). See category Business Regulation and Commerce, topic Commercial Code.

See note at head of Digest as to 1998 legislation covered.

See Topical Index in front part of this volume.

CORPORATIONS . . . *continued*

Stock Transfer Tax.—None.

General Provisions of Colorado Business Corporation Act.—C. 1 (Art. 101).

Filing Requirements.—§1.20 (7-101-201). Document filed may be true photographic, xerographic or similar copy and may be signed by any authorized person. Signature of each person constitutes acknowledgment, under penalties of perjury, that document is act of signer or corporation and that facts in document are true. (7-101-201[9]). Documents may be filed by facsimile transmission. (7-101-210). Articles filed with Secretary of State. See subhead General Supervision, supra.

Forms.—§1.21 (7-101-202). §1.21 of Model Act modified to provide that Secretary of State may prescribe forms for documents, and if so must furnish them. However: (a) use of forms not mandatory unless Secretary of State specifically requires use; and (b) requirement that form be used does not preclude inclusion in document of any item not prohibited, nor require inclusion of item not required. Except for resignation of registered agent, must note or be accompanied by address for returning filed copy.

Effective Time and Date of Filed Documents.—§1.23 (7-101-204). If document specifies delayed effective date, document may be prevented from becoming effective by delivering to Secretary of State, prior to earlier of specified effective date or 90th day after document is filed, certificate of withdrawal, executed in same manner as document being withdrawn, stating: (a) document revoked by appropriate corporate action or court order and is void; and (b) in case of court order, that order entered by court having jurisdiction. (7-101-204[3]).

Correcting Filed Documents.—§1.24 (7-101-205). Articles of correction may be filed by any person who may execute documents or who executed corrected document. (7-101-205[3]).

Filing Duty of Division.—§1.25 (7-101-206). Secretary of State has ten days to return document it refuses to file. (7-101-206[3]).

Appeal from Division's Refusal to File Document.—§1.26 (7-101-207). Appeal within 45 days to district court of county of principal office, or, if none in state, where registered office is located, or, if none in state, district court of City and County of Denver. (7-101-207[1]).

Certificates Issued by Secretary of State.—§1.28 (7-101-209). Secretary of State will issue certificate that sets forth any facts of record in office of Secretary of State. (7-101-209[1]).

Penalty for Signing False Documents.—§1.29 not adopted. See subhead Filing Requirements, supra.

Powers of Division.—§1.30 (7-101-301). See subhead General Supervision, supra.

Definitions.—§1.40 (7-101-401). "Delivery" to Secretary of State means actual receipt by Secretary of State. (7-101-401[12]). "Principal office" means office, in or out of state, designated by corporation as principal office in most recent document on file with Secretary of State providing such information, including notice of change of principal office. (7-101-401[25]). "Proceeding" includes arbitration or mediation. (7-101-401[26]). Adds definitions of "address", "affiliate", "assumed corporate name", "bylaws", "cash" and "money", "control", "corporate name", "effective date", "mail", "receive", "street address", "registered agent", "registered office".

Notice.—§1.41 (7-101-402). Notice by publication or broadcast not listed. If three successive notices to shareholder returned as undeliverable, no further notices necessary until another address made known to corporation.

Number of Shareholders.—§1.42. Not included.

Incorporation.—C. 2 (Art. 102).

Incorporators.—§2.01 (7-102-101). Incorporator who is natural person must be at least 18 years old.

Articles of Incorporation.—§2.02 (7-102-102). Articles must also set forth: address of corporation's principal office, and consent of initial registered agent to appointment (unless provided in accompanying document). For corporations formed after 1958, cumulative voting is mandatory for election of directors unless statement denying it is included in articles. For provisions limiting liability of directors, see 7-108-102. Any matter conditioned on provision in bylaws satisfied if provision present either in articles or bylaws. (7-102-102[5]).

Liability for Preincorporation Transactions.—§2.04 (7-102-104). Persons acting without good faith belief that they have authority jointly and severally liable.

Paid in Capital Requirements.—None.

Organization of Corporation.—§2.05 (7-102-105). Organizational meetings permissive, rather than mandatory. Incorporators may adopt bylaws. (7-102-105[1][a]).

Bylaws.—§2.06 (7-102-106). Adoption permissive, rather than mandatory. Board may adopt; if no board, incorporators may; if neither board nor incorporators adopt, shareholders may.

Purposes and Powers.—C. 3 (Art. 103). Corporations may appoint, in writing, agents or attorneys-in-fact to convey real estate. (7-103-105).

Name.—C. 4 (Art. 104).

Corporate Name.—§4.01 (7-104-101). Omits "words or abbreviations of like import in another language." Name must not be deceptively similar to name of Colorado corporation, limited partnership, limited liability partnership, limited liability limited partnership, limited partnership association or limited liability company; name of any foreign corporation, foreign limited liability company or foreign limited partnership association if registered with Secretary of State; name under which foreign corporation, foreign limited partnership, foreign limited liability company, foreign limited liability partnership or foreign limited partnership association is authorized to do business in Colorado; name reserved with Secretary of State; trade name or trademark registered; or name of dissolved corporation for 120 days after dissolution. Similar name may be used with written consent of other user if names are distinguishable in Secretary of State's records. (7-104-101[3]).

Reserved Name.—§4.02 (7-104-102). Name reservation may be renewed.

Registered Name.—§4.03 (7-115-107). Foreign corporation may register name through end of year if name not deceptively similar to name described in 7-104-101(2), by filing application for registration with Secretary of State. Registration may be renewed each year and may be assigned.

Office and Agent.—C. 5 (Art. 105).

Registered Office and Registered Agent.—§5.01 (7-105-101). Corporation may not serve as its own registered agent. (7-105-101[2]).

Shares and Distributions.—C. 6 (Art. 106).

Reverse Stock Split.—(7-106-105). Permits reverse split with vote of each class to be reverse split and each other voting group that is entitled, under articles, to vote. If articles amended (e.g., to change number of authorized shares or par value), must follow procedures for amendment of articles.

Subscriptions for Shares.—§6.20 (7-106-201). Corporation's acceptance of preincorporation subscription, and authorization of issuance pursuant thereto, subject to provisions for issuance of shares. (7-106-201[2]).

Issuance of Shares.—§6.21 (7-106-202). Future services not permitted consideration. (7-106-202[2]). Promissory notes acceptable only if full-recourse, negotiable and secured by collateral other than shares issued with fair market value equal to note amount. (7-106-202[5]). Unless prohibited by articles or bylaws, shares may be issued for less than any par value. (7-106-202[6]).

Liability of Shareholders.—§6.22 (7-106-203). Good-faith transferee without notice not liable for any unpaid consideration for shares. (7-106-203[3]).

Share Dividends.—§6.23 (7-106-204). Bylaws or, in absence of bylaw, board, may fix future record date. (7-106-204[3]).

Share Options and Other Rights.—§6.24 (7-106-205). Subject to articles, corporation may create and issue options and other rights for purchase of shares, assets or obligations of corporation. Terms of options may include restrictions that preclude or limit exercise, transfer, or receipt of options by persons owning or offering to acquire percentage of outstanding voting securities of corporation, or any transferee, or provide that such persons receive shares, assets or obligations different from other holders of such options. (7-106-205[2]). Provisions of 7-106-205 apply to all options notwithstanding date of grant. (7-106-205[3]).

Form and Content of Certificates.—§6.25 (7-106-206). Certificates may contain other information corporation considers necessary or appropriate. Only one officer's signature required.

Restrictions on Transfer or Registration of Shares or Other Securities.—§6.27 (7-106-208). Restriction may affect shares issued before restriction adopted if holders of shares acquire with knowledge or otherwise consent to restriction. (7-106-208[1]).

Shareholders' Preemptive Rights.—§6.30 (7-106-301). For corporations existing on June 30, 1994, shareholders have preemptive rights except as otherwise provided in articles and except that rights do not exist (i) to acquire shares issued to directors, officers or employees after shareholder approval; (ii) to acquire shares for other than cash; (iii) for holders of preferred stock; (iv) for holders of common stock where nonconvertible preferred stock is issued; (v) for holders of nonvoting common stock where voting common is issued; (vi) for shares of corporation incorporated before Jan. 1, 1959 that are acquired by corporation and are not cancelled or restored to status of authorized but unissued shares (and any such shares existing on June 30, 1994 or acquired thereafter not deemed restored to status of authorized but unissued shares). (7-117-101[3]—[6]).

Corporation's Acquisition of Its Own Shares.—§6.31 (7-106-302). If articles prohibit reissuance of acquired shares, corporation shall file amendment to articles without shareholder action to reduce number of authorized shares by amount equal to number of shares acquired by corporation. (7-106-302[2]).

Distributions to Shareholders.—§6.40 (7-106-401). Board may fix record date only if no applicable bylaw. Unless otherwise provided in articles or bylaws, statement of par value of shares does not limit distributions. (7-106-401[7]).

Unclaimed Distributions.—(7-106-402). If corporation has mailed three successive distributions to shareholder's address in corporate record and distributions returned as undeliverable, no further attempt need be made until another address made known to corporation, at which time all distributions accumulated must be mailed to shareholders.

Shareholders.—C. 7 (Art. 107).

Annual Meeting.—§7.01 (7-107-101). Failure to hold annual meeting at time fixed in bylaws or by board resolution does not work forfeiture or dissolution of corporation. (7-107-101[3]).

Special Meeting.—§7.02 (7-107-102). If not otherwise fixed, record date for determining shareholders entitled to demand special meeting is earliest date of demand or 60 days prior to date first written demand received by corporation, whichever is later. (7-107-102[2]).

Action Without Meeting.—§7.04 (7-107-104). Unless articles require action at meeting, shareholder action may be by written consent of all shareholders entitled to vote. Must be received by corporation and may be transmitted electronically unless otherwise provided in bylaws. Action effective as of date corporation receives writings describing and consenting to action signed by all shareholders entitled to vote on action, unless all writings specify another date as effective date. (7-107-104[2]). Shareholder may deliver written revocation of consent before last writing necessary to effect action is received. (7-107-104[3]). §7.04(d) of Model Act not adopted. District court of county of corporation's principal (or if none, registered) office may specify record date for consents and enter other appropriate orders. (7-107-104[7]).

Notice of Meeting.—§7.05 (7-107-105). If number of authorized shares to be increased, 30 days' notice required. (7-107-105[1]).

Meetings by Telecommunication.—(7-107-108). Unless otherwise provided in bylaws, shareholders may participate in meetings by any means of communication by which all persons participating can hear each other. Shareholders so participating deemed to be present at meeting.

Shareholders' List for Meeting.—§7.20 (7-107-201). Shareholders' list available for inspection beginning on earlier of ten days before meeting for which list prepared or two business days after notice of meeting given and continuing through meeting and

---

See note at head of Digest as to 1998 legislation covered.

See Topical Index in front part of this volume.

CORPORATIONS . . . *continued*
adjournments. (7-107-201[2]). Provision requiring shareholder to copy list at own expense omitted. (7-107-201[2]). Corporation may charge for copying. (7-116-103[3]). If court orders inspection or copying of list, unless corporation proves it refused inspection or copying in good faith because it had reasonable basis for doubt about right of shareholder to inspect/copy: (a) court must order corporation to pay shareholder's costs, including attorney's fees; (b) court may order corporation to pay shareholder for damages incurred; and (c) court may grant shareholder other remedies. Court may impose restrictions on use of list by shareholder. (7-107-201[5]).

Voting Entitlement of Shares.—§7.21 (7-107-202). Each fractional share entitled to corresponding fractional vote. (7-107-202[1]). §7.21(b) of Model Act modified; "special circumstances" exception replaced with exception for order by court upon finding that purpose of subsection would not be violated. (7-107-202[2]).

Proxies.—§7.22 (7-107-203). Without limiting ways in which shareholder may appoint proxy, following ways valid: (a) appointment form; (b) electronic transmission providing written statement of appointment. (7-107-203[2]). Copy or facsimile of appointment may be used in lieu of original appointment. (7-107-203[4]). Appointment coupled with interest may include enumerated persons or their designees. (7-107-203[5]). Revocation of appointment does not affect right of corporation to accept proxy's authority unless: (a) corporation had notice of appointment coupled with interest and notice of interest extinguished received by corporation's secretary before proxy exercises authority; or (b) other notice of revocation received by secretary before proxy exercises authority. (7-107-203[7]). Corporation not required to recognize appointment made irrevocable if it has received writing revoking appointment signed by shareholder or attorney-in-fact, notwithstanding that revocation may be breach of obligation of shareholder to third person. (7-107-203[8]).

Shares Held by Nominees.—§7.23 (7-107-204). Corporation may also recognize in beneficial owner rights or privileges other than voting. (7-107-204[2][b]).

Corporation's Acceptance of Votes.—§7.24 (7-107-205). Procedures regarding corporation's acceptance of votes apply as well to proxy appointment revocations. (7-107-205[1]). Corporation may also accept name signed not corresponding to shareholder name if acceptance otherwise proper under rules established by corporation. (7-107-205[2][f]).

Quorum and Voting Requirements for Voting Groups.—§7.25 (7-107-206). Quorum may not be fewer than one-third of votes entitled to be cast. (7-107-206[1]).

Greater Quorum or Voting Requirements.—§7.27 (7-107-208). If authorized in articles, may be created by bylaw adopted by shareholders.

Voting for Directors—Cumulative Voting.—§7.28 (7-107-209). At each election of directors, each shareholder entitled to vote at election has right to vote for as many persons as are directors to be elected and for whose election shareholder has right to vote, unless articles provide otherwise. Cumulative voting provisions in effect if required per 7-102-102(3). Articles may provide that shares otherwise entitled to vote cumulatively may not be so voted unless notice of meeting so states or shareholder with right to cumulate votes gives notice not less than 48 hours before meeting of intent to cumulate votes. (7-107-209[2]). In election of directors, that number of candidates equaling number of directors to be elected having highest number of votes are elected. (7-107-209[4]).

Voting Trusts.—§7.30 (7-107-301). Trustee must promptly inform corporation of changes in beneficial interest list and amendments to voting trust agreements. (7-107-301[1]). Extension of voting trust valid for no more than ten years, unless signed within two years before expiration date, in which case valid for up to ten years after expiration date. (7-107-301[3]).

Shareholder Agreements.—§7.32 of Model Act not adopted.

Procedure in Derivative Proceedings.—C. 7D of Model Act not adopted. Summary of 7-107-401 and 402 follows. No derivative action may be brought unless plaintiff was shareholder at time of transaction complained of, or received shares by operation of law from such shareholder. In action begun after 1958, if court finds that action was begun without reasonable cause, it must require plaintiff pay costs of defense (but not attorneys fees); and if plaintiff holds less than 5% of outstanding shares (unless valued greater than $25,000), corporation may require plaintiff to give security for its costs (but not attorneys fees). If court finds that action was begun without reasonable cause, corporation has recourse to such security in amount determined by court.

Directors and Officers.—C. 8 (Art. 108).

Requirement for and Duties of Board of Directors.—§8.01 (7-108-101). §8.01(c) of Model Act not adopted. Except as otherwise provided in articles, corporation must have board, and articles may provide that other persons perform duties of board. Directors must be natural persons at least 18 years old. Bylaws may prescribe other qualifications. (7-108-102).

Number and Election of Directors.—§8.03 (7-108-103). Number of directors (or range of numbers) fixed in accordance with bylaws. If range established, number may be changed within range by shareholders or board. §8.03(b) of Model Act not adopted.

Election of Directors by Certain Classes of Shareholders.—§8.04 (7-108-104). Applies to series as well.

Terms of Directors Generally.—§8.05 (7-108-105). Terms of initial directors expire at first shareholders' meeting at which directors elected, unless board has staggered terms. (7-108-105[1]). Term of director elected by board to fill vacancy expires at next election at annual shareholders meeting. Term of director elected by shareholders to fill vacancy is unexpired term of predecessor, unless predecessor was elected by board to fill vacancy, in which case term is unexpired term of last predecessor elected by shareholders. (7-108-105[4]). After expiration of term, director continues to serve until successor elected and qualifies. (7-108-105[5]). Director whose term has ended may deliver to Secretary of State for filing statement to that effect. (7-108-105[6]). See subhead Filing Requirements, supra.

Staggered Terms for Directors.—§8.06 (7-108-106). Omits condition precedent of nine or more directors to institute staggered terms. Terms of two or three years, as case may be, begin upon expiration of initial staggered terms.

Resignation, Removal of Directors.—§§8.07, 8.08, 8.09 (7-108-107; 7-108-108; 7-108-109). Director who is removed or resigns may deliver to Secretary of State for filing statement of resignation or removal. See subhead Filing Requirements, supra.

Vacancy on Board.—§8.10 (7-108-110). Unless articles provide otherwise, if vacant office held by director elected by voting group: (a) if one or more directors elected by same voting group, only they are entitled to vote to fill vacancy if filled by directors; and (b) only holders of shares of that voting group entitled to vote to fill vacancy if filled by shareholders. (7-108-110[2]).

Action Taken Without Meeting.—§8.21 (7-108-202). Action taken without meeting at time last director signs writing describing action taken, unless, prior to that time, any director has revoked consent. (7-108-202[2]). Action taken without meeting effective at time taken, unless directors establish different effective date. (7-108-202[3]).

Waiver of Notice.—§8.23 (7-108-203). Waiver of notice should be delivered to corporation for filing with corporate records, but delivery and filing not conditions to its effectiveness. (7-108-203[1]). If special notice of purpose of meeting was required, director does not waive notice by attendance or participation if he objects to transacting business with respect to purpose for which notice was required and does not vote for action taken with respect to such purpose. (7-108-203[2]).

Quorum and Voting.—§8.24 (7-108-205). Quorum of directors not less than majority of number fixed, or if not fixed, of number in office immediately before meeting begins. (7-108-205[2]).

Committees.—§8.25 (7-108-206). Board may authorize committee or any officer to approve issuance or sale of shares or determine designation and rights, preferences and limitations of class or series of shares. (7-108-206[4][h]).

Director Conflict of Interest.—§8.31 of Model Act not adopted. Summary of 7-108-501 follows. Loans, guaranties or other transactions with directors and certain related entities ("conflicting interest transactions") not void or voidable and do not give rise to injunction or damages if (a) material facts disclosed or known to board or committee that approves transaction in good faith by vote of majority of disinterested directors (though less than quorum); (b) material facts disclosed or known to shareholders who approve transaction in good faith; or (c) transaction fair to corporation. Definition excludes transactions between 100% parent and subsidiary.

Loans to Directors.—§8.32 of Model Act not adopted. Loans and guaranties to directors and certain related entities permitted only after ten days notice of transaction to shareholders entitled to vote if transaction were submitted to vote of shareholders.

Limitation of Liability of Directors.—(7-108-402). If provided in articles, corporation shall eliminate or limit director liability for monetary damages for breach of fiduciary duty, except liability for breach of duty of loyalty, acts or omissions not in good faith or involving intentional misconduct or knowing violation of law, unlawful distributions, or transaction from which director derives improper personal benefit. Directors and officers not personally liable for torts of employees unless they were personally involved or committed criminal offense.

Liability of Directors for Unlawful Distributions.—§8.33 (7-108-403). Amount of contribution from each shareholder who knowingly accepted unlawful distribution is amount of distribution to shareholder that exceeds what could have been distributed to that shareholder without violating law governing distributions or articles of incorporation. (7-108-403[2][b]).

Required Officers.—§8.40 (7-108-301). Officers must be natural persons at least 18 years old. (7-108-301[1]). Officers may be appointed by board or in any other manner as board or bylaws provide. (7-108-301[2]).

Resignation and Removal of Officers.—§8.43 (7-108-303). If officer's resignation made effective at later date, board may fill vacancy and provide that successor not take office until effective date or removal officer at any time prior to effective date and fill resulting vacancy. (7-108-303[3]). Officer who resigns or is removed or whose appointment expires may deliver to Secretary of State for filing statement of resignation. (7-108-303[5]). See subhead Filing Requirements, supra.

Indemnification Definitions.—§8.50 (7-109-101). Definition of "director" as used in this part includes individual who while director of corporation was serving as associate, manager, member, proprietor or fiduciary or similar position of another corporation, person, or employee benefit plan. (7-109-101[2]).

Authority to Indemnify Directors.—§8.51 (7-109-102). §8.51(a)(2) of Model Act modified to provide that director's conduct as to employee benefit plan for purpose director did not reasonably believe to be in interests of plan beneficiaries deemed not to be in good faith. (7-109-102[2]).

Determination and Authorization of Indemnification of Directors.—§8.55 (7-109-106). Corporation may not advance expenses to director unless authorized in specific case after written affirmation and undertaking received and required determination made. (7-109-106[1]). §8.55(b)(4) modified to provide that determination be made by all shareholders. (7-109-106[3]). If corporation indemnifies or advances expenses to director in proceeding by or in right of corporation, notice must be given to shareholders with or before notice of next shareholders meeting or before action by written consent of shareholders (if taken at instigation of board). (7-109-110).

Indemnification of Officers, Employees, Fiduciaries, and Agents.—§8.56 (7-109-107). Also applies to fiduciaries of corporation. Requirement in §8.56(1) and (2) of Model Act that officer, employee, fiduciary, or agent not be director omitted. (7-109-107[1]).

Insurance.—§8.57 (7-109-108). Applies as well to fiduciaries of corporation. Insurance may be procured from any insurance company designated by board, whether formed under laws of state or not, including company in which corporation has interest.

Limitations on Indemnification of Directors.—§8.58 (7-109-109). Contract referred to in §8.58 of Model Act does not include insurance policy. (7-109-109[1]).

See note at head of Digest as to 1998 legislation covered.

See Topical Index in front part of this volume.

CO – 3

CORPORATIONS . . . *continued*

Amendment of Articles of Incorporation and Bylaws.—C. 10 (Art. 110).

Amendment by Board of Directors.—§10.02 (7-110-101). §10.02(1) of Model Act not adopted. Board may adopt amendment to change corporate name in connection with reinstatement following administrative dissolution. (7-110-102[2]).

Amendment by Board of Directors and Shareholders.—§10.03 (7-110-103). Notice need be given only to shareholders entitled to vote on amendment. (7-110-103[4]). Bylaws may require greater vote, if adopted by shareholders. (7-110-103[5]). For corporations in existence on June 30, 1994, unless articles establish vote required to amend articles, amendment requires vote by each voting group entitled to vote, by $^2/_3$ of all votes entitled to be cast by that group. (7-117-101[7]). Amendment to articles of such corporation to reduce vote required (which may not be less than would be required to take action if action were taken by corporation formed on or after July 1, 1994) for actions described in 7-117-101(7) to (10) (amendment to articles, merger or share exchange, disposition of substantially all assets and dissolution) requires same vote as such actions require in 7-117-101(7) to (10). (7-110-103[5]). For corporations formed after June 30, 1994, unless articles, bylaws adopted by shareholders or proposing board or proposing shareholders require greater vote, amendment must be approved by shareholders by vote required for other shareholder action.

Amendment Before Issuance of Shares.—§10.05 (7-110-105). Incorporators may adopt amendments only if no board appointed.

Articles of Amendment.—§10.06 (7-110-106). §10.06(b) of Model Act modified. If amendment adopted by shareholders, articles of amendment must include statement that number of votes cast for amendment by each voting group entitled to vote separately was sufficient for approval by that group. (7-110-106[1][f]).

Restated Articles of Incorporation.—§10.07 (7-110-107). Incorporators may restate if no shares issued and no directors appointed. (7-110-107[1]). If shareholder approval required, notice need be given only to shareholders entitled to vote on restatement. (7-110-107[3]). Information on separate certificate required by §10.07(d) of Model Act should be set forth in restatement; no separate certificate need be filed. (7-110-107[4]). §10.07(f) of Model Act not adopted.

Amendment of Bylaws by Board of Directors or Shareholders.—§10.20 (7-110-201). Board may not amend bylaw if law or articles reserve power exclusively to shareholders or if bylaw expressly prohibits board from doing so. (7-110-201[1]).

Merger and Share Exchange.—C. 11 (Art. 111).

Merger.—§11.01 (7-111-101). Plan of merger must set forth any amendment to articles of surviving corporation to be effected by merger. (7-111-101[2]).

Action on Plan.—§11.03 (7-111-103). Corporation need only give notice of shareholder meeting to shareholders entitled to vote. (7-111-103[4]). Bylaws adopted by shareholders may require greater vote. (7-111-103[5]). Unless articles of corporation existing on June 30, 1994 establish vote required, merger or share exchange requires approval by each voting group entitled to vote, by $^2/_3$ of all votes entitled to be cast on proposal by that group. If corporation incorporated before July 1, 1978, each share (unless redeemable and called for redemption under 7-107-202[4]) entitled to vote even if articles provide otherwise, unless articles amended after June 30, 1978, by same vote that would have been necessary at time of amendment to approve plan, so as to restrict or eliminate right of such share to vote on plan. (7-111-101[8]). Plan of merger or share exchange may be abandoned at any time before effective date. (7-111-103[9]). If merger or share exchange abandoned after articles of merger or share exchange filed by Secretary of State specifying delayed effective date, merger or share exchange may be prevented from becoming effective by delivering to Secretary of State for filing, prior to specified effective date, statement of abandonment stating that by appropriate corporation plan abandoned. (7-111-103[9]).

Merger of Parent and Subsidiary.—§11.04 (7-111-104). Parent corporation may merge subsidiary into self or self into subsidiary. (7-111-104[1]). Board must adopt and shareholders approve, if shareholders so required, plan of merger. (7-111-104[2]). Plan of merger must set forth: (a) names of parent and subsidiary and of surviving entity; (b) terms and conditions of mergers; (c) manner and basis of converting shares of each corporation; (d) any amendments to articles of surviving corporation to be effected by merger; and (e) any other provisions relating to merger deemed desirable. (7-111-104[2]). Vote of shareholders of subsidiary not required with respect to merger. If subsidiary will be surviving corporation, approval of shareholders of parent must be sought. If parent will be surviving corporation, no vote of its shareholders required if vote of shareholders of surviving corporation would not be required under 7-111-103(7); otherwise, vote of parent's shareholders required. (7-111-104[3]). §§11.04(d) and (e) of Model Act not adopted. Effective date of merger may not be earlier than date on which all shareholders of subsidiary waived mailing requirement or ten days after date parent mailed copy or summary of plan of merger to each shareholder or subsidiary who did not waive mailing requirement. (7-111-104[5]).

Articles of Merger or Share Exchange.—§11.05 (7-111-105). §11.05(a)(3) of Model Act modified. If shareholder approval required, articles of merger or share exchange must include statement that number of votes cast for plan by each voting group entitled to vote separately was sufficient for approval by that voting group. (7-111-105[1][c]). If merger of parent and subsidiary, articles of merger must set forth: (i) statement that immediately prior to merger parent owned at least 90% of outstanding shares of each class of subsidiary; and (ii) effective date of merger and statement that effective date complies with law. (7-111-105[1][d]). Articles of merger or share exchange effective on stated effective date, or if earlier, on 90th day after filing; must be executed by each party, except that in parent-subsidiary merger, need only be executed by survivor. (7-111-105[2], [3]).

Effect of Merger or Share Exchange.—§11.06 (7-111-106). Transfer to and vesting of property in surviving corporation occurs by operation of law. No consent or approval of any person required unless specifically required in event of merger by law or express provision in contract or order. (7-111-106[1][b]).

Merger or Share Exchange with Foreign Corporation.—§11.07 (7-111-107). Foreign corporation wishing to merge must also provide address of principal office. (7-111-107[1][c]). §11.07(b) of Model Act not adopted. Once merger or share exchange takes effect, surviving corporation must: (a)(i) maintain registered agent in state to accept service of process for parties merged in survivor, or (ii) be considered to have authorized service on it at principal office; (b) promptly pay dissenting shareholders or corporation party to merger or share exchange amount to which entitled under dissenters' rights provisions; and (c) comply with foreign corporation provisions if it is to transact business in state. (7-111-107[2]). See subhead Foreign Corporations, infra.

Conversion to or Merger with Other Kind of Entity.—Corporation may convert to or merge with other types of entities. (7-90-201).

Redomestication as Domestic Insurer.—(7-111-108). Foreign insurer may submit three copies of articles of redomestication to commissioner of insurance and attorney general for their approval; then to be filed with Secretary of State.

Sale of Assets.—C. 12 (Art. 112).

Sale of Assets Other Than in Regular Course of Business.—§12.02 (7-112-102). Disposition of property in connection with dissolution, other than in regular course of business, requires shareholder approval, but if pursuant to court order not subject to shareholder approval. (7-112-102[1]). If corporation entitled to vote or otherwise consent, other than in regular course of business, with respect to disposition of property of another entity which it controls, and if interests held by corporation in other entity constitute all or substantially all property of corporation, then corporation can consent to transaction only if board proposes and shareholders approve consent. (7-112-102[2]). Notice of meeting at which transaction will be voted upon need be given only to shareholders entitled to vote on transaction. (7-112-102[5]). §12.02(e) of Model Act modified to provide that unless Act, articles, bylaws adopted by shareholders, or board required greater vote, transaction must be approved by each voting group entitled to vote on transaction by majority of all votes entitled to be cast on transaction by that voting group. (7-112-102[6]). Unless articles of corporation existing on June 30, 1994 establish vote required, transaction requires approval by each voting group entitled to vote, by $^2/_3$ of all votes entitled to be cast on transaction by that group. (7-117-101[9]).

Dissenters' Rights.—C. 13 (Art. 113).

Definitions.—§13.01 (7-113-101). "Interest" compounded annually at statutory rate set forth in 5-12-101, currently 8%. (7-113-101[5]).

Right to Dissent.—§13.02 (7-113-102). Shareholders entitled to dissent whether or not entitled to vote. (7-113-102[1]). Model Act provisions of §13.02(a)(3) denying dissenters' rights in case of sale of assets for cash whereby net proceeds will be distributed to shareholders within one year not adopted. Model Act §13.02(a)(4)(iii) not adopted. Shareholders may dissent from disposition of all or substantially all property of entity controlled by corporation if shareholders entitled to vote upon consent of corporation to disposition. (7-113-102[1][d]). No right to dissent if shares listed on national securities exchange or NASDAQ National Market or held of record by more than 2,000 holders, provided that shareholders receive only shares of another corporation listed on national securities exchange or NASDAQ National Market or held of record by more than 2,000 holders and cash in lieu of fractional shares. Shareholder may dissent from reverse split if shares will be reduced to fractional share that is acquired for cash or voided as scrip.

Dissent by Nominees and Beneficial Owners.—§13.03 (7-113-103). Corporation may require that when record shareholder dissents with respect to shares held by beneficial shareholders, each beneficial shareholder must certify to corporation that both he and record shareholders of all shares owned beneficially by him have asserted or will assert dissenters' rights as to all shares not limited in ability to exercise dissenters' rights. Certification requirement must be stated in dissenters' notice. (7-113-103[3]).

Notice of Dissenters' Rights.—§13.20 (7-113-201). §13.20 modified to provide that if proposed corporate action creating dissenters' rights submitted to vote at shareholders' meeting, meeting notice must be sent to all shareholders of corporation as of applicable record date, whether or not entitled to vote at meeting. Notice must state shareholders are or may be entitled to assert dissenters' rights. Notice must be accompanied by copy of Art. 113 of Act and materials required to be given shareholders entitled to vote on proposed action at meeting. Failure to give notice as required to shareholders does not affect any action taken at shareholders' meeting for which notice was to have been given, but any shareholder who is not given notice is not precluded from demanding payment because of failure to give notice of intent to demand payment. (7-113-201[1]). If proposed corporate action creating dissenters' rights authorized without meeting of shareholders, any solicitation of shareholder to execute written consent to action without shareholder meeting must be accompanied or preceded by written notice stating shareholders are or may be entitled to assert dissenters' rights, by copy of Art. 113 of Act, and by material required to be given to shareholders entitled to vote on proposed action if proposed action were submitted to vote at shareholders' meeting. Failure to give written notice to shareholders not entitled to vote does not affect any action taken for which notice was to have been given. (7-113-201[2]).

Notice of Intent to Demand Payment.—§13.21 (7-113-202). If proposed corporate action creating dissenters' rights authorized without meeting of shareholders, shareholder who wishes to assert dissenters' rights may not execute writing consenting to proposed corporate action. (7-113-202[2]).

Dissenters' Notice.—§13.22 (7-113-203). Dissenters' notice must: (a) state that corporate action authorized and effective date; (b) state address at which corporation will receive payment demands and address at which certificates for certified shares must be deposited; (c) inform holders of uncertificated shares to what extent transfer of shares will be restricted after payment demand received; (d) supply form for demanding payment, which requests dissenter to state address to which payment made; (e) set date by which corporation must receive payment demand and certificates for certificated shares, not less than 30 days after date dissenters' notice given; (f) state any requirement that beneficial shareholders must certify to corporation that dissenters' rights are asserted as to all shares beneficially owned by them for which dissenters' rights may be asserted; and (g) be accompanied by copy of Art. 113 of Act. (7-113-203[2]).

Procedure to Demand Payment.—§13.23 (7-113-204). §13.23(a) and (b) of Model Act substantively modified. Shareholder who wishes to assert dissenters' rights according to terms of dissenters' notice must: (a) deliver to corporation payment demand,

CORPORATIONS . . . *continued*
which may be payment demand form supplied per 7-113-203(2)(d) or another writing; and (b) deposit certificates for certified shares in accordance with terms of dissenters' notice. (7-113-204[1]). Shareholder who demands payment retains all rights of shareholder except right to transfer shares, until effective date of proposed corporate action giving rise to exercise of dissenters' rights and has only right to receive payment for shares after effective date of corporate action. (7-113-203[2]). Except as provided in 7-113-207 or 7-113-209(1)(b), demand for payment is irrevocable. (7-113-204[3]).

Payment.—§13.25 (7-113-206). Payment made to shareholder on later of effective date of corporate action and receipt by corporation of payment demand. (7-113-206[1]). Balance sheet and statements sent with payment must include statement in changes in shareholders' equity and statement of cash flow and be audited, if corporation customarily provides such statements to shareholders. (17-113-206[2][a]).

Special Provisions Relating to Shares Acquired After Announcement of Proposed Corporate Action.—§13.27 (7-113-208). Corporation may require shareholder to certify in writing whether he acquired beneficial ownership before date of first announcement to media or shareholders of proposed corporate action.

Dissolution.—C. 14 (Art. 114).

Authorization of Dissolution Prior to Issuance of Shares.—§14.01 of Model Act not adopted. If corporation has not issued shares, majority of directors, or if no directors majority of incorporators, may authorize dissolution. (7-114-101).

Authorization of Dissolution After Issuance of Shares.—§14.02 of Model Act not adopted. Corporation dissolved on expiration of period of duration stated in articles, without filing of articles of dissolution. (7-114-102.5; 7-114-103[4]). After shares issued, board must propose dissolution to shareholders. (7-114-102[1]). Corporation need only give notice of shareholder meeting to shareholders entitled to vote. (7-114-102[4]). Proposal to dissolve must be approved by each voting group entitled to vote separately on proposal, by majority of all votes entitled to be cast on proposal by that voting group, unless greater vote required by articles, bylaws adopted by shareholder, or board. (7-114-102[5]). Unless articles of corporation existing on June 30, 1994 establish vote required, dissolution or revocation of dissolution requires approval by each voting group entitled to vote, by $2/3$ of all votes entitled to be cast on proposal by that group. If corporation incorporated before July 1, 1978, each share (unless redeemable and called for redemption under (7-107-202[4]) entitled to vote even if articles provide otherwise, unless articles amended after June 30, 1978, by same vote that would have been necessary at time of amendment to approve plan, so as to restrict or eliminate right of such share to vote on plan. (7-117-101[10]).

Articles of Dissolution.—§14.03 (7-114-103). Articles of dissolution must also set forth: address of principal office, or if none, statement that none and address to which service of process may be mailed; if dissolution authorized by board of incorporators, statement to that effect; any additional information required by Secretary of State. §14.03(a)(3) and (4) modified. If dissolution authorized by shareholders, articles of dissolution must include statement that number of votes for proposal by each voting group entitled to vote was sufficient for approval by that group. (7-114-103[1]). After effective date of dissolution, corporate name of dissolved corporation must include words "a dissolved Colorado corporation" and year of dissolution. (7-114-103[3]).

Revocation of Dissolution.—§14.04 (7-114-104). §14.04(c)(6) modified. Articles of revocation of dissolution must set forth, if revocation approved by shareholders, statement that number of votes for proposal by each voting group entitled to vote was sufficient for approval by that group. (7-114-104[3][f]). No delayed effective date may be specified. (7-114-104[4]).

Disposition of Known Claims by Notification.—§14.06 (7-114-106). Written notice to known claimants must be given within 90 days after effective date of dissolution (7-114-106[2]); and must state that unless sooner barred by other state statute limiting action, claim barred if action to enforce claim not begun by deadline stated in notice, which may not be less than two years after notice given (7-114-106[2][d]). Failure of dissolved corporation to give notice to any known claimant does not affect disposition of any claim by other known claimant. (7-114-106[4]). Action to enforce claim may be civil action or arbitration. (7-114-106[5]).

Disposition of Claims by Publication.—§14.07 (7-114-107). Notice must state that unless sooner barred by other state statute limiting action, action barred if action to enforce not begun within five years after publication or, if later, within four months after claim arises. (7-114-107[2][c]). Disposition of claims by publication applies to all claims, known or unknown, due or to become due, absolute or contingent, liquidated or unliquidated, except where required to be disposed of under 7-114-106. (7-114-107[4]). Action to enforce claim may be civil action or binding arbitration. (7-114-107[4]). §14.07(d)(2) of Model Act modified to provide that claim may be enforced against shareholder of dissolved corporation, if assets distributed in liquidation; but shareholder's total liability may not exceed total value of assets distributed to him, as value determined at time of distribution. Any shareholder required to return any portion of value of assets entitled to contribution from all other shareholders. Contribution must be in accordance with shareholders' respective rights and interests and may not exceed value of assets received in liquidation. (7-114-108[1][b]). Dissolved corporation must maintain registered office to accept service of process or be deemed to have authorized service at principal office or address for service set forth in articles of dissolution or as changed by notice delivered to Secretary of State. (7-114-109[1]).

Grounds for Administrative Dissolution.—§14.20 (7-114-201). No 60 day grace period before Secretary of State may proceed to dissolve corporation.

Procedure for and Effect of Administrative Dissolution.—§14.21 (7-114-202). Secretary of State may (but not required to) dissolve corporation when grounds exist after expiration of 60 days following service of notice. (7-114-202[2]). Secretary of State dissolves corporation by serving written notice on corporation, stating effective date, and delivering copy of notice to last registered agent. (7-114-202[2]). If not reinstated within 120 days, corporate name must include words "a dissolved Colorado corporation" and year of dissolution. (7-114-202[3]). Administrative dissolution terminates authority of registered agent. (7-114-202[4]). Upon dissolution, Secretary of State becomes agent of dissolved corporation for service of process. (7-114-202[5]).

Reinstatement Following Administrative Dissolution.—§14.22 (7-114-203). Application for reinstatement must also include: address of registered office and name of registered agent (7-114-203[1][e]); other information required by Secretary of State (7-114-203[1][f]); written consent to appointment by designated registered agent (unless in accompanying document) (7-114-203[2]).

Grounds for Judicial Dissolution.—§14.30 (7-114-301). Attorney general, shareholder or creditor may bring action to liquidate corporation under judicial supervision, in case of dissolution by voluntary or administrative action. (7-114-301[4]).

Procedure for Judicial Dissolution.—§14.31(d) of Model Act not adopted. Action by shareholder or creditor for judicial dissolution must be brought in district court of county where principal office or registered offices located, or if none in state, in Denver district court. (7-114-302[1]).

Decree of Dissolution.—§14.33 (7-114-304). Decree of dissolution may be appealed as in other civil proceedings. (7-114-304[3]).

Election to Purchase in Lieu of Dissolution.—§14.34 of Model Act not adopted.

Deposit with State Treasurer.—§14.40 of Model Act modified. (7-114-401). Cash from assets of dissolved corporation that should be transferred to creditor, claimant or shareholder who cannot be found or is not legally competent deposited with state treasurer in accordance with Uniform Unclaimed Property Act. See category Property, topic Absentees, subhead Escheat.

Foreign Corporations.—C. 15 (Art. 115).

Authority to Transact Business Required.—§15.01 (7-115-101). Foreign corporation may not transact business in state until application for authority to transact business filed with Secretary of State. (7-115-101[1]). Applies to foreign corporations that conduct business governed by other statutes only to extent this part of Act not inconsistent with those other statutes. (7-115-101[1]). Section does not affect right to subject foreign corporation to jurisdiction of courts. (7-115-101[4]).

Consequences of Transacting Business Without Authority.—§15.02 (7-115-102). In addition to corporation, no person may maintain proceeding on corporation's behalf until application filed. (7-115-102[1]). Civil penalty for transacting business without authority: up to $5,000; officers and agents of corporation who participate in unauthorized transactions subject to civil penalty up to $1,000. (7-115-102[3]). Court must issue injunction in addition to or instead of civil penalty. (7-115-102[4]).

Application for Authority to Transact Business.—§15.03 (7-115-103). Application for authority to transact business must also set forth: date corporation commenced or expects to commence transacting business in state (7-115-103[1][g]); additional information required by Secretary of State (7-115-103[1][h]). Certificate of existence must be dated within 90 days prior to filing application for authority to transact business. (7-115-103[2]). Application for authority to transact business, or accompanying document, must contain written consent to appointment by registered agent. (7-115-103[3]).

Corporate Name and Assumed Corporate Name of Foreign Corporation.—§15.06 (7-115-106). §15.06 of Model Act modified. Foreign corporation whose name does not meet requirements for domestic corporate name must assume name that does. (7-115-106[1]). See subhead Name, catchline Corporate Name, supra. Foreign corporation may use deceptively similar name by filing either: (a) signed written consent, if name changed to make name distinguishable, or (b) judgment establishing prior right. (7-115-106[2]). If foreign corporation changes name to one not meeting name requirements, it must use assumed name and amend application for authority to transact business. (7-115-106[3]).

Registered Office and Registered Agent of Foreign Corporation.—§15.07 (7-115-108). Foreign corporation may not serve as own registered agent. (7-115-108[2]).

Resignation of Registered Agent of Foreign Corporation.—§15.09 (7-115-110). §§15.10(b)(2) and (3) of Model Act not adopted.

Withdrawal of Foreign Corporation.—§15.20 (7-115-201). §§15.20(b)(3), (4), (5), and (c) of Model Act not adopted. Application of withdrawal must also contain: address of principal office, or statement that corporation will not maintain principal office and address where process may be served; all trade or assumed names used by it, with statement that they are cancelled; additional information required by Secretary of State. (7-115-201[2][b], [e], [f]).

Service on Withdrawn Foreign Corporation.—(7-115-202). Withdrawn foreign corporation must either: (a) maintain registered agent in state, or (b) be considered to have authorized service of process to address of principal office or address in application for withdrawal. (7-115-202[1]). Service perfected at earliest of date withdrawn corporation receives process, date shown on signed return receipt, or five days after mailing. (7-115-202[2]). Means of service described not exhaustive. (7-115-202[3]).

Grounds for Revocation.—§15.30 (7-115-301). No 60 day grace period before Secretary of State has grounds for revocation of authority to transact business.

Records and Reports.—C. 16 (Art. 116).

Corporate Records.—§16.01 (7-116-101). Mandatory records include records of all waivers of notices of meetings of shareholders, board or committees. Shareholder record must have names and addresses, in form that permits preparation of shareholder list: (a) arranged by voting group and class or series; (b) alphabetically within each class or series; and (c) showing address of and number of shares of each class and series held by shareholder. (7-116-101[3]). §16.01(e)(3) of Model Act not adopted.

Inspection of Records by Shareholders and Directors.—§16.02 (7-116-102). Waivers of notices included in material subject to inspection and copying. (7-116-102[2][a]).

Scope of Inspection Right.—§16.03 (7-116-103). Corporation may charge reasonable amount for copying, but may not charge for information respecting shares.

Court-Ordered Inspection.—§16.04 (7-116-104). If court orders inspection or copying of records, unless corporation proves it refused in good faith with reasonable basis for doubt about right to inspect or copy, court may order corporation to pay shareholder for damages incurred; in case of records that shareholder is entitled to inspect or copy

See note at head of Digest as to 1998 legislation covered.

See Topical Index in front part of this volume.

CO – 5

CORPORATIONS . . . *continued*

under 7-116-104(2), court may order corporation to pay inspection and copying charges; court may grant any other legal remedy. (7-116-104[3]).

Financial Statements for Shareholders.—§16.20 (7-116-105). Financial statements, if any, required to be sent only on written request of shareholder.

Information Respecting Shares.—(7-116-106). Upon written request of shareholder, corporation must mail information respecting shares, whether or not information also on shareholder's share certificate.

Other Reports to Shareholders.—§16.21 of Model Act not adopted.

Annual Report for Secretary of State.—§16.22 (7-116-107). Corporate report filed with Secretary of State. See subhead Filing Requirements, supra. §§16.22(a)(5), (6) and (7) of Model Act not adopted. Secretary of State must deliver copy of prescribed form of corporate report to corporation in second calendar year after year incorporated or application for authority to transact business of foreign corporation filed, and thereafter, every two years. (7-116-107[2]). §16.22(c) of Model Act not adopted. Corporate report must be delivered to Secretary of State by end of second calendar month following calendar month in which report form mailed by Secretary of State. Corporation complies if proves to satisfaction of Secretary of State that report mailed. (7-116-107[3]). Corporation may deliver to Secretary of State for filing amendment to corporate report reflecting any change in information contained in corporate report as last amended. (7-116-107[6]).

Statement of Person Named as Director or Officer.—(7-116-108). Person named as director or officer of corporation in corporate report or other document on file with Secretary of State, may, if he does not hold named position, file statement setting forth: (a) name; (b) corporation's name; (c) information identifying report; and (d) date on which he ceased to be director or officer, or statement he did not hold position.

Interrogatories by Secretary of State.—(7-116-109). Secretary of State may propound interrogatories to foreign or domestic corporation subject to Act and to officers and directors to determine compliance with Act. Interrogatories must be answered in writing within 30 days after mailing. Corporation failing to answer is guilty of misdemeanor with fine of not more than $500. Officer or director failing to answer or who signs document filed with Secretary of State knowing it to be false in any material respect guilty of misdemeanor with fine of not more than $1,000.

Transitional Provisions.—C. 17 (Art. 117).

Application to Existing Domestic Corporations.—§17.01 (7-117-101). Effective date July 1, 1994. Applies to all corporations existing on June 30, 1994. Provisions of prior Act retained for existing corporations with respect to preemptive rights (7-117-101[3]; see subhead Shares and Distributions, catchline Shareholders' Preemptive Rights, supra), voting on amendments to articles (7-117-101[7]; see subhead Amendment by Board of Directors and Shareholders, supra), voting on mergers and share exchanges (7-117-101[8]; see subhead Merger and Share Exchange, supra); voting on dispositions of all or substantially all assets (7-117-101[9]; see subhead Sale of Assets Other Than in Regular Course of Business, supra); and voting on dissolution (7-117-101[10]; see subhead Authorization of Dissolution After Issuance of Shares, supra).

Repeal.—§17.05 not adopted. Colorado Model Business Corporation Act (title 7, Arts. 101 to 117) replaces repealed Colorado Corporation Code (title 7, Arts. 1 to 10).

Effective Date.—§17.06 (7-117-105). Effective date July 1, 1994. See subhead Application to Existing Domestic Corporations, supra.

Taxation of Corporate Property.—Generally, corporate property is taxed like individual property. See category Taxation, topic Taxes.

Franchise Tax.—Colorado does not impose franchise tax. See, however, category Taxation, topic Taxes, subhead Income Tax.

Professional Corporations.—Professional persons entitled to form professional corporations include: accountants (12-2-117), architects (12-4-110), chiropractors (12-33-124), dentists (12-35-101), engineers (12-25-104), optometrists (12-40-125), physical therapists (12-41-124), physicians and surgeons (12-36-134), podiatrists (12-32-101), psychologists (12-43-118). Attorneys are permitted to form professional service corporations by Supreme Court Rule. See category Legal Profession, topic Attorneys and Counselors.

Cooperative Housing Corporations.—Nonprofit cooperative housing corporation may be formed by any three or more adult residents for purpose of providing stockholders with right to occupy, for dwelling purposes, house or apartment owned or leased by corporation. (38-33.5-101).

Deeds.—See category Property, topic Deeds.

Model Non-Profit Corporation Act adopted with significant variations, effective Jan. 1, 1968. (7-20-101). Applies to nonprofit corporations organized before Jan. 1, 1968, pursuant to 7-40-101 or 7-50-101 and which have elected to accept it. (7-20-103).

Limited Liability Companies.—See topic Limited Liability Companies.

JOINT STOCK COMPANIES:

Provisions of 7-20-105 and 7-51-101 to 113 apply to joint stock associations organized before Jan. 1, 1968 for religious, benevolent or educational purposes, unless such associations elected to be governed by Nonprofit Corporation Act. (7-20-101 to 108). Other types of joint stock companies not authorized by statute.

Professional Corporations.—See topic Corporations, subhead Professional Corporations.

LIMITED LIABILITY COMPANIES:

Colorado Limited Liability Company Act.—(7-80-101 to 913).

Date of Adoption.—Apr. 18, 1990.

General Supervision.—Secretary of State.

Purposes.—Limited liability companies may be organized for any lawful business. (7-80-103).

Powers.—Very broad, include all powers necessary or convenient to effect purposes for which limited liability company may be organized. (7-80-104).

Name.—Must contain "limited liability company" or "LLC"; "limited" may be abbreviated "Ltd." and "company" may be abbreviated "Co." Name may not contain any word or phrase indicating or implying company is organized for any purpose not permitted by Act or articles of organization. Name may not be same as or deceptively similar to any name duly registered or reserved under applicable law, provided that restrictions against use of deceptively similar names shall not apply if organizer files with secretary of state either (i) written consent of such other corporation or holder of reserved or registered name if one or more words are added, altered or deleted to make name distinguishable from reserved or registered name, or (ii) certified copy of final decree of court of competent jurisdiction establishing prior right of applicant to use name in Colorado. (7-80-201). Names may be reserved for 120 days by submitting application and $10 to secretary of state, and initial reservation may be renewed for additional 120 days by submitting additional $10. (7-80-202).

Formation.—One or more natural persons 18 years of age or older must execute and file articles of organization with secretary of state. (7-80-203).

Articles of organization must include name of limited liability company and, if known, principal place of business, name and business address of registered agent for service of process, if management is vested in managers name and business address of initial manager or managers, if management is vested in managers statement to that effect, and name and business address of initial member or members if management is vested in members. (7-80-205). Duplicate originals of articles must be filed with secretary of state. (7-80-205).

Amendment to Articles of Organization.—Articles must be amended when there is (i) change in name of company, or (ii) false or erroneous statement in articles. Amendments must be signed and verified by manager and may be signed on his behalf by attorney in fact. Duplicate originals of amendment must be delivered to secretary of state with filing fee. (7-80-209).

Members are owners of limited liability companies. (7-80-102). Members may be natural persons or entities. After filing of articles, additional members may be admitted only upon receipt of written consent of all members unless written agreement provides otherwise. (7-80-108, 7-80-701). Interest of member constitutes personal property and may be assigned, provided that assignee shall have no right to participate in management or become member unless all members of company so consent unless written agreement provides otherwise. (7-80-108). Transferee is entitled only to receive his share of profits, losses and distributions. (7-80-702). Members are not liable for debts, obligations or liabilities of company. (7-80-705). Judgment creditors of members have only rights of assignee of interest. (7-80-703). Unless agreed otherwise, annual meetings of members must be held. (7-80-107, 7-80-707). Majority of members entitled to vote shall constitute quorum at meeting of members and, if quorum is present, affirmative vote of majority of members represented at meeting and entitled to vote shall be act of members, unless otherwise provided in operating agreement. Members may act by unanimous written consent. (7-80-711).

Operating Agreement.—Members may enter into operating agreement governing affairs of company and conduct of its business. (7-80-102). Operating agreement may grant to all or specified group of members right to consent, vote, or agree, on per capita or other basis, upon any matter. (7-80-706).

Management responsibility may be vested in members or one or more managers. If management is vested in manager or managers, articles or operating agreement may apportion management responsibility or voting power. Manager need not be resident of Colorado or member of company unless articles or operating agreement so requires. (7-80-401). Number of managers shall be fixed by or in manner provided by articles or operating agreement except as to number constituting initial manager or group of managers, which shall be fixed by articles. (7-80-402). Managers shall be elected by majority of members unless articles or operating agreement provide otherwise. (7-80-402). Classification of managers permitted. (7-80-403). Vacancies may be filled by written agreement of majority of remaining managers. (7-80-404). Managers may be removed by vote of majority of members then entitled to vote at election of managers. (7-80-405). Manager is obligated to perform duties in good faith in manner which he reasonably believes to be in best interests of company and with such care as ordinarily prudent person in like position would use under similar circumstances. Manager has no authority to act in contravention of either articles or operating agreement. Every manager is agent of company for purpose of its business. Act of every manager binds company unless manager so acting otherwise lacks authority to act and person with whom he is dealing has knowledge that manager has no such authority. (7-80-406). Indemnification of managers, employees and agents permitted. (7-80-410).

Records.—Company must maintain specified financial and other records at registered office. Such records are subject to inspection and copying at reasonable request of, and at expense of, any member during normal business hours. (7-80-411).

Capital.—Contributions of members may be in cash, property or services rendered or promissory note or other obligation to contribute cash or property or to perform services. (7-80-501). Promise to contribute to company is enforceable against member if in writing, and may not be waived without consent of all members. (7-80-502). Profits and losses of company will be allocated among members and among classes of members in manner provided in operating agreement and, if operating agreement does not so provide, profits and losses must be allocated on basis of value (as stated in company records) of contributions made by each member. (7-80-503). Distributions of cash or other assets will be allocated among members and among classes of members in manner provided in operating agreement and, if operating agreement does not so provide, distributions must be made on basis of value (as stated in company records) of contributions made by each member. (7-80-504).

Distributions.—Members entitled to distributions only to extent set forth in operating agreement. (7-80-601). Member does not have right to demand or receive any distribution except in cash. (7-80-604). Member may not receive distribution from

LIMITED LIABILITY COMPANIES . . . *continued*
company except to extent that, after giving effect to distribution, fair value of company's assets exceeds its liabilities. (7-80-606). Members are liable under certain circumstances if they receive return of their contribution. (7-80-607).

Resignation.—Unless prohibited in written operating agreement, member may resign at any time by giving written notice. If resignation violates operating agreement, company may recover damages from resigning member. Upon resignation, member is entitled only to receive share of profits to which such member would have been entitled if it had not resigned, unless operating agreement provides otherwise. (7-80-602).

Registered Agent.—Company must maintain registered agent and file report with secretary of state of any change in registered agent or his business address within 15 days. (7-80-302).

Reports.—Each domestic and foreign limited liability company must file periodic reports with secretary of state indicating name of company (and, in case of foreign company, state of organization), name and business address of registered agent (and, in case of foreign company, address of principal office in state of its organization) and name and address of each manager or member. Reports due biannually. Penalties are imposed if reports are not filed. (7-80-303 to 305).

Dissolution.—Company will be dissolved upon unanimous agreement of all members, or death, retirement, resignation, expulsion, bankruptcy or dissolution of member, or occurrence of any other event which terminates continued membership of member, unless business of limited liability company is continued by consent of remaining members. (7-80-801). Voluntary and involuntary dissolution is governed by 7-80-801 to 811.

Foreign limited liability companies are recognized and must qualify to do business in Colorado. (7-80-901 to 913).

PARTNERSHIPS:

General.—Colorado has adopted Uniform Partnership Act (1994) (Colorado Uniform Partnership Act [1997], 7-64-1012 to -64-1206) effective Jan. 1, 1998 with revisions relating primarily to limited liability partnerships and limited liability partnerships. Colorado Uniform Partnership Act (1997) will govern partnerships formed after effective date and partnerships that elect to be governed. (7-64-1025). Partnerships formed prior to effective date that do not elect to be covered by Colorado Uniform Partnership Act (1997) continue to be governed by Uniform Partnership Act. (Colorado Uniform Partnership Law, 7-60-101 to -60-143).

Partnership or other unincorporated association may sue or be sued in its common name. (13-50-105). See category Intellectual Property, topic Trademark and Tradenames, subhead Tradenames for filing requirements as to partnership name.

Colorado Deviations from Uniform Partnership Act (1994).—Domestic partnership may be converted into domestic limited partnership or foreign limited partnership. (7-64-902). Domestic limited partnership may be converted into domestic partnership or foreign partnership. (7-64-903). Unless lesser vote is provided for in partnership agreement, conversion of limited partnership into partnership requires approval of all partners. (7-64-903). Non-consenting limited partner to conversion of limited partnership to partnership or merger with another partnership considered to have withdrawn from partnership but not considered to be wrongfully withdrawn. (7-64-903, 7-64-905).

Partnership presumed to have been formed in jurisdiction in which it has its chief executive office. (7-64-106). Law of Colorado governs relationships among partners and partnerships, as well as liability of partners in registered limited liability partnership. (7-64-106). Duties of partner to partnership pertain to all transactions connected with formation, conduct or liquidation of partnership. (7-64-404). Upon partner request, partnership dissolved by judicial determination upon showing that partnership is not reasonably likely to pay liabilities against which it has obligation to indemnify dissociated partner. (7-64-801). Partnership agreement may only be amended by unanimous consent. (7-64-401).

Limited Partnerships.—Colorado has adopted Uniform Limited Partnership Act (1916) (Colorado Uniform Limited Partnership Law of 1931, 7-61-101 to 130) and Uniform Limited Partnership Act (1976 with 1985 amendments) (Colorado Uniform Limited Partnership Act of 1981, 7-62-101 to 1201) with numerous minor variations. Limited partnerships electing registration governed by Colorado Uniform Partnership Act (1997), and partnerships not making election governed by Colorado Uniform Partnership Law. (7-62-1104). Out-of-state limited partnerships must register with Secretary of State before transacting business in Colorado. (7-62-902).

Colorado Uniform Limited Partnership Act of 1981 applies to all limited partnerships formed on or after Nov. 1, 1981. (7-62-1101). Limited partnership formed prior to Nov. 1, 1981 governed by provisions of Colorado Uniform Limited Partnership Law of 1931 unless it elects to be governed by Colorado Uniform Limited Partnership Act of 1981. Election must be made in manner provided. (7-62-1103). In case not provided for in Colorado Uniform Limited Partnership Act of 1981, provisions of Colorado Uniform Partnership Law, or Colorado Uniform Partnership Act (1997), shall apply. (7-62-1104).

Provisions that have been added to Colorado version of Uniform Limited Partnership Act (1976 with 1985 amendments) include following: provisions to expand words or abbreviations that must appear in name to indicate limited partnership or limited liability limited partnership status (7-62-102), to permit renewal of reservation of name for additional periods of 120 days (7-62-103) and to provide for mergers and consolidations of limited partnership (7-62-210). Permits majority of limited partners to admit additional general partner upon withdrawal of last remaining general partner where partnership agreement does not provide for such appointment, unless prohibited by partnership agreement; and permits district court for county in which registered agent is located to admit additional general partner upon application by any limited partner after such withdrawal, unless limited partnership was formed before June 3, 1997 and any partner prior to June 2, 1998 delivers written election to general partner against application of such provision. (7-62-401; 7-62-801). In addition, Colorado provides that in absence of appointment of agent for service of process, service will be made on Secretary of State for either domestic limited partnership (7-62-108) or foreign limited partnership (7-62-909). Certificate of limited partnership must contain statement that there are at least two partners, at least one of whom is limited partner (7-62-201[1][d]), need not specify dissolution date and may specify effective date within 90 days after filing (7-62-201). Colorado extends liability for false statement in certificate to any general partner who knew when he executed certificate that statement was false. (7-62-207).

In derivative action by limited partner, Colorado requires, in addition to elements that must be established under Uniform Limited Partnership Act (1976 with 1985 amendments), that limited partner establish that general partner's decision not to sue constitutes abuse of discretion or conflict of interest. (7-62-1001). Court may require plaintiff who brings derivative action without reasonable cause to pay costs and fees other than attorneys fees. (7-62-1002). Limited partnership may require plaintiff in derivative action who owns less than 5% or $25,000 to give security for costs and expenses. (7-62-1003).

Limited Liability Partnerships, Limited Liability Limited Partnerships, Limited Partnership Associations.—Partnership may register as limited liability partnership and limited partnership may register as limited liability limited partnership. (7-64-1002[1]). Limited liability partnership is for all purposes partnership. (7-64-202[1]). Limited partnership association may be formed with indefinite duration. (7-63-104). Foreign limited liability partnership or foreign limited liability limited partnership may register as such with Secretary of State. (7-64-1002[2]). Foreign limited liability partnership or foreign limited liability limited partnership may not transact business in Colorado or maintain any court action in Colorado until it is registered. (7-64-1002[5]).

Registration statement for limited liability partnership or limited liability limited partnership, domestic or foreign, must contain: partnership name, address of chief executive office; if its chief executive office is not located in Colorado, name and street address of registered agent, and declaration that it is domestic or foreign limited liability partnership or limited liability limited partnership. (7-64-1002[1] and [2]). Registered limited liability partnership and limited liability limited partnership without chief executive office within Colorado must maintain registered office and registered agent who is individual resident, domestic corporation, or registered foreign corporation. (7-64-1113). Partnership or limited partnership that has registered for limited liability is for all purposes same entity that existed before it registered. (7-64-1002). Name of limited liability partnership must contain words limited liability partnership or abbreviation L.L.P. or LLP, and name of limited liability limited partnership must contain words limited liability limited partnership or abbreviation L.L.L.P. or LLLP. (7-64-1003[1][A]).

Except as provided in written partnership agreement, person is not liable, directly or indirectly, or through indemnification, contribution, assessment or otherwise, solely by being partner, for partnership obligations incurred while partnership is limited liability partnership. (7-64-306).

Except for reasonable compensation for current services, general partner of limited liability partnership or limited liability limited partnership may not receive distribution from partnership when liabilities of partnership exceed fair value of partnership assets. (7-64-1004). General partner liable to limited liability partnership or limited liability limited partnership for six years for general partner contributions improperly returned to general partner. (7-64-1005). Courts must apply corporate case law regarding piercing corporate veil to determine personal liability of general partners of limited liability partnership or limited liability limited partnership. (7-64-1009).

Requirements for filing partnership, limited partnership, limited liability partnership and limited liability limited partnership documents established. (7-64-1103). Secretary of State to establish partnership forms (7-64-1104) and fees (7-64-1105). Effective time and date of documents (7-64-1106) and procedures for correcting filed documents (7-64-1107) established. Partnership may change registered office or registered agent by filing with Secretary of State statement including partnership name, street address of current registered office, address of new registered office, name of current registered agent, name and written consent of new registered agent, and statement that after change street address of registered agent will be identical to business office of registered agent. (7-64-1114).

Colorado Corporations and Associations Act.—Various entities may convert to or merge with other types of entities. (7-90-201).

BUSINESS REGULATION AND COMMERCE

BANKS AND BANKING:

Uniform Commercial Code adopted. See topic Commercial Code. Uniform Consumer Credit Code adopted. See topic Consumer Credit.

Banking Days.—Defined to mean that part of any day, excluding Sat., Sun., and holidays, on which bank is open to public for carrying on substantially all of its banking functions. (4-4-104). Bank may determine to dispense with or restrict its hours on Sat. (11-6-103).

Regulated by.—Colorado Banking Code of 1957 is based on Model State Banking Code of American Banker Association. (Tit. 11, arts. 1-11). Banking corporations, including savings banks, and all national banks to extent applicable (11-1-102[2]; 11-1-105), are governed by this Code. General Corporation Code otherwise generally applicable. (11-11-110). Separate provisions govern nonbanking trust companies (11-23-101 to 125), savings and loan associations (11-40-101 to 11-47-120), credit unions (11-30-101 to 124) and industrial banks (11-22-101 to 706). See appropriate subheads, infra.

Division of banking exercises general control over all state banks. (11-2-101[1]). Within division there is banking board and bank commissioner. (11-2-101[2], 11-2-102[1]). Board exercises all policy-making and rule-making authority for division, and commissioner is responsible for internal administration thereof (11-2-103.5), including organization, merger, consolidation, conversion, sale of assets, liquidation, dissolution, and reorganization (11-1-105, 11-2-103). Board may delegate to commissioner any power, duty or function of board relating to adjudicatory determinations, but has power to review and affirm, reverse or modify any adjudicatory determination so delegated. (11-2-103.5[2]). Review of decision of board is vested in district court or court of

See note at head of Digest as to 1998 legislation covered.

See Topical Index in front part of this volume.

CO – 7

BANKS AND BANKING . . . *continued*
appeals. (11-2-105). Every state bank must file three reports annually with commissioner, detailing resources and liabilities (11-2-109[1]) and annual loan report stating aggregate dollar amounts of loans not later than Aug. 31 of each year for 12-month period ended preceding June 30 (11-7-112). Changes in voting stock control of state banks require prior application to banking board for approval. (11-2-109[4], [5]). Commissioner makes examination of state banks as often as directed by banking board. (11-2-108[1]). Costs of examinations and administrative expenses of division are assessed against state banks in proportion to their assets. (11-2-114).

Stockholders.—When banking board has reason to believe capital of any state bank is inadequate, it shall cause bank to assess stockholders pro rata to make good such deficiency and if any stockholder fails to pay such assessment bank may sell his stock at public auction or private sale to make good such assessment. (11-3-104[1]). If assessment not paid within time period specified in order (not to be less than 30 days), commissioner, with approval of board, may proceed with liquidation or reorganization. (11-3-104, 11-5-102 to 105).

Shareholders of every state bank are individually responsible equally and ratably for debts of bank to extent of double amount of stock ownership at par value (in addition to amount invested in such shares) unless bank is member of federal deposit insurance corporation. (11-3-105).

Branch Banking.—Losing its title as country's only unit banking state, Colorado adopted broad in-state branching legislation (11-25-101 to 107) in 1991 applicable to all "financial institutions", defined to include commercial banks, industrial banks, savings and loan associations, federal savings banks and their respective holding companies. Provisions include (1) conversion of any or all affiliated institutions to branches; (2) limited de novo branching (one branch per bank, industrial bank and savings and loan) until Jan. 1, 1997 and unlimited branching thereafter; (3) one or more additional de novo branches in "economically depressed" area (as defined in statute) upon prior approval of appropriate state regulatory agency; and (4) authority for all affiliated Colorado financial institutions to contract on behalf of each other to receive deposits, close and service loans, and receive payments on loans, without becoming branch banks.

Interstate Banking and Branching.—Pursuant to interstate banking law (11-6.4-101 to 104), Colorado bank holding company may acquire control of out-of-state state holding company or bank and out-of-state holding company may acquire control of Colorado holding company or bank. Acquisitions by out-of-state holding companies limited to Colorado holding companies and banks in operation for at least five years at time of acquisition of control. Out-of-state holding company may not acquire Colorado holding company or bank if acquisition would result in control of more than 25% of aggregate deposits in all federally-insured Colorado financial institutions.

Interstate branching in any form was prohibited in Colorado prior to June 1, 1997. Since then Colorado banks in existence at least five years may be acquired and converted into branches, but under no circumstances may out-of-state banks or bank holding companies establish de novo branches or acquire branches of existing banks.

Insurance.—Subject to laws and rules applicable to state or national banks, as case may be, banks may act as agent in solicitation and sale of insurance. (11-6-101[2]).

Nonbank Banks.—Prohibited within state as to ownership by domestic or foreign bank holding company or other "company". (11-6.3-101).

Deposits.—Banks may receive deposits from minors. (11-6-104). Joint deposits may be paid to either depositor, deemed in joint tenancy with right of survivorship. (11-6-105). Multiple-person accounts, including P.O.D. accounts, are governed by 15-15-201 to 227, part of Colorado Probate Code. See category Estates and Trusts, topic Wills.

Maximum annual rate of interest payable by state banks on all types of deposits or accounts may be set by board regulation or, in absence thereof, by applicable federal law. (11-6-102). Depositor must object to statement of his account within one year. (11-6-106). See topic Commercial Code. Bank need not recognize adverse claim to deposit in absence of court order or posted bond. (11-6-107).

Unclaimed Deposits.—Upon liquidation of state bank, such funds shall be held six years by commissioner and then paid over to county treasurer. (11-5-101, 11-5-104[11]). Colorado has also adopted version of Uniform Unclaimed Property Act, which requires financial institution that holds money and intangible property belonging to customers to file reports with and deliver property to state treasurer at specified intervals. (38-13-101 to 134). See category Property, topic Absentees, subhead Escheat.

Trust Companies.—Regulated by Trust Company Act. (11-23-101 to 125). Trust companies have powers to: Act in any fiduciary or representative capacity, act as transfer agent, registrar, escrow agent, or attorney-in-fact and receive, manage, and apply sinking funds; maintain and rent safekeeping facilities; maintain savings deposits, time deposits, and certificates of deposit for investment of fiduciary funds and other accounts for which trust company is empowered to act, and pay interest thereon at rates permitted state banks under 11-6-102(3), but all such deposits must be insured by federal deposit insurance corporation (11-23-103.5); exercise same investment powers as individual fiduciary under like circumstances; accept and execute any fiduciary business permitted by laws of Colorado or any other state and U.S. and establish common trust funds as provided by 11-24-101 to 107; take oaths and execute affidavits by oath or affidavit of specified officers; act as agent in solicitation and sale of insurance under rules of state insurance commissioner (11-23-103[3]); act as investment adviser under any applicable law; and do and perform any other acts necessary or proper to exercise foregoing powers; but are otherwise prohibited from conducting banking business and cannot use word bank in their names. (11-23-103).

Uniform Common Trust Fund Act adopted. (11-24-101).

Savings and Loan Associations.—Regulated by Savings and Loan Association Law (Tit. 11, arts. 40 to 46) administered by state commissioner of financial services (11-44-101). May branch to same extent as other financial institutions. See subhead Branch Banking, supra. Broad corporate powers (11-41-112), but business is to be primarily accumulation of funds through sale of shares, notes, debentures, acceptance of savings deposits, loan or investment of funds to its members to acquire real estate, make improvements and pay off encumbrances. (11-40-103). May act as agent in solicitation and sale of insurance under rules of financial services board and state insurance commissioner. (11-41-112[1]). Unless authorized by commissioner, savings and loan association may not act as fiduciary, other than as escrow agent. (11-41-112.5). Investments limited to specified categories. (11-41-114[1]). In general, may accept deposits, borrow money and make loans to same extent as federal savings and loan associations. (11-41-114[2], 11-41-119).

Credit Unions.—Regulated by state's credit union statutes (11-30-101 to 124) administered by state commissioner of financial services (11-30-124). Credit union has power to receive deposits, accept share drafts, make loans to members, make investments, hold individual retirement accounts, belong to central credit union, merge, dissolve, with commissioner approval sell any portion of its assets or purchase assets of another credit union, and generally engage in any activity that federally chartered credit union may engage in. (11-30-104).

Industrial banks are governed by state law (11-22-101 to 706), administered by state banking board (11-22-101). Generally, they may make all types of loans (11-22-107) but may carry only savings deposits, which must be insured by federal deposit insurance corporation (11-22-701). May act as agent in solicitation and sale of insurance under rules of state insurance commissioner (11-22-106[6]) and may branch to same extent as other financial institutions. See subhead Branch Banking, supra.

BILLS AND NOTES:

Uniform Commercial Code adopted. See topic Commercial Code.

Uniform Consumer Credit Code adopted. See topic Consumer Credit.

Judgment notes have been held to be enforceable in Colorado but are not in common use. Judgments so obtained will be vacated upon showing of meritorious defense. (160 Colo. 523, 418 P.2d 289). Uniform Consumer Credit Code renders void any authorization to confess judgment on claim arising out of consumer loan, credit sale or lease. (5-2-415, 5-3-407).

Attorney fee collection clauses are valid and enforceable if reasonable in amount (28 Colo. App. 441, 476 P.2d 292) and include fees incurred on appeal (635 P.2d 882). Uniform Consumer Credit Code authorizes reasonable attorney's fee not in excess of 15% of unpaid debt after default on consumer loans, credit, sales or leases referred to attorney not salaried employee of creditor. (5-3-404, 5-2-413).

Bad Checks.—Person who draws check not paid upon presentment is liable to holder for amount of check plus actual damages, or amount of check plus any posted or contractual charge not exceeding $20 and any collection agency cost equal to 20% of check's face value. If total amount due is not paid within 15 days after written notice of nonpayment on presentment, drawer is liable to holder for treble amount of check but not less than $100. Certain statutory exceptions apply. Court costs and reasonable attorney fees are recoverable by prevailing party. (13-21-109).

Special Defenses.—Assignee of consumer paper subject to claims and defenses of buyer against seller or lessor even if assignee is holder in due course. (5-2-403). See topic Consumer Credit.

BILLS OF LADING:

See topic Carriers.

BROKERS:

Towns and cities may tax, license and regulate brokers, provided that they do not interfere with persons required by law to sell property at auction. (31-15-501[p]).

Real Estate Brokers.—No person, firm, partnership, limited liability company, association, or corporation may engage in business or capacity of real estate broker or real estate salesperson unless license is obtained from real estate commission. (12-61-102). Licensing statute does not require one to have broker's license to negotiate on own behalf. (12-61-101[4][d]; 697 P.2d 34). Broker and salesperson are defined by statute. (12-61-101). Real estate commission shall no longer issue real estate salesperson license, effective Jan. 1, 1997. (12-61-103.5[1]). Transition from real estate salesperson to broker is governed by 12-61-103.5(2) and (3).

To collect finder's fee or commission, one who brings together buyer and seller must have real estate license if subject matter of sale involves change in ownership of interest in real estate. (196 Colo. 503, 593 P.2d 314). Broker's right to commission limited by statute. (12-61-201 to 203).

Broker must be at least 18 and must meet educational requirements and pass written examination under supervision of commission. (12-61-103). Special requirements apply to operation of independent brokerage practice and employment of brokers. (12-61-103[6]). Mandatory insurance is required. (12-61-103.6).

A nonresident may become a licensed real estate broker by complying with statute, but need not maintain place of business in this state if definite place of business maintained in another state. (12-61-107[1]). Every applicant must file irrevocable consent to service of process in any cause of action arising in Colorado by service on secretary of state. (12-61-107[2]).

Examination and license fees are as set forth in 12-61-110 and 12-61-111.5. Continuing education requirements are as set forth in 12-61-110.5. Unless commission establishes procedures for renewal on anniversary date, broker or salesperson license expires on Dec. 31 of first year. Each renewal is for three years. (12-61-110[4]). Licenses may be suspended or revoked, or licensee may be fined or censured by commission on various grounds (12-61-113; 12-61-306) after hearing (12-61-114). Subpoena power provided (12-61-120), penalty for failure to obey (12-61-121), and injunction power (12-61-122).

Recovery fund established to provide limited compensation to victims of negligence, fraud, willful misrepresentation, or conversion of trust funds by broker or salesman. (12-61-301 to 308; 708 P.2d 488). For purpose of recovery fund procedure, real estate salesmen licensed at time claim for relief arose deemed to have appointed secretary of state agent for service although no longer licensed in Colorado. (196 Colo. 473, 586 P.2d 1335).

See note at head of Digest as to 1998 legislation covered.

See Topical Index in front part of this volume.

CO – 8

BROKERS . . . *continued*

Person who solicits fee or consideration from prospective tenant for furnishing information concerning availability of real property must be licensed as real estate broker. (12-61-101[2][j]).

Broker relationships in real estate transactions governed by statute. (12-61-801 to 12-61-811). Dual agent, limited agent, single agent, buyer's agent, landlord's agent, seller's agent, tenant's agent, subagent and transaction-broker are each defined by statute (12-61-802) and respective duties and obligations of each established by statute (12-61-804 to 12-61-810).

Agricultural Broker.—Those who engage in business of soliciting or negotiating sales of farm products between vendor and purchaser are regulated by statute (12-16-101 to 118; must be licensed by commissioner of agriculture (12-16-104); and be bonded or file irrevocable letter of credit (12-16-106).

Securities Broker.—See topic Securities.

Uniform Commercial Code adopted. (4-1-101 to 4-11-102). See topic Commercial Code.

BULK SALES:

See topic Commercial Code; category Debtor and Creditor, topic Fraudulent Sales and Conveyances.

CARRIERS:

The public utilities commission is vested with power and authority to adopt all necessary rates, charges, and regulations to govern and regulate all rates, charges, and tariffs of every public utility of state; also with power to correct abuses, prevent unjust discriminations and extortions in such rates, charges, and tariffs, and generally to supervise and regulate all public utilities (except for utilities exempted by state constitution). (40-3-102). Common carriers are public utilities. (40-1-103[1][a]). Commission has full jurisdiction in home rule cities. (Colo. Const. art. XXV). Property carriers by motor vehicle, luxury limousines, charter or scenic buses, children's activity buses, and off-road scenic charters are subject to special provisions. (40-16-101 to 110). Certain nonprofit transportation of persons and operators of amusement rides also excluded from definition of public utility. (40-1-103 & 40-1.1-104).

Licenses.—See category Transportation, topic Motor Vehicles.

Rates.—No public utility may, without commission approval, directly or indirectly, provide free service, or service at rates greater or less than rates set by commission.(40-3-105). There are special provisions for rate regulation of rail carriers.(40-2-119, 120; 40-3-104 to 106). Emergency telephone access at discounted rates available for low-income individuals. (40-3.4-101 to 111).

Discrimination.—Unreasonable differences in rates and services of public utilities prohibited. (40-3-106). Common carrier, unlike contract carrier, must convey for all desiring its transportation. (40-1-102; 192 Colo. 537, 561 P.2d 1252).

Limiting Liability.—Carriers are liable for damages incurred as result of certain statutory violations. (40-9-103[1]). Carriers are liable as insurers of property received for transportation. (40-9-103[2]). Rail carrier may establish rates under which liability is limited to valuation declared by shipper or agreed upon by shipper and carrier and which provide for deductibles. (40-9-103[3]).

Liability of carrier for goods lost in transit is measured by full actual loss caused by carrier. (663 P.2d 621).

Common carrier by railroad in the state is liable for injury to or death of employee resulting wholly or partly from negligence of any officer, agent or employee of carrier. Carrier may not exempt itself from liability by contract. Contributory negligence is not bar, although it may diminish recovery so long as employer's violation of state or federal statute did not contribute to death or injury. Employee may not be held to have assumed risk. Injury or death arising out of and in course of employment is presumptive evidence of negligence of carrier. (40-33-101 to 109).

Penal statute makes carriers liable for damages not exceeding $10,000 nor less than $3,000 per person killed if death is caused by negligence, unskillfulness or criminal intent of officer, agent, servant or employee, or defect or insufficiency in conveyance. (13-21-201). Damages are punitive, not compensatory. (57 Colo. 90, 140 P. 463). Alternatively, wrongful death action for compensatory damages may be brought, with $250,000 noneconomic damages limitation or $50,000 solatium in lieu of noneconomic damages. (13-21-202, 203, 203.5). If wrongful act, neglect or default causing death constitutes felonious killing, then there is no limitation on damages. (13-21-203).

Uniform Commercial Code adopted. See topic Commercial Code.

Bills of lading must be issued for all intrastate shipments. Carrier cannot exempt itself from liability by terms of bill of lading, but it is not liable for greater sum than value fixed in bill of lading if such valuation is stated. (40-9-103[2]). Otherwise, Uniform Commercial Code governs. Optional language in U.C.C. §7-403 not adopted. See topic Commercial Code.

Hazardous Materials.—See category Transportation, topic Motor Vehicles.

Liens.—Carrier has lien on property transported at request of owner for reasonable transportation and storage charges. (38-20-105). Otherwise, Uniform Commercial Code governs. See topic Commercial Code.

Motor Vehicle Carriers.—See category Transportation, topic Motor Vehicles.

COMMERCIAL CODE:

Uniform Commercial Code has been adopted. Code is designated as Tit. 4 of Colorado Revised Statutes. Colorado Revised Statute section numbers contain that title number followed by Uniform Commercial Code article and section numbers, e.g., 4-1-101.

Action on Official Text and Amendments.—1962 Official Text adopted (with variations discussed below) effective July 1, 1966.

1966 Official Amendments and Optional Amendments adopted (with variations discussed below), effective Jan. 1, 1978, to §§2-702 and 3-501.

1972 Official Text of Art. 9 and related sections adopted (with variations discussed below) effective Jan. 1, 1978.

1973 Official Amendment to §8-102(3) adopted effective Apr. 9, 1973.

1977 Official Amendments to Art. 8 adopted (with variations discussed below) effective July 1, 1981. 1977 conforming amendments to Art. 8 adopted (with variations discussed below) effective July 1, 1985.

1977 Official Amendments to Art. 1, 5 and 9 adopted (with variations discussed below) effective July 1, 1985.

1987 Official Text of Art. 2A and conforming amendments to Arts. 1 and 9 as amended in 1990 adopted effective July 1, 1992.

1990 Official Text of Art. 4A and confirming amendment to §1-105(2) adopted effective Apr. 12, 1990.

1990 Official Text repealing Art. 6 adopted effective July 1, 1991.

1990 Revised Art. 3 and Amended Art. 4 with conforming amendments to Revised Art. 3 adopted (with variations discussed below) effective Jan. 1, 1995.

1995 Revised Art. 5 and Revised Art. 8, each with conforming amendments adopted (with variations discussed below) effective July 1, 1996.

Material Variations from Official Text, Omissions, and Action on Optional Provisions.—Listed below by Code section number are material variations made in Colorado from official text (including variations from official amendments adopted as set forth above), sections omitted, and action taken with respect to optional provisions in Colorado:

§1-109—Deleted.

§1-201—Added "(23.5) 'Livestock' means horses, mules, registered cattle, range cattle, cattle carrying one or more Colorado recorded brands, and sheep."

§1-209—Optional section adopted.

§2-102—After words "does not apply to" inserted "(a)". Added new subsection "(b) The donation, whether for or without valuable consideration, acquisition, preparation, transplantation, injection, or transfusion of any human tissue, organ, or blood or component thereof for or to a human being."

§2-318—Alternative A adopted with following modifications: Deleted "natural person who is in the family or household of his buyer or who is a guest in his home if it is reasonable to expect that such person may" and inserted instead "person who may reasonably be expected to." Deleted "in person."

§2-326—Added "(5) The provisions of this section shall not apply to the placement of works of fine art on consignment, which shall be governed by the provisions of article 15 of title 6, C.R.S."

§2-401—Added "(5) Notwithstanding any other provision of this section, when livestock have been delivered under a contract of sale, if on the accompanying brand inspection certificate or memorandum of brand inspection certificate the seller has conspicuously noted that payment of the consideration for the sale has not been received, title does not pass until payment is made."

§2-403—Added "(1.5) Notwithstanding any other provision of this section when livestock have been delivered under a transaction of purchase and on the accompanying brand inspection certificate or memorandum of brand inspection certificate the seller has conspicuously noted that payment of the consideration for the transaction has not been received, the buyer does not have power to transfer good title to a good faith purchaser for value until payment is made."

§2-511—Added "(4) (a) When livestock has been delivered under a transaction of purchase and on the accompanying brand inspection certificate or memorandum of brand inspection certificate the seller has conspicuously noted that payment of the consideration for the transaction has not been received, the seller shall send a certificate of payment stating that payment has been made either within ten days after receipt of a check drawn and payable within the United States or, in any other case, within three business days after payment has been made.

"(b) Unless otherwise agreed, when payment has been made, the buyer shall have a specifically enforceable right to the unqualified certification of payment from the seller and, where the seller has failed to provide the certification of payment in accordance with the provisions of this subsection (4), the seller will be deemed to have failed to make delivery of the livestock."

§2-725(1)—Last sentence changed to read: "This period of limitation may not be varied by agreement of the parties."

§2.5-103(e)—$25,000 limit.

§2.5-216—Alternative C adopted.

§2.5-305(1)—Modified to give same rights to buyer or sublessee from any transferor.

§2.5-306—Lien takes priority over interest "of the party to the lease at whose instance the services or materials were furnished, but does not take priority over any such interest of the other party to the lease contract."

§2.5-506(1)—Action must be commenced within time period prescribed by 13-80-101 and limitation period may not be varied by parties.

§2.5-518(2)—Added "(ii) interest on the amount computed under clause (i) of this subsection (2) from the date of commencement of the term of the new lease agreement until the date of entry of judgment at the same rate used in computing present value, and"; renumbered original (ii) as (iii).

§2.5-519(1)—Added following present value measure of damages "plus interest in the remainder so computed from the date of default until the date of entry of judgment at the same rate used in computing present value,".

§2.5-527(2)—Added new "(iii) interest on the amount computed under clause (ii) of this Subsection (2) from the date of commencement of the term of the new lease until the date of entry of judgment at the same rate used in computing present value and"; renumbered original (iii) as (iv).

§2.5-528(1)—Added new "(iii) interest on the sum of the amounts described in clauses (i) and (ii) of this subsection (1) from the date of default to the date of entry of judgment at the same rate used in computing present value, and"; renumbered original (iii) as (iv).

§2.5-528(2)—"At his or her option, lessor may recover from the lessee as damages for a default of the type described in subsection (1) of this section, in lieu of the damages recoverable under said subsection (1)," damages described in original. Requirement of inadequacy deleted.

See note at head of Digest as to 1998 legislation covered.

See Topical Index in front part of this volume.

COMMERCIAL CODE . . . *continued*

§2.5-533—Added with no code counterpart: "*Other measure of damages.* Notwithstanding any other provision of this Article, except as otherwise provided with respect to damages liquidated in the lease agreement (Section 4-2.5-504) or otherwise determined pursuant to agreement of the parties (Sections 4-1-102(3) and 4-2.5-503), a party to a lease contract, at his (or her) option, may recover for the other party's default, in addition to or in lieu of the damages expressly authorized by this Article, such additional or different damages as may be necessary to put such party in as good a position as if the other party had performed in accordance with the lease contract, determined in a reasonable manner."

§3-121—Alternative B adopted.

§3-312(b)(iv)—After sentence ending ". . . made in the declaration." add new sentence: "The warranty is made to the obligated bank and any person entitled to enforce the check."

§3-312(c)—After "under subsection (b)(4) and" add ", after the claim became enforceable,".

§3-404(d)—Removed "substantially" from "that failure substantially contributes".

§3-405(b)—Removed "substantially" from "that failure substantially contributes".

§3-406(a) and (b)—Removed "substantially" from "that failure substantially contributes".

§4-104(a)(3)—After "any day" added ", excluding Saturday, Sunday and holidays,".

§4-106—Optional language not adopted; alternative B adopted.

§4-202(a)(2)—Optional language adopted.

§4-212(b)—Optional subsection adopted.

§4-405(a)—Substituted "a determination" for "an adjudication" preceding "of incompetence" in first and second sentences.

§4-405(b)—Added at the end of subsection "or unless prohibited by section 39-23-139, C.R.S. 1973."

§4-406(a)—Added new sentence at end of subsection: "If the bank does not return the items, it shall provide in the statement of account the telephone number that the customer may call to request an item or legible copy thereof pursuant to subsection (b) of this section."

§4-406(b)—Added new sentence at end of subsection: "A bank shall provide, upon request and without charge to the customer, at least two items or a legible copy thereof with respect to each statement of account sent to the customer."

§5-115—Adopted "cause of action" alternative.

§§6-101-6-111—Repealed effective July 1, 1991.

§6-112—Right under §§6-101-6-111 arising before repeal valid until July 1, 1992.

§7-204(4)—Subsection not adopted.

§7-403(1)(b)—Optional language not adopted.

§9-103(2)(a)—Language "Except to the extent that motor vehicle titles are governed by section 42-6-131, C.R.S.," added at beginning of subsection.

§9-110—Deleted "or real estate." Added after word "sufficient" "if it specifically identifies and itemizes in the security agreement what is described as to consumer goods, and." Added after word "described" at end of section "as to all other personal property."

§9-201—Deleted word "small" preceding word "loans" in second sentence.

§9-203—Renumbered subsections (2), (3), and (4) to (3), (4), and (5), and added new subsection (2): "No security interest in consumer goods owned by a married person and used primarily for family or household purposes, other than a security interest in property referred to in section 4-9-302(3) or any purchase money security interest, shall be enforceable unless such security agreement is signed by both husband and wife if they are residing together at the time the security interest is created."

§9-203(4) [4-9-203(5)]—Blank filled in as follows: "other statutes regulating loans and retail installment sales, such as the 'Uniform Consumer Credit Code' and article 9 of title 8, C.R.S.;".

§9-206(1)—Words "or decision" after word "statute" deleted from first sentence.

§9-208(1)—Added word "either" after word "returned" in first sentence, and after word "debtor" at end of first sentence added "or to any other person designated by the debtor in such statement."

§9-208(2)—Third sentence amended to read: "If the secured party without reasonable excuse fails to comply he is liable for any loss thereby caused to the debtor or to any other person designated by the debtor to receive the statement referred to in subsection (1) of this section; and if the debtor has properly included in his request a good faith statement of the obligation or a list of the collateral or both, the secured party may claim a security interest only as shown in the statement against persons misled by his failure to comply." Added to fourth sentence after word "debtor" "or to any other person designated by the debtor to receive the statement referred to in subsection (1) of this section."

§9-301(2)-Deleted "ten" and substituted "twenty," effective for all purchase money security interests arising on or after July 1, 1990.

§9-302(3)(b)—Deleted words "the following statutes of this state" and substituted: "Any certificate of title statute of this state covering automobiles, trailers, mobile homes, boats, farm tractors, or the like."

§9-307(1)—Inserted "(a)" after figure "(1)" and added new subsection: "(b)(I) A security interest in farm products and the rights of a secured party, a buyer of farm products, a commission merchant, or a selling agent, as defined in the Federal 'Food Security Act of 1985' (7 U.S.C. Sec. 1631) pertaining to such products, shall be subject to the provisions of such Act. (II) For purposes of section 1324(e)(1) of the Federal 'Food Security Act of 1985', 'receipt' by a buyer of farm products, a commission merchant, or a selling agent of notice of a security interest created by a seller means the earlier of actual receipt of the notice by said parties or refusal by said parties to accept delivery of the notice. Actual receipt or refusal to accept delivery may be proven in any manner, including, without limitation, a statement of delivery or attempted delivery and refusal signed by the delivering party, acknowledgement of receipt signed by the accepting party, or return receipt showing delivery or refusal to accept delivery from the United States postal service, or courier or other delivering party."

§9-307(2)—After words "consumer goods" added "having an original purchase price not in excess of two hundred fifty dollars."

§9-307—Also added following subsections having no Code counterpart: "(4) Notwithstanding subsection (1) of this section, a buyer of farm products may take free of or subject to a security interest as determined by subsection (1) of this section, article 9.5 of this title, and other applicable Colorado law, and section 1324 of the federal 'Food Security Act of 1985', P.L. 99-198, to the extent it preempts applicable Colorado law.

§9-310—Amended to read: "When a person in the ordinary course of his business furnishes services or materials with respect to goods subject to a security interest, a lien upon goods in the possession of such person given by statute or rule of law for such materials or services does not take priority over a perfected security interest unless a statute expressly provides otherwise."

§9-311—Added at end of section "but this section shall not be construed as inconsistent with criminal sanctions now or hereafter applicable to transactions involving collateral or as justifying any transfer which would otherwise be a violation of law."

§9-312(4)-Deleted "ten" and substituted "twenty," effective for all purchase money security interests arising on or after July 1, 1990.

§9-401(1)(a)—Repealed effective July 1, 1996.

The following §9-401(b) was adopted having no Code counterpart: "(b)(I) The proper place to file in order to perfect a security interest is as follows: (A) when the collateral is timber to be cut or is minerals or other substances of value which may be extracted from the earth or accounts subject to subsection (5) of section 4-9-103, or when the financing statement is filed as a fixture filing (section 4-9-313) and the collateral is goods which are or are to become fixtures, then in the real estate records in the office of the county clerk and recorder in the county where the real estate concerned is located; (B) in all other cases, in the office of the secretary of state or in the office of the county clerk and recorder of any county." (II) This paragraph (b) is effective July 1, 1996.

§9-401(3)—Alternative subsection (3) not adopted.

§9-401(4)—Amended to read: "The rules stated in section 4-9-103 govern whether the law of this state determines whether filing is necessary in this state."

§9-401(5)—Office of secretary of state designated as place to file.

§9-402(1)—Divided §4-9-402(1) into subsections 1(a) and 1(b). Inserted "(b)" before sentence beginning "When the financing statement covers timber to be cut or covers minerals . . ."

§9-402(1)(a)—Revised first sentence to read as follows: "A financing statement is sufficient if it contains the names of the debtor and the secured party, an address of the secured party from which information concerning the security interest may be obtained, a mailing address of the debtor, and a statement indicating the types, or describing the items of collateral." After first sentence added following: "A financing statement must contain the social security number of the debtor or, in the case of a debtor doing business other than as an individual, the federal internal revenue service taxpayer identification number of such debtor." Effective Apr. 24, 1997, revised third sentence to read as follows: "Subject to section 4-9-413(1), a financing statement may be filed before a security agreement is made or a security interest otherwise attaches."

§9-402(1)(b)—In first sentence deleted "the like (including oil and gas)" and substituted: "other substances of value which may be extracted from the earth." In second sentence, deleted word "above" and substituted after word "information," phrase "required by paragraph (a) of this subsection (1)"; also deleted requirement that financing statement be signed by debtor. Deleted last sentence.

§9-402(2)—Deleted effective July 1, 1996.

§9-402(3)—Effective Apr. 24, 1997, below address of debtor added "Social security number or federal tax identification number of debtor . . . ."

§9-402(3)(3.)—Deleted "the like (including oil and gas)" and substituted: "other substances of value which may be extracted from the earth."

§9-402(3)(4.)—Deleted "(use whichever . . . . Signature of Debtor (or Assignor) is applicable) . . . . Signature of secured party (or Assignee)".

§9-402(4)—Revised first sentence to read as follows: "A financing statement may be amended by the filing of an amendment" (deleted requirement that it be signed by both debtor and secured party). After first sentence added following: "An amendment that deletes collateral covered by a financing statement shall be signed by the secured party and if such amendment is filed electronically it shall be signed electronically, pursuant to section 9-413(2)."

§9-402(5)—Deleted "the like (including oil and gas)" and substituted: "other substances of value which may be extracted from the earth." First optional language "[for record]" not adopted; second optional language ["sufficient . . . of this state]" adopted.

§9-402(6)—Divided §9-402(6) into subsections 6(a) and 6(b). Inserted "(b)" before sentence beginning "No fee with reference to the financing statement . . ." Subsections 6(a), (b), (c) and (d) changed to subsections 6(a)(I), (a)(II), (a)(III) and (a)(IV), and revised subsection 6(a)(III) to read as follows: "The mortgage complies with the requirements for a financing statement as set forth in this section; except that said mortgage is not required to include the social security number or federal taxpayer identification number of the debtor or a recital that said mortgage is to be filed in the real estate records; and".

§9-402(7)—In second sentence, deleted word "his" and substituted "the debtor's."

§9-402(8)—Added at end of subsection: "or, contains an incorrect debtor social security number or taxpayer identification number."

§9-403(3)—Made existing §9-403(3) subsection 3(a). Revised first sentence of subsection 3(a) to read as follows: "Subject to section 4-9-412 and paragraph (b) of this subsection (3), a continuation statement may be filed by the secured party within six months prior to the expiration of the five-year period specified in subsection (2) of this section." Revised second sentence of subsection 3(a) to read as follows: "Any such continuation statement must identify the original statement by filing office, file number, and date of filing." Revised fifth sentence of subsection 3(a) amended to read: "Unless a statute on disposition of public records provides otherwise and except as provided in subsection (6) of this section, the filing officer may remove a lapsed statement from the files and destroy it or a microfilm or other photographic record thereof after one year after the lapse." Effective July 1, 1996: (a) in second sentence deleted requirement that continuation statement be signed by secured party, (b) deleted third sentence, and (c) in seventh sentence added "or she" after "he". Added new subsection 3(b) that reads as follows: "(b) Any continuation statement filed on or after July 1, 1996, including one

See note at head of Digest as to 1998 legislation covered.

See Topical Index in front part of this volume.

CO – 10

COMMERCIAL CODE . . . *continued*
that was perfected by filing with both the offices of the secretary of state and a county clerk and recorder, continues the perfection in all of the collateral listed on the filing. The filing of a single continuation statement shall maintain the effectiveness of financing statements that name identical collateral but have been filed in multiple locations."

§9-403(5)—Not adopted. Fees governed by Art. 11.

§9-403(6)—Added at end of subsection: "Financing statements covering goods of a transmitting utility shall not be destroyed except pursuant to a specific statute for the disposition of such records."

§9-403(7)—Deleted "the like (including oil and gas)" and substituted "other substances of value which may be extracted from the earth." Optional language adopted.

§9-404(1)—Blank filled as follows: "January 1, 1978." Deleted "including payment of the required fee." (a) In first, second and fourth sentences deleted word "he" and substituted phrase "the secured party", and (b) deleted third sentence. Added at end of subsection: "A termination statement shall be signed by the secured party, and if such statement is filed electronically it shall be signed electronically, pursuant to section 9-413(2)."

§9-404(2)—Last sentence amended to read: "Unless a statute on disposition of public records provides otherwise, the filing officer may remove the originals of the financing statement and of any related continuation statement, statement of assignment, and statement of release or any microfilm or other photographic record thereof from the files at any time after one year after receipt of the termination statement." Added at end of subsection: "Unless a statute on disposition of public records provides otherwise, the filing officer may remove the original of the termination statement or any microfilm or other photographic record thereof from the files at any time after five years of receipt thereof."

§9-404(3)—Deleted. (See §11-102.)

§9-405(1)—Deleted last sentence concerning filing fees. (See §11-102.)

§9-405(2)—Deleted "the like (including oil and gas)" and substituted: "other substances of value which may be extracted from the earth." Deleted next to last sentence concerning filing fees. (See §11-102.) Effective July 1, 1996, in first sentence, deleted word "his" and substituted "the secured party's"; deleted requirement that assignment by secured party must be signed by secured party of record. In third sentence first time "he" appears, deleted it and substituted word "and"; second and third times "he" appears, deleted it and substituted "the filing officer". In first sentence, deleted word "written," and after second sentence added: "Such separate statement of assignment shall be signed by the secured party, and if such statement is filed electronically it shall be signed electronically, pursuant to section 4-9-413(2)."

§9-406—Deleted last sentence concerning filing fees. (See §11-102.) In first sentence deleted "by his signed statement"; deleted third sentence; in fourth sentence deleted word "he" and substituted "the filing officer." After second sentence added: "The statement of release shall be signed by the secured party, and if such statement is filed electronically it shall be signed electronically, pursuant to section 4-9-413(2)."

§9-407(1)—Optional provision adopted.

§9-407(2)—Deleted references to filing fees in second and last sentence. (See §11-102.) After "particular debtor," section amended to read: "any other statement, and any federal tax lien notice, and if there is, giving the date and hour of filing of each such statement or notice and the names and addresses of each secured party or grantee therein. Upon request the filing officer shall furnish a copy of any filed financing statement, any other statement, or any tax lien notice."

§9-410—Repealed.

Added following §9-412 with no official text counterpart: "*Refiling required.* (1) A financing statement or continuation statement filed before July 1, 1996, which has not lapsed by December 31, 1997, shall lose its perfection and priority rights unless a new continuation statement is filed on or after July 1, 1996, but on or before December 31, 1997, which identifies the original statement by county, file number, and date and time of filing, and lists the collateral of the original filing and includes a statement that the original financing statement is still effective. The filing of a new continuation statement shall preserve the priority of the original filing and shall be effective for five years from the expiration date of the original filing or any continuation statement filed before July 1, 1996. (2) The effectiveness of a financing statement or continuation statement filed before July 1, 1996, that lapses after July 1, 1996, but before December 31, 1997, may be continued by the filing of a continuation statement in accordance with section 4-9-403 (3). If the effectiveness of a financing statement or continuation statement is continued by the filing of a continuation statement before July 1, 1996, such financing statement or continuation statement must be continued by the timely filing of a further continuation statement, as required by subsection (1) of this Section. (3) For purposes of the refiling provisions of this Section only, a continuation statement does not have to be filed during the period beginning July 1, 1996, to December 31, 1997, when the only collateral on a financing statement is timber to be cut; minerals or other substances of value which may be extracted from the earth; fixtures; a mortgage or deed of trust effective as a fixture filing; collateral, including fixtures, of a transmitting utility; or accounts subject to Section 4-9-103(5)."

Added following §9-413 effective Apr. 24, 1997, with no official counterpart: "*Authorization to file financing statement - liability for unauthorized filing - electronic signatures.* (1)(a) No person shall file a financing statement or amendment that adds collateral covered by a financing statement unless the debtor authorizes such filing in a signed writing. Any such statement or amendment that is filed electronically shall be signed electronically, pursuant to subsection (2) of this section. Upon signing a written security agreement a debtor authorizes the secured party to file a financing statement and amendments covering the collateral described in the security agreement and any proceeds of said collateral.

(b) Any person who files a financing statement or amendment in violation of paragraph (a) of this subsection (1) is liable to the debtor for five hundred dollars and any loss sustained by the debtor as a result of such unauthorized filing.

(2) Any amendment that deletes collateral covered by a financing statement, termination statement, separate statement of assignment or statement of release of collateral and is filed electronically, shall include an electronic signature of the secured party that complies with procedures adopted by the filing officer with whom such filing is made. Such procedures shall require, at a minimum, that the name and address of the secured party appear on such filing when it is retrieved electronically or in printed form. An electronic signature may consist of an access code or any other identifying word or number assigned by a filing officer that is unique to a particular filer." (See also: §§38-35-201 to 204 "Spurious Liens and Documents".)

§9-503—Added "or provided in this section" following "otherwise agreed." Added following subsection having no Code counterpart: "(2) If the collateral is a mobile home or trailer coach as defined in Section 42-1-102(82), C.R.S., and is used and occupied by the debtor as a place of residence, the secured party may take possession of the collateral pursuant to this section without judicial process only if there is clear and convincing evidence that the debtor has vacated or abandoned the collateral or the debtor voluntarily surrenders the collateral to the secured party.

§9-503(3)—Repealed.

Added following §9-503.5, with no official text counterpart: "*Secured party's liability when taking possession after default—legislative declaration.* (1) The general assembly recognizes that in the past certain debtors may have been disadvantaged by the actions of repossessors and that such debtors were then unable to obtain just redress for their losses in the courts: The creditor who initiated the action by employing or contracting with the repossessor was shielded from liability because the repossessor was categorized by the courts as an independent contractor. The general assembly wishes to ensure that the repossessor is bonded or that the secured party or assignee is held responsible at law as a principal under the general principles of agency law for the actions of a repossessor who is acting at the behest of the creditor in the event that no bond has been posted. (2) A secured party or such party's assignee who wishes to recover or take possession of collateral upon default, including a motor vehicle repossessed pursuant to section 42-6-143, C.R.S., shall contract to recover or take possession of collateral only with a person who is bonded for property damage to or conversion of such collateral in the amount of twenty-five thousand dollars. Such bond shall be filed with and drawn in favor of the attorney general of the state of Colorado for use of the people of the state of Colorado and shall be revocable only with the written consent of the attorney general pursuant to rules and regulations promulgated by the office of the attorney general. The office of the attorney general may charge a fee to be paid by the person filing such bond in order to cover the direct and indirect costs incurred by such office in fulfilling its duties under the provisions of this section. (3) A secured party or such party's assignee who employs or contracts with a person who has not complied with the requirements specified in subsection (2) of this section shall be liable as principal for the actions of any person the secured party or assignee employs or contracts with to recover or take possession of the collateral after default as provided in section 4-9-503 in the same manner as if such person were the agent of the secured party or assignee, whether or not such person has been or may be deemed to be acting as an independent contractor in law. (4) A repossessor shall not engage in repossessing, recovering, or removing collateral or personal property on behalf of a secured creditor or assignee without first disclosing to such secured creditor or assignee whether such repossessor is bonded pursuant to this article. Any person who fails to disclose or misrepresents to a secured party such person's bonded status or fails to file such bond with the attorney general, shall be in violation of the 'Colorado Consumer Protection Act', Article 1 of Title 6, C.R.S., and shall be subject to remedies or penalties or both pursuant thereto. (5) Any person who knowingly falsifies a repossessor bond application or misrepresents information contained herein commits a Class 1 misdemeanor and, upon conviction thereof, shall be punished as provided in Section 18-1-106, C.R.S. (6) All moneys collected pursuant to this section shall be collected by the Attorney General who shall transmit such moneys to the state treasurer, who shall credit the same to the General Fund."

§9-504(6) and (7)—Repealed.

§9-506(2)—Repealed.

§9-508—Repealed.

Colorado adopted Art. 9.3 having no Code counterpart: 4-9.3-101.

§9.3-101—"*Short title.* This article shall be known and may be cited as the 'Central Indexing System Act.'"

§9.3-102—"*Definition.* As used in this article, unless context otherwise requires: (1) 'board' means Central Indexing System board."

§9.3-103—"*Central indexing system board.* [This Section provides for the appointment of an eleven member board which shall be responsible for creation and implementation of the central indexing system. This Section also sets forth the powers and duties of the board with respect to implementation and maintenance of the central indexing system.]

§9.3-104—"*Central indexing system.* (1) On the earliest practical date, the board shall implement the Central Indexing System under the supervision of a designee of such board.

(2) The indexing of a document pursuant to this article shall not constitute notice for purposes of section 38-35-109, C.R.S."

§9.3-105—"*Central indexing system cash fund—creation—repeal.* [This Section provides for the allocation and use of filing fees collected from commercial filings, including a one dollar surcharge on all commercial filings to be used to fund costs associated with creation and maintenance of the central indexing system. Subsections (1), (2), (3) and (4) of this Section are repealed, effective December 31, 2000.]"

§9.3-106—"*Duties of filing officer.* (1) The office of the secretary of state or any county clerk and recorder receiving a filing to perfect a security interest or agricultural lien pursuant to article 9 of this title shall transmit a copy of such filing, including all required elements of a financing statement as stated in section 9-402 (1), whether received electronically or by hard copy, to the Central Indexing System in a timely manner.

(1.5) Except as authorized by Section 38-35-202, C.R.S., a filing officer shall not reject a document submitted for filing under this title unless:

(A) the filing party has failed to submit the proper fee; or

(B) the filing officer determines that the document is illegible and cannot be indexed by the debtor's name.

(2) For purposes of this section, 'timely manner' means that (a) Filings received before noon on any business day will be transmitted to the Central Indexing System no

See note at head of Digest as to 1998 legislation covered.

See Topical Index in front part of this volume.

COMMERCIAL CODE . . . *continued*
later than the end of the following business day; (b) Filings received after noon will be transmitted to the Central Indexing System no later than the end of the second business day following the day of receipt.

(3) This section shall take effect July 1, 1996."

§9.3-107—"*Immunity.*" (1) Except in cases of willful misconduct or bad faith, the Department of Revenue and central indexing system board contractors and contractors' employees shall be exempt from personal liability as a result of an error or omission in receiving, entering, storing, or providing information or performing their duties as required by this Title.

(2) Any error or omission described in subsection (1) of this Section shall constitute a tort and not a breach of any express or implied contract."

Colorado adopted Art. 9.5, having no Code counterpart:

§9.5-101—"*Short title.* This article shall be known and may be cited as the 'Central Filing of Effective Financing Statement Act'."

§9.5-102—"*Legislative declaration.* The general assembly finds, determines, and declares its intent to adopt a central filing system for security interests relating to farm products pursuant to section 1324 of the federal 'Food Security Act of 1985', P.L. 99-198. The general assembly further finds, determines and declares that upon the certification and operation of this central filing system, security interest holders shall use such system in lieu of any other notice provided by section 1324 of the federal 'Food Security Act of 1985' for farm products used or produced in the state of Colorado which are included in the central filing system, except as otherwise allowed by this article or required by law."

§9.5-103—"*Definitions.* As used in this article, unless the context otherwise requires:

(1) 'Board' means the state central indexing system board, created in article 15 of title 35, C.R.S. Reference to art. 15 of title 35, C.R.S. is amended to refer to §4-9.3-103.

(2) 'Buyer of farm products' or 'buyer in the ordinary course of business' means a person who, in the ordinary course of business, buys farm products from a person engaged in farming operations who is in the business of selling farm products.

(3) 'Central filing system' means a system for filing effective financing statements or notice of such financing statements on a statewide basis and which has been certified by the secretary of the United States department of agriculture pursuant to section 1324 of the 'Food Security Act of 1985'.

(4) 'Commission merchant' means any person engaged in the business of receiving any farm product for sale, on commission, or for or on behalf of another person.

(5) 'Crop year' means: (a) For a crop grown in soil, the calendar year in which it is harvested or to be harvested; (b) For animals, the calendar year in which they are born, acquired or owned; (c) For poultry or eggs, the calendar year in which they are sold or to be sold.

(6) 'Debtor' means a person who owns a product and subjects it to a security interest, whether or not that person owes a debt to the secured party.

(7) 'Effective financing statement' means a statement that: (a) Is an original or reproduced copy thereof; (b) Is signed, unless the statement is filed by electronic transmission, and filed with the office of the board or its designee by the secured party; (c) Is signed by the debtor unless the statement is filed by electronic transmission; (d) Contains: (I) The name and address of the secured party; (II) The name and address of the debtor, which, in the case of a natural person, shall have the surname appear first, and, in the case of a corporation or other entity not a natural person, shall have the name appear beginning with the first word or character not an article or punctuation mark; (III) The social security number of the debtor or, in the case of a debtor doing business other than as an individual, the federal internal revenue service taxpayer identification number of such debtor; (IV) A description of the farm products by categories included in subsection (8) of this section subject to the security interest created by the debtor including: The amount of such products, unless all of a particular farm product is subject to the particular security interest; identification of each county, utilizing the county code or other numeric method of identification used to identify the county established by the board; where the farm product is produced or stored or to be produced or to be stored, and the crop year, unless every crop year for the duration of the effective financing statement is subject to the particular security interest; (V) Further details of the farm product subject to the security interest if needed to distinguish it from other farm products owned by the same person but not subject to the particular security interest; and (VI) Such other additional information as the board may require to comply with section 1324 of the federal 'Food Security Act of 1985', or to more effectively carry out the purposes of this article; (e) Shall be amended in writing within three months after any material change, similarly signed and filed, to reflect material changes. Such amendment and material change shall be signed by the secured party, and if such amendment is filed electronically it shall be signed electronically, pursuant to section 4-9-413(2). However, if the security interest is terminated as to one or more of the farm products shown on the filed effective financing statement and the effective financing statement is to remain effective as to one or more other farm products, an amendment shall be filed showing such partial termination within thirty days after termination of such security interest, and if the affected secured party fails to file an amendment showing such partial termination within the thirty-day period, he shall be liable to the debtor for one hundred dollars, and, in addition, for any loss caused to the debtor by such failure; (f) Remains effective for a period of five years from the date of filing subject to extensions for additional periods of five years each by filing a continuation statement within six months before the expiration of the current five-year period as provided in section 4-9.5-106; (g) Lapses on either the expiration of the effective period of the statement or the filing of a notice of termination signed by the secured party that the statement has terminated, whichever occurs first, as provided in section 4-9.5-107; (h) May, for any given debtor, cover more than one farm product located in more than one county; (i) May cover more than one debtor or one trade or assumed name of one debtor; (j) Is accompanied by the requisite filing fee, established pursuant to art. 9.3 of this title; (k) Is on a form prescribed by the board; and (l) Substantially complies with the requirements of this subsection (7) even though it contains minor errors that are not seriously misleading."

(8) " 'Farm product' shall mean an agricultural commodity, a species of livestock used or produced in farming operations, or a product of such crop or livestock in its unmanufactured state, that is in the possession of a person engaged in farming operations. 'Farm product' shall include, but is not limited to, apples, artichokes, asparagus, barley, cantaloupe, carrots, cattle and calves, chickens, corn, cotton, cucumbers, dry beans, eggs, fish, flax seed, fur-bearing animals, grapes, hay, hogs, honey, honeydew melon, horses, legumes, milk, muskmelon, oats, onions, pecans, popcorn, potatoes, pumpkins, raspberries, rye, seed crops, sheep and lambs, silage, sorghum grain, soybeans, squash, strawberries, sugar beets, sunflower seeds, sweet corn, tomatoes, trees, triticale, turkeys, vetch, walnuts, watermelon, wheat, and wool. The board may add other farm products in addition to those lists specified in this subsection (8) if such products are covered by the general definition contained in this subsection (8).

(9) 'Food Security Act of 1985' means P.L. 99-198, as amended: Section 1324 thereof has been codified at section 1631 of Title 7 of the United States Code.

(10) 'Person' means any individual or any partnership, corporation, trust, or any other business entity.

(11) 'Receipt' and other forms of the word 'receive' means the earlier of actual receipt or the tenth day after deposit in the United States mails, first-class mail, postage prepaid.

(12) 'Registrant' or 'registered buyer' means any buyer of farm products, commission merchant or selling agent, who has registered with the board pursuant to section 4-9.5-104(4).

(13) 'Secured party' means a person in whose favor there is a security interest.

(14) 'Security interest' means an interest in farm products that secures payment or performance of an obligation.

(15) 'Selling agent' means any person, other than a commission merchant, who is engaged in the business of negotiating the sale and purchase of any farm product on behalf of a person engaged in farming operations."

§9.5-104—"*Central filing system.* (1) The board shall be responsible for the design, implementation, and operation of a central filing system for effective financing statements. The system shall provide a means for filing effective financing statements or notices of such effective financing statements. The system shall include requirements: (a) That an effective financing statement be filed in the office of the board or its designee; (b) That the board or its designee record the date and hour of the filing of effective financing statements; and (c) That the board or its designee shall assign a file number to each effective financing statement.

(2) The board or its designee shall compile all such statements or notices into a master list: (a) Organized according to farm product; (b) Arranged within each such farm product: (I) In alphabetical order according to the last name of the individual debtors or, in the case of debtors doing business other than as individuals, the first word in the name of such debtors; (II) In numerical order according to the social security number of the individual debtors or, in the case of debtors doing business other than as individuals, the federal internal revenue service taxpayer identification number of such debtors; (III) Geographically by county; and (IV) By crop year; (c) Containing the information referred to in section 4-9.5-103(7)(d).

(3) (a) The board or its designee shall cause the information on the master list to be published in lists: (I) By farm product arranged alphabetically by debtor; and (II) By farm product arranged numerically by the debtor's social security number for individual debtors or, in the case of debtors doing business other than as individuals, the federal internal revenue service taxpayer identification number of such debtors. (b) If a registered buyer or other interested person so requests, the list or lists for such buyer or person may be limited to any county or group of counties where the farm product is used or produced or to any crop year or years or a combination of such identifiers.

(4) All buyers of farm products, commission merchants, selling agents, and other persons may register with the board or its designee to receive lists described in subsection (3) of this section. Any buyer of farm products, commission merchant, selling agent, or other person conducting business from multiple locations may be considered as one entity, at its option. Such registration shall be on an annual basis; except that the first registration shall be for calendar years 1988 and 1989. The board or its designee shall provide the form for registration which shall include the name and address of the registrant and the list or lists described in subsection (3) of this section which such registrant desires to receive. A registration shall not be completed until the form provided is properly completed and received by the board or its designee accompanied by the proper fee for the desired list or lists.

(5) (a) The lists as identified pursuant to subsection (3) of this section shall be distributed by board or its designee on a quarterly basis reflecting all then effective filings, calling attention to new filings, changes and terminations since the last list, and shall be in writing or printed, microfiche and computer-readable forms. The board or its designees may also distribute lists on an annual basis with three quarterly cumulative supplements reflecting all new filings, changes, and terminations since the last list, if it is cost-effective, requested by registered buyers, and permitted by applicable federal law. The board shall also provide for the distribution by the board or its designee of the lists in direct computer access form and establish reasonable charges therefor pursuant to article 9.3 of this title. The board may also develop other forms in which to distribute lists and establish charges therefor pursuant to article 9.3 of this title. The distribution shall be made by first-class mail, postage prepaid. A registrant is deemed to be registered only as to those products, counties, and crop years for which he requests a list. If the name of the seller of a farm product is not on a list requested and received by a registrant, the registrant shall have no liability under this article. Except as to those farm products for which the registrant has received direct notification of the existence of security interests pursuant to Section 1329(e)(1) and (g)(2)(A) of the federal 'Food Security Act of 1985'. The registrant may rely on the representation of the seller as to his identity, so long as the reliance is in good faith. (b) The board shall establish the dates upon which the quarterly distributions will be made, the dates after which a filing of an effective financing statement will not be reflected on the next quarterly distribution of lists, and the dates by which a registrant must complete a registration to receive the next quarterly list."

(6) "The board or its designee shall remove lapsed and terminated effective financing statements or notices of such financing statements from the master list prior to preparation of the lists required to be distributed by subsection (5) of this section.

See note at head of Digest as to 1998 legislation covered.

See Topical Index in front part of this volume.

COMMERCIAL CODE . . . *continued*

(7) The board shall apply no later than January 1, 1989, to the secretary of the United States department of agriculture for certification of the central filing system."

§9.5-105—"*Confirmations.* (1) Oral and written inquiries regarding information provided by the filing of effective financing statements may be made at the office of the board's designee between the hours of 8:30 A.M. and 5 P.M. on business days.

(2) Deleted.

(3) Deleted.

(4) Deleted.

(5) A buyer of farm products, whether or not registered, may rely conclusively on an oral or written confirmation received pursuant to this section, regardless of any errors or omissions committed by the board or its designee in the preparation or issuance of the confirmation. If the board or its designee confirms orally or in writing to such buyer that the name of the seller is not on the list for a specified product, such buyer shall have no liability under this article and the buyer may rely on the representation of the seller as to his identity, so long as the reliance is in good faith."

§9.5-106—"*Continuation statements.* (1) A continuation statement may be filed within six months prior to the expiration of the five-year period of an effective financing statement. Any such continuation statement shall identify the current effective financing statement by file number. Upon timely filing of the continuation statement, the effectiveness of the statement shall be continued for five years after the last date to which the filing was effective, whereupon it shall lapse unless another continuation statement is filed prior to such lapse. If an effective financing statement exists at the time insolvency proceedings are commenced by or against the debtor, the effective financing statement shall remain effective until termination of the insolvency proceedings and thereafter for a period of sixty days or until the expiration of the five-year period, whichever occurs later. Succeeding continuation statements may be filed in the same manner to continue the effectiveness of the original statement."

"(2) An effective financing statement filed before July 1, 1996, that has not lapsed by December 31, 1997, shall lose its perfection and priority rights unless a new continuation statement is filed on or after July 1, 1996, but on or before December 31, 1997. Any such continuation statement shall identify the original statement by filing office, file number, and date of filing. The filing of such continuation statement shall preserve the priority of the original filing and shall be effective for the later of five years after the expiration of the original filing or the expiration of any continuation statement filed before July 1, 1996.

(3) The effectiveness of an effective financing statement filed before July 1, 1996, that lapses after July 1, 1996, but before December 31, 1997, may be continued by filing a continuation statement in accordance with this section. If such continuation statement is filed before July 1, 1996, such effective financing statement or continuation statement shall be continued by the timely filing of a further continuation statement, pursuant to subsection (2) of this section."

§9.5-107—"*Notice of termination.* (1) Whenever there is no outstanding secured obligation and no commitment to make advances, incur obligations or otherwise give value, the secured party shall, within thirty days file with the board or its designee a notice of termination of the effective financing statement and provide notice to the debtor of such filing, unless the debtor otherwise requests. If the affected secured party fails to file a termination statement within the thirty-day period, he shall be liable to the debtor for one hundred dollars, and, in addition, for any loss caused to the debtor by such failure.

(2) (a) The notice of termination of an effective financing statement shall: (I) Be signed by the secured party, and if such notice is filed electronically it shall be signed electronically, pursuant to section 4-9-413(2); (II) Identify the effective financing statement to be terminated by file number; and (III) state that the effective financing statement is to be removed from the master list.

(b) Termination shall be effective as of the date and hour of filing the notice with the board or its designee."

§9.5-108—"*Filings generally.* (1) The board or its designee or, pursuant to section 4-9.5-104(1)(a), the county clerk and recorder or the secretary of state shall accept for filing all filings pursuant to this Title during regular business hours. The board or its designee or, pursuant to section 4-9.5-104(1)(a), the county clerk and recorder or the secretary of state shall record the date and hour of the filing of such statements. In the event of an electronic filing made other than during the regular business hours of the filing office, the date of filing shall be the day on which such office next commences business, and the hour of filing shall be the commencement of business on such day. All filings made pursuant to this Title that are filed as paper documents and not electronically shall be filed in duplicate, and one copy of the statement shall be returned to the filing party stamped to show the time of receipt thereof."

(2) A document filed pursuant to this article shall not constitute notice for purposes of Section 38-35-109, C.R.S."

(3) Any termination, amendment, assignment, or release of collateral filing made pursuant to this article shall include the signature of the secured party, and if such filing is made electronically it shall be signed electronically, pursuant to section 4-9-413(2).

§9.5-109—"'*Food Security Act of 1985'.* Whether a buyer of farm products takes subject to a security interest shall be determined by section 1324 of the federal 'Food Security Act of 1985' and applicable provisions of Colorado law."

§9.5-110—"*Fees—rules and regulations.* (1) Deleted.

"(2) The board is hereby authorized to adopt such rules and regulations as are necessary to carry out the provisions of this article, and to conform the central filing system to the requirements of the federal 'Food Security Act of 1985'.

(3) The board may contract with one or more public or private parties to perform some or all of its duties under this article, except that the board may not delegate the power to make rules or regulations, conduct public hearings, prescribe forms, and establish services and fees therefor."

§9.5-111—"*Penalties.* Any debtor or third party who provides any false or misleading information concerning the name of the owner of any farm products or the existence of any security interest affecting farm products with the intent to deprive the secured party of any of his or her security under the security interest or to defraud or mislead the buyer of any farm product as to the existence of the security interest or fails to pay to the secured party any moneys realized out of the sale of collateral in violation of any security agreement and with the intent to deprive the secured party of such party's rights thereto, or makes a filing that does not include the authorized signature of the secured party as required by section 4-9.5-108(3), shall be deemed to have violated section 18-5-206, C.R.S., and shall be subject to the penalties described in said section. Any penalty so collected shall be deposited into the central filing system fund for administering the central filing system pursuant to this article."

§9.5-112—"*Severability of provisions.* If any provision of this article disqualifies the central filing system for certification by the United States department of agriculture pursuant to the federal 'Food Security Act of 1985', the particular provision shall be null and void and shall not affect any other part of this act. If any provision of this article becomes null and void by operation of this section, the central filing system shall not become certified or effective until after the board conducts a public hearing with notice to all affected parties regarding any such hearing."

§10-101(1)—Specific calendar date set as effective date: July 1, 1966.

§10-101(2)—Colorado placed what appears in official text as §10-102(2) in §10-101 as subsection (2).

§10-102—Deleted.

§10-103—Amended to read: "Except as provided in section 4-10-104, all statutes, acts, and parts of acts inconsistent with the provisions of this title are hereby repealed as of July 1, 1966."

§10-104(2)—Blank completed with "or modify part 6 of article 1 of title 15, C.R.S., being" and "cited as" deleted.

Effective Date and Transition Provisions.—

Art. 11 of 1972 Official Amendment (§§11-101 through 11-108) was adopted and renumbered 4-10-201 through 4-10-208.

§11-101 [4-10-201]—Amended to read: "The 1978 amendments as defined in section 4-10-202(2) shall become effective at 12:01 a.m. on January 1, 1978."

§11-102 [4-10-202]—Amended to read: "As used in this part 2, unless the context otherwise requires: (1) '1966 code' means this title as originally enacted and as amended prior to January 1, 1978. (2) '1978 amendments' means the amendments to this title enacted by House Bill No. 1400, chapter 62 of the Session Laws of Colorado 1977. (3) '1978 code' means this title on and after January 1, 1978."

§11-103 [4-10-203]—Amended to read: "Transactions validly entered into after June 30, 1966, and before January 1, 1978, and which were subject to the provisions of the 1966 code and which would be subject to the provisions of the 1978 amendments if they had been entered into after January 1, 1978, and the rights, duties, and interest flowing from such transactions remain valid after the latter date and may be terminated, completed, consummated, or enforced as required or permitted by the 1978 code. Security interest arising out of such transactions which are perfected when the 1978 amendments become effective shall remain perfected until they lapse as provided in the 1978 code and may be continued as permitted by the 1978 code, except as stated in section 4-10-205."

§§11-103 through 11-108 [4-10-203 through 4-10-208]—New U.C.C. referred to as "1978 amendments" or "1978 code"; old U.C.C. referred to as "the 1966 code"; effective date of old U.C.C. given as June 30, 1966; effective date of new U.C.C. given as Jan. 1, 1978.

§11-206[4-10-206]—Effective July 1, 1996, deleted requirement that financing statement must be signed by either debtor or secured party.

Forms.—See end of Colorado Digest. All financing statements required to be filed with secretary of state must be typewritten and must include debtor's tax identification number. All filings must be in duplicate (one original plus one copy). Secretary of State prefers filings on Colo. $8^{1}/_{2}$ x 11 inch form, but will accept other forms if they include all required Colorado information, i.e., county code, collateral codes, EFS information, etc.

Filing Fees.—

Colorado adopted Art. 11, with no official text counterpart, dealing with fees. *Note,* pursuant to §4-9.3-105 there is a $1 surcharge on any and all filings and recordings made with division of commercial recordings, in addition to amount shown below.

§11-102—"Fees for filing, indexing, and furnishing data pursuant to sections 4-9-403 to 4-9-408. (1) The filing officer shall charge a uniform fee in accordance with the following schedule:

(a) For filing, indexing, and furnishing filing data for an original financing statement, pursuant to section 4-9-403: $15.

(a.5)(I) For filing a continuation statement between July 1, 1996, and December 31, 1997: $5.

(II) For filing, indexing, and furnishing filing data for a continuation statement, except between July 1, 1996, and December 31, 1997: $15.

(b) For filing and indexing a separate statement of assignment pursuant to section 4-9-404 (1): $15.

(c) For filing and indexing a termination statement pursuant to section 4-9-404 (2): $15.

(d) For filing, indexing, and furnishing filing data for a financing statement indicating an assignment of a security interest in the collateral described in the statement, pursuant to section 4-9-405 (1): $15.

(e) For filing, indexing, and furnishing filing data for a separate written statement of assignment, pursuant to section 4-9-405 (2): $15.

(f) For filing and noting a statement releasing all or a part of any collateral described in a filed financing statement, pursuant to section 4-9-406: $15.

(g) (I) For issuance of a certificate, pursuant to section 4-9-407 (2): Five dollars for the first year searched, plus two dollars for each additional year searched.

(II) For furnishing a copy of any filed financing statement or other statement, pursuant to section 4-9-407 (2): One dollar twenty-five cents per page, plus one dollar for certifying such copy and affixing the seal thereto.

(2) Deleted.

(3) When a document is not submitted on a standard form established by the central indexing system board for such purpose, the filing officer shall charge a five-dollar fee in addition to any other fee imposed pursuant to this section for filing, indexing, and

COMMERCIAL CODE . . . *continued*
furnishing data pursuant to subsections (1)(a), (1)(a.5)(II), (1)(b), (1)(c), (1)(d), (1)(e), and (1)(f) of this section."

§35-15-105—"*Fees for filing documents relating to effective financing statements pursuant to article 9.5 of title 4.* (1) The board shall establish fees and charges in amounts necessary to defray the anticipated costs of the central filing system. The board shall design, implement, and operate the central filing system in such a manner as to keep costs to a minimum while providing the state-of-the-art, cost effective services contemplated in article 9.5 of title 4, C.R.S. The fees and charges may be adjusted by the board from time to time as necessary or appropriate, but shall not exceed the maximums for the specific services described in subsection (2) of this section. The board is encouraged to develop additional methods of providing the services contemplated in article 9.5 of title 4, C.R.S., with the same or better manner and at lower costs.

(2) The board shall establish pursuant to subsection (1) of this section fees and charges for the following services not to exceed the amounts indicated:

(a) For filing an effective financing statement pursuant to article 9.5 of title 4, C.R.S., $15;

(b) For filing a continuation statement, partial release, assignment of or amendment to an effective financing statement pursuant to article 9.5 of title 4, C.R.S., $15;

(c) For filing a termination statement for an effective financing statement pursuant to article 9.5 of title 4, C.R.S., $15;

(d) For registering as a buyer of farm products, commission merchant, or selling agent pursuant to article 9.5 of title 4, C.R.S., no charge;

(e) For distributing the master list or portions thereof to buyers of farm products, commission merchants, and selling agents, or for providing such master list or portions thereof to other interested parties pursuant to article 9.5 of title 4, C.R.S., in photocopy, microfiche, or computer-readable form, such reasonable charges as may be developed by the board to cover the actual cost of providing the lists in the form requested;

(f) For issuing an oral and follow-up written confirmation of the existence of an effective financing statement pursuant to article 9.5 of title 4, C.R.S., $15 per debtor;

(g) For permitting a physical inspection of all filings of effective financing statements pursuant to article 9.5 of title 4, C.R.S., no charge; and

(h) For issuing a written confirmation in response to a written request of the existence of any effective financing statement on file pursuant to article 9.5 of title 4, C.R.S. $15 per debtor."

See also topics: Banks and Banking, Bills and Notes, Brokers, Carriers, Contracts, Factors, Frauds, Statute of, Sales, Securities, Warehousemen; categories Business Organizations, topic Corporations; Civil Actions and Procedure, topic Limitation of Actions; Debtor and Creditor, topics Assignments, Fraudulent Sales and Conveyances, Liens, Pledges; Documents and Records, topics Records, Seals; Mortgages, topic Chattel Mortgages.

CONSIGNMENTS:

See topic Sales.

CONSUMER CREDIT:

Uniform Consumer Credit Code (1969 Act) adopted, effective Oct. 1, 1971. Code is given Colorado Revised Statutes (C.R.S.) title number 5, and section numbers contain said title (and article) citation followed by numerical part of Uniform Consumer Credit Code citation, e.g., 5-1-101.

Official text of Code as promulgated by sponsoring organizations (1969 version) is in effect except for variations set out below.

Material Variations from Official Text.—

§1-106—Deleted.

§1-108—Deletes "consumer related sales and loans" from restrictions on maximum charges.

§1-109—Section adopted having no Code counterpart reading: "Discrimination prohibited.—No consumer credit sale, consumer lease, or consumer loan regulated by this title shall be denied any person, nor shall terms and conditions be made more stringent, on the basis of discrimination, solely because of race, creed, religion, color, sex, marital status, national origin, or ancestry. This section shall not apply to any consumer credit sale, consumer lease, or consumer loan made or denied by a seller, lessor, or lender whose total original unpaid balances arising from consumer credit sales, consumer leases, and consumer loans for the previous calendar year are less than one million dollars."

§1-201(4)—Deleted "or extortionate extensions of credit" and substituted, "or modification thereof."

§1-201(11)—Subsection adopted having no Code counterpart reading: "For the purpose of subsections (1), (2), and (3) of this section, 'receive' means obtained as a result of physical delivery, transmission, or communication to one who has actual or apparent authority to act for the seller, lessor, or lender in this state whether or not approval, acceptance, or ratification by any other agent or representative of such seller, lessor, or lender in some other state is necessary to give legal consequence to the sale, lease, or loan transaction."

§1-201(12)—Subsection adopted having no Code counterpart reading: "Territorial application. (12) With respect to a consumer credit sale or consumer loan to which this code does not otherwise apply by reason of subsections (1) to (11) of this section, if, pursuant to a systematic solicitation in this state, a person who is a resident of this state sends a signed writing evidencing the obligation or offer of the person to a creditor in another state and receives the goods or services purchased or the cash proceeds of the loan in this state: (a) The seller may not contract for or receive charges exceeding those permitted by this code; (b) The lender, whether licensed or not, may not contract for or receive charges exceeding those permitted by this code for supervised lenders; and (c) The provisions on powers and functions of the administrator (part 1 of article 6 of this code) shall apply as though the consumer credit sale or consumer loan were made in this state."

§1-201(13)—Subsection (13) adopted having no Code counterpart which reads as follows: "Territorial application. (13) Notwithstanding any other provision of this section, this code applies to any insurance premium loan made to a resident of this state."

§1-202(2)—Amended to read: "Except as otherwise provided in the article on insurance (article 4 of this code), the sale of insurance if there is no legal obligation to pay instalments of the premium and the insurance may terminate or be cancelled after nonpayment of an instalment of the premium;".

§1-202(5)—Is repealed.

§1-202(6)—Subsection adopted having no Code counterpart reading: "The disclosure of rates and charges in connection with transactions in securities and commodities accounts by a broker-dealer registered with the securities and exchange commission."

§1-202(7)—Subsection adopted having no Code counterpart reading: "Loans made, originated, disbursed, serviced or guaranteed by an agency, instrumentality, or political subdivision of the state pursuant to article 3.1 of title 23, C.R.S. 1973."

§1-202(8)—Subsection adopted having no Code counterpart reading: "A commercial credit plan as defined in section 5-12-107 and extensions of credit made pursuant thereto, unless the agreement evidencing the plan expressly states that it is subject to the provisions of this Code applying to (a) consumer credit sales or loans (section 5-2-601 and section 5-3-601); or (b) sales other than consumer credit sales (section 5-2-605).

§1-203(1)—Blanks filled in as follows: "The court of record of any judicial district in this state"; "the Colorado rules of civil procedure or by"; and "in the court of record."

§1-301(6)—Added at end of subsection: "A printed heading in capitals (as: WARRANTY) is conspicuous, and language in the body of the form is conspicuous if it is in larger or other contrasting type or color. In a telegram, any stated term is conspicuous."

§1-301(6.5)—New subsection adopted reading: "Consumer credit transaction means a consumer credit sale or consumer loan, or a refinancing or consolidation thereof, or a consumer lease."

§1-301(6.7)—Subsection adopted having no Code counterpart reading: "Consumer Insurance Premium Loan means a consumer loan which is also an insurance premium loan."

§1-301(7.5)—New subsection adopted reading: " 'Dwelling' means a residential structure or mobile home which contains one to four-family housing units, or individual units with condominiums or cooperatives."

§1-301(8)—Added "fees" after word "salary."

§1-301(8.3)—New subsection adopted reading: "Insurance premium loan means a loan that: (a) Is made for the sole purpose of financing the payment by or on behalf of an insured of the premium on one or more policies or contracts issued by or on behalf of an insurer; (b) Is secured by an assignment by the insured to the lender of the unearned premium on the policy or contract; and (c) Contains an authorization to cancel the policy or contract so financed."

§1-301(8.5)—New subsection adopted reading: " 'Investment purpose' means that primary purpose of the credit sale or loan is for future financial gain rather than for a present personal, family, or household use."

§1-301(9.5)—New subsection adopted reading: " 'Material disclosures' means disclosures, as required by this code of annual percentage rate; method of determining credit service charge or loan finance charge, as applicable, and balance upon which credit service charge or loan finance charge, as applicable, will be imposed; amount of credit service charge or loan finance charge, as applicable; amount to be financed; total of payments; number and amount of payments; and due dates or periods of payments scheduled to repay indebtedness."

§1-301(9.7)—New subsection adopted reading: " 'Mobile home' means dwelling which is built on chassis designed for long-term residential occupancy, which is capable of being installed in permanent or semipermanent location, with or without permanent foundation and with major appliances and plumbing, gas, and electrical systems installed but needing appropriate connections to make them operable, and which may be occasionally drawn over public highways, by special permit, as unit or in sections to its permanent or semipermanent location."

§1-301(12)—Amended to read: "Payable in instalments" means that payment is required or permitted by agreement to be made in more than four periodic payments, excluding a down payment. If any periodic payment other than the down payment under an agreement requiring or permitting two or more periodic payments is more than twice the amount of any other periodic payment, excluding the down payment, the consumer credit transaction is 'payable in instalments.' "

§1-301(16)—Deleted "a person related to that person, or others licensed or franchised to do business under his business or trade name or designation" and inserted in its place: "or from that person and any other person."

§1-301(18)—Definition adopted having no Code counterpart reading: "A business day is any calendar day except Sunday, New Year's day, the third Monday in January observed as the birthday of Dr. Martin Luther King, Jr., Washington-Lincoln day, Memorial day, Independence day, Labor day, Columbus day, Veteran's day, Thanksgiving and Christmas."

§1-303—Adds references to definitions of "Business day," "Consumer credit transaction," "Consumer insurance premium loan," "Dwelling," "Insurance premium loan," "Investment purpose," "Material disclosures," "Mobile home," "Receive," and "Residence," and omits references to definitions of "Consumer related loan," "Consumer related sale," "Contested case," "License," "Licensing," "Party," "Regulated lender," "Regulated loan," and "Rule."

§2-102—Amended to read: "This article applies to consumer credit sales, including home solicitation sales, and consumer leases; in addition, part 6 of this article applies to sales other than consumer credit sales and the provisions concerning credit card surcharges (section 5-2-109(3)) apply to all sales and leases."

§2-103—Omits reference to definition of "consumer related sale."

§2-104(1)—Added reference to "mobile home" following "services" in introductory phrase.

§2-104(1)(a)—Inserts "or arranged" following "granted."

§2-104(1)(c)—Inserted "mobile home" after "services", added "or" before "household", and deleted "or agricultural" before "purpose."

See note at head of Digest as to 1998 legislation covered.

See Topical Index in front part of this volume.

CO – 14

CONSUMER CREDIT . . . *continued*

§2-104(1)(e)—Added new clause at end of subsection reading: "or, if the debt is secured by a mobile home which is used as the primary residence of the debtor, the amount financed does not exceed fifty-two thousand, five hundred dollars."

§2-104(2)(b)—Added language: "Except as required by the 'Federal Consumer Credit Protection Act' " and deleted "except as provided" at beginning of subsection; added "a mobile home or a sale of" prior to "an interest in land."; changed percent from ten to twelve percent; deleted period at end of subsection, added comma and following language: "or, notwithstanding the rate of the credit service charge with respect to the sale of an interest in land, the sale is secured by a first mortgage or deed of trust lien against a dwelling to finance the acquisition of that dwelling. For the purposes of this paragraph (b), 'dwelling' means any improved real property or portion thereof that is used or intended to be used as a residence and contains not more than four dwelling units, and 'first mortgage or deed of trust' means a mortgage or deed of trust having priority as a lien over the lien of any other mortgage or deed of trust on the same dwelling and subject to the lien of taxes levied on that dwelling."

§2-104(2)(c)—Added subsection without Code counterpart reading: "A sale for a business, investment or commercial purpose, or".

§2-104(2)(d)—Added subsection without Code counterpart reading: "A sale primarily for an agricultural purpose."

§2-104(3)—Omitted.

§2-105(7)—Added "only" after "precomputed" and added additional clause reading: "or if any portion of the credit service charge is prepaid and the amount of that portion of the credit service charge either computed in advance or prepaid constitutes more than one-half of the total credit service charge applicable to the sale, refinancing, or consolidation."

§2-106(1)—Amended to read "(1) 'Consumer lease' means a lease of goods and includes any insurance incidental to the lease and any other services merely incidental to upkeep or repair of the goods."

§2-106(1)(a)—Added "or" before "household" and deleted "or agricultural."

§2-106(3)—Omitted.

§2-109—Amended to read: "(1) 'Credit service charge' means the sum of all charges payable directly or indirectly by the buyer and imposed directly or indirectly by the seller as an incident to or as a condition of the extension of credit, whether paid or payable by the buyer, the seller, or any other person on behalf of the buyer, to the creditor or a third party, including any of the following types of charges which are applicable: Time price differential; service, carrying, or other charge, however denominated; premium or other charge for any guarantee or insurance protecting the seller against the buyer's default or other credit loss; and charges incurred for investigating the collateral or credit worthiness of the buyer or for commissions or brokerage for obtaining the credit. The term does not include charges as a result of default, additional charges (5-2-202), delinquency charges (5-2-203), or deferral charges (5-2-204). (2) A discount offered by a seller for the purpose of inducing payment by cash, check, or other means not involving the use of a seller or lender credit card shall not constitute a credit service charge if such discount is offered to all prospective buyers and its availability is disclosed to all prospective buyers clearly and conspicuously in accordance with regulations of the administrator. (3) No seller or lessor in any sales or lease transaction or any company issuing credit or charge cards may impose a surcharge on a holder who elects to use a credit or charge card in lieu of payment by cash, check, or similar means. A surcharge is any additional charge imposed at the time of the sales or lease transaction by the merchant, seller, or lessor that increases the charge to the buyer or lessee for the privilege of using a credit or charge card. For purposes of this section, charge card includes those cards pursuant to which unpaid balances are payable on demand."

§2-110—First sentence restructured as follows after "may include": "the cash price of accessories, or related services such as delivery, installation, servicing, repairs, alterations, and improvements; and, if individually itemized, may also include (1) applicable sales, use, and excise and documentary stamp taxes, and (2) amounts actually paid or to be paid by the seller for registration, certificate of title or license fees."

§2-201(2)(a)—Changed percentages as follows: (i) 25%, (ii) 20%; changed amounts as follows: (i) $630.00; (ii) $630.00 and $2,100.00; (iii) $2,100.00.

§2-201(2)(b)—Changed 18% to 21%.

§2-201(6)—Added "but is less than five hundred dollars, or fifteen dollars when the amount financed is five hundred dollars or more."

§2-201(7)—Omitted.

§2-202(1)(d)—Added: "Annual charges, payable in advance, for the privilege of using a seller credit card or similar arrangement;" and

§2-202(1)(e)—Added: "The following changes if agreed to by the parties:

(i) A charge, not to exceed the greater of two dollars or two and one-half percent of the amount advanced, for each cash advance transaction made pursuant to a seller credit card; and

(ii) A fee, not to exceed twenty dollars, assessed upon return or dishonor of a check or other instrument tendered as payment."

§2-202(1.5)—Added: "No credit service charge may be assessed on any charge listed in paragraph (e) of subsection (1) of this section."

§2-202(3)—Amended to read: "With respect to a debt secured by an interest in land, reasonable closing costs are additional charges."

§2-203(1)(a)—Amount changed to ten dollars.

§2-203(2)—Language "until ten days after the deferred due date" added at end of second sentence.

§2-203(4)—Subsection adopted having no Code counterpart reading "The parties to a revolving charge account may contract to impose a delinquency charge on any minimum payment due in connection with a billing cycle that remains unpaid ten days after such minimum payment's scheduled due date. No delinquency charge may be collected on any minimum payment due which is paid in full within ten days after the scheduled due date, even though an earlier minimum payment was not paid in full. Payments shall be applied first to the current portion of the minimum payment due and then to any delinquent portion of the minimum payment due. No delinquency charge shall exceed fifteen dollars, and no more than one delinquency charge shall be collected on any minimum payment due regardless of the period of time during which the payment remains in default. A delinquency charge may be collected anytime after it accrues if no other delinquency charge has been collected on the same unpaid amount. A seller shall not assess a delinquency charge unless the delinquency charge is assessed within ninety days after the scheduled due date of the delinquent minimum payment. A seller who has imposed a delinquency charge pursuant to this subsection (4) shall notify the buyer in writing either before, on, or with the next periodic statement after the delinquency charge has been assessed of the amount of the delinquency charge. No credit service charge shall be assessed on the delinquency charge."

§2-204(5)—Subsection adopted having no Code counterpart reading: "A deferral charge made according to this section is earned pro rata during the period in which no instalment is scheduled to be paid by reason of the deferral and is fully earned on the last day of that period."

§2-207(2)—Amended to read: "A charge may be made in each billing cycle which is a percentage of an amount no greater than the average daily balance of the account in the billing cycle for which the charge is made, which is the sum of the amount unpaid each day during that cycle, divided by the number of days in that cycle; the amount unpaid on a day is determined by adding to any balance unpaid as of the beginning of that day all purchases and other debits and deducting all payments and other credits made or received as of that day."

§2-207(3)—First sentence amended to read: "If the billing cycle is monthly, the charge may not exceed one and three-quarters percent of the amount pursuant to subsection (2) of this section."

§2-207(4)—Amended to read: "Notwithstanding subsection (3) of this section, if there is an unpaid balance on the date as of which the credit service charge is applied, the seller may contract for and receive a minimum credit service charge not exceeding fifty cents."

§2-207(5)—Code text deleted and subsection adopted having no Code counterpart reading: "The parties may contract to use any method of determining the amount to which the rate of credit service charge is applied if the amount so determined does not exceed the amount permitted in subsection (2) of this section."

§2-208(1)—Language added at end of first sentence: "if the expenditure is reasonable to protect the risk of loss or damage to the property and if the seller has mailed to the buyer, at his last known address, written notice of his nonperformance, has given the buyer reasonable opportunity after such notice to so perform, and, in the absence of performance, the seller has made all expenditures on behalf of the buyer in good faith and in a commercially reasonable manner."

§2-209—Added after "in full": "or in part if payment is no less than five dollars."

§2-210(1)—In first sentence, word "otherwise" added after "except as", and words "subsection deleted and replaced by "by this section".

§2-210(3)—Repealed, reenacted and amended to read: "(a) Except as otherwise provided in this section, the unearned portion of the credit service charge is a fraction of the credit service charge of which the numerator is the sum of the periodic balances scheduled to follow the computational period in which prepayment occurs; and the denominator is the sum of all periodic balances under either the sale agreement or, if the balance owing resulted from a refinancing (5-2-205) or a consolidation (5-2-206), under the refinancing agreement or consolidation agreement. (b) With respect to a precomputed transaction entered into on or after Oct. 28, 1975, and payable according to its original terms in more than 61 instalments, or on any precomputed transaction entered into on or after January 1, 1982, the unearned portion of the credit service charge is, at the option of the creditor, either: (I) That portion which is applicable to all fully unexpired computational periods as originally scheduled, or if deferred, as deferred, which follow the date of prepayment. For this purpose the applicable charge is the total of that which would have been made for each such period, had the consumer credit sale not been precomputed, by applying to unpaid balances of principal, according to the actuarial method, the annual percentage rate of charge previously stated to the debtor pursuant to the provisions on disclosure (part 3 of this article) based upon the assumption that all payments were made as originally scheduled, or if deferred, as deferred. The creditor, at his option, may round the annual percentage rate to the nearest one-half of one percent if such procedure is not consistently used to obtain a greater yield than would otherwise be permitted; or (II) the total credit service charge minus the earned credit service charge. The earned credit service charge shall be determined by applying the annual percentage rate previously stated to the debtor pursuant to the provisions on disclosure (part 3 of this article) according to the actuarial method to the actual unpaid balances for the actual time the balances were unpaid up to the date of prepayment. If a delinquency or deferral charge was collected, it shall be treated as a payment. (c) In the case of a sale of an interest in land or a consumer credit sale secured by an interest in land, reasonable sums actually paid or payable to persons not related to the seller for customary closing costs included in the credit service charge shall be deducted from the credit service charge before the calculation prescribed by this subsection (3) is made."

§2-210(6)—Amended to read: "Except as otherwise provided in subsection (3)(b) of this section, if a deferral (5-2-204) has been agreed to, the unearned portion of the credit service charge is the portion thereof attributable according to the sum of the balances method to the period from the first day of the computational period following that in which prepayment occurs, except that the numerator of the fraction is the sum of the periodic balances, after rescheduling to give effect to any deferral, scheduled to follow the computational period in which prepayment occurs. A separate rebate of the deferral charge is not required unless the unpaid balance of the transaction is paid in full during the deferral period, in which event the creditor shall also rebate the unearned portion of the deferral charge."

§2-210(7)—Language added to beginning of sentence: "Except as otherwise provided in subsection (3)(b) of this section,".

§2-301(4)—Deleted "this Part" and substituted " 'the Federal Consumer Credit Protection Act.' "

§2-302(2)(c)—Subsection adopted having no Code counterpart reading: "No evidence of indebtedness shall be signed when it contains blank spaces to be filled in after execution, except that this provision shall not apply to serial numbers or other identifying marks which are not available for description at the time of execution of such evidence of indebtedness."

See note at head of Digest as to 1998 legislation covered.

See Topical Index in front part of this volume.

CO – 15

CONSUMER CREDIT . . . *continued*

§2-302.5—Added: "Disclosure requirements in connection with solicitation or application. (1) Notwithstanding any provision of this Article to the contrary, a seller shall disclose in a clear and conspicuous manner the following information in any application to open a revolving charge account for any person and in any solicitation to open such an account without requiring an application:

(a) Each annual percentage rate applicable to extensions of credit under the account;

(b) Where an extension of credit under the account is subject to a variable rate, the fact that the rate is variable the annual percentage rate in effect at the time of delivery to the prospective buyer, and how the rate is determined;

(c) Where more than one rate applies, the range of balance to which each rate applies; and

(d) Any annual charge imposed for the issuance or availability of such account, including any account maintenance fee or other charge imposed based on activity or inactivity during the billing cycle."

§2-302(3)(b)—Deleted "this part" and substituted: "said sections."

§2-304(5)(c)—After "in paragraph (a) or (b)" added: "of this subsection (5)."

§2-306(2)(b)—Deleted "not included in the cash price" and substituted "if not individually itemized in the cash price."

§2-306(2)(e)—Same substitution as in §2-306(2)(b) above.

§2-306(2)(f)—Same substitution as in §2-306(2)(b) above.

§2-306(2) (o)—Subsection adopted having no Code counterpart reading: "If the property includes a motor vehicle and the contract does not provide for automobile liability insurance, the following clause shall be in the contract in capital letters and boldface type: 'THIS CONTRACT DOES NOT PROVIDE FOR AUTOMOBILE LIABILITY INSURANCE, AND SAID BUYER ALSO STATES THAT HE HAS, HE HAS NOT (STRIKE WORDS NOT APPLICABLE) IN EFFECT AN AUTOMOBILE LIABILITY POLICY AS DEFINED IN SECTION 42-7-103(2), COLORADO REVISED STATUTES 1973, ON THE MOTOR VEHICLE SOLD BY THIS CONTRACT.' "

§2-307(1)—Amended to read: "The unpaid balance, including accrued charges, before refinancing;".

§2-312—Repealed.

§2-402—Deleted after "multiple agreements" the following: "with intent to obtain"; and substituted "with respect to a single consumer credit sale for the purpose of obtaining." Inserted new sentence having no Code counterpart between first sentence and second sentence: "Dividing a single consumer credit sale between a husband and wife shall be presumed to be a violation of this section."

§2-403—Amended to read: "Assignee subject to claims and defenses. (1) With respect to a consumer credit sale or consumer lease, except one primarily for an agricultural purpose, an assignee of the rights of the seller or lessor is subject to all claims and defenses of the buyer against the seller or lessor arising from the sale or lease of goods or services, notwithstanding that the assignee is a holder in due course of a negotiable instrument issued in connection with the consumer credit sale or consumer lease. (2) A claim or defense of a buyer specified in subsection (1) of this section may be asserted against the assignee under this section only to the extent of the amount owing to the assignee with respect to the sale or lease of the goods or services as to which the claim arose at the time the assignee has written notice of the claim or defense. (3) For the purpose of determining the amount owing to the assignee with respect to the sale or lease: (a) Payments received by the assignee after the consolidation of two or more consumer credit sales, except pursuant to a revolving charge account, are deemed to have been first applied to the payment of the sales first made; if the sales consolidated arose from sales made on the same day, payments are deemed to have first been applied to the smallest sale; (b) Payments received upon a revolving charge account are deemed to have been first applied to the payment of the credit service charges in the order of their entry to the account and then to the payment of debts in the order in which the entries of the debts are made to the account. (4) An agreement may not limit or waive the claims or defenses of a buyer under this section."

§2-404—Reserved for future use.

§2-405—Insert after "agricultural purpose,": "one involving a sale of an interest in land used for residential purposes and secured by a first deed of trust, mortgage, or similar first lien interest,". Deleted "earlier" and substituted "all other regularly." Deleted "without penalty" and added "at the creditor's prevailing rates for such type credit if the buyer meets the creditor's normal credit standards, and if the creditor is, at that time, in the business of extending such credit." Added after first sentence following nonuniform language: "The seller shall disclose this right in writing to the buyer at the time the sale is entered into." Deleted the second sentence and added at end of last sentence: "or to any irregular payment due within 45 days after the consummation of the transaction as to which payment no credit service charge has been made. This section shall not apply to a transaction of a class defined by rule of the administrator as not requiring for the protection of the buyer his right to refinance as provided in this section."

§2-407(2)—Added at end of subsection: "This subsection (2) does not apply to a security deposit for a consumer lease."

§2-407(4)—Omitted.

§2-410—Last sentence deleted.

§2-413—Added at end of first sentence of Alternative B: "or such additional fee as may be directed by the court."

§2-416(2)—Amended to read: "(a) Except as otherwise provided in paragraph (b) or (c) of this subsection (2), whenever any term of a revolving charge account is changed or the required minimum periodic payment thereon is increased, the seller shall mail or deliver written notice of the change, at least one billing cycle before the effective date of the change, to each buyer who may be affected by the change.

(b) The notice required by paragraph (a) of this subsection:

(2) Shall be given in advance, but need not be given one billing cycle in advance, if the change has been agreed to by the buyer or if the change is an increase in a credit service charge periodic rate, or other charge permitted under section 5-2-202 as a result of the buyer's delinquency or default.

(c) The notice otherwise required by paragraph (a) of this subsection (2) is not required if the change:

(i) Results from the buyer's delinquency or default, but is not of a kind listed in paragraph (b) of this subsection (2);

(ii) Results from an agreement related to a court proceeding or arbitration;

(iii) Is a reduction of any charge or component thereof; or

(iv) Is a suspension of future credit privileges or termination of a revolving charge account."

§2-416(3)—Amended to read:

"The notice provisions of subsection (2) of this section shall not apply if:

(a) The buyer after receiving notice in writing of the specific change agrees in writing to the change;

(b) The buyer elects to pay an amount designated on a billing statement (subsection (2) of section 5-2-310) as including a new charge for a benefit offered to the buyer when the benefit and charge constitutes the change in terms and when the billing statement also states the amount payable if the new charge is excluded;

(c) The change involves no significant cost to the buyer; or

(d) The agreement provides limitations on changing of terms which are more restrictive than the requirements of subsection (2) of this section."

§2-417—Subsection adopted having no code counterpart reading: "The use of a revolving charge account by a buyer, or by any person authorized by the buyer, constitutes the buyer's acceptance of the seller's offer of credit and creates a binding contract on the seller's terms then in effect. Such terms may be modified in the future as agreed by the parties and subject to the requirements of this Article, including, but not limited to, the notice requirements of section 5-2-416(2)."

§2-418—Subsection adopted having no code counterpart reading: "If a deposit reservation fee, or other advance payment is to be charged to a revolving charge account or revolving loan account for lodging or motor vehicle rental services to be provided in the future in this state, the seller shall not charge such advance payment to the buyer's account without first notifying the buyer, either orally or in writing, and giving the buyer the opportunity to reject the services."

§2-501—Amended to read: " 'Home Solicitation sale' means a consumer credit sale of goods or services, except primarily for an agricultural purpose, in which the seller or a person acting for him personally solicits the sale, and the buyer's agreement or offer to purchase is given to the seller or a person acting for him at a residence. It does not include a sale made pursuant to a preexisting revolving charge account, a sale made pursuant to prior negotiations between the parties at a business establishment at a fixed location where goods or services are offered or exhibited for sale, a transaction conducted and consummated entirely by mail or telephone, or a sale which is subject to the provisions of the 'Federal Truth-in-Lending Act' on the consumer's right to rescind certain transactions."

§2-502(5)—Amended to read: "The buyer may not cancel a home solicitation sale if, by separate dated and signed statement that is not as to its material provisions a printed form and describes an emergency requiring immediate remedy, the buyer requests the seller to provide goods or services without delay in order to safeguard the health, safety, or welfare of natural persons or to prevent damage to property the buyer owns or for which he is responsible, and".

§2-502(6)—Repealed.

§2-503(1)—Added sentence at end: "A copy of any writing required by this subsection (1) to be signed by the buyer, completed at least as to the date of the transaction and the name and mailing address of the seller, shall be given to the buyer at the time he signs the writing."

§2-503(2)—Amended to read: "The statement shall either: (a) Comply with any notice of cancellation or a similar requirement of any trade regulation rule of the federal trade commission which by its terms applies to the home solicitation sale; or (b) Appear under the conspicuous caption 'BUYER'S RIGHT TO CANCEL,' and read as follows: 'If you decide you do not want the goods or services, you may cancel this agreement by mailing a notice to the seller. The notice must say that you do not want the goods or services and must be mailed before midnight of the third business day after you sign the agreement.

The notice must be mailed to: . . . . (insert name and
. . . .' "
mailing address of seller)

§2-503(3)—Added at end "; except that the buyer's right of cancellation shall expire three years after the date of the consummation of the home solicitation sale, notwithstanding the fact that the seller has not complied with this part 5."

§2-504—Amended to read: "Restoration of down payment. (1) Within ten days after a notice of cancellation has been received by the seller or an offer to purchase has been otherwise revoked, the seller shall tender to the buyer any payment made by the buyer, any note or other evidence of indebtedness, and any goods traded in. A provision permitting the seller to keep all or any part of any goods traded in, payment, note, or other evidence of indebtedness is in violation of this section and unenforceable. (2) If the down payment includes goods traded in, the goods shall be tendered in substantially as good condition as when received by the seller. If the seller fails to tender the goods as provided by this section, the buyer may elect to recover an amount equal to the trade-in allowance stated in the agreement. (3) Until the seller has complied with the obligations imposed by this section the buyer may retain possession of goods delivered to him by the seller and has a lien on the goods in his possession or control for any recovery to which he is entitled."

§2-505(1)—In first sentence, subsection renumbered (3). After "by the buyer" added: "and allowing for ordinary wear and tear or consumption of the goods contemplated by the transaction."

§2-505(3)—Amended to read: "If a home solicitation sale is cancelled, the seller is not entitled to compensation for any service he performed pursuant to it."

§2-602—Omitted.

§2-603—Omitted.

§2-604—Omitted.

§2-605—Deleted "or a consumer related sale."

§3-102—Omitted "regulated and" preceding, and "in addition, part 6 of this article applies to consumer related loans" following, "supervised loans." Added at end of first

CONSUMER CREDIT . . . *continued*
sentence "and the provisions concerning credit card surcharges (section 5-3-110) apply to all sales and leases."

§3-103—Definitions deleted: "Consumer related loan," "Regulated lender"; and "Regulated loan."

§3-104(1)—Added at beginning: "Except as provided in subsection (2) of this section and". Inserted after "loan made": "or arranged."

§3-104(1)(b)—Deleted "or agricultural" and added "or" before "household purpose."

§3-104(1)(d)—Added new clause: "or, if the debt is secured by a mobile home which is used as the primary residence of the debtor, the principal does not exceed Fifty-two Thousand Five Hundred Dollars."

§3-104(2)—Amended to read: "Unless the loan is made subject to this code by agreement (section 5-3-601), 'consumer loans' does not include: (a) A loan for a business, investment, or commercial purpose; (b) A loan primarily for an agricultural purpose; or (c) a reverse mortgage as defined in section 11-38-102 C.R.S."

§3-105—Amended to read: "(1) Unless the loan is made subject to this Code by agreement (section 5-3-601) and except as provided with respect to disclosure (section 5-3-301), and debtors' remedies (section 5-5-201), and powers and functions of the Administrator (part 1 of article 6 of this Code), 'consumer loan' does not include a loan secured by a mobile home or a 'loan primarily secured by an interest in land', if at the time the loan is made the value of this collateral is substantial in relation to the amount of the loan, and the rate of the loan finance charge does not exceed twelve percent per year calculated according to the actuarial method on the unpaid balances of the principal on the assumption that the debt will be paid according to the agreed terms and will not be paid before the end of the agreed term or does not exceed thirteen percent per year, calculated in the same manner, if the loan is executed on or after July 1, 1979, but no later than July 1, 1981, or, notwithstanding the rate of the loan finance charge, the loan is secured by a first mortgage or deed of trust lien against a dwelling to finance the acquisition of that dwelling or to refinance by amendment, payoff, or otherwise, an existing loan made for that purpose including a refinance loan, other than a precomputed loan as defined in section 5-3-107(2), providing additional sums for any purpose whether or not related to acquisition or construction; except that as to any refinance loan in the form of a revolving loan account which is in whole or in part for purposes other than acquisition or construction, section 5-3-408 shall apply. For the purposes of this section, a 'loan secured by a first mortgage or deed of trust lien against a dwelling to finance the acquisition of the dwelling' includes a loan secured by a first mortgage or deed of trust lien against a dwelling to finance the original construction of such dwelling or to refinance any such construction loan, 'dwelling' means any improved real property, or portion thereof, that is used or intended to be used as a residence and contains not more than four dwelling units, and 'first mortgage or deed of trust' means a mortgage or deed of trust having priority as a lien over the lien of any other mortgage or deed of trust on the same dwelling and subject to the lien of taxes levied on that dwelling. (2) With respect to loans secured by a first mortgage or deed of trust lien against a dwelling to refinance an existing loan to finance the acquisition of the dwelling and providing additional sums for any other purpose which are not subject to this Code pursuant to subsection (1) of this section, the lender shall disclose to the debtor that the refinance loan creates a lien against the dwelling or property and that the limits set forth in section 5-3-404 on the amount of attorney fees that a lender may charge the debtor are not applicable."

§3-107(2)—Added "only" after "precomputed." Added following clause at end of sentence: "or, if any portion of the loan finance charge is prepaid, the amount of that portion of the loan finance charge either computed in advance or prepaid constitutes more than one-half of the total loan finance charge applicable to the loan, refinancing, or consolidation."

§3-107(3)(c)(i)—Deleted "if not included in (a)."

§3-109(1)—Amended after "as an incident to" and before "including any" to read: "or as a condition of the extension of credit, whether paid or payable by the debtor, the lender, or any other person on behalf of the debtor to the lender or to a third party;" deleted "irrespective of the person to whom the charges are paid or payable, unless the lender had no notice of the charges when the loan was made."

§3-110—Added new section having no Code counterpart reading: "Surcharges on credit transactions—prohibition on. No seller or lessor in any sales or lease transaction or any company issuing credit or charge cards may impose a surcharge on a holder who elects to use a credit or charge card in lieu of payment by cash, check, or similar means. A surcharge is any additional amount imposed at the time of the sale or lease transaction by the merchant, seller, or lessor that increases the charge to the buyer or lessee for the privilege of using a credit or charge card. For purposes of this section, charge card includes those cards pursuant to which unpaid balances are payable on demand."

§3-201(1)—Percentage changed to "twelve percent."

§3-201(3)—First sentence amended to read as follows: "Except as provided in subsection (7) of this section, the term of a loan, for the purposes of this section, commences with the date the loan is made."

§3-201(4)(a)—Percentages changed to "twelve percent" and "one percent."

§3-201(4)(b)—Percentages changed to "twelve percent" and "one percent."

§3-201(4)(c)—Amended after "may contract for and receive" to read: "a minimum finance charge not to exceed fifty cents." Delete remainder of subsection.

§3-201(6)—Added new subsection having no Code counterpart reading: "Notwithstanding subsection (1) of this section, the lender, in connection with a consumer loan other than a loan pursuant to a revolving loan account, may contract for and receive a minimum loan finance charge of not more than $25."

§3-201(7)—Added new subsection having no Code counterpart reading: "With respect to insurance premium loan, the term of the loan commences on the earliest inception date of a policy or contract of insurance, payment of the premium on which is financed by the loan."

§3-202(1)(e)—Previous subsection having no Code counterpart repealed.

§3-202(1)(f)—Added new subsection having no Code counterpart reading: "The following charges if agreed to by the parties:

(i) A charge, not to exceed the greater of two dollars or two and one-half percent of the amount advanced, for each cash advance transaction made pursuant to a lender credit card; and

(ii) A fee, not to exceed twenty dollars, assessed upon return or dishonor of a check or other instrument tendered as payment."

§3-202(1.5)—Added new section having no Code counterpart reading: "No finance charge may be assessed on any charge listed in paragraph (f) of subsection (1) of this section."

§3-202(3)—Deleted: "For the purpose of disclosure and advertising (part 3 of this article)" and substituted: "With respect to a debt secured by an interest in land."

§3-203(1)(a)—Amount changed to "ten dollars."

§3-203(2)—Added reference to nonuniform §3-203(5). Added at end of second sentence: "until ten days after the deferred due date."

§3-203(4)—Added at end of first sentence: "; and the terms of the converted loan shall be no less favorable to the debtor than the terms of the original loan."

§3-203(5)—Omitted uniform subsection and added following: "(a) Except as provided in paragraph (b) of this subsection (5), with respect to a consumer loan, refinancing, or consolidation which is not precomputed, including a revolving loan account, the parties may contract for a delinquency charge on any instalment not paid in full within ten days after its scheduled due date in an amount not exceeding fifteen dollars; except that the provisions of this paragraph (a) shall not apply to a revolving loan account for which a lender credit card is issued by the lender to the debtor. (b) With respect to a consumer loan, refinancing, or consolidation which is not precomputed and which is secured by an interest in land, including a revolving loan account, the parties may contract for a delinquency charge on any instalment not paid in full within ten days after its scheduled due date in an amount not exceeding five percent of the unpaid amount of the instalment. (c) A delinquency charge under paragraph (a) or (b) of this subsection (5) may be collected only once on an instalment regardless of how long the instalment remains in default. A delinquency charge may be collected at the time it accrues or at any time thereafter. No delinquency charge may be collected on an instalment which is paid in full within ten days after its scheduled instalment due date, even though an earlier maturing instalment or a delinquency charge on an earlier instalment may not have been paid in full. A lender who has imposed a delinquency charge pursuant to this subsection (5) shall notify the debtor in writing of the amount of the delinquency charge assessed before the due date of the next scheduled payment. A lender shall not assess a delinquency charge unless the delinquency charge is assessed within thirty days of the scheduled due date of any instalment not paid in full. (d) For purposes of this subsection (5), payments are applied first to current instalments and then to delinquent instalments. No finance charge may be assessed on any delinquency charge. For the purposes of this subsection (5), for revolving loans, an instalment is the minimum payment which the debtor is required to make during any billing cycle, excluding any past-due amount from any previous billing cycle."

§3-203(6)—Added new subsection having no code counterpart reading "The parties to a revolving loan account for which a lender credit card is issued and which is not secured by an interest in land may contract to impose a delinquency charge on any minimum payment due in connection with a billing cycle that remains unpaid ten days after such minimum payment's scheduled due date. No delinquency charge may be collected on any minimum payment due which is paid in full within ten days after the scheduled due date, even though an earlier minimum payment was not paid in full. Payments shall be applied first to the current portion of the minimum payment due and then to any delinquent portion of the minimum payment due. No delinquency charge shall exceed fifteen dollars, and no more than one delinquency charge shall be collected on any minimum payment due regardless of the period of time during which the payment remains in default. A delinquency charge may be collected anytime after it accrues if no other delinquency charge has been collected on the same unpaid amount. A lender shall not assess a delinquency charge unless the delinquency charge is assessed within ninety days after the scheduled due date of the delinquent minimum payment. A lender who has imposed a delinquency charge pursuant to this subsection (6) shall notify the debtor in writing either before, on, or with the next periodic statement after the delinquency charge has been assessed of the amount of the delinquency charge. No finance charge shall be assessed on the delinquency charge."

§3-204(5)—Added new subsection having no Code counterpart reading: "A deferral charge made according to this section is earned pro rata during the period in which no installment is scheduled to be paid by reason of the deferral, and is fully earned on the last day of that period."

§3-206.5—Added new section having no Code counterpart reading: "Prepaid loan finance charge. (1) Subject to the provisions of subsection (2) of this section, a lender may contract for the payment by the debtor of a prepaid loan finance charge; except that the total loan finance charge contracted for and received by the lender shall not exceed that permitted for consumer loans pursuant to section 5-3-201, or for supervised loans pursuant to section 5-3-508, whichever is appropriate. (2) With respect to a refinancing pursuant to section 5-3-205, or consolidation pursuant to section 5-3-206, of a previous consumer loan, refinancing, or consolidation, for which a prepaid loan finance charge was imposed, if said refinancing or consolidation is consummated within one year of the previous transaction, a new prepaid loan finance charge may be imposed: (a) Only on that portion of the aggregate principal resulting from the refinancing or consolidation which exceeds the unpaid balance of the previous transaction, determined in accordance with the provisions of section 5-3-205 or section 5-3-206, whichever is appropriate; or (b) On the aggregate principal resulting from the refinancing or consolidation; except that any unearned portion of the prepaid loan finance charge imposed in connection with the previous transaction shall be rebated to the debtor in accordance with the actuarial method as defined in section 5-1-301 and applicable rules adopted by the administrator."

§3-208(1)—Added at end of first sentence: "if the expenditure is reasonable to protect the risk of loss or damage to the property and if the lender has mailed to the debtor, at his last known address, written notice of his nonperformance, has given the debtor reasonable opportunity after such notice to so perform, and, in the absence of performance, the lender has made all expenditures on behalf of the debtor in good faith and in a commercially reasonable manner."

See note at head of Digest as to 1998 legislation covered.

See Topical Index in front part of this volume.

CO – 17

CONSUMER CREDIT . . . *continued*

§3-209—Added after "in full": "or in part if payment is no less than five dollars, the unpaid balance of a consumer loan, refinancing or consolidation, at any time without penalty. A payment in the amount of a scheduled installment, other than the last scheduled installment, not identified by the debtor as a partial prepayment shall not be deemed to be a partial prepayment regardless of when the payment is made if the amount equals the next scheduled installment. If such a payment is applied by the lender to the scheduled installment, the payment shall be deemed to have been made on the due date for the scheduled installment to which it was applied."

§3-210(1)—In first sentence, after "except as" added "otherwise", and deleted "subsection (2) of" and replaced with "this section".

§3-210(2)—Amended after "may not exceed" to read: "the lesser of the amount of loan finance charge contracted for or twenty-five dollars."

§3-210(3)—Amended to read: "(a) Except as otherwise provided in this section, the unearned portion of the loan finance charge is a fraction of the loan finance charge of which the numerator is the sum of the periodic balances scheduled to follow the computational period in which prepayment occurs, and the denominator is the sum of all periodic balances under either the loan agreement or, if the balance owing resulted from a refinancing (5-3-205) or a consolidation (5-3-206), under the refinancing agreement or consolidation agreement. (b) With respect to a precomputed transaction entered into on or after Oct. 28, 1975, and payable according to its original terms in more than 61 instalments, or on any precomputed transaction entered into on or after January 1, 1982, the unearned portion of the loan finance charge is, at the option of the lender, either: (I) that portion which is applicable to all fully unexpired computational periods as originally scheduled, or if deferred, as deferred, which follow the date of prepayment. For this purpose the applicable charge is the total of that which would have been made for each such period, had the consumer loan not been precomputed, by applying to unpaid balances of principal, according to the actuarial method, the annual percentage rate of charge previously stated to the debtor pursuant to the provisions on disclosure (part 3 of this article) based upon the assumption that all payments were made as originally scheduled, or if deferred, as deferred. The lender, at his option, may round the annual percentage rate to the nearest one-half of one percent provided that such procedure is not consistently used to obtain a greater yield than would otherwise be permitted, or (II) The total loan finance charge minus the earned loan finance charge. The earned loan finance charge shall be determined by applying the annual percentage rate previously stated to the debtor pursuant to the provisions on disclosure (part 3 of this article) according to the actuarial method to the actual unpaid balances for the actual time the balances were unpaid up to the date of prepayment. If a delinquency or deferral charge was collected, it shall be treated as a payment. (c) In the case of a loan primarily secured by an interest in land, reasonable sums actually paid or payable to persons not related to the lender for customary closing costs included in the loan finance charge shall be deducted from the loan finance charge before the calculation prescribed by this subsection (3) is made."

§3-210(6)—Amended to read: "Except as otherwise provided in subsection (3)(b) of this section, if a deferral (5-3-204) has been agreed to, the unearned portion of the loan finance charge is the portion thereof attributable according to the sum of the balances method to the period from the first day of the computational period following that in which prepayment occurs; except that the numerator of the fraction is the sum of the periodic balances, after rescheduling to give effect to any deferral, scheduled to follow the computational period in which prepayment occurs. A separate rebate of the deferral charge is not required unless the unpaid balance of the transaction is paid in full during the deferral period, in which event the creditor shall also rebate the unearned portion of the deferral charge."

§3-210(7)—Language at beginning added: "Except as otherwise provided in subsection (3)(b) of this section,".

§3-302(2)(c)—Added subsection without Code counterpart reading: "No evidence of indebtedness shall be signed when it contains blank spaces to be filled in after execution, except that this provision shall not apply to serial numbers or other identifying marks which are not available for description at the time of execution of such evidence of indebtedness."

§3-302.5—Added section without Code counterpart reading: "Disclosure requirements in connection with solicitation or application. (1) A lender shall disclose in a clear and conspicuous manner the following information in any application to open a revolving loan account for which a seller credit card is issued for any person and in any solicitation to open such an account without requiring an application:

(a) Each annual percentage rate applicable to extensions of credit under the account;

(b) Where an extension of credit under the account is subject to a variable rate, the fact that the rate is variable the annual percentage rate in effect at the time of delivery to the prospective debtor, and how the rate is determined;

(c) Where more than one rate applies, the range of balance to which each rate applies; and

(d) Any annual charge imposed for the issuance or availability of such account, including any account maintenance fee or other charge imposed based on activity or inactivity during the billing cycle.

(2) The disclosure requirements of this section do not apply to:

(a) Revolving loan accounts secured by an interest in land or to overdraft lines of credit tied to deposit accounts at depository institutions, even if lender credit cards or check guarantee cards are issued in connection with such accounts; or

(b) Lines of credit for which check guarantee or debit cards are issued that may be used only at automatic teller machines."

§3-306(2)(b)—Deleted "if not included in (a)."

§3-311—Repealed.

§3-402—Added after "for an agricultural purpose" and preceding "one pursuant to a revolving loan": "one involving a loan the primary security for which is an interest in land used for residential purposes and secured by a first deed of trust, mortgage or similar first lien interest,". Deleted "earlier" and substituted "all other regularly". Added after "it is due" following language: "at the creditor's prevailing rates for such type loan if the debtor meets the creditor's normal credit standards and the creditor is, at that time, in the business of making such loans," and deleted "without penalty." Added new sentences at end of first sentence in uniform text: "The lender shall disclose this right in writing to the debtor at the time the loan is entered into. These provisions do not apply to the extent that the payment schedule is adjusted to the seasonal or irregular income of the debtor. "This section shall not apply to a transaction of a class defined by rule of the administrator as not requiring for the protection of the debtor his right to refinance as provided in this section."

§3-403(1)—Amended to read: "A lender may not take an assignment of earnings of the debtor, other than commissions or accounts receivable payable to the debtor for services rendered, for payment or as security for payment of a debt arising out of a consumer loan. An assignment of earnings in violation of this section is unenforceable by the assignee of the earnings and revocable by the debtor."

§3-404—Added at end of first sentence of Alternative B: "or such additional fee as may be directed by the court."

§3-408(2)—Amended to read:

(a) Except as otherwise provided in paragraph (b) or (c) of this subsection (2), whenever any term of a revolving loan account is changed or the required minimum periodic payment thereon is increased, the lender shall mail or deliver written notice of the change, at least one billing cycle before the effective date of the change, to each debtor who may be affected by the change.

(b) The notice required by paragraph (a) of this subsection (2) shall be given in advance, but need not be given one billing cycle in advance, if the change has been agreed to by the debtor or if the change is an increase in a loan finance charge, periodic rate, or other charge permitted under Section 5-3-202 as a result of the debtor's delinquency or default.

(c) The notice otherwise required by paragraph (a) of this subsection (2) is not required if the change:

(i) results from the debtor's delinquency or default, but is not of a kind listed in paragraph (b) of this subsection (2);

(ii) results from an agreement related to a court proceeding or arbitration;

(iii) is a reduction of any charge or component thereof; or

(iv) is a suspension of future credit privileges or termination of a consumer loan."

§3-408(3)—Amended to read:

"The notice provisions of subsection (2) of this section shall not apply if:

(a) The debtor after receiving notice in writing of the specific change agrees in writing to the change;

(b) The debtor elects to pay an amount designated on a billing statement (subsection (2) of section 5-3-309) as including a new charge for a benefit offered to the debtor when the benefit and charge constitutes the change in terms and when the billing statement also states the amount payable if the new charge is excluded;

(c) The change involves no significant cost to the debtor; or

(d) The agreement provides limitations on changing of terms which are more restrictive than the requirements of subsection (2) of this section."

§3-409—Amended to read: "A lender may not use multiple agreements with respect to a single consumer loan for the purpose of obtaining a higher loan finance charge than would otherwise be permitted by this article or to avoid disclosure of an annual percentage rate pursuant to the provisions on disclosure and advertising (part 3 of this article). Dividing a single consumer loan between a husband and wife shall be presumed to be a violation of this section. The excess amount of loan finance charge is an excess charge for the purposes of the provisions on the effect of violations on rights of parties (5-5-202) and the provisions on civil actions by administrator (5-6-113)."

§3-411—Added new section without Code counterpart reading: "The use of a revolving loan account by a debtor, or by any person authorized by the debtor, constitutes the debtor's acceptance of the lender's offer of credit and creates a binding contract on the lender's terms then in effect. Such terms may be modified in the future as agreed by the parties and subject to the requirements of this Article, including, but not limited to, the notice requirements of Section 5-3-408(2)."

§3-501(1)—Omitted.

§3-501(2)—Omitted.

§3-501(3)—Renumbered (1); deleted "regulated loan" and substituted "consumer loan including a loan made pursuant to a revolving loan account;" percentage changed to "twelve percent."

§3-501(4)—Renumbered (2).

§3-502(2)—Deleted rest of sentence after "supervised loans."

§3-503(1)—Amended after "contain" to read: "such information as the administrator may reasonably require."

§3-503(2)—Amended by adding after last sentence thereof: "In determining financial responsibility of an applicant proposing to engage in making consumer insurance premium loans, the administrator shall consider the liabilities the lender may incur for erroneous cancellation of insurance."

§3-503(3)—Added to first sentence after "denied": "or objections filed." Added to second sentence after "denied": "or objections filed, and, in the case of a denial."

§3-503(4)—Added new subsection without Code counterpart reading: "The administrator may issue additional licenses to the same licensee upon compliance with all the provisions of this code governing issuance of a single license. A separate license shall be required for each place of business. Each license shall remain in full force and effect until surrendered, suspended, or revoked."

§3-503(5)—Added new subsection without Code counterpart reading: "No licensee shall change the location of any place of business without giving the administrator at least fifteen days prior written notice."

§3-503(6)—Amended by adding after last sentence thereof: "For purposes of this subsection (6), an insurance premium loan is made at the lender's business office."

§3-503(6)—Added new subsection without Code counterpart reading: "A licensee shall not engage in the business of making supervised loans at any place of business for which he does not hold a license, nor shall he engage in business under any other name than that in the license. For the purposes of this subsection (6), an insurance premium loan is made at the lender's business office."

§3-504(1)—Deleted from end of first sentence: "for a period not in excess of 6 months."

See note at head of Digest as to 1998 legislation covered.

See Topical Index in front part of this volume.

CONSUMER CREDIT . . . *continued*

§3-504(1)(a)—Amended to read: "The licensee has willfully violated this code or any rule or order lawfully made pursuant to this code; or has committed violations through negligence or error and after reasonable notice by the administrator has not adopted procedures reasonably designed to prevent such negligence or error; or."

§3-505(3)—Added new subsection having no Code counterpart reading: "The administrator may impose a penalty of $5 per day on any licensee failing to make a timely report."

§3-506(1)—Added "the administrator" to first sentence prior to "deems appropriate": Second sentence changed, substituting "supervised lender or any supervised financial organization" for "regulated lender." Third sentence changed, substituting "the administrator" for "he."

§3-506(2)—First sentence changed by substituting "the lender's" for "his," inserting "or her" between "his" and "representative," and adding the following to the end of the sentence: "except that the lender shall make the records available for examination at the administrator's office or at any other location the administrator deems appropriate, at the cost of the lender, if the administrator determines that the examination of the records at the location where the records are maintained endangers the safety of the examiner or that there are not adequate facilities at the location where the records are maintained to conduct the examination." Second sentence changed by adding "or her" after "his." New clause (b) added: "The administrator may require any lender whose records are located within the state to make its records available for examination at the administrator's office or at any other location the administrator deems appropriate, at the cost of the lender, if the administrator determines that the examination of the records at the location where the records are maintained endangers the safety of the examiner or that there are not adequate facilities at the location where the records are maintained to conduct the examination."

§3-506(3)—Substituted "the administrator's" for "his" and "that" for "which."

§3-506(4)—Bracket completed with "District Court in the City and County of Denver."

§3-507—Amended to read: "Except as otherwise provided, the provisions of sections 24-4-102 to 24-4-106, C.R.S. 1973, apply to and govern all administrative action taken by the administrator pursuant to this code."

§3-508(2)—Added at beginning of sentence: "Except for a loan pursuant to a revolving loan account." Changed $300 in (a)(I) to $630; (a)(II) changed $300 but not to exceed $1,000 to $630 - $2,100; (a)(III) changed $1,000 to $2,100. Changed rate in (b) from 18% to 21%.

§3-508(3)—Added new subsection without Code counterpart reading: "(a) Except as provided in paragraph (b) of this subsection (3), the loan finance charge for a loan pursuant to a revolving loan account, calculated according to the actuarial method, may not exceed 21% per year on the unpaid balance of the principal. (b) The finance charge obtained from a revolving loan account resulting from the purchase of goods or services may not exceed 18% per year on the unpaid balance of principal, calculated according to the actuarial method, unless the lender provides the debtor the privilege of paying all charges for the purchase of such goods or services, without loan finance charge, within 25 days after the date of the statement first reflecting such charges. The lender may condition the exercise of this privilege upon the debtor's payment of the full balance due as shown on the statement within 25 days."

Official §3-508(3) renumbered §3-508(4). "(c) Notwithstanding paragraph (a) of this subsection (3), if there is an unpaid balance on the date as of which the loan finance charge is applied, the lender may contract for and receive a minimum finance charge not exceeding fifty cents."

§3-508(4)—Renumbered (5) and inserted introductory clause reading: "Except as provided in subsection 8 of this section."

§3-508(5)—Renumbered (6) and amended, substituting in second sentence: "subsections (2) and (3) of this section" for "subsection (2)." Same substitution made under (a).

§3-508(6)—Omitted.

§3-508(7)—Added new subsection having no Code counterpart reading: "Notwithstanding the provisions of subsection (2) of this section, the lender, in connection with a supervised loan other than a loan pursuant to a revolving loan account, may contract for and receive a minimum loan finance charge of not more than $25."

§3-508(8)—Added new subsection having no Code counterpart reading: "With respect to an insurance premium loan, the term of the loan commences on the earliest inception date of a policy or contract of insurance, payment of the premium on which is financed by the loan."

§3-509—Repealed.

§3-510(1)—Changed $1,000 to $2,000.

§3-510(2)—Amended to read: "For the purposes of this section, on revolving loan accounts, the principal shall be determined by the limit in the amount of credit made available to or for the account of the debtor if that limit is established by an expressed written commitment by the lender and if the lender does not retain the right to unilaterally reduce that credit limit, except in the event of default."

§3-511(1)—Substituted "Supervised loans" for "Regulated loans." Changed "$1,000" to "$2,100" and in (a) and (b), changed "$300" to "$630".

§3-511(2)—Omitted.

§3-512—Amended to read as follows: "(1) A licensee who is authorized to make supervised loans under section 5-3-503 shall not engage in the business of making sales of goods, other than real estate or insurance, at any location where supervised loans are made. The word 'location' as used in this section means the entire space in which supervised loans are made and said location must be separated from any location in which merchandise is sold or displayed by walls which may be broken only by a passageway to which the public is not admitted. (a) A sale of goods or services pursuant to a lender credit card or similar arrangement made at a place of business other than that of a licensee does not violate this section. (b) An occasional sale of property used in the ordinary course of the business of the licensee does not violate this section. (c) A sale of items repossessed by the licensee does not violate this section." Added new paragraph having no Code counterpart reading: "(d) The sale of goods by a pawnbroker who is authorized to make supervised loans under section 5-3-503 does not violate this section."

§3-513—"Supervised loans" substituted for "regulated loans."

§3-514(1)—Amended first sentence to read: "With respect to a supervised loan the agreement may provide for the payment by the debtor of reasonable attorney's fees not in excess of fifteen percent of the unpaid debt after default and referral to an attorney not a salaried employee of the lender."

§3-514(2)—Omitted.

§3-602—Omitted.

§3-603—Omitted.

§3-604—Omitted.

§3-605—Amended to read as follows: "With respect to a loan that is specifically exempt from the rate ceilings of this code by the provisions of section 5-3-105, the parties may contract for the payment by the debtor of any loan finance charge up to a rate not to exceed an annual percentage rate of 45%. The rate of the loan finance charge shall be calculated on the unpaid balances of the debt on the assumption that the debt will be paid according to its terms and will not be paid before the end of the agreed term."

§4-102(1)—Amended to read: "This article applies to insurance provided or to be provided in relation to a consumer credit sale (section 5-2-104), a consumer lease (section 5-2-106), or a consumer loan (section 5-3-104)."

§4-102(2)—Repealed as of July 1, 1977.

§4-102(3)—Amended to read: "This article supplements and does not repeal the 'Credit Insurance Act,' Article 10 of Title 10, C.R.S. The provisions of this code concerning administrative controls, liabilities, and penalties do not apply to persons acting as insurers, and the similar provisions of said credit insurance act do not apply to creditors and debtors."

§4-103(1)(a)—Added after "Insurance": "as to which a credit service charge or loan finance charge is imposed and ".

§4-103(2)—Amended to read: " 'Credit insurance act' means the 'Credit Insurance Act', Article 10 of Title 10, C.R.S."

§4-108—Amended to read: "(1)(a) Except as provided in subsection (3) of this section, an appropriate refund or credit of unearned premiums shall be made to the person entitled thereto with respect to any separate charge made to the debtor for insurance if: (I) The insurance is not provided or is provided for a shorter term than that for which the charge to the debtor for insurance was computed; or (II) The insurance terminates prior to the end of the term for which it was written because of prepayment in full of the indebtedness or the insurance terminates for any other reason. (b) All consumer credit insurance shall terminate upon prepayment in full of the indebtedness. (2) If a refund or credit of unearned premiums is required pursuant to the provisions of subsection (1) of this section: (a) The original creditor, if he is the holder of the indebtedness at the time of prepayment, shall either promptly make the appropriate refund or credit or shall promptly notify the debtor and the insurer in writing that a refund or credit is due. Upon the receipt of notice that a refund or credit is due, the insurer shall promptly make an appropriate refund or credit of unearned premiums pursuant to the provisions of section 10-10-110(2), C.R.S. For the purposes of this section, 'original creditor' means the person to whom the indebtedness was initially payable, and 'insurer' means every person engaged as principal, indemnitor, surety, or contractor in the business of making contracts of insurance, excluding any licensed insurance agent. (b)(I) The assignee, if the indebtedness has been assigned, shall either promptly make the appropriate refund or credit or shall promptly notify the debtor, the original creditor, and the insurer, if known, in writing that a refund or credit is due. For the purposes of this section, 'assignee' means a person other than the original creditor who at the time of prepayment holds the indebtedness. (II) The original creditor, upon receipt of notice pursuant to subparagraph (I) of this paragraph (b), shall either promptly make the appropriate refund or credit or shall promptly notify the insurer in writing that a refund or credit of unearned premiums is due. (c) The insurer, upon the receipt of notice that a refund or credit is due pursuant to paragraph (a) or (b) of this subsection (2), shall make an appropriate refund or credit of unearned premiums pursuant to the provisions of section 10-10-110(2), C.R.S., and subsection (1) of this section. (d) An assignee or original creditor gives notice pursuant to this section upon delivery or mailing of the notice to the last address provided to him. Once an original creditor or an assignee has notified the appropriate party, as provided in paragraph (a) and (b) of this subsection (2) the original creditor and the assignee shall have no further obligations. (3) This article does not require a refund or credit of unearned premiums, if: (a) All refunds and credits due to the debtor under this article amount to less than one dollar; or (b) The charge for insurance is computed from time to time on the outstanding balance of the indebtedness and the charge relates to only one premium period. (4) Except as otherwise required, a refund or credit is not required because: (a) The insurance is terminated by payment of proceeds under the policy; or (b) The original creditor or assignee pays or accounts for premiums to the insurer in the amounts and at the times determined by the agreement between them; or (c) The original creditor or assignee receives directly or indirectly under any policy of insurance a gain or advantage not prohibited by law. (5) If a single type of insurance is terminated by the payment of proceeds under the policy pursuant to paragraph (a) of subsection (4) of this section, a refund or credit of unearned premiums for all other types of consumer credit insurance issued on the same indebtedness shall be made if so required by the provisions of this section and section 10-10-110(2), C.R.S. (6) A refund or credit required by subsection (1) of this section is appropriate as to amount if it is computed according to a method prescribed or approved by the commissioner of insurance or a formula filed by the insurer with the commissioner of insurance at least thirty days before the debtor's right to a refund or credit becomes determinable, unless the method or formula is employed after the commissioner of insurance notifies the insurer that he disapproves it."

§4-109—Amended by addition of "or lessor" after "creditor" each time it appears in section and by addition of "or lessee" after "debtor" each time it appears in section.

§4-112(2)—Amended to read: "Sections 24-4-102 to 24-4-106, C.R.S. 1973, apply to and govern all administrative action taken by the commissioner of insurance pursuant to this section."

§4-201(3)—Substituted "thirty days" for "15 days."

See note at head of Digest as to 1998 legislation covered.

See Topical Index in front part of this volume.

CO – 19

CONSUMER CREDIT . . . *continued*

§4-203(2)—Substituted "title 10, C.R.S. 1973" for optional language "Insurance Code." Added sentence reading as follows: "A premium rate or schedule of premium rates shall be deemed reasonable for all purposes under this code if the rate or schedule produces or reasonably may be expected to produce a ratio of earned premium (minus not to exceed forty percent for commission or compensation, whether or not actually paid) divided into claims incurred of sixty-six and two-thirds percent."

§4-301(3)—Changed second amount to $630.

§4-301(4)—Omitted.

§4-304—Amended by adding following sentence at beginning of section "This section does not apply to an insurance premium loan."

§5-102—Deleted "and in addition" after "consumer loans." Added at end "and to unconscionability (section 5-5-108)."

§5-103(1)—Added sentence reading: "A buyer is not liable for a deficiency unless the seller has disposed of the goods in accordance with the provisions on the disposition of collateral of the 'Uniform Commercial Code' (part 5 of article 9 of title 4, C.R.S. 1973)."

§5-103(2)—Amended to read: "If the seller repossesses (with or without the aid of judicial process) or voluntarily accepts surrender of goods which were the subject of the sale and in which he has a security interest, the parties obligated are not personally liable to the seller for the unpaid balance of the debt arising from the sale of a commercial unit of goods of which the cash sale price was $2,100 or less, and the seller's duty to dispose of the collateral is governed by the provisions on the disposition of collateral of the 'Uniform Commercial Code' (part 5 of article 9 of title 4, C.R.S. 1973)."

§5-103(3)—Added after words "If the seller repossesses": "(with or without the aid of judicial process)." Substituted "two thousand, one hundred dollars" for "$1000." Amended after "or less" to read: "the parties obligated are not personally liable to the seller for the unpaid balance of the debt arising from the sale, and the seller's duty to dispose of the collateral is governed by the provisions on disposition of collateral of the 'Uniform Commercial Code' (part 5 of article 9 of title 4, C.R.S. 1973)."

§5-103(4)—Added "5-2-408" to section citation.

§5-103(5)—Added "misused, abused, or" before "wrongfully damaged." Added "in writing" after "demand." Added new sentence reading: "Nothing in this section shall limit or restrict the remedies of the holders of a security interest for damage to the collateral because of conversion, destruction, or other wrongful acts."

§5-103(6)—In introductory paragraph and paragraph (a) substituted: "took possession of" for "repossessed".

§5-103(7)—Omitted.

§5-103.5—Added new section having no Code counterpart reading: "Insecurity and impaired collateral. (1) If a seller or lender takes possession of any collateral because he deems himself insecure or because he feels his collateral is impaired, and the seller or lender fails to prove that, at the time possession was taken, the seller or lender, in good faith, had reasonable cause to believe that he was insecure or that his collateral was impaired: (a) The seller or lender shall be liable to the buyer or borrower for court costs and attorneys' fees as determined by the court; and (b) The buyer or borrower shall not be liable for any credit service or loan finance charge incurred during the period he is without use of the collateral."

§5-104—Amended after "may not" to read: "replevin goods, except motor vehicles, of the debtor with the use of force from a dwelling upon an ex parte order of court, or attach unpaid earnings of the debtor by garnishment or like proceedings."

§5-105(2)(b)—Substituted "thirty times" for "forty times."

§5-105(4)—Added new subsection without Code counterpart reading: "It shall not be necessary for any individual to claim the exemptions for that portion of the aggregate disposable earnings which are not subject to garnishment as set forth in subsection (2) of this section, and such exemption from garnishment shall be self-executing in any garnishment procedure."

§5-105(5)—Added new subsection without Code counterpart reading: "This section does not repeal, alter, or affect other statutes of this state prohibiting garnishments or providing for larger exemptions from garnishments than are allowed under this section."

§5-108—Amended, adopting 5-108, UCCC, 1974 Final Draft with following material alterations:

§5-108(4)—Omitted.

§5-108(5)—Renumbered (4) and succeeding subsections accordingly.

§5-108(5)(a)—Changed "consumer" to: "debtor." Deleted: "or criminal prosecution."

§5-108(5)(b)—Changed "consumer" to: "debtor."

§5-108(5)(d)—Amended to read after "economic status by": "(I) Disclosing information affecting the debtor's reputation for credit worthiness with knowledge or reason to know that the information is false; (II) Orally communicating with the debtor's employer before obtaining a final judgment against the debtor, except: As permitted by statute; or to verify his employment; or to ascertain his whereabouts; or to request that the debtor contact the creditor; (III) Disclosing to a person, with knowledge or reason to know that the person does not have a legitimate business need for the information; or in any way prohibited by statute, information affecting the debtor's credit or other reputation; or (IV) Disclosing information concerning the existence of a debt known to be disputed by the debtor without disclosing that fact;".

§5-109—Added new sections having no Code counterpart reading: "Notice to cosigners and similar parties. (1) No natural person, other than the spouse of such person, shall be obligated as a cosigner, comaker, guarantor, endorser, surety, or similar party with respect to a consumer credit transaction, unless before or contemporaneously with signing any agreement of obligation or any writing setting forth the terms of the debtor's agreement, the person receives a written notice that contains a completed identification of the debt he may have to pay and reasonably informs him of his obligation with respect to it. Such written notice may be set forth in the debtor's agreement of obligation or in a separate writing. For the purposes of this section, the words 'cosigner,' 'comaker,' 'guarantor,' 'endorser,' or 'surety' mean a natural person who, by agreement and without compensation, renders himself liable for the obligation of another in a consumer credit transaction, and the terms 'agreement' and 'debtor's agreement' mean the original underlying agreement. (2) A clear and conspicuous notice in substantially the following form complies with this section: NOTICE. You agree to pay the debt identified below although you may not personally receive any goods, services, or money. You may be sued for payment although the person who receives the goods, services, or money is able to pay. This notice is not the contract that obligates you to pay the debt. Read the contract for the exact terms of your obligation. IDENTIFICATION OF DEBT YOU MAY HAVE TO PAY

(Name of Debtor)

(Name of Creditor)' (Date)' (Kind of Debt)'

I have received a copy of this notice

(Date)'

(Signed)

(3) The notice required by this section need not be given to a seller, lessor, or lender who is obligated to an assignee of his rights. Compliance with the disclosure requirements of 16 C.F.R. 444.3, contained in proposed 12 C.F.R. 227.14 as published in 49 Fed. Reg. 47041 *et seq.*or proposed 12 C.F.R. 535.3 as published in 50 Fed. Reg. 1863 and following shall constitute an alternative means of compliance with the notice provisions of this section. (4) A person entitled to notice pursuant to this section shall also be given a copy of any writing setting forth the terms of the debtor's agreement and of any separate agreement of obligation signed by the person entitled to the notice."

§5-110—Added new section having no Code counterpart reading: "Receipts; statements of account; evidence of payment. (1) The creditor shall deliver or mail to the debtor, without request, a written receipt for each payment by coin or currency on an obligation pursuant to a consumer credit transaction. A periodic statement showing a payment received by the creditor complies with this section (1). (2) Upon written request of a debtor, the person to whom an obligation is owed pursuant to a consumer credit transaction, other than one pursuant to a revolving charge or loan account, shall provide a written statement of the dates and amounts of payments made within the 12 months preceding the month in which the request is received and the total amount unpaid as of the end of the period covered by the statement. The statement shall be provided without charge, twice during each year of the term of the obligation. If additional statements are requested, the creditor may charge not more than $10 for each additional statement. (3) Within 30 days after a debtor has fulfilled all obligations with respect to a consumer credit transaction, other than one pursuant to a revolving charge or loan account, the person to whom the obligation was owed, shall deliver or mail to the debtor written evidence acknowledging payment in full of all obligations with respect to the transaction and written evidence of release of any security interest and termination of any financing statement held, retained, or acquired by the creditor."

§5-111—Added new section corresponding to 5-110, UCCC 1974 Final Draft with following material alterations: §5-110(1)—Changed "consumer" to: "debtor"; at end of second sentence changed reference to: "as defined in section 5-1-201(7)."; added "or the mobile home" after "goods." §5-111 amended to conform substantially with 5-110, UCCC 1974 Final Draft.

§5-112—Added new section corresponding to 5-111, UCCC, 1974 Final Draft with following material alterations: §5-111(1)—Changed "consumer" to: "debtor"; renumbered section 5-110 to section 5-111. Deleted at end of first sentence following: "20 days after a notice of the consumer's right to cure (section 5-110) is given,". §5-111(2)—Deleted language following "same obligation" and preceding "after a creditor."; added "other than defaults on an obligation secured by a mobile home." Section reference renumbered as above. At end of first sentence added: "with respect to any subsequent default that occurs within 12 month of such notice." In second sentence deleted language ", in open-end credit," and substituted: ", in connection with revolving charge and loan accounts,". In same sentence deleted: "unpaid balance of" and substituted: "debtor's." Added new sentence as follows: "With respect to defaults on the same obligation which is secured by a mobile home, this section gives the debtor no right to cure and imposes no limitation on the creditor's right to proceed against the debtor or goods that are collateral with respect to any third default that occurs within 12 months of such notice." §5-111(3)—Deleted reference to section 1.07; deleted language following "thereafter" and preceding "enforcing" and language following "enforcing" and preceding "the obligation".

§5-111(4)—Substituted new subsection: "This section shall not apply to consumer credit transactions which are payable in four or fewer instalments."

§5-202(1)—Amended to read as follows: "If a creditor has violated the provisions of this code applying to limitations on the schedule of payments or loan term for supervised loans (section 5-3-511), or authority to make supervised loans (section 5-3-502), the debtor is not obligated to pay the credit service charge or the loan finance charge, and has a right to recover from the person violating this code or from an assignee of that person's rights who undertakes direct collection of payments or enforcement of rights arising from the debt a penalty in an amount determined by the court not in excess of three times the amount of the credit service charge or loan finance charge. With respect to violations arising from consumer credit transactions made pursuant to revolving charge or loan accounts, no action pursuant to this subsection (1) may be brought more than two years after the violation occurred. With respect to violations arising from other consumer credit transactions, no action pursuant to this subsection (1) may be brought more than one year after the due date of the last scheduled payment of the agreement with respect to which the violation occurred."

§5-202(2)—Repealed.

§5-202(7)—Added after "error": "notwithstanding the maintenance of procedures reasonably adopted to avoid the error." Deleted reference to subsection 2.

§5-202(9)—Added subsection having no Code counterpart reading: "If a creditor repeatedly fails to provide a debtor with a statement of an annual percentage rate or credit service or loan finance charge as and to the extent required by the provisions on disclosure (part 3 of article 2 and part 3 of article 3) of this code and has received written notice from the administrator of such repeated failure, any such subsequent failure by the creditor shall relieve any debtor receiving such defective disclosure from any obligation to pay any credit service charge or loan finance charge in connection with such consumer credit sale or consumer loan."

§5-203(2)—Changed "fifteen days" to "sixty days."

See note at head of Digest as to 1998 legislation covered.

See Topical Index in front part of this volume.

CONSUMER CREDIT ... *continued*

§5-203(7)—Added new subsection having no Code counterpart reading: "No provision of this section or section 5-5-302 imposing any liability shall apply to any act done or omitted in good faith in conformity with any rule, regulation, interpretation, or written response to a person pursuant to a written request on behalf of such identified person by the administrator or the board of governors of the federal reserve system pursuant to the 'Federal Consumer Credit Protection Act,' notwithstanding that, after such act or omission has occurred, such rule, regulation, interpretation, or written response is amended, rescinded or determined by judicial or other authority to be invalid for any reason."

§5-203(8)—Added new subsection having no Code counterpart reading: "The multiple failure to disclose to any person any information required under this code to be disclosed in connection with a single account under a revolving charge or loan account, other single consumer credit sale, consumer loan, or other extension of consumer credit shall entitle the person to a single recovery under this section, but continued failure to disclose after recovery has been granted shall give rise to rights to additional recoveries."

§5-204(1)—Inserted "any property which is used as a dwelling" after "acquired in" and before "of the person" in substitution for "an interest in land which is used or expected to be used as the residence."

§5-204(2)—Changed "ten days" to "twenty days." Added at end of subsection: "The procedures prescribed by this subsection (2) shall apply except when otherwise ordered by a court."

§5-204(5)—Enacted substantially nonuniform provision reading: "This section does not apply to: (a) a transaction in which a mortgage, deed of trust, purchase money security interest arising under an instalment sales contract, or equivalent consensual security interest is created or retained against the debtor's dwelling to finance the acquisition or initial construction of such dwelling; (b) a transaction which constitutes a refinancing or consolidation (with no new advances) of the principal balance then due and any accrued and unpaid credit service charges or loan finance charges of an existing extension of credit by the same creditor secured by an interest in the same property; (c) a transaction in which an agency of a state is the creditor; or (d)(I) advances under a pre-existing, open end credit plan if a security interest has already been retained or acquired and such advances are in accordance with a previously established credit limit for such plan." Previous subsection having no Code counterpart repealed.

§5-204(6)—Added new subsection having no Code counterpart reading: "A debtor's right of rescission shall expire three years after the date of consummation of the transaction or upon the sale of the interest in land, whichever occurs earlier, notwithstanding the fact that the disclosure required under this section or any other material disclosure required under this code have not been delivered to the debtor."

§5-206—Section adopted having no Code counterpart reading: "Civil liability for discrimination.—If a person has failed to comply with section 5-1-109, the person aggrieved by such failure to comply has a right to recover actual damages from such person, but in no event less than one hundred dollars for actual and exemplary damages nor more than one thousand dollars for actual and exemplary damages. In the case of a successful action to enforce such right of recovery, the aggrieved person shall recover the costs of the action together with reasonable attorney's fees as determined by the court."

§5-301(1)—Amended after "upon conviction" to read: "shall be punished by a fine not to exceed five thousand dollars or by imprisonment in the county jail not to exceed one year, or by both such fine and imprisonment."

§5-301(2)—Amended as in §5-301(1) above.

§5-301(3)—Amended after "upon conviction" to read: "shall be punished by a fine not to exceed one thousand dollars."

§5-301(4)—Added new subsection without Code counterpart reading: "Any person who violates the provisions of this section and by the same act or acts violates the provisions of section 18-15-104 or 18-15-107, C.R.S. 1973, or both, shall be prosecuted for the violation of either or both of said sections and not for a violation of this section."

§5-302—First paragraph amended to read: "A person is guilty of a misdemeanor and upon conviction shall be punished by a fine not to exceed five thousand dollars, or by imprisonment in the county jail not to exceed one year, or by both such fine and imprisonment, if he willfully and knowingly."

§6-102(1)—Amended to read as follows: "Make or solicit consumer credit sales, consumer leases, consumer loans, or insurance premium loans; or".

§6-103—Completed to read as follows: " 'Administrator' means the assistant attorney general to be designated by the attorney general, with the advice and consent of the commission on consumer credit. Any district attorney may, with the consent of the administrator, exercise the powers and perform the duties of the administrator as provided in section 5-6-104(1)(a) and (1)(b) and section 5-6-105 to 5-6-115."

§6-104(1)(e)—Added at beginning of sentence: "With approval of the commission on consumer credit." Deleted "when specifically authorized by this code" and substituted: "to carry out the specific provisions of this code, including but not limited to lowering or increasing the amount of filing fees required pursuant to Sections 5-6-203 and 5-10-805, but not with respect to unconscionable agreements or fraudulent or unconscionable conduct."

§6-104(1)(g)—Added new subsection having no Code counterpart reading: "Enforce the provisions of article 14.5 of title 12, C.R.S."

§6-104(3)(a)—Added "and regulations" after "repealing rules."

§6-104(3)(b)—Added "and regulations" after "repealing rules."

§6-104(4)—Amended to read: "No liability is imposed under this code for an act done or omitted in good faith in conformity with a rule, regulation, interpretation, or written notice response to a person pursuant to a written request on behalf of such identified person by the administrator, notwithstanding that after the act or omission the rule, regulation, interpretation, or written response may be amended or repealed or be determined by judicial or other authority to be invalid for any reason."

§6-105(3)—Added new sentence reading: "The administrator may recover from a supervised financial organization his reasonable costs incurred in such investigation,

suit, or other official action as part of any relief granted the administrator by a court of competent jurisdiction."

§6-106(1)—Substituted "reasonable cause" for "probable cause." Added new sentence reading: "In any civil action brought by the administrator as a result of such an investigation, the administrator may recover the reasonable costs of making the investigation if he prevails in the action."

§6-107—Amended to read: "Except as otherwise provided, the provisions of sections 24-4-102 to 24-4-106, C.R.S. 1973, apply to and govern all administrative action taken by the administrator pursuant to this article or the provisions on supervised loans (sections 5-3-501 to 5-3-514) of part 5 of the article on loans (part 5 of article 3 of this title)."

§6-108(1)—Added at end of first sentence: "or of rules or regulations promulgated in accordance therewith." Second sentence completed as follows: "in the district court under section 24-4-106, C.R.S. 1973."

§6-108(4)—First sentence amended, after "subject to", to read: "appellate review in the same manner and form and with the same effect as in appeals from a final judgment or decree in any other civil action."

§6-110—Added after Act ["Code"]: "or rules or regulations promulgated thereunder."

§6-111(1)(b)—Deleted: "or" at end.

§6-111(1)(b.5)—Added new paragraph having no Code counterpart reading: "Conduct of any of the types specified in paragraph (a) or (b) of this subsection (1) with respect to transactions that give rise to or lead persons to believe they will give rise to consumer credit transactions; or".

§6-111(3)(d)—Deleted: "and" at end.

§6-111(3)(e)—Added: "and" at end.

§6-111(3)(f)—Added new paragraph having no Code counterpart reading: "Any of the factors set forth in section 5-5-108(4)."

§6-111(3.5)—Added subsection having no Code counterpart reading: "The administrator may bring a civil action to restrain a creditor or a person acting in his behalf from engaging in a course of making or arranging consumer loans to enable debtors to buy or lease from a particular seller or lessor goods or services, a principal purpose of which course of action is to avoid giving the debtors those rights which they would have had if the transactions were entered into as a consumer credit sale if: (a) The lender is a person related to the seller or lessor, unless the relationship is remote or is not a factor in the transaction; (b) The seller or lessor guarantees the loans or otherwise assumes the risk of loss by the lender upon the loans; (c) The loans are conditioned upon the debtor's purchase or lease of the goods or services from the particular seller or lessor, but the lender's payment of proceeds of the loan to the seller or lessor does not in itself establish that the loan was so conditioned; or (d) The lender, before he makes the consumer loan, has knowledge or, from his course of dealing with the particular seller or lessor or his records, notice of substantial complaints by other buyers or lessees of the particular seller's or lessor's failure or refusal to perform his contracts with them and of the particular seller's or lessor's failure to remedy his defaults within a reasonable time after notice to him of the complaints."

§6-112—Deleted "for appropriate temporary relief" and added "for a temporary restraining order or, upon notice, a preliminary injunction." Substituted in second sentence "any such temporary restraining order or preliminary injunction" for "any temporary relief or restraining order."

§6-113(1)—Substituted in next-to-last sentence "two years" for "one year."

§6-114—Added to end of sentence: "but this will not prevent a defendant from requesting a jury trial under the Colorado rules of civil procedure."

§6-116—Omitted.

§6-202(1)—Added new sentence after first sentence reading: "Persons subject to this part 2 on October 1, 1971, shall file notification with the administrator on or before January 31, 1972, and, thereafter, on or before January 31 of each year."

§6-202(1)(g)—Deleted "regulated or" and "or both."

§6-203(1)(a)—Amended to read: "A person required to file notification shall with the first notification and on or before Jan. 31 of each year thereafter pay to the administrator a nonrefundable annual notification fee of twenty dollars; except that a supervised lender other than a supervised financial organization shall pay with the filing of the first notification and on or before Jan. 31 of each year thereafter a nonrefundable annual license fee of four hundred dollars for each license issued and except that a person licensed pursuant to part 5 of article 3 of this title which does not make consumer loans and which is licensed pursuant to article 14 of title 12, C.R.S. 1973, shall pay with the filing of the first notification and on or before Jan. 31 of each year thereafter a nonrefundable annual notification fee of twenty dollars for each license issued pursuant to part 5 of article 3 of this title."

§6-203(1)(b)—Added subsection having no Code counterpart reading: "A person engaged in making consumer credit sales shall be required to pay the notification fee specified in this subsection (1) only if he: (I) charges a credit service charge; or (II) assigns the right to receive payment to any other person."

§6-203(2)—Deleted language at beginning of this clause and substituted: "Persons required to file notification who are sellers, lessors, or lenders other than a supervised financial organization or other supervised lender shall pay an additional nonrefundable annual volume fee on or before January 31 of each year in the amount of 12 dollars for each one hundred thousand dollars, . . ."

§6-203(3)—Amended to read: "Except as to a supervised financial organization or other supervised lender, persons required to file notification who are assignees shall pay an additional nonrefundable annual volume fee on or before January 31 of each year in the amount of 12 dollars for each one hundred thousand dollars, or part thereof, of the unpaid balances at the time of the assignment of obligations arising from consumer credit sales, consumer leases, and consumer loans made in this state or taken by assignment during the preceding calendar year, but an assignee need not pay a volume fee with respect to an obligation on which the assignor or other person has already paid a volume fee."

§6-203(4)—Added subsection having no Code counterpart reading: "The administrator may impose a penalty of $5 per day on any person failing to comply with this

CONSUMER CREDIT . . . *continued*

section; except that if the fees required by this section are paid on or before March 31 of each year, no penalty shall be imposed."

§6-203(5)—Added subsection having no Code counterpart reading: "If a licensee fails to pay the prescribed fee on or before March 1 of any year, such person's license may be revoked by the administrator. The licensee shall be informed of the action by the administrator pursuant to section 5-3-504(4)."

§6-203(6)—Added subsection having no Code counterpart to read as follows: "In addition to the other fees required by this section, a supervised lender other than a supervised financial organization shall pay an additional nonrefundable annual volume fee on or before January 31 of each year in the amount of $10 for each $100,000, or part thereof, in excess of $2,000,000 of the original unpaid balance arising from consumer insurance premium loans made to residents of this state within the preceding calendar year and held by the lender for more than 30 days after the inception of the loan giving rise to the obligation. A refinancing of a loan resulting in an increase in the amount of an obligation shall be considered a new loan to the extent of the amount of the increase."

§6-203(7)—Added subsection having no Code counterpart reading: "Notwithstanding the amount specified for any fee in this section, the Administrator by rule or as otherwise provided by law may reduce the amount of one or more of the fees if necessary pursuant to section 24-75-402 (3), C.R.S., to reduce the uncommitted reserves of the fund to which all or any portion of one or more of the fees is credited. After the uncommitted reserves of the fund are sufficiently reduced, the administrator by rule or as otherwise provided by law may increase the amount of one or more of the fees as provided in section 24-75-402 (4), C.R.S."

§6-204—Added new section without Code counterpart reading: "Cash fund created. On and after July 1, 1989, all fees collected under this code and under article 10 of this title shall be deposited to the credit of the uniform consumer credit code cash fund, which fund is hereby created, and all monies credited to such fund shall be used for the administration and enforcement of this code, article 10 of this title and article 14.5 of title 12, C.R.S. Interest earned on such fund shall be credited to the general fund. The general assembly shall make annual appropriations out of such fund for the administration and enforcement of this code, article 10 of this title and article 14.5 of title 12, C.R.S."

§6-301(1)—Inserted "nine" as number of members.

§6-301(2)—Term of office "three years." Second sentence amended to read: "Of those members first appointed, three shall be appointed for a term of one year, three for a term of two years, and three for a term of three years."

§6-301(3)—Added after "reimbursement of": "actual and necessary."

§6-303—Added to end of second sentence: "or administrator, or a quorum of the council."

§6-304—Repealed.

§6-401—Added new section without Code counterpart reading: "Commission on consumer credit created. There is hereby created in the department of law a commission on consumer credit which shall consist of three members. The members of the commission shall be the attorney general, two members to be appointed by the governor, one to represent the interests of the business and insurance industries, and one to represent the interests of the consumer, both of whom shall serve at the pleasure of the governor. Each appointed member shall be paid thirty dollars per day for each day of active service. Members of the commission shall serve without additional compensation, but are entitled to reimbursement of actual and necessary expenses incurred in the performance of their duties. The commission shall be the policy-making body for purposes of implementing this code."

§6-402—Added new section without Code counterpart reading: "Commission rules—quorum—meetings—annual report—review and amend rules and regulations of administrator. (1) The commission may adopt rules for conducting its proceedings and for electing a chairman. Any two members of the commission shall constitute a quorum for transacting commission business. The commission and the administrator shall meet together at a time and place designated by the chairman at least once each quarter during the year to carry out the purposes of this code. The commission may meet at such other times as may be called by its chairman or by a quorum of the commission. Complete minutes of each meeting shall be kept and filed in the department of law and shall be available for public inspection during office hours. (2) The commission may review, repeal, amend, or modify any rule or regulation adopted or promulgated by the administrator pursuant to section 5-6-104(1)(e)."

Colorado has utilized Art. 7, which is reserved in Uniform Code, as follows:

§7-101—*Scope.*—Provisions of this article apply to insurance premium loans.

§7-102—"*Form of Insurance Premium Agreement.* An agreement pursuant to which an insurance premium loan is made shall contain the names of the insurance agent or broker negotiating each policy or contract and of the insurer issuing each policy or contract, the number and inception date of the premium for each policy or contract, the date on which the term of the loan begins, and a clear and conspicuous notice that each policy or contract may be cancelled if payment is not made in accordance with the agreement. If a policy or contract has not been issued by the time the agreement is signed, the agreement may provide that the insurance agent or broker may insert the appropriate information in the agreement and, if he does so, shall furnish the information promptly in writing to the insured."

§7-103—"*Notice of Cancellation.*—If a default exists on an insurance premium loan and any right to cure which exists has expired without cure being effected, the lender may give notice of cancellation of each insurance policy or contract to be cancelled. If given, the notice of cancellation shall be in writing and given to the insurer who issued the policy or contract and to the insured. The insurer, within two business days after receipt of the notice of cancellation, together with a copy of the insurance premium loan agreement if not previously given to him, shall give any notice of cancellation required by the policy, contract, or law and, within ten business days after the effective date of the cancellation, pay to the lender any premium unearned on the policy or contract as of that effective date. Within ten business days after receipt of the unearned premium, the lender shall pay to the debtor indebted upon the insurance premium loan any excess of

the unearned premium received over the note owing by the debtor upon the insurance premium loan."

§9-101(1)—Blank completed as "October 1, 1971."

§9-101(2)—Deleted "the Part on Regulated and Supervised Loans" and added "the provisions on supervised loans." Completed blank as follows: "on July 1, 1971."

§9-102—First sentence amended to read: "Notwithstanding the repeal and reenactment of articles 2 and 3 of Chapter 73, C.R.S. 1963, by this code, all persons licensed or otherwise authorized under the provisions of articles 2 or 3 of this chapter 73, C.R.S. 1963, immediately prior to October 1, 1971, are licensed to make supervised loans under this code pursuant to the provisions on supervised loans of the article on loans (part 5 of article 3 of this title), and all provisions of said sections apply to the persons so previously licensed or authorized."

Sections or Subdivisions of Code omitted from Colorado Consumer Credit Code.—All adjustments of dollar amounts omitted, including: §§2-104(3); 2-106(3); 2-201(7); 2-203(4); 2-207(5); 2-407(4); 2-602(4); 3-104(2); 3-508(6); 3-511(2); 3-514(2); 3-602(3); 4-301(4); 5-103(7).

§2-404—Reserved for future use.

§3-501(1).

§3-501(2).

Optional Provisions Adopted or Not Adopted.—

§1-108(3)—Optional language adopted.

§1-108(4)—Optional language adopted.

§1-203—Optional language adopted.

§2-404—Reserved for future use.

§2-413—Alternative B adopted with modifications.

§3-404—Alternative B adopted with modifications.

§4-102(3)—Optional language adopted with modifications.

§4-112(2)—Optional language adopted with modifications.

§6-104(1)(g)—Optional language not adopted.

§6-116—Optional language not adopted.

§6-401—Optional Part 4 not adopted.

CONSUMER PROTECTION:

Advertising.—False or misleading advertising of credit with respect to consumer credit sale, lease or loan is prohibited under Consumer Credit Code. (5-2-313, 5-3-312). False or misleading statements in advertisement or sale of real property subject to provisions of Colorado Consumer Protection Act. (660 P.2d 1295). Bait and switch advertising and other activities constitute deceptive trade practices prohibited under Colorado Consumer Protection Act. (6-1-101 to 6-1-115). Promotion of pyramid scheme is class 1 misdemeanor on first conviction and class 5 felony on second or subsequent conviction. Bait advertising is class two misdemeanor. (18-5-303). Misleading advertising of meats and frozen foods intended for storage prohibited. (35-33-103). False advertisement of food, drug, device or cosmetic prohibited. (25-5-403[e]).

Assignment of Wages.—See category Debtor and Creditor, topic Assignments.

Buyers' Clubs.—Contracts for membership in buyer's clubs are regulated. (6-1-105[1][bb]).

Bulk Foods.—Sanitary maintenance and protection of bulk foods and equipment used to display and disperse bulk foods is regulated. (25-4-1301).

Closing and Settlement Services.—Such services are regulated by statute. Only collected funds may be disbursed at closing. (38-35-125).

Collection agencies are required to obtain license. Their communication and contact with customers is regulated. (12-14-101).

Consumer Credit Reporting Agencies.—Activities of consumer credit reporting agencies are regulated. (12-14.3-101).

Credit Services Organizations.—Activities of credit services organizations are regulated. (12-14.5-101).

Dairy Products.—Standards, inspection, and other public safety measures of dairy products and frozen desserts are regulated. (25-5.5-101).

Dance Studios.—Activities of dance studios are regulated. (6-1-105[1][w]).

Debt Management Organizations.—Activities of debt management organizations are regulated. (6-1-105[1][nn]).

Dietitians.—Deceptive trade practice to represent oneself as dietitian unless have appropriate credentials. (6-1-105[1][ee.5]).

Health Clubs.—Activities of health clubs are regulated. (6-1-105[1][t]).

Hearing Aids.—Dispensing of hearing aids is regulated. (6-1-105.5).

Home Solicitation Sales.—See topic Consumer Credit. (5-2-501 to 505).

Labeling and Packaging.—All labels of consumer commodities, as defined in 25-5-402(4), must conform to requirements for declaration of net quantity of contents of federal Fair Packaging and Labeling Act, unless exempted from federal Act. (25-5-419). Misleading packages prohibited; except as otherwise provided, commodity in package form must bear definite, plain and conspicuous declaration of quantity and, when package not sold on premises where packed, name and place of business of manufacturer, packer or distributor. (35-14-118, 119).

Loan Finders.—Activities of loan finders are regulated. (18-15-109).

Manufactured Homes.—Certain actions in connection with sales of manufactured homes are regulated. (6-1-105[1][qq]).

Misrepresentations of Academic or Honorary Degrees.—Misrepresentation concerning academic or honorary degrees is prohibited. (6-1-105[1][dd]).

Misrepresentation of Quantity or Price.—Misrepresentation of quantity (35-14-110) or price (35-14-111) of commodity or service prohibited.

Mortgage Loans.—Mortgage brokers must escrow fees earned only upon closing of loan. (38-40-101). Mortgage lenders must give written disclosure of settlement costs and conditions to guaranties of loan terms. (38-40-102). Mortgage services must give

CONSUMER PROTECTION . . . *continued*
notice of transfer of servicing responsibilities and annual report of loan activities, must respond to written inquiries for information, and must pay real property taxes on or before due date or be liable for penalties and interest. (38-40-103).

Motor Vehicle Sales.—Certain disclosures are required prior to sale of motor vehicle. (6-1-105[1][ii]).

Motor Vehicle Sales Involving Financing.—Certain actions involving financing of motor vehicle sales will constitute deceptive trade practice. (6-1-105[1][ff]).

Motor vehicle rental contracts are regulated with regard to collision damage waiver provisions. (6-1-201).

Motor Vehicle Repairs.—Certain activities in connection with motor vehicle repairs are regulated. (42-9-101 et seq.).

Motor Vehicle Service Contracts.—Issuance of motor vehicle service contracts is regulated. Issuer must obtain policy of insurance backing issuer's contractual liability. (42-11-102; 6-1-105).

Occupational Therapist.—Deceptive trade practice to represent oneself as occupational therapist unless have appropriate credentials. (6-1-105[1][ee]).

Optician.—Deceptive trade practice to represent oneself as certified optician unless have appropriate credentials. Scope of services regulated. (6-1-105[1][ee.8]).

Pet Animal Facilities.—Activities of pet animal facilities are regulated. (6-1-105[2][oo]).

Plain Language Statute.—None.

Product Liability.—One who sells article to be used as food impliedly warrants its fitness for purpose for which sold. (147 Colo. 358, 363 P.2d 667). Doctrine of res ipsa loquitur recognized. (137 Colo. 544, 328 P.2d 88). Seller's warranty, either express or implied, extends to any person who may reasonably be expected to use, consume, or be affected by goods. (4-2-318). Negligence or wilful misconduct required to recover for damages from impure blood. (13-22-104). Doctrine of strict liability in tort recognized with statutory limitations. (190 Colo. 57, 544 P.2d 983; 13-21-401 to 406; 13-21-501 to 505).

Promotional Merchandise.—Offering of prizes or free merchandise in connection with solicitation is regulated. (6-2-105).

Prize Notification.—Statements of prize winnings or eligibility to win are regulated. (6-1-105[1][jj]).

Radon.—Misrepresentation of radon test results is prohibited. (6-1-105[1][ll]).

Rental Purchase Agreements are regulated. (5-10-101; 6-1-105[1][ee]).

Replacement Automobile Crash Parts.—Sale of nonoriginal equipment crash repair parts is regulated. (10-3-1301).

Seeds.—Colorado Seed Act adopted and effective July 1, 1993. (35-27-101, et seq.). Deceptive trade practice to hold oneself out as being authorized to perform any action under act which requires registration without registering (6-1-105, 35-27-113[3][e]), soliciting to perform any of acts for which registration is required without registering (6-1-105, 35-27-113[3][f]), or making false, misleading, deceptive or fraudulent advertisements about specific lot of seed (6-1-105, 35-27-113[3][i]). Act is to be repealed as of July 1, 1999. (35-27-127).

Soil and Hazard Analyses.—Developer of residential property must give purchaser written report of soil conditions 14 days before closing. (6-6.5-101).

Telephone Solicitations.—Prevention of Telemarketing Fraud Act adopted and effective July 1, 1993. (6-1-301 et seq.). Unlawful telemarketing practices include failure to register with state as commercial telephone seller (6-3-303, 6-3-304); failure to allow cancellation at any time before expiration of three business days after purchaser's receipt of goods, services or property (6-3-304); failure to refund payments within 30 days of cancellation of goods or services, if possible, or return of goods (6-3-304); failure to disclose cancellation rights to purchaser (6-3-304); misrepresentation that any person has won contest, sweepstakes or drawing, or that person will receive free goods, services, or property (6-3-304); representing goods, services or products as free when seller charges fee for providing or delivering them (6-3-304); referencing compliance with act without informing purchaser that such compliance does not constitute governmental approval (6-3-304); and engaging in deceptive trade practices as defined by Consumer Protection Act (6-1-105, 6-1-105.5, 6-3-304). It is deceptive trade practice for telephone solicitor to fail to identify self, who solicitor represents and purpose of call within first minute of conversation or repeatedly call or engage in telephone conversation repeatedly or continuously with intent to annoy or harass. (6-1-105[1][p]). Attorney general's office may petition court for restraining orders and injunctions (6-1-110, 6-1-305), and civil penalties (6-1-112, 6-1-305). Violations may also lead to misdemeanor prosecutions (6-1-305), and civil actions by private parties for damages to $250,000 and for costs and reasonable attorney fees (6-1-113, 6-1-305).

Time Share Arrangements.—Misrepresentations in advertisement or sale of vacation time shares are prohibited. Seller must afford purchaser five-day right of rescission and contract must contain notice of such right. (6-1-105[1][s]).

Unsolicited Electronic Communications.—Deceptive trade practice to solicit Colorado consumer by fax or electronic mail without including toll-free telephone number or e-mail address to cancel further transmissions; deceptive trade practice to sell fax numbers or e-mail addresses without notice to consumers or allowing consumer to prevent sale. (6-1-105[1][p.5], [p.7]).

Unsolicited Goods.—Person receiving unsolicited goods has right to refuse to accept delivery and is not bound to return goods to sender. Goods addressed to or intended for recipient are gift to recipient. Sending bill or dunning communication for unsolicited goods constitutes class two petty offense. (6-6-101 to 6-6-103).

Uniform Deceptive Trade Practices Act adopted with modifications. It makes it unlawful to knowingly engage in deceptive trade practices which include misleading representations, advertisements and sales. (6-1-102). Deceptive trade practices also include representing goods as guaranteed without clearly and conspicuously disclosing nature and extent of guarantee, material conditions or limitations imposed by guarantor, manner in which guarantor will perform, and identity of guarantor. (6-1-105).

Remedies.—Attorney general may make examination for violations, take testimony and make copies of evidence. Attorney general can seek to enjoin deceptive practices and sue for civil penalties. Private civil actions for damages and attorneys fees are available against one who has acquired money or property by use of deceptive trade practices. (6-1-113).

Uniform Consumer Credit Code adopted. See topic Consumer Credit.

Usury.—See topic Interest.

Colorado has opted out of subsection 501(a)(1) of P.L. 96-221 removing the limits on the rate or amount of interest, discount points, finance charges, or other charges which may be charged, taken, received, or reserved with respect to loans, mortgages, credit sales, and advances made to apply in this state. (5-13-101).

Colorado has opted out of §511 of P.L. 96-221 setting interest rates on business and agricultural loans. (5-13-102).

Colorado has opted out of §524 of P.L. 96-221 which prescribes interest rates for small business loans. (5-13-103).

Wheelchairs.—Certain activities in connection with sales and services are regulated (6-1-401 et seq.) and specified express warranties required (6-1-403).

CONTRACTS:

Common law generally prevails. Seal or scroll is not necessary to proper execution of conveyance of real property. (38-30-118). Scroll has same effect as seal. (38-30-125).

By statute those 18 years old and older can legally contract as an adult but such obligation shall not be considered a family expense of person's parents. (13-22-101). See categories Documents and Records, topic Seals; Family, topic Infants.

Legislative Department Contracts.—Contract to which house of representatives is party must be approved by speaker of house; contract to which senate is party must be approved by president of senate; contract to which both house of representatives and senate are parties must be approved by both speaker of house and president of senate; contract to which legislative council, office of legislative legal services, joint budget committee, office of state auditor, or commission on uniform state laws is party must be approved by chairperson or vice chairperson of governing committee of such agency. (2-2-320[1]). For other approval requirements, see 2-2-320(2).

Public Construction Contracts.—Special provisions exist for retentions and payments in construction contracts, with public entities, exceeding $80,000. (24-91-101 to 110).

Marriage Contracts.—No contract to marry made within or outside Colorado will give rise to cause of action, and any contract made in settlement of any claim under such contract to marry is void. (13-20-202, 203, 204). These provisions, however, do not affect common law principles governing gifts made on condition of marriage. (198 Colo. 36, 596 P.2d 61).

Contracts to Make Will.—Contract to make or not to revoke will or devise executed after July 1, 1974 can be established only by provisions of will stating material provisions of contract, express reference in will to contract and extrinsic evidence proving terms of contract or writing signed by decedent evidencing contract. (15-11-701, effective until 7/1/95; 15-11-514, thereafter).

Uniform Commercial Code adopted. See topic Commercial Code.

FACTORS:

Uniform Commercial Code adopted. See topic Commercial Code.

License Requirements.—Commodity handler dealing in farm products must have annual state license; must keep records of consignments and sales; and must file bond. (12-16-101). See topic Brokers, subhead Agricultural Broker.

Liens.—Factors have general lien for advances made. (21 Colo. App. 494, 123 Pac. 110).

There is no statutory provision apart from Uniform Commercial Code for filing or recording in order to protect rights of consignor or lien of factor or commission merchant.

See also topic Sales, subhead Consignments.

FRANCHISES:

No special legislation.

FRAUDS, STATUTE OF:

Contracts for leasing for period longer than one year or for sale of land or any interest therein, are void unless contract or memorandum thereof, expressing consideration, is in writing and subscribed by lessor or seller. (38-10-108). No trust or power over in any way relating to lands can be created, granted, assigned, surrendered or declared, except by operation of law, or by deed or conveyance in writing, subscribed by party creating, granting, assigning, surrendering or declaring it. (38-10-106). However, statute of frauds does not prevent declaration of constructive trust. (198 Colo. 36, 596 P.2d 61). If court imposes constructive trust, oral agreement to reconvey real property is enforceable, despite statute of frauds. (197 Colo. 306, 592 P.2d 792).

Following are void unless agreement or memorandum thereof is in writing and subscribed by party to be charged therewith: Every agreement that by its terms is not to be performed within year from making thereof; every special promise to answer for debt or default of another; every agreement, promise or undertaking made upon consideration of marriage, except mutual promises to marry. (38-10-112). However, no debtor or creditor may file or maintain action on credit agreement involving more than $25,000 in principal unless agreement is in writing and signed by party against whom enforcement is sought. (38-10-124). Oral listing contracts for sale of real estate are valid (43 Colo. App. 467, 608 P.2d 830), as are oral settlement agreements (698 P.2d 1369), if to be performed within one year. Also, courts of equity may compel specific performance of agreements in cases of part performance. (38-10-110).

See note at head of Digest as to 1998 legislation covered.

See Topical Index in front part of this volume.

CO – 23

FRAUDS, STATUTE OF . . . *continued*

Uniform Commercial Code adopted. (4-1-101 to 11-102). See topic Commercial Code.

Sale of Goods.—Contract for sale of goods for price of $500 or more is not enforceable unless there is some writing signed by party to be charged or party's agent, sufficient to indicate contract for sale made between parties; writing is not insufficient because it omits or incorrectly states term agreed upon, but contract is not enforceable beyond quantity of goods shown in writing. However, no writing is necessary between merchants if written confirmation of contract has been received, and receiving party fails to object within ten days. Such contract is also enforceable if: (i) Goods are to be manufactured specially for buyer and are not suitable for sale to others in ordinary course of seller's business, and seller, before notice of repudiation, makes substantial beginning toward manufacture or commitment for procurement; (ii) payment for goods has been made and accepted or goods have been received and accepted; or (iii) party to be charged admits in litigation that contract for sale was made. (4-2-201).

Lease contract requiring total payments of $1,000 or more, excluding payments for option to renew or buy, is not enforceable unless there is some writing signed by party to be charged or party's agent, sufficient to indicate lease contract made between parties and to describe goods leased and lease term; writing is not insufficient because it omits or incorrectly states term agreed upon, but contract is not enforceable beyond quantity of goods shown in writing. Lease contract without such is also enforceable if: (i) Goods are to be manufactured specially for buyer and are not suitable for lease or sale to others in ordinary course of lessor's business, and lessor, before notice of repudiation, makes substantial beginning toward manufacture or commitment for procurement; (ii) goods have been received and accepted; or (iii) party to be charged admits in litigation that lease contract was made. (4-2.5-201).

Sale of Securities.—Contract for sale of securities is not enforceable unless: (1) There is some writing signed by party to be charged or party's agent or broker sufficient to indicate contract made for stated quantity of described security at defined or stated price; or (2) delivery of certificated security or transfer instruction has been accepted, or transfer of uncertificated security has been registered and transferee has failed to send written objection to issuer within ten days after receipt of initial transaction statement confirming registration, or payment has been made, but contract enforceable only to extent of such delivery, registration or payment; or (3) written confirmation within reasonable time of contract of sale or purchase sufficient against sender under (1) has been received and receiving party fails to object within ten days; or (4) party to be charged admits in litigation that contract was made for sale of stated quantity of described securities at defined or stated price. (4-8-319).

Security Agreement.—If collateral is not in possession of secured party, and subject to other Uniform Commercial Code provisions, security interest is not enforceable against debtor or third parties unless security agreement signed by debtor with description of collateral and, in case of crops or timber to be cut, description of land concerned, and unless value has been given and debtor has rights in collateral. No security interest in consumer goods used primarily for family or household purposes and owned by married person, residing with spouse when security interest created, other than purchase money security interest or certain other exemptions, is enforceable unless security agreement is signed by both spouses. Transaction is also subject to other statutes regulating loans and retail installment sales, such as Consumer Credit Code. In event of conflicting statutory provisions, such other statute controls. (4-9-203).

Sale of Personal Property Not Otherwise Covered.—Contract for sale of personal property other than goods, securities, or security agreements is not enforceable beyond $5,000 in amount or value of remedy unless there is some writing signed by party to be charged or party's agent indicating that contract for sale has been made between parties at defined or stated price and reasonably identifying subject matter. (4-1-206).

INTEREST:

Legal rate is 8%. (5-12-101). For money or property which has been "wrongfully withheld", prejudgment interest rate 8%, compounded annually, or rate which fully recognizes gain or benefit realized by person withholding money or property. Interest payable from date money or property wrongfully withheld or after it becomes due until date of payment or when judgment entered, whichever occurs first. (5-12-102[1]). Where no agreement, creditor allowed 8% from date due on any instrument or mutual settlement of accounts. (5-12-102[2]). Statute also intended to apply to damaged property. (666 P.2d 1117). Maximum rate that may be contracted for, except on loans hereinafter mentioned, is 45% per annum, calculated as annual percentage rate with all finance charges taken into account. (5-12-103). Criminal penalties for knowingly exceeding 45% annual percentage rate. (18-15-104). Rate for personal injuries set by secretary of state. (13-21-101[3-4]). Agreements in advance to pay interest on interest or compound interest are not prohibited or limited by public policy. (5-12-103[3]). Interest on consumer loans may not exceed 12% except for certain types or amounts of loans, unless made by supervised lender. (5-3-201, 508). (See topic Consumer Credit.) No interest which may accrue to savings and loan associations may be deemed usurious. (11-41-115[4]). Real estate lender may not increase loan's interest rate in excess of 1% per annum upon sale of residence. (38-30-165). Federal law preempts state law in area of interest rate increases in federal loan agreements. (649 P.2d 323).

Uniform Consumer Credit Code adopted. See topic Consumer Credit.

Credit Service Charge for Consumer Credit Sales.—For closed-end accounts, rate may not exceed greater of: (1) Sum of following amounts: 25% per year on unpaid balance not exceeding $630, 20% per year on balance over $630 but not exceeding $2,100, and 15% per year on balance over $2,100; or (2) 21% per year on unpaid balance. (5-2-201). For revolving charge accounts with monthly billing cycle, maximum rate is 1¾% of adjusted balance per month; for nonmonthly billing cycle accounts, maximum rate is pro-rated from that applicable to monthly cycle accounts. (5-2-207). (See topic Consumer Credit.)

Judgment.—Interest runs on Colorado judgments from date of entering until satisfaction at normal rate specified in contract or instrument and, if normal rate variable, then at rate in effect on date of judgment, but if no rate is specified, then at 8% compounded annually. (5-12-102[4]). Interest on judgments which appealed by judgment debtor in civil case where no written agreement, greater of 8% and rate certified by secretary of state, compounded annually, from date of entry of judgment until paid. (5-12-106[1]). Certified rate based on 2% above discount rate for commercial banks at federal reserve in Kansas City using government bond or other eligible paper as security, rounded to nearest full percent. (5-12-106[2]). If judgment modified or reversed with direction to enter judgment in trial court, interest on amount of final judgment from date of first entry of judgment. (5-12-106[1][b]). See also category Civil Actions and Procedure, topic Judgments.

Mechanics' Liens.—See category Debtor and Creditor, topic Liens.

LICENSES, BUSINESS AND PROFESSIONAL:

Licenses required for many businesses and occupations, under various statutes. See specific topics.

Collection Agency.—Collection agencies, solicitors, debt collectors and collection managers must register with and obtain license from collection agency board to be renewed annually. (12-14-115, 120, 121). Must maintain liquid assets of not less than $2,500 more than amounts due to agency's clients (12-14-123), and bond must be posted (or evidence of savings account, deposit or certificate of deposit must be presented) in sum of at least $12,000 (12-14-124). Solicitor of accounts and debt collector employed by collection agency must register with board. (12-14-125, 126). Board may conduct investigations of agencies. (12-14-130). Licensee must maintain trust account in which deposited at all times amounts sufficient to pay all amounts due to clients, submit upon request of board complete set of all form notices and form letters, maintain office in state open to public with at least one full-time employee, keep board informed of any changes in location or name and certain ownership or management changes and refrain from use of certain collection tactics. (12-14-122, 123, 128). Decisions of board may be judicially reviewed pursuant to Administrative Procedure Act. (12-14-130).

MONOPOLIES, RESTRAINT OF TRADE AND COMPETITION:

Restraint of Trade and Commerce.—Contracts or combinations in nature of trust or conspiracy in restraint of trade or commerce are illegal. Contracts, combinations, etc., intended to restrain or prevent competition in supply or price of commodity; or which control price or limit quantity of commodity; or monopolize or attempt to monopolize trade, are illegal. (6-4-101).

Mergers.—Acquisitions which may lessen competition, are illegal. (6-4-107).

Monopolization and attempted monopolization declared illegal. (6-4-105).

Exemptions.—Certain labor, agricultural and horticultural organizations excluded. Human labor not commodity. (6-4-103). Health care peer review committees immune from suit for good faith professional review actions resulting in denial or restriction of physician privileges. Sole remedy for unreasonable anticompetitive conduct is complaint before state board of medical examiners which may set aside peer review committee action. (6-4-103, 12-36-118, 12-36.5-101 to 106). Voluntary process of state approval of health care cooperative agreements with hospitals and corresponding antitrust exemption. (24-32-2701 to 2715).

Illegal Agreements.—Agreements made by conspirator which are connected with any violation are void; conspirator may not recover on agreements and payments to conspirator made under agreements can be recovered. Four year statute of limitations. (6-4-106).

Enforcement.—Violators are subject to both criminal prosecution punishable by fine (up to $100,000 for individual and $1,000,000 for business entity) and imprisonment (6-4-102, 104, 107); and civil suits for injunction and single damages (6-4-105, 108).

Unfair Practices Act.—Area or location discrimination in sale of goods or services, selling goods or services below cost, and secret rebates, are unlawful. (6-2-103, 105, 108).

Area Discriminations.—It is unlawful, with intent to destroy competition of competitor or prevent competition of potential competitor, to discriminate in price (including rebates and other devices) in goods or services between different areas or locations. Exceptions for differences in grade, quality, quantity and transportation cost, and meeting competition. Some regulated public utilities excluded. Special provisions apply to motion pictures and written material. (6-2-103).

Sales Below Cost.—It is unlawful, for purpose of injuring competitors or destroying competition, to sell, or offer or advertise to sell, goods or services below cost or give them away. (6-2-105). Exceptions in certain cases for close out sales; sales of seasonable, perishable or damaged goods; judicial sales; and meeting competition. Persons renovating personal property excluded. (6-2-110). Cost, which includes overhead, is defined (6-2-105, 106, 113) and proof of cost examined (6-2-106, 107, 112, 115). Meeting competition defined. (6-2-115).

Secret Rebates.—Secret payment or allowance of rebates, refunds, commissions, or unearned discounts, monetary or otherwise, or discriminatory and secret extension of special services or privileges, to injury of competitor and where tending to destroy competition, unlawful. (6-2-108).

Illegal Contracts.—Contracts made by person in violation of above provisions illegal; no recovery thereon may be had. (6-2-109).

Enforcement.—Violators are subject to both criminal prosecution punishable by fine and imprisonment (6-2-116); and civil suits for injunction and treble damages (6-2-111). Officer, director or agent who assists or aids person or business entity in violation of above provisions equally liable; in prosecution, it is sufficient to prove unlawful intent of person or entity for which he acts. (6-2-104).

Other Provisions.—Unlawful to advertise goods not available. (6-2-114). Use of other deceptive trade practice is prima facie evidence of intent to injure competitors and destroy or lessen competition. (6-1-105[2]).

NEGOTIABLE INSTRUMENTS:

Uniform Commercial Code adopted. See topics Commercial Code; Bills and Notes.

RESTRAINT OF TRADE:

See topic Monopolies, Restraint of Trade and Competition.

SALES:

Uniform Commercial Code adopted. See topic Commercial Code.

Bill of sale for livestock must definitely describe property sold in manner required by statute and guarantee to defend title against all lawful claims. (35-54-103). Livestock bill of sale laws not superseded by U.C.C.; passage of title to livestock is accomplished by compliance with 35-54-101 to 106. When neither party has complied, U.C.C. governs passage of title. (687 P.2d 962). There are no statutory limitations on size of type in printed contracts of sale.

Consignments.—(4-2-326). Work of fine art consigned by artist to dealer for exhibition or sale not subject to claims, liens or security interests of consignee's creditors, provisions of U.C.C. notwithstanding. (6-15-102[3]).

Conditional sales governed by Art. 9, Uniform Commercial Code. See topic Commercial Code.

Bulk Sales.—See topic Commercial Code.

Sales of Motor Vehicles.—See category Transportation, topic Motor Vehicles.

Retail credit sales are governed by 5-1-101 to 9-103, Uniform Consumer Credit Code.

Sales of Secondhand Property.—Every "secondhand dealer" must make record (on form designed by Colorado bureau of investigation or reasonable facsimile thereof) of each sale or trade of secondhand property which equals or exceeds $30 in value. Record must be mailed/delivered to local law enforcement agency within three days of sale or trade; copy of record must be maintained for one year and must be available for inspection by peace officers. (18-13-114). Secondhand dealer must keep and preserve for period of three years all invoices of goods and merchandise purchased for resale and such invoices must be open for examination by department of revenue or any peace officer. (18-13-117).

Consumer Protection.—See topic Consumer Protection

Uniform Consumer Credit Code adopted. See topic Consumer Credit.

SECURITIES:

Title of Act; Supervision.—Colorado Securities Act; administered by Securities Commissioner, Division of Securities, 1580 Lincoln Street, Suite 420, Denver, Colorado 80203.

Effective Date.—July 1, 1990. Offerings begun before that date and completed by Jan. 1, 1991 generally governed by prior statute. (11-51-802). Broker-dealers and sales representatives registered or exempt prior to July 1, 1990 became automatically licensed on that date.

Regulatory Powers of Supervising Authority.—It is unlawful for any person to offer or sell any security in Colorado unless security is registered, security is exempt, or transaction is exempt. (11-51-301).

Securities to Which Act Applicable.—"Security" means note, stock, treasury stock, bond, debenture, evidence of indebtedness, certificate of interest or participation in profit-sharing agreement, collateral-trust certificate, preorganization certificate of subscription, transferable share, investment contract, voting-trust certificate, certificate of deposit for security, certificate of interest or participation in oil, gas, or mining title or lease or in payments out of production under such title or lease, or, in general, any interest or instrument commonly known as "security" or any certificate of interest or participation in, temporary or interim certificate for, guarantee of, or warrant or right to subscribe to or purchase any of above. "Security" does not include insurance or endowment policy or annuity contract under which insurance company promises to pay sum of money either in lump sum or periodically for life or some specified period. "Investment contract" need not involve more than one person nor be limited to circumstances where there are multiple investors who are joint participants in same enterprise.

Exempt Securities.—Following securities are exempt from registration under 11-51-307: (1) Securities issued or guaranteed by U.S. or state or political subdivision or agency or instrumentality thereof or any certificate of deposit for any of them; (2) securities issued or guaranteed by Canada or province or political subdivision or agency or instrumentality thereof, or by other foreign governments with which U.S. maintains diplomatic relations; (3) securities representing interests in or debt of or guaranteed by depository institutions organized under U.S. law, or organized and supervised under any state's law; (4) securities issued or guaranteed by federal credit union or Colorado credit union or industrial loan or similar association; (5) securities issued or guaranteed by certain railroads, other common carriers, public utilities or holding companies thereof; (6) securities listed or approved for listing on notice of issuance on New York stock exchange, American stock exchange, Midwest stock exchange, Pacific stock exchange, PBW or Boston stock exchange or Chicago board of options exchange, or securities designated or approved for designation on notice of issuance in NASDAQ-national market system; or securities of equal or senior rank to such listed or approved security or called for by subscription rights or warrants so listed or approved, or any warrants or rights to purchase any of them; (7) securities issued by person organized and operated not for private profit but exclusively for religious, educational, benevolent, or charitable purposes or as chamber of commerce or trade or professional association and offered or sold to bona fide constituent or member of such organization or association, if no direct or indirect commission or remuneration is paid in connection with offer or sale except to licensed broker-dealer; or securities issued by cooperative association engaged in sale or production of electricity and regulated by Colorado public utilities commission; (8) commercial paper arising out of current transaction or proceeds of which have been or are to be used for current transactions and which evidence obligation to pay cash within nine months of date of issuance, exclusive of days of grace, or renewal of such paper which is likewise limited, or guarantee of such paper or of such renewal; (9) securities issued in connection with employee's stock purchase, savings, pension, profit-sharing, or similar benefit plan; (10) securities issued by cooperative association as defined in 7-55-101; (11) securities of certain registered investment companies or unit trusts; and (12) other securities exempted by rule of securities commissioner. (11-51-309).

Exempt Transactions.—Following transactions are exempt from registration under 11-51-308: (1) Isolated nonissuer transactions whether or not through broker-dealer; (2) nonissuer distributions of outstanding securities: (a) if recognized securities manual contains name of issuer, names of issuer's officers and directors, balance sheet of issuer as of date within 18-month period immediately preceding date of distribution, and profit and loss statement for either fiscal year preceding that date or most recent year of operations, (b) if securities have fixed maturity or fixed interest or dividend provisions and there has been no default by issuer during current fiscal year or within three preceding fiscal years, or during existence of issuer and predecessors if less than three years, in payment of principal, interest, or dividend on any security of issuer, (c) if any class of securities of issuer is registered under §12 of Securities Exchange Act of 1934, (d) if issuer is investment company registered under Investment Company Act of 1940, or (e) if issuer of securities has filed and maintained with securities commissioner, for not less than 90 days next preceding transaction, such information as securities commissioner may specify by rule and has paid exemption fee; (3) nonissuer transactions effected by or through licensed broker-dealer pursuant to unsolicited order or offer to buy, if either confirmation of transaction delivered to customer clearly states that transaction was unsolicited or broker-dealer obtains written acknowledgement signed by customer that transaction was unsolicited and copy of confirmation or acknowledgment is preserved by broker-dealer for such period as securities commissioner may, by rule, require; (4) transactions between issuer or other person on whose behalf offering is made and underwriter or among underwriters; (5) transactions in bonds or other evidences of indebtedness secured by mortgage, security interest, or deed of trust or by agreement for sale of real estate or chattels, if entire mortgage, security interest, deed of trust, or agreement together will all bonds or other evidences of indebtedness secured thereby is offered and sold as unit; (6) transactions by executor, administrator, sheriff, marshal, receiver, trustee in bankruptcy, guardian, or conservator; (7) transactions executed by bona fide pledgees without purpose of evading provisions of statute; (8) offers or sales to financial or institutional investors or to broker-dealers, whether purchaser is acting for itself or in fiduciary capacity; (9) transactions not involving any public offering; (10) transactions pursuant to offering of securities directed to not more than 20 persons (other than than those designated in [8] above) in Colorado and sold to not more than ten buyers (other than those designated in [8]above) in Colorado during any period of 12 consecutive months, whether or not offeror or offerees or buyers are then present in Colorado, if: (a) seller reasonably believes that all buyers in Colorado (other than those designated in [8] above) are purchasing for investment, and (b) no commission or other remuneration is paid or given directly or indirectly for soliciting any prospective buyer in Colorado (other than those designated in [8] above) except to licensed broker-dealer or sales representative; (11) offers or sales of preorganization certificates or subscriptions if no commission or other remuneration is paid or given directly or indirectly for soliciting any prospective subscriber, if number of subscribers does not exceed 25, and if no payment is made by any subscriber; (12) transactions pursuant to offers to existing security holders of issuer, including persons who are holders of convertible securities, nontransferable warrants, or transferable warrants exercisable within not more than 90 days of their issuance, if no commission or other remuneration (other than standby commission) is paid or given directly or indirectly for soliciting any security holder in Colorado except to licensed or exempt broker-dealer; (13) transactions involving offers to sell, but not sales, if: (a) registration or offering statement or similar document as required under Securities Act of 1933 has been filed with securities and exchange commission, but is not effective, (b) registration statement, if required, has been filed under 11-51-303, but is not effective, and (c) no stop order of which offeror is aware has been entered by securities commissioner or securities and exchange commission; (14) transactions involving offers to sell, but not sales, if: (a) registration statement has been filed under 11-51-304 but is not effective, and (b) no stop order of which offeror is aware has been entered by securities commissioner; (15) transactions in which security holders vote for certain reclassifications of securities, mergers, consolidations or similar plans of acquisition, or for transfers of assets if (a) plan provides for dissolution of entity whose security holders are voting, (b) securities will be distributed to securities holders, (c) board or similar representative causes such dissolution or distribution within one year after such vote, or (d) such transfer of assets is part of preexisting plan for distribution of securities (11-51-201[13][g]); (16) offers or sales of securities in compliance with exemption from registration with securities and exchange commission pursuant to regulations adopted under 3(b) or 4(2) of Securities Act of 1933 and issuer files with securities commissioner notification of exemption, upon such form as securities commissioner may prescribe, and pay exemption fee; and (17) other transactions exempted by rule of securities commissioner (11-51-309). Transactions exempt under Securities Act of 1933 (except intrastate offerings) also exempt in Colorado. (11-51-311).

Registration of Securities.—Securities for which registration statement has been filed under Securities Act of 1933 may be registered by filing. (11-51-303). Securities may be registered by qualification. (11-51-304). If issuer has principal office and majority of full-time employees in Colorado, if at least 80% of proceeds are to be used in Colorado, and if gross proceeds less than $1,000,000 in any 12 month period, limited offering registration procedure may be used. (11-51-304[6]).

Licensing of Dealers, Brokers, and Others.—In order for broker-dealer, sales representative, investment adviser or investment adviser representative to transact business in Colorado, such person must be licensed. (11-51-401). Exam may be required by securities commissioner for broker-dealer not registered under Securities Exchange Act of 1934 and for sales representative acting for such broker-dealer (11-51-405), and for investment adviser representative.

Following broker-dealers are exempt from license requirement under 11-51-402(1): (1) Broker-dealers registered as broker-dealers under Securities Exchange Act of 1934 who have no place of business in Colorado if business transacted in Colorado as broker-dealer is exclusively with issuers in transactions involving their own securities, other broker-dealers licensed or exempt from licensing in Colorado, except when acting as clearing broker-dealer for such other broker-dealers, financial or institutional investors,

See note at head of Digest as to 1998 legislation covered.

See Topical Index in front part of this volume.

CO – 25

SECURITIES . . . *continued*
individuals who are existing customers of broker-dealer and whose principal places of residence are not in Colorado, and during any 12 consecutive months, not more than five persons in Colorado, excluding persons described above; and (2) other broker-dealers securities commissioner by rule or order exempts. Following sales representatives are exempt from license requirement under 11-51-402(2): (1) Sales representatives employed or otherwise engaged by exempt broker-dealer; (2) sales representatives employed or otherwise engaged by issuers in effecting transactions only in certain exempt securities (including government, depository institution, credit union and cooperative association securities); (3) sales representatives employed by issuers in effecting transactions only with employees, partners, officers, or directors of issuer or of parent or subsidiaries of issuer, if no commission or other similar compensation is paid or given directly or indirectly to sales representative for soliciting employee, partner, officer, or director in Colorado; (4) licensed real estate brokers or salesmen trading only in securities comprised of notes, bonds, or evidences of indebtedness secured by mortgages or deeds of trust on real estate, where brokers or salesmen act as agent for buyer or seller of real estate securing note, bond, or evidence of indebtedness being traded and is neither issuer nor affiliated with or under direct or indirect control of issuer or affiliate of issuer of note, bond, or evidence of indebtedness (11-51-402[3]); and (5) other sales representatives securities commissioner by rule or order exempts. Following investment advisers are exempt from license requirement under 11-51-401(5): (1) those exempt from Federal registration; (2) those whose only clients in Colorado are: other investment advisers; Federal registered advisers; broker-dealers; depository institutions; insurance companies; employee benefit plans with assets of not less than $1,000,000; other institutional investors other than local government investment pool trust funds, as securities commissioner by rule or order exempts; (3) those with not more than five clients during preceding 12 months, other than those specified in (2); (4) other investment advisers securities commissioner by rule or order exempts. Investment adviser representatives employed by or otherwise associated with exempt investment adviser are exempt from license requirement.

Liabilities.—Injunctive action by securities commissioner, including damages or other equitable relief. (11-51-602). Securities commissioner may issue consent orders, summary stop orders and orders to show cause. (11-51-606). Criminal penalties for willful violations. (11-51-603). Civil liability for consideration paid with interest at statutory rate from date of payment, costs and reasonable attorney fees, less income received on security, upon tender of security, or for damages if buyer no longer owns security. (11-51-604). Damages are amount recoverable on tender, less value of security when buyer sold it, and interest at statutory rate from date of sale. No liability for failure to file notification of exemption or pay fee for transactions exempt under 3(b) or 4(2) of Securities Act of 1933. Same civil liability for violation of broker-dealer and sales representative licensing requirements, with limited exceptions. (11-51-604[2][b]). Same civil liability for sales in which untrue statements of material facts are made or material facts omitted (buyer not knowing of untruth or omission), unless seller sustains burden of proof that he did not know and in exercise of reasonable care could not have known of untruth or omission. (11-51-604[4]). For violations of anti-fraud provisions made recklessly, knowingly or with intent to defraud, such legal or equitable relief as court deems appropriate. (11-51-604[3]). Controlling persons are liable for violations of registration and broker-dealer and sales representative licensing requirements unless they sustain burden of proof that they did not know, and in exercise of reasonable care could not have known, of existence of facts by reason of which liability is alleged to exist. Controlling persons are liable for violations of anti-fraud provisions unless they sustain burden of proof that they acted in good faith and did not, directly or indirectly, induce acts constituting violation or cause of action. Any person who knows that another person is liable under anti-fraud provisions and who gives substantial assistance to such conduct is liable to extent as such other person. (11-51-604[5]). Contribution may be sought on basis of actual relative culpability of persons jointly liable. (11-51-604[13]). In case of certain willful violations of securities commissioner orders, Denver District Court may impose contempt sanctions. (11-51-604[14]).

Rescission offer made by written offer before suit to refund consideration paid with interest at statutory rate from date of payment, less income received on security. If made when buyer owned security, buyer may not sue if buyer fails to accept offer within 30 days. If buyer no longer owns security, buyer may not sue unless buyer rejects offer in writing within 30 days. (11-51-604[9]).

Statute of Limitations.—In civil actions for violation of registration and broker-dealer and sales representative licensing requirements, two years after contract of sale. In civil actions for violation of anti-fraud provisions, three years from discovery of facts giving rise to cause of action or after discovery should have been made by exercise of reasonable diligence, and in no event more than five years after purchase or sale. (11-51-604[8]). In criminal actions, five years from commission of offense.

Special District Bonds.—Bonds issued by special districts must be registered unless exempt. (11-59-106).

Nonrated Public Securities Report.—State, political subdivisions thereof and other public corporate bodies that issue nonrated public securities must file annual information report with Department of Local Affairs for years ending on or after Dec. 31, 1991. Excludes conduit financings. (11-58-101).

Uniform Transfer on Death Security Registration Act adopted. (15-15-301).

Uniform Simplification of Fiduciary Security Transfers Act adopted. (15-1-601).

STATUTE OF FRAUDS:

See topic Frauds, Statute of.

TRUST RECEIPT SECURITY:

Uniform Commercial Code adopted. See topic Commercial Code.

WAREHOUSEMEN:

Uniform Commercial Code adopted. See topic Commercial Code.

CITIZENSHIP

ALIENS:

Aliens may not vote or hold office as governor, lieutenant governor, secretary of state, state treasurer, attorney general, senator, representative, justice, judge or district attorney or be elected or appointed to any civil or military office in state. (Colo. Const., art. IV, §4; art. V, §4; art. VI, §§8, 11, 13-16; art. VII, §§1, 6). No unemployment benefits may be paid on basis of services performed by alien not lawfully admitted into U.S. for permanent residence or to perform such services or permanently residing in U.S. under color of law at time services were performed. (8-73-107[7][a]). Alien not eligible for public assistance unless is legal immigrant otherwise eligible in all respects for citizenship, and if has resided in U.S. less than three years is not eligible for old age pension without showing his sponsor lacks sufficient resources to meet needs of alien. (26-2-111[1][a], [2][c]). Department of revenue may not issue driver's license to illegal alien. (42-2-104[3][e]). Failure to advise alien criminal defendant of immigration consequences of guilty plea is ineffective assistance of counsel, entitling alien to new trial. (Colo. Const., Art. II, §16; 746 P.2d 534, 524).

Property.—Aliens, who are or may become bona fide residents of state, may acquire, inherit, possess, enjoy and dispose of property, real and personal, as native born citizens. (Colo. Const., art. II, §27). No person is disqualified as heir, devisee, grantee, lessee, mortgagee, assignee, or other transferee because he or person through whom he claims is or has been alien. (15-11-111).

CIVIL ACTIONS AND PROCEDURE

ACCORD AND SATISFACTION:

Governed by common law. Executory accord does not bar cause of action to collect original debt without evidence of express acceptance as satisfaction thereof, unless there is intent that performance of accord agreement is condition precedent to discharge of original agreement. (163 Colo. 408, 431 P.2d 14; 642 P.2d 47). Executory accord suspends performance of original obligation until accord is breached or satisfied. (689 P.2d 1166). Non-dischargeable judgment against one defendant operates as accord and satisfaction as to plaintiff and that defendant, but not as to remaining defendant who was not party to judgment. (695 P.2d 317). Satisfaction of corporate obligation by one director discharges obligation of other directors who were jointly liable on same claim. (770 P.2d 1352).

Uniform Commercial Code adopted. See category Business Regulation and Commerce, topic Commercial Code.

Compromise.—If claim is disputed, lesser amount paid in compromise discharges liability. (6 Colo. 162). Acceptance and negotiation of check tendered in full satisfaction of obligation discharges underlying obligation notwithstanding restrictive endorsement. (680 P.2d 1342). Uniform Commercial Code 1-207 (4-1-207) does not alter rule concerning "conditioned" checks, but restrictive endorsement on check giving partial refund of security deposit is void under 38-12-103(7). (737 P.2d 417). Settlement agreements and general releases of liability are void if entered into between person who was injured and receiving treatment as result of occurrence which might give rise to liability and person whose interest is adverse to injured party, if agreement or release is obtained within 30 days from date of injury. (13-21-301).

Uniform Consumer Credit Code adopted. See category Business Regulation and Commerce, topic Consumer Credit.

Pleading.—Must be affirmatively pleaded as a defense. (Rule 8[c]).

ACTIONS:

Rules for civil action are based upon Colorado Rules of Civil Procedure. See topic Practice. Additional rules for civil actions are set forth in Rules of County Court Civil Procedure.

Equity.—No separate equity jurisdiction. However, traditional equitable grounds must be shown for equitable relief.

Forms of Action.—There is but one form of action known as "civil action." (Rule 2). Special forms of pleadings in habeas corpus, mandamus, certiorari, quo warranto, prohibition, scire facias and other remedial writs are abolished. (Rule 106[a]).

Conditions Precedent.—No general rule. See particular topics.

Commencement.—Civil action is commenced by filing complaint with court or serving summons and complaint upon defendant. If action is commenced by service of summons and complaint, complaint must be filed within ten days after service, or service of summons shall be deemed to be ineffective and void without notice. In such case court may, in its discretion, tax reasonable sum in favor of defendant to compensate defendant for expense and inconvenience, including attorney's fees, to be paid by plaintiff or his attorney. Ten-day filing requirement may be expressly waived by defendant and shall be deemed waived upon filing of responsive pleading or motion to complaint without reserving issue. (Rule 3[a]). Court has jurisdiction from filing of complaint or service of summons and complaint, provided that if more than ten days elapses after service upon defendant before filing complaint, jurisdiction as to defendant shall not attach by virtue of service. (Rule 3[b]). See also topics Process, Pleading.

Mandatory Arbitration.—No civil action filed in any judicial district after July 1, 1991, is subject to mandatory arbitration. (13-22-402). Local court rules may require nonbinding alternative dispute resolution procedures.

Parties.—Action must be prosecuted in name of real party in interest. Executor, administrator, guardian, conservator, trustee of express trust, party with whom or in whose name contract has been made for benefit of another, or party authorized by statute may sue in his own name without joining with him party for whose benefit action is brought. (Rule 17[a]). Partnership or unincorporated association may sue or be sued in its common name. (Rule 17[b]).

See note at head of Digest as to 1998 legislation covered.

See Topical Index in front part of this volume.

CO – 26

ACTIONS . . . *continued*

Person subject to service must be joined if in his absence complete relief cannot be afforded those already parties or if he claims interest in subject of action and disposition of action in his absence may either endanger that interest or create a risk of further liability to present parties to action. (Rule 19[a]). If such person cannot be joined, court must determine whether interests of justice require dismissal. (Rule 19[b]). Persons having joint interest must be joined on same side, except that one who should be joint plaintiff but refuses to join may be made defendant or an involuntary plaintiff. (686 P.2d 1357; Rule 19[a]). Joined party must be dismissed from action if he objects to venue and his joinder would make venue improper. (Rule 19[a]). Court may order parties to be dropped or added. Misjoinder of parties is equivalent to dismissal without prejudice of claim against that party. (Rule 21; 641 P.2d 916). Leave of court may be required to add or replace parties even though no responsive pleading has been filed. (641 P.2d 916).

All persons asserting any right to relief in respect of or arising out of same transaction or occurrence may join as plaintiffs, and all persons against whom any such right is asserted may be joined as defendants, provided, in either case, that some question of law or fact common to all of them will arise in the action. (Rule 20[a]). All or any persons jointly and severally liable may be sued in same action. (Rule 20[c]).

In actions affecting real property, no persons claiming under or through named defendant need be made parties, unless interest shown of record, but are bound by judgment. Persons in possession must be joined in action to recover actual possession. (Rule 105[b]; 38-35-114).

Pretrial Procedure Prior to Jan. 1, 1995.—In every action except juvenile, mental health, marriage dissolution proceedings and mandatory arbitration unless ordered by court, disclosure certificate must be filed 180 days after case is at issue but no later than 90 days before trial whichever is first. (Rule 16[a]). Limited disclosure certificate supplementation. (Rule 16[b]). Disclosure certificate binding. (Rule 16[c]). Discovery cut-off 30 days prior to trial. (Rule 16[f]). Expert witness summaries due 80 days before trial. (Rule 16[g]).

Pretrial Procedure as of Jan. 1, 1995.—In every action except domestic relations, juvenile, mental health, probate, water law, forcible entry and detainer, and expedited actions, lead counsel shall confer with each other about nature and basis of claims and matters to be disclosed pursuant to Rule 26(a)(1) no later than 15 days after case is at issue, shall accomplish Rule 26(a)(1) disclosures no later than 30 days after case is at issue, shall explore possibilities of prompt settlement or resolution of case no later than 35 days after case is at issue, and shall file proposed case management order no later than 45 days after case is at issue. (Rule 16[b]). Case is at issue when all parties have been served and all pleadings permitted by Rule 7 have been filed or defaults or dismissals have been entered against nonappearing parties, or such other time as court shall direct. (Rule 16[b]). Proposed trial management order shall be filed no later than 30 days prior to date scheduled for trial or such time as court shall direct. (Rule 16[c]). There are limited rights to modify or diverge from case management orders and trial management orders. (Rules 16[b] and [c]). No less than seven days prior to trial, each party shall identify witnesses to be called, order they are to be called, and their anticipated length of testimony. (Rule 16[c][4]). Set of proposed jury instructions and verdict forms shall be filed with courtroom clerk jointly by counsel for parties no later than three days prior to trial. (Rule 16[d]). For further details, consult Rules 16, 26, 29, 30–34, 37, 121-1-11, 121-1-12, 121-1-15, and 121-1-19, as amended to take effect Jan. 1, 1995.

Class Actions.—Any action may be maintained as class action if court finds that requirements of Rule 23 have been met. (Rule 23[b]). Class action cannot be compromised or dismissed without court approval. (Rule 23[e]). Judgment may only include members of class. (34 Colo. App. 405, 527 P.2d 899). Uniform Class Actions Act not adopted.

Intervention may be of right or permissive as defined by Rule 24. In absence of showing that he is not adequately represented by existing parties to action, taxpayer cannot intervene as matter of right in action brought or defended by municipality. (152 Colo. 567, 384 P.2d 96).

Interpleader.—Plaintiff or defendant exposed to multiple liability may interplead claimants. (Rule 22).

Third Party Practice.—Defendant may bring in third party who is or may be liable to him for all or part of plaintiff's claim and plaintiff may proceed similarly with respect to counterclaim. Unless third-party plaintiff files his complaint within ten days after service of his answer, he must obtain permission from court on motion with notice to all parties. (Rule 14.)

Joinder of Causes of Action.—A party may join as many claims, legal or equitable, as he has against an opposing party either as independent or alternate claims. (Rule 18[a]).

Splitting Causes of Action.—See subhead Severance of Actions, infra.

Consolidation of Actions.—Court may consolidate pending actions involving common question of law or fact or may order joint hearing or trial of any or all issues. (Rule 42[a]).

Consolidated Multidistrict Litigation.—Actions involving common question of law or fact that are pending in different judicial districts may be transferred to any judge for hearing or trial provided that any jury trial is held in place prescribed by Rule 98 and that actions are consolidated in accordance with Rule 42. (Rule 42.1[b]).

Motions for transfer may be initiated by panel on consolidated multidistrict litigation or by party in any action in which transfer may be appropriate. (Rule 42.1[c]).

Panel will rule on motions for transfer and will transfer actions if one judge hearing all of actions will promote just and efficient conduct of actions and will serve ends of justice. (Rule 42.1[g]).

Severance of Actions.—Court may order separate trial of any issue or of any number of claims, cross-claims, counterclaims or third-party claims. (Rule 42[b]).

Stay of Proceedings.—In order for pendency of one action to be ground for stay of another action, suits must be identical such that disposition in one will determine all issues in other. (132 Colo. 144, 285 P.2d 831).

Abatement and Revival.—All causes of action except libel or slander survive and may be brought or continued after death of party in favor of or against whom accrued. (13-20-101[1]). Claim for exemplary damages expires with death of personal injury plaintiff. (42 Colo. App. 141, 594 P.2d 1064). Must serve personal representative of deceased defendant and file claim against estate within time and in manner required for other claims against estate. (13-20-101[2]). See also category Estates and Trusts, topic Executors and Administrators.

Limitation of.—See topic Limitation of Actions.

Small Claims.—See category Courts and Legislature, topic Courts.

Termination of Actions.—Actions, counterclaims, cross-claims or third party claims may be dismissed voluntarily or by court upon defendant's motion for failure to prosecute or failure to comply with Rules or court order. Involuntary dismissal operates as adjudication upon merits unless court specifies otherwise, except that dismissals for failure to prosecute (Rule 121) that do not specify are deemed without prejudice (Rule 41).

Prohibited Actions.—All civil causes of action for breach of promise to marry, alienation of affections, criminal conversation, and seduction are abolished (13-20-202), although this abolition does not extend to affect common law principles governing gift made on condition of marriage, with condition broken by donee (198 Colo. 36, 596 P.2d 61). Actions based on flight of aircraft over lands or waters within state are prohibited unless other than nominal damage results or irreparable damage is probable. (13-21-118). Action by individual for bodily injury caused by motor vehicle accident where medical expenses are $2,500 or less is prohibited. (10-4-714). See category Transportation, topic Motor Vehicles, subhead No-Fault Insurance.

Administration.—See category Estates and Trusts, topic Executors and Administrators.

Direct actions against insurer not authorized by statute. See category Transportation, topic Motor Vehicles, subhead Direct Actions.

APPEAL AND ERROR:

Appeal to supreme court and court of appeals governed by Colorado Appellate Rules, which are patterned on Federal Rules of Appellate Procedure. See also topic Certiorari and category Courts and Legislature, topic Courts.

Matters Appealable.—Appeal to appellate court may be taken from: final judgment of any district, superior, probate or juvenile court; judgment and decree, or any portion thereof, in proceeding concerning water rights; order refusing, granting, modifying, cancelling, affirming or continuing in whole or in part conditional water right, or determination that reasonable diligence or progress has or has not been shown in enterprise granted conditional water right; order granting or denying temporary injunction; and order appointing or denying appointment of, or sustaining or overruling motion to discharge, receiver. (App. Rule 1[a]). Matters designated by statute to be reviewable by writ of error are now reviewed on appeal. (App. Rule 1[c]).

Interlocutory orders in civil cases are generally unappealable, although supreme court will exercise original jurisdiction where judicial discretion has been abused and damage to party could not be cured on appeal. (196 Colo. 102, 581 P.2d 302). Where alternative theories asserted and one theory dismissed, such dismissal is not decision on entire claim for relief and therefore not appealable. (682 P.2d 501). Dismissal of complaint against one of multiple defendants on ground of lack of personal jurisdiction may be certified under Rule 54(b) as appealable final judgment. (685 P.2d 769).

Supreme Court.—Appeal lies directly to supreme court in: (a) Cases in which statute, municipal charter provision, or ordinance has been declared unconstitutional; (b) cases concerned with decisions or actions of public utilities commission; (c) water cases involving priorities or adjudications; (d) cases appealed from county court to district court; (e) writs of habeas corpus; (f) summary proceedings in connection with elections (13-4-102[1]); and (g) cases in which sentence of death has been imposed (13-4-102[1][h]; App. Rule 4[d]).

Extent of Review.—Ordinarily, confined to questions of law and sufficiency of evidence. For exceptions, see subheads To District Court and To County Court, infra.

Judgment or Order on Appeal.—Appellate court may affirm, reverse or modify judgment or order, and may remand for further proceedings. (App. Rule 35).

To Court of Appeals.—Court of appeals has initial appellate jurisdiction over appeals from final judgments of district court, and probate and juvenile courts of Denver, except as to matters listed in (a) through (g) in subhead Supreme Court, supra. It also has initial jurisdiction to review awards or actions of industrial claim appeals office, orders of banking board granting or denying charters for new state banks, decisions of state personnel board, actions and orders of state grievance board, final decisions and orders of civil rights commission and real estate commission, decisions of board of education in proceedings for dismissal of teacher, and all final actions and orders appropriate for judicial review of board of engineers and professional land surveyors, podiatry board, board of assessment appeals, state electrical board, board of chiropractic examiners, board of nursing, board of pharmacy, passenger tramway safety board, coal mine board of examiners, Colorado state board of architects, examining board of plumbers, directors of division of registration and racing commission. Court of appeals has initial jurisdiction over appeals from actions of board of medical examiners and board of dental examiners granting, revoking or suspending licenses or placing holder thereof on probation and actions of board of optometric examiners in refusing to grant or renew, revoking or suspending license, issuing letter of admonition, or placing on probation and to review final actions and orders of Colorado state board of psychologist examiners, state board of social work examiners, state board of marriage and family therapist examiners, state board of nursing in division of registrations in department of regulatory agencies, state board of licensed professional counselor examiners, Commissioner of Insurance, and final actions and orders of Department of Revenue relating to penalties for violations of statutes relating to sale of cigarettes and tobacco products to minors. (13-4-102[2]).

Certification of Cases to Supreme Court.—Court of appeals, prior to final determination, may certify any case before it to supreme court for its determination. Supreme

See note at head of Digest as to 1998 legislation covered.

See Topical Index in front part of this volume.

APPEAL AND ERROR . . . *continued*

court may accept certification or remand to court of appeals. (13-4-109[1]&[2]). Supreme court may decide any case pending before court of appeals by ordering certification (13-4-109[3]), granting writ of certiorari (App. Rule 50[a]), or requiring transfer (App. Rule 50[b]).

Limitation on Taking Appeal.—Filing of motion for post-trial relief is not condition precedent to appeal. All post-trial motions for relief must be filed within 15 days of date of judgment, or such greater time as court may allow, including motion for new trial based on newly discovered evidence. (Rule 59). Generally, notice of appeal required by App. Rule 3 must be filed with appellate court and advisory copy served on trial court within 45 days of entry of judgment or order being appealed from. (App. Rule 4[a]). Filing timely post-trial motion terminates running of time for filing appeal, and time begins to run anew with denial of motion. Court must determine any post-trial motion within 60 days of filing such motion; otherwise, motion deemed denied for all purposes upon expiration of 60-day period and time for appeal commences as of that date. (Rule 59[j]). Timely filing of notice of appeal is mandatory and jurisdictional, and parties to appeal may not stipulate to amend or waive this jurisdictional requirement. (36 Colo. App. 181, 538 P.2d 1343). App. Rules 10 and 11 set time limits for designation and transmission of record on appeal.

Stay of Proceedings.—Application for stay of judgment, approval of supersedeas bond or order affecting injunction during pendency of appeal must ordinarily be made first in trial court. However, motion for such relief may be made to supreme court or court of appeals, but must recite reason for so proceeding. (App. Rule 8[a]). Appellate court may condition relief upon filing of bond or other appropriate security in trial court. Court may dispense with or limit amount of bond in case of fiduciary, where fiduciary bond is sufficient, and bond need not be furnished by public officers or bodies or charitable and educational institutions of state. (App. Rule 8[b]&[c]).

Appeal Bond.—Unless appellant exempted by law or has filed supersedeas bond which includes security for payment of costs on appeal, bond for costs on appeal or equivalent security in sum of $250 must be filed in civil cases with notice of appeal, unless trial court fixes different amount. (App. Rule 7).

See topic Practice.

To District Court.—Appeals from final judgments of county courts and municipal courts of record are taken to district court for judicial district in which county or municipal court is located. Appeals are based upon record made in trial court. (13-6-310; 13-10-116[2]). On review of trial court judgment, district court reviews case on record, and may affirm, reverse, remand, or modify judgment, or may remand case for new trial with such instructions as it may deem necessary, or it may direct that case be tried de novo before district court. (13-6-310). Motion for new trial is not a prerequisite to appeal. (Rule 359[a]). If motion for new trial is filed, it must be in writing and be filed within 15 days of entry of judgment. (Rule 359[b]). If motion is made, only matters raised in motion shall be considered on appeal. Notice of appeal must be filed in trial court within 15 days after date of entry of judgment (unless motion for new trial is made, in which event time for appeal is extended to 15 days after disposition of motion [Rule 359]), with appeal bond (or cash deposit) which must also be filed with court clerk within 15 days. (13-6-311, Rule 411). If bond is used, it must be furnished by corporate surety authorized and licensed to do business in Colorado, or by one or more sufficient private sureties. Bonds are conditioned to pay costs and judgment amount if appealing parties fail, and must be approved by judge or clerk. Appellant must docket appeal and pay docket fee within 30 days after filing notice of appeal. Appellant must deposit estimated fee for preparing record with clerk. After filing of notice, bond, and estimated record fee, county court must recall any execution issued. Record transcript or stipulation must be prepared within 40 days after judgment. Parties have 15 days after notification of completion of record to file objections thereto. Record is certified by trial judge and filed with clerk of district court by clerk of trial court. Appellant must file brief within 20 days after such filing and appellee may file answering brief within 20 days after service of appellant's brief, unless court extends time for filing. (13-6-311[4], Rule 411).

To County Court.—Appeals from municipal courts not of record are made to county courts where trial is de novo. (13-10-116[1]).

BONDS:

Sureties.—Any bond executed as surety by company qualified as provided in statutes constitutes full compliance with any law, charter, ordinance, rule or regulation requiring that bond be executed by one or more sureties or that sureties be residents, householders or freeholders or possess any other qualifications. (10-4-301). Statutory requirement of surety bond as condition to licensure or authority to conduct business or perform duties may, in certain situations, be satisfied by qualified savings account or certificate of deposit. (11-35-101; 11-35-101[1]; 11-35-101.5). When surety given pursuant to C.R.C.P., surety submits himself to jurisdiction of court. (Rule 65.1).

Actions on bonds in civil actions follow the same rules as other civil actions.

CERTIORARI:

In Supreme Court.—Writs of certiorari lie to review judgments of court of appeals (13-4-108), cases pending in court of appeals (App. Rule 50), and determinations of district court on cases appealed from county court (13-6-310). Certiorari granted by supreme court within its judicial discretion only when special and important reasons exist therefor, (App. Rule 49). Additionally, court of appeals may review decisions of industrial claim appeals panel in workers' compensation cases under Arts. 40 to 47 of Title 8, C.R.S. by writ of certiorari.

Procedure.—Petition, proof of service, certified transcript of record below, and filing fee (petitioner, $150; respondent, $75) must be filed with clerk of supreme court. (App. Rule 51).

Review of Court of Appeals Judgment.—Petition for rehearing must first be filed with court of appeals. (13-4-108[1]). Certiorari petition must be filed within 30 days after denial of rehearing, except in workers' compensation and unemployment insurance cases, where petition must be filed within 15 days. (App. Rule 52[b]).

Review of Case Pending in Court of Appeals.—Certiorari petition may be filed by either party or by stipulation of parties. Transfer may be requested by court of appeals or required by supreme court. (App. Rule 50[b]).

Review of District or Superior Court Judgment.—Certiorari petition must be filed within 30 days after final judgment. (App. Rule 52[a]).

In District Court.—Relief in nature of certiorari may be obtained in district court where any governmental body or officer or lower judicial body exercising judicial or quasi-judicial functions exceeded its jurisdiction or abused its discretion and no plain, speedy and adequate remedy exists. (Rule 106[a][4][II]).

Procedure.—Initiated by complaint in district court. (Rule 106[a][4][II]). If no time within which review may be sought is provided by statute, complaint seeking review under Rule 106(a)(4) must be filed in district court within 30 days after final decision of body or officer. Timely complaint may be amended at any time with leave of court for good cause shown. (Rule 106[b]). Thirty-day time limitation is jurisdictional. (807 P.2d 541).

See also topic Appeal and Error.

CHARITABLE IMMUNITY:

See topic Damages.

COSTS:

Civil.—Except where express provision therefor by statute or court rule, costs in civil action (Rule 54[d]) and on appeal (App. Rule 39[a]) awarded to prevailing party, unless court in exercise of sound discretion otherwise directs. Costs may be imposed against state, its officers or agencies only where permitted by law. (Rule 54[d]; App. Rule 39[b]). Costs may be assessed against public entity sued pursuant to Governmental Immunity Act. (718 P.2d 221).

Procedure.—Bill of costs must be filed within 15 days of judgment or such greater time as court may allow. (Rule 121, §1-22). Costs may be taxed by clerk on one day's notice, subject to review by court upon motion served within five days after clerk's taxing. (Rule 54[d]). On appeal, following costs are taxed in appellate court, upon itemized and verified bill of costs filed within 14 days after entry of judgment: cost of printing or producing copies of briefs, copies of records and docket fees. (App. Rule 39[c]). All other costs on appeal taxed in trial court. (App. Rule 39[e]).

Recoverable Costs.—Items that may be taxed as costs include, without limitation, docket fees, jury fees and expenses, sheriff's fees, expert witness charges, mileage fees, witness fees, photocopying fees, costs of depositions for perpetuating testimony, service of process fees and attorneys' fees when authorized by statute or court rule. (13-16-122). Recoverable costs on appeal include costs of printing or producing copies of briefs or copies of records, docket fees, preparing and transmitting record, reporter's transcript, and premiums for bonds. (Rule 39[c], [e]). Attorneys' fees recoverable upon motion for frivolous, groundless or vexatious actions or if action interposed for delay or harassment or if attorney or party unnecessarily expanded proceeding. (13-17-102). If appeal is frivolous, appellate court may award damages, including attorneys' fees and single or double costs. (App. Rule 38[d]; 40 Colo. App. 556, 580 P.2d 825).

Security For Costs.—Cost bonds required for injunction (Rule 65), receiver (Rule 66), attachment (Rule 102), replevin (Rule 104) and election contests (1-10-304). Cost bonds required if suit brought by nonresident. (13-16-101). Cost bonds may be required if court concludes resident plaintiff unable to pay costs of suit. (13-16-102). Cost bond of $250, or as otherwise fixed by trial court, required for appeal. (App. Rule 7). If action is voluntarily dismissed by plaintiff, and subsequently recommenced, court may order payment of costs in previous action and stay proceedings pending compliance. (Rule 41[d]).

Liability of Attorney.—Attorneys' fees recoverable against attorneys for frivolous, groundless or vexatious action or if action interposed for delay or harassment or if attorney or party unnecessarily expanded proceeding. (13-17-102). Attorney for nonresident plaintiff liable for costs in case dismissed for failure to file cost bond. (13-16-102).

Criminal.—Costs paid by state if defendant acquitted or unable to pay (16-18-101) and by defendant if convicted (Crim. Rule 32[c]). Additional costs taxed defendant for victim compensation fund where defendant convicted or judgment and sentence deferred. (24-4.1-119).

DAMAGES:

Compensatory Damages.—Common law generally governs compensatory damages. However, comparative negligence as described in subhead Comparative Negligence, infra, applies in negligence cases. Recovery for noneconomic loss or injury (such as pain, suffering, emotional distress, impaired quality of life) ordinarily shall not exceed $250,000 against each defendant (866 P.2d 1361) and damages for derivative noneconomic loss or injury ordinarily shall not be awarded to persons suffering indirect harm or injury (13-21-102.5[3]). However, direct noneconomic damages may be increased up to but no more than $500,000, and derivative damages awarded up to but no more than $250,000, if court finds they are justified by clear and convincing evidence. (13-21-102.5[3]). These limitations shall not be disclosed to jury, but shall be imposed by court before judgment. (13-21-102.5[4]). Recovery for physical impairment or disfigurement not limited. (13-21-102.5[5]). See also subhead Mitigation, infra. Collateral source rule changed. Injured plaintiff who receives gratuitous benefits from collateral source will have recovery reduced by amount of benefits. (13-21-111.6). Ski Safety Act of 1979 amended to limit damages against ski area operators to $1,000,000 present value; also $250,000 cap on noneconomic damages and derivative claims. (33-44-103).

Wife has same right as husband for loss of consortium in tort actions. (14-2-209). But see 13-21-102.5(3). Damages in action for wrongful death limited, except where cause of death is felonious killing, in which case there is no limitation on damages recoverable. (13-21-102.5[2][b], 201 to 203, 203.5). See also category Estates and Trusts, topic Death, subhead Action for Death.

Joint and several liability abolished in any action brought as result of death or injury to person or property. (13-21-111.5). No defendant liable for amount greater than degree or percentage of negligence or fault attributable to that defendant. Exception:

DAMAGES . . . *continued*

Joint liability shall be imposed on two or more persons who consciously conspire and deliberately pursue common plan and design to commit tortious act. (13-21-111.5[4]). Consideration of degree or percentage of negligence or fault of nonparties to action authorized. (13-21-111.5). 13-20-602 Certificate of Review required to designate licensed health care provider as nonparty at fault. (13-21-111.5[3]). Special verdict procedure specified. (13-21-111.5).

Medical Malpractice.—13-64-101 effective as to acts and omissions occurring on and after July 1, 1988. Statute: (a) Provides for periodic payments where award of future damages exceeds present value of $150,000 and allows court discretion to allow periodic payments for future damages of less than that amount. (13-64-203). It specifies method of funding of periodic payments and how such periodic payments are determined and handled (13-64-207), including attorney fees (13-64-205); (b) provides cap on damages of $1,000,000 present value per patient, which includes any derivative claim by any other claimant and not more than $250,000 present value per patient (including any derivative claim by any other claimant) attributable to noneconomic loss or injury (13-64-302). For actions filed on or after July 1, 1995, interest on damages from date action accrues to date of filing (13-21-101) is deemed to be part of damages awarded, and subject to limitations of 13-64-101(1) and 13-64-101(2). Court may increase limit by present value of economic losses if, upon good cause shown, court determines that present value of lost earnings, medical or other health care costs would make imposition of limitation unfair (13-64-302); (c) provides for minimum qualifications of persons who testify as expert witness and prohibits expert in one medical subspecialty to testify against physician in another subspecialty unless standards of care and practice in two fields are similar (13-64-401); (d) provides that written notice must be given to health, sickness or accident insurance providers and their rights of subrogation recognized through specified procedures, and provides for waiver of those rights if written notice of claim not filed with Court 90 days after receipt of notice from plaintiff (13-64-402); (e) permits voluntary agreements between patient and health care providers to submit malpractice disputes to binding arbitration under certain specified safeguards, provides required language of agreement, including right of patient to rescind such agreement by written notice to health care provider within 90 days after signature if person is not hospitalized, or within 90 days after discharge from hospital if hospitalization was contemplated (13-64-403). Health care provider cannot withhold services because of person's refusal to sign agreement containing provision for binding arbitration (13-64-403); (f) makes special provisions and limits liability for health care professionals and health care institutions involved in labor, delivery or immediate postdelivery care and vaccine-related injury or death (13-64-502). In actions against licensed professional or acupuncturist plaintiff must file review certificate within 60 days after service or complaint dismissed. (13-20-602[4]). Review certificate is representation that another professional qualified under 13-64-401 has been consulted, and that consulted professional has concluded that claim does not lack substantial justification under 13-17-102(4). If certificate of review (13-20-602) filed rebuttably presumed that claim not frivolous or groundless (13-17-102[2.1]). For actions filed on or after Feb. 1, 1999, review certificate must be filed for each company that employed licensed professional or acupuncturist, even if licensed professional or acupuncturist is not named as party. (13-20-602[b]). Rule 11 still applicable.

Ad Damnum Clause.—Rule 8(a) amended by Colo. Supreme Court prohibits statement of dollar amounts in prayer for relief in civil damage complaints as of and after Jan. 1, 1987.

Exemplary damages may be awarded where injury to person or property attended by circumstances of fraud, malice or willful and wanton conduct. (13-21-102). Willful and wanton defined by statute to mean conduct purposefully committed which actor must have realized as dangerous, done heedlessly and recklessly, without regard to consequences, or rights and safety of others. (13-21-102[1][b]). Exemplary damages require proof beyond reasonable doubt. (13-25-127). Ordinarily exemplary damages may not exceed actual damages, but court may increase them up to treble amount of actual damages on basis of willful or wanton conduct during pendency of case, or reduce or strike if deterrent effect accomplished, conduct ceased or purpose for such damages otherwise served. (13-21-102). Exemplary damages may not be awarded in administrative or arbitration proceedings. (13-21-102[5]). Exception: Punitives authorized in medical malpractice arbitrations. (13-64-403[1.5]). Income or net worth of party may not be considered. (13-21-102[6]). May recover treble amount of check, draft, or order fraudulently made, plus costs and reasonable attorneys' fees. (13-21-109). Effective July 1, 1990, exemplary damages may not be plead in initial claim against health care provider; only added after sufficient discovery; (13-64-302.5); no exemplary damages against health care provider for use of any drug or product approved by state or federal regulatory agency (13-64-302.5), or used in accord with standard of care, and with informed consent (13-64-302.5[a][b]); no punitives against health care professional as result of acts of others unless acts specifically directed to be done or ratified (13-64-302.5).

Assumption of Risk.—Defense of assumption of risk reinstated (13-21-111.7) and shall be considered in apportioning negligence pursuant to Colorado Comparative Negligence Act (13-21-111).

Comparative Negligence.—Contributory negligence not bar to recovery if negligence of person seeking recovery not as great as negligence of person against whom recovery is sought. Damages allowed are reduced in proportion to amount of negligence attributable to each person seeking recovery. (13-21-111). Negligence of multiple defendants is to be combined when compared against plaintiff's negligence and damages may be recovered from multiple defendants found liable unless plaintiff was 50% or more at fault. (660 P.2d 883). Each defendant severally liable in proportion to his percentage of fault as found by trier of fact—no joint and several liability among tortfeasors. (13-21-111.5). Exception: Joint liability shall be imposed on two or more persons who consciously conspire and deliberately pursue common plan and design to commit tortious act. (13-21-111.5[4]). Negligence of settling nonparty or nonparty named by defendant may be considered in apportioning fault. (13-21-111.5[3][b]). Assumption of risk is factor in apportioning fault. (13-21-111.7). Jury is not to be told effect of its special verdict and findings as to comparative fault; 13-21-111(4) repealed,

and therefore, prior case law applies. (526 P.2d 295). Exception: For civil actions commenced after July 1, 1987, trial court shall instruct jury on effect of its finding of degree or percentage of negligence or fault between plaintiff and defendant(s), but not as to allocation of fault among two or more defendants. (13-21-111.5[5]). On July 1, 1990, liability of ski area operators (33-44-103) and equine sponsors (13-21-120) limited because of risks and dangers inherent in those sports.

In products liability action, person seeking recovery not barred by his own negligence. Damages reduced in proportion to amount of negligence attributable to person seeking recovery. (13-21-406[1]).

See also category Estates and Trusts, topic Death, subhead Action for Death.

Charitable immunity—Doctrine of charitable immunity bars levy of execution which would deplete trust funds. (419 P.2d 312).

Sovereign Immunity.—Doctrine of sovereign immunity abolished, and recognized in Colorado only to extent provided for by statute. (24-10-102). Application of sovereign immunity bars claim against public entity. (24-10-108). Sovereign immunity does not bar actions for damages for injuries resulting from: (1) Operation of motor vehicle, owned or leased by public entity, by public employee in course of employment (except certain emergency vehicles); (2) operation of certain public facilities; (3) dangerous condition of public buildings and certain other public facilities; (4) dangerous condition of public highway, road, or street which physically interferes with movement of traffic. (24-10-106). Public entity may waive immunity by adopting prospective resolution, and likewise may withdraw waiver. (24-10-104). Providing services or adopting policies or regulations does not create duty of care in public entity. (24-10-106.5). Person claiming injury by public entity or public employee must file detailed written notice within 180 days of discovery of injury as jurisdictional prerequisite to any action. (24-10-109). Liability of all public employees or entities limited to $150,000 per person and $600,000 per occurrence, unless increased by governing body. (24-10-114). Judgment may be claimed against State in excess of maximum limits, but State not liable for payment of excess unless approved by bill of State Legislature. (24-10-114). Actions against public employees for acts or omissions during performance of their duties and within scope of their employment, subject to notice requirements and damage limitations. (24-10-118). Allegations in complaint against public employee of willful and wanton conduct must set forth specific factual basis or be subject to dismissal. (24-10-114). Notice under Whistle Blower Statute is governed by 180-day limitation. (24-10-109; 752 P.2d 559).

Just compensation clause of constitution creates exception to sovereign immunity (601 P.2d 1082). Public entity not liable for exemplary or punitive damages or for outrageous conduct. (24-10-114[4]). Employees not liable for punitive or exemplary damages. (24-10-118[1][c]). Public entity liable for costs of defending employee if employee acting within scope of employment. (24-10-110[1.5]). Department of Personnel controls defense of claims against state. (24-30-1504). State self-insured and recovery on claims against state arising after Sept. 15, 1985, only through risk management fund. (24-30-1501, 1510). State claim board manages risk management fund (24-30-1509) and has limited power to settle claims (24-30-1515). Promise to indemnify or hold public entity harmless from entity's own negligence void as against public policy. (13-50.5-102[8]).

Guest Statute.—Repealed effective Apr. 9, 1975. (L. 75, §1, p. 1568).

Alcoholic Beverages.—Common law cause of action against commercial vendor or social host abolished, and liability for each statutory action limited to $150,000. (12-46-112.5; 12-47-128.5). Commercial vendor liable only where alcohol served willfully and knowingly to underage or visibly intoxicated person. Social host liable only where alcohol served willfully and knowingly to underage person. (12-46-112.5; 12-47-128.5).

Health Care.—No member of hospital utilization review committee liable for damages to patients by reason of recommendations made in exercise of proper function of committee unless willful or reckless disregard for patient's safety is shown. (13-21-110[1]). Persons providing mental health care to violent persons are exempt from liability in some circumstances. (13-21-117).

Good Samaritan Rule.—Doctrine of assumed duty abolished; persons volunteering assistance or services exempted from civil liability for their good faith acts and omissions. (13-21-116). Includes teachers, coaches, trainers, etc. who perform service or assistance for any program, organization, service group, social, recreational group, nonprofit corporation serving young persons or providing sporting programs. (13-21-116[2.5][a]). Young persons means 18 years of age or less. (13-21-116[2.5][b]. No civil liability for rendering uncompensated emergency medical services (13-21-108) or for mine rescue (13-21-114). 13-21-108(1) amended to clarify limitation of liability not applicable if physician renders emergency care to existing patient.

Nonprofit Corporations.—Assets of any nonprofit corporation which would, but for statutory provisions governing nonprofit corporations, be immune form levy and execution shall nonetheless be subject to levy and execution to extent such nonprofit corporation would be reimbursed by proceeds of liability insurance policies carried by it were judgments levied and executed against its assets. (7-20-108). Member of board of directors not liable for official acts or omissions unless willful or wanton. (13-21-116[2][b]).

Dams and Reservoirs.—Owners and operators of water storage reservoirs liable only for negligence. (37-87-104[1]). No negligence if state engineer's 100-year flow predictions are followed (37-87-102[3.7]), and state engineer and staff not liable for errors in calculations (37-87-115). Stockholders, officers, directors not liable if owner is adequately insured under statute. (37-87-104[3]).

Landowners.—Liability of owner or possessor of real property for injuries occurring on his land determined under statute. 13-21-115 declared unconstitutional by 779 P.2d 856 (1989), and reenacted in 1990 as new 13-21-115. Landowner's duty of care varies with plaintiff's purposes for being on land. (13-21-115).

Minors.—Parents with malicious or willfully destructive children under 18 years of age living with them shall be responsible for their actual damage to extent of $3,500, plus costs and attorneys' fees. (13-21-107). See also category Family, topic Infants.

See note at head of Digest as to 1998 legislation covered.

See Topical Index in front part of this volume.

DAMAGES . . . *continued*

No-Fault Insurance.—See category Transportation, topic Motor Vehicles, subhead No-Fault Insurance.

Firearms and Ammunition.—Recovery in products liability action against maker or seller of firearms or ammunition must be based on actual defect in design or manufacture of product. (13-21-501 to 505).

Damages for Blowing Soil.—Where damages are caused by blowing soil, 35-72-101 et seq. provide special rules for bringing actions for recovery of such damages.

Uniform Contribution Among Tortfeasors Act.—Adopted. (13-50.5-101 to 106). *Material Variations from Text:*

§2—replaced with following: "The relative degrees of fault of the joint tortfeasors shall be used in determining their pro rata shares." (13-50.5-103).

§4(a)—replaced with following: "It does not discharge any of the other tortfeasors from liability for their several pro rata shares of liability for the injury, death, damage, or loss unless its terms so provide; but it reduces the aggregate claim against the others to the extent of any degree or percentage of fault or negligence attributable by the finder of fact, pursuant to section 13-21-111 (2) or (3) or section 13-21-111.5, to the tortfeasor to whom the release or covenant is given; and". (13-50.5-105).

Mitigation.—Failure to mitigate damages is affirmative defense which must be pleaded and proven by defendant. (Rule 8[c]; 549 P.2d 1087). Evidence of nonuse of seatbelt by driver and front seat passengers in motor vehicle equipped with safety belt system is admissible in civil action to reduce damages recoverable for pain and suffering resulting from injuries sustained in accident. (42-4-236[7]).

Attorneys' Fees and Costs.—In any civil action of any nature commenced or appealed, court may award attorneys' fees if it finds that party brought or defended action which was substantially frivolous, groundless or vexatious, was interposed for delay or harassment, or that attorney unnecessarily expanded proceeding by improper conduct. (13-17-101 to 106). Court has discretion to award attorneys' fees for frivolous claim. (712 P.2d 491). If appellate court determines that appeal is frivolous, it may award just damages and single or double costs to appellee. (C.A.R. 38[d]; 674 P.2d 363). If plaintiff does not substantially prevail against public employee in action for exemplary damages, Court shall award attorney fees against plaintiff or plaintiff's attorney or both. (24-10-110[5]). Attorney's fees may be awarded in breach of trust actions to make injured party whole. (657 P.2d 992). Also see Rule 11, C.R.C.P. Rebuttable presumption not frivolous or groundless if (13-20-602) certificate of review filed.

See also topic Costs.

Baseball.—Spectators at professional baseball games presumed to know of and to assume inherent risks of injury, including risks of being struck by baseball or baseball bat (13-21-120[4][a]); assumption of inherent risks is complete bar and defense to suit against owner of team or stadium (13-21-120[4][b]), except when owner (a) fails to use reasonable effort to design, alter, and maintain stadium in reasonably safe condition; (b) intentionally injures spectator; or (c) fails to post notice required by statute (13-21-120[5][6]). Effective Jan. 1, 1994.

Statutory Interest.—See topic Interest.

DEPOSITIONS AND DISCOVERY:

Federal Rules of Civil Procedure are basis for Colorado Rules of Civil Procedure. See topic Practice.

Uniform Foreign Depositions Act not adopted.

Within State For Use Within State.—Federal Rules of Civil Procedure adopted with modifications. Limitation on number of depositions to one deposition of each adverse party and two other persons. (Rule 26[b][2][A]).

Within State for Use Elsewhere.—When deposition authorized by court of record outside Colorado, district court of county where witness resides or is found may issue subpoena commanding witness to appear and testify. Subpoena enforced in same manner as subpoena for case pending in Colorado court. (13-90-111).

Outside of State for Use within State.—See subhead Commissions, infra.

Perpetuating Testimony.—Deposition to perpetuate testimony may be taken when applicant expects to be party to action in this state or when proof of some fact is necessary to perfect title to property or to establish any other matter which it may thereafter become material to establish. Proceeding is commenced by filing verified petition in district court. Order allowing examination must be served personally (Rule 4[e]) on persons named in petition as expected adverse parties. If expected adverse parties are stated to be unknown and real property is to be affected by testimony, copy of order must be served on county clerk and recorder of county in which property is located and published for not less than two weeks in some newspaper to be designated by court. (Rule 27[a][1]). Testimony taken must be signed and sworn to in writing by each witness and certified by court. Any personal service required by Rule must be given at least ten days before testimony is to be taken. If any witness is absent from county in which proceedings are pending, court must designate some person authorized to administer oaths to take and certify his testimony. (Rule 27[a][2]). Such deposition may at any time thereafter be used in trial in which petitioner or any successor in interest is party, or between any parties in trial in which it is material to establish facts which such testimony proves or tends to prove where witness giving deposition is unable to be present at trial. (Rule 27[a][4]).

Where permitted by court, depositions may be taken at any time within 30 days from entry of judgment or during pendency of appeal to perpetuate testimony for use in further proceedings. (Rule 27[b]).

Before Whom Taken.—Depositions may be taken within U.S., or any territory or possession subject to dominion of U.S., before officer authorized to administer oath by laws of Colorado, of U.S. or of place where examination is held or before person appointed by court in which action is pending. (Rule 28[a]). Depositions of persons in military service may be taken anywhere by commissioned officer in active service of U.S. (24-12-104[1]). No deposition may be taken before relative, employee, attorney or counsel of any party, or one who is financially interested in action. (Rule 28[b]).

Commissions.—Commission or letters rogatory shall be issued when necessary, on application and notice, and on terms that are just and appropriate. Both commission and letters rogatory may be issued in proper cases. Officers may be designated in commission either by name or descriptive title. Clerk shall issue commission in form prescribed by jurisdiction where deposition is to be taken, such form to be prepared by party seeking deposition. Original sealed deposition shall be filed and sealed and commission shall so inform officer. (Rule 28[c]).

Examination of Witnesses.—Federal Rules of Civil Procedure adopted with no material variations.

Return.—Federal Rules of Civil Procedure adopted with no material variation.

Form.—Full instructions as to captions, certificates, etc., accompany commissions and are printed on back side of dedimus issued by clerk of court.

Compelling Attendance of Witnesses.—Attendance of witnesses may be compelled by subpoena, but Colorado resident may be required to attend deposition only in county wherein he resides, is employed or transacts business in person or such other convenient place as court directs. Nonresident of Colorado may be required to attend within 40 miles of place of service or in county where he resides, is employed, or transacts business in person or such other convenient place as court directs. (Rule 45[a], [d][2]).

Subpoenas must be issued by clerk of court in which case is docketed or by counsel whose appearance has been entered. (Rule 45[e]). Written objection to inspection or copying must be made within ten days of service or before time for compliance if earlier. (Rule 45[d][1]). Notice of deposition must be given to all parties. (Colorado Ethics Opinion No. 86).

Depositions on Written Questions.—Party desiring to take depositions on written questions must serve them on every other party with notice stating name and address of person who is to answer them and name or descriptive title and address of officer before whom deposition is to be taken. Within 20 days thereafter, parties so served may serve cross-questions on all other parties. Within ten days thereafter latter may serve redirect questions on all other parties. Within ten days after being served with redirect questions party may serve recross questions. (Rule 31[a]).

A copy of notice and copies of all questions served must be delivered by party desiring to take deposition to designated officer, who will take questions as provided in Rule 30 and certify and file or mail deposition attaching thereto copy of notice and questions received by him. (Rule 31[b], [c]).

Depositions on Oral Examination.—Federal Rules of Civil Procedure adopted with modification limiting number of depositions to one deposition of each adverse party and two other persons. (Rule 26[b][2][A]). Reasonable notice of deposition must not be less than five days. (121-1-12[1]).

EQUITY:

See topic Actions.

EVIDENCE:

Witnesses.—(13-90-101 to 210).

Generally no person is incompetent as witness because of interest in action (subject to exceptions, e.g., deadman's statute [13-90-102]), conviction for crime (though conviction for felony within five years may be shown to affect credibility), or religious belief. (13-90-101). Persons of unsound mind may not testify. Children under ten years who appear incapable of understanding facts or relating them truly may not testify, except in proceedings for child abuse, sexual abuse, sexual assault, or incest, when child able to testify as to facts or events in language appropriate to child of that age. (13-90-106).

See also topic Depositions and Discovery.

Privileged Communications.—Communication to attorney, clergyman, physician or registered professional nurse (except in proceedings before certain review boards, suits brought by patient, proceedings involving allegations of child abuse [19-3-311], certain insured claims based on nurse's actions, and certain civil actions involving injuries occurring during labor, delivery, or immediate postdelivery period), public officer, certified public accountant, licensed psychologist, professional counselor, marriage and family therapist, social worker, counselor to victims of domestic violence or sexual assault, or unlicensed psychotherapist privileged if made in confidence and in connection with professional relationship. (13-90-107). Confidential communications with certain employees of same also privileged. (13-90-107). Physician-patient privilege applies even to essential witness in criminal proceedings. (195 Colo. 386, 578 P.2d 647). Psychologist-client and physician-patient privileges extend to information disclosed for purpose or diagnosis or treatment but not to information disclosed for purpose of preparing for litigation. (785 P. 2d 132). Communication between patient and physician, registered professional nurse, licensed mental health professional, or certified school psychologist not privileged if it results in child abuse report under 19-3-304. (19-3-311). Communication to or knowledge of state or local health department employee or any health care provider or facility, third-party payor, physician, clinic, laboratory, blood bank, or other agency as to report or investigation concerning individual with AIDS infection privileged unless individual subject to public health order or restrictive action. (25-4-1404). Newspersons have privilege against disclosure of news information gathered or received from others except in certain circumstances such as where news information based on newsperson's personal observation of crime if substantially similar news information cannot reasonably be obtained by any other means. (13-90-119). Communication made in official confidence to confidential intermediary privileged when public interest would suffer by disclosure. (13-90-107[1][i]). Qualified interpreter of communications between hearing-impaired person and another, one of whom is privilege-holder under 13-90-107, cannot be examined without written consent of privilege-holder. (13-90-107[1][h]). Psychologist-patient privilege, like physician-patient privilege, is not qualified, and once privilege attaches only basis for disclosure is expressed or implied waiver. (668 P.2d 3). In civil case, implied waiver of privilege occurs by privilege-holder's assertion of his physical or mental condition as basis for claim or affirmative defense. (668 P.2d 3). In criminal case, defendant who places

See note at head of Digest as to 1998 legislation covered.

See Topical Index in front part of this volume.

CO – 30

EVIDENCE . . . . *continued*

mental condition at issue by pleading not guilty by reason of insanity under 16-8-103, asserting affirmative defense of impaired mental condition under 16-8-103.5, or raising question of incompetency to proceed under 16-8-110, waives privilege as to his communications with physician or psychologist made during exam or treatment for such mental condition for purposes of trial or hearing on issue of mental condition. (16-8-103.6).

Husband and Wife.—Communication by one spouse to other generally privileged.(13-90-107[1][a][I]). Privilege does not apply to proceeding involving allegations of child abuse (19-3-311[2]), suit between spouses, criminal suit for crime committed by one against other, or criminal suit against one or both of spouses for alleged offense occurring before marriage (13-90-107[1][a][I]). Privilege does not apply to communications made to aid commission of future crime or present continuing crime.(13-90-107[1][a][III]). Above privilege does not apply to any of certain felony proceedings, in which case spousal communications intended to be confidential are privileged.(13-90-107[1][a][II]).

Communications or Transactions with Persons Since Deceased or Incompetent.—Generally no interested person can testify adversely to representative or heir of deceased or incompetent concerning matters to which such deceased or incompetent, whether present or not, was party, unless representative introduces evidence of same, or except in certain cases. (13-90-102[1]). Examination of witness incompetent under statute is waiver of incompetency as to other adverse witnesses on same subject matter. (625 P.2d 364). Statute does not apply to facts occurring after death. (13-90-102[1][a][I]). Statute does not apply to interested party testifying about facts occurring prior to death and outside presence of deceased. (13-90-102[1][a][II]). Statute also does not apply to rebuttal evidence in any form once any witness has been permitted to testify concerning conversation or transaction with deceased or incompetent. (13-90-102[1.5]).

Self-Incrimination.—No person can be compelled to testify against himself in criminal case. (Const., Art. II, §18). State's attorney may petition court for order compelling witness' testimony over claim of privilege against self-incrimination, but such testimony, and information derived from it, may not be used against such witness in any criminal case, except prosecution for perjury, false statement or otherwise failing to comply with order. (13-90-118).

Compelling Attendance.—See topic Depositions and Discovery.

INJUNCTIONS:

Application for, hearing on and granting of injunctions are covered by the general rules governing actions of a civil nature.

Jurisdiction generally is in district court (Rule 65), county court being able to issue injunctions only in very limited circumstances when there is danger of threat or assault against person (County Court Rule 365).

Prerequisites.—Federal Rules of Civil Procedure adopted without material variation. See topic Practice.

Procedure.—Federal Rules of Civil Procedure adopted without material variation.

Bond.—Federal Rules of Civil Procedure adopted without material variation.

Preliminary Injunction.—Federal Rules of Civil Procedure adopted without material variation.

Mandatory Injunction.—May obtain mandatory injunction if restraining doing of act will not effectuate relief. (Rule 65[f]).

Temporary Restraining Order.—Federal Rules of Civil Procedure adopted without material variation.

Matrimonial Actions.—Rule inapplicable to suits for dissolution of marriage, legal separation, maintenance, child support, or custody of minors. In such suits, court may make prohibitive or mandatory orders without notice or bond, as may be just. (Rule 65[h]).

JUDGMENTS:

Colorado Rules of Civil Procedure are based on Federal Rules of Civil Procedure. (Vol. 12, Colo. Rev. Stat.). See topic Practice.

Judgments may be either interlocutory or final. (Rule 54[b]). See category Debtor and Creditor, topic Attachment.

Docketing.—Immediately on rendition of any judgment, clerk is required to enter same in register of actions. (Rules 58[a] and 79[d]).

Declaratory Judgments.—Uniform Act adopted. (13-51-101 et seq.; Rule 57).

Default Judgments.—Federal Rules of Civil Procedure adopted with following immaterial variations to Rule 55. In all civil actions court may enter judgment based upon affidavit of party seeking affirmative relief. (13-63-101[1]). Rule governs listing of documents which must be filed with motion for entry of default judgment. (Rule 121, §§1-14). Court may, upon own motion, require such supporting evidence as it deems necessary in addition to affidavit or require formal hearing on any and all issues. (13-63-101[2]).

Offer of Judgment.—Repealed Rule 68 and substituted Offer of Settlement Procedure 13-17-202.

Lien.—Judgments are liens on personal property of judgment debtor from time execution thereon is delivered to proper officer. Personal property lien only in county where execution delivered. Judgments are liens upon real estate within any county as soon as transcripts thereof, certified by the clerk of the court rendering the same, are filed of record in the office of the county recorder. Lien continues six years from entry of judgment. (13-52-102). Any person, including title insurance company, making representations concerning existence of judgment lien on real property has duty to make bona fide effort to determine whether person against whom judgment obtained is same person who holds real estate. Liability for not less than $100 nor more than $1,000 for actual and exemplary damages plus costs and attorney's fees for failure to make bona fide effort. (13-52-102[4]). Judgment debtor's lien against joint tenant attaches to

interest of only joint tenant debtor, and terminates if joint tenant debtor dies prior to attachment or levy having been made upon his interest. (660 P.2d 13).

Revival.—A judgment may be revived against one or more judgment debtors on motion alleging date of judgment and amount unsatisfied. The clerk thereupon issues a notice requiring judgment debtor to show cause within ten days after service thereof why the judgment should not be revived. Revived judgment must be entered within 20 years after entry of original judgment, and may itself be revived in same manner. (Rule 54[h]). Court loses jurisdiction to revive judgment, unless done within 20 years after entry of judgment revived, even if motion requesting revival is filed within 20-year period. (697 P.2d 799). Filing transcript of entry of revivor before expiration of lien in judgment docket with clerk and recorder operates to continue lien of judgment for same period as original lien. (Rule 54[h]).

Judgments by Confession.—Provision authorizing confession of judgment on claim arising out of consumer credit sale or consumer lease (5-2-415) or consumer loan (5-3-407) is void.

Assignment.—No particular form necessary.

Judgments by Consent.—Court has some discretion in entering judgment by consent. (126 Colo. 298, 248 P.2d 825).

Satisfaction in whole or part of money judgment may be entered in judgment record (Rule 79[d]) upon execution returned satisfied in whole or part, or upon acknowledgment of such satisfaction filed with clerk, made in manner of acknowledgment of conveyance of real property by judgment creditor, or by judgment creditor's attorney of record unless revocation of authority previously filed, or by signing such satisfaction, attested by clerk, upon judgment record by one authorized to execute acknowledgment of satisfaction. (Rule 58[b]).

Form

Form of Satisfaction.—For and in consideration of the sum of . . . . Dollars and . . . . Cents paid to me by . . . . . . , the defendant in the above entitled action, full satisfaction is hereby acknowledged of a certain judgment rendered in said . . . . . Court, in the above entitled action, on the . . . day of . . , 19. . ., in favor of . . . . . . , the plaintiff in the said action, and against the said defendant, for the sum of . . . . Dollars and . . . . Cents, besides . . . . . . Dollars and . . . . . . Cents, costs, and recorded in Book . . . of Judgments, at page . . . of the Records of said Court, and I hereby authorize and direct the Clerk of said Court to enter of record satisfaction of said judgment in said action.

Witness my hand and seal this . . . day of . . ., 19. . . .

. . . .

Presumption of Satisfaction.—Judgments of courts of record are presumed to be satisfied in 20 years, but may be revived as provided above so as to be continued beyond that time. Execution may issue thereon at any time within 20 years, or after, if revived. (13-52-102; Rule 54[h]).

Vacation or Modification.—Covered by Rules 59, 60 and 61. Rule 59 differs materially from Federal Rules of Civil Procedure in that it lists six grounds on which motion for new trial will be granted and requires affidavits in some cases.

Foreign Judgments.—An official record kept within U.S. or within a territory or possession subject to dominion of U.S. may be evidenced by a copy, attested by the officer having legal custody of the record, or by his deputy, and accompanied by a certificate that such officer has custody. If the office in which the record is kept is within U.S. or within territory or possession subject to dominion of U.S., certificate may be that of judge of court or record of district or political subdivision in which record is kept, authenticated by seal of court, or may be made by any public officer having seal of office and having official duties in district or political subdivision in which record is kept, authenticated by seal of his office. (Rule 44[a][1]). Other official records may be evidenced by copy, attested by person authorized to make attestation and accompanied by final certification as to genuineness of signature and official position of attesting person or of any foreign official whose certificate of genuineness relates to attestation or is in chain of certificates relating to attestation. If office in which record is kept is in foreign country, certificate may be made by secretary of embassy or legation, consul general, consul, vice-consul, or consular agent, or by any officer in foreign service of U.S. stationed in foreign state or country in which record is kept. (Rule 44[a][2]). Final certification is unnecessary if record and attestation are certified as provided for in treaty or convention to which U.S. and foreign country in which official record is located are parties.

In case the office or officer authenticating any document has no official seal, authentication by official publication or by seal is dispensed with. (Rule 44[d]).

If a foreign jurisdiction has a reciprocal provision, Colorado courts will recognize orders, judgments, and decrees therefrom in cases of divorce, dissolution of marriage, legal separation, separate maintenance, annulment, declaration of invalidity of marriage, or for support of minor children or spouse, and after personal service of process (see topic Process), may amend, modify, set aside, and enforce same, including awards of temporary alimony, support money and attorneys' fees. (14-11-101).

Uniform Enforcement of Foreign Judgments Act has been adopted. (13-53-101 et seq.). Fee for filing foreign judgment $90.

Material Variations from Official Text.—

§2—adds "court which would have had jurisdiction over the original action had it been commenced first in this state" at end of sentence beginning "A copy"; omits sentence beginning "The Clerk"; inserts "in which filed" preceding "and may be enforced" in sentence beginning "A judgment". (13-53-103).

Uniform Foreign Money-Judgments Recognition Act has been adopted. (13-62-101 et seq.).

Material Variations from Official Text.—

§1—adds "which governmental unit has entered into a reciprocal agreement with the United States recognizing any judgment of a court of record of the United States, or any state, district, commonwealth, territory, insular possession thereof, or the Panama Canal Zone, the Trust Territory of the Pacific Islands, or the Ryukyu Islands, and providing for

JUDGMENTS . . . *continued*
procedures similar to those contained in the article" at end of sentence beginning " 'Foreign state' ". (13-62-102[1]).

Judgment Notes.—See category Business Regulation and Commerce, topic Bills and Notes.

Summary Judgment.—Federal Rules of Civil Procedure, Rule 56 adopted with minor variations.

LIMITATION OF ACTIONS:

Actions are barred unless commenced within the following periods after the respective causes of action accrued:

Eighteen years: To recover real property, except as hereinafter mentioned (38-41-101); on public securities (11-55-107).

Fifteen years: To foreclose mortgage (38-39-205) except as limited by extinguishment of lien at time right to sue to enforce payment of underlying debt is barred (38-39-207, 730 P.2d 308). See also category Mortgages, topic Mortgages of Real Property, subhead Foreclosure.

Ten years: To enforce or procure any right or title to real property under contract of sale or bond for deed, by person not in possession. (38-41-116, 117).

Seven years: To recover real property where: (a) Defendant is and has been in possession for that time under claim and color of title, made in good faith, and has paid all taxes during that period; (b) the land is vacant and defendant holds under claim of title and has paid all taxes; or (c) title or right under which defendant claims has been of record for seven years, unless such record has been annulled by proper judicial proceedings or plaintiff has been deprived of possession within two years of commencement of actions (38-41-108, 109, 111); to question or set aside purported foreclosure (38-29-208); to commence civil action for relief under Colorado Uniform Controlled Substances Act, 18-18-101 through 18-18-605 (18-18-603).

Six years: Actions to recover liquidated debt or unliquidated, determinable amounts of money; for rent in arrears; to enforce rights in instrument securing payment of debt; to recover damages for nonpayment of negotiable instrument upon presentment under 13-21-109, except rights to treble damages under 13-21-109(2) (see subhead Two Years, infra); actions in replevin to recover personal property encumbered by instrument securing debt and actions by Public Employees' Retirement Association to collect unpaid contributions from employers (13-80-103.5); actions for damages to persons or property and against architects, contractors, builders or builder vendors, engineers, or inspectors caused by design, planning, supervision, inspection, or construction after substantial completion of improvement (13-80-104), (see subhead Two Years, infra); civil actions based on sexual assault or sexual offense against child, time running from date disability is removed under 13-81-101(1) or six years after cause of action accrues, whichever occurs later (13-80-103.7).

Five years: Action for recovery of land sold for taxes (39-12-101); actions for forfeiture, seizure or recovery of personal property for violations of outfitter licensing requirements under 12-55.5-110, abatement of public nuisance under 16-13-301, under contraband forfeiture act 16-13-501, under organized crime control act 18-17-106, and violations of 42-5-107 (13-80-103.8), and for violations of Colorado Commodity Code (11-53-101 to 11-53-210).

Four years: Civil actions for violations of Colorado Antitrust Act of 1992, 6-4-101 to 6-4-122, after facts giving rise to such are discovered or should have been discovered with reasonable diligence. (6-4-118).

Three years: Civil actions: on contract not otherwise covered including actions under Uniform Commercial Code, except as provided in 13-80-103.5; all actions for fraud or deceit except as provided in 13-80-102(1)(j) and 13-80-103(1)(f) or (1)(g) (see subheads Two Years and One Year, infra); for determination of paternity; for breach of trust or fiduciary duty; under Uniform Consumer Credit Code, except 5-5-202(6); of replevin or for taking, detaining or converting goods or chattels, except as provided in 13-80-103.5 (see subhead Two Years, infra); under Colorado Rental Purchase Agreement Act (5-10-101 to 5-10-1001); under Motor Vehicle Financial Responsibility Act (42-7-101 to 42-7-510); under Colorado Auto Accident Reparations Act (10-4-701 to 10-4-724); accruing outside Colorado if limitation of place where action accrued is greater than Colorado limitation; of debt under 40-30-102; for recovery of erroneous refunds of any tax under 39-21-102 (13-80-101); actions for fraud, misstatements of material fact or omission of material fact in sale or purchase of security, after facts giving rise to such action are discovered or should have been discovered with reasonable diligence, but in no event more than five years after such purchase or sale (11-51-604[8]); against land surveyor licensed under tit. 12, art. 25, part 2, for damage from negligent or defective land survey, from time negligence or defect was discovered or should have been discovered with reasonable diligence and concern (13-80-105); for misappropriation of trade secret under Uniform Trade Secrets Act (7-74-107); for collection of various fuel, tobacco, sales, use or severance taxes and charges on oil and gas production (39-21-107[1]); tort actions for bodily injury or property damage arising from motor vehicle use, except for strict liability or failure to warn provided in 13-80-102(1) or 13-80-106; to commence action or arbitration of "uninsured motorist" insurance claim after cause of action accrues (13-80-107.5).

Two years: Civil actions: of every kind in action not otherwise covered; for tort except as otherwise provided; for strict or absolute liability, or failure to warn; against persons or organizations in veterinary medicine; against any public or governmental entity or employee for which insurance coverage is provided under 24-14-105, except as provided in 13-80-103 (see subhead One Year, infra); actions against field labor contractors for violation of wage laws under 8-4-123; upon liability, other than forfeiture or penalty, created by federal statute which prescribes no limitation; for fraud or deceit in used car sales under 42-6-208; to recover damages for three times face amount of negotiable instrument under 13-21-109(2) (13-80-102); after action accrues under 13-80-108(1), against health care institutions and health care professionals for action arising in tort or contract, but in no case shall such action be brought more than three years after act or omission giving rise to action, unless (1) act or omission was knowingly concealed or consisted of leaving object in patient, in which case action must be commenced within two years after discovery, (2) physical injury and cause are not known or could not be known through exercise of reasonable diligence, (3) action is on behalf of minor under eight years who was under six years on date of action or omission giving rise to action, which must be brought before minor attains eight years of age or (4) action is on behalf of person otherwise under disability under 13-81-101, in which case 13-81-103 applies (13-80-102.5); against employer for personal injury or death in course of employment (8-2-204); after claim for relief arises against architects, contractors, builders or builder vendors, engineers or inspectors for recovery of damages for deficiency in design, planning, inspection, supervision or construction of real property improvement or for injuries to persons or real or personal property caused by such deficiency, but in no case shall such action be brought more than six years after substantial completion of real property improvement, unless action arises in fifth or sixth year after substantial completion, in which case must commence within two years of when it arises (13-80-104); actions to recover mining or placer claims, from commencement of actual possession obtained under tax deed (39-12-102); actions, except those under 4-2-725, against manufacturer or seller of product for injury or damage resulting from construction, design, labeling or failure to warn or protect against hazard in use or misuse of product (13-80-106); actions against manufacturer, seller or lessor of new manufacturing equipment, but not later than seven years after such equipment was first used for intended purpose unless claim arises from hidden defects or prolonged exposure to hazardous material or from intentional misrepresentation or fraudulent concealment by manufacturer, seller or lessor of material fact proximately causing death, injury or property damage, but such limit does not apply to certain claims under express written warranties extending beyond two years and arising during warranty period (13-80-107); actions against ski area operator for injury to person or property arising out of operation of ski area (33-44-111); actions after date of contract of sale against seller of unregistered security or unlicensed broker-dealer (11-51-604[8]).

One year: For assault and battery, false imprisonment, libel or slander; against sheriff, coroner, police or other law enforcement authority; for statutory penalty or forfeiture but not claims for exemplary damages (634 P.2d 1036); and except for forfeitures related to certain criminal activities (see subhead Five Years, supra); under Motor Vehicle Repair Act 42-11-101 to 42-11-109; for all actions under tit. 12, art. 20; for fraud, misrepresentation, concealment or deceit under 12-20-113 or for negligence, fraud, willful misrepresentation or conversion of trust funds under 12-61-303, alleging liability for penalty arising from class A or B traffic infractions as defined in 42-4-1501 (13-80-103); to enforce terms of any building restriction on real property (38-41-119); to make demand on another insurer for initial arbitration proceedings under Auto Accident Reparations Act after first payment of benefits (10-4-717); to commence enforcement of hospital lien (38-27-103).

Six months: To give notice to public authority of claim after discovery of injury (638 P.2d 816; 24-10-109); to commence action to foreclose mechanic's lien after last labor performed or material furnished or after completion of structure or other improvement (38-22-110); to commence action to foreclose lien on oil wells or oil field equipment after filing of lien statement (38-24-105).

Three months: To commence action to foreclose harvester's lien on grain and harvested crops after filing of lien statement (38-24.5-107); to commence action to foreclose mechanics' lien on personal property after charges for work are due (38-20-107).

Two months: To commence action to foreclose liens of innkeepers, agistors, common carriers and mechanics on personal property after charges for work or rent are due. (38-20-107).

No Right of Recovery.—Actions also are barred and no right exists to recover damages for personal injury sustained during commission of or immediate flight from commission of felony, provided person causing injuries acted under reasonable belief that physical force was reasonable and appropriate to prevent injury or to prevent commission of felony. (13-80-119).

Uniform Commercial Code adopted. See category Business Regulation and Commerce, topic Commercial Code.

Accrual of Cause of Action.—Generally, accrual of cause of action is controlled by statute in effect at time claim for relief first arose (115 Colo. 358, 174 P.2d 346), but subsequent amendment may be applied retroactively where no deprivation of due process (663 P.2d 1066). Causes of action are deemed to accrue at following times: for injury to person, property, reputation or status and for uninsured motorist action at time injury and cause are known or should have been known by exercise of reasonable diligence; for wrongful death on date of death; for fraud, deceit, breach of contract, warranty or trust, or for wrongful possession of personal property, at time such fraud, deceit, breach or wrongful possession is discovered or should have been discovered by reasonable diligence; for debt or performance on date such debt or performance becomes due; for balance due on open account at time of last proved item; for any other cause of action for loss or damage when loss or damage is discovered or should have been discovered by reasonable diligence; and for penalties when determination of overpayment or delinquency giving rise to penalties are no longer subject to appeal; for recovery of erroneous refunds of any tax under 39-21-102 on date refund is issued; on date of traffic infraction for penalty arising from class A or B traffic infractions as defined in 42-4-1501; for unpaid employer contributions by Public Employees' Retirement Association, when nonpayment is discovered or should have been discovered by exercise of reasonable diligence (13-80-108); for injury in course of employment, at date of injury or, if death results, at date of death (8-42-204); to bring action on express or resulting trust, at time claimant attains, or reasonably could have attained, notice of trustee's use of trust property in manner inconsistent with claimant's interest; to establish constructive trust, at time claimant is aware, or reasonably should be aware, of facts which would make reasonable person suspicious of wrongdoing asserted as basis of trust (198 Colo. 477, 601 P.2d 1376). Uniform Commercial Code governs accrual of certain actions against bank for unauthorized signature or alteration of instrument for payment of money (4-4-406); certain actions on commercial paper (4-3-122); actions under bulk sales provisions (4-6-111); and actions for breach of contract for sale of

See note at head of Digest as to 1998 legislation covered.

See Topical Index in front part of this volume.

CO – 32

LIMITATION OF ACTIONS . . . *continued*
goods (4-2-725). Damage to land from water seepage, when property is first visibly affected. (163 Colo. 575, 431 P.2d 1007).

Absence or Concealment.—Statute does not run in favor of defendant while he is absent from state or in hiding. (13-80-118). Tolling statutes remedial, and not given retroactive application in absence of express direction from General Assembly. (660 P.2d 510).

Death.—No statute running on cause of action of decedent which had not been barred at date of death shall bar cause of action surviving death sooner than one year after death. (13-80-112, 15-12-109). See topic Actions, subhead Abatement and Revival.

Disabilities.—If person entitled to bring action is under 18 years, insane, imprisoned, or absent from U.S. at time cause of action accrues, such person may bring action within time respectively limited after disability is removed. (13-81-103). Special provisions regarding removal of disability in cases of sexual assault on minors. (13-80-103.7). Claim for injury is considered to accrue on date injury and its cause is known or should have been known by exercise of reasonable diligence. (13-80-108[1]). Special provisions regarding redemption rights of owners of real property conveyed by tax deed to another. (39-12-104). Statute of limitations is not tolled if person was not imprisoned until after cause of action accrued. (34 Colo. App. 223, 524 P.2d 1394).

Persons under legal disability when a cause of action concerning real property accrues and also when the period of limitation applicable to such action expires may bring action within two years after such expiration, but not later. (38-41-112; 109 Colo. 467, 126 P.2d 1036).

If a person under disability has, when a cause of action in his favor accrues, a legal representative, or a representative appointed by instrument in writing giving him power to take action to enforce a right, the statutory period runs as though there were no disability; if a legal representative for such person is appointed after cause of action has accrued, the period runs from time of such appointment provided that two years from such time are allowed. (13-81-103). If disability of any person is terminated before expiration of period of limitation and no legal representative has been appointed for him, then such person shall be allowed to take action within period fixed by statute of limitation which would apply in similar case to person not under disability, or within two years after removal of disability, whichever period expires later. (13-81-103).

If person under disability dies before disability is removed and before cause of action has become barred, and if cause of action survives, executor or administrator may sue within one year after such death. (13-81-103).

New Promise or Part Payment.—A new promise in writing or a partial payment will remove the bar of the statute, but only as to the promisor or payor and not as to joint obligors. (13-80-113, 114, 116).

Causes Barred in State of Origin.—Uniform Conflict of Laws-Limitations Act has been adopted. (13-82-101 to 107).

Commencement of a New Action Upon Involuntary Dismissal.—If action which was commenced within allowable period is terminated because of lack of jurisdiction or improper venue, plaintiff or his personal representative may commence new suit on said action within 90 days after termination of original action or within period otherwise allowed, whichever is later. (13-80-111).

Pleading.—Defense of statute of limitations must be set forth affirmatively. (Rule 8[c]).

Contractual Limitations.—Shorter than statutory limitations established by contract are enforceable if reasonable. (53 Colo. 416, 128 P. 449). No contractual variation permitted for contract for sale of goods. (4-2-725).

Setoffs.—Limitation provisions of 13-80-101 to 119 apply to debt or contract alleged, by way of setoff, by defendant, except that counterclaim or setoff arising out of transaction that is subject of opposing party's claim must be commenced within one year after service of complaint by opposing party.

PARTITION:

Any person having interest in real or personal property may maintain action to partition same. (38-28-101).

Jurisdiction and Venue.—Court is empowered to make complete adjudication of rights of all parties to property (38-28-103), and may make such orders as it deems necessary to completely adjudicate every question concerning title, rights and interest of all persons known or unknown, in being or not, and may direct payment and discharge of liens, have property sold free of liens or may apportion liens among persons to whom partition is made (38-28-110). Process, practice and procedure shall comply with Colorado rules of civil procedure. (38-28-104). Venue shall be in county where subject of action or substantial part of it is situated. (Rule 98[a]).

Proceedings.—All persons having any interest must be made parties (38-28-102) and court must make complete adjudication of rights of all (38-28-103). Upon entry of order for partition, court appoints one or more commissioners who view property and make partition thereof in writing assigning each party his share. Report is presented to court for confirmation and parties may file objections within time permitted by court. (38-28-105).

Partition in Kind or Sale.—If commissioner reports and court finds that partition cannot be made without manifest prejudice to rights of interested party, court may direct public sale upon such terms as court may fix. Notice of sale given in same manner as required for sales of real estate upon execution. (38-28-107). Report of person making such sale must be confirmed by court and then court directs execution of proper instruments of conveyance and distribution of net proceeds of sale and any undistributed income from such property. (38-28-108).

PLEADING:

Federal Rules of Civil Procedure form the basis for Colorado's pleading rules. (Rules 7 through 16). See topic Practice. Colorado Rule 10(d) contains specific provisions regarding format of pleadings, including designations for courts, paper size, line spacing and order of identifying document information.

Pleadings Permitted.—Federal Rules of Civil Procedure adopted with exception that reply to affirmative defense permitted and court may order any pleading in addition to those enumerated. (Rule 7[a]).

Complaint.—Federal Rules of Civil Procedure adopted with exception that parties may commence action without pleading by filing agreed statement of facts supported by affidavit. (Rule 7[d]). No dollar amount shall be stated in prayer for relief. (Rule 8[a][3]). See topic Practice.

Answer.—Federal Rules of Civil Procedure adopted with exception that mitigating circumstances reducing damages must be affirmatively pleaded. (Rule 8[c]). For pleading requirements regarding mandatory arbitration, see topic Practice.

Counterclaim or Set-Off.—Federal Rules of Civil Procedure adopted with addition of provisions for claims against assignees and personal representatives and process for removal to district court if counterclaim exceeds jurisdictional limit of superior court. (Rule 13[j], [k]and [1]). No dollar amount shall be stated in prayer for relief. (Rule 8[a][3]).

Reply.—Federal Rules of Civil Procedure adopted with no material variation.

Affidavits of Merits.—Not used in Colorado.

Affidavits of Defense.—Not used in Colorado.

Filing.—In cases where rules do not expressly require filing and service of paper subsequent to original complaint and filing alone required, paper must be served on adverse party within 48 hours of filing; if service alone required, paper must be filed before serving or within reasonable time thereafter. Deposition transcripts, discovery requests and responses not filed until used in court proceedings. (Rule 5[d]).

Proof of Claims.—No statutory provision. Uniform Enforcement of Foreign Judgments Act adopted. (13-53-101 to 108). Fee of $75 required to be paid to clerk of court by person filing foreign judgment. (13-53-106).

Demurrer.—Demurrers, pleas and exceptions for insufficiency of a pleading shall not be used. (Rule 7[c]).

Amended or Supplemental Pleadings.—Federal Rules of Civil Procedure adopted with no material variation. (Rule 15).

Motion for Separate or More Definite Statement.—Before responding to pleading or, if no responsive pleading is permitted, within 20 days after service of pleading upon him, party may file motion for statement in separate counts or defenses, or for more definite statement, of any matter not averred with sufficient definiteness to enable him to prepare his responsive pleading. (Rule 12[e]).

Verification or affidavits need not accompany pleadings (Rule 11) except petitions or motions for depositions to perpetuate testimony (Rule 27[a][1]), temporary restraining order (Rule 65[b]), contempt (Rule 107[c]), service by mail (Rule 4[g]), service by publication (Rule 4[h]), entry of default and default judgment (Rule 55[a], [b] and Rule 121[1-14]), new trial on specified grounds (Rule 59[a], [c]) and order authorizing sale under power and response thereto (Rule 120[a], [c]).

Every pleading of party represented by attorney must be signed by attorney, who shall also state his address and party's address. Attorney must state his supreme court registration number on initial pleading filed by him. Party who represents himself must sign his pleading and state his address. (Rule 11). See subhead Frivolous Claims, infra.

Service.—See topic Process. Federal Rules of Civil Procedure adopted with no material variation. (Rule 5[a] and [b]).

For purposes of service a resident attorney must be associated as an attorney of record with any foreign attorney practicing in any courts of Colorado. (Rule 5[b]).

Time.—Defendant must file answer or other response within 20 days after service of summons and complaint or within 30 days if, pursuant to special order, copy of complaint was not served with summons or summons was served out of state, or by publication; party served with cross-claim or counterclaim, or desiring to reply to affirmative defense, must file reply within 20 days. If pleading ordered by court, reply must be filed within 20 days after entry of order. If court denies motion under Rule 12 or Rule 98 or postpones disposition until trial on merits, responsive pleadings shall be filed within ten days after notice of court's action. Upon grant of motion for more definite statement or statement in separate counts or defenses, responsive pleading must be filed within ten days after service of more definite statement or amended pleading. (Rule 12[a]). Upon grant of motion to change venue, responsive pleading must be filed within ten days of docketing action in court to which action removed or, where motion to change venue denied, responsive pleading must be filed within ten days of order so denying. (Rule 98[e][2]).

Demand for trial by jury must be made within ten days after service of last pleading directed to issue (Rule 38[b]); if party has demanded trial by jury for only some issues, any other party may, within ten days after service of demand, demand trial by jury for other issues (Rule 38[c]).

Motion for new trial must be filed within 15 days after entry of judgment, unless court grants longer period. (Rule 59[a]). Filing of motion for post-trail relief is not condition precedent to appeal or cross-appeal, and filing of such motion does not limit issues that may be raised on appeal. (Rule 59[b]). Affidavit supporting motion for new trial required, except when motion based on grounds of excessive or inadequate damages or error in law. Opposing party has 15 days after service to file opposing affidavits; this period may be extended by stipulation or leave of court. (Rule 59[d]). Within time allowed parties, court may order new trial on its own initiative. (Rule 59[c]).

Computation of time controlled by Rule 6 which adopts Federal Rules of Civil Procedure with exceptions that when period of time prescribed is less than seven days, intermediate Sats., Suns. and legal holidays excluded from computation; legal holidays include Colorado day and general election day.

Small Claims.—See category Courts and Legislature, topic Courts.
See also topic Damages.

See note at head of Digest as to 1998 legislation covered.

See Topical Index in front part of this volume.

CO – 33

PLEADING ... *continued*

Frivolous Claims.—Sanctions for any pleading that is substantially frivolous, groundless, or vexatious. (Rules 11, 121-1-15[7]; 13-17-102). Signature of attorney on pleading constitutes certificate by him that he has read pleading, that to best of his knowledge, information and belief formed after reasonable inquiry, it is well grounded in fact and is warranted by existing law or good faith argument for extension, modification, or reversal of existing law, and that it is not interposed for improper purpose, such as to harass or to cause unnecessary delay or needless increase in cost of litigation. Sanctions for violation include costs and attorneys fees incurred because of pleading. Sanctions not imposed if voluntary dismissal or withdrawal occurs within reasonable time after knowledge that party would not prevail on claim, action, defense, or motion. (13-17-102).

PRACTICE:

Practice in courts of record is governed by Colorado Rules of Civil Procedure which in most instances, are similar to Federal Rules of Civil Procedure. (Vol. 7, Colorado Revised Statutes). Practice before administrative agencies is governed in most cases by Colorado State Administrative Procedure Act. (24-4-101 to 108). As of Apr. 1, 1988, all local court rules abolished and only reinstated with specific permission of Supreme Court. No local rules in effect. Colorado Rule 121 sets forth statewide practice including procedures for: Entry of appearance and withdrawal; special admission of out-of-state attorneys; jury fees; access to court files; settings for trials or hearings; consolidation; dismissal for failure to prosecute; continuances; matters related to discovery; default judgments; determination of motions; pretrial procedure and settlement; jury instructions; bonds in civil actions; and other administrative matters.

Mandatory Arbitration.—Mandatory arbitration pilot project terminated July 1, 1991.

Requests for Admission of Facts.—Federal Rules of Civil Procedure adopted except presumptive limit of 20 requests. (Rule 36[a]; Rule 26[b]).

Small Claims.—See category Courts and Legislature, topic Courts.

See topics Actions, Appeal and Error, Certiorari, Depositions and Discovery, Injunctions, Judgments, Limitation of Actions, Partition, Pleading, Process, Replevin, Venue; categories Civil Actions and Procedure, topic Evidence, subhead Witnesses; Debtor and Creditor, topics Attachment, Creditors' Suits, Executions, Garnishment, Receivers; Family, topic Divorce.

Case Management.—In cases filed on or after Jan. 1, 1995, (except domestic relations, juvenile, mental health, probate, water law, forcible entry and detainer, sales under powers, or other expedited hearings) lead counsel must meet 15 days after case is at issue and discuss claims, defenses, and disclosure obligations. (Rule 16[b]). Case is at issue when all parties served and pleadings permitted under Rule 7 filed. Within 35 days after case is at issue, lead counsel must explore possibilities of settlement and begin to develop proposed Case Management Order. Case Management Order due 45 days after case is at issue. To extent possible, counsel shall agree to contents of Case Management Order, with disputed matters noted. Case Management Order shall include in specified format estimated length of trial, Rule 26 disclosures, witnesses and exhibits, discovery schedule, time to join parties and amend pleadings, anticipated pretrial motions, and settlement possibilities. (Rule 16[b]). Court approves Order at Case Management conference, and it becomes binding, except by consent of parties or Court order. (Rule 16[b][3]).

Counsel also must confer and develop Trial Management Order, which is due 30 days before trial. (Rule 16[c]). It must include in specified format statement of claims and defenses, stipulated facts, pretrial motions, legal issues, itemization of damages, proposed trial efficiencies, and identification of witnesses and exhibits. (Rule 16[c][1]). Court approves this Order, and it is binding. (Rule 16[c][3]). Counsel also must confer and develop jury instructions and verdict forms. (Rule 16[d]).

In domestic relations cases filed after July 1, 1995, parties and counsel must meet and confer in good faith before temporary orders may be heard. (Rule 16.2[b]). No later than 20 days prior to hearing, counsel and parties shall meet and discuss child custody, parenting time, child support, property distribution, other substantive issues, development of trial management certificate, and settlement. (Rule 16.2[d][1]). Trial management certificate shall be filed ten days prior to trial or hearing, and in specified format shall address nature of hearing, pretrial motions, stipulations and undisputed facts, disputed issues and points of law, witnesses, exhibits, financial affidavits and child support guidelines, and alternative dispute resolution. (Rule 16.2[d][2-4]).

Disclosure Duties.—In cases filed on or after Jan. 1, 1995, (except domestic relations, juvenile, mental health, probate, water law, forcible entry and detainer, sales under powers, or other expedited hearings), each party must provide to other parties name of each individual likely to have discoverable information, listing and copy or description of all documents relevant to facts alleged with particularity in pleadings, damage computation, and any relevant insurance agreement. (Rule 26 [a][1]). Disclosure must be made within 30 days after case is at issue. (Rule 16[b]). Unless otherwise specified in Case Management Order, expert testimony must be disclosed by plaintiff no later than 120 days before trial, and by defendant 30 days later. (Rule 26[a][2]). Rebuttal expert testimony must be disclosed 20 days after disclosure of expert evidence which it is meant to rebut. All disclosures must be signed, and signature constitutes attestation that disclosure is complete and correct. (Rule 26[g][1]). Court can compel disclosure or order sanctions if party fails to comply with disclosure obligations. (Rule 37[a][2][A]).

In domestic relations cases filed after July 1, 1995, disclosure obligations generally parallel those under Rule 26. Under Rule 26.2, however, parties must disclose information typically important in domestic relations cases, including financial affidavit, income tax returns, evidence of wages, and pension or profit-sharing information. (Rule 26.2[a][1]). Initial disclosures are due 20 days after response, disclosures regarding expert testimony are due 60 days prior to hearing, and disclosures regarding rebuttal expert testimony are due 20 days after other party's expert disclosures. (Rule 26.2[a][1-2]). Parties rather than attorneys sign mandatory disclosures. (Rule 26.2[g][1]).

For cases filed before Jan. 1, 1995, but after Apr. 1, 1988, (mental health, marriage dissolution, mandatory arbitration and trials de novo following mandatory arbitration), each party shall file with court and serve on all other parties disclosure certificate within 180 days after case is at issue but no later than 90 days before trial, whichever occurs first. (Rules 16[a] and 121[1-18]). Case is "at issue" tenth day after last pleading permitted under Rule 7 has been filed and served. See Rule 16 for required contents of certificate. Limited supplementation of disclosure certificate permitted no later than 80 days prior to trial for certain matters. (Rule 16[b]). Appropriate sanctions available, including preclusion of issues, witnesses, experts or particular evidence at trial, upon showing of bad-faith failure to disclose initially or to supplement promptly disclosure certificate. Expert witness reports or summaries shall be served on all parties no later than 80 days before trial. (Rule 16[g]). Report or summary shall set forth opinions of expert and basis for each opinion. No later than 15 days after receipt of supplemental designation of expert witness, opposing party may designate opposing or rebuttal expert to meet expert opinion first learned of in supplemental disclosure certificate. Rule 16 also governs status conferences and case management orders. (Rule 16[d], [e]).

Discovery.—Broad powers of discovery are provided. (Rules 26-37). In cases filed on or after Jan. 1, 1995, unless otherwise ordered by court, party may depose each adverse party once, take two other depositions, propound 30 interrogatories, and make 20 document requests and 20 requests for admission. In domestic relations cases filed after July 1, 1995, same discovery limits apply, but parties can additionally propound unlimited number of pattern interrogatories or document requests. (Rule 26.2[b][2]). See topic Depositions and Discovery.

Limited Discovery.—For cases filed before Jan. 1, 1995, any party may, at any time, file request for limited and simplified discovery. If such request not opposed in next responsive pleading, or within 30 days after service of such request by written response, discovery limited to three depositions by each party, one set of up to 30 interrogatories upon each adverse party, and one set of requests for admissions not exceeding 20 in number. Discovery governed by Rule 26.1 must be completed no later than 30 days before trial. If request for limited discovery is opposed, court determines whether limited discovery provisions apply. In making determination, court may consider whether factual and legal issues involved are appropriate for limited discovery, extent and expense of discovery anticipated, amount in controversy, number of parties and whether any party would be prejudiced. (Rule 26.1). Parties must supplement and amend responses. See also topic Depositions and Discovery.

PROCESS:

Process runs in the name of "The People of the State of Colorado" and is based on Federal Rules of Civil Procedure. See topic Practice. (Colo. Const., art. VI, §22).

Summons may be signed and issued by clerk, under seal of court, or by plaintiff's attorney. Separate, additional or amended summons may issue against any defendant at any time. All other process must be issued by clerk, except as otherwise provided by Rules. (Rule 4[b]).

Contents of Summons.—Summons must state name of court, names or designations of parties, county in which brought, must be directed to defendant, state time in which defendant must appear and defend and that failure to do so may subject him to judgment by default. If served by publication, summons must state money or relief demanded. Summons must state name, address, and registration number of plaintiff's attorney, if any, and if not, plaintiff's address. Except for service by publication or other court order, complaint must be served with summons, and if such other order issues, it must be served with summons. (Rule 4[c]).

Who May Serve.—Process may be served: (1) Within state by sheriff, or his deputy, or by any other person over age of 18 not party to action; (2) at any other place, by sheriff, constable, bailiff, their deputies or by other officer having like powers of political subdivision where service made; or by person authorized by Colorado law to take acknowledgments in such political subdivision to deeds conveying real estate in Colorado; or by person qualified to practice law in such place or by person commissioned by court in which action pending. (Rule 4[d]).

Personal service within the state may be made as follows: (1) On a natural person over the age of 18 by delivering a copy personally or leaving copy at his usual place of abode with some member of family over age of 18, or at usual place of business with stenographer, bookkeeper or chief clerk, or by delivering copy to agent authorized by appointment or by law to receive service of process. (2) On natural person between ages of 13 and 18 by delivering copy to him and copy to his father, mother, or guardian, or if there be none in state by delivering copy to any person in whose care or control he may be or with whom he resides or in whose service he is employed; upon natural person under age 13 by delivery of copy to his father, mother, or guardian. (3) On person for whom conservator has been appointed by delivering copy thereof to such conservator. (4) On partnership or unincorporated association by delivering copy to one or more of partners or associates, or managing or general agent thereof. (5) On private corporation by delivering copy to any officer, manager, general agent, or registered agent for process. If no such officer or agent can be found in county in which action is brought, such copy may be delivered to any stockholder, agent, member or principal employee found in such county. If service be on person other than executive officer, secretary, general agent or registered agent for process, clerk of court must mail copy of process to corporation at its last known address, at least 20 days before default is entered. (6) On municipal corporation by delivering copy thereof to mayor, clerk or deputy clerk of such corporation. (7) On county by delivering copy to county clerk or his chief deputy. (8) On school district by delivering copy to clerk or one of directors of district. (9) On state by delivering copy thereof to attorney general, or to any employee in his office designated by him to accept service of process. (10) On officer, agent, or employee of state, acting in his official capacity, by delivering copy thereof to officer, agent, or employee, and by delivering copy to attorney general, or to any employee in his office designated to accept service of process. (11) Upon department or agency of state by delivering copy thereof to principal officer, chief clerk, or other executive employee thereof and by delivering copy to attorney general, or to any employee in his office designated by him to accept service of process. (Rule 4[e]). For all purposes day of

PROCESS . . . *continued*

service upon officer, agent, employee, department or agency shall control, except that failure to serve copies upon attorney general within three days of service upon officer, agent, employee, department or agency shall extend time within which officer, agent, employee, department or agency may file responsive pleading for 60 days beyond time otherwise provided by rules. (Rule 4[e][10][C]). See topic Pleading, subhead Time.

Personal service outside state may be made: (1) On natural person over age 18 in action if person served is resident of Colorado or nonresident of Colorado who has submitted to or has become subject by law to jurisdiction of Colorado by delivering copy of process and pleading on which it was issued to such person; (2) on person other than natural person, who is domiciled in Colorado or who has submitted to or become subject by law to jurisdiction in Colorado by delivering copy of process and pleading on which it was issued as provided for personal service in Colorado; or (3) in any action affecting specific property or status or in any other proceeding in rem without regard to residence of person served by delivering copy of process, together with copy of pleading in manner provided for personal service in Colorado. (Rule 4[f]).

Jurisdiction of Courts.—Engaging, either in person or by agent, in transaction of any business within this state; commission of tortious act within this state; ownership, use, or possession of any real property situated in this state; contracting to insure any person, property, or risk residing or located within this state at time of contracting; or maintenance of matrimonial domicile within state if one party to marriage continues without interruption to be domiciled within state, submits such person and, if natural person, his personal representative to jurisdiction of courts of this state, concerning any cause of action arising from such acts. (13-1-124).

Service by mail or publication is allowed only in cases affecting specific property or status or other proceedings in rem. (Rule 4[g]). Service by mail or publication not permitted in personal injury action seeking compensatory damages even if defendant willfully conceals himself from service. (709 P.2d 1383). Registered mail as used in Colorado statutes includes certified mail. (2-4-401[12]).

Service by mail may be secured on a person who is without the state of Colorado on motion to the court verified by the oath of the party or someone in his behalf for an order for service by mail. Motion must state address of person being served and facts showing why service by mailing is advisable. Court may hear motion ex parte and direct clerk to send copy of process and pleading to person being served. Such service becomes complete on filing of clerk's proof, together with the return receipt showing delivery of the registered letter and signed by addressee. (Rule 4[g][1]).

Service by publication may be had on (1) Unknown persons; (2) domestic corporations which cannot be served because no person can be found on whom such service can be made; (3) foreign corporations when they have not appointed registered agent or agent cannot be found at registered office, (4) nonresidents, including persons who have departed from state without intention of returning, persons who conceal themselves to avoid service, or persons whose whereabouts are unknown and who cannot be served personally in state. (Rule 4[g]). Publication as means of service of process may be secured by filing verified motion for order of publication with specified information which court may grant following ex parte hearing if satisfied that due diligence has been used to obtain personal service within state or that efforts to obtain such service would have been of no avail. Publication is made for four weeks in newspaper published in county in which action pending or if none, designated paper in adjoining county. Within 15 days after order of publication clerk must mail copy of process to each person whose last known address has been stated in motion. Service becomes complete on day of last publication. (Rule 4[h]).

Refusal of Service.—If person to be served refuses to accept process, service shall be sufficient if person serving states name of process and offers to deliver copy. (Rule 4[k]).

Long Arm Statute.—See subhead Jurisdiction of Courts, supra.

Nonresident Motorist.—See category Transportation, topic Motor Vehicles.

Proof of Service.—If service is made by sheriff or deputy, proof is by certificate with statement as to date, place, and manner of service. If service is made by any other person, proof is by person's affidavit with same statement. If service is by mail, proof is by certificate of clerk showing date of mailing and date return receipt was received. If service is by publication, proof is by affidavit of publication, together with certificate of clerk as to mailing of copy of process where required. Proof also may be by duly acknowledged written admission or waiver of service by person to be served. (Rule 4[i]).

Amendment.—The court may, at any time and on such terms as it deems just, allow any process or proof of service thereof to be amended unless it clearly appears that material prejudice would result to the substantial rights of the party against whom the process issued. (Rule 4[j]).

REPLEVIN:

Rule 104, Colorado Rules of Civil Procedure.

County Court Rule 404 is substantially similar to Rule 104, but jurisdiction is limited to recovery of property of value not exceeding $10,000. (C.R.S. §13-6-104).

Plaintiff in an action to recover possession of personal property may at any time before trial claim delivery of such property to him. Although Rule 104 does not specify that demand be made, Colorado case law indicates demand must precede replevin when person in possession acquired property in good faith by purchase or when necessary to terminate defendant's right of possession or to confer that right on plaintiff, but demand may be made after commencement of action for possession. (9 Colo. 390, 12 P.434; 41 Colo. 164, 91 P.1110). Common law writs of replevin are archaic under current law and practice, since Rule 104 normally contemplates only issuance of show cause order followed by preliminary hearing prior to issuance of order for possession. (72 F.464). Purpose of Rule 104 prejudgment replevin hearing is to ensure that defendant's constitutional property rights are not jeopardized by unduly summary claim and repossession proceedings (601 P.2d 626). Although district court sits as court of general jurisdiction in action to replevin personal property, its powers are limited in Rule 104 prejudgment hearing to deciding issue of which party, with reasonable probability, is entitled to possession, use, and disposition of property pending final adjudication of claims of parties. (601 P.2d 626). Court conducting hearing under Rule 104 lacks jurisdiction to affect possessory rights in any property not brought within its purview by duly issued order to show cause, and jurisdiction over parties and subject matter does not authorize trial court to enter under Rule 104 whatever remedial orders it deems necessary to finally adjust equities between parties. (601 P.2d 626).

Proceedings.—Where delivery is claimed, plaintiff must by verified complaint or by complaint and affidavit under penalty of perjury show court following: (1) That plaintiff is owner of property claimed or entitled to possession thereof and source of such title or right; if plaintiff's interest is based upon written instrument, a copy thereof must be attached; (2) that property is being detained by defendant against plaintiff's claim of right to possession, means by which defendant came into possession thereof, and specific facts constituting detention against right of plaintiff to possession; (3) particular description of property, statement of its actual value, and statement to his best knowledge, information and belief concerning location of property and of residence and business address, if any, of defendant; (4) that property has not been taken for tax assessment or fine pursuant to statute, or seized under an execution against property of plaintiff; if so seized, that it is by statute exempt from such seizure. (Rule 104[b]).

Court must examine complaint and affidavit, and upon being satisfied that it meets above requirements, it must issue an order directed to defendant to show cause why property should not be taken from defendant and delivered to plaintiff. Such order shall fix time and date of hearing thereof. Hearing date must not be more than ten days from date of issuance of order and order must have been served at least five days prior to hearing date. Such order shall inform defendant that he may file affidavits on his behalf with court and may appear and present testimony in his behalf at time of such hearing, or that he may, at or prior to such hearing, file with court a written undertaking to stay delivery of property, in accordance with Rule 104(j) and that, if he fails to appear at hearing on order to show cause or file an undertaking, plaintiff may apply to court for an order requiring sheriff to take immediate possession of property described in complaint and deliver same to plaintiff. Summons and complaint, if not previously served, and order must be served on defendant and order must fix manner in which service shall be made which shall be by service in accordance with provisions of Rule 4, or in such manner as court may determine to be reasonably calculated to afford notice thereof to defendant under circumstances appearing from complaint and affidavit. (Rule 104[c]).

Subject to limitations of §5-104 of Uniform Consumer Credit Code, as modified (5-5-104), prohibiting prejudgment replevin of most goods in connection with collection actions arising out of consumer credit transactions, upon examination of complaint and affidavit and such other evidence or testimony as court may thereupon require, court may issue order of possession prior to hearing, if probable cause appears that any of following exist: (1) Defendant gained possession of property by theft; (2) property consists of one or more negotiable instruments or credit cards; (3) by reason of specific, competent evidence shown, by testimony with personal knowledge of affiant or witness, property is perishable, and will perish before any noticed hearing can be had, or that defendant may destroy, dismantle, remove parts from, or in any way substantially change character of property, or defendant may conceal or remove property from jurisdiction of court to sell property to innocent purchaser; or (4) that defendant has by contract voluntarily and intelligently and knowingly waived his right to hearing prior to losing possession of property by means of court order. (Rule 104[d]).

Where an order of possession has been issued prior to hearing under provisions described above, defendant or other persons from whom possession of said property has been taken, may apply to court for an order shortening time for hearing on order to show cause, and court may upon such application shorten time for hearing, and direct that matter be heard on not less than 48 hours notice to plaintiff. (Rule 104[d]).

Before prehearing order of possession can issue under Rule 104(d), bond must be filed by plaintiff with such surety as court may require in amount set by court in its discretion, but not to exceed double value of property as stated in affidavit, for return of property to defendant, if such return thereof be ordered, and for payment to defendant of any sum that may from any cause be recovered against plaintiff. (Rule 104[e]). Written exception to sureties on any bond required must be taken by party within two days after notice thereof or objection waived. Language of Rule 104(e) "any sum that may from any cause be recovered" concerning amount of bond covers only claims of possession and loss thereof and not underlying claims unrelated to possession or loss of property at issue. (586 P.2d 243).

At hearing on order to show cause, court must make preliminary determination which party is, with reasonable probability, entitled to possession of property, pending final adjudication. Court may require bond in such amount and with such surety as will protect rights of parties. Failure of defendant to be present does not constitute default in main action. (Rule 104[g]).

In addition to issuance of order to show cause or in lieu of immediate issuance of order for prehearing possession, court may issue such temporary orders, directed to defendant, prohibiting or requiring such acts with respect to property as may appear to be necessary for preservation of rights of parties and status of property. (Rule 104[f]).

Contents of Possession Order.—Order of possession shall describe specific property to be seized, and shall specify location or locations where there is probable cause to believe property or some part thereof will be found. It shall direct sheriff to seize same as it is found and to retain it in his custody. Order shall inform defendant that he has right to except to sureties or amount of bond upon undertaking or to file a written undertaking for redelivery of such property. (Rule 104[h]).

Sheriff shall forthwith take property if it be in possession of defendant or his agent, and retain it in his custody; except that when personal property is then occupied as a dwelling, sheriff shall take constructive possession of property and shall remove its occupants and take property into his actual custody at expiration of ten days after issuance of order of possession, or at such earlier time as property shall be vacated. (Rule 104[h]).

Sheriff May Break Open Building; When.—If property or any part thereof is in a building or enclosure, sheriff is to demand delivery of property, announcing his identity, purpose, and authority under which he acts. If property is not voluntarily delivered, he is to cause building or enclosure to be broken open in such manner as he reasonably

REPLEVIN . . . *continued*
believes will cause least damage to building or enclosure and take property into his possession. (Rule 104[i]).

Return to Defendant.—At any time prior to hearing on order to show cause, or before delivery of property to plaintiff, defendant may require return thereof upon filing with court written undertaking, in amount set by court at its discretion not to exceed double value of property and executed by defendant and such surety as court may direct for delivery of property to plaintiff, if such delivery be ordered, and for payment to plaintiff of such sum of money as may for any cause be recovered against defendant. (Rule 104[j]).

Claims of Third Persons.—Person other than defendant or plaintiff claiming property may intervene under provisions of Rule 24, and in event of a judgment in his favor, he may also recover such damages as he may have suffered by reason of any wrongful detention of property. (Rule 104[m]).

Precedence on Docket.—All proceedings brought to recover possession of personal property must, upon request of any party thereto, be given precedence by courts in which such actions are pending over all other civil actions, except actions to which special precedence is otherwise given by law, in manner of setting of same for hearing or trial, and in hearing or trial thereof, to end that all such actions shall be quickly heard and determined. (Rule 104[o]).

Judgment.—In an action to recover possession of personal property, judgment for plaintiff may be for possession or value in case where delivery cannot be had and damages for detention. If property has been delivered to plaintiff, and defendant claims a return thereof, judgment for defendant may be for return of property, or value thereof where return cannot be had and damages for taking and withholding same. Rule 13 relating to counterclaims applies to replevin actions. (Rule 104[p]).

Trial of principal action in which replevin order is issued proceeds in same manner as ordinary civil action. It is not affected by fact that property involved has been replevied or by plaintiff's failure to prevail on claim for prejudgment order of possession under Rule 104.

SEQUESTRATION:

No legislation.

STAY OF EXECUTION:

See topic Appeal and Error; category Debtor and Creditor, topic Executions.

SUBMISSION OF CONTROVERSY:

Actual justiciable controversy may be submitted, without pleadings on agreed statement of facts, supported by affidavit to court of competent jurisdiction, which may render judgment thereon as in action. (Rule 7 [d]).

Office of Dispute Resolution.—Persons are eligible for mediation services through state office of dispute resolution after having filed complaint in civil action in county or district court. Proceedings regarded as settlement negotiations, and statements made therein of limited discoverability and admissibility at trial. Agreements reduced to writing and presented to court as stipulation, and if approved, are enforceable as order of court. (13-22-301 to 313). Subject to certain limitations, any court of record may refer any case to early neutral evaluation by court appointed evaluator to narrow, eliminate, or simplify issues, or refer case to mediation, or other alternative dispute resolution procedures. (13-22-302 to 313).

VENUE:

Subject to exceptions below, actions may generally be tried in any county where any defendant resides at commencement of action, or in county where plaintiff resides when service is made upon defendant in such county; or on nonresident defendant, in any county where defendant may be found or in county designated in complaint. If defendant is about to depart state, action also may be brought in county where plaintiff resides or in county where service is made. (Rule 98[c][1]). Substance, rather than form, of action controls venue determination. (702 P.2d 262).

Real Property, Franchises and Utilities.—Actions affecting real property, franchises and utilities must be tried in county in which subject of action, or substantial part thereof, is situated. (Rule 98[a]).

Penalties and Public Officials.—Action to recover statutory penalty or against public officials must be brought in county where claim, or part thereof, arose. (Rule 98[b]). Claim for injunctive relief against public official arises in county in which public body had its official residence. (187 Colo. 113, 528 P.2d 1305).

Injunction to Stay Proceedings.—Action to stay suit or judgment must be brought in county where judgment was obtained or suit is pending. (Rule 98[d]).

Consumer Contracts.—Consumer contract is transaction by person primarily for personal, family or household purposes, involving $25,000 or less. (Rule 98[c][3][A]). Action on consumer contract must be brought in county where contract was entered into by any defendant, where any defendant resides at commencement of action or resided when contract entered into or on nonresident defendant, in any county where defendant may be found or in county designated in complaint. (Rule 98[c][3][B]). If defendant is about to depart state, action also may be brought in county where plaintiff resides or in county where service is made upon such defendant. (Rule 98[c][3][B]). Contract provision in consumer contract fixing venue in place unauthorized by rule is void. (Rule 98[c][3][C]). Debt collectors covered by provisions of federal "Fair Debt Collection Practices Act" must comply with venue provisions in 15 U.S.C. 1692(i). (Rule 98[c][3][D]).

Other Contracts.—Except for consumer contracts, contract action also may be brought in county where contract to be performed as well as in counties covered by general venue provisions. (Rule 98[c][2], [4]). Action on book account or for goods sold and delivered also may be tried in county where plaintiff resides or goods were sold. (Rule 98[c][2]).

Torts.—Tort action may be brought in county where tort committed as well as in counties covered by general venue provisions. (Rule 98[c][5]).

Interpleader action may be brought in county where claimant resides as well as in counties covered by general venue provisions. (Rule 98[c][6]).

Change of venue may be granted if action is brought in improper county or when convenience of witnesses and ends of justice would be promoted. (Rule 98[f]). If district court concludes, upon motion of party, that fair trial could not be obtained in county, venue must be changed. (Rule 98[g]). Venue also may be changed upon agreement of all parties. (Rule 98[i], [j]). Party obtaining change of venue is only entitled to one change upon same grounds. (Rule 98[k]).

COURTS AND LEGISLATURE

COURTS:

United States District Court.—Clerk's office: 1929 Stout Street, Room 145, Denver 80294.

Docket Fee.—On commencement of civil action, fee of $150 is required. One district covers entire state.

Court sits at Denver. Court sits when required at Boulder, Pueblo, Grand Junction, Montrose, Durango and Sterling. All papers should be filed at Denver. Court has enacted Local Rules of Practice; copies available from clerk's office.

Supreme Court.—Court consists of seven justices, who may sit en banc or in department. No decision of any department becomes judgment of court unless concurred in by at least three justices.

Docket Fee.—$150 for appellant or petitioner; $75 for appellee or respondent.

Court has jurisdiction to review some final judgments of court of appeals, district, probate, county and juvenile courts by writ of error, appeal or certiorari; it also has power to issue certain original writs. Court may review any death sentence. (App. Rule 4[e]).

Court sits at Denver. See category Civil Actions and Procedure, topic Appeal and Error.

Court of Appeals.—Court consists of 16 judges who sit in divisions of three judges. (13-4-103).

Docket Fee.—$150 for appellant or petitioner; $75 for appellee or respondent.

Bond for Costs.—$250 for civil cases, unless trial court fixes different amount.

Court has initial jurisdiction over appeals from final judgment of district courts, and probate and juvenile courts of Denver, except: Cases involving constitutionality of statutes, charters, and ordinances, cases involving public utilities commission, water priority and adjudication cases, writs of habeas corpus, post conviction relief when death sentence imposed (13-1-102[h]) and cases appealed from county court to district court, certain summary proceedings described in 13-14-102(g).

Court also has initial jurisdiction to review awards or actions of industrial claims appeals office, orders of banking board granting or denying charters for new state banks, decisions of medical examiners and of board of dental examiners refusing to grant, revoking or suspending licenses or placing holder thereof on probation, decisions of board of education dismissing teacher, final decisions and orders of civil rights commission, and orders or decisions of numerous other administrative agencies, boards or licensing authorities. (13-4-102).

Cases may be certified to supreme court for public interest, expedience and importance of legal principles involved. (13-4-109). See category Civil Actions and Procedure, topic Appeal and Error.

District Courts.—These courts have original jurisdiction of all causes at law and in equity, including divorce cases. They have original jurisdiction to try all criminal cases, whether involving a felony or a misdemeanor, and exclusive original jurisdiction in criminal cases where penalty may be death. They have appellate jurisdiction in all cases commenced in county courts. They have exclusive jurisdiction for certain water matters which are heard by designated water judges. (37-92-203). There are 22 districts.

Docket Fee.—As set forth in 13-32-101 to 113.

Districts.—For list of counties that are within particular judicial district, as well as names of court seats, see Colorado Courts' official website, www.courts.state.co.us.

County courts are courts of record established in each county. Jurisdiction is statewide, subject to venue provisions. County courts have original jurisdiction in hearings concerning impoundment of motor vehicles. (24-33.5-213.5). County courts have original jurisdiction concurrent with district courts in civil actions involving claims not exceeding $10,000, and counterclaims not exceeding $10,000. County courts also have concurrent jurisdiction with district courts in actions of forcible entry, forcible detainer, and unlawful detainer, where judgments for damages, rent, etc. do not exceed $10,000, exclusive of costs, interest and attorney's fees. (13-6-104). County courts have jurisdiction in petitions for change of name or issuance of delayed or corrected birth certificates, and to issue peace bonds and restraining orders to prevent assaults and threatened personal harm and in actions to foreclose liens under 38-20-101 et seq. County courts have only limited jurisdiction, and have no power over matters of probate, mental health, matters of divorce, annulment or separate maintenance, matters affecting children (including adoption, support, guardianship, custody, dependency and delinquency), matters affecting boundaries or title to real property, or original injunction proceedings (except as specifically authorized), such as orders to enforce restrictive covenants on residential property. (13-6-105). County courts have original criminal jurisdiction in misdemeanor or petty offense actions, including misdemeanor traffic offenses (42 Colo. App. 187, 591 P.2d 600), arising under state law, except in cases involving children over which Denver juvenile court or district courts of state have exclusive jurisdiction. They may issue warrants, conduct preliminary examinations, issue bindover orders, and admit persons to bail in both felony and misdemeanor matters. Appeals from county courts are to district court. Appellant must file notice of appeal and appeal bond with county court, within 15 days after date of entry of judgment appealed from. (13-6-301 to 311; C.R.C.P. 411).

Courts sit at county seat of each county (see subhead District Courts, supra).

See note at head of Digest as to 1998 legislation covered.

See Topical Index in front part of this volume.

CO – 36

COURTS . . . *continued*

Docket Fee.—$31 for plaintiff; and $26 for defendant.

Probate Courts.—A probate court, court of record, has been established for city and county of Denver, having original and exclusive jurisdiction over administration, settlement and distribution of estates of decedents, wards, and absentees, granting of letters testamentary, of administration, of guardianship and by conservatorship; administration of guardianships of minors and incompetent persons, and conservatorship of incompetents and absentees, lunacy proceedings, determination of heirship, administration of testamentary trusts, and all other probate matters. (13-9-101 to 122).

In all other counties, such probate and estate jurisdiction rests in district courts.

Small Claims Courts.—In each county court there is division designated as small claims court. Small claims courts have original jurisdiction concurrent with county and district court in civil actions involving claims and counterclaims not exceeding $5,000 exclusive of interest and costs. (Rule 508; 13-6-403). Small claims courts are not courts of general jurisdiction and only have jurisdiction specifically conferred by law. Small claims courts do not have jurisdiction over matters excluded from county court jurisdiction, matters involving claims of defamation by libel or slander, actions of forcible entry, forcible detainer or unlawful detainer, actions in replevin, actions for specific performance, class actions, and actions seeking prejudgment remedies, injunctive relief, except actions to enforce restrictive covenants on residential property when compliance will not exceed $5,000, exclusive of interest and costs (13-6-403), traffic violations and other criminal matters or awards of body execution. Unless party objects, cases are heard and decided by appointed referees who are attorneys admitted to practice in Colorado or county judges. Individuals represent themselves before small claims court, and organizations by active officers, partners, directors or full time employees. (13-6-407). Attorneys may appear and take part in filing, prosecution or defense of any matter in small claims court only when acting pro se or when active, full-time employee, general partner, officer, or member of association, union, or corporation which is party to action. (13-6-407). However, if defendant files written request not less than seven days before appearance date stating that he desires to be and will be represented by attorney, and upon payment of additional docket fee, clerk of small claims court shall transfer claim to county court, where matter will be tried under rules and procedures of small claims court. Thereupon, plaintiff may also be represented by attorney. If defendant fails to appear or appears without attorney after transferring claim to county court, and court finds transfer was made for purpose of delay, court may award plaintiff any costs and attorney's fees occasioned by delay. If plaintiff learns defendant will be represented by attorney in small claims court, plaintiff may transfer action to county court if plaintiff will be represented by attorney as consequence. (Rule 503). Purpose of small claims court is to provide inexpensive, speedy, and informal resolution of small claims in forum in which rules of substantive law apply, but rules of procedure, pleadings and technical rules of evidence do not.

Trials are conducted to do justice between parties. Unless parties agree at or prior to trial that there shall be no appeal and that decision of referee or judge be final and binding on both parties, appeals may be taken pursuant to county court rules. No plaintiff may file more than two claims per month, or 18 claims per year in any county. Each claim filed must certify number of claims filed in that month, and for year in small claims court of that county. State supported institutions of higher learning may file no more than 30 claims per month in all small claims courts of State. (13-6-411). Procedure applicable is governed by Rules of Procedure For Small Claims Courts, Rules 501 to 521.

Docket Fee.—Docket fees vary depending on size of claim asserted, up to maximum of $42 for claimant and $38 for defendant.

Municipal Courts.—All incorporated cities and towns must have a municipal court having exclusive original jurisdiction of all cases arising under ordinances of city within which it is organized. If a court of record, appeal is to district court or superior court if established. If not court of record, appeal is to county court or superior court if established and tried de novo. (13-10-101 to 125).

Juvenile Courts.—Juvenile court, court of record, has been established having original jurisdiction in over proceedings involving neglected, dependent or delinquent children under 18, and persons who contribute to such conditions, and over proceedings in adoption, custody, support, relinquishment, guardianship, and other disposition of children under 18, and care and protection of such children from neglect, cruelty or abuse. (Const., Art. 6, §15). Legislature has established comprehensive system of juvenile justice. (19-2-101 to 1004). Generally, in cases of violation of municipal ordinances, penalty for which may be jail sentence, or state law not amounting to felony, juvenile court has exclusive jurisdiction if under 18. Other courts retain jurisdiction in matters of custody by writ of habeas corpus, determination of custody, support, etc., incidental to other causes, and property or estates of children.

Office of Dispute Resolution.—Persons are eligible for mediation services through state office of dispute resolution before or after having filed complaint in civil action in county or district court. Proceedings regarded as settlement negotiations, and statements made therein of limited discoverability and admissibility at trial. Agreements reduced to writing and presented to court as stipulation, and if approved, are enforceable as order of court. (13-22-301 to 310). Any court of record may refer case to mediation. (13-22-311).

LEGISLATURE:

Meets annually no later than second Wed. in Jan. Regular sessions limited to 120 calendar days. (Const., art. 5, §7).

Special or extraordinary sessions may be called by governor or by written request of two-thirds of members of each house. (Const., art. 5, §7).

Initiative and referendum both provided for. (Const., art. 5, §1; 1-40-101 to 134).

Lobbyists must register and file disclosure statements with secretary of state. (24-6-302, 303).

REPORTS:

Decisions of supreme court through Sept. 1980 term are published in Colorado supreme court reports, beginning with volume 1 and ending with volume 200. Court of appeals was abolished in 1915 and re-established in 1970. Pre-abolition decisions reported in Colorado court of appeals reports, Vols. 1-27. Newly created court of appeals decisions, reported in Vols. 28-44, are published on selective basis as determined by majority of all court of appeals judges.

Pursuant to 13-2-124, Supreme Court has designated West Publishing Company as official reporter of decisions of supreme court and court of appeals. Opinions of both courts as printed in Pacific reporter and Colorado reporter are official reports for all cases announced by supreme court subsequent to last cases appearing in volume 200 of Colorado supreme court reports and all cases of court of appeals selected for official publication subsequent to last cases appearing in volume 44 of Colorado court of appeals reports. Only caption material and text of all opinions announced by both courts constitute official report; synopses, headnotes and key numbers provided by publisher merely informational. Court of appeals decisions which are not selected for official publication but are published in Pacific reporter must bear legend to such effect. (App. Rule 35[f]). Advance sheets of opinions of both courts published monthly in The Colorado Lawyer, official publication of Colorado Bar Association.

Digest is Colorado digest (West Pub. Co.) 35 volumes with annual supplements, containing digests of all Colorado supreme court and court of appeals decisions and federal decisions arising in Colorado.

STATUTES:

Colorado Revised Statutes 1997 has displaced all prior compilations. Colorado Revised Statutes 1997 are cited as "C.R.S."

Administrative Procedures.—State Administrative Procedure Act applicable to rule making and licensing procedures. (24-4-101 to 108).

Administrative Regulations.—Code of Colorado Regulations (CCR) is official publication of rules and regulations of agencies of executive branch. (24-4-103).

Uniform Acts of the National Conference of Commissioners on Uniform State Laws which have been adopted, some, if not all with variances, modifications or omissions, are: Alcoholism and Intoxication Treatment (1973); Anatomical Gift (1969); Arbitration (1975); Act to Secure the Attendance of Witnesses from Without a State in Criminal Proceedings (1972); †Bus. Corp. (1958); Certification of Questions of Law (1970); Child Custody Jurisdiction (1973); †Commercial Code (1965); †Common Interest Ownership (1991); †Common Trust Fund (1947); Conflict of Laws-Limitations (1984); †Consumer Credit Code (1971); Contribution Among Tortfeasors (1977); Controlled Substances (1990 Version) (1992); Criminal Extradition (1953); †Deceptive Trade Practices (1966 version) (1969); Declaratory Judgments (1923); Determination of Death (1981); Disposition of Community Property Rights at Death (1973); Division of Income for Tax Purposes (1968); †Durable Power of Attorney (1973); Duties to Disabled Persons (1973); Enforcement of Foreign Judgments (1969); †Evidence (1979); Facsimile Signatures of Public Officials (1969); †Federal Lien Registration (1988); Fiduciaries (1923); Foreign Money Claims (1990); Foreign Money-Judgments Recognition (1977); †Fraudulent Transfer (1991); †Guardianship and Protective Proceedings (1988); Insurers Liquidation (1955); International Wills (1989); Interstate Arbitration of Death Taxes (1953); Interstate Compromise of Death Taxes (1953); Interstate Family Support (1993); Judicial Notice of Foreign Law (1967); †Jury Selection and Service (1971); Limited Partnership (1916 Version) (1931), (1985 Version) (1986); Management of Institutional Funds (1973); Mandatory Disposition of Detainers (1969); †Marriage and Divorce (1971, 1973); Multiple-Person Accounts (1990); †Non-Profit Corp. (1967); †Parentage (1977); Partnership (1997); Photographic Copies of Business and Public Records as Evidence (1955); †Principal and Income (1955); †Probate (1973); †Prudent Investor (1995); †Reciprocal Transfer Tax (1943); Recognition of Acknowledgments (1969); Rendition of Accused Persons (1972); †Securities (1961); Simultaneous Death (1967); Statutory Construction (1973); Statutory Form Power of Attorney (1992); Statutory Rule Against Perpetuities (1991); †Testamentary Additions to Trusts (1967); Trade Secrets (1986); Transboundary Pollution Reciprocal Access (1984); Transfers to Minors (1984); †Unclaimed Property (1987); Veterans Guardianship (1945).

For text of Uniform Acts falling within the scope of the Martindale-Hubbell Law Digests see Uniform and Model Acts section.

† Adopted with significant variances, modifications, or omissions. See appropriate topics as to Acts within scope of Digests volume.

Other Uniform Acts adopted are: Transfer on Death Security Registration (1990).

UNIFORM LAWS:

For list of Uniform Acts in force in this state see topic Statutes. For text of Uniform Acts within the scope of the Martindale-Hubbell Law Digests see Uniform and Model Acts section.

CRIMINAL LAW

CRIMINAL LAW:

Most statutes relating to criminal procedure are contained in C.R.S., Title 16 (Criminal Proceedings), articles 1 to 13 being Code of Criminal Procedure; Title 17 (Parole and Corrections); Title 18 (Criminal Code); Title 19 (Children's Code); Title 42 (Vehicles and Traffic) (see category Transportation, topic Motor Vehicles). Colorado supreme court has power to prescribe rules of pleading, practice and procedure in criminal cases in all courts (13-2-109), and has adopted Colorado Rules of Criminal Procedure (Court Rules, Vol. 7B, C.R.S.).

Indictment or Information.—Felony cases are begun by grand jury indictment, complaint filed in county court, or information filed in district court. (16-5-101). Misdemeanor cases are begun by filing complaint in county court.

See note at head of Digest as to 1998 legislation covered.

See Topical Index in front part of this volume.

CRIMINAL LAW . . . *continued*

Bail.—All persons shall be bailable before conviction except persons accused of capital offense, when proof is evident or presumption is great, or persons alleged to have committed crime of violence while on parole, probation, bail, or after two previous felony convictions, or one previous felony conviction if for crime of violence, appealing conviction or awaiting sentencing for crime of violence, when proof is evident or presumption is great and public would be placed in significant peril. (16-4-101). Burden is upon prosecution to establish that such proof is evident or presumption is great. (16-4-101). Excessive bail forbidden. (Const., Art. 2, §20). Juvenile has only qualified right to bail. (623 P.2d 1253).

After conviction, either before or after sentencing, defendant may be released on bail as matter of discretion. (16-4-201).

Uniform Act for Out-of-State Parolee Supervision in effect. (24-60-301 to 309).

Uniform Criminal Extradition Act in effect. (16-19-101 to 132).

Uniform Mandatory Disposition of Detainers Act in effect. (16-14-101 to 108). When prisoner substantially complies with provisions of Act and prosecution has actual notice of prisoner's request, it is within trial court's discretion to dismiss pending charges under Act. (742 P.2d 302).

Uniform Act to Secure the Attendance of Witnesses From Without a State in Criminal Proceedings in effect. (16-9-201 to 205).

Other Acts.—Crime Victim Compensation Act in effect. (24-4.1-100.1 to 124). Interstate Compacts and Agreements are found at Title 24, Art. 60.

DEBTOR AND CREDITOR

ASSIGNMENTS:

Uniform Commercial Code adopted. See category Business Regulation and Commerce, topic Commercial Code.

Instrument Transferring Title.—Rights, except for contractual rights involving matters of personal trust or confidence or for personal services (122 Colo. 79, 220 P.2d 864), debts and/or choses in action are freely assignable. Except for requirements of Uniform Commercial Code for negotiable instruments and securities, no special form of instrument and no acknowledgment or witnesses required to transfer title.

Filing.—Filing necessary only when required to perfect assignment of accounts, contract rights or general intangibles under Commercial Code as against third parties; in which case file in office of secretary of state (or, on and after July 1, 1996, in office of clerk and recorder of any county) except: (a) When accounts or general intangibles arise from or relate to sale of farm products by farmers, file in county of debtor's residence (for organization, place of business or, if more than one, chief executive office) and with central filing system board (4-9.5-104) and payment of annual maintenance fee set by board; and (b) when accounts resulting from sale of timber to be cut or minerals or the like (including oil and gas) at wellhead or minehead, file in real estate records in county where real estate concerned is located. (4-9-401).

Recording.—See category Property, topic Deeds, subhead Recording. Where a recorded instrument constituting a promise or obligation for the payment of money and giving a lien on real estate as security therefor purports to bear on its face or back an assignment, this is prima facie evidence of the fact of assignment whether or not such purported assignment has been acknowledged. (38-35-102).

Notice to obligor not necessary to complete assignment as between assignee and assignor. (14 Colo. 58, 23 P. 88). Object of notice is to inform debtor that his creditor has divested himself of right to collect and invested assignee with that right. (6 Colo. 508).

Effect.—Assignee receives rights and remedies of assignor and is subject to defenses and claims good against assignor which arose prior to notice of assignment. (175 Colo. 406, 487 P.2d 1333).

Assignment of wages not already earned at time of assignment, or of any other sum to become due to assignor, is not valid against assignor's creditors who have had no actual notice of the assignment at time it is made unless same is recorded in county wherein wages are to be earned or such sums are to become due within five days from date thereof. (8-9-103). No such assignment, except for child support, is valid if assignor is married and residing with spouse unless spouse joins in assignment which is duly acknowledged before person authorized to take acknowledgments. (8-9-104). No assignment of wages by employee to any person for benefit of such employee is valid. All assignments of wages must be in writing and for fixed and definite part of wages earned or to be earned within 30 days from date of assignment. Assignments post- or ante-dated are void. (8-9-101). Copy of assignment must be given or sent by registered mail to employer within five days after execution and copy given to assignor. (8-9-102). If creditor of assignor contests assignment, assignee has burden of proof to sustain validity thereof. (8-9-105). Checkoffs for union dues and payroll deductions authorized by employee for medical, hospital, stock-purchase, savings, insurance, charities, credit unions, banks, savings and loans, or any other financial institution, or other similar purposes, or for rent, board and subsistence provided in connection with employment if authorization is revocable, are exempt from these provisions. (8-9-106, 107). All assignments of wages are subject to provisions of Uniform Consumer Credit Code. (8-9-101). Assignment of workmen's compensation benefits is regulated by statute. (8-42-124).

Uniform Commercial Code specifically exempts transfer of claim for wages, salary or other compensation of employee from application of Art. 9 of Code. (4-9-104[d]).

Uniform Consumer Credit Code adopted. See category Business Regulation and Commerce, topic Consumer Credit.

ATTACHMENT:

Actions in Which Allowed.—In courts of record attachments allowed, if cause exists, in actions on express or implied contracts, or in tort actions if tort committed against person or property of resident. (Rule 102).

Courts Which May Issue Writ.—District or county court (Rule 102; 13-56-102) may issue writs of attachment.

In Whose Favor Writ May Issue.—Any party may have nonexempt property of party against whom claim is asserted attached. (Rule 102[a]).

Against Whom Writ May Issue.—Writ may issue against: (1) Foreign corporation without certificate of authority to do business; (2) defendant who has been absent from state for four months, or whose whereabouts are unknown, or who is nonresident of state, if all reasonable efforts to obtain in personam jurisdiction over defendant have failed; (3) defendant who conceals himself to evade service of process; (4) defendant who is about to remove his property from state with intent to delay creditors; (5) defendant who has fraudulently conveyed property to delay creditors; (6) defendant who has fraudulently concealed property to delay creditors; (7) defendant who is about to convey property to delay creditors; (8) defendant who is about to fraudulently conceal or dispose of property to delay creditors; (9) defendant who has departed or is about to depart from state with intention of removing property from state. (Rule 102[c]).

Claims on Which a Writ May Issue.—See supra, subhead Actions in Which Allowed.

Grounds.—See supra, subhead Against Whom Writ May Issue.

Proceedings to Obtain.—In court of record, to obtain writ of attachment, plaintiff must file affidavit stating nature and amount of claim and that cause exists for attachment. (Rule 102[b]). Defendant, by affidavit, may at any time before trial traverse plaintiff's affidavit, and if plaintiff shall establish reasonable probability of one of causes alleged in affidavit, attachment shall be sustained. Hearing on defendant's traverse shall be held within seven days from filing with at least two days' notice to plaintiff. (Rule 102[n]). If hearing on traverse shows that evidence does not prove cause alleged in plaintiff's affidavit, but another cause, then on motion plaintiff's affidavit may be conformed to proof. (Rule 102[o]).

Attachment Bond.—In court of record, plaintiff must give bond in amount set by court not exceeding double amount claimed, conditioned that, if court finds plaintiff not entitled to attachment, plaintiff will pay costs awarded defendant and damages sustained by wrongful attachment. (Rule 102[d]). Whenever it appears to court that bond is insufficient, court may order another one and if plaintiff fails to comply within 20 days, writ of attachment must be dismissed. (Rule 102[x]).

Levy.—In court of record sheriff to whom writ directed must execute upon real estate by filing copy of writ together with description of property attached with county recorder, and upon personal property by taking it into custody. (Rule 102[h]).

Indemnity.—Sheriff must require undertaking of corporate surety company or two sureties for full value of attached property before releasing any property held under any writ of attachment. (Rule 102[v]).

Lien.—Attachment liens on real estate last six years unless judgment satisfied sooner (13-56-103), and certificate that levy has been made upon real estate must be filed in office of recorder in county where land is situate (13-56-101).

Release of Property.—In court of record writ of attachment will not issue if defendant gives sufficient security to pay judgment (Rule 102[a], Rule 102[f]); after writ of attachment has been levied defendant may post bond in sum fixed by sheriff, not less than value of property attached, and upon posting this bond property subject to attachment must be released (Rule 102[v]).

Sale.—Where perishable property attached, any party to the action may apply to court for sale thereof, and upon sale proceeds must be deposited with court clerk. (Rule 102[q]).

Third Party Claims.—In a court of record no final judgment may be rendered until expiration of 30 days from date levy made, and any creditor within 30 days may file affidavit setting forth his claim against defendant, and must then be made party plaintiff with same remedies as original plaintiff (Rule 102[k][1]), and judgment creditor may, upon motion without filing affidavit, be made party plaintiff having like remedies as original plaintiff (Rule 102[k][2]). When additional creditor is made party, dismissal by first attaching creditor of his cause of action does not operate as dismissal as to any other creditor. (Rule 102[l]).

Priorities.—Upon final judgment each creditor takes pro rata from money realized from attachment proceedings, provided that when property is attached while defendant is removing same or secreting same for purpose of defrauding creditors, court may allow creditors whose diligence procured property priority over other attachments or judgment creditors. (Rule 102[m]). Any third person claiming property attached may intervene and, in case judgment is in his favor, may recover damages by reason of attachment. (Rule 102[p]).

Vacation or Modification.—Allowed in attachment proceedings as in other actions. (Rule 102[y]).

See also topics Executions, Garnishment, Exemptions.

CREDITORS' SUITS:

Creditor's suit may be joined in a single action with suit on the claim itself. Thus, a plaintiff may state a claim for money and a claim to set aside conveyance fraudulent as to him without first obtaining judgment establishing claim for money. (Rule 18[b]).

Relief obtained through action may to great extent be obtained through supplementary proceedings (Rule 69[d], [e] [f], and [g]) (see topic Executions), but such proceedings are not adapted to reach disputed property of judgment debtor, as no contested title can be determined therein (89 Colo. 292, 1 P.2d 924).

Under Rule 69(a), post-judgment writ of garnishment can be issued without writ of execution preceding it. (40 Colo. App. 179, 570 P.2d 1320). (See topic Garnishment.)

Uniform Commercial Code adopted. See category Business Regulation and Commerce, topic Commercial Code.

Creditor with security interest in both real and personal property may, in case of default, proceed simultaneously against personalty and realty. (4-9-501; 632 P.2d 282).

Creditor can recover prejudgment and postjudgment interest. (5-12-102).

See note at head of Digest as to 1998 legislation covered.

See Topical Index in front part of this volume.

CO – 38

CREDITORS' SUITS . . . *continued*

Liens for state sales taxes are first and prior liens upon goods and business fixtures of or used by any retailer and take precedence over other creditor's claims of whatever kind, including Uniform Commercial Code Art. 9 security interest. (39-26-117; 632 P.2d 1053).

Uniform Fraudulent Transfer Act adopted, effective July 1, 1991. See topic Fraudulent Sales and Conveyances.

EXECUTIONS:

All goods and chattels, lands, tenements and real estate of every person against whom any judgment is obtained in court of record, either at law or in equity, are liable to be sold on execution to satisfy said judgment (13-52-102[1]) except such property as is specifically exempted (13-54-102).

Exemptions.—See topic Exemptions.

Issuance.—Execution from a court of record may issue 15 days after judgment unless further stay granted. (Rule 62[a]). It may issue to any county within state. (13-52-110).

Lien.—Execution is a lien on goods and chattels of debtor in such county from the time it is placed in hands of sheriff, who must indorse on execution the time when he received it and make his return within 90 days. (13-52-111; 19 P. 839).

Levy.—Except for property exempt by law from execution, judgment creditor may elect on what property execution levied, however, real estate on which judgment debtor resides must be taken last. (13-52-101). See category Civil Actions and Procedure, topic Damages, subhead Nonprofit Corporations.

Return.—All executions returnable 90 days after date of issue, unless sale is pending. Sheriff or officer must endorse back of writ with hour and date of receipt and enter information in public records. (13-52-111).

Priorities.—Liens entitled to priority in accordance with respective dates of their delivery to sheriff or officer. (13 Colo. 491, 22 P. 804).

Sales.—Must be public sale after advertisement of personalty for ten days (13-57-101) and real estate for 20 days (13-56-201). Sale may be set aside or other action taken where sale results in unconscionable condition. (636 P.2d 1280).

Redemption.—(Art. 39 of Title 38, C.R.S., 1982 Repl. vol., as am'd, is repealed and recodified in Art. 38 of Title 38, effective Oct. 1, 1990). Within six months from date of sale, owner or any person who might be liable on deficiency on agricultural real estate may redeem premises sold by paying to proper officer sum for which property was sold, with interest, taxes and other proper charges. (38-38-302[3]). Agricultural real estate is any parcel of real estate none of which is either plotted as subdivision in incorporated town, city or city and county, or valued and assessed as agricultural land. (38-38-302[4]). Redemption period for nonagricultural property is 75 days as to mortgages, deeds of trust, or other liens, or for execution or levy sales. (38-38-302[1]). If last day of redemption period Sat., Sun., legal holiday, or courthouse closed due to inclement weather, period extends to next business day. (38-38-302[5]). Certificate of redemption must be executed and recorded and money so received paid to holder of certificate of purchase. (38-38-302[2]). Senior encumbrancer or lienor of record may redeem within ten days from expiration of redemption period provided there is no redemption within that period. Subsequent encumbrancers and lienors in succession have five-day periods to redeem according to priority by paying all redemption amounts theretofore paid with interest plus liens of such redeeming encumbrances or lienors, or if none, amount for which property was sold plus interest. (38-38-303[1]&[4]). Person so redeeming is entitled to certificate of redemption. (38-38-304[3]). Lienor or encumbrancer must file notice of intent to redeem lien priority, attaching recorded or filed instruments evidencing lien, and advising of intention to redeem within applicable redemption period. (38-38-303[2]). Calendar dates of redemption periods are fixed and determined at expiration of redemption period, and such dates will not be advanced. (38-38-303[3]). Lienor must pay amount required to redeem and must deliver affidavit showing amount owing on lien from last day of owner's redemption period including accrued per diem amount thereafter. (38-38-303[4]). Upon expiration of period of redemption allowed owner and lienors, sheriff or public trustee must execute deed to holder of certificate of purchase or to last redeeming lienor. Such deed vests title free and clear of all liens recorded subsequent to recording of lien on which sale was based. (38-38-501). Statute applies to foreclosure of mortgages, trust deeds, or liens by execution or levy. (38-38-302[1]). Redemption rights apply to installment land contracts. (38-38-305[3]). Redemption rights may not be waived prior to default. (38-38-301[2]).

Stay of Execution.—There is an automatic stay of execution for 15 days after entry of judgment in district court. (Rule 62[a]). Interlocutory or final judgment in action for injunction or in receivership action is not so stayed. (Rule 62[a]). Trial court may suspend, modify, restore or grant injunction on such terms as it considers proper for security of rights of adverse party. (Rule 62[a], [c], [d]). There is no automatic stay of execution in county court. (County Court Rule 362).

Court may, in its discretion and on such conditions for security of adverse party as are proper, stay execution of, or any proceedings to enforce, judgment pending disposition of motion for new trial, for relief from judgment or order, for judgment in accordance with motion for directed verdict, for amendment to findings or for additional findings, or pending filing and determination of application to Supreme Court for supersedeas. (Rule 62[b], [d]). Posting of supersedeas bond is condition precedent to stay of enforcement of judgment. (814 P.2d 869).

As to stay pending writ of error, see category Civil Actions and Procedure, topic Appeal and Error.

Supplementary Proceedings.—At any time after entry of final money judgment, judgment creditor may cause subpoena or subpoena to produce to be served (as provided under Rule 45) requiring judgment debtor to appear before court, master or referee to answer concerning his property. (Rule 69[e]). If judgment debtor fails to appear after being properly served, judgment creditor may request court to issue bench warrant ordering sheriff to arrest judgment debtor and bring him before court for further proceedings under Rule. (Rule 69[e][2]). Subpoenas and subpoenas to produce require conspicuous notice that failure to appear will result in arrest. (Rule 69[e][1]). Judgment creditor may also serve written interrogatories. (Rule 69[d]).

At any time after entry of final money judgment, on proof that person has property of judgment debtor or is indebted to him in amount exceeding $500 not exempt from execution, court may issue subpoena or subpoena to produce to such person to appear before court, referee, or master at specified time and answer concerning same, or court may order property of judgment debtor, not exempt from execution, in hands of such debtor or any other person or due to judgment debtor to be applied towards satisfaction of judgment. (Rule 69[f], [g]).

Body Execution.—In tort actions, when specifically pleaded in summons and complaint, and where verdict or findings state that defendant was guilty of malice, fraud, wilful deceit or negligence consisting of reckless or wilful disregard of rights or safety of others, defendant may be imprisoned up to one year at plaintiff's expense unless plaintiff shows by affidavit he is poor and unable to pay costs of such imprisonment. No execution shall issue if judgment has been paid or if decedent has been convicted in criminal prosecution for same tort. (13-59-103, 105). Statute held unconstitutional in 746 P.2d 542; Civil Rule 101 governing body executions repealed.

See also topics Attachment, Exemptions, Garnishment.

EXEMPTIONS:

In addition to homestead exemption every person is entitled to hold exempt from levy, attachment, execution and garnishment issued out of any court large number of enumerated articles, most of which are limited as to value, said articles including wearing apparel; jewelry; personal library, family pictures and school books; burial sites; household goods; food; fuel; certain livestock and implements in case of farmers; tools of trade; motor vehicles used for business purposes or by elderly or disabled debtor for purposes of obtaining medical care; professional library; house trailer; moveable structure; mobile home; certain military pensions; life insurance proceeds; casualty insurance proceeds if lost property exempt; compensation under victim reparation law; utility security deposits; proceeds derived from personal injury claim unless claim arose from treatment of such injuries and funds from pension, retirement or deferred compensation plans, including ERISA plans, IRAs and Keogh plans. (13-54-102). Other exemptions (some limited as to value or subject to conditions) are: Cemetery company property (7-47-106); workmen's compensation benefits (8-42-124); employment security benefits (8-80-103); delinquent insurance company assets (10-3-556); group life insurance proceeds (10-7-205); sickness and accident insurance benefits (10-8-114); benefits paid by fraternal benefit society (10-14-403); constitutional state officers' fees or salaries (exempt from garnishment only) (13-61-101); teachers' retirement benefits (22-64-120); state employees' retirement benefits and public employees' retirement benefits (24-51-212, 24-54.7-108); public assistance payments (26-2-131); public police pension benefits (31-30-313, 31-30-616, 13-54-102); and firemen's pension payments (31-30-412, 31-30-518, 13-54-102).

Debts Against Which Exemptions Not Allowed.—No property is exempt in action to enforce obligation for purchase money thereof, or from sale for payment of any taxes legally assessed. (13-54-103, 105). Effective July 1, 1996, and applicable to all civil actions filed after that date, all property of person who has committed felonious killing shall be subject to attachment or levy in satisfaction of judgment awarded as result of such felonious killing. (13-54-102[4]).

Necessity of Claiming Exemption.—Debtor must claim exemption within ten days after being served with notice of levy or seizure. (13-55-101). In case of garnishment, debtor must attempt to resolve disputes regarding exemption of earnings within five days after receipt of writ of continuing garnishment, and must claim exemptions regarding property other than earnings within ten days after receipt of notice of exemption and pending levy. (13-54.5-108). In non-garnishment cases, failure to claim exemption conclusively constitutes waiver. (13-55-107).

Exemption statutes apply only to civil actions and cannot defeat a levy for fines and costs arising out of criminal prosecutions. (68 Colo. 110, 187 P. 729).

Earnings.—Maximum amount subject to garnishment, levy or attachment is lesser of 25% of disposable earnings or amount by which disposable earnings exceeds 30 times federal minimum wage (13-54-104[2][a][I]) or, solely with respect to enforcement of debts for fraudulently obtained public assistance, lesser of 35% of disposable earnings or amount by which disposable earnings exceeds 30 times federal minimum wage (13-54-104[D][a][II]). Maximum amount to enforce support order where debtor supporting another spouse or dependent child is 50% of disposable earnings, otherwise 60% of disposable earnings; if support payments more than 12 weeks in arrears maximums increase to 55% and 65%. (13-54-104[3][b]). Funds from workers' compensation benefits, unemployment insurance benefits, or pension, retirement or deferred compensation plans, interest, dividends, partnership distributions, tips and insurance proceeds to extent such proceeds are in lieu of wages are subject to garnishment only for arrearages in child support. (13-54-104[1][b][II]). Payments due or received from third parties to cover child's health care costs, but not yet applied to health care costs, are subject to garnishment by state medical assistance program to enforce judgment for medical support. (13-54-104[1][b][III]). Maximums do not apply to bankruptcy court orders under c. 13 nor to state or federal tax debts. (13-54-104[3][a]). Disabled persons may be subject to lesser garnishments by court order. (13-54-104[3][b][iii]). See category Business Regulation and Commerce, topic Consumer Credit for exemptions applicable to certain consumer debts.

See also topic Garnishment.

Child Support Obligations and Payments Exempt.—Effective May 22, 1994, any past or present payment received arising from child support obligation or as child support is exempt from levy under any writ of attachment or execution issued on or after that date. (13-54-102.5[1]). Child support payments are exempt only if they are deposited in custodial account for benefit of child and such payments, and any interest thereon, are not commingled with any other funds. (13-54-102.5[2]).

Waiver.—Stipulation in note waiving right of exemption void as against public policy. (79 Colo. 537, 246 P. 789).

Homestead Exemption.—See topic Homesteads.

See note at head of Digest as to 1998 legislation covered.

See Topical Index in front part of this volume.

CO – 39

EXEMPTIONS . . . *continued*

Exemptions in Bankruptcy.—Exemptions in 11 U.S.C. §522(d) are denied to residents of Colorado. (13-54-107).

FORECLOSURE:

See topic Liens; categories Business Regulation and Commerce, topic Commercial Code; Civil Actions and Procedure, topic Limitation of Actions; Mortgages, topic Mortgages of Real Property.

FRAUDULENT SALES AND CONVEYANCES:

A conveyance of any interest in land made to defraud prior or subsequent bona fide purchasers is void. (38-10-101). Transfer of realty or personalty in trust for transferor is void as against existing creditors. (38-10-111). Except as provided by Uniform Commercial Code (4-2-402), or except when evidence of transaction is included in central registry maintained with respect to transactions relating to title or is duly noted on certificate of title by issuing authority, or is included in records of proper filing office for security interest (4-9-401), or is transaction described in 4-9-302(1) or (2); sale by vendor or assignment of personalty in possession of vendor or assignor is presumed fraudulent as against creditors or bona fide purchasers of vendor or assignor, unless followed by immediate delivery and actual and continued change of possession (38-10-114).

Uniform Fraudulent Conveyance Act not adopted.

Uniform Fraudulent Transfer Act adopted and became effective on July 1, 1991. (38-8-101 et seq.). Transfer of property is fraudulent as to present or future creditor if it was made: (1) With actual intent to delay or defraud or (2) without receiving reasonably equivalent value in exchange and debtor making transfer was engaged in business for which remaining assets were unreasonably small or intended to incur debts beyond his ability to pay as they become due. (38-8-105). Transfer of property is fraudulent as to present creditor if it was made without receiving reasonably equivalent value in exchange for transfer and debtor making transfer was either insolvent at time or became insolvent as result of transfer. (38-8-106). Transfer of property is also fraudulent as to present creditor if it was made to insider for antecedent debt, debtor was insolvent at that time, and insider had reasonable cause to believe that debtor was insolvent. (38-8-106). To avoid transfer for intentional fraud, transferee must participate in or have knowledge of transferor's fraudulent intent. (86 Colo. 595, 284 P. 337). Transactions between spouses or relatives are presumed fraudulent. (65 Colo. 400, 177 P. 965; 827 P.2d 615). Transferee may be held personally liable in damages for value of fraudulently transferred property. (164 Colo. 206, 433 P.2d 772).

Remedies.—See topic Creditors' Suits; category Business Regulation and Commerce, topic Consumer Credit.

Criminal Liability.—Willful participation in a fraudulent conveyance to defeat or impair security interest is punishable as crime. (18-5-206).

Uniform Commercial Code adopted. See category Business Regulation and Commerce, topic Commercial Code.

Bulk Sales.—Uniform Commercial Code, Article 6 (4-6-101 et seq.), governing bulk transfers, repealed effective July 1, 1991. (4-6-101 to 111). See category Business Regulation and Commerce, topic Commercial Code.

Colorado Consumer Protection Act adopted with modifications. (6-1-101 to 115 et seq.). See category Business Regulation and Commerce, topic Consumer Protection.

GARNISHMENT:

In 1984, Colorado enacted new statutes (13-54.5-101 to 111) applicable to garnishments after Jan. 1, 1985, which are implemented by Rule 103. Rule 103 is exclusive process for garnishment and provides five different types of writs: (1) Writ of continuing garnishment; (2) writ of garnishment with notice of exemption and pending levy; (3) writ of garnishment for support; (4) writ of garnishment-judgment debtor other than natural person; and (5) writ of garnishment in aid of writ of attachment. All writs must be served as provided in Rule 4. Rule 103 contains very detailed instructions on execution of various writs. Although summary of highlights of Rule 103 follows, complete Rule should be consulted before proceeding with garnishment. Forms pertaining to writs are contained in Appendix of Colorado Rules of Civil Procedure. Forms 26-34. To determine earnings and other property subject to garnishment, see topic Exemptions.

Writ of Continuing Garnishment.—Provides exclusive procedure for withholding earnings of judgment debtor to successive pay periods for payment of judgment debt other than judgment for support. (13-54.5-101[1]). Writ of continuing garnishment to recover fraudulently obtained public assistance, whenever served, has priority over any other continuing garnishment, other than continuing garnishment for support. (13-54.5-104[1][C]). See subhead Writ of Garnishment for Support, infra. Writ will be lien and continuing levy against nonexempt earnings owed by garnishee to judgment debtor at time of service of writ (13-54.5-103), as well as nonexempt earnings of judgment debtor for 90 days following service of writ or for 90 days following expiration of any writs with priority. (13-54.5-104). Such lien will terminate before 90 days if underlying judgment is vacated, modified, or satisfied in full, or writ is dismissed, except when such writ is suspended for specific period of time by judgment creditor upon agreement with judgment debtor. Such agreement must be in writing and filed by judgment creditor with clerk of court where judgment was entered. Garnishee also must receive copy. (13-54.5-102[2]; Rule 103, §1[f][1], [j]). Judgment creditor must serve two copies of writ on garnishee, one of which garnishee must deliver to judgment debtor. (13-54.5-105; Rule 103, §1[d]).

Writ of Garnishment (on Personal Property Other than Earnings of Natural Person) with Notice of Exemption and Pending Levy.—Provides exclusive procedure by which personal property of any kind (other than earnings of natural person) in possession or control of garnishee is required to be held for payment of judgment debt. (Rule 103, §2[a]). Writ issues after entry of judgment when writ of execution may issue; writ with notice will be issued by clerk of court upon request. (Rule 103, §2[c]). Under such writ, any indebtedness, intangible personal property, or tangible personal property capable of manual delivery, other than earnings of natural person, owed to, or owned by, judgment debtor, and in possession or control of garnishee at time of service of such writ upon garnishee, will be subject to garnishment. (Rule 103, §2[c]). Proceeds of federally guaranteed student loans are also not subject to garnishment for antecedent debt. (769 P.2d 1058).

Writ of Garnishment for Support.—Provides exclusive procedure for withholding earnings of judgment debtor for payment of judgment debt for child support arrearages, child support debts, maintenance when combined with child support or maintenance. (Rule 103, §3[a][1]). Writ of garnishment for support is continuing and requires garnishee to withhold, pursuant to law, portion of earnings subject to garnishment at each succeeding earning disbursement interval until judgment is satisfied or garnishment released by court or released in writing by judgment creditor. (Rule 103, §3[f][1]). Writ of garnishment for support has priority over any writ of continuing garnishment notwithstanding fact such other writ may have been served upon garnishee previously. (Rule 103, §3[f][2]).

Writ of Garnishment—Judgment Debtor Other than Natural Person.—Provides exclusive procedure by which personal property (of any kind) of judgment debtor other than natural person is required to be held by garnishee. (Rule 103, §4[a]).

Writ of Garnishment in Aid of Writ of Attachment.—Provides exclusive procedure through which personal property of defendant in attachment action (other than earnings of natural person) is required to be held by garnishee. (Rule 103, §5[a]). After issuance of writ of attachment in accordance with Rule 102, writ of garnishment will be issued by clerk of court on request. Under such writ of garnishment, plaintiff in attachment may garnish personal property of any description, except earnings of natural person, owed to, or owned by, such defendant in attachment in possession or control of garnishee. (Rule 103, §5[c]).

Judgment Debtor's Objection—Written Claim of Exemption—Hearing.—If judgment debtor objects to initial or subsequent calculation of amount of exempt earnings, judgment debtor shall have five days from receipt of copy of writ of garnishment or calculation of amount of exempt earnings for subsequent pay periods, within which to resolve issue of such miscalculation by agreement with garnishee. If not resolved, judgment debtor may file written objection setting forth, with reasonable detail, grounds for such objection. (13-54.5-108[1][a]; Rule 103, §6[a]). When garnishee, pursuant to writ with notice, holds personal property of judgment debtor, other than earnings, which judgment debtor claims to be exempt, judgment debtor, within ten days after being served copy of such writ, will make and file written claim of exemption with clerk of court in which judgment was entered. (13-54.5-108[1][b]; Rule 103, §6[b]). Upon filing of objection or claim of exemption, court in which judgment was entered will set time for hearing of objection or claim of exemption which will be not more than ten calendar days after filing of objection or claim of exemption. (13-54.5-109[1][a]; Rule 103, §6[c][1]).

Failure of Garnishee to Answer (All Forms of Garnishment).—If garnishee, having been served with any form of writ provided for by Rule 103, fails to answer within time required, clerk of court will enter default against such garnishee upon request. (Rule 103, §7[a]).

Traverse of Answer (All Forms of Garnishment).—Judgment creditor, plaintiff in attachment or intervenor in attachment may file traverse of answer to any form of writ provided by Rule 103, provided such traverse filed within greater time period of 20 days from date that such answer should have been filed with court, or 20 days after such answer was filed with court. Failure to timely file traverse deemed as acceptance of answer as true. (Rule 103, §8[a]).

Intervention (All Forms of Garnishment).—Any person who claims interest in any personal property of any description of judgment debtor or defendant in attachment, which property is subject of any answer made by garnishee, may intervene as provided in Rule 24 at any time prior to entry of judgment against garnishee. (Rule 103, §9).

Set-Off by Garnishee (All Forms of Garnishment).—Every garnishee is allowed to claim as set-off and retain or deduct all demands or claims on part of garnishee against any party to garnishment proceedings, which garnishee might have claimed if not summoned as garnishee. (Rule 103, §10).

Garnishee Not Required to Defend Claims of Third Persons (All Forms of Garnishment).—Garnishee with notice of claim of third person in any property of any description of judgment debtor or defendant in attachment which is subject of any answer made by garnishee in response to any form of writ provided for by Rule 103 will not be required to defend on account of such claim, but must state in answer that garnishee has notice of such third party claim. (Rule 103, §11[a]).

Release and Discharge of Garnishee (All Forms of Garnishment).—Judgment against garnishee will release and discharge such garnishee from all claims or demands of judgment debtor or defendant in attachment to extent of all sums paid or property delivered by garnishee pursuant to judgement. (Rule 103, §12[a]).

Garnishment of Public Body (All Forms of Garnishment).—Any writ provided in Rule 103 wherein public body is designated as garnishee, must be served upon officer of such body whose duty it is to issue warrants, checks or money to judgment debtor or defendant in attachment, or, such officer as public body may have designated to accepted service. (Rule 103, §13).

HOMESTEADS:

Every homestead in state occupied as home by owner or family is exempt from execution and attachment arising from debt, contract or civil obligation, but only to extent of $30,000 actual cash value in excess of any liens or encumbrances. (38-41-201).

Limitation of Value.—$30,000. (38-41-201).

Limitation of Area.—None.

Debts or Liabilities against Which Exemptions Not Available.—Taxes (13-54-105); debt for purchase price (13-54-103); mobile home loans, debts, or obligations

See note at head of Digest as to 1998 legislation covered.

See Topical Index in front part of this volume.

CO – 40

HOMESTEADS . . . *continued*
incurred prior to Jan. 1, 1983 (38-41-201.6); however, another exemption may be claimed on mobile home which is not subject to this date limitation (13-54-102[o][II]). See topic Exemptions.

Designation of Homestead.—Homestead exemptions shall be deemed created and may be claimed if occupancy requirements (38-41-203) and type of property requirements (38-41-205) are met. Mobile home meeting certain requirements is homestead entitled to exemption. (38-41-201.6). For homestead to apply to debts or obligations incurred before July 1, 1975, owner of property or owner's spouse must record in clerk's office of county where situate written acknowledged instrument describing such property, setting forth nature and source of owner's interest and stating that owner is homesteading such property. (38-41-202[2]).

Claim of Exemption.—Homestead entry is not retroactive and exemption must have attached or been entered prior to specific levy or lien on land to be effective. (100 Colo. 247, 67 P.2d 73).

Although written claim of valid homestead exemption is not required, better practice is to interpose a claim by filing with clerk of court of record where writ was issued within ten days after property levied upon, seized or taken into possession by officer. (15 Colo. 223, 25 P. 183).

Waiver of Exemption.—Any person purchasing or redeeming pursuant to foreclosure sale under mortgage, deed of trust, or other lien containing waiver of homestead rights acquires property free of homestead rights and without compliance with 38-41-206 (requiring filing by creditor of affidavit regarding value of property and minimum sale price in relation to value). (38-41-212[1]). Any person purchasing or redeeming pursuant to foreclosure sale under mortgage, deed of trust or other lien, except in case of tax sale under Art. 11 of Title 39, C.R.S., which contains no waiver of homestead rights will be subject to homestead rights. (38-41-212[2]).

Loss of Exemption.—Property is exempt only while occupied as a home by owner thereof, or his or her family. (38-41-203; 685 P.2d 260).

Alienation or Encumbrance.—Homestead created by automatic provisions of 38-41-202(1) may be conveyed or encumbered by owner without signature of spouse, how ever, if created by filing, both husband and wife must execute conveyance or encumbrance of their respective interests. (38-41-202[3],[4]). Both may be done in same instrument. Conservator may convey for incompetent upon court order. (38-35-118[1], [4]).

Levy on Homestead.—Before proceeding against homesteaded property, creditors must file with county clerk affidavit showing description and value of property, that fair market value of property less any prior liens or encumbrances exceeds amount of homestead exemption fixed in 38-41-201, that no previous execution arising out of same judgment has been levied on property, and also appraisal of property by independent qualified appraiser. (38-41-206[1]). Property must bring more than 70% of value shown on affidavit or sale is terminated. (38-41-206[2]).

Proceeds of sale are exempt for one year if kept separate from other moneys and can be identified. If used in acquiring another home, homestead carries over to new property, except against lien of vendor or purchase money mortgagee. (38-41-207).

Rights of Surviving Spouse and Family.—Decedent's spouse or minor children, or both, are entitled to decedent's homestead exemption. (38-41-204, 685 P.2d 260). Homestead exemption inures to spouse and minor children if joint tenants of decedent. (38-41-208[1]). Exemption is in addition to allowance to widow and minor children of decedent and preferences granted to dependents of protected persons under articles 10 to 20 of title 15, C.R.S. 1973. (38-41-211).

LIENS:

Liens are given to farmers, ranchers, agistors, feeders, herders of cattle, veterinarians and livery stable keepers upon stock in their keep. (38-20-102[1]). No partido or share contracts (where livestock delivered to be kept on shares for period of time at end of which they, or any number are returned, as provided by contract) are valid, except between parties to contract, unless contract filed or recorded in office of county clerk and recorder of deeds in county where livestock is to be kept. (35-54-106).

Keepers of hotels, motels, inns, boarding houses and trailer courts have liens upon personal property of tenants on premises. (38-20-102[2]). Motor vehicles excepted.

Persons renting rooms, apartments or trailer space for housekeeping purposes of tenants have liens on personal property of tenant on premises. (38-20-102[3][a]). Some personal property excepted.

Common carriers of personal goods and passengers and any person who stores personal goods at owner's request have liens on personal property for reasonable charges. (38-20-105). Any person has lien on articles of personal property for making, repairing or altering same at request of owner. (38-20-106). Liens asserted under 38-20-106 terminate if lien holder does not commence judicial action within 90 days after charges, or final installment thereof, are due and payable. Liens under 38-20-102, 38-20-105 and 38-20-106.5 terminate after 60 days. Period of limitation may be extended for as much as 30 days by agreement between parties. (38-20-107; 41 Colo. App. 433, 586 P.2d 243). Agency or other authority issuing building permit for improvement, repair, restoration, or remodeling of or for construction of addition to residential property must send statutory notice to property. (38-22-105.5). Mechanic who surrenders possession of repaired motor vehicle upon payment by check, draft, or order for payment may have lien restored if check, draft, or order is not honored for full payment or is dishonored. (38-20-106.5).

Removal and storage of abandoned vehicles is provided for in 42-4-1102, 1103, 1108 and 38-20-116 is not applicable. (42 Colo. App. 347, 593 P.2d 1387).

Person performing service on property, such as dry cleaning clothes, and storage thereof, has special lien on customers' property serviced, dependent on possession. (38-21-101, 103).

Persons performing labor or furnishing materials in connection with drilling of oil, gas, or other wells have liens on property. (38-24-101; 624 P.2d 355). Lien statement must be filed within six months after furnishing labor or materials. (38-24-104). Lienholder must commence suit in district court within six months of filing lien statement. (38-24-105).

Person harvesting grain or other crops for use or benefit of others has lien upon grain and other crops harvested. (38-24.5-101 to 108). Notice of lien must be served within ten days after harvesting, and lien must be filed within 20 days after notice. (38-24.5-103[1]).

Hospitals have lien for services rendered to injured person upon net amount payable to such person, his heirs, assigns or legal representatives as damages for negligence or wrongful act of another, whether by settlement, compromise or judgment, but not upon amounts payable under Workers' Compensation Act. (38-27-101).

Owners of self-service storage facilities have liens on all personal property of occupant located at facility. (38-21.5-102).

Person filing pleading claiming affirmative relief affecting title to real property may record notice of lis pendens creating lien against property. (Rule 105 [f]).

Attorneys (see category Legal Profession, topic Attorneys and Counselors) and common carriers (see category Business Regulation and Commerce, topic Carriers) have liens.

Uniform Commercial Code adopted. See category Business Regulation and Commerce, topic Commercial Code.

Uniform Federal Tax Lien Registration Act adopted. (38-25-101 to 107).

Material Variations from Official Text.—

New section added which reads as follows:

"This Article applies only to federal tax liens and to other federal liens notices of which under any act of Congress or any regulation adopted pursuant thereto are required or permitted to be filed in the same manner as notices of federal tax liens"; (38-25-101.5).

New section added which reads as follows:

"Notices of liens, certificates, and other notices affecting federal tax liens or other federal liens must be filed in accordance with this Article"; (38-25-102[1][a]).

§1(a)—omits "taxes" and inserts "obligations" preceding "payable to the United States"; (38-25-102[1][b]); omits "filed" and inserts "recorded" preceding "in the office"; (38-25-102[1][b]); omits "a federal tax lien" and inserts "the liens" following "real property subject to"; (38-25-102[1][b]).

§1(b)—inserts "whether tangible or intangible" following "property" in opening paragraph; (38-25-102[2]); inserts "federal" after "notices of" and omits "taxes" and inserts "obligations" preceding "payable"; (38-25-102[2]).

§1(b)(1)—omits "tax" preceding "lien"; (38-25-102[2][a]); inserts "whose principal executive office is in this state" following "partnership"; (38-25-102[2][a]).

New sections added which read as follows:

"(b) if the person against whose interest the lien applies is a trust that is not covered by paragraph (a) of this subsection (2), in the office of the Secretary of State; (c) if the person against whose interest the lien applies is the estate of the decedent, in the office of the Secretary of State;"; (38-25-102[2][b][c]).

§1(b)(2)—inserts "the notice of lien shall be recorded" after "in all other cases,"; omits "taxpayer" and inserts "person against whose interest the lien applies" preceding "resides"; omits "filing" and inserts "recording" preceding "of the notice of lien"; (38-25-102[2][d]).

§2—omits "of notices of liens, certificates, or notices of compromise affecting tax liens" and inserts "or by any official or entity of the United States responsible for the filing or certifying of notice of any other lien," after "delegate"; (38-25-103).

§3(a)—omits "tax" after "federal"; "omits "notice of compromise" and inserts "a refiling of notice of federal lien"; (38-25-104[1]).

§3(a)(2)—omits "file it alphabetically or enter it in an alphabetical index" and inserts "record and index in the real estate records in accordance with the provisions of §§30-10-408 and 30-10-409, C.R.S."; omits "the serial number of the district director of internal revenue" and inserts "the title and address of the official or entity certifying the lien"; omits "of tax, interest, penalties, and costs" and inserts "appearing on the notice of lien" after "amount"; (38-25-104[1][b]).

§3(c)—omitted and replaced with "If a refiled notice of federal tax lien referred to in subsection (1) of this section or any of the certificates or notices referred to in subsection (2) of this section is presented for recording to any county clerk and recorder, such clerk and recorder shall enter the refiled notice or the certificate with the date of recording in the index in accordance with the provisions of Sections 30-10-408 and 30-10-409, C.R.S." (38-25-104[3]).

§3(d)—omits "federal tax" preceding "lien"; omits "on or after July 1, 1969" and inserts "under this Article"; omits "tax" after "federal" and before "lien"; omits last two sentences beginning with "The fee for a certificate" and inserts "The fee for the issuance of a certificate by the secretary of state shall be determined and collected pursuant to section 24-21-104(3), C.R.S., and the fee for the issuance of a certificate by a county clerk and recorder shall be the same as provided in section 4-11-102(1)(g)(I), C.R.S. Upon request the filing officer shall furnish a copy of any notice of federal tax lien or notice or certificate affecting a federal tax lien. The fee for furnishing and for certifying such copy and affixing the seal thereto shall be determined and collected pursuant to section 24-21-104(3), C.R.S., if furnished by the secretary of state, and the said fee shall be the same as provided in section 4-11-102(1)(g)(II), C.R.S., if furnished by a county clerk and recorder. (38-25-104[4]).

§4—replaced with, "(1)(a) A fee shall be charged for filing and indexing each notice of lien or certificate or notice affecting the lien: (I) For a tax lien on real estate; (II) For a lien on tangible and intangible personal property; (III) For a certificate of discharge or subordination; (IV) For all other notices, including a certificate of release or nonattachment. (b) The fee charged by a county clerk and recorder for filing and indexing each notice of lien or certificate or notice affecting the lien shall be five dollars. (c) When the filing officer is the secretary of state, the fees required by this subsection (1) shall be determined and collected pursuant to section 24-21-104(3), C.R.S.". (38-25-105); inserts "or other appropriate federal officials" after "internal revenue"; (38-25-105).

New section added which reads as follows: "Prior to the time of the filing of a notice of lien in the office of the secretary of state or the county clerk and recorder, as the case

See note at head of Digest as to 1998 legislation covered.

See Topical Index in front part of this volume.

CO – 41

LIENS . . . *continued*
may be, the same shall not be valid as against any mortgagee, purchaser, or judgment creditor. (38-25-106).

§5—omits "so interpreted" and inserts "applied"; omits "laws of those states which enact" and inserts "law with respect to the subject of this Article among enacting"; (38-25-107).

Enforcement of Liens.—A special lien for cleaning services on clothing, household goods, or any other items may be enforced by sale after 90 days. Notice to owner is required if owner's address was given at time property was delivered. Whether or not address was given at time property was delivered, such property may be disposed of after 180 days without notice to owner. (38-21-102, 103, 104). Other liens may be enforced by sale after shorter period. (38-20-107 to 113).

Mechanics' Liens.—(38-22-101 to 133). Whoever does any work or furnishes any material or equipment by contract express or implied with owner of any land, his agent or contractor, for construction, enlargement, alteration or repair of any building or other structure upon such land, shall have lien on land and buildings for amount and value of such work, materials, or equipment with interest at contract rate, or in absence of contract rate, at 12%. (38-22-101[1][5]). Owner of single-family, owner occupied residence has affirmative defense to any action to enforce lien if owner has paid amount sufficient to satisfy owner's contractual and legal obligations, including purchase price or contract amount plus all additions, to general contractor. (38-22-102[3.5]). In bankruptcy, once mechanics' lien perfected, relates back to date work commenced. (38 Bankr. 148). Owner's interest in property may be subjected to lien for unauthorized improvements made with owner's knowledge or for improvements authorized by landlord or vendor in lease or contract, unless owner posts notice that his interest will not be subject to lien. (38-22-105; 640 P.2d 1130). Payments made by owners prior to commencement of work or prior to time when due shall not be valid to defeat, diminish, or discharge any lien except to contractor or person to whom payment was made. (38-22-102[2][3]). However, exception is made when liened property is single-family dwelling unit. (38-22-102[3.5], 113[4]). Laborer on modular home later placed on real property of owner has no lien on real property. (34 Colo. App. 117, 523 P.2d 137). Lumber supplier of home building material seller has no lien on buyer-landowner's property. (715 P.2d 329). Mechanics' lien statute does not apply to public property (1997 Colo. LEXIS 524) or to partner's claim for improvements to partnership property (42 Colo. App. 281, 599 P.2d 262). In order to preserve any lien, notice of intent to file lien must be served upon owner and principal contractor at least ten days before filing lien statement, and affidavit of such service must be filed with lien statement. (38-22-109[3]; 653 P.2d 90). For residential property, agency issuing building permit must deliver prescribed notice, either directly to owner, or by mail addressed to property. (38-22-105.5[1][2][7]). Notice not required for new residential construction or for property with more than four living units. (38-22-105.5[3]). Laborers who have not furnished materials must file lien with clerk and recorder of county wherein land is situated after last labor for which lien claimed has been performed and before expiration of two months after completion of building or structure; all other lien claimants must file lien before expiration of four months after day on which last labor was performed or last material furnished by such lien claimant; within applicable time for filing lien statement, extension to four months after completion of structure or six months after filing of notice, whichever comes first obtained by filing notice of potential lien claim. (38-22-109[10]). Special rules apply to bona fide purchasers of single or double family dwellings. Liens may be assigned (38-22-117), and suit to foreclose same must be commenced within six months from time of completion of building or structure, performance of last work or furnishing of last materials. Mechanics' lien is extinguished upon claimant's failure to initiate action within statutory six-month period. (38-22-110; 656 P.2d 1321). Subject to limitation of six months after completion of improvements, lien is valid for a year, with yearly extensions if affidavit filed stating improvements have not been completed. (38-22-109). Liens are foreclosed in essentially same manner as mortgages. Proceeding is in rem (38-22-113[3]) and provision is made for service by publication. (38-22-115). Filing of notice of lis pendens must accompany action to enforce materialman's lien. (38-22-110; 153 Colo. 109, 384 P.2d 938). Laborers have priority as to proceeds of sale. Somewhat different provisions apply to liens on mines and mining property, railways, public roads and repair of ditches (38-23-101 to 110), oil, gas and other wells (38-22-104; 38-24-101 to 111). Liens on mining property do not attach against owner for work done or material furnished to lessee. (38-22-104). Statutory proceeding equitable in nature—no right to jury trial. (643 P.2d 31). Remedial portions of mechanics' lien statutes are liberally construed but those statutory provisions upon which right to existence of lien depends and with respect to acts necessary to perfect lien are strictly construed. (660 P.2d 925). Mechanics' lien may be extinguished if it is shown that there is no reasonable probability that amount claimed is due or if it is shown that lien claimant had both knowledge and intent to cheat or defraud in claiming such amount. (36-22-128; 38-22-123). Disbursers have duties to check filings, ascertain amounts due, etc. (38-22-126). Provisions for performance bonds included. (38-22-129 to 133).

Public Works.—General contractor for public works for state, county, city, school district or other political subdivision, whose contract exceeds $50,000, must file bond for faithful performance of contract and payment of claims for labor and material (but not equipment) used. (38-26-106). If labor or material claim is filed prior to final settlement, enough to satisfy is withheld for 90 days, during which period claimant may commence suit and file lis pendens with governing body. (44 Colo. App. 467, 615 P.2d 68). If suit not so commenced contractor receives money. (38-26-107). General contractor for public works for county, city, town or school district must file bond for labor and materials used. Suit may be commenced on bond within six months of completion of project. (38-26-105). Suppliers of labor and of materials have preferred positions in terms of demands upon retained funds in public works contracts. (655 P.2d 860).

State Tax Lien.—See category Taxation, topic Property Taxes.

Unemployment Contribution Lien.—State has first and prior lien for payment of unemployment contributions upon real and personal property of employer. (8-79-103[1]).

Vendors' liens are recognized. (44 Colo. 495, 99 P. 758; 63 Colo. 22, 164 P. 504).

Requirements for Filing Liens.—All instruments which create liens on real property except mechanics' liens and judgment liens shall include street address or comparable identifying numbers, if any. (38-35-122).

Redemption from foreclosure of liens, see topic Executions.

For other liens see topics Attachment, Executions, Homesteads; categories Business Regulation and Commerce, topics Banks and Banking, Carriers, Factors; Civil Actions and Procedure, topic Judgments; Legal Profession, topic Attorneys and Counselors; Mortgages, topics Chattel Mortgages, Mortgages of Real Property; Property, topic Landlord and Tenant; Taxation, topic Income Tax; Transportation, topic Motor Vehicles. Collateral security, see topic Pledges. Liens on exempt property, see topic Exemptions.

See also topic Creditors' Suits.

PLEDGES:

Common law of pledges applies except as stated below.

Uniform Commercial Code adopted. See category Business Regulation and Commerce, topic Commercial Code.

Uniform Consumer Credit Code adopted. See category Business Regulation and Commerce, topic Consumer Credit.

RECEIVERS:

A receiver may be appointed by the court in which an action is pending: (1) Before judgment, provisionally, on application of either party, when he establishes a prima facie right to the property, or to an interest therein, which is the subject of the action and is in possession of an adverse party, and such property, or its rents, issues and profits are in danger of being lost, removed beyond the jurisdiction of the court or materially injured or impaired; (2) by or after judgment, to dispose of the property according to the judgment, or to preserve it during appellate proceedings; (3) in other cases where proper and in accordance with established principles of equity. (Rule 66). Receiver may also be appointed under statute where action to foreclose mortgage, deed of trust, or other instrument securing indebtedness has been commenced and it appears that security is inadequate, or property may be damaged or removed so as to render security inadequate (38-38-601), or after foreclosure and during redemption period to prevent waste (38-38-602). Action must be pending before court in order for it to appoint receiver (672 P.2d 221), but application for receiver may be sole claim for relief (Rule 66[d]). Appointment of receiver is within discretion of trial court. (703 P.2d 1314).

Proceedings.—Motion may be made to appoint a receiver and when such motion is based on facts not appearing of record, the court may direct that the matter be heard on affidavits, oral testimony and/or depositions. (Rule 43[e]).

Qualification.—Receiver must take an oath and furnish bond approved by court and executed to the people of the State of Colorado with sufficient surety in such sum as the court directs. (Rule 66).

Compensation.—There is no statute governing compensation of receivers.

REDEMPTION:

See topics Executions, Liens; categories Mortgages, topic Mortgages of Real Property; Taxation, topic Property Taxes, subhead Redemption and Actions to Recover Property.

SUPPLEMENTARY PROCEEDINGS:

See topic Executions.

DISPUTE RESOLUTION

ALTERNATIVE DISPUTE RESOLUTION:

Mandatory Dispute Resolution.—In matter involving or expected to involve litigation, attorneys are required to advise clients of alternative forms of dispute resolution. (Rule 2.1 of Rules of Professional Conduct). Court, in its discretion, may refer case to any form of alternative dispute resolution, but involuntary referrals not permitted where one of parties claims to have been victim of physical or psychological abuse. Court may exempt referral where compelling reason for exemption is demonstrated by motion filed within five days of referral. (13-22-312, 313[1]). Referral not authorized where injunction is only remedy sought. (13-22-312, 313[6]). Local court rules may govern referrals. Parties shall affirmatively state in case management order submitted to court that they have discussed settlement and describe their future efforts to effectuate settlement. (Rule 16[b][1][vii]). Court, on request of party, may conduct settlement conference. Judge who is assigned to case shall not conduct conference, and discussions at settlement conferences shall not be disclosed to judge who presides at trial. (§1-17 of Rule 121).

Voluntary Dispute Resolution.—Office of Dispute Resolution established as part of Colorado Judicial Department to provide mediation services on voluntary basis. (13-22-305). Statements made in mediation are not admissible in evidence or subject to discovery except (i) with consent; (ii) where there is intent to commit crime, bodily injury or safety of child is threatened; (iii) where statute requires; or (iv) where relevant to action alleging willful or wanton conduct of mediator. (13-22-307). Settlement agreement, if approved by court, enforceable as order of court. (13-22-308). Any pending court hearing shall be continued if parties and mediator so request and represent to court that they are engaging in good faith mediation. (13-22-311[3]). Mediation of workman's compensation matters prior to administrative hearing permissible upon consent of all parties. (8-43-205).

See also topic Arbitration and Award.

ARBITRATION AND AWARD:

Colorado recognizes statutory (13-22-201 to 507) and common-law arbitration (52 Colo. 121, 117 P. 896). In addition, arbitration may be effected under Rule 109 of Rules of Civil Procedure. Uniform Arbitration Act adopted, but applies only to agreements

See note at head of Digest as to 1998 legislation covered.

See Topical Index in front part of this volume.

CO – 42

ARBITRATION AND AWARD . . . *continued*

made on or after effective date of July 14, 1975. (13-22-222). Colorado's Arbitration Act contains additional provision that arbitrator shall not give undue weight to hearsay, improper or unsubstantiated evidence (13-22-207[d]); application to vacate, modify or correct award must be made within 30 days of delivery of award (13-22-214[2], 215[1]); if application to vacate award predicated upon fraud or undue means, application must be made within 30 days after applicant knew or should have known of undue means (13-22-214[2]).

Form and Requisites of Submission.—Agreement to arbitrate and submission must be written for statutory arbitration. (13-22-203). Submission may be oral for common law arbitration. (52 Colo. 121, 117 P. 896).

Enforceability of Arbitration Agreements.—For statutory arbitration, written agreement to submit existing controversy or to arbitrate future disputes is valid, enforceable and irrevocable except upon grounds for revocation of any contract. (13-22-203). Arbitration is favored and doubts regarding arbitrability must be resolved in favor of arbitration (38 Colo. App. 360, 559 P.2d 255), but right to arbitration may be waived (612 P.2d 92).

Role of Court.—District court determines arbitrability of dispute (13-22-204) and may grant preliminary injunctive relief to preserve status quo pending arbitration (672 P.2d 1015). If dispute is arbitrable, court shall order arbitration and stay action involving arbitrable issue or, if issue is severable, court shall stay arbitrable issue and order arbitration. (13-22-204). Court may stay arbitration upon showing there is no agreement to arbitrate. (13-22-204).

Powers of Arbitrators.—Arbitrators determine questions of fact and law (642 P.2d 922) and administer oath (13-22-209). Arbitrators may issue subpoenas for attendance of witnesses and production of documents and may permit deposition of witnesses who cannot be subpoenaed or who are unable to attend hearing. (13-22-209).

Medical Malpractice Arbitrations.—Under Health Care Availability Act, C.R.S. 13-64-403, exemplary or punitive damages may be awarded by arbitrator with respect to medical malpractice claims, subject to certain procedural requirements set forth in C.R.S. 13-64-302.5. Agreement to arbitrate medical malpractice claims may also be declared invalid if agreement to arbitrate fails to meet certain statutory criteria. (C.R.S. 13-64-403[10]).

Wage Claim Act Arbitrations.—Anti-waiver provision of Wage Claim Act, C.R.S. 8-4-125, prohibits employers from requiring employees to submit disputes over compensation to arbitration. (903 P.2d 1126).

Award and Enforcement.—Statutory arbitration award must be written and signed by arbitrators joining in award. (13-22-210). Confirmation upon filing of award with district court (13-22-213), unless vacated (13-22-214) or modified (13-22-215).

Trial de novo clause allowing insured or insurer to demand trial on merits after arbitration where award exceeds specified limit is unenforceable. (952 P.2d 342).

Damage Limitations.—Unless otherwise provided by law, exemplary damages may not be awarded in administrative or arbitration proceedings, even if award or decision is enforced or approved in action commenced in court. (C.R.S. 13-21-102[5]).

Judgment on Award.—For statutory arbitration, judgment entered upon order confirming, modifying or correcting award. (13-22-216). Common-law award reduced to judgment by civil suit. (76 Colo. 409, 232 P. 680).

DOCUMENTS AND RECORDS

ACKNOWLEDGMENTS:

Uniform Recognition of Acknowledgments Act has been adopted. (12-55-201 to 211). Uniform Act supplements but does not supersede other statutes dealing with acknowledgments. (12-55-209).

May be taken by following officers:

Within State.—Any instrument—notary public. (12-55-110). Instruments affecting interest in or title to real estate—judge, clerk or deputy clerk of any court of record; clerk and recorder of any county or his deputy; any notary public. (38-30-126[1]).

Fees for taking acknowledgments are as follows: Judge, clerk or deputy clerk of court of record, $1 (13-32-104); county clerk and recorder, $2 (30-1-103); notary public, not to exceed $5 ($2 prior to Jan. 1, 1999) for each acknowledgment (12-55-121).

Outside State but within U.S. or any Territory Thereof.—Any instrument—see Uniform Recognition of Acknowledgments Act. Instruments affecting interest in or title to real estate—secretary of state or territory; clerk of court of record having seal; notary public; commissioner of deeds; any other officer authorized by laws of state or territory to take acknowledgments. (38-30-126[2]).

Outside United States.—Any instrument—see Uniform Recognition of Acknowledgments Act. Instruments affecting interest in or title to real estate—judge, clerk or deputy clerk of any court of record, or chief magistrate or other chief executive officer of any province, colony, island possession, bailiwick, or mayor or chief executive officer of any city, town, borough, county or municipal corporation having seal, of foreign kingdom, empire, republic, state, principality, province, colony, island possession or bailiwick; or any ambassador, minister, consul, vice consul, consular agent, vice-consular agent, charge d'affaires, vice-charge d'affaires, commercial agent, vice-commercial agent, or diplomatic, consular or commercial agent or representative or deputy thereof of any government; and, additionally, if within any colony, island possession or bailiwick belonging to or under control of U.S., any judge, clerk or deputy clerk of any court of record, chief magistrate or other chief executive officer, mayor or chief executive officer of any city, town, borough, county, or municipal corporation having seal, or notary public. (38-30-126[3]-[4]).

Persons in or with U.S. Armed Forces.—See subheads Uniform Recognition of Acknowledgments Act, supra and Forms, infra; and topic Notaries Public.

General Requirements as to Taking.—Person acknowledging instrument affecting title to real property must be personally known to officer or be identified by credible person known to such officer. (38-35-101). Effective Jan. 1, 1999, if taken by notary public, person acknowledging instrument must do so while in physical presence of such notary public, and must be personally known to such notary public or such notary public must receive satisfactory evidence of identity. (12-55-110[4]). See also Uniform Recognition of Acknowledgments Act.

General Requirements of Certificate.—Acknowledgment certificates must be under seal of officer taking acknowledgement and date of expiration of officer's commission must be stated if taken by notary public. (12-55-112; 38-35-101).

Married Women.—No special requirement.

Foreign Acknowledgments.—Uniform Recognition of Acknowledgments Act adopted. See also subheads Outside State but within U.S. or any Territory Thereof, Outside United States.

Effect of Acknowledgment.—Acknowledgment of instrument affecting title to real estate constitutes prima facie evidence of proper execution and, if properly recorded, of due delivery. (38-35-101).

Proof by Subscribing Witness.—Where an instrument is not acknowledged, execution thereof may be proved by testimony of a subscribing witness taken and reduced to writing by an officer authorized to take acknowledgments and subscribed by subscribing witness. (38-30-136).

Authentication.—When instrument affects title to real property, certificate of officer not specifically named in statute taking acknowledgment outside state but within U.S. must be authenticated by clerk of court of record where officer resides. (38-30-126[2]). See also Uniform Recognition of Acknowledgments Act.

Forms.—Following form is statutory for all instruments affecting title to real property, whether made by individual or corporation. (38-35-101). See also Uniform Recognition of Acknowledgments Act for other forms.

Form

State of . . . . , County of . . . . ss. The foregoing instrument was acknowledged before me this . . . . day of . . . ., 19. . . ., by . . . ., (if by natural person or persons, insert name or names; if by person acting in representative or official capacity or as attorney-in-fact, insert name of person as executor, attorney-in-fact or other capacity or description; if by officer of corporation, insert name of such officer or officers as the president or other officers of such corporation, naming it). Witness my hand and official seal.

. . . .
Title of Officer.
My commission expires . . . .

Form for acknowledgment before officer in Armed Forces (24-12-104):

Form

The foregoing instrument was acknowledged before me this . . . . day of . . . ., 19. . . ., by . . . ., serving in or with the armed forces of the United States. The undersigned further certifies that he is a commissioned officer of the rank stated below and is in the active service of (or performing inactive-duty training in) the armed forces of the United States. (Signature, rank and branch of service or subdivision thereof.)

Validating Acts.—Any instrument affecting title to real property, whether acknowledged, unacknowledged or defectively acknowledged, after being recorded in county where real property is located is notice to all persons claiming interest in such real property. (38-35-106[1]). Any instrument which has remained of record in county for ten years, although unacknowledged or defectively acknowledged is deemed to have been properly acknowledged. (38-35-106[2]).

Alternative to Acknowledgment or Proof.—No statutory provision.

AFFIDAVITS:

Affidavit may be sworn to before any court, judge, clerk and deputy clerk within jurisdiction of court, before certain officers in armed forces and before notary public in any county. (24-12-103; 24-12-104). They may be sworn to within or without state before any officer authorized by law to take and certify acknowledgment of deeds conveying lands. (Rule 108). See topic Acknowledgments for fees.

General Requirements.—Affiant must swear to, or affirm (24-12-101; 24-12-102) affidavit, before same person who takes it (12-55-205). See generally, Uniform Recognition of Acknowledgments Act. (12-55-201 to 211).

Use of affidavits in evidence is permitted, as authorized in specific statutory provisions or rules of procedure, such as acknowledgments relating to real property (38-35-104) or depositions before action (Rule 27-a). If they affect title to real property they may be recorded. (38-35-109).

Form.—No prescribed form of jurat. Form in general use: "Subscribed and sworn to before me this . . . . . day of . . . ., 19. . . . . . My commission expires . . . ." followed by signature and seal of notary public.

Alternative to Affidavit.—No statutory provision.

NOTARIES PUBLIC:

Qualification.—Every applicant for appointment as notary must take affirmation set forth in 12-55-105, and meet qualifications of 12-55-104 (U.S. citizen; qualified elector; read and write English; no felony conviction) and submit handwritten sample of signature of legal name.

Appointment and Term.—Appointments are by secretary of state; term is four years. (12-55-103).

Seal.—Notary must have rubber stamp or embosser seal and affix same to acknowledgments. (12-55-112[2]).

Powers.—Notary may take acknowledgments, administer oaths and affirmations, certify that copy of document is true copy, take depositions and perform any other act permitted by law. Notary is disqualified from performing any notarial act if he receives

NOTARIES PUBLIC . . . *continued*

any property or interest exceeding in value his fee or if he is party to transaction. (12-55-110). Cannot notarize any blank document. (12-55-110[3]).

Journals.—Notary must keep journal of his acknowledgments to instruments affecting title to real property. (12-55-111).

Fees are provided by statute. Fees of notaries public may be, but shall not exceed, $5 for each acknowledgment, except as otherwise provided by law.

Misconduct.—Notary who knowingly and willfully, violates his duties is guilty of official misconduct, class 2 misdemeanor, which results in his liability to any person damaged thereby. (12-55-116).

Commissioners of deeds have general notarial powers. (38-30-130 to 133). Fees are same as for notaries public. (38-30-134).

Authentication.—See topic Acknowledgments.

Commissioned officers of U. S. Armed Forces have general notarial powers. (24-12-104).

RECORDS:

Records relating to real property are kept by county clerk and recorder of county where property is located. Uniform Commercial Code adopted. (4-1-101 to 11-102). See category Business Regulation and Commerce, topic Commercial Code, and subhead Filing Under Commercial Code, infra, for places for filing personal property records. Uniform Federal Lien Registration Act adopted. (38-25-101 to 107).

Recordable Instruments.—All deeds, powers of attorney, agreements or other instruments conveying, encumbering or affecting title to real property, certificates and certified copies of orders, judgments and decrees of courts of record may be recorded. (38-35-109[1]). All must be recorded to be valid against any person with any kind of rights who first records, except parties to instrument and those with notice. In all cases in which instrument may be filed with county clerk and recorder, filing is deemed equivalent to recording. (38-35-109[1]). Filing notice of lis pendens is notice to all persons thereafter acquiring any interest in property described. (38-35-110). Clerk and recorder may, however, refuse to accept for recording any spurious lien or spurious document. (38-35-202[1]).

Place of Recording.—Recording is in office of clerk and recorder of county where land is situated. (38-35-109[1]). *For list of counties and county seats, see first page for this state in volume containing Practice Profiles Section.*

Requisites for Recordings.—Acknowledgment or proof by witnesses not required. (38-35-106[1]). All documents of title, including instruments creating liens on real property, except mechanics' and judgment liens, should include immediately preceding or following legal description street address or comparable identifying numbers for property if displayed on property or any building (38-35-122[1]), but failure to do so does not render document invalid (38-35-122[3]). Any instrument creating lien on real property, except mechanics' liens, when recorded shall include current mailing address of lienor and lienee. Lienor of judgment lien shall place such addresses on document. (38-35-123[1]). Failure to state mailing address does not render document or its recordation invalid. (38-35-123[2]). No deed will be recorded without notation of grantee's legal address, but acceptance of deed in violation of statute does not make deed invalid. (38-35-109[2]). Power of attorney must be recorded in same office as instrument executed by attorney-in-fact. (38-30-123). Any person who offers to have recorded or filed in office of clerk and recorder any document purporting to create lien against real property knowing or having reason to know document is forged, groundless, contains material misstatement or false claim, or is otherwise invalid, is liable to owner for greater of $1,000 or actual damages together with reasonable attorneys' fees. Any grantee or person purportedly benefited by such recorded document who willfully refuses to release document of record upon request of owner is liable to owner for greater of $1,000 or actual damages, together with reasonable attorneys' fees. (38-35-109[3]).

Uniform Simplification of Land Transfers Act not adopted.

Recording Fees.—Recording fee schedule is as follows (30-1-103) plus $1 per document surcharge through Dec. 31, 2000 (4-9.3-105[3], [4]):

Taking and certifying affidavit	$ 2.00
Certificate and seal, each	1.00
Filing bond and license	5.00
Certificate of magistracy under seal	2.00
Taking acknowledgments	2.00
Recording town and other plats and all documents larger than 8½" x 14"	10.00 per sheet
Entering subsequent taxes paid in tax sale record	5.00 each certificate
Entering certificate of redemption in tax sale record	5.00 each certificate
Recording all other documents	5.00 per page plus 0.25 per mining claim named therein

Foreign Conveyances or Encumbrances.—Instrument affecting title to real property executed and acknowledged in language of foreign country where executed may be recorded only if accompanied by sworn translation into English. (38-30-140). For validity of foreign conveyances or encumbrances, see category Property, topic Real Property, subhead Foreign Conveyances or Encumbrances.

Effect of Record.—No unrecorded instrument is valid against any person with any kind of rights who first records, except between parties and those who have notice thereof. (38-35-109[1]). Recording statute classified race-notice. (38-35-109[1]). Proper

acknowledgment and recording of any instrument relating to real property is prima facie evidence of due delivery, despite lapse of time between date of instrument and date of recording. (38-35-101[4]). Recorded instruments acknowledged in proper form may be proved in evidence by certified copy of record without further proof of execution. (38-35-104). Unacknowledged or defectively acknowledged instrument of record ten years deemed properly acknowledged. (38-35-106[2]). No spurious lien or spurious document shall affect property longer than 30 days after filing or recording, unless action to enforce lien is commenced and notice of lis pendens is filed or recorded. (38-35-203[1]).

Torrens Act.—Uniform Land Registration Act adopted. (38-36-101 to 199). Owner may apply for registration of land (38-36-101) to district court of county where land is situated and court may inquire into condition of title to and any interest in land and may make all orders and decrees necessary to determine, establish and declare title or interest, legal or equitable, as against all persons, known or unknown, and all liens and encumbrances thereon and to declare order, priority and preference as between them and to remove all clouds from title. (38-36-108). Court will refer application to examiner of titles who shall examine title, search records and file report, including certificate of examiner's opinion on title. (38-36-118). Based on report and results of hearing, if necessary, court will issue decree of confirmation of title, and registration shall be entered that binds land and quiets its title. (38-36-130). Every person receiving certificate of title pursuant to decree and each subsequent purchaser of registered land who takes for value and in good faith shall hold land free from all encumbrances except those noted in last certificate of title in office of registrar of titles and except rights and encumbrances specified by statute. (38-36-133[1]). Thereafter, no title in derogation of that of registered owner may be acquired by prescription or adverse possession (38-36-137), and subsequent encumbrances or changes in title must be registered with registrar and on original and duplicate certificates of title and will take effect only from time of registration, and new certificates of title shall be issued to subsequent owners of land (38-36-159 to 182). Schedule of registration fees is provided by statute. (38-36-198).

Transfer of Decedent's Title.—Transfer of decedent's title to real estate is shown of record by recording personal representative's deed describing, in case of testate estates, will and time and place of probate, and in case of intestate estates, death of decedent. (15-12-711, 907, 908). In all cases, deed should recite date of appointment of personal representative and should note state documentary fee. (15-12-714, 910).

Certified copy of letters, release of Colorado and U.S. estate tax liens should also be recorded. If no personal representative has been appointed, marketable title cannot be conveyed until creditors' claims are barred one year after decedent's death. (15-12-803[1][a][III]).

In addition, for nonresident decedent, certified copy of authenticated foreign letters of appointment and foreign official bond, as filed with and certified by Colorado court (see category Estates and Trusts, topic Wills, subheads Foreign Executed Wills and Foreign Probated Wills, as to testate nonresidents), and releases of Colorado and U.S. estate tax liens should be recorded. (15-13-204).

In case of joint tenancy, copy of death certificate and releases of Colorado and U.S. estate tax liens should be recorded. (38-31-102). Deed executed and delivered by one joint tenant, but not recorded until after his death, is effective to sever joint tenancy; rebuttable presumption of delivery created by recording relates back to execution of deed. (188 Colo. 303, 535 P.2d 197).

Filing Under Commercial Code.—Office of clerk and recorder in county of debtor's residence or if debtor is not resident of state, then in any county, designated as place of filing security interests in consumer goods, farm equipment or farm products, including crops growing or to be grown, farm products that have become inventory and accounts and general intangibles arising from sale of farm products. All financing statements covering farm products filed after July 1, 1994 must also be filed with state central filing system board, in Colorado department of agriculture, as more fully described in 4-9.5-101 to 112. (4-9-401[1][A]). Financing statement for fixtures filed as fixtures, timber to be cut, minerals or other substances of value extracted from earth, or accounts relating thereto, or crops growing or to be grown should be filed in real estate records in office of clerk and recorder in county where real estate is situated. (4-9-401[1][B]). In all other cases, filing required at office of secretary of state or, effective July 1, 1996, in office of county clerk and recorder of any county. (4-9-401[1][C]). Filings to be made with secretary of state should be mailed to: Secretary of State, UCC Division, 1560 Broadway, Suite 200, Denver, Colorado 80202.

Colorado adopted an Art. 11, with no official text counterpart, dealing with fees. Filing fees are $15 per standard form document (or $5 per standard form continuation statement filed between July 1, 1996 and Dec. 31, 1997) plus $5 when nonstandard form is used (4-11-102), plus $1 per document surcharge through Dec. 31, 2000 (4-9.3-105[3], [4]).

See category Business Regulation and Commerce, topic Commercial Code.

Vital Statistics.—State registrar in department of public health and environment administers state system of registration of births and deaths (25-2-103) and will furnish to applicant with direct and tangible interest certified copy of any registered birth or death certificate (25-2-117, 25-2-121). Fee is $12 for first copy and $6 for each additional copy ordered at same time, subject to change annually. Address: Vital Records, 4300 Cherry Creek Dr. South, Denver, CO 80222-1530.

Establishing Records.—If birth or death in state has not been recorded, delayed recording may be accomplished with submission of such evidence and compliance with such regulations as required by state registrar, who may be contacted at above address. (25-2-114).

SEALS:

It is not necessary to proper execution of any conveyance affecting real property that same shall be executed under seal of grantor, nor that any seal or scroll or other mark be set opposite name of grantor. (38-30-118). Private corporation, authorized by law to convey, mortgage or lease any of its real estate, may convey, mortgage or lease same by instrument under its common seal. (38-30-144). Any instrument to which maker affixes scroll, by way of seal, shall be of same effect as if sealed. (38-30-125).

See note at head of Digest as to 1998 legislation covered.

See Topical Index in front part of this volume.

SEALS . . . *continued*

Whenever any law, rule, or regulation requires use of seal, it is sufficient that rubber stamp with facsimile of seal required is placed or stamped upon document with indelible ink. (12-55-211).

Uniform Commercial Code adopted. See category Business Regulation and Commerce, topic Commercial Code.

TORRENS ACT:

See topic Records.

EMPLOYMENT

EMPLOYER AND EMPLOYEE:

See topic Labor Relations.

LABOR RELATIONS:

Director of division of labor, department of labor and employment, has jurisdiction over any employer-employee dispute affecting conditions of employment, or wages or hours, only when employer and employee request such intervention or when dispute, according to executive director, affects public interest. (8-1-125). Strike or lockout in industry affected with public interest may not occur prior to or during investigation, hearing or arbitration of dispute by director. (8-1-126). Persons participating, inciting or encouraging such strike or lockout guilty of misdemeanor. (8-1-129).

Combinations of employees to secure fair treatment from employers, better wages and conditions, or for purpose of aiding and protecting interests of employees in any other lawful manner are not unlawful. (8-2-101). Combinations may not prevent or intimidate employees from continuing employment by displays of force or threats of bodily or financial injury, nor boycott or intimidate employer. (8-2-101). Unlawful for employer to attempt to prevent employees from joining or continuing membership in union or political party (8-2-102), or from participating in politics (8-2-108). Violations are misdemeanors. (8-2-103, 108). Noncompetition covenant in employment contract is void and unenforceable, except when included in contract for sale of business or business assets, in limited instances when protecting trade secrets (44 Colo. App. 155, 609 P.2d 1125), when included in contract provision for recovery of education and training expenses when employee served employer less than two years, or when applied to executive and management personnel, officers and professional staff thereto (8-2-113[2]; 680 P.2d 1339). Covenant may not restrict physician's right to practice medicine, but may provide for damages. (8-2-113[3]). Valid covenants must be reasonable in both duration and geographic scope; court may modify overly broad covenant or decline to enforce. (681 P.2d 546).

Employer may not maintain blacklist or notify any other employer that any current or former employee has been blacklisted by such employer for purpose of preventing such employee from obtaining employment. (8-2-114[1]). However, any employer that, upon request by prospective employer or current or former employee, provides fair and unbiased information about current or former employee's job performance is presumed to be acting in good faith and shall be immune from civil liability for such disclosure and consequences of such disclosure. (8-2-114[2][a]).

Hours of Labor.—Except in emergencies, eight-hour day is maximum for cement and plaster manufacturing plants. (8-13-110). Varying provisions exist as to hours for workers at mining and smelting operations and fire departments. (8-13-101 to 103, 107, 108, 111). Criminal penalties for violations. (8-13-103, 108, 111). Colorado Minimum Wage Order No. 20 should be consulted for other issues regarding hours of labor and wages.

Wages.—All nonpublic employers must pay employees at least monthly unless there is mutual agreement for another period. Agricultural employees may not agree otherwise. (8-4-105). Statute excepts independent contractors. (8-4-101[5]). Statute does not apply to profit-sharing plans, pension plans or other deferred compensation programs. (8-4-105[3]). Employer must post written notice of paydays. (8-4-107). $50 per day penalty payable to state for each refusal to pay each employee on time. (8-4-109[1]). Greater of 50% penalty or ten days' wages payable to employee for refusal to pay discharged employee at time of termination, unless employer's accounting unit is not then operational, or refusal to pay quitting employee at next regular pay day, unless employer had good faith legal justification therefor. Penalty inapplicable where employee not available to receive payment or fails to make written demand within 60 days. (8-4-104). When dispute over amount of wages due, employer must pay undisputed sum on timely basis. (8-4-110). Attorney fees available to prevailing party under 8-4-104 or 8-4-105. (8-4-114). Employer may set-off debt of employee (8-4-104[2]), and shortages due to theft by employee under certain circumstances (8-4-101[7.5]).

Wages must be paid in cash or by negotiable instruments, payable on demand. (8-4-102). Use of scrip prohibited. (8-4-102). District Attorneys may enforce requirements. (8-4-112).

Certain mining employers, before commencing work in any period for which payment of wages is to be made, are required to have funds or readily saleable securities on hand or on deposit to pay such wages. (8-4-103). Definite places for payment of wages in event of termination of employment established, and definite times for payment of wages in event of strikes specified. (8-4-108).

Employer may not discriminate on basis of sex in payment of wages or salary to employees. (8-5-102). Commission hearing and judicial review similar to procedures under Workmen's Compensation Act available for enforcement. (8-5-103).

Director has authority to set minimum wage rates for different occupations. (8-6-105, 106, 107, 109, 111). Employer's failure to pay minimum wage is misdemeanor and employee working for less may have action for difference from minimum despite any contract with employer.

Assignment of wages, see category Debtor and Creditor, topic Assignments.

Child Labor.—Employment of children is governed by Colorado Youth Employment Opportunity Act of 1971. (8-12-101 to 117). Children nine and over are permitted enumerated and similar employments including certain types of delivery, shoe-shining, gardening, snow shoveling, and caddying. (8-12-106). Children 12 and older are permitted to engage in enumerated and similar employments including door-to-door selling, babysitting, operation of division of labor approved power-driven lawn equipment, operation of power-driven snow removal equipment, and certain agricultural work. (8-12-107). Children 14 and older are permitted to engage in enumerated and similar employment including nonhazardous manufacturing, public messenger service, operation of automatic enclosed elevators, janitorial service, office work, warehousing, nonhazardous construction and repair, retail food service, certain jobs in gasoline stations, restaurants, hotels, or motels, and jobs relating to parks and recreation. (8-12-108). Children 16 and over are allowed to use motor vehicles. (8-12-109). Children under 18 may not, except under certain circumstances, work in enumerated hazardous employments, including operation of certain boilers, work at certain elevations, manufacture, transportation, or storage of explosives, mining, logging, any occupation which would expose them to radiation, operation of certain power-driven machinery, livestock slaughter, manufacture of brick or clay products, wrecking or demolition, roofing and excavation. (8-12-110[2]). Exceptions are provided for minors over age 14 employed in certain programs or with specified training. (8-12-110[1]). Director may grant exemptions from provisions of Act under certain circumstances. (8-12-104).

No child under age 16 is permitted to work in excess of six hours if next day is school day. (8-12-105[2]). No child under age 16 may work during school hours, unless child has school release permit. (8-12-105[2], 8-12-113). No child under age 16 may work between 9:30 p.m. and 5:00 a.m. unless as babysitter or next day is not a school day. Children under 18 may not work more than eight hours in one day or 40 hours in one week, with certain exceptions for children over 14 in seasonal employment relating to perishable products. (8-12-105).

Employers may require proof of age. (8-12-111). Children age 14 and age 15 may apply for school release permit. (8-12-113). Employers and those having legal responsibility for minors are subject to fines, and to fines and imprisonment for subsequent violations of Act. (8-12-116).

Discrimination.—Antidiscrimination Act adopted. (24-34-301 to 802). Discrimination against employees on basis of race, creed, color, sex, age, national origin, ancestry, disability, or, in certain cases, marriage to coemployee, is unlawful. (24-34-402). Discrimination against "otherwise qualified" worker on basis of handicap is unlawful, unless no reasonable accommodation for handicap can be made by employer, handicap actually disqualifies person, and handicap has significant impact on job. (24-34-402). Termination of employment for engaging in lawful activity off employer's premises is unlawful, unless restriction relates to bona fide occupational requirement, is reasonably and rationally related to employment activities and responsibilities of particular employee or employee group, or is necessary to avoid conflict of interest or appearance thereof. (24-34-402.5). Employer and insurer liable for sex discrimination when insurance offered employees excluded benefits for normal pregnancy. (759 P.2d 1358). Discrimination charges must be filed within six months of complained-of act. (24-34-403). Unlawful for publicly-financed employer to discriminate on basis of handicap unless disability prevents performances of work. (43 Colo. App. 446, 614 P.2d 891; 24-34-801[1]).

Labor Unions.—Union security provisions between employer and union are unfair labor practices unless approved in secret ballot election by over half of bargaining unit employees eligible to vote or three-quarters of employees voting, whichever is greater. (8-3-108[1][c][I]). Union-security provision in effect as of June 29, 1977 may be ratified by agreement between employer and union, and certified by director of labor but is subject to deauthorization election upon petition by at least 20% of employees covered. (8-3-108[1][c][II]). Division of labor and state courts have authority to resolve disputes regarding unfair labor practices arising out of such elections or petitioning. (8-3-110; 199 Colo. 182, 606 P.2d 441). Union-security agreement in building and construction industry may be certified by director. (8-3-109[3]). Promises to join, not to join, or to withdraw from labor or employer organization unenforceable. (8-3-119).

Obtaining workmen by false representations, false advertising, etc., or by failing to advise of strike lockout or other current labor trouble illegal and misdemeanor (8-2-104); actual damages and attorney fees are recoverable for violation thereof (8-2-107). Blacklisting of employees (8-2-110, 111, 114) and publishing notices of boycott (8-2-112) are misdemeanors (8-2-115). There are numerous statutes dealing with certain classes of labor and conditions of employment (i.e. mines, child labor, women, etc.).

No public employment relations law, but public employers have authority to enter into collective bargaining contracts not in conflict with existing statutes. (191 Colo. 411, 553 P.2d 793).

Although public employee is not entitled to due process in discharge if employment contract is for indefinite term, discharge is unlawful if effected contrary to statute or charter. (43 Colo. App. 60, 598 P.2d 527).

Procedural and substantive rights of public school teachers are governed by statute. (22-63-101 to 403). Based upon chief administration officer's recommendation, school board may choose not to renew probationary teacher. (22-63-203[4]). Probationary full-time teachers automatically reemployed for next academic year unless school board gives contrary written notice on or before June 1. (22-63-203[3]). Teacher may be dismissed for good and just cause, in accordance with statutory procedures. (22-63-301 to 302).

Labor Disputes.—Governed by Labor Peace Act. (8-3-101 to 123). Act proscribes various unfair labor practices. (8-3-108). Division of labor, department of labor and employment administers Act and holds hearings regarding unfair labor practices. (8-3-110). State courts have no jurisdiction to enjoin peaceful picketing in labor dispute. (155 Colo. 54, 392 P.2d 601; 8-3-118).

Arbitration, see categories Civil Actions and Procedure, topic Actions, subhead Mandatory Arbitration; Dispute Resolution, topic Arbitration and Award.

Workers' Compensation Act (8-40-101 to 8-47-209) administered by division of workers' compensation, department of labor and employment (8-47-101).

Employers and Employees Subject to Act.—Every person, association, firm or corporation, including public service corporations, personal representatives, assignees, trustees and receivers, that has one or more persons in same business or employment under

See note at head of Digest as to 1998 legislation covered.

See Topical Index in front part of this volume.

CO – 45

LABOR RELATIONS . . . *continued*
any express or implied contract of hire (except common carriers by railroad and other employers for whom rule of liability has been established by U.S. [8-41-201] and employers of part-time domestic servants, part-time home and certain business repair or maintenance employees and elected or appointed advisors of eleemosynary, charitable, fraternal, religious or social groups receiving less than $750 per year [8-40-302]) are subject to provisions of Act. (8-40-203). Public employers also covered by Act. (8-40-203). Employer in bona fide cooperative education or student internship program subject to Act, but if student-employees do not receive pay or remuneration, educational institution sponsoring students must provide insurance coverage or agree to pay employer's insurance costs. (8-40-302[7]). Independent contractor who fails to obtain insurance cannot sue under Act. (8-41-401). $15,000 cap on damages to independent contractor. (8-41-401). Lessors and contractors-out are generally considered employers of employees of their lessees and contractors, and are liable to pay compensation for injury or death suffered by lessees, sublessees, contractors, and subcontractors and their employees or employees' dependents. (8-41-401). However, when lessee, sublessee, contractor, or subcontractor has workers' compensation insurance for its employees, it and its employees and insurer have no right of contribution or action of any kind against lessor or contractor. (8-41-401). Anyone contracting with landowner or lessee to perform specified farming or ranching operation must maintain insurance coverage for his employees. (8-41-401). Certain owners and occupants of residential real property exempted from employer status under Act for work contracted-out on home. (8-41-402). Lessor or sublessor renting or leasing real property to lessee or sublessee for purpose of lessee's or sublessee's business excluded from requirements of article. (8-41-403). Employer loaning services of employee normally liable for compensation for any injury or death to loaned employee. (8-41-303). Definition of employee is very broad and includes persons in service of both public and private employers, with some exceptions. (8-40-202, 301). Off-duty police officer, deputy sheriff, or firefighters injured while performing temporary emergency duty outside jurisdiction continues to be treated as employee of his jurisdiction. (43 Colo. App. 10, 601 P.2d 648; 29-5-109). Members of volunteer fire departments deemed employees, including retired firefighters receiving pension benefits who volunteer after retirement. (8-40-202). Student teacher is considered to be employee of school district in which student teacher is working, not of sponsoring institution. (22-62-105[2]). Public officials who receive no compensation for services may be excluded from coverage of Act if their employer files notice at least 45 days in advance of policy year in which exclusion is to be effective and notifies public officials of exclusion. (8-40-202[1][a][I][B]). Certain corporate officers and members of limited liability companies may reject coverage. (8-41-202). Commission real estate brokers excluded. (8-41-301[2]) Most prison inmates are excluded. (8-40-301).

Election.—Employer not otherwise covered elects to accept by securing compensation insurance for employees in conformity with Act (8-40-302[5]) and such election by employer constitutes surrender of all other rights and remedies, statutory or common law, on account of personal injuries or death of employee, and binds employee and employee's personal representative, successors, heirs or assigns. (8-41-104). Apparent inconsistency concerning employee's right to elect not to come under Act. (8-41-103, 104). Employee may elect between compensation or common law remedy if his employer uninsured at time of accident. (674 P.2d 1011). Defenses of assumed risk, negligence of fellow servant, and negligence of injured employee not available to uninsured employer. (8-41-101 to 103). Employee may elect to sue third party responsible for injury, and insurer will be subrogated to extent compensation benefits paid to employee. (8-41-101 to 103). Third party has no right to indemnification or contribution from employer. (749 P.2d 431).

Due Process.—By acquiescence in industrial commission procedures until an adverse decision was given, defendant waived any claimed denial of due process. (178 Colo. 65, 495 P.2d 546).

Notice.—Employer must give notice of injury for which compensation and benefits payable within ten days thereafter, or immediate notice in case of death or of accident in which three or more employees are injured, to division on forms prescribed by division. Two copies must be either delivered or sent by registered mail to division office in Denver. If notice not given by employer, any person may give notice. (8-43-101, 103). Right to compensation or benefits is barred unless notice of claim for compensation given by employee or someone on his behalf within two years after injury or after death resulting therefrom, provided such limitation does not apply if claimant has received compensation or division finds within three years after injury or death that reasonable excuse for failure to file existed and employer's rights have not been prejudiced thereby (8-43-103[2]), and further provided that if death or disability results from exposure to radioactive sources or uranium, or from asbestosis, silicosis, or anthracosis, notice must be given within five years (8-43-103[3]). If employer with notice of injury fails to submit required report to division of labor, statute of limitations barring claim for compensation shall not begin to run until filing of report. (8-43-103[2]; 720 P.2d 571). Report of accident filed by employer is insufficient substitute for employee's notice of claim. (43 Colo. App. 521, 608 P.2d 366). Employee or someone in his behalf must report injury in writing to employer within four days of occurrence of injury or within 30 days of first manifestation of occupational disease. If employee is physically or mentally unable to give notice, supervisor or manager with notice of injury shall give such written notice to employer. (8-43-102). Employer must keep record of all injuries which result in fatality to, or permanent physical impairment of, or lost time from work for injured employee in excess of three shifts or calendar days. (8-43-101).

Procedure and Hearing on Claim.—Employer or his insurer must give written notice admitting or contesting liability to Division and injured employee or dependents of deceased within 20 days after knowledge of injury which disables employee for more than three shifts or three calendar days or which causes death or permanent physical impairment. (8-43-203; 676 P.2d 1196). Notice must reference claimant's obligations under 8-42-113.5. (8-43-203[1][b]). Penalty attached for failure to file timely admission or denial. (8-43-203[2]). Admission of liability must include notification that claimant may contest admission. (8-43-203[2]). If liability is admitted, such notice must specify amount, to whom paid, period of and type of disability for which compensation will be paid and payment thereon must be made forthwith. (8-43-203[2]). Admission of liability for final payment of compensation shall include statement that this is final admission, that claimant may contest, to whom to contest, and that claimant must contest and request hearing within 30 days or case closed. (8-43-203[2]). Hearings to determine controversies shall be conducted by division director or appointed administrative law judge. (8-43-201, 207). Any party, or Division director or administrative law judge, may request pre-hearing conference not less than ten days before hearing. (8-43-207.5). Any party may, within 20 days of decision, petition for review by director or administrative law judge who may make supplemental order. (8-43-301). Any party may petition commission for review of supplemental order within 20 days of issuance. (8-43-301[6]). Commission has 60 days in which to issue order. Commission may not disturb findings of fact if supported by substantial evidence. (8-43-301[8]). Any party dissatisfied with commission's order may commence action for judicial review in court of appeals, within 20 days of final order. (8-43-301[10], 307). Review of court of appeals judgment by supreme court is limited to summary review of questions of law. (8-43-313). If commission does not issue order in 60 days, party has 30 days to commence action for judicial review in court of appeals. (8-43-301[11]). Unless petition for review is filed, order, corrected order, or supplemental order is final. (8-43-301[1]). Restrictive standard to reopen case. (8-43-303). Employer or insurer violating Act or lawful order under Act subject to fine of up to $500 per day for each such offense, 75% payable to aggrieved party and 25% payable to subsequent injury fund. (8-43-304, 305). Defense to penalty may be established if violation cured within 20 days and applicant for penalty cannot show alleged violator knew or reasonably should have known of violation. (8-43-304[4]).

Benefits available for injury caused by certain job-related mental impairment. (8-41-301[2]).

Benefits unavailable where claimant not within scope of employment at time of injury. (677 P.2d 416).

Scale of compensation is established for all injuries or death, based upon the earnings of the injured person. (8-42-102 to 117). Certain widows, widowers, and minor children presumed wholly dependent. (8-41-501). Intoxication and willful failure to adhere to safety standards reduce award by 50%. (8-42-112). Employer who continues to pay full wages to temporarily disabled employee may be reimbursed, if insured, or receive credit, if self-insured, for amount of statutory compensation otherwise due employee. (8-42-124[8]). As to computation of earnings, see 8-42-102. Disability and death benefits may be reduced by part or all of amounts of federal disability insurance or employer-financed pension plan or disability payments to employee. (8-42-103[1][c] and [d]). Employee required to give notice of receipt of such amounts and employer or insurer may recover overpayments for such amounts not originally reflected in benefit calculation. (8-42-113.5). Unemployment insurance will reduce total or partial disability payments. (8-42-103[1][f]).

Compensation for death is payable to decedent's dependents as determined as of time of injury, with exception for dependent children who are students between 18 and 21 years old. (8-41-503). Requirement in 8-42-115 that death benefits be paid to subsequent injury fund if employee not survived by dependents does not deprive non-dependent heirs of property. (196 Colo. 30, 580 P.2d 794). Death benefits terminate upon happening of following, and survive to remaining dependents, if any: (a) Remarriage of widow or widower; (b) death of any dependent; (c) when child or brother or sister of deceased reaches 18 years, with exception as provided in 8-41-501; (d) expiration of six years after death in case of partial dependents. (8-42-120). Some benefit available upon remarriage if no dependent children. (8-42-120). Insurer who makes support payments on claim is entitled to reimbursement out of judgment recovered in wrongful death action from third party tortfeasor. (39 Colo. App. 251, 567 P.2d 806).

Enforcement of Awards.—Awards constitute lien upon assets of employer and bear interest at 8% per annum from date payments are ordered to be made. (8-43-410). Failure to comply with order of department renders guilty party subject to penalty of up to $500 per day for each such offense, 75% payable to aggrieved party and 25% payable to subsequent injury fund. (8-43-304, 305). Attorney general or district attorney has duty to enforce awards at request of department. (8-43-401).

Attorneys' Fees.—Standards for reasonable fees. (8-43-403).

Insurance is permitted: (a) With Colorado Compensation Insurance Authority; (b) with stock or mutual corporations authorized to transact business of Workmen's Compensation Insurance in Colorado; (c) by procuring self-insurance permit from executive director or insurance commissioner. (8-44-101). Employer liable for 50% penalty for failure to comply with insurance provisions or failure to pay judgment. (8-43-408). Employer may appeal calculation of experience modification factors and classification assignment decisions made by insurance provider. (8-55-101).

Department may impose fine against employer or may issue cease and desist order and obtain injunction against continuance of employer's business if he fails effectively to insure. (8-43-409).

Intentional wrongs arising out of and in course of employment covered. (8-41-301; 645 P.2d 1300).

Sexual assault covered if arising out of and in course of employment. (759 P.2d 17).

Occupational Diseases.—Disability or death from occupational disease compensated under Workers' Compensation Act. (8-41-301).

Unemployment Compensation.—Employment Security Act adopted. (8-70-101 to 8-82-105). Covers full-time employees generally, with statutory exceptions for certain agricultural labor, domestic service employees, casual labor, family employees, U.S. government employees, employees of educational institutions, hospital employees, newspaper deliverers, salesmen, insurance agents, nonprofit organization employees, U.S. citizens performing services for American employers outside of U.S., and others. (8-70-103[11], 122, 125 to 140.2). Illegal aliens are not eligible for benefits. (8-73-107[7]). Benefits available for persons unemployed through no fault of their own. (8-73-108[1]). Benefits available to claimant terminated because of addiction to alcohol or drugs under limited circumstances, but award charged to unemployment compensation fund, not employer's account. (8-73-108[4][b]). Reduced awards available in appropriate circumstances. (8-73-108[5]). Severance payments, even when given for release of claims, may reduce and postpone benefits. (8-73-110). Claimant ineligible where unemployment due to strike in which employee has direct interest. (8-73-109; 669 P.2d 1049). Full award available where employer disregards its own discharge policy. (677

See note at head of Digest as to 1998 legislation covered.

See Topical Index in front part of this volume.

CO – 46

LABOR RELATIONS . . . *continued*
P.2d 447). Employee leasing company considered employing unit provided it has certain rights and responsibilities pursuant to employee leasing contract. (8-70-114[2]). Statutes should be consulted for numerous other conditions bearing on eligibility determination.

Benefit rates for totally unemployed persons generally are 60% of 1/26 of wages paid during two consecutive quarters base period in which such total wages were highest, with a maximum of one-half of average weekly earnings in all covered Colorado industries as published by U.S. bureau of labor statistics and minimum of $25. (8-73-102). Maximum award recoverable is for 26 weeks. (8-73-104). Employee may be eligible for full award or reduced award. (8-73-108).

Procedure and Appeal.—Initial determination of entitlement by deputy. (8-74-102). Interested parties, dissatisfied with deputy's decision, may obtain hearing of disputed claim before hearing officer. (8-74-103). Parties may appeal from hearing officer's decision to industrial claim appeals panel. (8-74-104). Party dissatisfied with panel's decision must petition panel for review of initial decision before appeal to court of appeals. (8-74-107). Employer with interest that could be adversely affected by outcome is indispensable party for perfecting appeal. (620 P.2d 65). Factual findings of panel conclusive as to unemployment compensation issues if supported by substantial evidence in absence of fraud. (8-74-107[4]). Determinations made during course of unemployment proceeding are not binding upon any other agency or court. (8-74-108).

Employment-At-Will/Wrongful Discharge.—Employment terminable at will of either party absent fixed term contract. (35 Colo. App. 1, 530 P.2d 984). Employment at will presumed, but implied contract can be found in handbooks or manuals distributed to employees based on acceptance by continued employment or prejudicial reliance. (731 P.2d 708; 903 P.2d 820). Under certain circumstances, contract not implied where handbook contains disclaimers. (799 P.2d 458; 711 F. Supp. 570; 670 F. Supp. 1517; but see, 765 P.2d 619). Promises may override disclaimer. (765 P.2d 619). Implied contract found on basis of letter offer of employment. (914 P.2d 909). Requirement of "good cause" for discharge will not be implied. (593 F.Supp. 1279). Wrongful discharge tort unavailable where statutory remedy exists (684 P.2d 265); public policy exception recognized where employee fired for filing workmen's compensation claim (770 P.2d 1367) or for refusing to violate statute (765 P.2d 619). Termination of employment for engaging in lawful activity off employer's premises is unlawful, unless restriction relates to bona fide occupational requirement, is reasonably and rationally related to employment activities and responsibilities of particular employee or employee group, or is necessary to avoid conflict of interest or appearance thereof. (24-34-402.5).

ENVIRONMENT

ENVIRONMENTAL REGULATION:

General Supervision.—Most environmental regulation within ambit of Department of Public Health and Environment, air, water, and hazardous waste management divisions. Board of Health oversees solid waste management. Department of Natural Resources responsible for mine reclamation.

Air Quality Control.—Ambient air standards and emission control regulations promulgated by air quality control commission. (25-7-108, 109). Air pollutant emission notices and permits required for new emissions. (25-7-114). Stationary sources of air pollution must pay annual emission fee unless exempted. (25-7-114.7). Construction and operating permits required. (25-7-114.2 and -114.3). Hazardous air pollutant control and reduction program established. (25-7-109). Air Quality Science Advisory Board created (25-7-109.4) to offer opinions on issues that arise under hazardous air pollutant control program (25-7-109.3). Accidental release prevention program established. (25-7-109.6). Open burning prohibited in designated areas unless permit obtained. (25-7-123). Small business stationary source technical and environmental compliance assistance program established. (25-7-109.2). Program to reduce and to prevent exposure of public to asbestos. (25-7-501 to 512). Automobile inspection and readjustment program instituted (42-4-301); proposed emissions standards of vehicle exhaust gases adopted by air quality control commission (42-4-306). Program consists of basic emission (42-4-302) and enhanced emission program (42-4-301). Biennial emission control inspection for 1982 and newer vehicles and annual inspection for 1981 and older models. (42-4-310). If vehicles not in compliance with emission standards, adjustments and repairs to be performed. (42-4-310). Standards for emissions from motor vehicles and motorcycles powered by gasoline or other fuel and from diesel-powered motor vehicles established. (42-4-412). Visible diesel emissions prohibited, effective Jan. 1, 1987, subject to fine as misdemeanor traffic offense. (42-4-413). Diesel inspection program established for Front Range counties. (42-4-401). Includes diesel-fueled motor vehicles with four wheels or more. Does not include off-road diesel-powered vehicles, heavy construction equipment, farm or ranch vehicles, or collectors' items. (42-4-401[5]). As of Jan. 1, 1990 no diesel vehicle can be sold, registered or re-registered unless certificate of emission control has been issued within past year. (42-4-406). Requirements for inspectors and inspection stations detailed. (42-4-407 to 409). Heavy duty diesel fleets of nine or more are exempted (42-4-411) unless owner commits two excessive violations in 12-month period (42-4-414[3][c]). Inspection program to be fully implemented for heavy-duty diesel trucks by Jan. 1, 1987. (42-4-414). In order to reduce carbon monoxide and particulate emissions from gasoline powered motor vehicles, Nov. 1 through Feb. 14, motor vehicle fuel sold in AIR Program area (Front Range counties) must have at least 2.7% oxygen content by weight (15% by volume MTBE shall be considered equivalent to 2.7% oxygen content by weight and 10% by volume denatured ethanol shall be considered equivalent to 3.5% oxygen content by weight). (5 Code Colo. Reg. 1001-16). Alternative fuels financial incentive program established. (25-7-106.9). Air quality control commission has promulgated rules and regulations for controlling emissions from new wood stoves. (5 Code Colo. Reg. 1001-6). Regulations detail, among other things: requirements for sale; certification procedure; emission standards, quality control and testing; labeling requirements; and standard method for measuring emissions. Certification required for sale of wood stoves after Jan. 1, 1987. (25-7-405). Boards of county commissioners must enact building code provisions to minimize emissions from fireplaces. (30-28-201[2]). Resale of used noncertified wood-burning devices prohibited unless device meets stringent standards adopted by commission. (25-7-405.5).

Air pollution limitations enforced and state program administered by air quality control division. (25-7-111). Private citizen may request investigation of suspected discharge. (25-7-112). Following conference compliance order issued; opportunity for hearing if requested within 20 days. (25-7-115). Compliance orders enforceable by injunction. (25-7-121). Delayed compliance orders may be issued. (25-7-118). Division or commission determinations judicially reviewable. (25-7-120). Civil penalties provided for violation of Air Quality Control Act. (25-7-115; 25-7-122; 25-7-123). Criminal penalties also available. (25-7-122.1).

State regulations for prevention of significant deterioration set forth. (25-7-201). Certain areas have been designated pristine areas for sulfur dioxide; increases in sulfur dioxide concentrations in such areas limited to increases for Class I areas under federal act. (25-7-209). Air quality related values program for Class I areas established. (25-7-1001 to 1008).

Lead-based paint abatement program enacted. (25-7-1101 to 25-7-1107). Air quality control commission to promulgate rules to implement "Residential Lead-based Paint Hazard Reduction Act". (25-7-1103). Air pollution control division to implement training and certification requirements. (25-7-1104[1]). Division may delegate implementation and enforcement to local health and building departments. (25-7-1104[2]). Division may commence enforcement action. (25-7-1106).

Water Quality Control.—Waters of state classified by water quality control commission. (25-8-203). Water quality standards developed. (25-8-204). Water quality designations established. (25-8-209). State program administered, and enforcement and permitting conducted by water quality control division. (25-8-302, 303). Discharge of pollutants into state waters from point source without permit prohibited. (25-8-501). Program for prevention of groundwater pollution from agricultural chemicals established. (25-8-205.5). Permits required for discharge of all pollutants except agricultural wastes. (25-8-501 to 508). Service of notice required for violations of orders, permits or control regulations. (25-8-602). Cease and desist orders issued after written notice of violation. (25-8-605). Clean up orders may be issued. (25-8-606). Injunctions are available. (25-8-607). Civil and criminal penalties authorized. (25-8-608, 609).

Department of Public Health and Environment authorized to require disinfection or treatment of drinking water supplied to public. (25-1-107[1][x]). Board may promulgate standards for contaminants or substances if no federal standard exists. (25-1-107[2][d]). Laboratory certification program established for ensuring competent testing of drinking water. (25-1-107[1][x.5]).

Minimum standards established for regulation of individual sewage disposal systems. (25-10-104, 105). Regulations enforced primarily by local health departments and boards of health. (25-10-109). Permit required before construction or modification of structure not serviced by sewage treatment works. (25-10-111). Permits may be prohibited in certain areas after public hearings before local board of health. (25-10-110).

Solid Waste Disposal.—Solid waste disposal sites and facilities require certificate of designation to operate. (30-20-102, 103). Minimum standards established. (30-20-110). Governing body having jurisdiction over area where site is or is proposed to be shall review application to maintain solid waste disposal facility. (30-20-103). Certificate of designation revocable for improper maintenance of facility. (30-20-112). Local authorities may enforce local solid waste ordinances. (30-20-114). Violation of solid waste disposal statute is misdemeanor punishable by fine and/or imprisonment. (30-20-114). Civil penalties provided for violation of Act. (30-20-113). Legislature recycling of plastics statute enacted. (25-17-101 to 105; 8-19.5-101; 39-22-114.5, 309). Waste tire recycling development fee program implemented on Jan. 1, 1994. (27-17-202).

Hazardous Waste Disposal.—State Hazardous Waste Siting Act enacted. (25-15-200.1). Colorado given implementation authority under "Resource Conservation and Recovery Act" on Nov. 2, 1984, and under "Hazardous and Solid Waste Amendments" on July 14, 1989. (25-15-301 to 316). Hazardous waste disposal sites require certificate of designation to operate. (25-15-201). Infectious waste statute enacted. (25-15-401 to 407). Department of Public Health and Environment, through waste management division, regulates hazardous waste management. (25-15-301). Permit required for treatment, storage, or disposal of hazardous wastes. (25-15-303). Rules and regulations promulgated by hazardous waste commission. (25-15-302). Statute providing for regulation of underground storage tanks containing regulated substances enacted. (8-20.5-201 to 209; 8-20.5-401 to 407). Statute providing for regulation of aboveground storage tanks containing fuel product enacted. (8-20.5-301 to 304). State inspector of oils promulgates and enforces regulations for underground and aboveground storage tank. (8-20.5-202, 302). Abandonment of vehicle containing hazardous material or intentionally spilling hazardous material on public property prohibited. (42-20-113). Any deed for property used for disposal of hazardous waste, subject to federal, state permit, certificate of designation or interim status must contain notation that property has been used for hazardous waste disposal. (25-15-303[4]). Criminal and civil penalties provided for violation of hazardous waste statutes. (25-15-212, 309, 310). Statute enacted to limit environmental third party liability for lenders. (13-20-701 to 703).

Department of Public Health and Environment authorized to participate in federal implementation of "Comprehensive Environmental Response, Compensation, and Liability Act of 1980" (CERCLA). (25-16-101). State accepts provision requiring payment of necessary state share of response costs. (25-16-104). Effective July 1, 1985, hazardous substance response fund established in state treasury to provide state's necessary share of costs of cleaning hazardous waste sites. (25-16-104.6). Natural resource damage recovery fund created. (25-16-104.7). Solid waste user fee imposed as of Jan. 1, 1986. (25-16-104.5). Voluntary cleanup of contaminated property authorized. (25-16-301 to -311).

Pollution Prevention Advisory Board created. (25-16.5-104). Duties include providing policy guidance, coordination and advice in development and implementation of pollution prevention activities program. (25-16.5-105 to -106). Technical assistance program to award grants. (25-16.5-107). Pollution prevention fees assessed on certain facilities. (25-16.5-108).

Hazardous Materials Transportation Act of 1987 enacted. (42-20-101). Permit required for motor vehicles requiring placarding under 49 C.F.R. 172 or 173 to transport

See note at head of Digest as to 1998 legislation covered.

See Topical Index in front part of this volume.

CO – 47

ENVIRONMENTAL REGULATION . . . *continued*
hazardous materials. (42-20-201,202). Criminal and civil penalties authorized. (42-20-204). State patrol, in consultation with local authorities, designates which public roads can be used for transportation of hazardous materials. (42-20-301). Persons deviating from designated routes are subject to penalties. (42-20-305). Persons who transport or cause to be transported certain hazardous materials must have proof of liability insurance. (40-20-202; 8 Code Colo. Reg. 1507-8).

Safe transportation of nuclear material regulated by statute. (42-20-401). All vehicles carrying nuclear materials are subject to inspection. (42-20-404). Permit is required to operate motor vehicle carrying nuclear materials upon public roads of Colorado. (42-20-501[1]). Each carrier must submit permit application prior to beginning transportation. (42-20-501[2]). State requires permit fees and fees for each shipment. (42-20-502). Criminal (42-20-405) and civil (42-20-406, 407) penalties are provided for as well as injunctive relief (42-20-408). Any person who causes release of nuclear material being transported is strictly liable for all injuries and damages from release. (42-20-509).

Regulation of transportation and management of low-level radioactive wastes provided by Rocky Mountain Low-Level Radioactive Waste Compact entered into with neighboring states. (24-60-2201). Nuclear and radioactive wastes may not be disposed of underground except on finding of no significant pollution by division of administration of Department of Public Health and Environment through water quality control division. (25-8-506). Board of health to regulate naturally occurring radioactive material once federal regulations are promulgated. (25-11-104).

Roadside Advertising.—State Outdoor Advertising Act enacted. (43-1-401). Erection and maintenance of advertising devices adjacent to state highways regulated by statute. (43-1-402). Rules and regulations developed by Department of Transportation for enforcement of roadside advertisement laws. (43-1-404, 407). Department authorized to institute appropriate action in court to prevent or remove violation. (43-1-417). Violation of roadside advertising provisions misdemeanor punishable by fine. (43-1-417). Permit required for erection or maintenance of nonconforming advertising devices, directional advertising devices, advertising devices in certain areas zoned industrial or commercial, and advertising devices on bus bench or bus shelter. (43-1-407).

Noise Control.—Statewide standards for noise level limits for various time periods and areas established. Noises prohibited constitute public nuisance. (25-12-101; 30-15-401[1][m]). Maximum permissible noise levels established on decibel basis for residential, commercial, light industrial and industrial zones. (25-12-103). Exemptions for aircraft or other activities subject to federal noise control law, use of property for vehicle speed or endurance events, use of property for manufacturing or maintaining machine-made snow and use of property by not-for-profit entities for public events. (25-12-103). Separate rules for motor vehicles. (25-12-106; 30-15-401[m][I]). Residents may bring action to abate and prevent public nuisance. (25-12-104). Violation of injunction against public nuisance deemed contempt of court punishable by fine for each day of offense. (25-12-105).

Other.—State Recreation Land Preservation Act enacted. (25-13-101). Minimum controls to prevent degradation of natural environment of recreational mountain areas established. (25-13-102). Facilities for sewage disposal to be provided by operator of campground. (25-13-106). Water supplies to campground to be conformed to requirements of standards, rules and regulations adopted by board. (25-13-108). Enforcement by different authorities. (25-13-111). Discharge of untreated sewage, deposit or burial of refuse except in provided receptacles, use of cleansers and defacing or cutting of rocks, trees, and shrubbery prohibited in public recreation areas. (25-13-105). Violation of provisions against discharge of untreated sewage, etc., in public recreation area constitutes misdemeanor punishable by fine. (25-13-114). Environmental self-evaluation privilege established. (13-25-126.5).

Local authorities may establish more stringent laws in areas of local air pollution (25-7-128), individual sewage disposal systems (25-10-104), noise abatement (25-12-108), and control of outdoor advertising (43-1-416).

Uniform Transboundary Pollution Reciprocal Access Act adopted. (13-1. 5-101). Any person in reciprocating jurisdiction injured by pollution originating in Colorado has same right to relief as if injury occurred within state. (13-1.5-104). State law to be applied. (13-1.5-105). Defense of sovereign immunity limited. (13-1.5-108).

Penalties.—See subheads Air Quality Control, Water Quality Control, Solid Waste Disposal, Hazardous Waste Disposal, Roadside Advertising, Noise Control, Other, supra, and Reclamation, infra.

Permits.—See subheads Air Quality Control, Water Quality Control, Solid Waste Disposal, Hazardous Waste Disposal, Roadside Advertising, supra, and Reclamation, infra.

Reclamation.—Colorado Mined Land Reclamation Act enacted. (34-32-101). Regulation of other mined land (non-coal) reclamation under Art. 32, Tit. 34 as follows. Operator of any proposed mining operation must obtain permit from mined land reclamation office or board. (34-32-109). Permit authorizes mining operations on affected land for life of mine. (34-32-112). Reclamation required on all affected land and application for permit must include detailed reclamation plan. (34-32-112). Duties of operator established. (34-32-116). Operator required to supply personal and financial warranty. (34-32-117).

Any operation affecting less than ten acres and extracting less than 70,000 tons of mineral or overburden per year subject to provisions of section concerning limited impact operations. (34-32-110). Any operation affecting less than ten acres which is conducted for sole purpose of obtaining materials for highway, road or similar type project under federal, state, county, town or special district contract may be entitled to special permit. (34-32-111). Law governing operations affecting fewer than two acres enacted. (34-32-110[1]).

Prospecting must be preceded by notice of intent to conduct prospecting operations including description of measures to reclaim any affected lands and posting of financial warranty. (34-32-113).

Board or office may issue cease and desist order for any violation of Act, notice, permit or regulation. (34-32-123, 124). Attorney general may bring suit in district court to enjoin failure to comply with cease and desist order. (34-32-124[3]). Violation of permit provision may result in suspension, modification or revocation of permit. (34-32-124[6]). Board may request attorney general to institute proceedings to secure or recover amounts warranted by forfeited financial warranties. (34-32-118).

Colorado Land Reclamation Act for the Extraction of Construction Materials enacted. (34-32.5-101). Regulation of reclamation for extraction of construction materials under Art. 32.5, Tit. 34 as follows. Construction material is defined as rock, clay, silt, sand, gravel, limestone, dimension stone, marble and shale. (34-32.5-103). Operator required to obtain reclamation permit for new operation after July 1, 1995 from mined land reclamation office or board. (34-32.5-109).

Expedited permitting procedures for operations of less than ten acres. (34-32.5-110). Special permit for operations to commence within specified short period of time and affecting less than 30 acres. (34-32.5-111). Notice to conduct exploration operations must be filed with board. (34-32.5-113). Duties of operators established. (34-32.5-116). Performance and financial warranties are required. (34-32.5-117).

Forfeiture of financial warranties for violation of cease and desist order, default under performance warranty or failure to maintain financial warrant in good standing. (34-32.5-118). Board can issue order for forfeiture and can request attorney general to secure or recover amounts warranted. (34-32.5-118). Board may issue cease and desist order for any violation of Act, notice, permit or regulation. (34-32.5-124). Attorney general may bring suit in district court to enjoin for failure to comply with cease and desist order. (34-32.5-124[3]).

Colorado Surface Coal Mining Reclamation Act enacted. (34-33-101). Regulation of surface coal mine reclamation under Art. 33, Tit. 34 as follows. Permit is required to conduct surface coal mining and reclamation operations. (34-33-109). Surface activities incident to underground mining and in situ operations included. (34-33-103[26]). Extraction by landowner or lessee for own noncommercial use, and extraction incident to government financed highway construction excluded from permit requirement. (34-33-129). Exploration permits required. (34-33-117). Permit applications submitted to office of mined land reclamation. (34-33-110). Permits to require operators to rehabilitate, restore or replace residential dwellings or noncommercial buildings damaged be subsidence form underground coal mining or compensate owner. (34-33-121). Colorado mine subsidence protection program established to protect owners of private residential structures against damages caused by land subsidence from underground coal mines. (34-33-133.5).

All permits require that mining operation be conducted so as to meet environmental protection performance standards (34-33-120) unless experimental practices are authorized by board and approved by secretary of interior (34-33-134).

Board and office are empowered to make on-site inspections and persons adversely affected by mining operations may request inspection be held. (34-33-122). Office is authorized to order cessation of all mining operations or that portion relevant to violation where inspection discloses infractions creating imminent danger to health or safety or significant imminent environmental harm, and to issue notice of violation for other violations. When necessary to abate imminent danger or harm, affirmative obligations may also be imposed. Failure to abate violation set forth in notice of violation is grounds for ordering cessation of all mining operations or portion relevant to violation. If office determines permit improvidently issued, office authorized to impose additional permit conditions or issue order to show cause why permit should not be suspended or revoked. (34-33-123). Notices of violation and cessation orders may be appealed to board for review. (34-33-124). Provision also is made for assessing civil penalties. Civil penalties are required if cessation order issued. Failure to correct violation is ground for assessing civil penalty of up to $750 or more. (34-33-123[8][i]). Willful and knowing violations are grounds for fine and imprisonment; corporate officers or agents may be assessed civil penalties and may be fined or imprisoned for willfully and knowingly authorizing, ordering or carrying out certain violations. (34-33-123[10]). Judicial review available for board orders on civil penalties and permit suspensions and revocations. (34-33-128).

ESTATES AND TRUSTS

ADMINISTRATION:

See topic Executors and Administrators.

CLAIMS:

See topic Executors and Administrators; category Civil Actions and Procedure, topic Pleading.

DEATH:

Common law presumption of death after seven years' absence and diligent search is generally followed. (84 Colo. 71, 268 P. 529).

Determination of Death.—Individual is determined to be dead if he or she has sustained irreversible cessation of circulatory and respiratory functions, or has sustained irreversible cessation of all functions of entire brain, including brain stem. Determinations made in accordance with accepted medical standards. Uniform Determination of Death Act adopted. (12-36-136).

Living Will (Right to Accept or Reject Medical or Surgical Treatment).—See topic Wills.

Survivorship.—Uniform Simultaneous Death Act reenacted (1973). (15-11-613).

Action for Death.—Right of action exists where death is caused by negligence, unskillfulness or criminal intent of operator of conveyance of persons or freight for hire (13-21-201) or by wrongful act, neglect or default where, absent death, such action would have been actionable by decedent (13-21-202). Plantiff must elect to proceed under 13-21-201 or 13-21-202. (13-21-203). In first year after death, action lies exclusively in spouse or, upon written election of spouse, in spouse and heir or heirs. In second year after death, action lies in spouse alone, heir or heirs alone or in spouse and heirs. If no surviving spouse, without regard to year, action lies in heir or heirs, or if

See note at head of Digest as to 1998 legislation covered.

See Topical Index in front part of this volume.

CO – 48

DEATH . . . *continued*
none survive, in parents. (13-21-201[1][a], [b], [c]). Punitive damages are not recoverable. (150 Colo. 110, 371 P.2d 422). Judgments recovered under 13-21-201, 13-21-202 or 13-21-203 are owned by deceased's heirs at law, and person bringing action is liable to other heirs for their shares. (144 Colo. 597, 357 P.2d 649).

Action must be brought within two years from date of death. (13-80-102[1][d], 13-80-108[2]). Limitation period will not apply to action arising out of use of motor vehicle. Limitation period may be tolled by statute. (690 P.2d 1248).

Recovery under 13-21-201 never less than $3,000 or more than $10,000. (13-21-201). For actions accruing before Jan. 1, 1998, generally, recovery under 13-21-202 for noneconomic loss or injury limited to $250,000. For actions accruing on or after Jan. 1, 1998, generally, recovery under 13-21-202 is limited to $250,000, adjusted annually for inflation from 1989. (13-21-102.5[3][c]). If wrongful act constitutes felonious killing (15-11-803[1][B]), there is no limitation on damages recoverable (13-21-203). Plaintiff may sue for solatium of $50,000 in lieu of noneconomic damages. (13-21-203.5). For actions accruing on or after Jan. 1, 1998, award for solatium is adjusted annually for inflation from 1989. (13-21-203.7).

Remedy for death of employee, see category Employment, topic Labor Relations.

For special action against carriers, see category Business Regulation and Commerce, topic Carriers, subhead Limiting Liability.

For survival of action, see category Civil Actions and Procedure, topic Actions, subhead Abatement and Revival.

Death Certificate.—Official certificate of death may be obtained from registrar in department of public health, for fee set annually, see topic Records, subhead Vital Statistics. (25-2-117, 25-2-121). Address: Colo. Dept. of Health, Vital Records, 4300 Cherry Creek Dr. S., Denver, CO 80246-1530. Phone: (303) 756-4464. Certificate may only be obtained by someone with direct and tangible interest in information. (25-2-117). Direct and tangible interest defined as significant legal relationship to person who is subject of record. (184 Colo. 282, 519 P.2d 1189). See category Documents and Records, topic Records, subhead Vital Statistics.

Uniform Anatomical Gift Act.—Adopted. (12-34-101). See topic Wills.

DESCENT AND DISTRIBUTION:

See also topics Executors and Administrators and Wills.

Intestate Succession.—1990 Amendments to Uniform Probate Code adopted with modifications. Rules apply to any part of decedent's estate not effectively disposed of by will or otherwise. (15-11-101). Portion not passing to surviving spouse (see subhead Surviving Spouse, infra) (or entire intestate estate if no surviving spouse) passes to: descendants per capita at each generation; if no surviving descendant, to parents equally if both survive or to surviving parent; if no surviving descendant or parents, to surviving descendants of parents or either of them per capita at each generation; if no surviving descendant, parent, or descendant of parents, to grandparents or surviving descendants of grandparents, per capita at each generation; if none of above relatives survive, birth children or parents may make claim within 90 days of death. (15-11-103). Survivorship by 120 hours is required. (15-11-104). One related to decedent through two lines is entitled to only single share based on relationship entitling him to larger share. (15-11-113).

Survivorship.—Uniform Simultaneous Death Act reenacted (1973). (15-11-613).

Representation.—Per capita at each generation defined at 15-11-106. For example, if one of decedent's three children survives and other two each leave decedent's grandchildren who survive, surviving child gets 1/3 and all grandchildren split other 2/3 in equal shares.

Surviving Spouse.—Surviving spouse's share of intestate estate is: All if no descendant or parent of decedent survives; if no descendant survives, but one or both parents survive, first $200,000 plus 75% of balance; if decedent has surviving descendants: (i) all if decedent's and spouse's surviving descendants are all descendants of both decedent and surviving spouse, (ii) if decedent has other surviving descendants, first $100,000 if and only if all such surviving descendants are adults, and 50% of balance, and (iii) if only surviving spouse has other surviving descendants, first $150,000 and 50% of balance. (15-11-102). Surviving spouse has right to elect to take up to 50% (5% for each year of marriage) of augmented estate as defined in 15-11-202 if decedent domiciled in Colorado. (15-11-201[1]). Certain supplemental elective share up to $50,000 may apply. (15-11-201[2]). (See topic Wills, subhead Election.) Surviving spouse is entitled to exempt property and family allowance whether or not elective share taken. (15-11-206 and 15-11-201[3]). If decedent not domiciled in Colorado, spouse's right to elective share of property in Colorado governed by law of decedent's domicile at death. (15-11-201[4]). One divorced from decedent or whose marriage to decedent has been annulled is not surviving spouse unless remarried to decedent. (15-11-802[1]). Rights of election and to property allowance, family allowance and homestead exemption may be waived, before or after marriage, by writing signed by waiving spouse after fair disclosure. (15-11-207).

Half Blood.—Relatives of half blood inherit same share they would inherit if they were of whole blood. (15-11-107).

Posthumous Children or Other Issue.—Relatives of decedent conceived before death but born thereafter and living at least 120 hours inherit as if born in lifetime of decedent. (15-11-108).

Illegitimates.—For purposes of intestate succession, individual is child of birth parent unless birth parent's relationship is extinguished by adoption. (15-11-114) (See subhead Adopted Children, infra.) However, birth parent may not inherit from or through child if birth parent has not acknowledged child or has refused to support child. (15-11-114[3]).

Adopted Children.—Adopted person is deemed child of adopting parents and not of natural parents, except that adoption by spouse of birth parent does not affect that parent's relationship with child. (15-11-114[2]). See also subhead Intestate Succession, supra, for limited additional rights of birth children.

Determination of Heirship.—Where no action has been brought for administration of estate within one year after death, alleged heir or devisee or person claiming interest derived from alleged heir or devisee (15-12-1301) may petition appropriate court in county of decedent's residence to determine heirs or devisees (15-12-1302). Among other requirements, verified petition must include statements that: (a) one year has passed since decedent's death; and (b) estate administration not granted in Colorado or, if granted, estate settled without determination of descent or succession of all or part of decedent's property. Petition may include more than one decedent if related by successive interests in property. (15-12-1302). Court must determine standing of petitioner to bring action, heirs and devisees of decedent, owners by inheritance of property, description of property, and other pertinent facts. (15-12-1305). Adjudication of heirship required in formal testacy and intestacy proceedings. (15-12-401, 15-12-409). See topic Wills, subhead Probate, regarding jurisdiction and venue.

Advancements.—Property given to heir during decedent's lifetime treated as advancement against heir's share of intestate estate only if declared in contemporaneous writing by decedent or acknowledged in writing by heir. Property valued as of date of death or date heir came into possession or enjoyment, whichever occurs first. If recipient does not survive decedent, property does not affect intestate share of recipient's descendants unless declaration or acknowledgment provides otherwise. Heir who has received from intestate more than heir's share not required to refund except where necessary to fund surviving spouse's elective share of augmented estate. (15-11-109; 15-11-203).

Election.—See subhead Surviving Spouse, supra and topic Wills, subhead Election.

Renunciation/Disclaimer.—Devisees and heirs or their fiduciary, attorney-in-fact or agent, may disclaim partial or entire interest in estate by filing, within time limits prescribed by 15-11-801(2), written and signed instrument containing description of property or interest disclaimed. (15-11-801).

Escheat.—Undistributed balance at time of final settlement of decedent's estate, because heirs unknown, unqualified or no takers exist, is paid to state treasurer. In addition, any fiduciary possessing unclaimed moneys for which proper receipt cannot be obtained may turn such moneys over to state treasurer. State treasurer must retain funds, subject to claims of persons entitled thereto, for period of 21 years. If no claim asserted within 21 year period, such balance becomes property of state and is transferred to public school fund. (15-12-914).

ESTATES:

See category Property, topic Real Property.

EXECUTORS AND ADMINISTRATORS:

Except in Denver, where a probate court has been established, jurisdiction of administration of estates is in district courts. (15-10-201[10]).

Venue for first proceedings after decedent's death is county of decedent's domicile or residence or, if decedent neither domiciled in nor resident of Colorado, any county where property of decedent located at time of death. Venue for subsequent proceedings is same as first proceedings unless initial proceeding transferred. (15-12-201).

Uniform Probate Code adopted, with substantial modifications, effective July 1, 1974. Code is given Colorado Revised Statutes (C.R.S.) Tit. number 15, Arts. 10 to 17. 1975 Amendments to Code adopted with modifications. 1990 Amendments to Code adopted with modifications.

Preferences in Right to Administer.—Persons not disqualified have priority for appointment as personal representative in following order: Person with priority as determined by probated will; surviving spouse, if devisee; other devisees; surviving spouse; other heirs; 45 days after death, any creditor. (15-12-203[1]).

Eligibility and Competency.—Persons under age 21 and persons found unsuitable by court in formal proceedings not qualified to be personal representative. (15-12-203[6]).

Qualification.—Personal representative qualifies by filing with appointing court any required bond and statement of acceptance of duties. (15-12-601).

Exemption from Bond.—

Informal Proceedings.—No bond required of personal representative except: Upon appointment of special administrator; where specifically required by will; or if determined by court to be desirable upon demand pursuant to 15-12-605 by one with interest or claim in excess of $5,000. (15-12-603[1]).

Formal Proceedings.—Bond may be required by court order at time of appointment of personal representative. Bond not required if waived by will unless court finds bond desirable upon request of interested party. Bond required by will may be dispensed with by court if found to be unnecessary. (15-12-603[2]).

Issuance of Letters.—Letters of appointment must be issued by court in formal and informal appointment proceedings. (15-12-103). If no local administration or application therefor pending, domiciliary foreign personal representative may file authenticated copies of appointment and of bond in county where property located (15-13-204) and may exercise powers of local administrator, subject to general rules for nonresidents (15-13-205). See topic Wills, subhead Probate regarding jurisdiction and venue.

Removal.—Personal representative may be removed by court for cause at any time. Court may commence proceedings upon own motion or petition of interested person. Notice of proceedings must be given to personal representative and such other persons as court orders. Cause exists when removal would be in best interests of estate, or if shown that personal representative or person seeking appointment intentionally misrepresented material facts in proceedings leading to appointment, that personal representative disregarded order of court, has become incapable of discharging duties of office, mismanaged estate, or failed to perform any duty. (15-12-611). Attorney's fees awarded to successful representative in suits for removal but not beneficiary seeking removal for his or her benefit alone. (713 P.2d 412).

Special Kinds of Administration.—Supervised administration authorized by 15-12-501, under which no distributions may be made without prior order of court. (15-12-

See note at head of Digest as to 1998 legislation covered.

See Topical Index in front part of this volume.

CO – 49

EXECUTORS AND ADMINISTRATORS . . . *continued*

504). Court may appoint special administrator upon petition of interested person and finding after notice and hearing that appointment necessary to preserve or properly administer estate. Prior to appointment of or after termination of appointment of personal representative registrar may appoint special administrator upon application of interested person when necessary to protect estate. (15-12-614). Special administrator appointed by registrar has duty to collect, manage, account for, preserve and deliver to personal representative assets of estate. (15-12-616). Special administrator appointed by court has power of personal representative as limited by court. (15-12-617).

Public Administrators.—Probate or district court in each judicial district may appoint public administrator to administer estate of decedent where no individual can be found to administer estate by virtue of being nominated by will to act as personal representative or entitled to receive portion of decedent's estate as heir or devisee. Court may appoint public administrator to act as conservator, temporary or special conservator, trustee or other fiduciary of any estate with assets requiring protection. Payment of administrative fees and costs of public administrator has priority over all other claims and exempt property or family allowances. (15-12-619 to 623).

Inventory and Appraisal.—Personal representative must, within three months of appointment, send copy of inventory of property owned by decedent at time of death, showing fair market value and type and amount of existing encumbrances to interested persons who request it, or may file original inventory with court. (15-12-706).

General Powers and Duties.—Representative has all powers specified in Colorado Fiduciaries' Powers Act (15-1-801) to extent consistent with will or order of court in formal proceeding (15-12-715), including power to mortgage or lease assets not otherwise specifically bequeathed or devised (15-1-804[2][g], [h]). Duties of personal representative include: settle and distribute estate expeditiously (15-12-703); inform heirs and devisees of appointment within 30 days after appointment (15-12-705); inventory and appraise assets (15-12-706); possess and control estate (15-12-709). See subheads Notice of Appointment, infra, and Inventory and Appraisal, supra.

Notice of Appointment.—Within 30 days of appointment, representative other than special administrator must give notice of appointment by mail or delivery to heirs and devisees. Failure is breach of duty but does not invalidate appointment. (15-12-705).

Notice to Creditors.—Unless one year or more has elapsed since date of death of decedent, representative must publish notice to creditors once a week for three successive weeks in newspaper of general circulation in county. Representative may give written notice to any creditor. (15-12-801).

Presentation of Claims.—All claims which arose before decedent's death must be presented as to creditors barred by publication, within time in published notice; as to creditors barred by written notice, within time set in written notice; as to all creditors, within one year of decedent's death. Claims arising at or after death must be presented within four months after arising or, if claim based on contract with personal representative, within four months after personal representative's performance due. Excepted are enforcement of mortgages, pledges or other liens; actions to establish decedent's or representative's liability covered by liability insurance; and collection of compensation for services rendered and reimbursement for expenses advanced by or for personal representative, attorney or accountant. (15-12-803).

Proof of Claims.—No particular form of proof of claim is prescribed. Claimant may present claim by mailing or delivering to personal representative or filing in court written statement including basis and amount of claim, name and address of claimant, description of contingent or unliquidated nature of claim and any security held for claim. (15-12-804).

Approval or Rejection of Claims.—Claims approved or rejected by representative. Claims disallowed by appropriate notice are barred unless claimant files petition for allowance or commences proceeding within 60 days of mailing of notice of disallowance. (15-12-806). Failure of representative to disallow claim (15-12-806[1]) generally amounts to allowance of claim. (633 P.2d 1100).

Payment of Claims.—Representative may pay claims after making provision for statutory allowances, claims already presented and unbarred claims which may yet be presented (including costs and expenses of administration). (15-12-807).

Priorities.—(1) Property held by deceased as fiduciary or trustee; (2) costs of administration; (3) reasonable funeral expenses; (4) debts and taxes preferred under Federal law; (5) expenses of last illness; (6) debts and taxes preferred under Colorado law; (7) claims of department of human services for medical assistance, per 26-4-403.3(5); and (8) all other claims. (15-12-805). All payments, except (1) above subject to statutory allowances. See subhead Allowances, infra.

Sales.—See subhead General Powers and Duties, supra.

Actions by Representative.—Representative may prosecute and defend claims for protection of estate. (15-12-709). Claim by decedent not barred by statute of limitations at his death may not be barred sooner than one year after death. (15-12-109).

Actions Against Representative.—Actions arising and not barred by statute of limitations before death of decedent are barred against representative unless claims are presented in accordance with 15-12-803. Any statute of limitations not measured by death or advertisement of claims against decedent is suspended during four months following death. (15-12-802). Claim in writing must be presented (delivered or mailed to representative or his attorney or filed with court), or action must be commenced in any court having jurisdiction over representative. (15-12-804; 666 P.2d 1109). See subhead Presentation of Claims, supra.

Allowances.—If decedent was domiciled in Colorado, following are available: (1) Exempt property allowance of $15,000, payable from estate in form of cash or other property, to surviving spouse, or divided among dependent children if no spouse survives. Exempt property allowance is exempt from and prior to all claims against estate except administration and funeral expenses and family allowance. (15-11-403). (2) Family allowance to surviving spouse, children under 18 and dependent children. Family allowance is exempt from and prior to all claims against estate except administration and funeral expenses. (15-11-404). Statutory allowances are not chargeable

against any share passing to spouse or children by decedent's will, unless will provides otherwise. (15-11-403, 404). Statutory allowances are in addition to and not in lieu of homestead exemption. (38-41-211). Statutory allowances and homestead exemption may be waived, in whole or in part, before or after marriage, by writing signed by waiving party after fair disclosure and such waiver will be enforced as long as all conditions of 14-2-307 are satisfied. (15-11-207).

Widow's Quarantine.—None.

Intermediate Accounting.—Representative must file annual interim accountings in supervised administration unless otherwise ordered by court. (Probate Court Rule 30).

Final Accounting and Settlement.—Estate may be settled by: (1) Petition for order of complete settlement (15-12-1001); (2) petition under informally probated will (15-12-1002); (3) except when under court prohibition or supervision, verified statement of representative that personal representative has fully administered estate by payment, settlement or other disposition of lawful claims, expenses of administration and estate, inheritance and other death taxes and distributed assets to persons entitled (15-12-1003).

Consent Settlement.—Representative may compromise claims against estate. (15-12-813).

Distribution.—Special provisions relating to distribution. (15-12-901 to 916). See also topic Descent and Distribution.
Unsupervised Administration.—Representative may settle and distribute estate without court order but may present questions to court. (15-12-704).
Supervised Administration.—Representative may not distribute without court order. (15-12-504). Partial distribution may be ordered by court during pendency of supervised administration upon application. (15-12-505).

Distribution If Abroad.—No statutory provisions.

Liabilities.—Unless provided in contract, representative is not liable on contract unless he fails to reveal representative capacity, but is liable for obligations and torts during administration if personally at fault. (15-12-808).

Compensation of Representatives.—Representative is entitled to reasonable compensation for services. Personal representative may renounce compensation set forth in will and be entitled to reasonable compensation unless compensation is set by contract with decedent. (15-12-719).

When Administration Unnecessary.—Any successor may collect personal property owed decedent at death by affidavit asserting as follows: Net estate is $27,000 or less; ten days have elapsed since death; there are no pending proceedings to appoint personal representative, and successor has right to payment. (15-12-1201).

Small Estates.—If estate inventory value, minus liens and encumbrances, is less than personal property held by decedent as fiduciary or trustee, exempt property allowance, family allowance, administration expenses, funeral expenses and expenses of last illness, representative may make immediate distribution and close estate by filing verified statement that: (1) Estate did not exceed items above; (2) representative has distributed estate to those entitled thereto; and (3) representative has sent copy of closing statement to all distributees and to all creditors, neither paid nor barred, and has furnished full written accounting of administration to distributees affected thereby. (15-12-1203, 1204). If no proceedings involving representative are pending in court one year after filing of closing statement, representative's appointment is terminated. (15-12-1204).

Foreign Executors and Administrators.—As to assets in Colorado, upon filing authenticated copies of appointment, foreign personal representative may exercise all powers of local personal representative and may maintain actions subject to any conditions imposed on nonresidents generally (15-13-204, 205), but only if no administration or petition for administration is pending in Colorado. (15-13-204, 206). Petition for Colorado administration terminates power of foreign personal representative. (15-13-206).

Uniform Fiduciaries Law adopted. (15-1-101).

Uniform Principal and Income Act adopted. (15-1-401).

Uniform Statutory Rule Against Perpetuities adopted. (15-11-1101).

Uniform Anatomical Gift Act.—See topic Wills.

FIDUCIARIES:

See topics Executors and Administrators, Trusts; category Family, topic Guardian and Ward.

PROOF OF CLAIMS:

See topic Executors and Administrators; category Civil Actions and Procedure, topic Pleading.

TRUSTS:

Uniform Probate Code adopted with substantial modifications, effective July 1, 1974. 1975 Amendments to Code adopted with modifications. 1990 amendments to Uniform Probate Code adopted with modifications. Sections pertaining to administration of trusts are 15-16-101 to 401. Amendments dealing with succession without administration have not been adopted. Uniform International Wills Act adopted. (15-11-1001 to 1011).
Registration; When Required.—Trustee of trust having its principal place of administration in Colorado must register trust in court in county of principal place of administration within 30 days after his acceptance of trust. Unless otherwise designated in trust agreement, principal place of administration is trustee's usual place of business where records pertaining to trust are kept, or at trustee's residence if he has no such place of business. In case of co-trustees, principal place of administration, if not otherwise designated in trust instrument, is usual place of business of corporate trustee if there is but one corporate trustee, or usual place of business or residence of individual trustee who is professional fiduciary if there is but one such person and no corporate co-trustee, and otherwise usual place of business or residence of any of co-trustees as agreed upon by them. (15-16-101[1]).

See note at head of Digest as to 1998 legislation covered.

See Topical Index in front part of this volume.

TRUSTS . . . *continued*

Registration not required if, in another jurisdiction in which trust is being administered, trustee cannot obtain release and if registration in Colorado would be inconsistent with foreign court's retained jurisdiction. (15-16-101[1]). Registration not required of trust which has no asset other than rights to receive property upon occurrence of some future event, or which is nominally funded with assets having value of $500 or less, until occurrence of such event or until assets having value in excess of $500 are deposited therein. (15-16-101[2]). Registration not required for fully and presently revocable inter vivos trust until grantor's power to revoke is terminated, nor is registration required if all assets of such trust become then distributable outright to beneficiaries. (15-16-101[3]). Only one registration required for trust which divides corpus into multiple trusts, or multiple testamentary trusts created by one will. (15-16-101[4]), Registration not required for trust created under 15-14-409.5 and 15-14-409.6. (15-16-101[s]).

Effect of Registration.—By registering trust, or accepting trusteeship of registered trust, trustee submits personally to jurisdiction of court in any proceeding initiated by interested parties pertaining to internal affairs of such trust. Beneficiaries also subject to jurisdiction of court in such proceedings, provided proper notice given to them. (15-16-103).

Effect of Failure to Register.—Any trustee failing to register trust is subject to personal jurisdiction of court where trust could have been registered. Any trustee failing to register within 30 days of written demand by settlor or beneficiary subject to removal and denial of compensation or surcharge. Any trustee who wrongfully and wilfully fails to register trust within 30 days of his acceptance of trust required to be registered may have imposed civil penalty of $100 per day for each day trustee fails to register trust, not to exceed $1,000. (15-16-104).

Life insurance policy may designate as beneficiary trustee of existing living or testamentary trust and such trust may be valid though there is no corpus other than trustee's right to receive insurance proceeds. (15-15-101[2]).

Trustee as Beneficiary Under Will.—Trust without funds or corpus whose only right is to receive benefits under will at settlor's death is valid. (15-15-101[2]).

Eligibility and Competency.—Foreign corporate trustee is required to qualify as foreign corporation doing business in Colorado if it maintains principal place of administration of any trust within Colorado. Foreign co-trustee not required to qualify solely because its co-trustee maintains principal place of administration in Colorado. Unless otherwise doing business in Colorado, local qualification by corporate or individual foreign trustee not required in order for that foreign trustee to receive distributions from local estate, or to hold, invest in, or manage or acquire property in Colorado or to maintain litigation. (15-16-105).

General Powers and Duties of Trustee.—Except as otherwise provided by terms of trust, trustee must deal with trust assets as prudent man dealing with property of another and, if trustee has special skills or is named trustee on basis of representations of special skills or expertise, he is under duty to use those skills. (15-16-302). Except as otherwise provided by terms of trust, trustee shall invest and manage trust assets as prudent investor would by considering purposes, terms, distribution requirements and other circumstances of trust. Trustee who has special skills or is named trustee on basis of representation of special skills, is under duty to use those skills. (15-1.1-102). See Colorado Fiduciaries' Powers Act for list of general powers. (15-1-804).

Investments.—Uniform Prudent Investor Act adopted. (15-1.1-101 to 15-1.1-115). See also 15-1-301 to 308.

Securities in Name of Nominee.—Fiduciary may hold securities in name of nominee. (15-1-804[2][o]).

Bequests and Devises to Inter Vivos Trusts.—See topic Wills.

Uniform Common Trust Fund Act.—Adopted. (11-24-101 to 107).

Revised Uniform Principal and Income Act.—Adopted. (15-1-401 to 417).

Gifts to Minors.—Uniform Transfers to Minors Act adopted. (11-50-101 to 126). See category Family, topic Infants.

Uniform Fiduciaries Act.—Adopted. (15-1-101 to 113).

Uniform Simplification of Fiduciary Security Transfers Act.—Repealed.

Perpetuities.—See category Property, topic Perpetuities.

Pour Over Trusts.—See topic Wills, subhead Testamentary Dispositions.

Renunciation.—For renunciation, by beneficiary, of benefits under testamentary trust, see topic Wills, subhead Renunciation/Disclaimer. Beneficiary of nontestamentary instrument or his fiduciary may disclaim, in whole or part, right of succession or transfer to him of any property, real or personal, or interest therein, by filing or delivering written disclaimer within time and at place provided in 15-1-902. (15-1-901).

Charitable; Amendment.—Trustee of charitable trust with consent of all beneficiaries allowed to amend governing instrument to conform to provisions of §§508(e), 664, 2055(e) and 2522(c) of Internal Revenue Code. (15-1-1002[3]).

Charitable: Enforcement.—Attorney General empowered to enforce trusts. (24-31-101[5]).

Trusts in land, except trusts arising by operation of law (38-10-107), must be in writing signed by party creating, granting, assigning, surrendering or declaring same or by his lawful agent authorized in writing (38-10-106).

Conveyances of real estate to trustee must name beneficiary and define trust, or refer to public record where such matters appear in county in which land is situated, otherwise shall not be notice of trust or of representative capacity of grantee. (38-30-108). Trustees must file affidavit with county clerk setting forth name of trust and names and addresses of trustees before trust can deal in any interest in real property. (38-30-166).

Upon death of sole or surviving trustee of express written trust affecting real property which does not provide for successor, trust vests in Public Trustee of county in which such real estate is situated, provided that district court may appoint new trustee upon application of any party in interest. (38-34-104).

WILLS:

See also topics Descent and Distribution, Executors and Administrators.

Uniform Probate Code adopted, with substantial modifications, effective July 1, 1974. Code is given Colorado Revised Statutes (C.R.S.) Tit. number 15, Arts. 10 to 17, and section numbers contain said Title citation followed by numerical part of Uniform Probate Code citation, with Art. 1 changed to 10, Art. 2 changed to 11, etc., e.g., §1-101 is 15-10-101. In many instances, however, Colorado statute uses letters for subsections where Uniform Probate Code uses numerals, and numerals where Uniform Probate Code uses letters. All references to homestead allowances in Uniform Probate Code were omitted from Colorado statute. 1990 amendments to Uniform Probate Code adopted with modifications.

Testamentary Dispositions.—Persons 18 years of age or older and of sound mind may make wills. (15-11-501). Testator may dispose of property in any manner testator wishes, subject, however, to right of surviving spouse to elect against will (see subhead Election, infra). There are no limitations as to date of will or amount in relation to what may be given to religious, charitable, etc. institutions. Testator may devise or bequeath property to written trust, and terms of such trust instrument shall govern property even though trust may be amended or revoked after execution of will or after death of testator. (15-11-511). Will may refer to written statement to dispose of tangible personal property not otherwise specifically disposed of by will. (15-11-513).

Execution.—Will must be in writing, signed by testator, or in testator's name by someone in testator's presence and at testator's direction. (15-11-502). Will must be signed by at least two persons either prior to or after testator's death, each of whom signed within reasonable time after he or she witnessed either signing or testator's acknowledgment of signature of will. (15-11-502).

Holographic Will.—Will which does not comply with 15-11-502, valid as holographic will, whether or not witnessed, if signature and material provisions are in handwriting of testator. (15-11-502).

Writings Intended as Wills.—Although will not executed in compliance with 15-11-502, will is valid if proponent establishes by clear and convincing evidence that decedent intended document to constitute will. (15-11-503).

Nuncupative Will.—Not recognized.

Self-proved Will.—Any will may be simultaneously executed, attested, and made self-proved by acknowledgment thereof by testator and affidavits of witnesses, each made before officer authorized to administer oaths under laws of state where execution occurs and evidenced by officer's certificate, under official seal, in form and content substantially as follows (15-11-504):

Forms

I, ..., the testator, sign my name to this instrument this . . . . . . day of . . . ., and being first duly sworn, do hereby declare to the undersigned authority that I sign and execute this instrument as my will and that I sign it willingly (or willingly direct another to sign for me), that I execute it as my free and voluntary act for the purposes therein expressed, and that I am eighteen years of age or older, of sound mind, and under no constraint or undue influence.

. . . .
Testator

We, ..., ..., the witnesses, sign our names to this instrument, being first duly sworn, and do hereby declare to the undersigned authority that the testator signs and executes this instrument as [his] [her] will and that [he] [she] signs it willingly (or willingly directs another to sign for [him] [her]), and that [he] [she] executes it as [his] [her] free and voluntary act for the purposes therein expressed, and that each of us, in the conscious presence of the testator, hereby signs this will as witness to the testator's signing, and that to the best of our knowledge the testator is eighteen years of age or older, of sound mind, and under no constraint or undue influence.

. . . .
Witness

. . . .
Witness

THE STATE OF . . . .
COUNTY OF . . . .
Subscribed, sworn to and acknowledged before me by . . . ., the testator, and subscribed and sworn to before me by . . . ., and . . . ., witnesses, this . . . . . . day of . . . .
(SEAL)

. . . .
(Signed)

. . . .
(Official capacity of officer)

An attested will may at any time subsequent to its execution be made self-proved by acknowledgment thereof by testator and affidavits of witnesses, each made before officer authorized to administer oaths under laws of state where acknowledgment occurs and evidenced by officer's certificate, under official seal, attached or annexed to will in form and content substantially as follows:
THE STATE OF . . . .
COUNTY OF . . . .
We, ..., ..., and . . . ., the testator and the witnesses, respectively, whose names are signed to the attached or foregoing instrument, being first duly sworn, do hereby declare to the undersigned authority that the testator signed and executed the instrument as the testator's will and that [he] [she] had signed willingly (or willingly directed another to sign for [him] [her]), and that [he] [she] executed it as [his] [her] free and voluntary act for the purposes therein expressed, and that each of the witnesses, in the conscious presence of the testator, signs the will as witness, and that to the best of [his] [her] knowledge the testator was at that time eighteen years of age or older, of sound mind and under no constraint or undue influence.

. . . .

See note at head of Digest as to 1998 legislation covered.

See Topical Index in front part of this volume.

WILLS . . . *continued*

Testator

. . . .
Witness

. . . .
Witness

Subscribed, sworn to and acknowledged before me by . . . ., the testator, and subscribed and sworn to before me by . . . . and . . . ., witnesses, this . . . . . . day of . . . .

. . . .
(Signed)

. . . .
(Official capacity of officer)

Revocation.—Will or any part thereof is revoked by a subsequent will which revokes prior will or part of such will expressly or by inconsistency or by its being burned, torn, canceled, obliterated, or destroyed, with intent and for purpose of revoking it, by testator or by another person in testator's presence and at testator's direction. (15-11-507). Cancellation of duplicate original raises presumption that testator intended to cancel original will in possession of another. (619 P.2d 91). 15-11-507 permits will or part thereof to be revoked by performing revocatory act on will.

Individual who is divorced from decedent or whose marriage to decedent has been annulled, is not surviving spouse unless, by virtue of remarriage, he or she is married to decedent at time of death. (15-11-802).

Revival.—If subsequent will that wholly revoked previous will is revoked by revocatory act under 15-11-507(1)(b), previous will remains revoked unless it is evident from circumstances of revocation of subsequent will or testator's contemporaneous or subsequent declarations that testator intended previous will to take effect. (15-11-509[1]). If subsequent will that partly revoked previous will is revoked by revocatory act under 15-11-507(1)(b), revoked part of previous will is revived unless it is evident from circumstances of revocation of subsequent will or testator's contemporaneous or subsequent declarations that testator did not intend revoked part to take effect. (15-11-509[2]). If subsequent will that revoked previous will in whole or part is revoked by another, later will, previous will remains revoked in whole or part, unless it appears from terms of later will that testator intended previous will to take effect. (15-11-509[3]).

Testamentary Gifts to Subscribing Witnesses.—Will or any provision thereof is not invalid because will is signed by an interested witness. (15-11-505).

Bequests and Devises to Inter Vivos Trusts.—See subhead Testamentary Dispositions, supra.

Testamentary Guardians.—See category Family, topic Guardian and Ward.

Probate.—Jurisdiction over probate matters is vested in probate court in Denver and district court in other counties. (15-10-302). Venue for first informal or formal testacy or appointment proceedings after decedent's death is in county where decedent was domiciled or resided at time of death or, if decedent was neither domiciled in nor resident of this state, in any county where property of decedent was located at time of death. (15-12-201). Interested persons have right to choose either formal or informal procedures in probate of estate (15-12-301 to 311 and 15-12-401 to 414) and to petition court for supervised administration (15-12-501 to 505) or determination or heirs, devisees and property interests by special proceeding (15-12-1301 to 1309).

Contest.—Informal probate can be contested by petition to prevent or set aside informal probate. (15-12-401). In formal probate proceedings, written objections must be filed. (15-12-404). After formal probate order, vacation or modification may be sought by (1) proponents of later-offered will, if without knowledge of its existence at first proceeding or if without knowledge and without actual notice of first proceeding, (2) heirs (in case of order of intestacy and determination of heirs) without knowledge of death, heirship or notice of proceedings, or (3) others for good cause. Time for filing petition to vacate or modify depends on proceedings used in first probate. (15-12-412, 413).

If alleged decedent not dead, may always recover property from personal representative, and from distributees if equitable. (15-12-412[2]).

Except for fraud, creditor's actions against distributees to recover property improperly distributed are barred one year after decedent's death. Any other claimant is barred three years after decedent's death or one year after distribution, whichever is later. (15-12-1006).

Legacies.—Personal representative in formal or informal probate may petition court for order directing distribution at any time after time for presenting claims has expired. Interested party may petition one year after appointment and must wait until after time for presenting claims. (15-12-1001, 1002). Except in supervised probate, personal representative may distribute without court approval. Personal representative may file closing statement with court no earlier than six months after appointment or one year after date of death, whichever occurs first. (15-12-1003).

Ademption.—Ademption of securities and certain specific devises is limited by 15-11-605, 606. Ademption by satisfaction occurs only if expressly stated in will or contemporaneous writing by testator, or if devisee acknowledges satisfaction in writing. (15-11-609).

Abatement.—Unless will has express or implied abatement order, shares of distributees abate in following order without difference between real and personal property: (1) property not disposed of by will; (2) residuary devises; (3) general devises; and (4) specific devises. (15-12-902).

Unclaimed Legacies.—See topic Descent and Distribution, subhead Escheat.

Lapse.—If devisee fails to survive testator and is grandparent or descendant of grandparent of testator, following apply, except as provided below: (1) If devise not in form of class gift, substitute gift is created in devisee's surviving descendants, who take per capita at each generation; (2) if devise is in form of class gift other than gift to "issue", "descendants", or class described by similar language, substitute gift is created in deceased devisee's surviving descendants. Words of survivorship like "if he survives me" are not, in absence of additional evidence, sufficient indication of intent contrary to these rules. Foregoing substitute gifts are superseded by alternate devise in will only if expressly designated devisee of alternate devise is entitled to take under will. (15-11-603). Except as provided in 15-11-603, if devise other than residuary devise fails for any reason, it becomes part of residue. (15-11-604[1]). Except as provided in 15-11-603, if residue is devised to two or more persons and share of one of residuary devisees fails for any reason, that share passes to other residuary devisee, or to other residuary devisees in proportion to their interests in residue. (15-11-604[2]).

Children.—Except as provided below, if testator fails to provide in will for child born or adopted after execution of will, omitted child receives share of estate as follows: (1) If testator had no living child when will executed, omitted child receives intestate share unless will devised all or substantially all of estate to other parent of omitted child and that parent survives testator; or (2) if testator had one or more children living when will executed and will devises property to one or more then living children, omitted child entitled to receive share of estate that child would have received had testator included all omitted children with children to whom devises were made under will and had given equal share of estate to each child. For this purpose, portion of testator's estate in which omitted child may share is limited to devises made to testator's then living children under will. Above rules not applicable if will shows omission intentional or testator provided for child outside will and statements of testator or other evidence show that transfer was intended to be in lieu of testamentary provision. (15-11-302).

Election.—Notwithstanding provisions of testator's will, surviving spouse may, within nine months after date of decedent's death or six months after will admitted to probate, whichever is later, elect to take possession of up to one-half of decedent's augmented estate by filing in court and mailing or delivering to personal representative, if any, petition for elective share. (15-11-201; 15-11-205[1]). Amount of elective share is determined by length of time spouse and decedent were married to each other. (15-11-201[1]). Court may extend time for election for cause shown upon petition of spouse made within nine months after decedent's death. (15-11-205[2]). In case of spouse who is incapacitated, court shall set aside elective share amount in trust for support of spouse. Upon surviving spouse's death, unexpended trust property shall be transferred under residuary clause, if any, of predeceased spouse's will, as if that predeceased spouse died immediately after surviving spouse or to predeceased spouse's heirs. (15-11-206). Election negates will provision regarding payment of taxes as administrative cost; taxes apportioned after calculation of elective share as in 15-12-916(2). (708 P.2d 476).

Contribution.—Where surviving spouse elects to take elective share (15-11-201), property already received by surviving spouse is charged against elective share, and decedent's probate estate and certain of decedent's non-probate transfers to others are so applied that liability for unsatisfied balance of elective share amount is equitably apportioned among recipients of decedent's probate estate and of that portion of decedent's non-probate transfers to others in proportion to value of their interests therein. (15-11-203[1] and [2]). Where omitted child takes share of estate under 15-11-302(1)(a), devises abate as provided in 15-12-902. (15-11-302[4]). Where omitted child takes share of estate under 15-11-302(1)(b), devises to testator's children who were living when will was executed abate ratably. (15-11-302[1][b][IV]).

Renunciation/Disclaimer.—Person to whom interest in property devolves may disclaim it by filing, within time limits and at places prescribed by 15-11-801(2), written disclaimer in form prescribed by 15-11-801(3). (15-11-801).

Exoneration.—Specific devise passes subject to any mortgage interest existing at date of death, without right of exoneration, regardless of general directive in will to pay debts. (15-11-607).

Foreign Executed Wills.—Written will is valid if its execution complies with law at time of execution of place where executed, or law of place where testator is domiciled, has place of abode or is national, either at time of execution or at time of death. (15-11-506). Uniform International Wills Act adopted. (15-11-1001 to 1011).

Foreign Probated Wills.—See topic Executors and Administrators for material variances from articles 3 and 4 of Uniform Probate Code, and those articles pertaining to probate of estate.

Living Will (Right to Accept or Reject Medical or Surgical Treatment).—Competent adults may, if procedural requirements met, execute declaration directing life sustaining procedures and artificial nourishment to be withheld or withdrawn if, at future time, declarant in terminal condition and either unconscious or otherwise incompetent to decide if medical procedure should be accepted or rejected. (15-18-101 to 113 and 15-18.6-101 to 108). Health care provider may rely upon medical treatment decision of proxy decision-maker selected in accordance with proper procedure. (15-8.5-101 to 103).

Simultaneous Death.—See topic Death, subhead Survivorship.

Testamentary Trusts.—See topic Trusts.

Uniform Anatomical Gift Act.—Adopted. (12-34-101 to 109).

Uniform Statutory Rule Against Perpetuities adopted. (15-11-1101 to 1107).

FAMILY

ADOPTION:

Any child (under 18) (19-5-201) or adult (14-1-101), may be adopted. With court approval person 18 or over and under 21 may be adopted as child. (19-5-201). Minor with court approval or any person over 21 may petition for adoption of minor, provided married person must petition jointly with spouse unless such spouse is birth parent of or has previously adopted child. (19-5-202). Any person may petition for adoption of adult. (14-1-101). Birth parent may specify adoptive applicant for placement. (19-5-206).

See note at head of Digest as to 1998 legislation covered.

See Topical Index in front part of this volume.

ADOPTION . . . *continued*

Consent Required.—Adoption of a person under 18 requires written and verified consent of (1) court-appointed guardian if parents deceased; (2) parent in stepparent adoption where other parent is deceased or his rights in child have been terminated or relinquished or where other parent has abandoned child for period of one year or more or has failed without cause to provide reasonable support for one year or more, (3) parent no longer having custody as result of divorce proceeding where it is spouse of parent having custody who seeks to adopt, (4) parent or parents in stepparent adoption where child is conceived and born out of wedlock. (19-5-203[1]). Written consent of person to be adopted required if 12 or over. (19-5-203[2]).

In order to comply with due process of law, grounds underlying termination order must be established by clear and convincing evidence. (654 P.2d 312).

When child placed for adoption by department of human services, child placement agency or individual, written consent of such person and notices received under 24-60-1801 to 1803 must be filed with petition to adopt. (19-5-207).

If placement for adoption occurred in another state department of human services must submit statement as to whether placement was carried out by placement agency authorized by other state's laws to make placement. (19-5-203[g]). If custody acquired in another state adoption requires verification by department of human services, child placement agency or attorney for petitioner that custody was acquired by proceedings or written consent complying with this or other state's laws and verification by department of human services that custody acquired by proceedings sanctioned by federal immigration and naturalization service whenever authorized or advised by federal law. (19-5-203[1][h] and [i]).

Adoption decree from foreign country may be declared valid upon petition by state resident if child is permanent resident or naturalized citizen of U.S. (19-5-205).

Interstate Compact on Placement of Children enacted. (24-60-1801).

No person may transport child into state for foster care or adoption without notice to and consent of department of human services. Notice must contain: (a) Name, date, birthplace of child; (b) identity and address of parent or guardian; (c) identity and address of person transporting child; (d) name and address of person to whom child is transported; (e) full statement of reasons and evidence of authority for placement. (26-6-104[5]).

Conditions Precedent.—Court order terminating or decreeing voluntary relinquishment of all parental rights required in cases other than where consents and statements described above are required. (19-5-203).

Written report showing general health and background of child and suitability of proposed petitioner must also be filed. (19-5-207). Except for stepparent adoptions and where placement for adoption has been made by court, if consent and report required by 19-5-207 is not filed with petition, court must order investigation and report. (19-5-209).

Jurisdiction.—Juvenile court in Denver and juvenile division of district courts elsewhere have exclusive original jurisdiction. (19-1-104[1][g]).

Venue.—Petition may be filed in county where petitioner(s) reside, or where licensed child placement agency is located. (19-5-204).

Petition for adoption of child must be verified by petitioner and substantially entitled: "In the matter of the petition of . . . . for the adoption of a child." Must contain: (a) Name, date and place of birth, race, and place of residence of each petitioner, including maiden name of adopting mother and date of marriage, if any, of petitioners; (b) name, date and place of birth, and place of residence, if known by petitioner, of child to be adopted; (c) relationship, if any, of child to petitioner; (d) full name by which child to be known after adoption; (e) full description of child's property, if any; (f) names of child's parents and address of each living parent, if known to petitioner; (g) names and addresses of guardian of child and/or estate of child, if any have been appointed; (h) name of agency or person to which custody of child has been given by proper court order; (i) length of time child has been in care and custody of petitioner or petitioners; (j) names of other children, natural and adopted, living and dead, of adopting parents; and (k) residence and occupation of each petitioner at or about time of birth of child. (19-5-208). Petition must be accompanied by standardized affidavit of amounts charged by any person or agency for adoption. (19-5-208[4]).

Proceedings.—Denver juvenile court requires one year waiting period after date of marriage for stepparent adoption. Petition must be filed not later than 30 days after child is first placed in home of adoptive applicants for purpose of adoption unless court finds reasonable cause or excusable neglect for delay. (19-5-208). Hearing closed to public and in court's discretion to child to be adopted if under 12, but court may interview child. (19-5-210[5]). No person may give or receive money or other consideration in connection with relinquishment and adoption except attorneys fees and other fees approved by court. Violation of this section is misdemeanor. (19-5-213).

Decree.—After hearing, court may continue petition, dismiss petition, or no sooner than six months from date of hearing unless time extended or shortened by court for good cause shown, may enter final decree of adoption. (19-5-210). In certain stepparent adoptions final decree may be entered at time of hearing but hearing may not be held less than 30 days after notice is served on other parent. (19-5-203[1][d][II]). Before making final decree, court must be satisfied as to: (1) Availability of child for adoption, (2) good moral character, ability to support and educate, and suitableness of home of petitioner, (3) mental and physical condition of child as proper subject for adoption in proposed home and (4) fact that best interest of child will be served by proposed adoption. (19-5-210[2]).

Name by which child to be known after adoption must be stated in petition and that name, not former, is stated in final decree. (19-5-208[2][d]; 19-5-210[3]).

Effect of Adoption.—After entry of final decree, person adopted is entitled to all rights and privileges and subject to all obligations of child born in lawful wedlock. Birth parents are divested of all legal rights and obligations and adopted child is free from all legal obligations, including maintenance, to birth parents; but adoption of child by spouse of birth parent has no effect on relationship between child and that birth parent. (19-5-211).

For purposes of intestate succession, adopted person is child of adopting parent and not of birth parents, unless there are no surviving heirs under 15-11-103(1) through (5), and surviving birth child or birth parent files claim within 90 days of decedent's death. (19-5-104[4]; 19-5-211[2]; 15-11-114[2]; 15-11-103).

With exception of equitable adoption for intestate succession (170 Colo. 465, 463 P.2d 305), this statute is only method of legal adoption (185 Colo. 400, 525 P.2d 1148).

Setting Aside Adoption.—Motion to vacate final decree for jurisdictional or procedural defects must be filed within 90 days of entry of final decree. Motion to vacate final decree by reason of fraud must be filed within one year of entry of final decree, except in cases of stepparent adoption. (19-5-214). Requirements of due process under both federal and state constitutions take precedence over statutory enactments. (163 Colo. 122, 428 P.2d 909).

Adoption of Adults.—Person desiring to adopt person over 18 as heir at law may file petition in juvenile court of county of petitioner's residence or residence of person sought to be adopted and summons is served on person sought to be adopted. Such person must file answer within time required by summons either consenting or disclaiming desire for such adoption. If disclaimer filed, petition is dismissed; if consent filed, decree is entered declaring such person to be heir at law of petitioner. Consent to be given by adult to be adopted, but if such person non compos mentis at time consent may be given by conservator or other representative. Such decree may or may not change name of such adopted person. Jurisdiction and procedure same insofar as practicable as for adoption of children. (14-1-101).

Registry Established.—State registrar of vital statistics maintains confidential registry of consenting adult adoptees and birth parents who authorize release of information to each other. (25-2-113.5).

Access to Information.—Any adult adoptee or adoptive parent may obtain specified "nonidentifying information" such as physical description, educational background and medical information concerning birth parents to extent information is available through State Department of Human Services. (19-5-402).

COMMUNITY PROPERTY:

Not in Colorado.

DISSOLUTION OF MARRIAGE:

Governing statute is based on Uniform Marriage and Divorce Act. Unless otherwise provided, Rules of Civil Procedure govern process, service thereof, practice and procedure. (14-10-105).

Grounds for Dissolution.—Irretrievable breakdown of marriage relationship. (14-10-106). Irretrievable breakdown is finding of fact and must be proven as essential element of action. (189 Colo. 499, 542 P.2d 845).

Grounds for Legal Separation.—Same as for dissolution of marriage. Decree granted in this form if one party so requests and other does not object. (14-10-106). Converted to dissolution of marriage after six months on motion of either party and proof of notice to other party. (14-10-120).

Maintenance.—Without regard to marital misconduct, court may grant, for either spouse, only upon finding that spouse seeking maintenance order lacks sufficient property and is unable to support self through appropriate employment or is custodian of child whose circumstances make it appropriate that custodian not seek employment. (14-10-114).

Citizenship and Residence Requirements.—One spouse must have been domiciled in state for 90 days next preceding commencement of action. (14-10-106).

Jurisdiction.—District court has exclusive jurisdiction over all actions for dissolution of marriage, legal separation, maintenance. District court entering decree has continuing jurisdiction to enforce child support orders through contempt power but different district court has no jurisdiction to punish contempt absent change of venue. (629 P.2d 1074). If out-of-state respondent waives court's lack of personal jurisdiction, court has jurisdiction both over subject matter and parties, and must divide marital property. (647 P.2d 693).

Venue.—Proper venue lies in county in which respondent resides at commencement of action or in county in which petitioner resides when service is made on respondent in such county. (Rule 98[c]).

Process.—Same as in other civil actions. Where personal service cannot be obtained, service by one publication may be ordered, and default judgment may be entered 30 days after publication. (14-10-107).

Pleading.—Petitioner must allege irretrievable breakdown of marriage, and set forth residence and length of residence in state of each party, date and place of marriage, date on which separation of parties occurred, names, ages and addresses of any living children of marriage and whether wife is pregnant, any arrangements as to custody and support of children and maintenance of spouse, and relief sought. (14-10-107).

Practice.—Rules of Civil Procedure govern, except as otherwise specifically provided. (14-10-105). Decree may not be entered absent court finding that 90 days or more have elapsed since it acquired jurisdiction over respondent, either by service of pro cess, or by respondent joining as copetitioner or otherwise entering appearance. (14-10-106). Appeals from district court to court of appeals lie as in all other civil cases.

By affidavit of either or both parties if no minor children and wife not pregnant, or both spouses represented by counsel have entered into separation agreement as to custody and child support; and adverse party properly served; and no genuine issue of material fact; and no marital property or parties have entered into property division agreement. Will not shorten statutory waiting period for entry of decree and court may require formal hearing on own motion. (14-10-120.3).

Judgment or Decree.—Court must make finding that marriage is irretrievably broken or continue matter for further hearing for not less than 30 days nor more than 60 days. At adjourned hearing, court must make finding whether marriage irretrievably broken. (14-10-110).

See note at head of Digest as to 1998 legislation covered.

See Topical Index in front part of this volume.

DISSOLUTION OF MARRIAGE . . . *continued*

Temporary Maintenance.—In proceeding for dissolution of marriage, legal separation, child custody or declaration of invalidity, or proceeding for disposition of property, maintenance or support following dissolution of marriage, court may order temporary debt payments, use of property, maintenance, custody, child support or attorneys fees on motion of either party. (14-10-108 to 114).

Restraining Order.—Provision is made for restraining orders, temporary injunctions, and enforcement thereof. (14-10-107 to 109). Unless grounds independent of marriage relationship exist, court is without authority to grant permanent injunction under 14-10-108. (44 Colo. App. 355, 618 P.2d 692).

Allowance for Prosecution of Suit.—Costs and attorney's fees may be granted. (14-10-119).

Permanent Maintenance.—In proceeding for dissolution of marriage or legal separation or in separate proceeding for maintenance after dissolution of marriage, court may make reasonable and just order for maintenance of either spouse only if it finds spouse lacks sufficient property and is unable to secure sufficient employment to maintain self or is custodian of child whose circumstances make it appropriate that custodian not seek employment (14-10-114), and may require payment to clerk of court as trustee or to family support registry and enforce payment by contempt or collection proceedings or by any other proceeding available under laws of state (14-10-117). Written agreement as to maintenance executed before or during marriage enforceable unless unconscionable at time enforcement sought. (14-2-307). Except where decree expressly precludes or limits modification, court which rendered decree may modify provisions for maintenance as to future installments upon showing of changed circumstances so substantial and continuing as to make terms unconscionable. Where decree expressly precludes modification, court can modify provisions for maintenance only on showing of fraud or overreaching. (38 Colo. App. 319, 558 P.2d 450). Modification can only be made upon motion at time when circumstances have changed and no automatic presumption as to unconscionability can be made in original decree. (44 Colo. App. 355, 618 P.2d 692). Unless otherwise agreed in writing or expressly provided in decree, death of either party or remarriage of party receiving maintenance terminates obligation to pay future maintenance. (14-10-122). Carrying life insurance in favor of former spouse may be required as maintenance device. (44 Colo. App. 305, 612 P.2d 1161). Whether maintenance shall be awarded in lump sum or periodic payments is in discretion of court. (190 Colo. 491, 549 P.2d 404). Court may award maintenance as tool to balance equities and compensate spouse whose work enabled other spouse to obtain education, but such tool is available only where statutory requirements of need are met. (641 P.2d 300).

Division of Property of Spouses.—Property distributed upon dissolution or legal separation by giving each spouse his or her separate property and then dividing marital property in proportions as court deems just. (14-10-113). Court to disregard marital misconduct and consider contributions (including contributions as homemaker), value of property set aside for each spouse, increase, decrease or depletion of separate property, and economic circumstances of each party. (14-10-113). Property acquired in first marriage and given to spouse in divorce settlement remains separate property if parties remarry. (632 P.2d 1048). Written agreement executed before or during marriage but prior to filing of dissolution generally enforceable as to property division. (14-2-301 to 310). Not enforceable if execution involuntary or disclosure of property or obligations at time of execution incomplete. (14-2-307).

Change of Wife's Name.—Court may restore the wife's maiden name. (13-15-101, 102).

Custody of Children.—Court must determine custody, after considering specified factors, in accordance with best interests of child. (14-10-124). Court may interview child to determine wishes of child. (14-10-126). Court may order joint custody. (14-10-123.5). Court may modify custody decree only on finding that circumstances have changed and that modification serves best interest of child. Modification of sole custody. (14-10-131). Modification to or from joint custody. (14-10-131.5). Motion for modification cannot be filed within two years of prior motion for modification unless child at physical or emotional risk. (14-10-131). Requirement that changed circumstances be found may not be modified by private agreement. (42 Colo. App. 198, 591 P.2d 1043). Court is not limited to inquiry as to legal right by which child is held, but must determine broad question of what will best serve child's interest. (186 Colo. 381, 527 P.2d 811). Court is not to presume that sex of any person proposed as custodian enables that person better to serve interests of child. (14-10-124[3]). Court may allow custodial parent to remove child from state of Colorado permanently if custodial parent shows that there is sensible reason to leave state. Burden shifts to non-custodial parent to demonstrate that removal is not in child's best interest. (834 P.2d 1287). In any child custody case, grandparent of child may seek court order granting him legal custody or reasonable grandchild visitation rights. (19-1-117). Court may award custody of child to interested person not party to action. (631 P.2d 1183). If parent is absent or leaves home because of spouse abuse by other parent, such absence or leaving not to be considered in determining best interests of child. (14-10-124[4]).

Visitation.—Term "visitation" has been changed to "parenting time" throughout the act when visitation refers to time non-custodial parent spends with his or her child.

Uniform Child Custody Jurisdiction Act adopted. (14-13-101).

Material Variations.—

§5(b)—Permits notice by publication; requires 20 days notice before hearing and clerk must post notice for 30 days. Number of times publication is required governed by Rule 4(h). (42 Colo. App. 270, 592 P.2d 1354).

§§18-22—Contain provisions without counterpart in Act relating to payment of costs.

Under UCCJA, when Colorado is home state, it has jurisdiction to modify sister state's decree in best interests of children. (643 P.2d 783).

Allowance for Support of Children.—Guidelines and schedule of basic child support obligations establish rebuttable presumption of amount and allocation of support based on combined gross income of parents, number of children, and custody arrangements. (14-10-115). Court may deviate from guidelines where inequitable, but must specify reasons for deviation. (14-10-115). Court may in proceeding for dissolution of marriage, legal separation, maintenance or child support make such order as may be reasonable and just for support of children dependent upon parents for support. (14-10-115). Unless otherwise emancipated, child support terminates at age 19, unless parties otherwise agree, child is mentally or physically disabled, or child is still in high school or its equivalent. Court may order parents to contribute to child's post-secondary education up to age 21 or upon obtaining undergraduate degree, whichever occurs first. Court may not order child support and contribution for post secondary education for same child. (14-10-115[1.5]). Defines gross income for determination of child support. (14-10-115[7]). Provision of decree respecting support may be modified only as to installments accruing subsequent to motion for modification. (14-10-122[1]; 44 Colo. App. 502, 614 P.2d 913). Rebuttable presumption that child support shall not be modified unless basis for modification will result in change of child support amount by 10% or more. (14-10-122[1]). May be lump sum charge against real property of father. (189 Colo. 103, 536 P.2d 1135). Upon request of any party or upon court's own motion, court shall order wage assignment. (14-14-107). Wage assignment order mandatory unless defense asserted that allegedly delinquent payment not due or was paid. (692 P.2d 329). Obligation to support survives death of parent. (14-10-122[3]). Court may order that income from gift made to children during marriage shall not reduce support payments later imposed on donor parent. (42 Colo. App. 433, 598 P.2d 524). Orders which resolve financial rights and obligations of parties, including issues of child support, even on temporary basis, are final for purposes of review. (650 P.2d 1352). Effects of inflation proper factors for consideration in action for child support modification, but there must be proper proof of rate of inflation and its specific effects on petitioner's circumstances. (635 P.2d 933). County and state child support enforcement units may certify past-due amounts of child support to Internal Revenue Service without court order for judgment or verified entry of judgment for purposes of intercepting federal tax refund. Court shall order immediate deductions from income for child support (14-14-111) absent good cause shown or written agreement of parties. Notice to deduct income for family support binding on employer. (14-14-111[4]). Lottery prize proceeds (26-13-118) and state income tax refunds (26-13-111) subject to offset for delinquent child support.

Child support enforcement procedures set forth in 14-14-101 to 111.

Uniform Interstate Family Support Act adopted without material variations. Effective Jan. 1, 1995. (14-5-101 to 903). Adds new sections without counterparts in Act relating to venue (14-5-1001), arrest of obligor (14-5-1002), duty of officials of Colorado as responding state (14-5-1003), proceedings not to be stayed (14-5-1004), declaration of reciprocity (14-5-1005), interstate central registry (14-5-1006), and enforcement of interstate income withholding (14-5-1007).

§201—Subsection (7) omitted.

§301—State Department of Social Services is state information agency.

§701—Parentage is determined by applying Uniform Parentage Act.

Remarriage.—Either party may remarry after final decree of dissolution of marriage and time for appeal has expired. An appeal not challenging finding of irretrievable breakdown does not delay finality of decree as to dissolution of marriage and parties may remarry pending such appeal. (14-10-120[1]).

Notice.—Notice provisions governed by Colorado Rules of Civil Procedure, Rule 4. (14-10-105; 620 P.2d 62). Court clerk required to give notice of entry of dissolution decree to department of health, office of registrar of vital statistics; information made public on request. (14-10-120[3]).

Separation Agreement.—Terms, other than those providing for custody, support, and visitation of children, are binding upon court unless found to be unconscionable. Terms of agreement set forth in decree may be enforced by all judgment remedies, including contempt, but not as contract terms. Agreement terms must be set forth in decree, unless agreement provided otherwise, in which case decree must identify agreement and indicate finding that it is not unconscionable. (14-10-112). Where terms of agreement incorporated in decree are uncertain, parol evidence is admissible to show intention of parties. (44 Colo. App. 252, 611 P.2d 590).

Defenses.—Failure to establish case and lack of jurisdiction are only defenses. All earlier existing defenses abolished by statute. (14-10-107[5]).

Marriage Counseling.—Provided for on a voluntary basis. (14-12-101).

DIVORCE:

See topic Dissolution of Marriage.

GUARDIAN AND WARD:

Jurisdiction over guardianship and conservatorship proceedings is in probate court in Denver, district courts elsewhere, and in juvenile courts with respect to children under juvenile court's jurisdiction by reason of Children's Code. (15-14-102; 19-1-104). Venue for guardianship proceedings for minor is where minor resides or is present. (15-14-205). Venue for guardianship proceedings for incapacitated person is where person resides or is present, or, if admitted to institution pursuant to court order, venue is also in county where court sits. (15-14-302). Venue for conservatorship proceedings is where protected person resides or, if person does not reside in state, where he has property. (15-14-403).

Uniform Probate Code adopted, with substantial variations from official text. (15-10-101 to 15-17-101). Sections pertaining to protection of persons under disability and their property are 15-14-101 to 15-14-611. 1975 Amendments not adopted.

Selection of Guardian.—Parent of unmarried minor may appoint guardian by will or other instrument. (15-14-202). Parent of incapacitated person may appoint guardian by will or other writing. (15-14-301[1]). Spouse of incapacitated person may appoint guardian by will or other writing and has priority over parent. (15-14-301[2]). Minor 14 or older or incapacitated person may prevent appointment of guardian or cause termination of previously accepted appointment by filing with court in which will is probated, or written instrument filed, written objection to appointment. (15-14-203, 301[5]).

Appointment of Guardian.—If legal custody of or decision-making responsibility for minor is suspended by prior court order, if minor is abandoned or if parents,

See note at head of Digest as to 1998 legislation covered.

See Topical Index in front part of this volume.

GUARDIAN AND WARD . . . *continued*

custodial person or person with decision-making responsibility requests, court may appoint guardian whose appointment would be in best interests of minor. (15-14-204). Persons having priority for appointment are: Person nominated by minor, if minor is 14 or older; person appointed by will or written instrument of parent; and any other interested person. (15-14-206).

Upon petition by incapacitated person or any person interested in his welfare, court may appoint guardian if incapacity is proved by clear and convincing evidence and appointment is necessary or desirable as means of providing continuing care and supervision. (15-14-303, 304). Priority for appointment given to: Person nominated by incapacitated person in writing prior to incapacity, spouse, adult child, parent or person nominated by will or other writing signed by deceased parent, any relative with whom incapacitated person resided for more than six months prior to filing of petition, nominee of person caring for or paying benefits to incapacitated person. (15-14-311).

Person to be protected, any person interested in his estate, affairs, or welfare, including parent, guardian, or custodian, or any person adversely affected by lack of effective management of his property or affairs, may petition for appointment of conservator. (15-14-404). Court may appoint as conservator individual, trust company, or bank with general power to serve as trustee, with priority given as follows: Fiduciary appointed or recognized by court of other jurisdiction where protected person resides; nominee of protected person, if 14 or over and has mental capacity to make intelligent choice, or nominee of adult protected person named in writing prior to time need for protective proceeding arose; spouse; adult child; parent or person nominated by will of deceased parent; relative with whom protected person resided for more than six months prior to filing of petition; nominee of person caring for or paying benefits to protected person. (15-14-410).

Eligibility and Competency.—Any person 21 or older, resident or nonresident, may be appointed guardian of minor. (15-14-206). Any competent person 21 or older or suitable institution may be appointed guardian of incapacitated person. (15-14-311). Any person 21 or older, trust company or bank with general power to serve as trustee may be appointed conservator of estate of protected person. (15-14-410).

Qualification.—No statutory provision regarding oath or bond of guardian of person of minor or incapacitated person. Court may require conservator of estate to furnish bond. (15-14-411, 412). Guardian of minor or incapacitated person must file written acceptance of appointment with court in which will is probated or written instrument filed. (15-14-202, 301). By acceptance of appointment guardian or conservator submits to personal jurisdiction of court in any proceedings related to guardianship or protected estate. (15-14-208, 305, 413).

Inventory.—Conservator must file with appointing court complete inventory of estate of protected person within three months after appointment. (15-14-418).

Powers and Duties.—Subject to limitation by appointing court, guardian of person has same powers and duties as parent respecting unemancipated child, except not required to provide for ward from own funds and not liable to third persons for acts of ward solely by reason of parental relationship. (15-14-209, 312). Subject to enlargement or limitation by appointing court (15-14-426), conservator has powers and duties conferred by law, including Colorado Fiduciaries' Powers Act (15-1-801 to 807), on trustees in administration of protected estate and distribution for support, education, care, or benefit of protected person and dependents (15-14-424, 425).

Investments.—See category Estates and Trusts, topic Trusts, subhead Investments.

Securities in Name of Nominee.—See category Estates and Trusts, topic Trusts, subhead Securities in Name of Nominee.

Real Estate.—Conservators' powers governed by Colorado Fiduciaries' Powers Act. (15-1-801 to 807).

Liabilities of Guardian.—Guardian of minor is not liable for injury to ward by reason of consent to medical or other professional care, unless consent by parent would have been illegal. (15-14-209[3]). Conservator may be sued in fiduciary capacity on contracts entered into as conservator, on obligations arising from ownership and control of estate, and on torts committed in administration. Conservator is individually liable on contracts entered into as conservator only if he fails to reveal representative capacity and identify estate in contract, and on obligations of estate and torts committed in administration only if personally at fault. (15-14-429).

Accounts.—Guardian must report condition of his ward and of ward's estate subject to his possession or control, as required by court or court rule. (15-14-209[2], 312[1]). Conservator must file accounting upon his resignation or removal, on termination of protected person's minority or disability, and at other times as court may direct. (15-14-419).

Termination of Guardianship.—Guardianship of minor terminates on death, resignation, or removal of guardian, or on minor's death, adoption, marriage, or majority. (15-14-210). Guardianship of incapacitated person terminates on death, incapacity, removal, or resignation of guardian, death or termination of incapacity of ward, or denial of probate of informally probated will appointing guardian. (15-14-306, 307). Conservatorship is terminated on death, resignation, or removal of conservator, or on determination that minority or disability of protected person has ceased. (15-14-415, 430).

Insane Persons.—Provisions relating to incapacitated persons apply to mentally impaired or deficient persons. (15-14-101[1]). Unless stated in court order, mentally ill person does not forfeit any legal right or suffer legal disability. (27-10-104).

Foreign Guardian.—If no local conservator has been appointed and no petition in protective proceeding is pending in this state, upon filing authenticated copies of his appointment and any official bond already filed or additionally required, domiciliary foreign conservator may exercise as to assets in this state all powers of local conservator and may maintain actions and proceedings subject to any conditions imposed upon nonresident parties generally. (15-14-432).

Transfers to Minors.—See topic Infants.

Uniform Fiduciaries Act adopted. (15-1-101 to 113).

Uniform Simplification of Fiduciary Security Transfers Act repealed.

HUSBAND AND WIFE:

With respect to holding, selling and conveying property, suing and being sued, carrying on business and contracting, married woman may act as if sole. (14-2-201, 202, 203, 207, 208).

Disabilities of Married Women.—Chief common law disabilities have been removed. (42 Colo. 367, 94 P. 360). Right to maintain separate domicile. (14-2-210).

Separate Property.—Married woman retains property owned at marriage; rents, issues, profits, and proceeds thereof; and property which comes to her by descent, devise, or bequest, or gift of any person, except her husband, including some gifts from her husband, as her sole and separate property and such property not subject to disposal of her husband or liable for her husband's debts. (14-2-201).

Liability for Debts.—Property of both spouses is liable for family expenses and education of children, jointly and severally (14-6-110), except that common law governs if husband and wife living separate and apart at time expense was incurred (65 Colo. 70, 173 P. 544).

Liability for Torts.—Husband not liable for torts committed by wife without his presence and in which he in no manner participated. (42 Colo. 367, 94 P. 360). Wife may be sued for torts in same manner as if she were unmarried. (14-2-202). Judgments, decrees or orders may be enforced against wife, as if sole. (14-2-208).

Contracts.—Wife may contract debts in her own name and upon her own credit, and may execute notes, bonds, and other instruments in writing, and enter into any contract, as if sole. (14-2-208). There is no statutory prohibition against her becoming bound as surety.

Antenuptial Contracts.—See subhead Marital Agreements, infra.

Domestic Abuse.—Municipal court of record, county and district courts authorized to issue restraining orders and emergency protection orders to prevent domestic abuse. (14-4-102, 103). Violation of order is class 1 or class 2 misdemeanor. (18-6-803.5[2][a]). Peace officer has duty to use reasonable means to enforce orders, including arrest of restrained person upon probable cause for knowing violation. (18-6-803.5[3]). Special sentencing provisions apply for crimes involving domestic violence. (18-6-801).

Actions.—Wife may sue or be sued as if sole. (14-2-202; Rule 17b). Wife may sue husband in tort (97 Colo. 19, 46 P.2d 740) and either spouse may sue to recover separate property from other spouse (87 Colo. 607, 290 P. 285). Wives have same right for loss of consortium as is afforded husbands in like actions. (14-2-209).

Agency.—Either spouse may act as agent for other. Agency of one spouse to act for other may be proved by less convincing evidence than is required to establish agency between strangers. (139 Colo. 496, 340 P.2d 869).

Conveyance or Encumbrance of Property.—Neither spouse requires the consent or joinder of the other in order to convey or encumber his or her separate property (14-2-207) except homestead (38-35-118). See category Debtor and Creditor, topic Homesteads.

Marital Agreements.—Agreement enforceable without consideration if in writing and signed by both parties (14-2-303) as to rights and obligations of parties in property of either or both parties; acquisition, disposition, management and control of property; disposition of property upon separation of parties, dissolution of marriage, death of either party or other event; spousal maintenance; making of will or trust or other arrangement to carry out provisions of agreement; ownership and disposition of life insurance; rights and obligations regarding employee benefit or retirement plans (except as prohibited by federal law); choice of law; and any other matter not in violation of public policy or criminal statute. (14-2-304[1]). Marital agreement may not adversely affect right of child to support. (14-2-304[3]). Agreement may be signed by prospective spouses in contemplation of marriage or by present spouses if signed by both parties prior to filing of action for dissolution. (14-2-302[1]). Agreement unenforceable against party who did not execute agreement voluntarily (14-2-307[1][a]), or if before execution of agreement such party was not provided with fair and reasonable disclosure of property or financial obligations of other party (14-2-307[1][b]). Provisions as to maintenance of spouses upon dissolution unenforceable if, at time enforcement sought, such provisions are unconscionable as matter of law. (14-2-307[2]).

Maintenance and Support.—Person failing to support spouse or children under 18 years old, or who willfully fails, refuses or neglects to provide proper care, food or clothing in case of spouse or child's sickness, or who willfully fails to pay expenses of child legally inmate of state, county or children's home in state, or any parent who willfully leaves child with intent to abandon or any man who willfully neglects, fails or refuses to provide proper care, food and clothing to mother of his child during childbirth and attendant illness shall be deemed guilty of class 5 felony. (14-6-101). It is affirmative defense that inability to provide such support, care and maintenance is due to physical incapacity or other good cause. (14-6-101). Obligation of mother equal to that of father to provide care of child. (186 Colo. 65, 525 P.2d 457). Proceedings instituted by complaint filed in any court of record by prosecuting attorney or other appropriate agency or in county court of county where offense committed. (14-6-104). Venue is in county where child or spouse is present. (14-6-106). In any proceeding for above mentioned offenses, either spouse is competent witness against other spouse and no consent is required. (14-6-105). Extradition is provided for. (14-6-103).

Husband is not guilty of criminal violation for failure to support if wife refuses without just cause to live with him. (64 Colo. 209, 170 P. 956).

Uniform Interstate Family Support Act (1992 Act) adopted effective Jan. 1, 1995. (14-5-101 to 14-5-1007). See topic Dissolution of Marriage.

Material Variations.—

§101(6) modified: " 'Income-withholding order' means an order or other legal process to withhold support from the income of the obligor directed to an obligor's employer, employers, or successor employers or other payor of funds as described in section 14-14-107 relating to wage assignments and in section 14-14-111 relating to immediate deductions for family support obligations." (14-5-101[6]).

See note at head of Digest as to 1998 legislation covered.

See Topical Index in front part of this volume.

HUSBAND AND WIFE . . . *continued*
Added Part 10, Colorado Implementation Provisions. (14-5-1001 to 14-5-1007).

Community property system does not obtain in Colorado.

Uniform Disposition of Community Property Rights at Death Act(1973 Act) adopted. (15-20-101).

Material Variations.—

§3—Sentence beginning "With respect to property" omitted.

§4—Added "or by a trustee of an inter vivos trust created by the decedent" before "title of the surviving spouse" and substituted "The personal representative shall have no" for "Neither the personal representative nor the court in which the decedent's estate is being administered has a".

§5—Added following subsections having no Act counterpart: "(2) Written demand in this section and in section 15-20-105 shall be made by a surviving spouse, the spouse's successor in interest, or the decedent's heirs or devisees not later than six months after the decedent's will has been admitted to probate, or not later than six months after the appointment of an administrator if there is no will, or not later than six months after the decedent's death if the property to which this article applies is held in an inter vivos trust created by the decedent; and written demand by a creditor of the decedent shall be made not later than six months from the decedent's date of death. (3) Written demand in this section and in section 15-20-105 shall be delivered in person or by registered mail to the personal representative. As used in this article, the personal representative may also mean the trustee of an inter vivos trust created by the decedent who has legal title to, or possession of, the property to which this article applies."

INFANTS:

For purposes of Colorado Revised Statutes, age of majority for both sexes is 21 except where otherwise provided expressly by statute. (2-4-401[6]). Among statutory exceptions are statute that deems age of emancipation to be 19 for purposes of termination of child support absent specified conditions (14-10-115[1.5][a]) and statutes that deem person otherwise competent to be of legal age at age 18 to: (1) Enter into any legal contractual obligation and be bound to same extent as any other adult person, but such obligation not considered family expense of parents of person who entered into contract under 14-6-110; (2) manage his estate in same manner as any other adult person, except for custodial property given or held under terms of Colorado Uniform Transfers to Minors Act or property held for protected person; (3) sue and be sued to same extent as any other adult person, without necessity for guardian ad litem or someone acting in his behalf; (4) make decisions in regard to his own body and body of his issue, whether natural or adopted by such person, to full extent allowed to any other adult person; (5) register for and vote at all elections. (13-22-101; 1-2-101[1]).

Adoption.—See topic Adoption.

Emancipation.—Common law rules govern. Presumption of emancipation arises at age of majority. (667 P.2d 1374). Presumption of emancipation invalid when child incapable of supporting himself by reason of physical or mental disability. (667 P.2d 1374). In situations to which presumption inapplicable, emancipation is question of fact. (492 P.2d 81). To determine whether child emancipated, trier of fact should consider whether child financially independent of parents; whether child established domicile separate from parents; whether child maintains relationships incompatible with subordinate position in parents' family; whether evidence reveals domestic situation radically inconsistent with parental control over child. (564 P.2d 961; 629 P.2d 1069; 670 P.2d 31).

Disabilities.—Common law rules govern generally. Specific statutory disabilities include: (1) Children under ten cannot testify in court if unable to relate facts accurately or truly, except in any proceeding involving child abuse, sexual abuse, assault or incest when child can relate facts in language appropriate to child's age (13-90-106); (2) children under 18 cannot work in mines except in office, janitorial or food service capacities or other non-extraction, preparation or production activities (34-24-104); children under 21 cannot serve, purchase or possess alcohol in certain locations (12-47-128). Minor 16 or over may contract for property and liability insurance. (10-4-104).

Ratification of Contracts.—Common law rules govern. Executed contracts are binding until avoided while executory contracts, except for necessaries, are not binding until affirmed. (87 Colo. 301, 287 P. 284). Partly executed contracts are considered executory. (17 Colo. 506, 30 P. 245). No new consideration is needed to ratify and language relied on may be oral or written; however, acts or words or both must amount to new promise, simple acknowledgment being insufficient. (17 Colo. 506, 30 P. 245). Child may ratify by acts recognizing contract within reasonable time after attaining majority. (623 P.2d 370).

Children's Code.—Whenever it appears that child is within court's jurisdiction, any person may refer matter to district attorney, who shall determine whether interests of child or community require further action. (19-2-510[1]). Children's Code is to be construed favorably to best interests of child and society. (182 Colo. 157, 511 P.2d 898).

Jurisdiction.—Juvenile court has exclusive original jurisdiction in most proceedings concerning delinquent children; neglected or dependent children; legal custody, guardianship or custodianship of children otherwise within court's jurisdiction; termination of parent-child relationship; issuance of orders of support; determination of parentage; adoption of person of any age; judicial consent to marriage, employment or enlistment; treatment or commitment of mentally ill or disabled children; petitions for review of need for placement. (19-1-104).

Venue.—Delinquency proceedings in county where alleged violation took place. (19-2-105). Proceedings for support in county where child is physically present or resides or where obligor parent resides, or where public assistance paid. (19-6-102). Adoption proceedings in county where petitioner resides or where placement agency is located. (19-5-204). Proceedings to determine parentage in county where child or respondent resides or is found or where public assistance paid or, if respondent deceased, where probate of his estate could be commenced. (19-4-109). Child support enforcement unit may establish noncontested paternity in administrative procedure. (19-4-109; 26-13.5-101).

Support.—Any person may commence support proceedings by filing verified petition with court prior to 21st birthday of child. (19-6-101). Upon finding that respondent has obligation to support child, court may order respondent to pay support reasonable under circumstances. (19-6-104). Non-parent obtaining legal custody not obligated to continue to serve as legal custodian and provide support after loss of physical custody in marriage dissolution action. (580 P.2d 836). Genetic tests and other tests of inherited characteristics are usable to determine parentage and may overcome presumption of legitimacy. (13-25-126). Spouse who adopts children of other spouse is obligated to support said children even though dissolution of marriage occurs soon after decree of adoption. (629 P.2d 1108). See topic Dissolution of Marriage, subhead Allowance for Support of Children.

Parental Responsibility.—Any person, entity or political subdivision may recover damages up to $3,500, plus court costs and attorneys' fees, from parents of child under 18, living with parents, who maliciously or willfully destroys property, and any person may recover same from parents of child under 18, living with parents, who knowingly inflicts bodily injury. (13-21-107). Parents of unemancipated minor who shoplifts from mercantile establishment liable to owner for actual damages plus penalty of $100 to $250. (13-21-107.5). Parent of child under 18 required to give affidavit of liability for child to obtain driver's license or instruction permit. Subsequent negligence or willful misconduct of child under 18 while driving motor vehicle imputed to parent who signed affidavit. (42-2-108).

Actions.—Court must appoint guardian ad litem to protect child's interests in all dependency or neglect cases involving abuse (19-1-111[1]) and in hearing to determine involuntary termination of parent-child relationship for child and for minor parent (19-3-602). Court may appoint guardian ad litem in: (1) Delinquency proceeding (19-1-111[2]); (2) proceeding under School Attendance Law of 1963 (19-1-111[2]); (3) proceeding for review of placement (19-3-701[4]); (4) action to determine parentage (19-4-110). In proceeding to hospitalize child for mental health services, if child under 15 and ward of department of human services, guardian ad litem must be appointed. (27-10-103[3.1]). Uniform Probate Code adopted, with substantial modifications, effective July 1, 1974. 1975 Amendments adopted with modifications. 1982 amendment dealing with succession without administration has not been adopted.

Termination of Parental Rights.—Parent-child relationship may be terminated where child has been adjudicated dependent or neglected and has been abandoned or child has been adjudicated dependent or neglected and no appropriate treatment to address unfitness of parents can be devised. (19-3-604). Act provides extensive criteria and procedures for termination of parental rights by court order upon filing of written motion alleging factual grounds for termination and subsequent hearing. (19-3-602[1]). Motion must be filed at least 30 days before hearing. (19-3-602[1]). Court order terminates all rights and obligations except rights of child to inherit from parent and to receive benefits from third parties, including Indian tribes. (19-3-608).

See topic Guardian and Ward.

Uniform Transfers to Minors Act adopted. (11-50-101). Age of majority under Act is 21. (11-50-102).

Uniform Securities Ownership by Minors Act not adopted.

Uniform Child Custody Jurisdiction Act adopted. (14-13-101). See topic Dissolution of Marriage.

Uniform Interstate Family Support Act adopted. (14-5-101). See topic Dissolution of Marriage.

Uniform Parentage Act adopted with material variations. (19-4-101). Order in dissolution of marriage proceeding concerning parentage issue reversible if court fails to follow procedures in Uniform Parentage Act. (689 P.2d 726, 854 P.2d 1346). Uniform Parentage Act provides no basis for obtaining genetic testing for purpose of providing basis for diagnosing problems minor child may encounter. (197 Colo. 510, 595 P.2d 223). Failure of Uniform Parentage Act to grant right to bring action for determination of paternity to claiming birth father with respect to child born to birth mother during her marriage to another violates equal protection clause of Federal and Colorado Constitutions as well as equal rights amendment to Colorado Constitution. (200 Colo. 345, 615 P.2d 666).

Assessment of costs and attorney fees against state human services department required to bring paternity action is not precluded by supremacy clause of U.S. Constitution. (647 P.2d 239).

MARRIAGE:

Governing statute is based on Uniform Marriage and Divorce Act. (14-2-101 to 113).

Consent Required.—Parents or guardian or judge of juvenile court must give consent for each party over 16 but less than 18. If under 16 party must have consent of parents or guardian and judge of juvenile court. (14-2-106[1][a][I], 108).

Medical Examination.—None required after July 1, 1989.

License may be obtained from county clerk upon appearance of one party, payment of fee, and presentation of: Application signed by both parties; proof of age or consent; and proof that marriage not prohibited. (14-2-106). License is valid for 30 days (14-2-107).

Waiting Period.—None.

Marriage may be solemnized by judge, retired judge or court magistrate, public official who has power or parties to marriage, or by any mode of solemnization recognized by any religious denomination or Indian nation or tribe. (14-2-109).

Report of Marriage.—Person solemnizing marriage must complete certificate and forward to county clerk within 60 days; thereafter late fees are assessed. (14-2-109[1]).

Record.—See category Documents and Records, topic Records, subhead Vital Statistics.

Common Law Marriage.—Recognized. (130 Colo. 225, 274 P.2d 605).

See note at head of Digest as to 1998 legislation covered.

See Topical Index in front part of this volume.

MARRIAGE . . . *continued*

Proxy Marriage.—Authorized. (14-2-109[2]).

Marriage by Written Contract.—Not authorized.

Prohibited Marriage.—Marriage prohibited when entered into: Prior to dissolution of party's earlier marriage to another; between ancestor and descendant, or brother and sister, whether whole or half blood; between uncle and niece or aunt and nephew, whether whole or half blood, except as permitted by aboriginal cultures. (14-2-110[1]). Children of prohibited marriage are legitimate. (14-2-110[2], 14-10-111[4]). Putative spouse of prohibited marriage has rights. (14-2-111).

Foreign Marriage.—Marriage contracted outside Colorado valid by laws where contracted or domicile of parties also valid in Colorado. (14-2-112).

Annulment.—District court declares marriage invalid upon application of specified party if marriage was void where contracted, is prohibited, or if party: Lacked capacity to consent because of infirmity, incapacity, alcohol or drugs; was incapable of consummating marriage through intercourse; was under age and lacked consent; or married due to fraud, misrepresentation, duress, jest or dare. (14-10-111[1]). Time limits for actions for declaration of invalidity variously six months, one year, and 24 months, but in no case after death of other party to marriage unless brought by child of marriage prior to final settlement of estate. (14-10-111[2], [3]). No decree shall be entered unless one of parties has been domiciled in state for 30 days preceding action or unless marriage contracted in state. (14-10-111[7]). Provisions applicable to dissolution apply to declaration of invalidity. (14-10-111[6]). Children of invalid marriage are legitimate. (14-10-111[4]).

INSURANCE

INSURANCE COMPANIES:

Division of insurance within department of regulatory agencies charged with execution of laws relating to insurance and has supervisory authority over business of insurance in Colorado. (10-1-103[1]). Commissioner of insurance is head of division of insurance. Commissioner appointed by governor subject to senate confirmation. (10-1-104[1]). Most regulatory laws are collected in C.R.S. Tit. 10. Declaratory judgment petitions may be accepted by Commissioner pursuant to Regulations 86-2, 3 CCR 702-12.

Reserves.—Following must maintain certain reserves or minimum surplus: Life insurance companies (10-7-101, 310); state employees and officials group benefit plans (24-50-613); title insurance companies (10-11-110); employers mutual liability insurance companies (10-12-210); interinsurance groups (10-13-107); fraternal benefit societies (10-14-604); preneed funeral contracts (10-15-107); nonprofit hospital and health service corporations (10-16-310); prepaid dental care plans (10-16-505, 506); and health maintenance organizations (10-16-411, 412).

Deposits.—Cash or securities representing statutory minimum paid in capital or guaranty fund requirements for life, fire, casualty, multiple line and title insurance companies stated in 10-3-201. Requirements for nonadmitted insurers in 10-5-108.

Deposit requirements for other companies stated in Article relating to such companies. Examples include: Captive insurance companies (10-6-116); employers mutual liability insurance (10-12-211); preneed funeral contracts (10-15-107); nonprofit hospital and health service corporations (10-16-310[2]); prepaid dental care plans (10-16-505); health maintenance organizations (10-16-412); and interinsurance (10-13-107). Fund deposits are required of alien and foreign companies, except life insurers. Such deposits held for benefit of all policyholders of such insurer in all states. Credit allowed for deposits in other states. (10-3-302).

Fees Paid to Commissioner.—Fees paid by every entity regulated by Division of Insurance transacting business of insurance in state contained in 10-3-207 include: $500 for investigating and processing initial application for authorization or licensure; annual fee between $500 and $3,345 depending upon volume of insurance written; and other reasonable fees for administrative services. (10-3-207).

Other Fees and Taxes.—See category Business Organizations, topic Corporations. After filing articles with secretary of state, no further filing is required in that office other than amendments to articles. (10-3-108). Employers' mutual liability companies pay secretary of state filing fee in amount equal to filing fee for domestic corporations capitalized at $75,000. (10-12-203). Foreign and domestic companies pay costs of commissioner's examination outside of state. (10-1-110[5]).

Rates and rating organizations are covered in 10-4-401 to 10-4-421 for all kinds of insurance except reinsurance, life and annuities, sickness and accident, nonprofit hospital and health services, health maintenance organization services, credit life and other credit insurance and surplus lines insurance. Mutual liability in 10-12-208. Commissioner does not have power to approve rates conditionally. (41 Colo. App. 380, 585 P.2d 929).

Legislative policy favors expeditious handling of liability claims. (10-4-101). Voluntary partial payment of liability claims may be made without admission of liability. (10-4-103). Cancellation, nonrenewal, decreases in coverage, limits on some types of liability, and increases in premiums on most policies are restricted. (10-4-107 to 110.7; 10-4-601 to 611). Insurance companies required to participate in joint underwriting association authorized to issue commercial liability insurance otherwise unavailable. (10-4-1101 et seq.). Rating organizations and rate advisory organizations authorized. (10-4-408, 410). Anticompetitive behavior prohibited. (10-4-415). Colorado insurance guaranty association and life and health insurance protection association provide mechanism for payment of covered claims and for avoidance of loss to policyholders because of insolvency of insurer. (10-4-502 et seq.; 10-20-101 et seq.). Uninsurable health plan available. (10-8-501 et seq.). Assigned risk available for motor vehicle insurance. (10-4-412).

Surplus line insurance (i.e., coverage placed with approved nonadmitted insurer) is regulated. (10-5-101 to 119).

Captive insurance companies authorized and regulated. (10-6-101 to 130).

Insurance sales by financial institutions covered in 10-2-601 et seq.

Reports and Statements.—Annual financial statement of insurance company is due commissioner on Mar. 1 (10-3-208) and synopsis of statement, together with certificate of authority must be published in newspaper (10-3-109). Loss and expense experience and certain other data must be reported. (10-4-404). Fraternal benefit society annual statement is due commissioner Mar. 1. (10-14-602). Interinsurance reports are covered in 10-13-108. Insurance holding company systems are regulated under 10-3-801 to 814.

Policies are regulated in detail. Seal is not required but secretary must attest. (10-1-116). Life policy requirements are in 10-7-102. Mutual protective associations in 10-12-101. Assessment accident associations in 10-3-123. Group life in 10-7-201. Preneed funeral contracts in 10-15-101 et seq. Fraternal benefit societies in 10-14-101 et seq. Mandatory health care coverage provisions in 10-16-101 et seq. Description forms required for each health benefit plan or Medicare supplemental coverage policy in 10-16-108.5. Medicare supplement policies or certificates issued on or after July 1, 1989, in 10-18-101 to 109. Long-term care insurance in 10-19-101 to 115. Risk management programs mandated for commercial policies in 10-4-420. Coordination of benefits provisions are permissible in group health plans in accordance with Rule 86-3, 3 CCR 702-12. Suicide after one year is no defense to payment of policy unless policy specifically limited to accidental death. (10-7-109). Group life insurer may pay certain verifiable expenses incident to last illness or death of insured. (10-7-202). Policy may designate trustee named in inter vivos or testamentary trust as beneficiary. (15-15-101[2]). Claims-made policies are regulated in 10-4-419 and 10-5-119. Reasonable policy conditions on recovery enforceable (683 P.2d 1212, Colo. App. 1984), but such conditions cannot reduce statutorily mandated no fault coverage (620 P.2d 29, Colo. 1980). Limitations placed on nonrenewability of individual health benefit plans (10-16-201.5) and automobile insurance policies (10-4-604). Procedures for denial of health plan benefits covered in 10-16-113.

Standard Nonforfeiture and Valuation Act adopted. (10-7-301 to 316). Standard Nonforfeiture Law for Individual Deferred Annuities adopted. (10-7-501 to 510).

Unfair Competition and Prohibited Discrimination.—Following are unfair methods of competition and unfair trade practices: Misrepresentations and false advertising of insurance policies, but misrepresentation may not be construed where written comparison of policies is made factually disclosing relevant features and benefits for which policy is issued and by which informed decision can be made; false information and advertising generally; defamation; boycott, coercion and intimidation; using stock and advisory board contracts as inducement to insurance; unfair discrimination including discrimination between individuals of same class and equal expectation of life with respect to life insurance or annuities; unfair discrimination between individuals of same class or between neighborhoods within municipality and of essentially same hazard; any classification solely on basis of marital status or sex unless for purpose of insuring family units where justified by actuarial statistics; any classification solely on basis of blindness, partial blindness, or specific physical disability unless based upon unequal expectation of life or expected risk of loss different than that of other individuals; denial of health care coverage based on participation in certain recreational activities; failure to comply with all provisions of 10-3-1104.5 regarding HIV testing; rebates; unfair claim settlement practices; failure to maintain complaint handling procedures; misrepresentation in insurance applications; requiring any insured or claimant to submit to any polygraph test concerning any application or claim; violation or noncompliance with any insurance law; failure to make full refund or credit of all unearned premiums upon termination of insurance coverage; requiring or otherwise inducing health care provider to utilize arbitration agreements with patients; violations of or noncompliance with any provision of Model Quality Replacement Parts Act; issuing claim-made or automobile policy form that does not comply with statute; reducing benefits by adding exclusionary rider except in specified circumstances; failure to comply with provisions of 10-16-108.5 and 10-16-105 regarding health benefit plans; violation of 25-1-801 et seq. regarding patient access to medical records. (10-3-1104).

Consumer Protection Standards Act for the Operation of Managed Care Plans establishes requirements for creation and maintenance of provider networks. (10-16-701 et seq.).

Agents and Brokers.—Soliciting for unauthorized companies is forbidden. (10-3-104). Qualification, pre-licensing education, examination, licensing and continuing education of insurance producers is required. (10-2-201 et seq.). ("Insurance producers" defined in 10-2-103, 10-2-105.) License required for public insurance adjusters. (10-2-417). Commissioner authorized to enter into reciprocal agreements with other states regarding licensing requirements. (10-2-501 et seq.). Commissioner shall set reasonable fees by rule. (10-2-413).

Insurance producers' fiduciary responsibilities relating to premiums set out in 10-2-704. Grounds and procedures for disciplinary actions against insurance producers set out in 10-2-801 et seq.

Reinsurance Intermediary Model Act and Managing General Agents Act adopted. (10-2-901 et seq.; 10-2-1001 et seq.).

Process Agent.—Commissioner must be appointed in writing as attorney for service of process on foreign companies. (10-3-107, 10-14-118).

Investments.—Domestic insurance companies may invest their funds in categories of assets described in Tit. 10, Art. 3. All permitted investments admitted assets except to extent quantitative limitations exceeded. Subject to specific exceptions insurance companies may own nonadmitted assets. (10-3-213[1]). Required to reasonably diversify investments and maintain sufficient degree of liquidity. (10-3-213[2]).

Foreign insurance companies must procure certificate of authority from commissioner. (10-3-105). Insurance agencies must file with commissioner list of individual insurance producers. (10-2-406). Certified copy of charter and financial statement must be filed with commissioner. (10-3-108). Foreign insurer authorized to transact business in Colorado may become domestic insurer. (10-3-125). Certificate of authority required for foreign fraternal benefit society transacting business in state. (10-14-608). No insurance company owned or financially controlled by another state can do business in Colorado except as provided in 10-3-105.

See note at head of Digest as to 1998 legislation covered.

See Topical Index in front part of this volume.

INSURANCE COMPANIES . . . *continued*

Retaliatory Laws.—If state of domicile of insurance company imposes more onerous fees, taxes, etc., than does Colorado, such company may be subject to same in Colorado, except for taxes, if such company maintains a home or regional home office in state. (10-3-209[2]).

Premium Tax.—Insurance companies are taxed on premiums collected or contracted for in this state less reinsurance premiums on Colorado business, amounts refunded under credit life, credit accident and health insurance policies terminated prior to maturity date of indebtedness and (for other than life companies) payments to policyholders as return premiums. Rate of tax is 2.20% for 1996, then reduced by .05% annually until 2000, when rate will remain at 2.00%. (10-3-209). If, however, companies maintain home or regional home offices in state, tax is 1%. If domestic company with its principal place of business in Colorado has 30% of its assets invested in bonds or warrants of Colorado or municipality therein, there is no tax on policies issued prior to 1959 where premium is fixed and contractually binding on company. Section should be consulted for other exceptions. (10-3-209[1]). Insurance companies liable for more than $5,000 in taxes pay quarterly estimates of such taxes. (10-3-209[3]). Fraternal and benevolent associations organized and doing business under Colorado law are exempt from all but real estate and office equipment taxes. (10-14-504).

Insurers' Rehabilitation and Liquidation Model Act.—Provides comprehensive scheme for rehabilitation and liquidation of insurance companies; governs conduct of delinquency proceedings against insurers. (10-3-501 to 559).

Direct Actions Against Insurer.—See category Transportation, topic Motor Vehicles, subhead Direct Actions.

No-Fault Insurance.—See category Transportation, topic Motor Vehicles, subhead No-Fault Insurance.

Plain Language.—See category Business Regulation and Commerce, topic Consumer Protection.

SURETY AND GUARANTY COMPANIES:

Insurance company shall not do business in state unless it possesses specified combined minimum in cash capital or guaranty fund and accumulated surplus in cash or marketable securities. (10-3-201). Foreign companies not maintaining home office or regional home office in state must appoint commissioner of insurance as agent for service of process. (10-3-107).

INTELLECTUAL PROPERTY

TRADEMARKS AND TRADENAMES:

Trademark means any word, name, symbol, device or combination thereof adopted and used to identify goods or services of an individual, firm, partnership, corporation, association, union or other organization and to distinguish them from others. (7-70-101).

Registration.—One who adopts and uses trademark in Colorado may apply for registration on form furnished by secretary of state setting forth at least following: Name and business address of applicant and, if corporation, applicant's state of incorporation; appointment by nonresident applicant or foreign corporation applicant not licensed to do business in Colorado of secretary of state as agent for service of process in any action relating to registration; specification of statutory classes of goods or services; identification of goods or services in connection with which mark is used and mode or manner in which mark is used on those goods or services; date of first use of mark anywhere and date mark was first used in Colorado by applicant or his predecessor; and statement that applicant believes himself to be owner of mark and that no other person has right to use mark in Colorado in identical or confusingly similar form. Application must be signed and verified by applicant or by officer or agent of applicant (or manager or managers of limited liability company) and must be accompanied by specimen or facsimile of mark. Application must be filed in duplicate with payment of fees provided by statute for filing and recording application and for issuing certificate of registration. (7-70-102). Registration is effective for ten years and, upon application within six months prior to expiration of term and payment of renewal fee, may be renewed for like terms. (7-70-104).

Any person who believes he will be damaged by registration of trademark may bring action to cancel registration upon enumerated grounds. Prevailing party in cancellation action may be awarded reasonable attorney's fees. (7-70-108).

Assignment.—Assignable, by instruments in writing, with good will of business. May be filed with secretary of state with required fee. Assignment is void against subsequent purchaser for value unless recorded with secretary of state within three months or prior to subsequent purchase. Registrant changing its name required to file change of name statement with secretary of state and pay statutory filing fee; new certificate of registration reflecting name change will be issued upon request and payment of statutory fee. (7-70-105).

Protection Afforded.—In addition to enforcement of rights acquired at common law (7-70-113), registrant may sue to enjoin manufacture, use, display or sale of counterfeits or imitations of registered mark; court may require payment to owner of profits derived or damages suffered; order surrender for destruction of existing imitations or counterfeits (7-70-112); and in its discretion may award prevailing party reasonable attorney's fees (7-70-111, 112).

Person who uses in Colorado name, mark, or device to indicate ownership of articles or supplies such as coats, aprons, or other garments and towels, table linens, or other kindred articles and supplies designed and intended for reuse in normal course of trade by such person may file with secretary of state verified statement setting forth: Name and business address of person filing statement; nature of its business; and type of articles or supplies in connection with which name, mark, or device is used, accompanied by quadruplicate copies, specimens, or facsimiles of same and payment of fee provided by statute. Secretary of state will then issue certificate to person filing statement reflecting information so filed, which certificate is assignable. Misuse of, failure to return, defacement, or trafficking in articles or supplies upon which name, mark, or

device so filed with secretary of state is used by any person without consent of owner of such supplies or articles constitutes misdemeanor punishable by fine and/or imprisonment. (7-73-101-109).

Tradenames.—Every person, general partnership or other business organization doing business in Colorado under any name other than personal name of its owner or owners must register and annually renew such tradename with department of revenue. Corporations, limited liability companies, general partnerships registered as registered limited liability partnerships and limited partnerships, including limited partnerships registered as limited liability limited partnerships, operating under tradename must register tradename with secretary of state as described below, but not with department of revenue. (24-35-301[1]). Registration with department of revenue includes tradename, address of principal place of business in Colorado, and names and addresses of persons, general partnership, or other business organization doing business under tradename. (24-35-301[2]). Each county clerk and recorder will receive from department of revenue all registrations. (24-35-302). Penalty for failure to comply is fine up to $500 and inability to sue for collection of certain debts. (24-35-303, -304).

Corporation, limited partnership, limited liability company, limited liability partnership or limited liability limited partnership may operate under tradename by filing with secretary of state certificate setting forth: (1) name of entity; (2) location of principal office; (3) tradename; (4) brief description of kind of business to be carried on under tradename. (7-71-101[2]). Tradename submitted to secretary of state shall (1) not be same or deceptively similar to name of any entity on file with secretary of state, any name which has been reserved or registered with secretary of state or corporate or tradename of dissolved corporation during 120 day period following dissolution of such corporation, and (2) not so resemble any non-abandoned trademark registered with secretary of state, that it is likely to cause confusion or mistake or to deceive when used in connection with goods or services of owner of such registered trademark. Secretary of state shall charge and collect fee which is determined and collected in accordance with 24-21-104(3). (7-71-101[5]). Penalty for lack of compliance is inability to prosecute suits for collection of debts, until assumed name certificate is filed. (7-71-102).

Uniform Deceptive Trade Practices Act (1966 Revision) adopted, with numerous variations, omissions, and additional matter. (6-1-101 to 114).

TRADE SECRETS:

Uniform Trade Secrets Act adopted.

LEGAL PROFESSION

ATTORNEYS AND COUNSELORS:

The state bar is not integrated.

Jurisdiction Over Admission.—Supreme court is vested with jurisdiction to admit attorneys to practice of law (12-5-101), and has promulgated Rules Governing Admission to the Bar (Rule 201). Members of bar are appointed to "law committee" and "bar committee" to aid court in passing on applicants. (Rule 201.2).

Eligibility.—No person may be denied license to practice law on account of race or sex. (12-5-102). Applicant must be mentally stable and morally and ethically qualified for admission. (Rule 201.6). Determinations of mental instability or ethical or moral disqualification are reviewed by inquiry panel of bar committee. After 15 days notice, applicants may be interviewed by inquiry panel. Upon written request applicant may appeal adverse determination to formal hearing panel. (Rules 201.7 through 201.10). Membership in professional organization or bar association not prerequisite to licensure. (12-5-101).

Registration as Law Student.—Law student interns may appear and participate in civil and criminal proceedings under certain circumstances. (12-5-116.1 to 116.5; Rule 226).

Classification of Applicants.—Class A: Those who have been admitted to bar of another state, territory or district of U.S. and who have actively practiced for five of seven years immediately preceding application in Colorado. "Practice" includes private practice of law, employment by corporation or other entity, teaching in A.B.A. approved law school, employment by U.S. government, state or political subdivision in position requiring performance of specified legal services, or as judge or similar official, provided such position is available only to lawyer. (Rules 201.3, -.5). Class B: All other applicants. (Rule 201.3).

Educational Requirements.—Class A applicants must have obtained first professional law degree from A.B.A. approved law school. (Rule 201.5[1]). Class B applicants (see subhead Classification of Applicants, supra) must have received by time of written examination first professional law degree from A.B.A. approved law school, or first professional law degree from state approved law school, if applicant is admitted to bar of another state, territory, or district of U.S. and has actively practiced for five of seven years immediately preceding application in Colorado, or first professional law degree from law school in common law, English-speaking nation if applicant is admitted to bar of nation where first professional degree was received and has actually practiced for five of seven years immediately preceding application in Colorado. (Rule 201.5).

Effective July 1, 1992, all Class A and B applicants must have achieved scaled score of at least 85 on Multi-State Professional Responsibility Examination within two years before acceptance of application for admission in Colorado. (Rule 201.5[3]).

Petition for Admission.—Applications must be made on forms furnished by board. (Rule 201.4[1]). They may be obtained from Executive Director, State Board of Law Examiners, 600 Seventeenth Street, Suite 520-S, Denver, CO 80202.

Class B applications must be received or postmarked on or before first day of Dec. preceding Feb. bar exam or on or before first day of May preceding July bar exam. Fees for all applicants to be fixed by court must accompany application and may be paid by cash, bank cashier's check or money order. (Rule 201.4[2], -[3]). Bar committee may require additional evidence of applicant's mental stability and moral and ethical qualifications reasonably related to standards for admission it deems appropriate, including

See note at head of Digest as to 1998 legislation covered.

See Topical Index in front part of this volume.

ATTORNEYS AND COUNSELORS . . . *continued*

current mental status examination. Costs of mental status examination or obtaining additional information required by bar committee borne by applicant. (Rule 201.6).

Examination.—Law committee gives examinations twice a year (in Feb. and July) in Denver. (Rule 201.2). Decision of law committee as to whether examinee has passed or failed bar examination will be final. Beginning 20 days after results are mailed and ending on 60th day thereafter, any unsuccessful examinee will be entitled to inspect examinee's answers to essay portion of examination. No inspection of multi-state bar examination is permitted. (Rule 201.13).

Multi-state bar examination used. Additional local subjects that may be tested are: business associations (including agency, partnership, and corporations), civil procedure, commercial transactions (including Uniform Commercial Code, creditors' rights, and sales), family law, public law (including administrative law and constitutional law), wills, estates, and trusts.

Residency Requirements and Oath.—Applicants must take oath of admission no later than 18 months after approval of application (Class A) or after announcement of passing exam (Class B). (Rule 201.14).

Clerkship.—No requirement for any period of clerkship.

Admission Without Examination.—No examination required for applicants in Class A (see subhead Classification of Applicants, supra). (Rule 201.3[4]). Full-time commissioned officer and U.S. judge advocate stationed in Colorado may be admitted temporarily without exam only for purposes of practice as judge advocate. (Rule 201.3[3]).

Admission Pro Hac Vice.—Attorney from an adjacent state who has business in any court in this state may be admitted on motion for purpose of transacting such business and none other. (12-5-113; Rule 221). But resident attorney, on whom pleadings and other papers may be served, must be associated as attorney of record with any foreign attorney. (Rules 5[b]; 221).

Admission Before State Agencies.—Any attorney in good standing from any other U.S. jurisdiction may be admitted to practice before any state agency at discretion of administrative hearing officer. (Rule 221.1).

License.—No person may practice law without license. (12-5-101). Amount of license fee shall be as prescribed by supreme court under rules for admission to bar. (12-5-103).

Registration Fee.—Every attorney admitted to practice (including judges, those admitted on provisional or temporary basis and those admitted as judge advocate) must pay annual fee of $115 (effective Jan. 1, 99, $195) on or before Feb. 28; provided that fee for attorney during first three years after first admission to practice is $75 (effective Jan. 1, 99, $155). Annual fee for attorney on inactive status $25 (effective Jan. 1, 99, $50). Annual fee is collected by clerk of supreme court. Any attorney who fails to pay required fee is summarily suspended 30 days after mailing of notice of delinquency unless excused on grounds of financial hardship. (Rule 227).

Registration Statement.—All persons required to pay annual registration fee must file on or before Feb. 28 of every year a statement on a form prescribed by clerk, setting forth (a) date of admission to Colorado supreme court, (b) registration number, (c) current residence and office addresses, and (d) such other information as clerk may direct. In addition to statement, every attorney must file supplemental statement of change in information previously submitted within 30 days of such change. (Rule 227).

Attorney who has retired or is not engaged in practice shall file notice in writing that he or she desires to transfer to inactive status and discontinue practice of law. Upon filing such notice, attorney is no longer eligible to practice law but must continue to file required statements annually. Attorney must pay $25 annual fee until age 65. (Rule 227). Attorney need not comply with continuing legal education requirements. (Rule 260.6[11]). Attorney wishing to resume practice must file application, pay registration renewal fee and meet any post-graduate study requirements determined to be applicable. (Rules 227, 260.2[5], 260.6[11]).

Qualification.—An attorney must take oath prescribed by supreme court. (Rule 201.14).

Disabilities.—Attorney may not become surety in any bond authorized by statute to be taken for payment of any sum of money in court in default of principal, without consent of judge of district first having approved such surety. (12-5-117).

Liabilities.—See category Civil Actions and Procedure, topic Costs.

Compensation.—Rules of Professional Conduct require reasonable fees (Rule 1.5[a]), limit fee sharing (Rule 1.5[d]), prohibit referral fees (Rule 1.5[e]), and permit contingent fees in accordance with Colorado Rules of Civil Procedure (Rule 1.5[c]). No contingent fee agreement shall be enforceable unless there has been substantial compliance with Supreme Court Rules governing contingent fees, which, in part, prohibit such agreements in certain classes of cases and require that permissible contingent fee arrangements be reduced to writing. (c. 23.3, Rules Governing Contingent Fees, Rules 1-7).

Lien.—Attorneys have liens upon any money, property, choses in action, claims or demands of their clients in their hands, and on judgments obtained by them, for compensation for professional services; must file notice with clerk of court; after giving such notice lien attaches to moneys due client in hands of adverse party, and also to any papers of clients which have come into their possession in course of employment. This lien is enforceable by proper civil action. (12-5-119, 120).

Disbarment or Suspension.—(Rules 241.1 through 242.26). Rules provide, among other things, for 25-member grievance committee (18 of whom must be members of Colorado Bar), full time committee counsel to be appointed by committee, grounds for discipline and procedure. See also 12-5-108, -114.

Unauthorized Practice.—No person may practice as attorney unless admitted to bar by supreme court and licensed thereby. Unlicensed person who holds himself out as

attorney is guilty of contempt. (12-5-108, 112). Corporations, except professional service corporations (Rule 265), cannot practice law (99 Colo. 50, 59 P.2d 468). Professional corporations and limited liability companies, except professional service companies (Rule 265), cannot practice law. Supreme Court has exclusive jurisdiction to define practice of law and prohibit unauthorized practice. (Rules 228 to 240.1). See also, Rules of Professional Conduct, Rules 5.4(d) and 5.5.

Mandatory Continuing Legal Education.—Attorneys must take 45 "units," as accredited by board of continuing legal education every three years, at least seven units of which must be devoted to legal ethics. Noncomplying attorneys are subject to summary suspension. (Rule 260; but see Rules 260.6[5], [13]). Attorneys admitted to Colorado bar after Jan. 1, 1979, must satisfy "basic legal skills curriculum." (Rule 260.2[3]). All attorneys admitted after Jan. 1, 1995 must satisfy four of the seven-unit ethics requirement during first compliance period by completing required professionalism course presented by Colorado Bar Association. (Rule 260.2[4]).

Professional Service Companies.—Supreme Court Rule permits lawyers licensed to practice in Colorado to form "professional companies" for practice of law under specified conditions. "Professional companies" includes professional corporations, limited liability companies, limited liability partnerships, registered limited liability partnerships, and joint stock companies. Name must contain words "professional company", "professional corporation", "limited liability company", "limited liability partnership", "registered limited liability partnership", or abbreviations thereof that are authorized by law. Officers, directors, shareholders, partners, members, or managers must be duly licensed persons actively engaged in practice of law except as permitted by Supreme Court Rule. Professional company required to carry professional liability insurance. Usual standards of professional conduct apply to professional company and anyone acting on its behalf. (Rule 265).

Attorney Ethics.—Effective Jan. 1, 1993, Supreme Court adopted ABA Model Rules with modifications, titled Colorado Rules of Professional Conduct. Until Jan. 1, 1993, Colorado Code of Professional Responsibility in effect.

MINERAL, WATER AND FISHING RIGHTS

MINES AND MINERALS:

Hardrock mining on federal lands regulated mainly by federal laws, but varied by local law as to acts of location, size of claims, notice and recording. Federal laws may preempt local laws which interfere with party's right to validate claims under federal law. (652 P.2d 1050).

Mineral Estate and Royalties.—Severance of mineral interest creates two separate and distinct freehold estates. (125 Colo. 267, 243 P.2d 412). Conveyance of royalty interest in minerals creates real property interest. (38-30-107.5). Modifies Corlett v. Cox. (138 Colo. 325, 333 P.2d 619). Reservation of overriding royalty interest is real property interest for nonresident tax purposes. (182 Colo. 337, 513 P.2d 208; 886 P.2d 652). Unless otherwise agreed, payments to persons entitled to share of proceeds from oil or gas must begin within six months of first production sold and minimum information which must accompany payments is prescribed by statute. (34-60-118.5).

Lode and placer claims may be located and, by compliance with the law regarding discovery of valuable minerals, location, posting of notice and recording, may be held until mineral patent is applied for by performing annual labor, called "assessment work" or payment of annual claim rental. Amount of assessment work required is $100 per annum for each claim. (34-43-101 to 116; 7 Colo. 443, 4 P. 752). Location of mineral claims other than claims for coal and oil shale may be made upon unleased mineral lands belonging to state subject to additional requirements. (36-1-140).

State-owned minerals, including stone, coal, oil and gas and geothermal resources, may be leased from state board of land commissioners. (36-1-113, 36-1-147).

State Legislation.—Director of division of minerals and geology in department of natural resources is responsible for directing activities of office of active and inactive mines. (34-20-101, 34-21-101 to 110). Annual report detailing production and other information due Jan. 31. (34-24-101). Notification required prior to opening or abandoning mine. (34-24-105). Geothermal resources regulated (37-90.5-101 to 108) and must be specifically mentioned in deed or presumed not included in references to minerals or mineral rights (38-35-121).

Inspection of Mines.—Effective July 1, 1988, inspection of nonproducing mines and mines that are open to public controlled solely by federal legislation, Mine Safety and Health Act, P.L. 95-164. (34-20-101 to 34-25-101). Nonproducing "tourist mine" inspected by office of active and inactive mines. (34-21-110). Certificates of competency required to work certain positions in coal mines issued by coal mine board. (34-22-105). Permit required to store, transport or use explosives and operate diesel machinery underground. (34-24-103). Abandoned workings must be covered or fenced. (34-24-110).

Oil and Gas.—Underground storage of natural gas by gas public utilities is authorized and procedure for condemnation for that purpose provided. (34-64-101 to 107). Oil and gas conservation commission regulates activities of all producers to prevent waste, regulate size of drilling units and protect public health, safety and welfare. (34-60-101 to 126). Counties and home-rule charter municipalities may regulate by laws not in conflict with operation of state regulations or intent of state legislature. (830 P.2d 1045; 830 P.2d 1061). In addition to $75 filing and service fee, conservation charge not to exceed one and one-half mills and environmental response fund charge not to exceed two-tenths of one mill on each dollar of market value of production is payable. (34-60-106[1][f], 34-60-122). Oil and gas may be leased from state through state board of land commissioners. (36-1-113). Oil and gas leases have implied covenants to drill, to develop after discovery, to operate diligently and prudently, including marketing during primary term, and to protect against drainage. (109 Colo. 401, 125 P.2d 964; 808 P.2d 358).

See also generally, "Fuel Products." (8-20-101 to 8-20-414).

Mineral leases which contain options to purchase must so state in title thereof (38-42-101, 103); otherwise lessor may elect to have option voided and nonetheless keep

MINES AND MINERALS . . . *continued*

any money paid for lease (38-42-102). Lessee of recorded mineral lease is obligated to record surrender thereof within 90 days after forfeiture or expiration thereof. (38-42-104). If lessee neglects or refuses to do so, lessor may sue and recover $100 plus costs and attorney's fees. (38-42-105).

Record notice of lessee's interest in oil, gas, or other mineral lease expires six months after expiration of primary or definite term unless lessee has recorded affidavit claiming extension. (38-42-106).

Taxes.—Severance tax instituted on nonrenewable resources. (39-29-101 to 115). Coal, oil and gas, metallic minerals, oil shale, and molybdenum have separate severance taxes imposed in addition to property taxes. (39-29-103 to 107). Tax on gross income derived from production or extraction of crude oil, natural gas, carbon dioxide, and oil and gas from deposits in state levied at rate of 2%, 3%, 4% and 5% respectively for incomes under $25,000; $25,000-99,999; $100,000-299,999; $300,000 and over. (39-29-105[1]). Credit against ad valorem taxes on such resources except oil wells producing less than ten barrels per day average, effective Jan. 1, 1985. (39-29-105[2]). Credit against local government portion of severance tax available for certain taxpayer contributions made to assist local governments in solving impact problems from new mining operations. (39-29-107.5).

Mining surface disturbance subject to control of Colorado Mined Land Reclamation Board and permit requirements. (34-32-101 to 34-33-137). Act amended effective July 1, 1993 to regulate operations using toxic or acidic chemicals for metallurgical extraction or exposing or disturbing acid or toxic forming materials. (34-32-103).

See also category Environment, topic Environmental Regulation.

MORTGAGES

CHATTEL MORTGAGES:

Uniform Commercial Code adopted. Chattel mortgages governed by Art. 9 of Uniform Commercial Code. See category Business Regulation and Commerce, topic Commercial Code.

Manufactured Homes.—Security interest in manufactured (i.e., mobile) home to be effective as valid lien against third persons, must be filed for public record with county clerk and recorder (manager of revenue in City and County of Denver) and noted on certificate of title. (38-29-125[1]; 38-29-128; 38-29-129; 42-1-210). Perfection of security interest in manufactured home held for sale or lease which constitutes inventory as defined in C.R.S. §4-9-109 is governed by provisions of Art. 9 of Uniform Commercial Code. (38-29-125[2]). Mortgage enforceable if certificate of title, whether issued in Colorado or another state, bears adequate notation to apprise purchaser, creditor or mortgagee of existence of mortgage at time third person acquires right in manufactured home. (38-29-127). Priority of mortgages governed by first-to-file rule. (38-29-134). If mortgagee repossesses manufactured home, must notify law enforcement agency within 12 hours (police department, town marshall or other local law enforcement agency if repossession takes place in incorporated city or town, and county sheriff if repossession takes place in unincorporated area) of fact of repossession, identity of owner and identity of mortgagee or assignee. (38-29-142).

Motor Vehicles.—See category Transportation, topic Motor Vehicles, subhead Liens, for requirement as to perfection of security interest in motor vehicle.

Execution and Requisites.—Governed by Art. 9, Uniform Commercial Code. (4-9-203; 4-9-402). See category Business Regulation and Commerce, topic Commercial Code.

Filing.—Art. 9 of Uniform Commercial Code governs necessity (4-9-302) and place (4-9-401) of filing.

Forms.—Forms following and at end of this Digest have either been approved by Secretary of State and County Clerk and Recorders Association or have been suggested for use.

Form

Security Agreement.—
Debtor:
  Name: . . . .
  Address:
    Residence . . . .
          No.   Street   City   State
    Business . . . .
          No.   Street   City   State
Secured Party:
  Name: . . . .
  Address: . . . .
          No.   Street   City   State

Debtor, for consideration, hereby grants to Secured Party a security interest in the following property and any and all additions, accessions and substitutions thereto or therefor (hereinafter called the "COLLATERAL"): . . . . To secure payment of the indebtedness evidenced by . . . . certain promissory note . . . of even date herewith, payable to the Secured Party, or order, as follows: . . . .
DEBTOR EXPRESSLY WARRANTS AND COVENANTS:

1. That except for the security interest granted hereby Debtor is, or to the extent that this agreement states that the Collateral is to be acquired after the date hereof, will be, the owner of the Collateral free from any adverse lien, security interest or encumbrances; and that Debtor will defend the Collateral against all claims and demands of all persons at anytime claiming the same or any interest therein.

2. The Collateral is used or bought primarily for:
☐ Personal, family or household purposes;
☐ Use in farming operations;
☐ Use in business.

3. That Debtor's residence is as stated above, and the Collateral will be kept at . . . .
No. and Street   City   County   State

4. If any of the Collateral is crops, oil, gas, or minerals to be extracted or timber to be cut, or goods which are or are to become fixtures, said Collateral concerns the following described real estate situate in the . . . . County of . . . . and State of Colorado, to wit:

5. Not to sell, transfer or dispose of the Collateral, and promptly to notify Secured Party of any change in the location of the Collateral within the State of Colorado and not to remove the same from the State of Colorado without the prior written consent of the Secured Party.

6. To pay all taxes and assessments of every nature which may be levied or assessed against the Collateral.

7. Not to permit or allow any adverse lien, security interest or encumbrance whatsoever upon the Collateral and not to permit the same to be attached or replevined.

8. That the Collateral is in good condition, and that he will, at his own expense, keep the same in good condition and from time to time, forthwith, replace and repair all such parts of the Collateral as may be broken, worn out, or damaged without allowing any lien to be created upon the Collateral on account of such replacement or repairs, and that the Secured Party may examine and inspect the Collateral at any time, wherever located.

9. That he will not use the Collateral in violation of any applicable statutes, regulations or ordinances.

UNTIL DEFAULT Debtor may have possession of the Collateral and use it in any lawful manner, and upon default Secured Party shall have the immediate right to the possession of the Collateral.

DEBTOR SHALL BE IN DEFAULT under this agreement upon the happening of any of the following events or conditions:

(a) default in the payment or performance of any obligation, covenant or liability contained or referred to herein or in any note evidencing the same;

(b) the making or furnishing of any warranty, representation or statement to Secured Party by or on behalf of Debtor which proves to have been false in any material respect when made or furnished;

(c) loss, theft, damage, destruction, sale or encumbrance to or of any of the Collateral, or the making of any levy, seizure or attachment thereof or thereon;

(d) death, dissolution, termination of existence, insolvency, business failure, appointment of a receiver of any part of the property of, assignment for the benefit of creditors by, or the commencement of any proceeding under any bankruptcy or insolvency laws of, by or against Debtor or any guarantor or surety for Debtor.

UPON SUCH DEFAULT and at any time thereafter, or if it deems itself insecure, Secured Party may declare all Obligations secured hereby immediately due and payable and shall have the remedies of a secured party under Article 9 of the Colorado Uniform Commercial Code. Secured Party may require Debtor to assemble the Collateral and deliver or make it available to Secured Party at a place to be designated by Secured Party which is reasonably convenient to both parties. Expenses of retaking, holding, preparing for sale, selling or the like shall include Secured Party's reasonable attorney's fees and legal expenses.

No waiver by Secured Party of any default shall operate as a waiver of any other default or of the same default on a future occasion. The taking of this security agreement shall not waive or impair any other security said Secured Party may have or hereafter acquire for the payment of the above indebtedness, nor shall the taking of any such additional security waive or impair this security agreement; but said Secured Party may resort to any security it may have in the order it may deem proper, and notwithstanding any collateral security, Secured Party shall retain its rights of setoff against Debtor.

All rights of Secured Party hereunder shall inure to the benefit of its successors and assigns; and all promises and duties of Debtor shall bind his heirs, executors or administrators or his or its successors or assigns. If there be more than one Debtor, their liabilities hereunder shall be joint and several.

Dated this . . . . day of . . . ., 19. . .
Debtor:

. . . .
. . . .

MORTGAGES OF PERSONAL PROPERTY:

See topic Chattel Mortgages.

MORTGAGES OF REAL PROPERTY:

Mortgages and deeds of trust to private trustee or that secure obligations other than evidence of debt may be foreclosed only through courts. (38-39-101). Most common security instrument is deed of trust to public trustee which may be foreclosed by public trustee under statutory procedure (38-38-101) or through courts. Sale by public trustee also requires legal holder of indebtedness to obtain order authorizing sale from courts. (38-38-105; Rule 120). Public trustees are appointed for all first and second class counties and in all other counties county treasurer is public trustee. (38-37-102).

Foreclosure through public trustee is available if obligation secured is evidence of debt, such as note or bond (38-39-101), but release may not be granted unless original cancelled note or statutory substitute is delivered to public trustee (38-39-102). (See subhead Release, infra.)

Execution.—Mortgages must be signed by obligor or attorney-in-fact, but seals and witnesses are unnecessary. (38-30-118). Powers of attorney must be acknowledged and recorded. (38-30-123). Although mortgages and deeds of trust by corporation need not bear corporate seal to be valid, seal is customary. Acknowledgment is not necessary for validity but is necessary for presumption of proper execution (38-35-101[3]) and, together with recording, for presumption of due delivery (38-35-101[4]).

Recording.—Recording is necessary for validity as against persons with any kind of rights except those who are parties to unrecorded instrument or who have notice thereof

See note at head of Digest as to 1998 legislation covered.

See Topical Index in front part of this volume.

MORTGAGES OF REAL PROPERTY . . . *continued*
prior to acquiring their rights. (38-35-109[1]). Recording may be done at any time but is notice to third parties without other notice only from date of recording. Recording statute classified as race-notice. (38-35-109[1]). Recording must be in office of clerk and recorder in county where property is located. (38-35-109[1]). Instruments conveying title to state or political subdivision must be recorded in office of clerk and recorder in county where property is located within 30 days of conveyance. (38-35-109.5). If instrument may be filed by law, filing in office of county clerk and recorder where property is situated is equivalent to recording. (38-35-109[1]).

Recording Fees.—Recording fee is $5 per page. (30-1-103[1]).

Taxes.—None.

Trust Deeds.—Deeds of trust to public trustee are commonly used instead of mortgages because they may be foreclosed under power of sale as well as through judicial foreclosure. Because delivery of original evidence of debt, such as note or bond, is required for release, is imperative that owner of debt retain original. See subheads Release; Foreclosure; Forms; infra. Public trustee has no responsibility for determining amount or reasonableness of bid at foreclosure sale, allowable costs and expenses, amount necessary for reinstating loan or redeeming property, or description of property in partial release. (38-37-104[4]).

Future Advances.—No statutory restrictions but instrument must refer to same.

Priorities.—Rule in Colorado is first in time, first in right except as modified by recording statute that unrecorded encumbrance is not notice to any person with any kind of rights who first records, unless person is party or has notice prior to acquiring his rights. (38-35-109[1]). Colorado rule may be supplemented or avoided by agreements between secured parties as to priority. (620 P.2d 58).

Subordination Agreements.—No statutory restriction.

Assignment.—See category Debtor and Creditor, topic Assignments.

Release.—Mortgage shall be released by separate instrument of release executed with formality required for conveyances. (38-39-104). Deed of trust to public trustee shall be released by filing with public trustee written request for release signed and acknowledged by owner of evidence of debt and accompanied by original or certified copy of deed of trust and original cancelled evidence of debt. (38-39-102). If original evidence of debt cannot be produced, public trustee may accept corporate surety bond, indemnification agreement from title insurance company, or indemnification agreement together with certified resolution from certain enumerated financial institutions indemnifying it against damages resulting from release. (38-39-102[3]). If original evidence of debt cannot be produced and owner of evidence of debt is member of group of certain enumerated financial institutions, public trustee may accept from such owner certification contained in request for release or partial release to effect that such owner is such financial institution, that original evidence of debt is not being produced, and that owner agrees that it is obligated to indemnify public trustee. (38-39-102[3.5]). Public trustee's fee for execution and acknowledgment of release is $10 (38-37-104[1]) and fee for recording release is $5 per page (30-1-103). Same procedure is followed for partial release of deed of trust except that evidence of debt is not cancelled. If purpose of deed of trust has been partially or fully satisfied but indebtedness has not been paid, then release may be obtained by exhibition of original evidence of debt or statutory substitute and statement on request for release that purpose of deed of trust has been partially or fully satisfied. (38-39-102[2]).

Satisfaction.—Satisfaction of mortgage may be entered only by separate release deed or instrument of release executed with formalities required of conveyance. (38-39-104).

Discharge.—See subhead Release, supra.

Foreclosure.—Foreclosure under deed of trust to public trustee is initiated by legal holder of indebtedness electing to enforce instrument by declaring violation of any covenant of deed of trust and filing with public trustee two executed copies of written notice of election and demand for sale signed by legal holder of indebtedness or attorney or agent with original evidence of debt, such as note or bond, or bond in amount one and one-half times face value of evidence of debt, original or certified copy of deed of trust, certificate executed by beneficiary under deed of trust or legal holder of indebtedness secured, or agent or attorney for such beneficiary or holder which states name and address of current owner of property to best knowledge of person executing such certificate, affidavit of principal balance due and list of names and addresses to which all notices required by statute must be mailed. (38-38-101). Public trustee shall advertise premises for sale in accordance with terms of sale specified in deed of trust (38-38-101[4]), and shall, within ten days, record notice of election and demand for sale (38-38-101[3]). Period of advertising notice of sale is four weeks (once each week for five successive weeks) in newspaper of general circulation in county where property is situated, unless longer period of advertising is provided in deed of trust. (38-38-101[6]). If county where property is located has no newspaper of general circulation, then newspaper printed wholly or partially in adjoining county and having general circulation in county where property is located may be used. (24-70-103). Foreclosure sale must be held not less than 45 days and not more than 60 days (or such longer period as provided in deed of trust) after recording notice of election and demand for sale with county clerk and recorder, unless extended in accordance with statute. (38-38-108). Within ten days after first publication of notice, public trustee shall mail printed copy of notice to grantor of deed of trust and to each person who has acquired interest in property subsequent to recordation of deed of trust. (38-38-101[7][a]). Such notice need only be given to grantor and other parties of record and is good against all others claiming through grantor even if indebtedness is claim against estate of deceased or incompetent. (38-38-505). Beneficiary may cause foreclosure sale date to be postponed. Postponement of foreclosure sale postpones statutory deadlines for cure. (661 P.2d 1161; see subhead Right to Cure, infra.) Beneficiary may terminate foreclosure proceedings by filing written withdrawal of notice of election and demand for sale, which shall be recorded. (38-38-101[11]). All costs of foreclosure shall be borne by grantor. (38-38-107). Excess proceeds of sale shall be held in escrow by public trustee during redemption period (38-38-111, see subhead Redemption, infra) and then paid first to last redeeming lienor up to amount due on such lien and balance to junior lienors who have duly filed intent to redeem in order of priority and finally to owner of record as of day of sale if owner claims excess within five years or, if he does not, to county general fund (38-38-111[2]). Public trustee sale may be enjoined where amount and priority of claims in dispute. (Rules 105 and 120; 626 P.2d 724). Fees payable to public trustee are fixed by statute. (38-37-104).

Foreclosure under mortgage is largely matter of contract, subject to applicable court rules and statutes. In action to foreclose mortgage, court may adjudicate and determine rights, titles, interests, claims and demands adverse and paramount to such mortgage or remove clouds from title to mortgaged property. (Rule 105[a]). Person claiming under or through named defendant need be made party only if his interest is shown of record or he is in actual possession and action seeks recovery of possession. (Rule 105[b]).

Person who has filed pleading seeking affirmative relief affecting title to real property may file notice of lis pendens in office of recorder of county where property is located, containing names of parties and describing claim made and property, and lis pendens shall be constructive notice from time of its filing to 45 days from earlier of entry of final judgment in trial court or entry of order determining that property will not be affected by judgment on issues then pending. (Rule 105[f]). If timely notice of appeal filed while lis pendens in effect, lis pendens remains in effect until otherwise ordered. (Rule 105[f][4]).

All foreclosures require court order authorizing sale under power of sale which may be satisfied by motion and order under Rule 120. Verified motion requesting such court order which describes instrument containing power of sale and property and specifies default or other facts claimed to justify invocation of power of sale, and to which copy of instrument is attached shall be filed with district court. If obligation secured by deed of trust is not consumer obligation as defined in Rule 120(f), proceeding may be heard in any county. (Rule 120[f]). Motion shall also state to lienor's knowledge and belief names of each person who has interest in property and who would be materially affected by order with his last known address. If power is contained in deed of trust to public trustee, then motion need state only names and addresses of grantor and current record owner, of those with record interest in property prior to recording of notice of election and demand for sale but subsequent to recording of deed of trust, and of persons believed to be personally liable on indebtedness. Hearing shall be set not less than seven days before sale date (661 P.2d 1161), and movant shall serve notice on persons named. Any interested person who disputes movant's entitlement to order authorizing sale may file and serve response verified by oath. (Rule 120[c]). Scope of inquiry in Rule 120 proceeding is limited to existence of default or other circumstances authorizing exercise of power of sale and other issues required by Soldiers' and Sailors' Relief Act of 1940, as amended. (Rule 120[d]). Court may consider all relevant evidence, including possible oral modification of written loan instruments, to determine whether there is reasonable probability that default exists. (665 P.2d 613). Scope of court's inquiry does not include determination of amount or whether attorneys' fees can be recovered. (662 P.2d 483). Court shall summarily grant or deny motion upon determination of reasonable probability of default and propriety of sale and shall approve it if sale was conducted in conformity with order. Action for wrongful foreclosure not governed by foreclosure statute of limitations. (620 P.2d 56).

Mortgage payable in installments may be wholly or partially foreclosed as to any one or more past due installments plus sums advanced for taxes, insurance, liens, assessments or similar charges, but no more than one partial foreclosure proceeding may be brought in any 12-month period. (38-38-201).

Attorneys' fees in any foreclosure action based upon one or more past due installments without declaring whole amount due may not exceed 10% of sum for which property is foreclosed. (38-38-201[1][a]). Foreclosure does not affect lien of mortgage for balance of obligation. (38-38-201[1][g]). Holder of indebtedness may exercise acceleration option in mortgage notwithstanding partial foreclosure. (38-38-201[2]).

Redemption from sale under court order is governed by same rules as redemption from execution sale. (38-38-301).

Right to Cure.—When default is nonpayment, owner or party liable on indebtedness may cure by filing written notice of intention to cure with officer conducting sale at least seven days prior to sale and by paying all delinquent principal and interest (exclusive of accelerated amounts), costs, expenses, late charges, attorney and other fees incurred by holder of indebtedness in connection with foreclosure to such officer by noon on day before date of sale. (38-38-104). When default is failure to furnish balance sheets or tax returns, default may be cured by providing required balance sheets, tax returns or other adequate evidence of financial condition provided all sums currently due under evidence of debt have been paid and all costs, expenses, late charges, attorney and other fees incurred by holder of indebtedness in connection with foreclosure are paid. (38-38-104). If deed of trust or mortgage being foreclosed was recorded on or after Oct. 1, 1990, any holder of interest junior to lien being foreclosed shall be entitled to cure. (38-38-104). Notice of this right shall be mailed to grantor and owners of property within ten days after recording notice of election and demand for sale if instrument showing their interest was recorded subsequent to recording of deed of trust but prior to recording of notice of election and demand for sale. (38-38-103). Where suit is brought on promissory note alone and not to foreclose, debtor has no statutory or equitable right to cure default. (597 P.2d 1043). Debtor may exercise right to cure more than once. (612 P.2d 1149).

Sales.—Anyone purchasing land under foreclosure sale of trust deeds or mortgages or sale under execution or order of court and who has received certificate of purchase may pay any special or general taxes, ditch or water assessments, insurance premiums, interest, costs and expenses of defending, protecting and maintaining property and holder's interest therein, and sums due on prior lien or encumbrance and, upon filing receipts with officer making sale, shall have additional claim against lands sold which is added to amount due on redemption. (38-38-301; 38-38-302).

Within ten working days after later of expiration of all redemption periods or receipt of certificate of purchase or certificate of redemption and all statutory fees, public trustee or sheriff shall deliver deed to holder of certificate of purchase or lienor last redeeming, confirming sale. (38-38-501). Any deed executed by officer conducting sale is prima facie evidence of compliance with all statutory requirements for sale, of execution of deed and of recitals contained in deed. (38-38-504).

See note at head of Digest as to 1998 legislation covered.

See Topical Index in front part of this volume.

CO – 61

MORTGAGES OF REAL PROPERTY . . . *continued*

Holder of any debt secured by deed of trust being foreclosed, or his attorney or agent, may submit bid to public trustee in writing instead of appearing personally to buy property at sale. Bid, substantially in form prescribed by statute, must be received by public trustee before 12:00 noon on or before day prior to sale and be signed by debt holder or his attorney or agent. (38-38-106).

Title vests in grantee of sheriff's or trustee's deed free and clear of all liens and encumbrances recorded or filed subsequent to recording or filing of lien on which foreclosure sale is based. (38-38-501).

Certificate of purchase may be assigned by endorsement. (38-38-403). Receiver may be appointed to preserve property pending foreclosure of mortgage or deed of trust if security clearly inadequate or premises in danger of being materially injured or reduced in value as security by removal, destruction, deterioration, accumulation of prior liens or otherwise. (38-38-601[1]). Foreclosure sale through court action or public trustee shall be held not less than 45 days after commencement of foreclosure action. (38-38-108).

Deficiency Judgments.—No statutory restriction.

Moratorium.—None.

Redemption.—Notice of redemption rights must be given to grantor of trust deed or mortgage, subsequent owners of record, persons who might be liable for deficiency, and persons having right to redeem as shown by interest recorded subsequent to recording of deed of trust and prior to recording of notice of election and demand for sale. (38-38-103). Owner or any person liable on deficiency may redeem premises within 75 days after sale under mortgage, trust deed or other lien or execution and levy, or six months for agricultural real estate (defined as not platted for subdivision or not located within incorporated town, city or city and county, or not valued and assessed as agricultural land), by payment of sum for which property sold and interest from date of sale at default rate specified in instrument and taxes and other charges paid. (38-38-302).

In appropriate circumstances, extension of statutory period of redemption is within equity powers of court, even after redemption period has expired and public trustee's deed or sheriff's deed has issued. (665 P.2d 613). If owner redeems, sale is annulled and premises remain subject to all liens which would have existed absent sale except discharge of lien of foreclosed deed of trust or mortgage. (38-38-304[1]). If redemption is made by person liable on deficiency on foreclosed lien, then sale is annulled and person so redeeming shall own lien redeemed to its full extent including costs he paid, and person redeeming remains liable for deficiency. (38-38-304[2]). If owner does not redeem, then junior encumbrancers or lienors may redeem in succession according to priority of lien within five days each (ten days in case of senior most junior encumbrancer or lienor) by payment of amounts owner paid or would have paid to redeem, or redemption amounts previously paid with interest, and amounts of all liens prior to his. (38-38-303[1]). Lienors and encumbrancers may redeem only if they file notice of intention to redeem with officer conducting sale and lien appears of record prior to expiration of owner's period of redemption. (38-38-303[2]). Last lienor redeeming shall receive payment from escrow of proceeds not to exceed amount of his lien and excess proceeds shall be paid to owner of record as of date of foreclosure sale. (38-38-306). If lienor redeems, his recorded certificate of redemption acts as assignment to him of estate and interest acquired by purchaser at sale subject to rights of persons entitled to redeem subsequently. (38-38-304[3]).

Lessee is considered lienor and, if subsequent lienor redeems from lessee then he takes subject to lease. (38-38-305). Judgment creditor has no right to redeem unless judgment is made lien of record. (38-38-306).

Duration of Lien.—No lien created by mortgage, deed of trust or other written instrument securing payment of indebtedness shall remain longer than 15 years after final principal payment was due and payable as shown by such recorded instrument and thereafter shall have no more effect than unrecorded instrument (38-39-201) unless extended by recordation within 15-year period of written instrument signed by beneficiary, owner or legal holder of indebtedness describing mortgage and date to which it is extended (38-39-202). Recording date considered due date if instrument recorded is silent. (38-39-201). Extension is limited to maximum of 30 years beyond original maturity date. (38-39-202[2]). Recordation of notice of pending foreclosure proceedings extends period until final disposition of proceedings. (38-39-204). Once lien has expired, public trustee and other officers of state have no authority to act and no foreclosure action may be brought. (38-39-205). Lien is also extinguished when right to bring action to enforce payment of underlying obligation is barred. (38-39-207). Statute of limitations on promissory note is six years and runs from date of maturity (13-80-108[4]; 48 P. 276) or, in case of demand note, date of execution (705 P.2d 533).

No action to question or set aside any foreclosure where purchaser took possession may be maintained after seven years from date of deed issued pursuant to foreclosure. (38-29-208).

Action for wrongful foreclosure not governed by foreclosure statute of limitations. (620 P.2d 56).

Unreasonable Restraint on Alienation.—Following practices are prohibited by statute when applied to real property utilized as residential dwelling units except motels, hotels or nursing homes (38-30-165): Acceleration of maturity of indebtedness on sale or transfer of real estate or on assumption of indebtedness unless transferee is reasonably determined to be financially incapable of retiring indebtedness; increase of interest rate more than 1% per annum on occurrence of such events except that such limitations do not apply to federally chartered savings and loans (502 F. Supp. 658); charge, collect or attempt to collect fee greater than $^1/_2$ of 1% of outstanding principal amount not including charges appertaining to sale; or enforcement of any provisions in mortgage, deed of trust or real estate security instrument executed on or after July 1, 1975 which are contrary to these prohibitions. (38-30-165[1]). Security interests excepted from this section are those in which indebtedness is matured by secretary of department of housing and urban development on multiple-family housing projects in accordance with federal housing administration regulations and those interests held by one not regularly engaged in business of making real estate loans. (38-30-165[4], [5]). If party assuming indebtedness declines to agree to increased interest rate, he may prepay indebtedness without penalty or increased interest within 60 days after assumption; if he does not timely make such prepayment, he thereafter must proceed in accordance with increased interest rate from date of assumption and prepayment term in instrument of indebtedness. (38-30-165[6]). Except as provided by 38-30-165, due-on-sale provisions are per se reasonable restraints on alienation. (661 P.2d 257).

Forms.—Statutory short form of mortgage is as follows:

Forms

. . . ., whose address is . . . ., County of . . . . and State of . . . . hereby mortgages to . . . ., whose address is . . . ., County of . . . . and State of . . . ., to secure the payment of . . . . dollars, due as follows: . . . . the following described real property in the County of . . . ., and State of Colorado, to wit: . . . . with all its appurtenances, and warrants the title to the same subject to . . . . .

Signed this . . . . day of . . . . 19. . . . . (38-30-117[1]).

Such mortgage should be acknowledged. (See category Documents and Records, topic Acknowledgments.) Street address of encumbered property and current mailing address of grantor and grantee (or beneficiary of deed of trust) should appear on face of instrument and assessor's schedule or parcel number may appear, but failure to state address, assessor's schedule or parcel number, county or state of residence or current mailing address of grantor or grantee does not affect validity. (38-30-117[2], 38-35-122, 38-35-123[2]).

Every such mortgage when properly executed is a mortgage to secure the payment of the moneys therein specified, and if it contains the words, "and warrants the title to the same," it is construed as warranting covenants of seisin, right to convey, against encumbrances except as stated in instrument, and quiet enjoyment (38-30-113[2]); but if the words, "and warrant the title to the same," are omitted, no such covenants are implied. (38-30-117[3]).

There are many forms of public trustee deeds depending upon circumstances. Following is one form which is occasionally used with variations containing addition of waiver of homestead and provision for receivership in case of default.

This Indenture, made this . . . . day of . . . ., 19. . . ., between . . . ., whose address is . . . . County of . . . ., State of Colorado, part . . . . of the first part, and the Public Trustee of the . . . . County of . . . ., State of Colorado, party of the second part, Witnesseth:

That Whereas, The part. . . . of the first part ha. . . . executed . . . .h. . . . promissory note . . . . bearing even date herewith, for the . . . . principal sum of . . . . Dollars, payable to the order of . . . ., whose address is . . . ., on or before . . . ., with interest thereon from date until maturity at the rate of . . . .% per annum, interest payable. . . .

And Whereas, The said part. . . . of the first part . . . . desirous of securing said promissory note . . . . in whose hands soever the said note may be.

Now Therefore, The said part. . . . of the first part for the purpose aforesaid, do . . . . hereby grant, bargain, sell, and convey unto said Public Trustee the following described property situate in the . . . . County of . . . ., State of Colorado, to-wit:

To have and to hold in trust nevertheless that in case of default (specify as appropriate), the beneficiary hereunder or the legal holder of the indebtedness secured hereby may declare a violation of any of the covenants herein contained and elect to advertise said property for sale and demand such sale, then, upon filing notice of such election and demand for sale with the Trustee, who shall upon receipt of such notice of election and demand for sale cause a copy of the same to be recorded in the recorder's office of the county in which said real estate is situated, it shall and may be lawful for the Trustee to sell and dispose of the same at public auction at the (specify) door of the Court House in the County of (specify), State of Colorado, for the highest and best price the same will bring in cash, four weeks' public notice having been previously given of the time and place of such sale, by advertisement, weekly, in some newspaper of general circulation at that time published in said county of (specify) (insert covenants and agreements, if any, as: seisin; against encumbrances; for insurance; taxes, expenses of release; attorneys' fees in case of foreclosure; and option of beneficiary that debt become due on default or breach of covenant).

In Witness Whereof, The said party . . . . of the first part has . . . . hereunto set . . . . hand. . . . and seal. . . . the day and year first above written.

Form of Release.—A form of release of a deed of trust in common use is as follows:

Know All Men by These Presents, That whereas, ... of the County of . . . ., State of Colorado, by . . . . certain Deed of Trust, dated the . . . . day of . . . ., 19. . . ., and duly recorded in the office of the County Clerk and Recorder of . . . . County, State of Colorado, on the . . . . day of . . . ., 19. . . ., in book . . . . of said . . . . County Records, on page . . . . conveyed to the Public Trustee in said . . . . County, certain real estate in said Deed of Trust described, in trust to secure the payment of indebtedness referred to therein.

And Whereas, The said . . . . has . . . . paid and fully satisfied said note . . . ., together with all interest and charges thereon, according to . . . . tenor:

Now, Therefore, At the request of the legal holder of the indebtedness secured by said Deed of Trust, and in consideration of the premises, and the payment of the statutory sum, the receipt of which is hereby acknowledged, I . . . . as the public Trustee in said . . . . County, do hereby remise, release and quitclaim unto . . . . the said . . . . and . . . . heirs and assigns forever, all the right, title and interest which I have in and to the said real estate, as such Public Trustee, in said Deed of Trust mentioned, and more particularly described as follows: to-wit: . . . . situate, lying and being in the County of . . . ., State of Colorado.

To Have and to Hold the Same, Together with all and singular the privileges and appurtenances unto the said . . . . heirs and assigns forever. And further, that the said Trust Deed is, by these presents, to be considered as fully and absolutely released, cancelled and forever discharged.

Witness my hand and seal, this . . . . day of . . . ., 19. . . . .

. . . .

As the Public Trustee in said . . . . County.

. . . . as the Public Trustee in said . . . . County.

Please execute this release, the indebtedness secured by the above mentioned Deed of Trust having been fully paid.

. . . .

See note at head of Digest as to 1998 legislation covered.

See Topical Index in front part of this volume.

MORTGAGES OF REAL PROPERTY . . . *continued*

(To be signed and acknowledged by the legal holder of the indebtedness secured by said deed of trust).

The same form may be used for a release of a mortgage by substituting "Mortgage" for "Deed of Trust", by substituting name of mortgagee for references to Public Trustee and by omitting request to Public Trustee to execute release.

Partial Release of Deed of Trust.—Form in common use is identical to Release of Deed of Trust except for addition of "And whereas, by the terms of said Deed of Trust partial releases are to be made from time to time upon certain conditions as in said Deed of Trust set forth, and whereas, said conditions have been performed as to the real estate hereinafter described."

Chattel Mortgages.—See topic Chattel Mortgages.

Homestead Exemption.—See category Debtor and Creditor, topic Homesteads.

Uniform Consumer Credit Code.—See category Business Regulation and Commerce, topic Consumer Credit.

Public Trustee Sale Bid.—Written bids submitted in public trustee sales must itemize all amounts due under note and deed of trust and all allowable expenses, including appraisal fees, attorney fees and costs, and are required to be substantially in following form:

BID

To: _____
Public Trustee of the County of ____, State of Colorado.
Date: _____
____ whose mailing address is ____ bids the sum of $__ in your Sale No. __ at the Public Trustee's Sale to be held on the __ day of ___, 19_.

The following is an itemization of all amounts due to the owner of the evidence of debt secured by the [deed of trust][mortgage] [lien] being foreclosed.

Principal	$_____
Interest	_____
Late Charges	_____
Less Impound Account Credit	_____
Plus Impound Account Deficiency	_____
Title or Abstracting Charges	_____
Docket Fee	_____
Appraisal Fee	_____
Postage	_____
Photocopies	_____
Attorney Fees	_____
Telephone Charges	_____
Other [Describe the nature of such costs or expenses]:	_____
Total Due Holder	_____
Public Trustee's Fee and Costs	_____
Total	_____
Bid	_____
Deficiency	_____

I enclose herewith the following:
1. Order Authorizing Sale.
2. Check to your order in the sum of $__ covering the balance of your fees.
3. Other: _____.
Please send us the following:
1. Original Certificate of Purchase.[1]
2. Promissory Note (cancelled or with deficiency noted thereon).[1]
3. Refund Check for overpayment of Public Trustee costs if any.
4. Other:

(Name of Foreclosing Party, agent, or attorney)

By _____
Address _____
Telephone _____
Footnote [1] Delete as case may be.

PROPERTY

ABSENTEES:

There is no general provision affecting rights or liabilities of absentees or nonresidents. For particular related provisions, see following: categories Business Organizations, topic Corporations; Civil Actions and Procedure, topics Limitation of Actions, Process; Debtor and Creditor, topic Attachment; Estates and Trusts, topics Death, Executors and Administrators; Family, topic Husband and Wife; Transportation, topic Motor Vehicles.

Care of Property.—See category Family, topic Guardian and Ward.

Process Agent.—Secretary of state is agent for nonresident corporations unless corporation appoints or maintains agent in state. (7-9-119). Secretary of state is agent for limited partnership unless limited partnership appoints or maintains agent in state. (7-62-108, 909). Secretary of state is agent for limited liability partnership and limited liability limited partnership unless same appoint or maintain agent in state. (7-60-144, 7-64-1002[5]). Process may be served via certified or registered mail, sent directly to principal office of limited liability company, unless limited liability company appoints or maintains agent in state. (7-80-306[2]). Owners of lands registered under Torrens Title Registration Act must appoint agent residing in state. (38-36-114).

Escheat.—Uniform Unclaimed Property Act adopted with modifications, effective July 1, 1987. (38-13-101 to 134). If there is no known qualified taker of interest in decedent's estate, personal representative reduces interest to cash and that interest is held by state treasurer for 21 years, subject to claims of persons legally entitled to it. (15-12-914[1]). At end of 21 year period, interest becomes property of state. (15-12-914[3]). Any person, corporation or other entity holding unclaimed moneys in fiduciary capacity may pay such moneys to state treasurer to be held in same manner, such payment discharging such person from further liability. (15-12-914[2]). Dividends remaining unclaimed after approval of final report of liquidation of savings and loan association may be transferred to commissioner of savings and loan associations, who may elect, after six years, to pay such dividends over to state treasurer to be held for 21 years prior to escheat. (11-41-132).

Voting.—Any registered elector who expects to be absent from precinct or unable to attend polls may cast absentee voter's ballot. (1-8-101 to 128). In absence of claim of fraud, undue influence, or intentional wrongdoing in election, standard in determining validity of absent voter ballots is whether absent voter affidavits substantially comply with statutory requirements for absentee voting. (670 P.2d 749).

ADVERSE POSSESSION:

Character of Possession.—Possession must be actual, adverse, hostile, under claim of right, exclusive and uninterrupted for statutory period. (164 Colo. 278, 434 P.2d 414). However, if claimant is in actual possession of land under claim and color of title, made in good faith, and pays all legally assessed taxes and both possession and payment of all legally assessed taxes continue for seven successive years (38-41-108) or if lands are vacant and unoccupied and claimant pays all legally assessed taxes for seven successive years and holds color of title in good faith (38-41-109), then claimant acquires legal ownership to extent of his paper title. Possession may be tacked where there is privity of possession. (38-41-108, 109; 116 Colo. 221, 179 P.2d 671). Possession necessary to establish title to property need not always be personal possession, but may be established by conduct of another authorized by adverse claimant. (635 P.2d 926). Execution of written agreement acknowledging exclusive title and right to use in another prior to running of applicable statute of limitations constitutes fatal interruption of period of adverse possession. (628 P.2d 166). Standard of proof is "preponderance" of evidence. (13-25-127[1]; 768 P.2d 701). No adverse possession of property owned by state, county, city or municipality. (38-41-101[2]). Adverse possession of surface is not adverse possession of severed mineral estate. (119 Colo. 561, 206 P.2d 600).

Duration of Possession.—Title may be obtained by 18 successive years of adverse possession without color of title (38-41-101) or after seven years of possession under color of title made in good faith and payment of all legally assessed taxes for seven successive years, to extent of paper title (38-41-108) or after seven years of payment of legally assessed taxes and color of title held in good faith for vacant and unoccupied lands, to extent of paper title (38-41-109).

Easements.—Easements may be obtained by adverse possession for 18 years. (116 Colo. 221, 179 P.2d 671). Possession may be tacked. (152 Colo. 342, 382 P.2d 191). Solar easement cannot be acquired by prescription. (38-32.5-101). All roads over private lands used adversely without interruption or objection for more than 20 years become public highways. (43-2-201[1][c]). Mere footpath across unenclosed vacant lands in urban area is not public highway. (687 P.2d 1299).

Title to property acquired by adverse possession matures into absolute fee interest after running of applicable statute. (38-41-101; 181 Colo. 435, 510 P.2d 336). Transfer of property thereafter only effected by validly executed deed, adverse possession, or other legal means. (632 P.2d 644).

Disabilities.—Disabilities in existence when cause of action accrued and which are still in existence when applicable limitation period has run entitle disabled person to two additional years in which to commence action, after which his rights are cut off. (38-41-112).

CONVEYANCES:

See topic Deeds.

CURTESY:

Abolished. (15-11-112).

DEEDS:

See topic Real Property for types of estates.

Execution.—Deeds may be signed by grantor or by attorney in fact under recorded power of attorney. (38-30-113, 38-30-123). Acknowledgment is not required for validity of deed or for recording (38-35-106[1]), but acknowledgment in statutory form is prima facie evidence of proper execution (38-35-101[2]). Powers of attorney may be acknowledged and proved like deed. (38-30-124).

See also topic Real Property; categories Debtor and Creditor, topic Homesteads, subhead Alienation or Encumbrance; Documents and Records, topic Acknowledgments; Family, topic Husband and Wife, subhead Conveyance or Encumbrance of Property.

Execution by Corporation.—Common method of conveyance for private corporation is execution by president, with attestation by secretary. Private corporation authorized by law to convey, mortgage or lease property may use standard form of execution or may convey by instrument under its common seal, subscribed by its president, vice president or other head officer. (38-30-144[1]). If latter method of conveyance is used, instrument shall be deemed to have been executed in usual course of business and shall be binding on corporation as against bona fide purchasers, encumbrancers and other persons relying on instrument. (38-30-144[2]). Alternatively, domestic or foreign corporations may appoint agents or attorneys-in-fact to convey real estate and it is not necessary to affix corporate seal to any conveyance so executed. (7-3-103).

Recording.—All deeds and other instruments affecting title to real property are within jurisdiction of recording act. (38-35-109[1]). Recording statute classified race-notice. (38-35-109[1]). Recording is not necessary for validity of rights as between parties and third persons with notice, but unrecorded document is not valid against any other person who first records. (38-35-109[1]). There is no time limit for effective

See note at head of Digest as to 1998 legislation covered.

See Topical Index in front part of this volume.

DEEDS . . . *continued*
recording (38-35-101[4]), except that conveyances to state, county or municipality must be made within 30 days of conveyance (38-35-109.5), but recording must be in office of county clerk and recorder in county where property is situated (38-35-109[1]). All documents of title should include immediately preceding or following legal description street address or comparable identifying numbers for property if displayed on property or any building (38-35-122[1]), but failure to state address does not render document invalid nor render title unmarketable if legal description appears in deed (38-35-122[3]). Any deeds or other instruments containing newly created legal description of real property must include name and address of person who created such legal description, but failure to state such name and address does not render such instrument invalid or not recordable and does not confer liability upon person who prepared such instrument. (38-35-106.5). Legal description controls if variance or ambiguity exists by including street address. (38-35-122[2]). Clerk and recorder's office will not record any deed which does not include notation of grantee's legal address. (38-35-109[2]). If instrument is executed by attorney-in-fact, power of attorney must be recorded in same office to show grantor's assent. (38-30-123). If instrument may be filed by law with county clerk and recorder, then filing with county clerk and recorder is equivalent to recording and, recording thereof in office of such county clerk and recorder shall be equivalent to filing thereof. (38-35-109[1]). State and local employees may either accept or reject for recording or filing any spurious document (38-35-202[1]), and such employees are relieved from any liability for either accepting or rejecting for recording or filing any document such employee believes in good faith to be spurious document (38-35-202[2]). Spurious document is one that is forged, groundless, fraudulent or otherwise patently invalid. (38-35-201[3]). Spurious document is only valid for 30 days following its recording or filing. (38-35-203[1]). Any person who offers to have recorded or filed in office of county clerk and recorder any document purporting to create lien against real property, knowing or having reason to know that such document is forged, groundless, contains material misstatement or false claim, or is otherwise invalid, shall be liable to owner of such real property for sum of not less than $1,000 or for actual damages caused thereby, whichever is greater, together with reasonable attorneys' fees. Any grantee or other person purportedly benefited by such recorded forged, groundless, or false document who willfully refuses to release such document of record upon request of owner of real property affected shall be liable to owner for damages of not less than $1,000, together with reasonable attorneys' fees. (38-35-109[3]). Instrument may be recorded whether or not acknowledged or properly acknowledged. (38-35-106[1]). Recordation of acknowledged instrument is prima facie evidence of due delivery. (38-35-101[4]). Unacknowledged or defectively acknowledged deed which has remained of record for ten years is deemed properly acknowledged. (38-35-106[2]).

Deeds or other instruments affecting title to real property and acknowledgment or proof of execution thereof written in foreign country and language may be recorded only if accompanied by sworn translation. If so translated, instrument may be read in evidence and recorded as if it were written in English language, but translation is not conclusive upon any party desiring to question correctness thereof. (38-30-140).

Recording Fee.—See category Documents and Records, topic Records.

Operation and Effect.—Deed is deemed to convey estate in fee simple unless limited expressly or lesser estate is conveyed by operation of law. (38-30-107). Deed is valid conveyance of after-acquired title if it purports to convey fee simple absolute; grantor is deemed to hold title in trust for his vendee. (38-30-104). Person claiming right or title to land may convey his interest even if he is out of possession or if there is adverse possession against him. (38-30-105). All conveyances carry right to immediate possession unless future day is specified. (38-30-120). Water rights, except where held as ownership of stock in ditch company, must be conveyed with same formalities as real estate. (38-30-102). Estate in joint tenancy is created only by express declaration in instrument of conveyance that property is conveyed in joint tenancy, except when conveyance is to executors, trustees or fiduciaries. (38-31-101). Conveyance to grantee named in representative capacity shall also name beneficiary and define source of representative's authority, or refer to recorded or filed writing containing such information by citing recording or filing information. Failure to do so will be deemed description of person only and not notice of his representative capacity. (38-30-108).

Livery of seisin is unnecessary. (38-30-103). If conveyance would have been of estate in fee tail at common law, that grantee shall be deemed to be seized of estate in fee simple. (38-30-106). Affixation of scroll by way of seal shall have same effect as seal. (38-30-125).

Covenants.—Statutory form of warranty deed deemed to contain covenants of seisin, right to convey, freedom from encumbrances, warranty of peaceable possession. (38-30-113[2]). Covenants of seisin, peaceable possession, freedom from encumbrances, and warranty in instrument of conveyance run with premises and inure to benefit of subsequent purchasers and encumbrancers. (38-30-121). Warrantee may not sue warrantor once possession has been actually delivered until party menacing warrantee's possession has begun proceedings to obtain possession and warrantor has had notice and refused to defend. (38-30-122). Statutory form of special warranty deed contains covenant that grantor will warrant and defend title against persons claiming title by, through or under grantor. (38-30-115). Statutory forms of bargain and sale and quitclaim deeds contain no warranties. (38-30-115, 116).

See also categories Business Regulation and Commerce, topic Frauds, Statute of; Mortgages, topic Mortgages of Real Property.

Taxes.—See category Taxation, topic Real Estate Conveyance Tax.

Forms.—Deeds may be substantially in following forms:

Warranty Deed.— . . . ., whose street address is . . . ., City or Town of . . . ., County of . . . . and State of . . . ., for the consideration of . . . . Dollars, in hand paid, hereby sell(s) and convey(s) to . . . . whose street address is . . . ., City or Town of . . . ., County of . . . . and State of . . . ., the following real property in the County of . . . . and State of Colorado, to wit: . . . . with all its appurtenances and warrant(s) the title to the same, subject to . . . .

Signed this . . . . day of . . . ., 19. . . . . .

Such deed may be acknowledged. (38-30-113[1]).

Special Warranty Deed.—Deed executed according to above form with phrase "and warrant the title against all persons claiming under me" is special warranty deed. (38-30-115).

Bargain and Sale Deed.—Deed executed according to above form with words, "and warrant the title to the same," omitted therefrom has the same force and effect as a bargain and sale deed, without covenants of warranty, at common law and will pass after-acquired title of grantor. (38-30-115).

Quitclaim Deed.—A deed executed according to the above form with the word "quitclaim," substituted for "convey," and the words "and warrant the title to the same," omitted therefrom, is a deed of quitclaim. (38-30-116).

See category Environment, topic Environmental Regulation, subhead Hazardous Waste Disposal, for requirements for deeds of property used for disposal of hazardous wastes.

DEEDS OF TRUST:

See category Mortgages, topic Mortgages of Real Property.

DOWER:

Abolished. (15-11-112).

ESCHEAT:

Uniform Unclaimed Property Act was passed with modifications, effective July 1, 1987. (38-13-101 to 134). Act includes unclaimed intangible property held in fiduciary capacity. (38-13-108). See category Business Regulation and Commerce, topic Banks and Banking, subhead Unclaimed Deposits.

See also topic Absentees; category Estates and Trusts, topic Descent and Distribution.

LANDLORD AND TENANT:

Uniform Commercial Code Art. 2A.—Not adopted.

Kinds of Tenancy.—Tenancies may be at will or at sufferance, periodic, or for certain term.

Leases for a longer period than one year must be in writing. (38-10-108). All manufactured home leases must be in writing. (38-12-202). Witnesses are not necessary. Acknowledgment is not necessary for validity or for recording but is necessary for presumption of proper execution (38-35-101[2]) and, together with recording, for presumption of due delivery (38-35-101[4]).

Security Deposits.—Landlord must return security deposit in full within one month of termination of tenancy or term, or surrender and acceptance of premises, whichever is later, unless lease extends period up to 60 days (38-12-103[1]), or within, generally, 72 hours if termination due to hazardous gas condition (38-12-104). Security deposit cannot be retained for ordinary wear and tear. If actual cause exists for retaining deposit, landlord must deliver to tenant written statement of reasons for retention and difference between amount retained and amount deposited. (38-12-103[1]). Statement may be mailed to tenant's last known address. (38-12-103[1]). Failure to provide statement forfeits landlord's right to retain any part of security deposit. (38-12-103[2]). Landlord is liable for treble damages, reasonable attorneys' fees, and court costs for willful retention of security deposit in violation of statute (38-12-103[3][a] and [b]) unless court finds landlord acted in good faith (194 Colo. 160, 570 P.2d 532). Tenant must give seven days notice of intent to file legal proceeding. (38-12-103[3][a]). Statute of limitations for treble damages is one year. (13-80-104). Statute of limitations for recovery of deposit and attorneys fees is six years. (193 Colo. 391, 566 P.2d 1073). Landlord has burden of proving withholding was not wrongful. (38-12-103[3][b]). Upon cessation of his interest in dwelling, landlord must transfer deposited funds to his successor in interest and give notice of transfer to tenant or return funds to tenant. (38-12-103[4]). Requirements regarding security deposits apply to short term rentals of condominium units as well as other residential premises.

Manufactured home lease security deposits may not exceed statutory limits. (38-12-207). Such deposits must be deposited in separate account administered by landlord as private trustee. (38-12-209 [2][b]).

Recording is not necessary even as against third persons where tenant is in possession (55 Colo. 287, 134 P. 107) and is never necessary as between parties or those with actual notice (38-35-109). If recorded, lease should include street address or comparable identifying numbers immediately preceding or following legal description. (38-35-122[1]). Failure to include address does not invalidate instrument (38-35-122[3]).

Rent.—Obligation to pay rent is governed by common law. In absence of express provision in lease to contrary, tenant not obligated to pay future rents if tenant vacates in compliance with landlord's notice to pay or quit premises. (660 P.2d 907).

Rent Control.—Counties and municipalities may not enact rent control legislation on private residential property. (38-12-301).

Lien.—Landlord renting furnished or unfurnished rooms or apartments for tenants' housekeeping purposes has lien upon tenants' household furniture, goods, appliances and other personal property, excluding specified items, and personal effects, for amount of unpaid board, lodging or rent and reasonable costs of enforcement, but not attorneys' fees. (38-20-102[3][a]). Landlord must allow tenant access to premises to remove property not covered by lien. (38-20-102[3][b]). If tenant has not vacated premises, landlord may enter to assert lien and may peaceably assert dominion over property covered by lien. If landlord's assertion substantially interferes with tenant's right to reasonably occupy and enjoy premises, lien is forfeited and tenant has action for damages. (38-20-102[3][c]). Lien terminates if not foreclosed in 60 days after charges become due. (38-20-107). If charges for which lien is given are not paid within 30 days after due and payable, landlord may file foreclosure action in county or district court of county in which lease was executed or entered into or in which tenant resided at time lease was entered into or at time foreclosure action commenced. Landlord need not file foreclosure action if property held falls within statutory definition of abandoned property. (38-20-107[3], 116). Summons issued by court clerk upon filing of complaint,

See note at head of Digest as to 1998 legislation covered.

See Topical Index in front part of this volume.

CO – 64

LANDLORD AND TENANT... *continued*
commanding tenant to file answer and appear before court at specified time and date no less than three nor more than five days from date of issuance, and giving notice of consequences of failure to answer. (38-20-108). After receiving judgment, landlord may sell property at public auction for cash after giving ten days notice of sale by publication and after delivering copy of notice to owner of property or mailing copy to his usual place of abode if he does not reside in county. (38-20-109[1]). Landlord may retain amount of charges and costs, including maximum of $90 for storage, and must return excess and unsold property to owner. (38-20-109[1]). Lienor may purchase at sale. (38-20-111). Lien does not bar landlord's right of action for charges remaining after sale. (38-20-113). Court may order accelerated sale if property may deteriorate or is expensive to keep. (38-20-109[2]).

Injuries.—Lessor liable for injuries outside premises caused by dangerous activity on premises, notwithstanding lessor's relinquishment of control under lease. (44 Colo. App. 429, 618 P.2d 706; 768 P.2d 1260).

Consent to Assignment.—Lease assignable unless covenant to contrary. (175 P.2d 392). Covenant requiring consent is enforceable. (540 P.2d 1149; 699 P.2d 1343; 731 P.2d 700). Whether landlord unreasonably withheld consent is question of fact based upon standard of conduct of reasonably prudent person, and cannot be based upon arbitrary considerations of personal taste, convenience, sensibility or racial reasons. (638 P.2d 824).

Termination of Tenancy.—Notice is not required for a term certain. Law presumes tenancy at will after assent of owner is shown. Tenancy for a year or more requires three months notice of termination; tenancy for six months to a year, one months notice; tenancy for one to six months, ten days notice; tenancy for one week to one month, tenancy after substantial violation or tenancy at will, three days notice; and tenancy of less than one week, one days notice. Notice shall describe property and time of termination and shall be signed by person giving notice or his agent or attorney. (13-40-107). Notice may be served by delivery to tenant or another occupant of premises, by leaving with member of tenant's family more than 15 years old residing in or in charge of premises, or by posting in conspicuous place if no one is on premises when service is attempted. (13-40-108). Special rules for manufactured home parks. (38-12-201 to 217). Foreclosure on property terminates recorded junior or subordinated leases (864 P.2d 116; 867 P.2d 111), and unrecorded junior lease if lessee named and notified in foreclosure. (38-38-101[7][a]). Developer who converts existing multi-unit dwelling into condominium units must notify each residential tenant of dwelling of such conversion in accordance with statutory provision. (38-33-112). Tenant can vacate premises and terminate lease if landlord fails to repair hazardous gas condition within, generally, 72 hours of written notice of condition. (38-12-104[3], [4]).

Manufactured home leases may be terminated only upon written notice containing specified information (38-12-202), and only for reasons limited by statute (38-12-203 to 205).

Abandonment.—Two requisite elements of abandonment include act of abandonment and intent to relinquish premises. Landlord can take possession of abandoned lease premises without resort to legal process. (623 P.2d 49).

Holding Over.—Landlord/tenant holdover doctrine discussed, 864 P.2d 116. See also subhead Proceedings to Recover Possession, infra.

Dispossession.—See subhead Proceedings to Recover Possession, infra.

Distress.—See subhead Proceedings to Recover Possession, infra.

Proceedings to Recover Possession.—Proceedings to recover possession may be brought for forcible entry, forcible detainer, or unlawful detainer. (13-40-109). Unlawful detainer includes tenant at will or at sufferance holding over after termination (13-40-104[1][c]), tenant holding over without permission after default in rent payment and after three days written notice demanding payment or possession (13-40-104[1][d]), and tenant holding over after substantial violation or without landlord's permission in breach of other covenant or condition of lease and after three days written notice requiring possession (13-40-104[1][d.5], [e], [e.5]). Agreement under which tenant holds possession must not contain waiver by tenant of three days notice requirement. (13-40-104[1][d]). In absence of clear lease language preserving tenant's liability for unaccrued rent, notice to pay rent or quit premises constitutes election by landlord to terminate unless tenant's subsequent rent payment renders notice ineffective. (660 P.2d 907; 684 P.2d 957). Notices required must state grounds for right to possession and must be signed. (13-40-106).

Proceedings commenced by filing written complaint in district or county court describing property, grounds for recovery, name of person in possession or occupancy, and prayer for recovery of possession. Complaint may also include prayer for rent due or to become due, for present and future damages, and for costs and other relief. (13-40-110). Court clerk or plaintiff's attorney issues summons for defendant to appear in five to ten days or take default judgment. (13-40-111). Personal service may be had as in any civil case. If personal service can't be had by person qualified under Colorado Rules of Civil Procedure to serve process, such person may serve by posting summons and complaint on premises. If personal service not obtained, plaintiff must mail, no later than next day following day on which he files complaint, copy of summons or if alias summons is issued, copy of alias summons, and copy of complaint to defendant at premises by postage-paid, first class mail. Personal service or service by posting must be made at least five days before day for appearance specified in summons. (13-40-112). Defendant must file written answer, at or before time specified for appearance, describing grounds for claim for possession, presenting all defenses, and admitting or denying all material allegations of complaint. (13-40-113[1]). If service by posting, judgment may be only for restitution, but court may continue case until personal service obtained. (13-40-115[1]). If personal service obtained, judgment may be for restitution, rent, damages and costs. (13-40-115[2], 13-40-123). Prevailing party entitled to recover damages, reasonable attorney fees and costs. (13-40-123). If plaintiff's action, upon trial, is dismissed or if plaintiff fails to prove right to possession of premises, defendant gets judgment and execution for his costs. (13-40-116). Writ of restitution cannot be issued until 48 hours after entry of judgment. (13-40-122). If either party appeals, all proceedings shall be stayed (13-40-117[2], and if defendant appeals, he shall deposit with trial court all rents found due and specified in judgment, and thereafter deposit with appellate court all future rents as they come due. Penalty for failure to pay such rents due is appellate court's affirmance of judgment with costs. (13-40-118). If appellee believes he may suffer serious economic harm during appeal, he may petition court for additional undertaking by appellant and court shall order such undertaking only after hearing and upon finding substantial likelihood of economic harm to appellee not protected by appeals bond and deposit of rent. (13-40-117[3]).

Discrimination in rental or lease of housing or refusal to show, rent, or lease housing by any person with right of ownership or possession on account of race, creed, color, sex, marital status, familial status, religion, national origin, ancestry or disability is prohibited (24-34-502[1][a]), except that "housing" does not include any room offered for rent or lease in single family dwelling maintained and occupied in part by owner or lessee as his household (24-34-501[2]), and familial status does not apply to housing for older persons (24-34-502[7]), nor to certain private individual owners of single family houses (24-34-502[8]). Remedies include administrative conciliation proceeding, injunctive relief and cease and desist order. (24-34-306, 508).

Uniform Residential Landlord and Tenant Act.—Not adopted.

Rental Location Agents.—See category Business Regulation and Commerce, topic Brokers.

PERPETUITIES:

Common law rule against perpetuities has been superseded by statute in Colorado. (15-11-1101 to 1107). Colorado statute is intended to effectuate provisions of Uniform Statutory Rule Against Perpetuities Act. (15-11-1107[1]).

Rule against perpetuities has no application to transfers in trust of not more than $25,000 for purpose of creating or maintaining grave, tomb, monument, etc. (38-30-110).

Rule against perpetuities does not apply to trust for benefit of employees or their beneficiaries or pension, stock bonus, disability, death benefit or profit sharing plan existing on Sept. 29, 1951. (38-30-111, 112).

PERSONAL PROPERTY:

Joint tenancy in personal property created by declaration of joint tenancy in instrument evidencing ownership. (38-11-101).

POWERS OF ATTORNEY:

Attorneys in Fact.—A conveyance or mortgage of real estate may be executed by attorney in fact acting under power of attorney, provided power is recorded, in same offices in which conveyances themselves are required to be recorded. (38-30-123). Power of attorney authorizing agent to receive principal's workmen's compensation benefits generally void. (8-42-124).

Formalities.—Power of attorney for conveying, leasing or releasing interests in real property may be acknowledged or proved in same manner as deeds. (38-30-124).

Revocation.—If power of attorney contains words showing intent of principal that authority conferred is exercisable notwithstanding disability, then it is exercisable notwithstanding disability, incapacity, or later uncertainty as to whether principal is dead or alive. (15-14-501). Power of attorney not containing such words not revoked so long as attorney acts in good faith without actual knowledge of death, disability or incompetence of principal. (15-14-502).

Uniform Durable Power of Attorney Act.—Adopted with significant modifications. (15-14-501, 502).

Colorado Patient Autonomy Act authorizes principal to grant to agent medical durable power of attorney to consent to or refuse medical treatment on behalf of principal. (15-14-503 to 509).

Uniform Statutory Form Power of Attorney Act.—Legislatively sanctions prescribed form of power of attorney for broad range of powers (15-1-1302) and interprets scope of agent's empowerment for each type of power (15-1-304 through 15-1-1317).

Members of Armed Forces.—No special statutory provision.

Other Provisions.—Statutes also provide generally for applicability and duration of agency instruments, duties of agents, reliance by third parties on agency instruments and related matters, and form agent's affidavit regarding power of attorney. (15-14-601 to 611).

REAL PROPERTY:

Joint tenancy and tenancy in common are recognized. Tenancy by entirety is not. (62 Colo. 461, 163 P. 76). Except when real property is conveyed or devised to executors, trustees or fiduciaries, tenancy in common presumed unless declared in instrument conveying or will devising property that property conveyed or devised in joint tenancy. (38-31-101). Grantor may be one of grantees in such instrument of conveyance. (38-31-101).

Grant deemed to be in fee simple unless limited by express words, or by operation of law; no words of inheritance necessary. (38-30-107). Estates in fee tail are abolished; persons who would have taken at common law take in fee simple. (38-30-106).

Rule in Shelley's Case.—Colorado supreme court has assumed, without deciding, rule is in force. (71 Colo. 401, 207 P. 332).

Foreign Conveyances or Encumbrances.—All instruments affecting title to real estate acknowledged or proved in another state before a notary public or other officer empowered by laws of Colorado to take acknowledgments, if the form of acknowledgment is in substantial compliance with laws of state where taken or with requirements in Colorado (see category Documents and Records, topic Acknowledgments), are deemed prima facie to have been properly acknowledged before proper officers and such instruments or record thereof are prima facie evidence of execution, acknowledgment and delivery thereof. (38-35-105). Instruments affecting title to real property executed in any foreign country may be executed and acknowledged in language of such foreign country but may only be recorded if such instruments accompanied by sworn translation

See note at head of Digest as to 1998 legislation covered.

See Topical Index in front part of this volume.

CO – 65

REAL PROPERTY . . . continued

thereof into English, and acknowledgment or proof of execution, as translated, has same effect as if written in English, except not conclusive in challenge to correctness of translation. (38-30-140).

Condominiums.—Estates, rights and interests in areas above surface of ground, whether or not contiguous to it, are severable from land and are recognized estates, rights and interests. (38-32-101). Condominium ownership and interval ownership of property is recognized. (38-33-102, 38-33.3-201, 38-33-110). Developers must notify residential tenants of condominium conversion. (38-33-112). Uniform Condominium Act has not been adopted.

Cooperatives.—Cooperative housing corporations may be formed by any three or more adult residents of Colorado associating themselves to form non-profit corporation, specific purpose of which must be to provide each stockholder with right to occupy, for dwelling purposes, house or apartment in building owned or leased by such corporation. (38-33.5-101). Corporation may have only one class of stock outstanding; interest of each stockholder deemed estate in real property rather than personal property. (38-33.5-102). Bylaws of cooperative housing corporation must provide that no less than 80% of gross income of property in any taxable year be derived from tenant-stockholders. (38-33.5-103[1]). Bylaws must also provide that each tenant-stockholder be credited with his proportionate payment of real estate taxes and interest paid or incurred and depreciation on real and personal property related to lands and improvements thereon. (38-33.5-103[2]).

Common Interest Ownership Act applies to condominiums, cooperatives and planned communities, imposes requirements for creation, alteration and termination of such common interest communities (38-33.3-201 through 38-33.3-222) and makes provisions for management (38-33.3-301 through 38-33.3-319), including allowable lien of homeowners' association for six months' unpaid association assessments, with priority over other liens, except taxes (38-33.3-316). Large planned community of at least 200 acres and approved for development of at least 500 residential units and 20,000 square feet of commercial use may be exempted from certain provisions. (38-33.3-116.3).

Discrimination in housing because of disability, race, creed, color, sex, national origin, marital status, familial status, religion, or ancestry by any person is prohibited. (24-34-502). Before start of construction of residential project including seven or more residential units, contract must be made with municipality or county where project located to guarantee that specific number of units be constructed for access by persons with disabilities. (9-5-112).

Soil Analysis.—Soil and hazard analysis report of land and site recommendations developed for new residence must be provided to purchaser by builder or developer at least 14 days prior to closing. For sites with significant potential for expansive soils, buyer must be supplied with additional pertinent information. (6-6.5-101). Failure to so provide subjects builder or developer to $500 fine payable to purchaser. (6-6.5-101[2]).

Uniform Simplification of Land Transfers Act has not been adopted.

See also topics Adverse Possession, Curtesy, Deeds, Dower, Landlord and Tenant; categories Business Regulation and Commerce, topic Securities; Civil Actions and Procedure, topic Partition; Debtor and Creditor, topic Homesteads; Family, topic Husband and Wife; Mortgages, topic Mortgages of Real Property.

TRUST DEEDS:

See category Mortgages, topic Mortgages of Real Property.

TAXATION

ADMINISTRATION:

Department of revenue, headed by executive director and including division of enforcement, administers and enforces state taxes other than property tax. (24-35-101). Colorado division of property taxation, headed by property tax administrator, charged with assisting and cooperating in administration of all property tax laws, supervising activities of assessors, reviewing methods used by assessors and county boards of equalization, issuing manuals for appraisers and administering program to computerize assessments. (39-2-109, 109.5). Board of assessment appeals reviews and hears appeals from decisions of property tax administrator, county boards of equalization, county assessors, and county commissioners. (39-2-125).

Constitution requires annual study of county assessor compliance with constitutional assessment standards and mandates corrective action by state board of equalization. (Const., Art. 10, §3[2]; 39-1-105.5).

Statutes exempting property not specified in constitution void. (Const., Art. 10, §6, para. 3). Levy must be uniform on all nonexempt property within jurisdiction of levying authority. (Const., Art. 10, §3[1][a]).

Certificate of Taxes Due.—All public entities required to provide taxpayer or person authorized by taxpayer on 30 days' request certificate of taxes due from taxpayer and copies of returns or summary of tax payments for current and preceding three years. (38-25.5-102, -103). General taxes on real property excluded. (38-25.5-102[4]).

Interest on deficiencies for taxes administered by department is computed at prime rate reported by Wall Street Journal on July 1 of preceding year plus three points. (39-21-110.5). Department must waive three points in excess of prime if taxpayer pays deficiency within 30 days, unless deficiency results from willful neglect or failure to pay tax. (39-21-109[1.5]). Payment of deficiency under protest does not prevent taxpayer from protesting deficiency administratively.

Penalties.—Any person who willfully evades any tax administered by department in addition to other penalties provided by law is guilty of class 5 felony and shall be punished as provided in 18-1-105, and/or by fine of not more than $100,000 ($500,000 for corporation) together with costs of prosecution. (39-21-118). Included among penalties for failure to comply with Colorado tax provisions are following:

Income Tax.—Penalties ranging from $5 to 150% of tax due for failure to pay tax, failure to file return, fraudulent or willful failure to file return, and fraudulent or willful filing of false return. (39-22-621).

Penalties are cumulative and are collected at same time and in same manner as tax. (39-22-621[2][i]).

If failure of person which may have subjected him to penalties listed above was due to good cause, in judgment of director, director may waive or reduce any of such penalties. (39-22-621[2][j]).

Any person who willfully fails to make return, keep required records or supply required information, in addition to other penalties, will be fined and/or imprisoned as provided in 39-21-118. (39-22-621[3]).

Any person required to file timely annual information report shall be subject to fine of $50 for each failure. (39-22-601[9]).

Any person who willfully fails to collect, account for or pay over taxes required to be collected, accounted for or paid over or who willfully fails to pay any tax, or in any manner evades or defeats any tax or payment thereof, in addition to other penalties, will be fined and/or imprisoned as provided in 39-21-118. (39-22-621[3]).

Estate Tax.—Following penalties apply: (1) For failure to timely pay—greater of $15 or 5% of amount of tax due for first month with additional 5% for each succeeding month to maximum of 20%; (2) willful or fraudulent failure to file—greater of $75 or 100% of tax; (3) filing fraudulent return—greater of $100 or 150% of tax; (4) failure to timely pay after assessment, determination, and notice—15% of tax; (5) fraudulent failure to pay tax when due or attempt to evade payments—150% of tax; (6) failure to file within extension granted by director—5% of tax due with additional 5% for each succeeding month to maximum of 20%. (39-23.5-110). Any person who willfully fails to file return, files fraudulent return, or fails to pay tax will be fined and/or imprisoned as provided in 39-21-118. (39-23.5-113).

Sales Tax.—See topic Sales and Use Taxes, subhead Sales Tax.

Use Tax.—See topic Sales and Use Taxes, subhead Use Tax.

Real and Personal Property Taxes.—See topic Property Taxes.

Gasoline and Special Fuel Tax.—Specific penalties for violations concerning gasoline and special fuel tax include greater of $30 or 10% of taxes due with additional 1/2% for each succeeding month to maximum of 18% plus interest for failure to file statement or filing false statement. (39-27-105[2]; -205[5]). Penalty for distributor's refusal to file sworn statement required by 39-27-105(1) or for incorrect or fraudulent statement or tax return is 30% plus interest pursuant to 39-21-110.5. (39-27-105[3]). Penalty to nondistributor or nonsupplier for not filing statement when special fuel is diverted within state ranges from $5,000 to $15,000. (39-27-205[3.8], [8]). Penalty for importing special fuel without license or single-trip permit also ranges from $5,000 to $15,000 plus revenue agents may detain shipment until excise tax is paid. (39-22-205[3.5], [8]). Willful refusal or failure to report or pay gasoline or special fuel tax punishable by fine and/or imprisonment as provided in 39-21-118. (39-27-108, -208). Violator may also be subject to suspension or loss of license and injunction against selling gasoline. (39-27-120, -217).

Cigarette and Tobacco Products Taxes.—Any wholesaler or retailer selling cigarettes without stamps is subject to fine and/or imprisonment as provided in 39-21-118 (39-28-108[1]); distributor or agent who sells or distributes tobacco products without license or who willfully violates provisions is subject to fine and/or imprisonment for class 5 felony (39-28.5-110[1]); and any person who neglects or refuses to pay cigarette or tobacco tax assessed additional penalty equal to 10% with 1/2% for each succeeding month up to maximum of 18% plus interest at rate computed under 39-21-110.5. (39-28-108[2]; 39-28.5-110[2]).

ALCOHOLIC BEVERAGE TAX:

Liquor Taxes.—

Fermented malt beverages (containing not more than 3.2% alcohol by weight) may be manufactured and sold only under licenses granted by executive director of department of revenue (12-46-104) and local licensing authority (12-46-107). Fees for manufacturers, importers, wholesalers and retailers set out in 12-47-501. Licensing authorities will charge application fees to cover expenses. (12-46-105, 107).

Excise tax of 8¢ per gallon (or equivalent unit volume tax applied to metric measure) imposed on fermented malt beverages; manufacturer or wholesaler receiving beverage from out of state primarily liable. Tax is due on 20th of month following first sale; manufacturers and wholesalers must file monthly returns on 20th with state licensing authority and department of revenue. (12-47-503[4]).

Excise tax on liquors sold or offered for sale in state is 8¢ per gallon (or equivalent unit volume tax applied to metric measure) on all malt liquors; 7.33¢ per liter on all vinous liquors (plus surcharge of 4¢ to 6¢ per liter); 60.26¢ per liter on all spirituous liquors. Tax payable by manufacturer or first licensee receiving liquor in Colorado, unless proof liquor sold out of state. (12-47-503).

Annual liquor license fees payable to department of revenue range from $25 to $1,025 depending on type of license and/or establishment, plus application fees. (12-47-501). Following additional annual license fees are payable to city, town or county where licensee is located: Retail liquor stores, drug-stores, and beer and wine licenses, $150 if located within any city, or town or city and county; $250 if located elsewhere; resort hotel beer and wine licenses, $200; hotels, taverns, racetracks and restaurants licenses, $325; clubs licenses, $100; bed and breakfast permit, $25. (12-47-505).

BUSINESS TAXES:

Corporate Tax.—See category Business Organizations, topic Corporations, subhead Taxation of Corporate Property. Officers of corporation willfully evading any tax are subject to penalty equal to 150% of tax evidenced and other penalties provided by law. (39-21-116.5).

Franchise Taxes.—See categories Business Organizations, topic Corporations; Insurance, topic Insurance Companies.

See note at head of Digest as to 1998 legislation covered.

See Topical Index in front part of this volume.

CIGARETTE AND TOBACCO PRODUCTS TAXES:

Tax of 10 mills per cigarette levied and paid by licensed wholesalers. (39-28-103). Stamp affixed on cigarette packages evidence of payment of taxes. (39-28-104). Municipalities may impose additional taxes on cigarettes. (39-28-112). Sales to U.S. government, sales in interstate commerce, or transactions where U.S. Constitution forbids taxation are exempt. (39-28-111). Each wholesaler must file monthly report by tenth day of following month. (39-28-109). Department may read and inspect approved metering machines monthly and determine amount of tax due. (39-28-105[2]).

Tax imposed on sale, use, consumption, handling, or distribution of all tobacco products other than cigarettes, in Colorado at rate of 20% of manufacturer's list price. (39-28.5-102). License required for distributors at $10 annual fee. (39-28.5-104). Distributors must file report and pay tax minus 3[1]/3% collection discount on 20th day of month following month when purchase made. (39-28.5-106).

ESTATE TAX:

Colorado estate tax (39-23.5-101 et seq.) is based on credit for state death taxes allowable under federal estate tax (Internal Revenue Code §2011). Gross estate has same meaning as under federal law. (39-23.5-102[9]).

Amount of Tax.—For domiciliaries, estate tax is federal credit reduced by lesser of: (i) Death tax on property of domiciliary paid to other states allowable as credit against federal estate tax, or (ii) federal credit times ratio of value of gross estate less value of property of domiciliary over value of gross estate. (39-23.5-103). For nondomiciliaries, estate tax is fraction of federal credit attributable to value of property included in nondomicilary's gross estate which is located in Colorado. (39-23.5-104; -105).

Tax on generation-skipping transfers imposed at maximum amount allowable as credit under Internal Revenue Code §2604 multiplied by ratio of property located in Colorado included in generation-skipping transfer over value of all property included in generation-skipping transfer. (39-23.5-106).

Property Subject to Tax.—Property of domiciliary includes real property in Colorado whether in trust or otherwise, all tangible personal property except that having actual situs outside Colorado, and all intangible personal property. Real property outside Colorado in personal trust is not included. (39-23.5-103[3]). Property located in Colorado of nondomiciliary includes real property in Colorado whether in trust or otherwise, and tangible personal property having actual situs in Colorado. Intangibles with actual or business situs in Colorado are not included (39-23.5-104[3]), except intangibles of domiciliary of foreign country located within or subject to protection of Colorado shall be included (39-23.5-105[3]). For generation-skipping transfer tax, property in Colorado includes real and personal property in state and intangible property of trust administered in Colorado. (39-23.5-106[3]).

Taxable Transfers.—Transfers as defined in Internal Revenue Code §2001 (39-23.5-102[17]) and generation-skipping transfers for which federal credit for state taxes is allowable under Internal Revenue Code §2604 (39-23.5-102[8]).

Tax Returns and Payment.—No Colorado return need be filed by persons required to file if gross estate or generation-skipping transfer does not require filing federal return. Persons required to file must file return and pay tax due on or before date federal return must be filed. If return not filed, executive director may make such return and assessment based on available information. Personal representative may elect to extend time for filing and payment in accordance with federal rules on extension. (39-23.5-107; -108).

Amended Returns.—If amended federal return is filed, personal representative must immediately file amended Colorado return together with any additional tax due, plus interest, subject to extensions. Personal representative must notify department of revenue of final determination of federal tax due in respect of any gross estate or generation-skipping transfer and pay any additional Colorado tax due within 60 days after such determination, subject to extension. (39-23.5-111).

Criminal Acts.—Any person who willfully fails to file Colorado estate tax return or who willfully files false return will be punished as provided in 39-21-118. (39-23.5-113).

Persons Liable.—Persons required to file are liable for tax due to extent of value of property actually received. If tax not paid when due, transferees and beneficiaries are liable for tax due to extent of value of property received. No personal liability with respect to estates of decedents dying, or generation-skipping transfer, on or after July 1, 1980, for purchasers, mortgagees, pledgees, transferees, or holders of security interest in such property if transfer was for value. (39-23.5-114). Unless otherwise provided in will, and subject to certain exceptions, tax will be apportioned among all persons interested in estate. (15-12-916[2]).

Procedures for Collection.—Department of revenue may institute proceedings and represent state in all matters for collection of tax, interest, and penalties in courts, or in any other manner. No distraint and sale proceedings may be instituted until final agency action no longer subject to judicial review. (39-23.5-115).

Apportionment Against Inter Vivos Disposition.—There is no statute providing for apportionment.

Interstate Cooperation.—Uniform Acts on Interstate Arbitration and Interstate Compromise of Death Taxes were adopted in 1953 as one law entitled "The Uniform Act on Interstate Compromise and Arbitration of Inheritance Taxes". (39-24-101 et seq.). See Part III for text of Acts.

GASOLINE AND SPECIAL FUEL TAX:

Excise tax in lieu of all other taxes (39-27-111,-207) imposed and collected on: (1) Gasoline sold or used in state for any purpose (39-27-102); and (2) special fuel sold or used in state for propulsion of motor vehicles on state highways (39-27-202). Any distributors, suppliers, importers, exporters, carriers or blenders holding license must file statement by 25th day of month concerning shipments received for gasoline or special fuels acquired from any source whatsoever during preceding calendar month. (39-27-105,-205). Statement concerning gasoline may be submitted electronically. (39-27-105[f]). Nondistributors using or possessing supplies of gasoline in state over amount in vehicle tanks must report such use or possession and pay excise tax. (39-27-107). Tax imposed on gasoline at 20¢ per gallon or fraction thereof through Dec. 31, 1990 and 22¢ thereafter. (39-27-102[1][a][II]). For special fuel, rate is 20.5¢per gallon or fraction thereof through Dec. 31, 1989, 18¢ from Jan. 1, 1990 to Dec. 31, 1991 and 20.5¢ thereafter. (39-27-202[1][c]).

Credit or refund of gasoline tax allowed for destruction of 100 gallons or more by causes beyond control of distributor or transporter and for gasoline purchases of 100 gallons or more by federal government and political subdivisions of state. (39-27-103[1], [2]). Refund of tax on 20 or more gallon purchase or use of gasoline allowed for: (1) Operation of stationary gas engines, (2) motor vehicles operated on or over fixed rails, (3) farm machinery used on farms or ranches for agricultural purposes, (4) motorboats, (5) any non-highway related commercial use, (6) scheduled aircarriers or commuter airlines and (7) 50% credit for licensed agricultural applicator aircraft. (39-27-103[3]). Refund of special fuel tax on 20 or more gallon purchase or use of gasoline allowed for non-highway use and vehicle with power take-off unit. (39-27-203). Special fuels tax does not apply to motor vehicles using liquefied petroleum gas or natural gas and displaying decal. (39-27-202[5]). Operators of such vehicles pay $70-$125 fee in lieu of tax unless vehicle is operated for exclusively nonprofit functions. (39-27-202[5]; [7]).

Unlawful to distribute, supply, import, export, carry or blend gasoline or special fuel without license issued by executive director. (39-27-104,-204). Applicant for license to distribute or refine gasoline must show evidence of savings account, deposit or certificate of deposit meeting requirements of 11-35-101 or surety bond or negotiable certificate of deposit. Executive director fixes amount of required security. (39-27-104[2][a]). Distributor of special fuels must post surety bond in sum of approximately two times estimated monthly tax liability as security for tax payment. (39-27-204[4][a]).

GIFT TAX:

Colorado does not impose gift tax. However, former gift tax law (39-25-101 et seq.) remains in effect for transfers by gift occurring before Jan. 1, 1980 until all moneys due under it are collected (39-25-120).

Liability.—Tax is personal liability of donor, and of donee to extent of gift. (39-25-110[2][a]). Tax is lien on all taxpayer's property for ten years. (39-25-110[2][a]). Lien not valid against mortgagees, pledgees, purchasers or judgment creditors until filed. (39-25-110[2][a]). Executive director has one year from filing to determine amount of tax due or accept return as filed, unless taxpayer intended to evade tax by false filing. (39-25-111). If taxpayer fails to furnish information requested by executive director, tax determined at highest rate at which tax could be computed. (39-25-118).

INCOME TAX:

Colorado income tax law (39-22-101 et seq.) is patterned after federal income tax provisions. Generally, terms have same meaning as when used in comparable context in federal tax law. (39-22-103[11]). Persons otherwise required to file return whose only activity in Colorado is sales may be able to elect gross receipts tax in lieu of income tax. (39-22-104[5]).

Individuals.—Resident individuals, estates, and trusts, taxed at rate of 5% on federal taxable income determined under Internal Revenue Code §63 subject to following adjustments: Federal taxable income increased by (1) federal net operating loss deductions carried over from years beginning prior to Jan. 1, 1987, (2) interest income excluded from gross income pursuant to Internal Revenue Code §103(a) less amortization of premium on obligations of any state or political subdivision thereof, other than interest income on obligations of Colorado or its political subdivisions issued on or after May 1, 1980, or before if such interest specifically exempt from income taxation under law authorizing issuance of such obligations, (3) deduction allowed by Internal Revenue Code §402(e)(3), (4) for years beginning on or after Jan. 1, 1992 amount equal to deduction claimed for state income taxes pursuant to Internal Revenue Code §164(a)(3), (5) expenses incurred at certain restricted membership clubs, and (6) amounts withdrawn from medical savings accounts pursuant to 39-22-504.7(3)(b)(II) or (III). (39-22-104[3]). Federal taxable income decreased by (1) interest income on U.S. obligations and its possessions and qualified Colorado investment deposits to extent included in federal taxable income, (2) certain portions of gains or losses from sale or other disposition of property having higher adjusted basis for Colorado income tax purposes than for federal income tax purposes, (3) amounts necessary to prevent taxation of annuity or other income or gain properly taxed under Colorado law for prior tax years to taxpayer or certain related parties, (4) net operating loss deduction allowed under 39-22-504 to extent carried over from taxable year beginning prior to Jan. 1, 1987, (5) refund or credit for overpayment of income taxes imposed by Colorado or other taxing jurisdiction to extent included in gross income for federal income tax purposes but not previously allowed as deduction for Colorado income tax purposes, (6) certain amounts received as pensions or annuities from any source, to extent included in federal adjusted gross income or otherwise included in adjustments to federal taxable income, up to $20,000 per year if recipient is 55 years of age or older or if benefits are received because of death of original recipient, (7) for years beginning after June 30, 1995, amount for qualifying capital gains (39-22-518), (8) amounts contributed to medical savings account by employer pursuant to 39-22-504.7(2)(e) if not claimed as deduction by taxpayer and income distributed for qualified beneficiaries pursuant to qualified state tuition programs. (39-22-104[4]).

For income tax years commencing after Jan. 1, 1990 but prior to Jan. 1, 1993 health insurance fund surcharge of $2 to $4 imposed on returns with federal adjusted gross income over $15,000. (39-22-117).

Nonresidents are taxed on Colorado nonresident federal taxable income. (39-22-109). Colorado nonresident federal taxable income is federal taxable income, modified as in case of resident, derived from sources within state. (39-22-109[2][a]). Income is derived from Colorado sources if attributable to: Ownership of interest in real or tangible property in Colorado; business, trade, profession or occupation carried on in Colorado; use or disposition of intangible personal property to extent employed in business, trade, profession or occupation carried on in Colorado; distributive share of partnership, limited liability company, estate or trust income, gain, loss, and deduction derived from

See note at head of Digest as to 1998 legislation covered.

See Topical Index in front part of this volume.

INCOME TAX. . . *continued*
Colorado sources; and share of subchapter S corporation income, gain, loss, credit and deduction allocable or apportionable to Colorado. (39-22-109[2][a]). Compensation paid by U.S. to servicemen residing but not domiciled in state is not income derived from sources within Colorado. (39-22-109[2][b]). Nonresident's federal itemized or standard deduction and federal exemption deduction allowed in ratio of Colorado adjusted gross income to federal adjusted gross income. (39-22-109).

Part year residents taxed on federal taxable income relating to period of residence in Colorado and on remaining portion of federal income as nonresident if income received from Colorado sources for that period. (39-22-110).

Credits against tax payable are allowed to resident individuals for taxes on Colorado net income accrued to another state subject to certain limitations. (39-22-108[1]). Individuals engaged in business in Colorado also allowed certain other credits allowed corporations. See subhead Corporations, infra.

Alternative minimum tax (AMT) imposed in addition to income tax on individuals, estates, and trusts. AMT tax equal to excess of (a) 3.75% of AMT tax base over (b) regular tax computed under 39-22-104. AMT tax base equals federal alternative minimum taxable income under Internal Revenue Code §55, reduced by §55 federal exemptions, with same adjustments required by 39-22-104 for regular tax, except that no state or local interest income added back and any interest income from debt of Colorado or political subdivision thereof that is included in federal alternative minimum taxable income is subtracted. (39-22-105[1]). Credit against AMT allowed equal to 18% of federal §53 credit for years beginning after Jan. 1, 1988. (39-22-105[3]).

Nonresidents apportion AMT and credit against AMT in ratio of modified federal alternative minimum taxable income from Colorado sources to total from all sources. (39-22-105[4]).

Partnerships are not subject to tax (39-22-201), although return must be filed (39-22-601[5]). Partners are taxed in individual capacities. (39-22-201 et seq.). Limited liability partnerships and limited liability limited partnerships authorized. (7-60-144).

Limited liability companies must file return. (39-22-601[4.5]). LLC that qualifies as partnership under Internal Revenue Code §761(a) is defined as partnership for tax purposes. (39-22-103[5.6]).

Corporations, both domestic and foreign, are taxed on net income derived from sources within state. (39-22-301[1]). Small business corporations which have election in effect under subchapter S of Internal Revenue Code not subject to corporate tax. (39-22-302; 320 et seq.). S corporation may elect to pay tax on behalf of nonresident shareholders. (39-22-601[2.5][e]). Corporation doing business in Colorado and in other state may elect to attribute income to Colorado (24-60-1301, Art. 3) by either: (1) Apportioning entire net income according to two-factor (property, revenue) formula (39-22-303), or (2) allocating nonbusiness income and apportioning business income according to three-factor apportionment (property, payroll, sales) formula pursuant to Multi-State Tax Compact (24-60-1301, Art. 4). Executive director may vary apportionment formula to prevent inequity or income distortion, or distribute or allocate income and deductions among corporations owned or controlled by same interests; this may require filing of combined report or consolidated return. (39-22-303[5]-[6], [11]). Changes in method of apportioning income may limit ability to deduct net operating loss carryovers. (39-22-504[5]). Income from outside of U.S. not includable in combined report if 80% or more of corporation's property and payroll is assigned to locations outside of U.S. (39-22-303[8]). Amount of foreign source income considered in apportionment formula varies according to federal tax treatment of foreign taxes paid. (39-22-303[10]). Two or more members of affiliated group may elect to file combined return or may be required to file combined return if three of six listed objective unitary facts exist for current and two preceding tax years. (39-22-303[11][a]).

Net income of corporations means federal taxable income, as defined in Internal Revenue Code for taxable year, with certain modifications including certain of those applicable to federal taxable income of resident individual, as specified in 39-22-104. (39-22-304).

Taxable income of corporation taxed: (1) For tax years commencing after July 1, 1991 but before July 1, 1992, at (a) 5% of Colorado net income of $50,000; or less or (b) $2,500 plus 5.2% of Colorado net income over $50,000, (2) for tax years commencing on or after July 1, 1992, but before July 1, 1993, at (a) 5% of Colorado net income over $50,000 or less or (b) $2,500 plus 5.1% of Colorado net income over $50,000. For tax years commencing on or after July 1, 1993, taxable income of corporation taxed at 5% of Colorado net income. (39-22-301[1][d]).

Credits against tax payable are allowed for payments of estimated taxes (39-22-609[2]), for overpayments of tax (39-21-108[3]-[4]), to all taxpayers for portion of federal investment tax credit that would have been allowed had federal credit not been repealed for investment in depreciable property used in Colorado (39-22-507.5), to all taxpayers for portion of enterprise zone credit which is triple allowable federal investment credit or 3% of total qualified investment (39-22-507.5[12]; 39-30-104), for new employee credit to taxpayers establishing qualifying new business facility in Colorado (39-22-508.2; -508.3), for qualified job training programs to improve skills of enterprise zone employees (39-30-104[4]), for qualified school to work program (39-30-104[5]), for research and experimental expenditures in enterprise zones (39-30-105.5), for contributions to enterprise zone administrator to implement zone's economic development plan (39-30-103.5), for rehabilitation of historic properties from tax year 1991 to 2000 (39-22-514) or vacant building in enterprise zones (39-30-105.6), for investments in plastic recycling technology (39-22-114.5; 309), to corporations credit for increase in purchases of Colorado coal (39-22-308); 20% of cost to purchase qualified equipment utilizing post-consumer waste from tax year 1991 to 1996 (39-22-515); 5% of purchase price of up to 50 business cars or trucks licensed in Colorado that use clean burning alternative fuel (39-22-516); 20% of cost to purchase qualified property for use in child care center or family care home (39-22-517); 10% of investment in qualified school-to-career program (39-22-520); 20% of cost (for first two years) of providing child care services, health or dental insurance, job training, or transportation to and from work for employees on public assistance (39-22-521) and 25% of total value of monetary or in-kind contributions to promote child care in Colorado (39-22-121).

Child care expense credit for tax years on or after Jan. 1, 1998 will vary depending upon state revenues and individual income. (39-22-119). Part-year residents must pro rate tax. (39-22-119[4]). Excess credit may not be carried forward. (39-22-119[2]). Person receiving state child care assistance, except to extent of unreimbursed out-of-pocket expenses that result in federal credit for child care expense, is not allowed child care expense credits allowed under 39-2-119(1) and (1.5). (39-22-119[3]).

Certain persons and corporations whose sole activity in state consists of making sales which result in annual gross receipts of not more than $100,000, and who do not own or rent real estate in Colorado, may pay tax of 1/2 of 1% on annual gross receipts in lieu of income tax. (39-22-104[5]).

Returns must be made to executive director by 15th day of 4th month following close of taxable year. (39-22-608[2]). Returns must be filed by every individual whose adjusted gross income is equal to or greater than his Colorado standard deduction plus his Colorado exemptions (whether exemptions are attributable to individual, to his spouse if filing jointly, or to being age 65 or older); every fiduciary for such individuals, for resident estate, or trust whose income exceeds $850 multiplied by annual inflation factor, or for nonresident estate or trust whose taxable income exceeds its Colorado exemption; every corporation subject to taxation; and every partnership, limited liability company and every person who is required by federal rules to file annual reports concerning tips or remuneration from services or direct sales. (3-22-601).

Tax is payable when return is due. Executive director may grant extension of time for payment (39-22-609).

Withholding.—Effective Jan. 1, 1994, Department determines whether employer is quarterly, monthly, weekly or seasonal filer based on review of Colorado withholding tax reported in preceding 12 month period July 1 through June 30 ("lookback period"). If less than $7,000 in tax was reported in lookback period taxpayer is quarterly filer. Returns are due Apr. 30, July 31, Oct. 31 and Jan. 31. If at least $7,000 in tax but not more than $50,000 was reported taxpayer is monthly filer. Returns are due on or before 15th day of following month. If $50,000 or more in tax was reported taxpayer is weekly filer. Tax must be remitted by third business day following Fri. Employers who do not operate entire calendar year are seasonal filers. Returns are due on or before 15th day of following month of operation. Weekly filers must remit tax by electronic funds transfer. Others remit by check with coupon or by electronic transfer. (39-22-604[4][a]-[b]; Dep't of Rev. Pub. 1872). Before date established by §6071 of Internal Revenue Code, currently Mar. 15 of following year, employer must submit annual statement summarizing withholding information for each employee to department. Penalty for failure to provide annual statement for each employee is $5 to $50 in addition to civil and criminal penalties. (39-22-604[6]).

Persons making payment of winnings subject to federal withholding must withhold 4% of such winnings. (39-22-604[17]; Dep't of Rev. Reg. 39-22-604.17).

Employer holds deducted amounts in trust for state. State has lien senior to all other liens on employer's assets and on property used in employer's trade or business to secure payment upon delinquency. (39-22-604[7][a]). However, exemption certificate may be obtained for property subject to mortgage, etc., if bond posted (39-22-604[7][b]), and equipment leased to employer may be exempted if reasonably identifiable from lease and employer has no right to acquire it (39-22-604[7][c]).

Certain entities providing closing and settlement services required to withhold 2% of sales price or net proceeds, from sale of Colorado real property interests to certain nonresidents. (39-22-604.5).

Estimated Tax by Individuals.—Every individual, resident or nonresident, whose estimated tax for current year can reasonably be expected to exceed allowable credits by $1,000 must file state declaration and pay state estimated tax that executive director may prescribe, less amounts to be withheld and anticipated credits. (39-22-605[1]). If prior to Apr. 1, taxpayer expects estimated tax to exceed $1,000, he must file declaration on or before Apr. 15 of tax year. If taxpayer first expects estimated tax to exceed $1,000 after Apr. 1 but before June 2, declaration is due on or before June 15. If taxpayer first expects estimated tax to exceed $1,000 after June 1 but before Sept. 2, declaration is due on or before Sept. 15. If taxpayer first expects estimated tax to exceed $1,000 after Sept. 1, declaration is due on or before Jan. 15 of next tax year. (39-22-605[2][a]). If declaration is filed on or before Apr. 15, estimated tax is paid in four equal installments due on date declaration is filed, June 15, Sept. 15, and Jan. 15 of next year. (39-22-605[2][b][I]). If declaration is filed after Apr. 15 and before June 16, estimated tax is paid in three equal installments due on date declaration is filed, Sept. 15, and Jan. 15 of next tax year. (39-22-605[2][b][II]). If declaration is filed after June 15 and before Sept. 16, estimated tax is paid in two equal installments due on date declaration is filed and Jan. 15 of next tax year. (39-22-605[2][b][III]). If declaration is filed after Sept. 15, estimated tax is paid in full on date declaration is filed. (39-22-605[2][b][IV]).

For tax years commencing on or after Jan. 1, 1987, underpayments of estimated tax deemed not to have occurred if taxpayer payments and credits pursuant to filed declaration equal or exceed taxpayer's actual Colorado tax liability before allowable credits for preceding tax year or 70% of taxpayer's Colorado tax liability before allowable credits for current tax year. (39-22-605[4]).

Estimated Tax by Corporations.—Every corporation must file declaration of estimated tax if its tax for current year can reasonably be expected to exceed $5,000. (39-22-606[1][a]). Estimated tax is based on computation of tax on expected income, less $5,000, and amounts expected to be withheld from oil and gas royalty payments. (39-22-606[1][b]). Declaration generally due by Apr. 15. (39-22-606[2]). First installment due at time declaration filed, other installments due on 15th of June, Sept., and Dec. (39-22-606[4][b]).

INHERITANCE TAX:

Colorado does not impose inheritance tax. However, former inheritance tax law (39-23-101 et seq.) remains in effect for estates of decedents dying before Jan. 1, 1980 until all moneys due under it are collected (39-23-170).

See note at head of Digest as to 1998 legislation covered.

See Topical Index in front part of this volume.

CO – 68

OIL, GAS AND OTHER MINERALS SEVERANCE TAX:

See category Mineral, Water and Fishing Rights, topic Mines and Minerals.

OLD AGE PENSION FUND TAX:

Following fees assessed and allocated to old age pension fund: additional 10% of fees due and payable on incorporation of corporation or association for profit; and additional 10% of inheritance taxes payable. (26-2-113[2]).

PROPERTY TAXES:

Is imposed on all real and personal property not expressly exempted (39-1-102[16]) including partial interests (39-1-106) and severed mineral interests (39-1-104.5).

Exemptions.—There are numerous constitutional and statutory exemptions from state property tax, including, among others: Property used solely and exclusively for strictly charitable purposes (Const., Art. 10, §5; 39-3-101); household furnishings not used for production of income (39-3-102; Const., Art. 10, §3[1][c]); personal effects never used to produce income (39-3-103; Const., Art. 10, §3[1][c]); ditches, canals and flumes if used to irrigate owner's lands (39-3-104); property of state, counties, cities, towns, other municipal corporations and public libraries (39-3-105; Const., Art. 10, §4); property owned and used exclusively for religious purposes (39-3-106; Const., Art. 10, §5); property owned and used exclusively for nonprofit schools (Const., Art. 10, §5; 39-3-107); nonresidential property of nonprofit health care facilities or domestic water companies (39-3-108; Const., Art. 10, §5); property owned and used by nonprofit community corrections agency for community correctional facility or program (39-3-108.5); certain residential property used as integral part of church, charitable health care facility, school or other exempt institution (39-3-109); property used as integral part of qualifying child care center (39-3-110); certain property of qualifying fraternal and veterans organizations (39-3-111); certain property of qualifying health care providers who provide medical health care service to poor (39-3-111.5); certain residential property of qualifying orphanages and homes for disabled, elderly or homeless (39-3-112; 39-3-112.5); certain in-construction residential property that will be used for charitable purposes (39-3-113); nonprofit cemeteries (39-3-117); intangible personal property including computer software (39-3-118); inventories (39-3-119); personal property if value of all taxpayer's personal property is less than $2,500 (39-3-119.5); mobile homes while in dealer inventory (39-5-203[3][a]); livestock (39-3-120); agricultural and livestock products (39-3-121); agricultural equipment (39-3-122); works of art, literary materials or artifacts loaned to governmental entity or to library, gallery or museum of charitable organization, while on loan (39-3-123); property leased by exempt governmental entity to which it can take title at end of lease with no (or nominal) payment (Const., Art. 10, §4; 39-3-124); horticultural improvements resulting from planting of trees are disregarded in assessing land value until earlier of 30 years or trees becoming economically useful (39-3-126); certain property used to hold county fairs (39-3-127); personal property rented for 30 days or less similar in nature to merchandise inventories (39-1-102[7.2]); airport authorities classified as political subdivisions by general assembly (41-3-102; 41-3-107; 681 P.2d 945); nonproducing unpatented mining claims that are possessory interests in real property by virtue of leases from U.S. (Const., Art. 10, §3[1][b]); and possessory interests (39-3-136).

Generally taxpayer does not need to apply to department to have property granted exempt status. Exempt status, however, will not be recognized under §§39-3-106 to 39-3-113 and 39-3-116 until exempt status applied for and granted by property tax administrator. (39-2-117[2]). Initial filing fee for exemption application is $75. (39-2-117[1]). After initial exemption is granted annual reports and $25 fee must be filed by Apr. 15. (39-2-117[3][a][I]). Delinquent annual reports accepted between Apr. 15 and July 1 with additional $50 late fee. If report not filed by July 1, exemption is forfeited. (39-2-117[3][a][II]). Annual report not required of previously exempt fraternal or veterans organizations if declaration filed that nonexempt use is below certain hour limit or gross income levels. (39-2-117[3][a][I]). Religious organizations receive special considerations. (39-2-117[3][a][III]). If any property subject to exemption under 39-3-106 to 39-3-113 is used by other than owner, both owner and user must be exempt for property to be exempt from tax. (39-3-116). Use of exempt property for nonexempt purposes does not destroy exempt status if non-qualifying use is less than 208 hours annually, adjusted for partial usage where applicable, and does not generate $10,000 or more in income derived from any unrelated trade or business and does not generate $10,000 or more in annual rental income. (39-3-106.5).

Apportionment required if real property becomes (or ceases to be) exempt during year or if portion becomes exempt. (39-3-129 to 132). No proration of property tax for personal property. (39-3-129[1]; 130).

Tax Deferral for Elderly.—Taxpayer over 65 years old may elect to defer property taxes on home he owns and occupies. (39-3.5-101 et seq.). Deferral continues until taxpayer dies, moves, sells or uses property to earn income. (39-3.5-110). Deferral amount becomes lien junior to prior mortgages and deeds of trust, senior to subsequent encumbrances. (39-3.5-105[4]). State treasurer pays deferred amount to county treasurer, whereupon right to payment and to enforce lien vests in state treasurer. (39-3.5-106, 107).

Tax Deferral for Nongaming Property.—Certain property owners in local jurisdictions that have developed nongaming property tax deferral program may file nongaming property tax deferral claim and defer portion of their property taxes. (39-3.9-103). Available only for tax years in which property taxes exceed 130% of taxes paid on property for immediately preceding year. (39-3.9-102[1]). Lien for deferred taxes and interest attaches on date certificate of deferral is issued. (39-3.9-103[9]). Deferral is discontinued upon owner's death, cessation of business, sale of property, other disqualification of property. (39-3.9-103[5]).

Tax Work-Off for Elderly.—Taxing entities may establish work-off programs that allow taxpayers over 60 years old to work for taxing entity in lieu of paying money for real property taxes on homestead. (39-3.7-102).

Motor Vehicles.—Graduated specific ownership taxes apply in lieu of ad valorem taxes to motor vehicles, trailers, and self-propelled construction equipment, other than mobile homes, inventory and such items undergoing manufacture. (Const., Art. 10, §6).

Statutes classify vehicles and set tax rates. (42-3-101 et seq.). Specific ownership tax does not apply to: Government property (42-3-103[1]); property leased to state or subdivision if department approves lease agreement (42-3-103[2]); one noncommercial vehicle owned by U.S. armed forces disabled veteran (42-3-103[5]); one noncommercial vehicle owned by certain former U.S. armed forces prisoners of war (42-3-103[6]); or property owned or leased by entities exempt from ad valorem tax (42-3-103[7]).

Assessment.—Residential real property (excluding hotels and motels) and mobile home parks valued for assessment at 21% of actual value through 1985. (Const., Art. 10, §3; 39-1-104; 39-1-102[4.5]). Thereafter percentage adjusted to maintain constant ratio from year to year of residential property valuation for assessment to all property valuation for assessment. For tax year 1998, percentage is 9.74%. (39-1-104.2[3]). Producing mines and lands or leaseholds producing oil or gas valued for assessment as portion of value of actual annual or average annual production of unprocessed material. All other taxable property valued for assessment at 29% of actual value. (Const., Art. 10, §3[1][b]; 39-1-104).

Exempt school, church, and charitable-use real property assessed and valued as is otherwise exempt property used by person or entity seeking profit. (39-3-105).

Assessor lists all taxable property in county on assessment date except public utility property. (39-5-101). Real property in cities and towns and mining claims listings based on municipal and land office records. (39-5-103; 103.5; 39-6-103). For 1998, level of value will be value for 18 months preceding July 1, 1996. After 1998, level of value will be based on 18 months preceding a date one year after level of value date used in previous year. Oil and gas properties valued without regard to base year. (39-1-104[12]). Land and most improvements valued separately. (39-5-105). Taxpayer must list all taxable personal property on schedule furnished by assessor or face penalty up to 25% of value of omitted property. (39-5-107; 39-5-116). Disclosure of information to assessor may be compelled by court order. (39-5-119). Failure to obtain schedule does not impair assessor's valuation. (39-5-118). Owners and operators of mines and oil or gas leaseholds must supply production and sales information. (39-6-106; 39-7-101).

Actual value must be determined using cost, market, and income approaches to appraisal, except for residential real property (only market approach used); agricultural lands (earning or productive capacity used) (Const., Art. 10, §3[1][a]); and after Jan. 1, 1999, nongaming property located in district where gaming is authorized (39-1-103[18][a]). Primary indicator for valuation of superfund water treatment facility is income approach. (39-1-103[16][a]). No presumption of correctness attaches to assessing authority's determination of actual value. (Const., Art. 10, §20). Sales by lenders and governmental entities not automatically excluded in market approach. (Const., Art. 10, §20). Where cost, market, and income approaches fail to produce actual value of real property, value determined by comparison of surface use to property with similar surface use (except nonproducing oil, gas, and mineral interests which must use income approach capitalizing annual net rental income at appropriate market rate). (39-1-101). Five sales of reasonably similar property required to establish market for use of market approach for oil shale mineral interests. (39-1-103[8][a][II]). Special rules apply for use of income approach for nonproducing oil shale interests. (39-1-103[12]). Other special rules govern valuation for assessment of: Oil and gas leaseholds and producing mines (Const., Art. 10, §3[1][b]; 39-7-101 et seq.; 39-6-106); nonproducing mines (39-1-103[11]; 39-6-111); public utilities (39-4-101 et seq.); water rights (39-5-105); newly constructed taxable buildings in growth impacted counties (39-5-132); and mobile homes (39-5-201 et seq.). Special provisions set or apportion assessed value of movable equipment (39-5-113) and destroyed property (39-5-117).

Review of Assessment.—Notice of valuation of real property must be mailed annually by assessor by May 1. (Const., Art. 10, §20; 39-5-121[1]). Protests must be postmarked by May 27 or submitted in person by June 1. (39-5-121[1]). Notices of change in value of tangible personal property must be sent by June 15 and protests must be postmarked by June 30 or submitted in person by July 5. (39-5-121[1.5]). Initial hearings before assessor on taxpayer protests begin on first working day after notices are mailed for real property, June 15 for personal property. (39-5-122[1], [2]). Denials may be appealed first to county board of equalization for real property by July 15 or, after Jan. 1, 1999, in large counties electing alternate protest procedure, by Sept. 15, for personal property by July 20 (39-5-122[3]; 39-8-106, 107), then, within 30 days of decision, to either board of assessment appeals (39-2-125[1][c]), district court of county where property is located (39-8-108[1]) or to binding arbitration (39-8-108[1]; 108.5). Taxpayer may appeal adverse decision by board of assessment appeals or district court to court of appeals pursuant to appellate rules and Administrative Procedure Act. (39-8-108[2]; 24-4-106). County can appeal adverse decision on basis that it is either matter of statewide concern, would result in significant reduction of total assessed valuation or contains procedural errors or errors of law. (39-8-108[2]). Above procedure for individual taxpayer; no class certification. State board of equalization may review decision of board of assessment appeals only with regard to valuation of classes and subclasses of property. (39-9-103). Complaints relating to valuation of classes and subclasses of property may also be filed with property tax administrator (39-2-111; 39-2-114) who may petition state board of equalization for reappraisal (39-2-111; 39-2-114). Decisions of state board of equalization subject to judicial review. (39-9-108; 24-4-106). Public utilities are valued by property tax administrator and utility or county may protest value by June 15. (39-4-108[1]; [2]). If protest denied, utility or county may appeal to board of assessment appeals (39-2-125[1][b][I]) and thereafter to court of appeals (39-4-109).

Taxpayer may request administrative abatement or refund if taxes were levied erroneously or illegally because of erroneous valuations, levy irregularity, clerical error or overvaluation. (39-10-114[1]). Petition for abatement or refund must be filed within two years after Jan. 1 of year following year in which taxes were levied. (39-10-114[1]). Abatements may not be granted on overvaluation grounds for years prior to 1988, or if property valuation was protested at time of valuation. (39-10-114).

Payment.—Taxes payable Jan. 1, and delinquent on June 16, payable to county treasurer. (39-10-102). Treasurer required to mail statement of taxes due. (39-10-103). Payment may either be in full before last day of Apr. or in two equal installments due last day of Feb. and June 15. (39-10-104.5). Interest and penalties apply for late payment. (39-10-104.5). Unit operator of hydrocarbon wells must remit tax for all fractional interests or be liable for tax. (39-10-106[2]). Unit operator may withhold from

---

PROPERTY TAXES . . . *continued*

royalty payments or arrange for purchasers of well output to do so. Operator remains liable unless fractional interest owner provides inaccurate revenue information to unit operator. (39-10-106).

Incentive Payments.—Taxpayer establishing qualifying new business facilities in designated enterprise zones may negotiate incentive payments for property located in such zones. (39-30-107.5).

Collection.—Tax collected by county treasurer (39-10-101), who prepares list of delinquents (39-10-109) and publishes it one time in Sept. (39-10-110). Treasurer may institute action to collect unpaid taxes (39-10-111; 39-10-112), and to prevent removal or transfer of taxable personal property (39-10-113; 4-6-101 et seq.). Treasurer may employ collection agency to collect unpaid taxes. (39-10-112[1][a]). Collection agency is selected through bid process and cannot be paid more than one-third of amount recovered. (39-10-112[1][b]). Treasurer may accept partial payments for delinquent personal property taxes pursuant to written payment plan. (39-10-110.5).

Lien.—Attaches on assessment date, Jan. 1, at 12 noon, on real and personal property (including tax liens levied on new construction in growth impacted counties) (39-1-107[1]; 105), and is perpetual prior lien thereafter until paid in full. Lien for general taxes that are deferred replaced by new lien when tax deferral for elderly elected. (39-3.5-102[c]). Lien for deferred taxes and interest attaches when certificate of nongaming property tax deferral is issued. (39-3.9-103[9]).

Sale.—At any time after Oct. 1, county treasurer, after mailing and publishing notice of delinquency, shall enforce collection of delinquent taxes on personal property, and on mobile homes and public utility property, by distraint, seizure, and sale. (39-10-111[1], [11]; 39-5-202). Notice of amount demanded and time and place of sale must be furnished owner (39-10-111[2]), and published or posted (39-10-111[3]). Time fixed for sale must be within ten days of notice, but may be adjourned for not more than 30 days. (39-10-111[4]). Sale is by public auction, with property offered at minimum price, including taxes, penalty interest and costs of advertising and seizure. (39-10-111[5]). Levying county may cause county to which property has been removed to seize and sell it (39-10-111[1][b]) or may seize property to prevent removal from county (39-10-113). County may employ collection agency or sue taxpayer if property cannot be located or if sale proceeds inadequate to pay tax. (39-10-112).

In case of sales of tax liens on real property, notice of delinquency is mailed to owner delinquent in taxes no later than Sept. 1. (39-11-101). Twenty days after mailing, treasurer lists lands subject to sale, together with notice of sale. (39-11-101). Notice of sale is then published and posted at least four weeks before sale date, for period of four weeks. (39-11-102). Sales to commence on or before 2d Mon. in Dec., (39-11-109), unless, for any cause, due publication and sale cannot be had by that time, in which case property may be sold at subsequent time (39-11-110). If no bids, tax lien is sold to county, city, town, or city and county for amount of taxes, interest, and costs. (39-11-108). Sales are for cash (39-11-111) to highest bidder; bid must equal or exceed taxes, interest, and costs (39-11-115). If bidder fails to pay, tax lien may be resold or bidder sued. (39-11-116). Treasurer gives purchaser certificate of purchase (39-11-117) which is assignable (39-11-118), and which may be exchanged for tax deed at expiration of three years (39-11-120) after notice to persons in possession and record owner, if possible, and publication if actual notice not possible (39-11-128). Owners of easement concerning common areas of subdivision are "record owners" and must be notified or tax deed void. (689 P.2d 720). Tax deed is prima facie evidence of regularity of sale, when acknowledged and recorded. (39-11-136). Suits to quiet title by holder under tax deed are authorized by statute (39-11-133), and are common practice to make tax title merchantable.

Redemption and Actions to Recover Property.—Real property for which tax lien was sold for taxes may be redeemed by owner or his agent, or "any person having legal or equitable claim therein." (39-12-103). Holder of tax sale certificate may redeem from sale subsequent to time of issuance of his certificate. (39-12-103). Redemption may be made at any time before execution of treasurer's deed to purchaser, his heirs or assigns, upon payment to treasurer, to be held by him subject to order of purchaser, of amount of taxes, penalty interest, and costs for which tax lien on property was sold, with interest from date of sale at statutorily determined rate, plus all taxes accruing after sale paid by purchaser and endorsed on certificate, with interest on such interest. (39-12-103[3]). Person under legal disability when tax deed issued may redeem within lesser of nine years from recording of tax deed or two years from removal of disability. (30-12-104). Undivided interest may be redeemed by paying ratable amount of sum necessary to redeem whole. (39-12-113). Assessor shall ascertain such proportionate redemption amount on request. (39-12-113).

Mobile home owners may redeem within one year of date of sale if home on leased land, three years if on owned land. (39-10-111[10]). Redemption period is 60 days if value of mobile home is less than $1,000. (39-10-111[12]).

Five year limitation period for suit to recover land for which tax deed issued, commencing with execution and delivery of deed. (39-12-101). But, taxpayer who was under legal disability when deed issued may sue during extended redemption period. (39-12-101). Limitation period two years from actual possession under tax deed for mining claims. (39-12-102).

RACING TAX:

Is imposed on receipts derived from pari-mutuel wagering on races of greyhounds and horses. (12-60-701 to 706). Through July 1, 1994, 5% tax is imposed on gross receipts derived from pari-mutuel wagering at race or simulcast race of greyhounds. (12-60-701[1]). After July 1, 1994, tax is 4.5%. Tax of 3/4% imposed on gross receipts of pari-mutuel wagering at race or simulcast race of horses. Tax for operation of class B track is greater of (1) actual cost of regulation up to $2,500 per race day or 3/4% of gross receipts at race. (12-60-701[2][a][I]). Additional 1/4% tax on certain gross receipts from pari-mutuel wagering at races of horses is paid to Colorado State University for racing-related equine research. (12-60-701[2][a][II]). Additional 1/2% or 1 1/2% tax on gross receipts from pari-mutuel wagering at races of horses is paid to department for horse breeders' and owners' awards. (12-60-701[2][b]). Except for breeders' tax which is remitted day of race, all taxes and accompanying returns are due to department on business day following race. (12-60-705). Failure to file return or pay tax is penalized $15 per failure or 10% of tax plus penalty interest of 1/2% per month not to exceed 18%. Regular interest charged on tax due at rate set in 39-21-110.5. (12-60-705[4]).

REAL ESTATE CONVEYANCE TAX:

Documentary fee when consideration paid by purchaser, inclusive of amount of any liens or encumbrance, exceeds $500. (39-13-102). Computed at rate of 1¢ for each $100 or major fraction thereof. (39-13-102[2]). No deed will be recorded unless fee paid. (39-13-105). Declaration of sales price required. (39-14-102).

SALES AND USE TAXES:

Sales Tax.—Tax at rate of 3% (39-26-106) is imposed upon purchase price of certain retail sales of tangible personal property, telephone, telegraph, gas, electric and steam service, meals at place regularly furnishing meals to public (39-26-104), portion of factory-built housing (except subsequent sales of such housing after once subject to tax) (39-26-114[10]), and lodging except when there is written agreement for 30 consecutive days' lodging (39-26-114[1][a][VI]).

Purchase price includes all amounts paid by consumer, excluding any direct taxes and excluding fair market value of property exchanged if exchanged property is to be sold thereafter in usual course of retail business or if exchanged property is vehicle exchanged for another vehicle, and both vehicles subject to state licensing, registration or certification requirements. (39-26-102[7]). Sales price is gross value of all materials, labor, service, and profit included in price charged customer. (39-26-102[12]). Tax is added to sales price and, except for liquor by drink, separately stated. (36-26-106[2]). Misdemeanor to represent to customer that tax absorbed by seller or not added to sale. (39-26-108). Motor vehicle may not be registered nor certificate of title issued until tax paid. (39-26-113). Refunds of amounts erroneously paid may be sought under procedures of 39-26-114(2).

Statutory Exemptions.—There are numerous exemptions from state sales tax, including, among others: Sales to governmental units (39-26-114[1][a][I]); sales to charitable organizations (39-26-114[1][a][II]); sales prohibited from taxation under constitution or laws of U.S. or Colorado and sales to noncorporate residents of adjoining states where such sales within 20 miles of Colorado boundary and not taxed by adjoining state (39-26-114[1][a][III]); cigarettes (39-26-114[1][a][IV]); prescription drugs and certain medical appliances (39-26-114[1][a][V]; sales of lodging to permanent resident of hotel, lodging house, etc. (39-26-114[1][a][VI]); certain fuels subject to other fuels taxes or used on farms and ranches (39-26-114[1][a][VII]; [XV]); sales to nonprofit schools (39-26-114[1][a][VIII]); certain trucks and trailers (39-26-114[1][a][IX]; [X]); sales to interstate railroads for track maintenance (39-26-114[1][a][XI]); certain leases of tangible personal property that are for less than three years if lessor pays tax on acquisition (39-26-114[1][a][XII]); products that are temporarily in Colorado for testing, modification and inspection prior to ultimate use out of state (39-26-114[1][a][XIV]); sales to contractors and subcontractors for use in building or repairing public facilities owned and used by governmental units, charitable organizations and nonprofit schools (39-26-114[1][a][XIX]); food (39-26-114[1][a][XX]); electricity and certain fuels for residential use (39-26-114[1][a][XXI]); commercial aircraft used in interstate commerce (39-26-114[1][a][XXII]); tangible personal property permanently affixed as component part of aircraft (39-26-114[1][a][XXIII]); tangible personal property affixed as component part of railroad car or equipment (39-26-114[1][a][XXIV]); locomotives, freight cars, railroad work equipment and other railroad rolling stock used in interstate commerce (39-26-114[1][a][XXV]); Internet access services from May 1, 1998 to and including Apr. 30, 2001; certain livestock and all farm close-out sales (39-26-114[5]); feed, bedding, seeds and orchard trees (39-26-114[6]; [8]); sales not exceeding 15¢ from registered and complying vending machines (39-26-114[7]); 48% of first purchase price, and 100% of purchase price on subsequent sales, of factory-built housing (39-26-114[10]); sales of manufacturing machinery, machine tools or parts over $500 (39-26-114[11]); part of price paid for nonautomotive lubricating oil (39-26-114[13]); refractory materials and carbon electrodes for manufacture of iron and steel, and inorganic chemicals for processing vanadium-uranium ores (39-26-114[14]); sale of certain precious metal bullion and coins prior to Apr. 17, 1995 (39-26-114[17]); occasional sales by charitable organizations (39-26-114[18]); all sales and purchases of tangible property used as component parts in manufacturing goods which are then donated by manufacturer with aggregate value over $1,000 to tax exempt organizations (39-26-114[20]); sale of pre-press preparation printing materials (39-26-102[19]); certain sales of electricity and fuel for industrial uses (39-26-102[21]); sale of automobiles to nonresidents for use outside Colorado (39-26-113[5]); purchases of machinery or tools over $500 used exclusively in enterprise zone (39-30-106[1]). Taxpayers establishing qualifying new business facilities in enterprise zone may negotiate refund of other sales tax levied in zone. (39-30-107.5). Strong presumption that taxation is rule and exemption exception. (665 P.2d 626). State-chartered credit unions not exempt. (Id.).

Collection of Tax.—Seller at retail must obtain license from executive director with annual renewal. Executive director may revoke for violation of sales tax law. (39-26-103[4]). Seller liable for tax and must make monthly report of sales and remit 3% tax, less 3 1/3% of tax retained to cover collection and remittance expenses. (39-26-105). Seller must also remit any excess over 3% collected. (39-26-112). Credit seller generally may return and remit as payments received. (39-26-111). Executive director may, at seller's written request, accept reports at other intervals to prevent hardship. (39-26-109). Seller with two or more locations may file combined returns. (39-26-110).

Penalties and Enforcement.—Seller must keep record of sales adequate to determine amount due. (39-26-116). Tax due becomes lien on taxpayer's goods and business fixtures and on business property leased to taxpayer unless exempted. (39-26-117). Penalty for underpayment due to negligent or knowing disregard of regulations 10% of deficiency, 100% if due to fraud with intent to evade, plus interest and penalty interest in each case. (39-26-115). Refusal to file or filing fraudulent return felony punishable by fine, imprisonment or both, as provided in 39-21-118. (39-26-120; -121). If taxpayer neglects or refuses to file, executive director may estimate tax, add interest and penalty and, following notification, levy on and distrain taxpayer's property. (39-26-118). Penalty and interest may be waived for good cause. (39-26-118[9]). Action to collect tax

See note at head of Digest as to 1998 legislation covered.

See Topical Index in front part of this volume.

CO – 70

SALES AND USE TAXES . . . *continued*

must begin within three years from date tax due, unless seller fails to file return or files false or fraudulent return with intent to evade tax, in which case action to collect tax may be begun at any time. (39-26-125).

Use Tax.—3% imposed upon storage or acquisition charges or costs for privilege of storing, using or consuming any articles of tangible personal property purchased at retail. (39-26-202). Property not subject to tax includes: Property subject to sales tax, property held for resale in state in regular course of business, motor fuel, property of nonresident temporarily in state, property of U.S. or Colorado and its political subdivisions used in governmental capacity, property of charitable organizations used in conduct of regular charitable functions, personalty acquired outside of state and used by nonresident acquiring residency, personalty having value less than $100 purchased by resident outside of state, certain machinery or machine tools used in manufacturing, food purchased in grocery stores for consumption at home, electricity, coal, gas, fuel, oil and coke used in residences, certain precious metal bullion or coins, Internet access services, storage, use or consumption of aircraft used in interstate commerce, and storage, use or consumption of tangible personal property permanently affixed as component part of aircraft, storage, use or consumption of tangible property used as component parts in manufacturing goods which are then donated by manufacturer with aggregate value over $1,000 to tax exempt organizations. (39-26-203). Payments of tax must be made to department of revenue on 20th of each month following month in which cumulative tax due is in excess of $300, Jan. 20 of year following if less than $300 for calendar year. (39-26-204).

If taxpayer neglects or refuses to make return, executive director makes appealable determination of tax due plus 10% penalty and interest for delinquency period. (39-26-204[5]). Willful failure to make return or to pay tax felony punishable by fine, imprisonment or both, as provided in 39-21-118. (39-26-206). Penalty interest accrues on unpaid tax and executive director may, through attorney general, sue to recover tax plus interest. (39-26-207). Tax constitutes prior lien on property unless exempted. (39-26-205). Automobile may not be registered or certificate of title issued until tax paid. (39-26-208).

Action to collect tax must begin within same time period applicable to sales tax. (39-26-210).

Local Sales and Use Tax.—Statutory cities and counties may levy sales and use taxes on tax base similar to state sales and use tax base. Local tax rate when combined with state tax rate cannot exceed 7%. Regardless of combined rate limit, local tax rate may always be 1% or less. (29-2-108[1]). Home rule cities may impose sales and use taxes on broader base and at higher rates. (29-2-107).

STAMP TAX:

No general documentary stamp tax. See subheads Real Estate Conveyance Tax; Liquor Taxes, infra.

TRANSPORTATION TAXES:

Highway Compensation Tax.—See category Transportation, topic Motor Vehicles, subhead Motor Vehicle Carriers.

UNEMPLOYMENT COMPENSATION TAX:

Imposed on employers. (8-76-101).

"Employer" is defined to include any employing unit with one or more employees, unless exempt. (8-70-103).

Tax applies only to wages or other remuneration not in excess of $7,000 per annum to any individual in calendar year 1983, $8,000 for calendar years 1984-1986, $9,000 for calendar year 1987, and $10,000 for calendar years 1988 and thereafter. (8-70-103[26]). Rate is 1% first year and thereafter based on benefit experience of employer. (8-76-103).

TRANSPORTATION

MOTOR VEHICLES:

Executive director of Colorado department of revenue has general supervision (42-1-201): Executive Director, Colo. Dep't. of Revenue, 1375 Sherman Street, Denver, CO 80261.

Vehicle Equipment Safety Compact adopted. (24-60-901 to 912).

Driver License Compact adopted. (24-60-1101 to 1107).

Vehicle Registration and Licenses.—All vehicles, except those exempted by 42-3-104, must be registered (42-3-103) within 45 days of purchase; vehicles previously registered in another state must be registered within 30 days of Colorado residency. Registration expires at end of each 12-month registration period (42-3-102) or on transfer of vehicle (42-3-126). Generally, vehicle must be registered in county of owner's residence. (42-6-139).

Certain persons eligible for extended temporary registration. (42-3-103.5).

Numbered plates must be displayed front and rear and registration card carried in vehicle. (42-3-112, 123). Registration fee is payable in accordance with 42-3-134. In addition, specific ownership tax imposed on vehicles in lieu of personal property taxes. (42-3-105 to 111). Various exemptions from payment of fees available. (42-3-104, 134). Designated government officers and dealers required to verify vehicle information by physical inspection. (42-3-105[1][b]).

Operator's License Required.—Persons licensed in following manner: (A) Any person at least 21 years old, as driver; (B) any person at least 18 years old but not yet 21 years old, as provisional driver; (C) any person at least 16 years old but not yet 18 years old, as minor driver. (42-2-104). Following classes of operator's licenses established: Class A includes any vehicle or combination of vehicles except bus or motorcycle; Class B includes any single vehicle except bus or motorcycle, and will permit licensee to tow one other vehicle of less than 10,000 pounds; Class C is basic driver's license and permits operation of any two-axle vehicle, but does not permit operation of vehicles described in Class A, B, S, or M, and does permit towing of one other vehicle or trailer

of less than 10,000 pounds gross vehicle weight; Class M permits only operation of motorcycles and motor-driven cycles and can be sole classification of license or can be added as endorsement to any other class; Class S permits operation of vehicle which is equipped for carrying ten or more persons (but does not permit operation of school buses). (1 Code Colo. Reg. 204-6). Any class driver's license authorizes operating motorized bicycle (moped). (42-2-103). Commercial licenses regulated by 42-2-401 to 408. License, permit or identification card must be exhibited on demand. (42-2-115).

New residents have 30 days to obtain license. (42-2-102[2]). Exemption for persons operating federally owned military vehicle while serving in U.S. armed forces. (42-2-102[1][a]). Exemption for nonresident student, 16 years or older with valid out-of-state license. (42-2-102[1][f]).

Department of revenue authorized, upon specific statutory conditions, to cancel, suspend, or revoke operator's license. (42-2-122 to 135). In general, unlawful use or possession of license is misdemeanor. (42-2-136). Penalties imposed for driving without valid license (42-2-101) or with license under restraint (42-2-138). Habitual offenders of laws may have their licenses revoked. (42-2-201 to 208).

Titles.—Certificate of title required before certificate of registration or license plates may be issued. (42-6-106). Such certificate may be obtained by filing verified application with director through county motor vehicle office upon form provided and by presenting evidence of ownership. (42-6-116). If applicant cannot show right to certificate by sufficient evidence, certificate may nevertheless issue, provided applicant furnishes director with his statement setting forth source of title to, and liens against, vehicle and sufficient security or surety bond. (42-6-115). Certificate of title is prima facie evidence of matters recited therein and that person named therein is lawful owner. (42-6-107[2]). If certificate lost, duplicate may be issued by Director. (42-6-135). Mobile home titles governed by separate statutes administered by director. (38-29-101 to 143).

Sales.—Transfer of motor vehicle must be accompanied by delivery to transferee of certificate of title. (42-6-109). Within 45 days, transferee must present certificate to director, together with application for new certificate and transfer fee of $6.50, whereupon new certificate will be issued. (42-6-110, 137). Upon transfer by dealer of new motor vehicle, dealer must execute bill of sale to transferee together with manufacturer's certificate of origin. Upon presentment thereof to director by transferee, new certificate of title may be obtained. (42-6-113). Upon transfer of motor vehicle by bequest, inheritance, operation of law or lien or mortgage foreclosure, director may issue new certificate of title upon receipt of proper application and upon surrender of old certificate of title or presentation of other proof of ownership. (42-6-114).

Any transfer of motor vehicle without complying with Act is misdemeanor. (42-6-142). Altering or forging certificate of title or knowing use or transfer thereof is felony. (42-6-143). Sunday sales of motor vehicles prohibited. Violation constitutes misdemeanor. (12-6-302, 303).

Sales subject to regulations. (1 Code Colo. Reg. 205-1).

Terms of installment sales regulated by Uniform Consumer Credit Code. (5-1-101 to 2-605). Motor vehicle dealers, used motor vehicle dealers, salesmen, wholesalers, distributors, auctioneers, manufacturers and factory representatives licensed by motor vehicle dealer licensing board. (12-6-101 to 126). Applicants for licenses must post surety bond and appoint agent for service of process in state. (12-6-111, 112, 115[6]). Right of action against dealers, salesmen, wholesalers, auctioneers, manufacturers and factory representatives for fraud or commission of certain prohibited acts, including deceptive trade practices. (12-6-122, 6-1-101 to 205). Certain deceptive trade practices prohibited in sale of motor vehicles. (6-1-105, 42-6-202).

Repairs.—No repairs on covered motor vehicle may be performed by repair garage without provision of written cost estimate and written consent of customer, except written consent may be waived by customer where vehicle has been towed to garage or left at garage outside of business hours or by specific statutory written waiver, but repairs made under such waiver will be limited to $100 maximum. (42-9-104). When estimate has not been waived, repair charges will be limited to cost estimate plus 10% or $25, whichever is less, unless customer gives written or oral consent to additional charges before performance of additional work. (42-9-105). Certain deceptive and unfair practices relating to repair of motor vehicles prohibited. (42-9-111). Statutory violation may result in criminal conviction; aggrieved customer may recover damages including attorney fees and costs. (42-9-112).

Liens.—Transactions creating security interests in motor vehicles (other than mobile homes) held for sale or lease which constitute inventory governed generally by Art. 9, Uniform Commercial Code. (4-9-101 to 507). Security interests in motor vehicles not constituting inventory governed only by certificate of title statute. (42-6-120). To be valid against third persons, holder of chattel mortgage must file signed original or signed duplicate original of mortgage or copy thereof; authorized agent thereupon files mortgage for record, notes mortgage upon certificate of title and forwards same to director, who issues new certificate containing description of mortgage. (42-6-121 to 123). Such mortgage may remain lien for eight years after filing, after which time lien may be extended for successive three year periods. (42-6-127). No mortgage on motor vehicle recorded in any other state valid against third persons having no actual notice thereof unless certificate of title to such vehicle bears notation adequate to apprise such third persons of existence of mortgage. (42-6-133).

Any mechanic or other person who performs repairs at request of owner shall have lien upon vehicle for amount due for such repairs or material furnished and for all costs incurred in enforcing lien for so long as person who performed repairs maintains possession or, if vehicle has been released, upon receipt of payment in form of check, draft, or order for payment which is not honored for full payment or is dishonored. (38-20-106, 106.5).

Identification Marks.—Except for legitimate repairs, removal, alteration, or obliteration of vehicle identification number, manufacturer's number, or engine number, as well as knowing possession of vehicle on which these numbers have been tampered with, is felony. (42-5-102[2]).

Size and Weight.—Regulated by 42-4-501 to 512.

Lights Required.—Regulated by 42-4-204 to 222.

See note at head of Digest as to 1998 legislation covered.

See Topical Index in front part of this volume.

MOTOR VEHICLES ... *continued*

Equipment Required.—Regulated by 42-4-223 to 237. Child restraints mandated. (42-4-236). Drivers and front seat passengers required to use safety belts. (42-4-237).

Inspection.—No safety inspection program. Annual emissions control inspection required for vehicles registered in certain heavily populated locations. (42-4-304[20]). Comprehensive legislation and regulatory program enacted regarding motor vehicle emissions (42-4-301 to 316; 5 Code Colo. Reg. 1001-15 to 17), including provisions permitting buyers to return vehicles out of compliance with emissions standards to motor vehicle dealers for repair or refund (42-4-309). See also category Environment, topic Environmental Regulation.

Traffic Regulations.—Provisions regarding driving, overtaking and passing. (42-4-1001 to 1012). Provisions regarding vehicle speed. (42-4-1101 to 1105). Provisions regarding parking and backing. (42-4-1201 to 1211). Provisions regarding towing of abandoned vehicles. (42-4-1801 to 1815). Provisions regarding other traffic offenses. (42-4-1401 to 1413). Provisions regarding penalties and procedure. (42-4-1701 to 1718).

Any person operating motor vehicle in Colorado deemed to consent to (i) blood or breath test for alcohol and (ii) blood, saliva or urine test for drugs. (42-4-1301[7][a]). For purposes of prosecution, alcohol levels at the time of the alleged offense give rise to the following presumptions: not under influence and ability not impaired if less than or equal to .05; ability impaired, but other evidence necessary for proving under influence if greater than .05 but less than .10; under influence if greater than or equal to .10. (42-4-1301[5]). Driving includes "actual physical control"; person in driver's seat of motor vehicle with ignition key in on position is in actual physical control. (804 P.2d 873). Miranda warnings need not be given prior to performing driver roadside sobriety test in connection with routine traffic stop. (719 P.2d 1091). Roadside sobriety test can be administered only with probable cause or consent and cannot be compelled (633 P.2d 1071); however, revocation of license for specified violations or refusal to take sobriety test mandated (42-2-126[2][a][II]). Chemical test need only be requested within "reasonable time". (766 P.2d 665). Breath tests not automatically inadmissible due to lack of evidence of testing officer's certification. (753 P.2d 239). Mandatory license revocation prescribed for conviction of driving under influence. (42-2-125[1][b]). Mandatory revocation of commercial driver's license for possession or knowing transportation of illegal drugs. (42-2-405[2]).

Accidents.—Driver of car involved in accident causing injury to person or property must stop, give name, address and car registration and render reasonable assistance to injured including carrying victim or causing victim to be carried to medical assistance. (42-4-1602, 1603). Driver of car striking unattended vehicle must locate its owner or attach thereto note giving name, address and registration number of vehicle. (42-4-1604). All accidents causing injury to person or property must be reported immediately to nearest police authority. (42-4-1606). If personal injury, death or any property damage results, operator or owner must report in writing to director within ten days. (42-4-1606[2], 42-7-202).

Vehicular Homicide and Assault.—Driver guilty of vehicular homicide if he operates or drives motor vehicle recklessly or while under influence of alcohol or drugs and such conduct is proximate cause of death of another. (18-3-106). Driver guilty of vehicular assault if he operates or drives motor vehicle recklessly or while under influence of alcohol or drugs and such conduct is proximate cause of serious bodily injury to another. (18-3-205).

Liability of Owner.—Family car doctrine recognized. (63 Colo. 365, 167 P. 966). However, adoption of no-fault insurance (see subhead No-Fault Insurance, infra) and elimination of joint and several liability (see category Civil Actions and Procedure, topic Damages) may also affect liability of owner.

Guest Statute repealed effective Apr. 9, 1975. (1975, c. 379).

Financial Responsibility.—Motor Vehicle Financial Responsibility Act (42-7-101 to 609) provides that driver's license may be suspended if person at fault in an accident fails to furnish director adequate security for satisfaction of any liability arising out of accident up to $35,000, and proof of financial responsibility in future (42-7-301). Future responsibility may be shown by certificate of insurance coverage, deposit of money or securities, or posting of bond. (47-7-408). License may also be suspended where liable party fails to satisfy judgment within 30 days, or fails to comply with terms of order of restitution made as condition of probation in criminal proceeding arising from use or operation of motor vehicle. (42-7-401).

The "free from any fault" exception to requirement of posting security by an uninsured motorist following an accident means no reasonable possibility of a judgment being rendered against him, and motorist has burden of bringing himself within that exception. (179 Colo. 270, 499 P.2d 1169).

Insurance.—See subhead No-Fault Insurance, infra.

No-fault insurance adopted. (10-4-701 to 725). Insurance required for every owner of motor vehicle who operates it in state; noncompliance sanctions imposed by Motor Vehicle Financial Responsibility Act (see subhead Financial Responsibility, supra). (10-4-705). Policy must provide: legal liability coverage for injury or death up to $25,000 per person and $50,000 to all persons in one accident, and $15,000 for property damage;

compensation for medical expenses and certain nonmedical costs up to $50,000 per person; rehabilitative benefits up to $50,000; 100% of first $125 per week of loss of gross income and reduced percentages of further gross income, up to payment of $400 per week, for up to 52 weeks; compensation for essential services injured person would have performed without income; and compensation to estate of deceased of $1,000. Alternatively, insurers may offer basic personal injury protection policy deemed to provide required minimum coverages to individuals with annual gross income less than $20,000. (10-4-706). In lieu of owner's insurance policy, requirements of 10-4-705 may be satisfied by obtaining operator's policy meeting statutory requirements. (10-4-706.5). Tort actions not allowed unless motor vehicle accident causes death; dismemberment; permanent disability; permanent disfigurement; reasonable need for treatment and rehabilitation costs over $2,500 or, if ridership arrangement involved, over $5,000; loss of earning capacity beyond 52 weeks; or economic loss in excess of minimum coverage. (10-4-714). Policy must allow insured to assign payments due under policy to licensed health care provider. (10-4-708.4). No limitation on actions against intentional tortfeasors, persons not complying with statute or persons subject to products liability tort claims. (10-4-715). Person with more than 25 registered motor vehicles can qualify as self-insurer. Statute sets forth reasons for canceling certificate of self-insurance. (10-4-716). Proof of insurance required. (42-4-1409). Underinsured and uninsured coverage must be offered. (10-4-609).

Foreign vehicles, properly licensed in home state, may operate without Colorado license, except that vehicle carrying goods or persons for hire must have Colorado license but only in accordance with registration reciprocity between Colorado and foreign state. (42-3-128).

Nonresident Operators.—Nonresident over 16 having in his possession operator's license issued by his home state may operate vehicle as private operator. (42-2-102[c]).

Actions against Nonresident.—Service of process personally made outside state in action arising from transaction of any business; ownership, use, or possession of any real property; contracting to insure any person, property or risk; maintenance of matrimonial domicile; agreeing to dispute resolution through arbitration or similar means within state; or commission of tortious act within state gives state court jurisdiction over person served. (13-1-124, 125).

Direct actions not authorized by statute.

Snowmobiles.—No person shall operate or have in his possession snowmobile in state unless registered and licensed by division of wildlife. (33-14-102).

Motor Vehicle Carriers.—

Common carrier transporting persons or property must obtain certificate of convenience and necessity from public utilities commission (40-10-104), unless in interstate commerce in which case registration, but no certificate, is required (40-10-120). Filing fee $35 for intrastate and $15 for interstate commerce. Fee for transfer of certificate or registration $35 for intrastate commerce and $5 for interstate commerce. (40-10-109). Carriers must also pay $5 identification fee per vehicle every year. (40-2-110.5). Common carrier must file liability insurance policy or surety bond. Policy limits or bond amount must comport with regulations of commission. (40-10-110). Common carrier does not include ridesharing arrangements, carriers of household goods, luxury limousines, charter or scenic busses, offroad scenic charters, children's activity bus, motor vehicle carrier exempt from regulation as public utility, commercial transport of ashes, trash, waste, rubbish, garbage, industrial waste products or other discarded materials, except sludge and fly ash, nonemergency transportation of persons with disabilities, hearses, ambulances or emergency vehicles. (40-1-102[3]; 40-10-104; 40-16-101).

Contract carrier in interstate commerce must register with public utilities commission (40-11-115). If in intrastate commerce must obtain permit from commission (40-11-103). Filing fees parallel those for common carriers. (40-11-108). Must file liability insurance policy or surety bond in compliance with commission regulations. (40-11-109). Exceptions from regulation generally coincide with exceptions to common carrier regulation. In addition, "contract carrier" excludes common carriers and carriage of friend or neighbor on trip. (40-11-101[3], -102[2]). Commission has power and duty to prescribe minimum rates for contract carriers in competition with common carriers. (40-11-105). Commission has promulgated numerous regulations regarding contract carriers. (4 Code Colo. Reg. 723-23).

Towing carriers must obtain permit from public utilities commission. (40-13-103). Fee for permit $10. (40-13-104). Insurance or surety bond required. (40-13-105).

Person injured by violation of statutes hereinbefore cited may apply to court of competent jurisdiction for enforcement by injunction or other proper process; such person also has cause of action in damages. (40-10-115[4], 40-11-113[4], 40-13-112[4]).

Certain Transported Materials.—Transport of hazardous and nuclear materials subject to detailed regulations. (42-20-101 to 511).

Highway Compensation Tax.—In addition to regular registration and license fees, carriers subject to various passenger-mile and ton-mile taxes. (42-3-134). Certain interstate carriers may apply for special 72-hour laden weight registration in lieu thereof. (42-3-134[15]).

Gasoline Tax.—See category Taxation, topic Gasoline and Special Fuel Tax.

Ownership Tax.—See category Taxation, topic Property Taxes.

COMMERCIAL CODE FORMS
See also categories Business Regulation and Commerce, topic Commercial Code and Mortgages, topic Chattel Mortgages.

COLORADO UCC-1 FINANCING STATEMENT
(See instructions on back)
Standard Form Effective May 1, 1998
Total Fee = $16, includes Surcharge

1st DEBTOR
Name (Last, First):
SSN/FED Tax ID:
Street: Check One:
City, State, Zip: Business ☐
                                          Individual ☐

2nd DEBTOR (Put Additional Debtors on attachment)
Name (Last, First):
SSN/FED Tax ID:
Street: Check One:
City, State, Zip: Business ☐
                                          Individual ☐

CHECK ONLY ONE (If no box is checked, it will be filed in UCC only)

☐   File in **UCC ONLY**
☐   This statement is to be recorded in the real estate records **ONLY.**
☐   This statement is to be filed in UCC **AND** recorded in the real estate records.
      (Requires an additional recording fee.)
☐   The debtor is a transmitting utility.

1st SECURED PARTY (Put Additional Secured Parties on attachment)
Name (Last, First):
Street:
City: State, Zip:

ASSIGNED PARTY (Put Additional Assigned Party on attachment)
Name (Last, First):
Street:
City, State, Zip:

FOR UCC FILINGS (Fill in collateral codes from UCC Codes)

RETURN COPY TO
Name:
Street:
City, State, Zip:

FOR AGRICULTURAL LIEN NOTIFICATION

Name of the Record Owner of the real property containing the collateral is: _____
(See Instruction 13)

Check if this filing is intended as EFS notification ☐
Enter EFS collateral code, County Code and crop years covered.
If all years are covered, leave from and to dates blank.

EFS Code   County Code   From   To

(Use if collateral codes do not adequately describe collateral.
Attach additional pages if necessary)

COMPLETE DESCRIPTION OF COLLATERAL

_____
Debtor Signature(s) (See Instruction 14)

_____
Printed Name(s)

_____
Title

_____
Secured Party Signatures (See Instruction 14)

_____
Printed Name(s)

_____
Title

Contact Phone/FAX

COLORADO UCC-1 INSTRUCTIONS

1. Type the form in Upper Case.

2. Type only one debtor name in each debtor field. For more than two debtors, attach a separate sheet.

3. Do **NOT** use D/B/A, A/K/A or F/K/A with a debtor's name. If the debtor uses a tradename, or goes by another name, list it as a separate debtor. For example, if John Brown does business as Brown's Auto Body Shop, list John Brown as an individual debtor and Brown's Auto Body Shop as a second debtor.

4. Do **NOT** use titles, i.e. Dr., Rev., Esq., etc. in individual names.

5. Do **NOT** use the same social security number for two separate individual debtors. If the debtor uses a tradename, the social security number of the debtor may be used as the tax identifier for the tradename. If a social security number or Federal Tax ID number has not been received as of the time of filing, put "Applied For" in the appropriate field, but you must submit a UCC-3 Amendment upon receipt of the number.

6. Check the "Business" box if the debtor is a business entity. Check the "Individual" box if the debtor is an individual.

7. If you check the box that the document is to be filed in both the UCC and Real Estate records, the Clerk and Recorder may charge you a separate filing fee for the real estate recording.

8. List UCC collateral by code in the spaces provided. List UCC collateral only once, regardless of the number of debtors on the financing statement. A financing statement may be filed with the Colorado Secretary of State or the clerk and recorder for any county for most types of collateral under Colorado law. When the financing statement covers timber to be cut or minerals or other substances of value which may be extracted from the earth, or accounts subject to subsection (5) of section 4-9-103 C.R.S., or when the financing statement is filed as a fixture filing and the collateral is goods which are or are to become fixtures, the filing must be made in the Clerk and Recorder's office of the county where the real estate is located. If you inserted the collateral code for "Consumer goods", you should insert a specific description of the collateral in the "Complete description of Collateral" section of this form.

9. An "EFS" filing is one in which the collateral consists of specific farm products. If this box is checked, the secured party wants to be named as a joint-payee on the check from the buyer of farm products to the producer.

10. If the "EFS" box is marked, you must list one or more of the EFS codes. For each EFS code, you must list all of the counties, by two-digit code, where the farm products are located. Provide a crop year "from" and "to" date only if "all crop years" is not applicable.

11. Pursuant to subsection (3) of section 4-11-402 C.R.S., additional sheets describing the collateral may be attached to the filing, however, a filing officer may charge an additional $5.00 nonstandard form fee if more than a single page is filed or if the Colorado Central Indexing System approved form is not used.

12. This form may be filed in any of the sixty-three county clerks and recorders' offices or with the Secretary of State except as set forth in item 8 above.

13. If this financing statement is to be recorded in the real estate records, a description of the real property must be included in this form and, if the debtor does not have a record interest in the real property, the name of the record owner must be described in this form.

14. Colorado does not require debtor or secured party signatures on UCC-1's. **HOWEVER, IF THE FILING IS MARKED AS AN "EFS", THE SIGNATURE OF THE DEBTOR IS REQUIRED UNDER FEDERAL REGULATIONS.**

15. This form may be filed electronically. For more information on electronic filing, contact your county clerk.

COUNTY CODES

12 Adams	18 Delta	59 Jackson	21 Montrose	50 San Miguel
30 Alamosa	01 Denver	11 Jefferson	15 Morgan	39 Sedgwick
10 Arapahoe	58 Dolores	45 Kiowa	09 Otero	61 Summit
48 Archuleta	47 Douglas	26 Kit Carson	56 Ouray	43 Teller
22 Baca	44 Eagle	41 Lake	54 Park	27 Washington
29 Bent	34 Elbert	20 La Plata	37 Phillips	03 Weld
07 Boulder	04 El Paso	06 Larimer	57 Pitkin	19 Yuma
31 Chaffee	14 Fremont	05 Las Animas	17 Prowers	
46 Cheyenne	24 Garfield	33 Lincoln	02 Pueblo	95 *Out-of-state*
51 Clear Creek	60 Gilpin	13 Logan	49 Rio Blanco	99 *Sec of State*
25 Conejos	53 Grand	08 Mesa	23 Rio Grande	
38 Costilla	40 Gunnison	62 Mineral	28 Routt	
36 Crowley	63 Hinsdale	42 Moffat	35 Saguache	
52 Custer	16 Huerfano	32 Montezuma	55 San Juan	

UCC COLLATERAL CODES

10 Accounts	12 General Intangibles	40 Equipment	500 Fixtures
(Includes accounts	15 Chattel Paper	50 Farm Products	550 Inventory
receivable and	20 Consumer goods	60 Investment Property	570 Minerals and the like
contract rights)	34 Documents	70 Instruments	750 Standing timber

FARM PRODUCT CODES

110 Cattle & Calves	146 Quail	234 Safflower	320 Honeydew	422 Celery
112 Angora	148 Semen	236 Seed crops	melon	424 Cucumbers
114 Beefalo	150 Sheep & lambs	238 Silage (specify)	322 Nectarines	426 Eggplant
116 Buffalo	152 Turkeys	240 Sorghum grain	324 Peaches	430 Green peas
118 Chickens	154 Wool	242 Soybeans	326 Pears	438 Green beans
120 Ducks	156 Other Livestock	244 Sugar beets	328 Plums	440 Lettuce
122 Eggs	(specify)	246 Sunflower seeds	330 Pumpkins	442 Okra
124 Elk	210 Hay	248 Trees (specify)	332 Strawberries	444 Onions
125 Emus	212 Barley	250 Triticale	334 Raspberries	446 Pecans
126 Fish (specify)	214 Corn	252 Vetch	336 Muskmelon	448 Peppers
128 Fur animals	216 Dry beans	254 Wheat	338 Watermelon	450 Radishes
130 Geese	218 Flax seeds	256 Other Field	340 Other Fruits	452 Snap beans
132 Hogs	220 Honey	Crops (specify)	(specify)	454 Squash
134 Horses	222 Legumes	310 Apples	410 Artichokes	456 Sweet corn
136 Llamas	224 Millet	312 Apricots	412 Asparagus	458 Tomatoes
138 Milk	226 Oats	314 Cantaloupe	414 Broccoli	460 Turnips
140 Mules	228 Popcorn	316 Cherries	416 Cabbage	462 Walnuts
142 Ostriches	230 Potatoes	318 Grapes	418 Carrots	464 Other Vege-
144 Pheasants	232 Rye		420 Cauliflower	tables (specify)

COLORADO UCC-3 STATEMENT OF CHANGE
(See instructions on back)
Standard Form Effective May 1, 1998
Total Fee = $16 (See Instructions)

1st DEBTOR
Name (Last, First):
SSN/FED Tax ID: Check One:
Street: Business ☐
City, State, Zip: Individual ☐

2nd DEBTOR (Put Additional Debtors on attachment)
Name (Last, First):
SSN/FED Tax ID: Check One:
Street: Business ☐
City, State, Zip: Individual ☐

1st SECURED PARTY (Put Additional Secured Parties on attachment)
Name (Last, First):
Street:
City: State, Zip:

ASSIGNED PARTY (Put Additional Assigned Party on attachment)
Name (Last, First):
Street:
City, State, Zip:

RETURN COPY TO
Name:
Street:
City, State, Zip:

The name of the record owner of the real property
containing the collateral is:

_____

DESCRIPTION OF AMENDMENT/ASSIGNMENT

INFORMATION CONCERNING ORIGINAL FILING
Original Filing Number:
Date of Original Filing:
Two Digit Code for County/Secretary of State where Original Document was Filed:
County Book/Page Number (If used by County):
Real Estate Recording Number:

CHECK ONLY ONE (If no box is checked, it will be filed in UCC only)

☐ File in **UCC ONLY**
☐ This statement is to be recorded in the real estate records **ONLY.**
☐ This statement is to be filed in UCC **AND** recorded in the real estate records.
    (Requires an additional recording fee).
☐ The debtor is a transmitting utility.

Check if this filing is intended as EFS notification ☐
Enter EFS collateral code, County Code and crop years covered.
If all years are covered, leave from and to dates blank.

EFS Code	County Code	From	To

Check Box for Appropriate Transaction(s)

☐ TERMINATION

☐ CONTINUATION

☐ AMENDMENT (Describe in adjacent space)

☐ RELEASE OF COLLATERAL

☐ PARTIAL ASSIGNMENT

☐ TOTAL ASSIGNMENT

Secured Party Signatures (See Instruction 12)

_____

Debtor Signature(s) (See Instruction 12)

_____   Printed Name(s)

Printed Name(s)

_____   Title

Title

Contact Phone/FAX

COLORADO UCC-3 INSTRUCTIONS

1. Type this form in Upper Case.

2. Type only one debtor name in each debtor field. For more than two debtors, attach a separate sheet.

3. Do not use the same social security number for two separate individual debtors. If the debtor uses a tradename, the social security number of the debtor may be used as the tax identifier for the tradename.

4. Check "Business" if the debtor is a business entity or "Individual" if the debtor is an individual.

5. Type the original filing number from the filing office where the original was filed. Type the two digit county code or 99 for Secretary of State.

6. An "EFS" filing is one in which the collateral consists of specific farm products and the secured party wants to be named as a joint payee on the check from the buyer of farm products to the producer.

7. If the "EFS" box is marked, you must list one or more of the EFS collateral codes. For each EFS code, you must list all of the counties, by two-digit code, where the farm products are located. Provide a crop year "from" and "to" date only if "all crop years" is not applicable.

8. Check the box for the appropriate amendment type. The filing fee is $16.00 per transaction. However, the Secretary of State and some County filing officers do not charge per transaction. Check with your filing officer for the appropriate fee.

9. When the financing statement covers timber to be cut or covers minerals or other substances of value which may be extracted from the earth, or accounts subject to subsection (5) of section 4-9-103 C.R.S. or when the financing statement is filed as a fixture filing and the collateral is goods which are or are to become fixtures, the filing must be made in the Clerk and Recorder's office of the county where the real estate is located. However, if you check the box "File in UCC and real estate records", notification of the security interest relating to real estate will also appear on the Central Indexing System. The Clerk and Recorder may charge you a separate filing fee for the real estate recording.

10. Pursuant to subsection (3) of section 4-11-102 C.R.S. additional sheets describing the amendment or describing collateral to be affected may be attached to the filing, however, a filing officer may charge an additional $5.00 nonstandard form fee if more than a single page is filed or if the Colorado Central Indexing System approved form is not used.

11. For all collateral other than fixtures, minerals and the like, accounts on minerals and timber to be cut, this document may be filed in any one of the sixty-three Colorado counties, or at the Secretary of State's office. If this Statement of Change is to be recorded in the real estate records, a description of the real property must be included in this form and, if the debtor does not have a record interest in the real property, the name of the record owner must be described in this form.

12. Colorado law does not require the signature of the debtor on any type of UCC filings. However, the secured party must sign all amendments that delete collateral, terminate a filing, assign a filing or release collateral. **If this filing is marked as an "EFS", it must be signed by the debtor to comply with federal regulations**.

13. This form may be filed electronically. For more information on electronic filing, contact your county clerk.

COUNTY CODES

12 Adams	18 Delta	59 Jackson	21 Montrose	50 San Miguel
30 Alamosa	01 Denver	11 Jefferson	15 Morgan	39 Sedgwick
10 Arapahoe	58 Dolores	45 Kiowa	09 Otero	61 Summit
48 Archuleta	47 Douglas	26 Kit Carson	56 Ouray	43 Teller
22 Baca	44 Eagle	41 Lake	54 Park	27 Washington
29 Bent	34 Elbert	20 La Plata	37 Phillips	03 Weld
07 Boulder	04 El Paso	06 Larimer	57 Pitkin	19 Yuma
31 Chaffee	14 Fremont	05 Las Animas	17 Prowers	
46 Cheyenne	24 Garfield	33 Lincoln	02 Pueblo	95 *Out-of-state*
51 Clear Creek	60 Gilpin	13 Logan	49 Rio Blanco	99 *Sec of State*
25 Conejos	53 Grand	08 Mesa	23 Rio Grande	
38 Costilla	40 Gunnison	62 Mineral	28 Routt	
36 Crowley	63 Hinsdale	42 Moffat	35 Saguache	
52 Custer	16 Huerfano	32 Montezuma	55 San Juan	

UCC COLLATERAL CODES

10 Accounts (Includes accounts receivable and contract rights)	12 General Intangibles	40 Equipment	500 Fixtures
	15 Chattel Paper	50 Farm Products	550 Inventory
	20 Consumer goods	60 Investment Property	570 Minerals and the like
	34 Documents	70 Instruments	750 Standing timber

FARM PRODUCT CODES

110 Cattle & Calves	146 Quail	234 Safflower	320 Honeydew melon	422 Celery
112 Angora	148 Semen	236 Seed crops		424 Cucumbers
114 Beefalo	150 Sheep & lambs	238 Silage (specify)	322 Nectarines	426 Eggplant
116 Buffalo	152 Turkeys	240 Sorghum grain	324 Peaches	430 Green peas
118 Chickens	154 Wool	242 Soybeans	326 Pears	438 Green beans
120 Ducks	156 Other Livestock (specify)	244 Sugar beets	328 Plums	440 Lettuce
122 Eggs		246 Sunflower seeds	330 Pumpkins	442 Okra
124 Elk	210 Hay	248 Trees (specify)	332 Strawberries	444 Onions
125 Emus	212 Barley	250 Triticale	334 Raspberries	446 Pecans
126 Fish (specify)	214 Corn	252 Vetch	336 Muskmelon	448 Peppers
128 Fur animals	216 Dry beans	254 Wheat	338 Watermelon	450 Radishes
130 Geese	218 Flax seeds	256 Other Field Crops (specify)	340 Other Fruits (specify)	452 Snap beans
132 Hogs	220 Honey			454 Squash
134 Horses	222 Legumes	310 Apples	410 Artichokes	456 Sweet corn
136 Llamas	224 Millet	312 Apricots	412 Asparagus	458 Tomatoes
138 Milk	226 Oats	314 Cantaloupe	414 Broccoli	460 Turnips
140 Mules	228 Popcorn	316 Cherries	416 Cabbage	462 Walnuts
142 Ostriches	230 Potatoes	318 Grapes	418 Carrots	464 Other Vegetables (specify)
144 Pheasants	232 Rye		420 Cauliflower	

COLORADO SECRETARY OF STATE
1560 BROADWAY STE 200
DENVER CO 80202-5169

UCC-11

UNIFORM COMMERCIAL CODE
SEARCH REQUEST FOR
INFORMATION OR COPIES

Debtor Name and Address	Requesting Party Name and Address	Office Use
ssn/tax id	**Phone**	

☐ **INFORMATION REQUEST:** Filing officer, please furnish certificate showing whether there is on file any presently effective financing statement, any other statement, or any federal tax lien notice naming the debtor(s) listed above, give the date and hour of filing of each such statement, and the names and addresses of each secured party or grantee as such information may be available.

☐ **COPY REQUEST:** Filing officer please furnish certificate and copies of any presently effective financing statement, any other statement, or any federal tax lien notice naming the debtor(s) listed above. If individual filing is required to be certified, there will be a $1 charge per filed document.

☐ **SPECIFIC COPIES: (NO CERTIFICATE GIVEN)** Please furnish copies of the specific file numbers listed below, including all attachments thereto. On Specific Copy requests, please provide both original and amendment file numbers.

☐ **CERTIFIED COPIES: (NO CERTIFICATE GIVEN, SPECIFIC COPIES ONLY)** Please furnish copies of the requested statement(s) or tax lien notice(s) of the file numbers listed below. There will be a charge of $1 per filing certification.

Requesting Party Signature _____

Original File #	Amendment File #	Amendment File #

SERVICE DESIRED: ☐ Standard. $15 per debtor name plus $1 per page per copy request
☐ Expedited. $50 per debtor name plus standard fees.

SELECT ONLY ONE: ☐ Mail when ready
☐ Call for pick-up (at phone) _____
☐ Fax return (at phone) _____ ($7 fee - limit 20 pages)

Rev:08/03/93

UCC-11 INSTRUCTIONS

1. This document **MUST** be typed in UPPER CASE.
2. There is one debtor section on this form. You may enter **ONLY** one name per section, either personal or business, but not both. Enter complete address and Federal Tax id# or SSN. If more space is needed, use additional 8.5" x 11" sheets with name, complete address, and Federal Tax ID or SSN of debtor(s).
3. Uniform Commercial Code request for information or copies from Secretary of State will be complete searches, at a fee of $15 for each business or debtor name. Restricted dates will only apply to providing copies of filed documents. Please note a complete search will be performed. Copies are $1 per page, plus $1 for certification for each file number. County fees are generally $1.25 per page but you should check with the UCC Filing Manual or the county clerk.
4. Only those names and addresses of debtors listed above will be searched. If a specific address is requested for debtor, only that address will appear on the completed search. If no address is listed, all addresses found in our data base will be included on the completed search. The certification date on the certificate is the most recent date which has been completely processed and appears in the Uniform Commercial Code records.
5. More detailed information and instructions are available in the UCC Filing Manual. This commercially available manual is priced at $10. It has detailed instructions on how to fill out the forms and warns of the most common errors that cause rejections.
6. Questions may be addressed by calling (303) 894-2200 - ext 3 from 8:30 am to 5:00 pm.
7. There are three options in Colorado on where to record liens. The collateral or security used determines where to file:

Collateral	Filing Office
Agricultural products (Liens may require a UCC filing with the county).	Central Filing Systems, Inc. 1301 Pennsylvania St. - Box #5 Denver, Co 80203 (303) 831-0623
Farm Equipment, accounts or general intangibles arising from or relating to the sale of farm products by a farmer; consumer goods; timber to be cut or minerals which may be extracted from the earth; goods which are or are to become fixtures.	County Clerk of county where debtor lives or where collateral is. See the county list in the UCC Filing Manual.
All other collateral	Secretary of State

8. The state has a prepaid account system which will allow many functions to be handled via faxed requests. For more information, contact the Secretary of State at (303) 894-2251 or fax a request to (303) 894-2242.
9. This form may be photo copied.

CONNECTICUT LAW DIGEST REVISER

Sorokin, Gross & Hyde, P.C.
One Corporate Center
Hartford, Connecticut 06103-3291
www.sorokin.net
Telephone: 860-525-6645
Fax: 860-522-1781
E-mail: Sorokin @ Micro-Net.com

Reviser Profile

History: Sorokin, Gross & Hyde, P.C. is a medium-sized (23-attorney) law firm with one office in downtown Hartford, one in Rocky Hill, Connecticut and one in Simsbury, Connecticut. The firm was formed in 1989 through the merger of Sorokin & Sorokin, P.C. and Gross, Hyde & Williams, one of the oldest continuous law partnerships in Connecticut.

Practice: The firm has a comprehensive and diverse practice with numerous areas of specialization. For administrative purposes, the firm is divided into several practice groups: commercial transactions and business insolvency; real estate; tax, pension, probate and estate planning; corporate law and securities; litigation; employment; government relations; and general and administrative matters. Within these groups the firm handles matters such as secured, asset based and unsecured lending, commercial and residential real estate transactions, real estate syndications, private placements, venture capital, general corporate matters for existing clients and start-up businesses, banking, labor and employment, computer law issues, federal and state administrative agencies, and legislative lobbying.

Sorokin, Gross & Hyde, P.C. has over 30 administrative personnel including six paralegals.

Client Base: Sorokin, Gross & Hyde, P.C. provides complete services for clients of all sizes in numerous industries across the Northeast Region.

Firm Activities: Sorokin, Gross & Hyde, P.C. strongly supports the involvement of its members in professional and civic organizations. Members of the firm are affiliated with state and national bar associations and professional organizations, as well as various arts, charity, and local civic groups. Firm members lecture to local and national business and legal associations, and serve as authors and editors for both state and national publications. Members of the firm have served as faculty members at local colleges and universities including: University of Connecticut School of Law, New York Law School, University of Bridgeport School of Law, University of Hartford, and Hartford Graduate Center. Members have also served regularly as appointed and elected members at various levels of state and local government.

Management: Sorokin, Gross & Hyde, P.C. is managed by a five-member Executive Committee.

Significant Distinctions: Major distinctions of the firm began with its conception. The three original principals of Gross, Hyde & Williams were Judge Loren Waldo—a member of the General Assembly, member of Congress, and Superior Court Judge; Richard Hubbard—a member of Congress, and Governor of the State of Connecticut; and Alvan Hyde—a member of the General Assembly. These distinctions continue. One former partner is now a United States District Court Judge, one partner served as Mayor of Hartford, and another former partner, who had served as Magistrate for the United States District Court for the District of Connecticut, is now a Superior Court Judge. Two partners are listed in The Best Lawyers in America. Sorokin, Gross & Hyde, P.C. is the Reviser for the Connecticut Law Digest.

CONNECTICUT LAW DIGEST

(The following is a list of all Categories and Topics, including cross-references, covered in this Digest.)

CONNECTICUT LAW DIGEST

Revised for 1999 edition by

SOROKIN, GROSS & HYDE, P.C., of the Hartford Bar.

(Citations, unless otherwise indicated, refer to sections of the General Statutes, Revision of 1958, as codified through January 1, 1995. "c." citations refer to chapters of the General Statutes. "PA -_" citations refer to Public Acts of the legislature passed during the session year noted in the citation. Citations to 1996 legislation include all enactments through the February regular session. "Const." citations refer to Article and section of the Connecticut Constitution of 1965. "C.P.B." citations refer to the Connecticut Practice Book and indicate sections thereof. Parallel citations to the Atlantic Reporter begin with 53 Conn. "CLJ" refers to the Connecticut Law Journal, cited by volume and number. "CGS" refers to Connecticut General Statutes.)

Note: This revision covers all legislation passed by the Governor through October, 1998.

INTRODUCTION

GOVERNMENT AND LEGAL SYSTEM:

The State of Connecticut is a constituent state of the United States of America. For further discussion of the U.S. federal system, see Introduction to the Federal Government of the United States at the beginning of this volume. A great many laws are promulgated by the federal government of the United States and are not reflected in the topics below. See the Introduction to this volume for references to the federal law topics covered.

Like all but one of the United States, Connecticut has a common law legal system, with roots in English common law. For information on the courts and legislature of Connecticut, see category Courts and Legislature.

HOLIDAYS:

Legal holidays are: Jan. 1, 1st Mon. occurring on or after Jan. 15, Feb. 12, 3d Mon. in Feb., last Mon. in May, July 4, 1st Mon. in Sept., 2d Mon. in Oct., Nov. 11, Dec. 25, and any day appointed by Governor or President for thanksgiving, fasting, or religious observance. When holiday occurs on Sun., next Mon. is holiday; holiday on Sat., preceding Fri. is holiday. (1-4).

Certain contracts (e.g., those made by car dealers or contractors) are voidable if made on Sun. upon return of consideration. (52-207, 53-300a, 53-301, 53-302a, 53-303b to 53-303e, 53-303f). Contracts affecting real property not voidable. (53-300a).

OFFICE HOURS AND TIME ZONE:

Connecticut is in the Eastern Standard (GMT −05:00) time zone. Office hours are generally from 9 a.m. to 5 p.m.

BUSINESS ORGANIZATIONS

AGENCY:

In general, the common law governs. Statutes govern agents of student athletes. (PA 97-120; 20-553-20-558).

ASSOCIATIONS:

Formation.—Voluntary associations are formed by agreement among members. Except for agricultural or horticultural societies (29-119 et seq.) and fraternal benefit societies (38-206 et seq.), there are no statutes relating specifically to their formation or dissolution.

Rights and Powers.—Association holds property by its members as individuals, and member who abandons association abandons his interest in its property. (19 Conn. 154, 166).

Associations as such cannot hold legal title to land (44 Conn. 260), and conveyances should be to trustees (47-6). However, a devise to an association operated for purposes of public charity will not be allowed to fail for want of a devisee. (17 Conn. 181, 187).

Association is treated as employer separate from its members for purposes of fair employment practices (31-122, 31-275); workers' compensation (31-275); and labor relations (31-101).

In becoming a member of an association, one submits himself to its jurisdiction, and consents to abide by its law, rules and usages as an incident of membership. (58 Conn. 552, 557, 20 Atl. 671).

Liabilities.—Where the association is formed to engage in business for profit, the members are liable as partners; but where the association is nonprofit, authorization or ratification is prerequisite to member liability. (119 Conn. 681, 179 Atl. 201).

Voluntary associations and their members, as individuals, are liable to be sued in civil actions both in contract and tort, but no civil action, except under a contract, may be brought against the members of such association without joining such association, if it is located or has property subject to attachment in this state. (52-76). Individual property of members is not liable to attachment or levy unless they are joined. Judgment must be satisfied first from personal property of association and then from property of any member against whom judgment was rendered. Attachment liens on personal property of members shall not expire until two months, and on real estate four months, after levy of execution against personal property of associations. Judgments in actions of tort may be satisfied out of real estate of association. (52-292).

Professional Associations.—Any three or more persons licensed or authorized to practice a profession by State, may associate to practice such for profit, if articles of association of members provide that the association has three of the following four attributes: (a) Continuity of life so that death, insanity, bankruptcy, retirement, resignation or expulsion of any member will not cause dissolution; (b) centralized management so that any one or more but less than all manage the operations; (c) limited liability; and (d) free transferability of interests. Such articles of association must be signed by all members and recorded with the Secretary of State (fee $25) and office of Town Clerk in town wherein association has its principal offices. Such association may become professional service corporation. (34-82).

See also topic Corporations, subhead Professional Corporations.

CORPORATIONS:

For unincorporated organization, see topic Associations.

Connecticut has enacted Connecticut Business Corporation Act (33-600 through 33-998, am'd 98-137) substantially changing current provisions regarding stock corporations. Effective date of new legislation is Jan. 1, 1997.

Provisions in stock corporation's certificate of incorporation already in effect on Jan. 1, 1997 which were permissible under then-existing law, but are contrary to, inconsistent with, or in addition to permissible provisions under new law, will continue to govern. (33-601).

Stock Corporations.—One or more persons (33-635) may form corporation for any lawful business except that of state bank and trust company, savings bank, industrial bank, building and loan association, telegraph, gas, electric light, water or cemetery company, or which shall need to condemn lands or occupy highways, except telephone company. (33-645). But this section does not prohibit formation of corporation for transaction of any business in any other state which business is not prohibited by laws thereof. No corporation may be formed for purpose of transacting business of insurance company or surety or indemnity company, unless (1) it is affiliate of insurance company chartered by, incorporated, organized or constituted within or under laws of this state, and (2) at time of filing of its articles of incorporation, there is also filed certificate issued by insurance commissioner pursuant to §33-646 authorizing formation of corporation. No corporation shall have power to transact in this state business of insurance company or surety or indemnity company until it has procured license from insurance commission in accordance with provisions of §§38a-41. There is no requirement as to citizenship or residence of incorporators.

Articles of incorporation must be filed, showing: Name; authorized capital; street address of corporation's initial registered office and name of initial registered agent at that office; and name and address of each incorporator. (33-636). Articles may contain any other provisions regulating corporation and must be signed by one incorporator and filed in office of Secretary of State (33-608).

Corporate existence commences upon filing of articles of incorporation by Secretary of State; filing by Secretary of State conclusive evidence of incorporation in all courts, except as against state in action to cancel or revoke certificate of incorporation. (33-637).

Corporate name must contain "corporation," "company," "incorporated," "limited," or "Societa per Azioni" or abbreviation "corp.," "co.," "inc.," "ltd." or "S.p.A." if formed after Jan. 1, 1961 and must not describe corporate powers, purposes or authority which corporation does not possess. (33-655). Secretary of State examines name reservation application and if available, name may be reserved for 120 days from date of filing with Secretary of State (33-656), fee $30 (33-167). Any existing corporation may register name with Secretary of State if name is such as to distinguish it upon state records. (33-657). Must be annually renewed for following year between Oct. 1 and Dec. 31, fee, $30. (33-288). No informal name clearance authorized.

Taxes and fees incident to organization are: On filing articles of incorporation, or articles of amendment to increase capital, or on merger or consolidation franchise tax of 1¢ per share up to and including first ten thousand authorized shares, one-half cent per share for each authorized share in excess of 10,000 shares up to and including 100,000 shares, 1/4¢ per share for each authorized share in excess of 100,000 shares up to and including 1,000,000 shares, and 1/5¢ per share for each authorized share in excess of 1,000,000 shares. Minimum franchise tax is $150. (33-618).

Amendments.—A corporation may amend its articles of incorporation at any time, so long as amended articles contain only such provisions as would be lawful in new certificate of incorporation filed at time of making such amendment. (33-795).

Amendments to articles may be made in the following manner: (a) unless existing articles provide otherwise, board of directors, without shareholder approval, may amend articles (1) to extend duration of corporation, (2) to delete names of initial directors, (3) to delete name of original registered agent, (4) to change authorized shares of outstanding class into greater number of whole shares if corporation has only shares of that class outstanding, (5) to change corporate name to substitute word or words required by 33-655 or to add, delete or change geographical attribution for name, or (6) to make any other change expressly permitted by Connecticut Business Corporations Act to be made without shareholder action (33-796); (b) where shareholder action required, at shareholder meeting by majority vote (unless existing articles require greater vote) of those entitled to vote, after recommendation approving change from board of directors, and notice to shareholders (both voting and nonvoting) (33-797).

By-laws shall be promulgated initially by incorporators or board of directors and may contain any provision for managing business and regulating affairs of corporation not inconsistent with law or existing articles of incorporation. (33-640). Emergency

---

See note at head of Digest as to 1998 legislation covered.

See Topical Index in front part of this volume.

CORPORATIONS . . . *continued*

by-laws, for use in case of catastrophic event preventing assembly or quorum of board of directors, authorized. (33-641).

Organization.—Before or after incorporation, board of directors (if named in articles of incorporation) or incorporator(s) (if board not named) shall hold organizational meeting to complete organization by electing board (if necessary). Board shall complete organization by appointing officers and adopting by-laws. (33-639, am'd PA 97-246).

Any two or more offices may be held by the same person. (33-763). Officer performs duties set forth in by-laws. (33-764). Officers may be removed, with or without cause, but without prejudice to their contract rights, if any. Mere appointment or election for specified term does not of itself create contract rights. (33-766, 33-767).

Directors.—A corporation may have board of directors consisting of one or more individuals. Directors need not be residents of this state or shareholders of corporation unless by-laws so require. (33-736). Articles of incorporation may provide for classification of directors either as to their term of office or as to their election by one or more classes of shareholders exclusively or both. (33-738). Terms of initial directors expire at first shareholders meeting at which directors are elected. Unless terms are staggered, all other directors' terms expire at next annual meeting of shareholders. (33-739). Terms may be staggered in up to five groups of directors, with terms expiring at successive annual meetings. (33-740).

Directors shall manage or direct management of corporation subject to any provisions contained in articles of incorporation (33-735), or shareholder agreement (33-717).

Directors' committees are authorized if allowed by -laws, to exercise all such authority as may be delegated to them by board of directors. (33-753). Directors' meetings may be held either within or without State by any means of communication by which all directors may simultaneously hear each other at meeting. Director shall cease to be in office on: (1) Death; (2) resignation; (3) removal from office pursuant to bylaws; (4) court order removing him by reason of incompetency; or for any other lawful cause. (33-741–33-743).

Liability of Directors.—Directors may be personally liable for willful nonpayment of taxes collected under sales tax and admission, cabaret or due tax. (12-414a; 12-547a). Director is not liable for any action taken as director, or any failure to act, if he or she performed duties of director (1) in good faith; (2) with care ordinarily prudent person in like position would exercise under similar circumstances; and (3) in manner director reasonably believes to be in best interests of corporation. (33-756). In discharging duties, director entitled to rely upon reports, data, and statements if prepared and presented by (1) corporate officers whom director reasonably believes to be competent and reliable; (2) legal counsel, public accountant, or other persons as to matters director reasonably believes to be within professional or expert competence of individual; or (3) committee of board of directors if director reasonably believes committee merits confidence. Director is deemed not to be acting in good faith if he or she has knowledge concerning issue in question which makes reliance unwarranted. (33-756).

Indemnification of Directors and Officers.—Indemnification may be mandatory, discretionary, or prohibited depending upon circumstances. Detailed statutory provisions govern. (33-770 through 33-778, am'd PA 97-246).

Stock.—Shares may but need not be represented by certificates. If shares issued without certificates; corporation must send shareholder written statement of required information. (33-677). Each certificate must set forth (1) the name of the corporation; (2) a statement that the corporation is organized under the laws of this State; (3) name of person to whom issued or that same is issued to bearer; (4) number, class and designation of series, if any. Where there is more than one class of stock authorized certificate must summarize differing rights, preferences, or limitations, or state that corporation will furnish to stockholder on request and without charge, full or summary statement of designations, rights, terms, limitations and preferences of various classes. (33-676).

Before issuance of shares, board of directors must determine that consideration received or to be received for shares is adequate. (33-672). Consideration for shares may consist of any tangible or intangible property or benefit to corporation, including cash, promissory notes, services performed, contracts for services to be performed or other securities of corporation.

A corporation may purchase its own shares which thereupon become or revert to authorized but unissued shares (concept of "treasury" shares abolished). (33-684).

Preemptive Rights.—Except for corporations in existence prior to Jan. 1, 1997 whose articles of incorporation do not prohibit preemptive rights, such rights do not exist unless articles of incorporation specifically provide for same. (33-683).

Voting.—Stockholders may vote in person or by proxy, and each share entitles its owner to one vote. Redeemable shares are not entitled to vote after notice of redemption mailed and sum sufficient to redeem deposited to pay holders. (33-705). Holders of debt securities of corporation may have voting rights, if articles of incorporation so provide. (33-705[e]).

Voting Trusts.—One or more stockholders of any corporation may by written agreement transfer stock to a voting trustee, vesting in such trustee right to vote thereon for a period not exceeding ten years. Copy of such agreement must be promptly filed in principal office of corporation in Connecticut. All or some of parties to voting trust may extend same for additional terms of ten years by executing written agreement to that effect. Extension affects only those who are parties thereto. (33-715).

Transfer of Stock.—Governed by Uniform Commercial Code. (Tit. 42a).

Tender offers must comply with Connecticut Tender Offer Act. (36b-40 to 36b-52). No person shall make tender offer, or acquire equity securities pursuant to such offer, unless registration statement is filed with bank commissioner or exempted by him. Copy must be sent by certified or registered mail to principal office of target company and terms thereof publicly disclosed. (36-347c). Registration statement must: (1) Be submitted on forms prescribed by bank commissioner, (2) be accompanied by consent of offeror to service of process, and (3) contain information specified in 36b-43. Filing fee: $500. (36b-49). Tender offer defined generally as offer to acquire equity security of target company if after acquisition offeror would be record or beneficial owner of more than 10% of any class of outstanding equity securities of target company. (36b-41[8]).

Stockholders.—52-572j governs derivative actions by shareholders or members.

Meetings of Stockholders.—Within two business days after notice of each stockholders' meeting, complete list of stockholders entitled to notice is required to be prepared, which must be opened to inspection. (33-704). Annual stockholders' meetings may be held either within or without this state as may be provided in by-laws. (33-695). At least ten and not more than 60 days written notice of all meetings must be given. (33-699).

Directors have power to fix record date for determination of stockholders entitled to notice and vote if a by-law does not fix such date. The period between meeting date and record date may not exceed 70 days. (33-701).

Special meetings must be called if demanded by board of directors, person authorized by articles of incorporation, or upon written request of holders of at least one-tenth of outstanding stock entitled to vote at that meeting.

Dividends.—Distributions may be made to shareholders subject to restrictions in articles of incorporation and subject to following: (1) no distribution is permissible if corporation would not be able to pay its debts as they become due in usual course of business; or (2) corporation's total assets would be less than sum of total liabilities plus amount needed, upon dissolution, to satisfy preferential rights of those shareholders not receiving distribution but whose rights are superior to those receiving distribution. (33-687).

Unclaimed Dividends.—See category Property, topic Absentees, subhead Escheat.

Reports.—Every corporation, except banks, trust companies, insurance, or surety companies, building and loan associations, and public service companies shall file annual report with Secretary of State. (33-953).

First such report is to be filed within 30 days after organization meeting. Each annual report must be filed as provided by regulations of Secretary of State.

The report must contain: The name of the corporation; its principal office; names and respective business and residence addresses of the directors and officers unless good cause (including personal security considerations) excuses disclosure. (33-953).

Failure to File.—Corporation which fails to file its annual or biennial report on or before due date is in default.

Secretary of State shall not accept report until any default for failure to file prior report is cured. If report does not conform to law, Secretary of State may return it for correction along with any fee submitted with it. If not corrected on or before due date, corporation shall be in default and late filing fee is assessed unless report is filed within 18 days of rejection by Secretary of State. (33-954).

Dissolution.—A corporation may be dissolved: (1) By board of directors and shareholders (33-881); (2) by decree in judicial proceedings to liquidate corporate assets (33-896); (3) by forfeiture action by Secretary of State. (33-890). In normal case, dissolution by resolution requires affirmative vote of majority of voting power of shares entitled to vote thereon and recommendation by Board of Directors. Other shareholder voting proportions may be established by articles of incorporation. Articles of dissolution in required form must be filed with Secretary of State. (33-882). Dissolution may be revoked within 120 days. (33-883). Superior Court may, by judicial decree, dissolve corporation (1) in proceeding brought by shareholder, if is established that (A) directors are deadlocked, shareholders cannot break deadlock, and irreparable injury to corporation is threatened, or affairs can no longer be conducted to shareholders' advantage generally, because of deadlock, (B) directors or those in control are, have, or will act illegally, oppressively, or fraudulently, (C) voting shareholders are deadlocked and have failed for two consecutive annual meetings, to elect successors to directors whose terms have expired, or (D) corporate assets have been misapplied or wasted; (2) in proceeding brought by creditor (A) if creditor has claim against corporation reduced to judgment and execution on judgment has been returned unsatisfied and corporation is insolvent, or (B) corporation has admitted in writing that creditor's claim is due and owing and corporation is insolvent. (33-896). In event of proceeding brought by shareholder, corporation or one or more non-petitioning shareholders may elect to purchase shares of petitioner at fair value, to be determined by agreement or by court order. Election to purchase must be made within 90 days after filing of petition to dissolve or at such later time as court in its discretion may allow. (33-900).

Administrative dissolution may occur when Secretary of State determines corporation has failed to maintain registered agent or agent cannot be found. Upon issuance of notice to corporation of impending administrative dissolution, corporation has three months to file new appointment of agent. (33-890). Corporation has three years to apply for reinstatement after administrative dissolution (33-892), which application must be accompanied by documentation and fees necessary to cure default.

Procedure on Dissolution.—If dissolution is by action of board of directors and shareholders, corporation may publish notice in newspaper published in this state and having general circulation in town of corporation's principal office. Any action, suit or proceeding against dissolved corporation for any right or claim existing at, or for any liability incurred prior to, dissolution shall be barred if not commenced within three years after last publication of notice above provided for. However, corporation may shorten this period of limitation as to known creditors and claimants as follows: Written notice shall be sent to all known claimants of corporation warning them to present their claims. Such notice to creditors shall state to whom, at what place and time limit within which, which time limit shall not be less than 120 days after date of mailing such notice, such claims are to be presented. Notice shall also state expressly that claims not presented as therein provided will be barred. Claims of known claimants not thereafter presented within 120 days are barred. If claim presented, and corporation rejects claim, claimant has 90 days from rejection to bring court action to enforce claim.

See note at head of Digest as to 1998 legislation covered.

See Topical Index in front part of this volume.

CORPORATIONS . . . *continued*

Upon discharge of all obligations, a dissolved corporation may distribute assets to its stockholders, but no final liquidating distribution may be made without first obtaining current statements from both the State Tax Commissioner and the State Unemployment Compensation Administrator to the effect that all current and future corporate obligations to these two offices have been satisfied. (33-885).

Involuntary dissolution.—If the corporation is dissolved by court order, the court may appoint a receiver, to wind up the business. Such receiver, may be a director or other corporate officer. The court may limit the period for presentation of claims to four months, dissolve the corporation and take such other action as it deems advisable to expedite the dissolution and determine the rights of parties. (33-898).

Consolidation or Merger.—Corporations may merge or consolidate in accordance with detailed provisions. (33-815 through 33-821; 33-840 through 33-845).

Dissenter's Rights.—Certain fundamental changes trigger right of shareholder to demand payment for shares upon surrender of same. These actions are: (1) consummation of merger if shareholder approval was required; (2) consummation of share exchange in which corporation's shares will be acquired; (3) sale of all or substantially all of corporate assets other than in usual course of business, if shareholder entitled to vote on same, except for court-ordered sale or sale pursuant to which net proceeds will be distributed to all shareholders within one year after sale; (4) amendment to articles of incorporation that materially and adversely affects dissenter's rights because it: (a) alters or abolishes preferential right, (b) creates, alters or abolishes redemption right, (c) alters or abolishes preemptive right to acquire shares, (d) excludes or limits voting rights, other than by dilution through issuance of shares with similar rights, or (e) reduces dissenter's holdings to fraction of share if fraction is subsequently to be acquired for cash. (33-856). Corporation considering action which will trigger dissenter's election must notify affected shareholders of their rights, and give shareholders not less than 30 nor more than 60 days to demand payment for shares. If shareholder demands payment for shares, corporation must offer what it determines to be fair value for shares. Dissenter may accept or reject offer. If rejected, dissenter must make counter-offer, which corporation must pay or, alternatively, corporation must start court action within 60 days of receiving dissenter's demand. (33-864 et seq.).

Corporations Without Capital Stock.—Governed by Connecticut Non-Stock Corporation Act (PA 96-256, not yet permanently codified) which follows closely provisions of Connecticut Business Corporations Act.

Corporate Powers.—Unless its articles of incorporation provide otherwise, every corporation has perpetual duration and succession in its corporate name and has same powers as individual to do all things necessary or convenient to carry out its business and affairs, including without limitation power: (1) to sue and be sued, complain and defend in its corporate name; (2) to have corporate seal, which may be altered at will, and to use it, or facsimile of it, by impressing or affixing it or in any other manner reproducing it; (3) to make and amend by-laws, not inconsistent with its articles of incorporation or with laws of this state, for managing business and regulating affairs of corporation; (4) to purchase, receive, lease or otherwise acquire, and own, hold, improve, use and otherwise deal with, real or personal property, or any legal or equitable interest in property, wherever located; (5) to sell, convey, mortgage, pledge, lease, exchange and otherwise dispose of all or any part of its property; (6) to purchase, receive, subscribe for or otherwise acquire, own, hold, vote, use, sell, mortgage, lend, pledge or otherwise dispose of, and deal in and with shares or other interests in, or obligations of, any other entity; (7) to make contracts and guarantees, incur liabilities, borrow money, issue its notes, bonds and other obligations, which may be convertible into or include option to purchase other securities of corporation, and secure any of its obligations by mortgage or pledge or any of its property, franchises or income; (8) to lend money, invest and reinvest its funds, and receive and hold real and personal property as security for repayment; (9) to be promoter, partner, member, associate or manager of any partnership, joint venture, trust or other entity; (10) to conduct its business, locate offices and exercise powers granted by §§33-600 to 33-988, inclusive, within or without this state; (11) to elect directors and appoint officers, employees and agents of corporation, define their duties, fix their compensation and lend them money and credit; (12) to pay pensions and establish pension plans, pension trusts, profit sharing plans, share bonus plans, share option plans and benefit or incentive plans for any or all of its current or former directors, officers, employees and agents; (13) to make donations for public welfare or for charitable, scientific or educational purposes; (14) to transact any lawful business that will aid government policy; and (15) to make payments or donations, or do any other act, not inconsistent with law, that furthers business and affairs of corporation.

Emergency corporate powers, for use in event of catastrophic event preventing assembly of quorum of board of directors, authorized. (33-648). Such powers may (1) modify lines of succession to accommodate incapacity of any director, officer, employee, or agent; and (2) relocate principal office, or designate alternate principal office.

Fees.—Secretary of State shall charge and collect following fees for filing documents and issuing certificates: (1) Filing application to reserve, register or renew registration of corporate name, $30; (2) filing transfer or reserved corporate name, $30; (3) filing articles of incorporation, including appointment of statutory agent, $50; (4) filing change of address of registered agent or change of statutory agent, $25; (6) filing amendment to articles of incorporation, $50; (7) filing restated articles of incorporation, $50; (8) filing articles of merger or share exchange, $30; (9) filing articles of correction, $50; (10) filing certificate of surrender of special charter and adoption of general articles of incorporation, $50; (11) filing articles of dissolution, $25; (12) filing articles of revocation of dissolution, $25; (13) filing certificate of administrative dissolution, $25; (14) filing annual report, $75 except as otherwise provided in §§33-953 and 33-954; (15) filing application of foreign corporation for certificate of authority to transact business in this state and issuing certificate of authority, $50; (16) filing application of foreign corporation for amended certificate of authority to transact business in this state and issuing amended certificate of authority, $50; (17) filing application for withdrawal of foreign corporation and issuing certificate of withdrawal, $50; (18) filing application for reinstatement, $75; and (19) filing corrected annual report, $50.

Miscellaneous Charges.—Secretary of State shall charge and collect following miscellaneous charges: (1) At time of any service of process on Secretary of State as statutory agent of corporation, which amount may be recovered as taxable costs by party to suit or action causing such service to be made if party prevails in suit or action, plaintiff in process so served shall pay $25; (2) for preparing and furnishing copy of any document, instrument or paper filed or recorded relating to corporation: For each copy of each such document thereof regardless of number of pages, $25; for affixing his certification and official seal thereto, $5; (3) for preparing and furnishing his certificate of existence or authorization under §33-636, which certificate may reflect any and all changes of corporate names and date or dates of filing thereof, $60; and (5) for other services for which fees are not provided by general statutes Secretary of State may charge such fees as will in his judgment cover cost of services provided.

Foreign Corporations.—Each foreign corporation shall pay to Secretary of State license fee of $225 at time of filing its application for certificate of authority to transact business in this state, and annually thereafter on or before last day of calendar month in which falls anniversary of day of issuance of its certificate of authority, until such time as it has filed certificate of withdrawal from state or its certificate of authority to transact business in this state has been revoked.

Reports.—Every corporation, except banks, trust companies, insurance or surety companies, building and loan associations, or public service companies shall file annual report with Secretary of State. (33-953).

First such report of corporation shall be filed within 30 days after its organization meeting. Subsequent annual reports shall be filed at times provided by Secretary of State's regulations.

Nonstock corporations which are charitable in nature (except those granted exemption in §17-21h) and which seek to solicit funds from general public are required to register with and are regulated by Department of Consumer Protection (17-21g).

Close Corporations.—§11 modifies CGS §12-719(c)(3) regarding S-Corps and shareholders' pro rata share (CGS §12-726; HB 5681; PA 98-262). "S-Corporation" definition includes any subsidiary of such corporation that is qualified subchapter S subsidiary (I.R. Code §1361[b][3][B]; HB 5679; PA 98-244, §5).

Foreign corporations may purchase, hold, mortgage, lease, sell and convey real and personal estate in this state, but may not engage in banking insurance or public utilities business unless empowered to do so by some general or special law of this state.

No foreign corporation shall transact any business within the state without first obtaining a certificate of authority from the Secretary of State. (33-920).

A foreign corporation may not be appointed administrator. (74 Conn. 625, 51 Atl. 609). It may be appointed executor or trustee if, but not unless, state of its domicile extends a like privilege to Connecticut corporations, if its charter authorizes it so to act, if it is expressly so named and if it appoints Secretary of State its agent for service of process. (45-191).

Qualification.—In order for a foreign corporation to procure a certificate of authority to do business within this state, it must make application to the Secretary of State. Such application shall be made on forms procured from the Secretary of State and shall set forth: (1) The name of the corporation and the state under the laws of which it is incorporated; (2) the date of incorporation and the period of duration of the corporation; (3) the address of the principal office of the corporation in the state under the laws of which it is incorporated and the address of the executive offices of the corporation; (4) the address of the proposed principal office of the corporation in this state, if any; (5) name of its registered agent at that office; and (6) names and respective residence addresses of directors and officers of corporation. (33-922).

Application shall be accompanied by certificate, attesting to corporation's legal existence at time of execution of application in state of incorporation, and required license fee. (33-922).

See also subhead Foreign Limited Partnership—Authority to do Business, infra.

Agent for Process.—Foreign corporation with office or place of business in this state (except insurance and surety companies) must appoint in writing registered agent, who may be (A) individual who resides in this state; or (B) domestic or foreign corporation whose business office is identical to registered office. (33-926).

Failure to comply may result in fine of $165 per month or part thereof, plus all fees and taxes (with interest) which would have been imposed on such corporation had it duly applied for and received certificate of authority. Attorney General may bring action to recover fees and penalties, including action to restrain such corporation from transacting business until penalties have been paid. Noncomplying corporation may not be plaintiff in action in this state except upon compliance and payment. (33-921, am'd PA 97-228).

See also supra, subhead Taxes and Fees.

Reports.—Foreign corporations authorized to conduct business in Connecticut must file with Secretary of State annual reports similar to those required of domestic corporations. (PA 96-271).

Foreign Limited Partnership—Authority to do Business.—In order for foreign limited partnership to procure certificate of authority to do business within this state, it must make application to Secretary of State. Such application shall be made on forms procured from Secretary of State and shall set forth: (1) Name of foreign limited partnership under which it proposes to register and transact business in state; (2) state and date of its formation; (3) general character of business it proposes to transact; (4) name and address of agent for service of process on foreign limited partnership which shall be either: (a) Secretary of State, or (b) individual resident of state or domestic corporation or foreign corporation authorized to do business in this state; (5) address of office required to be maintained in state and its organization by laws of that state; (6) name and business address of each general partner; (7) address of office at which is kept list of names and addresses of limited partners and their capital contributions; and (8) date foreign limited partnership commenced transacting business in this state. Any

See note at head of Digest as to 1998 legislation covered.

See Topical Index in front part of this volume.

CT – 3

CORPORATIONS . . . *continued*

foreign limited partnership which transacts business in this state without registering with Secretary of State as required shall be levied fine in sum of $2,000. (34-38g).

Corporation business tax is imposed on most corporations doing business in state at rate of 10.75% of net income. Phased rate reduction to 7.5% is ongoing. (12-214, am'd PA 93-74). Companies subject to tax shall file declaration of estimated tax by June 15 if preceding year's tax or estimate of current year's tax obligation exceeds $1,000. (12-242b). Commencing Jan. 1, 1997, tax phased out over five years as to Subchapter S corporations, but net income of Subchapter S corporations distributed to individual shareholders that is no longer taxed is subject to personal income taxes.

Out of state corporations whose only contact with Connecticut is participation as limited partner in investment partnership are exempt. (PA 96-197). HB-5679; PA 98-244, §6 modifies CGS §12-214 regarding exemptions from imposition of taxes; includes non-U.S. corporation whose sole activity in Connecticut consists of trading in stocks or securities for its own corporation is exempt. (I.R. Code §§7701[2][5]; 864[b][2][A][ii]).

Any company subject to tax imposed by 12-214(a) shall pay, for each such income year additional tax in amount equal to 15% of tax calculated under subsection (a) for such income year, without reduction of tax so calculated by amount of any credit against tax. (12-214[b]).

Minimum franchise tax is imposed (if greater than that based on income mentioned above), and it is larger of following: (1) $3^1/10$ mills per dollar of invested capital which is specially defined; (2) flat sum of $200 for each income tax year. (12-219).

Building and loan associations, savings and loan associations, mutual savings banks, telephone companies, production credit associations, every company engaged in business of carrying passengers for hire over highways of this state in common carrier motor vehicles, and all other corporations doing business in this state which are subject to federal income tax, except insurance companies, domestic international sales corporations, housing corporations, railroads, other public utility companies, political campaign organizations, and companies engaged in research, manufacture or sale of alternative energy systems, are required to pay this tax (12-214) except, however, minimum tax is lower (12-219).

Banks in general are required to pay only tax measured by income, but all other corporations subject to this tax must pay the higher tax. (12-219).

Nonprofit Corporations.—Unrelated business income of nonprofit corporations is taxable. (PA 92-124).

Net income is computed in same manner as required for federal tax, except that no deductions are allowed for federal tax paid on income or profit, losses of prior years, interest from government and municipal securities, specific exemptions, or interest paid. (12-213).

Where corporation business is not carried on wholly within this state only such proportion of net income as is attributable to business done in state or such proportion of net worth as is allocated to state is taxed. To apportion corporation must conduct business in other state. Detailed provisions for allocation are contained in statutes. (12-218, am'd 96-197).

Additional credit of 5% may be obtained for expenditures for industrial waste treatment facilities. (12-217d).

Exemption from Property Tax.—Corporations paying franchise tax pay no property tax on intangible personal property.

Returns and Payments.—Corporation subject to this tax must file annual return with, and pay tax to, Commissioner of Revenue Services on or before Apr. 1. (12-222; 12-233). Corporation, where tax of preceding income year or expected tax of income year did or may exceed $1,000, must file with Commissioner by 15th day of ninth month of said income year declaration of estimated tax, but if expectation occurs after last day of eighth month, declaration must be filed by 15th day of 12th month. HB-5679; PA 98-244, §7 modifies CGS §12-222 regarding requirements for filing tax return. §8 modifies CGS §12-2232 regarding taxpayers included in consolidated federal tax return may elect to file combined return with other companies subject to tax who are included in federal tax return; such election shall be in effect per initial income year and for subsequent years until revoked. Payments required: by 15th day of third month of income year, 30% of required amount; by 15th day of sixth month, 40%; by 15th day of ninth month, 10%; by 15th day of 12th month, 20%. §9 modifies CGS §12-242d regarding quarterly payments; "required annual payment" redefined; recapture of reductions in required installments; calculation of annualized income installments; applicable percentages for quarterly installments set forth. Company failing to make such payments on account must pay by due date. For late filing of return, 1% per month interest, plus penalty of 10% of tax due for negligent or intentional failure to file and 25% penalty for fraud. Criminal sanctions for failure to file return or falsify same may include fine up to $5,000 and/or imprisonment up to five years. (12-229 to 12-235). Consolidated returns may be filed in some circumstances. (12-223a).

Tax Credit.—Corporation business tax credit for new manufacturing or economic development activities. Applicable to income years of corporations commencing on or after Jan. 1, 1993. (PA 92-250). Business tax exemption to promote development of aero-derived gas-turbines. (12-214). 12-632(i) is repealed. Total amount of business tax credits to which business firms entitled may not exceed four million dollars per fiscal year. Two million dollars out of total allowable tax credit may be granted to business firms eligible for tax credits per 12-635. (PA 97-251). Order for claiming tax credits. (HB-5679; PA 98-244 §10 [new]). SB-541; PA 98-261, §4 repeals PA 98-244 (§10) Order delineated for claiming more than one tax credit to which corporation may be entitled; at no time may credit be claimed more than once. (CGS §12-217t). HB-5681; PA 98-262, §2 modifies CGS §12-217p(h) regarding conditions precedent to five years carry forward/back of investment tax credit. §10 modifies PA 97-295(1)(f) regarding fixed capital held by corporation for more than three years and for which corporation has claimed tax credit; recapture of credit. §13 modifies PA 97-295(21) regarding taxpayer or business eligible for tax credit per statute may carry remaining tax credit forward to any income year on or after 1/1/98. (See CGS §§ 12-217c, 12-217d, 12-252a, 12-252b, 12-265b, 12-265c, 176-740.)

Computer Equipment Tax Credit.—Effective with respect to all personal property taxes paid on account of equipment appearing on grand list of Oct. 1, 1994 and

subsequent lists, 100% credit afforded to corporations for personal property taxes paid on computer equipment, including printers, peripherals, and bundled software. Credit available only after all other available credits have been exhausted, and cannot be used in lieu of quarterly estimated income tax payments or to pay interest or penalties on account of overdue taxes. (12-217t).

Enterprise Zones.—Abatements and credits are available to entities which establish new facilities and new jobs in towns and cities with enterprise zones, based on sliding scale. (PA 96-239).

Model Non-Profit Corporation Act not adopted.

Deeds.—See category Property, topic Deeds.

Private Foundations.—Charitable corporation deemed "private foundation" under federal Internal Revenue Code authorized to make necessary expenditures to avoid federal taxes, and prohibited from actions endangering charitable status. (33-281c).

Professional Corporations.—See also topic Associations, subhead Professional Associations. Individual members of a profession (dentists, naturopaths, physicians and surgeons, optometrists, architects, professional engineers, landscape architects, land surveyors and attorneys-at-law, veterinarians, certified public accountants and public accountants and chiropractors) offering professional service are generally authorized to incorporate and become shareholders. (33-182a to 33-182j; see also 20-298b[b]).

No such professional corporation may render services thereunder unless rendered through its duly licensed practitioners (33-182d), and corporate shield in no way diminishes otherwise professional responsibility and liability (33-182e).

Opthalmologists and Optometrists included in law. (PA 97-153).

No such professional corporation shall engage in any business other than professional service for which it was incorporated. (33-182f).

Restriction is placed on transfer of stock, mergers, and corporate name shall contain words "Professional Corporation" or "P.C." (33-182g-i).

Limited Liability Companies.—See topic Limited Liability Companies.

JOINT STOCK COMPANIES:

A corporation organized under the general law is a "joint stock company" as distinguished from a "corporation" chartered by the General Assembly. (89 Conn. 583, 94 Atl. 984; 84 Conn. 618, 80 Atl. 791). In practice and throughout statutes both are, in general, spoken of as corporations.

There are no statutes relating to unincorporated associations having transferable shares of stock. See topic Associations.

Professional Corporations.—See topic Associations, subhead Professional Associations.

LIMITED LIABILITY COMPANIES:

Connecticut Limited Liability Company Act (PA 93-267), effective Oct. 1, 1993, recognizes entity. Numerous refinements enacted. (34-100 et seq. and PA 97-70). Limited Liability Company (LLC) formed by filing "articles of organization" with Secretary of State. (PA 93-267, §10). Company name, which may be reserved, must contain words "Limited Liability Company" or abbreviations LLC or L.L.C. (34-100, et seq.). Owners set forth respective rights and obligations in "operating agreement" (34-100 et seq. and PA 97-70), similar to partnership agreement. Owners are "members", not stockholders or partners. Any member may bind LLC as any partner binds partnership, unless articles invest management in one or more managers, equivalent to corporate board of directors. (PA 93-267, §16). Interest in LLC may be given in exchange for property, services, promissory note or promise to provide services. (PA 93-267, §26). Allocation of profits and losses per operating agreement. Absent express provision, value of contribution determines allocation. (PA 93-267, §§28, 29). Absent provision in operating agreement, no member may transfer interest without consent of majority in interest of members, excluding interest of transferor. (PA 94-217). Upon death, dissolution, or bankruptcy of member, LLC dissolved unless majority in interest of remaining members consent to continue enterprise, absent operating agreement provision to contrary. (34-119, PA 97-70). LLC generally deemed to be "person" for purposes of numerous definitional statutes. (PA 95-79).

PARTNERSHIPS:

Uniform Partnership Act (1994) adopted. (34-39 to 34-80). (See category Courts and Legislature, topic Statutes, subhead Uniform Acts.) Additional section (34-82) authorizes professionals who cannot incorporate to form special partnership which permits taxation as corporation and allows creation of qualified pension plans; this section provides also for incorporation of professional associations (34-82).

Receivership of Partnership.—See category Debtor and Creditor, topic Receivers.

Limited Partnership.—Revised Uniform Limited Partnership Act adopted, 1979. (34-9 to 34-38n). Secretary of State may propound any limited partnership under act to interrogatories to ascertain compliance with act which must be answered within 30 days. Failure to answer in timely fashion results in fine. (PA 90-228, §4). See category Courts and Legislature, topic Statutes, subhead Uniform Acts.

Limited Liability Partnerships.—Effective Jan. 1, 1996, new entity known as "Limited Liability Partnership" or "LLP" authorized. Registration and regulations closely tracks that of Limited Liability Companies (see topic Corporations). LLP partners are liable for LLP contracts and obligations, but exempt from personal liability for LLP's debts, obligations, and liabilities arising from negligence, wrongful acts, or misconduct committed in course of LLP's business by another LLP partner, employee, agent, or representative not under their direct supervision or control. (PA 94-218).

Authority to do Business.—See topic Corporations, subhead Foreign Limited Partnership—Authority to do Business.

See note at head of Digest as to 1998 legislation covered.

See Topical Index in front part of this volume.

BUSINESS REGULATION AND COMMERCE

BANKS AND BANKING:

Effective Jan. 1, 1995, former Title 36 codification will be divided into Title 36A, "The Banking Law of Connecticut," and Title 36B, "The Securities and Business Investment Laws of Connecticut," containing Connecticut Tender Offer Act, Uniform Securities Act, and Business Opportunity Investment Act. (PA 94-122).

New codification creates new general category "Connecticut banks", encompassing state bank and trust companies, savings banks, and savings and loan associations. Formerly separate provisions concerning each type of bank's organization, administration, mergers, conversions, general powers, permissible loans and investments have been unified so as to apply to all "Connecticut banks", generally by adopting least restrictive former provision. §1 modifies CGS §36a-70 regarding application to organize Connecticut bank; when approved, temporary certificate issued is valid for 18 months and may be extended after hearing. §2 modifies CGS §36a-125 regarding merger of two or more Connecticut banks into one, resulting bank shall not commence business unless insurable accounts and deposits are insured by FDIC or successor (CGS §§33-700; 36a-34; 33-855–33-872); mutual savings banks shall not merge or consolidate if resulting bank is to be capital stock bank unless prior to or during merger or consolidation, mutuals have converted to capital stock banks (CGS §36a-136; HB-5280; PA 98-260).

Act expands banks' authority to open limited branches, requires prior notice for closing branches, streamlines and simplifies procedures for interim banks, and adds new application fees in connection with these activities.

Provisions of this new codification are expressly provided to control over any inconsistent provision of Connecticut general corporate laws in Title 33 (see topic Corporations).

Banking Commissioner has general supervisory powers. (36-10). Commissioner must report annually to governor and joint standing committee on banks on his administration of C. 662c of general statutes. (36-13). Connecticut has adopted Truth in Lending Act (36-393), virtually identical to Federal Truth in Lending Act, and exemption from Federal Act has been obtained. Banking Commissioner is charged with enforcement of state Act. Home Mortgage Disclosure Act prohibits discrimination in mortgage lending and requires financial institutions to report to bank commissioner and public certain information regarding loans. (36-443 et seq.). Banking Commissioner's right to involuntarily liquidate state branches of foreign banks. (PA 97-160).

Investigation and Processing Fees.—Fees payable to Department of Banking for various investigations and processing are as follows: (A) establishment or sale of branch or relocation of main office, $2,000; (B) establishment of mobile branch, establishment of limited branch, or relocation of branch, $1,500; (C) establishment and use of satellite device, $150; (D) merger, consolidation, purchase of assets, or assumption of liabilities, organization of holding company $2,500 for two institutions or $5,000 if three or more institutions are involved; (E) organization of Connecticut bank, $15,000; (F) processing notice of closing of branch, reasonable fee not to exceed $2,000. (PA 36a-65).

Uniform Commercial Code adopted. (Title 42a).

Interstate banking is governed by 36-552 of general statutes. Nation-wide system of interstate banking was implemented in 1990. New rules regarding interstate banking. (PA 97-160).

Under regulation of Banking Commissioner, savings banks may sell or issue without charge negotiable checks or drafts drawn by or on them and payable by or through any bank accepting commercial deposits. (36-133). Savings banks or savings and loan associations may issue credit cards. (36-104n, 182b).

Upon qualification as savings and insurance bank, savings bank may create separate insurance department and issue life insurance to residents or persons regularly employed in Connecticut or wife or child of person regularly employed in state. (36-42). As of Jan. 1, 1988, savings bank or employee selling insurance must be licensed under 38-72. (36-142, §4[c]). Maximum face value of $100,000 for one individual. Maximum face value of $200,000 for one individual under group policy. No person may have savings bank life insurance in excess of aggregate face value of above limits. (36a-285, am'd PA 97-34).

Branch banks, including limited service branches, may be established and operated by state banks and trust companies. (36-59; 36-129). Branch banking by private bankers (36-161), and foreign banks, unless national association with main office in Connecticut or authorized under c. 662c, are prohibited (36-59).

General powers of Connecticut banks fully described by statute. (PA 94-122, §115).

Interstate merger transactions between Connecticut banks and out-of-state banks, and de novo interstate branching, permitted prior to June 1, 1997 by special legislation passed in response to federal Riegle-Neal Interstate Banking and Branching Efficiency Act of 1994. (PA 95-155).

Loan Limits.—See 36-65(1), 36-98b(a), 36-179c(a), PA 94-122, §118.

No savings bank or state bank and trust company may have on savings deposit an amount in excess of $300,000 exclusive of interest or dividends credited on such deposit. (36-104).

State banks and trust companies (except those legally engaged in such business on Jan. 1, 1907) may not engage in the title insurance and guarantee business. (36-60).

State bank and trust company, building or savings and loan association or savings bank may act as trustee or custodian of individual retirement account under internal revenue code. Account's funds must be limited to savings, time and certificates of deposit, with indebtedness of self-employed members of retirement plans shown in notes. (36-73a).

Automated banking devices permitted subject to regulation. (36-193a to 36-193h). Subject to regulations of U.S. Treasury Department, banks and savings and loans may serve as Treasury tax and loan depositories. (36-9q).

State banks with assets greater than $2 million may provide home banking services to customers. Any electronic transfer of funds by such services are governed by 15 U.S.C. §1693. (PA 90-223).

Check cashing services, other than those regulated by federal or state banking law, must be licensed by Banking Commissioner. Maximum fee for cashing state check to welfare recipient is 1% of amount of check. Commissioner shall establish maximum fees for cashing check, draft, or money order drawn on depository institution. No check cashing service shall cash item in excess of $2,500. (21-211 to 21-219). Issuers of electronic payment instruments must be licensed. (PA 98-192).

Withdrawals.—Any savings bank or savings department of state bank and trust company (36-106) may, despite any contrary provisions in its charter or by-laws, require three months notice of depositor's intention to withdraw funds, and Commissioner may extend period. Despite such notice requirement such bank may within notice period pay out such sums weekly or at other intervals to depositors as it may deem prudent. Where depositor withdraws all funds before end of earning period, financial institution must pay interest on pro rata basis from first earning period day to withdrawal date. (PA 89-117).

Where a depositor in savings bank or state bank and trust company dies prior to compliance with his order for payment of funds out of his account, payments thereunder not to exceed $500 may be made within 30 days of date of order, or at any time until actual notice of death. (36-112). Commercial Banks may pay checks of a dead or incompetent customer for a period of ten days after such event, regardless of knowledge of such fact. (42a-4-406).

No institution may impose before Sept. 1, 1990, hold periods on checks deposited in customer accounts which exceed one business day if drawn on same institution, three business days if drawn on in-state institution, five business days if drawn on out-of-state institution unless depository institution has reason to believe check will not clear. Banking commissioner may extend maximum time limitations. (36-9v). Time limits do not apply to items deposited when opening account, provided customer is so informed. (36-9v). Except as otherwise provided, on and after Sept. 1, 1990 each institution must comply with applicable provisions of Expedited Funds Availability Act, 12 USC 4001 et seq. (36-9v).

Financial institutions must accept identity card issued by Connecticut Department of Motor Vehicles as identification sufficient to establish account. (PA 93-8).

Statements of Account.—Bank may charge account of apparent drawer of forged, raised or altered check with full amount thereof unless, within one year from time of rendering statement showing payment of such check, customer notifies bank of such forgery or alteration. (36-77). Depositor may not question correctness of statement of account except within seven years after its rendition. (36-76). Disclosure of interest rates paid on time deposits and various account charges regulated by statute. (36-27c, am'd PA 93-168).

Unclaimed Deposits.—Savings, demand or matured time deposits presumed abandoned after five years of total inactivity. Checking accounts after five years and contents of safe deposit boxes five years after expiration of last rental period. (3-57a).

Holding institution must give notice to record owner of such property within one year prior to time such presumption arises, and if property still unclaimed must pay or deliver it over to State Treasurer within 90 days after presumption arises. (3-65a; 3-65a[b]). Thereafter, such sums are treated as abandoned property (see discussion under category Property, topic Absentees, subhead Escheat).

Commercial Bank Deposits and Collections governed by Uniform Commercial Code. (42a-4-101 to 42a-4-504). Optional Provisions of 1962 Official Code Text adopted include: 4-106, bracketed material omitted; included bracketed material in 4-202. (Conn. 42a-4-202).

Investments and Loans.—Permissible investments are detailed in 36a-276. There are percentage limits on investments in debt and/or equity instruments.

Foreign banks cannot do business in this state, except that they can make mortgage loans in-state, secured by in-state real estate. (36-5a). New England bank holding companies may establish or acquire ownership of any Connecticut bank, savings bank, savings and loan or holding bank, provided Banking Commissioner finds that benefit to public clearly outweighs anticompetitive effects of transaction. (36-5a; 36-553 to 36-556). Any New England bank, bank holding company, savings bank, or savings and loan which acquires such control shall comply with 42-133C. (PA 87-205, §4). If any New England bank ceases to be New England bank and does not become Connecticut state bank, Commissioner may order immediate divestiture of ownership of stock of Connecticut bank acquired by it. After Mar. 30, 1990, Commissioner must order immediate divestiture. (36-553).

Building or savings and loan associations are regulated by 36-172 to 36-193.

Federal savings and loan association having its place of business here may convert to a state building or savings and loan association by following specified procedure. (36-191).

Credit unions for the purpose of accumulating payments on shares from their members and making loans therefrom to members, are under and regulated by 36-194 to 36-224.

Must be licensed annually on June 30 by Commissioner, which license is revocable for cause after hearing. (36-195). Credit unions may merge, with approval of Commissioner. (36-223c). Credit union organized in another state may do business as credit union in Connecticut with approval of Commissioner. (PA 85-208).

All credit unions shall have and maintain share insurance as provided by Federal Credit Union Act. Failure to obtain and maintain share insurance shall terminate its corporate existence. (36-200[i]).

Trust Companies.—SB-235; PA 98-258 defines out-of-state trust company as one chartered to act as fiduciary but not chartered in Connecticut, banks, out-of-state banks, Connecticut credit unions, federal credit unions or out-of-state credit unions (CGS §36a-2); amendment of savings deposit definition (CGS §36a-2); includes out-

---

See note at head of Digest as to 1998 legislation covered.

See Topical Index in front part of this volume.

BANKS AND BANKING . . . *continued*
of-state trusts whose trustees are corporations acting as fiduciaries as those entities which are exempt from application of licensure requirement (CGS §§36a-380—36a-381-386; 395; 45a-206); redefines permissible investment (CGS §§36a-596; 36a-2); out-of-state trust companies may establish offices to do business in Connecticut as long as states chartering them permit such business (CGS §§36a-425; 33-920; 33-1210; 34-223; 34-429); employees must be bonded; Commissioner may examine out-of-state trust companies' practices at companies' expense; such companies must give notice of events which affect their control, transfers of all or substantially all accounts out of state, or closing of their offices.

HB-5280; PA 98-260, §3 modifies CGS §36a-135 regarding conversion of certain mutual banks and savings and loans may convert into other mutual banks and savings and loans if they comply with certain laws, rules and regulations; converted institution shall not commence business unless insurable accounts and deposits are insured by FDIC or successor. §4 modifies CGS §36a-136(j) regarding conditions for approval of merger. §5 modifies CGS §36a-137 regarding requirements for conversion of capital stock Connecticut or federal banks into similarly organized entities except capital stock federal banks cannot convert into another capital stock federal bank; FDIC or successor agency insurance required. §6 modifies CGS §36a-138 regarding conditions for approval of conversion; FDIC or successor agency insurance required. §7 modifies CGS §36a-185 regarding requirements for approval of offer, invitation, request, agreement or acquisition of beneficial ownership of holding companies and banks (CGS §36a-184); offer, etc., shall be disapproved under certain circumstances.

Additionally, §8 modifies CGS §36a-192(b) regarding requirements and means of reorganizing mutual savings bank or mutual savings and loan association to form mutual holding company. (CGS §§36a-125; 36a-193). §9 modifies PA 97-209, §4 regarding requirements and means of expanding powers of community banks to operate within CGS §36a-7(r)(3) as Connecticut bank. §10 modifies PA 97-209, §5 regarding requirements for conversion of Connecticut credit unions or federal credit unions into mutual savings banks or mutual savings and loans or mutual community banks. (CGS §36a-70[r]). §11(new) regarding Commissioner of Banking has discretion to hold hearings regarding application filed with Commissioner and otherwise regarding matters within his discretion; Commissioner shall hold hearings regarding acquisition of beneficial ownership of holding companies and banks (CGS §36a-184) if bank or holding company so named files written request, statement of issues which, if proven, would constitute grounds for disapproval (CGS §§36a-184; 36a-185).

Bank holding companies, defined as companies holding 25% or more of voting shares of any state bank and trust company, or private bank, or controlling selection of majority of directors of such bank, or selection of majority of officials of bank holding company, are regulated. (PA 83-132). Among other things, acquisition plan must be filed with Bank Commissioner. Person acquiring more than 10% of bank or bank holding company must file acquisition statement, including specified information as to his background and intentions. (36-419, 36-420 to 36-429, 36-430). Sale or purchase of all or substantially all of assets and business of institution requires prior approval of two-thirds of shareholders, voting members, or corporators as applicable. (36-12a, am'd 93-59).

Mutual holding company may be formed by reorganizing mutual savings bank or mutual savings and loan association. Accomplished when mutual savings institution establishes subsidiary capital stock savings bank or savings and loan association with at least 51% of its stock owned by mutual holding company. Any reorganized savings institution shall commence business with minimum capital stock of $1,000,000 with capital surplus at least equal in amount. Capital stock and surplus must be paid for before business may commence. Application must be submitted to commissioner for approval. Insurable amount must be insured by FDIC or FSLIC. Mutual holding company may exercise all powers of mutual savings and loan except deposit-taking powers. Acquisition rules are same as for bank holding companies. (PA 85-330).

Director's Liability.—Article of incorporation or charter of banking institution may contain provision limiting personal liability of director to institution or its members or its stockholders for monetary damages for breach of duty as director to amount that is not less than compensation received by director for serving institution during year of violation if such breach did not (1) involve knowing and culpable violation of law by director; (2) enable director or associate, as defined in subdivision 3 of §33-374d of general statutes, to receive improper personal economic gain; (3) show lack of good faith and conscious disregard for duty of director to institution under circumstances in which director was aware that his conduct or omission created unjustifiable risk of serious injury to institution; (4) constitute sustained and unexcused pattern of inattention that amounted to abdication of director's duty to institution; or (5) create liability under §36-9 of general statutes.

Issuing Secondary Mortgage Loans.—Any person who engages in secondary mortgage loan business in this state as lender or broker without obtaining license required under this chapter, as amended by this act, shall be assessed civil penalty of not more than $2,000 for each violation. Each secondary mortgage loan negotiated, solicited, placed, found or made without license shall constitute separate violation. Attorney General may bring action in Superior Court to force provisions of this section. (90-184, §2b). Any lender who fails to comply with provisions of this act shall be liable to borrower in amount equal to sum of (1) amount by which total of all loan fees, points, commissions, transaction fees, other prepaid finance charges, and brokers fees and commissions exceeds 10% of principal amount of loan; (2) 10% of principal amount of loan or $2,500, whichever is less; and (3) costs incurred by borrower in bringing action under this section, including reasonable attorneys' fees, as determined by court, provided no such lender shall be liable for more than amount specified in this subsection in secondary mortgage loan transaction involving more than one borrower. (90-184, §5b).

BILLS AND NOTES:

Governed by Uniform Commercial Code, particularly 42a-3-101 to 42a-3-805. In §42a-3-121 Connecticut adopted Alternative A as Set Forth in 1962 Uniform Commercial Code Official Edition. (§3-121 of Official Edition).

Wagering Contracts.—The validity of a negotiable instrument held by a person who acquired the same for value and in good faith without notice of illegality in the consideration is not affected by the fact that the instrument was based on a wagering contract. (52-553).

Attorney Fees.—If note contains provision for payment of reasonable attorneys fees, they may be advanced as item of costs. (19 Conn. Sup. 422, 116 A.2d 447).

Special Defenses, Consumer Instruments.—Holder in due course subject to defenses of buyer against seller if buyer has made written demand on seller. Same rule applies to notes arising from "consumer service" transactions payments which include supply of accommodations, exercise and health club programs, instruction or education, and any work for personal, family, or household purposes. (52-572g).

Dishonored Checks.—Payee of dishonored check may impose service charge not to exceed $20. Additionally, drawer shall be liable to payee for damages in addition to face amount of check in event that drawer does not pay full face amount of check within 30 days of second written demand for payment. (52-565a).

BILLS OF LADING:

See topic Carriers.

BILLS OF SALE:

See topic Sales.

BLUE SKY LAW:

See topic Securities.

BROKERS:

Uniform Commercial Code adopted. (Title 42a).

Insurance brokers must be licensed by Insurance Commissioner. (See category Insurance, topic Insurance Companies.) Brokers of securities must be registered with Bank Commissioner. See topic Securities.

Keeping a "bucket shop" is unlawful. (53-313 to 53-315).

Real estate brokers are licensed by Department of Consumer Protection after investigation of character. (20-311; 20-314; 20-315 to 20-319; 20-320 to 20-324, §§1-4; 20-325, 20-325a; 20-325b to 20-329bb). Grounds for refusal of license (20-316, 20-316 [c]), and for suspension or revocation (20-320), after notice and hearing (20-321) as specified. Nonresident brokers must be licensed but are extended reciprocity if licensed by state with similar reciprocal requirements and if no disciplinary proceeding or unresolved complaint is pending against him/her. (20-317). Technical Revisions to c. 392 (Real Estate Brokers and Salespersons) and c. 400g (Real Estate Appraisers). (PA 98-10).

Real estate brokers and salesmen must pay fees to a real estate guaranty fund, which is held by real estate commission, and anyone aggrieved by fraud, embezzlement, etc., of real estate broker, may recover from such fund up to $25,000 for any one transaction or claim. (20-324a to 20-324j).

Unsecured Loan Brokers.—Advance fees prohibited. (PA 92-67, §§1-7).

See also topic Commercial Code.

BULK SALES:

See category Debtor and Creditor, topic Fraudulent Sales and Conveyances. Article 6 of Uniform Commercial Code repealed. (PA 93-107).

CARRIERS:

Uniform Commercial Code adopted. (Title 42a).

Supervision.—Common carriers are subject to regulation and supervision by Public Utilities Control Authority as to rates, routes, adequacy and safety of equipment and facilities, method of operation, prevention of accidents at crossings, large financial matters, etc., and must report accidents to Public Utilities Control Authority and file annual reports with Authority. Appeal lies from Public Utilities Control Authority to Superior Court. (16-1 to 16-50x).

Rates must be sufficient to cover operating costs, attract capital and maintain financial integrity (16-19; 16-19a; 16-19b; 16-19c to 16-19h, 16-19i to 16-19x; 16-19y to 16-22; 16-41[a]), freight rates for short haul may not exceed rate for longer haul over same route (16-69); nor may any one or more connecting carriers be discriminated against in rates or in facilities furnished for cooperative handling of passengers and freight (16-65). Carrier may be required to establish requisite connections and operate cars delivered to it by connecting carrier. (16-63).

Liens.—Railroad may not charge storage for less than two consecutive days excluding Sundays and holidays. (16-172). Lien for transportation and storage charges exists if company delivers to consignee on request a copy of a bill of charges as same appears on way-bill held by company. (16-173).

Bills of Lading.—Governed by Uniform Commercial Code. (Tit. 42a).

Motor Vehicle Carriers.—See category Transportation, topic Motor Vehicles.

See also topic Commercial Code.

COMMERCIAL CODE:

Uniform Commercial Code adopted, effective Oct. 1, 1961. By amendment Conn. has adopted 1962 Official Text. (42a-1-201). 1972 Official Amendments adopted. 1990 Official Amendments adopted.

Connecticut has adopted the following options in the 1962 Official Text, and made following other changes.

Art. 1-209—1966 Official Optional Amendment not adopted.

Art. 2-318—1966 Official Optional Amendment not adopted. Connecticut text of §2-318 (42a-2-318) is as follows:

"A seller's warranty whether express or implied extends to any natural person who is in the family or household of his buyer or who is a guest in his home if it is

See note at head of Digest as to 1998 legislation covered.

See Topical Index in front part of this volume.

CT – 6

COMMERCIAL CODE ... *continued*

reasonable to expect that such person may use, consume or be affected by the goods and who is injured in person by breach of warranty. This section is neutral with respect to case law or statutory law extending warranties for personal injuries to other persons. A seller may not exclude or limit the operation of this section."

See also topic Sales, subhead Blood, Human Tissue, or Organs.

Art. 2-702—1966 Official Amendment adopted.

Art. 3-121—Alternative A adopted. (42a-3-121).

Art. 3-501—1966 Official Amendment not adopted.

Re Art. 3—See topic Bills and Notes, subhead Special Defenses, Consumer Instruments, for nonnegotiability.

Art. 4-104(c)—"Banking Day" for purpose of midnight deadline does not include Saturday.

Art. 4-106—Bracketed material omitted. (42a-4-106).

Art. 4-107(2)—Item or deposit received on a day not a banking day treated as received on opening of next banking day.

Art. 4-202—Bracketed material in paragraph 4-202(1)(6) included. (42a-4-202[1][6]).

Art. 4-212—Bracketed material in paragraph 4-212(2) included. (42a-4-212[2]).

Art. 4A-101 to 108—Adopted 1990. (90-202, §1).

Art. 4A-201 to 212—Issue and acceptance of payment orders, adopted. (90-202, §2).

Art. 4A-301 to 305—Execution of sender's payment order by receiving bank, adopted. (90-202, §3). §33 modifies CGS §42a-9-305—Security interest in letters of credit and letters of advice may also be perfected by taking possession of collateral. (HB-6001; PA 98-1).

Art. 4A-401 to 406—Payment, adopted. (90-202, §4).

Art. 4A-501 to 506—Adopted. (90-202, §5).

Art. 5-107—Last seven words of 5-107(2) included (not an option but these words omitted in Massachusetts enactment of Code). (42a-5-107[2]).

Art. 5-112—Bracketed material included. (42a-5-112[b]).

Art. 5-113—Subsections (a) and (b) of subsection 2 included (not listed as option but omitted in Massachusetts enactment of code). (42a-5-113).

Art. 5-114—Bracketed material (Optional provisions 5-114[4] and [5] included. (42a-5-114).

For purposes of Art. 6, municipal tax collector considered a creditor. (42a-5-113).

Art. 6 repealed. (PA 93-107).

Art. 7-209—1966 Official Amendment not adopted.

Art. 7-403—Bracketed provisions in Official Draft (7-403[1][c]) are excluded.

Art. 8.—Revised as to Investment Securities. (PA 97-182; am'd by PA 98-93).

Art. 9-103—Connecticut has repealed 42a-9-103.

Art. 9-105—1966 Official Optional Amendment not adopted.

Art. 9-106—1966 Official Optional Amendment not adopted.

Art. 9-301—Time for perfection of purchase money security interest increased from ten to 20 days after collateral comes into debtor's possession.

Art. 9-302—§5 is added which varies method of perfection for certain public utility companies and carriers. (42a-9-302[5]).

Art. 9-304—*Financing Statements.* Financing statements and related instruments filed prior to effective date of act are valid despite error or omission of execution date. (S.A. 97-6, §8; H.B. 6402; 42a-9-304).

Art. 9-401(1)—First Alternative of 1972 Official Amendments adopted. (42a-9-401[1]).

Art. 9-401(3)—Alternative Subsection (3) of 1972 Official Amendments not adopted.

Art. 9-403(5)—Am'd to exempt public officials from fees. (42a-9-403[5]).

Art. 9-407—This section included in Connecticut enactment of Code. (42a-9-407[2]). Filing, indexing, and certain other fees, $5. (42a-9-401 to 407).

Certain further changes were made in the code, to dovetail the provisions of the Code with the existing Connecticut Retail Installment Sales Financing Act (42-83 et seq.) and Uniform Motor Vehicle Certificate of Title and Anti-Theft Act (§§14-165 et seq.). Sections affected include: 42a-9-203, §2 added (requirements of §§42-83 et seq. govern where item is subject to requirements of both §§42-83 et seq. and Art. 9), 42a-9-409.

1973 Official Amendment adopted.

1977 Official Amendments not adopted.

Forms.—See end of this Digest.

See also topics: Banks and Banking, Bills and Notes, Brokers, Carriers, Contracts, Factors, Frauds, Statute of, Sales, Securities, Warehousemen; categories Business Organizations, topic Corporations; Civil Actions and Procedure, topics Accord and Satisfaction, Limitation of Actions; Debtor and Creditor, topics Assignments, Fraudulent Sales and Conveyances, Liens, Pledges; Documents and Records, topics Records, Seals; Mortgages, topic Chattel Mortgages.

CONDITIONAL SALES:

See topic Sales.

CONSIGNMENTS:

See topic Factors.

CONSUMER PROTECTION:

Department of Consumer Protection.—Generally responsible for food quality and purity, labeling, weights and measures. (21a-1 to 21a-12; 43-3). Under 42-144 to 42-149, which prohibits referral or multi-level sales schemes and declares contracts for same void, Department empowered to investigate same, and to secure injunction and or restitution via attorney general in superior court action.

Unfair Trade Practices.—Unfair and deceptive acts as defined by Federal Trade Commission Act prohibited. (42-110a to 42-110q). Commissioner of consumer protection empowered to promulgate rules and regulations, conduct investigations and hearings, and to issue cease and desist orders, enforcing them through court action. Award

of attorney's fees against violators. (PA 94-15). Court may order restitution, revocation of license to do business or appointment of receiver. Wilful violation punishable by civil penalty of up to $5,000 for each violation. Private parties may also institute actions under Act. Jury trial specifically authorized by statute. (PA 95-123).

Consumer Collection Agencies.—Actions of third-party collection agencies retained by creditors strictly controlled. (42-127 to 42-133a).

State Child Protection Act.—Act defines hazardous and banned substances and prohibits placing in commerce or receipt of any misbranded or banned hazardous substance or tampering with labeling of any such substance. First offense is Class C misdemeanor, with civil penalty up to $500 for each offense, second offense or offense committed with intent to defraud punishable by sentence of up to one year imprisonment and $3,000 fine. (21a-335 to 21a-346).

Credit Transaction Discrimination.—Unlawful for any creditor in credit transaction to discriminate on basis of sex, age, race, color, religious creed, national origin, ancestry, marital status, mental retardation, blindness, or physical disability against anyone 18 years of age or older. (36-437). For violating Act, creditor held liable for actual damages and punitive damages of up to $1,000. (36-438a).

Fair Credit Reporting.—Various safeguards and procedures to protect and allow consumer to dispute and rectify derogatory credit reports. (36a-696, am'd PA 95-104).

Check Cashing Services.—See topic Banks and Banking.

Conn. Anti-Trust Act.—Patterned after Federal anti-trust act, Conn. legislation prohibits contract, combination, or conspiracy: in restraint of any part of trade or commerce, to monopolize, attempt to monopolize or monopolization. Act specifies certain acts as unlawful without limiting violations to those specified and places enforcement responsibility under attorney general. Injunctive relief, treble damages and civil penalties of up to $250,000 are provided for in Act. (35-25 to 35-71).

Diet Companies.—New rules regarding disclosures, cancellations and rebate of contract price for diet programs. (42-280).

Extended Warranties.—Providers and procedures for such warranties regulated by statute. (PA 93-258).

Truth in Lending Act.—Requires complete disclosure of all finance charges and closing costs in any consumer credit transaction, including true annual percentage rate at time of down payment or, for real estate transaction, at time of creditor's commitment. Where real property of obligor is used as security in consumer credit transaction, obligor may rescind transaction at any time until midnight of third business day following consummation of transaction or delivery of required disclosures, whichever is later. Unless corrected within 15 days after discovery, any creditor who failed to provide proper disclosure, is liable for any actual damage sustained plus costs of collection, including reasonable attorney fees. In addition, in individual action, creditor is liable for twice finance charge up to $1,000 or minimum of $100. In class action, no minimum recovery and total recovery limited to $500,000 or 1% of net worth of creditor. (36-393 to 36-417).

Home Solicitation Sales Act.—No home solicitation sale agreement effective if not signed and dated by buyer or if seller: (1) Fails to furnish buyer with copies of completed receipts and contracts at time of sale. Contract must: (a) Be in same language as was used in sales presentation; (b) show address of seller; (c) inform buyer of right to cancel transaction within three business days. (2) Fails to furnish buyer with completed form captioned "Notice of Cancellation". (3) Includes in receipt or contract any confession of judgment or waiver of buyer's rights. (4) Fails to orally inform buyer of right to cancel or misrepresents such right. (5) Fails to honor valid notice of cancellation within ten business days of receipt. (6) Transfers note or other evidence of indebtedness to third party within five business days of sale. (42-135a).

Transfer of note or other evidence of indebtedness given by buyer in home solicitation sale is assignment only and transferee takes subject to all defenses and claims of buyer against seller arising under act. Note must include specified statement that instrument is not negotiable. (42-136). Buyer may cancel until midnight of third business day after signing, and seller must thereafter return all payments and/or notes within ten business days. (42-138). Buyer must return goods within 20 days upon demand of seller, at buyer's address. (42-139). Referral sale schemes prohibited. (42-140). Violation of Act punishable by imprisonment up to 90 days and/or $500 fine, and constitutes unfair or deceptive act or practice as defined by 42-110b. (42-141).

Home Improvement Act.—No home improvement contract is valid unless it: (1) Is in writing; (2) is signed by homeowner and contractor; (3) contains entire agreement; (4) contains date of transaction; (5) contains name and address of contractor; (6) contains starting and completion dates; and (7) is entered into by registered salesman or registered contractor. Home improvement contracts are subject to requirements of Home Solicitation Sales Act. (20-418 to 20-431). Contractor may still recover reasonable value of services if court determines denial of recovery would be inequitable. (PA 93-215).

Uniform Food and Drug and Cosmetic Act (not proposed by Nat. Conf. of Commissioners on Uniform State Laws) adopted. (21a-91 to 21a-120).

Labeling of dangerous toys required. (21a-337, am'd PA 92-127).

Unsolicited Goods.—Voluntary and unsolicited sending of goods not actually ordered or requested by recipient deemed unconditional gift. (42-126b). Trial offers include written procedures to cancel products or services. (PA 98-109).

Credit Cards.—Fine of not more than $100 for sending unsolicited credit card or charge plate. (53-311a).

Facsimiles.—No person shall use machine that electronically transmits facsimiles to transmit unsolicited advertising material which offers to sell goods or services. Persons aggrieved by violation may bring civil action to enjoin further violation and to recover damages, costs, attorney fees or $200 whichever greater. (PA 89-103).

Plain Language.—Every consumer contract, in which consumer leases residence or receives up to $25,000 in credit, but excluding mortgages, real estate deeds, insurance

See note at head of Digest as to 1998 legislation covered.

See Topical Index in front part of this volume.

CONSUMER PROTECTION ... *continued*

policies or securities documents, must be written in plain language. Provides subjective and objective tests for determining compliance, and exempts real property descriptions and language expressly required by court, statute or regulation. Consumer contract violating this chapter is enforceable, but creditor or seller is liable for statutory damages of $100 plus $100 attorney's fees. (42-151 to 42-158).

Lemon Law.—Manufacturer must repair or replace vehicle which does not conform to express warranties. (42-179). If motor vehicle does not conform to warranties, it is presumed reasonable number of attempts undertaken to conform vehicle to warranties. No claim may be used unless at least one attempt to repair nonconformity has been made by manufacturer or agent, or manufacturer agent has refused to repair such nonconformity. (42-179[e]). Consumer grievances may be brought to arbitration panel of department of consumer protection if manufacturer has not established approved dispute settlement procedure. (42-181). Term "consumer" does not include lessee who purchases vehicle at end of lease term pursuant to lease contract option. (42-220). Resale, transfer or lease of motor vehicle returned pursuant to lemon law must be disclosed as "manufacturer buyback". (42-179[g]).

Malpractice Insurance.—Health care providers, including physicians, osteopaths, chiropractors, podiatrists, and naturopaths required to maintain malpractice insurance in minimum amount of $500,000. Failure to do so grounds for license denial or revocation. (PA 94-71).

Property Condition Disclosure.—Effective Jan. 1, 1996, person offering for sale, exchange, or lease with purchase option, residential property consisting of four dwelling units or less must provide prospective buyer with written "condition report" in form to be developed by Commissioner of Consumer Protection. Form will cover such issues as: radon, lead, environmental matters, subsurface sewage disposal. If seller fails to provide report, seller must credit purchaser $300 toward purchase price. Transfers exempt from requirement are: (1) sales between or among existing co-owners; (2) transfers to certain family members without consideration; (3) court-ordered transfers; (4) new construction; (5) transfers by executors, administrators, trustees, or conservators; (6) governmental transfers; (7) deeds in lieu of foreclosure, or transfers pursuant to foreclosure by sale; (8) transfers pursuant to exercise of option obtained prior to effective date. (PA 95-311).

Telemarketers, sweepstakes promotions, buying clubs, telecommunication services regulated. (42-284 et seq.; PA 98-148).

Utility Companies.—SB-498; PA 98-254 sets forth requirements for notice of termination of utility services. (CGS §16-262d).

See also topics Interest, Sales; category Insurance, topic Insurance Companies.

CONTRACTS:

See topic Bills and Notes; categories Documents and Records, topic Seals; Family, topic Infants.

Wagering contracts void except for regulated State lottery, off-track betting facilities, and pari-mutuel systems (52-533; 12-557 to 12-582), but see topic Bills and Notes. Referral sales contracts offering rebate contingent upon procuring additional contracts are unlawful and void. (42-146). Home solicitation sales regulated by statute and voidable at any time before midnight of third business day following signing of contract at election of buyer. (42-137). Contracts for illegal sale of alcoholic liquors are void. (30-103). Negative option service contracts by home improvement contractors are void. (20-429).

Uniform Commercial Code adopted, effective Oct. 1, 1961. (Title 42a). By amendment, Connecticut has adopted 1962 Official Text. See topic Commercial Code.

19-6a makes any agreements exempting owners and contractors from liability for negligence void and unenforceable. (19-6a). See topic Monopolies, Restraint of Trade and Competition.

FACTORS:

Governed by Uniform Commercial Code. (Tit. 42a).

FRANCHISES:

No franchisor shall, directly or through any officer, agent or employee, terminate, cancel or fail to renew franchise, except for good cause, including, but not limited to franchisee's refusal or failure to comply with any material and reasonable obligation of franchise agreement. See 42-133f section (e). Franchisor shall give franchisee written notice of such termination, cancellation or intent not to renew, at least 60 days in advance with cause stated; provided, in event franchisor elects not to renew, franchisor shall give franchisee written notice of such intent not to renew at least six months prior to expiration of current franchise agreement. Provisions of this section shall not apply (1) where alleged grounds are voluntary abandonment by franchisee, in which event, notice may be given 30 days in advance of termination, cancellation, or failure to renew, (2) where alleged grounds are conviction of franchisee in court of competent jurisdiction of offense punishable by term of imprisonment in excess of one year and directly related to business conducted pursuant to franchise, such notice may be given any time following conviction and shall be effective upon delivery and written receipt of such notice.

If franchise which is subject of notice of termination, cancellation or failure to renew is operated on premises leased by franchisor to franchisee under lease which terminates upon termination of franchise, if franchisor seeks to terminate lease, notice shall be served and shall expressly state that lease shall terminate upon termination of franchise.

Upon termination of any franchise, franchisee shall be allowed fair and reasonable compensation by franchisor for franchisee's inventory, supplies, equipment and furnishings.

Notwithstanding provisions of §52-550, no franchise entered into or renewed on or after Oct. 1, 1973 whether oral or written shall be for term of less than three years and for successive terms of not less than three years thereafter unless cancelled, terminated or not renewed.

Franchisor may elect not to renew franchise which involves lease by franchisor to franchisee of real property and improvement, in event franchisor (1) sells or leases such real property and improvements to other than subsidiary or affiliate of franchisor for any use; or (2) sells or leases such real property to subsidiary or affiliate of franchisor who shall not use real property for operation of same business of franchisee; or (3) converts such real property and improvements to use not covered by franchise agreement; or (4) has leased such real property from person not franchisee and lease from person is terminated or not renewed. (42-133f).

Uniform Franchise and Business Opportunities Act not adopted.

FRAUDS, STATUTE OF:

No action can be maintained upon an agreement of an executor or administrator to answer damages out of his own estate, or against any person upon any promise to answer for the debt, default or miscarriage of another; or upon any agreement made in consideration of marriage; or upon any agreement for the sale of real estate or any interest in or concerning it (except lease for one year or less in pursuance of which lessee actually occupies leased premises); or upon any agreement that is not to be performed within one year, unless such agreement, or a memorandum thereof, be in writing and signed by the party to be charged therewith, or his agent (52-550), contracts for sale of personal property are governed by Uniform Commercial Code (42a-1-206; 42a-2-201; 42a-8-319).

INTEREST:

Judgments.—Legal rate of accrual as addition to debt in absence of agreement to contrary is 8%. (37-1). This rate is collectible on past due obligations, running accounts, and judgments. Interest recoverable as damages in civil action at rate of 10%. Reasonable and just interest on compensation awarded for taking property by eminent domain. (37-3a).

Maximum Rates.—Contract to pay interest in excess of 8% need not be in writing, but loans at greater rate than 12% prohibited (37-4), except by national bank, state bank or trust company or wholly owned subsidiary, except on consumer loans, federal or state savings and loan association, or credit union or federal credit union (37-9), duly licensed small loan company (36-233), or pawnbroker (21-44) or on real estate mortgage for sum in excess of $5,000 or in commercial loans in excess of $10,000, or on obligations or loans made by state, local government, or public agencies (37-9). Maximum for financing purchase of new cars, boats, or recreational vehicles is 16%, on used is 18%. (37-9). Maximum on loans by institution of higher education to students is greater of: Rate allowed in 37-4 or 5% above current discount rate on 90-day commercial paper. (37-9). This limitation may not be evaded by taking note for greater amount than actually loaned (37-5) nor by charges for inquiries, expenses, etc. (37-6).

Borrower cannot recover back or set-off interest paid in excess of 6%. (37-2 but see 37-1, 37-3a). Whenever maker of note is nonresident or mortgage security is located in another state, resident obligee or holder may recover any agreed rate of interest not exceeding legal rate in state where contract made or mortgage security located. (37-3a).

Small Loans.—Every person, partnership or corporation licensed under Small Loan Act may loan up to $15,000 excluding charges and may receive thereon charges on loans not exceeding $1,800 at per annum rate not to exceed $17 per $100 on that part of cash advance not exceeding $600, and $11 per $100 on any remainder, on loans exceeding $1,800 charges not to exceed $11 per $100, and proportionally at those rates over longer or shorter term of loan. Such charges must be computed at time loan is made on full amount of cash advance, must be added to cash advance, resulting sum becoming face amount of note and all payments, except for default and deferment charges are deemed applied to unpaid installments. Default periods and deferred payment and charges are regulated (36a-555). Credit life insurance may not be made condition of small loan. (36-234).

No one may make loan of money or credit in amount below $15,000 and receive or contract for greater rate of interest, charge or consideration than 12% with some exceptions. (CGS §36a-555; HB 5429; PA 98-264).

Pawnbrokers may charge 5% per month on loans not exceeding $15; 3% per month on loans exceeding $15 but not exceeding $50; and 2% per month on loans exceeding $50. Monthly rate may be charged for fractions of a month. (21-44).

Credit Cards.—After effective date of Act, retail seller may apply maximum interest 1½% per month on average daily balance or unpaid balance at end of billing cycle. (42-133c).

Usury.—No action may be brought to recover principal or interest or any part thereof on any loan at a rate of interest exceeding that permitted by law, or upon any cause arising from the negotiation of such loan. (36-243). But this does not prevent national bank, state bank, federal or state savings and loan association, which has acquired negotiable instrument in good faith and for value, without notice of illegality in consideration, from recovering principal thereof and interest thereon. (37-9). Accommodation indorser may contest usurious note same as maker might. (102 Conn. 34, 127 Atl. 907).

LICENSES, BUSINESS AND PROFESSIONAL:

Licenses and permits from different authorities, on varying conditions, and at various fees are required for a large number of occupations and activities. Municipality or district health department may withhold or revoke any license or permit from business enterprise more than one year delinquent in municipal personal property tax. (12-146a). Licenses for specific occupations are governed by Titles 12 and 20. Technical revisions to Title 20. (PA 98-3). Amendments to Acupuncturist licensing requirements. (PA 98-9, amending 20-206bb).

See note at head of Digest as to 1998 legislation covered.

See Topical Index in front part of this volume.

LICENSES, BUSINESS AND PROFESSIONAL... *continued*

Marriage and Family.—Therapists, sanatarians, speech pathologists, podiatrists, opticians, acupuncturists, clinical social workers and massage therapists must be licensed. (20-195, 20-50, 20-74, 20-146). Physical therapists, occupational therapists and practical nurses must be licensed. (20-70a, am'd 97-15).

Alcohol and Drug Counselors.—One who has Masters degree and is certified by The Department of Mental Health and Addiction Services shall be deemed licensed alcohol and drug counselor. One who does not have Masters degree must obtain certification and will then be deemed certified alcohol and drug counselor. Methods of obtaining certification are delineated in statute as are exceptions to licensure and certification and penalties for noncompliance. (CGS §§19A-14, 19A-88, 20-740-20-74r, 17a-4502; SB 426; PA 98-247).

Clinical Social Workers.—SB 426; PA 98-247 limits those who may hold themselves out as licensed clinical social workers; prescribes licensing requirements, exceptions to licensing and renewal procedures. (CGS §§20-195q, 20-1950).

Bounty Hunters.—Governed by PA 97-287.

Child day care centers and homes are regulated. (19a-77, 79, PA 98-71).

Chiropractors seeking license renewal required to participate in continuing education programs. (20-32, am'd PA 95-31).

Commercial travelers need not be licensed. (21-27).

Counselors and Marriage and Family Therapists.—Governed by 19a-14, amended by PA 98-43.

Collection Agencies—Governed by 36a-805-809.

See also category Insurance, topic Insurance Companies, subhead Agents, Brokers and Adjusters.

Paramedics.—Governed by PA 97-287.

Business Assistance.—HB 5716; PA 98-246 established one-stop business registry in Department of Economic and Community Development; allows joint contracts between DECD, Office of Policy and Management with private entities to implement registry. Such registry will provide information and forms to those doing business in State or intending to do business. (CGS §32-349).

Established Connecticut Water Guarantee Fund to issue or make advance commitments to issue guarantees of loans or other investments. Limitations on guarantees which would result in issued and outstanding guarantees to exceed four times amount available in fund plus unpaid parts authorized by DECD. (CGS §32-261).

Pharmacy technician regulations require registration and fee. (PA 98-31).

MONOPOLIES, RESTRAINT OF TRADE AND COMPETITION:

State antitrust law in effect; restraint of trade and monopolization of any part of trade or commerce unlawful. (35-24 to 35-43).

Fairness in Franchising Act.—42-133e to 42-133h. See topic Franchises.

Unfair Sales Practices.—Sales practices determined to be unfair or deceptive by Federal Trade Commission Act rules or regulations are prohibited. Cigarettes are also governed by special provisions. (12-322 to 12-326).

Unfair competition and trade practice affecting intrastate commerce in food, drugs, devices, and cosmetics are restricted by 21a-93; 21a-128. Regulatory power is vested in Commissioner of Food and Drugs. (21a-115). Unfair competition and trade practices in advertisement and sale of alcoholic liquors are prohibited. (30-63 et seq.). State minimum mark-up law on liquor sales repealed. (38-68a to 30-68c). Unfair drug and pharmaceutical trade practices regulated. (38-174). Unfair merchandising schemes regulated by Commissioner of Consumer Protection, enforced by Attorney General. (42-144 to 42-150). Acquisition or merger of banks must be approved by Banking Commissioner . (36-553 to 36-557).

Standard marketing contracts with duly organized cooperative marketing corporations requiring members to sell for a period of time, not over ten years, exclusively to or through the corporation are valid (33-212); liquidated damage provisions are enforceable and corporation may obtain injunction against threatened or actual breach and is entitled to decree of specific performance (33-213).

Petroleum product franchisors are subject to special regulation. (42-133j to 42-133n).

Electrical distribution companies to be restructured and unbundled as of Oct. 1, 1998. (PA 98-28).

NEGOTIABLE INSTRUMENTS:

See topic Bills and Notes.

RESTRAINT OF TRADE:

See topic Monopolies, Restraint of Trade and Competition.

SALES:

Governed by Uniform Commercial Code. (Tit. 42a, especially 42a-2-101—42a-2-725). Note should be taken of fact that 42a-2-725 provides a four year statute of limitations for causes of action governed by Article 2 of Code.

Conditional Sales.—

Filing.—Conn. has central filing with Secretary of State under Uniform Commercial Code for all documents except those pertaining to motor vehicles, which are filed with Motor Vehicle Commissioner (Uniform Motor Vehicle Certificate of Title and Anti-Theft Act [14-165—14-211]) and fixtures, which are filed in town where real estate is located. Conditional sales contracts filed prior to Oct. 1, 1961, need not be refiled and continue to be effective for three years after final payment date stated in conditional sales contract. (16-290). For schedule of fees see category Documents and Records, topic Records.

Retail credit sales, home solicitation and referral sales specially regulated. (42-134 to 42-143).

Retail Installment Sales Financing.—Special provisions govern retail installment contracts or installment loan contracts including "consumer goods" and "equipment" as defined in 42a-9-109(1) and (2) of Uniform Commercial Code made after Oct. 1, 1947 on chattels personal having sale price of $6,000 or less. (36-244i). Detailed restrictions are imposed upon form and contents of such contracts (38-57; 42-96), upon foreclosure, including retaking possession, notice of intention of retake, redemption, resale, etc. (42-98), upon anticipation of payments and refund therefor (45-88; 42-96) and upon renewals and extensions of such contracts (42-97). Connecticut Truth in Lending Act, virtually identical to Federal Truth in Lending Act, has been adopted. (36-393 to 36-417). Fair Credit Billing Act also adopted. (36-417a to 36-417y).

In cases not governed by the retail installment sales financing act, the relative rights of buyer and seller are governed by the contract terms, which normally allow vendor to reclaim possession upon default (76 Conn. 221, 56 Atl. 494), or bring action to recover the purchase price. If latter course is followed, sale becomes absolute and vendor cannot thereafter reclaim. (118 Conn. 220, 171, Atl, 658). If vendor has right under contract to sell property after repossession upon default and recover any deficiency, he may not retain property and still get deficiency judgment (117 Conn. 251, 167 Atl. 734), but may sue for balance due after resale (116 Conn. 364, 165 Atl. 203). 42-84a and 42-84b concern errors in retail transactions.

Interest rate cap on certain open end credit plans. See topic Interest, subhead Credit Cards.

Consumer Protection.—See subhead Retail Installment Sales Financing, supra. See also topic Consumer Protection, subhead Home Solicitation Sales Act.

Bulk Sales.—Art. 6 of Uniform Commercial Code repealed. (PA 93-107).

Sales of Motor Vehicles.—See category Transportation, topic Motor Vehicles.

Product Liability.—Connecticut has abolished necessity for privity in breach of warranty actions; no requirement in negligence cases. (148 Conn. 710, 174 A.2d 294).

Unsolicited Merchandise.—See topic Consumer Protection, subhead Unsolicited Goods.

Blood, human tissue, or organs not goods subject to sale, but medical services, and implied warranties or merchantability and fitness not applicable. (19a-280).

SECURITIES:

Uniform Securities Act adopted. (36b-2 to 36b-33). See Uniform and Model Acts section for text of Uniform Securities Act. Act, as adopted in Connecticut, does not permit registration of securities by notification, and contains lengthier lists of exempted securities (§22[6]) and exempted transactions (§22[6]) than Uniform Act. Penalties in event of violations specifically include restitution and disgorgement of profits. (36b-2 to 36b-33, am'd PA 98-162).

Supervision of Act conferred upon bank commissioner.

Uniform Commercial Code adopted, Tit. 42a. See topic Commercial Code.

Tender Offers.—See category Business Organizations, topic Corporations.

Uniform Fraudulent Transfer Act.—(52-557).

Uniform Simplification of Fiduciary Security Transfers Act not adopted.

Uniform Securities Ownership by Minors Act not adopted.

Fairness and Franchising Act.—42-133e to 42-133h. See topic Franchises.

STATUTE OF FRAUDS:

See topic Frauds, Statute of.

TRUST RECEIPT SECURITY:

Governed by Uniform Commercial Code (Tit. 42a) recordation is with Secretary of State, or in case of motor vehicles, with Motor Vehicle Commissioner. (14-165 to 14-211).

WAREHOUSEMEN:

Any person may establish and maintain a public warehouse and receive commodities for storage, but receipts may not be issued unless conspicuous "Public Warehouse" sign is displayed on front of building where commodities are stored. (40-1).

Bonds.—No statutory provisions.

Licenses.—No statutory provisions.

Warehouse Receipts.—Governed by Uniform Commercial Code. (42a-7-101 to 42a-7-603). Under optional provisions provided by Official Text of Code (1958) Connecticut excluded bracketed material in 7-403.

CITIZENSHIP

ALIENS:

Any alien, whether or not resident in U.S. has same rights relative to real estate in this state as citizen hereof. Prior transfers of real estate to aliens validated. (PA 85-211). Under "most favored nation" provisions of treaties most aliens may now inherit realty as well as personalty and may otherwise acquire land for any purpose. Any person who has legal settlement in some other state who becomes pauper may be deported. Land inherited by nonresident alien must be sold to avoid escheat. (17-269; 45-249).

Permit to carry or sell pistol or revolver may not be issued to alien. (29-28). No person, firm or corporation shall sell at retail, deliver or otherwise transfer any pistol or revolver to any alien. (29-33).

See note at head of Digest as to 1998 legislation covered.

See Topical Index in front part of this volume.

CIVIL ACTIONS AND PROCEDURE

ACCORD AND SATISFACTION:

Agreement to accept lesser sum in full payment of amount due is enforceable if founded on new contract based on new consideration with unmistakable mutual assent to the satisfaction. (109 Conn. 244, 146 Atl. 288).

Compromise.—Claim subject to actual good faith controversy may be compromised by acceptance of lesser amount. (85 Conn. 50, 81 Atl. 972).

Pleading.—Accord and satisfaction must be specially pleaded. (C. P. B. 10-50; 83 Conn. 241, 252, 76 Atl. 533).

See category Business Regulation and Commerce, topic Commercial Code.

ACTIONS:

See also topic Submission of Controversy.

Equity.—Remedies at law and in equity may be enforced in the same suit. (52-97).

Forms of Action.—Common law forms are discontinued and one form of civil action provided. (52-91).

Conditions Precedent.—In action for negligence against party bound to keep road, sidewalk or bridge in repair, following written notice of injury is required: against municipality, 30 days if injury due to ice or snow, two years from date of injury in all other cases (13a-149, am'd PA 86-338, §13); against Commissioner of Transportation, 60 days (13a-144; 13a-149); 90 days notice to Commissioner of Transportation (PA 76-222§1). In civil action against health care provider for personal injury or wrongful death, attorney party filing action must make reasonable inquiry that there are grounds for good faith belief that there has been negligence in care or treatment of claimant. (52-190a).

Commencement.—Action is commenced by legal process consisting of writ of summons or attachment, accompanied by complaint. (52-89). Service upon defendant is considered commencement of action. Attachment or garnishment may be made after hearing held pursuant to prejudgment remedy procedure unless defendant: Is avoiding service of process; is about to leave state or remove property from state; is fraudulently conveying assets or has waived hearing (in commercial transactions only). (52-278a to 52-278g). See also topic Process; category Debtor and Creditor, topic Attachment.

Parties.—When parties are numerous, one may represent all. (52-105). Where complete determination cannot be had without the presence of other parties court may direct that such other parties be brought in; if person not party has interest or title which judgment will affect, court, must, on his application, direct him to be made party. (52-107). New parties may be added and summoned in, and parties misjoined may be dropped, by order of court, at any stage of action. (52-108). If action is commenced in name of wrong person as plaintiff, court may allow any other person to be substituted or added as plaintiff if satisfied that it was so commenced through mistake and that change is necessary for determination of dispute. (52-109). When counterclaim raises questions affecting interests of third parties, defendant may cause them to be summoned in as parties. (52-110). In commencing civil action by or against partnership plaintiff may, within first three days of court, amend without costs, by inserting names of partners. (52-112).

Persons in whom any right to relief in respect to, or arising out of, the same transaction or series of transactions is alleged to exist jointly or severally may be joined as plaintiffs; separate trials allowable for proper cause. (52-104).

Release of a joint tortfeasor does not discharge other tortfeasors except to extent release so provides. (52-572e[b]).

Intervention.—In any action in which property has been attached, any person may appear and defend in the name of the defendant on filing an affidavit that he is creditor of defendant and has good reason to believe that amount claimed by plaintiff at commencement of action is not due and that he, creditor, is in danger of being defrauded by recovery by plaintiff. (52-86).

Interpleader is expressly provided for in case of goods in possession of warehouseman (40-18) or carrier (41-23), or between claimants to a condemnation award (48-21), or, between insured and municipal, state, or nonprofit hospital or ambulance owner as to amount due by reason of accident not covered by Workmen's Compensation Act (49-73).

Action in nature of interpleader is permitted whenever any person has any money or other property in his possession which is claimed by two or more persons. (52-484).

Joint Debtors.—A discharge of one joint debtor purporting to discharge him only does not discharge the others, who may still be sued and who may defend as though the action were brought against all. (52-142).

Joinder of Causes of Action.—Several causes of action may be united in the same complaint but, to be so united, they must all be brought to recover either: (1) Upon contract, express or implied; (2) for injuries, with or without force, to person and property, or either, including a conversion of property to the defendant's use; (3) for injuries to character; (4) upon claims to recover real property, with or without damages for the withholding thereof, and the rents and profits of the same; (5) upon claims to recover personal property specifically, with or without damages for the withholding thereof; (6) upon claims arising by virtue of a contract or by operation of law in favor of or against a party in some representative or fiduciary capacity; or (7) upon claims, whether in contract or tort, or both, arising out of the same transaction or transactions connected with the same subject of action. The several causes so united must not only belong to one of these classes but, excepting actions for the foreclosure of mortgages or liens, must affect all the parties to the action and not require different places of trial. They must also be separately stated. The same union is permissible in counterclaim and set-off. (52-97).

Severance of Actions.—The court has power to sever causes of action joined as aforesaid if it deems severance wise. (52-97).

Abatement.—No right of action or pending action (except civil actions on a penal statute or actions which are rendered useless by the death of any party thereto) is lost or abated by death of any party, but survives in favor of or against his personal representative, or may be continued by or against such personal representative. The personal representative of a deceased plaintiff may enter and prosecute the suit within six months of death. Plaintiff may within one year after death of any defendant apply to court for order to substitute defendant's personal representative. (52-599).

Action will not abate by reason of death (after death is noted on record) of co-plaintiff or co-defendant. (52-600). In any action by or against personal representative, public officer or trustee, as such, in case of his death, his successor in office may enter and prosecute, or be cited in to defend. (52-601; 52-602). Successor to public officer may bring any action which would have accrued to predecessor in his official capacity. (52-603).

Limitation of.—See topic Limitation of Actions.

Termination of Actions.—Actions may be terminated by judgment, dismissal for failure to prosecute with diligence (C. P. B. 14-3), nonsuit, or default (C. P. B. 17-20).

Small Claims.—See category Courts and Legislature, topic Courts.

Direct Actions Against Insurer.—See category Transportation, topic Motor Vehicles, subhead Direct Action.

Action Against State.—Claims against State must be filed with Claims Commissioner within one year of occurrence. (4-160). Claims Commissioner may authorize suit against State. (4-160). Medical malpractice claims against State shall be authorized for suit after claim and good faith certificate are filed. (PA 98-76).

Actions Between Spouses.—See category Family, topic Husband and Wife, subhead Actions.

APPEAL AND ERROR:

Courts of Appellate Jurisdiction.—Appeals from any final judgment or action of Superior Court, except small claims matters, which are not appealable, and under certain other statutes taken to Appellate Court within 20 calendar days after issuance of notice of judgment.

Zoning cases may be appealed to Appellate Court only upon certification by two judges of Appellate Court. Appeal period is: five days in summary process (landlord/tenant eviction) matters; seven days in applications to dissolve mechanics' lien and prejudgment remedy matters, and in certain zoning issues related to standing.

Appeals of serious felony convictions, decisions declaring state or federal statute or constitutional provision unconstitutional, and judicial review matters bypass Appellate Court and are heard by Supreme Court. Supreme Court may exercise discretion to transfer sufficiently important cases from Appellate Court docket to its own docket for determination.

Decisions of Appellate Court are appealable to Supreme Court only upon certification by three justices of Supreme Court. (51-197f, am'd 96-179).

Appeals lie from probate courts to Superior Court, in which case Superior Court tries case de novo. (45-288). Appeals lie from workmen's compensation commissioners to Compensation Review Division. (31-301). Appeals also lie from various special boards and commissioners to Superior Court. For example, Superior Court has exclusive jurisdiction of appeals from any municipal board, officer or commission and from liquor control commission. (52-7). Appeals on questions of law only lie from superior courts to Supreme Court.

Appeals to Appellate and Supreme Courts are in large measure governed by rules of court and not by statute. (C.P.B. 60-1 to 86-2). Appeal to Supreme Court must be filed within 20 days after issuance of notice of rendition of judgment, and must be accompanied by $400 bond or recognizance guaranteeing payment of costs; at time appeal is filed, record and entry fees of Supreme Court must be paid. (C.P.B. 61-10, 62-7, 52-259).

Writs of error for errors in matters of law only may be brought from judgments of superior court to Supreme Court. (52-272). Such writ must be allowed and signed within two weeks after rendition of judgment complained of. No writ may be brought in any civil or criminal proceeding for correction of any error which might have been reviewed by appeal. (52-273). It must include special and precise assignment of errors relied upon; no others will be heard by court.

Reservation of questions of law for advice of Supreme Court or Appellate Court is permitted, upon consent of all parties to record, in all cases in which appeal could lawfully have been taken to said court had judgment been rendered therein. (52-235).

Appeals to Inferior Courts.—In general method of appeal from compensation commissioners to superior court is same as method of appealing to Supreme Court. In general other appeals to inferior courts are analogous to bringing of an original action.

Appeal from probate is to superior court (§45a-186) and must be taken within 30 days, except that parties who had no notice to be present and were not present may appeal within 12 months (§45a-187); minors without guardian or guardian ad litem may appeal within 12 months after coming of age, and nonresidents who had no legal notice to be present and were not present may appeal within 12 months, or within one month of receipt of actual legal notice given by executor, administrator, or trustee (§45a-188).

Fees.—For appeal to Supreme or Appellate Court, $250, plus $50 record fee to Appellate Court. For each civil cause in Superior Court, $185, except $75 for case in Superior Court when sole claim for relief is damages less than $2,500. (§52-259).

Stay of Execution.—Stay of execution until final determination of cause, which is incident of appeal (52-264), applies to every judgment in civil action providing for recovery of damages or requiring performance of act (C.P.B. 61-11).

BONDS:

When one is required to give a bond by statute a surety is requisite. (1-26 and C. P. B. 8-10). In action on bond in penal amount judgment may be entered only for what is equitably due and where breach has been partial, scire facias may be brought to obtain further judgments up to face of bond with interest. (52-238).

See note at head of Digest as to 1998 legislation covered.

See Topical Index in front part of this volume.

CT – 10

BONDS... *continued*

Professional bondsmen are required to obtain license from State Police Commissioner, fee, $100 (29-145; 29-146), and are limited in fees they may charge (29-151).

CERTIORARI:

Applies to appeals from Appellate Court to Supreme Court and, in zoning cases, to appeals from Superior Court to Appellate Court. See topic Appeal and Error.

CHARITABLE IMMUNITY:

See topic Damages.

COMMISSIONS TO TAKE TESTIMONY:

See topic Depositions and Discovery.

COSTS:

Costs are fixed by statute (52-240 to 52-254, am'd PA 85-271, §§2, 5; 52-257) and rule of court (C.P.B. 18-1 to 18-19) and are taxed by clerks of several courts. Costs allowed are small but include nominal indemnity for proceedings before trial and trial of issue of fact, entry fees, witness fees, travel expenses, expenses of depositions and judicial sales, title examination, fees paid experts, jury fees, etc. If court finds in any criminal or civil matter that party is indigent, court shall waive costs which shall be paid by state. (52-259b, am'd PA 90-261, §14). Premiums upon bonds provided pursuant to statute rule or order of court or stipulation of parties, including bonds in lieu of or in release or dissolution of attachment, are allowed as costs in reasonable amount. (52-257).

Bonds for cost are made requisite to validity of complaints in civil actions by nonresident and by residents unless the attorney signing the writ is satisfied of the ability of the plaintiff to pay the same. (52-185). Amount of such bond is usually $150 in Superior Court, $75 in other courts; but larger bond may be ordered by court.

No costs are taxed in any court in proceedings under Workmen's Compensation Act except where appeal for vexation or delay. (31-301c).

DAMAGES:

Common Law generally prevails.

Punitive Damages.—Treble damages may be assessed for knowingly cutting or destroying timber on land of another except damages five times reasonable value may be assessed for cutting any tree to be used as Christmas tree (52-560); theft (52-564); injury to highway markers or milestones (52-567).

Double damages allowed for forgery (52-565) and intentionally throwing down fences and gateways (52-569).

In actions for libel, if plaintiff proves malice in fact or that defendant failed to retract libel, after request in writing, he may recover actual expenses of his action less taxable costs.(52-237; 92 Conn. 236, 102 A. 640).

Person prosecuting civil action without probable cause liable for double damages (treble damages if prosecuted with malicious intent). (52-568).

Parental Liability for Torts of Child.—Parent or guardian of unemancipated minor child liable for minor's willful or malicious misconduct up to the amount of $5,000. Statute does not affect any other rights which may exist against minors themselves. (52-572).

Comparative negligence rule adopted; economic or noneconomic damages may be reduced in proportion to percentage of negligence attributable to recovering party; if more than one person liable, each person against whom recovery is allowed shall be liable to claimant only for his share of recoverable economic and noneconomic damages. (52-572h). Neither contributory negligence nor comparative negligence bar recovery in strict tort liability. (52-5721). In recovery for economic or noneconomic damages over $200,000 parties may agree to payment schedule or court will order lump sum payment. (52-225d).

Right of contribution exists in persons paying more than their equitable share of damages. Action must be brought within two years. (52-572h).

Charitable Immunity.—Defense abolished. (52-557[d]). Person who serves as uncompensated director, officer or trustee of tax-exempt organization is immune from civil liability if acting in good faith and within scope of employment, unless reckless, willful or wanton. (52-557m).

Sovereign Immunity.—Claims Commissioner may authorize suit against State. Action must be brought within one year of authorization. Any applicable statute of limitation is tolled until date authorization to sue is granted. Jury not allowed. (4-160). Political subdivisions of state shall be liable for certain negligent acts. (PA 86-338, §13).

See category Criminal Law, topic Criminal Law; Estates and Trusts, topic Death, subhead Action for Death; Transportation, topic Motor Vehicles, subhead Accidents.

DECLARATORY JUDGMENTS:

See topic Judgments.

DEPOSITIONS AND DISCOVERY:

Within State for Use Within State.—Parties to civil action may take testimony from any person by deposition after giving written notice to adverse party. Court order is required to take deposition of prisoner, or if initiator of action seeks to take deposition within 20 days of commencement of proceedings. However, court order not required if initiator states that person to be examined is about to leave state. Depositions may be taken by judge, clerk of any court, justice of peace, notary public, or commissioner of superior court. Witness must be cautioned to speak whole truth and carefully examined; must subscribe depositions and make oath thereto before authority taking same, and such authority must attest same and certify that adverse party or his agent was present (if so) or that he was notified; and must also certify reason for taking such deposition, seal it up, direct it to court where it is to be used, and deliver

it, if desired, to party at whose request it was taken. Party on whose behalf deposition of adverse party is taken shall be subject to having his deposition taken on behalf of such adverse party. (52-148a to 52-148d). Testimony of any expert medical witness may be taken by deposition in lieu of expert appearing at hearing. (52-149a).

Uniform Foreign Depositions Act not adopted.

Within State for Use Elsewhere.—Taken in same manner as if to be used in Connecticut. (52-148e).

Outside of State for Use Within State.—Depositions taken outside of state by notary public, commissioner appointed by Connecticut Governor or magistrate having power to administer oaths. If taken in foreign country may also be taken by any foreign minister, secretary of legation, consul or vice consul appointed by U.S. or any person appointed by him for that purpose and having authority under laws of country where taken. Official character of such person may be proved by certificate from secretary of state of U.S. (52-148c).

Commissions.—Court in which action is pending may commission person to take out-of-state deposition. Person so commissioned has power to administer oaths and take testimony. (52-148c).

Compelling Attendance.—Subpoena and capias are available to compel attendance of deponent before commissioner or others authorized to take deposition. (52-148e).

Notice.—Party desiring to take deposition of any person must give written reasonable notice to every other party. If whereabouts of adverse party is unknown, deposition may be taken after such notice as court may direct.

Form.—The following may be used:

Form

A.B. vs. C. D. . . . . . . Court, ... County, Connecticut.

I, ... of the town of . . . . . County of . . . . . and State of Connecticut, of lawful age, being duly cautioned, examined and sworn, depose and say:

The deposition may be by questions and answers or in narrative form, and may be in handwriting of witness or magistrate, but must not be written by any party to the action, nor his attorney. (52-150). Cross-examination should be headed: Cross-examination on the part of the plaintiff (or defendant) by . . . . . and examination in rebuttal and reply should be similarly indicated. Papers referred to in the deposition and annexed as exhibits should be signed by the witness and magistrate. Objections to testimony should be minuted by the magistrate; but magistrate cannot exclude any question as inadmissible. Adjournments may be had from time to time, not necessarily to the next day. The fact of adjournment should be noted.

Return of magistrate should read:

State of . . . . Town of . . . .
County of . . . . ss.

Personally appeared the above named . . . . . signer of the foregoing deposition, and after having been duly cautioned to speak the whole truth, and carefully examined, did subscribe the same and make oath before me that the same contains the truth, the whole truth, and nothing but the truth.

The foregoing deposition is taken pursuant to the annexed notice at the request of the (plaintiff or defendant), to be read on the trial of an action pending before the . . . . . . Court within and for the County of . . . . . and State of Connecticut, in which action . . . . . . plaintiff, and . . . . . . defendant. The cause of taking this deposition is (the witness resides out of the State) or (other cause as the case may be). The adverse party was notified to be present at the taking of this deposition, and was (or was not) present threat (by his attorney). (Official signature and seal). The magistrate should then seal up the package and endorse thereon: To the Clerk of the . . . . . . Court, County of . . . . . (the town), Connecticut. The deposition of X., Y. and Z. to be used in said cause: Taken, sealed up and addressed by me, John Doe, notary public. In the care of . . . . . Esq.

The package may be then enclosed in another cover and addressed to its destination in usual manner for mailing, or may be delivered to care of the party or his attorney taking the same.

Perpetuation of Testimony.—In addition to the depositions taken in connection with pending actions because of the inconvenience of testifying at the trial, depositions may be taken for the purpose of perpetuating testimony concerning any matter which is or may be the subject of a suit, the person desirous of perpetuating such testimony presenting a petition in writing to any judge of the superior court upon due notice to other persons interested. The judge may prescribe the times and places for taking the depositions and may appoint a commissioner to take them. Fee $3 per day. (52-156).

EQUITY:

See topic Actions.

EVIDENCE:

See topic Depositions and Discovery.

Witnesses.—Witness is not disqualified because of his interest in outcome of action as party or otherwise or of his disbelief in existence of supreme being, or of his conviction of crime, but such interest or conviction may be shown for purpose of affecting his credibility. (52-145). Adverse parties or their agents in civil action or probate proceeding may be compelled to testify. (52-178). Counsel for any party may argue during closing arguments that adverse influence should be drawn from another party's failure to call witness who has been proven available to testify; however, court shall not instruct jury of same. (PA 98-50). Witness must possess some sense of moral responsibility, justly comprehend and appreciate nature, purpose, and obligation of oath or affirmation and have intelligent understanding of facts to be developed, and no child is conclusively presumed to be disqualified as witness. (104 Conn. 585, 134 Atl. 73).

Employer shall not coerce or penalize employee because employee obeys legal subpoena to appear before court in criminal proceeding. Violation by employer results

EVIDENCE . . . *continued*

in criminal contempt and fine not more than $500 or imprisonment for not more than 30 days or both. Employee has action for damages. (54-856).

See also topic Depositions and Discovery.

Privileged Communications.—Reports, notices, and records of Commissioner of Labor on serious accidents to employees (31-40; 31-40a) and reports and communications of members of Armed Forces of State in line of duty (27-99) are privileged. Conversations of juvenile court judge with child or youth whose case is before court are privileged. (17-67). Communication between student and professional employee of board of education re drugs or alcohol privileged. (10-154a). Communications between person and clergyman privileged. (52-146b). Information disclosed to states' attorney for purpose of enabling him to perform duties of his office is privileged. (128 Conn. 124, 20 A.2d 613).

Information provided to bail commissioner for release is confidential. (54-63d).

Communications between attorney and client are normally privileged, but there are exceptions. (71 Conn. 576, 42 Atl. 654).

Communications or records may be disclosed to commissioner of health services in connection with any inspection, investigation or examination of institution pursuant to 19a-490 and 19a-498.

Husband and Wife.—In a criminal case the accused and the spouse of the accused are competent witnesses, and spouse may elect or refuse to testify for or against accused, except that when wife has received personal violence from her husband for which action is brought or is spouse of one who is charged with violation of §§53-21, 23, 25, 304, 53a-70, 70a, 71, 83-88 of C.G.S., she may be compelled to testify. (54-84[a]). Wife may be compelled to testify in action brought against her husband for necessaries furnished her while living apart from him. (52-146). Communications between husband and wife are normally privileged, but there are exceptions; not privileged if overheard. (47 Conn. 518; 49 Conn. 378).

Communications or Transactions with Persons Since Deceased or Incompetent.—In actions by or against representatives of deceased persons and by or against beneficiaries of life or accident insurance policy insuring person deceased at time of trial, the relevant entries, memoranda and declarations of the deceased are admissible, and in action by or against representative of deceased persons in which any trustee or receiver is adverse party, relevant testimony of deceased given at his examination, upon application of trustee or receiver, is admissible. (52-172). Whenever entries and written memoranda of deceased would be admissible in favor of his representatives, such evidence is admissible in favor of any person claiming title under or from the decedent. (52-173). Where party to action at time of trial is mentally ill, or unable to testify because of incurable sickness, failing mind, old age, infirmity or senility, his relevant entries or memoranda, made while sane, are admissible. Whenever such evidence of such mentally ill person would be admissible in his favor in action to which he was party, evidence may be admitted in favor of any person claiming under or from mentally ill person. (52-175).

Self-incrimination.—No person may be compelled to give evidence against himself, except as otherwise provided by statute, nor may such evidence when given be used against him (51-35) and right of witness not to answer self-incriminating question may be claimed by him or his counsel (52-199). There are number of exceptions to self-incrimination rule in official investigations and proceedings, in most of which cases there is immunity from prosecution as to matters disclosed. (2-47; 16-8; 54-85; 45-262; 31-95). In criminal action accused is competent witness and may testify or refuse to do so, but neglect or refusal to testify may not be commented upon to court or jury. (54-84).

Immunity.—In criminal case involving narcotics, arson, bribery, gambling, election law violations, felonious crimes of violence or any violation of tit. 25, superior court may grant immunity to witness claiming self-incrimination on application by state's attorney. (54-47a, am'd PA 85-611, §8).

Mediation.—Limitations on disclosure of written or oral communications obtained during mediation. (PA 98-59).

INJUNCTIONS:

Jurisdiction.—Any court of equity jurisdiction or any judge thereof, when court is not in session, may on motion grant and enforce writs of injunction in all actions for equitable relief. (52-471).

Procedure.—The facts alleged must be verified by oath of the plaintiff or some competent witness (52-471), and temporary injunction will not issue until party making application has given bond, with surety satisfactory to court, to opposite party to answer all damages in case plaintiff fails to prosecute action to effect (52-472).

Issuance.—Injunctions may be granted immediately, if circumstances demand, or court may cause immediate notice that defendant show cause why injunction should not be granted. (52-473).

Dissolution.—Any such judge who has granted temporary injunction may hear motion to dissolve same, or designate another judge therefor. (52-475).

See also category Employment, topic Labor Relations.

JUDGMENTS:

Judgment of court is final, but execution may not issue for at least ten days. (C.P.B. 61-11, 61-13, 61-14, 66-6). Clerk of any court, may, when directed by court, make up, amend, and complete any imperfect or unfinished record in such manner as court may direct. (51-52a).

Judgments by Confession.—Lender under Small Loan Act may not take confession of judgment (36-236), nor is provision for confession of judgment in retail instalment contract or instalment loan contract valid or enforceable (42-88).

Judgment by consent is as conclusive as one upon controverted facts (135 Conn. 405, 65 A.2d 577) and ordinarily cannot be appealed from or reviewed on writ of error (110 Conn. 208, 147 Atl. 675).

Summary judgment may be entered in any action to recover a debt or liquidated demand in money, with or without interest arising (a) on a negotiable instrument, a

contract under seal or a recognizance; (b) on any other contract, express or implied, excepting quasi contracts; (c) on a judgment for a stated sum; (d) on a statute where the sum sought to be recovered is a fixed sum or in the nature of a debt; (e) on a guaranty, whether under seal or not, when the claim against the principal is in respect of a debt or liquidated demand and in any other action; (f) for the recovery of specific chattels, with or without a claim for withholding the same; (g) to quiet and settle title to real estate or any interest therein; and (h) to discharge any claimed invalid mortgage, lien, caveat, or lis pendens. (51-15; C.P.B. 17-44). Judgment may enter, upon motion supported by such documents as may be appropriate, unless defendant within 15 days after motion and affidavit shows by affidavit facts sufficient to entitle him to defend. (C.P.B. 17-45). If action is by or against corporation, affidavit of officer is sufficient. These rules also apply to counterclaims.

Declaratory Judgments.—Superior court may, in any action or proceeding, declare rights and legal relations on request, and such declaration has force of final judgment. (52-29).

Default Judgments.—Where process has been duly served on defendant and returned to court and defendant does not appear on or before second day after return day, judgment by default may be entered against him. (52-84).

Default judgment may enter where party fails to plead according to the rules and orders of court (52-119) after notice and hearing (52-121). Default may also enter for failure to give proper bond for prosecution (52-186), if nonresident defendant in realty action does not give proper cost bond (52-188), or if notice of intention to suffer a default is filed (51-55).

If resident defendant is absent from state at commencement of action and does not enter appearance, case is continued for 30 days and if defendant does not then appear, judgment by default may be entered. In case of nonresident defendant case is continued for three months and notice of pendency of action by publication or otherwise ordered, or may authorize any person duly empowered to serve process by the laws of the foreign jurisdiction in which such defendant resides to serve upon such defendant a copy of the summons, complaint, and order of notice and such person shall make affidavit of his doings thereon on the original order or notice; and if defendant does not appear within such period judgment by default may be entered. (52-87).

If defendant or his counsel fails to appear after default, damages and special damages may be proven by affidavit. (52-221a).

Offer of judgment may be filed with clerk of court before trial in action on contract or for recovery of money only. (52-193). If written acceptance filed within ten days, court renders judgment against defendant for sum named and costs accrued to date of offer. (52-194). If acceptance not filed offer is not admissible in evidence and unless plaintiff recovers more than sum offered he is liable for all costs after date of offer, including reasonable attorney's fees not exceeding $350. (52-195). For claims accruing after Oct. 1, 1976, following applies: Plaintiff may file offer and if not accepted by defendant within 30 days it is considered rejected. Plaintiff may file new offers until trial and all offers are included in record of case. If, at trial, plaintiff recovers amount equal to or greater than that stated in offer, court will add to amount so recovered 12% interest on amount contained in offer, computed from date offer was filed. (52-192a).

Vacation or Modification.—Judgment rendered or decree passed on default or non-suit may be vacated within four months after rendition, and case reinstated, upon verified complaint showing reasonable cause, or that good cause of action or defense existed at time of judgment and party prevented by mistake, accident, or other reasonable cause from appearing to make this defense. (52-212).

Judgment may not be abated, suspended, set aside, or reversed for any kind of circumstantial error, mistake, or defect, if the person and cause may be rightly understood and intended by the court (52-123), but may be vacated for prejudicial irregularity (120 Conn. 235, 180 Atl. 507). Judgment of strict foreclosure may be opened and modified. (49-15).

Lien.—Judgments are not liens upon property of defendant except property which has been attached in the action, in which case the lien continues against personal property for 60 days and against real estate for four months after final judgment, if execution is levied within those periods. (52-328). One owning unsatisfied judgment at any time may cause to be recorded in town clerk's office in any town where defendant owns real estate certificate of claim of lien, setting forth action, judgment, amount due thereon, and describing real estate. Such judgment from time of filing such certificate will constitute lien upon such real estate, and if filed within four months from date of judgment against real estate attached in said suit lien will hold from date of attachment. Lien remains in force for 20 years and may be foreclosed or property redeemed like real estate mortgage. (52-380a). If not foreclosed within 20 years, automatically released. (49-40a; 49-40b).

For form which may be used to release or discharge judgment lien see category Mortgages, topic Mortgages of Real Property.

Assignment.—Assignee of judgment may cause judgment lien to be recorded (52-380a), and may sue in his own name (82 Conn. 213, 72 Atl. 1083). See also category Debtor and Creditor, topic Assignments.

Satisfaction, in whole or in part, is entered by clerk of court on record. (52-356a, am'd PA 85-613, §§131, 154). If judgment is returned unsatisfied there may be examination of debtor. (52-397). Judgment is presumed satisfied after 20 years. (74 Conn. 652, 51 Atl. 857).

Action on Judgment.—To predicate suit upon judgment requires complete and final judgment and one upon which execution may issue. (57 Conn. 329, 18 Atl. 254).

Title to real estate may be passed by decree of court of equitable jurisdiction, which decree, when recorded in land records of town where land lies is as effectual to transfer land as deed of party or parties holding title. (52-22).

Foreign Judgments.—Limitation period on contracts does not apply to action on foreign judgments. (52-576).

Uniform Enforcement of Foreign Judgments Act adopted. (52-604 to 52-609).

JUDGMENTS . . . *continued*

Uniform Foreign Money-Judgments Recognition Act adopted with modification that, upon appeal or showing of grounds for stay, court shall stay enforcement provided defendant furnishes security for satisfaction of judgment. (PA 88-39).

Judgment Notes.—See category Business Regulation and Commerce, topic Bills and Notes.

Release of Judgment Against Joint Tortfeasors.—See topic Actions, subhead Parties.

LIMITATION OF ACTIONS:

The statutes limit the time within which actions may be brought, as follows:

Forty years: To foreclose town lien against real property of pauper. (17b-125).

Twenty-five years: On action based upon judgment for money damages rendered in court of this state, except in small claims actions where time limit is 15 years. (52-598).

Twenty years: To reclaim property which has been deposited with state as abandoned property. (3-70a[a]).

Fifteen years: To recover real property (52-575), to foreclose judgment lien (time running from recordation) (49-36).

Seven years: After substantial completion of an improvement to real property, on action against architects, professional engineers, and architectural designers by anyone other than possessor of improvement. (52-584a).

Six years: On simple or implied contract, sealed or unsealed written contract, or account (52-576); against surety on probate bond, time running from final settlement and acceptance of account of principal (52-579); against city or town for damages caused by change in grade or excavation of highway (52-578).

Five years: Recovery of distributed property of heir presumed dead. (§45a-446). To enforce judgment rendered in small claims.

Four years: Under Uniform Commercial Code on breach of contract for sale (including actions in warranty) regardless of knowledge of breach. Parties by agreement may reduce limitation period to one year but may not extend it beyond four years. (42a-2-725).

Three years: On express oral contract not governed by Uniform Commercial Code (52-581); for torts except those hereinafter specified (52-577; 52-577a); bastardy proceedings from date of birth or date of cessation of support whichever is later (52-435; 52-435a); petition for new trial (52-582); nuisance (121 Conn. 579, 186 Atl. 629; 20 Conn. Supp. 31, 120 Atl. 156); after actual or constructive knowledge of violation of private real property restriction recorded in land records of municipality in which property is located, other than easements, utility lines, park or open space land (52-575a); on strict liability action against manufacturer or seller (time running from discovery of injury; however no action may be brought later than ten years from the date manufacturer or seller last parted with possession or control of product, except nonemployee claimant may escape ten year "statute of repose" by proving harm occurred during useful safe life of product) (52-577a); for indemnification (running from date and determination of action, by judgment or settlement, against party seeking indemnification) (PA 93-370, §1).

Two years: For death or injuries resulting in death (running from when injury sustained, discovered, or should have been discovered; no more than three years from act or omission) (52-555); for injury to person, or to real or personal property, caused by negligence, or by reckless or wanton conduct, or by malpractice of a physician, surgeon, dentist, hospital, or sanitarium, but counterclaim may be interposed in action brought within two years at any time before pleadings finally closed (52-584); against sheriff, constable or deputy for neglect (52-583); for payment of remuneration for employment payable periodically, except this limitation will be tolled upon filing complaint with labor commissioner pursuant to 52-596; for libel or slander (52-597); against commissioner of transportation for damages for injuries sustained on state highways or sidewalks (notice or commencement of action with 90 days of injury required, however) (13a-144); for sale or offer of security employing untrue statements or material omissions (running from sale) except period altered to one year from discovery of fraud or misrepresentation, if done intentionally in connection with sale of limited partnership interests not required to be registered under Securities Act of 1993 (but not more than five years from sale) (36b-29, am'd 93-169).

One year: For forfeiture under penal statute (52-585); scire facias against garnishee (52-586). One year limitation applies to action for loss or expense resulting from injury to person other than plaintiff. (83 Conn. 503, 77 Atl. 950).

Against municipality, volunteer fireman's or policeman's negligence (7-308); on bond substituted for artificer's lien (49-67). Action after entry into lands (52-575); on negotiable note obtained by fraud where holder given written notice of fraud, time running from date of notice (52-588); against surety on bond or recognizance for costs only or on appeal bond in civil actions, or bail bond, time running from final judgment in suit in which bond or recognizance given (52-587); against adjoining owner for purchase of division fence, time running from division and appraisal (47-49); against liquor seller where purchaser does damage, if 60 days notice given (up to 120 days of time between death or incapacity and appointment of executor, administrator, conservator or guardian excluded in calculating whether 60 day notice requirement met) (30-102). Under executory contract to sell real estate, action must be begun within one year after date for performance under contract or within 18 months of date of execution if no performance date established. (47-33a). Action against State must be brought within one year of authorization by claims commissioner. (4-160).

Six months: For forcible entry and detainer (52-589).

Four months: On claim disallowed by executor, administrator, administrator de bonis non, guardian, conservator, or trustee required to account to court of probate, time running from date written notice of disallowance given. If creditor dies within four months and before suit is brought, further period of four months from death allowed. This period does not apply in tort cases. (45a-398, 45a-402, 45a-399). On claim to set aside judgment rendered upon default or nonsuit (52-212). On claim for apportionment by defendant in tort action, measured from return date in original complaint (stated as 120 days, not four months). (PA 95-111).

Three months: On claims disallowed against bank selling assets, time running from receipt of written notice of disallowance. (36a-210).

Sixty days: On action to contest validity of municipal bond, time running from vote approving sale (7-386).

Two weeks: Writ of Error. (52-273).

New Action.—Where an action begun within the period of limitations fails for matter of form, or judgment is arrested or reversed, new action may be begun within one year of such failure or reversal of judgment, although statute of limitations would otherwise have run by that time. Where action begun or continued against executor or administrator fails, new action must be begun within six months (52-592); and where action fails because of naming wrong defendant, new action may be begun within one year of such failure (52-593).

When judgment in favor or plaintiff suing in representative character or for benefit of third persons is reversed on ground of mistake in complaint or improper parties thereto and time for new action expires during suit, parties for whose special benefit action brought may bring new action in individual names within one year after judgment reversed, if original action could have been so brought. (52-591).

Actions Not Specifically Provided For.—There is no general limitation statute for actions not specifically provided for.

No limitation on town claim for reimbursement for support of pauper or persons mentally ill (17b-122).

Foreign Causes of Action.—Connecticut limitation statutes apply to suit brought in Connecticut, unless foreign cause of action arose under foreign statute which not only creates the liability and remedy but imposes the limitation thereon. (131 Conn. 671, 42 A.2d 147).

Absence of or Concealment by Defendant.—Time during which defendant is out of state (52-590) or fraudulently conceals existence of cause of action (52-595) is excluded from computation; however, excluded time may not exceed seven years.

Absence of plaintiff from state has no effect on running of statute. (24 Conn. 432).

Disability of Plaintiff.—In actions to recover possession of real estate plaintiff, if a minor, non compos mentis or in prison, may bring action within five years next after removal of disability or his heirs may bring such action within five years after his death. (52-575). Ordinary actions based on contracts (except book debts and actions based on express oral contracts) where plaintiff is legally incapable of bringing action when right of action accrues, may be brought within three years next after plaintiff has become legally capable of bringing such action. (52-576). Limitation on suit on probate bonds does not apply to infant parties in interest. (52-579). Except as aforesaid, there is no provision tolling running of limitations during incapacity of plaintiff.

Death of Plaintiff.—If right of action survives death and time has not expired, the executor or administrator has one year after the death of claimant. (52-594). See category Estates and Trusts, topic Death.

Suspension.—Running of statute is suspended by presentation of claim to solvent estate of deceased person until written disallowance of claim or expiration time allowed by court for presentation of claims, whichever is earlier, if limitation period would otherwise expire within time so allowed by court. (45a-402).

If process delivered to sheriff by date statute runs and served within 15 days thereafter, cause of action preserved. (52-593a).

Revival of barred claims by new promise or part payment is a matter governed by common law except that in an action against the representative of a deceased person a new promise will not take the case out of the statute of limitations unless the same be in writing, signed by the party to be charged, but this does not alter the effect of part payment. (52-176).

Contractual limitations, if not unreasonably short, are permissible. (90 Conn. 226, 96 Atl. 926; 91 Conn. 57, 98 Atl. 353). Insurance company may not limit time for suit against it on: (1) Fidelity or surety bond for less than three years, (2) construction performance bond or payment bond for less than three years, (3) uninsured motorist provisions on policy for less than two years, (4) all other policies for less than one year. (38a-290).

Statute tolled if, prior to judgment, attorney ceases to be member of bar, or becomes physically, mentally, or otherwise disabled, for 30 days. (52-235b).

Pleading.—Defense of limitation statutes must be raised by answer, unless complaint anticipates such defense, then raised by demurrer. (114 Conn. 731, 159 Atl. 657). Creditor appearing and defending in name of a defendant may not plead the statute of limitations. (38a-290).

Abandonment.—Statute of limitations for recovery of money or property shall not affect presumption of abandonment, duty to file report, or duty to turn over to State Treasurer. (3-73b).

PARTITION:

When title to property is vested in two or more persons, either ordinarily is entitled to partition or sale (14 Conn. 360), but parties may enter into reasonable agreement which will expressly, or impliedly, bar them from seeking partition, nor will partition be granted when it would violate trust or defeat its purpose (110 Conn. 516, 148 Atl. 358). To lose right to partition cotenant must have been ousted of possession. (133 Conn. 424, 52 A.2d 2). Interest of joint tenant with right of survivorship treated the same as interest of tenant in common. (47-14a to k).

Jurisdiction and Venue.—Courts of equitable jurisdiction may order partition of real property: (1) When held in joint tenancy, tenancy in common, coparcenary, or by tenancy in tail, and may appoint committee for that purpose (52-495); or (2) when any deceased tenant in common, joint tenant or coparcener has devised freehold interest to any person with contingent interest to any other person, born or unborn (52-496). Jurisdiction of court is determined by value of property. (50 Conn. 256). No partition or

See note at head of Digest as to 1998 legislation covered.

See Topical Index in front part of this volume.

CT – 13

PARTITION . . . *continued*

sale may be made of any property belonging to estate being settled in probate court until estate is ready for distribution. (52-503). But when person dies owning undivided interest in property, not specifically devised or bequeathed, probate court, during settlement of estate, may order partition upon petition of personal representative and owner of major portion of other interest therein. (45-257a).

Partition in Kind or Sale.—Court may order sale instead of partition when sale would better promote the interests of the owners. (52-500). Probate court may also order sale when it would better promote interests of owners, or when estate cannot be beneficially divided for purposes of distribution. (45-257a).

Proceedings.—In proceeding in probate court (which has jurisdiction in cases involving estates only), there must be public notice of hearing unless all parties in interest sign petition. (45-257a). Upon sale, court may make any orders necessary to protect rights of all parties and carry sale into effect, order distribution of proceeds, and make orders relative to custody or investment of shares of unknown parties. (52-502; 45-257a).

Decree of partition of real property must be recorded in town where land lies. (52-497; 45-257a).

PLEADING:

Code system prevails, and each pleading must contain plain and concise statement of material facts, such statement being divided into paragraphs numbered consecutively. (C.P.B. 10-1). Detailed rules on pleading are contained in Connecticut Practice Book. (C.P.B. 10-1 to 10-79). Electronic filing of pleadings to be permitted after rules are promulgated by judges of Superior Court. (PA 98-13).

Pleadings Allowed and Their Order.—(1) Complaint, (2) motion to dismiss complaint, (3) request to revise complaint, (4) motion to strike complaint, (5) answer, (6) request to revise answer, (7) motion to strike answer, (8) reply to special defenses. (C.P.B. 10-6).

Complaint accompanies process and must contain statement of facts constituting cause of action, demand for relief, allegation that matter is within court's jurisdiction and statement that amount, legal interest, or property in demand is less than $15,000 or is not less than $15,000 exclusive of interests and costs. If amount, legal interest or property is less than $5,000 or less than $2,500, statement shall be included in complaint. In contract action for only money damages under $15,000, demand must state whether remedy is based on express or implied promise. (52-91; C.P.B. 10-20).

Counterclaim or set-off may be made subject of separate trial upon order of court. (52-97). In action for recovery of debt, defendant may set-off mutual debts in certain cases. (52-139). Set-off is allowed in some suits by assignee of non-negotiable chose in action. (52-140). In action for trespass to property other than action for taking property exempt from execution and in action for tort unaccompanied with force when injury is consequential, debts, except those acquired by purchase or assignment after cause of action accrued, may be set off. (52-141). Set-off is also allowed where one joint debtor has been discharged. (52-142).

Motion to dismiss used to assert: (1) Lack of jurisdiction over person or subject matter, (2) improper venue, (3) insufficiency of process or service of process. If defendant contests jurisdiction may file motion within 15 days after entering general appearance. Motion must always be supported by memo of law. (C.P.B. 10-31).

Request to revise used to obtain: (1) More particular statement of adverse party's pleading, (2) deletion of part of pleading, (3) separation of causes of action, or (4) any other correction in adverse party's pleading. (C.P.B. 10-35).

Reply to special defenses may admit some allegations and deny others or by general denial put defendant upon proof of all material facts alleged therein.

Motion to strike pleading must distinctly specify reason or reasons why pleading is insufficient. (52-92).

Amendments are freely permitted. (52-130; 52-138).

Affidavits verifying cause of action, amount due, and belief of no defense, are required in action for summary judgment, under Practice Act. See topic Judgments. Affidavit as to military service in case of nonappearing defendant is required when default judgment is sought. Motion to reopen judgment of default or nonsuit must be verified. (52-212).

Filing.—Pleadings must be in writing and filed with Clerk of Court. (104 Conn. 322, 133 Atl. 99). Copies of all pleadings must be mailed to all parties appearing of record. Certification of same must be made over signature of individual counsel.

Time to Plead.—Beginning with return day of writ, pleadings must advance at least one step every 15 days. (C.P.B. 10-8). When pleading is amended, adverse party may plead within 15 days, or if he has already pleaded, alter his pleading within ten days. (C.P.B. 10-61).

Pleadings in summary process are dealt with in 52-134.

Appearance must be entered on or before the second day after return date or default may be entered. (52-84).

Plaintiff has a right to amend within 30 days after return day. (C.P.B. 10-59).

Claims on open accounts should be presented with the names and residences of debtor and creditor and a statement of the account, with dates; which information is sufficient for institution of the action.

Small Claims.—See category Courts and Legislature, topic Courts.

PRACTICE:

Practice and procedure are regulated by Practice Act, Titles 51, 52 and 54, and court rules contained in Connecticut Practice Book. Supreme Court, Appellate Court and Superior Court judges have power to make orders and rules on practice and procedure. (51-14).

Equity and law are distinct in substance but the distinction between actions at law and suits in equity and the forms of these actions have been abolished. (52-91).

Discovery.—In any civil action the court, upon motion, may order disclosure of facts or records by any party, material to the mover's cause of action or defense and within the knowledge, possession or power of the adverse party. (52-197; 52-199). Court may deny disclosure which is mere fishing expedition or which would result in unjustifiable delay. (114 Conn. 165, 158 Atl. 219; 166 Conn. 501, 353 A.2d 800). Rules for discovery are contained in Connecticut Practice Book. (C.P.B. 13-1 to 13-32).

Independent action for discovery in equity still exists. (126 Conn. 382, 11 A.2d 800; 166 Conn. 501, 353 A.2d 800).

Demand for Admission of Facts.—Any party to a civil action may, by written notice, request another party to admit the existence and due execution of a material document, saving all just exceptions. If opposing party unreasonably neglects or refuses to make this admission within reasonable time, costs of proving such document shall be paid by party neglecting or refusing, to make admission regardless of result of action. (52-206).

Direct Actions Against Insurer.—See category Transportation, topic Motor Vehicles, subhead Direct Action.

Small Claims.—See category Courts and Legislature, topic Courts.

See also topics Actions, Appeal and Error, Depositions and Discovery, Injunctions, Judgments, Pleading, Process; category Debtor and Creditor, topics Attachment, Executions, Garnishment.

PROCESS:

Process in civil actions is a writ of summons or attachment. (§52-45a). Form at §52-45b.

General Requisites.—Writ must describe parties, court to which it is returnable, return day, and date and place for filing appearance, must be accompanied by complaint. Such writ must be signed by commissioner of Superior Court, or judge or clerk of court to which it is returnable. (52-45a). Attorneys of state in good standing are commissioners of Superior Court and have power to issue subpoenas. (51-85). Return day for action is any Tues. of any month. Return day in any summary process action may be any Mon. through Sat., except holiday. All process shall be made returnable not later than two months after date of process and shall designate place where court is to be held. (52-48). Process to Superior Court must be served at least 12 days and returned at least six days before return day. (52-46; §51-347).

Who May Serve.—Service may be made by a sheriff, his deputy, a constable, and, under certain stated conditions, by an indifferent person. (52-50). If any officer commences service of process within his precincts, he may complete attachment or service outside his precincts, or may deliver process to officer of other precinct for service upon any defendant or garnishee residing in such precinct. (52-56).

Personal Service on Individual.—Service of a writ of summons is made by officer reading it and accompanying complaint in hearing of defendant or by leaving an attested copy thereof with him, or at his usual place of abode in state. If service at place of abode, return of process must note address where left. (52-54). Person domiciled in or subject to jurisdiction of courts of state may be served without state by anyone qualified to serve, or by attorney of place of service. (52-57a).

Personal Service on Incompetent.—Service of process on any person confined in any institution for mentally ill or mentally deficient is made by sending a copy of writ and complaint by registered mail to Commissioner of Welfare at Hartford and a copy to institution where person confined or by service upon superintendent of institution where person confined. (§4-68f).

Personal Service on Domestic Corporation.—Service is made upon any officer, teller, general or managing agent, manager, or upon any director resident in the state. If no such officer can be found, service may be made upon any person in charge of the business of the corporation or any person who is in charge of the principal office of the corporation. (52-57).

Personal Service on Partnership.—Service may be made by serving one partner personally in state or, if none of partners are state residents, service may be made on Secretary of State, provided copies of writ and complaint are mailed by certified or registered mail, return receipt requested, to every partner not personally served. (52-57).

Personal Service on Association.—Service of process against a voluntary association may be made upon the presiding officer, secretary or treasurer. If these officers are nonresident and the association is doing business or carrying out its operations or functions within the state, service may be made by serving the Secretary of State at least 12 days before return day, and by mailing another true and attested copy to the defendant by registered mail with an endorsement thereon of service upon the Secretary of State. (52-57).

Personal Service on Foreign Corporation.—Service may be made upon the same officers or agents as for a domestic corporation, or upon the Secretary of State, or with any clerk having charge of the corporation department of his office, if foreign corporation doing business in state has appointed him its agent pursuant to 33-929. Each foreign corporation must designate agent for service of process before transacting business in state. (33-926). Constructive service upon Secretary of State for corporations doing business in state who have not registered with Secretary of State provided. (33-929).

Personal jurisdiction over nonresident individual or foreign partnership, or his or its executor or administrator, may be exercised where he or it, in person or through an agent: (1) Transacts business in state; or (2) commits tortious act other than defamation of character in state; or (3) commits tortious act outside state causing injury to person or property within state, if (a) regular doing or solicitation of business, persistent conduct, or revenue from within state, or (b) in interstate commerce, and expects or should expect act to have consequences in state; or (4) interest in real property in state. Jurisdiction based on any of these acts does not confer jurisdiction for unrelated cause of action. (52-59b). Constructive service on Secretary of State and registered or certified mailing to defendant's last known address required. (52-596).

See note at head of Digest as to 1998 legislation covered.

See Topical Index in front part of this volume.

PROCESS . . . *continued*

Personal service on nonresident fiduciaries in any action founded or arising from acts or omissions as executor, administrator, conservator, guardian, or trustee may be made by leaving a true and attested copy with the judge of probate in the district where the estate is in settlement. (52-61). Process against a foreign corporation acting as executor or trustee in this state may be served upon the Secretary of State. (§45a-206).

Personal Service on Municipalities or State.—Process may be served in action against town, upon its clerk, assistant clerk, manager, or one of its select men; against city, upon its clerk, assistant clerk, mayor or manager; against school district, upon its clerk or one of its committee; against other municipal or quasi-municipal corporation, upon its clerk or its chief presiding officer, or managing agent (52-57), against state or any institution, board, commission, department, or administrative tribunal thereof, upon leaving true and attested copy of process and complaint with Attorney General, or at his office in Hartford (52-64).

Personal Service Outside the State.—Personal service outside the state is not equivalent to an appearance or to a submission to the jurisdiction of the court. (89 Conn. 214, 93 Atl. 232).

Substituted Service.—Any licensed operator or owner of registered motor vehicle, who or whose car has caused injury and upon whom it is impossible to make service at his address on file in the motor vehicle department, may be served with process by leaving true and attested copy of process with motor vehicle commissioner, with certification by officer of impossibility of service, and by sending by registered mail a similar copy to the defendant at the address on file in the motor vehicle department. (52-63). Nonresident causing boat to be operated on Connecticut waters is deemed to have appointed Commissioner of Agriculture as his agent for service of process, true and attested copy of such process to be sent to his last known address by registered or certified mail. (15-140a). Quo warranto information against nonresident usurping office in Connecticut corporation may be served on him personally or by leaving copy with resident secretary or treasurer of corporation, or if no such resident officers, service may be made upon attorney general. (52-65).

Writ of error against nonresident defendant may be served by leaving true and attested copy with, or at the usual abode of, his attorney. (52-276).

Out-of-state creditor foreclosing mortgage or mechanic's lien can be served by serving his attorney and mailing copy by certified or registered mail to defendants at his last known address. (52-59c).

Service by Publication.—The judge or clerk may make such order as is reasonable in regard to notice to be given of the institution or pendency of all complaints, writs of errors and appeals from probate, when the adverse party, or parties, reside out of the state, or when the names and residences of such parties are unknown, and such notice given and proved is sufficient service and notice. (52-68). Such service is valid in all actions which are substantially proceedings in rem. (89 Conn. 214, 93 Atl. 232). Order need not require publication of recital of details pertinent to application which are not essential parts of notice to be given. Either return of any officer authorized to serve process or affidavit of any person showing that publication was made as directed is sufficient to prove publication of notice. (52-52).

For special provisions for banks, foreign insurance companies and corporations, nonresident motorists or aviators, or nonresident fiduciaries, see the appropriate categories and topics.

Service of Process of Foreign Attachment.—When any corporation is named as the agent, trustee, or debtor of the defendant in an action commenced by process of foreign attachment, service may be made by some proper officer by leaving true and attested copy with, or at the usual place of abode of, its secretary or clerk or any agent or clerk employed by such corporation to keep its accounts, when corporation is engaged in transacting business in any other town than that in which its secretary or clerk resides. (52-335). Whenever a bank or trust company is named as garnishee, process is served by leaving a copy with any officer or teller at the garnishee's principal office during its regular hours of business. (52-337). Service on a branch of such bank or trust company, if located in a town different from the principal office and named as garnishee must be made at such branch as above described. (52-337). When the garnishee does not reside in the state, but is engaged in the transaction of business herein by an agent, process may be served on such garnishee by leaving a true and attested copy with the agent. (52-338). When a partnership is named as garnishee, service is made by leaving a copy of the process with, or at the usual place of abode of, the members of such partnership, or acting partner or partners, agent or agents. (52-339).

Long Arm Statute.—See subhead Personal Jurisdiction Over Nonresident Individual or Foreign Partnership, supra.

Proof of Service.—Return of officer must state compliance with requirements of law. (5 Conn. 400). Officer serving process must endorse thereon items of his fees, with number of miles traveled by him. (52-70).

Failure of Defendant to Appear.—In any case where a civil action is begun against a defendant absent from the jurisdiction at the time of service of process, if such defendant does not enter his appearance the action in the case of residents must be postponed for 30 days before default may be taken; in the case of nonresidents it must be postponed for three months, and further notice by publication may be given, or foreign process served, but this provision does not apply to quiet title actions nor to certain equitable actions against the estate of deceased persons nor to nonexistent individuals or foreign partnerships over whom court has personal jurisdiction pursuant to 52-59b(a)(4) and is served process pursuant to 52-59b(c). (52-87). Action need not be postponed more than 12 days beyond date of receipt of actual notice by defendant. (52-88).

Nonresident Motorist.—See category Transportation, topic Motor Vehicles.

REPLEVIN:

The action of replevin may be maintained to recover any goods or chattels in which plaintiff has general or special property interest with a right to immediate possession, and which are wrongfully detained from him in any manner, together with damages for detention. (52-515).

Proceedings.—Replevin writ must contain an affidavit by the plaintiff or other credible person, stating the true value of the goods and that the plaintiff is entitled to immediate possession, and a bond of a person of responsibility, with at least one surety, in double the sworn value of the property, must be furnished by plaintiff. (52-518). Suggested form of writ, affidavit, and bond is provided. (52-519). Special provisions also govern pleadings and defenses. (52-522; 52-525).

Writ must be served within three days after replevy, and replevying officer must retain replevied property in his custody for 24 hours after leaving copy of process with defendant, unless defendant endorses on writ that he is satisfied with amount and sufficiency of bond. If defendant is not satisfied, he may, before return day, bring motion for new bond. If order for new bond is not complied with, or officer does not comply with law, replevin writ is null and void. (52-521). Defendant may defend on ground that third person was entitled to possession without connecting himself with latter's title. If plaintiff's right to possession is in issue, he must prove it, and may also show damages for detention, and if defendant counterclaims for damages for replevin, he may show them. (52-525).

Repossession.—No statutory provision.

Judgment for the plaintiff is for his damages and costs, and if for the defendant for a return of the property and his damages and costs (52-529) but no judgment for return of goods, or for damages, may be given under mere denial, nor may judgment for return be rendered if defendant files disclaimer or has not filed counterclaim seeking return of goods replevied (52-526).

Property attached may be replevied in certain instances. (52-517).

SEQUESTRATION:

No statutory provision for sequestration.

SERVICE:

See topic Process.

STAY OF EXECUTION:

See topic Appeal and Error; category Debtor and Creditor, topic Executions.

SUBMISSION OF CONTROVERSY:

Parties to a question in difference which might be the subject of a civil action between them may, without action, agree upon a case containing the facts upon which the controversy depends and submit it to any court in the county in which either of them resides, in which a suit might have been brought, together with an affidavit of the parties or their attorneys that the controversy is real and the proceeding is in good faith. The court upon payment of court and clerk fees may hear the case and render judgment, which may be enforced in the same manner as if it had been rendered in an action. (52-406). Judgment may be appealed upon questions of law. (52-407). All costs incurred in such amicable suit are borne equally by contesting parties. (52-254).

VENUE:

(c. 895).

Land actions concerning title or trespass are brought in superior court in judicial district where land is with enumerated exceptions. (51-345).

Consumer transactions shall be brought in county or judicial district within which defendant resides or within which transaction occurred. (51-345).

All other civil actions, except where provision otherwise is made, are brought in judicial district where plaintiff or defendant dwells, if either or both are inhabitants of state. If neither is inhabitant of state action is brought in judicial district where: (A) Injury occurred, (B) transaction occurred, or (C) property is located or lawfully attached. (51-345). Small claims actions are brought in geographical area, established pursuant to 51-27, within which defendant resides or is doing business or within which transaction occurred. (51-349a). In summary process actions, plaintiff may elect to bring action in geographical district where defendant resides, or where leased premises or trailer located or if defendant is corporation, where it has office or place of business, or if defendant is non-resident where plaintiff resides or where land lies. (51-349). Support actions brought in geographical area, established under 51-27a, in which party to be supported resides or where party to provide support resides. (§46b-215). Civil Actions generally, see 51-345; 51-349. See category Courts and Legislature, topic Courts.

Foreclosure or redemption suit, with minor exceptions, is brought in county or judicial district where land is located; if land crosses dividing line, in either county or judicial district. (51-345).

Action by trustee for sale of land when trust cannot be executed is brought in superior court of county where land is located. (52-498). Action by trustee for sale of land to promote interest of beneficiaries is brought in superior court of county within which probate court admitting will is located. (52-499).

Foreign corporation suit against inhabitant of state is brought in town or county where one of defendants resides, but corporation organized under laws of United States and located in any town in state may sue before same courts in which any inhabitant of town may sue. (51-27a).

Action on savings bank insurance or annuity policy must be brought in county where issuing bank is located. (§36a-285).

Action to compel arbitration is brought in superior court of county in which one of parties resides or, if concerning land controversy, in county in which land is situated. (52-410).

Habeas Corpus application is brought in county in which person is claimed to be confined illegally. (52-466, am'd PA 86-186, §16).

VENUE . . . *continued*

Juvenile court petition concerning delinquent children is heard in district where delinquency occurred or, like other juvenile court petitions, in district where child resides. (§46b-150).

Change of name complaint is brought in superior court of county in which person resides. (52-11).

Change of Venue.—Jury case in superior court may be transferred to any other county, if, upon motion, judge finds that cause of justice requires such transfer, any case may be transferred to another county or from one circuit court to another by agreement of parties, and chief court administrator may order transfer on his own motion in any case when required for efficient operation of courts and to insure prompt and proper administration of justice. (51-347[a], [b]). No cause shall fail on ground that it has been made returnable to improper location. (51-351).

COURTS AND LEGISLATURE

COURTS:

United States District Court.—Bridgeport Office of Clerk: 915 Lafayette Boulevard 06604; Hartford Office of Clerk: 450 Main Street 06103; New Haven Office of Clerk: 141 Church Street 06510.

Supreme Court.—Supreme Court is highest court in state and sits for direct appeal in certain matters including those where Superior Court declares invalid state statute or provision of state constitution and on certain criminal judgments. Uniform Certification of Questions of Law Act adopted. (PA 85-111).

Judges of Supreme Court are by law also judges of Superior Court, but judges of Superior Court are not judges of Supreme Court. If, by reason of sickness or otherwise, a quorum cannot be had Chief Justice may call to bench temporarily judge of Superior Court. (51-199; 51-207). Panel assigned to hear appeal to Supreme Court may include no more than one judge referee (i.e. retired justice or judge) who previously sat as justice or judge of either Supreme or Appellate Court. (PA 95-80).

Court sits at Hartford.

Appellate Court.—Appellate Court consists of nine judges, who are also judges of Superior Court, and who sit in panels of three or en banc at times and in such locations as may be necessary. Panel assigned to hear appeal to Appellate Court may include no more than one state referee (i.e. retired justice or judge) who previously sat as justice or judge of either Supreme or Appellate Court. (PA 95-80). Appeals from final judgments or actions of Superior Court, not within Supreme Court jurisdiction, are taken to Appellate Court.

Determination by Appellate Court is final except that review of final decision by Supreme Court is available if appellate panel certifies on its own motion such appeal, or Supreme Court certifies on petition by aggrieved party or appellate panel which heard matter. (51-197a to 51-197f).

Superior Court.—There is Superior Court for State of Connecticut which holds terms and sessions in each county of state.

Jurisdiction.—Superior Court has jurisdiction in all criminal matters and in all civil matters in law and equity and over administrative appeals. Superior Court has jurisdiction in all causes of action, except actions over which courts of probate have original jurisdiction. (51-164s).

Return day of writ is any Tues. not later than two months after date of writ. (52-48). Must be served upon defendant at least 12 days before return day (52-46), and returned to court at least six days before return day (§51-347).

Small Claims.—All claims for money damages of $2,500 or less, except for libel or slander, may be brought before small claims division without writ or formal pleadings, on payment of entry fee of $30. (51-15; 52-259). Venue is same as in ordinary civil actions. Magistrates may hear small claims matters. (PA 85-464, §3). Statement of claim is made to clerk and is entered in docket in concise untechnical form. Service is made by registered mail. Actual cash disbursements of prevailing party for entry, mailing, witness and officer's fees must be allowed as costs. Further costs, not exceeding $25, may be awarded by special order of court against any party who has in any way sought to hamper party or court in securing speedy determination of cause. Any party interested in cause, other than plaintiff, may secure transfer to regular docket upon motion prior to date of hearing provided such motion is accompanied by affidavit stating that good defense exists to claim and, when appropriate, that jury trial is desired, and provided further that moving parties comply with such terms as are fixed by judge, which must at least provide for payment of entry and jury fee. (52-259[a]). Whenever plaintiff prevails after defendant has transferred to regular docket, court may allow plaintiff his costs, plus reasonable attorney's fees. (52-251a).

Parties may, by agreement, submit controversy to commissioner for speedy hearing. At hearing commissioner not bound by rules regarding admissibility of evidence. (52-549).

Probate Courts.—Probate courts have jurisdiction in all matters pertaining to probate of wills, settlement of estates of deceased persons and insolvent debtors, trusts, adoption, estates and persons of minors and incompetents and commitment of insane. Amendments to Act. (PA 98-52). Appeals lie to superior court. They have no stated terms for holding their courts, but sit daily, weekly, or whenever occasion requires, at discretion of judge. State is divided into a large number (over 100) of probate districts—many including only one small town. Judges are elected by people quadrennially and are not necessarily lawyers. Judge of probate, if a lawyer, may not appear as attorney in any probate court in any contested matter (§45a-25); and partner or associate of probate judge may not practice in that judge's court (§45a-26).

Certain acts of the probate court concerning jurisdiction of nonresident decedents, orders of sale of real estate by non-statutory means, limitation of time for presentation of estate claims, orders for sale of real property not consummated within ten years, are all validated. (S.A. 97-6, §7; H.B. 6402).

Probate Court Costs.—Costs charged by probate courts are uniform and governed by statute. (45a-106, 107). Estate settlement charges based on percentage of gross taxable estate, with specified adjustments. (45a-107). Basic costs payable to courts of probate for any proceeding other than in connection with settlement of estate of deceased person or periodic accounts of trustees, guardians, conservators or other fiduciaries shall be as follows: Except for such proceedings for which basic costs are specified in subdivisions (2), (3), and (4) of this subsection in general statutes, there shall be payable to court of probate with respect to each application, petition or motion filed with court to commence matter before it, entry fee of $100 which shall be paid by person making application, petition or motion. (45a-106). Additional fees authorized for lengthy matters.

Court of probate, may upon request of fiduciary responsible for filing account, issue certificate, prior to acceptance of final administration account, if it is in best interests of parties (45a-450).

Judge Referees.—PA 98-245, §13 modifies CGS §§52-434 regarding appointment, designation, compensation and duties of trial judge referees.

JUSTICES OF THE PEACE:

Office still exists. However, justices have been stripped of most of their former authority. There are specific provisions concerning term and number of justices each municipality must have, (9-183a, 9-183b, 9-184, 51-95, PA 93-155, PA 94-230).

LEGISLATURE:

In odd numbered years, meets in Jan. and must adjourn by June of same year. Any business appropriate to legislature may be acted on in these sessions. In even numbered years, meets in Feb. and must adjourn by May in same year. In even year session, cannot consider business other than budgetary revenue and financial matters, bills and resolutions raised by committees of General Assembly and matters certified by Speaker of House of Representatives and President pro tempore of Senate to be of emergency nature. (Const. 3, 2). Governor may call Special Session. No provision for initiative or referendum.

Lobbyists activities regulated by Code of Ethics, including detailed registration provisions. (1-84; 1-79; 1-80[a], [b]; 1-81; 1-82; 1-91; 1-92; 1-93; 1-93a; 1-93b to 1-101). Lobbying activities by ex-legislators curtailed. Legislators elected in 1994 will be unable to lobby for one year after term expires. (2-16a, am'd 93-156).

Ethics Reform.—Changes to legislation concerning goods and services given to public officials and state employees. (H.B. 8005; PA 97-6; 1-79; 1-84[j], [k], [m]; 1-91[g]; 1-96[e]; 1-97; 53a-147; 53a-148; 1-79a; 1-92; 1-93a; 1-83; 1-84b and 9-333[b]).

Campaign Finance.—Changes and additions to campaign finance legislation concerning campaign contributions and reporting requirements. (1-79; 1-91; Cross ref. 9-333j; 9-333j[c]; 9-333k; 9-333h; 9-333b; 9-3331; 9-333e; 9-333a; 9-333n[d] and [e]; 9-333m; 9-333f; 1-79[e]; 1-91[g]; and 9-333w).

Receipt of "Soft Money" Funds Banned.—State parties and political committees organized for ongoing political activities are prohibited from receiving "soft money" funds from national political parties. (PA 98-7).

REPORTS:

Reports are: Kirby, 1 vol. (1786-88); Root, 2 vols. (1796-1797); Day, 5 vols. (1802-1813); Connecticut Reports, the current series, beginning with vol. 1 reports Supreme Court decision; Connecticut Appellate Reports reports Appellate Court decisions from Nov. 1983 to date; Connecticut Supplement reports Superior and Common Pleas decisions of note from 1935 to date; Connecticut Circuit Court Reports report Circuit Court cases, 1963-1974. (52-21). Weekly editions of Connecticut Law Tribune and Connecticut Law Reporter report Superior Court decisions and offer periodic bound volumes collecting decisions.

Digests are: Baldwin's, vol. 1 (pub. 1870); vol. 2 (pub. 1892); Index Digests—Andrews & Fowler (pub. 1896) covering Kirby to 63 Conn., and Maltbie & Townshend (pub. 1924) covering 64 to 97 Conn.; Phillips (pub. 1934) covering 97 Conn. to 117 Conn.; Phillips (pub. 1937) covering 118 Conn. to 121 Conn.; Phillips (pub. 1940) covering 122 Conn. to 125 Conn.; Philips (pub. 1945) covering Kirby to 130 Conn., with supplement covering 131 Conn. to 161 Conn. Dowling (pub. 1982). Digest to each volume of official reports appears at back of volume. Connecticut and Atlantic Digest, with annual pocket parts, covers all Connecticut cases.

STATUTES:

Latest revision is General Statutes, Revision of 1958, Revised to 1991.

Uniform Acts which have been adopted and the years of adoption are: Acknowledgement (1961); Aircraft Financial Responsibility (1959); Anatomical Gift (1969); Certification of Questions of Law (1985); Child Custody Jurisdiction (1978); Code of Military Justice (1967); Commercial Code (1959); Common Interest Ownership Act (1983); Controlled Substances (1972); Criminal Extradition (1957); Enforcement of Foreign Judgments (1973); Federal Tax Lien Registration Act, Revised (1967); Foreign Money-Judgments Recognition Act (modified, 1988); Fraudulent Transfer (1991); Interstate Arbitration of Death Taxes (modified, 1947); Interstate Compromise of Death Taxes (modified, 1947); Interstate Family Support (1998); Judicial Notice of Foreign Law (1918); Land Sales Practices (1969); Limited Partnership Act, Revised (1976) Version (1979); Management of Institutional Funds (1973); Motor Vehicle Certificate of Title and Anti-Theft Act (1957); Partnership Act (1994); Photographic Copies of Business and Public Records as Evidence (1961); Principal and Income (1958); Proof of Statutes (1947); Prudent Investor (1997); Reciprocal Enforcement of Support 1952 version (1953); Recognition of Acknowledgments (1969); Securities (1977); Simultaneous Death (1943); State Administrative Procedure, Revised (1971); Statutory Rule Against Perpetuities (1989); Testamentary Additions to Trusts (1961); To Secure Attendance of Witnesses from Without a State in Criminal Proceedings (1937); Trade Secrets (1983) (N.B. 1985 amendments not adopted.); Transboundary Pollution Reciprocal Access (1992); Transfers to Minors (1995).

See note at head of Digest as to 1998 legislation covered.

See Topical Index in front part of this volume.

STATUTES . . . *continued*

No Uniform Acts adopted with significant variations or modifications, except for Uniform Securities Act, as to which see topic Securities and Uniform Common Interest Ownership Act, as to which see category Property, topic Real Property.

Uniform Commercial Code has been adopted. (Conn. Gen. Statutes, Tit. 42a-1-101 to 42a-10-104). Art. 6 (Bulk Sales) repealed. (PA93-107).

For text of Uniform Acts falling within the scope of the Martindale-Hubbell Law Digests see Uniform and Model Acts section.

UNIFORM LAWS:

For list of Uniform Acts in force in this state see topic Statutes. For text of Uniform Acts within the scope of the Martindale-Hubbell Law Digests see Uniform and Model Acts section.

CRIMINAL LAW

BAIL:

See topic Criminal Law.

CRIMINAL LAW:

New Penal Code (Tit. 53a) became effective Oct. 1, 1971. Most sections of old penal code (Tit. 53) were repealed but some remain in effect. Criminal procedure was formerly provided for by Tit. 54 but some procedural sections are included in Tit. 53a. Tit. 54 still in effect. Procedure primarily governed by C. P. B. 592-1022.

Many basic elements of criminal liability and defenses set out in statutory form. (53a-4 to 53a-23).

In addition to usual defenses, certain new "affirmative defenses" available, which defendant must prove by preponderance of evidence. (53a-12).

Felonies divided into Class A, B, C, D, and unclassified, and capital felonies carrying death penalty. (53a-25). All felony sentences are indeterminate, with court setting maximum and minimum based on class of felony. (53a-35).

Misdemeanors divided into Class A, B, C, and unclassified (53a-26), with appropriate definite sentence (53a-36).

Conditional discharge may be imposed as sentence, with less restriction than probation. (53a-28 to 53a-33).

No degrees of murder. Certain classes of murder carry death penalty: (a) Murder of policeman or corrections officer; (b) murder by one hired for pecuniary gain; (c) murder by defendant previously convicted of intentional murder or murder committed while committing a felony; (d) murder by prisoner under life sentence; (e) murder by a kidnapper; (f) where illegal sale of cocaine, heroin or methadone, directly causes death of buyer; (g) murder committed in course of commission of 1st degree sexual assault; (h) murder of two or more persons at same time or in course of single transaction. (53a-54b).

Death Penalty.—Carried out by lethal injection. (54-100, am'd PA 95-16). Imposed only after separate penalty phase hearing focusing upon aggravating/mitigating factors.

Rape Shield Law.—(10-182j[d]).

Stalking Law.—(PA 92-237).

Child Pornography Law.—(PA 95-143).

Registration of Sexual Offenders.—Criminal History Searches new fee schedule. (CGS §29-11 am'd by PA 97-182; PA 98-111; HB 5334; PA 98-170).

Jury Trials.—No trial by jury in criminal actions where maximum penalty is fine of $199. (54-82b).

Indictment or Information.—No person charged by state shall be put to plea or held to trial for any crime punishable by death or life imprisonment unless court at preliminary hearing determines there is probable cause to believe offense charged has been committed and that accused person committed it. Accused person may knowingly and voluntarily waive probable cause hearing. (54-46a). Prosecution by complaint or information in other cases. (54-46).

Accused arrested upon bench warrant issued by superior court.

Bail.—All offenses bailable except capital offenses in which proof evident or presumption great. (Const 1, 8; 159 Conn. 264, 268 A.2d 667). Any person arrested and charged with Class A, B, C, or D felony, with certain exceptions, shall be released on bail if court can be reasonably assured of appearance of arrested person in court and that safety of others will not be endangered. Conditions of release found sufficient to meet these specifications are: (1) Execution of written promise to appear without special conditions; (2) execution of written promise with nonfinancial conditions; or (3) execution of bond. (54-63d). Bail Commissioner may impose restrictions regarding travel and activities. (PA 97-53). Court may also order person to submit to drug testing and to participate in program of drug treatment if it has reason to believe person is drug dependent. Result of this test will not be admissible in any criminal proceeding. Courts may also consider following factors to determine whether arrested person will appear in court or if safety of another person will be in danger: (a) Nature, and circumstances of offense; (b) person's previous convictions; (c) person's past record of appearance in court proceedings after being admitted to bail; (d) person's family ties; (e) person's employment record; (f) person's financial resources, character and mental condition; (g) person's community ties; (h) number and seriousness of charges pending against arrested person; (i) weight of evidence against arrested person; (j) arrested person's history of violence; (k) whether arrested person has previously been convicted of similar offenses while released on bond; and (l) likelihood, based upon expressed intention of arrested person, that such person will commit another crime while released. (54-64a). Prisoner who has not made bail appears in court at least every 45 days for review of amount of bail. Prisoner detained pursuant to bench warrant of arrest, arraignment, sentencing or trial for class D felony or misdemeanor, appears in court at least 30 days for review of amount of bail. (54-53a). Any person who has not made bail may be heard at any time by court upon motion for modification of bail. (54-53a).

Parole.—Commissioner of Correction shall not release from confinement to supervised home release program any prisoner convicted and incarcerated after 10/1/91 unless such prisoner has served at least 25% of sentence. As of 10/1/92 prisoners must serve at least 40% of sentence before being released into such programs. Commission may petition to waive such requirements in order to reduce inmate population to acceptable size. On 6/30/93 new requirements for eligibility for home release programs go into effect. (18-100).

Compensation.—Innocent victims of crime or their dependents are sometimes eligible for compensation. (54-143; 54-201 to 54-217, 54-211).

Firearms.—No person should store loaded firearm if they have reason to know minor is likely to gain access to firearm without parent or guardian's permission unless person keeps firearm in reasonably secure place or carries it on his person. Person is guilty of criminally negligent storage of firearm, class D felony, when he violates this provision and minor obtains firearm and causes death or injury to himself or others unless minor obtains firearm as result of unlawful entry. (29-37i).

Retail Sale of Firearms.—Any person, firm or corporation selling firearms shall provide trigger lock, gun lock, and written warning against unlawful storage penalties, as well as post at their service counter same written warning. Violators will be fined not less than $500. (29-37b).

Person who sells, delivers or provides firearm who knows or should know that transferee will use firearm in criminal activity is liable as principal. (53a-8).

In or on school property class D felony. (53a-217b).

Purchase, sale, and transfer of pistols, revolvers, and assault weapons, all as defined, strictly regulated. Waiting periods, eligibility requirements, and mandatory sentencing for violations all provided for. (29-27 to 29-38, am'd PA 98-129).

Crime Victims' Compensation.—No award of compensation to victim will be provided if offender is unjustly enriched. If commission has reason to believe that offender will be unjustly enriched by award greater than $250, commission shall investigate any relationship between victim and offender and financial responsibilities and resources of victim and offender. Compensation will be awarded for crimes committed outside state provided victim is resident of this state and state in which crime occurred does not have program for compensation. (54-211). There is Office of Victim Advocate. (PA 98-231).

Juvenile Matters.—HB 5696; PA 98-256, §1 modifies CGS §97-319 regarding child defined as one under 16 years or over 16 years who prior to reaching 16 violated federal, state, local or municipal law or ordinance; child may be convicted as delinquent if he has violated such laws except ordinance regulating behavior of child in family with service needs, violated Superior Court Orders or conditions of probation. §2 modifies CGS §46b-121k regarding establishment of secure or supervised residential facilities for juveniles referred by court. §3 modifies CGS §46b-127 regarding transfer from juvenile to regular criminal docket. File to remain sealed until end of tenth working day after arraignment in regular criminal docket. State attorney may file motion for transfer to juvenile docket not later than ten days after arraignment for proceedings in accordance with statute.

By motion of juvenile prosecutor and order of court case may be transferred from juvenile to regular criminal docket if above conditions met. Court in regular criminal docket may return case to juvenile docket not later than ten working days after date of transfer and proceeding.

If case remains in regular criminal docket, child to be tried and sentenced as if 16 years of age. If action dismissed or nolled, or if child not guilty of charge transferred for or any lesser included offense, child to resume status as juvenile until 16 years of age. §4 modifies CGS §46b-133 regarding photograph, name and custody status of juvenile arrested for capital or class A felony may be disclosed to public (see 46b-124).

Upon arrest or referral for commission of delinquent act, and child isn't placed in detention or referred to diversionary program, officer shall serve written complaint and summons on child and parent, guardian or other person in control of child.

When population of juvenile detention center exceeds or equals maximum capacity, detention supervisor to admit child only if, inter alia, child is subject of order to detain or outstanding custody order.

§5 modifies CGS §46b-33 substituting "count" for "charge"; §6 modifies CGS §46b-140 regarding required residence and prohibited acts of child under probation; §7 modifies CGS §46b-146 regarding conditions for erasure of child's record; §10 modifies CGS §46b-121 regarding juvenile matters included in criminal session; §11 modifies CGS §46b-137 regarding confessions and statements made by child to police or juvenile court official; and §12 modifies CGS §54-761 regarding disclosure of records of youth adjudged and youthful offender on or after Oct. 1, 1995.

Note: §8 (new) regarding court discretion to modify or enlarge probation or suspended commitment; service of court order; terms of alternative incarceration programs; arrest or notice to appear for violation of conditions of probation or suspended commitment; penalties for violation; §9 (new) regarding notice of and provision of medical/dental services to child; and §13 (new) regarding CPR training of persons who directly supervise child.

Welfare and Benefits.—HB 5650; PA 98-263, §16 modifies CGS §18-88 regarding food service for inmates; §17 modifies CGS §18-992 regarding inmate education and assistance; §18 modifies CGS §18-99b regarding establishment of schools for inmates.

DEBTOR AND CREDITOR

ASSIGNMENTS:

Uniform Commercial Code adopted. (Title 42a).

The assignee and equitable and bona fide owner of any chose in action, not negotiable, may sue thereon in his own name (42-123; 52-118), or at common law in assignor's name (102 Conn. 425, 435, 129 Atl. 221). Partial assignments are valid in equity, and rights thereunder may be enforced by suit to which assignor is party. (C. P. B. 95).

Benefits under Workmen's Compensation Law (49-73), unemployment compensation benefits, aid to dependent children (17-99), embalmer's licenses (22-18) and liquor permits (30-14) are not assignable.

ASSIGNMENTS . . . *continued*

Instrument Transferring Title.—An assignment of a chose in action should be in writing. (42-123). There are no statutory requirements for witnesses and acknowledgment.

Filing and Recording.—No requirements except as imposed by Commercial Code (Title 42a) or by trademark law. (35-11a).

Accounts Receivable.—Governed by applicable provisions of Uniform Commercial Code. (Title 42a).

Earnings.—Wages, salaries, commissions and other earnings may not be assigned except for payment of union dues and support in public welfare cases. (52-361[g]). See also topic Executions, subhead Supplementary Proceedings.

ATTACHMENT:

Constitutionality.—See Pinsky v. Duncan, 898 F.2d 852 (2d Cir. 1990), affd. Connecticut v. Doehr, 111 S.Ct. 2105, 115 L.Ed 2d 1, 500 U.S. . . . (1991), where ex parte attachment of real estate as permitted under then effective version of §52-278e found to violate due process.

Actions in Which Allowed.—Upon original writ in any action for recovery of money, but no attachment may be made in action for slander, libel, or invasion of privacy except upon court order. (52-279, 10a-24). Plaintiff, or defendant on counterclaim may obtain attachment. (52-278a to 52-278g; 52-278e).

In Whose Favor Writ May Issue.—There is no distinction in favor of local creditors.

Against Whom Writ May Issue.—Writ may issue against either resident or nonresident defendant. No prejudgment attachment may be issued against municipal officer for act or omission while acting in discharge of his duties unless malicious, wanton or wilful. (52-278e).

Claims on Which Writ May Issue.—It is not necessary that the claim sued on should be insured or payable within the state.

Grounds.—Attaching party at hearing must show probable cause that his claim will be sustained. (52-278d).

Proceedings to Obtain.—Plaintiff must apply for prejudgment remedy, submit affidavit and serve defendant with application at least four days prior to required hearing. Temporary restraining order may be obtained. (52-278c). Hearing's purpose is to ascertain: (1) whether probable cause exists that judgment will be obtained by plaintiff in amount sought or in greater amount, considering any defenses, counterclaims, or setoffs; (2) whether insurance available to adequately secure any judgment; (3) whether property sought is exempt from attachment; (4) if court grants remedy, whether plaintiff should post bond to protect defendant from damage caused by prejudgment remedy or whether defendant can post bond in lieu of attachment or remedy sought. (52-278d, am'd 93-431). Upon motion for disclosure defendant may be ordered to disclose property in which he has interest sufficient to satisfy prejudgment remedy. (52-278n). Effective Jan. 1, 1994, applicant seeking attachment of any prejudgment remedy without prior notice of hearing must show that there is reasonable likelihood that defendant: (a) has evaded or will evade service of process; (b) is about to leave Connecticut or remove property sought to be attached from state; or (c) had made or will make fraudulent conveyance. (52-278e, am'd PA 93-431).

In determining whether to authorize prejudgment remedy sought and in what amount, reviewing court must consider any known defenses, counterclaims or set-offs. (52-278c, am'd 93-431).

Process served upon defendant prior to hearing or after issuance of order authorizing remedy sought must include court-prescribed "notice and claim form" specifying defendant's right to: (a) contest remedy sought as improper or excessive, due to available defenses, set-offs, or counterclaims; (b) demonstrate availability of liability insurance to cover any judgment; (c) ask court to require applicant to post bond to cover damages caused by prejudgment remedy; (d) ask court to allow defendant to post bond in lieu of remedy sought; (e) claim property sought to be attached as exempt under applicable law. (52-278d, am'd 93-431).

Procedure not applicable to commercial transactions, as defined, where written waiver previously secured, but process notifying defendant of attachment or other remedy pursuant to waiver must contain prescribed notice of rights to hearing to contest remedy. (52-278f, am'd 93-431).

Defendant asserting set-off, counterclaim for money damages or plaintiff after commencement of action may obtain attachment on application and hearing as provided above. (52-282).

Attachments secured prior to May 30, 1973 shall retain their effectiveness by filing a motion for a hearing. (52-278g).

Post-Judgment Remedies.—Post-Judgment Remedies Act represents comprehensive update of creditor remedies and debtor protections, including new discovery rights, equitable enforcement procedures, and exemption notice and claim provisions. (52-347 to 52-400c). Money judgment may be enforced against any property of judgment debtor unless property is exempt. Amount of judgment may include statutory fees and costs, interest and any allowable attorney's fees. (52-350f). Judgment creditor may obtain discovery from judgment debtor, certain third persons, or from any financial institution pursuant to statute's procedures. (52-351b). Disputes between judgment debtor or creditor and third persons concerning interests in personal property sought to be levied on may be heard by Superior Court. (52-356c).

Forms.—Following forms are to be used:

Forms

Application for Prejudgment Remedy.—(C.P.B. Form 101.5).
To the Superior Court for Judicial District of . . . .
The undersigned represents:
1. That . . . . . is about to commence an action against . . . . . of . . . . . (give name and address of defendant) pursuant to the attached proposed unsigned Writ, Summons, Complaint and Affidavit.

2. That there is probable cause that a judgment will be rendered in such matter in favor of the applicant and to secure the judgment the applicant seeks an order from this court directing that the following prejudgment remedy be issued to secure the sum of $. . . . .:
a. To attach the following described (real) property of the defendant located in the town of (name of town) and further described as follows: (insert description)
b. To garnishee . . . . ., as he is the agent, trustee, debtor of the defendant and has concealed in his hands the goods, effects and estate of the defendant and is indebted to him.
c. (Other Type of Prejudgment Remedy Requested.)

　　　　　　　　　　　　　　　Name of Applicant
　　　　　　　　　　　　　　　By . . . .
　　　　　　　　　　　　　　　　His Attorney
　　　　　　　　　　———————————

Order.—(C.P.B. Form 101.5).
The above application having been presented to the court, it is hereby ordered, that a hearing be held thereon on . . . . . at . . . . . a.m. and that the plaintiff give notice to the defendant of the pendency of the application and of the time when it will be heard by causing a true and attested copy of the application, the proposed unsigned writ, summons, complaint, affidavit and of this order to be served upon the defendant by some proper officer or indifferent person on or before . . . . ., and that due return of service be made to this court.
Dated at . . . . . this . . . . . day of . . . . ., 19. . . .
. . . .
　　　　　　　　　　　　　　　　　Clerk of the Court
　　　　　　　　　　———————————

Summons.—(C.P.B. Form 101.5).
To the Sheriff of the County of . . . . ., his deputy, or either constable of the Town of . . . . ., in said County,
Greeting:
By authority of the State of Connecticut, you are hereby commanded to serve a true and attested copy of the above application, unsigned proposed writ, summons, complaint, affidavit and order upon . . . . ., of . . . . . . by leaving the same in his hands or at his usual place of abode on or before . . . . .
Hereof fail not but due service and return make.
Dated at . . . . . this . . . . . day of . . . . ., 19. . . .
　　　　　　　　　. . . . .
　　　　　　　　　　Commissioner of the Superior
　　　　　　　　　　　　　　　Court
　　　　　　　　　　———————————

Times for Issuance of Writs.—Attachment may issue on commencement of action or anytime thereafter upon court order or pursuant to temporary restraining order. (52-278b). See subhead Proceedings to Obtain, supra.
When the court cites in a new party to an action pending before it, it may include in such citation an order for a supplemental attachment against the property of such new party. (52-103).
Upon amendment of defective process, if court after notice and hearing finds that parties had notice of pendency of action and have not been prejudiced by the defect, attachment made by original process is preserved as though proper from date of service of original process. (52-72).

Property Subject to Attachment.—Attachment may be levied on any estate of defendant not exempt. (52-279; 52-280). As to exempt property, see topic Exemptions.
Equitable interests (114 Conn. 79, 157 Atl. 638), future interests (71 Conn. 149, 41 Atl. 284), and partial interests in land (68 Conn. 1, 35 Atl. 804) are subject to attachment if sufficiently definite to be capable of appraisal; but security interests such as interest of vendor or mortgagee may be reached only by garnishing debt secured and filing certificate of garnishment for record with town clerk for town where the land is situated (52-346). Income from trust fund, if available to defendant by terms of trust (see category Estates and Trusts, topic Trusts), may be availed of by equitable decree requiring trustee to pay income to creditor. (52-321). Interest of partner in partnership property may be attached, but any party to action or partner may, by bill in equity, cause dissolution of attachment and division of partnership property on equitable principles. (52-299).
Fixtures of telephone, telegraph, light or power companies are attachable in manner and effect the same as real estate by lodging a certificate of attachment with the Secretary of State. (52-287).
Public Servants.—No attachments of property of municipal officials, policemen, members, teachers, or employees of board of education or members of any other municipal board or commission, in action involving official conduct, except on court order, or, in case of policeman, on dismissal. (52-279).

Levy.—Attachment is made under order of court after hearing. (52-89; 52-90; 52-278a to 52-278g). Sheriff or constable makes attachment by serving writ of attachment on defendant, and, in case of personal property by seizing and removing property where practicable (52-280; 107 Conn. 300, 140 Atl. 354), and, in case of real estate (52-285) or leaseholds (52-286) by lodging in office of town clerk in town where real estate is located certificate that he has made such attachment and true and attested copy of process authorizing same (52-285).
Estate of nonresident defendant is attached as above described, a copy of the process being left with the agent or attorney of the defendant within the state, or in the absence of such agent or attorney, with the person in charge or possession of the estate attached; if there is no person in charge or possession of the estate attached, the court may order reasonable notice to be given to the defendant, and such notice, having been given and proved, is deemed sufficient service of process, and such attachment thereupon becomes effective. (52-284). Not applicable to garnishments. (79 Conn. 15, 17, 63 Atl. 641; 52-88).
Shares of stock in a corporation, together with the dividends due thereon, may be attached by the officer leaving attested copies of the process and complaint at the office of the corporation, and the officer in charge thereof must issue to him a certificate of the

ATTACHMENT . . . *continued*
amount of stock owned, the incumbrances thereon and the dividends due; but no such attachment shall be valid until the stock certificate be seized by the officer, or be surrendered to the corporation. (52-289).

Attachments of certain cumbersome articles not moveable without manifest injury may be effectual without removal thereof if properly filed within 48 hours in town clerk's office in town where property situated and with secretary of state. In some cases, posting on building containing property required. (52-283).

Lien.—Attachment constitutes lien on property attached to secure payment of attaching creditor's claim, and priority of levy of attachment gives priority of lien. (36 Conn. 578). Real estate attachment is not lien after 15 years unless reduced to judgment and judgment lien filed. (52-327).

Attachment holds until the execution is levied, provided the levy is made within 60 days after final judgment when personal estate is attached. No real estate that has been attached may be held subject to attachment to respond to judgment obtained in suit, either against debtor or any other creditor, unless judgment creditor places judgment lien on real estate within four months after final judgment. (52-328).

Sale.—Upon order of court, perishable property or property difficult or expensive to care for and preserve levied on under attachment may be sold (52-293), provided the plaintiff gives bond with surety in double the value of such property, conditioned on prosecution to effect and payment of damages sustained by sale at less than appraised value (52-294). Proceeds of such sale are paid into court and are there subject to attachment by other creditors. (52-297). Defendant may take proceeds at any time during suit upon giving bond with surety conditioned on refund in event of adverse judgment. (52-298).

Priorities.—Where several attachments of the same property are made, the debt and costs of suit of the first attaching creditor must first be fully satisfied, and subsequent attaching creditors are paid in the order of their several attachments. (85 Conn. 573, 578, 84 Atl. 119; 36 Conn. 578).

Property of Nonresidents.—The property of a nonresident defendant may be attached in the same manner as other property is attached except that the writ and complaint is served by leaving a copy with the defendant's agent or attorney in state, if known and by giving such notice to said defendant as court, on application made to it, shall require. (52-284).

Release of Property.—Defendant may secure release of attached property and dissolution of attachment lien upon substitution of surety bond or lien on other property which has equal or greater net equity value than amount secured by attachment (52-304); all persons interested may be heard in relation to amount and sufficiency of bond or substitute lien, and amount must equal value of estate which process directed to be attached, except in tort action for unliquidated damages in which case reasonable bond or substitute lien is sufficient (52-307). Lien on real estate of surety on bond may be obtained by filing in office of Town Clerk. (49-86). Release may also be obtained by court order following hearing in probable cause. (52-278a to 52-278g).

Dissolution.—When attachment of record is for any reason of no effect, any person interested in estate may require plaintiff (52-322) or clerk of court (52-324) to file certificate of dissolution with Town Clerk. If plaintiff fails to execute and deliver a release within 30 days after demand, he is liable to person aggrieved at $100 per week, up to $5,000 or in amount equal to loss sustained by aggrieved person, whichever is greater. (49-8, 49-13).

When the attachment is dissolved, the defendant must file a certificate of dissolution signed by the plaintiff or the plaintiff's attorney with the town clerk if real estate was attached, with the served officer of the corporation if corporate stock was attached, or with the garnishee in case of goods or effects in hands of garnishee, before the corporation or garnishee can be held liable for refusing to transfer stock, pay debts or return goods and effects. (52-310).

Bond.—By application to court defendant may secure dissolution of attachment lien upon substitution of a surety bond or lien on other property which has equal or greater net equity value than amount secured by attachment. (52-304). Amount and sufficiency of bond or substitute lien are subject to hearing, but amount must equal value of estate which process directed to be attached, except in action of tort for recovery of unliquidated damages where court may take bond or substitute lien for amount deemed reasonable. (52-307).

CREDITORS' SUITS:

Since legal and equitable remedies can be granted in the same action, a creditor can in the same complaint have judgment for his debt and also the equitable aid necessary to reach intangible assets; therefore, the former creditor's bill is ordinarily unnecessary. (100 Conn. 712, 124 Atl. 715). See also topics Executions, Fraudulent Sales and Conveyances.

EXECUTIONS:

Money judgment may be enforced against any property of judgment debtor, unless exempt property, by execution or foreclosure of real property lien. Clerk of court rendering judgment must receive application from judgment creditor before issuing execution through sheriff, deputy sheriff or constable.

Exemptions.—Natural person's exempt property listed in 52-352b. See topic Exemptions. Executions must be accompanied by exemption claim form when served.

Levy and Sale.—The officer in levying execution must first make demand of the sum due and upon refusal of the judgment debtor to pay, he then levies the execution on nonexempt personal property other than debts due from banks or earnings. Officer advertises for sale and sells such personal estate so levied after 20 days, or if property be perishable or livestock, after shorter period. (52-356a[b]). If personal estate sufficient to satisfy judgment cannot be found, officer may levy execution on real property of debtor held in his own right through judgment lien. (52-380a).

Execution on Bank Account.—An execution may be granted against any debts due judgment debtor not natural person from any banking institution, including federal credit union, and upon service at any office such institution must, before its midnight deadline, pay to serving officer amount of such indebtedness not exceeding amount due on such execution. Failure to pay renders institution personally liable for such amount. (52-367a). Upon receipt of execution, banking institution immediately segregates funds, and sends notice to debtor, including exemption claim form. Debtor must claim exemption within 15 days to avoid payment by banking institution to executing creditor. If exemption claimed, court conducts hearing to determine validity of claim. (52-367b).

Execution on Cumbersome Articles Not Moveable Without Manifest Injury.—Notice of such levy must be posted on the outer door of building in which the property is located; such property is held by such levy as effectually as if it had been removed. (52-356a).

The owner of a judgment may, instead of taking out execution, file a judgment lien on debtor's land and foreclose same. (52-355a). See category Civil Actions and Procedure, topic Judgments.

Stay of Execution.—In all actions, there is automatic stay of execution until time to take appeal has expired and on appeal or notice thereof such stay is extended until final determination, unless on contrary order of court. (C. P. B. 4065-4067, 4107).

When in foreign attachment it appears that debt garnished is not yet due the defendant, execution must be stayed until it becomes due. (52-386).

Satisfaction.—Each clerk of court to whom an execution is returned after service must note on the margin or on the record of the judgment upon which it was issued whether and to what extent such execution was satisfied. (52-356a).

No redemption from an execution sale.

Supplementary Proceedings.—A judgment debtor against whom execution is returned unsatisfied may be examined touching his property and means before a judge of superior court or court of common pleas, which would have jurisdiction of an action on said judgment or before a committee appointed by such judge. (52-397). Debtor will not be excused from answering on ground that it might show him party to any fraud, or fraudulent conveyance, but his answers cannot be used against him in any criminal proceeding except for perjury (52-398), and on refusal to appear or answer he may be committed for contempt. (52-399).

When creditor seeks satisfaction of his claim out of wages of debtor, the court, as part of, or after, its final judgment in the action, may make reasonable orders, and modify the same from time to time, for payments to be made by the judgment debtor into court toward satisfaction of such judgment. On failure to obey order, judgment creditor may on application to court obtain execution on salary or wages, which when served on employer of judgment debtor becomes a lien on debtor's wages or salary. Wage execution limited to lesser of: (a) 25% of disposable earnings, or (b) disposable income which exceeds higher of 40 times minimum wage or full minimum fair wage in 31-58. (52-361a). Priority of levy of execution gives priority of lien. Employer (whether private individual, corporation, the state or a subdivision thereof) who fails to pay out under such execution becomes personally liable to judgment creditor. (52-361a).

Body Execution.—In contract action in which defendant might have been arrested on mesne process (52-355; see Arrest) or in any tort action (111 Conn. 225, 149 Atl. 770) or in action based on fraud in contracting debt, concealing property from legal process, or refusal to disclose rights of action so that same can be taken by foreign attachment (52-362), judgment creditor may, by writ of execution, have defendant arrested and held for payment of judgment if officer cannot find sufficient personal estate to satisfy judgment (52-369).

EXEMPTIONS:

Exempt property: (1) Necessities; (2) tools, books, instruments, farm animals and livestock feed necessary for occupation, profession or farming operation; (3) burial plot; (4) public assistance payments; (5) health and disability insurance payments; (6) health aids; (7) workers' compensation, social security, veterans and unemployment benefits; (8) court approved payments for child support; (9) military equipment of member of armed forces; (10) one motor vehicle to value of $1,500; (11) wedding and engagement rings; (12) residential utility deposits; (13) certain payments under pension plan and the like (PA 92-215); (14) alimony and support to certain extent; (15) award under Crime Reparations Act; (16) sickness or incapacity benefits exempt; and (17) insurance money due on exempt property (52-352b, am'd PA 92-94, §§2, 3).

Substitution.—Debtor who does not own articles specifically exempted may not hold other articles or money exempt in lieu thereof.

Earnings.—For exemption of wages, see topic Garnishment.

Liquor permits are exempt. (30-14).

Homestead Exemption.—See topic Homesteads.

FORECLOSURE:

See topic Liens; category Mortgages, topics Chattel Mortgages, Mortgages of Real Property.

FRAUDULENT SALES AND CONVEYANCES:

All conveyances made with intent to avoid any debt or duty belonging to others are void as against those persons only, their heirs and representatives, to whom such debt belongs. (52-552).

Remedies.—Injured creditor may attach or levy execution on property as property of debtor, or may proceed in equity to set aside conveyance, which equitable proceeding may be joined with his suit on the debt. (68 Conn. 384, 36 Atl. 813; 100 Conn. 712, 124 Atl. 715).

Deed from husband to wife not presumed to lack consideration. (76 Conn. 197, 56 Atl. 558).

Uniform Fraudulent Conveyance Act not adopted.

Bulk Sales.—Governed by the Uniform Commercial Code. (42a-6-101, 42a-6-110). Connecticut has adopted less stringent option re bulk sales than Code. See category Business Regulation and Commerce, topic Commercial Code.

GARNISHMENT:

Garnishment proceedings, called the process of "foreign attachment" in this state, may be had against any person who as agent or trustee holds property belonging to the defendant or who is indebted to him. (52-329).

Property Which May Be Reached.—In general, effects, debts, legacies or distributive shares belonging to defendant may be garnisheed. Debtor's interest in note secured by mortgage may be garnisheed. (52-346; 52-278a). Amounts in checking accounts in excess of $5,000 may be garnisheed only on court order for good cause shown. (52-289a). See topic Exemptions.

Earnings.—Wages may not be garnisheed but in lieu thereof extraordinary supplementary proceedings in aid of collection therefrom are provided. See topic Executions.

Jurisdiction.—Garnishment may be directed subject to requirements of 52-278a in any civil action in which judgment or decree for payment of money may be rendered. (52-329).

Proceedings to Obtain.—Plaintiff inserts in his writ a direction to officer to leave a true and attested copy of writ and complaint with garnishee at least 12 days before return day. (52-329).

Service.—See category Civil Actions and Procedure, topic Process.

Answer of Garnishee.—Garnishee, in the writ, may be summoned to appear on return day and disclose under oath whether he has property of defendant or is a debtor of defendant. (52-330). A disclosure to the sheriff at the time of service is usually sufficient, although the plaintiff if he desires may examine the garnishee in court. (52-331).

Practice.—From time of serving such process on garnishee, any debt owing by him to defendant, and any property held by him belonging to defendant shall be secured in hands of garnishee to pay such judgment as plaintiff may recover. (52-329).

Adverse Claims.—If a negotiable note is garnisheed and defendant has notice of garnishment he is liable to plaintiff in a civil action for fraud if he transfers note to bona fide purchaser, but bona fide purchaser is protected. (52-341). If scire facias is brought to recover a debt or effects taken by garnishment, the defendant having notice of any assignment of the property may give notice to all persons claiming as assignees that such scire facias is pending so that they may appear and defend. (52-387).

Judgment.—If after judgment is recovered the garnishee fails to pay the judgment to the amount of such debt or to produce such property after demand made by the officer with the execution in hand, so that execution may be levied on it, the garnishee becomes personally liable to the plaintiff in the amount of such debt not exceeding the amount of the judgment, such liability being enforced by scire facias proceedings instituted by the plaintiff as a separate action against the garnishee. (52-381).

HOMESTEADS:

"Homestead", defined as owner-occupied real property or mobile manufactured home used as primary residence, exempt from attachment to value of $75,000, provided value to be determined as fair market value less amount of any statutory or consensual lien which encumbers it. (52-352b, am'd PA 93-301).

JUDGMENT NOTES:

See category Business Regulation and Commerce, topic Bills and Notes.

LEVY:

See topics Attachment, Executions.

LIENS:

Uniform Commercial Code adopted. (Title 42a).

Equitable liens are governed by common law.

Board or Lodging.—When there has been any special agreement regarding the price for board or lodging the keeper of the boarding or lodging house has a lien on the baggage and effects of the boarder or lodger, and if his bill is not paid within 60 days his effects may be sold and the proceeds applied on the debt. (49-68). Hotel keepers have similar liens, but may sell the goods after 30 days after advertising the sale in a newspaper for three days commencing at least five days before the sale. (49-69).

Remainderman having vested interest in real property has lien for costs of necessary repairs and improvements and may apply to probate court during continuance of life estate, or within 60 days thereafter, for ascertainment of amount and for sale of so much of estate as will repay sum advanced. (45-258).

Hospitals receiving state aid or owned or operated by a municipality or by state may have a lien on accident and liability policies. (49-73).

Municipal liens on proceeds of fire insurance for taxes and demolition expenses allowable (49-73a-i; 12-172). Tax or municipal liens upon real estate, continued by certificate on land records, are invalid if no action is taken within 15 years of recording date. (12-175, am'd PA 85-396, §2).

Vessels are subject to lien for claim of not less than $50 for work, materials, and expenses connected with building, repairing, mooring, dockage or storage. Vessel lien must be filed with Secretary of State within 60 days after ceasing furnishing goods or services, and it is subordinate to previously filed security interests. (49-55; 49-55c). Upon satisfaction of claim or judgment for defendant, must be released within ten days upon request. (49-56a).

Water rent lien, where municipal or private corporation by law may have lien on real estate, continues one year from time rent due, unless proper certificate filed on land records before year expires, in which case lien continues two years from date of filing. (49-72).

Release of Artificer's Lien.—Owner of personal property held by bailee for hire or by one having legal or equitable interest therein claiming lien thereon may apply for dissolution of lien upon substitution of bond with surety. If no application made within three months from completion of work by bailee, bailee may sell upon giving prescribed statutory notice. If property is car, notice must also be given motor vehicle commissioner. (49-61).

Succession Lien.—There is no fee for certificate of release of lien for succession tax. (12-364).

Mechanics' Liens.—Any person having claim for labor or material furnished in construction or repair of any building or in improvement of any lot or site development or subdivision of any plot of land by virtue of contract with or by consent of owner exceeding $10 in amount, may have lien on same, land on which it stands, or lot or plot of land. (49-33).

Total amount of mechanics' liens cannot exceed total amount which owner has agreed to pay for building and its appurtenances or for development of lot or plot of land; if they exceed this amount lienors other than original contractor must first be paid in full and, if necessary, prorate any loss. In determining the amount, owner is credited with whatever payments he has made in good faith to the original contractor before receiving notice of the lien. No payment made in advance of the time stipulated in the original contract is considered as made in good faith, unless written notice of intention to make such payment is given at least five days before such payment is made to all persons known to have furnished materials or rendered services. (49-36).

Certificate of Lien.—Although mechanics' liens originate as of date of beginning of services or furnishing materials, they are not valid unless lienor, within 90 days, after he has ceased performing work or furnishing materials, files certificate of lien in office of town clerk for town in which property involved is situated, which certificate must be recorded with deeds of land and, prior to or within same time, but not later than 30 days after filing such certificate, serves true and attested copy of such certificate upon owner. This certificate must be under oath and must describe premises and state amount claimed, name or names of person against whom lien is being filed, date of origin of lien and that amount claimed is justly due. (49-34). If certificate does not contain name of owner, town clerk must index it according to such information as he can obtain. (7-28).

Notice of Lien.—Validity of lien is also destroyed if lienor, not being original contractor or subcontractor whose contract is in writing, does not give written notice to owner at some time after origin of lien and before expiration of 90 days after ceasing to work or furnish materials that he intends to claim such lien. (49-35).

Proceedings to Discharge or Reduce.—Owner may make application to Superior Court for hearing to determine whether lien should be discharged or reduced and must serve lienor with such application at least four days before hearing. Entry fee of $20 required. At hearing lienor must first establish probable cause to sustain validity of lien. Court may: (1) Deny application if probable cause to sustain validity of lien established; or (2) order lien discharged if (A) probable cause to sustain its validity not established, or (B) by clear and convincing evidence its invalidity established; or (3) reduce amount of such lien if amount found to be excessive by clear and convincing evidence; or (4) order lien discharged or reduced conditioned upon posting of bond with surety sufficient to indemnify lienor. Order automatically stayed for seven day appeal period during which party taking appeal may file application requesting further stay. Upon hearing court must, upon motion of party taking appeal, set amount of bond with surety sufficient to indemnify adverse party for damages resulting from stay and must grant stay if bond given. Order of discharge, reduction, or stay effective upon recording certified copy thereof in office of town clerk in which certificate of lien originally recorded. Similar procedure available to any party to pending action for foreclosure of lien by motion to court. (49-35a-c).

Forms.—Following forms are to be used (49-35a):

APPLICATION FOR DISCHARGE OR
REDUCTION OF MECHANIC'S LIEN

To the . . . . . . Court of . . . . . .

The undersigned represents:

1. That . . . . . . is the owner of the real estate described in Schedule A attached hereto.

2. That the names and addresses of all other owners of record of such real estate are as follows:

3. That on or about . . . .
(date) (name of lienor)
of . . . . placed a mechanic's lien on such real estate and
(address of lienor)
gave notice thereof.

4. That there is not probable cause to sustain the validity of such lien (or: That such lien is excessive).

5. That the applicant seeks an order for discharge (or reduction) of such lien.

(Name of Applicant)
By . . . .
His attorney

ORDER

The above application having been presented to the court, it is hereby ordered, that a hearing be held thereon at . . . . . . on . . . . . . at . . . . . . a.m. and that the applicant give notice to the following persons: (Name and addresses of persons entitled to notice) of the pendency of said application and of the time when it will be heard by causing a true and attested copy of the application, and of this order to be served upon such persons by some proper officer or indifferent person on or before . . . . . . and that due return of such notice be made to this court.

Dated at . . . . . . this . . . . . . day of . . . . . . 198. . . .

SUMMONS

To the sheriff of the county of . . . . . ., his deputy, or either constable of the town of . . . . . ., in said county,

Greeting:

By authority of the State of Connecticut, you are hereby commanded to serve a true and attested copy of the above application and order upon . . . . . ., of . . . . . . by leaving the same in his hands or at his usual place of abode (or such other notice as ordered by the court) on or before . . . . . .

See note at head of Digest as to 1998 legislation covered.

See Topical Index in front part of this volume.

CT – 20

LIENS... *continued*

Hereof fail not but due service and return make. Dated at . . . . . . this . . . . . . day of . . . . . . 198. . . .

. . . .
Commissioner of the Superior Court

Duration of Lien.—Lien will not continue longer than one year from date of perfection of lien unless proceedings are commenced to foreclose same, and lis pendens recorded with town clerk, within one year of date or recording, or within 60 days of any final disposition of appeal, whichever is later. (49-39). If time limit not met, lien automatically extinguished. (49-39).

Priorities.—The lien originates as of the time of commencement of such services or the furnishing of such materials and is entitled to priority over all incumbrances originating subsequent thereto except other mechanics' liens. If an incumbrance not a mechanic's lien originates subsequent to the origin of one set of mechanics' liens and prior to another set, the order of priority is: (1) Mechanics' liens originating prior to the intervening incumbrance; (2) the intervening incumbrance; (3) mechanics' liens originating subsequent to the intervening incumbrance. If lienor releases or waives claim of priority over such incumbrance, lien is classed with, and has not priority over, liens originating prior to such incumbrance. (49-33).

Enforcement.—Mechanic's lien may be foreclosed in same manner as a mortgage. (49-33h).

Release or Discharge.—For form which may be used to release or discharge mechanic's lien see category Mortgages, topic Mortgages of Real Property.

Railroad Property.—Similar liens may be had against railroad properties for materials or labor furnished under contract with the railroad company, certificate of which should be filed in the office of the Secretary of State. (49-38).

Public Works.—General contractor on public construction job exceeding $25,000 must furnish bond in amount of contract with surety for protection of persons supplying labor and material, providing no bond required for any general bid where total estimated cost of labor and material is less than $25,000 or for any sub-bid where total estimated cost of labor and material is less than $50,000. (49-41). Suit may be brought on bond by unpaid persons if payment not made within 90 days after last labor was done or last material furnished. Any person who furnishes labor or materials, including one having contract with sub-contractor but not with principal, may sue on bond provided he gives proper notice to surety and to principal within 180 days from date of performing last labor or supplying last material. (49-42). Suit on bond must be brought within one year after last labor performed or material supplied by plaintiff. (49-42[b]). If sub-contractors' work is set forth in requisition or estimate for payment, 180-day and one-year limitations period run from payment date to contractor, rather than date of last work or material supplied. (49-42, am'd PA 94-188). Public works contracts must require payment of subcontractors by general contractors within 30 days. If payment not made within 30 days, subcontractor must set forth his claim, and ten days thereafter general contractor liable for interest at 1% per month and, at subcontractor's written demand, must place claimed amount plus interest in bank escrow account. Contractor may refuse to fund escrow on ground that subcontractor failed to perform but is liable for subcontractor's attorney's fees and interest if litigation or arbitration determines that subcontractor in fact performed. General contractor must require each subcontractor to pay amounts due to its subcontractor or materialmen within 30 days of subcontractor's receipt of payment. (49-41a).

Dissolution of Liens on Real Estate.—Owner or any one interested in real estate may apply to judge of superior court or court of common pleas to dissolve lien thereon and substitute therefor bond. If certified copy of judge's order is filed with town clerk where real estate is situated within ten days lien is dissolved. Suit upon bond must be brought within one year. (49-37). Principal or surety on bond may make application to court for hearing to determine whether lien for which bond was substituted should be declared invalid or reduced in amount. (49-37). See catchline Proceedings to Discharge or Reduce, supra, for procedure and issues upon hearing.

Redemption.—There is no right to redeem property after a sale to enforce a lien.

For various other liens, see 7-118; 14-150; 15-75; 15-76; 16-129; 17-25; 17-280; 17-281; 20-325a; 40-60; 49-60; also topics Attachment, Pledges; categories Business Regulation and Commerce, topics Banks and Banking, Carriers, Factors; Civil Actions and Procedure, topic Judgments; Legal Profession, topic Attorneys and Counselors; Mortgages, topics Chattel Mortgages, Mortgages of Real Property; Property, topic Landlord and Tenant; Taxation, topic Taxes.

MECHANICS' LIENS:

See topic Liens.

PLEDGES:

Uniform Commercial Code adopted. (Tit. 42a). Governs most Pledge Relationships.

Pawnbrokers must obtain license and are regulated as to records, reports, interest, and sale of pledged property. (21-39; 21-46).

RECEIVERS:

Receivers may be appointed by any court of equitable jurisdiction as auxiliary to action for equitable relief. (73 Conn. 587, 48 Atl. 759). See topic Executions; categories Business Organizations, topic Corporations; Business Regulation and Commerce, topic Banks and Banking; Insurance, topic Insurance Companies.

Proceedings.—Application is made in court where action pending, or if such court is not in session, to Superior Court, and appointment is made after due notice is given. (52-504). Superior Court in judicial district where partner resides or partnership property is located may appoint receiver when partnership has been dissolved and partners cannot agree on settlement of its affairs. (52-509). Superior Court, on application of any partner or party to action, may appoint receiver in action in which partnership assets have been attached to secure claim against individual partner. (52-299). Commencement of proceedings for appointment of corporation or partnership receiver dissolves all

attachments, and all executions not completed, made within 60 days, but they revive if property is subsequently taken from receiver so that it cannot be subject to order of court, or if receivership is terminated. Legal costs of attaching or levying creditor before receivership are preferred claim if claim upon which attachment is founded is allowed in whole or in part. (52-514). See also categories Business Organizations, topic Corporations; Business Regulation and Commerce, topic Banks and Banking; Insurance, topic Insurance Companies.

Receiver may be appointed for association, community, or corporation organized wholly or partly for support of its members and having property upon which members depend for support (52-505) or for credit union (36-214).

Qualification.—Receiver must file bond with surety payable to state, in amount ordered by court before assuming duties (52-506), but state bank or trust company need not file bond unless so ordered (36-57).

Powers and Duties.—Receiver of corporations has right to possession of all its books, papers, and property, may bring or defend actions, and do all other acts necessary in execution of his trust. Under order of court he may have power of directors to call in subscriptions of stock. (52-507). Partnership receiver is entitled to possession of all its property, subject to order of court (52-511) which has power over management of partnership and disposition of its property (52-510).

Reports.—Receiver must file semi-annual reports of his doings in April and October. (52-508).

Removal.—Court may remove receiver at its pleasure, and fill vacancy in event receiver is removed, dies, or declines to act. (52-513).

REDEMPTION:

See topics Executions, Liens; categories Civil Actions and Procedure, topic Judgments; Mortgages, topic Mortgages of Real Property; Taxation.

SUPPLEMENTARY PROCEEDINGS:

See topic Executions.

TRUSTEE PROCESS:

See topic Garnishment.

USURY:

See category Business Regulation and Commerce, topic Interest.

DISPUTE RESOLUTION

ALTERNATIVE DISPUTE RESOLUTION:

Variety of court-sanctioned and independent programs exist to encourage resolution of civil disputes without necessity of full-scale trial on merits before judge or jury. All are voluntary. By court rule (P.B. 546T), parties may stipulate to pursue program of alternative dispute resolution, and court will stay judicial proceedings for period not to exceed 90 days. See also category Civil Actions and Procedure, topic Evidence, subhead Witnesses, catchline Mediation.

ARBITRATION AND AWARD:

An agreement in any written contract or in a separate writing executed by the parties to any written contract or in the articles of association or by-laws of an association or corporation to which both parties are members to arbitrate any controversy which may arise between them in the future, or an agreement in writing between two or more persons to submit to arbitration any controversy existing between them at the time of the agreement to submit, is valid, irrevocable and enforcible except when sufficient cause at law or equity exists for the avoidance of written contracts generally. (52-408).

Uniform Arbitration Act not adopted.

Unicitral Model Law on International Commercial Arbitration is enacted. (PA 89-179).

Court proceedings may be stayed upon motion of any party to the arbitration agreement who is willing to proceed with such arbitration, when it appears that an agreement to arbitrate has been made. (52-409).

Compelling Proceeding with Arbitration.—If one party to an arbitration agreement neglects or refuses to proceed with the arbitration thereunder, the other party may apply to the superior court having jurisdiction for an order directing the parties to proceed with the arbitration in compliance with their agreement. (52-410).

If the agreement to arbitrate contains no method of appointing an arbitrator or if the method so provided for any reason fails to name an umpire, any party may apply to the superior court having jurisdiction for the appointment of an arbitrator. (52-411).

Attendance of Witnesses and Production of Documents.—Any arbitrator or umpire or any other person qualified to issue subpoenas in civil actions may issue subpoenas for attendance of witnesses and production of documents at arbitration hearings. (52-412).

Hearing.—All the arbitrators must meet and act together during the hearing, but, when met, a majority, or, in the event of an equal division of opinion, the presiding arbitrator (51-183e) may determine any question. If additional arbitrator is selected or appointed after evidence is heard, matter must be reheard unless such rehearing is waived in writing. (52-414).

Assistance of Court.—Upon request of all the parties to the arbitration, the arbitrator must make application to any designated court or judge for a decision on any issue, provided such parties agree that such decision shall be final and bind the arbitrator. (52-415).

Time for Rendering Award.—If time within which an award must be rendered is not fixed in agreement, arbitrator must render award within 30 days after completion of hearings or submission of additional material after hearings. Award thereafter made is

---

ARBITRATION AND AWARD . . . *continued*

void unless parties expressly, in writing, extend time in which award may be made. (52-416).

Court Action on Award.—At any time within one year after the rendition and notification of an award by arbitrators, either party may apply to superior court in judicial district in which one of parties resides (or, if controversy concerns land, in county in which land is situated) for order confirming award, which award court must confirm unless it vacates, modifies or corrects it. (52-417). Award shall be vacated if procured by fraud, corruption or undue means, if partiality or corruption on part of any of arbitrators is evident, if arbitrators have been guilty of misconduct in refusing to postpone hearing or to hear material evidence or if arbitrators exceeded or imperfectly executed their powers. If vacated, court may order rehearing by arbitrators if time for rendering award has not expired. Notice of application to vacate award of State Board of Mediation and Arbitration shall be made to Board and Attorney General within five days of filing. (52-418). Superior court may modify or correct award in event of evident material mistake on their own principles upon application of any party to arbitration. (52-419). Any motion to vacate, modify or correct award must be made within 30 days of notice of award to moving party. (52-420). If award is confirmed it may be enforced (52-421) and is subject to appeal (52-423) in same manner as any judgment of superior court.

Arrest on Execution.—See category Debtor and Creditor, topic Executions.

DOCUMENTS AND RECORDS

ACKNOWLEDGMENTS:

Uniform Acknowledgment Act adopted. (1-28 to 1-41). See category Courts and Legislature, topic Statutes, subhead Uniform Acts.

May be taken by following officers or in accordance with Uniform Acknowledgments Act.

Within state: judge of U.S. or state court of record; clerk of superior or district court or court of common pleas; justice of peace (in county for which elected); secretary of school fund (3-47); commissioner of superior court (51-85); in conveyance of real estate, notary public (anywhere in state); town clerk or assistant town clerk. Not necessary that seal of office be affixed. (47-5A). Fee shall not exceed $1 plus 15¢ for each mile of travel. (3-95). Social workers, social worker trainees, paralegals, and certified legal interns performing duties within Public Defender Services Commission, and any state trooper or member of local police department may take acknowledgment with reference to any statement made by or to police. (PA 96-58).

Without state but within U.S.: in conveyance of real estate, any officer authorized to take acknowledgments of deeds in state or territory where taken; commissioner appointed by Governor of Connecticut and residing in such state or territory. (4-21; 47-5A).

Without U.S.: in conveyance of real estate, ambassador, minister, chargé d'affaires, consul, vice consul, deputy consul, consul general, vice consul general, deputy consul general, consular agent, vice consular agent, commercial agent or vice commercial agent of U.S.; notary public or justice of peace or any other public officer before whom oaths may be taken or acknowledgments made, of country where taken within territorial limits of his jurisdiction. (47-5A).

Officers in U. S. Armed Forces.—Acknowledgment of any person in U. S. Armed Forces may be taken by any officer of such forces of the rank of Second Lieutenant, Ensign or higher. No authentication of officer's certificate is required but he must endorse thereon his rank and command to which he is attached. (27-137).

Uniform Recognition of Acknowledgments Act adopted (1-57 to 1-65), whereby, in addition to recognition accorded by any of above cited statutes: Notarial acts performed outside state by following recognized: (1) Notary public of place where act performed; (2) judge, clerk, or deputy clerk of court of record of place where act performed; (3) officer of U.S. Foreign Service, consular agent, or other person authorized by U.S. Department of State; (4) commissioned officer or other authorized person, in case of person in or with armed forces, merchant seaman, or dependents; or (5) anyone else authorized to perform notarial acts in place performed.

Proof of Authority.—Classifications (1) through (4) above: Signature, rank or title, and serial number, if any, sufficient. Person authorized by foreign country: U.S. foreign service officer resident in U.S. certifies authority of person holding such an office; or official seal affixed; or title and indication of authority appears in digest of foreign law or customarily used list. Notarial act by any other person: Certificate of clerk of court of record of place of act.

Following short forms may be used:

Forms
(1) For an individual acting in his own right:
State of . . . .
County of . . . .
The foregoing instrument was acknowledged before me this (date) by (name of person acknowledged.)
(Signature of person taking acknowledgment)
(Title or rank)
(Serial number, if any)
(2) For a corporation:
State of . . . .
County of . . . .
The foregoing instrument was acknowledged before me this (date) by (name of officer or agent, title or officer or agent) of (name of corporation acknowledging) a (state or place of incorporation) corporation, on behalf of the corporation.
(Signature of person taking acknowledgment)
(Title or rank)
(Serial number, if any)
(3) For a partnership:

State of . . . .
County of . . . .
The foregoing instrument was acknowledged before me this (date) by (name of acknowledging partner or agent), partner (or agent) on behalf of (name of partnership), a partnership.
(Signature of person taking acknowledgment)
(Title or rank)
(Serial number, if any)
(4) For an individual acting as principal by an attorney in fact:
State of . . . .
County of . . . .
The foregoing instrument was acknowledged before me this (date) by (name of attorney in fact) as attorney in fact on behalf of (name of principal).
(Signature of person taking acknowledgment)
(Title or rank)
(Serial number, if any)
(5) By any public officer, trustee, or personal representative:
State of . . . .
County of . . . .
The foregoing instrument was acknowledged before me this (date) by (name and title of position).
(Signature of person taking acknowledgment)
(Title or rank)
(Serial number, if any)

Interest in a corporation or a voluntary association does not disqualify a person from witnessing or taking the acknowledgment of the grantor in deeds to or from such corporation or the trustees of such association. (47-6).

Married women acknowledge like other persons; no special requirements.

Proof by Subscribing Witness.—Proof by a subscribing witness in lieu of an acknowledgment is not provided for in Connecticut.

Authentication.—Secretary of State authenticates signatures of judges and clerks and clerks of superior court, of state's attorneys and sheriffs, and of clerks and assistant clerks appointed by judges of superior court. (3-96). Fee $25. (3-99).

See also topic Notaries Public.

Validating Acts.—Any duly recorded instrument pertaining to or affecting any interest in real property, the acknowledgment of which was not completed, or was erroneously taken or recited, or was taken by a person without authority, or where such authority was not stated or authenticated, or where no acknowledgment was taken, was validated by 1967 Special Act.

Form.—The following form may be used:

Form
State of . . . . . . , County of . . . . ss. (City where taken) (Date).
Personally appeared John Jones, president of the A. B. Company, signer and sealer of the foregoing instrument, and acknowledged the same to be his free act and deed, and the free act and deed of said A. B. Company, before me . . . .
Or, Personally appeared John Doe and Anne Doe, signers and sealers of the foregoing instrument, and severally acknowledged the same to be their free act and deed, before me . . . .
(Official seal). . . . . (Official title)

See also forms contained in Uniform Acknowledgments Act. (1-28 to 1-41).

Alternative to Acknowledgment or Proof.—No statutory provision.

AFFIDAVITS:

Affidavits may be sworn to before notary public, or any magistrate authorized to administer oaths in place where they are made, but should have annexed certificate of official capacity from clerk of court of record. (47-5a).

No particular form is prescribed. Person objecting to taking oath may execute affidavit on solemn affirmation. (1-23).

Affidavits are generally used in ex parte proceedings such as uncontested divorces, uncontested foreclosures, injunction and receivership proceedings, where a finding of fact may be based on an affidavit. Files, records, votes and proceedings of any court, community, corporation, society or public board having a clerk may be proved by sworn copies. (52-171).

Alternative to Affidavit.—No statutory provision.

NOTARIES PUBLIC:

Term begins on date of appointment and ends five years later on last day of month of appointment unless notary is suspended or resigns. Certificate of oath must be recorded by town clerk of town in which notary resides within 30 days. (3-92). Notary must be at least 18. (3-91). Notary who ceases to reside within state must resign immediately by filing with Secretary of State signed, written notice of resignation. (PA 90-154, §16).

Appointments.—Secretary of State may appoint as notary public any person who: (1) Is 18 years of age or older; (2) is resident of state of Connecticut at time of application and appointment, or has one's principal place of business in Connecticut; (3) passes written examination approved or administered by secretary; (4) submits application accompanied by: (a) application fee of $60, and (b) recommendation of individual who has personally known applicant for one year. Secretary may deny application based on: (1) Applicant's conviction of felony or crime involving dishonesty or moral turpitude; (2) revocation, suspension or restriction of notary public appointment or professional license issued to applicant by this state or any other state; or (3) applicant's official misconduct whether or not any disciplinary action has resulted. (3-94b).

Reappointments.—Notary public may apply for reappointment on form provided by secretary with fee of $60 after being notified by secretary 90 days prior to expiration of previous term. (PA 90-154, §4).

See note at head of Digest as to 1998 legislation covered.

See Topical Index in front part of this volume.

NOTARIES PUBLIC . . . *continued*

Police Notaries.—Secretary of State may appoint as notary publics any number of state police majors, captains, lieutenants and sergeants. Secretary shall not charge any such person application fee. Notary appointed under this section shall exercise his authority only on administration of oaths and affirmations in taking of acknowledgments as pertain to official police matters. Upon terminating employment with state police notary appointed under this section shall immediately resign in writing. (PA 90-154, §5).

Behavior in Office.—Notary public shall not influence person to enter into or refrain from lawful transaction. Notary public shall not unreasonably refuse to perform notarial acts. Notary public is disqualified from performing notarial act if notary is: (1) Signatory of or named in document that is to be notarized; (2) will receive directly from transaction any commission, fee, advantage, right, title, interest, cash, property or other consideration that exceeds in value statutory fee permitted for performing notarial act; or (3) is legally related to person for whom notarial act is to be performed. Notary public shall not: (1) Notarize any document that contains statement known by such notary to be false; (2) notarize blank document; (3) perform any official action with intent to deceive or defraud; or (4) use notary title or seal in endorsement or promotional statement for any product, service, contest, or other offering. Notary public, except those appointed within state police, may keep and use official notarial seal. In completing notarial act notary public shall sign on notarial certificate only his or her own name. If notary public utilized notarial seal, notary shall affix impression in notarial seal which shall include: (1) Notary's name exactly as it appears on notary certificate of appointment; (2) words "notary public" and "Connecticut"; and (3) "My Commission Expires" with commission expiration date following. If notary does not utilize notarial seal or stamp words "notary public" and "My Commission Expires" shall be typed or printed legibly by notary near notary's official signature. (PA 90-154, §§6-11).

Liability.—Notary public shall be liable to any person for all damages proximately caused to that person by notary's official misconduct. Employer of notary shall be liable to any person for any damages proximately caused to that person by notary's official misconduct related to employer's business if employer directed, encouraged, consented to, ratified or approved notary's official misconduct. Employer of notary shall also be liable to notary for all damages recovered from notary as result of official misconduct that was coerced by threat of employer if threat was made in reference to particular notarial act or implicitly by employer's previous actions. Employer shall also be liable to notary for damages caused by demotion, dismissal or other action resulting from notary's refusal to commit official misconduct. (PA 90-154, §12).

Powers of Secretary of State.—Secretary may deliver written official warning and reprimand to notary as result of such notary's official misconduct or on any ground for which application for employment as notary may be denied. Lapse of appointment as notary shall not stop or preclude any investigation into such notary's conduct by secretary. Within 30 days after resignation, revocation or suspension of notary's certificate of appointment secretary shall notify all town clerks within state of such resignation, revocation or suspension. (PA 90-154, §13).

Powers.—Notaries may administer oaths (1-24), take acknowledgments on deeds with or without his seal (47-5a), take depositions (52-148c), issue subpoenas to deponents (52-148e), and at request of Commissioner appointed to take testimony, may issue subpoenas or capias, and on failure of witness to appear and testify, may commit him to prison (52-155).

Notary may exercise functions of office at any place in state. (3-91).

Notarial seal is normally sufficient evidence of his official capacity. (38 Conn. 230).

Certificate of authority and official acts of notary may be given by clerk of town where notary resides or is employed. (3-92). Fee $10 for recording commission and oath of notary; $2 for certifying under seal to official character of notary. (7-34a[a]).

Fees.—Fee for any act performed by notary in accordance with provisions of general statutes must not exceed $2, plus additional 25¢ for each mile of travel. (3-95). For taking acknowledgment of any instrument or signing and issuing subpoena or capias, 25¢; for administering oath out of court, 10¢. $2 fee is charged by superior court for recording certificate and oath, and for certificate of authority. (52-259[a]).

Commissioners of deeds for other states, District of Columbia, and any U. S. territory, are appointed by Governor for term of five years from date of commission. (4-21). Before exercising powers Commissioner must file with Secretary an affidavit of faithful performance of duties. He has power to take acknowledgments of deeds and other instruments required to be acknowledged, administer oaths or affirmations, examine witnesses and take depositions for use in courts of state. (4-21).

Officers of U. S. Armed Forces, in active service, may take acknowledgments. (1-38). See topic Acknowledgments.

Legal officers and officers of rank of Lt. Comm. or Major or above may administer oaths to persons serving in armed forces and their spouses. (1-24; 3-91).

RECORDS:

Town clerks have charge of records relating to real property. (7-24; 7-25).

Filing Under Commercial Code.—Uniform Commercial Code governs most personal property records with respect to security interests and personalty which are filed with Secretary of State (30 Trinity Street, UCC Division, Hartford, CT 06106), except motor vehicles subject to Uniform Certificate of Title and Anti-Theft Act which are filed with Commissioner of Motor Vehicles, and fixtures which are filed with Town Clerk. Fees for filing with Secretary of State are as follows: Financing statements, $25; Statement of Continuation, Partial Release, Assignment, (UCC-3), $25, Termination Statement (#3 copy of Original UCC-1), $25; Request for Information (UCC-11), $25; Request for Copies (first three pages), $5, each additional page, $5; Certification (additional fee), $5; financing statement covering timber to be cut or covering minerals or the like, including oil and gas or accounts subject to subsection (5) of 42a-9-402 or when financing statement is filed as fixture filing and collateral is goods which are or are to become fixtures, $6 in addition to appropriate filing fee; Bulk Transfer—Notice of Affidavit of No Creditors, $20; Bulk Transfer—Schedule of Property and List of Creditors, first two pages, $25; Lien Notice, $25, Copy, $20, Release, $25; Notice of Attachment, $25; Releases of Attachment, $25. (PA 89-251, §183). Submit all fees for different types of transactions on separate checks.

Inspection of Statements filed with secretary of state, $25 per debtor filed in alphabetical index. (42a-9-403).

Recordable Instruments.—Conveyances of land, mortgages, assignments and liens on real estate must be recorded with the clerk of the town in which the land lies, in order to be effectual against any other person than the grantor and his heirs (47-10), and same is true of leases for more than one year or which provide for renewal thereof or option to purchase real estate involved (47-19). Defectively executed deeds, land sale contracts and other instruments creating equitable interest in land, in which land is adequately described, may be recorded, and thus be notice of equitable interest created. (47-17).

Validation of Acts and Deeds.—No assessment list completed prior to effective date of act will be deemed invalid because assessor failed to perform certain enumerated duties and tasks with respect to the list. (S.A. 97-6, §1[a]; H.B. 6402).

No assessment list completed prior to effective date of act will be deemed invalid because board of tax review or its member(s) failed to perform certain enumerated duties and tasks with respect to the list. (S.A. 97-6, §1[b]; H.B. 6402). No tax lien with certificate recorded prior to effective date of act will be deemed invalid due to certain enumerated acts or omissions of municipal officials and/or employees. (S.A. 97-6, §1[d]; H.B. 6402).

No vote or action fixing tax rates providing discounts for early payment, nor collection proceedings thereunder will be deemed invalid. (S.A. 97-6, §1[e]; H.B. 6402).

Related legislation pertaining to tax assessment/collection errors and omissions. (S.A. 97-6, §1[f]; H.B. 6402).

Lis Pendens.—Notice of lis pendens may be recorded in actions affecting real property. (52-325). Notice of lis pendens prohibited if based on allegation of illegal, invalid, or defective transfer of real estate interest unless court claim concerning such transfer contains date of challenged transfer and transfer occurred fewer than 60 years before court claim. (PA 93-4, Oct. Special Session). Notice expires after 15 years unless rerecorded. (PA 87-360). Certain railroad conveyances must be filed with Secretary of State. (16-59).

In addition, the following instruments affecting title to land must be recorded in office of town clerk for town where land lies: probate certificate of freedom from claim for succession taxes in case of joint ownership of real property (12-363; 12-364); certificate of change of name of person or corporation (47-12, 13); certificate of attachment (7-30; 52-285); certificate of judgment lien (52-380a; 49-46a); certificate of garnishment of mortgage debt (52-346); certificate of tax lien (12-173); certificate of foreclosure (49-16); certificate of satisfaction of judgment of foreclosure (49-21); certificate of mechanic's lien (49-34; 49-39); certificate of appointment of conservator (45-74); certificate of taking land by appraisal (47-15). Liens in favor of U.S. may be recorded. (49-36; 49-32). Development maps may be filed. (7-34a[a]). Public service companies must file any maps prepared in connection with acquisition of any interest in real property. (16-50a). Electric light, water, gas, power and railway company mortgages may be recorded with Secretary of State instead of with various town clerks. (16-59; 49-5).

See further, as to other instruments which must be filed or recorded, categories Business Organizations, topics Corporations, Partnerships, subhead Limited Partnership; Business Regulation and Commerce, topic Banks and Banking; Debtor and Creditor, topic Liens; Insurance, topic Insurance Companies; Intellectual Property, topic Trademarks and Tradenames; Property, topic Landlord and Tenant.

Requisites for Recording.—Instruments that must be recorded on land records must be signed by grantor with his own hand or with his mark with his name thereto annexed, or by his attorney, and attested by two witnesses with their own hands and acknowledged by the grantor or his attorney to be his free act and deed. (47-5).

Recording Fees.—$7.50 for recording first page of statutory form warranty deed, quit claim deed, mortgage deed, or assignment of mortgage. $5 for each additional page of such documents. $1 for each marginal notation of assignment of mortgage. (7-34a[a]). For each page or part thereof of other documents $10 for first page and $5 for subsequent page or part thereof. (17-34a[1]). Page must not exceed 8 1/2 x 14 inches. $1 additional for any document without typed, printed or stamped names of persons executing, witnessing or acknowledging instrument; $5 additional where no current mailing address; $5 for filing survey map; $5 for indexing survey or map ($15 if subdivision map); and $5 for filing any other document. (7-34a[a]). Additional $5 fee is charged for recording certain documents with respect to which data must be submitted to state tax commissioner. (7-34a[a]). $10 fee for recording commission and oath of notary public; $2 for certifying under seal to official character of notary. (7-34a[a]).

Foreign Conveyances or Encumbrances.—A conveyance, mortgage, release of mortgage or lien of real estate located in Connecticut, or any power of attorney authorizing another to convey any interest in Connecticut land, executed and acknowledged in another state or territory in accordance with the laws of that state or territory or in accord with laws of this state is valid. (47-7).

Effect of Records.—Land records constitute constructive notice. (109 Conn. 433, 146 Atl. 843). Conveyances, mortgages, assignments, and other instruments affecting title must be recorded in order to be valid against subsequent purchasers or incumbrancers, and one who relies in good faith upon record title apparently complete is protected against any claimed interests not of record of which he has no notice. (117 Conn. 558, 169 Atl. 192). Time of recording, in most instances, determines priority of claim, but deed recorded in reasonable time after delivery prevails over attachment made after delivery but prior to record. (40 Conn. 83).

Torrens Act.—Not adopted.

Transfer of Decendent's Title.—In case of death of the owner, mortgagee, or lienor of real estate situated in Connecticut, administration of the estate, either domiciliary or ancillary, is necessary to clear the title of his heirs or devisees. The executor or administrator must, within two months after qualification, file with the town clerk for the town where real estate is situated a certificate stating death of the owner, his

RECORDS . . . *continued*

residence and whether he left a will. (45-259). After completing settlement of estate, executor or administrator must obtain from probate court certificate of devise or descent, describing land and probate proceedings with reference thereto and method by which land was divided, set out or descended to persons entitled thereto, which certificate must be filed with town clerk for town where land lies within one month after acceptance of final account. (45-286).

Vital Statistics.—Records of births, upon affidavit of mother or father, deaths and marriages are filed in office of registrar of vital statistics of town where they occur. (7-42). Statutes govern contents, indices, etc., of records. (7-36, 7-45). No fee required for filing; fee of $15 for certified copy of certificate of birth and $15 for certification of birth registration. (7-74). Such fees not required of state or federal agencies. Fee for marriage license, $10 plus $20 surcharge. (7-73). Certified copy of death certificate, $5. (7-74). Burial or removal permit, $3. (7-73).

Establishing Birth Records.—Any adult, or the guardian of the person of any minor, for whose birth no certificate is on file, may, with two other persons having knowledge of facts, make affidavit as to facts required, which are as follows: name, place and date of birth, sex, name of father, maiden name of mother, age, color, residence and birthplace of each of parents, occupation of father, number of child, name and address of medical attendant, and any other information required by State Department of Health. Affidavit must be filed with town clerk in town of birth, who thereupon prepares certificate, or if registrar finds affidavit unsatisfactory, probate court will, on hearing after application, order registrar to issue a certificate based on facts found by probate court. (7-57). No certificate may contain any reference to illegitimacy. (7-42).

As to birth certificate in adoption cases, see category Family, topic Adoption.

Medical records must be disclosed to patient or representative with authorization. (19a-490a). Fee for copy of records limited. (19a-490). Limitations on disclosure. (PA 98-18).

SEALS:

All instruments executed by any person or corporation not having an official or corporate seal, purporting and intended to be specialties or under seal, and not otherwise sealed than by addition of the word "seal" or the letters "L.S." or in case of an official or corporate seal, by an impression of the seal upon the paper are deemed to be sealed instruments, and received in evidence as such (52-179) but word "seal" or letters "L.S." do not make an instrument a specialty unless instrument itself purports to be one (110 Conn. 413, 148 Atl. 367).

Corporation Seal.—Duly organized corporation has power to make and use a common seal and alter the same at pleasure.

Effect of Seal.—Presence of seal imports consideration, but real consideration may be inquired into. (97 Conn. 193, 116 Atl. 239). Contract under seal may be varied by parol agreement. (121 Conn. 163, 183 Atl. 887).

TORRENS ACT:

Not adopted in Connecticut.

VITAL STATISTICS:

See topic Records.

EDUCATION

COMPUTER TRAINING:

§37 modifies CGS §10-145b(1) regarding at least 15 hours of continuing education requirement for certified employees of local and regional boards of education shall be in computer training.

EMPLOYMENT DIVERSITY:

HB 5118; PA 98-252, §13 modifies CGS §10-220(a) regarding each local or regional board of education that must develop and implement written plan for minority staff recruitment. (CGS §10-4a[3]).

EMPLOYMENT

EMPLOYER AND EMPLOYEE:

See topic Labor Relations.

LABOR RELATIONS:

Working conditions and wages are under supervision of Commissioner of Labor and Factory Inspection and Wage Board. (31-1 to 31-76h). Labor disputes are under supervision of Board of Mediation and Arbitration and State Board of Labor Relations. Fair employment practices are under supervision of Commission on Human (not Civil) Rights. (460a-60, et seq., formerly 31-122; 31-222[a][1][d]; 31-237i; 31-237j, 31-245, 31-247; 31-248). Information and notices regarding carcinogens required to be posted by employer. (31-40[d],[e],[f]). Employer required to notify employees of electronic monitoring; does not apply to criminal investigations. Civil fines up to $3,000 per offense. (PA 98-142).

Discrimination.—HB 5673, PA 98-245, §1 modifies CGS §46a-57 regarding appointment and compensation duties and authority of hearing officers of CHRO; §2 modifies CGS §46a-86 regarding procedure following filing of two discriminatory practice complaints with CHRO; answers to complaints and review of allegations and investigation; probable or no cause determinations; §3 modifies CGS §46a-832 regarding dismissal of complaint; §4 modifies CGS §46a-84 regarding certification of complaint, hearing and answer; §5 modifies CGS §46a-942 regarding appeals from decisions of hearing officers; §6 modifies CGS §46a-100 regarding commencement of Superior Court action; §7 modifies CGS §46a-101 regarding releases from CHRO jurisdiction; §9 modifies CGS §46a-54 regarding powers and duties of CHRO; §10 modifies CGS §46a-68h regarding issuance of orders per CGS §46a-56; show cause motions; §11 modifies CGS §46a-68i regarding rights of appeal regarding orders per CGS §46a-68h; and §12 modifies CGS §46a-52(c) regarding appointment of CHRO executive director.

Note: §8 (new) regarding pending complaints; requests for hearings.

Hours.—Eight hours of labor in any one day is a legal day's work unless otherwise agreed. (31-21). No person is required to work for more than 7½ consecutive hours without 30 consecutive minutes for meal. Exemption from requirements possible if compliance is adverse to public safety, duties of position performed only by one employee, etc. Provisions do not apply to employees of board of education of any town or school district. (PA 89-71). No mechanic in state institution may work more than eight hours a day except in case of emergency. (5-73). Contract for construction or repair of public building must provide that no person may work more than eight hours a day or more than 40 hours a week on such work, but in emergency Comptroller may suspend this limitation. (31-57).

Contract for construction or repair of state bridge must contain similar 48-hour limitation, which may be suspended by commissioner of transportation. (31-56). Employee in state institution, except one employed in professional capacity may work only an average of 48 hours per week during any six weeks period, except in case of unavoidable emergency. (5-73). See also catchline Minors, Elders 66 or Over, Handicapped, Disabled Veterans, infra.

Minors, elders 66 or over, handicapped, disabled veterans, not permanent salaried employees in executive, administrative or professional positions, normally may not work in any manufacturing or mechanical establishment more than nine hours in one day or 48 hours in a calendar week, but under certain conditions exception may be made (31-12), in mercantile establishment, not more than eight hours a day, nor more than six days a week, nor more than 48 hours a week, but here also Commissioner may make exception (31-13). Hours in which above may work in public restaurant, dining room, barber shop, hair dressing or manicuring establishment, amusement or recreational establishment, bowling alley, shoe shining establishment, billiard or poolroom or photographic gallery are limited. (31-18). Night work in manufacturing, mechanical or mercantile establishment by minors under 18 between 10 P.M. and 6 A.M. is forbidden unless Governor suspends this limitation or unless minor has graduated from secondary institution. (31-14). Night work by minor in messenger service also is limited. (31-16). Minors under 16 may not be employed in any manufacturing, mercantile, mechanical or theatrical industry, restaurant, bowling alley, shoe-shining establishment or barber shop (31-23[a]), nor in certain hazardous employments (31-24), nor in operation of elevator (31-25). Fifteen year-old minors may be employed in mercantile establishment as baggers, stock clerks, or cashiers. Hours strictly limited during school year. (31-23[b]).

Minor may not be employed in occupation pronounced hazardous by State Department of Health or Department of Labor and Factory Inspection unless 16 or over and either apprentice in bona fide apprenticeship course in manufacturing or mechanical establishment, vocational school or public school, or vocational or secondary school graduate. (31-23[b]). Employer of minor must also obtain certificate from this Board. (10-193; 31-23[c], am'd PA 86-333, §§26, 32). Statutes as to hours and conditions of minors apply to home workers. (31-30). Minors under 18 may not work in tavern or other permit premises except package store. (31-81; 31-90a). Minors under 14 may not be employed in agriculture, and hours and conditions for minors under 16 employed in agricultural work are strictly regulated. (22-13; 22-14).

Charitable Work.—State employees may accrue additional vacation time for each full year employee participates in Big Brother and Big Sister Programs. Eligibility for additional vacation time shall be determined. (HB 5718; PA 98-257).

Hazardous Conditions.—Private, state and municipal employees have right to act concerning hazardous conditions. (PA 91-33).

Industrial Homework.—Person using residential building for manufacturing must obtain license from Commissioner (31-29), and all homeworkers must obtain permits (31-33). Terms and conditions of such work are regulated. (31-29 to 31-33). Minimum wage $3.75 as of Oct. 1, 1987, $4.25 as of Oct. 1, 1988. (31-58[j]).

Wages.—Minimum wage is $5.75, effective Jan. 1, 1999 and $6.15, effective Jan. 1, 2000. (PA 98-44). Industrial employees must be paid weekly the wages earned within eight days of such payment: if employee leaves voluntarily, he must be paid in full on next regular pay day, and if discharged, on next business day after discharge but upon application, labor commissioner may waive requirements as to any particular weeks and may permit less frequent but at least monthly, payments. (31-71i). Discrimination in amount of compensation paid an employee on account of sex is prohibited. (31-75). Employer withholding wages because of express agreement as to notice before leaving is subject to fine. (31-70). Employer may not deduct or receive refund as fee for severing or continuing employment (31-73) nor may employer make discount or deduction from wages when they are paid at earlier time than that at which such wages would regularly have been paid (31-74). Promissory notes to pay employer if employee leaves employment before certain date are prohibited as condition of employment. Agreements requiring employee to repay loans, observe conditions of sabbatical leaves, or comply with programs bargained for collectively are not prohibited. (31-51r, am'd PA 87-42).

Regular deduction of specified amount for payment of union dues in accordance with contract between employer and employees or their collective bargaining agent is allowed. (52-361a; 52-361[g]).

Workmen on construction, remodeling or repair of public building must be paid prevailing wage for same work in town where building is located unless total cost of all work is less than $200,000. (31-53).

Claim for wages due from corporation or partnership in receivership or from insolvent debtor for labor within three months of receivership or insolvency proceedings are preferred up to $600. (33-115; 52-512). In insolvent estates claim for wages due from deceased for work within three months of death are entitled to 4th priority. (45-229). Where unpaid wages of decedent are less than $5,000, employer may pay them directly to next of kin, physician, or funeral director under certain circumstances. (45-266).

For assignment of wages, see category Debtor and Creditor, topic Assignments.

See note at head of Digest as to 1998 legislation covered.

See Topical Index in front part of this volume.

CT – 24

LABOR RELATIONS . . . continued

Where Commissioner finds that any substantial number of workers in any occupation, other than domestic service or farm labor, are receiving less than reasonable wages, he may appoint a wage board to report on establishment of minimum fair wage rate of not less than the federal minimum wage per hour for that occupation. (31-59). Board consists of equal number of representatives of employees, employers and public, has full powers of investigation, and reports minimum fair wage standard with reasonable differentiations as to type of work, employee, locality, etc. (31-61). Upon acceptance of report by Commissioner and proper hearing after notice he issues appropriate order to carry report into effect. (31-62). Person aggrieved by order may seek review in Superior Court. (31-63). Orders may be reconsidered (31-64) or modified (31-65). Any deficiency in wages paid below minimum fixed by order may be recovered in civil action by employee or by Commissioner as trustee for employee, and agreement to work for less is no defense. (31-68).

Retirement Benefits.—(PA 98-251). Changes to qualification requirements for teachers (CGS §§10-183e; 10-183g; 10-183i); survivorship and monthly benefits (CGS §10-183h).

Family and Medical Leave.—As of July 1, 1991 maximum leave for employees of employers with 75 or more employees, with family or medical reasons shall be 16 weeks of unpaid leave within any two year period. (PA 89-382). Many provisions of Federal Family and Medical Leave Act adopted. (PA 96-140).

Drug testing of applicants and employees regulated. (PA 87-551).

Labor Unions.—No "right to work" legislation enacted.

Labor disputes may be submitted by parties to State Board of Mediation and Arbitration with written statements of grievances and complaints upon promise to stay at work without strike or lockout until Board renders decision, but such promise is not binding unless written decision rendered within ten days after investigation completed. No panel of said board may consider any claim that issue before panel is improper for arbitration unless party making claim has notified opposing party and chairman of panel of claim, in writing, at least ten days prior to hearing date, except panel may consider claim if it determines there was reasonable cause for failure to comply with notice requirement. (31-97). In case of strike or lockout, actual or seriously threatened, Board must endeavor to effect settlement, and may inquire into causes of trouble and issue subpoenas. (31-99). Powers and duties of Board in case of strike or lockout may be exercised or performed in case of dispute that has not reached strike or lockout stage, upon request of either party. (31-95).

Picketing of residences is forbidden. (31-120). No employer, except state or any political subdivision thereof, or employee organization involved in labor dispute shall hire any member of municipal police department in town in which dispute taking place for protection or other duties related to dispute during period of dispute. (31-48c).

Occupational Licenses.—Any person, who engages in or practices work or occupation that requires license without license or apprentice permit, or willfully employs or supplies for employment, without license shall be fined not more than $100. (20-341).

Unfair employment practices involving racial, marital status, age, sex, physical disability, mental retardation, genetic information or religious discrimination by employers, unions or others are prohibited. (31-126, PA 98-180). Commission on Human Rights and Opportunities has power to investigate such practices (31-125), hear complaints of persons aggrieved by such practices and issue cease and desist orders. Complaints must be filed within 180 days of alleged act of discrimination, except that any complaint based on 4-61o(a) must be filed within 30 days. (31-127). Orders may be enforced by injunction or otherwise, and person aggrieved by Commission order may appeal within 30 days after mailing of notice of final decision, to superior court for judicial district of Hartford-New Britain or judicial district wherein aggrieved resides. (31-128[d]; 52-48; 52-49). Commission must rule within 90 days of close of evidence. (PA 96-241).

Whistleblower protection provided by 31-51m, but action alleging violation must be brought within 90 days of discharge. Whistleblower protection applies to state departments and agencies and quasi-public agencies (4-61dd), public service companies, public holding companies, nuclear regulatory commission licensees (16-8a, am'd PA 98-68).

Labor Relations Act gives employees the right of self-organization, to form, join or assist labor organizations, to bargain collectively, and to engage in concerted activities. (31-104). It is an unfair labor practice for an employer (1) to spy upon employees' activities in the exercise of their rights; (2) to engage in blacklisting activities; (3) to interfere with formation or administration of any employee organization or contribute support to it by any means, except that employer may permit employee to confer with him during working hours without loss of time or pay; (4) to require employee or potential employee to join company union or to refrain from participation in labor organization of his own choosing; (5) to encourage membership in company union or discourage membership in labor organization by discrimination in regard to hire or tenure or any term or condition of employment, but employer may agree with labor organization to require membership therein as condition of employment if organization is representative of employees under Act; (6) to refuse to bargain collectively or discuss grievances with representative of employees, subject to provisions of Act; (7) to discharge or discriminate against any employee because he has participated in proceeding under Act; (8) to do any other acts which restrain, coerce or interfere with employees in exercise of their rights under Act. (31-105).

The Board of Labor Relations supervises and regulates the method and procedure for selection of exclusive employee representative for purposes of collective bargaining. When petitioned, Board has power to investigate question of representation through agent, order elections, certify results. (31-106[b]; 5-275[a]; 7-471). When petitioned, Board has power of clarification or modification of existing unit. (PA 91-255). Board has power to prevent unfair labor practices, including power to hold hearings, issue findings, order cessation of unfair practices, to withdraw recognition or refrain from bargaining with company union, and order reinstatement with or without back pay, but Board may not require as condition of taking action or issuing order that employees on strike or engaged in any other lawful concerted activity shall discontinue strike or

activity. (31-107). Board may petition Superior Court for enforcement of its orders and for appropriate temporary relief or restraining order, Superior Court has exclusive jurisdiction to review final orders of board. (31-109). Persons subject to National Labor Relations Act, Federal Railway Labor Act unless federal agency declines to assert jurisdiction, political subdivisions, charitable, educational or religious organizations and persons engaged in farming, are not "employees" under Act. (31-101).

Willful interference with Board's functions or with employees' right to select representative is punishable by fine or imprisonment or both. (31-111).

Injunctive relief in labor disputes is strictly limited (31-113) and may be used only in certain cases. (31-115). Liability of unions and union officers for unlawful acts of individuals is restricted. (31-114). Injunction may not be made permanent unless plaintiff proves written notice to Commissioner of willingness to submit dispute to arbitration or mediation. (31-117). Person aggrieved by issuance or denial of temporary injunction in labor dispute may appeal to Appellate Court on question of law. (31-118).

Workers' Compensation Act (31-275 to 31-355a) is administered by Workers' Compensation Commission, 16 person board, one who serves as chairman (31-276[a]). Employer-employee advisory board to assist chairperson. (PA 91-339, §3). ·

Persons Included.—Employee is any person employed, either within or without state, including municipal employees and members of General Assembly. But term excludes out-workers, casual employees, members of employee's family unless said family member's wages or salary are included in payroll upon which insurance premium is based, persons performing services around private dwellings not regularly employed more than 26 hours per week and corporate employees electing not to be covered by provisions of this Act and persons not resident in Connecticut but injured in state, unless person spends 50% or more of time in state or is working under contract of employment to be performed in this state (31-275). Employer is not liable unless injury can be traced to employment other than through weakened resistance or lowered vitality nor for accidental injury due to habitual use of alcohol or narcotic drugs nor due to willful misconduct of employee. Policemen and firemen covered portal to portal. (31-275). "Injury" deemed not to include; (A) injury which results from voluntary participation in any activity of social or recreational nature such as athletic events, parties, picnics which employer pays some or all expenses of; (B) mental or emotional impairment not arising from physical injury or occupational disease; (C) mental or emotional impairment which results from personnel action (transfer, promotion, demotion, termination). (31-275).

Employer is not liable for action in damages, the employee's exclusive remedy being under this Act. Common law may provide for damages for intentional tort by employer. Employer who fails to provide worker's compensation insurance or to adequately self-insure potential liability to workers may be sued. (31-284, am'd 96-65). Each employer must either furnish Compensation Commission satisfactory proof of solvency and financial ability to pay injured employee, or insure his full liability. Willful failure to comply with this provision results in fine of not more than $1,000 for each failure. (31-275).

Construction design professional and his employees not liable for injury on construction project for which compensation is payable under this chapter, except for negligent preparation of design plans or specifications, or unless responsibility expressly assumed by contract. (31-293).

Any person, firm, association or corporation which suffers damages as result of competitive bid for project involving construction, repair, remodeling, alteration, conversion or renovation of building or structure not being accepted due to another person, firm, association or corporation knowingly violating provisions of c. 567 or 568 of general statutes, may bring action for damages in Superior Court. For purposes of action brought pursuant to this section, employee status shall be determined by applicable provisions of Internal Revenue Code of 1986, or any subsequent corresponding Internal Revenue Code of U.S. as from time to time amended. (PA 90-273).

If principal employer has work done, which is a part or process of his trade or business, on or about premises under his control, by a contractor, or through him by a subcontractor, he is liable to pay compensation to same extent as if work were done without intervention of such contractor or subcontractor. Principal employer does not have immunity from civil action to recover damages for personal injury or wrongful death unless he has paid injured employee or his dependents workers' compensation benefits. (31-291). When worker temporarily lent to another by employer, latter under Act continues to be employer of such worker while he is so lent or hired by another. (31-292).

When injuries are sustained under circumstances rendering the employer liable under the Act and some third person liable at common law, either employer or employee may sue the third person, but must notify the other in writing who may join in the suit. Failure to so join the suit abates action of nonjoining party. If the employer and employee are thus joined in the suit against the negligent third person the damages recovered go first to reimburse the employer for the compensation which he has paid or become obligated to pay and the balance goes to the employee. Compromise by either with third person does not affect rights of other unless assented to. Workers' compensation insurers, unions, and union members are immune from third party liability for failure to furnish safety inspections incident to providing workers' compensation insurance. (31-293).

Injured employee must forthwith notify employer of fact of injury, and commissioner may reduce award proportionate to any prejudice sustained by employer by such failure. (PA 91-32, §10). No proceeding for compensation may be maintained unless written notice of claim is given within one year from date of accident or within three years of occupational disease symptom. If employer wishes to contest liability for injury, he must notify commissioner of this fact within 20 days of time he first has knowledge of injury or death. (31-297; am'd PA 91-32, §16). To contest liability for injury or death which occurs on or after effective date of this Act, employer must notify commission within 28 days of receiving written notice of claim. Provided employer commences payment of compensation on or before 28 days of notice of claim, employer shall have additional period of one year from notice to contest liability. (31-294c). However, if death has resulted within two years from date of accident or symptom, dependent of decent employee may make claim within said two year period, or within one year of death. (PA 91-32, §10[a]). Notice to employer must give name and address of injured

LABOR RELATIONS . . . *continued*

party, date and place of accident, and nature of injury or disease. On notice of injury, employer is required to provide competent medical care from list of approved physicians maintained by commission. If employer fails to do this medical care may be obtained by employee and charged to employer. Medical reports must be furnished employer, employee or his attorney. If employee refuses medical care, his rights under this act are suspended during such refusal. (PA 91-32, §§12, 13).

No compensation is payable under this act for total or partial incapacity of three days or less. If incapacity is more than three but less than seven days, compensation begins at expiration of just three days. If incapacity is more than seven days, compensation runs from date of injury. The day of injury does not count as a day of incapacity and employee must be paid full wages for that day. (31-295; am'd PA 91-32, §15).

If employer and employee reach settlement agreement, such must be approved by commissioner. Employee's request for hearing on proposed discontinuance or reduction of benefits is given priority over requests for hearings on other matters. If commissioner finds that employer reduced or discontinued any payments without approval, employer shall be required to make such payments with interest, at rate of 1¼% per month or portion thereof. (31-296; am'd PA 90-116). If no agreement is reached, commissioner may be notified by either party. Commissioner then schedules hearing on matter within ten days' notice to both parties. Hearings are held in town where employee lives, if possible. (31-297; am'd PA 91-32, §16). Hearing is informal and both parties and/or their attorneys may appear. Commissioner not bound by rules of evidence or procedure. No fees are taxed, but commissioner must allow subpoenaed witnesses usual fees and traveling expenses to be paid by person in whose behalf subpoena was issued. If liability or extent of disability is contested and employee prevails, he may recover reasonable fees paid physicians or surgeons for X-rays, medical tests, and testimony and ⅕ of weekly compensation (as computed under Workers' Compensation Act) for each day of attendance at hearing. (31-298, am'd PA 85-65; PA 91-32, §17). As soon as possible but no later than 120 days after conclusion, commissioner must notify each party of his findings and award. Appeal therefrom must be taken within ten days. If no appeal, execution may be made as in Superior Court actions. Payments due from voluntary agreement, award or second injury fund must be paid on or before tenth business day after date of agreement or award. (31-300). Where commissioner finds adjustment of claim has been unduly delayed, he may add interest at rate prescribed in §37-3a and reasonable attorney's fee. If payments of compensation are unduly delayed, commissioner may add interest at rate of 12% per annum and reasonable attorney's fee. (31-300). Payments not begun within 35 days after filing of written notice are presumed unduly delayed unless notice to contest is filed in accordance with 31-297. (31-300). Commissioner may allow successful claimant to be reimbursed for medical deposition/testimony costs. (PA 97-106).

Employer may not discontinue payments awarded on account of total or partial incapacity, if employee claims incapacity continues, without giving commissioner and employee notice of proposed discontinuance and obtaining commissioner's written approval. Upon notification, commissioner must render decision within 14 days and notify parties within seven days of decision. If commissioner finds for employer, employee must refund payments received from date of notice to decision. Employer who last employed successful claimant liable for compensation. Commissioner may apportion liability to prior employers. (31-299[b]). Where commissioner finds for employee, he must allow reasonable attorney's fee and interest at rate prescribed in §37-3a on discontinued payments. (31-300). Appeal from commissioner lies to compensation review division by filing in office of commissioner from which award originated. Such actions are privileged. No costs are taxed. (31-301).

A husband or wife living with spouse at time of injury or receiving support regularly from spouse, a child under 18, or child over that age but physically or mentally incapacitated from earning, living with, or receiving regular support from, deceased parent, are conclusively presumed to be totally dependent. In all other cases questions of dependency shall be determined in accordance with the facts. Within 30 days of stopping disability benefits because of disabled employee's death, employer sends form notifying deceased employee's dependents of possible death benefits. Commissioner will approve form by Oct. 1, 1998. (PA 98-104).

The compensation payable in case of death is (1) Burial expenses $4,000 if death arises out of and in course of employment or from occupational disease where employee died on or after Oct. 1, 1988. If there is no person wholly or partially dependent upon deceased, burial expenses will be paid to person who assumes responsibility of paying funeral expenses; (2) to those wholly dependent on deceased weekly compensation of 75% of average weekly after-tax earnings of deceased at time of injury, but not less than $20 nor more than maximum benefit rate set forth in Act for totally incapacitated employees; (3) if spouse is sole surviving presumptive dependent, then shall receive compensation until death or remarriage; (4) if presumptive dependent spouse and presumptive dependent children, all of which children are either children of surviving spouse or living with such spouse, payments will be made as in (2) above. However, if any such children are neither children of surviving spouse nor living with such spouse, share payments will be made to each such dependent, or his guardian, not living with presumptive dependent spouse; (5) if compensation being paid to surviving spouse terminates for any reason, or there is no surviving dependent spouse at time of death, but there are presumptive dependent children, they must be paid as class for maximum of 780 weeks, or until all children reach 18 years of age (22 years of age for unmarried full-time students; 22+ years of age for same earning postsecondary degree) and are physically and mentally capable of earning their own living whichever is sooner; (6) payments to partial dependents must be paid according to their relative degree of dependence, for 312 weeks or until dependency ceases, whichever occurs sooner. (31-306; 31-308). Dependents of any deceased employee injured on or after Jan. 1, 1974 and deceased not later than Nov. 1, 1991 must be paid compensation retroactively to date of employee's death. Cost of payment paid by employer or his insurance who shall be reimbursed from second injury fund as provided in 31-354. (31-306).

Compensation for total incapacity is 75% of average weekly after-tax earnings at time of injury but not more than 100%, nor less than 20%, of average production wages for

all workers in state for year in which injury occurred as determined by Labor Commissioner. (31-307; 31-309).

If employee is partially incapacitated, compensation amounts to 75% of difference between after-tax wages currently earned by employee in position comparable to position previously held by injured employee and after-tax amount he is able to earn thereafter, but not to exceed 100% of state's average weekly wage. Compensation continues for actual period of partial disability or 520 weeks, whichever is less. Certain awards are designated for specified injuries, i.e., loss of master arm, 75% of average weekly after-tax earnings for 208 weeks; loss of one leg at or above knee, 75% of average weekly after-tax earnings for 155 weeks, etc. (31-308). Regulatory definitions of both disfigurement and scarring have been codified. (PA 91-339, §1). If injury caused by employer's violation of health and safety regulations result in total incapacity to work, employee shall receive 100% of average weekly earnings. (31-307). Any award for compensation pursuant to §31-308 shall be paid to employee, or in event of such employee's death, to surviving spouse, if no spouse, to dependents in equal shares or if no dependents, to children in equal shares. (31-308).

Provisions require employer to keep record of injuries (31-316), prevent employer from avoiding law by contractual or other devices (31-290), provide for retention of employee at suitable, full-time work while being rehabilitated (31-313), and provide for Commissioner approval of attorneys' and physicians' fees (31-319).

Employees with pre-existing physical defects may by contract execute acknowledgment of physical defect in cases where such physical defect contributes in material degree to injury. (31-325).

Employee entitled to hearing before commissioner, upon employee's claim that employer failed to provide suitable, full-time work during rehabilitation. (31-313, am'd PA 86-166).

Employee with previous disability who incurs second disability in course of employment, resulting in permanent disability, may recover for total disability, even if greater than second disability. Second Injury and Compensation Assurance Fund created to supplement employee's compensation payments. (31-349 to 31-355a). Second Injury Fund also provides payments for cost of living adjustments for permanently totally disabled worker. (31-310). Second Injury Fund also pays cost of accident and health insurance for employee receiving compensation payments whose employer shuts down or moves operations from Connecticut on or after Jan. 1, 1985 and fails to provide coverage or proof of financial ability and solvency. (31-349). Fund liable for cost of insurance coverage equivalent to employee's coverage prior to relocation or shutdown of employer's operations, beginning on date custodian is notified and continuing as long as individual receives workers' compensation pursuant to chapter. (31-349). Second injury fund closed to claimants whose injuries occur on or after July 1, 1995. (31-349, am'd 95-277).

Provision is made for the formation of employer mutual companies to insure in compensation cases. (31-328 to 31-338).

Employers who fail to obtain coverage or furnish proof of financial ability and solvency may be fined not more than $1,000 (31-284), and attorney general may bring civil action to enjoin employer from entering into any employment contracts to employ additional employees until employer complies (31-284). Employer who willfully and repeatedly fails to comply with workers' compensation provisions may be enjoined from conducting business in Connecticut pending compliance. (PA 93-228).

Employers with high incidence of injuries required to form health and safety committees. (PA 93-228).

Employers failing to conform with other provisions of the act may be fined not more than $250. (31-285).

Municipal Employee Benefits.—HB 5650; PA 98-263, §6 modifies CGS §3-122 regarding relief for police officers injured/rendered ill in line of duty and dependents of police officers killed in line of duty; §7 modifies CGS §3-123 regarding relief for firefighters and their dependents. §8 modifies CGS §5-144 regarding relief for state officers/general assembly members and their dependents; §9 modifies CGS §5-145 regarding notification of injury of state employee; §10 modifies CGS §5-259(2) regarding insurance for certain state/municipal employees; and §11 modifies CGS §5-192t regarding relief to dependents of tier II employees.

Fraudulent Claims.—Any person making false claim for benefits through intentional misrepresentation or nondisclosure, or any person or employer intentionally aiding another in making such claims shall be guilty of class C felony if amount of benefits claimed is less than $2,000. If amount exceeds $2,000, such person is guilty of class B felony and will also be liable for treble damages in civil proceeding under 52-564. (PA 90-244).

Workers' compensation fraud unit under supervision of chief state's attorney has been established. (PA 92-173).

Unemployment Compensation.—Unemployed person whose prior services fall within scope of 31-222 et seq. is eligible for weekly benefits if: (1) He has made claim under 31-240 and has registered for work at designated public employment bureaus; (2) he is able and willing to work, and is making reasonable efforts to get work; (3) he has earned from employer subject to provisions of Unemployment Compensation Act (31-222 et seq.) at least 40 times his benefit rate for total unemployment during base period of his current benefit year as defined in 31-230; (4) he has been totally or partially unemployed as defined in 31-228 and 31-229 for one week, called waiting week, during which, although eligible, he has received no benefits under any provisions of Act (31-235). Individual disqualified from receiving benefits if discharged for committing larceny. (31-236). Employee may not be penalized or discriminated against for filing claim for benefits. (PA 88-169).

SB500; PA 98-169 eff. 7/1/98 includes: §1 Self-sufficiency measurement established to assist in education, training and employment; §2 Department Social Services to administer Employment Services Program for persons receiving benefits under Temporary Assistance For Needy Families Program; §§3, 4 and 5 regarding assessment of eligibility and pilot programs for recipients.

See also category Taxation, topic Unemployment Compensation Tax.

See note at head of Digest as to 1998 legislation covered.

See Topical Index in front part of this volume.

ENVIRONMENT

ENVIRONMENTAL REGULATION:

General Supervision.—

Department of Environmental Protection, headed by Commissioner of Environmental Protection has broad jurisdiction over air, water, and other natural resources (22a-2 et seq.) and has consolidated jurisdiction over areas such as water resources, coastal area management (22a-90 to 22a-112), air pollution, noise pollution (22a-67), litter control (22a-27; 22a-80; 22a-89), pesticide control (22a-46 to 22a-66z), parks, and fisheries and game formerly regulated by variety of agencies (22a-5), harvested and nonharvested wildlife, chemical discharges (PA 90-77).

Council on Environmental Quality, appointed by governor, speaker of house and president pro tempore of senate, submits annual environmental quality report to governor, has consultative and advisory authority concerning state agency construction plans, and refers citizen complaints to appropriate agency. Council on environmental quality within Department of Environmental Protection for administrative purposes only.

Power Facility Evaluation Council reviews plans for electric transmission lines, fuel transmission lines, and associated facilities for environmental compatibility. (16-50gw). Land acquisition or construction cannot commence without certificate of environmental compatibility and public need from council. (16-50k).

Emergency Response Commission reviews and processes chemical information and notifications made pursuant to Emergency Planning and Community Right-to-Know Act, 42 USC 11001 et seq., and makes recommendations for state enforcement of that Act's provisions. (PA 88-246, §§4-9).

Endangered species program established to conserve, protect, restore and enhance any endangered or threatened species and essential habitat. (PA 89-224).

Wildlife.—

Licenses.—§26-35 is repealed and substituted. All hunting and fishing licenses will expire on last day of year issued and may not be altered, transferred or lent to another. Licensees may be required to temporarily surrender license in wildlife study areas. All licensees must file written, annual report describing wildlife killed or trapped. Licensees may not carry pistols or revolvers. (PA 97-250, §1; Subst. S.B. 857; 26-35).

Wildlife Refuges.—§26-101 is repealed and substituted. Upon obtaining written consent, Commissioner may establish wildlife refuges on private land. Such areas may be closed to hunting or public use if necessary to manage wildlife or for public safety. Notice to be posted near boundaries of area. (PA 97-250, §2; Subst. S.B. 857; 26-101).

Commissioner.—§26-3 is repealed and substituted. Commissioner of Wildlife Protection has authority to enforce laws, enter orders and employ and train personnel to ensure protection and safety of wildlife. (PA 97-250, §3; Subst. S.B. 857; 26-3). May also establish regulations for management of salmon; migratory game birds. (26-48a).

Damage Control.—§26-82 is repealed and substituted. Land owners or lessees may obtain damage permits enabling them to hunt wildlife causing damage to their property. Such hunting and distribution of animals is regulated by statute. (PA 97-250, §4; Subst. S.B. 857; 26-82).

Deer Management.—§26-862 is repealed and substituted. Establishes regulations for deer management, including type of weapon, permits required, prohibited hunting days, and penalties for violation of regulations. (PA 97-250, §5; Subst. S.B. 857; 26-86c).

Weapons.—§26-86c is repealed and substituted.

Permits may be issued for bow and arrow hunting to qualified applicants. (PA 97-250, §6; Subst. S.B. 857; 26-86c).

Hunter Education.—§§26-31 and 26-61 are amended.

Persons whose hunting licenses have been suspended for hunting safety violations must successfully complete remedial hunter education course prior to restoration or reinstatement. (PA 97-250, §§7-8; Subst. S.B. 857; 26-31; 26-61). One who has caused death of person or non-wild animal, or damaged property may have license suspended and must successfully complete remedial hunter education course. (26-62).

Protected Rivers Act (PA 94-150) restricts activities in river corridors, designated by Commissioner to be eligible and worthy of protection.

Traprock ridges, as defined, may be protected by setback regulations, if adopted by local zoning authorities, to control development. (8-2, am'd 95-239).

Solid Waste Management.—Solid Waste Commission established. (22a-57). See also PA 97-124 for minor revisions.

Resource Recovery Facilities.—Commissioner must determine need before issuing permits for resource recovery facilities. (PA 87-556; PA 89-386; PA 90-179). Commissioner shall monitor emissions, conduct dioxin studies, inspect facilities, establish qualifications for operators. (22a-193). Resource recovery authority. (22a-261).

Solid waste law with regard to disposal, recycling and tipping fee fund are governed by 22a-225 of general statutes. (PA 90-312). New rules regarding disposal of grass clippings and directory publications. (PA 97-102).

Recycling.—State-wide plan to be developed. (PA 87-544; PA 88-231; PA 89-385).

Biomedical Waste.—Each generator must submit to commissioner name of person contracted to dispose of biomedical waste, amount of waste and site of disposal. (22a-213a).

Radioactive Waste.—Creation of hazardous waste management service. (PA 91-337).

Notification of Chemical Spills.—Department of Health Services shall cause all information concerning discharge, spillage, uncontrolled loss, seepage or filtration of oil or petroleum or chemical liquids or solid, liquid or gaseous products or hazardous wastes upon any land or into any of waters of state or into any offshore or coastal waters which may result in threatened danger to public health to be transmitted to Commissioner of Environmental Protection, and Chief Executive Officer and local Director of Health of municipality in which such discharge, spillage, uncontrolled loss, seepage or filtration occurs. Such information shall be proved in timely manner. (19a-47).

Prohibited Acts of Pollution.—Causing air pollution to a degree that is injurious to public welfare, health, or property or unreasonably interferes with enjoyment of life or property (22a-170; 22a-184); pollution of, or discharge of wastes into (22a-427), or discharge of sewage into (26-26), waters, in violation of regulatory statutes (22a-422 to 22a-453), discharge into class A waters of less than tertiary treated sewage (26-26a); failing to report oil spills in state waters (22a-425; 22a-450); operation of motor vehicles so as to produce noise exceeding decibel level set by commissioner of motor vehicles, which shall not exceed maximum set by federal law (14-80a); violate statutes concerning registration and use of pesticides (22a-63); violate regulations to be established re noise pollution (22a-67); dumping refuse at other than proper facilities (22a-250; selling products packaged in or composed in whole or in part of polystyrene foam if foam manufactured using any controlled substance (PA 89-227); placing used batteries in mixed municipal solid waste (PA 90-248); operating woodburning facility in violation of regulatory statutes (PA 90-264).

Enforcement.—

Air Pollution.—Commissioner of Environmental Protection enforces commission regulations by order. (22a-177; 22a-178). Hearing may be held after order issued, and after hearing, order may be affirmed, modified, or revoked. (22a-178). If Commissioner issues order to two or more persons including landowner and person causing pollution or creating or maintaining potential air pollution source, each such person shall be jointly and severally liable. If commissioner has reasonable cause to believe that any person has violated any regulation, order or permit, he may issue order to such person to investigate by monitoring, production of records, or any other means, source of air pollution. (22a-178). Action may be brought in superior court to impose civil penalties and/or for injunction. (22a-180). Commissioner develops internal performance evaluation program to provide for planning and monitoring of programs and annually submits reports to joint standing committee of general assembly outlining departments progress and assessing state's air quality. (PA 90-150, §2). Commissioner may, upon showing of cause, modify, revoke or suspend any permit. Grounds for doing so include violation of c. 446c, or any regulation, permit or order adopted or issued thereunder or misrepresentation of facts at any time by holder of permit. (PA 90-150, §4).

Water Pollution.—Commissioner enforces by orders prohibiting or abating water pollution (22a-416 to 22a-434), and commissioner can request attorney general to bring action for injunction (22a-435). Commissioner can also apply to attorney general to bring injunction action against installation or maintenance of new discharge into state waters without permit. (22a-430). Violations of state regulations or authorized municipal regulations concerning inland wetlands and water courses can be restrained by Superior Court or ordered corrected or removed. (22a-44). Commissioner may issue order to municipality or person(s) responsible for pollution, to provide potable drinking water. (22a-471). Commissioner may file notice of contaminated well on land records of town. (PA 87-395). Control of discharge of sewage from vessels is regulated by PA 90-173.

Endangered Species.—Commissioner enforces by orders prohibiting taking, killing, injuring or reducing likelihood of survival of species. (PA 89-224, §10).

Declaratory and equitable relief available to attorney general, any governmental authority, or any private party against any other such party. (22a-16). Court may grant permanent or temporary relief on showing of unreasonable pollution, or impairment or destruction of public trust in air, water, or other natural resources. (22a-17; 22a-18). It is affirmative defense that no feasible and prudent alternative, and conduct is consistent with public health, safety, and welfare. (22a-17). Proceeding is supplemental to administrative proceedings, and court may remand to administrative agency (22a-18; 22a-20), but if administrative procedure inadequate, court action may be maintained. (22a-20).

Environmental Use Restriction.—Commissioner empowered to establish new interest in title to contaminated land entitled "environmental use restriction" to prohibit activities on or uses of particular parcel which may increase exposure to pollutants and environmental hazards. Restriction, once executed by owner and Commissioner, requires subordination of all other interests (including mortgages) and runs with land. Termination/release provided for on stated terms and conditions. Violation of restriction can result in civil penalty up to $25,000 per day. (PA 94-198).

Fees.—Commissioner may require payment of fee to cover cost of reviewing application, monitoring compliance with state or federal permit and providing status reports concerning compliance. (22a-6).

Penalties.—

General Civil Penalties may be imposed by Commissioner of Environmental Protection up to $25,000 per violation per day. (22a-6b).

Air Pollution.—For not taking preventative or corrective measures after tenth day following deadline in commission order, up to $5,000 per week. If any person fails to comply with any protective provision of order within six months, and (1) no request from such person for hearing on such order is pending, (2) time for making such request has expired, and (3) commissioner determines that noncompliance is not due to factors beyond control of person, commissioner will request Attorney General to bring action in superior court for injunctive relief to secure compliance with order. (22a-180). For open air burning violation, up to $50 for first violation or up to $200 for subsequent violations. Any person who willfully or with criminal negligence violates any provision of this chapter shall be fined or imprisoned or both. Any person who knowingly makes any false statement representation, or certification in any application, record, report, plan or other document filed or required to be maintained under this chapter shall upon conviction be fined or imprisoned or both. (22a-175). If commissioner finds that (1) violation of terms of permit issued pursuant to §22a-174 exists and (2) person alleged to be committing such violation has received written notification of two violations in preceding year, Commission will require emission test of air contaminant source at expense of source and if results indicate noncompliance, order requiring abatement will be issued. (22a-178).

Any Water Pollution Statute.—Knowing violation, up to $10,000 per violation or per day. Criminal violation of statutes, up to $25,000 per day for each day of violation and/or imprisonment up to one year, subsequent violations, up to $50,000 per day for each day of violation and/or imprisonment up to two years. Responsible corporate officers are not immune to penalties. (22a-438). Violation of inland wetlands or water courses statutes or regulations punishable by civil penalty up to $1,000 for each day of violation. For willful or knowing violation up to $1,000 per day, up to six months in prison

See note at head of Digest as to 1998 legislation covered.

See Topical Index in front part of this volume.

ENVIRONMENTAL REGULATION . . . *continued*
or both. For subsequent violation up to $2,000 per day or up to one year in prison or both. (22a-44).

Solid Waste.—For knowing violation of provision, regulation, order or permit under chapter, civil penalty not to exceed $25,000. (22a-226). $100,000 or less fine for violation of 22a-226 which puts another in imminent danger of death or serious bodily injury. (22a-226). Penalties for illegal disposal of solid waste at landfill operated by municipality, may be established by municipality as long as they do not exceed $1,000 for first offense, $2,000 for second and $3,000 for any subsequent offense. (PA 90-216). Appeals must be made pursuant to 7-125b, §6.

Any Pesticide Statute.—Knowing violation by commercial applicant, up to $5,000 and/or imprisonment up to one year; knowing violation by private applicant, up to $1,000 and/or imprisonment up to 30 days. State may bring suit to recover civil penalty up to $2,500 per day for each violation. (22a-63).

Oil Spill or Hazardous Material Pollution.—Responsible party liable to state for costs and expenses over $5,000 in controlling and removing and for 1½times costs and expenses if negligent. Also responsible for reimbursement for short-term and long term provision of potable drinking water. (22a-451, am'd PA 97-241). Liable to private party for removal of oil if spill was due to negligence. (22a-452). State may bring suit to recover costs of detecting, controlling, abating violations of pollution statutes. Civil penalties established. (22a-6a).

Voluntary Site Remediation.—Under certain limited circumstances, in areas where groundwater has been classified as GB or GC (i.e. not suitable for public drinking water supply) and no prior enforcement orders have been issued, landowner, lessor, or lender may undertake voluntary remediation of spill without direct DEP involvement, but with DEP approval. Studies and remediation plans conducted or overseen by pre-approved contractors pursuant to DEP guidelines, and certified as such by said contractors, will be accepted without prior approval. DEP may agree to exempt landowner, lessor, or lender from liability for acts or omissions prior to date of clean-up. Exemption, known as covenant not to sue, may be transferred with land.

HB 5430; PA 98-253: §1 modifies PA 97-109 regarding municipalities and allows them to agree to abate property tax due from property owner for seven years if owner agrees to site assessment, demolition and remediation contingent upon such action continuing; abatement terminates on sale/transfer; recapture may be required; forgiveness may be granted; approval of abatement or other actions required; notification of decisions to act; §2 modifies CGS §22a-134(l) regarding transfer of establishment clarifying that transfer does not include conveyance of parcel which prior to July 1, 1997 had been developed solely as residential and has not changed or conveyance of parcel to entities operating under c. 130 or 132 or to urban rehabilitation agency (§8-292), to municipality (§32-225), to Connecticut Development Authority or its subsidiaries; §3 modifies CGS §22a-133m regarding new section "h"—joint identification by Environmental Protection and Department of Economic and Community Development commissioners of urban community sites which have or may have environmental contamination which if remediated and developed would improve urban environment; §4 modifies CGS §22a-133aa regarding covenant not to sue property owner or prospective purchaser if detailed plan of remediation has been approved by Environmental Protection Commissioner; includes "owner" within text of statute; covenant not to sue precludes action against holder of covenant to remediate unless property not remediated per approved plan or if environmental land use restriction has not been recorded or if there is failure to comply with restrictions; purchaser or owner shall pay fee equal to percentage of property value; §5 modifies CGS §22a-133bb regarding conditions for issuance of covenants not to sue between commissioner of environmental protection and prospective purchasers or owners; conditions upon which commissioner shall enter into covenant not to sue; upon compliance with statutory requirements, covenants not to sue shall issue not later than 45 days after compliance; §7 modifies CGS §32-11a regarding establishment of subsidiaries to encourage and carry out remediation development and financing; §8 modifies CGS §32-23pp regarding State policy to encourage pollution prevention and remediation; §9 modifies CGS §32-23qq regarding Environmental Assistance Revolving Loan Fund and issuance of grants, loans and credits; §10 modifies CGS §32-23rr regarding definition of remediation activities; §13 modifies CGS §22a-133x regarding addition of owners of contaminated property located in a GA or GAA grounduster classification area. *Note:* §6 (new) regarding exceptions to liability for lenders; §11 (new) Regional Economic Development Assistance Revolving Fund; and §12 (new) regarding exceptions to liability for licensed environmental professionals hired or retained by municipalities.

Underground Storage Tank.—Clean-up Fund established. Responsible party liable to state for costs and expenses less than $10,000 or more than $1,000,000 with exceptions. (PA 91-254).

Littering.—$250 fine; for dumping refuse at other than proper facility, fine up to $10,000. (22a-250).

Note: Effective Jan. 1, 1980, 22a-77-79 provide that all beverage containers shall be recyclable, having refund value of 5¢ or more.

Hazardous Waste Tax imposed upon generators of hazardous waste. See category Taxation, topic Environmental Taxes, subhead Hazardous Waste Tax.

Violation of hazardous waste program up to $25,000 per day. (22a-131). "Minor" violations of hazardous waste laws, as defined, which may be addressed by violator within 30 days on expedited basis, may, after certification by commissioner, escape further enforcement action or liability. (PA 95-56).

Biomedical Waste.—Violation of any provision of c. 446d or 446k of general statutes fined $25,000 or less for each offense. (22a-213).

Endangered Species.—For committing, taking part in or assisting in violating §§26-40c, 26-40d, fined up to $1,000 or imprisoned up to six months for each offense. Taking of each species deemed separate offense. (26-40f).

Asbestos Dumping.—No person shall dump, discard or otherwise dispose of more than one cubic foot of any substance containing asbestos or asbestos-containing material, as defined in §19a-332 of general statutes, except at solid waste facility which has been granted permit pursuant to §22a-208a of general statutes. Any person who knowingly violates any provision of this act or §22a-208a of general statutes, any permit issued under this section or under §22a-250(c) or (d), or regulation adopted under §22a-209 or §22-231 or any order issued pursuant to §22a-225, shall be fined not more than $25,000 per day for each day of violation or imprisoned not more than one year, or both. Subsequent conviction for any such violation shall carry fine of not more than $50,000 per day for each day of violation or imprisonment for not more than two years, or both (PA 90-163).

Permits.—

Air Pollution.—Exemption from regulations may be granted by permit from Commission on Environmental Protection if no danger to public health and safety, and compliance would produce hardship. (22a-183). Relative interests of applicant and public must be balanced. (22a-183; 22a-176). New contaminant source may not be installed or employed without permit from Air Pollution Control Commission. (22a-174; 22a-184). Applicant for permit must give written notification to people whose property abuts applicant's land within ten days of filing application. Applicant must send written notification to Commissioner. Commissioner must not make decision on application less than 45 days after receipt of written notification. (22a-174). Each source of air pollution must register biannually with Commissioner. (22a-174). Upon presentation of petition signed by at least 25 persons, or upon request of any person if activity is subject to Federal Clean Air Act, public hearing will be held. (PA 95-165).

Waters.—Any new discharge into state waters requires permit from Commission on Environmental Protection; satisfactory treatment plan required for new discharge which might cause pollution. Permit lasts ten years except 30 years for discharges into subsurface sewerage disposal systems. Detailed permit procedures. (22a-430). Discharges not reasonably expected to cause pollution are exempt from permit but must be registered with Commissioner. (PA 87-235, §1). Permit for operation on inland wetlands or water courses requires permit from Commissioner of Environmental Protection. (22a-36 to 22a-45). There shall be no discharge of sewage from any vessel in no discharge zone.

Oil.—Terminals for loading or discharge of oil from vessel must be licensed annually by Commission on Environmental Protection. (22a-449). Permit valid for fixed term not exceeding five years is needed for business of collecting or disposing of waste oil. (22a-454). (SB 5530; PA 98-171 repeals CGS §22a-54[e].) Permit required for aerial spraying of pesticides.

Notice.—Commissioner may require any applicant for any permit provided for under Title 22a to post conspicuous notice on site of activity for which permit is being sought. (PA 94-85).

Hazardous waste facilities strictly regulated. (22a-115 through 22a-125). Hazardous Waste Management Service will prepare state plan for low-level radioactive waste disposal. (PA 87-540; PA 88-243). Commissioner shall discover and evaluate hazardous waste sites and clean up with state funds, if necessary, seeking reimbursement from responsible party. (PA 87-561). Significant fees triggered by transfers of hazardous waste establishments requiring remediation. (22a-134e, am'd PA 93-277). Commissioner shall charge each nuclear powered commercial electric power generating plant $40,000 annual fee to monitor radiation released. (22a-135). Fund established to assist state in disposal of low-level radioactive waste, financed by tax on Nuclear Regulatory Commission licensees. (PA 88-243). Commissioner may adopt regulations for storage of hazardous substances near water courses. (PA 89-209).

Transfer Act.—Special disclosure rules govern "transfers" of "establishments". "Establishment" is: (A) dry cleaner in operation at any time on or after May 1, 1967; (B) furniture stripping establishment in operation at any time on or after May 1, 1967; (C) vehicle body repair shop or vehicle painting shop in operation at any time on or after May 1, 1967; or (D) any real property or business operation which, at any time on or after Nov. 19, 1980, generated 100 kilograms of hazardous waste in any one month. "Transfer" is any transaction or proceeding through which establishment undergoes change of ownership, but does not mean (A) conveyance or extinguishment of easement; (B) conveyance pursuant to foreclosure; (C) deed in lieu of foreclosure; (D) conveyance of mortgage or other security interest; (E) lease renewal; (F) conveyance, assignment, or termination of lease for period of less than 25 years; (G) conveyance by probate court decree; (H) conveyance to surviving joint tenant, or by intestate succession, or to trustee, administrator, or executor under will or testamentary trust; (I) corporate reorganization not substantially affecting ownership; (J) original issuance of stock by entity which owns establishment; (K) transfer of stock representing less than majority interest; (L) immediate family transfers; (M) conveyance of portion of parcel upon which portion no establishment is or was located and no spill occurred, provided portion is 50% or less of entire parcel, or written notice of such proposed partial conveyance is provided to DEP 60 days prior to closing of transfer; (N) conveyance of service station; or (O) conveyance of land continuously used as residence since July 1, 1997 or before.

Prior to transfer of establishment, transferor must deliver to transferee Form I negative declaration (no spill has ever occurred on-site), or Form II declaration (spill occurred, but complete, approved remediation was carried out); either form must be filed with DEP within ten days after transfer. If transferor cannot execute Form I or Form II, some party must execute either Form III (either environmental conditions are unknown or spill has occurred, and certifying party agrees to investigate and remediate as needed) or Form IV (spill occurred, remediation done except follow-up monitoring, and further remediation, if indicated by monitoring, will be performed by certifying party). Form III or Form IV to be filed with DEP within ten days after transfer. (22a-134 et seq.; am'd PA 95-183).

Establishments requiring remediation will be remediated either: (A) pursuant to prior DEP review and approval; or (B) by licensed environmental professionals, who will subsequently verify remediation performed to applicable standards.

Various fees are required at time of filing of Form I, II, III, or IV declarations, based on sliding scale keyed to projected remediation costs. (22a-134e, am'd PA 95-183).

Newsprint Recycling.—Percentage of recycled fiber contained in newsprint used by all publishers governed by statute. If percentages specified are not achieved by publishers as to dates specified, Commissioner of Environmental Protection may levy fines against publishers as well as printers. Each newsprint user must also submit annual report to Commissioner of Environmental Protection indicating percentage of recycled fiber used in preceding calendar year. Commissioner of Environmental Protection may

See note at head of Digest as to 1998 legislation covered.

See Topical Index in front part of this volume.

ENVIRONMENTAL REGULATION ... *continued*

exempt publisher or printer from compliance with provisions in this statute for particular reasons. (PA 90-224).

Lead Paint.—Lead Poisoning Prevention and Control Act (19a-111) requires abatement of defective surfaces in residential buildings where children under age six reside. Act also has reporting requirements for exposure to lead. (19a-110; PA 98-66). Intact surfaces also must be abated if child resident exhibits elevated blood-lead concentration. Abatement contractors must be licensed by state. (20-475).

ESTATES AND TRUSTS

ADMINISTRATION:

See topic Executors and Administrators.

ADVANCEMENTS:

See topic Descent and Distribution.

ALLOWANCES:

See topic Executors and Administrators.

CLAIMS:

See topic Executors and Administrators; category Civil Actions and Procedure, topic Pleading.

DEATH:

One absent and unheard of for seven years is presumed dead and administration may be granted on his estate. Former bond and five year waiting period for distribution abolished. (45a-329). Where beneficiary has been unheard of for seven years trustee may settle estate and pay it over to remainderman on latter filing in probate court bond with surety for return of trust estate to trustee or his successor if beneficiary should return within 13 years. (45a-483).

Survivorship.—Uniform Simultaneous Death Act has been adopted. (45a-440).

Deaths of husband and wife are presumed to be simultaneous when there is no evidence to indicate priority of death, except as set forth in 45a-440a.

Action for Death.—The right of action for injuries resulting in death survives to the executor or administrator of the person killed. (52-599). Action must be commenced within two years from date when injury is first sustained or discovered and in no event may action be brought more than three years from date of act or omission complained of. (52-555). All damages recovered for injuries resulting in death, after payment of costs and expenses of suit, all expenses of last illness and all funeral bills, expenses of administration, claims against estate, and such amount for support of surviving spouse or family of deceased during settlement of estate as court of probate may allow, shall be distributed as personal estate in accordance with last will and testament of deceased, or if intestate in accordance with laws governing intestacy. Recovery not subject to transfer or succession taxes. (45a-448).

Actions Against Health Care Providers.—Standard of care for health care providers is that level of care, skill, and treatment which, in light of all relevant surrounding circumstances, is recognized as acceptable and appropriate by reasonably prudent similar health care providers. (52-184c).

Death certificate may be obtained from Registrar of Vital Statistics of town where person died. (7-62b). Certified copy of death certificate is $5. (7-74). Burial or removal permit is $3. (7-73).

Commission on Medico-Legal Investigations established to act through chief medical examiner to investigate violent, sudden, suspicious, employment related, etc., deaths. (19a-400 to 19a-414).

Anatomical Donations.—(19a-279a to 19a-2791; 19a-279b am'd by PA 98-172). See also topic Wills, subhead Living Wills.

DECEDENTS' ESTATES:

See topics Descent and Distribution, Executors and Administrators, Wills; category Debtor and Creditor, topic Homesteads.

DESCENT AND DISTRIBUTION:

Subject to interests of surviving spouse, real and personal estate descends and is distributed as follows, each class of which a member is living taking to exclusion of subsequent classes: (1) Children and representatives of deceased children, advancements being taken into consideration (45a-438) (child in gestation at time of intestate's death inherits equally with prior born children); (2) parent or parents, provided such parent has not abandoned minor child and continued such abandonment until time of death; (3) brothers and sisters and their representatives; (4) next of kin of equal degree, no representation being permitted, and kinship being reckoned according to civil law (relatives of half and whole blood share equally); (5) stepchildren and their representatives. (45a-439).

Issue of deceased children, brothers or sisters take by representation, even though there be no surviving child, brother or sister of the intestate. (See 25 Conn. 387; 115 Conn. 239, 161 Atl. 94.)

Real property subject to life use of husband or wife, remaining at end of term, is distributed as above provided, or may be so distributed during term subject to life interest. (45a-439).

Surviving spouse or conservator or guardian of his or her estate of intestate decedent takes as follows: if no surviving issue or parents of deceased, entire estate; if no surviving issue but deceased parents alive, $100,000 plus three-quarters of remainder; if issue of deceased survive and are all issue of surviving spouse, $100,000 plus one-half of remainder; if issue of deceased survive who are not issue of surviving spouse, one-half of estate absolutely. (45a-437). Issue shall include children born out of wedlock and

issue of children who qualify for inheritance under provisions of 45a-438 of general statutes. Share of surviving spouse may be set out in realty or personalty or both. Probate court can set out allowance for support during settlement. (45a-436). Different rules govern where marriage was contracted prior to June 20, 1877.

Surviving spouse is not entitled to statutory share of estate or to elective or intestate share where, without sufficient cause, spouse has abandoned other spouse and continued abandonment to time of death. (45a-436a).

As to election to take against will, see topic Wills.

Except as provided in 45a-731, individual is child of his genetic parents, regardless of marital status of such parents. With respect to child born out of wedlock, father shall be considered parent if father and mother marry after child's birth, father has been adjudicated father of child by court of competent jurisdiction, father has acknowledged under oath in writing that he is father of child, or after death of father or child, paternity is established by Probate Court by clear and convincing evidence that father acknowledged in writing that he is father of child and openly treated this child as his. (45a-438[b]).

Adopted Children.—See category Family, topic Adoption.

Person convicted as principal or accessory to murder or capital felony may not inherit from his victim. (45a-447).

Advancements.—Children or other descendants who have received estate by advancement of the intestate in his or her lifetime, or their representatives, take only so much of the estate as will, together with such advancements, make their share equal to what they would have been entitled to receive had no such advancement been made. (45a-438).

Disclaimers of interests in property are regulated by statute. (PA 45a-578 to 45a-585).

Escheat.—On failure of heirs estate shall be presumed to be abandoned and shall escheat to state (45a-452), subject to reclamation (3-70a).

See also topic Executors and Administrators.

ELECTION:

See topic Wills.

ESTATES:

See category Property, topic Real Property.

EXECUTORS AND ADMINISTRATORS:

Estates of decedents dying on or after Oct. 1, 1987 are subject to 1987 amendments regarding: Notice requirements, filing periods and order of preference of claims.

Jurisdiction of administration of decedent's estate is in court of probate of district where decedent was domiciled at his death (45a-283) or where estate or part of estate of nonresident decedent (45a-287) is found.

Original probate or administration may not be granted after ten years unless for a good cause. (45a-330).

Appointment and Qualification.—Executor named by will, if found by probate court to be willing and able to serve, qualifies by filing bond. If no executor is named, or if executor named is dead or unwilling or unable to serve and no alternate or successor has been named, probate court appoints administrator c.t.a. If executor or administrator c.t.a. dies in office, resigns or is removed, and no alternate or successor has been named, probate court appoints administrator d.b.n. c.t.a. (45a-290). Executor or administrator c.t.a. is ex officio administrator of intestate portion of estate. (45a-291).

No oath of office is taken.

Bond with resident surety or authorized surety company is required of representative, amount usually being double the value of the personalty. (45a-139, 45a-289). Where will directs that no bond be required of executor, probate court shall excuse posting of any bond if no objection to will is filed, but amount of any bond required may be not less than double debts or amount of penalty and succession tax, whichever is greater. Bond may be reduced after interim accounting. (45a-289).

Preferences in Right to Administer.—Administration of intestate estates (45a-290), and of testate estates when it becomes necessary to appoint administrator c.t.a., is granted to surviving spouse or next of kin (unless there is will and they are not interested in such will) or, on their refusal or incapacity or reasonable objection by creditor or heir, to such other person as court deems proper.

Temporary administrator with limited powers may be appointed without notice pending probate of will or appointment of administrator. (45a-316).

Eligibility.—Married woman may be executor or administrator and husband is not liable for her acts or defaults. Nonresident may serve as executor or administrator (45a-396) and foreign corporation may be executor under some circumstances, but not administrator (see category Business Organizations, topic Corporations). As to appointment of process agent by foreign corporation or nonresident individual, see category Property, topic Absentees. (45a-206).

Allowance in court's discretion may be ordered out of and during settlement of an estate for support of surviving spouse and family with provision for: allowance to run for a fixed period or entire period of settlement; payment of lump sum; vesting of allowance in spouse regardless of remarriage or death; or for ultimately charging all or part of allowance against spouse or family member supported (45a-320) and property of deceased spouse exempt from execution may be set out to surviving spouse where estate is insolvent (45a-435). As matter of practice such allowances are usually granted ex parte unless hearing is specifically requested.

Notice and Limitation to Creditors.—If estate is settled as solvent, the probate court, on original appointment or qualification of representative, limits time (not less than three nor more than 12 months) within which claims must be presented to representative. Notice is published by publishing same in a newspaper having circulation in subject probate district, or both, and by such other notice as court may direct. For cause

---

See note at head of Digest as to 1998 legislation covered.

See Topical Index in front part of this volume.

EXECUTORS AND ADMINISTRATORS . . . *continued*
shown upon hearing after public notice, court may limit further time for presentation of claims, not exceeding period which it might originally have limited. (45a-395).

With respect to estates where settlement was commenced six years or more prior to effective date of 1997 Amendment, no creditor will be deemed to have filed claim outside of order of limitation where estate fiduciary has failed to provide notice of limitation period to creditor or has failed to make sworn return of order to court. (S.A. 97-6, §4; H.B. 6402).

Applies to Decendents Dying on or after Oct. 1, 1987.—Notice to creditors by newspaper publication within 14 days after appointment of first fiduciary. State agencies from which decedent or family received aid or care shall be notified by certified mail and may present claims within 90 days or be forever barred. Fiduciary and beneficiaries may notify specific creditors giving such creditors at least 90 days to present claims or be forever barred from recovery unless creditor requests and is granted extension from probate court. No claim may be presented more than two years from date claim arose (if it arose after decedent's death) or from appointment of first fiduciary (or after statute of limitations applicable to claim expires). (45a-353 to 45a-357).

Estate Represented Insolvent.—If estate is represented insolvent and it is deemed expedient by court to settle it as such, two or more commissioners are appointed by court to receive and pass on claims, and time is similarly limited within which claims may be exhibited to them. Representative must give similar public notice of time and place of commissioners' meeting and send copy thereof to each known creditor within ten days of their appointment. (45a-406 to 45a-407).

An estate not represented as insolvent at the start may be represented as such after the time limited for presentation of claims has expired, in which event, if deemed expedient commissioners are appointed and, without further limitation (unless found necessary), claims presented to representative are committed to commissioners and passed on by them. (45a-408; 45a-407).

When it appears that the estate is no more than sufficient to pay expenses of administration, funeral, last sickness, taxes, and allowances for family and surviving spouse, the court may decree its settlement without commissioners. (45a-409).

Applies to Decedents Dying on or after Oct. 1, 1987.—Probate court will determine at hearing if estate is insolvent. Newspaper notice shall be published within 14 days after insolvency determined. Fiduciary shall notify all creditors allowing creditors 210 days to present claims or be forever barred unless creditor requests and is granted extension by probate court. (45a-390 et seq.).

Presentation of Claims.—Claims must be presented (by all creditors whether resident or nonresident) in writing and, if required by representative or probate court, with affidavit of creditor (45a-391) within time limited therefor, or within such further time as court may limit to permit late presentation in deserving cases, such further limitation not to extend more than 30 days beyond one year from date of first limiting decree (45a-395).

Applies to Decedents Dying on or after Oct. 1, 1987.—Claims in writing to fiduciary or court of probate. Fiduciary may require affidavit proving justice of claim. Personal delivery or mail allowed. Date determined by date of receipt or of mailing if properly addressed. (45a-358).

Debts Absolutely Due and Owing.—Claims for debts absolutely due and owing (whether matured or not matured) which are not so presented, are absolutely barred, unless, in the case of an insolvent estate, the claimant can show some estate of the deceased not included in the inventory. (45a-395).

Debts Not Absolutely Due and Owing.—Claims against solvent estates not absolutely due and owing may be presented within four months of their accrual, and if so presented claimant may collect out of estate remaining after payment of claims duly presented (no notice necessary if claim is subject of action pending in any court against decedent) (45a-395) or, if distribution has taken place, may charge legatees or distributees, or may procure probate sale of real property in hands of heirs or devisees or purchasers from them (86 Conn. 462, 85 Atl. 682; 102 Conn. 644, 129 Atl. 854; 6 Conn. 258), but no such sale may be had after heir or devisee has sold to bona fide purchaser for value except within first ten years after decedent's death (45a-327).

Tort Claims.—No requirement of notice in case of tort claims on which action is pending in court at time of death. If person against whom a claim founded in tort dies on day applicable statute of limitations expires or within 30 days prior to such day, period of 30 days from appointment of executor or administrator allowed to file suit. (45a-395).

Actions Pending at Death.—Where action on claim was pending at time of debtor's death, such claim need not be presented if, within one year after the death, action is properly continued against executor or administrator under survival statute. (52-599; 98 Conn. 201, 118 Atl. 915).

Secured claim need not be presented to protect security but must be presented to participate as to excess over security. If a creditor has security against an insolvent estate, the commissioners appraise such security and the representative notifies the creditor of the valuation thus placed on the security and the amount of the claim allowed. Unless within 15 days after such notice the creditor files in court a written relinquishment of the security he is entitled to a dividend only on the amount of his claim allowed in excess of the appraised value of the security. (45a-412).

Applies to Decedents Dying on or after Oct. 1, 1987.—If fiduciary fails to reject, allow, or pay claim within 90 days of presentation, claimant may give fiduciary notice to act. Failure to act within 30 days from such notice will be deemed rejection of claim. (45a-360).

Aggrieved claimant of solvent estate may file suit within 120 days from date of rejection or make application to court of probate within 30 days of rejection to hear and decide claim. Claimant of insolvent estate may apply to probate court to hear and decide grievance within 30 days of rejection. (PA 87-384, §§11, 12, 29).

If representative is nonresident, claims may be left with judge of probate. (45a-396).

Proof of Claims.—All claims must be presented in writing and, if required by representative or probate court, with affidavit of proof signed by creditor. (45a-391). The following form may be used for proof of claims:

Form

To . . . . . . Administrator of the estate (or executor of the will) of . . . . . . late of . . . . . deceased. The subscriber represents that: (1) The above named deceased was at the time of his death, and his estate is still, justly and truly indebted to the subscriber in the sum of . . . . . . dollars, with interest thereon from . . . . . . day of . . . . . ., 19. . . ., at . . . . . . per cent per annum. (2) The nature and consideration of said debt is as follows: Merchandise as per itemized statement filed herewith and made part hereof (or promissory notes, copies of which are filed herewith and made part hereof, etc.). (3) No part of said debt has been paid and there are no setoffs or counterclaims to the same. (4) The subscriber has not nor has any person by his order, for his use, had or received any manner of security for said debt except as follows: . . . . . . Wherefore, the subscriber presents a claim to you as administrator of the estate (or executor of the will) of said deceased for the sum of . . . . . . dollars and . . . . . . cents and with interest from the . . . . . . day of . . . ., 19. . . . .
(Conn. Probate Practice, §500).

. . . .

Approval or Rejection of Claims.—Representative should notify creditor of disallowance of claim, which notice in the case of insolvent estate must be given within six days after the return of commissioners' report (45a-413) and in case of solvent estate should, for representative's protection, be given no later than 30 days after expiration of time limited for presentation of claims (45a-397; 45a-402).

Commissioners of insolvent estates must file with probate court a report of their doings as soon as practicable after expiration of time limited for presentation of claims, which report must contain a list of claims with the amounts, presented, allowed and disallowed. (45a-413).

Any claimant who has presented claim (45a-391; 45a-396 to 45a-398) and has not received written notice of disallowance of claim within 30 days following end of limitation period for presenting claims may bring suit within four months of notice to executor that claimant intends to bring suit. (45a-400; 45a-401).

Applies to Decedents Dying on or after Oct. 1, 1987.—Creditor of secured claim may only share in estate with respect to excess of claim over value of security unless creditor elects in writing to relinquish security. Fair market value of security determined by fiduciary may be challenged in probate court within 30 days. (45a-379).

Payment of Claims.—*Real estate* is subject to being appropriated for payment of claims, but only by taking out administration on the estate, following which the executor or administrator sells the real estate at probate sale and brings the proceeds into the administration account. (83 Conn. 75, 75 Atl. 93; 60 Conn. 63, 22 Atl. 488).

If estate is insufficient, the order of appropriation of assets for payment of claims is: (1) personal estate not specifically bequeathed; (2) real estate not specifically devised; (3) personal estate specifically bequeathed; (4) real estate specifically devised. (71 Conn. 521, 42 Atl. 641; 60 Conn. 63, 22 Atl. 488).

In insolvent estate, the claims are paid in the following order: (1) Funeral and administration expenses; (2) debts due for last illness; (3) taxes due the state or the United States; (4) wages due for personal services performed within three months of the decease; (5) other preferred claims; (6) all other debts pro rata. (45a-392).

Applies to Decedents Dying on or after Oct. 1, 1987.—Preference of claims in settlement of decedent's estate: (1) Funeral expenses; (2) expenses of settling estate; (3) claims for last illness of decedent; (4) taxes and claims of state and U.S.; (5) personal wages due laborers or mechanics within three months prior to decedent's death; (6) other preferred claims; (7) all other claims in proportion to respective amounts. (45a-365).

Actions on Claims.—Payment of claim allowed but not paid may be enforced by suit on representative's bond (45a-654) or by application for removal of representative for neglect of duty (45a-242).

Claimant against solvent estate whose claim has been disallowed may apply within 30 days of notice of disallowance to probate court for hearing upon same or appointment or one or more commissioners to decide upon claim. If application for hearing or appointment of commissioner denied, creditor may bring suit within four months after denial of application. Appeal is to Superior Court. (45a-193; 45a-402; 45a-401).

Claimant against insolvent estate whose claim has been disallowed by commissioners has choice of two remedies: (1) To file, within 14 days, written objections to the acceptance by the probate court of the commissioners' report, which report may be rejected only for misconduct of commissioners affecting validity of report as whole (45a-413); (2) if his claim exceeds $50, to appeal from doings of commissioners to Superior Court within one month of acceptance of report by probate court (45a-190).

Actions pending at death may be revived or continued against executor or administrator and right of action against deceased person survives against executor or administrator (52-599); but no suit thereon (except for taxes, expenses of last sickness and funeral expenses) may be brought if estate is in settlement as insolvent estate (45a-414), and creditor of solvent estate may not sue representative within time allowed for presentation of claims unless representative has given written notice of disallowance. (45a-402).

Applies to Decedents Dying on or after Oct. 1, 1987.—Claimant of solvent estate may file suit against fiduciary within 120 days of rejection of claim. Suit may be brought against beneficiaries if claims are unsatisfied. (45a-368).

No suit shall be brought against fiduciary of insolvent estate except as provided in 45a-380. (45a-382).

Inventory and Appraisal.—An inventory and appraisal of all the decedent's property, except foreign real estate, must be made and sworn to by the representative and filed in the probate court within two months after his qualification. This time may be extended by court, for cause shown, but not to exceed four months from qualification. (45a-341). Failure to file within time limited is grounds for removal of fiduciary. (45a-342). Appraisal is at fair market value by fiduciary. (45a-341).

In case of nonresident decedent, the inventory must list all property, real and personal, located within this state.

Administration and Distribution of Estate.—The following steps are usually taken by executors and administrators after qualification and compliance with order of notice to creditors:

See note at head of Digest as to 1998 legislation covered.

See Topical Index in front part of this volume.

CT – 30

EXECUTORS AND ADMINISTRATORS . . . *continued*

(1) Publish notice to creditors within ten days after order of notice. (45a-395).

(2) Apply to probate court for authority to continue decedent's unincorporated business (45a-328), unless such authority is contained in will (106 Conn. 602, 138. Atl. 795).

(3) Record death notice in each town where real estate is situated within two months after qualification. (45a-322).

(4) Return inventory and appraisal within two months of qualification. (45a-341).

(5) Within nine months after death file with probate court a report of any transaction which may be a taxable transfer inter vivos or by survivorship. (12-359). See category Taxation, topic Estate Tax.

(6) Take custody of the real estate not specifically devised or occupied by the family of deceased as a dwelling house, bringing the income therefrom into the account as personal property (45a-321), and sell or mortgage real estate only on probate court order and on furnishing special bond, unless executor or administrator is authorized bank or trust company (45a-169), if such sale or mortgage is requisite to pay claims or legacies (45a-427), or is otherwise reasonable (45a-169), such sale being public or private (45a-164) on such notice as court directs. Where deceased owned undivided interest in real estate not specifically devised, representative may, by petition joined by owners of major portion of other interests therein, procure partition thereof by committee of three appointed for that purpose by probate court, which committee must file return of their doings with court. Subject to court's approval, portion set over to estate thereafter will be treated same as if it had come to deceased by partition during his life. (45a-169).

(7) Take custody of and title to the personal property, selling it as required or expedient. (45a-162). Upon written application of fiduciary, after notice and hearing, if court finds it would be for best interest of parties in interest, it may authorize person other than fiduciary to sell any of deceased's personal estate, upon posting of bond. Such sale may be public or private; if public upon such notice, and if private upon such terms, as court may direct; and at any sale so made fiduciary may be purchaser. (45a-169).

(8) Within 30 days of expiration of time limited for presentation of claims, in case of solvent estate, file with probate court a sworn return stating that notice was given creditors as required, listing claims presented and amounts allowed or disallowed. (45a-397).

(9) Where for the best interests of estate, compromise doubtful or disputed claims in favor of or against the estate, first procuring probate court order therefor. (45a-151).

(10) As a general rule pay funeral expenses, expenses of last sickness, and allowance for support of family or surviving spouse without delay.

(11) So far as estate will obviously permit, pay specific and cash bequests and claims.

(12) Within nine months of date of death, unless time extended, file with tax commissioner and probate court a succession tax return. (12-359[a]). See category Taxation, topic Succession and Transfer Tax.

(13) *Final Account.*—File final account usually within one year of appointment, on which the representative is charged with the amount of inventory, additions thereto, gains thereon, income, etc., and is credited with his expenses, compensation, allowance to family, claims paid, loss on inventory, legacies paid, etc., and estate on hand for distribution. After notice to parties in interest probate court passes on propriety of account, subject to appeal to superior court and if necessary orders it corrected, and this action renders res judicata all matters covered by account. (62 Conn. 218, 25 Atl. 109). No resignation may be accepted until representative has fully and finally accounted as above. (45a-242). Where representative dies during distribution, final account in somewhat different form must be prepared by his executor or administrator. Partial accounting prior to final account is sometimes filed but this is open to collateral attack on hearing on final account. (56 Conn. 1, 12 Atl. 513; 45-270 to 45-288).

(14) *Distribution.*—At time of acceptance of final account procure probate court order of distribution, ascertaining heirs and distributees of intestate estate and of testate estate so far as will may leave them necessary to be defined. (45a-431). For settlement of will contests see 45a-434.

(15) Distribute property to heirs or distributees and file return of distribution with probate court. (45a-434).

(16) On acceptance by probate court of return of distribution, deliver possession of the real estate as indicated therein, transfer the personal estate as indicated therein, pay the amount of the succession and estate taxes, if not already paid, and file a return of distribution with the probate court, in the nature of a supplemental account, showing that this has been done.

(17) Within 30 days of acceptance of final account, file with town clerk for town where real estate is located certificate of devise, descent or distribution. (45a-450). See category Documents and Records, topic Records.

(18) If additional estate is afterward discovered, administer on it without further appointment, filing supplemental account of doings with reference thereto. (16 Conn. 310).

Distribution if Abroad.—Where legatee or distributee is not within territorial limits of the U. S., any probate court may order such property converted into available funds and paid to the State Treasurer, to be invested by him, and to be held pending such further order as the probate court may make. (45a-449).

When a testator orders an estate to be divided among two or more devisees or legatees without appointing any person to divide it, or if he appointed persons to divide it who refuse or are unable to do so, or where in any will any estate or interest is given to two or more persons jointly, and the same is susceptible of a division, the executor or other fiduciary charged with the administration of the estate makes the division, provided the court before which such will was proved may, in its discretion, during the settlement of the estate of the testator, on its own motion or on the request of any one interested, appoint three disinterested persons to make the division; and such division, when accepted by the court, is binding on all persons interested; but, if the devisees, legatees or heirs are legally capable of acting and make a division in writing, in the manner provided for the division of intestate estates, such division is valid. (45a-434).

Intestate estates, after deducting expenses and charges, are distributed by the administrator or other fiduciary charged with the administration of the estate; provided the court of probate may, in its discretion, on its own motion or upon application by any interested person, appoint three disinterested persons to make the distribution; but if all the persons interested in the estate are legally capable of acting, and make and file in such court a division of the same, made, executed and acknowledged like deeds of land, such division, being recorded in the records of such court, constitutes a valid distribution of such estate. When it appears that a legatee, distributee or beneficiary living outside the United States or its possessions would not have the benefit, use, or control of property due him, probate court may order property to be converted into funds and paid to State Treasurer to be held and invested by him subject to further order of such court or to be held for purchase of food, clothing, medicine and necessities of life and periodic transmittal of same to legatee or beneficiary. (45a-449).

Liabilities of Executors and Administrators.—Representative may obtain practical immunity from errors in judgment in selling personal property paying or compromising claims and making other payments by obtaining probate court's approval in advance. (45a-202). Person with claim against representative for money paid or services rendered to estate may sue representative or his successor and such claims may be ordered paid out of estate, but this does not prevent claimant from electing to hold representative personally liable for debts contracted for estate or from holding representative liable for any balance which estate is insufficient to pay. (52-202).

Limitation.—When claim against representative as such cannot be adjusted, the claimant must bring suit within four months of notice of disallowance. (45a-399 to 45a-401).

Applies to Decedents Dying on or after Oct. 1, 1987.—Following final distribution of all assets known to fiduciary any suit on unsatisfied obligation is against beneficiary. Fiduciary is not chargeable for any assets distributed in good faith after 150 day period has elapsed. (45a-356).

Compensation to executor or administrator is allowed on his final account at such amount as is claimed by him if found by probate court to be reasonable, there being no statutory rate of compensation. (98 Conn. 374, 119 Atl. 341). In practice, executors and administrators, particularly corporations, often compute their compensation on the basis of a fixed percentage of the gross estate administered.

Foreign Executors and Administrators.—Ordinarily the executor or administrator at the place of residence will be favored for appointment as ancillary administrator in this state. (49 Conn. 411). Ordinarily foreign executors and administrators have no standing in this state unless qualified either as ancillary executors or administrators. (2 Root 462). However, payment of a debt to a foreign executor or administrator not qualified in this state is a lawful payment. (32 Conn. 308). A foreign executor or administrator of a deceased mortgagee may release or assign a mortgage without obtaining ancillary appointment, on filing with clerk of town where the land is located a certificate of appointment. (49-12). Foreign corporations duly qualified to act as executor or testamentary trustee may hold stocks in name of nominee upon compliance with statutory conditions. (45a-207). See category Business Organizations, topic Corporations, subhead Foreign Corporations, as to foreign corporation acting as executor or administrator.

See also Wills, subhead Foreign Probated Wills.

Distribution Without Administration.—Where administration is not taken out within 30 days after decedent's death, corporate stocks or bonds, bank deposits, equities in building or savings and loan shares, wages due, death benefits from insurance policies, personal property, tangible or intangible or unreleased interest in mortgage, not exceeding $20,000 in aggregate, left by decedent, may be paid to husband, wife, next of kin, creditor to whom debt is due for last sickness of decedent or undertaker, on application, without administration. (45a-273). If value of decedent's property exceeds claims against estate, and decedent left will providing for distribution different from that under laws of intestate succession, excess is paid in accordance with terms of will. If decedent left no will, or if will provides for distribution same as under laws of intestate succession, excess is distributed as though decedent died intestate. (45a-273).

Applies to Decedents Dying on or after Oct. 1, 1987.—When court determines assets of deceased do not exceed expenses of funeral, settling estate, last sickness, taxes and claims of government (excluding allowance for family support), it may order settlement. (45a-383).

When Administration Unnecessary.—See subhead Distribution Without Administration, supra.

Small Estates.—See subhead Distribution Without Administration, supra.

Third parties having knowledge as to any estate before the probate court may be summoned upon the written application of any person having interest in any matter or upon court's own motion to give testimony under oath relating to such matter. (45a-129).

Attendance may be compelled by subpoena and capias. (45a-129).

Incorporation by Reference.—Testator can incorporate by reference certain broad powers for executors or administrators c.t.a. or administrators c.t.a., d.b.n. or their successors or ancillary fiduciaries without setting forth powers at length. (45a-234). Also, other further powers can be specifically and individually incorporated. (45a-235). See also topic Trusts, subhead Incorporation by Reference.

Uniform Fiduciaries Act not adopted.

Uniform Principal and Income Act not adopted. See topic Trusts, subhead Accounting.

Uniform Prudent Investor Act adopted. (PA 97-140).

Uniform Simplification of Fiduciary Security Transfers Act.—Not adopted.

Uniform Anatomical Gift Act repealed but see topic Death, subhead Anatomical Donations. (19a-270a to 19a-2791). Signed statement or donor card is prima facie evidence of good faith attempt to conform to donor's intent and physician or health care provider or facility not civilly or criminally liable if they abide by statutes or another State's law. (SB 545; PA 98-172—repeals and substitutes CGS §19a-279b).

See note at head of Digest as to 1998 legislation covered.

See Topical Index in front part of this volume.

FIDUCIARIES:

See topics Executors and Administrators, Trusts; category Family, topic Guardian and Ward.

INTESTACY:

See topic Descent and Distribution.

PROOF OF CLAIMS:

See topic Executors and Administrators; category Civil Actions and Procedure, topic Pleading.

TRUSTS:

Kinds.—Inter vivos trusts are mostly within jurisdiction of courts of equity, which also have some jurisdiction with probate courts over testamentary trusts. (102 Conn. 96, 128 Atl. 292).

Charitable trusts may be created by deed or by will (45a-514) and need not designate a particular charitable purpose, provided the trustee or any other person has the power to select, from time to time, the charitable purpose, and no gift or bequest in trust accompanied by such power of selection is void for uncertainty (45a-515). Gift by deed or will to charitable community trust may incorporate by reference terms and conditions of any existing written charitable community trust, and no gift or bequest so made is void for uncertainty or invalid for failure of community trust to comply with statutes on wills. (45a-516). Community trustee must render annual account to probate court. (45a-517). Where current market value of charitable trust is under $150,000 steps may be taken to terminate trust. (45a-520). See catchline Private Foundations, infra.

Cemetery trust for perpetual care or improvement of a cemetery or lot therein is valid, and may be received by town, ecclesiastical society or cemetery association. (19a-299; 73 Conn. 56, 46 Atl. 278).

Common trust funds held by any fiduciary under stated conditions are valid. (36a-365).

Employees' trust funds created by employer as part of stock bonus, pension, disability, death benefit, or profit-sharing plan is exempt from rule against perpetuities and suspension of power of alienation, and income may be accumulated in accordance with terms of trust. (45a-505-508).

Life insurance and annuity proceeds may be held by company in trust upon such terms and restrictions as to revocation by insured and control by beneficiaries and with such exemptions from claims of creditors of beneficiaries other than insured as are agreed to in writing by company and insured. (38a-453, 38a-454). Insurance trust agreement with third person as trustee is not a testamentary trust. (119 Conn. 570, 177 Atl 742).

Spendthrift trust must give trustee power to accumulate or express authorization to withhold income, or income must be expressly given for support of beneficiary or his family, or else income is liable in equity for claims of creditors. (52-321; 95 Conn. 216, 111 Atl. 182). Settlor cannot create such trust for his own benefit. (129 Conn. 220, 27 A.2d 166).

Constructive trust arises by operation of law and is founded on fraud, actual or constructive, misrepresentation, imposition, circumvention, artifice, concealment, or abuse of confidential relations. (121 Conn. 153, 183 Atl. 394).

Resulting or presumptive trust rests upon presumed intention of parties to create a trust. (94 Conn. 350, 109 Atl. 249).

Dry or simple trust is conveyance in trust without further duties or directions to trustee and beneficiary has right of possession and can compel trustee to execute necessary conveyances. (93 Conn. 402, 106 Atl. 326).

Naked trust is recognized, and trustee has none of ordinary duties of trustee as to care of property. (56 Conn. 284, 15 Atl. 791).

Precatory trust requires clear intent to make expectation of testator binding upon donee, certainly as to subject matter of the expectation, and certainly as to the object to be benefited. (86 Conn. 516, 86 Atl.7).

Statutory trusts authorized and governed by Connecticut Statutory Trust Act. (34-500 to 34-547).

Private Foundations.—If charitable trust considered "private foundation" under federal Internal Revenue Code, authorized to make necessary expenditures to avoid imposition of taxes, and trustees prohibited from certain acts endangering charitable status under Internal Revenue Code. (33-281c).

Creation.—Where donor by inter vivos agreement wishes to establish voluntary trust by appointing a third person as trustee, he must make such a transfer of the property that nothing remains to be done on his part to make the gift effective. (131 Conn. 307, 39 A.2d 895). Express trust in real estate must be in writing (124 Conn. 140, 198 Atl. 577). Trusts of personal property may be created verbally, by direct and express statements, or by implication from the circumstances showing intention of donor to be creation of trust. (104 Conn. 169, 132 Atl. 902). Trust under a will may not be created by oral declarations. (86 Conn. 516, 86 Atl. 7). Declaration of trust arises when owner of property without making any transfer declares that he holds property in trust. (82 Conn. 504, 74 Atl. 781). Connecticut has adopted Uniform Testamentary Additions to Trusts Act. (45a-260).

Appointment of Trustee.—Donor or testator can appoint trustee and determine how to fill vacancy, but surviving trustee cannot appoint successor unless instrument or will so provides. (84 Conn. 494, 80 Atl. 758). Probate court in district where estate is, when no provision is made by law or in inter vivos instrument for contingency of death, refusal to act or resignation of trustee, and in district where will proved when in testamentary trust no trustee is appointed or trustee dies, becomes incapable, refuses to accept or resigns, may appoint suitable person to fill the vacancy. (45a-474). Superior court may also appoint trustee of inter vivos trust and may appoint testamentary trustee where trust would otherwise be defeated. (60 Conn. 314, 22 Atl. 945; 60 Conn. 32, 22 Atl. 447). Upon death, resignation, or removal of testamentary trustee for incapacity, neglect, or waste, court of probate may fill vacancy unless will provides otherwise.

(45a-242). Legal title vests in successor upon appointment and qualification, and certificate of appointment on land records in town where property is situated is evidence that legal title is vested in him. (45a-476).

Superior court may suspend powers of trustee of inter vivos trust during his war service and appoint substitute. (45a-479). Probate court may appoint foreign trustee of nonresident life tenant as trustee in Connecticut (45a-477), may appoint trustee of life estate in personalty where no trustee named, if life tenant does not give bond (45a-451) and may appoint trustee of estate of person who has disappeared (45a-478). Upon sale of undivided interest in estate, probate court may appoint trustee for any unknown or unascertained party entitled to share in proceeds. (45a-326).

Eligibility and Competency.—Corporations other than national and state banks may not act as trustee without specific legislative authority and license from Bank Commissioner. (36a-380 to 36a-386). Foreign corporation authorized by its charter to act as trustee and named as trustee in will of Connecticut resident or nonresident leaving property in state or so named by any person or persons to whom power of appointment of trustee was granted in such will, or so named by any corporation may qualify and act as testamentary trustee if state of its domicile extends similar privilege to Connecticut corporation, if it appoints Secretary of State and probate judge its agents for service of process. (45a-206; 52-60). National bank may act as trustee. (94 Conn. 648, 110 Atl. 54). Judge of probate may not appoint as trustee any corporation of which he is director or salaried officer unless such corporation has been nominated by testator or trustor. Nonresident may act as trustee, but appointment does not take effect until he appoints probate judge his agent for service of process. (52-60). Probate court can reject trustee nominated by testator for any cause impeaching his integrity or capacity. (54 Conn. 325, 8 Atl. 136).

Qualification.—Trustee qualifies upon accepting trust and giving necessary bond, and qualification dates from time bond filed and not from when bond approved by probate court. (73 Conn. 435, 47 Atl. 665). Testamentary trustee appointed by testator or trustee appointed by probate court to fill vacancy must give bond with surety, unless will provides otherwise, and refusal to give bond is deemed a refusal to accept or perform duties of trustee. Public or charitable corporation or cemetery association as trustee may give bond without surety. (45a-473). When will requires no bond or bond is deemed insufficient by probate court, court, upon application by interested party, may require trustee to furnish sufficient probate bond. (45a-473). Trustee for missing person must give bond before taking charge of estate (45a-478), as must successor trustee (45a-242). Probate bond need not be required of state bank or trust company or foreign bank or trust company which has qualified and been approved as trustee. Court may also dispense with bond requirement if not needed for protection of interested parties. (45a-169).

Removal of Trustee.—Trustee may be removed for being incapable of executing trust, for neglect, and for wasting estate, upon motion of probate court, or complaint of interested party or surety on his bond, and all suits in favor or against trustee removed survive to successor. (45a-242). Trustee may also be removed for failure to substitute new bond, for mismanagement, for failure to give additional bond (45a-141), and for failure to file succession tax return in time (12-359[a]). Insolvency or bankruptcy of trustee individually is not of itself ground for removal. (117 Conn. 573, 169 Atl. 602). Trustee may appeal from probate court decree of removal. (45a-243). Trustee removed must file account and turn over estate to successor, and probate court may enforce delivery to successor in same manner as court of equity might do. (45a-244; 80 Conn. 459, 68 Atl. 990).

General Powers and Duties of Trustees.—Courts of equity possess broad powers to advise trustees concerning their powers and duties, including construction of trust instrument, but will not interfere in exercise of discretionary powers in absence of fraud, bad faith, or abuse of discretionary power. (116 Conn. 588, 165 Atl. 807). Fiduciary appointed or whose appointment was approved by probate court may receive authority from it to compromise and settle (45a-151) and to arbitrate claims (45a-153). Trustee shall allocate receipts and expenditures to principal or income of trust in accord with terms of trust or with provisions of this act or, if neither is applicable, with what is reasonable and equitable. (45a-215). If claim against fiduciary required to account to probate court is disallowed, claimant must commence suit against trustee within four months after receiving written notice of disallowance. (45a-399). Trustee of estate of deceased nonresident may execute release of mortgage of Connecticut real estate provided he files certificate of appointment with release. (49-12). Payment or delivery of property by trustee in good faith under proper probate court order and before appeal is taken from such order does not make him liable for such money or property although the order is later reversed, vacated, or set aside. (45a-202). Testamentary trustee must pay real estate taxes due from estate before making final settlement of his account. (45a-333). Claim for moneys paid or services rendered estate in hands of trustee may be paid out of estate, but if estate is not sufficient, claimant may bring civil action against trustee for balance or may hold trustee liable to his personal responsibility for any debt contracted in execution of trust. (52-570a). Trustee having personalty subject to property tax must file return (12-45) and if not done, he forfeits to town where return should be made 2% of cash value of taxable property for each year of such neglect (12-46). Trustee is liable for estate tax due on property received by him until it is paid. (12-392). Trustee of inter vivos or testamentary trust may divide single trust into two or more separate trusts if division is in best interest of beneficiaries. Procedures for division set forth by statute. (45a-488).

Trustees of "private foundations" under federal Internal Revenue Code prohibited from certain acts endangering charitable status. (33-281c).

Sales and Mortgages.—Trustee has broad power under authority of probate court to mortgage and sell property. (45a-162 to 45a-169). When real estate is held in trust created by deed or will, and by reason of change of circumstances or in condition of real estate since creation of trust, execution of trust in exact accordance with trust is impossible or there would be failure to secure objects intended in trust, superior court in county where land is located may order sale of it. (52-498). Superior court may also order sale of real estate when it will best promote interest of trust beneficiaries. (52-499). Use of word "trustee" following name of grantee in deed, with or without name of cestui appearing, and without any other language expressly limiting powers or

TRUSTS . . . *continued*
interest of grantee does not, in absence of separate instrument duly executed and recorded defining powers of grantee, affect right of grantee to sell, mortgage, or otherwise dispose of real estate in same manner as if word "trustee" had not been used, and transferee or mortgagee from grantee is not liable for claim of any undisclosed beneficiary or for application of any money paid by him. (47-20).

Investments.—Trust funds, unless otherwise provided in trust instrument, may be invested in such real estate mortgages as savings banks in this state may be authorized by law to invest in, or may be deposited in savings banks incorporated by this state or in savings departments or state banks and trust companies located in this state, or may be paid into accounts of savings and loan associations located in this state insured by Federal Savings and Loan Insurance Corporation, or may be invested in any bonds, stocks including mutual funds registered under Federal Investment Company Act of 1940, or other securities selected by trustee with care of prudent investor. Trustee may, unless otherwise provided in trust investment, invest in securities of open-end or closed-end management investment company or investment trust registered under Investment Company Act of 1940. (45a-209). Banking institution acting as fiduciary may purchase up to 10% of issue of state or municipal bonds or securities underwritten by it or affiliate provided such bonds or securities are within top four rating categories recognized by state Banking Commissioner, beneficiaries receive annual disclosure that banking institution has interest in underwriting of bonds or securities, and purchase is made with care of prudent investor. (45a-203).

Funds may be kept invested in same securities as when received by fiduciary unless court directs, or trust instrument provides, otherwise. (45a-204). Temporarily uninvested funds may be deposited by trust company in bank. (36a-384). Funds over $1,000 and held for 30 days must be invested in income-producing media with rate of return at least equal to highest publicly-announced rate paid by such banking institution on similar deposits (36a-351).

Trustee cannot invest in purchase of shares on margin (89 Conn. 226, 93 Atl. 526), nor ordinarily make permanent improvements to real estate, in absence of authority in instrument creating the trust (109 Conn. 187, 145 Atl. 648), nor may trustee make personal loans from fund without security (130 Conn. 332, 33 A.2d 540). In a proper case courts can modify legislative or will provision as to trust fund investments. (133 Conn. 89, 48 A2d 266). Court will not interfere with investments made by trustee with discretionary power, unless there is bad faith, fraud, or abuse of discretion. (116 Conn. 588, 165 Atl. 807).

Common law requirement that security should disclose on its face that it is held in a particular trust renders impracticable investment of trust funds in participating mortgages. (121 Conn. 558, 186 Atl. 543).

Investments held by state bank and trust company or national banks as trustee must be segregated and not mingled with other assets and must clearly set forth the fiduciary capacity of the bank; but such bank as trustee may hold stock in name of nominee without mention of trust, if co-fiduciaries given prior consent, fiduciary retains possession of stock certificate and maintains adequate records indicating ownership, except may be held by clearinghouse. Fiduciary is personally liable for any loss resulting from act of nominee in connection with stock so held. (36a-352).

Fiduciary, with consent of probate court, may subscribe for and take shares of increased capital stock to which estate is entitled or may sell and transfer right to subscribe to such stock. (45a-205).

Accounting.—Allocations between principal and income are governed by Principal and Income Act. (45a-214 to 45a-227). Upon foreclosure, premises foreclosed or proceeds of sale are held by trustee in same manner for benefit of same persons and for same purposes as money secured by mortgage would be if collected without foreclosure, and if premises are not sold, are to be distributed or disposed of to persons who would have been entitled to money if collected. (49-18). Premises acquired upon conveyance or foreclosure by trustee become principal asset in lieu of mortgage and tenant for life or limited term is entitled to income from such property from date of its acquisition. (45a-480).

Probate court has jurisdiction over interim and final accounts of testamentary trustees and trustees appointed by such court. Probate court, upon application of trustee, may take jurisdiction of an inter vivos trust accounting, which jurisdiction is limited only to such account or, upon its own motion, court may appoint auditor to examine accounts. Probate court may grant beneficiary of inter vivos trust petition for accounting by trustee(s) if: (A) beneficiary has interest in trust entitled to accounting, (B) cause shown for accounting, (C) petition not to harass. Court has jurisdiction if: Trustee of trust resides in its district, principal place of business in district where corporate trustee, any of trust assets maintained or evidence of intangible property of trusts situated in district, or settlor resides in district. (45a-175). Such trustees, except those excused by will creating trust, must render account under oath at least once every three years, and such account must show fully how principal of trust is invested and items of income and expenditure. (45a-177). If amount held in trust is less than $2,000, or in case of corporate fiduciary under supervision of bank commissioner or any other fiduciary bonded by surety company authorized to do business in this state less than $10,000 no account is required unless ordered by court. (45a-177). But requirement of account every three years does not preclude probate court from ordering other accounts from time to time. (92 Conn. 286, 102 Atl. 586). Court may adjust and allow account after hearing upon notice to interested parties. (45a-178). Trustees of charitable community trust are subject to same requirements as to annual accounts. (45a-517). Probate court may require accounting from trustee for missing person. (45a-478). Surety upon any bond taken by probate court, or interested party, may apply for order requiring trustee to exhibit condition of estate held by him. (45a-143). When testamentary trustee dies before completion of accounting for his trust, his executor or administrator must settle account of decedent. (45a-180).

A hearing must be held on all final accounts (45a-179), and no resignation of trustee will be accepted until trustee has fully and finally accounted to probate court. (45a-242).

Uniform Trustees' Accounting Act not adopted.

Compensation.—Trustee of an express trust is entitled to reasonable compensation, but trustee of a resulting trust is not. (135 Conn. 584, 67 A.2d 409). There is no statute regulating the fees of trustees and matter of compensation is within discretion of appropriate court. (124 Conn. 472, 200 Atl. 809). Ordinarily a trustee is not entitled to compensation in addition to that fixed in the trust instrument or by statute, but may be allowed an additional sum for special and extraordinary services outside and beyond the general duties of the trust. (120 Conn. 322, 180 Atl. 469).

Discharge.—Trustee must file final account and have it accepted by probate court when trust is under jurisdiction of such court, before he can make distribution. (98 Conn. 471, 120 Atl. 317). He must also make distribution and have the return of distribution accepted by the court. (92 Conn. 286, 102 Atl. 586). Upon termination of trust, a testamentary trustee may, unless the will creating the trust provides otherwise, after settling his final account, deliver the property to the remainderman upon order of the probate court, without returning it to the estate of the decedent. (45a-481). For judicial termination of a trust, all parties must be sui juris and request it, all interests must have vested, and the design and object of the trust must be accomplished, and termination must not disturb restrictions put on by trustor. (125 Conn. 640, 7 A.2d 652; 90 Conn. 63, 96 Atl. 149). If assets of charitable trust are less than $150,000, beneficiary or trustee may terminate. (45a-520[b]). Probate court may terminate non-spendthrift trust if value is less than $40,000 and continuing trust is uneconomic or not in best interest of beneficiaries. (45a-484).

Gifts to Minors.—See category Family, topic Infants. See also category Family, topic Adoption, subhead Effect of Adoption.

Common trust funds provided for. (36a-365).

Uniform Principal and Income Act.—See supra subhead Accounting.

Uniform Fiduciaries Act not adopted.

Uniform Simplification of Fiduciary Security Transfers Act not adopted.

Accumulations.—Except in cases where charity is beneficiary, it is illegal to accumulate more than period measured by rule against perpetuities. (132 Conn. 96; 42 A.2d 796).

Perpetuities.—See category Property, topic Perpetuities.

Taxation of Income.—See 12-701.

Pour Over Trusts.—See topic Wills, subhead Bequests and Devises to Inter Vivos Trusts.

Incorporation by Reference.—Testator or settlor can incorporate numerous broad trustee powers enumerated in 45a-233(c); 45a-234; additionally, certain other further trustee powers can be specifically and individually incorporated by reference. (45a-235). See also topic Executors and Administrators, subhead Incorporation by Reference.

WILLS:

All persons of the age of 18 years and of sound mind may dispose of their estate by will. (45a-250).

Testamentary disposition is not restricted, and except for spouse's right to elect statutory share (see subhead Election, infra) will may dispose of all testator's property. There is no restriction as to amount which may be given to religious or charitable institutions. Devise purporting to convey all real estate of testator is construed to convey all real estate belonging to him at time of his decease, unless will clearly shows contrary intent. (45a-261). Any person may, by will, deed or other instrument, give, devise or bequeath property, real or personal or both, to any trustee or trustees, and may provide in such instrument that such property so given, devised or bequeathed shall be held in trust and income or principal applied in whole or in part for any charitable purpose. Donor or testator is not required to designate in such will, deed or other instrument particular charitable purpose or class of purposes for which such property shall be used or such income applied. Any such gift, devise or bequest is valid and operative, provided donor or testator gives to trustee or trustees thereof or to any other person or persons, power to select, from time to time and in such manner as such donor or testator may direct, charitable purpose or purposes to which such property or income thereof shall be applied. (45a-515, 47-2).

Execution.—Will or codicil is not valid unless it is in writing, subscribed by testator and attested by two witnesses, each of whom must subscribe in presence of testator, but a will executed in compliance with laws of state or country where executed may be admitted to probate here and is effectual to pass any estate situated in this state. (45a-251). It is unnecessary that witnesses should subscribe in each other's presence. (57 Conn. 182, 17 Atl. 926).

Uniform International Wills Act adopted. (50a-1 to 50a-9).

Attestation.—The following is sufficient:

Form

Subscribed, sealed and declared to be his last will and testament by the said . . . . . . in the presence of us, who, in his presence, and at his request, and in the presence of each other, have hereunto subscribed our names as witnesses this . . . . . . day of . . . . . . A. D., 19. . .

. . . . .of. . . .(city). . . . . .(state) . . . . . .
. . . . .of. . . . .
. . . . .of. . . . .

Any or all attesting witnesses may make and sign an affidavit before any officer authorized to administer oaths in or out of this state, stating facts required to prove the will in court, which affidavit should be written on the will or on a paper annexed thereto, and oath of witness so taken will be accepted as though made in court. (45-166). Affidavit may be in following form:

State of
County of } ss. (name of city) (date)

Then and there personally appeared the within named . . . . . ., ... and . . . . . . who, being duly sworn, depose and say: That they witnessed the execution of the within will of the within named testator, ...; that said testator subscribed said will and declared the same to be his last will and testament in their presence; that they thereafter subscribed the same as witnesses in the presence of said testator and in the presence of

See note at head of Digest as to 1998 legislation covered.

See Topical Index in front part of this volume.

WILLS . . . *continued*
each other and at the request of said testator; that the said testator at the time of the execution of said will appeared to them to be of full age and of sound mind and memory, and that they make this affidavit at the request of said testator.

. . . .

. . . .

. . . .

Subscribed and sworn to before me,

. . . .

(seal)

Notary Public.

Holographic will executed in Connecticut is not admissible. But such a will properly made outside the state is valid. (86 Conn. 630, 86 Atl. 664).

Nuncupative will executed in Connecticut is invalid. (74 Conn. 304, 50 Atl. 744).

Revocation.—Will executed before Jan. 1, 1997 is completely revoked by subsequent marriage, divorce, or dissolution of marriage, or birth or adoption of child or birth of child by heterologous artificial insemination or artificial insemination with semen of donor, as defined in 45-69f-n, if no provision for such event is made therein. As to wills executed after Dec. 31, 1996, subsequent marriage, dissolution of marriage, or birth or adoption of child will not revoke unaffected provision of will; surviving spouse receives intestate share if will executed before marriage and makes no provision for surviving spouse, unless it appears omission was intentional or testator appears to have provided for surviving spouse by other means; subsequent dissolution of marriage (including annulment but not including legal separation) revokes all testamentary dispositions or appointments of property to former spouse, and nominations as guardian, trustee, conservator, or other fiduciary; in cases where testator is without living children when will is executed, but subsequently has or adopts child or children, child or children receives intestate share, unless will gives all or substantially all to other parent, who survives testator; in cases where child or children at time of execution of will are provided for, but subsequently born or adopted child is omitted, omitted child receives share equal, as nearly as possible, to share each child receives under will, reduced proportionately if necessary, unless omission appears intentional or omitted child was provided for by other means; if it appears that testator's intention was to provide only for testator's then-living children, subsequently born or adopted child receives intestate share. (45a-257a-f). It cannot be revoked in any other manner except by burning, canceling, tearing or obliteration by testator or some person in his presence by his direction, or by later will or codicil. (45a-257).

Revival.—A will is not revoked by the mere execution of a subsequent will, although the latter contains a revocatory clause, and if the later will is destroyed by testator with knowledge that the former will is still in existence, that will, if allowed to stand until death of testator, is revived. (98 Conn. 21, 118 Atl. 454).

Testamentary gift to subscribing witness or spouse of subscribing witness is void unless will or codicil is legally attested without the signature of such witness or unless the devisee or legatee is an heir of the testator, but the competence of such witness is not affected by the gift. The interest of any witness in any community, church, society, association, or corporation, beneficially interested in any such gift does not affect the gift or the competency of witness. (45a-258).

Bequests and Devises to Inter Vivos Trusts.—Devise may be made by will to trustee of a trust established or to be established by any person provided the separate trust instrument is identified and is a written instrument executed at same time or before testator's will or is in a valid will or codicil thereto, regardless of date of such will or codicil. Devise is not invalid because trust is amendable or revocable or was amended after execution or death of testator. (45a-260). Devise to trust will not render trust or any part thereof subject to probate jurisdiction where not otherwise subject. (45a-259).

Uniform Testamentary Additions to Trusts Act adopted. (45a-260).

Probate.—Will is probated in court of probate of district where testator was domiciled at his death, and every person having knowledge of his designation in will as executor of testator's estate must present will in that court within 30 days after testator's death. (45a-283). If testator lived out of state, will may be proved in any district in which estate conveyed or any part of it is, but if there is such estate in more than one district first court in which proceedings are commenced has jurisdiction over all property of deceased in state. (45a-287). Upon application for admission of will to probate, court must hold hearing with notice to all parties known to be interested in estate (normally surviving spouse, executor if any, and known heirs-at-law), unless all such parties sign and file written waiver of notice, or unless court for cause dispenses with such notice. Finding that estate is only large enough to pay administration and funeral expenses and expenses of last illness is sufficient cause to dispense with notice. (45a-286).

Self-proved Wills.—See subhead Attestation, supra.

Contest.—Will is contested in probate proceedings, and the probate court must allow the executor his reasonable expenses of defending the will in that court, whether or not the will is admitted. If appeal is taken to Superior Court from order admitting or refusing to admit the will, executor is also allowed his reasonable expenses in maintaining or defending the appeal. These expenses are charged pro rata against the respective shares of the beneficiaries under the will and the distributees of the estate. (45a-294). Acts of executor in settling estate during pendency of appeal are valid to same extent as if no appeal had been taken, but executor may pay no legacies while appeal pending. (45a-296).

Legacies.—All pecuniary legacies are a charge on real property not specifically described and devised if personal property is insufficient for their payment, unless will directs otherwise. Specific legacies may not be taken or sold for payment of debts and charges against estate when there is other real or personal property, sufficient and available therefor and not specifically devised or bequeathed, but real property may be sold in lieu thereof, when necessary for this purpose, unless will directs otherwise. (45a-426). Encumbrances on real property or life insurance of decedent are chargeable to property or proceeds of policies and not to estate, unless expressly indicated, or to testamentary or named beneficiaries. (45a-266). Land specifically devised is not subject to payment of debts until other assets are exhausted. (120 Conn. 77, 179 Atl. 479).

Legacies are normally payable one year after death, and bear 6% interest thereafter, but there are exceptions to this rule. (53 Conn. 102, 22 Atl. 678). If will provides time of payment, interest runs from that time. (121 Conn. 106, 183 Atl. 400). Specific legacies are entitled to the income therefrom from date of death. (106 Conn. 19, 137 Atl. 20). No legacies may be paid while appeal from admission of or refusal to admit will to probate is pending. (45a-296).

Bequest of use for life or term of years of livestock, wearing apparel, and other personal property which will necessarily be consumed by using gives legatee an absolute estate in such property. (45a-267).

Total ademption occurs when the testator gives the legatee in his lifetime what he left him in his will or when before his death he so deals with the subject of the bequest as to render it impossible to effect the transfer or payment which the will directs. (75 Conn. 683, 55 Atl. 171). A specific legacy or devise is adeemed when the testator disposes of the property in his lifetime, whatever may have been his motive or intent in doing so. (133 Conn. 725, 54 A.2d 510). Ademption of a general legacy payable out of general assets of estate depends upon the intent of the testator. (56 Conn. 240, 13 Atl. 414).

Unclaimed Legacies.—See subhead Lapse, infra, and topic Descent and Distribution, subhead Escheat.

Lapse.—When a devisee or legatee who is the child, grandchild, brother or sister of the testator dies before the testator, and the will makes no provision for this contingency, the issue of the devisee or legatee take the devise or legacy. (45a-441). If a specific devise of real property in will executed after Oct. 1, 1947, is void or lapses or for any other reason fails to take effect, it passes under residuary clause unless will provides otherwise. (45a-442). Lapsed bequest of personalty also falls into residue. (97 Conn. 245, 116 Atl. 182). Lapsed gift of portion of residue passes by intestacy. (101 Conn. 142, 125 Atl. 253).

Children living when will is executed may be disinherited by mere failure to mention them. (45a-257; 45a-257b). See also category Family, topic Adoption, subhead Effect of Adoption.

Election.—Provision in will for surviving spouse is taken to be in lieu of statutory share in estate unless contrary intention clearly appears from will. But in any such case surviving spouse may elect to take statutory share in lieu of provision of will. Surviving spouse must, by signed written notice to probate court within 150 days of appointment of first fiduciary, elect to take one-third of estate for life. In absence of such election spouse is deemed to have accepted will and is barred of statutory share. Statutory share is set out by administrator of estate or by person appointed by probate court and may consist of both personal and real property. (45a-436).

Contribution.—When spouse elects to take statutory share in lieu of provision in will, general legacies are taken to satisfy that share, before specific devises or legacies are disturbed. (120 Conn. 77, 179 Atl. 479). When any estate bequeathed or devised to any person is taken for payment of debts and charges, all other legatees and devisees must contribute their proportional part to person from whom estate was taken. (45a-429). This section applies only when will is silent or intent uncertain (68 Conn. 201, 36 Atl. 38), and only in favor of specific legatees or devisees who have been deprived of property by judicial sale (71 Conn. 521, 42 Atl. 641; 77 Conn. 705, 60 Atl. 664).

Foreign executed wills may be admitted to probate in this state. See subhead Execution, supra.

Foreign probated wills conveying property in state may be proved in state by filing for record in probate court in district in which any of property is located (1) a duly authenticated and exemplified copy of will and of record of proceedings proving and establishing it and (2) complete statement of property of deceased in state. If copies are admitted, after hearing upon notice, they have the same effect as if will originally proved in such court. (45a-288).

Living Wills.—Physician or hospital will not be liable for damages or subject to criminal prosecution for withholding or removing life support system if patient is legally incapacitated, and decision to withhold life support system is based on best medical judgment of attending physician in accordance with usual and customary standards of practice; attending physician determines patient to be in terminal condition, or in consultation with physician qualified to make neurological diagnosis who has examined patient and deems patient to be permanently unconscious and attending physician considers patient's wishes concerning withholding or withdrawal of treatment. In determining wishes of patient, attending physician shall consider wishes of patient as expressed in document executed in accordance with 19a-575 and 19a-575a. (19a-571).

Simultaneous Death.—Uniform Simultaneous Death Act adopted. (45a-440).

Uniform Anatomical Gift Act repealed but see topic Death, subhead Anatomical Donations. (19a-279a to 19a-279l).

Testamentary Guardian.—See category Family, topic Guardian and Ward, subhead Foreign Guardians.

Testamentary Trusts.—See topic Trusts.

FAMILY

ADOPTION:

Unless child is to be adopted by new spouse of one already parent (45-61i), child must be free for adoption, i.e., have no living parents or all parental rights have been terminated under Connecticut law (45-61j).

Child may be given for adoption by: Statutory parent appointed after parental right terminated, single parent or guardian. (45-61i). Married persons must join in adoption, unless probate court finds sufficient reason for nonjoinder. (45-62).

Application and agreement of adoption filed in court of probate for district where adopting parent resides or in district where main office or any local office of statutory

ADOPTION . . . *continued*

parent is located. (45-63). Court of probate must upon motion of any party except adopting parent or may on its own motion or that of adopting parent transfer case to Superior Court. (45-61c).

Petition for validation of foreign adoption if necessary to obtain U.S. citizenship may be filed with court of probate. (45-63).

Termination of Parental Rights.—See topic Infants. Continuing jurisdiction conferred on court in pre-adoptive proceedings (17a-112) does not confer continuing jurisdiction on court for purposes of reopening judgment terminating parental rights (52-212a and PA 93-51). Motion to open decree terminating parental rights may not be granted if final decree of adoption has been issued. (PA 93-170). Foster parents have right to comment in proceedings regarding custody of children formerly in their care. (PA 98-185).

Proceedings.—Adoption is instituted by filing application in court of probate, together with written agreement of adoption in duplicate. Application shall include declaration that to best of knowledge and belief of declarant there is no other proceeding pending or contemplated in any court affecting child's custody or detailing nature of such proceeding and averring that it will not interfere with adoption. Probate court shall then request commissioner of children and youth services or child-placing agency to make investigation and written report to it within 90 days. On return of such report to court, hearing is held upon agreement, at which time court may deny application, enter final decree approving adoption, enter interlocutory decree, or order further investigation. If interlocutory decree is entered, hearing on final approval or disapproval must be held not less than 12 nor more than 13 months from institution of proceedings. At such hearing, adoption may be approved, disapproved or continued for further investigation as hereinbefore described. While interlocutory decree is in effect, child is deemed for all purposes to have been adopted. (45-63). Where stepparent or certain blood relatives adopting, procedure slightly different, and probate court may waive notice to, and report by, Commissioner of Children and Families or child placing agency. (45-63a).

Change of name of adoptee, as requested by the adopting parents, may be made by any court of probate as part of its final decree. (45-66a).

Records of adoption are confidential; no person other than adopting parents or adopted person, or person whose guardian or parents were removed, if over 18, for cause shown, may have access thereto except upon order of court. (45-68m). However, genetic parents, including person claiming to be father, who was not party to termination of parental rights proceedings, and adult biological siblings may make written request for release of identifying information. If adopted person consents, information may be released. (PA 95-179). New birth certificate listing adopting parents shall be issued. (7-53, am'd PA 94-26).

An adult younger than adopter may be adopted, but not without consent of husband or wife, if any, of adoptee. (45-67; 45-68).

Effect of Adoption.—Upon the entry of a final decree approving the adoption, an adopted child inherits from its adopting parents and their relatives and not from its natural parents and their relatives, and the adopting parent inherits from such child, except that when one parent has died and surviving parent has remarried, adoption by person with whom such remarriage is contracted does not bar child from inheriting from relatives of deceased parent. (45-67). Custody and support of adopted children governed by same rules as pertain to natural children. (46b-58). Words "child," "issue," "decedent," "heir," "grandchild" or their plurals used in any will or trust agreement executed after Oct. 1, 1959 include legally adopted persons unless such document indicates contrary intention. (45-64a). When surviving parent of child remarries, or when mother of child born out of wedlock marries, or when single person who has adopted child marries, other party to such remarriage or marriage may adopt such child, and such child, whether minor or adult, then inherits from such adopting parent and relatives instead of from relatives of any parent deceased at time of such adoption. (45-67).

Hard-to-Place Child.—If so designated by Commissioner of Children and Families, adoption shall be subsidized. (17-44 a-d). Adoption fees waived. (45-17a[h]).

ALIMONY:

See topic Dissolution of Marriage.

COMMUNITY PROPERTY:

System does not obtain in Connecticut.

DESERTION:

See topic Husband and Wife.

DISSOLUTION OF MARRIAGE:

Governing statute is Tit. 46b.

Grounds for dissolution of marriage are: finding that marriage has broken down irretrievably, or that parties have lived apart for a continuous period of at least 18 months due to incompatibility and no reasonable prospect of reconciliation exists, or for any of following: adultery, fraudulent contract, willful desertion for a year with total neglect of duty, seven years' absence unheard from, habitual intemperance, intolerable cruelty, sentence to imprisonment for life, any infamous crime involving a violation of conjugal duty and punishable by imprisonment for more than a year, or legal confinement because of mental illness for an accumulated period of at least five years within the six-year period next preceding complaint. (46b-40).

Legal Separation.—On petition of party who would be entitled to dissolution of marriage, court may decree legal separation having effect of dissolution of marriage except that parties are not free to remarry. Procedure and power of court are same as for dissolution of marriage. Parties may resume marital relations on filing with clerk of court their written declaration of such resumption, signed, acknowledged and witnessed. If relations are not resumed, either party may petition court for final decree of divorce. (46b-51). Wife who is separated from her husband through no fault of her own may

obtain equitable decree for support. (114 Conn. 575, 159 Atl. 489; 111 Conn. 124, 149 Atl. 246).

Process is same as in ordinary civil actions (46b-45), except that when any married person has been convicted of offense against chastity, which offense would be ground for dissolution of marriage or annulment of marriage, any person aggrieved may petition Superior Court within four months of conviction, and, upon notice to person so convicted, such court may grant dissolution of marriage, annulment, or such other relief as it may determine; but right to apply to civil side of said court for similar relief is preserved in such circumstances. (46b-48). When ground of action is mental illness, copy of writ and complaint must be served on adverse party, conservator of adverse party, if any, and welfare commissioner in Hartford. (46b-47).

Pleading.—Complaint claiming dissolution of marriage must state date and place of marriage, jurisdictional basis of court, whether or not there are minor children of parties, and, if so, date of birth of each and name of any individual or agency presently responsible by virtue of judicial award for custody or support of any such child. (46b-40; C. P. B. 453).

Defendant may counterclaim for dissolution.

Either party may submit request for conciliation, court may order conciliator named after which two mandatory consultations are required. (46b-53).

If, during pendency of dissolution or annulment of marriage, wife is pregnant, she may so allege in pleadings. Parties may in their pleadings allege and answer that child born of pregnancy will or will not be issue of marriage. (46b-45a).

Amendment to complaint for dissolution stating ground for dissolution arising subsequent to commencement of action may be permitted by court. (C. P. B. 455).

Citizenship Requirement.—None.

Residence.—Complaint may be filed any time after either party has established residence. Decree granting dissolution or legal separation granted if: (1) One party has been resident for year preceding filing of complaint; (2) either party was domiciled in state at time of marriage and has returned with intention of remaining permanently; (3) cause of dissolution arose after removal of either party to state. (46b-44).

Any plaintiff who has served or is serving with Armed Forces or Merchant Marine and who was a resident of this state at time of his or her entry into Armed Forces, shall be deemed to have continuously resided in this state during time he or she served with forces or Merchant Marine. (46b-44).

Jurisdiction.—Superior court shall have exclusive jurisdiction of all complaints seeking decree of annulment, dissolution of marriage or legal separation. (46b-42).

Time for Hearing and Decree.—No complaint may be heard or final decree granted until 90 days after return day; except whenever dissolution of marriage is claimed under a cross-complaint, amended complaint or amended cross-complaint. Such case may be heard and a decree granted thereon after expiration of 90 days from date on which original complaint in such action is made returnable and 20 days after such cross-complaint, amended complaint or amended cross-complaint has been filed. The 20-day delay does not apply (a) when waived by opposing counsel or (b) defendant not appearing, and amendment does not set forth a cause of action or one not contained in original complaint. (46b-67).

Temporary Orders.—Court may enter temporary order at any time after return date of writ awarding alimony and support pendente lite to either party. Court may also award exclusive use of family home or any other dwelling unit which is available for use as residence (PA 93-7) to either party. (46b-83).

Decree.—Final decree is entered as soon as issues are determined; no interlocutory decree.

Agreements concerning custody, support, alimony, etc., scrutinized by court for fairness. If written agreement approved, incorporated in decree; if disapproved, court makes other orders. (46b-66).

Evidence.—Where parties make oral or written stipulation that marriage has broken down irretrievably and they have submitted an agreement concerning custody, care, education, visitation, maintenance or support and alimony and disposition of property, testimony of either party, uncorroborated by other evidence is sufficient to permit a finding by court. (46b-51). In case of action claiming dissolution of marriage on ground of habitual intemperance, it is sufficient if cause of action is proved to have existed until time of separation of parties. In case of willful desertion for a year, with total neglect of duty, furnishing of financial support does not, in absence of other evidence, disprove total neglect of duty. (46b-32).

Alimony.—Either party may be ordered to pay alimony and support while suit pending. (46b-83). Court may assign definite portion of either party's estate to other, in addition to which, alimony may be granted to either spouse. (46b-81). Attachment to secure financial interest available by court order after hearing and notice whether or not money demand made in complaint; or by filing lis pendens on land records where real estate located including names of parties, nature of complaint, court, date of complaint and description of real property, provided, notice of lis pendens may be discharged by substitution of bond with surety. (46b-80).

Periodic alimony may be continued, set aside or modified by court upon showing of substantial change in circumstances by either party whether or not contemplated at dissolution, unless agreement specifies changes which will not alter agreement. (46b-86).

Lump sum alimony cannot be modified. (179 Conn. 277, 426 A.2d 271).

Division of Property of Spouses.—Superior Court may assign to either husband or wife all or part of estate of other. Court may pass title to real property to either party or to third person or may order sale of such real property, without any act by either husband or wife, when in judgment of court it is proper mode to carry decree into effect. (46b-81[a]).

In fixing nature and value of property, if any, to be assigned, court shall consider length of marriage, cause of dissolution, age, health, station, occupation, amount and sources of income, vocational skills, employability, estate, liabilities, and needs of each of parties and opportunity of each for future acquisition of capital assets and income.

DISSOLUTION OF MARRIAGE . . . *continued*

Court shall consider contribution of each of parties in acquisition, preservation or appreciation in value of their respective estates. (46b-81[c]).

Court has broad discretion under 46b-81 in assigning property upon dissolution of marriage. (173 Conn. 273, 377 A.2d 260).

Name.—Woman may have name changed to her birthname or former name after dissolution decreed. (46b-63).

Paternity.—If wife is pregnant during pendency of dissolution of marriage and parties disagree as to whether husband is father of child, court shall hold hearing within reasonable time after child's birth to determine paternity. (46b-45a).

Custody of Children.—Decree assigning custody of minor children, whether or not adopted, to either party or both jointly may be made pending suit or after termination thereof, and amended at any time. (46b-56).

Uniform Child Custody Jurisdiction Act adopted. (46b-90 to 46b-114).

Support of Children.—

Uniform Interstate Family Support Act.—Effective Jan. 1, 1998. (PA 97-1; S.B.3002). Petitions to be filed with Family Support Magistrate Division; administrative and non-judicial functions may be performed by Superior Court Support Enforcement Division. (§3). Comprehensive act pertaining to extent of jurisdiction to enforce/modify orders of support (§§5-10); priority of multiple support orders (§§11-13); registration of support orders (§14); standing to maintain support proceeding (§15); choice of laws (§16); distribution of information and orders (§17); notice (§§18-19); enforcement assistance (§20); legal representation (§21); negligent enforcement contingencies (§22); information resources (§23); content of petition for support or modification (§24); confidentiality (§25); assessment and allocation of fees (§26); personal jurisdiction (§27); conclusiveness of paternity (§28); introduction of evidence (§29); interstate dissemination of information (§30); interstate discovery (§31); disbursement and maintenance of records of proceeds (§32); issuance of support orders (§33); administrative enforcement of support orders (§34); registration of foreign order for enforcement (§§35-37); calculation of obligation under orders (§38); notice to party of registration of foreign order (§39); contesting validity of registered order and burden of proof (§§40-41); confirmation of registered order (§42); modification of foreign order and subsequent enforcement (§§43-45); enforcement of modified order (§46); paternity determination (§47); demand and extradition of violators (§§48-49).

§§51-57 modify existing sections of following statutes:
§51 modifies 16b-745(b) re: reasonableness of order;
§52 modifies 46b-46(b) re: jurisdiction over nonresident;
§53 modifies 46b-49 re: closed hearing;
§54 modifies 46b-62 re: payment of attorney's fees;
§55 modifies 46b-69 re: marriage dissolution, annulment, separation;
§56 modifies 46b-160 re: paternity;
§57 modifies 46b-170 re: withdrawal of petition;
§58 modifies 46b-172 re: acknowledgment of paternity and support;
§59 modifies 46b-179a re: recordation of paternity judgments;
§60 modifies 46b-179b re: recognition of foreign paternity judgment;
§61 modifies 46b-179c re: notice of paternity judgment;
§62 modifies 46b-179d re: appeal from foreign paternity judgment;
§65 modifies 46b-215 re: enforcement of reasonable orders;
§66 modifies 46b-215b re: payment guidelines;
§67 modifies 46b-231 re: Family Support Magistrate's Act;
§69 modifies 52-57 re: service of process;
§70 modifies 52-251d re: attorney's fees for state;
§71 modifies 52-362 re: income withholding (also 52-362f);
New §73 re: dissemination of and procedures for enforcing foreign income withholding order.

Child Support Reform (PA 97-7; S.B. 3001) effective July 11, 1997. Institution modification of procedures to assist in locating parents and other persons who have deserted children and may be liable for support. (S.B. 3001; PA 97-7; 42-18; 7-42; 7-48; 7-50; 7-62b).

Following are new sections:

§6 re: voluntary acknowledgments of paternity (18b-27; 17b-90; 17b-137; 17b-179; 17b-745; 19a-42[c]; 36a-42; 362-43[c]; 382-497a[e]; 46b-25; 46b-84);

§18 re: reports identifying paternity are admissible without further foundation than certification by creator or custodian (46b-160; 46b-168);

§21 re: persons must submit to paternity testing unless otherwise excused (46b-171; 46b-172; 46b-172a[f]; 46b-215; 46b-231; 52-251d[a]; 52-362; 52-362d; 52-362e);

§31 re: defines past due support (46b-220; 46b-221);

§34 re: recordation of social security numbers (46b-69b; 46b-231[m]);

§36 re: family support magistrate may order parenting education participation (46b-164).

Welfare Reform.—Effective July 1, 1997. (H.B. 8003; PA 97-2).

General legislation to research and implement procedures to streamline aid to families and financial assistance to municipalities, modifies numerous provisions of existing law. See amendments to cc. 1b, 4, 7-10, 12, 16a, 17b, 18a, 19a, 19b, 31, 32, 36a, 38a, 42, 45a, 54, 62, 54 and 97.

New sections are as follows:

§117 (rental assistance for elderly) (19a-122b);
§119 (computerized information/case management system);
§120 (employment assistance program);
§121 (enhancing effectiveness of employment services);
§123 (conviction of substance abuse/possession);
§144 (qualified aliens eligible for [temporary] assistance) (17b-352; 17b-353; 17b-272; 8-11g; 8-115a[2]);
§§157-159 (establishment of registry of persons terminated from employment due to abuse/neglect and terms of employment of those persons) (2c-2b[a]; 42-207; 10-303[2]; 17b-113; 17b-115; 17b-180—17b-182; 17b-680 to 17b-688a; 17b-689a; 17b-690 to 17b-693; 17b-811).

Remarriage.—No restrictions. Divorced person applying for marriage license must present certified copy of dissolution decree. (46b-31; 46b-26). Remarriage of husband does not affect his obligation to pay alimony (116 Conn. 632, 166 Atl. 67) but remarriage of wife terminates her right to alimony (112 Conn. 256, 152 Atl. 302) unless decree specifies otherwise.

Foreign Divorces.—Certain foreign matrimonial judgments become judgments of court of this state upon filing certified copy of judgment in court of this state. (46b-70).

Effect of Divorce on Will.—See category Estates and Trusts, topic Wills.

Annulment of Marriage.—See topic Marriage.

Provisions for Maintenance of Wife or Children in Case of Nonsupport.—See topic Husband and Wife.

DIVORCE:

See topic Dissolution of Marriage.

GUARDIAN AND WARD:

Father and mother are joint guardians of their children under age of 18. If unfit, either or both may be removed upon application to probate court by any adult relative (blood or marriage) of child, by court on own motion, or by counsel for child. (45-43, 45-43a). Probate court will appoint guardian of minor's estate, if he has one, which guardian may be same as guardian of his person or different one. (45-47). Trust companies may be guardians of estates but not of person. (36-57). Court of probate may determine visitation rights to any person removed as guardian temporarily pending hearing. (45-44; 45-44e, 45a-612, am'd 93-62).

Parent, spouse, or guardian of minor may not receive or use minor's property exceeding $5,000 in value until formally appointed guardian of estate. (45-49).

Incapable Persons.—Statutory provision made for guardianship (called conservatorship) of incapables. (45-70 through 45-77a). "Incapable" defined as person with physical or mental infirmities rendering him unable to adequately manage his own affairs. (45-70a). Duties of conservator similar to duties of guardian. Include duty to support family of incapable. (45-75). If no suitable conservator can be found, Commissioner on Aging or Commissioner of Human Resources shall accept appointment as conservator of any "incapable" 60 years or older. (45-70g). Incapable may be restored to capacity upon court hearing and upon death of incapable, property turned over to estate. Conservatorship may be terminated if court determines ward has no assets. (45-77).

19a-458 to 19a-458f provides procedures and details powers needed to investigate cases of abuse of mentally retarded persons.

Standby Guardian.—Parent or guardian may designate standby guardian for minor child using specified form of affidavit, for period of up to one year, such designation to take effect upon occurrence of specified contingency, including but not limited to mental incapacity, physical disability, or death of principal. (45a-624d, am'd PA 95-50).

Foreign Guardians.—When any personal property in this state belongs to a nonresident who has a guardian of his estate appointed under the laws of his place of residence, such guardian may, by application to the probate court for the district where the property is located and on showing that the property is not subject to debts in this state and that he has provided a proper bond, remove such property to the state of residence of ward. (45-55).

Foreign guardian may remove proceeds of sale of real estate upon like procedure. (45-55; 45-56).

Surviving parent may by will appoint a guardian or guardians of person and estate of minor and guardian(s) may be nonresidents. (45-51[a], am'd PA 86-200, §1; PA 86-264, §5).

Noncustodial parent may appoint guardian for child by will if (1) child is minor; (2) custodial parent dies; and (3) probate court has not already appointed different guardian. (PA 96-98).

Real Estate.—Guardians may lease (45-52, am'd PA 86-200, §4), partition (45-57), mortgage or sell real property under order of probate court (45-238).

Gifts to Minors.—See topic Infants.

Uniform Fiduciaries Act not adopted.

Uniform Simplification of Fiduciary Security Transfers Act not adopted.

Child Custody.—See topic Dissolution of Marriage.

HUSBAND AND WIFE:

Rights and Disabilities.—Married women are subject to none of common law disabilities associated with that status.

Separate Property.—Wife's separate earnings are her sole property and she may contract with her husband or third persons, may convey and receive conveyance of real and personal property and may sue and be sued in her own name, her property being subject to attachment and execution. (46b-36).

Actions.—Husband and wife may transact business with each other and one spouse may act as attorney in fact for other. Wife may sue or be sued by her husband in contract or tort. (88 Conn. 42, 89 Atl. 889; 103 Conn. 583, 131 Atl. 432). In civil actions arising out of personal injury or property damage as a result of which husband of plaintiff has made or will be compelled to make expenditures or has contracted indebtedness, amount of such expenditures or indebtedness may be recovered by plaintiff, provided a recovery by plaintiff bars claim of husband, except in an action in which husband is a defendant. (52-204). Spouses may bring action against one another for negligence in operation of motor vehicle even if accident happened in state which would bar action. Rights, including standard of care, determined as if injury occurred in Connecticut. (52-572d). Any adult person who has been subjected to threat of present physical pain or physical injury by his or her spouse may apply to superior court for relief. (46b-15).

HUSBAND AND WIFE... *continued*

Agency.—Both spouses liable for necessary family expenses. Joint duty of each spouse to support family. No action maintained against either spouse during or subsequent to separation for any liability of other spouse if spouse who is liable for support has provided other spouse with reasonable support. (46b-37).

Special rules for abandoned spouses. (46b-37).

Antenuptial Contracts.—Governed by Connecticut Premarital Agreement Act, effective Oct. 1, 1995. (PA 95-170).

Conveyances.—Either spouse may freely dispose of his or her property, inter vivos, without the other spouse joining in the conveyance. (46b-36; 68 Conn. 91, 35 Atl. 783; 71 Conn. 233, 41 Atl. 773).

All the foregoing applies where the marriage occurred on or after Apr. 20, 1877. Where the marriage occurred before that date, the common law disabilities of coverture apply in somewhat modified form.

Desertion or Nonsupport.—If person neglects to furnish reasonably necessary support to his spouse, minor child or parent under 65, when physically and otherwise capable of doing so, he is subject to imprisonment of not more than one year, but execution of sentence may be suspended by court on condition of payment of support commensurate with necessities of case and abilities of individual. Failure to pay is punishable as contempt and in addition thereto or in lieu thereof, priority execution may be issued. (53-304). See category Criminal Law, topic Criminal Law.

Uniform Reciprocal Enforcement of Support Act (1952 version) has been adopted. (17-327 to 17-355b). Civil enforcement is by Superior Court.

Community property system does not obtain in Connecticut.

INFANTS:

Any person under age 18 years is minor, except as otherwise provided by statute. (1-1d). In regards to Liquor Control Statutes, any person under age 21 years is minor. (30-1[20]. Infants are liable for reasonable value of necessaries. (42-2). In general common law as to liability on contracts obtains. Infants may sue only through next friend, but married minor may prosecute or defend dissolution of marriage or legal separation in his or her own name. (46b-43). No civil nor criminal judgment nor juvenile court proceeding, nor probate proceeding against infant is legal unless guardian ad litem has been appointed by court. (45-54). Minor may sue parent for tort in motor vehicle actions. (52-572[c]).

A minor 15 years old or more may contract for life, health and accident insurance upon his own life for his (or her) own benefit or for that of his father, mother, husband, wife, child, brother or sister. (38-157).

Place of public accommodation may not restrict mother's right to breast-feed child. (46a-64).

HIV Testing and Treatment.—Parental consent not required for HIV testing and treatment. (PA 92-119, §1).

Parental Responsibility.—Parent or guardian of unemancipated minor who wilfully or maliciously causes personal or property damage is liable for such damage up to $5,000. (52-572).

Minor charged with commission of any offense must be accompanied in court by parent or guardian, unless court waives. (54-199).

Any veteran or other person eligible for a loan pursuant to the Servicemen's Readjustment Act of 1944 may enter into and contract in this state for a loan or loans pursuant to such Act although he is a minor. The claim of infancy may not be pleaded in any action arising out of any such loan. (36-4).

Uniform Transfers to Minors Act adopted. (PA 95-117).

Uniform Securities Ownership by Minors Act not adopted.

Termination of Parental Rights.—Probate court may terminate parental rights upon petition of: (1) Either or both parents; (2) guardian; (3) selectman of any town having charge of any foundling; (4) officer of any child-care or child-placing agency; or (5) blood relative of child when child has been deserted; if over age of 12, child's consent is necessary. (45-61c). Contested cases may be transferred to Superior Court. Notice of hearing on petition must be given to all interested parties including father of minor child born out of wedlock if paternity has been acknowledged or adjudicated. If either or both parents contest termination, commissioner of child and youth services must make investigation and report. (45-61c, 45-61d).

Court may terminate parental rights if in best interest of child and it is found that parent voluntarily and knowingly consents to termination, or that child has been abandoned or abused. Court order terminates all rights and responsibilities except child's right of inheritance and religious affiliation. (45-61a to 45-61h).

Motion to open or set aside judgment terminating parental rights may not be granted if final decree of adoption has been issued prior to filing of motion. (PA 93-170).

Adoption.—See topic Adoption.

Alcoholic Beverages.—Drinking Age is 21 for both sexes. (30-1[20]).

Notice of Child Abuse.—In case of single, custodial parent or guardian, notice of substantiated child abuse complaint must be given by Department of Children and Families by certified mail to custodial and non-custodial parents and guardian of child. Content of notice is proscribed by Act and proof of service must be obtained. (PA 98-173; Substitute HB 5282).

Education.—SB 61, PA 98-168 concerns programs and financing pertaining to special education including but not limited to benefits and grants (CGS §§10-66ee; 10-74d; 10-76a; 10-262h; 10-262i; 10-2641); custodial/institutionalized children (CGS §10-76d[e][2]); access and support (CGS §10a-54); financial responsibility (CGS §10-253[b]); school profile reports (CGS §10-220); review/reporting procedures (CGS §10-66gg); advisory board/judicial oversight (CGS §10-76i; PA 98-168, §11); interdistrict programs (CGS §10-266j; PA 98-168, §§23, 25); classification of children (CGS §10-17[f]). *Note:* new provisions concerning procedures for determining educational needs (PA 98-168, §5); grants (PA 98-168, §§10, 17); accessing resources (PA 98-168, §7); and minority teacher incentive programs (PA 98-168, §13).

All persons providing interpretation services for hearing impaired shall register annually with Commission on the Deaf and Hearing Impaired. Interpreters must pass written tests, be certified and satisfy continuing education requirements. There are additional requirements for interpreters in medical and legal fields. (CGS §§46a-27, et seq.; 51-245; 51-245a; HB 5118; PA 98-252).

MARRIAGE:

Consent Required.—If either party is under supervision or control of a guardian or conservator, written consent of such guardian or conservator signed in the presence of one witness and acknowledged before a notary public must be filed with the registrar. If either party is a minor, written consent similarly witnessed and acknowledged must be given by parent or guardian; if minor is under 16 years, written consent of judge of probate of district where minor lives is also required. (46b-30). Person married without required consent acquires no right by marriage in property of any person who is under supervision of conservator at time of marriage. (46b-29).

License.—Persons intending to be married must obtain certificate from Registrar of Vital Statistics in town in which such marriage is to be celebrated. It is sufficient that the application for certificate be signed and sworn to by one party if, before certificate is granted, the other party signs and swears to the application before the Registrar. If applicant has been divorced or marriage dissolved, certified copy of divorce or dissolution decree or certificate from clerk of court issuing decree must be presented. (46b-31).

Certificate is license for authorized person to perform marriage within town named and is good for 65 days after issuance. (46b-24).

Fee for marriage license is $10 plus $20 surcharge. (7-73). See category Documents and Records, topic Records, subhead Vital Statistics.

Serological Test.—Application for certificate will not be accepted until Registrar receives statement from licensed physician that female applicant under age of 50 and capable of pregnancy has been given standard blood test for rubella. (46b-26). Judge of probate for district within which marriage is to be celebrated may waive this requirement by written decision that public policy or physical condition of either party so requires. (46b-27).

Waiting Period.—Certificate may not be issued until fourth day after filing of application unless probate judge certifies that public policy or physical condition of either party requires earlier marriage. (46b-27).

Ceremonial Marriage.—Marriage must be solemnized by judge, justice of the peace, or ordained or licensed clergyman belonging to this or other state so long as he continues in work of the ministry. No public official, his assistant or deputy legally authorized to issue license may perform marriage under license issued by such official assistant, or deputy. Marriages celebrated by any other person are void, but any marriage solemnized according to the forms and usages of any religious denomination shall be valid. All marriages that were performed before effective date of this act and otherwise valid except that justice of peace was unauthorized are valid. (46b-22a, am'd PA 85-83, §§1, 2; PA 89-4).

Report of Marriages.—Person performing the ceremony must certify upon the license the fact, time, and place of such marriage and return it to issuing Registrar before end of first week of month next succeeding the marriage. (46b-34). Such certificate is prima facie evidence of the facts stated therein. (46b-35). Registrar must record certificate and send certified copy to state health commissioner. (7-42).

Record.—See category Documents and Records, topic Records, subhead Vital Statistics.

Common law marriages are not recognized. (165 Conn. 277, 334 A.2d 437). No decision on local recognition of out-of-state common law marriage.

Proxy marriages are not authorized.

Marriages by written contract are not authorized.

Prohibited Marriages.—Relatives nearer than first cousins may not marry, and incestuous marriage is void. (46b-21). Common law determines voidable marriages.

Foreign marriage, where one party is Connecticut citizen, is valid if celebrated in conformity with law of country of marriage, provided each party would have legal capacity to contract such marriage in this state. (46b-28). Any party where foreign matrimonial judgment rendered must file certified copy of marriage judgment in state that such judgment is final. Certificate must have full name and last known address and name and address of court in foreign state where judgment rendered. Foreign matrimonial judgment becomes judgment of court where filed and enforced in same manner as any like judgment of court of state. (PA 89-3).

Annulment.—When marriage from any cause is void or voidable under Connecticut law, or law of state of celebration, Superior Court must declare such marriage void and may make such order as to children, who shall be deemed legitimate, or alimony as it might in a proceeding for dissolution of marriage. (46b-40, 46b-60). Spouse of person convicted in any court of offense against chastity which would be ground for annulment may, within four months, petition Superior Court for annulment. (46b-48).

Connecticut Premarital Agreement Act governs such agreements effective Oct. 1, 1995. (PA 95-170).

MARRIED WOMEN:

See topics Husband and Wife, Marriage; categories Civil Actions and Procedure, topic Evidence, subhead Witnesses; Debtor and Creditor, topic Homesteads; Documents and Records, topic Acknowledgments; Estates and Trusts, topics Executors and Administrators, Wills; Property, topic Dower.

See note at head of Digest as to 1998 legislation covered.

See Topical Index in front part of this volume.

HEALTH

HEALTH CARE:

Before earlier of execution of contract for continuing care, or transfer of money or other property to provider, provider shall deliver to contracting party or his legal representative conspicuous statement notifying prospective resident that: (1) contract is investment which may be at risk; (2) provider's ability to meet its contracted obligations depends on its financial performance; (3) prospective resident is advised to consult attorney or other professional advisor; and (4) Department of Social Services does not guarantee security of investment. (CGS §§17b-520; 17b-535; 17b-524; 17b-525; 42-152; HB 5648; PA 98-250). *Note:* §23 of PA 98-250 modifies CGS §17b-522.

INSURANCE

INSURANCE COMPANIES:

The business of insurance in general is governed by Title 38, and is under the supervision of the Insurance Commissioner. (38-4). See also c. 592 (Hospital Service Corporations); c. 593 (Medical Service Corporations).

Insurance Commissioner has general supervision over domestic, foreign and nonresident companies, and insurance agents, solicitors, brokers and adjusters, and has duty to see that laws relating to insurance are faithfully executed, as well as enforcing provisions of Titles 38 and 38a through his or her enumerated powers of those powers reasonable and necessary to protect public interest. (38-4). Whenever all parties to claim for medical malpractice agree, they may request insurance commissioner select nonbinding pretrial screening panel. (38-19b to 38-19f). Commissioner may conduct investigations and hearings concerning insurance. (PA 86-95, §2). Division of Consumer Affairs shall review and mediate complaints. (PA 87-515, §1). Insurance department maintains brokered transactions guaranty fund from which any resident aggrieved by action of insurance broker or unlicensed person engaged in business of insurance may recover compensation not exceeding $25,000. (PA 89-106).

Each company doing business in Connecticut must, by Mar. 1 of each year, file with commissioner, on forms prescribed by him, report of its condition on preceding Dec. 31. In addition to annual report, Commissioner may require quarterly or even more frequent reports. (38-24; 33-160). If he finds that company is doing business in illegal or improper manner (as, for instance, by granting rebates or other inducements not included in policy [38-59] by issuing false or misleading information as to terms of policies or financial condition [38-55; 38-56] by using unauthorized policy forms, or failing to meet capital, surplus, reserve and deposit requirements) or if he finds that company is failing to adjust and pay losses and obligations when due, except claims to which in his judgment there is substantial defense, he may order discontinuance of such practices or payment of such losses and obligations. (38-8). Enforcement of such order is provided for by power of revocation of license in case of foreign or nonresident company (38-20), and by power to cause receivership and dissolution in case of domestic company (38-9).

Commissioner shall review conduct of domestic insurance company within 30 days of change of control and must give written approval before company can engage in specified transactions for up to three years. (PA 87-302).

When Governor declares existence of banking emergency affecting local companies, Commissioner, with approval of Governor, may issue and enforce such regulations for management and operation of insurance companies as may be for the protection of policy holders and stockholders. (38-17).

License.—No insurance company (domestic, nonresident, or foreign) may do business in state without a license from Commissioner. Application for license must include certified copy of charter, evidence of compliance with laws of state or country where organized, and statement of financial condition with evidence of its correctness. Before license may be issued, there must be compliance with laws as to process agent, capital and deposit requirements, etc. License expires on May 1 following date of issue, is renewable annually, and for cause may be suspended, revoked, or reissued. Insurance company which writes or receives more than 10% of premiums from employees of employer who controls insurer cannot be licensed. (38-20). Commissioner may refuse or revoke license to company incorporated in state or country refusing permission to Connecticut company to do business on certificate of solvency and good management issued by him and on compliance with reasonable laws of that state or country as to deposits of money or securities, until his certificate is recognized. (38-22).

Any foreign insurer admitted to do business in state for purpose of writing insurance may become domestic insurer. Any domestic insurer may transfer its domicile and become foreign insurer. (PA 91-232).

Issuance of burial contracts or certificates constitutes insurance (38-32), but guarantee of workmanship and materials by seller of property does not (38-31). State bank and trust company may not engage in insurance business. (36-60).

Risk retention groups must be chartered and licensed under state's insurance laws. (PA 87-135, §2).

Unauthorized insurers, doing insurance business in Connecticut, deemed to have appointed secretary of state agent for process in any action by insurance commissioner or state, and insurance commissioner agent for all other process. To file pleading in court or administrative proceeding, unauthorized insurer must post cash, securities, or bond with surety; or become authorized. Contracts of such insurer are unenforceable, and fines are provided for doing unauthorized insurance business. (38-263 to 38-272).

Investigators, adjusters, and insureds involved in unauthorized insurance must report to commissioner of revenue services. 4% premium receipts tax plus penalties for nonpayment, imposed on such an insured. (38-371).

Capital and Surplus Requirements.—No fire, marine, or casualty insurance company can be initially licensed to do business in Conn., unless it complies with following requirements: To transact fire, marine, accident, health, workmen's compensation, liability, fidelity and surety, or title insurance, company must have capital of $500,000. Must also have paid-in surplus of $250,000 for fire and marine insurance, and $500,000 for other lines. To transact mortgage guaranty insurance, company must have capital of $2,000,000 and paid-in surplus of same amount. (38-93). To transact more than one of above forms of insurance, company must meet total minimum requirements, as to capital and surplus, of all forms to be transacted, except no need to have more than $2,000,000 capital and $2,000,000 surplus in aggregate. (38-93[b]). Nonresident or foreign life insurance company must have capital and surplus funds of $3,000,000 to be initially licensed. (38-130a).

Mutual insurance company may be licensed to transact any or all forms of insurance when net surplus of such company is at least as great as capital and surplus requirements for companies with capital stock. (38-93; 38-130a).

Prohibited Communications.—No insurer may knowingly send or permit to be sent any written communication or oral statement to any person known or believed to have claim for bodily injury or wrongful death that affirmatively advises against need for or discourages retention of attorney. (PA 97-58).

Foreign Insurance Companies.—See infra, subheads Deposits; Risk Limits.

Foreign insurance companies are to be treated as domestic companies for purposes of state taxes. (PA 90-196).

Deposits.—Where other states require deposits of securities with Connecticut state officer before doing business in such other states, State Treasurer may be depository for domestic insurance companies, and may issue certificates of deposits. Legal title to securities deposited is transferred to him in trust, but company may receive income from these securities. (38-43). He must return deposit to company when all policies paid, cancelled, or reinsured and all liabilities extinguished or assumed by another company (38-46), or deliver them to receiver in case of receivership (38-47).

Foreign insurance company to transact fire, marine or casualty insurance must furnish certificate showing it has cash deposit with treasurer of this state, or proper officer of some other state, of not less than minimum capital and surplus requirements for similar nonresident insurance companies, or $750,000, whichever amount is less. (38-93[b]).

Trusteed surplus of foreign insurance company, for purposes of Connecticut insurance laws, consists of aggregate value of its money or securities deposited as above, plus real estate mortgages legal for investment by such companies in states where land lies, plus all other assets in United States in which similar domestic insurance companies may invest, after deducting for losses, liabilities, and unearned premiums. Such mortgages and other assets must be held by United States citizen trustees approved by Commissioner for benefit of policyholders and creditors. (38-94). Trustees are appointed by company and are subject to examination by the Commissioner. (38-95).

Reserves.—Every company transacting business in state must at all times maintain reserves equal to amount of its liability under all its policies, computed according to statute or requirements of Commissioner, to protect policyholders and secure solvency of company. (38-25).

Life insurance companies' reinsurance reserves are computed by Commissioner after receipt of each annual report by valuing all outstanding policies upon net premium basis, according to company valuation standard, but must equal legal minimum standards prescribed by statute. Minimum standard varies, depending upon date policy issued. (38-130). Companies transacting health, accident and liability insurance in Connecticut must maintain premium reserve equal to unearned portion of gross premiums charged for covering the risks. (38-164). Surety company doing business in state must report amount of its reserve fund as a liability in its annual statement. (38-176). Companies transacting livestock insurance and mutual companies transacting boiler insurance must maintain premium reserves on all policies in force equal to unearned portion of gross premiums charged for covering risks. (38-183; 38-184).

Risk Limits.—No foreign insurance company may insure against loss by fire or inland navigation, nor expose itself to any such loss by any one risk, for any greater amount in proportion to its capital than may domestic companies. (38-111). No risk of stock fire company doing business in state, after deducting portion reinsured in another company authorized to do business in Connecticut, may exceed 10% of its paid-up capital and surplus. One risk of mutual fire company doing business in state, after deducting reinsurance, may not exceed 10% of total of net surplus and two and one-half times the amount of its total cash premiums or premium deposits in force. In no event, however, may risk exceed amount authorized by charter, by-laws, or directors. (38-110).

Liability of surety company for one person, corporation, etc. limited to one-tenth of its paid-up capital and surplus unless excess over this amount covered by indemnifying security. (38-177). No one risk of mutual boiler insurance company may exceed 10% of its net assets. (38-185).

Rates.—Rating organizations permitted, but regulated, and all insurers must be given equal access to services of rating organizations. No insurers may agree between or among themselves to set same rates. Insurance Commissioner is responsible for determining whether rates or rating schedules are neither excessive nor inadequate according to statutory standards. (38-201a to 38-201s; 38-20lr; 10-289; 7-10). Division of rate review shall review and determine if rates violate statutory requirements. (PA 87-515, §1). Any insurance company delivering medical supplement policies which seeks to increase rates must file request with insurance department 60 days prior to proposed effective date of increase. After public hearing, Insurance Commissioner must approve or deny request within 45 days of its receipt. (PA 90-81).

Discrimination.—No company, agent, or broker may pay or allow any premium rebate, or any special favor in dividends or benefits or other inducement not specified in the policy. (38-59). Casualty and liability rates may not be unfairly discriminatory. (38-177). Similar prohibition applies to life insurance (38-149); nor may life insurance company discriminate against persons of African descent (38-150). If application of colored person refused, affidavit of examining physician stating grounds of refusal must be furnished applicant. (38-151). No discrimination solely because of blindness. (38-61[12], [13]). Another unfair practice would be discrimination against offspring of female parent who was exposed to diethylstilbestrol (DES). (38-61[13]).

Person or company selling real or personal property or engaged in business of financing the purchase of real or personal property or of lending money on the security of real or personal property may not require as condition to such sale, financing or

See note at head of Digest as to 1998 legislation covered.

See Topical Index in front part of this volume.

CT – 38

INSURANCE COMPANIES . . . *continued*
lending that purchaser or borrower must negotiate insurance on property through particular company, agent, or broker. (53-323).

Declination, cancellation or non-renewal of policy for auto insurance is prohibited if based upon: (1) Race, religion, nationality or ethnicity of applicant; (2) lawful occupation of applicant; (3) principal location of insured motor vehicle; (4) age, sex or marital status or applicant; (5) fact that applicant got insurance before through residual market; (6) another insurer previously declined to insure applicant; (7) first or second accident within current experience period which applicant or insured was not convicted and not at fault (38-175x); or declination, cancellation or non-renewal of health insurance is prohibited if based on genetic information (PA 97-95). No surcharge for any motor vehicle liability or physical damage insurance premium may be assigned for (1) accident involving property damage not exceeding $1,000; (2) first accident with property damage exceeding $1,000 which would result in surcharge to policy of insured within insurers safe driver plan; (3) any violation of §14-219 unless it results in suspension or revocation of license; (4) less than three violations of §14-218a within any one year period; (5) any accident caused by any operator other than named insured, relative residing in named insured household or person who customarily operates insured vehicle. (38-201[c]).

Agents, brokers and adjusters and casualty adjusters must be licensed by Commissioner. (38-71; 38-72; 38-77). License issued after May 1, 1956, continues in force until cancelled, suspended or revoked if insurance company annually notifies commissioner of names of agents whose licenses it wishes to continue. (38-72). License holder must notify Commissioner within 30 days of changes of address, employer, home, or licensed members of firm as stated in license application. (PA 87-20). In addition to required qualifications of good moral character and financial responsibility applicable to all applicants, new applicants for title insurance license must show that he/she is commissioner of Superior Court in good standing. (38-72). Agent for Risk Retention Group must be licensed according to 38-72. (PA 87-135, §14). License may be suspended or revoked for cause, or fine of up to $1,000 imposed, and person aggrieved by such action or by refusal to grant or reissue license may within 30 days, take privileged appeal to court of common pleas in Hartford. (38-74). Appeal is to Superior Court of Hartford County or judicial district wherein aggrieved resides. (38-74). Temporary agent's license may be issued to executor, administrator, conservator or next of kin of deceased or disabled licensed agent. (38-76).

Brokered Guaranty Fund.—Insurance department shall establish and maintain brokered transactions guaranty fund from which residents aggrieved by action of insurance agent or unlicensed person in insurance business may recover if approved by department. (PA 89-106, §1). Any licensed insurance broker or agent or person who receives license for first time on Oct. 1, 1989 must pay $10 fee credited towards fund. (PA 89-106, §2).

Insurance Administrator's license may be issued upon application to Commissioner, examination and filing of $150,000 bond. Fee for biannual renewal, $100. License may be suspended or revoked for cause, or fine of up to $1,000 may be imposed. Administrator cannot act as such without written agreement with insurer or party using his services. Detailed records of all transactions must be maintained for inspection and audit by Commissioner. (PA 88-298).

Excess line brokers license may be issued upon application after examination and filing of $25,000 surety bond (38-83) to licensed insurance agent domiciled or maintaining an office in this state, authorizing licensee to procure insurance through insurer not licensed to do business here. Fee for application and for annual renewal, $250. Commissioner may suspend or revoke license for cause shown after notice and hearing. Appeal from such action must be in accord with §4-183, except venue is in Hartford-New Britain district. Appeals shall be privileged as to order of trial assignment. (38-78). Detailed records of each such policy must be kept and report made to Commissioner in affidavit form of each such policy within 30 days after issuance. See infra, subhead Taxation. (38-78).

Except for the foregoing, no person may solicit or procure insurance except on his own person or property, or do any business by or with any insurer not authorized to do business in state (38-70) and any person making contract of insurance on behalf of company not authorized to do business in state is personally liable to insured for performance of contract (38-90). Company or agent may not pay commission to unlicensed agent or broker (38-91; 38-92), but licensed agents may share commissions (38-75).

Insurance agent, other than industrial life insurance agent, receiving only commissions for service is exempt from unemployment compensation. (31-222[a][5][K]).

Penalty for soliciting business for unlicensed insurance or surety company is $100 or six months imprisonment or both. (38-70).

Unfair competition and deceptive practices are prohibited for both agents and insurers. (38-60 to 38-63).

Process Agent.—No nonresident or foreign insurance company may, directly or indirectly, issue policies, take risks or transact business in this state, until it shall have first appointed in writing the Insurance Commissioner to be its attorney in this state, upon whom all lawful process, in any action or proceeding against it, may be served with the same effect as if the company was a domestic corporation. Such power of attorney must agree that it will remain in effect as long as any policy or liability remains outstanding in this state. Certificate of appointment must be certified and authenticated. (38-23). Commissioner, when thus served, collects $25 fee from plaintiff and must mail copy to secretary or resident manager of company. (38-49). Commissioner may appoint person in his office upon whom, in his absence, service may be made. (38-6).

Merger.—With approval of Insurance Commissioner, a domestic insurance company may merge or consolidate with another insurance company, provided a Connecticut corporation results. Prior to approval, Commissioner may hold hearing and must satisfy himself that interests of policy holders and stockholders, if any, are protected. (38-42; 38-36). Procedure follows general corporation law or special charter provision, if any. (38-42; 33-423[e]).

With approval of Commissioner after written notice to all stockholders of both companies and after advertised hearing and prior approval of stockholders, a domestic insurance company may issue its authorized capital stock in exchange for outstanding stock of another insurance company, or partly for stock and partly for cash. If, immediately prior to exchange, domestic company owns beneficially or of record 90% or more of voting securities of other company, prior approval of stockholders not required. After Commissioner has approved merger, consolidation of insurance and exchange of stock, copy of director's agreement as to terms together with commissioner's approval thereof must be filed in office of Secretary of State. (38-35).

Acquisition of subsidiary by mutual life insurance company authorized where subsidiary in business complementary to insurance, where company owns majority of subsidiary, and no more than 10% of assets invested in subsidiaries (38-146a).

Acquisition.—Anyone proposing to acquire a total of 10% or more of voting power in an insurance company must file with Commissioner, the company, and have distributed to stockholders of company, specified extensive data concerning his background, financial condition, and intentions. After public hearing, Commissioner must approve or disapprove proposal. (39a-L).

Insurance Holding Company Systems.—Insurance companies which are part of such systems must register with Commissioner if not similarly registered in another state, and they are regulated as to transfers among affiliates and fair dealing among affiliates. (38-39g to 38-39h[d]).

Reports.—See supra, subhead Insurance Commissioner.

Insolvency, Receivership and Dissolution.—Commissioner, on application to Superior Court in Hartford, may become ancillary receiver of foreign or nonresident company in receivership. (38-18).

Connecticut insurance guaranty association comprised of licensed insurance companies, which must become members, conducts business of insolvent companies, including premium rebates and claim adjustment. (38-273 to 38-289).

Connecticut Life and Health Insurance Guaranty Association comprised of life insurors, health insurors and annuity insurors fulfills obligations of insurors which are insolvent or may be unable to fulfill contractual obligations by guaranties, payments of contractual obligations, loans, etc. Funded by assessments on member insurors. (38-301 to 38-318).

Policies.—No nonresident or foreign company may issue or deliver policy or make insurance contract, unless such policy or contract is issued through and countersigned by lawfully constituted and licensed resident agent, but this does not apply to life insurance, certificates of fraternal benefit societies, reinsurance or insurance on rolling stock of common carrier or to property in transit, or to bid bonds issued by any surety insurer in connection with public or private contracts. (38-21).

Insurance company doing business in state may not limit time within which suit may be brought against it or with respect to (d) of this paragraph, any claim shall be submitted to arbitration on: (a) Fidelity or surety bond to period less than three years from time of loss; (b) construction performance bond to period less than three years from date when claimant last performed work; (c) construction payment bond to period less than three years from date when claimant last performed work; (d) uninsured motorist provisions of policy for period of less than two years from date of accident; and (e) all other policies to period less than one year from time loss occurred. (38-27).

Fire insurance companies may also cover windstorm, tornado, hail, frost and other risks of damage to property or of liability for damage to property from the elements, from war, from explosion (except steam boiler), from collisions, from burglary and theft, etc., and may effect reinsurance of any such risk taken by them. (38-107).

Domestic mutual and stock companies writing fire, marine, casualty, fidelity and surety, or boiler and machinery insurance may issue participating and nonparticipating policies. (38-30).

Standard form of fire policy is specified. (38-97; 38-101; 38-102; 38-103). No condition is valid unless stated in body of policy. (38-105). If policy is issued by a mutual, co-operative or reciprocal insurer having special regulations with respect to the payment by the policyholder of assessments, such regulations must be printed upon the policy. (38-99). Domestic companies may use, in other states, forms complying with local laws. (38-106). Policy may be cancelled at any time at request of insured with refund of excess of paid premium above customary short rate for expired time. Company may not cancel without 30 days written notice accompanied by reason therefor and return of excess of paid premium above pro rata premium for expired term. Where cancellation for nonpayment of premium, at least ten days written notice of cancellation accompanied by reason therefor. (38-98). Where owner obtains fire policy payable to mortgagee and fails to file proof of loss, mortgagee, upon notice, must render proof of loss in statutory form within 60 days thereafter. Insured must render proof of loss within 60 days after occurrence of loss. (38-98).

Mass marketing of personal lines of property and casualty insurance authorized for employees, officers, directors, and partners of same employer, labor union members, credit union members, and professional associations. Guaranteed issue with limited exceptions. (38-185m to 38-185u).

Life insurance company may not discriminate in premium, dividends, benefits, terms for conditions between insurants of same class and expectation of life, nor may company, agent, sub-agent or broker make any contract with insured regarding the insurance not plainly expressed in policy (38-149) nor may policy be dated back to produce lower premium (38-156). However, companies may insure on group plan with special rates for such policies, but must keep mortality experience for group assureds separate and report separately to Commissioner on annual report. (38-153). Domestic life companies may also issue annuities (38-154), and insure against loss of life or personal injury from any cause and loss of time from sickness (38-155) and may insure minors 15 years of age or over with same effect as if of age (38-157). Educational, ecclesiastical, benevolent, charitable and eleemosynary corporations may be made beneficiaries. (38-159). Company may hold policy proceeds under trust agreement, with such exemption from claims of creditors and such control by beneficiary as may be agreed, and need not segregate trust fund. (38-162). Beneficiary of life policy, except insured, is entitled to policy proceeds as against representative or creditor of insured unless policy or designation of beneficiary was procured in fraud of creditors, in which event policy proceeds become part of estate of insured so far as necessary to pay debts and administration expenses. In so far as premiums have been paid in fraud of creditors, such amount plus interest must

See note at head of Digest as to 1998 legislation covered.

See Topical Index in front part of this volume.

CT – 39

INSURANCE COMPANIES . . . *continued*
be deducted from policy proceeds and become part of estate of insured. However, company may safely pay beneficiary unless given notice of fraud claimed and unless suit is brought to establish claim within three months thereafter. (38-161). Individual life policies in this State require notice to insured that policy may be cancelled by return to company or agent by mail within ten days of insured's receipt of policy. (38-157a).

Viatical settlements are permitted and monitored by statute. (PA 97-202).

Accelerated Life Insurance.—Any life insurance company or fraternal benefits society doing business in Connecticut may issue accelerated benefits life insurance policies and certificates, riders or endorsements to existing life insurance policies which provide accelerated benefits. Such policy shall not include policy providing for disability, income protection coverage or long term care coverage. Death benefits may not be reduced more than amount of accelerated benefits paid plus any applicable actuarial discount appropriate to policy design if policy is without additional premium payments. When accelerated benefit is paid amount paid may be considered as: (1) Pro rata reduction in cash value or death benefits; or (2) lien against death benefit of contract and access to cash value shall be restricted to any excess of cash value over sum of other outstanding loans and lien. Accidental death benefit in policy shall not be affected by payment of accelerated benefit. All accelerated benefits policies shall comply with following disclosure requirements: Face of every accelerated benefits policy shall contain: (a) description of coverage which uses terminology "accelerated", and (b) following statement: "benefits as specified under this policy will be reduced upon receipt of accelerated benefit". Insurance Commissioner may adopt such regulations as he deems necessary for purpose of governing accelerated life insurance policies. (PA 90-200, §1).

Unclaimed funds held by any life insurance company doing business in the state upon matured policy are covered by 3-58a.

Health and accident insurance policy forms must have Commissioner's approval, subject to appeal to superior court. (38-165). They must express entire consideration therefor, must indicate effective and termination dates, must not purport to insure more than one person except when issued to the head of a family to cover expenses incurred by him on behalf of sickness or injury of self, spouse or children, must contain certain standard provisions and no inconsistent provisions, may contain certain additional standard optional provisions, and size of printing of various parts is specified. (38-166; 38-167). However, policies issued by foreign and nonresident companies may contain language required by state of incorporation, and policies issued by domestic companies for use elsewhere may comply with law of state where used. (38-167). Falsity of statement in application is not bar to recovery unless such false statement materially affected either acceptance of risk or hazard assumed. (38-169). Acknowledgment of notice, furnishing forms for proof of loss, accepting proofs, or investigation is not waiver of policy defense. (38-170).

There are standard forms for health and accident policies written in this state. No group accident, health or medical services policy may contain an offset provision as defined by 38-174j. (10-66c; 38-166; 38-174). Where husband and wife work for same employer and are covered by group policy, neither required to pay any premium not resulting in greater coverage than if policy provided to only one spouse. (38-262g, 38-262h).

Coverage of physically or mentally handicapped dependent children must be continued under individual and group health insurance policies and membership hospital and medical insurance contracts, despite termination of coverage provision in policy. If child is and continues to be (1) incapable of self-support and (2) chiefly dependent upon policy holder for support. Proof of these elements is required. (38-174e; 38-174f).

Provision made for insurance policies to provide coverage for single full time students beyond age of 19. (38-174r).

Small employers, as defined in 38a-564, may group together solely for purpose of securing group health insurance coverage.

Group medical benefit contracts must cover mental or nervous conditions to limited extent. (10-66c; 38-174d). Coverage for individual and group health insurance policies must provide coverage for laboratory and diagnostic tests for diabetes and in some cases provide coverage for treatment of diabetes. (PA 97-268). Every major medical expense policy in state on or after effective date of act shall provide home health care to residents whose benefits are no longer provided under Medicare or any other plans. (38-174k). Individual health care plan must be available to all residents except those 65 or older and eligible for medicare. (38-372). Insurers must offer group hospital or medical plans providing coverage of expenses incurred for comprehensive rehabilitation services. (38-174p). Health insurance benefits applicable for children must apply to new born child from moment of birth. (38-262d[a]). Every group hospital or medical expense insurance policy or service plan contract delivered, issued for delivery or renewed on or after Oct. 1, 1989 must provide benefits for preventive pediatric care for children covered by policy at following approximate age intervals: every two months from birth to six months, every three months from nine to 18 months, annually from two years to six years. (PA 89-101). Individual, surviving spouse and dependents losing eligibility in group medical plans may qualify for continued group coverage for limited period. (38-262d[a]). Insurers shall provide required minimum coverage for tumor removal and leukemia treatment, including outpatient chemotherapy, reconstructive surgery and nondental prosthesis. (38-262[i]). All health and hospitalization policies must include coverage for services provided by veterans' homes and hospitals. (PA 88-68). Insurers must provide required minimum benefits for mammographic examinations to any woman covered under policy. (PA 88-124, §1). Insurers must provide required minimum benefits for mastectomy and breast reconstruction after mastectomy. (PA 97-198). Insurers must offer group hospital or medical plan coverage of expenses for diagnosis and treatment of infertility, including in-vitro fertilization procedures. (PA 89-120). Insurers must provide same coverage for chiropractic services licensed under c. 372 of general statutes as provided by physician if services treat condition covered by policy and are within services chiropractor licensed to perform. (PA 89-112). Employers who deduct from employees' wages for group hospital or medical insurance and fail to procure coverage are liable for benefits to same extent as insurer or hospital or medical insurance company had insurance been procured. Corporate officers responsible for procuring coverage for employees and who willfully fail to procure coverage are personally liable for benefits same as if coverage had been procured. Personal liability imposed only if amount owed employee cannot be collected from corporation. (PA 89-69). No medical benefits issued by insurance company, hospital service corporation, medical service corporation or health care center may require covered individual to obtain prescription drugs from mail order pharmacy as condition of obtaining benefits for such drugs. (PA 89-374).

Failure to Pay Claims.—Insurers must pay undisputed claims within 45 days or pay 15% interest on said claim, plus applicable penalties. Each insurer must annually report to commissioner percentage of claims interest was paid on and total amount of interest payments. (38-61).

Policies issued in violation of law are valid but are construed in accordance with law. (38-168). Certain statutes on health and accident insurance do not apply to liability or workmen's compensation insurance, group policies, certain life insurance policies, fraternal benefit societies, insurance issued in conjunction with automobile liability policy, and accident ticket policies. (10-66c; 38-174).

Health Care Fraud.—Person intentionally making false statements to support claim for health insurance subject to penalties for larceny. (PA 87-481).

Plain Language.—All insurance policies must be made readable. Tests for readability include Flesch reading ease test. All filings must include certification by officer of insurer that policies meet test requirements. This chapter does not increase risk assumed by insurer.

See also category Business Regulation and Commerce, topic Consumer Protection.

Liability Insurance.—Insurer against liability on account of death, personal injury or damage to property becomes absolutely responsible whenever a liability covered by the policy arises, and if a judgment against the assured is not satisfied within 30 days after it becomes final, the judgment creditor is subrogated to rights of insured on policy and may sue insurer. (38-175).

Company writing commercial risk insurance must submit annual report beginning June 1, 1988 concerning earnings, losses, and reserves. (PA 87-515, §2).

Professional liability insurance means contracts for (1) physicians and surgeons, (2) hospitals, (3) lawyers, (4) dentists, (5) architects and engineers, and such other categories as Insurance Commissioner shall provide. (PA 90-90, §2).

Insurer must give 90 days notice before cancelling or refusing to renew professional liability policy. (38-185w[e]). Any individual, partnership, corporation or unincorporated association providing professional liability insurance coverage for its employee shall furnish each insured employee upon cancellation or discontinuance of such professional liability insurance notice of cancellation or discontinuation of such insurance. Such notice shall be delivered to insured employee not less than 45 days next preceding effective date of cancellation or discontinuation. This section shall apply to any of above individuals, partnerships, corporations or unincorporated association which substitute one policy providing such professional liability insurance coverage for another such policy with no interruption in coverage. In event of failure to furnish notice, individual or entity shall be liable for benefits to same extent as professional liability insurer would have been liable if coverage had not been cancelled or discontinued. (PA 90-63).

Automobile Liability Insurance.—See category Transportation, topic Motor Vehicles, subheads No-Fault Insurance and Proof of Financial Responsibility. Automobile liability insurance can be cancelled only for certain reasons, and notice of cancellation with reason specified must be given at least 45 days before effective date of cancellation. (38-175f to 38-175), and not renewed unless 60 days notice is given (PA 86-98, §§1, 6).

No-Fault Insurance.—See category Transportation, topic Motor Vehicles, subhead No-Fault Insurance.

Workers' compensation insurance companies must report all risks to Board of Workers' Compensation Commissioners, and cancellation does not become effective until one week after filing of notice of cancellation with appropriate Compensation Commissioner. (31-348).

Title Insurance.—No corporation can insure or guarantee titles to Connecticut realty except subject to and in accordance with its insurance laws generally. No corporation doing title insurance business or mortgage guaranty insurance business may do any other line of business. (38-29). Title insurer shall have such minimum capital and surplus as is required by statute. (38-93). Net retained liability of title insurer for single risk on property located in this state, whether assumed directly or as reinsurance, may not exceed 50% of sum of its total surplus to policyholders and reserve, less value assigned to title plants, as shown in most recent annual statement of insurer on file in office of commissioner. (PA 90-218, §7). General guidelines for title insurance in state of Connecticut were substantially revised in PA 90-218.

Retaliatory Law.—Where any state or country or political subdivision imposes upon Connecticut companies doing business therein taxes, fees, obligations, prohibitions or restrictions more onerous than those imposed by the laws of Connecticut on foreign or nonresident insurance companies doing business in this state, companies of such state or country doing business in Connecticut are subject to the same fees, obligations, etc., as are imposed by such state or country upon Connecticut companies, but this does not apply to ad valorem taxes on real or personal property or to personal income taxes or fees for agents' licenses or special purpose assessments. (12-211). Insurance companies organized under laws of foreign nations which do not regulate insurance companies in the same manner as the several states of the United States, shall be deemed to be organized under laws of state of its entry into U.S. (38-50; 12-58).

Fees.—For each annual license issued to domestic insurance companies, $10; for receiving and filing annual reports of domestic insurance companies, $25; for filing all documents prerequisite to the issuance of a license to domestic insurance companies, $175; for filing any additional paper required by law, $15; for each certification of valuation, organization, reciprocity or compliance, $20; for each certified copy of license to a company, $20; for each certified copy of report or certificate of condition of a company to be filed in another state, $20; for amending a certificate of authority, $100; for each license issued to an agent of a domestic insurance company, $40, and to agent of any other insurance company, $5; for each license issued to rating organization, $100; for each license issued to insurance broker, $88; for each license issued to public

See note at head of Digest as to 1998 legislation covered.

See Topical Index in front part of this volume.

INSURANCE COMPANIES... *continued*

adjuster, $125; for each certificate requested, whether issued or not, that license has been issued to agent, broker, or adjuster, $13 (38-50); for deposit of securities by domestic company with State Treasurer, $150 annually, and for examination of such securities outside Treasurer's office, $10 plus travel, both payable to state (38-45); for accepting service of process, $25 payable by plaintiff to Commissioner (38-49); for issuing license to broker, $88, to public adjuster, $100 (38-50); for issuing license to casualty adjuster, $20 per year (38-77); for issuing excess line broker's license, $250, for renewing every two years excess line broker's license, $500 (38-80); all payable to Commissioner (38-50).

Taxation.—Domestic insurance companies pay a tax of 2¹/₂% of net direct life insurance premiums written before July 1, 1973 on property or risks located or resident in this state and 2³/₄% of all other net direct premiums. Tax on all net direct premiums after June 30, 1973 is 2%,(12-39a, am'd PA 93-74). Effective Jan. 1, 1995, rate drops to 1.75%. There are credits against tax. This franchise tax is in addition to excise tax on investment income imposed by 12-202; 12-203. Newly licensed insurance companies incorporated in another state or foreign country, must pay commissioner of revenue services, within 45 days after license becomes effective, tax on net direct premiums received for preceding five years from policies written on property or risks located in this state, except marine insurance, at rate in effect for each of those years. HB 5679; PA 98-244, §4 modifies CGS §12-205 regarding annual returns to be filed in Mar. and provides information regarding officers, principal place of business subsidiaries, interest, dividends, premiums, gross income, deductions from gross income; tax due and payable on Mar. 1st. Foreign insurance companies doing business in state must, annually, pay tax of 2% of all net direct premiums from instate policies, except marine insurance. Upon ceasing to transact new business in state, company must continue to pay tax upon renewals at rate applicable at time of cessation of business. (12-210). Excess line broker must pay to Commissioner each Mar. 1st 4% of gross premiums charged insureds by insurers for excess line insurance, less amount of return premium. This tax does not apply to any policy issued to state or municipality. (38-84).

Such companies may also be subject to retaliatory tax. See supra, subhead Retaliatory Law.

Foreign insurance companies must file estimated tax return and remit estimated tax due on June 15 and Dec. 15 of each year. (12-210). Any insurance company aggrieved by action by Commissioner may apply for hearing within one month after notice of such action. (12-208). Company may appeal tax levied to superior court of Hartford. (12-208).

Assessment insurance companies are governed by special provisions. (38-120; 38-129; 38-130; 38-149 to 38-205).

Savings bank life insurance is governed by special provision. (36-142). See category Business Regulation and Commerce, topic Banks and Banking.

Insurers Controlled by Lending Institution or Bank Holding Company.—Cannot insure real or personal property securing loan by lending institution or bank holding company if loan contingent on such insurance. (38-76c).

Certified insurance consultants may not use that title or similar titles unless licensed as an insurance consultant. Examination is required for such a license. Insurance consultants must give written statements of services rendered and receipts for fees. (38-92c to 38-92j).

Uninsured children and youth covered by special government funded "Husky Plan" for medical coverage. (PA 98-8 amending PA 97-1).

Insurance premium finance companies licensed and regulated. (38-290 to 38-300).

Direct Actions Against Insurer.—See category Transportation, topic Motor Vehicles, subhead Direct Action.

Indemnification of directors, officers, and employees of mutual insurance companies allowed on much the same terms as corporate personnel. (38-27b). See category Business Organizations, topic Corporations, subhead Indemnification of Directors and Officers.

Personal liability of director of mutual insurance company allowed on much same terms as corporate directors. (PA 89-322). See category Business Organizations, topic Corporations, subhead Directors.

SURETY AND GUARANTY COMPANIES:

Such corporations are under the supervision of the Insurance Commissioner, and are governed to a considerable extent by the laws applicable to insurance companies. See topic Insurance Companies.

Financial Guaranty Insurance Act subjects companies issuing surety bonds, indemnity contracts and similar guaranties to substantial license, reporting, and disclosure requirements concerning financial strength, over and above applicable insurance company requirements. (PA 93-136).

Rights and Powers.—Domestic, and nonresident surety companies authorized to do business in the state, upon production of evidence of solvency and credit satisfactory to officer authorized to approve bond, may be accepted as surety upon the bond of any person or corporation required by laws of state to execute a bond. (38-178). Whenever any bond is required by law, it must be a bond with surety. (1-26). Surety company may be released from its liability on a bond on the same terms and conditions as are prescribed by law for release of individual sureties. (38-179). Company executing bond as surety may not deny its corporate power to execute such instrument or to assume such liability, in any action to enforce its liability under bond. (38-180). Liability of surety company for one person is limited. (38-177). Reasonable sum for expense of procuring surety company as surety on a bond may be allowed in settlement of accounts. (38-181).

Rates on surety and guaranty bonds are regulated. (38-201b).

Reports.—Each surety company doing business in state must file annual report, in which gross amount of risks are classified as commissioner directs, and reserve fund is

classified as liability. Commissioner may order cessation of business for failure to report or for taking excessive risks. (38-176).

Agents.—Any person acting as agent of nonresident or foreign surety company before it has complied with all requirements of law is subject to $1,000 fine (38-182) and person acting as agent without license or without being reported as agent of any particular company is also subject to fine (38-70). For other requirements, see topic Insurance Companies.

Nonresident or foreign surety company to do business in the state must have a capital of at least $500,000 and a paid-in surplus of not less then $500,000. Mutual surety company must have net surplus at least as great as capital and surplus requirements for stock companies. Company must also furnish certified copy of its charter, copy of its last annual report, and certificate showing cash deposit to this or other state of minimum capital requirement. (38-93). For other requirements, see topic Insurance Companies.

Taxation.—No special taxes. See topic Insurance Companies.

Managed Care.—New requirements exist for submitting information to Insurance Commissioner regarding managed care plans. (PA 97-99).

INTELLECTUAL PROPERTY

TRADEMARKS AND TRADENAMES:

Trademarks and Servicemarks.—(Note: 35-18a is based on Model State Trademark Bill of U.S. Trademark Association with certain modifications). See also 35-11a and for tradenames see 35-1.

A trademark or service mark (including titles, character names and other distinctive features of radio or television programs), used in conjunction with or on and to identify such goods or services distributed or offered within this state, may be registered with Secretary of State, such registration being effective for five years (ten years if registered prior to Oct. 1, 1993), renewable thereafter for like term, and open for public inspection. Nonuse for two consecutive years shall be prima-facie evidence of abandonment. (35-11e, am'd 93-152).

Registration.—Application for registration must be made to Secretary of State, stating: Applicant's name and business address; goods or services with and manner in which mark is used; date when mark was both first used and used within this state; that no other person has a right to use such a mark in this state either in identical form or in such near resemblance as to cause confusion or deceive; and whether an application(s) has been made to U.S. Patent Office, giving full particulars including filing date(s), serial number(s) and status thereof. Application must be signed, verified and accompanied by three specimens or photographs showing mark as actually used in commerce. (35-11c, am'd 93-152).

Secretary of State may refuse to register such mark if: Deceptive, scandalous, misdescriptive, falsely connective with or disparaging of persons, institutions or beliefs; or if primarily a surname, or geographically descriptive, or comprising the name, signature or portrait of a living person without consent; or if likely to cause confusion or mistake. Mandamus may be used to compel registration where refusal to register is improper. (35-18d). Right to use trademark is assignable by duly executed instrument, but is good only against assignor unless recorded with Secretary of State three months after execution or three months prior to subsequent purchase of a bona fide purchaser for value without notice.

Assignment.—Any registered mark is assignable with goodwill of business in which mark is used. Assignment shall be by instruments in writing duly executed and filed in Office of Secretary of State with payment of $25 transfer fee for each mark assigned plus $5 for each additional mark. (35-11f; 35-18f).

Fees.—A fee of $50, payable to Secretary of State, is required with every application or renewal (35-11c; 35-11e). Fee of $25 for each mark assigned must accompany assignment documentation.

Protection Afforded.—Any person, who used a copy or imitation of any registered trade or service mark on or in advertising or distributing any goods or services with knowledge that such is intended to deceive, cause confusion or mistake, or who, on behalf of himself or any other person, procures registration by knowingly making false representations in any manner, is liable for all damages sustained or profits. An aggrieved party may enjoin wrongful manufacture, use, display or sale of an imitation or counterfeit mark and may, notwithstanding absence of competition or confusion, enjoin use of any mark likely to injure business reputation or dilute the distinctive quality of a registered mark. Court may award damages of three times actual profits and reasonable attorney's fee if acts are done with knowledge or in bad faith. (35-11i, am'd 93-152).

Persons who, fraudulently and with intent to deceive, apply a registered trademark to goods other than those which the trademark is designed and appropriated to protect, are subject to criminal penalty. (35-18a).

Any person or corporation manufacturing, bottling or selling soda, mineral, or aerated waters, near beer, ginger ale, milk, cream or other beverages or medicines, medicinal preparation, perfumery, oils, compounds or mixtures in bottles, cans, jars, siphons, boxes or cases with his name or other marks or devices handed, stamped, engraved, etched, blown, impressed or otherwise produced thereon, or any person engaged in business of supplying towels, coats, aprons, or toilet cabinets to others for hire with his name or other marks or devices thereon may register and renew a description of name, mark or devices used with Secretary of State. (35-19). Use of such name, mark, or device without written consent of owner results in criminal penalties. (35-20).

State Board of Education is authorized to obtain patents, trademarks, and copyrights. (10-4f).

Trade Union Labels, etc.—Persons, trade associations or trade unions desiring to mark goods as products of their labor may secure the exclusive right to use a label, trademark, term, design, device or form of advertisement distinguishing the goods by filing two copies, counterparts or facsimiles thereof for record with the Secretary of State and obtaining from him a certificate of record, fee $1. (35-18a). Unauthorized use of such mark thereafter is forbidden. (35-18h). Any society, association, incorporated

TRADEMARKS AND TRADENAMES . . . *continued*

club, or labor union may in similar manner secure exclusive use of its insignia, flag, ribbon, badge, rosette, seal, button or emblem. (35-18a). Persons thus securing right to exclusive use of such label, mark, etc., may obtain injunction against, or damages, sustained on account of unauthorized use. (35-18h).

Infringement.—Any person who reproduces or counterfeits registered mark without consent of registrant shall be liable for damages. Owner may enjoin wrongful use of such mark if there is likelihood of injury to business reputation or dilution of distinctive quality of mark. Treble damages may be available. (35-11i).

Incontestable Right.—Where mark has been in use for five years, right to use mark in commerce shall be incontestable. (35-11m).

Tradenames.—Person or corporation conducting or transacting business in the state under an assumed name or under any designation, name, or style, corporate or otherwise, other than the real name of the person or persons conducting such business must file with the town clerk in the town in which such business is conducted an acknowledged certificate executed by all persons doing such business, stating the name under which the business is conducted and the names and addresses of each person conducting business. Filing fee is prescribed in 7-34a(a). This provision does not apply to use of partnership name or designation if it includes true surname of at least one of partners nor to limited partnership if it has filed certificate as provided in 34-10. Failure to comply with this provision results in fine or imprisonment. (35-1).

A partnership, common law trust, association, or individual using a tradename may not use as part of its name the word "bank," "banking," "bankers," "trust," "savings," except the word "bankers" or "trust" may be used when qualified and immediately preceded by the word "investment" if not followed by the word "company" or "corporation." This provision does not apply to a charitable or athletic association or a state bank, or building and loan associations. (35-2).

Name of brand, tradename or other distinctive characteristic by which liquors are bought and sold must be registered with, and approved by liquor control commission. (30-74).

A motor vehicle may not be registered under a tradename unless a certified copy of certificate is filed in office of Commissioner. (14-12).

TRADE SECRETS:

Uniform Trade Secrets Act has been adopted in State of Connecticut. Act was adopted in 1983. (PA 83-344, §1). Connecticut Uniform Trade Secrets Act has not incorporated 1985 amendments to Uniform Trade Secrets Act, as shown in Volume 14 of Uniform Laws Annotated, Master Edition. Act is codified in §35-50 through §35-58 of Connecticut General Statutes Annotated.

Definitions are encoded in §35-51 of C.G.S.A.

Injunctive Relief.—Actual or threatened misappropriation may be enjoined under application to any court of competent jurisdiction. Injunction shall be terminated when trade secret has ceased to exist, but injunction may be continued for additional reasonable period of time in order to eliminate commercial advantage that otherwise would be derived from misappropriation. (35-52).

Damages.—In addition to or in lieu of injunctive relief, complainant may recover damages for actual loss caused by misappropriation. Complainant also may recover for unjust enrichment caused by misappropriation that is not taken into account in computing damages for actual loss. If court finds willful and malicious misappropriation, court may award punitive damages in amount not exceeding twice any award made. (35-53).

Protection of Trade Secrets by Court.—In action under this chapter court shall preserve secrecy of alleged trade secret by reasonable means, which may include granting protective orders in connection with discovery proceedings, holding in-camera hearings, sealing records of action and ordering any person involved in litigation not to disclose alleged trade secret without prior court approval. (35-55).

LEGAL PROFESSION

ATTORNEYS AND COUNSELORS:

State bar is not integrated.

Jurisdiction Over Admission.—State Bar Examining Committee, consisting of 24 members appointed by judges of Superior Court, assisted by Standing Committees on Recommendations for Admission in each county, has jurisdiction over admissions. (C. P. B. 9-20). Admission of attorneys is exclusive province of judicial branch, and attempts by legislative branch to control it are unconstitutional. (148 Conn. 177; 169 A.2d 654).

Eligibility.—Applicant for admission to bar must satisfy Bar Examining Committee that he is citizen of U. S., or of country which allows U. S. citizens to become members of its bar on same terms as its citizens, 18 years of age, and that he is of good moral character. (C. P. B. 16). Bar Examining Committee may receive confidential information from State Police Bureau of Identification. (29-16). Such information includes state, multistate, and federal criminal records and any cost incurred by State Police Bureau of Identification will be paid for by State Bar Examining Committee. (29-11).

Examination.—Multi-State Bar Examination is used. Transfer of scores from other jurisdictions not accepted. (Bar Examining Committee, P.O. Box 1964, New Haven, 06509).

Annual examinations are held in New Haven on those dates on which National Multi-State examination is given. First day's exam consists solely of Multi-State questions, second day contains two three-hour essay sessions. There is no limitation to number of times applicant may take examination. State Bar Examining Committee shall develop and implement procedure to adapt administration of exam to needs of persons with disabilities. (51-81).

Registration as Law Student.—Applicant must file with administrative director of bar examining committee application to take examination and for admission to bar. Committee shall determine fee for application. (C.P.B. 16).

Educational Requirements.—

Legal.—Applicant must show that he has obtained a bachelor of laws or equivalent degree from a law school accredited by committee or obtained a master of laws degree for postgraduate work acceptable to committee at a law school accredited by committee, having already obtained a bachelor of laws or equivalent degree at a law school for work acceptable to committee. He must also have passed course in professional responsibility in accordance with committee regulations, or passed committee-administered examination in professional responsibility. (C. P. B. 16).

Petition for Admission.—Should be made to Clerk of Superior Court in judicial district where applicant intends to practice.

Clerkship.—There is no requirement of serving clerkship for a specified time before admission.

Admission Without Examination.—Applicant who has practiced five years in highest court of original jurisdiction in state with approved standards (ten years if he has once failed Connecticut Bar examination), meets general requirements, including U. S. citizenship or alien lawfully residing in U.S., is of good moral character and has passed course or examination in professional responsibility in accordance with or administered by committee's regulations, respectively, intends that major portion of time devoted to practice shall be in Connecticut and pays fee that committee will from time to time determine, may obtain temporary license for one year without taking examination. (C. P. B. 21, 22).

If, since admission, applicant is engaged for major portion of year in practice of law in Connecticut and intends to continue so to practice, temporary license may be made permanent on motion to court between 30 and 60 days before expiration of such temporary license. (C. P. B. 23).

Compensation.—If contingent fee agreed to, it shall be exclusive method of payment and shall not exceed percentages in 52-251c (b). Fee shall be percentage of: (a) Damages awarded and received by claimant or (b) settlement amount. Expenses incurred, other than ordinary office expenses, are not included in fee. (52-251c). Letter to new clients required setting forth terms and scope of engagement.

Client Solicitation.—Limitations placed upon written communications to prospective client for purpose of obtaining professional employment. Shall take effect Oct. 1, 1993. (PA 92-245).

Misconduct.—Statewide Grievance Committee exists to review allegations of attorney misconduct; committee comprised of lawyers and lay persons; procedures for hearing and determination of complaints specified. (51-90).

Disbarment or Suspension.—Superior Court for just cause may suspend or disbar attorney, (C.P.B. 28-31).

Unauthorized Practice.—No person not duly admitted to the bar may practice law, solicit employment for a lawyer or hold himself out to the public as being a lawyer. (51-88).

Professional Association or Corporation.—See category Business Organizations, topic Associations, subhead Professional Associations, and topic Corporations, subhead Professional Corporations.

Taxation.—See category Taxation, topic Professional Taxes, subhead Attorneys and Judges.

MINERAL, WATER AND FISHING RIGHTS

FISHING RIGHTS:

Commercial fisheries may be required to provide information to Department of Environmental Protection. (PA 97-79). Licensing requirements for commercial fisheries. (PA 97-133). Limitations on fishing methods. (PA 97-145).

MINES AND MINERALS:

No special legislation as to operation and taxation. Nonresident alien may acquire, hold and convey land for mining purposes upon certain conditions. (PA 85-211). Regulation on refining of oils repealed. (7-404).

Aquaculture and dredging activities regulated by state; permit required. (22a-361; PA 98-63).

MORTGAGES

CHATTEL MORTGAGES:

Governed by Uniform Commercial Code. (Tit. 42a). Conn. has central filing with Secretary of State, except in case of motor vehicles, which are filed with Motor Vehicle Commissioner (14-173) pursuant to Uniform Certificate of Title and Anti-Theft Law (14-165 to 14-211; 14-174d; 14-192c; 14-197c) and fixtures which are filed in town where real estate is located. Chattel mortgages filed prior to Oct. 1, 1961 need not be refiled and are effective for three years after date of final payment as provided in original chattel mortgage. Filing fee is $25; $25 fee for filing termination statement.

Retail Instalment Sales Financing.—Any security agreement made after Oct. 1, 1947, evidencing an agreement to pay the retail purchase price of goods having a cash price of $25,000 or less (42-83[b][3]) in instalments over period of time is subject to special restrictions as to form and content (42-88 to 42-96; 42-91), foreclosure, including repossession, redemption, resale, etc. (42-98), renewals and extensions (42-97), and anticipation of payments (42-96).

Concealment of mortgaged property with intent to place it beyond control of mortgagee is a crime carrying a penalty of three months imprisonment or $500 fine. (53-129a).

Sale of the mortgaged property without informing the vendee of the existence of the mortgage subjects mortgagor to imprisonment of not more than three months, fine of $500 or both. (53-129a).

See note at head of Digest as to 1998 legislation covered.

See Topical Index in front part of this volume.

CHATTEL MORTGAGES . . . *continued*

Forms.—Forms below and at end of this Digest are in general usage. However, any form containing pertinent information is accepted by filing office. No prescribed or officially suggested form for security agreement.

Form

SECURITY AGREEMENT

(Date)

. . . ., a corporation having

Name of Corporation

its office and principal place of business at . . . .

Address

in the City of . . . ., County of . . . ., and State of . . . .
(hereinafter called "Debtor"), hereby grants to . . . .
. . . . (hereinafter called "Secured Party"),
Name and description of Corporation,
a security interest in the following property (hereinafter called the "Collateral"):
(Herein insert brief description of security interest created).
Upon failure or refusal of the Debtor to repay the Secured Party such sums as may be due it, the Secured Party may, at its exclusive option, declare any and all obligations immediately due and payable whether or not said obligations shall have matured and shall have the rights and remedies of a secured party under the Uniform Commercial Code.

Debtor	Secured Party
. . . .	. . . .
Name	Name
By	By . . . .
Its	Its

COLLATERAL SECURITY:

See category Debtor and Creditor, topic Pledges.

MORTGAGES OF PERSONAL PROPERTY:

Uniform Commercial Code adopted. (Title 42a). Filings are with Secretary of State only excepting motor vehicles, which are filed with Department of Motor Vehicles under Uniform Motor Vehicle Certificate of Title and Anti-Theft Act, and fixtures which are filed in town where fixtures located.

See also topic Chattel Mortgages.

MORTGAGES OF REAL PROPERTY:

Mortgage conveys title and leaves only an equitable title to redeem. (51 Conn. 64). As to variable rate mortgages and deferral of interest see 36-9g.

Execution.—Mortgages are executed, attested, acknowledged and recorded like deeds of land (see category Property, topic Deeds), and are usually warranty deeds with conditional clause of defeasance added. Statutory form may be used which incorporates by reference following mortgage convenants: "The mortgagor convenants with the mortgagee that he is lawfully seized in fee simple of the mortgaged premises; that the same are free from all encumbrances, except as therein set forth; that he has good right, full power and lawful authority to sell and convey the same to the mortgagee and that he, the mortgagor, and his heirs and assigns, executors and administrators shall and will warrant and defend the same to the mortgagee and his heirs and assigns forever against the claims and demands of all persons except as therein set forth," and following statutory condition: "Provided, and this conveyance is made upon the express condition, if the mortgagor or his heirs, executors, administrators or assigns shall pay to the mortgagee or his heirs, executors, administrators or assigns the principal and interest of that certain promissory note or notes secured by this deed, at the time provided in said promissory note or in this deed, and shall also pay all taxes and assessments of every kind levied or assessed upon or in respect of the mortgaged premises or upon the note or notes secured thereby, then this deed, and also said promissory note, shall be absolutely void; otherwise the same shall remain in full force and effect." (47-5; 47-5a). See subhead Forms, infra.

Recording.—Mortgages, assignments, and releases must be recorded with the clerk of the town in which the land lies, to be effective against any other person than the grantor and his heirs. (47-36a-1, o-r, 47-10). Reasonable time is allowed to record. (91 Conn. 421, 99 Atl. 1045). See category Documents and Records, topic Records.

Lending institution may record master form containing lengthy standard terms, then record only portions of individual mortgages, incorporating standard terms on master form. (49-5a).

Mortgages of electric light, power and similar utility companies, covering lines in more than one town, may be recorded in the office of the Secretary of State, provided a certificate containing the names of mortgagor and mortgagee, the date of the mortgage and the fact that the mortgage is recorded with the Secretary of State is recorded with the town clerk of each town wherein any of the lines covered by the mortgage are located. (49-31c).

Recording Fees.—See category Documents and Records, topic Records.

Taxes.—No tax upon recording. See also category Taxation.

Trust Deeds.—Statutes as to mortgages apply.

Insurance.—No mortgage lender shall require any prospective mortgagor to obtain fire insurance policy in excess of replacement value of covered premises as condition for granting of such mortgage. (36-94). Any lender that requires borrower to pay for mortgage insurance must disclose to borrower in writing (1) purpose of insurance to protect lender from loss because of default by borrower, (2) insurance required as condition for loan and conditions which may release borrower and (3) good faith estimate of initial cost and monthly cost if any. Provisions not applicable to any first mortgage loan insured or guaranteed by any agency by federal government or any state or municipal government or quasi-government agency where mortgage insurance is required in connection with loan. (PA 89-95, §2a).

Future Advances.—First mortgages to secure future advancements of money for construction or repairs of buildings or improvements, including site improvements, are valid to secure money actually advanced in accordance with its provisions, up to amount of full loan authorized, with same priority as if it had been advanced at time mortgage was delivered if mortgage contains description of loan in substantially statutory form. Time for completing buildings or improvements may be changed by recorded instrument signed by parties, and priority not affected. In event of default, mortgagee may complete work and add cost to mortgage, up to face amount. Time and amount of future advances may be at sole discretion of mortgagee or advances may be by stage payments. (49-3).

Subsequent advancements for repairs on mortgaged property may be made to original mortgagor or subsequent owner but cannot exceed difference between debt at time of advancement and original mortgage debt, nor can time of repayment in original mortgage be extended. These provisions apply only to mortgages executed and recorded after Oct. 1, 1947. For mortgages executed and recorded after Oct. 1, 1955, advancements for any purpose may be made to original mortgagor or successor under open-end mortgages, but stated amount of indebtedness cannot be exceeded nor time of repayment in original mortgage lengthened and mortgage must be clearly headed "open-end mortgage" and specifically allow advancements. Written notice to mortgagee destroys priority of advancements made subsequent to such notice. (49-2).

Open End Mortgages.—49-2(c); 49-4b(a).

Priorities.—See subhead Redemption, infra.

Subordination Agreements.—Mortgage may be subordinated to subsequent mortgages even though subordination agreement does not contain terms or provisions of subsequent mortgages. (49-31c). Construction and effect of lien waiver depends upon intent of parties and circumstances. Waiver may relinquish all lien or claim of lien, or merely waive priority of lien. (101 Conn. 92, 125 Atl. 367).

Assignment.—Whenever any obligation secured by mortgage shall be assigned in writing which describes mortgage, and is executed, attested and acknowledged as provided for deeds of land, title held by virtue of mortgage vests in assignee. (49-10). Statutory Form may be used. See subhead Forms, infra. Mortgagor has good faith defense for payments to assignor without notice of assignment. (PA 98-147).

Release.—Upon satisfaction of a mortgage or bona fide offer to satisfy or partially satisfy same in accordance with terms of mortgage, mortgagee must execute and deliver a release to extent of such satisfaction, and if mortgagee fails to do so within 60 days of receipt of written request, mortgagee is liable to aggrieved party at rate of $200 for each week of such failure after this 30 day period, but not for more than total of $5,000 or amount equal to loss sustained by aggrieved party as result of failure, whichever is greater. (49-8, am'd PA 95-102). If mortgagee fails to execute and deliver release within 60 days of payoff, attorney or title insurance agent may, on behalf of mortgagor or his assigns, execute and record affidavit attesting mortgage has been paid off, more than 60 days have elapsed since said payoff, affiant has given mortgagee 15 days notice, in writing, of intention to execute affidavit, states names and recording information on mortgage, and provides proof that payment has been received. Such affidavit, when recorded, shall constitute release. (49-8a, am'd PA 95-102). Mortgage of real and personal property, judgment lien, mechanic's lien or power of attorney for conveyance of land may be released by instrument in writing executed, attested, and acknowledged like land deed, and short form of release is sufficient. (49-9[a]). Partial release of mortgage may be effected by quit-claim deed (see category Property, topic Deeds) or by short form release stating extent to which such mortgage is partially released with sufficiently definite and certain description of that part of property being released. (49-9[b]).

After 17 years of undisturbed possession and non-recognition of mortgage, mortgagor or person owning his interest may bring action in superior court of county where land located seeking judgment that mortgage invalid as lien. Such judgment is granted if no evidence is offered of any act in recognition of its existence as valid mortgage and must be recorded within 30 days in town where property located; thereafter no action to enforce a title under such mortgage may be maintained. (49-13).

Executor, administrator, spouse, next-of-kin, guardian, or other person deemed suitable by court may on payment, satisfaction or sale of mortgage debt, release legal title. (49-11). Executor, administrator, trustee, conservator or guardian of deceased may release or assign mortgage on Connecticut real estate, provided he files with clerk of town where land is located certificate of appointment and qualification from court having jurisdiction of estate. (49-11).

Real property passing through estate will not be exonerated from mortgage unless specifically and clearly indicated that testator's intention was to have mortgage exonerated. (45-175a).

Mortgage to, or lien in favor of, state or its treasurer may be released by treasurer under his hand and official seal. (47-8).

Railroad mortgages are governed by special provisions. (16-216; 16-227).

Trustees under mortgage or deed of trust, other than national banks and state banks and trust companies, where the notes or bonds secured by mortgage are sold as investments (36-249) must register with Bank Commissioner, submit to examination by him, file annual reports before Jan. 30, pay annual fee of $25 (36-250), keep assets and records in trust name, and are subject to injunction and removal for violation of statute or in case of insolvency (36-253). Such trustees have power, unless expressly forbidden, to accept conveyance of mortgaged property instead of foreclosing, but may not release right to deficiency judgment without consent of investors. After acquiring title to property by deed or foreclosure, and in stated instances to obtain funds to protect property, they may mortgage it to any Connecticut savings bank, or to any other bank under supervision of Commissioner. (36-252).

Debt secured by mortgage or lien includes: (1) Insurance premiums, taxes and assessments paid by mortgagee, and payments of interest and principal due on prior mortgage or lien to protect interest of subsequent mortgagees or lienor; (2) advances

See note at head of Digest as to 1998 legislation covered.

See Topical Index in front part of this volume.

CT – 43

MORTGAGES OF REAL PROPERTY . . . *continued*
made by mortgagee as outlined under subhead Future Advances, supra; (3) interest paid currently or to accrue. Accrued interest is added to principal mortgage debt. (49-2).

Agreements concerning expenses and attorneys fees contained in note or mortgage for collecting debt or foreclosing mortgage or in protecting lien of mortgage are valid but are construed to allow fair compensation only, and court may determine amount allowed even though agreement specifies larger amount. (49-7).

Strict foreclosure is by suit in equity against owner of equity of redemption and subsequent lienors, brought to Superior Court of county where land located. Amount of matter in demand is amount of debt described in mortgage. (52-38). Court in its judgment fixes conditions on which redemption may be had by ascertaining debt due and fixing time within which owner or subsequent lienors must pay or be forever barred. Such judgment may, on written motion of any person having interest therein, be opened or modified upon such terms as court deems reasonable, but judgment may not be opened after title has become absolute in any incumbrancer. (49-15).

On failure to redeem within the time limited, title becomes absolute in mortgagee, whereupon he must record within one month in town where land lies a certificate of foreclosure describing premises, mortgage, foreclosure proceedings and date title became absolute, or else is subject to fine. (49-16). If plaintiff demands possession in foreclosure action, court may issue execution of ejectment against person in possession if party to action, or transferee or lienor who is bound by judgment by virtue of lis pendens. (49-22). In absence of contrary mortgage provision possession may be obtained by peaceable entry (117 Conn. 218, 167 Atl. 728) or by ejectment independently of or prior to foreclosure (2 Conn. 1), but tender of debt with interest and costs of suit is bar to further prosecution of ejectment (49-23).

Right to foreclosure is not barred by running of statute of limitations on debt (119 Conn. 355, 176 Atl. 880), but is barred by adverse possession for 15 years after right to foreclose arose (76 Conn. 223, 56 Atl. 524).

Foreclosure Protection.—Mortgagee of owner-occupied one or two unit residential dwelling may apply for limited protection from foreclosure, if income requirements met (i.e., unemployment or "underemployment"). Protection may include mandatory restructuring.

Sale.—Mortgage or other lien may, upon motion of any party and in discretion of court, be foreclosed by decree of sale instead of strict foreclosure (49-24), in which event court appoints committee to make sale, directs manner and time of sale, and appoints three appraisers. If plaintiff is paid judgment debt and costs before sale, all further proceedings stayed. (49-25). If redemption is not thus made, committee after sale and its ratification by court executes deed to purchaser, which vests in him same estate as in strict foreclosure, and is valid only against all parties to action, and court may order possession be given him as well as issue execution of ejectment. (49-26). Proceeds of sale are distributed to persons specified in supplemental judgment, but if mortgagee is purchaser he need only bring into court excess of proceeds over judgment debt, interest and costs. (49-27). Judgment and cost of mortgagee are first paid out of proceeds, and parties receiving balance are allowed costs. (49-29).

Deficiency Judgment and Other Enforcement of Debt.—Foreclosure is a bar to any further action upon the debt against persons liable for payment who are or could have been made parties to foreclosure (49-1), but debt may be enforced in separate action either prior to or during strict foreclosure (102 Conn. 644, 129 Atl. 854). Expiration of law day, without redemption, results in appropriation of property (120 Conn. 16, 179 Atl. 339) and further action on debt is then barred if value of property at that time is equal to or in excess of debt (109 Conn. 329, 146 Atl. 724). Statutory provision for appraisal and deficiency judgment is not exclusive remedy against persons made parties in foreclosure suit. (49-14; 91 Conn. 586, 101 Atl. 332).

In foreclosure by sale, other proceedings for collection of debt are stayed during pendency of suit. If proceeds of sale exceed appraised value but are not sufficient to pay debt, deficiency judgment may be rendered against any person liable to pay debt who is party to suit. Such deficiency judgment abates other proceedings for collection of debt. If property is sold for less than appraised value, no judgment for deficiency in foreclosure or in other proceedings may enter against person on whose motion sale is ordered, nor may unpaid portion be collected by any other means, until one-half of difference between appraised value and sale price has been credited on debt as of date of sale. (49-28).

Redemption may be had until day set for redemption in strict foreclosure has passed or until sale in foreclosure by sale has been made, but not after those dates nor after 15 years after mortgagee has taken possession in assertion of his right thereto as mortgagee. Junior encumbrancer as to part of land may redeem as to whole. (49-20).

Priorities are determined in strict foreclosure by foreclosure judgment which assigns to owner of equity and junior encumbrancers in the reverse order of priority successive days in which to redeem, and such redemption by any such person is subject to the lien of those encumbrancers whose days for redemption are subsequent to his, but cuts off the lien or title of those whose days for redemption are prior to his. (49-19). Person redeeming must obtain from one receiving payment a certificate of satisfaction of the foreclosure judgment, which must be filed in court, and certified copy of certificate of satisfaction, and of judgment must be recorded with town clerk. (49-9). In foreclosure by sale priorities are determined by supplemental decree directing disposition of proceeds of sale. (49-27).

Uniform Act.—Connecticut has adopted its version of Uniform Common Interest Ownership Act. Act is comprehensive regulation of all common interest communities, including condominiums, cooperatives, and planned communities. (47-200 et seq.).

Forms.—The following may be used:

Forms

Mortgage: To all people to whom these presents shall come, greeting:

Know ye, That . . . . . . of . . . . . . for the consideration of . . . . . . full satisfaction of . . . . . . do give, grant, bargain, sell and confirm unto the said . . . . . . his heirs, successors, or assigns (description of premises).

To have and to hold the above granted and bargained premises, with the appurtenances thereof, unto . . . . . . the said grantee . . . . . . heirs and assigns forever, to . . . . . . and their own proper use and behoof. And also, ... the said grantor . . . . . . do . . . . . for . . . .sel. . . . heirs, executors, and administrators, covenant with the said grantee . . . . . . heirs and assigns, that at and until the ensealing of these presents, ... well-seized of the premises, as a good indefeasible estate in fee simple; and have good right to bargain and sell the same in manner and form as is above written; and that the same is free from all encumbrances whatsoever . . . .

And furthermore, ... the said grantor. . . . do by these presents bind . . . . sel . . . . and . . . . . . heirs forever to warrant and defend the above granted and bargained premises to . . . . . . the said grantee . . . . . . heirs and assigns, against all claims and demands whatsoever.

The condition of this deed is such, that whereas the said grantor . . . . justly indebted to the said grantee . . . . . . in the sum of . . . . . . dollars, as evidenced by . . . . . . promissory note for . . . . . . dollars, of even date herewith, payable to said grantee . . . . . . or order, as follows: . . . . . .

Now therefore, if said note shall be well and truly paid according to its tenor, then this deed shall be void, otherwise to be and remain in full force and effect.

In witness whereof, ... have hereunto set . . . . . . hand and seal . . . . . . this . . . . . . day of . . . . . ., in the year of our Lord 19. . .

Signed, sealed and delivered . . . . (L. S.)
in the presence of
. . . .
. . . .
(Acknowledgment).

Mortgage, Statutory Form:

MORTGAGE DEED

. . . .
of . . . . to
secure payment of . . . . dollars with interest payable as provided in a certain promissory note dated . . . . . . with final maturity on . . . . . . grant to . . . . of . . . . with MORTGAGE COVENANTS . . . .

(Description and Encumbrances, if any and any additional provisions)

This mortgage is made upon the STATUTORY CONDITION
Signed this . . . . day of . . . ., 19 . . .
Witnessed by: . . . .
. . . .
(Acknowledgment)

Assignment: Know all men by these presents, that . . . . . . of the Town of . . . . . ., County of . . . . . . and State of Connecticut, in consideration of the sum of . . . . . . Dollars, lawful money of the United States, to . . . . . . in hand paid by . . . . . . of the Town of . . . . . ., County of . . . . . . in said State, at or before the ensealing and delivery of these presents, the receipt whereof is hereby acknowledged, ha. . . . granted, bargained, sold, assigned, transferred and set over, and by these presents do. . . . grant, bargain, sell, assign, transfer and set over unto the said . . . . . . a certain indenture of mortgage, made and executed by . . . . . . in favor of . . . . . . bearing date the . . . . . . day of . . . . . . in the year nineteen hundred and . . . . . . and recorded in . . . . . . Town Records, Vol. . . . . . ., Page . . . . . ., to which reference may be had for a more particular description of said mortgage and of the land therein described, together with the debt, note and obligation therein described, and the money due or to become due thereon with the interest.

To have and to hold the same unto the said . . . . . . h. . . . heirs and assigns forever, subject only to the proviso in said indenture of mortgage mentioned: And . . . . . . do hereby make, constitute and appoint the said . . . . . . true and lawful attorney, irrevocable in . . . . . . name or otherwise, but at . . . . . . proper cost and charges, to have use and take all lawful ways and means for the recovery of the said money and interest; and in case of payment, to discharge the same as fully as might or could do if these presents were not made.

In witness whereof, ... have set . . . . . . hand and seal this . . . . . . day of . . . . . ., in the year of our Lord 19. . .

Signed, sealed and delivered . . . . (L. S.)
in the presence of
. . . .
. . . .
(Acknowledgment).

Assignment, Statutory Forms:

ASSIGNMENT OF MORTGAGE

. . . .
of . . . . for
consideration paid, assign to . . . . all interest in a mortgage from . . . . to . . . . dated . . . . and recorded in Volume . . . . at Page . . . . of the . . . . Connecticut Land Records.
Signed this . . . . day of . . . ., 19. . .
Witnessed by: . . . .
. . . .
(Acknowledgment)

ASSIGNMENT OF MORTGAGE (49-10[a]).

Know all men by these presents, that . . . . . . of . . . . . . in the County of . . . . . . and State of . . . . . . does hereby grant, bargain, sell, assign, transfer and set over a certain (mortgage, assignment of rent or assignment of interest in a lease) from . . . . . . to . . . . . . dated . . . . . . and recorded in the records of the Town of . . . . . . County of . . . . . . and State of Connecticut, in book . . . . . . at page . . . . . . In witness whereof . . . . . . have hereunto set . . . . . . hand and seal, this . . . . . . day of . . . . . . A.D. . . . .

See note at head of Digest as to 1998 legislation covered.

See Topical Index in front part of this volume.

MORTGAGES OF REAL PROPERTY . . . *continued*
Signed, sealed and
delivered in the
presence of
                                                                              (Seal)
(Acknowledgment).
                          _____

Release.—(49-9[a]): Know all men by these presents, that . . . . . of . . . . in the county of . . . . . and state of . . . . do hereby release and discharge a certain . . . . . from . . . . . to . . . . dated . . . . and recorded in the records of the town of . . . . . in the county of . . . . and state of Connecticut, in book . . . . at page . . . .

In witness whereof . . . . . . have hereunto set . . . . . . hand and seal, this . . . . . . day of . . . ., A.D. . . . . .
Signed, sealed and delivered
in the presence of
                                                                              (Seal)
. . . .
. . . .
(Acknowledgment).
                          _____

The above form also may be used to discharge a chattel mortgage, or a mechanic's lien. (49-9[a]).

Chattel Mortgages.—See topic Chattel Mortgages.

PROPERTY

ABSENTEES:

Every civil action in which the defendant shall be an inhabitant of this state but shall be absent from State at commencement of action and shall continue to be absent until after return day, without having entered any appearance therein, shall be continued or postponed for 30 days by order of court; and, if defendant shall not then appear and no special reason be shown for further delay, judgment by default may be entered against him. If defendant is not inhabitant or resident of this state at commencement of action and does not appear therein, court shall continue or postpone it for period of three months, and may, if it deem further notice advisable, direct further notice of pendency of action to be given to defendant by publication in some newspaper; or may authorize any person duly empowered to serve process by laws of foreign jurisdiction in which such defendant resides to serve upon defendant copy of summons and complaint and of order of notice; any such person serving process in foreign jurisdiction shall make affidavit of his actions concerning process on original order or notice; and, if upon expiration of said three months, defendant shall not then appear and no special reason be shown for further delay, judgment may be rendered against defendant by default. Upon expiration of three month continuance, it shall be presumed prima facie that no special reason for further delay exists. Continuance or postponement under this section shall not be granted, or if granted, shall terminate if actual notice is shown. (52-87).

Any such continuance must terminate and cause may be brought to trial whenever court finds that absent defendant has received actual notice of pendency of action at least 12 days prior to such finding. (52-88).

Care of Property.—When any person having property shall have disappeared so that after diligent search his whereabouts cannot be ascertained, court of probate in district in which he resided or had his domicile at time of his disappearance or, if such person shall have resided outside of this state, then in district in which any of his property is situated within this state, upon proper application shall, after public notice and hearing thereon, appoint trustee of estate of such person. (45-87).

Escheat.—Money or property of another held for specified period of total unexplained inactivity is presumed to be abandoned. (3-57a-3-64a).

Holder must notify record owner of such money or property within one year prior to time such presumption arises, and, if property still unclaimed, must turn same over to State Treasurer within 90 days after presumption arises. Except upon request of a holder of 200 or more items in each category of unclaimed funds, Treasurer may approve aggregate reporting where each of the items is less than $25 and cost of reporting would be disproportionate. Holder so electing assumes responsibility for any valid claim made within 20 years. (3-65a). State Treasurer must thereafter comply with certain further notice requirements (3-65a) and reduce to cash (3-68a). If still unclaimed, money is paid over to general fund of State. (3-69a). Any person claiming interest in property surrendered to treasurer may claim property, or proceeds from sale, at any time thereafter. Any person claiming interest in such property must file certified claim with Treasurer including facts upon which party claims to be entitled to recover money or property. (3-70a[a]). After termination of this last period, provision is made for action in rem to formally bar further claim. (3-65a). See also categories Business Regulation and Commerce, topic Banks and Banking, subhead Unclaimed Deposits; Estates and Trusts, topics Descent and Distribution, subhead Escheat, Wills, subhead Unclaimed Legacies; Transportation, topic Motor Vehicles, subhead Proof of Financial Responsibility, catchline Return of Security.

ADVERSE POSSESSION:

In order to gain title by adverse possession, the owner must be kept out of possession for 15 uninterrupted years by open, visible and exclusive possession of adverse possessor and his privies without license from or consent of owner. (171 Conn. 149, 367 A.2d 1380; 156 Conn. 510, 244 A.2d 385; 52-575). User must be as one's own, but need not be under claim of title. (83 Conn. 627, 78 Atl. 432; 108 Conn. 5, 142 Atl. 400). Title by adverse possession cannot be obtained to railways or canal land (47-26), nor by or against railroad or street railway (47-27), nor against state (56 Conn. 517, 16 Atl. 548).

To interrupt adverse possession, owner must (a) serve, in manner provided for service of legal process, notice of intent to dispute adverse possessor's claim, (b) record notice on land records, and (c) within one year of recordation, commence legal action to settle title. (52-575, am'd PA 96-249).

Conveyance or lease of any building, land or tenement of which the grantor or lessor has been ousted by the entry and possession of another is void, unless made to the person in possession. (47-21).

Disabilities.—Where owner, at time his title accrues, is legally incapable by reason of minority, insanity, imprisonment, etc., title of adverse possessor is not good until five years after owner's death or restoration to capacity. (52-575).

Easements may be acquired by 15 years adverse, exclusive, open, visible, continuous user as of right and not in subordination to owner. (47-37; 124 Conn. 398, 200 Atl. 330). User may be exclusive though in common with owner. (105 Conn. 722, 728, 136 Atl. 684). Right to keep, maintain or enjoy any window or light may not be acquired by adverse possession so as to prevent owner of adjoining premises from erecting any building thereon. (47-25). Owner may prevent acquisition of easement by prescription, no matter for how long user may continue after such notice, by serving notice on person claiming easement that his right thereto is denied, and recording same on land records of town where land lies (47-38); or if owner of dominant tenement is unknown, notice may be conspicuously posted on dominant estate and copy thereof served on person to whom estate was last assessed for tax purposes (47-40).

CONDOMINIUMS:

See topic Real Property.

CONVEYANCES:

There are certain instances in which conveyance documentation will not be deemed invalid despite errors or omissions in its creation or administration. (S.A. 97-6, §3[a-c]; H.B. 6402).

CURTESY:

No curtesy where marriage took place after Apr. 20, 1877.

DEEDS:

See topic Real Property for types of estates.

All conveyances of land must be in writing subscribed with or without seal by grantor with his own hand, or with his mark with his name thereto annexed, or by his attorney authorized for that purpose by power executed and acknowledged in manner provided for conveyances, and attested by two witnesses with their own hands and acknowledged by grantor or by such attorney to be his free act and deed or using Power of Attorney form in 47-5(b). (47-5).

Any conveyance of land situated in this state, executed and acknowledged in any other state in conformity with laws of such state, or with laws of this state, is valid, provided officer taking acknowledgment indicates date of expiration of current commissions. (47-7).

Deed by person ousted of possession is void. (47-21).

If marriage took place on or after Apr. 20, 1877, it is not necessary for spouse to join in execution of deed. See also category Family, topic Husband and Wife.

Only time wife need join in deed is when she is an actual party to the transaction.

Corporate deed must be executed in name of corporation by agent appointed by directors, attested by two witnesses, subscribed by duly authorized person and acknowledged. Person interested in corporation may be witness or take acknowledgment. (47-5; 47-6).

Recordation in town where land lies is necessary to render deed effectual against creditors and bona fide purchasers for value. If deed is executed under power of attorney this must be recorded with deed. (47-10).

As to recording generally, effect of recording defective instrument and recording fees, see category Documents and Records, topic Records.

Taxes.—See category Taxation, topic Property Taxes, subhead Real Estate Conveyance Tax.

Forms.—Following statutory short forms for warranty deeds and quit-claim deeds have been adopted. (47-36c):
Warranty Deed
. . . . . of . . . . . . for consideration paid, grant to . . . . . . of . . . . . . with WARRANTY COVENANTS
          (Description and Encumbrances, if any and any additional provisions)
Signed this . . . . . . day of . . . . . ., 19. .
Witnessed by: . . . .
                                                     . . . .
(Acknowledgment)
                          _____

Quit-Claim Deed
. . . . . . of . . . . . . for consideration paid, grant to . . . . . . of . . . . . . with QUIT-CLAIM COVENANTS
          (Description and Encumbrances, if any and any additional provisions)
Signed this . . . . . . day of . . . . . ., 19. .
Witnessed by: . . . .
                                                     . . . .
(Acknowledgment)
                          _____

Above statutory short forms incorporate following covenants:

Deed following form entitled "Warranty Deed" shall, have effect of conveying title in fee simple to grantee, with covenants of grantor to grantee, for himself and for his heirs, executors and administrators: (1) That at time of delivery of such deed he is lawfully seized in fee simple of granted premises, (2) that granted premises are free from all encumbrances except as therein set forth, (3) that he has good right, full power and lawful authority to sell and convey same to grantee and (4) that grantor shall, and his heirs, executors and administrators shall, warrant and defend granted premises to grantee and his assigns forever against claims and demands of all persons, except as therein set forth. (47-36d, e).

                          _____

DEEDS . . . *continued*

Deed entitled "Quit-Claim Deed" shall have effect of conveyance to release of all releasor's right, title and interest in and to property described therein except as otherwise limited therein, but without any covenants of title. (47-36f, g).

Statutory forms also exist for mortgage deeds, assignments of mortgages, conservators' deeds, testamentary trustees' deeds, executors' deeds, and administrators' deeds. (47-36c, O-r).

Establishment of new statutory short forms does not preclude use of following forms:

Warranty Deed: To all People to whom these Presents shall come. Greeting: Know Ye, That . . . . . . for the consideration of . . . . . received to . . . . . . full satisfaction of . . . . . . do give, grant, bargain, sell and confirm unto the said . . . . . ., heirs, successors and assigns, To Have and to Hold the above granted and bargained premises, with the appurtenances, thereof, unto . . . . . . the said grantee, heirs and assigns forever, to . . . . . . and their own proper use and behoof. And also . . . . the said grantor . . . . . . do for . . . .sel. . . . heirs, executors and administrators, covenant with the said grantee, ... heirs and assigns, that at and until the ensealing of these presents . . . . . . well seized of the premises, as a good indefeasible estate in fee simple; and have good right to bargain and sell the same in manner and form as is above written; and that the same is free from all incumbrances whatsoever . . . . And Furthermore, the said grantor. . . . do by these presents, bind . . . .sel. . . . and . . . . . . heirs forever to warrant and defend the above granted and bargained premises to . . . . . . the said grantee. . . . heirs and assigns, against all claims and demands whatsoever.

In Witness Whereof . . . . . . have hereunto set . . . . . . hand and seal this . . . . . . day of . . . . . . in the year of our Lord, 19—.

Signed, sealed and delivered in presence of

. . . . L. S.

(Acknowledgment)

Quitclaim Deed: Know all Men by these Presents: That . . . . . . for divers good causes and considerations thereunto moving, especially for . . . . . . received to . . . . . . full satisfaction of . . . . . . have remised, released and forever quit-claimed and do by these Presents for . . . . . . and successors, heirs justly and absolutely remise, release, and forever Quitclaim unto the said Releasee . . . . . . successors, heirs and assigns forever all such right and title as . . . . . . the said Releasor have or ought to have in or to . . . .

To Have and to Hold the premises, unto . . . . . . the said Releasee and to . . . . . . successors, heirs and assigns, to the only use and behoof of the said Releasee . . . . . . successors, heirs and assigns forever, so that neither . . . . . . the said Releasor nor any other person or persons in . . . . . . name and behalf shall or will hereafter claim or demand any right or title to the premises or any part thereof, but they and every one of them shall by these presents be excluded and forever barred.

In Witness Whereof . . . . . . have hereunto set . . . . . .hand and seal this . . . . . . day of . . . . . . in the year of our Lord, 19. . .

Signed, sealed and delivered in presence of

. . . . L. S.

(Acknowledgment)

DEEDS OF TRUST:

See category Mortgages, topic Mortgages of Real Property.

DOWER:

No dower where marriage occurred after Apr. 20, 1877.

ESCHEAT:

See topic Absentees, subhead Escheat; categories Business Regulation and Commerce, topic Banks and Banking, subhead Unclaimed Deposits; Estates and Trusts, topics Descent and Distribution, subhead Escheat, Wills, subhead Unclaimed Legacies; Transportation, topic Motor Vehicles, subhead Proof of Financial Responsibility.

LANDLORD AND TENANT:

General rights and liabilities of parties are governed by 47a-1 to 47a-21. Tenant is liable for waste. (52-563).

Leases.—Lease for life or for a term exceeding one year or which contains renewal provision or option to purchase is not effectual against persons other than parties to the lease or their heirs, successors or personal representatives unless either the lease itself or a notice thereof is written, executed, attested, acknowledged and recorded as a deed of land (47-19). Reasonable time is allowed to record lease. (76 Conn. 44, 55 Atl. 670). Actual possession of tenant probably is not notice of unrecorded lease. Lease for term exceeding one year, or for term of one year to begin in future, is not enforceable against either party if not in writing, signed by party to be charged or his agent. (52-550; 86 Conn. 32, 84 Atl. 104). Parol leases reserving monthly rental where no time for termination is agreed on are for one month only. (47a-3d). Lease which does not fix definite term is month to month tenancy, unless rent is paid weekly, then tenancy is week to week. (47a-3[c]). Lease shall not provide that tenant waives certain rights and remedies nor that tenant is liable for attorneys fees in excess of 15% of amount of judgment in any action where money damages awarded. (47a-4).

Lease for any term of any building or land of which lessor has been ousted by the entry and possession of another is void unless made to the person in actual possession. (47-21). Foreign corporation may lease real estate in state (33-136), and guardians may lease ward's real estate for period not extending beyond minority of the ward, upon approval of probate court (45-52). Leasehold interests in real estate are attachable. (52-286). Leases under terms of franchise agreement regulated. (42-133f, g).

Landlord required to place advanced rent or each security deposit in separate bank account and pay interest at rate indexed to average rate paid by insured commercial banks on savings deposits, but in no event less than 1.5%. (47a-21, am'd PA 93-33). Landlord liable for twice value of security deposit for failure to refund within 30 days

after termination of lease. (47a-21[d]). Security deposit may not exceed two months rent. In case of tenant who is 62 or older said security deposit shall not exceed one month's rent and tenant may request return of excess amount. (47a-21[b]). Security deposit exempt from attachment and execution by creditor of landlord. (47a-21[c]). Landlord liable for civil penalties for leasing premises without certificate of occupancy.

Rent.—State rent control has expired but several cities have local rent control. Both husband and wife are liable for rent of premises occupied by them as their residence. (46b-37). If tenement house is occupied for human habitation in violation of state building code, no rent is recoverable by owner or lessee on such premises for period of such unlawful occupation, and no action or special proceedings may be maintained therefor. (19a-362). If landlord fails to provide essential services, tenant, after notice to landlord, may: (1) Procure such essential service and deduct cost from rent; or (2) procure substitute housing during absence of essential service; or (3) terminate tenancy and recover quarter of two months rent or double damages if landlord's failure to provide was willful. (47a-13). If tenement becomes uninhabitable through no fault of tenant, he is not liable for rent. If only portion becomes unusable, tenant may vacate that part and rent will be reduced accordingly. (47a-14). If rent is unpaid for nine days after due (four days after due if one-week tenancy), landlord may terminate rental agreement according to 47a-23 to 47a-23b (47a-15a). If premises used for sale of illegal drugs landlord may elect to evict under violation of subsection h of §47a-11. Burden on tenant to show that he did not have knowledge of nuisance. (47a-15).

Rents deposited with receiver to remedy housing code violations, lack of heat, running water, electricity, light, sewage disposal, or other dangerous conditions, upon judgment in special form of class action by tenants. (47a-14a to 47a-14g). Landlord can avoid by undertaking work and posting security. (47a-14f).

Lien.—Boarding or lodging houses (49-68) and hotels (49-69) have liens by statute against baggage and effects of boarder or guest.

Termination of Tenancy.—Conviction of lessee for illegal use of premises renders lease void and lessee subject to ouster by summary process without notice. (52-539). Where tenement becomes uninhabitable through no fault of tenant, he may terminate tenancy. (47a-12; 47a-14).

Holding over after expiration of term of original lease is no evidence of agreement for a further lease. (47-22).

Dispossession.—Under state law, use of summary process to recover possession is strictly limited. (47a-23; 47a-23a; 47a-23c; 47a-25; PA 98-61). When specified grounds exist, action may be brought, but there is five-day stay of execution and, on issuance of writ of error (47a-36), further stay of six months or more may be granted at end of which additional nine month stay may be granted if dwelling unit declared conversion condominium (47a-39). It is affirmative defense if plaintiff brought action in retaliation for defendant seeking to remedy, by lawful means, illegal condition of premises or for complaining to fair rent commission or if municipal agency filed notice, complaint, or order regarding violation, or if defendant requested plaintiff make repairs, or is affiliated with tenant's union. (47a-33).

Special rules for abandonment by occupants. (PA 92-171, §8).

Special rules of pleading apply to action. Defendant must appear within two days of return date and pleadings must move forward each two days thereafter. (47a-26[a]-[f]). On motion and without hearing, unless defendant files objection within five days of filing of motion, court shall order defendant to deposit with court, within ten days of filing of motion, use and occupancy payments equal to last agreed upon rent during pendency and appeal of eviction action. If defendant files objection, court may order defendant to turn over to court use and occupancy payments during pendency and appeal of eviction action. Last agreed-upon rent shall be prima facie evidence of fair rental value. Party claiming different amount shall have burden of proving that it is not said fair rental value. (47a-26[a]-[f]).

Summary process judgment binds named defendants and occupants whose presence is known or should be known and who are properly named or served. Persons claiming not to be subject to summary process may file claim prior to execution. (PA 87-507, §3; PA 92-171, §6).

Other Remedies.—Availability of summary process does not prevent the use of common law remedies such as ejectment. (47a-34). Forcible entry or ejectment subject to double damages. (52-465). Lockouts by landlord criminal violation. (53a-214). Intentional damage to landlord's property subjects tenant to criminal sanctions. (53a-117e and 53a-117f; am'd PA 98-107).

Distraint does not obtain in Connecticut.

Discrimination.—Lessors of public accommodations prohibited from discriminating on basis of age, race, creed, color, national origin, ancestry, sex, marital status (except cohabitation of single males and females), mental retardation, or physical disability, including blindness and deafness. No landlord or his agent shall refuse to rent to any tenant or potential tenant because such tenant occupies or intends to occupy dwelling unit with minor children. Does not apply to one or two family homes, owner-occupied building, with four or less units, or if rental would violate local, state, or Federal law, or condominium bylaw. (46a-64; 46a-64a; 46a-98a; 46a-51[8]; 46a-54; 46a-86[c]; 46a-91[a]; 46a-64c).

Note: HB 5650; PA 98-263 enacted following new sections: §2 regarding establishing state-wide electronic database regarding availability of housing for disabled and status of units; §3 regarding grants-in-aid to public and private operators of housing for elderly to employ supervisors and implement programs to assist residents; based on need and availability of matching funds; §4 regarding employment of resident service coordinators; and §15 regarding federally or other publicly funded housing grants.

§5 of PA 98-263 modified CGS §29-252a(b) regarding conditions precedent to construction/renovation of state buildings.

Mobile Home Parks.—Special rules (21-70), including provision allowing association of mobile home owners to purchase park from owner intending to close or sell (PA 93-283).

Lead Paint Abatement.—See category Environment, topic Environmental Regulation.

LEASES:

See topic Landlord and Tenant.

PERPETUITIES:

Uniform Statutory Rule Against Perpetuities adopted, 1989. (PA 89-44). In applying rule to interest in real or personal property created before effective date of this act, limited to take effect at or after termination of one or more life estates in, or lives of, persons in being when period of rule commences to run, validity of interest determined on basis of facts existing at termination of such one or more life estates or lives. For purposes of this rule, interest which must terminate not later than death of one or more persons is life estate although it may terminate at earlier time. If interest created before effective date of this act would violate rule against perpetuities as amended because such interest is contingent upon any person attaining or failing to attain age in excess of 21 years, age contingency shall be reduced to 21 years. (45-95, 45-96).

Rights of entry and reverters extinguished if contingency does not occur within 30 years. (45-97). Estates granted for charitable uses (47-2) and charitable trusts (45-79) are not within the rule against perpetuities (109 Conn. 529, 147 Atl. 181; 123 Conn. 549, 196 Atl. 785). Certain employees' trust funds are exempt from the rule against perpetuities and suspension of the power of alienation. (45-100, 45-100f).

PERSONAL PROPERTY:

No statutory authorization for tenancy by entireties in personal property. See comparable legislation with regard to real estate in 47-14a.

POWERS OF APPOINTMENT:

A power of appointment is a power of disposition given to a person over property not his own by someone who directs the mode in which power shall be exercised, by a particular instrument. (131 Conn. 307, 39 A.2d 895). Power restricted as to appointee is a special power. (133 Conn. 221, 50 A.2d 168). Right reserved by insured to change beneficiary is in nature of power of appointment. (120 Conn. 633, 182 Atl. 472). Donee of general or special power to appoint absolute estate may appoint lesser one unless such exercise would violate intent of donor of power. (133 Conn. 221, 50 A.2d 168). Except to extent otherwise expressly provided in instrument creating power, donee of power of appointment over trust may appoint any or all property subject to power in further trust and create further special powers of appointment. (45-123a-c).

Donee of special power to appoint must not appoint property to himself, his estate, his creditors or creditors of his estate. May appoint to anyone not expressly excluded from class of permissible appointees. (PA 92-73).

"General Power of Appointment" defined for succession and transfer tax by 12-345b.

Exercise.—Method prescribed in instrument creating power must be strictly followed in its exercise (84 Conn. 494, 80 Atl. 758) and to constitute a valid exercise, the intention of the donee must be clear (127 Conn. 359, 17 A.2d 8). Donee of general or special power to appoint absolute estate may appoint lesser one unless such exercise would violate intent of donor of power. (133 Conn. 221, 50 A.2d 168).

Legal effect of attempt to exercise power of appointment depends upon law of residence of donor of power. (111 Conn. 594, 151 Atl. 252).

Creditors of donee who has exercised general power of appointment may reach property subject to this power (111 Conn. 594, 151 Atl. 252), but this doctrine does not apply in favor of a corporate surety (124 Conn. 416, 200 Atl. 567)

Release of power is governed by c. 783. Under this chapter a power includes all powers which are in substance and effect a power of appointment regardless of language used in creating it. Such power whether or not coupled with an interest, whether or not existing July 8, 1943, and whether held by donee in individual or fiduciary capacity may be released wholly or partially by donee unless otherwise expressly provided in instrument creating the power. (45-120, 45-121).

Method of Release.—Power may be released by delivery of written release executed by donee, for consideration or under seal, to any person who could be adversely affected by exercise of power, to person holding in trust property subject to power, or in case of power created by will, by filing release in probate court in which will proved. Release of power is not valid as to land in state subject to power, except as against releasor and persons having actual notice of release unless, in case of power created by will or other written instrument, it is acknowledged like a deed and recorded in land records of town where land is located, and, in case of power created by will, it is also filed in probate court. (45-121). Such release is effective to extent provided therein. (45-122).

Effect Upon Other Donees.—Release by one donee, unless instrument creating power otherwise provides, does not prevent or limit exercise or participation in exercise by other donee or donees of a power exercisable by two or more persons in conjunction or successively. (45-123).

Taxation.—See category Taxation, topic Succession and Transfer Tax.

POWERS OF ATTORNEY:

Attorneys in Fact.—No special form is required for letters of attorney but powers of attorney to convey real estate must be witnessed and acknowledged like deeds. (47-5).

While no specific form of power of attorney is required, State has adopted statutory short form power of attorney (1-42 to 1-56) allowing incorporation by reference of extremely broad attorney powers. Party using statutory form grants broad powers to attorney unless specific power is specifically excluded. Power of attorney may, under certain circumstances, survive subsequent incompetence of principal, but will terminate upon appointment of conservator. (45-69o). Connecticut recognizes "springing" power of attorney, taking effect upon occurrence of specified contingency. (PA 93-203).

Power of attorney executed in another state in accordance with laws of that state or with laws of this state authorizing one to convey real estate in this state is valid. (47-7). Power of attorney must be recorded with deed. (47-10).

Agent is not liable for acting under power of attorney from person in U. S. Armed Forces, after death of principal, where agent acted in good faith without knowledge of such death. (45-92).

REAL PROPERTY:

Proprietor in fee simple has absolute and direct dominion. (47-1).

Fee tail estate becomes fee simple in issue of first donee in tail. (47-3).

Rule in Shelley's Case is abolished, and grant or devise to a person for life and then to his heirs invests the grantee with a life estate only. (47-4).

Collateral warranty of land, made by one who had no estate of inheritance in the land at the time of making such warranty, is void as against his heirs. (47-4).

Implied warranties upon sale of newly constructed single family dwelling include: (1) Freedom from faulty materials; (2) construction according to sound engineering standards; (3) construction in workmanlike manner; (4) fitness for habitation; and, if purchaser reveals purpose and relies on vendor's skill and judgment, (5) fitness for purpose. Warranties may be expressly excluded or modified by sale contract if unit completed. (47-116 to 118).

Joint tenancy is recognized, but presumption against same and conveyance to more than one person is deemed to create tenancy in common unless words "as joint tenants," which mean joint tenants with right of survivorship, follow names. (47-36a). Conveyance to joint tenants shall be deemed to be in survivorship. (47-14a). Joint tenancies may be converted into tenancy in common by conveyance (47-14c); mortgage (47-14e); attachment and execution (47-14f); or dissolution of marriage (47-14g) of interest of one or more but less than all joint tenants.

Tenancies by the entirety are not recognized. (11 Conn. 337).

Perpetuities.—Act adopting Uniform Statutory Rule Against Perpetuities is enacted. (PA 89-44). See topic Perpetuities.

Uniform Act.—Connecticut has adopted Uniform Common Interest Ownership Act. Act is comprehensive regulation of all common interest communities including condominiums, cooperatives, and planned communities. (47-200 et seq.).

Condominiums.—Condominium Act of 1976 (47-68a to 47-90c) now in effect for method of establishing real property ownership of individual units in multi-unit structures popularly known as condominium. There are certain instances in which condominium documentation will not be deemed invalid despite errors or omissions in its creation or administration. (S.A. 97-6, §1[a-d]; H.B. 6402).

Time Sharing Plans.—Defined and governed by 42-103.

Maps and Plans.—No deed, mortgage, lease or other instrument recorded prior to effective date of act will be deemed invalid despite errors or omissions with respect to maps and plans. (S.A. §5; H.B. 6402).

Action to quiet title may be brought by any person claiming title to or any interest in land against all persons asserting adverse claims, including unknown persons whose possible claims are described by plaintiff. (47-31).

Rights of entry and reverters extinguished if specified contingency does not occur within 30 years (for instruments effective after Oct. 1, 1955). (45-97).

In ejectment defendant may recover value of improvements made in good faith, or plaintiff may confirm title in defendant and be awarded such sum as defendant equitably ought to pay therefor. (47-30).

Foreign Conveyances or Encumbrances.—Conveyance, mortgage, release of mortgage or lien of real estate located in state, and power of attorney authorizing conveyance of such real estate, executed and acknowledged in another state in accordance with laws of that state as to real estate are valid. (47-7).

Systematic Sales of Lots Located Outside Connecticut.—Seller must accept service through secretary of state, post bond, produce prospectus and other information, apply for license and pay fee, and deliver prospectus to customer. (20-329a to 20-329m).

Claims of title to real property good if unbroken 40 years prior to date marketability is to be determined. (47-33a to 47-33k). Some question among bar concerning whether title searches should nevertheless still be taken back 60 years. All actions taken by certain municipal and/or administrative entities with respect to real property will be deemed valid despite errors or omissions in compliance with notice provisions where no appeal from action is pending or time for such appeal has not expired. (S.A. §6[c]; H.B. 6402).

Limitation on enforceability of land use restrictions, see category Civil Actions and Procedure, topic Limitation of Actions, subhead Three Years.

Property Acquired with State Financial Assistance.—Nonprofit corporations holding title to real property acquired with state financial assistance may convey titles to such structures and improvements on real property to low income families, limited equity cooperatives, or other corporations so long as: (1) Property is only used for low income housing; (2) nonprofit corporation retains title to real property upon which such structures and improvements are situated; and (3) nonprofit corporation shall have first option to purchase any structures and improvements transferred at below market price. (8-214d).

See also topics Curtesy, Deeds, Dower, Landlord and Tenant; categories Civil Actions and Procedure, topic Partition; Debtor and Creditor, topic Homesteads; Documents and Records, topic Records; Family, topic Husband and Wife; Mortgages, topic Mortgages of Real Property.

Conveyance Disclosure Requirements.—Psychologically impacted property means effect on property from occupant infected or suspected of being infected with human immune deficiency syndrome, or from being suspected site of homocide, other felony or suicide. Existence of any fact which may have psychological impact on purchaser or lessee is not material fact that must be disclosed in real estate transaction, nor shall cause of action arise against owner for failure to disclose that property has been psychologically impacted. If purchaser or lessee advises owner in writing that knowledge of psychological impact is important to his or her decision to purchase or lease property, owner shall report any findings or advise purchaser by writing of his refusal to disclose such information. (PA 90-141).

Definition of displaced person who is required to move from real property due to displacement by agency or governmental entity no longer includes business which is so

See note at head of Digest as to 1998 legislation covered.

See Topical Index in front part of this volume.

REAL PROPERTY . . . *continued*

required to move, but which has also reached end of its lease term or has been evicted for nonpayment of rent as long as agency acquired property at least ten years prior to move. (CGS §8-267; PA 98-246).

Planning and Zoning.—There are certain instances in which conveyance of title in subdivision will not be deemed invalid despite errors or omissions in subdivision approval. (S.A. §6[b]; H.B. 6402).

TRUST DEEDS:

See category Mortgages, topic Mortgages of Real Property.

TAXATION

ADMINISTRATION:

Commissioner of Revenue Services has general supervision over the administration and enforcement of tax laws. (12-2).

At their option, state and local authorities may allow payment of taxes, penalties and interest by credit card. (12-39r; 12-141a).

In general, any partial payment of taxes applied first to any penalties (unless waived), then interest on tax, then taxes due, in that order. (12-39h). Beginning with taxes due after July 1, 1995, accrual of interest on overdue taxes is limited to amount of tax liability, instead of liability plus applicable penalty.

Uniform system of enforcement of taxes due the state (other than inheritance or succession tax) permits, where not otherwise provided for, the addition of a 10% penalty 30 days after due date or $50 whichever amount is greater and interest at 1¼% per month (12-35), acceleration of due date by commissioner or other enforcement agency where delay would in his opinion jeopardize collection (12-36), and enforcement of tax with penalty and interest and costs by (1) Civil action brought by Attorney General; (2) levy on taxpayer's property by sheriff, constable or any person or employee of state collection agency designated for such purpose by commissioner or other enforcement agency in manner provided for collection of property tax by tax collector (12-35; 12-36); (3) foreclosure of tax lien, if one has been provided for, by ordinary foreclosure action in name of state (12-36). Prosecution for wilful failure to pay tax or file return must be within three years of violation. (PA 97-203).

Penalties.—See topics/subheads detailing particular taxes.

Comity.—Attorney General authorized to bring suit in other states for delinquent taxes and to collect delinquent succession and transfer taxes, and political subdivisions can sue in other states for delinquent. Same privilege accorded other states in courts of this state if they allow Connecticut to sue. (12-387a to 12-387c). Commissioner of Revenue Services authorized to enter into agreements with other states for reciprocal enforcement of tax laws. (12-34c). Definitions of "taxpayer", "claimant state", "taxes", "refund", "tax officer" for purposes of collection of taxes to different state; conditions upon which refunds may be withheld and paid to another state; certification of out-of-state obligation, notification. (PA 98-244, §2 [new]).

Appeals.—Two judges of Superior Court will be designated to hear only appeals from various orders, decisions and disallowances of Commissioner of Revenue Services under variety of tax statutes. (12-391). HB 5681; PA 98-262, §1 modifies CGS §12-391 regarding orders from which appeals may be taken. HB 5679; PA 98-244, §3 modifies CGS §12-39m regarding posting bond during objection to assessment. (CGS §12-39h).

Dissemination of Information.—HB 5679; PA 98-244, §1 modifies CGS §12-15 regarding employees of state and of others who have access to tax returns shall not disclose or inspect return information except in accordance with Act and statutes.

HB 5679; PA 98-262, §23 (new) regarding deficiency assessments of taxes payable to municipalities; notice and hearing; written objections; interest rate of 1% per month from date tax due and payable; penalty of greater of $50 or 10% of tax assessed in event of negligent or intentional disregard of provisions of c. 223; if intent to evade or defraud, penalty shall equal 25% of deficiency assessment; no more than one penalty per same tax period. If no timely appeal made, Commissioner may collect taxes as if due state per §12-35 and as if such term expressly included taxes, penalties and interest. (§§12-39g[2]; 12-739[a]).

ADMISSIONS AND CLUB DUES:

Tax is imposed equal to 10% paid as dues or fees to social, athletic or sporting clubs. Organization is exempt if its dues are $100 or less. (12-543).

Exemptions for organizations controlled by charitable or religious organizations, government agencies, or nonprofit educational institutions, or organizations operating under lodge system, or college fraternities. (12-543).

Collection procedures and penalties are same as under subhead Amusement Tax, above. (12-544 to 556; 33-286).

If corporation fails to file return or pay admissions, cabaret or dues tax and it cannot be collected from corporation, and if responsible corporate officer willfully made that failure, officer is personally liable for full tax. (12-547a).

ALCOHOLIC BEVERAGE TAX:

Tax is levied on sale of alcoholic beverages by distributors within state. Tax does not apply to sales to licensed distributors, sales in course of which beverage is transported to point outside of state or sales of malt beverages consumed on premises covered by manufacturer's permit. (12-435). By distributor is meant any person or his backer, who holds wholesaler's or manufacturer's permit under Liquor Control Act. (12-433). Such distributor must obtain license from Commissioner of Revenue Services and only licensed distributor may import alcoholic beverages or sell untaxed wine. (12-436). Licensed distributors must file with Commissioner of Revenue Services, before last day of each month, returns computing tax for preceding calendar month (12-437) and must pay tax with return or submit to penalty of 10% of tax due or $50 whichever is greater plus interest at rate of 1% per month (12-439 and 12-440). Criminal sanctions for failure

to file return or falsify same may include fine up to $5,000 or imprisonment up to five years or both. (12-452). Uniform system of enforcement of taxes due state is applicable, and tax is lien on all property used in business, but such lien has priority only from time of filing certificate of lien with town clerk. Purchaser of business becomes liable for seller's tax. (12-441). Where Connecticut beverages are taxed in another state at rate greater than beverages manufactured in that state, additional tax in same proportion is levied on sale in Connecticut of beverages manufactured in that other state. (12-451). Tax upon storage or use within State of any untaxed alcoholic beverages in possession of person other than licensed distributor or carrier for transit from without State to licensed distributor within State. (12-435b). Any advertisement for sale of untaxed alcoholic beverages for use and consumption in this state shall contain words on container or be announced "These alcoholic beverages are subject to the payment of the Connecticut alcoholic beverage use tax and Connecticut use tax and may be subject to seizure as contraband goods." (12-435c).

PA 98-244, §24 modified CGS §12-540, excludes from definition of "cabaret or other similar place" places where Karaoke is performed alone without Karaoke performer; nor does it include room in restaurant where permits for beer or beer and wine only have been issued. (CGS §§30-22[b]; 30-22[c]; 30-22[e]).

AMUSEMENT TAX:

Amusement tax of 10% is imposed upon any person paying admission to certain amusements except for admission charges less than $1, or for motion picture shows less than $4.50. (12-541). Tax does not apply to organizations exempt from federal income taxes or organizations determined similar by Commissioner of Revenue Services. (12-541).

Each collector must file return for preceding month with tax commissioner last day of next month, or else is subject to penalty of 10% of tax due or $50 whichever is greater plus interest at rate of 1% added interest per month. (12-547). Tax must be paid with return. If commissioner determines deficiency, penalty of 10% of deficiency (or $50 whichever is greater) plus 1% added interest per month. (12-548). Criminal sanctions for wilful failure to file return or falsify same may include fine up to $5,000 or imprisonment up to five years or both. (12-551). Collector may appeal to commissioner within 30 days after tax determined in writing. (12-553). Collector may appeal within one month of commissioner's order to Superior Court at Hartford. (12-554).

Municipality may impose 10% tax on charge for admission to any pari-mutuel or off-track betting facility located within municipality. Where tax is imposed, return and tax due on 20th of each month. Penalty for failure to pay tax when due is $10 plus 10% of tax, plus 1% of amount due for each additional month's delay. (12-579; 12-581).

BUSINESS TAXES:

Industrial Waste Facilities.—(12-217d; 12-247b; 12-252b; 12-258c; 12-265c). (repealed by PA 97-295 effective July 8, 1997, but remaining tax credits carry forward).

Child Day Care Credit.—Any business firm which desires to subsidize its employees for child day care from licensed providers or desires to pay or incur expenditures for facilities for establishing child day care facility may apply to commissioner of human resources for allocation for tax credit. (12-634).

Hospitals must pay quarterly taxes upon gross earnings, as defined. Current rate is 9.25%, and is being phased down to 6.25%, effective Oct. 1, 1999. (12-263b). PA 98-244, §12 modifies CGS §12-263b regarding taxation of gross earnings of hospital at rate of 11% in each taxable quarter for taxable quarters commencing prior to 10/1/96; 9¼% on or after 10/1/96; 8¼% on or after 10/1/97 but pre-10/1/98; 7¼% on or after 10/1/98 but pre-10/1/99; and 6¼% on or after 10/1/99; returns file quarterly and signed by principal officer.

Gross Revenue Tax on Petroleum Companies.—Any petroleum company including any corporation, partnership, limited partnership, association, individual or any fiduciary thereof engaged in refining and distribution of petroleum products shall pay quarterly tax of 5% on gross earnings in each taxable quarter derived from sale within state of petroleum products except number 2 heating oil and propane gas used for residential heating. Any company that imports or causes to be imported into Connecticut petroleum products for its use and consumption, other than company that is already subject to and has paid petroleum products gross earnings tax on such petroleum products, must pay quarterly tax at rate of 5% of consideration given, or contracted to be given, for such petroleum product is consideration for all such deliveries during quarterly period for which tax is to be paid exceeds $100,000. "Use" includes sale of imported petroleum products in regular course of business. (Act 3 [S.B. 2010], §146). Within 30 days of due date for tax imposed under §12-587, one third of total amount of tax due shall be credited by treasurer to Underground Storage Tank Petroleum Clean Up Fund to be used by Commissioner of Environmental Protection. (PA 89-373). Tax imposed under this Act shall be in addition to any other tax imposed by Connecticut for which petroleum company is liable. Returns must be filed on last day of month succeeding Jan., Apr., July and Oct. for prior quarter. Failure to do so results in penalty of 10% of tax due for negligent or intentional failure to file and 25% penalty for fraud. If return is more than three months late Commissioner of Revenue Services may estimate tax and add 25% or $50 penalty. Criminal sanctions for wilful failure to file return or falsify same may include fine up to $5,000 and/or imprisonment up to five years. Commissioner has broad investigatory powers and can examine returns up to three years after filing. Interest on overdue taxes 1% per month. Unpaid taxes shall be lien against all real estate of company within state. Petroleum company shall not increase wholesale rack prices to compensate for this tax. Superior Court in Hartford has jurisdiction over all complaints arising under this Act. (12-587 to 12-602).

Tire Fee.—All retailers of tires required to pay fee of $2 per tire upon sale, (PA 93-74, §47). *Note:* Fee repealed, effective July 1, 1996. (PA 94-4, May Sp. Sess.).

CAPITAL GAINS TAX:

Capital gains tax imposed on gains of taxpayer during taxable year from sales or exchanges of capital assets (not otherwise exempt in 12-506) at rate of 4.5%. (12-506). Tax will not apply to gains received, accrued or credited on or after Jan. 1, 1992. (Act 3

CAPITAL GAINS TAX ... *continued*
[S.B. 2010], §156) corresponding to date when personal income tax became fully effective.

CIGARETTE AND TOBACCO TAXES:

Cigarette Tax.—25 mills for each cigarette held for sale, payment being evidenced by dealers and distributors affixing to packages stamps purchased from Tax Commissioner, who will redeem unused stamps. (12-296 to 12-339b, am'd 93-74). Additional excise tax of 1.5 mills per cigarette imposed on distributors, effective July 1, 1994. Any written advertisement in this state for sale of untaxed cigarettes for use and consumption in this state shall contain words "These cigarettes are subject to the payment of the Connecticut cigarette use tax and the Connecticut use tax and may be subject to seizure as contraband goods." (12-292). PA 98-262, §21 repeals CGS §12-299 regarding metering machines.

Tobacco.—Tax imposed on all tobacco products held in state by any person, taxed at rate of 20% of wholesale sales price or wholesale value if no price set. Tax imposed on distributor or unclassified importer at time tobacco product manufactured, purchased, imported, received or acquired in state. Each distributor or unclassified importer must obtain license issued by commissioner before manufacturing, purchasing, importing, receiving or acquiring any tobacco products in state. Fee for distributor's license, $100. There shall be no fee for unclassified importer's license. Each distributor and unclassified importer shall keep complete and accurate records of all tobacco products. (PA 89-251, §§26, 32; am'd PA 90-115). Procedures for claiming refund of tax overpayments. (PA 98-262, §4 [new]).

ENVIRONMENTAL TAXES:

Hazardous Waste Tax.—Generators of hazardous waste must pay 5¢ per gallon of metal hydroxide sludge and 6¢ per gallon of any other hazardous waste plus additional charges but no assessment is paid if total assessment would be less than $20 per year. (22a-132). Department of Environmental Protection to develop plan of assessment upon Nuclear Regulatory Commission licensees for financing of state low-level radioactive waste disposal fund. Note: Imposition and collection of this tax to end June 30, 2001. (22a-132, am'd 95-92).

Recycling Tax.—Owners of resource recovery facilities or mixed municipal solid waste landfills shall pay $1 per ton of solid waste processed or disposed of. Failure to do so will result in penalty of 10% of amount due. Owners must also submit quarterly returns. (PA 90-235).

ESTATE TAX:

Estate tax is imposed on the transfer of the estate of each person dying resident in this state, equal to the amount by which Federal credit allowed for such taxes under the provisions of the Federal Revenue Code in force at date of decedent's death exceeds the total estate, inheritance, legacy, transfer and succession taxes actually paid to the states and territories of the United States (including this state) in respect to the estate of such decedent. (12-391). This tax is due at date of taxable transfer and payable nine months thereafter. (12-392). Commissioner of Revenue Services assesses this tax on basis of information contained in succession tax returns to probate court, appeal lying from Commissioner to Superior Court for judicial district of Hartford. (12-391). Administrative provisions of succession tax law are applicable to this tax so far as adapted to it except no lien for estate tax. (12-395). Tax remains applicable only so long as credit allowed under 1986 Federal Internal Revenue Code continues to be allowed. (12-396).

Federal and state estate taxes are equitably prorated among persons interested in estate, in absence of will provision to the contrary. (12-401).

§12-364 is repealed and substituted. Where Commissioner has determined that joint tenant has died and that succession tax is assured or not due, release of lien may issue conclusively releasing property from succession tax lien. Certificate may be recorded with town clerk where real property is situated upon finding by Commissioner that tax payment is adequately assured by bond, other security or surety, or payment of tax or appointment of bonded executor or administrator. Commissioner may adopt regulations prescribing circumstances under which probate court may issue lien release certificate. (12-364; PA 97-3).

§12-366 is repealed and substituted. Succession tax lien in favor of state is not valid against lienor, creditor, mortgagee, bona fide purchaser or judgment creditor without notice until recorded or filed with town clerk. Commissioner may adopt regulations prescribing circumstances under which probate court may discharge lien by payment of tax. (12-366; PA 97-3).

§12-378 is repealed and substituted. Where probate judge does not believe estate is taxable, judge may send written opinion to Commissioner with tax return. After 60 days, judge's opinion is conclusive evidence that estate's real property is tax-free with respect to deceased. If on or before sixth day, Commissioner files objection or appraised value is raised or taxability is increased by more than $1,000, court may correct errors in opinion. After 60 days, judge may issue certificate. (12-378; PA 97-3).

§12-382 is repealed and substituted. One who transfers or permits transfer of property subject to taxation, without consent of Commissioner; and if no administration granted by probate court, and has actual knowledge of transferor's death, is liable for penalty three times tax found due. (12-382; PA 97-3).

Valuation Date.—Estate is taxed on value as of date of death. (141 Conn. 257, 105 A.2d 654).

Interstate Co-operation.—Commissioner of Revenue Services may compromise (12-372) or arbitrate (12-374) with taxing authorities of other states when domicile of decedent is in dispute.

Apportionment Against Inter Vivos Dispositions.—Connecticut has statutes allowing proration. (12-400 to 12-405).

Nonresident Estate.—Any fiduciary of nonresident estate in excess of $20,000 (as reported on Federal Fiduciary Tax Return) shall be deemed "taxpayer" for purposes of 12-405c, 405d, or 405k. (12-405c).

"Fiduciary" means executor or administrator of resident or nonresident estate, whether or not such executor or administrator is taxpayer. (12-405a[h]).

Commissioner has been granted broad investigatory and enforcement powers in estate tax areas. (12-405c; 12-405d).

Regulations under §§12-405e to 12-405i eliminate estimated estate taxes under said statute.

GASOLINE TAX:

On or after July 1, 1998, 32¢ per gallon of fuel sold, 31¢ per gallon of gasohol sold, payable by distributors to state treasurer for account of consumers, computed on basis of monthly reports filed with Motor Vehicle Commissioner on 25th of each month. (12-458). Fuel consumption by industrial customers and vessels primarily engaged in interstate commerce is subject to taxes at different rates. (12-458). Aviation fuel is not subject to tax. (12-462).

Provision is made for refund of state tax to school, airport bus operators, to those who purchased fuel for use other than propelling of motor vehicles over highway, to U.S. Government, governmental agencies, ambulances owned by hospitals or civic nonprofit organizations, high occupancy commuter vehicles owned or leased by transit district, taxicab owners and livery service operators. (12-459). PA 98-262, §8 modifies CGS §12-462(a) regarding circumstances under which Commissioner licenses dealers to purchase tax exempt fuel from distributors and sell it directly. PA 98-244, §20 modifies CGS §12-458b regarding distributors of fuel who are contractors performing contract services for municipality or school district in this state may file tax returns and pay tax quarterly, not monthly. §21 modifies CGS §12-459(b) by changing month for filing claims for fuel tax refunds from Mar. to May.

INCOME TAX:

Personal Income Tax.—Tax is imposed on Connecticut taxable income of each resident individual, trust or estate at rate of 1.5% for tax years beginning on or after Jan. 1, 1991 and prior to Jan. 1, 1992, and at rate of 4.5% of such Connecticut taxable income for tax years beginning after 1991 and before 1996. Effective Jan. 1, 1996, tax is reduced slightly with 3% rate applied to lowest income bracket, irrespective of taxpayer class or total income level. Initial 3% bracket further increased effective Jan. 1, 1997. (12-700, am'd PA 95-160, am'd PA 97-309). Tax is imposed on Connecticut taxable income derived from or connected with sources within Connecticut of each nonresident individual, estate and trust. Part-year residents included as well. PA 98-244, §28 modifies CGS §12-704 regarding credit to taxpayers for tax imposed by another state; notice required for changes in tax paid to other states due to change in income or corrections to returns; time for notice; concession of accuracy of determinations of identification of errors; notice of differences in tax credits due to other state taxes; Commissioner may, by regulation, prescribe exemptions; §29 (new) regarding taxation of income earned by athletes, entertainers, or performing artists from closed circuit and cable television transmissions of special events taking place in this state but only to extent such transmissions were received or exhibited in this state; §33 modifies CGS §12-733(b) by providing that if any taxpayer omits from his income tax return income derived from source in this state, notice of deficiency assessment may be mailed to him within six years after return is filed.

Connecticut Adjusted Gross Income.—Defined as federal adjusted gross income with Connecticut modifications. (12-701[a][20]).

Personal Exemptions.—Any individual who files federal income tax return for such tax year as unmarried individual or as married individual filing separately is entitled to personal exemption of $12,000. However, if taxpayer's Connecticut adjusted gross income for tax year exceeds $24,000, exemption is reduced by $1,000 for each $1,000 or fraction by which taxpayer's adjusted gross income for tax year exceeds $24,000. In no case can reduction exceed 100% of exemption.

Heads of households are allowed personal exemption of $19,000. If such taxpayer's Connecticut adjusted gross income for tax year exceeds $38,000, exemption is reduced by $1,000 for each $1,000 or fraction by which taxpayer's adjusted gross income exceeds $38,000. Reduction cannot exceed 100% of exemption.

Taxpayers filing joint return and surviving spouses are entitled to personal exemption of $24,000. If such taxpayer's adjusted gross income exceeds $48,000, exemption is reduced by $1,000 for each $1,000 or fraction by which taxpayer's adjusted gross income exceeds $48,000. Reduction cannot exceed 100% of exemption. (12-702).

Credits.—Individuals are allowed tax credit in amounts ranging from 75% to 1% of tax due depending on filing status and Connecticut adjusted gross income. (PA 94-4, May Sp. Sess.). Commencing with 1996 income year, varying credit available for actual property taxes paid on primary residence or privately-owned motor vehicles. (PA 95-160, am'd PA 98-110).

Rebate.—For 1998 income years, individuals received income tax rebate up to $150 of actual tax paid for property taxes paid on primary residence or privately owned motor vehicles. (PA 98-110).

Withholding.—Employers maintaining office or transacting business in Connecticut and making payment of any wages subject to personal income tax must deduct and withhold tax from such wages for each payroll period. (12-705). Withholding returns and payments are due at same time employer is required to pay federal withholding taxes. (12-707).

Payment of Tax.—Returns and payment of tax are due on or before 15th day of fourth month following close of taxpayer's tax year. (12-719). Underpayments bear interest at rate of 1% per month. (12-722). Penalties for underpayment exist. (12-722). PA 98-244, §30 modifies CGS §12-723 notwithstanding §12-735. No penalty for nonpayment of excess tax due if such unpaid tax is no greater than 10% of tax shown on return and balance due is paid on or before extension date. PA 98-244, §31 modifies CGS §12-727(b) regarding if taxpayer's federal income tax return is modified by authorized entity, taxpayer must provide notice of charge/correction to Commissioner by filing amended return within 90 days after final determination and concede accuracy of determination or challenge errors. Commissioner may redetermine tax and taxpayer shall be required to pay tax for any taxable year without regard to statutes of limitation otherwise applicable. PA 98-244, §32 modifies CGS §12-732(b) by providing that if

See note at head of Digest as to 1998 legislation covered.

See Topical Index in front part of this volume.

INCOME TAX . . . *continued*
taxpayer complies with CGS §12-704 and timely files amended tax returns and is entitled to refund, such claim shall be deemed timely regardless of statute of limitations.

Estimated Tax.—If taxpayer's Connecticut taxable income or, in case of nonresident, such taxpayer's Connecticut taxable income derived from or connected with sources within this state, can reasonably be expected to exceed $200, taxpayer is required to make declaration and payment of estimated tax. No taxpayer is required to make such declaration if tax on taxpayer's Connecticut taxable income, other than $200 from wages can reasonably be expected not to exceed tax withheld. Declaration of estimated tax must be filed on or before Apr. 15 of tax year, and payments of estimated tax are due at time of filing declaration and on or before 15th day of June, Sept. and following Jan. Declaration of estimated tax is due later in year and fewer installments are required if requirements for reporting and paying estimated tax are first met later in year. (12-722).

Estate Income and Gift Tax.—Connecticut estate income tax does not apply to income of any estate for any income year beginning on or after Jan. 1, 1991. Tax had been imposed to absorb maximum credit allowed against federal estate tax.

For calendar year 1991 and each year thereafter, tax is imposed on transfer of property by gift during tax year by any individual resident or nonresident. However, for 1991 only, tax is imposed only on those gifts that are transferred on or after Sept. 1, 1991. (12-640). Tax does not apply to transfer of any tangible personal property and real property having situs outside Connecticut. (12-641).

Gift tax rate ranges between 1% if amount of taxable gifts is not over $25,000, and 6% if amount of taxable gifts is over $200,000. Tax is to be paid by donor. (12-642). Returns and payments are due on or before Apr. 15 following close of calendar year during which gift was made, except, where gift is made during calendar year when donor dies, filing deadline is governed by applicable federal gift tax deadline. (12-645; 12-644). Credit against succession tax for gift tax paid with respect to gifts includable in donor's gross taxable estate. (12-648). Exemption from transfer taxes (gift or succession) provided for "annual exclusion gifts" made ($10,000 per year per donee; $20,000 with spousal gift splitting). (12-643).

Electronic Funds Transfer.—PA 98-244, §27 modifies CGS §12-687 regarding taxes withheld from income electronically transferred by employer and time for crediting tax; imposition of penalty for untimely tax payments. (CGS §12-39a).

Dividend and interest income tax increases from 0.75% to 9.5% on adjusted gross income starting at $54,000 and is imposed along with capital gains tax. Similar conditions of taxpayer liability apply as in capital gains tax imposition. (12-506). Tax will not apply to dividends and interest received, accrued, or credited on or after Jan. 1, 1992, corresponding to date when personal income tax became fully effective.

Other Income Taxes.—

Corporation Business Tax.—See category Business Organizations, topic Corporations.

Insurance Companies.—See category Insurance, topic Insurance Companies.

Railroad and street railway corporations must pay on or before July 1 annual tax upon gross earnings from all sources of operation in state. (12-249). Street railway rate is 3%. Rate for other railways varies from 2% to 3½% depending on extent to which operating net income exceeds 8% of gross earnings. If operating net income does not exceed 8% of gross earnings, rate is 2%, if it exceeds 8%, but not 10% rate is 2¼%, etc. Allocation formula is used where only part of railway lies in state. (12-251). Certain railroads may qualify for tax exemption upon certification by PUC if net income is less than 12% of gross earnings, upon payment of $20 fee. (12-251). PA 98-244, §11 modifies CGS §12-250 regarding taxation of railway operating revenues; return to be filed 7/1 and signed by Treasurer and specify operational information as of 12/31 or portion of year in which company did business including assessed value of property.

Taxes on gross earnings are in lieu of all other taxes, except that real estate, when not used exclusively for railroad purposes, is taxed locally. (12-255). Amount of such real estate taxes is deducted from amount of tax on gross earnings. (12-251). Owners of securities of such corporations incorporated in state are exempt from tax thereon. (12-255).

Annual return must be filed with Commissioner of Revenue Services on or before July 1. (12-250). Companies may file objections with commissioner to apportionment method in 12-249. (12-268a). Interest on unpaid tax is 10% (or $50 whichever is greater). (12-268d). Penalty for fraudulent filing not more than $1,000. (12-268e). Fiduciaries responsible for filing and tax payments. (12-268b).

Water, gas, electric and power companies must pay quarterly tax upon gross earnings from operations in state. Company that sells water is not taxable unless it is water company as defined under public utility control statutes defined in §16-1. (12-264). Rate of tax of 5% of gross earnings (rate of 4% for seller or distributor of gas or electricity to be used for light, heat or power), but deduction may be made of all sales of water, steam, gas, and electricity to other public service corporation for resale, and of sales of appliances using water, steam, gas, or electricity, whether or not such purchasers are Connecticut public service corporations or Connecticut municipal utilities. (12-265). Public utility sales of natural gas as motor vehicle fuel exempt from gross earnings tax through 1999. (12-264). If part of business is outside state, portion of gross earnings, represented by ratio of miles of water or steam pipes, gas mains or electric wires operated within state to total number of miles operated is subject to tax. (12-265). This tax is in lieu of all state license or income taxes and of all taxes upon intangibles.

Quarterly return with payment must be filed on or before last day of Jan., Apr., July, and Oct. of each year. (12-264). Commissioner determines tax and notifies company of amount before June 15. It is payable on July 15 and is lien on property on account of which tax is laid until paid, and takes precedence over any other incumbrance. Unpaid taxes bear interest of 1½% per month. Interest rate drops to 1% per month, effective July 1, 1995. (12-268h). Company may appeal action of Commissioner within 30 days to superior court of county in which taxpayer is located. (12-33). PA 98-244, §13 modifies CGS §12-264 regarding taxation of utility companies; returns to be signed by Treasurer or authorized agent or officer and must specify gross earnings, name and type of utility, miles of pipeline operated on first and last calendar days of prior year.

Express, telegraph, telephone, cable companies and community antenna television systems must pay annual tax upon gross earnings from operations in state. (12-256). Rate for express companies is 2%; for telegraph and cable companies, 4½%; for telecommunications companies subject to competition or not subject to regulation, 6½% (PA 86-410, §2); for telecommunications companies subject to rate regulation and in markets in which competition is prohibited, tax equals assessed personal property of company times median mill rate for all towns in state (12-256; 12-258). PA 98-262, §12 modifies CGS §12-80a regarding taxation of telecommunications service providers and election of manner of taxation dependent upon whether taxpayers were subject to tax under c. 211 or 219. Allocation is made where company also has operations without state. (12-256). This tax is in lieu of all other taxation in state upon such companies and upon companies furnishing, leasing, or operating railroad cars, and upon tangible and intangible personal property used in such business. Real estate here is assessed and taxed locally. (12-30).

Company must file annual return with payment for last calendar year on or before Apr. 1. (12-256). Company may appeal within one month to superior court in county where taxpayer is located. (12-33). If tax not paid, it bears interest at 1½% per month until paid.

Air carriers which make landing or take-offs in state are subject to corporation business tax. (12-248). Special provision governs allocation of income attributable to business done in state. (12-244). Real and personal property, except flight equipment, is taxed locally in accordance with applicable law. (12-245).

Returns must be filed on calendar year basis unless books closed on a fiscal basis with approval of Civil Aeronautics Board. (12-246). Certain provisions of corporation business tax are made expressly applicable. (12-248). See category Business Organizations, topic Corporations.

Motor Vehicles.—Liability for property tax for motor vehicles registered between Oct. and Apr. of assessment year; pro rata taxation if motor vehicle registered after Oct. (CGS §12-71b; PA 98-261).

INHERITANCE TAX:

No tax denominated as such, but see under topics Succession and Transfer Tax, and Estate Tax.

MEALS TAX:

See topic Sales and Use Taxes.

MOTOR VEHICLE TAXES:

Road Tax.—Motor carriers using Connecticut highways are subject to road use tax at rate equal to gasoline tax per gallon of fuel burned on Connecticut highways, but are credited for amounts of fuel purchased within state. (12-478 to 12-493).

Automobile Rental Surcharge.—Effective Jan. 1, 1996, surcharge equal to 3% of total amount charged to rent private passenger vehicle for period of less than 31 days is to be collected and remitted by lessor. (12-692). Motor vehicle repair shops exempted. (12-692[a][2]). PA 98-262, §9 modifies CGS §12-692 regarding change in definition of "rental company" to exclude entities licensed as new car dealer, repairer or limited repairer or as used car dealer that is not primarily engaged in business of renting passenger motor vehicles without driver in Connecticut to lessees; "lessee" defined as one who leases passenger motor vehicle from rental company for personal use; registration and titling fees where rental company rents vehicle from another and then re-leases vehicle.

OLD AGE ASSISTANCE TAX:

Old age assistance tax has been repealed.

PROFESSIONAL TAXES:

Professional Tax.—Members of numerous specified professions (e.g., medicine, accounting, etc.) pay annual license fee. (Tit. 20).

See also subhead Attorneys and Judges, infra.

Attorneys and judges subject to annual tax of $450 due Jan. 1. Chief court administrator and judges of Superior Court notified of failure to pay. $25 penalty and 1¼% per month interest for nonpayment. If removed from roll of attorneys or retired or in armed forces, not liable for tax. (51-81b).

PROPERTY TAXES:

Property tax applies to all real estate located in Connecticut (12-64); all tangible personal property located in Connecticut seven months of year, except goods in transit owned by nonresident having no office or place of business in this state (12-43; 12-59) and all other tangible personal property owned by residents of Connecticut (12-71), except certain property specifically exempted (12-81).

Assessment.—Real estate including air space is subject to tax in town where located. (12-64). Personal property of resident is taxed in town of residence. (12-43). Tangible property of nonresident is taxed in town where it is located. (12-71). Property of trading or mechanical business is assessed in name of owner in town where business is carried on. (12-58).

Manufacturers, retailers and wholesalers taxed on average inventory but current statutes provide for gradual phase out of this portion of tax. (12-81 et seq.).

Each taxpayer must, on or before Nov. 1 of each year, file with the assessors of the town in which the property is taxable, on the form provided him, a list of his taxable property owned as of the preceding Oct. 1 (12-42) except in certain municipalities wherein the assessors' office has established a listing system approved by Commissioner of Revenue Services (12-41). Assessors may require owners of rental income property to disclose annual rental income and operating expenses on or before June 1. (12-63c). In case of business organization with goods for sale, average monthly quantity of goods on hand during preceding year, instead of amount on hand on Oct. 1, must be listed. (12-58). For failure to file this taxpayer is liable to 25% increase in assessment. (12-53; 12-111). Assessors fill in on list valuation of this property at "its present true

See note at head of Digest as to 1998 legislation covered.

See Topical Index in front part of this volume.

CT – 50

PROPERTY TAXES . . . *continued*

and actual value" or at uniform percentage of true and actual valuation (12-64), revalue property at least every four years (12-62; 12-62a[a]-[d]; 12-62e), add property improperly omitted (12-53), notify taxpayer of any additions to list or increases in valuation over prior years (12-53; 12-55), examine persons failing to file lists as required (12-54), make out lists for those failing to file lists (12-53), arrange all lists thus prepared in alphabetical order (which set of lists constitutes "grand list") and lodge grand list, together with abstract of lists, with town clerk for public inspection, all on or before Jan. 31 next following date for filing lists (12-55), unless extension not exceeding one month is granted by Commissioner of Revenue Services (12-117). Commencing Oct. 1, 1997, town-wide reassessment by physical inspection of taxable real estate must be undertaken at least every 12 years, and adjusted every four years, without examination, using statistical data, as necessary. (12-62).

Review of Assessment.—Board of assessment appeals of each town meets during month of Mar. each year (12-110) to review doings of assessors in behalf of taxpayers appealing to board for relief, or on its own motion (12-111), and prepares, after due notice to affected taxpayers, supplemental lists showing additions or deductions of items and increases or decreases in valuation (12-111; 12-115), resulting from board's deliberations, all of which duties board must complete no later than last business day of Mar. (12-110); unless extension not exceeding one month is granted by Office of Policy and Management (12-117). Board of assessment appeals of each town also meets at least once in Sept. solely to hear appeals relating to motor vehicle assessments. This duty must be completed before last business day of Sept. (12-110; 12-112). Property owner appealing assessment must do so in writing prior to Feb. 20th, unless extension granted to municipality to complete reassessment pursuant to statute, in which case deadline for appeal to Board of assessment appeals is Mar. 20. (12-111, am'd 96-1). Board of assessment appeals to schedule hearing during Mar. and provides minimum of seven days' notice to taxpayer. Board need not schedule hearing on commercial, industrial, apartment, or utility property assessed at more than $500,000. (12-111, am'd 95-283). Appeal from local board to superior court which may grant equitable relief to persons aggrieved. (12-118). Appeal must be brought within two months of board's determination. Venue is judicial district in which property at issue is located. (12-117a, am'd 96-261).

Credit.—Persons over 65 with total annual income under $20,000 if married and under $16,200 if unmarried are entitled to credit based on amount of their "qualifying income." Also applies to person over 50 who is surviving spouse of previously qualified taxpayer. (12-170a [d], [h]; 12-170aa[b]). Municipalities may provide property tax relief to residents 65 or over and residents eligible because of disability. (12-129n). PA 98-262, §19 modifies CGS §12-129b regarding reduction in payment of real property taxes by owner, tenant for life or tenant for term of years if certain conditions are satisfied. (CGS §§12-48, 12-129c, 12-170aa). Appeals must be brought within two months of board's determination. In addition, tax benefit to owners of damaged buildings who provide for their complete demolition. (12-64a). PA 98-262, §15 modifies PA 97-295, §7 regarding residents subject to tax per CGS §12-701(a)(1) are entitled to tax credit regarding liability under c. 229 for all or portion of property tax due and paid during taxable year on primary residence or motor vehicle as set forth; "property tax" defined as amount of property tax exclusive of interest, fees or charges thereon for which taxpayer(s) are liable. Property tax first becomes due, if due and payable in single installment, on date designated by municipality, if due and payable in two or more installments, on date designated by municipality or, at election of taxpayer, on date designated by municipality or date on which earlier installment was due and payable.

Exemptions.—Land owned or held in trust by religious, charitable, scientific, educational, literary, historical, agricultural and cemetery organizations exempt under 12-81 et seq.; and from which no income is derived, is exempt from taxation though not in actual use for purposes of organization if construction of buildings or improvements is in progress. Land of such organizations not used exclusively for purposes of organization, but leased, rented or used for other purposes is not exempt. If only portion of land or building is used exclusively for organization purposes, only that portion is exempt. Assessors determine portion exempt. (12-89; 12-90[a]). For still other exemptions see: 12-81 et seq. 12-91; 12-92; 12-104; 12-107a. In general exemption lost upon acquisition of property by another taxpayer and acquiring taxpayer is liable for pro rata portion of tax for part of year of his ownership. (12-81a). *Note:* §18 (new) of PA 98-262 exempts from property tax of commercial fishing apparatus subject to c. 208 taxation if value exceeds $500. PA 98-262, §20 modifies CGS §12-170f(a) regarding renters may be entitled to reduction in rent or utility bills if over age of 65 or have permanent total disability; application for procedures and time restraints.

Members of the Armed Forces.—Member of armed forces entitled to property tax exemption of motor vehicle garaged outside state. (12-81[51], [52], [53]). Connecticut residents who are presently members of armed forces and who were in service between certain specified dates are entitled to $1,000 veterans' exemption. See subhead Veterans' Exemption, infra. (12-81[19]). Disabled service-persons receive larger exemption depending on degree of disability. (12-81[20]). If exemption greater than amount of property, excess may be applied to property of serviceperson's spouse, widow, widower or minor child. (12-81[20]).

U.S. Army Instructors.—Regular army personnel assigned as Connecticut National Guard instructors get $1,000 exemption and an additional $2,000 exemption for certain property and equipment used in performance of duties. (12-81[28]).

Veterans' Exemption.—Persons who served as members of U.S. or armed forces of any government signatory of United Nations Declaration of Jan. 1, 1942 between certain specified dates are entitled to a $1,000 tax exemption (12-81[19]); upon proper proof of service (12-93). Disabled veterans receive larger exemption, depending upon degree of disability. Such exemption may be applied upon property of veteran's spouse, widow, widower or minor child if he or she lacks said amount of property. If death was due to service and occurred while on active duty, exemption is $3,000. (12-81 et seq.).

Abatement.—A corporation unable to secure working capital loan from a United States Government Agency because of real or personal property taxes assessed may apply to town for abatement, which may be granted only with approval of Commissioner of Revenue Services. Withdrawal of loan application or failure to receive loan applied for rescinds abatement. (12-125).

Payment and Collection.—After completion of the work of the board of relief, the town levies a tax on the grand list as supplemented, at such rate as is necessary to raise requisite revenue. (12-122). The town then gives to the tax collector of the town a signed rate bill showing proportion due from each taxpayer, accompanied by a warrant ordering collection. (12-130). Payment date is fixed by town, which may provide for installment payments. (12-142). Usual last date for payment of whole or first installment is June 1 of year following year of assessment, with unpaid installments due quarterly or semiannually thereafter. Any property tax due in any municipality of state in amount not in excess of $100 must be paid in single payment. (12-144). Tax collector may accelerate time for payment if he believes delay will jeopardize collection. (12-163).

When final day for payment of any tax occurs on Sat., Sun. or legal holiday, payment may be made without interest or penalty on following business day. (12-169).

Collection may be made by any tax collector, sheriff, deputy sheriff or constable of the municipality where the tax is due upon proper warrant or alias tax warrant in any part of the state. (12-135).

Tax Identification Numbers.—Municipal tax collectors are authorized to obtain social security and tax identification numbers to identify taxpayers (CGS §12-148); Commissioner of Revenue Services shall furnish to town tax assessors list of names/addresses of motor vehicle owners, and vehicle registration numbers, tax identification and/or social security numbers (CGS §14-163; PA 98-261).

Lien.—Real estate tax is prior lien on taxed real estate from assessment date until one year from payment date unless continued (12-172), which may be done by collector causing to be recorded by proper town clerk certificate of lien, after which continuation lien remains good for 15 years from continuation date (12-175).

Personal property tax is lien on taxpayer's goods in Connecticut. Lien has priority over all subsequently perfected liens except certain security interests, and is effective for ten years from filing date. (12-35).

Receiver of Rents.—Where owner is delinquent on property taxes with respect to income-producing property, municipality may petition superior court for appointment of receiver to collect rents or use and occupancy payments. Receiver, upon collection, applies proceeds as follows: (1) current taxes; (2) current utility charges; (3) receiver's fees and costs; (4) municipality's reasonable legal fees; (5) delinquent taxes; (6) such other obligations and/or parties as court may direct. (12-163a).

Sale.—Property tax may be enforced by collector by levy on and sale of taxpayer's personal property in manner of executions or, if person property proves insufficient, collector may levy upon real property (12-155), but his sale of real property must be advertised in manner provided and all owners and encumbrancers must be notified by registered mail (12-157). Taxes become debt enforceable by action in name of community in whose favor assessed. (12-161). Real estate tax lien may be enforced by levy and sale, if completed during life of lien (12-172) by foreclosure in manner of mortgage foreclosures (12-181) or by summary foreclosure proceedings in nature of action in rem when market value of realty is less than encumbrances on property and not more than $50,000 (12-182). No redemption from tax sale is provided for.

By action of selectmen of town, mayor and aldermen of city, or warden and burgesses of borough, collection may be deferred for unusual financial or other circumstances of the taxpayer, and while so deferred interest will not run. (12-174).

Refund for overpayment of property tax may be obtained on application in writing to tax collector within three years. (12-129).

Penalties.—Failure to file list of taxable property may result in 25% additional assessment. (12-42). Failure to pay property taxes on time results in assessment of interest at rate of 1½% per month or fraction thereof. (12-145). Provision also made for lien of real estate (12-173) and foreclosure thereof with tax sales (16-256d). Assessor, if authorized by ordinance, may waive 25% penalty. List of waivers must be published. (12-119a).

Apportioning in Eminent Domain.—When condemning authority apportions real property taxes in manner other than customary, amount of taxes condemned must pay in excess of usual apportionment is element of damages. (48-14a).

Real Estate Conveyance Tax of .50% and .11% of consideration for interest in real property conveyed by such deed, instrument or writing, credited to state general fund and general revenue of municipality, respectively when consideration for interest or property conveyed equals or exceeds $2,000. (12-494). No tax imposed on deeds enumerated in 12-498 or deeds of principal residence of person approved for assistance under 12-129b or 12-170a or deeds of property located in enterprise zone designated in 32-70. (12-498). PA 98-262, §16 modifies CGS §12-170d(b) regarding determining qualifying income; if married renter applies for grant, and is legally separated on 12/31 preceding date of application, he may apply as unmarried person for purposes of qualifying income; §17 modifies CGS §12-170aa(b) regarding reduction of property tax for qualifying residents over age of 65. PA 98-244, §22 modifies CGS §12-498(a) regarding exemption of taxation of certain deeds per §12-494. No tax imposed on transfer of burial rights to cemetery lot. (12-497a). If conveyance of real property used for any purpose other than residential use at time of conveyance tax shall be imposed at 1% of consideration for interest in real property conveyed and if conveyance is of residential estate for which consideration is in excess of $800,000 tax shall be imposed at ½% of consideration up to and including amount of $800,000; rate of 1% on portion over $800,000. (12-494[b]). Tax of .50% of consideration for interest in real property conveyed to financial institution which holds mortgage on such real property which has been delinquent for not less than six months. (12-494[b]). Tax of .11% imposed on any sale or transfer of controlling interest in any entity which possesses interest in real property in state when value of interest so conveyed equals or exceeds $2,000. Tax payable by person conveying such controlling interest. Return and payment due from sale or transfer due on or before last day of month following month sale or transfer occurred. (12-638b; 12-638c). Conveyance tax between 1% and 10% on sale of open space land within ten years of initial classification, and conversion of such land to other uses taxable as conveyance. Said tax also applied upon sale of farm or forest land within

See note at head of Digest as to 1998 legislation covered.

See Topical Index in front part of this volume.

PROPERTY TAXES . . . *continued*
ten years of initial classification or purchase by vendor. (12-504[a]). Said tax also applied if controlling interest in property also sold or conveyed. (12-6381).

REAL ESTATE CONVEYANCE TAX:

See topic Property Taxes, subhead Real Estate Conveyance Tax.

REVISED UNIFORM FEDERAL TAX LIEN REGISTRATION ACT:

Revised Uniform Federal Tax Lien Registration Act adopted. (49-32a).

SALES AND USE TAXES:

Sales Tax.—Imposed upon retailers for privilege of "making any sales . . . . ." (12-407; see also 12-408[1]). "Sale" and "selling" mean and include: (a) Any transfer of title, exchange or barter, in any manner of tangible personal property for consideration; (b) any withdrawal of tangible personal property from place located for delivery to point in this state for purpose of sale; (c) producing, fabricating, processing, printing or imprinting of tangible personal property for consideration for materials used but not limited to, computer programming, sign construction, photofinishing, duplicating, and photocopying (*Note:* sales tax on computer and data processing services being phased out over six years in 1% increments beginning July 1, 1997 [12-408(1)]); (d) furnishing and distribution of tangible personal property for consideration by social clubs, etc.; (e) furnishing, preparing, serving food, meals, drinks, for consideration; (f) transaction which transfers possession of property but not title as security for payment of price; (g) transfer for consideration of title of tangible personal property produced, fabricated, or printed to special order of customer or publication, including but not limited to computer programming, sign construction, photofinishing, duplicating, and photocopying; (h) transfer for consideration of occupancy of any room or rooms of hotel or lodging house for 30 consecutive days or less; (i) rendering of certain services for consideration, specified in 12-407; (j) leasing or rental of tangible personal property; (k) rendering of telecommunications service as defined in subsection 26 of 12-407; (l) rendering of community antenna television service so defined in subsection 27 of 12-407 (am'd PA 97-316); (m) rendering of transportation service as defined in subsection 28 of 12-407; (n) transfer for consideration of space for purpose of storing or mooring any noncommercial vessel; (o) business services for evaluating, preventing, or treating hazardous waste, or contaminants of air, water, or soil that are not hazardous wastes. Tax on coin operated telephones shall be computed to nearest multiple of 5¢ except if tax midway, higher multiple applies. (PA 89-251, §7). PA 98-262, §3 modifies CGS §12-330e by changing term "distributor" to "importer" regarding penalties for failure to comply with statute. §5 modifies CGS §12-408(2) regarding refund of tax paid by retailers to be reimbursed by taxing consumers, collecting sums and depositing in special trust for state; credit for tax will be allowed within three years unless special waiver obtained. PA 98-244, §15 modifies CGS §12-407(12) by including in definition of "retailer" persons who make retail sales of items of tangible personal property from outside state to destination within state and do not maintain place of business in state who repair or service such items, under warranty, in state, either directly or indirectly through agent, independent contractor or subsidiary. §16 modifies CGS §12-407(15) by including in definition of "engaged in business" retailer who meets requirements of §15 above. Services taxed are exclusive of services by employee for his employer. (12-407[2]). Renovation and repair services provided to other than industrial, commercial or income-producing real property: paving of any sort, painting or staining, wallpapering, roofing, siding and exterior sheet metal work. Amusement and recreation services included in Major Group 79 of Standard Industrial Classification (SIC) Manual are subject to tax, excluding any such service provided by government, state of Connecticut (or subdivisions), nonprofit charitable hospitals, or charitable or religious organizations. Photographic studio services, tax preparation services, and miscellaneous personal services included in Industry Group 729 of SIC Manual. Rendering of transportation service for consideration is exclusive of any such service rendered by employee for his employer. Tax does not apply to transportation services rendered by any person along regular, scheduled route or any person causing to be operated taxicab or commercial motor vehicle. (PA 92-17, §24).

Rate of sales tax is 6% of gross receipts, except that differing rate of gross receipts is imposed on: (a) Sales of machinery used exclusively in manufacturing process, (b) rendering of certain services specified in 12-407; 12-408, (PA 98-244, §17 states sales tax rate is 4½% of gross receipts for sale of motor vehicles to members of armed forces of U.S. on full-time active duty in this state who are residents of another state per 50 App. USC 574 or to such individuals and their spouses. [12-408(1)].), and (c) sales of 8¢ or less, provided records acceptable to Commissioner of Revenue Services are maintained. Commissioner of Revenue Services is authorized to permit alternative method of reporting sales tax by multiplying total receipts by 94.3% to determine what portion thereof represents sales tax. (12-414[3], am'd PA 89-251, §200; Act 3 [S.B. 2010], §119). Exemptions: Sales of tangible personal property and services to U.S., State of Connecticut or any political subdivisions thereof, or its or their respective agencies; (2) sales or services which State of Connecticut is prohibited from taxing under federal constitution; (3) sales, furnishing, or service of gas (including bottled gas), electricity when delivered to consumers through mains, lines, pipes or bottles and used in residential building or directly in agricultural production fabrication of finished products to be sold or industrial manufacturing plant provided exemption only allowed at metered building, location or premise at which not less than 75% of gas, or electricity consumed is used for production, fabrication or manufacturing; sale or furnishing of telephone service and community antenna television and cable service; sale, furnishing or service of water, steam, telegraph, when delivered through mains, lines, pipes, or bottles (12-412, am'd PA 89-251, §12); (4) sale of medicine, syringes and needles only by prescription and certain non-prescription drugs or medicines including those used to treat eye diseases (12-412[48]); (5) sales or services to and by nonprofit charitable hospitals; (6) subscription newspapers and magazines (12-412[6], am'd Act 3 [S.B. 2010]); (7) sales or services to charitable and religious organizations, and educational institutions; (8) sales of cigarettes (which are taxed under different formula); (9) children's clothing; (10) personal services (except those described in 12-407[2]); (11) sales of livestock and poultry, equines, except horses racing at commercial racetrack in Connecticut, feed, seeds, plants and fertilizer; (12) sales of certain food products (PA 98-262, §6 modifies CGS §12-412(13) regarding definition of "food products", "meal" and "eating establishment"); (13) motor vehicle fuel (which is taxed under different formula) and domestic fuel; (14) containers (12-412[14]); (15) sales and storage or use of any equipment that becomes ingredient or component part in fishing industry or industrial plant where finished product may be sold (12-412[18]); (16) sale of and storage, use and consumption of tangible personal property for use in agricultural production; production materials which become part of tangible personal property to be sold or are used directly in agricultural production or in process of manufacture of tangible personal property to be sold; also materials used in furnishing power, gas, steam, water or electricity when delivered to consumers through mains, lines or pipes; (17) sales of and repair services related to oxygen, blood, crutches, wheel chairs, hearing aids, artificial limbs, supports, life support equipment, etc.; (18) flyable aircraft and equipment; (19) sale or consumption of tangible personalty for control or elimination of air pollution; (20) sales of U.S. and Connecticut state flags; (21) municipal publications such as zoning regulations, etc., and library book sales; (22) sales, under $5 by public libraries or by municipality at auction; (23) sales for not more than $20 by nonprofit youth organizations and schools (12-412); (24) sale of tangible personal property to and by senior citizen organizations; (25) sales of and storage, use, other consumption of tangible personal property acquired for incorporation, use or consumption in operation of moderate and low income facilities constructed by nonprofit housing organizations; (26) sales and storage, use and consumption of ambulance type motor vehicles used exclusively as such, except transportation for payment; (27) sales of and storage, use or other consumption of any equipment designed exclusively for use by persons who are deaf or blind for purposes of communication by telephones; (28) sales or installation of alternative energy systems including their parts and components, prior to 7/1/85, primary purpose of which is reducing use of conventional energy sources; (29) sales of any replacement parts for machinery to any business entity located in any enterprise zone (12-412[43]); (30) sales of services used to determine human health (12-412[41]); (31) sales of vessels designed exclusively for use in commercial fishing (45-70c[a]); (32) sales of aircraft held for resale by certain air carriers (12-411; 12-412, 12-412[40]); (33) sales of home delivered meals to elderly, disabled, and other homebound persons (12-412[46]; 12-412[13]); (34) sale of clothing or footwear less than $50 (12-412[47]); (35) property tax on leased motor vehicles paid by lessee; (36) motion picture leasing or rental; (37) sales of certain services by corporate shareholder or partner in joint venture for new or experimental products with corporation or partnership; (38) any sale of cloth or fabric for noncommercial sewing; (39) sales of certain products used in care of diabetes; (40) sales of personal property by funeral establishment up to $2,500; (41) sales of item for not more than $100 made by gift shops located in nonprofit nursing homes, convalescent homes or adult day care centers provided profit from sales are retained for benefit of patients (12-412); (42) sale of aviation fuel used in experimental testing (12-412); (43) sale of motor vehicle to nonresident (12-412); (44) sale, storage, use of ambulance licensed under 19a-180 (12-412); (45) receipts from purchase of any motor vehicle, snowmobile, vessel or aircraft other than from licensed motor vehicle dealer, snowmobile dealer, licensed marine dealer or aircraft retailer shall not be included in measure of sales tax but purchaser shall pay use tax on total purchase price (12-431); (46) sales of and storage, use, other consumption of equipment used directly in production and cleaning of computer discs (12-412); (47) sales, rentals and leasing of commercial trucks, truck tractors, tractors and semitrailers, and vehicles used in combination therewith, which: (a) have gross vehicle weight rating in excess of 26,000 lbs., or (b) are operated actively and exclusively for carriage of interstate freight pursuant to certificate or permit issued by Interstate Commerce Commission (Act 3 [S.B. 2010], §117); (48) machinery, equipment, tools, materials and supplies used exclusively in production of printed material by commercial printer are exempt from tax. Also exempt are machinery, equipment, tools, materials and supplies used exclusively in production of typesetting, color separation, finished copy with type proofs and artwork or similar content mounted for photomechanical reproduction, or other similar products to be sold for use in production of printed materials (Act 3 [S.B. 2010], §117); (49) sale of any part of machine purchased exclusively for purpose of assembling machine for use directly in manufacturing production process; (50) sale, storage or use of aviation fuel for aviation purposes; (51) on or after July 1, 1993, sale, storage or use of aircraft repair or replacement parts; (52) on or after July 1, 1993, sale of aircraft repair services; (53) on or after July 1, 1993, sale, storage or use by aircraft manufacturer of materials, tools, fuel, machinery and equipment used in facility; (54) sale, storage or use of bunker fuel oil, intermediate fuel, marine diesel oil and marine gas oil for use in vessel displacing 4,000 dead weight tons; (55) sale, storage or use of special equipment installed in motor vehicle for exclusive use of person with physical disabilities (Act 3 [S.B. 2010], §117; PA 92-17, §29); (56) on or after July 1, 1996, sales and services provided to private water company for use in maintaining, operating, managing, or controlling any water distribution system or plant that services 50 or more customers (PA 94-4, May Sp. Sess.); (57) on or after July 1, 1997, sales tax for boat repair and maintenance services is phased out in two steps, eliminated entirely on July 1, 1999.

Retailer must make return and pay tax to Commissioner of Revenue Services quarterly on last day of month succeeding close of calendar quarter. (12-414, am'd PA 85-316, §§1, 7). Reimbursement for tax is collected by retailer from consumer, with certain exceptions. Nonresident contractor who enters into contract for tangible personal property to be consumed in State of Connecticut shall deposit with commissioner 3% of total amount to be paid under contract or furnish guarantee bond in that amount to secure payment of sales tax. Person dealing with nonresident contractor shall deduct 3% from payment of contract or secure guarantee bond in that amount and pay over same to commissioner. (12-430).

If corporation fails to file return or pay sales tax and it cannot be collected from corporation, and if responsible corporate officer willfully made that failure, officer is personally liable for full tax. (12-414a).

Changes and additions to sales tax collection and proceeds allocation. (S.B. 3004; PA 97-11; 32-305). Payment of up to 50% of assessed tax actually collected to another state's revenue agent if information provided by that agent was instrumental in making assessment. (§§12-407, 12-416; PA 98-244, §19 [new]).

See note at head of Digest as to 1998 legislation covered.

See Topical Index in front part of this volume.

CT – 52

SALES AND USE TAXES . . . *continued*

Use Tax.—Excise tax is imposed on storage, acceptance, consumption or any other use in this State of tangible personal property purchased from any retailer, for storage, use or other consumption in this State, or for any service as described in 12-407, at rate of 6% except: (a) at rate of 5½% for repair or replacement parts for use in agricultural or manufacturing machinery as in 12-412, (b) 4½% rate for motor vehicles sold to armed forces member on full time active duty in state but permanent residence out-of-state, (c) 12% of rent paid for hotel room not exceeding 30 days, (d) vessels purchased from any retailer and used in state by out-of-state resident, lesser of (1) 6% of sales price of (2) percentage payable as use tax in purchaser's state of residence (12-411[1], am'd PA 89-123; 12-408[1]); also except: (1) Storage, acceptance, consumption or other use in this state of property, gross receipts from sale of which are required to be included in measure of sales tax; (2) exemptions under sales tax; (3) storage, use or other consumption in this state of property purchased from any unincorporated agency or instrumentality of U.S. except (a) any property reported to Surplus Property Board of U.S. as surplus by any owning agency, and (b) any property included in any contractor inventory; (4) individual purchase of tangible personal property where price does not exceed $25, provided purchase is for personal use or consumption, and not for use in business or trade (12-413). Retailer must make returns and payments same as in case of sales tax. (12-411). Excise tax of 4½% of sale price of vehicle purchased for storage, acceptance, consumption or use in this state by one in armed forces of U.S. on full-time active duty in this state who is resident of another state per 50 App. USC 574 or to such individual and spouse. (12-411[1]; PA 98-244, §18). §25 of PA 98-244 modifies CGS §12-587 regarding companies subject to quarterly petroleum tax; changes to definitions of "company", "gross earnings", "first sale of petroleum products in this state", exempt gross earnings; tax rates. (CGS §§12-412; 16a-22c; 14-344d). §26 of PA 98-244 modifies CGS §12-587a regarding companies liable for tax on gross earnings from first sale of petroleum products within this state for export and sale outside of state. (CGS §12-587[b]).

Penalties.—(Apply to both Sales and Use Taxes.)

Deficiency assessment may be made by Commissioner to bear interest at 1¼% per month to date of payment. Additional 10% penalty on amount of assessment imposed if negligent or intentional failure to file and 25% penalty for fraud. (12-415). Jeopardy assessments (12-418) and liens of real estate (14-420) are provided as collection methods. Criminal sanctions for failure to file return or falsify same may include fine up to $5,000 and/or imprisonment up to five years. (12-428). Minimum prison sentence of one year. (PA 94-4, May Sp. Sess.). PA 98-262, §7 modifies CGS §12-415(7) regarding notices of deficiency to be mailed within three years after last day of month following period for which tax is proposed to be assessed or within three years of filing return.

Dry Cleaners Surcharge.—Effective July 1, 1994, surcharge of 1% of gross retail receipts levied on all dry cleaners using tetrachlorethylene or Stoddard solvent or other chemicals for cleaning clothing or furniture. Proceeds are to be applied to new Dry Cleaning Establishment Remediation Account, available for grants to fund containment, mitigation, and/or remediation of dry cleaner-related pollution. Payments and return due quarterly, beginning with quarter commencing July 1, 1994. (12-263m).

STAMP TAX:

None, except on cigarettes. No stamps required on corporate stock or other instruments.

SUCCESSION AND TRANSFER TAX:

Succession and transfer tax (***NOTE:*** Succession and transfer tax will be phased out over several years, beginning with respect to deaths occurring after Jan. 1, 1997, and will be completely eliminated with respect to deaths occurring after Jan. 1, 2005.) Imposed on transfer, in trust or otherwise, by residents or nonresidents, of all real estate located in Connecticut, all tangible personal property having situs in Connecticut, and (in case transferor is Connecticut resident but not otherwise) all other tangible personal property not having actual situs without this state and all intangible personal property. (12-340). Tax applies only to transfers: (a) By will; (b) by intestate succession; (c) in contemplation of death (transfers made within three years prior to death being presumed to be so made); (d) by gift or grant intended to take effect in possession or enjoyment at or after death of transferor (including any transfer where transferor retains for life or other period not ascertainable without reference to his death, or for period of such duration as to evidence intention that he should retain or receive for his life (1) possession or enjoyment of income from, or right to income from property or (2) right, either alone or in conjunction with any person, to designate person who shall possess or enjoy property or income therefrom) (but does not include property where decedent retained reversionary interest which valued actuarially immediately before death, would not amount to more than 5% of value of property transferred); (e) in payment of claim arising from contract (except antenuptial agreement) made during obligor's life, but payable by its terms at or after his death (12-341; 12-341b); (f) in trust where settlor reserves powers of revocation, alteration or amendment, revesting trust res in settlor (to extent of value of property subject to such powers) (12-345); (g) by succession to jointly owned property by rule of survivorship, but tax is only on fractional share owned by decedent which is determined by dividing value of property by number of joint owners; (h) by transfer deemed to have taken place when decedent has at time of death general power of appointment irrespective of whether exercised, or exercises power of appointment as in (c) or (d) or if exercises power of appointment by creating new power of appointment (12-345c). "General Power of Appointment" defined in 12-345b. See also topic Powers of Appointment. In case of joint checking or savings accounts and U.S. war or savings bonds, payable to survivor, only fractional share in excess of $5,000 is taxable, but this does not prevent taxation in whole or in part under (c) or (d). (12-48). Payment of life or accident insurance proceeds to beneficiary thereof, including trustee under inter vivos or testamentary trust or to trustee of life insurance trust, whether revocable or not, and including proceeds payable to decedent's estate, is not taxable transfer. (12-342). If property is transferred to executor or trustee in lieu of commission or allowance for services, excess of value of property above amount of commission payable in absence of such transfer is taxable. (12-346).

Exemption from state succession taxes for certain transfers of open-space land is described in 12-347(c).

Transfers to the United States, any state or territory or political subdivision thereof, the District of Columbia, public institutions for exclusively public purposes, Connecticut corporations or institutions receiving money appropriations from the Legislature; transfers to any strictly non-profit making organization incorporated or organized under the laws of Connecticut or any other state whose laws provide a similar exemption of transfers to similar Connecticut organizations, formed for charitable, educational, literary, scientific, historical or religious purposes, provided the property transferred is to be used for such purposes; and transfers in trust for the care of cemetery lots, are exempt. (12-347).

Valuations.—Fiduciary or transferee determines valuations of gross estate which shall be fair market value as of decedent's date of death or date it was transferred. Commissioner of Revenue Services or any interested party may file an objection within 120 days thereafter and if none, fiduciary's determination stands. Commissioner may file objections to fiduciary's return. Commissioner has 60 days in which to modify request by fiduciary for extension of time in which to file his return. (12-359[b], [c]). In ascertaining value of property transferred inter vivos, deduct any consideration in money's worth given for transfer. (12-341). Payments from qualified pension trust plans, retired serviceman's benefit protection plans, Social Security, Railroad Retirement Act plans or self-employed pension plans made after decedent's death are excluded from gross estate. (12-349). PA 98-244, §14 modifies CGS §12-349 regarding gross estate calculations; gross estate is fair market value of all property transferred subject to tax under Part I except value of real property classified as farm land (CGS §12-107c) under certain circumstances including, but not limited to, ownership at time of death.

Deductions.—In case of a resident transferor, net taxable estate is determined by deducting from gross taxable estate: ante-mortem claims, personal property taxes assessed and income taxes accrued prior to death, amount of mortgages and tax liens on decedent's Connecticut property, funeral expenses, allowance to dependents, executors', administrators', attorneys' and probate fees, other administration expenses except those chargeable to income, and net taxable estate passing to surviving spouse. (12-350). State and federal inheritance, succession, estate, and transfer taxes are not deductible. (12-351). But see topic Estate Tax.

If transferor died after July 1, 1949, not resident in Connecticut the deductions are similar except that ordinarily no deduction for ante-mortem claims, accrued income, personal property taxes accrued, income taxes accrued, capital losses, inheritance, succession, estate or transfer taxes payable to other states and countries or federal government, are allowed; and the deduction for administration expenses is limited to those incurred in the Connecticut ancillary proceedings, and includes fees of Connecticut administrator or executor and of Connecticut attorneys. (12-352). Where domiciliary estate is insolvent, amount of Connecticut estate necessary to be taken to pay claims and domiciliary administration expenses will be exempt from Connecticut succession tax. (12-352).

In case of transfer other than by will or intestate succession deduction allowed only for property includable in decedent's gross taxable estate to extent transferee has actually paid deductible items. (12-350). Federal and state estate, inheritance, succession, and transfer taxes are not deductible, but reasonable fees for Connecticut attorneys may be deducted. (12-350; 12-352).

Exemptions and Computation of Tax.—Entire property transfer of which is subject to tax at transferor's death (viz., net taxable estate passing by will or intestate succession, ascertained as above, plus property subject to inter vivos taxable transfers and to taxable succession by survivorship) is divided into three classes according to relationship which beneficiaries bear to decedent. There is a single exemption for each class and rates of tax on excess over exemption vary according to amount transferred to class as a whole (not according to amount transferred to each beneficiary). Tax is computed on entire amount passing to class and apportioned among members of class according to amount passing to each member. Classification, exemptions and rates are as below. (12-344; see 93 Conn. 648, 107 Atl. 506; 178 Conn. 81, 420 A.2d 1160).

Rates.—See 12-344 for current rates of tax and exemption amounts. Succession and transfer tax being phased out over 1997 to 2005. But see topic Estate Tax.

Reports.—Within two months after appointment of fiduciary of estate, an inventory of decedent's assets is filed with Probate Court. For a resident, inventory includes all assets of decedent except real property outside state, and for nonresident, inventory includes only real and tangible personal property located in this state and all intangible property if Connecticut proceeding is not ancillary to that in another state. Only one extension of two additional months may be granted if good cause shown. (45-202). Within nine months after learning of death of transferor, fiduciary, beneficiary or donee concerned in transaction which may be taxable transfer inter vivos must file with probate court having jurisdiction of administration of transferor's estate, copy of instrument evidencing transfer or, if there is none, written statement of details of transaction; and unless taxability or nontaxability is conceded, probate court decides question of taxability. (12-359).

Filing of reports as to inter vivos transfers may be dispensed with by probate court, upon request, where such transfers are of cash, bank accounts or U.S. savings bonds and all other property subject to tax is less than the applicable tax exemption. Inventory or appraisal of cash, bank accounts, or U.S. savings bonds may also be waived in certain cases. (12-360; 12-361).

Within six months after transferor's death, unless time is extended, fiduciary (or transferee) must file with Probate Court a statement (in duplicate) containing all items necessary for correct computation of tax, indicating which items (including non-probate items) are conceded taxable. Probate Court, within ten days after receipt, must forward a copy of this report to Commissioner of Revenue Services who, within 120 days thereafter, may file objection. If fiduciary and commissioner cannot agree, either may file application for Probate Court hearing on commissioner's objections, and decree of Probate Court shall be conclusive unless appeal is taken. Extensions for filing return may be requested by fiduciary before due date to commissioner and if commissioner does not grant request within 30 days, fiduciary may ask Probate Court for extension.

See note at head of Digest as to 1998 legislation covered.

See Topical Index in front part of this volume.

SUCCESSION AND TRANSFER TAX . . . *continued*

Failure to file return when due shall be grounds for summary dismissal of fiduciary. (12-359). §12-358 is repealed and substituted. Probate clerks submit uniform report monthly to Commissioner of Revenue Services along with letters testamentary or administration containing required information, certified copies of all wills submitted to probate and returns pursuant to §12-359. (PA 97-3).

Certificate of Nontaxability.—If no tax is due, commissioner shall issue certificate of nontaxability and no final accounting shall be issued without such certificate. (12-378). Probate Court, however, may issue certificate of nontaxability if such is its opinion, and if commissioner does not object within 60 days thereafter, no tax shall be due from estate. (12-378).

Determination of Tax.—Within 120 days of receipt of tax return (or if objection is filed by Commissioner of Revenue Services, within 60 days after objection is settled) tax commissioner shall file computation of tax with Probate Court and fiduciary. If fiduciary objects to computations, he must file objection with Probate Court within 60 days thereafter, and Probate Court thereupon shall make tax computation after hearing. Computations of commissioner shall be conclusive if no objection is made. (12-367).

Collection and Penalties.—Taxes: (a) Not paid within six months of transferor's death bear interest thereafter at 12% per annum, if time for payment is extended, 11¼% per annum, if extension expires then 12% per annum (12-376[a]); (b) are lien on land transferred, to extent of tax on transfer of that land, from date of filing of certificate of lien in appropriate town clerk's office (12-366); (c) are personal debt of fiduciary to extent of value of property received by him and of transferee to extent of proportion of tax chargeable to transfer to him (12-384); (d) are to be retained by executor or administrator out of estate distributed and, in absence of contrary provisions in will, charged pro rata to distributees receiving taxable transfers (12-376a; 12-385); (e) are to be collected, if necessary, by fiduciary from transferees liable therefor by probate sale of such portion of transferred property as is necessary to satisfy tax on transfer thereof (12-385). Refunds to estate for overpayment accrued at .67% per month. (12-376[a]).

Where a nonresident decedent leaves an estate in Connecticut that state will protect the domiciliary state in the collection of its inheritance tax if that state furnishes similar protection to Connecticut. Such protection is afforded by Commissioner of Revenue Services furnishing domiciliary state with full information pertaining to estate, by refusing to accept final account of executor or administrator until he has furnished proof of payment of such foreign inheritance tax, and by authorizing foreign tax authorities to petition for accounting and for decree ordering transmission to fiduciary of domiciliary state of sufficient personal property to secure payment of such tax. (12-371).

Refunds.—Where refunds due overpayment shall bear interest at rate of .67% per month. (12-367).

UNEMPLOYMENT COMPENSATION TAX:

Application of chapter to employers governed by detailed provisions. (31-222 to 31-275). Employers subject to c. 374 and to taxation under title IX of federal social security act must pay Commissioner of Labor and Factory Inspection contributions (not deductible from wages) generally equal to 5.4% of payroll (no tax on wages in excess of $4,200 yearly to any individual), but rate subject to adjustment in accordance with 31-225a(d).

Contributions are payable quarterly or more often as Commissioner may determine, and employer must furnish information reports. (31-225). Past due contributions bear interest for each month (31-265) and payment may be enforced by uniform method of collecting state taxes (31-266). In case of employer's insolvency or termination of employer's corporate existence, claim for contributions has priority over all other claims except taxes. (31-267). In case of failure to file report when due or error in report, Commissioner may determine amount of contribution, subject to appeal to superior court for judicial district of Hartford-New Britain within 30 days. (31-270). Knowing failure to pay contribution is Class A misdemeanor. (31-273).

The amount due is a lien, from the due date until discharged by payment, against all the property of the employer within the state whether real or personal, except such as is exempt from execution, including debts to the employer, and a certificate of such lien without specifically describing such real or personal property signed by the administrator or the executive director may be filed in the office of the clerk of any town in which such real property is situated or, in the case of personal property in office of secretary of state, which lien shall be effective from date on which it is recorded. (31-266).

Definition of "compensation" excludes compensation received from certain charitable organizations. (31-222 et seq.).

TRANSPORTATION

MOTOR VEHICLES:

Commissioner of Motor Vehicles has general supervision. (14-3). Department of Motor Vehicles, 60 State Street, Wethersfield, Connecticut 06109.

Vehicle registration is renewed every two years. No motor vehicle registration may be renewed by commissioner for any private passenger motor vehicle unless applicant signs and files statement that he or she will maintain minimum security required by §38-327. Such form shall contain name of applicant's insurance company and his policy number. (14-12b). Registration certificate must be carried with car (14-13[b]), and number plates furnished by Commissioner displayed on rear (14-18[a]). Vehicle validly registered in another state may be driven for 60 days on its old registration following owner's establishment of residence in this state. (14-12). However, Connecticut resident may be fined after 60 days for failing to register vehicle in Connecticut. (PA 98-33). "Emancipated minors shall be deemed over 18 years of age for purpose of registering motor vehicles." (14-12). Registrations expire in accordance with schedules established by Commissioner. (14-22). No registration passed until applicant supplies insurance identification card. (14-12c, d, f; 14-21b; 14-213b; 38-319a[b]). Mere operation of unregistered vehicle is not negligence nor nuisance. (114 Conn. 262, 158 Atl. 545). Operation of unregistered vehicle may result in forfeiture. (PA 98-215).

Trailers require special permit. (14-263).

Motorcycles are specially regulated. (14-50; 14-80). High mileage motor vehicles are specifically regulated in part. (14-1[66]; 14-12b; 14-14; 14-34[a]; 14-49[y]; 14-286; 38-319; 38-319a; 38-323[a]; 7-479e[d]; 14-103b;).

Snowmobiles and all terrain vehicles regulated by municipalities. (14-390). Registration specifically regulated. (14-381; 14-382).

Farm vehicles required to register every two years. No farm registration issued to person operating farm that has less than $1,000 gross annual sales. (14-49).

Members of Armed Forces.—Upon induction of vehicle owner into armed forces, he may surrender vehicle registration and receive pro rata rebate (14-23), no other exemption.

Operator's License.—Driver License Compact enacted. Effective Jan. 1, 1993.

Each motor vehicle operator's license shall be renewed quadrennially from date of operator's birthday. Beginning 7/1/99, Commissioner of Motor Vehicles shall screen vision of each operator prior to every other renewal of license unless operator submits results from screening done by licensed professional. Any person failing vision test will not have their license renewed until they pass. (14-41). Where license belongs to individual 65 years of age or older, it may, at discretion of licensee, be renewed for either two- or four-year period (14-41a; 14-50). No motor vehicle license may be issued to any person between 16 and 18 years of age unless certificate prescribed by commissioner signed by parent of applicant or guardian, or spouse or uncle or aunt. Applicants between 16 and 18 required to obtain learner's permit and successfully complete course in motor vehicle operation and complete course of not less than five hours on safe driving practices including minimun of two hours on alcohol and drug education. (14–36, am'd PA 97-1). Valid operator's license of another state is good for period of 60 days following establishment of residence by owner thereof (14-36), notice of renewal of license (14-41d).

Motorcycles.—No person under 18 may operate or be passenger on motorcycle without protective headgear which conforms to minimum specifications in Code of Federal Regulations Title 49, §571.218. (PA 89-242). Any applicant issued learner's permit must wear protective headgear. Any applicant who has not yet had Connecticut motorcycle license within preceding two years must demonstrate to Commissioner or agent that applicant is knowledgeable of motorcycles, laws concerning motorcycles, other motor vehicles and rules of road. Any applicant under 18 years of age must also demonstrate he has successfully completed novice motorcycle training course. (14-40a).

Boating.—No resident, person owning real property or vessel in state shall operate on waters of state vessel required to be registered pursuant to c. 268 unless individual has obtained certificate of boating operation from Commissioner. Certificate valid for life of person issued to. No certificate shall be issued unless applicant successfully passed equivalency examination prepared and administered by Commissioner or has successfully completed course in safe boating operation approved by Commissioner. Any applicant under 20 years of age required to successfully complete course. (PA 89-388). Certificate required to be on board or on person at all times. No person less than 12 years of age shall operate motor powered vessel unless accompanied by person more than 18 who has been issued certificate. (PA 89-388, §4).

Members of Armed Forces.—Examination waived for two years after separation from military service under certain circumstances. (14-36). Fee waived for Connecticut resident member of armed forces during military service and for two years thereafter. (14-50c).

Dealers and repairers, except dealers in boat trailers, must be licensed by Commissioner (14-51 to 14-65; 10-153m; 14-65b, c, d), and may obtain distinguishing number plates which may be used on all commercial vehicles owned by them or in their custody (14-59). Leasing companies are also licensed. (14-15).

Uniform Motor Vehicle Certificate of Title and Anti-Theft Act adopted. (14-165 to 14-211). Note: Certain technical amendments have been made in uniform law to dovetail it with appropriate sections of Uniform Commerical Code. (14-165; 14-167; 14-185).

Titles.—Upon transfer of ownership, registration expires, but upon death of owner registration continues until end of registration year or until transfer. Registered owner must return certificate of registration and number plate or plates within 24 hours unless another car registered for remainder of year. (14-16a).

Sales.—Sale of motor vehicle must be evidenced by order signed by buyer and seller and by invoice, both of which must contain make, year of model, whether sold as new or used, and on invoice identification number, deposit (words specifying type of deposit required, i.e., "not refundable," "conditionally refundable," or "unconditionally refundable"), cash selling price, finance charges and statement as to insurance, allowance on and description of car traded in, and specific statement as to guarantee. (14-62). See category Taxation, topic Sales and Use Taxes, subhead Use Tax. New motor vehicle warranties regulated. (42-179, and PA 97-6).

Used car dealers must furnish buyer, at sale, with title, assignment and warranty of title, disclosure of any liens, security interest in or other encumbrances on vehicle. (14-62).

Liens.—Filed with State Department of Motor Vehicles. See Uniform Motor Vehicle Certificate of Title and Anti-Theft Act. (14-165 to 14-211).

Identification Marks.—It is a misdemeanor to remove, deface, obliterate or change any factory, serial or other identification number or mark. Any officer discovering a vehicle with its factory or serial number mutilated must take vehicle and operator into custody. (14-149). As of Jan. 1, 1990 each new car dealer must offer purchaser optional service of etching indentification number of vehicle on windshield and each window in vehicle. (PA 89-313).

Operation Prohibited.—By person under age of 16 (49-36); by person under influence of intoxicating liquor or drugs (14-227a); by one whose license has been suspended or revoked (14-215); by minor unless vehicle properly insured (14-216).

Prohibited acts are, among others, speeding (14-218a; 14-219), reckless driving (14-224), overcrowding (14-257), racing (14-224), solicitation of rides on other than limited access highways (53-181), stopping vehicle to solicit alms or make sales (53-180), leaving vehicle in dangerous condition (14-228), operation at unreasonably slow speed

MOTOR VEHICLES . . . *continued*
(14-220), stealing number plates or inserts (14-147), tampering with odometer (14-145), tampering with vehicle and larceny (53a-119b), operate vehicle at any time during periods of precipitation without illuminating lighted lamps (14-96a), carrying children in back of pick-up truck or open bed truck having gross weight of 7,500 pounds or less without approved restraint, except in parade or for farming or recreational hayride (PA 93-116).

Period of Continuous Operation.—Operator of commercial or public service vehicle who has been continuously on duty for 12 hours must thereafter have at least eight hours off duty; if he has been on duty 16 hours in any 24-hour period he must then have at least ten hours off duty. (14-274).

Size and Weight Limits.—Regulated by 14-262 to 14-270 (am'd PA 98-196). Commissioner of Public Safety and Motor Vehicles regulates hours and staffing of weigh stations. (CGS §§14-27a, et seq.; PA 98-248).

Lights Required.—Regulated by 14-96a to 14-97b.

Equipment Required.—Regulated by 14-80 to 14-106. Seat belts are required on all new cars sold or registered in state. As of Jan. 1, 1986, all drivers and any front seat passenger must wear seat belts and driver is responsible for front passengers between ages of four and 16 wearing seat belts. (14-100a). Child restraint systems (approved by Department of Motor Vehicles) must be used on all children under age of four. Tamper-resistant odometer required on 1971 and later models. (14-106a; 14-106b). Various motorcycle regulations (re: brakes, height of handlebars, etc.) are described in 14-80. Additional motor vehicle equipment regulations (re: wheels, windshield, and license plates) are described in 14-80b; 14-99f; 14-99g; 14-18. See also subhead Operator's License, catchline Motorcycles, supra.

Inspection.—Commissioner may establish and maintain a system of voluntary examination of equipment of motor vehicles registered in this state by approved automobile dealers and garages. (14-103). As of Jan. 1, 1981 all vehicles registered in this state shall be inspected annually for exhaust emissions in accordance with rules and regulations established by Commissioner. (14-100c). Sticker requirement for tinted windows after factory delivery. (PA 92-9, §3). Motor vehicles ten model years or older must be inspected upon transfer of ownership prior to new registration. (14-16a, am'd 97-236). Certain vehicles exempted from emissions inspection. (PA 97-82).

Accidents.—Operator causing injury to person or property must stop, render needed assistance and give name, address, and operator's license and registration number to officer, injured person or witness, if requested. (14-224; 14-225). Accident causing death, personal injury or $1,000 property damage to property of any one person must be reported to Commissioner by all operators involved within five days. Commissioner of Transportation shall forward to Commissioner of Motor Vehicles copy of accident reports where person is killed or involving school bus or public service vehicle. Commissioner of Motor Vehicles may then investigate any accident reported with assistance of state police. (14-108). Operator causing injury to or death of dog must report to owner, police officer or motor vehicle inspector. (14-226). Driver who deliberately or recklessly violates rules of road may be subject to double or treble damages for resulting injuries. (14-295).

Liability of Owner.—Owner is not generally liable for negligence of operator except in case of agency, of which there is a rebuttable presumption. (52-183). Owner of rented car is liable for damage by operator, if operator would have been liable. (14-154a). Family car doctrine is adopted and where operator is husband, wife, parent or child of owner car is presumed to be operated as family car within scope of general authority from owner. (52-182).

Guests.—No statutory restriction of liability for injury to guest.

Proof of Financial Responsibility.—Unless operator and/or owners of a motor vehicle in any manner involved in an accident involving death, injury, or damage to property of any one person in excess of $400 (1) has in effect an automobile liability policy (minimum limits $20,000 per person. $40,000 per accident bodily injury or death and $5,000 property damage, except that for motor vehicles registered in another state security may be deposited for difference with respect to vehicle involved) or (2) is covered as to such accident by a liability policy if not owner or (3) is, in judgment of Commissioner, covered as to such accident by any other form of liability policy or bond, or qualifies as a self-insurer or operator for a self-insurer (registered owner of more than 25 motor vehicles approved and certified by the Commissioner), Commissioner or his designee holds a hearing and determines whether there is a reasonable possibility judgment(s) may be recovered against such owner or operator. If such possibility found, such owner and/or operator must, within 20 days after filing accident report, furnish evidence satisfactory to Commissioner that (1) he has been released from liability or (2) has been finally adjudicated not to be liable or (3) has executed a duly acknowledged written agreement providing for payment of an agreed amount in instalments with respect to all claims resulting from accident. (14-117).

Suspension and Security.—If such evidence is not so filed with Commissioner, he determines amount of security which is sufficient in his judgment to satisfy any judgment for damages that may ensue, and unless security in such sum is deposited with him, he must suspend license of each operator and all registrations of each owner in default in depositing security. In case of a nonresident owner or operator, privilege of operation or use of any motor vehicle within this state is suspended and certified copy of record of such action is forwarded to proper official of other state. (14-117).

Notice of Suspension.—In all cases, Commissioner must give such operator and/or owner ten days written notice of contemplated suspension including statement of amount of security required. (14-117).

Exemption from Security and Suspension.—In addition to exemption arising from insurance coverage, security and suspension requirements do not apply: (1) to the operator or owner of a motor vehicle involved in an accident wherein no injury or damage was caused to the person or property of anyone other than such operator or owner; (2) to the operator or owner of a motor vehicle legally parked at the time of the accident; (3) to the owner of the vehicle if, at time of accident, it was being operated or had been parked without his permission, express or implied; or (4) was legally stopped at a stop sign or stop light or at the direction of a police officer or in a line of traffic including at least three motor vehicles; (5) if other driver has been convicted of manslaughter or similar charge arising out of such accident; (6) if, prior to date when Commissioner would otherwise invoke suspension, evidence of release from liability, final adjudication of nonliability, or agreement for payment, as above described, has been filed with him; (7) motor vehicles owned by the United States, this state or any political subdivision of this state; and (8) public service motor vehicles or busses subject to 14-29(a), (b) (except as to filing of accident reports [14-119]).

Duration of Suspension.—Suspension of license, registration and operating privilege continues until: (a) deposit of required security is made; (b) two years have elapsed following date of accident and evidence satisfactory to Commissioner has been filed with him that no action for damages arising out of such accident has been instituted; (c) satisfactory evidence has been filed of release from liability, final adjudication or agreement for payment, as above described. If operator or owner has no license or registration or is a nonresident, he is not allowed a license or registration until he complies with Act to same extent as would have been necessary had he held license or registration at time of accident. (14-120).

Reciprocity.—Commissioner is enjoined to take necessary action to secure security or suspension of license or registration of nonresident if law of other state provides such action. Upon receipt of certification that operating privilege of resident of this state has been suspended in another state pursuant to a law providing for deposit of security for payment of judgments arising out of a motor vehicle accident, under circumstances which would require suspension of a nonresident's operating privilege had the accident occurred in this state, and if the law of such other state contains reciprocal provisions, the Commissioner must suspend the license of such resident if he was the operator and all of his registrations if he was the owner. Suspension continues until evidence of compliance with laws of other state relating to deposit of security is furnished. (14-121).

Security is in such form and amount as Commissioner may require but in no case in excess of $20,000 per person for death or personal injury and $1,000 for property damage. If Commissioner deems amount excessive, he may reduce same within six months of accident. (14-122). Such security is placed in the custody of the State Treasurer and is applicable to the payment of law judgments for damages rendered against the person on whose behalf the deposit was made and arising out of the action in question or to the payment of agreed settlements. (14-123).

Return of security occurs upon filing with Commissioner of satisfactory evidence of release from liability, final adjudication, or agreement for payment, as above described, or upon running of statute of limitations with no action pending or judgment unpaid. Security deposits unclaimed escheat to state ten years after deposit date. (14-123).

Judgment requires immediate suspension of license and registration or operating privilege, continuing until such judgment is stayed, satisfied, or discharged in full. (14-125).

Transfer of title while registration suspended pursuant to financial responsibility statute is prohibited until Commissioner is satisfied that transfer is proposed in good faith and not for purpose or effect of defeating purposes of statute. Rights of conditional vendor, chattel mortgagee or lessor are protected. (14-126).

Criminal penalties are imposed for failure to file accident report, giving false information or forged or unauthorized evidence of proof of financial responsibility, failure to deliver to Commissioner license and/or registration promptly upon suspension, and for violation of any other provision of statute. (14-133).

Insurance exemption above described is not available unless policy is issued by company authorized to do business in this state, except in case of motor vehicle not registered in this state on effective date of policy in which case policy is effective if in sufficient amount and if unauthorized company executes a power of attorney authorizing the Commissioner to accept service on its behalf in any action upon such policy arising out of such accident. (14-117).

Appeal from any act or order of Commissioner lies to Superior Court for county in which such person resides, or for Hartford County, at instance of any party in interest. Court determines whether appeal stays such order or decision, and may modify, affirm or reverse in whole or in part. Appeals taken under this section have precedence over non-privileged cases in respect to order of trial. (14-114).

Other Financial Liability.—Proof also is required of owners who permit their cars to be operated by persons under 18 years old (14-216), owners who are under 18 years old, except for registration of private passenger vehicle as described in 38-319(g) (14-14), and owners or lessees of public service motor vehicles (14-29[a], [b]), and may be required of any owner or operator who has violated certain laws or whose driving record is such that Commissioner deems such proof necessary for protection of others. Owner or operator failing to furnish required proof forfeits registration and operator's license. Nonresident forfeits privilege of operating in state. (14-111 to 14-112).

Owner or lessee of public service vehicle must insure liability for personal injury or death up to maximum of $300,000 for each vehicle depending on seating capacity, and for property damage $10,000 or procure certificate of financial responsibility from Commissioner of Transportation. (14-29; 14-26[c]). Other owner or operator must furnish to Commissioner of Motor Vehicles proof of responsibility up to $20,000 per person; $40,000 per accident for personal injury or death and $10,000 for property damage. Proof may consist of certificate of licensed Connecticut insurance agent that sufficient insurance has been issued, bond with professional surety or individual surety owning real estate or sufficient cash deposit with State Treasurer. (14-112).

Such insurance or bond must be non-cancellable except upon ten days written notice to Commissioner. Bond constitutes lien in favor of state upon real estate of any surety, which lien exists in favor of holder of judgment on account of damage caused by operation of car, upon notice to town clerk in town where land is located. Insurance company named in agent's certificate must notify Commissioner of renewal, or of cancellation or termination of policy at least ten days before cancellation or termination. Bond or deposit is held to satisfy any execution issued in damage suit against owner or operator for operation of vehicle, and is only subject to attachment or execution in action for damages resulting from operation of vehicle. If judgment against bond principal is not satisfied within 30 days, plaintiff may for his own use and at own expense bring action in name of state against surety. (14-112[a]; 14-112[f], [g]).

See note at head of Digest as to 1998 legislation covered.

See Topical Index in front part of this volume.

MOTOR VEHICLES . . . *continued*

Insurer Designated Repair Shops.—Insurance companies prohibited from designating repair shops for motor vehicle repairs. (38a-354).

No-Fault Insurance.—Former no-fault thresholds and reparation benefits were repealed, effective Oct. 1, 1993. (PA 93-297).

Insurance policies must contain provision conforming coverage to that required by other governments in U.S. and Canada while vehicle is operated therein and must specify whether coverage is provided for rented vehicles. (38-175b).

Foreign Vehicles.—Reciprocity of motor vehicle registration as between the states is recognized. (14-12b; 14-34a).

Nonresident operator over 16 years old, who may legally operate motor vehicles in home state or country, may operate any motor vehicle (except public service vehicle) in Connecticut, without registration or operator's license, for same time that home state or country accords similar privilege to Connecticut residents, but if operator is under 18, vehicle must be insured for $20,000 for personal injury and $1,000 for property damage. (14-39; 14-40; 14-40a).

Actions Against Nonresidents.—Nonresident causing motor vehicle to be operated in the state is deemed to have appointed Commissioner of Motor Vehicles his agent on whom process may be served in any civil action for damages for negligence of such person, his agent or servant, while operating in the state. Service on Commissioner has same validity as if process served personally upon nonresident. True and attested copy must be served upon Commissioner at least 12 days before return day, and similar copy with indorsement of service on Commissioner must be sent by registered mail to nonresident at his last known address. Death of nonresident does not revoke appointment of Commissioner. (52-62).

Direct Action.—Not authorized.

Actions Between Spouses.—See category Family, topic Husband and Wife, subhead Actions.

Motor vehicle carriers, including motor busses, school busses, taxicabs, and livery vehicles must be specially registered. (14-26; 14-44). Carrier means any local or regional school district, any educational institution providing elementary or secondary education or any person, firm or corporation under contract in such district or institution engaged in business of transporting school children. (PA 90-112, §3). On and after 7/1/91, no motor vehicle having (1) wheel base of less than 101 inches, or (2) convertible top or open body, may be used by carrier for transportation of students under age of 21 years to and from school. General registration to cover more than one vehicle may be issued, but $10,000 bond may be required. Before registration owner must have certificate of public convenience and necessity from Department of Transportation and furnish proof of financial responsibility. (14-26). Each motorbus, taxicab, livery vehicle must carry number plates which indicate vehicle is licensed by Commissioner. (14-27). Public service operators must obtain special license; must be 18, already hold regular operator's license, show good character and no criminal record, be fingerprinted and must pass examination to determine ability to operate public service vehicle, except no physical examination is required of operator complying with safety regulation of U.S. Dept. of Transportation. (14-44). Driver disqualified if operating commercial vehicle with blood alcohol ratio of 4/100 of 1% or more. (14-44k). Nonresident operators must also obtain special license, unless holding valid, out-of-state public service operator's license and not engaged in intra-state commerce. (14-39). School bus operators are regulated. (14-276). Each serious accident involving school bus or student transportation vehicle as defined in §14-212 of general statutes must be reported to Commissioner of Motor Vehicles. Serious accident means any accident in which (1) any occupant of

school bus or student transportation vehicle is killed, or (2) fire occurs in, or there is rollover of, school bus or student transportation vehicle. (PA 90-112, §1).

Owner or operator of busses traveling in state between points out of state or between points in state and points out of state are under jurisdiction and regulation of Department of Transportation (16-313) and must obtain permit and certificate of public convenience and necessity. Motor Vehicle Commissioner has jurisdiction over registration and lighting and licensing of operators of such busses. (14-273[a], 16-309 to 16-317). Carrier shall require each person whom it intends to employ to operate school bus, as defined in §14-275, or student transportation vehicle, as defined in §14-212, to submit to urinalysis drug test in accordance with provisions of §31-51v and §31-51w. No carrier may employ any person who has received positive test result for such test which was confirmed as provided in subdivisions (2) and (3) of §31-51u.

Owners of such vehicles are common carriers and subject to regulation by Department of Transportation as to rates, public convenience and necessity, routes (in case of motor buses) and adequacy of service. They must obtain from said Department certificate of public convenience and necessity or, in case of livery service, permit describing character of service, and in case of motor busses, permit describing routes and terminals. (16-329; 14-27; 16-309, 16-314a, 16-320). Busses purchased for fixed route service by transit district or state-subsidized entity after 4/18/88 must be equipped with mechanical lift or other device to provide access to persons with disabilities. (PA 88-62).

Persons engaged in motor transportation of property for hire must obtain permit from Department of Transportation, which will issue only after finding of public necessity and convenience and after proof of financial responsibility; and such carriers are subject to regulation by Commission as to rates, routes, adequacy and necessity of service, etc. (16-253, 16-284, 16-286, 16-304, 16-308). Five persons may be carried on daily round trip for hire without permit from Department of Transportation, or livery license if transportation is between place of residence and place of employment. In addition, corporation or employee may operate for hire vehicles for 15 passengers to and from place of employment without permit or livery license. (16-328). "Motor vehicle in livery service" means and includes every motor vehicle used by any person, association or corporation in business of transporting passengers for hire except motorbuses, taxicabs and those hired through contract with federal or state agency. (13b-101).

Many types of vehicles are specifically excepted from these provisions. (16-284). Interstate carriers for hire must obtain permit and are subject to regulation as to routes and terminals. (14-261a; 16-313). All busses, however owned, are deemed to be common carriers, and as such subject to regulation by Department of Transportation. (16-312a, 313).

There is a Department of Transportation with general authority in motor carrier area. (Tit. 13b).

School Bus.—Each school bus and student transporting vehicle shall display lighted head lamps while transporting school children. (14-281a).

Snowmobiles and all-terrain vehicles must be registered. (14-380; 14-381; 14-388).

Safety.—At request of municipal legislative body, State Traffic Commission or local traffic authority may designate any part of state highway as school zone and post signs; Superior Court jurisdiction over violations. (CGS §§14-218a; 14-219; PA 98-252, §64 [new]).

Gasoline Tax.—See category Taxation, topic Gasoline Tax.

RAILROADS:

See category Business Regulation and Commerce, topic Carriers.

COMMERCIAL CODE FORMS
See also categories Business Regulation and Commerce, topic Commercial Code; Mortgages, topic Chattel Mortgages.

Financing Statement.—Form UCC-1

This FINANCING STATEMENT is presented to THE SECRETARY OF THE STATE for filing pursuant to the Uniform Commercial Code.		3. Maturity date (if any):
1. Debtor(s) (Last Name First) and address(es)	2. Secured Party(ies) and address(es)	For Filing Officer (Date, Time, Number, and Filing Office)

4. This financing statement covers the following types (or items) of property:

Check ☒ if covered: ☐ Proceeds of Collateral are also covered ☐ Products of Collateral are also covered   No. of additional sheets presented:

Filed with: State of Connecticut, Secretary of the State, Uniform Commercial Code Div., State Office Bldg., Hartford 15, Conn.

By: . . . .   By: . . . .
        Signature(s) of Debtor(s)   Signature(s) of Secured Party(ies)

Termination Statement—Form UCC-1, page 3.

TERMINATION STATEMENT:
This statement of termination of financing is presented to a filing officer for filing pursuant to the Uniform Commercial Code. The Secured Party certifies that the Secured Party no longer claims a security interest under the financing statement bearing the file number shown above.

Dated: . . . . 19 . .   By: . . . .
                                       (Signature of Secured Party or Assignee of Record—Not Valid Until Signed)

Statement of Continuation, Partial Release, Assignment, Etc.—Form UCC-3

This STATEMENT is presented to THE SECRETARY OF THE STATE for filing pursuant to the Uniform Commercial Code.		3. Maturity date (if any):
1. Debtor(s) (Last Name First) and address(es)	2. Secured Party(ies) and address(es)	For Filing Officer (Date, Time, Number, and Filing Office)

This statement refers to original Financing Statement No. . . . .
Dated . . . . 19 . . .

A. Continuation . . . . . ☐	B. Partial Release . . . . ☐	C. Assignment . . . . ☐	D. Other: . . . . ☐
The original financing statement between the foregoing Debtor and Secured Party, bearing the file number shown above, is still effective.	From the collateral described in the financing statement bearing the file number shown above the Secured Party releases the following:	The Secured Party certifies that the Secured Party has assigned to the Assignee whose name and address is shown below, Secured Party's rights under the financing statement bearing the file number, shown above in the following property:	

Dated: . . . . 19 . . . .   By: . . . .
                                          (Signature of Secured Party)

See note at head of Digest as to 1998 legislation covered.

See Topical Index in front part of this volume.

DELAWARE LAW DIGEST REVISER

Richards, Layton & Finger
Post Office Box 551
(One Rodney Square)
Wilmington, Delaware 19899
Telephone: 302-658-6541
Fax: 302-658-6548

Reviser Profile

Richards, Layton & Finger, one of Delaware's oldest firms, was founded in the early 1900s and has grown to become Delaware's largest firm with a local, regional and national practice. The firm currently has approximately 80 lawyers.

The firm has a full-service practice, emphasizing corporate law, litigation, partnership law, limited liability company law, trust law, bankruptcy, real estate, tax, estates, estate planning and complex financial transactions. Since over half of the Fortune 500 corporations of the United States are incorporated in Delaware, the firm's practice has a dynamic national focus as well as an established and growing local and regional base. Since its inception, the firm has played a significant part in many of the most important cases decided in Delaware, including litigation involving corporate takeovers and acquisitions, commercial and other general civil matters, major litigation, corporate bankruptcies, trust and will construction, and interpretation of Delaware business and tax laws.

The firm is organized into four departments: (1) Corporate (including mergers and acquisitions, counselling of directors and management, corporate structuring, and corporate and securities litigation); (2) Business (including limited partnerships, limited liability companies, business trusts, complex financing arrangements including leveraged leases and collateralized mortgage obligations, commercial, banking, municipal bonds, real estate, environmental, labor and bankruptcy matters); (3) Litigation (including complex litigation, injunctive proceedings, business litigation, bankruptcy litigation, product liability, intellectual property litigation, environmental litigation, labor and employment, medical malpractice and real estate litigation); and (4) Tax (including federal and state tax, ERISA, trusts, estates, estate planning and probate law).

The lawyers of Richards, Layton & Finger are leaders in the profession and in the community. One member is a past President of the Delaware State Bar Association and a Fellow of the American College of Trial Lawyers. The head of the firm's Tax Department is a Past-President of the American College of Trust and Estate Counsel, two members of the firm are Fellows of the American College of Tax Counsel and two members of the firm are Fellows in the American College of Trust and Estate Counsel. One member of the firm serves on the Board of Governors of the American College of Real Estate Lawyers, while another is a Fellow of both the American College of Real Estate Lawyers and the American College of Mortgage Attorneys. One firm member currently serves on the Board of The American Judicature Society. The head of the firm's Bankruptcy Group is a member of the American College of Bankruptcy. Several of the firm's lawyers are members of various American and Delaware Bar Association committees including those which involve corporation, limited partnership business trust, and other business laws. One member is presently the chair of the Commercial Law Section of the Delaware State Bar Association and another member is vice-chair of the Intellectual Property Section. Several members were past chairs of the Corporation, Commercial, Estates and Trust, Environmental Law, Health Law, Labor and Employment Law, New Lawyers, Taxation and Real Property Sections of the Delaware State Bar Association. Firm lawyers have written extensively and have been active in drafting Delaware's state-of-the-art General Corporation Law, Revised Uniform Limited Partnership Act, Business Trust Act, and Limited Liability Company Act and Tax Legislation. Another member of the firm has published and lectured extensively on legal opinions and is one of the members of the drafting group which prepared a national accord and related report with respect to legal opinions. The firm's corporate lawyers have written a multi-volume treatise entitled "The Delaware Law of Corporations and Business Organizations," which is considered a standard reference work on Delaware corporate law. Firm members routinely appear on national continuing legal education programs. Several former members of the firm have become judges, law professors and cabinet members for the State government. Two members are experienced in higher levels of the public sector: one as a United States Congressman, Governor of Delaware and candidate in 1988 for the Republican nomination for President of the United States, and the other as Secretary of State of Delaware and head of Delaware's Division of Corporations.

Richards, Layton & Finger is a member of several law firm networks including Lex Mundi, a global organization of independent law firms, and The State Capital Law Firm Group. Members of Lex Mundi and The State Capital Law Firm Group practice independently and not in a relationship for the joint practice of law.

DELAWARE LAW DIGEST

(The following is a list of all Categories and Topics, including cross-references, covered in this Digest.)

DELAWARE LAW DIGEST

Revised for 1999 edition by

RICHARDS, LAYTON & FINGER, of the Wilmington Bar.

(Citations, unless otherwise indicated, are to the Delaware Code (1974 Revision) by Title and Section or Chapter (c.) number. Del. indicates Delaware Reports. Del. Ch. indicates Delaware Chancery Reports. Del. L. indicates Delaware Laws not codified. Parallel citations to the Atlantic Reporter begin with 12 Del. and 6 Del. Ch. After 220 A.2d only Atlantic Reporter cited. "Supr. Ct. Rule" indicates Supreme Court Rule. "Super. Ct. Civ. Rule" and "Super. Ct. Crim. Rule" indicate Superior Court Rules. "Ch. Ct. Rule" indicates Chancery Court Rule. "J.P. Civ. Rule" indicates Justice of Peace Court Rule. "C.P. Ct. Civ. Rule" indicates Court of Common Pleas Rule. "DRE" indicates Delaware Uniform Rules of Evidence rule. Reference to court rules without designation of court indicates similar or identical Superior Court and Court of Chancery Rules.)

NOTE: This revision covers legislation adopted and approved by the Governor through July 23, 1998, (Volume 71, Chapter 490, Laws of Delaware).

INTRODUCTION

GOVERNMENT AND LEGAL SYSTEM:

The State of Delaware is a constituent state of the United States of America. For further discussion of the U.S. federal system, see Introduction to the Federal Government of the United States at the beginning of this volume. A great many laws are promulgated by the federal government of the United States and are not reflected in the topics below. See the Introduction to this volume for references to the federal law topics covered.

Like all but one of the United States, Delaware has a common law legal system, with roots in English common law. For information on the courts and legislature of Delaware, see category Courts and Legislature.

HOLIDAYS:

Legal Holidays are: Jan. 1; 3d Mon. in Jan.; 3d Mon. in Feb.; Good Friday; last Mon. in May; July 4; first Mon. in Sept.; 2d Mon. in Oct.; Nov. 11; 4th Thurs. and Fri. in Nov.; Dec. 25; Sats.; day of general election as it biennially occurs; and in Sussex County, Return Day, 2d day after general election, after 12:00 Noon. (1-501).

Saturday is legal holiday for all state offices except police, employees assigned to rotating hours or shiftwork and Department of Public Safety; for latter, all Saturdays, except last two of each quarter. (29-5104).

Holiday Falling on Sunday.—Next Monday a holiday. (1-501).

Holiday Falling on Saturday.—If legal holiday other than Sat. falls on that day, Fri. preceding is legal holiday. (1-501).

Legality of Transactions on Holiday.—Holiday, as opposed to Sabbath, is not dies non. (40 A. 1124). Transactions and legal proceedings done on any of enumerated legal holidays listed in 1-501 are not thereby rendered invalid. (1-502).

OFFICE HOURS AND TIME ZONE:

Delaware is in the Eastern (GMT −05:00) time zone. Office hours are generally from 9 a.m. to 5 p.m.

BUSINESS ORGANIZATIONS

AGENCY:

Common law rules govern.

ASSOCIATIONS:

No general statute governing unincorporated associations.

Formation.—No unincorporated association may transact business in state unless individual names of all concerned are first certified by an officer of the association to prothonotary of each county. (6-3104). Requisites of certificates are same as in case of limited partnership. See topic Partnerships.

Rights and Powers.—No statutory provisions.

Liabilities.—See subhead Actions, infra.

Actions.—Unincorporated association of persons, including a partnership, may sue and be sued in its common name. Judgment recovered in such a case is a lien and may be executed by levy, attachment, seizure and sale of personal or real estate of association or of persons composing same as if they had been made parties defendant by their individual names. (10-3904). Class actions may be brought by or against members of unincorporated association. (Ch. Ct. Rule 23.2).

Dissolution.—No statutory provisions. Absent agreement, withdrawal of part of membership will not effect dissolution. (39 Del. Ch. 221, 163 A.2d 242).

Professional Associations.—See topic Corporations, subhead Professional Corporations.

CORPORATIONS:

Incorporation is under general law, except for municipal or banking corporations, and those for charitable, penal, reformatory or educational purposes sustained in whole or part by state. (8-101 et seq.; Const., art. IX, §1). There are special provisions applicable to public utility corporations operating in Delaware. (26-201 et seq.). Corporations organized prior to 1897 must accept provisions of present constitution before amending or renewing their charters. (Const., art. IX, §2). General Corporation Law, as amended to date (8-101 et seq.), provides for incorporation of any lawful business except those prohibited by law. Following provisions, unless otherwise noted, are from that law. (Model Business Corporation Act not adopted.)

General Supervision.—Secretary of State, Division of Corporations, P.O. Box 898, Dover, DE 19903, exercises general supervision over corporations.

Purposes.—See subhead Certificate of Incorporation, infra.

Name.—For requirements as to corporate name, see infra, subhead Certificate of Incorporation.

It is informal practice of Delaware Secretary of State to reserve corporate name upon oral or written request for 30 days. If, during said 30 day period, another party should file certificate seeking reserved name, party first reserving said name is accorded 24 hours within which to file its own certificate of incorporation under reserved name or lose right to use reserved name. Reservation may be extended for additional 30 day period upon request.

Term of Corporate Existence.—Corporate existence begins when certificate is filed, and fees and taxes are paid. (8-103[c], 106). Unless limited, corporate existence is perpetual. (8-102[b][5]). If dissolved, existence continues three years, or longer as Court of Chancery directs, after dissolution for winding up its affairs. (8-278).

Incorporators.—Any person, partnership, association or corporation or combination, regardless of residence, domicile or state of incorporation may incorporate. (8-101). If persons to serve as directors until first annual meeting not named in certificate of incorporation, incorporators, until directors elected, may do whatever necessary and proper to perfect organization, including adoption of by-laws and election of directors. (8-107).

Certificate of incorporation must state name, which must distinguish it upon records in office of Secretary of State from names of other corporations organized, reserved or registered as foreign corporations or foreign limited partnerships under laws of Delaware; except with written consent of other foreign corporation, domestic, or foreign limited partnership and contain one of following words: association, company, corporation, club, foundation, fund, incorporated, institute, society, union, syndicate or limited, or abbreviation co., corp., ltd. or inc., or words or abbreviations of like import in other languages in roman letters (requirement may be waived upon filing certificate stating total assets more than $10 million) may only contain word bank if entity is bank reporting to State Bank Commissioner, to subsidiary of bank or savings association, or corporation regulated under 12 U.S.C. §1841 et seq., or 12 U.S.C. §1461; word bank may be used in context clearly not referring to banking business or in otherwise abusive manner; address (including street, number, city and county) of registered office in state and name of registered agent; nature of business, "engage in any lawful act or activity for which corporations may be organized under the General Corporation Law of the State of Delaware" is sufficient; number of shares with their par value, or that they have no par value; description of classes of stock; where there is more than one class of stock, number and par value of shares of each such class; powers, preferences, rights, qualifications, limitations, restrictions of any class or series of any class of stock, fixing of which by certificate of incorporation is desired; name and mailing address of incorporators; if power of incorporators to terminate upon filing of certificate of incorporation, names and mailing addresses of persons to serve as directors until first annual stockholder meeting or until successors elected and qualify. (8-102[a]).

Certificate of incorporation may state any provisions, not contrary to state law, for management of business and conduct of affairs of corporation and for creating, defining, limiting and regulating powers of corporation, directors and stockholders; any provision required or permitted in by-laws; authorization of binding compromise or arrangement of debts due creditors and rights of stockholders and agreement for reorganization on application to court by corporation, creditor, stockholders, receivers, or trustees in liquidation upon majority vote of three-fourths in value of class affected and approval by court; grant of preemptive rights to stockholders to subscribe to additional issues (otherwise, no preemptive rights exist); requirement for any corporate action of vote of larger portion of stock, any class or series, or any securities having voting power, or of larger number of directors than required by statute; limitation of corporation's existence to specified date (otherwise, corporation is perpetual); imposition of personal liability for debts of corporation on stockholders to specified extent and upon specified conditions (otherwise, stockholders not personally liable except as may be by reason of own conduct and acts); elimination or limitation of director's personal liability to corporation or stockholders for monetary damages for breach of fiduciary duty as director provided no such elimination or limitation for breach of director's duty of loyalty, for acts or omissions not in good faith or intentional misconduct or knowing violation of law, for liability under 8-174, for transactions where director derived improper personal benefit. (8-102[b]).

Certificate of incorporation need not state any powers conferred on corporations by General Corporation Law. (8-102[c]).

Corporations without capital stock must state that they have no authority to issue stock and conditions of membership. (8-102[a][4]).

Copies.—Original delivered to Secretary of State. No copies required. (8-103[c][1]).

Signatures.—Incorporators, if directors not named within. (8-103[a][1]).

Acknowledgment.—See category Documents and Records, topic Acknowledgments, subhead Forms, catchline Secretary of State.

Filing and Recording of Certificate.—Filed with Secretary of State. Copy recorded in office of recorder of county in which registered office located except certificate of dissolution under 8-391(a)(5). (8-103[c][5]). As to filing fee, see subhead Incorporation Tax or Fee, infra.

CORPORATIONS . . . *continued*

Correcting Filed, Inaccurate Documents.—Any document containing incorrect record of corporate action, or defectively or erroneously executed, may be corrected by filing with Secretary of State a certificate of correction or by filing corrected instrument. (8-103[f]). Secretary of State not liable for defectively filed document. (8-103[g]).

Incorporation Tax or Fee.—To Secretary of State on filing certificate of incorporation: For authorized par value stock, 2¢ per share up to 20,000; 1¢ per additional shares up to 200,000; 2/5¢ per additional share in excess of 200,000 shares. For authorized stock without par value, 1¢ for each share up to 20,000; 1/2¢ for each share in excess of 20,000 up to 2,000,000; 2/5¢ for each share in excess of 2,000,000; in no case less than $15. Par value stock defined in $100 units for purposes of taxation. (8-391[a][1]). Fee for receiving, filing and indexing certificate, $25. (8-391[a][7], [b]). In addition to fees charged under 8-391(a) there shall be paid to Secretary of State for all services described in 8-391(a) additional $500 if two hour service is requested, up to $200 if same day service is requested or up to $100 if 24 hour period service is requested. (8-391[h]).

Fee for Certifying and/or Copying.—$20 for each document certified, plus $1 per page if Secretary of State provides copy of document. (8-391[a][10]).

Recording fee payable to recorder, according to length of certificate. In all counties, fees are established by ordinance. (9-9617, 9619).

Failure to Pay Fee or Tax.—In connection with filing any instrument or certificate with Secretary of State, failure to pay appropriate fee or tax upon demand may cause corporation to cease to be in good standing and to lose right to file subsequent instruments or certificates with Secretary of State. (8-391[i]).

License to Do Business.—No provisions, as such. General licensing provisions for particular occupations actually transacting business in state appear in 24 et seq.

Organization meeting must be held by incorporator or incorporators or by board of directors if initial directors named in certificate of incorporation to adopt by-laws, elect directors (if meeting is of incorporators), elect officers (if meeting is of directors), do any other acts to perfect organization, and transact any business coming before meeting. Any action permitted at meeting may be taken without meeting if incorporators or directors sign instrument stating action taken. Two day written notice of meeting necessary. Notice need not be given anyone attending meeting or signing waiver. Meeting may be held anywhere. (8-108).

Paid-In Capital Requirements.—None.

Amendment of Certificate.—Certificate may be amended to change corporate name; change, enlarge or diminish nature of business or corporate powers and purpose(s); increase, decrease or reclassify authorized capital stock; cancel or change right of holders of any class shares to receive dividends which have accrued but have not been declared; create new classes of stock with rights and preferences prior and superior or subordinate and inferior to authorized stock; change period of duration; make any change provided that amended provisions are lawful and proper to insert in original certificate as of time of filing of amendment. (8-242[a]). If certificate requires greater vote by directors, or holders of any class or series of stock or securities with voting power than is required by any section of statute, such provision can be altered only by such greater vote. (8-242[b][4]).

For corporation with capital stock, amendment is effected by resolution of directors, followed by vote of majority of outstanding voting shares at meeting called by board of directors for purpose of voting on proposed amendment or at annual meeting. Resolution adopted may grant directors authority to abandon proposed amendment, notwithstanding prior stockholder approval. In addition, class vote provided where any proposed amendment would adversely alter or change preferences, special rights or powers of one or more classes of stock or series of stock. Certificate setting forth amendment and its adoption must be filed with Secretary of State and recorded in county where registered agent is located. In case of corporations without capital stock, certificate may require approval of a specified percentage of members; otherwise procedure differs but slightly. (8-242[b], [c]).

Increase or Decrease of Authorized Capital Stock.—Directors may issue capital stock at any time within amount authorized in certificate. (8-161). Authorized capital stock may be increased by amendment of certificate. (8-242[a][3]). Authorized capital may be reduced, by resolution of board of directors, if assets remaining after such reduction are sufficient to pay any debts for which payment has not been otherwise provided. (8-244).

On filing of certificate of amendment increasing authorized capital stock, tax is payable equal to difference between tax computed at foregoing rates upon total authorized capital stock of corporation including proposed increase, and tax computed at foregoing rates upon total authorized stock excluding proposed increase, in no case less than $30. Tax for filing certificate of amendment reducing authorized capital stock is $30. (8-391[a][2-3]). Fee for receiving, filing and indexing certificate, $50. Certifying and recording fees, as set forth above, apply. Expedited service available for additional charge of up to $100 if 24 hour service is requested, up to $200 if same day service is requested, and $500 if two hour service is requested. (8-391[a][7]).

By-laws.—Original or other by-laws may be adopted, amended, or repealed by incorporators, by initial directors if named in certificate, or, before corporation has received any payment for any of its stock, by its board of directors. After corporation has received any payment for any of its stock, power to adopt, amend or repeal shall be in stockholders entitled to vote or in directors if authorized by certificate (latter does not divest stockholders of power to adopt, amend or repeal by-laws). They may contain any provision, not inconsistent with law or certificate, relating to business of corporation, conduct of its affairs, its rights or powers, or rights or powers of stockholders, directors, officers or employees. In nonstock corporation, power to adopt, amend, or repeal by-laws resides in members entitled to vote or in governing body if charter permits. (8-109).

Emergency by-laws for enemy attack, atomic disaster, catastrophe, or similar emergency conditions, are authorized. (8-110).

Stock.—If shares of stock are owned by nonresidents, they are not taxable in Delaware. (Const., art. IX, §6).

Stock; common, preferred or special, may be with or without par value. (8-151[a]). No-par value stock may be issued for such consideration as may be fixed by directors or by stockholders (if provided by certificate). (8-153[b]).

Stock; common, preferred or special, with or without par value, may be issued in classes or in series within classes, each class or series having such voting powers, preferences, rights, qualifications, limitations, or restrictions as stated in certificate of incorporation, amendment thereof or in resolution of directors providing for issue pursuant to authority expressly stated in certificate. (8-151[a]). If issued under resolution of directors, "certificate of designations" fully stating rights and privileges must be filed with Secretary of State and copy recorded in same manner as certificate of incorporation. (8-151[g]).

Stock of any class or series may be made redeemable at option of corporation or stockholder provided corporation shall have outstanding shares of at least one class or series with full voting powers not subject to redemption. (8-151[b]). Only such stock may be made redeemable. (8-160). Any redeemable stock may be redeemed at such times and prices as are stated in certificate of incorporation or resolution of directors providing for issue. Such stock may be redeemed for cash, property or rights, including securities of same or another corporation. (8-151[b]). Redeemed stock is not considered outstanding for voting purposes. (8-160[d]).

Stock may be purchased or otherwise acquired by corporation unless capital is or will become impaired. Stock redeemable at option of corporation may not be purchased for a price greater than redemption price. Corporation may exchange a debt security for its stock as long as capital is not impaired. (8-160[a]).

Corporation may retire any shares of its capital stock that are issued but not outstanding. Retired shares resume status of authorized and unissued shares unless certificate of incorporation provides otherwise. If certificate of incorporation prohibits reissuance of retired shares, certificate so stating must be filed in accordance with 8-103. (8-243). No reduction of capital may be made unless assets remaining are enough to pay debts. (8-244[b]).

Stock of any class or series is convertible into or exchangeable for any other class or series of stock as stated in certificate or resolution of directors providing for issue. (8-151[e]).

Uncertificated Stock.—Any stock of any class or series may, by resolution of board of directors, be represented by uncertified shares. However, every stockholder upon request is entitled to stock certificate, notwithstanding such resolution. (8-158).

Stock certificates must be signed, facsimile sufficient, by chairman or vice-chairman of board or president or vice-president and treasurer or assistant treasurer or secretary or assistant secretary of such corporation. Any or all of signatures may be facsimiles. (8-158).

Issuance of Stock.—Stock may be issued only for cash, labor done, personal property, real property or leases thereof. (Const., Art. IX, §3). Stock so issued is deemed fully paid and nonassessable if: (1) Par or stated value allocated to capital is paid in full by type of consideration named above; or (2) balance or "surplus" consideration is supported by binding obligation. Board of directors may issue stock as partly paid shares pursuant to 8-156. (8-152).

Directors may require payment on 30 days notice, and may sue for payment, or sell, or forfeit stock if payment is not made. (8-163-164).

Transfer of Stock.—Governed by Art. 8, Uniform Commercial Code. (6-8-101 et seq.). Record date for determination of stockholders of record may be not more than 60 nor less than ten days before meeting. If no record date fixed, date shall be at close of business on day next preceding day on which notice is given, or, if notice waived, at close of business on day next preceding day on which meeting is held. (8-213[a]).

For purposes other than meetings, record date shall not precede date upon which resolution fixing record date is adopted and which date shall not be more than ten days after resolution date. If no record date, date shall be when first written consent is received by corporation or if prior action taken by board, date shall be at close of business on day board adopts resolution taking such prior action. (8-213[b]).

Restrictions.—Written restriction on transfer of security is enforceable if noted conspicuously on security or in notice sent to holders of uncertificated shares pursuant to 8-151(f) and against any person with actual knowledge. Restriction may be imposed by certificate, by-laws, or agreement among security holders or among such holders and corporation. Restriction may obligate holder to offer security to corporation, other holders or any other person; may obligate corporation, any holder, or any person to purchase security; may require corporation's or holders' consent to transfer; or may prohibit transfer to designated persons. Other lawful restrictions on transfer or registration of transfer of securities may be allowed. (8-202).

Business Combinations with Interested Stockholders.—Corporation may not engage in business combination with interested stockholder for three years following time such stockholder becomes interested stockholder, unless: (a) Prior to such time, board approved business combination or transaction by which stockholder became interested stockholder, (b) upon such time, interested stockholder owned 85% or more of outstanding voting stock at time transaction commenced (excluding shares owned by directors who are officers and by certain employee stock plans), or (c) upon or after such time, business combination is approved by board and stockholders authorize by vote at annual or special meeting, and not by written consent, of at least two-thirds of outstanding voting stock not owned by interested stockholder. Such restrictions shall not apply to corporation when: (a) Original certificate of incorporation expressly rejects statutory restrictions, (b) within 90 days of Feb. 2, 1988 (effective date of statute), board permanently amends by-laws expressly rejecting restrictions, (c) majority of voting shares amends by-laws (which board cannot further amend) or certificate of incorporation expressly rejecting restrictions, (amendment is effective immediately if corporation has never had class of voting stock described in [d] below and certificate of incorporation of corporation has never elected to be governed by this section, otherwise amendment not effective until 12 months after its adoption and not applicable to business combination and person or entity becoming interested stockholder on

See note at head of Digest as to 1998 legislation covered.

See Topical Index in front part of this volume.

DE – 2

CORPORATIONS . . . *continued*
or prior to date of adoption), (d) no class of voting stock is listed on national securities exchange, authorized for quotation on NASDAQ, or held of record by more than 2,000 stockholders, unless any of foregoing results from act of interested stockholder or as result of transaction by which stockholder becomes interested stockholder, (e) stockholder becomes interested stockholder inadvertently and subsequently divests, and would not have been interested stockholder (except for inadvertent acquisition) for three year period before business combination involving such stockholder, (f) business combination with interested stockholder is proposed subsequent to public announcement of, and prior to consummation or abandonment of, merger, sale of 50% or more of corporate assets, or tender offer for 50% or more of voting stock, or (g) business combination is with interested stockholder who became interested stockholder at time when restrictions in this section did not apply by reason of (a) through (d) above, provided, however, that this paragraph (g) shall not apply if at time such interested stockholder became interested, certificate of incorporation provided that any amendment to certificate of incorporation shall not apply to restrict business combination between corporation and interested stockholder if interested stockholder became such prior to effective date of amendment. For purposes of statute, "business combination" and "ownership" of voting stock are broadly defined. Chancery Court has exclusive jurisdiction over foregoing matters. (8-203).

Uniform Securities Ownership by Minors Act not adopted.

Uniform Simplification of Fiduciary Security Transfers Act adopted (12-c. 43) and not repealed by Art. 8, Uniform Commercial Code (6-10-104[2]).

Uniform Commercial Code adopted. (Title 6). 6-8-317(1) changed to retain existing Delaware statutes as to attachment and sequestration of securities. See category Business Regulation and Commerce, topic Commercial Code.

Stock Transfer Tax.—None.

Stockholders Actions.—Stockholder may recover from corporation amount paid by stockholder for any debt of corporation for which corporation is liable under Tit. 8. (8-326). In derivative action, stockholder must aver that he was stockholder at time of transaction of which he complains or that stock thereafter devolved upon him by operation of law. (8-327). Complaint must allege demand upon directors or reason for no demand. (Ch. Ct. Rule 23.1). Action may be settled or dismissed only with court approval. (Ch. Ct. Rule 23). Stockholder in derivative or class action must fairly and adequately protect interests of class. (Ch. Ct. Rule 23).

Stockholders' Liabilities.—Personal liability for debts of corporation may be imposed to extent and upon conditions specified in certificate; otherwise not liable except as may be by reason of own conduct or acts. (8-102[b][6]). If stock not fully paid, stockholder liable up to sum necessary to complete amount of unpaid balance of consideration for which shares issued. (8-162[a]). No person holding unpaid shares as collateral security shall be personally liable but person pledging shares shall be liable. (8-162[d]). No reduction of capital shall release any liability of any stockholder whose shares have not been fully paid. (8-244[b]).

Stockholders' meetings may be held at such times and such places, either within or without state, as by-laws provide. (8-211[a]).

Unless directors are elected by written consent in lieu of annual meeting, annual meeting is required by statute. (8-211[b]). Unless certificate of incorporation provides otherwise, stockholders may act by written consent to elect directors. (8-211[b]). However, if such consent is less than unanimous, action by written consent may be in lieu of annual meeting only if all directorships which directors could be elected at annual meeting are vacant and are filled by such action. (8-211[b]). Failure to hold meeting will not affect otherwise valid corporate acts or work a forfeiture or dissolution of corporation. (8-211[c]). Chancery may order holding of overdue meeting upon application of any stockholder or director. (8-211[c]).

For record date, see subhead Transfer of Stock, supra.

Written notice required of any meeting at which stockholders required or permitted to take action. (8-222[a]). Notice must state place, date and hour of meeting and purpose(s) of special meeting. (8-222[a]). Notice must be given at least ten and not more than 60 days before meeting. (8-222[b]). (See also, however, subheads Sale or Transfer of Corporate Assets, and Merger and Consolidation, infra.) No notice necessary for adjourned meeting unless adjournment for more than 30 days, new record date fixed, or time and place of adjourned meeting not announced at meeting where adjournment taken. (8-222[c]). Any notice required by statute, certificate of incorporation or by-laws may be waived in writing either before or after meeting. (8-229). Attendance at a meeting is waiver of notice except attendance to object at beginning of meeting that it is not lawfully called or convened. (8-229). Neither business to be transacted nor purpose of any regular or special meeting need be specified in any written waiver unless required by certificate of incorporation or by-laws. (8-229).

Vote on any particular action required or permitted to be taken at meeting of stockholders or members of non-stock corporation, may be dispensed with if that number necessary to approve particular action at meeting consent thereto in writing, and consents are delivered to corporation's registered office in state, principal place of business, or to officer having custody of book recording proceedings of shareholder meetings. (8-228). No notice need be given to any person with whom communication is unlawful. (8-230[a]). No notice need be given to any stockholder or member of non-stock corporation to whom notice has been mailed to his or her address as shown on records of corporation and returned undelivered if: (a) Two consecutive annual meetings and all notices of meetings and actions by written consent between such annual meetings, or (b) all and at least two dividend or interest payments (if sent by first-class mail) during 12 month period. (8-230[b]).

Stock ledger is only evidence of stockholders who are entitled to vote or to examine stock ledger. (8-219[c]). List of stockholders must be open for inspection by any stockholder, for any purpose germane to meeting, during business hours, in city where meeting to be held, at least ten days before meeting and during meeting. (8-219[a]).

One vote allowed for each share unless otherwise provided in certificate of incorporation. (8-212[a]). Voting may be by proxy granted by stockholder in writing or by some form of electronic transmission to persons acting as proxy. (8-212[b]-[c]). Irrevocable proxies recognized. (8-212[e]). Certificate of incorporation may authorize cumulative voting for all elections of directors or for elections held under specified circumstances. (8-214).

Corporation shall appoint inspector or alternate to (a) ascertain outstanding shares and voting power, (b) determine shares represented and validity of proxies and ballots, (c) count votes, (d) determine and retain challenges to inspector's decisions, (e) certify determination of shares represented at meeting and count of votes. (8-231[a]-[b]). No voting changes after polls close, unless Chancery Court determines otherwise. (8-231[c]). Unless certificate of incorporation or bylaws provide, section does not apply if no voting stock is listed on national securities exchange, authorized for interdealer quotation, or held of record by more than 2,000 stockholders. (8-231[e]).

Voting Trusts.—Stockholders may, by agreement in writing, create voting trust for any period. Copy of agreement and any amendments must be filed in registered office of corporation in Delaware, open to inspection of any stockholder or beneficiary of agreement. Certificates of stock or uncertified stock shall be issued to voting trustee to represent any stock of original issue deposited with trustee. Certificates of stock or uncertificated stock deposited under said agreement shall be cancelled and new certificates or uncertificated stock issued to voting trustees, in which certificates, if any, and on stock ledger, it must appear that they are issued under agreement. Voting trustees may vote in person or by proxy, but incur no liability as stockholder, trustee, or otherwise, except for individual malfeasance. Majority of voting trustees determine manner of voting, unless otherwise provided in agreement; if equally divided, vote shall be divided equally among trustees. (8-218[a]).

Voting Agreements.—Any amendment to voting trust agreement shall be made by written agreement. (8-218[b]). Signed and written agreement between stockholders may provide for shares to be voted as provided in agreement or as parties agree. (8-218[c]).

Directors.—Board of directors must consist of one or more members (as designated in certificate or bylaws). Each director shall hold office until his successor is elected or until his earlier resignation or removal. (8-141[b]). Directors need not be stockholders unless required by certificate of incorporation or bylaws. (8-141[b]). Directors may be divided into one, two or three classes with staggered terms. (8-141[d]). Directors may be removed by holders of majority of shares, with or without cause. Cause must be shown for: (1) Classified board unless certificate of incorporation provides otherwise, or (2) corporations having cumulative voting if votes cast against removal are sufficient to elect director if cumulatively voted at election of entire board or, if there be classes of directors, at election of director's class. (8-141[k]).

Unless directors are elected by written consent, directors are elected at annual meeting of stockholders. (8-211[b]). Election is by written ballot unless otherwise provided in certificate of incorporation. (8-211[e]). Failure to hold annual meeting or to elect sufficient directors to conduct business of corporation will not affect otherwise valid acts or work forfeiture or dissolution of corporation. (8-211[c]). Chancery may compel holding of annual meeting under certain circumstances. (8-211[c]). Unless otherwise provided in certificate of incorporation or by-laws, majority of directors in office, although less than a quorum, may fill vacancies or newly created directorships. (8-223[a][1]). If no directors in office, any officer, stockholder or executor, administrator, trustee, guardian or other fiduciary of a stockholder may call special stockholder meeting or apply to Chancery to order an election. (8-223[a][2]).

Upon application of any stockholder, Chancery may appoint custodian(s) to continue business of corporation and not to liquidate its affairs and distribute its assets, except when Court shall otherwise order and except in cases arising under paragraph (3) of subsection (a) of this section or paragraph (2) of subsection (a) of 352 of this title. (8-226).

Directors' meetings may be held outside of state, unless otherwise restricted by certificate of incorporation or by-laws. (8-141[g]). Majority of total number of directors constitutes quorum unless certificate of incorporation or by-laws require greater number. (8-141[b]). Unless certificate provides otherwise, by-laws may provide for quorum of less than majority but in no case less than one-third of total number of directors except where board of one director authorized. (8-141[b]). Certificate of non-stock corporation may provide for quorum of less than one-third members of governing body. (8-141[j]). Vote of majority of directors present at meeting at which quorum is present is act of board unless certificate of incorporation or by-laws provides otherwise. (8-141[b]). Any action required or permitted to be taken at any meeting of board may be taken without meeting if all members consent in writing and writings filed with board minutes. (8-141[f]). Interested directors may be counted in quorum of meeting which authorized transaction. (8-144[b]). Participation of interested director in meeting will not void transaction if material facts as to his interest or relationship are disclosed or known to board and shareholders who approve in good faith, or if transaction is fair as of time it is authorized by board, committee or shareholders. (8-144[a]).

Powers and Duties of Directors.—Business of every corporation is managed by or under direction of board of directors except as provided in certificate. (8-141[a]). When authorized by majority vote of stockholders, directors may sell, lease or exchange all or substantially all corporate assets, including goodwill and franchises, for money or other property, including stock and securities. (8-271[a]). Notwithstanding stockholder authorization or consent, board of directors may abandon such proposed sale, lease or exchange without further action by stockholders, subject to rights, if any, of third parties under any contract relating thereto. (8-271[b]). Except as certificate of incorporation provides otherwise, directors may mortgage or pledge assets without stockholder consent. (8-272).

Committees (of corporations incorporated prior to July 1, 1996) of one or more directors may, to extent provided in resolution of board or by-laws, exercise powers of board in management of business. Committees may not amend certificate of incorporation (but may adopt certificate of designation), adopt merger agreement, recommend asset sales, dissolution, or revocation of dissolutions or amend by-laws and may not authorize issuance of stock or declare dividend unless specifically authorized by by-laws, resolution appointing committee, or certificate of incorporation. (8-141[c][1]).

See note at head of Digest as to 1998 legislation covered.

See Topical Index in front part of this volume.

DE – 3

CORPORATIONS . . . *continued*
For corporations incorporated on or after July 1, 1996, and corporations incorporated prior to July 1, 1996 that by resolution elect to be governed by §(2), committees may be designated with resolution passed by majority of whole board. Such committees may have powers and authority board delegates, but may not approve, adopt or recommend to stockholders action required by this chapter to be submitted for stockholder approval, and may not adopt, amend or repeal by-laws. (8-141[c]).

Liabilities of Directors.—Directors are fully protected in relying in good faith upon records of corporation or reports made to corporation by any officer or by person director reasonably believes is expert selected on behalf of corporation by board. (8-141[e]). Directors jointly and severally liable for payment of unlawful dividend and for unlawful stock purchase or redemption unless dissent or absence from meeting is noted in minutes. (8-174[a]). Where certificate of incorporation so provides, liability for breach of fiduciary duty may be limited or eliminated, provided that such provision shall not eliminate or limit liability of director (i) for any breach of director's duty of loyalty to corporation or its stockholders; (ii) for acts or omissions not in good faith or which involve intentional misconduct or knowing violation of law; (iii) under §174 of title 8; or (iv) for any transaction from which director derived improper personal benefit. (8-102[b][7]). See topic Process.

Indemnification of Directors and Officers.—Corporation may indemnify any person who was or is a party or is threatened to be made a party to any threatened, pending or completed action, suit or proceeding, whether civil, criminal, administrative or investigative (other than action by or in right of corporation), by reason of fact he is or was a director, officer, employee or agent of corporation or serving another corporation at request of corporation, against expenses (including attorneys' fees), judgments, fines, and amounts paid in settlement, actually and reasonably incurred by him if he acted in good faith and in manner he reasonably believed to be in or not opposed to best interests of corporation and, with respect to criminal action or proceeding, had no reasonable cause to believe his conduct unlawful. Lack of good faith not presumed from settlement or nolo contendere plea. (8-145[a]). Indemnification of expenses (including attorney's fees) allowed in derivative actions except no indemnification in respect to any claim, issue or matter as to which any such person has been adjudged to be liable unless Chancery decides indemnification is proper. (8-145[b]). To extent any such person succeeds on merits or otherwise in defense of action referred to in subsections (a) and (b) of this section, such person shall be indemnified against expenses (including attorney's fees). (8-145[c]). Determination that person to be indemnified met applicable standard of conduct is made by board of directors by majority vote of directors not party to such action, suit or proceeding or, if there are no such directors, by committee of directors designated by majority vote of directors, even though less than quorum, or if such directors so direct, by independent legal counsel or by stockholders. (8-145[d]). Expenses (including attorneys' fees) may be paid in advance upon receipt of undertakings to repay by director or officer if it is ultimately determined that such person is not entitled to be indemnified by corporation. (8-145[e]). Corporation may purchase indemnity insurance. (8-145[g]). Right of indemnification provided by section continues as to person who has ceased to be director, officer or agent unless otherwise provided in authorization. (8-145[j]). Court of Chancery has exclusive jurisdiction for advancement of expenses or indemnification. (8-145[k]).

Officers.—Any number of offices may be held by same person unless certificate of incorporation or by-laws provide otherwise. Corporation may have such officers as are desired, chosen in such manner and holding office for such terms as prescribed by by-laws or determined by directors. One officer shall record proceedings of stockholder and directors' meetings in book for that purpose. Vacancies are filled as provided in by-laws; otherwise by directors. Failure to elect officers annually will not dissolve corporation. (8-142).

Liabilities of Officers.—No statutory provisions respecting liability of officers.

Registered Office.—Every corporation must maintain registered office in state. It need not be same as place of business. (8-131[a]). Corporation may change registered office to any other place in state by resolution of board of directors. (8-133). Certificate of change must be filed with Secretary of State and recorded in county in which new office located. (8-133).

Registered Agent.—Every corporation must maintain registered agent in state. (8-132[a]). Agent may be any of corporation itself, individual resident in this State, domestic corporation (other than corporation itself), limited partnership, limited liability company, domestic business trust, or foreign corporation authorized to transact business in this State, provided that each has business office identical with office of registered agent which generally is open during business hours to accept service of process and perform agent functions. (8-132[a]). Corporation may change its registered agent to any other person or corporation including itself. (8-133). Certificate of change must be filed with Secretary of State and recorded in county of new registered office. (8-133). Registered agent may change its name or address of registered office by filing certificate with Secretary of State. (8-134). Registered agent may resign and appoint successor by filing certificate with Secretary of State. (8-135). Corporation must ratify and approve substitution. (8-135). If registered agent resigns without appointing successor, resignation not effective for 30 days after filing of certificate. (8-136[a]). Certificate must state that agent notified corporation of resignation by mail or delivery to corporation's last known address, and set forth date of notice. Notification must be at least 30 days before filing of certificate. (8-136[a]). Corporation must appoint new registered agent within 30 days of filing of certificate of resignation by registered agent, or Secretary of State will declare its charter forfeited. (8-136[b]). If it is foreign corporation, Secretary of State will forfeit its authority to do business in state. (8-136[b]). If no new registered agent is designated as provided, service of legal process against corporation shall be upon Secretary of State. (8-136[c]).

Powers of Corporations.—Corporation has power to have perpetual succession by its corporate name, unless certificate of incorporation limits period of duration; to sue or be sued; to have corporate seal; to purchase, receive, take by grant, gift, devise, bequest or otherwise, lease, or otherwise acquire, own, hold, improve, employ, use and otherwise deal in and with real or personal property, or any interest therein, wherever situated, and to sell, convey, lease, exchange, transfer or otherwise dispose of, or mortgage or pledge, all or any of its property and assets, or any interest therein, wherever situated; to appoint officers and agents and pay them; to adopt, amend and repeal by-laws; to wind up and dissolve itself; to conduct business and have offices and exercise its powers within or without state; to make donations for public welfare or for charitable, scientific or educational purposes; to be incorporator, promoter or manager of other corporations; to participate with others in any corporation, partnership, limited partnership, joint venture or other association, or in any transaction, undertaking or arrangement which participating corporation would have power to conduct by itself, whether or not such participation involves sharing or delegation of control with or to others; to transact any lawful business in aid of governmental authority; to make contracts, including contracts of guaranty and suretyship, incur liabilities, borrow money, issue notes, bonds and other obligations, and secure any of its obligations by mortgage, pledge or other encumbrance of all or any of its property, franchises and income; to lend money, invest and reinvest its funds, and take, hold and deal with real and personal property as security for payment of funds so invested; to pay pensions and establish and carry out pension, profit sharing, stock option, stock purchase, stock bonus, retirement, benefit, incentive and compensation plans, trusts and provisions for any and all directors, officers and employees and for those of its subsidiaries; to provide insurance for its benefit on life of any directors, officers or employees or on life of any stockholder to acquire at his death his shares of its stock (8-122); to indemnify its officers, directors, employees, agents or persons serving at request of corporation and to purchase liability insurance (8-145); to lend money to or guarantee any obligation of any officer or employee; including officers and employees who are directors, with or without interest and security (8-143); to merge or consolidate (8-251); to deal in securities of other corporations or entities and exercise all rights of ownership, including right to vote (8-123). No act of corporation and no conveyance or transfer of property is invalid by reason of fact corporation was without capacity or power to do such act. (8-124). Banking powers expressly denied. (8-126).

Dividends.—Subject to any restrictions in certificate of incorporation, directors may pay dividends out of surplus or, if no surplus is available, out of net profits for fiscal year in which dividend is declared and/or preceding fiscal year. (8-170[a]). No dividends may be declared while capital is impaired to extent that it amounts to less than aggregate amount of capital represented by issued and outstanding stock of all classes having preference on distribution of assets. (8-170[a]). Dividends may be paid in cash, in property, or in shares of corporation's capital stock. (8-173). If dividend is paid in shares of theretofore unissued capital stock, amount not less than aggregate par value of par value shares being declared as dividend (or amount determined by board of directors for shares without par value) must be transferred from surplus to capital account by resolution of board of directors. (8-173). No such transfer is required if additional shares are distributed pursuant to stock split or division rather than as dividend. (8-173).

Unclaimed Dividends.—Part III, c. 11, subc. IV of Tit. 12. (12-1197). See topic Absentees, subhead Escheat.

Sale or Transfer of Corporate Assets.—Board of directors or governing body as authorized by affirmative vote of majority of voting stock at stockholders' meeting called upon at least 20 days notice or by written consent of majority of voting stock or by majority of members of non-stock corporation having right to vote for election of members of governing body may sell, lease or exchange all or substantially all of corporate assets. (8-271[a]). Consideration may include money or other property, including stock or securities of any other corporation. (8-271[a]). Notwithstanding stockholder authorization or consent to proposed sale, lease or exchange of corporation's property and assets, board of directors may abandon such proposed sale, lease or exchange without further action by stockholders or members, subject to rights, if any, of third parties under any contract relating thereto. (8-271[b]). See also subhead Business Combinations with Interested Stockholders, supra.

Books and Records.—Any records maintained in regular course of business, including stock ledger, books of account, and minute books, may be kept by any information storage device if readily convertible into legible form. (8-224). Stockholder of record, in person or by attorney or agent, may, upon written demand under oath stating purpose, inspect for any proper purpose stock ledger, list of stockholders and other books and records and make copies and extracts. (8-220[a]). Proper purpose means purpose reasonably related to such person's interest as a stockholder. (8-220[ba]). If corporation refuses inspection, stockholder may apply to Chancery to compel it. (8-220[c]). Certificate of incorporation may confer upon bond and debenture holders same right of inspection. (8-221). Director may examine stock ledger, list of stockholders and other books and records for purpose reasonably related to his position as director. (8-220[d]).

Reports.—On or before 1st day of Mar., Delaware corporation must make annual franchise tax report to and on form designated by Secretary of State. Report must be signed by corporation's president, secretary, treasurer or other proper officer, or by any director, or by any incorporator if directors not yet elected. Individual's signature shall be prima facie evidence that he is authorized to certify report. Title or position of signer must be designated. Report must contain following information: Location of registered office in Delaware; name of agent upon whom process against corporation may be served; location of principal places of business of corporation without Delaware; names and addresses of all directors and not more than two officers, including officer signing report, and when their terms expire; number of shares and par value per share of each class of capital stock having par value and number of shares of each class of stock without par value which corporation is authorized to issue and number of shares of each class of stock actually issued, if any; and, if exempt from taxation for any cause, specific facts entitling corporation to exemption. If corporation fails to file report, or pay franchise tax, Secretary of State determines amount of franchise tax and corporation must pay $50 to be treated as addition to tax. (8-502). Corporation may file with franchise tax report statement of total amount of gross assets, including goodwill. Filing of such statement permits corporation to pay franchise tax according

See note at head of Digest as to 1998 legislation covered.

See Topical Index in front part of this volume.

CORPORATIONS . . . *continued*
to formula in 8-503(a)(2). (8-503[b]). See subhead Franchise Tax, infra. Corporations which owe franchise tax cannot be issued certification of good standing. (8-502[g]).

Corporate Bonds or Mortgages.—Corporation may issue bonds, and may secure any obligation by mortgage. (8-122[13]). Bondholders may be granted same rights as stockholders have to vote and to inspect corporate books, accounts and records. Certificate of incorporation may provide that holders of debt securities shall be deemed to be stockholders for any voting purposes and it may place exclusive power to vote in hands of bondholders (8-221) except as to class votes on charter amendments that would increase or decrease aggregate number of authorized class shares or their par value, or that would alter powers, preferences or special rights so as to affect them adversely (8-242[b][2]). Usury may not be pleaded in defense to any action on bond, note or other evidence of indebtedness. (8-330). Except to extent certificate of incorporation provides otherwise, authorization or consent of stockholders not necessary to mortgage or pledge corporate property or assets. (8-272).

Merger and Consolidation.—Any two or more Delaware corporations may merge pursuant to resolution of board of directors (8-251[a], [b]) approved by vote of majority of total number of outstanding shares of capital stock of each corporation. Stockholder vote may be at annual or special meeting. Notice must be mailed to each stockholder at least 20 days prior to meeting. Certified agreement must be filed with Secretary of State and recorded in county in which registered office of surviving corporation is located. (8-251[c]). In lieu of filing full agreement, surviving or resulting corporation may file certificate of merger or consolidation executed in accordance with 8-103. (8-251[c]). Agreement may contain provision permitting termination or certain modifications of agreement at any time prior to time that agreement (or certificate in lieu thereof) filed with Secretary of State becomes effective in accordance with 8-103, by board of any constituent corporation notwithstanding approval of stockholders. (8-251[d]). Except to extent certificate of incorporation provides otherwise, no vote of stockholders of surviving corporation necessary: (1) If agreement does not amend certificate of incorporation of surviving corporation, (2) if each share of surviving corporation outstanding prior to merger is to be identical or treasury share of surviving corporation after merger, and (3) either no shares of common stock of surviving corporation and no shares, securities or obligations convertible into such stock are to be issued or delivered under plan of merger, or authorized unissued shares or treasury shares of common stock of surviving corporation to be issued or delivered under plan of merger plus those initially issuable upon conversion of any other shares, securities or obligations to be issued or delivered under plan do not exceed 20% of shares of common stock of constituent corporations outstanding prior to merger. No vote of stockholders is necessary if no shares of stock of such corporation have yet been issued. (8-251[f]). Notwithstanding majority vote requirements of 8-251(c), no vote of shareholders of constituent corporation is necessary to authorize merger with or into single direct or indirect wholly owned subsidiary corporation if requirements of 8-251(g) are met. (8-251[g]).

Surviving or resulting corporation possesses all rights, privileges, powers and franchises and is subject to all restrictions, disabilities and duties of each constituent corporation. All property and debts of each corporation are vested in surviving or resulting corporation. All rights of creditors and liens upon property survive. (8-259[a]). Merger does not abate actions against any constituent corporation. (8-261). Surviving or resulting corporation may issue bonds to cover payments or obligations in effecting merger and may mortgage its franchise, rights, privileges and property to secure bonds. (8-260).

Delaware corporation may merge or consolidate with one or more foreign corporations if law of state of incorporation of foreign corporations permits. (8-252[a]). If surviving or resulting corporation is to be governed by laws of another state, it must consent to be served with process in Delaware in any proceeding for enforcement of any obligation of any constituent Delaware corporation or of any obligation of surviving or resulting corporation arising from merger, including suit for appraisal rights under 8-262. (8-252[d]). Corporation shall irrevocably appoint Secretary of State as its agent to accept service of process. (8-252[d]). Delaware corporation may merge or consolidate with non-U.S.A. corporation if its laws permit and if surviving or resulting corporation is Delaware corporation. (8-252[a]).

Parent company may merge with or into 90% or more owned subsidiary on filing certificate setting forth resolution of board of directors (8-253[a]); but, if Delaware corporation party to merger is not wholly owned by parent, stockholders have appraisal rights under 8-262. (8-253[d]). (See subhead Appraisal, infra.) And, if parent corporation is not surviving corporation, approval of majority of outstanding stock of parent is necessary. (8-253[a]). Unless forbidden by laws of state under which joint stock association was formed, corporation may merge with joint stock companies on filing and recording of agreement, in accordance with 8-251 or 8-255 or on filing of certificate of merger or consolidation executed in accordance with 8-103. (8-254).

Two or more non-stock corporations may merge (8-255[a]) as may non-stock with stock corporations regardless of whether any is profit or nonprofit (8-257[a]). Domestic corporation may merge or consolidate with one or more limited partnerships, except for limited partnerships formed under laws of state which forbid such merger or consolidation. (8-263). Mergers of mutual insurance companies governed by 18-5521.

Filing Tax.—On filing of certificate of consolidation or merger, tax is equal to difference between tax computed on total authorized stock of corporation created by merger or consolidation, and that computed on total authorized capital stock of constituent corporations, minimum tax being $75. This tax shall be in addition to any required under any law of this state for noncorporate entity in connection with filing of certificate of merger or consolidation. (8-391[a][4]). Secretary of State may permit extension of credit for taxes or fees so required. (8-391[e]). Secretary shall retain from taxes and fees collected sum sufficient at all times to provide fund of at least $500, but not more than $1,500, out of which he may refund excess payments. (8-391[f]).

Dissolution.—If corporation has not issued shares or commenced business, majority of incorporators or directors, if they have been named or elected, may surrender corporation's rights and franchises by filing with Secretary of State certificate that no shares of stock have been issued or business has not been begun; that no part of capital has been paid or, if some has been paid, that amount less disbursements for necessary expenses has been returned; that if corporation has begun business but has not issued shares, all debts have been paid; that if corporation has not begun business but has issued certificates that all issued stock certificates have been surrendered and cancelled; and that all rights and franchises of corporation are surrendered. Upon filing certificate in accordance with 8-103, corporation is dissolved. (8-274). Filing tax is $40, or $10 if corporation has no assets and has ceased doing business; and has paid only minimum franchise tax under 8-503; and has paid all franchise taxes or fees due through end of year in which dissolution certificate filed. (8-391[a][5]).

Dissolution of any corporation may be effected by resolution of directors followed by approval of majority of outstanding voting stock at stockholder meeting for which notice has been mailed to each stockholder having voting power. Dissolution may also be effected in certain instances by unanimous written consent of shareholders having voting power. Certificate of dissolution must be filed with Secretary of State in accordance with 8-103. (8-275).

No corporation may be dissolved or merged until all franchise taxes due or assessable have been paid by it. (8-277).

Corporate existence continues for three years, or longer period as Chancery directs, after dissolution for prosecuting and defending suits, settling business, disposing of property, discharging liabilities and distributing assets to stockholders. (8-278). Chancery may appoint one or more directors as trustees or may appoint receivers to wind up business. (8-279). Suits begun by or against corporation prior to or within three years after dissolution shall proceed until fully disposed of. (8-278).

Joint Venture Having Two Stockholders.—If stockholders each own 50% of stock and are unable to agree on desirability of discontinuing venture, either stockholder may file with Court of Chancery petition and proposed plan for discontinuance along with certificate that petition and plan have been transmitted in writing to other stockholder. If stockholders do not file within three months certificate that plan agreed to and within one year certificate that distribution of assets completed, Court may dissolve corporation and appoint trustees or receivers to wind up affairs. Either or both periods may be extended by agreement of stockholders with certificate filed in Chancery prior to expiration of period. (8-273).

Revocation.—At any time within three years, or such longer period as Chancery may have directed, following voluntary dissolution, revocation thereof may be effected by resolution of directors, and majority vote at noticed special meeting of outstanding stockholders entitled to vote before dissolution. Certificate stating name of corporation, names and addresses of officers and directors, and affirmative vote of majority of stockholders or in lieu of vote written consent of stockholders must be acknowledged and filed with Secretary of State. Secretary of State's certificate that corporation has revoked dissolution will be recorded in county of registered office by the State. (8-311).

Insolvency and Receivers.—When corporation becomes insolvent Court of Chancery, on application of any creditor or stockholder, may appoint one or more persons to be receivers for corporation, to take charge of its affairs, to collect debts and property due, to prosecute and defend all claims and suits, and to appoint agents to act for corporation for so long as Chancery deems necessary. (8-291). Appointed receivers are vested with all title and rights of corporation. Receiver must file copy of appointment within 20 days with recorder in each county in which corporation owns real estate. (8-292). Receiver must file full itemized inventory of all assets in office of Register in Chancery in county in which proceeding is pending and complete inventory of all assets and accounting of all debts due. (8-294).

All creditors must prove under oath respective claims against corporation and cause same to be filed within time fixed by Rules of Court of Chancery. Creditors failing to do so within time prescribed by this section or by order of Court may be barred from participating in distribution of assets of corporation. Notice of such time by publication or otherwise may be required by Court. (8-295). Within 30 days after receiving notice of claim from Chancery, receiver, if not satisfied with validity of claim, must notify creditor of disputed claim. Receiver shall require creditors whose claims are disputed to submit themselves to examination in which creditors will produce books relating to claims as required. Creditors or claimants may appeal from disallowance to Chancery within 30 days. (8-296).

Chancery may order receiver to sell property which will deteriorate in value and is encumbered by liens. (8-297). Chancery, before distributing assets, must first allow for reasonable compensation to receiver for services, administrative expenses and court costs out of assets of insolvent corporation. (8-298). Receiver, upon application to court, shall be substituted as party plaintiff in place of corporation. No action against receiver shall abate because of death, but shall be continued against successor or against corporation if no new receiver is appointed. (8-299).

Employees of insolvent corporation have lien upon assets for wages due, not exceeding two months wages, which will be paid prior to any other debts of corporation. "Employee" not construed to include officers of corporation. (8-300).

Liquidation of insolvent corporation may be discontinued if it is established that cause for liquidation no longer exists. Chancellor may dismiss proceedings and direct receiver to redeliver all remaining assets to corporation. (8-301).

Reorganization.—Any plan of reorganization pursuant to any U.S. statute confirmed by court of competent jurisdiction may be carried out pursuant to said plan and decree or order without further action by directors or stockholders. (8-303).

Forfeiture of Charter.—Charter may be forfeited in Chancery for abuse, misuse or nonuse of its powers, privileges or franchise on motion of Attorney General in county of registered agent or upon relation of proper party in county of corporation's registered agent. No proceeding for nonuse will be brought during first two years of incorporation. (8-284[a], [c]). Charter may also be revoked for failure to pay franchise tax for one year (8-511) or for failure to appoint new registered agent within 30 days of filing of certificate of resignation by registered agent (8-136[b]).

Renewal or Revival of Certificate of Incorporation.—Any corporation may, at any time before expiration of time limited for its existence, and any corporation whose certificate of incorporation has become inoperative for nonpayment of taxes, has expired for failure to renew same or has been renewed invalidly, has expired due to

See note at head of Digest as to 1998 legislation covered.

See Topical Index in front part of this volume.

DE – 5

CORPORATIONS . . . *continued*
nonappointment of successor registered agent within 60 days after resignation by registered agent, may at any time procure renewal or revival of its certificate of incorporation by filing with Secretary of State certificate stating: Name of corporation and date of filing of its original certificate of incorporation, name and office address of registered agent; whether renewal is to be perpetual, and, if not, length of its existence; in case of renewal before expiration of time limited for its existence, date when such renewal is to commence, which must be prior to date of expiration of old certificate of incorporation; that corporation was duly organized in Delaware; date when certificate would expire or other facts showing certificate has been forfeited or become void; that certificate is filed by authority of those on board at time certificate expired or those elected to replace such directors. Renewal or revival validates all lawful acts done before or during period when certificate of incorporation was inoperative or void. All franchise taxes, penalties and interest due at time certificate of incorporation became void or expired must be paid, but in case of corporation which has been inoperative for more than five years, it shall instead pay sum equal to three times amount of annual franchise tax that would be due and payable by such corporation for year in which renewal or revival is effected, computed at then current rates. (8-312[a]-[e], [g]).

Close Corporations.—If certificate of incorporation states in heading that it is a close corporation (8-343) and provides that all issued stock is not to be held by more than thirty persons, that all issued stock is subject to one or more restrictions on transfer permitted by 8-202, and that corporation does not offer any stock at "public offering" within meaning of Securities Act of 1933, as amended, then corporation may be organized as close corporation. (8-344). Existing corporation may become close corporation by amending certificate of incorporation to comply with 8-342. Amendment must be approved by vote of two-thirds of outstanding shares of each class of stock. (8-344). Corporation may terminate status as close corporation by amending certificate of incorporation to delete provisions required by 8-342. (8-346). Amendment must be approved by vote of two-thirds of outstanding shares of each class of stock unless certificate requires greater than two-thirds vote to terminate. (8-346). If any of provisions required by 8-342 are breached, corporation's status as close corporation is terminated unless within 30 days of breach or within 30 days of its discovery, whichever is later, corporation files certificate in accordance with 8-103 stating breached provision has ceased to be applicable, furnishes copy of this certificate to each stockholder, and takes steps necessary to correct situation threatening its status as close corporation, including refusal to register wrongfully transferred stock. (8-348). Upon suit by corporation or stockholder, Chancery may enjoin or set aside any act inconsistent with provisions required by 8-342. (8-348).

If stock certificate conspicuously notes qualifications or number of persons entitled to be holders of record and stock is issued or transferred in breach of qualifying conditions, person taking is presumed to have notice of ineligibility. (8-347[a][c]). Corporation may then refuse to register transfer unless all stockholders consent to transfer or corporation amends certificate of incorporation as provided by 8-346. (8-347). If restriction on transfer shall be found not authorized by 8-202, corporation has option for 30 days after judgment setting aside transfer is final, to acquire restricted security at price agreed on by parties, if no agreement is reached, or at fair value as determined by Chancery. (8-349).

Written agreement among majority of stockholders is not invalid on grounds of restricting discretion or powers of directors. Agreement places liability for managerial acts or omissions on stockholders who are parties to agreement, rather than directors as long as agreement in effect. (8-350). Certificate of incorporation may provide business of close corporation to be managed by stockholders. No meeting of stockholders must be called to elect directors. Unless context requires otherwise, stockholders are deemed directors for applying provisions of corporate law, and are subject to all liabilities of directors. Certificate of incorporation may be amended to include such provision if all incorporators and subscribers or all holders of record of stock with or without voting power so authorize. Amendment to delete such provision must be adopted by holders of majority of outstanding stock with or without voting power. If such provision in effect, it must be noted conspicuously on each stock certificate. (8-351).

No written agreement among stockholders or provision of certificate of incorporation or by-laws is invalid on ground it is attempt to treat corporation as partnership. (8-354).

Certificate of incorporation may grant to any stockholder or holders of any specified number or percentage of shares option to have corporation dissolved. Stockholder must give written notice of exercise of option to all other stockholders and 30 days thereafter dissolution shall commence. (8-355[a]).

Certificate may be amended to include provision under 8-355(a) by affirmative vote of holders of all outstanding stock with or without voting power unless certificate authorizes such amendment by at least two-thirds vote. (8-355[b]). If such provision is in effect, it must be noted conspicuously on each stock certificate. (8-355[c]).

Chancery may appoint custodian of insolvent corporation upon application of any stockholder if stockholders are deadlocked or if petitioning stockholder has right of dissolution under 8-355. In lieu of custodian, Chancery may appoint provisional director. (8-352). Provisional director may also be appointed regardless of solvency, in certain cases where directors are deadlocked. (8-353). Provisional director must be impartial and cannot be stockholder or creditor of corporation or affiliate. Provisional director has same rights and powers as elected director until removed by court, by majority vote of shareholders, or by two-thirds vote of class of shareholders which filed application for his appointment. (8-353[c]).

Appraisal.—If proposed merger for which appraisal rights are provided is to be submitted at stockholder meeting, corporation must give at least 20 days notice to each stockholder of record on record date of meeting who is entitled to appraisal, and must include copy of 8-262(d)(1). Each stockholder electing appraisal must make written demand prior to vote on merger. Demand sufficient if it reasonably informs corporation of stockholder's identity and his intent to demand appraisal. Notice must be given to stockholders who have demanded appraisals. (8-262[d]). Similar procedure for action where there is no meeting (8-228), or for shares of subsidiary Delaware corporation where parent merges with or into 90% to 100% owned subsidiary (8-253). Appropriate notice of appraisal rights must be given within ten days after merger. (8-262[d][2]). Any stockholder who has complied with foregoing may, within 120 days after merger, petition Court of Chancery demanding valuation of stock of such stockholder, but stockholder may withdraw demand and accept offered terms within 60 days after merger. (8-262[e]). Upon application of stockholder for appraisal proceeding, court may order all or part of expenses, including attorney's fees and expenses of experts, to be charged pro rata against value of shares entitled to appraisal. (8-262[j]). Appraisal not available to holders of shares of any class of stock which are registered on national securities exchange or designated as national market system security on interdealer quotation system by National Association of Securities Dealers, Inc. or held of record by more than 2,000 stockholders or to stockholders of corporation surviving merger if merger did not require vote of stockholders of surviving corporation as provided in 8-251. (8-262[b][1]). (See subhead Merger or Consolidation, supra.) Above restrictions on appraisal not applicable to holders of class or series of stock of constituent corporation if under terms of merger or consolidation pursuant to 8-251, 252, 254, 257, 258, 263 and 264, such holders are required to accept for such stock anything except: (a) stock of corporation surviving or resulting from merger or consolidation, (b) stock of any other corporation which at record date were either registered on national securities exchange or designated as national market system security on interdealer quotation system by National Association of Securities Dealers, Inc. or held of record by more than 2,000 stockholders, (c) cash in lieu of fractional shares of corporation described in (a) and (b), or (d) combination of stock and cash in lieu of fractional shares as set forth in (a), (b), and (c). (8-262[b][2]). Corporation in charter may provide for appraisal in transactions other than mergers. (8-262[c]).

Foreign Corporations.—No foreign corporation may do business in state until it files with Secretary of State a certificate evidencing its corporate existence and stating name and address of its registered agent, its assets and liabilities and authorized business it proposes to do in this state, and pays fee of $80. (8-371[b]). Secretary of State will insure name of foreign corporation is distinguishable from other entities in Delaware. (8-371[c]). Certificate of Secretary of State is prima facie evidence of company's right to do business in state. (8-371[c]).

Change of registered agent affected by filing certificate with Secretary of State listing name and address of registered agent and revocation of previous agents. (8-377[a]). Registered agent may resign by filing signed statement with Secretary of State including post office address of main or headquarters office. (8-377[b]). If registered agent dies or is not in state or resigns, foreign corporation must substitute, designate and certify to Secretary of State replacement within ten days. (8-377[c]). Certificate containing all charter amendments and all articles of merger or consolidation must be filed with Secretary of State within 30 days of amendment or merger. (8-372[a]-[b]).

Exceptions.—Foreign corporation is not deemed to be doing business in state and need not comply with 8-371 and 8-372 if it is mail order business accepting orders outside state; if it employs salesmen in state but approves orders outside state, with all goods shipped from outside state, and no sales, repairs, or replacements made from stock in state; if it delivers into state under contract made outside state equipment whose installation requires skilled supervision and furnishes such supervision as provided by contract; if it is any other business operation wholly interstate in character; if it is insurance company doing business in state; if it creates, as borrower or lender, or acquires evidences of debt, mortgages or liens on real or personal property; if it secures or collects debt or enforces any rights in property by securing same. (8-373).

Annual report must be filed on or before June 30 each year with Secretary of State. Report must be made by president, secretary, treasurer, or other authorized officer or by two directors or by any incorporator if directors not elected. Report must state address of registered office in Delaware and name of registered agent; address of main or headquarters place of business outside state; names and addresses of all directors and officers and their terms; date of next annual stockholder meeting for election of directors; number of shares of each class of authorized capital stock and par value if any; number of shares of each class actually issued; amount of capital invested in real and other property in state and tax paid thereon; if exempt from tax in state, specific facts entitling exemption. (8-374). Filing fee is $50, with $50 penalty for failure to file. (8-391[a][8]). Failure to file report within any two year period may result in termination of right to do business in state. (8-375).

Service of process upon qualified foreign corporation may be made on registered agent or, if there is no such agent, on any officer, director or other agent of corporation then in state. If such service is impossible, service may be made upon Secretary of State and additional $50 fee will be assessed to plaintiff. (8-376). Service of process upon corporation not qualified to do business in Delaware as foreign corporation, but transacting business in state may be made on Secretary of State. Provisions of 8-373 shall not apply in determining whether any non-qualifying foreign corporation is transacting business in state for purpose of service of process. (8-382).

Unqualified foreign corporation, doing business in this state, may not maintain any action or special proceeding in state until it has become authorized to do business in state and has paid state all fees, penalties and franchise taxes for period business done without authority. Failure to qualify will not prevent foreign corporation from defending any action or special proceeding in state or impair validity of any contract or act. (8-383).

Powers.—Foreign corporation with requisite certificate of incorporation or by-laws may act as executor, guardian, trustee or other fiduciary under testamentary instrument probated in state when and to extent that laws of its state of organization confer like powers on corporation organized in Delaware. (8-380). No foreign corporation shall have banking powers. (8-379). Foreign corporation owning lands in state may exercise all rights and privileges of ownership to same extent as if incorporated in state. (25-305).

Withdrawal.—Foreign corporation qualified to do business in state may withdraw by filing with Secretary of State address to which process against corporation may be mailed and (1) certificate executed in accordance with §103, surrendering authority to do business; or (2) certified copy of certificate of dissolution; or (3) certified copy of

See note at head of Digest as to 1998 legislation covered.

See Topical Index in front part of this volume.

DE – 6

CORPORATIONS . . . *continued*
order or decree of dissolution. (8-381). Filing tax and fees of $10 must be paid. (8-391[a][6]).

Penalties.—Chancery may enjoin any foreign corporation from doing business in state if corporation not qualified or if certificate of authority secured by false or misleading representations. (8-384). Foreign corporation doing business of any kind in state without complying with provisions for foreign corporations subject to fine of $200 to $500 for each offense. Agent of any foreign corporation doing any business in state before corporation has complied subject to fine of $100 to $500 for each offense. (8-378).

Filing of any required instrument with Secretary of State abolishes need to file with Recorder of Deeds of County. (8-385).

Franchise Tax.—(Contained in 8-c. 5). Every corporation must file franchise tax report with Secretary of State on or before first day of Mar. (8-502[a]). (For contents of report see subhead Reports, supra.) Filing fee $20. Corporate name reservation fee by telephone, $10. (8-391[a][17], [23]).

Following classes of corporations are exempt from general franchise tax: banking corporation, savings bank, building and loan association, religious, charitable, educational, or any corporation for drainage and reclamation of lowlands, or any company, association or society which exists to assist sick, needy or disabled, to defray funeral costs, or care for families after death. (8-501). Railroad car, telephone, cable and telegraph, express, insurance and utility and pipeline companies are subject to franchise taxes. (8-501). For banking organizations, franchise tax is calculated by multiplying .56 and net income and reduced by: (1) gross securities losses; (2) net income from foreign branch offices taxable elsewhere; (3) net income from international branch offices; (4) gross income from international transactions, minus deductions or expenses; (5) gross income of international banking facility; (6) interest income from volunteer fire companies; and (7) any examination fee paid to office of State Bank Commissioner. Franchise tax is imposed on "taxable income" of banks, trustees, and national banks. (5-1101). See category Business Regulation and Commerce, topic Banks and Banking, subhead Taxation.

Failure to file report or pay tax subjects corporation to tax amount in accordance with §503 as determined by Secretary of State, plus penalty of $50. (8-502[c]).

If corporation fails to make annual report and to pay franchise tax, Secretary of State may investigate and refer matter to Attorney General for proceedings under 8-284 for revocation of charter. (8-502[e]). Unpaid franchise tax will prevent issue of certificate of good standing. (8-502[g]).

If corporation neglects or refuses for period of one year to pay franchise taxes assessed against it, charter of corporation shall be void and all powers conferred by law upon corporation are declared inoperative, unless Secretary of State had given further time for good cause shown. (8-510).

Domestic corporations pay annual franchise tax to Secretary of State based on whichever of two following formulas results in smaller tax: (1) Where authorized capital stock does not exceed 3,000 shares, $30; where authorized capital stock exceeds 3,000 shares but is not more than 5,000 shares, $50; where authorized capital stock exceeds 5,000 shares but is not more than 10,000 shares, $90; and further sum of $50 on each 10,000 shares or part thereof; (2) $30, where assumed no-par capital of corporation does not exceed $300,000; $50 where assumed no-par capital exceeds $300,000 but is not more than $500,000; $90, where such assumed no-par capital exceeds $500,000 but is not more than $1,000,000; and further sum of $50 for each $1,000,000 or part thereof of such additional assumed no-par capital. "Assumed no-par capital" is determined by multiplying number of authorized shares of capital stock without par value by $100. To tax attributable to assumed no-par capital add tax of $200 on each $1,000,000 or fraction thereof in excess of $1,000,000 of assumed par value capital for par value shares; assumed par value capital arrived at by dividing total assets by total number of issued shares of all denominations, and multiplying resulting quotient by number of authorized par shares. When quotient is less than par value of any class of authorized par value shares, "assumed par value capital" is determined by multiplying number of shares of each class by par value, and number of authorized shares having par value to be multiplied by quotient shall be reduced by number of shares whose par value exceeds quotient; and where, to determine assumed par value capital, it is necessary to multiply class or classes of shares by quotient and also to multiply class or classes of shares by par value of shares, assumed par value capital of corporation shall be sum of products of multiplications. If total assumed par value capital is less than $1,000,000, tax bears same relation to $200 as assumed par value capital bears to $1,000,000. (8-503[a]). Minimum tax for any taxable year $30, maximum $150,000. (8-503[c]). "Total assets" are defined as those reported on IRS Form 1120 Schedule L or on replacement schedule designated by Secretary of State, if Schedule L is no longer in use. (8-503[i]).

Regulated investment company may compute its tax under (1) or (2) above or on basis of $200 per $1,000,000 of average gross assets or fraction thereof, whichever is least, but in no case is tax to exceed $65,000. (8-503[h]).

Inactive companies which have stated in their annual reports that they are not engaged in any business pay only one-half of usual tax for inactive period. (8-503[f]).

Taxes become payable on Mar. 1, except for corporations whose current estimated franchise tax liability is $5,000 or more, in which case return and tax payable quarterly based on preceding year's liability: 40% of estimated tax due 6/1, 20% due 9/1, 20% due 12/1, and 20% due 3/1. If unpaid on due dates, tax bears interest at 1½% per month thereafter. (8-504). Failure to pay taxes within one year voids charter. Secretary of State may allow extension of time for payment where good cause shown, in which case certificate must be filed stating reason for failure to pay. (8-510).

Where entire assets of corporation are in unfriendly country from which it is impossible to remove them or withdraw income or with which communication is illegal, tax may be abated at Secretary of State's discretion. (8-518).

Income Tax.—See category Taxation, topic Income Tax.

Professional Corporations.—May be formed by persons performing personal services to public which require obtaining of a license or other legal authorization and which formerly by reason of law could not be performed by corporation. Such persons may include architects, certified or other public accountants, chiropodists, chiropractors, dentists, doctors of medicine, optometrists, osteopaths, professional engineers, veterinarians, and, subject to Supreme Court Rules, attorneys. (8-601, 603). Other than rendering professional services for which it specifically incorporated, owning real estate or making investments or mortgages, professional corporations may not conduct any business. (8-609).

Deeds.—See category Property, topic Deeds.

Model Non-Profit Corporation Act not adopted.

Limited Liability Companies.—See topic Limited Liability Companies.

JOINT STOCK COMPANIES:

Business Trusts.—Recognized by statute as alternative form of business organization designed primarily as means of protecting and managing property. (12-3801[a]). Substantial contractual flexibility permitted in structuring of governing instrument. (12-3801[f]). At least one trustee must be resident of State or have principal place of business in State unless business trust is registered investment company. (12-3807[a], [b]). Each business trust must file certificate of trust with Secretary of State, signed by all trustees (12-3811), containing name of trust, name and business address of at least one trustee meeting requirements of 12-3807, and effective date of certificate if not effective upon filing. (12-3810). Filing fee is $100. (12-3813[a][2]). Certificate cancelled upon completion of winding up and termination of trust, and certificate of cancellation or amendment must be filed with Secretary of State. (12-3810[d]). Name of trust may be reserved. (12-3814[d]).

LIMITED LIABILITY COMPANIES:

Delaware Limited Liability Company Act ("Act") effective Oct. 1, 1992, permits formation of limited liability company ("LLC"). (6-18-101-1109).

Certificate of Formation Requirements.—One or more persons may form LLC. (18-101). To form, one or more authorized persons must execute certificate of formation ("Certificate"), which must be filed with Secretary of State ("Secretary"). Certificate must state LLC's (a) name, (b) address of registered office and name and address of registered agent for service of process, and (c) other desired provisions. (18-201).

Name.—LLC's name must include words "Limited Liability Company" or abbreviation, "L.L.C." or designation "LLC". LLC's name must be distinguishable from name filed by any other entity reserved, registered, formed or organized under Delaware law or qualified to do business or registered as foreign corporation, foreign limited partnership or foreign LLC in Delaware, unless written consent of other entity is obtained and filed with Secretary. (18-102). Name may be reserved by filing executed application and filing fee of $75 (18-1105[a][1]) with Secretary (18-103).

Purpose.—LLC may carry on any lawful business purpose other than banking or insurance operations whether or not for profit. (18-106).

Registered Office and Registered Agent.—LLC must maintain registered office in Delaware. LLC must maintain resident agent in Delaware to accept service of process. Agent's office must be identical with LLC's registered office and must be open during normal business hours. Change of address of LLC's registered office or of identity of LLC's registered agent must be filed with Secretary along with fee of $50. (18-104; 18-1105[a][2]).

Amending Certificate.—Amendment of Certificate must state (a) name of LLC and (b) amendment to Certificate. Certificate of amendment is filed with Secretary and is effective on filing date, unless later time is specified.

False statements or outdated information in Certificate must be amended promptly by manager, or, if there is no manager, by any member aware of error or change. (18-202).

Powers.—LLC may carry on any lawful business, purpose or activity except insurance or banking operations. LLC may exercise all powers and privileges granted by Act or any other law or by its limited liability company agreement ("Agreement"), together with any powers incidental thereto. (18-106).

Limited Liability Company Agreement.—Written or oral agreement of member or members as to affairs of LLC and conduct of its business. (18-101). Any action to interpret, apply, or enforce Agreement, duties of LLC to managers and members, duties of managers and members to LLC, duties among managers and members, or rights and restrictions of LLC may be brought in Court of Chancery. (18-111).

Limited Liability Company Interest.—LLC interest ("Interest") is member's share of profits and losses of LLC and member's right to receive distributions of LLC's assets. (18-101).

Limited Liability.—Unless Agreement provides otherwise, no member or manager of LLC is personally liable for LLC's obligations solely by reason of being member or manager. (18-303).

Management.—Unless otherwise provided in Agreement, LLC shall be managed by its members in proportion to their then current percentage or other interest in LLC's profits owned by all of members, with decision of those owning more than 50% of such percentage or interest controlling. Agreement may provide for management, in whole or in part, by manager, chosen by members as provided in Agreement. Unless Agreement provides otherwise, each member and manager has authority to bind LLC. LLC may have more than one manager. (18-402). Manager who is also member has rights and powers, and is subject to restrictions and liabilities, of manager and, except as provided in Agreement, is subject to restrictions and liabilities of member to extent of his participation in LLC as member. (18-403). Agreement may provide for classes or groups of managers and specify their relative rights, powers and duties. Agreement may provide for taking of action, including amendment of Agreement, without vote or approval of any manager or class or group of managers. Unless prohibited by agreement, managers may take action by written consent to act by proxy. (18-404).

Manager and member are protected by good faith reliance on LLC's records, and upon other information presented to LLC by any of its managers, members, officers, committees or employees, or by any other person, as to matters manager reasonably

LIMITED LIABILITY COMPANIES . . . *continued*
believes are within such person's professional or expert competence and who has been selected with reasonable care by or on behalf of LLC. (18-406). Agreement may specify penalties or consequences for failure of manager to comply with terms of Agreement or upon happening of specified events. (18-405).

Upon application of member or manager, Court of Chancery may determine validity of admission, election, appointment, or withdrawal of manager as well as right of person or persons to serve as managers. (18-110). Unless Agreement provides otherwise, members and managers may delegate rights and powers to manage and control. (18-407). Such delegation shall not alter manager's or member's power to control LLC.

Members.—Person may become member of LLC and receive interest therein without making contribution or being obligated to make contribution to LLC. Unless Agreement provides otherwise, person may become member without acquiring interest in LLC. (18-301). Contribution of member to LLC may be in cash, property, services or promissory note or other obligation to contribute cash, property or services. (18-501). Member failing to contribute agreed property or services for any reason must, at option of LLC, contribute cash equal to agreed value (as stated in LLC's records) of contribution not made. Unless Agreement provides otherwise, member's obligation to make contribution or return money or other property paid or distributed in violation of this chapter may be compromised only by consent of all other members. Creditors may under certain circumstances enforce member's obligation to make contribution or return money or other property to LLC regardless of consented compromise. Member's LLC interest may be reduced for failure to pay contribution obligation if agreement so provides. (18-502).

Profits and losses of LLC shall be allocated among members, and among classes or groups of members, as provided in Agreement. In absence of Agreement, profits and losses shall be allocated on basis of agreed value (as stated in LLC's records) of contributions made by each member to extent received by LLC and not returned. (18-503).

Unless Agreement provides otherwise, distributions shall be made to members, and among classes or group of members on basis of agreed value (as stated in LLC's records) of contributions made by each member to extent received by LLC and not returned. (18-504). No obligation of member or manager to LLC shall be subject to defense of usury. (18-505).

Distribution not allowed if, after distribution, all liabilities of LLC, other than liabilities to members on account of their interests and liabilities for which recourse of creditors is limited to specified property of LLC, exceed fair value of its assets, except that fair value of property subject to liability for which recourse of creditors is limited must be included in assets of LLC only to extent that fair value of that property exceeds that liability. If member knowingly receives improper distribution, LLC may recover amount for up to three years. (18-607). After three years such member shall not be subject to liability under this chapter unless action to recover sum was commenced before expiration of three-year period and such member was found liable as result of that action.

Member's interest is personal property and member has no interest in specific property of LLC. (18-701). Member's interest is assignable in whole or in part except as provided in Agreement. Unless provided in Agreement, assignment of interest does not entitle assignee to become or exercise any rights of member; however assignment entitles assignee to share in such profits, losses, distributions, allocation of income, gain, loss, deduction or credit or similar item to which assignor was entitled, to extent assigned. Member ceases to be member and to have power to exercise any rights or powers of member upon assignment of all his interest. Unless Agreement provides otherwise, pledge of, or granting of security interest, lien or other encumbrance in or against any or all of interest of member shall not cause member to lose membership or power to exercise any rights or powers thereof. Agreement may state that interest in LLC may be provided by certificate of membership issued by LLC. Unless agreement provides otherwise, assignee is not liable as member solely because of assignment. Unless Agreement provides otherwise, LLC may acquire any interest of member or manager, after which interest will be deemed canceled. (18-702). Assignee of member may become member as provided in Agreement and upon (a) approval of all members of LLC other than assignor, or (b) compliance with any procedure specified in Agreement. (18-704). Assignee who becomes member has rights and powers to extent assigned and is subject to restrictions and liabilities as provided in Agreement. Assignee-member is subject to assignor's liability to make contribution under 18-502, but not under subchapter VI of this chapter. Assignee not subject to liabilities including that of assignor to make contribution under 18-502 if assignee did not know about obligations at time he became member and such obligations could not be ascertained from Agreement.

Service of Process, Manager or Member.—Manager or liquidating trustee may be served with process even if he is not manager or liquidating partner at time suit is commenced. Serving as manager or liquidating trustee is consent to appointment of LLC's registered agent, or Secretary of State being such person's agent upon whom service of process may be made. Serving as manager or liquidating trustee shall also constitute consent that service of process in compliance with this section is valid and of legal force as if served upon such manager or liquidating trustee. (18-109[a]). In Agreement or other writing, manager or member may consent to non-exclusive jurisdiction of courts of, or arbitration in, specified jurisdiction, or exclusive jurisdiction of courts of, or exclusivity of arbitration in, Delaware, and to be served with legal process in manner prescribed in such Agreement or writing. (18-109[d]).

Records.—Member may, subject to reasonable standards as set forth in Agreement or otherwise established by manager or, if no manager, then by members, obtain from LLC upon reasonable demand for any purpose reasonably related to member's interest as member of LLC: (a) information regarding status of LLC's business and financial condition, (b) LLC's federal, state and local income tax returns for each year, (c) current list of name and last known business, residence or mailing address of each member and manager, (d) copy of any written Agreement and Certificate and amendments thereto, as well as copies of any written powers of attorney by which such documents have been executed, (e) information regarding amount of cash and description and statement of agreed value of any other property or services contributed by each member and which each member has agreed to contribute in future, and date on which each became member, and (f) any other information that is reasonable. (18-305[a]). Manager may also examine any of foregoing for purpose reasonably related to his position as manager. (18-305[b]).

Manager may keep confidential from members for reasonable period of time any information which manager reasonably believes to be in nature of trade secrets or other information disclosure of which manager in good faith believes is not in best interest of LLC or could damage LLC or its business or which LLC is required by law or agreement with third party to keep confidential. (18-305[c]).

Any action to enforce any right under §18-305 shall be brought in Court of Chancery which is vested with exclusive jurisdiction to determine whether person seeking information under §18-305 is entitled to such information. (18-305[f]). Court of Chancery may order LLC to permit member access to information of subsection (a) (3) on condition that member first pay cost of obtaining information. Court may impose other conditions, limitations and restrictions it finds appropriate.

Derivative Actions.—Member may bring action in Court of Chancery on behalf of LLC to recover judgment in its favor if: (a) managers or members with authority to do so have refused to bring action; or (b) if effort to cause those members or managers to bring action is not likely to succeed (18-1001); and (c) plaintiff is member at time of bringing suit; and (d) plaintiff is member at time of transaction of which he complains; or (e) plaintiff's status devolved upon him by operation of law or by terms of Agreement from person who was member at time of transaction. (18-1002). Complaint shall state with particularity effort, if any, of plaintiff to secure initiation of action by manager or reasons for not making such effort. (18-1003). If derivative action is successful, in whole or in part, by judgment, compromise or settlement, court may award plaintiff reasonable expenses, including attorney's fees, from any recovery in such action or from LLC. (18-1004).

Resignation.—Member may resign from LLC only at time and in manner specified in Agreement. Unless provided for in Agreement, member may not resign prior to dissolution and winding up of LLC. (18-603). Upon resignation from LLC, member is entitled to receive such distribution as is provided in Agreement. Except as otherwise provided, member shall receive, within reasonable time after resignation, fair value of his interest as of date of resignation based upon his right to share in distributions from LLC. (18-604).

Voting.—Agreement may provide for classes or groups of members and their relative rights, powers and duties. Agreement may grant to all or certain identified members or specified class or group of members right to vote separately or with all or any class or group of members or managers, on any matter. Voting by members may be on per capita, number, financial interest, class, group or any other basis. Agreement may provide for taking of action, including amendment to Agreement, without vote or approval of any member or class or group of members. Unless otherwise provided, members may vote by proxy or in person. (18-302). Upon application of member or manager, Court of Chancery may determine results of any vote pursuant to Agreement. (18-110). Court may also determine appointment, election, removal or resignation of LLC manager.

Merger and Consolidation.—LLC may merge with or into one or more domestic LLC or "other business entities" formed or organized under laws of Delaware or any other state or foreign country or other foreign jurisdiction, with such domestic LLC or other business entity as agreement shall provide being surviving or resulting domestic LLC or other business entity. Unless Agreement provides otherwise, merger or consolidation must be approved by members or, if there is more than one class or group of members, then by each class or groups of members, in either case, by members who own more than 50% of then current percentage or other interest in LLC's profits owned by all members or by members in each class or group interests, rights or securities of domestic LLC may be exchanged for same in entity resulting from merger or consolidation. Entity surviving or resulting in or from merger must file certificate of merger or consolidation with Secretary and include detailed information required by Act. If certificate calls for future effective date and Agreement is subsequently terminated or amended to change date, then certificate must be filed so indicating. Upon effectiveness of merger, surviving or resulting entity succeeds to all rights, powers and privileges, and all property, real, personal and mixed, and all debts, of merged entities, as well as all other things and causes of action belonging to such merged entities. Unless otherwise agreed, merger or consolidation of domestic LLC shall not require that LLC wind up its affairs under §18-303 or pay its liabilities and distribute its assets under §18-804. (18-209). Corrections to defective, inaccurate certificates may be filed in certificate of correction or new corrected certificate may be filed. (18-211).

Agreement may provide for contractual appraisal rights available to any class or group of members in connection with LLC agreements, mergers, consolidations or sale of all or substantially all LLC's assets. (18-210).

Domestication.—Non-U.S. entity may become domesticated LLC upon approval of jurisdiction governing internal affairs of entity and upon filing with Secretary certificate of domestication which states: (i) Date on which and jurisdiction where entity came into being; (ii) name of entity immediately prior to filing of certificate of domestication; (iii) name of limited liability company set forth in certificate of formation that complies with §18-201 and has been executed by one or more authorized persons in accordance with §18-204; (iv) future effective date of domestication as LLC if not to be effective upon filing of certificate of domestication; and (v) jurisdiction that constituted seat, siege social, or principal place of business of non-U.S. entity immediately prior to filing of certification of domestication. (18-212). Domestication as U.S. LLC is not deemed to affect obligation and liabilities of entity prior to domestication.

Transfer.—Domestic LLC may transfer to any jurisdiction, other than any state, that permits transfer to, domestication or continuance in such jurisdiction of LLC, and, in connection therewith, may elect to continue as domestic LLC, which must be approved in writing by all of managers and members of LLC, and which shall occur

See note at head of Digest as to 1998 legislation covered.

See Topical Index in front part of this volume.

DE – 8

LIMITED LIABILITY COMPANIES . . . *continued*
upon filing of certificate of transfer or certificate of transfer and continuance with Secretary which shall state: (i) name of LLC; (ii) date of filing of original certificate of formation; (iii) jurisdiction to which LLC shall transfer or be domesticated; (iv) future effective date or time of transfer or domestication, if not upon filing of certificate; (v) approval of transfer or continuance in accordance with §18-213; (vi) agreement to service of process in Delaware and appointment of Secretary as agent to accept service of process; (vii) address to which service of process shall be sent by Secretary; and (viii) in case of continuance as domestic LLC, statement of continuance. (18-213). Transfer or domestication out of Delaware does not affect liabilities incurred prior to transfer.

Conversion.—Any other entity, other than incorporated business, may convert to domestic LLC upon: (i) approval of LLC agreement in matter provided for by document governing internal affairs of entity; (ii) filing of certificate of conversion to LLC that has been executed by one or more authorized persons in accordance with §18-204; and (iii) filing of certificate of formation that complies with §18-201 and has been executed by one or more authorized persons in accordance with §18-204. (18-214).

Service of Members.—LLC agreement may establish or provide for establishment of designated series of members, managers or LLC interests having separate rights, powers and duties with respect to specified property, losses or obligations of LLC. (18-215).

Conversion from LLC.—LLC may convert to other business entity as authorized by LLC agreement if not included or prohibited by LLC agreement, by approval of members, or if more than one class or group of members then by each group or class of members, each of which must own more than 50% of then current percentage or other interest in profits of LLC owned by all of members or by members in each class or group. (18-216).

Dissolution and Winding Up.—LLC is dissolved and its affairs wound up upon first to occur of following: (a) expiration of period stated in Agreement; (b) happening of events specified in Agreement; (c) unless Agreement provides otherwise, written consent of members, or, if more than one class or group of members, then by each group or class of members, in either case, by members who own more than two-thirds of then current percentage or other interest in profits of LLC owned by members in each class or group; (d) at such time as there are no members, provided that, unless otherwise provided in Agreement, personal representative of last member agrees in writing to continue LLC and to admit personal representative of last member or its nominee or designee as member of LLC within 90 days of event that terminated membership of last member or other such period provided for in Agreement. Unless otherwise provided, death, resignation, bankruptcy or dissolution of any member shall not result in winding up of LLC's affairs; upon occurrence of such event LLC shall continue with dissolution unless after 90 days LLC members or those who own more than 50% interest agree in writing to dissolve LLC (18-801); (e) entry of decree of judicial dissolution upon application by or for member or manager. (18-801, 802). Unless Agreement provides otherwise, manager who has not wrongfully dissolved LLC or, if none, members or person approved by members, in either case, by members who own more than 50% percent of the then current percentage or other interest in profits of LLC owned by all members or by members in each class or group, as appropriate, may wind up LLC's affairs. Court of Chancery may wind up LLC's affairs upon application of any member or manager, his representative or assignee, and upon cause shown. Court may appoint liquidating trustee in connection therewith. (18-803[a]). Upon winding up, assets distributed in following order: (a) to creditors of LLC, including members or managers who are creditors, to extent otherwise permitted by law, in satisfaction of liabilities of LLC (whether by payment or reasonable provision for payment thereof) other than liabilities for distributions to members and former members under 18-601 ("Interim distributions") and 18-604 ("Distributions upon resignation"); (b) unless Agreement provides otherwise, to members and former members in satisfaction of liabilities for distributions under 18-601 and 18-604; (c) unless Agreement provides otherwise, return of members' contributions and subsequently respecting their interests, in proportions in which members share in distributions. Dissolved LLC shall pay or make provision to pay all known claims and obligations. If assets are insufficient to pay them in full, such claims and obligations shall be paid or provided for according to their priority. Liquidating trustee shall not be liable (personally) to claimants of dissolved LLC. (18-804). Certificate of formation shall be cancelled upon dissolution and completion of winding up. Upon dissolution and completion of winding up or upon conversion of domestic LLC under 18-216, certificate of cancellation shall be filed with Secretary containing: (a) name of LLC; (b) date Certificate was filed; (c) reason for cancelling; (d) future effective time of cancellation, if not upon time of filing; (e) any other information person filing for cancellation determines. (18-203).

Foreign LLC Qualification.—Foreign LLC's internal affairs and liability of its members and managers governed by law of state, territory, possession, or other jurisdiction or country of organization. Foreign LLC will not be denied registration in Delaware based on any difference between laws of LLC's place of organization and Delaware law. Foreign LLC may carry on same business, purpose or activity and shall possess same powers and privileges, together with any powers incidental thereto, as Act grants to domestic LLCs. (18-901). Before doing business in Delaware, foreign LLC must register with Secretary. To register, foreign LLC must pay requisite fee and set forth: (a) its name and, if different, name under which it proposes to register and do business in Delaware; (b) state, territory, possession or other jurisdiction or country where formed; (c) date of its formation; (d) statement by authorized person attesting to its validity under laws of its state as of filing date; (e) nature of business or purposes to be conducted or promoted in Delaware; (f) address of registered office and name and address of registered agent to receive service of process; (g) statement appointing Secretary as its agent for service of process; (h) date it first did or intends to do business in Delaware. (18-902).

Construction and Application of Chapter and LLC Agreement.—Rule that statutes in derogation of common law are to be strictly construed does not apply to this chapter. Policy of chapter is to give maximum effect to principle of freedom of contract and to enforceability of Agreements. (18-1101).

To extent that, at law or in equity, member or manager or other person has duties (including fiduciary duties) and liabilities relating thereto to LLC or to another member or manager: (a) any such member or manager or other person acting under Agreement shall not be liable to LLC or to any such other member or manager for member's or manager's or other person's good faith reliance on provisions of Agreement; and (b) member's or manager's or other person's duties and liabilities may be expanded or restricted by provisions in Agreement. (18-1101).

PARTNERSHIPS:

Uniform Partnership Act has been adopted. (6-c.15).

Registered Limited Liability Partnerships.—Delaware Registered Limited Liability Partnership Act adopted and became effective Aug. 1, 1994. (6-1502; 6-1544). Delaware registered limited liability partnership ("DLLP") is type of general partnership in which all partners are liable for all contractual debts and obligations of partnership, but partner is not personally liable either directly or indirectly, by way of indemnification, contribution, assessment or otherwise, for debts, obligations and liabilities of or chargeable to partnership or another partner or partners, whether arising in contract, tort, or otherwise. (6-1502[7]; 6-1515[a], [b]). Partner, however, remains personally liable for his or her own negligence, wrongful act, or misconduct or negligence, wrongful act, or misconduct of person under his or her direct supervision or control. (6-1515[c]).

In addition to requirements for forming general partnership (6-c.15), in order to form and organize DLLP, application must be filed with Delaware Secretary of State and renewal application must be filed on annual basis to maintain this special status (6-1544[a], [b]). Partnership becomes registered limited liability partnership at time of filing or on date specified in application. DLLP must also pay fee of $100 per partner per year with maximum annual registration fee of $120,000 per partnership. (6-1544[c]). DLLP must carry minimum of $1,000,000 of liability insurance or specifically designate and segregate $1,000,000 of funds, in form designated by statute, for satisfaction of judgments against partnership or its partners based on kinds of negligence for which liability is limited. (6-1546[a], [d]). DLLP must have registered agent and office in Delaware. (6-1549).

Name of DLLP must be registered with Delaware Secretary of State. Name must include words "Registered Limited Liability Partnership", "LLP", or "L.L.P." as last words or letters of its name. Name of LLP must be such as to distinguish it from other DE business entities; may register under similar or identical name only with written consent of other entity. Right to exclusive name may be transferred or cancelled to another person by filing notice of transfer or cancellation with Secretary of State. (6-1545). DLLP can reserve exclusive right to name for renewable periods of 120 days for $75 fee. (6-1548). DLLP is not required to comply with Delaware trade names statute. (6-1544[h]).

Registration of General Partnership Name.—See category Intellectual Property, topic Trademarks and Tradenames.

Limited Partnerships.—Revised Uniform Limited Partnership Act adopted with certain modernizing modifications. (6-c.17). Limited partnership ("LP") may engage in any lawful business, purpose, or activity, whether or not for profit, except granting policies of insurance, assuming insurance risks, and banking. (6-17-106[a]). LP may indemnify and hold harmless partners or other persons subject to provisions of LP agreement. (6-17-108).

LP agreement may be written or oral, and may provide that person may be admitted as limited partner or may become assignee of LP interest, and become bound by LP agreement, by execution of LP agreement or any writing evidencing intent to be bound by LP agreement, or by compliance with conditions for becoming limited partner or assignee in LP agreement and request that LP records reflect such admission or assignment. Such request may be made orally, in writing or by other act such as payment for LP interest. (6-17-101[11]).

Certificate of LP must be executed by all general partners. Limited partners need not execute certificate. Certificate must state name of LP, address of registered office, name and address of registered agent for service of process, and name and address of each general partner. (6-17-201).

Merger or consolidation of domestic LP with or into one or more LPs or other business entities is permitted, pursuant to agreement of merger or consolidation. Merger must be approved by all GPs and LPs; if more than one class or group of LPs, then by each group/class or those who own more than 50% of interests of limited partnership owned by limited partners. Surviving entity must file certificate of merger or consolidation with Secretary of State. Domestic LP or other business entity, as agreement provides, shall be surviving or resulting domestic LP or other business entity. (6-17-211).

Broad voting rights may be exercised by limited partners, under statutory "safe harbors" or pursuant to LP agreement or other agreement, without limited partners being deemed as participating in control of business of LP. (6-17-303). Limited partner has right, enforceable by Chancery Court, to LP information reasonably related to interest as limited partner, except that trade secrets or other confidential information may be withheld by general partners. (6-17-305). Classes or groups of limited partners, with varying rights and powers, permitted pursuant to LP agreement. (6-17-302).

Admission of additional general partner after filing of LP's initial certificate requires consent of all partners, unless LP agreement provides otherwise. (6-17-401). General partner ceases to be general partner upon occurrence of statutorily-defined "event of withdrawal". (6-17-402). General partner may contractually modify liability to other partners and to LP. (6-17-403). Classes or groups of general partners, with varying rights and powers, permitted pursuant to LP agreement. (6-17-405). General partner may withdraw from LP upon occurrence of events specified in partnership agreement or with written notice at any time, notwithstanding 6-17-402, though LP may recover against such partner if withdrawal violates LP agreement. Agreement may state that GP does not have right to withdraw. (6-17-602).

See note at head of Digest as to 1998 legislation covered.

See Topical Index in front part of this volume.

DE – 9

PARTNERSHIPS . . . *continued*

Failure to make required contribution to LP may result in penalty to partner's interest in LP, or in specific performance against partner, pursuant to LP agreement. (6-17-502). Contribution may be cash, property, services rendered, or obligation to contribute same. (6-17-501). LP agreement may provide for allocations of profits and losses, and distributions of cash and assets to partners. (6-17-503, 504).

Wrongful distribution to partner who knew that distribution violated statute makes partner liable to LP for amount of distribution. (6-17-607).

Assignment of LP interest, in whole or in part, may be governed by LP agreement. (6-17-702). Assignment does not dissolve LP or give assignee rights and powers of partner, but gives assignee right to distributions and share in profit and losses to extent assigned. Assignee may become limited partner pursuant to LP agreement or if all partners consent. (6-17-704).

Dissolution of LP may occur: (i) upon events specified in LP agreement; (ii) by written agreement of all general partners, and consent of limited partners, or if more than one class or group of limited partners, then by each class or group, in either case, by limited partners who own more than two-thirds of then current percentage or other interests in profits of LP; (iii) following withdrawal of general partner, and remaining general partners, if any, may not, pursuant to LP agreement, or do not, continue LP; provided that, LP agreement may permit majority of limited partners to appoint new general partner and continue business; or (iv) by entry of decree of judicial dissolution or there are no limited partners at time. (6-17-801, 802). Upon application of partner, Chancery Court may appoint liquidating trustee for purpose of winding up business. (6-17-803). Dissolved LP must pay, or establish reasonable reserves for payment of, all claims and obligations known or unknown likely to become known to LP within ten years after date of dissolution. Liquidating trustee winding up LP's affairs in compliance with this section shall not be personally liable to claimants of LP because of his actions in winding up of partnership affairs. (6-17-804[b]). Certificate of cancellation of LP must be filed with Secretary of State. (6-17-203).

Foreign LP must register with Secretary of State before doing business in State. (6-17-902[a]). Foreign LP or other foreign business entity is not deemed to be doing business in State solely by reason of its being partner in domestic LP. (6-17-902[b]).

Derivative action may be brought in Chancery Court by limited partner if general partners have refused to bring action or effort to cause general partners or assignee of limited partner to bring action is futile. (6-17-1001).

Annual tax of $100 required of each domestic LP and foreign LP registered to do business in State. (6-17-1109). Failure to pay tax shall result in both loss of good standing and right of access to courts (6-17-1109[g], [k]) and may result in loss of right to transact business in State (6-17-1109[i]).

BUSINESS REGULATION AND COMMERCE

BANKS AND BANKING:

Uniform Commercial Code adopted. (6-Art. 4). See topic Commercial Code.

Regulation by.—Banks and trust companies are regulated by Tit. 5.

Banks and trust companies except savings banks and national banks, are created under corporation law for State banks and trust companies. (5-701). Banking powers may not be exercised by corporations formed under general corporation law (8-126) or by foreign corporations (8-379). Any bank or trust company, if authorized by charter, may open Delaware branch office upon authorization of State Bank Commissioner. (5-770[a][1]). Any bank or trust company having paid-in capital and surplus exceeding $1,000,000 may open branch office outside state upon issuance of certificate by State Bank Commissioner. (5-771[a]). Banks and trust companies are allowed reasonable time to commence business. (5-734).

Exercise of bank powers is subject to regulation by State Bank Commissioner. (5-761[b]).

Minimum of three persons, including two Delaware citizens and residents, required to create corporation to form bank or trust company. (5-722).

Banks and trust companies doing business in Delaware may not merge or consolidate with other banks or trust companies without approval by State Bank Commissioner. (5-751[a]).

No acquisition of any Delaware bank or trust company is permitted without minimum of 60 days prior written notice of such proposed change in control to State Bank Commissioner, who shall have authority to approve or disapprove such acquisitions. (5-160[a]).

Stockholders.—Private property of stockholders not subject to payment of corporate debts unless otherwise provided in articles of association. (5-747). No stock issued until par value fully paid in cash, and no business transacted until all stock subscribed for and paid for in cash. (5-746).

Deposits.—Deposits for minors, decedents, joint deposits (payable to either or to survivor), and deposits in trust governed by 5-920, 922-924.

Unclaimed Deposits.—See category Property, topic Absentees, subhead Escheat.

Collections.—Uniform Commercial Code adopted. (6-4-301-303).

Trust Companies.—General powers of corporation organized under 5-c.7 set forth at 5-761. Trust companies established under 5-c. 7 authorized to act as fiduciaries (5-765) and as corporate agents (5-766).

Uniform Common Trust Fund Act not adopted, but common fund investments by bank or trust company authorized to act as fiduciary are permitted in accordance with statutory regulations. (12-3307[a]).

Foreign Banks.—Banking powers generally denied to foreign corporations. (8-379). However, under certain conditions, foreign banks may transact business in State. Foreign bank authorized by its charter and under laws of its country of organization may apply to State Bank Commissioner for certificate of authority to establish and maintain foreign bank agency. (5-1402, 1403). Such authorized foreign banks may engage in general banking business subject to statutory and administrative restrictions on authority to exercise fiduciary powers and to engage in general deposit-taking business. (5-1404). In addition, foreign banks with U.S. branches may engage in interstate branching by merger with Delaware banks in same manner as out-of-state banks. (5-1432, 1433). Foreign bank's ability to compete with existing banking institutions in State subject to restrictions. (5-1403).

Credit Card Institutions.—State chartered credit card institutions are allowed if they engage only in credit card operations, do not accept demand deposits or deposits that depositor may withdraw by check or similar means for payment to third parties or others, do not accept any savings or time deposits of less than $100,000, maintain only one office that accepts deposits, do not engage in business of making commercial loans, and are excepted from definition of "bank" in Bank Holding Company Act of 1956, as am'd, 12 U.S.C. §1841 et seq. (5-1501). Effective Sept. 29, 1997, these credit card institutions may convert to banks, upon filing application with State Bank Commissioner. (5-1544, 793).

Securities Powers.—Bank or trust company may engage in sale, distribution and underwriting of, and deal in, stocks, bonds, debentures, notes or other securities. (5-761[a][12]). Such securities activity is not subject to investment limitations on banks and trust companies. (5-910[2]).

Investments.—Bank or trust company may without approval of State Bank Commissioner invest up to 50% of its capital, surplus, and undivided profit in real estate suitable for conduct of its business. Such amount includes money invested in other organizations holding real estate for use in conduct of business, but excludes any investment made prior to July 1, 1933. (5-762-911).

No bank or trust company shall hold more than 10% of capital stock of any other bank or trust company without approval of State Bank Commissioner. (5-769).

Acquisition of Existing Savings Banks.—Under certain conditions, out-of-state savings institution, out-of-state savings and loan holding company or out-of-state bank holding company (or any subsidiary of such institution) may acquire Delaware savings bank or a Delaware savings and loan holding company. (5-832). Any institution proposing to make such acquisition must apply to State Bank Commissioner for approval. (5-832, 833).

Agency.—Delaware state bank can act as agent on behalf of any affiliated insured depository institution with approval of State Bank Commissioner. (5-796A).

Loans to person or association are limited to percentage of lender's total capital. (5-909[a]). Limit does not apply to loans secured or guaranteed by U.S. or State obligations, or those secured by certain commercial instruments or segregated deposit. Limit also does not apply to loans arising from discount of commercial or consumer paper or to sale of federal funds to F.D.I.C. insured banks or to purchase of securities under agreement to resell. (5-909[b]). Bank or trust company may make loans to directors and executive officers in amounts exceeding lesser of $500,000 or 5% of bank's total capital only after borrowers submit statement of financial condition and loan is approved by majority of whole board of directors or majority of whole empowered committee. (5-909[d]).

Delaware and federal banks may extend credit under revolving credit plan and may take such security as collateral as may be acceptable to bank. No borrower loan limits, unless imposed by charter or law. (5-942). Periodic interest may be charged pursuant to plan agreement (5-943), and bank may apply variable interest rates to all outstanding balances (5-944). In addition to or in lieu of interest, bank may impose membership fee, transaction charges, periodic charge for period of outstanding credit, service fees, expensive reimbursements or other fees incident to plan, returned payment charges, documentary evidence charges, stop payment fees, over-limit charges, prepayment charges authorized by 5-945(b), automated teller machine charges, and any other fees and charges set forth in plan, subject to limitations of 5-c.9. (5-945[a]). None of aforementioned charges imposed in addition to or in lieu of interest shall be deemed void as penalty or otherwise unenforceable. (5-945[c]). Different terms on purchase and loan balances may be utilized. (5-946). If bank provides overdraft checking, customary charges imposed on negative balances chargeable to borrower's account may be treated as loan even if charge not mentioned in plan agreement. (5-947). Bank may allow borrower to defer monthly installments (5-948), require borrowers under listed circumstances to obtain insurance (5-949), charge any borrower late fee as interest for delinquent installments (5-950), collect attorneys' fees and costs of collection, where agreement so provides (5-951), amend terms of plan if agreement so provides, and upon borrower's continued use, apply changes to entire outstanding balance (5-952).

Delaware and federal banks may extend closed-end credit subject to bank charter and legal limitations. (5-962). Periodic interest may be charged pursuant to loan agreement (5-963), and variable interest rates may apply to all outstanding balances pursuant to agreement (5-964). In addition to or in lieu of periodic interest, bank may charge loan fees, points, finders' fees, front-end and periodic charges (but in case of individual borrower, agreement must provide for such charges), returned payment charges, documentary evidence charges and fees for services rendered or expenses incurred by bank in connection with loan. (5-965). Bank may permit borrower to defer installment payments and charge as interest deferral charges (5-966), may require borrowers under listed circumstances to obtain insurance (5-967), may charge late fee for payments in default; individual borrower pays late fee only if agreement so provides (5-968). Bank may charge individual borrower for attorneys' fees and collection costs where agreement so provides. (5-971). If individual borrower fully prepays loan bearing precomputed interest, bank must refund unearned interest as calculated under actuarial method (5-969[b]); individual borrower not subject to prepayment charge except as provided in residential mortgage loan agreement (5-969[e]). Terms of loans to nonindividual borrowers regarding extended or deferred payment, prepayment and refinancing charges, late charges, attorneys' fees, and collection costs are matters of contract. (5-972).

All terms, conditions, and other provisions relating to plan or in agreement governing plan, other than those which are interest under revolving credit and closed-end credit subchapters, are deemed material terms. (5-955, 975).

See note at head of Digest as to 1998 legislation covered.

See Topical Index in front part of this volume.

DE – 10

BANKS AND BANKING . . . continued

Revolving credit plans between bank and individual borrower, and agreement, bond, note, or other evidence of loan between bank and individual borrower are governed by Delaware law. (5-956, 976).

Regulation of mortgage loan brokers governed by 5-c.21.

Merger, Consolidation and Conversion.—State or national bank may merge or convert into resulting national bank pursuant to approval by 2/3 of each class of voting stock of state bank. (5-782). Any dissenting shareholders shall have right to receive value of their shares at time of merger in cash, value to be determined by appraisal. (5-788).

State or national bank may merge to result in Delaware state bank or national bank may convert into Delaware state bank. (5-783). Merger requires approval from board of directors of each merging bank (5-784[a]) and State Bank Commissioner (5-784[b]). Commissioner approval automatic if no action taken within 30 days. (5-784[c]). Following approval, procedure for merger will be in manner prescribed by c. 1 of Title 8 which governs merger or consolidation of Delaware corporations. (5-785). Stockholders dissenting from merger have right to receive value of their shares at time of merger in cash, value to be determined by appraisal. (5-788). Conversion of national bank into Delaware state bank also subject to approval of State Bank Commissioner; approval automatic if no action taken within 30 days. (5-786).

Effective Sept. 29, 1997, any credit card institution formed under c. 15 of Title 5 may convert to Delaware state bank upon filing application with State Bank Commissioner. (5-793[a]). Building and loan association with voting stock regulated by c. 17 of Title 5 may convert into Delaware state bank pursuant to filing application with Commissioner and following 45-day notice and comment period. (5-794).

In both mergers and conversions into state bank, if resulting state bank is not to exercise trust powers, State Bank Commissioner shall not approve merger or conversion until satisfied that adequate provision has been made for successors to fiduciary positions held by merging banks or converting bank. (5-789). If merging or converting state bank has assets or conducts business not conforming with Delaware law, it may be allowed reasonable time to conform. (5-790). Resulting bank may not value assets higher than they were valued before merger or conversion on books of merging or converting bank without approval of State Bank Commissioner. (5-791). Any application for merger or conversion requires payment of fee to Commissioner. (5-792).

Delaware state or national bank may merge or consolidate with out-of-state bank when Delaware bank is resulting bank. (5-795C, D). Delaware state or national bank that is at least five years old may merge or consolidate into out-of-state state bank pursuant to same procedures required for merger of Delaware state banks. (5-795F). Delaware state or national bank at least five years old may merge or consolidate into out-of-state national bank pursuant to procedures required by laws of U.S. (5-795E). Commissioner may approve merger in which resulting bank has concentration of more than 30% of total insured deposits in state. (5-795H). Commissioner may approve emergency merger of failing Delaware state bank with out-of-state bank, even when Delaware state bank is less than five years old. (5-795G). Offices of merging bank may continue as branch offices of resulting bank. (5-795B[a]). State Bank Commissioner's approval is required for additional branch offices in Delaware of resulting banks that are out-of-state banks. (5-795B[b]). Commissioner may examine branch offices, require periodic reports and enter into cooperative agreements with other regulatory authorities. (5-795J). Commissioner may also promulgate regulations for examination of branches. (5-795L).

See also subhead Bank Holding Companies, catchline Acquisitions, infra.

Taxation.—Franchise tax is imposed on taxable income of banking organizations and trust companies. Taxable income is computed by formula which represents net operating income before taxes plus net securities gains or losses before taxes, minus net operating income before taxes of subsidiaries and certain foreign branch offices, multiplied by factor of .56. (5-1101). Rate of tax is 8.7% of taxable income not exceeding $20,000,000; 6.7% on $20,000,000-$25,000,000; 4.7% for $25,000,000-$30,000,000; 2.7% in excess of $30,000,000; 1.7% for years beginning after Dec. 31, 1996, in excess of $650,000,000. (5-1105[a]). All banking organizations, trust companies, and federal savings banks not headquartered in but maintaining branches in state, are subject to franchise tax, but exempt from Delaware corporation income tax, occupational taxes, and taxes on income, capital and assets; but real estate owned not exempt. (5-1109). Affiliated finance companies taxed on basis of their capital base. (30-6303).

Any claim for assessment or credit or refund on such taxes is subject to three-year statute of limitations. (5-1111, 1112). However, in case of fraudulent return with intent to evade tax or failure to file return, tax may be assessed at any time. (5-1111[b]).

Building and loan associations subject to annual franchise tax of net operating income at same rate as provided for banking organizations, above. (5-1801). Upon failure to pay tax, tax due becomes lien in favor of State on property and rights thereto. (5-1803).

Bank Holding Companies.—State Bank Commissioner empowered to regulate Delaware bank holding companies. (5-855). Delaware corporation regulated under Federal Bank Holding Company Act or Federal Savings and Loan Holding Company Act may use "trust" in corporate name without being subject to regulation by State Bank Commissioner. (8-395).

Acquisitions.—After Sept. 29, 1995, out-of-state bank holding company or subsidiary may acquire more than 5% of voting share or substantially all assets of any bank located in Delaware without having to satisfy listed requirements or submit application to Commissioner. (5-803[b]; 5-804[c]). Out-of-state holding company must file with Commissioner, upon Commissioner's request, all reports required under §13 or 15(d) of Securities Exchange Act of 1934, as amended, excluding portions not available to public. (5-805).

Out-of-state bank holding company or subsidiary may acquire or retain ownership or control of bank or bank holding company located in Delaware; provided that out-of-state bank holding company proposing such acquisition makes application to State Bank Commissioner. (5-843, 844). Commissioner may approve acquisition even if it would result in concentration of at least 30% of total insured deposits in State in same

out-of-state bank holding company together with any affiliated insured depository institution. (5-843[b]).

See also subhead Merger, Consolidation and Conversion, supra.

Bidco.—"Bidco" is business and industrial development corporation licensed under c. 33 of Title 5, "Delaware Bidco Act". (5-3301, 3303). Bidco provides financing and management assistance to business firms. (5-3322[a]). State Bank Commissioner supervises and regulates Bidco. (5-3306).

BILLS AND NOTES:

Uniform Commercial Code adopted. (6, Art. 3). See topic Commercial Code.

Judgment Notes.—May be entered without declaration or cognovit, but confession of judgment is subject to procedures in Super. Ct. Civ. Rule 58.1. (10-2306, 3908). See, however, topic Consumer Protection.

Attorney's Fee Clauses.—Enforceable up to 20% of amount adjudged for principal and interest. (10-3912).

BILLS OF LADING:

See topic Commercial Code.

BLUE SKY LAW:

See topic Securities.

BROKERS:

Every person in business of buying and selling for other persons for profit is broker. (30-2301[a][4]).

Licenses.—Broker must obtain license from Department of Finance before engaging in business. (30-2101, 2301). Fee is $75 plus surtax plus 0.384% of gross receipts, plus $25 for each additional branch or location. (30-2301).

Real Estate Brokers.—Must obtain licenses. Fee for agent is $75 plus surtax plus 0.384% of gross receipts, plus $25 for each additional branch or location. (30-2301[a][18], [d]). Brokers and salesmen must also obtain certificates of registration from State Real Estate Commission. (24-2906). License fees for brokers, including nonresidents, and salespersons computed by Division of Professional Regulation at beginning of calendar year. (24-2908). Prior to licensing, nonresident broker applicants shall consent to service of process. (24-2909[b]).

Uniform Commercial Code adopted. See topic Commercial Code.

BULK SALES:

Uniform Commercial Code (Art. 6) repealed.

CARRIERS:

Public Service Commission empowered to regulate and fix rates. (26-201[a]).

Uniform Commercial Code adopted. (6, Art. 7). See topic Commercial Code.

Rates.—Sixty days notice to Commission prior to rate change required. Commission either upon complaint or own initiative may enter upon hearing. (26-304).

Discrimination.—Unjust, unreasonable, unduly preferential, unjustly discriminatory rates and practices prohibited. (26-303[a]).

Limiting Liability.—Can generally be limited by contract, but emphasis placed on notice. (22 Del. 15, 64 A. 252).

Bills of Lading.—Uniform Commercial Code adopted. (6, Art. 7). See topic Commercial Code.

Liens.—Subject to provisions of Uniform Commercial Code, charges may be collected out of proceeds of sale of goods within 60 days after demand and after notice of sale published in local newspaper and printed on handbills. (25-3501).

COMMERCIAL CODE:

Uniform Commercial Code adopted. (Title 6). With the addition of Title 6, statutory numbering corresponds to Official Text.

Material Variations from Official 1995 Text.—

2-316(5)—Blood, blood plasma or tissue or organs shall not be considered commodities subject to sale or barter, but shall be considered medical services.

2A-309(9)—Section omitted.

2A-506(1)—Parties in original lease contract may reduce period of limitation to no less than one year, where not consumer lease.

3-118(h)—Does not affect state common law pertaining to instruments under seal.

Revised Art. 5—Not adopted.

Art. 6—Repealed.

Revised Art. 6—Not adopted.

8-102(11)—Spelling of defined term differs from official UCC spelling. UCC version defines term "Indorsement," Delaware Code defines term "Endorsement."

8-501(c)—Acting under §8-501, security holder and intermediary not in collusion in violation of §8-504.

8-601—This Act takes effect on Jan. 1, 1998.

8-602—Not adopted.

Delaware Code §8-602(b)—Grace period for improperly perfected security interest is one year.

Delaware Code §8-602(c)—Security interests with respect to uncertificated interests in general and limited partnerships that are perfected by Jan. 1, 1998 will remain perfected until lapse or continuation as provided by Art. 9.

Delaware Code §8-602(d)—If only filing of financing statement remains to perfect already perfected certificated security after Jan. 1, 1998, security interest is perfected for three years thereafter.

8-110(d)—Issuers organized under Delaware law cannot specify law of another jurisdiction.

See note at head of Digest as to 1998 legislation covered.

See Topical Index in front part of this volume.

COMMERCIAL CODE . . . continued

8-112(a), (b)—Add "Except to the extent otherwise provided or permitted by sections 169 and 324 of Title 8, sections 365, 366 and Chapter 35 of Title 10, and Subsection (d) hereof."

9-103(6)(f)—If debtor changes jurisdiction, debtor has four months or until expiration of perfection in first jurisdiction to obtain perfection in new jurisdiction.

9-105(1)(d)—Credit device account defined.

9-106—"Account" also refers to any credit devise account.

9-111—Repealed.

9-302(2)—Registered grain buyers defined; registration by Secretary of State; may not be subject to liens on grain crop purchases.

9-312(4)—Priority of purchase money security interest in collateral occurs if purchase money security interest is perfected at time debtor receives possession of collateral or within 20 days.

9-401(6)—Notwithstanding defective execution, Secretary of State not liable for filings.

9-407—Receiving information from Filing Officer in 24 hours add $25, complete in same day add $50, complete in two hours add $75. For notification of lapse add $25.

Alternate Provisions and Options.—
1-105—1995 Amendment not adopted.
1-209—Section not adopted.
2-318—Alternative B adopted but omitting "in person".
2-512(1)(b)—1995 Amendment not adopted.
2A-103(1)(e)—Optional language not adopted.
2A-216—Alternative C generally followed.
4-106—Alternative B adopted.
5-114(2)—Strike "8-306" and substitute "8-108".
7-204(4)—Omitted.
7-209(3)(b)—Subsection not adopted.
7-403(1)(b)—Bracketed words omitted.
8-112(a), (b)—Insert "Except to the extent otherwise provided or permitted by §§169 and 324 of Title 8, §§365, 366 and chapter 35 of Title 10" at the beginning of each section.
9-104(m)—1995 Amendment not adopted.
9-105(3)—1995 Amendments not adopted.
9-106—1995 Amendment not adopted.
9-304(1)—1995 Amendment not adopted.
9-305(1)—1995 Amendment and textual edits not adopted.
9-401(1)—First alternative subsection adopted.
9-401(3)—Alternative subsection adopted.
9-402(1)—Last sentence omitted.
9-402(5)—Second optional phrase adopted.
9-403(7)—Optional language adopted.
9-407—Adopted.
Blanks in Official Text are filled in as follows:
9-203(4)—"Subchapter II of Chapter 9 of Title 5, relating to bank revolving credit; Subchapter III of Chapter 9 of Title 5, relating to bank closed end credit; Credit 21 [Repealed] of Title 5, relating to small loans; Chapter 29 of Title 5, relating to financing the sale of motor vehicles; Chapter 26 of Title 6, relating to interest; Chapter 43 of Title 6, relating to retail instrument sales; Chapter 44 of Title 6, relating to home solicitation sales; and Chapter 23 of Title 24, relating to pawnbrokers and junk dealers". 9-401(1)(b)—"Secretary of State"; 9-403(5)—"$25"; "$50"; "$25"; 9-404(3)—"$25"; "$50"; 9-405(2)—"$25"; "$50"; 9-406—"$25"; "$50"; 9-407(2)—"$25"; "$35"; "$2" "(min. $5)".

Permanent Editorial Board's Recommendations for Amendments.—
§2-702—1996 Official Amendment not enacted.
§3-501—1996 Official Amendment not enacted.
§7-209(3)(b)—1966 Official Amendment not enacted.

Permanent Editorial Board's Recommendations for Optional Amendments.—
§1-209—1966 Official Optional Amendment not enacted.

Filing Fees.—See category Documents and Records, topic Records, subhead Filing Under Uniform Commercial Code. See also categories Debtor and Creditor, topic Assignments; Mortgages, topic Chattel Mortgages.

See Uniform and Model Acts section of this volume for 1962 Official Text of Uniform Commercial Code and later Official Amendments and Official Optional Amendments.

Forms.—See end of this Digest.

See also topics: Banks and Banking, Bills and Notes, Brokers, Carriers, Contracts, Factors, Frauds, Statute of, Sales, Securities, Warehousemen; categories Business Organizations, topic Corporations; Civil Actions and Procedure, topic Limitation of Actions; Debtor and Creditor, topics Assignments, Fraudulent Sales and Conveyances, Liens, Pledges; Documents and Records, topics Records, Seals; Mortgages, topic Chattel Mortgages; Property, topic Leases.

CONDITIONAL SALES:

See topic Commercial Code.

CONSIGNMENTS:

See topic Commercial Code.

CONSUMER PROTECTION:

Home Solicitation Sales.—General Provisions interpreted to protect consumers from high-pressure tactics and resultant inequities found in certain ambiguous or misleading contracts, poor quality merchandise and quick discounting of evidence of indebtedness. (6-4401). "Door-to-door sale" defined as sale, lease or rental of at least $25, where seller or its representative personally solicits, and buyer's agreement is made at other than place of seller's business. Sale or rental of real property, insurance or registered securities excluded. Telephone sales included unless buyer initiates transaction conducted entirely by mail or telephone. (6-4403).

Seller must furnish buyer with completed receipt or copy of contract, in same language used in oral sales presentation, containing conspicuous statement of buyer's right to cancel within three business days (Sat., Sun., legal holidays excluded); and completed form in duplicate of Notice of Cancellation, as described. Seller must inform buyer orally of right to cancel, may not misrepresent it, and must honor Notice of Cancellation. Contract may not contain confession of judgment or waiver of rights. (6-4404). Enforcement by Consumer Protection Division of Department of Justice. (29-2517).

Credit Cards.—Credit cards may not be distributed unless requested, or unless 14 days notice given of intent to issue, containing conspicuous legend of right to refusal, and prepaid preaddressed envelope or card upon which refusal can be indicated. Use constitutes acceptance; no liability prior to use; subchapter does not apply to issuance of renewal or substitute cards. (6-2542). Violators subject to fine of $100-$500 per offense, or appropriate injunction. (6-2543, 2544).

Advertising.—Merchandise may not be advertised, publicly and falsely, and with intent to deceive, advertise or otherwise represent that goods, are or were, in whole or in part, as being property of insolvent or bankrupt or their assignee, or as in whole or in part damaged by fire or accident of any kind. (6-2501). Violators fined $100. (6-2503).

Consumer Fraud.—General provisions (6-2511-2527) construed liberally to protect consumers from unfair or deceptive merchandising (6-2512).

Unlawful to use deception, fraud, false pretense, false promise, misrepresentation, or concealment, suppression, or omission of any material fact with intent that others rely in connection with sale or advertisement, whether or not any person has been misled, deceived or damaged. (6-2513). Attorney General on Superior Court order may serve investigative demand on any person believed to be engaged in unlawful practice (6-2514), and may institute action in Court of Chancery to enjoin it (6-2522), or for other appropriate relief Court of Chancery may grant including appointment of receiver (6-2523, 2524). Willful violators fined no more than $10,000 per violation. (6-2513[c]). Consumer Protection Fund established. (6-2527).

Products Liability.—Uniform Commercial Code adopted and preempts products liability actions where applicable. Seller's liability under warranty may extend to third parties. (6-2-318).

Retail Credit Sales.—General regulatory provisions for retail installment sales. (6-c.43). Regulatory provisions cannot be waived. (6-4302). Retail installment contract must be dated, in writing, and printed portion in at least eight point type. (6-4303). Delinquency charges limited to $5 or 5% of installment, whichever is less. (6-4308). Seller must furnish buyer signed copy of contract (6-4309) unless contract made by telephone or mail without solicitation of salesman (6-4310). Contracts may not contain provisions whereby buyer agrees not to assert claims or defenses or waives rights of action or remedies against seller, or whereby maturity of contract may be accelerated in absence of buyer's default. (6-4311). Service charges are regulated. (6-4315, 4317). Generally, service charge may be specified in retail sales contracts. (6-4315). (See topic Interest.) Buyer may pay contract in full at any time and receive refund of any unearned prepaid service charge. (6-4322). Retail installment accounts may be established. (6-4334-4343). Deferral of installment and deferral charges allowed. (6-4324). Minimum service charge of $1 may be established. (6-4337). For special provisions regarding automobile installment sales, see 5-c.29. Uniform Commercial Code adopted as to installment deliveries. (6-2-612).

Uniform Deceptive Trade Practices Act adopted. (6-2531 et seq.).

Attorney General may institute proceedings to halt fraudulent and deceptive merchandising practices. (6-2514 et seq.). Person likely to be damaged by deceptive trade practice of another may be granted injunction against it; court may also award attorney's fees to prevailing party in exceptional circumstances. (6-2533[a], [b]). Victim of deceptive trade practice may recover treble damages. (6-2533[c]). Attorney General may seek remedies for violations of §2532. (6-2533[d]).

"Unsolicited goods" may be returned without penalty or treated as gift. (6-2505).

Plain Language.—No statutory provision.

See topics Interest, Sales.

CONTRACTS:

Uniform Commercial Code adopted. (6-1-101 et seq.). Special statutes on Motor Vehicle financing (5-c.29) and retail installment sales (6-c.43). See topics Sales, Commercial Code; categories Documents and Records, topic Seals; Family, topic Infants.

FACTORS:

Uniform Commercial Code adopted (compare with 25-c.35). See topic Commercial Code.

License Requirements.—There is a state merchants' license fee. (30-2901 et seq.).

Liens.—Where factor has lien under existing law, failure to pay for goods within 60 days exposes goods for public sale. (25-3501-03).

Consignment Agreements.—Uniform Commercial Code adopted. See topic Commercial Code.

FRANCHISES:

Definitions.—Franchised distributor is individual, partnership, corporation or unincorporated association with place of business within State that purchases or takes on consignment products bearing trademark or trade name of manufacturer, producer or publisher for selling to retail outlets; or sells in or through retail outlets products bearing trademark or trade name of no more than three manufacturers, producers, publishers, trademark or trade name licensors; or purchases, or takes on consignment books, magazines, journals, newspapers or other publications for selling to retail outlets, or operates service or filling station, store, garage or other place of business

FRANCHISES . . . *continued*

for sale of motor fuel for delivery into service tank or tanks of any vehicle propelled by internal combustion engine. Franchisor is individual, partnership, corporation or unincorporated association that distributes or sells to franchised distributors, for itself or others, products bearing trademark or trade name of manufacturer, producer or publisher; or licenses use of trademarks or trade names to franchised distributors; or distributes or sells books, magazines, journals, newspapers and/or other publications to one or more franchised distributors; or produces or refines petroleum products or produces any automotive products sold by service station. Franchise is contract or other arrangement governing business relationship within State between franchised distributor and franchisor where franchised distributor pays more than $100 to enter into contract, provided, franchise distributor operating service or filling station, store, garage, or other place of business for sale of motor fuel for delivery into vehicle tanks not required to have paid consideration. Products are tangible items for sale irrespective of their nature, including publications. (6-2551).

Unjust Termination.—Termination of or failure to renew franchise deemed unjust if termination or failure to renew is without good cause or in bad faith. (6-2552[a], [b]). Provision of franchise permitting franchisor to terminate or fail to renew franchise which does not specify grounds, construed to permit franchisor only to terminate justly or justly fail to renew. (6-2552[c], [d]). Refusal of franchisor to renew lease for property except upon payment of unreasonable or excessive rent or other charge in light of use to which property has been placed by franchisor and/or franchisor's interest in such property deemed unjust termination of franchise. (6-2552[jj]).

Remedies.—Franchised distributor entitled to recover damages from franchisor and obtain order from Court of Chancery enjoining termination or failure to renew franchise if franchisor unjustly terminates or unjustly fails to renew, or threatens or attempts unjustly to terminate or unjustly to refuse to renew franchise. (6-2553[a]). Pending issuance of such order, franchised distributor shall be entitled to order enjoining such termination pendente lite, in case of failure to renew they may get mandatory order extending franchise pendente lite. Franchised distributor entitled to recover damages from franchisor, including loss of profits, and obtain order from Court of Chancery directing franchisor to deal with franchised distributor on fair and competitive terms, if franchisor unjustly refused to deal with franchised distributor with whom franchisor has been dealing for at least two years. (6-2553[b]). Damages include but not limited to: portion of franchised distributor's tangible assets in State used with respect to terminated or unrenewed franchise, loss of goodwill, loss of profits, other damages as allowed by State and attorney's fees and costs. (6-2553[c]).

Notice for Termination or Election to Not Renew.—90 days notice must be given when terminating or electing not to renew franchise notwithstanding franchise agreement to contrary. (6-2554).

Uniform Franchise and Business Opportunities Act not adopted.

FRAUDS, STATUTE OF:

Uniform Commercial Code adopted. (6, -Art.2). See topic Commercial Code.

Contracts and Agreements Generally.—No action may be brought to charge any person upon any agreement made upon consideration of marriage, or upon any contract or sale of lands, tenements, or hereditaments, or any interest in, or concerning them, or upon any agreement that is not to be performed within space of one year from making thereof, or to charge any person to answer for debt, default, or miscarriage of another, in any sum of $25 and upwards, unless contract is reduced to writing, or some memorandum, or notes thereof, are signed by party to be charged therewith, or some other person thereunto by him lawfully authorized in writing; except for goods, wares and merchandise, sold and delivered, money loaned and other matters which are properly chargeable in account, in which case oath or affirmation of plaintiff, together with record regularly and fairly kept, shall be allowed to be given in evidence in order to charge defendant with sums therein contained (6-2714[a]), subject to provisions of Uniform Commercial Code. Contract, promise, undertaking or commitment to loan money or to grant or extend credit, or any modification thereof, greater than $100,000, not primarily for personal, family, or household purposes, made by person engaged in business of lending or arranging lending of money or extension of credit shall be invalid unless it or some note or memorandum thereof is in writing, subscribed by charged party or by party's agent. For purposes of this section, contract, promise, undertaking or commitment to loan money secured solely by residential property consisting of one to four dwelling units shall be deemed to be for personal, family or household purposes. (6-2714[b]).

A promise to pay for the default, debt or miscarriage of another for a sum under $5 is good if proved by the oath or affirmation of the persons to whom such promise is made. (6-2712). Where sum is between $5 and $25, oath or affirmation of one credible witness, or some memorandum, or note in writing signed by party to be charged is required. (6-2713). Where sum is $25 or more, writing signed as above stated is necessary (6-2714[a]), subject to provisions of Uniform Commercial Code.

Agreements as to Wills.—No action may be brought against the personal representative or heirs of a deceased person upon any agreement to make will or give legacy or make devise unless such agreement was reduced to writing, or some memorandum thereof was signed by person whose personal representative or heir is sought to be charged or someone authorized in writing, by decedent, to sign for him. This does not apply to agreements made prior to May 1, 1933. (6-2715).

Demises.—No demise, except in writing, is effective for a longer time than one year. (25-5106[a]).

Sales of Goods.—No sale of any goods or chattels shall be good except against the vendor, unless a valuable consideration for same is paid or secured to be paid, and unless goods and chattels are actually delivered into possession of vendee as soon as convenient after sale. If goods come into and continue in possession of vendor, he will be liable to demands of all creditors. (6-2711).

Uniform Commercial Code adopted. See topic Commercial Code.

Part performance of a parol contract within the Statute of Frauds removes the bar of statute; and part payment of price, if acknowledged in writing, is such part performance. (10 Del. Ch. 63, 84 A. 878).

INTEREST:

Maximum Rate.—Legal interest rate for loans insured by Federal Housing Administration is 5% over Federal Reserve discount rate. Where rate agreed upon in writing, lawful rate may be up to 5% over Federal Reserve discount rate. (6-2301[a]). No limit on rate of interest where loan exceeds $100,000 and is not secured by mortgage against borrower's principal residence. (6-2301[c]). Bank may charge and collect periodic interest (i) under revolving credit plan on outstanding unpaid indebtedness in borrower's account, and (ii) in respect of loan, at such periodic percentage rate as agreement provides. (5-943 and 5-963). Licensee may charge and collect interest (i) under revolving credit plan on outstanding unpaid indebtedness in borrower's account, and (ii) in respect of loan, at such periodic percentage rate as agreement provides. (5-2216 and 5-2229). Retail seller or holder of retail installment contract may charge and collect finance charge in respect of retail installment transaction and may calculate such finance charge in manner and at rate or rates specified in contract. (5-2908[a]). Service charge on retail installment sale calculated in manner and at rate specified in sales contract. (6-4315). Service charge on outstanding unpaid indebtedness in buyer's retail installment account calculated in manner and at rate specified in agreement governing retail installment account. (6-4337).

Judgments.—Interest runs on judgments at legal rate. (25 Del. Ch. 388, 22 A.2d 865).

Open Accounts.—Payment of money bears interest from date of its entry, but equitable consideration may affect such rule in particular case. (31 Del. Ch. 76, 66 A.2d 425).

Usury.—When rate of interest exceeds lawful rate, debtor is not required to pay excess. If whole debt is paid with interest exceeding lawful rate, debtor may recover three times amount of excess interest or $500 whichever is greater, by action brought within one year of payment. (6-2304[b]). No corporation, limited partnership, business trust or limited liability company, and no association or joint stock company having any powers and privileges of corporations not possessed by individuals or partnerships, may interpose defense of usury. (6-2306). Individual indorser or guarantor to corporate note may not assert usury defense when statute prevents corporate maker from doing so. (325 A.2d 108).

LICENSES, BUSINESS AND PROFESSIONAL:

Practically all pursuits and occupations are licensed in this state. (30-c.23 et seq.).

Commercial Travelers.—Persons engaging in business as "transient retailers" subject to $25 license fee and gross receipts tax of .720% for goods and services rendered within Delaware which exceed $3,000. (30-2905[f] & [g]).

For various other license fees, see category Taxation, topic License Fees.

Collection Agencies.—Collector of commercial accounts, except attorney, is classified as mercantile agent and must procure license from Division of Revenue. Fee $75 plus $25 for each additional place of business. (30-2301[a(13)]; 30-2905[a]).

MONOPOLIES, RESTRAINT OF TRADE AND COMPETITION:

Contracts, combinations, conspiracies or trusts in restraint of trade are unlawful and civilly actionable by Attorney General. No criminal provisions or private right of action, but Attorney General may sue as parens patriae. (6-c.21). Exemptions for certain labor, agricultural and horticultural associations, public utilities, nonprofit institutions, securities dealers, banking institutions, and persons acting pursuant to Insurance Code or regulations. (6-2104).

Unfair Trade Practices.—Price discrimination between geographical sections intended to destroy or prevent competition is misdemeanor, and is punishable by fine of not less than $200, nor more than $5,000 and/or maximum imprisonment of one year. (6-2504).

Resale Price Agreements.—See category Intellectual Property, topic Trademarks and Tradenames.

NEGOTIABLE INSTRUMENTS:

Uniform Commercial Code adopted. (6-c.1-101). See topic Commercial Code.

RESTRAINT OF TRADE:

See topic Monopolies, Restraint of Trade and Competition.

SALES:

Uniform Commercial Code adopted. (6-1-101 et seq.) Special regulatory provisions apply to financing of motor vehicle sales. (5-c.29). Printed portion of motor vehicle sales contracts must be at least eight-point type and portions must be in ten-point bold type. (5-2907[b]).

Contracts of Sale.—See topics Frauds, Statute of, Commercial Code, Consumer Protection.

Conditional Sales.—Uniform Commercial Code adopted. See topic Commercial Code.

Bulk Sales.—See topic Commercial Code.

Sale of Motor Vehicles.—See category Transportation, topic Motor Vehicles.

Consumer Protection.—See topic Consumer Protection.

Bills of Sale.—No special requirements.

Retail Credit Sales.—See topic Consumer Protection.

Products Liability.—Strict liability not available where plaintiff covered by warranties. (373 A.2d 218). Strict liability recognized in bailment-lease situation. (353 A.2d 581).

SECURITIES:

Uniform Commercial Code adopted. (6-1-101 et seq.).
Blue Sky law contained in 6-7301 et seq.

Supervision.—Securities Commissioner, Division of Securities, Department of Justice, Carvel State Office Building, 5th Floor, 820 N. French Street, Wilmington, Delaware 19801. (6-7325).

Regulatory Powers of Supervising Authority.—Commissioner may: (1) Issue stop order (6-7308[a]); (2) deny, suspend, revoke or cancel any registration of broker-dealer or investment adviser (6-7316); (3) suspend trading in any security for ten days (6-7318[b]); (4) initiate public or private investigations (6-7319[a]); (5) seek injunction under specified conditions (6-7320); (6) require escrow of proceeds from sale of securities (6-7321). Orders of Commissioner are subject to review in Court of Chancery upon filing of complaint within 60 days after order is entered. (6-7324).

Prerequisites to Sales or Offerings.—Registration required unless exempted. (6-7304, 6-7309, 6-7312).

Securities to Which Act Applicable.—"Security" means any note; stock; treasury stock; bond; debenture; evidence of indebtedness; certificate of interest or participation in any profit-sharing agreement; collateral-trust certificate; pre-organization certificate or subscription; transferable share; investment contract, including pyramid promotion which includes any plan or operation for sale or distribution of property, services, or any other thing of value wherein a person for consideration is offered an opportunity to obtain benefit based in whole or in part on inducement, by himself or by others, of additional persons to purchase same or similar opportunity; voting-trust certificate; certificate of deposit for security; certificate of interest of participation in oil, gas or mining title or lease or in payments out of production under such title or lease; options on commodities; or, in general, any interest or instrument commonly known as a "security," or any certificate of interest or participation in, temporary or interim certificate, for, receipt for guarantee of, or warrant or right to subscribe to or purchase, any of foregoing. "Security" does not include any insurance or endowment policy or annuity contract under which an insurance company promises to pay money either in a lump sum or periodically for life or some other specified period. (6-7302[13]).

Exempt Securities.—Any security: (1) Issued or guaranteed by governmental body, including valid obligations of certain foreign governments; (2) any interest in, debt of, or debt guaranteed by Federal or state chartered banks, federal savings and loan associations, or any trust company, building and loan associations and insurance companies licensed to do business in Delaware; (3) any security issued or guaranteed by Federal credit union, or credit union, industrial loan association or similar association licensed to do business in Delaware; (4) any security issued or guaranteed by certain governmentally regulated companies; (5) any security, including warrants and subscription rights therefor listed on certain national and regional exchanges and any other security of same issuer which is of senior or substantially equal rank; (6) any security issued by certain nonprofit organizations; (7) any commercial paper, renewal or guarantee thereof, proceeds of which are for current transactions and due within nine months; (8) any investment contract issued by employee's pension plan, etc., provided written notice is given to Commissioner; (9) any security issued by agricultural cooperative organized under 3-c. 85, or foreign cooperative association authorized to do business in Delaware; (10) any security traded pursuant to NASDAQ for which Commissioner has determined registration not necessary for protection of investors. (6-7309[a]).

Exempt Transactions.—(1) Any isolated transaction by non-issuer whether effected by broker-dealer or not; (2) any non-issuer transaction by registered agent of registered broker-dealer, and any resale transaction by sponsor of unit investment trust registered under Investment Company Act of 1940, in security of class that has been outstanding in hands of public for at least 90 days, provided certain conditions exist; (3) any non-issuer transaction through registered broker with unsolicited offer to buy, but Commissioner may require customer to acknowledge on specified form sale was unsolicited; (4) transactions between issuers and underwriters or among underwriters; (5) unitary sales of bonds or other evidences of indebtedness secured by chattel or real mortgage or deed of trust or by agreement for sale of real estate or chattels; (6) any transaction by enumerated fiduciaries; (7) any transaction by bona fide pledgee without any purpose of evading Act; (8) any offer or sale to financial institutions, institutional investors or to broker-dealer; (9) any transaction by offeror not involving more than 25 persons in state within any consecutive 12 month period where seller reasonably believes that domestic purchasers are buying for investment expanded to include sales to not more than 35 purchasers by Rule 9(b) (9) (I) of Regulations promulgated by Del. Securities Commissioner. See Blue Sky Rep. (CCH) ¶ 15, 109 and 419; (10) any offer or sale involving preorganization certificates or subscriptions to ten or fewer persons, provided no remuneration is paid and no payment is made by solicited subscribers; (11) any transaction pursuant to offer to existing security holders of issuer if no remuneration other than standby commission is paid or issuer first files notice and Commissioner does not object within next five full business days; (12) any offer (but not sale) of security for which registration statement has been filed and no stop order is in effect or pending and offeror complies with §7306 (d); (13) any offer or sale of security by or through registered broker-dealer if such offer or sale is not for benefit of issuer or 10% beneficial owner of outstanding voting securities of issuer, and no administrative stop order or injunction is in effect with respect to security offered or any security of same class. (6-7309[b]). These exemptions may be denied or revoked by Commissioner. (6-7309[c]).

Registration of Securities.—

Coordination.—Any security for which a registration statement has been filed under Securities Act of 1933 in connection with same offering may be registered by coordination. (6-7305[a]). Detailed registration statement must be filed, and filing fee paid (except registration renewals for open investment companies). (6-7305[b]).

Qualification.—Security may be registered by qualification. (6-7306[a]). Detailed registration statement required. (6-7306[b]).

Registration of Broker-Dealers, Investment Advisers and Agents.—No broker-dealer, investment adviser, or agent may transact business in Delaware unless registered. (6-7313[a]). Initial application and each annual renewal application must be accompanied by $250 filing fee for broker-dealers and investment advisers, and $50 for initial, transfer or renewal registration as agent. (6-7314[c]). Commissioner may require minimum capital for registered broker-dealers. (6-7314[e]). Broker-dealers and investment advisers must maintain such records, report such information, and submit to such audits as Commissioner by rule shall prescribe. (6-7315[a], [d]). Certain advisory and contractual practices of investment advisers prohibited. (6-7317).

Bonds.—Commissioner may require registered broker-dealers, agents and investment advisers to post surety bonds in amounts as Commissioner may prescribe. (6-7314[f]).

Advertisements.—Commissioner may require filing of sales and advertising literature for nonexempt securities and transactions. (6-7312).

Criminal Penalties.—Willful violator may be fined up to $200,000 or imprisoned not more than five years, or both. (6-7322[a]). Five year statute of limitations. (6-7322[d]).

Civil Liabilities.—Any person who offers, sells or purchases a security by means of any untrue statement of a material fact or any omission of a material fact necessary in order to make statements made, in light of circumstances under which they are made, not misleading (buyer or seller not knowing of untruth or omission), and who does not sustain burden of proof that he did not know, and in exercise of reasonable care could not have known of untruth or omission and any person who offers or sells security in violation of any registration requirement or stop order, is liable to person buying or selling security from or to him, who may sue either at law or in equity to recover consideration paid for security, together with legal interest from date of payment, costs, and reasonable attorneys' fees, less amount of any income received on security, upon tender of security, or for damages if he no longer owns security. (6-7323[a]). Three year statute of limitations runs from date of sales contract. (6-7323[e]).

Tender Offers.—See category Business Organizations, topic Corporations.

Pyramid Sales.—Sales device whereby person is granted franchise license which he may further perpetuate upon condition that he part with money, property or other thing of value is pyramid or chain distribution scheme. (6-2561[1]). Use of such scheme is unlawful, regardless of limitations. (6-2561-2564, 2513).

Uniform Simplification of Fiduciary Security Transfers Act adopted under title "Uniform Act for Simplification of Fiduciary Security Transfers" (12-c.43), not repealed by Uniform Commercial Code (6-10-104[2]).

Uniform Securities Ownership by Minors Act not adopted.

STATUTE OF FRAUDS:

See topic Frauds, Statute of.

TRUST RECEIPT SECURITY:

See topic Commercial Code.

WAREHOUSEMEN:

Uniform Commercial Code adopted. See topic Commercial Code.

Licenses.—Annual general service license fee is $75. (30-2301[b]). Fee is $25 for each additional place of business. (30-2301[a]. There shall be added to license fee calculated under paragraph (1) of 30-2301(d) surtax in amount of 10% of license fee calculated under said paragraph said surtax to be reduced by nonrefundable credit of $30 per month; provided, however, that any unused credit may not be carried backward or forward into any other month and may not be applied against license fee calculated under paragraph (1) of 30-2301(d). (30-2301[d][4]).

CITIZENSHIP

ALIENS:

Property.—Real and personal property situate in state may be taken, acquired, held and disposed of by aliens in same manner as by citizens of state. (25-306). Good title may be derived to property passing by succession to or from alien. (25-307). All prior conveyances to or from aliens are validated. (25-308). No person disqualified as heir because of alienage. (12-507).

CIVIL ACTIONS AND PROCEDURE

ACCORD AND SATISFACTION:

Common law rules govern (42 Del. 432, 36 A.2d 40) except as modified by Uniform Commercial Code. See category Business Regulation and Commerce, topic Commercial Code.

Compromise.—Acceptance of payment tendered in full settlement constitutes accord and satisfaction if claim is subject to bona fide dispute as to amount owing. (34 Del. Ch. 354, 104 A.2d 378).

Pleading.—Must be set forth as affirmative defenses in chancery court. (Ch. Ct. Rule 8[c]).

ACTIONS:

To a great extent, suits in equity follow the common law forms. Court Rules governing suits at law are analogous to Federal Rules. See also topics Submission of Controversy and Practice.

Equity.—Distinction between legal and equitable remedies is fully observed. (32 Del. Ch. 413, 85 A.2d 724).

ACTIONS . . . *continued*

Forms of Action.—The one form of legal action is known as civil action. (Ch. Ct. Rule 2).

Conditions Precedent.—No general requirements.

Commencement.—See topic Process.

Parties.—Assignees of bonds, specialties and notes in writing may sue in their own name. All assignments of bonds or specialties shall be under hand and seal, and executed before one credible witness. (6-2702). Person to whom contract, express or implied, has been transferred or assigned, either in accordance with statute or with common law, may sue thereon in his own name. (10-3902). Superior Court and Court of Chancery have similar rules 17a, and identical rules 19a (except Chancery rule is subject to Rule 23 dealing with class actions), 20a and 21; these rules are identical to corresponding federal rules (except for difference noted above, modification of rule 17a for state purposes and Federal Rule 20(a) includes any vessel, cargo or other property subject to admiralty process in rem as defendants who can be joined in one action) and cover real party in interest, necessary joinder, permissive joinder, and misjoinder.

Class Actions.—Uniform Class Actions Act not adopted. Maintainable in equity and at law. (Ch. Ct. Rule 23). Special class action rules for derivative actions by shareholders (Ch. Ct. Rule 23.1) and actions against unincorporated associations (Ch. Ct. Rule 23.2). Complaint must allege that plaintiff was shareholder or member at time of transaction of which he complains. It must also allege her efforts to obtain action she desires from directors and reasons for failure to obtain action or not making effort. (Ch. Ct. Rule 23.1).

Action against members of unincorporated association as class may only be maintained if representative parties will adequately protect interests of association. (Ch. Ct. Rule 23.2).

Intervention is a matter of right by motion (1) when statute confers unconditional right to intervene; or (2) when applicant claims interest relating to property or transaction which is subject of action. (Ch. Ct. Rule 24).

Interpleader.—Court may order interpleader of third person in law action if defendant brings subject matter of case into court, disclaims interest, and alleges interest of third party. (10-3910). Interpleader is a recognized remedy in equity also. (Ch. Ct. Rule 22).

Third Party Practice.—Defendant, or plaintiff if counterclaim filed, may cause complaint to be served on third party defendant any time. Within ten days after answer leave of parties not required. Thereafter leave of court required upon notice to all parties involved. (Ch. Ct. Rule 14; 10-6306).

Joinder of Causes of Action.—Claims against opposing party may be freely joined. (Rule 18).

Splitting Causes of Action.—Suit by partial assignees of chose in action must be in solido unless maker consented to assignment. (22 Del. Ch. 309, 2 A.2d 128).

Consolidation of Actions.—Courts may consolidate actions when common questions of law or fact are involved. (Ch. Ct. Rule 42[a]).

Severance of Actions.—Courts may order separate trials of claims and issues to avoid delay, embarrassment, additional expense, or prejudice. (Ch. Ct. Rule 20[b], 42[b]).

Stay of Proceedings.—No special provision for stay while action pending and before judgment.

Abatement and Revival.—An action will not abate upon the death of one or more of several plaintiffs or defendants but may be prosecuted by or against the surviving plaintiff or defendant if the cause of action survives. (10-3702). Substitution of parties in event of death is governed by Ch. Ct. Rule 25(a). In case of death of party plaintiff, suggestion of such death is entered of record; in case of death of party defendant scire facias is necessary. (Const., art. IV, §23). All personal causes of action, except for defamation, malicious prosecution or upon penal statute, survive to or against personal representatives of deceased party. (10-3701). Pending action for personal injury survives death of plaintiff and personal representatives may be substituted. (10-3704). See category Estates and Trusts, topic Executors and Administrators.

Small Claims.—See category Courts and Legislature, topic Courts.

Termination of Actions.—Plaintiff may voluntarily dismiss by (i) filing notice of dismissal prior to service of answer, or motion for summary judgment (except in replevin); or (ii) by filing stipulation of dismissal signed by all parties who have appeared in action. (Super. Ct. Rule 41[a][1]). Otherwise dismissal only upon order of court. (Rule 41[a][2]). Same rules applicable to counterclaim, crossclaim, or third party claim. (Rule 41[c]). Action may be dismissed for inaction for one year. (Ch. Ct. Rule 41[e]). Thirty day notice of dismissal is sent to parties in actions pending in court for six months during which time there have been no proceedings taken. (Super. Ct. Rule 41[e]). Equity rule is subject to Chancery Court Rules 23, 23.1, and 23.2.

Administration.—See category Estates and Trusts, topic Executors and Administrators.

Prohibited Actions.—No action permitted against party opposing land use application through judicial review by another party to review as result of seeking such review. (9-2699, 4999, 6999). See category Property, topic Real Property, subhead Judicial Review of Land Use Application.

Limitation of.—See topic Limitation of Actions.

Direct Actions Against Insurer.—See category Transportation, topic Motor Vehicles, subhead Direct Actions.

APPEAL AND ERROR:

From Courts of General Jurisdiction.—Writs of error may be taken, from Superior Court and from Court of Chancery to Supreme Court. (Const., art. IV, §11).

From Minor Courts.—Appeals lie to Court of Common Pleas in civil cases from justices of peace where demand or judgment exceeds $5 and is given without referee trial (10-9570), and cases are tried de novo according to usual or required mode of procedure. (250 A.2d 507). Appeals taken within 30 days to Superior Court in county from which final order, ruling, decision or judgment was rendered and such appeals are on record and not de novo. (10-1326). Notice of appeal from Court of Common Pleas is filed with Prothonotary within 15 days of entry of judgment. (10-1326, 9571; 415 A.2d 497). Appeals from Family Court on matters of divorce, property division, separate maintenance and alimony are to Supreme Court. (13-515, 1522). Appeal from child support order of Family Court is to Superior Court. (412 A.2d 319).

Appeals from inferior courts to Superior Court are allowed in criminal cases where fine or imprisonment exceeds $100 or one month (Const., art. IV, §28) but all motor vehicle convictions are appealable to Court of Common Pleas (21-708).

Appeals may be taken from Register of Wills to Court of Chancery. (57 Del. L., c. 402, §4).

Time.—Appeals from final decree of Chancery Court (10-145) or final judgment of Superior Court in civil or criminal action (10-147-48) must be filed in Supreme Court within 30 days. Appeals from an interlocutory order, judgment or decree of Chancery or Superior court to Supreme Court must be filed within 30 days after entry (10-143); failure to appeal from such an order will not bar objection to such order upon appeal from final judgment (10-144); from a decree of register of wills to Court of Chancery within six months (12-1309); in partition cases, within three months (25-750); and exceptions to account of executor or administrator within three months after notice given (12-2302[d]). Appeals from Family Court to Supreme Court involving civil proceeding must be within 30 days of order appealed; to Superior Court involving criminal proceeding within 30 days of order appealed. (10-143, 1051).

Appeals from justices of peace to common pleas courts to Superior Court must be taken within 15 days from day of giving judgment. (10-9571). Appeals from Common Pleas Courts to Superior Court must be taken within 30 days of giving of judgment. (10-1326).

Disability usually tolls the above periods, (10-146).

Appeal considered filed when received and filed by Office of Clerk, not when mailed. (554 A.2d 778).

Appeal Bond.—Court of Common Pleas establishes supersedeas bond requirements (10-9571); amount of supersedeas bond must be sufficient to cover judgment plus interest and court costs (Ct. Civ. Rule 62[c]).

Stay of Proceedings and Supersedeas.—Appeals to Supreme Court do not stay proceedings in court below unless bond is filed, conditioned for prosecution of appeal to effect. (Const., art. IV, §24). In civil cases, bond binds principal obligor to pay judgment money, including damages for delay. Approval of bond is contingent on service and filing of notice of appeal in appellate court. (Supr. Ct. Rule 32[c]).

Extent of Review.—Supreme court generally confines its review to questions of law and the existence of evidence to support findings of fact although some flexibility exists in equity if factual issue unresolved by record. (34 Del. Ch. 267, 103 A.2d 234).

Character of Hearing.—Review, except appeals to Superior Court from justices of peace, where trial de novo provided. (250 A.2d 507).

Judgment or Order on Appeal.—Supreme Court Rule 19 governs mandates and contemplates special form of mandate where appropriate.

BONDS:

Official bonds and official obligations as well as those ordered by court are recorded. (9-9114, 9610; 10-375). Judgments on bonds are not liens on real property until filed with Prothonotary. (10-4718).

Sureties.—Domestic and foreign companies must comply with provisions regulating insurance companies. (18-7701). See category Insurance, topic Insurance Companies.

Enforcement.—Persons injured by breach of condition of public bond may bring suit in name of State, but for their own use. (10-7502).

CERTIORARI:

Jurisdiction.—Supreme Court can issue writs of certiorari to Superior Court and Court of Chancery. Federal courts as well as highest appellate court of other states can certify questions of law to Delaware Supreme Court. (Const., art. IV, §11; 10-142). Superior Court can issue writs of certiorari necessary for bringing action to such court. (10-562).

Grounds.—Writ lies to correct errors of law, to review proceedings not conducted according to law and to restrain an excess of jurisdiction. (42 Del. 198, 29 A.2d 369).

Proceedings.—From courts of general jurisdiction; see topic Appeal and Error.

In appeals where action is tried de novo: Action is commenced in Superior Court upon filing with Prothonotary praecipe, certified transcript of record and deposit for costs and fees. (Super. Ct. Civ. Rule 3).

Review.—Review on certiorari is confined to the record. (42 Del. 198, 29 A.2d 369).

CHARITABLE IMMUNITY:

See topic Damages.

COMMISSIONS TO TAKE TESTIMONY:

See topic Depositions and Discovery.

COSTS:

Party for whom final judgment is given in court of law in any civil action, or on writ of error, shall recover costs of suit, to be awarded by court. (10-5101).

See note at head of Digest as to 1998 legislation covered.

See Topical Index in front part of this volume.

COSTS . . . *continued*

Subject to express provision in statute, Super. Ct. Civ. Rules, or Rules of Supreme Court, costs allowed to prevailing party as matter of course unless court directs otherwise. (Super. Ct. Civ. Rule 54[d]).

Costs will follow judgment of court. (Supr. Ct. Rule 20).

Upon affirmance of judgment by Supreme Court, costs of appellee to be added to his costs in first judgment. (10-5107).

Generally, party prevailing on appeal from justice of peace recovers costs both from action before justice and from appeal. (10-5110).

Prepayment of Costs or Fees by Nonresidents.—No Prothonotary, Register in Chancery, clerk of any court, or justice of peace is compelled to issue any writ or other original process in civil action, or any writ of execution on any judgment, in favor of person not resident of state, unless costs of issuing such writ shall be first paid. Likewise no sheriff, coroner or constable shall be compelled to execute any such writ until his legal fees are paid. (10-3102).

Security for Costs.—Usual initial deposit to begin suit in Chancery is $100; if three or more defendants, usual deposit is $200. (Ch. Ct. Rule 3[bb]). Justice of Peace Court requires $16 initial deposit. (J.P. Civ. Rule 4A). Initial deposit in Court of Common Pleas is $50. In Court of Common Pleas jury trial, deposit equals amount required in Superior Court currently, $100. (C.P. Ct. Civ. Rules 3[e], 109; Super. Ct. Civ. R. 77[h]). Superior Court filing fee is $125 plus Sheriff's service. (Super. Ct. Civ. Rule 77[h]). In Chancery, Superior and Common Pleas Court, out-of-state plaintiff may be made to post security for costs. (Ch. Ct. Rule 3[c]; Super. Ct. Civ. Rule 3[f]; C.P. Ct. Civ. Rule 3[f]). In Family Court, filing fee is $40 and $75 for divorce and annulment cases. (Fam. Ct. Civ. R. 3[c]).

Where any party unnecessarily swells record or causes unnecessary expense, court may, in its discretion, tax such expenses against offending party, regardless of outcome of action. (Ch. Ct. Rule 54[e]; Super. Ct. Civ. Rule 54[e]; C.P. Ct. Civ. Rule 54[e]).

At any time pending action for debt or damages, defendant may bring into court sum for discharging same, together with costs then accrued, and plaintiff not accepting same, if upon final decision, plaintiff shall not recover greater sum than that so paid into court or recover any costs accruing after such payment, except where plaintiff is executor or administrator. (Const., art. IV, §22).

DAMAGES:

Common law generally prevails as to compensatory damages except as modified in category Transportation, topic Motor Vehicles, subhead No-Fault Insurance and in this topic, subhead Medical Malpractice. Punitive damages allowed only where act is malicious, willful or wanton. (24 Del. 107, 75 A. 1014, aff'd, 78 A. 401).

Charitable Immunity.—Charitable corporations responsible for own legally careless actions and subject to doctrine of respondeat superior. (46 Del. 350, 83 A.2d 753).

Comparative negligence rule adopted. (10-8132).

See also category Estates and Trusts, topic Death, subhead Actions for Death.

Sovereign Immunity.—Waived (18-6511) only for claims in state court (406 F.Supp. 4) and only when claim covered by state insurance program (316 A.2d 236). See also State Tort Claims Act which provides limited immunity and indemnity. (10-c.40).

Uniform Contribution Among Tortfeasors Act.—Adopted. (10-6301-6308).

No-Fault Insurance.—See category Transportation, topic Motor Vehicles, subhead No-Fault Insurance.

Medical Malpractice.—Court may deduct from medical malpractice award, and pay to plaintiff amount covering plaintiff's attorney's fees, litigation expenses, past health care expenses, leaving rest of award to be paid in set monthly installments, including interest on unpaid balance, except as it is necessary to release more money to cover continuing medical expenses. If plaintiff dies within 20 years of award, and before all installments have been paid, court deducts from balance due amount for future pain and suffering and medical care, and remainder is paid to plaintiff's estate. (18-6864). Evidence of public collateral source of compensation for injuries to person seeking damages for such injuries in medical malpractice action, and changes in marital, financial or other status of such persons, except those regarding life insurance or private compensation or benefits, may be introduced and considered by trier of fact. (18-6862). Punitive damages may be given only by special, separate award of trier of fact, which must find that injury was maliciously intended or was result of willful or wanton misconduct. (18-6855). See also category Courts and Legislature, topic Courts, subhead Superior Court, catchline Jurisdiction—Medical Malpractice; also topic Limitation of Actions; category Insurance, topic Insurance Companies.

DECLARATORY JUDGMENTS:

See topic Judgments.

DEPOSITIONS AND DISCOVERY:

See also topic Practice.

Rules of Court, 26, 28-32, 37 based on corresponding federal rules.

Uniform Foreign Depositions Act not adopted.

Within State for Use Within State.—Parties may obtain discovery regarding any matter, not privileged, which is relevant to subject matter involved in pending action, whether it relates to claim or defense of party seeking discovery or to claim or defense of any other party. Not grounds for objection that information sought will be inadmissible at trial if information sought appears reasonably calculated to lead to discovery of admissible evidence. (Ch. Ct. Rule 26[b][1]).

Within State for Use Elsewhere.—Commissions issued by courts of other jurisdictions are honored and Prothonotary of Superior Court will issue subpoena or subpoenas duces tecum and Superior Court may proceed to enforce obedience in same manner as in case of subpoena initially issued by court itself. (10-4311).

Outside of State for Use Within State.—Rules of Court based upon Federal Rules. Same as within state except applicant may have to pay attendance expense and fee of one attorney for adversary if proposed deposition at place more than 150 miles from courthouse where action was commenced. (Ch. Ct. Rule 30[h]). See also subheads Before Whom Taken; Commissions, infra.

Outside of County.—In civil debt actions, witness outside of county may answer depositions upon written questions before justice of peace of county where he resides. (10-9531). Register of Wills has similar power. (12-2503).

De Bene Esse.—Court rules providing for use of depositions modeled after Federal Rules. (Ch. Ct. Rule 26). But Federal Rule 27, Deposition Before Action or Pending Appeal, not adopted in Delaware.

Uniform Act to Secure Attendance of Witnesses From Without a State in Criminal Proceedings adopted.

Perpetuating Testimony.—Any person interested in perpetuating testimony respecting boundaries may file petition in Chancery, naming tenants and owners of adjoining land, and commission will issue to one or more persons to take depositions on interrogatories filed after ten days written notice of filing thereof. (25-1102). See also Rules of Court based upon Federal Rules.

Before Whom Taken.—Depositions may be taken: (1) in U.S., (a) before officer authorized to administer oaths by laws of place where examination is held, or (b) before person or officer appointed by court in which action is pending, through notice, commission, or letters of request; (2) in foreign country, (a) pursuant to applicable treaty or convention, (b) pursuant to letter of request, (c) on notice before person authorized to administer oaths by law of place in which examination is held, or (d) before person commissioned by court. (Ch. Ct. Rule 28). Parties may make any desired arrangements by stipulation. (Ch. Ct. Rule 29).

Commissions.—Court of Chancery may award commissions for taking answers and examining witnesses, in all causes brought before it. (10-368).

Compelling Attendance of Witnesses.—Party issuing notice of deposition may serve subpoena upon person to be deposed, commanding latter to give testimony. Such subpoena may also command person to whom it is directed to produce and permit inspection of books, papers, documents or tangible things; but this person may object to such inspection, move to quash subpoena, request costs, or move for protective order pursuant to Ch. Ct. Rule 26(c). Attendance of witnesses and production of documents or tangible things outside Delaware may be compelled by whatever means available under laws of place where examination is held. (Ch. Ct. Rule 45).

Examination of Witnesses.—Rules of Court based upon Federal Rules.

Return.—Completed deposition is examined and signed by witness, and officer certifies that it is true record of testimony. Officer then seals deposition and transmits it to attorney who arranged for transcript or recording. Party taking deposition shall give prompt notice of its filing to all parties. Officer shall retain copy of recording. (Ch. Ct. Rule 30[e], [f]).

Form

Return of person taking deposition orally: I, ..., the officer before whom the foregoing deposition was taken, do hereby certify that the witness whose testimony appears in the foregoing deposition was duly sworn by me, and that said deposition is a true record of the testimony given by said witness; that I am neither attorney nor counsel for, nor related to or employed by any of the parties to the action in which this deposition is taken, and further that I am not a relative or employee of any attorney or counsel employed by the parties hereto or financially interested in the action.

See also topic Practice.

EQUITY:

See topic Actions.

EVIDENCE:

Delaware has enacted Uniform Rules of Evidence based on Federal Rules of Evidence with modifications based, in part, on Uniform Rules of Evidence. (DRE).

See also subhead Witnesses, infra; topic Depositions and Discovery.

Witnesses.—Every person, including parties and interested persons, competent except as otherwise provided in Rules of Evidence. (DRE 601).

A party to the record may interrogate unwilling or hostile witness by leading questions, and may call adverse party or person for whose immediate benefit action is brought or defended or officer or director of any corporation, partnership or association which is adverse party and interrogate, impeach and contradict witness as if called by adverse party. Witness may be cross-examined, contradicted and impeached by or on behalf of adverse party also. (Ch. Ct. Rule 43).

See also topic Depositions and Discovery.

Husband and wife may testify for or against each other in criminal cases and in civil cases unless testifying as to confidential communication and privilege is asserted. (DRE 504).

Communications or Transactions with Persons Since Deceased or Incompetent.—Delaware Dead Man's Statute (10-4302) superseded by DRE 601 which provides that every person is competent to be witness.

Privileged Communications.—Attorney-client privilege recognized. (DRE 502). Priest-penitent privilege recognized as to certain communications made to clergyman in his professional capacity. (DRE 505). Physician and psychotherapist-patient privilege recognized. (DRE 503). Other privileged information provided for in Art. V of DRE. Reporters' Privilege Act adopted. (10-4320-26).

Self-Incrimination.—Accused shall not be compelled to give evidence against himself. (U.S. Const. amend. V).

Compelling Attendance.—See topic Depositions and Discovery.

See note at head of Digest as to 1998 legislation covered.

See Topical Index in front part of this volume.

INJUNCTIONS:

Generally, see Rules of Court of Chancery based upon Federal Rules. (Ch. Ct. Rule 65).

Jurisdiction.—Court of Chancery has jurisdiction to hear all matters and causes in equity. (10-341). Court has all of jurisdiction that was possessed by high court of chancery in England. (26 Del. Ch. 344, 28 A.2d 676).

President judge or any associate judge of Superior Court and of Orphans' Court has power during absence of chancellor and all vice-chancellors to grant restraining orders and preliminary injunctions pursuant to laws of Court of Chancery. (Const. 1897, art. IV, §14).

Prerequisites.—See subhead Temporary Injunction, infra.

Procedure.—Application for injunction may be filed after complaint filed; motion to dissolve injunction may be made at any time. (Ch. Ct. Rule 65). See subhead Temporary Injunction, infra.

Bond.—No restraining order or preliminary injunction shall issue except upon giving of security by applicant in such sum as court deems proper, for payment of costs and damages which may be suffered. (Ch. Ct. Rule 65[c]).

Temporary Injunction.—A preliminary injunction will not be ordered without notice, and unless it be specifically prayed for, or by affidavit-supported motion. (Ch. Ct. Rule 65[a]).

Temporary restraining order will not issue unless prayed for. Nor will one issue without notice unless immediate and irreparable injury, loss or damage will probably result and applicant's attorney certifies in writing efforts to give notice and reasons why notice should not be required. (Ch. Ct. Rule 65[b]).

If a preliminary injunction or restraining order be issued, defendant may, upon two days' notice to plaintiff, appear before Court, put in his answer, under oath or affirmation, for purpose of moving to dissolve or modify injunction. (Ch. Ct. Rule 65[b]). (Rules of Court based upon Federal Rules.) See also topic Practice.

JUDGMENTS:

Generally, see 10-c.47, Court Rules based on Federal Rules. See topic Practice.

Judgment by confession, entered on obligation containing warrant for confession of judgment, is not entered as final judgment until defendant is given written notice by certified mail of hearing to determine whether defendant understandingly waived his right to notice and opportunity to be heard. (10-2306[b]). In case of defendant who was nonresident when he signed confession authorization, plaintiff must file with Prothonotary affidavit signed by defendant setting forth authorization of judgment in specific county, sum of money for which judgment may be entered, contact with State in transaction, and defendant's mailing address and residence where he would most likely receive mail. (10-2306[c]). Defendant is not deemed to have waived right to present defenses of which he had no knowledge at time of signing authorization, or which arose after that time; and stay of execution is given until defendant gets hearing on these defenses. (10-2306[j]). Warrant of attorney may furnish provision for collateral security. (10-2306[a]). See also Super. Ct. Rules 58.1-58.3 and category Business Regulation and Commerce, topic Consumer Protection.

Judgments by Consent.—Valid absent mutual mistake or proof that judgment does not reflect agreement. (364 A.2d 826; Super. Ct. Rule 60[b]).

Judgments on Pleadings.—Court Rules based on Federal Rule. (Ch. Ct. Rule 12c).

Summary Judgments.—Court Rules based on Federal Rule. (Ch. Ct. Rule 56).

Declaratory Judgments.—Except where State Constitution provides otherwise, courts have power to declare rights and other legal relationships, whether or not further relief is prayed for. Such declaration has effect of final judgment. (10-6501 and Court Rules based on Federal Rules).

Default Judgments.—In actions upon bills, notes, bonds or other instruments of writing for payment of money or for recovery of book accounts, on foreign judgments, and in all actions of scire facias on recognizances, judgments or mortgages, plaintiff, if he notates demand on complaint and files instrument or judgment, has right to require defendant to answer all allegations of complaint by affidavit explaining specific nature of each defense and factual basis thereof. (10-3901[a] [b]). When party against whom judgment for affirmative relief is sought has failed to appear, plead, or otherwise defend, default judgment may be entered. (Super. Ct. Rule 55[b]).

Offer of Judgment.—Any time more than ten days before trial begins, party defending against claim may serve upon adverse party offer to allow judgment to be taken against defending party to effect specified in offer, with costs then accrued. If within ten days after service of offer, adverse party serves written notice offer is accepted, either party may then file offer and notice of acceptance and proof of service thereof and clerk will enter judgment. Offer not accepted deemed withdrawn and evidence of it not admissible except to determine costs. If judgment finally obtained by offeree not more favorable than offer, offeree must pay costs incurred after making of offer. Fact that offer is made but not accepted does not preclude subsequent offer and when liability has been determined by verdict or judgment, but extent thereof has not, party adjudged liable may make offer. (Super. Ct. Rule 68).

Docketing.—Judgment dockets are kept by the prothonotary. (10-2304, 4731).

Vacation or Modification.—Court may relieve party from final judgment for following reasons: (1) Mistake, inadvertence, surprise or excusable neglect; (2) newly discovered evidence; (3) fraud, misrepresentation or misconduct of adverse party; (4) void judgment; (5) judgment has been satisfied, released or discharged, or prior judgment on which it is based has been reversed or vacated, or equity demands that it no longer have prospective application; or (6) any other reason justifying relief from operation of judgment. (Super. Ct. Rule 60).

Lien.—Judgments shall bind lands only from time of actually entering or signing them. (10-4702). Judgments of Justice of Peace Courts become lien on property when filed in Superior Court on transfer. (10-9569[b]).

Lien effective for period of ten years after day following entry of judgment and may be renewed and continued by written agreement signed by plaintiff and defendant, or by scire facias sued out within ten years. (10-4711).

The lien attaches to equitable as well as legal interests in land, except in the case of an active trust. (7 Del. 476).

A judgment binds all personal property of the debtor for three years from the time of levy by sheriff, provided such levy occurs within 60 days after execution writ is delivered to sheriff. (10-5081). To extent that this provision conflicts with 6-2-403, this provision has been superseded. (343 A.2d 599).

Revival.—After ten years a judgment may be revived by scire facias, and becomes a lien from the time of such revival. (10-4711, 4715).

Assignment.—No statutory provisions.

Subrogation.—When surety pays judgment entered against principal and surety, creditor must mark the judgment to the use of the surety. (18-7712[a]).

Satisfaction of judgment must be entered on record forthwith and signed by holder or his attorney. (10-4751[a], 4753). Fine of not more than $500 (10-4751[b]) and liability for civil damages of $10 to $500 unless special damages to larger amount were proved (10-4754) for willful failure to enter satisfaction.

Form

Form of Power of Attorney to Satisfy Judgment: Whereas .... had and received full payment and satisfaction of the above stated judgment ...... Therefore, ... do hereby authorize and empower ...... in ...... County and State last aforesaid, to enter satisfaction for ...... and in ...... name as ...... attorney, of and on the aforesaid judgment, debt, interest and costs, and for so doing this shall be his sufficient warrant and authority.

In witness whereof ...... have hereunto set ...... hand and seal this ...... day of ...... A.D. ....

Actions.—Action against liable officers, directors or stockholders based on unsatisfied judgment against corporation can be maintained only after judgment against corporation and execution are returned unsatisfied. (8-325[b]). After 20 years rebuttable presumption of satisfaction arises. (50 Del. 424, 132 A.2d 60). Status of appeal is matter of defense. (21 Del. Ch. 9, 186 A. 916). Beneficiary must prove validity of jurisdiction in action on judgment. (43 Del. 298, 46 A.2d 643).

Foreign Judgments.—Foreign judgments, properly proven, may be filed in office of any Prothonotary of this State. (10-4782). Affidavit must be filed by judgment creditor. (10-4783[a]). No execution of foreign judgment until 20 days after filing. (10-4783[c]).

Uniform Enforcement of Foreign Judgments Act.—Adopted. (10-4781-4787).

Uniform Foreign Money-Judgments Recognition Act.—Adopted. (10-4801-4808).

LIMITATION OF ACTIONS:

Actions must be brought within following periods, which run, except where otherwise noted, from time cause of action accrues:

Twenty Years.—Entry on real property (10-7901); seisin or possession (10-7902); collection of state inheritance or estate taxes (10-8129).

Seven Years.—Action upon official obligation of escheator, against either principal or sureties, after seven years from expiration of his term of office. (10-8105). Return of commissions to mark and bound lands are conclusive if action challenging location of such lands is not brought within seven years. (10-8122).

Six Years.—Actions against either principal or surety on recognizance of sheriff or testamentary or administration bond (10-8101); limitation period running from time of recognizance or bond; action on promissory notes, bills of exchange or acknowledgment under hand of party of subsisting demand (10-8109); action resulting from deficiency in construction, supervision or planning of improvement in real property, from whichever of several specified dates is earliest (10-8127[b]).

Five Years.—See category Employment, topic Labor Relations, subhead Workers' Compensation Act.

Four Years.—Action for breach of any contract for sale of goods. Parties by agreement may reduce to not less than one year but may not extend. (6-2-725). Uniform Commercial Code adopted. Action for fraudulent transfer generally. (6-1309[1], [2]).

Three Years.—Actions: on guardian bond, from end of guardianship; against surety in recognizance taken in Chancery with condition for payment of appraised value or purchase money of lands or tenements, from time when last money mentioned in condition fell due (10-8103); on official bond (10-8104); for trespass, to regain possession of personal chattels, for damages for detention of personal chattels, to recover debt not evidenced by record or instrument under seal, arising out of contractual or fiduciary relations and based on detailed statement of mutual credit or debit demands, based on promise, based on statute, or to recover damages from injury unaccompanied with force or resulting indirectly from act of defendant, subject to exceptions set forth in other listed sections applying to some of these actions (10-8106); waste (10-8112); antitrust (6-c.21).

Two Years.—Actions for wrongful death, injury to personal property (10-8107) or personal injuries (10-8119), with certain possible exceptions in suits brought against construction contractors (10-8127), on corporate officers' bonds (10-8114).

Medical Malpractice.—Action for personal injuries must be brought within two years from date of injury, except that in case of injury that could not through reasonable diligence have been discovered by injured person within two years of injury, action may be brought within three years of injury, and except that child under six has time allowed him under above provisions, or until his sixth birthday, whichever is later, in which to bring action. (18-6856).

See note at head of Digest as to 1998 legislation covered.

See Topical Index in front part of this volume.

LIMITATION OF ACTIONS ... *continued*

See also category Employment, topic Labor Relations, subhead Workers' Compensation Act.

One Year.—Civil actions for forfeiture under penal statute (10-8115); actions on wage claims (10-8111); certain penalty refunds to public improvement contractors (29-6911[4]). Negligence action against Mayor and Council of Wilmington or any departments, officers, agents or employees thereof, for death or personal or property injuries, may only be brought if Mayor is notified of injury in writing within one year from its occurrence. (10-8124). Action for fraudulent transfer to insider with reasonable cause to believe that debtor was insolvent. (6-1309[3]).

See also category Employment, topic Labor Relations, subhead Workers' Compensation Act.

Eight Months.—Claims against decedent's estate. (12-2102[a]).

Six Months.—Certain property valuations and assessments (10-8125). Bulk transfers and Sales, formerly under Uniform Commercial Code. (6-6-111 repealed). Claims against decedent's estate arising at or after death. (12-2102[b]).

Sixty Days.—Challenge of zoning or land subdivision ordinance from time notice of adoption of ordinance is published in newspaper. (10-8126).

Uniform Commercial Code adopted. See category Business Regulation and Commerce, topic Commercial Code.

Medical Malpractice.—See subhead Two Years, catchline Medical Malpractice, supra.

Actions Not Specifically Provided For.—Action on sealed instrument, presumption of payment arises after 20 years. (23 Del. Ch. 45, 2 A.2d 85). No general limitation for actions not specifically provided for.

New Actions.—In personal action, where there is insufficient service by any unavoidable accident, or by neglect of officer in charge, where writ is abated or action is defeated by death of party, or for any matter of form, where judgment is not given on verdict for plaintiff because of error on face of record, or where judgment for plaintiff is reversed on appeal, new suit may be commenced for same cause of action within one year after abatement, determination or reversal of original action. (10-8118).

Accounts.—Three year limitation under 10-8106 does not begin on mutual running accounts as long as they are open and current. (10-8108).

Foreign Causes of Action.—Action cannot be brought on cause of action arising outside Delaware after expiration of statute of limitations of jurisdiction where cause of action arose or of Delaware, whichever is shorter, except that Delaware statute of limitations applies where person in whose favor cause of action accrued was Delaware resident at time of accrual. (10-8121).

Disabilities of Plaintiff.—Generally, except in case of personal injuries, statutory period does not run while the plaintiff is an infant or insane, and action not barred until three years after disability ceases. (10-8116). Action for entry on real property may be brought within ten years after disability removed, notwithstanding 20 years specified in 10-7901 and 10-7902. (10-7903).

Absence or Concealment of Defendant.—Absence from state prevents running of statute of limitations against plaintiffs (10-8117), as does concealment of acts on which action is based (27 Del. Ch. 33, 29 A.2d 801).

Interruption of Statutory Period.—If after cause of action accrues, defendant departs and remains out of state, statutory period interrupted until return to state. (10-8117).

Revival of Barred Claims.—Statute of limitations will be started over and debt revived if liable party issues oral or written acknowledgment of debt. (2 Marv. 332, 43 A. 166).

Contractual Limitations.—Limitation to less than three years in life insurance policy prohibited. (18-2926).

Pleading.—Statute must be specially pleaded as affirmative defense. (Ch. Ct. Rule 8c).

PARTITION:

Jurisdiction and Venue.—Where two or more persons hold land as joint tenants or tenants in common or have interest therein either in possession or remainder, or as parceners under Delaware intestate laws, any one or more of lawful age or guardian of any minor may present petition for partition to Chancery Court of county where land is situate. (25-721[a]).

Proceedings.—Upon petition of any such person of lawful age or of guardian of such as are not of lawful age Chancery Court shall order summons in partition to be issued unless others interested and not joining petition show cause why such petition should not be granted. (25-721[b]). After issuance of summons, all parties must receive service of summons either by party petitioning for partition or by Court before decree of partition is ordered. (25-722).

Upon return of summons, if parties summoned do not appear, or appear but fail to show sufficient cause against making partition, Court will enter decree that such partition be made among parties interested, and court may then direct that commission be issued, authorizing three commissioners to go upon premises and make just partition thereof, or if partition would be detrimental to interests of parties entitled, to make no partition, but appraise premises at true value, and return, if land, with survey of premises made by skillful surveyor by them to be appointed. (25-724).

Upon return of commissioners, if it appears that partition of premises has been made, and such partition is approved by Chancery Court, final decree is entered that partition shall remain firm; such proceedings and decree are conclusive upon parties and all claiming under them. (25-726).

Partition in Kind or Sale.—If from return of commissioners it appears that no partition of premises has been made and return is approved by Court or if partition of said premises is detrimental to interests of parties entitled, court makes order for sale of same by trustee at public vendue to highest bidder therefor, upon notice of time and place of said sale as prescribed in order. After sale is approved by Court, and purchase money paid into Court, or secured as Court directs, Court orders deed to be executed by trustee, conveying said premises to purchaser. (25-729).

PLEADING:

Superior Court and Chancery rules are modeled on Federal Rules of Civil Procedure and have the same rule numbers. See topic Practice.

Pleadings Permitted.—Rules modeled on Federal Rules. (Ch. Ct. Rules 7, 8, 9, 10, 11, 12, 13, 15).

Complaint must contain short and plain statement of claim and demand for relief. (Ch. Ct. Rule 8[a]; Super. Ct. Civ. Rule 8[a]). In actions on notes or other written instruments, and in actions of scire facias plaintiff may file with complaint, affidavit of demand. (Super. Ct. Civ. Rule 3[b]).

Answer must admit or deny the averments of the complaint unless party is without knowledge sufficient to do so. (Ch. Ct. Rule 8[b]; Super. Ct. Civ. Rule 8[b]).

Counterclaim or Set-Off.—Pleading shall state as counterclaim any claim against opposing party arising out of same transaction or occurrence unless claim involves third parties over whom court does not have jurisdiction or claim is subject of another pending action and may state as counterclaim any claim against opposing party not arising out of same transaction or occurrence. (Ch. Ct. Rule 13[a], [b]; Super. Ct. Civ. Rule 13[a][b]).

Reply.—After defendant has answered, plaintiff or defendant will answer defendant's crossclaim or counterclaim, if any. (Ch. Ct. Rule 7[a], [b]; Super. Ct. Civ. Rule 7[a]).

Demurrer.—No longer in use. (Ch. Ct. Rule 7[c]). Purpose accomplished by motion to dismiss, for judgment on the pleadings or motion for summary judgment. (Ch. Ct. Rules 12[b], [c], 56; Super. Ct. Civ. Rule 12[b], [c], 56).

Amended or Supplemental Pleadings.—Rule modeled after Federal Rule. (Ch. Ct. Rule 15; Super. Ct. Civ. Rule 15).

Affidavits of Defense.—In all actions in Superior Court upon bills, notes, bonds, or other written instruments for payment of money, or for recovery of book accounts, on foreign judgments, actions of scire facias on recognizances, judgments or mortgages, plaintiff may require defendant to answer allegations of complaint by affidavit setting forth specific nature and character of defense and factual basis therefor by specific notation on face of complaint that those allegations must be answered by affidavit, provided plaintiff shall have filed with its complaint copy of written instrument that is subject of action, etc. (10-3901[a], [b], [c]). If plaintiff complies with above and defendant fails to respond to designated allegations by affidavit filed with answer, designated allegations will be deemed admitted and default judgment may be entered. (10-3901[d]). Upon judgment for plaintiff in accordance with above, defendant may have stay of execution for six months upon giving proper security. (10-3901[e]). Judgment in default may be opened for trial upon giving of security and showing cause. (10-3901[f]).

Bill of Particulars.—No longer in use. When a pleading is too vague or ambiguous to respond to, opposing party may move for a more definite statement before pleading. (Ch. Ct. Rule 12[e]; Super. Ct. Civ. Rule 12[e]).

Verification.—Not required generally. (Ch. Ct. Rule 11; Super. Ct. Civ. Rule 11).

Service.—Rule providing service on attorney modeled after Federal Rule. (Ch. Ct. Rule 5[b]; Super. Ct. Civ. Rule 5[b]).

Filing and Delivery.—A copy of any pleading must be filed with Court and delivered or mailed to adverse party or adverse party's attorney. (Ch. Ct. Rule 5[a][b]). Adverse party is not required to plead, answer or reply till 20 days after being served. This does not apply in Superior Court actions of certiorari, ditch returns, mechanics liens, and appeals under Rule 3(c). (Ch. Ct. Rule 12[a]; Super. Ct. Civ. Rule 12[a]).

Time.—Court rules based on Federal Rules of Civil Procedure. (Ch. Ct. Rule 6; Super. Ct. Civ. Rule 6).

Small Claims.—See category Courts and Legislature, topic Courts.

Proof of Corporate Existence.—Plaintiff may require defendant to deny allegation of incorporation by affidavit filed with answer, by specific notation of need for denial by affidavit within paragraph alleging corporate existence. Such affidavit may be made by president, secretary, treasurer or any director of any corporate defendant. Where plaintiff complies with above, failure of defendant to file affidavit with answer will be admission of corporate existence. Any defendant denying existence of corporation shall state to best of defendant's knowledge whether there is any corporation which is related to subject matter of complaint. (10-3915).

Proof of Partnership.—Plaintiff may require defendant to deny allegation of partnership by affidavit filed with answer, by specific notation of need for denial by affidavit within paragraph alleging partnership and stating to best of defendant's knowledge and belief whether there is any partnership in relation to subject matter of action and who are partners therein. Where plaintiff complies with above, failure of defendant to file affidavit with answer will be admission of partnership existence. (10-3914).

Denial of Signature.—Plaintiff may require defendant to deny allegation that defendant's signature appears on written instrument at issue, which is filed with plaintiff's complaint, by affidavit filed with answer by specific notation of need for denial by affidavit within paragraph alleging such. Where plaintiff complies with above, failure of defendant to file affidavit with answer will be admission of signature. (10-3917).

PRACTICE:

No code of civil practice. Practice governed generally by Court Rules based upon Federal Rules. Local deviations from Federal Rules are too numerous to mention but are largely minor. Equity and law courts are separate and distinct, but appeal lies to the

PRACTICE... *continued*

Supreme Court from the Court of Chancery as well as Superior Court. See category Courts and Legislature, topic Courts. (Const., art. IV).

Discovery.—Rules resemble Federal rules in both law and equity courts, but omit Rules 26(f), 27 and 37(e) (Ch. Ct. only) and (f) and retain Rule 32(c) (Ch. Ct. only). (Ch. Ct. Rules 26-37; Super. Ct. Civ. Rule 36).

Demand for Admission of Facts.—Provided for by Rule resembling Federal Rule. (Ch. Ct. Rule 36).

Direct Actions Against Insurer.—See category Transportation, topic Motor Vehicles, subhead Direct Actions.

Small Claims.—See category Courts and Legislature, topic Courts.

See also topics Actions, Appeal and Error, Depositions and Discovery, Injunctions, Judgments, Pleading, Process; category Debtor and Creditor, topics Attachment, Executions, Garnishment.

PROCESS:

Civil action is commenced by filing complaint and, in Superior Court, a praecipe directing issuance of writ by Prothonotary. (Ch. Ct. Rule 3; Super. Ct. Civ. Rule 3).

General Requisites.—Bears date of day issued (Super. Ct. Civ. Rule 4[c]) and is returnable within 20 days (Super. Ct. Civ. Rule 4[g]).

By Whom Issued.—Issued by Prothonotary in Superior Court or Register in Chancery. (Super. Ct. Civ. Rule 4[a]; Ch. Ct. R. 4[a]).

Who May Serve.—Served by sheriff or if he is disqualified by coroner. (Super Ct. Civ. Rule 4[d]; Ch. Ct. R. 4[c]). For justice of peace, by constable, sheriff, deputy sheriff, coroner or any other person authorized by statute. (J.P. Civ. Rule 5[e]).

Personal service on individual is effective if made on defendant personally or left at his usual place of abode with a person of suitable age and discretion residing therein or to agent appointed for service of process. (Super. Ct. Civ. Rule 4[f][1][I]). In case of justices of peace, if service is not made, it is returnable on fourth day preceding date of appearance. (J.P. Civ. Rule 5[h]).

Personal Service on Infant.—For persons under age of 18 service at law is on guardian of individual in this state; if no such guardian, service is upon adult with whom infant resides or who provides infant's place of abode. (Super. Ct. Civ. Rule 4[f][1][II][b]).

Personal Service on Incompetent Persons.—Service at law of incompetent person is on that person's trustee or guardian in same manner as upon individual; if there is no guardian or trustee, service is upon adult with whom incompetent person resides or who provides incompetent person's place of abode. (Ch. Ct. Rule 4[d]; Super. Ct. Civ. Rule 4[f][1][II][c]).

Personal Service on Partnership or Association.—Partnership or unincorporated association subject to suit under common name may be served by delivering copy of process to any officer or agent authorized to receive service. (Super. Ct. Civ. Rule (4[f][1][III]).

Personal Service on Domestic Corporation.—Service on domestic corporation made by delivering copy personally to any officer or director in state or to registered agent of corporation in this State or by leaving it at dwelling house or usual place of abode in this State of any officer, director or registered agent or at registered office or other place of business in this State. If registered agent is corporation, service may be made on its president, vice-president, secretary, assistant secretary or any director. Service by leaving copy must be delivered at least six days before return date in presence of adult person and officer serving process must state manner of service in his return. If after due diligence, service cannot be made as above provided, it may be made on Secretary of State; plaintiff must pay to Secretary of State $50 costs. (8-321).

Service may also be made in accordance with 10-3111 on president or head officer if residing in state and if not, on any officer, director or manager.

Personal Service on Foreign Corporations.—When a cause of action arises in the state against any corporation incorporated outside of this state, and there is no president or head officer of such corporation or any officer, director or manager thereof resident in this state, nor any certified agent for the service of process resident in this state, process against such corporation may be served upon any agent of such corporation then being in the state. (10-3111[a]).

Service of process on foreign corporation qualified to do business in state may be made on registered agent or, if there is none, on any officer, director or other agent then in state, or if process cannot be so served by due diligence, then upon Secretary of State to whom plaintiff shall pay $50 fee. (8-376). If any foreign corporation transacts business in state without qualifying to do so, service of process may be made on Secretary of State; plaintiff must pay to Secretary of State $50 costs. (8-382).

Service on foreign insurance company, see category Insurance, topic Insurance Companies.

Personal Jurisdiction by Acts of Nonresidents.—As to cause of action arising from: Transaction of business in state; contract to supply services or things in state; tortious injury in state caused by act or omission in state; tortious injury in or outside state caused by act or omission in state, where defendant regularly does or solicits business in state; interest in, use or possession of real property in state; or contract to insure or act as surety for, or on, any person, property, risk, contract, obligation or agreement located, executed or to be performed within state at time contract is made, unless parties otherwise provide in writing, courts may exercise personal jurisdiction over nonresident or his personal representative and nonresident is deemed to have appointed Secretary of State as agent for acceptance of legal process. (10-3104[b], [c]).

Service of legal process may be made upon Secretary of State along with $2 fee. Within seven days after filing of return of service of process, plaintiff or his representative must send by registered mail to nonresident defendant notice consisting of copy of process and complaint served upon Secretary of State. (10-3104[d], 3112[b]).

Service by Mail.—Service by registered mail is permitted on nonresident motorists (10-3112[b]); on defendants in divorce actions where no personal service is had if combined with service to address petitioner avers is most likely where respondent will receive mail (13-1508[d]); on unauthorized insurers doing business in state if mailed by Commissioner (18-2105[a]); and on nonresident directors (10-3114[b]).

Substituted Service.—Court may in special cases direct another or additional mode of service. (Ch. Ct. Rule 4[c]).

Service on nonresident executor or administrator may be made on the Register of Wills. (12-1506).

Service by publication in Chancery may be by order of Chancellor upon application and affidavit that defendant cannot be served and is intentionally avoiding such service. (10-365).

In any suit against corporation whose officers reside out of state, process may be served by publishing substance thereof in newspaper of this state and of state where head officer resides, 20 days before return thereof. (10-3111[b]). In divorce suit against resident or nonresident defendant, where it is unlikely that jurisdiction can be acquired over defendant other than by publication, Clerk of Family Court shall cause summons to be published once in newspaper of general circulation in county where action is pending. Service shall also be sent by registered mail to last known address of defendant. (13-1508).

Long Arm Statute.—See subheads Service by Mail, Personal Jurisdiction by Acts of Nonresidents, and Service by Publication, supra.

Proof of Service.—If service is not made by officer or his deputy such person's return shall be verified. (Ch. Ct. Rule 4[g]). Further pleading may not be filed unless receipt of service of a copy is endorsed thereon by parties served or an affidavit of service is filed. (Ch. Ct. Rule 5[f]).

Nonresident Motorist.—See category Transportation, topic Motor Vehicles.

Service on Nonresident Directors of Delaware Corporation.—Acceptance of election or appointment, by nonresident after Sept. 1, 1977 or by resident who thereafter removes his residence from state, as director, trustee or member of governing body of Delaware corporation, and serves as such after June 30, 1978, is deemed to have consented to appointment of registered agent of corporation, or, if none, Secretary of State, as agent upon whom process may be served in all civil actions brought in state, by or on behalf of or against corporation, in which such director is necessary or proper party, or in any action for violation of his duty in such capacity, whether or not he continues to so serve. In addition to service of process on registered agent or Secretary of State, Prothonotary or Register in Chancery of court in which action is pending must mail process within seven days of such service to such director at corporation's principal place of business and at his residence or last known address. Time within which such director must respond computed from date of such mailing. (10-3114[a], [b], [c]).

REPLEVIN:

Action of replevin is founded on general or special property of plaintiff and his immediate right of possession of property. It lies only for goods and chattels which may be subject of property and only where party has right of immediate and exclusive possession. (26 Del. 84, 80 A. 975). It also lies to recover goods and chattels seized by virtue of any process of execution, or attachment, with damages and costs for taking and detention thereof, against officer seizing same, security being given, as in other cases by plaintiff in replevin, before delivery to him of goods and chattels replevied. Plaintiff in such case must not have been defendant in execution or attachment. Goods unlawfully detained from owner, or person entitled to possession thereof may be recovered by civil action. (10-3905, 3906).

Proceedings.—Except when rule to show cause is necessary any matter shall be initiated by motion following complaint or petition. (Super. Ct. Civ. Rule 64.1). Affidavit of demand not necessary; bringing of action is sufficient demand. (10-3907).

Repossession.—Defendant may give return bond within a reasonable time and retain the goods. (3 Del. 113).

Claims of Third Persons.—Defendant may disclaim ownership if, under oath, right of ownership is attributed to third person not party to action, who has sued or is expected to sue for same. Court may then order plaintiff to interplead with such third person making such person a party to action. (10-3910).

Judgment or Order.—Judgment includes any order from which writ of error or appeal lies. (Super. Ct. Civ. Rule 54).

SEQUESTRATION:

Sequestration available in Court of Chancery to compel appearance of resident defendant who avoids personal service. (10-365). Sequestration available for nonresident defendants, subject to minimum contact requirements. (10-366). See topic Process.

Property subject to sequestration includes legal and equitable interests in both real and personal property. (28 Del. Ch. 1, 35 A. 2d 831).

Situs of ownership of capital stock of Delaware corporation is Delaware except for taxation purposes. (8-169). Provision for attachment of stock. (8-324, 10-c.35). See category Debtor and Creditor, topic Attachment.

Uniform Commercial Code adopted. 8-317 modified to retain existing Delaware law. (6-8-317). See category Business Regulation and Commerce, topic Commercial Code.

SERVICE:

See topic Process.

STAY OF EXECUTION:

See topic Appeal and Error; category Debtor and Creditor, topic Executions.

SUBMISSION OF CONTROVERSY:

Any persons willing to become parties to amicable action may enter into agreement in writing for that purpose. On filing such agreement with Prothonotary, he shall docket action in Superior Court and action shall be treated thereafter as if defendant had appeared to summons issued against him by plaintiff. (10-3109).

VENUE:

Change of Venue.—Criminal defendant may request transfer to another county where prejudice would prevent fair trial. (Super. Ct. Crim. Rule 21[a]).

COURTS AND LEGISLATURE

COURTS:

United States District Court.—Clerk's office: 844 King St., Wilmington 19801. *Filing fee* of $150 is required in all civil actions.

Court sits at Wilmington.

Supreme Court.—Consists of five justices. Quorum of justices is three. (Supr. Ct. Rule 2[a]). If quorum unavailable Chief Justice or next in rank by seniority shall designate lower court judge to temporarily fill vacancy. No judge shall be designated to sit in any cause on which he sat below. (Const., art. IV, §12).

Jurisdiction.—Has appellate jurisdiction over criminal causes where penalty is death or exceeds one month imprisonment or $100 fine. (Const., art. IV, §11). Has jurisdiction over appeals by state where accused has been granted new trial after verdict, or other post-conviction relief, or in any action collaterally attacking criminal judgment, or order declaring any act of General Assembly unconstitutional. (Const., art. IV, §11[1][c]; 10-9902[d-f]). Has jurisdiction of appeals by state in criminal cases where order below based on invalidity or construction of statute on which indictment founded or on lack of jurisdiction of court below (10-9902); or in its discretion where there is substantial question of law or procedure. (10-9903). Has jurisdiction of appeals in civil cases as to final judgments, certain interlocutory decrees and other proceedings of Court of Chancery and Superior Court. (Const., art. IV, §11). Has jurisdiction of appeals from Family Court for adoption proceedings (13-917) and proceedings to terminate parental rights (13-1110).

Court sits at Dover.

Court of Chancery.—

Jurisdiction.—Court has jurisdiction of all cases in equity (10-341), and may not determine any matter where sufficient remedy may be had by common law or statute before any other Delaware Court (10-342). Jurisdiction of appeals of Orphans' Court and Register of Wills transferred to Court of Chancery pursuant to Const. art. IV, §32 (384 A.2d 627), except adoptions and terminations of parental rights (13-902; 13-1102).

Court sits in New Castle County, at Wilmington; in Kent County, at Dover; in Sussex County, at Georgetown.

Special sessions may be held in chambers at discretion of chancellor.

Superior Court.—One judge constitutes quorum (Const., art. IV, §5); quorum is two in election law violation cases in Superior Court. (Const., art. V, §8).

Jurisdiction.—Superior Court has jurisdiction of real, personal and mixed civil causes at common law (Const., art. IV, §7), and has original and concurrent jurisdiction over all crimes, except where jurisdiction is exclusively vested in another court (11-2701[c]). Superior Court has jurisdiction of appeals from Common Pleas in civil cases (10-1323), appeals from convictions before Alderman or Mayor except where sentence was imprisonment not exceeding one month, or fine not exceeding $100 (11-4503[a]), and criminal cases (11-5301[c]; 10-9902). Court also entertains civil (10-9570) and defendants' criminal appeals (10-9505) from Justice of Peace Courts. Same rules governing State appeals to Supreme Court (see subhead Supreme Court, catchline Jurisdiction, supra) also apply to State appeals to Superior Court. (10-9902).

Jurisdiction—Medical Malpractice.—All health care malpractice claims must be brought in Superior Court. (18-6802[a]). Any party to malpractice suit has right to convene malpractice review panel (18-6802[b]), which may receive evidence (18-6807), conduct hearing (18-6808) and give opinion, which is prima facie evidence before Superior Court (18-6811[c]); but Superior Court will review opinion at behest of party aggrieved by it (18-6811[d]), who may call witnesses who appeared before panel to appear in Court (18-6812). See also subhead Medical Malpractice under categories Civil Actions and Procedure, topics Damages, Limitation of Actions; Insurance, topic Insurance Companies.

Courts of Common Pleas.—

Jurisdiction.—Court of Common Pleas has jurisdiction over all civil actions at law, where amount in controversy, exclusive of interest does not exceed $50,000 but there is no limitation of jurisdiction of any amount sought by way of counterclaim, crossclaim or third party claim (10-1322); and has original jurisdiction over all misdemeanors including those over which justice of peace has jurisdiction, jurisdiction of Court of Common Pleas being concurrent with that of justice of peace except: (1) Those committed within City of Wilmington, (2) those over which another court has exclusive jurisdiction (11-2701). No jury trial in civil action (10-1327), but party other than one bringing suit may demand jury trial on issue for which there is jury trial right, in which case action will be removed to Superior Court (10-1328). Except as otherwise provided, defendant has jury trial right in criminal cases, criminal jury trials in New Castle County being removed to Superior Court. (11-5301[a]). Court has same power as Superior Court to make rules, issue and endorse writs and processes, compel attendance of witnesses, require security for costs from nonresident plaintiffs, and require production of all necessary evidence. (10-1324). Court of Common Pleas also entertains civil appeals from Justice of Peace Courts. (10-9570).

Family Court has exclusive original civil jurisdiction in proceedings concerning: dependent, neglected or delinquent children; any child charged with violation of any Delaware law except first or second degree murder, kidnapping, unlawful sexual intercourse in first degree or other specifically excepted crimes; enforcement of any Delaware law for protection of children and education of children or handicapped; divorce and annulment; child support liens. Delinquency based on alleged violation of Titles 11, 16 or 21 which would otherwise be within original jurisdiction of Family Court shall be within criminal jurisdiction of Superior Court if charges are joined with felony pending against same child in Superior Court. Proceedings relative to parental notice of abortion under Subchapter VIII, c. 17, Title 24. (10-921). Court has exclusive original criminal jurisdiction in any proceeding concerning: mistreatment of child; offenses or crimes, except felonies, by one member of family against another; offenses, except felonies, committed against peace officer during family altercation; violation of child labor laws; desertion or failure to support, interference with custody, incest, exposing children to gambling, violation of protective order and sale of alcohol, tobacco or weapons to children. If offenses may be properly joined with felony, they are within jurisdiction of Superior Court. Court has concurrent criminal jurisdiction with Justice of the Peace Courts in curfew violation proceedings. (10-922).

Registers' (or Probate) Courts.—Each Register of Wills holds Register's Court. (Const., art. IV, §31). Jurisdiction of appeals was transferred to Court of Chancery. (384 A.2d 627).

Justices of the Peace Courts.—Justices of peace severally have jurisdiction, throughout State, of all causes of action arising from obligation, or express or implied promise, or warranty, or contract, for payment of money, rent, or delivery of produce, chattels, goods, wares or merchandise; or contract, or agreement, for personal labor, hire or service; or for any penalty, or forfeiture, incurred under provisions of any statute, or of any by-law, or ordinance, authorized by statute; where matter in demand does not exceed $15,000, which sum excludes any penalty arising in any obligation, or contract, or interest due on any cause of action within this jurisdiction. (10-9301). Also have jurisdiction concurrent with Superior Court of actions of trespass, trespass on case, replevin and detinue where damages claimed, or value of property in controversy, is $15,000 or less. (10-9303; 10-9304). Justices of peace have original jurisdiction of certain misdemeanors (11-2702) and may act as committing magistrates (11-5911). Accused may have case originally before Mayor or Alderman or Justice of Peace transferred to Court of Common Pleas. (11-5303; 11-5901).

Municipal Court abolished effective on Apr. 14, 1998.

Small Claims Courts.—See subheads Courts of Common Pleas, and Justices of the Peace Courts, supra.

LEGISLATURE:

Annual sessions: from 2d Tues. in Jan. but not beyond last day in June; session may begin at a different time or extend beyond last day of June by call of Governor or of presiding officers of both Houses. (Const., art. II, §4).

Special or extraordinary sessions may be called by the Governor or presiding officers of both Houses. (Const., art. II, §4).

Initiative and Referendum.—No provision for, except that voters of each district of State decide by referendum whether bingo is to be legal within district. (Const., art. II, §17A).

Lobbyists.—Every lobbyist must register with State Public Integrity Commission. (29-5832). Every employer of lobbyist must furnish to lobbyist written and signed authorization to act which must be filed with Commission at time of registration. (29-5833). No lobbyist shall be employed pursuant to compensation agreement that permits more than half of compensation to be contingent upon outcome of legislative or administrative action. (29-5834). Lobbyists must file, on or before 20th day of month following each calendar quarter, written report containing certain required information. (29-5835). Violation of lobbyist registration provisions is misdemeanor. (29-5837).

REPORTS:

Delaware law reports consist of: Harrington's reports, 5 vols. 1832-1855; Houston's reports, 9 vols. 1855-1893, Marvel's reports, 2 vols. 1893-1897; Pennewill's reports, 7 vols. 1897-1909; Boyce's reports, 7 vols. 1909-1920; W. W. Harrington's reports, 9 vols. 1919-1939; Terry's reports, 11 vols. 1939-1958; Storey's reports, 9 vols. 1958-1966; Houston's criminal reports, 1 vol. 1856-1879; Bates' chancery reports, 4 vols. 1814-1873; Chancery reports consist of vols. 1-43, 1892-1968. Delaware Decisions are also reported in Atlantic Reporter. As of Jan. 1, 1969, above Delaware reports were discontinued and Delaware official reporter is Delaware Reporter which is captioned as and cited as appropriate volume of Atlantic Reporter.

Digests.—Delaware digests consist of: Ridgely's Digest, covering Harrington's reports I to V inclusive, Del. Chancery I to V. Houston's reports I to VI inclusive, Houston's Criminal Cases Vol. I; and Marvel's Delaware Corporations and Receiverships, 6th Ed., covering all cases under Delaware corporation law as amended through 1939, and all decisions relating to receiverships of Delaware corporations; Wooley on Delaware Practice, 2 vols. (1906). Delaware and Atlantic Digest, with pocket parts supplement, covers reported Delaware cases.

STATUTES:

Delaware Code is a compilation of revised statutes up to 1974.

Uniform Acts adopted are: Alcoholism and Intoxication Treatment (1979) (16 Del.C. §§2201 to 2232); Anatomical Gift (1970) (trans. 1990) (16 Del. C. §§2710-2719); Arbitration (1972) (10 Del.C. §§5701 to 5725); Child Custody Jurisdiction (1976) (13 Del.C. §§1901 to 1925); Child Protection From Domestic Violence (1994) (13 Del.C. §§701A to 711A); Commercial Code (adopted 1977 Revision of Art. 8 and 1972 Revision of Art. 9) (1967) (6 Del.C. §§1-101 to 11-109); Contribution Among Tortfeasors (1949) (10 Del.C. §§6301 to 6308); Controlled Substances (1972) (16 Del.C. §§4701-4796); Criminal Extradition (1937) (11 Del.C. §§2501 to 2530); Deceptive Trade Practices (1964 Act) (1965) (6 Del.C. §§2531 to 2536); Declaratory Judgments (1981) (10 Del.C. §§6501 to 6513); Determination of Death (1986) (1990) (24 Del. C. §1760); Disclaimer of Transfers by Will, Intestacy or Appointment (1982) (12 Del.C. §§601 to 608); Disclaimer of Transfers Under Nontestamentary Instruments

STATUTES ... *continued*

(1982) (12 Del.C. §§601 to 608); Durable Power of Attorney (1982) (12 Del.C. §§4901 to 4905); Enforcement of Foreign Judgments (1986) (10 Del.C. §§4781 to 4787); Facsimile Signatures of Public Officials (1971) (29 Del.C. §§5401 to 5406); Federal Tax Lien Registration (1973) (25 Del.C. §§4801 to 4805); Foreign Money-Judgments Recognition (1997) (Fraudulent Transfer (1996) (6 Del.C. §§1301 to 1311); †Insurers Liquidation (1968) (18 Del.C. §§5901 [2] to [13], 5902, 5903, 5913 to 5920); Interstate Family Support (1994) (13 Del.C. §§601-691); †Limited Partnership (1976 Act) (1973) (6 Del.C. §§17-101 to 17-1111); Management of Institutional Funds (1974) (12 Del.C. §§4701 to 4708); Notarial Acts, Uniform Law on (1984) (29 Del.C. §§4321 to 4328); Parentage (1983) (13 Del.C. §§801 to 819); Partnership (1947) (6 Del.C. §§1501 to 1553); Rules of Evidence (1980) (D.R.E. 101 to 1103); Securities (1956 Act) (1973) (6 Del.C. §§7301 to 7330); Simplification of Fiduciary Security Transfers (1963) (12 Del.C. §§4301 to 4311); Simultaneous Death (1945) (12 Del.C. §§701 to 707); State Antitrust (1979) (6 Del.C. §§2101 to 2114); To Secure Attendance of Witnesses from Without a State in Criminal Proceedings (1937) (11 Del.C. §§3521 to 3526); Trade Secrets (1982) (6 Del.C. §§2001 to 2009); Transfers to Minors (1996).

Uniform Commercial Code adopted. See category Business Regulation and Commerce, topic Commercial Code.

For text of Uniform Acts falling within the scope of the Martindale-Hubbell Law Digests see Uniform and Model Acts section.

†Adopted with significant variations or modifications. See appropriate topics.

UNIFORM LAWS:

For list of Uniform Acts in force in this state see topic Statutes. For text of Uniform Acts within the scope of the Martindale-Hubbell Law Digests see Uniform and Model Acts section.

CRIMINAL LAW

BAIL:

See topic Criminal Law.

CRIMINAL LAW:

For general provisions concerning crimes, see 11-c.1-5 and 15. For general procedure see 11-c.17-45; Rules of Superior Court based on Federal Criminal Rules. For jurisdiction and procedure of Family Court, see 10-c.9.

Indictment or Information.—No person may, for any indictable offense, be proceeded against criminally by information except in cases arising in land or naval forces or in militia while in active service. (Const., art. I, §8). Proceedings may be begun by indictment, by complaint, or by arrest where arrest is permissible without warrant. (Super. Ct. Crim. Rule 3[a]). Capital offense may be prosecuted only by indictment, and except as otherwise provided by State Constitution, other offenses within exclusive jurisdiction of Superior Court must be prosecuted by indictment, unless defendant waives indictment, in which event case may proceed by information. (Super. Ct. Crim. Rule 7[a]).

Proceedings in Municipal Court of City of Wilmington are by information. (11-5701). Prosecution of adults in Family Court is by either information or complaint. (10-1021).

Bail.—Person arrested and charged with any crime, other than capital crime, shall be released (a) upon his own recognizance, or (b) upon unsecured personal appearance bond, or (c) upon secured bond, as determined by court. (11-2104[a]). If accused furnishes surety, court may impose any of conditions under 11-2108, including specific consideration for safety of victim and community. (11-2104[b]). Superior Court will immediately revoke bail and incarcerate any person convicted of felony which carries mandatory jail sentence. (11-2104[c]). Family Court Master or Judge may restrict freedom of person released on bail. (10-1021). Capital crimes are not bailable, unless defendant discharges burden of proving that there is good ground to doubt truth of accusation. (11-2103). Purpose of bail system is to assure appearance and protect safety of community. (11-2105). Court may restrict person released on bail from having contact with victim. (11-2108[a][5]). Persons violating bail provisions are subject to separate criminal penalties. (11-2113[c]). Excessive bail prohibited. (Const., art. I, §11).

Uniform Criminal Extradition Act adopted. (11-2501-2530).

Uniform Law for Out-Of-State Parolees' Supervision adopted. (11-4358-4359).

Uniform Agreement on Detainers, as proposed by Council of State Governments, adopted. (11-2540-2550).

DEBTOR AND CREDITOR

ASSIGNMENTS:

All bonds, specialties, and notes in writing, payable to any person, or order, or assigns, may be assigned, or indorsed, and the assignee, or indorsee, his executors, administrators, or assigns, may again assign, or indorse the same, as often as may be desired, subject to provisions of Uniform Commercial Code. (6-2702, 2703). See category Business Regulation and Commerce, topic Commercial Code.

Filing required for assignments of chattel mortgages (6-9-302), subject to provisions of Uniform Commercial Code.

Recording required for mortgage assignments (9-9608), subject to provisions of Uniform Commercial Code.

Notice of an assignment in the office of the recorder of deeds constitutes constructive notice of such assignment as against all persons.

Instruments Transferring Title.—Deeds may be proved by acknowledgment or in court by one or more subscribing witnesses. (25-122).

Effect.—Assignors, or indorsers, or their executors, or administrators cannot release or discharge any sum due by such bonds, specialties, or notes, after date of such assignment. (6-2702).

Assignment of Wages.—Excluded from secured transaction requirements under Uniform Commercial Code. (6-9-104[d]).

Action by Assignee.—A person to whom a contract, express or implied, has been transferred or assigned, either in accordance with a statute or with the common law, may sue thereon in his own name. (10-3902). Assignability of unperfected mechanics' lien is not authorized under existing law and may not be permitted. (435 A.2d 730).

Assignment Of Workmen's Compensation.—Prohibited. (19-2355).

Uniform Commercial Code adopted. See category Business Regulation and Commerce, topic Commercial Code.

ATTACHMENT:

Actions in Which Allowed.—In both foreign and domestic attachment actions the writ will issue in contract or in tort.

Courts Which May Issue Writ.—In foreign and domestic attachment, Superior Court has jurisdiction in any amount exceeding $50 (10-3501, 3506; 3507) and justices of peace up to $15,000 (10-9583). Common Pleas Court has jurisdiction similar to Superior Court. (10-1324).

In Whose Favor Writ May Issue.—Any plaintiff may secure attachment where proper grounds therefor are shown (10-3501-07), even if writ is to be issued against nonresidents or foreign corporations (10-3506-07). Provision is made for attachment of shares of corporate stock or any interest therein. (8-324).

Against Whom Writ May Issue.—Domestic writs may be issued against residents of Delaware (10-3501) and corporations doing business in Delaware (10-3502[a][b]). Foreign writs may be issued against nonresidents (10-3506) or foreign corporations (10-3507). Banks, trust companies, savings institutions and loan associations, except only as to wage attachment against wages of employee, and building and loan associations doing business in state are exempt. (10-3502[b]; 5-1708). Insurance companies are liable only as to amounts claimed or payable under policy. (10-3502[c]).

An unincorporated association including a partnership is liable to attachment in any action in its common name. (10-3504[a]).

Claims on Which Writ May Not Issue.—Property title to which has not yet passed to judgment debtor not subject to attachment (52 Del. 397, 158 A.2d 809); lessee's interest in personal property cannot be attached (367 A.2d 658).

Grounds.—Writs of both domestic attachment against a resident or a domestic corporation and writs of foreign attachment against nonresident or foreign corporation may issue by order of court, on proof satisfactory to court. Affidavit is satisfactory for this purpose. (Super. Ct. Rule 4[b]).

Domestic writs may issue against a resident or domestic corporation, except banks, trust companies, savings institutions and loan associations, upon proof satisfactory to court that defendant cannot be found or that defendant is justly indebted to plaintiff in amount over $50, and that he has absconded, is about to leave state, or has left state, with intent to defraud creditors or elude process. (10-3501-02).

Foreign writs may issue against a nonresident upon proof satisfactory to court that defendant cannot be found, that plaintiff has good cause of action against defendant in amount exceeding $50, and that defendant resides out of state. (10-3506). Foreign writs may issue against foreign corporation upon proof satisfactory to court that defendant is a corporation not created by, or existing under laws of Delaware, and that plaintiff has a good cause of action against defendant in an amount exceeding $50. (10-3507).

Procedure to Obtain.—Affidavit filed in Superior Court with complaint setting forth statutory grounds and other facts required by court rules. (Super. Ct. Rule 4[b][1]).

Attachment Bond.—No mesne writ of attachment will be issued until plaintiff gives bond conditioned that if suit is not prosecuted with effect, or if judgment rendered therein is in favor of defendant, plaintiff will pay any and all costs which may be awarded to a defendant, together with any and all damages, not exceeding amount of the bond, which a defendant in the suit may have sustained by reason of such attachment. Amount and surety discretionary with Superior Court. (Super. Ct. Rule 4[b][2]).

Levy is to cover both real and personal property. (10-3508). Lessee's interest in personal property cannot be levied on in satisfaction of judgment against lessee. (367 A.2d 658).

Indemnity.—Statute gives Superior Court power to issue orders concerning indemnity. (10-3512). See subhead Attachment Bond, supra.

Lien.—Writ is a lien on goods and chattels actually levied on from time of levy. (276 F. 724).

Priorities.—Writs of attachments are to be executed by sheriff in order in which received by him. If several against same defendant are received together, priority is assigned according to their respective numbers. (10-5082, 5084).

Release of Property.—The writ may be discharged by furnishing security to the amount of the value of the attached property or the amount claimed in the suit, whichever is the lesser. (Super. Ct. Rule 4[b][3][B]). If nonresident enters general appearance and moves to release property, court must so order unless plaintiff shows other circumstances which threaten satisfaction of any judgment obtained and unless plaintiff gives bond in amount at least equal to current value of property. (Super. Ct. Rule 4[b][3][A]).

Sale.—If attached property is perishable, court may order attaching officer to sell same. No sale without court order. (Super. Ct. Rule 4[b][9]).

ATTACHMENT . . . *continued*

Third Party Claim.—See category Civil Actions and Procedure, topic Actions, subhead Third Party Practice.

Vacation or Modification.—Nonresident may generally get property released on general appearance; property in any event will be released on furnishing security. (Super. Ct. Rule 4[b][3]).

CREDITORS' SUITS:

Court of Chancery has jurisdiction of creditors' bills for equitable relief. There is no special legislation regulating these suits. See topic Executions; also topic Fraudulent Sales and Conveyances.

EXECUTIONS:

Kinds of Execution.—Governed generally by statute and Court Rules based upon Federal Rules. Execution fieri facias is usual selling writ for personalty, and is seizing writ for realty. Venditioni exponas is usual selling writ for realty. (10-4951). The writ of levari facias is the selling writ for land actions begun by scire facias. (10-4961).

Personal property must be exhausted before real property can be seized and real estate is subject to execution and sale where no sufficient personal estate can be found. (10-4901).

Exemptions.—See topic Exemptions.

Time for Issuance.—If a judgment is final and has not been satisfied, and if there is no stay of execution, execution may issue at any time within five years after judgment is rendered. (10-5072[a]).

Stay of Execution.—Upon judgment before court against freeholder for sum exceeding $5 besides costs, there may be stay of execution for six months, if defendant makes application within five days after judgment and unless creditor in judgment or other credible person files affidavit before justice "that he has good ground to apprehend and does verily believe that if the stay of execution be allowed, the sum due by the judgment will be lost." (10-9544). Plaintiff may file transcript of his judgment in Superior Court and judgment so transferred will become lien upon any real estate of defendant in same manner as judgments obtained in Superior Court. (10-9546). Execution on judgment for more than $5, besides costs, will also be stayed for nine months if security with approved surety is given that judgment will be satisfied at expiration of this time. (10-9545).

In all cases where a judgment by default for want of an affidavit of defense is taken, a stay for six months will be granted if security is given to pay the judgment, interest and costs. (10-3901[e]).

Lien.—Execution of lien binds all goods and chattels within bailiwick, which are levied upon within 60 days. No levy upon goods and chattels, made by virtue of execution process, is of any force or effect as against subsequent execution levied upon same goods and chattels for longer period than three years from making of such first-mentioned levy. (10-5081).

Levy.—Valid levy necessitates a seizure, actual or constructive. Inventory and appraisal constitute constructive seizure of personalty. Constructive seizure of realty is effected by filing a description of lands with writ and making return. (42 Del. 510, 39 A.2d 17).

Return.—In a court of record, execution is returnable before the rising of court on the second day after the return day mentioned in the writ. (10-5041).

In a court of a justice of the peace, execution is returnable on a day certain, not more than 60 nor less than 30 days after date of issue, but a return of nulla bona or "no goods" may be made after two days from date of issue. (10-9547[b]).

Priorities.—If several executions against same defendant are delivered same day, first delivered has priority. If several executions against same defendant are delivered together, they have priority according to respective numbers. (10-5082).

Claims of Third Party.—If real property of third party is sold under execution and deed granted purchaser, such deed is on trust or any person having right may be otherwise relieved. (10-4980).

Satisfaction.—(See category Civil Actions and Procedure, topic Judgments, subhead Satisfaction of Judgment.) No judgment is deemed paid or satisfied merely on evidence of levy. (10-5072[b]).

Sale.—Sales by order of court are at public auction, to highest and best bidder, and subject to confirmation. (10-4971-4976).

Public notice of sale of goods and chattels by sheriff or coroner, under execution process, and of day, hour, and place thereof, must be given by advertisements posted, at least ten days before day of sale, in five, or more, public places in county, two in hundred of defendant's residence, if he resides in county; and one must at least ten days before day of sale, be delivered to defendant, and one to each plaintiff in execution, and to each plaintiff in any other execution, at time in hands of sheriff or coroner, or left at usual place of abode of such defendant and plaintiffs respectively; and if any plaintiff in any such execution resides out of county such advertisement must be delivered to attorney of such plaintiff, and one advertisement must be transmitted to such plaintiff by mail, at post office nearest his place of abode; and advertisement must, at least ten days before day of sale, be delivered to defendant's landlord, or his agent, if there be such residing in county. This section and §4971 do not apply to execution issued by justices of peace or Court of Common Pleas. (10-4972).

Time of Sale.—Goods and chattels, taken in execution by a sheriff, or coroner, may not be sold until the expiration of 30 days after the levy thereon and notice thereof to the defendant; goods of perishable nature, or those that will create charge by keeping, may by order of court be sold sooner. (10-4971).

Public notice of sale of lands and tenements under execution process must be given by advertisements posted, at least ten days before day of sale, in ten of most public places of county, where premises are situated, setting forth day, hour and place of sale, and what lands and tenements are to be sold, and where they lie. One of said advertisements must be posted in hundred in which premises are located, and one, in each of hundreds which immediately adjoin said hundred; like advertisement must be

delivered ten days before day of sale to defendant, or left at his usual place of abode, if he has known place of abode in county; if defendant does not reside in county, notice is served on tenant, or if there is no tenant, it is left at mansion house or other public place on premises. Same provisions apply to land as to chattels in respect of notices to each plaintiff in execution. Notices of sale must be published for two weeks previous to sale in two newspapers of county wherein land lies, with not more than three insertions per week in any one newspaper. (10-4973[a]).

Redemption.—There is no statutory provision for redemption under Delaware law.

Supplementary Proceedings.—Discovery by deposition, interrogatories and requests for production available to judgment creditor in aid of judgment or execution under rule of court. (Super. Ct. Rule 69[aa]).

Body Execution.—No writ of capias ad satisfaciendum may be issued upon any judgment in civil action against any person until writ of fieri facias on said judgment has issued, and it appears by return thereon that defendant has no property within county sufficient to pay debt or damages, or there is affidavit to same effect; nor may it issue until plaintiff files affidavit of fraud. Affidavit must also allege debt of more than $50. (10-5051-2). Person arrested may move for investigation of specifications on issue of fraud. (10-5053).

EXEMPTIONS:

Every person residing within this state has exempt from execution or attachment process, or distress for rent, following articles of personal property: Family Bible, school books, family library, family pictures, seat or pew in any church, lot in any burial ground, all wearing apparel of debtor and his family, and in addition to articles hereinbefore specifically named, shall have exempt tools, implements and fixtures necessary for carrying on his or her trade or business, not exceeding in value $75 in New Castle and Sussex Counties, and $50 in Kent County. All sewing machines owned and used by seamstresses or private families are exempt but this provision does not apply to persons who keep sewing machines for sale or hire. All pianos, piano playing attachments and organs leased or hired by any person residing in this state are exempt, but owner is to give notice of hiring of piano or organ to landlord, or his agent. (10-4902).

Head of family exemption provided for in 10-4903 declared unconstitutional. (380 A.2d 985).

Benefits paid by any benefit society are exempt from attachment, garnishment and other process and cannot be taken in any way to pay any debt or liability of any member or beneficiary. (18-6218).

Substitution.—No provision.

Debts Against Which Exemptions Not Allowed.—Personal property is not exempt from taxation or sale for taxes. (10-4910). See also supra, second introductory paragraph of this topic.

Necessity of Claiming Exemption.—Exemptions allowed to head of family may be claimed by husband and wife jointly or by either with the written consent of the other, or half may be claimed by each spouse. (10-4904).

Waiver of Exemptions.—Personal property exemption may be waived by husband and wife jointly. (10-4912).

Earnings.—85% of any Delaware resident's wages for labor or services are exempt from mesne or execution attachment, except when process is for fine, costs or taxes owed to State. Only one attachment may be made on any amount of wages due, and creditor causing attachment to be made has priority until judgment for which attachment was made has been fully paid. Wages includes salaries, commissions, and any other remuneration employer pays employee, but does not include payments made for services of person who is master of his own time and effort. (10-4913). Attachments for support of spouse and minor children are not subject to limitations of 10-4913. (460 A.2d 525).

Exemption of wages cannot be waived. See also topics Garnishment, Attachment.

FORECLOSURE:

See topic Liens; categories Business Regulation and Commerce, topic Commercial Code; Mortgages, topic Mortgages of Real Property.

FRAUDULENT SALES AND CONVEYANCES:

Uniform Commercial Code adopted. See category Business Regulation and Commerce, topic Commercial Code.

Uniform Fraudulent Transfer Act has been adopted. (6-1301 et seq.).

Remedies.—Under this chapter, cause of action for fraudulent transfer or obligation is extinguished unless action is brought (a) under §1304(a) within four years after transfer or obligation occurred, or, if later, within one year after transfer or obligation was or could reasonably have been discovered; (b) under §§1304(a)(2) or 1305(a) within four years after transfer was made or obligation incurred; or (c) under §1305(b), within one year after transfer was made or obligation incurred.

Bulk Sales.—Uniform Commercial Code bulk transfers provision repealed. (70 Del. L. 439, §1).

GARNISHMENT:

On any judgment of court of record, in addition to any other execution, writ of attachment may be issued containing order for summoning as garnishees any persons indebted to, or holding property of judgment debtor. Perishable goods or goods creating charge by keeping seized under writ may be sold by order of court. (10-5031).

In attachment, individuals or corporations (except banks, trust companies, savings institutions and loan associations for attachment other than wage attachment of employee) may be summoned as garnishees and proceedings had thereafter to subject property held by them belonging to debtor, or debts owed by them to debtor, to writ. Insurance companies are not liable to attachment except as to moneys due in consequence of happening of risk provided in insurance policy or wage attachments of

GARNISHMENT . . . *continued*

employees. (10-3502). Banks and trust companies are exempt from equitable order restraining disbursement of funds. (517 A.2d 259). Unlawful for employer to dismiss employee because employer summoned as his garnishee. (10-3509).

Property Which May Be Reached.—Goods, chattels, rights, credits, moneys, effects, lands and tenements may be attached under this chapter. (10-3508). See also topic Exemptions.

Jurisdiction.—In Superior Court, Court of Common Pleas, Justice of Peace or Family Court.

Proceedings to Obtain.—Same as foreign attachment. (10-5031).

Answer of Garnishee.—Garnishee must serve answer within 20 days of service of process specifying what goods, chattels, rights, credits, money or effects of defendant, if any, he has in his possession or custody. (Super. Ct. Rule 5[aa][2]). Answer of garnishee in execution attachment, at option of plaintiff, may be taken by affidavit before anyone authorized to administer oaths, and when so taken, it is docketed in same manner, and has same effect, as if taken in open court. (10-5032).

Practice.—Follows foreign attachment practice. (10-5031).

Adverse Claims.—No statutory provision.

Judgment is pleadable in bar by garnishee in action by defendant in execution attachment against him. (10-5031).

Earnings.—Wages of employee of the state or any county, district or municipality thereof are subject to garnishment. (10-3503[a]). Employee includes any person performing any form of work for State, county, district or municipality for compensation. (10-3503[b]).

As to wages generally, see topic Exemptions.

HOMESTEADS:

No legislation.

JUDGMENT NOTES:

See category Civil Actions and Procedure, topic Judgments, subhead Judgment by Confession.

LEVY:

See topics Attachment, Executions.

LIENS:

Uniform Commercial Code adopted. See category Business Regulation and Commerce, topic Commercial Code.

Garage Keeper.—Hotelkeeper, innkeeper, garage owner, auction service or other person who for price has custody or care of any vehicle, who makes repairs on or who provides services, supplies or materials for same, has lien on vehicle to secure payment of price. (25-3901). If price remains unpaid, in whole or in part, 30 days after it became due lienor may apply to Justice of Peace Court for authorization of sale. Court will notify owner, who may request hearing. (25-3903). Owner may file action in replevin at any time, in accordance with 10-c.95. (25-3908).

Mechanics' Liens.—Law contained in 25-c.27. Any person or persons having performed or furnished labor or material, or both, to amount exceeding $25 in or for erection, alteration, or repair of any structure, in pursuance of any contract, express or implied, with owners of such structure, or with agent of such owner, or with any contractor or subcontractor who has contracted for erection, alteration or repair of same, and for furnishing of whole or any part of materials therefor, may obtain lien upon such building, and upon ground upon which same is situated. (25-2702[a]). No lien shall be obtained on land or structure which is used solely as residence of owner, when said owner has made full or final payment in good faith to contractor with whom he contracted for construction or repair. (25-2707). Unperfected lien not assignable. (435 A.2d 730).

Statement of Claim.—Every person entitled to benefits conferred by 25-c.27, and desiring to avail himself of lien provided for, must, within time specified, file statement of claim in office of Prothonotary of Superior Court in and for county wherein such structure is situated. (25-2712).

Any contractor who has contracted directly with owner or reputed owner of any structure and has furnished both labor and material shall file no statement of his claim until after expiration of 90 days from completion of such structure; and such contractor must file his statement within 30 days after expiration of 90 days. All other persons embraced within provisions of this chapter and entitled to avail themselves of liens, must file statement of their respective claims within 90 days from completion of labor performed or from last delivery of materials furnished by them respectively. (25-2711).

Statement must set forth: Names of plaintiff or claimant, owner or reputed owner of structure, and contractor; name of contractor and whether contract of claimant was made with such owner or his agent or with such contractor; amount or sum claimed to be due; description of labor done or materials furnished with bill of particulars annexed; time when said labor or furnishing of said materials was commenced and finished; location and description of structure; that said labor was performed, or said materials were furnished on credit of said house or structure; amount of claim (which must exceed $25), and that neither amount nor any part thereof has been paid to claimant; and time of recording of first mortgage upon such structure which is granted to secure existing indebtedness or future advances. Claimant must make affidavit to truth and correctness of claim and of facts stated therein. (25-2712).

Discharge.—Lien may be discharged during proceedings by deposit with court of cash or approved security. (25-2729).

Judgment obtained upon such claim becomes a lien upon such building, house or structure, and upon the ground upon which the same is situated, and relates back to the day upon which labor was begun or furnishing of said material was commenced or

time immediately following recording of first mortgage on conveyance in nature of first mortgage and takes priority accordingly. (25-2718).

Proceedings to recover amount of any claim are by writ of scire facias, in form prescribed by Superior Court. (25-2714).

Execution of judgments for mechanics lien is by writ of levari facias. (25-2719).

Lien on Vessels.—Mechanics' liens may be placed for labor or materials furnished in the construction or alteration of a vessel within this State; affidavit and bill of particulars must be filed within one year after such repairs. (25-2726).

If proceeds of sale are not sufficient to pay all liens in full, proceeds are divided ratably without priority or preference. (25-2720).

Personal action against owner, contractor, or other contracting parties may be maintained before, after, or at time of mechanics' lien proceedings and judgment on one does not bar judgment on other. But monies paid on one such judgment may be ordered by court to be credited on other. (25-2721, 2725).

Public Works.—Simultaneous with execution of formal contract successful bidder shall execute bond to State or contracting county in sum equal to 100% of contract price. In event of default, money from bond will be used by Department of Transportation. Agency may reduce or waive bond if stated in bid specifications. (29-6927[b][f]).

For other liens mentioned or discussed elsewhere in this digest, see topics Attachment, Executions, Exemptions, Homesteads; categories Business Regulation and Commerce, topics Carriers, Commercial Code; Civil Actions and Procedure, topic Judgments; Mortgages, topic Mortgages of Real Property; Property, topic Landlord and Tenant; Taxation, topic Property Taxes, subhead Liens.

Redemption.—There is no statutory right of redemption of property sold in foreclosure of liens thereon.

MECHANICS' LIENS:

See topic Liens.

PLEDGES:

Uniform Commercial Code adopted. (6-Art. 9). See category Business Regulation and Commerce, topic Commercial Code.

RECEIVERS:

Jurisdiction.—Court of Chancery has jurisdiction as at common law respecting receivers in general. This jurisdiction has been broadened to include receivers for corporations. (Ch. Ct. Rules 148-168).

Proceedings.—Upon bill filed, chancellor may appoint receiver pendente lite and issue rule requiring defendant to show cause why receiver should not be appointed or continue. (Ch. Ct. Rule 149).

Eligibility and Competency.—No person may be appointed sole receiver who does not at the time of appointment reside in the State of Delaware. (Ch. Ct. Rule 150).

Upon dissolution of any corporation, Court of Chancery, upon application of any creditor, stockholder, director of corporation, or other person, who, in court's discretion, shows good cause therefor, may either appoint one or more of directors thereof as trustees, or appoint one or more persons as receivers. (8-279).

Qualification.—Receiver must give bond with surety to be approved by court. (Ch. Ct. Rule 149).

Powers and Duties.—In general, are at discretion of chancellor. (Ch. Ct. Rule 148). Receiver appointed by chancellor for any Delaware corporation is vested by operation of law without act or deed, with title to all corporate property, real, personal or mixed, except real estate situate outside state. (8-292[a]).

Compensation is fixed by chancellor after notice to creditors. (Ch. Ct. Rules 164-167).

Discharge is effected by chancellor upon petition of receiver after final distribution. (Ch. Ct. Rule 168).

REDEMPTION:

See topics Executions, Liens; categories Mortgages, topic Mortgages of Real Property; Taxation, topic Property Taxes, subhead Redemption.

SUPPLEMENTARY PROCEEDINGS:

No provision for.

TRUSTEE PROCESS:

See topic Garnishment.

USURY:

See category Business Regulation and Commerce, topic Interest.

DISPUTE RESOLUTION

ALTERNATIVE DISPUTE RESOLUTION:

Mandatory Dispute Resolution.—

Rule 16.1 Compulsory Arbitration.—Pretrial arbitration required for all civil cases filed in Superior Court or Court of Common Pleas for which trial is available, monetary damages sought, and nonmonetary claims insubstantial, except those in which counsel for party requesting damages certifies that damages exceed $100,000 for Superior Court claims, and $15,000 for Court of Common Pleas claims. (Super. Ct. Civ. Rule 16.1; C.P. Ct. Civ. Rule 16.1; Super. Ct. Form 32). Any case, however, may be submitted to pretrial arbitration pursuant to Rule 16.1 by agreement of all parties. (Super. Ct. Civ. Rule 16.1; C.P. Ct. Civ. Rule 16.1). All claims should indicate whether case is arbitration or non-arbitration case in caption beneath civil action number. (Super. Ct. Civ. Rule 16.1; C.P. Ct. Civ. Rule 16.1; Super. Ct. Form 31).

ALTERNATIVE DISPUTE RESOLUTION . . . *continued*
Claims involving equitable relief will not be referred to arbitration. (Super. Ct. Civ. Rule 16.1[a]; C.P. Ct. Civ. Rule 16.1[a]).

Procedure.—All arbitration cases referred to arbitration within ten days after filing of all initial responsive pleadings of all parties. (Super. Ct. Civ. Rule 16.1[b]; C.P. Ct. Civ. Rule 16.1[b]). Arbitrator may be appointed by agreement of parties through stipulation filed with Court no later than ten days after case is referred to arbitration. (Super. Ct. Civ. Rule 16.1[d][2]; C.P. Ct. Civ. Rule 16.1[d][2]). If parties fail to file stipulation, Court will select arbitrator assigned from list of arbitrators as provided by Rule 16.1. (Super. Ct. Civ. Rule 16.1[d][3]; C.P. Ct. Civ. Rule 16.1[d][3]). All discovery requests may be filed, but responses to discovery are stayed until and unless request for trial de novo is made. (Super. Ct. Civ. Rule 16.1[e]; C.P. Ct. Civ. Rule 16.1[e]).

Hearing.—Arbitration hearing shall be scheduled and held by arbitrator within 40 days of appointment. (Super. Ct. Civ. Rule 16.1[f][1]; C.P. Ct. Civ. Rule 16.1[f][1]). Arbitrator shall give each party at least ten days' written notice of hearing if date is not agreed to by all parties. (Super. Ct. Civ. Rule 16.1[f][2]; C.P. Ct. Civ. Rule 16.1[f][2]). Rules of court in which action filed apply to proceeding to compel attendance of witnesses and production of documents and testimony is under oath unless waived by both parties. (Super. Ct. Civ. Rule 16.1[f][5] & [6]; C.P. Ct. Civ. Rule 16.1[f][5] & [6]). Delaware Uniform Rules of Evidence used as guide to admissibility of evidence, but evidence may be submitted and considered if it possesses probative value under reasonable person standard. (Super. Ct. Civ. Rule 16.1[f][7]; C.P. Ct. Civ. Rule 16.1[f][7]). Copies or photographs of all exhibits except impeachment exhibits must be delivered to arbitrator and all parties at least ten days prior to hearing. (Super. Ct. Civ. Rule 16.1[f][7]; C.P. Ct. Civ. Rule 16.1[f][7]). Arbitrator shall consider all such exhibits so delivered, unless adverse party notifies all parties five days prior to hearing that there is issue of authenticity of exhibit. (Super. Ct. Civ. Rule 16.1[f][7]; C.P. Ct. Civ. Rule 16.1[f][7]). Arbitrator can refuse to receive into evidence any exhibits not submitted through this process. (Super. Ct. Civ. Rule 16.1[f][7]; C.P. Ct. Civ. Rule 16.1[f][7]).

Award and Enforcement.—Arbitrator shall issue written arbitrator's order to parties within five days following hearing. (Super. Ct. Civ. Rule 16.1[g][1]; C.P. Ct. Civ. Rule 16.1[g][1]). Judgment has same force and effect as civil judgment of court in which action filed except that it is not subject to appeal. (Super. Ct. Civ. Rule 16.1[g][1]; C.P. Ct. Civ. Rule 16.1[g][1]). Arbitrator's order will be entered as order of judgment by Superior Court upon motion of party after time for requesting trial de novo has expired. (Super. Ct. Civ. Rule 16.1[g][1]; C.P. Ct. Civ. Rule 16.1[g][1]).

Appeal.—Judgment of arbitrator not appealable. (Super. Ct. Civ. Rule 16.1[g][1]; C.P. Ct. Civ. Rule 16.1[g][1]). Party, however, may demand trial de novo within 20 days after filing of arbitrator's order. (Super. Ct. Civ. Rule 16.1[h][1]; C.P. Ct. Civ. Rule 16.1[h][1]). Trial de novo is only remedy of any party in case subject to Rule 16.1. (Super. Ct. Civ. Rule 16.1[h][1]; C.P. Ct. Civ. Rule 16.1[h][1]). Upon request of trial de novo, case is placed on calendar of Court and treated for all purposes as if arbitration had not occurred. (Super. Ct. Civ. Rule 16.1[h][2]; C. P. Ct. Civ. Rule 16.1[h][2]). Court shall not admit evidence that there has been arbitration proceeding, nor may it use any other evidence from arbitration proceeding except recorded testimony given at arbitration hearing may be used in same manner as testimony taken at deposition in trial de novo. (Super. Ct. Civ. Rule 16.1[h][3]; C.P. Ct. Civ. Rule 16.1[h][3]). If party demanding trial de novo fails to obtain verdict from Superior Court more favorable than arbitrator's order, moving party shall be assessed fees and costs of arbitration and arbitrator's compensation. (Super. Ct. Civ. Rule 16.1[h][4]; C.P. Ct. Civ. Rule 16.1[h][4]).

Family Court Mediation.—In all proceedings requesting relief in form of support and all proceedings involving custody and visitation, mediation conference with parties shall be held by Court staff mediator to identify specific areas at issue to attempt amicable settlement of all unresolved issues or to limit those issues which must be submitted to Court for determination. (Fam. Ct. Civ. Rule 16[a][1] & [b][1]). No trial for either custody or support scheduled prior to completion of mediation process unless Court, upon application of either party or Court staff mediator, orders proceeding referred to judicial scheduling. (Fam. Ct. Civ. Rule 16[a][1] & [b][1]).

Procedure.—Prior to mediation conference, each party may be required to complete written report in form approved by Court. (Fam. Ct. Civ. Rule 16[a][3] & [b][3]). For support cases, Rule 16(a) financial report is required. (Fam. Ct. Civ. Rule 16[a][3]). For custody or visitation cases, Court will inform each party whether written report is required. (Fam. Ct. Civ. Rule 16[b][3]). If matter is not resolved at mediation conference, interim order will be entered.

Hearing.—If matter is not resolved, parties will immediately appear before master for entry of this interim order in support cases. (Fam. Ct. Civ. Rule 16[a][4]). Immediate appearance may be waived if trial before master of action is to be held within ten days of mediation conference. (Fam. Ct. Civ. Rule 16[a][4]). For visitation cases, if agreement cannot be reached, mediator shall recommend interim contact schedule. (Fam. Ct. Civ. Rule 16[b][4]). Recommendation will be reviewed by judge and, if approved, will become interim order of contact without prejudice to either party pending full hearing. (Fam. Ct. Civ. Rule 16[b][4]). If recommendation is not approved, hearing before judge shall be scheduled on expedited basis. (Fam. Ct. Civ. Rule 16[b][4]). Failure of either party to comply with requirements of mediation conference may result in imposition of appropriate sanctions. (Fam. Ct. Civ. Rule 16[a][7]).

Voluntary Dispute Resolution.—Uniform Arbitration Act adopted. (10-5701-5725). See topic Arbitration and Award.

Family Court Voluntary Arbitration.—Voluntary binding arbitration available in all matters involving property division, spousal support, and alimony. (Fam. Ct. Civ. Rule 16.1). Arbitration not available in protection from abuse, custody and/or visitation proceedings. (Fam. Ct. Civ. Rule 16.1[a]). Election to pursue arbitration by both parties constitutes waiver of right to trial. (Fam. Ct. Civ. Rule 16.1[b]). Parties can select arbitrator or judge will do so from list of attorneys who have significant and current experience in Family Court, if parties have not done so. (Fam. Ct. Civ. Rule 16.1[c] & [d]). Arbitrator to be compensated $100 per hour, not to exceed $1,000. (Fam. Ct. Civ. Rule 16.1[e]). Arbitration to be held within 40 days of appointment of arbitrator. (Fam. Ct. Civ. Rule 16.1[f]). Rules of Family Court apply to compel attendance of witnesses and production of documents. (Fam. Ct. Civ. Rule 16.1[i]). Unless waived by parties, testimony is under oath. (Fam. Ct. Civ. Rule 16.1[j]). Arbitrator to issue decision within ten days of conclusion of hearings. (Fam. Ct. Civ. Rule 16.1[n]).

Interim Rule 16.2 Voluntary Mediation.—Any civil matter pending in Superior Court docket is eligible for voluntary mediation. (Super. Ct. Civ. Rule 16.2). Cases are referred to mediation by election of parties or on guidelines established by Office of Mediation Services. (Super. Ct. Civ. Rule 16.2).

Procedure.—Once mediation is elected, all parties and at least one attorney for each represented party must participate in mediation conference. (Super. Ct. Civ. Rule 16.2[b]). Both parties must complete and file mediation conference statement ten days prior to scheduled mediation. (Super. Ct. Civ. Rule 16.2[c]). At some time prior to commencement of mediation conference, all parties must enter into written consent identifying methods by which parties will attempt mediation. (Super. Ct. Civ. Rule 16.2[d]). Written consent form must include rights and obligations of parties to mediation conference and confidentiality of conference. (Super. Ct. Civ. Rule 16.2[d]). All memoranda, work product and other material contained in case files of mediator or anything that occurs at mediation considered confidential. (Super. Ct. Civ. Rule 16.2[e]). However, mediation agreement, if one is reached, is not confidential unless agreed by parties. (Super. Ct. Civ. Rule 16.2[e]).

Hearing.—Mediation conference is intended to be informal proceeding lasting from one to four hours. (Super. Ct. Civ. Rule 16.2[h]). Mediator should assist parties to reach resolution of dispute through discussion and negotiation. (Super. Ct. Civ. Rule 16.2[h]). If agreement is unable to be reached, mediator should officially terminate mediation conference. (Super. Ct. Civ. Rule 16.2[h]). No party is bound by anything said or done at conference unless settlement is reached. (Super. Ct. Civ. Rule 16.2[h]).

Award and Enforcement.—If parties in mediation conference reach agreement, agreement is reduced to writing and signed by parties and mediator. (Super. Ct. Civ. Rule 16.2[i]). Agreement will be binding on all parties to agreement and, upon filing by mediator, will become part of Court record. (Super. Ct. Civ. Rule 16.2[i]). If parties choose to keep terms of agreement confidential, stipulation of dismissal may be filed in alternative. (Super. Ct. Civ. Rule 16.2[i]).

Settlement Week.—Rule 16.2 also provides for annual settlement week in each county. (Super. Ct. Civ. Rule 16.2[j]). Settlement week lasts for two weeks during one calendar year, and any person meeting mediator eligibility requirements may be asked to serve as voluntary mediator. (Super. Ct. Civ. Rule 16.2[j]). Goal of settlement week is to reduce backlog of civil cases pending on Superior Court docket. (Super. Ct. Civ. Rule 16.2[j]).

Summary Proceedings.—To be eligible for Summary Proceedings, there must be at least $100,000 in controversy as to one party although upon application of parties, Court may agree to apply summary proceedings rules to actions involving lesser amounts. (Super. Ct. Civ. Rule 124[b] & [c]). One party must be Delaware citizen, corporation or other business entity. (Super. Ct. Civ. Rule 124[b]). Personal injury claims may not be brought as summary proceedings. (Super. Ct. Civ. Rule 124[b]). All parties to summary proceeding must agree to matter being tried as such. (Super. Ct. Civ. Rule 124[b]). Agreement may be written or by stipulation. (Super. Ct. Civ. Rule 124[b]).

Procedure.—Summary proceedings can be initiated in one of two ways. Where all parties agree prior to filing of complaint to treatment of litigation as summary proceeding, action may be filed as such. (Super. Ct. Civ. Rule 124[b]). Complaint must state that summary proceedings requested, amount in controversy, that one party is Delaware citizen or corporation, and that defendant agrees to summary proceedings. (Super. Ct. Civ. Rule 125[a][3]). In alternative, action pending in Superior Court or in any other court may be converted into summary proceeding if action initially could have been brought as summary proceeding and court consents. (Super. Ct. Civ. Rule 125[b]). Expedited pleading schedule used in summary proceedings. (Super. Ct. Civ. Rule 126). Within 55 days after service of complaint, briefing on motion to dismiss will be completed. (Super. Ct. Civ. Rule 126[c]). Expedited discovery schedule is also used. (Super. Ct. Civ. Rule 127). Each party limited to ten interrogatories and ten requests for admissions, including subparts. (Super. Ct. Civ. Rule 127[b] & [e]). Depositions are limited to opposing party's identified witnesses and affiants and four other persons. (Super. Ct. Civ. Rule 127[d]). Litigants are also required to identify documents they intend to rely upon at trial and witnesses they intend to call at trial, and plaintiffs must identify all persons consulted in preparation of complaint or answer to counterclaim at early stage in discovery. (Super. Ct. Civ. Rule 127[a]). All depositions must be completed within 120 days of filing of last answer, and all discovery must be completed within 180 days of filing of last answer. (Super. Ct. Civ. Rule 127[d] & [h]). There is no motion for summary judgment in summary proceeding. (Super. Ct. Civ. Rule 128).

Contractual Provisions.—Agreement in contract to use Summary Proceedings to resolve any disagreements about contract will be upheld if requisite amount is in controversy.

Hearing.—Parties have option to submit matter without using witnesses. (Super. Ct. Civ. Rule 129). Under this option, expedited briefing schedule is used. All briefing is completed within 75 days of close of discovery. (Super. Ct. Civ. Rule 129[a]). When live witnesses are used at trial, trial will commence within 30 to 60 days after close of discovery and trial should be completed in five days. (Super. Ct. Civ. Rule 130[b]). Parties then file simultaneous post-trial briefs limited to 50 pages within ten days after trial. (Super. Ct. Civ. Rule 130[b]). Court's decision is rendered 30 days after filing of final brief or 30 days after oral argument. (Super. Ct. Civ. Rule 130[c]). Goal is to have final decisions rendered from ten months to one year from filing of complaint.

Appeal.—Cases treated as summary proceedings may be appealed directly to Delaware Supreme Court. No interlocutory appeals may be taken in case treated as summary proceeding. Appeals from cases tried as summary proceedings also expedited.

See note at head of Digest as to 1998 legislation covered.

See Topical Index in front part of this volume.

DE – 24

ALTERNATIVE DISPUTE RESOLUTION . . . *continued*

Voluntary Alternative Dispute Resolution.—(6-7701-7721). Dispute must involve at least $100,000 and not be subject to summary proceedings under 8-211, 215, 220, or 225. Initiation of ADR under this statute toll statute of limitations applicable to proceedings until 14 days after conclusion of ADR. (6-7720). Statute ceases to have any effect if litigation is commenced concerning dispute. (6-7721).

Procedure.—Any person can file certificate with Secretary of State accompanied by filing fee of $1,000 or in case of business entity organized in Delaware, filing fee is $100. (6-7703-7706). Certificate must state that each person signing agrees to follow provisions of statute. In addition, persons who have not filed certificate can agree to be bound to Voluntary Alternative Dispute Resolution Act if other party has filed certificate and agreement or contract incorporates (by reference or otherwise) agreement to be bound by ADR. (6-7703[b]). ADR may be revoked by filing certificate stating such intent accompanied by appropriate filing fee. (6-7707).

ADR Specialist is chosen by party initiating proceedings if proceeding is conducted in Delaware, so long as other party agrees that ADR Specialist is acceptable. (6-7709[a]). If dispute is not submitted for resolution in Delaware, then ADR Specialist is chosen by one of two ways. If there are only two parties to dispute, ADR Specialist is chosen by party who initiated proceedings from panel of three qualified persons who reside or have office in state of incorporation of other party or jurisdiction where other party resides according to other party's ADR certificate. (6-7709[b][1]). If there are more than two parties, party who initiated proceedings chooses panel of three ADR Specialists where greatest number of other parties either are incorporated or reside as before. (6-7709[b][2]). This list of ADR specialists is distributed with notice to other parties required by 6-7710. Other parties then choose acceptable ADR Specialist from list. In dispute with more than two parties, ADR Specialist chosen by greatest number of parties is selected. (6-7709[d]).

Proceedings are started by sending written notice to all interested parties. (6-7710). Other parties who have not filed certificate with Secretary of State can agree to be bound by proceedings by participating in process of selecting ADR Specialist. (6-7711).

Hearing.—Parties can agree to adopt different rules, but statute provides for following rules. (6-7714). No later than seven days prior to ADR, each party submits statement of position (limited to 25 pages) and supporting documents. (6-7714[a]). At ADR, each party has one hour to present position. (6-7714[b]). Other party can have up to one hour to question presenting party. (6-7714[b]). After presentation, ADR Specialist will attempt to resolve dispute by meeting with parties either together or separately until close of regular business hours. (6-7714[c]). Parties can agree to continue discussion after this time until settlement or impasse is reached. (6-7714[d]). If settlement is reached, it must be reduced to writing as soon as possible and will be binding on both parties. (6-7715). If no settlement is reached or impasse is declared, ADR Specialist will declare ADR concluded. (6-7715).

All ADR proceedings are confidential and any statements made or materials produced at ADR are not subject to discovery nor subject to waiver of any applicable privilege. (6-7716). But documents which otherwise would have been discoverable are still treated as discoverable despite their introduction at ADR. (6-7716).

Enforcement of ADR Rights.—Right to ADR may be enforced by any court with jurisdiction over parties. Filing of certificate with Secretary of State is consent to have Chancery Court enforce this right. (6-7719[a]). Party forced to enforce its right to ADR may recover reasonable attorneys' fees. (6-7719[b]). Party failing to pay fees for ADR Specialist is subject to suit for three times fees plus attorneys' fees incurred in such litigation. (6-7719[c]).

ARBITRATION AND AWARD:

Uniform Arbitration Act adopted. (10-5701-5725). Act does not apply to labor contracts if employees represented by contract negotiated by any labor organization or collective bargaining agent or representative. (10-5725).

Form And Requisites Of Submission.—Written agreement to submit to arbitration necessary. (10-5701). Appointment of arbitrator by method provided by agreement. If no method provided or method fails, court will appoint arbitrators upon application of party. (10-5704). Notice of intent to arbitrate must be served on other party, specifying agreement under which arbitration is sought, serving notice of 20 days to apply to enjoin arbitration (10-5703[c]) and setting time and place of arbitration (10-5706).

Contracts To Arbitrate Future Disputes.—Written agreements are valid. (10-5701).

Rescission.—No statutory provision.

Powers of Arbitrators.—Majority of arbitrators may compel attendance of witnesses, production of documents and evidence and administer oaths. Arbitrator or attorney may issue subpoena. (10-5705, 5708). Arbitrators shall appoint time and place for hearing and cause notification to be served not less than five days before hearing. All arbitrators are to conduct hearing, but majority may determine any question and render final award. (10-5706).

Mandatory Arbitration.—No statutory provision.

Award and Enforcement Thereof.—Court of Chancery enforces agreements and enters judgment on awards. (10-5702). Exception: Award of money damages becomes a judgment enforced by Superior Court and constitutes lien on realty in county where award made. (10-5718). Award by confession available for money due at any time before award otherwise made. Basis for award is written statement verified by each party authorizing award. Award must be made within three months of verification and entered on judgment roll by arbitrators or agent named to designate arbitrators. (10-5710). Court of Chancery must confirm award within one year unless grounds urged for modifying, vacating or correcting award. (10-5713).

Death or Incompetency of Party.—Where party to written agreement to submit dies, proceedings may be begun or continued upon proper notice to administrator, executor, or, in case of real estate, devisee or distributee. (10-5722).

State and municipal governments may enter into and be bound by written arbitration agreements. (10-5724).

Statute of Limitations.—Claim barred from arbitration where it would be barred if submitted to state court. (10-5702[c]).

DOCUMENTS AND RECORDS

ACKNOWLEDGMENTS:

Uniform Law on Notarial Acts adopted. (29-4321 to 4328).

Within State.—Acknowledgment or proof of deed may be made in Superior Court, or before any judge, notary public, two justices of peace for same county, or Mayor of City of Wilmington. Fee, 75¢. (25-122, 128). Acknowledgment may be made in Superior Court by attorney by virtue of power in or separate from instrument, if power be first proved. (25-122).

Outside State but Within United States.—Acknowledgment or proof of deed may be made before any U.S. circuit or district judge, any judge of court of record of any state, territory or country, mayor or chief officer of any city or borough, any commissioner of deeds, or any notary public of any state or territory or of District of Columbia by certificate endorsed upon or annexed to deed; or by certificate of clerk, or other officer of court, if certified by judge, seal of her court may be affixed to her certificate or certificate of attestation of clerk or keeper of seal. (25-129).

Outside the United States.—Acknowledgment or proof of deed may be made before any U.S. consul general, consul, vice-consul, consular agent or commercial agent of U.S. at places of their official residences. (25-129).

Persons in or with U. S. Armed Forces.—Acknowledgment by member of U.S. Armed Forces or of merchant seaman outside U.S., or person on war duty outside U.S. may be taken by any commissioned officer of rank of second lieutenant or higher in Army, Marine Corps, or Air Force or ensign or higher in Navy or Coast Guard. Such officer must sign certificate of acknowledgment and state his or her rank and branch of service. (25-130). See topic Notaries Public.

General Requirement as to Taking.—Notarial officer taking acknowledgment must determine from personal knowledge or satisfactory evidence that person appearing before officer and making acknowledgment is person whose true signature is on instrument. (29-4322[a]). Such officer has satisfactory evidence if person is personally known to officer, is identified upon oath or affirmation of credible witness personally known to officer or is identified on basis of identification documents. (29-4322[f]).

General Requirements of Certificate of Notarial Acts.—Date of expiration of commission, if any, is necessary if notarial officer is notary public, but omission may be subsequently corrected. Notarial act must be evidenced by signed and dated certificate by notarial officer. Certificate must also include identification of jurisdiction, title of office of notarial officer, and may include official stamp of office. (29-4327[a]). Certificate of notarial act sufficient if it meets requirements of 29-4327(a) and in form set forth in 29-4328, in form otherwise prescribed by law of State or by-laws or regulations applicable in place in which notarial act performed, or sets forth actions of notarial officer which are sufficient to meet requirements of designated notarial act. (29-4327[b]).

Married Women.—Deed of married woman, executed during coverture, concerning lands or tenements, must be acknowledged by her. (25-102). Deed binds her, her heirs, and all claiming by and under her to special warranty deed. (25-102). If married woman abandoned without just cause any judge certifying must so state. (25-124).

Attorneys in Fact.—Uniform Durable Power of Attorney Act adopted. (12-4901-4905).

Corporations.—Corporate acknowledgment may be by president, or other presiding officer or vice president or assistant vice-president duly authorized by resolution or by legally constituted attorney before any state or federal district or circuit court judge, notary public or two justices of the peace of the same county. (25-127).

Foreign Acknowledgments.—See subheads Outside State but Within United States, and Outside the United States, supra.

Effect of Acknowledgment.—Duly certified acknowledgment of deed or letter of attorney does not constitute instrument evidence without recording, unless deed is one taken and certified upon private examination of married woman. (25-155).

Proof by Subscribing Witness.—Deed may be acknowledged by any party to deed in Superior Court or before any judge in state, notary public, two justices of peace for same county, or Mayor of Wilmington. Deed can also be acknowledged in Superior Court by attorney, by virtue of power in or outside it, if power is first proven in court. Deed may be proved in Superior Court by one or more of subscribing witnesses. (25-122).

Certification of acknowledgment is made by clerk, or Prothonotary, judge, notary public, justice of peace before whom proof is taken. (25-123).

Alternative to Acknowledgment or Proof.—No statutory provision.

Forms.—Following short form certificates of notarial acts (29-4328) are sufficient for purposes indicated, if completed with information required by §4327(a) of this title:

Form

For an acknowledgment in an individual capacity:

State of . . . .
County of . . . .
This instrument was acknowledged before me on . . (date) . . by . . (name(s) of person(s)).

. . . .
(signature of notarial officer)

(Seal, if any)

. . . .
(title and rank)
(my commission expires: . . .)

See note at head of Digest as to 1998 legislation covered.

See Topical Index in front part of this volume.

ACKNOWLEDGMENTS . . . *continued*

Form

For an acknowledgment in a representative capacity:
State of . . . .
County of . . . .
This instrument was acknowledged before me on . . (date) . . by . . (name(s) of person(s)) as . . . . . . (type of authority, e.g. officer, trustee, etc.) of . . (name of party on behalf of whom instrument was executed).

. . . .
(signature of notarial officer)

(Seal, if any)

. . . .
(title and rank)
(my commission expires: . . .)

Form

For verification upon oath or affirmation:
State of . . . .
County of . . . .
Signed and sworn to (or affirmed) before me on . . (date) . . by . . (name(s) of person(s) making statement).

. . . .
(signature of notarial officer)

(Seal, if any)

. . . .
(title and rank)
(my commission expires: . . .)

Form

For witnessing or attesting a signature:
State of . . . .
County of . . . .
Signed and attested before me on . . (date) . . by . . (name(s) of person(s)).

. . . .
(signature of notarial officer)

(Seal, if any)

. . . .
(title and rank)
(my commission expires: . . .)

Form

For attestation of a copy of a document:
State of . . . .
County of . . . .
I certify that this is a true and correct copy of a document in the possession of . .

. . . .
(signature of notarial officer)

(Seal, if any)

. . . .
(title and rank)
(my commission expires: . . .)

Secretary of State.—If instrument to be filed with Secretary of State must be acknowledged, person or one of persons signing must acknowledge, before person authorized by law of place of execution to take acknowledgments, that it is, as case may be, his or corporation's deed and act and that facts stated therein are true. If person taking acknowledgment has seal of office, it shall be affixed to instrument. (8-103[b]).

Validating Acts.—Defective acknowledgment does not affect validity. (25-132).

AFFIDAVITS:

Ordinarily a notary public or commissioner of deeds is proper person to take affidavits for either residents or nonresidents. Any judge, justice of the peace, or notary public has authority, in any case in which an oath or affirmation is necessary or proper, to administer such oath or affirmation. (10-5301). Officer of Armed Forces may take affidavits for military personnel. (25-130). See topic Acknowledgments.

General Requirements as to Administration.—No statutory requirement concerning knowledge of identity by person taking oath.

General Requirements of Jurat.—Official seal must be affixed but certificate of authority not required.

Use of Affidavit.—Miscellaneous statutory uses. Use in motion for summary judgment as in federal rules. See Rule 56.

Alternative to Affidavit.—No statutory provision.

Form

State of . . . . County of . . . . SS: Be it remembered that on this . . . . day of . . . . A.D. 19. ., personally came before me, the Subscriber, a Notary Public for the State and County aforesaid, ... being duly sworn, did depose and say:

. . . .

Sworn to and subscribed before me the day and year aforesaid.

. . . .
Notary Public

NOTARIES PUBLIC:

Qualification.—Must be at least 18 years of age and provide: evidence of good character and reputation; a reasonable need for a notary commission; and legal residence in Delaware. Appointment revocable for cause by Governor. (29-4301[b], [d]).

Authentication.—See topic Acknowledgments.

Seal must show name, official title and date of appointment. Possible removal by Governor for failure to comply. (29-4309).

Powers and Duties.—Usual duties of office. Power to take acknowledgments. Must ensure identity of person whose signature he is certifying by requiring identification. (29-4308).

Territorial Extent of Powers.—Statewide.

Term of Office.—Two year commission (fee $50), four year renewal (fee $75) at option of Governor. (29-4306).

Fees for certification under hand and notarial seal for applicant for registration of motor vehicle or motor vehicle license may not exceed 50¢ for first and 25¢ for each additional. (21-318[a]; 29-4310[a]). Acknowledgment of deed 50¢; certifying affidavit 25¢. (29-4310[a]).

Commissioners of deeds in any other jurisdiction may take acknowledgment and proof of deed. (25-129[b]).

Officers of U.S. Armed Forces.—Notarial acts for a member of U.S. Armed Forces or merchant seaman or a person on war duty outside U.S. may be performed by an officer in active service of rank of second lieutenant or higher in Air Force, Army or Marine Corps, or Ensign or higher in Navy or Coast Guard. (25-130[a]). Such officer must sign certificate as to oath, etc., and state his rank and branch of service. (25-130[d]).

RECORDS:

There is Recorder of Deeds in each county. *For list of Counties and County Seats see first page for this state in Volume containing Practice Profiles Section.*

Uniform Commercial Code adopted. See category Business Regulation and Commerce, topic Commercial Code.

Recordable Instruments.—It is duty of each county recorder to record within reasonable time, deeds, indentures, letters of attorney relating to land, mortgages, releases of lien of mortgages, leases, releases, assignments, conditional sales and leases of railroad and railway equipment and rolling stock, oaths of office, plots and descriptions, appointments of deputy registers of wills, certificates of commissioners and agreements of owners bounding and marking lands, petitions and orders for sheriff's deeds, all instruments authorized or directed by law, to be recorded or lodged by recorder of deeds, including certificates of discharge regularly issued to veterans. No fee shall be charged for recording any certificate of discharge. (9-9605[a]).

Place of Recording.—Deed or letter of attorney concerning lands or tenements shall, with certificate of acknowledgment or proof certified, be recorded in recorder's office for county wherein such lands or tenements or any parts thereof are situated. (25-151).

Requisites for Recording.—No deed or other instrument conveying land may be recorded without words "prepared by" followed by name and address of person who drafted or prepared deed for recording. Information required by this subsection shall appear on first page of instrument to be recorded. Recorder of Deeds for Kent County shall not accept for recording until received payment of all state and municipal realty transfer tax due on transfer, with exception of City of Dover realty transfer tax. Any municipality which imposed realty transfer tax may continue to impose tax. (9-9605[h], [i]). Deed or instrument concerning land has no effect on lands other than those mentioned in document located in county where document is recorded. (25-152). Faulty acknowledgment will not invalidate properly recorded instrument. (25-132).

Recording Fees.—Fees in each county are established by ordinance. (9-9617-9619).

Filing under Uniform Commercial Code.—When collateral is timber to be cut, minerals, or the like, goods which are or are to become fixtures, filing should be made in same place where mortgage on property would be recorded. In all other cases, filing should be in office of Secretary of State. (6-9-401[1]). Uniform filing fee, for statements in standard form is $25; otherwise $50. Additional $25 if statement subject to 6-9-402(5) (timber, minerals, fixture filings). (6-9-403[5]).

Foreign Conveyances or Encumbrances.—See category Property, topic Real Property.

Effect of Not Recording.—Deed concerning lands or tenements has priority from time of recording, without respect to time it was signed, sealed or delivered. (25-153). Failure to record within 15 days of execution of any writing transferring title or possessory interest, renders document unenforceable in Delaware courts. (25-158). Upon recordation and payment of any and all taxes, penalties and other charges hereto, document rendered unenforceable by statute shall be renewed and reviewed with same force and effect as if it had never been unenforceable.

Torrens system of land registration has not been adopted.

Transfer of decedent's title to real estate to his heir or devisee sufficiently shown by probate record of will or administration.

Vital Statistics.—Reports of births, deaths, and marriages must be filed in Office of Vital Statistics or as otherwise directed by State Registrar. (16-3121, 3123, 3125). Reports of adoption must be filed with state registrar. (16-3126[a]). Fee for searches of records and issuance of certificates shall reflect cost of doing such work, but shall not exceed $10. (16-3132[a]).

Establishing Records.—State Registrar of Vital Statistics may register any unrecorded birth, marriage, divorce or fetal death, death on production of evidence thereof satisfactory to him. (16-3129).

See note at head of Digest as to 1998 legislation covered.

See Topical Index in front part of this volume.

SEALS:

Distinction between sealed and unsealed instruments at common law is recognized. (24 Del. Ch. 436, 15 A. 2d 177). No statutory requirement for seals on private instruments. Deed valid regardless of grantor's seal. (25-131).

"L. S." or "seal," written, printed or typed, is sufficient seal.

Uniform Commercial Code adopted. (6-1-101 et seq.).

Corporate Seals.—Corporation may have a corporate seal. (8-122[3]).

Effect of Seal.—Failure of consideration is defense to action on sealed contract, but lack of consideration is not. (262 A.2d 648).

TORRENS ACT:

Not adopted.

VITAL STATISTICS:

See topic Records.

EMPLOYMENT

EMPLOYER AND EMPLOYEE:

See topic Labor Relations.

LABOR RELATIONS:

Department of Labor is charged generally with administering labor laws of state, directing attention of Attorney General to violation of such laws, investigating labor conditions generally, proposing rules to Industrial Accident Board, promoting voluntary arbitration, mediation and conciliation of labor disputes, promoting voluntary apprenticeship through cooperation with U.S. Department of Labor, and making regulations for internal administration of Department. (19-105[a]).

Hours of Labor.—Children under 16 will not be allowed to work before 7:00 a.m. or after 7:00 p.m. (9:00 p.m. from June 1 through Labor Day), nor more than four hours in any day when school is in session, eight hours in any day when school is not in session, 18 hours in any week when school is in session, 40 hours in any week when school is not in session and six days in any week. (19-506[d], [e]). Children under 18 shall not spend more than 12 hours in combination of school and work hours per day, shall have at least eight consecutive hours of nonwork, nonschool time each 24-hour day and shall not work more than five hours continuously without nonworking period of at least one-half hour. (19-507[c], [d], [e]).

Wages.—Employer must not knowingly pay any warrant or order due any person for borrowed money where more than lawful interest received or charged. Employer can be fined $1,000-$5,000 for violation. (19-701[a],[b]). Railroads must pay employees bi-weekly except executives, administrators and professionals. (19-702[a]).

Minimum wage law adopted. (19-c.9). Minimum wage of not less than federal minimum wage for all employees in any occupation (19-902[a]) except those receiving gratuities of more than $30 per month, in which case gratuities may constitute amount equal to tip credit percentage, as set by federal government (19-902[b],[c]), Dept. of Labor may set lower rate for aged or handicapped workers (19-905) and learners or apprentices (19-906).

Employer must pay wages by cash or check on regular paydays at least once each month (19-1102[a]) and at specified times after discharge, resignation or suspension for labor dispute (19-1103[a]). If employer, without reasonable grounds, fails to pay wages, employer can be held liable for liquidated damages in amount of 10% of wages not paid. (19-1103[b]). Provisions for liability of contractors for wages (19-1105); payment of wages due to family of deceased employee (19-1106); withholding of wages generally prohibited except as provided (19-1107); differential rate of pay based on sex prohibited (19-1107A); duty of employer to notify employee of rate, time and place of payment and maintenance of wage and hour records (19-1108); and payment or providing of benefits and wage supplements (19-1109). Statutory rules governing payment of wages and benefits cannot be waived by private agreement. (19-1110).

Liens.—In New Castle County all claims that may become due or growing due for labor or services rendered by any mechanic, laborer, clerk or other employee of any person or persons, chartered company or association employing laborers, clerks or mechanics in any manner whatsoever, shall be a first lien on all real and personal property of such employer or employers, and shall be first to be satisfied out of proceeds of sale of such property, whether made by an officer or an assignee of such employer or employers or otherwise, for sum equal to wages of one month but not to exceed $50. (10-4931[a]).

Where a domestic or foreign corporation doing business in Delaware becomes insolvent, employees, not including officers, doing labor or service in regular employ of such corporation, have lien upon assets thereof for amount of wages due to them not exceeding two months which shall be paid prior to any other debt or debts of said corporation. (8-300).

Child Labor.—Children under 14 forbidden to be employed or to work (19-505); children under 16 forbidden to be employed or to work during prescribed school days or in dangerous occupation (19-506). Hours and occupations are restricted for children under 18. (19-507). Special permits available for children under 16 to work as models, performers or entertainers. (19-508). See also subhead Hours of Labor, supra.

Female Labor.—Provisions on female labor repealed.

Discrimination.—Discrimination by employer or employment agency on basis of race, marital status, color, age, religion, sex or national origin prohibited. (19-711). Penalty for violation $1,000-$5,000 fine. Jurisdiction of violations with Equal Employment Review Board. (19-718).

Labor Unions.—Employees have right to bargain collectively with employers through representatives of their own choosing in order to change wages or other conditions of work. (19-913). Public employees have right to organize (19-1303), but not to strike (19-1316). No "right to work" law.

Conditions of Workplace.—"Right to know" legislation enacted, granting employees exposed to hazardous chemicals in workplace right to know what chemicals they are exposed to. (16-2415[a]). Standards mirror OSHA regulations. Employers required to provide training for employees on how to protect themselves from chemical hazards in workplace (16-2410, 16-2415[a]), and required to provide appropriate personal protective equipment (16-2415[a]). Penalties for violation not to exceed $500 per violation. (16-2413[c]).

Labor Disputes.—It is unlawful for any person, firm or corporation, not directly involved in a labor strike or lockout, to recruit any person for employment, or to secure or offer to secure for any person employment, when the purpose of such action is to have such person take place in employment of employees in industry where labor strike or lockout involving recognized labor organizations exists. (19-703[a]). Does not apply to Delaware State Employment Service or United States Employment Service or to any person, firm or corporation engaged in production, handling or processing of agricultural commodities. (19-703[a]). Penalty for violation $1,000-$5,000 fine. (19-703[b]).

Employment Records.—Employees have right to inspect personnel files, including performance evaluations. (19-732). Inspection to take place during regular business hours. (19-732). Employer may require employee to file written request to inspect files. (19-732). Employee may not copy files, but may take notes. (19-733). Inspection may be limited to once every calendar year. (19-733). Employer may be fined $1,000-$5,000 for each violation of statute. (19-735).

Workers' Compensation Act.—Industrial Accident Board has jurisdiction of cases arising under Workers' Compensation Act. (19-3201[a]). Appeals heard by Superior Court. (19-2350[a]).

No compensation unless injury arises out of and in course of employment, and incapacitates employee from earning full wages for three days, unless incapacity extends to seven days, except for surgical, medical and hospital services, medicines and supplies, and funeral benefits, all of which shall be paid from and including first day of injury. (19-2321). Workers may receive benefits for permanent injury relating to hearing or vision loss even though not incapacitated for three days. (19-2321). Employer must pay for medical services. (19-2322[a]). Compensable occupational diseases are covered. (19-2301[4]).

If employer and injured employee, or dependents in case of death, reach agreement as to benefits, memorandum of such agreement, if signed by parties and filed and approved by Board, shall be binding. (19-2344). Award by Accident Board shall be conclusive in absence of fraud, except that Board may, not more than once in six months, review any agreement or award where it is alleged that incapacity of injured employee has changed, and except that either party shall have right to appeal to Superior Court within 20 days. (19-2347, 2349). Claims are barred after two years unless there is compensation agreement or petition to Board. (19-2361[a]). Where payments made under agreement approved by Board or by award of Board, no statute of limitation shall take effect until five years after last receipted payment made. (19-2361[b]).

Provisions for total or partial disability from work and schedules for permanent disability, disfigurement and death benefits are contained in Act. (19-2324 et seq.). Reasonable attorneys' fees for employee awarded compensation, in amount of 30% of award or $2,250 whichever is smaller. (19-2320[g][1]).

Act applies to employer and employee in any employment where one or more employees engaged, except as otherwise indicated. (19-2306[a]). Act does not apply to domestic servants who earn less than $750 in cash in any three month period, and only applies to farm workers if employer carries insurance to pay for benefits. (19-2307). Act does not apply to State or subdivisions of it unless government unit in question elects to be covered. (19-2309). Volunteer fire and ambulance companies may elect to be bound. (19-2312[b], [d]). Act does not apply to employees injured or killed while engaged in interstate or foreign commerce if covered by federal law. (19-2310).

Every employer must be insured by approved corporation or furnish proof of ability to pay direct compensation, and must periodically present such evidence to Board. (19-2372[a]; 19-2374[a]).

Occupational Diseases.—Claims for compensation for occupational disease must be filed with Board within one year of time employee realized that disability might have resulted from employment (19-2361[c]), and within five years of last compensation payment (19-2361[b]). See subhead Workers' Compensation Act, supra.

Employers' Liability Act.—Employer and employee are bound by Act to pay and accept compensation, regardless of negligence, and to exclusion of other remedies. (19-2304).

Unemployment Compensation.—Administered by Department pursuant to 19-cc.31, 33. Generally, unemployed individual eligible if: (1) He has registered to work at an employment office; (2) he has made a claim for benefits; (3) he is able to work, available for work, and actively seeking work; (4) he participates in reemployment services; and (5) he has, during his base period, been paid wages equal to not less than 36 times his weekly benefit amount. Benefits are based on service in employment. (19-3314, other details there appearing). Disqualifications for benefits include voluntary termination of employment by employee without good cause attributable to such work, discharge for just cause, refusal to accept work for which reasonably fitted, strikes, receipt of unemployment benefits from another governmental entity, fraudulent statements to Department, incarceration, physical inability to work, temporary break in athletic employment, illegal alien status. (19-3315). Delaware Unemployment Compensation Law is in conformity with federal law.

Individual's weekly benefit amount for claims beginning July 1, 1983 is 1/78 of his total wages paid during three quarters of his base period in which total wages were highest, with minimum benefit of $20 and maximum benefit of 66 2/3% of statewide average weekly wage as defined in 19-3302(22). (19-3313[b]). Computations for increase in maximum weekly benefit amount shall commence with new claims filed to establish benefit year commencing after effective date of increase. (19-3313[b][5]). Computation of benefits is determined by balance in Unemployment Insurance Trust Fund. (19-3313[e], [g]). Each eligible individual, unemployed in any week, shall be

LABOR RELATIONS . . . *continued*

paid sum equal to his weekly benefit amount less wages payable which exceed greater of $10 or 50% of his weekly benefit amount. (19-3313[j]). Individual filing new claim for unemployment compensation shall, at time of filing, disclose whether or not he or she owes uncollected over issuance of food stamps. Department will notify state food stamp agency of individual owing on food stamp obligation. Department shall deduct or withhold from any unemployment compensation payable to individual who owes uncollected over issuance of food stamp coupons. (19-3313[o]). Contribution employer must pay to Unemployment Compensation Fund is average industry contribution rate in that employer's standard industrial classification category or 5.4% of wages he pays during year. (19-3348). No employer assigned assessment rate shall have rate less than 1%. (19-3348[i]).

WORKERS' COMPENSATION LAW:

See topic Labor Relations.

ENVIRONMENT

ENVIRONMENTAL REGULATION:

General Supervision.—Department of Natural Resources and Environmental Control, 89 Kings Highway, P.O. Box 1401, Dover, DE 19903, has responsibility for managing use of air, land, water and underwater resources. (7-6001[b] [2]). Division of Air and Waste Management and Division of Water Resources; and Council on Environmental Control are agencies thereof. (29-8014-8015). Environmental Appeals Board decides all appeals from any order of Secretary of Department. (7-6008).

Prohibited Acts of Pollution.—Any of following activities undertaken without permit from Department Secretary: causing or contributing to discharge of air contaminant, or of water pollutant into surface or ground water; causing or contributing to withdrawal of ground or surface water; collecting, transporting, storing, processing or disposing of solid wastes; constructing, maintaining or operating pipeline or appurtenance; constructing any water facility; planning or constructing any highway which may contribute to air or water pollution; constructing, installing, replacing, modifying, or using any equipment which is intended to prevent or control air or water pollution, or to withdraw ground or surface water for treatment and supply, or which is for disposal of solid waste. No issuance of building, placement, storage or occupancy permit until owner obtains permit for underground discharge of wastewater and withdrawal of groundwater. (7-6003).

Enforcement.—Secretary may order person violating any rule, regulation, order, permit condition, or provision of 7-c. 60 to cease and desist, but such order expires after 30 days and may be suspended by injunction or withdrawn by Secretary. (7-6018). Public hearing on violation held at least 20 days after notice to violator by registered mail and publication. Alleged violator may appear either personally or by counsel and produce evidence on his behalf. Secretary may administer oaths, examine witnesses and issue notices of hearings and subpoenae requiring testimony of witnesses and production of documents. Subpoenae also issued at request of violator. If subpoena or notice of hearing is disobeyed, Secretary may apply to Superior Court for order requiring appearance and testimony at hearing to be taken. Secretary to make findings of fact and give order, with reasons. (7-6006). Secretary's decision may be appealed within 20 days to Environmental Appeals Board. (7-6008[a]). Board decision may in turn be appealed to Superior Court within 30 days. (7-6009[a]).

Penalties.—

Civil.—If violation completed, civil penalty imposed by Superior Court of $1,000 to $10,000 for each completed violation; each day of continued violation considered separate violation. If violation completed and substantial likelihood it will reoccur, Secretary may seek permanent or preliminary injunction or temporary restraining order in Court of Chancery. (7-6005[b][1]). After written notice to violator, Secretary may impose administrative penalty of maximum of $10,000 for each day of violation. (7-6005[b][3]). Person violating chapter or order liable for Department expenses of abatement, control, and cleanup, including legal expenses. (7-6005[c]).

Criminal.—Willful violation of statute, permit condition or regulation imprisonment for not more than five years and $2,500 to $25,000 fine for each day of violation, negligent violation of same $2,500 to $25,000 for each day of violation. Knowingly false statement, $500 to $10,000 and/or maximum of six months' imprisonment; Superior Court has jurisdiction. (7-6013).

Permits.—No permit granted unless county or municipality having jurisdiction first approves by zoning procedures. (7-6003[c]). Must apply for permit; public hearing if request meritorious, to be held within 75 days of receiving request or if in best interest of State, to be held within 90 days of receiving application. (7-6004).

Land Use Planning.—Quality of Life Act of 1988 adopted to encourage most appropriate use of land, water and resources. Land development must conform to comprehensive land use plans to be adopted by each county. (9-cc. 26, 49, 69). See category Property, topic Real Property, subhead Land Use Planning.

ESTATES AND TRUSTS

ADMINISTRATION:

See topic Executors and Administrators.

ADVANCEMENTS:

See topic Descent and Distribution.

ALLOWANCES:

See topic Executors and Administrators.

DEATH:

Presumption of death arises from seven consecutive years absence not accounted for. (12-1105).

Right to Terminate Treatment.—See topic Wills, subhead Living Wills.

Death With Dignity.—See topic Wills, subhead Living Wills.

Living Wills.—See topic Wills, subhead Living Wills.

Right to Die.—See topic Wills, subhead Living Wills.

Survivorship.—Uniform Simultaneous Death Act has been adopted in pre-1953 form. (12-701 et seq.).

Uniform Survival and Death Act.—Not adopted.

Actions for Death.—

Survival of Actions.—Action for damages for negligently inflicted personal injuries survives death of plaintiff, and may be continued by plaintiff's personal representative. (10-3704). Generally, all causes of action survive except defamation, malicious prosecution, and actions upon penal statutes to and against person to or against whom accrued. (10-3701).

Wrongful Death.—Where death is caused by wrongful act of another, person injured as result of that death may institute action for damages not limited to pecuniary losses. (10-3721-3725). No statutory limitation of amount which may be recovered. Two year limitation applies for wrongful death and damage to personal property. Cause of action in asbestos-related death accrues when plaintiff has knowledge that death is attributable to asbestos exposure. (10-8107).

See also topic Executors and Administrators, subhead Actions.

Death Certificate.—See category Documents and Records, topic Records, subhead Vital Statistics.

Uniform Anatomical Gift Act adopted. (16-2701-2730). See topic Wills.

DECEDENTS' ESTATES:

See topics Descent and Distribution, Executors and Administrators, Wills.

DESCENT AND DISTRIBUTION:

Uniform Probate Code.—Not adopted.

Entire intestate estate if there be no surviving spouse, or excess over share of such spouse, descends and is distributed: (a) To issue of decedent, per stirpes; (b) if there is no surviving issue, to decedent's parent or parents equally; (c) if there is no surviving issue or parent, to brothers and sisters and issue of each deceased brother or sister, per stirpes; (d) if there is no surviving issue, parent or issue of a parent, then to next of kin of decedent, and to issue of deceased next of kin, per stirpes; (e) property passes to two or more such persons as tenants in common. (12-503).

Surviving Spouse.—Intestate share of surviving spouse is: (1) If there is no surviving issue or parents of decedent, entire estate; (2) if there is no surviving issue but decedent is survived by parent or parents, first $50,000 of intestate personal estate, plus one-half of balance of intestate personal estate, plus life estate in intestate real estate; (3) if there are surviving issue all of whom are issue of surviving spouse also, first $50,000, plus one-half of balance of intestate personal estate, plus life estate in intestate real estate; (4) if there are surviving issue, one or more of whom are not issue of surviving spouse, one-half of intestate personal estate, plus life estate in intestate real estate. (12-502).

Half Blood.—Relatives of half blood inherit same share as they would if of whole blood. (12-506).

Posthumous children, if born alive, take as if born before death of parent. (12-505).

Illegitimate children or their issue share real and personal estate of mother in same manner as legitimate children or their issue. (13-1303). Property of intestate illegitimate without lawful issue passes to mother, if living, or to her heirs. (13-1302).

Adopted Children.—See category Family, topic Adoption.

Determination of Heirship.—No special proceedings provided. Action at law for distributive share authorized. (12-3101). Chancery Court given jurisdiction to make decree of distribution on application. (12-2331 et seq.).

Advancements.—If person dies intestate as to all his estate, property given in his lifetime to heir is treated as advancement against latter's share of estate only if declared in contemporaneous writing by decedent or acknowledged in writing by heir to be advancement. For this purpose, property advanced valued as of time heir came into possession or enjoyment of property or as of time of death of decedent, whichever first occurs. If recipient fails to survive decedent, property not taken into account in computing intestate share to be received by recipient's issue, unless declaration or acknowledgment provides otherwise. (12-509). For treatment of advancement upon partition of joint estates, see 25-721.

Election.—Surviving spouse has right of election to take elective share of amount equal to 1/3 share of elective estate, less amount of all transfers to spouse by decedent. Elective share may be satisfied in cash or in kind, and is valued at date of distribution. (12-901).

Renunciation.—Legatee may renounce (315 A.2d 625, aff'd, 328 A.2d 141), but beneficiary of spendthrift trust may not be able to renounce (43 Del. Ch. 124, 219 A.2d 576).

Escheat.—If intestate leaves neither heirs nor any known kindred who can inherit, entire estate, both real and personal, escheats. (12-1101). See also topic Executors and Administrators.

ESTATES:

See category Property, topic Real Property.

EXECUTORS AND ADMINISTRATORS:

Whether matter is litigated in Chancery or Superior Court depends on whether action is at law or in equity. But almost all suits relating to decedents' estates are brought in Chancery which has exclusive jurisdiction to determine same. Register of Wills' function is mostly clerical. Specific statutory grants of authority to Chancery or to Register of Wills are mentioned under appropriate subheads.

Preferences in Right to Administer.—Administration is granted in following order: (1) spouse of decedent, children of decedent, parents of decedent, siblings of whole and half blood of decedent or their nominee; (2) if no person under (1) is living and competent, or (3) if no petition for grant of letters is filed within 60 days from date of death, qualified person will be determined by Register of Wills. (12-1505).

Eligibility and Competency.—Letters testamentary, or of administration, are not granted to minor, one who is mentally incapacitated, or one convicted of crime disqualifying from taking oath. (12-1508).

No statutory prohibition of appointment of nonresidents.

Married woman may be executrix or administratrix and has same power as femme sole. Her husband has no right to participate in administration and is not liable for her acts or defaults unless he is party to her bond and then only as such party. (13-313).

Personal representative of deceased executor or administrator shall not represent (unless expressly appointed) and shall have no personal liability or responsibility with respect to estate being executed or administered by decedent, other than to notify Register of Wills of death of decedent's executor or administrator. (12-1507[b]). See also subhead Foreign Executors or Administrators, infra.

Qualification.—No bond is required of personal representative prior to receiving letters unless expressly required by will or ordered by Court of Chancery. (12-1522). Persons receiving letters of administration or letters testamentary must give bond. (12-1502; 12-1505).

Personal representative must take oath to perform duties of office with fidelity. (12-1509).

Issuance of Letters.—No one may act as executor or administrator of domiciliary decedent's estate without letters testamentary or letters of administration. (12-1501). Register of Wills normally grants both types of letters. (12-1502, 1504). When parties cannot agree on administrator, Chancery Court may pick one. (12-1505[c]).

Removal.—Chancery Court may remove executor or administrator neglecting his duties. (12-1541). Upon removal or resignation from office, or death or incapacity of sole executor, or administrator, or if there are several of all of them, administration shall be granted to successor administrator or administrators as though it were original administration. (12-1507[a]).

Whenever an executor or administrator is removed, or dies before he closes estate of deceased, his co-executor, or co-administrator, or his successor, is entitled to receive all unadministered effects, including books and papers which, at time of removal or death are in his hands. (12-1543).

Special Kinds of Administration.—Upon removal or resignation, or death or incapacity of administrator, administration will be granted to successor under same regulations as original administration. (12-1507[a]).

If named executor is dead, or fails to give necessary bond, or renounces or is incapacitated, administration with will annexed must be granted in accordance with 12-1503 and 12-1504. (12-1502[b]).

Ancillary Administration.—Same rules governing administration generally also apply to local administration of estate of nonresident decedent, both in respect to procedures followed and rights of parties. (12-1568).

Public Administrators.—No provision.

Inventory and Appraisal.—Must be filed within three months after the grant of letters testamentary or of administration, with Register of Wills. (12-1905[a]). Personal representative may employ one or more qualified and disinterested appraisers to assist. (12-1904).

General Powers and Duties.—Executor acquires title to property of deceased, and it is his duty to collect everything due estate, pay debts and distribute residue under directions of will. (30 Del. Ch. 592, 65 A.2d 484).

Notice of Appointment.—Notice of grant of letters given by Register of Wills. Same requirements as for notice to creditors, below.

Notice to Creditors.—Within 40 days from grant of letters, notice to creditors to present their claims must be given. Notice is by advertisement posted in the county court house and by publication at least once a week for three successive weeks in one or more designated newspapers; except register may in his discretion give notice by posting only where gross personal estate does not exceed $20,000 and gross real and personal estate does not in aggregate exceed $25,000. (12-2101).

Presentation of Claims.—All claims against estate arising before decedent's death are barred unless presented pursuant to 12-2104 within eight months of decendent's death, whether or not notice under 12-2101 was given. (12-2102[a]). All claims against estate arising at or after decedent's death are barred within six months after they arise, unless presented pursuant to 12-2104, except that claims based on contract with personal representative are barred unless presented within six months after performance by personal representative is due. (12-2102[b]). Claim based on bond secured by mortgage on real estate is barred unless claim has been presented to executor or administrator within eight months of decedent's death. (12-2102[e]).

Above limitations, except that for claim based on secured bond, do not apply to claims for legacies or shares of decedent's estate; and none of above limitations apply to proceedings to establish liability of decedent or of personal representative to extent of liability insurance coverage (12-2102[d], [f]), to matters claimed in proceedings pending against decedent at time of death (12-2104), or to debts of which executor or administrator is deemed to have notice, namely, mortgages and such judgments as would be liens against real estate at date of death of decedent, which are recorded in county where letters were granted (12-2103).

Claim may be presented by: (1) Sending written statement of claim to personal representative, or (2) filing statement of claim with Register of Wills, or (3) beginning proceeding against personal representative in any court where he is subject to jurisdiction. (12-2104).

If no letters granted for ten years after death, all claims barred except mortgages and judgments which shall be controlled by applicable law. (12-2109).

Form for Proof of Claim.
STATEMENT OF CLAIM **(Chancery Ct. Rule 191)**

1. Name of deceased . . . .
2. Name and address of claimant . . . .
3. Amount of claim . . . .
4. Statement as to basis of claim . . . .
5. Copy of any written obligation signed by decedent, if available . . . .
6. Date obligation became due or, if not yet due, state date on which obligation becomes due . . . .
7. If obligation is contingent or unliquidated, so state and explain . . . .
8. State whether claim is secured or unsecured and, if secured, describe security . .
9. Statement that claim is being filed within time set forth in 12-2102 . . . .

Approval or Rejection of Claims.—Representative may reject claims and if rejected they will be barred unless action is begun within three months of written notice of rejection delivered in person or sent to last known address of claimant. In case of unliquidated or contingent claim, or claim not presently due, executor or administrator may consent to, or Chancery Court may order, extension of three-month period, but not beyond statute of limitations. (12-2102[c]).

Three-month limitation does not apply to claims for legacies or shares of decedent's estate, or to proceedings to establish liability of decedent or of personal representative to extent of insurance coverage. (12-2102[d], [f]).

Payment of Claims.—Executor has one year from date of letters for settling decedent's estate except where circumstances justify longer period. (12-2311). If person files petition claiming interest in estate and if it appears that portion of estate may be distributed to that person, Chancery Court may reserve part for contingent liability against estate. (12-2335).

Priorities.—After all administration expenses, fees and commissions have been paid, claims are paid in following order: Surviving spouse's allowance; funeral expenses; child support arrears or retroactive support due as of date of death; reasonable bills for medicine and medical attendance during last sickness; wages for up to one year of servants employed in household or farm; state taxes; rent not exceeding one year; judgments against deceased; recognizances, mortgages, and other obligations of record for payment of money; obligations and contracts under seal; contracts under hand for payment of money or delivery of goods, wares or merchandise; and lastly other demands. (12-2105[a]). See also subhead Sales, catchline Application of Proceeds; Order of Payment of Debts, infra.

Whenever executor or administrator is unable to determine between two or more creditors order of preference to be given to their respective demands, he may upon petition to Chancery Court have parties in interest summoned to appear, and upon hearing duly had, Court of Chancery determines order of preference to be given to respective demands; upon compliance with such determination petitioner and his sureties are discharged from all further liability in respect to said preferences. (12-2106).

Sales.—When personal estate is insufficient to pay debts administrator may petition Court of Chancery of county wherein real estate is situated for an order for its sale. Specific procedure provided when land situated in more than one county. (12-2701[a], [c]). There must be ten days notice of petition to parties interested. (12-2701[b]).

Compelled Sale.—Creditor may apply to Chancery Court of county where letters were granted for citation of executor or administrator to show cause why executor or administrator should not petition for order of sale under 12-2701; and if it appears that creditor will be remediless without sale of real estate, court may order executor or administrator to file petition for sale. (12-2702). Chancery Court may also order executor or administrator to sell real estate where it appears generally that there is not enough personalty to pay decedent's debts. (12-2704).

Manner of Sale.—Sale must be by public auction, or by private sale approved by Chancery Court. Where sale is by public auction, executor or administrator is to give notice of it by advertisements made by clerk, describing land to be sold, and time and place of sale. Advertisements are to be posted at least ten days before sale at places specified by court. Court may also order other kinds of notice. (12-2706).

Return of Sale.—Executor or administrator returns proceedings to Chancery Court after order of sale has been made, and if return is approved he makes deed to buyer. But court will not order deed made until purchase money has been paid. (12-2708[a], [e]).

Application of Proceeds; Order of Payment of Debts.—Money from sale, after charges allowed by Chancery Court have been deducted, is applied to debts of decedent in following order. First Class: Judgments against decedent which, before sale, were liens on premises sold, and recognizances and mortgages decedent executed for payment of money or interest, not dependent on contingency, and which, before sale, were liens on premises sold. Preference among judgments, mortgages and recognizances of this class is according to legal priority of lien. Where recognizance, obligation or mortgage has been executed by decedent other than for absolute payment of money or interest, and is by its own force lien on premises sold, and in proceeding on such recognizance, obligation or mortgage, sum has been assessed as payable by virtue of recognizance, obligation or mortgage, and judgment has been given at time of sale, then sum assessed also is within first class, and stands in priority, and is preferred in payment, according to date of obligation or recognizance, or of depositing of mortgage. Second Class: All other debts against decedent, priority being determined by 12-2105. (See subhead Priorities, supra.) (12-2710).

Where will devises real estate to be sold without authorizing anyone to make sale, or if named executor authorized by will to make sale becomes unavailable, then person having execution of will may sell real estate. (12-2719[b][d]).

See note at head of Digest as to 1998 legislation covered.

See Topical Index in front part of this volume.

EXECUTORS AND ADMINISTRATORS . . . *continued*

Private Sale.—Administrator can sell personalty at private sale if price is reasonable. (16 Del. Ch. 445, 143 A. 489).

Actions:

By and Against Representative.—All causes of action except defamation, malicious prosecution or actions on penal statutes, survive to and against executors and administrators of person to, or against whom, cause of action accrued. (10-3701). No suit abates by death of party, where cause of action survives; executor or administrator of dead plaintiff may prosecute suit, and executor or administrator of dead defendant may be made party to suit through service of scire facias. (Const., Art. IV, §23). See also topic Death, subhead Actions for Death; category Civil Actions and Procedure, topic Actions, subhead Abatement and Revival.

Presentation of claim against estate in accordance with 12-2104 is condition precedent to action thereon against executor or administrator. (12-3121). Otherwise there is no suspension of right to sue. For time limits, see subhead Presentation of Claims, supra.

Interruption of Statute of Limitations.—If statute of limitations on action against estate had not expired during decedent's lifetime, period of limitations is extended to six months from date of death. If claim is filed within proper time, and suit is brought within three months of notice of rejection of claim by executor, or administrator, statute of limitations is no defense. (10-8113).

Allowances.—Executor or administrator must pay to surviving spouse, upon demand made within six months from granting of letters, or nine months from date of death, whichever occurs first, cash up to $2,000. This allowance is considered debt of estate and property may be sold to pay allowance in same manner as other debts. (12-2308). Allowance has priority over other debts, including funeral expenses and expenses of last illness, and taxes. (12-2105).

Widow's Quarantine.—No provision.

Accounting and Settlement.—Executor or administrator must account each year until estate is closed. (12-2301[a]). Except where circumstances justify longer period, executor or administrator has one year from date of his letters for settling estate; until expiration of that time he is not required to make distribution or be chargeable with interest on assets in his hands. But if any part of estate carries interest or is productive, he must account for interest or produce. (12-2311).

Consent Settlements.—No statutory provision.

Disclaimers.—Person, or representative of deceased, incapacitated or protected person with right to any property interest may disclaim interest, in whole or in part, by delivering written irrevocable disclaimer within nine months of creation of present interest or within nine months of event determining taker of indefeasibly vested future interest. (12-601 et seq.).

Distribution.—Executor, administrator, or one claiming an interest in the estate may, after account filed, petition Chancery Court for decree of distribution. After due notice and hearing, court may enter decree of distribution binding on executor, administrator and persons claiming interests in the estate. (12-2332-35).

Distribution to Infant or Beneficiary Abroad.—Where person entitled to distributive share of personal estate cannot receive it because infant or absent from state, then money due may be deposited in bank to credit of person entitled (12-2315) and if residue of intestate personal estate, distributive share, or trust fund cannot be paid because, absent from state, unknown, or incompetent, then upon petition Court of Chancery may order money to be paid into court (12-2316). Register of Wills may appoint conservator to take charge of estate of which missing or captured serviceman is beneficiary. (12-4101).

Compensation of Representatives.—Provided by Rule 192 of Court of Chancery. (12-2305).

When Administration Unnecessary.—If value of entire personal estate, not including exempt or jointly owned property, does not exceed $20,000, decedent's spouse, grandparent, relative who is lineal descendant of grandparent of decedent, personal representative of any of foregoing who is deceased, or guardian or trustee of any of foregoing who is incapacitated or trustee of trust created by decedent, or funeral director licensed in state, shall be entitled to receive personal estate for purposes of distribution without appointment of representative, provided that 30 days have elapsed since death, no petition for appointment of representative is pending or has been granted, all known debts have been provided for, decedent did not own solely owned real estate located in Delaware, surviving spouse's allowance has been paid, provided for, waived, or has expired by lapse of time and affidavit showing compliance with these conditions is furnished. (12-2306).

Small Estates.—See subhead When Administration Unnecessary, supra.

Foreign Executors or Administrators.—Domiciliary foreign personal representative only has power if there is no administration or pending application therefor in Delaware. (12-1567). In this case, at any time after 60 days from death of nonresident decedent, person holding property of decedent or owing debt to him may pay debt or deliver property to domiciliary foreign personal representative, if representative presents proof of his appointment and specified affidavit (12-1562) and such tender releases tenderor to same extent as if made to local representative (12-1563). Where there is no local ancillary administration or pending application therefor, domiciliary foreign personal representative may file with Register of Wills in county in which property of decedent is located exemplified copies of his appointment and of any official bond he has given (12-1565), and may thus exercise as to assets in Delaware all powers of local personal representative, provided that he complies with Delaware law governing notice to creditors and filing of inventory and appraisal (12-1566). However, application for local administration ends power of foreign personal representative under 12-1566, except that Court of Chancery may allow foreign representative to keep limited powers to preserve estate. (12-1567).

Nondomiciliary, or foreign corporation, may only be granted letters testamentary or of administration if it files with Register of Wills irrevocable power of attorney designating Register as agent upon whom process may be served. (12-1506). See also topic Wills, subhead Foreign Probated Wills.

Uniform Fiduciaries Act not adopted.

Revised Uniform Principal and Income Act adopted in part, with significant changes. (12-c. 61).

Uniform Simplification of Fiduciary Security Transfers Act adopted (12-c.43) and not repealed by Art. 8, Uniform Commercial Code (6-10-104 [2]).

Uniform Anatomical Gift Act adopted. (16-2710).

FIDUCIARIES:

See topics Executors and Administrators, Trusts; category Family, topic Guardian and Ward.

Delaware Uniform Simplification of Fiduciary Security Transfers Act (12-c.43) relieves transfer agents from duty to inquire into authority of fiduciary. This is not repealed by Art. 8, Uniform Commercial Code. (6-10-104[2]).

INTESTACY:

See topic Descent and Distribution.

PROOF OF CLAIMS:

See topic Executors and Administrators.

TRUSTS:

Rules of common law as of 1776 generally apply.

Kinds.—All kinds including any lawful business or activity, whether for profit or not, formed as business trusts are recognized. (12-3801[a]).

Spendthrift trusts recognized and certain limited assignments therefrom are authorized. (12-3536).

Creation.—Trusts are created by will, deed or operation of law.

Business Trusts.—See category Business Organizations, topic Joint Stock Companies. (12-3801 et seq.).

Appointment of Trustee.—Trust will not fail because of lack of trustee. Chancellor will name trustee when necessary. (12-3501 et seq.).

Eligibility and Competency.—Court of Chancery has general supervisory jurisdiction. (12-3501 et seq.). No prohibition of foreign trustees.

Qualification.—Court determines amount and type of surety for court appointed trustee, unless waived by required instrument creating trust, or unless Court waives it for cause. (Ch. Ct. Rule 109). Court may waive surety on bond in case of trust companies. (5-917).

Removal of trustee is a matter of discretion with Chancery Court. (27 Del. Ch. 8, 29 A.2d 591).

Sales.—On petition of trustee, Chancellor may in his discretion authorize sale of trust property unless expressly prohibited by instrument creating trust. (12-3533).

Investments by fiduciaries are regulated by 12-3302 so-called "prudent investor" rule. Bank or trust company acting as trustee may retain its own stock unless expressly forbidden by trust instrument. (12-3305). Bank or trust company may use fiduciary funds to purchase from its commercial department mortgages acquired within preceding year, earmarked for trust investment at acquisition, and appraised within ten days prior to purchase by trust department; provided interest and taxes are current at time of purchase. (12-3308). Trustee, banks or trust companies may invest trust assets in common trust funds created and managed by such trustee. (12-3307).

Securities in Name of Nominee.—Trustee, other than bank trustee or clearing corporation, must hold securities in fiduciary name unless provided otherwise in governing instrument. Bank, clearing corporation, or trust company may hold securities in name of nominee. (12-3309).

Gifts to Minors.—See category Family, topic Infants. (12-c. 45).

Bequests and Devises to Inter Vivos Trusts.—See topic Wills, subhead Bequests and Devises to Inter Vivos Trusts.

Uniform Simplification of Fiduciary Security Transfers Act adopted (12-c. 43) and not repealed by Art. 8, Uniform Commercial Code (6-10-104[2]).

Accounting.—Trustees appointed by Chancellor and testamentary trustees must submit accounting showing all receipts or disbursements with respect to assets to Court for approval. First accounting shall be filed within one year from appointment of trustee and further accountings must be filed at least every two years or at any other time Court deems appropriate. (Ch. Ct. Rule 114). Trustees of inter vivos trust receiving property by will must account only if required by Court of Chancery. (12-3521).

Compensation is set by Ch. Ct. Rule 132 subject to modification by Chancery Court.

Revised Uniform Principal and Income Act adopted with significant changes. (12-c. 61).

Uniform Fiduciaries Act not adopted.

Uniform Common Trust Fund Act.—Not adopted, but see subhead Investments, supra.

Accumulations.—No statutory limitation, as such; but see 12-3521-3525 on accounting and distribution of trust funds.

Perpetuities.—See category Property, topic Perpetuities.

Pour Over Trusts.—See topic Wills, subhead Bequests and Devises to Inter Vivos Trusts.

Renunciation.—Beneficiary of spendthrift trust may not be able to renounce. (43 Del. Ch. 124, 219 A.2d 576).

See note at head of Digest as to 1998 legislation covered.

See Topical Index in front part of this volume.

WILLS:

Any person aged 18 years or more and of sound and disposing mind and memory may make will of both real and personal property. (12-201).

Testamentary disposition is not limited; testator may be arbitrary if he wishes.

Execution.—The will, whether of personal or real estate, if in writing and signed by testator, or by some person subscribing testator's name in his presence and by his express direction, and attested and subscribed in testator's presence by two or more credible witnesses, is valid (12-202), or if signed will is in compliance with law at time and place of execution or at time and place of testator's domicile at execution or death (12-1306). Will need not be signed in presence of witnesses. (295 A.2d 755).

Form of Attestation Clause

Signed, sealed, published and declared by . . . . . . the testator as and for his last will and testament in the presence of us who at his request, in his presence and in the presence of each other, have hereunto subscribed our names as witnesses.

Holographic wills must meet requirements of all wills. (12-202).

Nuncupative Wills.—Statutory authorization repealed. (12-202).

Revocation.—Will not altered or revoked except by cancelling by testator, or by some other person in his presence and by his express direction, or by a subsequent valid will, or by writing signed by testator, or by some person subscribing testator's name in his presence and by his express direction, and attested and subscribed in his presence by two or more credible witnesses. This does not apply to implied revocation. (12-208). If after executing will, testator is divorced or his marriage annulled, divorce or annulment revokes any disposition or appointment of property made by will to former spouse, any provision conferring general or special power of appointment in former spouse, and any nomination of former spouse as executor, trustee, guardian or other fiduciary unless will expressly provides otherwise. Property thus prevented from passing passes as though spouse failed to survive deceased. (12-209).

Testamentary Gifts to Subscribing Witnesses.—Such gifts are valid. (28 Del. 450, 94 A. 760).

Testamentary Guardian.—See category Family, topic Guardian and Ward, subhead Selection of Guardian.

Probate.—Custodian of a will must deliver it to Register of Wills for county in which he resides within ten days from time he receives information of death of testator and if in willful default thereof, is liable for damages to anyone harmed thereby. (12-1301).

Will shall be proved before Register of Wills of county in which testator was domiciled at time of his death. If he was not domiciled in this state, it may be proved before Register of any county in this state wherein are any goods, chattels, rights, credits, or lands, of deceased. To be effective to prove transfer of any property or to nominate executor, will must be declared to be valid by admission to probate. (12-1302).

Inheritance Tax.—Repealed as of 7/1/98. (12-2304).

Self-proved Wills.—Attested will may be self-proved by acknowledgment thereof by testator and affidavits of witnesses made before officer authorized to administer oaths under laws of Delaware and evidenced by that officer's certificate. (12-1305).

Contest.—Caveat may be received by Court of Chancery at any time before proof of instrument but must be followed within ten days by bond in such sum as court may determine. Hearing is before Court of Chancery. (12-1308). After proof, review within six months is available before Court of Chancery to anyone who did not appear and was not cited. (12-1309).

Bequests and Devises to Inter Vivos Trusts.—Pour over trusts recognized by statute. Trust instrument may be amended subsequent to making of will. (12-211).

Legacies must be paid within one year of first appointment of personal representative if no time for payment is fixed by will (12-2312) and after expiration of year a legatee may maintain suit to compel payment of his legacy if sufficient assets exist. (12-3101).

Except as provided in connection with elective share of surviving spouse who elects to take elective share, shares of distributees abate, with personal property to be abated prior to real property within each class, in following order: (1) property not disposed of by will; (2) residuary bequests and devises; (3) general bequests and devises; (4) specific bequests and devises; unless will expresses order of abatement or purposes of testator require different order of abatement. (12-2317).

Unclaimed Legacies.—Estate of intestate dying without heirs escheats to State under 12-1101-1116. Where legatee unknown or cannot be found legacy paid into Court of Chancery. Any such property unclaimed after five years shall, subject to court's discretion, be considered abandoned, and two months after publication of that fact, will escheat to State. (12-1160-63). See also topic Executors and Administrators, subhead Distribution to Infant or Beneficiary Abroad; category Property, topic Absentees.

Lapse.—Unless will provides otherwise, if devisee or legatee who is grandparent or lineal descendant of grandparent of testator is dead at time of execution of will, fails to survive testator, or is treated as if he predeceased testator, issue of deceased devisee or legatee who survived testator by 120 hours take in place of deceased devisee or legatee, per stirpes. This does not apply to devisees or legatees under class gift. (12-2313). Lapsed devise or bequest falls into residue. (31 Del. Ch. 247, 70 A.2d 1).

Children.—Afterborn children for whom no will provision is made shall take intestate portion unless will directs otherwise. (12-301).

Election.—Surviving spouse has right of election to take an elective share of amount equal to $^1/_3$ of elective estate, less amount of all transfers to surviving spouse by decedent and less certain debts. (12-901-03; see also 12-908). Right of election of surviving spouse may be exercised by him only during his lifetime. (12-904). Surviving spouse who elects to take his elective share must file petition for elective share in Court of Chancery within six months after grant of letters testamentary or administration. (12-906).

Contribution.—In case of birth of child after execution of will or election of widow to take against the will, legatees and devisees contribute proportionately if residue of the estate is insufficient. (12-302, 908).

Foreign Probated Wills.—Will of person domiciled outside this state at time of death, concerning real estate or property located in this state, may be admitted to probate and recorded in this state. If such will was admitted to probate where testator domiciled, admission and recording in this state shall be accomplished by filing as provided in §12-1307. If such will was not admitted to probate in jurisdiction of testator's domicile and if not rejected from probate there for cause which would be valid grounds under laws of this state, admission and recording in this state shall be accomplished by proving such will in accordance with §§1302-05. In either case, such will shall then have same force and effect as if originally proved and allowed in this state. Copy must be properly verified. (12-1307). See also topic Executors and Administrators, subhead Foreign Executors and Administrators.

Renunciation.—Legatee may renounce. (315 A.2d 625, aff'd, 328 A.2d 141).

Construction.—A devise of real estate, without words of limitation, is construed to pass fee simple, or other whole estate or interest, which testator could lawfully devise in such real estate, unless contrary intention appears by will. (12-205).

After-acquired land passes as if possessed at making of will, unless contrary intention appears by will. (12-206).

Living Wills.—Competent adults are entitled to refuse medical treatment, including artificial nutrition and hydration, if death is imminent or they are in state of permanent unconsciousness. Such refusal may be by means of dated, written advance health-care directive. Such competent adult may also appoint agent to make health-care decisions. Directive must be signed by declarant, or by another person in declarant's presence, and at declarant's expressed direction and witnessed by two or more adults. No witness may (i) be related to declarant by blood, marriage, or adoption; (ii) be entitled to any portion of declarant's estate by will or intestacy; (iii) have present or inchoate claim against estate of declarant; (iv) have direct financial responsibility for declarant's medical care; or (v) be employee of, or have controlling interest in, hospital or health care facility in which declarant is patient. Each witness must state in writing that he is not disqualified for any of above reasons. Directive effective upon determination declarant lacks capacity. If withdrawing life-sustaining procedure, must determine declarant lacks capacity and has qualifying condition. Directive ceases effect upon recovered capacity. Directive can be revoked in whole or in part by competent adult. Agent shall make health care decision after consulting with attending physician. Agent's decision shall conform with declarant's instructions, and if not known, should conform as closely as possible under circumstances or in best interest of declarant. Agent's decision should take into account: declarant's values, likelihood of recovered capacity or death, burden and benefit of treatment to declarant, and oral or written statements previously made by declarant. Agent's decision is effective without judicial approval. Directive may include declarant's nomination of guardian. Revocation of directive must be made by signed writing or in manner which communicates intent to revoke. Intention must be memorialized in writing, signed and dated. Any person informed of revocation must communicate same to declarant's supervising healthcare provider. Decree of annulment, divorce or dissolution of marriage revokes spouse designation as agent. Earlier directive is revoked to extent of conflicts with subsequent directives. Initiation of emergency treatment presumed to represent suspension of directive. (16-2501 et seq.).

Uniform Anatomical Gift Act adopted. (16-2710-19).

Simultaneous Death.—See topic Death, subhead Survivorship.

Testamentary Trusts.—See topic Trusts.

FAMILY

ADOPTION:

Unmarried person or husband and wife jointly, who are not legally separated or who are not living apart from each other, or divorced or legally separated person, being resident in Delaware, and being over 21, may petition Family Court for order authorizing adoption of minor child or children. (13-903). Placement made with regard to religion specified by either natural parent in notarized statement made prior to placement. Placement made without regard to religion if religion not known, or there is no religion, or natural parents declare indifference. (13-911[a]). If proposed adoptive parent is stepparent or blood relative, no restriction regarding religious affiliation. (13-911[b]). If restriction in 13-911(a) will create hardship in obtaining placement, it may be waived by court. (13-911[c]). Except where petitioner is stepparent or blood relative, no petition may be presented unless child has been placed for adoption by Department of Services for Children, Youth and Their Families or agency licensed by it. (13-904).

No nonresident child may be brought into state for adoption or placement without approval of Department of Services for Children, Youth and Their Families. (13-926 and 31-307).

Conditions Precedent.—Generally, decree may be rendered only after continual residence of one year of adoptee with adopter under supervision of Department of Services for Children, Youth and Their Families, Division of Child Protective Services or authorized agency. Petition may be filed after six months supervision on recommendation of Department of Services for Children, Youth and Their Families or licensed agency. (13-913).

Consent Required.—Written consent, notarized and attached to petition, must be given by Department of Services for Children, Youth and Their Families or licensed or authorized agency in which parental rights exist. (13-907-08). If adoption by stepparent or blood relative, consent of natural parents required, but consent of alleged natural father need not contain admission of paternity. (13-908). Consent by child required if 14 years (may be waived by court). (13-907). Consent may be withdrawn by petition within 60 days of date of filing of adoption petition containing consent. (13-909). Courts may dispense with requirements and make interpretations subject to best interest of child. (13-932).

See note at head of Digest as to 1998 legislation covered.

See Topical Index in front part of this volume.

DE – 31

ADOPTION . . . *continued*

Jurisdiction of adoption proceedings rests in Family Court. (13-902).

Venue is in the county wherein petitioner resides or placing agency is located. (13-902).

Petition must state: Name, address and marital status of petitioners; sex and birthdate of child; relationship of petitioners to child; name of person or organization required to consent and basis of right; date of placement in adoptive home or if adoption by stepparent, date of marriage of natural parent to adopting stepparent; name to be assumed. Unless legal termination of parental rights has occurred, petition must state: name and residence of parents of child; marital status of mother at child's conception and birth; and if not married or her husband is not natural father, affidavit by mother, including name and last known address of natural father, or statement that mother knows natural father's name but is unwilling to disclose it, or that she does not know natural father's name, or name of natural father and statement that mother has never known his address. (13-906).

Exchange of identifying information before adoption is final permitted by consent of birth parent(s), adoptive parent(s), and Department of Services for Children, Youth and Their Families in best interest of child. Adoptee over 14 must consent. (13-929[a]). After finalization, Department of Services for Children, Youth and Their Families may exchange identifying information only with consent of all parties required under 13-961-65 or court order. (13-929[b]).

Proceedings.—Family Court must order investigation and report by Department of Services for Children, Youth and Their Families, licensed or authorized agency, and render decision on petition within 60 days from receipt of report. If decision is favorable, final decree of adoption is entered; if unfavorable, hearing must be ordered if requested by any petitioner. (13-912, 915[a]). Court may order further investigation. (13-912[d]).

Decree must state child's original name, name by which child is to be known, sex and age of child. (13-915[c]).

Name.—Name to be assumed by child upon adoption must be included in petition. (13-906[6]).

Effect of Adoption.—Decree of adoption terminates rights and duties between the natural parents and child, and creates between the adoptive parents and adoptee all rights and duties of parent-child relationship. (13-919). Upon entry of decree, adoptee and natural parents and relatives lose rights of inheritance running to and from each other; adoptee and adoptive parents and their relatives acquire rights of inheritance running to and from each other. (13-920[a], [b]). Adoption after will gives adoptee rights of after-born child. (13-920[c]).

Setting Aside Adoption.—Irregularities in proceedings cured by expiration of two years from entry of decree, and validity of decree not subject to attack thereafter. (13-918).

Adoption of Persons 18 or Older.—Effectual by decree entered upon signed petition of adopters to Family Court in county where petitioner or adoptee resides and after appearance and consent of adoptee. (13-951-53).

Termination of parental rights effected upon petition to Family Court by mother, father or presumed father, both parents, blood relative of child, authorized agency or Department of Services for Children, Youth and Their Families. (13-1104).

ALIMONY:

See topic Divorce.

COMMUNITY PROPERTY:

System does not obtain in Delaware.

DESERTION:

See topic Husband and Wife.

DISSOLUTION OF MARRIAGE:

See topic Divorce.

DIVORCE:

This subject is governed by 13-c. 15. Uniform Marriage and Divorce Act adopted in part.

Grounds.—Court to grant divorce when marriage is irretrievably broken and reconciliation is improbable, which is deemed to occur when there is: (1) Voluntary separation; (2) separation caused by respondent's misconduct, including but not limited to adultery, bigamy, conviction of serious crime, physical or oral abuse of petitioning spouse or children, desertion, homosexuality, refusal to perform marriage obligations, contracting venereal disease, and habitual alcoholism or drug abuse; (3) separation caused by respondent's mental illness; (4) separation caused by incompatibility. (13-1503, 1505).

Grounds for Legal Separation.—Legal separation does not exist.

Residence.—Action may be brought for divorce where either party has been resident of state continuously for six or more months immediately preceding commencement of action. (13-1504).

Jurisdiction.—Exclusively in Family Court. (13-1504).

Venue.—County of either party's residence. (13-1507[c]).

Process.—Service may be made by Sheriff upon respondent personally or respondent's agent by (1) delivery or (2) appearance of respondent or (3) appearance of counsel for respondent. If petition avers jurisdiction over respondent can only be acquired through mailing and publication, copy of summons must be sent by registered or certified mail, return receipt required, or if by publication, notice must be published once in newspaper of general circulation. (13-1508[a]-[d]).

Pleading.—(a) If petitioner avers marriage irretrievably broken and respondent does not deny it, such fact is presumed, and court shall so find, unless controverted by evidence, after hearing at which only petitioner need testify. If court not satisfied from evidence that marriage irretrievably broken, it shall deny petition. (13-1517[a]). If contested, court may order voluntary counseling to determine if marriage is irretrievably broken. (13-1517[b]).

(b) Petition must set forth, among other things, that residency requirements for jurisdiction have been met; whether there have been any previous matrimonial proceedings between parties; that marriage is irretrievably broken, and how it is to be characterized; and relief prayed for. (13-1507[b]).

Respondent may file counterclaim for divorce or annulment, and may seek interim relief, alimony, disposition of property, attorney's fees, resumption of former name or any other relief available to petitioner. If there are living children, respondent shall submit affidavit regarding children's rights. (13-1511).

Practice.—All hearings and trials are held before court without jury, or by master, privately, unless for reasons appearing sufficient to court. (13-1516). Parties must be separated not less than six months prior to date of hearing to grant divorce decree. (13-1507[e]). Free access of parties to all records and evidence. Court has discretion to appoint disinterested attorney, with fee taxed as part of court costs. (13-1516).

Judgment or Decree.—Decree granting or denying petition for divorce or annulment is final when entered, subject to right of appeal. (13-1518[a]).

Temporary Alimony.—Either party may file motion, along with or after petition for divorce, for temporary alimony. Also available in action for annulment. (13-1509[b][1], 1512[a]).

Allowance for Prosecution of Suit.—Court may order party to pay part or all costs to other party of maintaining or defending suit. (13-1515).

Permanent Alimony.—Court may award alimony to party if evidence shows dependence of party, lack of property, or inability of party to provide self-support. Party is eligible for alimony up to period of 50% of term of marriage, except for parties married 20 years or longer, no time limit. Party awarded alimony has obligation to seek vocational training and employment. Death, remarriage or cohabitation of party receiving alimony extinguishes alimony rights, unless parties otherwise agree. Party may waive right to alimony by contract. (13-1512).

Division of Property of Spouses.—See subhead Division of Marital Property, infra.

Division of Marital Property.—Upon request of either party in divorce or annulment proceeding, court shall divide equitably all marital property without regard to marital misconduct as it deems just. (13-1513).

Change of Wife's Name.—Upon request of a party court may issue order permitting such party to resume her maiden name, or that of a former husband. (13-1514).

Custody of Children.—Family court has discretionary power concerning custody of children, during and after divorce, and may revise orders from time to time. (13-721-732). Delaware has adopted The Child Protection From Domestic Violence Act. (13-701A-711A).

Allowance for Support of Children.—Duty to support child under 18 rests primarily upon his parents (13-501), and Family Court, which has exclusive original jurisdiction of support actions (13-507), may order defendant to make support payments into Division of Child Support Enforcement, directly to dependent, or to guardian (13-513). Court may order either party to pay support to other party as may seem reasonable. (13-513).

Family Court has exclusive original jurisdiction relating to support and maintenance actions involving children. (13-507). Award governed by special formula. (13-514).

Uniform Child Custody Jurisdiction Act.—Adopted. (13-1901-1925)

Uniform Parentage Act.—Adopted. (13-801-819).

Uniform Reciprocal Enforcement of Support Act.—Repealed and replaced by Uniform Interstate Family Support Act. (13-601-691).

Uniform Interstate Family Support Act.—Adopted. (13-601-691). *Note:* Replaced Uniform Reciprocal Enforcement of Support Act.

Remarriage.—No restriction on remarriage after decree of divorce has become final and appeal is pending only with respect to relief, other matters incidental or collateral. (13-1518).

Foreign Divorces.—Full faith and credit shall be given to decree of annulment or divorce by court of competent jurisdiction in another state, territory or possession of U.S. (13-1521).

Uniform Divorce Recognition Act.—Not adopted.

Separation Agreements.—Agreements between husband and wife relating to support or adjustment of property rights will be upheld, though in contemplation of divorce, if free of collusion and not directly conducive to procurement of divorce. Law prefers private settlement of marital obligations at time of separation. (287 A.2d 413, aff'd, 336 A.2d 216). Family Court has jurisdiction over such agreements. (13-507[a]).

GUARDIAN AND WARD:

Jurisdiction to appoint and remove guardians for disabled person in Court of Chancery. (12-3901; 3908). Superior Court has jurisdiction to appoint guardians for disabled person and approve settlement in connection with single-transaction matter arising out of tort claim for disabled person. Upon entry of order appointing guardian and approving settlement, jurisdiction is transferred to Chancery. (12-3901[k]).

Selection of Guardian.—In its discretion Chancery Court may appoint two or more persons, one or more to have care of person of disabled person and other(s) to have care and management of property; or court may appoint one guardian for both person and property. When guardian of person is sought, ward entitled to representation by counsel. (12-3901; 12-3903).

Sole surviving parent may by deed or last will name guardian of person, property or both of child, who must be appointed if there be no just cause to contrary. (12-3902[b]). In practice nonresidents are not appointed guardians of property.

See note at head of Digest as to 1998 legislation covered.

See Topical Index in front part of this volume.

GUARDIAN AND WARD... *continued*

Minor over 14 years of age, whose parents have not otherwise effectively provided for guardianship, may choose guardian and court will appoint person so chosen if there be no just cause to contrary. But court may appoint guardian according to its discretion when minor is under age 14, neglects to choose guardian, or is resident out of state. (12-3902[c][d]).

No one has any authority to act as guardian unless he has been appointed by Chancery Court. (12-3902[a]).

Eligibility and Competency.—No statutory provision.

Appointment of Guardian.—Chancery Court may appoint guardian for any disabled person upon filing of proper petition. (12-3901).

Public Guardian.—Court of Chancery may, at its discretion, appoint public guardian for persons disabled for reasons other than minority. (12-3991-3997).

Qualification.—Every person appointed guardian shall, unless requirement is waived by court, become bound, with surety, to disabled person in penal sum to be fixed by court. (12-3905[a]). Where petitioner is public agency, court may order that guardian need not give bond either with or without surety. (12-3905[d]).

Inventory by guardian or trustee is required within 30 days of appointment. Inventory shall include personal knowledge of fair market value. (Ch. Ct. Rule 110). Court may order appraisal if unsatisfied with inventory. (Ch. Ct. Rule 111). Supplemental inventory is required for property received after initial inventory. (Ch. Ct. Rule 110). Upon terminating guardianship (Ch. Ct. Rule 180-C) or upon request of interested party court may require full accounting. (Ch. Ct. Rule 115).

Powers.—Guardian of person may exercise powers, rights and duties of parent to care for ward. (12-3922). Guardian of property has power to: collect, hold and retain assets; receive additions to estate; invest estate assets; deposit estate funds in bank; sell or exercise stock rights; vote stock; insure assets; pay taxes; make payment for ordinary repairs to disabled person's dwelling; prosecute or defend actions; execute instruments; and hold securities. (12-3923).

Investments.—12-3971-3975 governs Chancery Court's power to invest funds for minors; 12-3923 governs guardian's power to invest. For investment by fiduciaries generally, see category Estates and Trusts, topic Trusts, subhead Investments.

Securities in Name of Nominee.—See category Estates and Trusts, topic Trusts, subhead Securities in Name of Nominee.

Real Estate.—Guardian can sell ward's real estate only on order of court. (12-3951, 3954). Court may permit sale to be partially or wholly on credit. (12-3953).

Liabilities of Guardian.—If guardian does not render true accounts of his guardianship, or if, upon termination of guardianship, he does not deliver to ward all property in his possession due ward, or if he does not faithfully perform his duties as guardian, then he forfeits bond. (12-3905[a]).

Accounts.—Guardian of property must fully account for all money, effects and property of disabled person that have come into his possession; guardian of person has no duty to account. (12-3941). Accounts are filed, adjusted and settled in Chancery Court. (12-3942). Guardian must render account of his guardianship at end of one year from his appointment, and afterwards as Chancery Court shall require but no more than once in two years unless there is special occasion. (12-3943).

Termination of guardianship occurs when ward turns 18. (12-3909). Court of Chancery may remove guardian for any sufficient cause, and guardian may be allowed to resign if Chancery deems proper. (12-3908).

Gifts to Minors.—See topic Infants.

Insane Persons.—Appointment of guardian for persons disabled by mental incapacity is by Court of Chancery except as noted above; all provisions concerning disabled persons apply. (12-3901).

Foreign Guardians.—Foreign or alien guardian duly appointed in another state, whose nonresident minor ward has property in Delaware has all rights and power of a guardian appointed by Chancery Court upon his recording with Register in Chancery certificate of appointment setting forth facts of appointment, security entered into and that guardian is vested with care and management of ward's estate with authority to receive and liability as guardian to account for same. Foreign guardian may petition Court for additional powers upon giving such security as Court directs. (12-3904).

Uniform Fiduciaries Act not adopted.

Uniform Simplification of Fiduciary Security Transfers Act adopted (12-c.43) and not repealed by Art. 8, Uniform Commercial Code (6-10-104[2]).

HUSBAND AND WIFE:

Disabilities of Married Women.—None by statute.

Separate Property.—Married woman holds all her property as separate estate and may sell, convey, assign, transfer, devise, bequeath, encumber or otherwise dispose of same. (13-311; 449 A.2d 1055, aff'd, 461 A.2d 696).

Contracts.—Married woman may enter into contracts with any person, sue, or be sued, or make a will, as though femme sole. (13-311).

Actions.—Husband and wife can sue each other at law (630 A.2d 1096), and equity will entertain jurisdiction of such actions in proper cases (38 Del. Ch. 220, 149 A.2d 320). See also subhead Contracts, supra.

Conveyance or Encumbrance of Property.—Deed of lands or tenements woman executes while married is valid as if she were sole, if she acknowledges having executed deed. (25-102).

Married woman who has been abandoned by her husband without just cause, may sell, or otherwise dispose of her real property as though single, provided that conveyance, or other instrument, be acknowledged before chancellor, or Superior Court judge. In such case, in addition to usual certificate of acknowledgment, it must be certified that it has satisfactorily appeared to judge who took acknowledgment, that person who executed instrument had been abandoned without just cause. (25-107, 124).

See also subheads Contracts, Separate Property, supra; and category Property, topic Curtesy.

Desertion and Nonsupport.—Duty to support spouse rests upon other spouse. (13-502). Spouse is bound by support order during pendancy of divorce appeal, since divorce decree appealed on its merits is not final until affirmed. (476 A.2d 1096). Duty to support child under 18, and child under 19 who is high school student, whether born in or out of wedlock, rests primarily with parents, and equally upon each. (13-501; 403 A.2d 1121). Where parents unable to provide minor child's minimum needs, stepparent or person who cohabits in relationship of husband and wife with parent of minor child is under duty to supply these needs, but only during cohabitation and while child makes residence with such stepparent. (13-501). Family Court has exclusive original jurisdiction. (13-507). If court, after notice to defendant and hearing to show cause, concludes defendant violated terms of support order for spouse or child, it may punish defendant for contempt and may attach wages. (13-516[a]). If attachment of wages is impractical, court shall require defendant to enter into bond to Court. (13-516[e]). Order terminates by operation of law when child reaches 18 years of age, or at 19 if still in high school; however obligation for payment of past due support shall not terminate until paid. (13-517). For court order of support payments, see topic Divorce, subhead Allowance for Support of Children.

Uniform Interstate Family Support Act adopted. (13-601 et seq.).

Uniform Parentage Act adopted. (13-c.8). If party to action filed under this chapter requests name of child be changed by order of Court, party must file motion setting forth position of parties to action, reason for request and if child is over 14 years, position of child on having name changed. Court shall grant motion if it is in best interest of child and is consistent with Court's determination of existence or nonexistence of parentage. (13-819).

Community property system does not obtain.

INFANTS:

Minor or infant is person under 18, and adult is person 18 or older. (1-302). See also subhead Disabilities, infra.

Emancipation.—Person reaching age of 18 is deemed to be of full legal age. (1-701). Competent person 18 or older may prosecute, defend, settle or dismiss any action at law or in equity, without guardian or other legal representative, and may himself be appointed guardian ad litem or other legal representative for person under 18 (10-3923); has full capacity to contract and is responsible for his contracts unless declared legally incompetent for reason other than age (6-2705); and may make any conveyance of or transaction relating to real estate without interference of guardian (25-312).

Disabilities.—Persons under 21 may not buy alcoholic beverages. (4-904). Males under 18 and females under 16 may not marry; and female under 18 may only marry with consent of parent or guardian or, if minor has no parent, with consent of Family or Superior Court Judge, or one of their appointees. Age limitations not applicable if male and female acknowledge under oath that they are parents or prospective parents of child. If female pregnant, must present doctors' certificate so stating. (13-123). Operator's license for motor vehicle not issued to persons under 16. (21-2707). Certificate of title for motor vehicle not issued to person under 18 without consent of parent or guardian. (21-2306[d]). Minor may not change name without consent of one parent or guardian. (10-5902). Persons under 17 may not have access to material defined as harmful to minors (11-1365), and those under 18 may not buy or be given tobacco by anyone but their parent or guardian (11-1116). Persons intoxicated or under 21 may not buy deadly weapons made for defense of one's person. (24-903). Minors are incapable of making wills of real or personal estate (12-201). Child under 14 may not be employed. Children between 14 and 15 are restricted as to time of day and number of hours per week they can work, and certain work is restricted to those over 16. (19-504-508). See category Employment, topic Labor Relations, subhead Child Labor.

Adoption.—See topic Adoption.

Contracts.—Uniform Commercial Code adopted. See category Business Regulation and Commerce, topic Commercial Code.

Ratification of Contracts.—Common law principles apply. (4 Del. 75).

Bank Deposits.—Any banking institution may receive money on deposit from or in name of minor. Such deposit is held for benefit of depositor as though adult (5-920[a]) and in all transactions with banking institution, minor is subject to same obligations, equities, and defenses as adult (5-920[c]). Similar provision for investment by minor in building and loan association. (5-1917).

Actions.—In Chancery Court no proceeding is deferred because of infancy of party unless court otherwise orders. Disinterested guardian or trustee appears for infant; otherwise, appearance is by guardian ad litem. (Ch. Ct. Rule 17 [c]). In Superior Court, representative sues or defends on behalf of infant; if there is no duly-appointed representative, infant may sue by next friend or guardian ad litem. (Super. Ct. Rule 17 [c]).

Suit for collection of county taxes on real and personal estate may be brought against guardian or trustee of infant owner or guardian ad litem or trustee ad litem. (9-8702). Parent, guardian or next friend of minor who has claim for labor or services rendered, as per 10-4931, may bring action on claim. (10-4934).

Support of Minor.—Duty to support minor rests primarily and equally with parents. (13-501[a], [c]). Where parents unable to support minor child's minimum needs, duty to support resident minor rests with stepparent or person cohabiting with parent. (13-501[b]). Duty to support child over 18 who is high school student and likely to graduate continues until child is 19 or graduates, whichever first occurs. (13-501[d]). Family Court has broad power to require support where duty to support found. (13-513).

Uniform Interstate Family Support Act.—Wholly adopted in all relevant aspects. (13-601 et seq.).

Interstate Compact on Juveniles is adopted. (31-c. 52).

Uniform Transfers to Minors Act adopted. (12-c. 45). Age of majority for purpose of Act is 21. (12-4501). Transfer made under Delaware Act if one or more of donor

---

See note at head of Digest as to 1998 legislation covered.

See Topical Index in front part of this volume.

INFANTS . . . *continued*
transferor, minor or custodian is Delaware resident or if custodial property is located in Delaware. (12-4502[e]).

Uniform Parentage Act adopted. (13-c. 8).

Uniform Securities Ownership by Minors Act not adopted.

Parental Responsibility.—Parents are liable (up to $5,000) for property intentionally or recklessly destroyed or damaged by their children under 18 who live with them. (10-3922). Negligent operation of automobile by minor is imputed to person signing license application. (21-6105). See topic Adoption, subhead Termination of Parental Rights.

MARRIAGE:

Minimum Ages.—Males 18, females 16. Age limitations not applicable if male and female acknowledge under oath that they are parents or prospective parents of child. If female pregnant, must have doctor's certificate so stating. (13-123).

Consent Required.—Where female under 18, written consent of parents or guardian, with two reputable witnesses, required. (13-123).

Medical Examination.—None required.

License is required and must be obtained from the county clerk of peace for $10 fee. (13-108). Both applicants must appear in person except in case of critical illness. Doctor may appear as proxy. (13-120). License becomes void if ceremony is not performed within 30 days from date of its issuance. (13-107). False answer by applicant is perjury. (13-127). Divorced applicant must file with clerk of peace certified copy of decree or certificate of divorce. (13-101).

Waiting Period.—License must be obtained at least 24 hours (or 96 hours if both parties nonresidents) before ceremony. Clerk of peace may shorten or lengthen time for good cause. (13-107).

Serological Tests.—None required.

Ceremonial marriages must be solemnized in presence of two reputable witnesses by clergyman or minister of any recognized religion, members of State Supreme Court, Superior Court, Family Court, Chancery, Court of Common Pleas, and Justice of the Peace Court, clerks of peace, chief deputy or deputy, or, if at least one of parties is Delaware resident, by Mayor of Wilmington. They may be solemnized according to forms and usages of any religious society. (13-106).

Reports of Marriages.—Marriage Record Book kept by issuing officer is open for public inspection and may be admitted as evidence in any court of record. (13-119).

Record.—See category Documents and Records, topic Records, subhead Vital Statistics.

Common law marriages in Delaware are not valid (31 Del. 303, 114 A. 215), but common law marriage of nonresidents, contracted outside of Delaware and valid where contracted, will be recognized (299 F. Supp. 192).

Proxy Marriages.—No provision.

Marriages by Written Contract.—No provision.

Prohibited Marriages.—Between: Persons and their ancestors, descendants, brothers, sisters, uncles, aunts, nieces, nephews, or first cousins (13-101[a]); parties to marriage contracted or solemnized outside of Delaware will be punished in same manner as those parties who contracted their marriage within Delaware, when legal residence of either party is in Delaware, and parties thereto live and cohabit as husband and wife within Delaware. (13-104).

Annulment.—Court shall enter annulment of marriage entered into under any of following circumstances: (1) Party lacked capacity to consent to marriage at time marriage was solemnized, either because of mental incapacity or infirmity, or because of influence of alcohol, drugs or other incapacitating substances; (2) party lacked physical capacity to consummate marriage by sexual intercourse and other party did not, at time marriage was solemnized, know of incapacity; (3) party was less than legal age and did not have consent of his parents or guardian or judicial approval as provided by law; (4) one party entered into marriage in reliance upon fraudulent act or representation of other party, which fraudulent act or representation goes to essence of marriage; (5) one or both parties entered into marriage under duress exercised by other party, or a third party, whether or not such other party knew of such exercise of duress; (6) one or both parties entered into marriage as a jest or dare; or (7) marriage is prohibited and void or voidable as provided in 13-101. (13-1506[a]).

Decree of annulment may be sought by any of following persons, and petition filed within times specified, but in no event may decree of annulment be sought after death of either party to marriage, except as provided: (1) For paragraphs (1), (4), (5) or (6), supra, by either party to marriage who was aggrieved by condition or conditions, or by legal representative of party who lacked capacity to consent, no later than 90 days after petitioner obtained knowledge of described condition; (2) for paragraph (2), supra, by either party no later than one year after petitioner obtained knowledge of described condition; (3) for paragraph (3), supra, by underaged party, his parent, or guardian, no later than one year after date marriage entered into; (4) decree of annulment for reason set forth in paragraph (7), supra, may be sought by either party, by legal spouse in case of bigamous, polygamous or incestuous marriages, by appropriate state official, or by child of either party at any time prior to death of either party or prior to final settlement of estate of either party and discharge of personal representative, executor, or administrator of estate, or prior to six months after order of distribution is made under 12-c.23. (13-1506[b]).

Children born of an annulled marriage are legitimate. Marriages annulled so declared as of date of marriage. (13-1506[c]).

Provisions relating to property rights of spouses are applicable to annulment. (13-1506[d]).

Separation as defined in 13-1503(7) not applicable to annulment proceedings. (13-1506[e]).

If living children, petitioner must submit affidavit that petitioner has read or been advised of children's rights. (13-1507[g]).

Family Court has jurisdiction over all divorce and annulment proceedings. Party must have resided in State for six consecutive months immediately preceding commencement of action. (13-1504).

Voidable Marriages.—Voidable at instance of innocent party, subject to judicial approval, where either party was: of unsound mind, mental patient not having certificate from mental hospital superintendent, infected with any communicable disease unknown to innocent party, venereally diseased, habitual drunkard, confirmed user of narcotic drug, divorced and lacking necessary certificate or copy of decree, or on probation or parole and lacking necessary consent. (13-101[b]).

MARRIED WOMEN:

See topics Husband and Wife, Marriage; categories Civil Actions and Procedure, topic Evidence, subhead Witnesses; Documents and Records, topic Acknowledgments; Estates and Trusts, topics Executors and Administrators, Wills; Property, topic Dower.

INSURANCE

INSURANCE COMPANIES:

Regulated by Title 18 of Code.

Supervised by Insurance Commissioner, Dover, DE. (18-301-332). Powers and duties of Commissioner include promulgation of regulations (18-311[b]) acting as hearing officer (18-325[a]), subject to Administrative Procedures Law (29-c. 101); and conducting examinations of every insurer licensed in State at least every five years (18-318[a]).

Rates.—Rates for casualty insurance, including workmen's compensation; all forms of motor vehicle insurance; surety insurance; fire, marine and inland marine insurance on risks located in Delaware; and for health, group health, blanket health, and Medicare supplement insurance and health service corporations regulated by 18-c. 25. (18-2502). Insurers must file with Commissioner every manual, minimum, class rate, rating schedule and rating rule (18-2504), or join licensed rating organization which makes such filings (18-2510). Rates shall not be excessive, inadequate, or unfairly discriminatory. (18-2501, 2503). Insurer may file and use rates, but if Commissioner finds that filing does not meet requirement, he must specify reasons and grant hearing within 20 days after written request. (18-2507). Must file rates 90 days prior to proposed effective date, and such filings are deemed effective unless disapproved by Commissioner within 45 days of receipt of filing. (18-2506). Commissioner may also suspend or modify requirement of filing as to any kind of insurance, rates for which cannot practicably be filed before they are used. (18-2505). Contracts must be in accord with filings or in accord with 18-2505 (exemptions) or 18-2509 (excess rates). See generally 18-c. 25.

Annual statements of financial condition, transactions and affairs must be filed with Commissioner by Mar. 1, in each year for year ending Dec. 31. Statements must be verified by two principal officers; if reciprocal insurer, by oath of attorney in fact or like officer if corporation. Annual statement form approved by, and requirements of, National Association of Insurance Commissioners must be adhered to. Statement of alien insurer must be verified by its U.S. manager. (18-526). See also subhead Medical Malpractice, infra.

Policies are regulated as follows: Life insurance and annuity contracts, 18-c. 29; group life insurance, 18-c. 31; health insurance contracts, 18-c. 33; group and blanket health insurance, 18-c. 35; consumer credit insurance, 18-c. 37; casualty insurance contracts, 18-c. 39; motor vehicles, no-fault insurance, 21-2118; property insurance contracts, 18-c. 41; surety insurance contracts, suretyship contracts, 18-c. 43, 77; title insurance contracts, 18-c. 45.

Trade practices are regulated in 18-c. 23 by defining and prohibiting unfair competition and unfair or deceptive acts. Unfair discrimination in value of insurance policies and premiums based upon race, color, religion or national origin is prohibited. (18-2304[22]).

Rebates.—Rebates in any form prohibited unless expressly authorized by law. (18-2304[14][15]).

Liens.—Property owner who fails to furnish demanded proof of fire insurance to lienholders after 30 days notice forfeits right to insure to lienholders who can insure and collect proceeds. (25-4701-4702).

Agents and Brokers.—In order to do business in state, must be licensed. (18-c. 17). Unless specifically exempted (18-1724) written examination is required (18-1725). Where nonresident agent's state imposes stricter requirements on Delaware agent than Delaware law would otherwise impose on out-of-state agent, Delaware applies that state's own requirements against its agent in Delaware. (18-532, 1723).

Process Agent.—Every insurer must appoint Commissioner its attorney to receive process before Commissioner authorizes it to do business in state. Service of process on foreign insurance companies must be made on Commissioner. (18-524).

Investments.—Insurer's investments are regulated. (18-c. 13).

Foreign Insurer.—Insurer formed under Delaware law or located in this state must have certificate of authority from Commissioner to solicit or transact insurance in foreign jurisdiction. (18-505). Insurer must be incorporated stock or mutual insurer or reciprocal insurer of same general type as domestic insurers; must maintain reserves as required by 18-c. 11; must not transact business on assessment plan, stipulated premium plan or any similar plan; must not transact workmen's compensation insurance unless approved by Industrial Accident Board; must not transact a kind of insurance in this State unless authorized to transact such insurance in state or country of domicile. (18-507). May not be owned or controlled by any government or governmental agency. (18-508). Foreign insurance companies may make investments as permitted by laws of domicile if of a quality substantially equal to that required under 18-c. 13 for similar funds of like domestic insurers. (18-1329).

For deposit requirements see 18-513. For application for certificate of authority see 18-515.

See this topic generally.

See note at head of Digest as to 1998 legislation covered.

See Topical Index in front part of this volume.

DE – 34

INSURANCE COMPANIES . . . *continued*

Retaliatory Laws.—Taxes, licenses, fees, fines, penalties, deposit requirements or other requirements imposed on Delaware insurers seeking to do business in any state or foreign country which are more onerous than Delaware requirements for insurers of such other state or country shall be imposed upon insurers of such other state or country seeking to do business in Delaware. (18-532).

Premium Tax.—Each insurer must file with Commissioner by Mar. 1 report showing, except for wet marine and transportation insurance, gross direct premium income, including policy, membership and other fees, assessments and all other considerations for insurance, received during next preceding year on account of insurance contracts, other than workmen's compensation and employer's liability, covering property, subjects or risks located in this State (with proper proportionate allocation of premiums as to such subjects in this State insured under policies covering subjects in more than one state), after deducting: (1) amount of returned premiums on cancelled policies (but not including return of cash surrender value of life insurance policies); and (2) unabsorbed portion of any deposit premium, and amount returned to policyholders as dividends and similar returns. Report must be verified by president, secretary or other responsible officer. Considerations received for annuity contracts not to be included in gross direct premium income and not to be subject to premium taxes. (18-702[a]).

Domestic insurers must include, excepting wet marine and transportation insurance, gross amount of premiums and other considerations for direct insurance from mail solicitations of business in a state or province of Canada, in which insurer is not admitted to transact insurance, covering persons, property, subjects or risks located in such state or province, on which no premium tax is paid and no surplus line tax is payable to such other state or province, and shall make similar deductions as above. (18-702[b]).

Amount of tax is $1^3/4\%$ of net premiums. (18-702[c]). 25% of estimated tax liability for current year must be paid each Apr. 15, June 15, Sept. 15, and Dec. 15, with remaining balance paid on Mar. 1 of following year. (18-702[d]). Certain wet marine and transportation insurers must file report with Commissioner and pay 5% of taxes shown on report. Report due on June 1. (18-702[e]).

Gross Premium Tax.—Every insurer transacting insurance in state other than workmen's compensation, wet marine, and transportation insurance must on Mar. 1 each year pay tax of $1/4\%$ on gross premiums received and assessments collected from insurance of every kind upon persons, property or risks located within state. (18-707). Tax on wet marine and transportation insurance underwriting profits shall be 5% of taxable profit ascertained as provided in 18-702(e).

Every insurance carrier insuring employers against liability for injury to or death of employees is subject to tax of 2% of all workers' compensation or employers' liability premiums received from business within state, less returned premiums or cancelled policies and premiums on reinsurance received from other insurance carriers. This tax is in lieu of all other taxes on such premiums. Mutual companies are taxed on gross premiums and not credited with unabsorbed premiums or dividends. 25% of estimated tax liability is payable to Secretary of Finance on Apr. 1, June 15, and Sept. 15 of current year, and remaining balance due on Mar. 1 of following year. (19-2391-92; 18-704).

Privilege Tax.—Domestic insurers, other than mutual insurer doing business on assessment premium plan up to $95,000 per year based on gross receipt, due and payable at same time as premium tax and estimated payments as provided in 18-702. (18-703). Against this may be credited $1,500 for each $100,000 gross compensation paid by domestic insurer in Delaware. Any insurer which writes 50% or more of total premiums on property or persons in state is exempt from privilege tax. (18-703).

Political Contributions.—No insurer shall directly or indirectly pay or use, or offer, any money or property to aid any candidate for Insurance Commissioner, or for nomination, reimbursement or indemnification of any person for money so used. Any officer, director, agent or stockholder who aids, abets, or consents to any contributions and also any person who knowingly solicits or receives such contribution subject to fine of up to $1,000 and imprisonment of up to one year. (18-2304[6]).

Direct Actions Against Insurer.—See category Transportation, topic Motor Vehicles, subhead Direct Actions.

Uniform Insurers Liquidation Act.—Adopted. (18-5920).

No-Fault Insurance.—See category Transportation, topic Motor Vehicles, subhead No-Fault Insurance.

Unfair Practices.—Governed by 18-c. 23. Discrimination between insureds of equal risk prohibited. (18-2304[13], [15]). Discrimination in medical policies, not reflection of available government subsidies, against insureds over 65 prohibited. (18-2315). Refusal to issue accident or health policy on basis of blindness or deafness prohibited. (18-2316). Tying arrangements prohibited to bank and trust companies engaged in selling of insurance products under 5-761[a]. (18-2304[23]).

Health Service Corporations.—Health service corporations subject to supervision of Commissioner. (18-c. 63).

Medical Malpractice.—Temporary Joint Underwriting Association, for purpose of issuing medical malpractice insurance, is established by Delaware Malpractice Law. Membership consists of two categories, Delaware casualty insurers, and Delaware health insurers and certain health service corporations, second category only having liabilities to association when association's aggregate losses reach certain point. Insurers within statutory definitions must be members of association as condition of continued authority to sell insurance in Delaware. (18-6830). However, association only begins underwriting each category of health care provider upon Insurance Commissioner's finding that health care malpractice insurance is not reasonably available in voluntary market for that type of health care provider. (18-6830[f]). Authorization of association to underwrite given category does not exclude others from issuing same coverage. Association's grant is limited to providing insurance for two years after it begins underwriting operations. (18-6830). Association is nonprofit; final premium for all its policy-holders being set to equal administrative expenses, loss and loss adjustment expenses, and taxes, and reasonable allowance for contingencies and servicing.

(18-6832[d]). All licensed health care providers are entitled to apply for coverage from Association. (18-6834). Maximum authorized coverage is $1,000,000 for each claimant under one policy and $3,000,000 for all claimants under one policy in one year. (18-6830[h]). Rates and rating plans of association are subject to 18-c. 25 (18-6832[c]), and Association must file annual statement on or before Mar. 1 with Insurance Commissioner (18-6838).

SURETY AND GUARANTY COMPANIES:

Organization.—Surety companies must receive certificate of authority from Insurance Commissioner as provided in 18-505 to transact insurance in State. (18-7701). Certain capital funds required in cash or cash equivalent. (18-511).

Reports.—Annual statements and supplemental reports required to conform with National Association of Insurance Commissioner's Annual Statement, unless prescribed or permitted by this title or Commissioner. (18-526). See topic Insurance Companies, subhead Annual Statements.

Rights and Powers.—Scope of surety insurance defined at 18-905(a). Transaction of surety insurance does not confer power on insurer to guarantee titles to real estate. (18-905[b]).

Foreign Companies.—See topic Insurance Companies, subhead Foreign Insurer.

Taxation.—See topic Insurance Companies. No special taxes imposed on surety and guaranty companies as such.

INTELLECTUAL PROPERTY

TRADEMARKS AND TRADENAMES:

What May Be Used.—Any mark not: deceptive, defamatory of any persons, national symbols, institutions or beliefs, immoral, containing flag or coat of arms of government or political subdivision, primarily descriptive or deceptively misdescriptive of goods or services, primarily geographical in description, primarily consisting of surname, or referring to or picturing any living individual without his written consent, or resembling mark registered or used. (6-3303).

Registration.—Applicant may fill out form setting forth name and business address, state of incorporation, goods or services for which mark will be used, manner in which mark will be used, class in which goods or services will fall, dates when mark first used anywhere and first used in Delaware, statement that owner has clear right to mark. Form shall be signed, verified and filed with Secretary of State accompanied with facsimile of mark in duplicate and filing fee of $25. (6-3304). Secretary shall issue certificate of registration upon receipt of $10 fee. (6-3305[c]).

Duration.—Term of ten years, renewable indefinitely, with $25 fee. (6-3306).

Assignment.—Instrument of assignment may be filed with $25 fee. (6-3307).

Infringement.—Any usage or copying without consent. (6-3312).

Protection Afforded.—Injunction, destruction of counterfeits, accounting and damages. (6-3314).

Resale Price Agreements.—Repealed by 60 Del.L. 470.

Tradenames.—Partnership or person using tradename or title which does not include Christian name and surname of each partner or person using such tradename, must file certificate in office of Prothonotary of each county where business is carried on, showing tradename or title and Christian name and surname of each partner or person using such tradename, and date of organization of firm, with attached affidavit of one of partners or person using tradename to effect that facts stated are true. (6-3101). Filing fee, $5. (6-3103). Change of membership in partnership or firm must be registered in like manner within ten days after change. (6-3102).

TRADE SECRETS:

Uniform Trade Secrets Act adopted. (6-2001-6-2009).

Complaints must be brought no later than three years after misappropriation of trade secret has been or should have been discovered. (6-2006). Court may enjoin actual or threatened misappropriation, and it may require royalty payments or compel affirmative acts to protect trade secrets. (6-2002). Complainants also may seek damages for actual loss and unjust enrichment. (6-2003). Exemplary damages are available for willful and malicious misappropriations. (6-2003). Court may award attorney's fees for willful and malicious misappropriations, or in cases where either party has made claims or defenses in bad faith. (6-2004). In any proceedings, court must take reasonable precautions to protect trade secrets. (6-2005; 505 A.2d 30).

LEGAL PROFESSION

ATTORNEYS AND COUNSELORS:

State bar is not integrated.

Jurisdiction over Admission.—Admission to bar is by Supreme Court on recommendation of board of 16 examiners, members of bar, who are appointed by court. (Supr. Ct. Rules 51, 52).

Eligibility.—21 or older, of good moral character, vouched for by preceptor, baccalaureate degree or equivalent from accredited college or passed Board approved examination; graduate of ABA approved law school, passed bar examination prescribed by Board, completed five-month clerkship in Delaware and attended preadmission instruction session. (Supr. Ct. Rule 52).

Registration As Law Student.—No requirement.

Educational Requirements.—Baccalaureate degree or equivalent from accredited college or university, or successful completion of examination to be determined by Board. Baccalaureate law degree or equivalent from ABA approved law school. (Supr. Ct. Rule 52[a][4], [5]).

See note at head of Digest as to 1998 legislation covered.

See Topical Index in front part of this volume.

ATTORNEYS AND COUNSELORS ... *continued*

Petition for Admission.—Formal application for admission to bar must be made in open court before Supreme Court or in Chambers of any Justice of Court. (Supr. Ct. Rule 54). Procedures prior to formal court application governed by Rules of Board of Bar Examiners and include written application. (Supr. Ct. Rule 52[b]).

Examination.—Applicants for admission must take examination prepared by Board of Bar Examiners. (Supr. Ct. Rule 52[a][6]). This examination is given each year on days designated by Board. (Board of Bar Examiners Rule BR-11). Examination includes Multistate Bar Exam and essay questions from following subjects as selected by examiners: agency, constitutional law, contracts, corporations, criminal law (including Delaware Criminal Code), equity, evidence, partnerships, procedure, property, torts, trusts, uniform commercial code, wills. Professional conduct examination is also required. (Board of Bar Examiners Rule BR-12[a], [b]).

Admission Without Examination.—No longer permitted. (Supr. Ct. Rule 52[a][6]).

Admission Pro Hac Vice.—Permitted. (Supr. Ct. Rule 71).

Clerkship.—Five months in Delaware with five-year member of bar, or with judge of listed courts, or in offices listed, or in office otherwise approved by Board. (Supr. Ct. Rule 52[a][8]).

Licenses.—$75 annual general service fee. (30-2301[b]).

Privileges.—Attorney-client privilege recognized. (DRE 502).

Attorney Ethics.—ABA Model Rules of Professional Conduct adopted. (Del. Rule Prof. Conduct).

Disabilities.—No attorney or other officer of court shall be taken as special bail or surety in any case, but he or she may be principal. (Supr. Ct. Rule 83).

Liabilities.—See category Civil Actions and Procedure, topic Costs.

Compensation.—Attorney must not accept compensation for representing client from one other than client without client's permission, unless client consents after consultation and there is no interference with attorney's independence of judgment or with client-attorney relationship. (Del. Rul. Prof. Cond. 1.8[f]).

Disbarment or Suspension.—Administered by Supreme Court in proceedings instituted by court appointed Board on Professional Responsibility. (Supr. Ct. Rules 62, 63).

Unauthorized Practice.—Punishable as contempt. (386 A.2d 652).

Mandatory Continuing Legal Education.—Members of bar and judiciary must complete minimum of 30 hours of actual instruction in approved legal education during each two year period. Recently admitted attorneys must, within four years of admission to bar, attend each of basic courses in practice established by Continuing Legal Education Committee. (Supr. Ct. Rule 70; Del. Rul. Mand. Cont. Leg. Educ. Rule 4).

Specialty Certification Requirements.—No requirements.

Professional Association (or Corporation).—See category Business Organizations, topic Corporations, subhead Professional Corporations.

MINERAL, WATER AND FISHING RIGHTS

MINES AND MINERALS:

Governor and Department of Natural Resources and Environmental Control have authority to lease public lands for mining and exploration, and Department has regulatory power. (7-4510, 4511).

Submerged and Tide Lands.—Secretary of Department of Natural Resources and Environmental Control, and Governor, empowered to lease such lands approved by State for exploitation. (7-6102). Permits required for surveys. (7-6103, 6104). Pertinent records of lessee must be available to Secretary and State Geologist upon request. (7-6105). Public hearing required before lease. (7-6107). Lease shall be for minimum of ten years (7-6111), and for not more than six sq. miles or 3,840 acres (7-6109). Royalty not less than 12¹/₂% of gross production (7-6112); not less than $1 per long ton sulphur (7-6135). Annual rent not less than 25¢ an acre. (7-6114). Performance and compliance bonds required. (7-6115). Lease not assignable without Secretary's prior written consent. (7-6123). Secretary may cancel lease for failure to exploit. (7-6126). Pollution, contamination and impairment of public or wildlife use prohibited, lessees held to high standard of care. (7-6119). Secretary may offer to lease, has discretion to accept or reject bids. (7-6128). Permission of Secretary required for joint exploration. (7-6134). Secretary may promulgate rules, regulations and orders (7-6138); civil and criminal penalties can be imposed for violations. (7-6142).

Operation of Mines.—No statutory provisions.

Safeguarding of Employees.—No statutory provisions.

Inspection of Mines.—No statutory provisions.

Taxes.—No special taxes.

MORTGAGES

CHATTEL MORTGAGES:

Uniform Commercial Code adopted. (6, Art. 9).

Filing.—Uniform Commercial Code adopted (6-9-101), requirements not applicable for liens on motor vehicles filed under 21-2331-2341 (21-2333).

Taxation.—No statutory provision.

Motor Vehicles.—Security interests in motor vehicles must be noted on certificate of title. (21-2332). No additional filing required under Commercial Code (21-2333) unless motor vehicle held by debtor as inventory held for sale (21-2334).

Forms.—Since each security agreement is unique there is no general security form in use. Out-of-state forms accepted. Officially recognized forms are as set forth at end of this Digest.

MORTGAGES OF PERSONAL PROPERTY:

See topic Chattel Mortgages; category Business Regulation and Commerce, topic Commercial Code.

MORTGAGES OF REAL PROPERTY:

Mortgage, although in form of conveyance, does not vest legal title in mortgagee, but is merely security for debt. (5 Del. Ch. 200). Usual practice is to have mortgage secure bond or note, which may have warrant of attorney for confession of judgment.

Married woman may validly execute bond or mortgage without husband's consent, and husband not liable thereon unless party thereto. (25-2104).

Execution of bond or mortgage by person at least 18 years old is valid. (25-2102). Mortgages are considered as personal property. (42 Del. Ch. 394; 213 A.2d 57).

Execution.—Should be signed, acknowledged and attested by one witness (25-2101), as a matter of proof. Must be under seal to form basis for action scire facias sur mortgage or to be recognized in court of law, although court of equity will disregard technical defect in determining rights between debtor and creditor. (457 A.2d 734).

Recording.—Mortgages should be filed with Recorder of Deeds in county wherein property is located. Mortgage duly executed and acknowledged operates as valid lien from time of recording. (25-2106).

Taxes.—No tax on mortgages or recording thereof. See subhead Recording Fees, infra.

Recording fees depend on length. New Castle County, Kent County and Sussex County, $6 document fee. (9-9607, 9617, 9619).

Trust Deeds.—No statutory provision.

Future Advances.—If expressly stated therein, mortgage may secure not only existing debt but also any obligatory or optional future advances. (25-2118[b]). Mortgage has priority as to such advances over any lien subsequent in time to recording of mortgage. (25-2118[b]). Total debt secured by mortgage at any one time must not exceed maximum principal amount which must be specified in mortgage or other such recorded instrument. (25-2118[a]). Mortgage or other instrument given for purpose of creating lien on real property may secure disbursements and other advances thereunder for payment of taxes, assessments, maintenance charges, or insurance. (25-2118[b]).

Priorities.—Except for purchase money mortgages, mortgage has priority from time of proper recording. (25-2106, 2108). If two or more mortgages, or conveyances in nature of mortgages, of same premises, are lodged in and recorded in same office at same time, they shall stand in priority in relation to each other, according to their respective recording date and time. (25-2107).

Purchase money mortgages on same land have priority according to times of record in proper office. If recorded at same time no priority between them. (25-2108).

Purchase money mortgage recorded within five days after recording of deed of conveyance has priority over prior judgments and other liens against mortgagor. (25-2108).

Subordination Agreements.—Commonly used; no applicable statutory provision.

Assignment must be attested by one witness. (25-2109).

Release.—Release by mortgagee or his assigns of part of mortgaged premises is not release or discharge of any other part of land included in mortgage. Such release must be under hand and seal of releasor, acknowledged like deed, and becomes effective upon date of filing in recorder's office of county where lands lie. (25-2110).

Partial payments on the principal of a mortgage must be entered once every three years, on the margin of the record, by the holder, on tender of legal fees to him. (25-2117[a]). Pursuant to procedures, civil damages of $100 for failure to comply. (25-2117[b]).

Satisfaction.—Satisfied mortgages must be so entered forthwith on record. Penalties for wilful failure to enter satisfaction: fine up to $1,000 (25-2111); liability for civil damages up to $500 or larger special damages where alleged and proved (25-2114). On application (properly sworn to) to Superior Court, rule may be obtained ordering mortgagee or obligee or their executors, administrators or assigns to appear on day fixed by court, and show cause, if any, why such mortgage or judgment shall not be marked satisfied of record. (25-2115[a]). Upon return of rule, court may direct recorder to mark it satisfied. (25-2115[b]). In New Castle and Sussex Counties, fees for satisfaction of mortgage shall be established by ordinance. (9-9617). Same for Kent County. (9-9619). Recorder of Deeds of each county shall collect surcharge of $5 for each document filed for Housing Development Fund and $1 for Government Records Management Improvement Fund. (9-9607[b]).

Discharge.—No statutory provision.

Foreclosure.—Ordinary method of foreclosure is to sue out writ of scire facias in Superior Court of county wherein mortgaged property is located. (10-5061[a]). Upon issuance of writ, it shall be served and returned in same manner as original summons. (10-3105). If defendant fails to appear on proper date, judgment entered that plaintiff shall have execution by levari facias directed to proper officer. (10-5063).

Sales.—Under a levari facias, mortgaged premises taken in execution and, following notice given, exposed to public sale. (10-5065). Upon confirmation of such sale, premises conveyed by deed to purchaser. (10-5065). Any surplus from proceeds of sale after satisfying costs, prior liens, mortgage, and any inferior liens returned to mortgagor. (10-5067). If no sale for want of bidders, return made accordingly, and a liberari facias may issue and be executed. (10-5065).

Deficiency Judgments.—No specific provision. Any deficiency must be recovered by independent proceeding on debt instrument which was secured by mortgage. Where bond or note contains warrant of attorney to confess judgment, mortgagee may proceed on bond or note by applying to prothonotary to enter judgment by confession, following written notice to obligor. (10-2306).

Redemption.—No equity or redemption after foreclosure sale confirmed by court. (10-5066).

Mortgage may be in the following form:

See note at head of Digest as to 1998 legislation covered.

See Topical Index in front part of this volume.

MORTGAGES OF REAL PROPERTY . . . continued
Forms

This Mortgage, Made this . . . . . . day of . . . . . . in the year of Our Lord one thousand nine hundred and . . . . . ., Between . . . . . .

Whereas, the said . . . . . . in and by . . . . certain Obligation . . . . . . duly executed, bearing even date herewith, stand . . . . . . bound unto the said party . . . . of the second part, in the sum of . . . . . . current lawful money of the United States of America, payable . . . . . . together with costs and counsel fees, under the terms and conditions therein expressed.

Now this Mortgage Witnesseth, That the said party. . . . of the first part, for and in consideration of the aforesaid debt of . . . . . . dollars and for the better securing payment of the same, with interest as aforesaid and costs and counsel fees, do. . . . hereby grant and convey unto the said party. . . . of the second part, All . . . . . .

And it is hereby expressly provided and agreed, that if any action, suit, matter or proceeding be brought for the enforcement of this mortgage or the accompanying bond, and if the plaintiff or lien holder in said action, suit or proceeding shall recover judgment in any sum, such plaintiff or lien holder shall also recover as reasonable counsel fees . . . . . . per centum of the amount decreed for principal and interest, which said counsel fees shall be entered, allowed and paid as a part of the decree or judgment in said action, suit or proceeding.

Provided Always, nevertheless, that if the said party of the first part . . . . . . or his Assigns, shall and do well and truly pay, or cause to be paid, unto the said party of the second part . . . . . . or his Assigns the aforesaid debt of . . . . . . dollars on the day and time hereinbefore mentioned and appointed for the payment thereof, with interest, then and from thenceforth, as well this present indenture, and the estate hereby granted, as the said recited Obligation shall cease, determine, and become void and of no effect, anything hereinbefore contained to the contrary thereof, in anywise notwithstanding.

In witness whereof, etc.

Sealed and delivered in presence of:
. . . .(Seal).

(Acknowledgment).

Assignment may be in the following form: Know all men by these presents, that . . . . . . Mortgagee named in the Indenture of Mortgage hereinafter mentioned, for and in consideration of the sum of . . . . . . to . . . . . ., in hand, paid by . . . . . . at and before the time of the execution hereof, the receipt whereof is hereby acknowledged, ha. . . . granted, bargained, sold, assigned, transferred, and set over, and by these presents do. . . . grant, bargain, sell, assign, transfer, and set over unto the said . . . . . . Heirs, Executors, Administrators and Assigns, a certain Indenture of Mortgage, bearing date the . . . . . . day of . . . . . . A. D. 19. . . . executed by . . . . . . unto the said . . . . . . and Recorded in the office for Recording of Deeds, &c., in and for . . . . . . County, and State of Delaware, in Mortgage Record . . . . . . Vol. . . . . . ., Page . . . . . . &c., ... also the Bond in said mortgage recited, and all moneys, principal and interest, due or to become due thereon and thereby secured, or intended so to be as aforesaid, and all . . . . . . therein mentioned and described.

Together with the rights, members and appurtenances thereto belonging, and all . . . . . . Estate, Right, Title and Interest therein. To Have and To Hold all and singular the premises hereby granted and assigned, or mentioned or intended so to be unto the said . . . . . . Heirs, Executors, Administrators, and Assigns, forever . . . . . .

Subject nevertheless to the right and equity of redemption (if any there be) of the said Mortgagor . . . . . . Heirs and Assigns in the same.

In Witness Whereof, the said . . . . . . ha. . . . hereunto set . . . . . . hand and affixed . . . . . . seal the . . . . . . day of . . . . . . in the year of Our Lord one thousand nine hundred and . . . . . .
. . . .(Seal.)

Sealed and delivered in the presence of:
. . . .
(Acknowledgment).

Release of part of property may be in following form: Know All Men by these Presents, ... that the said . . . . favoring the request of the said . . . . and for and in consideration of the sum of . . . Dollars, to . . . in hand, paid by the said . . . the receipt whereof is hereby acknowledged hath and by these presents, both for . . . and assigns, remise, release, and forever quit claim, unto the said . . . and assigns, all that portion of the above mentioned and described property, bounded and described as follows, to wit: And the said . . . for . . . and assigns, both hereby covenant and agree, that . . . or they shall not and will not at any time hereafter, proceed against the said portion of the above mentioned and described property, by legal process or otherwise, nor look to the same or any part thereof for the payment of any part of the principal or interest of the sum of money secured by the said Indenture of Mortgage, nor disturb, molest, or put to charge or damage, the present or future owner or owners, occupier or occupiers of the said hereby released portion of the aforesaid property, for or by reason of the said Indenture of Mortgage, or anything connected with it.

Provided, nevertheless, that nothing herein contained shall effect the said Indenture of Mortgage, or its legal validity, or the other remaining portion of the said above mentioned and described property, not expressly hereby released therefrom.

In Witness Whereof, The said . . . hath caused its corporate name by . . . its . . . President to be hereunto set, and the common or corporate seal of the said corporation to be hereunto affixed, duly attested by its Secretary, the . . . day of . . . A.D. 19. . . . Sealed and Delivered in the Presence of:
. . . .(Seal).

(Attested)

Power of Attorney to Satisfy Mortgage may be in following form: Know all men by these presents that I, ..., of the City of . . . . . ., ... County and State of . . . . . ., have made, constituted and appointed, and by these presents do make, constitute and appoint . . . . . ., of . . . . . ., my true and lawful attorney, for me and in my name, place and stead, to enter satisfaction upon the record of a certain mortgage executed by . . . . . . unto me for a real debt of . . . . . . Dollars, said mortgage bearing date . . . . . .,

and recorded in the office of the recording of deeds, etc., at . . . . . ., in and for . . . . . . County, State of . . . . . ., in Mortgage Record . . . . . . Volume . . . . . . Page . . . . .; giving and granting unto my said attorney full power and authority to do and perform all and every act and thing whatsoever requisite and necessary to be done in and about the premises, as fully, to all intents and purposes, as I might or could do if personally present, with full power of substitution and revocation; hereby ratifying and confirming all that may said attorney or substitute shall lawfully do, or cause to be done, by virtue hereof.

In witness whereof, I have hereunto set my hand and seal, this . . . . . . day of . . . . . ., 19. . . . .
. . . .(Seal.)

Chattel Mortgages.—See topic Chattel Mortgages.

PROPERTY

ABSENTEES:

Common law rules govern. See also category Estates and Trusts, topic Death.

Care of Property.—No statutory procedure.

Process Agent.—No statutory procedure.

Escheat.—Estate of intestate dying without heirs escheats to state under 12-1101. Escheat of certain abandoned property such as bank deposits that have remained unclaimed for over five years (12-1170), postal savings system accounts (12-1220), funds from life insurance company doing business in state and owed to person or corporation residing in state (12-1180), and certain court funds on unclaimed property (12-1160), and other unclaimed property (12-1197), governed by 12-1130-1224. Reporting must take place on or before Mar. 1 of each year. (12-1199). Remittance or delivery must take place within 90 days of reporting. (12-1201). State Escheator examines records of people, business organizations, and organizations for compliance. State Bank Commissioner examines banks. (12-1155). See categories Business Organizations, topic Corporations, subhead Unclaimed Dividends; Estates and Trusts, topic Wills, subhead Unclaimed Legacies.

ADVERSE POSSESSION:

Character of Possession.—No fixed rule; common law standards of adversity, exclusivity, hostility, openness, notoriety, and continuity apply. (16 Del. Ch. 410, 147 A. 165).

Duration of Possession.—Actions for recovery of real property must be brought within 20 years of their accrual. (10-7901).

Easements.—Continuous adverse use of a way over another's land for 20 years establishes an easement by prescription. (26 Del. Ch. 94, 22 A.2d 519). There is no prescriptive right to light and air. (24 Del. Ch. 86, 6 A.2d 614).

Disabilities.—Person under disability when the right accrues may have further time up to ten years after removal of disability. Disabilities are infancy, mental illness and imprisonment. (10-7903).

State Property.—Title or interest in real property belonging to state cannot be acquired by adverse possession. (7-4519). Former statute (7-4501) which permitted such adverse possession except in case of state owned salt marsh, beach or shore has been repealed.

CONVEYANCES:

See topic Deeds.

CURTESY:

Estate of curtesy abolished. (12-511).

DEEDS:

Words "grant and convey," in any deed, unless specifically limited operate as special warranty against grantor and his heirs and all persons claiming under him. This also applies to short form of deed and mortgage, valid by statute, unless words are specifically restricted. (25-121[b]). See topic Real Property for types of estates.

Execution.—Deed may be acknowledged by any party to it before any judge of State, or notary public, or before two justices of peace from same county, or before judge of Wilmington Municipal Court, or before Mayor of Wilmington or may be proved in court by one or more of subscribing witnesses. (25-122). Legal instrument which may be recorded, and which has been duly executed, but which has not been properly acknowledged, is nevertheless valid. (25-132). Instrument conveying or alienating lands, signed before Jan. 1, 1974, properly acknowledged, but not under seal, not including certain key language, is nevertheless valid. (25-131).

For circumstances in which spouse must join, see category Family, topic Husband and Wife, subhead Conveyance or Encumbrance of Property. See also topics Dower, Curtesy; category Documents and Records, topic Acknowledgments.

Deed of corporation may be executed and acknowledged before any Delaware or federal judge, notary, two justices of peace of same county, by president or other presiding officer, or vice-president, duly authorized by resolution of directors, trustees or other managers, or by legally constituted attorney of corporation. (25-127).

Recording not necessary to validity as between parties. (28 Del. 497, 94 A. 903). Deed has priority from time of recording in office of recorder of county in which land is situated. (25-151, 153). Acknowledgment or proof is prerequisite to recording. (25-151). See also category Documents and Records, topic Records.

Recording Fee.—Depends on length of instrument. Fee in New Castle, Kent and Sussex Counties established by ordinance. (9-9617-9619; New Castle County Code §2-27).

See note at head of Digest as to 1998 legislation covered.

See Topical Index in front part of this volume.

DEEDS . . . *continued*

Operation and Effect.—Lands, tenements and hereditaments may be aliened and possession transferred by deed without livery of seisin; and legal estate will accompany use and pass with it. (25-101). See also introductory paragraph under this topic.

Taxes.—Realty transfer tax of 2% of value of property represented by document, payable at time of making, execution, delivery, acceptance or presenting for recording of document, except when actual value of property transferred is less than $100. (30-5902[a][b]). Exceptions for will; nonresidential leases; residential leases not more than five years; mortgages; conveyance between corporation operating Slum Clearance and Redevelopment Authority Law project and shareholders thereof; conveyance to non-profit industrial development agency and between such agency and industrial corporation; conveyance between spouses, or between former spouses after divorce of property acquired before divorce, or between parent and child or child's spouse; conveyance to trustee, nominee or straw party for grantor as beneficial owner, or for beneficial ownership of another where exception from tax would be applicable if such beneficiary were grantee, or from trustee, nominee or straw party to beneficial owner; conveyance without consideration between parent corporation and wholly owned subsidiary; correctional deed without actual consideration; conveyance to or from State, U.S., or any of their instrumentalities, agencies or political subdivisions and University of Delaware; conveyance to or from corporation or partnership where grantor or grantee owns stock or interest in same proportion to interest in real estate conveyed provided that conveyance does not result from liquidation of corporation unless stock of corporation being liquidated has been held by grantor or grantee for more than three years; conveyance to or from partnership, where grantor or grantee owns interest in same proportion to interest in real estate conveyed provided that partnership can only convey to partner who has held interest in partnership for more than three years; trade, between homeowner and builder, of old residence as part consideration for new; conveyance from purchase money mortgagor to lender holding such mortgage, which is genuinely in default, by sheriff's sale or in lieu thereof; conveyance to religious organization of real estate not to be used for commercial purposes, provided, that only portion of tax paid by religious organization holding title to real estate is exempt; conveyance to or from volunteer fire company, provided that only that portion of tax payable by fire company is exempt; bona fide pledge of stock or partnership interests as loan collateral or any transfer of publicly traded stock; conveyances where owners of real property own 80% or more of beneficial interest in real estate or where owners own less than 80% of beneficial interest if no contrary regulations promulgated by Secretary of Finance; conveyance of mobile home provided (30-5401) taxes have been paid; conveyance without consideration to federal tax-exempt organization; conveyance to nonprofit conservation organization when property for open space preservation (30-5401[u]). Tax credit is given to licensed real estate broker for transfer of residential property transferred to him within preceding year as part consideration for purchase of other residential property. (30-5403). Similar 1% on transfer of all real property in City of Wilmington, in addition to State tax. (Wilm. City Code §§44-81 through 44-88). Other municipalities may have, and some do have, additional transfer tax of up to 1%. Realty transfer tax of 1% of amounts exceeding $10,000 of cost of construction on land must be paid as prerequisite to obtaining building permit for land when contract for construction on land is entered into within one year of land transfer. (30-5402).

Form.—Long form valid; short form authorized by 25-121 as follows:

Form

This Deed made this ...... day of ......, A. D. ...., between A.B., of ...., party of the first part, and C.D. of ...... party of the second part.

Witnesseth, that the said party of the first part for and in consideration of the sum of ...., the receipt whereof is hereby acknowledged, hereby grants and conveys unto the said party of the second part.

ALL
(Description of premises).
(Recital of title).

In witness whereof, the said party of the first part hath hereunto set his hand and seal.
..........(Seal).

Sealed and Delivered in The Presence of
....
....

DEEDS OF TRUST:

See category Mortgages, topic Mortgages of Real Property.

DOWER:

Estate of dower abolished. (12-511).

ESCHEAT:

See topic Absentees, subhead Escheat; category Estates and Trusts, topics Descent and Distribution, subhead Escheat, Wills, subhead Unclaimed Legacies.

LANDLORD AND TENANT:

Kinds of Tenancy.—Normal common law tenancies.

Leases.—Rental agreement includes all agreements, written or oral, establishing or modifying terms, conditions, rules, regulations, or other provisions concerning use and occupancy of rental unit. (25-5141[21]). Rental agreements not in writing or not signed by landlord and tenant (25-5110[c]) effective for no longer than one year (25-5107[a]). If no term specified, it is month-to-month. (25-5106[b]). Where landlord accepts rent without reservation and without signing written rental agreement tenant has signed and tendered to him, or where tenant takes possession and pays rent without reservation, without signing rental agreement landlord has signed and tendered to him, rental agreement has same effect as if signed by both parties. (25-5110[a], [b]). Rental agreements cannot waive or require any indemnification for any landlord liability arising under law. (25-5301[a][3]). Retaliatory evictions and rent increases are generally prohibited. (25-5516). Confession of judgment provisions authorizing person other than tenant to confess are void. (25-5301[a][2]). Landlord must supply and maintain fit rental unit. (25-5305[a]).

See also category Taxation, topic Lease Tax.

Security Deposit.—If rental agreement requires deposit, maximum deposit equals one month's rent on lease of or tenancy that has lasted one year or longer. (25-5514[a][2]). Failure to return security deposit with itemized list of damages within 20 days is waiver of claim for damages and entitles tenant to return of double amount of deposit. (25-5514[f], [g]). Landlord must supply tenant with receipt for money paid as application fee not exceeding greater of 10% of monthly rent or $50 and maintain appropriate record for at least two years. (25-5514[d]). Tenant must allow landlord reasonable access to unit for inspection, upkeep, and exhibition of premises and tenant may install new lock at own cost as long as tenant supplies landlord with key, new lock fits into system already in place and tenant does not damage door. (25-5509[a]).

Rent.—Except for purposes of payment, rent shall be uniformly apportionable on daily basis. (25-5501[c]). Landlord must give minimum 60 day written notice of rent increase and effective date thereof. (25-5107[a]). Tenant is deemed to have accepted increase if has not responded within 45 days of end of term. Tenant liable for wrongful quitting (25-5507[d]) if response is not made (25-5901). Tenants may petition for receivership, after five days notice to landlord if there exists lack of heat, running water, light or electricity, sewage facilities or other condition imminently dangerous to health and if such duty is imposed by rental agreement and/or governmental authority. (25-5901; see also 5902-5907).

Recording.—See category Documents and Records, topic Records.

Lien.—No lien on behalf of landlord in personal property of tenant is enforceable, except under Self-Service Storage Facility Act (25-4903, 5120) or against commercial tenant except pursuant to rental agreement (25-6301[a]).

Termination of Tenancy.—Where no term is provided, term is month-to-month. (25-5106[b]). Rental agreement may be terminated by either party upon minimum of 60 days notice prior to end of term. (25-5106[c]). Where tenant is required to move because of employment, active duty in U.S. military, admission to senior citizen housing facility or subsidized rental unit, death or serious illness of tenant or member of immediate family residing with tenant requiring permanent change, tenant may terminate upon 30 days written notice. (25-5314[b]).

Holding Over.—If there is rental agreement for term of one or more years and landlord does not give notice in writing of intention to terminate to tenant or tenant does not give like notice to landlord, 60 days or more before end of term, 45 days or more before end of term, such rental agreement becomes lease by month and all stipulations of rental agreement continue in force but this provision does not apply to leases of farm lands. (25-5108). Tenant remaining in rental unit beyond term of rental agreement or after landlord exercises right of termination must pay landlord sum not exceeding twice monthly rental under previous agreement, computed and prorated on daily basis, for each day he remains in possession as well as other losses incurred by landlord as determined by hearing before any court of competent jurisdiction. (25-5515[b]).

Notice required to be served personally or by leaving copy in presence of adult person at either landlord's or tenant's abode, or with landlord's agent. (25-5513[a]).

In lieu of personal service, notice may also be sent by registered, certified or 1st-class mail as evidenced by certificate of mailing. Return registry receipt is prima facie evidence. (25-5113[b]).

Dispossession.—Should tenant breach any rule or covenant material to rental agreement, and not comply with landlord's written notice to remedy it within seven days or breach constitutes material breach of code, ordinance or statute, landlord may bring summary proceeding for possession (25-5513[a]) in court which handles civil cases. Summary proceeding to recover possession may be maintained in Justice of Peace Court (25-5701), where, inter alia: tenant illegally continues in possession after expiration of lease; tenant wrongfully fails to pay entire rent; tenant has breached lawful obligation relating to use of premises; defendant wrongfully ousted petitioner who is rightful tenant of unit; defendant holds over for more than five days for various reasons; tenant is convicted of class A misdemeanor or felony which caused or threatened to cause irreparable harm to person or property; tenant refuses to yield possession after unit rendered partially or wholly unusable by fire or casualty and landlord requires possession to effect repairs; or rental agreement for commercial rental unit provides for such action (25-5702).

Distress.—Landlord right of distress is abolished, except pursuant to rental agreement for commercial unit; in that event, must be action at law. (25-6301[a]). No distress shall remain in force for more than 60 days; goods not sold within that period shall be discharged from distress levy. (25-6303[e]). Written rental agreement authorizing person other than tenant to confess judgment against tenant void and unenforceable. (25-6104). Landlord's remedy for tenant's failure to pay rent is action for possession or rent alone following demand and notice in writing. (25-5502[b]).

Uniform Residential Landlord and Tenant Act.—Not adopted.

LEASES:

Uniform Commercial Code adopted. (6-Art.2A). See category Business Regulation and Commerce, topic Commercial Code.

Leases of Real Property.—See topic Landlord and Tenant.

PERPETUITIES:

Common law rule against perpetuities is in force. (28 Del. Ch. 303, 42 A. 2d 784). Charitable uses are not within the rule. (2 Del. Ch. 392, aff'd, 2 Del. Ch. 421).

For purpose of rule against perpetuities all powers of appointment are deemed to have been created at time of exercise of such power and not at time of creation thereof; and no estate or interest is void under rule unless void if created at date of exercise of power of appointment. (25-501).

Accumulations.—See category Estates and Trusts, topic Trusts, subhead Accumulations.

See note at head of Digest as to 1998 legislation covered.

See Topical Index in front part of this volume.

PERSONAL PROPERTY:

Tenancy by entirety may exist. (32 Del. Ch. 381, 88 A. 2d 126).

POWERS OF ATTORNEY:

Common law rules govern, except where changed by particular provisions of UCC. (6-1-103), and as changed by durable power of attorney authorized in 12-c.49. Power of attorney given in writing shall be exercisable notwithstanding principal's subsequent disability or incapacity if it denotes as such. (12-4901).

Attorneys in fact can be empowered to sell and otherwise dispose of real estate if power is acknowledged or proved. (25-171; 25 Del. Ch. 1953).

Formalities.—Acknowledgment of deed by attorney may be made before any judge, notary public or two justices of the peace when letter of attorney is acknowledged, certified, and recorded, provided letter authorizes such acknowledgment or grants authority to sell or dispose of premises. (25-172).

Revocation.—Disability or incapacity of principal does not terminate agency of anyone acting under durable power of attorney. (12-4902). Death of principal does not terminate agency of anyone acting in good faith or other person who, without actual knowledge of such death, acts under written power of attorney, durable or otherwise. (12-4904[a]).

Persons in Military Service.—Agency created by power of attorney in writing by principal who is or becomes member of armed forces, merchant seaman outside U. S. or person on war duty abroad shall not be revoked by death of principal until actual knowledge or notice of death received by agent or one dealing with agent. (25-174[a]).

REAL PROPERTY:

Person holding estate in fee tail may convey in fee simple by duly acknowledged deed. (25-302).

Permanent leasehold estates, renewable forever, are regarded as fee simple estates and subject to same modes of alienation and same rules of descent and distribution if grantor of leasehold interest has released all his rights to rent charged upon leasehold. (25-304).

Both joint tenancies and tenancies in common recognize conveyance of real estate. (25-311). Statutory presumption in favor of tenancies in common, except with regard to executors and trustees; joint tenancy created only through express statement. (25-701).

A grant, conveyance or devise to husband and wife gives them an estate by the entirety as at common law. (8 Del. Ch. 404, 68 A. 450).

See also topics Curtesy, Deeds, Dower, Landlord and Tenant; categories Civil Actions and Procedure, topic Partition; Family, topic Husband and Wife; Mortgages, topic Mortgages of Real Property.

Rule in Shelley's Case is recognized. (25 Del. Ch. 404, 22 A. 2d 380).

Foreign Conveyances or Encumbrances.—Deed, concerning lands, may be acknowledged or proved, or may be taken out of state. (25-129). See category Documents and Records, topic Acknowledgments.

Condominiums.—A Unit Property Act has been adopted relating to division of real property into units; unit owner has leasehold interest in land and fee simple interest in other common elements. (25-c. 22).

Land Use Planning.—Quality of Life Act of 1988 adopted to establish and implement comprehensive land use planning programs to guide and control land development. Each county must adopt or revise comprehensive land use plan and regulations to implement plan. No land development permitted unless in conformity with comprehensive land use plan. Each county must adopt capital improvements plan to provide for construction and expansion of public facilities. Each county must report to State every two years on success or failure of plan. (9-cc. 26, 49, 69). See category Environment, topic Environmental Regulation, subhead Land Use Planning.

Judicial Review of Land Use Application.—Person or association which opposes land use application through means of judicial review is not liable to any party to such review as result of seeking such review. (9-2699, 4999, 6999). See category Civil Actions and Procedure, topic Actions, subhead Prohibited Actions.

TRUST DEEDS:

See category Mortgages, topic Mortgages of Real Property.

TAXATION

ADMINISTRATION:

Contractors License.—Contractors must obtain annual license ($75 fee) and remit gross receipts tax of 0.624%. $50,000 deduction allowed on monthly aggregate gross receipts. If gross receipts not in excess of $750,000 during lookback period, $150,000 deduction allowed on quarterly aggregate gross receipts. If contract in excess of $50,000 person shall initiate license application prior to, or in conjunction with, submission of bid. (30-2502).

Wilmington Wage Tax.—Individual residing in Wilmington or there employed is taxed on earned income at rate of 1.25% of income earned per year. (Wilmington City Code §44-107).

Nonresident Bonds.—Nonresident person or firm doing business in state must file surety bond of variable amount with Department of Finance payable to state to guarantee payment of income taxes, occupational or business licenses, unemployment compensation contributions and income taxes withheld from wages of employees, together with any penalties and interest thereon. Secretary of Finance may waive bond. Penalty not more than $10,000 per occurrence for failure to comply with bond requirement. Knowing or willful failure to file surety bond is misdemeanor offense and punishable by maximum fine of $3,000 and/or maximum imprisonment of six months. (30-375).

Penalties.—See topics detailing various taxes.

BUSINESS TAXES:

Affiliated (Captive) Finance Company Tax.—Affiliated Finance Company (corporation whose activity within Delaware is limited to issuance of commercial paper or other debt obligations and use of proceeds to make loans to or to purchase receivables from one or more of its affiliated corporations) (30-6301), is taxed through annual license fee issued by Secretary of Finance (30-6302).

Rates.—Fee is based on capital base. If base is $0-$99,999,999.99, fee is $10,000; if base is $100,000,000-$224,999,999.99, fee is $15,000; if base is $225,000,000-$749,999,999.99, fee is $25,000; if base exceeds $750,000,000, fee is $50,000. (30-6303).

Payment.—Tax is due on or before Apr. 30 each year, or as soon thereafter as corporation commences operations. (30-6304).

Banks.—In lieu of Delaware corporate income tax, bank, trust company, other banking organization and any subsidiary corporation of banking organization is liable for Delaware franchise tax on taxable income. For this purpose, "taxable income" is defined as 56/100 of 1% of net operating income before taxes, with certain modifications. Maximum rate is 8.7% of taxable income not in excess of $20 million, and minimum rate is 2.7% of taxable income in excess of $30 million. See category Business Regulation and Commerce, topic Banks and Banking.

Franchise Taxes.—See category Business Organizations, topic Corporations. Corporation incorporated in Delaware, if not exempt, is required to pay annual franchise tax. Delaware law provides that number of classes of corporations are exempt from franchise tax. More significant exemptions are for banking corporations, savings banks and building and loan associations. In no case will franchise tax for full taxable year be more than $150,000 nor less than $30.

Insurance Companies.—In lieu of Delaware corporate income tax, insurer doing business in Delaware, other than workmen's compensation insurer or wet marine and transportation insurer, is liable for basic tax of $1^3/_4$% on gross premiums received, less allowable deductions, and additional tax of $1/_4$ of 1% on gross premiums received, less allowable deductions. Insurers chartered under Delaware law (other than certain mutual insurers) having annual gross receipts of $1 million or more are also required to pay annual Delaware "privilege taxes" ranging from minimum of $10,000 to maximum of $95,000.

See category Insurance, topic Insurance Companies.

Taxation of Banks.—See category Business Regulation and Commerce, topic Banks and Banking.

Taxes on Insurance Companies.—See subhead Insurance Companies, supra and category Insurance, topic Insurance Companies.

CIGARETTE AND TOBACCO PRODUCTS TAXES:

Tobacco Product Tax.—12 mills per cigarette; tobacco products other than cigarettes 15% of wholesale price. (30-5305[a], [b]).

ESTATE TAX:

There is imposed on estate of every resident of Delaware dying on or after Jan. 1, 1999, estate tax. Amount of estate tax is amount of credit allowable under provisions of federal estate tax laws for estate, inheritance, legacy and succession taxes paid to any state reduced by portion of state death taxes paid by decedent to another state. (30-1502, 1503). Estate tax would only apply to decedents having estates large enough to require filing federal estate tax return (currently persons having gross estate in excess of $625,000 and increasing through year 2006 to $1,000,000).

Apportionment.—In absence of testamentary or other direction estate taxes are apportioned among beneficiaries. (12-c. 29).

Payment.—Tax payable to Department of Finance within nine months from date of decedent's death. Interest accrues thereafter at 1% per month. (30-1504).

Apportionment Against Inter Vivos Dispositions.—State and Federal estate taxes apportioned on pro rata basis among persons interested in estate to whom property is or may be transferred unless decedent has directed otherwise. Persons interested in estate include all persons who have received or may be entitled to receive any property or interest required to be included in gross estate or any benefit in such property received by will, intestacy, transfer, trust, estate, interest, right, power or relinquishment of power. (12-2901).

Interstate Co-operation.—Delaware has statutory procedure for compromising or arbitrating taxes in cases where there is dispute with other state over domicile of decedent at time of death. (30-1702).

EXCISE TAXES:

Public Accommodations Tax.—Excise tax imposed at rate of 8% on rental of hotel, motel or tourist home rooms. (30-6102[a]).

Payment.—Operators must pay tax collected to Department of Finance not later than 15th day of month following month of collection. (30-6104).

Penalties.—Interest at rate of 1% per month charged on payments made after prescribed due date. (30-6104).

GASOLINE TAX:

23¢ per gallon. (30-5110). Certain sales are exempt. (30-5111).

GIFT TAX:

Repealed with respect to gifts made on or after Jan. 1, 1998. (71 Del. Laws, c. 130, §1).

INCOME TAX:

(Contained in 30-c. 11 and c. 19.) Levied on entire taxable income of individual residents and nonresidents of state. (30-1102, 1121-2).

See note at head of Digest as to 1998 legislation covered.

See Topical Index in front part of this volume.

INCOME TAX . . . *continued*

Taxable income is taxable federal adjusted gross income modified as herein set forth, less deductions and exemptions hereinafter set forth. (30-1105, 1121). Modifications: add (1) interest qualifying under 26 U.S.C. §103, (2) dividends paid by regulated investment company qualifying under 26 U.S.C. §852(b)(5), (3) amount of any depletion allowance taken under 26 U.S.C. §611 as determined under 26 U.S.C. §613, and (4) deduction in excess of $30,000, for net operating loss carryback under 26 U.S.C. §172; subtract (1) interest or dividends on obligations of U.S., its territories and possessions, and its instrumentalities exempt from state income tax under federal law, (2) amounts, not to exceed $2,000 for separate return, $4,000 for joint return, provided certain conditions of age or disability and maximum income are met, (3) retirement plan, pension and IRA income not exceeding $3,000, for persons under age 60 and $5,000 for 60 or older, to be adjusted yearly, (4) social security benefits paid by federal government, to extent included in federal adjusted gross income, (5) amount of wages paid or incurred which is disallowed as deduction by IRS under 26 U.S.C. §280C, (6) federally-taxed benefits from participation in travelink program, (7) deductions consistent with 26 U.S.C. §172, (8) distributions received from certain retirement or compensation plans, to extent they are applied to books, tuition or fees at institution of higher learning attended by person or dependents under age 26, so long as amounts have been included in federal adjusted gross income; add or subtract from federal adjusted gross income any share of fiduciary adjustments applicable under 30-1134. (30-1106).

Deductions.—Residents may deduct standard deduction unless election to itemize. (30-1107). For taxable periods ending before Jan. 1, 1998, standard deduction of resident individual is $1,300, and of husband and wife filing jointly is $1,600, and filing separately is $800. For taxable periods beginning after Dec. 31, 1998, standard deduction of resident individual is $3,250, and of husband and wife filing jointly is $4,000, and filing separately is $2,000. $2,500 added to standard deduction in certain circumstances. (30-1108). Itemized deductions equal sum of itemized deductions allowable on federal return minus: (1) amount thereof representing Delaware income taxes; (2) income taxes paid to other states or their subdivisions if taxpayer credits such amounts under 30-1111(a); plus (i) portion of state employee automobile reimbursement allowance allowed as charitable deduction for federal tax purposes; (ii) amount paid for health insurance by self-employed person, less amount allowed as deduction pursuant to 26 U.S.C. §162(1); (iii) 12% of itemized deductions. (30-1109[a]). Husband and wife may itemize only if both do so. (30-1109[b]). Amount of itemized deductions representing income taxes imposed by Delaware, another state, or District of Columbia equals amount of such taxes reduced by amount of such taxes multiplied by percentage determined under §68(a) of Internal Revenue Code. (30-1109[c]). Delaware adjusted gross income of individual means such individual's federal adjusted gross income with modifications under §30-1106. (30-1123-4).

Exemptions.—For tax years beginning after Dec. 31, 1995, residents allowed personal credit of $100 for each personal exemption against individual's tax. Additional $100 allowed for residents over age 60. (30-1110). Part-time resident taxpayers have election to (1) report tax as resident for taxable year, or (2) report tax as nonresident for taxable year. (30-1125).

Credits.—Resident taxpayer allowed credit for income taxes paid to any other state on income earned therein which is also taxable in Delaware subject to limitation. (30-1111).

Members of Armed Forces.—Compensation paid nonresident by U.S. for military service not Delaware source income. (30-1124[g]).

Rates.—For years after Dec. 31, 1996 and before Jan. 1, 1999, rates are as follows: 3.1% of taxable income in excess of $2,000, but not in excess of $5,000; 4.85% of taxable income in excess of $5,000, but not in excess of $10,000; 5.8% of taxable income in excess of $10,000, but not in excess of $20,000; 6.15% of taxable income in excess of $20,000, but not in excess of $25,000; 6.45% of taxable income in excess of $25,000, but not in excess of $30,000; 6.9% of taxable income in excess of $30,000. (30-1102[a][7]).

For tax years after Dec. 31, 1998, rates are as follows: 2.6% of taxable income in excess of $2,000, but not in excess of $5,000; 4.3% of taxable income in excess of $5,000, but not in excess of $10,000; 5.2% of taxable income in excess of $10,000, but not in excess of $20,000; 5.6% of taxable income in excess of $20,000, but not in excess of $25,000; 5.95% of taxable income in excess of $25,000, but not in excess of $60,000; 6.4% of taxable income in excess of $60,000. (30-1102[a][8] as am'd by 71 Del. Laws c. 347).

There is additional tax on lump sum distributions as that term is defined under Federal law 26 U.S.C. §402(e)(4). (30-1102).

Returns and Payment.—Returns and payment must be made to Department of Finance on or before Apr. 30 for calendar year taxpayers. (30-1168).

Extensions for Filing Returns.—Director of Division of Revenue may grant reasonable extension of time for payment of income tax or estimated tax, or for filing any return, declaration, statement or other required document. (30-511[a]).

Estimated Tax.—Resident and nonresident individual or trust must declare estimated tax where his Delaware estimated tax is expected to exceed $100. (30-1169). Payment of estimated tax required on or before same dates as for federal estimated tax except that State Tax Commissioner may establish other dates. (30-1170). Director's Ruling 72-3 requires first payment by date of Delaware Personal Income Tax Return (Apr. 30 unless it falls on Sat., Sun. or legal holiday).

Refunds.—Taxpayer may apply in writing, stating specific grounds, to State Tax Commissioner, Tax Appeal Board and Superior Court, in order named, as provided, for refund under certain conditions, within three years from date return was filed or within two years from time tax is paid. (30-539; 30-544; 30-331).

Penalties and Interest.—Interest accrues at 1% per month (30-533[a]); penalty for failure to file return of 5% of tax due multiplied by number of months return has not been timely filed, not to exceed 50%; penalty for failure to pay tax (in whole or in part) is .5% of tax due multiplied by number of months tax has not been paid, not to exceed 25%; penalty for failure to file partnership returns or to furnish information required on such return is $25 times number of partners in tax year, limited to maximum of five months or $10,000 (30-534); penalty for underpayment of estimated tax 1.5% per month (30-535[b]-[c]); negligence penalty of 20% of deficiency (30-536[a]); fraud penalty of additional 75% of deficiency due to fraud (30-535[a]). Willful failure to pay tax, to collect or account for taxes, or make, sign or certify return or supply required information or make, sign, certify false or fraudulent return or supply false or fraudulent information, penalty of not more than $3,000, in addition to any other amounts prescribed plus any criminal penalties; these penalties in addition to all other penalties. (30-535[f]-[g]). Interest at 1% per month computed on tax from last date prescribed for payment (without regard to any extension of time) until date of payment; on penalties in addition to tax only from date of notice and demand, none if payment made within ten days of notice and demand. (30-533[a], [d], [e]).

Withholding of Income Tax.—Willful furnishing of false or fraudulent withholding tax statement or failure to furnish, civil penalty equal to total amount of tax evaded plus penalty of not more than $3,000. (30-535[f], [g]). Penalty for failure to pay amount shown as tax on any withholding return filed, unless due to reasonable cause, .5% per month, not to exceed 25%. (30-534[a], [b]). Negligence penalty for failure to pay, 20% of deficiency. (30-536[a], [b]).

Corporations.—Unless specifically exempted, foreign and domestic corporations are subject to 8.7% tax on income from business and property within state. (30-1902[a]). Exemptions include those corporations whose activities within Delaware are confined to maintenance and management of their intangible investments or intangible investments of trusts registered as investment companies under 15 U.S.C. §80a-1 and collection and distribution of income from such investments or from tangible property physically located outside Delaware. (30-1902[b][8]). S corporations are also exempt. (30-1902[b][9]). Every corporation, not exempt, must file return, regardless of amount. (30-1904[e]). Tax deduction of 5% of tax paid or $50,000 (30-2004), whichever is less, for investment in neighborhood assistance in impoverished areas (30-2005). Tax credit and license fee reduction allowed for taxpayers establishing new business facilities in state which will employ five or more persons and for new business facility investments of $200,000 or more. (30-2011[a]-12).

Penalties and Interest Re Corporation Income Tax.—Interest on amount unpaid at date prescribed for payment, 1% per month. (30-533[a]). Penalty for underpayment of tentative tax or installment of estimated tax, 1.5% per month. (30-535[a], [b]). Penalty for failure to file return, unless due to reasonable cause, 5% per month, not to exceed 50%. (30-534[a]). Penalty for failure to pay amount on timely filed return, .5% per month, not to exceed 25%. (30-534[b]). Negligence penalty of 20% of deficiency in addition to deficiency. (30-536[a], [b]). Fraud penalty of 75% of deficiency in addition to deficiency. (30-535[a]). Fine of not more than $3,000 plus any criminal penalties for willful failure, neglect or refusal to file return. (30-535[f]). In addition, $500 penalty will be assessed for any false statement for which there was no reasonable basis. (30-535[g]). Willful refusal to file tax return or make available any books, papers, records or memoranda for examination, Director may apply to Superior Court for order requiring return to be filed. Refusal to obey order may be held in contempt of Court. (30-559).

INHERITANCE TAX:

Inheritance tax repealed. Effective for decedents dying after Dec. 31, 1998. (71 Del. Laws c. 353).

LEASE TAX:

On lessee, 1.92% of rent under lease of tangible personal property, except household property, hospital property, any medical or remedial equipment leased by or to elderly, ill, injured or handicapped persons and manufacturing equipment under leveraged leases in which rental payments guaranteed in whole or part by Economic Development Administration, add surtax of 10%. (30-4302). This section does not apply to leases used in agricultural production. (30-4302[a][3]). Any lessor who is not also retailer licensed under 30-2905 (from which 50% of gross receipts are derived) must pay $75 license fee plus $25 for each additional place of business, renewable yearly. Lessor must also pay license tax of .288% of gross yield of leases in excess of $150,000 to be paid quarterly, add surtax of 10% reduced by $30 nonrefundable monthly credit. (30-4305).

LICENSE FEES:

Manufacturers Tax.—Annual license fee for manufacturers doing business in state of $75 for each place of business, plus .24% of gross receipts payable monthly on preceding month's receipts plus 10% surtax reduced by $100 nonrefundable credit ($1,000,000 deduction allowed). If taxable gross receipts during lookback period defined in 30-2122 do not exceed $300,000, fee is payable quarterly. (30-2702). Manufacturers of steam, gas or electricity for heat, light or power and producers of farm products are exempt. (30-2703). Manufacturers also entitled to exemption for cost of manufacturing intermediate products in any new or expanded facility. (30-2704).

Mercantile Tax.—Annual license fee of $75 plus: (1) for wholesalers, monthly tax of .384% of aggregate gross receipts over $50,000 from goods sold within state, plus .24% of taxable gross receipts from sale of petroleum products, plus $75 for each additional place of business, plus 10% surtax reduced by $30 per month nonrefundable credit plus additional tax as provided in 7-9114 (30-2902); (2) for food processors, .192% of aggregate gross receipts over $50,000 from goods sold within state, plus $75 for each additional place of business, plus 10% surtax reduced by $30 per month nonrefundable credit (30-2903); (3) for commercial feed dealers, .096% of aggregate gross receipts over $13,000 from goods sold within state, plus $75 for each additional place of business, plus 10% surtax reduced by $30 per month nonrefundable credit (30-2904); (4) for retailers, .72% of aggregate gross receipts over $50,000 from sales and services within state, plus $25 for each separate branch or business location, plus 10% surtax reduced by $60 per month nonrefundable credit plus additional tax as provided in 7-9114 (30-2905); (5) for restaurant retailers, .624% of aggregate gross receipts over $50,000 from goods sold within state, plus $25 for each separate branch or location, plus 10% surtax reduced by $60 per month nonrefundable credit (30-2906); (6) for farm

See note at head of Digest as to 1998 legislation covered.

See Topical Index in front part of this volume.

DE – 40

LICENSE FEES . . . *continued*
machinery retailers, .096% of aggregate gross receipts over $50,000 from goods sold within state, plus $75 for each additional place of business, plus 10% surtax reduced by $30 per month nonrefundable credit (30-2907); (7) for grocery supermarket retailers, .384% of first $2 million and .72% thereafter of aggregate gross receipts from sales within state allowing deduction of $50,000, plus $25 for each separate branch or location (30-2908). Sale of unprocessed agricultural products exempt; sale of motor vehicle by dealer to user exempt; retail sale of off premises consumption of alcohol exempt; goods delivered outside of state by retailer on which out-of-state retail sales tax paid exempt; commercial crabbers exempt; activities related to conduct of horse racing meetings exempt; nonprofit organizations exempt from federal income tax exempt from §§2905, 2906. Some artists, craft persons, handicapped peddlers and some senior citizens also exempt. (30-2909).

Occupational Licenses and Fees.—Various annual occupational license taxes (30-2301[a], [b]), plus .384% of aggregate gross receipts in excess of $50,000, plus 10% surtax reduced by $30 per month nonrefundable credit; unused credit may not be carried into any other month or applied against license fee (30-2301[d][1], [4]). Number of occupations and businesses are specifically exempt from payment of general occupational and services gross receipts tax, including most notably Delaware investment companies, banks, insurance companies, public utilities, savings and loan and building and loan associations, nonprofit organizations exempt from federal income tax, real estate mortgage investment conduits and Delaware business trusts registered as investment companies under Investment Company Act of 1940.

PROPERTY TAXES:

All taxes shall be uniform upon same class of subjects within territorial limits of authority levying tax and shall be levied and collected under general laws passed by general assembly. County Councils of New Castle and Sussex Counties and levy court of Kent County may exempt similar real property within their respective counties as in their opinion will best promote public welfare; incorporated municipalities may do likewise within said municipalities. Agricultural property given limited tax exemption. (Const., art. VIII, §1).

Taxable Property.—All real property, liable to taxation and assessment by counties at same tax rate, defined in 9-8101 to include land, buildings, improvements and special betterments.

Personal property, whether tangible or intangible, is not taxable by counties or other political subdivisions. (9-8103). However, certain transfers of real property are taxable by counties. (9-8102).

Exemptions.—Real property belonging to state, or U.S., or any county of state, or any municipality thereof and held for public use, or any church or religious society, and not held as investment, or any college or school and used for educational or school purposes, shall not be liable for state and local taxes except as otherwise provided. Any corporation created for charitable purposes and not held by way of investment is exempt from taxation, by local state governments. (9-8105; Const., art. VIII, §1).

Any person, resident of state, age 65 or over, having income not in excess of $3,000 per year and residing in dwelling house or mobile home owned by him, has real property tax exemption for such property up to $5,000 assessed value. No such exemption shall be in addition to any other exemption to which person entitled. Exemption not applicable where person's spouse lives on property and has income in excess of $3,000 per year. (9-8132r). Mobile home owners meeting foregoing criteria may be entitled to exemption as determined by County Council. (9-8363).

No individual real property tax exemption for members of armed forces or veterans.

Land and improvements held by church, religious society, charitable corporation, or nonprofit organization, devoted to housing elderly pursuant to §231 National Housing Act, not taxable by any county or political subdivision provided that at least 75% of dwelling units on property are inhabited by elderly and entire property operated on nonprofit basis. (9-8151). Special assessment payable in lieu of taxes of not less than 10% of gross rentals less utilities and social services. (9-8156).

Assessment.—Real property is assessed at its true value in money. (9-8306[a]).

Methods of assessment and collection vary in different counties but in general taxes are levied for county, poor, school, and if property is situated in municipality, municipal purposes.

Review of Assessment.—Each county has board of assessment which makes and revises assessments and hears appeals from existing assessments. (9-8311).

Payment due on July 1 in New Castle County; June 1 in Kent County; May 1 in Sussex County. (9-8601). Penalty of 6% for failure to pay by Sept. 1st in New Castle County, additional penalty of 1% per month after Sept. 30. (9-8604[a], [1]). Penalty of 1.5% per month in Kent and Sussex Counties after Sept. 30th. (9-8604).

Collection.—Real estate taxes are collected by receiver of taxes and county treasurer for Kent County (9-8401; 9-8421) and Department of Finance for Sussex and New Castle Counties (9-7004; 9-1301).

Liens.—All state, county and municipal taxes; all charges for water, sewer, garbage or other services and assessments for installation of curbing, sidewalks, sewer lines or water mains constitute lien upon all real estate of taxable person in county in which taxes and/or charges imposed; fines imposed by any court for local building, housing or sanitation code violation greater than $100 per property are assessed which lien is prior to all other liens. (25-2901).

In Kent and Sussex Counties, lien for county and state taxes remains lien for period of two years from first day of July of year in which tax is imposed; school taxes for two years from 10th of Aug. of year in which tax is imposed, town or municipal taxes for two years from date prescribed by charter for delivery of duplicate to collector. In New Castle County, tax liens on real estate endure for ten years from first day of July of year for which tax is levied or until tax is collected so long as real estate remains property of person who was owner at time tax was assessed. (25-2903).

Sales.—Procedure as to sales varies in different counties, sales in Kent and Sussex Counties governed by 9-8771. In New Castle County, Office of Finance may institute by motion proceedings or proceed by attachment. (9-8741-9-8757).

Redemption.—No sale for taxes in Kent and Sussex Counties shall be approved by court, and no deed shall be made until expiration of one year from time of sale within which time owner, his heirs, executors or administrators, shall have power to redeem land on payment to purchaser of amount of purchase money, 20% interest and cost of deeds to Receiver of Taxes and County Treasurer or Director of Finance. (9-8776).

In New Castle County owner at any time within 60 days after sale is confirmed by Superior Court, if action has begun by attachment, may pay to purchaser amount of purchase price plus 15% to redeem real estate. (9-8758).

Penalties.—Failure of any person owning or having care, management or control of real property liable to assessment, to deliver to Board of Assessment within ten days after time limited to do so, particular account of such property shall be fined not more than $100. Prosecution may be stayed by filing return and paying sum of not more than $10 plus costs. (9-8319[a], [c], [d]). Persons swearing to false returns, guilty of perjury. (9-8323). Any violation of provisions for valuation and assessment for which no other penalty provided, punishable by fine of $100 and/or imprisonment for not more than one year. (9-8326).

REALTY TRANSFER TAX:

Realty transfer tax is imposed on value of property upon transfer of real property. Certain transfers are excluded. At state level it is generally 2% but will not exceed 1.5% if municipality or county where such property is located imposes transfer tax of 1.5%. (30 ch. 54). See category Property, topic Deeds.

SALES AND USE TAXES:

No general sales or use tax.

STAMP TAX:

No stamp tax on corporate stock. Stamp tax on realty transfers, see category Property, topic Deeds.

UNEMPLOYMENT COMPENSATION TAX:

Every employer of one or more employees must contribute to State Unemployment Compensation Fund at average contribution rate for each industrial classification established by Federal Secretary of Labor (5.4% for unclassified employers 1985 and beyond). (19-3348). There is no payment by employees. (19-3346). Following are excluded from benefits of Act and employers thereof not liable for contributions with respect to such employments: Some agricultural laborers; students employed by university in which they are enrolled and which they regularly attend; minor in employ of parent or individual in employ of child or spouse; individual employed by any government or political subdivision of Delaware; individual employed by charitable organization; employees of carriers engaged in interstate commerce; service by officer of building and loan association, labor union, political or social club, etc. when service is part-time and remuneration is less than $75 in calendar quarter; insurance or real estate agent paid only by commission; any full-time student employed in instructional work program; any patient employed in hospital; anyone employed so as to be eligible for unemployment compensation program set up by Act of Congress; elected, appointed or fee-compensated officials; direct sellers as defined by §3508 of Internal Revenue Code. (19-3302). Fund is to be administered by State Treasurer as custodian under direction of Department of Labor. (19-3162). Contributions are payable at times prescribed by Department of Labor. (19-3345).

UNIFORM FEDERAL TAX LIEN REGISTRATION ACT:

Adopted. (25-4801-25-4805).

TRANSPORTATION

MOTOR VEHICLES:

General supervision in Department of Public Safety (21-301 et seq.); Secretary of Department of Public Safety appoints a Director of Division of Motor Vehicles, Highway Administration Center, Dover, DE 19901 to head Division of Motor Vehicles. (29-8203).

Vehicle License.—No unregistered vehicle may be operated, except for temporary operation while registration application pending or vehicle being towed. (21-2101). Registration issued by Department of Public Safety through Division of Motor Vehicles. Vehicles are registered for 24 months, 12 months or six months and effective date of registration shall be date vehicle is titled, except that trailer or semi-trailer not under fleet account may obtain license for period of from one to 12 months. If vehicle is registered after 15th of month, effective date is 16th day of month. Effective date for issuance of vehicle registration will be date vehicle is titled. Any newly manufactured motor vehicle or trailer with gross registered weight of 10,000 lbs. or less, not previously registered, may be registered for three years—effective date being first day of month when vehicle is registered. Fees shall be calculated by using rates in effect during prorated or extended registration. (21-2109). Registration of commercial vehicles, trailers or farm trucks may be renewed for three months, six months, one year or two years; where annual safety inspection waived, registration of trailer with gross registered weight of 4,000 lbs. or less may be renewed for three years. (21-2110). Registration expires on transfer (21-2501) but such registration may be transferred upon payment of $15 fee (21-2503). Transferee shall make application for new certificate of title within 30 days of purchase of vehicle (21-2503) or be subject to $25 penalty fee (21-2508). Manufacturer's gross vehicle weight rating must be supplied, and cannot be exceeded, for registration of vehicles at gross vehicle weight of 26,000 pounds or greater. (21-2105[a]). Vehicles and fire apparatus which were manufactured prior to Jan. 1, 1993 that are owned or used by organized fire company within Delaware are not subject to this

MOTOR VEHICLES . . . *continued*
provision. (21-2105[k]). Number plate, which must be at least 12 inches from ground, must be attached to rear of motor vehicle except on tractor trailers, which must display them on front. (21-2126). Certain disabled veterans exempt from registration fee limited to one vehicle at any one time. (21-2164). No statutory exemption for members of Armed Forces.

Operator's license required (21-2701); renewable every five years with fee of $12.50 and late fee of $1.15 (21-2715[a], [c]). Licenses issued by Division of Motor Vehicles. (21-2702). Operator of motorcycle or motorbike or other 2-wheeled motor-driven vehicle must be licensed and pass special examination. (21-2703). Upon application and fee of $35 person licensed for three consecutive years may, upon Secretary's discretion, get permanent license which is good until revoked, cancelled or suspended. (21-2716). Examinations required of all applicants, except Department may waive examination for renewal applicants. (21-2713[a], [b]). Permits to learn to drive with licensed operator over age of 25 are granted, valid for 60 days; person who is at least 15 years, ten months old but less than 18, applicant for permit must be enrolled in or have completed approved course in driver's education or received license and completed approved instruction in another state. (21-2710). Members of Armed Forces having valid license from state of domicile are excepted. Persons operating farm machinery exempt from requirements. (21-2705). Uniform Commercial Driver License Act in effect. (21-c. 26).

Age Limits.—No license issued to any person under age 16 (21-2707) application for temporary instruction permits and Class D operator's license for persons 18 or older (21-2712). If applicant is under 18, he must have completed approved driver education course; if course was in another state, he must have been licensed in said state. (21-2707[b][8]). For Class A, CDL Class A, Class B or CDL Class B license, applicant must be at least 18. (21-2707[a][1]). For school bus driver, applicant must be at least 18 years of age with one year of driving experience. (21-2708[b][1]).

License shall be suspended for period of at least one year for refusal to submit to chemical test if motorist is stopped for suspicion of driving under influence of alcohol or other drugs. (21-2742). Road blocks permitted to be used by police as stop checks.

Titles.—Vehicle owner must obtain from Department a certificate of title showing any liens or encumbrances; certificate valid with vehicle transfer. (21-c. 23). Within 30 days of final payment on any lien, certificate shall be signed and lien register shall be amended to reflect that lien has been satisfied. (21-2339).

Sales.—On sale or transfer, holder of certificate of title must endorse assignment on back thereof, with warranty of title and further statement of liens or encumbrances. Transferee must then present such certificate endorsed and assigned to Department, accompanied by transfer fee of $15, and make application for new certificate of title. (21-2510[a], [b], [c]). Financing of sale regulated by 5-c. 29.

Liens.—Every application for certificate of title shall contain section where applicant must disclose any and all liens on vehicle to be titled. Duplicate original of agreement whereby lien or encumbrance is sought to be secured on motor vehicle must be permanently attached to application for title certificate, but requirement waived if Department already has lien information or information available on out-of-state title being exchanged for Delaware title. (21-2331). Certificate must state owner's title and all liens and encumbrances on vehicle. (21-2332). If certificate, at time, is outstanding and valid, and is not assigned or transferred, certificate of title must be returned to Department together with application for placing and recording any new lien or encumbrance upon motor vehicle; such application must be accompanied by duplicate original of written instrument evidencing lien or encumbrance and $10 fee; upon filing of application and entering of claim, certificate of title will be returned. (21-2335). Such liens and encumbrances entered upon certificate of title and recorded in lien register shall be notice to all creditors. (21-2337).

Identification Marks.—Misdemeanor to remove or falsify vehicle's identification number. Felony to remove or falsify identification number willfully and with intent to conceal or misrepresent identity of vehicle, bicycle or engine. Misdemeanor to knowingly buy, sell, receive or dispose of vehicle or engine with false identification number. (21-6705). Felony to knowingly buy, sell, receive, possess or dispose of vehicle, bicycle or engine knowing that identification number of vehicle or engine has been removed or falsified and with intent to conceal or misrepresent identity of engine or vehicle. (21-6705[a-d]). Felony to be in possession of certain motor vehicle documents unaccompanied by 75% of vehicle described. (21-6710). Felony to remove or alter warranty, identification plate or confidential vehicle identification number. (21-6709). Felony to alter or forge Department of Motor Vehicle documents or identification plate. (21-2316).

Operation Prohibited.—Operator's license not issued to persons whose license suspended during period of suspension; persons whose license is revoked until expiration of one year after revocation; persons determined to be habitual drunkards or addicted to narcotics; persons adjudged mentally ill, idiots, etc., unless Department is satisfied as to competence; persons whose mental or physical disability makes them incapable of exercising control over motor vehicle; delinquents; epileptics, unless person's attending physician licensed in State certifies infirmity controlled; or persons who are unable to read and understand road signs; or persons subject of outstanding capias or bench warrant from Family Court for child support delinquency. (21-2707[b]).

Size and Weight Limits.—Regulated by 21-c. 45.

Equipment Required.—Regulated by 21-c. 43.

Lights Required.—Regulated by 21-4316, 4331-4358.

Inspection is required for purpose of determining that a vehicle is safe and in fit condition for operation. Inspection is held at one or more places in each county. (21-2141-2142).

Traffic Regulations.—Rules of the Road. (21-c.41).

Accidents.—Driver must stop and give name, address, registration number and driver's license number to injured person or occupants of motor vehicle, or to owner of property with which he collides, render assistance to injured and, where there is personal injury, property damage apparently exceeding $500, or where driver involved in incident appears to be under influence of drugs or alcohol, report accident to police agency with primary jurisdictional responsibility at once. (21-4201-3[a]). Nonresident involved in accident involving damage to property or person may not remove vehicle from state without posting security for double estimated damages sustained by any person, firm or corporation involved, damages to be determined by reputable repairman and posted with Justice of Peace. (21-2927[a], [b]).

Liability of Owner.—Owner engaged in business of renting vehicles who does not carry proper insurance policy insuring renter shall be jointly and severally liable with renter for damages caused by renter's negligence in operating vehicle. This provision creates no right of action by any passenger in rented vehicle against owner. (21-6102[a], [b], [c]). Any person who has signed license application for person under 18 shall be jointly and severally liable for damages arising out of such person's negligent operation of vehicle. (21-6105[a]). Owner who knowingly permits person under 18 to operate vehicle shall be jointly and severally liable for damages caused by latter's negligence. (21-6106).

Guests.—Guest Statute repealed by 64 Del. Laws, c. 59, §1, eff. 6/23/83.

Financial Responsibility.—See subhead No-Fault Insurance infra.

See also supra, subhead Accidents.

Insurance.—See subhead No-Fault Insurance, infra.

Requirement of Insurance.—No owner of vehicle required to be registered in State, other than self-insurer, may operate or authorize to be operated such vehicle unless owner has following minimum insurance coverage: (1) Indemnity from legal liability for property damage, bodily injury, or death arising out of ownership, use or maintenance of vehicle, to limit, exclusive of interest and costs of Delaware Financial Responsibility Law; (2) $15,000 for one person, $30,000 for all persons injured in accident to cover general medical expenses, funeral expenses, loss of earnings, and substituted services. Funeral expenses not to exceed $5,000 per person. Coverage in §2 is applicable to occupants of owner's vehicle and pedestrians, but not to occupants of other motor vehicles; (3) minimum limit of $10,000 for damage to property other than motor vehicle; (4) damage to insured motor vehicle, including loss of use, not to exceed actual cash value of vehicle and $10/day up to $300 for loss of use. (21-2118[a]). No owner of vehicle operated in State shall operate or authorize operation of vehicle unless owner has insurance equal to minimum required by State or jurisdiction where vehicle is registered. (21-2118[b]).

Only insurance policies issued by State-authorized companies shall satisfy requirements set forth above. (21-2118[c]). Coverage may be more extensive than minimums set forth above. (21-2118[d]). Persons eligible for benefits under subsections (2) and (3) precluded from pleading or introducing into evidence, in any suit against tortfeasor, damages compensable under subsections (2) and (3). (21-2118[h]). Insurer required to arbitrate claim upon request of party claiming damages. Request must be made in writing and mailed to Insurance Commissioner. Losing party has right, where procedures followed, to appeal de novo in Superior Court. (21-2118[j]). Director may adopt rules and regulations. (21-2118[z]).

Foreign vehicles duly registered in home state or country and displaying proper license plates may be operated in Delaware without local registration or payment of any fees (21-2112[a]) but if owner takes up Delaware residence, registration must be obtained within 60 days. (21-2102[a]). Exemption for vehicle owned by citizen of foreign nation only if that nation grants reciprocal privilege to U.S. citizens. Privilege does not apply to vehicle used by nonresident in course of doing business in this State unless home state grants reciprocal privilege to Delaware residents. (21-2112[b], [c], [d]).

See also supra, subhead No-Fault Insurance.

Nonresident over age of 16 having home state operator's license may drive in Delaware without examination or license. (21-2706[a]). If home state requires no license, he must obtain Delaware license, except that he may operate his own vehicle for period up to 30 days in any one year if it is registered in his home state. Driver must display home state license plate on vehicle and have in his possession registration card. (21-2706[b]). Driver's License Compact adopted. (21-c.81).

See also supra, subhead No-Fault Insurance.

Action against nonresident or his executor or administrator arising out of operation of motor vehicle may be commenced by service of process on Secretary of State with $2 fee, provided that notice is sent to defendant and other procedures complied with. (10-3112). Operation of car in state is implied designation of Secretary of State as agent for service of process. (10-3112[a]). Provisions apply to resident who departs State subsequent to accident and remains absent for 30 days. (10-3113).

Direct Actions.—No provision permitting direct action by injured person against insurer.

Motor Vehicle Carriers.—Supervision of operation is by Public Service Commission as to rates. (See category Business Regulation and Commerce, topic Carriers.) Size and weight of loads supervised by Division of Motor Vehicles. (21-c.45; 29-8207).

Motor Vehicle Taxes.—Real property tax on mobile homes. See category Taxation, topic Property Taxes, subhead Taxable Property.

Motor vehicle document fee on sale, transfer or registration in State of any new or used motor vehicle, truck tractor, trailer or motorcycle. (30-3002[a]). If purchase price less than $400, then uniform rate of $8. If $400 to $500, fee $13.75. Fee increased by $2.75 per additional $100 of purchase price or fraction thereof above $500. (30-3002[c]). No document fee for renewal registration in name of same owner, for sales or transfers for purpose of resale, for delivery of trailer outside State to nonresident where sales tax paid, for registration in State of vehicles bought and registered out of State, if sales tax was paid in other State not more than 90 days prior to registration in Delaware, for fleet registration of truck tractors and trailers obtained outside State, for vehicles used by State, its agencies and departments, or any state political subdivision, or American Legion, Veterans of Foreign Wars, any volunteer fire company or Delaware Civil Air Patrol, American Red Cross, Salvation Army or for vehicle meeting requirements of school bus and under contract to school district. (30-3002[a]). Purchase price evidenced by notarized bill of sale. (30-3002[b]).

Gasoline Tax.—See category Taxation, topic Gasoline Tax.

See note at head of Digest as to 1998 legislation covered.

See Topical Index in front part of this volume.

DE – 42

MOTOR VEHICLES ... *continued*

Motor carriers fuel tax imposed on liquid fuel consumed, calculated on amount of fuel used on Delaware highways (computed as ratio of miles driven in Delaware over total miles driven by motor carrier). (30-5203; 30-5207).

RAILROADS:

See category Business Regulation and Commerce, topic Carriers.

See note at head of Digest as to 1998 legislation covered.

See Topical Index in front part of this volume.

COMMERCIAL CODE FORMS

See also categories Business Regulation and Commerce, topic Commercial Code; Mortgages, topic Chattel Mortgages.

Financing Statement—UCC Form No. 1

State of Delaware

UNIFORM COMMERCIAL CODE—FINANCING STATEMENT—FORM UCC-1

This FINANCING STATEMENT is presented to a Filing Officer for filing pursuant to the Uniform Commercial Code.

If to be filed with Recorder of Deeds indicate Tax Parcel No.(s). _____

No. of additional sheets presented_____ .

PARTIES	PARTIES

Debtor (or Assignor) (last name first if individual) and mailing address:

Secured Party(ies) (last name first if individual) and address:

Debtor (or Assignor) (last name first if individual) and mailing address:

Assignee (if any) of Secured Party(ies) and address of Assignee:

This statement is filed without the Debtor's signature to perfect a security interest in collateral (check X in applicable box(es))

☐ Already subject to a security interest in another jurisdiction when it was brought into this State.

☐ Already subject to a security interest in another jurisdiction when the Debtor's location changed to this State.

☐ Which is proceeds of the original collateral described below in which a security interest is perfected.

☐ Acquired after a change of name, identity or corporate structure of Debtor.

☐ As to which the filing has lapsed.

By: _____
Signature of Secured Party(ies)   Title
(Required only if item is checked)

Special Types of Parties (check X in applicable box(es))
☐ The terms "Debtor" and "Secured Party" mean "Lessee" and "Lessor", respectively.
☐ The terms "Debtor" and "Secured Party" mean "Consignee" and "Consignor", respectively.
☐ Debtor is a Transmitting Utility.
☐ Debtor acting in representative capacity (e.g., as trustee).

Filed With:

Prepared By (Name And Address):

☐ Check to request Continuation Statement notice for additional fee.

This Financing Statement covers the following types (or items) of property: Check only if applicable: ☐ Products of collateral are also covered.

If the collateral is crops, the crops are growing or to be grown on the following described real estate:

If the collateral is (a) goods that are or are to become fixtures; (b) timber to be cut; or (c) minerals or the like (including oil and gas) or accounts resulting from the sale thereof at the wellhead or minehead, the description of the real estate concerned is: (check X in applicable box(es))

☐ Fixtures   ☐ Timber   ☐ Minerals or accounts resulting from sale thereof at wellhead or minehead

And this Financing Statement is to be filed in the real estate records where a mortgage on such real estate would be recorded. If the Debtor does not have an interest of record, the name of a record owner is:

By: _____
Signature of Debtor (or Assignor)   Title

By: _____
Signature of Debtor (or Assignor)   Title

THIS SPACE FOR USE OF FILING OFFICER
(DATE, TIME, NUMBER, FILING OFFICER)

See note at head of Digest as to 1998 legislation covered.

See Topical Index in front part of this volume.

Statement of Continuation, Assignment, Termination, etc.—UCC Form No. 3

State of Delaware

UNIFORM COMMERCIAL CODE FORM UCC-3

STATEMENT OF CONTINUATION, ASSIGNMENT, TERMINATION, ETC.

This STATEMENT is presented to a filing officer for filing pursuant to the Uniform Commercial Code:

1A. Debtor (Last Name First and Address):	2. Secured Party(ies) and Address(es)*	For Filing Officer (Date, Time and Filing Office)
1B. Debtor (Last Name First and Address):		

* If other than the secured party of record is indicated, this Form UCC-3 must be accompanied by a separate written statement of assignment (on separate Form UCC-3 or substantially similar form) signed by the secured party of record, and the required fee paid.

3. This statement refers to original Financing Statement bearing File No.

Filed with _____ Date Filed _____ 19 _____

4. Put an "X" in the correct box. (Check only <u>one</u> box per form)

A. ☐ Continuation. The original financing statement between the debtor and secured party, bearing file number shown above, is still effective.

B. ☐ Assignment. The secured party's rights under the financing statement bearing file number shown above have been assigned to the assignee whose name and address appears in Item 5.

C. ☐ Partial Assignment. The secured party's rights under the financing statement bearing file number shown above have been assigned in part to the assignee whose name and address appears in Item 5 (indicate in Item 5 the portion of collateral being assigned).

D. ☐ Amendment. Financing Statement bearing file number shown above is amended as set forth in Item 5. (Assignment of rights of the secured party should be by written statement of assignment on a separate Form UCC-3 or substantially similar form, and not by amendment. Assignment of Debtor's interest should be by amendment using this form.)

E. ☐ Release. The secured party releases all collateral from the financing statement bearing file number shown above.

F. ☐ Partial Release. The secured party releases the collateral described in Item 5 from the financing statement bearing file number shown above.

G. ☐ Termination. The secured party no longer claims a security interest under the financing statement bearing file number shown above.

5.

By _____
    Signature of Debtor   Title
    (necessary only if item 4D is applicable)

By _____
    Signature of Secured Party   Title

By _____
    Signature of Debtor   Title
    (necessary only if item 4D is applicable)

By _____
    Signature of Secured Party   Title

See note at head of Digest as to 1998 legislation covered.

See Topical Index in front part of this volume.

Request for Copies or Information.—UCC Form No. 11.

Present in DUPLICATE to: ☐

_____ COUNTY RECORDER OF DEEDS

_____ , DELAWARE

Present to: ☐
UNIFORM COMMERCIAL CODE DIVISION
OFFICE OF THE SECRETARY OF STATE
DOVER, DELAWARE

Del. UCC Form No. 11

CHECK ONE

☐ 2 Hour Request

☐ Same Day Request

☐ 24 Hour Request

☐ Regular Request

REQUEST FOR COPIES OR INFORMATION

DEBTOR

NAME: _____

Indicate Representative Capacity, If Any (e.g., Trustee). State Name and Date of Document Creating Representative

CAPACITY: _____

ADDRESS: _____
No.   Street   City   State   Zip

PARTY REQUESTING COPIES OR INFORMATION

NAME: _____

ADDRESS: _____
No.   Street   City   State   Zip

☐ Please furnish certificate listing all presently effective financing statements naming the above debtor, giving date and hour of filing of each such statement and names and addresses of each secured party named therein.

☐ Please furnish certificate listing all presently effective federal tax lien statements naming the above debtor.

☐ Please furnish certified copies of the following (indicate all or specific filings listed below):

☐ Please furnish copies of the following (indicate all or specific filings listed below):

FILE NUMBER	DATE AND HOUR OF FILING	NAME AND ADDRESS OF SECURED PARTY

TIME OF SEARCH _____

DISTRICT OF COLUMBIA LAW DIGEST REVISER

Margaret L. Moses
Loyola University Chicago
School of Law
One East Pearson Street
Chicago, Illinois 60611
Telephone: 312-915-6430
Fax: 312-915-7201
Email: mmoses@luc.edu

Reviser Profile

Margaret L. Moses is a member of the bars of the District of Columbia, New York, New Jersey, and South Carolina. She is Assistant Professor of Law at Loyola University Chicago School of Law.

Ms. Moses is a graduate of Columbia Law School, and has practiced in France and Italy, as well as the U.S. Before joining the Loyola faculty, she represented clients in many areas of the world engaged in international business transactions. Her areas of practice included corporate, commercial, international, litigation, and arbitration. She is also a former chair of the International Section of the New Jersey State Bar Association, a member of the American Law Institute, and an arbitration panel member of the American Arbitration Association and NASD.

DISTRICT OF COLUMBIA LAW DIGEST

(The following is a list of all Categories and Topics, including cross-references, covered in this Digest.)

DISTRICT OF COLUMBIA LAW DIGEST

Revised for 1999 edition by

MARGARET L. MOSES, of the District of Columbia and New Jersey Bars.

(Citations herein, unless otherwise indicated, refer to sections of the Code of the District of Columbia, 1981 edition with 1998 Supplement to December 31, 1997; Sup. Ct. Civ. R. refers to Rules of Civil Procedure for the District of Columbia Superior Court. DCMR refers to District of Columbia Municipal Regulations, and DCRR refers to District of Columbia Rules and Regulations. DCMR is gradually replacing DCRR. DCR refers to District of Columbia Register. Sup. Ct. Cr. R. refers to Rules of Criminal Procedure for D.C. Superior Court. Parallel citations to the Federal Reporter begin with 49 App. D. C.)

Note: This revision reflects 1997 and 1998 enacted legislation published in the DCR through June 1, 1998.

INTRODUCTION

GOVERNMENT AND LEGAL SYSTEM:

The District of Columbia is a special district created by the U.S. Congress, which retains ultimate legislative authority over its legal system. For more information on the courts and legislature of the District of Columbia, see category Courts and Legislature. For further discussion of the U.S. federal system, see Introduction to the Federal Government of the United States at the beginning of this volume. A great many laws are promulgated by the federal government of the United States and are not reflected in the topics below. See the Introduction to this volume for references to the federal law topics covered.

HOLIDAYS:

Legal holidays are: Jan. 1, 3d Mon. in Jan., 3d Mon. in Feb., last Mon. in May, July 4, 1st Mon. in Sept., 2d Mon. in Oct., Nov. 11, 4th Thurs. in Nov., Dec. 25, every Sat. after noon, any day of inauguration of President in every 4th year (5 U.S.C. §6103; §1-613.2, am'd 1986, D.C. Act No. 6-227; §28-2701 am'd 1985) and any day appointed by President of U.S. as day of public feasting or thanksgiving. All day Sat. is holiday for banking institutions and building associations. (§28-2701, am'd 1985).

Holiday Falling on Sun. or Sat.—Whenever any legal holiday falls on Sun., next succeeding day is holiday. Whenever any legal holiday falls on Sat., other than day of inauguration of President, next preceding day is holiday. (§28-2701, am'd 1985).

Legality of Transactions on Holiday.—There is no statute or judicial decision declaring illegal or void transactions made on a Saturday, Sunday or legal holiday.

OFFICE HOURS AND TIME ZONE:

The District of Columbia is in the Eastern Standard (GMT −05:00) time zone. Office hours are generally from 9 a.m. to 5 p.m.

BUSINESS ORGANIZATIONS

AGENCY:

Common law rules govern.

ASSOCIATIONS:

See topic Corporations, subhead Professional Corporations.

CORPORATIONS:

Governing statutes are §§29-101-1148 of Code, District of Columbia Business Corporation Act of 1901 (§§29-101-240), District of Columbia Business Corporation Act of June 8, 1954, as am'd (§§29-301 et seq.) and District of Columbia Nonprofit Corporation Act of Aug. 6, 1962. (§§29-501 et seq.).

Act of June 8, 1954, is patterned after the Model Business Corporation Act (see Uniform and Model Acts section) prepared by Committee on Corporate Laws of Section of Corporation, Banking and Business Law of American Bar Association in 1946. It does not repeal any existing statutes or special acts of Congress under which corporations have been created in past. Effective Dec. 5, 1954, corporations for profit must be organized under Act of June 8, 1954. Corporations formed before effective date of 1954 Act may continue to function under Business Corporation Act of 1901, but are required to (1) maintain registered office in D.C., (2) appoint registered agent, and (3) file two-year reports with Mayor. (§§29-398, 29-214). Corporations for profit organized prior to July 1, 1978, may be incorporated or reincorporated under said Act. (§29-399.42).

Legislative Formation.—Corporation may be formed by special Act of Congress. Any person other than a Senator or Representative who intends to present to Congress a bill for an act of incorporation or amendment of charter must give notice by publishing copy of bill at least once a week for four successive weeks in District newspaper approved by Council of District of Columbia, last publication to be made at least 14 days prior to presentation of bill. (§29-102).

Statutory Formation.—Separate statutory provisions are made for organization of corporations for profit (§§29-301 et seq.), nonprofit corporations (§§29-501 et seq.), religious societies (§§29-901-916), insurance companies (§§35-101-2015), trust, loan, mortgage, safe deposit and title corporations (§§26-401-436), fraternal benefit associations (§§35-1201-1228), cooperative associations (§§29-1101 et seq.); and professional corporations (§§29-601 et seq.).

General Supervision.—Mayor of District of Columbia and District of Columbia Council are charged with administration and enforcement of Act of June 8, 1954 (§29-399.21) and of Act of Aug. 6, 1962 (§29-594). Functions of Mayor and Council under both Acts have been delegated to Department of Consumer and Regulatory Affairs, for administration by Corporation Division of Department, 614 H St., N.W., Washington, D.C. 20001.

Purposes.—Corporations for profit may be organized under Act of June 8, 1954, for any lawful purpose or purposes, except banking, life insurance, acceptance and execution of trusts, railroads, or building and loan associations. (§29-303). Other kinds of corporations may be organized for purposes and under statutes indicated under subhead Statutory Formation, above.

Name must contain word "corporation," "company," "incorporated," or "limited," or abbreviation thereof. Must not contain any word or phrase indicating that it is organized for any purpose other than a purpose contained in the articles; must not be the same or similar to the name of any domestic corporation or of any foreign corporation authorized to do business in District; must not indicate or state that it is organized under an Act of Congress. May be reserved for 60 days by filing application. No procedures specified for initial clearance of name. Reserved name may be transferred to another person or corporation by filing notice of transfer. (§§29-308, 309).

Term of corporate existence may be perpetual. (§29-304).

Incorporators.—Corporations for profit, one or more; nonprofit corporations, three or more (§§29-346, 529); religious societies, not more than ten trustees (§29-902); trust, loan, mortgage, safe deposit and title corporations, 25 or more citizens of U.S. (§26-401); insurance companies, seven or more persons (§35-601); fraternal benefit associations, nine or more persons, at least one-third of whom are residents of District (§35-1207).

Articles of Incorporation.—In case of corporations for profit, must be signed and filed by incorporator(s), and must state name of corporation, period of its duration, its purpose or purposes, aggregate number of shares and number of shares and any par value thereof in each class, preferences and rights of each class of shares, minimum amount of capital for starting business (not less than $1,000), statement of variations between any different series of same class of shares, statement of any authority of board of directors to establish series and fix preferences and rights, and any provision regarding preemptive rights, any provision for regulation of internal affairs, address of initial registered office and name of initial registered agent, number and names and addresses of directors, and name and address of each incorporator. (§§29-346, 347). Separate but similar provisions are made for nonprofit corporations (§§29-529, 530) and for professional corporations (§29-606). Certificate of incorporation, in case of other corporations, must be signed and acknowledged by incorporators.

In case of trust, loan, mortgage, etc., corporations must state name, purposes, term, number of directors, names and residences of officers, amount of capital stock and subdivision into shares (§26-404).

Filing of Articles or Certificate.—Must be delivered in duplicate original to Mayor, who retains one original and issues certificate of incorporation to which is affixed the other duplicate original. Said certificate is delivered to incorporators or their representatives. (§29-348).

Incorporation Fees.—Corporations for profit organized under Act of June 8, 1954, must pay as an initial license fee, upon filing of articles, $.02 per each of first 10,000 authorized shares, $.01 per each of next 50,000 authorized shares, and $.005 per remaining authorized shares. Par value of stock with par value other than $100, number of shares is determined by dividing aggregate par value by 100. Minimum initial license is $20. In event of increase of authorized capital additional license fee is charged equal to difference between license fee computed on total number of shares including increase and license fee computed on total number of shares excluding increase, but in no case less than $10. (§29-399.22).

Filing Fees.—Corporations for profit: articles of incorporation, merger or consolidation, domestication, reincorporation, $100; amended or restated articles, $100; intent to dissolve, $25; articles of dissolution, $50; change of address, change of registered agent, $25; reservation of corporate name, $25. (§29-399.22).

Nonprofit corporations organized under Act of Aug. 6, 1962: articles, $30; amendment to articles, $25; election to accept act, $30; application for reservation of name, $25; for indexing each document, $20; certificate of good standing, $10; filing amended report, $25. (§29-593). Nonprofit two-year report fee is $50 (§29-593[19]); penalty for failure to file is $30 (§29-592).

Each domestic corporation and each foreign corporation authorized to do business in District of Columbia will pay two-year report fee of $500. (§29-399.22). Corporation which fails to file two-year report within time prescribed is subject to penalty of $25. (§29-399.29).

Organization.—With respect to corporations for profit organized under Act of June 8, 1954, corporate existence begins upon issuance of certificate of incorporation; and organization meeting of the board of directors must be held in United States at call of majority of directors, on five days notice by mail, for purpose of adopting by-laws, electing officers and transacting any other proper business. (§§29-349, 351).

Paid-in Capital Requirements.—Minimum amount of capital with which corporation may commence business must not be less than $1,000. (§§29-347, 350).

Amendment of articles of incorporation, including increase or decrease of authorized shares or par value thereof, may be accomplished (1) prior to acceptance of subscriptions by directors, by filing amendment in duplicate signed by all original incorporators, and (2) after acceptance of such subscriptions by (a) resolution of

See note at head of Digest as to 1998 legislation covered.

See Topical Index in front part of this volume.

CORPORATIONS . . . *continued*
directors directing amendment to be submitted to meeting of stockholders, (b) written notice of not less than ten nor more than 50 days, of such meeting to shareholders, and (c) affirmative vote of holders of at least two-thirds of outstanding shares entitled to vote, unless articles of incorporation provide for vote of less than two-thirds, in which case, effective vote cannot be less than simple majority. Filing fee for amendment, $100. (§§29-326, 352, 353, 354, 355, 399.22).

By-Laws.—Power to make, alter, amend, or repeal is vested in board of directors unless reserved to shareholders by the articles. (§29-324).

Shares may be divided into one or more classes with or without par value, with such designations, preferences, voting powers, special or relative rights, limitations, restrictions or qualifications as shall be stated in the articles. (§29-313).

Certificates representing shares must be signed by the president or a vice-president; must state all limitations and restrictions upon transferability or that corporation will furnish a statement thereof without charge; must state all designations, preferences, limitations, and relative rights of each authorized class of shares or that corporation will furnish a statement thereof without charge; must state par value or that without par value; that corporation is organized under laws of District of Columbia; name of person to whom issued; number and class of shares of which represented. By resolution of board of directors, some or all classes or series of stock may be uncertificated. Rights and obligations of holders of uncertificated shares are identical to holders of certificated shares, unless otherwise provided by law. Corporation must send to registered owner written notice of information required to be stated on certificates or that corporation will furnish information without charge. (§29-320).

Issuance of Shares.—Shares may be issued for such consideration, not less than par value, as fixed by directors. Consideration may be money, other property, labor or services actually performed for corporation. Promissory notes or future services are not payment. (§§29-316, 317).

Transfer of Shares.—In order to determine shareholders directors may close books for not more than 50 days and for at least ten days immediately preceding shareholders meeting. (§29-328). Transfer generally governed by Uniform Commercial Code. See category Business Regulation and Commerce, topic Commercial Code. Art. 8 of Code deals with investment securities, and replaces Uniform Stock Transfer Act.

Uniform Simplification of Fiduciary Security Transfers Act (§§28-2901-2909) remains in force and prevails over inconsistent provisions of Art. 8 of U.C.C. (§28:10-104).

Stock Transfer Tax.—None.

Shareholders owning an aggregate of at least 5% of all outstanding shares may (1) examine, in person or by agent, at any reasonable time, for any proper purpose, corporation's record of shareholders and make extracts therefrom, and (2) inspect sworn statement by corporate officer of corporation's affairs within 30 days after written request for such sworn statement stating purpose thereof. Any shareholder may inspect and copy such sworn statement. (§29-345).

Shareholder Actions.—Shareholder may bring derivative action to enforce right of corporation by filing complaint which alleges that (a) plaintiff was shareholder at time of transaction complained of, (b) action not collusive to confer jurisdiction, and (c) particular efforts plaintiff made to obtain action from directors. (Sup. Ct. Civ. R. 23.1).

Shareholders' Liability.—A holder of or subscriber to shares has no obligation to corporation or its creditors, other than to pay corporation full consideration for shares owned. Assignee of shares in good faith, having no notice that full consideration has not been paid, is not liable for any unpaid portion of consideration. (§29-322).

Shareholders' Meetings.—May be held within or without District, as may be provided in by-laws. Annual meeting must be held for election of directors. Written or printed notice stating place, day and hour of meeting, and, in case of special meeting, the purpose, must be delivered personally or by mail not less than 10 nor more than 50 days prior to meeting, unless by-laws specify different period. Each outstanding share entitled to one vote on each matter submitted to vote. Shareholder may vote by proxy executed in writing. Proxy valid for 11 months unless otherwise provided and revocable by shareholder. Articles may provide for cumulative voting. (§§29-325, 326, 327, 333).

Voting trusts may be created for period not to exceed ten years. Counterpart of agreement must be deposited with corporation at its registered office and is subject to examination by shareholders. (§29-330).

Directors.—Number, which may be one or more, is fixed by by-laws except first board which is fixed by articles. Directors are chosen annually, and need not be shareholders, unless articles or by-laws so provide. Vacancies by reason of increase may be filled by annual or special meeting of shareholders; other vacancies are filled by majority of remaining directors. (§§29-332, 333, 335).

Classes.—By-laws may provide for two or three classes of directors who shall have staggered terms. (§29-334).

Directors Meetings.—May be held within or without District as may be provided by by-laws or directors' resolution, or by means of telephone conference, and upon such notice as may be provided in by-laws. Majority of directors is quorum unless greater number required by articles or by-laws. (§§29-336, 338, 339).

Powers and Duties of Directors.—Manage the business and affairs of corporation, declare dividends and establish reasonable compensation for directors and officers. (§§29-332, 340).

Liabilities of Directors and Officers.—Directors who vote for dividend or distribution of assets contrary to Act of June 8, 1954, or contrary to articles, or which would render corporation insolvent or reduce net assets below stated capital, or during liquidation without adequate provision for payment of all obligations of corporation, are jointly and severally liable to corporation for amount of such dividend or assets in excess of that which could have been paid without violation of Act of June 8, 1954 or articles, or to extent that corporation is rendered insolvent, its net assets reduced below stated capital or obligations of corporation not paid. Directors who vote for loan to officer or director of corporation are jointly and severally liable to corporation for amount of such loan until repaid. (§29-342). No statute authorizing articles of incorporation to limit liability of directors or officers. However, Nonprofit Corporation Act provides that if nonprofit corporation (a) is exempt from Federal taxation under §501(c)(3) of Internal Revenue Code and has total annual expenses of less than $100,000 or (b) maintains liability insurance with coverage limits of not less than $200,000 per individual claim and $500,000 per total claims from same occurrence, officers, directors and trustees of nonprofit corporation who are not compensated are immune from civil liability for acts or omissions occurring on or after Mar. 17, 1993, except where injury results from willful misconduct, commission of crime, receipt of improper personal benefit, or act or omission not in good faith and beyond scope of authority of corporation. This provision does not exempt nonprofit corporation from liability for conduct of volunteer, but corporation's liability is limited to applicable limit of insurance coverage. (§29-599.15). Personal liability of employees of nonprofit corporations for acts and omissions occurring on or after Mar. 17, 1993 is limited to amount of total compensation received by employee during 12 months immediately preceding act or omission for which liability is imposed, except where injury or damage results from willful misconduct, commission of crime, receipt of improper personal benefit, or act or omission not in good faith and beyond scope of authority of corporation. This limitation of liability does not apply to licensed professional employees operating in professional capacity and does not exempt corporation from liability, but nonprofit corporation's liability is limited to extent of applicable limit of insurance coverage. (§29-599.16).

Statute of limitations on actions against directors for liability under District of Columbia Business Corporation Act is three years. (§29-342).

Officers.—There must be a president, and such other officers, if any, as prescribed in by-laws, and as may be elected by board of directors or chosen in such manner as prescribed by by-laws. (§29-343).

Indemnification of Directors and Officers.—Corporation may indemnify present or former directors and officers against expenses actually and necessarily incurred in connection with defense of any action, suit, or proceeding in which they are made party by reason of being or having been directors or officers, except in matters in which they are adjudged liable for negligence or misconduct in performance of duty. (§29-304).

Registered office must be maintained in District of Columbia. Need not be corporation's place of business. (§29-310).

Registered agent must be maintained in District. May be individual resident in District, whose business office is identical with registered office, or corporation authorized by articles to act as such agent and authorized to transact business in District having business office identical with the registered office. Registered agent's consent to appointment must be demonstrated either by written statement of agent or by written certification of incorporator(s) that agent has consented. Registered agent is agent for service of process. (§§29-310, 312).

General Powers of Corporation.—Corporation may sue and be sued, have a seal, purchase or acquire and own real or personal property, sell or mortgage or otherwise dispose of property, lend money to employees other than to its officers and directors, own shares or obligations of other corporations, make contracts and incur liabilities, conduct its business in United States or any foreign country, invest its surplus funds, acquire its own shares, make charitable contributions, have all powers necessary and convenient to effect corporate purpose. Defense of ultra vires limited to proceedings by shareholder against corporation to enjoin doing of act or transfer of property by or to corporation, by corporation against incumbent or former officers or directors, or by Mayor to dissolve corporation or to enjoin transaction of unauthorized business. (§§29-304, 305, 307).

Dividends may be declared by directors except (a) no dividend when corporation is or would then be insolvent or net assets are or would then be less than stated capital, (b) dividends are payable from paid-in surplus or surplus arising from surrender of any of its shares only upon shares having a preferential right to receive dividends, (c) upon payment of stock dividend, surplus equal to par value or stated value thereof must be transferred to stated capital. (§29-340).

Unclaimed Dividends.—Dividends are presumed abandoned if unclaimed, or if no communication, etc. within five years. (§42-209). See category Property, topic Absentees, subhead Escheat.

Sale or Transfer of Corporate Assets.—Disposition of substantially all corporate assets, if made in usual and regular course of business, may be upon such terms as authorized by directors. If disposition of substantially all assets of corporation not in usual and regular course of business, must be recommended by directors and authorized by two-thirds of outstanding shares of each class entitled to vote, unless articles of incorporation provide for vote of less than two-thirds, in which case, effective vote cannot be less than simple majority. (§§29-374, 375).

Books and Records.—Corporation must keep correct and complete books and records of account and minutes of proceedings of its shareholders and board of directors; must keep record of its shareholders at its registered office or place of business or at office of its transfer agent or registrar. (§29-345).

Reports.—Corporation must file with Mayor on prescribed forms, on or before Apr. 15 of every second year from date of incorporation, if there has been no change in material facts, two-year report stating (1) name, address of registered office and name of its registered agent, (2) address of principal office in District if other than its registered office, (3) names and addresses of directors and officers, (4) brief statement of character of business, (5) statement of aggregate number of authorized shares, itemized by classes, (6) statement of aggregate number of issued shares, itemized by classes. (§29-398). Two-year report fee of $500 payable at same time. (§29-399.22).

Nonprofit corporation must file on or before Jan. 15 of each second year from date of incorporation. (§29-584).

Merger and Consolidation.—Any two or more domestic corporations may merge into one of such corporations or consolidate into a new corporation. Plan must be approved by majority of board of directors and by two-thirds of outstanding shares of

See note at head of Digest as to 1998 legislation covered.

See Topical Index in front part of this volume.

DC – 2

CORPORATIONS . . . *continued*
each class of each corporation, unless articles of incorporation provide for vote of less than two-thirds; in which case, effective vote cannot be less than simple majority. Articles of merger or of consolidation in duplicate must be then executed by president or vice-president of each corporation and delivered to Mayor, who issues certificate of merger or of consolidation with duplicate original articles attached and delivers same to surviving or new corporation or its representatives. Foreign and domestic corporations may merge or consolidate if permitted by laws of state in which foreign corporation is organized; each corporation must comply with laws of place in which organized; and surviving or new corporation is in general treated as foreign or domestic corporation depending upon jurisdiction by whose laws it is to be governed. Domestic corporation(s) and domestic partnerships, domestic limited partnership(s) or domestic limited liability companies (LLCs) may merge or consolidate, and domestic corporation(s) and domestic partnerships, limited partnership(s) or LLC(s) of any state of U.S. may merge or consolidate if not prohibited by laws of that state. No member of domestic LLC that is party to merger will become personally liable for liabilities of any other person or entity unless member approves agreement of merger or otherwise consents to becoming personally liable. Dissenting shareholders are entitled to be paid fair value of shares. Filing fee for articles, $100. If surviving or new corporation is domestic, license fee computed on number of authorized shares is payable. (§§29-364-373, 399.22).

Dissolution.—Corporation may be voluntarily dissolved (1) by its incorporators within year after issuance of certificate of incorporation if it has not commenced business nor issued shares, or (2) by majority of board of directors and two-thirds of outstanding shares entitled to vote, unless articles of incorporation provide for vote of less than two-thirds, in which case, effective vote cannot be less than simple majority, or (3) by written consent of all shareholders. If by incorporators, articles of dissolution are filed with Mayor, who issues certificate of dissolution. If by corporation or shareholder consent, statement of intent to dissolve is filed with Mayor, and after liquidation of affairs of corporation, articles of dissolution are filed with Mayor, who issues certificate of dissolution. (§§29-376-387).

Corporation may be dissolved involuntarily by Superior Court in action instituted by Mayor if: (a) Franchise was procured through fraud, (b) corporation has exceeded or abused authority, (c) corporation has failed for 30 days to appoint and maintain registered agent, or (d) corporation has failed for 30 days after change of registered office or registered agent to file with Mayor statement of such change. (§29-388).

Insolvency and Receivers.—Superior Court has full power to liquidate assets and business of corporation in dissolution proceedings, and issue injunctions and appoint receivers in connection therewith. (§29-390, 391).

Appraisal.—Shareholders dissenting from merger or consolidation of corporation are entitled to payment of fair value of shares upon compliance with statutory procedures. (§29-373).

Close Corporations.—Close corporation is corporation organized under Business Corporation Act of 1954, as amended, which elects to become close corporation and thereby becomes subject to §§29-399.54—29-399.69 of Act. Articles of incorporation must contain heading stating that it is close corporation, and must provide (1) corporation's stock shall be represented by certificates, and shall be held by no more than 35 persons; (2) all stock shall be subject to one or more of restrictions on transfer permitted under §29-320 of Act; (3) corporation shall make no public offering of its stock. Existing corporation may become close corporation upon amending its articles of incorporation, by vote of at least two-thirds of each class of stock, to comply with statutory requirements. (§§29-399.54—29-399.57).

Corporation may voluntarily terminate its status as close corporation by amending its articles of incorporation by two-thirds vote of each class of stock of its shareholders to delete provisions required to become close corporation; however, articles may require vote greater than two-thirds to terminate status as close corporation. Any such provision may not be amended except by vote not less than that required to terminate status as close corporation. Corporation may involuntarily lose its status as close corporation if it breaches any statutory conditions which are not remedied within 30 days in accordance with statutory procedures. (§§29-399.59, 399.61).

If stock of close corporation is issued or transferred in breach of qualifying conditions, corporation may refuse to register transfer of stock into name of transferee. (§29-399.60).

Agreement among shareholders holding majority of outstanding stock is not invalid on grounds that it may restrict discretion of directors. Effect will be to shift liability for acts and omissions from directors to majority shareholders to extent power of board is controlled or limited by agreement. Articles of incorporation may provide that business of corporation may be managed by shareholders rather than by board of directors. (§§29-399.63, 399.64).

Court may, in certain circumstances, appoint receiver, custodian or provisional director of close corporation. (§§29-399.65, 399.66).

Foreign corporations must obtain certificates of authority from Mayor before transacting business in District. No foreign corporation is entitled to procure such certificate to transact business of banking, insurance, acceptance and execution of trusts, operation of railroads, or building and loan association, such corporations being admitted to do business in District pursuant to laws relating to such business. Application for such certificate is made in duplicate to Mayor on forms supplied by Mayor, and must set forth (a) Name and state of organization, (b) if necessary, one of words "corporation," "company," "incorporated" or "limited" or abbreviation thereof, for use in District, (c) date of incorporation and period of duration, (d) address of principal office in state of organization, (e) address of proposed registered office in District and name of proposed registered agent, (f) statement of business it proposes to transact in District, (g) names and addresses of directors and officers, (h) any additional pertinent information. Certified copy of articles of incorporation and all amendments must be attached. Filing fee is $150. No restrictions on right to hold real property. (§§29-399, 399.1, 399.4, 399.5, 399.22).

Foreign corporations, other than those that limit their activities to investing in loans secured by real estate, which transacts business in District without certificate of authority may not sue in District of Columbia courts until certificate is obtained, are deemed to have appointed Mayor their agent for service of process, shall be guilty of misdemeanor, shall be liable for all fees and charges they should have paid plus penalty not in excess of $500, and may be liable for civil fines, penalties, and fees. Annual reports on prescribed forms and annual report fee of $100 must be delivered on or before Apr. 15 each year to Mayor. To surrender authority to do business, foreign corporation must file application on prescribed forms for withdrawal with Mayor, and receive certificate of withdrawal (fee, $25). (§§29-399, 399.9, 399.13, 399.14, 399.15, 399.20, 399.22, 399.30).

Foreign corporation may become domestic corporation by filing articles of domestication with Mayor. (§29-399.52). Foreign corporation with name confusingly similar to name of corporation already conducting business in D.C. may qualify to do business under fictitious name unless it engages in same type of business as similarly named corporation. (§§29-399.2).

Taxation.—See category Taxation.

Professional corporations may be formed by persons rendering professional personal service pursuant to license including services performed by certified public accountants, attorneys, architects, practitioners of healing arts, dentists, optometrists, podiatrists and professional engineers. (§29-601 et seq.). Professional corporation may merge with another domestic professional corporation or domestic limited liability company (LLC) if both are organized to render same professional services, or which, if not same, could otherwise be rendered by single professional corporation or LLC. No member of domestic LLC that is party to merger will become personally liable for liabilities of any other person or entity unless member approves agreement of merger or otherwise consents to becoming personally liable. (§29-613).

Deeds.—See category Property, topic Deeds.

Model Non-Profit Corporation Act.—Adopted, with modifications. (§§29-501-599.14).

JOINT STOCK COMPANIES:

No statute.

As to professional corporations, see topic Corporations, subhead Professional Corporations.

LIMITED LIABILITY COMPANIES:

District of Columbia Limited Liability Company Act of 1994 became effective July 23, 1994.

Formation.—One or more persons may form limited liability company (LLC) by signing articles of organization and filing with Mayor (Department of Consumer and Regutory Affairs, Business Regulation Administration, Corporations Division). (§29-1302).

Powers.—LLC may exercise all powers necessary to effect purposes. May also, subject to any restrictions in articles of organization or operating agreement, indemnify any member, agent, manager, or employee against any claims except willful misconduct or recklessness. (§29-1303).

Name shall contain words "limited liability company" or abbreviation "L.L.C." Professional limited liability company shall contain words "professional limited liability company" or abbreviation "P.L.L.C." Name must not be deceptively similar to names of other companies or partnerships, domestic or foreign, transacting business in District. Fictitious name may be adopted by filing statement with Mayor, provided that foreign LLC may not adopt fictitious name for use in transacting business in District if that foreign LLC has name that is same as, or deceptively similar to, company or partnership already engaged in District in same business as foreign LLC. (§29-1304). Exclusive use of LLC name may be reserved for 60 day period, and may be renewed for successive 60 day periods, by applying to Mayor. (§29-1305).

Articles of organization shall contain following matters: (1) Name of LLC; (2) latest date on which LLC is to be dissolved; (3) address of LLC's registered office, name of registered agent, and evidence of registered agent's consent. Articles must be executed and filed with Mayor, along with filing fees. LLC is formed as of later of (1) time established in articles of organization, or (2) when articles are delivered to Mayor for filing. If articles do not conform to act and are not brought into conformance within 20 days after notification of nonconformance has been given, LLC deemed never to have been formed. (§29-1306). Articles may be amended, unless otherwise provided by articles or by operating agreement, by those members with voting rights holding at least majority of interest in profits of LLC. Articles of amendment must be executed and filed with Mayor, and must set forth (1) name of LLC; (2) text of each amendment adopted; (3) date of each amendment's adoption; and (4) statement that amendment was adopted by vote of members in accordance with LLC's articles of organization and applicable law. (§29-1307).

Registered Office and Registered Agent.—Must be maintained in District and may be changed. Registered agent's written consent must be filed with Mayor. Resignation, which must be in writing and filed with Mayor, is effective 30 days after receipt of notice by Mayor, or upon appointment of successor agent, whichever occurs first. (§§29-1309-1311).

Partnership Conversion to LLC.—General partnership may be converted to LLC if approved by all general partners. Limited partnerships may be converted to LLC by approval of majority in interest of limited partners or by number or percentage of partners specified for conversion in applicable partnership agreement. General partner who becomes member of LLC as result of conversion remains liable as general partner for any liability incurred by general partnership or limited partnership before conversion took effect. Limited partner remains liable for obligations incurred prior to conversion by limited partnership to extent provided by law of state in which limited partnership was organized. After conversion, title to real estate and other property remains vested in converted entity without reversion or impairment, liabilities continue as liabilities of converted entity, and any pending proceeding may be continued as if conversion had not occurred. (§29-1313).

See note at head of Digest as to 1998 legislation covered.

See Topical Index in front part of this volume.

LIMITED LIABILITY COMPANIES... *continued*

Liability to Third Parties.—Except as act or articles of organization specifically provide otherwise, no member, manager, employee or agent of LLC is personally liable for debts, obligations or liabilities of LLC. Member of Professional Limited Liability Company (PLLC) is personally liable only for negligent or wrongful act or misconduct committed by such member, or by any individual working under such member's supervision and control. Member of LLC is not proper party to proceeding by or against LLC except for enforcement of member's rights against or liability to LLC, or as part of derivative action on behalf of LLC. (§§29-1314-1315, 1343-1347).

Property.—LLC may acquire, hold and convey real or personal property. (§29-1316).

Management is vested in members, except to extent that articles of organization provide for management of LLC by manager or managers. Articles or operating agreement may provide for classes or groups of members with relative rights, powers and duties, and may provide for taking of action, including amending articles of organization or operating agreement, without vote or approval of any member or class or group of members. Articles or operating agreement may grant right to vote separately or with class on any matter to all or certain identified members of class. Voting may be on per capita, number, financial interest, class, group, or other basis. If not otherwise provided in articles or operating agreement, (1) members shall vote in proportion to respective interests in LLC profits; (2) decisions must be approved by members with voting rights holding at least majority of interests in profits of LLC. Articles or operating agreements which provide voting rights may set forth provisions relating to such rights, such as notice, waiver of notice, quorum requirements, action without meeting, establishing record date, etc. (§29-1317). Articles or operating agreement may delegate full or partial responsibility to one or more managers, who need not be residents of District or members of LLC. Managers shall be selected and removed by members. Vacancies shall be filled by members with voting rights holding at least majority of interests in profits of LLC. Similarly, managers can be removed with or without cause by voting members with majority of interests. Unless otherwise provided in articles or operating agreement, any action permitted to be taken by managers of LLC may be taken upon majority vote of managers. (§29-1319).

Operating Agreement is not mandatory but normally regulates affairs of LLC, conduct of its business and relations of its members. May contain any provisions not inconsistent with laws of District or articles of organization. May provide for penalties or specified consequences for members or managers for nonperformance of obligations or noncompliance with terms of operating agreement. Initial agreement must be agreed to by all current members. Unless otherwise provided in articles or operating agreement, members with voting rights holding majority of interest in profits must approve any amendment. (§29-1318).

Limitation of Liability.—In any proceeding brought by or in right of LLC or brought by or on behalf of members of LLC, liability may be limited in articles of organization or operating agreement, except if manager or member engaged in willful misconduct. (§29-1320).

Business Transactions with Members.—Member or manager may transact business with LLC, and, subject to other applicable law, has same rights and obligations as person who is not member or manager, unless otherwise provided in articles or operating agreement. (§29-1321).

Records.—LLC must keep at principal office names and addresses of members, copies of articles of organization and operating agreement, copies of federal, state and local tax returns for three years, and, unless contained in operating agreement, description of contributions of members, times or events which may trigger additional contributions, right to any distributions, and events which would trigger dissolution. Subject to reasonable standards as may be set forth in articles or operating agreement, member has right to inspect and copy, at own expense, LLC records required to be maintained by this section. (§29-1322).

Contributions, Profits and Losses.—Contributions may consist of anything of value. Profits and losses are allocated among members in manner provided in articles of organization or operating agreement. In absence of operating agreement or applicable provision therein, profits and losses shall be allocated on basis of value of member's contribution, to extent received by LLC and not returned. (§§29-1323-1324).

Distributions.—Unless otherwise provided in articles or operating agreement, distributions shall be made on basis of value of member's contribution. (§29-1325). Upon resignation, unless otherwise provided in articles or operating agreement, member is entitled to receive fair value of interest as of date of resignation. Any damages caused by member's breach of operating agreement or by wrongful conduct may be set off by LLC against amount otherwise distributable. (§29-1327). Member has no right to demand nor any obligation to accept distribution in any form other than cash, unless otherwise provided in articles or operating agreement. (§29-1328). LLC cannot make distribution if it cannot pay debts as they come due. (§29-1329). After two years from date of wrongful distribution, member who receives such distribution shall have no liability to LLC. (§29-1330). Member entitled to receive distribution has status of and is entitled to all remedies available to creditor of LLC with respect to such distributions. (§29-1331).

Transferability of Interests.—LLC interest is considered personal property (§29-1333), and as such is assignable in whole or in part. Full membership interest is transferred by assigning both governance rights and financial rights. Financial rights assignable unless restricted as provided in §29-1337. Governance rights may be assigned from one member to another member without consent of any other member, unless restricted by articles or operating agreement. (§29-1336). Governance rights may be assigned to non-member if approved by members with voting rights holding at least majority of interests in profits, unless further restricted by articles or operating agreement. Assignment of financial rights does not dissolve LLC, and does not entitle or empower assignee to become member, to exercise any governance rights, to receive any notices from LLC, or to cause dissolution. (§29-1335). Written restriction on assignment of financial or governance rights, unless noted conspicuously in records of

LLC, is ineffective against person without knowledge of restriction. (§29-1337). Deceased member's executor may exercise all rights of member for purpose of settling such member's estate or administering such member's property. (§29-1339).

Merger.—LLC may merge with or into one or more District or foreign LLC's or other business entities. Unless otherwise provided in articles or operating agreement, approval of merger by members holding majority of interests in profits required; if surviving entity does not afford limited liability, unanimous approval of voting and nonvoting members required. Interests in LLC that is constituent part to merger may be exchanged for or converted into cash, property, interests in surviving entity or any other entity. (§29-1340). Articles of merger, agreement of merger and effect of merger addressed. (§§29-1341-1342).

In any merger of partnership with LLC, no member of domestic LLC that is party to merger will become personally liable for liabilities of any other person or entity unless member approves agreement of merger or otherwise consents to becoming personally liable. (§41-428).

Dissolution.—LLC dissolved by (i) judicial decree; (ii) events specified in articles or operating agreement; (iii) unanimous consent of members with voting rights, or (iv) death, retirement, resignation, expulsion, bankruptcy, or dissolution of member. However, LLC is not dissolved if (A) there are at least two remaining members or one remaining member and new member is admitted, and (B) either (1) within 90 days of event terminating membership of member, remaining members with voting rights unanimously consent to continuation, or (2) there is compliance with procedures in articles or operating agreement for continuation. (§29-1347). Member may apply to Superior Court of District for decree of dissolution if not reasonably practicable to carry on business in conformity with articles or operating agreement. (§29-1348). Articles of dissolution, winding-up and distribution of assets addressed. (§§29-1349-1351).

Foreign LLC must register with Mayor prior to transacting business in District. Foreign LLC may not be denied registration because of differences between laws of state of formation and District laws. Subject to District law, formation, internal affairs, and liability of members of foreign LLC are governed by laws of state of formation. (§§29-1352-1353). By doing business in District, foreign LLC assents to laws of District. (§29-1361). Procedure of registration, cancellation of registration, transaction of business without registration, transactions not constituting doing business, merger, and related matters addressed. (§§29-1353-1362).

Fees.—Payable to Mayor as follows: Registration of foreign LLC, $150; filing articles of organization, merger, amendment, correction, dissolution, cancellation, certificate of correction, document effecting merger, petition for reinstatement, $100; filing change of registered agent or registered office, application to reserve or renew reservation of name, notice of transfer of name reserved, statement of fictitious name, $25. (§29-1363).

Annual Reports and Annual Registration Fees.—Foreign and domestic LLC must file annual report with Mayor before June 16th of each year on forms prescribed and furnished by Mayor. Annual registration fee of $50 must be paid at time of filing. Failure to file report or pay fee for two consecutive years results in articles of organization being declared void for domestic LLC and certificate of registration being revoked for foreign LLC. (§§29-1364-1366). Procedures for carrying out such penalties, fines for doing business after revocation of authority, procedures for reinstatement, and other related matters addressed. (§§29-1367-1372).

Transaction of Business Outside District.—Intent of Council that LLC formed under act be recognized outside of District, and, subject to reasonable registration requirements, be granted protection of full faith and credit under §1 of Art. IV of U.S. Constitution. (§29-1373).

Taxation.—LLC shall be classified as partnership unless classified otherwise for federal income tax purposes, in which case LLC shall be classified in same manner as classified for federal income tax purposes. Member shall be classified as either resident or nonresident partner unless classified otherwise for federal income tax purposes, in which case shall have same status as for federal income tax purposes. (§29-1374).

Regulation of Professionals.—Except for §29-1314 (relating to liability to third parties), act not intended to restrict authority of any regulatory body to license individuals rendering professional services within District or to regulate practice of any profession. (§29-1375).

PARTNERSHIPS:

Uniform Partnership Act of 1996 (§§41-151.1-161.6) in effect Apr. 9, 1997 for partnerships formed after that date, or for partnerships that elect to be governed by act. After Jan. 1, 1998, act governs all partnerships. (§41-162.3). Uniform Partnership Act of 1962 is repealed, effective Jan. 1, 1998. (§§41-101-148).

Limited Liability Partnership.—Partnership may become Registered Limited Liability Partnership (LLP) by filing application with Department of Consumer and Regulatory Affairs stating: (1) name of LLP; (2) address of principal office; (3) name and address of registered agent and written permission of registered agent; (4) number of partners; (5) brief statement of business in which LLP engages; and (6) statement that LLP will maintain required insurance coverage. Application to be executed by majority in interest of partners or by one or more partners authorized by majority in interest of partners. Registration effective for one year after date registration is filed, unless voluntarily withdrawn by majority in interest of partners. (§41-143). Limited partnership may become LLP by (1) obtaining approval by vote necessary to amend limited partnership agreement, except where such agreement expressly considers contribution obligations, then by vote necessary to amend those provisions; (2) filing statement of qualification under §1001(c) of Uniform Partnership Act of 1996; and (3) complying with requirements of §§1002-1004 of that Act. (Law 234, 44 DCR 2592).

Name shall contain words "Registered Limited Liability Partnership" or abbreviation "L.L.P." as last words or letters of name. (§41-144).

Insurance.—LLP must carry at least $100,000 liability insurance of type designed to cover errors, omissions, negligence, incompetence, or malfeasance for which liability

See note at head of Digest as to 1998 legislation covered.

See Topical Index in front part of this volume.

PARTNERSHIPS . . . *continued*
is limited, or coverage in minimum amount of not less than amount carried by individual partner carrying greatest amount of individual liability insurance, whichever is greater. If insurance requirements are complied with, they shall not be admissible or be made known to jury in determining issue of liability. (§41.145).

Limited Liability.—Partner in LLP not individually liable for debts and obligations of LLP arising from errors, omissions, negligence, incompetence, or malfeasance committed in course of business by second partner or representative of LLP not working under supervision or direction of first partner at time errors, omissions, negligence, incompetence, or malfeasance occurred, unless first partner: (1) was directly involved in specific activity in which errors, omissions, negligence, incompetence, or malfeasance were committed; or (2) had written notice or knowledge of errors, omissions, negligence, incompetence, or malfeasance that were committed at time of occurrence. Limitation on liability does not affect joint liability of partner for debts and obligations of LLP arising from any cause not specified in section limiting partner's liability, nor does it affect liability of LLP assets for LLP debts and obligations. (§41-146).

Foreign LLP.—Foreign LLP may conduct business in District upon filing legally sufficient application. Foreign LLP and liability of its partners shall be governed by laws of state or jurisdiction of its organization. Foreign LLP may not be prohibited from conducting business in District by reason of any difference between laws of state or other jurisdiction under which it is organized and laws of District. (§41-147).

Full Faith and Credit.—LLP may do business in other jurisdictions of U.S. or in any foreign country. Intent of D.C. Council that legal existence of LLP be recognized outside boundaries of District and that LLP be granted full faith and credit. (§41-148).

Limited Partnership.—Uniform Limited Partnership Act of 1987 in effect. (§§41-401-499.25).

BUSINESS REGULATION AND COMMERCE

BANKS AND BANKING:

Uniform Commercial Code adopted. Article 4A—Funds Transfers (1989 text), adopted effective Apr., 1992. Article 2A—Leasing adopted effective July 22, 1992. Revised Article 3—Negotiable Instruments, and revised Article 4—Bank Deposits and Collections, adopted effective Mar. 23, 1995. See topic Commercial Code.

Except for national banking association organized under laws of U.S., only corporation may conduct business of bank of deposit and such corporation (unless in business prior to Mar. 4, 1933) must be organized under provisions of D. C. Code. (§26-103).

Supervision.—All banks (except national banks), savings banks, savings companies, and trust companies and other financial institutions in D.C., including regional and nonregional interstate bank holding companies doing or seeking to do business in D.C. are under supervision of Superintendent of Banking and Financial Institutions (or Mayor until Superintendent appointed). (§§26-101-103; Law 6-107, §3[a][8]; §26-802.1). Nonnational D.C. banks no longer subject to examination by Controller of Currency or compelled to comply with Federal Reserve System regulations. (Law 6-107, §2[k]; §26-102[c][3]).

Deposits.—Deposits in names of two or more persons, including husband and wife, payable to either or survivor, may be paid to either whether others be living or not; and receipt of person to whom deposit is paid is complete release and discharge of bank. (§26-201).

Notice to bank of adverse claim to deposit is not effectual to cause bank to recognize adverse claimant unless adverse claimant either: (1) Procures restraining order or other court process or (2) executes bond to indemnify bank from all liability, loss, damage, costs and expenses on account of payment of adverse claim. Notice to bank of adverse claimant is effectual, however, where person to whose credit deposit stands is fiduciary for adverse claimant, and adverse claimant's affidavit shows reasonable cause to believe that fiduciary is about to misappropriate said deposit. (§26-203).

On death of trustee bank may, in absence of further notice as to terms of trust, pay trust deposit to trust beneficiary or his legal representative. (§26-204).

Unclaimed Deposits.—Any demand, savings, or matured time deposit with District bank, and any sum payable on certified check, draft, money order or like instrument is presumed abandoned if no communication etc. from owner within five years. (§42-206). Any sum payable on traveler's check issued by bank or financial organization in District is presumed abandoned if no communication etc. from owner within 15 years. (§42-206). See category Property, topic Absentees, subhead Escheat.

Collections.—Uniform Commercial Code adopted. See topic Commercial Code.

Safe deposit boxes in names of two or more persons, including husband and wife, with right of access to either or survivor, may be opened and contents removed by any of such persons whether others be living or not; and in case of such removal banking institution is exempt from liability. (§26-202).

Trust companies are organized under the provisions of §§26-401-436 of Code, subject to approval of D. C. Council (§26-405) and supervision of Superintendent of Banking and Financial Institutions (Law 6-107, §2[k]; §26-408).

Uniform Common Trust Fund Act adopted. (§§26-301-304).

Foreign Banks.—No branch of a foreign banking institution may be opened without consent of Superintendent of Banking and Financial Institutions. (§26-103[b]).

International Banking Facilities.—No international banking facility may be established in District of Columbia without consent of Comptroller of Currency. (§26-103[h]).

Interstate Banking.—Regional Interstate Banking Act of 1985 allows for reciprocal banking activities among District of Columbia and 11 Southeastern states. Amendment to Interstate Banking Act clarifies that local law applies equally to acquisition of D.C. bank holding company or D.C. bank by regional bank holding company or by D.C. bank holding company, so long as conditions of §26-802(a) are met. (§26-802). Amendments allow nonregional bank holding companies to acquire D.C. banks or D.C. bank holding companies, subject to approval of D.C. Council and Superintendent of Banking and Financial Institutions. (§26-806.1). Nonregional bank holding companies seeking such approval must commit to make loans and lines of credit available to low-to-moderate income D.C. residents in amount equal to greater of 0.0625% of total assets (three years following acquisition) or $50,000,000, with maximum required commitment of $100,000,000. Other economic development commitments also required. Letter of credit to D.C. government to secure obligations also required. (§26-806.1). Nonregional banks doing business in D.C. may not obtain reciprocal regional banking privileges. Banking and Branching Act of 1996 permits interstate banking, branching and consolidation, and conversion of banks pursuant to federal Riegle-Neal Interstate Banking and Branching Efficiency Act of 1994. (§§26-1001-1011).

D.C. Savings and Loan Acquisition Amendment Act of 1988 allows for reciprocal activities by savings and loan associations and savings and loan holding companies in District of Columbia and 15 southern and eastern states. (§§26-901-916, Oct. 1988). Permits regional associations or holding companies to acquire D.C. associations (§26-902) or establish D.C. branches (§26-903) on approval of Superintendent. Economic development commitments required. (§26-904). Nonregional associations or holding companies seeking such approval must commit to make loans and extend credit to residents and small businesses in low-to-moderate-income areas in amount equal to or greater than .0625% of total assets (within three years following acquisition), in addition to other economic development and service commitments. Letter of credit to D.C. government to secure obligations also required. (§26-905).

Insurance Requirements.—Bank or trust company established pursuant to Amendments to Interstate Banking Act of 1985 required to insure with FDIC. Savings & Loan Association established pursuant to Amendments to Interstate Banking Act of 1985 required to insure with FSLIC. (§26-807.1).

Registered Agent.—Regional and nonregional bank holding companies seeking to acquire D.C. bank or bank holding company required to designate registered agent; D.C. Mayor acts in absence of same. (§26-807[b]).

Taxation.—Financial institutions are, as of July 1, 1981, subject to tax on certain personal property held on that date and each succeeding July 1, at rate of 10% per annum. (§§47-2510, 1522).

In addition, financial institutions are subject to franchise tax, as are corporations. (§47-1807.1). See category Taxation, topic Income Tax, subhead Corporations and Financial Institutions.

Foregoing is in lieu of all other taxes except on real estate.

BILLS AND NOTES:

Uniform Commercial Code adopted. See topic Commercial Code.

Days of grace not provided for.

Bad Checks.—It is a misdemeanor to make or utter, with intent to defraud, check or draft in an amount less than $100 with knowledge at time of making, drawing, uttering or delivering that maker or drawer has not sufficient funds in or credit with bank on which drawn for payment in full on presentation. Offense is punishable by imprisonment for not more than one year, fine of not more than $1,000, or both. Offense is felony, punishable by imprisonment of one to three years, fine of not more than $3,000 or both, if amount of instrument is $100 or more. (§22-1410). Making drawing, uttering, or delivery of such check or draft, payment of which is refused by drawee on account of insufficient funds is prima facie evidence of drawer's knowledge of insufficiency and intent to defraud, unless he pays holder full amount due on check, etc., within five days after notice of nonpayment. (§22-1410).

Attorney fee clauses are enforceable as indemnity for a reasonable fee. (31 A. 2d 673 [D. C. Ct. of Appeals]).

BILLS OF LADING:

See topic Carriers.

BILLS OF SALE:

See topic Sales; category Mortgages, topic Chattel Mortgages.

BLUE SKY LAW:

See topic Securities.

BROKERS:

Real estate brokers and salesmen must be licensed. (§45-1926). Single act constitutes doing business. (§45-1926). Certain exemptions are granted to fiduciaries acting under court order if not regularly engaged in real estate practice, public officers, attorneys; owners or lessors of real estate acting in regular course of managing their investments; employees of brokers engaged in clerical functions only; as well as trustees or auctioneers acting under authority of power of sale in mortgage or similar instrument; and banks, trust companies, building and loan or savings and loan associations or insurance companies (but not title companies) engaged in transaction of business as fiduciary. (§45-1931). No suit for compensation may be brought by broker or salesman without proof of due licensing. (§45-1926). Duties of brokers, salespersons, and property managers, including duty to disclose brokerage relationship, are set forth in Real Estate Licensure Amendment Act of 1996. (§45-1934.1). See subhead Licenses, infra.

Mortgages brokers and lenders must also be licensed. Mortgage Broker and Lender Act of 1996. (§§26-1001-1014). Act exempts, inter alia, chartered or incorporated banks, trust companies, savings bank, savings and loan associations, and credit unions, as well as insurance companies authorized to do business in District, any corporate instrumentality or agency of U.S. government, and persons not in business of making or brokering mortgages loans. (§26-1002).

See note at head of Digest as to 1998 legislation covered.

See Topical Index in front part of this volume.

DC – 5

BROKERS . . . *continued*

Licenses.—Applicants for real estate license must be 18 years of age, able to read, write and understand English, high school graduate or holder of high school equivalency certificate, have furnished Mayor with certificate of completion of course of study prescribed by Mayor, and have passed examination required by Mayor. If applicant furnishes evidence of education from other sources, Mayor may waive educational requirements in whole or in part. No license may be issued to one whose application has in District or elsewhere been rejected for reasons other than failure to pass required examination within one year, or whose license in District or elsewhere is suspended at time application is filed, or whose license has been revoked within three years. No real estate broker's license may be issued unless applicant has been licensed and actively engaged in business as real estate broker or salesperson in District or elsewhere for two years prior to application unless applicant provides proof of equivalent experience acceptable to Mayor. (§45-1927). Licenses issued to individuals may not be transferred to others. (§45-1932). Licenses will not be issued to firms or corporations unless applicant is organized pursuant to applicable laws, every individual engaged in broker activities is licensed and every branch office is managed by licensed broker. (§45-1932.1). Licenses may be revoked for substantial misrepresentations, false promises, false advertising, incompetence, fraud, commingling of escrow funds, and other acts. (§45-1936). Mayor must suspend license and convene revocation hearing within 30 days of conviction of crime involving fraud. (§45-1941). Biannual fees: Brokers, $180 for first license; $160 for renewal license; salespersons, $180 for first license; $100 for renewal license.

Applicant for mortgage broker or lender license must satisfy Superintendent of District of Columbia Office of Banking and Financial Institutions that its members, officers, directors and principals are of good moral character and have sufficient financial responsibility, experience and fitness to engage in business as mortgage lender or broker, must warrant that business will be conducted lawfully, honestly, fairly and efficiently, and must capitalize business by having at least $200,000 if lender, and at least $10,000 if broker. (§26-1003). Applicant must file surety bond and pay fees of $1,100. (§26-1003).

Insurance agent or broker must obtain license from Commissioner of Insurance and Securities. Applicant for insurance broker's license must have at least two years experience as insurance agent or in comparable employment during three years prior to date of application. Applicants for license as insurance agent or insurance broker must pass written examination. (§§35-1312-1334).

BULK SALES:

See category Debtor and Creditor, topic Fraudulent Sales and Conveyances.

CARRIERS:

Persons.—Washington Metropolitan Area Transit Commission, created by compact of District, Md. and Va., regulates the transportation of persons, for hire, in the metropolitan Washington area and the carriers performing such service. (§1-2411 et seq.). Commission may prescribe or suspend rates, regulations or practices of the carriers. Certificates of public convenience and necessity are required. Rates must be just, reasonable and nondiscriminatory. Tariffs showing rates and, if required by Commission, regulations and practices of the carriers must be filed with Commission and kept open to public inspection. Commission's authority does not extend to transportation of persons by water, air, or rail; by federal government or signatories; of school children or teachers; transportation by regular route primarily outside metropolitan Washington area; or by certain carriers subject to I.C.C. Appeal from orders of Commission lies to U.S. Court of Appeals for Fourth Circuit or District.

Washington Metropolitan Area Transit Authority, created by amendment of Washington metropolitan area transit regulation compact of District, Md. and Va., has responsibility to plan, develop, finance, and cause to be operated by private companies or persons mass transit facilities (including rail rapid transit) in National Capital region, and to coordinate operation of public and privately owned or controlled transit facilities and serve other regional purposes. Authority has sole jurisdiction over service, rates and fares of transit facilities which it owns or controls, but has no jurisdiction over functions of Washington Metropolitan Area Transit Commission. U.S. District Courts and courts of Md. and Va. have concurrent original jurisdiction of all actions by or against Authority.

Other.—Public Service Commission of D. C., appointed by Mayor with advice and consent of City Council (§43-401 et seq.), supervises street railroads, transportation of freight or property from one point to another within District of Columbia and any common carrier performing such service (§§43-209, 211, 222, 409, 503, 602; §§44-201). Appeal lies to D. C. Court of Appeals from any order or decision of Commission. (§43-905).

Rates must be reasonable, just and non-discriminatory; certification required. (§43-402, 501). Schedule of rates, tolls and charges must be filed with P.S.C., and must remain in force until set aside by P.S.C. (§43-523). Copy of schedule must be available for public inspection at every station and office of carrier (§43-525), with new schedules made available ten days prior to effective date (§43-528). Changes in rates may be made on written application therefor after hearing and investigation with reasonable notice thereof to all interested persons. (§43-601).

Bills of Lading.—Are governed by the Federal Bill of Lading Act (49 U.S. Code §§81-124), which is in effect local law in District. Uniform Commercial Code is in effect. See topic Commercial Code.

Liens.—After failure for six months to claim or to pay charges on baggage or other property transported by or deposited with a common carrier, carrier may sell such baggage or other property at public auction after giving three weeks notice of time and place, once a week for three successive weeks, in a newspaper published in the District. (§44-101). On application verified by affidavit that residence of owner or consignee is unknown or that such baggage or other property is perishable or showing other cause rendering delay impracticable, Superior Court may authorize sale on such terms as it deems desirable. (§44-102).

Liability to Employees.—A carrier is liable to an employee, or in case of his death, to his representative for benefit of widow or next of kin for any damage which may result by reason of negligence. (§44-401). Contributory negligence or insurance contracts of employee no bar to recovery. (§§44-402, 403). One year statute of limitations applies. (§44-404).

Conduct of Public.—Conduct of passengers and occupants aboard public passenger vehicles regulated by §44-223 et seq.

Motor Vehicle Carriers.—See category Transportation, topic Motor Vehicles.

COMMERCIAL CODE:

Uniform Commercial Code (1962 text) has been adopted, effective Jan. 1, 1965, and 1977 Official Amendments (Article 8), effective Mar. 16, 1993. Code appears as Subtitle I of Title 28 of the District of Columbia Code. Article 4A—Funds Transfers (1989 text), adopted effective Apr., 1992. Article 2A—Leasing, adopted effective July 22, 1992. Revised Article 3—Negotiable Instruments, and revised Article 4—Bank Deposits and Collections, adopted effective Mar. 23, 1995. Revised Article 5—Letters of Credit, adopted effective Apr. 9, 1997. Revised Article 6—Bulk Sales, adopted effective Apr. 9, 1997. Revised Article 8—Investment Securities, adopted effective Apr. 9, 1997. Citation follows that of the Official Text of U.C.C. prefixed by 28; *e.g.*, Art. 1, §1 of U.C.C., cited in U.C.C. as "1-101," is cited: "D. C. Code 28:1-101."

Material Variations.—Material variations from the 1962 and 1972 Official Texts are:

§1-103, U.C.C.—Age of capacity to contract is 18 years.

§1-201(14a), U.C.C.—"District" means District of Columbia, and "state" includes District.

§2-316, U.C.C. re exclusion or modification of warranties does not apply to sale of consumer goods or services. §28:2-316.1 renders unenforceable any modification by seller of any implied warranties of merchantability or fitness for particular purpose. Particular defects and limitations, however, are excluded from this section if noted conspicuously in writing. Manufacturer of consumer goods cannot limit consumer's remedies for breach of express warranties unless manufacturer provides reasonable and expeditious means of performing warranty obligations.

§3-302, U.C.C.—Modified by §36-1004(j)(2) which provides that promissory notes executed under employment agency agreements not held in due course beyond 120 days.

§9-114(3), U.C.C.—Art dealers selling artists' work on consignment basis are trustees for benefit of artists; trust property is not subject to claims, liens, or creditors of art dealers.

§9-302(3), U.C.C.—Modified to exclude from filing requirements (i) property subject to statute of U.S. providing for national or international registration or certificate of title, or specific place of filing, (ii) motor vehicles, other than those held in inventory for sale (see topic Motor Vehicles, subhead Liens), and (iii) property subject to certificate of title statute of another jurisdiction requiring indication of security interest on certificate.

§9-401(1), U.C.C.—In all cases, proper place for filing security interests is Recorder of Deeds.

§9-504, U.C.C.—Subsection (3) modified to restrict debtor from renouncing after default right to notice of sale of collateral, in cases involving consumer goods.

§9-505, U.C.C.—Subsection (2) modified to restrict debtor from renouncing after default right to require disposition of collateral by secured party, in cases involving consumer goods.

Optional Provisions.—Following options and alternatives have been elected:

§2-318, U.C.C.—Alternative A elected.

§4-106, U.C.C.—Alternative A elected.

§6-102, U.C.C.—Alternative B elected.

§7-204(4), U.C.C.—Omitted.

§7-403(1)(b), U.C.C.—Material in brackets omitted.

§9-401(1), U.C.C.—Special language.

§9-407, U.C.C.—Section adopted.

§10-104(2), U.C.C.—Substance of optional section adopted.

Permanent Editorial Board's Recommendations for Amendments.—

§2-702.—1966 Official Amendment adopted effective Sept. 13, 1982.

§7-209.—1966 Official Amendment adopted effective Sept. 13, 1982.

Permanent Editorial Board's Recommendations for Optional Amendments.—

§1-209.—1966 Official Optional Amendment not enacted.

§2-318.—1966 Official Optional Amendment not enacted.

1972 Official Amendments.—Adopted effective Sept. 13, 1982.

1973 Official Amendment.—Not adopted.

1977 Official Amendments.—Not adopted.

Secured Transactions under Code.—No official form of financing statement adopted. Requirements are as in 1962 and 1972 Official Texts. For place of filing and fees, see category Documents and Records, topic Records.

See also topics: Banks and Banking, Bills and Notes, Brokers, Carriers, Contracts, Factors, Frauds, Statute of, Sales, Securities, Warehousemen; categories Business Organizations, topic Corporations; Civil Actions and Procedure, topic Limitation of Actions; Debtor and Creditor, topics Assignments, Fraudulent Sales and Conveyances, Liens, Pledges; Documents and Records, topics Records, Seals; Mortgages, topic Chattel Mortgages.

CONDITIONAL SALES:

See topic Sales.

CONSIGNMENTS:

See topic Factors.

See note at head of Digest as to 1998 legislation covered.

See Topical Index in front part of this volume.

CONSUMER PROTECTION:

Revolving Credit Accounts.—Where seller or financial institution extends credit to buyer, whether pursuant to credit card or other specified credit arrangement, unpaid balances are debited to account, credit service charge is computed on outstanding unpaid balance, and buyer has privilege of paying balances in full or in installments, monthly credit service charge may not exceed 2% of outstanding balance. Changes in certain account terms require specified advance notice of change and must provide buyer option to repay existing debt under former account terms, unless buyer incurs additional debt after effective date of change. (§§28-3701, 28-3702).

Consumer Credit Sales and Installment Loans.—Chapter 38 of Title 28 of D. C. Code, applying to actions to enforce rights arising from consumer credit sales not exceeding $25,000 and to direct installment loans as used in §28-3308 (not including loans secured on real estate or direct motor vehicle installment loans), provides various protections for debtors, including (a) prohibition of balloon payments, assignment of earnings, authorization to confess judgment, attorney fees for creditors in excess of 15%, and negotiable instruments in consumer credit sales; (b) subjecting assignee to all claims and defenses of consumer not exceeding amount owing at time of assignment; (c) subjecting lender who makes direct installment loan to consumer to all claims and defenses of consumer not exceeding amount of loan if lender acts at express request of seller and participates in preparation of loan documents or is controlled by or under common control with seller or gives compensation to seller for arranging loan; and (d) regulating cross-collateral arrangements, referral sales, creditor remedies, consumer remedies and debt collection practices. C. 33 of Tit. 28 provides additional debtor protection, including: (a) Right to request twice yearly statements of past payments and unpaid principal; (b) limiting late charges to 5% of late payment; (c) prohibiting misleading practices by lenders; (d) prohibiting hidden acceleration clauses and clauses waiving c. 33 rights (e.g., by advertising or offering services without intent to provide them, or by failing to state material fact); and (e) right of action for lender violations of c. 33, including right to seek punitive damages and reasonable attorney fees.

Home Solicitation Sales.—Where seller of service or goods, other than farm equipment, engages in personal solicitation of sale at or near residence of buyer, buyer has right to cancel home solicitation sale until midnight of third business day after day on which buyer signs agreement or offer to purchase. Cancellation occurs when buyer gives written notice to seller at address stated in agreement, and such notice is given when properly deposited in mail. Except under specified conditions buyer must be informed of right of cancellation. Written waiver by buyer of right to cancel is effective where buyer has requested seller to provide goods or services without delay because of emergency, seller has commenced performance, and goods cannot be returned in substantially as good condition as when received. Within ten days of cancellation, seller must tender to buyer any payments or evidences of indebtedness from buyer, and no cancellation fee may be charged. Goods become property of buyer if seller does not demand their return within reasonable time after cancellation (section presumes 40 days to be reasonable time). (§28-3811).

Telephone Automatic Dialing Sales Prohibited.—It is prohibited to solicit sales or survey information for purposes of sales by means of automatic dialing or push-button or tone activated address signaling telephone system with prerecorded message. Exemptions: Government agency using system for emergency purposes; preexisting business relationship between party calling and party called and call concerns goods, services or real property previously purchased or ordered. Penalty of $1,000 for first violation; $5,000 for each subsequent violation. (§43-1418[a]-[b]).

Prescription Drug, Hearing Aid and Health Spa Sales.—Pharmacies must conspicuously display poster, provided by Department of Consumer and Regulatory Affairs, and must conspicuously post price list of 100 most commonly used prescription drugs, and prices of pharmacy's professional and convenience services, and may dispense, under certain conditions, lowest priced therapeutically equivalent drug to any purchaser presenting prescription for brand name drug. (§33-701 et seq.). Hearing aid dealers must be registered with and approved by Department of Consumer and Regulatory Affairs and must post and/or make available for inspection retail price list of all hearing aids for sale. Hearing aid sales can be made only within three months following purchaser's medical clearance and hearing test examination, except that purchaser may waive examination under certain circumstances, and all such sales must be made with 30-day money-back written guarantee. Each hearing aid sale must also be accompanied by receipt that meets several minimum requirements. (§§28-4001 et seq.). Health spas must register with Department of Consumer and Regulatory Affairs, post with Department bond, irrevocable letter of credit, or cash of no less than $50,000, or, under certain circumstances, $25,000, and annually evidence to Department that bond or letter of credit remains in force. Health spa sales may be cancelled by purchaser within 15 days because of death, illness, injury, or change of residence or change in location of spa. (§28-3817).

Sales of Checks, Drafts, or Money Orders.—Except in case of banks, credit unions, trust companies, and certain building and loan and savings and loan associations, persons engaged in business of selling checks, drafts, personal money orders or certain other instruments for transmission of money must be specifically licensed by District of Columbia. Those applying for license must meet certain net worth, bonding, and other qualifications, are subject to investigation to determine whether qualifications are met, and must submit annual licensing fees. No licensee or his agent may charge fee for selling or cashing checks in excess of 1% of face amount thereof, or 50¢, whichever is greater. (§47-3101 et seq.).

Lay Away Plans.—Sales of consumer goods pursuant to plan whereby three or more agreed payments must be made prior to transfer of such goods are subject to certain disclosure, cancellation, and fee provisions. Buyer may cancel and obtain full refund within two weeks after executing plan. After two weeks, cancellation fee of lesser of 8% of purchase price or $16 may be charged. If seller defaults on delivery of goods, full refund in addition to amount equal to cancellation fee is due. If buyer fails to make timely payment, notice of delinquency must be sent, and, after 14 days, seller may deduct $1 from amount paid by buyer and refund balance. Acceleration of payments is prohibited. Disclosure of payment schedule, statement that goods will be retained by seller until final payment, statement of refund and exchange policies, and description of certain statutory provisions governing plan must precede execution of plan. Written receipt and description of goods identified in plan must accompany or, in certain circumstances, follow all payments. (§28-3818).

Employment Services.—Person who for fee provides employment services to employers or job-seekers must register with, and obtain license from, Mayor of District of Columbia. Persons who receive fees from job-seekers must post bonds with Mayor as follows: Employment agencies and employment counsellors ($100,000 or $50,000, depending on average fee and volume); job-listing services ($5,000). Employment agency and counsellor contracts with job-seekers must be in writing and meet type-size, plain language and notice requirements. Job-seekers may cancel such contracts by written notification within three days of signing. (§36-1001 et seq.).

Rental Housing Locators.—Person who for fee provides information about rental units available for rent must register with Department of Consumer and Regulatory Affairs. Locator must update information and may only provide information concerning units publicly held out as available for rent or where given permission to do so by unit owner/manager. Rental housing locator contracts must be in writing and in compliance with accuracy, notice, and refund requirements. (§28-3819).

Prohibited Conditions for Accepting Check or Credit Card.—Seller may request but not require consumer to produce credit card as condition of accepting check, nor require address and telephone number of consumer as condition of accepting credit card. Seller may not imprint credit card information on face or back of check, nor record number of credit card as condition to accepting check. (§47-3152). Aggrieved party may institute suit for actual damages or $500, whichever is greater, plus attorneys' fees. (§47-3151 et seq.).

Natural Disasters.—Restrictions on raising prices of goods or services during period of natural disaster. Fine of up to $1,000 and revocation of license or permit for violation. (§28-4101 et seq.).

Uniform Deceptive Trade Practices Act, adopted. (§28-3904).

Investment Advisers Act of 1992.—Regulates investment advisers, i.e., persons who are in business of providing advice as to securities for compensation. Excluded are banks, lawyers, accountants, engineers, teachers, publishers and certain other occupations or fiduciary positions. Act prohibits fraud, deceit, and unethical conduct as may be defined by Public Service Commission of District of Columbia. Investment adviser is required to register with Commission, maintain prescribed records and preserve them for three years. Commission is authorized to investigate, take evidence and subpoena witnesses, conduct hearings, deny, suspend or revoke registration, and obtain contempt orders and injunctions from court. Under private right of action, party proving violation of antifraud provisions can recover (1) consideration paid for advice, plus interest, (2) actual damages proximately caused, (3) attorneys' fees and costs. Action must be brought within two years after rendering of investment advice, except in case of fraud, for which actions may be brought within two years from date person discovered or should have discovered fraud. Violators are also subject to civil and criminal penalties. (§§2-2631-2652). Public Service Commission's rules of practice and procedure apply to Act. (17 DCMR c.18 §1823). Effective 2/03/95.

Department of Consumer and Regulatory Affairs has broad powers to receive and investigate complaints, issue summonses and subpoenas, hold hearings, take testimony under oath, issue cease and desist orders with respect to trade practices determined to be in violation of District law by Department and appoint private attorneys from D.C. bar to take action in name of Department. (§§28-3902 et seq.). Department also regulates street vendors, (24 DCMR §500 et seq.).

Plain Language.—No universally applicable plain language statute.

See topics Sales, subhead Retail Credit Sales, Interest, subheads Maximum Rate and Usury, Commercial Code, subhead Material Variations; categories Insurance, topic Insurance Companies, subheads Policies and Rates; Transportation, topic Motor Vehicles, subheads Titles and Sales and Automobile Consumer Protection.

CONTRACTS:

Uniform Commerical Code adopted. See topic Commercial Code; categories Documents and Records, topic Seals; Family, topic Infants.

FACTORS:

Factor's liens are now regulated by Uniform Commercial Code. See topic Commercial Code.

License Requirements.—Commission merchants dealing in food must obtain annual license. (§47-2827).

FRANCHISES:

District of Columbia Franchising Act of 1988, which became effective Mar. 16, 1989 (D.C. Code, §§29-1201-1208) is repealed, (D.C. Law 12-86, 45 DCR 1172, §1002, effective Apr. 29, 1998).

District of Columbia has not adopted Uniform Franchise and Business Opportunities Act.

No person or entity may operate cable television system within District without first obtaining franchise pursuant to Cable Television Communications Act of 1981 (§43-1801 et seq.), as amended by Cable Television Franchise Amendment Act of 1996 (Law 11-210, 44 DCR 2405).

FRAUDS, STATUTE OF:

No estate of inheritance or for life or for a longer term than one year in any real property in the District, and no declaration or limitation of uses in the same for any of such estates, may take effect except by deed signed and sealed by grantor, declarant or lessor, or by will. (§45-306). Estate in real property attempted to be created for more than one year in manner other than by deed is estate by sufferance. (§28-3501).

FRAUDS, STATUTE OF ... *continued*

No action may be brought to charge executor or administrator upon special promise to answer for damages out of his own estate or to charge defendant upon any special promise to answer for debt, default, or miscarriage of another person, or to charge person upon agreement made in consideration of marriage, or upon contract or sale of real estate, or upon any agreement that is not to be performed within one year of making it, unless agreement upon which such action is brought is in writing, which need not state consideration, and is signed by party to be charged or person authorized by him. (§28-3502).

Statute of frauds is applicable to contracts for sale of goods for $500 or more, with exceptions, as set forth in Uniform Commercial Code. (§28:2-201). See topic Commercial Code.

Equitable doctrines of promissory estoppel, equitable estoppel, and waiver by admission are applied by local courts.

INTEREST:

In absence of agreement, legal rate is 6% per annum. (§28-3302).

Maximum Rate.—D. C. Code sections cited in this paragraph are as amended by Interest Rate Ceiling Amendment Act of 1983 (D. C. Law 5-62), effective Mar. 14, 1984. By contract in writing, 24% per annum may be charged. (§28-3301). Interest rate ceiling established by §28-3301 is subject to, and in some cases, is preempted or rendered inapplicable by, §§501-529 of Depository Institutions Deregulation and Monetary Control Act of 1980. (12 U.S.C. §§86a, 1730g, 1735f-7, 1785, and 1931d; 15 U.S.C. §687). Any loans secured by deed of trust on residential real property or security interest in stock or membership certificate in cooperative housing or assignment by way of security of borrower's interest in proprietary lease lien or right of tenancy is subject to following requirements: (a) Loan is both contracted for and consummated after effective date of said Act of 1983 and no written commitment to make loan at rate lower than 24% was issued by lender to borrower prior to such effective date, (b) loan may be prepaid by borrower at no penalty at any time following expiration of three years from execution of loan transaction, and within three years from execution of loan transaction no prepayment charge shall be contracted for or received which exceeds amount equal to two months advance interest on aggregate amount of all prepayments in excess of one-third of amount of original loan transaction made in any 12 month period, (c) any borrower who, on date of execution of loan transaction, has made down payment equalling 20% or more of total purchase price of property or who has equity interest in property equal to or greater than 20% of fair market value of property must not be required by term of loan to make advance payments of real estate taxes or casualty insurance premiums to enable lender to have funds on hand for disbursement of payment of such taxes or insurance premiums, and such borrower must be furnished with separate statement, in writing, which clearly and conspicuously set forth his right to pay such taxes and insurance premiums directly, and (d) prior to execution of loan transaction, lender must furnish borrower with separate statement, in writing, which complies with disclosure statements of Truth-in-Lending Act and regulations and interpretations thereunder, and, where applicable, separate statement, in writing, which complies with disclosure provisions of Alternative Mortgage Transaction Parity Act of 1982, and regulations and interpretations thereunder. (§28-3301 [b], [c], [f]). However, any federally insured bank or savings and loan association doing business in District of Columbia may charge interest up to 24% per annum or finance charge which, if expressed as annual percentage rate, does not exceed 24% per annum on direct installment loan (other than loan directly secured on real estate) (§28-3308); and such bank or association may charge interest up to 24% per annum or finance charge which, if expressed as annual percentage rate, does not exceed 21% per annum on direct motor vehicle installment loan (§§28-3601 to 3602).

Judgments.—Interest at rate of 4% is allowed on judgments against District of Columbia or its officers or employees acting within scope of their employment. Where judgment is not against District of Columbia or its officers or employees acting within scope of their employment, or where rate of interest is not fixed by contract, interest is 70% of rate of interest set by Secretary of Treasury pursuant to §6621 of Internal Revenue Code of 1986 (100 Stat. 2085; 26 U.S.C. §6621) for underpayments and overpayments of tax to Internal Revenue Service, rounded to nearest full percent, or if exactly 1/2 of 1%, increased to nearest full percent; provided that court may lower such rate of interest for good cause shown or upon showing that judgment debtor in good faith is unable to pay judgment (§28-3302).

Open Accounts.—While there are no statutes directly appertaining to the rate of interest on open account, where there is no rate of interest agreed upon between the parties, there are some decisions which hold that interest may be awarded, in the discretion of the jury, after the account is overdue, as part of the damages suffered, and where the suit is for a liquidated sum, interest may be awarded from the date the account becomes due.

Small Loans.—It is illegal to engage in the business of lending money at a rate of interest greater than 6% without procuring a license as a moneylender. With such a license, lawful rate, set by c. 23 of Tit. 28, may be charged, which must cover all fees and expenses except those attendant upon foreclosure; such interest may not be deducted from principal when the loan is made. (§§26-701, 705). The Small Loans Act does not apply with respect to any loan: (1) To corporation unable to plead usury, (2) secured on real estate outside District, (3) to borrower residing, doing business or incorporated outside District, or (4) greater than $25,000. (§26-712).

Usury.—In the case of small loans, the penalty for usury is loss of interest and one-fourth of the principal, fine of $300 and imprisonment for not less than 30 days or more than 90 days, and restitution of property illegally obtained; in other cases, forfeiture of interest. (§§26-705; 26-707; 28-3303). Usurious interest paid may be recovered. (§28-3304).

Cooperative associations formed under D.C. Cooperative Association Act are exempt from D.C. laws regulating licenses for loans and interest rates, in loans for members in connection with utility operations (§29-1143); and D.C. Council is authorized to exempt from the 6% interest limitation any mortgage or loan insured or guaranteed under National Housing Act or Chapter 37 of Title 38, U.S. Code, interest rate of which is subject to regulation by an officer or agency of Federal Government (§28-3307). D.C. Council has granted such exemption. (D.C. Law 2-140).

Lenders are authorized to contract for or receive any rate of interest on loans in excess of $1,000 if borrower is not-for-profit corporation or religious society under c. 9 of Tit. 29 of D.C. Code, or if loan is made for purpose of acquiring or carrying on business or acquiring real or personal property as investment or carrying on investment activity. (§28-3301[d], as am'd by Interest Rate Ceiling Amendment Act of 1983, effective Mar. 14, 1984).

LICENSES, BUSINESS AND PROFESSIONAL:

Licenses and license fees are required of persons engaged in most trades and businesses (§§47-2808-2840) including street vendors (§47-2834, 24 DCMR §502), and health professions (2-3301.1 et seq.), real estate brokers and salesmen (§45-1926), mortgage brokers and mortgage lenders (§§26-1001-1014), and insurance agents and brokers (§§35-1321-1334). All businesses must obtain either Class A license (requiring inspection) or Class B license (not requiring inspection) from Business License Center of Department of Consumer and Regulatory Affairs. (§§47-2851.1—2851.17). Council has power by legislation to impose license fee sufficient to cover cost of inspection supervision, regulation, or other activity or expenditure on any occupation not specifically provided for (§47-2842). License fees for hospitals and other health care facilities are set forth in 22 DCMR §§2013, 3114. In most instances, application for license is made to Mayor. (§47-2801). However, where special board commission, or office has been set up, as in real estate (§§45-1921 et seq.), architecture (§§2-241 et seq.), banking (see topic Brokers, for mortgage brokers and mortgage lenders), insurance (see category Insurance, topic Insurance Companies), and most professional or quasi-professional occupations (§§2-101 et seq., §2-3305.5), application is made to appropriate board. See Title 17 DCMR (Business, Occupations and Professions).

With exception of licenses or permits required pursuant to Construction Code Approval and Amendments Act of 1976 (§5-1301 et seq.), or any license or permit determined by Mayor to be necessary to remedy unsafe and hazardous condition that presents immediate threat to public health or safety, District government will not issue or reissue any license or permit to any applicant if applicant owes more than $100 in outstanding debt to District as result of fines, penalties or interest assessed pursuant to Litter Control Administration Act of 1985 (§6-2901 et seq.), Illegal Dumping Enforcement Act of 1994 (§6-2911 et seq.), or Department of Consumer and Regulatory Affairs Civil Infractions Act of 1985, or as result of past due taxes. Clean Hands Before Receiving a License or Permit Act of 1996. (§47-2861-2866). Mayor may also, upon 30 days notice, revoke or refuse to issue driver's license or any professional or business license to parent more than 60 days behind in child support payments. If obligor is member of D.C. Bar, Clerk of Court shall send written notice to Board of Professional Responsibility so that appropriate action may be taken. Child Support Enforcement and Licensing Compliance Amendment Act of 1995. (§30-525).

Every person engaged in certain enumerated professions, including certified public accountants, lawyers, architects, registered professional engineers, persons licensed as interior designers, and persons licensed, certified, or registered to practice medicine, dentistry, optometry, acupuncture, chiropractic, podiatry, or psychology shall file for professional license with Mayor, by Dec. 1, each year; fee is $250. (§§47-1814.1, 1814.1a). Exemptions for employees of local, state or national government, employees of certain international organizations, inactive attorneys, pro bono legal services attorneys, attorneys employed by nonprofit organizations serving indigent clients, and retired judges. (§47-1814.1a).

Collection Agencies.—See topic Consumer Protection, subhead Consumer Credit Sales and Installment Loans.

MONOPOLIES, RESTRAINT OF TRADE AND COMPETITION:

The Sherman Anti-Trust Act and similar federal legislation apply in the District to intrastate as well as interstate transactions. (U. S. Code, T. 15, §3; 286 U. S. 427).

District of Columbia Antitrust Act also became effective Mar. 5, 1981. (D. C. Code, §§28-4501-4518). This Act parallels §§1 and 2 of Sherman Act (U. S. Code, T. 15, §§1, 2) prohibiting contracts, combinations or conspiracies in restraint of trade, and monopolization, conspiracy to monopolize, or attempt to monopolize. Federal court interpretations of comparable statutes can be used as guide in construing Act. Violation is misdemeanor, punishable by fine not exceeding $50,000 and/or imprisonment not exceeding one year. Individual directors, officers and agents who intentionally order, authorize or ratify violations are subject to criminal penalties. Private parties may bring treble damage actions and seek injunctions or other equitable relief. Indirect purchasers may recover damages, contrary to rule of Illinois Brick Co. v. Illinois, 431 U. S. 720; and defendants may assert "pass-on defense," contrary to rule of Hanover Shoe, Inc. v. United Shoe Machinery Corp., 392 U. S. 481. Corporation Counsel may bring action for damages on behalf of District government, seek injunctive or equitable relief, or bring parens patriae action on behalf of District residents. Act has four year statute of limitations for civil actions. Under District of Columbia Criminal Statute of Limitations Act of 1982 (D. C. Law 4-104, codified at D. C. Code §23-113), three year statute of limitations applies to criminal actions. Corporation Counsel has authority to issue "civil investigative demand" similar to that authorized under Federal statute for Department of Justice. Act excludes certain organizations from coverage, including nonprofit labor, agricultural or horticultural organizations seeking to carry out their legitimate objectives; religious, charitable, literary, and educational organizations; regulated industries and monopolies to extent their activity is specifically regulated, permitted, or required by any regulatory body, agency or commission acting under authority of District or Federal law; and Washington Metropolitan Area Transit Authority. Nonprofit cooperative association does not violate D.C. Antitrust Act if its activities comply with D.C. Cooperative Association Act. (D.C. Code, §§29-1101-1147).

D.C. Code, §33-742, relating to "Prescription Drug Price Information" treats as restraint of trade any interference with: (1) Disclosure of information relating to

See note at head of Digest as to 1998 legislation covered.

See Topical Index in front part of this volume.

MONOPOLIES, RESTRAINT OF TRADE AND COMPETITION . . . *continued*
prescription drugs, including price information; (2) retail drug price-setting, substitution, or marketing policy or action; and (3) supply of prescription drugs to pharmacies, government agencies, health insurers, or other purchasers. These purchasers may bring treble damages actions for such interference.

Fair Trade Act.—See category Intellectual Property, topic Trademarks and Tradenames.

NEGOTIABLE INSTRUMENTS:

See topic Bills and Notes.

RESTRAINT OF TRADE:

See topic Monopolies, Restraint of Trade and Competition.

SALES:

Uniform Commercial Code in effect. Art. 2 replaces Uniform Sales Act. See topic Commercial Code.

Bills of Sale.—No statutory provisions as to form or necessity of bill of sale.

Retail Credit Sales.—Credit service charge not exceeding 2% per month may be charged by seller of goods or services or by financial institution pursuant to credit card or other arrangement between seller or financial institution and retail buyer. Seller or financial institution may impose or increase any credit service charge, change method of computing balance, or increase required minimum periodic payment, provided seller or financial institution: (1) Mails written notice of change to buyer at least 30 days prior to effective date of change; and (2) permits buyer to repay under existing terms any debt incurred prior to effective date of change. (§§28-3701, 3702). Requirements as to form of such written notice are specified in §28-3702.

Consumer Protection.—See topic Consumer Protection.

Conditional Sales are among the devices governed by Art. 9 of Uniform Commercial Code, dealing with secured transactions. See topic Commercial Code.

Bulk Sales.—See category Debtor and Creditor, topic Fraudulent Sales and Conveyances.

Sales of Motor Vehicles.—See category Transportation, topic Motor Vehicles.

Sales of Cigarettes.—Under Cigarette Sales Below Cost Act of 1994, no individual or entity doing business in District of Columbia may, for purpose of injuring competitors or destroying competition, sell, offer for sale, or advertise for sale cigarettes for less than cost, either at retail or wholesale. (§28-4521 et seq.).

International Sales of Goods.—See Part VI of this volume, Selected International Conventions.

SECURITIES:

Federal Securities Act (15 U.S.C. §77a) governs both intrastate and interstate transactions in the District.

"Blue Sky" law or D. C. Securities Act is substantially same as Uniform Securities Act (1956 Act), except that provisions relating to: (1) Investment advisers and investment advice, (2) registration of securities, and (3) prohibition against use of private information for personal benefit by government officials administering Act are omitted. Act also contains provisions for civil penalties in lieu of criminal penalties that are not in Uniform Act. Act provides for licensing of broker-dealers and agents, with licensing requirements same as registration under Uniform Act. Minimum capital requirement of broker-dealer is variable, and conforms with Securities Exchange Act Rule 15-c3. Initial or renewal license fee for broker-dealer firm is fixed by Department of Insurance and Securities Regulations. (§2-2604). Licenses must be renewed once each year. (§2-2603). Act is administered by Department of Insurance and Securities Regulation. (§2-2616).

"Bucket shopping" is unlawful (§22-1510), and if any dealer in securities fails, within 24 hours after demand, to furnish to a customer for whom he has executed a purchase or sale of securities a written statement containing name of buyer or seller, time, place and price, such neglect is prima facie evidence of bucketing. (§22-1512).

Uniform Commercial Code in effect. (§28:1-101 et seq.). See topic Commercial Code.

Uniform Simplification of Fiduciary Security Transfers Act adopted. (§§28-2901-2909). Act prevails over inconsistent provisions of Art. 8 of Uniform Commercial Code. (§28:10-104). See topic Commercial Code.

Uniform Transfers to Minors Act in effect since 3/12/86. (§§21-301-324). See category Family, topic Infants.

Investment Advisers Act regulates investment advisers and establishes procedures for registration and monitoring. (§2631 et seq., 15 DCMR §1800 et seq.). See topic Consumer Protection.

STATUTE OF FRAUDS:

See topic Frauds, Statute of.

TRUST RECEIPT SECURITY:

Trust receipts are among the devices governed by Art. 9 of Uniform Commercial Code. See topic Commercial Code.

WAREHOUSEMEN:

Warehouse receipts and other documents of title and rights, duties and liabilities of warehousemen are governed by Uniform Commercial Code. Art. 7 of Code replaces Uniform Warehouse Receipts Act. See topic Commercial Code.

CITIZENSHIP

ALIENS:

Property.—Restrictions on ownership of real property by aliens contained in 48 U.S.C. §§1501-07 are made expressly applicable to District of Columbia (§§45-1301); however, under 48 U.S.C. §1502, as construed in Larkin v. Washington Loan and Trust Co., 31 F.2d 635 (D.C. Cir.), cert. denied, 279 U.S. 867 (1929) there is no restriction on ownership of land by aliens in District of Columbia.

See also categories Employment, topic Labor Relations; Estates and Trusts, topic Executors and Administrators, subhead Eligibility and Competency.

CIVIL ACTIONS AND PROCEDURE

ACCORD AND SATISFACTION:

By judicial construction, the tender of a sum in settlement of a disputed item or items and the acceptance by the creditor, even though the latter receive it only on account, operates as an accord and satisfaction. (291 A.2d 187; 32 App. D. C. 392).

Compromise.—Any one of several joint debtors when their debt is overdue may make a separate composition or compromise with a creditor. (§16-2106).

Pleading.—Accord and satisfaction must be pleaded affirmatively if relied upon.

Uniform Commercial Code adopted. See category Business Regulation and Commerce, topic Commercial Code.

ACTIONS:

The Federal Rules of Civil Procedure (1938), as amended, govern all actions in the District Court except as provided therein. (See Rule 81, F. R. C. P.).

Superior Court has adopted rules that are substantially identical to Federal Rules, and that abolish forms of action and distinction between law and equity, and permit joinder of any legal or equitable claims in one proceeding. (§11-946; Sup. Ct. Civ. R. 1-2, 18).

Condition Precedent.—No action may be maintained against District of Columbia for unliquidated damages to person or property unless notice thereof is given in writing to Mayor within six months of injury, reporting approximate time, place, cause and circumstances thereof. Report by police department is sufficient. (§12-309).

Commencement.—Every civil action is commenced by filing a complaint with court, whereupon clerk issues summons. See topic Pleading; also topic Practice.

Abatement and Revival.—On the death of any person in whose favor or against whom a right of action has accrued for any cause, right of action survives in favor of or against legal representative of deceased. (§12-101). No pending action abates if right of action survives. If action has been commenced, death of decedent may be suggested to court and his legal representative may be substituted in his place and stead. (§12-102. See Rule 25[a] F. R. C. P.).

Actions commenced against the head of a Department or Bureau and other United States or District of Columbia officers in an official capacity, do not abate because of death of such officers, and successor in office is automatically substituted as defendant. (Rule 25[d] F. R. C. P.).

Limitations of.—See topic Limitation of Actions.

Small Claims.—See category Courts and Legislature, topic Courts.

Direct Actions Against Insurer.—No statutory provisions.

APPEAL AND ERROR:

From U.S. District Court.—Appeal lies from any final order, judgment, or decree and from certain interlocutory orders of U.S. District Court to U.S. Court of Appeals for District of Columbia Circuit or, in certain cases, to U.S. Court of Appeals for Federal Circuit, see 28 U.S.C. §1295, as matter of right, but notice of appeal in civil cases must be filed within 30 days after entry of order, judgment, or decree; if U.S. or officer or agency thereof is party, notice of appeal may be filed by any party within 60 days after such entry; and notice of appeal in criminal cases shall be filed within ten days after entry of order or judgment. (28 U.S.C. 1291, 1292[a], 2107; Rule 4, F.R.A.P.). Appeal also lies, but not as matter of right, in case of certain interlocutory orders of U.S. District Court certified to involve controlling question of law, but petition for permission to appeal must be filed within ten days after entry of order. (28 U.S.C. 1292[b]; Rule 5, F.R.A.P.). Appeal does not lie to U.S. Court of Appeals from decision or order of U.S. District Court which may be reviewed directly by U.S. Supreme Court.

Federal Rules of Appellate Procedure, as supplemented by local rules, regulate appeals from U.S. District Court to Court of Appeals. District Court may require appellant to file bond or provide other security in such form and amount as it finds necessary to ensure payment of costs on appeal in civil case. (Rule 7, F.R.A.P.). To obtain stay on appeal, supersedeas bond may be necessary. (Rule 8, F.R.A.P.).

From Superior Court.—Appeal lies from any final judgment and certain interlocutory orders of Superior Court of District of Columbia to District of Columbia Court of Appeals, as a matter of right, but notice of appeal must be filed within period specified below (§11-721[b], [a][2]); except that judgments of Small Claims and Conciliation Branch of Superior Court and judgments in Criminal Division of Superior Court where penalty imposed is fine of less than $50 for offense punishable by imprisonment of one year or less, or by fine of not more than $1,000, or both, are reviewable only upon granting of application for allowance of appeal (§11-721[c]). Appeal also lies, but not as matter of right, in case of certain rulings and orders certified by Superior Court to involve controlling question of law. (§11-721[d]). Note that District of Columbia Court of Appeals also may answer questions of law certified to it by U.S. Supreme Court, any U.S. Court of Appeals or highest appellate court of any State, if there are involved in proceeding before certifying court questions of District of Columbia law which may be determinative of cause and as to which there appears to be no controlling precedent in decisions of District of Columbia Court of Appeals. (§11-723).

See note at head of Digest as to 1998 legislation covered.

See Topical Index in front part of this volume.

APPEAL AND ERROR . . . *continued*

Appeals are governed by rules of District of Columbia Court of Appeals. Notice of appeal as of right in civil cases must be filed within 30 days after entry of judgment or order, and notice of appeal in criminal cases must be filed within 30 days after entry of order or judgment, except as otherwise specified by District of Columbia Code. (Rule 4). Application for appeal when required pursuant to §11-721(c) must be filed within three days from date of judgment or order. (Rule 6). Application for permission to appeal from ruling or order described in §11-721(d) must be filed within ten days after entry of order. (Rule 5). To obtain stay on appeal, bond may be required. (Rule 8).

From District of Columbia Court of Appeals.—Final judgments and decrees of District of Columbia Court of Appeals in civil cases are reviewable only by U.S. Supreme Court pursuant to 28 U.S.C. 1257. (§11-102).

From U.S. Court of Appeals.—Judgments of U.S. Court of Appeals for District of Columbia Circuit may be reviewed by U.S. Supreme Court pursuant to 28 U.S.C. 1254.

BONDS:

A bond signifies an obligation in a certain sum or penalty, subject to condition, on breach of which it is to become absolute and enforcible by action. (§28-2501). An undertaking signifies an agreement entered into by a party to a proceeding upon which judgment in same suit may be entered against said party and his sureties. (§28-2501). In all cases, except with respect to bond in attachment before judgment (51 App. D. C. 109, 276 Fed. 631), where a bond is required from a fiduciary or from any party to a cause in District Court or Superior Court such bond must be in form of an undertaking, under seal, in an amount fixed by court, conditioned as required by law, sureties therein submitting themselves to jurisdiction of court and undertaking to perform judgment or decree of court and that, upon default, damages may be ascertained in such manner as court may direct in cause or proceeding (§16-601).

Sureties.—Court bonds, except supersedeas and undertakings required by §40-407, may be approved by clerk of District Court and clerk of Superior Court by consent of where surety is a corporation holding Treasury authority to do business in District and having process agent therein. In all other cases, approval of Court is required, and two days written notice of application for approval must be served on all parties. No member of bar in active practice or other officer of court will be accepted as surety. (Dist. Ct. Rule 116; Sup. Ct. Civ. R. 77-II[a][3] and 303[b] and [c]).

Enforcement.—The court is vested with jurisdiction to enter such judgments and orders against the principal and sureties, or any of them, upon an undertaking, as law and justice shall require, but any party having a cause of action under such an undertaking may elect to pursue his ordinary remedy by suit. (§16-601). Counsel fee may be allowed in proceeding to recover damages on bond or undertaking for restraining order or injunction. (§15-111). Damages recovered as against surety on penal bond may not exceed penalty of bond. (§28-2502).

CERTIORARI:

Supreme Court and all courts established by Act of Congress may issue all writs (including certiorari) necessary or appropriate in aid of their respective jurisdictions. (28 U.S.C. §1651).

The Supreme Court of the United States may review any case in U.S. Court of Appeals for District of Columbia Circuit or D.C. Court of Appeals by writ of certiorari granted upon petition of any party to any civil or criminal case, as specified in 28 U.S.C. 1254 and 1257. (28 U.S.C. 1254 and 1257).

CHARITABLE IMMUNITY:

See topic Damages.

COMMISSIONS TO TAKE TESTIMONY:

See topic Depositions and Discovery.

COSTS:

Except when express provision is made either in appropriate statute or in rule, costs are allowed as of course to prevailing party unless court directs otherwise. (Sup. Ct. Civ. R. 54[d]). Costs allowable in U.S. District Court and procedure for filing bill of costs are governed by Dist. Ct. Rule 214. Persons financially unable to pay costs may, with approval of court, file and prosecute cases without prepayment of fees and costs or security therefor. (§§15-712, 16-3903, Sup. Ct. Civ. R. 54-II).

Security for Costs.—Nonresident plaintiff may be required to give security for costs, or by order of court a satisfactory deposit may be made with the clerk in lieu of an undertaking to pay costs. (§§15-711, 703).

DAMAGES:

Common law generally prevails, except as to actions of replevin. (§16-3710, 3711).

Charitable Immunity.—Doctrine not a defense against claim of strangers or beneficiaries to charity. (130 F.2d 810; 251 F.Supp. 614).

Comparative Negligence Rule.—Not adopted.

DECLARATORY JUDGMENTS:

See topic Judgments.

DEPOSITIONS AND DISCOVERY:

Circumstances under which depositions in the District Court may be employed and procedure therein are governed by rules 26-32 and 37 of the Federal Rules of Civil Procedure as am'd.

Superior Court of District of Columbia has adopted rules pertaining to depositions substantially same as those of Federal Rules of Civil Procedure. (Sup. Ct. Civ. R. 26-32 and 37).

Within District for Use Elsewhere.—(a) Federal Rules of Civil Procedure govern for depositions to be used in United States District Courts; (b) when a commission is issued by any court of a state for taking testimony of witnesses within District, such testimony may be taken by leave of a judge of U.S. District Court or District of Columbia Superior Court in manner prescribed by rules applicable to court from which leave is obtained. (§14-103; Sup. Ct. Civ. R. 28-I[b]).

Without District for Use Therein.—Judge of District Court or of Superior Court may appoint a person to take deposition of nonresident witnesses whose testimony is required in a civil action pending in District of Columbia. (§14-104; F.R.C.P. 28; Sup. Ct. Civ. R. 28-I[a]).

Perpetuating Testimony.—Governed by Sup. Ct. Civ. R. 27, which is virtually identical to Fed. R. Civ. P. 27.

Before Whom Taken.—Governed by Sup. Ct. Civ. R. 28, which is virtually identical to Fed. R. Civ. P. 28.

Compelling Attendance of Witnesses.—Witnesses may be compelled to attend deposition by subpoena, which will be issued by clerk upon proof of service of notice to take deposition. Proof of service is made by filing copy of notice of deposition and certification of date of service and persons served with clerk. Subpoena may command witness to produce documents and tangible things within scope of examination. Person to whom subpoena is directed may serve written objection to production of requested documents within ten days of service or time for compliance, whichever is shorter. If objection is so made, production will not be compelled unless court order is obtained by party serving subpoena. Resident of district in which deposition is to be taken may be required to attend examination only in county wherein he resides or is employed or transacts business, or at some other convenient place fixed by order of court. Nonresident of district may be required to attend only in county wherein he is served with subpoena, or within 40 miles of place of service, or at some other convenient place fixed by order of court. (Sup. Ct. Civ. R. 45).

Examination of Witnesses.—Governed by Sup. Ct. Civ. R. 30(c), which is substantially similar to Fed. R. Civ. P. 30(c).

Uniform Foreign Depositions Act not adopted.

EQUITY:

See topic Actions.

EVIDENCE:

See topic Depositions and Discovery.

Witnesses.—Parties may testify on their own behalf in both civil and criminal proceedings, except as hereinafter stated.

Officer of corporation party is competent. (56 App. D.C. 327, 13 F.2d 299). Persons convicted of crime are not thereby incompetent. (§14-305).

Privileged Communications.—Professional communications to attorney are privileged. (97 U.S. App. D.C. 254, 230 F.2d 222). Professional communications to physicians or surgeons or mental health professionals as defined in §6-2001 et seq. are privileged except: (1) In criminal cases where accused is charged with causing death of, or inflicting injuries upon, human being, and disclosure is required in interest of public justice, (2) as evidence relating to mental competence or sanity of accused in criminal trial where insanity defense is raised or in pre- or post-trial proceedings where issue arises, (3) as evidence relating to mental competence or sanity of child alleged to be delinquent, neglected, or in need of supervision in proceeding before Family Division of Superior Court, or (4) as evidence relating to alleged fraud with respect to services provided under District's medical assistance program. (§14-307). Professional communications to ministers of religion are privileged. (§14-309).

Husband and wife are competent, but not compellable, to testify for or against each other in either civil or criminal cases, but may not testify to confidential communications made by one to the other during marriage. (§14-306).

Children.—For child called as witness in delinquency proceeding, and ordered to testify despite claim of privilege against self-incrimination, no testimony or other information compelled under such order or derived from such testimony or other information may be used against witness except in proceeding for perjury, false statement, or failure to comply with order. (§16-2339).

Communications or Transactions with Persons since Deceased or Incompetent.—In any civil action against a person legally incapable of testifying or against the committee, trustee, executor, administrator, heir, legatee, devisee, assignee, or other representative of a deceased person or of the person so incapable of testifying, no judgment shall be rendered in favor of the plaintiff founded on the uncorroborated testimony of the plaintiff or his agent as to any transaction with, declaration or admission of the deceased or incapable person. In such action if the plaintiff or his agent testifies as to any such transaction, declaration or admission, no entry, memorandum or declaration by the deceased or incapable person shall be excluded as hearsay. (§14-302).

Compelling Attendance.—District Court is a federal court and as such may compel attendance of a witness from anywhere in U.S. in a criminal case and within 100 miles in a civil case. Superior Court may compel attendance of witnesses if found anywhere in District of Columbia, or outside District and within 25 miles of place of hearing or trial. In criminal case in which felony is charged, Superior Court may compel attendance of witness from anywhere in U.S. (§11-942). Attendance of witnesses found within District in criminal proceeding in state court and attendance of witnesses found within state in criminal proceedings in District may be compelled under District of Columbia Uniform Act to Secure Attendance of Witnesses from Without a State in Criminal Proceedings. (§§23-1501-1504).

INJUNCTIONS:

Federal Rules of Civil Procedure (Rule 65), Dist. Ct. Rule 205, and Federal Rules of Appellate Procedure (Rule 8) govern issuance of injunctions and temporary restraining orders in U.S. District Court and U.S. Court of Appeals for District of Columbia

INJUNCTIONS . . . *continued*
Circuit. Superior Court has jurisdiction to issue injunctions and temporary restraining orders in cases which may properly be filed in that court. (Sup. Ct. Civ. R. 65).

JUDGMENTS:

Procedure with respect to judgments is controlled by Federal Rules of Civil Procedure which govern District Court and to which Superior Court adheres closely.

Declaratory judgments may be had pursuant to provisions of 28 U.S.C. 2201, F. R. C. P. No. 57, and Sup. Ct. Civ. R. 57.

Lien.—Every final judgment or decree for payment of money of District Court or of Superior Court for 12 years from date of filing and recording in Office of Recorder of Deeds, and every recognizance taken by said District Court or Superior Court when entry or order of forfeiture is filed and recorded in Office of Recorder of Deeds, is a lien on all freehold and leasehold estates, legal and equitable, of defendants bound by such judgment, decree or recognizance, in any lands, tenements or hereditaments in District, whether such estates be in possession or be reversions or remainders, vested or contingent. (§15-102).

Effect and operation of a judgment or decree, including lien thereby created and all remedies for its enforcement, are extended for a period of 12 years from date of an order reviving said judgment or decree when said order is issued within 12 years after either rendition of the judgment or decree or after date of a previous revival order. (§15-103).

Revival.—There is no provision for revival of dormant judgments.

Assignment.—In Superior Court, judgment or money decree may be assigned in writing. Upon filing of assignment in clerk's office, assignee may maintain action or sue out execution in his own name. (§28-2301).

Uniform Enforcement of Foreign Judgments Act adopted. (§§15-351-357).

Uniform Foreign Money-Judgments Recognition Act adopted. (§§15-381-388).

Uniform Foreign-Money Claims Act adopted. (§§15-901-914).

LIMITATION OF ACTIONS:

Actions must be brought within the following periods after the respective causes of action accrue:

Fifteen Years: For recovery of lands, tenements or hereditaments. (§12-301).

Twelve Years: On bonds, single bills, covenants or other instruments under seal. (§12-301).

Ten Years: To recover damages for personal injury, injury to real or personal property, or wrongful death resulting from defective or unsafe condition of improvement to real property. (§12-310). Limitation does not apply to any action based on contract or any action brought against owner or person in actual possession or control of such real property or any manufacturer or supplier of equipment or machinery installed upon real property or any action brought by District of Columbia government. (§12-310).

Five Years: On any executor's or administrator's bond. (§12-301). For assessment of District income tax if return omits substantial gross income. (§47-1812.10). For recovery of damages for injury to real property from toxic substances including products containing asbestos. Period runs from date injury is discovered or with reasonable diligence should have been discovered. (§12-301).

Four Years: Action for breach of any contract for sale of goods must be commenced within four years after cause of action accrues. Limitation period may be reduced to not less than one year by agreement. (§28:2-725). Uniform Commercial Code in effect. See topic Commercial Code.

Three Years: On any simple contract, express or implied, for injury to any real or personal property, for recovery of personal property or damages for its unlawful detention. (§12-301). For assessment of District income and personal property taxes where return properly filed; for collection of income or franchise tax, from date of assessment if properly made (§47-1812.10); for collection of income tax from decedent's estates, running from date of return (§47-1812.10).

One Year: For any statutory penalty or forfeiture, for libel, slander, assault, battery, mayhem, wounding, malicious prosecution, false arrest or false imprisonment or violation of D. C. Mental Health Information Act (§12-301); for actions for injury, illness or wrongful death based upon exposure to asbestos, running from date of disability or discovery that disability was caused by exposure (§12-311); for death by wrongful act occurring in District (§16-2702); for usurpation of office (§16-3548); against common carrier for injury or death of one of its employees (§44-404); for collection of hospital lien from proceeds of accident case (§38-303). See also category Debtor and Creditor, topic Liens.

Six Months: Statutory notice in action for unliquidated damages against District. (§12-309). See category Estates and Trusts, topic Wills, subhead Contest.

Actions Not Specifically Provided For.—No action, the limitation of which is not otherwise specially provided for, shall be brought more than three years from its accrual. (§12-301).

Actions by United States.—Limitations in §§12-301, 12-302, 12-305, and 12-307 do not apply to action in which U.S. is real plaintiff. (§12-308).

Disabilities of Plaintiff.—Period runs from date of removal of disability except in cases for recovery of lands, tenements or hereditaments or upon instruments under seal in which cases the period is extended to five years after removal of disability. (§12-302). In actions to quiet title obtained by adverse possession, rights of infants or others with disabilities are saved for period of two years after removal of disabilities, with maximum saving period of 22 years over all. (§16-3301; 21 App. D. C. 295).

Absence or Concealment of Defendant.—If when a cause of action accrues against a resident, he is out of the District or has absconded or concealed himself, the period limited for the bringing of the action shall not begin to run until he comes into

the District or while he is so absconded or concealed, and if after the cause of action accrues he absconds or conceals himself, the time of such absence or concealment shall not be computed as part of the period within which action must be brought. (§12-303).

Action against Decedent's Estate.—In action against estate of deceased person, interval between such death and six months after date of first publication of notice of appointment of personal representative, not to exceed two years, is not counted. (§12-305).

Interruption of Statutory Periods.—Where bringing suit has been stayed by court order or statutory prohibition, the time of the stay is not counted as part of the time limited for commencement of the action. (§12-304). Upon payment of any part of the principal or interest on a debt past due, the statute begins to run anew from the date thereof. (1 App. D.C. 123).

Revival of Barred Claims.—In actions of debt or upon case grounded upon any simple contract, no acknowledgment or promise by words only shall be deemed sufficient evidence of a new or continued contract to extend statute or deprive any part of benefit thereof, unless such acknowledgment or promise shall be made or contained by or in some writing, to be signed by party chargeable thereby; this provision, however, not to lessen effect of payment of any principal or interest. Judgment may be recovered against one joint contractor, executor or administrator, although action against co-obligor be barred by statute. Endorsements of payment upon promissory notes, bills of exchange, or other writings made by or on behalf of party to whom such payment shall purport to be made, shall not be deemed sufficient proof of such payment so as to take case out of operation of statute of limitations. (§28-3504). For estate of decedent, unless contrary intent is expressly indicated as will, no claim which was barred by any statute of limitations at time of decedent's death shall be allowed or paid. (§20-902).

Foreign Causes of Action.—D. C. statute controls limitation on suit brought on foreign cause of action (65 App. D. C. 281, 82 F.2d 887) except statutory right of action (177 F.2d 654) and suit on foreign judgment is barred if barred where judgment was obtained (§12-307).

Contractual limitations are permitted, except that action on policy of life insurance may not be limited to less than three years. (§35-529).

Pleading.—Defense of Statute of Limitations must be pleaded (64 App. D. C. 131, 75 F.2d 650), except where action is brought on a statute conditioned on suit being brought within prescribed period (40 App. D. C. 391). See also Federal Rules of Civil Procedure.

PARTITION:

Jurisdiction.—Superior Court may decree a partition of any lands on complaint of any tenant in common or joint tenant. (§16-2901).

Proceedings.—Any party may file complaint for partition. Infant acts by his guardian or next friend, and person non compos mentis by his committee. (§16-2901).

Partition in Kind or Sale.—If it appears that the lands cannot be divided without loss or injury to the parties interested, the court may decree a sale thereof and a division of the proceeds. (§16-2901).

Accounting for Rents and Profits.—In case of partition, any tenant in common who may have received rents and profits of property to his own use may be required to account to his cotenants, and any amounts found due on accounting may be charged against share of party owing same. (§16-2901).

PLEADING:

Pleading in U.S. District Court is governed by Federal Rules of Civil Procedure and, as to form, U.S. District Court for D. C. Rule 106.

Pleading in Civil Division of Superior Court is governed by Superior Court Rules of Civil Procedure which are generally similar to Federal Rules of Civil Procedure on pleading. Suits solely for recovery of money in amount of $2,000 or less are initiated in Small Claims Branch of Superior Court by filing a brief Statement of Claim in a prescribed form (§11-1321, Sup. Ct. Rules-Small Claims 3). No answer or other pleading is required in this branch. (Sup. Ct. R.-Small Claims 5).

Frivolous Claims.—Prohibited by court rule modelled on F.R.C.P. Rule 11. (Sup. Ct. Civ. R. 11).

Probate.—Pleadings in uncontested matters in Probate Division of Superior Court are governed by statute or rules of that Division, and in general resemble equity practice. Superior Court Rules of Civil Procedure, however, are applicable to contested matters in probate division.

PRACTICE:

Federal Rules of Civil and Criminal Procedure govern all proceedings in U.S. District Court except certain statutory matters. Proceedings in District of Columbia Superior Court are governed by Superior Court Rules of Procedure for Civil, Criminal, Family, Tax and Probate Divisions of that court respectively.

See also topics Actions, Appeal and Error, Depositions and Discovery, Injunctions, Judgments, Pleading, Process; category Debtor and Creditor, topics Attachment, Executions, Garnishment.

Small Claims.—See category Courts and Legislature, topic Courts.

Direct Actions Against Insurer.—See topic Actions.

PROCESS:

All process is issued by clerk of court. In U.S. District Court summons and complaint may be served by anyone who is not party to litigation and is not less than 18 years of age or by first-class mail to be accompanied by two copies of Form 18-A, Notice and Acknowledgment for Service by Mail, one of which is to be executed and returned by person served to person requesting service. U.S. Marshal is authorized to serve summons on behalf of indigent persons proceeding under 28 U.S.C. §1915,

See note at head of Digest as to 1998 legislation covered.

See Topical Index in front part of this volume.

PROCESS . . . *continued*
seamen proceeding under 28 U.S.C. §1916, on behalf of U.S. and in certain other circumstances pursuant to court order. Additionally, service of summons and complaint must be made within 120 days after filing of complaint or Court may sua sponte or upon motion dismiss complaint. Subpoena may be served by Marshal or by any person not less than 18 years of age and not party or by registered or certified mail. (F.R.C.P. 4 and 45; U.S. Dist. Ct. Rule 208). In Superior Court process other than summons and subpoena may be served by Marshal or by any competent person over 18 who is not party to suit. (Sup. Ct. Civ. R. 4). Summons may be served by person not less than 18 years old and not party, by U.S. Marshal on behalf of U.S. or pursuant to court order, or (except in case of infant, incompetent or out-of-state government) by certified or registered mail or by first-class mail accompanied by two copies of Form 1-A, Notice and Acknowledgment For Service by Mail, with self-addressed, postage-prepaid return envelope. (Sup. Ct. Civ. R. 4[c]). Subpoena may be served by Marshal, by any person not party not less than 18 years old, or by registered or certified mail. (Sup. Ct. Civ. R. 45[c]).

Who May Serve.—See introductory paragraph.

Time of Service.—All papers after complaint required to be served on party, other than those covered in Civil Rule 12-I(e), must be filed with Court either before service or within five days after service. (Sup. Ct. Civ. R. 5[d]). Civil Rule 5 also permits waiver of filing of depositions upon oral examination, interrogatories, requests for admission, and other discovery materials upon order of Court.

Personal Service on Individual.—By serving him personally, or by leaving copies at his dwelling or usual place of abode with some person of suitable age and discretion residing therein, or by serving agent authorized by appointment or by law to receive service of process. (Sup. Ct. Civ. R. 4[d][1], identical to Fed. R. Civ. P. 4[d][1]).

Personal service on infant under the age of 16 must be made on the infant, as well as the person with whom he resides. (§13-332).

Personal service on incompetent person must be made on the person non compos mentis and upon his committee. (§13-333).

Personal Service on Foreign Corporations.—In actions against foreign corporations doing business in the District all process may be served on the agent of such corporation or person conducting its business or, in case he is absent and cannot be found, by leaving a copy at the principal place of business in the District, or, if there be no such place of business, by leaving the same at the place of business or residence of such agent in said District. (§13-334).

When a foreign corporation transacts business in the District, without having any place of business or resident agent therein, service may be made upon any officer or agent or employee of such corporation in the District, as to suits on contracts entered into or to be performed, in whole or in part, in the District or torts committed in the District. (§13-334).

Service may be had on Mayor where foreign corporation fails to appoint or maintain a registered agent or transacts business without a certificate of authority. (§29-399.9[b]).

Personal service on domestic corporation may be made in same manner in which foreign corporation may be served. (Sup. Ct. Civ. R. 4[d][3], identical to Fed. R. Civ. P. 4[d][3]).

Personal service on partnership, whether general or limited, may be had only by service on partners. (607 F. Supp. 220).

Service by Publication.—Publication may be substituted for personal service upon any defendant who cannot be found and who is shown by affidavit to be a nonresident, or to have been absent from the District for at least six months, or against the unknown heirs or devisees of deceased persons, in suits for partition, divorce or annulment, child custody, attachment, foreclosure, enforcement of liens, establishment of title to real estate by possession, or proceedings in rem. (§13-336). Service by publication provision is affected by recent D.C. adoption of Uniform Child Custody Jurisdiction and Marital or Parent & Child Long-Arm Jurisdiction Amendments Act of 1982 ("Act"). (D.C. Code, Tit. 16, c. 45). Under Act, service by publication is allowed pursuant to Superior Court direction if other prescribed means of notification are ineffective. (§16-4505). Other prescribed means of service include personal delivery in manner prescribed for service of process within District; in manner prescribed by law of place in which service of process is made; and by registered or certified mail, return receipt requested. In such cases, personal service outside District may be made by any person not party to or otherwise interested on nonresident defendant out of District of Columbia, which service has same effect as order of publication duly executed. (§13-337). Return must be made under oath in D. C. unless person making service is authorized to serve process where service is made, and such return must show time and place of such service and that defendant so served is nonresident of District. Cost and expense of such service of process out of District must be borne by party at whose instance made and not taxed as costs unless made by some authorized officer, when actual and usual cost of such service may be taxed. (§13-337).

Long Arm Statute (§§13-401-434) is modeled on Uniform Interstate and International Procedure Act and gives D. C. courts personal jurisdiction over persons outside D. C., and permits personal service of process upon them outside D. C., if person or corporation is domiciled or organized in D. C. or maintains principal place of business in D. C. as to any claim for relief, or as to a claim for relief arising from person's transacting business in D. C., contracting to supply services in D. C., causing tortious injury in D. C., having an interest in, using or possessing real property in D. C., or insuring or acting as surety for any person, property or risk in D. C. Additionally, D.C. courts have personal jurisdiction over persons involved in claims arising from marital relationship if plaintiff resides in D.C. and D.C. was matrimonial domicile or cause of action to pay spousal support arose in D.C., and over persons involved in claims affecting parent child relationship if person is alleged parent of child conceived in D.C., child resides in D.C., or person has resided with child in D.C. Finally, D.C. courts may exercise personal jurisdiction if there is any basis consistent with U.S. Constitution. (§§13-401-434).

Nonresident Motorist.—See category Transportation, topic Motor Vehicles.

REPLEVIN:

The common law rules determine the right to the writ.

Proceedings.—To institute action in replevin, plaintiff must file complaint (§16-3702) accompanied by affidavit of plaintiff, his agent, or attorney stating that: Plaintiff is entitled to recover possession of chattels, defendant has seized and detains chattels and chattels were not taken upon writ of replevin between parties (§16-3703). At time of filing complaint, plaintiff shall enter into undertaking, with surety, to abide by and perform judgment of court. (§16-3704).

Judge may authorize issuance and execution of writ of replevin: (1) At conclusion of hearing at which both parties are heard or (2) without prior adversary hearing when plaintiff can establish by affidavit of sworn testimony that there is immediate danger that defendant will destroy or conceal property in dispute. (Sup. Ct. Civ. R. 64-II[f]). Immediately upon issuance of writ of replevin by Civil Clerk's office, U.S. Marshal may take possession of property described in writ. If writ is issued without prior adversary hearing, hearing shall take place on fifth court day after execution of writ. (Sup. Ct. Civ. R. 64-II[f]).

Repossession.—After marshall has taken possession, defendant may, on one day's notice to plaintiff or his attorney, move to have writ of replevin vacated and property returned to defendant's possession prior to final judgment in action. If motion is granted, court may require defendant to enter into undertaking, with surety, to abide by judgment of court. (§16-3708; Sup. Ct. Civ. R. 64-II[f]).

Judgment or Order.—Where defendant has eloigned goods sued for, plaintiff's damages shall be full value of goods taken (amount discharged if goods returned within ten days after judgment), and damages for detention. (§§16-3710, 3713). Court may instruct jury to assess damages as may compel return of goods. (§16-3712). If judgment is for defendant, goods, if delivered to plaintiff, shall be returned to defendant with damages for their detention. If goods are not returned, defendant shall recover for damages he has sustained. (§16-3711).

Under Art. 2 of Uniform Commercial Code.—Where seller fails to deliver goods or repudiates contract, buyer has right of replevin for goods identified to contract if, after reasonable effort, he is unable to effect cover for such goods, or circumstances reasonably indicate that such effort will be unavailing. (§§28:2-711, 716). See category Business Regulation and Commerce, topic Commercial Code.

SEQUESTRATION:

District Court and Superior Court, for purposes of executing decree or compelling obedience thereto, may order immediate sequestration of real and personal estate of defendant, or such part thereof as may be necessary to satisfy decree and may order payment and satisfaction out of sequestered estate and effects, according to intent of decree. (§15-320).

Property of defendant failing to pay alimony is subject to sequestration by court and income from such property may be applied to payment of alimony. (§16-911). Probate court may order sequestration of real and personal property of person who has failed to appear to testify. (§§16-3103, 3104).

SERVICE:

See topic Process.

STAY OF EXECUTION:

See topic Appeal and Error; category Debtor and Creditor, topic Executions.

SUBMISSION OF CONTROVERSY:

There is no statutory provision but in practice, cases in which jury trials may be had, may be tried without the intervention of the jury, either upon a stipulation containing an agreed statement of facts or providing for the taking of testimony.

VENUE:

There is no provision for change of venue. Since there are no political or judicial subdivisions of District venue of all actions is otherwise in proper court in District. If one judge is disqualified, another judge of same court may hear matter.

COURTS AND LEGISLATURE

COURTS:

Preliminary Note: District of Columbia constitutes a separate Federal judicial circuit and district. U.S. Court of Appeals for this circuit and U.S. District Court for this district derive their Federal judicial power from Article III of Constitution and therefore parallel U.S. Courts of Appeals and U.S. District Courts for other Federal circuits and districts. They have traditionally had additional power derived from Art. 1 §8, Clause 17 of Constitution, but this local jurisdiction was transferred to D. C. Court of Appeals and D. C. Superior Court by D. C. Court Reform and Criminal Procedure Act of 1970 (P. L. 91-358).

United States Court of Appeals for the District of Columbia Circuit.—Clerk's office: U.S. Court House, Washington, D. C. 20001.

Jurisdiction.—This Court as one of 13 U.S. Courts of Appeals has full appellate jurisdiction of such courts in cases, both civil and criminal, originating in U.S. District Court for District of Columbia. (28 U.S.C. §1291). In addition, U.S. Court of Appeals for D. C. Circuit has jurisdiction in review by petition judgments of D. C. Court of Appeals which involve violations of criminal laws of U.S. not applicable exclusively to D. C. (§11-301). Court of Appeals also has jurisdiction concurrently with other U.S. Courts of Appeals to review decisions of Tax Court of U.S. (26 U.S.C. §7482), and to review or enforce orders of several Federal commissions, boards, agencies and officers, such as Securities and Exchange Commission, Interstate Commerce Commission, National Labor Relations Board, Federal Trade Commission, Secretary of Treasury,

See note at head of Digest as to 1998 legislation covered.

See Topical Index in front part of this volume.

COURTS . . . *continued*
Board of Governors of Federal Reserve System, Administrator of Wage and Hour Division of Department of Labor. (See list in Historical and Revision Notes to 28 U.S.C. §1291.) Court has exclusive appellate jurisdiction to review orders of Federal Communications Commission in cases involving radio and television licenses. (47 U.S.C. §402).

Court has jurisdiction to issue extraordinary writs of mandamus, prohibition and like, when necessary in aid of its appellate jurisdiction. (28 U.S.C. §1651).

Right of appeal to U.S. Supreme Court, except under 28 U.S.C. §§1252 (§1252, repealed—Pub.L. 100-352, §1, June 27, 1988, 102 Stat. 662), 1254(2), from decisions of Court of Appeals has been abolished. Review of case in Court, other than by appeal, is by petition for writ of certiorari or certification of question of law by Court of Appeals. (28 U.S.C. §1254).

There are ten circuit judges and two senior circuit judges on Court. Court, pursuant to practice prescribed in 28 U.S.C. §46 for all of U.S. Courts of Appeals, sits in panels of three judges, although Court may sit en banc if majority of circuit judges of circuit in active service so determine.

United States District Court for the District of Columbia.—Address: U.S. Court House, Washington, D. C. 20001, (202) 273-0555.

Jurisdiction.—This court has all original jurisdiction of U.S. District Courts in states. This court also has criminal jurisdiction over local crimes joined in same indictment or information with any Federal offense. (§11-502). It has jurisdiction in civil actions against foreign state (28 U.S.C. §1332), and power to grant relief in nature of mandamus in original proceedings against cabinet officers and other Federal officials in their capacity as such, who may be considered officially present in District of Columbia (28 U.S.C. §§1361, 1391).

Divisions.—Cases are assigned randomly. See Local Rule 403.

Fees.—Filing fee of $120 must be paid at commencement of all civil actions. (28 U.S.C. §1914). For filing fees in bankruptcy cases, see 28 U.S.C. §1930.

District of Columbia Court of Appeals.—Address: 500 Indiana Avenue, N. W., Washington, D. C. 20001.

Jurisdiction.—This Court has jurisdiction over appeals from all divisions of D. C. Superior Court. Court also has jurisdiction to review decisions of agencies of D. C., D. C. Redevelopment Land Agency, and of D. C. Mayor and D. C. Council acting in quasi-judicial capacity. (§§11-721, 722). Court also has jurisdiction to answer questions of law certified to it by U.S. Supreme Court, U.S. Court of Appeals, or highest appellate court of any State. (§11-723).

District of Columbia Superior Court.—Address: 500 Indiana Avenue, N. W., Washington, D. C. 20001.

Jurisdiction.—This Court has jurisdiction of all civil actions not within exclusive jurisdiction of Federal court in D. C. or jurisdiction of U.S. District Court for D. C. under §11-501. (§11-921). Small Claims and Conciliation Branch of Civil Division of Superior Court has exclusive jurisdiction over cases within Superior Court jurisdiction which are for recovery of money only, not exceeding $2,000, except that cases affecting interest in real property may not be brought in Branch. (§11-1321).

Family Division of Superior Court has exclusive jurisdiction over all actions for divorce, legal separation, annulment of marriage, support of spouse or minor children, custody of minor children, adoption, paternity, proceedings related to commitment of mentally ill or substantially retarded, matters involving delinquency, dependency and neglect of children under 18, and determinations and adjudications of property rights, both real and personal, in various domestic relations actions, irrespective of any jurisdictional limitation otherwise imposed upon Court. (§11-1101). In addition, Family Division has jurisdiction in matters involving delinquency, dependency and neglect of children under 18 (§11-1101) and compulsory education law (§31-413).

Tax Division of Superior Court has exclusive jurisdiction to hear appeals from assessment of any tax imposed by D.C. or from disallowance of or failure to act on claim for refund of District taxes. (§11-1201). In case of income tax, appeal may be made from additional assessment or disallowance of claim for refund, within six months of notice of assessment or disallowance. (§47-1815.1). Real estate taxes may be appealed within six months after Oct. 1 of year for which tax assessed, provided taxpayer has first made proper administrative appeal. (§47-825). All other taxes may be appealed from within six months of assessment, provided taxpayer has first paid such tax, penalties and interest due. (§47-3303).

Criminal Division has jurisdiction over cases involving violation of laws applicable exclusively to D. C. In cases in which U.S. District Court for D. C. has jurisdiction, Superior Court may act with respect to bail and pretrial detention. (§11-923). See Sup. Ct. Cr. Rule 40.

Clerk of Superior Court and such Deputy Clerks as may, in writing, be designated by Clerk of Court and approved by Chief Judge, are authorized to celebrate marriages in D. C. (§30-106).

Superior Court administers Crime Victims Compensation Program, issuing necessary rules and regulations, and appointing 15 member Crime Victims Compensation Advisory Commission. (§§3-421-438).

Fees.—Filing fees differ depending upon whether action is in Civil Division, Small Claims and Conciliation Branch or Landlord and Tenant Branch. (Sup. Ct. Civ. R. 202).

LEGISLATURE:

Congress retains ultimate legislative authority over District of Columbia pursuant to U.S. Const., art. I, §8 but has delegated broad legislative powers to Council of District of Columbia (§§1-204, 227) subject to several express limitations (§§1-206, 207, 233 and 47-313). Thirteen members of Council are elected by registered qualified electors of District for four-year term, and vacancies are filled by special election. (§1-221). Neither time for regular council sessions nor power to call special or extraordinary sessions is statutorily prescribed; Council adopts rules governing regular and special sessions at beginning of each two-year Council period. (annot. to §1-227). Council may enact emergency legislation, which shall be effective for period not to exceed 90 days. (§1-229[a]). Majority of Council members present and voting is required to pass legislation. (§1-229[a]). Majority of Council constitutes quorum. (§1-229[c]). D. C. Charter (Tit. IV of Act of Dec. 24, 1973, 88 Stat. 785, P.L. 93-198) may be amended by passage of act by Council with subsequent ratification by majority of qualified D.C. electors voting in referendum and submission of such act to both Houses of Congress unless Congress enacts into law joint resolution disapproving such amendment within prescribed 35-calendar-day period. (§1-205). Initiative or referendum may be proposed by petition of 5% of registered electors of District of Columbia, provided that total signatures include 5% of registered electors in at least five wards. (§§1-281, 282). Council may also call special election to take advisory referendum vote on any proposition upon which Council desires to take action. (§1-229[b]). Members of Council are immune from liability for any speech or debate made in course of their legislative duties. (§1-223).

REPORTS:

Circuit Court (1801-1863): 1-5 Cranch C. C., 1-2 Hayward & Hazelton. Supreme Court, General Term (1863-1893): 6-7 D. C. (by Mackey), 1-3 MacArthur (8-10 D. C.), MacArthur & Mackey (11 D. C.), 1-9 Mackey (12-20 D. C.), 21 D. C. (by Tucker & Clephane). Court of Appeals (1893 to date): Appeal Cases, D. C. (App. D. C.) Vols. 1-74, (U. S. App. D. C.) Vols. 75 et seq.: beginning with Vol. 49 App. D. C., also in Federal Reporter, Vols. 258-300, and Second Series, Vol 1 et seq. District Court decisions of Federal importance are reported in Federal Supplement beginning with Vol. 16. Decisions of the District of Columbia Court of Appeals are reported in the Atlantic Reporter, commencing with Vol. 31A.2d. Other decisions or notes thereof are reported in Washington Law Reporter, which has quasi-official status.

Digests.—Cranch (1 to 5 Cranch); Maupin (1 Cranch to 14 App. D. C.); Torbert 1 vol. and 3 vol. supplement (1 App. D. C. to 59 App. D. C.); District of Columbia Digest (Washington Law Book Co.-West Pub. Co.), with pocket parts, 1658 to date, including Maryland decisions prior to 1801.

STATUTES:

The latest official compilation presently available is District of Columbia Code, 1981 edition as modified by various replacement volumes and subsequent pocket parts.

In addition, many acts of Congress contained in the U. S. Code or statutes at large are in effect local laws in the District, though not contained in the District Code. All statutes relating to procedure, to the extent in conflict therewith, have been superseded by the Federal Rules of Civil Procedure (1938) as amended.

Uniform Acts in force are: Anatomical Gift* (1968 Act) (1970); Arbitration* (1977); Attendance of Witnesses from Without a State in Criminal Proceedings (1952); Business Corporation (A.B.A.) (1954); Certification of Questions of Law* (1986); Child Custody Jurisdiction* (1983); Commercial Code* (1963); Common Trust Fund (1949); Conservation Easement (1986); Controlled Substances* (1981); Determination of Death (1981); Disposition of Unclaimed Property (1966 Act) (1980); Durable Power of Attorney (1987); Enforcement of Foreign Judgments* (1990); Fiduciaries (1928); Firearms (1932); Foreign-Money Claims (1996); Foreign Money-Judgments Recognition (1996); Fraudulent Transfer (1996); Guardianship and Protective Proceedings (1988); Interstate and International Procedure* (1970); Interstate Family Support (1996); Limited Partnership* (1976 Act) (1987); Management of Institutional Funds* (1977); Model State Administrative Procedure (1961 Act)* (1969); Non-Profit Corporation (A.B.A.) (1962); Notarial Acts* (1991); Partnership (1997); Premarital Agreement (1996); Reciprocal Enforcement of Support (1950 Act)* (1957); Securities* (1964); Simplification of Fiduciary Security Transfers (1960); Simultaneous Death (1966); Testamentary Additions to Trusts (1963); Trade Secrets* (1989); Transfers to Minors* (1986).

* Indicates with modifications.

For text of Uniform Acts falling within the scope of the Martindale-Hubbell Law Digests, see Uniform and Model Acts section.

UNIFORM LAWS:

For list of Uniform Acts in force in the District see topic Statutes. For text of Uniform Acts within the scope of the Martindale-Hubbell Law Digests, see Uniform and Model Acts section.

CRIMINAL LAW

BAIL:

See topic Criminal Law.

CRIMINAL LAW:

Statutes as to criminal law are embraced in District Code (§§22-101-3901) and acts of Congress. Police or municipal regulations are made by District of Columbia Council. Common law offenses existing in Maryland on Feb. 27, 1801, not repealed or modified by statute, are applicable. (26 App. D. C. 382).

In the District Court the Federal Rules of Criminal Procedure apply. Separate rules, patterned after Federal Rules, apply in Superior Court. These other procedural provisions are in District Code. (§§23-101-1504; 24-103-905).

Offenses, except by juveniles not prosecuted as adult offenders, punishable by imprisonment for more than one year are prosecuted upon indictment in either District Court or Superior Court depending on felony charged, unless defendant, after advised of charge and his rights, waives prosecution by indictment in open court. Any other offense may be prosecuted by indictment or by information in either court depending on crime charged. (§§11-502, 11-923, 23-301).

Prosecution of offenses of disorderly conduct or obscene acts are conducted in name of District of Columbia by corporation counsel. Prosecution for violation of police or municipal ordinances or regulations, or penal statutes in nature thereof, where punishment cannot exceed fine only, or imprisonment for not more than one year, are

CRIMINAL LAW . . . *continued*

conducted in name of District of Columbia by corporation counsel. All other prosecutions are conducted in name of U.S. by U.S. Attorney. (§23-101). As practical matter, serious misdemeanors are prosecuted by U.S. Attorney.

Bail.—District Code §§23-1321-1332 replaces Federal Bail Reform Act in District of Columbia. Conditions of bail are fixed by a judicial officer in his discretion. Upon a proper showing pretrial detention may be ordered. Trial judge may modify or revoke pretrial bail. (459 A.2d 134 [D. C. 1983]).

Jury Trial.—Valid verdict may be returned by 11 jurors, in extraordinary circumstances where court finds it necessary to excuse juror for just cause after jury has retired to consider verdict. (§16-705[c]).

Probation and Parole.—Imposition of sentence of probation in District Court governed by federal law. (18 U.S.C. §§3561-3562). Probation in Superior Court authorized by District Code. (§16-710). Parole, probation, and good time credit procedures governed by District Code. (§§24-103-209, -428-434).

Sex Offender Registration.—Sex offenders convicted of (1) sexual abuse or other sexual offense against minor or (2) sexually violent offense, and sexually violent predators, and any person released from confinement as sexual psychopath, must register current address with Metropolitan Police Department. Registration information may be disclosed to public in cases where needed for public protection. (§§24-1101-1117).

Extradition is governed by 18 U.S.C. §3182 and District Code §§23-701-707. Chief Judge of Superior Court exercises executive authority in extradition matters. (§23-704).

DEBTOR AND CREDITOR

ASSIGNMENTS:

In general, such rights of action as survive are assignable. See category Civil Actions and Procedure, topic Actions.

A judgment or money decree may be assigned in writing, and upon the assignment thereof being filed in the clerk's office the assignee may maintain action or sue out execution on said judgment in his own name. (§28-2301).

Any bond or obligation under seal for payment of money may be assigned in writing by obligee therein named, and assignee may maintain action thereon in his own name. (§28-2302).

All nonnegotiable written agreements for payment of money, including nonnegotiable bills of exchange and promissory notes, or for delivery of personal property, open accounts, debts, and demands of liquidated character, except claims against U.S. or salaries of public officers, may be assigned in writing, so as to vest in assignee right to sue in his own name. (§28-2303).

Uniform Commercial Code adopted. See category Business Regulation and Commerce, topic Commercial Code.

Filing is unnecessary except in case of judgments. (See subhead A Judgment or Money Decree, supra.) Filing is required in connection with secured transactions. (See infra, subhead Secured Transactions.)

Recording is generally unnecessary. However, assignment of recorded lien on motor vehicles, if in writing and acknowledged, should be recorded with representative of Recorder of Deeds in office of Director of Vehicles and Traffic. (§40-1008).

Notice is unnecessary between the parties, but may be necessary to preserve rights as against third parties. As to secured transactions, see infra, subhead Secured Transactions.

Wages or Salary.—A contract attempting to assign unearned salary or wages is unenforceable. It is a misdemeanor to demand or receive such an assignment from a debtor or to notify an employer of it. (§28-2305).

Secured Transactions.—(1) Except as otherwise provided in §28:9-104 on excluded transactions, this article applies: (a) To any transaction (regardless of its form) which is intended to create security interest in personal property or fixtures including goods, documents, instruments, general intangibles, chattel paper or accounts; and also (b) to any sale of accounts or chattel paper. (2) This article applies to security interests created by contract including pledge, assignment, chattel mortgage, chattel trust, trust deed, factor's lien, equipment trust, conditional sale, trust receipt, other lien or title retention contract and lease or consignment intended as security. (§28:9-102).

ATTACHMENT:

Attachments may be levied on the lands and tenements and personal chattels of defendant not exempt by law, whether in defendant's or a third person's possession, whether defendant's title is legal or equitable, and upon his credits in hands of third person whether due and payable or not, and upon his undivided interest in partnership. (§16-507).

While attachment may be issued upon a judgment in aid of execution (§16-542), the following pertains to attachment before judgment:

Actions in Which Allowed.—In any action for the recovery of specific personal property, or a debt, or damages for the breach of a contract, express or implied. (§16-501).

Courts Which May Issue Writ.—District and Superior courts. (§§16-501, 533).

In Whose Favor Writ May Issue.—Any plaintiff.

Against Whom Writ May Issue.—Any defendant.

Claims on Which Writ May Issue.—On matured claims (§§16-501, 507) or claims where debt is not due and payable (§16-503, 507[a]).

Grounds for attachment are that defendant (1) Is a foreign corporation or a nonresident or has been absent from District for at least six months; (2) evades service of ordinary process by concealing himself or temporarily withdrawing himself from District; (3) has removed, or is about to remove, some or all of his property from District so as to defeat just demands against him; (4) has conveyed, disposed of, assigned or secreted his property, or is about to do so, in fraud of creditors; or (5) fraudulently contracted debt or incurred obligation. (§16-501[d]).

Proceedings to Obtain.—An affidavit must be filed by plaintiff showing grounds for his claim, his right to recover, and if action is to recover specific personal property, nature and value of such property and probable amount of damages; and, if action is for debt, amount thereof; and, if action is for damages on contract, showing in detail breach of contract and actual damage. (§16-501).

If the debt is not yet due the affidavit of the plaintiff must be substantiated by testimony of one or more witnesses showing amount and justice of claim, time it will become due, and must also show either that defendant has removed, is removing or that he intends to remove a material part of his property from District to defraud creditors. Judgment may not be entered before debt matures. (§16-503).

Attachment Bond.—Plaintiff must file a bond with security approved by clerk of court with penalty of twice amount of his claim or value of specified property to be levied upon, whichever lower. (§16-501). Officer who serves writ, U. S. marshal, may require appraisal of specified property and refuse to execute writ when appraised value exceeds half of bond amount.

Levy.—An attachment is sufficiently levied on real estate by said real estate being described by the marshal in an indorsement on the writ of attachment to the following effect:

Levied on the following estate of the defendant, A. B., to wit: (here describe property) this . . . . day of . . . .

                                                C. D. Marshal.

and by serving upon the person, if any, in possession of the property copy of writ bearing such indorsement and notice to defendant and person in possession of property to appear. (§16-508).

An attachment is levied on personal chattels by the marshal taking the same into his possession and custody unless the defendant or person in possession gives an undertaking, in which event attachment is sufficiently levied by the taking of the undertaking. (§16-509).

An attachment is levied on credits of defendant in hands of garnishee or upon undivided interest in partnership by serving garnishee or partner with copy of writ and interrogatories and a notice that any property or credits in his possession are attached. (§16-511).

Lien.—Attachment is a lien on property from the date of delivery of the writ to the marshal. (§16-507).

Priorities are according to the dates when the attachments were delivered to the marshal. (§16-507).

Release of property or credits may be secured by defendant or person who had possession of property or credits, by furnishing an undertaking with security to be approved by the court to pay any judgment recovered against him. (§16-510).

Sale.—After judgment of condemnation, specific property may be sold under writ of fieri facias to satisfy demand of plaintiff. (§16-525). Prior to final decision, court may order sale of property if perishable or if for other reasons sale appears expedient. (§16-518).

Third Party Claims.—A third party may file a petition in the cause claiming the personalty attached, and the matter must be tried to determine the ownership. (§16-523).

Vacation or Modification.—Defendant (§16-506), as well as a garnishee where attachment is based on fraudulent conveyance (§16-529), may contest right of plaintiff to writ by filing affidavits traversing facts set forth in plaintiff's affidavits. Motion to quash writ may be heard on three days notice (§16-506). Also, defendant or any garnishee may plead to attachment, and raise issue to be tried by court. (§16-520).

Interrogatories.—Garnishee may be required to answer interrogatories under oath concerning defendant's property in his possession or his indebtedness to defendant. In addition to answers to written interrogatories required of him, garnishee may, on motion, be required to appear in court and be examined orally, under oath, touching any property or credits of defendant in his hands. (§16-521). Plaintiff may traverse such answers and have issue tried by court. (§16-522).

Judgment.—If defendant has been served with process, final judgment may not be entered against garnishee until action against defendant is determined. (§16-524[b]). Where plaintiff recovers judgment against defendant, plaintiff may have judgment of condemnation of property attached or of proceeds from sale of property (§§16-524, 525) or judgment of condemnation against garnishee for amount of defendant's credits in his hands or where undertaking has been provided judgment of condemnation of property and against garnishee and his sureties (§§16-526, 527). If judgment is rendered for defendant, garnishee may be discharged and recover costs. (§16-524[b]).

Payment of salary or earnings before due for the purpose of preventing or avoiding an attachment or garnishment against them is void as to an attaching creditor. After the service of a writ of attachment or garnishment on a judgment against an employer, any advance payment of salary or earnings made within a period of six months after the service of the writ or before an earlier satisfaction of the judgment is, as to an attaching creditor, presumed to be for the purpose of avoiding the attachment. (§16-513).

Wage Attachment.—See topic Garnishment.

CREDITORS' SUITS:

Creditor's bill is necessary to reach debtor's equity in real estate, except to extent that new combined or supplementary procedures may be available under Federal Rules of Civil Procedure. Judgment of U.S. District Court or Superior Court is lien on judgment debtor's interest in real estate from date such judgment is filed and recorded in office of Recorder of Deeds. (§15-102). Enforcement of judgment against equitable

CREDITORS' SUITS . . . *continued*

interests may be had by civil action. (§§15-102, 16-532). See also topics Executions, and Fraudulent Sales and Conveyances.

EXECUTIONS:

Every final judgment for payment of money by District Court and by Superior Court may be enforced by execution, provided that execution on judgment may be levied on real estate only after judgment is filed and recorded in Office of Recorder of Deeds. (§§15-101, 311).

Kinds of Execution.—The ordinary writ of execution is the writ of fieri facias. (§15-311).

Exemptions.—See topic Exemptions.

Time for Issuance.—In civil action, execution may issue after ten days and within three years after entry of judgment (§15-302, modified by F.R.C.P. 62; Sup. Ct. Civ. R. 62), but execution on judgment may be levied on real estate only after judgment filed and recorded in Office of Recorder of Deeds (§15-311).

Stay.—In District Court, stay of execution is governed by Federal Rules of Civil Procedure. Superior Court stay of execution is governed by Rules of Court.

Lien.—Writ of fieri facias issued by District Court or Superior Court becomes lien on personal property of judgment defendant, not exempt by law, and his equitable interest in chattels in his possession upon delivery to marshal. (§15-307).

Levy.—Execution is levied on personal property by the marshal taking the same into his possession and custody unless the defendant or person in possession gives an undertaking, in which event the execution is sufficiently levied by taking the undertaking.

Levy on real property is made by an endorsement on the writ to the following effect:
Levied on the following estate of the defendant, A. B., to wit: (here describe the property) this . . . . . . day of . . . .

C. D., Marshal.

and by serving a copy of the writ bearing such endorsement and notice to defendant to appear, upon person, if any, in possession of property. (§§16-508, 509).

Real property or rent may not be seized for debt if present goods and chattels of debtor are sufficient to pay debt and debtor stands ready to satisfy it. (§15-323).

Levy or judicial lien is invalid on property in possession of bailee where negotiable document of title is outstanding without surrender thereof or injunction against its negotiation (§28:7-602) or upon security or any share or other interest evidenced thereby without seizure of certificate except at source when certificate surrendered to issuer (§28:8-317).

Return.—Writs are returnable by the marshal on or before 60 days after its date. (§15-302).

Priorities between different executions are determined according to the times when the liens thereof attach.

Claims of Third Persons.—As to personalty, claims of third persons may be determined by suit against marshal for false levy (§15-317, 521) or replevin (§15-524); as to realty, affidavit will stay issuance of writ of habere facias possessionem and title may be settled in action for ejectment (§15-318).

Sales.—Writ of fieri facias may be levied on nonexempt property or legal interest or estate of judgment debtor. (§15-311). After appraisal, property levied on, except money, is sold at public auction upon notice by advertisement; ten days notice being requisite as to personalty, as to realty notice must be as provided in 28 U.S.C. §2002. (§15-314). The equitable interest in chattels may be levied upon and lien so obtained may be enforced by civil action. (§15-313). See topic Creditors' Suits.

Redemption.—No right of redemption of property sold under execution. (§15-316).

Supplementary Proceedings.—Writs of attachment and garnishment may be issued (§§16-542, 544) and other proceedings authorized by the Federal Rules of Civil Procedure may be employed.

EXEMPTIONS:

A resident householder or a nonresident householder earning the major portion of his livelihood in the District is entitled to hold exempt from attachment or execution a number of designated articles of personal property, in some instances limited as to value. (§15-501[a]).

Debts Against Which Exemptions Not Allowed.—No exemption (except as to wearing apparel, beds, bedding and household furniture for debtor and his family) extends to attachments or executions for debts due for wages of servants, common laborers or clerks. (§15-501[b]).

Waiver of Exemption.—By judicial decision, debtors cannot waive exemption by agreement. (1 Mackey [12 D.C.] 303).

Necessity of Claiming Exemption.—Notice of claim or motion to quash process may be filed in the cause by debtor or spouse or garnishee; and after due notice court must promptly pass on matter. (§15-503[d]).

Earnings other than wages, insurance, annuities, or pension or retirement payments, not otherwise exempted, not to exceed $200 each month, of a resident, or nonresident earning major portion of livelihood in the District, who provides the principal support of a family, for two months next preceding the issuance of any writ or process against him, from any court or officer of and in the District, are exempt from attachment, levy, seizure, or sale upon such process. Where husband and wife are living together, the aggregate of such earnings, insurance, etc., of the husband and wife determine the exemption of either in cases arising ex contractu. This exemption is $60 a month for persons not providing support of a family; also wearing apparel of such persons not exceeding $300 in value and mechanic's tools not exceeding $200 in value are exempt. (§15-503). Wages, salary, earnings and other income of a prisoner participating in a D. C. work release program are not subject to garnishment or

attachment while in hands of an employer or Mayor. (§24-466). See also topic Garnishment.

Wages of nonresidents, who do not earn major portion of such wages in District, in any case arising out of contract or transaction entered outside of District, shall be exempt to same extent as provided by law of states wherein such persons reside. (§15-503[c]).

Insurance.—Proceeds of disability and group life insurance policies are exempt. (§§35-522-523). Proceeds of life insurance policies are exempt in hands of beneficiary or assignee except as to premiums paid in fraud of creditors. (§35-521).

Public assistance (§3-215.1) and unemployment compensation (§46-119[b][1]) benefits (so long as not commingled with other funds of recipient) are exempt from attachment or execution. No exemption for unemployment compensation benefits used to pay debts for necessaries furnished to recipient, his spouse or dependents during time when recipient was unemployed. (§46-119[b][1]).

Encumbrances.—No deed of trust, assignment for benefit of creditors, bill of sale, or mortgage upon any exempted articles, is binding or valid unless signed by spouse of debtor, who is married and living with his or her spouse. (§15-502).

FORECLOSURE:

See topic Liens; category Mortgages, topic Mortgages of Real Property.

FRAUDULENT SALES AND CONVEYANCES:

Uniform Fraudulent Transfer Act adopted. (§§28-3101-3111). Transfer is fraudulent as to present or future creditor if transfer made or obligation incurred with intent to hinder, delay, or defraud any creditor, or without receiving reasonably equivalent value and debtor (A) was engaged or about to engage in transaction for which remaining assets of debtor were unreasonably small in relation to transaction or (B) intended to incur debts beyond debtor's ability to pay as they became due. Statute provides number of factors to be considered in determining debtor's actual intent. (§28-3104).

Transfer is fraudulent as to creditor whose claim arose before transfer was made if debtor made transfer without receiving reasonably equivalent value and debtor was insolvent or became insolvent as result of transfer. Transfer fraudulent as to creditor whose claim arose before transfer was made if transfer made to insider for antecedent debt, debtor was insolvent, and insider had reasonable cause to believe debtor was insolvent. (§28-3105).

Various remedies available to creditors include avoidance of transfer to extent necessary to satisfy creditor's claim, attachment, injunction, appointment of receiver, or other necessary remedy. (§28-3107). Transfer generally not voidable against person who took in good faith and for reasonably equivalent value, or against any subsequent transferee. (§28-3108).

Bulk Sales.—Uniform Commercial Code, Art. 6, governs. (§28:6-101 et seq.). See category Business Regulation and Commerce, topic Commercial Code.

Vendee must notify Department of Finance and Revenue by registered mail 15 days before taking possession of property sold and for failure to comply he is personally liable for any gross sales tax unpaid by vendor. (§47-2022).

GARNISHMENT:

Property of a debtor in possession of third person may be levied upon by a writ of attachment either before or after judgment. (§§16-542, 501). For practice and procedure before judgment see topic Attachment.

Property Which May Be Reached.—After judgment the writ may be levied upon the debtor's goods, chattels and credits. (§16-544).

Jurisdiction.—Both District Court and Superior Court may issue writ. (§§16-501, 533).

Proceedings to Obtain.—Attachment may be issued upon judgment either before or after or at same time with fieri facias. (§16-542). Plaintiff may submit interrogatories in writing, in such form as may be allowed by rules or special order of court, to be served upon any garnishee, asking about property of defendant in his possession or charge, or indebtedness of his to defendant. (§16-552).

Answer of Garnishee.—Garnishee must answer interrogatories within ten days of service. (§16-552).

Practice.—In addition to the answers to the interrogatories, the garnishee may be required, on motion, to appear in court for oral examination. (§16-552). Where the garnishee answers that he has no property or credits of the defendant in his possession or less than the amount of plaintiff's judgment, the plaintiff may traverse the answer and the issue may be tried. A jury trial will be granted if demanded. (§§16-521, 522, 551-553). Losing plaintiff shall be required to pay garnishee's costs and attorney fee. (§16-553).

Adverse Claims.—Any garnishee or stranger who may make claim to attached property may file answer defending against attachment, or any person may file motion and affidavit in cause setting forth his claim, interest or lien and trial will be had on issues raised, by jury if demanded. (§16-551, 554).

Judgment.—If a garnishee admits credits or if the same are found after trial, judgment will be entered against him for the amounts admitted or found not exceeding plaintiff's judgment and costs. If the garnishee fails to answer the interrogatories or fails to appear and show cause why a judgment of condemnation should not be entered, judgment will be entered against him for the whole amount of plaintiff's judgment and costs. (§16-556).

Wage Attachment.—Attachment after judgment on wages becomes a lien and remains a continuing levy upon gross wages due or to become due to extent of (1) 25% of disposable wages that week, or (2) amount by which disposable wages for that week exceed 30 times Federal minimum hourly wage prescribed by §6(a) of Fair Labor Standards Act of 1938 (29 U.S.C. 206), whichever is less. In case of wages for any pay period other than a week, Mayor shall by regulation prescribe equivalent

See note at head of Digest as to 1998 legislation covered.

See Topical Index in front part of this volume.

GARNISHMENT . . . *continued*

multiple. Only one attachment on wages may be satisfied at a time. Attachments have priority in order delivered to marshal. (§16-572).

In case of judgment for alimony or maintenance, however, limitation is 50% of all gross wages due or to become due to any such person for pay period or periods ending in any calendar month. Execution upon such judgment shall, in discretion of court, have priority over other attachments. (§16-577).

No attachment or garnishment on wages may be made before judgment except as otherwise provided in District of Columbia Child Support Enforcement Amendment Act of 1985 or as provided in §16-916 dealing with alimony. (§16-583).

No employer shall discharge employee for reason that creditor of employee has subjected or attempted to subject unpaid earnings of employee to garnishment (§16-584), but holder served with notice of withholding may deduct additional $2 for expenses (§16-583).

Employer-garnishee must withhold and pay to judgment creditor, within 15 days after employee-debtor's last pay period in each calendar month, amount represented by his lien during such calendar month (§16-573), and judgment creditor must file with court: (1) Receipt every three months showing amount received and balance due on judgment and (2) final receipt, with copy to employee-garnishee, and (3) must obtain vacation of judgment within 20 days after payment in full (§16-574). Judgment for amount of lien may be entered against any employer-garnishee who fails to make any required payment. (§16-575). Attachment lapses if defendant-employee resigns or is dismissed unless reinstated or re-employed within 90 days. (§16-576). On written notice of court proceeding attacking attachment or judgment, employer must stop all payments except child support payments, which require judicial termination order. (§16-573[b]).

Earnings in excess of the statutory exemption (see topic Exemptions) are subject to garnishment.

HOMESTEADS:

No homestead law.

JUDGMENT NOTES:

See category Business Regulation and Commerce, topic Bills and Notes.

LEVY:

See topics Attachment, Executions, Garnishment.

LIENS:

Uniform Commercial Code is in effect. See category Business Regulation and Commerce, topic Commercial Code.

Mechanics and artisans have possessory lien on personal property for work done thereon and materials furnished therefor. (§38-124).

Liverymen have a lien on animals left in their charge until all charges for care, keep and board are paid; notice of intention to detain such animals being first delivered to the owner. (§38-201).

Garage keepers have a lien similar to that of livery stable keepers. (§38-202).

Hotels, motels, innkeepers, etc. have a lien upon, and may retain possession of, any personal property belonging to guests for amount due up to $1,000. If guest fails to pay within 30 days, establishment may sell property at public sale after proper notification and newspaper advertisement, and proceeds shall be used to cover expenses of storage and sale, and discharge of lien. If motor vehicle is retained, notification must be sent to any person with recorded security interest lien, or other claim on vehicle. (§34-102).

Hospitals are permitted to enforce liens for services on recoveries in accident cases (§38-301), by filing written notice thereof in Office of Recorder of Deeds and mailing copy of such notice to person alleged to be liable and his insurance carrier (§38-302). Such liens are not valid against anyone suffering injuries under District's Employee's Compensation Act or Workmen's Compensation Act. (§38-301).

District of Columbia has lien on tort recovery by injured police and firemen to or for whom District has paid benefits as result of injury for which tort recovery is had. (§4-504).

For other liens see topics Attachment, Executions; categories Business Regulation and Commerce, topics Carriers, Commercial Code; Civil Actions and Procedure, topic Judgments; Legal Profession, topic Attorneys and Counselors; Mortgages, topic Mortgages of Real Property; Property, topic Landlord and Tenant; Taxation, topic Property Taxes, subheads Liens and Sale; Transportation, topic Motor Vehicles.

Enforcement.—In case of liverymen and garage keepers, articles may be sold at public auction after newspaper notice (§38-203); and in case of mechanics or artisans, if value of articles retained is not more than $50 same may be sold at public auction after demand for payment and newspaper advertisement (§38-125); but if value exceeds $50, procedure to enforce lien must be by civil action in nature of petition in equity (§38-126). In case of hotels, motels, innkeepers, etc., personal property may be sold at public sale after demand for payment and newspaper advertisement. (§34-102).

Mechanics' Liens.—Mechanics' liens upon buildings and the lot of ground on which the same may stand will lie in favor of contractors, subcontractors, material men, and laborers, who file in the Office of the Recorder of Deeds, during the construction, or within three months after the completion of such building, any improvement or addition thereto, or placing therein, or in connection therewith, of any engine, machinery, or other thing, so as to become a fixture, a notice of their intention to hold a lien on the property declared liable to such lien, setting forth the amount due or to become due, and specifically the amount claimed, name of party against whose interest lien is claimed and description of property to be charged. If person claiming lien is subcontractor or person claiming under original contractor, he must serve notice upon owner of property on which lien is claimed, by leaving copy thereof with him or

his agent, or if neither can be found, by posting same on premises, and on his failure to do so, or until he shall do so, owner may make payments to his contractors according to terms of his contract, and to extent of such payments, lien of principal contractors will be discharged, and amount for which property is chargeable reduced. (§38-101-108).

Mechanics' liens have priority over all mortgages, judgments, deeds of trust, liens and encumbrances attaching subsequent to the commencement of the work, except that purchase money mortgages will have priority, if recorded within ten days from the date of acknowledgment. (§38-109).

Mechanics' liens are enforced by suit to be commenced within one year after filing of notice of lien or within six months from the completion of the building or repairs, and on failure to do so, the lien ceases to exist, unless the claim is not due, in which case action must be begun in three months after it becomes due. (§38-115).

Those claiming under a subcontractor are not entitled to a mechanics' lien. (§38-103; Battista v. Horton, 128 F.2d 29 [D.C. Cir. 1942]).

Public Works.—Any contractor for construction, alteration, or repair of any public building or public work of District, where contract for same exceeds $25,000, must furnish: (1) Performance bond, and (2) payment bond for protection of all persons supplying labor and material. Every person who has furnished labor or material and not been paid in full within 90 days has right to sue on payment bond for unpaid amount and to prosecute said action to final judgment for amount due. Any person having direct contractual relationship with subcontractor only shall have said right of action on payment bond upon written notice to contractor. Every suit shall be brought in name of District in Superior Court, but no such suit shall be commenced after one year from last day labor or material was furnished. (§1-1104-1106).

Those furnishing labor or material for federal public works may come within protection of U. S. Code, T. 40, §§270a-270d.

Redemption.—There is no right of redemption of property sold in satisfaction of a lien.

Wage Lien.—See topic Garnishment.

MECHANICS' LIENS:

See topic Liens.

PLEDGES:

Pledges are among the devices governed by Art. 9 of Uniform Commercial Code. See category Business Regulation and Commerce, topic Commercial Code.

There is a statute known as the "Loan Shark Act" regulating loans on personal property and the like. (§§26-701-712).

RECEIVERS:

This subject is governed by statutory and general equitable principles. Receiver may sue to set aside fraudulent transaction. (§28-3103).

Pursuant to D. C. statute, receiver may be appointed to take possession of assets of a person violating §2-2601 et seq., dealing with security agents and brokers (§2-2611); of property which has been attached (§16-518); of assets of bank that has discontinued operations for 60 days or is in liquidation (§26-103); of assets on dissolution of corporations (§§29-391-405); and of rents for master-metered apartment building when utility payments are delinquent (§43-543). Receiver may also be appointed under certain conditions to operate nursing home or other similar facility in order to safeguard rights of its residents. (§§32-1411-1420). Action wherein receiver has been appointed shall not be dismissed except by order of court. (Fed. R. Civ. P. 66; Sup. Ct. Civ. R. 66).

REDEMPTION:

See topics Executions, Liens; categories Mortgages, topic Mortgages of Real Property; Taxation, topic Property Taxes, subhead Redemption.

SUPPLEMENTARY PROCEEDINGS:

See topic Executions.

TRUSTEE PROCESS:

See topic Garnishment.

USURY:

See category Business Regulation and Commerce, topic Interest.

DISPUTE RESOLUTION

ALTERNATIVE DISPUTE RESOLUTION:

Mandatory Dispute Resolution.—In District of Columbia Superior Court all civil cases except those in certain categories (e.g., landlord-tenant, constitutional, injunctive, declaratory judgment) are required to proceed through one of three forms of alternative dispute resolution ("ADR"), namely, mediation, nonbinding arbitration, or case evaluation. DC court rules provide that scheduling order to be issued by assigned judge early in case will "ordinarily specify. . .a time period in which mediation or other alternative dispute resolution proceedings will be held." (Sup. Ct. Civ. R. 16[b]). In practice, judges allow parties to choose one of three ADR forms at scheduling conference. If arbitration is chosen, that process is scheduled to take place in period immediately following scheduling conference. If mediation or case evaluation is chosen, it is scheduled to take place after discovery is completed and before pretrial conference. "Neutrals" who conduct ADR proceedings are volunteer attorneys who have been trained by court. ADR programs are administered by Multi-door Dispute Resolution Division of Superior Court.

Voluntary Dispute Resolution.—In U.S. District Court for District of Columbia, ADR is voluntary. §3 of Civil Justice Expense and Delay Reduction Plan (adopted by

---

ALTERNATIVE DISPUTE RESOLUTION . . . *continued*

order of Court on Nov. 30, 1993) requires parties to meet and confer, shortly after case is filed, as to, among other things, determine whether case should go through ADR. Parties must report their views to judge who, if parties wish to use ADR, will refer case for mediation by court-appointed volunteer mediator. Mediation program is administered by Office of Circuit Executive of U.S. Court of Appeals for District of Columbia Circuit. Circuit Executive's Office also administers similar voluntary mediation program for appellate cases.

See also topic Arbitration and Award.

ARBITRATION AND AWARD:

The U.S. Arbitration Act (9 U.S.C. §§1-15) covers all contracts made subsequent to 1925 involving "commerce" in District of Columbia and containing written provision to settle controversy by arbitration.

Probate court has power, with consent in writing of both parties, to arbitrate, or to refer dispute to arbitrator, between personal representative and third persons; if reserved by parties, exceptions as to matters of law may be filed to award; said award when confirmed by court is conclusive between parties. (§16-3111).

Superior Court.—Small Claims and Conciliation Branch has authority with consent of all parties to settle cases by arbitration and conciliation. (§11-1322). Judges may also act as arbitrators either alone or in conjunction with other persons under §11-1322 or under U.S. Arbitration Act (9 U.S.C. §§1-14).

Uniform Arbitration Act adopted. (§§16-4301-4319 as am'd by D. C. Law No. 3-85).

DOCUMENTS AND RECORDS

ACKNOWLEDGMENTS:

Uniform Law on Notarial Acts adopted. (§§45-621-628). May be taken by following officers:

Within District: Judge of any court, employee of any local court designated by chief judge, clerk of District Court, notary public, (§1-810; §§11-742, 945). Fee, $2 for each signature required for seal and writing of certificate. (§1-813). Acknowledgment may be taken by notary public, judge, clerk, or deputy clerk of any D.C. court, or any other person authorized by law. (§45-623[a]).

Outside District but within United States: Notary public, judge, clerk, or deputy clerk, or any other person authorized by law. (§45-624[a]). In Puerto Rico and Philippine Islands, deeds and other instruments affecting land in D.C. may be acknowledged by notary public or any officer having ex officio powers of notary public, but acknowledgment must be accompanied by certificate of Executive Secretary of Puerto Rico or Governor, or Attorney General of Philippine Islands that notary is such. (§45-606). In Guam, Samoa and Canal Zone, deeds and other instruments affecting land in D.C. may be acknowledged by judge, notary public or any officer having ex officio powers of notary public, but acknowledgment must be accompanied by certificate of Governor or Acting Governor that notary is such. (§45-605).

Outside United States: Deeds made outside U.S. may be acknowledged before judge, notary public, or any secretary of legation or consular officer, or acting consular officer of U.S. (§45-604).

In Philippine Islands acknowledgment may be taken by notary public or any officer having ex officio powers of notary public, but acknowledgment must be accompanied by certificate of Governor or Attorney General that notary is such. (§45-606).

Person in Armed Forces.—As to notarial powers of officers, see topic Notaries Public.

General Requirements as to Taking.—Officer must have personal knowledge of identity of acknowledger, or same must be proved by oath or affirmation of credible witnesses or on basis of identification documents. (§45-622[a], [d]). Attorney cannot execute or acknowledge deed of conveyance by individual. (§45-601). No notary may take acknowledgment in connection with matter in which he is employed as counsel, attorney or agent, or in which he is interested. (§1-801).

General Requirements of Certificate.—All requirements for certificates found in Uniform Law on Notarial Acts adopted. (§45-627).

Married women acknowledge like other persons. Married women acknowledge like other persons for post Apr. 10, 1869 acknowledgment. (§45-609). Nothing in statute requires separate examination.

Proof by Subscribing Witness.—There is no statutory provision of proof of such instrument by affidavit of subscribing witness.

Authentication.—Signature and title of person who took acknowledgment are prima facie evidence that signature is genuine and person holds designated title. (§§623-625).

Notary Licenses and Authentication (Rm. 230, 717 14th Street, N.W. 20005) is proper office to authenticate certificates of acknowledgment taken by notaries public in District for use elsewhere. Fee $5 for certificate to be used in U.S.A.; $6 for certificate to be used outside U.S.A. Checks payable to "District of Columbia Treasurer".

Form.—Acknowledgment in individual capacity shall be sufficient if completed with information required by §45-627(a) in following form (§45-628):

Form

State of . . . .
(County) of . . . .
This instrument was acknowledged before me on (date) by (name(s) of person(s))

. . . .
(Signature of notarial officer)
(Seal, if any)
. . . .
Title (and Rank)
[My commission expires: . . . . .]

Acknowledgment in representative capacity shall be sufficient if completed with information required by §45-627(a) in following form (§§45-628, 621):

Form

State of . . . .
(County) of . . . .
This instrument was acknowledged before me on (date) by (name(s) of person(s)) as (type of authority, e.g., officer, trustee, etc.) of (name of party on behalf of whom instrument was executed.)

. . . .
(Signature of notarial officer)
(Seal, if any)
. . . .
Title (and Rank)
[My commission expires: . . . . .]

Alternative to Acknowledgment.—No statutory provision.

Validating Acts.—Certain irregular acknowledgments made in foreign countries prior to March 3, 1879, are validated (§45-607); and certain defective acknowledgments on deeds recorded prior to Jan. 1, 1969, are validated (§45-608); certain deeds made prior to Jan. 1, 1902, cannot be invalidated for lack of acknowledgment (§§45-611-12).

AFFIDAVITS:

May be taken by the following officers:

Within District: May be taken before a United States Magistrate (28 U.S.C. §636), notary public (§1-810), any judge of any court of District (28 U.S.C. §459), or any employee of any court authorized by chief judge of District of Columbia Court of Appeals (§11-742). Each judge and employee of Superior Court authorized by chief judge may administer oaths and affirmations and take acknowledgments. (§11-945). (Note that any Clerk of U.S. court and his deputies may take acknowledgments or administer oaths and affirmations. [28 U.S.C. §953].)

Outside District: May be taken before U.S. Magistrate (28 U.S.C. 636), any federal judge (28 U.S.C. 459), clerk of any U.S. court (28 U.S.C. 953), or any U.S. consular officer or embassy or legation secretary within their limits (22 U.S.C. 4215, 4221).

Persons in U. S. Armed Forces.—As to notarial powers of officers, see topic Notaries Public.

General Requirements as to Administration.—Notary public is disqualified to administer oath in connection with matter in which he is employed as counsel, attorney or agent, or in which he is interested before any U.S. government department. (§1-801).

Use of Affidavit.—No statutory provision permitting use of affidavits in evidence, but rules of court (see, e.g. Superior Court, Criminal Procedure, Rule 45[d]) or Federal Rules of Civil Procedure require or permit their use in many preliminary or interlocutory matters. Corporations generally may execute affidavits by officer, agent or attorney.

Form

Usual form of jurat: Subscribed and sworn to before me this . . . . . . day of . . . . . ., 19. . . . . Notary Public, D. C. (Seal).

Alternative To Affidavit.—No statutory provision.

Affidavits to be used in a court proceeding should bear the titles of the court and of the cause.

NOTARIES PUBLIC:

Appointment is made by Mayor. (§1-801).

Eligiblity.—A notary must be a resident of the District of Columbia or have his sole place of business or employment there. (§1-801).

Qualification.—A notary must take oath and give bond of $2,000. (§1-803).

Seal.—Notary must provide a seal to authenticate official acts. (§1-804).

Powers.—He may take depositions, acknowledgments, affidavits to be used before any court, judge or officer within District, administer oaths, certify papers (§1-810), protest negotiable instruments (§1-807, 808), etc.

Fees.—$2 for any notarial act including administering oath, taking affidavit including jurat and seal, and each signature required in taking acknowledgment of proof of deed or other instrument including seal and writing of certificate. (§1-813).

Authentication.—See same subhead under Acknowledgments.

Persons in or with U. S. Armed Forces.—The following persons on active duty or performing inactive-duty training are authorized to exercise general powers of a notary public for members of any of Armed Forces and for persons employed by or accompanying Armed Forces in certain places outside U. S.:

All judge advocates, summary courts-martial, adjutants, assistant adjutants, acting adjutants, personnel adjutants, commanding officers of the Navy, Marine Corps, and Coast Guard, staff judge advocates and legal officers, acting or assistant staff judge advocates and legal officers, and all other persons designated by regulations of the Armed Forces or by statute. (10 U. S. C. §936, am'd 1986).

RECORDS:

Record all deeds, contracts, and other instruments in writing affecting title or ownership of real estate or personal property in District with Recorder of Deeds, 515 D Street, N.W., Washington, D.C. 20001. (§45-901).

Record plats and subdivisions of all private property in District with Office of the Surveyor, 614 H Street, N.W., Rm. 605, Washington, D.C. 20001. (§1-905).

Record corporation and partnership documents with Department of Consumer & Regulatory Affairs, Corporations Division, 614 H Street, N.W., Rm. 407, Washington, D.C. 20001. (§§41-421, 426).

Filing Under Commercial Code.—Filing officer under Art. 9 of Uniform Commercial Code is Recorder of Deeds. (§§28:9-401[1], 45-901). See infra subhead Recorder's

See note at head of Digest as to 1998 legislation covered.

See Topical Index in front part of this volume.

RECORDS . . . *continued*

Fees, catchline Fees for Filing Under Uniform Commercial Code; also category Business Regulation and Commerce, topic Commercial Code.

Requisites for Filing or Recording.—Except for instruments (including financing statements) filed pursuant to Art. 9 of Uniform Commercial Code, or c. 10 of tit. 40 of D. C. Code, no instrument affecting title or ownership of real or personal property may be recorded unless acknowledged and certified. (§§45-803, 901). Instruments under Art. 9 are not recorded, but filed and indexed (§42-101), and, like instruments relating to motor vehicle liens under c. 10 of tit. 40, require neither acknowledgment nor certification. (§45-901). Deed conveying fee simple interest in real property may not be recorded until all delinquent real property taxes and interest and penalties related to real property have been paid. (§45-926). Does not apply to real property under Distressed Properties Improvement Act (§45-2584) or Homestead Housing Preservation Program (§45-2704). All parties with interest in particular real property must notify Recorder of Deeds if change of name or address occurs. Penalty of up to $300 for noncompliance, (§45-801.4).

Recorder's Fees.—

Real Property Documents.—For recording any deed of trust affecting real property, $15 for first three pages, and $5 for each additional page or fraction thereof; for recording other real property documents including deeds, releases, leases, agreements, security agreements (land), condominium agreements, covenants, covenants not to encumber, or foreclosures (real property and condominium), $15 for first two pages, and $5 for each additional page or fraction thereof. (36 DCR 6853-55). Surcharge of $5 must be paid before any document is accepted for recordation at Recorder of Deeds. (§45-909.1). For recording plat of subdivision when survey performed by private surveyor, $75 per sheet; for recording condominium plat and plans when survey performed by private surveyor, $300 flat fee plus $15 per sheet. (39 DCR 5745-49).

Corporation and Partnership Documents.—For filing certificate of limited partnership, $70. (35 DCR 2540). For filing application of registration of limited liability partnership (domestic and foreign), $150. (17 DCMR §3505). For filing articles of incorporation, $100 for profit corporation and $12 for nonprofit corporation (this includes filing, indexing and license fees). (§§29-399.22, 593).

General Documents.—For recording mechanic's lien, mechanic's lien release, mechanic's lien undertaking, hospital lien, U.S. tax lien, U.S. tax lien release, judgment, judgment release, bill of sale (chattels), security agreement (chattels), terminations, affidavits, or powers of attorney, $15 for first two pages, and $5 for each additional page or fraction thereof. (36 DCR 6853).

Search, Reproduction, and Certification.—Search for real property or general document certificate, $30; each additional general document certificate search for same debtor, free. Certificate reproduction, $2.25 per page; for certified copies add $2.25 for certificate and seal. (36 DCR 6853).

Fees for Filing Under Uniform Commercial Code.—For filing original financing statement, continuation statement, statement of assignment, termination statement or release, $15 for first two pages, $5 for each additional page and $15 per additional debtor. Search, reproduction and certification fees are same as above. (36 DCR 6853).

Real Estate Transfer and Recordation Taxes.—See category Taxation, topic Real Estate Conveyance Tax.

Effect of recording or filing is to affect third persons with constructive notice of instrument. See categories Mortgages, topic Mortgages of Real Property; Property, topics Deeds, Landlord and Tenant.

Torrens Act has not been adopted for the District.

Transfer of Decedent's Title.—For decedents who die on or after Jan. 1, 1981—Upon request of distributee, personal representative of decedent must execute instrument of distribution as evidence of distributee's title. Distribution of real property may be effected by quit claim deed. Deed must be indexed in grantor index under decedent's name and personal representative must pay all costs of recordation as cost of administration of estate. (§20-1103). See category Estates and Trusts, topic Executors and Administrators, subhead Foreign Executors or Administrators.

Vital Statistics.—

Birth and death certificates must be filed with Registrar of Vital Records, Vital Records Branch, 9th Floor, 613 G Street, N.W., Wash., D.C. 20001 (§§6-205, 211), where certified copies thereof may be obtained (§6-220). Fees for certified copies of vital records are as follows (39 DCR 492, as am'd):

	Fee	
Birth Certificate (computer record)	$ 12	
Birth Certificate (long form giving time of birth and age of parents)	18	
Delayed Birth Record	20	
Death Certificate	12	
Legal Change of Name	18	
Legitimation	18	
Adoption	20	
Certificate of Search	12	(for each three years searched, according to current practice)
Adjudgment of parentage	18	
Correcting birth or death records.	18	

Establishing Birth Record.—In case of persons having no recorded birth certificate, a delayed birth certificate may be obtained upon filing with Registrar of Vital Records application on official form with one or more supporting documents, such as hospital or physician's records, baptismal or other church records, affidavits, etc. (§§6-207, 208).

Marriage records are kept by Marriage Bureau of Superior Court, 500 Indiana Ave., N.W., Rm. 4485, Washington, D.C. 20001. Fee for certified copy of marriage license, $10. (§30-114; Sup. Ct. General Family R. C).

Divorce records are kept by Divorce Division of Superior Court, 500 Indiana Ave., N.W., Rm. 4335A, Washington, D.C. 20001. Fee for certified copy of divorce decree, 50¢ per page and $5 for certified seal. (§11-1101; Sup. Ct. General Family R. C).

SEALS:

Necessity, sufficiency and effect of seal are governed by common law. Seals are contained in all forms given by the Code. The symbol "L.S." or the word "Seal" written, printed or typed is a sufficient seal on any instrument.

Uniform Commercial Code in effect. See category Business Regulation and Commerce, topic Commercial Code.

TORRENS ACT:

Not adopted.

VITAL STATISTICS:

See topic Records.

EMPLOYMENT

EMPLOYER AND EMPLOYEE:

See topic Labor Relations.

LABOR RELATIONS:

Labor relations are governed by the National Labor Relations Act, which applies in the District to intrastate as well as interstate commerce. (29 U.S.C. §§141-187). Federal anti-injunction act controls District Court in labor disputes. (29 U.S.C. §§101-115).

Hours of Labor.—No statute regulating hours of labor.

Payment of wages must be made in money or check payable on demand, at least twice a month on regular paydays designated in advance, except that employer, by contract or custom, may continue to pay wages at least once a month. (§36-102). Unless otherwise specified in collective agreement with bona fide union (a) employer must pay to discharged employee wages earned not later than next working day, but employer allowed four days where employee responsible for employer's moneys, (b) employer must pay quitting employee his wages due upon earlier of next regular payday or within seven days, (c) employer must pay suspended employee wages earned not later than next regular payday, (d) upon failure to pay such wages, employer is liable to employee for an additional 10% of unpaid wages for each working day in default not to exceed unpaid wages. (§36-103). Where amount of wage in dispute, employer must pay wages conceded to be due. (§36-104). Collection of unpaid wages is supervised by Minimum Wage and Industrial Safety Board. Employer with more than ten employees must pay full-time employees usual compensation, less any fees received by employee, for jury service of five days or less. (§15-718).

Employee Trusts.—See category Property, topic Perpetuities.

Child Labor.—Minors under 14 may not be employed in gainful occupation, except in home or on farm, and except minors ten or over distributing newspapers outside school hours. (§36-501). Except as previously noted, persons under 18 may not be gainfully employed more than six days or 48 hours per week or more than eight hours per day. Minors 16 or 17 may not be employed between 10 P.M. and 6 A.M. Minors under 16 cannot be employed between 7 P.M. and 7 A.M. except that during summer evening hour is 9 P.M. (§36-502). Minors under 18 must obtain work permits from Board of Education to engage in gainful employment. (§§36-506-511). Employment of minors in dangerous occupations (§36-503), and in certain specific occupations (§§36-504, 505) is prohibited.

Minimum Wages.—District of Columbia Minimum Wage Act applies to all employers in District of Columbia, with exception of United States or District of Columbia, and provides that minimum wage shall be minimum wage set by U.S. government from time to time, plus $1. It also provides for time and one half regular rate for all hours in excess of 40 hours per week. Minimum wage and overtime provisions are not applicable to employee employed in executive, administrative or professional capacity, or in capacity of outside salesperson, as such terms are defined under Fair Labor Standards Act; or to newspaper delivery boy or casual babysitter in residence of employer; and overtime provisions do not apply to seafarer, railroad employee, any salesperson, part-sperson or mechanic primarily engaged in selling or servicing automobiles or trucks, car wash employee, any parking lot attendant or airline employee who voluntarily exchanges work days with another employee to utilize air travel benefits. (§§36-220.1, 220.2, 220.3). Handicapped workers are covered, with some exceptions. (§36-220.2[d]).

Special rules apply to employees who receive gratuities or commissions. (§36-220.2[e-g]).

Mayor is authorized to make and revise regulations, investigate, require production of information and attendance and testimony of witnesses for public hearing. (§§36-220.4, 220.5, 220.6).

Every employer subject to Act or any regulation or order issued thereunder must make and keep for not less than three years a record of (1) Name, address and occupation of each of his employees; (2) record of date of birth of any employee under 19; (3) rate of pay and amount paid each pay period; (4) hours worked each day and each work week by each employee; and (5) such other information as prescribed by Mayor. Every employer is required to furnish each employee at time of each payment of wages an itemized statement showing date of wage payment, gross wages paid, deductions from and additions to wages, net wages paid, hours worked during pay period, and any other information prescribed by Mayor. (§36-220.7).

Any person willfully violating Act is subject to criminal prosecution and upon conviction to fine of not more than $10,000 or imprisonment for not more than six

---

See note at head of Digest as to 1998 legislation covered.

See Topical Index in front part of this volume.

LABOR RELATIONS . . . *continued*
months, or both, provided no person shall be imprisoned except for conviction of second offense. (§36-214).

Any employee may sue on his own behalf and/or for other employees similarly situated for any unpaid wages provided for under Act and additional amount as liquidated damages. Employer who shows that his omission to pay required wages was in good faith may in discretion of court escape payment of liquidated damages. Court in employee's action shall allow reasonable attorney fees and costs to prevailing employee. City likewise may sue to recover any unpaid wages on behalf of employee upon written request by employee and assignment of his wage claim. Statute of limitations shall be three years after accrual of claim. (§§36-220.11, 220.12).

Public Works.—Employees of contractors erecting public works or buildings for District or U.S. must be paid at rate of wages prevailing in District for similar work, as determined by Secretary of Labor. (40 U.S.C. §276a). Wages are to be computed on basis of eight hour day and 40 hour week, with hours in excess of either being compensated at one and one-half times basic rate of pay. (40 U.S.C. §328).

Family and Medical Leave.—Employee is entitled to family leave in certain cases involving birth, adoption, or serious health condition and to medical leave in certain cases involving serious health condition. (§§36-1301-1317).

Unemployment Compensation.—An insured worker who has been paid within base period (four of last five calendar quarters completed prior to start of benefit year which commences on filing claim) wages of at least $1,300 in one quarter, $1,950 in at least two quarters and total wages for base period equal to 1½ times highest wages in any quarter during period is eligible to receive benefits if he: (1) Is able and available for work, (2) has registered and inquires for work at employment office, (3) has been unemployed for at least one week, (4) has made minimum of two contacts for new work in such week and (5) files claim for benefits. (§§46-108, 110 as am'd by D.C. Law 5-3). Eligibility of pregnant or recently pregnant women is governed by same standards as others and that pregnancy creates no presumption of inability to work. (§46-111[h]). Benefits are unavailable to aliens who are not lawfully admitted for permanent residence at time services upon which benefits are to be received were performed. (§46-110[9]). Individual who fails without good cause to attend training or retraining course, or participate in job counseling or other reemployment services ineligible for benefits. (7 D.C.M.R., §314). "Additional Benefits Program" consisting of two five-week phases of benefits is available to individual who: (1) Has received all requested benefits available under §46-108; (2) has satisfied requirements of §46-108 for eligibility; (3) provides (during Phase 1) tangible evidence of systematic and sustained effort to obtain work by making contact with at least three new employers on at least three days; and (4) provides (during Phase 2) tangible evidence of systematic and sustained effort to obtain work by making contact with at least five new employers on at least three days. (§46-108[h][2]). Individual judged by cooperating employer not to be job ready shall be referred to job counseling, training, or retraining. (§46-108[h][2][E]).

Workers' Compensation.—Compensation for disability or death resulting from injury to employees is governed by District of Columbia Workers' Compensation Act of 1979. (§§36-301-345 as am'd by D.C. Law 8-198). Licensed real estate sales persons and brokers under written contract as independent contractors are not covered by this Act under certain circumstances. (§36-301, as am'd by D.C. Law 10-169). Administration of workers' compensation is shifted to District government. This act parallels provisions of Longshoremen and Harbor Worker's Compensation Act (33 U.S.C. §§901-950) but differs from it in major respects: (1) Disability is defined solely in terms of physical or mental incapacity resulting in loss of wages; (2) maximum permissible compensation is equal to District's average weekly wage of insured District employees or $396.78, whichever is greater; (3) cost of living increases in benefits are limited to 5%; (4) compensation rates for disability are altered; (5) method of determining employee's average weekly wage is changed; (6) no compensation awards for disability can be made after death of injured employee; (7) employer or insurer is no longer required to provide substantial evidence of employee's lack of entitlement to compensation; (8) modified award is effective from date of modification, not date of injury; and (9) fund is established to cover costs of administering Act. Pre-1980 claims are covered by Longshoremen and Harbor Worker's Compensation Act, as amended subsequent to May 17, 1928. (§§36-301-345 as am'd by D.C. Law 8-198).

Occupational Safety and Health.—Employers shall furnish employees with places and conditions of employment that are free from recognized hazards likely to cause death, serious physical harm or illness, and shall comply with all promulgated occupational safety and health rules and orders. (§§36-1201-24).

Employers' Liability Act.—See category Business Regulation and Commerce, topic Carriers.

Discrimination.—Employers, employment agencies and labor unions prohibited from discrimination in matters relating to employment on basis of race, color, religion, national origin, sex, age, marital status, personal appearance, sexual orientation, family responsibilities, disability, matriculation, or political affiliation under Human Rights Act of 1977, as amended by D.C. Law 10-129. (§§1-2512-2514). Mandatory mediation process precedes formal investigation of complaint by Office of Human Rights. (§1-2544). If complaint not resolved, and Office finds probable cause after investigation, it will permit 60 days for conciliation. If no conciliation, Office will certify case to Commission for public hearing. (§1-2546). Private cause of action must be filed in court within one year of unlawful discriminatory practice, or discovery thereof. Timely filing with Office tolls running of one year statute of limitation during period complaint is pending before Office. (§1-2556). Rules governing complaints of discrimination in District of Columbia are set forth at 4 DCMR §100 et seq., as amended, Dec. 1996. (44 DCR 6569). No person may discriminate against employee or applicant on basis of use by employee or applicant of tobacco or tobacco products; however, enforcement of workplace smoking restrictions permitted or required by law is not precluded by this section. (§6-913.3). District government agencies must submit to Mayor and Council, affirmative action hiring plans. (§1-508).

D.C. Procurement Practices Act of 1985, as amended, prohibits (a) employer interference with employee disclosure of false claims, and (b) retaliation against employee who disclosed information to government or law enforcement agency. (§1-1188.16).

WORKERS' COMPENSATION LAW:

See topic Labor Relations.

ENVIRONMENT

ENVIRONMENTAL REGULATION:

(References to DCMR are to District of Columbia Municipal Regulations.)

General Supervision.—District of Columbia Council and Mayor of District of Columbia have delegated administrative control over environment to Department of Consumer and Regulatory Affairs; Department of Public Works; and Department of Environmental Services. (D.C. Register, Vol. 18, No. 3, pp. 91-93, Aug. 9, 1971). These Departments administer regulations issued by District of Columbia Council and Mayor pursuant to District of Columbia Air Pollution Control Act of 1984 (§6-904 et seq.), pursuant to statutory provisions of District of Columbia Code relating to solid waste disposal (§§6-501-604), pursuant to District of Columbia Phosphate Soaps and Detergent Restriction Act of 1985 (§6-971 et seq.), and pursuant to District of Columbia Noise Control Act (20 DCMR §§3000-3199.1). Department of Public Works also administers Hazardous Waste Management Act of 1977 as am'd by D.C. Law 8-66 (§§6-701-714); Solid Waste Management and Multi-Material Recycling Act (§§6-3401 et seq.) and Litter Control Administration Regulations (24 DCMR §1380 et seq.). Regulations concerning water pollution are issued pursuant to federal statutes made specifically applicable to District of Columbia (33 U.S.C. 1251 et seq.), pursuant to Water Pollution Control Act of 1984 (§6-921 et seq.), pursuant to Wastewater System Regulation Amendment Act of 1985 (§6-951 et seq.), and pursuant to provisions of District of Columbia Code relating to control and use of harbor facilities (§22-1701) and protection of life, health, and property (§1-319). District of Columbia also regulates transportation of hazardous materials (§6-3301) and, through Department of Public Works, recycling procedures (§§6-3407-3408). District of Columbia also subscribes to Potomac River Basin Compact (§§7-1301-1302), interstate agreement to coordinate resource planning and action among Maryland, Pennsylvania, Virginia, West Virginia, and District of Columbia; except that Congress has refused to consent to §(F)(2) of art. II of amended compact, dealing with establishment of certain water quality standards (§7-1302[a]). District of Columbia also maintains Soil and Water Conservation District to conduct, inter alia, surveys, investigations and research. (§1-2801-2813). District of Columbia also requires preparation of Environmental Impact Statements pursuant to Environmental Policy Act of 1989. (§6-981 et seq.).

Prohibited Acts of Pollution.—

Air Pollution.—Air Pollution Control Act of 1984 amended in 1993 to establish standards complying with National Ambient Air Quality Standards. Use of certain fuel oils and coal (20 DCMR §§801-802); discharge of nitrogen oxides over permitted levels (20 DCMR §804); improper transfer, discharge and storage in improper containers of volatile organic compounds, petroleum products and other designated substances and activities (20 DCMR §§700-713); particulate emission above permitted levels (20 DCMR §600); blowing soot from fuel-burning equipment fired by solid fuels (20 DCMR §600); use of unapproved incinerators (20 DCMR §602); visible and particulate emissions above permitted levels (20 DCMR §§603, 606); open-burning (20 DCMR §604); permitting fugitive dust into outdoor atmosphere (20 DCMR §605); automobile exhaust emissions above permitted levels (18 DCMR §§750-753); emission of odorous pollutants (20 DCMR §903); smoking in places frequented by public (§6-913-913.1); failing to post no smoking signs in such places (§6-914); use of rotary cup burner (20 DCMR §601); discharge into atmosphere of sulfur oxides above permitted levels (20 DCMR §803); engine idling (20 DCMR §900); escape of visible fumes or smoke from motor vehicle for more than permitted time (20 DCMR §901); sale of gasoline with excessive amount of lead (20 DCMR §902).

Alternative Fuels Technology Act of 1990 and c.9 of Title 20 of DCMR amended in 1994 by Clean Fuel Fleet Vehicle Program and Alternative Fuels Incentives Amendment Act of 1994, to conform district law and regulations to requirements of Title II of Clean Air Act. (See Law 10-201, 41 DCR 7178, effective 3/14/95.) Clean Air Act Compliance Fee of $20 per month is imposed on certain parking spaces to discourage single-occupant vehicle, home-to-work travel. (§§47-2731-33).

Noise Pollution.—Emission of sound above maximum permissible levels, said levels varying with time, place and source of occurrence (§1-315 note; 20 DCMR §3001.1); emitting sound determined by Mayor to constitute noise disturbance (20 DCMR §3000.14); offering for sale new motor vehicle that exceeds maximum noise limits (20 DCMR §3110.1); alteration of vehicle's exhaust system to increase noise emitted above permissible limits, or operation of such vehicle (20 DCMR §3112); failure to comply with Act's notice of violation provisions (20 DCMR §3010.9); failure to comply with emergency order of mayor to reduce or discontinue act creating sound level likely to be injurious to public health, welfare and enjoyment of life and property (20 DCMR §3011.2); interference with sound measurement authorized by statute (20 DCMR §3012.1); keeping or owning dog that disturbs neighborhood or any person (D. C. Law 3-17, §3); and operation of refuse collection vehicle within 300 feet of residential, special purpose or water front zone at nighttime (D.C. Law 6-93).

Water Pollution.—Throwing or depositing matter in Potomac River (§22-1702, 21 DCMR §700.4); depositing deleterious matter in Rock Creek or Potomac River (§§22-1703); maliciously making water supply impure (§22-3118); engaging in land disturbing activity without approved erosion and sedimentation control plan (21 DCMR §502.1); discharge of petroleum or waste in D. C. waters from vessel (D. C. Law 1-25, §11); discharge of waste from vessels berthed at marina, dock or basin (21 DCMR §540.1); throwing gravel, etc. into canal (24 DCMR §1000); discharging pollutants into District waters except as provided under §6-926 (§6-922); discharging sanitary sewage, wash or process water, oil laden bilge water, refuse or litter from watercraft (§6-926[m]); discharging harmful material into sanitary or combined sewer (§6-927[c]);

See note at head of Digest as to 1998 legislation covered.

See Topical Index in front part of this volume.

DC – 19

ENVIRONMENTAL REGULATION . . . *continued*
discharging hazardous substances, pollutants, or nuisance materials into public spaces (§6-927[d]); discharging of used motor oil to any sewer (§6-927[e]); storing pollutant or hazardous substance before approval of spill prevention and cleanup plan (§6-930); not testing underground storage tank containing oil, gasoline or other pollutants for leaks (§6-930); tampering and misuse of wastewater system (§6-955); discharging certain substances into wastewater system (§6-955, 20 DCMR 1501.1); installing septic tanks (§6-956[g]); and installing or using earth pit privies (§6-956[g]). Solid waste disposal regulations also prohibit disposal of solid waste in Potomac River or other waters of District of Columbia. (21 DCMR §700.4).

Hazardous Waste.—Construction, alteration, or operation of hazardous waste treatment or disposal facilities, or generation, storage, transportation, treatment or disposal of hazardous waste without permit or in violation of regulations (§6-703); hazardous waste reduction priority (§6-701); identification of major hazardous waste generators (§§6-732-733); fees for generation of hazardous wastes (§6-736); waiver of fees upon certain conditions (§6-736). District of Columbia has adopted 40 C.F.R. Parts 260-265, 270, and 124 (Subpart A) with appropriate amendments (20 DCMR §4000); and instituted procedures governing transportation of hazardous materials (§6-3301 et seq.).

Lead-Based Paint.—Entity or individual shall not do following in violation of Lead-Based Paint Abatement and Control Act of 1996 (§§6-997.1-14): Conduct lead-based paint activity; undertake lead-based paint abatement project; or provide training to others who conduct lead-based paint activities. Person must not apply lead-based paint or glaze to any surface, including but not limited to interior and exterior surfaces of residence, building bridge or other structure, fixture, household appliance, cooking, drinking, or eating utensil, furniture, toy or other article for use by children; nor to any paved surface. Entity or individual must not sell or transfer any object to which lead-based paint or glaze had been applied. (§§6-977.3). Criminal penalties include fine not to exceed $1,000 for 1st offense, $5,000 for subsequent offense, and $500 per day civil penalty. (§§6-977.12-13). Procedures for accreditation of training programs and for certification of individuals and business entities engaged in lead-based paint activities, and standards for conducting lead-based paint activities are set forth in 20 DCMR §806. (45 DCR 20).

Low-level Radioactive Waste.—Generators of low-level radioactive waste must annually register with D.C. and pay fees to reimburse D.C. for costs associated with disposal of such waste. (§6-3701 et seq., 20 DCMR 2120.1). Citizen suits provision to enforce (§6-3705); failure to register (§6-3703).

Solid Waste.—Disposal of waste in a manner not designated in regulations (§§6-507, 6-508, §6-2912; 21 DCMR §§700-799); failure to obtain, or violation of, permits or licenses required by regulations (§6-501; 21 DCMR §700); failure to follow appropriate recycling procedures (§6-3407).

No person may operate open solid waste facility (i.e. where solid waste is stored or processed outside fully enclosed building or structure). No person may construct or operate solid waste facility except in accordance with permit issued by Mayor. Fee for initial permit is $10,000. Permit valid for three years. Renewal fee is $9,000. In addition, solid waste facility charge imposed at rate of $4 per ton, except for construction and demolition wastes which are $2 per ton. Periodic reports required. Fines up to $25,000, as well as possibility of suspension or revocation of permit for failure to submit reports. Mayor has right to inspection of operations and records, and to establish rules and regulations to implement act. (§6-3452-3458). Full Environmental Impact Statement is required for construction of any new solid waste facility or substantial modification of existing structure. (§6-990.1).

Phosphate Cleaners.—Sale, use, or furnishing of cleaning agent with more than trace quantity of phosphorous compound except for enumerated uses (§6-972); sale, use or furnishing of cleaning agent exceeding 8.7% of elemental phosphorous by weight (§6-972).

Asbestos.—To qualify for asbestos abatement permit or license, person or business entity must comply with Asbestos Licensing and Control Act of 1990 (§6-991 et seq.), as amended, and rules set forth in 20 DCMR §§800, 899.

Environmental Impact.—District of Columbia Environmental Policy Act of 1989 (§§6-981 et seq.) requires preparation of environmental impact statement for actions likely to have significant effect on environment.

Enforcement.—

Air Pollution.—Mayor may inspect premises and records of operation. (20 DCMR §101.1). Mayor may issue orders for compliance. (20 DCMR §102). Criminal penalties are available. (20 DCMR §105). Mayor may modify, revoke, or terminate permits. (20 DCMR §202). Persons aggrieved by administrative decisions may seek review in District of Columbia Court of Appeals. (§11-722). Restrictions on smoking in public places may be enforced by citizen suits for injunctive relief (§6-915) or by civil and criminal penalties (§6-916).

Noise Regulations.—Mayor may issue notices of violation (20 DCMR §3010) and emergency orders (20 DCMR §3011) requiring violators to reduce sound emissions to permissible levels. Any aggrieved person may complain to Metropolitan Police Department which shall enforce Act. (20 DCMR §3013). D.C. may seek civil penalties ($300 fine) or criminal penalties (imprisonment not to exceed ten days) for violation of noise pollution statute (20 DCMR §3013); citizens may bring civil actions to enjoin noise pollution or enforce noise regulations against violators or to require Mayor to perform non-discretionary acts (20 DCMR §3014).

Water Pollution.—Under Water Pollution Control Act of 1984, Mayor may monitor and inspect facilities (§6-935); may issue compliance orders and assess civil penalties (§6-937); may institute civil action for injunctive relief and civil penalties (§6-938); and may seek criminal penalties. Under Water Quality Monitoring Regulations, Department of Consumer and Regulatory Affairs may impose self-monitoring of water quality conducted in accordance with quality assurance manual to be organized in specific format. (21 DCMR c.19 §§1900-04, 1999). Citizens may institute civil actions as well. (§6-939). Under Wastewater System Regulation Amendment Act of 1985, Mayor may enter to inspect (§6-958); may issue compliance orders (§6-960); may revoke permits (21 DCMR §1509); may seek injunctive relief or civil or criminal penalties (§§6-961, 6-964) and may set and collect charges or fees necessary to ensure compliance (§6-957). District of Columbia may seek criminal penalties for violations of statutes prohibiting dumping in Potomac River. (§§22-1702, 22-1703a). Dept. of Consumer and Regulatory Affairs may issue orders to correct current erosion and to compel compliance with permits. (21 DCMR §§504-505). Enforcement procedures are set forth in 21 DCMR §§2200.1-2206.9.

Solid Waste.—District of Columbia may seek civil or criminal penalties for violators of solid waste laws and regulations, including seizure and forfeiture of motor vehicle used in violating act. (§§6-508, 6-604; 6-2902; 6-2912; 6-3417). Mayor, through Dept. of Public Works, enforces litter control. (§6-2902).

Recycling.—After Jan. 1, 1994, sellers or distributors of paper products must sell or distribute paper products composed of minimum percentage of recycled content. (§§6-3403-23). Newspaper recycling mandatory. (§6-3407).

Hazardous Wastes.—D.C. may enter and inspect hazardous waste facilities, take samples, and inspect records. (§6-707). If violations are found, violator's permit may be suspended or revoked (§6-709); orders may be issued requiring corrective measures (§6-711); injunctive relief and civil or criminal penalties may be sought (§§6-710-711). Financial guarantor of violator may be liable if violator is bankrupt or beyond court jurisdiction. (§6-714). Mayor may also seek civil or criminal penalties for illegal dumping of hazardous wastes and violation of procedures relating to transportation of hazardous materials. (§§6-2912; 6-3304). Mayor may waive hazardous waste and toxic chemical fee if business has successfully implemented source reduction techniques. (§6-736).

Phosphate Restrictions.—Mayor may seek criminal penalties. (§6-974).

Underground Storage Tanks.—Owner of underground tank shall notify Mayor of its existence. (§6-995.2). Any person knowing of leak must notify Mayor (§6-995.3). Until new rules issued, installation of new underground storage tanks prohibited absent certain exceptions. (§6-995.4). Underground storage tank trust fund created to undertake corrective action. (§6-995.5). Businesses installing, removing or testing tanks must be licensed. (§6-995.6). Right of entry, inspection, analyses, and corrective action. (§6-995.8).

Penalties.—Violators of Air Quality Regulations (20 DCMR §§100-999) are subject to a fine not to exceed $5,000 or imprisonment for term not to exceed 90 days or both (20 DCMR §105); each day of continuing violation is separate offense. Violators of prohibition against smoking in certain public places are subject to fine not to exceed $50 for first offense; violators of obligation to post no smoking signs are subject to fine of up to $300 for each day of violation. Violators of noise pollution statute are subject to fine of not more than $300 or imprisonment for not more than ten days or both, each day of violation constituting separate offense. (20 DCMR §3013). Violators of water pollution statute are subject to civil penalties of up to $50,000 per violation and up to $250,000 for willful violations. Each violation constitutes separate offense. (§6-938). Violators are also subject to fine of not less than $2,500 nor more than $25,000 for each day of violation or imprisonment for not more than one year or both for first conviction; more severe penalties may be imposed for repeat convictions. Violators of wastewater statute are subject to civil penalties of up to $10,000 or imprisonment up to one year or both for intentional, willful, or reckless violation. Each day of violation constitutes separate offense and penalties apply to each separate offense. (§6-964). Violators of §22-1702, relating to deposit of matter in Potomac River, are subject to fine not to exceed $100 or imprisonment not exceeding six months, or both. Violators of §22-1703, relating to depositing deleterious matters in Rock Creek or Potomac River, are subject to fine of $300 or imprisonment not to exceed 90 days, or both. Violators of §22-3118, relating to making water impure, are subject to fine of not less than $500 nor more than $1,000 or imprisonment for not less than one year nor more than three years. Violators of regulations governing soil erosion (see supra under subhead Prohibited Acts of Pollution) are subject to fine of not more than $300 or imprisonment of not more than ten days. (21 DCMR §508). Each day of continuing violation is separate offense. Violators of §§6-505 to 6-510 concerning construction and use of incinerators are subject to fine of not more than $100 or imprisonment of not more than 60 days or both. (§6-508). Violators of certain provisions of Litter Control Act are subject to fines set forth in 21 DCMR §§700 et seq., and 24 DCMR 101 et seq. Violators of hazardous waste statute and regulations are subject to civil penalties of up to $25,000 with each day of violation constituting separate offense. Knowing violators are subject to up to $25,000 fine or up to one year in prison or both for each violation. (§6-711). Person who knowingly disposes of hazardous waste in violation of §6-2912(a) is guilty of felony, and subject to fine for each offense of up to $25,000, and up to five years in prison. (§6-2912[b][3]). Violations of solid waste disposal are subject to fine not to exceed $1,000 or imprisonment not to exceed 90 days or both. Person who disposes of solid waste for commercial purpose is guilty of felony and subject to fine for each offense of up to $25,000, or up to five years in prison or both. (§6-2912[b][2]). Each day of continuing violation is separate offense. (21 DCMR §§700.6-700.7). Person who knowingly disposes of medical waste in violation of §6-2912(a) is guilty of felony and subject to fine for each offense of up to $25,000, and up to five years in prison. (§6-2912[b][4]). Violators of restrictions on transportation of hazardous materials may be subject to fine of $100 to $10,000, up to one year imprisonment, or both. Violators may also be subject to permit suspension. Each day of continuing violation is separate offense. (§6-3304). Violators of recycling provisions are subject to fines and denial of issuance or renewal of license to engage in collection of solid wastes; Mayor may also refuse to collect or dispose of wastes not treated as required. (§6-3417). Violators of anti-litter regulations (D. C. General Police Regs., Tit. §35, Art. 3; 14 DCMR §§800-803; 21 DCMR §§700, 701) may be referred to D. C. Environmental Health School for remedial education (Org. Action No. 73-73). Violators of restrictions on phosphate cleaners are subject to fine of up to $15 for using prohibited cleaning agent and fine of up to $500 for selling at retail or furnishing prohibited cleaning agent. (§6-974). Violators of D.C. Underground Sewage Tank Act of 1990 (§6-1001 et seq.) subject to cease and desist order; fines of up to $25,000 per day (§6-1009), suspension of licenses (§6-1010) and citizen suit (§6-1011).

Permits.—District of Columbia, before issuing permits for building, demolition or construction activities must ensure that appropriate erosion prevention measures have been taken. (21 DCMR §503). No agency shall issue any permit for construction, expansion or operation of any cogeneration facility until Public Service Commission

See note at head of Digest as to 1998 legislation covered.

See Topical Index in front part of this volume.

ENVIRONMENTAL REGULATION ... *continued*
has established appropriateness standards and procedure through which entity can demonstrate that proposed facility meets appropriateness standards. (§43-2002). Approval must be obtained before installing incinerators and other disposal systems (21 DCMR §713.6); permit is required for installation of privies other than water closets connected with sewer (§6-602); permit is required to modify existing stationary sources of air pollution, to construct new sources, and to operate such sources (20 DCMR §§200-299); licenses are required for commercial collection and transportation of solid wastes by vehicle (21 DCMR §710); permit is required to discharge hazardous substance or pollutant from point source (§6-926); permit is required for dredging and filling activities on underwater land (§6-926); permit is required for real estate construction to control pollution from nonpoint sources (§6-926); permit is required for construction and operation of water treatment facilities (§§6-933, 6-934); permit is required for significant industrial users to discharge into wastewater system (21 DCMR §1502); permit is required to construct, alter or operate hazardous waste treatment or disposal facility or to generate, store, transport, treat or dispose of hazardous wastes (§6-703); and (under temporary authority) District of Columbia may impose fees and charges for issuance of wastewater pretreatment permits (§6-957). Variances from air pollution control act statute may be obtained upon application to Mayor (20 DCMR §103); variances and temporary exemptions from noise control statute may be obtained upon application to Mayor (20 DCMR §§3005-3007); variances from solid waste disposal requirements may be obtained from Director of Dept. of Public Works (21 DCMR §718); and exemptions from phosphate cleaner restrictions may be obtained from application to Mayor (§6-972).

Generally, business entities engaged in abatement of asbestos must be licensed and permitted, and employees engaged in abatement projects must be licensed. (§6-991.4). In cases of emergency and under certain conditions involving removal of resilient floor covering materials, licenses and permits are not required.

ESTATES AND TRUSTS

ADMINISTRATION:
See topic Executors and Administrators.

ADVANCEMENTS:
See topic Descent and Distribution.

ALLOWANCES:
See topic Executors and Administrators.

CLAIMS:
See topic Executors and Administrators.

DEATH:
A rebuttable presumption of death arises from unexplained absence for seven years. (§14-701).

Survivorship.—Uniform Simultaneous Death Act is in force. (§§19-501 et seq.).

Action for Death.—The executor or administrator of a person whose death was caused by wrongful act, neglect, or default of another, occurring in District, may bring action against wrongdoer for damages, provided action is brought within one year of death. Damages recovered (except amount specified by verdict or judgment for reasonable expenses of last illness and burial) do not form part of estate or become subject to debts of deceased, but inure to benefit of surviving spouse and next of kin according to allocation made in verdict or judgment or, in absence of such allocation, according to District statute of distribution, and are assessed only with reference to injury caused by such death to persons entitled to distribution. (§§16-2701-2703).

For survival of action on death, see category Civil Actions and Procedure, topic Actions, subhead Abatement and Revival.

Certified Copies of Death Certificates.—See category Documents and Records, topic Records, subhead Vital Statistics.

Uniform Anatomical Gift Act adopted. (§§2-1501-1508).

Living Wills.—See topic Wills, subhead Living Wills.

DECEDENTS' ESTATES:
See topics Descent and Distribution, Executors and Administrators, Wills.

DESCENT AND DISTRIBUTION:
Family Allowance.—Upon death of any person, surviving spouse entitled to $10,000 family allowance out of personal estate of decedent. Allowance exempt from all debts of decedent and subject only to payment of funeral expenses not exceeding $750. If no surviving spouse, any surviving minor children entitled to allowance. Allowance is in addition to respective shares of surviving spouse and children. (§19-101).

Real Estate.—Real property of intestate descends, subject to any rights of dower (see category Property, topic Dower), to those persons entitled on intestacy to personal property, and such persons take as tenants in common and in same proportions as for personal property. (§19-301).

Personal Property.—Surviving spouse of intestate is entitled to receive personal property subject to distribution as follows: If there are children or their descendants, one-third; if no children or their descendants, but parents or their descendants, one-half; if no children, parents, or descendants of either, all. (§§19-302-304).

The surplus after distribution to surviving spouse, or if no surviving spouse, all personal property subject to distribution, passes as follows, each class of which member is living taking to exclusion of subsequent classes: (1) To children, and descendants of deceased children by representation; (2) to parents equally or their survivor; (3) to brothers and sisters, and descendants of deceased brothers and sisters by representation;

(4) to collateral relatives in equal degree, per capita; (5) to grandparents, or such of them as survive, equally. (§§19-305-312).

Surviving Spouse.—See subheads Family Allowance, Real Estate, and Personal Property, supra.

Half Blood.—There is no distinction between whole and half blood. (§19-315).

Posthumous Children or Other Issue.—Any child or descendant of intestate born after death of intestate has same right of inheritance as if born before his death. (§19-314).

Children born out of wedlock and their heirs take both real and personal estate from mother or from their father if parenthood has been established, or from each other, or from heirs of each other in same shares as if born in wedlock; and mother and father if parenthood has been established and their respective heirs are capable of inheriting from such children. (§19-316). Antenuptial children of parents who marry, and which children are acknowledged by man, are legitimated and capable of inheriting and transmitting property. (§19-318).

Adopted Children.—See category Family, topic Adoption.

Advancements to a child or other descendant are taken into account. If advancement is equal to or greater than distributive share, child or descendant is excluded from any further share but is not liable to refund any amount advanced. Where advancement is less than share, descendant inherits only so much as to make equal share. Surviving spouse can take no advantage by advancements being brought into reckoning. (§19-319).

Election.—Surviving spouse loses dower right unless election to take dower filed with probate court within six months after letters of administration issued for intestate deceased spouse. (§19-113[b]).

Escheat.—In absence of surviving spouse, and relatives within fifth degree, counting from common ancestor to more remote, real and personal property subject to distribution escheats to District for benefit of poor. (§19-701).

See also topic Executors and Administrators.

ESTATES:
See category Property, topic Real Property.

EXECUTORS AND ADMINISTRATORS:
Probate Division of the District of Columbia Superior Court has jurisdiction of administration of estates of decedents.

Code citations refer to Tit. 20 of Code of District of Columbia 1981 edition. Tit. 20 of Code was completely rewritten by District of Columbia Probate Reform Act of 1980 (D.C. Law 3-72), and extensively amended by Probate Reform Act of 1994, (D.C. Law 10-241), which amendments apply to estates of decedents opened on or after July 1, 1995. For questions pertaining to estates of decedents opened prior to this date, refer to Title 20 of Code as it existed prior to D.C. Law 10-241.

Preferences in Right to Administer.—Order of priority in appointment of personal representative, successor personal representative and special administrator is: Personal representative named in will; surviving spouse or children of intestate decedent or surviving spouse of testate decedent; residuary legatees; children of testate decedent; grandchildren; parents; brothers and sisters; next of kin; other relations; largest creditor who applies for administration; any other person. (§20-303[a]). Whole blood is preferred to half blood in equal degree, and descending to ascending. (§§20-303[a][2][A], [B]).

Eligibility and Competency.—Letters will not be granted to any person who has filed renunciation of right to administer, or is under 18, or has mental illness, or is under conservatorship, or has been convicted of felony, or is alien not lawfully admitted for permanent residence, or is judge of any court established under laws of U.S. or is employee of any District of Columbia Court unless such judge or employee is surviving spouse or is related within third degree. (§20-303[b]). Nonresidents and foreign corporations having trust powers may act provided they file with Register of Wills power of attorney designating Register as agent for service of process and notices. (§20-303[b][7]).

Supervised and Unsupervised Probate.—Under District of Columbia Probate Reform Act of 1994, all probate is unsupervised unless decedent's will directs supervised probate or court finds good cause for supervised probate. (§§20-312, 401-406). During unsupervised administration, any interested person or personal representative may petition court for supervised administration, or court itself may initiate such action for good cause. (§20-403b). During supervised administration, filing of signed waivers by all interested persons shall be treated as change to unsupervised administration. Filing of subsequent demand for filing of inventories and accounts by any such interested person is treated as change back to supervised administration. (§20-403a).

Supervised personal representatives have unrestricted powers unless letters of appointment enumerate constraints. (§20-404). Supervised administration is terminated when final account approved, or when personal representative obtains order from court. (§§20-405, 1301[a]). Unsupervised personal representatives do not file inventories or accounts, are exempt from requirements for supervised representatives, and are subject to court only after good cause shown for court intervention. (§20-401[b]). Unsupervised administration terminates when Certificate of Completion filed with court by personal representative (§20-735), or automatically three years after appointment, unless extended. (§20-1301[c]).

Qualification.—Each personal representative, whether in supervised or unsupervised administration, is required to file: (a) Statement of acceptance of duties of office, (b) any required bond, and (c) written consent to personal jurisdiction in any action brought in District of Columbia, and, in case of nonresident personal representative, irrevocable power of attorney designating Register of Wills as person upon whom notices and process may be served. (§20-501, 303[b][7]).

Each personal representative must give bond, except domestic banks and trust companies and national banks, unless excused by decedent's will or written waiver of all

EXECUTORS AND ADMINISTRATORS . . . *continued*
interested persons, for benefit of all interested persons and creditors. Where so excused or waived, by one or more interested persons, no bond shall be given, except upon written demand by interested person or creditor having interest or claim in excess of $1,000 for bond in amount of such interest or claim. (§§20-502[a], [b]).

Issuance of Letters.—Letters must be issued to personal representative by Register of Wills, and must contain: (a) Name and address of court, (b) name of decedent and personal representative, (c) date of appointment of personal representative, (d) date will was admitted to probate, (e) signature of Register and seal of court, (f) date letters were issued, and (g) whether administration is supervised or unsupervised, and, if supervised, any limitations on powers of personal representative. (§20-503).

Form

LETTERS OF ADMINISTRATION

To all persons who may be interested in the estate of . . . ., deceased:
Administration of the estate of the deceased has been granted on . . . . to . . . . (and the will of the deceased was probated on . . . .).

This administration (is) (is not) (strike inapplicable language) subject to continuing supervision of the court. The powers of the personal representative (are not limited) (are limited as follows: . . .)

The appointment is in full force and effect as of this date.

(SEAL)

Witness: . . . .
Dated: . . . .
Register of Wills.
(§20-504).

Removal.—Personal representative may be removed for misrepresentation of material facts in proceedings for appointment, willful disregard of court order, inability to discharge duties and powers effectively, mismanagement of property, and failure without reasonable excuse to perform any material duty. (§20-526).

Special Kinds of Administration.—Provision is made for appointment of special administrator when necessary to protect property, or upon termination of appointment of personal representative and prior to appointment of successor. (§20-531[a]).

Public Administrators.—No provision.

Inventory and Appraisal.—Personal representative must file, within three months of appointment, inventory of real and personal property owned by decedent. Following articles are not included in inventory: Wearing apparel other than furs and jewelry, food for consumption by family, family pictures, family Bibles. All property must be appraised. Personal representative must use standing appraisers, or for good cause shown, special appraisers. However, personal representative may appraise debts, bank accounts and corporate stocks listed on any national and regional exchange or sold on over-the-counter market. (§20-711, 712).

General Powers and Duties.—Personal representative has duty and all powers necessary to collect, manage and preserve property, to pay debts, and to settle and distribute estate in accordance with will or laws relating to intestacy or administration. (§§20-701, 702, 741).

Notice of Appointment to Heirs, Legatees and Creditors.—Within 20 days after appointment, personal representative must publish notice of appointment once a week for three successive weeks in Washington Law Reporter and any other publication court may order. (§20-704).

Form

" 'To all persons interested in the estate of . . . .

" 'This is to give notice that the undersigned, ... whose address is . . . . was, on . . . . . . appointed personal representative of the estate of . . . . who died on . . . . . ., (with) (without) a will, and that the personal representative will serve in (supervised) (unsupervised) administration.

" 'All persons having any objection to such appointment (or to the probate of the decedent's will) shall file an objection with the Register of Wills on or before . . . . . . (6 months from the date of the first publication of notice under this section).

" 'All persons having claims against the decedent shall present their claims to the undersigned or file their claims with the Register of Wills on or before 6 months from the date of the first publication of this notice.

" 'Any claim not so filed on or before such date, shall be unenforceable thereafter.

" 'Any person who is related to the decedent and who does not receive notice of this appointment by mail within 25 days shall so inform the Register of Wills including such person's name, address, and relationship to the decedent.

. . . .
" 'Personal representative.

" 'Date of first publication:' "
. . . . . .

(§20-704[a]).

Within 20 days after appointment, personal representative must send by registered or certified mail to heirs and legatees and creditors who are reasonably identifiable text of first newspaper notice of appointment and certain general information in form prepared by Court (§20-704[b]) within 90 days after appointment personal representative (supervised or unsupervised) must certify to Register that required notices have been given (20-704[b-1]).

Presentation of Claims.—Except as provided by statute with respect to claims of U.S. and District of Columbia, all claims against decedent's estate, whether due or to become due, absolute or contingent, liquidated or unliquidated, founded on contract or other basis, are barred unless presented within six months after date of first publication of notice of appointment; and all claims against estate based on conduct of or contract with personal representative are barred unless action is commenced against estate within six months of date claim arose. (§20-903[a]).

Proof of Claims.—Claimant must present claim against decedent's estate by delivering or mailing, return receipt requested, verified written statement of claim to personal representative with copy to Register of Wills or to Register with copy to personal representative. (§20-905[a]).

Form.—Statement of claim must state: (1) Name and address of claimant, (2) basis of claim, (3) amount claimed, (4) if not yet due, when due, (5) if contingent, nature of contingency, and (6) if secured, description of security. (§20-905[b]).

Approval or Rejection of Claims.—For claims duly presented within time limit of six months, personal representative must notify claimant: (1) That claim has been allowed in stated amount, (2) that claim has been disallowed in whole or in part and advising claimant of procedures and time limitations for contesting such disallowance, or (3) that personal representative will petition Court to determine whether claim should be allowed. Claim is forever barred to extent of disallowance unless claimant files verified complaint within 60 days after mailing of notice of disallowance. If no action by personal representative, claimant may file verified complaint. (§20-908[a], [b]).

Payment of Claims.—Personal representative must within eight months from date of first publication of notice of appointment, unless Court extends time, pay claims allowed against estate. (§20-909[a]). If unsecured proven claim is not yet due, or contingent or unliquidated claim becomes due or certain before distribution of estate, and claim has been established by proceeding, it is paid in same manner as presently due claims of same class. (§20-911[a]). Provision made for other cases of unsecured claims or secured future claims. (§20-911[b]-[c]). Secured creditor who surrenders security must be paid full amount. (§20-912[a]). Secured creditor who does not surrender security must be paid full amount of claim less amount realized from security or value of security. (§20-912[b]).

Priorities.—If assets of estate are insufficient to pay all claims in full, after funeral expenses not exceeding $1,500, personal representative must make payment in following order: (1) Family allowance not exceeding $10,000, (2) claims for rent in arrears for which attachment might be levied by law, (3) judgments and decrees of courts in District of Columbia, (4) all other claims. (§20-906[a]). For solvent estates where will makes no provision for funeral expenses, $5,000 authorized for funeral expenses, but heirs and legatees may waive limitation. (§20-907).

Sales.—Personal representative is empowered to sell real and personal property without court order. (§20-741[6]). Any interested person may move Court to have priority placed on sale of any real or personal property; and upon filing of such motion, no sale shall take place until all interested persons have been given notice and Court after hearing has made appropriate order. (§20-703).

Actions by Representative.—Personal representative may prosecute or submit to arbitration actions, claims or proceedings in any appropriate jurisdiction for benefit of estate, including commencement of any personal action that decedent might have commenced. (§20-741[18]).

Actions against Representative.—Personal representative may defend or submit to arbitration actions, claims or proceedings in any appropriate jurisdiction for benefit of estate. (§20-741[18]). No proceeding to enforce claim against estate may be revived or commenced before appointment of personal representative. After appointment, and until estate is closed, procedures described under subheads Presentation of Claims, Proof of Claims, Approval or Rejection of Claims, and Payment of Claims must be followed. After estate has been closed, creditor whose claim has not been barred may recover directly from persons to whom property has been distributed up to amount of distribution or from personal representative individually, provided that any such claim is barred one year from date of distribution, or 30 or 60 days from date of receipt of notice and copy of final account (§§20-726, 736; §§20-901, 1302, 1303). No execution upon or levy against any property of estate under any judgment against decedent or personal representative is permitted. (§20-914).

Allowances.—$10,000 to surviving spouse or to surviving minor children. (§19-101[a], [b]).

Quarantine.—Surviving spouse may reside rent-free in chief house of deceased spouse for 40 days after latter's death, during which time dower must be assigned. (§19-102[a]).

Intermediate Accountings.—Supervised personal representative must file his first account within one year and one day of first publication of notice of appointment, and must file subsequent accounts thereafter every nine months until final account. (§20-724[a]).

Final Accounting and Settlement.—No time limit specified.

Consent Settlement.—Supervised personal representative is excused from filing inventories and accounts if each heir or legatee signs written waiver filed with Register of Wills. (§20-731[a]).

Distribution.—Subject to will and needs of administration, personal representative must distribute in kind subject to following: (a) Specific legatee must receive object of legacy, (b) family allowance may be satisfied by value in kind if person entitled has not demanded payment in cash and residuary legatee does not object, (c) residuary estate must be distributed in kind if no objection and it is practicable to distribute undivided interests. (§20-1102). For intestate property, see topic Descent and Distribution; for legacies, see topic Wills.

Liabilities.—Personal representative, whether supervised or unsupervised, is fiduciary who, in addition to specific duties expressed in Tit. 20 of D. C. Code, is under general duty to settle and distribute estate in accordance with will or laws relating to intestacy as would prudent person in such matters. (§20-701[a]). Supervised personal representative must distribute all assets in his possession or control within 30 days of approval of final account (§20-701.1).

Compensation.—Personal representative is entitled to reasonable compensation. (§20-751). Courts will not review compensation of personal representatives, attorneys or agents unless heir or legatee complains. Upon notice and hearing, court may review reasonableness of compensation. If court determines fees were excessive, and orders refund, that alone cannot be basis for finding misappropriation of funds or violation of

---

See note at head of Digest as to 1998 legislation covered.

See Topical Index in front part of this volume.

DC – 22

EXECUTORS AND ADMINISTRATORS . . . *continued*
ethics or disciplinary rules. (§20-753). Factors court considers include: (1) Reasonable relationship of proposed compensation to work, (2) estimate of costs and any change in costs, (3) reasonableness of time spent including hours and usual hourly compensation, (4) nature and complexity, and results achieved, (5) whether time limitations have been met, or reasons for any delay. (§§20-751, 753).

When Administration Unneccesary.—When only assets consist of not more than two motor vehicles and all debts and taxes are paid, title may be transferred without administration. (§20-357; §40-102[d]). Also, see subhead Small Estates, infra.

Small Estates.—Small estates consisting of property not in excess of $15,000 may be administered under simplified procedures. Personal representative is not required to be represented by attorney or to give bond, and is not entitled to receive commission. (§§20-351-354).

Foreign Executors or Administrators.—Foreign personal representative of non-domiciliary is not required to obtain letters in District of Columbia for any purpose. (§20-341[a]). If estate has property in District of Columbia, foreign personal representative must file with Register of Wills copy of his appointment and copy of will (§20-341[b]), and publish notice of appointment once a week for three consecutive weeks (§20-343[a]). Foreign personal representative may exercise powers of office and may sue and be sued in District. (§20-342).

Uniform Fiduciaries Act adopted. (§§21-1701-1712).

Uniform Principal and Income Act not adopted.

Uniform Simplification of Fiduciary Security Transfers Act adopted. (§§28-2901-2909). Act prevails over inconsistent provisions of Art. 8 of Uniform Commercial Code. (§28:10-104). See category Business Regulation and Commerce, topic Commercial Code.

FIDUCIARIES:

See topics Executors and Administrators, Trusts; category Family, topic Guardian and Ward.

INTESTACY:

See topic Descent and Distribution.

PROOF OF CLAIMS:

See topic Executors and Administrators; category Civil Actions and Procedure, topic Pleading.

TRUSTS:

Equitable principles governing trusts under common law are generally applied, absent statute on subject.

Kinds.—Express, resulting, and constructive trusts recognized following common law principles.

Creation.—Governed by common law generally. (464 A.2d 87).
All declarations or creations of trust of real estate are void unless in writing, signed by the person making the same, or made in his will. (§28-3503).
Writing is essential to create any trust effective against third parties such as creditors. (104 A.2d 835).
Any resulting or constructive trust, or any conveyance of real estate by which a trust or confidence may arise by implication or construction of law, or be transferred or extinguished by an act or operation of law is of same effect as under common law without any requirement of writing. (§28-3503).

Appointment of Trustee.—No statutory provision.

Eligibility and Competency.—Domestic business corporations not organized as trust companies under §26-401 may not accept trusts. (§29-303). Foreign corporations may not accept trusts unless they comply with requirements applicable to domestic trust companies. (§26-435).

Qualification.—No statutory provision.

Removal of Trustee.—No statutory provision.

General Powers and Duties of Trustees.—No statutory provision.

Sales.—No statutory provision.

Investments by testamentary and other trustees, except those who have been appointed by or are under supervision of the court, are not subject to regulation by statute or rule of court. All fiduciaries subject to order of court may make such investments as would be made by prudent men subject to terms of instrument. (Sup. Ct. Civ. R. 306).

Securities in Name of Nominee.—No statutory authorization.

Bequests and Devises to Inter Vivos Trusts.—See topic Wills, subhead Bequests and Devises to Trusts.

Accounting.—No statutory provision.

Compensation.—No statutory provision.

Discharge.—No statutory provision.

Uniform Common Trust Fund Act adopted. (§§26-301-304).

Uniform Principal and Income Act not adopted.

Gifts to Minors.—See category Family, topic Infants.

Uniform Fiduciaries Act adopted. (§§21-1701-1712).

Uniform Simplification of Fiduciary Security Transfers Act adopted. (§§28-2901-2909). Act prevails over inconsistent provision of Art. 8 of Uniform Commercial Code. (§28:10-104). See category Business Regulation and Commerce, topic Commercial Code.

Accumulations.—See category Property, topic Perpetuities.

Perpetuities.—See category Property, topic Perpetuities.

Pour Over Trusts.—See topic Wills, subhead Bequests and Devises to Trusts.

Renunciation.—No statutory provision.

WILLS:

Any person at least 18 years of age may make valid will and testament or codicil if at time of its execution or acknowledgment he or she was of sound and disposing mind and capable of executing valid deed or contract. (§18-102).

Testamentary Disposition.—All real and personal property that might pass by deed or gift, or that would descend to decedent's heir or other representatives in case of intestacy, are subject to disposal by will or codicil. (§18-301). No statutory restrictions on devises to religious or charitable institutions.
Will executed after Jan. 1, 1902 which, by words of general import, devises all of testator's estate or property operates as valid devise of real property acquired by testator after execution of will, unless contrary intention appears therefrom. (§18-305).

Execution.—All wills and testaments (other than valid nuncupative wills [§18-107]) must be in writing and signed by testator or by some other person in his presence and by his express direction and must be attested and subscribed in presence of testator by at least two credible witnesses, or else they are void. (§18-103).

Attestation Clause.—The form of attestation clause in general use is:

Form
Signed, sealed, published and declared by the above named testator, ..., as and for his last will and testament, in our presence, and we, at his request, in his presence and in the presence of each other, have hereunto subscribed our names as attesting witnesses, on the day and year last hereinbefore written.

Holographic wills not executed and attested in accordance with statute are void.

Nuncupative wills are void, except that soldiers in active service and mariners at sea may dispose of personal property by such will during their last sickness, if oral will proved by two witnesses asked to act as such by testator and reduced to writing within ten days. (§18-107).

Revocation.—No will or codicil, or any part thereof, may be revoked, except by later will or codicil or other writing declaring such revocation; by burning, cancelling, tearing, or obliterating such will or codicil with intent to revoke by testator or in his presence and by his direction and consent; or by implication of law. (§18-109).
However, the common law rule that marriage and the birth of a child capable of inheriting revoke a prior will, if both occurred after the execution thereof, is in force in the District. (79 U.S. App. D. C. 354, 147 F.2d 880). A divorce with property settlement presumptively revokes will in favor of former spouse. (435 A.2d 379).

Revival.—No will, codicil, or any part thereof, once in any manner revoked, can be revived, other than by reexecution or by a codicil. (§18-109).

Testamentary gifts to subscribing witnesses are void, but such witnesses are competent to prove will. Such witnesses may take portion of testamentary gift entitled to in case of intestacy. (§18-104).

Bequests and Devises to Trusts.—"Pour Over" trusts permitted. Bequests and devises may be made to inter vivos trust or testamentary trust. Unless will or codicil provides otherwise, inter vivos trust may be amended subsequent to testator's will; termination of trust by its terms will not invalidate bequest; and revocation of inter vivos trust prior to death of testator will invalidate bequest. (§18-306).

Testamentary Guardian.—See category Family, topic Guardian and Ward, subhead Selection of Guardians.

Probate.—See topic Executors and Administrators. Custodian of will or codicil must file instrument with Register of Wills or Probate Court or deliver to executor named in instrument within 90 days following death of testator. (§18-111).
Probate proceedings are commenced by filing with Probate Division of District of Columbia Superior Court petition for probate, which shall include: Information specified in §20-304 (for standard or abbreviated proceeding) or §20-352 (for small estate proceeding) and original of will, or copy if original previously filed.
Supervised and Unsupervised Probate.—See topic Executors and Administrators.
Standard Probate Proceeding.—Petitioner must give notice to all known interested persons and shall publish notice each week for two successive weeks in newspaper of general circulation in District of Columbia, and shall state whether administration is supervised or unsupervised. (§20-323). Unless Court orders otherwise, proof of execution will be made by affidavits of witnesses in form provided in §20-324(c). Following proof of execution, Court will enter order admitting will to probate and appointing one or more personal representatives, or determining that decedent died intestate. Court may order that administration will be supervised as provided in §20-402. (§20-324[b]).
Abbreviated Probate Proceeding.—Proceeding may be conducted without prior notice required for Standard Probate, and due execution of will will be presumed, and will may be admitted to probate either: (a) If will appears to have been duly executed and contains recital by attesting witnesses of facts establishing due execution; or (b) upon verified statement of such facts by any person having personal knowledge of circumstances of execution, whether or not such person was attesting witness. (§§20-311, 312).
Small Estate Proceeding.—If property of decedent subject to administration in District has value of $15,000 or less, property may be administered as small estate. (§20-351). Petition must be verified and must be filed by person eligible for appointment as personal representative of estate. (§20-352). If Court determines that petition (and any other information required to be filed) is accurate, Court will appoint personal representative, direct payment of allowable funeral expenses and family allowance, direct such sales of property as may be necessary to pay funeral expenses and family allowance, and, if any property remains, admit will to probate, and direct issuance of notice. (§20-353). Personal representative must report to Court immediately any property of decedent discovered after petition. (§20-355).
Creditors filing claims in excess of $500 constitute interested persons. (§20-101[d][1][E]). All creditors known or reasonably identifiable must be sent notice by personal representative within 20 days of appointment. (§20-704[b]). Any interested

WILLS . . . *continued*

person or creditor having interest or claim in excess of $1,000 may make written demand that personal representative give bond in amount of person's or creditor's interest or claim. (§20-502[a-1]).

Fraud.—Person injured by fraud may obtain appropriate relief from any person who benefitted from fraud, other than bona fide purchaser. Proceeding must be commenced within two years after discovery of fraud, but no later than five years after commission of fraud as against non-perpetrator of fraud. Person convicted of fraud in probate proceeding is subject to penalties under District of Columbia Theft and White Collar Crimes Act of 1982. (§20-108.1).

Self-proved Wills.—See subhead Probate, catchline Abbreviated Probate Proceeding, supra.

Living Wills.—Any person 18 years or older may execute declaration, in form and with witnesses specified by statute, directing withholding or withdrawal of life-sustaining procedures in event of terminal illness. (§§6-2421-2430). Likewise, any adult may execute enforceable durable power of attorney for health care. (§§21-2201-2213).

Contest.—Except with respect to small estates (for which 30-day period may become applicable under §20-353[b]), any person may contest validity of will by filing verified complaint within six months of publication of notice of appointment or reappointment of personal representative. Any person filing such complaint must give notice to all other interested persons. (§20-305).

Legacies may be distributed during administration and must be distributed within 30 days of approval of final account, unless time extended by Court. (§§20-701[b], 20-741[t]). If specifically bequeathed item not part of estate, legacy generally fails, unless testator clearly evidenced intent that proceeds of sale of item during lifetime would stand in its place. (439 A.2d 516).

Unclaimed Legacies.—All intangible personal property held in fiduciary capacity for benefit of another person is presumed abandoned if no communication etc. from owner within five years after it becomes payable. (§42-211). See category Property, topic Absentees, subhead Escheat.

Lapse.—If legatee or devisee predeceases testator, leaving issue surviving at testator's death, such issue take their ancestor's bequest or devise, unless will evidences contrary intent. If there are no issue of deceased legatee or devisee, lapsed legacy or devise included in any residuary devise or bequest. (§18-308).

Children.—Surviving children are entitled, in absence of surviving spouse, to allowance of $10,000 out of personal estate of decedent. (§19-101). For doctrine of implied revocation of will in event of birth of child after execution of will, see subhead Revocation, supra.

Election.—A devise or bequest to a surviving spouse bars his or her share (other than intestate share of any property undisposed of by decedent's will) in decedent's estate (including dower rights, if any) unless it be otherwise expressed in will (§19-112) or unless he or she files written renunciation in probate court within six months after will is probated (§19-113). By so renouncing, surviving spouse becomes entitled to share of decedent's estate to which he or she would have been entitled had decedent died intestate (with dower if elected in lieu of real estate), but not in excess of more than one half of net estate bequeathed and devised or, if dower elected, not more than one half of net personal estate bequeathed and dower share in real estate devised. (§19-113[e]). If decedent has made no devise or bequest to surviving spouse or if nothing passes by such devise or bequest, surviving spouse is entitled to either take dower under §19-113(b) or to take legal share without filing written renunciation. (§19-113[d]). If surviving spouse does not renounce, he or she is entitled to receive benefit of all provisions in his or her favor in will of deceased spouse and takes intestate share in any estate of decedent undisposed of by will. (§19-114).

Foreign Executed Wills.—No statutory provisions.

Foreign Probated Wills.—See topic Executors and Administrators, subhead Foreign Executors or Administrators.

Foreign executed or foreign probated will must comply with District statute in order to pass title to real estate in the District. However, filing of certified foreign probated will in office of Register of Wills is sufficient to pass title to such real estate. (§14-504). (See category Documents and Records, topic Records.)

Simultaneous Death.—See topic Death, subhead Survivorship.

Testamentary Trusts.—See topic Trusts.

Uniform Anatomical Gift Act (1968) adopted. (§§2-1501 to 1511).

FAMILY

ADOPTION:

Adoption is governed by Tit. 16, §§301-315.

Any person, provided spouse (if any) joins in petition or (if spouse is natural parent of adoptee) consents thereto, may petition Superior Court for adoption of any minor or adult. If marital status of petitioner changes after time of filing petition and before time of decree of adoption is final, petition must be amended accordingly. (§16-302, 303).

Consents Required.—If adoptee is over 18 years old, only consent required is that of adoptee. (§16-304[f]).

If adoptee is minor, consent required of adoptee (if 14 or over), and also (a) both parents, if both are alive; or (b) living parent of adoptee, if one of parents is dead; or (c) court appointed guardian of adoptee; or (d) licensed child-placing agency or Mayor in cases where parental rights have been terminated by court of competent jurisdiction or by release of parental rights to Mayor or licensed child-placing agency in accordance with consents obtained pursuant to (a) through (c) above and adoptee has been lawfully placed under care and custody of such agency or Mayor; or (e) Mayor in any situation not provided for above. (§16-304[b]).

Conditions Precedent.—See infra, subhead Decree.

Jurisdiction is conferred on Superior Court (Family Division) if petitioner is legal resident of, or has actually resided at least one year prior to filing of petition in, D. C., or if adoptee is in legal care, custody or control of Mayor or licensed child-placing agency. (§11-1101[9]; §16-301).

Petition must state name, sex, date and place of birth of adoptee; names, addresses and residences of natural parents (if known) except that information regarding natural parents need not be set forth in adoption proceeding which is consented to by Mayor or licensed child-placing agency; name, address, age, business or employment of petitioner, and name of employer (if any) of petitioner; relationship (if any) of adoptee to petitioner; race and religion of adoptee, or natural parents or parent; race and religion of petitioner; date that adoptee commenced residing with petitioner; and any change of name which may be desired. If any facts are unknown to petitioner, petitioner shall state this fact. (§16-305). Petition need not contain information concerning race and religion if petitioner is spouse of natural parent of adoptee and natural parent joins in petition or consents thereto. (§16-308).

Proceedings.—Immediately upon filing of petition, notice of adoption proceedings by summons, by registered letter, or otherwise as court may direct, must be given to persons whose consent is necessary, except that persons who have formally consented, shall be held to have waived requirement of notice. (§16-306). Upon filing of petition, Court shall direct Mayor or licensed child-placing agency to investigate and report findings with recommendations within 90 days or such other time as extended by Court. (§§16-307, 309[a]). Whenever adoptee is adult or petitioner is spouse of natural parent and natural parent consents or joins in petition, court may dispense with investigation, report, and interlocutory decree. (§16-308).

Decree.—Court may enter final or interlocutory decree of adoption when it is satisfied that adoptee is suitable for adoption by petitioner, petitioner is fit and able to give adoptee proper home and education, adoption is in best interest of adoptee, and adoption form has been completed by petitioner pursuant to §10 of Vital Records Act of 1981. (§16-309[b]). Final decree of adoption may not be entered until adoptee has lived with adopting parents for six months. (§16-309[c]). Court may enter interlocutory decree which automatically becomes final on date specified (not less than six months nor more than one year from entry of interlocutory decree) unless set aside for cause shown. (§16-309[d]). All adoption proceedings are confidential. (§16-309[f]).

Finality of Decree.—Any attempt to invalidate final adoption decree by reason of jurisdiction or procedural defect, must be filed within one year following effective date of final decree. (§16-310).

Name.—Family name of adoptee must be changed to that of adopter unless decree provides otherwise, and the given name of adoptee may be fixed or changed at same time. (§16-312[c]).

Effect of Adoption.—Adoption establishes relation of natural parent and natural child between adopter and adoptee for all purposes, including mutual rights of inheritance and succession. All rights and duties between adoptee, natural parents, their issue, collateral relatives, etc., are cut off, except when natural parent is spouse of adopting parent. (§16-312[a]).

Sealing of Papers.—Records and papers, from filing of petition, are sealed and may not be inspected by any person, including parties to the proceeding, except upon order of court, and only then when the court is satisfied that welfare of child will be promoted or protected. (§16-311).

Setting Aside Adoption.—See subhead Finality of Decree, supra.

Birth Certificates.—Upon issuance of final adoption decree unless otherwise requested in petition, Registrar shall make new record of birth in new name with names of adopters and seal original birth certificate and order of Court. (§16-314).

Surrogate parenting contracts are prohibited and unenforceable. Violators are subject to civil penalty not in excess of $10,000, and/or imprisonment of not more than one year. (§§16-401, 402).

ALIMONY:

See topic Divorce.

COMMUNITY PROPERTY:

System not in effect.

DESERTION:

See topics Divorce, Husband and Wife.

DISSOLUTION OF MARRIAGE:

See topic Divorce.

DIVORCE:

This subject is governed by Tit. 16, §§901-924 of 1981 Edition of D. C. Code, as am'd.

Grounds for Absolute Divorce.—(1) Both parties to marriage have mutually and voluntarily lived separate and apart without cohabitation for six months next preceding commencement of action; (2) both parties have lived separate and apart without cohabitation for one year next preceding commencement of action. (§16-904[a]). For purposes of (1) and (2), parties who have pursued separate lives, sharing neither bed nor board, shall be deemed to have lived separate and apart from one another even though they reside under same roof or separation is pursuant to court order. (§16-904[c]). Upon application of party who has been granted decree of legal separation, court may enlarge decree to absolute divorce if it finds (based on affidavits) that no reconciliation has taken place or is probable and separation has continued voluntarily and without interruption for six-month period or without interruption for one year. (§16-905[b]).

Grounds for Legal Separation.—(1) Both parties have mutually and voluntarily lived separate and apart without cohabitation; (2) both parties have lived separate and apart without cohabitation for period of one year next preceding commencement of

DIVORCE . . . *continued*

action; (3) adultery; or (4) cruelty. (§16-904[b]). For purposes of (1) and (2), parties who have pursued separate lives, sharing neither bed nor board, shall be deemed to have lived separate and apart from one another even though they reside under same roof or separation is pursuant to court order. (§16-904[c]).

Citizenship Requirements.—No statutory provisions.

Residence Requirements.—No action for divorce or legal separation shall be maintainable unless one of parties to marriage has been bona fide resident of D.C. for at least six months next preceding commencement of action. Member of U.S. Armed Forces residing in D. C. for period of six continuous months during period of service shall be deemed D. C. resident for purposes of this section only. (§16-902).

Jurisdiction is vested in Family Division of Superior Court. (§11-1101; §16-901). Court has jurisdiction over person for claims relating to marital or parent/child relationship if: (a) Plaintiff resides in District when suit is filed; (b) person is personally served with process; and (c) in cases related to marital relationship, parties were domiciled in District immediately prior to separation, or cause of action for spousal support arose under District law or agreement executed in District; or (d) in cases relating to parent/child relationship, child was conceived in District and person is parent or alleged parent, or child resides in District as result of act, directive or approval of person, or person has resided with child in District. (§13-423[a][7]).

Process.—By personal service within or without jurisdiction or by publication if defendant cannot be found and if it appears by affidavit that defendant is nonresident or has been absent from District for six months. (§§13-336, 337).

Pleading.—Governed by Superior Court Rules of Family Division. Where adultery is alleged, person with whom act is alleged to have been committed must be named defendant and served with process. (§16-917). Practice permits defendant to file counterclaim for divorce or separation.

Practice.—Proceedings same as in other civil action causes except that no decree will be rendered on default without proof, and no admission in answer will be taken as proof of grounds charged in complaint, which must be proved by other evidence. (§16-919). Practice also requires that determination be made by court whether to appoint attorney for absent defendant prior to entry of decree by default. Where court deems necessary, disinterested attorney may be appointed to defend, his compensation to be determined by court and assessed to parties as court directs. In child custody case, court may appoint disinterested attorney to appear for child and represent his best interest. (§16-918).

Judgment or Decree.—No decree of divorce, or granting absolute divorce, is effective until expiration of time for noting appeal, or if notice of appeal entered, until disposition of appeal. (§16-920).

Temporary Alimony.—Court may require payment of alimony during pendency of suit for maintenance of spouse and minor children. (§16-911[a][1]).

Allowance for Prosecution of Suit.—Money for conduct of case, including counsel fees, may be granted during pendency of suit to spouse, whether plaintiff or defendant. (§16-911[a][1]).

Permanent Alimony.—Court may require payment of alimony. (§§16-912, 913). Jurisdiction of cause is retained to enter further orders where alimony has been granted. (§16-914[a]). Modification of alimony may not be retroactive. (§30-504[c]). There is no statutory provision for termination of alimony upon remarriage. If spouse obtains foreign ex parte decree of divorce, then, upon personal service of that spouse in D.C., other spouse may obtain court decree for maintenance and suit money. (§16-916[b]).

Division of Property of Spouses.—See subhead Property of Spouses, infra.

Property of Spouses.—In absence of valid antenuptial or postnuptial agreement or decree of legal separation disposing property of spouses, upon entry of final decree of divorce, each party is assigned his sole and separate property acquired prior to marriage and his sole and separate property acquired during marriage by gift, bequest, devise or descent; and all other property accumulated during marriage is distributed regardless of whether title is held individually or in form of joint tenancy or tenancy by entirety. This property shall be distributed in equitable, just and reasonable manner after considering such factors as: duration of marriage, age, health, occupation, employability, assets, debts, provisions for custody of minor children, etc. (§16-910). During pendency of action for divorce, Court may sequestrate property if spouse fails or refuses to pay alimony (§16-911[a][3]), enjoin disposition of spouse's property to avoid collection of allowances so required (§16-911[a][2]), and, if party under court order to make payments is in arrears, Court may order party to make assignment of part of salary, wages, earnings or income to person entitled to receive payments (§16-911[a][4]).

As to effect of divorce on dower right, see category Property, topic Dower.

Change of Wife's Name.—In granting decree of absolute divorce, court may, upon party's request, restore party's birth-given or other previous name. (§16-915).

Custody of Children.—Court may determine who shall have care and custody of infant children either during or after proceeding and will retain jurisdiction of cause for future orders relative thereto. In determining care and custody of infant children, best interest of child shall be primary consideration. There is rebuttable presumption that joint custody is in best interest of child, except where judicial officer has found intrafamily offense, child abuse, child neglect or parental kidnapping has occurred. (§§16-911[a][5], 914[a]).

Allowance for Support of Children.—Court may order payment by father or mother of sufficient funds for support of minor children (including medical insurance whenever available at reasonable cost) either before or after entry of final decree. (§§16-911[a][1], 912, 916). Guidelines set forth presumptive guidelines for payment of support; establish Guideline Commission. (§16-916.1-2). Where duty of support exists, expedited hearing will be held and temporary support may be ordered. (§16-924). Court may require bond, security or other guarantee to secure overdue support obligations. (§16-916[e][1]). Court may in certain circumstances order payments withheld from earnings. (§30-505). Parent more than 60 days behind in child support payments may, upon 30 days notice, have drivers' license or any professional or business license revoked or nonrenewed by Mayor. (§30-525). Court will retain jurisdiction of cause for entry of future orders concerning support. (§16-914[a]). Modification of child support may not be retroactive. (§30-504[c]).

Legitimacy of Issue.—Child's relationship to its mother is established by its birth to her. Child's relationship to its father is established by providing by preponderance of evidence that he is father. Statute establishes presumptions as to relationship of child to its father. (§16-909).

Remarriage.—There is no prohibition of remarriage after decree has become absolute.

Foreign Divorces.—No statutory provisions.

Separation agreements to settle financial affairs of spouses who are not able to maintain harmonious marriage relationship are encouraged and will be enforced in absence of fraud, duress, concealment, or overreaching. (App. D.C., 317 A.2d 521).

Annulment of Marriage.—See topic Marriage.

Antenuptial Contracts.—See topic Husband and Wife.

GUARDIAN AND WARD:

Superior Court (Probate Division) has exclusive jurisdiction to appoint guardians of infants' estates. (§§11-921; 21-101-104, 106).

Selection of Guardians.—Father and mother are natural guardians of person of minor children, and on death or incapacity of either, natural guardianship of person devolves upon survivor, provided that either may, by deed or last will, appoint guardian of property subject to approval of proper court of District; guardianship of person and of property are each subject to power of court of competent jurisdiction to appoint some other person guardian when welfare of children requires it. (§§21-101, 105).

Testamentary Guardian.—Every father or mother, whether of full age or not, when other parent is dead, may, by last will and testament, appoint guardian of person to have care, custody, and tuition of his or her infant child, other than married infant; and if person so appointed shall refuse trust, Probate Court may appoint another person in his place. (§21-102). Nonresident may act as testamentary guardian. (§21-110).

Selection by Court.—If an infant has neither natural nor testamentary guardian, a guardian of the person may be appointed by the probate court in its own discretion or on the application of a next friend of such infant. (§21-103).

When infant under 18 becomes entitled to or acquires real or personal property, Probate Court may appoint guardian of his estate, who may be either guardian of his person or different person. (§21-106). If infant is under 14, father or mother, or spouse if infant is married to person 18 years or older, is entitled to preference, if deemed suitable by court. (§21-107).

Selection by Infant.—If infant is over age of 14, he is entitled to select his guardian, and if one had been appointed before he attained age of 14 he may select new guardian, subject, in both cases, to approval of court. Such guardian is under same obligations as if selected by court. When infant marries, he or she may select his or her spouse as guardian of his or her estate, with approval of court. (§§21-108, 109).

Eligibility and Competency.—The only direct statutory limitation is a prohibition against any person, except trust companies, acting as guardian of the person of more than five infants at one time, unless such infants are members of the same family or as guardian of the estates of more than five infants unless such infants are entitled to share in same estate. (§§21-103[b], 106[c]).

Appointment of Guardian.—Except in the cases of natural and testamentary guardians of the person, appointment of guardians is made by the proper court as stated above.

Qualification.—Every guardian appointed by court, except corporations authorized to act as guardians and testimentary guardian, unless otherwise directed by appointing will, before entering upon or taking possession of or interfering with estate of infant, must execute bond in such penalty, and with such surety or sureties, as court shall approve. (§21-115). At any time court may require additional bond and revoke appointment of guardian refusing to give such bond. (§21-117).

Inventory.—Every guardian, within three months after the execution and approval of his bond, is required to return to the court, under oath, an inventory of the real and personal estate of his ward and probable annual income thereof. (§21-142).

Powers and Duties.—Guardians of the persons have the care, custody and tuition of their wards. (§21-102). Guardians of the estate have control of the property of their wards, subject to direction and approval of Probate Court. (§§21-141, 143).

Investments.—Investment of funds is controlled by Rule No. 306 of Superior Court under statutory authority. (§16-3108).

Securities in Name of Nominee.—See category Estates and Trusts, topic Trusts.

Real Estate.—Whenever it appears that sale of realty is necessary for maintenance or education of ward, probate court may decree a sale. (§21-147). Whenever it appears that interests of ward will be promoted by sale, exchange or lease of realty, court may authorize such action by decree. (§§21-148-156). Likewise, where it appears to court that it is to infant's benefit to raise money by mortgage for his maintenance, for improvements or to discharge encumbrances, court may authorize such action. (§21-157).

Liabilities of Guardian.—There is no statutory provision summarizing or limiting the possible liability of guardians.

Accounts.—It is the duty of a guardian to manage the estate for the best interests of the ward, and once in each year, or oftener if required, to settle an account of his trust, under oath. He must account for all profits or increase of ward's estate and annual value thereof. His commission cannot exceed 5% of amounts collected, if and when disbursed. (§21-143).

On arrival of any ward at age of 18 years guardian must exhibit final account of his trust to court, and must deliver up, agreeably to court's order, to ward all property of said ward in his hands, and on his failure so to do his bond may be put in suit by party interested, and he may be attached, as herein elsewhere provided. (§21-158).

See note at head of Digest as to 1998 legislation covered.

See Topical Index in front part of this volume.

DC – 25

GUARDIAN AND WARD . . . *continued*

Termination of Guardianship.—Natural or appointive guardianships of person cease when person reaches 18 years of age or marries. (§21-104). Guardianships of estates of infants cease when wards reach 18. (§21-158).

Mentally Ill or Incapacitated Persons.—Guardianship, protective proceedings and durable power of attorney governed by §§21-2001-2085.

Foreign Guardians.—Guardian of nonresident infant, appointed by court of another state, may obtain ancillary letters by petition to probate court, proof of authority and posting of same security required from resident, whereupon he may collect assets or institute court proceedings in District. (§§21-111, 112).

Gifts to Minors.—See topic Infants.

Uniform Fiduciaries Act adopted. (§§21-1701-1712).

Uniform Simplification of Fiduciary Security Transfers Act adopted. (§§28-2901-2909). Act prevails over inconsistent provisions in Art. 8 of Uniform Commercial Code. (§28-10-104[2]).

HUSBAND AND WIFE:

The rights, duties and powers of married persons as between themselves and with respect to other persons remain as at common law except to the extent modified by statute.

Disabilities of Married Persons.—Marriage does not remove any of disabilities respecting property or contractual matters affecting minor. (§30-201). Otherwise, disabilities have generally been removed.

Separate Property.—Each spouse may hold property separately of other and dispose and convey it as if unmarried. No spouse shall be liable because of any contract or tort in which spouse has not directly or indirectly participated, except for debts incurred for necessaries for either of them or their dependent children. (§30-201).

For dower and curtesy rights, see category Property, topic Dower.

Contracts.—Fact that person is married shall not impair such person's ability to contract or engage in any trade occupation, or business. (§30-201).

Antenuptial Contracts.—Uniform Premarital Agreement Act adopted. (§30-141 et seq.). Premarital agreement must be in writing and signed by both parties. It is enforceable without consideration, and becomes effective upon marriage. (§§30-142, 144).

Actions.—Fact that person is married shall not impair such person's ability to engage in civil litigation of any sort (whether tort, contract or otherwise) with or against anyone, including such person's spouse, to same extent as unmarried person. (§30-201).

Agency.—Husband and wife relationship, in and of itself, does not establish principal-agent relationship, but neither does it prevent such relationship. (158 A.2d 681).

Conveyance or Encumbrance of Property.—Fact that person is married shall not impair such person's ability to acquire from anyone, and to hold and dispose of in any manner, as his or hers, property of any kind, to same extent as unmarried person. (§30-201). For release of dower see category Property, topic Dower.

Desertion and Nonsupport.—See subhead Uniform Reciprocal Enforcement of Support Act, infra.

Uniform Reciprocal Enforcement of Support Act (1952 version of 1950 Act) with local modifications is in force. (§§30-301-326, 30-501-531). Such modifications include mandatory withholding of earnings or other income for original or modification of support order effective after Oct. 1, 1990, if obligation enforceable under federal Title IV-D program (42 USC §§651-669), unless Court finds good cause not to or parties agree in writing to alternative payment method, or in cases of 30-day or more support payment arrearages (§30-507); expedited hearings to establish or modify child support obligations (§16-924); provisions for reimbursement for money expended for support of dependents by political subdivisions (§30-305) (but subordinated to caretaker's rights [§30-503(a)]); for representation of plaintiff by Corporation Counsel or private counsel (court appointed or at plaintiff's expense) (§30-308); and omission of §§5 and 6 and 33 through 38 of Act relating to criminal enforcement and registration of foreign support orders. §§39 and 40 of 1968 Act relating to registration and effect of foreign support orders are in force. (§§30-325, 326).

Community Property.—System does not obtain in District of Columbia.

Domestic Partnerships.—Two unmarried individuals may register as "domestic partnership" and obtain certain benefits otherwise reserved to married persons. (§36-1401 et seq.).

INFANTS:

Infants, including minor married women, become of age at 18. (§30-401). Person of 18 may make will. (§18-102). Person under 21 may not purchase, attempt to purchase, possess, or drink any alcoholic beverage in D.C. (§25-130).

Emancipation.—There are no statutory provisions for emancipation. See topic Guardian and Ward as to cessation of guardianship. Minor parent may consent to health care for child (DCMR Tit. 22, §600.3 [1986]), yet minor is liable for payment for services (22 DCMR §601.1).

Disabilities.—Infants are subject to common law disabilities to contract except for health care.

Consent to Health Care.—Minors of any age may consent to health care for pregnancy or its lawful termination, substance abuse, psychological disturbance, and sexually transmitted diseases. (22 DCMR §600.7). Minors are liable for payment for such care if consented to by self. (22 DCMR §601.1). Parent or legal guardian may convey authority necessary for another adult person to consent to medical treatment on behalf of minor. (§16-4901).

Ratification of Contracts.—Person cannot be charged with ratification of debt incurred during infancy (except for necessaries) unless, after reaching full age, acknowledgment or promise to pay was made in writing signed by party to be charged. (§28-3505). No time limit for ratification provided by statute.

Actions.—Infant may sue or defend by duly appointed representative. Where there is no representative, infant may sue by next friend or guardian ad litem appointed by Court or Court shall make whatever order it deems proper to protect infant. (§13-332; Sup. Ct. Civ. R17[c]).

Curfew.—Person under 17 cannot remain in public place or establishment during curfew hours. Curfew hours are from 11 p.m. - 6 a.m. Sun.-Thurs.; 12:01 a.m. - 6 a.m. Sat. and Sun.; except during July and Aug., when curfew hours are 12:01 a.m. - 6 a.m. every night. (§6-2182). No person under 18 with valid D.C. drivers license can drive after midnight, except as provided in §6-2183. (§40-301).

Custody.—Uniform Child Custody Jurisdiction Act adopted. (§16-4501).

Parental Responsibility.—Parents not responsible for injuries resulting from wrongful act of minor child unless parent is negligent in exercise of parental supervision and such negligence has specific relation to act complained of. (34 A.2d 257). Parent can be held responsible for permitting minor to remain in public place or establishment during curfew hours. (§6-2183). Court may hold parents and guardians in contempt for not participating in court-ordered proceeding or program. (§16-2305[b]).

Delinquency, Neglect, Supervision.—District may take custody if reasonable grounds exist to believe child neglected or in need of supervision. (§§16-2309, 2320, and 2337). When child has been placed in secure detention prior to fact finding hearing pursuant to §§16-2310-2313, fact finding hearing shall commence not later than 30 days from date of detention, unless child is charged with murder, assault with intent to kill, first degree sexual abuse, burglary in first degree, or robbery while armed, in which case fact finding hearing shall commence not later than 45 days from date of detention. (§16-2310[e]). Any person under 21 who falsely misrepresents age for purpose of procuring alcohol shall be deemed guilty of misdemeanor and fined for each offense not more than $300, and in default of payment of fine shall be imprisoned not exceeding 30 days. (§25-130). Health care professionals and law enforcement professionals must notify Department of Human Services if reasonable cause to believe child is abused. (§2-1352). Courts have discretionary authority to order parenting classes and family counseling for families of juveniles involved in neglect, delinquency, and person in need of supervision proceedings. (§16-2320). Expulsion from District public schools for not less than one year required of any student who brings weapon into school, absent extenuating circumstances. (§31-451).

Uniform Transfers to Minors Act adopted. Age of majority is 18. (§§21-301-324).

Adoption.—See topic Adoption.

Uniform Securities Ownership by Minors Act not adopted.

Support of Minor.—All court orders effective after Oct. 1, 1990 that direct payment of child support must provide that arrearages equal to 30 days of support payments shall be withheld from earnings or other income. (§30-505). See topic Husband and Wife, subhead Uniform Reciprocal Enforcement of Support Act.

Termination of Parental Rights.—Parental rights may be terminated when in best interests of child. (§§16-2320, 2353). Motion for termination of parental rights may be filed by District or by child through child's legal representative where child has been adjudicated neglected for at least six months, abandoned, or if parents cannot be located for three months prior to fact-finding hearing. Court order terminates all rights and obligations except right of child to inherit from parent. (§16-2361).

See also topic Divorce and category Debtor and Creditor, topic Garnishment.

Establishment of Paternity.—Conclusive presumption of paternity is established (i) if father acknowledges paternity in writing; or (ii) upon genetic test result and affidavit from laboratory certified by American Association of Blood Banks, indicating 99% probability that putative father is child's father. (§16-909.1). District must give full faith and credit to paternity determinations by other states. (§16-909.2). Public and private birthing hospitals are required to operate hospital-based program that provides services to facilitate voluntary acknowledgment of paternity for child of unmarried woman. (§16-909.3).

Surrogate Parenting Contracts.—See topic Adoption.

MARRIAGE:

Marriage is governed by Tit. 30, §§101-121.

Age of consent, males and females, 16. (§30-103[4]).

Consent Required.—Consent of parent or guardian required where male or female under 18, unless previously married. Such consent may be given personally or by writing attested by witness and proved to satisfaction of clerk. (§30-111).

Medical Examination.—License application must be accompanied by physician's (or other authorized person's) statement that applicant, within 30 days of application, has been found by standard blood test not to be infected with syphilis in such stage that disease can be transmitted to another. (§30-117). If person is unable for financial reasons to obtain services of physician (or other authorized person) for blood test and required statement, any medical officer of D.C. Dept. of Human Services is authorized to conduct test and provide statement at no cost to such person. (§30-119). Any information obtained from any laboratory blood test required under §30-117 is confidential. (§30-120). See also subhead License, infra.

License required. Issued by clerk of Superior Court, who must, before issuing same, examine applicant under oath as to relevant facts. In case of previous divorce, facts must be disclosed but copy of proceedings need not be furnished. (§§30-110). License may not issue until three days have elapsed since date of application. (§30-109) and must be addressed to individual who is to perform ceremony (§30-112). License fee, $35. (Super. Ct. C.V. R.—Family Division, R.C.). Superior Court judge may waive three-day waiting period and medical examination requirement in case of public policy or emergency. (§30-118).

Ceremonial Marriage.—Every marriage must be solemnized according to law.

Every minister of any religious society approved or ordained according to ceremonies of his religious society, whether his residence be in District or elsewhere in U.S., may be authorized by any judge of Superior Court to celebrate marriages. Marriages may also be celebrated by any judge or justice of any court of record or by clerk or approved

MARRIAGE . . . *continued*
deputy clerks of Superior Court. Marriages of members of any church or religious society which does not by its custom require intervention of a minister for celebration of marriages may be solemnized in manner prescribed and practiced in any such society. License in such case is issued to, and returns made, by a person appointed by such church or religious society for that purpose. (§30-106).

Penalties are imposed for solemnizing marriage without delivery of license, and solemnization of marriage by unauthorized person. (§§30-107-108).

Reports of Marriages.—Return must be within ten days to clerk's office of Superior Court by person solemnizing marriage (§30-112); penalty of $50 may be imposed for failure to make return (§30-113).

Record.—See category Documents and Records, topic Records, subhead Vital Statistics.

Common Law Marriages are recognized. (303 F.2d 408).

Proxy Marriages.—No provision.

Marriages by Written Contract.—No provision.

Prohibited Marriages.—The following marriages are prohibited and are absolutely void ab initio, without being so decreed, and their nullity may be shown in any collateral proceedings: (1) Marriage of a man with his grandmother, grandfather's wife, wife's grandmother, aunt, mother, stepmother, wife's mother, daughter, wife's daughter, son's wife, sister, granddaughter, son's son's wife, daughter's son's wife, wife's son's daughter, wife's daughter's daughter, niece; (2) marriage of a woman with her grandfather, grandmother's husband, husband's grandfather, uncle, father, stepfather, husband's father, son, husband's son, daughter's husband, brother, grandson, son's daughter's husband, daughter's daughter's husband, husband's son's son, husband's daughter's son, nephew; (3) marriage of person previously married and whose previous marriage has not been terminated by death or divorce. (§30-101).

The following marriages are illegal, and are void from the time when their nullity is declared by decree: (1) Marriage of an idiot or of a person adjudged to be a lunatic; (2) any marriage the consent to which of either party has been procured by force or fraud; (3) any marriage either of the parties to which shall be incapable, from physical causes, of entering into the married state; (4) when either of the parties is under the age of consent (16 years of age). (§30-103).

Foreign Marriages.—Marriages prohibited in the District and entered into in another jurisdiction by persons domiciled in the District may be decreed to be void as if celebrated in the District. (§30-105).

Annulment.—Decrees of nullity will be entered if parties are within prohibited degree of relationship, if either party's previous marriage is still in effect; if either party was insane or under age of consent or physically incapable of entering into marriage state, or if marriage was procured by force or fraud. But marriage may not be annulled on ground that party was a lunatic or under age of consent if there has been voluntary cohabitation after discovery of lunacy or attainment of legal age. (§§16-903, 904). Otherwise, there is no statutory limitation of time within which action to avoid marriage on ground of nonage must be brought.

A proceeding to declare the nullity of a marriage may be instituted, in the case of an infant under the age of consent, by such infant, through a next friend, or by the parent or guardian of such infant; and in the case of an idiot or lunatic, by next friend. But no such proceedings may be instituted by any person who, being fully capable of contracting marriage, has knowingly and willfully contracted any marriage declared illegal by foregoing sections. (§30-104).

Final decree annulling a marriage is not effective until expiration of time for noting appeal, and, if notice of appeal entered, until final disposition of appeal. (§16-920).

Practice in annulment actions is similar to that in actions for divorce or separation. See topic Divorce.

No action for annulment of marriage performed outside District is maintainable unless at least one party is bona fide resident of District at time of commencing action. If marriage performed in District, residence of parties is not considered in determining whether action for annulment is maintainable. (§16-902).

Child born in wedlock or born out of wedlock is legitimate child of its father and mother and is legitimate relative of its father's and mother's relatives by blood or adoption. (§§16-907, 908).

Antenuptial Contracts.—See topic Husband and Wife.

Domestic Partnerships.—Two unmarried individuals may register as "domestic partnership" and obtain certain benefits otherwise reserved to married persons. (§36-1401 et seq.).

MARRIED WOMEN:

See topics Husband and Wife, Marriage; categories Civil Actions and Procedure, topic Evidence, subhead Witnesses; Documents and Records, topic Acknowledgments; Estates and Trusts, topics Executors and Administrators, Wills; Property, topic Dower.

INSURANCE

INSURANCE COMPANIES:

Department of Insurance and Securities Regulation, headed by Commissioner of Insurance and Securities, has charge of insurance matters generally. (§§35-121, 401). All insurance companies (except D. C. Insurance Guaranty Assn.), domestic, foreign and alien, stock, mutual or fraternal, are required, under penalty, to obtain annual license (fee $200) issued by Commissioner which shall date from first of month in which application is made, and expire on following Apr. 30. (§§47-2603, 2604). Each company is also required to file annual statement before Mar. 1 concerning its operations for previous year, to pay $50 filing fee (§47-2606) and to contribute to Insurance Regulatory Trust Fund, amount assessed by Mayor. Payment must be made within 30 days of mailing date of Notice of Assessment. Minimum annual assessment is $1,000. (§35-2703). Each company must also file report disclosing material acquisitions and dispositions of assets or material nonrenewals, cancellations or revisions of ceded reinsurance agreements within 15 days after end of month in which transaction occurred (§35-4101), and must file annual financial statement substantially in form adopted by National Association of Insurance Commissioners ("NAIC"), by Mar. 1st with Mayor and with NAIC, and audited financial report. (§§35-3401, 3202, 3203). Each domestic insurer shall file report of its Risk-Based Capital ("RBC") levels as of end of calendar year just ended, in form required by RBC Instructions of National Association of Insurance Commissioners ("NAIC"), with Commissioner, with NAIC, and with Commissioner in any state in which insurer is authorized to do business, if requested to do so in writing by such Commissioner. (§§35-4601-4613). Commissioner issues certificates of authority to companies that comply with statutory requirements, and may revoke or suspend same for noncompliance with requirements. (§§35-404, 405).

There are special requirements regarding stock, dividends, voting, directors, investments, capital surplus, merger or consolidation, etc. (§§35-601-649).

Chief governing statutes are the Life Insurance Act of 1934 as am'd (§§35-301-802 [§§35-425-428 repealed by Insurance Agents and Brokers Licensing Revision Act of 1996, Law 11-227]). Fire and Casualty Act of 1940 as am'd (§§35-1501-1562 [§35-1521 amended by African Development Bank and Asian Development Bank Investment Amendment Act of 1990, D.C. Law 8-141, §§35-1508-1510 repealed by Insurers Rehabilitation Act of 1993, Law 10-35; §35-1511 repealed by Required Annual Financial Statements and Participation in the NAIC Insurance Regulatory Information System Act of 1993, Law 10-42; §35-1513 repealed by Law on Examinations Act of 1993, Law 10-49, and §§35-1534, 1536-41, 1547-49 repealed by Insurance Agents and Brokers Licensing Revision Act of 1996, Law 11-227]), Act (of 1962) for Regulation of Credit Life Insurance and Credit Accident and Health Insurance as am'd (§§35-1001-1012), Compulsory/No-Fault Motor Vehicle Insurance Act of 1982 as am'd (§§35-2101-2114), Life Insurance Amendments Reform Act of 1984 as am'd (§§35-531-536), Prohibition of Discrimination in Provision of Insurance On Basis of AIDS Test Act of 1986 (§§35-221-229), Drug Abuse, Alcohol Abuse, and Mental Illness Insurance Coverage Act of 1986 (§§35-2301-2311), Holding Company System Act of 1993 (§§35-3701-3714, Law 10-44), which repealed Holding Company System Regulatory Act of 1974 (§§35-2001-2015), Insurers Rehabilitation and Liquidation Act of 1993 (§§35-2801-2855), Property and Liability Insurance Guaranty Association Act of 1993 (§§35-3901-3915, Law 10-51) which repealed District of Columbia Insurance Guaranty Association Act (§§35-1901-1917), Insurance Agents and Brokers Licensing Revision Act of 1996 (§§35-1321-1334), Fraternal Benefit Societies Act of 1998 (§35-1231 et seq.), and Reciprocal Insurance Company Conversion Act of 1998 (§§35-3741—3750).

Extensive regulatory system was enacted in 1993, establishing standards in many areas, for example, with respect to managing general agents (§§35-3001-3006), for identifying insurance companies deemed to be in hazardous financial condition (§§35-3501-3503), to authorize Commissioner of Insurance and Securities to take over companies for protection of interests of insureds, claimants, creditors and general public (§§35-2801-2857), for reinsurance intermediaries to act, and duties of insurers utilizing services of insurance intermediary (§§35-3101-3110), for transacting business when insurance broker has controlling interest in insurer with which business is to be placed (§§35-4001-4008) and for calculating premiums to be charged by taxicab insurers (26 DCMR c. 8, §§801, 805), effective 4/14/95. Legislation also regulates formation and operation of risk retention groups (§§35-2901-2912), provides for examining activities, operations, financial conditions and affairs of all persons transacting business of insurance and subject to its laws (§§35-3601-3608), and permits life insurance companies to offer modified guaranteed contracts (§35-639). 1996 legislation affords mutual insurance companies opportunity to convert to stock company (§§35-4201-4215), and opportunity to reorganize by directly or indirectly forming insurance holding company upon mutual plan, and continuing corporate existence of reorganized insurance company as stock insurance company subsidiary to holding company or to holding company's subsidiary. (§§35-3721-3728). 1996 laws also provide means for foreign insurance company to become domestic insurer, and for domestic insurer to transfer domicile to another state (§§35-4301-4305), and permit U.S. branch of non-U.S. insurer to use District as state of entry to transact insurance in U.S. (§§35-4401-4407). 1998 laws regulate benefit contracts offered by fraternal benefit societies (orders or lodges without capital stock, whether incorporated or not, operating for benefit of members and their beneficiaries). (§35-1231 et seq.). In addition, reciprocal insurance company can be converted into stock insurance company when it forms mutual insurance holding company that directly or indirectly owns insurance company. (§§35-3741—3750).

Policies.—Standard provisions are specified for life, annuity and endowment, group life, and accident and health policies. Policy forms delivered or issued for delivery in District after Mar. 14, 1987 must qualify under policy simplification standards. (§§35-531, am'd 1987, 532, am'd 1987, 533, am'd 1987, 534-536). Certain provisions are forbidden in life insurance policies, but policy of any company not organized in District may contain any provisions required by laws of state or organization. (§§35-503, am'd 1987, 504-505, 507, am'd 1987, 513-517, 528, 529, 1101-1104). Copy of application for life insurance must be delivered with policy, in default of which no defense is allowed in respect of error in application. (§35-203). Wagering policies are illegal. (§35-1432). Credit life insurance and credit accident and health insurance are subject to regulation. (§§35-1001-1012). Financing of insurance premiums is also regulated. (§§35-1551-1562). Certain health insurance policies and contracts must provide coverage for treatment of drug abuse, alcohol abuse and mental illness. (§§35-2301-2311). Individual and group health insurance policies are required to cover preventive and primary care for dependent children up to 18 years of age. (§35-1102).

As to exemption of proceeds, see category Debtor and Creditor, topic Exemptions.

Rates, in general, are controlled by the Commissioner of Insurance and Securities. (§§35-205, 1601-1609, 1701-1710).

Reserves, or reserve liabilities, for all outstanding life insurance policies and annuity and pure endowment contracts of every life insurance company doing business in District are valued annually by Commissioner of Insurance and Securities, except that in case of foreign insurance company such valuation is limited to its insurance transactions in U.S. (§35-501). Every insurance company must submit annually opinion of qualified

INSURANCE COMPANIES . . . *continued*
actuary as to whether reserves are computed accurately and comply with all applicable laws. (§35-3801).

Discrimination.—On fire, marine or casualty policies, discrimination between individual risks of the same class or hazard is prohibited. (§35-1533). Nor may any life company discriminate between individuals of the same class or equal expectation of life. (§35-520). No insurer may deny coverage or withhold payments on grounds that subscriber or policyholder is eligible for Medicaid. (§§3-701, 1.359.1). No insurer may deny enrollment of child under health plan of parent on grounds that child (1) was born out of wedlock; (2) was not claimed as dependent on parent's federal tax return; or (3) was not residing with parent or in insurer's service area. (§1-359.1). On health, disability or life insurance policies, insurers may not discriminate based on factors used to predict development of acquired immune deficiency syndrome, nor may policies contain any limitation of benefits with respect to AIDS-related illness or death. (§35-223). Insured who tests positive for AIDS under testing protocol certified by Commissioner of Public Health may appeal test result to Commissioner of Insurance and Securities, who may order insurer to disregard positive result. (§35-224).

Rebates of premiums or special favors or advantages in dividends are prohibited. (§§35-520; 35-1534).

Agents and Brokers.—Any person, whether resident or nonresident, may obtain license to solicit insurance business or act as insurance broker or agent in the District on payment of statutory fees (brokers and general agents, $50; agents and solicitors, $10 for each company represented). Officers and traveling representatives of life insurance companies receiving salary instead of commission need not be licensed. (§§35-1301, 1302, 402, 425, 428).

Every contract of insurance, except title and ocean marine, on any person, property, business activity or insurable interest in the District must be written through policy-writing agents or authorized salaried employees licensed in the District. (§35-1534). No part of commission on any such contract may be paid to a person not licensed in the District, except for reinsurance and other minor exceptions. (§35-1535). (Where no company authorized to do business in District will write contract, license can be obtained to do business with unauthorized company [§35-1544].) Policy-writing agents, or soliciting company agents must be residents of District or maintain principal place of business therein. Nonresidents may obtain licenses as brokers or salaried company employees. Resident and nonresident brokers must post corporate surety bond with Superintendent in amount of not less than $10,000 for benefit of persons defrauded. Examination required for license but requirement may be waived for those licensed before Nov. 8, 1940, or nonresident brokers licensed elsewhere. (§35-1536). Annual license fees: Policy-writing agent or salaried company employee authorized to sign policies and solicit, $100, renewal fee, $100, without regard to number of companies represented; with additional charge of $10 for each individual member, in excess of two, named in license; for soliciting agent, $50 for each company, renewal fee $50; resident or nonresident brokers, $100, unless also paying $50 fee as policy-writing agent or salaried company employee, in which case $10 only; soliciting agent or salaried company employee authorized to solicit but not sign, $50 for each company represented but not to exceed $100; for employee authorized to solicit and sign, $75; license to procure lines in unauthorized companies, $100, annual renewal fee, $100. (§35-1545).

Process Agent.—The Commissioner of the Department of Insurance and Securities Regulation must be appointed agent for service of process by every domestic company not having its home office in District, every foreign or alien company doing business in District or soliciting, selling or writing insurance on any resident thereof through U.S. mails and every fraternal benefit association doing business in District and not having its principal office in District and not being organized under laws of U.S. relating to District. Failure to authorize service on Commissioner does not invalidate such service. (§§35-423, 1205, 1527).

Foreign Insurers.—Domicile of insurer organized or formally located in foreign country is insurer's principal place of business in U.S., except for Canadian insurers, whose domicile is Canadian province where insurer's headquarters are located. (§47-2602). Under certain conditions, Mayor may impose retaliatory taxes, fees, fines, deposits, obligations or restrictions against insurers of other states and foreign countries that impose similar burdens on District insurers. However, this retaliatory authority does not apply to personal income taxes, ad valorem taxes on real and personal property and special assessments charged by state in connection with insurance, other than property insurance. (§47-2610).

Foreign life companies generally are subject to same requirements as domestic companies doing same business. They are required to file certified copy of charter, obtain certificate of authority, etc. (§35-701).

Taxation.—In lieu of all other taxes except real estate taxes and insurance license fees, domestic and foreign insurance companies doing business in District must pay annually, before Mar. 1, a sum equal to 1.7% of net premium receipts and policy and membership fees from District business. (§§35-105, 47-2608). Each company which had premium tax liability for preceding year of $1,000 or more must remit before June 1 amount equal to one-half tax liability for preceding year. (§35-105). Each company which had tax liability for preceding year of $2,000 or more must pay at least part of its tax equal in amount to 84% of its tax liability for preceding year in three installments during calendar year in which premiums and fees are received, paying any remainder by Mar. 1 of following calendar year. Net premium receipts are arrived at by deducting from gross receipts sum of premium returns, reinsurance premiums and dividends paid. (§47-2608).

Direct Actions Against Insurer.—See category Civil Actions and Procedure, topic Actions.

SURETY AND GUARANTY COMPANIES:

Surety and guaranty companies may be formed under corporation law by not less than 25 persons. Minimum of $1,000,000 capital is required. Certificate must be presented to District Council which has power and discretion to grant or refuse charter. (§§26-401 et seq.).

The federal statutes under which surety companies may be authorized to do business are applicable here. (§26-809.1). Clerk of each court has list of surety companies authorized. Powers of attorney must be filed by these companies with clerk of District Court to authorize their agents to sign bonds in District.

Taxation.—Foreign and domestic surety and guaranty companies pay tax of 3% of gross receipts from District of Columbia sources in lieu of corporate income tax. (§47-2502).

INTELLECTUAL PROPERTY

TRADEMARKS AND TRADENAMES:

Subject governed generally by federal trademark law. Local statute fixes misdemeanor criminal penalty for violation of trademark. (§22-1402). Trademark counterfeiting is punishable upon first conviction by fine not exceeding $1,000 or by imprisonment for not more than 180 days, or both. Subsequent convictions carry greater penalties. (§22-752). Special statutes govern voluntary registration, and protection of, trademarks and tradenames on beverage bottles, milk containers, containers for beverages composed principally of milk, and labor union labels. (§§48-101-102, 48-201-211, 48-301-307, 48-401-403).

Resale Price Agreements.—No "Fair Trade Act" permitting resale price agreements with respect to trademarked commodities has been enacted with specific reference to the District of Columbia.

Tradenames.—There is no requirement of registration of a tradename or business name.

TRADE SECRETS:

Uniform Trade Secrets Act adopted effective Mar. 16, 1989; applies to misappropriations after that date. (D.C. Code, §§48-501-510). Significant modification that excepts out disclosures of trade secrets relating to pesticide use and violations of occupational health and safety regulations to D.C. government officials. (D.C. Code §48-510).

LEGAL PROFESSION

ATTORNEYS AND COUNSELORS:

Effective Apr. 1, 1972, Bar of District of Columbia became unified under rules of District of Columbia Court of Appeals, under authority of District of Columbia Court Reform and Criminal Procedure Act of 1970. (§§11-2501-2504).

Jurisdiction over Admission.—District of Columbia Court of Appeals has jurisdiction over admission to practice in District of Columbia and over censure, suspension and disbarment of members of District of Columbia bar. (§§11-2501-2504).

Eligibility.—Any applicant must demonstrate good moral character and general fitness to practice law. (D.C. Ct. of App. Rule 46[d]).

Registration as Law Student.—Not required.

Educational Requirements.—Each applicant shall have graduated from an ABA approved law school or, in case of graduation from a nonapproved law school, have received credit for 26 semester hours of study at an approved law school. (D.C. Ct. of App. Rule 46[b][3],[4]).

Petition for Admission.—Must be typewritten and addressed to Court on form to be prescribed by Bar Committee. (D.C. Ct. of App. Rule 46[b][2][i], [c][1]). Nonrefundable fees of $100 (plus separate specified amount payable to National Conference of Bar Examiners) for applicants for examination, and $400 (plus separate fee to National Conference of Bar Examiners) for admission without examination. (D.C. Ct. of App. Rule 46[b][2][ii], [c][2]).

Examination.—To be conducted by Bar Committee twice yearly (Feb. and July) at Washington, D. C. (D.C. Ct. of App. Rule 46[b][1]). Except for extensions granted for exceptional cause shown, applications for admission by examination must be filed by Jan. 4 for Feb. examination and May 23 for July examination. (D.C. Ct. of App. Rule 46[b][2][i]). Examination includes Multistate Bar Examination as well as essay examination on subjects including administrative law, contracts, agency, Uniform Commercial Code, equity, business associations, conflicts of law, evidence, torts, wills, trusts, administration of estates, family law, real and personal property, civil and criminal procedure, constitutional law, criminal law, and tax law. (D.C. Ct. of App. Rule 46[b][8]). Multistate Professional Responsibility Examination is required, and applicants must receive minimum grade as determined by Committee on Admissions. (D.C. Ct. of App. Rule 46[b][5]). Multistate Bar Examination scores from other jurisdictions may be transferred. (D.C. Ct. of App. Rule 46[b][8][i][A],[ii]). Committee may in its discretion give notice of application by publication in newspaper or posting of public notice. (D.C. Ct. of App. Rule 46[d]).

Clerkship.—Not required.

Admission without Examination.—Any person may, upon proof of his or her good moral character as it relates to practice of law, be admitted without examination, provided that such person: (i) Has been active member in good standing of bar of court of general jurisdiction in any state or territory of U.S. for period of five years immediately preceding filing of application; or (ii) (A) Has been awarded J.D. or LL.B. degree by law school which, at time of awarding of degree, was approved by American Bar Association; (B) has been admitted to practice of law in any state or territory of U.S. upon successful completion of written bar examination and has received scaled score of 133 or more on Multistate Bar Examination which State or territory deems to have been

See note at head of Digest as to 1998 legislation covered.

See Topical Index in front part of this volume.

DC – 28

ATTORNEYS AND COUNSELORS ... *continued*

taken as part of such examination; and (C) has passed Multistate Professional Responsibility Examination. Application for admission under this subparagraph (ii) must be made within 25 months from date of such Multistate Bar Examination. (D.C. Ct. of App. Rule 46[c][3]).

Special Legal Consultant.—Court may, in its discretion, license to practice as Special Legal Consultant applicant who has been in good standing as attorney in foreign country for five of eight years preceding application, has good moral character, intends to maintain office to practice as SLC in District of Columbia, and is at least 26 years of age. Unless court waives requirement, applicant for license must file with Bar Committee typewritten application, certified check for $350, certificate from highest authority over professional discipline in applicant's foreign country, letter of recommendation from executive body of such authority or from judge of foreign country's highest court, and summary of opportunities for attorneys to practice in foreign country. Authenticated translation required for non-English materials. Court may, in its discretion, waive or vary these provisions. Bar Committee may investigate applicant or require report from National Conference of Bar Examiners concerning applicant's fitness. Court may consider whether D.C. bar member would have practical opportunity to give legal advice in foreign country. (D.C. Ct. of App. Rule 46[c][4][A-C]).

Scope of Practice.—Licensed SLC may render legal services, but may not: Appear in court (except upon admission pro hac vice) or prepare pleadings; prepare wills or instruments relating to real property, administration of estates, marital relations or child custody; render advice on laws of District of Columbia, U.S., or any state without advice of SLC's duly qualified counsel; hold self out as member of Bar, or use any title other than "Special Legal Consultant", title in foreign country or name of firm in foreign country, in each case only in conjunction with name of foreign country. (D.C. Ct. of App. Rule 46[c][4][D]). SLC is subject to ABA Code of Professional Responsibility and must file with court clerk written commitments to observe such Code, and to notify clerk of resignation from practice, censure or suspension in foreign country, evidence of professional liability insurance, and designation of court clerk as agent for service of process. Service of process made by delivering to clerk's office duplicate copies of process and $10, one copy to be delivered to SLC. SLC not member of D.C. Bar but considered affiliate of D.C. Bar, subject to conditions applicable to active or inactive member, and shall upon being licensed take oath to demean self uprightly and according to law. (D.C. Ct. of App. Rule 46[c][4][E][F]).

Admission Pro Hac Vice.—Attorney not a member of D. C. Bar may request special permission to appear in a particular proceeding. (D. C. Ct. of App. Rule 49[c][1]; Sup. Ct. Civ. R. 101[a][3]. In Sup. Ct. such attorney (unless he is State Attorney General or his designee) must be joined of record by D. C. Bar member who shall sign all papers. (Sup. Ct. Civ. R. 101[a][3]-[5]). D. C. Court of Appeals permits no more than five such appearances in any calendar year. (D. C. Ct. of App. Rule 49[c][1]).

Law Students' Limited Practice Privileges.—Law student who has completed 41 semester hours of law school may, as part of a law school clinical program, engage in limited practice of law in Superior Court in connection with any civil case (including any family and/or juvenile proceeding) and any criminal case (not involving a felony), on behalf of any indigent person who has consented in writing to that appearance, provided that a supervising lawyer has approved such action and also entered his appearance. Any such eligible law student may also appear in any criminal case on behalf of the U.S. or District of Columbia with written approval of U.S. Attorney or Corporation Counsel and supervising attorney. (D. C. Ct. of App. Rule 48[a]-[e]; Sup. Ct. Civ. R. 101[e]; Sup. Ct. Crim. Rule 44-I[f]). Such student may participate in oral argument in any appeal in presence of supervising attorney, provided appellant's and supervising attorney's written consents filed with clerk. (D.C. Ct. of App. Rule 48[d][2]).

Professional License Fee.—Annual fee of $250. (§§47-1814.1).

Privileges.—No statutes exempting lawyers from arrest or service of process or as witnesses.

Disabilities.—Attorney in active practice may not be surety on bond requiring approval of court or clerk. (Sup. Ct. Civ. R. 303[c]).

Compensation.—Attorneys are not prohibited from charging their clients reasonable compensation in addition to taxable costs. (§15-701). Attorney for District of Columbia may not retain attorney fees taxed as costs in litigation in which D.C. is party. (§15-702).

Liens.—Common law rule applies.

Attorney Ethics.—D.C. Rules of Professional Conduct (adopted effective 1-1-91). Significant variations from ABA Model Rules of Professional Conduct reflected in Rule 1.4 (specific requirement that client to be informed of settlement offer or proffered plea bargain); Rule 1.5 (written fee agreements mandatory; contingent fees permitted in domestic relations matters); Rule 1.6 (retains approach of Code of Professional Responsibility to confidentiality; permits lawyer to reveal client confidences and secrets under certain circumstances; defines government lawyer's client as employing agency; requires lawyers to exercise reasonable care to prevent employees, associates and others from revealing client confidences); Rule 1.7 (general rule on conflicts of interest, differs substantially from Model Rule); Rules 1.9 and 1.10 (conflicts of interest with former clients; imputed disqualification of lawyers who change law firms; Rule 1.17 (Model Rule relating to sale of law practice omitted); Rule 3.3(b) (deals differently with lawyer's duties in relation to false evidence and perjury); Rule 3.6 (trial publicity, different standard for prohibiting public comments); Rule 3.7 (lawyer as witness, exempts government lawyers from disqualification if other agency lawyers testify); Rule 3.8 (special responsibilities of prosecutor, differs substantially from Model Rule); Rule 4.2 (communication with opposing parties, includes specific provisions relating to communications with nonparty employees of organizations, including government); Rule 5.4(b) (permits partnership or other affiliation with nonlawyers under certain circumstances); Rule 7.1 (advertising, expands Rule 7.1 as compared to Model Rule; Model Rules 7.2, 7.3 and 7.4 omitted); and Rule 9.1 (not included in Model Rules, prohibits lawyers from discriminating in employment).

Disbarment or Suspension.—Disbarment proceedings are instituted and handled by Board on Professional Responsibility which makes recommendations to D. C. Court of Appeals. (D.C. Bar Rule XI). D.C. Court of Appeals, Federal courts of D.C. and Superior Court may censure, suspend or disbar member for cause. (§§11-2502-2504).

Unauthorized Practice.—No person shall regularly engage in practice of law in District of Columbia or in any manner hold himself out as authorized or qualified to practice law in District of Columbia unless he is enrolled as active member of D. C. Bar. (D.C. Ct. of App. Rule 49[b]). Rule does not apply to practice before federal courts, government agencies, commissions, executive departments, etc. (D.C. Ct. of App. Rule 49[c]).

Professional Association or Corporation.—See category Business Organizations, topic Corporations, subhead Professional Corporations.

MINERAL, WATER AND FISHING RIGHTS

MINES AND MINERALS:

No statute.

MORTGAGES

CHATTEL MORTGAGES:

Chattel mortgages are among security devices governed by Uniform Commercial Code, Art. 9. No particular form of Financing Statement or Security Agreement under the Code has received official approval. Requirements of Financing Statement are as set forth in 1962 Official Text of Uniform Commercial Code. See category Business Regulation and Commerce, topic Commercial Code.

Motor Vehicles.—For special provisions, see category Transportation, topic Motor Vehicles, subhead Liens.

COLLATERAL SECURITY:

This subject is governed by Art. 9 of Uniform Commercial Code.

MORTGAGES OF PERSONAL PROPERTY:

See topic Chattel Mortgages; category Business Regulation and Commerce, topic Commercial Code.

MORTGAGES OF REAL PROPERTY:

Mortgages are not in use in the District. Deeds of trust, conveying title to trustees, for the benefit of parties secured are in use.

Execution.—Mortgages and deeds of trust are executed, acknowledged, and recorded same as absolute deeds. (§45-701).

Recording.—In order to be effective against creditors and subsequent bona fide purchasers and mortgagees without notice, mortgages and deeds of trust must be recorded in office of recorder of deeds. (§§45-701, 801).

Recording Fees.—See category Documents and Records, topic Records.

Foreclosure.—No court proceedings are required to foreclose a deed of trust. (§45-715). Written notice by certified mail, return receipt requested, to owner of encumbered property, with copy to Mayor of District, is required at least 30 days prior to foreclosure sale under power of sale provided by security instrument. (§45-715). If length of notice and terms of sale are not prescribed by instrument or are not left therein to discretion of trustee, any person interested in sale may apply to court, before advertisement, to determine same. (§45-715). Residential mortgage debtor, not more than once in any two consecutive calendar years, may cure his default and prevent foreclosure sale at any time after receipt of written notice up to five business days prior to commencement of bidding at sale. (§45-715.1). There is no right of redemption after sale.

Form of Deed of Trust.—The form of the deed of trust is as follows (§45-501).

Form

This deed, made this . . . . . . day of . . . . . ., in the year . . . . . ., by me, ... of . . . . . ., witnesseth, that whereas (here insert consideration), I, the said . . . . . ., do grant unto . . . . . ., of . . . . . ., as trustee, the following property (here describe it) in trust for the following purposes (here insert the trusts and any covenant that may be agreed upon). Witness my hand and seal.

. . . . (Seal).

Substitution of Trustee.—Trustee in deed of trust may be replaced by written agreement of grantor and secured party (or their successors) appointing substitute trustee. Agreement to be executed same as deed, and substitution becomes effective as to third persons when notice of appointment (signed, sealed and acknowledged by parties) is recorded. (§45-714).

Release.—Deed of trust may be validly released as lien on real property by one of following:

1. Deed of trust securing lost, misplaced or destroyed promissory note which has been fully paid and satisfied may be released by recording among Land Records affidavit by holder of note. (§45-718.2[c][1]).

"FORM OF RELEASE AFFIDAVIT
FOR LOST, MISPLACED, OR DESTROYED PROMISSORY NOTE
"KNOW ALL MEN BY THESE PRESENTS:
"THAT I, the undersigned, hereby certify under penalties of perjury that:
"1. I was the last known holder of a certain promissory note (or the trustees named in the original deed of trust or substitute trustees appointed by an instrument of substitution recorded in the land records);

See note at head of Digest as to 1998 legislation covered.

See Topical Index in front part of this volume.

MORTGAGES OF REAL PROPERTY . . . *continued*

"2. Despite diligent search, I have been unable to locate the original promissory note which has been lost, misplaced or destroyed, (if the holder add: and neither the promissory note nor any interest therein has been transferred, assigned or negotiated to any other person);

"3. The promissory note has been fully paid and satisfied; and

"4. The deed of trust dated (date) securing said promissory note granted by (grantor) in favor of (trustee(s)) securing (grantee) and recorded in the land records on (date) in Liber , at Folio , as instrument no. and constituting a lien upon that piece or parcel of land located in the District of Columbia and known as:

"LOT in SQUARE , (additional legal description, ex. subdivision) as per plat recorded in Liber at Folio among the land records is hereby RELEASED.

"WITNESS the hand and seal of the undersigned [noteholder/trustee/substitute trustee] this day of,.

....

"STATE/DISTRICT of)
) ss:
"COUNTY of)

"I, the undersigned, a Notary Public in and for the aforesaid do hereby certify that party to and who is personally well known to me as the person who executed the foregoing Release Affidavit dated the day of _____, , personally appeared before me in said jurisdiction and acknowledged the same to be his/her/its act and deed. Given under my hand and seal, this day of , and: My commission expires:

                                    Notary Public

2. Original promissory note, marked "paid" or "cancelled" by holder, may be recorded, along with affidavit stating promissory note is fully paid or satisfied and releasing deed of trust as lien on real property described in deed of trust. (§45-718.2[c][2]).

"FORM OF RELEASE AFFIDAVIT
TO ACCOMPANY PROMISSORY NOTE

"KNOW ALL MEN BY THESE PRESENTS:

"THAT I, the undersigned, hereby certify under penalties of perjury that:

"1. I am [the last known holder of the attached promissory note marked "Paid" or "canceled"] or [an officer of the undersigned title insurance company] or [a validly licensed title insurance agent] which disbursed funds in payment of the promissory note;

"2. the attached promissory note has been fully paid, canceled or satisfied; and

"3. the deed of trust dated (date) securing said promissory note granted by (grantor) in favor of (trustees) securing (grantee) and recorded in the Land Records on (date) in Liber , at Folio , as instrument no. and constituting a lien upon that piece or parcel of land located in the District of Columbia and known as:

"LOT in SQUARE , (additional legal description, ex. subdivision) as per plat recorded in Liber at Folio among the Land Records is hereby RELEASED.

"WITNESS the hand and seal of the undersigned [noteholder/trustee/substitute trustee] this day of .

....

"STATE/DISTRICT of)
) ss:
"COUNTY of)

"I, the undersigned, a Notary Public in and for the aforesaid do hereby certify that party to and who is personally well known to me as the person who executed the foregoing Release Affidavit dated the day of   , , personally appeared before me in said jurisdiction and acknowledged the same to be his/her/its act and deed. Given under my hand and seal, this day of , and: "My commission expires:

                                    Notary Public.".

3. Certificate of satisfaction executed by beneficiary, mortgagee, assignee, or trustee, stating deed of trust is released, may be recorded. (§45-718[c][3]).

"CERTIFICATION OF SATISFACTION

"KNOW ALL BY THESE PRESENTS:

"That (name, title), representing (beneficiary), does hereby certify and acknowledge, under penalties of perjury, that the promissory note or other evidence of indebtedness secured by that certain mortgage/deed of trust made by to , mortgage/trustee(s), dated and recorded as Instrument No. among the Land Records of the District of Columbia, which encumbers the real property described in Exhibit A attached hereto, has been fully paid and satisfied and that was, at the time of satisfaction, the holder of the promissory note or other evidence of indebtedness and that the lien of the said mortgage/deed of trust is hereby released.

"The property encumbered by said mortgage/deed of trust is described as follows:

"WITNESS the hand and seal of the party making this certification this day of, .

....

"(ACKNOWLEDGMENT).

_____

PROPERTY

ABSENTEES:

Care of Property.—If one domiciled in District, obligated to support one in District, or having property in District has disappeared, and individual has property that will be wasted or dissipated unless management is provided or money is needed for support, care, and welfare of individual or those entitled to his/her support, individual to be protected or other interested person may file petition in Superior Court seeking appointment of conservator or other protective order. After hearing, court may appoint conservator or make other appropriate orders. Court, directly or through conservator, has wide authority to manage property, including authority to convey or release interests in property, enter contracts and make gifts. (§21-2051-2077).

Process Agent.—No statutory provisions regarding right or duty to appoint agent for service of process. However, court rules permit appointment of agent to receive service of process (F. R. C. P. 4; Sup. Ct. Civ. R. 4), and in certain cases, service may be by publication (§§13-336, 341) or by personal service outside District (§13-337).

Escheat.—Uniform Disposition of Unclaimed Property Act of 1980 requires annual report of abandoned personal property by holder thereof. Such report as of prior June 30 must be filed with District of Columbia before Nov. 1. Delivery of abandoned property so reported must be made to District of Columbia within six months after Nov. 1. (§§42-201-242).

See categories Business Organizations, topic Corporations, subhead Unclaimed Dividends; Business Regulation and Commerce, topic Banks and Banking, subhead Unclaimed Deposits; and Estates and Trusts, topic Wills, subhead Unclaimed Legacies.

See category Estates and Trusts, topic Descent and Distribution, subhead Escheat.

ADVERSE POSSESSION:

Character of Possession.—Must be actual, continuous, open, and exclusive, attended with such manifest intention of holding and continuing the possession as will make that possession notorious to everyone interested in reclaiming the property to the rightful ownership. (13 App. D. C. 30). If action is to recover unimproved property, it is not necessary for defendant to show that premises had been enclosed, but it is sufficient to show equivalent of possession by actual enclosure that defendant has regularly paid taxes upon same and was only person exercising control thereof. (§16-1113).

Duration of Possession.—No action may be brought for the recovery of lands, tenements or hereditaments after 15 years from the time the right to maintain such action accrued. (§12-301).

Quieting Title.—When title to real estate has become vested in any person by adverse possession, holder thereof may file a complaint in Superior Court to have title perfected, in which complaint it is sufficient to allege that plaintiff holds title to such real estate and same has vested in him, or in himself and those under whom he claims, by adverse possession; and it is unnecessary to make parties defendants other than those persons appearing to have claim or title adverse to plaintiff. (§16-3301). Upon showing of facts at trial establishing title by adverse possession, decree must be entered, copy of which may be recorded in office of recorder of deeds. If process is returned not to be found, subject to rights of those under legal disability, notice by publication may be substituted, and if it is unknown whether person who would be adverse party is living or dead, or in case of decedent, whether he died testate or left heirs or whose heirs or devisees are unknown, process may be had by publication. (§16-3301).

Disabilities.—The rights of those under legal disability are saved for a period of two years after the removal of their disability; but the entire period during which such rights shall be preserved may not exceed 22 years from the time such right accrued, either in plaintiff or in those under whom he claims. (§16-3301).

CONVEYANCES:

See topic Deeds.

CURTESY:

Abolished with respect to wife dying after Nov. 29, 1957. (§19-102). But see topic Dower, as to both husband and wife.

DEEDS:

See topic Real Property for types of estates.

Execution.—Deed must be signed and sealed. (§45-501, 801). The statute does not require signature of witness, but it is customary to have officer taking acknowledgment sign as witness. Deed properly sealed and delivered is valid without acknowledgment; but acknowledgment is necessary to entitle deed to be recorded. (§45-803; 59 App. D. C. 369, 42 F.2d 604).

Deed of an individual may not be executed or acknowledged by attorney. (§45-601). See also topics Curtesy, Dower; and category Family, topic Husband and Wife, subhead Conveyance or Encumbrance of Property.

Corporations.—Deed of a corporation must be signed with name of corporation by its president or other officer, must have its seal attached, and must be acknowledged by attorney-in-fact appointed for that purpose, under corporate seal, by power of attorney embodied in deed or separate therefrom, and annexed to and recorded with deed. (§45-502).

Recording is not necessary to validity as between parties; but, deeds must be recorded with recorder of deeds in order to take effect as to creditors and subsequent bona fide purchasers and mortgagees without notice. (§45-801). Recorder may not accept for recording any deed not executed and acknowledged by grantor. (§45-803). See also category Documents and Records, topic Records.

Recording Fees.—See category Documents and Records, topic Records.

Operation and Effect.—Any deed conveying real estate in the District or any interest therein or declaring or limiting any use or trust thereof, takes effect and passes title from the time of delivery, except as to creditors and subsequent purchasers and mortgagees without notice, as to whom it takes effect upon delivery to the recorder of deeds for the purpose of recordation. (§45-801). When more than one deed of the same property is made to bona fide purchasers for value without notice, the deed first recorded is preferred. (§45-802). A covenant binds covenantor and privies without so stating. (§45-503).

No words of inheritance are necessary to create a fee simple, but every conveyance of real estate shall be construed to pass a fee simple or entire estate of grantor unless contrary intention appears by express terms or is necessarily implied. (§45-401). "Grant" and "bargain and sell" are construed to pass whole estate unless there are limitations showing different intent. (§45-402).

DEEDS . . . *continued*

Form.—The following is a form of deed in fee simple (§45-501):

Form

This deed, made this . . . . . . day of . . . . . ., in the year . . . . . ., by me, ..., of . . . . . ., witnesseth, that in consideration of (here insert consideration), I, the said . . . . . ., do grant unto (here insert grantee's name), of . . . . . ., all that (here describe the property).

Witness my hand and seal.

. . . . (Seal)

(Acknowledgment).

There is no statutory form of warranty deed, but the Code gives statutory effect to the following short phrases as if the longer common law form had been used: "that he will warrant generally the property hereby conveyed" (or, following granting words, "with general warranty"), "that he will warrant specially the property hereby conveyed" (or, following granting words, "with special warranty"), "that the said grantee shall quietly enjoy said land," "that he has done no act to encumber said land," and "that he will execute such further assurances of said land as may be requisite." (§§45-504-508).

DEEDS OF TRUST:

See category Mortgages, topic Mortgages of Real Property.

DOWER:

Dower in case of wife intermarried to deceased husband before Nov. 29, 1957 or of both husband and wife if spouse dies on or after Mar. 16, 1962, entitles surviving spouse to one-third interest for life in real estate of which deceased spouse seized (by legal or equitable title) during coverture. No dower attaches to land held in joint tenancy while joint tenancy exists. All statutory rights and incidents of dower apply to only surviving wife where intermarried to deceased husband before Nov. 29, 1957, but apply to both husband and wife where spouse dies on or after Mar. 16, 1962. (§19-102).

See also category Estates and Trusts, topic Executors and Administrators, subhead Quarantine.

Release.—Spouse may release dower by joining in other spouse's deed or by separate conveyance to one claiming under other spouse, if releasing spouse is over eighteen. (§19-107a).

Bar.—Jointure before marriage is bar to dower if expressly made and declared to be in satisfaction of whole dower. (§19-105).

Divorce.—Court may retain to spouse obtaining divorce his or her right of dower. (§16-912).

Election.—Intestate share of surviving spouse in real estate is in lieu of dower unless he or she files written election in probate court within six months after letters of administration issued, to take dower. (§19-113). As to election between dower or intestate share and testamentary provision, see category Estates and Trusts, topic Wills.

ESCHEAT:

See category Estates and Trusts, topic Descent and Distribution.

LANDLORD AND TENANT:

Except to extent modified by statute or agreement common law governs rights and liabilities growing out of the relation.

Rent Control.—Rental Housing Act of 1985 (§45-2501 et seq.) regulates rents of most residential units. Most lessors must file annual registration statements including base rent charged, determined by statute. (§45-2515[f]). Any charges to lessee above base rent must be within statutory rent ceiling. (§45-2516). Tit. III of Act (§45-2531 et seq.) establishes tenant assistance program to fund rental housing of qualifying lessees. Tit. V (§45-2551 et seq.) sets conditions which must be met before eviction can occur, and Tit. VII (§45-2571 et seq.) provides for relocation assistance under certain conditions funded by lessor. Finally, Act sets penalties for violation of any of its provisions (§45-2591), including treble damages against lessor for specified violations (§45-2591[a]) and recovery of attorneys fees (§45-2592), and also authorizes civil actions for certain purposes (§45-2528).

Kinds of Tenancy.—The following tenancies are permitted: estates for years (§45-218); estates by sufferance (§45-220); estates from month to month or from quarter to quarter (§45-221); estates at will (§45-222). Estates said to be from year to year are good for one year only. (§45-219). Estates which at common law were construed to be from year to year, such as where a tenant for years holds over, and all verbal hirings by the month or at any specified rate per month are deemed estates by sufferance. (§45-220).

Leases.—Estates for longer than one year must be created by deed signed and sealed and delivered by lessor or by will. (§45-306). Execution, acknowledgment and certification are necessary for validity of lease and for recording. (§§45-801, 45-803).

Recording or lack thereof does not affect validity of lease as between the parties (§45-801) or as to persons having actual notice of its existence (46 App. D.C. 363). It is required for constructive notice. (§45-801). For requirements as to form, acknowledgment and place for recording, see topic Deeds.

Lien.—The landlord has a tacit lien upon such of the tenant's personal chattels on the premises as are subject to execution for debt, to commence with the tenancy and continue for three months after the rent is due, and until the termination of any action for such rent brought within said three months. This lien may be enforced by attachment issued upon affidavit that the rent is due and unpaid, or if not due, that the defendant is about to remove or sell all or some part of said chattels, or by judgment against the tenant and execution to be levied on said chattels, or any of them, or by action against any purchaser of said chattels with notice of lien, in which action the plaintiff may have judgment for the value of the chattels purchased by the defendant, not exceeding the rent in arrears. (§§45-1413-1414).

Termination of Tenancy.—Tenancies from month to month, quarter to quarter, at will or at sufferance are terminable by 30 days notice in writing to quit delivered to tenant or to some person of proper age on premises, or, if that is impossible, by posting on premises in conspicuous place and sending to occupant of premises. Where estate is determined by its own limitation, no notice to quit or otherwise is required. (§§45-1401-1406). Rental Housing Act of 1985 requires 30-180 days notice depending on reason for eviction and permits eviction only for certain specified reasons even after expiration of lease or rental agreement so long as tenant continues to pay rent. (§45-2551). Act applies to most evictions, notwithstanding lesser notice requirements in §§45-1401-1406. Retaliatory action by landlord in rent control cases is prohibited. (§45-2552).

Holding Over.—Tenants holding over are treated as tenants at sufferance. (§45-220).

Dispossession.—Suit for possession may be brought by written complaint on oath of person entitled to same before Superior Court, and a summons served at least seven days, exclusive of Suns. and legal holidays, before date set for trial. (§§16-1501-1502).

Distress.—Common law right of distress is abolished.

See also category Business Regulation and Commerce, topic Consumer Protection.

LEASES:

See topic Landlord and Tenant.

PERPETUITIES:

Except in the case of gifts or devises to charitable uses, every future estate, whether of freehold or leasehold, whether by way of remainder or without a precedent estate, and whether vested or contingent, is void in its creation, if it suspends, or may by possibility suspend, the power of absolute alienation, for a longer period than during the continuance of not more than one or more lives in being and 21 years thereafter. (§45-302). These provisions equally apply to limitations of chattels real and personal property. (§45-223, 303).

Provision for accumulations is valid. (75 App. D.C. 48, 123 F.2d 924).

Pension, profit sharing, stock bonus, annuity, disability, death benefit, or other employee trusts established by employers for distribution of income or principal or both do not violate laws against perpetuities, restraints on alienation, or accumulation of income. (§45-307).

PERSONAL PROPERTY:

Tenancy by the entirety exists. (41 App. D. C. 525).

POWERS OF ATTORNEY:

As to conveyance by attorney, see topic Deeds.

Uniform Durable Power of Attorney Act.—Adopted. (D.C. Code §§21-2081—21-2085).

REAL PROPERTY:

Estates in the District shall be of inheritance, for life, for years, at will and by sufferance. (§45-201). The estate tail has been abolished. (§45-202).

Every estate granted or devised to two or more persons in their own right, including estates granted or devised to husband and wife, is a tenancy in common, unless expressly declared to be a joint tenancy; but every estate vested in executors or trustees, as such, is a joint tenancy, unless otherwise expressed. (§45-216). Estate in joint tenancy or by entireties may be created by conveyance in which one or more of grantors is also grantee. (§45-216). Conveyance to husband and wife as joint tenants creates tenancy by entireties. (41 F. Supp. 634).

Condominium Ownership.—Condominium Act of 1976 (§§45-1801 et seq.) regulates in detail creation and governance of condominiums. Condominiums created after March 8, 1991, governed by Condominium Act of 1976 Reform Amendment Act of 1990 which contains more elaborate regulations. (§§45-1801-72). Rental Housing Conversion and Sale Act of 1980, as amended by Extension and Amendment Act of 1994, and by Reenactment and Amendment Act of 1995, regulates conversion of rent controlled property to condominiums and cooperatives. (§45-1601 et seq.).

Rule in Shelley's Case has been abolished. (§45-403).

Transactions.—The Real Estate Transaction Amendment Act of 1990 amends Real Estate Licensure Act to discourage discrimination against owners and occupants of real property, including individuals with AIDS.

See also topics Curtesy, Deeds, Dower, Landlord and Tenant; categories Business Regulation and Commerce, topic Frauds, Statute of; Civil Actions and Procedure, topic Partition; Debtor and Creditor, topics Fraudulent Sales and Conveyances, Homesteads, Liens; Estates and Trusts, topic Descent and Distribution; Family, topic Husband and Wife; Mortgages, topic Mortgages of Real Property; Taxation, topic Taxes.

TRUST DEEDS:

See category Mortgages, topic Mortgages of Real Property.

TAXATION

ADMINISTRATION:

Most taxes are assessed, collected and otherwise administered by Department of Finance and Revenue and are uniform throughout District of Columbia. (Organization Order No. 3, Amendment No. 1, Order of Commissioner No. 67-24, Dec. 13, 1967, as am'd; Order of Commissioner No. 69-96, Mar. 7, 1969).

Economic Development Zones that are established are qualified for tax and other development incentives. (§5-1401-06).

Penalties.—
Income Tax.—

See note at head of Digest as to 1998 legislation covered.

See Topical Index in front part of this volume.

ADMINISTRATION . . . *continued*

Civil Penalties: Failure to file return or to pay tax within time prescribed by law and failure of employer to withhold taxes or to make quarterly return or to remit withheld tax: addition of 5% of tax or amount of taxes that should have been properly withheld or paid over for each month or fraction thereof that failure continues, not to exceed 25% in aggregate, except if failure to file was due to reasonable cause. (§§47-1813.1, 47-455). Underestimate of tax: If estimated tax plus withholding payments total less than 90% of tax due under §47-1806.3, then there is added to tax amount equal to difference between tax payments and 90% of tax due, or 1½% per month of difference between tax payments and tax due, whichever is lesser. (§47-1813.1). Underestimate of tax (corporation, financial institution or unincorporated business): Penalty of 1½% per month on amount of underpayment for period of underpayment. (§47-1812.14). Deficiencies: Interest on deficiencies to be assessed at rate of 1½% per month or portion thereof from date prescribed for payment of tax to date deficiency is assessed. Interest is also assessed at same rate for period of extension granted for payment of deficiency. (§§47-1813.2, 47-453). Deficiency—additions: Where deficiency is due to fraud, addition equal to 75% of underpayment and 50% of interest under §47-453 will be assessed. (§§47-1813.3, 47-456). Nonpayment—additions: For failure to pay tax or any part thereof on or before prescribed date, there is imposed interest of 1½% per month or portion thereof on unpaid amount until it is paid. For failure to pay tax or any part thereof before expiration of extension period, there is imposed interest of 1½% per month or portion thereof on unpaid amount from expiration date of extension until payment. (§§47-1813.4, 47-453). Interest at rate of 1½% per month or any portion thereof is assessed during any extension period. (§47-1813.5). Substantial underpayment—addition: For understatement of tax greater than 10% of tax required to be shown on return or report or $2,000 except if due to reasonable cause, tax equal to 20% of amount of any underpayment attributable to understatement is added. (§47-454).

Deficiencies or Additions—Interest: Where deficiency or any interest or additions are not paid within ten days from date of assessment interest in amount of 1½% per month or portion thereof on unpaid amount is assessed until payment. (§§47-1813.4[b], 47-453).

Criminal Penalties: Willful violation: any person who willfully refuses to pay or collect any tax or to make a return, or to keep records, or to supply information, or who makes a false or fraudulent return, or who willfully attempts in any manner to defeat or evade the tax is guilty of a misdemeanor and fined not more than $5,000 or imprisoned for not more than one year, or both, together with costs of prosecution. (§47-1813.6[a]). Negligent violation: Effective for years beginning after Dec. 31, 1976, any person who negligently fails to pay or collect any tax or to make return, keep records, or to supply information is guilty of misdemeanor and may be fined not more than $3,000 or imprisoned for not more than six months or both. (§47-1813.6[b]). Concealment of assets: Any person who, in connection with compromise of tax, willfully conceals property or receives, destroys, mutilates or falsifies any record, or makes under oath any false statement relating to estate or financial condition of taxpayer or to person liable for tax, shall be fined not more than $5,000 or imprisoned for not more than one year, or both. (§47-1812.13[b]).

Property Taxes.—Penalty of 5% of tax per month or fraction thereof, not to exceed 25% in aggregate, for failure to file return or to pay tax within prescribed time except if failure was due to reasonable cause. (§§47-1531, 47-455). Penalty of 20% of underpayment attibutable to understatement of tax if understatement exceeds greater of 10% of tax required to be shown on return or report or $2,000. (§§47-451, 47-454). Penalty for underpayment due to fraud equal to 75% of underpayment and 50% of interest payable under §47-453. (§§47-1531, 47-456). Interest on tax not paid by prescribed date of 1½% per month or fraction thereof until date paid. (§§47-1531, 47-453). Violation of personal property tax law: penalty not to exceed $500. (§47-1603). Negligent failure to notify Mayor of termination of eligibility for Homestead Exemption subjects owner to penalty of not more than $1,000 or 180 days in prison or both. Penalty for willful failure to notify is not more than $5,000 or one year in prison, or both, (§47-850).

License Tax.—Penalties for violation of any provision of General License Law or regulations promulgated thereunder: fine of not more than $300 or imprisonment for not more than 90 days. Same penalty applies for failure to file any information required by the law, or any regulation promulgated thereunder, or for making any false or misleading statement in the filing of such information. (§47-2846).

Non-Regulatory Professional License.—Annual license fee, which varies from profession to profession, imposed on certified public accountants, lawyers, architects, registered professional engineers, persons licensed as interior designers, and persons licensed, certified, or registered to practice medicine, dentistry, optometry, acupuncture, chiropractic, podiatry, or psychology. (§47-1814.1). Failure to file return for or to pay annual fee: revocation of license (§47-1814.4), or refusal to issue or renew license (§47-1814.5). Failure to obtain license: fine of not more than $300 for each violation with provision that each and every day during which violation continues shall constitute a separate offense. (§47-1814.6).

Annual Reports of Corporations.—For failure to pay two year report fee when due, interest is to be assessed at rate of 5% per month until paid (§29-399.22[e]) and penalty of $25 may be assessed by Mayor. (§29-399.29). Failure to pay fee or file report for two consecutive years: if domestic corporation, articles of incorporation shall be void; if foreign corporation, certificate of authority shall be revoked. (§29-399.23). If corporation continues to operate after revocation, it shall be deemed guilty of misdemeanor punishable by fine not to exceed $500 and responsible persons may be imprisoned for not exceeding one year, or alternative civil fines, penalties and fees may be imposed. (§29-399.25).

Alcoholic Beverage Taxes.—For violation of provisions of the law there is provided penalty of a fine of not more than $1,000 or imprisonment for not more than one year, or both. Additional penalty of not more than $5,000 or imprisonment for not more than three years, or both, for willful failure to file return or to perform any other required act within time prescribed. Alternative civil fines, penalties and fees may be imposed. (§25-132).

Gasoline Tax.—Interest and penalties imposed by §§47-453-458 discussed under subhead Penalties, catchline Property Taxes, supra, apply. (§47-2316). Also, if failure to file is not shown to be due to accident or justifiable oversight, license will be revoked. (§47-2303). For negligent failure to file, penalty is fine of not more than $1,000 or imprisonment for not more than six months, or both. For willful failure, penalty is fine of not more than $5,000 or imprisonment for not more than one year, or both. (§47-2310).

Cigarette Tax.—For violation of any provisions of Act, or regulations issued thereunder, license may be suspended or revoked. (§47-2404[f]). For violation of provisions of §47-2405, involving transportation of cigarettes, fine of up to $25 for each 200 contraband cigarettes or three years imprisonment, or both. (§47-2405[c]). For violations involving counterfeiting, forging or altering tax stamps, fine of up to $10,000, or imprisonment for up to five years, or both. (§47-2406[f]). Interest and penalties imposed by §§47-453-458 discussed under subhead Penalties, catchline Property Taxes, supra, apply. (§47-2411.1). Willful failure to pay tax, make return, keep records, or supply information required punishable by fine of up to $5,000, or imprisonment up to three years, or both, in addition to other penalties. (§47-2414[a]). Violations of chapter for which no specific penalties provided punishable by up to $1,000 fine, or up to one year imprisonment, or both. (§47-2414[b]). Chapter also provides for seizure of contraband and associated personalty. (§47-2409).

Deed Recordation Tax.—Criminal Penalties: For violation of any provision of act or any rules or regulations thereunder for which no specific penalty is provided, fine of not more than $1,000 or imprisonment not more than one year, or both. Criminal penalties are provided for fraudulent use, removal or alteration of stamps, and a violator thereof is guilty of a felony and shall be fined not more than $5,000 or imprisoned not more than three years, or both. (§§45-940-941). Failure to file correct return within prescribed time results in penalty of 5% of tax per month, not to exceed 25%, except that penalty may be waived where failure is due to reasonable cause and not to neglect. Interest on deficiencies is assessed at rate of one-half of one per cent per month or portion thereof from date prescribed for payment of tax to date deficiency is assessed. Interest at rate of one-half of one per cent per month or portion thereof, is assessed during any extension period and for any time after expiration of an extension period until payment of deficiency. If deficiency is due to negligence or intentional disregard, but without intent to defraud, a penalty of 5% of the deficiency will be assessed. If deficiency is due to fraud with intent to evade tax, a penalty of 50% of the deficiency will be assessed. Interest on deficiencies or interest or additions to the tax is imposed at rate of one-half of one per cent per month or portion thereof from due date until payment. (§45-929).

Sales and Use Taxes.—

Sales Tax: Interest and penalties imposed by §§47-453-458 discussed under subhead Penalties, catchline Property Taxes, supra, apply. (§47-2411.1). Failure to file return when due, fine of not more than $1,000 or imprisonment of not more than six months, or both, for each failure. Willful failure to file return, fine of not more than $5,000 or imprisonment of not more than one year, or both. (§47-2028). Failure to obtain registration certificate, fine of not more than $50 for each day. (§47-2026). For advertisement of absorption of the tax or that tax will not be added to price or will be refunded, penalty provided is fine of not more than $500 or imprisonment for not more than six months, or both. (§47-2014).

Use Tax: The above sections, except for §47-2026, are made applicable to use tax law by §§47-2209 and 47-2213.

Taxes on Utilities.—Penalty of $500, or in default of such payment, imprisonment not to exceed six months is imposed for any violation of §§47-2501, imposing gross receipts, real estate and franchise taxes upon utilities. (§47-1603). Interest and penalties imposed by §§47-453-458 discussed under subhead Penalties, catchline Property Taxes, supra, apply. (§47-2411.1).

Insurance Companies.—For failure to pay a tax a penalty of 8% per month until paid is assessed. (§47-2609).

Inheritance and Estate Taxes.—Penalty for failure to file return within prescribed time and for filing false or fraudulent return imposed by §§47-453-458 discussed under subhead Penalties, catchline Property Taxes, supra. (§47-3718). Interest for extension of time or for additional tax due to amended return imposed by §§47-453-458 discussed under subhead Penalties, catchline Property Taxes, supra. (§§47-3705, 47-3708). Willful failure to pay tax, or make a return or to supply any information: misdemeanor punishable by fine of not more than $1,000 or imprisonment for not more than one year, or both. (§47-3718).

Unemployment Compensation.—Employer contributions, failure to pay when due: interest at rate of 1½% per month or fraction thereof from due date until paid. (§46-105[c][1]). If contributions are not paid or wage reports are not filed by specified time, there is to be added penalty of 10% of amount due, but such penalty shall not be less than $100, and may be waived for good cause shown. (§46-105[c][2]). For failing to disclose material fact to avoid payment of any or all employer contributions required or for failure or refusal to pay contributions or other payment: Fine of not more than $1,000 or imprisonment of not more than six months, or both. (§46-120).

ALCOHOLIC BEVERAGE TAXES:

Alcoholic beverages tax imposed on wine, champagne, spirits, alcohol and beer. Returns must be filed monthly by holders of manufacturer's or wholesaler's license. (§§25-124, 138).

BANK TAX:

See category Business Regulation and Commerce, topic Banks and Banking.

CIGARETTE TAXES:

Cigarettes are taxed at rate of 3.25¢ per cigarette. (§47-2402[a]).

GASOLINE TAXES:

Tax at rate of 20¢ per gallon. In addition to Federal tax, imposed on purchaser and collected by seller. (§§47-2301-2325).

GIFT TAX:

None.

See note at head of Digest as to 1998 legislation covered.

See Topical Index in front part of this volume.

DC – 32

INCOME TAX:

Income tax is imposed by the District of Columbia Income and Franchise Tax Act of 1947 (§§47-1801.1-47-1816.3) as am'd.

Income for D.C. income tax purposes generally has same meaning as under Internal Revenue Code of 1986 (gross income defined under I.R.C. §61; adjusted gross income defined under I.R.C. §62, in case of individual, estate, or trust). (§47-1803.2 as am'd by D.C. Law 7-29).

Individuals are taxable if they are residents of District. (§47-1806.3). "Resident" means every individual domiciled within District at any time during taxable year, and every individual maintaining place of abode within District for aggregate of 183 days or more during taxable year, whether domiciled in District or not. Resident does not include any elective official of U.S. Govt. or any employee of elected official in legislative branch of U. S. Govt. if such employee is bona fide resident of state of residence of such elective official, or any official of executive branch whose appointment was by President and confirmed by Senate and serving at pleasure of President or any Justice of U.S. Supreme Court, unless such officials or Justices are domiciled in District on last day of taxable year. In determining whether individual is resident, such individual's absence from District for temporary or transitory purposes shall not be viewed as changing his domicile or place of abode. (§47-1801.4[17]).

Personal exemptions are allowed to residents in same manner as allowed under §151 of Internal Revenue Code 1986 with following changes: (a) There is no exclusion of certain income of handicapped dependents as described in §501(c)(5) of Tax Reform Act of 1986, and no inflation adjustment for years after 1989 as described in §501(d)(3) of Tax Reform Act of 1986; (b) for purposes of this section, exemption amount shall be $1,370. Taxpayers who qualify as head of household shall be allowed additional exemption. Likewise, additional exemption shall be allowed for taxpayer who is blind or has attained age of 65 at close of his or her taxable year, and additional exemption for spouse of taxpayer if spouse is blind or has attained age of 65 at close of taxable year of taxpayer and, if spouse, for calendar year in which taxable year of taxpayer begins, has no gross income and is not dependent of another taxpayer, except that if spouse dies during such taxable year determination regarding blindness shall be made as of time of death. (§47-1806.2).

Individual who is a resident of D. C. for entire taxable year is taxable on his entire income (after deductions, exemptions and credits). Individual who becomes domiciled in D. C. during calendar year is taxable on amount of income received from and after date he becomes a resident of District. Individual who changes his domicile to a place outside D. C. on or before Dec. 31 is taxable as a resident for that portion of taxable year during which he is domiciled in District. In case of a change in resident status during taxable year, personal exemptions and credits are prorated according to number of months during which taxpayer resided in District, and only those deductions actually paid while a resident of District are allowed. (Instructions, Form D-40). Above rules relating to taxpayers who change their residency during taxable year have been promulgated as a result of U.S. Court of Appeals decision in District of Columbia v. Davis, 125 App. D. C. 311, 371 F.2d 964 (1967), cert. denied 386 U.S. 1034 (1967).

For taxable years beginning after Dec. 31, 1987, tax is determined in accordance with following: For taxable income not over $10,000, 6% of taxable income; for taxable income over $10,000 but not over $20,000, $600, plus 8% of excess over $10,000; and for taxable income over $20,000, $1,400, plus 9.5% of excess over $20,000. (§47-1806.3).

Method of determination of taxable income, deductions, and credits, is substantially same as under Internal Revenue Code of 1986, as amended.

Multistate taxpayers' state and local income tax liability, including apportionment of tax bases and settlement of apportionment disputes, is determined under Multistate Tax Compact Act of 1981. (§§47-441-446).

Estates and trusts are "resident" if decedent at time of death or creator at time of creation was domiciled in D. C., and, if "resident," are taxed at same rates as individuals. In lieu of exemption for trusts, there is credit against net income of $100. (§§47-1809.1-1809.5).

Corporations and financial institutions, foreign or domestic, are subject to franchise tax for privilege of engaging in business within D. C., and of receiving income from sources within District (except as exempted under §47-1802.1), at rate of 9.5% for taxable years beginning after Dec. 31, 1994 for any taxable period on taxable income derived from District sources. (§§47-1807.2, -1810.2). Surtax is 2.5% for taxable periods beginning Sept. 30, 1992 and additional surtax of 2.5% for taxable period beginning Oct. 1, 1994. (§47-1807.2). Following are not considered income derived from District sources: (a) Dividends (in case of any corporation) and interest (in case of corporation not engaged in trade or business in District) received from corporation subject to District income tax or from insurance company subject to District premium tax under §§47-2601-2611 as am'd by D.C. Law 6-42, (b) in case of corporation organized under Bank Holding Company Act of 1956 as am'd 1970, dividends received from corporation subject to District income tax or from financial institutions and public utilities subject to taxation under §47-2501, 34 DCR 689 and interest (in case of any such bank holding company not engaged in trade or business in District) received from such financial institutions or public utilities (but all dividends received by financial institution from corporation not subject to District franchise tax and all interest received by financial institution are deemed business income, see §47-1810.1), and (c) income derived from sale of tangible personal property by corporation or unincorporated business not doing business within District (except for certain sales to federal government). (§47-1810.1). Dividends received from subsidiary corporation for whom parent provides services deemed to be business income subject to apportionment. (§47-1810.1). Nonetheless, in computing net income for corporation, deduction allowed for all dividends received on or after Mar. 1, 1997 from wholly-owned subsidiary. (§47-1803.3). Income derived by corporation, financial institution, or unincorporated business not carrying on trade or business within District (as defined in §47.1801.4,[6][A]), shall not be considered income from D.C. sources, with exception for income from sales to U.S. not excluded under §47-1803.2(a)(2)(I).

Rules prescribed for allocation of income and deductions between District and foreign sources where income is derived from sources within and without D.C. (§47-1810.2).

Corporations exempt include insurance companies and surety and guaranty companies which pay gross receipts, etc., taxes under other provisions of D. C. laws. (§47-1802.1 [7]).

See also category Business Regulation and Commerce, topic Banks and Banking.

Unincorporated businesses, as defined in §47-1808.1, are subject to franchise tax for privilege of engaging in business within D.C., and of receiving income from sources within District except as exempted under §47-1802.1, at rate of tax of 9.5% for any taxable period ($100 minimum tax) on taxable income derived from District sources. (§47-1808.3). Surtax is equal to 2.5% of franchise tax and separate and additional surtax is also equal to 2.5%. (§47-1808.3). Income derived from D. C. sources determined in same manner as corporate tax. Exemptions: $5,000. (§47-1808.4). Tax not applicable to professional corporations incorporated under D.C. Professional Corporation Act (see D.C. Law 6-16, repealing §29-621 after it was declared invalid in Bishop v. District of Columbia, 401 A.2d 955, aff'd 411 A.2d 997 [D.C. App. 1980]).

Exempt Organizations.—Organizations exempt from income and franchise tax are determined under §47-1802.1.

Withholding at Source.—Employers making payment of wages to employees (except employees who are not considered as residents) are required to withhold taxes from such wages. (§§47-1812.8, -1801.4[24]). Provision is also made for filing of declarations of estimated tax by individuals (§47-1812.8) and by corporations and unincorporated businesses (§47-1812.14). District Council may, by rules and regulations, require any person subject to jurisdiction of District to withhold and pay to Mayor, amount not in excess of 5% of all income payable by such person to any foreign corporation or unincorporated business. Any excess over tax of such corporation, as finally determined, must be refunded. (§47-1812.8[a]).

Returns and Payment.—Return must be filed with Mayor, by Apr. 15 following close of calendar year (or three and one-half months after close of fiscal year); and total amount of tax due must be paid to Mayor, at time of filing return. (§47-1812.7).

INHERITANCE AND ESTATE TAXES:

Inheritance and estate tax is imposed by §§47-3701 et seq.

Property Subject.—All real and tangible and intangible personal property having taxable situs in District is subject to inheritance and estate tax, whether decedent is resident or nonresident. (§§47-3702-3703).

Intangible property not used in trade or business has taxable situs only at domicile of owner. (§§47-3702-3703).

Valuation is based on value as determined for federal estate tax purposes under Internal Revenue Code, in effect for federal estate tax purposes on Jan. 1, 1986. (§47-3701[13]).

Tax on transfer of taxable estate of every resident (as defined in §47-3701[10]) having its taxable situs in District is amount of "federal credit" (maximum amount of credit for state death taxes allowable by §2011 of Internal Revenue Code). (§§47-3701[4], 3702[a]). If real or tangible personal property of resident is located outside District and is subject to death tax imposed by another state for which credit is allowed under §2011 of Internal Revenue Code, amount of tax due is credited with lesser of: (a) Amount of death tax paid other state that qualifies for credit against federal estate tax, or (b) amount computed by multiplying federal credit by fraction, numerator of which is value of part of gross estate over which other state has jurisdiction, and denominator of which is value of gross estate. (§47-3702[b][2]).

Tax on transfer of taxable estate of every nonresident having its taxable situs in District is amount computed by multiplying federal credit by fraction described above. (§47-3703).

Returns and Payment.—Personal representatives of estate subject to tax must file with Mayor, within ten months after death of decedent: (a) Return for District inheritance and estate tax, and (b) copy of federal estate tax return. (§47-3705[a]). Tax due must be paid by personal representative before distribution of estate and no later than date return must be filed. (§§47-3705[c], 3713). Personal representative personally liable for unpaid tax if he distributes property of estate without having paid or secured tax due. (§47-3712).

Penalty for delinquency in filing return is assessed against estate. (§47-3718[a]).

Compromise.—Where Mayor claims that decedent was domiciled in District at time of death and taxing authorities in other state(s) claim domicile in their state(s), Mayor may compromise inheritance and estate tax imposed by District tax act. (§47-3704).

Lien.—District has lien for all inheritance and estate taxes, including related penalties and interest, on all property that decedent dies seized or possessed of which is subject to tax. (§47-3711).

PREMIUM TAX:

See category Insurance, topic Insurance Companies.

PROPERTY TAXES:

Taxable Property.—Taxes on real and personal property are imposed for tax year beginning Oct. 1 for real property and July 1 for personal property. (§§47-802[7], 47-1522[e]).

Tax on intangible personal property was repealed in 1939.

Tax on average stock in trade of merchants was repealed effective July 1, 1974. (§47-1507 as am'd by D.C. Law 6-212, §24).

Exemptions.—Real property of certain designated ownership and use is exempt. (§47-1002). Transfer of title into revocable trust and transfer to beneficiary of revocable trust are exempt under certain conditions. (§§47-850[e 2A], 863[d], 902). Exempt personalty includes that of any corporation, and any community chest fund or foundation, organized exclusively for religious, scientific, charitable, or educational purposes, including hospitals, no part of net earnings of which inure to benefit of any private

See note at head of Digest as to 1998 legislation covered.

See Topical Index in front part of this volume.

DC – 33

PROPERTY TAXES . . . *continued*

shareholder or individual, except that organization shall have first obtained certificate from Mayor stating that it is entitled to exemption. (§47-1508, as am'd).

Rates for real property are set each year for each class of property. (§§47-501, 812). Five classes of property are established for tax purposes: Class 1—owner-occupied residential property of less than five dwelling units; Class 2—nonowner-occupied residential rental property; Class 3—improved commercial real property including hotels and motels; Class 4—improved real property not in Classes 1-3, and certain unimproved real property not in Classes 1-3; Class 5—real property not in Classes 1-4 and certain unimproved real property not in Classes 1-4 (§47-813 as am'd by D.C. Law 8-160). Class 1 property owners, 65 years or older, whose annual household adjusted gross income is less than $100,000, are eligible for 50% decrease in property tax liability (§47-863).

Rate for tangible personal property is $3.40 for each $100 of assessed value. (§47-1522).

Assessment.—Effective July 1, 1975, assessment procedures are governed generally by §§47-820-828. Property to be assessed at least once every three years at estimated market value as of Jan. 1 preceding tax (fiscal) year. (§47-820). Mayor to appoint assessors, and to compile preliminary assessment roll and to notify each taxpayer of his assessment not later than Mar. 1 of each year. (§§47-821-825.1). Owner may petition for administrative review of assessment, equalization, valuation or classification on or before Apr. 1 following date of notice of proposed assessment. Mayor has authority to change assessment or classification in accordance with final determination made on petition. Owner aggrieved by final determination may appeal to Board of Real Property Assessment and Appeals within 30 days of date of notice of final determination. (§47-825.1). Board to assure assessment at estimated market value, and to raise or lower assessment if it finds preliminary assessment deviates from estimated market value by more than 5%. (§47-825.1[g]). Mayor will estimate assessment roll and submit it to Council of D.C. on same date proposed real property tax rates are published. (§47-825.1[h]).

Public Advocate for Assessments and Taxation may appear before or intervene in proceedings before Board of Real Property Assessments and Appeals, Superior Court, and Court of Appeals on behalf of interest of public and taxpayers, or may demand hearing if it deems public interest involved. (§47-825.2).

Assessment of tangible property, other than automobiles, is based on return prescribed by Mayor. Taxpayer shall not file return before July 1, but shall file return before Aug. 1. (§47-1524). For failure to file timely return, for failure to pay tax within time required, or for filing fraudulent return, penalties and interest shall be added to tax in accordance with title III of Tax Amnesty Act of 1986. (§47-1531). Mayor may require person, upon notice, to file return, render under oath statements, or keep records sufficient to show whether or not person is liable for personal property and extent of liability, if any. (§47-1525).

Review of Assessment.—Review of most taxes imposed by District may be obtained by payment of tax in full, and appeal to Superior Court (§47-3303), from which appeal lies to Court of Appeals (§47-3304). In case of income tax, appeal may be made from deficiency assessment, after payment of assessed tax, interest and penalties, or from disallowance of claim for refund, within six months of assessment or disallowance. (§47-1815.1). Real estate taxes may be appealed within six months after Mar. 30 of year for which tax assessed provided taxpayer who received written notice of assessment prior to Mar. 30, has first appealed to Board of Real Property Assessments and Appeals. (§47-825.1).

Payment.—All property taxes are payable to District of Columbia Treasurer, and are due in semiannual installments on Mar. 31 and Sept. 15 (in case of real property taxes) (§47-811) and during month of July (in case of personal property taxes) of fiscal year for which they are imposed (§47-1524). If any real property tax, or any installment thereof, is not paid within time prescribed, there shall be added to such tax or installment penalty of 10% of unpaid amount plus interest on unpaid amount at rate of 1¹/₂% per month or portion of month until real property tax or installment is paid. (§47-811). Owners occupying family dwelling houses may elect to pay in four installments (§47-1101), and time of payment may be extended by Collector of Taxes of District, in its discretion, not to exceed 90 days (§47-1102). Certain owners may defer payment of portion of real property tax increases. (§47-845).

Liens.—All personal property and property rights are subject to distraint for nonpayment of personal property taxes (§47-1702), and in absence of goods and chattels to distrain District of Columbia Treasurer may levy on real estate (§47-1601). Furthermore, on nonpayment of personal property taxes, Department of Finance and Revenue, ten days after demand, may file certificate of delinquent tax with Recorder of Deeds, which has effect of a lien created by Superior Court judgment until tax with interest and penalties is paid. (§47-1706).

Sale.—List, prepared annually by Assessor of District, of all real property taxes in arrears on Oct. 1, is published according to D. C. Council regulations, together with notice of sale, which is fixed by District Council to begin not less than three weeks after first publication. (§47-1301). Persons bidding enough to cover delinquent taxes, penalties and costs receive tax certificate and not less than 6 months nor more than one year thereafter, if there has been no redemption, may request issuance of tax deed conveying absolute title to property. (§47-1304[a][e]). If bids are insufficient, property must be bid in by District which may thereafter sell at private sale, issue tax certificate therefor on payment of taxes, costs and charges, or proceed to enforce tax lien by judicial proceeding in Superior Court, but minimum period of redemption under any such procedure is six months. (§§47-1304, 1312). District is also authorized to take deed in fee simple on property so bid off by it and not redeemed within six months, and under Council regulations may sell property to urban homesteaders. (§§47-847, 848). Certain properties also may be brought to tax sale under District's Homestead Housing Preservation Program. (§45-2704). Owner of real property with delinquent taxes may not bid on property at tax sale unless owner first pays all delinquent taxes, applicable penalties and costs assessed against property. (§47-1320).

Redemption.—Owner may redeem at any time within six months by payment of tax, penalties, costs and 1% per month interest, or, if no application for deed is made by holder of certificate within one year, may redeem by payment of taxes, penalties and costs and interest at the rate aforesaid for first six months and 6% per annum for three years thereafter (§47-1304). Minors or persons under disability are allowed until one year after majority or removal of disability to redeem, on payment of purchase money and intervening taxes paid, with 8% interest added. (§47-1304). Owner can also redeem at any time prior to sale when District takes judicial proceeding to enforce lien (§47-1312), or prior to issuance of deed in fee simple pursuant to §47-847. Redemption period under Homestead Housing Preservation Program is six months. (§§47-847, 47-1304, §45-2704).

REAL ESTATE CONVEYANCE TAX:

Separate transfer and recordation taxes are imposed. Transfer tax: 1.1% of consideration for transfer. (§47-903). Recordation tax: 1.1% of total consideration paid when deeds are presented for recording. Deed evidencing transfer of economic interest is taxed at 2.2% of higher of assessed value or sales price allocable to real property, and security interest instrument is taxed at 1.1%of debt secured by interest in real property. (§§45-923, 924). Exemptions include deeds securing debts, deeds of release, deeds to entities exempt from real property taxation, certain intra-family deeds and deeds evidencing economic interest in improved real property owned by cooperative housing association (§45-922) and certain conservation easements (§45-2402). There is also exemption when partnership converts to limited liability company, so long as membership and allocation of profits and losses do not change for 12 months following conversion, other than by death of member or involuntary dissolution. (§29-1313).

SALES AND USE TAXES:

Sales Tax.—5.75% of gross receipts of any vendor from retail sale (including snack food and food sold from vending machines) or rental of tangible personal property (with certain exemptions) and of certain selected services, except that such tax is: (a) 10.5% with respect to room charges by hotels, etc., (b) 9% with respect to rental vehicles, spiritous or malt liquors, beers and wines consumed on premises where sold, and food prepared for immediate consumption whether or not consumed on premises where sold, 8% with respect to spiritous or malt liquors, beer and wine sold for consumption off premises where sold, (c) 12% with respect to parking or storage of motor vehicles. (§§47-2002). In addition to 10.5% sales tax, there is imposed tax of $1.50 for every occupancy of hotel room in District, with certain exemptions. (§47-3202).

Payment in Lieu of Sales Tax.—All street vendors will make payments of $375, on or before 20th of every Jan., Apr., July and Oct., in lieu of collecting and remitting sales tax. (§47-2002.1).

Use Tax.—In general, sale of certain selected services in District of Columbia, as well as all tangible personal property purchased from vendor or retailer, for storage, use or consumption in District, upon which sales tax has not been paid, are subject to use tax of 5.75%, unless exempted or specifically treated. (§47-2202).

Utilities Gross Receipts.—Gas, electric lighting, telephone or telecommunications company including both toll telecommunications companies and wireless telecommunications companies, and deliverers of heating oil to end user must pay 10% of gross receipts from sale of public utility services or commodities. (§§47-2501, 3902-3903). Utility companies are also subject to real property, personal property and corporate income tax. (§47-2501[c]).

Telecommunications companies must pay 10% of monthly gross charges from sale of toll telecommunication service that originates or terminates in District and for which charge is made to service address located in District, regardless of where charge is billed or paid. (§47-3902).

As to tax on: Gross earnings of banks, see category Business Regulation and Commerce, topic Banks and Banking; premium receipts and membership fees of insurance companies, see category Insurance, topic Insurance Companies; gross receipts of surety and guaranty companies, see category Insurance, topic Surety and Guaranty Companies.

Employment.—Sales and use taxes imposed on procurement of job seeker for employer or procurement of employment for job seeker. (9 DCMR §490-493).

STAMP TAX:

None, except on sale of cigarettes. (§§47-2401-2417).

UNEMPLOYMENT COMPENSATION TAX:

Employers of one or more persons for any period (§46-103) must pay monthly (§46-105) contributions to D. C. Unemployment Compensation Board at standard rate in effect for current year. (§46-103). Rate is subject to adjustment based on experience. (§46-103[c]). No tax on employees. (§46-103[d]). Exemptions include: Casual labor not in course of business, inter-family employment, charitable corporations, insurance agents on commission. (§46-101[2]).

USE TAX:

See topic Sales and Use Taxes.

TRANSPORTATION

MOTOR VEHICLES:

Department of Transportation has general supervision. (§40-703[D]).

Vehicle registration required, expiring on dates established by Mayor (§40-102[b]) or on sale or transfer of vehicle (§40-102[d]), issued by Department of Transportation (§40-102[a]). Vehicles qualifying for International Registration Plan ("IRP"), which lists D.C. as established place of business, must declare D.C. as base of jurisdiction for purpose of IRP and obtain base plate from D.C. (§40-123).

Operator's permit required, renewable every four years. Persons under sixteen may not be licensed. Single form for issuance, renewal or correction of driver's permit may

MOTOR VEHICLES . . . *continued*
also be used as application for voter registration, to be forwarded by Mayor to Board of Elections and Ethics. (§40-301). Special license required for any person operating commercial motor vehicle. (§§40-1801-09).

Titles and Sales.—A certificate of title must be obtained before license plates and vehicle registration will be issued. (§§40-703[d], 702[c]). Certificate of title is issued by Department of Transportation upon application in form prescribed by Mayor and payment of sum not to exceed $10 and excise tax (certain vehicles exempt) from 6% to 7% (depending on weight) of fair market value of such vehicle or trailer at time such certificate is issued. (§40-703[j]).

Maximum finance charges for retail installment sales of motor vehicles where seller holds security interest are regulated by statute, which gave D. C. Council authority to make regulations with respect to such sales including provisions governing form and substance of security instruments, requiring equal and regular installment payments, permitting prepayment with refund of unearned charges, and governing maximum charges, insurance, methods of sale of repossessed vehicles, and examination of books of seller. (§§40-1101-1110).

Automobile Consumer Protection.—If new motor vehicle (not including buses sold for public transportation, motorcycles, motor homes, or motorized recreational vehicles) does not conform to all warranties during first 18,000 miles of operation or first two years of use, whichever is earlier, manufacturer or dealer shall correct condition at no charge to consumer, unless condition does not significantly impair vehicle or is result of abuse, neglect, or unauthorized modifications. (40-1301 et seq.). If manufacturer or dealer is unable to correct condition after reasonable number of attempts, consumer has option to receive exchange of comparable motor vehicle or refund of full purchase price. If vehicle is returned to manufacturer, Department of Public Works must be notified and will note return on certificate of title.

Claims for refund or replacement must be submitted to Board of Consumer Claims Arbitration within Department of Consumer and Regulatory Affairs. Arbitration decisions are subject to de novo review in D.C. Superior Court. Purchasers must receive written notification of consumer protection rights from manufacturer or dealer, and waiver or limitation of those rights is void. (§§40-1302[f], 1303).

Used motor vehicle dealers must provide prospective purchasers with written notification of damage to or material defect in vehicle. Noncompliance provides purchaser with cause of action for any resulting damages or injuries first before Board of Consumer Claims Arbitration and then in D.C. Superior Court and subjects dealer to criminal or civil fines and revocation of license. (§40-1305).

Liens.—Except between the parties, or as to persons with notice, liens not valid until entered on certificate of title (§40-1002) by recorder of deeds (§40-1003). See category Documents and Records, topic Records. Filing provisions of Uniform Commercial Code are not applicable for perfecting lien as to third parties. (§§28:9-203, 302; 40-1002). Security agreement or other instrument creating security interest is to be filed, but notation of lien on certificate of title is required for validity of lien as to third persons. Holder of first unsatisfied lien has right to possession of certificate of title. (§40-1010). Recorder maintains index under trade name and engine, serial or identification number of vehicles. (§40-1014).

Traffic Offenses.—Minor infractions are subject to administrative adjudication, under supervision of Department of Transportation. (§40-601). Functions of Department of Transportation were transferred to Department of Public Works by Reorganization Plan No. 4 of 1983, effective Mar. 1, 1984.

Operation Prohibited.—By person under influence of liquor (assumed with blood alcohol content of .10% or urine content of .13%) or any drug (§40-716), or by unlicensed individuals (§40-301) except nonresidents licensed in compliance with laws of their states, or driving vehicles registered under law of state not requiring operator's permit (§40-303).

Impounded or Immobilized.—Motor vehicle left upon public or private property, other than public highways, without owner's consent may be impounded; owner or other authorized person may repossess or secure release upon: (1) Depositing collateral required for appearance in Superior Ct., or depositing amount of potential fine (not to exceed $25) and penalty for each unsettled violation or warrant, and (2) paying $75 towing fee and reasonable storage fee. Vehicle abandoned on private property and subject to impoundment may be towed only if (1) notice of violation is issued against vehicle; (2) removal is done pursuant to valid work order; (3) private property owner makes reasonable efforts to notify owner of whereabouts of removed vehicle and means of obtaining vehicle; and (4) vehicle is towed to site within District reasonably safe from vandalism, and redeemable for reasonable cost. (§§40-812, 813). Abandoned vehicle not reclaimed can be sold at public auction. (§40-812.2).

Implied Consent Act.—Any operator of a motor vehicle in District is deemed to have given consent to two chemical tests of his blood, breath or urine, whichever arresting police officer or any other appropriate law enforcement officer shall elect. Operator can object to particular test only on valid religious or medical grounds. Refusal to submit means no test shall be given, but will result in revocation of license for 12 months. (§§40-501-507).

Size and Weight Limits.—Regulated by District of Columbia Municipal Regulations, Tit. 18, Vehicles and Traffic, Apr. 1981.

Equipment Required.—Regulated by District of Columbia Municipal Regulations, Tit. 18, Vehicles and Traffic, Apr. 1981.

Mandatory Seat Belts.—Driver and passenger sitting next to door in front seat of motor vehicle shall wear properly adjusted and fastened safety belt. (§40-1602). Any child between three and 16 years old being transported in motor vehicle must be properly restrained in child restraint seat or safety belt. (§40-1203).

Lights Required.—Regulated by District of Columbia Municipal Regulations, Tit. 18, Vehicles and Traffic, Apr. 1981.

Inspection, for which fee is levied, is required prior to registration. (§§40-201-207). Motor vehicles and trailers will be inspected for safety and emissions biennally. (18 DCMR, c.6, §601). Owners of all motor vehicles subject to unresolved emissions recall notices issued after Nov. 1, 1998, in order to pass inspection must provide proof that necessary repairs were completed. (18 DCMR §619).

Accidents.—Driver must stop and give name and address, and name and address of owner of vehicle, to someone at scene of accident, or if no one present, to police. Heavy fine and loss of driver's permit penalty for failure if accident involves personal injury or substantial property damage. (§40-716).

Liability of Owner.—Where motor vehicle is operated by any person other than the owner with the owner's consent, the operator is deemed to be the agent of the owner and proof of ownership is prima facie evidence that vehicle was operated with consent of the owner. (§40-408).

Liability of District.—District is now precluded from asserting defense of governmental immunity in damage action where vehicle owned or controlled by District is driven by District employee acting within scope of employment. However, where emergency vehicle on emergency run is involved, District is liable only for gross negligence. (§1-1212).

No action against District employee is permitted unless District specifically defends on ground of no action within scope of employee relationship. (§1-1215).

Claimant is required to give statutory notice within six months, and may not sue until six months after claim made. (§1-1213).

Guests.—There is no statute restricting liability for injury to a gratuitous guest.

Proof of Financial Responsibility.—Persons who have been convicted of or forfeited bail for certain motor vehicle offenses or who have failed to pay judgments upon causes of action arising out of ownership, maintenance, or use of registrable vehicles are required to deposit proof of financial responsibility for future, i.e., proof that motor vehicle is insured under Compulsory/No-Fault Motor Vehicle Insurance Act of 1982, §35-2101 et seq. (§§40-434, 435). In case of final conviction or forfeiture of bond for driving while intoxicated, homicide by means of motor vehicle, leaving scene of accident without giving assistance, reckless driving involving personal injury, any felony involving use of motor vehicle, or conviction of or forfeiture of bail for one of these offenses, license and registration of such person shall be suspended unless person has previously given or shall then give proof of financial responsibility for future with respect to such vehicles. (§40-437).

Foreign Vehicle.—Nonresident is not required to register. (§40-303).

No-Fault Insurance.—D.C. has adopted "No-Fault" insurance as to personal injury (Sept. 18, 1982). (§35-2101 et seq.). All motorists must carry and all insurers selling motor vehicle insurance in District must offer property damage liability, uninsured motorist coverage, and third-party liability coverage for accidents occuring outside District. In addition, all insurers must offer motorists optional personal injury protection and underinsured motor vehicle coverage. (§§35-2103, 2104, 2106).

Optional personal injury coverage of three types available to motorists: (1) At least $50,000 and up to $100,000 per victim for medical expenses; (2) at least $12,000 and up to $24,000 for loss of work; and (3) $4,000 for funeral benefits. Such coverage, when obtained by motorist, shall be provided without regard to, and irrespective of, negligence, freedom from negligence, fault, or freedom from fault on part of any person. (§35-2104).

Accident victim who seeks personal injury protection benefits must so notify insurer within 60 days of accident. Where accident victim elects to receive personal injury protection benefits, victim may then maintain civil action based on liability with respect to injury only if victim's damages exceed available benefits, or if motor vehicle was operated in such way as to cause death or permanent or long-term impairment. (§35-2105). Statute of limitations for recovery of personal injury protection benefits is three years from date of injury. (§35-2111). Parties with insurance coverage dispute may opt to have dispute resolved by Board of Consumer Claims Arbitration for District of Columbia. (§35-2105). Disputed claims for automobile physical damage must be arbitrated in accordance with terms of Nationwide Intercompany Arbitration Agreement. (§35-2105[i]).

No-fault insurance policy may be cancelled or suspended only for nonpayment of premium due or for suspension or revocation of insured's license or registration. Written notice to insured of cancellation or nonrenewal is required at least 30 days before effective date. (§35-2109).

Uninsured Motorist Fund consisting of monies assessed among all insurers shall be administered by Mayor for purpose of awarding compensation to injured accident victim who would not otherwise be compensated for his or her loss. (§35-2114).

Violations of chapter may result in fine of $300 to $500, license suspension for up to 30 days and/or imprisonment of up to 30 days for first offense, or fine of $500 to $1,000, license suspension for up to 60 days and/or imprisonment of up to 90 days for each subsequent offense. (§35-2113).

Bicycles.—Operators of bicycles have same rights and duties as do operators of other vehicles, except as otherwise expressly provided by DCMR and except for duties imposed on operators of vehicles by DCMR which could have no reasonable application to bicycle operator. (18 DCMR §§1200.3-1201.1).

Nonresident operator, who has complied with laws of another state is not required to register for 30 days following entrance. (§40-303[a]). Thereafter nonresident drivers licensed under States having reciprocal motor vehicle relations with District may obtain reciprocity sticker for further 180-day period and are then required to register in accordance with general law. (§40-303[b][2]). Otherwise, nonresident is required to register at end of initial 30-day period. (§§40-303[b][1], 40-102, 40-301).

Actions Against Nonresidents.—In action against nonresident arising out of any accident or collision in which said nonresident or his agent was involved while operating motor vehicle on public highway in District, process may be served by placing copy and fee of $2 in hands of Mayor, provided (1) plaintiff must first file in court undertaking for expense of defense, including reasonable attorney's fee, to reimburse defendant on failure of plaintiff to prevail, and (2) notice of such service and copy of process must be sent forthwith by registered mail to defendant and return receipt appended to writ, or such notice be served by publication. (See category Civil Actions and Procedure, topic Process.) Defendant may be granted such continuances as may be necessary to afford

See note at head of Digest as to 1998 legislation covered.

See Topical Index in front part of this volume.

DC – 35

MOTOR VEHICLES . . . *continued*

him reasonable opportunity to defend action and no default judgment may be granted until at least 20 days have elapsed after service and notice were completed. (§40-407).

Direct Actions Against Insurer.—See category Civil Actions and Procedure, topic Actions.

Motor Vehicle Carriers.—Taxicab rates within the District are subject to regulation by Public Service Commission (§§43-203, 211, 523), but meters may not be required. Taxicabs must carry liability insurance. (§40-1714). It is crime for taxicab passenger to avoid or attempt to avoid payment of lawful fare. (§43-314). See category Business Regulation and Commerce, topic Carriers.

Gasoline Tax.—See category Taxation, topic Gasoline Taxes.

RAILROADS:

See category Business Regulation and Commerce, topic Carriers.

WATERCRAFT:

Operation of any vessel or watercraft, including, but not limited to, water skis, aquaplane, surfboard, personal water craft or similar device is prohibited when person is under influence of intoxicating liquor or any controlled substance. Penalties for first offense include fine not to exceed $500, imprisonment for not more than 90 days, or both. Higher penalties for subsequent offenses. (§§25.127a.1-a.7).

See note at head of Digest as to 1998 legislation covered.

See Topical Index in front part of this volume.

FLORIDA LAW DIGEST

(The following is a list of all Categories and Topics, including cross-references, covered in this Digest.)

FLORIDA LAW DIGEST

Revised for 1999 edition by

JARRET C. OELTJEN, Professor, Florida State University College of Law, of the Florida Bar.

Citations refer to Florida Statutes 1997 and 1998 Supp. R. C. P. indicates Florida Rules of Civil Procedure. F. P. R. indicates Florida Probate Rules. F. L. R. P. indicates Florida Family Law Rules of Procedure. Session laws are cited by year and chapter number (e.g., 98-96). Statute specifies codification procedures and official Florida law. (11.242). See also category Courts and Legislature, topic Reports.

Note: The 1999 Edition includes statutory revisions contained in 1998 Florida Session Laws.

INTRODUCTION

GOVERNMENT AND LEGAL SYSTEM:

The State of Florida is a constituent state of the United States of America. For further discussion of the U.S. federal system, see Introduction to the Federal Government of the United States at the beginning of this volume. A great many laws are promulgated by the federal government of the United States and are not reflected in the topics below. See the Introduction to this volume for references to the federal law topics covered.

Like all but one of the United States, Florida has a common law legal system, with roots in English common law. For information on the courts and legislature of Florida, see category Courts and Legislature.

HOLIDAYS:

Legal holidays are: Sundays, Jan. 1, Jan. 15 (Birthday of Martin Luther King), Jan. 19 (Birthday of Robert E. Lee), Feb. 12 (Lincoln's Birthday), Feb. 15 (Susan B. Anthony's Birthday), 3d Mon. in Feb. (Washington's Birthday), Apr. 2 (Pascua Florida Day), Good Friday, Apr. 26 (Confederate Memorial Day), last Mon. in May (Memorial Day), June 3 (Birthday of Jefferson Davis), June 14 (Flag Day), July 4, 1st Mon. in Sept. (Labor Day), 2d Mon. in Oct. (Columbus Day), Nov. 11 (Veterans' Day), general election day, 4th Thurs. in Nov. (Thanksgiving Day), Dec. 25, Shrove Tuesday also known as "Mardi Gras" (in counties where carnival associations are organized for celebrating same). (683.01). When legal holiday falls on Sun., following Mon. is holiday. (683.01[2]).

Service or execution on Sun. of any writ, process, warrant, order, or judgment is void, unless person liable to have any such service or execution upon him intends to withdraw himself from state in which case such service may be obtained upon affidavit of person requesting service or execution. (48.20). Warrants for arrest may be lawfully served any day and at any time of day or night (901.04; 1956 Op. Atty. Gen. 056-327), and search warrants may be lawfully served on Sun. if expressly authorized in warrants. (933.101).

OFFICE HOURS AND TIME ZONE:

Most of Florida is in Eastern (GMT −05:00) time zone; the western half of Florida Panhandle (northwestern Florida) is in Central (GMT −06:00) time zone. Office hours are generally from 9 a.m. to 5 p.m.

BUSINESS ORGANIZATIONS

AGENCY:

Common law governs.

ASSOCIATIONS:

Provisions exist for creation of Agricultural Cooperative Marketing Associations (c. 618), Limited Agricultural Associations (604.10), for Nonprofit Cooperative Associations of three or more persons engaged in certain specified agricultural businesses (c. 619), Motor Vehicle Service Agreement Companies (634.011-634.281), Condominium Associations (c. 718), Home Warranty Associations (634.301-634.348), Florida Insurance Guaranty Association, Incorporated (631.55), Capital Stock Associations (c. 665), Mobile Home Owner Associations (723.075-723.0791), Service Warranty Associations (634.401-634.444), Fraternal Benefit Societies (632.601-.638). §634.041, provides that in order to qualify and hold license to issue service agreements, service agreement company must maintain, among other criteria, minimum net assets of $500,000.

Foreign unincorporated joint stock associations may, in lieu of filing authenticated copy of any charter, Certificate of Incorporation, or Articles of Incorporation, qualify to do business in state by filing authenticated copy of Articles of Association with Secretary of State and otherwise qualifying in same manner as foreign corporation, including payment of all fees, taxes, and other charges so prescribed, and appointment of resident agent. (c. 622)

Professional Corporations.—See topic Corporations, subhead Professional Corporations.

CORPORATIONS:

Corporation Law of Florida was completely rewritten effective July 1, 1990. Model Business Corporation Act was basis for Florida Business Corporations Act. C. 608 reenacted effective Apr. 21, 1982 relating to limited liability companies. Corporations not for profit are governed by Florida Not For Profit Corporation Act, c. 617, which was substantially revised effective July 1, 1991.

General Supervision.—Vested in Department of State, division of corporations. (20.10 and 607.0130).

Purposes.—Corporation may be organized for any lawful purpose or purposes, except when in conflict with regulations and statutes controlling specific types of businesses. (607.0301).

Name must include word "corporation" or "incorporated" or abbreviation, affix, prefix, suffix or word clearly indicating corporation and may not imply corporation is organized for other than permitted purpose or connected with state or federal government agency and must be distinguishable from all other filed or registered names. (607.0401). Model Act also allows word "limited". (§4.01). Name of business corporation may not include word "co-operative" unless it has complied with provisions of c. 618. (618.27). Fictitious name must be filed with Department of State. (865.09). See category Intellectual Property, topic Trademarks and Tradenames, subhead Tradenames. No formal name clearance procedure. For fees, see subhead Filing Fee, infra.

Incorporators.—One or more persons, or domestic or foreign corporation, partnership, limited partnership or association, may act as incorporator or incorporators by signing and delivering to Secretary of State articles of incorporation. (607.0201). There are no requirements that incorporator be citizen or resident of Florida.

Term of corporate existence is perpetual unless otherwise specified. (607.0302).

Articles of incorporation must be executed by incorporator(s) (607.0120) and must include corporate name, street address of principal office if known, and, if different, mailing address of corporation, authorized capital stock and name and street address of initial registered agent and written acceptance required by §607.0501(3), and name and address of each incorporator. (607.0202). Articles of incorporation must authorize one or more classes of shares that together have unlimited voting rights and that are together entitled to receive net assets of corporation on dissolution. (607.0601). Any of following provisions, if applicable, must be included in articles: classes of stock, their par value, preferences, limitations and relative rights of each class; terms and beginning date of corporate existence if other than date of filing of articles of incorporation (607.0203); shareholders' preemptive rights; and number, name and address of initial board of directors, if one exists. Articles may also include any other lawful provisions relating to corporation's powers, conduct of its affairs, officers, and rights and duties of stockholders and directors. (607.0202).

Filing of Articles.—Articles of incorporation must be delivered to Department of State. (607.0201). Corporate existence shall commence upon filing, unless articles designate date, which may be on subscription and acknowledgment date if articles filed within five business days of said date (excluding legal holidays), or articles may postpone commencement of existence for up to 90 days after filing. (607.0123, 607.0203).

Correcting Filed Documents.—Documents filed with Department of State may be corrected within ten days of filing if document contains incorrect statement, was defectively executed, attested, sealed, verified or acknowledged, by filing articles of correction that describe document and its filing date and specifying incorrect statement and reason it is incorrect or manner in which execution was defective and by correcting incorrect statement or defect. (607.0124). Articles of correction are filed with Department of State and are effective on effective date of document they correct except as to persons who rely on uncorrected document and who are substantially and adversely affected by correction. (607.0124[3]).

Filing fee for articles of incorporation is $35, filing fee for amendment to articles of incorporation is $35. Filing fee for articles of merger or share exchange is $35 for each party to merger or consolidation. Filing fee is $35 for application of foreign corporation for authority to transact business in state, filing amended application of foreign corporation for authority to transact business in state, filing application of foreign corporation for withdrawal, or articles of revocation of dissolution. Fee for certificate of domestication of foreign corporation is $50. Filing fee is $600 for application for reinstatement following administrative dissolution. Filing fee is $61.25 for filing annual report. Supplemental corporate fee in amount of $138.75 is imposed on corporations authorized to transact business and required to file annual report. Filing fee is $87.50 for filing application for, or renewal of, registered name. Filing fee is $35 for filing certificate designating registered agent, changing resident agent. Fee for agent's statement of resignation from dissolved corporation is $35; for resignation from active corporation, $87.50. Fee for furnishing certified copy of any document, instrument, or paper relating to corporation, is $52.50. Fee for application for certificate of status is $8.75. Filing fee for any other corporate document, statement or report, $35. (607.0122).

License to Do Business.—Foreign corporation must apply for certificate of authority to transact business. (607.1501).

Paid in Capital Requirements.—No minimum capital requirement established by statute.

Certificate Evidencing Filing.—Department of State's filing of articles of incorporation is conclusive proof incorporators complied with all conditions precedent and corporation incorporated under c. 607, except against state in proceeding to cancel or revoke certificate of incorporation or for involuntary dissolution of corporation. (607.0203). Certificate attached to copy of document filed by Department of State is conclusive that original document is on file with Department. (607.0127). Anyone may apply to Department of State for Certificate of Status which may be relied upon as conclusive evidence that domestic or foreign corporation is in existence or is authorized to transact business in Florida. (607.0128).

See note at head of Digest as to 1998 legislation covered.

See Topical Index in front part of this volume.

CORPORATIONS . . . *continued*

Amendment to Articles of Incorporation.—Corporation may amend its articles, to add or change provision that is required or permitted in articles or to delete provision not required in articles. (607.1001). Unless articles provide otherwise, Board of Directors may amend articles without shareholder vote to extend duration of corporation if it was incorporated at time when limited duration was required by law; delete names and addresses of initial directors or initial registered agent; delete any other information that is solely of historical interest; change each issued and unissued authorized share of outstanding class into greater number of whole shares if it is only class outstanding; or delete authorization of class or series of shares authorized pursuant to §607.0602, if no shares of such class have been issued; change par value for class or series of shares; or provide that if corporation acquires its own shares, shares belong to corporation and constitute treasury shares until disposed of or canceled. (607.1002). All other amendments must be recommended by Board, (unless Board determines that conflict of interest exists), submitted to vote at meeting of shareholders, and approved by affirmative vote of majority of shares entitled to vote thereon, unless greater vote is required, and by any special voting groups entitled to vote pursuant to §§607.0725 and 607.0726. Unless otherwise provided in articles, shareholders of corporation having 35 or fewer shareholders may amend without act of directors at meeting for which notice of changes to be made is given. (607.1003).

Amendments adversely affecting one class of stockholders must be separately approved by such class. (607.1004). Restated articles of incorporation may be adopted by board of directors without vote of stockholders. (607.0122; 607.1007). If restatement includes one or more amendments to articles requiring shareholder approval it must be adopted pursuant to §607.1003 and contain information required under §607.1006.

Increase or decrease of authorized stock is accomplished by amending articles of incorporation upon vote by holders of outstanding shares. (607.1004, 607.1002). See also subhead Filing Fee, supra.

By-Laws.—Power to adopt, alter, amend or repeal by-laws vested in board of directors, unless reserved to shareholders by articles of incorporation (607.0206, 607.1020) or by-law to be adopted, amended or repealed fixes greater quorum or voting requirement for shareholders (607.1020). Shareholders have right to amend or repeal by-laws in any event. (607.1020). By-laws fixing greater shareholder quorum or voting requirements may be adopted, amended or repealed only upon such greater vote or quorum. (607.0121, 607.1022). By-laws fixing greater quorum or voting requirements of directors may be amended or repealed only by shareholders if initially adopted by shareholders, but if initially adopted by directors, then either shareholders or directors. (607.1022). By-laws may contain any provisions for regulation and management of affairs of corporation not inconsistent with law or certificate. (607.0206). Florida now permits directors to determine, if articles so provide, before issuance of any shares of class or series, relative rights of such class or series of shares within limits of 607.0601. (607.0602).

Stock authorized may consist of one or more classes, and may have par value or no par value, with designations, preferences, limitations and relative rights as prescribed by articles of incorporation. (607.0601). Corporations may issue fractional shares, and scrip in registered or bearer form. (607.0604). Florida permits directors to determine, if articles so provide, relative rights of class or series of shares before issuance of any shares of class or series. (607.0602).

Emergency By-Laws.—Directors may adopt emergency by-laws, unless articles provide otherwise, to be effective if quorum of directors cannot readily be assembled because of catastrophic event. (607.0207). Emergency by-laws may provide for procedures for calling directors' meeting, quorum requirements, designation of additional or substitute directors during such emergency. Emergency by-laws are subject to amendment or repeal by shareholders. Regular by-laws consistent with emergency by-laws remain in effect during emergency; emergency by-laws become ineffective after emergency ends. (607.0207[3]). Corporate action taken in good faith in accordance with emergency by-laws binds corporation and may not be used to impose liability on corporate director, officer, employee or agent. (607.0207[4]). Emergency powers of directors operating pursuant to emergency by-laws are set out at 607.0303.

Issuance of Stock.—Corporation may issue stock described in its articles of incorporation. (607.0603). Board of Directors may authorize shares to be issued for consideration consisting of any tangible or intangible property or benefit. Prior to issuance of shares, Board of Directors shall make conclusive determination as to adequacy of consideration relating to whether shares are validly issued, fully paid and nonassessable. (607.0621). Par value stock may be issued for value not less than par value of shares as determined from time to time by board of directors. However, if articles of incorporation reserve right to determine consideration to shareholders, then majority vote of shareholders entitled to vote thereon is required unless articles require greater vote.

Shareholders have no preemptive rights unless provided in articles of incorporation. (607.0630). Shareholders of corporations in existence prior to Jan. 1, 1976 having preemptive rights, continue to have such preemptive rights unless certificate of incorporation is amended to alter or terminate those rights. (607.0630). Model Act contains procedure relative to preemptive rights and reacquisition of shares.

See also category Taxation, topic Stamp Tax, subhead Documents.

Stock Certificates.—Shares may but need not be represented by certificates. (607.0625). Certificates must be signed manually or by facsimile by officers designated in by-laws or by board of directors and may be sealed with corporate seal. (607.0625). Florida allows issuance of shares without certificates, as long as required information is communicated in writing. (607.0626).

Certificates representing shares issued by corporation authorized to issue shares of more than one class must set forth or summarize upon face or back of certificate, or state that corporation will furnish to shareholders upon request and without charge full statement of, designations, preferences, limitations and relative rights of such shares, and if corporation is authorized to issue any preferred or special class in series, variations in relative rights and preferences between such shares. (607.0625). Certificates representing shares restricted as to sale, disposition or other transfer must state such restrictions set forth or summarized upon certificate, or state that corporation will furnish to shareholders upon request and without charge full statement of, such restrictions. (607.0627).

Transfer of Stock.—Uniform Commercial Code adopted. (cc. 670-680). See category Business Regulation and Commerce, topic Commercial Code. Stockholder agreements imposing reasonable restrictions on transfer are valid, but should be authorized by articles of incorporation. (76 So.2d 478).

See also category Taxation, topic Stamp Tax, subhead Documents.

Stock Transfer Tax.—Taxed only on original issue. (201.05). See category Taxation, topic Stamp Tax, subhead Documents.

Uniform Securities Ownership by Minors Act.—Not adopted.

Uniform Simplification of Fiduciary Security Transfers Act adopted (c. 610) and takes precedence over Uniform Commercial Code (671.304[2][b]).

Stockholders' Liabilities.—Holder of or subscriber for shares of corporation under no obligation to corporation or creditors to pay for shares other than obligation to pay corporation unpaid portion of consideration for which shares were issued. Pledgee or fiduciary holder of stock not personally liable as shareholder but pledgor or other person transferring such shares as collateral shall be considered holder thereof for purposes of liability under §607.0622. Ordinarily shareholders are not liable for debts of corporation. (607.0622).

Stockholders' Meetings.—Notice stating place, day and hour of meeting, and in case of special meeting, purpose(s) for which meeting called, must be given to stockholders with right to vote not less than ten nor more than 60 days before meeting, which may be held within or without state. (607.0705, 607.0701, 607.0702). If corporation has not held annual meeting for 13 month period (15 months, or six months after end of fiscal year under Model Act), or if corporation has failed to hold special meeting properly demanded by shareholder pursuant to §607.0702, any shareholder may apply to circuit court to order such meeting to be held. (607.0703). Unless otherwise provided in certificate of incorporation, action may be taken without meeting, notice or vote, if consent in writing setting forth action taken is signed by minimum number of votes necessary to authorize such action at meeting. (607.0704). Actions without meeting are effective only upon delivery to corporate secretary or authorized custodian of corporate records of one or more written consents describing action taken, dated and signed by approving shareholders having requisite number of votes of each voting group entitled to vote thereon. Such corporate actions are effective only if taken within 60 days of earliest written consent delivered. (607.0704[1]). Written consents may be revoked in writing prior to receipt by corporation of minimum number of consents necessary to authorize proposed action. Notice of such action taken must be given within ten days to shareholders who have not consented or who are not entitled to vote thereon. (607.0704[3]).

Notice must be in writing, unless oral notice is expressly authorized by articles or by-laws and is reasonable under circumstances, and may be communicated by telephone, telegraph, teletype, other form of electronic communication, or by mail. (607.0141). Written notice by domestic or foreign corporation authorized to transact business in Florida to its shareholder is effective when mailed postpaid and correctly addressed to shareholder's address, and notice to such corporation may be addressed to its registered agent at its registered office or to its secretary at its principal office. (607.0141). All other notices are effective at earliest of (i) receipt, (ii) five days after deposit in U.S. mail, properly addressed and postpaid, (iii) date of return receipt if by registered or certified mail, (iv) time communicated, if oral notice, (v) time specified for particular circumstances under c. 607, or (vi) time specified in articles or by-laws if less stringent than required under c. 607.

Voting.—Unless articles of incorporation provide otherwise, voting for directors is not cumulative and each stockholder is entitled to one vote for each share standing in his name on books. (607.0728, 607.0721[1]). Majority of shares constitutes quorum unless articles specify otherwise but in no event shall quorum consist of less than 1/3 of shares entitled to vote. (607.0803). Majority of shares in series or class of voting as series or class constitutes quorum. (607.0727[1]). Shares entitled to vote as group pursuant to §607.0725 may only take action if quorum is present at meeting; majority is quorum of such group unless otherwise provided in articles. Stockholders may vote by proxy appointed by written instrument and proxy is valid for 11 months from date of signing unless otherwise provided therein. Proxy is revocable unless holder thereof falls within one of statutory classifications. (607.0722).

Control-Share Acquisition.—Florida has adopted control-share acquisition statute that was based and similar in form to Indiana control-share acquisition statute that was upheld by U.S. Supreme Court. (607.0902). Statute limits ability of person or group of persons to vote stock of corporation, if person or group of persons have voting power to elect directors of corporation and person or group of persons control at least one-fifth of corporation's stock. Articles of incorporation and by-laws of corporation can exclude corporation and its shareholders from §607.0902's application. Additionally, several other exceptions to statute's requirements are set forth in §607.0902.

Voting trusts may be created by entering into written agreement, depositing copy with corporation, and transferring shares to trustee. (607.0730).

Affiliated Transactions.—Unless requirements of §607.0901 are complied with, affiliated parties (as defined in quoted statute) are prohibited in certain situations from obtaining stock by sale, lease, exchange, mortgage, pledge or other disposition.

Tender Offers.—See category Business Regulation and Commerce, topic Securities, subhead Tender Offers.

Stockholders' Derivative Actions.—Plaintiff must have been, or acquired shares from, shareholder at time of transaction complained of. Complaint must be verified and allege with particularity rejected demand on directors to obtain action. Court may dismiss derivative proceeding if one of specified groups makes good faith determination that derivative suit is not in corporation's best interest. If court finds action was commenced without reasonable cause it may assess costs, including reasonable attorneys fees, against plaintiff. (607.07401).

See note at head of Digest as to 1998 legislation covered.

See Topical Index in front part of this volume.

CORPORATIONS . . . *continued*

Directors.—Corporation is managed by one or more directors (607.0803) who need not be residents of state or shareholders of corporation unless otherwise provided in articles of incorporation. (607.0801). Corporation having 35 or fewer shareholders may dispense with or limit authority of board of directors by describing in its articles of incorporation who will perform some or all of duties of board of directors. (607.0801[3]). Stockholders elect directors at annual meeting. (607.0701). Directors may be divided into not more than three classes with number of directors in each class being as nearly equal as possible (607.0806[1]), whose terms of office shall expire at different times. Corporations existing prior to July 1, 1990 may continue to have four classes of directors and continue to serve staggered terms pursuant to articles or by-laws. (607.0806[2]). Vacancies are filled, until next election of directors, by affirmative vote of majority of remaining directors or by shareholders. (607.0809).

Executive Committee.—By resolution board may designate executive committee from among its members unless prohibited in articles of incorporation or by-laws. (607.0825). Such committees shall or may exercise all authority of Board except approval or recommendation to shareholder of actions required to be approved by shareholders, filling board vacancies, adoption, amendment or repeal of by-laws, reacquisition of corporation shares, and issuance or contract for sale of shares or determination of rights of such shares, except within limits specifically prescribed by Board. (607.0825).

Directors' meetings may be held within or without state. (607.0820). Regular meeting may be held with or without notice as prescribed in by-laws. (607.0822[1]). Special meeting shall be held upon at least two days notice unless otherwise provided in by-laws. Attendance of director at meeting constitutes waiver of notice thereof, unless attendance is for express purpose of objecting to manner in which meeting has been called. (607.0823). Attendance may be by any means of communication by which all directors participating may simultaneously hear each other. (607.0820[4]). Majority of members of board constitutes quorum, unless articles of incorporation or by-laws provide otherwise, but in no event may number constituting quorum be less than 1/3 of number of directors. (607.0824). Vote of majority of members present at meeting at which quorum is present constitutes action of board, unless otherwise provided. (607.0824). Directors may act by unanimous written consent without meeting, unless otherwise provided in articles of incorporation or by-laws. (607.0821).

Liabilities of Directors.—Director has no liability by reason of being director if director has discharged duties in good faith, in manner director reasonably believes to be in best interests of corporation and with that degree of diligence, care and skill which ordinarily prudent person would exercise under similar circumstances in like position. (607.0830). In discharging such duties, director is entitled to rely on information, opinions, reports or statements, including financial statements and other financial data prepared by certain officers and employees of corporation, counsel, public accountants and certain other professionals, or committee of board on which director has not served as to matters within its designated authority. (607.0830).

Unless director complies with above standard, director who votes for or assents to declaration of dividend or other distribution of assets to shareholders made in violation of §607.06401, is liable to corporation (607.0834); although Florida provides for mandatory indemnification of reasonable expenses upon successfully defending action, indemnification is permissive but not mandatory for substantive liability (607.0850[1]-[3]). Procedures for indemnification are set forth in §607.0850.

Director against whom claim for improper distribution is successfully asserted is entitled to contribution from other directors and shareholders who voted for, or concurred in action upon which claim is asserted. (607.0834[2]).

Officers.—Corporation shall have officers described in its by-laws or appointed by Board of Directors. (607.08401). Two or more offices may be held by same person. Officer has such authority and performs such duties as may be provided in by-laws, or determined by resolution of board not inconsistent with by-laws. Officers serve at pleasure of Board of Directors. (607.0842). Officers may be removed by Board of Directors at any time, with or without cause. (607.0842).

Registered Office and Registered Agent.—Every corporation must maintain registered office in this state and registered agent, which agent may be individual resident in this state whose business office is identical with such registered office or foreign or domestic corporation or not for profit corporation authorized to transact business or conduct its affairs in Florida having business office identical with such registered office. (607.0501). Does not apply to corporations otherwise required to designate insurance commissioner and treasurer as attorney for service of process, savings associations or savings and loan associations subject to c. 665, banks and trust companies subject to Florida banking code, savings banks and industrial savings banks. (607.0501). Each registered agent and each successor registered agent appointed pursuant to §607.0502 on whom process may be served must file statement with Department of State accepting appointment simultaneously with being designated, unless agent signed document making appointment. Such acceptance shall state that registered agent is familiar with and accepts obligations of that position. (607.0501). Corporation may not maintain any action in court of Florida until corporation complies with §607.0501 or §607.1507. Filing fee for certificate designating registered agent is $35. (607.0122[7]).

General powers of corporations conferred by statute. (607.0302).

Political contributions are not prohibited but limited in amount by c. 106.08.

Ultra vires no defense. (607.0304). Lack of capacity may be asserted in proceeding by corporation against incumbent or former officers and directors of corporation or in proceeding by attorney general to enjoin corporation from transaction of unauthorized business or to dissolve corporation. (607.0304[2]).

Dividends.—Board of directors may authorize and corporation may make distributions to its shareholders, subject to restrictions in articles, unless corporation would not be able to pay its debts as they become due in usual course of business or corporation's total assets would be less than sum of its total liabilities plus (unless articles permit otherwise) amount that would be needed to satisfy preferential rights of shareholders whose preferential rights are superior to those receiving distribution. (607.0640). If distribution is based upon fair valuation of assets, distribution shall be identified as distribution based upon current valuation of assets, and amount per share paid on basis of such valuation shall be disclosed to shareholders. (607.0640).

Unclaimed Dividends.—See category Property, topic Absentees, subhead Escheat.

Sale, Lease or Exchange of all Assets.—Corporation may sell, lease, exchange or otherwise dispose of all, or substantially all of its property in ordinary course of business upon director approval unless articles require shareholder approval. (607.1201). Dispositions otherwise than in ordinary course of business must be approved by directors and authorized by majority of shareholders and any voting group entitled to vote unless articles require greater vote. (607.1202). Corporation shall notify each shareholder of record and notice shall specify rights of dissenting shareholders to be paid fair value for their shares and other specified information. (607.1202). Dissenting stockholders who object in writing prior to taking of vote on proposed corporate action and do not vote in favor of such action, or if action was by written consent make written demand within 20 days of notice of authorization by written consent, can demand fair cash value of stock, but only if stock not registered on national securities exchange, designated as national market system security on interdealer quotation system by National Association of Securities Dealers, Inc. or record stockholders are less than 2,000 unless articles of incorporation provide otherwise. (607.1320, 607.1302). Model Act does not so limit dissenters' rights. Unless otherwise provided in articles of incorporation, directors may, without stockholder consent, mortgage or pledge any or all corporate property and assets to secure corporate obligations. (607.1201). Transactions constituting distributions are governed by §607.06401 not by §607.1202.

Stock books and records, including minutes of proceedings of shareholders, board of directors, and executive committees, must be kept and made available for inspection by shareholders during regular business hours upon five business days written notice. Shareholder of corporation is entitled to inspect and copy during regular business hours excerpts from minutes of any meeting, accounting records of corporation, record of shareholders, and any other books or records upon five business days written notice and if demand is made in good faith, she describes her purpose and records she desires to inspect, and records are directly connected with that purpose. (607.1602). Corporation may deny any demand for inspection if demand was made for improper purpose or if demanding shareholder has, within two years preceding demand, sold or offered for sale any list of shareholders of corporation or any other corporation or improperly used any information secured through any prior examination of corporate records. (607.1602). Shareholder may not sell or otherwise distribute any information or records inspected, except to extent such use is for proper purpose. (607.1602). Persons violating foregoing provision shall be subject to civil penalty of $5,000. (607.1602). Unless modified by shareholder resolution, within 120 days of close of each fiscal year corporation shall furnish its shareholders annual financial statements that include balance sheet, income statement and statement of cash flow for that year. (607.1620). If corporation indemnifies or advances expenses to any director, officer, employee or agent under 607.0850 otherwise than by court order or action by shareholders or by insurance carrier, corporation shall report indemnification or advance in writing to its shareholders. (607.1621).

Annual Reports.—All domestic and foreign corporations authorized to do business in this state must file after Jan. 1 and before July 1 of each year annual report (607.1622) and pay filing fee of $61.25 (607.0122[19]) to Department of State. Corporation failing to file may not maintain or defend any action in any court in this state and may be subject to dissolution or cancellation of certificate of authority to do business. (607.1622[8]). On or before Apr. 1 of each year, all corporations doing business in Florida must give their Florida stockholders of record as of preceding Dec. 31 written notice reflecting value of each class of stock subject to annual tax. (199.062). (See category Taxation, topic Intangible Personal Property Tax, subhead Annual Information Reports.) On or before June 30 of each year, copy of such notice must be filed with state. (199.062).

Corporate Bonds or Mortgages.—Issuance by board of directors authorized. No need of shareholder approval unless required by articles of incorporation. (607.1201).

Merger and Share Exchange.—Two or more Florida corporations may merge (607.1101) or engage in share exchange (607.1102). To effect merger or share exchange, board of each corporation must adopt and submit to stockholders plan of merger or plan of share exchange. (607.1101, 607.1102 and 607.1103). Proposed plan of merger or plan of share exchange must be approved by vote of majority of stockholders unless otherwise provided. (607.1103). Notwithstanding foregoing, unless required by articles of incorporation, vote of shareholders of surviving corporation on plan of merger is not required if plan does not amend articles of incorporation of surviving corporation; each share of stock of surviving corporation outstanding immediately before merger becomes identical share of surviving corporation; and, shares of voting stock of surviving corporation to be issued pursuant to plan plus those initially issuable upon conversion of any other shares or obligations to be issued pursuant to plan will not exceed 20% of shares of voting stock of surviving corporation outstanding immediately prior to effective date of merger. (607.1103[7]).

Parent corporation owning at least 80% of outstanding shares of each class of subsidiary corporation may merge such subsidiary into itself, may merge itself into subsidiary, or such subsidiary into another subsidiary without approval of shareholders of any of corporations. (607.1104). Directors shall adopt plan of merger setting forth name of parent and subsidiary; manner and basis of converting shares of parent or subsidiary; provision for pro rata issuance of shares of subsidiary to holders of shares of parent corporation upon surrender of certificates therefor; clear and concise statement that shareholders of subsidiary who, except for provisions of §607.1104, would be entitled to vote and who dissent from merger pursuant to 607.1320, may be entitled to be paid fair value of their shares. (607.1104).

Foreign and domestic corporations may merge or enter into share exchange if, in merger, merger is permitted by foreign jurisdiction and, in share exchange, corporation, shares of which will be acquired, is domestic corporation. (607.1107). Where foreign or domestic corporation is surviving or acquiring corporation it must comply

See note at head of Digest as to 1998 legislation covered.

See Topical Index in front part of this volume.

CORPORATIONS . . . *continued*
with Florida law with respect to filing articles of merger or share exchange (607.1105), and, where merged corporation or corporation whose shares are acquired is domestic corporation, it must comply with applicable Florida law with respect to adoption of plans of merger and share exchange, shareholder notification and voting. (See generally §§607.1101-607.1104.)

Merger or share exchange becomes effective upon filing of articles with Department of State unless articles specify later date. (607.1105[1]). Dissenting stockholders who object in writing prior to taking of vote on proposed corporate action, do not vote in favor of such action, and make written demand within 20 days of receipt of notice that corporate action which is objectionable has been authorized, which demand shall state shareholder's name and address, number, class and series of shares as to which he dissents and demand for payment of fair value. (607.1302; 607.1320).

Dissolution.—Voluntary dissolution may be accomplished by incorporators or directors before commencement of business or issuance of shares (607.1401), or by written consent of all shareholders at any time (607.1402[6]), or by board of directors proposal approved by vote of majority of stockholders (607.1402). In all cases, articles of dissolution must be prepared setting forth name of corporation, date dissolution was authorized, statement that number of shareholder votes cast was sufficient for dissolution, if applicable. (607.1403). Corporation is dissolved upon effective date of its articles of dissolution. (607.1403). Dissolved corporation continues its corporate existence but may not carry on any business, except that appropriate to wind up and liquidate its business and affairs. (607.1405). Name of dissolved corporation shall not be available for assumption or use by another company until 120 days after effective date of dissolution. (607.1405[4]).

Corporation may be dissolved involuntarily by decree of circuit court for county in which principal office or, if none, registered office of corporation is located in action filed by department of legal affairs when it is established that corporation procured its articles of incorporation through fraud, or corporation has exceeded authority conferred upon it by law (607.1430, 607.1431); in proceeding by shareholder if directors are deadlocked and shareholders are unable to break deadlock and irreparable injury to corporation is threatened, or shareholders are deadlocked and have failed to elect successor directors, (607.1430[2]), in proceeding by shareholder or group of shareholders in corporation having 35 or fewer shareholders if corporate assets are being misapplied or wasted causing material injury to corporation or directors or those in control have acted, are acting or are reasonably expected to act in manner that is illegal or fraudulent (607.1430[3]), or in proceeding by creditor if creditor's claim is reduced to judgment which remains unsatisfied and corporation is insolvent or corporation has admitted in writing claim is due and owing and corporation is insolvent. (607.1430[3]). Corporation may be dissolved administratively by order of Department of State if corporation has failed to file its annual report or pay annual report filing fee, has failed for 30 days to appoint and maintain registered agent in this state, has failed for 30 days after change of its registered office or registered agent to file statement of such change, has failed to answer truthfully and fully interrogatories propounded by Department of State or corporation's period of duration has expired. (607.1420). Notice must be given 60 days before proposed administrative dissolution. (607.1421). Corporation dissolved by Department of State may be reinstated by application and payment of fees. (607.1422).

Receiver or custodian may be appointed by circuit court in judicial proceeding to dissolve corporation. (See 607.1432, 607.1434.) Court may also appoint provisional director, order purchase of complaining shareholder's shares or grant other equitable relief as court in its discretion deems appropriate. (607.1434, 607.1435, 607.1436).

Appraisal.—In case of disagreement as to fair cash value of stock of stockholder who dissented from sale of assets or consolidation or merger and demanded payment of value of stock, corporation, or if it fails to do so, stockholder may petition circuit court for determination of value. (607.1320). Court may appoint appraisers to recommend decision on fair value. (607.1320[7]).

Limited Liability Company.—See topic Limited Liability Companies.

Close Corporations.—No separate provisions for close corporations.

Foreign Corporations.—Certificate of authority to do business in state is required. (607.1501). To procure certificate of authority, corporation must file certificate of existence issued from authorized officer of jurisdiction of incorporation evidencing its incorporation, translated under oath if in foreign language. (607.1503[2]). Application, must include name of corporation, jurisdiction, and date of incorporation, duration of corporation, street address of principal business office, address of registered office in state and name of resident agent, name and usual business addresses of its current directors and officers, and such other facts as may be required by Department of State. (607.1503[1]). Authority to transact business continues until surrendered, suspended or revoked. (607.1505, 607.1520). Foreign corporation doing business in Florida without certificate of authority cannot maintain any action in Florida courts until certificate obtained. (607.1502). Failure to obtain authority to transact business does not impair validity of any contract, deed, mortgage, security interest or act of corporation and does not prevent such corporation from defending any proceeding in this state. (607.1502[5]). Corporations transacting business without certificate are liable to state for all fees and taxes that would have been imposed had such corporations duly qualified and such corporations are liable to state for penalty of not less than $500 nor more than $1,000 for each year or part thereof during which they so transact business. (607.1502[4]).

See subheads Annual Reports, and Filing Fee, supra.

See also category Property, topic Real Property.

Surrender of Authority.—Withdrawal is effected by filing with Secretary of State application for certificate for withdrawal on forms provided by Secretary stating: Name of corporation, jurisdiction of incorporation, that corporation is not transacting business in state and surrenders authority to do so, revocation of authority of registered agent and naming Secretary of State as agent for service of process, mailing address for mailing copy of any process and commitment to notify Department of State of future change in mailing address. (607.1520). Application must be accompanied by $35 fee. (607.0122[16]).

Foreign Boycott.—Effective Oct. 1, 1977, Florida corporations and corporations doing business in state are prohibited from cooperating in various specified ways with foreign boycotts that discriminate on basis of person's sex, race, color, religion, ancestry, or national origin or on basis of person's lawful business associations. (542.34).

Corporate privilege tax previously called capital stock tax was redesignated annual report filing fee as of Apr. 14, 1972. (See subhead Annual Reports, supra.)

Corporate Income Tax.—All references herein to Internal Revenue Code are to U.S. Internal Revenue Code of 1986, as amended and in effect on Oct. 1, 1998.

Corporation income tax of 5½ is imposed on all corporations. Taxpayers subject to alternative minimum tax liability under §55(b)(2) of Internal Revenue Code of 1986 subject to 3.3% state tax on alternative minimum taxable income less exemption amount, as computed under Internal Revenue Code of 1986. (220.11[2], 220.13[2][k]). All domestic corporations and all foreign corporations qualified to do business in Florida or actually doing business in Florida are subject to income tax. Among those entities subject to tax are limited liability corporations (608), corporations not for profit (617), agriculture cooperative marketing associations (618), professional service corporations (621), foreign unincorporated associations (622), private school corporations (623). Not included are state or public fairs or expositions. (615, 616; 220.03). Exemption allowed of $5,000 or lesser amount which will provide State with amount equal to maximum federal income tax credit. (220.14). Subchapter S corporations (§1361 of Internal Revenue Code) are subject to tax at corporate level in same manner as they are taxed for federal income tax purposes under §1363 of Internal Revenue Code. (220.13[2][i]). Income tax generally administered by Department of Revenue. (220.51). Returns with certain exceptions required to be filed and tax paid at place designated by Department of Revenue on first day of fourth month after close of tax year or 15th day following due date for filing of related federal return. (220.222). Return required by any taxpayer liable for Florida income tax or required to file Federal income tax return regardless of whether taxpayer is liable for Florida income tax. (220.22). Florida partnership having partner subject to tax under c. 220 is required to file information return by first day of fifth month following close of tax year. (220.22; 220.222). All taxpayers are required to notify Department of Revenue with respect to any deficiency or adjustment made on federal income tax return and file certified copy of such change. (220.23[1]). Failure to notify Department of Revenue of any deficiency or adjustment and as required in §220.23 subjects taxpayer to penalty for late filing of returns described below. Returns for DISC (§6011[c][2] of Internal Revenue Code) are due by first day of tenth month following close of tax year. (220.222). Penalties in regard to Florida corporate income tax are similar to federal penalties, i.e., penalty for late filing is 10% of tax due per month up to maximum of five months (220.801). Interest accruing on taxes not paid at rate, determined semi-annually, which is based on average prime rate charged by commercial banks to large businesses during prior six month period (220.807; 220.809). Interest on overpayments of tax accrues from date taxpayer files written notice with Department of Revenue at same rate as interest on underpayments and is payable to taxpayer unless overpayment is refunded within three months after date upon which written notice is filed, in which case no interest is allowed. (220.723). Criminal penalties provided for willful violation of Florida corporate income tax code. (220.901; 220.903; 220.905). Penalty for incomplete return in amount of greater of $300 or 10% of tax due, up to $10,000. (220.211).

Corporate income for purposes of state income tax is based on corporate income determined for federal income tax purposes. (220.12). Business and nonbusiness income apportioned separately. Nonbusiness income is allocated based upon location, situs, or place of use of underlying assets. Business income is apportioned based upon formula described below. Statute provides for certain adjustments to income. For example, added back to income for Florida income tax purposes is federal deduction for state income tax and interest not subject to federal income tax under §103(a)(1) of Internal Revenue Code. (220.13[1][a]). Subtracted from Federal income tax are certain deductions allowed for Federal income tax, i.e., net operating losses, which relate to years prior to Florida income tax and foreign source and dividends. (220.13[1][b]). Special rules are provided for reporting installment sales which decrease taxable income from sales consummated in years prior to enactment of income tax statute. (220.13[1][c]). Special rules are provided for life insurance companies (220.13[2][a]); mutual insurance companies (220.13[2][b]); regulated investment companies (220.13[2][d]); corporations filing consolidated returns (220.13[2][f], see also 220.131); cooperative corporations or associations (220.13[2][g]); and organizations exempt under §501(a) of Internal Revenue Code (220.13[2][h]). Because of limited space it is not possible to mention adjustments in any detail or all of adjustments; therefore, statute must be consulted. Apportionment formula is provided at §§220.15 and 220.16. Generally, apportionment of business income is based on formula to determine income subject to Florida income tax, arrived at by using 25% of ratio of real and personal property owned and rented in Florida to total of such property everywhere, 25% of ratio of compensation paid in Florida to total compensation everywhere, 50% of ratio of taxpayer's Florida sales to total sales everywhere. (220.15). In applying apportionment and formula, special rules applicable to tax years beginning after Dec. 31, 1986 apply in determining what constitutes "property" and "sales" of financial organizations. (220.131; 220.15). Apportionment methods for insurance companies and taxpayers furnishing transportation services are separately provided. (220.151). Apportionment method under 220.15 rather than 220.151 applies to insurance companies and taxpayers furnishing transportation services if such taxpayers are members of affiliated group which has elected to file Florida consolidated return. (220.131[5]). Special formulas are provided for when 220.15 and 220.151 do not fairly reflect Florida income. (220.152).

Nonbusiness income allocated as follows: Net rents and royalties of Florida real property and capital gains and losses from sales of Florida real property allocable to Florida; net rents and royalties from tangible personal property are allocable to Florida if and to extent such property utilized in Florida or in their entirety if taxpayer's commercial domicile is Florida and taxpayer not organized under or taxable in state

---

See note at head of Digest as to 1998 legislation covered.

See Topical Index in front part of this volume.

FL – 4

CORPORATIONS . . . *continued*
where such property utilized; capital gains and losses from sales of tangible personal property allocable to Florida if such property was located in Florida when sold or taxpayer's commercial domicile is Florida and taxpayer not taxable in state where such property was located; if taxpayer's commercial domicile is Florida, interest, dividends and capital gains and losses from sales of intangible property allocable to Florida. (220.16). As in case of adjustments to income, apportionment statute must be consulted.

Tax credit of 20% of initial cash investment in export finance corporation made on or before June 30, 1992, in amount not to exceed 50% of taxpayer's tax is allowed. (220.188[2], [3]). Also statewide limit for such credit of $5,000,000 for all taxpayers in all taxable years. (220.188[3]). Export finance corporation means corporation organized pursuant to Part VI of c. 288. (220.03gg). Also tax credits for gasohol development (220.182), enterprise zone jobs (220.181), enterprise zone property (220.182), community contribution (220.183), hazardous waste facility (220.184) and Florida alternative minimum tax (220.186).

Declaration of estimated tax where estimated tax can reasonably be expected to exceed $2,500 must be filed. (220.24). Declaration of estimated tax is required to be filed by first day of fifth month of tax year and be paid in four equal installments, first installment being due when declaration is filed, second due on first day of seventh month of tax year, third due on first day of tenth month of tax year and final due on or before first day of next tax year. (220.33). Extensions for filing and paying tax are provided for (220.222[2]), but tentative tax based on estimation of tax due is required (220.32).

Tax year and method of accounting are same as those for federal income tax purposes. (220.42, 220.41). Taxpayer may elect to use percentage of completion (Treas. Reg. 1.451-3[b][1]) for reporting income if completed contract election in effect for federal income tax purposes (220.42[3]).

Emergency excise tax (EET) of 2.2% of amount equal to 2.5 times remainder of 40% of deductions allowed under §168 of Internal Revenue Code, exclusive of deduction allowed under §168(B)(3), for assets placed in service after Dec. 31, 1980 and before Jan. 1, 1987. (221.01[2]). Taxpayer must file estimated, tentative and final returns on combined corporate tax/emergency excise tax return and declaration forms as prescribed by Department of Revenue in order for corporate income tax administrative provisions relating to tentative and estimated taxes to apply to combined payments and tax liabilities. (221.04).

Banking institutions are subject to state franchise tax. (220.63). Under statute, franchise tax base is bank's adjusted federal income tax as defined in §220.13 less $5,000. (220.63[3]).

Taxation of Corporate Stock.—See category Taxation, topics Intangible Personal Property Tax, Stamp Tax, subhead Documents.

Franchise Tax.—See subhead Corporate Privilege Tax, supra.

Corporations not for profit may be organized for any lawful purpose not for pecuniary profit and not specifically prohibited to corporations under laws of Florida. (617.0301). One or more persons, including corporations, partnerships and other entities, may act as incorporators by delivering articles of incorporation to Department of State for filing. (617.02011). Articles must state name (including "corporation", "incorporated", "corp." or "inc."), purposes, address of principal office and mailing address, manner in which directors are to be elected or appointed, any provision which limits corporate powers authorized by act, address of initial registered office and name and written acceptance of initial registered agent, and name and address of each incorporator. (617.0202). Fees for filing documents and issuing certificates are as provided in §607.0122. (617.0122).

Professional Corporations.—
Professional Service Corporation Act (c. 621) allows one or more individuals legally authorized to perform same professional services within state to incorporate for sole purpose of rendering same professional services (621.05). Special provisions limit issuance and transfer of stock (621.09); impose personal liability on officer, employee or agent for negligent or wrongful acts or misconduct committed by him or by person under his or her direct supervision and control (621.07); and permit corporate name to contain names of some or all shareholders which may contain the last names of deceased former individual shareholders or of a predecessor corporation or partnership, and shall contain designation "chartered," "professional association," or "P.A.," provided that it may do business under corporate name without such designation if it is registered under fictitious name law (621.12). Corporation organized for profit may convert to Professional Service Corporation. (607.1805). Provisions of c. 607 govern when not in conflict with c. 621. (621.13).

Deeds.—See category Property, topic Deeds.

JOINT STOCK COMPANIES:

No statutory provision for organization in Florida. Florida Statutes do expressly recognize validity of business trusts, however. See subhead Business Trusts, infra.

Business trusts may engage in any business except banking or security business. (609.01).

Creation.—Business trusts are created by deed or declaration of trust, which is sworn to by chairman of board of trustees and filed with Department of State with $350 filing fee (609.02), after which certificate of authority is issued (609.03). Settlor of business trust transfers assets to trustees who then manage business for benefit and profit of beneficiaries, usually called shareholders, who hold certificates evidencing beneficial interests in trusts.

Continuity.—Perpetual existence unless otherwise provided in declaration of trust.

Sale of Shares.—It is unlawful to sell shares of business trust without certificate of authority. (609.04). Certificates held by shareholders of business trust are freely transferable. However, before sales may be made to public, business trust must register under Florida Blue Sky laws (609.05) and business trust certificates are "securities" subject to regulation under federal securities laws.

Liability.—Shareholders of business trust have no personal liability to either trust or its creditors other than for payment of agreed purchase price for their shares. (609.07).

Merger.—Upon filing corporate articles of merger with $350 filing fee, business trust can be merged with corporation which is wholly owned by trust. In such merger, corporation survives and trust disappears. Dissenting shareholders are not entitled to any appraisal rights unless provided in declaration of trust. (609.08).

Taxation.—For state ad valorem tax purposes, shares of Florida business trust are treated as personal property, regardless of nature of trust assets. (609.051).

Foreign unincorporated associations have option to qualify to transact business in Florida with Secretary of State. (622.01-.07).

Professional Corporations.—See topic Corporations, subhead Professional Corporations.

LIMITED LIABILITY COMPANIES:

Limited Liability Companies may be organized for any lawful purpose. (608.403). One or more persons must file articles of organization with Department of State (608.405) and pay appropriate fee (608.452). Articles must state name (including "limited company" or "L.C."; "limited liability company" or "L.L.C.") (608.406), period of duration (not to exceed 30 years), purpose, address, name and address of registered agent, cash and value of property contributed, agreed additional contributions, terms and conditions of admission of additional members, survival provisions, statement that company is to be managed by manager, and name and address of manager (608.407). Transferee of interest has no right of management absent unanimous written approval of company members. (608.432). Liability of member limited to: (1) difference between its contribution to capital and amount stated in articles of organization as having been contributed; (2) any unpaid contribution to capital which it agreed in articles of organization to make in future. (608.435). Members not otherwise liable for any debt, obligation or liability of company. (608.436).

PARTNERSHIPS:

Florida has adopted 1994 Revised Uniform Partnership Act, effective Jan. 1, 1996. Partnerships formed before Jan. 1, 1996, that do not elect to be governed by RUPA subject to UPA. (620.81001-.91).

Service of process on one co-partner binds all. (48.061). Under certain circumstances of departure of partners from state, or concealment by nonresident partners, service may be made on Secretary of State. (48.181).

See category Intellectual Property, topic Trademarks and Tradenames, subhead Tradenames.

Limited Partnership.—Revised Uniform Limited Partnership Act 1986 adopted with certain modifications. (620.101-620.192). Fees of Department of State under this Act codified at 620.182.

BUSINESS REGULATION AND COMMERCE

BANKS AND BANKING:

Uniform Commercial Code adopted. (cc. 670-680). See also subhead Deposits, infra, concerning stop payment orders. See topic Commercial Code.

Florida Banking Code, cc. 658-663 provides for organization, consolidation, merger, conversion, dissolution, reorganization, liquidation, and powers of banks and trust companies.

Regulated by.—Application for and operation as bank, trust company, or international banking corporation in Florida is subject to approval of Department of Banking and Finance (658.19) and must be coordinated with appropriate federal regulatory agencies (658.22). Finally, within three months after needed approvals, duly executed articles of incorporation and filing fee for Department of State must be submitted to Department of Banking and Finance, which will subsequently file articles of incorporation with Department of State if it approves application for and operation as bank, trust company or international banking corporation. (658.23). Any bank or trust company incorporated pursuant to this chapter shall have one main office, which shall be located within State. (658.26).

Deposits.—May only be accepted by Florida chartered bank or national bank authorized to do business in Florida. (655.005; 655.922). Deposits may be made or withdrawn by minors. (655.77). Unless otherwise expressly provided in contract, agreement, or signature card executed in connection with opening of account, account in name of two or more persons may be paid to or on order of any of such persons. (655.78). It is presumed that joint account proceeds are to be paid to survivor or, in event of incompetency, to guardian of such survivor. (655.79). Agents may be designated to withdraw funds from convenience accounts. (655.80).

Remote Financial Service Units.—Banks, savings and loan associations and credit unions authorized to do business in Florida or having principal place of business in Florida may use facilities of such number of remote financial service units at such locations as such institution may determine. Owner of remote financial service units may share use of any remote service terminal with other financial institutions. Any bank not having its principal place of business and office in Florida may not utilize any remote financial service unit unless such bank does not take deposits by use of remote unit; such bank does not hold title to remote service unit; and remote service unit has as its owner, among other requirements, one or more banks each of which has its principal office or place of business in Florida, or is accessible by such bank or its customers only through computer or similar electronic systems used by, and use of which is controlled by, among other requirements, one or more banks each of which has its principal office or place of business in Florida. (658.65).

Unclaimed Deposits.—See category Property, topic Absentees, subhead Escheat.

See note at head of Digest as to 1998 legislation covered.

See Topical Index in front part of this volume.

FL – 5

BANKS AND BANKING . . . *continued*

Deposits and Collections.—Uniform Commercial Code adopted. (674.201-216).

Branching.—With approval of Florida Department of Banking and Finance, bank branches may be established within or outside state. (658.26).

Florida Reciprocal Banking.—Florida has revised Regional Reciprocal Banking Act of 1984, in 1994. New act, entitled Florida Reciprocal Banking Act, provides that entry into Florida by out-of-state bank holding company shall be only by acquisition of Florida bank or Florida bank holding company. Entry by interstate branching or by any other means is expressly prohibited. Out-of-state bank holding company is authorized to acquire Florida bank or Florida bank holding company upon approval by Department of Banking and Finance. Approval requires determination by Department that laws of state in which out-of-state bank holding company making acquisition has its principal place of business permit Florida bank holding companies to acquire banks and bank holding companies in that state and also requires determination by Department that Florida bank to be acquired has been in existence and continuously operating for more than two years. Department is authorized to subject acquisition to any conditions, restrictions, requirements, or other limitations that would apply to acquisition by Florida bank holding company of bank or bank holding company in state where out-of-state bank holding company making acquisition has its principal place of business. Prior to authorizing acquisition, Department must ensure that notice of intent to acquire has been published in newspaper of general circulation in counties in which bank to be acquired is located or that notice of intent to acquire has been mailed via certified mail to each person owning stock in bank to be acquired. (658.295).

Fiduciary Powers.—No corporation except bank, association (as defined in 665.012[1]), or trust company having Florida or federal charter authorized to conduct trust business and located in Florida and except national banking associations or federal associations located in Florida and authorized to conduct trust business is permitted to act as: (a) Personal representative of decedent; (b) receiver or trustee under appointment of any court; (c) assignee, receiver or trustee of insolvent person or corporation; or (d) fiscal agent, transfer agent, or registrar of any municipal or private corporation under certain circumstances. (660.41[1-4]).

See also subhead Remote Financial Service Units, supra.

Nonbank Banks.—Bank holding company prohibited from controlling institution in Florida that accepts federally insured deposits unless that institution is bank as defined by Bank Holding Company Act, 12 U.S.C. §1841(c) (i.e. accepts demand deposits and makes commercial loans). (658.296). No "company" as defined in Bank Holding Act that is not bank holding company as defined by Bank Holding Act may control bank. (658.296). Law "grandfathers" any "bank holding company" or other "company" as defined in Bank Holding Company Act from controlling institution in Florida that accepts federally insured deposits if bank holding company or other company controlled such bank on June 30, 1983.

Credit Card Banks.—Any domestic lender may organize credit card bank if certain requirements set forth in §658.995 are met. (658.995). Credit card bank is subject to supervision, regulation and examination of Department of Banking and Finance. Credit Card Bank shall not be considered "bank" for purposes of §§658.27-658.296. Subject to provisions of §658.995, any domestic lender, foreign lender or business organization may own credit card bank provided that, if credit card bank is to be organized under laws of this state, such bank shall be organized as provided in c. 658; applicant pays to Department fees required in §658.73; shares of bank are owned solely by domestic lender, foreign lender, or business organization; credit card bank accepts deposits only at single location in state; credit card bank maintains capital stock and paid in surplus in amount not less than $4,000,000; bank engages only in business of soliciting, processing, and making loans pursuant to credit card accounts; bank does not accept demand deposits or deposits that depositor has ability to withdraw by check or similar means for payment to third parties; credit card bank may accept savings or time deposits of $100,000 or more; bank must obtain insurance of its deposits by FDIC; and bank does not engage in business of making commercial loans. (658.995[3]).

International Banking.—International banking corporations organized under laws of foreign countries are authorized, upon approval of Florida Department of Banking and Finance, to establish in Florida international administrative office, international bank agency or representative office. (663.06). General powers of international administrative offices, international bank agencies and representative offices are set forth in §§663.063, 663.061 and 663.062. International bank agency may, if authorized by rule of Florida Department of Banking and Finance, exercise powers of federal agency under federal law. (663.061[3]). International banking corporation is authorized to transact only such limited business as is clearly related to, and is usual in, international or foreign business and financing international commerce. (663.06[7]). International bank agency is permitted to act as custodian and furnish investment management services to nonresident entities or persons and to resident entities or persons but only with respect to international or foreign investments. (663.061). Agency may not receive deposits unless such deposits are from: (i) Nonresident entities or persons whose principal place of business or domicile are outside U.S.; (ii) interbank deposits; or (iii) international banking facility deposits as defined in §655.071. (663.061).

International Development Banks.—Corporations organized, upon approval of Department of Banking and Finance, for purpose of promoting development in foreign countries by directly or indirectly making funding available to foreign business enterprises and foreign governments. (663.301). Such international development banks may make loans, extend credit or otherwise finance foreign business enterprises and foreign governments but may not: (a) Take deposits (except from foreign foundations, certain tax-exempt entities and foreign business enterprises), (b) offer deposit accounts other than those permitted to be offered by international banking agency; (c) exercise trust or fiduciary powers, (d) offer credit cards, (e) establish or use remote financial service units or (f) serve as depository of public moneys or serve as financial agent of state (663.309). Name of all such international development banks shall include words "Development Bank". Words "National", "Federal", "United States", "Insured" or "Guaranteed" may not be used, unless authorized by federal law. (663.307).

Trust Companies.—General rules applicable to trust business, whether undertaken by trust companies or trust divisions of banks or state or federal associations, are found at §§660.25—660.48. Bank, state or federal association conducting activities of fiduciary is not "finance company", but may conduct fiduciary activities, upon approval, through "trust department." (660.33). General powers of trust companies and departments enumerated in §660.34. Trust companies or departments may act as agents or advisors to other trust companies or departments. (660.36). Special provision for substitution of fiduciaries. (660.46).

Upon approval of Department of Banking and Finance and stockholders, members and/or directors, as may be applicable, trust companies or trust departments may establish trust service office. (660.33).

Fees and Assessments.—Application and examination fees for banking activities are detailed in §658.73.

BILLS AND NOTES:

Uniform Commercial Code adopted. (cc. 670-680). See topic Commercial Code.

Judgment Notes.—Not recognized, except to extent that nonrecognition violates full faith and credit clause. See 442 So.2d 182, finding 55.05 unconstitutional to extent it prohibits enforcement of foreign confessed judgment. Provision for entry of judgment appears severable, not invalidating note. (55.05).

Attorney Fee Clause.—Provision for payment of attorney's fee to holder of note in event of default is enforceable to extent required to indemnify holder as to attorney's fee he has paid or becomes obligated to pay. Reasonableness of fee is to be determined by the court unless specific sum not to exceed 10% of principal is stipulated. (135 So. 521; 687.06).

BILLS OF LADING:

See topic Carriers.

BILLS OF SALE:

See topic Sales.

BLUE SKY LAW:

See topic Securities.

BROKERS:

Uniform Commercial Code adopted. (cc. 670-680). See topic Commercial Code. Real estate brokers and salespersons are registered, examined, and licensed by Florida Real Estate Commission of Department of Professional Regulation. (475.04, .15, .181). Mortgage brokers and solicitors are licensed and regulated by Department of Banking and Finance. (494.003-494.0043). Insurance agents: See category Insurance, topic Insurance Companies. Securities dealers and brokers: See topic Securities. For procedures regarding securities brokers who have pleaded guilty or nolo contendere to fraud, see §215.684. Commission merchants: See topic Factors.

Real Estate Brokers and Salespersons.—Parties acting as real estate brokers or salespersons must be licensed. (475.001). Definition of broker includes any person who is general partner, officer, or director of partnership or corporation which acts as broker and includes anyone, unless exempt under §475.011 or §721.20, who lists or sells one or more time-share periods per year in one or more time-share plans. (475.01[1][c]). Such brokers must have valid broker's license and must disclose all material aspects of transactions. Qualifications of applicants for licensure are set forth in §§475.17 and 475.80. Salespersons and brokers must fulfill post-licensure education requirements consisting of Commission-approved courses. (475.182). Brokers are subject to discipline for failure to deposit certain money in appropriate escrow account. (475.25). Brokers are subject to discipline for failing to give notice and obtain consent regarding representation. (475.25). Brokers are subject to discipline for violating Uniform Standards of Professional Appraisal Practice. (475.25; 475.611). No contract for commission or compensation is valid unless broker or salesperson is licensed. (475.41). Statute provides for civil and criminal liability for prohibited activities. (475.42). Broker and salespersons render professional service and are professionals for purposes of §95.11(4)(a). (475.01).

Mortgage Brokerage.—Parties acting as mortgage brokers or operating mortgage brokerage business must be licensed. (494.0033; 494.0031). Individual mortgage broker must be associate of mortgage brokerage business. (494.0033). "Act as a mortgage broker" means, for compensation or gain, accepting application for mortgage loan, soliciting mortgage loan for borrower or negotiating mortgage loan for lender, or offering to do any of above. (494.001[2]). To license mortgage brokerage business, business must have qualified principal broker. (494.0035). No person may receive fee for acting as mortgage brokerage business except pursuant to written agreement between business and borrower. (494.0038). Law provides penalties for violating provisions of Act. (494.0041).

Yacht and Ship Brokers.—Governed by c. 326. Provides that broker who intentionally fails to comply with provisions concerning establishment of, deposit into, or withdrawal from trust accounts commits third degree felony. Failure to establish trust account or to place funds therein shall constitute prima facie evidence of intentional and purposeful violation (326.005). §326.006 gives to Division of Florida Land Sales, Condominiums, and Mobile Homes power to enforce c. 326.

BULK SALES:

See topic Commercial Code and category Debtor and Creditor, topic Fraudulent Sales and Conveyances. Art. 6 (Bulk Sales) of Uniform Commercial Code repealed.

CARRIERS:

Uniform Commercial Code adopted. (cc. 670-680). See topic Commercial Code for deviations from uniform text.

See note at head of Digest as to 1998 legislation covered.

See Topical Index in front part of this volume.

CARRIERS . . . *continued*

Florida Public Service Commission (350.011) has jurisdiction over intrastate rail rates and practices in accordance with standards and procedures of 49 U.S.C. §11501 et seq. It is responsibility of Department of Transportation to promote further development and improvement of transportation systems. (20.23).

Regional transportation authorities may be formed by any two or more political subdivisions to provide or contract for transportation facilities. (163.565 et seq.).

Semiannual fee upon railroad companies measured by 1/8 of 1% of gross operating revenues derived from intrastate business during preceding six month period is payable to Florida Public Service Regulatory Trust Fund within 30 days of end of each six month period. (350.113).

COMMERCIAL CODE:

Uniform Commercial Code (as reproduced in Part VI) was enacted by the 1965 legislature, effective Jan. 1, 1967. (cc. 670-680). 1966 amendments not adopted except 2-702(3). 1972 Official Text (Art. IX-Secured Transactions and Related Sections) adopted. 1977 Amendments (Investment Securities) adopted, effective Oct. 1, 1987. 1987 Official Text (Art. IIA-Leases) enacted, effective Jan. 1, 1991. (cc. 680, former provisions of cc. 680 either repealed or transferred to Part III of c. 671). 1990 Official Amendments (Art. IIA-Leases) enacted, effective Oct. 1, 1998. 1989 Official Text (Art. IVA-Fund Transfers) enacted, effective Jan. 1, 1992. (c. 670). 1990 Amendments (Art. III-Negotiable Instruments and Art. IV-Bank Deposits and Collections) enacted, effective Jan. 1, 1993. Art. VI-Bulk Transfers repealed, effective July 1, 1993. 1994 Official Text (Art. VIII-Investment Securities, Art. IX). Official Amendments enacted, effective Oct. 1, 1998. Section numbering corresponds generally with official text, but each U.C.C. article assigned in addition separate chapter number designation, thus: 7-308 becomes 677.308. Art. II A is c. 680; Art. IV A is c. 670, thus 2A-201 becomes 680.201 and 4A-108 becomes 670.108.

Deviations from Official 1962 Text, Arts. I-VIII; Optional Provisions.—

1-105, 1972 Official Text enacted. 1987 and 1989 Official Amendments adopted. Amended to conform to repeal of Art. IV.

1-201, 1972 Official Text enacted. 1977 Official Amendments not adopted. 1987 Official Amendments to 1-201(37) and 1990 Official Amendments to 1-201(20), (24), (43), (44) adopted.

1-209, 1966 Official Optional Amendment not adopted. 1972 Official Amendments to Article IX and Related Section not adopted in total.

2-207, 1972 Official Text enacted.

2-316 amended to exclude from transactions constituting "Sales" the "procurement, processing, storage, distribution, or use of whole blood, plasma, blood products and blood derivatives, for the purpose of injecting or transfusing the same into the human body for any purpose . . . . . ." and "The procurement, processing, testing, storing, or providing of human tissues and organs . . . ." No implied warranty that cattle or hogs are free from sickness or disease except not available where seller has knowledge.

2-318, 1966 Official Optional Amendment Alternative A enacted, but with words "or who is an employee, servant or agent of his buyer" inserted after "in his home."

2-702, 1966 Official Amendment enacted.

4-106, Alternative B selected.

4-403(a), insert "written" before "order"; omit "reasonable" before "certainty"; insert "by an officer of the bank during a banking day" after "received".

4-403(b), delete reference to oral stop payment orders.

4-403(c), insert new beginning sentence "The bank may be liable to its customer for the actual loss incurred by the customer resulting from the wrongful payment of an item contrary to a valid and binding stop-payment order or order to close an account."

5-103(1)(a), substitute, for second sentence, "A credit shall clearly state whether it is revocable or irrevocable and in the absence of such statement shall be presumed to be irrevocable."

5-114, optional subsections (4) and (5) omitted.

5-116, 1972 Official Text enacted.

7-209(3)(b), 1966 Official Amendment not enacted.

7-403(1)(b), optional portion enacted in cases "when value of such damage, delay, loss or destruction exceeds $10,000."

8-101 et seq., 1977 Revision adopted, effective Oct. 1, 1987. (Laws, c. 87-275).

Deviations from 1972 Official Text Arts. IX and XI; Optional Provisions.—

9-104(10), 679.104(10) was reenacted to make clear that Section 9-104(10) of Uniform Commercial Code-Secured Transactions be literally construed to exclude transferring of leasehold interests in land from provisions of Uniform Commerical Code-Secured Transactions.

9-105(1)(j) defines "mortgage" with reference to Ch. 697, F.S.; 9-105(1)(n) specifically includes telephone companies; 9-105(2) delete "construction mortgage-section 9-313(1)" and "fixtures filing—Section 9-313(1)."

9-110, includes proviso that instrument filed to protect security interest in crops or goods which are fixtures sufficient only if filing or recording constitutes constructive notice under laws applicable to filing or recording real estate mortgages.

9-203(4), refers to Chs. 516 and 520, F.S.

9-301, delete (4). Extends to 15 days time period for secured party to file under UCC with respect to purchase money security interests.

9-302(1)(a) includes security interest in possession of secured party under 679.304(1), 679.305.

9-305, delete "instruments, money".

9-307, delete (3).

9-312, Priority of purchase money security interest determined under subsection (5) if failure to perfect. Extends to 15 days period of time during which purchase money security interest with respect to UCC may be perfected under certain circumstances.

9-313, 1972 version not enacted. 1962 version modified and renumbered: 9-313(2) (679.313[2][b]) gives priority to security interest in fixtures after perfection of interest and affixation to real estate over persons thereafter acquiring interest in real estate. 9-313(3) (679.313[2][a]) delete "valid against all persons subsequently acquiring interests in the real estate except as stated in subsection (4), but". 9-313(4) not enacted. 9-313(5) (679.313[3][a]) delete "and (4)". Add subsection 679.313(3)(b) requiring secured party to give reasonable notice before removing collateral.

9-401, Variant of official second alternative enacted. See category Documents and Records, topic Records, subhead Filing Under Commercial Code. Consumer goods and farming equipment must be filed with Secretary of State. Local recording must be in county of debtor's place of business or chief executive office, or, if none, in county of debtor's residence. Subsections (2) and (3) are each qualified by following clause: "Except as is provided in §679.313(2),". Alternative Subsection (3) not enacted. Delete 9-401(6). New subsection (6) is added to provide transition rules for 1980 change in filing rules.

9-4011, Added as wholly nonuniform section dealing with sufficiency of filing, etc., as follows: Filing complete and sufficient only if recorded with appropriate clerk of the circuit court. Recording shall be in manner provided in cc. 965 and 28.

9-402, delete 9-402(6). 9-402(7) becomes Section 679.402(6); 9.402(8) becomes Section 679.402(7). Add new subsection (679.402[8]), providing that Department of State may promulgate uniform forms, and mandating additional $5.25 fee for use of nonconforming form. Section 679.402(6) amended by Laws, c. 87-256, adding additional sentence to end of section "A filed financing statement remains effective with respect to collateral transferred by the debtor even though the secured party knows of or consents to the transfer."

9-403, Subsection (4) modified to conform with 9-4011. In subsection (5), filing fees given by referring to cc. 15 and 18.

9-403(6), second sentence omitted. 9-403(7) also includes financing statements covering crops growing or to be grown.

9-404, No provision for filing termination statement with filing officer. 9-404(1), delete "covering consumer goods"; add "after July 1, 1992" in blank space provided; insert "Except for termination statements of financing statements filed under §679.402(2) and (5)," at beginning of penultimate sentence which currently begins "A termination"; delete "within one month or" in third line.

9-405(2), Substitute "time" for "hour"; substitute "a filing on goods which are or are to become fixtures" for "fixture filing"; and insert "crops or" before "timber". In last sentence omit "effective as a fixture filing (subsection (6) of section 9-402)."

9-406, Separate written statement of assignment by secured party not required for release of financing statements filed under 9-402(4) and (5). Refer to cc. 15 and 28, for fees.

9-407, Upon request filing officer shall provide certified copy of instrument filed under this Chapter. Fee for such service shall be as provided in cc. 15 and 28.

9-504(3), Secured party must give required notice to guarantors and except for consumer goods secured party must notify every other person having secured interest in collateral who has filed a financing statement indexed in name of debtor.

9-505, 1972 Official Text not adopted. 1962 Official Text modified to dispense with requirement to notify secured parties who have not filed financing statement and require written objection within 30 days from those entitled to notice. If debtor has renounced or modified his rights provided by subsection, secured party may retain collateral unless written objection is received.

9-506, Between "debtor" and "or any other secured . . ." insert ", any guarantor of the obligation secured,".

Filing fee blanks in U.C.C. art. 9 (c. 679) are filled by references to cc. 15 and 28. Secretary of State's fee for filing any financing statement "or other writing required or permitted to be filed by any provisions of chapter 679" is $25 for first page plus $2 for each subsequent page (includes termination statement filing fee). (15.091). See also 9-402(6) for additional fee for nonuniform forms. Secretary of State charges no additional fee for acknowledging filing of financing statement or other written instrument. (679.407[1]). Fee of clerk of circuit court for recording written instrument is $5 for first page plus $4 for each subsequent page. (28.24). Financing statement and any other instrument filed with clerk of circuit court pursuant to U.C.C. art. 9 entitled to be recorded "without oath, acknowledgment or proof of its execution" but required in all other respects to be "in the manner provided in [c. 695]for recording of conveyances of real property, and in the manner and upon the payment of fees as provided in [c. 28]." (679.4011). Effect of reference to c. 695 unclear but 695.03 dealing with acknowledgments by married women and service personnel inapplicable to c. 679. (695.031). See also category Mortgages, topic Chattel Mortgages, subhead Forms.

Financing statement not to be accepted for filing or recording "unless there appears thereon the notation that the [documentary] taxes required by [c. 201] have been paid on the promissory instruments secured by said financing statement and will be paid on any additional promissory instruments, advances or similar instrument that may be secured by said financing statement." (201.22). See category Taxation, topic Stamp Tax, subhead Documents.

See also category Documents and Records, topic Records, subhead Filing Under Commercial Code.

Deviations from 1987 Official Text, Art. IIA; Optional Provisions—2A-101 et seq.—enacted, numbered at c. 680. F.S., former provisions of Art. X—either repealed or transferred to Part III of c. 671. (Laws, c. 90-278).

2A-101, et seq., 1990 Official Amendments.

2A-104, subsection (1)(a) inserts are "chapter 319 or chapter 328".

Subsection (1)(b) insert is "(680.1051)".

2A-106, in subsection (1), inserts "or in which the lease is executed by the lessee" following "to be used." (680.1061).

2A-108, deleted subsections (2) and (4); and amended subsection (3) to read: "before making a finding of unconscionability under subsection (1) the court, on its own motion or that of a party, shall afford the parties a reasonable opportunity to present evidence as to the setting, purpose and effect of the lease contract or clause thereof." (680.1081).

2A-201, amended subsection (1)(a) to read "In a lease contract that is not a consumer lease, the total payments to be made under the lease contract, excluding payments for options to renew or buy, are less than $1,000.00; or". (680.201).

See note at head of Digest as to 1998 legislation covered.

See Topical Index in front part of this volume.

FL – 7

COMMERCIAL CODE... *continued*

2A-209, added subsection (4) of amended version 2A-209 in conformity with 1990 amendment, but 1990 official amendments not made to subsections (1), (2) and (3). (680.209).

2A-216, 1987 official alternative A enacted. (680.216).

2A-219, in subsection (1), inserts ", unless the loss resulted from the lessee's negligence" following "pass to the lessee." (680.219).

2A-221, deleted phrase "that is not a consumer lease" appearing after phrase "except in a finance lease." (680.221).

2A-308, in subsection (1), insert "or voids the lease contract" following "fraudulent" and "and does not void the lease contract" at end thereof. Amended subsection (2) to read: "nothing in this chapter impairs the rights of creditors of a lessor if the lease contract is made under circumstances which under any statute or rule of law apart from this chapter would constitute the transaction, a fraudulent transfer or voidable preference." (680.308).

2A-309, in subsection (4)(a), substitutes "a fixture filing covering the fixtures is filed or recorded" for "the interest of the lessor is perfected by a fixture filing."

2A-311, becomes 680.32.

2A-406, deleted phrase "is not a consumer lease" from subsection (1)(b). (680.406).

2A-407, adopted addition of subsection (3) in conformity with 1990 official amendment. (680.407).

2A-501, omits reference to 1-106(1) in subsection 4. (680.501).

2A-506, amended subsection (1) to refer to limitations period in c. 95, subject to right of parties to lease that is not consumer lease to reduce period of limitation to not less than one year. (680.506).

2A-514, insert at beginning of text of each subsection (a) and (b), "To justify rejection or to establish default".

2A-516, deleted phrase "except in the case of a consumer lease" from subsection (3)(b). Added subsection (6) as follows: "subsection (3) shall not apply to a consumer lease." (680.516).

2A-517, omits subsections (2) and (3). (680.517).

2A-518, amends subsection (3) to read: "if a lessee's cover is by lease agreement that qualifies for treatment under subsection (2) the lessee may elect to proceed under subsection (2) or section 680.519. If a lessee's cover is by lease agreement that for any reason does not qualify for treatment under subsection (2) or is by purchase or otherwise, the lessee may recover from lessor as if the lessee had elected not to cover."

2A-519, subsection (1) reads: "(1) Except as otherwise provided with respect to damages liquidated in the lease agreement (§680.504) or otherwise determined by agreement of the parties (§§671.102[3] and 680.503), if a lessee elects not to cover or a lessee elects to cover and the cover is by lease agreement, whether or not the lease agreement qualified for treatment under §680.518(2), or is by purchase or otherwise, the measure of damages for nondelivery or repudiation by the lessor or for rejection or revocation of acceptance by the lessee, is the present value as of the date of the default of the then market rent minus the present value as of the same date of the original rent, computed for the remaining lease term of the original lease agreement together with incidental and consequential damages, less expenses saved in consequence of the lessor's default."

2A-527, in subsection (2)(b) inserts "of the commencement of the term of the new lease agreement." following "the present value as of the same date".

Subsection (3) reads: "(3) If the lessor's disposition is by lease agreement that qualifies for treatment under subsection (2), the lessor may elect to proceed under subsection (2) or §680.528. If the lessor's disposition is by lease contract that for any reason does not qualify for treatment under subsection (2), or is by sale or otherwise, the lessor may recover from the lessee under §680.528 as if the lessor had elected not to dispose of the goods." (680.527).

2A-528 omits word "for" between "damages" and "default" near end of first paragraph of subsection (1).

2A-529, subsection (1)(a) reads:

"(a) For goods accepted by the lessee and not repossessed by or effectively tendered back to the lessor and for conforming goods lost or damaged after risk of loss passes to the lessee (§680.219):"

Subsection (4) reads:

(4) "Payment of the judgment for damages obtained pursuant to subsection (1) entitles the lessee to the use and possession of the goods not then disposed of for the remaining lease term in accordance with the lease agreement, provided that the lessee complies with all other terms and conditions of the lease agreement."

At end of subsection (5) "or" has been changed to "and."

2A-532, omits "or other law". (680.532).

Deviations from 1989 Official Text Art. IVA; Optional Provisions.—

4A-101, et seq., enacted and numbered at c. 670.

Deviations from 1990 Official Text Arts. III and IV; Optional Provisions.—Adopted revision of Art. 3 and amendments to Art. 4, effective Jan. 1, 1993. All Art. 3 provisions and several Art. 4 are codified with additional "1" at end to distinguish them from former sections which were repealed when revision and amendments were adopted, e.g., 3-302 becomes 673.3021 rather than 673.302. Florida subsections are (1), (2), (3), etc. and sub-sections are (a), (b), (c), etc., e.g., 3-310(c)(1) becomes 673.3101(3)(a).

3-104, add new subsection "(11) A warrant of this state is not a negotiable instrument governed by this chapter." Revise introduction to section to read "Except as provided in subsections (3), (4), and (11),".

3-118, official text deleted and reference is made to general statute of limitations in c. 95.

3-415(a), 1993 amendment not adopted.

4-101 et seq., amendments to conform Art. 4 to revised Art. 3 were adopted. If Art. 4 section was amended, it kept same number; if old section was replaced, new section number has added "1" to distinguish it from repealed section, e.g., 4-106 now becomes 674.1061 but 4-105 remains 674.105.

4-106, Alternative B adopted.

4-111, official text deleted and reference is made to general statute of limitations in c. 95.

4-403, first sentence of subsection (a) is significantly amended to read: "A customer or any person authorized to draw on the account if there is more than one person may stop payment of any item drawn of the customer's account or close the account by a written order to the bank describing the item or account with certainty received by an officer of the bank during a banking day and at a time and in a manner that affords the bank a reasonable opportunity to act on it before any action by the bank with respect to the item described in §674.303." First sentence of subsection (b) reads; "A stop-payment order is effective for 6 months." Insert following as first sentence in subsection (c): "The bank may be liable to its customer for the actual loss incurred by the customer resulting from the wrongful payment of an item contrary to a valid and binding stop-payment order or order to close an account."

Forms.—See end of this Digest.

See also topics: Banks and Banking, Bills and Notes, Brokers, Carriers, Contracts, Factors, Frauds, Statute of, Sales, Securities, Warehousemen; categories Business Organizations, topic Corporations; Civil Actions and Procedure, topic Limitation of Actions; Debtor and Creditor, topics Assignments, Fraudulent Sales and Conveyances, Liens, Pledges; Documents and Records, topic Records; Mortgages, topic Chattel Mortgages.

CONDITIONAL SALES:

Uniform Commercial Code adopted. (cc. 670-680). See topics Commercial Code, Sales; category Mortgages, topic Chattel Mortgages.

CONSIGNMENTS:

Uniform Commercial Code adopted. (cc. 670-680). See topics Commercial Code, Factors; category Mortgages, topic Chattel Mortgages.

CONSUMER PROTECTION:

Consumer Protection Generally.—(c. 501). Prohibits delivery by mail, or other means, of unsolicited credit cards (501.011), prohibits certain restrictions on service station credit cards (501.0115), regulates "health studios" (501.012) (repealed Oct. 1, 2000), restricts certain telephonic sales calls to consumers, and provides certain requirements for unforceability of contracts made pursuant to telephonic sales call (501.059), controls use of nonionzing radiations and lasers (501.122), requires labeling of art or craft material containing toxic substances (501.124), regulates consumer unit pricing (501.135), regulates placement in escrow of deposits received for purchase of residential dwelling units (501.1375), indicates standards for advertising of movie previews or trailers (501.138), posting of signs by retail establishments indicating no-refund policy (501.142), requires labeling of bedding that contains used materials (501.145), and regulates home solicitation sales. Creates penalties for tampering with, or attempting or conspiring to tamper with, consumer product. (501.93). Deceptive and unfair trade practices Act (501.201 et seq.) makes unfair or deceptive acts or practices unlawful in broadly defined group of consumer transactions. Act to be interpreted and administered consistently with Federal Trade Commission Act. (501.204, 501.205). State Governor and cabinet have power to adopt rules implementing Act. (501.205). Civil penalty of not more than $10,000 imposed for each violation committed with actual or implied knowledge, in actions brought by Department of Legal Affairs or state attorney. Penalty may be waived if full restitution or reimbursement made or actual damages paid to injured consumers. (501.2075). Retailer not liable to injured consumer for claims made by manufacturer not known by retailer to violate Act. (501.211[2]). Act does not apply to personal injury claims and other specified matters. (501.212). Division of Consumer Services may investigate complaints and bring actions for violation of certain provisions of c. 501. (501.911). See also topic Monopolies, Restraint of Trade and Competition, subhead Fraudulent Practices.

Home solicitation sales, leases, and rentals of consumer goods or services with purchase price in excess of $25 are regulated and permits are required. With limited exceptions for insurance and farm equipment, contract of sale must be written and contain statutory notice of buyer's right to cancel. Buyer has right to cancel until midnight of third business day after day buyer signs agreement or offer to purchase. Buyer's cancellation may be evidenced by written notice, telegram or mail to seller. Certain duties are placed on businesses conducting home solicitation sales and various practices are prohibited. (501.021-.055).

Bingo.—Provides for conditions for conduct, limitations of use, and permitted uses of proceeds. (849.0931).

Game promotions are regulated comprehensively by Department of State. (849.094).

Credit Cards.—Fraudulent factoring of credit card transactions is unfair or deceptive trade practice under c. 501, Part II. (817.62).

Dance Studio Act.—Provides for registration and other regulations as to dance studios. (501.143).

Solicitation of Contributions Act.—Governs solicitation of public contributions and is regulated extensively by Division of Consumer Services of Department of Agriculture and Consumer Services. (496.401 et seq.). Charitable organization, unless exempted by 496.406, which intends to solicit contributions in Florida by any means must, prior to engaging in any such solicitation, file registration statement with Division of Consumer Services (496.405). Fee must be paid with such registration in amount specified in 496.405(4). Charitable organization that is required to register must file annual report for immediately preceding fiscal year, such report to include information specified in 496.407. Registration and duties of professional solicitors is governed by 496.410 through 496.412. Any person who willfully and knowingly

See note at head of Digest as to 1998 legislation covered.

See Topical Index in front part of this volume.

FL – 8

CONSUMER PROTECTION . . . *continued*
violates provisions of Solicitation of Contributions Act commits felony of third degree, and for any subsequent conviction, commits felony of second degree. (496.417). In addition to other remedies provided by law, Department of Legal Affairs may bring civil action to enforce provisions of 496.401 et seq.

False Advertising.—There are criminal penalties for misleading and false advertising. (817.45).

False Claims of Academic Degree.—There are criminal penalties for making false claims of academic degree or title. (817.567).

State Lottery.—Governed by Department of Lottery. (24.104 et seq.).

Unsolicited Merchandise.—Recipient has no obligation to return or accept delivery and may dispose of same as if they were gifts. (570.545).

Deceptive and Unfair Trade Practices Act.—Purpose is to make state regulation of consumer sales practices consistent with established policies of federal law relating to consumer protection. (501.201 et seq.).

Bottled Water.—Operation of bottled water plants, and transportation and sale of bottled water regulated by Department of Health and Rehabilitative Services. (381.294). Any person operating bottled water plant or transporting water into or within state without permit shall be guilty of second degree misdemeanor. (381.294[7]).

Water Vending Machine Protection Act.—Provides licensing procedures and establishes standards for water vending machines. (500.459). Any person seeking to operate water vending machine must first obtain operator's permit for fee not to exceed $200. (500.459[3]). Any person who operates water vending machine without permit shall be guilty of second degree misdemeanor. (500.459[7]).

Florida Motor Vehicle Repair Act.—Requires written repair estimates, unless waived by customer; repair shops must prepare and maintain bills and repair records in prescribed form and make replaced parts available for customer inspection. (559.901 et seq.).

Motor Vehicle Sales Warranties (Lemon Law).—Manufacturer has duty to conform new motor vehicle with all applicable express warranties. (681.101 and 681.103). Dispute-settlement procedure established for consumers to file claims when vehicle does not conform with express warranties. (681.104 and 681.108). If consumer resorts to manufacturer's certified dispute-settlement procedure and decision is not rendered or performed within 40 days, consumer may apply to division to have dispute removed to board for arbitration. (681.109, 681.1095). Consumer shall have option of filing action to recover damages, costs, and attorney's fees. (681.112). It is contrary to public policy to attempt to disclaim or limit rights of consumer under act. (681.115). Violation by manufacturer of this chapter is unfair or deceptive trade practice as defined in part II of c. 501. (681.111).

Credit Agreement.—Subject to numerous exceptions contracts for payment of interest at rate higher than 18% per annum simple interest are usurious. (687.02). See topic Interest.

Public Lodging Telephone Surcharges.—Public lodging establishments which impose surcharge for any telephone calls must post notice in conspicuous place by each telephone from which call which is subject to surcharge may originate. Any public lodging establishment not posting such notice may be fined or have its license suspended or revoked. (509.2015).

Motor Vehicle Registration.—Tax collectors in several counties of state, as authorized agents of Department of Highway Safety and Motor Vehicles, shall issue registration certificates to applicants in accordance with rules of Department. Any person or entity representing itself to be authorized agent of Department of Highway Safety and Motor Vehicles for registration purposes is guilty of unfair and deceptive trade practice as defined in c. 501, Part II. (320.03).

Plain Language.—No plain language statute.

Sale of Dogs and Cats.—There are requirements for administering tests, vaccines and anthelmintics to dogs and cats offered for sale within state, or transported into state for sale. Certificate of veterinary inspection shall accompany each such dog and cat offered for sale, and shall list all vaccines and deworming medications administered to each such dog or cat. Certain remedies are available to consumer if dog or cat is later found by licensed veterinarian to have been unfit for purchase due to illness, disease, congenital disorder, or breed, sex or health of animal was misrepresented to consumer. Requires pet dealers to provide consumers with written notice of their rights at time of sale. (585.95).

Agriculture regulated by Department of Agriculture and Consumer Services. Authorizes Division of Consumer Services to seek injunctions and other relief on behalf of consumer when violations of state consumer protection laws have occurred, or when public health, safety or welfare is endangered by any consumer product or service. Hearing shall be held within three days after commencement of such proceedings by Division. Nurserymen, stockdealers, agents and plant brokers must obtain certificate or registration before selling or distributing any nursery stock in this state. (581.131). Maximum annual registration fee shall be $460. (585.131). Department of Agriculture and Consumer Services may enter, inspect, and test any premises and animals where such animals exist, which are suspected of harboring biological or chemical residues, where such residues present likelihood that resultant meat and poultry products would be adulterated. (585.68).

It is third degree felony for any person to sell or transport undenatured pet food for human consumption. (585.85).

Senior Citizens and Handicapped Persons.—Civil penalty of up to $10,000 can be imposed upon any person who engages in activities that victimize senior citizens or handicapped persons. (501.2077).

Florida Telemarketing Act.—(501.601 et seq.). Prior to doing business in Florida, person who engages in commercial telephone solicitation must obtain license from Department of Agriculture and Consumer Services (501.605), for fee not to exceed $1,500 (501.605[5][b]). Contract made pursuant to commercial telephone solicitation is not valid and enforceable against purchaser, unless in writing, matches description of goods or services as that principally used in telephone solicitation, contains name, address, telephone number, and registration number of commercial telephone seller, total price of contract, detailed description of goods or services being sold, contains specified disclaimer, does not exclude any oral or written representations made by commercial telephone seller, and complies with all other applicable laws. (501.615[1]). Purchaser may give notice of cancellation to commercial telephone seller in writing within three business days after receipt of written confirmation of sale from seller. (501.615[4]). Any person who engages in any act that is violative of Florida Telemarketing Act is liable for civil penalty of not more than $10,000 for each violation (501.619), and various criminal penalties may be imposed as provided in 501.623.

See also topic Sales.

Commercial Weight-Loss Practices Act.—Sets forth standards for conduct of weight-loss programs for profit and warnings that must be given to participants. (501.057—501.0581).

CONTRACTS:

See categories Documents and Records, topic Seals; Family, topic Infants.

Uniform Commercial Code adopted. (cc. 670-680). See topic Commercial Code.

FACTORS:

Uniform Commercial Code adopted. (cc. 670-680). See topic Commercial Code.

Persons selling (except at retail) produce or other articles (except lumber, naval stores, or any consignment sold in less quantities than original packages) as factors or commission merchants must send sales account and check to consignor within seven days of sale, and should sale be unsatisfactory to party furnishing produce or articles, then at request commission house shall furnish, within five days, names and residences of purchaser of produce or article; and consignor also generally allowed access to factor's books and records. (522.06).

Artists and Art Dealers.—Specific statutory provisions govern relationship between artist and art dealer (686.501 et seq.), and provide for required contract provisions and priority for artist notwithstanding other provisions of Uniform Commercial Code (686.503). Violation is punishable as second degree misdemeanor. (686.506).

Liens.—See topic Commercial Code.

Consignment Agreements.—Generally treated as secured transactions governed by Uniform Commercial Code. (See 672.326; 679.114.) See topic Commercial Code.

Miscellaneous.—False representations as to prevailing market price, etc., to obtain consignment of Florida produce is punishable by fine and imprisonment. (817.14).

FRANCHISES:

Uniform Franchise and Business Opportunities Act has not been adopted.

Business Opportunity.—Sale of Business Opportunities Act adopted in 1979. (559.80-559.815). Act requires seller of business opportunities to file disclosure statement with Division of Consumer Services (559.805[1]); prominently display advertisement identification number (if required) in all written advertisements, promotional material, and contracts (559.805[2]); annual filing fee of $300. (559.805[4]). Defined as sale or lease of any products, equipment, supplies, or services to enable purchaser to start business for which purchaser is required to pay $500 or more to seller, where seller represents he will provide locations for use of vending machines or the like (559.801[1][a]); if applicable, purchase products made by purchaser (559.801[1]); guarantee in writing that purchaser will derive income from opportunity exceeding price paid (559.801[1]); or provide sales program or marketing program, for fee, from which purchaser will derive income (559.801[1]). Business opportunity does not include sale of ongoing business where owner intends to sell business opportunities "no more than five in number" nor does it include not-for-profit sale of sales demonstration equipment for $500 or less, or sales training course for $500 or less, or sale and lease of laundry and dry cleaning equipment. (559.801[1][b]).

Bond/Trust Requirement.—Seller of business opportunity representing that seller will derive guaranteed income or that seller will refund all or part of purchase price or repurchase products if buyer is unsatisfied (559.801[1][a][3]) required to obtain surety bond, trust account or guaranteed letter of credit of not less than $50,000 in favor of Division of Consumer Services (559.807).

Prohibited Acts.—Seller of business opportunity may not, among other things, misrepresent prospect of success of proposed business activity, misrepresent known required business investment, misrepresent amount of profits buyer can expect or assign "exclusive territory" encompassing same area to more than one purchaser. (559.809).

Remedies.—Failure to comply with provisions of Act regarding proper disclosures or delivery of equipment or supplies within 45 days of delivery date or if contract content does not comply with statutory requirements, Act allows purchaser to rescind contract within one year of execution date. (559.813). Private right of action for damages created for purchaser injured by seller's breach of contract or violations under Act including attorney's fees (559.813[3]), as well as injunction or other relief by state action (559.813[5]).

Fraudulent Practices.—C. 817 makes unlawful, when selling or establishing franchise or distributorship, misrepresentations regarding prospects of success of proposed or existing franchise, known required total investment or efforts to sell or establish more franchises or distributorships than is reasonable for market to sustain. (817.416). Violations of chapter permit investors to recoup moneys invested in such franchises or distributorships, attorney's fees and reasonable costs. (817.416[3]).

Specific Products.—Certain products and markets given separate substantive treatment, among them beer sales and distribution (563.022), motor vehicle franchise agreements (320.6405) and cable television franchises (166.046).

See note at head of Digest as to 1998 legislation covered.

See Topical Index in front part of this volume.

FL – 9

FRAUDS, STATUTE OF:

No action shall be brought in following cases, unless agreement or promise, or some note or memorandum thereof, be in writing and signed by party to be charged or someone by him lawfully authorized: (1) Whereby to charge executor or administrator upon any special promise to answer for or pay any debt or damages out of his own estate; (2) or whereby to charge defendant on any special promise to answer for debt, default or miscarriage of another; (3) or on agreement made upon consideration of marriage; (4) or on any contract for sale of lands, tenements and hereditaments or of any uncertain interest therein or concerning them or for any lease thereof for more than one year; (5) or upon any agreement not to be performed within one year from making; (6) or to charge any health care provider upon any guarantee, warranty or assurance as to results of any medical, surgical or diagnostic procedure performed by any licensed physician, osteopath, chiropractor, podiatrist, or dentist. (725.01).

Contracts for sale of lands, tenements or hereditaments, or of any uncertain interest in or concerning these must be in writing and signed by party to be charged therewith. (725.01).

Contract for Sale of Personalty.—See topic Commercial Code.

Uniform Commercial Code adopted. (cc. 670-680). See topic Commercial Code.

Part Performance.—Equitable doctrine of part performance of oral agreements within the statute of frauds is recognized but not for personal service contracts. (315 So.2d 518).

Credit agreement must be in writing, express consideration, set forth relevant terms and conditions and be signed by creditor and debtor in order to be enforceable by debtor. (687.0304).

Subscriptions for Periodicals.—No person is liable to pay for any newspaper, or other periodical unless he subscribes for or orders same in writing. (725.03).

INTEREST:

Where interest shall accrue without special contract, rate shall be set by Comptroller of State (687.01, 55.03); permitted by contract in writing, any rate up to and including 18% per annum simple interest (687.02); if loan or contract exceeds $500,000 in amount or value, then not in excess of 25% rate prescribed by §687.071 (687.02).

Consumer Finance Loans.—Person, copartnerships or corporations (excluding banks, savings banks, trust companies, building and loan associations, credit unions or industrial loan and investment companies and bonafide pawnbrokers) specifically licensed to engage in business of making consumer finance loans of $25,000 or less may charge 30% on first $2,000; 24% on amount over $2,000 and not exceeding $3,000; 18% on amount exceeding $3,000 and not exceeding $25,000. (516.031[1]). Such licensees may also offer lines of credit subject to same requirements as are applicable to loans in respect of interest rates and charges, but may not issue credit cards. (516.02[3]). Annual percentage rate of any loan under this chapter may equal but not exceed rate required by Federal Truth in Lending Act and Regulation Z of Board of Governors of Federal Reserve System to be disclosed. When loan is subject to two or more interest rates, licensee may charge single annual percentage rate applied to each periodic principal balance by actuarial method producing at maturity same total amount of interest otherwise permitted. (516.031[1]). No security interest on land for any loan less than $1,000. Except for those charges enumerated in §516.031(3)(a) and bad check charges provided for in 516.031(3) (b), no other charges shall be charged. (516.031[3]). If all or part of new loan is unpaid principal of prior loan, then new principal may not include more than 60 days unpaid interest which has accrued on prior loan. (516.031[5]). Splitting loans to obtain greater finance charges is not permitted (516.031[4]). Interest on defaulted loans may be in amounts as provided in §516.031(1) for 12 months and thereafter interest shall not exceed 18% per annum. (516.035). No licensee shall charge interest greater than 18% for loans of more than $25,000 in the aggregate to same borrower or other person who may be jointly or severally liable to licensee for more than $25,000. If loan of $25,000 or less used to discharge preexisting debt for goods or services to provider of goods or services, licensee may charge such person 18% interest on guaranty of such loan. Acceptance of one or more such guarantees shall not affect rights of licensee to charge primary borrower charges authorized by §516.031. (516.21[1]).

Interest on sale of motor vehicles regulated by Motor Vehicle Sales Finance Act. (520.01 et seq.).

Judgments and decrees entered after Oct. 1, 1981, shall bear interest at rate set by Comptroller of State (55.03[1]), unless rate of interest was established by written contract or obligation (55.03[1]). Judgments not indicating rate of interest, or referencing statutory rate of interest (55.03[1]), will not be docketed or collected by county sheriffs (55.03[4]). Judgments and decrees on evidences of indebtedness of county or special road and bridge districts or incorporated city or town or taxing district bear interest at 5% or at lower rate if such provided for in such evidence of indebtedness. (55.04).

Municipal Bonds.—Interest on same not to exceed 7¹/₂% per annum. (159.08[1]).

Requirement of Receipt.—On receiving payment lender, other than bank, trust company, savings and loan association or insurance company, must give receipt, dated same day as payment, stating amount paid and whether principal or interest, and signed by person receiving payment. Entire interest forfeited by refusal to give such receipt. In lieu of providing such receipt, lender may furnish to borrower annual statement showing interest paid on loan during previous year as well as balance of loan, unless payment is made in cash or request of receipt made in writing. (687.08, 687.10).

Purchase of Assignment of Wages.—Where payment of $25,000 or less for any assignment of wages or compensation is less than amount of wages or compensation assigned, payment is deemed loan and excess is deemed interest until date when such compensation is payable and subject to laws relating to interest rates and usury. (516.26). Wage assignments prohibited. (516.17).

Usury.—Charge of more than 18% per annum interest to individual or corporation unlawful, and if loan exceeds $500,000 in amount or value, then charge of more than 25% prescribed by 687.071 is unlawful (687.01-.03) but provision not applicable to sales of bonds in excess of $100 and mortgages securing same or money loaned on bonds, or on certain loans for which commitment to insure or guarantee is given by FHA, VA, and other federal agencies. (687.03) Provision inapplicable to alien borrowers in connection with international or foreign business. (687.13). Where usurious interest charged, all interest is forfeited and where such interest is collected, double such collected interest forfeited. Penalty provision inapplicable to holder in due course of negotiable paper unless holder had actual notice before purchase or usury appears on face of instrument, or if prior to action or filing of defense by borrower or receipt by lender of notice that usury has been charged or collected, lender notifies borrower of usurious overcharge and refunds same plus interest on overcharge. (687.04). Person or company which lends money, extends credit, sells or leases goods may pursuant to contract charge on delinquency up to 5% on each installment which is in default for at least ten days. Charge not deemed interest or finance charge and may not be included when determining limits on charges. (687.03[2][c]).

Criminal Usury.—Extension of credit at annual rate of 25%-45% is second degree misdemeanor, punishable by imprisonment (60 days) and/or fine ($500). (687.071[2], 775.082[4], 775.083[1]). Extension of credit at annual rate in excess of 45% is third degree felony, punishable by imprisonment (five years) and/or fine ($5,000). (687.071[3], 775.082[3], 775.083[1]). Keeping of books and records for loans at annual rate of 25% or more is separate crime (first degree misdemeanor, one year and/or fine $1,000. (687.071[5], 775.082[4], 775.083[1]). If loan or forbearance is criminal, debt is not enforceable. (687.071[7]).

LICENSES, BUSINESS AND PROFESSIONAL:

Numerous professions are required to be licensed by and are regulated by Florida Department of Professional Regulation. (c. 455 et seq.). These professions include hypnosis (c. 456), acupuncture (c. 457), medical practice (c. 458), osteopathy (c. 459), chiropractic (c. 460), podiatry (c. 461), naturopathy (c. 462), optometry (c. 463), nursing (c. 464), pharmacy (c. 465), dentistry (c. 466), midwifery (c. 467), miscellaneous professions including speech-language pathology, nursing home administration, occupational therapy, radiologic technology, respiratory therapy, auctioneers, talent agencies, community association management, athlete agents, dietetics and nutrition practice, employee leasing companies, water and wastewater operators and building code administrators and inspectors (c. 468), asbestos abatement (c. 469), funeral directing, embalming and direct disposition (c. 470), engineering (c. 471), land surveying (c. 472), public accountancy (c. 473), veterinary medicalpractice (c. 474), real estate brokers, salespersons and appraisers (c. 475), barbering (c. 476), cosmetology (c. 477), electrolysis (c. 478), outdoor advertising (c. 479), massage practice (c. 480), architecture and interior design and landscape architecture (c. 481), pest control (c. 482), health testing services (c. 483), dispensing optical devices and hearing aids (c. 484), physical therapy practice (c. 486), pesticides (c. 487), commercial driving schools (c. 488), contracting (c. 489), psychological services (c. 490), clinical counseling and psychotherapy services (c. 491), geology (c. 492), and private investigators, private security and repossession services (c. 493). Licenses are also required for mortgage brokers (c. 494), yacht and ship brokers (c. 326), motor vehicles (c. 320), operators of motor vehicles (c. 322) and sale of alcoholic beverages (c. 561).

Practically all business and professional pursuits are required to pay a license tax. This tax is imposed in addition to permit, etc. or other regulatory fees. (205.013 et seq.). Licenses are issued for only one year, are due and payable on or before Sept. 30 of each year and expire on Sept. 30 of succeeding year. If Sept. 30 falls on weekend or holiday, tax shall be due and payable on or before first working day following Sept. 30. (205.053). Business licenses may be transferred upon payment of transfer fee of up to 10% of annual license tax but not less than $3 nor more than $25. (205.033). License taxes are levied by local county or municipality, and license must be procured from them. (205.032, 205.043).

Licenses not renewed when due and payable are subject to delinquency penalty of 10% for month of Oct. plus 5% penalty for each succeeding month until paid. Total penalty shall not exceed 25% of occupational license fee. (205.053).

Commercial Travelers.—There is no license tax against commercial travelers as such, but agents of certain businesses must pay a license fee.

MONOPOLIES, RESTRAINT OF TRADE AND COMPETITION:

Florida Antitrust Act of 1980 (542.15 et seq.) prohibits every contract, combination, or conspiracy in restraint of trade or commerce (542.18) and monopolization, attempts to monopolize, and conspiracies or combinations to monopolize (542.19). Language similar to §§1, 2 of Sherman Act (construed in pari materia with federal antitrust law—542.32).

Combinations affecting price or sale of meat (c. 544), and motor vehicle financing (c. 545) are prohibited or regulated by special provisions.

Penalties.—Knowing violation of §§542.18 or 542.19 is felony. Knowing violation includes one who knowingly aids in or advises such violation. (542.21[2]). Alternative civil penalty is provided. (542.21[1]). Private actions for treble damages are authorized. (542.22[1]).

Contracts in Restraint of Trade.—All contracts in restraint of trade are void except for following: (1) Person selling goodwill of business or any shareholder selling or otherwise disposing of all his shares in corporation may agree with buyer, and employee, independent contractor or agent may agree with employer not to carry on similar business or solicit employer's old customers within reasonably limited time and area and for so long as buyer or employer continues like business therein; (2) partners may agree on dissolution of partnership that all or some will not carry on similar business within reasonably limited time and area; (3) licensee, or any person deriving title from licensee, of use of trademark or service mark and business format or system identified by that trademark or service mark may agree with licensor to refrain from carrying on or engaging in similar business and from soliciting old

See note at head of Digest as to 1998 legislation covered.

See Topical Index in front part of this volume.

MONOPOLIES, RESTRAINT OF TRADE AND COMPETITION . . . *continued*

customers of licensor within reasonably limited time and area, so long as licensor or any person deriving title from licensor continues to carry on like business. (542.33). Such agreements may be enforced by injunction except where injunction would be contrary to public health, safety or welfare or in any case where injunction would enforce unreasonable covenant not to compete or where there is no showing of irreparable injury. (542.33[2][a]).

Unfair Discrimination and Competition.—Any person doing business in state, and engaged in production, manufacture, sale or distribution of any commodity in general use, who, for purpose of destroying competitor's business in any locality, discriminates between different sections, communities, or cities of state by selling at lower rate in one than in another, after allowing for differences in grade, quality and transportation costs, is guilty of unfair discrimination, unless such discrimination is made in good faith to meet competition. (540.01[1]). Unfair discrimination is punishable as misdemeanor. (540.06).

Fraudulent Practices.—Certain actions are labeled fraudulent or deceptive and penalties for their violation are provided. (c. 817; c. 501, Part II). These include false pretenses, unauthorized subleasing of automobiles, misrepresentations of academic standing or association with any postsecondary educational institution, and credit card crimes. (c. 817). Use of telephone and other communications, media and devices in scheme to defraud is prohibited. (817.034).

Misbranded and adulterated foods, drugs, cosmetics prohibited. (cc. 499; 500).

Posting different gasoline prices at same retail service station for same grade of gasoline is unlawful. (526.121[1]). Price differential permitted if one pump self-service and other attendant operated or between cash and credit sales. (526.121[2]).

Unfair competition and deceptive trade practices, as defined by administrative regulations, which must not be inconsistent with provisions of §5(a)(i) of 15 U.S.C. §45(a)(1) as incorporated by federal courts, or inconsistent with rules, regulations and decisions of Federal Trade Commission, are proscribed. Civil and criminal penalties provided for violation. (501.201-.213). See also topic Consumer Protection.

Resale Price Agreements.—Florida Fair Trade Law (541.001-.09), repealed by c. 75-15. Now covered by Florida Antitrust Act of 1980, §§542.18-.19 (construed in pari materia with federal antitrust law-542.32).

NEGOTIABLE INSTRUMENTS:

Uniform Commercial Code adopted. (cc. 670-680). See topic Commercial Code.

RESTRAINT OF TRADE:

See topic Monopolies, and Restraint of Trade and Competition.

SALES:

Uniform Commercial Code adopted. (cc. 670-680). See topic Commercial Code.

Contracts of Sale.—See topic Frauds, Statute of.

Bills of Sale.—Seals and acknowledgments not required. (See category Documents and Records, topic Seals.) A bill of sale intended to secure payment of money is deemed to be a mortgage. (697.01). Bills of sale may be recorded in the office of clerk of circuit court. (28.222). See category Documents and Records, topic Records.

Retail Installment, Motor Vehicle and Home Improvement Sales.—Content of contracts, effective interest rate, solicitation of, collections on account of, etc., regulated by The Retail Installment Sales Act. (520.30-.42). Biennial license fee and maintenance of agent in Florida for service of process are required. Somewhat similar provisions with respect to sales of motor vehicles and home improvements are in Motor Vehicle Sales Finance Act (520.01-.13) and Home Improvement Sales and Finance Act (520.60-.992). All foregoing laws conform with federal truth in lending legislation, but with certain additional purely local requirements.

Consumer Protection.—See topic Consumer Protection.

Home Solicitation Sales.—See topic Consumer Protection.

Game promotions are regulated comprehensively by department of legal affairs. (849.094).

Unsolicited Merchandise.—Recipient has no obligation to return or accept delivery and may dispose of same as if they were gifts. (570.545).

Bulk Sales.—U.C.C. Art. 6 repealed.

Resale Price Agreements.—See topic Monopolies, Restraint of Trade and Competition.

Sales of art including consignment sales and required warranties, regulated by statute. (686.501 et seq.).

See also topic Consumer Protection; category Debtor and Creditor, topic Fraudulent Sales and Conveyances.

SECURITIES:

Uniform Securities Act has not been adopted, but Florida Securities and Investor Protection Act is in effect (c. 517) and takes precedence over any inconsistent provision of Uniform Commercial Code (671.304[2]). See topic Commercial Code. See also "Sale or Lease of Business Opportunities Act". (§§559.80-559.815).

Supervision is by Department of Banking and Finance. (517.03).

Regulatory Powers of Supervising Authority.—Department has rule making power and power to enforce statute in courts and administratively. (517.03). Department of Banking and Finance may revoke or suspend security's registration or may deny application if its appears that issuer or control person of issuer is insolvent, has violated any provision of which issuer has notice, has engaged or is about to engage in fraudulent transactions, has been found guilty of fraudulent act in connection with sale of securities, has demonstrated any evidence of unworthiness, is subject to injunction or administrative stop order prohibiting sale of security, issuer's application under §517.081 exhibits inequitable terms, or issuer failed to timely complete application for registration. (517.111).

Prerequisites to Sales or Offerings.—Securities may not be sold or offered for sale within Florida, unless of class exempt under §517.051 or sold in exempt transaction under §517.061 all of which exemptions are self-executing and do not require registration under §517.07, or are federal covered securities or are registered pursuant to this subsection. (517.07). Provisions regarding fraud and concealment (517.301), false representations (517.311) and boiler rooms and prohibited practices (517.312) do apply to exempt transactions under 517.061 and 517.051. (517.312).

Securities and Investments to which Act Applies.—Security defined to include notes, stock, treasury stock, bonds, debentures, evidences of indebtedness, certificates of interest or participation, whiskey or commodity warehouse receipts, certificates of interest or participation in profit sharing agreements or oil, gas, petroleum, mineral or mining titles or leases, collateral trust certificates, reorganization certificates, investment contracts, certificate of deposits, certificate of deposit for security, preorganization subscription, any transferable share, investment contract, or beneficial interest in title to property, profits, or earnings, interests in or under profit sharing or participation agreement or scheme, any option contract which entitles holder to buy or sell amount of underlying security at fixed price within specified period of time, and all rights to subscribe to or purchase any securities. (517.021[17]).

For purpose of false representations and other prohibited practices, investment means any commitment of money or property, not otherwise security, in expectation of receiving economic benefit, but excluding certain sales. (517.301[2]).

Exempt Securities.—Registration provisions of Act do not apply to: Securities issued by U.S., any State, territory, possession or political subdivision, or by most foreign nations and political subdivisions thereof, or by national banks and certain other banks and associations and corporations created by U.S.; nor to certain securities issued or guaranteed by railroads and other regulated public utilities; nor to securities issued by religious, educational, charitable and other similar corporations, provided that offers or sales of such securities may be made only by offering circular containing full and fair disclosure of all material information in accordance with statutory and regulatory provisions; nor to any security issued or guaranteed by bank, trust company, savings institution or building or savings and loan association, international development bank or credit union when said entity is subject to examination, supervision or control of State of Florida or Federal Deposit Insurance Corporation or National Credit Union Association. (517.051). Initial subscriptions for equity securities of bank, trust company, saving institution or building or savings and loan association will be exempt if such institution is subject to examination, supervision or control of State of Florida; nor to securities (other than common stock) outstanding for at least five years without default in payment of fixed return; nor to securities issued by nonprofit Florida agricultural cooperatives when sold to persons principally engaged in production or sale of agricultural products; nor to any insurance or endowment policy or annuity contract or optional annuity contract, or self-insurance agreement issued by corporation, insurance company, reciprocal insurer, or risk retention group subject to supervision of insurance commissioner, bank commissioner or any agency or officer performing functions, of any state or territory of U.S., or District of Columbia. (517.051).

Exempt Transactions.—Following are generally exempt (517.061) but may be subject to statutory notice, escrow and other conditions: Sales by trustee in bankruptcy and judicial sales; sales by certain fiduciaries, by pledgees and mortgagees; isolated sales neither by nor for issuer or underwriter; distributions by unincorporated and incorporated issuers of securities to existing security holders as stock dividend or other distribution out of earnings or surplus; issuance of securities by unincorporated and incorporated issuers to security holders or creditors in reorganization proceedings; any transaction involving distribution of securities of issuer exclusively among its own security holders where no commission paid; sales to banks, trusts, trust companies, brokers and dealers, investment companies as defined by Investment Company Act of 1940; or pension or profit sharing trust or qualified institutional buyer, whether any of such entities is acting in its individual or fiduciary capacity; sale of securities from one corporation to another, which securities have sales price over $50,000, when buyer and seller corporations have assets in excess of $500,000; sales or exchanges with other corporations or their security holders in connection with mergers; issuance of notes or bonds in connection with acquisition of real property or renewals thereof, if such notes or bonds are issued to sellers of, and are secured by all or part of, real property acquired; exchanges pursuant to conversion rights; sale by issuer of its own securities to not more than 35 persons in state within any consecutive 12 month period if certain conditions met; sales by Florida and national banks whose profit therefrom does not exceed 2%; transactions by registered dealers at or near current market price if issuer registered under §13 or §15(d) of Securities Exchange Act of 1934 if securities are dealt in on any stock exchange registered under Securities Exchange Act of 1934; cooperative apartments; unsolicited purchases or sales by registered dealers; sale of securities under employer-sponsored pension or profit-sharing plan when offered only to employees of sponsoring organization, or to employees of controlled subsidiaries; sale by or through registered dealer of certain securities options; and certain sales for purpose of constructing rental housing. (517.061).

Registration of Securities.—Registration is by qualification on Department's prescribed forms, and payment of filing fee of $1,000 (517.081) or by notification (517.082) ($1,000 filing fee) upon request of issuer or any registered dealer. Registration by notification is not available for securities offering price of which was $5 per share or less, unless listed on registered stock exchange or through NASDAQ, or unless such securities are of same issuer and of senior or substantially equal rank to securities so listed. (517.082[3]). If issue found not to be fraudulent, terms of sale fair, just and equitable and issuer's business not based on unsound business principles, securities may be sold (517.081[7]), but Department may regulate commissions (517.081[5]), require escrow of promotional stock (517.181) and otherwise condition registrations.

See note at head of Digest as to 1998 legislation covered.

See Topical Index in front part of this volume.

SECURITIES . . . continued

Registration of Dealers, Salesmen, Investment Advisers and Branch Offices.—No person may engage in such business unless application is first filed with and approved by Department. (517.12). With few exceptions, every dealer shall be registered with SEC. (517.12[16]). Federally regulated advisors must file with Department copy of documents required to be filed with Securities Exchange Commission, along with consent to service of process and $200 filing fee, per year, expiring on Dec. 31 unless renewed. (517.1201). Any branch office from which such business is conducted must be registered with Department. (517.12[5]). Department may require examination. (517.12[8]). Registrations may be refused, suspended, restricted or revoked for stated causes after notice and hearing. (517.161). Registration of associated persons is specific to dealer or investment advisor identified at time registration is approved and previously registered associated persons are required to file new application for registration when that person seeks to be associated with new securities dealer or investment advisor. (517.1205). Application fee for dealer or investment advisor $200, associated person $20, plus cost of fingerprint card if current card not on file with NASD. (517.12[10]). Dealers and investment advisors to pay $100 fee for each office in Florida, except principal office. (517.12[10]). Each dealer, investment adviser and branch office required to keep record of currency transactions in excess of $10,000. (517.12[14]).

Liabilities and Remedies.—Federal statutory civil remedies for purchasers or sellers made applicable. (517.241[3]). Purchaser of securities sold in violation of Act may void same and recover price of security or investment, interest and attorney's fees from seller and all officers and agents who participated or aided in sale (517.211), but such rights generally conditional on prior tender back to seller. See category Civil Actions and Procedure, topic Limitation of Actions. Purchaser may be entitled to relief from Securities Guaranty Fund. (517.131). §517.241(2) which preserves person's statutory and common law right to bring court action for any act involving sale of securities found invalid under supremacy clause (453 So.2d 858) because of conflict with Federal Arbitration Act 9 U.S.C. §§1 to 14 (1976). Ability to bring action to court subject to Federal Arbitration Act 9 U.S.C. §§1 to 14 (1976).

Violation of Act is third degree felony or first degree felony, depending on size of damages. Violator may be assessed fine equal to triple damages caused or profit gained. (517.302).

Tender Offers.—No specific provisions.

Florida Uniform Land Sales Practices Law adopted with significant modifications including major revisions in 1988. (c. 498).

Uniform Simplification of Fiduciary Security Transfers Act adopted (c. 610), and takes precedence over Uniform Commercial Code (671.304[2]).

Uniform Securities Ownership by Minors Act not adopted.

Uniform Commercial Code adopted. (cc. 670-680). See topic Commercial Code.

STATUTE OF FRAUDS:

See topic Frauds, Statute of.

TRUST RECEIPT SECURITY:

Uniform Commercial Code adopted. (cc. 670-680). See topic Commercial Code.

WAREHOUSEMEN:

Uniform Commercial Code adopted. (cc. 670-680). See topic Commercial Code.

Bonds.—No provisions with respect to bonds of warehousemen.

CITIZENSHIP

ALIENS:

Generally aliens may not vote (97.041), hold certain public offices (Const., art. 4, §5; art. 3, §§2, 15), or serve on juries (40.01).

Alien may not be disqualified from practicing occupation or profession regulated by state solely because of alien status. (455.10).

Unauthorized Employment.—It is unlawful for any person knowingly to employ, hire, recruit or refer for private or public employment within state, alien who is not duly authorized to work by immigration laws or U.S. Attorney General. (448.09[1]). First violation for unauthorized employment shall be punishable by civil fine of not more than $500. (448.09[2]). Person who subsequently violates statutes will be guilty of second degree misdemeanor, and each subsequent violation will constitute separate offense. (448.09[3]). (*Note:* This statute must be considered in relation to Federal Immigration Reform and Control Act of 1986, which provides comprehensive scheme of employer sanctions for unauthorized employment of illegal aliens.)

Property.—Aliens eligible to become citizens of U.S. have same rights as to ownership, inheritance and disposition of property as citizens. (Const. art. 1, §2).

Personal representative of nonresident alien decedent whose gross estate included property located in state must file executed copy of federal estate tax return with Department of Revenue. (198.13).

Proceedings.—In any proceeding affecting property, special rules apply to notice or service of process upon person, firm or corporation located in any territory under control of any country which is at war with U.S. Copy of notice or service of process must be sent by registered or certified mail to Alien Property Custodian, Washington, D. C., but failure to send such copy does not invalidate proceedings. (48.131).

Arrest.—Official arresting an alien must notify nearest consul or other officer of nation of which alien is a citizen if U.S. has diplomatic relations with that nation. (901.26).

Convicted Offenders.—Governor or his designee is authorized to consent to transfer of convicted alien offender to country of which offender is national when treaty is in effect between U.S. and foreign country providing for such transfer. (944.596).

Felony Records.—Clerk committing alien to any state or county institution for conviction of felony must furnish any records pertaining to case to U.S. Immigration officer upon request. (943.0535).

Unemployment Compensation—Alien Agricultural Workers.—State law conformed to changes in federal law postponing coverage of alien agricultural workers. This act applies to agricultural labor services performed after Dec. 31, 1992 by individual who is alien admitted to U.S. to perform agricultural labor services pursuant to 214(c) and 101(a) (15) (H) of Immigration and Nationality Act, and shall operate retroactively to Jan. 1, 1986. (443.036[19][e][3]). Aliens, felony records—clerk of court committing alien to any state or county institution for conviction of felony must furnish any records pertaining to case to U.S. Immigration officer upon request. (943.0535).

CIVIL ACTIONS AND PROCEDURE

ACCORD AND SATISFACTION:

Common law rules govern.

Pleading.—Accord and satisfaction must be affirmatively pleaded. (R. C. P. 1.110[d]). Avoidance of accord and satisfaction must also be pleaded. (R. C. P. 1.100[a], R. C. P. 1.110[d]).

Uniform Commercial Code adopted. See category Business Regulation and Commerce, topic Commercial Code.

ACTIONS:

Rules of Civil Procedure are similar to Federal Rules of Civil Procedure.

Forms of Pleadings.—Forms of action and technical forms for seeking relief and of pleas, pleadings, or motions are abolished. (R.C.P. 1.110[a]).

Conditions Precedent.—Generally there are no conditions precedent to institution of actions. However as to some causes of action or actions against certain parties there are such conditions. (See, e.g., 713.06; 768.28[6][b]; 770.01). In pleading performance or occurrence of conditions precedent, it is sufficient to aver generally that all conditions precedent have been performed or have occurred. (R.C.P. 1.120[c]). Action may not be instituted against state, state agency or subdivision unless claim is first presented in writing to both appropriate agency and Department of Insurance within three years from when claim accrues. Claimants against municipalities and Spaceport Florida Authority need not notify Department of Insurance. (768.28[6][a]).

Commencement.—See topics Process, Pleading. (R.C.P. 1.050).

Parties.—Every action may be prosecuted in name of real party in interest and all persons having an interest in subject of the action or relief demanded may join as plaintiffs, and any person may be made a defendant who has or claims an interest adverse to plaintiff. (R.C.P. 1.210 [a]). Executor, administrator, guardian, trustee of express trust, party with whom or in whose name contract has been made for benefit of another or party expressly authorized by statute may sue in own name without joining party for whose benefit action is brought. (R.C.P. 1.210 [a]). Any person may at any time be made party if his presence is necessary or proper to complete determination of cause. (R. C. P. 1.210[a]). Misjoinder of parties is not ground for dismissal of action. (R.C.P. 1.250 [a]). Any claim against party may be severed and proceeded with separately. (R.C.P. 1.250 [a]). Parties may be dropped or added by court on motion or of its own initiative at any stage of action on such terms as are just. (R. C. P. 1.250[b]). See also c. 46; R. C. P. 1.230 (interventions); 1.240 (interpleader); 1.260 (survivor and substitution of parties).

Class Actions.—One party may maintain any claim or defense on behalf of all members of class when: (1) Class members are so numerous that separate joinder of each member is impractical; (2) questions of law or fact raised by representative party are common to those of each class member; (3) claim or defense of representative party is typical of those of each class member; and (4) representative party can fairly and adequately protect and represent interest of each class member. (R. C. P. 1.220[a]).

After control of condominium association is obtained by owners other than developer, association may represent unit owners in matters of common interest. (R. C. P. 1.221).

Uniform Class Action Act not adopted.

Interventions.—Anyone claiming interest in pending litigation may at any time be permitted to assert right by intervention but intervention shall be in subordination to, and in recognition of, propriety of main proceeding, unless ordered by court. (R. C. P. 1.230).

Interpleader.—Persons having claims against plaintiff may be joined as defendants and required to interplead when their claims are such that plaintiff is or may be exposed to double or multiple liability. (R.C.P. 1.240). Defendant exposed to similar liability may obtain interpleader by crossclaim or counterclaim. (R.C.P. 1.240). No objection to joinder that claims do not have common origin or that plaintiff denies liability to any or all claimants. (R. C. P. 1.240).

Third Party Practice.—Similar to Federal Rules. Defendant may also assert any other claim against third party that arises out of transaction or occurrence that is subject matter of plaintiff's claim. (R.C.P. 1.180). Defendant need not obtain leave of court if he files third party complaint not later than 20 days after his answer is originally served. (R.C.P. 1.180). Otherwise, defendant must obtain leave on motion and notice to all parties to action. (R.C.P. 1.180).

Joinder.—Causes of action, of whatever kind, by and against same parties in same right, may be joined in same suit. (R. C. P. 1.110[g]). Several causes of action may be joined and claims aggregated to confer jurisdiction only if such claims are related. (86 Fla. 376, 98 So. 140; 100 Fla. 489, 129 So. 816).

Consolidation and Severance.—When actions involving common question of law or fact are pending before court, it may order joint hearing or trial of any or all matters

ACTIONS . . . *continued*
at issue or consolidation of all actions. (R. C. P. 1.270[a]). Court may also order separate trial of any claim, cross-claim, counter-claim or third party claim or of any separate issue or of any number of claims or issues to further convenience or avoid prejudice. (R. C. P. 1.270[b]; see also R. C. P. 1.170[i]).

Stay of Proceedings.—No general provisions governing stays. Court may grant stay of execution or other process based on final judgment for good cause on motion and notice to all adverse parties. (R.C.P. 1.550[b]). See also topic Appeal and Error.

Abatement and Revival.—All actions survive death of party and may be commenced, prosecuted or defended in name of person prescribed by law. (46.021; see also R.C.P. 1.260[a]). If party dies and claim is not thereby extinguished, court may order substitution of proper parties. Unless motion for substitution made within 90 days after death is suggested upon record by service of statement of fact of death, action shall be dismissed as to deceased party. Where action survives to surviving plaintiff, or against surviving defendant, if there be two or more plaintiffs, or defendants, one or more of whom dies, action does not abate, but upon suggestion of death, it proceeds in favor of or against surviving parties. (R. C. P. 1.260[a]). Claim must be filed with estate pursuant to 733.702. Generally, actions which have not been prosecuted for period of one year shall be dismissed by court on its own motion or on motion of any interested person, whether party to action or not, after notice to parties unless stipulation staying action is approved by court or stay order has been filed or party shows good cause in writing at least five days before hearing on motion seeking dismissal. (R. C. P. 1.420[e]). Marriage of woman shall not cause action to abate. (708.08).

Limitation of.—See topic Limitation of Actions.

Small Claims.—See category Courts and Legislature, topic Courts.

Prohibited Actions.—Actions for breach of contract to marry, alienation of affections, seduction or criminal conversation, are abolished. (771.01).

Estate Administration.—See category Estates and Trusts, topic Executors and Administrators.

Direct Actions Against Insurer.—See category Transportation, topic Motor Vehicles.

APPEAL AND ERROR:

Appellate jurisdiction of Supreme Court, district courts of appeal, and circuit courts set forth in Florida constitution, Art. 5. Rules governing appeals in such courts are prescribed by Supreme Court in Florida Appellate Rules.

To Supreme Court.—Appeals from trial courts may be taken directly to Supreme Court, as matter of right, only from judgments imposing death penalty and decisions of district courts of appeal declaring invalid state statute or provision of state constitution, and when provided by general law, from final orders in proceedings for validation of bonds or certificates of indebtedness and actions of statewide agencies relating to rates or service of utilities providing electric, gas, or telephone service. (Rule 9.030, App. Rules). See topic Certiorari.

To District Courts of Appeal.—Appeals may be taken of right to district courts of appeal from final orders of trial courts not directly reviewable by supreme court or circuit court and nonfinal orders of circuit courts which concern venue or which grant, continue, modify, deny or dissolve or refuse to modify or dissolve injunctions, or which determine jurisdiction of person, right to immediate possession of property, right to immediate monetary relief or child custody in domestic relations matters, of issue of liability in favor of party seeking affirmative relief, or whether party is entitled to arbitration and administrative action when provided by general law. (Rule 9.030, App. Rules). See topic Certiorari.

Certain questions certified to District Court of Appeal as being of great public importance may be accepted by district court.

To Circuit Courts.—Circuit courts have appellate jurisdiction over final orders of lower tribunals as provided by general law, nonfinal orders of lower tribunals which concern venue or which grant, continue, modify, deny, or dissolve or refuse to modify or dissolve injunctions, or which determine jurisdiction of person, right to immediate possession of property, right to immediate monetary relief or child custody in domestic relations matters, of issue of liability in favor of party seeking affirmative relief, or whether party is entitled to arbitration and administrative action when provided by law. (Rule 9.030, App. Rules). See topic Certiorari.

Limitations.—Appeals from final decisions, orders, judgments or decrees must be commenced within 30 days from rendition of final decision, order, or judgment appealed from. (Rule 9.110, App. Rules). Appeals from partial final judgments may be taken immediately or after final judgment entered. Appeal must be taken when partial final judgment disposes of entire case as to any party within 30 days of rendition. (Rule 9.110[k] App. Rules). Filing of timely motion for new trial or rehearing, to alter or amend, for judgment in accordance with prior motion for directed verdict, n.o.v., in arrest of judgment, or challenge to verdict, tolls time for filing notice of appeal and notice of appeal filed within 30 days of denial of motion is timely. (Rule 9.020[h], App. Rules).

Bonds.—A bond is not required in an appeal except to make the appeal operate as a supersedeas. (Rule 9.310, App. Rules). State or political subdivision need not give bond unless required by order of court. (Rule 9.310, App. Rules).

Stays.—Appeal operates as supersedeas if appellant applies to trial court for stay. Court may require bond, other conditions, or both. If appeal is from money judgment or decree, stay is automatic on posting bond conditioned to satisfy judgment or decree or any modification thereof not increasing its amount, including costs, interest, fees, and damages for delay equal to principal amount of judgment plus twice statutory rate of interest on judgments on total amount upon which party has obligation to pay interest. Timely filing of notice operates as stay pending review of award by deputy commissioner on claim for birth-related neurological injury. (Rule 9.310, App. Rules).

Notice of Appeal.—Two copies of notice are filed with clerk of lower tribunal within 30 days of rendition of order together with filing fee prescribed by law except in appeal of administrative action where appellant shall pay fee and file second copy of notice with court. (Rule 9.110[b], [c], [d], App. Rules).

BONDS:

Many special districts and authorities have authority to issue bonds. Advance Refunding Law provides for issuance of bonds. (c. 132).

Sureties.—See category Insurance, topic Surety and Guaranty Companies.

Ballroom dance studios receiving advance payment from customers in excess of $250 and in business under same ownership less than three years, or entering retail installment contracts for dance studio services or lessons must maintain mechanism for ensuring customer refunds in form of bond issued by surety company admitted to do business in Florida, irrevocable letter of credit, or guaranty agreement secured by certificate of deposit. (501.143[5]). Department may require any ballroom dance studio that has operated or is operating in violation of this section or Department rules to post security bond not to exceed $25,000. (501.143[7][c]).

Certain health studios which sell contracts for health studio services must maintain bond of $50,000 and file it with Department of Agriculture and Consumer Services. In lieu of maintaining bond, health studio may furnish to department irrevocable letter of credit from any bank in amount of $50,000, or guaranty agreement which is secured by certificate of deposit in amount of $50,000. Health studio which collects payments for services monthly is exempt from bond. In addition, bond may be reduced if health studio proves that aggregate dollar amount of all current outstanding contracts is less than $5,000. (501.016).

Contractors.—Municipality or county may require bond not to exceed $5,000 for construction contractors (489.131[3]) and electrical contractors (489.537[3]).

Building Construction Standards–Plumbing.—Counties may elect to require any person who desires to engage in plumbing activities within county to file with Clerk of Circuit Court $5,000 bond conditioned upon said person complying with minimum requirements of State Plumbing Code. (489.131).

Educational and Ancillary Plant Construction Funds (235.42).—Encumbrances of funds for authorized projects may include proceeds received under resolution approved by State Board of Education authorizing issuance of public education capital outlay bonds pursuant to Art. XII, §9(a)(2), Fla. Const. (235.42).

Florida Housing Finance Corporation Act (420.501 et seq.) provides that negotiated sale of revenue bonds issued on corporation's behalf is preferable to public sale and that Division of Bond Finance is authorized to negotiate such sale with corporation-designated underwriters. (420.509[12] et seq.). Bonds issued to provide financing for construction of project must be secured in manner corporation determines will reasonably protect interests of Corporation and shareholders. (420.508[3][a][4]). Discrimination is prohibited by sponsor while bonds are outstanding for purpose of funding or financing sponsor's project. (420.516). "Finder" is one who acts as intermediary between issuer of bonds and managing underwriter for purpose of influencing any transaction in purchase of bond. (420.509[14]). If bond proceeds are used to finance housing project under §420.509, 20% of tenants must have annual income under 80% of state or county median income, whichever is higher. (420.509[19]). Pursuant to Florida Affordable Housing Guarantee Program (420.5092), corporation may issue revenue bonds to establish guarantee fund. Such revenue bonds shall be primarily payable from annual debt service reserves, interest earned on funds, fees, charges, reimbursements or other revenue sources. Revenue bonds may only be issued once validated by provisions of c. 75. (420.5092[10]). Maximum total of revenue bonds issued by corporation is $200 million. (420.5092[11]).

Allocation of private activity bonds (Internal Revenue Code §103[n]) provided for in c. 159 (Part VI).

Registered Public Obligations Act (c. 279) requires bonds and other evidence of indebtedness to be registered in order to be exempt from federal income taxation (279.03).

State Lands–Petroleum Exploration and Production Bond Trust Fund.—Board of Trustees may require surety or property bond from lessee of public lands before lessee may commence extraction in any manner of petroleum or petroleum products from said public lands. (253.571).

Title Insurance–Agents.—Title insurance agency must either deposit securities with Department of Insurance or post surety bond with Department with market value of no less than $35,000 payable to damaged insurer making claim on bond. (626.8418[2]).

Transportation.—Issuance of state bonds to finance or refinance cost of acquiring real property or state bridge construction is authorized by §215.605(1).

Water Resources—Revenue Bonds.—Powers and authorities of districts to issue revenue bonds, including, but not limited to, bonds to finance stormwater management system as defined by §373.403, and to enter into contracts incidental thereto, and to do all things necessary and desirable in connection with issuance of revenue bonds, shall be coextensive with powers and authority of municipalities to issue bonds under state law. (373.584).

CERTIORARI:

District courts and circuit courts may issue writs of certiorari except for those cases in which direct appeal of non-final orders is permitted; see topic Appeal and Error. (App. Rule 9.030).

Application for writ of certiorari must be within 30 days of decision sought to be reviewed and procedure is governed by Florida appellate rules. (App. Rule 9.100).

Supreme Court may, in its discretion, review certain matters, under Const. art. 5, §3 and App. Rule 9.030, although such review is not technically by certiorari. Supreme Court does not have certiorari jurisdiction. Such discretionary jurisdiction may be sought to review decisions of district courts that: expressly declare state statute valid;

See note at head of Digest as to 1998 legislation covered.

See Topical Index in front part of this volume.

FL – 13

CERTIORARI . . . *continued*

expressly construe provision of state or federal constitution; expressly affect class of constitutional or state officers; expressly and directly conflict with decision of another district court or Supreme Court on same point of law; pass upon question certified to be of great public importance or in direct conflict with decisions of other district courts. Discretionary jurisdiction also to review orders and judgments of trial courts certified by district courts to require immediate resolution by Supreme Court and of great public importance or to have great effect on proper administration of justice. Supreme Court also may review questions of law certified by U.S. Supreme Court or court of appeals that are determinative of case and for which there is no controlling precedent of Supreme Court of Florida. (Const. art. 5, §3; App. Rule 9.030).

CHARITABLE IMMUNITY:

See topic Damages.

COMMISSIONS TO TAKE TESTIMONY:

See topic Depositions and Discovery.

COSTS:

Costs in cases at law generally are recovered by prevailing party; they are included in judgment. (57.041). Premiums on bonds or other security are allowed as part of costs along with necessary costs for court reporting services and any sales or use tax due on legal services provided to such party. (57.071). However, court may exercise discretion in awarding costs in equity matters. Costs on appeal are recoverable by prevailing party. (App. Rule 9.400).

In all criminal cases, cost of prosecution, including investigative costs, must be included in judgment rendered against convicted person. (938.27). Additional cost of $20 must be imposed on any person, except political subdivision, who pleads guilty or nolo contendere to, or is convicted of, any violation of law or ordinance in which victim is handicapped or elderly. (938.09).

Security for Costs.—Nonresident plaintiff or resident plaintiff who removes himself or his effects from state must, after suit is instituted, file bond with surety of $100 conditioned for payment of all costs and charges which may be adjudged against him in court in which suit is brought. (57.011).

Liability of Attorney.—Failure to file nonresident cost bond within 30 days of commencement of suit or removal from state gives defendant right, after 20 days notice to plaintiff (within which time bond may be filed), to dismiss suit or hold plaintiff's attorney liable for all plaintiff's costs and charges. (57.011).

Attorney's Fees.—Court shall award reasonable attorney's fee to prevailing party in civil action where there was complete absence of justiciable issue of either law or fact raised by losing party (57.105[1]); if contract contains provision allowing attorney fees to party when he is required to take action to enforce contract, court may also allow reasonable attorney fees to other party when that party prevails in any action with respect to contract (57.105[2]); if court finds complete absence of justiciable issue of either law or fact raised by defense, court may award prejudgment interest (57.105[1]).

See also In Re Statewide Uniform Guidelines for Taxation of Costs in Civil Actions, Florida Supreme Court Administrative Order (Oct. 28, 1981).

In certain instances, fees and costs can be recovered by prevailing entities in action initiated by department to enforce department order (120.69[7]) and by small business parties in other administrative actions (57.111).

In actions by state against persons for failure to comply with professional licensing requirements, prevailing party may recover fees and costs, and state, if it prevails, may also obtain reasonable costs of investigation. (455.228). In addition, state may impose administrative penalty not to exceed $5,000 per incident. If state is required to seek enforcement of department cease and desist order, it shall be entitled to collect its attorneys' fees and costs, together with any costs of collection. (455.228).

Person who suffers pecuniary loss or is otherwise affected adversely by failure of motor vehicle manufacturer, distributor, importer or dealer to comply with statutory licensing requirements may recover costs and fees. (320.697).

Costs and fees may be recovered by party seeking access to public records that have been improperly withheld. (119.12).

In any civil litigation involving violation of telephone solicitation statute, prevailing party, shall receive his reasonable attorneys' fees and costs from non-prevailing party. For any civil litigation initiated by Department of Legal Affairs, involving violation of telephone solicitation statute, court may award to prevailing party reasonable attorneys fees and costs if court finds that there was complete absence of justiciable issue of either law or fact raised by losing party or if court finds bad faith on part of losing party. (501.059[9]).

Prevailing party may be entitled to fees and costs resulting from consumer transaction involving violation of Florida Deceptive and Unfair Trade Practices Act. (501.2105).

Condominium association not entitled to fees and costs in unit foreclosure action for unpaid assessments where notice of foreclosure not given to unit owner at least 30 days prior to filing of foreclosure action. Fees and costs also not recoverable where unit owner pays all unpaid assessments prior to entry of final judgment of foreclosure. (718.116[6][b]).

Failure of tractor or farm equipment manufacturer, distributor, or wholesaler to repurchase inventory from dealer upon termination of franchise agreement, entitles dealer to fees and costs in maintaining action on repurchase obligation. (686.407[5]).

Prevailing party in action brought to enforce terms and conditions of prepaid health clinic contract is entitled to recover fees and costs. (641.454).

Any person who causes seizure of non-counterfeit goods shall be liable for costs, and, if seizure was instituted in bad faith, attorney's fees incurred in defending against seizure. (506.09[3]).

Fees and costs may be recovered by any person who brings action for injury caused by discharge or other condition of pollution into or upon any waters or lands of State. (376.313[5]).

Fees and costs may be awarded in action premised on unreasonable refusal to comply with statutory way of necessity. (704.04).

DAMAGES:

Just compensation is hallmark for legal damages under Florida common law. (464 F.2d 267). Exemplary or punitive damages may be imposed where private injuries partake of public wrongs. (340 So.2d 922). See subhead Punitive Damages, infra.

Misleading Advertising.—Prevailing party in civil action for misleading advertising shall be awarded costs including reasonable attorney's fees and may be awarded punitive damages in addition to actual damages proven. (817.41).

Citrus Canker.—Destruction of citrus to eradicate citrus canker was valid exercise of state's police power. However, it is also a taking which requires just compensation to be paid by state to owners of healthy plants. Statute awards damages in place of all liability of state. Amount of damages are awarded based on table included in statute. Citrus Canker Compensation Trust Fund and Office of Citrus Canker Claims are established. Some claimants are also entitled to attorney's fees. (602.015-602.099).

Collateral Source of Indemnity.—Damages awarded to claimant shall be reduced by total amounts paid for benefit of claimant from collateral sources such as: insurance (except life), or disability, from either public or private sources except when subrogation right exists. Reductions shall be offset by amounts paid by claimant or his family to secure any collateral source benefit. (768.76). Governmental and charitable benefits available to general public admissible for jury consideration when determining future care costs. (452 So.2d 514).

Comparative Fault.—Judgment against each party liable in action shall be based on party's percentage of fault; doctrine of joint and several liability only applies to economic damages and parties whose fault equals or exceeds claimant's fault. This section does not apply to pollution or intentional tort cases or actions in which total amount of damages does not exceed $25,000. (768.81).

Comparative Negligence Rule.—Adopted effective July 10, 1973. (280 So.2d 431). Effective June 12, 1975, contribution among tortfeasors provided in all causes of action then pending and thereafter filed. (768.31[7]).

Charitable Immunity.—Doctrine abrogated. (145 Fla. 360, 199 So. 344).

Agriculture and Forestry.—Various damages may be recovered by buyer for deficiencies or shortages in commercial fertilizer. (576.061). Damages may be recovered from fertilizer manufacturer by purchaser of mixed plant fertilizer for deficiencies in primary, secondary or micro plant nutrients where actual amount of nutrients falls significantly below level guaranteed by manufacturer. Where plant nutrient deficiency is found, purchaser may recover three times commercial value of deficiency. (576.061). Double damages may be recovered for knowingly using recorded lumber mark, brand or stamp. (706.05).

Libel and Slander.—Only actual damages can be recovered against newspaper, periodical or broadcast station if newspaper or periodical prints fair and equally conspicuous correction, apology and retraction within certain specified times after receipt of notice of alleged false and defamatory statements or against broadcast station if correction, apology, or retraction is broadcast at comparable time so long as libelous article or slanderous broadcast was published in good faith, its falsity was due to honest mistake, and reasonable grounds existed for believing statement true. (770.02).

Equal Rights.—Any person who discriminates on basis of sex, marital status, or race in areas of lending money, granting credit, or equal pay for equal services performed is liable for compensatory and punitive damages, plus reasonable attorney's fees. (725.07).

Motor Vehicles.—Person who suffers pecuniary loss or is otherwise affected adversely by failure of motor vehicle manufacturer, distributor, importer or dealer to comply with statutory licensing requirements may recover treble damages and reasonable attorney's fees. (320.697).

Minors.—Parents may be held liable for actual damages and taxable court costs, for malicious or willful destruction or theft of property by minors under age 18 living with parents. (741.24).

Open Pits or Holes.—Double actual damages recoverable from individual or company leaving unenclosed pits or holes. (768.11).

Payment Methods.—In any action in which award of future economic losses exceeds $250,000, court may order that it be made by lump-sum payment or with periodic payments secured by bond. (768.78).

Pollution.—Persons polluting air or water which results in damage to animal or plant life or air or water are jointly and severally liable to State for such damage and costs of investigating same and for costs of restoration plus civil penalty up to $10,000 per offense, except where damage caused by use of state-approved chemicals for control of aquatic weeds or algae performed in accordance with state standards, permits and label instructions and not done negligently. (403.141).

Punitive Damages.—Pleading of claim for punitive damages shall not be permitted in civil action unless there is reasonable showing by evidence in record or proferred by claimant which would provide reasonable basis for recovery of such damages. (768.72). Award for punitive damages in civil action based on negligence, strict liability, products liability, commercial misconduct, professional liability or breach of warranty that involves willful, wanton or gross misconduct shall not exceed three times amount of compensatory damages awarded to each claimant, except class actions (768.73[1][a]). However, if jury awards punitive damages in excess of that amount, and claimant demonstrates by clear and convincing evidence that award is not excessive in light of facts, award above three times amount of compensatory damages permitted. (768.73[1][b]). Jury shall not be informed as to provisions of statute. (768.73[8]). Employer is not liable for punitive damages by virtue of doctrine of respondeat superior unless employee's tortious conduct is wanton or willful and employer is shown to be negligent in retaining employee. (393 So.2d 545).

See note at head of Digest as to 1998 legislation covered.

See Topical Index in front part of this volume.

DAMAGES . . . *continued*

Replevin.—See topic Replevin.

Solicitation of Orders.—Treble damages may be assessed for solicitations by statement or invoice, without appropriate warning, of payments for goods not yet ordered or services not yet performed. (817.061).

Dishonored Checks.—If check, draft, or other order of payment is dishonored because of lack of funds, credit, or account, and if drawer fails to pay within 30 days of written demand, damages are amount of item plus triple amount of item but in no event less than $50. Drawer also liable for court costs and reasonable attorney fees. (68.065[1]).

Stolen Property.—Person injured by any person who knowingly obtains or uses property of another with intent to either temporarily or permanently deprive other person of right to property or appropriate property to his own use is entitled to threefold damages sustained if proved by clear and convincing evidence. In addition, such person shall also recover attorney's fees and court costs in trial and appellate courts. Punitive damages are not recoverable and claimant must make written demand for damages prior to filing suit. Defendant may recover attorney's fees and court costs upon finding that claim was without substantial fact or legal support. (772.11 and 812.014).

Strict Liability in Tort.—Doctrine as expounded in ALI Restatement 2d of Torts §402A is adopted. (336 So.2d 80).

Obstruction of Drainage Canals.—Person wilfully obstructing drainage canal or damaging drainage facility is liable to injured party for actual damages, and to state drainage district for double cost of removing obstruction or repairing facility. (298.66[1]).

Life Care Contracts.—Act authorizes any purchaser or nominee of, or subscriber to continuing care agreement, injured by violation of Act to bring action for recovery of damages plus reasonable attorneys fees. (651.13).

No-Fault Insurance.—See category Transportation, topic Motor Vehicles, subhead No-Fault Insurance.

See also category Estates and Trusts, topic Death, subhead Actions for Death.

Sovereign Immunity.—State, or subdivision thereof waives sovereign immunity up to policy limits of its insurance coverage. (768.28[5]; 497 So.2d 934). And, sovereign immunity is only waived where employee is acting within scope and course of his employment and not acting in bad faith or with malicious purpose. (768.28; 417 So.2d 658). State's waiver of sovereign immunity extends to claims for contribution. Notice requirements of 768.28 are condition precedent to maintaining action against state, its agencies and subdivisions or employee of state, its agencies and subdivisions.

Uniform Contribution Among Tortfeasors Act adopted. (768.31).

DECLARATORY JUDGMENTS:

See topic Judgments.

DEPOSITIONS AND DISCOVERY:

Taking and use of depositions are regulated by Florida Rules of Civil Procedure which are patterned after Federal Rules of Civil Procedure.

Deposition Pending Action.—Any party to suit of civil nature has right at any time after commencement of action to take deposition of any person, including a party for purpose of discovery and use as evidence, except that leave of court must be obtained if notice of taking is served by plaintiff within 30 days after such commencement or if person to be deposed is in prison. (R.C.P. 1.310). Deposition of expert expected to testify at trial allowed without motion or order of court. (R.C.P. 1.280[b][4][A]). Deposition of expert not expected to testify only upon showing of exceptional circumstances under which it is impracticable for party seeking discovery to obtain facts or opinions by other means. (R.C.P. 1.280[b][4][B]). See R.C.P. 1.390(b).

Use of Depositions.—May be used at trial or upon hearing of motion or interlocutory proceeding so far as admissible under rules of evidence against any party present or represented at taking of deposition or who had notice thereof or an officer, director or managing agent authorized to testify. May also be used against a witness who is not a party for impeachment or for any purpose if witness is unavailable to testify. Deposition of expert witness may be used regardless of availability. (R.C.P. 1.330).

Depositions by Telephone.—Upon motion court may order that testimony at deposition may be taken by telephone. (R.C.P. 1.310[b][7]). Witness deposed by telephone must be sworn by person in witness's presence and who is qualified in that location to administer oath. (R.C.P. 1.310[c]).

Deposition Before Action.—Deposition of any person regarding any matter that may be cognizable in any court of this state may be taken by any person after filing of verified petition upon court order granting petition. (R.C.P. 1.290[a]).

Deposition Pending Appeal.—Upon motion and leave of court, may be taken to perpetuate testimony for subsequent proceedings if appeal has been taken or if time for taking appeal has not expired. (R.C.P. 1.290).

Before Whom Taken.—Depositions may be taken before any notary public, judicial officer or other officer authorized to take acknowledgments or proof of executions of deeds or by any person appointed by court in which action is pending. (R.C.P. 1.300).

By Stipulation.—Before any person, at any time or place by written stipulation. (R.C.P. 1.300).

Persons Disqualified.—Unless by stipulation, no deposition may be taken by a relative, employee, attorney, counsel of any party, or relative or employee of such counsel, or one financially interested in action. (R.C.P. 1.300).

Videotaping.—Any deposition taken upon oral examination may be recorded on videotape without leave of court. Party intending to videotape deposition shall state his intention in his notice and give name and address of video operator. Videotaped depositions must also be recorded stenographically unless otherwise agreed by parties. Counsel for videotaping party must permit viewing of tape by opposing party and provide copy of tape at expense of any requesting party. (R.C.P. 1.310[b][4]).

Within State for Use Outside State.—When a person authorized to administer oaths by Florida law is appointed by a court of record of another state, jurisdiction or government as a commissioner to take testimony of a named witness in this state, such witness may be compelled to attend and testify by a witness subpoena issued by clerk of circuit court. (R.C.P. 1.410).

Uniform Foreign Depositions Act adopted. (92.251).

Outside State for Use Within State.—Upon parties' stipulation, depositions may be taken before any person at any time or place upon any notice and in any manner, and may be used like other depositions. (R.C.P. 1.300[c]). In foreign country depositions may be taken: (1) on notice before person authorized to administer oaths in place of examination, (2) before person commissioned by court, or (3) pursuant to letter rogatory. (R.C.P. 1.300[b]). Depositions taken outside Florida for use in Florida should conform to procedural and formal requirements of Rules 1.290(a)(2), 1.300, and 1.310, R.C.P.

Compelling Attendance of Witnesses.—Attendance of witnesses may be compelled by subpoenas as provided in Rule 1.410. (R.C.P. 1.310). Clerk of court in which deposition to be taken may subpoena witnesses. Failure of witness to obey subpoena may be deemed a contempt of the court. (R.C.P. 1.410). Disinterested witnesses must be reimbursed for costs incurred in producing documents pursuant to subpoena. (92.153).

Interrogatories to Parties.—Without leave of court, interrogatories may be served on plaintiff after commencement of action and on any other party with or after service of process and initial pleading upon that party. Form interrogatories are required where they have been adopted by Supreme Court. (R.C.P. 1.340[a]). Interrogatories are limited to 30 absent leave of court. (R.C.P. 1.340[a]). Each interrogatory is answered separately and fully in writing under oath, unless objected to in which event reasons for objection are stated instead of answer. Answers must be signed by person making them and objections signed by attorney making them. Party to whom interrogatories were directed serves copy of answer and any objections within 30 days after service of interrogatories, except that defendant may serve answers or objections within 45 days after service of process and initial pleading upon that defendant. Court may allow shorter or longer time. Party submitting interrogatories may move for order under R.C.P. 1.380(a) with respect to any objection to or other failure to answer interrogatory. (R.C.P. 1.340).

Interrogatories may relate to any matter that can be inquired into under Rule 1.280(b), and answers may be used to extent permitted by rules of evidence except as otherwise provided in R.C.P. 1.340(b). Interrogatory otherwise proper is not objectionable merely because answer to interrogatory involves opinion or contention that relates to fact, calls for conclusion or asks for information not within personal knowledge of party. Party responds to such interrogatory by giving information he has and source on which information is based. Such qualified answer may not be used as direct evidence for or impeachment against party giving answer unless court finds it otherwise admissible under rules of evidence. If party introduces answer to interrogatory, any other party may require him to introduce any other interrogatory and answer that in fairness ought to be considered with it. (R.C.P. 1.340).

When answer to an interrogatory may be derived or ascertained from records of party to whom interrogatory has been directed or from examination, audit or inspection of records, or from a compilation, abstract or summary based on records and burden of deriving or ascertaining answer is substantially same for party serving interrogatory as for party to whom it is directed, answer to interrogatory may specify records from which answer may be derived or ascertained and offer to party serving interrogatory reasonable opportunity to examine, audit or inspect records and to make copies, compilations, abstracts or summaries. (R.C.P. 1.340).

Answers made by a party are not binding on a co-party. (R.C.P. 1.340).

Interrogatories are so arranged that a blank space is provided after each separately numbered interrogatory. Space is reasonably calculated to enable answering party to insert answer within space. If sufficient space is not provided, answering party may attach additional papers with answers and refer to them in space provided in interrogatories. Original of interrogatories is served on party to whom interrogatories are directed and copies are served on all other parties. Notice that interrogatories have been served, stating date of service and name of party to whom directed, must be filed with court. Completed interrogatories are served upon party originally propounding interrogatories and copy is served upon all parties. Original or copy of answers may be filed by any party, or court may order copy filed, when court should consider answers in determining any matter before it. (R.C.P. 1.340).

Depositions Upon Written Questions.—After commencement of action any party may take testimony of any person by deposition upon written questions. (R.C.P. 1.320[a]).

EVIDENCE:

Evidence questions governed by Florida Evidence Code (c. 90), applicable to criminal proceedings related to crimes committed after July 1, 1979, and to civil actions and all other proceedings pending on or brought after Oct. 1, 1981. Florida Evidence Code based on Federal Evidence code.

Witnesses.—Evidence Code adopted, based on Federal Rules of Evidence, applicable to criminal proceedings related to crimes committed after Oct. 1, 1981, to civil actions, and all other proceedings pending on or brought after Oct. 1, 1981.

Privileged Communications.—Confidential communications between husband and wife, lawyer and client, clergy and penitent, psychotherapist and patient, sexual assault counselor and victim, domestic violence advocate and victim, and accountant and client recognized (90.502-.5055); privilege with respect to trade secrets also recognized (90.506). Privilege can be waived by voluntary disclosure (90.507), but not when compelled erroneously by Court or made without opportunity to claim privilege (90.508).

See note at head of Digest as to 1998 legislation covered.

See Topical Index in front part of this volume.

FL – 15

EVIDENCE... *continued*

Transactions with Persons Since Deceased or Incompetent.—With limited exceptions, no person interested in action or proceeding against personal representative, heir-at-law, assignee, legatee, devisee, or survivor of deceased person, or against assignee, committee or guardian of mentally incompetent person, shall be examined as witness regarding any oral communication between interested person and person who is deceased or mentally incompetent at time of examination. (90.602).

Expert testimony may be taken by deposition at any time before trial and may be used at trial, regardless of place of residence of witness or whether he is within 100 miles from place of trial or hearing, or is out of state. (R.C.P. 1.390, but see R.C.P. 1.280[b][4], regarding limitations on discovery of expert testimony.)

Self-incrimination.—No person is compelled in any criminal matter to be a witness against himself. (Const. art. 1, §9). Persons are not excused from testifying or producing evidence in certain prosecutions on self-incrimination grounds, but no testimony so given or evidence so produced may be received against person upon any criminal investigation or proceeding unless related to perjury. (914.04).

Compelling Attendance.—On application, clerk of court will issue subpoena directed to witness compelling attendance and testimony. Attorney of record may also issue subpoena. (R.C.P. 1.410[a]). Method of service of criminal trial witness subpoena upon federal, state or municipal employee closely controlled. (48.031[4]).

INJUNCTIONS:

See also topics Pleading, Practice.

Injunctions may be issued to prevent irreparable injury, where no adequate remedy at law exists, to abate nuisances, to stay proceedings at law, to prevent waste, to prevent multiplicity of suits and for other usual purposes.

Jurisdiction.—Circuit courts have jurisdiction to issue temporary and permanent injunctions. (26.012[3]).

Temporary injunctions may be granted without notice only if: (a) It appears from specific facts shown by affidavit or verified pleading that immediate and irreparable injury, loss or damage will result to movant before adverse party can be heard; (b) movant's attorney certifies in writing any efforts that have been made to give notice; and (c) affidavit states reasons why notice should not be required. (R. C. P. 1.610[a][1]). No evidence other than affidavit or verified pleading shall be used to support application unless adverse party appears or has received reasonable notice of hearing. (R.C.P. 1.610[a][2]). Every temporary injunction granted without notice shall be endorsed with date and hour of entry and shall be filed forthwith in clerk's office and shall define injury, state findings by court why injury may be irreparable, and give reasons why order was granted without notice if none was given. (R.C.P. 1.610[a][2]). Temporary injunction shall remain in effect until further order of court. (R.C.P. 1.610[a][2]).

Bond.—No temporary injunction shall be entered unless bond is given by movant in amount court deems proper, conditioned for payment of costs and damages sustained by adverse party if adverse party wrongfully is enjoined. (R. C. P. 1.610[b]). When injunction is issued on pleadings of municipality, state or any officer, agency or political subdivision thereof, court may dispense with bond. (R. C. P. 1.610[b]). No bond required for issuance of temporary injunction issued solely to prevent physical injury or abuse of natural person. (R.C.P. 1.610[b]; 741.30[3][b][dealing specifically with protection against domestic violence]).

Dissolution.—Party against whom temporary injunction has been granted may move to dissolve or modify at any time. Motion to dissolve or modify shall be heard within five days after movant applies for hearing on motion. (R. C. P. 1.610[d]).

Consolidation With Trial on Merits.—Court may consolidate hearing on temporary injunction with trial of action, pursuant to R.C.P. 1.270(a), which governs consolidation of pending actions involving common questions of law or fact.

Form and Scope.—Every injunction shall: (1) Specify reasons for entry, (2) describe in reasonable detail act(s) restrained without reference to pleading or another document, and (3) shall be binding on parties, their officers, agents, servants, employees and attorneys and on those persons in active concert or participation with them who receive actual notice of injunction. (R.C.P. 1.610[c]).

JUDGMENTS:

Final judgment determines rights of parties and disposes of cause on its merits leaving nothing more remaining to be done in cause. (48 Fla. 226, 37 So. 722). Interlocutory order or judgment leaves other issues in cause open for further judicial determination and does not finally determine or complete action. (138 Fla. 841, 190 So. 885; 153 Fla. 501, 15 So.2d 175).

Federal Rules of Civil Procedure in large part have formed basis of Fla. Rules of Civil Procedure relating to motions for new trials and rehearing; amendments of judgments (R. C. P. 1.530); relief from judgments (R. C. P. 1.540); discovery in aid of execution of judgments (R. C. P. 1.560); defaults and final judgments thereon (R. C. P. 1.500); dismissal of actions (R. C. P. 1.420).

Judgments by Confession.—Warrant of attorney to confess judgment executed after action brought is proper. (106 Fla. 582, 143 So. 633). Power of attorney to confess judgment executed within or without state prior to institution of action is invalid, void. (55.05). Foreign judgment by confession, if valid where rendered, enforceable in Florida courts. (164 So.2d 893; see 405 U.S. 174).

Judgments by Consent.—Judgment by consent of parties valid (126 Fla. 339, 171 So. 674); however, jurisdiction of subject matter cannot be conferred by consent.

Judgments on Pleadings.—After pleadings are closed, but within such time as not to delay trial, any party may move for judgment on pleadings. (R. C. P. 1.140[c]).

Summary Judgments.—Party asserting claim may move for summary judgment upon all or part of claim with or without supporting affidavits at any time after 20 days from commencement of action or after service of motion for summary judgment by adverse party. (R.C.P. 1.510[a]). Party against whom claim asserted may move for summary judgment at any time. (R.C.P. 1.510[b]).

Motion must be served at least 20 days prior to time fixed for hearing; 25 days if mailed. Motion must state with particularity grounds on which it is based and substantial matters of law to be argued. Adverse party may serve opposing affidavits by mailing five days or delivering two days prior to day of hearing. Judgment sought shall be rendered if pleadings, depositions, answers to interrogatories, admissions on file and affidavits, if any, show that there is no genuine issue of material fact and moving party is entitled to judgment as matter of law. Summary judgment, interlocutory in character, may be rendered on issue of liability alone although there is genuine issue as to amount of damages. (R. C. P. 1.510[c]).

Summary judgment may be awarded to nonmoving party. (70 So.2d 573). Summary judgment not favored in action based upon fraud. (139 So.2d 163).

Default Judgments.—Party seeking relief may have clerk enter default against party failing to file or serve any papers in action and may have court enter default against party failing to plead or defend as provided by rules. (R. C. P. 1.500[a] and [b]). Party may plead or otherwise defend at any time before default is entered. (R. C. P. 1.500[c]).

Final judgment after default may be entered by court at any time, but no judgment may be entered against infant or incompetent unless represented by guardian or representative who has appeared therein. Court may receive affidavits, make references, or conduct hearings as necessary and shall accord trial by jury when required by law. (R. C. P. 1.500[e]).

Declaratory judgments may be entered by circuit courts under act following substantially the Uniform Declaratory Judgments Act. (86.011-86.111).

Offer of Judgment.—Procedural provisions of §45.061 only govern causes of action accruing prior to Oct. 1, 1990. (608 So.2d 1). Procedural provisions of §768.79 govern causes of action accruing after Oct. 1, 1990; former R.C.P. 1.442 was repealed as of July 9, 1992. (608 So.2d 1). Attorney's fees recoverable against party who fails to obtain judgment at least 25% less than refused statutory offer, or by party who obtains judgment for at least 25% greater than refused statutory offer. (768.79).

Docketing.—Orders of dismissal and final judgments of courts in civil actions are recorded in official records. (28.29). Failure to record order or judgment does not affect its validity. (28.29).

Vacation or Modification.—Clerical mistakes in judgment may be corrected by court on its own initiative or motion of party. (R. C. P. 1.540[a]).

Court may, on motion made within reasonable time, not exceeding one year since judgment was entered, relieve party from judgment for following reasons: Mistake, inadvertence, surprise, or excusable neglect; newly discovered evidence which could not have been timely discovered and presented; fraud, misrepresentation, or other misconduct of adverse party. No time limit for motions based on fraudulent affidavits in marital cases. Court may, on motion made within reasonable time, relieve party from judgment for following reasons: Judgment is void; judgment has been satisfied, released, or discharged, or prior judgment on which it was based has been reversed or vacated or it is no longer equitable to give it prospective application. Independent action to relieve party from judgment is also permitted. (R. C. P. 1.540[b]).

Liens.—Judgment, order or decree becomes lien on real estate in any county where certified copy of it is recorded in official records or judgment lien record of county, whichever is maintained at time of recordation, and it shall be lien for period of seven years from date of recording. Recording original is insufficient. (55.10). Lien may be extended for additional period of seven years by re-recording certified copy of judgment, order, or decree within 90-day period preceding expiration of lien. If lien is extended, lien may be further extended by re-recording certified copy of judgment, order or decree within 90-day period preceding expiration of lien. In no event may lien upon real property created by this subsection be extended beyond 20 years. (55.081). For judgments recorded or rerecorded after Oct. 1, 1993, judgment or affidavit recorded simultaneously must contain address of person who has lien as result of judgment. (55.10[1]).

Any such lien may be transferred to other security by following certain prescribed steps. (55.10).

No money judgment or decree against municipal corporation is lien on its property, and no execution or writ in nature of execution may be issued or levied. (55.11).

Revival and Limitations.—Action on judgment of Florida court of record may be commenced at any time within 20 years. (95.11[1]). Action on judgment of Florida court not of record, or of federal court, or of court of foreign state or foreign country, may be commenced at any time within five years. (95.11[2][a]). Bankrupt or debtor discharged from debts under federal bankruptcy laws may employ special procedure to cancel and discharge prior judgments as matter of record. (55.145).

Stays.—No execution or other final process shall issue until judgment has been recorded nor within time for serving motion for new trial or rehearing, and if motion for new trial or rehearing timely served, until determined; provided execution may be issued upon special order of court. (R. C. P. 1.550[a]). Court before which execution or other process based on final judgment is returnable may stay execution or process and suspend proceedings thereon for good cause on motion and notice to all adverse parties. (R. C. P. 1.550[b]).

Assignment of a judgment carries with it cause of action on which it is based, together with all beneficial interests of assignor and its incidents. Assignee may use every remedy, lien, or security which assignor might have used to enforce judgment. Purchaser of a judgment with notice from a purchaser without notice, takes a good title. (56 Fla. 279, 47 So. 797). Consideration for assignment is ordinarily necessary. (47 Fla. 147, 35 So. 986). Clerk of Circuit Court is county recorder and is required to record all assignments of judgments entered by any Florida court or federal court having jurisdiction in Florida upon presentation of assignment and payment of service charge. (28.222).

Satisfaction.—Whenever judgment amount is fully paid, party to whom payment is made must execute and record written instrument acknowledging satisfaction and send recorded satisfaction to payer within 60 days or be liable for any attorneys fees and costs arising from failure to do so. (701.04).

See note at head of Digest as to 1998 legislation covered.

See Topical Index in front part of this volume.

JUDGMENTS . . . *continued*

Judgment may be satisfied by paying into registry of court total amount due with interest and costs of issuance of execution thereon. (55.141).

Judgments of U. S. Courts.—Judgments and decrees of the United States district courts of Florida, and certified copies thereof, are prima facie evidence, in state courts, of the entry and validity thereof. (92.06). Clerks of circuit courts must record certified copies of such judgments and decrees upon presentation of such copies and payment of service charge. (28.222[3][c]).

Foreign Judgments.—Foreign state judgments duly recorded with clerk shall have same effect and be subject to same defenses as Florida judgment provided procedures set out in this chapter are followed. Nothing herein shall impair judgment creditor to bring action to enforce judgment instead of proceeding under this Act. (55.502; 55.503). At time of recording foreign judgment, affidavit shall be recorded setting forth name, social security number, if known, and last known address of judgment debtor and judgment creditor. (55.505[1]). Clerk shall mail notice of recording to judgment debtor. Judgment creditor may mail notice, by registered mail return receipt, and record proof of mailing and if done, clerk's failure to mail notice of recording shall not affect enforcement proceedings. (55.502[2]). No enforcement of judgment or lien shall issue until 30 days after mailing or if action to stay is filed. (55.505[3]; 55.507). Court shall stay enforcement if judgment debtor files action contesting jurisdiction or validity of judgment within 30 days after judgment was recorded and records lis pendens directed towards foreign judgment. (55.509[1]). Grounds to stay enforcement of Florida judgment may be asserted to stay enforcement of foreign judgment provided same security for satisfaction is also required. (55.509[2]). Act is very similar to Uniform Enforcement of Foreign Judgments Act.

Uniform Enforcement of Foreign Judgments Act not adopted.

Judgment Notes.—See category Business Regulation and Commerce, topic Bills and Notes.

LIMITATION OF ACTIONS:

Uniform Commercial Code adopted. (cc. 670-680). Uniform Commercial Code statutes of limitation included in §95.11. See category Business Regulation and Commerce, topic Commercial Code.

All actions except for recovery of realty must be commenced in following periods. (95.11).

Twenty Years: On judgment or decree of a court of record in this state. (95.11[1]).

Five Years: (1) On judgment or decree of any court, not of record, of this state or any court of U.S. or of any other state or territory in U.S. or of a foreign country; (2) on legal or equitable action on obligation, contract or liability founded on written instrument; (3) on action to foreclose mortgage (95.11[2]); (4) on action for violation of False Claims Act (68.081 et seq.) or more than two years after when material facts were or should have been known, but in no event more than seven years (68.089).

Four Years: (1) Action founded on negligence; (2) relating to determinations of paternity with time running from date child reaches age of majority; (3) founded on design, planning or construction of real property improvement, with time running from date of actual possession by owner, issuance of certificate of occupancy, abandonment of construction if not completed, or date of completion or termination of contract between professional engineer, architect or licensed contractor and his employer (where latent defect is involved time runs from time defect is or should have been discovered but in any event within 15 years from issuance of certificate of occupancy, date of completion, abandonment if not completed, termination of contract to build, design or engineer improvement, whichever is latest—caveat: similar predecessor statute held unconstitutional [369 So.2d 572]); (4) to recover public money or property held by present or former public officer or employee and obtained during, or as result of, such office or employment; (5) for injury to person founded on design, manufacture, distribution or sale of personal property not permanently incorporated in improvement to realty including fixtures; (6) founded on statutory liability; (7) for trespass to realty; (8) for taking, detaining or injuring personal property; (9) to recover specific personal property; (10) legal or equitable action founded on fraud; (11) legal or equitable action on contract, obligation or liability not founded on written instrument, including action on sale and delivery of goods, wares and merchandise and store accounts; (12) to rescind contract; (13) for money paid to governmental authority by mistake; (14) for statutory penalty or forfeiture; (15) for assault, battery, false arrest, malicious prosecution, malicious interference, false imprisonment or any intentional tort except as provided under §95.11(4), (5), (7) and for any action not specifically provided for by statute. (95.11[3]).

Two Years: (1) Action for professional malpractice founded on tort or contract (period runs from time cause is or should have been discovered); limited to persons in privity with professional; (2) for wages or overtime, or damages, or penalties concerning wages or overtime; (3) for wrongful death; (4) special section for medical malpractice; (5) actions arising under Florida Securities Act (period runs from time facts giving rise to cause are or should have been discovered but not more than five years from date such violation occurred); (6) for personal injury caused by phenoxy herbicides while serving Armed Forces of U.S. from Jan. 1, 1962 to May 7, 1975 (period runs from time cause is or should have been discovered); (7) libel; (8) slander (95.11[4]); (9) disparagement of agricultural food products (865.065[4]). See category Family, topic Husband and Wife, subhead Actions. All claims against decedent or estate must be made within two years of decedent's death. (733.710). See also subhead Probate, infra.

One Year: (1) For specific performance of a contract; (2) to enforce equitable lien arising from furnishing of labor, services or material for improvement of realty; (3) action against guaranty association and its insured with period running from date of deadline for filing claims in order of liquidation; and (4) action to enforce claim on payment bond on which principal is subcontractor or sub-subcontractor as defined in §713.01, for private and public work, from last furnishing of labor, services or materials or from last furnishing of labor services or materials by general contractor if general contractor is principal on bond on same project, whichever is later. (95.11[5]).

For Tort Claims.—Statute (95.241) dispensing with notice of claim requirements before suing municipalities repealed. Local notice requirements should be checked before commencing suit.

For Tort Claims Based on Abuse.—Action founded on intentional torts based on abuse may be commenced at any time within seven years after age of majority, within four years after injured person leaves dependency of abuser, or within four years of discovery of injury and causal relationship between injury and abuse, whichever occurs later. (95.11[7]).

Claims Against State.—Actions against state or one of its agencies must be commenced within three years after action accrues and preceded by notice in writing to agency and Department of Insurance, provided that if claim is for contribution, it shall be presented within six months after judgment against tortfeasor seeking contribution has become final or, if no judgment has been rendered, within six months after tortfeasor seeking contribution has discharged or agreed to discharge common liability. (768.28[6]).

Real Property.—No action to recover real property or its possession shall be maintained unless person seeking recovery, his ancestor, predecessor or grantor, was seized or possessed thereof within seven years before commencement of action. (95.12). Same period of limitation applies to actions or defenses to an action founded on title to real property or rents, or service from it, but where title was derived from U.S. or State of Florida, limitation will not begin to run until title passed therefrom. (95.14).

After 20 years from recording of deed or probate of will purporting to convey real property, no person shall assert claim to such property against claimants under such deed or will or their successors in title. (95.231[2]).

After seven years from recording of conveyance executed by persons as heirs or devisees of decedent, no person, other than those whose names appear of record as devisees under will or as heirs in probate proceedings, may claim or recover property conveyed. (95.22).

After five years from recording of deed or probate of will purporting to convey real property where it appears person owning it attempted to convey it or devise it, absent fraud, adverse possession, or pending litigation; deed or will held to authorize conveyance or devise, or to convey or devise fee title, or any interest of person so signing instrument despite lack of seals, witnesses, defects in acknowledgment, release of dower. Instrument admissible in evidence. (95.231[1]).

Encumbrances, e.g., Mortgages.—If maturity ascertainable, lien terminates five years after maturity; if not ascertainable, lien terminates 20 years after date of instrument unless further recording states maturity, in which case five years after stated maturity. (95.281[1][a], [b]). For all obligations including taxes paid by mortgagee, five years. (95.281[1][c]). For mortgage extensions, five years after maturity; if maturity date not ascertainable then 20 years from date of mortgage. (95.281[2]).

Foreign Causes of Action.—No action may be maintained on a cause of action which arose outside of the state and is barred by limitations in the jurisdiction in which it arose. (95.10).

If person is declared incapacitated before expiration of limitations period and cause of action survives, action may be commenced by guardian of property after such expiration and within one year after appointment or time otherwise limited by law, whichever is longer. (744.394).

Computation of Time.—Generally, time within which action shall be begun runs from time cause accrues. Cause accrues when last element constituting cause occurs. For limitation purposes, last element constituting cause of obligation founded on note payable on demand or after date with no specific maturity date specified on note, and last element constituting cause against any person secondarily liable on any such obligation founded on such note, is first written demand for payment. (95.031[1]). On oral obligation to pay debt, cause accrues upon demand by creditor for payment and failure by debtor to pay. (95.031[1]; 483 So.2d 833). Limitations run from time cause of action accrues. In actions for products liability, or fraud, period runs from time facts giving rise to cause of action were discovered or should have been discovered in exercise of due diligence. Action for fraud is barred if not commenced within 12 years after date of commission of alleged fraud, regardless of date fraud was or should have been discovered. (95.031[2]).

When Limitations Tolled.—In general by: (1) Absence from state of person to be sued; (2) use by person to be sued of false name that is unknown to person entitled to sue so that process cannot be served on him; (3) concealment in state of person to be sued such as to prevent service of process; (4) adjudicated incapacity of person entitled to sue before cause of action accrued—must in any case be commenced within seven years from act or event giving rise to cause of action; (5) voluntary payments by alleged father of child in paternity suit; (6) payment of any part of principal or interest of any obligation or liability founded on written instrument; (7) pendency of any arbitral proceeding pertaining to dispute that is subject of action; (8) minority or adjudicated incapacity of person entitled to sue, during such time as no effective guardian exists, not to exceed seven years and not to apply to medical malpractice.

(1)—(3) above do not apply if service of process or service by publication can be made in manner sufficient to confer jurisdiction to grant relief sought. No disability other than above or as conferred in §95.091, probate code or guardianship law tolls statute. (95.051).

Revival.—A barred debt may be revived by acknowledgment or promise to pay in writing and signed by person to be charged. (95.04).

Contractual provisions which shorten limitations period are void. (95.03).

Pleading.—The defense of the statute of limitations must be pleaded affirmatively. (R. C. P. 1.110[d]). Where cause of action set forth in amended pleading is new, different, and distinct from that originally set up, new pleading is equivalent to

See note at head of Digest as to 1998 legislation covered.

See Topical Index in front part of this volume.

LIMITATION OF ACTIONS . . . *continued*
bringing of new action, and statute of limitations runs against new cause of action to time it is introduced into pleading. (63 Fla. 213, 58 So. 186).

Trade Secrets.—Action for misappropriation of trade secret under Uniform Trade Secrets Act must be brought within three years after misappropriation is or should have been discovered. (688.007).

Probate.—No claim arising before death against decedent's estate is binding on estate, personal representative or beneficiary unless presented within later of (1) three months after first publication of notice of administration or (2) 30 days of service of copy of notice of administration to creditor. (733.702).

Trustees.—Action against trustee for breach of trust by beneficiary who has received account or statement must be commenced within six months of receipt of account or statement; otherwise, within time provided in c. 95 generally.

Taxes.—Special provisions for expiration of tax liens are contained in 95.091.

PARTITION:

Partition proceedings are regulated by statute. (64.011-64.091).

Actions for partition are entertained in circuit courts. (26.012[2][c], see also 64.011). Laws applicable to partition of real property also applicable to personal property insofar as nature of property permits. (64.091).

Jurisdiction and Venue.—Suit must be brought in any county in which land or any part thereof lies. (64.022).

Scope.—Action may be filed by any one or more of several joint tenants, tenants in common, or coparceners against their cotenants, coparceners or others interested in lands to be divided. (64.031). Requirements of complaint prescribed in §64.041. Estate by entireties is not subject to partition during joint lives of husband and wife, so long as they remain married. (132 So.2d 623).

Partition in Kind or Sale.—If property cannot be divided without prejudice, it may be sold at public auction and proceeds divided. (64.071).

PLEADING:

Pleadings Permitted.—Rules of pleading are prescribed by Florida Rules of Civil Procedure which are patterned on Federal Rules of Civil Procedure. Allowed pleadings are: (1) complaint or petition, (2) answer, (3) counterclaim, (4) cross-claim, (5) answer to counterclaim, (6) answer to cross-claim, (7) third-party complaint, (8) third-party answer, (9) reply to affirmative defense. (R. C. P. 1.100, 1.110, 1.170, 1.180). Every pleading, motion, order or judgment or other paper shall have caption containing name of court, file number, name of first party on each side with indication of other parties, designation identifying party filing it and nature of paper. (R.C.P. 1.100[c][1]). All papers filed in action shall be styled as to indicate clearly subject matter of paper and party requesting or obtaining relief. (R.C.P. 1.100[c][1]). All averments of pleading must be made in consecutively numbered paragraphs. (R.C.P. 1.110[f]). Each claim or defense founded upon separate transaction or occurrence should be set forth in separate count or as separate defense. (R.C.P. 1.110[f]).

Complaint.—Claim for relief, whether original complaint, counterclaim, third party claim or cross-claim must set forth brief statement of grounds for jurisdiction, short and plain statement of ultimate facts showing entitlement to relief, and demand for relief. (R.C.P. 1.110[b]). Relief in alternative or of different types may be demanded. (R.C.P. 1.110[b]). Party may state legal or equitable claims as well as inconsistent claims. (R.C.P. 1.110[g]). Every complaint shall be considered to pray for general relief. (R. C. P. 1.110[b]). Instrument upon which action is brought, or copy thereof, must be attached to or incorporated in complaint, and any exhibit so attached becomes part of complaint for all purposes. (R. C. P. 1.130). Conditions precedent may be averred generally, but denial of performance or occurrence must be specific (R.C.P. 1.120[c]). Circumstances constituting fraud or mistake must be stated with particularity, but malice, knowledge or intent may be averred generally. (R. C. P. 1.120[b]). Averments of time and place are material and claims for special damages should be specifically stated. (R.C.P. 1.120[f] & [g]). It is unnecessary to specifically allege capacity or authority of party to sue or be sued or legal existence of party; rather, when such issue exists, it should be pled by specific negative averment. (R.C.P. 1.120[a]). In pleading official document or Act, it is sufficient to state document was issued or act done in compliance with law and in pleading judgment or decree it is sufficient to simply refer to judgment. (R.C.P. 1.120[d] & [e]).

Civil cover sheet (Form 1.997) must be filed with clerk at time initial complaint or petition is filed by party instituting action. (R.C.P. 1.100[c][2]). If civil cover sheet is not filed clerk will accept complaint for filing; but further proceedings shall be abated until civil cover sheet is filed. (R.C.P. 1.100[c][2]). Clerk shall complete civil cover sheet for party appearing pro se. (R.C.P. 1.100[c][2]).

Final disposition form (Form 1.998) must be filed with clerk by prevailing party at time of filing of order or judgment which disposes of action. (R.C.P. 1.100[c][3]). Clerk shall complete this form for pro se party or if action is dismissed for lack of prosecution under Rule 1.420(e). (R.C.P. 1.100[c][3]).

Answer.—The answer must state in short and plain terms defenses to each claim asserted, and shall admit or deny each of averments of complaint. (R. C. P. 1.110[c]). If pleader is without knowledge as to any averment of complaint, pleader shall so state and such statement acts as denial. (R.C.P. 1.110[c]). If only part of averment is denied, pleader shall specify what is true and deny remainder. (R.C.P. 1.110[c]). Answer or other response to claim for relief and any reply must be served within 20 days after service of document to which answer, response or reply is directed. (R.C.P. 1.140[a]).

Failure to deny, except averments as to amount of damages, when response is required, is to admit. (R.C.P. 1.110[e]). Answer may be general denial if pleader intends to deny all averments of complaint. (R.C.P. 1.110[c]). Affirmative defenses must be set forth in answer, or, if apparent on face of pleading to which motion is directed may be asserted as grounds for motion. (R.C.P. 1.110[d]). Inconsistent or alternative defenses may be filed. (R. C. P. 1.110[g]).

Counterclaim.—Counterclaims are allowed. (R. C. P. 1.170). Counterclaim arising out of transaction or occurrence that is subject matter of action is compulsory counterclaim and must be pleaded or is barred. (R.C.P. 1.170[a]). Any other counterclaim is permissive. (R. C. P. 1.170[b]). If counterclaim matures after original claim is filed, counterclaim should be presented with court approval by supplemental pleading; if counterclaim was inadvertently omitted, it should be presented with leave of court by amendment to pleading. (R.C.P. 1.170[e] & [f]).

Cross-claim or Third Party Practice.—Party may assert claim against co-party or against third party who might be properly brought into action if claim arises out of transaction or occurrence that is subject matter of original action or counterclaim or relating to any property that is subject of original action. (R.C.P. 1.170[g] and 1.180[a]). Cross-claim or third party claim may include claim that party is or may be liable for all or part of claim asserted in action against cross-claimant. (R.C.P. 1.170[g] and 1.180[a]). Party cannot bring third party claim more than 20 days after serving answer except by leave of court on motion with notice to all parties. (R. C. P. 1.180). Service of cross-claim on party who has appeared in action shall be made pursuant to Rule 1.080(b). Service of cross-claim against party who has not appeared in action shall be made in manner provided for service of summons. (R.C.P. 1.170[g]). Third party defendant may assert defenses to plaintiff's main claim and may assert any claims against plaintiff that arise out of transaction or occurrence sued on by plaintiff. (R.C.P. 1.180[a]). Plaintiff may sue third party defendant for any claim arising out of same transaction or occurrence of his main claim. (R.C.P. 1.180[a]).

Defenses.—Every defense, in law or fact, to a claim for relief in any pleading, whether a claim, counterclaim, cross-claim, or third party complaint must be asserted in responsive pleading thereto if one is required; except that following defenses may at option of pleader be made by motion: (1) Lack of jurisdiction over subject matter; (2) lack of jurisdiction over person; (3) improper venue; (4) insufficiency of process; (5) insufficiency of service of process; (6) failure to state cause of action; (7) failure to join indispensable parties. (R.C.P. 1.140[b]). Motion making any of these defenses must be made before pleading if further pleading is permitted and grounds for such defenses must be stated with particularity. (R. C. P. 1.140[b]). Party waives right to raise these defenses by motion unless service of motion is made under Rule 1.140, except motion for lack of jurisdiction over subject matter. Motion under Rule 1.140, except motion for judgment on pleadings or motion to strike pleading containing redundant, immaterial, impertinent or scandalous matter, alters time periods for filing answer. See subhead Service, infra. If court denies motion or postpones disposition until trial, responsive pleading must be served within ten days after notice of court's action, or if court grants motion for more definite statement, pleader must serve within ten days after service of more definite statement unless court fixes different time. (R.C.P. 1.140[a][2]). If court permits or requires amended or responsive pleading or more definite statement, pleading or statements shall be served within ten days after notice of court's action and responses to pleadings or statements shall be served with ten days of service of pleadings or statements. (R.C.P. 1.140[a][3]). If answer or third party answer contains affirmative defense and opposing party seeks to avoid it, opposing party must file reply containing avoidance. (R. C. P. 1.100[a]). Averments in pleading to which responsive pleading is required, other than those to amount of damages, are admitted when not denied in responsive pleading. (R.C.P. 1.110[e]). Averments in pleading to which no responsive pleading is required or permitted must be taken as denied or avoided. (R. C. P. 1.110[e]). Verified motion to strike is appropriate for any part of sham pleading and may be filed before cause is set for trial. (R.C.P. 1.150).

If pleading to which responsive pleadings is permitted is vague or ambiguous preventing responsive pleading, motion for more definite statement may be filed. (R.C.P. 1.140[e]). After pleadings are closed, party may move for judgment on pleadings. (R.C.P. 1.140[c]).

Amendments.—A party may amend once as a matter of course before a responsive pleading is served or, if no responsive pleading is permitted and action is not on trial calendar, amendment may be made at any time within 20 days after it is served. (R.C.P. 1.190[a]). Otherwise, leave of court or written consent of adverse party, must be obtained for amendments. (R.C.P. 1.190[a]). Pleading in response to amended pleading must be within ten days of service thereof unless court otherwise orders. (R.C.P. 1.190[a]). Court may permit amendments at any time. (R. C. P. 1.190[e]). If amendment relates to same conduct, transaction, or occurrence set forth in original pleading, amendment relates back to date of original pleading. (R.C.P. 1.190[c]). Upon motion and reasonable notice, court may permit party to serve supplemental pleading setting forth matters that occur after original pleading and court may permit adverse party to file response. (R.C.P. 1.190[d]).

Service.—Copies of all pleadings must be served on each party or party's attorney. (R.C.P. 1.080[b]). If service of initial process and initial pleading is not made upon defendant within 120 days after filing of initial pleading and party filing does not show good cause why service was not made within that time, action shall be dismissed without prejudice or that defendant dropped on court's own initiative after notice or on motion. (1.070[h]). Answer, answer to counterclaims and cross-claims, and reply must be served within 20 days of service of pleading to which they are directed. (R. C. P. 1.140[a][1]).

Filing.—All original papers must be filed with court prior to or immediately after service. (R. C. P. 1.080[d]).

Verification.—Pleadings not required to be verified or accompanied by affidavit except where rule or statute specifically so provides. (R. C. P. 1.030[a]).

Proof of Claims.—Claims for collection should be accompanied by all of the material facts on which claim is based, together with copies of notes, contracts, book entries and other documents which are basic to claim. (R.C.P. 1.130[a]). See also topic Judgments.

Small Claims.—See category Courts and Legislature, topic Courts.

Frivolous Claims.—Losing party and losing party's attorney must pay reasonable attorneys' fee to prevailing party if complete absence of justiciable issue of law or fact raised by complaint or defense of losing party; provided, however, losing party's

PLEADING . . . *continued*
attorney is not responsible if he relies on representations of client. (57.105[1]). See also Fla. Bar R. Professional Conduct, Rule 4-3.1. If defense fails to raise justiciable issue of law or fact, prejudgment interest also awarded. (57.105[1]).

PRACTICE:

Code.—Practice and procedure in all courts is governed by rules adopted by Supreme Court. (Const. art. 5, §2). In absence of applicable statute or rule, practice is based upon common law. The Florida Rules, while quite similar to the Federal Rules, require complaint to state a cause of action rather than grounds for relief. (R. C. P. 1.110[b]).

Equity.—There is one form of action known as "civil action." (R. C. P. 1.040).

Discovery.—Fla. Rules of Civil Procedure providing for discovery are very similar to and adopted from Fed. Rules for discovery prior to their amendment in 1970. (R. C. P. 1.280-1.390). Five days are added after service by mail. (R.C.P. 1.090[e]).

Direct Actions Against Insurer.—See category Transportation, topic Motor Vehicles, subhead Direct Actions.

Small Claims.—See category Courts and Legislature, topic Courts.

See also topics Actions, Appeal and Error, Depositions and Discovery, Injunctions, Judgments, Pleading, Process; category Debtor and Creditor, topics Attachment, Executions, Garnishment.

PROCESS:

Upon commencement of an action, clerk or judge issues an original summons. (R. C. P. 1.070[a]). In civil actions, process runs throughout state. (48.011). Defendant must respond with answer or proper motion within 20 days. (R. C. P. 1.140).

If summons is returned unexecuted or improperly executed as to any defendant, plaintiff is entitled to such additional summons as may be required to effect service. (R. C. P. 1.070[b]). Where there is more than one defendant, clerk must issue as many writs of summons against several defendants as directed by plaintiff. (R. C. P. 1.070[c]). Failure to make required proof of service does not affect validity of service. (R. C. P. 1.070[b]). Plaintiff must supply all necessary copies of documents to be served. (R. C. P. 1.070[e]).

Who May Serve.—All process shall be served by sheriff or by special process server appointed by sheriff of county where person to be served is found, or by certified process server as provided in §§48.25-48.31. Sheriff of each county may, in his or her discretion, establish approved list of natural persons designated as special process servers. (48.021, R. C. P. 1.070[b]).

Personal Service on an Individual.—In general, service of an original writ of summons is effected on the person to be served by delivering to him or her copy thereof together with copy of complaint or other initial pleading, or by leaving such copies at his or her usual place of abode with any person residing therein 15 years of age, or older, and informing such person of their contents. (48.031).

Witness subpoenas are to be served as above except, in criminal cases involving only misdemeanors, service may be made by certified U.S. mail to last known address of witness at least seven days prior to date of appearance. (48.031[3]).

Service of criminal witness subpoena on law enforcement officer for testimony in official capacity in criminal case may be made as provided in 48.031(1) or to designated supervisor if witness is still employed or is scheduled to work prior to date witness is required to appear. Service may also be made as provided in 48.031(3). (48.031[4][a], [b]).

Service on Minors.—By serving parent, guardian or other person appointed by court to represent minor as provided in §48.031. Service not necessary if guardian ad litem appears voluntarily or court orders appearance without service. (48.041). Minors who are or have been married shall be served as provided in 48.031(1).

Service on Incompetents.—By serving two copies of process to person who has care or custody of incompetent, serving legal guardian as provided in 48.031 or by serving guardian ad litem if one appointed. Service not necessary on guardian ad litem if he/she appears voluntarily or is ordered to appear without service. (48.042).

Service on State Prisoners.—Process against state prisoner shall be served on prisoner. (48.051).

Personal Service on Partnership.—In action against partnership service on one partner binds the others. (48.061). Judgment enforceable against partnership assets and individual assets of partner served. Service of process on one partner gives court jurisdiction over partnership and authorizes it to render judgment binding on partner served and partnership assets. Service on designated employee authorizes judgment binding against partnership assets, but not individual partner's assets. (48.061). For service of process on domestic or foreign limited partnerships, see 48.061(2) and (3).

Personal Service on Association.—In cases of nonresidents associated together in any type of association, including foreign corporations, transacting business in state or having office or agency in state, service of process concerning matters arising out of said business or agency may be had on resident agent, or if none, on Secretary of State. (48.181).

Personal Service on Nonresidents.—Service of process may be had in certain circumstances upon all nonresident persons or business organizations doing business in Florida (48.181); and process may be had in certain circumstances upon nonresidents who commit wrongful acts outside Florida, which cause injury within Florida (48.193-.194).

Service of Process for Possession of Premises.—In actions for possession of residential premises, if tenant cannot be found in county or there is no person 15 years of age or older residing at tenant's usual place of abode in county of residence, after at least two attempts to obtain service, summons may be served by attaching copy to conspicuous place on property described in complaint or summons; minimum time delay between two attempts shall be six hours. (48.183[1]). If landlord causes or anticipates causing service solely by attaching process to conspicuous place on property, then landlord shall provide clerk with additional copy of complaint and prestamped envelope addressed to defendant at premises. Clerk shall mail copy of summons, note fact of mailing in docket, and file certificate of same within court file. Service shall be effective on date of posting or mailing, whichever occurs later, and judgment for final removal of defendant may not be entered until at least five days from date of service. (48.183[2]).

Service on Nonresident Operator of Water Craft or Aircraft.—Service of process may be made on nonresident operator of water craft or aircraft in suit resulting from accident arising out of such operation within state by service on Secretary of State. (48.19).

Personal Service on Corporations Except Insurance Companies.—Process against domestic or foreign private corporation may be served: (a) On president, vice-president or other head of corporation; (b) in absence of any person described in paragraph (a), on cashier, treasurer, secretary or general manager; and in absence of all above; (c) on any director; and in absence of all above; (d) on any officer or business agent residing in Florida. (48.081). If foreign corporation has none of foregoing officers or agents in this state, service may be upon any agent transacting business in state. (48.081). As alternative, process may also be served on designated agent under 48.091. If service of process cannot be made on registered agent because of failure to comply with 48.091, service of process shall be permitted on any employee at corporation's place of business. (48.081). When corporation engages in substantial and not isolated activities within state, or has business office within state and is actually engaged in transaction of business therefrom, service upon any officer or business agent may personally be made pursuant to 48.081, and it is not necessary that action, suit, or proceeding against corporation arise out of any transaction or operation connected with or incidental to business being transacted within state. (48.081).

Service on any director of any corporation which was dissolved before July 1, 1990, as trustee, binds all directors. (48.101). Service on any other dissolved corporation must be in accordance with §48.081, relating to service on private corporations.

Method of Substituted Service on Nonresident.—By leaving or mailing by certified mail copy of process and $8.75 fee with public officer designated by law and sending notice of process and copy thereof forthwith to defendant or attorney, by registered or certified mail. Plaintiff must file return receipt and affidavit of compliance with court on or before return date or within such further time as court may allow. (48.161). For service on nonresident motor vehicle owners, service may be upon Secretary of State. (48.171).

Service on State.—When state has consented to suit, service shall be on state attorney or assistant state attorney for judicial circuit where action is brought and by sending two copies of process by registered or certified mail to Attorney General. (48.121).

Service on Alien Property Custodian.—Where proceeding before any court or administrative board involves property or interest therein and where service or notice is required to be made upon entity in country or territory with which U.S. is at war, copy of notice or process must also be sent by registered or certified mail to alien property custodian, addressed to him or her at Washington, D.C. Failure to mail such notice does not invalidate action or proceeding. (48.131).

Service on Labor Unions.—Process against labor organizations shall be served on president, officer, business agent, manager or person in charge of business of organization. (48.141).

Personal Service on Municipal Corporations.—Process against any municipal corporation, agency, board, or commission, department or subdivision of state or county which has governing board, council, or commission or which is body corporate, shall be served: (a) on president, mayor, chairman, or other head, (b) and in his absence: on vice president, vice mayor, vice chairman; (c) or in absence of all above: any member of governing board, council or commission. Process against such entities not corporate or having no governing board or commission is served on public officer being sued or chief executive officer of entity. In suit in which Department of Revenue is party, process must be served upon executive director of Department. (48.111).

Absent Defendants.—No provision is made for the service of personal process in actions at law upon defendants temporarily absent from this state. For a person concealing his or her whereabouts, see §§48.161; 48.181.

Service by publication is regulated by c. 49 under which such service may be had in enumerated proceedings in any state court unless personal service is required by constitution or statute of this state or U.S. Constitution. (49.011).

Defendants who may be served by publication are: (A) Natural persons and unknown persons claiming by, through, under or against them. (B) Any corporation or other legal entity whose domicile be domestic, foreign or unknown, and whether dissolved or existing or not known whether dissolved or existing, and unknown assigns, successors in interest, trustees or other parties claiming under them. (C) Any group, firm, entity or persons doing business or who have done business in Florida under name or title indicating or tending to indicate that same may be corporation or other legal entity. (D) All claimants under any such parties. (49.021).

Conditions Precedent.—To entitle plaintiff to such process, a sworn statement must be made in the original pleading or by supplementary affidavit by the plaintiff, his or her agent or attorney setting forth facts as to various classes of defendants as follows. (49.031).

(1) Natural person as defendant: (A) That diligent search and inquiry have been made to discover name and residence of defendant and that the same is set forth as particularly as is known. (B) Whether such person is over or under 18 years of age or that age is unknown. (C) That residence of such person is (a) unknown to affiant or (b) in state or country other than Florida, stating residence if known, or (c) in Florida, but that defendant has been absent from state for more than 60 days or conceals himself or herself so process cannot be served. (D) That affiant believes there is no person on whom Florida service of process would be binding. (49.041).

(2) Corporation as defendant: (A) That diligent search and inquiry have been made to discover true name, domicile, principal place of business and whether domestic,

PROCESS . . . *continued*
foreign or dissolved, and to discover true names and whereabouts of all persons upon whom service of process would bind corporation and that same is specified as particularly as known to affiant. (B) Whether or not corporation has ever qualified to do business in Florida unless it is shown to be Florida corporation. (C) That all officers, directors, general managers, cashiers, resident agents and business agents of corporation are (a) absent from state, (b) cannot be found within state, (c) conceal themselves so process cannot be served so as to bind corporation, (d) their whereabouts are unknown, or (e) that officers, etc., of corporation are unknown to affiant. (49.051).

(3) Parties doing business under a corporate name: (A) Name under which said parties have done business. (B) That after diligent search and inquiry affiant is unable to ascertain whether or not the organization was a corporation, either domestic or foreign. (C) Names and places of residence, if known, of all persons known to have been interested in such organization and whether or not other or unknown persons have been interested therein; or that after diligent search and inquiry all persons interested in such organization are unknown. (D) As to known persons that (a) they are absent from this state, or (b) cannot be found within this state, or (c) conceal themselves so process cannot be personally served or (d) their whereabouts are unknown. (49.061).

(4) Unknown parties as defendants: (A) That affiant believes there are persons who are or who may be interested in the subject matter of the suit, whose names after diligent search and inquiry are unknown. (B) Whether unknown parties claim as heirs, devisees, grantees, assignees, lienors, creditors, trustees or other claimants (a) by, through, against or under known person who is dead or not known to be either dead or alive, (b) by, through, against or under some corporation, domestic or foreign, that has been dissolved or which is not known to be existing or dissolved, (c) by, through, against or under some organization which did business under name indicating corporation, or (d) otherwise as case may be. In any case alleged against named defendant alleged to be dead or alive, dissolved or existing, any judgment, decree or order rendered against such defendant shall be as good, valid and effectual as if it had not been so stated. (49.071).

Notice of Suit.—On compliance with aforementioned requirements notice of suit must be issued by clerk or judge not later than 60 days after filing sworn statement, which notice must set forth: (A) Names of known natural defendants; names, status and description of corporate defendants; description of all unknown defendants claiming, by, through, against or under known defendants and other unknown defendants. (B) Nature of suit or proceeding. (C) Name of court where pending and abbreviated title of case. (D) Description of real property, if any, proceeded against. (49.08).

Return day: Notice must require defendant to file answer and serve copy upon plaintiff or his or her attorney on day fixed by notice, not less than 28 nor more than 60 days from date of publication of such notice. (49.09).

Publication: Notice must be published once each week for four consecutive weeks in a newspaper published in the county where the court is located and meeting the statutory requirements. Proof of publication is made by affidavit of owner, officer or employee of the newspaper having knowledge of the publication, which affidavit must set forth or have attached a copy of the notice and must state date of each publication. (49.10).

Posting in lieu of publication: If there be no newspaper published in the county, three copies of the notice must be posted at least 28 days prior to return day in three different conspicuous places in county, one of which must be front door of courthouse, and proof of posting must be made by affidavit of person posting, which affidavit must include a copy of notice and state date and places of posting. (49.11).

Mailing notice: If residence of party to be served is stated with more particularity than state or country, clerk or judge must mail a copy by U.S. mail, postage prepaid, to defendant within ten days after making or posting notice, and date of mailing must be noted on docket with copy of pleading for which notice was issued. (49.12).

Proof of Service.—Officers to whom process is directed shall note on it time received, time executed, manner of execution, name of person served and position he holds if served in representative capacity. Failure to so note invalidates service, except that amendment may be allowed, after which service is effective as though originally valid. Officer failing to state all facts in return subject to fine not exceeding $10, in court's discretion. (48.21).

Long Arm Statute.—See subhead Personal Service on Nonresidents, supra.

Termination of parental rights requires personal service of notice of date, time, and place of advisory hearing for petition to terminate parental rights and copy of petition on mother, legal custodian, relative, grandparent, father of child if child born during marriage, adopted or supported by father, person who has physical custody, or guardian ad litem. (39.801).

REPLEVIN:

Replevin is a statutory possessory action to recover possession of personal property wrongfully detained. (c. 78).

Any person whose personal property is wrongfully detained by another may have writ of replevin to recover property and damages sustained by reason of wrongful taking or detention. Notice of lis pendens may be filed and recorded as in other actions. (78.01).

Complaint.—Actions for replevin may be brought in any county in which property located, where contract was signed, where defendant resides or where cause of action accrued and in court which has jurisdiction of value of property sought to be replevied. (78.032). In order to obtain prejudgment writ of replevin, complaint must contain allegations: (1) Of description, value and location of property, (2) of ownership or right to possession of property, (3) of defendant's wrongful detention, means by which defendant came into possession thereof, and cause of such detention according to best knowledge, information and belief of plaintiff, (4) that property was not taken for tax, assessment or fine pursuant to law, and (5) that property was not taken under execution or attachment of plaintiff's property, or if so, that it is exempt. (78.055).

Without Prior Notice or Hearing.—Prejudgment writ of replevin without notice and hearing may be issued and property delivered forthwith if plaintiff clearly shows by specific facts in affidavit or verified petition nature and amount of claim and grounds for issuance of writ. From this, court must find that defendant is engaging in, or about to engage in, conduct placing property in danger of destruction, concealment, waste, removal from state or jurisdiction of court, or transfer to innocent purchaser or that defendant has failed to make payment as agreed. Petitioner must post bond in amount of lesser of twice value of goods subject to writ or twice balance remaining due. Defendant may obtain release of property by posting bond in amount of 1¼ amount due within five days after serving of writ, or by defendant's motion within ten days after serving writ unless petitioner proves grounds of writ. (78.068).

With Prior Notice and Hearing.—Unless waived under §78.075, notice by show cause order and hearing must be provided. If defendant waives notice and hearing in accordance with §78.075 court shall order clerk to issue writ. (78.065[1]). Otherwise, court shall promptly issue order to show cause why property should not be replevied. (78.065[2]). Order shall set hearing no sooner than five days from service and shall contain other items set forth in §78.065(2) (a)-(f). If defendant waives hearing court may order clerk to issue writ. (78.067[1]). Otherwise, if upon affidavits and showings of parties court determines underlying claim probably valid, court shall order clerk to issue writ for possession pending final adjudication. However, writ stayed if defendant files satisfactory bond equal to value of property. (78.067[2]). No bond is required of petitioner if this method of obtaining writ is utilized.

Officer executing writ shall deliver property to plaintiff forthwith unless writ directs otherwise. Defendant may obtain release of property within five days after seizure by posting 125% of amount due and owing with clerk, conditioned to have property forthcoming to abide by result of action, or on agreement for satisfaction of adverse judgment. (78.13).

Judgment or Order.—If judgment is rendered for the plaintiff, and the goods have been delivered to him, the judgment is for damages and costs. (78.18).

If for the plaintiff, and goods have been redelivered to defendant, the judgment is for the property itself and against the defendant and the sureties on his bond for the value thereof, such judgment to be satisfied by the recovery of the property, or of the amount adjudged against the defendant and his sureties. (78.19[1]).

If for defendant, and goods have been redelivered to him, judgment is against plaintiff for damages for taking, attorney fees, and costs. These remedies do not preclude any other remedies available under other laws. (78.20).

If for defendant, and goods have not been redelivered to him, judgment is for possession of property, for costs and against plaintiff for value of property and costs in same manner as provided in 78.19 for judgment in favor of plaintiff. Value of each article of goods replevied shall be determined as directed in §78.19. (78.21).

Execution.—Executing sheriff may break into home, building or enclosure where property concealed, if not delivered upon public demand by sheriff and if sheriff has reasonable grounds to believe property concealed therein. If sheriff has no reasonable grounds, plaintiff may petition court for "break order" directing sheriff to physically enter home, building or enclosure. Break order shall issue upon plaintiff showing probable cause. (78.10). If property in possession of defendant at issuance passes into possession of third person before execution, officer shall serve writ on both and amendments may be made later. (78.11). If property removed from jurisdiction before execution, officer shall deliver writ to proper officer in new jurisdiction who shall execute and deliver property to plaintiff. (78.12).

SEQUESTRATION:

Sequestration is of relatively small importance in Florida, but is specifically available to enforce judgments. (R.C.P. 1.570[c][1]-[3]). Sequestration is specifically available to preserve property in an equitable action where defendant is residing out of state or cannot be found at his usual residence. (68.03). Court shall require plaintiffs to give bond with surety, to abide by future orders made for restoring property to absent defendant upon his appearance in action. If plaintiff does not furnish bond, property shall remain under direction of Court or in hands of receiver or otherwise until property is disposed of as Court sees fit. (68.03[2]). Sequestration also available to enforce judgments against corporations if writ of execution cannot be satisfied out of property of corporation. (56.10). Although statute does not explicitly require hearing on creditor's affidavit, hearing is probably constitutionally required. (416 U.S. 600).

SERVICE:

See topic Process.

STAY OF EXECUTION:

See topic Appeal and Error; category Debtor and Creditor, topic Executions.

SUBMISSION OF CONTROVERSY:

No statutory provisions.

VENUE:

Suits except against nonresidents must be initiated in county where defendant resides, where cause of action accrued, or where property in litigation is located. (47.011). Suits against two or more defendants residing in different counties may be brought in any county in which any defendant resides. (47.021). Suits upon several causes of action may be brought in any county where one of causes of action arose. (47.041).

Venue of Receiverships.—Application for receiver of property must be made to circuit court of circuit in which principal place of business, residence or office of defendant is located. If property is located in more than one judicial circuit, court appointing receiver has jurisdiction over entire property for purposes of that action. (47.031).

Actions on Promissory Notes.—Action on unsecured promissory notes can be brought only in county in which note was signed by maker or one of makers, or in

See note at head of Digest as to 1998 legislation covered.

See Topical Index in front part of this volume.

FL – 20

VENUE... *continued*

which maker or one of makers resides. When note was signed by makers in more than one county, action may be brought in any such county where signed. (47.061).

Contractors of Public Buildings.—In addition to provisions of c. 47, actions brought after 5/17/77 by materialmen, etc. pursuant to §255.05 may be brought in any county where public work is being constructed or repaired. (255.05[5]).

Corporations.—Suits against domestic corporations must be commenced in county where corporation has or usually has an office for transaction of its customary business or where cause of action accrued, or where property in litigation is located. (47.051).

In the case of a foreign corporation doing business in this state, suit must be begun in a county wherein such company has an agent or other representative, where property in litigation is situated, or where cause of action accrued. (47.051).

Navigable Waters.—Courts having territorial jurisdiction extending to one bank of any navigable water have jurisdiction from shore to shore; and where different courts have territorial jurisdiction extending to opposite banks of any navigable water, such courts have concurrent jurisdiction across same from shore to shore. (47.071).

Trust Proceedings.—Actions and proceedings concerning trusts may be brought in any county where venue is proper under c. 47 or where beneficiary suing or being sued resides or has his principal place of business or in any county where trust has its principal place of administration. (737.202).

Replevin Actions.—See topic Replevin.

Change of Venue.—All courts have power to grant changes of venue. (47.091). Party desiring change of venue must file verified motion not less than ten days after action is at issue unless good cause is shown for failure to so file. Motion must set forth facts and be supported by affidavits of at least two reputable citizens of county not kin to defendant or attorney. Statutory grounds include inability to receive fair trial because: (a) Adverse party has undue influence over minds of inhabitants of county; (b) movant is odious to inhabitants of county. (47.101).

If adverse party denies allegations of motion, court must hear evidence. (47.111). Change of venue must be granted if it appears impracticable to obtain qualified jury in particular county. (47.121). For convenience of parties or witnesses or in interest of justice, any court of record may transfer any civil action to any other court of record in which it might have been brought. (47.122; but see 223 So.2d 94). Second change of venue may be granted but not back to original county. (47.131). Order granting change transfers cause to another court of same jurisdiction. If judge of such court is disqualified, some other court shall be selected. (47.141).

Transfer Fees.—Party requesting change of venue must pay required transfer fee. However, when action was initially filed in improper venue, initially filing party must pay filing fee required to file new action in court to which action is moved. Payment of such filing fee shall be considered transfer fee. (47.091).

Contract Provisions.—Contract provisions for venue are valid and enforceable. (196 So.2d 22).

COURTS AND LEGISLATURE

COURTS:

United States District Courts.—

Northern District.—Clerk's office: Tallahassee 32301, Pensacola 32501.

Cases to be filed in Gainesville division should be sent to Clerk's office Tallahassee, Florida as records for this division are held in Tallahassee. Cases and pleadings in Panama City division are to be filed in Pensacola clerk's office.

Fees.—For filing complaint, $120; for removing cause from state court, $120. Judicial Improvements and Access to Justice Act (Pub.L. 100-702), enacted in 1988, makes several changes in removal statutes. §1009(b)(3) deletes 28 U.S.C. 1446(d) and thereby abolishes bond requirement associated with removal. Bond requirement imposes cost that may be substantial to some litigants, and constitutes additional procedural complication. Bond is not required on filing action, and should not be required on removal.

Middle District.—Clerk's office: Jacksonville 32201, Tampa 33602, Orlando 32801, Ft. Myers, 33901. Cases and pleadings in Ocala Division should be filed in clerk's office in Jacksonville where records are kept for Ocala Division.

Fees.—For filing complaint $120; for removing cause from state court, $120. Judicial Improvements and Access to Justice Act (Pub.L. 100-702), enacted in 1988, makes several changes in removal statutes. §1009(b)(3) deletes 28 U.S.C. 1446(d) and thereby abolishes bond requirement associated with removal. Bond requirement imposes cost that may be substantial to some litigants, and constitutes additional procedural complication. Bond is not required on filing action, and should not be required on removal.

Southern District.—Clerk's office: Miami 33128 (filings for Miami and Key West divisions); Ft. Lauderdale 33301 (filings for Ft. Lauderdale division); West Palm Beach 33401 (filings for West Palm Beach and Ft. Pierce divisions).

Fees.—For filing complaint, $120; for removing cause from state court, $120. Judicial Improvements and Access to Justice Act (Pub.L. 100-702), enacted in 1988, makes several changes in removal statutes. §1009(b)(3) deletes 28 U.S.C. 1446(d) and thereby abolishes bond requirement associated with removal. Bond requirement imposes cost that may be substantial to some litigants, and constitutes additional procedural complication. Bond is not required on filing action, and should not be required on removal.

Note.—Divisions in Florida are not statutory but are created by rule of court and hence federal statutes relative to divisions are not always applicable to divisions in Florida. District Court is open at all times for admiralty and maritime cases.

Supreme Court shall hear appeals from final judgments of trial courts imposing death penalty and from decisions of district courts of appeal declaring invalid state statute or provision of state constitution.

Supreme Court may, through discretionary review, review any decision of district court of appeal that expressly affects class of constitutional or state officers, that passes upon question certified by district court of appeal to be of great public importance, or that is in direct and express conflict with decision of another district court of appeal, or of Supreme Court, questions of law certified by U.S. Supreme Court or U.S. Court of Appeals determinative of cause of action without controlling Florida Supreme Court precedent, any decision of district court of appeal that expressly declares valid state statute or expressly construes provision of state or federal constitution, and any order or judgment of trial court certified by district court of appeal in which appeal is pending to be of great public importance, or to have great effect on proper administration of justice throughout state, and certified to require immediate resolution by Supreme Court.

When provided by general law, Supreme Court must hear appeals from final judgments entered in proceedings for validation of bonds or certificates of indebtedness and must review actions of statewide agencies relating to rates or service of utilities providing electric, gas or telephone service.

Supreme Court may issue writs of mandamus and quo warranto to state officers and state agencies, writs of prohibition to courts, writs of habeas corpus, and all writs necessary for complete exercise of its jurisdiction. (Const., art. 5, §3).

District Court of Appeal.—Counties divided into five appellate districts. (26.021; 35.2; 35.05).

Appeals in each appellate district may be taken to court of appeals of such district as matter of right from all final judgments or orders of trial courts (excepting cases directly appealable to Supreme Court and cases where circuit courts have final appellate jurisdiction), and district courts have such powers of direct review of administrative action as may be provided by law. May consider certain certified questions from county courts. (See subhead Circuit Courts, infra.)

District Courts of Appeal or any judge thereof may issue writs of habeas corpus. District Courts of Appeal may issue writs of mandamus, certiorari, prohibition, and quo warranto, and all writs necessary to complete exercise of jurisdiction. (Const., art. 5, §4).

Fees.—$250 fee for each case docketed for filing of certified copy of notice of appeal or petition. (35.22[3]).

Circuit courts have exclusive original jurisdiction in all cases in equity including juvenile matters (except traffic offenses not punishable by law as felony as provided in cc. 39 and 316), in all cases at law not cognizable by county courts (Const., art. 5, §5) and in all probate matters, of all felonies and of all misdemeanors arising out of same circumstances as felony which is also charged, in all cases involving legality of any tax assessment or toll, in ejectment actions, and in all actions involving title, right of possession, or boundaries of real property (Const., art. 5, §20; 26.012). Circuit courts have appellate jurisdiction of appeals from county courts and municipal courts except appeals declaring invalid state statute or provision of state constitution, except orders and judgments of county court certified by county court to district court of appeal to be of great public importance and accepted by district court of appeals and appeals from final administrative orders of local government code enforcement boards. (26.012). Presiding judge in each Circuit exercises administrative supervision over all trial courts in that Circuit. (43.26).

Fees.—Sum of all service charges and fees permitted under §28.241 may not exceed $200. (28.241[1]). Service charge or fee may not be imposed upon party for responding by pleading, motion, or other paper to civil or criminal action, suit, proceeding, or appeal in circuit court. (28.241[4]).

County courts have original jurisdiction in all misdemeanor cases not cognizable in circuit courts, of all violations of municipal and county ordinances, of all actions at law accruing before July 1, 1980 where amount in controversy does not exceed $2,500, exclusive of interest, costs and attorney's fees, except those within exclusive jurisdiction of circuit courts, and of all actions at law accruing on or after July 1, 1980 where amount in controversy does not exceed $5,000, exclusive of interest, costs and attorney's fees, except those within exclusive jurisdiction of circuit courts, of all actions at law accruing on or after July 1, 1990 where amount in controversy does not exceed $10,000, exclusive of interest, cost and attorney's fees, except those within exclusive jurisdiction of circuit courts, and of all actions at law accruing on or after July 1, 1992 where amount in controversy does not exceed $15,000, exclusive of interest, cost and attorney's fees, except those within exclusive jurisdiction of circuit courts; party instituting any civil action, suit or proceeding pursuant to this schedule where amount in controversy exceeds $5,000 shall pay to clerk of county court filing fees and service charges in same amounts and in same manner as provided in §28.241; county court judges may hear matters involving dissolution of marriage under simplified dissolution procedure pursuant to Rule 1.611(c), Florida Rules of Civil Procedure or may issue final order for dissolution in cases where matter is uncontested; county court judges may hear all matters in equity involved in any case within jurisdictional amount of county court except as otherwise restricted by State Constitution or laws of Florida (34.01), as well as concurrent jurisdiction with circuit court in landlord/tenant cases which are within its jurisdictional limits, and jurisdiction of cases relating to right of possession of real property and forcible or unlawful detention of lands and tenements, except that circuit court also has jurisdiction if amount in controversy exceeds jurisdictional limits of county court or circuit court otherwise has jurisdiction as provided in §26.012 (34.011).

Fees.—Sum of all service charges and fees permitted under §34.041 may not exceed $200. Charge or fee may not be imposed upon party for responding by pleading, motion, or other paper to civil or criminal action, suit, or proceeding in county court or to appeal to circuit court. (34.041).

Probate Courts.—Probate jurisdiction is exercised by circuit courts. (26.012).

Fees.—Additional service charge of $2.50 on petitions seeking summary administration, family administration, formal administration, ancillary administration, guardianship, curatorship, and conservatorship, shall be paid to clerk for deposit into Court Education Trust Fund. (28.2401).

Juvenile Courts.—Juvenile jurisdiction is exercised by circuit courts. (26.012).

Municipal Courts.—Abolished Jan. 3, 1977. (Const. art. 5, §20; 77-119).

Small Claims Courts.—Jurisdiction is exercised by county courts. (34.01).

See note at head of Digest as to 1998 legislation covered.

See Topical Index in front part of this volume.

LEGISLATURE:

Regular Sessions.—Held on 1st Tues. after 1st Mon. in Feb. of each year, unless some other date fixed by law for each even-numbered year; session not more than 60 consecutive days or such other date as may be fixed by law. (Const. art. 3, §3[b] & [d]).

Organization Sessions.—Held on 14th day following each general election for exclusive purpose of organization and selection of officers. (Const. art. 3, §3[a]).

Special sessions may be called by proclamation of governor for limited purpose stated in proclamation or other executive communication, or for such purpose as is agreed to by two-thirds membership of each house; session shall not exceed 20 consecutive days unless extended by three-fifths vote of each house. (Const. art. 3, §3[c]).

Referendum required for: Amending state constitution (Const. art. 11, §5); calling convention to revise entire constitution (Const. art. 11, §4); consolidation (Const. art. 8, §3); transfer of local powers (Const. art. 8, §4); imposing or repealing prohibition in counties (Const. art. 8, §5).

Lobbyists.—Regulated by c. 11 relating to legislative organization, procedures and staffing (11.045-.062) and c. 112 relating to code of ethics for public officers and employees (112.3213-.3217).

REPORTS:

Decisions of Florida Supreme Court and Florida district courts of appeal are published in Southern Reporter, which, beginning with 37 So.2d 692, is official publication. Florida Reports, vols. 1-160, is official report prior to 37 So.2d 692, and covers most cases through Dec. 21, 1948. Decisions of circuit courts are published in Florida Supplement.

"FLW" refers to Florida Law Weekly, an advance sheet.

"FLW-Fed" refers to Florida Law Weekly Federal, advance sheet for Florida federal district court, appellate court and United States Supreme Court cases.

Digests.—West Publishing Co., Southern Digest and Florida Digest cover Florida decisions.

STATUTES:

Florida Statutes is revision, compilation and consolidation of general statutes of permanent nature carried forward under annual revision system. Florida Statutes are published biennially following each odd-year regular session, and Supplement is published following each even year regular session. Official text is contained in Florida Statutes 1995 and is best evidence of Florida law. Supplement does not contain official text but is prima facie evidence of law of Florida.

Repeal of Prior Statutes.—All statutes of general or permanent nature enacted at or prior to 1995 regular legislative session, and every part of such statute, not included in Florida Statutes 1997, as adopted by §11-2421, as amended were repealed (11.2422), unless recognized and continued in force by reference therein or in 11.2423 and 11.2424, as amended. Such repeal does not affect any rights accruing before such repeal or any civil remedy where suit is pending. (11.2425).

Session Laws.—Statutes enacted during 1996 and 1997 legislative sessions, published as 1996 and 1997 Session Laws, provide interim authority pending publication of 1997 Florida Statutes.

Unofficial Compilation.—Florida Statutes Annotated uses text of official Florida Statutes together with annotations, kept up to date by revised volumes, periodic pamphlets, and cumulative annual pocket parts, published by The Harrison Company, Atlanta, and by West Publishing Company.

Uniform Acts.—Act to Secure the Attendance of Witnesses From Without a State in Criminal Proceedings (1941); Anatomical Gift (1969); Arbitration (1992); Child Custody Jurisdiction Act (1977); Commercial Code (1967); Common Trust Fund (1941); Contribution Among Tortfeasors (1975); Declaratory Judgments (1943); Disposition of Unclaimed Property (1961); Federal Lien Registration Act (1992); Fraudulent Transfer (1988); Interstate Family Support (1996); Limited Partnership, Revised (1986); Management of Institutional Funds Act (1990); Partnership, Revised (1996); Principal and Income Act, Revised (1975); †Probate Code (1976); †Reciprocal Transfer Tax (1931); Simplification of Fiduciary Security Transfers (1961); Simultaneous Death (1941); Statutory Rule Against Perpetuities (1988); Testamentary Additions to Trusts (1961); Trade Secrets (1988); Transfers to Minors Act (1985); Florida Enforcement of Foreign Judgments Act is very similar to Uniform Act—some sections are identical.

Uniform Commercial Code enacted, effective Jan. 1, 1967. See category Business Regulation and Commerce, topic Commercial Code.

For text of Uniform Acts falling within the scope of the Martindale-Hubbell Law Digests see Uniform and Model Acts section.

† Adopted with significant variations or modifications. See relevant topics for discussion of Florida statutes.

UNIFORM LAWS:

For list of Uniform Acts in force in this state see topic Statutes. For text of Uniform Acts within the scope of the Martindale-Hubbell Law Digests see Uniform and Model Acts section.

CRIMINAL LAW

BAIL:

See topic Criminal Law.

CRIMINAL LAW:

Crimes generally: c. 775-c. 896.

Criminal procedure generally: c. 900-c. 942; Fla. Rules Crim. Pro. 3.010-3.851.

Indictment or Information.—Capital offenses must be tried on indictment by a grand jury; other offenses (with exceptions for juveniles' crimes) and persons on active duty in military may be tried on either indictment or information by prosecuting attorney under oath. (Const. art. 1, §15).

Bail.—All crimes are bailable by sufficient sureties except capital or life imprisonment offenses where proof of guilt is evident or presumption great. (Const. art. I, §14; Fla. Rule Crim. Pro. 3.131[a]). Bail must be revoked for commission and conviction of separate felony while free on appeal. (903.131). No bail permitted on appeal from felony unless defendant establishes that appeal is taken in good faith, on grounds fairly debatable, and not frivolous. (903.132[1]). Provided also that bail shall not be granted if such person had been previously convicted of felony committed prior to felony in question, and such person's civil rights have not been restored; or, if other felony charges are pending for which probable cause has been found at time request for bail is made. In no case may original appearance bond be continued for appeal. (903.132[3]; 903.132[3]). Because of increased risk and longer time considerations, there shall be new undertaking of bond for appeal. (903.132[3]). Denial of bail because of pending first degree felony charges for which probable cause has been found is appealable. (903.132[2]). Notwithstanding conditions for granting appellate review in bail matters, no person adjudged guilty of felony of murder in violation of §§782.04(2) or (3), kidnapping in violation of §787.01, sexual battery in violation of § 794.011(4), arson in violation of §806.01, selling, purchasing, manufacturing, delivering, or possessing with intent to sell, purchase, manufacture or deliver controlled substance in violation of §893.13, drug trafficking in violation of §893.135, or adjudged guilty of sexual battery in violation of §§794.011(2) or (3), must be admitted to bail pending review either by post-trial motion or appeal. (903.133).

Interstate Compact for Supervision of Parolees and Probationers in effect. (949.07-.08).

Uniform Criminal Extradition Act in effect. (941.01-.4).

Uniform Law on Fresh Pursuit in effect. (941.31-35).

Uniform Act to Secure the Attendance of Witnesses from Without a State in Criminal Proceedings in effect. (942.01-06).

Registration of Felons.—Persons convicted of a felony, in any federal or state court or foreign state or country except one who has had his civil rights restored, received full pardon, or has been released from incarceration, or other sentence or supervision for felony conviction for more than five years prior to such time for registration, must register with sheriff within 48 hours after entering any county of this state. (775.13). This law does not apply to parolee or probationer under supervision of U.S. Parole Commission or any federal probation officer who consents to presence of such person in Florida, nor to probationer under supervision of any federal probation officer in state, nor to one who is lawfully discharged from such parole or probation. (775.13). See 944.293, initiation of restoration of civil rights.

Failure of convicted felon to register shall constitute second degree misdemeanor. (774.13[6]).

DEBTOR AND CREDITOR

ASSIGNMENTS:

Uniform Commercial Code adopted. (cc. 670-680). See category Business Regulation and Commerce, topic Commercial Code.

Contractual rights are generally assignable unless restricted by public policy, statute or when contract involves personal trust and confidence of assignor or is prohibited by provision in contract. Civil actions by real parties in interest are authorized except as to assignment of chose in action not arising out of contract. It is not necessary for assignee in any suit upon an instrument assignable by law to set forth in declaration consideration upon which instrument was given or to prove such consideration or execution unless same is impeached by defendant under oath. Executor or administrator may, however, deny execution or consideration by plea not under oath. (68.06).

Mortgages may be assigned. (701.01). Assignment of mortgage on real property not effectual against creditors or subsequent purchasers, for valuable consideration, and without notice, unless assignment is contained in document which indicates assignment of mortgage in title and assignment is recorded. (701.02).

Liens, except those of laborers, may be assigned by lienor at any time before discharge. Assignment may be recorded in Clerk's Office. (713.19).

Statutory Retirement Benefits Not Assignable.—Most, if not all, statutory retirement benefits are not assignable, including those for firefighters (175.241), municipal police officers (185.25), state and county employees (122.15) and teachers (238.15). See 587 So.2d 151 regarding garnishment of such benefits for child support purposes under §§61.1301 and 61.046(4).

Instrument Transferring Title.—See category Business Regulation and Commerce, topic Frauds, Statute of.

Notice to debtor of assignment of debt or chose in action necessary to impose duty to pay assignee. If debtor pays assignor or subsequent assignee before receiving notice of initial assignment, debtor discharged.

ATTACHMENT:

Caution: Prejudgment attachment and garnishment remedies in other states having provisions similar to those in Florida have been declared unconstitutional. (419 U.S. 601).

Actions in Which Allowed.—Attachment lies before or after judgment in actions ex contractu in nature. (76.01 et seq.). Attachment not available in tort actions except those arising from navigation, direction or management of boats, vessels, etc. (76.32).

Courts Which May Issue Writ.—Attachments are required to be issued by judge of court which has jurisdiction of amount claimed by creditor, unless property to be

ATTACHMENT . . . *continued*
attached is being actually removed from state and creditor is unable to obtain process from proper court in time to prevent such removal, in which case any judge may issue writ, making same returnable to circuit or county court having jurisdiction of amount claimed. (76.03).

In Whose Favor and Against Whom Writ May Issue.—Any creditor may have an attachment against goods, lands and tenements of his debtor in a proper case. (76.01). No restrictions on foreign corporations or nonresidents.

Claims on Which Writ May Issue.—See subhead, Actions in Which Allowed, supra.

Grounds.—Attachment may be procured upon filing motion therefor, when grounds relied upon clearly appear from specific facts shown by verified complaint or separate affidavit and requirements of Fla. Stat. §§76.09-.11 are met. (76.08). When debt is due, motion shall state amount of debt that is actually due, and that movant has reason to believe that defendant will fraudulently part with his property before judgment, is actually removing his property out of State of Florida, is about to remove his property, resides out of state, is actually moving himself beyond limits of state, is about to move himself out of state, is absconding, is concealing himself, or is secreting or fraudulently disposing of his property, is actually removing himself beyond limits of judicial circuit in which he resides, or is about to so remove himself out of limits of such judicial circuit. (76.09; 76.04).

When Debt Not Due.—Motion must state amount of debt or demand; that it is existing debt; and must state specifically at least one of following special grounds: that debtor is actually removing his property beyond limits of state, that he is fraudulently disposing of property for purpose of avoiding payment of just debts or demands or fraudulently secreting property for such purpose. (76.10; 76.05). In addition, plaintiff must produce before officer granting attachment proof, by affidavit (other than his own) or otherwise, satisfactory to such officer, of existence of such special ground. (76.10).

When Attachment in Aid of Foreclosure of Mortgage on Personal Property.—Motion shall describe property on which mortgage exists, and state that complaint has been filed to foreclose mortgage, amount of debt secured by mortgage, that it is actually due, and that movant has reason to believe that property or part of same: (1) will be concealed or disposed of so that it will not be forthcoming to answer judgment or decree of foreclosure; (2) will be removed beyond jurisdiction of court; (3) is perishable and is being used and consumed; or (4) has been disposed of without consent of holder and owner of mortgage, stating who has property, if known, or that affiant does not know who has same. (76.11; 76.07). Where attachment is based on ground (4) and holder of property is unknown, attachment bond must be payable to state. (76.12). See also, Commercial Code c. 679, pt. 5.

Proceedings to Obtain.—Practice in suits commenced by attachments are same as other suits at law. See R. C. P. 1.010.

Attachment Bond.—No attachment may issue until person applying for same, his agent or attorney, has entered into bond, with surety, payable to defendant, in at least double debt or sum demanded, conditioned to pay all costs and damages which defendant may sustain in consequence of improperly suing out attachment. (76.12). See subhead When Attachment in Aid of Foreclosure of Mortgage on Personal Property, supra, regarding need for bond payable to state in certain foreclosure circumstances. (76.12).

Levy, Lien, Priorities.—Levy of a writ of attachment does not operate to dispossess tenant of any lands or tenements, but levy upon real or personal property binds property attached, except against preexisting liens. Levies upon same property under successive attachments have precedence as liens in order in which they are made. Levy binds real estate as against subsequent creditors or purchasers only from time of record by clerk of circuit court in lien book of notice of levy and description of property levied upon. (76.14).

Upon statement in motion that defendant has property in a county other than that in which suit is instituted, a writ of attachment may issue directed to sheriff or other proper officer of county where said property is, and said officer must execute writ and hold and dispose of property as in other cases. (76.16).

Release of Property.—Property attached may be restored to defendant or other person for him at any time after execution of writ upon giving of surety bond to officer levying attachment, payable to plaintiff in amount which exceeds by one-fourth value of property, determined by court, or which exceeds by one-fourth amount of claim, whichever is less (76.18), or upon defendant giving bond, with surety approved by officer, conditioned for payment to plaintiff of debt and all costs of action when such debt and costs are adjudicated payable to plaintiff (76.19).

Vacation or Modification.—Defendant may by motion obtain dissolution of writ and court shall set down such motion for immediate hearing and if any allegation in plaintiff's affidavit which is denied under oath in writing by defendant is not sustained and proved to be true, such court will dissolve attachment. Issue joined upon such denial may be tried by jury, upon demand of either party. (76.24).

Third Party Claims.—Attached property claimed by third persons may be replevied, or a claim interposed therefor by filing with officer levying attachment an affidavit made by claimant, his agent or attorney, that property claimed by him is his property, and by giving of a bond, payable to plaintiff, with surety to be approved by such officer in double value of goods claimed. (76.21; 56.16).

CREDITORS' SUITS:

Creditors' bills may be filed in chancery before creditors' claims have been reduced to judgment, but no such action shall be entertained unless plaintiff has first instituted separate action at law for collection of claims, and no final judgment will be entered until such claims have been reduced to judgment. (68.05).

See also proceedings supplementary to execution intended to give as full relief as creditors' suit. (56.29; 47 So.2d 769). See also R. C. P. 1.560 providing for discovery concerning assets in aid of judgment, decree or execution. See topic Executions.

EXECUTIONS:

Exemptions.—See topic Exemptions.

Issuance.—When issued, execution is valid and effective during life of judgment or decree on which it is issued. (56.021). When fully paid, officer executing it shall make his return and file it in court which issued execution. (56.021). If execution is lost or destroyed, party entitled thereto may have alias, pluries or other copies on making proof of such loss or destruction by affidavit and filing it in court issuing execution. (56.021).

Stay.—Upon affidavit showing illegality of issuance of an execution, and whether anything be due thereon, and filing of a bond with surety payable to plaintiff in double amount of execution or part of which stay is sought, enforcement thereof may be stayed. (56.15).

Lien.—Execution is lien on personal property effective from time of delivery of writ to sheriff. (73 Fla. 819, 75 So. 30). As general rule, lien binds all property, real or personal, which is subject of levy and sale. (80 Fla. 84, 85 So. 659, 56.061).

Levy.—All lands and tenements, goods and chattels, equities of redemption in real and personal property, interest in personal property in possession of vendee under retained title or conditional sales contract, and stock in corporations are subject to levy and sale under execution. (56.061). Mandamus lies to compel levy and sale. (56.26). See topic Exemptions.

Return.—Execution is returnable when satisfied. (56.041[1]). Unsatisfied executions may be returned 20 years after final judgment. (56.041[2]).

Claims of Third Persons.—Same as in Attachments, q.v.

Sale.—All sales of property under legal process must take place any day of week except Sat. and Sun., and continue from day to day until such property is disposed of. (56.22). Property not effectively disposed of at initial sheriff's sale may be readvertised upon receipt of additional deposit to cover costs incurred in connection with maintenance of property under legal process. (56.22). If no additional deposit is received by sheriff, property may be returned to defendant, or if defendant refuses to accept property, it may be returned to third party, such as lienholder, upon presentation of proper court order so directing, or if none of above can be accomplished, such property shall be disposed of as unclaimed or abandoned. (56.22). Notice of all such sales is given by advertisement, once each week for four successive weeks, in newspaper published in county in which sale is to take place, time of such notice may be shortened by court upon affidavit that property is subject to decay and will not sell for its full value if held until date of sale. (56.21). Copy of notice must be furnished to debtor or debtor's attorney by certified mail on or before date of first publication or of posting. Notice must be made in same manner upon owner of record of real property being levied upon. (56.21). On or before date of first publication or posting of notice of sale, copy of notice must be furnished by certified mail to attorney of record of judgment debtor or to judgment debtor at his last known address if he does not have attorney of record. Such notice is required even though default judgment was entered. When levying upon real property, notice of levy and execution sale must be made to property owner of record in same manner as notice to any judgment debtor. (56.21). When selling real or personal property, sale date must not be earlier than 30 days after date of first advertisement. (56.21).

Redemption.—There is no right of redemption of property sold under execution.

Supplementary Proceedings.—After execution returned unsatisfied, proceedings supplementary to execution are provided whereby execution creditor may examine judgment debtor, under oath, as to his property, business, or financial interests. Examination is before judge of court issuing execution or before master appointed by court. Burden is on debtor to prove bona fides of any transfer of personal property within one year to his wife, any relative or person in confidential relation. Judge may order any property of judgment debtor not exempt from execution, in hands of either himself or any other person or due judgment debtor, to be applied toward satisfaction of judgment debt. Reasonable attorney's fees may be taxed against debtor. (56.29). Circuit court has broad discretionary power in supplemental proceedings to enforce execution of judgment against defendant's property as substitute for creditor's bill in equity. (56.29[9]; 47 So.2d 769). See also R. C. P. 1.560, providing for discovery in aid of execution.

Body Execution.—Capias ad satisfaciendum abolished. (56.011).

EXEMPTIONS:

Generally exempt from legal process are: Damages for injuries or death in certain hazardous occupations (769.05), proceeds and cash surrender value of life insurance and proceeds of annuity contracts (222.13, 222.14), disability insurance benefits (222.18) (unless policy or contract was effected for benefit of creditors), firemen's pensions (175.241), subsidy payments made to participants in municipal police officers' retiree health insurance subsidy program (185.25), and certain pensions and funds of state and county employees (122.15) and teachers (238.15). (See also topic Garnishment.)

Debts Against Which Exemptions Not Allowed.—No property is exempt from sale for taxes or assessments or for the payment of obligations contracted for the purchase of said property.

Waiver of Exemption.—Generally, failure to make application for homestead tax exemption by Mar. 1, of any year shall constitute waiver of tax exemption privilege for that year. (196.011[1]). See topic Homesteads. Otherwise, there may be no general waiver of exemption, but specific liens may be created, against which exemption may not be claimed. (c. 713).

Wages owed to resident head of family including wages which are deposited in bank accounts and which can be traced and identified as wages are generally exempt from all legal process (222.11), but courts may remove or limit exemptions for payment of alimony or child support (61.12). "Head of family" includes any unmarried, divorced, legally separated or widowed person who is providing more than one-half of support for child or other dependent. (222.11). Exemption may be claimed by

See note at head of Digest as to 1998 legislation covered.

See Topical Index in front part of this volume.

FL – 23

EXEMPTIONS . . . *continued*

affidavit filed before issuing officer and by serving notice of same on creditor, who may deny same within two days in which case issue is tried. (222.12). Wage assignments to secure certain loans are not valid. (516.17). See also topic Garnishment.

FORECLOSURE:

See topic Liens; category Mortgages, topic Mortgages of Real Property.

FRAUDULENT SALES AND CONVEYANCES:

Uniform Commercial Code adopted. (cc. 670-680). Bulk Sales Law repealed. See category Business Regulation and Commerce, topic Commercial Code.

Uniform Fraudulent Conveyance Act not adopted.

Uniform Fraudulent Transfer Act adopted and became effective on Jan. 1, 1988. (726.101 et seq.). Transfer of property is fraudulent as to present or future creditor if made: (1) With actual intent to delay or defraud or (2) without receiving reasonably equivalent value in exchange and debtor making transfer was engaged in business for which remaining assets were unreasonably small or intended to incur debts beyond ability to pay as they became due. (726.105). Transfer of property is fraudulent as to present creditor if made without receiving reasonably equivalent value in exchange for transfer and debtor making transfer was either insolvent at time or became insolvent as result of transfer. (726.106). Transfer of property also fraudulent as to present creditor if made to insider for antecedent debt, debtor was insolvent at that time, and insider had reasonable cause to believe that debtor was insolvent. (726.106).

Remedies.—Relief under Uniform Fraudulent Transfer Act includes: (1) Avoidance of transfer to extent necessary to satisfy creditor's claim; (2) attachment against asset transfered or other property of transferee; (3) injunction against further disposition of asset transferred or other property; (4) appointment of receiver to take charge of asset transferred or of other property of transferee; or (5) any other relief circumstances may require. (726.108). Under common law, creditors of transferor may: (1) Place demand in judgment and levy on property allegedly fraudulently conveyed; (2) bring bill in equity to remove allegedly fraudulent conveyance as obstructing enforcement of judgment lien and have it set aside; or (3) bring action in nature of creditors bill to reach equitable assets. (106 Fla. 567, 143 So. 433).

Execution of Judgment.—When defendant in execution is on confidential terms with transferee of personal property, burden is on defendant to establish that transfer within one year prior to service of process was not done for purpose of hindering or defrauding creditors. (56.29[6][a]).

Bulk Sales.—Uniform Commercial Code article on bulk sales repealed effective July 1, 1993.

Fraudulent Sale of Franchises.—Any sale of franchise wherein seller intentionally misrepresents chances for success, total investment, or efforts to sell more franchises than is reasonable to expect market area to sustain is unlawful. If violation is proven, violator subject to punishment for second degree misdemeanor. Prevailing party in civil action is entitled to all monies invested in franchise or distributorship and in court's discretion, attorneys' fees. Dept. of Legal Affairs and Dept. of Agriculture and Consumer Services may sue for injunctive relief against franchise plans in violation of this section. (817.416).

False Pretenses and Frauds.—Fraudulent practices may be felony or misdemeanor and subject to injunction. (817.02-817.567). Deceptive and Unfair Trade Practices Act prohibits unfair methods of competition, unconscionable acts and unfair or deceptive practices in conduct of trade or business. (501.201-501.213). Persons who counterfeit, forge, alter or possess any ticket, token or paper designed for admission to any sports, amusements, concert or other facility offering services to public with intent to defraud may be guilty of first degree misdemeanor. (817.355). Game promotions and contests conducted in connection with sale of consumer goods or services are strictly regulated by statute. (849.094).

Credit Cards.—Person who knowingly makes false statement for purpose of procuring credit card, takes credit card from another without consent, retains possession of lost, mislaid or mistakenly delivered credit card, forges or alters credit card, or uses credit card for any fraudulent purpose is in violation of State Credit Card Crime Act (817.57-817.685) and may be guilty of first degree misdemeanor or third degree felony.

Fraudulent Advertising.—Any advertising or other offer of "free" goods must contain clear and conspicuous, complete disclosure of any condition or restriction on acceptance of gift. Commissioner of Agriculture or Attorney General may sue for injunctive relief. (817.415).

GARNISHMENT:

Garnishment is creditor's remedy whereby debtor's property, money or credits in possession or control of, or owing by another, garnishee, is applied to payment of debt pursuant to statutory process against debtor and garnishee. (77.01). Writ of garnishment is available whenever suit brought to recover debt or judgment is recovered. Writ covers any debt due defendant by third person and any tangible or intangible personal property of defendant in possession or control of third person. (77.01). Disposable earnings of head of family are exempt from garnishment if less than $500 week; if greater than $500 per week then exempt unless garnishee agreed otherwise in writing. Where wages are garnished, continuing writ of garnishment shall be issued to debtor's employer; employer entitled to collect $5 for first deduction and $2 each deduction thereafter for administrative costs. (222.11; 77.0305). Federal law preempts conflicting provisions to extent maximum allowed to be garnished exceeds lesser of 25% of person's disposable weekly earnings or amount of such weekly earnings exceeding 30 times federal minimum hourly wage. (297 So.2d 6; 15 U.S.C. §1673; 29 C.F.R. §§870.1-.57). Method of applicable exemptions to personal property set forth in 222.061. Other exceptions set forth in c. 222. Garnishment not available in tort action prior to judgment. (77.02).

Before judgment against defendant, writ of garnishment may be issued only by court or by clerk on order of court. To obtain writ, plaintiff, his agent or attorney shall file in court where action is pending verified motion or affidavit alleging by specific facts: (1) Nature of cause of action, (2) amount of debt, (3) that debt is just, due and unpaid, (4) garnishment is not sought to injure either defendant or garnishee, and (5) belief that after execution is issued defendant will not have in his possession in county where action pending sufficient tangible or intangible personal property on which levy can be made to satisfy plaintiff's claim. Motion or pleading need not negative any exemptions of defendant. (77.031[4]). Upon issuance, clerk shall mail defendant copy of writ which shall include notice of defendant's right to immediate hearing for dissolution of such writ pursuant to §77.07. Except where attachment has issued, no prejudgment garnishment shall issue until plaintiff gives satisfactory bond of double debt and payable to defendant conditioned to pay defendant all costs, damages and attorneys' fees from improper garnishment. Informality of garnishment bond shall not void bond or cause obligors to be discharged, even though garnishment is dissolved because of its informality. (77.031).

After Judgment.—Before writ will issue after judgment, plaintiff, his agent or attorney shall file motion (which shall not be verified or negative defendant's exemptions) stating amount thereof, and that movant does not believe that defendant has in his possession sufficient visible property subject to levy to satisfy judgment. Motion may be filed and writ issued either before or after return of execution. (77.03).

Answer.—Garnishee must serve answer to issued writ on plaintiff within 20 days after service, stating whether garnishee is indebted at time of answer or service of writ, or at any time between such times, and in what sum and what tangible or intangible personal property of defendant is in garnishee's possession or control at time of answer or service of writ, or at any time between such times, and whether garnishee knows of any other person indebted to defendant, or who may possess or control any property of defendant. Writ must also state amount in plaintiff's motion. (77.04; 77.06[2]). On failure to answer as required, default shall be entered against garnishee. (77.081[1]; R.C.P. 1.500[e]). Issued writ also requires garnishee to report in its answer and retain, subject to provisions of §77.19, any deposit, account, or tangible or intangible property in its possession or control. Answer of garnishee must state name and address of such others appearing to have ownership interest in property. (77.06[2]). If garnishee doubts in good faith whether property or indebtedness is to be included in answer, garnishee may include same without liability. (77.06[3]). Service of writ renders garnishee liable in any fiduciary or representative capacity held by him if specified in suit. (77.06[4]).

Notice.—Within five days after service of garnishee's answer on plaintiff, or after time period for garnishee's answer has expired, plaintiff shall serve copies of writ and answer on defendant and on any person disclosed in garnishee's answer to have any ownership interest in deposit, account or property controlled by garnishee. Plaintiff must also file and serve certificate of service and notice that recipients must move to dissolve writ within applicable time period in §77.07(2) or be defaulted and that there may be exemptions available as defense. (77.055).

Dissolution of Writ.—By motion filed and served within 20 days after date indicated in certificate of service, defendant or any party with ownership interest in property may obtain dissolution of writ, unless plaintiff proves grounds upon which writ was issued and, unless, if prejudgment writ, there is reasonable probability that plaintiff will receive final judgment in underlying action. If motion to dissolve is not timely filed and served, court shall strike motion. Court shall set such motion for immediate hearing and if writ is dissolved action shall proceed as if no writ had been issued. (77.07).

Deposit Required.—Before issuance of writ of garnishment, party applying for it must deposit $100 in registry of court which must be paid to garnishee on its demand at any time after service of writ for payment or part payment of attorney's fee. On rendering final judgment court shall determine and tax as costs garnishee's costs and expenses, including reasonable attorney's fee. Plaintiff may recover in this manner sums advanced and paid into registry of court, and if amount allowed by court is greater than amount of deposit, together with any offset, judgment for garnishee shall be entered against party against whom costs are taxed for deficiency. (77.28). Garnishee may claim pay of its witness out of debt or property, or if none, from plaintiff. (77.17).

Discharge of Garnishment.—At any time before judgment, defendant may secure release of property by giving bond to be approved by clerk or by court if no clerk, lesser of double amount claimed plus interest and costs or double value of property, conditioned to pay up to value of property, any judgment recovered against defendant plus interest and costs. If garnishee admits indebtedness in excess of plaintiff's claim, garnishee may after motion with notice to plaintiff be released from responsibility for any indebtedness except sum deemed by court to be sufficient to satisfy plaintiff's claim plus interest and costs. (77.24).

If plaintiff not satisfied with garnishee's answer, plaintiff may serve reply within 20 days thereafter denying allegations of answer. On failure of plaintiff to file reply, answer shall be taken as true, and on proper disposition of any assets disclosed garnishee is entitled to discharge from further liability on writ. (77.061).

If no reply is served garnishee may surrender goods, chattels or effects of defendant in garnishee's possession to sheriff and may pay any money or debt into registry of court. In such event or if garnishee prevails in trial of any reply and after proper disposition of property disclosed by answer, court shall discharge garnishee from further liability under writ. (77.082).

Judgment against garnishee on answer or after trial must be entered for amount of garnishee's liability determined by answer or trial, but not to exceed amount remaining unpaid on final judgment against defendant. (77.083). After garnishee's default, on entry of judgment for plaintiff, final judgment shall be entered against garnishee for full amount of plaintiff's claim against defendant with interest and costs. No final judgment against garnishee shall be entered before entry of, or in excess of, final judgment against original defendant with interest and costs. If claim of plaintiff is dismissed or judgment is entered against plaintiff, default against garnishee must be

See note at head of Digest as to 1998 legislation covered.

See Topical Index in front part of this volume.

FL – 24

GARNISHMENT ... *continued*

vacated and judgment for garnishee's costs entered. (77.081[2]). Court may subpoena garnishee to inquire about garnishee's liability to or possession of property of defendant. (77.083).

Earnings.—See topic Exemptions.

HOMESTEADS:

Homestead owned by natural person is entitled to exemption from forced sale under process and no judgment, decree or execution shall be lien thereon. (Const. art. 10, §4[a]; 196.031). Dependent spouse or dependent heirs are not necessary for homestead to apply. (531 So.2d 946). See category Property, topic Real Property.

Limitation of Value.—Only $1,000 of personal property is exempt. (Const. art. 10, §4[a][2]). See topic Exemptions. No limitation on value of real property plus improvements.

Limitation of Area.—One hundred sixty acres of contiguous land if not in a municipality or one-half acre of contiguous land if in a municipality, but no homestead may be reduced in area, without owner's consent, by reason of subsequent inclusion in a municipality. (Const. art. 10, §4[a][1]).

Improvements on real property are within exemption except that exemption in a city or town does not extend to more improvements or buildings than the residence of owner or his family. (Const. art. 10, §4[a][1]).

Debts or Liabilities Against Which Exemption not Available.—Exemption does not extend to sale for taxes or assessments thereon or payment of obligations contracted for purchase, improvement or repair of property desired to be exempted, or obligations contracted for house, field or other labor performed on realty. (Const. art. 10, §4[a]).

Designation of homestead before levy is accomplished by recording in office of clerk of circuit court, written statement, signed by person making statement designating property therein described as homestead. (222.01).

Claim of exemption after levy and before day of sale is made by written notice under oath to officer making levy describing therein homestead property, and remainder only will be subject to sale. (222.02).

Waiver or loss of exemption is possible only by abandonment (196.061), alienation (Const., art. 10, §4) or annulment (222.10), and waiver in promissory note or mortgage is unenforceable (89 So.2d 28). Rental of homestead constitutes abandonment. (196.061).

Alienation.—Owner of homestead real estate, joined by spouse if married, may alienate homestead by mortgage, sale or gift, and, if married, may by deed transfer title to an estate by the entirety with spouse. (Const. art. 10, §4[c]).

Proceeds of sale are exempt to extent intended to be reinvested in another homestead within a reasonable time. (137 So.2d 201).

Rights of Surviving Spouse and Family.—Homestead exemption inures to benefit of surviving spouse or heirs of owner. (Const. art. 10 §4[b]). Homestead descends as intestate property and may not be devised if owner is survived by spouse or minor child, except that homestead may be devised to spouse of owner if there is no minor child (732.4015); however, if spouse and lineal descendants survive, surviving spouse takes life estate with vested remainder to lineal descendants in being at death of decedent (732.401). Homestead is not included in property subject to elective share. (732.208).

Exemption from Taxation.—See category Taxation, topic Property (Ad Valorem) Taxes, subhead Exemptions.

Dower.—See category Estates and Trusts, topic Descent and Distribution.

Disclaimer.—See category Estates and Trusts, topic Descent and Distribution, subhead Disclaimer.

JUDGMENT NOTES:

See category Business Regulation and Commerce, topic Bills and Notes.

LEVY:

See topics Attachment, Executions.

LIENS:

Uniform Commercial Code adopted. (cc. 670-680). See categories Business Regulation and Commerce, topic Commercial Code; Mortgages, topic Chattel Mortgages.

Waiver, Loss or Extinguishment.—Liens may be waived expressly or by operation of law. Possessory liens are extinguished by loss of possession. (131 Fla. 277, 179 So. 882). Presumption is against waiver unless intent is clear. (104 Fla. 93, 139 So. 209). Failure to bring action on statutory lien within time provided by law extinguishes it. (99 Fla. 1151, 128 So. 801). Lien may be released by filing bond in accordance with §713.76.

Statutory liens are provided as follows and are not governed by Uniform Commercial Code except for certain priority questions. (679.104[3], .310).

Authorized marina may dispose of boat or vessel for price greater than 50% of fair market value of boat or vessel by nonjudicial sale pursuant to provision in written lease where nonpayment of rent for six months and compliance with certain notice provisions. (328.17).

For labor or services on personalty of another, on such personalty or that which is used in business, occupation or employment in which the labor or services are performed. (713.58). Procedures provided for enforcement of lien created under 713.58 for services on aircraft (329.51) and on motor vehicle (713.585).

For labor on machines, newspaper or printing material and work in hotels, on such machines, newspaper or printing material, and on furniture, furnishings and belongings of such hotels. (713.56).

For labor on logs and timber, on such logs and timber, and any article manufactured therefrom. (713.57).

For labor on crops, on those cultivated or harvested. (713.59).

For labor or services in ginning cotton. (713.595).

For labor on or for vessel, including masters, mates and members of the crew and stevedores, on such vessel or water craft. (713.60). For materials or supplies furnished for construction of vessel or water craft, on such vessel or water craft. (713.60).

For care and maintenance of horses and other animals, on such animals. (713.65).

For rendering professional services to animal by veterinarian on such animals. (713.655).

For materials furnished by ship chandler or storekeeper to ship, vessel, steamboat or water craft, on the same. (713.64).

For manufacturing, altering or repairing anything of value, on such article or thing. (713.61).

For furnishing logs, lumber, clay and other material for use in manufactory to be manufactured into articles of value, on such articles and those manufactured therefrom. (713.62).

For furnishing locomotives or other machine or parts to any railroad, telegraph or telephone line or other manufactory, on articles furnished. (713.63).

For recovering, towing, or storing vehicles mounted on wheels, whether motorized or not, in favor of person regularly engaged in such business, on such vehicle, provided that detailed notice provisions are complied with. (713.78).

For services of stallion and other breeding animals, upon the animal served and its get. (713.70).

For loans or advances of money or property by factor, merchant or other person to aid in planting, farming, timber getting or other business, upon the products, provided consent to lien is executed by borrower and filed for record in county where farming, etc. business is conducted. (713.71). See category Documents and Records, topic Records.

In favor of mobile home and recreational vehicle parks for rent due or advances of money or property, upon the personal property of the occupant. (713.77).

In favor of keepers of hotels, apartment houses, rooming houses and boarding houses, for board and lodging and for money advanced to guests or tenants, upon goods belonging to such guest or tenant. (713.67-.69; held unconstitutional, 399 F. Supp. 1138 [1975]).

In favor of furnisher of feedstuffs and bedding to owner of racehorses, racing dogs or polo ponies, for price of such supplies for one year, on all animals consuming them, which lien is superior to all other liens, recorded or unrecorded. (713.66).

In favor of Florida Board of Forestry, U. S. Government or other governmental authority, on lands covered by agreement between owner and such authority for prevention and control of fires and other forestry work, to extent of amount expended on behalf of, and not paid by, such owner. (589.13-.17).

For labor performed or material furnished in connection with drilling or operating of any oil or gas well or pipeline. (713.801-.825).

In favor of governing body of publicly owned airport, on aircraft landing there, for landing fees and other charges. (329.40).

Factor's Liens.—See category Business Regulation and Commerce, topic Commercial Code.

Foreign Judgments.—Foreign judgment shall not operate as lien until 30 days after mailing of notice by clerk. Applicability of any automatic stay is restricted.

RICO Lien.—During any civil proceeding under Florida RICO Act, investigative agency may file in any county RICO notice against any person, which creates lien in favor of state against any real property or beneficial interest then or thereafter owned by person in county where filed. (895.07). RICO lien lasts six years unless renewed or terminated. (895.08). Department of Legal Affairs may apply ex parte to Circuit Court for order authorizing RICO lien against real property in certain instances. (895.05[12]).

Acquisition of Statutory Lien.—

Persons in privity with owner: As to owner, lien is acquired by performance of work or furnishing materials. (713.74). No lien is acquired on personalty against purchaser or creditor without notice unless lienor has possession of property, but even then lien continues for only three months. (713.74).

Persons not in privity with owner: Written notice must be delivered to owner stating indebtedness or cautionary notice may be given, thereafter same provisions apply as for persons in privity. (713.75).

Enforcement of foregoing statutory liens may be by retention of possession of property not exceeding three months, or by suit in equity, ordinary suit at law, special proceeding at law or summary proceeding. (85.011-.051). Proceedings to enforce must be commenced within 12 months from record of lien or performance of work or furnishing materials if lien exists without recording. (85.051). Priority of such liens depends on time notice creating each was given or recorded, if recording is required. (713.73). Lien for performing labor or services on motor vehicle (713.58) may be enforced by sale of such vehicle, following compliance with detailed notice and hearing provisions (713.585).

Satisfaction.—Clerk of Circuit Court is county recorder and is required to record notices or claims of liens, including federal liens. (28.222). Whenever lien amount is fully paid, party to whom payment is made must execute and record written instrument acknowledging satisfaction and send recorded satisfaction to payer within 60 days, or be liable for any attorneys' fees and costs resulting from failure to do so. (701.04).

Mechanics' Construction Liens.—

Who may Acquire.—Architects, landscape architects, interior designers, engineers, or surveyors and mappers on real property improved by their services rendered in accordance with their contracts (713.03); materialmen, laborers, contractors in privity with owner of real property have liens to extent of contract (713.05); laborers, materialmen, subcontractors, "sub-subcontractors" not in privity who perfect their liens have liens to extent of contractor's contract with owner if lienor follows procedure of c. 713

See note at head of Digest as to 1998 legislation covered.

See Topical Index in front part of this volume.

LIENS . . . *continued*
(713.06). (See also catchline Whether or not Lien Limited to Amount Due Principal Contractor, infra.)

Subdivision Improvements.—Any lienor who performs services of furnishing materials to real property, making it suitable as site for improvements, is entitled to lien on the real property. If activity is on dedicated or to be dedicated property, e.g., streets, lien is on abutting property and distributed pro rata among lots benefitted. (713.04).

Property Subject.—Improvement, for direct contract price of $2,500 or less, subjects owner only to liens of contractor or of materialman or laborer in privity with him. (713.02[5]).

Lessor is not subject to liens for improvements contracted by lessee when lease or short form thereof that prohibits same is recorded, or where all of leases entered into by lessor on parcel of land prohibit such liability and notice meeting certain requirements is recorded. (713.10).

Contract made by one spouse for property owned by other or by both is deemed to be made for both or other spouse unless objection is recorded within ten days after objecting spouse learns of contract. (713.12).

In contract made by one without an interest in real property, lien attaches only to improvements which may be removed. (713.11).

Except as provided above, liens extend only to right, title, and interest of person who contracts for improvement. (713.10).

Notice of Commencement.—Owner or authorized agent, before actually commencing to improve real property or before recommencing an improvement after default or abandonment, must record notice of commencement and either post certified copy or notarized statement that notice of commencement has been filed along with copy thereof in protected conspicuous place on front of site. (713.13[1]).

Notice must give adequate description of real property (including legal description and street address), general description of improvement, name and address of owner (also of fee simple title holder if different), name and address of contractor, name and address of surety on payment bond and amount of bond, (if obtained), name and address of any person making loan for construction of improvements, (if applicable), and name and address within State of person other than himself who may be designated by owner as person upon whom notices or other documents may be secured (service upon person so designated constitutes service upon owner). Owner has option to designate additional person to receive copies of lienor's notices and if owner does so, name and address of such person must be included in notice of commencement. (713.13[1]).

If contract between owner and contractor named in notice of commencement expresses period of time for completion of construction greater than one year, notice of commencement must state that it is effective for period of one year plus any additional period of time. Any payments made by owner after expiration of notice of commencement are considered improper payments. Form for notices of commencement is set forth in statute. Copy of any bond must be attached at time of recordation of notice of commencement. Failure to attach copy of bond negates exemption provided in §713.02(6). However, if such bond exists but is not recorded, bond may be used as transfer bond pursuant to §713.24. Giving of notice of commencement is effective upon filing in clerk's office. Owner must sign notice and no one else may be permitted to sign in his stead. (713.13[1]).

Improvement described in notice of commencement must be commenced within 90 days after recording or notice is void. (713.13[2]).

Recording of notice of commencement does not constitute lien, cloud or encumbrance on real property, but gives constructive notice that claims of lien under statute may be recorded and may take priority as provided in §713.07. Posting of copy does not constitute lien, cloud, or encumbrance on real property nor actual or constructive notice of any of them. (713.13[3]).

Unless otherwise provided in notice of commencement, notice of commencement is not effectual in law or equity against conveyance, transfer, or mortgage of or lien on real property described in notice, or against creditors or subsequent purchasers for valuable consideration, after one year after date of recording. (713.13[5]).

Lender must, prior to disbursement of any construction funds to contractor, record notice of commencement in clerk's office; however, lender is not required to post certified copy of notice at construction site. Posting of notice at construction site remains owner's obligation. Failure of lender to record notice of commencement renders lender liable to owner for all damages sustained by owner as result of failure. Whenever lender is required to record notice of commencement, lender shall designate lender, in addition to others, to receive copies of notices to owner. Owner is given claim or right of action against lender for failure to record notice of commencement. (713.13[6]).

Notice of commencement must be given before owner can properly pay any money on account of direct contract to lienors not in privity with owner. If description of property in notice is incorrect and error (except for clerical errors when description listed covers property where improvements are) adversely affects any lienor, payments made on direct contract shall be improperly paid as to that lienor. (713.06[3][a]).

Authority issuing building permits must provide applicant with printed statement detailing notice requirement, construction lien law, and copies of form of notice of commencement. No liability of authority for failure to so provide. Reasonable fee may be assessed. (713.135). In addition to any other information required by issuing authority, all building permit applications contain name and address of owner, name and address of contractor, description sufficient to identify real property to be improved, and number assigned to building permit by issuing authority. (713.135). Issuing authority shall verify that either certified copy of recorded notice of commencement or notarized statement that notice of commencement has been filed for recording, along with copy thereof, has been posted in accordance with 713.13. In absence of such verification, issuing authority must not approve inspection. (713.135).

When Attach, Priority.—Liens for professional services (713.03) and for subdivision improvements (713.04) attach and take priority as of time of recordation of claim of lien (713.07[1]).

All other permissible liens attach and take priority as of time of recordation of notice of commencement. If notice of commencement is not filed, liens attach and take priority as of time claim of lien is recorded. (713.07[2]).

Any conveyance, mortgage, or demand recorded prior to time lien attaches, and any proceeds of any such mortgage (regardless of when disbursed), is prior to any lien. Any other conveyance, encumbrance or demand is inferior. (713.07[3]).

Priorities among lien claimants are: (a) Laborers, (b) persons other than contractor, (c) contractor. (713.06[4]). Each class must be satisfied in full in order. If funds are not sufficient to satisfy class, they are apportioned pro rata. (713.06[4][b]). Any person required to serve notice under 713.06(2)(a) who fails to do so in required time has no lien and may only seek payments from and be paid by party with whom he contracts.

Notice of Termination.—Owner may terminate period of effectiveness of notice of commencement by executing, swearing to, and recording notice of termination containing: (a) same information as notice of commencement; (b) recording reference for and date of notice of commencement; (c) date as of which notice of commencement is terminated (may not be earlier than 30 days after notice of termination is recorded); (d) statement specifying that notice applies to all of real property subject to notice of commencement or specifying portion of property to which it applies; and (e) statement that all lienors have been paid in full. Owner may rely on contractor's affidavit given under §713.06(3)(d) (except with respect to lienors who have already given notice) in connection with recording notice of termination, but notice of termination must be accompanied by contractor's affidavit. Owner may not record notice of termination except after completion of construction, or after construction ceases before completion and all lienors have been paid in full or pro rata in accordance with §713.06(4). If owner or contractor, by fraud or collusion, knowingly makes any fraudulent statement or affidavit, they are liable to any lienor who suffers damages as result of filing of fraudulent notice of termination. Notice of termination is effective at later of 30 days after recording or date stated in notice of termination provided notice is served pursuant to §713.132(1)(f) on contractor and each lienor who has given notice. (713.132).

Proceedings to Perfect Lien.—

(1) All lienors not in privity, except laborers, as prerequisite to perfecting and recording lien must serve notice to owner giving: (a) lienor's name and address, (b) adequate description of real property, (c) nature of services or materials furnished or to be furnished. Sub-subcontractors and materialmen to subcontractors must serve copy of notice to owner on contractor as prerequisite to perfecting and recording lien. Materialmen to sub-subcontractors must serve copy of notice to owner on contractor and subcontractor of sub-subcontractor as prerequisite to perfecting and recording claim of lien. Materialman to sub-subcontractor shall serve notice to owner on subcontractor if materialman knows name and address of subcontractor. Notice must be served not later than 45 days after commencing to furnish services or materials but, in any case, before date of owner's disbursement of final payment after contractor's affidavit has been furnished to owner. This notice is distinct from requirement for claim of lien, infra. (713.06[2][a]).

(2) All lienors, including laborers and persons in privity with owner must record a sworn claim of lien which shows: (a) Name and address, (b) name of person with whom he contracted or by whom employed, (c) labor, services, materials furnished and contract price or value, (d) description of real property, (e) name of owner, (f) dates first and last item furnished, (g) amount unpaid. If claim is by person not in privity with owner, date and method of service of notice to owner must be shown in claim (713.08[1]); (if claim is by person not in privity with contractor or subcontractor, date and method of service on contractor or subcontractor must be shown). Claim may be recorded any time during work or not later than 90 days after final furnishing of labor or materials or services by lienor. Claim must be recorded in clerk's office in each county in which real property affected is situated. (713.08[5]).

Claim must be served on owner or authorized agent within 15 days after recording, or is voidable to extent delay is prejudicial. (713.08[4][c]).

Service may be either in manner provided by law for service of process or by certain special methods. (713.18).

Whether or not Lien Limited to Amount Due Principal Contractor.—

(1) After notice has been given to owner, when any payment becomes due on direct contract except final payment, owner must see to payment of all claimants giving notice. If amount due under contract is less than total amount of claims, lienors properly giving notice under 713.06(2)(a) are to be paid pro rata (see catchline When Attach, Priority, supra). (713.06[3][c]).

(2) Before final payment, contractor must give affidavit to owner stating that all lienors have been paid or showing amounts due lienors. Owner must retain only "the final payment due under the direct contract" until contractor furnishes this affidavit. Owner must apply this fund first to make full payment to remaining unpaid lienors who have properly served notice and then to those unpaid lienors who are disclosed by affidavit and whose time for serving notice has not expired, all such payments to extent of unpaid sums under direct contract either in full or pro rata. Proper disbursement limits contractor's liability to amount of direct contract. (713.06[3][d]).

Payment Bond.—Owner may require contractor to furnish payment bond (form described in 713.23), with copy of bond to be posted at construction site and recorded in county public records. Failure to record bond voids exemption from mechanics' liens. Copy of payment bond must be attached to notice of commencement when it is recorded. Upon receipt, owner is exempt from liabilities under c. 713 (construction/mechanics' and miscellaneous liens), and c. 85 (statutory liens) except for posting notice of commencement, and lien of contractor. (713.02[6]). Owner is only exempt from provisions of c. 713 Part I (Construction/Mechanics' Liens) as to that direct contract under which bond is furnished. Lienors, except laborers, not in privity with contractor must serve notice on contractor within 45 days from commencing work, or 45 days from written notice of existence of fund by way of its inclusion in notice of commencement or otherwise, that he will look to bond for protection on his work. Any lienor not in privity with contractor must serve notice on contractor, if he has not been paid, not later than 90 days after final furnishing of labor, services or materials by lienor. Unless both notices served, no action against contractor may be maintained.

See note at head of Digest as to 1998 legislation covered.

See Topical Index in front part of this volume.

FL – 26

LIENS . . . *continued*

Conditional Payment Bond.—If contractor's written contractual obligation to pay lienors is expressly conditioned upon and limited to payments made by owner to contractor, duty of surety to pay lienors will be coextensive with duty of contractor to pay, if bond contains legend specified in §713.245 on front page. (713.245[1]). No action may be brought against contractor or surety after one year from date lien is transferred to bond. (713.245[2]). Owner's property not exempt from liens filed under this section, and lienors must fulfill requirements contained in section in order to preserve and perfect lien rights. (713.245[3]). Within 90 days after claim of lien is recorded for labor, services, or materials for which contractor has been paid, owner or contractor may record notice of bond as specified in §713.23(2), together with copy of bond, and sworn statement entitled "Certificate of Payment to the Contractor" in form set forth in §713.245(4). Any notice of bond recorded more than 90 days after recording of claim of lien shall have no effect as to that lien unless owner, contractor and surety all sign notice of bond. (713.245[4]). Clerk serves copy of notice, bond and certificate on contractor, surety and lienor, certifies to service, records notice, bond and certificate, and collects fee. (713.245[5]). Contractor may join in certificate of payment to contractor at any time by recording sworn statement entitled "Joinder in Certificate of Payment" in form specified in §713.245(6). Clerk serves joinder in certificate of payment on owner, surety and lienor, certifies to service, records joinder, and collects fee. (713.245[7]). If contractor disputes certificate of payment to contractor, contractor must record, not later than 15 days after date clerk certifies service of certificate, sworn statement entitled "Notice of Contest of Payment" in form set forth in §713.245(8). Clerk serves copy of notice to contest payment on owner, lienor and surety, certifies service, records notice, and collects fee. (713.245[9]). If contractor has signed certificate of payment to contractor or joinder in certificate, or contractor fails to record notice of contest of payment within 15 days after clerk certifies service of certificate of payment to contractor signed by owner, lien transfers to bond to extent of payment specified in certificate of payment to contractor. Surety may assert all claims or defenses of owner regarding validity of claim of lien or of contractor regarding amount due lienor. (713.245[10]). If notice of contest of payment specifies that contractor has been paid portion of amount due lienor, lien shall transfer to bond to extent of payment specified in notice of contest of payment. Surety may assert all claims or defenses of owner regarding validity of claim of lien or of contractor regarding amount due lienor. (713.245[11]). If there are any material misstatements of fact made by owner or contractor in any certificate of payment to contractor, or by contractor in any notice of contest of payment, person making material misstatement is guilty of felony of third degree. Penalties apply individually and to business entity if false certificate is signed in representative capacity. (713.245[12]). Certificate of payment to contractor and notice of contest of payment must be signed by owner or contractor individually if he is natural person, by general partner if owner or contractor is limited partnership, by partner if owner or contractor is general partnership, by president or vice-president if owner or contractor is corporation, or by any authorized agent if owner or contractor is any other type of business entity. (713.245[13]). In action to enforce lien, owner shall not be considered prevailing party solely because lien is transferred to conditional payment bond after action to enforce lien is brought. (713.245[14]).

Single claim is sufficient for most improvements to multiple units that are part of single project. (713.09).

Duration.—Lien continues for one year from recordation of claim, unless within that time action to enforce lien is commenced in court of competent jurisdiction. Owner can shorten to 60 days by filing notice of contest of lien. (713.22).

Waiver and Release.—Acceptance of unsecured note is not waiver unless expressly so stated in writing. Release may be in whole or in part of lien or whole or part of real property covered. Right to claim lien may not be waived in advance and may be waived only to extent of services furnished. This section also includes form for partial release of lien. (713.20[2][4]).

Discharge may be by properly executed and recorded: (1) Satisfaction of lien, (2) failure to bring action to enforce lien within one year, (3) recording in clerk's office original or certified copy of judgment or final decree, (4) order of circuit court requiring lienor to sue on lien within 20 days. (713.21).

Enforcement is in equity in circuit court by foreclosure and sale. Deficiency decree can be obtained. (713.28[3]). Claim of lien can be transferred from real property to other satisfactory security deposited with clerk. (713.24). Relief is cumulative to action at law or other existing remedies. (713.30). Prevailing party in action to enforce mechanic's lien is entitled to reasonable attorney's fees. (713.29).

Misapplication of Funds.—Person receiving payment on account of improving real property must apply such portion of payment to payment of all amounts due and owing for services, labor or materials which were furnished for improvement prior to receipt of payment (however payment may be withheld if in accordance with terms of contract or pursuant to bona fide dispute regarding amount due for services, labor or materials). Any person knowingly and intentionally failing to comply with this requirement is guilty of misapplication of construction funds, punishable as felony, degree of felony depending upon amount of payments misapplied. This section does not apply to mortgage bankers or their agents, servants or employees for their acts in usual course of business of lending or disbursing mortgage funds. (713.345). Person willfully making or furnishing affidavit containing false statement, relied upon, commits perjury. (713.35).

Public Works.—Contractor for public building or other public work must give bond for prompt payment of all persons supplying labor, material or supplies used in prosecution of work. Bond must state name and principal address of both principal and surety and must contain description of project sufficient to identify it. Bond must be in amount equal to awarded contract price and supplied by authorized surety company; except where contract price is $25,000 or less, $25,000 security may be in other forms. No bond required if work for state and contract $100,000 or less; bond at Department of Management Services' option if $100,000-$200,000. Claimant, except laborer, not in privity with contractor and who has not received payment for labor, materials or supplies, must have, in order to bring action against contractor or surety, furnished contractor with notice before commencing or not later than 45 days after commencing to furnish labor, materials or supplies that he intends to look to bond for protection,

and must deliver to contractor and surety within 90 days after performance of labor or after complete delivery of materials or supplies, written notice of such performance or delivery and of nonpayment. Notice of nonpayment may be served at any time during progress of work or thereafter but not before 45 days after first furnishing of labor, services, or materials, and not later than 90 days after final furnishing of labor, services, or materials by claimant; with respect to rental equipment, not later than 90 days after date that equipment was last on job site available for use. Action must be brought within one year from performance of labor or completion of delivery of materials or supplies. Claimant may not waive in advance his right to bring action under bond against surety. (255.05; 337.18).

Special Situations.—Mechanics' Construction Lien Law deals with numerous special situations, including notice of delivery requirements for assignment of lien, abandonment and recommencement of project, priority of claims in unused materials, and running accounts. (713.01-713.37).

Attachment Lien.—See topic Attachment.

Attorney's Lien.—See category Legal Profession, topic Attorneys and Counselors.

Collateral Security.—See topic Pledges.

Execution Lien.—See topic Executions.

Judgment Lien.—See category Civil Actions and Procedure, topic Judgments.

Landlord's Lien.—See category Property, topic Landlord and Tenant.

Liens on Exempt Property.—See topic Exemptions.

Liens on Homestead.—See topic Homesteads.

Real Estate Mortgage Lien.—See category Mortgages, topic Mortgages of Real Property.

Tax Lien.—See category Taxation, topic Property (Ad Valorem) Taxes, subhead Liens.

MECHANICS' LIENS:

See topic Liens.

PLEDGES:

Uniform Commercial Code adopted. (cc. 670-680). See category Business Regulation and Commerce, topic Commercial Code.

Collateral Security.—Person selling collateral security before debt becomes due and without authority of depositor is punishable by fine or imprisonment. (818.04).

RECEIVERS:

Receivers may be appointed to take custody of property or funds in dispute for purpose of preserving, managing, and/or properly disposing of such property at direction of court. (See e.g. 658.79.)

Jurisdiction.—Where property is located in more than one judicial circuit, application for receiver must be made in circuit court in which principal place of business, residence or office of defendant is located. (47.031). Thereafter, court appointing receiver has jurisdiction over entire property for purposes of that action. (47.031).

Proceedings.—Receiver appointed in accordance with rules 1.620 and 1.610, Fla. R. C. P., relating to injunctions and receivers, respectively.

Qualification.—Bonds of receivers may be required by chancellor under his general equity jurisdiction. See R. C. P. 1.620; 1.620(c).

Eligibility and Competency.—Receiver must be indifferent as between parties to dispute, as unbiased as court for whom he acts. (49 So. 502). Short of special circumstances or agreement between parties, party to cause will not normally be appointed receiver.

Powers and Duties.—Must file, in clerk's office, inventory under oath, of property under receiver's control within 20 days of appointment. Must file, unless court orders otherwise, every three months, inventory and accounting. (R.C.P. 1.620[b]). If receiver fails to so file, court must order filing and require receiver to pay expenses of order and proceeding from own funds. (R.C.P. 1.620[b]).

Compensation.—Duly authorized expenses and reasonable compensation are otherwise awarded by court from corpus of or income from property in question. (56 So. 699). Such costs and expenses have preference even over secured claims.

Discharge.—Upon completion of duties or upon showing of good cause, receiver is discharged by court.

Liquidators.—Department of Banking and Financing may appoint liquidator of state bank or trust company. (658.79). See category Business Regulation and Commerce, topic Banks and Banking.

Insurance Companies.—Under "Insurer's Rehabilitation and Liquidation Act", Dept. of Insurance is appointed receiver for insolvent insurer, upon application of Dept. (631.061).

REDEMPTION:

See topic Executions; categories Mortgages, topic Mortgages of Real Property; Taxation, topic Taxes.

SUPPLEMENTARY PROCEEDINGS:

See topic Executions.

TRUSTEE PROCESS:

See topic Garnishment.

USURY:

See category Business Regulation and Commerce, topic Interest.

DISPUTE RESOLUTION

ALTERNATIVE DISPUTE RESOLUTION:

Mandatory Dispute Resolution.—

Referral by Presiding Judge.—Judge may refer all or any part of contested civil matter to mediation (process whereby neutral third party facilitates resolution of dispute [§44.1011(2)]), or arbitration (process whereby neutral third person or panel considers facts and arguments presented by parties and renders decision which may be binding or nonbinding [§44.1011(1)]). (R.C.P. 1.700[a]; §§44.102; 44.103). Bond estreatures (time during which case is held in abeyance pending forfeiture of bond), habeas corpus and extraordinary writs, bond validations, civil or criminal contempt or other matters specified by administrative order of chief judge in circuit may not be referred to mediation or arbitration. (R.C.P. 1.710[b]; R.C.P. 1.800).

United States District Courts in Florida have also established court annexed mediation and arbitration processes. Rule 16.2, General Rules of the United States District Court for the Southern District of Florida; cc. 8 and 9, Rules of the United States District Court for the Middle District of Florida; Civil Justice Expense and Delay Reduction Plan of the United States District Court for the Northern District of Florida.

Mediation.—

Mediation Procedures.—Court-ordered mediation must be conducted in accordance with rules of practice and procedure. (§44.102[1]). Parties must agree upon certified or qualified mediator within ten days of order of referral (R.C.P. 1.720[f][1]) and if agreement is not reached, within ten days of expiration of selection period, plaintiff must file notice of non-agreement and court appoints certified mediator. (R.C.P. 1.720[f][2]; 44.102[5]). R.C.P. 1.720(f)(3) provides for appointment of substitute mediators in same manner. §44.102(5), R.C.P. 1.720(g) and administrative rules of court govern compensation of mediators. Mediator controls mediation and procedures to be followed. (R.C.P. 1.720[d]). Unless otherwise ordered, first mediation conference or arbitration hearing held within 60 days of order of referral. (R.C.P. 1.700[a][1]). Notice of conference date, time and place must be provided within 15 days after designation of mediator or arbitrator, unless order of referral specifies such information. (R.C.P. 1.700[a][2]). Mediation must be completed within 45 days of first mediation conference unless extended by court order or parties' stipulation. (R.C.P. 1.710[a]). However, mediator may adjourn conference at any time and may set times for reconvening notwithstanding above rule. (R.C.P. 1.720[c]). Time for completing mediation is tolled during any period in which mediation is interrupted pending resolution of party's motion for interim or emergency relief during mediation, which motion may be filed at any time. (R.C.P.1.720[a]). Absent court order or decision of mediator, mediation shall continue pending disposition of motion. (R.C.P. 1.720[a]).

Dispensing With Mediation.—Within 15 days of order of referral, party may move to dispense with mediation or arbitration if: same parties have previously mediated or arbitrated same issue pursuant to Florida law; issue presents question of law only; order of referral violates rules relating to issues excluded from mediation (R.C.P. 1.700[b]) or arbitration (R.C.P. 1.800) or for other good cause shown (R.C.P. 1.700[b]).

Deferring Mediation.—Within 15 days of order of referral, party may move to defer mediation or arbitration. Motion must set forth in detail facts and circumstances supporting deferral and be set for hearing prior to conference date. Mediation or arbitration is tolled until disposition of motion. (R.C.P. 1.700[c]).

Sanctions for Failure to Appear at Mediation.—Upon motion, sanctions against party failing to appear for duly noticed mediation conference, including award of mediator and attorneys' fees and other costs, may be imposed. (R.C.P. 1.720[b]). Party is deemed to appear upon presence of party or its representative with full settlement authority; party's counsel of record; representative or insurance carrier for any insured party with full authority to settle up to lesser of amount of plaintiff's last demand or policy limits. (R.C.P. 1.720[b]). R.C.P. 1.720(b) also defines presence of public entity of state.

Communication With Parties at Mediation.—Mediator may consult privately with any party or its counsel. (R.C.P. 1.720[e]). Party may communicate privately with its counsel. (R.C.P. 1.720[d]). Parties have right to keep communications disclosed in mediation confidential except with respect to disciplinary proceedings against mediators. (§44.102[3][4]).

Completion of Mediation.—If agreement is reached, it shall be written and signed by all parties and their counsel, if any. Agreement may be filed and if required by law shall be filed. Where agreement is not filed, stipulation of dismissal is filed. (R.C.P. 1.730[b]). Where no agreement is reached, mediator shall report lack of agreement to court without comment or recommendation. With parties' consent, report may indicate other pending matters. (R.C.P. 1.730[a]). Sanctions may be imposed in event of breach or failure to perform under agreement. (R.C.P. 1.730[c]). §44.102(6) provides for tolling of certain deadlines relating to offers of settlement and demands for judgment during mediation.

County Court Mediation.—Cases pending in Florida county courts are governed by R.C.P. 1.750 to extent of conflicting provisions in R.C.P. 1.700-1.730.

Family Mediation.—Issues in marriage dissolution and post-dissolution proceedings and in domestic proceedings between unmarried parents governed by F.L.R.P. 12.740.

Voluntary Dispute Resolution.—

Stipulation.—Parties to any contested civil matter may file written stipulation to mediate or submit to voluntary binding arbitration of any issue between them at any time. (R.C.P. 1.700[a], 44.104[1]). Court must incorporate stipulation into its order of referral. Filing application for binding arbitration tolls running of applicable statute of limitations. (44.104[6]).

Mediation.—See subhead Mandatory Dispute Resolution, supra and R.C.P. 1.700-1.750 and §44.102.

Voluntary Binding Arbitration.—Application for voluntary binding arbitration filed and fees paid to clerk of court. (44.104[5]). Within ten days of request for binding arbitration, court provides for appointment of arbitrator(s). Chief arbitrator must meet qualifications and training requirements required by 44.106. Court shall appoint arbitrator(s) as prescribed in stipulation providing for method of appointment of arbitrator(s), however, in absence of agreement or agreed method fails, court shall appoint arbitrator(s). (44.104[2][4]). Arbitrators set time and place for hearing (44.104[4]), and Chief Arbitrator has power to administer oaths, conduct proceedings and issue subpoenas for witnesses and production of documents (44.104[7]). Florida Rules of Evidence apply to proceedings. (44.104[9]). Hearing procedures are as agreed by parties before arbitration and in absence of agreement are established by Court. (R.C.P. 1.830[a]). Record and transcript may be made and used in subsequent proceedings. (R.C.P. 1.830[b]). Compensation is as set forth in agreement or as set by court in absence of agreement, but not less than $75 per day. (44.104[3]; R.C.P. 1.830[a]). Majority of arbitrators conducting hearing may decide any question and render decision. (44.104[8]). Arbitrator(s) shall render majority decision and notify parties in writing of decision within ten days of final adjournment of hearing. (R.C.P. 1.830[c]). Appeal shall be taken to circuit court within 30 days after service upon parties and is limited to review of record of: (a) arbitrator(s)' alleged failure to comply with applicable rules of procedure or evidence; (b) arbitrator(s)' alleged partiality or misconduct prejudicing right of any party; or (c) whether result is contrary to Florida or U.S. constitutions. Harmless error doctrine applies and no further appeal permitted unless constitutional issue presented. (44.104[10]; R.C.P. 1.830[c]). If no appeal is taken, decision referred to judge who may enter all orders and judgments required to conform to terms of decision. (44.104[11]; (R.C.P. 1.830[c]). Voluntary binding arbitration not applicable to child custody, visitation or support disputes or to rights of third party not party to arbitration. (44.104[12]).

ARBITRATION AND AWARD:

Uniform Arbitration Act adopted. (Florida Arbitration Code, 682.01-22).

Form and Requisites of Submission.—A party to agreement for arbitration subject to Code claiming the neglect or refusal of another party to comply therewith may apply to court for an order directing the parties to proceed with arbitration. (682.03[1]). Code does not apply to agreement or arbitration or award thereunder in which it is stipulated Code does not apply. (682.02).

Rescission.—An arbitration agreement complying with statute is valid, enforceable and irrevocable. (682.02).

Powers of Arbitrators.—Arbitrators or umpires may issue subpoenas for witnesses and for production of books, records, documents and other evidence; administer oaths; and permit depositions. (682.08).

Contracts to Arbitrate Future Disputes.—Two or more parties may agree in writing to submit to arbitration any controversy existing between them at the time of the agreement or include in a written contract a provision for settlement by arbitration of any future controversy relating to the contract. (682.02).

Award and Enforcement Thereof.—Award must be in writing, signed by arbitrators joining therein or by umpire, and delivered to each party personally by registered or certified mail, or as agreement provides. (682.09[1]). Upon application of party, court must confirm award, unless, within time limits specified, grounds are urged for vacating, modifying, or correcting award in accordance with §§682.13, .14. (682.12).

Judgment on Award.—Upon granting of order confirming, modifying or correcting award, judgment or decree is entered in conformity therewith and is enforced as any other judgment or decree. (682.15).

Court-ordered, nonbinding arbitration must be conducted in accordance with rules of practice and procedure. (44.103[1]). In absence of agreement of parties, court determines number of arbitrators and designates them within 15 days of order of referral. (Rule 1.810[a]). Cases assigned to arbitration assigned to arbitrator or to panel of three arbitrators from list of qualified persons maintained by Chief Judge of circuit. (Rule 1.810[a]; 44.104[3]). Chief Judge of circuit sets procedures for determining time and place of hearing and other procedures. (Rule 1.820[a]). Chief Arbitrator has authority to commence and adjourn arbitration hearing and carry out other duties prescribed by law, and may issue instructions for conduct of hearing which may be enforced by court order, administer oaths, conduct proceedings and issue subpoenas for witnesses and production of documents. (Rule 1.820[a]; 44.103). Rule 1.820 and administrative orders provide for conduct of arbitration hearing, presentation of evidence.

Selection and Compensation of Arbitrators.—Upon court's determination, cases assigned to arbitration assigned to arbitrator or panel of three arbitrators from list of qualified persons maintained by Chief Judge of circuit. (Rule 1.810[a]). Compensation of arbitrators set by Chief Judge and unless otherwise agreed by parties and court, shall not exceed $200 per day. (44.103[2]).

Completion of Arbitration.—Arbitration must be completed within 30 days of first arbitration hearing unless extended by court order, but no extension shall be for period exceeding 60 days from first hearing date. (Rule 1.820[g]). Arbitrator(s) render majority decision upon completion and notify parties in writing of decision within ten days of final adjournment of hearing. (Rule 1.820[g]). Decision and original of any hearing transcripts sealed and filed with clerk of court. (Rule 1.820[g]). Arbitration decision is final unless party files de novo motion for new trial within 20 days of service of decision on parties. (44.103[5]; Rule 1.820[h]). Arbitration decision not made known to judge if motion for trial is filed. (44.103[5]). If motion for trial is not timely made, decision referred to judge who may enter all orders and judgments required to conform to terms of decision. Orders are enforceable pursuant to contempt powers of court. (44.103[5]). If trial de novo is not favorable to party who filed, that party may be assessed arbitration costs, court costs, other reasonable costs including attorneys' fees, investigation, testimony and expert expenses incurred after arbitration hearing. (44.103[6]).

Sanctions For Failure To Appear at Arbitration.—When party fails to appear for arbitration hearing, hearing may commence and decision based upon facts and circumstances presented may be rendered. (Rule 1.820[e]).

See note at head of Digest as to 1998 legislation covered.

See Topical Index in front part of this volume.

ARBITRATION AND AWARD . . . *continued*

Florida International Arbitration Act governs arbitration between two or more persons at least one of whom is nonresident of U.S., or two or more residents if dispute involves contract, property or investment outside U.S. or bears some other relation to foreign country. (c. 684).

DOCUMENTS AND RECORDS

ACKNOWLEDGMENTS:

Uniform Acknowledgments Act not adopted, but provisions are similar to Uniform Acknowledgments Act.

To entitle any instrument concerning real property to be recorded, except secured transactions under Uniform Commercial Code, execution must be acknowledged by party executing it, proved by subscribing witness to it, or legalized or authenticated by civil-law notary or notary public who affixes his official seal. (695.03, 695.032). Acknowledgment may be taken by following officers (695.03):

Within State.—Generally: Judge, clerk or deputy clerk of any court; U.S. Commissioner or Magistrate; notary public. (92.50[1], 695.03[1]).

Outside State but Within U.S.—Generally: Judge or clerk of any U.S. state, territory or district court of record where taken, having seal; notary public or justice of peace with seal authorized by such state, territory or district to take acknowledgments. (92.50[2], 695.03[2]). For instruments concerning real property: Above list excepting deputy clerk; and adding U.S. Commissioner or Magistrate, master in chancery, registrar or recorder of deeds of state, territory or district where taken, having seal. If before notary public who does not affix seal, it is sufficient for notary to type, print or write on instrument, "I am a Notary Public of the State of (state) and my commission expires on (date)." (695.03[2]).

In Foreign Countries.—Generally: Judge or justice of court of last resort, notary public of country where taken; U.S. minister, consul general, chargé d'affaires, or consul resident in country where taken. Signature and seal of such individual required. (92.50[3], 695.03[3]). For instruments concerning real property: Above list excepting judge or justice of court of last resort; and adding commissioner of deeds appointed by Governor of Florida to act in foreign country or before any civil law notary or notary public having official seal, U.S. ambassador, envoy extraordinary, minister plenipotentiary, commissioner, vice consul, consular agent, or any other diplomatic or consular officer appointed to reside in country where taken; U.S. military or naval officer authorized by Laws or Articles of War of U.S. to perform duties of notary public. All acknowledgments require seal of acknowledging officer. (695.03[3]).

Person in or with U.S. Armed Forces, their spouses and persons whose duties require presence with such forces, wherever located, may acknowledge before any commissioned officer in active service with U.S. Armed Forces holding rank of Second Lieutenant, Ensign or higher. Certificate need not state place where taken and no seal or authentication is required if signature, rank and branch of service of such officer appears on instrument. (695.031, 92.51).

General Requirements as to Taking.—Officer taking acknowledgment shall know, or have satisfactory proof, that the person making the acknowledgment is the individual described in and who executed such instrument, or that the person offering to make proof is one of the subscribing witnesses to such instrument. (695.09).

Married Women.—No special requirements.

General Requirements of Certificate.—Officer's certificate shall contain and set forth substantially the matter required to be done or proved to make such acknowledgment effectual. (695.04).

Seals.—Whether the acknowledgment or proof is taken within or without this state, or outside the United States, the certificate must be under the seal of the court or officer before whom the acknowledgment or proof is taken. (695.03). Florida notary seal may be of rubber stamp or impression-type, but rubber stamp seal is official seal for use on paper document and impression-type may not be substituted therefor. (117.05). Armed Forces acknowledgment (695.031) and out-of-state U.S. notaries without seal (695.03), and electronic notarizations (117.20[2]) are only exceptions.

Proof by Subscribing Witness.—Instruments concerning real property may only be recorded on acknowledgment of executing party or on certificate of proof by subscribing witness before any officer authorized to take acknowledgments. (695.03).

Where the grantors and witnesses of any instrument which may be recorded are dead, or cannot be had, the judge of the circuit court, or the county judge for the county wherein the real property is situated, may take the examination of any competent witness or witnesses, on oath, to prove the handwriting of the witness or witnesses, or, where such proof cannot be had, then to prove the handwriting of the grantor or grantors, which shall be certified by the judge, and the instrument being thus proved may be recorded. (695.10).

Effect of acknowledgment is to conform to statutory requirement or to entitle instrument concerning real property to be recorded. (695.03).

Forms of Certificates.—Error in stating venue in acknowledgment to any deed or other instrument relating to real estate does not invalidate acknowledgment. (695.06). Notary must show expiration date of his commission, and Florida notary seal must include words "Notary Public—State of Florida", name of notary public, date of expiration of commission of notary public, and commission number. (117.05). Forms are as follows:

Forms

Acknowledgment by Person in Military Service:

On this . . . . . day of . . . . . ., 19. . . ., before me . . . . . ., the undersigned officer, personally appeared . . . . . ., known to me (or satisfactorily proven) to be serving in or with, or whose duties require his presence with, the Armed Forces of the United States, and to be the person whose name is subscribed to the within instrument, and acknowledged that he executed the same for the purposes therein contained, and the

undersigned does further certify that he is at the date of this certificate a commissioned officer of the rank stated below, and is in the active service of the Armed Forces of the United States.

(Signature and rank of commissioned officer and command or branch of service to which attached.) (695.031[2]).

Short Forms

(All short forms must be followed by signature of person taking acknowledgment, name of acknowledger typed, printed or stamped, his title or rank, and his serial number, if any.) (695.25).

By Individual Acting in Own Right:
State of
County of
The foregoing instrument was acknowledged before me this (date) by (name of person acknowledging) who is personally known to me or who has produced (type of identification) as identification. (695.25[1]).

For Corporation:
State of
County of
The foregoing instrument was acknowledged before me this (date) by (name of officer or agent, title of officer or agent) of (name of corporation acknowledging) a (state or place of incorporation) corporation, on behalf of the corporation. He/She is personally known to me or has produced (type of identification) as identification. (695.25[2]).

For Partnership:
State of
County of
The foregoing instrument was acknowledged before me this (date) by (name of acknowledging partner or agent), partner (or agent) on behalf of (name of partnership), a partnership. He/She is personally known to me or has produced (type of identification) as identification. (695.25[3]).

For Individual Acting as Principal by Attorney in Fact:
State of
County of
The foregoing instrument was acknowledged before me this (date) by (name of attorney in fact) as attorney in fact, who is personally known to me or who has produced (type of identification) as identification. (695.25[4]).

By Public Officer, Trustee, Personal Representative:
State of
County of
The foregoing instrument was acknowledged before me this (date) by (name and title of position), who is personally known to me or who has produced (type of identification) as identification. (695.25[5]).

Acknowledgment of Will.—See category Estates and Trusts, topic Wills.

Alternative to Acknowledgment or Proof.—No statutory provision.

Validating Acts.—There are curative acts as to certain defective acknowledgments under previous statutory requirements. (694.01-.15).

AFFIDAVITS:

Within State.—Judges, clerks or deputy clerks of any court of record in the state, including federal courts, U.S. commissioners and notaries public of this state, are authorized to take or administer oaths and affidavits which by law are required to be administered, except oaths to jurors and witnesses in court and such other oaths, affidavits and acknowledgments as are required by law to be taken or administered by or before particular officers. (92.50[1]).

Outside State but Within the United States.—In other states, territories and districts, oaths and affidavits may be taken or administered before any judge, clerk or deputy clerk or any court of record having seal or before any notary or justice of peace having seal provided such officer is authorized under laws of such state. (92.50[2]).

Outside the United States.—In foreign countries oaths and affidavits may be taken or administered by any judge of a court of last resort, or by a notary public of such foreign country, or by any minister, consul general, chargé d'affaires, or consul of U.S. residing in such country. Seal of officer or court must be affixed. (92.50[3]).

Persons in U.S. Armed Forces, their spouses, and persons whose duties require presence with such forces, may have oath taken or administered by any commissioned officer in active service of U.S. Armed Forces with rank of second lieutenant, ensign or higher, within or without U.S. Certificate showing date of oath and stating in substance that person appearing before officer made or signed instrument under oath is sufficient. Place need not be stated. No authentication is required if signature, rank, and branch of service or subdivision thereof of such officer appears on instrument, and such officer's action is prima facie evidence that person making oath or affidavit is within purview of act. (92.51).

General Requirements of Jurat.—Jurat must be authenticated by signature and official seal (except in case of Armed Forces officer) of officer or person taking or administering same, however judges and clerks may use seal of court. (92.50). Jurat must indicate affiant swore (or affirmed) affidavit before administering officer. (416 So.2d 1240, 1241 n.2). Authentication of officer's authority is not required. See topic Acknowledgments, subhead Authentication.

Use of Affidavit.—Affidavits may be used to verify pleadings, prove service of summons, notice or other process, obtain provisional remedy and support or oppose motions for summary judgment. (R. C. P. 1.510).

Form.—There is no prescribed form of certificate. The following is in general use:

See note at head of Digest as to 1998 legislation covered.

See Topical Index in front part of this volume.

AFFIDAVITS . . . *continued*

Form

State of . . . . . .
County of . . . . . .
On this day personally appeared before me, an officer duly authorized to administer oaths, ..., who being first duly sworn by me, states:
. . . .
Sworn to and subscribed before me this . . . . . day of . . . . . ., A.D. . . . . . .
(Seal of officer).
Signature of Notary Public, or other authorized officer. My commission expires . . . . . . (for notaries only).

Alternative to Affidavit.—No statutory provision.

NOTARIES PUBLIC:

Qualification.—Appointed by Governor for term of four years upon application prescribed by statute. Must be at least 18 years of age and legal Florida resident throughout term of appointment. Must give bond for $5,000, pay fee of $25, together with $4 surcharge which surcharge shall be used to educate notaries public, and take oath of office. No person may be automatically reappointed as notary public without recompleting full application process. (117.01).

Powers and Duties.—May administer oath when necessary to execution of document to be attested, protested or published under official seal. (117.03). May solemnize marriages and take acknowledgments of written instruments for record. (117.045). May attest to trueness of photocopy of original document. (117.045).

Territorial Extent of Powers.—May act anywhere within boundaries of state. (117.01).

Seals.—Notary seal is required to be affixed to all documents notarized. Seal must be of rubber stamp type and include words "Notary Public—State of Florida", name, date of expiration of commission of notary public and commission number. (117.05). See topic Acknowledgments, subhead Seals.

Fees.—Notary public fee may not exceed $10 for any one act, except with marriages for which fee may not exceed those provided by law to clerks of circuit court for same services. (117.05).

Officers of U.S. Armed Forces holding at least rank of second lieutenant (or equivalent) may take or administer oaths, affidavits, and acknowledgments when person involved is member of Armed Forces, spouse of member, or person whose duties require his presence with Armed Forces. (92.51).

Advertising.—Words "Notary Public" may not be translated literally in another language for advertisements, and if notary public is not attorney, any advertising for notarial services by notary public must disclaim ability to give legal advice and accept fees for giving legal advice. (117.05).

RECORDS:

Uniform Commercial Code adopted. (cc. 670-680). See categories Business Regulation and Commerce, topics Commercial Code, Sales; Debtor and Creditor, topic Liens, subheads Statutory Liens and Mechanics' Construction Liens; Mortgages, topic Chattel Mortgages; Property, topic Deeds.

Recordable Instruments.—Following shall be recorded upon presentation to clerk of Circuit Court: Instruments relating to ownership, transfer, encumbrances on or claims against real or personal property; notices of lis pendens; judgments of Florida courts or federal courts having jurisdiction in state; notices of federal tax liens and other liens in favor of U.S.; petitions, decrees of adjudication, and orders approving trustees' bonds in federal bankruptcy proceedings; that portion of certificates of discharge or separation from armed forces which indicates character of service, discharge or separation; any other document required or authorized by law to be recorded. (28.222[3]). Recordation is not necessary to make conveyances or judgments valid (695.01), but see subhead Effect of Record, infra. All instruments recorded in official records are open to public for inspection. (28.226[6]).

Place of recording is county where affected property is situated (28.222, 695.01-.015), except for certain commercial code filings (see subhead Filing Under Commercial Code, infra). Documents affecting property, including probate records, are filed with clerk of circuit court. (28.222-.223). *For list of Counties and County Seats see first page of this state in Volume containing Practice Profiles Section.*

Requisites of Recording.—To entitle any instrument concerning real property to be recorded, execution must be acknowledged by party making same and proved by subscribing witness or authenticated by civil law notary or notary public in order to be entitled to record. (695.03). Instruments purporting to contain agreement to purchase or sell real estate must be acknowledged by vendor in order to be entitled to record. (696.01). Assignment of contract of sale may not be recorded unless original contract entitled to record. (696.02). Any instrument affecting interest in or lien upon real estate (except instrument executed before July 1, 1991, court orders, plats, instruments prepared or executed by any public officer excluding notaries public, and instruments executed, proved, or acknowledged outside Florida) must contain name of each person who executed such instrument legibly printed, typewritten, or stamped on instrument immediately beneath that person's signature, post office address of each such person, legibly printed, typewritten, or stamped on instrument, name and post office address of natural person who prepared document or under whose supervision it was prepared, legibly printed, typewritten, or stamped on document, name of each witness to document legibly printed, typewritten, or stamped on document immediately beneath signature of such witness, name of any notary public or other officer authorized to take acknowledgments or proofs whose signature appears on document, legibly printed, typewritten, or stamped on document immediately beneath signature of such notary public or other officer authorized to take acknowledgment or proofs, three inch square at top right-hand corner for use by clerk of court, and on any instrument, other than mortgage conveying or purporting to convey any interest in real property, name and post office address of each grantee, legibly printed, typewritten, or stamped on document. (695.26). Failure to comply with this section does not impair validity of recordation or of constructive notice imparted by recordation. (695.26). Contract for sale of real property executed by agent or attorney may not be recorded until authority or power of attorney is recorded. (696.03).

Documentary tax stamps must be placed on instruments requiring same prior to recording. (201.01). See category Taxation, topic Stamp Tax, subhead Documents, for rates and instruments affected.

Foreign conveyance, encumbrance or other instrument to be recorded, must be acknowledged by party making same or proved by subscribing witness. If notary public of another state signing acknowledgment certificate does not affix seal, it shall be sufficient for notary public to type, print, or write by hand on instrument, "I am a Notary Public of the State of (state) and my commission expires on (date)." (695.03[2]). Certificates of acknowledgment or proof made in foreign countries must be under seal of authority taking acknowledgment or proof. (695.03[3]). See topic Acknowledgments for form and officers authorized to take same.

Effect of Record.—In order to create lien on real property certified copy of judgment must be recorded. (55.10[1]). Conveyances, transfers or mortgages of real property or of any interest therein and leases for term of one year or longer, in order to be good and effectual in law or equity against creditors or subsequent purchasers for valuable consideration and without notice, must be recorded (695.01), and in order for any such instrument made or executed by virtue of any power of attorney to be good and effectual in law or equity against creditors or subsequent purchasers for valuable consideration and without notice such power of attorney must also be recorded before accruing of right of such creditor or subsequent purchaser. (695.01). In general, owner of any interest in or lien upon real property who is not in actual possession must file statutory notice within 30 years after recording to assure that interest or lien is not extinquished by Marketable Record Title Act. (712.05).

All instruments which are authorized or required to be recorded in Official Records Book of Clerk of Circuit Court are deemed recorded from time official whose duty it is to record same affixes thereon consecutive official register number and are notice to all persons. Sequence of such official numbers shall determine priority of recordation. (695.11). As to personal property, financing statements filed and recorded pursuant to Uniform Commercial Code on or after Jan. 1, 1967 and prior to Jan. 1, 1980, which have not lapsed remain effective for period provided in 671.304, but not less than five years from date of filing. (679.4011, 679.403, 671.301).

Recording fees for deeds, contracts, mortgages and other instruments are $5 first page and $4 for each additional page and additional service charge of $1 first page and 50¢ each additional page shall be paid to clerk. (28.24[15]).

There are other service charges prescribed by statute for copying, indexing, mailing, and other services. (28.24).

Properly authenticated or certified copies of public records are admissible in evidence like originals. (90.955).

Federal tax lien notices and notices of other liens in favor of U.S. are to be filed in office of clerk of circuit court. (28.222[3][e]).

Lis Pendens.—In order for an action in state or federal courts to operate as a lis pendens, a notice of institution thereof, containing names of parties, time of institution of suit, name of court, a description of the property and a statement of relief sought must have been recorded in office of clerk of circuit court of county where property is situated. (48.23[1][a]).

Torrens Act has not been adopted in Florida.

Transfer of decedent's title to distributee is shown by instrument transferring asset from personal representative. (733.811). Title to Florida property owned by nonresident established by ancillary administration. (734.101-.102).

Vital Statistics.—Reports of births, including still births, deaths, marriages and divorces must be filed with Bureau of Vital Statistics. (382.008, -.013, -.015, -.017, -.018, -.019, -.021). Records of last known names and addresses of natural parents, adoptive parents and adoptee shall be maintained. Conditions for disclosure prescribed by statute. (63.162). Birth certificate may be filed when Florida residents adopt alien child. (382.017).

Copies of certificates of birth, death, marriage and dissolution of marriage for all counties may be obtained from Bureau of Vital Statistics, Florida Department of Health, P.O. Box 210, Jacksonville, Florida 32231 (Tel: 904-359-6911). Fee of $9 for each certified copy of birth certificate and $5 each for certified death, marriage, and dissolution of marriage certificates. Complete name and date are required; place is helpful. Searches are not less than $3 nor more than $5 for first calendar year, plus not more than $2 for each additional calendar year, up to maximum of $50 and entitle applicant to one certified copy without additional charge. (382.025). Marriage and dissolution certificates are available from June 6, 1927, to present. Prior to this date marriage certificates must be obtained from county judge and divorce decrees from clerk of court or county in which marriage or divorce occurred. Birth certificates are confidential and are available only to individual, his parents or any government agency for official purpose (382.025[2]); however, original certificate to adopted individual only upon court order (63.162); however, short form certificate of birth or birth card stating name, date and place but not parentage is available to other than individual or his parents (382.025). Birth certificates are confidential and exempt from provisions of §119.07(1). This exemption is subject to Open Government Sunset Review Act in accordance with §119.14. (382.025).

Delayed Birth Certificates.—Registration after one year is delayed registration. Department may register delayed certificate if department does not already have certificate of birth, death or fetal death on file, upon receipt of fee and proof as required by this section. (382.019[1]). Registrar may require supporting documents and other proofs and further regulate registration. (382.019[2]). Any person born in state may file petition in circuit court in county of residence or in alleged county of birth for delayed birth certificate. (382.0195).

See note at head of Digest as to 1998 legislation covered.

See Topical Index in front part of this volume.

RECORDS . . . *continued*

Termination of Pregnancy.—Physician, or director of any medical facility in which pregnancy is terminated, must submit monthly report containing number of procedures, reason for same and period of gestation at time of procedure to Department of Health. Reports submitted pursuant to this section shall be confidential and exempt from provisions of §119.07(1). This exemption is subject to Open Government Sunset Review Act in accordance with §119.14. (390.0112).

Filing Under Commercial Code.—Financing statements and statements as to continuation, termination, release and assignment are filed with office of UCC Bureau, Department of State, Tallahassee, FL (679.401[1][c]), except as follows: If collateral is farm products, or accounts, or general intangibles arising from or relating to sale of farm products by farmer, by recording in office of Clerk of Circuit Court in county of debtor's place of business, if he has one, in county of chief executive officer if has more than one place of business, otherwise in county of residence or, if debtor not resident of state, by recording in office of Clerk of Circuit Court in county where foregoing collateral located; and, if collateral is crops, by also recording in office of Clerk of Circuit Court in county where land on which crops are growing or to be grown located. Financing statement or continuation statement filed on foregoing collateral perfected only by filing with Department of State during period Jan. 1, 1980 until May 20, 1980 shall be effective as provided in 679.403; except that, said financing statement or continuation statement may be continued upon expiration by filing new financing statement conforming to 671.309(4) in appropriate office described above (679.401[6]); if collateral is timber to be cut, minerals or like (including oil and gas) or accounts subject to 679.103(5) or goods which are or are to become fixtures by filing in office where mortgage on land would be filed or recorded (679.401[1][b]). Generally, security interest in collateral of transmitting utility filed with office of Department of State. (679.401[5]). If collateral is motor vehicle for which certificate of title has been issued in this state, lien must be noted on certificate of title by Department of Highway Safety and Motor Vehicles. (319.27). If no Florida title has been issued, notice of lien can be filed with Department or county tax collector. See also category Transportation, topic Motor Vehicles.

Filed financing statement is effective for five years unless continuation statement filed within six months prior to lapse of original. Continuation statement will be effective for additional five years. (679.403[2]). Assignment of security interest must be filed in place where original was filed. (679.405[2]).

Certain fees relating to Commercial Code are as follows:

Recordation of UCC-1 with Secretary of State (15.091):
- $25.00 for 1 debtor/1 secured party; cost includes cost of termination statement
- $3.00 for each additional debtor, each additional secured party and each attached page
- $5.00 additional charge for non-approved form

Recordation of UCC-3 with Secretary of State (15.091):
- $12.00 for one debtor/one secured party
- $3.00 for each additional debtor, each additional secured party, and each attached page

UCC-11 with Secretary of State (15.091):
- Search: $20.00 per debtor name
- Copy: $1.00 per page
- Certified Copy: $10.00 for first ten file numbers; $10.00 each additional group of ten.

$24 for original or duplicate certificate of title plus $2 to note lien on title certificate (includes services for subsequent issue of corrected certificate on cancellation of lien when satisfied) for motor vehicle filing. (319.32).

$3 for assignment of lien by motor vehicle lienholder. (319.32[1]).

For recording fees of Clerk of Circuit Court, see §28.24.

See also category Business Regulation and Commerce, topic Commercial Code.

SEALS:

All bonds, notes, covenants, deeds, bills of exchange and other written instruments not under seal have same force and effect (so far as rules of pleading and evidence are concerned) as bonds and instruments under seal. (68.06). No seal is necessary to convey real property (689.01), or trust estates (689.06).

Uniform Commercial Code adopted. (cc. 670-680). See category Business Regulation and Commerce, topic Commercial Code.

Sufficiency of Seal.—A scrawl or scroll printed or written, affixed as seal to any written instrument shall be as effectual as seal. (695.07). "LS" can be a seal. (42 So. 457).

Effect of Seal.—Seal "imports" consideration (98 So.2d 791), but lack of consideration makes sealed contract unenforceable (4 Fla. 359; 6 Fla. 359).

Counties and Municipalities.—Governing body may adopt official seal; penalties provided for unauthorized use of official seal. (165.043).

Corporate Seal.—Unless articles provide otherwise, every corporation has perpetual duration in its corporate name and all powers necessary to conduct business, including to have corporate seal, alterable at will. (607.0302[2]).

TORRENS ACT:

Not adopted.

VITAL STATISTICS:

See topic Records.

EMPLOYMENT

EMPLOYER AND EMPLOYEE:

See topic Labor Relations.

LABOR RELATIONS:

Division of Labor, of Department of Labor and Employment Security charged with enforcement of labor laws. (450.121).

Hours of Labor.—No minor 15 years of age or younger shall be permitted to work before 7:00 A.M. or after 7:00 P.M. when school is scheduled for next day. Nor may child under 15 work more than three hours on day when school is in session unless there is no session of school on following day. During holidays and vacations minors 15 and under shall not be employed before 7:00 A.M. or after 9:00 P.M., for more than eight hours in any one day or for more than 40 hours in any one week. (450.081[1][b]). Minors 16 and 17 years of age shall not be employed before 6:30 A.M. or after 11:00 P.M. or for more than eight hours on any one day when school is scheduled for following day. (450.081[2]). When school is in session, minors 16 or 17 years of age shall not work more than 30 hours in any one week. (450.081[2]). On any school day, minors 16 and 17 years of age, who are not enrolled in vocational educational program, shall not be employed during school hours. (450.081[2]). No minor 17 years or younger shall be employed for more than six consecutive days in any one week. (450.081[3]). Minors 17 years or younger shall not be employed for more than four continuous hours without interval of at least 30 minutes. (450.081[4]). Provisions do not apply to child 16 years old or older who has graduated from high school, or child who holds valid certificate of exemption issued by school superintendent or his/her designee pursuant to §232.06, or child who qualifies for hardship exemption to be determined by school superintendent or his/her designee. (450.081[5]). Provisions do not apply to minors in domestic service in private home or farm work or pages in Florida Legislature. (def. 450.012). (450.081[5][b][c]). Special statutory provisions exist for employment of children by motion picture and television studios. (450.132).

Wages, unemployment compensation, and traveling expenses due at time of death are not subject to administration of estate and may be paid to specified parties. (222.15, .16).

Payment of wages may be made by check, draft, note or other acknowledgment of indebtedness. Instrument must be negotiable and payable in cash, on demand, without discount. (532.01).

Any person who issues coupons, tickets, tokens, or other devices in lieu of cash as payment for labor whether redeemable in goods or merchandise who shall on demand fail to pay same in current U.S. money on or after 30 days from issue shall be liable to pay full amount, with legal interest and 10% as attorneys' fees. (532.02). Direct deposit of wages or salary can be made to account of payee of wages or salary in any financial institution if authorized in writing by payee, however payee cannot be fired for refusing to sign such authorization for direct deposit. (532.04).

Children.—Employment of children under 13 prohibited with certain exceptions. (450.021). Children of age of ten years or younger are prohibited from selling or distributing newspapers, magazines and periodicals. (450.021). Persons under 18 may not be employed in any establishment which retails alcoholic beverages, with certain exceptions. (450.021). Persons under 18 may not be employed for any obscene, indecent or immoral purpose or for production of or depiction in any obscene materials. (450.151). Children under 16 cannot work in "hazardous occupations," as enumerated (450.061); unless employed as student learner 16 to 18 years old, enrolled in youth vocational program and employed under specified written agreement (450.161).

Farm Labor.—Department of Labor and Employment Security has authority to administer Federal Migrant and Seasonal Agricultural Worker Protection Act of 1983 and Florida Labor Registration Law, which extensively regulate farm labor and provide for civil and criminal penalties for violations. (c. 450).

Discrimination.—Florida Civil Rights Act prohibits discrimination in employment on basis of race, color, religion, sex, national origin, age, handicap, or marital status. (760.01). Act does not prohibit religious organizations from limiting employment opportunities within its organization to members of its religion or persons who subscribe to its beliefs. (760.10[9]). Act creates remedial procedures (760.11), and creates Commission on Human Relations (760.11). Commission has power to provide relief to persons discriminated against by employer and to award attorneys fees analogous to that available in suits brought under Tit. VII of Civil Rights Act of 1964, as am'd, 42 U.S.C. §2000e et seq. (760.11). Discrimination in wage rate based upon sex is prohibited. (448.07).

HIV.—No person may require individual to take Human Immunodeficiency Virus (HIV)-related test as condition of hiring, promotion, or continued employment, unless absence of HIV infection is bona fide occupational qualification for job in question. (760.50[3][a]). No person may fail or refuse to hire or discharge any individual, segregate or classify any individual in any way which would deprive or tend to deprive that individual of employment opportunities or adversely affect his status as employee, or otherwise discriminate against any individual with respect to compensation, terms or conditions or privileges of employment on basis of knowledge or belief that individual has taken human immunodeficiency virus test or results or perceived results of such test unless absence of HIV infection is bona fide occupational qualification of job in question. (760.50[3][b]). Person asserting that bona fide occupational qualification exists for HIV-related testing bears burden of proving that test is necessary to ascertain whether employee is able to perform duties of particular job in reasonable manner or whether employee will present significant risk of transmitting HIV infection to other persons in course of normal work activities, and there exists no means of reasonable accommodation short of requiring individual be free of human immunodeficiency virus infection. (760.50[3][c]). Every employer who provides or administers health or life insurance benefits shall develop and implement procedures to protect confidentiality of records relating to medical condition or status of employees receiving such insurance benefits or be liable for damages. (760.50[5]). Penalties for violation of this section are greater of $1,000 or actual damages; greater of $5,000 or actual damage for intentional or reckless violation; and reasonable attorneys' fees. (760.50[6]).

See note at head of Digest as to 1998 legislation covered.

See Topical Index in front part of this volume.

FL – 31

LABOR RELATIONS . . . *continued*

Labor Unions.—Employees have right to self-organization, and to engage in concerted activities for purpose of collective bargaining or other mutual aid or protection. (447.03).

Labor organizations may sue or be sued in their commonly used name. (447.11).

Public employees rights to organize and bargain collectively are governed by special provisions. (447.201-.609). Public Employees Relations Commission (PERC) established to handle all labor disputes between public employers and public employees having to do with organization and collective bargaining. (447.205). Legislature retains right to approve, rescind or amend rules promulgated by PERC. (447.607). PERC was given powers analogous to those of NLRB and analogous procedures were established for perfecting rights of public employers and employees. (447.201-.609). However, public employees are prohibited from striking and are subject to severe penalties for violating no strike statute. (447.505, .507). Strikes by public employees are also prohibited by Florida Constitution. (art. 1, §6).

Right to Work.—Right of persons to work cannot be denied on account of membership or nonmembership in any labor union. Right of employees to bargain collectively by and through a labor organization may not be denied. (Const., art. I, §6). Agency shop is outlawed as violating the right to work provision. (141 So.2d 269, aff'd 375 U.S. 96).

Worker's Compensation Law (440.01-.60) applies to employment by state and all political subdivisions, to all public and quasi-public corporations and to all private employments in which four or more employees are employed by same employer, or, with respect to construction industry, all private employment in which one or more employees are employed by same employer. Does not apply to domestic servants in private homes, agricultural farm labor, performed for farmer who employs five or fewer regular employees and fewer than 12 seasonal employees, labor under sentence of court to perform community services as provided in §316.193, and professional athletes. (440.02[15][c][3]). Term "employees" means every person engaged in any employment under any colorable form of contract, including officer of corporation remunerated in any fashion except those requesting exemption and volunteers other than those working for state or local governmental entity. (440.02[13]). However, volunteer fire fighters, who are responding to or assisting with fire or medical emergencies are considered employees. (440.02[15][b][3]). Term employees includes partner or sole proprietors who are actively engaged in construction industry unless they elect to be excluded from definition of employee by filing written notice of election as provided in §440.05. However, no more than three partners in partnership that is actively engaged in construction industry may elect to be excluded. (440.02[13][c]). Independent contractor who meets criteria specified in §440.02(14)(d)(1) is not considered employee. Employers having employees excluded from Law and corporate officer previously exempted may waive exclusion by proper notice thereof. (440.04-.05). No compensation is payable in respect of disability or death of employee covered by Federal Employer's Liability Act, Longshoremen's and Harbor Worker's Compensation Act or Jones Act. (440.09[2]). Act is applicable to occupational diseases. (440.151).

If employer with less than four employees chooses not to secure payments of compensation, employer must annually file affidavit stating that he has not secured payment of compensation under this statute and he must provide clear written notice to all employees of their lack of entitlement to benefits. (440.055).

All self-insurers, other than public utilities, and government entities, must join Florida Self-Insurers Guaranty Association, Inc. (440.385). Funds to cover costs of claims and administration are raised by assessment of members. Amount of assessments determined by Department of Labor and Employment Security. (440.385[3][c]). Any sums acquired by member by refund, dividend or otherwise from Association shall be payable within 30 days of receipt to Department of Revenue for deposit with Treasurer to credit General Revenue Fund. (440.385[13]). Self-Insurers Guaranty Association manages insolvency fund for member employers. (440.385[4]). Department of Labor and Employment Security has power to revoke power to self-insurer for failure to pay assessment or failing to comply with plan of operation. (440.385[6]).

Compensation for disability is minimum of $20 per week unless weekly wage is less than $20. Maximum shall not exceed amount equal to 100% of statewide average weekly wage for injuries occurring after July 31, 1979 or two-thirds of statewide average for injuries incurred before that date, figures adjusted to nearest dollar. (440.12, .14). Employer must furnish medical services and supplies. (440.13). No compensation, except payment for medical services and supplies, is allowed for first seven days of disability if total period of disability is 21 days or less. (440.12, .13, .20, .25). Subject to above limitation formula, compensation shall depend on variety of factors including severity and type of injury and activities of employee. (See 440.15.) Temporary total disability includes period necessary for training in use of artificial members and appliances. Compensation may be paid for temporary partial disability. (440.15[4]). If employee is eligible for social security benefits, worker's compensation benefits shall be secondary, sum of two benefits should not exceed amount of wage-lost benefits which would otherwise be payable. (440.15[3]). Injured worker requesting wage loss benefits for any period of unemployment has duty to make good faith efforts to obtain employment. (440.15[3][b][3]).

If death results from accident within one year thereafter or follows continuous disability and results from accident within five years thereafter, there are allowed actual funeral expenses not to exceed $5,000 and, following percentage of average weekly wages to following persons in following order of precedence: (1) To spouse if there is no child, 50% of average weekly wage until death; (2) to spouse, if there is one child or children, in addition, 16⅔% on account for child or children; in case of death of surviving spouse, 33⅓% for each child and judge of compensation claims may provide payment as it appears just and may pay entire amount to children; upon remarriage of surviving spouse, spouse shall be entitled to lump sum payment equal to 26 weeks of compensation at rate of 50% of average weekly wage (as provided in §440.012[2]) unless $100,000 limit has been exceeded, in which case surviving spouse shall receive lump sum payment equal to remaining available benefits in lieu of any further indemnity benefits. (440.16[b]). In no case shall surviving spouse's acceptance of lump sum payment affect payment of death benefits to other dependents (440.16[b][2]); (3) to child or children, if there is no spouse, 33⅓% for each child; (4) to parents, 25% to each during dependency; (5) to brothers, sisters, and grandchildren, 15% to each. (440.16[b]). Dependence of child, unless incapacitated from earning livelihood, terminates on attainment of age 18 or marriage or age 22 if full-time student in accredited educational institution. (440.16[2]). Payments in case of death cannot exceed 66⅔% of employee's weekly wages nor $100,000 and provision is made for allocation of payments among beneficiaries where full amounts stated in this paragraph are not payable. Surviving spouse also entitled to receive payment of postsecondary student fees for up to 1,800 classroom hours at area vocational-technical center, or student fees at any area community college for up to 80 semester hours. (440.16). If during period of disability employer continues to provide considerations such as board, rent, housing or lodging, value of same shall be deducted when calculating average weekly wage. (440.14).

If employer has reason to believe injury was drug or alcohol induced he may require employee to submit to testing. (440.09[7][a]).

Notice of injury or death must be given to carrier or self-insured employer within 30 days after date of same, and notice of injury resulting in death must be given by employer to Division by telephone or telegraph within 24 hours of actual knowledge of injury. Employer must notify carrier of injury to employee within seven days of actual knowledge of injury. (440.185). Within three days of receipt of notice of injury of employee which results in employee losing more than seven days of work, carrier must provide information brochure to employee setting out employee rights and benefits under law. (440.185[4]).

Claim for disability or death must be filed within two years after time of injury or death, except that where compensation is paid or remedial treatment furnished without an award, claim may be filed within two years after date of last payment or remedial treatment. (440.19). Claim must contain name and address of employee, name and address of employer, statement of time/date, place, nature and cause of injury or equivalent information to put division and employer on notice of identity of parties and nature of claim. (440.19).

Claimant injured by third party, or claimant's dependents, may accept compensation and sue third party. Amount recovered by claimant or dependents from third-party tortfeasor either by judgment or settlement before or after filing of suit, before claimant has accepted compensation or filed written claim for benefits, shall be setoff against any compensation benefits other than for remedial care, treatment and attendance as well as rehabilitative services. Amount offset shall be reduced by amount of court costs expended in prosecution of third-party suit, including reasonable attorney's fees. Employer or insurer who pays compensation is subrogated to employee's rights against third party to extent of amount paid. (440.39). 100% subrogation is constitutional. (402 So.2d 1273). If injured employee or his dependents fail to sue within one year, employer or insurer may sue. If employer or insurer does not bring suit within two years after cause arises, action reverts to employee. (440.39). Settlement by employee or dependents without notice to employer or insurer to participate affects only employee's claim. (190 So. 2d 426). Settlement by employer or insurer cannot be made without agreement of employee or dependents. (440.39). §440.20(12)(a) prohibition against release of employer-carrier's liability for future medical expenses is constitutional. (402 So.2d 518).

Act is administered by Division of Workers' Compensation of Department of Labor and Employment Security. Hearings and investigations are conducted by judges of compensation claims who have summary process power, with right of review by Industrial Relations Commission. (See 440.271, .29, .33, .44, .45.) Appeals shall be filed in accordance with rules of procedure prescribed by Supreme Court for review of all orders. Division shall be made party respondent to every such proceeding. (440.271). Actions by judges of compensation claims are not subject to review pursuant to Administrative Procedures Act (c. 120). (440.021). Judges of compensation claims can assess costs and can set attorney's fees based upon circumstances of action. (440.31, .34). Act makes it misdemeanor to render services in processing of application for fee not approved by judge of compensation claims. (440.34[6]). Legislative delegation of power to Division of Worker's Compensation to establish schedule for determining existence and degree of permanent impairment constitutional. (415 So.2d 1277). Provision is made for mediation conference. (440.25[3][b]).

Penalties may be imposed on employers with high frequency or severity of work related injuries. (440.56).

Occupational Diseases.—If employer and employee are subject to provisions of Act, death or disablement of employee which results from occupational disease shall be treated as industrial accident, with compensation to be provided according to Act. (440.151). However, employer shall only be liable where disease results from nature of employment in which employee was engaged, in that there was in that employment particular hazard of such disease or that incidence of such disease was substantially higher than in usual run of occupations and among population in general. No compensation shall be payable where employee falsely represents himself in writing as never having been previously disabled in any manner by the disease. Compensation shall be reduced proportionately where compensable disease is aggravated or in anywise contributed to by noncompensable disease. Only afterborn children of marriage existing at beginning of compensable disability may be compensated where death of employee leaves as survivor one whose relationship to deceased began after onset of first compensable disability. Occupational disease means disease solely due to peculiar characteristics of employee's trade, and disablement means partial or total incapacity to perform that trade. Employer in whose employment employee was last injuriously exposed to hazards of occupational disease, and insurance carrier bearing risk shall alone be liable for compensation, without right to contribution. (440.151). In case of occupational diseases, time of notice of injury or death provided in §440.185(1) extended to 90 days. (440.151[6]).

Unemployment Compensation.—Unemployed individuals entitled to benefits upon compliance with statutes. (c. 443). Penalties provided for noncompliance. (443.071). There are many exemptions such as agricultural labor, domestic service, casual labor, service in employ of school by student, service on vessel, service in employ of certain

See note at head of Digest as to 1998 legislation covered.

See Topical Index in front part of this volume.

FL – 32

LABOR RELATIONS . . . *continued*

familial relations, service in employ of foreign government, service solely for commission (real estate and insurance salesman, barber). (443.036). Weekly benefit amounts to ¹/₂₆ of total wages for insured work paid during quarter of base period in which total wages paid were highest, but not less than $32 nor more than $250 (amount raised to $275 for benefit weeks beginning Jan. 1, 1998). (443.111). For claims with benefit years beginning July 1, 1997, through Dec. 31, 1997, additional 5% of weekly benefit amount must be added for first eight compensable weeks of benefits paid, not to exceed $262 (for claims with benefit years beginning Jan. 1, 1998, through June 30, 1998, maximum is raised to $288). (443.111[3]). Weekly benefits are rounded down to nearest full dollar amount. (443.111[2][a]). State will deduct child support payment obligations from unemployment benefits and forward to appropriate state or local child support agency. (443.051[3]).

Employers who, for economic reasons, must lay off employees may instead file plan for shortened work week with Division of Employment Security which if approved will allow employees to draw benefits for time they are not working. (443.111[6]).

Hazardous Occupations.—(c. 769). Employers engaged in following hazardous occupations: Railroading, operating street railways, generating and selling electricity, telephone and telegraph business, express business, blasting or dynamiting, operating automobiles for public use, boating when propelled by steam, gas or electricity, are liable in damages for injuries to and death of their agents and employees caused by negligence of such employers, their agents and servants unless it is made to appear that ordinary and reasonable care and diligence have been exercised, presumption being against employer. (769.02).

As to such hazardous occupations, if both employee and employer or the agents and employees of the latter are both at fault, there may be a recovery, but the damages are assessed in proportion to the fault of each. Damages are not recoverable by an employee injured in part through his own negligence, and partly through the negligence of another employee, such employees being fellow servants, when both are jointly engaged in performing the act causing the injury and the employer is guilty of no negligence. Where the injury or death is caused by the consent of the employee, or by his own negligence, there is no liability against the employer. (769.03).

Where the injury or death is attributable to the negligence of the employer engaged in such hazardous occupations, employer's agents or servants, doctrine of assumption of risk does not apply. (769.04). Damages for injuries arising under such hazardous occupations are exempt from garnishment, execution and other processes. (769.05). Contracts limiting liability imposed by this law are invalid. (769.06).

Railroads.—Where railroad company employee is injured by equipment of railroad and injury is caused by negligence of another employee, without fault of injured employee, such employment is no bar to recovery. No contract restricting such liability is legal or binding. (768.07).

WORKERS' COMPENSATION LAW:

See topic Labor Relations.

ENVIRONMENT

ENVIRONMENTAL REGULATION:

General Supervision.—Department of Environmental Protection ("DEP"). (403.061). Duties and responsibilities previously with Department of Environmental Regulation and Department of Natural Resources were transferred to DEP in 1993, and statutory provisions revised to reflect these changes pursuant to 94-356. Supervision extends to underground water, lakes, drinking water, rivers, streams, canals, ditches, wetlands (403.91 et seq.) and coastal waters, as well as atmosphere (403.061). Provision is made for local pollution control programs (403.182) and their compliance with U.S. Environmental Protection Act Standards and Clean Air Act (403.061). Regulatory power regarding beaches and shores, preservation, restoration, and erosion, rests with Division of Beaches and Shores. (c. 161).

Pollution resulting from oil and other spillage from storage tanks and piping facilities between vessels, between onshore facilities and vessels, and between offshore facilities and vessels is dealt with in a separate chapter. (c. 376). State Underground Petroleum Environmental Response Act of 1986 requires registration of persons who cause taxable pollutants to be imported into Florida and imposes certain excise taxes. DEP empowered to administer Florida Petroleum Liability and Restoration Insurance Program which was created to provide restoration funding assistance to facilities regulated by and in compliance with DEP's petroleum storage tank rules. (376.3072[1]). Requirements for insurance are provided. (376.3072[2]).

Department of Environmental Protection regulates small pollution from above ground crude oil storage tanks, drilling for and production of oil, gas and other petroleum products and requires fees and bonds or other securities equitably allocated among interested parties for certain geophysical permits. (c. 377). Oil and mineral severance taxes fund Conservation and Recreation Lands Trust Fund within Department of Environmental Protection for acquisition of public lands. Department of Environmental Protection regulates building in coastal zones. (cc. 161, 163, 186, 380).

Water Resources Act creates water management districts to: Regulate consumptive use of water; protect existing uses; provide permit system; provide for annual dam inspection; regulate well construction; regulate impoundments, storage or other diversion of surface waters. Water Management District also created under §253.002. Permits are required. (c. 373). Permit not required for temporary construction, operation, or maintenance of water supply back pumping facilities for storage of surplus water if water emergency declared. Soil and Water Conservation Council advises Department of Agriculture and Consumer Services on soil and water conservation matters.

Environmental Land and Water Management Act of 1972 provides for comprehensive statewide land management and development and water quality control measures adopted. (c. 380). Counties are also authorized to setup "land authorities" to acquire land interests. (380.0666). Counties now able to provide alternative water supplies. (cc. 125, 153, 170, 180).

Disposition of lands now authorized by Preservation 2000 Act in certain situations. (259.101).

Development designated as "Florida quality development" exempt from certain regional impact requirements imposed upon projects with regional impact. (380.06).

Environmental Equity and Justice Commission established by 94-219. (§760.85). Southern Interstate Low Level Radioactive Waste Management Compact in effect. (404.30). Model Energy Efficiency Code in effect and provides for statewide conservation of energy by efficient design and use of buildings. Inland Protection Trust Fund created to pay for costs associated with field and laboratory testing and toxicological risk assessment of ground water contamination sites. (376.3071). Due to increasing backlog of reimbursement applications, legislature now prohibits reimbursement for rehabilitation work conducted after Mar. 27, 1995 unless person receives prior written approval from department. (95-2). Early Detection Incentive Program enacted to facilitate reporting and cleanup of tainted sites.

Greenways Coordinating Council to promote greenway (protected open areas for benefit of land and wildlife) support throughout Florida. (95-260).

Outdoor recreation and conservation is responsibility of DEP (375.021).

DEP promulgates rules for siting electrical power plants, for environmental precautions in operation thereof (403.501 et seq.), magnetic and electrical fields (403.061), and inspection of pollutant storage tanks (376.303).

Permits are required for construction, dredging, and filling on wetlands. (403.91 et seq.).

DEP empowered to establish rules for categorizing bodies of water as Outstanding Florida Waters worthy of special protection. (403.061[27]).

Department of Agriculture and Consumer Services researches, monitors and enforces pesticide and certain other hazardous substance regulations. (c. 487).

DEP governs issuance of permits for sanitary sewage systems. (403.087).

Prohibited Acts of Pollution.—Florida Air and Water Pollution Control Act forbids pollution (including noise) of air or waters in violation of rules or regulations adopted by Department of Pollution Control, or to violate or fail to comply with any order of Department. (403.161, 403.151). Local pollution control programs authorized if in compliance with Act. (403.182). Department is also authorized to develop standards for deep water commercial navigation, including water quality and dredging requirements. Pollution defined as presence in outdoor atmosphere or waters of state of any substances, contaminants, noise, or man-made or man-induced alteration of chemical, physical, biological, or radiological integrity of air or water in quantities or levels which are or may be potentially harmful or injurious to human health or welfare, animal or plant life, or property, or unreasonably interfere with enjoyment of life or property, including outdoor recreation. (403.031).

The Natural Gas Transmission Pipeline Siting Act forbids construction of natural gas transmission after Oct. 1, 1992 without first obtaining certification under statute. (403.9401 et seq.).

Pollution resulting from drilling for or producing oil, gas, or other petroleum products is prohibited. (377.371). Surety required to drill. (377.22[2][F]). Rules, conditions, and permits are imposed including prohibition on erection of structure for drilling or production within one mile seaward of coastline of state. (377.24).

Saltwater fisheries and products protected and regulated. (c. 370).

Surface Water Improvement and Management Act (373.451) provides for development of water improvement and management plans and regulation of construction at beach and water areas.

Enforcement.—By Department of Environmental Protection in accordance with procedures outlined in §403.121.

Department of legal affairs, political subdivision or municipality, or private citizen may maintain action for injunctive relief to prohibit violation of pollution laws or to compel governmental authorities to enforce such laws. (403.412).

Governing board of any water management district and any officer of district may enforce Water Resources Act. (373.129).

Penalties.—Anyone who commits a violation of c. 403 may be fined up to $10,000 for each offense, in addition to civil liability to state for damages to air, waters, or property, including animal, plant, and aquatic life. Each day of violation constitutes a separate offense. (403.141).

Civil penalty for drilling or producing oil and gas in violation of c. 377 up to $10,000 per offense; each day during which violation occurs constitutes separate offense. (377.37). Civil liability imposed for damages, costs of tracing source and clean-up costs. Negligence need not be shown in action by State. (377.37).

Up to $500 per day and up to 60 days in jail penalty imposed on persons violating regulations on well construction and use. (373.336, 775.082, 775.083).

Variances.—May be granted for certain enumerated reasons and upon compliance with procedure for application therefor. (403.201).

ESTATES AND TRUSTS

ADMINISTRATION:

See topic Executors and Administrators.

ADVANCEMENTS:

See topic Descent and Distribution.

ALLOWANCES:

See topic Executors and Administrators.

CLAIMS:

See topic Executors and Administrators; category Civil Actions and Procedure, topic Pleading.

See note at head of Digest as to 1998 legislation covered.

See Topical Index in front part of this volume.

DEATH:

Person who is absent from place of his last known domicile for continuous period of five years and whose absence is not satisfactorily explained after diligent search and inquiry [is] presumed dead. (731.103[3]).

Uniform Simultaneous Death Act has been adopted with some modifications. (732.601).

Actions for Death.—
Survival of Actions.—Wherever the act causing death is such as would, if death had not ensued, have entitled the injured party to recover damages therefor, then the person or persons who would have been liable in damages if death had not ensued, will be liable notwithstanding the death of the person injured. (768.19). Includes both ex contractu and ex delicto actions.

Wrongful Death.—Action maintained by decedent's personal representative for decedent's survivors and estate. (768.20). Recovery may include lost support and services, loss of companionship, mental pain and suffering of certain family members of decedent, and medical and funeral expenses plus certain other damages. (768.21).

Action for wrongful death must be commenced within two years from time of death of injured party. (95.11[4][d]).

Judgment for personal injuries rendered in favor of injured party while living bars subsequent wrongful death action based on same tortious conduct. (445 So.2d 1010).

Death Certificate.—See category Documents and Records, topic Records, subhead Vital Statistics.

Life-Prolonging Procedures.—Competent adult may, at any time, make written declaration or living will directing withholding or withdrawal of life-prolonging procedures in event person suffers from terminal condition. Declaration must be signed in presence of two subscribing witnesses, one of whom is neither spouse nor blood relative of declarant. If declarant physically unable to sign living will, one of witnesses must subscribe declarant's signature in declarant's presence and at principal's direction. (765.302[1]). See also 568 So.2d 4 (Fla. 1990). Florida also allows person to designate healthcare surrogate to make such decisions. (765.202; 765.204[5]).

Right to Die.—See subhead Life-Prolonging Procedures, supra and topic Wills, subhead Life Prolonging.

DECEDENTS' ESTATES:

See topics Descent and Distribution, Executors and Administrators, Wills; category Debtor and Creditor, topic Homesteads.

DESCENT AND DISTRIBUTION:

Uniform Probate Code adopted with significant variations. (cc. 731, 732).

Real (other than homestead) and personal property of intestate descends and is distributed as follows: (1) In absence of lineal descendants, to surviving spouse, (2) if all surviving lineal descendants are lineal descendants of surviving spouse, first $20,000 plus one-half of balance of estate to surviving spouse and other one-half of balance to lineal descendants, (3) if any of surviving lineal descendants is not lineal descendant of surviving spouse, one-half to surviving spouse and one-half to lineal descendants, (4) if no surviving spouse, entire estate to lineal descendants, or if none, (5) to father and mother equally, or survivor of them, or if none, (6) to brothers and sisters and descendants of deceased brothers and sisters, (7) if none of foregoing, one-half each to paternal and maternal kindred in following course: (a) Grandfather and grandmother equally, or survivor, (b) uncles and aunts and descendants of those deceased uncles and aunts, (c) if either no paternal or no maternal kindred, to such of kindred as survive in order aforesaid, (8) if no kindred of either part, then to kindred of last deceased spouse as if said spouse survived decedent and then died intestate entitled to estate. (732.101-103). See category Debtor and Creditor, topic Homesteads.

Descent is always per stirpes. (732.104).

Half Blood.—Half blood, collateral kindred of intestate inherit only half as much as those of whole blood; but if all are half blood they take whole parts. (732.105).

Out of Wedlock Children.—For purposes of intestate succession, person born out of wedlock is lineal descendant of mother and is one of natural kindred of mother's family. He is lineal descendant of father and one of natural kindred of father's family, if, and only if (i) natural parents were married before or after his birth even though marriage is void, (ii) paternity is established by adjudication or (iii) paternity is acknowledged in writing by father. (732.108).

Adopted Children.—For purposes of intestate succession, adopted person is lineal descendant of adopting parent and is natural kindred of all members of adopting parent's family. Adopted person is not lineal descendant of natural parent or kindred of natural parent's family except where person was adopted by natural parent's spouse or by certain close relatives after death of natural parents. (732.108).

Surviving Spouse.—Preexisting right to dower of widow of man who died prior to Oct. 1, 1973, shall be barred in any real property conveyed by her husband before his death without her relinquishment of dower, unless within three years after husband's death she records with clerk for county where real property is located instrument executed by her describing property in manner sufficient to give constructive notice if contained in recorded deed, and naming record owner of property, date of husband's death and his place of residence, and indicating that she has elected to take dower or that she may elect to do so. (732.213).

Right to Elective Share.—Surviving spouse of person who dies domiciled in Florida or guardian of property of surviving spouse has right to elect elective share of estate of deceased spouse. No elective share exists in Florida property of decedent not domiciled in Florida. (732.201, .205, .210).

Elective share consists of 30% of fair market value on date of death of all assets of decedent wherever located that are subject to administration, except real property not located in Florida, after deducting from total value of assets all valid claims paid or payable from estate, and all mortgages, liens, or security interests thereon. (732.206, .207).

Elective share is in addition to homestead and other exempt property and allowances otherwise provided. (732.208, 732.401-.403).

Unless otherwise provided by will, elective share is paid from assets passing under will which, but for election, would have passed outright to surviving spouse and to extent such assets are insufficient, then from assets in order of abatement prescribed in §733.805. If property must be sold to provide elective share, person otherwise entitled to property may pay amount assessed against property interest and receive property. (732.209).

If election is filed, remaining assets of estate after payment of elective share are distributed as though surviving spouse predeceased decedent. (732.211).

Election must be filed within four months from date of first publication of notice of administration but if proceeding occurs involving construction, admission to probate, or validity of will or on other matter whereby complete extent of estate subject to elective share may be in doubt, surviving spouse has 40 days from termination of all proceedings to elect. (732.212).

On petition of personal representative or surviving spouse and after notice and hearing, court shall determine amount of elective share and order payment in cash or in kind from assets of estate subject to elective share within time certain, but no distribution may be required until six months from date of death when no federal estate tax return is required or until return is timely filed when required. Order may provide for partial distributions. On petition of interested party after notice, court may suspend distribution of elective share or part thereof until final settlement of federal estate tax liability. Assets distributed in kind are distributed at fair market value on date of distribution. (732.214).

When election of elective share has effect of increasing estate taxes, share of surviving spouse bears additional tax. (732.215). However, where elective share qualifies for federal marital deduction and entire increase in estates taxes due is generated by nonmarital property passing to residuary beneficiaries, estate taxes are payable by residuary beneficiaries and not by surviving spouse in accordance with §733.817. (564 So.2d 1106).

Advancements.—Property given by total intestate prior to death to heir is advancement against heir's share only if declared as such in contemporaneous writing by decedent or acknowledged in writing by heir. If recipient does not survive decedent, such property shall not be taken into account in computing share to be received by recipient's descendants unless declaration or acknowledgment provides otherwise. (733.806).

Escheat.—If person dies and is not survived by any person entitled to his estate, his property escheats to state and proceeds of estate are paid to State Treasurer. In this event or in case of uncertainty, personal representative shall petition court for determination of beneficiaries within one year after issuance of letters of administration. Any person claiming to be entitled to estate may reopen administration within ten years after issuance of letters of administration. (732.107). See category Property, topic Absentees, subhead Escheat.

Unclaimed probate assets held by personal representative also escheat to state if funds deposited with state go unclaimed for ten years. (733.816). Claims by persons entitled to these assets must be made within ten years from date of deposit with State Treasurer. (733.816).

See also topic Executors and Administrators.

Disclaimer.—Beneficiary may disclaim his interest in any property which would pass to him by intestate succession, devise, descent of homestead, exempt property, family allowance, or life insurance (see 222.13), exercise or non-exercise of power of appointment exercisable by will, testamentary exercise or nonexercise of power of appointment exercisable either by deed or will, as beneficiary of testamentary trust, as beneficiary of testamentary gift to nontestamentary trust, as donee of power of appointment created by will, by succession to disclaimed interest, or in any other manner under testamentary instrument. Disclaimer may be made for minor, incompetent, incapacitated person or deceased beneficiary by guardian or personal representative, subject to court approval upon petition served on all interested parties. (732.801).

Unless decedent or donor of power of appointment has otherwise provided for possibility of disclaimer by beneficiary, disclaimed interest shall be distributed as if disclaimant had died immediately preceding decedent's death or such other event that has caused him to become finally ascertained as beneficiary or his interest to become indefeasibly fixed. Any interest in disclaimed property shall never vest in disclaimant. (732.801).

Form, Filing, Recording and Service.—To be disclaimer, writing shall declare disclaimer and its extent, describe interest in property disclaimed, be signed, witnessed and acknowledged in manner provided for conveyance of real property. Disclaimer is effective and irrevocable when instrument is recorded in office of circuit court of county in which estate of decedent is administered. If no administration has been commenced, recording may be made with clerk of any county where venue of administration is proper. Disclaimer must be recorded within nine months after event giving rise to right to disclaim, including death of decedent, or if disclaimant is not finally ascertained as beneficiary or interest has not become indefeasibly fixed in quality and quantity, then such disclaimer must be recorded not later than six months after event which would cause him so to become finally ascertained and interest to become indefeasibly fixed. (732.801).

Beneficiary's right to disclaim shall be barred if beneficiary is insolvent or by assignment, transfer, contract to assign or transfer, encumbrance, waiver, or judicial sale or other disposition pursuant to judicial process with respect to disclaimed property. Right to disclaim exists irrespective of limitation imposed on interest of disclaimant of spendthrift provision or similar restriction. (732.801).

ESTATES:

See category Property, topic Real Property.

EXECUTORS AND ADMINISTRATORS:

(See also topics Wills, and Descent and Distribution.)

EXECUTORS AND ADMINISTRATORS . . . *continued*

Uniform Probate Code adopted with significant variations. (cc. 731, 732).

Probate jurisdiction is in circuit court.

Venue of probate of wills and granting of letters of administration is: (a) In county where decedent had his domicile; (b) if decedent had no domicile in state, any county in which he was possessed of property; (c) if decedent had no domicile, and possessed no property in State, then in county where any debtor of decedent may reside. (733.101[1]). Married woman whose husband is alien or nonresident of Florida may establish or designate separate domicile in Florida. (733.101[2]).

Ancillary Administration.—Upon death of nonresident leaving assets in state, personal representative designated in will to administer Florida property, or domiciliary personal representative, may have ancillary letters issued to him, if qualified to act. After payment of administration expenses and claims, circuit court may order remaining property held by ancillary personal representative transferred to domiciliary personal representative or distributed to heirs or devisees. (734.102).

If assets in state do not exceed $25,000, domiciliary personal representative may determine question of claims in this state by filing with circuit court where property located authenticated copies of: (i) Probated will if testate estate; (ii) order admitting will to record; (iii) letters; and (iv) part of record showing beneficiaries. Court shall admit will to probate if it complies with §732.502(1) or (2). (734.1025[1]). Personal representative shall cause notice to be served and published according to §731.111. (734.1025[2]). If no claims, court will enter order that notice was duly given and all claims are satisfied. (734.1025[4]). If claim filed, court notifies domiciliary personal representative and sets hearing to appoint ancillary personal representative. (734.1025[5]).

Preference in appointment as personal representative is given in testate estates to: (a) Personal representative or successor nominated by will or pursuant to power in will; (b) person selected by majority in interest of persons entitled to estate; (c) devisee under will and if more than one applies, court may select one best qualified; and in intestate estates to: (a) Surviving spouse; (b) person selected by majority in interest of heirs; (c) heir nearest in degree, and if more than one applies, court may select one best qualified. Guardian of property of ward who if competent would be entitled to appointment or to select representative may exercise right to select personal representative. If no application is made by persons named above, court shall appoint capable person. (733.301).

Eligibility and Competency.—Any person sui juris who is resident of Florida at time of death of person whose estate he seeks to administer is qualified to act as personal representative, unless convicted of felony, mentally or physically unable to perform duties, or under age 18. (733.302, .303).

Nonresidents.—Person not domiciled in Florida cannot qualify as personal representative unless legally adopted child or adoptive parent, related by lineal consanguinity, or spouse, brother, sister, uncle, aunt, nephew, or niece of decedent or someone related by lineal consanguinity to any such person or spouse of person otherwise qualified. (733.304). Constitutionality of §733.304 upheld by Supreme Court of Florida. (390 So.2d 40; appeal dismissed 450 U.S. 961; Contra, 463 F. Supp. 661).

Removal of domicile from Florida, not being qualified under above exceptions, is cause for removal of personal representative. (733.504[11]).

Trust companies incorporated under laws of Florida, state banking corporations, state savings associations and national banking associations and federal savings and loan associations authorized and qualified to exercise fiduciary powers in Florida may act as personal representatives and curators. (733.305[1]).

See, however, category Business Regulation and Commerce, topic Banks and Banking.

Formal Administration.—Verified petition for administration may be filed by any interested person. If decedent was nonresident, petition must state whether domiciliary proceedings are pending in another state or country and name and address of foreign personal representative and court issuing letters. (733.202). Upon proof of will, if any, court appoints person entitled and qualified to be personal representative. After court determines amount of any bond required, and bond and any required oath or designation of and acceptance by resident agent are filed, letters are issued to personal representative. (733.401). See other subheads re formal administration of estates, infra.

Family Administration.—Family administration may be had in decedent's estate when value of gross estate at date of death for federal estate tax purposes is less than $60,000 and consists entirely of personal property or, if real property forms part of estate, when administration under c. 733 has proceeded to point that all claims have been processed or barred, provided intestate estate heirs at law consist solely of surviving spouse, lineal descendants or lineal ascendants or any of them, or in testate estate that beneficiaries under will consist of surviving spouse or lineal descendants, lineal ascendants or any of them, and that any specific or general devise to others is minor part of decedent's estate and that decedent's will does not direct formal administration under c. 733. (735.101). Upon petition and proof of will, and admitting will to probate, if any, if estate consists of personal property only, after hearing, order of family administration may be entered allowing immediate distribution of assets to persons entitled. Petitioners for order are personally liable for lawful claims against estate to extent of value of estate received by each petitioner, less exempt property. Any rightful heir or devisee not included in order may enforce his rights to share against those who procured order. If estate includes real property and administration under c. 733 has proceeded so all claims have been processed or barred, after hearing, order of family administration may be entered and personal representative authorized to distribute all assets to persons entitled. Upon satisfactory evidence that distribution has been made, order discharging personal representative is entered by court. (735.107).

Summary Administration.—Summary administration of decedent's estate may be had when value of entire estate subject to administration in Florida, less exempt property, does not exceed $25,000, or decedent has been dead for more than two years, provided that testate estate decedent's will does not direct formal administration under c. 733 (735.201). Estate may be administered in same manner as administration of any other estate or it may be administered by summary administration. (735.202). After filing of petition showing assets, estate is not indebted or that provision for payment of debts has been made, and proposed distribution to those entitled as surviving spouse, beneficiaries or creditors, and after court admits any will, order of summary administration may be entered allowing immediate distribution to persons entitled. Petitioners for order are personally liable for all lawful claims against estate to extent of assets received by each petitioner, exclusive of exempt property. (735.203, .206). Petitioners may publish and serve notice to creditors according to §731.111. (735.2063). Any rightful heir not included in order of summary administration may enforce his rights to share against those who procured order. (735.206). Any beneficiary not joining in or consenting to petition for summary administration must receive formal notice of hearing on petition. (735.209[2]).

Disposition of Personal Property without Administration.—No administration is required for estate of decedent leaving only personal property entire value of which does not exceed exempt property, preferred funeral expenses and reasonable and necessary medical and hospital expenses of last 60 days of last illness. Upon informal application by interested party, court if satisfied that requirements are met, may by letter or other writing under seal of court authorize payment, transfer or disposition of personal property to those persons entitled, and person, firm or corporation paying, delivering or transferring property under authorization is discharged from liability thereon. (735.301).

Curators.—Circuit court, when necessary, may appoint curator to take charge of estate of decedent until letters are granted. If person entitled to letters is resident of county where property is situated, curator may not be appointed until after formal notice to such person, unless there is danger of property being wasted or destroyed during delay. (733.501).

Public Administrator.—No provision for such.

Bonds.—Before letters of administration are issued, bond with surety must be filed. No bond is required where testator waived such requirement. Bond is in sum set by circuit court, payable to Governor and his successors, and conditioned to perform all duties as personal representative according to law. (733.402). Curators must give bond as court deems necessary. (733.501, 733.501[4]). No bond is required of bank or trust company authorized to act in Florida. (733.402). Court may waive requirement of filing bond, require personal representative or curator to give bond, increase or decrease bond, or require additional surety. (733.403[2]). Bond of others may be reduced or dispensed with under court order providing for deposit of part of or all personal assets of estate with bank or trust company doing business in Florida. (69.031).

Person Presumed Dead.—Where person has been absent and unheard from for five years, administration of person's estate may be granted after petition for administration request, and entry of order declaring death. (731.103, 733.209).

Inventory and Appraisal.—Within 60 days after issuance of letters, personal representative must prepare and file inventory, including estimated fair market value of each listed item at decedent's death. Copy must be served on surviving spouse, each heir at law in intestate estate, each residuary beneficiary in testate estate, any other interested person who requests it and Department of Revenue, and file proof of service. If personal representative learns of any property not included in original inventory or that estimated value or description indicated in original inventory for any item is erroneous or misleading, he must prepare and file amended or supplemental inventory and serve copy on each person on whom copy of original inventory was served, and file proof of service. Any original, amended or supplemental inventory filed shall be subject to inspection only upon order of court upon good cause shown. Initial opening of safe-deposit box of decedent and inventory of contents must be conducted in presence of employee of institution where box is located and personal representative. Both must verify contents by signing copy of inventory. Personal representative must file inventory with court within ten days after box is opened. (733.604[1]).

Personal representative may employ one or more appraisers, to appraise estate, who receive for their services reasonable compensation. (733.605).

Waiver and Consent.—Interested party, including fiduciaries, may waive, to extent of that person's interest, any right or notice or filing of any document, exhibit, or schedule required to be filed, and may consent to any action or proceeding which may be required or permitted by code. (731.302).

Notice of Administration.—Personal representative must promptly publish and serve notice of administration on surviving spouse and all beneficiaries known to him in manner provided for formal notice unless served under §733.2123, and he may serve other heirs or devisees under known prior will. Personal representative shall also promptly make diligent search to determine names and addresses of creditors of decedent who are reasonably ascertainable and shall serve on those creditors copy of notice within three months after first publication, unless creditor has already filed claim, creditor has been paid in full, or creditor's claim is listed in timely Personal Representative's Proof of Claim if personal representative notified creditor of that listing. Publication must be once a week for two consecutive weeks. Notice shall require all interested persons to file (a) all claims within later of three months of first publication or, as to any creditor required to be served with notice, 30 days after date of service of notice; notwithstanding foregoing, within two years after date of decedent's death, and (b) any objection by interested person that challenges validity of will, qualifications of personal representative, venue or jurisdiction of court within later of three months of first publication or 30 days after service of notice. (733.212). Department of Revenue may file claim subsequent to expiration of three months if filed within 30 days after service of inventory on Department of Revenue, or if amended or supplemental inventory is prepared, within 30 days after service of amended or supplemental inventory on department. (733.702). Notice shall contain name of decedent, file number of estate, designation and address of court, name and address of personal representative and his attorney, and shall state date of first publication. (733.212). Objections to will, personal representative, venue or jurisdiction by interested parties to whom notice was mailed that are not filed within later of three months after date of first publication of notice or 30 days after service of notice are

See note at head of Digest as to 1998 legislation covered.

See Topical Index in front part of this volume.

FL – 35

EXECUTORS AND ADMINISTRATORS . . . *continued*
barred. (733.212). Claims are barred as set forth under subheads Presentation and Statement of Claims, and Notice to Present Claims, infra. (733.702).

Sales.—Sale made under specific power in will to sell real property or general power in will to sell any asset is valid without authorization or confirmation of court. Real property of estate or any interest therein may be sold for cash or credit or for part cash and part credit, and without security for unpaid balances. Sale need not be justified by showing of necessity when made pursuant to power in will. (733.613). General power cannot be exercised arbitrarily and if power is limited, it can be exercised only as provided for or contemplated by will. (183 So.2d 849; 200 So.2d 547; 318 So.2d 509). Where no power of sale is given in will or decedent died intestate, petition for authorization or confirmation must be filed by personal representative setting forth reasons for sale, description of property, and price and terms of sale. (733.613).

Notice to Present Claims.—See subhead Notice of Administration, supra. (733.212). Unless proceedings are under ancillary, family or summary administration (c. 734 or 735) notice of administration must be published and served under §733.212, 733.701.

Presentation and Statement of Claims.—All claims must be in writing, with statement indicating basis, name and address of creditor, his agent or attorney and amount claimed; if claim is not yet due, date when it becomes due; if claim is contingent or unliquidated, nature of uncertainty; if claim is secured, description of security. Claim must be verified. Creditor must deliver original and copy of claim to clerk of court who serves copy on personal representative. (F.P.R. 5.490). Claim is presented when filed. (733.703). Claims on judgments against decedent must be filed in same manner as other claims. However, provisions for claims are not to be construed to prevent enforcement of mortgages, security interests, or liens encumbering specific property. (733.706).

Approval or Rejection of Claims.—Claim not objected to by personal representative or other interested person within four months of first publication of notice of administration or within 30 days from timely filing of claim, whichever occurs later, is deemed allowed but court may extend time for filing of objections by order entered in estate administration proceeding upon showing of good cause. If objection filed, person filing must serve copy of same on claimant or attorney for claimant, and personal representative. Claimant then limited to 30 days from such service within which to bring appropriate proceedings. (733.705). Personal representative cannot be compelled to pay any claim before five months after first publication of notice of administration and if any suit is brought within five months upon any claim not objected to, plaintiff although obtaining decree or judgment, shall receive no costs or attorney's fees. (733.705).

Disclaimer.—See topic Descent and Distribution, subhead Disclaimer.

Compromise or settlement of claims is permitted. (733.708).

Order of payment of expenses of administration and obligations of estate are: (1) Costs, expenses of administration, compensation of personal representatives and their attorneys' fees; (2) reasonable funeral expenses, not to exceed $6,000; (3) debts and taxes with preference under federal law; (4) medical and hospital expenses of last 60 days illness; (5) family allowance; (6) arrearage from court ordered child support; (7) debts after death by continuation of business, to extent of business assets; (8) all other claims including judgments before death and excess over sums for (2) and (4). If, after paying any preceding class assets are insufficient to pay next succeeding class, such latter claimants are paid pro rata. (733.707). Assets held in any trust created by decedent over which decedent held power to revoke as of time of death are liable for payment to decedent's creditors and for payment of estate administration expenses. (733.707[3]).

Limitations.—After two years from decedent's death, neither decedent's estate, or beneficiaries shall be liable for any obligation or on any cause of action against decedent whether or not letters have been issued, but this shall not apply to creditor who has filed claim or whose claim has been paid within said two years and does not affect lien of duly recorded mortgage or of person in possession of personalty or impair right to foreclose and enforce such mortgage or lien. (733.710).

Beneficiaries.—No legacy may be required to be paid or specific property surrendered until five months after grant of letters. No personal representative may be compelled to pay over or deliver or surrender property before final settlement of his accounts except on petition filed, showing that property or money claimed will not be required for expenses or prior claims, which petition may be filed by any beneficiary, and circuit court may require refunding bond if distribution is made before final settlement. (733.801, .802).

Unless general power of sale is conferred or contrary intention is indicated by will or assets are otherwise disposed of by statute, distributable assets of estate must be distributed in kind through application of specified provisions. (733.810). Whenever under any will or trust instrument executor or trustee is required to, or has option to, satisfy bequest, devise or transfer in trust to or for benefit of surviving spouse of decedent by transfer of assets in kind at values finally determined for federal estate tax purposes, such bequest, devise or transfer in trust shall be satisfied, in absence of contrary provisions in will or trust instrument, by distribution of assets, including cash, fairly representative of appreciation or depreciation in value of all property available for distribution in satisfaction of such bequest, devise or transfer. (733.810).

Interested persons may agree among themselves to alter interests, shares or amounts to which they are entitled, in written agreement executed by all who are affected, subject to rights of creditors and taxing authorities and rights of beneficiaries not parties to agreement. Trustees of testamentary trust are beneficiaries for purposes of this section which does not relieve trustees of duties to trust beneficiaries. (733.815).

As to prorating estate taxes, see category Taxation, topic Estate Tax, subheads Tax Upon Estates of Resident Decedents, Tax Upon Estates of Nonresident Decedents, Tax Upon Estates of Alien Decedents.

Where doubt exists as to rights or interests of beneficiaries, a petition may be filed to determine the same. (733.105).

Right of possession of decedent's real estate (except homestead) passes to personal representative. (733.607).

Specific devisee of encumbered real property entitled to have encumbrance paid from residue only when will shows intent. General direction in will to pay debts does not show such intent. (733.803).

Investments.—See topic Trusts.

Vendor Contracts.—Personal representative may fulfill contracts of decedent for sale, conveyance, or lease of real property in this state or personal property. (733.612[2]).

Allowances.—Surviving spouse, or, if none, minor children are entitled to, subject to perfected security interests, household furniture, furnishings and appliances in decedent's usual place of abode up to net value of $10,000, and personal effects up to net value of $1,000 (§4, Art. X of Florida Const.), Florida Prepaid College Program contracts, and automobiles, in addition to homestead property and family allowance. Such rights are in addition to any benefit or share passing to spouse or minor children by will unless will otherwise provides, or by intestate succession or elective share. Persons entitled to exempt property deemed to have waived their rights unless petition for determination of exempt property is filed within four months after first publication of notice of administration, or within 40 days after termination of proceedings involving construction, validity or admission of will to probate. (732.402). Surviving spouse and lineal heirs decedent was obligated to support or did support, including lineal ascendants and descendants, are entitled to reasonable family allowance not to exceed $6,000, to be paid to surviving spouse, if living, for use of spouse and lineal heirs, or if not, to lineal heirs or person having custody. (732.403).

Accounts.—Annual or periodic accountings are not required. Final accounting and petition for distribution and discharge must be filed within 12 months after issuance of letters for estates not required to file federal estate tax return, otherwise from date return is due, unless time is extended by court for cause shown after notice to interested persons. (733.901). Final accounting may be waived upon consent of all interested persons. (733.901[4]). In family administration and summary administration, petitions contain required accounting information. (735.103, .203). Removed personal representative must file accounting within 30 days after removal. (733.508).

Actions.—There is no suspension of right to sue on claims against estate, but if action is brought within five months on claim to which no objection has been filed, no costs or attorneys' fees are allowed. Action on claim objected to must be brought within 30 days from date claimant is served with such objection. (733.705[1]).

Closing Estate.—Final accounting and petition for distribution and discharge in formal administration must be filed and served on interested persons within 12 months after granting of letters for estates not required to file federal estate tax return, otherwise 12 months from date return is due, unless time is extended by court order on showing of cause after notice. If no objection to accounting or petition for discharge is filed within 30 days from date of service, or if service is waived, personal representative may distribute according to plan in petition without court order. If timely objection is filed, court shall determine plan of distribution. Upon receipt of evidence of proper distribution and payment or disposition of claims, court enters order discharging personal representative and releasing surety on any bond. (733.901).

Compensation.—Personal representatives, attorneys, accountants and other agents employed by personal representative are entitled to reasonable compensation. Testamentary provision for direct or conditional compensation of personal representative may be renounced by personal representative entitling him to reasonable compensation, unless there is contract with decedent regarding compensation. If personal representative is member of Florida Bar and has rendered legal services in connection with official duties, he is allowed reasonable compensation for same. (733.617). Compensation of personal representative may be increased or decreased by order of court upon petition of any interested party. (733.617[7]). Attorney's compensation presumed to be reasonable under sliding scale formula based upon size of decedent's estate for ordinary services. (733.6171[3]). In addition, attorney may be further compensated for extraordinary services rendered to or on behalf of estate including probate litigation, auditing, tax advice, post mortem estate planning, and preparation of federal estate tax return. (733.6171[4]).

Removal.—Personal representative may be removed and letters revoked for: (1) Adjudication of incompetency; (2) physical or mental incapacity; (3) failure to comply with order of court not superseded on appeal; (4) failure to account for sale of property, produce and exhibit assets when required; (5) wasting or maladministration of estate; (6) failure to give bond or security; (7) conviction of felony; (8) insolvency or appointment of receiver or liquidator for corporate personal representative; (9) conflicting or adverse interests held or acquired (not applicable to claim of elective share or family allowance and exemptions by surviving spouse); (10) revocation of probate of will designating personal representative; (11) removal of domicile from Florida if no longer qualified under §733.301-.309. (733.504).

Foreign executor or administrator who produces probate of will or letters of administration duly obtained in any state or territory of U.S., properly authenticated may maintain actions in courts of this state. Personal representatives appointed in any state or country may be sued in this state with reference to property in this state and may defend actions brought in Florida. (734.101).

Debtors residing in Florida, or whose property in Florida is subject to a lien or mortgage held by a nonresident decedent, may make payment to foreign personal representatives and persons holding possession of personalty may deliver it, provided no notice or demand has been given by locally appointed representative for 60 days after appointment of foreign representative. (734.101).

See also category Business Regulation and Commerce, topic Banks and Banking, subhead International Banking.

Uniform Fiduciaries Act not adopted.

Uniform Principal and Income Act (690.01-.15) replaced by revised Principal and Income Law effective Jan. 1, 1976 (738.01-738.15).

See note at head of Digest as to 1998 legislation covered.

See Topical Index in front part of this volume.

EXECUTORS AND ADMINISTRATORS . . . *continued*

Uniform Simplification of Fiduciary Security Transfers Act adopted (c. 610), and takes precedence over Uniform Commercial Code (671.304[2][b]).

Uniform Anatomical Gift Act adopted. (732.910–.922).

FIDUCIARIES:

See topics Executors and Administrators, Trusts; category Family, topic Guardian and Ward.

INTESTACY:

See topic Descent and Distribution.

PROOF OF CLAIMS:

See topic Executors and Administrators; category Civil Actions and Procedure, topic Pleading.

TRUSTS:

New probate and trust administration provisions effective Jan. 1, 1976. (cc. 731-738).

Kinds.—Inter vivos trusts, testamentary trusts, business trusts (609.01), resulting trusts (89 Fla. 457, 105 So. 106), constructive trusts (132 So.2d 198), Totten trusts (85 So.2d 726), life insurance trusts (733.808[1][a]), Illinois type land trusts (689.071), including inter vivos trusts in which certain powers are retained by settlor either singly or jointly with another (689.075), are recognized.

Creation and Appointment of Trustee.—All grants, conveyances, or assignments of trust or confidence in any lands, or of any interest therein, must be: (1) By deed signed and delivered in presence of two subscribing witnesses by grantor, conveyor, or assignor, or by his attorney or lawfully authorized agent; or (2) by last will and testament, or same will be void. (689.06).

Declaration of trusts in lands must be proved by some writing, signed by the party authorized by law to declare or create same, or by last will and testament. Implied and constructive trusts arising or resulting from conveyance of lands are not required to be in writing. (689.05). Valid trust in personalty may be created by deed, or may rest entirely in parol, or may be partly in writing and partly in parol. (73 Fla. 1120, 75 So. 860).

Note: Effective Oct. 1, 1995, testamentary aspects of trust are invalid unless trust instrument is executed by settlor with formalities for execution of will. (737.111). Testamentary aspects of trust created by nonresident are not invalid because trust does not meet requirements of this section, if trust is valid under laws of state or country where settlor was at time of execution. (737.111).

As to exercise of trust functions by corporation, see topic Executors and Administrators.

Trust Registration.—Repealed. (77-344).

Common Trust Funds.—See category Business Regulation and Commerce, topic Banks and Banking.

Eligibility of Foreign Trust Companies.—See category Business Regulation and Commerce, topic Banks and Banking, subhead International Banking.

Removal of Trustee.—Court has jurisdiction over administration and distribution of trusts, including, but not limited to, appointment or removal of trustee, review of trustee fees, review and settlement of interim or final accounts, ascertainment of beneficiaries, construction of trust instruments, and determination of existence or nonexistence of any immunity, power, privilege, duty or right. (737.201).

Trustee Compensation.—Attorney for trustee of revocable trust for use and benefit of grantor is entitled to reasonable compensation for legal services rendered in initial administration of trust. (737.2041). Unless otherwise agreed trustee's attorney is also allowed compensation for ordinary services at rate of 75% of schedule provided under §733.6171(3). (737.2041[2]).

Beneficiaries.—Every deed, conveyance, mortgage, or transfer of interest in real estate in which words "trustee" or "as trustee" are added to name of grantee, transferee, assignee or mortgagee, and in which no beneficiaries are named, nor nature and purpose of trust, if any, are set forth, is declared to grant fee simple estate, or to transfer interest of transferor, or full ownership in mortgage, unless contrary intention appears in instrument, and unless declaration of trust by grantee, transferee, assignee or mortgagee is recorded. (689.07).

Land Trusts.—See category Property, topic Deeds, subhead Land Trusts. See also §689.071.

Powers, Duties and Liabilities of Trustee.—From time of creation of trust until final distribution of trust assets, trustee has power to perform any act prudent trustee would perform for purposes of trust, without court authorization. Unless otherwise provided in trust instrument, trustee may perform but is not limited to, following activities: (a) To collect, hold, and retain trust assets until time for disposition even though they include assets in which trustee is personally interested; (b) to hold without liability any property received from settlor or property lawfully substituted therefor (except cash for reinvestment purposes), including power to exchange bank stock for holding company stock, whether or not permissible for investment of funds of particular trusts; (c) to receive additions to assets of trust and invest and reinvest trust assets in accordance with trust provisions or as provided by law; (d) to continue or participate in operation of any business or other enterprise and to effect any reorganization or liquidation of business or enterprise; (e) to acquire undivided interest in trust asset in which trustee holds undivided interest in any trust capacity; (f) to invest and reinvest trust assets in accordance with provisions of trust as provided by law; (g) if bank, to deposit trust funds in another department of same entity or in bank that is affiliated with trustee bank; (h) to acquire or dispose of asset for cash or on credit at public or private sale; to manage, develop, improve exchange, partition, change character of, or abandon trust asset or any interest in it; and to encumber, mortgage, or pledge trust asset for term within or extending beyond term trust in connection with exercise of any power vested in trustee; (i) to make ordinary or extraordinary repairs or alterations in buildings; (j) acquire or dispose of asset, manage, develop, or abandon trust asset, encumber, mortgage or pledge trust asset for term within or extending beyond term of trust; (k) subdivide, develop, or dedicate land to public use, make or obtain vacation of plats and adjust boundaries, adjust differences in valuation on exchange or partition, dedicate easements to public use without consideration; (l) to enter into lease for any purpose; (m) to enter into arrangement for exploration and removal of minerals or other natural resources; (n) to grant or obtain options concerning disposition or acquisition of any asset; (o) to vote or not vote security, pay calls, assessments, and other sums chargeable with respect to securities; (p) to sell or exercise stock rights, to participate in reorganization, consolidation, merger, dissolution, or liquidation; (q) to hold securities in name of nominee, but trustee is liable for any act of nominee; (r) to insure assets of trust and trustee; (s) to borrow and advance money in connection with administration of trust; (t) to pay, contest, settle, or release any claim; (u) to pay taxes, assessments, compensation of trustee, and other trust administration expenses; (v) to allocate items of income or expense to either trust income or principal, as provided by law; (w) to pay any sum distributable to beneficiary under legal disability, by paying beneficiary, legal representative or relative, or in case of minor, expending it for his benefit; (x) to effect distribution of property and money in divided or undivided interest and to adjust resulting differences in valuation; (y) to hire agents, even though they are trustee or associated with trustee, to advise and assist in administrative duties and to act without independent investigation upon their recommendations; (z) to prosecute or defend legal claims and actions; (aa) to execute and deliver all instruments that will accomplish or facilitate exercise of powers vested in trustee. (737.402).

From creation of trust until final distribution of assets from trust, unless otherwise provided in trust instrument, trustee has power, acting reasonably and for benefit of beneficiaries: (a) to inspect or investigate property held by trustee for purpose of determining compliance with environmental law affecting that property; (b) to take any action necessary to prevent, abate, or otherwise remedy actual or potential violation of environmental law affecting property held by trustee; (c) to refuse to accept property in trust if trustee determines that any property to be donated or conveyed to trustee either is contaminated with hazardous substance or is being used for activity involving hazardous substance; (d) to settle or compromise any claim against trust or trustee which involved alleged violation of environmental law; (e) to disclaim any power granted by any document, statute, or rule of law which may cause trustee or trust to incur liability under any environmental law; (f) to decline to serve or resign as trustee, if trustee believes conflict of interest exists; and (g) to charge against income and principal of trust costs associated with contaminated asset.

Note: Effective Jan. 1, 1996, trustee has duty to pay expenses and obligations of settlor's estate. (737.3054).

Note: Effective Oct. 1, 1995, trustee must file notice of trust with court of county of settlor's domicile and court having jurisdiction of settlor's estate. (737.308).

Where there are three or more trustees any power is exerciseable by majority. Dissenting trustee not joining in exercise of power, or dissenting trustee who joins in exercise of power but expresses dissent in writing at or before time of joinder, is not liable for result. (737.404).

With certain exceptions, if duty of trustee and his individual interest conflict in exercise of trust power, power may be exercised only by court authorization. (737.403).

Except as otherwise provided by trust instrument, trustee must meet standard that would be observed by prudent trustee dealing with property of another unless trustee has or is represented to have special skills which skills trustee is under duty to use. (737.302).

Trustee need not provide bond to secure performance unless required by trust instrument, reasonably requested by beneficiary, or found to be necessary by court. (737.304).

Unless otherwise provided, trustees are not personally liable on contracts, except contracts for attorneys' fees, properly entered into unless trustee fails to reveal representative capacity and identify trust estate in contract. If personally at fault trustee is personally liable for torts and obligations arising out of ownership or control of trust property. Contractual claims, except for attorneys' fees, may be asserted against trust by proceeding against trustee in trustee's fiduciary capacity whether trustee is personally liable or not. Issues of liability between trust estate and trustee may be determined in accounting, surcharge, indemnification or other appropriate proceeding. (737.306).

Conflict of Interest of Trustee.—Where inherent conflict of interest exists between trustee who is beneficiary and other beneficiaries of trust, unless terms of trust refer specifically to §737.402(4)(a) and provide expressly to contrary any of following powers conferred upon trustee (other than settlor or decedent of revocable or amendable trust or decedent's or settlor's spouse who is trustee of testamentary or inter vivos trust for which marital deduction has been allowed) cannot be exercised (1) to make discretionary distributions to such trustee, except to provide for that trustee's health, education, maintenance or support as described under I.R.C. 2041 and 2514, (2) to make discretionary allocations of receipts or expenses as between income and principal, unless such trustee acts in fiduciary capacity whereby such trustee has no power to enlarge or shift any beneficial interest, and (3) to make discretionary distributions of either principal or income to satisfy any legal support obligations of such trustee, or (4) to exercise any other power, including right to remove or replace any trustee, so as to cause powers enumerated in subparagraphs 1, 2 or 3 to be exercised on behalf of, or for benefit of, beneficiary who is also trustee. (737.402[4][a]). Any of above powers that are conferred upon two or more trustees may be exercised by trustees who are not so disqualified. If there is no trustee qualified, any party in interest (as defined in 737.402[4][c]) may apply to court of competent jurisdiction to appoint independent trustee. (737.402[4][a][3]).

§737.402(4)(a) applies to (i) any trust executed after June 30, 1991, (ii) any testamentary trust created under will executed after June 30, 1991 (unless terms of trusts applicable to [i] and [ii] refer specifically to this subsection and provide expressly to contrary), and (iii) any trust created under document executed before July 1, 1991, unless (a) if trust is revocable or amendable, settlor revokes or amends trust at any

See note at head of Digest as to 1998 legislation covered.

See Topical Index in front part of this volume.

FL – 37

TRUSTS . . . *continued*

time to provide otherwise, or (b) if trust is irrevocable, all parties in interest elect affirmatively not to be subject to application of this subsection. Such election must be made on or before later of July 1, 1994 or three years after date on which trust becomes irrevocable. (737.402[4][b]).

Small Trust Termination.—If market value of trust is less than $50,000, corporate trustee may terminate trust without court approval if continuation of trust would substantially hinder purposes of trust relative to costs of administering trust. Trustee is to comply with intent of settlor as near as possible and may enter into any agreement necessary to that end or to protect beneficiaries and trustee. (737.402[3]).

Investment of fiduciary funds regulated by §§518.01-.16. Fiduciary includes executor, administrator, trustee, guardian, etc., who has responsibility for money or property of another. (518.10). Prudent man rule used as standard for fiduciary conduct. (518.11). Court may permit fiduciary to deviate from will, etc. (518.13). Certain trustees may invest in money market mutual funds, mutual funds, and common trust funds.

In determining qualification of guardian's investments of funds received from Veterans' Administration, published statements of corporations or statements of reliable companies engaged in business of furnishing statistical information on bonds may be used. (518.01).

Trust Fund for Disabled or Mentally Ill.—Department of Health is required to establish umbrella trust fund for benefit of developmentally disabled and mentally ill persons in Florida. (402.175).

Securities in name of nominee permitted under §737.402.

Disclaimer.—See topic Descent and Distribution, subhead Disclaimer.

Uniform Trusts Administration Law repealed by Laws 1974 c. 74-106. Similar provisions in c. 737.

Uniform Principal and Income Act, Revised, adopted. (c. 738).

Uniform Fiduciaries Act not adopted.

Gifts to Minors.—See category Family, topic Infants.

Accounting.—Trust accounting law provisions incorporated in c. 737.

Uniform Simplification of Fiduciary Security Transfers Act adopted (c. 610) and takes precedence over Uniform Commercial Code (671.304[2]).

Attorney's Fees.—Attorney may recover fees from trust for litigation which benefited trust. (469 So.2d 903).

Accumulations.—See category Property, topic Perpetuities.

Perpetuities.—See category Property, topic Perpetuities.

Pour Over Trusts.—See topic Wills, subhead Devise to Trustee.

Charitable Trust.—Provisions adopted governing administration of charitable trusts. (737.501-737.512).

Limitation of Action Against Trustee.—Six month limitation period applies for bringing claims against trustee for breach of trust for beneficiary who has received final, annual or periodic account or other statement fully disclosing matter. Absent full disclosure, as provided in c. 95. (737.307).

Surcharge.—Trustees may be held individually liable for money damages due to breach of fiduciary duty in paying attorney's fees for personal defense out of trust fund. (462 So.2d 1122).

WILLS:

Uniform Probate Code adopted with significant variations.

See also topic Executors and Administrators.

Any person 18 or more years of age who is of sound mind may make will. (732.501).

Agreements to make will or devise, or to revoke will or devise, or not to make will or devise must be in writing and signed by agreeing party in presence of two attesting witnesses. (732.701).

Execution.—Every will must be in writing, and testator must sign his signature at end, or some other person in testator's presence and by his direction must subscribe testator's name to it, and execution or acknowledgment must be in presence of at least two attesting witnesses who must sign in presence of each other and in presence of testator. (732.502). Codicil must be executed with same formalities as will. (732.502[4]). No particular form or words required (732.502[3]); suggested form of attestation clause is as follows:

Form

Attestation Clause.—The foregoing instrument, was signed by . . . . . ., the testator, as his last will and testament, in our presence, and we, in his presence and in the presence of each other have hereunto subscribed our names as witnesses, this . . . . . . day of . . . . . . 19. . . .

. . . . residing at . . . .
. . . . residing at . . . .

Holographic Wills.—Not recognized. Properly executed will in testator's handwriting not considered holographic will. (732.502[2]).

Nuncupative Wills.—Not recognized. (732.502[1]).

Revocation.—Will or codicil or any part of either may be revoked by subsequent inconsistent will or codicil, or by other writing declaring revocation and executed with same formalities required for execution of wills, or by burning, tearing, canceling, defacing, obliterating, or destroying it with intent and for purpose of revoking it. (732.505-.506). Revocation of will also revokes all codicils thereto. (732.509).

Revival of Revoked Will.—Revocation of will revoking former will does not revive former will. Revocation of codicil to will does not revoke will, and in absence

of evidence to contrary it is presumed that in revoking codicil testator intended to reinstate provisions of will that were changed or revoked. (732.508).

Devise to Subscribing Witness.—Will or codicil, or any part of either, is not invalid because will or codicil is signed by interested witness. (732.504[2]).

Devise to trustee is valid if made to trustee of written trust in existence at time of making of will or by written trust subscribed concurrently with making of will, provided that such written trust is identified in will. Such devise is not invalid for any or all of following reasons: (1) Trust is amendable or revocable or both by any person; (2) trust has been amended or revoked in part after execution of will or codicil thereto; (3) trust or any amendment thereto was not executed in manner required for wills; (4) only trust res is possible expectancy of receiving devise under will or death benefits (as defined in 733.808) as named beneficiary, even though testator or other person has reserved all rights of ownership in such death benefits, including right to change beneficiary; (5) because of provisions of 689.075. (732.513).

Devises to Inter Vivos Trusts.—See subhead Devise to Trustee, supra.

Probate.—Circuit court has jurisdiction of probate of wills. (Const., art. 5, §5; 26.012). Any will may be proved upon oath of any attesting witness, or if they are incompetent or their testimony cannot be obtained within reasonable time, by oath of personal representative nominated by will, whether or not he is interested, or by any other person who is disinterested, by oath that he believes writing exhibited to be true last will of deceased. (733.201).

As to probate venue, see topic Executors and Administrators.

Will is ineffective to prove title to, or right to possession of, property of testator until admitted to probate in Florida or in state where decedent was domiciled. (733.103, 733.103[1]).

If original will of Florida resident has, through inadvertence, error, or omission, been admitted to foreign probate, Florida proceedings may be based on authenticated copies of foreign proceedings in lieu of original will, if original could have been admitted to probate in this state. (733.206).

In any collateral action or proceeding relating to devised property, probate of will in Florida is conclusive of its due execution, absence of fraud, duress, mistake or undue influence, competency of testator and fact that will was unrevoked on testator's death. (733.103, 733.103[2]).

Self-proved Wills.—Will or codicil executed in conformity with 732.502(1) and (2) may be made self-proved at time of execution or at any subsequent date by acknowledgment of it by testator and affidavits of witnesses, each made before officer authorized to administer oaths and evidenced by officer's certificate attached to or following will, in substantially following form (732.503):

Form

State of . . . .
County of . . . .

We, ... , ..., and . . . ., the testator and the witnesses, respectively, whose names are signed to the attached or foregoing instrument, having been sworn, declared to the undersigned officer that the testator, in the presence of witnesses, signed the instrument as his last will (codicil), that he (signed) (or directed another to sign for him), and that each of the witnesses, in the presence of the testator and in the presence of each other, signed the will as a witness.

(Signature of Testator)
(Signature of Witness)
(Signature of Witness)

Subscribed and sworn to before me by . . . ., the testator, and by . . . . and . . . ., the witnesses, on this . . . . day of . . . ., 19. . . .
(Signature and title of officer) (Seal)

Contest.—Any creditor or interested person who is apprehensive that will may be admitted to probate without her knowledge may file caveat in circuit court. (731.110[1]). After filing of caveat by creditor clerk shall notice caveator upon issuance of letters of administration. (F.P.R. 5.260[e]). After filing of caveat by interested person other than creditor no will may be admitted to probate without service of notice on caveator or designated agent. (F.P.R. 5.260[f]). Persons to whom notice of administration was served under §733.212 must file objections within later of three months following first publication of notice or, as to any person required to be served with copy of notice, 30 days after date of service. (733.212, 733.212[1][b]). Persons on whom formal notice of petition for administration is served by petitioner prior to issuance of letters and persons who have waived notice may not challenge validity of will, testacy of decedent, qualifications of personal representative, venue or jurisdiction of court, except in connection with proceedings before issuance of letters. (733.2123). Any interested person including beneficiary under prior will, except those barred under §733.212 or §733.2123, may, before final discharge of personal representative, petition court in which will was admitted to probate, for revocation of probate. Petition shall be served upon personal representative and all other interested parties by formal notice. (733.109, 733.109[1][b]).

Legacies.—See topic Executors and Administrators, subhead Beneficiaries.

Unclaimed Legacies.—See category Property, topic Absentees, subhead Escheat; and topic Executors and Administrators.

Testamentary Guardian.—See category Family, topic Guardian and Ward.

Lapse.—If a devisee or legatee is dead when will is made or dies before testator, testamentary disposition lapses unless will shows an intent to substitute another, except where such disposition is to grandparent or lineal descendant of grandparent of testator, in which case descendants of deceased devisee take per stirpes. (732.603). Where devise lapses voiding entire will, estate will be distributed according to laws of intestacy. (445 So.2d 622).

Pretermitted Heirs.—A will is not revoked by subsequent marriage of testator but in such case the surviving spouse is entitled to share as in case of intestacy unless will discloses a contrary intent or provision for spouse is made by will or marriage contract in contemplation of marriage. (732.507, 732.301, 418 So.2d 256). Child born or adopted

See note at head of Digest as to 1998 legislation covered.

See Topical Index in front part of this volume.

WILLS . . . *continued*

after execution of will shares as in case of intestacy unless will shows contrary intent or testator had one or more children when will was executed and devised substantially all his estate to other parent of pretermitted child. (732.301, 732.302, 732.507[1]).

Effect of Dissolution of Marriage.—Wills made by husband or wife whose marriage to each other has been dissolved subsequent to date of said will are made void by means of said dissolution of marriage insofar as said will affects surviving spouse whose marriage to testator has been dissolved. (732.507[2]).

Election between Elective Share and Testamentary Provision.—If election is filed, remaining assets of estate after payment of elective share are distributed as though surviving spouse had predeceased decedent. (732.211).

Surviving spouse has right to share of estate of deceased spouse. (732.201).

Foreign Executed Wills.—Will other than holographic or nuncupative will, executed by nonresident of Florida, is valid as will in Florida if valid under laws of state or country where testator was at time of execution. (732.502).

Foreign probated will of Florida resident may be admitted to probate in circuit court having jurisdiction, with same force and effect as though original had been probated in this state. Authenticated copies of will and foreign proof of will and order of probate, and of letters, if any, issued thereon, are filed in circuit court in lieu of original will, and same are prima facie evidence of execution thereof and its admission to foreign probate. (733.206[2]). In case of death of nonresident and probate in foreign state, domiciliary personal representative may, if qualified to act, be appointed ancillary personal representative in Florida. (734.102).

Foreign probated will of nonresident that devises real property in state or right, title, or interest to real property may be admitted to record in county where property is located, any time after two years from decedent's death or any time after domiciliary personal representative has been discharged, if no proceeding to administer estate in this state, provided will complies with §732.502 and will properly admitted in proper court of any state, territory, or country. Authenticated copy of foreign will, petition for probate, and order admitting will to probate must accompany petition to admit foreign will to record. When admitted to record, foreign will is valid and effectual to pass title to real property or right or interest in property as if will admitted to probate in this state. (734.104).

Health care advance directives adopted. (765.101-.401).

Simultaneous Death.—See topic Death.

Testamentary Trusts.—See topic Trusts.

Disclaimer.—See topic Descent and Distribution, subhead Disclaimer.

Life Prolonging.—Advance Directive, defined as witnessed written document or oral statement in which instructions are given by principal or in which principal's desires are expressed concerning any aspect of principal's health care, may instruct principal's physician to provide, withhold or withdraw life-prolonging procedures, or to designate another to make treatment decision for him in event that such person should be found to be incompetent and suffering from terminal condition. (765.101[1], 765.102[3]). Advance Directive includes, but is not limited to, designation of health care surrogate, living will, or orders not to resuscitate issued pursuant to §401.45. (765.101[1]). Statute contains form for designation of health care surrogate (765.203) and living will (765.303).

Uniform Anatomical Gift Act (732.910-.922) is in effect.

Anatomical gift may be made: (1) By will; or (2) by separate document signed and witnessed by two others. (732.914). Delivery of document is not necessary for gift to be valid. (732.914[2][a], 732.915). Gift is subject to amendment or revocation. (732.916). Donations may be made as part of driver license or identification card process. (732.921).

See also category Civil Actions and Procedure, topic Limitation of Actions.

FAMILY

ADOPTION:

(c. 63).

Any adult or unmarried minor birth parent except homosexuals may adopt minor or adult, but married person must be joined by other spouse in petition unless other spouse is parent and consents or failure to join or consent is excused. Adoptive parent(s) must be Florida resident(s). (63.042). Legislative intent to maintain sibling groups, whenever possible. (63.022[1]).

Jurisdiction and Venue.—Petition for adoption or for declaratory statement as to adoption contract is filed in circuit court of county where person applying for adoption resides or in which child resides or in which child-placing agency having custody of child is located. (63.102[2]).

Consent Required.—Mother, minor if more than 12 years of age, and father, if: (1) Minor conceived or born while father was married to mother; (2) minor is his child by adoption; (3) minor is established as his child by court proceedings; (4) he has filed acknowledgment with Department of Health; or (5) he has provided child with repetitive, customary support, must consent in writing unless consent is excused by court. (63.062). Consent may be required from person entitled to lawful custody or court having jurisdiction over minor. (63.062). Good faith, diligent efforts must be made to notify, and obtain written consent within 60 days after filing petition. (63.062[3]). If intermediary is involved in placement, he must inform those persons consenting that he represents adoptive parents, and provide written acknowledgment to that effect signed by those persons consenting to be adoptive parents. (63.085[1][f]).

Petition must be verified and state: (1) Date, birthplace, name to be given, date petitioner acquired custody, name of person placing minor; (2) name, age, place, duration of residence of petitioner, marital status, date and place of marriages, divorces and facilities, and resources; (3) value of property of person to be adopted; (4) facts

concerning those of which consent is required but outstanding and facts or circumstances that excuse lack of consent; (5) reasons for adoption. Following documents must be filed and attached to petition: Required consents, favorable preliminary home study, and surrender document. (63.112).

Preliminary study shall be made after report of intention to place minor. Favorable report may lead to placement of minor pending judgment. Unfavorable report may lead to petition for court determination. (63.092). Preliminary home study must be performed by licensed child-placing agency, licensed professional, or agency described in 61.20(2). (63.092).

Order of Adoption.—Hearing held after child lives with petitioner 90 days except when petitioner is spouse of natural parent, hearing may be held immediately on filing petition. (63.122). Petitioners and person to be adopted, if 12 years or over, required to attend hearing in person unless court upon showing of good cause excuses attendance of either. No interlocutory period. (63.142).

Effect of Adoption.—Effect of adoption is to make adopted child legal heir of adopting parents, entitled to all rights and privileges, and subject to all obligations, of child born in lawful wedlock. Adopted children regarded as natural brother or sister of natural children and other adopted children of adopting parents for inheritance purposes. All relationships terminated with natural parents, except natural parent who is petitioner or married to petitioner. (63.172). New birth certificate issued after entry of adoption judgment. (63.022)[h]). Where child is adopted by spouse of only living natural parent, or if both natural parents have died and child's brother, sister, grandparent, aunt or uncle adopts child, child's right of inheritance from deceased parent(s) and relationship with family of deceased natural parent is unaffected. (63.172). Adoption by natural parent's spouse does not terminate grandparental rights of visitation. (c. 752).

Setting Aside Adoption.—Irregularity or procedural defect presumed cured after one year from entry of final decree. (63.182).

Confidentiality.—All hearings held in closed court. Except by order of court for good cause shown, no disclosure of names is permitted absent written release by natural parent, adoptive parent (authorizing release of his name), adoptee 18 years or older, or if adoptee is less than 18 years, adoptive parent. No specific names or identifying information given in family medical history. All available nonidentifying information regarding adoptee and natural parents given to adopting parents prior or subsequent to finalization of adoption and to adoptee, upon request, after majority. (63.162).

Preplanned Adoption.—Contract for adoption of unborn child in return for any valuable consideration is illegal and void. (63.212[1][i]). Preplanned adoption is permissible if it is based on agreement which specifies certain terms. (63.212[1][i]2). Volunteer mother has absolute right to withdraw her consent for seven days following child's birth. (63.212[1][i]1.b).

State Registrar to maintain registry with last known names and addresses of natural parents, adoptive parents, and adoptee and any other identifying information which natural parents, adoptive parents or adoptee may wish to include in registry. Person entering information required to indicate to whom information may be released, which is limited to natural and adoptive mother and father, adoptee, natural siblings, and maternal or paternal natural grandparents. (63.165). Except as provided in this section, registry information is confidential and exempt from §119.07(1). Consent to release information may be made on behalf of minor adoptee by adoptive parents or by court after good cause shown. Any person may withdraw, limit, or otherwise restrict consent to release information at any time by notifying Department in writing. (63.165[1]). Department may charge reasonable fees. Department must make counseling available for fee to all seeking to use registry. (63.165[2]).

Subsidized Adoption Program.—Subsidy for prospective adoptive parents of children whose permanent custody has been awarded to Department of Health or to licensed child-placing agency and who have emotional ties with foster parents or who are unlikely to be adopted. Subsidies determined through agreement between adoptive parents and Department, and may be readjusted periodically depending upon changed circumstances. (409.166). Department authorized to reimburse, retroactive to 1/1/87, adoptive parents who participate in subsidized adoption program for children with special needs. Reimbursement for up to $1,000 in nonrecurring expenses relating to adoption. (409.166[6]). Adoption fees may be waived in certain cases. (409.166[5]).

Statewide Adoption Exchange.—To be maintained with photo listing, updated monthly to recruit adoptive families for children legally freed for adoption and permanently placed with Department of Health or to licensed child-placing agency. Child must be referred to adoption exchange within 30 days of permanent placement unless district determines otherwise, in which case child must be referred to adoption exchange within three months of permanent placement. (409.167).

ALIMONY:

See topic Dissolution of Marriage.

COMMUNITY PROPERTY:

System does not obtain in Florida.

DESERTION:

See topics Dissolution of Marriage, Husband and Wife.

DISSOLUTION OF MARRIAGE:

(c. 61).

Residence.—One of parties to marriage must have resided in state for six months before filing petition to obtain dissolution of marriage. (61.021). Actions may be brought against persons residing out of state. (61.061). No dissolution of marriage is from bed and board, but is from bonds of matrimony. (61.031). Term "residence" connotes domicile. (156 Fla. 104, 22 So.2d 580). Service of process on nonresidents may be obtained by publication. See category Civil Actions and Procedure, topic Process. However, service will not result in Court securing personal jurisdiction over

DISSOLUTION OF MARRIAGE . . . *continued*
nonresident. Because marriage is considered a separable subject matter, Court will dissolve marriage without adjudicating any support or property rights where personal jurisdiction has not been obtained over nonresident. See also topic Husband and Wife.

Grounds for dissolution of marriage are: (1) Marriage is irretrievably broken; or (2) mental incapacity of party if adjudged incapacitated for preceding period of at least three years in accordance with provisions of §744.331. (61.052).

Venue.—Proceeding may be brought in county where property in dispute located, county in which grounds for dissolution accrued, or where respondent resides. (47.011). If respondent is nonresident, proceeding may be brought in any county in state. (145 Fla. 705, 200 So. 78).

Pleading.—Defenses of condonation, collusion, recrimination and laches abolished. (61.044).

Practice.—Evidence need not be corroborated except to establish residency. Evidence of residency may be corroborated by affidavit of third party or by valid Florida driver's license, Florida identification card, or voters registration card. (61.052).

Mediation.—In any proceeding in which issues of parental responsibility, primary residence, visitation, or support of child are contested, court may refer parties to mediation in accordance with rules promulgated by Supreme Court. (61.183).

Parenting Class.—All parties to dissolution of marriage proceeding with minor children or modification of final judgment action involving shared parental responsibilities, custody, or visitation will be required to complete court-approved parenting course prior to entry of final judgment or order modifying final judgment, unless excused for good cause. (61.21).

Decree.—Final decree of dissolution of marriage is entered on determination of court that dissolution of marriage should be granted. There is no interlocutory decree.

No final decree of dissolution of marriage may be entered until at least 20 days after petition is filed, except when court is shown that injustice will result from delay. (61.19).

Temporary Orders.—During pendency of proceeding, court may make appropriate order for support and alimony of parties, preservation of their property, attorney's fees, and primary residence, custody, rotating custody, support, maintenance and education of minor children. Any protective injunction arising out of dissolution must be issued as separate order in compliance with c. 741 and not included in dissolution decree. (61.052).

Alimony and suit money pendente lite may be allowed any party on petition or by motion. (61.071). Alimony may be granted to either party, either rehabilitative or permanent in nature. Payments may be periodic or lump sum or both. (61.08). Court may issue income deduction order to employer providing income to person obligated to pay alimony or child support. (61.1301). Court may order any party required to pay alimony to purchase or maintain life insurance policy or bond. (61.08). Adultery of spouse may be considered. Court shall include findings of fact relative to enumerated factors in any award or denial of alimony. (61.08). Amount of alimony, maintenance or separate support may be increased or decreased by order of court when circumstances or financial ability of either party significantly changes. (61.08).

Division of Property of Spouses.—Equitable division of assets and liabilities by court, after considering relevant factors, including specified points. (61.075). Cut-off date for determining whether assets and liabilities are marital or nonmarital is earliest of date parties enter into valid separation agreement, such other date as may be expressly established by such agreement, or date of filing petition for dissolution of marriage. Valuation date of marital assets and liabilities determined by judge based on circumstances. Different assets may be valued as of different dates. If court awards cash payment for purpose of equitable distribution of assets, full amount awarded vests when judgment is awarded and award will not terminate upon remarriage or death of either party, unless otherwise agreed to by parties, but must be treated as debt owed from obligor or obligor's estate to obligee or obligee's estate, unless otherwise agreed to by parties. (61.075). Terms of valid property settlement agreement generally may not be modified by courts. (339 So.2d 681). In any contested dissolution of marriage action, wherein stipulation and agreement has not been entered and filed, any distribution of marital assets or marital liabilities shall be supported by factual findings in judgment or order based on competent substantial evidence with reference to specified factors. (61.075). Court may enforce antenuptial agreement to arbitrate dispute. (61.052).

Effect on Will.—Any provisions of will executed by married person, which provision affects spouse of that person, shall become void upon dissolution or annulment of marriage. After dissolution or annulment, any such will shall be administered and construed as if former spouse had died at time of dissolution or annulment of marriage, unless will or dissolution or judgment expressly provides otherwise. (732.507[2]).

Payment and Enforcement System.—

Central Depository.—Office of clerk of court shall operate depository. Fee shall be charged for receiving, recording, reporting, disbursing, monitoring or handling alimony or child support payments. Certified copies of payment records maintained by depository shall, without further proof, be admitted into evidence in any legal proceeding in this state. (61.181).

Support.—If person having ability to contribute to maintenance of his or her spouse and support of his or her minor children fails to do so, spouse who is not receiving support or who has custody of children may petition court for alimony and support for minor children without petitioning for dissolution of marriage and court shall enter such order as it deems just and proper. (61.09). Reasonable amount for attorney's fees, suit money and costs may be ordered. (61.16). Payment of child support on or after Jan. 1, 1985 shall be made through appropriate depository as provided for in 61.181, unless court orders otherwise. (61.13). Each order for child support must contain provision for health insurance for minor child when obligor has access at reasonable rate to group insurance. (61.13). If obligor fails to enroll child, payer of insurance shall be notified, shall enroll minor child as beneficiary in health plan and shall withhold any required premium from obligor's income. (61.13). Court may order any party required to pay child support to purchase or maintain life insurance policy or bond. Agreements for support, maintenance or alimony are subject to modification by court if circumstances or financial ability of either party changes. (61.14). Allowance for children before and after decree in discretion of court. Amount may be changed. (61.13, .14). Orders and judgments of court may be enforced and satisfied by attachment or garnishment for amounts due with respect to certain dissolution, alimony or child support proceedings. (61.12[1]). Disciplinary action against employee by employer to whom writ is issued solely because such writ is in effect shall constitute contempt of court. (61.12[2]). Professional licenses for certain occupations may be denied or suspended when licensee is delinquent in making child support payments. (61.13015). *Note:* Florida follows Uniform Interstate Family Support Act. (88.0011). See also topic Husband and Wife, subhead Desertion and Nonsupport.

Child Support Guidelines.—Presumptively establishes amount of child support. Court may order amount different from guidelines upon written or specified finding explaining why departure is just or appropriate. No change of circumstances need be proven to warrant modification of Title IV-D (Social Security) cases received pursuant to three-year review and adjustment cycle. (61.30).

Remarriage.—Both parties may remarry.

Children.—All matters relating to custody of minor children decided in accordance with Uniform Child Custody Jurisdiction Act and best interest of child. (61.1302-61.1348). Court required to order parental responsibility of minor to be shared by both parties unless detrimental to child. No presumption will arise in favor of or against request to relocate when primary residential parent seeks to move child and move will materially affect visitation with secondary residential parent. Factors court must consider are provided. (61.13[2]). Whether or not there is conviction of any offense of domestic violence or child abuse or existence of injunction for protection against domestic violence, court must consider evidence of spouse abuse as evidence of detriment to child and may award sole parental responsibility to abused spouse and may make visitation arrangements to protect child and abused spouse from further harm. Court shall consider evidence that parent has been convicted of felony of third degree or higher involving domestic violence as rebuttable presumption of detriment to child. If presumption is not rebutted, shared parental responsibility, visitation, residence of child, and decisions made regarding child, must not be granted to convicted parent. Division of responsibilities may be ordered if in best interest of child. Best interest of child to be determined on basis of all factors involved including those in §61.13. Father given same consideration as mother in determining custody regardless of age or sex of child. Court may award reasonable visitation to grandparents if in child's best interest. Grandparents have legal standing to seek judicial enforcement of such award. Termination of parental rights does not affect grandparents' rights. (61.13).

Where custody of minor child is at issue, court may request division of family services of Department of Health to make investigation and social study concerning all pertinent details relating to child and each parent and submit written report. (61.20).

In action for dissolution of marriage, modification, parental responsibility, custody or visitation, court may appoint Guardian ad Litem. (61.401).

Annulment of Marriage.—See topic Marriage.

Divorce A Mensa Et Thoro.—Florida courts are not authorized to enter decree of separation from bed and board, rather all divorces are absolute. (61.031).

DIVORCE:

See topic Dissolution of Marriage.

GUARDIAN AND WARD:

Guardianship governed by c. 744, Florida Guardianship Law, and "Veteran's Guardianship Law". It is modified version of Uniform Veterans' Guardianship Act.

Term "guardian" means person who has been appointed by court to act on behalf of ward's person or property, or both; and term "incapacitated person" means person who has been judicially determined to lack capacity to manage at least some of property or to meet at least some of essential health and safety requirements of such person. (744.102).

Jurisdiction and Venue.—Circuit court has exclusive jurisdiction of guardianship proceedings. (26.012[2][b]). Domicile of resident ward is county where ward resides. Venue for appointment of guardian is: (1) County where incapacitated person resides; or (2) if nonresident, in any county in this state where incapacitated person owns property; or (3) if neither, where any debtor of incapacitated person resides; (4) if incapacitated person is found in county other than county of residence, venue for appointment of guardian may be county where incapacitated person is found. Upon transfer of incapacitated person to county of residence, guardian may have venue of guardianship changed to county of residence and successor guardian may be appointed. If incapacitated person's residence changes to another county, venue may be changed. (744.201, .202).

Types of Guardianship.—Guardian ad litem may be appointed by court to represent interests of ward or ward's estate (744.102; P.G.R. 5.120), of abused child (61.401), or in dependent child proceedings (c. 39). In case where minor has claim for personal injury, property damage, or wrongful death in which gross settlement equals or exceeds $25,000, court shall appoint guardian ad litem to protect minor's interest before approval of settlement. (744.301). Father and mother, jointly or survivor, are natural guardians of their own and adopted children during minority and may without court appointment collect, receive, manage and dispose of real or personal property from estate, trust or life insurance not exceeding in any instance $5,000. (744.301). Parent, brother, sister, next of kin, or other person interested in welfare of minor, may petition court to appoint guardian. (774.3021). Resident guardian of property of nonresident may be appointed on petition of foreign guardian, next of kin or creditor. (744.308). Standby guardian of minor may be appointed by court upon petition or consent of both parents, natural or adoptive, if living, or of surviving parent, to assume duties of guardianship or limited guardianship upon death or adjudication of incapacity of last surviving natural or adoptive parent of minor. Currently serving guardian may petition court to appoint standby guardian of incapacitated person. (744.304). Foreign guardian is one appointed in another state or country and upon appointment may maintain or defend any action in

See note at head of Digest as to 1998 legislation covered.

See Topical Index in front part of this volume.

GUARDIAN AND WARD . . . *continued*
this state as representative of his ward and can manage property of nonresident ward. (744.102, -.306, -.307). Voluntary guardian is one appointed upon petition of resident or nonresident person who is unable by reason of age or physical infirmity to manage his property. (744.341). If petitioned for, court can order that only part of ward's property will be included in guardianship estate. (744.341[2]). Veteran's guardian is one appointed before payment of veterans' benefits to incompetent veteran or minor ward. (744.602, 744.613). Corporate guardian means corporation authorized to exercise fiduciary of guardianship powers in this state, including nonprofit corporate guardian. (744.102). Pre-need guardian may be named by written declaration by competent adult to serve in event of declarant's incapacity. (744.3045). Pre-need guardian may be nominated by written declaration by birth or adoptive parents. Rebuttable presumption that nominated pre-need guardian is entitled to serve. (744.3046).

Eligibility and Competency.—Any resident of this state who is 18 years of age or older is qualified to act as guardian of ward unless convicted of felony or who, from any incapacity or illness, is incapable of discharging duties of guardian, or who is otherwise unsuitable to perform duties of guardian. (744.309). Judge may not act as guardian of resident ward unless related to ward by blood, marriage, or adoption, or has maintained close relationship with ward or ward's family, and serves without compensation. (744.309[1][b]). Nonresident of state may serve as guardian of resident ward if related by lineal consanguinity; is legally adopted child or adoptive parent of ward; is spouse, sibling, uncle, aunt, niece or nephew of ward, or blood relative or spouse of person otherwise qualified. Trust company, incorporated under laws of this state, state banking corporation or state savings association authorized and qualified to exercise fiduciary powers in this state, or national banking association or federal savings and loan associations authorized and qualified to exercise fiduciary powers in this state, may act as guardian of property of ward. (744.309[4]). Nonprofit corporation organized for religious or charitable purposes and existing under laws of this state may be appointed guardian for ward. (744.309[5]). See also category Business Regulation and Commerce, topic Banks and Banking, subhead International Banking.

Proceedings for Appointment.—Petition for appointment verified by petitioner, must be filed showing name, age, residence and postoffice address of incapacitated person or minor; nature of incapacity, if any; extent of guardianship desired, either plenary or limited; residence and postoffice address of petitioner; names and addresses of next of kin of incapacitated person, or minor, if known to petitioner; name of proposed guardian; and previous relationship of proposed guardian to ward; and nature and value of property subject to guardianship; reasons why this person should be appointed guardian. If willing and qualified guardian cannot be located, petition must so state. (744.334). Court may appoint any person who is fit and proper and qualified to act as guardian, whether related to ward or not. Court shall give preference to appointment of person who (1) is related by blood or marriage to ward; (2) has educational, professional, or business experience relevant to nature of services sought to be provided; (3) has capacity to manage financial resources involved; or (4) has ability to meet requirements of law and unique needs of individual case. (744.312). Court shall also consider wishes expressed by incapacitated person as to who shall be appointed guardian; consider preference of minor who is age 14 or over; consider any person designated as guardian in will in which ward is beneficiary. (744.312). Upon petition, court may appoint guardian for minor without appointing examining committee or conducting adjudicatory hearing pursuant to 744.331. (744.342).

Qualification.—Oath must be filed and bond given with surety (except in case of corporate guardians) in amount fixed by court and not less than full value of cash and bearer securities, which may be reduced by Court for good cause. Court may waive bond if petitioner presents compelling reasons or court can require use of designated financial institution. (744.347, .351).

Powers and Duties.—Guardian of incapacitated person may exercise only those rights that have been removed from ward and delegated to guardian. Guardian of minor shall exercise powers of plenary guardian. (744.361[1]). Guardian shall file initial guardianship report within 60 days after letters of guardianship are signed and guardianship report annually. (744.361[2]-[3]). Guardian must implement guardianship plan. (744.361[4]). Unless court requires filing on calendar-year basis, guardian must file with court, annual guardianship report within 90 days after last day of anniversary month of guardian's appointment. (744.367). Guardian of property must take possession, file inventory and manage and invest assets for best interest of ward (744.361), and under order may compromise and settle claims by or against guardian of property of ward (744.387). Property of ward is held primarily for support, maintenance and education of ward but court may authorize use for dependents of ward. Any dependent of ward may petition court for order directing guardian to contribute to dependent's support from property of ward. (744.421). If ward is minor and parents are able to support, maintain and educate ward, guardian must not so use ward's funds unless directed by court. (744.397). After obtaining approval of court pursuant to petition for authorization to act, plenary guardian, or limited guardian within powers designated by court order may prosecute or defend claims or proceedings. (744.441). Court may authorize voluntary guardian to take possession of less than all of ward's property. (744.341).

Investments.—In making investments guardian must observe standards of prudent man dealing with property of another and if he has special skills or so represented, is under duty to use skills. (744.361[7]).

Custodian of Minors.—Custodians of minors do not have standing as interested parties to question settlement agreement entered into on behalf of minors by guardian of property. (Maceda v. Duhig, 474 So.2d 292).

Securities in Name of Nominee.—Without obtaining court approval, plenary guardian, or limited guardian within powers granted by order appointing guardian or by approved annual or amended guardianship report, may hold security in name of nominee or in other form without disclosing interest of ward, but guardian is liable for any act of nominee in connection with security so held. (744.444[15]). Guardian may redeem or sell liquid assets to pay for reasonable living expenses of ward. (744.444[10]).

Encumbering Property.—Where expedient or necessary the court may authorize guardian to borrow with or without security or on pledge or mortgage of ward's property. (744.441).

Sales.—Sale may be made upon court authorization based upon petition and hearing. Notice is not required for sale of perishable or deteriorating property. (744.441-.451).

Power of Election or Appointment.—After petitioning court for approval, plenary guardian, or limited guardian within powers granted by order appointing guardian or by approved annual or amended guardianship report, may execute power of appointment or other power, if best interests of ward requires such execution. (744.441[2]).

Annual Reports.—Each guardian of person must file with court annual guardianship plan within 90 days after last day of anniversary month of guardian's appointment unless court requires filing on calendar-year basis. Annual guardianship report of guardian of person must consist of annual guardianship plan. Each guardian of property shall file with court annual guardianship report on or before Apr. 1 of each year, unless court requires or authorizes filing on fiscal year basis. Report of guardian of property must consist of annual accounting. Unless otherwise directed, guardian of property may file first annual accounting on either fiscal year or calendar year basis and must notify court as to filing intentions within 30 days from date guardian issued letter of guardianship. All subsequent annual accountings must be filed for same period as first. Annual report shall be served on ward unless ward is minor under 14 or totally incapacitated and attorney for ward, if any. Guardian shall provide copy to any other person as court may direct. Within 30 days after annual report has been filed, any interested person, including ward, may file written objections to any element of report, specifying nature of objection. (744.367). If guardian fails to file guardianship report, court shall order guardian to file report within 15 days after service of order or show cause why guardian should not be compelled to do so. (744.3685).

Annual Accounting.—Each guardian of property must file annual accounting with court. Such accounting must contain full and correct account of receipts and disbursements, statement of ward's property on hand at end of accounting period and copy of annual or year's-end statement of all of ward's cash accounts from each of institutions where cash is deposited. (744.3678). Substantiating papers need not be filed but must be available for inspection at court's order and must be preserved for three years after discharge. (744.3678). Court may require production of evidence of property for inspection of any creditor or interested person. (744.373).

Resignation or Removal.—Upon petition and approval of court, guardian may resign after giving notice to surety and such other notice as court may require, but before being relieved guardian must file final reports and deliver assets to successor and acceptance of resignation does not relieve guardian or surety of liability previously incurred. Guardian of person must deliver to successor guardian copies of all medical and personal care records. (744.467). Guardian may be removed: (1) fraud in appointment; (2) for failure to discharge duties; (3) for abuse of powers; (4) for incapacity or illness, including substance abuse, which renders guardian incapable of discharging duties; (5) for failure to comply with order; (6) failure to return schedules or produce assets; (7) for waste, embezzlement or mismanagement; (8) for failure to give bond or security as required; (9) for conviction of felony; (10) for appointment of receiver trustee in bankruptcy or liquidator for corporate guardian; (11) for development of conflict of interest between ward and guardian; (12) for finding of probable cause made by Department of Health that guardian has abused, neglected or exploited ward; (13) for material failure to comply with guardianship report by guardian; (14) for failure to comply with rules for timely filing initial and annual guardianship reports; (15) for failure to fulfill guardianship education requirements; (16) for improper management of ward's assets; (17) for material change in ward's financial circumstances such that guardian is no longer qualified to manage finances of ward, or previous degree of management is no longer required; (18) for becoming disqualified after appointment; or (19) upon showing by one who did not receive notice of petition for adjudication of incapacity, when notice required, and who is related to ward within specified relationships for nonresident relatives, and who has not been previously rejected by court as guardian, that current guardian is not family member, and removal is in ward's best interest. Removal may be by circuit court on own motion or by petition of surety or other interested person or by ward. (744.474-.477). Removed guardian must, within 20 days, file final reports with court, successor guardian and ward and surrender assets to successor upon demand and may be subject to contempt for defaults. (744.511-.517).

Discharge.—When ward becomes sui juris or ward dies or is restored to capacity, or guardian has been unable to locate ward through diligent search, or for guardian of property, when property has been exhausted, guardian shall file final report and receive discharge. (744.521). If no objections are filed and it appears guardian has made full distribution and faithfully discharged duties, order of discharge and release are granted. If objections are filed, hearing is held. (744.527). With prior court approval, guardian may file final report and close guardianship in this state upon change of domicile of resident ward under conditions of §744.2025. (744.524). Guardian of person is discharged without further proceeding upon filing of certified copy of ward's death certificate. (744.521). Voluntary guardianship may be terminated by ward by filing notice with court. (744.341).

Appeals from final orders and decrees of circuit courts pertaining to guardianship matters may be taken to District Court of Appeal (Const., art. 5, §4[b]) pursuant to Florida Appellate Rule 9.110.

Insane Persons.—See subhead Proceedings for Appointment, supra. Upon death of incapacitated person, guardianship terminates and estate is settled as estate of any other decedent. See subhead Powers and Duties, supra. See also category Estates and Trusts, topics Wills, Descent and Distribution, and Executors and Administrators.

Foreign guardian producing authenticated orders of appointment may maintain or defend any action in this state as representative of ward; debtors may pay foreign guardian or deliver property to guardian after 60 days from appointment if no demand be made by guardian appointed in this state within such time (744.306); management of property of nonresident ward may be permitted by court following filing of petition showing appointment and sufficiency of security for protection of ward and designation

See note at head of Digest as to 1998 legislation covered.

See Topical Index in front part of this volume.

FL – 41

GUARDIAN AND WARD . . . continued

of resident agent (744.307). See category Business Regulation and Commerce, topic Banks and Banking, subhead International Banking.

Veteran's Guardianship.—Guardians appointed under Veteran's Guardianship Law must not be required to comply with annual reporting provisions of §744.367. (744.653).

Dependents of ward may petition for support from guardian. (744.625[1]). Benefits may be exempt from claims of creditors. (744.625).

Public Guardianship.—Where there is no willing and responsible person available to serve as guardian to incapacitated person and where private guardian cannot be afforded, public guardian will be provided. (744.702).

Appointment of Public Guardian.—Chief Judge shall appoint public guardian. Public guardian must have knowledge of legal process and knowledge of social services available to meet needs of incapacitated persons. Public guardian is appointed for term of four years. (744.703).

Powers and Duties of Public Guardian.—Public guardian may serve if there is no person willing or qualified to serve as guardian and if assets of ward do not exceed asset level for Medicaid eligibility, exclusive of constitutionally exempt property, and ward's income is less than $4,000 per year excluding social security, welfare, and certain state pensions, and ward's income from all sources does not exceed $30,000 per year. Public guardian is vested with all same powers as guardian under this chapter. Ward may not be committed to mental health treatment facility by public guardian without involuntary placement proceeding. (744.704). Ward's personal and medical records must not be disclosed. Within six months of public guardian being appointed to ward, public guardian shall submit report on efforts to locate appropriate person to act as guardian of ward and on ward's potential to be restored to capacity. Public guardian shall insure that each ward is seen by professional staff person at least four times per year. Ratio for professional staff to wards is 1 to 40 which chief judge may enlarge or reduce for good cause. (744.708). Upon taking office, public guardian shall file bond as prescribed in §45.011. (744.709). Public guardians shall not be required to file any other bonds. (744.351).

Disposition of Unclaimed Funds Held by Guardian.—Where guardianship has been terminated due to ward's death and property cannot be distributed because no estate proceeding has been instituted, then guardian of property may institute such proceeding. Where there has been termination of guardianship pursuant to §744.521 and guardian of property has been unable to locate ward through diligent search, court shall order guardian to sell property and deposit proceeds and cash already on hand with clerk of court. Clerk shall deposit funds in registry of court to be disposed of after posting statutory notice. After six months clerk shall deposit funds with state treasurer who shall then deposit funds to credit of public guardianship. Within ten years from date of deposit, upon written petition to court and notice to department of legal affairs, any person entitled to funds, after proof of such entitlement, may obtain court order directing payment of funds to him. Funds deposited and not claimed within ten years from date of deposit shall escheat to state for benefit of public guardianship. After depositing funds with clerk guardian of property may proceed with discharge. (744.534).

Gifts to Minors.—See topic Infants.

Uniform Fiduciaries Act not adopted.

Uniform Simplification of Fiduciary Security Transfers Act adopted (c. 610), and takes precedence over Uniform Commercial Code (671.304[2][b]).

See also category Property, topic Powers of Attorney.

HUSBAND AND WIFE:

Real or personal property may be held in name of either husband or wife or in names of both.

Disabilities of Married Women.—All disabilities removed. (Const., art. 10, §5).

Separate Property.—Married woman is empowered to manage and control her separate property without joinder or consent of husband. (708.08[1]).

Contracts; Conveyances.—Married woman is empowered to contract, sell, convey, transfer, mortgage, use and pledge her real and personal property and exercise all rights and power with respect thereto without joinder or consent of husband (708.08[1]) except homestead property (Const. art. 10, §4). Both spouses must join in sale, gift or mortgage of homestead property. Conveyance of real property, including homestead, by one spouse to the other conveys legal title as if parties not married and grantee need not execute conveyance (689.11[1]). Estate by entirety may be created by one spouse: (1) conveying to other by deed in which purpose to create estate is stated or (2) conveying to both spouses. (689.11[1]).

As to incompetent married persons, see topic Guardian and Ward.

Antenuptial Contracts.—Prenuptial contracts are enforceable by court. (61.052). Right of election of surviving spouse, rights of spouse as intestate successor or as pretermitted spouse, and rights of spouse to homestead, exempt property, waivable in prenuptial contract. (732.702[1]).

Actions.—Married woman is empowered to sue and be sued without joinder or consent of husband. (708.08). In action brought by man and wife for injury done to wife in respect to which she is necessarily joined as co-plaintiff, husband may join thereto claims of any nature in his own right. (46.031). Husband is not liable for torts of wife. (741.23). Doctrine of interspousal tort immunity is abrogated. (741.235). Each spouse may recover for loss of consortium if due to negligence of another. (248 So.2d 648). Married woman who conveyed or mortgaged her separate real property without joinder of husband before effective date of 1968 State Constitution had until June 2, 1985 to file notice of lis pendens and bring action based on nonjoinder of husband to contest validity of conveyance or mortgage. (708.08[2]).

Agency.—Either spouse may give power of attorney to other, may enter into contracts with other, and may become partner of other. (708.09).

Community Property.—This system does not exist in Florida.

Domestic Violence.—Injunction for protection against domestic violence is available between spouses, former spouses, persons related by blood or marriage, persons who are presently residing together as if a family or who have resided together in past as if a family, and persons who have child in common regardless of whether they have been married or have resided together at any time.

Ex parte temporary injunction shall be effective for fixed period not to exceed 15 days. Full hearing shall be set for date no later than date when temporary injunction ceases to be effective. Any injunction must be extended if necessary to remain in full force and effect during any period of continuance. (741.30[5][3][c]).

Willful violation of injunction for protection against domestic violence under certain circumstances may be considered misdemeanor of first degree. (741.28-741.31).

Desertion and Nonsupport.—It is a felony for a man to desert his wife or children or to willfully withhold support, and upon conviction thereof, he is punishable by imprisonment not exceeding five years subject to extended term if deemed habitual felony offender or by fine not exceeding $5,000 or both. (856.04[1]). Husband may not be prosecuted for such desertion or nonsupport when there exist grounds for dissolution of marriage and husband has provided for support of children. (856.04). See topic Dissolution of Marriage. Spouse may petition for alimony and support for children without petitioning for dissolution of marriage. (61.09). Spouse residing in state apart from spouse and minor children, whether at fault or not, may obtain adjudication of his financial obligations to his spouse and children and his custody or visitation rights. (61.10).

Uniform Interstate Family Support Act (88.0011-88.9031) replaced Revised Uniform Reciprocal Enforcement of Support Act. Enacted to minimize multiple order problem by providing means for one controlling support order at any time. Continuing exclusive jurisdiction. (88.2051). Recognition of controlling child support orders. (88.2071). Procedure when responding state has not enacted similar law. (88.3041). Employer must comply with income-withholding order of another state. (88.50211). Recognition of order modified in another state. (88.6121). Jurisdiction to modify child support order of another state when parties reside in this state. (88.6131). Notice to issuing tribunal of modifications. (88.6141).

INFANTS:

Disability of nonage removed for all persons of 18 years of age or older. (743.07[1]). Drinking age is 21. (562.11[1][a]).

Removal of Disabilities.—Marriage of minor removes disabilities, notwithstanding subsequent divorce or death of spouse. (743.01).

Disabilities are removed to permit participation in benefits of Home, Farm and Business Loans Act. (743.04). Disabilities are removed for minors 16 or older for purposes of borrowing money for own higher education. (743.05).

Contracts.—See subhead Removal of Disabilities, supra.

Actions.—Infant may sue through representative or by next friend if unrepresented or guardian appointed by court. (R.C.P. 1.210 [b]). All civil suits may be prosecuted in name of guardian. (R.C.P. 1.210[a]). Person who, through negligence, causes significant permanent injury to natural or adoptive parent of unmarried dependent resulting in permanent total disability shall be liable to dependent for damages, including for permanent loss of services, comfort, and companionship and society for acts of negligence occurring on or after Oct. 1, 1988. (768.0415).

Child Support.—Comprehensive child support and income deduction regulations and requirements. (61.046; 61.10; 61.12; 61.1301; 61.13015; 61.14 et seq.).

Bicycles and Mopeds.—Riders/operators under age of 16 required to wear helmets. (316.2065[3][d], 316.211[4]).

Parental Responsibility.—Parent is liable for torts of minor committed while in parent's custody, whether or not minor is personally liable. (710.119).

Gifts to Minors.—Florida Uniform Transfers to Minors Act adopted to replace Uniform Gifts to Minors Act. (c. 710).

Uniform Securities Ownership by Minors Act not adopted.

Child Abuse and Neglect.—C. 827 provides for criminal penalties for aggravated child abuse, child abuse, negligent treatment of children, persistant nonsupport, misuse of child support money, and sexual performance by child. (827.01 et seq.). Criminal penalties for possession of photographs, motion pictures, exhibitions, shows or other presentations including sexual conduct by child. (827.071).

Harm which constitutes "child abuse or neglect" means harm or threatened harm to child's physical or mental health or welfare by acts or omissions of person responsible for child. (415.503[10]). Comprehensive regulations as to placement of child in shelter. (39.402[3]).

Comprehensive child care regulation by state and local governments.

MARRIAGE:

Minimum Age for Marriage.—License cannot be granted without written parental (or guardian) consent unless both parties are at least 18, or unless party under 18 has been previously married, or both parents are dead or they have or are expecting child. (741.04, 741.0405). License cannot be granted to any persons under 16 without judicial permission unless they are parents or expectant parents. (741.0405).

Consent Required.—If either party is under 18, written and properly acknowledged consent of parents (or guardian) is required, unless both parents dead or party previously married, or they have or are expecting child. (741.04; 741.0405). Florida law removed disability of nonage from all persons 18 or older. (743.07).

License is required; issued by any county court judge or clerk of circuit court (741.01).

In order to obtain license, affidavit signed by both parties reciting their true and correct ages required. (741.04[1]). No license may be issued unless both parties filed written statement specifying whether premarital preparation course was completed and that both have read otherwise accessed information in Family Law Handbook. Failure to submit valid certification will delay effective date of marriage license for three days

See note at head of Digest as to 1998 legislation covered.

See Topical Index in front part of this volume.

MARRIAGE . . . *continued*
from application date (exceptions granted for nonresidents and hardships). (741.04[2], [3]).

Ceremony may be performed by ordained clergy or elders in communion with some church, any judicial officer, clerk of circuit court, or notary public. Within ten days after ceremony, person performing same must make certificate of same and transmit to office of county court or clerk of circuit court. Quaker marriages valid. (741.07-.08).

Artificial Insemination.—Any child born within wedlock who has been conceived by means of artificial or in vitro insemination is irrebuttably presumed to be child of husband and wife, provided that both husband and wife have consented in writing to artificial or in vitro insemination. (742.11).

Records of licenses issued and marriages performed must be kept by county court judge, or clerk of circuit court with whom original license and certificate must be filed. (741.09). After recordation, county court judge or clerk of circuit court must forward license to vital statistics office of Department of Health. (382.021). In absence of certificate, affidavit of two witnesses who were present that marriage was performed may be filed and recorded with same effect as certificate. (741.10).

See also category Documents and Records, topic Records.

Common law marriages entered into after Jan. 1, 1968 are invalid. (741.211).

Proxy Marriages.—Not recognized.

Prohibited Marriages.—Man may not marry woman to whom he is related by lineal consanguinity or his sister, aunt or niece. Corresponding prohibitions as to woman. (741.21).

Foreign Marriages.—No statutory provisions.

Annulment.—There are no statutory provisions as to annulment of marriage. The circuit court in chancery has jurisdiction where annulment is sought for nonage, incapacity, fraud, duress or other recognized legal cause. (77 Fla. 95, 80 So. 739; 83 Fla. 7, 90 So. 622; 120 Fla. 607, 163 So. 35).

MARRIED WOMEN:

See topics Husband and Wife, Marriage; categories Civil Actions and Procedure, topic Evidence, subhead Witnesses; Debtor and Creditor, topic Homesteads; Documents and Records, topic Acknowledgments; Estates and Trusts, topics Descent and Distribution, Executors and Administrators, Wills; Property, topic Powers of Attorney.

INSURANCE

INSURANCE COMPANIES:

Regulated by Insurance Code (cc. 624-632, 634-635, 641-642, 648, 651) and by general corporation laws (see category Business Organizations, topic Corporations) except where Code conflicts (628.041); incorporation of insurers subject to special requirements of 628.011 et seq. and as to fraternal benefit societies, 632.601 et seq. Proposed insurer must have permit to incorporate from Department of Insurance. (628.051–.071). Articles of incorporation and amendments must be approved by Department prior to formation of corporation or amendment, respectively. (628.091; 628.101). Capital requirements for insurers, c. 624.407 et seq. Special types of regulated insurers: (1) Fraternal benefit societies (c. 632); (2) motor vehicle service agreement companies and home warranty and service warranty associations (c. 634); (3) mortgage guaranty insurers (c. 635); (4) prepaid ambulance service plan offered by political subdivision exempt from insurance code (624.127); (5) health care service plans (c. 641); (6) continuing care contractors (c. 651); (7) legal expense insurers (c. 642); (8) nonprofit multiple employer welfare arrangements (624.436, 624.446); (9) commercial self-insurance fund (624.488); (10) bail bondsmen and runners (c. 648); (11) state fire marshal (c. 633). Exclusions from Florida Insurance Code regarding specific business entities. (624.01 et seq.). See Tort Reform & Insurance Act of 1986. (768.71-.81).

Supervision by Department of Insurance, head of which is Insurance Commissioner and Treasurer. (20.13).

Certificate of Authority.—Regulated by §624.401 et seq. Proposed insurer must first obtain a certificate of authority from Department. (624.401). Any person who engages in insurance activities without certificate commits felony of third degree. (624.401[4]). Capital funds requirements (624.407, 624.4075), policyholders surplus requirements (624.408) and deposit of securities requirements (624.411) must be met. Application for certificate must be filed as in §624.413. Department may suspend or revoke certificates for violation of code and other reasons. (624.418). Insurer, other than life insurer, desiring to surrender certificate, withdraw from state, or discontinue writing of certain kinds of lines of insurance must give 90 days notice to Department. (624.430).

Rates and rating organizations relating to property, casualty, and surety insurance are regulated by c. 627.011 et seq. C. 627 does not apply to reinsurance, except joint reinsurance (627.311); insurance against loss of or damage to aircraft, their hulls, accessories or equipment or against liability, other than workers' compensation and employer's liability, arising out of ownership, maintenance, or use of aircraft; insurance of vessels or craft and their cargoes, marine builders' risks, marine protection and indemnity, or other risks commonly insured under marine, as distinguished from inland marine, insurance policies, surplus lines insurance under §§626.913-.937. (627.021[2]). See §627.570 re: premium rates for group life insurance contracts. See §627.782-.783 re: title insurance rates.

Annual statements and other reports required must be filed with Department on or before Mar. 1. Quarterly statements covering periods ending on Mar. 31, June 30, and Sept. 30 shall be filed within 45 days after each such date. (624.424).

Policies.—Regulated by §§627.401-.429 and as follows for specific kinds of insurance: Life and annuities (627.451 et seq.); industrial life (627.501 et seq.); group life (627.551 et seq.); health insurance (627.601); group, blanket and franchise health insurance (627.651 et seq.); Medicare supplement policies (627.671 et seq.); credit life and disability (627.676 et seq.); property (627.701 et seq.); casualty and automobile liability (627.7261 et seq.); surety (627.751 et seq.); title (627.7711 et seq.); variable annuities (627.801 et seq.); premium finance agreements (627.826 et seq.); long term care insurance (627.9401 et seq.); financial guaranty insurance (627.971 et seq.).

Discrimination and Rebates.—Insurers may not discriminate (626.9541[1][g]), make rebates or give special benefits (626.9541[1][h]). Excepted from definition of discrimination and rebates are following practices: Paying bonuses to annuity and life insurance policy-holders; issuing life or disability insurance policies at reduced rates where payment is by preauthorized check or payroll deduction plan; readjustment of group insurance rates based on experience; issuing life or annuity insurance policies at rates less than usual rates of premiums for contracts such as group or employee insurance; making allowance for life insurance policies issued on industrial debt plan. (626.9541[1][h][2]). Certain discriminatory practices with respect to AIDS in life and health insurance prohibited. (627.429, 627.411, 627.6646). Payments of attorney's fees and agent's commission for services in connection with issuing title insurance specifically allowed. (626.9541[1][h][3][b]).

Insolvent and Defaulting Companies.—Liquidation, rehabilitation and priorities governed generally by c. 631. Florida Insurance Guaranty Association Act provides mechanism for payment of covered claims under certain policies when insurer becomes insolvent. (631.50, et seq.). Florida Health Maintenance Organization Consumer Assistance Plan provides for subscriber protection from insolvent HMOs. (631.811, et seq.).

Liens.—Cash surrender value of life insurance and annuity contracts generally exempt from legal process in favor of any creditor unless policy is effected to benefit creditor. (222.14).

Agents, solicitors, adjusters, service or customer representatives, administrators, and service companies must be licensed or appointed in accordance with provisions of §§626.011-.899.

Written examination is required, with several exemptions (626.221); Department may investigate character, background and fitness (626.201). Life insurance solicitation regulated. (626.99). General lines agent licenses regulated. (626.726 et seq.). Administrators regulated. (626.88-.899). Life agent and health agent not licensed as to other forms of insurance of same insurer must be 18 years of age and Florida resident. (626.785; 626.831). Nonresidents may be licensed as life agents and health agents if licensed as life or health agent in other state or province of Canada and other state or province of Canada accords same privilege to Florida residents, but nonresident agent must not have place of business, be officer, director, stockholder or partner of corporation or partnership doing business in Florida as life or health insurance agency. (626.792; 626.835). Different classes of adjusters provided for and varying qualifications specified. (626.851-.878). Nonresident may be licensed as general lines agent if nonresident's domicile extends reciprocal treatment. (626.741). Employees of Veterans Administration may not be life or health insurance agents. (626.788; 626.833).

Service of Process.—Each licensed insurer shall be deemed to have appointed Insurance Commissioner and Treasurer as its attorney to receive service for all legal process issued against it in any civil proceeding. (624.422). Service of process fee is $15. (624.502). Process statutes relating to various nonresident insurance agents are as follows: General lines (626.742) and health (626.836). Process statutes relating to various insurers are as follows: (1) Unauthorized foreign or alien insurers doing business by mail (626.906-907); (2) unauthorized insurers (626.937); (3) motor vehicle service agreement companies (634.151; 634.161); (5) home warranty associations (634.315). See also §48.151(3).

Investments regulated. (625.301-.340). See also §§518.15, 518.151; 518.152.

Standard valuation regulated. (625.121).

Foreign insurance companies must secure certificate of authority from Department (624.401), and meet special requirements (624.404). Application, including one certified copy of its charter, copy of its power of attorney, financial statement and by-laws, and report of most recent examination within three years preceding date of application, certificate of compliance from insurance supervisory official of domiciliary state, and certificate of officer having custody of deposit maintained by insurer in another state must be filed. (624.413). Deposit requirements are set forth in §624.411. Other relevant statutes: (1) Definition (624.06[2]); (2) investment requirements (625.340 et seq.); (3) deposits of foreign insurers not taxed (625.53[3]); (4) commissioner as receiver to conserve assets (631.071).

Retaliatory Laws.—Obligations or prohibitions imposed by another state on Florida insurers and agents doing business in such other state are imposed on insurers and agents of such other state doing business in Florida. (624.5091). Retaliation on nonresident agents (other than life and health agents). (626.711). Retaliation on general lines agents. (626.743). Domestic insurers are allowed certain credit against taxes under 624.509.

Local Agent Required.—Generally unlawful to issue life, annuity, property, casualty, or surety insurance except through local producing agent, properly licensed. (624.425-624.428).

Premium Tax.—Each insurer, except as to wet marine and transportation insurance taxed under §624.510, must pay premium tax by Mar. 1 for preceding calendar year based on 1% of gross receipts on local annuities and 1.75% of gross receipts on all other policies insuring Florida risks and residents except reinsurance. (624.509). Tax of 3/4 of 1% on gross underwriting profit is imposed on wet marine and transportation insurance. (624.510). Home Warranty Associations are subject to premium tax of 2% of gross premiums. (634.313).

Motor Vehicle Service Agreement Companies and Service Warranty Associations are not subject to premium tax but are subject to sales tax imposed by c. 212. (634.131, 634.415).

Fraternal benefit societies enjoy general exemption from taxes on insurance companies. (632.626).

Fire insurance premiums are subject to additional regulatory assessment of 1% of gross amount of premiums collected on fire insurance policies covering Florida property. (624.515-624.516).

See note at head of Digest as to 1998 legislation covered.

See Topical Index in front part of this volume.

FL – 43

INSURANCE COMPANIES . . . *continued*

License tax must be paid by each insurer annually, together with other fees and state and county license taxes for agents and solicitors. (624.501 et seq.). Fraternal benefit society, with membership restricted to physically disabled, insuring less than 200 members in Florida pays $25 annual license tax. (624.501[3]). Municipal corporations may impose taxes on agents and solicitors not to exceed 50% of state tax. (624.507).

No-Fault Insurance.—See category Transportation, topic Motor Vehicles.

Civil remedy provided for persons damaged by insurer's violations of various provisions of Insurance Code. (624.155).

SURETY AND GUARANTY COMPANIES:

For requirements to obtain certificate of authority to do business in state, see topic Insurance Companies.

Organization.—See topic Insurance Companies.

Rights and Powers.—Any surety company with currently effective certificate of authority to do business in state may be accepted on bond of any person or corporation required by laws of state to give bond, but additional surety may be required by official authorized to approve bond. (627.751-.759). Attorney's fees recoverable against surety in suits for breach of building or construction contract. (627.756, 627.428).

As to agents and solicitors, see topic Insurance Companies.

Foreign Companies.—See topic Insurance Companies; category Business Organizations, topic Corporations.

Taxation.—See topic Insurance Companies.

INTELLECTUAL PROPERTY

FICTITIOUS NAMES:

See topic Trademarks and Tradenames, subhead Tradenames.

TRADEMARKS AND TRADENAMES:

What May Be Used.—Common law rights in marks are preserved. (495.161). Registration Statute provides for registration of word, name, symbol, character, design, drawing or device or combination used for goods made or sold or services rendered or offered as, where applicable, trademark, service mark, certification mark, collective mark, or trade name. (495.021, 495.011). Certain exceptions are specified in §495.021.

Registration.—Any individual, firm, partnership, corporation, association, union or other organization who adopts and uses a mark may register same by filing verified application with Department of State on its form accompanied by specimen in triplicate and filing fee of $87.50 for each class of goods or services listed in 495.111 for which mark is used. (495.031). Registration effective for ten years and may be renewed for successive like terms for $87.50 fee per class six months prior to expiration of each term. (495.071).

Reservation.—Person with bona fide and good faith intention to use mark in connection with sale of goods and/or services in Florida, may reserve right to register mark, subject to limitations set forth in c. 495 by submitting Request for Reservation with Department of State on its form. (495.027). Mark may be reserved by requester for nontransferable, nonrenewable, 120-day period commencing from date requester files request and $50 per class fee. (495.027).

Assignment.—Registered marks are assignable in connection with sale of business by instrument in writing, and assignments are recordable with Department of State. Assignments are void against subsequent bona fide purchasers without notice of prior assignment unless recorded within three months after assignment or, if after three months, prior to recording of subsequent assignment unless subsequent bona fide purchaser records his assignment prior to or within ten days after prior assignment is recorded. (495.081). $50 filing fee with Department of State is required. (495.081).

Special statutory provisions exist for marks used in connection with certain beverages and medicines, etc. (506.01 et seq.), fruit and produce containers (506.19 et seq.), milk and ice cream (506.30 et seq.), shopping and laundry carts, dairy cases, egg baskets, bakery containers, and poultry boxes (506.503), or adopted by unions (506.06 et seq.).

Protection Afforded.—Common law rights preserved (495.161) but statutory rights to injunctions, damages and other remedies provided for in §495.141. Suits to enjoin may be brought and require defendants to pay up to three times their profits and up to three times all damages suffered by plaintiffs. (506.09). Court may order seizure of all counterfeit goods upon motion or ex parte application upon showing that goods are likely to be destroyed, sold or removed from court's jurisdiction and probability of success on merits upon posting of undertaking and may waive requirement of notice for ex parte proceedings. Persons causing seizure of goods which are not counterfeit are liable for damages, costs, punitive damages, if warranted, and, upon showing of bad faith, attorney's fees. Injunctive relief, damages, attorney's fees for prevailing party also available under Florida Deceptive and Unfair Trade Practices Act. (501.211). State may also enforce provisions of Florida Deceptive and Unfair Trade Practices Act. (501.201 et seq.). See, also, Regulations issued pursuant to §501.205.

Infringement.—Any person who uses, without registrant's consent, any reproduction, counterfeit, copy, or imitation of registered mark on any goods for sale, distribution, or advertising, will be civilly liable to registrant. Registrant cannot recover profits or damages unless acts committed with knowledge such mark intended to cause confusion or mistake, or to deceive. (495.131). Registrant may sue to enjoin manufacture, use, display, or sale of counterfeits. Court may grant injunction and require defendant to pay registrant all profits derived from and/or all damages suffered by reason of such wrongful use and costs. Court may also order counterfeits under defendant's control to be delivered to court officer or complainant to be destroyed. In assessing profits, complainant required to prove only defendant's sales; defendant must prove costs and deductions claimed. Court may assess up to three times actual damages. (495.141).

Tradenames.—Persons natural or artificial including corporations doing business under tradenames must comply with Fictitious Name Statute (865.09) which requires advertising such fictitious name at least once in newspaper in county of principal place of business. (865.09[3][d]). Noncompliance prohibits maintenance of suit in Florida courts and is misdemeanor. (865.09[9]). Processing fee is required. (865.09[12]).

Deceptive Trade Practices, Misbranding of Foods.—See category Business Regulation and Commerce, topic Monopolies, Restraint of Trade and Competition.

Florida Deceptive and Unfair Trade Practices Act.—(501.201-501.213). Unfair methods of competition, unconscionable acts or practices, and unfair or deceptive acts or practices in conduct of any trade or commerce are unlawful. (501.204). Great weight and due consideration given to interpretations of Federal Trade Commission and federal court interpretations of §5(a)(1) of Federal Trade Commission Act. Department of Legal Affairs may promulgate rules (501.205) and issue cease and desist orders after notice, complaint and hearing (501.208). State Attorney and Department have investigative powers (501.206) and may bring declaratory judgment actions and/or seek injunctions and damages on behalf of consumer(s) against one whose act or practice violates statute (501.207). Civil penalties for willful violations of act (501.2075) and increased penalties for violations involving senior citizens or handicapped persons (501.2077). Prevailing party may receive attorneys' fees. (501.2105). In addition, any individual harmed by violation may bring action and seek injunctive relief, damages, fees and costs. (501.211). All remedies are in addition to other remedies provided by law. (501.213). Exceptions provided for certain retailers (501.207, 501.211) and others (501.212).

TRADE SECRETS:

Records of Department of Agriculture, Division of Consumer Services.—Records are public except trade secrets are confidential and exempt from §119.07(1). (570.544[9]).

Public Service Commission.—If commission undertakes formal proceeding, any matter determined to be trade secret coming into its possession pursuant to inquiry shall be considered confidential and exempt from §119.07(1). (350.121).

Department of Health.—Records, reports and information obtained by any person under c. 381, unless otherwise provided by law, is available to public unless person providing such records, reports, or information can show to Department's satisfaction such material contains trade secrets. Such trade secrets are confidential and exempt from §119.07(1) and Const., art. 1, §24(a). (381.83).

LEGAL PROFESSION

ATTORNEYS AND COUNSELORS:

Name.—Official name is The Florida Bar. (Rules Regulating The Florida Bar, Rule 1-1).

Admission to practice is under exclusive jurisdiction of Supreme Court. (Const. art. V §15). Supreme Court by rule created Florida Board of Bar Examiners, which conducts character, fitness and general qualifications investigation and preparation and grading of written examination and recommends qualified candidates to the Supreme Court for admission. Applicant must be age 18 or older. Every applicant must show that he: (1) Has received academic Bachelor's Degree from college accredited by one of specified regional accrediting associations, and has graduated with LL.B. or J.D. from any law school approved (including provisionally) by American Bar Association or which is member of Association of American Law Schools; or (2) has practiced law ten years or longer in District of Columbia or some other state, and is member of some other bar, in which event he must furnish abstract of scope and character of his previous experience and practice, academic and legal training. (Rules of the Supreme Court Relating to Admission to Bar, arts. I, III, IV). Rules governing admission, information and applications may be obtained from Florida Board of Bar Examiners, Tallahassee.

Registration as law student within 180 days after beginning law school is required of persons intending to apply for admission; there are provisions for early registration with discount in amount of registration fee. (Rules of the Supreme Court Relating to Admission to Bar, Art. II).

Examination.—State bar examination includes Multistate Bar Exam, but scores from exams taken in other states are not accepted in Florida. Examination includes Florida essay and multiple choice questions. Successful completion of Multistate Professional Responsibility Examination also required. (Rules of the Supreme Court Relating to Admission to Bar, Art. IV, 3).

Fees.—Law student: $75 if filed within 180 days of start of law study; $100 if filed within 95 days; $200 if filed within 250 days; $500 if filed after 250 days. Examination fee: $375 in addition to above registration fees to convert registration to application for admission. Attorney applicant: $875 if not member of bar of any other jurisdiction for over 12 months; if member of bar of another jurisdiction more than one year but less than five years, $1,300; if more than five years but less than ten years, $1,600; if more than ten years but less than 15 years, $2,000; and if more than 15 years, $2,500.

Admission Pro Hac Vice.—Practicing attorney of another state, in good standing, who has professional business in a court of record may upon motion be permitted to practice for such business only. (Rules Regulating The Florida Bar, Rule 1-3.2[a]).

Probationary Matters.—Persons with prior histories of drug, alcohol or psychological problems may be admitted to membership in The Florida Bar upon appropriate conditions imposed by Supreme Court. Probationary period will be no longer than three years or for such indefinite period of time as Court may deem appropriate by conditions in its order. Probationary conditions may include, but are not limited to: Participation in rehabilitation program, periodic blood and urine analysis, periodic psychological examinations or supervision by another member of The Florida Bar. (Rules Regulating The Florida Bar, Rule 1-3.2[b]).

Unauthorized Practice.—Only active members of The Florida Bar in good standing may practice law, except as stated above. (Rules Regulating The Florida Bar, Rule 1-3.2[a]).

ATTORNEYS AND COUNSELORS . . . *continued*

Professional Corporations.—See category Business Organizations, topic Corporations, subhead Professional Corporations.

License.—Every attorney must be member of The Florida Bar and pay annual dues. (Rules Regulating The Florida Bar, Rule 1-7.3).

Liens.—There is no statute giving liens in favor of attorneys at law. Those created by common law, whether merely possessory or not, may be enforced in chancery.

Suretyship.—Attorney cannot be surety on official bond of state, county or city official or on bond of client in judicial proceedings. (454.20).

Discipline of attorneys is under exclusive jurisdiction of Florida Supreme Court. This responsibility is delegated to The Florida Bar subject to court's review. Bar board of governors appoints one or more grievance committees in each circuit to investigate misconduct. Procedure leading to judgment of disbarment, suspension, public reprimand, probation or other discipline is set forth in Rules Regulating The Florida Bar, c. 3.

Attorney ethics are governed by "Rules of Professional Conduct", c. 4 of Rules Regulating The Florida Bar. These ethical rules are derived from American Bar Association Model Rules of Professional Conduct with some modifications.

MINERAL, WATER AND FISHING RIGHTS

MINES AND MINERALS:

Department of Environmental Protection charged with administration, supervision, development and conservation of natural resources of state. (370.013). Department of Community Affairs is required to assess and report on state's energy resources, including availability of commercially developable and imported fuels. (377.703[3][e]4). Governor and cabinet, as Board of Trustees of Internal Improvement Trust Fund, may sell or lease any mineral located in, on, or under state land. (253.45).

Operation of Mines.—Permit issued by Division of Resource Management of Department of Environmental Protection required prior to exploration for, or extraction of, minerals pursuant to grant of oil, gas or mineral rights. (377.244-377.2408). Persons engaging in mining any mineral or subterranean product are required to provide necessary places of deposit for waste and débris, and must prevent escape of such waste and débris into streams and rivers. (533.01-.02).

Safeguarding of Employees.—Duly authorized representative of Department of Environmental Protection may conduct inspection of any property, premises or place, except building, on which reclamation operation is or will be conducted. (378.205, 378.405). No statutory provisions.

Inspection of Mines.—Duly authorized representative of Department of Environmental Protection may conduct inspection of any property, premises or place, except building, on which reclamation operation is or will be conducted. (378.205, 378.405).

Oil and Gas.—Division of Resources Management administers provisions of c. 377 relating to oil and gas conservation. Department of Environmental Protection is authorized to adopt rules and regulations governing all phases of exploration, drilling and production. (377.22). Criteria and conditions for Department's granting permits for drilling, exploring, or extracting through well holes, for surface exploration or extraction of oil, gas and minerals, and for conducting any other geophysical activity on privately owned or state owned lands are prescribed in §§377.241-.244. Governor authorized to join with other states in interstate compact to conserve oil and gas. (377.01). Department of Environmental Protection can order cycling, pooling or unitization of oil and gas fields to conserve resources. (377.28). Board of Trustees of Internal Improvement Trust Fund authorized to negotiate, sell and convey leasehold estates in and to such lands for purpose of development thereof and production therefrom, of oil and gas. (253.51). All leases made are upon sealed bids (253.53) after publication of notice that lease will be offered for sale (253.52).

Taxes.—Excise tax is levied on oil, gas and sulfur production. (211.01-.25). Mineral, oil and gas and other subsurface rights, when owned separately from surface, must be returned for separate assessment and tax on basis of just valuation. (193.481). Each producer of oil, gas or sulfur must file tax return on or before last day prescribed for payment of excise tax. (211.075). Criminal and civil penalties and interest charges are incurred on failure to pay tax or file return. (211.076, 211.25). Excise tax on severance of solid minerals, collected and distributed as provided in §§211.30-.34. Refund provided for restoration and reclamation. (211.32). Excise tax on severance of phosphate rock, its collection and distribution is separately addressed in §211.3103.

Termination of Easements.—Easements except those running to state, reserved in any instrument for purpose of mining, drilling, exploring or developing for oil, gas, minerals or fissionable materials may be extinguished by marketable record title pursuant to §712.04 unless excepted or not affected by §§712.03 and 712.04. May be protected from extinguishment by following procedures set forth in §§712.05 and 712.06. Statute intended to act retrospectively. (704.05).

MORTGAGES

CHATTEL MORTGAGES:

Uniform Commercial Code adopted and governs all transactions on and after effective date of Jan. 1, 1967. (cc. 670-680). See category Business Regulation and Commerce, topic Commercial Code for deviations from Official Text, optional provisions adopted, filing fees.

Forms.—For UCC-1, UCC-3 and UCC-11 forms, see end of this Digest.

Filing Fees.—See category Documents and Records, topic Records.

COLLATERAL SECURITY:

See category Debtor and Creditor, topic Pledges.

MORTGAGES OF PERSONAL PROPERTY:

See topic Chattel Mortgages; category Business Regulation and Commerce, topic Commercial Code.

MORTGAGES OF REAL PROPERTY:

Any indebtedness, howsoever evidenced, may be secured by mortgage. Mortgage is specific lien and not conveyance of legal title or right of possession. (697.02). Written instrument selling or conveying realty to secure payment of money, whether to creditor or to third person in trust for creditor, is deemed mortgage, provided, no such conveyance may be deemed mortgage, against bona fide purchaser or mortgagee, for value without notice, holding under grantee. (697.01).

Execution.—Notwithstanding certain exceptions, safe procedure and general practice are that all mortgages be signed in presence of two subscribing witnesses and acknowledged. But see 356 So.2d 785 (mortgage of homestead realty need not be signed in presence of witnesses). Mortgage should recite marital status and when mortgagor is married, spouse should join. Spouse must join in mortgage of homestead realty. (689.111).

Recording.—Mortgages of real property, although valid as between parties, in order to be valid and effectual against creditors or subsequent purchasers for valuable consideration and without notice, must be recorded in county in which property is situated. (695.01). In order to entitle mortgage to be recorded, execution thereof must be acknowledged by persons executing same (695.03), name and address of natural person who prepared instrument or under whose supervision it was prepared must appear on its face (unless instrument executed or acknowledged outside of Florida) (695.26), and intangible tax on mortgage must be paid to recording officer (199.135). Effective July 1, 1991, no mortgage will be recorded by clerk of circuit court unless name of each person who executed mortgage is legibly printed, typewritten or stamped immediately beneath signature of such person and post office address of each such person appears on mortgage. Also, name of each witness and notary public or other officer who acknowledged signature of instrument must be legibly printed, typewritten or stamped immediately below signature of such witness, notary public or other officer, and 3 inch square must be reserved for use by clerk of court at top right hand corner of instrument. (695.26). These requirements do not apply to instrument executed, acknowledged or proved outside Florida. (695.26[3][c]). Mortgagee must file statutory notice to assure that lien is not extinguished 30 years after recording by operation of Marketable Record Title Act. (712.01-.10).

Documentary stamp taxes shall be paid on all recordable instruments requiring documentary stamp tax prior to recordation. Notation should be made on note that tax has been paid on mortgage. (201.01). Effective Aug. 1, 1992, tax on mortgages is 35¢ on each $100 or fraction thereof of indebtedness or obligation secured by mortgage. (201.08). See category Taxation, topic Stamp Tax, subhead Documents, for rates and other information.

Recording Fees.—See category Documents and Records, topic Records.

Taxes.—Indebtedness secured by mortgage is taxed 2 mills on the dollar of just valuation payable one time at time instrument is recorded, in addition to stamp taxes. (199.133). See also category Taxation, topic Intangible Personal Property Tax, subhead Nonrecurring Tax Levy.

Trust deeds may be used to secure debt. As in case of mortgage, trust deed creates only lien, and legal title to property covered thereby does not pass. (c. 697).

Future Advances.—Mortgage may be given to secure future advances, when expressed therein, whether obligatory or otherwise, provided such advances are made within 20 years from date of such mortgage. (697.04[1][a]). Total amount of indebtedness may increase or decrease from time to time, but total unpaid balance at any one time may not exceed a maximum principal amount which must be specified in such mortgage, plus interest and any disbursements made for taxes, levies or insurance. (697.04[1][b]). Mortgagor may impose subsequent limitation on additional principal amounts by recorded instrument. (697.04[1][b]).

Assignment of Rents.—Mortgage or other instrument may provide for assignment of rents, and if such assignment is made, it is absolute upon mortgagor's default; and is operative upon written demand by mortgagee; mortgagee may apply to court to have all rents paid into court registry after payment of expenses necessary to protect, preserve and operate property including payment of real estate taxes and insurance pending adjudication of mortgagee's rights to such rents. (697.07).

Balloon Mortgages.—With exception of mortgages in transactions covered by Federal Truth-in-Lending Act in which mortgagor has received satisfactory disclosure statement, mortgage by purchaser to seller of real property pursuant to written agreement that provides that final payment will exceed periodic payments on mortgage debt, first mortgages, mortgages in effect prior to Jan. 1, 1960, mortgages periodic payments on which consist of interest only with entire original principal payable on maturity, mortgages created for term of five years or more, and mortgages securing extension of credit in excess of $500,000, every mortgage in which final payment or principal balance due and payable upon maturity is greater than twice amount of regular monthly or periodic payment is deemed balloon mortgage, and must have printed or clearly stamped thereon legend in substantially following form: THIS IS A BALLOON MORTGAGE AND THE FINAL PRINCIPAL PAYMENT OR THE PRINCIPAL BALANCE DUE UPON MATURITY IS $. . . . ., TOGETHER WITH ACCRUED INTEREST, IF ANY, AND ALL ADVANCEMENTS MADE BY THE MORTGAGEE UNDER THE TERMS OF THIS MORTGAGE. This legend, including principal balance due upon maturity shall be conspicuously printed or stamped at top of first page or face sheet of mortgage and also immediately above place for signature of mortgagor. Reference should be made to statute (697.05[3]) for penalties for failure to comply and for separate legend required for variable, adjustable or renegotiable balloon mortgages (697.05[2][a]; 697.05[2][c]).

Priorities.—The priority between mortgages is generally based upon priority of time. This priority may be varied by operation of the recording act. Subsequent mortgagees or

See note at head of Digest as to 1998 legislation covered.

See Topical Index in front part of this volume.

MORTGAGES OF REAL PROPERTY . . . *continued*
bona fide purchasers without actual notice who rely on the record title may acquire superior rights to prior mortgagee. (695.01[1]).

Subordination Agreements.—No special form required. Common law rules govern.

Assignment.—Assignments of mortgages are permitted (701.01), but as against creditors or subsequent purchasers for a valuable consideration and without notice they must be recorded and assignment document must indicate in its title that it is Assignment of Mortgage. (701.02). Assignment of mortgage does not assign debt, unless mortgage note is also assigned. (4 Fla. 283). Assignment of debt ipso facto carries with it security. (80 Fla. 84, 85 So. 659).

Limitations.—Special statute of limitations applies to encumbrances on real property. (95.281). See also category Civil Actions and Procedure, topic Limitation of Actions.

Extension.—No special form required, but it is advisable to have joinder therein by junior lienors and parties secondarily liable.

To Husband and Wife.—Any mortgage, or assignment of mortgage, to two persons who are husband and wife creates estate by entirety in mortgage and underlying obligation unless contrary intention appears in instrument. (689.115).

Satisfaction and Release.—Satisfaction or release of a mortgage must be in writing and acknowledged in manner provided for acknowledgment of deeds, and recorded by clerk of circuit court in official record book. No satisfaction or release by an assignee may be entered until an assignment has also been entered. (28.222; 701.04). Upon payment of recorded mortgage, failure to satisfy same of record for period of 30 days after written demand by person making payment constitutes misdemeanor of second degree. (701.05). Recorded satisfaction to be sent to person paying within 60 days of payment. Provision made for attorneys' fees. (701.04).

Foreclosure must be in equity without jury. Court shall sever for separate trial all counterclaims against foreclosing mortgagee. (702.01). Suit must be commenced within five years from maturity date, or 20 years from date of mortgage if maturity date is unascertainable from record unless within said 20 years mortgagee rerecords mortgage with obligation indicating maturity date or records copy of obligation secured by mortgage indicating maturity date with affidavit identifying mortgage by official recording data (limitations not applicable to railroad or public utilities mortgagors). (95.281).

Judge may appoint committee of three for protection of holders of bonds or units or certificates of beneficial interest in pending cause for foreclosure of mortgage or trust deed securing bonds where owners of bonds or beneficiaries of trust exceed ten, and no committee not appointed by judge may be heard. (69.021).

Deficiency decree is within discretion of court, but complainant may also have right to sue at common law for deficiency. (702.06).

Sales.—All sales of property under legal process shall take place at time, date and place advertised in required notice of sale (56.21) on any day of week except Sat. and Sun. (56.22). Reference should also be made to judicial sales procedure described in §45.031. Purchaser at foreclosure sale gets only such title as parties to suit had. (41 Fla. 241, 25 So. 678). Where holder of legal title is not made party in foreclosure proceedings, he is not deprived of his rights by sale of property. (61 Fla. 513, 55 So. 273). If amount bid at sale is inadequate and inequitably less than real value of property, sale should not be confirmed, but judge may order resale. (77 Fla. 825, 82 So. 292).

Redemption.—At any time before later of filing of certificate of sale by clerk of court or time specified in judgment, order, or decree of foreclosure, mortgagor or holder of any subordinate interest may cure mortgagor's indebtedness and prevent foreclosure sale by paying amount of monies specified in judgment, order, or decree of foreclosure, of if no judgment, order, or decree of foreclosure has been rendered, by tendering performance due under security agreement, including any amounts due because of exercise of right to accelerate, plus reasonable expenses of proceeding to foreclosure incurred to time of tender, including reasonable attorneys' fees of creditor. Otherwise, there is no right of redemption. (45.0315).

Florida Home Equity Conversion Act adopted to provide for state administration of home equity conversion mortgage program. (697.20-697.206).

Low-Income Emergency Home Repair Program (420.33-420.37) and Community Care for the Elderly Act (410.021-410.029) were adopted to assist eligible people especially elderly or physically disabled homeowners to make emergency repairs to their homes so they may continue living in their homes and to improve same through use of deferred loans from local governments.

Forms.—Following are forms of mortgage and assignment, partial release and satisfaction thereof by individuals and corporations (compliance with "Scrivener's Act" may be required, see subhead Recording, supra):

Mortgage for Execution by Individual.—The Mortgagors . . . ., in consideration of the principal sum specified in the promissory note hereafter described, received from . . . . ., the Mortgagee, hereby, on this . . . . ., mortgage to the Mortgagee the real property in . . . . County, Florida, described as: . . . . as security for the payment of the promissory note of which the following is a copy: . . . . [copy note, indenting, conforming signatures]. . . . . and agree:

1. To make all payments required by that note and this mortgage promptly when due.
2. To pay all taxes, assessments, liens and encumbrances on that property promptly when due. If they are not promptly paid the Mortgagee may pay them without waiving the option to foreclose, and such payments, with interest thereon from the date of payment at the same rate as specified in that note, shall also be secured by this mortgage.
3. To keep all buildings now or hereafter on that land insured against damage by fire and lightning in the sum secured by this mortgage, by an insuror satisfactory to the Mortgagee, the insurance policy to be held by and payable to the Mortgagee. If the Mortgagor shall not do so, the Mortgagee may do so without waiving the option to foreclose, and the cost thereof, with interest thereon from the date of payment at the same rate as specified in that note, shall also be secured by this mortgage. If any sum becomes payable under such policy, the Mortgagee may apply it to the indebtedness secured by this mortgage, or may permit the Mortgagor to use it for other purposes, without impairing the lien of this mortgage.
4. To commit, permit, or suffer no waste, impairment, or deterioration of the mortgaged property.
5. To pay all expenses reasonably incurred by the Mortgagee because of failure of the Mortgagor to comply with the agreements in that note or this mortgage, including reasonable attorneys' fees. The cost thereof, with interest thereon from the date of payment at the same rate as specified in that note, shall also be secured by this mortgage.
6. If any payment provided for in that note is not paid within thirty days after it becomes due, or if any agreement in this mortgage other than the agreement to make the payments is breached, the entire unpaid principal balance of that note shall immediately become due at the option of the Mortgagee, and the Mortgagee may foreclose this mortgage in the manner provided by law, and have the mortgaged property sold to satisfy or apply on the indebtedness hereby secured.
7. The rents and profits of the mortgaged property are also hereby mortgaged, and if proceedings to foreclose this mortgage shall be instituted, the court having jurisdiction thereof should appoint a receiver of the mortgaged property, and apply those rents and profits to the indebtedness hereby secured, regardless of the solvency of the Mortgagor or the adequacy of the security.

Signed in the presence of:

. . . .
(Witness)
Print Name: . . . .
. . . .
(Witness)
Print Name: . . . .

. . . . (Seal)
[As many lines for signature as there are mortgagors, with name and address of each typed under line for his signature]

State of . . . .
County of . . . .
(See category Documents and Records, topic Acknowledgments for individual form of acknowledgment.)

Mortgage for Execution by Corporation.—. . . . ., a corporation organized and existing under the laws of the State of . . . . ., the Mortgagor, in consideration of the principal sum specified in the promissory note hereafter described, received from . . . . . ., the Mortgagee, hereby, on this . . . . . ., mortgages to the Mortgagee the real property in . . . . . . County, Florida, described as: . . . . as security for the payment of the promissory note of which the following is a copy: . . . . [copy note, indenting, conforming signatures]. . . . . and agrees:

1. To make all payments required by that note and this mortgage promptly when due.
2. To pay all taxes, assessments, liens and encumbrances on that property promptly when due. If they are not promptly paid the Mortgagee may pay them without waiving the option to foreclose, and such payments, with interest thereon from the date of payment at the same rate as specified in that note, shall also be secured by this mortgage.
3. To keep all buildings now or hereafter on that land insured against damage by fire and lightning in the sum secured by this mortgage, by an insuror satisfactory to the Mortgagee, the insurance policy to be held by and payable to the Mortgagee. If the Mortgagor shall not do so, the Mortgagee may do so without waiving the option to foreclose, and the cost thereof, with interest thereon from the date of payment at the same rate as specified in that note, shall also be secured by this mortgage. If any sum becomes payable under such policy, the Mortgagee may apply it to the indebtedness secured by this mortgage, or may permit the Mortgagor to use it for other purposes, without impairing the lien of this mortgage.
4. To commit, permit, or suffer no waste, impairment, or deterioration of the mortgaged property.
5. To pay all expenses reasonably incurred by the Mortgagee because of failure of the Mortgagor to comply with the agreements in that note or this mortgage, including appellate costs and reasonable attorneys' fees. The cost thereof, with interest thereon from the date of payment at the same rate as specified in that note, shall also be secured by this mortgage.
6. If any payment provided for in that note is not paid within thirty days after it becomes due, or if any agreement in this mortgage other than the agreement to make the payments is breached, the entire unpaid principal balance of that note shall immediately become due at the option of the Mortgagee, and the Mortgagee may foreclose this mortgage in the manner provided by law, and have the mortgaged property sold to satisfy or apply on the indebtedness hereby secured.
7. The rents and profits of the mortgaged property are also hereby mortgaged, and if proceedings to foreclose this mortgage shall be instituted, the court having jurisdiction thereof should appoint a receiver of the mortgaged property, and apply those rents and profits to the indebtedness hereby secured, regardless of the solvency of the Mortgagor or the adequacy of the security.

(Name of Corporation)
By: . . . .
Print Name:
[Corporate Seal] Its . . . . President, Vice-President, or Chief Executive Officer
State of . . . . Address:
County of . . . .
(See category Documents and Records, topic Acknowledgments for corporate form of Acknowledgment.)

Assignment by Individual.—. . . . ., the holder of the mortgage executed by . . . . . to . . . . ., dated . . . . . and recorded in . . . . ., public records of . . . . . County, Florida, in

See note at head of Digest as to 1998 legislation covered.

See Topical Index in front part of this volume.

FL – 46

MORTGAGES OF REAL PROPERTY . . . *continued*

consideration of the sum of . . . . . received from . . . . ., hereby, on this . . . . ., assigns that mortgage and the note and debt described therein to . . . . .

. . . .
[As many lines for signature as there are holders, with name and address of each typed under line for his signature]

State of . . . .
County of . . . .
(See category Documents and Records, topic Acknowledgments for individual form of Acknowledgement.)

Assignment by Corporation.—. . . . ., a corporation organized and existing under the laws of the State of . . . . ., the holder of the mortgage executed by . . . . to . . . . ., dated . . . . . and recorded in . . . . ., public records of . . . . County, Florida, in consideration of the sum of . . . . . received from . . . . ., hereby, on this . . . . ., assigns that mortgage and the note and debt described therein to . . . . .

(Name of Corporation)
By: . . . .
Print Name:

[Corporate Seal]   Its . . . . President, Vice-President, or
                                Chief Executive Officer
State of . . . .   Address:
County of . . . .
(See category Documents and Records, topic Acknowledgments for corporate form of Acknowledgment.)

Partial Release by Individual.—. . . . ., the holder of the mortgage executed by . . . . . to . . . . ., dated . . . . . and recorded in . . . . ., public records of . . . . County, Florida, in consideration of . . . . ., hereby, on this . . . . ., releases from the lien of that mortgage the real property in that county described as:. . . . . . without impairing the lien of that mortgage on the remaining part of the property described in that mortgage.

. . . .
[As many lines for signature as there are holders, with name and address of each typed under line for his signature]

State of . . . .
County of . . . .
(See category Documents and Records, topic Acknowledgments for individual form of Acknowledgment.)

Partial Release by Corporation.—. . . . ., a corporation organized and existing under the laws of the State of . . . . ., the holder of the mortgage executed by . . . . . to . . . . ., dated . . . . . and recorded in . . . . ., public records of . . . . County, Florida, in consideration of . . . . ., hereby, on this . . . . ., releases from the lien of that mortgage the real property in that county described as: . . . . without impairing the lien of that mortgage on the remaining part of the property described in that mortgage.

(Name of Corporation)
By . . . .
Print Name:

[Corporate Seal]   Its . . . . President, Vice-President, or
                                Chief Executive Officer
State of . . . .   Address:
County of . . . .
(See category Documents and Records, topic Acknowledgments for corporate form of Acknowledgment.)

Satisfaction Executed by Individual.—. . . . ., the holder of the mortgage executed by . . . . . to . . . . ., dated . . . . . and recorded in . . . . ., public records of . . . . County, Florida, hereby, on this . . . . ., acknowledges full payment and satisfaction of that mortgage.

. . . .
[As many lines for signature as there are holders, with name and address of each typed under line for his signature]

State of . . . .
County of . . . .
(See category Documents and Records, topic Acknowledgments for individual form of Acknowledgment.)

Satisfaction Executed by Corporation.—. . . . ., a corporation organized and existing under the laws of the State of . . . . ., the holder of the mortgage executed by . . . . . to . . . . ., and recorded in . . . . ., public records of . . . . County, Florida, hereby, on this . . . . ., acknowledges full payment and satisfaction of that mortgage.

(Name of Corporation)
By: . . . .
Print Name:

[Corporate Seal]   Its . . . . President, Vice-President, or
                                Chief Executive Officer
State of . . . .   Address:
County of . . . .
(See category Documents and Records, topic Acknowledgments for corporate form of Acknowledgment.)

Chattel Mortgages.—See topic Chattel Mortgages.

PROPERTY

ABSENTEES:

Any person serving in or with Armed Forces, Red Cross, Merchant Marine or otherwise, during any period of time when state of hostilities exists between U.S. and any other power and for one year thereafter, who has been reported or listed as missing in action, interned in neutral country, beleaguered, besieged or captured by enemy is "absentee," as is any resident of Florida, or any person owning property in Florida, who disappears under circumstances indicating that he may have died, or may have disappeared as result of mental causes. (747.01).

Conservator of Absentee's Property.—Upon petition to circuit court by any person who would have interest in absentee's property or estate or who is dependent upon absentee for maintenance or support, notice will be given to all persons named in petition of hearing to determine absentee status. (747.03, 747.031). If court is satisfied that absentee status is appropriate, court has jurisdiction to appoint conservator where court finds conservator necessary. (747.02, 747.032). Conservator will have same powers and duties as guardian, and may be required by court to post bond. (747.035, 747.034 [744.38 and 744.39 referred to in 747.034 are repealed]).

Homestead Property.—Absentee considered incompetent for purposes of homestead exemption and restrictions on alienation. (747.011). See category Debtor and Creditor, topic Homesteads.

Summary Procedure.—Permits wife or next of kin if absentee has no wife to sell or transfer any of absentee's property which has gross value less than $5,000, or perform acts requiring absentee's consent in matters involving absentee's children or in any other matter in which gross value of subject matter is less than $5,000, to apply to circuit court for approval to sell, transfer, or perform. These acts may be done without full conservatorship; application may be made without attorney; and order may be entered without notice or hearing. Statutory pleading form provided. (747.051).

Nonconservator Procedure.—Where gross value of absentee's property is greater than $5,000, or in any other matter in which gross value of subject matter is greater than $5,000, spouse, or next of kin if no spouse, may petition circuit court for order authorizing action. Court may appoint guardian ad litem for absentee; hearing is required. Court may authorize action without having full conservatorship. (747.052).

Escheat.—

Uniform Disposition of Unclaimed Property Act adopted. (c. 717). Department of Banking and Finance shall administer and provide for enforcement of c. 717. (717.138). Unless filing date postponed after written request, all persons holding funds of $25 or more or other property must file verified reports before Nov. 1 each year as of June 30 next preceding, except in case of life insurance company, which must file before May 1 of each year as of Dec. 31 next preceding. (717.117).

C. 716 provides for escheat of all funds or other property having situs in state or belonging to resident, provides procedures for state to recover such funds or other property which are held by U.S. government. Provision is made for recovery by claimants within five years from receipt by state.

See also category Estates and Trusts, topic Descent and Distribution, subhead Escheat.

ADVERSE POSSESSION:

Character of Possession.—

Under color of title continued possession is required. For purpose of constituting adverse possession by any person claiming title founded upon written recorded instrument, or judgment or decree, land is deemed to have been possessed, where it has been usually cultivated or improved, or protected by substantial enclosure, or where it has been used for supply of fuel, or fencing timber for purpose of husbandry, or for ordinary use of occupant, or when known lot or single farm has been partly improved, portion of such farm or lot which may have been left not cleared or not enclosed according to usual course and custom of country, shall be deemed to have been occupied for same length of time as part improved or cultivated. Adverse possession commencing after Dec. 31, 1945 shall not be deemed adverse possession under color of title until instrument upon which claim of title is founded is recorded. (95.16).

Without color of title actual continued occupation is required. For purpose of constituting adverse possession by any person claiming title not founded upon written instrument, judgment or decree, land is deemed to have been occupied where it has been protected by substantial enclosure or where it has been usually cultivated or improved. To acquire title by adverse possession without color of title, claimant must make return of property for taxation within one year after his entry into possession and must pay all taxes and special improvement liens thereon before such taxes become delinquent. (95.18).

Duration of Possession.—Actual continued occupation without color of title or continued occupation and possession under color of title for seven years is necessary to confer title. (95.16; 95.18). However, 20 years after deed is recorded or will purporting to convey property is probated, no person can assert claim to property against claimants under deed or will or their successors in title. (95.231).

Easements may be created by prescription if there is a continuous, open and visible use, under an adverse claim of right, for 20 years. (100 So.2d 57).

Disabilities.—Rights of persons under disabilities are subject to being barred by Marketable Record Title Act. (712.04). See topic Real Property.

CONVEYANCES:

See topic Deeds.

CURTESY:

Curtesy abolished. (732.111). See category Estates and Trusts, topic Descent and Distribution, subhead Right to Elective Share.

See note at head of Digest as to 1998 legislation covered.

See Topical Index in front part of this volume.

DEEDS:

See topic Real Property for types of estates.

No estate or interest of freehold, or for a term of more than one year, in land may be created, assigned or released except by written instrument or will or by act and operation of law. (689.01).

Execution.—Deeds must be in writing, signed in presence of at least two witnesses, who attest the same by signing their names. (689.01). Seal is not necessary for execution of deed. (689.01).

Acknowledgment is not necessary to validity of deed. (689.01). However, to entitle any deed to be recorded execution must be acknowledged, proved by subscribing witness or legalized or authenticated by civil law notary or notary public who affixes official seal. (695.03). Deeds must contain name and address of each signatory legibly printed, typewritten or stamped beneath signature, name and address of natural person who prepared deed or under whose supervision it was prepared legibly printed, typewritten or stamped, name of each witness and notary public legibly printed, typewritten or stamped below signature, 3 inch square at top right-hand corner on first page and 1" by 3" space at top right-hand corner on each subsequent page for use by clerk, and name and address of each grantee legibly printed, typewritten or stamped. (695.26[1]). These requirements do not apply to instrument executed before July 1, 1991, decree, order, judgment or writ of any court, instrument executed outside of state, will, plat, and instrument prepared or executed by any public officer other than notary public. (695.26[3]). For circumstances in which spouse must join, see category Family, topic Husband and Wife; also category Debtor and Creditor, topic Homesteads.

Recording.—Deeds must be recorded in the county where the land conveyed is situated in order to be effective as against creditors and subsequent purchasers for a valuable consideration without notice. (695.01[1]). Grantees by quitclaim shall be deemed bona fide purchasers. (695.01[2]).

As condition precedent to recording of any deed transferring interest in real property, grantor or grantee or agent for grantee shall execute and file return with Clerk of Circuit Court. Return shall state parcel identification number maintained by county property appraiser in manner prescribed by department. Return shall state actual consideration paid for interest in real property. Return shall not be recorded, or otherwise become public record and shall be confidential as provided in §193.074 with certain exceptions provided in statute. This exemption is subject to Open Government Sunset Review Act in accordance with §119.14. Failure of any grantee or agent to execute and file such return does not impair validity of any deed transferring interest in real property but does subject any person who is required to file return with penalty. (§201.022).

For recording fee, see category Documents and Records, topic Records.

Operation and Effect.—Deed without words of limitation, such as heirs or successors, vests fee simple title or other whole estate or interest which grantor had power to dispose of when deed made unless contrary intention appears in deed. (689.10).

For effect of addition of words "trustee" or "as trustee" to name of grantee, see category Estates and Trusts, topic Trusts, subhead Beneficiaries.

Land trusts are recognized if the recorded instrument confers upon a trustee power to manage and dispose of realty. Permits persons to deal without inquiry of trustee's authority or provisions of unrecorded agreement. If interest transferred is within trustee's power as contained in recorded instrument, such interest is free of beneficiaries' claims and claims of dower. (689.07; 689.071).

Corporation may convey lands by deed sealed with the corporate or common seal and signed in its name by its president, vice-president or chief executive officer. (692.01). Corporations may also convey lands in same manner as individuals; that is with two witnesses and without necessity of seal. (689.01). Person signing must acknowledge in official capacity.

Tax.—There is excise tax on deeds at rate of 70¢ on each $100 of consideration (except in Dade County where tax is 60¢). Consideration includes money paid or agreed to be paid, discharge of obligation, and amount of any mortgage or other encumbrance whether or not indebtedness is assumed. (201.02). Required stamps must be placed on deed prior to recording, unless provisions of §§201.132 and 201.133 apply. See category Taxation, topic Taxes, subhead Stamp Taxes. In addition, charter counties have been authorized by Florida legislature to levy discretionary surtax on certain documents. Reference should be made to applicable county clerk's office of county where recording is to occur to determine whether surtax has been levied and if so, in what amount.

Curative acts have been passed validating certain defectively executed, acknowledged, or witnessed deeds and powers of attorney. (692.02; 694.01-.15; 695.03; 695.05-.06, 95.231).

Forms.—Warranty deed may be in following form:

Form

This indenture, made this _____ day of _____, A.D. _____ between ___ _____ of the county of _____ in the state of _____, party of the first part, whose post office address is _____, and _____, of the county of _____ ____, in the state of _____, party of the second part, whose post office address is _____, and whose Social Security Number is _____ witnesseth: that the said party of the first part, for and in consideration of the sum of _____ dollars, to him in hand paid by the said party of the second part, the receipt whereof is hereby acknowledged, has granted, bargained and sold to the said party of the second part, his heirs and assigns forever, the following described land, to-wit Parcel Identification Number _____

And the said party of the first part does hereby fully warrant the title to said land, and will defend the same against the lawful claims of all persons whomsoever. (689.02; 695.26).

. . . .

Print Name: . . . .
                                        Print Name: . . . .
. . . .

Print Name: . . . .

State of . . . .
County of . . . .
(See category Documents and Records, topic Acknowledgments for proper form of acknowledgment.)

This instrument was prepared by (name of natural person), (address).

All warranty deeds must include blank space for property appraiser's parcel identification number, which number, if available, shall be entered on deed before it is recorded and blank spaces for social security numbers of grantees named in deed, if available, which numbers may be entered on deed before it is recorded. Failure to include such blank spaces, or parcel identification number, or any social security number, or inclusion of incorrect parcel identification number or social security number, does not affect validity of conveyance or recordability of deed. Parcel identification number does not constitute part of legal description of property. Social security number shall not serve as designation of grantee. (689.02[2]).

Deeds executed substantially in this form are held to be warranty deeds with full common law covenants. (689.03).

Quitclaim deed may be in substantially same form except to substitute "remise, release and quitclaim" in place of words of grant and eliminate warranty clause.

DEEDS OF TRUST:

See category Mortgages, topic Mortgages of Real Property.

DOWER:

Dower and curtesy are abolished in Florida. (732.111).

See category Estates and Trusts, topic Descent and Distribution, subhead Surviving Spouse and Right to Elective Share.

ESCHEAT:

See topic Absentees, subhead Escheat; also category Estates and Trusts, topic Descent and Distribution, subhead Escheat.

LANDLORD AND TENANT:

Florida Statutes governing rights and liabilities of landlords and tenants is divided into three parts. (c. 83). Part I governs nonresidential tenancies, Part II governs residential tenancies and Part III governs self service storage space. Part I applies to all rentals for business and commercial purposes. Part II applies to all residential landlord-tenant relationships (excluding transient occupancies) including those for rental of structure that is furnished, with or without rent, as incident to employment for use as home, residence or sleeping place by one or more persons, structure for use as home, residence or sleeping place by one or more persons who maintain common household, and mobile home. (83.42-.43). Part II is patterned after Uniform Residential Landlord and Tenant Act.

Under Part II landlord is required to maintain residential premises in accordance with all building, housing and health codes and, if none applies, in good repair and safe condition. (83.51[1]). Landlord is additionally required to comply with certain statutory obligations of maintenance including extermination of certain rodents and insects, lock and keys, clean and safe condition of common areas, garbage removal and functioning facilities for heat during winter and hot and running water (83.51[2]), unless otherwise agreed in writing. (83.51[2][a]). Unless otherwise agreed in writing, at commencement of tenancy of single-family home or duplex, landlord shall install working smoke detection device. (83.51[2][b]). Unconscionable provisions in rental agreement are unenforceable. (83.45). Duties are also placed by Act on tenants to comply with housing codes and to keep premises clean and sanitary. (83.52). Tenants can raise any defense, other than payment, they may have to action for possession based upon nonpayment of rent but before such defenses can be raised they must deposit in registry of court rent claimed to be owed and rent which accrues during pendency of suit. Defense of material noncompliance of duty to maintain may only be raised by tenant if seven days have elapsed after written notice to landlord. (83.60).

Common law rules generally govern relationships with respect to nonresidential premises.

Kinds of Tenancies.—Tenancy at will is created unless there is a written lease signed by lessor in nonresidential tenancy. (83.01). If tenancy has been created by writing from period to period and term is unlimited, it shall be tenancy at will. (83.02). In residential tenancy, if rental agreement contains no provision as to duration of tenancy, duration is determined by periods for which rental is payable. (83.46[2]). Such tenancy runs from year to year, month to month or week to week, depending on period for which rent is payable. (as to nonresidential property 83.01; as to residential property 83.46). If, however, dwelling unit is furnished without rent as incident to employment and there is no agreement as to duration of tenancy, duration is determined by periods for which wages are payable. (83.46[3]).

Tenancy for fixed term is created by written agreement signed by lessor and, if for more than one year, lease must be witnessed by at least two subscribing witnesses. (689.01).

Tenancy at sufferance is created when any tenancy of written limited term expires and tenant holds over without renewing in writing. (83.04).

Recording.—Lease for one year or longer, to be effectual against creditors and subsequent purchasers for valuable consideration and without notice, must be recorded. (695.01). However, tenant's possession puts purchaser on inquiry as to his rights. (53 Fla. 1076, 43 So. 771).

Rent.—When a tenant refuses to surrender possession of premises at end of term of lease, landlord may demand double rent for duration of wrongful possession. (As to nonresidential property 83.06, as to residential property 83.58.) If tenant fails to pay rent when due, landlord has right to obtain possession. (As to nonresidential property 83.05, as to residential property 83.625.)

See note at head of Digest as to 1998 legislation covered.

See Topical Index in front part of this volume.

LANDLORD AND TENANT . . . *continued*

Security Deposits.—When residential lease deposit for advance rent or security is held by landlord, landlord must deposit in separate interest bearing or non-interest bearing account or post surety bond. If deposit is held in interest bearing account tenant shall collect interest of either 75% of annualized average interest rate payable on account or 5% per annum, simple interest, at landlord's option. If landlord posts surety bond he shall also pay to tenant simple interest of 5% per annum. Landlord must give notice within 30 days to tenant of manner in which deposit is being held. Upon termination of lease, landlord, within 15 days, must return deposit plus interest or notify tenant as to claim against deposit. If landlord fails to comply with statutory notice requirements for imposing claim upon tenant's security deposit, landlord forfeits right to impose said claim. Provisions do not apply to transient rentals by hotels or motels as defined by Florida law or in certain instances governed by federal law. Prevailing party in suit over security deposits entitled to costs and reasonable attorney's fees. (83.49).

Liens.—Landlords of business property have a lien for unpaid rent: (1) Upon agricultural products raised on the land; (2) upon all other property of lessee, his sublessee or assigns, usually kept on premises; (3) upon all other property of defendant. First class of liens are superior to all others; second class are superior to any others acquired subsequent to bringing of property on premises; third class dates from levying of distress warrant. (83.08).

Landlords of residential property have lien on all personal property of tenant located on premises. This lien is in addition to all other liens upon such property which landlord may acquire by law. (713.691[1]).

Termination of Tenancy.—Where tenancy is from year to year, it may be terminated by not less than three months for business premises or 60 days for residential premises notice prior to end of any annual period; tenancy from quarter to quarter, by not less than 45 days for business premises or 30 days for residential premises notice prior to end of any quarter, tenancy from month to month, by not less than 15 days notice for both business and residential premises prior to end of any monthly period; tenancy from week to week by not less than seven days notice for both business and residential premises prior to end of any weekly period. (83.03 & 83.57).

As to residential premises, landlord or tenant may terminate tenancy upon one or more of various grounds applicable to each, set forth in 83.56. Tenant is given statutory right to cure with respect to certain of tenant's defaults. (83.56). With respect to residential tenancies, landlord may terminate lease due to nonpayment of rent by tenant only if default continues for three days after written notice of intention to terminate is given by landlord to tenant. (83.56[3]). Tenant may raise defenses of noncompliance with 83.51(1), retaliatory conduct (83.64) or other defenses tenant may have (83.60).

Holding Over.—As to business premises, where tenant holds over in possession without renewal in writing, after term of written lease has expired, such holding over is deemed to be tenancy at sufferance and mere payment or acceptance of rent will not be construed to be renewal; but if such holding over is with written consent of lessor, it will be deemed tenancy at will. (83.04).

As to a residential premises, if tenant holds over and continues in possession after expiration of rental agreement without permission of landlord, landlord may recover possession of dwelling unit in manner provided for in 83.59, which includes right to a summary proceeding. (83.58). Landlord's agent is not permitted to take any action other than initial filing of complaint, unless landlord's agent is attorney. (83.59[2]).

Dispossession.—As to business premises, summary proceeding is provided by which landlord may obtain judgment for possession against tenant and writ directing sheriff to put landlord in possession. (83.21-.251).

As to residential premises after entry of judgment in favor of landlord for possession, clerk will issue writ commanding sheriff to put landlord in possession 24 hours after sheriff posts notice on premises (83.62) and landlord may not resort to self-help (83.59[3]).

Distress.—Not available to a landlord of residential property (713.69[3]) but can be resorted to by landlord of business property (83.11-.19). Defendant may have property restored by posting bond. (83.14). After judgment for plaintiff, property not restored to defendant may be sold after two advertisements, first being at least ten days before sale. (83.19).

Unlawful Entry, Forcible Entry and Unlawful Detainer.—These remedies are available to landlord of business premises (82.01-.101) but not to landlord of residential premises (82.02[2], 82.04[2], 82.081[2]).

Mobile Home Park Leases.—Florida Mobile Home Act (c. 723), which governs residential leases of mobile home lots where ten or more lots are available for rent. When fewer than ten lots, governed by Part II c. 83. (723.002[1]).

Mobile home owners have right to peaceably assemble in common areas, to canvas other owners regarding matters relevant to park association, to communicate among themselves and to invite public officers and candidates to speak before them. (723.054, 723.055). Mobile home owner or owner of lot in mobile home subdivision has right to sell home within park. (723.058). Purchaser, if otherwise qualifies, has right to assume seller's rental agreement and become tenant subject to reasonable approval of park owner. Rent to purchaser may be increased after term of assumed rental agreement if increase was disclosed before purchaser's occupancy. Lifetime leases are non-assumable unless so provided in rental agreement or transferee is lessee's spouse. (723.059). Mobile home owner must comply with building codes and park rules and regulations and keep lot clean. (723.023). Park owner must comply with building codes, maintain common areas and utility connections, provide access to common areas and enforce rules. (723.022).

Mobile Home Owners' Association.—If mobile home park owner offers his park for sale, officers of homeowners' association must be notified of offer, stating price and terms and conditions of sale. Tenants, through mobile home owner's association, have right to purchase park if they meet park owner's offer by executing contract within 45 days of mailing of notice. If contract is not executed and owner thereafter offers park at lower price than specified in notice, tenants have additional ten days to meet offer by executing contract. If owner receives bona fide offer to purchase park that he intends to consider or make counter offer to, he must notify officers of homeowners' association of offer and disclose price and material terms and conditions and consider any offer made by tenants. (723.071). Park owner may record affidavit attesting to his compliance with statute on which title examiners may rely. (723.072). Certain transfers, such as those to park owner's heirs, gifts, devises, transfers to affiliated corporations or from partnership to its partners, transfers in connection with financing park, and where park is exchanged for other real property, are exempted from provisions of this statute. (723.071). Similarly, owner of recreational facilities exclusively serving mobile home subdivision may not sell facilities without first giving right to homeowners' association. (723.074).

In order to exercise their purchase rights, mobile home park tenants shall form mobile home owners' association, which shall be for profit or not for profit corporation, in which written consent to be shareholders or members has been given in writing by at least two-thirds of mobile homes. (723.075). Statute provides content of association's articles of incorporation. (723.077). By-laws of association shall provide for administration by board of directors and shall provide for meetings of board and of members. (723.078). Statute provides further details for operation of association. (723.079). Any nonprofit association may conduct bingo games as provided in §849.0931. (723.079[8]).

Rental Agreements.—Agreement must be for at least one year and must contain lot rental amount and services included and all security payments held for more than three months must be handled pursuant to §83.49 (see subhead Security Deposits, supra). Lot rental amount may only be increased in accordance with §723.031(5). (723.031). Statute provides that court may refuse to enforce or limit any rental agreement, rental amount, rent increase or change found unreasonable. (723.033). Lot rental amount in excess of market rent as defined in §723.033(4) shall be considered unreasonable. (723.033[3]). Park owner must give mobile home owners 90 days' notice of rental increase, reduction in services or change in regulations. Procedure is established for meeting with owner to discuss proposed change, and for mediation if majority of mobile home owners state in writing that change is unreasonable. (723.037). Provision for dispute settlement provides for rules to be established to govern proceedings. (723.038). Any party may initiate action to enforce agreement arising from mediation which has been reduced to writing. (723.038[7]).

Eviction.—Park owner may evict mobile home owner only for nonpayment of rent for five days after written demand, conviction for violation of law deemed detrimental to health, safety or welfare of other residents, violation of park rule or rental agreement, change in land use (upon at least one year notice) or failure to qualify as tenant. Procedure established for park owner to file complaint in county where lot is situated to evict mobile home owner. Notice must be posted on premises and sent by certified or registered mail, return receipt requested, addressed to mobile home owner at last known address. (723.061). In action based on nonpayment of rent, mobile home owner may raise defense of noncompliance with statute. Statute provides procedure for payment of rent into court registry and for disbursement of funds to park owner. Failure to pay rent into court registry constitutes waiver of all defenses except payment entitling park owner to default. (723.063).

Disclosure.—Mobile home park owner of park with 26 or more lots shall file prospectus with Division of Florida Land Sales, Condominiums, and Mobile Homes before entering into enforceable rental agreement. Park owner must deliver copy of prospectus or offering circular to prospective lessee prior to entering into enforceable rental agreement. Upon delivery of prospectus, rental agreement is voidable by lessee for 15 days. (723.011). Statute prescribes information about park and park owner that must be in prospectus or offering circular. (723.012). Any person who relies upon false or misleading statement in advertising materials may rescind contract for purchase of mobile home or placement of mobile home in lot or collect damages. (723.017). Park owner cannot require mobile home owner to purchase equipment from him (723.043), to make improvements without disclosure prior to occupancy (723.042) or to pay more for utilities sold by park owner than was charged park owner (723.045) and cannot collect fees and assessments other than those which were previously disclosed (723.041).

Enforcement.—Division of Florida Land Sales, Condominiums and Mobile Homes has power to enforce statute. (723.005). Division may impose civil penalty against park owner or home owners' association for violation of law. (723.006). Any amounts collected will be credited to The Division's Trust Fund, created to defray Division costs of administering statute. (723.009).

Self Service Storage Space.—Lease of space for storage in building to tenants who have access to store and remove personal property is covered in Part III of c. 83, "Self-Storage Facility Act". (83.801-.809). Remedies for nonpayment of rent, and for post-judgment remedies, including sale of stored property are provided for. (83.805-.806).

LEASES:

See topic Landlord and Tenant.

PERPETUITIES:

Nonvested property interest in real or personal property is invalid unless when interest is created, it is certain to vest or terminate no later than 21 years after death of individual then alive or interest either vests or terminates within 90 years after its creation. (689.225[2][a]).

General power of appointment not presently exercisable because of condition precedent is invalid unless when power is created, condition precedent is certain to be satisfied or become impossible to satisfy no later than 21 years after death of individual then alive or condition precedent is satisfied or becomes impossible to satisfy within 90 years after its creation. (689.225[2][b]).

Rule is inapplicable to: Any interest which does not violate or is exempt by statute from common law rule; certain powers of trustees; and certain leases to commence in future, certain commitments to enter into lease with subtenants and leasehold mortgagees and certain options to purchase or lease. (689.225[5][a]).

With respect to any matter relating to validity of interest within rule against perpetuities, unless contrary intent appears, it shall be presumed that transferor of interest intended that interest be valid. (689.225[7]).

Statute applies to nonvested property interest or power of appointment that is created on or after Oct. 1, 1988 and power of appointment that was created before Oct. 1, 1988 but only to extent that it remains unexercised on Oct. 1, 1988. Nonvested property

See note at head of Digest as to 1998 legislation covered.

See Topical Index in front part of this volume.

FL – 49

PERPETUITIES ... *continued*

interest or power of appointment created by exercise of power of appointment is created when power is irrevocably exercised or when revocable exercise becomes irrevocable. (689.225[6]).

Upon petition of interested person, if certain conditions are met, court shall reform disposition in manner that closely approximates transferor's manifested plan of distribution. (689.225[4]).

PERSONAL PROPERTY:

Uniform Commercial Code adopted. (cc. 670-680). See category Business Regulation and Commerce, topic Commercial Code.

Personal property may be held by husband and wife as tenants by entirety. (689.15).

POWERS OF ATTORNEY:

Power of Attorney.—Conveyance may be made under recordable power of attorney, which must be recorded in order that conveyance will be given full effect. See topic Records.

Unknown death of grantor does not invalidate act by holder of power of attorney. (709.01).

Formalities of execution and acknowledgment are same as those for deed when real property is involved. See topic Deeds.

Durable Family Power of Attorney.—Principal may create durable power of attorney designating person as his attorney in fact by executing power of attorney. Power of attorney must be in writing, must be executed with same formalities required for conveyance of real property by Florida law, state relationship of parties, if any, and include words "This durable power of attorney shall not be affected by disability of the principal except as provided by statute" or similar words clearly showing principal's intent that power conferred shall be exercisable from date specified in instrument, notwithstanding later disability or incapacity of principal, unless otherwise provided by statute. Not-for-profit corporation organized for charitable or religious purposes in this state which has qualified as court-appointed guardian prior to Jan. 1, 1996, and which is tax-exempt under 26 U.S.C. §501(c)(3), may also act as attorney in fact. (709.08). Power of attorney is exercisable as of date of execution. Power of attorney may include authority for attorney-in-fact to arrange for and consent to medical, therapeutical, and surgical procedures for principal, including administration of drugs. All acts done by attorney in fact pursuant to power conferred during any period of disability or incompetence have same effect, and inure to benefit of and bind principal or his heirs, devisees, and personal representatives, as if principal were competent and not disabled. (709.08).

Durable power of attorney is nondelegable (except to transfer agent or similar person with authority to register any stocks, bonds or other securities), is valid until time principal dies, revokes power or is adjudged incompetent, unless court determines otherwise. (709.08). Durable power of attorney is temporarily suspended when petition to determine competence of or to appoint guardian for principal has been filed. Whenever emergency arises between time petition is filed and adjudication attorney-in-fact may petition court for permission to exercise power. (709.08). Property subject to durable power of attorney includes all real and personal property owned by principal, principal's interest in all property held in joint tenancy, principal's interest in all non-homestead property held in tenancy by entirety, and all property over which principal holds power of appointment. Attorney-in-fact is not permitted, when principal is married, to mortgage or convey homestead property without joinder of spouse or spouse's legal guardian, but joinder may be accomplished through exercise of power of attorney. (709.08).

Any third party may rely upon authority granted in durable power of attorney until third party has received notice as provided under 709.08(5). Third party who has not received notice under §709.08(5) may request affidavit from attorney-in-fact.

Generally, attorney-in-fact has full authority to perform, without prior court approval, every act authorized and specifically enumerated in durable power of attorney. (709.08[7]).

Deployment-Contingent Power of Attorney, which may be signed in advance and go into effect upon deployment of principal, are afforded full force and effect by Florida courts. (709.11).

Members of Armed Forces.—Terms "missing" or "missing in action" applied to grantors of powers in connection with any activity pertaining to hostilities in which U.S. is engaged, do not constitute actual knowledge or actual notice of death of principal and do not constitute revocation of agency. (709.01).

REAL PROPERTY:

All interests in real estate which were recognized by the common law are recognized in Florida, except that no real estate may be entailed. (689.14). The doctrine of survivorship as to joint tenancies has been abolished, unless the instrument shall expressly provide for it, but where property is conveyed to both husband and wife they are presumed to be seized of estate by entirety with resulting survivorship (66 Fla. 427, 63 So. 822) and in case of divorce former spouses become tenants in common and remain so even though they subsequently remarry (689.15).

Rule in Shelley's Case.—Abolished in Florida. (689.17).

Foreign conveyances or encumbrances when affecting Florida property, must be in conformity with laws of Florida, both as to validity of instrument and as to acknowledgment entitling instrument to record. (689.01, 695.03).

Condominium Act recognizes condominium form of real property ownership, prescribes rights and obligations of developers, rights and obligations of condominium association, phase condominiums, mixed-use condominiums, regulation and disclosure prior to sale of residential condominium, conversions to condominiums and method of creation, and rights and liabilities with respect thereto. (718.101-.312).

Cooperative Act.—Residential cooperatives recognized as form of real property ownership in which legal title vests in corporation and beneficial use is evidenced by ownership interests in association. (c. 719).

Homeowner's Association.—Certain types of homeowner's associations are regulated. (617.301-.312).

Liability for Improper Legal Description.—In any action relating to real property, court may award costs, attorneys' fees and actual damages to prevailing party that has been impaired by inaccurate or improper legal description in instrument prepared by another party. (697.10).

Marketable Record Title is defined by statute, as title held by any person having legal capacity to own land in Florida who alone, or with predecessors in title has been vested with any estate in land of record for more than 30 years. Person shall have marketable record title to such land free and clear of all claims except for exceptions defined in §712.03. (712.02). In general, owner of any interest in or lien upon land who is not in actual possession must file statutory notice every 30 years to assure that interest or lien is not extinguished. (c. 712). See categories Documents and Records, topic Records; Mortgages, topic Mortgages of Real Property.

Model Land Sales Practices Act adopted with substantial modifications including major revisions in 1988. (c. 498).

Bert J. Harris, Jr. Private Property Rights Protection Act adopted to provide relief for real property owners from certain government actions. (c. 70; 163.3181[4]; 163.3184[5]).

Foreign corporations and alien business organizations that own real property or mortgages on real property in Florida, whether or not they transact business in Florida, must maintain registered office and registered agent in Florida and file notice of same with Secretary of State. (607.0505). Reference should be made to §607.0505(1)(b) for penalties for failure to comply.

Time-Share Facilities.—Sales and operation of vacation plan, vacation club and time-share properties are regulated. (cc. 721, 475).

Local Strategic Plans.—There is to be state review and approval of local plans regarding land use that apply to areas of critical state concern (380.05) and of plans for developments of regional impact (380.06).

Deeds. See topic Deeds.

Rule Against Perpetuities.—Florida Uniform Statutory Rule Against Perpetuities enacted in 1988. (689.225).

See topic Deeds; categories Debtor and Creditor, topic Homesteads; Estates and Trusts, topic Descent and Distribution; Family, topic Husband and Wife.

TRUST DEEDS:

See category Mortgages, topic Mortgages of Real Property.

TAXATION

ADMINISTRATION:

State Taxes.—See topics Alcoholic Beverage Taxes, Cigarette and Other Tobacco Product Taxes, Estate Tax, Gasoline and Special Fuels Taxes, Income Tax, Oil and Gas Production Tax, Mineral Severance Tax, Pollution Abatement Authority Tax, Race Tracks and Jai Alai Frontons Tax, Sales and Use Taxes, Stamp Tax, and Unemployment Compensation Tax.

County, School and Municipal Taxes.—See topics Occupational License Tax, Property (Ad Valorem) Taxes, and Sales and Use Taxes, subhead Discretionary County Sales and Use Surtax.

Exemptions.—See individual topics.

Penalties.—See individual topics.

Interstate and Intergovernmental Cooperation.—Department of Revenue is authorized to make available, for official purposes, to proper officer of U.S. or any state information to comply with any formal agreement for mutual exchange of state information, to Bankruptcy Trustees, to law enforcement and prosecutorial agencies, and to others as provided by statute. All information sharing is subject to statutory confidentiality restrictions. (213.053).

Taxpayer Bill of Rights.—Guarantees that rights, privacy, and property of taxpayers are adequately safeguarded and protected during tax assessment, collection, and enforcement processes. For details, see statute. (213.015).

ALCOHOLIC BEVERAGE TAXES:

State excise tax on malt beverages, wines, and other alcoholic beverages paid by consumer and collected by manufacturer or distributor. Tax ranges from 48¢ per gallon of bulk beer to $9.53 per gallon of liquor containing over 55.780% alcohol. (cc. 563–565). State also imposes surcharge of 10¢ on each ounce of liquor and on each four ounces of wine, 6¢ on each 12 ounces of cider, and 4¢ on each 12 ounces of beer sold at retail for consumption on premises. (561.501).

CIGARETTE AND OTHER TOBACCO PRODUCT TAXES:

Cigarette Tax.—Imposed at varying rates dependent upon weight and length of cigarette and packaging. (210.02). Any person who possesses or transports unstamped packages of cigarettes for purpose of sale, or sells or offers to sell cigarettes in violation of 210.01-210.22, or willfully attempts to avoid or evade tax is guilty of misdemeanor of first degree. Alteration or forgery of stamps is felony of third degree. (210.18). Possession of less than 50 cartons of unstamped cigarettes is misdemeanor of second degree. Possession of more than 50 cartons of unstamped cigarettes creates presumption of knowledge that they are untaxed and is felony of third degree. All of above crimes are punishable as provided in 775.082, 775.083, or 775.084. (210.18).

Tobacco Product Tax.—Imposed upon all tobacco products in this state and upon any person engaged in business as distributor thereof at rate of 25% of wholesale sales price of such tobacco products. (210.30). "Tobacco products" means loose tobacco suitable for smoking; snuff; plug and twist tobacco; fine cuts and other chewing tobacco; shorts; refuse scraps; clippings, cuttings, and sweepings of tobacco, and other

See note at head of Digest as to 1998 legislation covered.

See Topical Index in front part of this volume.

CIGARETTE AND OTHER TOBACCO PRODUCT TAXES... *continued*
kinds and forms of tobacco prepared in such manner as to be suitable for chewing, but "tobacco products" does not include cigarettes, as defined by §210.01(1), or cigars. (210.25).

COAL SEVERANCE TAX:

See topic Mineral Severance Tax.

CORPORATE STOCK TAX:

See topics Intangible Personal Property Tax and Stamp Tax.

CORPORATE LICENSE TAXES:

See categories Business Organizations, topic Corporations; Business Regulation and Commerce, topics Banks and Banking, Licenses, Business and Professional.

ESTATE TAX:

Gross and net estate determined under applicable federal revenue act. (198.01). Where not otherwise provided for, rules of construction applicable to estate and inheritance tax laws of U.S. apply. (198.35). Department may compromise or settle any penalty imposed (198.18) and may sue to recover any tax, penalty or interest (198.25).

Tax Upon Estates of Resident Decedents.—Sum equal to amount by which credit allowable under federal estate, inheritance, legacy and succession taxes exceeds aggregate of all constitutionally valid estate, inheritance, legacy and succession taxes actually paid to several states (other than Florida). (Const. arts. 7, 5; 198.02).

Tax Upon Estates of Nonresident Decedents.—Tax on all realty situate and tangible personalty having actual situs in this state, intangible personalty having business situs in Florida, and stocks, bonds, debentures, notes and other securities or obligations of corporations organized under Florida laws, is equal to proportion of credit allowable under federal revenue act for estate, inheritance, legacy, and succession taxes actually paid to the several states as value of property taxable in Florida bears to value of entire gross estate. (198.03).

Tax Upon Estates of Alien Decedents.—Tax on all realty situate and tangible personalty having actual situs in, and intangible personalty physically present in this state is equal to proportion of credit allowable under applicable federal revenue act for estate, inheritance, legacy and succession taxes actually paid to several states as value of property taxable in Florida bears to value of estate taxable by U.S. Rules regarding situs detailed in statute. (198.04).

Residence.—Decedent residing in Florida for greater part of 12 consecutive months of 24 months prior to death, presumed to have died Florida resident. (198.015).

Generation-Skipping Transfer Tax.—If original transferor is resident of Florida, tax is amount by which credit allowable under federal generation-skipping transfer tax provisions for state legacy taxes exceeds aggregate of all constitutionally valid taxes actually paid on same transfer to other states. (198.021). If original transferor not resident of Florida at time of original transfer, but property transferred includes real or personal property in Florida, tax is equal to amount of credit allowable for state legacy taxes under I.R.C., reduced by proportion of total credit as value of transferred property taxable by all states other than Florida bears to value of gross generation-skipping transfer. (198.031). Person liable for payment of federal generation-skipping transfer tax is liable for Florida generation-skipping tax. Due upon taxable distribution or taxable termination as determined under federal provisions. Delinquent on day after last day allowed for filing return for generation-skipping transfer. If not paid before delinquent, interest is imposed at rate of 1% per month on unpaid portion. (198.155).

Notice.—Personal representative, within two months after decedent's death or after qualifying as such, must give written notice to Department on its form. (198.12).

Necessary Returns.—Personal representative of every estate required to file federal estate tax return, must file Florida return consisting of executed copy of federal return and any supplemental data necessary to determine correct Florida tax. Such return is made in case of every decedent who, at time of death, was not resident of U.S. and whose gross estate includes real property situated in Florida, tangible personal property having actual situs in Florida, and intangible personal property physically present within Florida. (198.13[1]). Every person required to file federal return reporting generation-skipping must file with Department on or before last date prescribed for filing federal return, return consisting of duplicate copy of federal return. (198.13). Department of Revenue must allow extension of time for filing return if personal representative files copy of approved Federal extension request with Department within 30 days after receiving approved Federal extension. (198.15). On failure to make return, or on making of false return, Department must make up return from its own knowledge and information, which will be prima facie good and sufficient for all legal purposes. (198.15).

Payment or Collection.—Tax due and payable by personal representative on or before last date prescribed by law for paying federal estate tax pursuant to initial federal estate tax return. Tax receipt must be given on any payment of tax. (198.19). Department of Revenue must extend time for payment of tax or any part of tax if time for paying Federal estate tax is extended, provided personal representative files with Department copy of approved Federal extension notice within 30 days after receiving such notice. (198.15). No extension for more than one year and aggregate of extensions not to exceed ten years. (198.15). If time for payment of tax is extended, interest accrues thereon at rate of 1% per month of amount due. (198.15).

Deficiency in tax or any tax payment not received by Department as provided in 198.15, will, in addition to other penalties, bear interest at rate of 1% per month of amount due. (198.16). Executor shall file written notice with Department within 60 days after final determination of deficiency in federal estate tax. (198.16). If deficiency is due to negligence or intentional disregard of law, with knowledge but without intent to defraud, penalty of 10% per annum, and if wilfully made with intent to defraud, penalty is 100% of total deficiency.

Assessment.—Taxes must be determined and assessed within four years after return was filed or within 90 days after assessment of deficiency in Federal Estate Tax may be made. (198.28). In case of fraud or failure to file return, tax may be assessed at any time. (198.28).

Refund by Department if tax paid in excess of amount due but no refund after four years from payment of tax, unless notice of final determination of federal tax is filed with Department within 60 days from such determination. (198.29).

Notice to and Discharge of Executor or Administrator.—Department must notify executor or administrator filing completed return and making application for determination of tax and discharge from personal liability of amount of tax due within one year, and on payment thereof executor or administrator is discharged from any personal liability for any additional tax thereafter found due; entitled to receive written discharge from Department. (198.19). Discharge does not release gross estate from lien of any additional tax while it remains in hands of executor or administrator, heirs, devisees, or distributees; but it does release estate after it has passed to bona fide purchaser for value. (198.19). Final account of executor or administrator of estate, value of which exceeds $60,000, will not be allowed unless such account shows all as paid. (198.26).

Waiver of Lien.—Department may release all property from lien if tax liability, if any, has been fully discharged. (198.22). Property of estate is discharged of liability for estate or inheritance taxes under this Act after ten years from date of filing notice of death of decedent with Department, or after ten years from date of filing estate tax return with Department, whichever is earlier, unless Department records notice of lien in office of clerk of circuit court in county where part of estate situated. (198.33). No lien for estate and inheritance taxes under this chapter continues for more than 20 years from death of decedent. (198.33).

Penalties.—

Knowingly making false statement, in any notice or return required to be filed, first degree misdemeanor. (198.39).

Failing to exhibit records, papers, etc. on request of Department or appointee, civil penalty not exceeding $500. (198.36).

Willfully failing to make return, keep any records or supply any information, as required by law, for purposes of computation, assessment or collection of tax, will constitute first degree misdemeanor. (198.37).

Failing to collect and truthfully account for and pay over tax, willfully attempting to evade or defeat tax or willfully aiding, assisting in, procuring, or advising preparation or presentation of false return, constitutes first degree misdemeanor. (198.40).

Forms and instructions for representatives of nonresident decedents may be obtained from Estate Tax Division, Department of Revenue of Florida; 5050 W. Tennessee St.; Tallahassee, Fl, 32399-0100.

GASOLINE AND SPECIAL FUELS TAXES:

Motor Fuel (and diesel fuel) tax per gallon includes following: 2¢ (4¢ for diesel) "constitutional fuel tax", 1¢ (gas) "county fuel tax", 1¢ (gas) "municipal fuel tax", 1¢ (gas & diesel) "ninth-cent fuel tax", between 1¢ and 11¢ (gas) (6¢ diesel) "local option fuel tax" levied per 336.025, "State Comprehensive Enhanced Transportation System Tax" (gas & diesel) levied per 206.608, and "fuel sales tax" (gas & diesel) as determined annually by Department at not lower than 6.9¢. (206.41[1], 206.87[1]).

Exemptions.—

Exemptions from motor fuel taxes include fuel contained in fuel tanks to propel motor vehicle into Florida from another state and fuel supplied by vehicle manufacturer, contained in tanks of new and untitled motor vehicle (206.41[3]), rocket fuel and certain aviation gasoline (206.42), and that sold to U.S. (206.62).

Exemptions from diesel fuel taxes are extensive and complex. See statutes, c. 206, pt. 2. (206.85-206.97).

Refunds.—Upon timely application, refunds for part of tax on motor and diesel fuel used by mass public transportation system operating within city, town, municipality, county, or transit authority region, as distinguished from over-the-road or charter transportation; for agricultural, aquacultural, or commercial fishing purposes; for municipality or county vehicles, for public or private school buses. Rights to refunds not assignable. (206.41[4], [5]; 206.8745). Ethanol dealers entitled to refund of tax on purchases of motor fuel used for denaturing. (206.626).

Detailed records open to inspection by Department, of each fuel purchase, must be kept by terminal supplier, importer, blender, exporter, or wholesaler. (206.41[5], 206.91).

Liability for Tax Payment.—Persons liable for tax payment detailed in statute. (206.413 & .414, 206.872).

Penalties for Willful Evasion of Payment of Motor Fuel Taxes.—$10 for every gallon of motor fuel involved or $1,000, whichever is greater, for first offense. Penalty shall increase with subsequent violations by multiplying penalty amount by number of prior violations. (206.413[3]).

Penalties Regarding Diesel Fuel Taxes.—See statutes, c. 206, pt. 2. (206.85-206.97).

Aviation fuel tax of 6.9¢ per gallon on aviation fuel (including kerosene not otherwise taxed or exempted) sold in this state, or brought into this state upon which tax has not been paid or lawfully assumed. Fuel taxed pursuant to this part shall not be subject to motor or diesel fuel taxes. (206.9825). Air carrier may make election under 212.0598 to use special tax base in computing tax, while using corresponding special tax rate under 212.9825(2). Additional rules for kerosene set out in statue. (206.9825[3][a]).

Liquefied Petroleum Gas or Compressed Natural Gas Decal Fees in Lieu of Tax.—Tax imposed by 206.87 not applicable to certain motor vehicles powered by alternative fuels for which decals are required and have been acquired. Decals transferable with change of ownership of vehicle and notice to Department. Sales of alternative fuel regulated. (206.877).

Diesel and Motor Fuel Commercial Use Tax.—Privilege tax upon every motor carrier for operating commercial motor vehicle upon state highways of this state at rate which includes minimum rates provided in pts. I, II, and IV of c. 206 on each gallon of diesel fuel or motor fuel used for propulsion within state. (207.003). Amount of fuel used within this state calculated using statutory formula. (207.005[2]).

See note at head of Digest as to 1998 legislation covered.

See Topical Index in front part of this volume.

FL – 51

GENERATION SKIPPING TAX:

See topic Estate Tax, subhead Generation-Skipping Transfer Tax.

GIFT TAX:

Florida has no gift tax.

INCOME TAX:

Income Taxed—Individuals.—Florida has no personal income tax.

Income Taxed—Corporations.—Florida's income tax is applicable to corporations only. See category Business Organizations, topic Corporations, subhead Corporate Income Tax.

INHERITANCE TAX:

See topic Estate Tax.

INTANGIBLE PERSONAL PROPERTY TAX:

Taxable Property.—All intangible personal property except notes and other obligations for payment of money, except bonds, which are secured by mortgage, deed of trust or other liens on real property situated in Florida. (199.032).

Intangible personal property is property which is not in itself intrinsically valuable but which derives its chief value from that which it represents, e.g., stocks or shares of incorporated or unincorporated entities, bonds, notes, and similar instruments and most leases of real property. (199.023[1]).

Annual Tax Levy.—Rate of 2.0 mills per dollar of just valuation (199.032), except on securities in Florida's Future Investment Fund for which lesser millage is assessed depending on Fund balance. (199.033).

Assessment and Valuation.—Property subject to annual tax at just valuation as of Jan. 1 of each year. Required methods of valuation outlined in statute. (199.103).

Credits Against Tax.—Banks and savings associations (defined in 220.62) entitled to credit of up to 33% of tax paid in immediately preceding year. (199.104, repealed, effective 12/31/99). Credits for up to 35% of costs of voluntary cleanup and rehabilitation of contaminated sites as defined in statute. (199.1055). Credits also given for intangible personal property taxes assessed by other states. (199.106).

Nonrecurring Tax Levy.—One-time assessment of 2 mills imposed upon just valuation of notes, bonds, and other obligations for payment to extent secured by mortgage, deed of trust, or other lien upon real property situated in Florida. Apportionment if taxable obligations also secured by out-of-state real property or personal property. (199.133). Rules regarding taxable situs given in statute. (199.175).

Future Advances.—If mortgage, deed of trust, or other lien secures line of credit or future advances, nonrecurring tax must be paid on initial obligations. As additional amount borrowed or future advance made, additional nonrecurring tax must be paid. Taxation of certain increases in indebtedness caused by interest occurring under adjustable interest rate limited. (199.143[1]). If borrower's residence secures line of credit, nonrecurring tax must be paid on full amount of line with no further tax due upon borrowing under line. (199.143[2]).

Assignment, replacement, assumption, or refinancing of obligation or mortgage, deed of trust, or other lien usually does not give rise to additional nonrecurring tax if obligation remains same (or less) and mortgage, deed of trust, or other lien, covers identical real property. (199.145).

Exemptions from Annual or Nonrecurring Tax.—Following intangible property, with certain limitations is exempt from taxation. See statutes for details.

Governmental property owned by Florida, any political subdivision or municipality. (199.183[1]).

Nonprofit Institutions.—Property owned by narrowly defined religious, educational, or charitable institutions. (199.183[2]).

Out-Of-State Banks and National Banks with Principle Office Out-Of-State.—Credit card receivables processed in Florida but owed by credit card holders domiciled outside of state. (199.183[3], 199.185[7]).

Other Exempt Organizations.—Banks, savings associations, and other similar institutions as listed in 220.62(1)–(4), and insurers (624.03), whether authorized or unauthorized (624.09), are exempt from annual tax (199.185[5], [8]). Charitable trust that pays 95% of income to tax-exempt (I.R.C. 501[c][3]) organization is exempt from 1 mill of annual tax (199.185[4]).

Personal Exemptions.—With respect to first mill of annual tax, every natural person has exemption of $20,000 of property, husband and wife filing jointly have exemption of $40,000. With respect to last mill, $100,000 of property is exempt, $200,000 for husband and wife filing jointly. Most agents and fiduciaries may not claim exemption on behalf of principals or beneficiaries. (199.185[2][a] & [b]). Widows, widowers, and persons who are blind or permanently disabled have limited additional $500 exemption from annual or nonrecurring tax. (199.185[3]).

Additional exemptions include property such as money; franchises; Florida or U.S. issued bonds, notes, or other obligations; property held in trust under certain retirement, welfare, or benefit plans; notes and other obligations, except bonds, secured by mortgage, deed of trust or other liens upon out-of-state real property; assets of corporation or units of trust registered under Investment Company Act of 1940; bank owned property issued in or arising out of international banking transactions; certain interests in real estate securitizations such as real estate mortgage investment conduits and financial asset securitization trusts; accounts receivable arising or acquired in ordinary course of business (exemption in three phases: 1/3 in 1999, 2/3 in 2000, all in 2001); certain employee stock options. (199.185[1]). Accounts receivable of Florida liquor distributor derived from out-of-state sales to out-of-state buyers are also exempt. (199.185[6]).

Annual tax return must be filed with Department on or before June 30 by all corporations authorized to or doing business in Florida, and any person, regardless of domicile, who on Jan. 1 owns, controls, or manages intangible personal property subject to tax. Character, description, and just valuation of all such property must be separately listed. Husband and wife may file joint return. No payment tax required if annual tax

after exemptions is less than $60. In such cases returns not required except from corporations not required to file report under 607.1622, agents or fiduciaries required by Department to file, and, until July 1, 2000, certain banking organizations. (199.052[1], [2]). Affiliated group of corporations may file consolidated return. (199.052[10]).

Trustees, Agents, Guardians, and Other Representatives.—Trustee of Florida-situs trust, personal representative or curator of Florida estate, and Florida resident with beneficial interest in foreign-situs trusts, are primarily responsible for filing return and paying tax. (199.052[5]-[7]). Guardian of property of Florida incompetent and custodian of Florida minor must file return and pay tax. (199.052[8]). Agent that has control or management of intangible personal property must report and pay intangible tax if principle fails to do so. (199.052[9]).

Banks and financial institutions filing returns for customers must file using "machine-sensible media". (199.052[16]).

Valuation.—Intangible personal property subject to annual tax at its just valuation as of Jan. 1. Statute sets forth methods of valuation for various types of property. (199.103).

Payment of Annual Taxes.—Except as otherwise provided by 199.052, owner of intangible property liable for payment of annual tax. Person required to file return, liable for tax if owner fails to pay. (199.052[13]). Due and payable on June 30, payment to be made upon filing of return. (199.042[1]). Corporations incorporated or qualified to do business in state, may elect to pay stockholders' annual tax. (199.057).

Discount Allowed for Early Payment.—4% for payment on or before last day in Feb., 3% for payment on or before Mar. 31, 2% for payment on or before Apr. 30, 1% for payment on or before May 31. (199.042[2]).

Payment of Nonrecurring Tax.—Due and payable when instrument presented for recordation. If not written or not presented for recording within 30 days of creation of obligation, then due and payable at end of that 30 days. Taxpayer solely liable for tax but may pass it on to borrower or mortgagor. Procedures spelled out in statute. (199.135).

Annual Information Reports.—

Corporate Report to Shareholders.—On or before Apr. 1, corporations doing business in Florida must give Florida shareholders of record, written notice of just value of each class of stock subject to annual tax. Corporations listed on public stock exchange or traded over-the-counter usually exempt from this requirement as are corporations that have elected under 199.057 to pay stockholders annual tax. (199.062[1]).

Corporate Report to Department.—On or before June 30 of each year, corporations must file with Department copy of any notice required to be sent to shareholders under 199.062(1). (199.062[2]).

Security dealers and investment advisers registered in Florida must file with Department, on or before June 30, position statement as of prior Dec. 31 for each customer whose mailing address is within state or statement that no securities held on account for any customer whose mailing address is in this state. See statute for details. Department may also require each customer be sent copy of Department's intangible tax brochure. (199.062[3]).

Property appraisers may be required to send to each owner of Florida property, copy of Department's intangible tax brochure. (199.062[3][b][2]).

Fiduciaries are required to serve Department with copy of each inventory required by law or court rule to be prepared or filed with court for decedents estates, trusts, or guardianships. Court cannot approve inventory until copy filed with Department. (199.062[4]).

Refunds.—Claim for refund may be filed within three years from date right to refund has accrued. (199.2325). Claims to be filed by taxpayer or taxpayer's heirs, personal representatives, successors, or assigns, and shall include such information as Department may require. (199.2325).

Interest.—If annual or nonrecurring tax is not paid, without regard to any extensions, interest on unpaid amount of 12% per year from due date of payment required. (199.282[2]).

Penalties.—

Delinquency penalty of 10% of delinquent tax per month from due date until paid, up to limit of 50% of total tax if any annual or nonrecurring tax is not paid. If required annual return not filed by due date, penalty of 10% of tax due per month during which annual tax return remains unfiled, up to limit of 50% of total tax. Combined total of above penalties cannot exceed 10% per month, up to limit of 50% of total tax due. (199.282[3]).

Omitted or Undervalued Property on Return.—Penalty of 10% of tax attributable to each omission and undervaluation. No delinquency or late filing penalty for undervaluation. (199.282[4]).

Late reporting penalties of $100 imposed upon corporation that does not comply with Information Report Requirements of 199.057(2) or 199.062(2). Securities dealer or investment dealers subject to penalty of $10 per customer position statement plus 1% of initial penalty (or $50, whichever is greater) for each month late. Minimum penalty of $100. (199.282[6]).

Not to be Enforced or Permitted to be Recorded.—Mortgages, deeds of trust, or other liens on Florida real property are enforceable or eligible for recording until nonrecurring tax has been paid and clerk has noted its payments. (199.282[5]).

Penalties for willful violation or failure to comply with taxing provisions constitute felony of third degree punishable as provided in 775.082, 775.083, or 775.084. (199.282). Any officer or director of corporation who willfully directs employee to fail to file or to pay tax or to evade, defeat or improperly account for tax, is liable for penalty equal to amount of tax not paid. (199.282[9]). Failure or refusal to file annual return or to make records available for inspection constitutes misdemeanor of first degree. (199.282).

MARIJUANA AND CONTROLLED SUBSTANCES TAX:

Florida does not have special tax for marijuana and other controlled substances.

See note at head of Digest as to 1998 legislation covered.

See Topical Index in front part of this volume.

MINERAL SEVERANCE TAX:

Levy.—Tax is levied upon every person in business of severing solid minerals as defined in 211.30(1).

Tax rates are as follows:

Phosphate rock is taxed at base rate of $135 per ton severed. Base rate is adjusted annually and communicated to affected producers. (211.3103[5], [6]).

Heavy minerals are taxed at base rate of $1.34 per ton severed for commercial use. Base rate is adjusted annually and communicated to affected producers. (211.3106[2], [3]).

Other solid minerals are taxed at rate of 8% of value of identified solid minerals severed. (211.31).

Exemptions.—

Solid minerals sold to governmental agencies in this state or those extracted by owner of site of severance to improve site. (211.3108[1], [3]).

Solid minerals except phosphate rock severed solely for direct application in agricultural uses. (211.31[4]).

Solid minerals except phosphate rock and heavy minerals upon which sales tax is ultimately paid to state. (211.31[2]).

Administration and Inspection of Records.—See statute for details. (211.33).

Delinquency Penalties and Interest and Tax Crimes.—See statutes for details. (211.33; 211.335).

MOTOR CARRIER FUELS TAX:

See topic Gasoline and Special Fuels Taxes.

MOTOR VEHICLE USAGE TAX:

See topic Sales and Use Taxes.

OCCUPATIONAL LICENSE TAX:

Annual local occupational license taxes imposed by county and municipality on certain businesses, professions, and occupations subject to certain exemptions. (c. 205). Failure to obtain required license punishable by fine of 25% of tax determined to be due, plus any other penalty provided by law or ordinance. (205.0532). Tax deemed regulatory and in addition to, but not in lieu of, local occupational license fees imposed under provisions of c. 205. (205.022). See 205.053 for provisions governing occupational licenses. See also topic Race Tracks and Jai Alai Frontons Taxes, subhead Occupational Licenses of Racetrack Employees.

OIL AND GAS PRODUCTION TAX:

Levy.—Tax is levied on every person who severs oil, gas, or sulfur in state for sale, transport, storage (not mentioned in gas section), profit, or commercial use. (211.02; 211.025; 211.026).

Tax rates are as follows:

Oil is taxed on value of oil produced and saved or sold during month. Small well oil and tertiary oil is taxed at 5% of gross value; all other oil, 8% of gross value. (211.02).

Gas is taxed on volume, in mcf (thousand cubic feet), or gas produced and sold or used by producer during month. Gas is taxed at base rate of $0.171 per mcf. Base rate is adjusted annually and communicated to affected producers. (211.025).

Sulfur is taxed on long tons of sulfur produced or recovered by producer during month from hydrogen sulfide gas contained in oil or gas production from well, measured in its molten, elemental state. Sulfur is taxed at base rate of $2.71 per long ton. Base rate is adjusted annually and communicated to affected producers. (211.026).

Exemptions.—

Oil or gas production used for lease operations on lease or unit where produced. (211.027[1]).

Oil or gas produced for period of 60 months from new field wells or for period of 48 months for new wells in existing fields, shut-in wells returned to service after 24 months, abandoned well or wellbore redrilled and recompleted, oil or gas produced from any horizontal well or having depth in excess of 15,000 feet. These exemptions will not be granted after June 30, 2002. (211.027[4]–[7]).

Gas returned to horizon in field where produced. Unsold gas vented or flared directly into atmosphere. (211.027[2], [3]).

Administration and Books and Records.—See statutes for details. (211.075; 211.09; 211.125).

Delinquency Penalties and Interest and Tax Crimes.—See statutes for details. (211.076; 211.25).

POLLUTION ABATEMENT AUTHORITY TAX:

Fuel and Other Pollutants Tax.—C. 206, pt. IV.

Coastal Protection.—Tax of 2¢ per barrel of "pollutant", other than petroleum products produced in or imported into this state until Coastal Protection Trust Fund ("Fund") equals or exceeds $50 million. Special provision for petroleum products. (206.9935[1]). Pollutants include any petroleum product; pesticides, ammonia, and chlorine; lead-acid batteries; and certain solvents. $50 million cap automatically increases to $100 million if offshore oil drilling approved. Tax ceases to be assessed when Fund reaches caps. If discharge of catastrophic proportions which could significantly reduce Fund, Secretary of Environmental Protection has authority to levy tax up to 10¢ per barrel to replenish and maintain Fund's balance. (206.9935[1]).

Water Quality.—Tax of from 2¢ to 5.9¢ per barrel (depending on type of pollutant) if unobligated balance of Water Quality Assurance Trust Fund falls below $3 million, until unobligated balance in fund exceeds $5 million, at which time tax of from 1¢ to 2.36¢ per barrel (depending on type of pollutant). If unobligated balance of fund exceeds $12 million, levy of tax shall be discontinued until unobligated balance of fund falls below $5 million. Persons producing or importing liquid mixture, claiming it is not subject to taxation as pollutant shall bear burden of proof. (206.9935[2]).

Inland Protection.—Tax of 30¢ per barrel of pollutant produced or imported into state until Inland Protection Trust Fund ("Fund") is between $100 million and $150 million. (206.9935[3]). If Fund exceeds $150 million, tax discontinued until unobligated balance reaches $100 million. If Fund goes below $100 million but remains above $50 million, tax increases to 60¢ per barrel. If Fund is $50 million or less tax goes up to 80¢ per barrel. See 206.9941 for exemptions. (206.9935[3]).

PROPERTY (AD VALOREM) TAXES:

Taxable Property.—Unless expressly exempted, all real and personal property in state, all personal property belonging to persons residing in state, and all leaseholds in governmental property are subject to taxation. (196.001).

Exemptions.—Taxpayers claiming exemptions must still file tax return. (196.193).

Application for Exemption.—With limited exceptions, claim for exemption must be filed with county property appraiser on or before Mar. 1 (196.011[1]), provided any person who is unable to file claim for exemption by reason of service in Armed Forces of U.S. may file claim through next of kin or other person authorized in writing (196.071). In lieu of annual application for exemption tax assessor may accept certified statement under oath that there has been no change in ownership or use of property since it was last determined to be fully exempt from tax for religious, literary, etc., purposes. (196.011).

Following are exempt from taxation:

Exempt Entities.—All property owned by exempt entity used exclusively for educational, literary, scientific, religious, charitable or government use, as defined in c. 196, is totally exempt. Property used predominately for such purposes is proportionately exempted. (196.192).

Care Facilities.—With certain restrictions, property used by hospitals, nursing homes, homes for special services (196.197), and homes for aged (196.1975).

Disabled Persons.—Property of certain permanently and totally disabled veterans (196.081), quadriplegics and other disabled persons who are required to use wheelchair or who are legally blind (196.101).

Property to value of $500 of every widow, widower, blind person or totally and permanently disabled person who is bona fide resident of Florida. (196.202).

Household goods and personal effects of persons residing and making permanent home in this state. Such property may be held individually, by entireties, jointly or in common with others. (196.181).

Renewal Energy Source and Historic Property.—With limits, for improved real property upon which renewable energy source device installed and operated (196.175) and for certain improvements made to historic properties (196.1997).

Inventory is exempt from ad valorem taxation. (196.185).

Goods in Transit.—Personal property manufactured or produced outside of Florida and brought into state for transshipment in interstate or foreign commerce is exempt. (192.032[4][a]).

Leaseholds in Governmental Property.—With limits, for certain leasehold interests in governmental property taxable under intangible personal property tax. (196.199).

Homestead property up to assessed tax valuation of $25,000 (except special assessments for benefits) of person who, on Jan. 1, has legal or beneficial title and makes it permanent residence or residence of others legally or naturally dependent upon such person; title to homestead may be held by entireties, jointly or in common with others and exemption may be apportioned among owners resident thereon as their interests appear; but no exemption in excess of $25,000 shall be allowed any one person or any one dwelling except that exemption up to $25,000 may be allowed on each owner-occupied apartment, condominium owner-occupied residential property. Exemptions allowed may not exceed proportionate assessed valuation of interest owned. (196.031).

Abandonment.—Except for member of Armed Forces of U.S., rental of entire dwelling previously claimed to be homestead is abandonment of homestead, but abandonment after Jan. 1 does not affect such exemption for that particular year. (196.061).

Assessment.—Ad valorem taxes on real and tangible personal property are assessed by all counties. (192.032). Each county has tax assessor and tax collector that have responsibility for assessment of property and collection of taxes. (192.001).

Assessment based on "just valuation". Assessment on Jan. 1 of each year. Factors to be considered: (1) Present cash value; (2) highest and best use in immediate future and present use; (3) location; (4) quantity and size; (5) cost and present replacement value of any improvement thereon; (6) condition; (7) income from property; and (8) net proceeds of sale, after deduction of all usual and reasonable fees and costs of sale and expenses of financing. (193.011). All assessments should be completed by July 1. (193.023). Separate assessment roll prepared for real and tangible personal property. (193.114). Separate rules for assessment of agricultural crops, nonbearing fruit trees and nursery stock (193.451), agricultural lands (193.461), oil, mineral and other subsurface rights (193.481), outdoor recreational or park lands and environmentally-endangered land (193.501), and pollution control devices (193.621). Agricultural property consisting of residence and curtilage must be assessed separately. (193.461[3][d]). All land against which state holds any tax sale certificate or other lien for delinquent taxes assessed for 1940 or prior years must be assessed as if no taxes were delinquent against such lands. (193.102).

Review of Assessment.—Value adjustment board for each county hears petitions filed pursuant to 194.011(3), complaints relating to homestead exemptions (196.151) or regarding exemption applications (196.011), and appeals concerning ad valorem tax deferrals (194.032). Petitioners may be represented by attorney and present testimony and other evidence. Hearings are to conform with c. 120. Circuit Court has jurisdiction over property taxation matters (194.171) including de novo appellate review of findings of property appraisal adjustment board (194.036[3]). Venue is Leon County regarding certain railroad property. (193.085). To obtain jurisdiction of court, taxpayer must pay amount admitted for contested year and each year thereafter. Verbatim record of proceedings is made and documentary evidence is preserved and made available to Department of Revenue. (194.034[1][c]). Procedures for property owner's challenge to assessment value are found at 194.011(3).

Levy.—Counties, school districts, and municipalities can each levy ad valorem taxes on assessed value of real and tangible personal property of up to 10 mills; most special

See note at head of Digest as to 1998 legislation covered.

See Topical Index in front part of this volume.

FL – 53

PROPERTY (AD VALOREM) TAXES..., *continued*

districts' millage is established by law upon vote of electors owning nonexempt freeholds. (Const., arts. 7, 9).

Collection.—Tax collector required to mail tax statement to each taxpayer appearing on assessment rolls whose post office address is known. (197.322).

Payment.—All taxes except intangible personal property taxes are due on Nov. 1, or as soon as assessment roll available to tax collector. (197.333).

Discounts for Early Payment.—4% in Nov. or within 30 days after mailing of original tax notice; 3% in Dec.; 2% in following Jan.; 1% in following Feb. (197.162). Taxes delinquent Apr. 1 of year following year assessed or 60 days from date of mailing of original tax notice, whichever is later. (197.333).

Property Tax Payment Deferral.—Persons qualifying for homestead exemption can defer portion of combined total of ad valorem taxes and certain non-ad valorem assessments tax which exceeds 5% of applicant's household income. (197.252). Must file annual application for deferral on or before Jan. 31 following year taxes assessed. (197.252[1]).

Liens.—Lien, superior to all others, exists on all real and personal property assessed for taxation. (197.122).

Delinquent Taxes.—No tax certificate or warrant shall be issued for property if petition contesting valuation of such property has not received final action by property appraisal adjustment board. (197.323[2]).

Tangible personal property upon which taxes are delinquent may be levied upon, seized, and sold by tax collector. Procedures and timelines for issuance of warrants for, levy upon, and seizure and sale of property are described in 197.413–197.417.

Delinquent Real Property Taxes.—Tax collector may sell tax certificates on lands on which taxes have not been paid. Procedure for sale of tax certificates is described in 197.432.

Redemption.—Tax certificates may be redeemed, or county held certificates purchased, at any time after issuance and before tax deed is issued or property is put on sale list. (197.472[1]). Procedure for redemption or purchase is described at 197.472. Procedures for issuance of tax deed described at 197.502 et seq.

PROVIDER TAX:

See topic Sales and Use Taxes.

RACE TRACKS AND JAI ALAI FRONTONS TAXES:

Administration and Collection.—Division of Pari-mutuel Wagering of Department of Business and Professional Regulation is to collect taxes and require compliance with reporting requirements. (550.0251).

Electronic Funds Transfers.—Permitholders may be required to remit taxes and fees by electronic funds transfers if taxes and fees amounted to $50,000 or more in prior reporting year. (550.0251[8]).

Penalties.—Administrative fine of not more than $1,000 for each count, may be imposed for violation of c. 550. (550.0251[10]). Civil penalty of up to $1,000 for each day payment not remitted. Failure to pay taxes or penalties may result in suspension or revocation of license or permit. (550.0951[6]).

Payment of various taxes by permitholders to division is to be made twice weekly. Monthly reports are also required. Details set out in statute. (550.0951[5]).

Daily License Fee.—Each permitholder, licensee or permittee conducting race meetings or jai alai games is to pay daily license fee on each live or simulcast pari-mutuel event of $100 for each horserace and $80 for each dograce and $40 for each jai alai game. (550.0951[1][a]). See statutes for limits on amount of tax payable. (550.0951[1]).

Admission tax equal to 15% of entrance admission charge or 10¢, whichever is greater, on each person attending event. No tax imposed on free passes. (550.0951[2]).

Tax on handle (aggregate of contributions to pari-mutuel pools) is as follows: for thoroughbred, harness, and quarter horse racing, 3.3% of handle; for dogracing, 7.6% of handle; for jai alai, 7.1% of handle; for intertrack wagering, from 2.4% to 3.3% depending on type of host facility and whether rebroadcast. Guest tracks that impose surcharge on each winning ticket pursuant to 550.6335 shall pay additional 5% of surcharge as tax. (550.0951[3]).

Breaks Tax.—Each permitholder conducting jai alai performances pays tax equal to breaks (portion of each pari-mutuel pool not distributed to contributors). (550.0951[4]).

Limitations, Exemptions, Qualifications on Taxes.—

Jai alai taxes are further qualified and limited by 550.09511.

Harness horse taxes are further qualified and limited by 550.09512. Any permit of harness horse permitholder who does not pay tax on handle for live performances for full schedule of live races during any two consecutive years is void and escheats to state to be reissued as initial permit to qualified applicant. (550.09512[3]).

Greyhound dogracing taxes are further qualified and limited by 550.09514. Also see 550.1625 as to dogracing.

Thoroughbred horse taxes are further qualified and limited by 550.09515. Any permit of thoroughbred horse permitholder who does not pay tax on handle for live performances for full schedule of live races during any two consecutive years is void and escheats to state to be reissued as initial permit to qualified applicant. (550.09515[3]).

Non-wagering permits, issued only for horseracing meets, are exempt from daily license fees and admission tax. (550.505).

Occupational Licenses of Racetrack Employees.—Each person connected with racetrack or jai alai fronton must purchase annual occupational license. Annual fee varies from $10 to $50 depending whether license is business, restricted, or unrestricted and whether restricted or unrestricted licenses are for professionals and managers or general employees. Certified public accountants and attorneys licensed to practice in this state are not required to have occupational license. See statute for details. (550.105).

REAL ESTATE CONVEYANCE TAX:

See topic Stamp Tax.

SALES AND USE TAXES:

Sales Tax.—6% on sales at retail and leases of tangible property (212.05); leases for storage, parking or docking spaces for motor vehicles and boats and transient rentals of residence as described in 212.02 (212.03); lease or rental of or license in real property subject to numerous statutory exceptions and regulations (212.031) and amusement admissions with certain exemptions and limitations (212.04).

Self-propelled or power drawn farm equipment used exclusively by farmer, tax on sales is 3% but tax on leases of such equipment is 6%. (212.083).

Vending Machines.—Sales from machines and sales to vending machine owners merit special provisions. (212.0515).

Convention Development Tax for revenue to promote tourism and use of hotel facilities by facilitating improvement and construction of convention centers. Each such tax is individually enacted, specifying types of local governments authorized to levy, rate or rates, maximum length of time of imposition, required procedure to secure voter approval, limitations of expenditures of collections, and other legislative requirements. (212.0305).

Collections.—Sales tax revenues collected from all retail dealers. (212.06[1]). No title, registration, or license will be issued for motor vehicle until sales tax paid when old title certificate is presented for new one. (212.06[10]).

Out-of-state dealer, e.g., catalogs, with requisite minimum contacts with state must collect tax when property is sold to purchaser in state. (212.0596).

Exemptions.—Following are examples only. For full range of exemptions, see 212.08.

Foods (including water) for human consumption (excluding candy) except when sold for immediate consumption on or off premises.

Feed for poultry, ostriches, racehorses, dairy cows, and other livestock.

Fuel used in home heating, used by railroads and ships when engaged in interstate commerce, used in generation of electric power or energy, or used for certain agricultural, aquacultural, or commercial fishing.

Purchases of machinery and equipment used to increase productive output (including machinery and equipment purchased to comply with federal procurement regulations) used in production of electrical or steam energy, used for processing recyclable materials, used in silicon technology production.

Medical, Etc.—Medicine, prosthetic and orthopedic appliances, guide dogs for blind.

School books and lunches and most other purchases by educational institutions, public and private.

Religious Materials.—Bibles, hymn books, prayer books, other religious publications, and sales to or by churches.

Isolated or occasional transactions by one not engaged in business. This exemption does not apply to motor vehicles or certain boats or aircraft or mobile homes. (212.022).

Use Tax.—6% on tangible personal property used, consumed or stored for use, but not sold in state. (212.05).

Sales Tax Exemptions apply also to use tax. (212.05).

Additional exemptions include electric power or other energy self-generated for direct use in manufacturing or processing tangible personal property for sale (212.06[1][b]) and certain vessels used by vessel manufacturers and dealers solely for demonstration, sales promotion, or testing (212.06[1][d]).

Discretionary County Sales and Use Surtax.—(212.054, 212.055). When legislatively authorized, county governing bodies may levy surtax on transactions subject to sales, use, services, rentals, admissions, etc. imposed by c. 212, pt. I. Tangible property sales amounts above $5,000 and long distance telephone service not subject to surtax. All legislative authorizations of surtax must be published in 212.055. Most surtaxes must be approved by local referendum.

Local Option Food and Beverage Tax.—Any county may impose following additional taxes: 2% on food, beverage, or alcoholic beverage sales in hotels and motels; 1% on food, beverage, or alcoholic beverage sales by licensees for sale of alcoholic beverages for consumption on premises. See statute for exemptions and other details. (212.0306).

Utility Services Gross Receipts Tax.—Persons receiving payment for any utility service must report by last day of each month to Department of Revenue, under oath of secretary or some other officer of total amount of gross receipts derived from business done within this state, or between points within this state, for preceeding month and, at same time, shall pay into state treasury sum of 2.5% such gross receipts. (203.01).

Exclusions.—Gross receipts do not include payments for natural gas sold to public or private utilities for resale or use in generation of electricity, for sale of electricity to utility for resale within Florida or pursuant to electrical interchange agreement, for sale of telecommunication services for resale within Florida, and receipts from sales or leases of telecommunications service for use in conduct of telecommunications service for hire. (203.01).

Tax May Be Billed as Line Item to Customer.—Customer fully liable for tax whether separately stated as line item or component of total bill. (201.01[5]).

Penalties.—Provider failing to remit tax imposed in this part, liable for tax and guilty of misdemeanor of first degree. (203.01[7]). Person who willfully violates provisions of c. 203, guilty of misdemeanor of first degree. In addition, penalty of 10% of unpaid tax for failure to timely report and pay tax if failure less than 31 days, plus additional 10% of unpaid tax for each additional 30 days; penalty may not be less than $10 or exceed total of 50% of any unpaid tax. If failure due to fraud, penalty shall be 100% of tax due and second degree misdemeanor. (203.01[2]). Interest on delinquent payments is 1% per month accruing from date due until paid. (203.06).

Gross receipts taxes on certain telecommunication services which originate but do not terminate in Florida or which terminate but do not originate in Florida, and charge for such services is billed or charged to Florida telecommunication number or device, telephone or number are taxable; tax computed using gross receipts tax provisions. (203.62). Failure to collect or remit tax constitutes first degree misdemeanor. (203.63).

See note at head of Digest as to 1998 legislation covered.

See Topical Index in front part of this volume.

SALES AND USE TAXES . . . *continued*

Franchise or License Taxes.—See categories Business Organizations, topic Corporations; Business Regulation and Commerce, topics Banks and Banking, Licenses, Business and Professional.

Tax on Deeds and Mortgages.—See topic Stamp Tax.

Excise Tax on Gas and Oil.—See topic Gasoline and Special Fuels Taxes, subheads Motor Fuel (and Diesel Fuel) Tax and Aviation Fuel Tax.

Hospital and Health Care Entity Tax.—Annual assessment (based on operating revenues for most recently completed fiscal year) against certain hospitals and health care entities equal to 1.5% of annual net operating revenues to be paid to Agency for Health Care Administration. Net operating revenue is gross revenue less deductions resulting from bad debts; contractual adjustments; administrative, courtesy, and policy discounts and adjustments; and offsets for restricted donations and grants for indigent care. Hospital defined in 395.002(11). Health care entities include ambulatory surgical centers licensed under 395.003, certain clinical laboratories including those licensed under 483.091, certain freestanding radiation therapy centers, and certain diagnostic imaging centers that are freestanding outpatient facilities. Within six months after end of entity's fiscal year, Agency shall certify amount of assessment to entity. Assessment shall be payable to and collected by Agency in equal quarterly amounts on or before first day of each calendar quarter. (395.701, 395.7015).

SPECIAL FUELS TAX:

See topic Gasoline and Special Fuels Taxes.

STAMP TAX:

Documents.—Tax on documents levied, collected and paid as follows (201.01–.24):

Deeds, instruments, or other writings whereby any real property or any interest therein is transferred (even if interest designated as personal property), 70¢ on each $100 of consideration therefor. Tax applies to document granting tenant-stockholder of condominium right to occupy apartment, to certain conveyances of real property to partner from partnership, and to documents conveying beneficial interest in lands pursuant to 689.071. (201.02). See also category Property, topic Deeds, subhead Tax.

Corporate certificates of stock (original issue, organization or reorganization) issued in Florida, 35¢ on each $100 of face value. Certificate without face value, 35¢ on each $100 of actual value. Tax to be shown on stock book not certificate. (201.05).

Bonds, debentures, or certificates of indebtedness issued by any person, and instruments and documents, however termed, issued by any corporation with interest coupons or in registered form, 35¢ on each $100 of face value thereof. When secured and only part of security is located in Florida, tax is proportionate. (201.07).

Promissory notes, nonnegotiable notes, written obligations to pay, including mortgages not securing separate notes or in connection with certain nonsecured retail sales, assignment of wages or other compensation, executed, sold, transferred or assigned in this state, and on renewals thereof, 35¢ per $100 of obligation. (201.08).

Filed or recorded mortgages, trust deeds, security agreements, or other evidences of indebtedness and for each renewal of same, 35¢ on each $100 of indebtedness or obligation evidenced thereby. See statute for rules dealing with future advances and multiple parties. (201.08). Required taxes must be paid, prior to recordation. For mortgages or trust deeds that do not incorporate certificate of indebtedness, notation is to be made on note or certificate that tax has been paid on mortgage or trust deed. (201.01).

Renewal note for existing promissory note, which extends or continues identical contractual obligations without enlargement, not subject to tax if renewal note has attached to it original promissory note with notation required by 201.133. Renewal note term which increases unpaid balance but which otherwise meets exemption criteria, taxable only on face amount of increase. Renewal note for revolving obligation which increases original face amount but which otherwise meets exemption criteria of this section is taxable only on increase. (201.09[1]). Note given in renewal of adjustable rate note or mortgage which has initial interest rate adjustment interval of not less than six months taxed only to extent of accrued interest upon which taxes have not been paid. (201.09[3]).

Financing statements under c. 679 of Uniform Commercial Code not accepted for filing unless notation thereon that taxes have been paid on promissory instruments secured by financing statement. (201.22).

Exemptions include receipts or other transaction record of use of credit card, charge card, or debit card and promissory notes executed for certain student financial aid (201.08); certificates of deposit issued by any bank, banking association, or trust company (201.10); certain foreign notes and other written obligations; drafts or bills of exchange arising out of certain transactions involving importation, exportation or foreign storage of goods, or for dollar exchange; documents, notes, financing statements, drafts, bills of exchange, or other taxable items used in conduct of international banking transaction, as defined in 199.023(11), (201.23); obligations to pay money issued by municipality, political subdivision, or agency of state (201.24); assignment, transfer, or other disposition, or any document, which arises out of rental, lease, or lease-purchase or real property agreement within §235.056(2) or (3). (201.24). No tax on transfer of marital home between spouses or former spouses pursuant to marriage dissolution action. (201.02). If promissory note not subject to taxation pursuant to 201.09(1), then mortgage, trust deed, etc. not subject to taxation. (201.09[2]).

Discretionary county surtax on taxable documents may be levied except for document involving single-family residence. (201.031).

Penalties.—

Failure to pay tax or otherwise illegally avoiding tax constitutes first degree misdemeanor. (201.17, 201.20).

Payment of Insufficient Amount of Tax or Improper Reporting.—Must pay tax not paid, penalty of up to 50% of tax not paid unless fraud in which case penalty equals 200% of deficiency, and interest accruing from date of recordation until paid at rate of 1% per month, based on tax not paid. Department may settle or compromise any interest or penalties. (201.17).

Illegal use of stamps constitutes felony of third degree. (201.18).

UNEMPLOYMENT COMPENSATION TAX:

Unemployment compensation tax is imposed on each employer or employing unit which has had in employment at least one individual for some portion of day in each of 20 different calendar weeks (whether or not consecutive), in current or preceding calendar year or has paid wages in any calendar quarter in excess of $1,500 in current or preceding calendar year. (443.036[19]). Standard rate of employer contribution is 2.7%, but experience rating of employer and size of compensation fund may reduce rate or increase it to maximum of 5.4%. (443.131). Division of Unemployment Compensation of Department of Labor and Employment Security requires quarterly returns and payments. (443.131). No contributions are exacted from employees. (443.131).

UNIFORM FEDERAL LIEN REGISTRATION ACT:

Adopted without substantive amendment. Removed gender-specific references applicable to human beings, effective July 1, 1997. (713.901).

USE TAX:

See topic Sales and Use Taxes.

TRANSPORTATION

MOTOR VEHICLES:

Department of Highway Safety and Motor Vehicles exercises general supervisory power in this area. Mailing address: Department of Highway Safety and Motor Vehicles, Kirkman Building, Tallahassee, Florida 32301.

Vehicle License.—Owners of motor vehicles as defined in §320.01 must register such vehicles with Department of Highway Safety and Motor Vehicles (320.02), and renew such registration annually (320.07), except certain business vehicles may be registered semiannually (320.0705). Registration may be withheld from owners whose license is suspended under cc. 318 or 322. (322.059). Registration plates are issued to owner or lessee, one for each vehicle, for five year period. (320.06). Replacement fees are $10, paid $2 each year in advance. (320.06). Validation sticker for life of plate in upper-left corner. (320.06). Sticker with year of expiration in upper-right corner. (320.06). Registration valid for not more than 12 months and expires midnight of last day of registration period. (320.06). Registration period begins first day of birth month of person whose name first appears on registration and ends last day of month preceding such birth month in succeeding year. (320.055). Renewal period is 30-day period ending at midnight on owner's date of birth. (320.055). Owner whose vehicle registration is expired for four months or less is subject to civil penalty and if more than four months, guilty of second degree misdemeanor. (320.07[3]). Validation stickers issued annually. (320.06). Advance renewal provided when absence anticipated. (320.071). License fees must be paid upon registration or reregistration in accordance with license plates available for certain vehicles in classification and weight of vehicle (320.08) and service charge of $2.50 must be paid (320.04). Personalized license plates available for certain vehicles. (320.0805). Mobile homes, as defined in §320.01(2), require annual license fee based upon length of vehicle which is in lieu of ad valorem taxes and special rates based on net weight are designated for certain recreational vehicle-type units, other than mobile homes as defined in §320.01(1)(b) (see 320.08[11]); payment evidenced by suitable license plate. (320.08, .081, .0815; Const. Art. 7, §1). Florida manufacturers of mobile homes must display certificate showing compliance with applicable standards of U.S.A. standard institute. (320.827). Trust fund exists from which judgments against recreational vehicle dealers may be satisfied. (320.781). Special license plate at special or no fee may be obtained by holders of amateur radio licenses (320.083), active members of Florida National Guard (320.089), active members of any branch of U.S. Armed Forces Reserve (320.089), former prisoners of war (320.089), survivors of Pearl Harbor (320.089), Purple Heart medal recipients (320.089), Congressional Medal of Honor winners (320.0893), certified emergency medical technicians (320.0898), certified paramedics (320.0898), firefighters (320.0898), law enforcement officers (320.0898), handicapped persons (320.0848), disabled veterans (320.084), members of Seminole and Miccosukee Indian Tribes (320.0841), veterans who are confined to wheelchairs (320.0842), wheelchair users (320.0843), and owners of ancient vehicles (320.086) and antique trucks (320.08[3]). In addition, licenses commemorating Challenger space shuttle, veterans, manatees, panthers, United States Olympic Committee, Girl Scouts, Boy Scouts, colleges in state and other causes and organizations are available for special additional fees. (320.08058). Motor vehicles owned or exclusively operated for benefit of certain organizations are exempt from licensing tax. (320.10). Port vehicles and equipment (320.525) as well as golf carts (320.105) exempt from certain registration and license requirements.

Driver's License.—Drivers must have license (322.03), except persons operating road and farm machinery, U.S. Government employees operating vehicles leased or owned by U.S. Government and certain nonresidents with valid noncommercial licenses may operate noncommercial (Class D, E) vehicles and persons driving golf carts. Drivers of commercial motor vehicles required to obtain commercial driver's license. (322.03[3]). Licenses issued by Department of Highway Safety and Motor Vehicles (322.14) for four year periods (322.15[2]). "Safe drivers" may renew for six years. (322.18[2]). All renewal driver's licenses issued only if applicant eligible. (322.18[5]). Application for commercial license includes tests of eyesight, hearing, road signs, knowledge of laws regulating driving under influence and safe driving of commercial vehicle of class applied for. (322.12[3]). Commercial driver's license fee of $50 (Class A, B, C) includes fee for driver education; $20 for noncommercial license (Class D, E). (322.21). Driver's licenses not issued to persons under 18, unless driver is 16 years of age prior to Jan. 1, 1990 (322.05) or is 16 years of age and enrolled in public or private school or other equivalent program (322.0601). Eligibility for driver's license may be delayed due to conviction of certain offenses. (322.055). Restricted licenses may be issued to persons at least 15 years of age and meet school attendance requirements unless otherwise ineligible due to conviction of certain offenses. (322.05, 322.056, 322.16). All licenses issued to person under 21 shall have distinguishing markings or

See note at head of Digest as to 1998 legislation covered.

See Topical Index in front part of this volume.

FL – 55

MOTOR VEHICLES... *continued*
color from all other licenses issued. (322.141[1]). Applicants who have insulin dependent diabetes may have their licenses so designated. (322.141[2]). Applicants for licenses must be examined unless otherwise qualified (322.12) and restrictions may be imposed on licenses (322.16). All applicants who have never been issued license in any jurisdiction must complete approved traffic law and substance abuse education program. (322.08[5]). Re-examination required of all licensees every three years for eyesight and hearing. Those with convictions in past three years also are tested for ability to read and understand highway signs and pavement markings regulating, warning and directing traffic. (322.121). Department of Highway Safety and Motor Vehicles may require licensed drivers to submit to examination or re-examination if believed to be incompetent or not qualified to be licensed, or upon recommendation for such re-examination by proper court, law enforcement agency, or physician; licensee may be required to submit medical reports about his physical or mental condition. (322.221). Drivers must sign licenses (322.14[1][a]) and have licenses in their immediate possession when operating vehicle, and they must be displayed to authorized officer or representative upon demand; provided licensee shall not be convicted for failure to do so if he shall produce in court or to clerk of court valid license existing at time of arrest (322.15[3], 322.15). Driver failing to produce license must allow fingerprint imprint on citation. Licenses are revoked upon driver's conviction of certain offenses and may be suspended upon certain grounds based on point system or multiple convictions of certain offenses. (322.26, .27 and 322.2615). Attendance at driver improvement course may be mandated upon occurance of certain accidents. (322.026[1]). Licenses may be restored to habitual offenders as defined in 322.264 upon petition after investigation of qualifications and fitness to drive. (322.331). Penalties are provided for driving while license suspended, revoked, cancelled or disqualified. (322.34). Implied consent to intoxication test; license may be suspended and operator of commercial vehicle may be disqualified if refusal to submit to such tests. (316.1932, 322.2615, 322.64). For DUI conviction, vehicle can be impounded or immobilized for ten to 90 days. No exemptions for members of Armed Forces. See, however, subhead Vehicle License, supra, as to members of Florida National Guard.

Identification cards may be issued upon application and payment of fee. (322.051).

Titles and Sales.—Certificate of title must be obtained by every owner except for mopeds, trailer or semitrailer with net weight less than 2,000 pounds, and motorized disability access vehicles from Department of Highway Safety and Motor Vehicles. (319.20; 319.21). Applicant must show that all sales or use taxes due on transfer are paid; current motor vehicle registration, if any required under 320.02, has been obtained; and where "RP" license issued, that applicant has informed tax assessor of county where mobile home to be situated. (319.23[7]). On sale or transfer, vendor must indorse on back of certificate of title assignment thereof with warranty and statement of all liens and incumbrances. (319.22; 319.27). Purchaser must immediately notify Department and arrange for transfer of registration. (319.22). Seller may notify Department of transfer of title to avoid civil liability arising from operation by another prior to surrender of certificate and reissue to purchaser. Seller's price and odometer disclosure statement must be indicated upon each certificate of title issued or transferred in order to be accepted by any officer of State. (319.22, 319.225). Criminal penalties relating to fraudulent dealings and improper use of title certificates, registrations and failure to complete or acknowledge odometer disclosure statement and other indicia of ownership are provided. (319.33, 319.225). It is unlawful, with certain exceptions, to tamper with, adjust, alter, change, set back, disconnect or fail to connect odometer of motor vehicle to reflect lower than actual mileage or to provide false information on odometer readings or to knowingly possess, sell, or offer for sale, conceal or dispose of motor vehicle with odometer that has been tampered with. (319.35).

License tags must be removed upon sale and delivery of second-hand motor vehicle. (320.271). Car dealers must obtain license to operate from Department of Highway Safety and Motor Vehicles as prescribed. (320.27).

Nonresident dealers not having permanent place of business in Florida must register all used motor vehicles, recreational vehicles or mobile homes brought into state for sale and must apply for certificate of title for vehicle at least ten days prior to offering for sale, advertising for sale or selling vehicle. (320.28).

Taxicabs, lease vehicles no longer in lease service after 4/29/1990, police vehicles, rebuilt vehicles, unless proper application certificate of title for rebuilt vehicle and Department inspection have been made, and the like, shall not be knowingly offered for sale, sold or exchanged until Department has stamped on registration certificate and certificate of title words stating such previous use. (319.14[1]).

Liens on vehicles are not enforceable against creditors or subsequent purchasers without notice unless sworn notice of lien is filed in office of Department of Highway Safety and Motor Vehicles, but there are certain exceptions to this rule. (319.27). Certificate of title is delivered to owner, or if lien exists, to first lienholder unless first lienholder directs otherwise. Motor vehicle dealers who purchase motor vehicle must satisfy outstanding lien within ten days of purchase; lienholder must deliver certificate of title indicating lien satisfaction or notify person satisfying lien that title not available within ten days of receipt of payment. (319.24[3]). If official towing or storage fees are 45 days delinquent, garage owner may auction car to satisfy lien. (713.585; 713.78). Liens for labor and services on personal property may be enforced by sale with proper notice after 60 days from completion of repair work. (713.585, 713.78).

Identification Marks.—Unlawful to knowingly buy, sell, receive, dispose of, conceal or possess any motor vehicle or major component part thereof, from which manufacturer's serial number or other number or identification mark has been removed, defaced, covered, altered or destroyed for purpose of concealment or misrepresenting identity of same. (319.30, 319.33).

Operation Prohibited.—No person, unless expressly exempted, can operate a vehicle unless he has a valid license. (322.03). See subhead Driver's License, supra. It is unlawful for any person who has blood alcohol level of 0.08% or above or who is under influence of alcoholic beverages, any chemical substance set forth in §877.11 or any substance controlled under c. 893 to extent that his normal faculties are impaired to drive or be in actual physical control of vehicle within this state. (316.193[1]). Department must approve and monitor traffic law and substance abuse education course (322.095[1]) that must be completed by all license applicants who have never been issued license in any jurisdiction (322.08[5]). Persons convicted of violations of §316.193 or similar violations in other states must complete substance abuse course. (322.03[2]). No person, except law enforcement officer, shall operate motor vehicle while wearing headset, headphone or other listening device other than hearing aid or other instrument to improve defective hearing, cellular telephone which provides sound in one ear, and operator of motorcycle headset approved by Department of Highway Safety and Motor Vehicles for purpose of communication with passenger or communication with persons in other vehicles by radio. (316.304). No person shall operate motor vehicle on street or highway while any sound making device, other than warning device, is above certain audible level except where sound making device is used for law enforcement, political or business purposes.

Size and Weight Limits.—Regulated by Chapter 316, Florida Uniform Traffic Control Law.

Equipment Required.—Regulated by Chapter 316, Florida Uniform Traffic Control Law. With certain exceptions, it is unlawful for any person to operate motor vehicle unless operator and passengers are restrained by safety belt or child restraint device. (316.614[4]).

Lights Required.—Regulated by Chapter 316, Florida Uniform Traffic Control Law.

Inspection.—Effective Jan. 1, 1991, motor vehicles registered in Florida in those counties electing to participate in inspection program (325.204), required to obtain vehicle inspection certificate, or waiver, within 90 days (with certain exceptions) of registration expiration (325.203). Inspection fee is $10, each vehicle entitled to one free reinspection after failing test. (325.214). Exempt vehicles: 1974 model year and older vehicles; golf carts; farm vehicles; mopeds, propane and natural gas powered vehicles; motorcycles; new motor vehicles for initial year only (325.203[4]) and any vehicle determined by Department of Environmental Protection to not significantly contribute to air pollution (325.211). Department of Environment Protection shall establish emission standards. (325.206). Vehicles failing inspection test must be repaired and reinspected. Waivers may exempt certain motor vehicles from inspection requirements for up to one year. (325.209). Repair shops only charge limited amounts for additional repairs needed to pass inspection. (325.210). Owners of 25 or more vehicles may apply for self-inspection. (325.213).

Accidents.—Operator of vehicle involved in an accident resulting in injury or death of any person or damage to a vehicle must immediately stop and give his name, address, registration number of the vehicle he is driving, and upon request exhibit his license to person injured or person attending any vehicle collided with and such person shall render reasonable assistance to person injured in accident. (316.062[1]). If vehicle collided with is unattended operator of colliding vehicle must stop and locate operator or owner of other vehicle and give him above information or leave same in conspicuous place and shall without unnecessary delay notify police. (316.063[1]). Accidents resulting in injury or death of any person or property damage to any vehicle or other property exceeding $500 must be immediately reported to local police department, county sheriff, or Florida Highway Patrol. (316.065[1]). Where bodily injury or death or where damage exceeds $500 to any vehicle or other property, operator of vehicle must forward written report to Department of Highway Safety and Motor Vehicles or traffic-records center within ten days unless investigating officer has made written report. (316.066[1]). Accident reports made by person involved in accident and statements made to complete such reports are not to be used as evidence in any trial. (316.066[4] and 324.051[1][b]). However, certain statements and test results are not confidential. (316.066[4]).

Liability of Owner.—Court adopted "dangerous instrumentality" rule, holding owner who consents to use of car by another liable for negligent damage done by car. Immaterial whether driver exceeded area or distance of owner's consent. (77 S.2d 468). Negligence or willful misconduct of minor under 18 years of age is imputed to person who signs such minor's application for license and that person and minor shall be jointly and severally liable for any damages caused by conduct. (322.09[2]).

Guests.—Guest statute repealed. (72-1).

Proof of Financial Responsibility.—Law enforcement officer who investigates accident must, within ten days of investigation, file written report of accident to Department of Highway Safety and Motor Vehicles, unless investigation will take more than ten days in which case preliminary copy of accident report must be forwarded to Department within ten days of occurrence, with final report to follow within ten days of completion of investigation. (324.051[1]). Department must suspend, after hearing, licenses of operators and registrations of owners of vehicles involved in accident resulting in bodily injury or death or damage of $500 or more to property, or nonresident's operating privilege, within 30 days from receipt of notice of accident; however, owner or operator will be exempt if vehicle was legally parked, vehicle owned by U.S., this State or political subdivision or Florida municipality, there has been adjudication of no civil liability by court, owner or operator has deposited with Department security in accordance with 324.061 and has complied with 324.031, concerning financial ability to respond to damages caused by accident or owner or operator had automobile liability policy in effect at time of accident or traffic conviction. (324.051[2][a] & [b]; 324.031; 324.061). Proof of ability to respond may be shown by automobile liability policy, surety bond, deposit of cash or securities, or by qualifying as self-insurer. (324.031). "For Hire" passenger transportation vehicles must show automobile liability policy. (324.031). Proof of personal injury protection insurance and property damage liability (and combination bodily injury and property damage liability for certain commercial vehicles) must be furnished upon registration and must be in possession of owner or registrant of vehicle when vehicle is in operation. (316.646, 320.02). For purposes of financial responsibility requirements, lessor of vehicle for term of one year or longer may not be deemed owner provided lessor requires lessee to maintain $100,000/$300,000 bodily injury and $50,000 property damage liability insurance or not less than $500,000 combined property damage and bodily injury liability. Required insurance may be obtained by lessor or lessee but if by lessee, combined coverage for bodily injury and property damage liability must contain at least $1,000,000 and providable by lessor's blanket policy. (324.021[9][b]).

See note at head of Digest as to 1998 legislation covered.

See Topical Index in front part of this volume.

FL – 56

MOTOR VEHICLES . . . *continued*

Insurance.—See subheads Proof of Financial Responsibility, supra and No-Fault Insurance, infra.

No-Fault Insurance.—Florida Motor Vehicle No-Fault Law (627.730-627.7405), requires medical, surgical, funeral and disability insurance benefits to be provided without regard to fault and to require motor vehicle insurance securing such benefits for motor vehicles required to be registered in this state and with respect to motor vehicle accidents, to limit damage claims for pain, suffering, mental anguish and inconvenience.

Person injured may recover to a limit of $10,000 without necessity of establishing negligence on part of anyone for 80% of all reasonable and necessary medical expenses, 60% of loss of gross income and death benefits to limit of $5,000 per individual. (627.736[1]). §627.736(1) held constitutional. (415 So.2d 12). Insurers may enter into contracts with "preferred providers" and may provide option to insured to elect use of such providers. (627.736[10]).

Recovery for pain, suffering, mental anguish, and inconvenience is allowed where injury results in significant and permanent loss of bodily function, permanent injury, significant permanent scarring or disfigurement, or death. (627.737[2]). Requirement of permanent injury before tort claim for pain and suffering may be brought held constitutional. (415 So.2d 12).

Foreign vehicle whose owner has complied with law of his residence and on which home registration number is conspicuously displayed may be operated without registration. (320.37[1]). This does not apply to foreign corporation doing business in state or to motor vehicle operated for hire, recreational vehicles or mobile homes located in state for at least six consecutive months, and commercial vehicles defined in 316.003(66). However, motor vehicle duly registered in another state or foreign country operated or proposed to be operated in this state by nonresident, except nonresident migrant farm worker as defined in 316.003(61), must be registered here within ten days after such nonresident accepts employment, engages in any trade, profession or occupation here or enters children to be educated in public schools here. (320.37, 320.38). Special rules apply for nonresident college or university students. (320.38).

Nonresident Operators.—State Department of Highway Safety and Motor Vehicles, Department of Transportation and Public Service Commission may negotiate and consummate with proper authorities of other states reciprocal agreements whereby residents of such other states, properly licensed there, may enjoy privileges and exemptions in operation of their motor vehicles in this state. (320.39). Every nonresident, spouse or dependent children, except nonresident migrant farm worker defined in 316.003(61), employed in any trade, profession or occupation in this state or who enters his children in public schools of this state shall obtain drivers license within 30 days thereafter if he operates motor vehicle on this state's highways. (322.031[1]). Nonresident at least 16 years old having operator's license in his home state or at least 18 years old having chauffeur's license in his home state exempt from obtaining operator's license. (322.04[1][c] & [d]). No other nonresident, exempt employee of U.S. Government while driving vehicle owned by U.S. Government on official business, any person operating road equipment or golf cart or person working for U.S. Government contractor (up to 60 days), is exempt from licensure requirements. (322.04).

Actions Against Nonresidents.—In a civil action against a nonresident operator or owner of a motor vehicle, or, if dead, against his personal representative, arising out of accident or collision in the state, in which such vehicle is involved, substituted process may be served by leaving or mailing copy certified mail for fee of $8.75, with or to Secretary of State; provided notice of such service and copy of process are forthwith sent by plaintiff or his attorney to defendant by registered or certified mail and defendant's return receipt and affidavit of plaintiff or his attorney of compliance with statute are filed in office of clerk of court in which action is pending. (48.171; 48.161). Like service may be had against resident removed or removing from State. (48.161; 48.171).

Notice of Service and copy of process also may be served on nonresident by sheriff where defendant found (and officer shall file return of service) or if defendant found in state by any qualified officer. (48.161; 48.171).

Motor Carriers.—Department of Transportation authorized to promulgate and enforce weight and safety regulations applicable to interstate motor carriers. (c. 316).

Motor Vehicle Taxes.—Motor vehicles, as property, subject only to license tax which is in lieu of all ad valorem taxes. (Const., Art. 7, §1). Certain vehicles of specified owners exempt from license tax but plates showing exempt status must be displayed. (320.10).

Gasoline Tax.—See category Taxation, topic Gasoline and Special Fuels Taxes, subhead Motor Fuel (and Diesel Fuel) Tax.

Lemon Law.—See category Business Regulation and Commerce, topic Consumer Protection, subhead Motor Vehicle Sales Warranties (Lemon Law).

RAILROADS:

See category Business Regulation and Commerce, topic Carriers.

See note at head of Digest as to 1998 legislation covered.

See Topical Index in front part of this volume.

COMMERCIAL CODE FORMS

See categories Business Regulation and Commerce, topic Commercial Code; Mortgages, topic Chattel Mortgages.

Financing Statement.—Form UCC-1.

NOTE: This is a two-part form. Send both parts to the Department of State for filing. If a copy of this form is needed prior to filing, make photocopies for your records.

IMPORTANT: Read instructions on back before filling out form.

STATE OF FLORIDA

UNIFORM COMMERCIAL CODE **FINANCING STATEMENT** FORM UCC-1 (REV. 1993)

This Financing Statement is presented to a filing officer for filing pursuant to the Uniform Commercial Code:

1. Debtor (Last Name First if an Individual)		1a. Date of Birth or FEI#	
1b. Mailing Address	1c. City, State		1d. Zip Code
2. Additional Debtor or Trade Name (Last Name First if an Individual)		2a. Date of Birth or FEI#	
2b. Mailing Address	2c. City, State		2d. Zip Code
3. Secured Party (Last Name First if an Individual)			
3a. Mailing Address	3b. City, State		3c. Zip Code
4. Assignee of Secured Party (Last Name First if an Individual)			
4a. Mailing Address	4b. City, State		4c. Zip Code

5. This Financing Statement covers the following types or items or property [include description of real property on which located and owner of record when required. If more space is required, attach additional sheet(s)].

6. Check only if Applicable: ☐ Products of collateral are also covered. ☐ Proceeds of collateral are also covered. ☐ Debtor is transmitting utility.

7. Check appropriate box: (One box must be marked) ☐ All documentary stamp taxes due and payable or to become due and payable pursuant to s.201.22 F.S., have been paid. ☐ Florida Documentary Stamp Tax is not required.

8. In accordance with s.679.402(2), F.S., this statement is filed without the Debtor's signature to perfect a security interest in collateral:

☐ already subject to a security interest in another jurisdiction when it was brought into this state or debtor's location changed to this state.

☐ which is proceeds of the original collateral described above in which a security interest was perfected.

☐ as to which the filing has lapsed. Date filed _____ and previous UCC-1 file number _____

☐ acquired after a change of name, identity, or corporate structure of the debtor.

9. Number of additional sheets presented: _____

This Space for Use of Filing Officer

10. Signature(s) of Debtor(s)

11. Signature(s) of Secured Party or if Assigned, by Assignee(s)

12. Return Copies to:

Name
Address
Address
City, State, Zip

FILING OFFICER COPY **STANDARD FORM—FORM UCC-1** Approved by Secretary of State, State of Florida

See note at head of Digest as to 1998 legislation covered.

See Topical Index in front part of this volume.

Continuation, Termination, Release and Assignment.—Form UCC-3.
NOTE: This is a two-part form. Send both parts to the Department of State for filing. If a copy of this form is needed prior to filing, make photocopies for your records.
IMPORTANT: Read instructions on back before filling out form.

STATE OF FLORIDA
UNIFORM COMMERCIAL CODE **STATEMENT OF CHANGE** FORM UCC-3 (REV. 1993)

This Statement of Change is presented to a filing officer pursuant to the Uniform Commercial Code:

1. Debtor (Last Name First if an Individual)		1a. Date of Birth or FEI#
1b. Mailing Address	1c. City, State	1d. Zip Code
2. Additional Debtor or Trade Name (Last Name First if an Individual)		2a. Date of Birth or FEI#
2b. Mailing Address	2c. City, State	2d. Zip Code
3. Secured Party (Last Name First if an Individual)		
3a. Mailing Address	3b. City, State	3c. Zip Code
4. Additional Secured Party (Last Name First if an Individual)		
4a. Mailing Address	4b. City, State	4c. Zip Code

5. This Statement refers to original Financing Statement bearing file number: _____ filed on _____.

6.
A. ☐ Continuation— The original Financing Statement between the Debtor and Secured Party bearing the file number shown above is continued.
B. ☐ Release— The Secured Party releases the collateral described in Block 7 below from the Financing Statement bearing the file number shown above. RELEASE DOES NOT TERMINATE LIEN AGAINST DEBTOR.
C. ☐ Full Assignment— All of the Secured Party's rights under the Financing Statement have been assigned to the assignee whose name and address is shown in Block 7 below.
D. ☐ Partial Assignment— Some of Secured Party's rights under the Financing Statement have been assigned to the assignee whose name and address is shown in Block 7. A description of the collateral subject to the assignment is also shown in Block 7.
E. ☐ Amendment— The Financing Statement bearing the file number shown above is amended as set forth in Block 7. (See instructions for signature requirements.)
F. ☐ Termination— The Secured Party no longer claims an interest under the Financing Statement bearing the file number shown above.
G. ☐ Other— _____.

7. Description of collateral released or assigned, Assignee name and address, or amendment. Use additional sheet(s) if necessary.

This space for use of Filing Officer

8. Signature(s) of Debtor(s): (only if amendment—see instructions)

9. Signature(s) of Secured party(ies):

10. Number of Additional Sheets Presented _____

11. Return Copy to:

Name
Address
Address
City, State, Zip

FILING OFFICER COPY **STANDARD FORM—FORM UCC-3** Approved by Secretary of State, State of Florida

See note at head of Digest as to 1998 legislation covered.

See Topical Index in front part of this volume.

Request for Copies or Information—Form UCC-11.

IMPORTANT—Read Instructions before filling out form.
Contact Filing Officer for fee schedule or additional information.

STATE OF FLORIDA
UNIFORM COMMERCIAL CODE—REQUEST FOR INFORMATION OR COPIES—FORM UCC-11 REV. 1981

INSTRUCTIONS
1. Please type all information on this form using a typewriter having a black inked or carbon ribbon.
2. See special instructions for completing Item Number 1.
3. Place an X in the appropriate box(es) of Items 2, 3, and 4, to indicate whether this form is being used as an Information Search Request or a Request for Copies.
4. If information or copies are requested from different filing offices, separate requests must be submitted to each filing officer.
5. For prompt services, enclose sufficient money to cover services requested. If there is any question as to the fees required, contact the filing officer.
6. Send in only the original and white duplicate copies. Retain the canary colored copy for your files. The original will be returned to you with the information requested.
7. Complete Item 6. This will be used as the mailing label for returning the requested information to you.

1. DEBTOR. Complete items B, C and D only if the debtor is to be searched as so specified. If left blank, the debtor will be searched at any location. Only one debtor per form.

This Space For Use of Filing Officer

A NAME

B STREET ADDRESS

C CITY

D STATE

2. ☐ INFORMATION SEARCH REQUEST. Filing officer, as of _____ 19____, (leave blank if wanted through the most current postings) please provide a computer printout of any presently effective financing statements and subsequently filed statements relating to the original filing naming the debtor above.

3. ☐ COPY REQUEST. Filing officer, please furnish _____ copy(ies) of each page of the statements listed in Item 5, below. (If you cannot provide file numbers, you must first request an Information Search Request.)

4. ☐ CERTIFIED COPY REQUEST. Filing officer, please furnish _____ certified copy(ies) of the statements listed in Item 5, below. (If you cannot provide file numbers, you must first request an Information Search Request.)

5. FILE NUMBER	DATE OF FILING	NAME(S) AND MAILING ADDRESS(ES) OF DEBTOR(S)

Filing Officer Response
The filing officer hereby provides the following notification based upon record postings through _____ 19____.

☐ SEARCH. The attached computer printout lists all active original filings and subsequent filings on the name and address as given above. We may have included some slight variations. However, if you know of any variations in the debtor's name and/ or address, you may wish to request another search.

☐ NO RECORD. After a thorough search of our records, we find no filings on the debtor name and address EXACTLY as given above. If you know of any variation in the debtor's name and/or address, you may wish to request another search.

6. Return information or copies to (requesting party information):

NAME
ADDRESS
CITY
STATE   ZIP CODE

7.

Signature of Requesting Party
Date _____ 19

STANDARD FORM—FORM UCC-11

FILING OFFICER

Approved by Secretary of State, State of Florida

See note at head of Digest as to 1998 legislation covered.
See Topical Index in front part of this volume.

GEORGIA LAW DIGEST REVISER

Alston & Bird LLP
One Atlantic Center
1201 West Peachtree Street
Atlanta, Georgia 30309-3424
Telephone: 404-881-7000
Telecopier: 404-881-7777

Washington, D.C. Office: 601 Pennsylvania Avenue, N.W., North Bldg., 11th Floor, 20004-2601.
Telephone: 202-508-3300. Telecopier: 202-756-3333.
Charlotte, N.C. Office: 1211 East Morehead Street, P.O. Drawer 34009, 28234-4009.
Telephone: 704-331-6000. Telecopier: 704-334-2014.
Raleigh, N.C. Office: 3605 Glenwood Avenue, Suite 310,
P.O. Drawer 31107, 27622-1107.
Telephone: 919-420-2200. Telecopier: 919-881-3175.
www.alston.com

Reviser Profile

Alston & Bird is a major U.S. law firm, with an extensive national and international practice. We have some 400 lawyers—with more in a single office than any other firm south of Manhattan and east of Houston— and we offer services in virtually every practice area from antitrust to utilities.

Alston & Bird has broad transactional and litigation experience in the areas of law that are defining the direction of business and the expansion of the global economy into the next century. Our international team is helping clients with joint ventures and alliances, acquisitions, licensing arrangements and manufacturing facilities in growing customer markets from Latin America to Europe to Asia. We're handling intellectual property and technology issues such as outsourcing, electronic commerce and data encryption for the Internet, and the preparation of legislation on digital signature issues. Our lawyers have handled project finance transactions that involve negotiating everything from foreign supply agreements to construction contracts. And we've developed multi-media environmental compliance programs for a wide variety of businesses.

The same extensive experience and strategic focus apply to all of our practices. In health care, we have helped set national policy, put together financing for mergers and acquisitions from Chicago to San Francisco, and are helping international manufacturers successfully defend bet-the-company product liability claims. Our real estate team has handled transactions in 46 states and is providing day-to-day strategic advice to some of the largest developers, hotel chains and investment funds in the world. In recent years, we've closed major corporate transactions at the rate of one every five days; last year we handled securities offerings at the rate of one every ten days. Our litigation teams have tried over 150 cases in the last few years and have been in arbitration or mediation more than 400 days during just the last two years.

A key element in our ability to offer this level of expertise is the grouping of our attorneys into focused, client-based skill teams rather than the large departments into which more traditional law firms are structured. So our litigation attorneys, for example, are organized into a series of teams focusing on securities, environmental matters, bankruptcy, labor and employment, construction, taxes and ERISA, complex and appellate matters, financial services, antitrust and investigations, medical malpractice and product liability. Because so many clients need health care corporate finance expertise, we assembled a special team that combined regulatory health care knowledge and the skills of our business combinations group. We anticipated the growth of businesses' state and local tax and international tax burdens and developed a superior skill base in these areas to enhance our tax team.

Among our partners are many who served in significant positions with federal agencies including the Justice Department, State Department, Treasury Department, Internal Revenue Service, Federal Deposit Insurance Corp. and Environmental Protection Agency. Attorneys who previously worked at Alston & Bird now are on the state and federal bench. And we have 23 lawyers listed in *Best Lawyers in America* and five members of the American College of Trial Lawyers.

Representative Clients: AFLAC, Inc., American Airlines, Inc., American Cancer Society Inc., AmvesCap PLC, Anacomp, Inc., Anheuser-Busch Companies Inc., The Arthritis Foundation, Atlantic Steel Industries, Inc., BancAmerica Robertson Stephens, Bass Hotels & Resorts, Baxter Healthcare Corporation, Beers, Inc., Boral Industries, Inc., Borden, Inc., Bose Corporation, Brunswick Corporation, B T Alex. Brown, CARE, Inc., Celpage, Inc., CGW Southeast and Affiliates, Charles Schwab & Co., Inc., Chubb Group of Insurance Companies, The Community Foundation for Greater Atlanta, Inc., Coopers & Lybrand LLP, Dorsey Trailers, Inc., Dry Branch Kaolin Company, Eastman Chemical Company, E.I. du Pont de Nemours and Company, Emory University and Emory Healthcare, Equifax Inc., The Equitable Life Assurance Society of the United States, Exxon Corporation, First Union Corporation, Fortis, Inc., Genuine Parts Co. Inc., Georgia Hospital Association, Georgia-Pacific Corporation, Gold Kist Inc., The Goodyear Tire & Rubber Co., Grady Health System, Greystone Realty Corporation, GTE Corporation, Industrial Developments International, Inc., J.C. Bradford & Company, Kaiser Permanente Medical Care Program, Komatsu America International Company, KPMG Peat Marwick LLP, Levi Strauss & Co., London International Group plc, MAG Mutual Insurance Co. Inc., Magellan Health Services, Inc., Medical University of South Carolina, Mohawk Industries, Inc., NationsBank Montgomery Securities, Morgan Keegan & Company, Inc., Municipal Electric Authority of Georgia (MEAG), Municipal Gas Authority of Georgia (MGAG), National Association for Stock Car Auto Racing, Inc. (NASCAR), National Data Corporation, NationsBank Corporation, New England Insurance Company, New York Life Insurance Company, Nissan Motor Manufacturing Corporation USA, Paragon Trade Brands, Inc., PhyCor, Premiere

Technologies, Inc., Primerica Financial Services, Inc., Printpack Inc., Provident Companies, Inc., The Prudential Insurance Company of America, Raymond James & Associates, Inc., Regions Financial Corporation, The Robinson-Humphrey Company, Inc., The Rouse Company, Sears, Roebuck & Co., SMS AG, Sofamor Danek Group, Inc., Southwire Company, SunTrust Banks, Inc. and Affiliates, Turner Broadcasting System, Technical Association of the Pulp and Paper Industry, Inc., Umbro International, Uniden America Corp., Union Planters Corporation, United Parcel Service, Vulcan Materials Co., Inc., Waffle House, Inc., and Watkins Associated Industries Inc.

GEORGIA LAW DIGEST

(The following is a list of all Categories and Topics, including cross-references, covered in this Digest.)

GEORGIA LAW DIGEST

Revised for 1999 edition by

ALSTON & BIRD LLP, of the Atlanta Bar.

(References, unless otherwise indicated, are to Official Code of Georgia Annotated, including Annual Pocket Parts, for Code of 1981, effective Nov. 1, 1982. For explanation of mode of citation see category Courts and Legislature, topic Statutes. Session laws are cited by year and page number. Parallel citations to the South Eastern Reporter begin with 77 Ga. and 1 Ga. App.)

Note: Legislature in recess at time of going to press. This Revision incorporates the 1998 Acts passed by the Assembly and approved by the Governor through March 19, 1998.

INTRODUCTION

ADMINISTRATIVE PROCEDURE:

Open Meetings.—All meetings of state, county and municipal departments, agencies, boards and other political subdivisions, school districts and certain nonprofit organizations receiving funds from tax revenues must be made public. (50-14-1[b]). Any official action taken at meeting not opened to public as required not binding. (50-14-1[b]). Law does not apply to volunteer groups organized for purpose of collecting information, making recommendations and rendering advice but which have no authority to make governmental decisions and act for state. (257 Ga. 398, 359 S.E.2d 913).

Press Access.—Visual and sound recording during open meetings permitted. (50-14-1[c]).

Exemption.—Open meeting rule does not apply to staff meetings held for investigative purposes (50-14-3[1]); deliberation and voting of State Board of Pardons and Paroles (50-14-3[2]); meetings of Georgia Bureau of Investigation or any other law enforcement agency (50-14-3[3]); meetings where agency discusses future acquisition of real estate (50-14-3[4]); meetings where hospital authority discusses staff privileges or granting of abortions (50-14-3[5]); meetings where agency discusses or deliberates on employment of, or disciplinary action against, public officer or employee (unless receiving evidence or hearing argument on charges filed to determine disciplinary action) (50-14-3[6]); adoption proceedings (50-14-3[7]); or meetings where board of trustees or investment committee of public retirement system discusses investment securities trading or portfolio positions (50-14-3[8]).

Jurisdiction.—Superior courts have jurisdiction to enforce compliance. (50-14-5).

Methods of Meeting.—Unless otherwise specifically prohibited, meetings may be conducted by teleconference or similar means. (50-1-5[a]).

GOVERNMENT AND LEGAL SYSTEM:

The State of Georgia is a constituent state of the United States of America. For further discussion of the U.S. federal system, see Introduction to the Federal Government of the United States at the beginning of this volume. A great many laws are promulgated by the federal government of the United States and are not reflected in the topics below. See the Introduction to this volume for references to the federal law topics covered.

Like all but one of the United States, Georgia has a common law legal system, with roots in English common law. For information on the courts and legislature of Georgia, see category Courts and Legislature.

HOLIDAYS:

Legal Holidays.—All public holidays designated by federal government and others designated by Governor. (1-4-1). State offices closed 12 days per year.

Following holidays are generally observed: New Year's Day (Jan. 1), Robert E. Lee's Birthday (Jan. 19), King Holiday (3d Mon. in Jan.), Presidents' Day (3d Mon. in Feb.), Confederate Memorial Day (Apr. 26), National Memorial Day (last Mon. in May), Independence Day (July 4), Labor Day (1st Mon. in Sept.), Columbus Day (2d Mon. in Oct.), Veterans' Day (Nov. 11), Thanksgiving Day (4th Thurs. in Nov.), Christmas Day (Dec. 25). Holidays falling on weekend are observed following Mon.

Religious Holidays.—Sundays only religious holidays. (1-4-2).

Legality of Transactions on Holidays.—Statute declaring certain acts and deeds occurring on religious holidays void, repealed. Sun. business activity regulated. (7-1-294).

Bank Holidays.—No statutory provision.

OFFICE HOURS AND TIME ZONE:

Georgia is in the Eastern (GMT −05:00) time zone. Office hours are generally from 9 a.m. to 5 p.m.

BUSINESS ORGANIZATIONS

AGENCY:

Common law rules apply generally, as codified in Tit. 10, c. 6.

Contract entered into by purported agent purporting to bind principal only is void where purported principal does not exist, and purported agent is individually liable to anyone misled thereby. (10-6-89).

Agent of nonresident, who returns property of agent's principal for taxation, is liable for tax. (48-5-14).

In sales by auction, auctioneer is agent for both parties so far as to dispense with further memorandum other than auctioneer's own entries. (11-2-328).

ASSOCIATIONS:

Formation.—Governed by specific provisions relating to type association contemplated.

Liabilities.—Unincorporated association may sue in its own name (9-2-24) and may be sued upon any claim which plaintiff may maintain against its members. (9-2-25). But individual property of members not subject unless member participated in transaction. (9-2-25). Volunteers for nonprofit associations' sports or safety programs not liable if acting in good faith within scope of duties and unless conduct amounts to willful and wanton misconduct or gross negligence. (51-1-20.1).

Actions.—May be maintained by and against association in name of association. (9-2-24 through -25). Process must be served on officer or agent of association designated in filing with Secretary of State. If no designation filed, then must be served on any officer or official member of association. Action maintainable in any county in which association does business or has in existence branch or local organization. (9-2-25).

Professional Associations.—May be formed under 14-10-1 et seq. for purpose of rendering any type of professional service which may be legally performed only pursuant to state license. (14-10-2).

Professional association means unincorporated association as distinguished from partnership. (14-10-2).

Formation is by any two or more licensed professionals who desire to associate for purpose of rendering one particular type of professional service and dividing gains therefrom. (14-10-3).

Articles of association must be executed and recorded with clerk of superior court in county in which association's principal office located. Recording fee is $20. (15-6-77). No other notice or publication required. (14-10-4). Articles may be amended or dissolved at any time by agreement of two-thirds of members at regular or special meeting and upon filing amendment or instrument of dissolution in same place articles filed. (14-10-4).

Name for association is at discretion of associators but must have suffix, "Professional Association," or "P.A." (14-10-4).

Rights and Powers.—Association may render only one specific kind of professional service and cannot engage in any other business. Association may own real or personal property appropriate for rendering its professional service and may invest its funds in real estate, mortgages, stocks, bonds, or any other type investment. (14-10-5). May render its services only through duly licensed officers, agents or employees. (14-10-6). May contract in its own name, take, hold and sell real and personal property in its own name and likewise sue and be sued. Conveyance in name of association executed by president and attested by secretary is conclusive against association, board of governors and members. (14-10-16).

Ownership.—Articles of association may provide for stock-type or nonstock organization. Membership, if nonstock, or stock or certificate of membership, if stock-type, is freely transferrable except as restricted in articles of association. (14-10-10). See catchline Membership, infra.

Membership may be sold or transferred only to licensed professional. (14-10-14). Member, shareholder, agent or employee who becomes legally disqualified to render professional services must sever all interest in or employment with association. Failure to do so subjects association to involuntary dissolution. (14-10-11). Stock purchase or membership limited to persons duly licensed to render same professional services; estate of member or shareholder may continue ownership during period of administration of estate. (14-10-10).

Management by board of governors elected by members or shareholders. Board elects officers, including president, vice-president, secretary and treasurer. President must be member of board. Board members and officers need not be professionals, but nonprofessionals may not participate in decisions constituting practice of profession. Members may promulgate bylaws or delegate that power to board in articles. Voting by members as provided in articles. (14-10-8).

Existence continued as separate entity independent of members or stockholders for period of time provided in articles or until dissolved by two-thirds vote, notwithstanding happening of events (death, incompetency, etc.) that would dissolve partnership. (14-10-9).

Liabilities.—Members or shareholders, including lawyers who practice as shareholders in professional corporations (see 266 Ga. 844, 471 S.E. 885), not individually liable for debts or claims against association unless such individual has personally participated in transaction giving rise to debt or claim. (14-10-7). Association assets not liable to attachment for individual debts of members or shareholders. (14-10-16).

Laws applicable to relationship between person furnishing professional service and person receiving such service, including liability arising out of such professional service and laws governing confidential relationships, are not modified. (14-10-7). Where applicable and not in conflict, laws governing corporations, not partnerships, apply. (14-10-18).

Taxation.—Taxed as corporations under income tax act. See category Taxation, topic Taxes.

Registered Office and Registered Agent.—Association must maintain registered office and registered agent. (14-10-18; 14-2-501). See topic Corporations, subhead Registered Office and Registered Agent.

Dissolution.—Assets of stock-type association applied first to payment of debts of association, secondly to shareholders. Assets of non-stock-type association distributed, or sold, and net proceeds distributed first to payment of association debts and, secondly, to members. (14-10-15).

See note at head of Digest as to 1998 legislation covered.

See Topical Index in front part of this volume.

ASSOCIATIONS . . . *continued*

See also topic Corporations, subhead Professional Corporations; category Estates and Trusts, topic Trusts, subhead Business Trust.

CORPORATIONS:

Georgia Business Corporation Code (Title 14) ("Code") is based primarily upon Revised Model Business Corporation Act (ABA, 1984), copy of which is printed in Uniform and Model Acts section.

Digest below does not apply to nonprofit corporations or to special category of corporations, including cooperatives chartered by Secretary of State, banking, trust, insurance, railroad, canal, navigation, express and telegraph companies (14-2-1701) or multi-level distribution companies (10-1-15), with nonprofit and special category corporations subject to statutory changes effective July 1, 1989.

General Supervision.—Power to grant incorporation for normal business corporations and close corporations is vested in Secretary of State. (Corporations Division, 2 Martin Luther King, Jr. Drive, Suite 315, West Tower, Atlanta, Georgia 30334). Secretary of State also grants charters for banking, trust, insurance, railroad, canal, navigation, express and telegraph companies.

Purposes.—Every corporation incorporated has purpose of engaging in any lawful business unless more limited purpose specified in articles of incorporation. (14-2-301).

Name.—Corporate name must include word corporation, company, incorporated, or limited or abbreviation corp., co., inc., or ltd., or words or abbreviations of like import in another language. Name must not contain any language implying organization for purpose not permitted by Code and articles of incorporation. Name must not be obscene. Name must not exceed 80 characters. (14-2-401). Name must be distinguishable upon records of Secretary of State from names of other corporations incorporated or authorized to transact business in state, corporate names reserved pursuant to Code, fictitious names adopted by foreign corporations authorized to transact business in state, corporate names of nonprofit corporations incorporated or authorized to transact business in state, names of limited partnerships or professional associations filed with Secretary of State, or names of limited liability corporations formed or authorized to do business in state. Corporation may apply to Secretary of State for authorization to use name that is not distinguishable upon records of Secretary of State from other names of record. Secretary of State must authorize use of nondistinguishable name applied for if other corporation consents to use of name in writing and files with Secretary of State amendment to articles of incorporation changing its name to name that is distinguishable. Corporation may use name (including fictitious name) of another domestic or foreign corporation that is used in state if other corporation is incorporated or authorized to transact business in state and proposed user has merged with other corporation, or proposed user has been formed by reorganization of other corporation, or other domestic or foreign corporation has taken steps required by Code to change its name to name that is distinguishable of record. Issuance of name means that name is distinguishable for filing purposes or records of Secretary of State; it does not affect commercial availability of name. (14-2-401).

Reservation of Name.—Person may apply to reserve use of corporate name, including fictitious name for foreign corporation whose name is not available. (14-2-402). If name available, name is reserved for applicant's use for nonrenewable 90-day period. (14-2-402). Person who has in effect name reservation may transfer reservation by notice to Secretary of State. (14-2-402). Foreign corporation may register its corporate name (or name with any required additions) (14-2-1506) provided name does not exceed 80 characters and name is distinguishable from other names of record (14-2-403). To register its corporate name, foreign corporation must file application with Secretary of State. When application effective, applicant has exclusive use of name. Applicant may file annual renewal applications to continue registration of name for following calendar year. If foreign corporation registers name, it may then qualify as foreign corporation or may consent in writing to use of name by corporation thereafter incorporated under Code or by another foreign corporation thereafter authorized to transact business in state. Name registration terminates when domestic corporation is incorporated or foreign corporation qualifies or consents to qualification of another foreign corporation under registered name. (14-2-403). No fee for name registration. (14-2-122). Availability of name may be determined without payment of fee by contacting Secretary of State by letter or telephone.

Term of Corporate Existence.—Corporations are granted perpetual duration and succession in their corporate names unless articles of incorporation or amendment thereto adopted on or after Apr. 1, 1969 provide otherwise. (14-2-302).

Incorporators.—One or more persons may act as incorporator or incorporators of corporation by filing articles of incorporation with Secretary of State. (14-2-201).

Articles of Incorporation.—Original and one exact or conformed copy required. (14-2-120). Articles of incorporation signed by incorporator(s) or by Chairman of Board of Directors, if any, must set forth: (1) authorized name; (2) number of shares authorized; (3) street address and county of corporation's initial registered office and name of initial registered agent at that office; (4) name and address of each incorporator; and (5) mailing address of initial principal office. Articles of incorporation may set forth: (1) names and addresses of initial directors; (2) provisions not inconsistent with law regarding (a) purpose(s) for which corporation is organized, (b) management of business and regulation of affairs of corporation, (c) definition, limitation, and regulation of powers of corporation, its board of directors, and shareholders, (d) par value for authorized shares or classes of shares, and (e) imposition and extent of shareholder personal liability for debts of corporation upon specified conditions; (3) any provision under Code required or permitted to be set forth in bylaws; (4) provision eliminating or limiting personal liability of director to corporation or its shareholders for monetary damages for any action taken, or any failure to take any action, as director, except liability for any appropriation, in violation of duty, of any business opportunity of corporation, for acts or omissions which involve intentional misconduct or knowing violation of law, for unlawful distributions (14-2-832), for improper personal benefit after date such provision becomes effective; and (5) provision permitting board of directors and individual directors, in addition to considering effects of any action on corporation or its shareholders, to consider interests of employees, customers, suppliers, and creditors of corporation, communities in which it is located and other factors such directors consider important, provided that such factors are discretionary to them and shall not be deemed to provide to any constituency any right to be considered. (14-2-202). Articles of incorporation need not set forth general powers (14-2-302) or emergency powers (14-2-303; 14-2-202). See subhead General Powers of Corporations, infra.

Filing of Articles of Incorporation.—No later than next business day after filing articles of incorporation, incorporator must deliver notice of incorporation in prescribed form, along with $40 publication fee, to publisher of newspaper which is official organ of, or newspaper of general circulation (not less than 60% paid circulation) in, county where initial registered office of corporation is to be located. (14-2-201.1). Notice must be published once a week for two consecutive weeks beginning within ten days of receipt of notice by newspaper. Failure to publish requisite notice does not invalidate incorporation of corporation or filing of articles of incorporation. (14-2-201.1). To file articles of incorporation, incorporator must deliver to Secretary of State: (1) completed Secretary of State Form BR-227; (2) undertaking to publish notice of filing of articles of incorporation as required by 14-2-201.1(b) (14-2-201.1); (3) one original and one exact or conformed copy of articles of incorporation signed by incorporator(s) (14-2-120); and (4) filing fee of $60 (14-2-122). Unless delayed effective date is specified, corporate existence begins when articles of incorporation are filed. Secretary of State's filing of articles of incorporation is conclusive proof that incorporators satisfied all conditions precedent to incorporation except in proceeding by state to cancel or revoke incorporation or involuntarily dissolve corporation. (14-2-203).

Correcting Filed Document.—Articles of correction may be filed with Secretary of State if filed documents contain incorrect statements or if documents were defectively executed, attested, sealed, verified or acknowledged. Articles of correction must: (1) describe document to be corrected or contain copy of document to be corrected; (2) specify incorrect statement and explain why it is incorrect or state reason execution was defective; and (3) correct incorrect statement or defective execution. Articles of correction are effective on effective date of document they correct except as to persons relying on uncorrected document and adversely affected by correction. (14-2-124).

Incorporation Fee.—None. See subhead Filing Fees, infra.

Filing Fees.—Fees for documents filed with Secretary of State or penalties: (1) articles of incorporation, $60; (2) application for certificate of authority for foreign corporation to transact business, $170; (3) annual registration, $15; (4) agent's statement of resignation, no fee; (5) certificate of judicial dissolution, no fee; (6) application for reservation of corporate name, no fee; (7) civil penalty for each year or part thereof during which foreign corporation transacts business in state without certificate of authority, $500; (8) statement of change of address of registered agent, $5 per corporation but not less than $20; (9) application for reinstatement, $100; and (10) any other document required or permitted to be filed under Code, $20. (14-2-122).

License To Do Business.—Corporate existence begins when articles of incorporation are filed unless delayed effective date is specified. (14-2-203). For authority to transact business for foreign corporations, see subhead Foreign Corporations, infra.

Organization.—If articles of incorporation name initial directors, initial directors must hold organizational meeting at call of majority of initial directors to complete organization of corporation by appointing officers, adopting bylaws, and carrying on any other business brought. If articles of incorporation do not name initial directors, incorporator(s) shall hold organizational meeting at call of majority of incorporator(s) to elect directors and complete organization of corporation or to elect board of directors who shall have responsibility for completing organization of corporation. Any of organizational tasks required or permitted to be taken by incorporators at organizational meeting may be taken by written consents describing action taken and signed by incorporators. (14-2-205). Organizational meeting may be held in or out of state. (14-2-205).

Paid-in Capital Requirements.—None. Code no longer requires receipt of $500 for issuance of shares prior to beginning business. Requirements related to par value, stated capital and capital surplus upon issuance of shares have been deleted.

Amendment of Articles of Incorporation.—Unless articles of incorporation require otherwise, board of directors may amend articles of incorporation without shareholder action: (1) to extend duration of corporation; (2) to delete names and addresses of initial directors; (3) to delete name and address of initial registered agent or registered office if annual registration form is on file with Secretary of State; (4) to delete name and address of incorporator(s); (5) to delete mailing address of initial principal office if annual registration on file; (6) to change each issued or each issued and unissued authorized share of outstanding class into greater number of whole shares if corporation has only shares of that class outstanding; (7) to change or eliminate par value of each issued and unissued share of outstanding class of stock if corporation has only shares of that class outstanding; (8) to change corporate name; or (9) to make any change expressly permitted by Code to be made without shareholder action. (14-2-1002).

Majority vote of shareholders generally required for amendment, unless greater vote or vote by voting groups required by articles of incorporation, board of directors, or Code. (14-2-1003). Shareholders of class are entitled to vote as separate voting group on proposed amendment to articles of incorporation if amendment would: (1) increase or decrease aggregate number of authorized shares of class (unless articles specifically authorize increase or decrease without shareholder vote); (2) effect exchange or reclassification of all or part of shares of class into shares of another class; (3) effect exchange or reclassification or create right of exchange of all or part of shares of another class into shares of class; (4) change designation, rights, preferences, or limitations of all or part of shares of class; (5) change shares of all or part of class into different number of shares of same class; (6) create new class of shares having rights or preferences to distributions or to dissolution that are prior, superior, or substantially equal to shares of class; (7) increase rights, preferences, or number of authorized shares of any class that, after giving effect to amendment, would have rights or

CORPORATIONS . . . *continued*

preferences with respect to distributions or dissolution that are prior, superior, or substantially equal to shares of class; (8) limit or deny existing preemptive right of all or part of shares of class; (9) cancel or otherwise affect rights to distributions or dividends that have accumulated but not yet declared on all or part of shares of class; or (10) cancel, redeem, or purchase all or part of shares of class. (14-2-1004).

Amendment accomplished by filing articles of amendment with Secretary of State setting forth: (1) name of corporation; (2) amendment; (3) provisions for implementing amendment if amendment provides for exchange, reclassification or cancellation of issued shares; (4) date of each amendment's adoption; (5) statement that shareholder action was not required, or that amendment was duly approved by shareholders in accordance with 14-2-1003. (14-2-1006).

Restatement of Articles of Incorporation.—Corporation may restate articles of incorporation by action of board of directors with or without shareholder approval. Restatement may include one or more amendments to articles, but if restatement includes amendment requiring shareholder approval, it must be adopted as provided in 14-2-1003. Restatement accomplished by filing articles of restatement with Secretary of State setting forth name of corporation and text of restated articles of incorporation including, or accompanied by certificate setting forth, following information: (1) whether restatement contains amendment to articles requiring shareholder approval, and, if it does not, that board of directors adopted restatement; or (2) information required by 14-2-1006 if restatement contains amendment to articles requiring shareholder approval. (14-2-1007).

Increase or Decrease of Authorized Capital Stock.—If authorized capital stock to be increased and corporation has only one class of outstanding stock, increase in authorized shares may be accomplished by amendment by action of board of directors. (14-2-1002). Other amendment to articles of incorporation must be approved by shareholders. (14-2-1003).

Bylaws.—May contain any provision for regulation and management of corporation not inconsistent with law or articles of incorporation. Incorporators or directors must adopt initial bylaws for corporation. (14-2-206). Bylaws adopted by incorporators or board of directors prior to or contemporaneously with issuance of corporation's shares constitute bylaws adopted by shareholders. (14-2-206[a]). Bylaws adopted by incorporators or board of directors prior to issuance of corporation's shares may be amended by incorporators or board of directors prior to issuance of corporation's shares. (14-2-1020[d]). Thereafter, directors may amend or repeal bylaws or adopt new bylaws unless such power is reserved to shareholders in articles of incorporation or in Code or unless shareholders, in amending or repealing particular bylaw, provide expressly that directors may not amend or repeal that bylaw. Shareholders may amend or repeal bylaws or adopt new bylaws. Bylaw limiting authority of directors or establishing staggered terms for directors may be adopted, amended, or repealed only by shareholders. (14-2-1020). Bylaws may also be amended to increase quorum or voting requirements for shareholders or for directors. (14-2-1021, -1022).

Shares of Stock.—Corporation may issue one or more classes of shares. If more than one class of shares is authorized, articles of incorporation must prescribe distinguishing designation for each class and, prior to issuance of shares of class, preferences, limitations, and relative rights of that class must be described in articles of incorporation. (14-2-601). All shares within class must have identical preferences, limitations, and relative rights except as varied among series. (14-2-602). Articles of incorporation must authorize one or more classes of shares that together have unlimited voting rights and must authorize one or more classes of shares that together are entitled to receive net assets of corporation upon dissolution. Voting rights and rights upon dissolution need not be vested in same class. Classes of shares may also have following characteristics: (1) conditional or limited voting rights (except to extent limited by Code); (2) redeemable, exchangeable or convertible (as specified in articles of incorporation) either at option of corporation, shareholder, another person, or upon designated event; (3) rights to distributions or dividends; or (4) preferences with respect to distributions upon grant of dividends or upon dissolution. (14-2-601).

Articles of incorporation may empower directors to determine, in whole or in part, preferences, limitations and relative rights (including voting rights) of any class of shares before issuance of any shares of that class or one or more series within class, and may designate number of shares within that series before issuance of any shares of that series. (14-2-602). Before issuing any shares of class or series designated by directors, corporation must file amendment with Secretary of State, effective without shareholder action, setting forth: (1) name of corporation; (2) text of amendment determining terms of class or series of shares; (3) date amendment was adopted; and (4) statement that amendment was duly adopted by directors. (14-2-602).

Corporation may issue number of shares of each class or series authorized by articles of incorporation. Reacquisition, redemption, or conversion of outstanding shares is subject to limitations on distributions generally. (14-2-603). See subhead Distributions, infra. If at time corporation issues shares or other securities that are redeemable or exchangeable or convertible into shares of another class, corporation does not have authorized and unissued shares sufficient to satisfy rights, granting of rights is not invalid solely by reason of lack of sufficient authorized but unissued shares to honor exercise of rights. (14-2-601).

Corporation may issue rights, options, or warrants with respect to shares of corporation whether or not in connection with issuance and sale of its shares or other securities. Directors shall determine terms upon which rights, options, or warrants are issued, their form and content, and consideration for issuance, and terms relating to exercise, including timing, conditions precedent and price for exercise. (14-2-624). Granting of such rights is not invalid solely by reason of lack of sufficient authorized but unissued shares to honor exercise of such rights. (14-2-624).

Stock Certificates.—If share is represented by certificate, certificate must state on its face: (1) name of issuing corporation and that it is organized under state law; (2) name of person to whom issued; and (3) number and class of shares and designation of series, if any. (14-2-625). Shares may be authorized without certificates. (14-2-626).

If corporation is authorized to issue different classes of shares or different series within class, reference on certificate to state of incorporation is treated as reference to articles of incorporation and its provisions governing designations, relative rights, preferences and limitations applicable to each class and variations in rights, preferences, and limitations determined for each series and authority of directors to determine variations for future series. Certificates may, however, describe designations, relative rights, preferences, and limitations or certificate may state that corporation will furnish shareholder this information upon request. Certificates must contain either original signature or signature by facsimile of one or more officers designated in bylaws or by directors. (14-2-625).

If shares are issued without certificates, corporation, within reasonable time after issue or transfer of shares without certificates, must send shareholder written statement containing information required on certificates by 14-2-625. (14-2-626). If articles of incorporation, bylaws, agreement among shareholders, or agreement between shareholders and corporation restrict transfer or registration of transfer of shares of corporation, restriction on transfer must be conspicuously noted on face of certificate or on face of information statement for shares issued without certificates in order to be enforceable against person without knowledge of restriction. Authorized restriction not noted on face of certificate or information statement is enforceable against person with knowledge of restriction. (14-2-627).

Issuance of Stock.—Directors have power, unless power is reserved to shareholders in articles of incorporation, to fix consideration for shares. Consideration for shares may consist of any tangible or intangible property or benefit to corporation including cash, promissory notes, services performed, contracts for services to be performed, or other securities of corporation. Prior to issuance of shares, directors must determine that consideration received or to be received for shares to be issued is adequate. Once corporation receives consideration set by directors, shares issued therefor are fully paid and nonassessable. (14-2-621). If corporation issues shares in exchange for contract for future services or benefits or promissory note, corporation may place such shares in escrow or make other arrangements to restrict transfer of such shares. If services are not performed, note is not paid, or benefits are not received, shares escrowed or restricted and distributions credited may be cancelled in whole or in part. (14-2-621).

Transfer of Stock.—Uniform Commercial Code generally governs. Restrictions on transfer of stock may be accomplished through articles of incorporation, bylaws, agreement among shareholders, or agreement between shareholders and corporation. Restriction on transfer or registration does not affect shares issued before restriction was adopted unless holders of shares are parties to restriction agreement or voted in favor of restriction. (14-2-627). Further, restrictions on transfer or registration of shares are valid and enforceable against holders or transferees if restriction is authorized by Code and its existence is noted conspicuously on front or back of certificate or is contained in information statement for shares issued without certificate. (14-2-627). Authorized restriction on transfer or registration of shares is one designed to: (1) maintain corporation's status when it is dependent on number or identity of its shareholders; (2) preserve exemptions under federal or state securities law; or (3) accomplish any other reasonable purpose. (14-2-627).

Restriction on transfer or registration of transferred shares may: (1) obligate shareholder to offer first to corporation or other persons opportunity to acquire restricted shares; (2) obligate corporation or other persons to acquire restricted shares; (3) require corporation, holders of any class of its shares, or another person to approve transfer of restricted shares; or (4) prohibit transfer of restricted shares to designated persons or classes of persons. Restrictions on transfer of shares or registration of transfer of shares also applies to securities convertible into, or carrying right to subscribe for or acquire shares. (14-2-627).

Corporation Reacquisition of Stock.—Corporation may acquire its own shares which then constitute authorized but unissued shares, unless articles of incorporation provide that reacquired shares become treasury shares or prohibit reissuance. Board of directors may amend articles of incorporation without shareholder action to provide that reacquired shares become treasury shares or to reduce amount of authorized shares for reacquired shares. (14-2-631).

Uniform Securities Ownership by Minors Act not adopted.

Uniform Simplification of Fiduciary Security Transfers Act adopted (53-12-320—53-12-330), and expressly stated to govern in case of inconsistency with Uniform Commercial Code (11-10-105).

Stock Transfer Tax.—None.

Preemptive Rights.—Shareholders of corporations (other than corporations described in following sentence), do not have preemptive rights to acquire corporation's unissued or treasury shares, if any, except to extent expressly provided in articles of incorporation. Shareholders of following corporations have preemptive rights unless their articles of incorporation expressly provide otherwise: (1) corporations electing statutory close corporation status and (2) corporations in existence on July 1, 1989, whose shareholders had such rights as of that date or whose articles of incorporation have been restated or amended on or after that date with notice to shareholders that such restatement or amendment would create preemptive rights. (14-2-630). 14-2-630 outlines basic preemptive rights of shareholders. Preemptive rights accompany all securities that are convertible into, or carry right to acquire, shares subject to preemptive rights. (14-2-630). Shares issued in violation of preemptive rights which are otherwise validly issued and outstanding are not subject to cancellation by reason of preemptive rights violation. (14-2-630). Statute of limitations for enforcing any liability for violation of preemptive rights is three years from discovery or notice of violation, but in no event more than five years after issuance giving rise to violation. (14-2-630).

Shareholders' Actions.—Derivative actions permitted in accordance with 14-2-740 through 14-2-747. In order to bring derivative action, shareholder must: (1) have been shareholder of corporation at time of act or omission complained of or have become shareholder through transfer by operation of law from one who was shareholder at that time; and (2) fairly and adequately represent interests of corporation in enforcing right of corporation. (14-2-741). Actions expressly authorized against directors for violation of duties or unlawful transactions. (14-2-831). Shareholder may maintain direct action

See note at head of Digest as to 1998 legislation covered.

See Topical Index in front part of this volume.

CORPORATIONS . . . *continued*
if shareholder has been injured in way which is different from other shareholders or independently of corporation. (264 Ga. 817, 450 S.E.2d 814).

Shareholders' Liabilities.—Purchaser of corporation's shares shall have no obligation to corporation or its creditors other than obligation to pay consideration for which shares were authorized to be issued or as specified in subscription agreement. Unless otherwise provided in articles of incorporation, shareholder of corporation is not personally liable for acts or debts of corporation except by reason of shareholder's own acts or conduct. (14-2-622).

Shareholders' Meetings.—May be held within or without state as provided in accordance with bylaws. If no location specified in accordance with bylaws, meetings must be held at corporation's principal office. Annual meeting required, but failure to hold annual meeting in accordance with bylaws does not affect validity of any corporate action. (14-2-701). Special meetings shall be held at call or demand of one of following: (1) directors or person or persons authorized to do so by articles of incorporation or bylaws; (2) holders of at least 25% of votes entitled to be cast on issue proposed to be considered at special meeting, or greater or lesser percentage as provided by articles of incorporation or bylaws; or (3) in case of corporation having 100 or fewer shareholders of record, 25% of shareholders or such lesser percentage as may be provided in articles of incorporation or bylaws, who are entitled to vote on any issue at proposed special meeting. (14-2-702). Demand for special meeting may be revoked if revocation received in writing by corporation before call of special meeting. (14-2-702). Notice of meetings stating date, time, and place must be given not less than ten and no more than 60 days before meeting to each shareholder entitled to vote at meeting unless waived in writing by shareholder. (14-2-705; -706). Any shareholder may waive notice either before or after meeting and shareholder's attendance at meeting is generally waiver to any objection regarding lack of notice or defective notice of meeting unless shareholder objects to holding meeting. (14-2-706). Notice of annual meeting need not disclose purpose(s) of meeting, unless Code or articles of incorporation require otherwise. Notice of special meetings, however, must include description of purpose(s) for meeting. (14-2-705).

Proxies permitted, but expire after 11 months unless otherwise provided in proxy. Execution of proxy may be accomplished by any reasonable means, including facsimile. Appointment of proxy is revocable by shareholder unless appointment form conspicuously states that it is irrevocable and appointment is coupled with interest. Appointments coupled with interest include appointment of: (1) pledgee; (2) person who purchased or agreed to purchase shares; (3) creditor of corporation who extended credit under terms requiring appointment; (4) employee of corporation whose contract requires appointment; or (5) party to voting agreement created under 14-2-731. (14-2-722). Appointment made irrevocable when coupled with interest (14-2-722[d]) is revoked when interest with which appointment is coupled is extinguished. Death or incapacity of shareholder appointing proxy does not affect right of corporation to accept proxy's authority unless notice of death or incapacity is received before proxy exercises authority. Transferee for value of shares subject to irrevocable appointment may revoke appointment if transferee did not know of its existence when it acquired shares and existence of irrevocable appointment was not noted conspicuously on certificate representing shares or on information statement for shares issued without certificates. (14-2-722).

Each outstanding share, regardless of class, is entitled to one vote on each matter voted on at shareholders' meeting except as provided in Code or except as provided by articles of incorporation. (14-2-721). No cumulative voting unless expressly provided in articles of incorporation. Directors are elected by plurality of votes cast by shares entitled to vote (when quorum present) unless articles of incorporation provide otherwise. (14-2-728).

Certain shareholder action may be taken without meeting by unanimous written consent of all shareholders entitled to vote or, if permitted by articles of incorporation, by written consent of number of shares otherwise necessary to authorize or take action at meeting. No written consent is valid unless consenting shareholder has been furnished same material that, under Code, would have been required to be sent in notice of meeting including notice of any applicable dissenter's rights of appraisal or written consent contains express waiver of right to receive material otherwise required to be furnished. If articles of incorporation provide for cumulative voting, action with respect to any election of directors may be taken without meeting only by unanimous written consent signed by all shareholders entitled to vote on election of directors. Written consent action of shareholders has effect of shareholder vote taken at meeting of shareholders and may be described as such in any document. Notice of nonunanimous action must be given to shareholders who did not participate in written consent within ten days after action taken without meeting. Written consents must bear date of each shareholder's signature. No written consent shall be effective unless corporation receives sufficient number of consents to take action within 60 days of earliest date appearing on any of such consents. Written consent may be revoked by writing to that effect received by corporation prior to its receipt of unrevoked written consents sufficient in number to take corporate action. Consent delivered to corporation shall become effective on date of delivery of last consent required to take action or such later date as it may provide. If Code requires notice of action by shareholders be given to shareholders not eligible to vote and action is taken without meeting, corporation must give its shareholders not eligible to vote written notice of action within ten days of taking action without meeting. Notice to such nonvoting shareholders as to shareholder consent actions must contain or be accompanied by same material that would have been required to be sent to nonvoting shareholders in notice of meeting at which proposed action would have been submitted to shareholders for action. (14-2-704).

After fixing record date for meeting, corporation shall prepare alphabetical list of names of all its shareholders who are entitled to notice of shareholders' meeting. Shareholder list must be available for inspection by any shareholder, his or her agent, or his or her attorney at time and place of meeting. (14-2-720). Corporation may establish procedure (subject to 14-2-723) by which beneficial owners of shares that are registered in name of nominee are recognized by corporation as shareholders. (14-2-723).

For quorum purposes, share is deemed present at meeting and for adjournments of that meeting (unless new record date is set or must be set for adjourned meeting), once share is represented for any purpose at meeting other than purpose of objecting to holding meeting or transacting business at meeting. Unless Code or articles of incorporation provide otherwise, majority of shares entitled to be cast on matter by voting group constitutes quorum of that voting group for action on that matter. Shares entitled to vote as separate voting group may take action on matter at meeting only if quorum of those shares exist with respect to that matter. If quorum exists, action on matter by voting group, as general rule, is approved if votes cast within voting group favoring action exceed votes cast opposing action, unless articles of incorporation, bylaw adopted by shareholders or Code require greater number of affirmative votes. (14-2-725). Election of directors governed by 14-2-728. If Code or articles of incorporation provide for voting by single voting group on matter, action on that matter is taken when voted upon by particular voting group. If Code or articles of incorporation provide for voting by two or more voting groups on matter, action on that matter is taken only when voted upon by each of those groups counted separately. Action may be taken by one voting group on matter even though no action is taken by another voting group entitled to vote on matter. (14-2-726). Articles of incorporation or bylaw adopted under 14-2-1021 may provide for greater or lesser quorum (not less than one-third) or greater voting requirement for shareholders (or voting groups of shareholders) than is provided by Code. Amendment to articles of incorporation or bylaws that changes or deletes greater quorum or voting requirement must meet same quorum requirements and must be adopted by same vote and voting groups required to take action under quorum and voting requirements prescribed in provision being amended. (14-2-727). Holders of majority of voting shares represented at meeting, whether or not quorum is present, may adjourn such meeting from time to time. (14-2-729).

Directors are elected by plurality of votes cast by shares entitled to vote in election at meeting at which quorum is present, unless otherwise provided for in articles of incorporation. No cumulative voting unless articles of incorporation provide otherwise. Shares otherwise entitled to be voted cumulatively at particular meeting may not be voted cumulatively unless meeting notice or proxy statement accompanying notice states that cumulative voting will be in effect or unless shareholder who has right to cumulate votes gives notice to corporation of intent to cumulate votes during meeting. (14-2-728).

Voting Trusts.—One or more shareholders may create voting trust by signing agreement setting out provisions of trust and transferring their shares to trustee. Once voting trust agreement is signed, trustee must prepare list of names and addresses of all owners of beneficial interests in trust together with number and class of shares each transferred to trust; trustee must deliver copy of list and agreement to corporation's principal office. Voting trusts are valid for no more than ten years, but may be extended. (14-2-730).

Shareholders' Agreements.—Two or more shareholders may agree to exercise their voting rights in accordance with written and signed agreement. Duration of agreement may not exceed 20 years. Agreements are renewable for periods not in excess of 20 years. Voting agreements are specifically enforceable. (14-2-731). Voting agreements created under 14-2-731 are not subject to provisions applicable to voting trusts. (14-2-730). Transferee of shares formerly held by shareholder who had entered into such agreement shall be bound thereby if transferee had notice of agreement. Such notice may include notation of existence of agreement on face or back of certificate representing shares or upon written statement required for shares without certificates. To extent that discretion or power of directors is controlled by any such shareholder agreement, directors are relieved from liability for managerial acts or omissions imposed on directors by law and liability is imposed upon shareholder assenting to agreement. (14-2-731). Amending shareholder voting agreement requires approval of all shareholders unless agreement provides otherwise. Unless shares of corporation are listed on national securities exchange or regularly quoted in markets maintained by securities dealers or brokers, no written agreement by all shareholders which relates to any phase of affairs of corporation shall be invalid as among shareholders on ground that it eliminates directors, authorizes director proxies or weighted voting rights for directors, or is attempt to restrict discretion or powers of board of directors in its management of corporation. (14-2-731).

Directors.—Minimum number of directors is one individual. Articles of incorporation or bylaws may authorize shareholders or directors to fix or change number of directors or may establish variable range for size of board of directors. After initial election or appointment of directors, directors are elected at each annual shareholders' meeting unless their terms are staggered pursuant to 14-2-806. If corporation has cumulative voting, any amendment of bylaws decreasing number or minimum number of directors must be adopted by shareholders, and no amendment of either articles of incorporation or bylaws decreasing number or minimum number of directors shall be effective when number of shares voting against proposal for decrease would be sufficient to elect director if voted cumulatively at annual election. (14-2-803). Articles of incorporation or bylaws may set minimum qualifications for directors, but Code only requires that directors be natural persons who are 18 years of age or older. (14-2-802). Directors are not required to be residents of State of Georgia. (14-2-802). Term of initial director expires at first shareholders' meeting at which directors are elected. Unless terms of directors are staggered pursuant to 14-2-806, terms of all directors expire at next annual shareholders' meeting. Interim directors shall be elected for unexpired term of their predecessors in office. Despite expiration of director's term, director serves until successor is elected and qualifies or until there is decrease in number of directors. (14-2-805).

Corporation may establish staggered board of directors through articles of incorporation or through bylaw adopted by shareholders. Staggered board may consist of two or three groups with each group containing one-half or one-third of total of directors. (14-2-806). When staggered board of directors is first implemented, terms of directors in first group expire at first annual shareholders' meeting after their election, terms of second group expire at second annual shareholders' meeting after their election, and

CORPORATIONS . . . *continued*

terms of third group, if any, expire at third annual shareholders' meeting after their election. Thereafter, directors are chosen for term of two or three years depending on number of groups of directors. (14-2-806). Unless articles of incorporation or bylaw approved by shareholders provides otherwise, vacancy on board of directors may be filled by: (1) shareholders; (2) or board of directors; or (3) majority of board of directors if number of remaining directors is less than quorum. If vacant office on board was held by director elected by voting group, only that voting group or remaining directors elected by that voting group are entitled to fill vacancy. (14-2-810).

Directors may create one or more committees and appoint members of board of directors to serve on those committees unless articles of incorporation or bylaws provide otherwise. Each committee may consist of one or more board members who serve at pleasure of board of directors. Board of director meetings and committee meetings governed by 14-2-820 through 14-2-824. Committee of board of directors may not: (1) approve or propose to shareholders action that Code requires shareholders to approve; (2) fill vacancies on board of directors or on any of its committees; (3) amend articles of incorporation; (4) adopt, amend, or repeal bylaws; or (5) approve plan of merger not requiring shareholder approval. (14-2-825).

Directors' Meetings.—Regular or special meetings may be held within or without state. Unless provided otherwise by articles of incorporation or bylaws, board of directors or committees may conduct regular or special meeting through use of any means of communication by which all directors may hear one another simultaneously; any director participating in such meeting is deemed present in person at meeting. (14-2-820). Regular meetings may be held with or without notice except as provided in bylaws or articles of incorporation. Unless articles of incorporation or bylaws provide longer or shorter period, special meetings of board of directors must be preceded by at least two days' notice of date, time, and place of meeting, but notice need not describe purpose unless required by articles of incorporation or bylaws. (14-2-822). Quorum of board of directors consists of majority of fixed number of directors if corporation has fixed board size or majority of number of directors prescribed or if no number is prescribed, majority of number in office immediately before meeting begins if corporation has variable-range size board; however, Code, articles of incorporation, or bylaws may require greater number for quorum of directors. Articles of incorporation or bylaws may provide lower quorum but not less than one-third of fixed or prescribed number of directors. (14-2-824). Written agreement meeting requirements of 14-2-731 may provide director with more or less than one vote, and, if so provided, references in Code to majority or other proportion shall refer to votes and not membership. (14-2-824). Directors may waive any required notice before or after date and time stated in notice. Waiver must be in writing, signed, and delivered to corporation for inclusion in minutes or filing with corporate records. Director's attendance at or participation in meeting waives required notice to him unless director, at beginning of meeting, raises objection to lack of notice and does not thereafter vote at meeting. (14-2-823). Unless articles of incorporation or bylaws provide otherwise, board action required or permitted by Code may be taken by unanimous written consent of directors and such consent action shall have effect of meeting and may be described as such in any document. (14-2-821).

Powers and Duties of Directors.—Business and affairs of corporation are managed by directors, subject to provisions of articles of incorporation, bylaws, or shareholders' agreements. Each corporation must have board of directors except as provided in provisions governing statutory close corporations (14-2-901 through 943) or as provided in written agreement pursuant to 14-2-731 (14-2-801).

Liabilities of Directors.—Directors must discharge their duties as director or as member of committee: (1) in good faith belief in best interest of corporation; and (2) with care ordinary prudent person in like position would exercise under similar circumstances. In discharging duties, director may rely on information, opinions, reports, or statements, including financial statements and other financial data if prepared or presented by: (1) one or more officers or employees of corporation whom director reasonably believes to be reliable and competent in matters presented; (2) legal counsel, public accountants, investment bankers, or other persons as to matters director reasonably believes are within person's professional or expert competence; or (3) committee of board of directors of which director is not member if director reasonably believes committee merits confidence. Director may not rely upon information if director has knowledge concerning matter in question that makes reliance unwarranted. If director performs duties of his or her office in compliance with above, director is not liable to corporation or to shareholders for any action taken as director or any failure to take action. (14-2-830).

Derivative proceeding may be brought within four years from time cause of action accrued by shareholder against one or more directors or officers of corporation: (1) to account for neglect or failure or other violation of his or her duties in management of corporation or disposition, acquisition, transfer or waste of corporate assets or misappropriation of corporate opportunity; or (2) to enjoin or set aside unlawful conveyance, assignment or transfer of corporate assets. (14-2-831).

Within certain limitations, corporation may limit or eliminate personal liability of director to corporation or shareholders by provision in articles of incorporation. See subhead Articles of Incorporation (14-2-202), supra.

Director may be personally liable for deceit for false statements in corporate documents made or authorized by director. (130 Ga. App. 407, 203 S.E.2d 597). Director who votes for or assents to distribution made in violation of 14-2-640 or articles of incorporation is personally liable to corporation for amount of illegal distribution in excess of amount allowed if it is established that director did not perform duties in compliance with 14-2-830. (14-2-832). Director who is held liable for unlawful distribution is entitled to contribution from every other director who could otherwise be held liable under 14-2-832 and from each shareholder for amount shareholder accepted knowing distribution was made in violation of 14-2-640 or in violation of articles of incorporation. Statute of limitations for challenging unlawful distribution is two years from date on which effect of distribution was measured. (14-2-832).

Officers.—Corporation has officers described in bylaws or appointed by directors in accordance with bylaws. Specific officer titles are not required. (14-2-840). Duties of each officer are set in bylaws or prescribed by directors or by direction of officer authorized by directors to prescribe duties of other officers. (14-2-841). Unless otherwise provided by articles of incorporation, bylaws or resolution of board of directors, chief executive officer (or president if no chief executive officer) of corporation has authority to conduct all ordinary business on behalf of corporation and execute any contract for which Code does not require board or shareholder approval. (14-2-841). Same individual may simultaneously hold more than one office in corporation. (14-2-840). Bylaws or directors must delegate to one of officers responsibility for preparing minutes of directors' and shareholders' meetings and for authenticating records of corporation. Duly appointed officer may appoint one or more officers or assistant officers if authorized by bylaws or directors. (14-2-840). Appointment of officer does not itself create contract right. (14-2-844). Directors may remove any officer at any time with or without cause. (14-2-843). Unless bylaws provide otherwise, any officer or assistant officer appointed by officer pursuant to 14-2-840(b) may be removed at any time with or without cause by any officer having authority to appoint such officer or assistant officer. (14-2-843).

Liabilities of Officers.—Officer with discretionary authority must discharge duties: (1) in manner believed in good faith to be in best interests of corporation; and (2) with care ordinary prudent person in like position would exercise under similar circumstances. When discharging duties as officer, officer is entitled to rely on information, opinions, reports, or statements, including financial statements and other financial data if prepared or presented by: (1) one or more officers or employees of corporation whom officer reasonably believes to be reliable and competent in matters presented; or (2) legal counsel, public accountants, investment bankers, or other persons as to matters officer reasonably believes are within person's professional or expert competence. Officer may not rely upon information if officer has knowledge concerning matter which would make reliance unwarranted. If officer performs duties in compliance with 14-2-842, officer is not liable to corporation or to shareholders for any action taken as officer. (14-2-842). Officer may be personally liable for deceit for false statement in corporate document made or authorized by officer. (130 Ga. App. 407, 203 S.E.2d 597).

Indemnification.—

Directors.—Corporation may generally indemnify director against liability incurred in legal proceeding if director conducted self in good faith and reasonably believed conduct in official capacity was in best interests of corporation or, if conduct not in official capacity, not opposed to best interests of corporation, and, in case of criminal proceeding, had no reasonable cause to believe conduct unlawful. (14-2-851). Corporation may not indemnify director in connection with proceeding by or in right of corporation in which director was adjudged liable to corporation or in connection with any other proceeding in which director was adjudged liable on basis that personal benefit was improperly received by director, except for reasonable expenses incurred if standard of conduct met. (14-2-851). Mandatory indemnification against reasonable expenses incurred is available to one who is or was director of corporation for situations in which director or former director was successful on merits or otherwise successful in defense of any proceeding to which director was party because he or she is or was director. (14-2-852). If authorized by articles of incorporation, bylaw, contract, resolution approved by shareholders by majority of votes entitled to be cast by persons other than interested directors, corporation may indemnify or obligate itself to indemnify director made party to proceeding, including proceeding brought by or in right of corporation, without regard to other limitations in Code, except that corporation may not indemnify director for any liability incurred in proceeding in which director is adjudged liable to corporation or is subjected to injunctive relief in favor of corporation for any of following situations: (1) for any appropriation, in violation of his or her duties, of any business opportunity of corporation; (2) for acts or omissions which involve intentional conduct or knowing violation of law; (3) for types of liability set forth in 14-2-832 (unlawful distributions) or (4) for any transaction from which director received improper personal benefit. (14-2-856). Code also permits corporation before final disposition of proceeding to advance expenses to directors who are parties to proceedings because he or she is director if: (1) director affirms in writing that director believes, in good faith, that he or she has met relevant standard of conduct in 14-2-851 or that proceeding involves conduct for which liability has been eliminated under articles of incorporation as authorized by 14-2-202; and (2) director undertakes, in writing, to repay any advances if it is ultimately determined that director is not entitled to indemnification. (14-2-853, 856).

Director of corporation who is party to proceeding because he or she is director may apply for indemnification or advance of expenses to court conducting proceeding or to another court of competent jurisdiction, and court shall order indemnification or advance of expenses if: (1) director is entitled to indemnification under Code; or (2) in view of relevant circumstances it is fair and reasonable to indemnify director or advance expenses to director. (14-2-854).

Corporation may not indemnify director pursuant to 14-2-851 unless corporation is authorized to make such indemnification and corporation has made determination in specific case that indemnification of director is permissible under circumstances because director has met relevant standard of conduct set forth in 14-2-851. Determination of whether corporation may indemnify director may be made: (1) if there are two or more disinterested directors, by majority vote of disinterested directors or committee of two or more disinterested directors appointed by majority of disinterested directors; or (2) by special legal counsel appointed in manner prescribed by statute; or (3) by holders of shares not owned by or voted under control of interested director. (14-2-855).

Officers, Employees and Agents.—Corporation may indemnify and advance expenses to officer who is party to proceeding to same extent as director and, if officer is not director or officer is party to proceeding on basis of act or omission committed solely as officer, to such further extent as may be provided by articles of incorporation, bylaws, resolution of board of directors or contract except for liability arising out of conduct described in statute. (14-2-857). Officer of corporation is entitled to mandatory indemnification under 14-2-852 and may apply to court to procure indemnification under 14-2-854 to same extent as director. (14-2-857). See subhead Directors, supra.

See note at head of Digest as to 1998 legislation covered.

See Topical Index in front part of this volume.

GA – 5

CORPORATIONS ... *continued*

Corporation may also indemnify and advance expenses to employee or agent who is not director to extent provided for by articles of incorporation, bylaws, general or specific action of directors or contract and not inconsistent with public policy. (14-2-857). Regardless of whether corporation would have power to indemnify officer, director, employee, or agent, corporation may purchase and maintain insurance on behalf of individual who is or was director, officer, employee, or agent of corporation. (14-2-858).

Directors' Conflicting Interest Transactions.—Part 6 of Art. 8 of Code regulates transactions between directors and corporation and subsidiaries of corporation. Director's conflicting interest transaction may not be enjoined, set aside, or give rise to award of damages or other sanctions in action by shareholder or by or in right of corporation, on ground of director's interest in transaction if: (1) director's action respecting transaction was at any time taken in compliance with 14-2-862 (transaction approved by majority vote of qualified directors on board or committee thereof after either required disclosure to board or committee or director with conflicting interest discloses to qualified directors existence and nature of conflicting interest, informs them of character and limitations imposed by any duty of confidentiality, and plays no part directly or indirectly in deliberations of committee on transaction); (2) shareholders' action respecting transaction was at any time taken in compliance with 14-2-863 (majority of votes entitled to be cast by holders of qualified shares cast in favor of transaction after receiving notice describing director's conflicting interest transaction, disclosing certain information including number and identity of persons holding or controlling vote, revealing which shares are, to knowledge of director, beneficially owned by director or related person of director); or (3) transaction, judged in circumstances at time of commitment, is established to have been fair to corporation. (14-2-861).

Registered Office and Registered Agent.—Corporation must continuously maintain in state: (1) registered office, which need not be its place of business; and (2) registered agent which may be individual who resides in state and whose business office is identical with registered office, domestic corporation or nonprofit domestic corporation whose business office is identical with registered office, or foreign corporation or nonprofit foreign corporation authorized to transact business in state whose registered office is identical with registered office. (14-2-501). Corporation may change its registered office or registered agent by filing with Secretary of State amendment to its annual registration that sets forth name of corporation, street address of its current registered office, street address of new registered office, name of current registered agent, name of new registered agent, and statement that after change(s) are made, street addresses of registered office and business office of registered agent will be identical. If registered agent changes street address of its business address, it may change street address of registered office of any corporation for which it is registered agent by notifying corporation in writing and by filing statement with Secretary of State setting forth change. (14-2-502).

General Powers of Corporations.—Unless articles of incorporation provide otherwise, every corporation has perpetual duration and has same powers as individual to do all things necessary or convenient to carry out business and affairs, including, without limitation, power: (1) to sue, be sued, complain and defend in corporate name; (2) to have corporate seal which may be altered at will and to use it, or facsimile of it, by impressing or affixing it or in any other manner reproducing it; (3) to make and amend bylaws, consistent with its articles of incorporation and with laws of state, for management and regulation of corporation; (4) to purchase, receive, lease, or otherwise acquire, hold, improve, use and otherwise deal with real or personal property or any legal or equitable interest in property, wherever located; (5) to sell, convey, mortgage, pledge, lease, exchange and otherwise dispose of all or any part of its property; (6) to purchase, receive, subscribe for or otherwise acquire, hold, vote, use, sell, mortgage, lend or otherwise dispose of and deal in and with shares or other interests in or obligations of, any other entity; (7) to make contracts and guarantees, incur liabilities, borrow money, issue its notes, bonds, and other obligations (which may convert into or include option to purchase other securities of corporation), and secure any of its obligations by mortgage, or pledge of any of its property, franchises or income; (8) to lend money, invest and reinvest its funds, and receive and hold real and personal property as security for repayment; (9) to be promoter, partner, member, associate or manager of any partnership, joint venture, trust or other entity; (10) to conduct its business, locate offices, and exercise powers granted by Code within or without state; (11) to elect directors and appoint officers, employees and agents of corporation, define their duties, fix their compensation, and lend them money and credit; (12) to pay pensions and establish pension plans, pension trusts, profit sharing plans, share bonus plans, share option plans and benefit or incentive plans for any or all of its current or former directors, officers, employees and agents; (13) to make donations for public welfare or for charitable, scientific or educational purposes; (14) to transact any lawful business that will aid governmental policies; (15) to provide insurance for its benefit on life or physical or mental ability of any person whose death or physical or mental disability might cause financial loss to corporation, or pursuant to contract concerning reacquisition of shares, or pursuant to contract as part of compensation arrangements or concerning principal obligor or guarantor; and (16) to make payments or donations or any other act not inconsistent with law that furthers business affairs of corporation. (14-2-302).

Unless restricted by articles of incorporation, corporation may exercise all above enumerated powers regardless of whether they are expressly permitted by articles of incorporation. (14-2-302).

Distributions.—Directors may authorize and corporation may make distributions to its shareholders subject to restrictions in corporation's articles of incorporation and certain restrictions imposed by 14-2-640. Corporation may not make proposed distribution if, after making distribution: (1) corporation would not be able to pay its debts as they come due in usual course of business or (2) corporation's total assets would be less than sum of its total liabilities together with (unless articles of incorporation permit otherwise) amount that would be needed, if corporation were to be dissolved at time of distribution, to satisfy rights of shareholders whose preferential rights are superior to those receiving distribution. Effect of distribution is measured depending on type of distribution. Directors may base determination that distribution is not prohibited by Code either on financial statements prepared on basis of accounting practices and principles reasonable in circumstances or on fair valuation or other method reasonable in circumstances. If directors do not fix record date then date of board authorization becomes record date. (14-2-640).

Unclaimed distributions are subject to Uniform Disposition of Unclaimed Property Act, as enacted in state. (44-12-190 et seq.).

Sale or Transfer of Corporate Assets.—Corporation may sell, lease, exchange or otherwise dispose of all or substantially all of its property on terms and conditions and for consideration determined by directors only if directors propose, and its shareholders approve, proposed transaction. Unless articles of incorporation, bylaws, or directors conditioning its submission of transaction require greater vote or voting by groups, transaction must be approved by majority of all votes entitled to be cast on transaction. (14-2-1202). Unless articles of incorporation require, no shareholder approval is required for following transactions if carried out under terms and conditions fixed by directors: (1) sale, lease, exchange or other disposition of all or substantially all of property of corporation if (a) corporation is insolvent and sale for cash or its equivalent is deemed advisable by board to meet liabilities of corporation or (b) corporation was incorporated for purpose of liquidating such property and assets; (2) mortgage, pledge, dedication to payment of indebtedness, whether with or without recourse, or encumbrance of any or all of corporation's property whether or not in usual or regular course of business; (3) transfer of any or all of corporation's property to wholly-owned subsidiary corporation; or (4) sale, lease, exchange or other disposal of less than all or substantially all of corporation's property (statutory presumption is that assets deemed to be less than substantially all of corporation's property if fair value of assets as of date of most recent available financial information does not exceed two-thirds of fair value of all assets of corporation, and annual revenues for most recent fiscal year for which such financial information is available represented or produced by such assets do not exceed two-thirds of total revenues of corporation). (14-2-1201).

Fair Price Requirements.—Found in Part 2 of Art. 11 of Code. Fair price provisions are designed to assure that shareholders will receive fair and equitable treatment in event of business combination between corporation and significant shareholder and are aimed at preventing inequities of two-tiered or front-end loaded takeover transactions.

Applicability.—If provided in bylaws, fair price provisions apply to any business combination. Fair price bylaw may be adopted at any time and in normal manner for adopting bylaws and shall apply to any business combination approved or recommended by directors after date of bylaw's adoption. Fair price bylaw revocable only by affirmative vote of two-thirds of continuing directors and majority of votes entitled to be cast by voting shares of corporation, other than interested shareholder and affiliates. Once repealed, corporation may not readopt fair price bylaw. No cause of action against directors for adoption or failure to adopt fair price bylaw. Fair pricing provisions inapplicable if, during three-year period immediately preceding consummation of business combination, interested shareholder has always been interested shareholder or has not increased percentage of ownership of any class or series of stock by more than 1% in any 12-month period. (14-2-1110 through 1113).

Requirements.—Business combination (as defined below) must be either: (1) unanimously approved by continuing directors, provided there are at least three (14-2-1111); (2) recommended by at least two-thirds continuing directors and approved by majority of votes entitled to be cast by holders of voting shares, other than shares held by interested shareholder and affiliates (14-2-1111); or (3) for fair price (14-2-1112). Fair price paid if four requirements met: (1) fair market value of consideration five days prior to consummation at least equal to highest of: (i) highest per share price (including brokerage commissions, transfer taxes, and soliciting dealers' fees) paid by interested shareholder in previous two years or in transaction in which it became interested shareholder, (ii) fair market value per share of stock, or (iii) if not common stock, highest preferential amount per share payable upon liquidation or dissolution; (2) consideration received is cash or same form as interested shareholder previously paid for largest number of shares; (3) after becoming interested shareholder and prior to consummation, unless approved by majority of continuing directors, corporation does not (i) fail to declare and to pay on regular date full dividend on preferred stock, (ii) reduce annual rate of dividends on common stock, (iii) fail to increase annual rate of dividends to reflect reclassification, recapitalization or reorganization, and (iv) increase interested shareholder's percentage ownership of any class or series of shares by more than 1% in any 12-month period; and (4) interested shareholder has not received disproportionate financial assistance or tax advantages from corporation or subsidiary relating to business combination or otherwise. (14-2-1112).

Scope.—Business combination is: (1) merger of corporation or any subsidiary with interested shareholder or other corporation which is or after merger would be affiliate of interested shareholder; (2) any share exchange with any interested shareholder or any corporation which is or after share exchange would be affiliate of interested shareholder; (3) any sale, lease, transfer, or other disposition not in ordinary course of business in one or more transactions in any 12-month period to any interested shareholder or any affiliate of any interested shareholder of at least 10% of corporation's or its subsidiary's net assets; (4) issuance or transfer by corporation or subsidiary to interested shareholder or affiliate in one or more transactions in 12-month period of equity securities with at least 5% of market value of all issued stock, except in exercise of rights offered pro rata to all shareholders; (5) adoption of any plan or proposal for liquidation or dissolution of corporation if interested shareholder or affiliate would receive anything other than cash; or (6) any reclassification of securities, recapitalization of corporation or merger or share exchange with subsidiary in one or more transactions in 12-month period which has effect of increasing by at least 5% proportionate amount of any class or series of stock of corporation or subsidiary owned by interested shareholder or affiliate. (14-2-1110). Interested shareholder is any person, other than corporation or its subsidiaries, that is beneficial owner of 10% or more of voting power of outstanding voting shares of corporation, or is affiliate of

---

See note at head of Digest as to 1998 legislation covered.

See Topical Index in front part of this volume.

CORPORATIONS . . . *continued*

corporation and, at any time within two-year period immediately prior to date in question, was beneficial owner of 10% or more of voting power of then outstanding voting shares of corporation. (14-2-1110). To determine whether person is interested shareholder, voting shares deemed outstanding does not include issuable but unissued voting shares. (14-2-1110). For purpose of statutory fair price requirements, affiliate is person that directly or indirectly controls or is controlled by or is under common control with specified person. (14-2-1110).

Business Combinations with Interested Shareholders.—Resident domestic corporation may not engage in business combination with any interested shareholder for period of five years following time that such shareholder became interested shareholder unless: (1) prior to such time, directors approve business combination or transaction which resulted in shareholder becoming interested shareholder, (2) in transaction which resulted in shareholder becoming interested shareholder, interested shareholder became beneficial owner of at least 90% of voting stock (excluding shares owned by directors, officers and their affiliates and associates; subsidiaries; and certain employee stock plans); or (3) subsequent to becoming interested shareholder, such shareholder became beneficial owner of 90% of outstanding voting stock (excluding shares owned by corporation's directors, officers, and their affiliates and associates; corporation's subsidiaries; and certain employee stock plans) and business combination was approved by holders of majority of corporation's voting stock entitled to vote, excluding from such vote (for purposes of fair pricing provisions only) stock held by interested shareholder or (i) directors, officers, and their affiliates and associates, (ii) corporation's subsidiaries, and (iii) certain employee stock plans maintained by corporation. (14-2-1132).

Except as set forth in 14-2-1131, definitions (including definition of interest shareholder) applicable to fair pricing provisions apply to provisions relating to business combinations involving interested shareholders of resident domestic corporations. (14-2-1131). Definition of business combination in 14-2-1131 substantially similar to definition in 14-2-1110 (summarized above).

Resident domestic corporation is corporation that is organized under laws of state and has at least 100 beneficial owners in state and either has: (1) its principal office located in state; (2) has at least 10% of its outstanding voting shares beneficially owned by residents of state; (3) has at least 10% of holders of its outstanding voting shares beneficially owned by residents of state; (4) owns or controls assets which represent lesser of (i) substantially all of its assets, or (ii) $25 million. (14-2-1131). For purpose of 14-2-1131, substantially all of corporate assets includes either one-half of value of corporation's assets or corporate assets located within state that generate more than one-half of total revenues of corporation on consolidated basis. (14-2-1131).

Limitation on ability of resident domestic corporations to engage in business combination with interested shareholder only applies if domestic resident corporation has incorporated such limitation in bylaws. (14-2-1133). Restrictions shall not apply if shareholder: (1) becomes interested shareholder inadvertently; (2) as soon as practicable divests sufficient shares; and (3) would not, at any time within five-year period immediately prior to business combination between resident domestic corporation and such shareholder, have been interested shareholder but for inadvertent acquisition. (14-2-1132).

Books and Records.—Corporation must keep: (1) permanent records of all meetings of shareholders and directors; (2) executed consents evidencing all actions taken by shareholders or directors without meeting; (3) record of all actions taken by committee of directors in place of board on behalf of corporation; (4) waivers of notice of all meetings of board of directors and its committees; (5) appropriate accounting records; and (6) record of shareholders in form that permits preparation of list of names and addresses of all shareholders in alphabetical order by class of shares showing number and class of shares held by each. Corporation's records must be maintained in written form or in other form capable of conversion into written form within reasonable time. (14-2-1601). Corporation must keep copy of following records: (1) articles or restated articles of incorporation and all amendments in force; (2) bylaws or restated bylaws and all amendments in force; (3) resolutions adopted by either shareholders or directors increasing or decreasing number of directors, classification of directors and names and addresses of all directors; (4) resolutions adopted by directors creating one or more classes or series of shares, and fixing relative rights, preferences, and limitations; (5) minutes of all shareholders' meetings, executed waivers of notice of meetings, and executed written consents evidencing all action taken by shareholders without meeting, for past three years; (6) all written communications to shareholders within past three years including financial statements; (7) list of names and business addresses of current directors and officer; and (8) most recent annual registration filed with Secretary of State. (14-2-1602). If shareholder gives corporation written notice of demand to inspect and copy records, shareholder may inspect and copy above records of corporation. Additional inspection rights may be available to shareholder who meets test of proper purpose reasonably relevant to legitimate interest as shareholder. Articles of incorporation or bylaws may limit additional right to inspection of records to only those shareholders owning 2% or more of shares outstanding. (14-2-1602). Scope of inspection rights is set forth in 14-2-1603. This section does not, however, affect right of shareholder to inspect records under 14-2-720 or power of court to compel production of corporate records for examination. (14-2-1602). If corporation improperly refuses to permit shareholder to inspect records, shareholder may invoke power of court to open records for inspection. (14-2-1604).

Reports.—Annual registration required of domestic corporations and foreign corporations authorized to transact business in state. Annual registration must show: (1) name of corporation, employer identification number issued by federal government, and state or country of incorporation; (2) street address and county of registered office and name of registered agent at that office in state; (3) mailing address of principal office; and (4) names and respective addresses of chief executive officer, chief financial officer, and secretary, or individuals holding similar positions. Each annual registration must be filed with Secretary of State between Jan. 1 and Apr. 1 (subject to change by Secretary of State). Initial annual registration of domestic corporation must be filed within 90 days after its articles of incorporation are delivered to Secretary of

State for filing, unless articles are delivered for filing subsequent to Oct. 1, in which case initial annual registration must be filed between Jan. 1 and Apr. 1 of year following year in which corporation's certificate of incorporation is issued by Secretary of State. (14-2-1622).

Corporation must prepare balance sheet and profit and loss statement showing results of operations during its fiscal year not later than four months after close of each fiscal year and in any case prior to annual meeting of shareholders. (14-2-1620). Such report must be available to shareholders of record upon written request. If financial statements prepared for other purposes, corporation must also furnish upon written request statement of sources and applications of funds and statement of changes in shareholders' equity for fiscal year. Financial statements must also include statement of basis upon which they were prepared. If public accountant reports on annual financial statements, such report must accompany financial statements. If financial statements are not reported upon by public accountant, statements must be accompanied by statement of president or person responsible for corporation's records stating reasonable belief that statements were prepared on basis of generally accepted accounting principles or other basis of preparation and describing any respects in which statements were not prepared on basis of accounting consistent with statements prepared for preceding year. (14-2-1620). If corporation indemnifies or advances expenses to director pursuant to 14-2-851 through 14-2-854, corporation must report indemnification or advance in writing to shareholders with or before notice of next shareholders' meeting. (14-2-1621).

Corporate Bonds or Mortgages.—Corporations are expressly empowered to issue bonds and to secure any obligations by mortgages. (14-2-302). See subhead General Powers of Corporations, supra. Shareholder approval not required to transfer all or part of assets as security for indebtedness. (14-2-1201).

Mergers and Share Exchanges.—

Merger.—One or more corporations may merge into another corporation if directors of each corporation adopt and its shareholders approve plan of merger. Plan of merger must set forth: (1) name of each corporation planning to merge and name of surviving corporation into which each other corporation plans to merge; (2) terms and conditions of merger; and (3) manner and basis of converting shares of each corporation into securities of surviving or any other corporation or into cash or other property in whole or in part. Plan of merger may also set forth amendments to articles of incorporation of surviving corporation and other provisions relating to merger. (14-2-1101). Shareholder approval of plan of merger by shareholders of surviving corporation or by shareholders of acquiring corporation in share exchange, however, is not necessary if: (1) articles of incorporation of surviving or acquiring corporation will not change; (2) each shareholder of surviving or acquiring corporation whose shares are outstanding immediately before effective date of merger will hold same number of shares, with identical designations, preferences, limitations, and relative rights immediately after merger or share exchange; and (3) number and kind of shares outstanding immediately after merger or share exchange plus any shares issuable as result of merger or share exchange will not exceed total number and kind of shares of surviving corporation authorized by its articles of incorporation immediately before merger or share exchange. (14-2-1103). Similarly, no shareholder approval required for parent to merge with 90% owned subsidiary (14-2-1104). Directors of parent must adopt plan of merger for merging subsidiary into parent which sets forth names of parent and subsidiary and manner and basis of converting shares of subsidiary into shares of parent or into other consideration. Within ten days after corporate action parent must mail copy or summary of plan of merger to each shareholder of subsidiary that has not waived mailing requirement in writing. Articles of merger or certificate of merger pursuant to 14-2-1104 relating to merger of subsidiary into parent may not contain amendments to articles of incorporation of parent. (14-2-1104).

Share Exchange.—Corporation may acquire all of outstanding shares of one or more classes or series of another corporation through share exchange if directors of each corporation adopt and its shareholders approve share exchange. Plan of share exchange must set forth: (1) name of corporation whose shares will be acquired and name of acquiring corporation; (2) terms and conditions of share exchange; and (3) manner and basis of exchanging shares. (14-2-1102).

Action on Plan.—Once directors adopt plan of merger or share exchange, directors of each corporation to transaction must submit plan for approval by shareholders. Directors must recommend plan to shareholders unless directors elect, because of conflict of interest or other circumstances, to make no recommendation and communicate basis for their election to shareholders with plan; and shareholders entitled to vote must approve plan. (14-2-1103). Corporation must notify each voting shareholder of proposed shareholders' meeting and notice must also set forth purpose(s) of meeting and must contain or be accompanied by copy or summary of plan. (14-2-1103). Unless Code, articles of incorporation, bylaws, or directors require greater vote or vote by voting groups, plan of merger or share exchange must be authorized by approval of: (1) majority of all votes entitled to be cast on plan by all shares entitled to vote on plan, voting as single group; and (2) majority of all votes entitled to be cast by holders of shares in each voting group entitled to vote separately on plan as voting group by articles of incorporation. Shares of class or series not otherwise entitled to vote on merger are entitled to vote on plan of merger if plan contains provision that would require action by class as separate voting group under 14-2-1004. Shares of class or series included in share exchange, but not otherwise entitled to vote on plan of share exchange are entitled to vote with each class or series constituting separate voting group. After merger or share exchange is authorized, and at any time before articles of merger or certificate of merger or share exchange is filed, plan of merger or share exchange may be abandoned without further shareholder action in accordance with procedures set forth in plan of merger or share exchange or, if none is set forth, in manner determined by directors. (14-2-1103).

Once plan of merger or share exchange is properly approved, surviving or acquiring corporation must file with Secretary of State articles of merger or share exchange setting forth plan of merger or share exchange and statement regarding shareholder approval. In lieu of filing articles of merger or share exchange that set forth plan of merger or share exchange, surviving or acquiring corporation may file certificate of

CORPORATIONS . . . *continued*
merger or share exchange which sets forth: (1) name and state of incorporation of each corporation which is merging or engaging in share exchange and name of surviving corporation; (2) in case of merger, any amendments to articles of incorporation of surviving corporation; (3) statement that executed plan of merger or share exchange is on file at principal place of business of surviving or exchanging corporation and stating address thereof; (4) that copy of plan of merger or share exchange will be furnished by surviving or exchanging corporation on request and without cost to any shareholder of any corporation that is party to merger or whose shares are involved in share exchange; (5) if shareholder approval was not required, statement to that effect; and (6) if shareholder approval was required, statement that merger or exchange was duly approved by shareholders. Merger or share exchange takes effect when articles or certificate of merger or share exchange is filed, unless delayed effective date is specified. (14-2-1105). When filing articles or certificate of merger or share exchange, surviving or acquiring corporation must deliver to Secretary of State statement that request for publication of notice of filing of articles or certificate of merger or share exchange, and payment therefore, will be made. No later than next business day after filing articles or certificate of merger or share exchange, surviving or acquiring corporation must deliver to publisher of newspaper which is official organ of or newspaper of general circulation (not less than 60% paid circulation) in county where registered office of surviving or acquiring corporation is to be located request to publish notice in prescribed form. Statute specifies form of notice required. Request for publication must include $40 payment of publication costs. Notice must be published once a week for two consecutive weeks commencing within ten days after receipt of notice by newspaper. Failure on part of surviving corporation to mail or deliver notice or payment therefor, or failure on part of newspaper to publish notice, will not invalidate merger or share exchange. (14-2-1105.1).

Effect of Merger.—When merger takes effect: (1) all corporations merge into surviving corporation and their separate existences cease; (2) title to all property owned is vested in surviving corporation without reversion or impairment; (3) surviving corporation has all liabilities of each corporation party to merger; (4) proceedings pending against any merged corporation may be continued as if merger did not occur or surviving corporation may be substituted in lieu of extinguished corporation; (5) articles of incorporation of surviving corporation are amended to extent provided in plan of merger; and (6) shares of each corporation party to merger that are to be converted into shares, obligations, or securities of their survivor are converted and former holders of shares are entitled only to rights provided in plan of merger or to their dissenters' rights of appraisal. When share exchange takes effect, shares of each acquired corporation are exchanged as provided in plan and former holders of shares are entitled only to share exchange rights provided in articles of share exchange or to their dissenters' rights of appraisal. (14-2-1106).

Merger or Share Exchange With Foreign Corporation.—Foreign corporations and domestic corporations may engage in merger or share exchange with domestic corporation if: (1) in merger, merger is permitted by law of state or country under which foreign corporation is incorporated and foreign corporation complies with such law in effecting merger; (2) in share exchange, corporation whose shares will be acquired is domestic corporation regardless of whether share exchange is permitted by law under which foreign corporation is incorporated; (3) foreign corporation complies with 14-2-1105 (filing of articles or certificate of merger or share exchange) if it is surviving corporation of merger or acquiring corporation of share exchange; and (4) each domestic corporation complies with 14-2-1101 through 14-2-1104 and if surviving or acquiring corporation of share exchange is domestic corporation, surviving or acquiring corporation complies with 14-2-1105 (filing of articles or certificate of merger or share exchange). (14-2-1107). Upon merger or share exchange taking effect, surviving or acquiring foreign corporation is deemed to appoint Secretary of State as its agent for service of process and is deemed to agree to promptly pay dissenting shareholders according to their dissenters' rights of appraisal. (14-2-1107).

Mergers with Other Entities.—Corporations may merge or engage in share exchanges with banking, insurance, railroad, trust, canal, navigation, express, and telegraph companies and other corporations whose charters have been granted by Secretary of State unless otherwise prohibited by law. (14-2-1108). Each merging or exchanging corporation must comply with provisions of Code except to extent merger or share exchange is governed by provisions governing other entity. If surviving entity is corporation organized under Code, time and effect of merger shall be as provided in Code. If, however, surviving entity is not organized under Code, time of effect of merger shall be as provided in Code except as provided by laws governing surviving entity. (14-2-1108).

Domestic corporations may merge with foreign or domestic nonprofit corporations, limited liability companies, joint-stock associations or limited partnerships pursuant to 14-2-1109 unless laws of foreign nonprofit corporation, limited liability company, association or partnership forbid merger with corporation. Approval of merger is as for domestic corporations. (14-2-1109).

Dissolution.—
Voluntary.—Corporation may be voluntarily dissolved by: (1) action by majority of incorporators or initial directors if corporation has not issued shares or has not commenced business (14-2-1401); or (2) majority vote of shareholders entitled to vote, unless articles of incorporation or directors (acting pursuant to 14-2-1402[c]) require otherwise (14-2-1402). Once proposal for dissolution is approved by shareholders pursuant to 14-2-1402, corporation must begin dissolution by filing with Secretary of State notice of intent to dissolve setting forth: (1) name of corporation; (2) date that dissolution was authorized; and (3) statement that dissolution was duly approved by shareholders if shareholder approval was required. (14-2-1403). Along with notice of intent to dissolve, corporation must deliver to Secretary of State undertaking that request for publication of notice to dissolve and payment of fee therefor will be made. 14-2-1403.1 prescribes form for notice of intent to voluntarily dissolve. Request for publication must include payment of $40 publication fee. (14-2-1403.1). After filing notice of intent to dissolve, corporation continues its corporate existence, but may not carry on any business except that business appropriate to winding up and liquidating its business and affairs. (14-2-1405). 14-2-1406 and 14-2-1407 set forth procedure for disposing of claims against corporation.

If notice of intent to dissolve has not been revoked (revocation procedures outlined in 14-2-1404) and when all known debts, liabilities, and obligations of corporation have been paid and discharged, or adequate provision made therefor, corporation may dissolve by filing with Secretary of State articles of dissolution setting forth: (1) name of corporation; (2) date on which notice of intent to dissolve was filed and statement that it has not been revoked; (3) statement that all known debts, liabilities, and obligations of corporation have been paid and discharged or that adequate provision has been made therefor; (4) statement that all remaining property and assets of corporation have been distributed among shareholders in accordance with their respective rights and interests or that adequate provision has been made therefor or that such property and assets have been deposited with Georgia Department of Administrative Services; and (5) statement that there are no actions pending against corporation in any court or that adequate provision has been made for satisfaction of any judgment, order, or decree. Once articles of dissolution are filed, corporation shall cease to exist, except for limited purposes. (14-2-1408).

Administrative.—Secretary of State may commence dissolution proceeding under 14-2-1421 to dissolve corporation if: (1) state Revenue Commissioner has certified that corporation has failed to file license or occupation tax return and that one year has expired since last day permitted for timely filing, but dissolution proceedings shall be stayed so long as corporation is contesting in good faith alleged grounds for dissolution; (2) corporation failed to deliver its annual registration to Secretary of State, together with all required fees and penalties within 60 days after report and penalties and fees are due; (3) corporation is without registered office or registered agent in state for 60 days or more; (4) corporation does not notify Secretary of State within 60 days that its registered agent or registered office has been changed, that its registered agent has resigned, or that its registered office has been discontinued; (5) corporation pays fee to Secretary of State as required by Code by check or other form of payment which is dishonored and corporation or its incorporator or agent does not resubmit payment within 60 days of notice of nonpayment issued by Secretary of State; or (6) any notice which is required to be published has not been published. (14-2-1420). 14-2-1422 provides procedure for corporation to apply for reinstatement following administrative dissolution.

Judicial.—Superior court has power to dissolve corporation: (1) in action by Attorney General if it is established that corporation obtained articles of incorporation through fraud or corporation has continued to exceed or abuse authority conferred upon it by law; (2) in shareholder action if it is established directors are deadlocked in management of (i) corporate affairs and deadlock cannot be broken by shareholder action and irreparable injury to corporation is threatened, (ii) directors or those in control of corporation have acted, are acting, or will act in illegal or fraudulent manner in connection with operation or management of business and such action is initiated by holders of at least 20% of outstanding shares of corporation, (iii) shareholders are deadlocked in voting power and have failed for at least two consecutive annual meeting dates to elect successors to directors whose terms have expired or would have expired, or (iv) corporate assets are being misapplied or wasted; (3) in creditor action if creditor's claim has been reduced to judgment, and execution on judgment has been returned unsatisfied and corporation is insolvent, or if corporation has admitted in writing that creditor's claim is due and owing and corporation is insolvent; or (4) in proceeding by corporation to have its voluntary dissolution continued under court supervision. (14-2-1430).

Receivership or Custodianship.—In judicial proceedings to dissolve corporation, court may appoint receivers to wind up and liquidate, or one or more custodians to manage, business and affairs of corporation. Court must hold hearing before appointing receiver or custodian. Powers and duties of receiver are ordered by appointing court. Receiver may dispose of all or part of corporate assets wherever located at public or private sale with court authorization, sue and defend in his or her own name as receiver, and exercise corporate powers through or in place of directors or officers to extent. (14-2-1432).

Close Corporations.—
Election of Close Corporation Status.—Corporation having 50 or fewer shareholders may elect close corporation status by amending articles of incorporation to include statement that corporation is statutory close corporation. Amendment electing close corporation status must be approved by holders of at least two-thirds of votes of each class or series of shares of corporation, voting as separate voting groups, whether or not otherwise entitled to vote on amendments. Shareholders voting against amendment for close corporation status are entitled to dissenters' rights of appraisal. (14-2-902).

Applicability.—Provisions governing close corporations apply to corporations and professional corporations (organized under Georgia Professional Corporation Act) electing close corporation status. (14-2-901).

Shares.—Each share or certificate issued by statutory close corporation must contain following legend:

> "The rights of shareholders in a statutory close corporation may differ materially from the rights of shareholders in other corporations. Copies of the articles of incorporation and bylaws, shareholders' agreements, and other documents, any of which may restrict transfers and affect voting and other rights, may be obtained by a shareholder on written request to the corporation."

If corporation issues shares without certificates, corporation must deliver notice to shareholders containing information in above legend. Corporation must provide, upon written request and without charge, copies of provisions that restrict transfer or affect voting or other rights of shareholders. (14-2-910).

Unless and to extent permitted by articles of incorporation or 14-2-912, interest in shares of close corporation may not, as general rule, be transferred. General prohibition against transfer does not apply to following (unless and to extent articles of incorporation provide otherwise): (1) transfer to issuer corporation or to any other holder of same class or series of shares; (2) transfer to members of shareholder's immediate family; (3) transaction approved in writing by all holders of corporation's

See note at head of Digest as to 1998 legislation covered.

See Topical Index in front part of this volume.

GA – 8

CORPORATIONS . . . *continued*
shares having general voting rights; (4) transfer to executor or administrator upon death of shareholder or to trustee or receiver as result of bankruptcy, insolvency, dissolution, or similar proceeding brought by or against shareholder; (5) transfer pursuant to merger or share exchange under Art. 11 of Code or exchange of existing shares for other shares of different class or series of corporation; (6) transfer pursuant to pledge as collateral for loan that does not grant pledgee any voting rights possessed by pledgor; or (7) transfer made after termination of close corporation status. (14-2-911). Attempt to transfer shares in violation of prohibition against transfer binding on transferee is ineffective. (14-2-913). Attempt to transfer shares in violation of prohibition against transfer which is not binding on transferee gives corporation option to purchase shares from transferee for same price and on same terms that transferee purchased them. (14-2-913).

14-2-912 provides procedure by which shareholder may transfer shares to eligible third party. Shareholder must first offer shares to corporation by obtaining written offer to purchase shares for cash from eligible third party purchaser. (Eligible third party purchaser is one who is eligible to become qualified shareholder under any federal or state tax statute applicable to corporation, one who agrees in writing not to terminate tax qualification without approval of remaining shareholders, and one whose purchase of shares will not impose personal holding company tax or similar federal or state tax or penalty on corporation.) Selling shareholder must deliver offer to corporation giving corporation opportunity to buy shares on same terms as eligible third party purchaser. Within 20 days after receipt of offer, corporation must call special shareholders' meeting to be held within 40 days to decide whether corporation should purchase all (but not less than all) of offered shares. To accept offer, affirmative vote of majority of shares entitled to vote (excluding votes in respect of shares covered by offer) is required. Corporation must deliver notice of acceptance to shareholder in writing within 75 days after receiving offer or else offer is rejected. If corporation makes counteroffer, shareholder must deliver to corporation written notice of acceptance within 15 days of receipt of counteroffer or otherwise counteroffer is rejected. Once offer or counteroffer is accepted, shares must be delivered within 20 days after effective date of notice of acceptance. Corporation accepting offer to purchase shares may allocate some or all of shares pro rata to those of its shareholders who desire to purchase shares unless all shareholders who desire to purchase approve different allocation of shareholders or to other persons. If corporation has more than one class or series of shares remaining, holders of class or series being purchased are entitled to first option to purchase shares, pro rata, which are not purchased by corporation. If offer to purchase shares is rejected, offering shareholder, for period of 120 days after corporation receives offer, is entitled to transfer to third person offeror all of offered shares in accordance with terms of offer. (14-2-912).

Articles of incorporation may provide for mandatory purchase by corporation of shares from shareholder who dies. Adding or repealing compulsory purchase provision requires vote of two-thirds of shares of each class or series of shares, voting as separate groups. Shareholder who votes against compulsory purchase provision is entitled to dissenters' rights. (14-2-914). 14-2-915 provides procedure for exercising mandatory purchase option. (14-2-915). Superior court of county where corporation's registered office is located may compel mandatory purchase. (14-2-916).

Governance.—Shareholders may agree in writing to regulate exercise of corporate powers, management of corporate business and affairs, and relationship among shareholders. Shareholders' agreement may: (1) eliminate board of directors; (2) restrict discretion or powers of board; (3) authorize director proxies or weighted voting rights; (4) provide that corporation be treated as partnership; or (5) create relationship among shareholders or between shareholders and corporation that would otherwise be appropriate only among partners. (14-2-920). Articles of incorporation or by-laws of close corporation may provide that holders of class or series may elect one or more directors. (14-2-921). Shareholders may also agree that certain directors shall have more or less than one vote. References to percentages of directors necessary to take action in Georgia corporation code shall take into account any such agreement. (14-2-824). Close corporation may operate without board of directors if articles of incorporation, bylaws approved by shareholders, or agreements between shareholders that are otherwise lawful contain statement to that effect. While close corporation is operating without board of directors, corporate powers are exercised by or under authority of shareholders. (14-2-922). Bylaws not necessary for close corporation if provisions required by law to be contained in bylaws are contained in either articles of incorporation or agreement among shareholders. (14-2-923). Unless articles of incorporation, bylaws, or authorized shareholder agreement provide otherwise, annual meeting date is first business day after 31st day of May. Close corporation does not have to hold annual meeting unless one or more shareholders delivers written notice to corporation requesting meeting at least 30 days prior to scheduled meeting date. (14-2-924). Failure to observe usual corporate formalities or requirements relating to exercise of corporate powers or management of its business and affairs is not grounds for imposing personal liability on shareholders or liabilities of corporation. (14-2-926).

Reorganization and Termination.—Plan of merger or share exchange that would terminate statutory close corporation status or plan of merger or share exchange that would result in close corporation being surviving or acquiring corporation requires approval of two-thirds of votes of each class or series of shares voting as separate voting groups regardless of whether holders are otherwise entitled to vote on plan. Sale, lease, exchange, or other disposition of all or substantially all property of close corporation requires approval of shareholders by two-thirds majority vote of each class or series of shares voting as voting groups, whether or not holders are otherwise entitled to vote on transaction. (14-2-930). Terminating close corporation status requires amendment to articles of incorporation. Amendment terminating close corporation status requires approval of at least two-thirds of votes of each class or series of shares, voting as separate voting groups, whether or not holders are otherwise entitled to vote on amendments. Shareholders voting against termination of close corporation status are entitled to dissenters' rights. (14-2-931). Effect of termination is that corporation is then subject to Code generally or Georgia Professional Corporation Act. Termination of close corporation status does not affect any right of shareholder or of corporation under agreement, articles of incorporation or by-laws unless otherwise invalidated by law. (14-2-932).

Dissolution.—Articles of incorporation, bylaws adopted by shareholders, or agreement among all shareholders may authorize one or more shareholders, or holders of specified number or percentage of shares, to dissolve corporation at will or upon occurrence or specified event or contingency. Unless otherwise provided in articles, bylaws adopted by shareholders or shareholders agreement, any amendment to articles or by-laws altering right of specified shareholders to dissolve corporation must be approved by all shareholders of corporation. (14-2-933).

Judicial Supervision.—Shareholder may petition superior court for relief of type described in 14-2-941 through 14-2-943 if: (1) directors or those in control have acted illegally, oppressively, fraudulently or prejudicially to petitioning shareholder in capacity as shareholder, director or officer; (2) directors or those in control are deadlocked in management of corporation's affairs, with shareholders are unable to break deadlock, and corporation is suffering or will suffer irreparable injury or business since affairs of corporation cannot be conducted to advantage of shareholders because of deadlock; or (3) ground for judicial dissolution exists. Shareholder may not pursue relief if shareholder previously agreed to forego judicial remedy or if shareholder pursued dissenters' rights. (14-2-940). Court may order ordinary relief (14-2-941), extraordinary relief such as share purchase (14-2-942) or dissolution (14-2-943). Court may also take specific remedial action such as cancellation of actions, alter provisions, remove or appoint officers and directors or provisional directors, appoint custodian or pay dividends or award damages to any aggrieved party. (14-2-941).

Dissenters' Rights-Appraisal.—Remedy available to shareholder dissenting from: (1) consummation of plan of merger if corporation required to obtain shareholder approval and shareholder entitled to vote on merger or if corporation was subsidiary that was merged into its parent pursuant to 14-2-1004; (2) consummation of plan of share exchange to which corporation is party if shares of corporation will be acquired and if shareholder is entitled to vote on plan of share exchange; (3) consummation of sale or exchange of all or substantially all of property of corporation if shareholder vote is required on sale or exchange; (4) amendment to articles of incorporation that materially and adversely affect rights in respect of dissenters' shares; or (5) any corporate action taken pursuant to shareholder vote to extent that provisions governing close corporations, articles of incorporation, bylaws, or resolution of directors provides that voting or nonvoting shareholders are entitled to dissent and obtain payment for their shares. (14-2-1302). Right to dissent governed by 14-2-1302; procedure for exercise of dissenters' rights governed by 14-2-1320 through 14-2-1332. Three year statute of limitations for actions by dissenters to enforce their dissenters' rights of appraisal. (14-2-1332).

Foreign Corporations.—Before transacting business, foreign corporation must obtain certificate of authority from Secretary of State. Statute sets out non-exhaustive list of activities not considered transacting business for purposes of qualification. (14-2-1501). Foreign corporation with certificate of authority has same rights and privileges under Code and is generally subject to same duties, liabilities and restrictions as domestic corporation. (14-2-1505).

Qualification.—Foreign corporations authorized to transact business in state on July 1, 1989 are subject to revised Code, but are not required to obtain new certificate of authority to transact business. (14-2-1702).

Foreign corporation must complete and file with Secretary of State application which sets forth: (1) name of foreign corporation or, if name is unavailable for use in state, corporate name that satisfies requirements of 14-2-1506; (2) name of state or country under whose law it is incorporated; (3) date of incorporation and period of duration; (4) mailing address of corporation's principal office; (5) address of corporation's registered office in Georgia and name of corporation's registered agent at that address; and (6) names and usual business addresses of corporation's current directors and officers. With application, foreign corporation must file duly authenticated certificate of existence (or document of similar import) from Secretary of State or other official having custody of corporate records in state or country where foreign corporation is incorporated. (14-2-1503). Fee for filing, $170. (14-2-122). $500 penalty for noncompliance for each year or part thereof during which corporation transacts business. (14-2-122). Failure to obtain certificate of authority renders corporation unable to maintain proceeding in any court in state until it obtains certificate of authority and may subject corporation or incorporators to civil penalties. Failure to obtain certificate of authority, however, does not impair validity of corporate acts or prevent corporation from defending any proceeding. (14-2-1502). Foreign corporation authorized to transact business in state must obtain amended certificate of authority if it changes corporate name, changes period of duration or changes state or country of incorporation. (14-2-1504). Application filing fee to register foreign corporation's name is $20. (14-2-122). Foreign corporation authorized to transact business in state must continuously maintain in state: (1) registered office; and (2) registered agent who may be individual resident of state and whose business office is identical with registered office, domestic corporation or nonprofit domestic corporation whose business office is identical with registered office, or foreign corporation or nonprofit corporation authorized to transact business in state whose business office is identical to registered office. (14-2-1507). Registered agent is corporation's agent for service of process, notice, or demand. Foreign corporation may be served by service upon Secretary of State together with service by registered or certified mail addressed to chief executive officer, chief financial officer or secretary of corporation (or person of comparable position) at its principal office if foreign corporation has no registered agent or registered agent cannot, with reasonable diligence, be served. (14-2-1510).

Foreign corporations domesticated under prior law have same legal status as corporations qualifying under Code, and all rights are preserved. (14-2-1540).

Withdrawal.—Foreign corporation may file application for certificate of withdrawal with Secretary of State: (1) setting forth name of foreign corporation and its state or country of incorporation; (2) stating that it is no longer transacting business in state and that it is surrendering its authority to transact business in state; (3) revoking authority of its registered agent to accept service on its behalf; and (4) appointing Secretary of State as its agent for service of process in any proceeding based on cause

See note at head of Digest as to 1998 legislation covered.

See Topical Index in front part of this volume.

CORPORATIONS . . . *continued*

of action arising during time it was authorized to transact business in state by providing mailing address to which copy of any process served be mailed and committing to notify Secretary of State of future changes in its mailing address. Once foreign corporation has effectively withdrawn, service of process on Secretary of State constitutes service of process on foreign corporation provided that copy of process is mailed to foreign corporation's chief executive officer, chief financial officer, secretary or person holding comparable position. (14-2-1520). Secretary of State may commence proceeding pursuant to 14-2-1530 through 14-2-1532 to revoke certificate of authority of foreign corporation under certain circumstances. (14-2-1530).

Reports.—Foreign corporations subject to same reporting requirements and annual registration statement requirements to which domestic corporations are subject. (14-2-1505). See subhead Reports, supra.

Taxation of Corporate Property.—Same as for taxation of property of individual. See category Taxation, topic Intangible Recording Tax, subhead Intangible Personal Property Tax.

Taxation of Corporate Stock.—See category Taxation, topic Intangible Recording Tax, subhead Intangible Personal Property Tax.

Income Tax.—See category Taxation, topic Taxes, subhead Income Tax.

License Tax.—Domestic and domesticated corporations organized for profit must pay annual license or occupation tax, amount of which is based on net worth, as follows (48-13-72, -73):

Corporations with Net Worth Including Issued Capital Stock, Paid-in Surplus and Earned

Surplus Not Exceeding $10,000			$ 10
Over	$ 10,000 not exceeding	$ 25,000	20
Over	25,000 not exceeding	40,000	40
Over	40,000 not exceeding	60,000	60
Over	60,000 not exceeding	80,000	75
Over	80,000 not exceeding	100,000	100
Over	100,000 not exceeding	150,000	125
Over	150,000 not exceeding	200,000	150
Over	200,000 not exceeding	300,000	200
Over	300,000 not exceeding	500,000	250
Over	500,000 not exceeding	750,000	300
Over	750,000 not exceeding	1,000,000	500
Over	1,000,000 not exceeding	2,000,000	750
Over	2,000,000 not exceeding	4,000,000	1,000
Over	4,000,000 not exceeding	6,000,000	1,250
Over	6,000,000 not exceeding	8,000,000	1,500
Over	8,000,000 not exceeding	10,000,000	1,750
Over	10,000,000 not exceeding	12,000,000	2,000
Over	12,000,000 not exceeding	14,000,000	2,500
Over	14,000,000 not exceeding	16,000,000	3,000
Over	16,000,000 not exceeding	18,000,000	3,500
Over	18,000,000 not exceeding	20,000,000	4,000
Over	20,000,000 not exceeding	22,000,000	4,500
Over	22,000,000		5,000

If corporation does not return income taxes to Georgia, tax period begins Jan. 1 and ends Dec. 31. (48-13-76). Otherwise, tax period same as that adopted for Georgia income tax purposes. Tax is computed on net worth as of first day of such period and tax is payable on same date. (48-13-76). Failure to file return and pay tax by 15th day of third calendar month beginning with first calendar month of tax period subjects corporation to penalty of 10% of tax imposed plus interest at rate of 1% per month from date tax due until tax paid. (48-13-78, -79; 48-2-40). First return of corporation coming into existence or otherwise becoming subject to tax shall be filed by 15th day of third calendar month beginning with first calendar month of tax period. (48-13-76, -78). If return is for period of less than six months, license tax is 50% of tax for entire year. (48-13-73). Payment of tax authorizes conduct of business in any county in Georgia. (48-13-78).

Business Trusts.—See category Estates and Trusts, topic Trusts, subhead Business Trust.

Professional Associations.—See topic Associations, subhead Professional Associations.

Professional Corporations.—Those licensed in professions of certified public accountancy, architecture, chiropractic, dentistry, professional engineering, land surveying, law, pharmacy, psychology, medicine and surgery, optometry, osteopathy, podiatry, veterinary medicine, registered professional nursing or harbor piloting may practice as professional corporation. (14-10-1 et seq.). Member (i.e., shareholder) may become liable for misdeeds of another member in certain circumstances. (250 Ga. 844, 302 S.E.2d 674).

Limited Liability Companies.—See topic Limited Liability Companies.

Deeds.—See category Property, topic Deeds.

Model Non-Profit Corporation Act.—Not adopted, but used as basis for Georgia Non-Profit Corporation Code. (14-3-101 et seq.).

JOINT STOCK COMPANIES:

Not provided for by statute.

Professional Associations.—See topics Associations, subhead Professional Associations; Corporations.

LIMITED LIABILITY COMPANIES:

Georgia Limited Liability Company Act ("Act") adopted. (14-11-100 et seq.).

Not a Corporation.—Limited liability company organized under Act is not corporation, but association closer in character and structure to limited partnership.

General Supervision.—Under Act, articles of organization and annual registration reports must be filed with Secretary of State.

Purposes.—Limited liability company formed under Act has purpose of engaging in any lawful activity unless more limited purpose is set forth in articles of organization or written operating agreement. (14-11-201[b]).

Powers.—Limited liability company has powers to do all things necessary to carry out its purpose, business and affairs. (14-11-202).

Name.—Must contain words "limited liability company" or "limited company" (certain abbreviations are also permitted). (14-11-207[a]). Name must be distinguishable on records of Secretary of State from name of any other corporation, limited liability company or limited partnership formed or authorized to transact business in state, from any nonprofit corporation, professional corporation, or professional association on file with Secretary of State, and from any name reserved or registered under Act. (14-11-207[a][2]). Any person may apply to Secretary of State to reserve use of name for nonrenewable 90-day period. (14-11-208[a]). Issuance of name means that name is distinguishable for filing purposes on records of Secretary of State and does not affect commercial availability of name. (14-11-207[b]).

Formation.—One or more persons may act as organizer(s) of limited liability company by delivering articles of organization to Secretary of State for filing. (14-11-203[a]). Organizer need not be member of limited liability company at time of formation or thereafter. (14-11-203[b]). At delivery of articles of organization, organizer(s) must provide to Secretary of State: (i) name and address of each organizer; (ii) street address and county of limited liability company's initial registered office and name of its initial registered agent at that office; and (iii) mailing address of limited liability company's principal place of business. (14-11-203[a][1]-[3]). If articles of organization conform to requirements of Act, existence of limited liability company commences at time of filing of articles of organization by Secretary of State or at time specified in articles, which time may not be later than 90th day following filing. (14-11-203[c]; 14-11-206[e][1], [2], [f]).

Articles of Organization.—Must provide the name of limited liability company. (14-11-204[a]). Optionally, articles may state that management of limited liability company is vested in one or more managers and may include any other provisions not inconsistent with law. (14-11-204[b]).

Filing of Articles.—Upon delivery of original and conformed copy of articles of organization and other required information, and payment of required filing fee ($75), Secretary of State files original articles, indicates such filing on copies, returns copies, and issues certificate evidencing that articles have been filed. (14-11-206[a], [g]; 14-11-1101[a][1]).

Amendment to Articles of Organization.—Articles of organization may be amended by delivering for filing to Secretary of State articles of amendment including: (i) name of limited liability company; (ii) date of filing of articles of organization; (iii) amendment to articles of organization; and (iv) date of effectiveness of amendment if later than filing date. (14-11-210[a], [b]). Filing fee for articles of amendment is $20. (14-11-1101[a][2]).

Restated Articles of Organization.—Articles of organization may be restated by delivering restated articles of organization for filing to Secretary of State. (14-11-210[c]). Filing fee for restated articles of organization is $75. (14-11-1101[a][1]).

Registered Office and Registered Agent.—Must continuously maintain registered agent for service of process who must be individual resident of State of Georgia, Georgia corporation or foreign corporation authorized to transact business in Georgia. (14-11-209[a], [b]). Must also continuously maintain registered office within State of Georgia which may, but need not, be its place of business. (14-11-209[a][1]). Address of business office of registered agent must be same as address of registered office. (14-11-209[a][2]). Registered office and agent may be changed by indicating such change on company's annual registration or by filing statement with Secretary of State (14-11-209[c]).

Management.—Unless otherwise provided in articles of organization or written operating agreement, management is vested in members. (14-11-304[a]). Members are agents of and can bind company unless management is vested in one or more managers, in which case manager is agent of and can bind company. (14-11-301[a][b]). Unless otherwise provided in articles or operating agreement, managers need not be natural persons or members and are elected and removed by majority of members (14-11-304[b]). Subject to provisions in articles or organization or operating agreement, managers have right and authority to manage affairs of limited ability company and to make all decisions with respect thereto. (14-11-304[a]).

Members and managers must act in good faith in best interests of company with care which ordinarily prudent person in like position would exercise under similar circumstances, but are not liable to company, its members or managers for any action taken in managing company if performed in compliance with prescribed standard of duty and care. (14-11-305[1]). Nonmanaging members have no duty to limited liability company or other members solely by reason of acting in his or her capacity as member. (14-11-305[1]). Members and managers may rely on information prepared or presented by specified persons. (14-11-305[2]).

Unless otherwise provided in articles of organization or operating agreement, managing members have one vote each and must take action by majority vote to decide any matter arising in connection with business and affairs of limited liability company. (14-11-308[a][1]). Unless otherwise provided in articles of organization or operating agreement, dissolution, merger, transfer of all assets (or at least two-thirds of value thereof), admission of new members, amendment of articles of organization or operating agreement, reduction of capital contribution obligations, distributions and continuation of limited liability company require unanimous vote or consent of members. (14-11-308[b]). Unless otherwise provided in articles or operating agreement, if management is vested in manager or managers, managers have one vote each and must decide every action by majority vote. (14-11-308[a][2]).

LIMITED LIABILITY COMPANIES . . . *continued*

Unless otherwise provided in articles of organization or written operating agreement, members or managers may take action by written consent without meeting, subject to specified requirements. (14-11-309[1]).

Limited Liability.—Member, manager, agent or employee of limited liability company is not liable for debts, obligations or liability of company solely by reason of being member, manager, agent or employee of company. (14-11-303).

Exoneration of Liability and Indemnification.—Member or manager has no liability to limited liability company or any other member or manager if he or she has relied in good faith on provisions of written operating agreement. (14-11-305[4][B]). Articles of organization or written operating agreement may eliminate or limit liability of member or manager except for intentional misconduct or knowing violation of law or for transaction in which member or manager received personal benefit in breach of written operating agreement. (14-11-305[4][A]).

Subject to any standards and restrictions set forth in articles of organization or written operating agreement, limited liability company may indemnify any member, manager or other person from claims arising in connection with company, except for claims related to intentional misconduct or knowing violation of law, or transaction in which member or manager received personal benefit in breach of written operating agreement. (14-11-306).

Application of Laws Imposing Liability.—Act does not alter any law with respect to disregarding legal entities, nor does it alter any law with respect to liability arising out of rendering of professional services. (14-11-314).

Interested Transactions.—Unless articles or written operating agreement provide that statutory provisions applying to conflicting interest transactions do not apply to company, conflicting interest transaction may not be enjoined, set aside, or give rise to award of damages or other sanctions if transaction was disclosed to members or managers voting on transaction, or transaction was established to have been fair to company. (14-11-307[c], [d], [e]).

Records.—Limited liability company must keep specified records and member may, at his or her expense, inspect and copy such records upon reasonable demand and obtain certain other information regarding business, affairs and financial condition of company. (14-11-313).

Contributions to Capital.—Contributions to capital may be in cash, tangible or intangible property, services rendered, promissory note or other obligation to contribute cash or property, or to render services. (14-11-401). Promise to make contribution to capital is not enforceable unless it is set out in articles of organization or written operating agreement that is binding on promisor or in another writing signed by promisor. (14-11-402[a]). Unless otherwise provided in articles of organization or written operating agreement, obligation to contribute to capital may be reduced or eliminated only with unanimous consent of members. (14-11-402[b]).

Allocations and Distributions.—Unless articles of organization or written operating agreement provide for manner of allocation of profits and losses to members, they are allocated equally among members. (14-11-403).

Unless articles of organization or written operating agreement provide for manner of allocation of distributions to members, distributions prior to and after dissolution of company are shared equally among members (14-11-404), may be made in cash only (14-11-406) and are subject to specified solvency requirements (14-11-407). Distributions prior to dissolution of company require approval of all members unless otherwise provided for in articles of organization or written operating agreement. (14-11-404). Member or manager who votes for or expressly consents to distribution made in violation of articles of organization, written operating agreement, or 14-11-407 is personally liable to company for amount of distribution that exceeds lawful distribution, subject to contribution entitlement from specified persons. (14-11-408). Statute of limitations for unlawful or excessive distributions is two years. (14-11-408[c]).

Transfers.—Interest in limited liability company is personal property, may be evidenced by certificate and, unless otherwise provided in articles of organization or written operating agreement, is assignable in whole or in part. (14-11-501, -502[1]). Assignment does not by itself dissolve company. (14-11-502[3]). Although membership interest may be freely assigned, assignee has no right to participate in management and affairs of company or exercise rights as member, unless other members unanimously consent or unless otherwise provided in articles of organization or written operating agreement. (14-11-502[3]; 14-11-503[1]). Assignee is entitled to share in distributions and allocations of profit and loss allocable to which assignor was entitled, to extent assigned. (14-11-502[2]).

Dissolution.—Limited liability company is dissolved and must be wound up upon first to occur of following: (1) arrival of time specified in articles or written operating agreement; (2) happening of events specified in articles or written operating agreement; (3) arrival of time approved by all members; (4) subject to contrary provision in articles or written operating agreement, 90 days after any event of member dissociation (14-11-601) unless limited liability company is continued by consent of all remaining members or as provided in articles or written operating agreement; or (5) entry of decree of judicial dissolution upon application by member under 14-11-603. (14-11-602). Member is entitled to receive fair value of his or her interest in company upon dissociation unless dissociation results in dissolution of company, is otherwise provided in articles of organization or written operating agreement, or is prohibited by other enumerated restrictions. (14-11-405).

Upon dissolution, statement of commencement of winding up may be delivered for filing with Secretary of State. (14-11-606). Company may then dispose of known claims against it by notifying its known claimants in writing of winding up proceedings and request that claimant submit his or her claim within stipulated deadline or be barred. (14-11-607). Dissolved company that has filed statement may publish request that persons holding claims against company present them to company. (14-11-608, -609).

Dissolved limited liability company may deliver to Secretary of State for filing certificate of termination stating name of company, that all known debts, liabilities and obligations have been paid, discharged, or barred, or that adequate provision has been made therefor, and that there are no actions pending against company in any court, or that adequate provision has been made for satisfaction of any pending claim(s). (14-11-610). Deeds or other instruments requiring execution after filing of certificate of termination may be signed by any person who had authority to wind up dissolved company. (14-11-611).

Derivative Action.—Member may bring action on behalf of company only if: (1) member is unable to cause company to sue on its own behalf; (2) member has demanded in writing that members or managers having authority cause company to sue on its own behalf; (3) 90 days have expired from date demand was made unless demand has been rejected earlier or unless irreparable injury would result to company by waiting for expiration of 90 days; (4) plaintiff is member at time of bringing action and was member at time of alleged wrong, or is assignee of member who was; and (5) plaintiff fairly and adequately represents interests of company in enforcing right of company. (14-11-801).

Conversion into Limited Liability Company.—Any corporation, limited partnership, or general partnership may elect to become limited liability company by delivering certificate of election to Secretary of State for filing setting forth statutorily required information. (14-11-212).

Merger.—Limited liability company may merge with or into one or more business entities pursuant to written agreement. (14-11-901[a]). If merger involves foreign entity, merger is permitted if law of jurisdiction under which foreign entity is organized also permits merger. (14-11-901[b]). Each constituent entity must adopt written plan of merger setting forth statutorily required information. (14-11-902). Unless articles of organization or written operating agreement provide otherwise, all members of limited liability company must authorize and approve plan of merger. (14-11-903[a]). Surviving entity must deliver to Secretary of State for filing articles of merger setting forth statutorily required information. (14-11-904).

Dissenters' Rights.—Unless otherwise provided by articles of organization or written operating agreement, record member of limited liability company may dissent from and obtain payment of fair value of his or her interest in company in event of following: (1) consummation of plan of merger if approval of less than all members is required and member is entitled to vote thereon; (2) consummation of transfer of all or substantially all of company's assets if approval of less than all members is required and member is entitled to vote thereon; (3) amendment of articles of organization that materially and adversely affects rights in respect of dissenter's membership in company; or (4) any company action taken pursuant to member vote to extent that articles of organization or written operating agreement provide that voting or nonvoting members are entitled to dissent and obtain payment for their membership interests. (14-11-1002[a]). Member entitled to dissent may not challenge company action creating his or her entitlement to dissent unless company action fails to comply with specified procedural requirements. (14-11-1002[b]). Statute of limitations applicable to enforcement of dissenter's rights is three years from date company action was taken. (14-11-1013).

Treatment of Foreign Limited Liability Companies.—Laws of the jurisdiction under which foreign limited liability company is organized govern its organization and internal affairs and liability of its managers, members, and other owners, regardless of whether foreign limited liability company procured or should have procured certificate of authority in State of Georgia. (14-11-701[a]). Must procure and receive certificate of authority from Secretary of State to transact business in State of Georgia (14-11-702[a]) and must maintain registered office and registered agent for service or process who must be either individual resident of State of Georgia, domestic corporation, or foreign corporation authorized to transact business in State of Georgia. (14-11-703[a], [b]). Once foreign limited liability company receives certificate of authority, it possesses substantially same rights and privileges and is subject to same duties, restrictions, penalties and liabilities as domestic limited liability company. Act provides non-exhaustive list of activities deemed not to constitute transacting business in State of Georgia. (14-11-702[b]). Failure to procure certificate of authority does not impair validity of contracts of foreign limited liability company and does not prevent it from defending in Georgia court, but prohibits it from maintaining action, suit or proceeding in Georgia court until company is authorized to transact business in State of Georgia. (14-11-711).

PARTNERSHIPS:

Uniform Partnership Act.—"UPA" adopted with certain modifications. (14-8-1 et seq.). Rules for determining whether property is considered partnership property differ from standard UPA. (14-8-8, -25). Section added authorizing filing of statement of partnership with clerk of superior court of any county. (14-8-10.1). Partnership may be sued in its common name. (14-8-15.1). Partnership terminates upon incorporation and commencement of business under corporation form. (14-8-31[a]). See 224 Ga. App. 88, 479 S.E.2d 474.

Revised Uniform Limited Partnership Act.—("RULPA") adopted with some variation; Georgia's Act is known as Georgia Revised Uniform Limited Partnership Act ("Act"). (14-9-100 et seq.). Act applies to all domestic limited partnerships formed on or after July 1, 1988, to previously existing domestic limited partnerships that so elect pursuant to Act, and to all foreign limited partnerships transacting business in state after July 1, 1988. (14-9-1201). In order to form limited partnership under Act, certificate of limited partnership setting forth certain information required by Act must be executed and filed with Secretary of State. (14-9-201). Corporation, limited liability company or general partnership may elect to become limited partnership by delivering to Secretary of State certificate of election, certificate of limited partnership and related statement setting forth information required by statute. (14-9-206.2). Domestic limited partnerships and foreign limited partnerships authorized to transact business in state must file annual registration with Secretary of State. (14-9-206.5). Instruments executed by domestic or foreign limited partnership conveying interest in real property located in state, when signed on behalf of such limited partnership by person purporting to be general partner thereof, are presumed to have been duly authorized by and binding upon limited partnership unless contrary limitations on authority of general partner are set forth in partnership's certificate of limited

See note at head of Digest as to 1998 legislation covered.

See Topical Index in front part of this volume.

GA – 11

PARTNERSHIPS . . . *continued*

partnership and copy of such certificate certified by Secretary of State is properly filed and recorded in office of clerk of superior court of county where real property is located. (14-9-106[c]). Subject to any limitations contained in partnership agreement, limited partnerships may indemnify any partner or any other person against any claims and demands except those arising from such person's intentional misconduct or knowing violation of law or from transaction in which such person received personal benefit in violation of partnership agreement. (14-9-108). Limited partner's right to inspect partnership records is subject to reasonable procedural standards in partnership agreement or as otherwise established by general partners, and such right may be exercised only for purposes reasonably related to limited partner's interest as limited partner. (14-9-305). Act permits, and provides framework for, mergers between domestic limited partnerships, and domestic or foreign limited partnerships, corporations and limited liability companies. (14-9-206.1). Limited partners who participate in management or control of limited partnership do not thereby become liable for partnership obligations. (14-9-303). General partner who ceases being limited partnership's general partner remains personally liable to any creditor who extended credit to partnership prior to time proper notice of such cessation is filed with Secretary of State. (14-9-602[d]). General partner is not personally liable as general partner for partnership debts incurred after such filing unless relevant creditor had, at time partnership debt was incurred, reasonable basis, as defined by Act, for believing that partner remained general partner. (14-9-602[e]). Promise to make contribution to capital of limited partnership is not enforceable unless made in writing. (14-9-502). Act supplements RULPA's provisions regarding withdrawal of general partners. (14-9-602). Limited partner may withdraw from partnership at time or upon occurrence of events specified in partnership agreement. (14-9-603). Assignee of partnership interest may become limited partner if and to extent partnership agreement so provides or all other partners so consent. (14-9-702, -704).

Out-of-State Partnerships.—No special requirements for out-of-state partnerships. Foreign limited liability partnerships and limited partnerships transacting business in state required to procure from Secretary of State certificate of authority. (14-8-45[a]; 14-9-902[a]). Certain activities which, in and of themselves, do not constitute "transacting business in Georgia" for purposes of Act are listed. (14-8-45[b]; 14-9-902[b]). Foreign limited liability partnerships and limited partnerships that are required to obtain certificate of authority to do business in state must continuously maintain in state agent for service of process. (14-8-46[a]; 14-9-902.1). Amendment to certificate of authority must be obtained from Secretary of State if partnership changes name or state of organization. (14-8-49; 14-9-905). Failure of foreign limited liability partnerships or limited partnerships transacting business in state to obtain certificate of authority does not impair validity of any contract or act of such foreign limited liability partnerships and limited partnerships or prevent such partnerships from defending any action, suit or proceeding in any state court, but such foreign limited liability partnerships and limited partnerships may not maintain action, suit or proceeding in state court and are subject to annual fine of $500. (14-8-54; 14-9-907).

Limited Liability Partnerships.—To become limited liability partnership, partnership must record limited liability partnership election containing certain information with clerk of superior court of any county in which partnership has office. (14-8-62). Partner in limited liability partnership is not liable either directly or indirectly for any debts, obligations or liabilities of or chargeable to partnership or any other partner solely by reason of being partner in such partnership. (14-8-15). Partner in limited liability partnership is not proper party to action against such partnership solely by reason of being partner in such partnership. (14-8-15).

PROFESSIONAL ASSOCIATIONS:

See topic Associations, subhead Professional Associations.

BUSINESS REGULATION AND COMMERCE

BANKS AND BANKING:

Uniform Commercial Code adopted. (Title 11). See topic Commercial Code.

Supervision and Regulation.—Regulated by 7-1-1 et seq. Law relating to financial institutions enforced and administered by Department of Banking and Finance. (7-1-60). Governor has power to declare banking holiday because of bank emergency. (7-1-111). Department may order financial institutions to restrict all or part of business during any financial emergency proclaimed by Governor. (7-1-112).

Transactions by Bank—Limitations On.—Limitations on bank loans: loan to single borrower not to exceed 15% of statutory capital base or 25% with good security (7-1-285); single maturity loans on real estate may not exceed 75% of fair market value; regularly amortized loans may not exceed 95% of fair market value (with certain exceptions) (7-1-286); loans to directors or officers in excess of $25,000 not permitted unless requirements of 7-1-491 are met and security is adequate. Limitations placed on holding of corporate securities by banks. (7-1-288). Purposes for which banks can hold real estate limited. (7-1-262, -263). Reserves to be fixed by regulation but not in excess of: 5% of total deposits for non-Federal Reserve savings bank, and 15% of demand deposits plus 5% of other deposits for non-Federal Reserve commercial bank; reserves for members of Federal Reserve System determined by Federal law; some reserves can be invested in certain approved obligations. (7-1-371).

Bank may not receive a pledge or other security interest in its own stock or securities. (7-1-288).

Shareholders' Liability.—Limited to amount constituting full consideration for shares or subscription. (7-1-430).

Qualifications of Directors.—All must be U.S. citizens. Majority must reside in Georgia or within 40 miles of office in Georgia offering complete banking or trust service. (7-1-480).

Share Certificates.—No certificate delivered until share or shares represented thereby are fully paid. (7-1-417).

Deposits in trust payable by bank on order of depositor without liability if before service of suit to enjoin. (7-1-352).

Deposit of Decedent.—Upon death of depositor intestate having deposit of not more than $10,000, financial institution is, subject to certain limitations, authorized to pay proceeds of such deposit to: (1) surviving spouse; (2) if no surviving spouse, to children pro rata; (3) if no children or surviving spouse, to father and mother pro rata; (4) if none of above, to brothers and sisters of decedent pro rata. (7-1-239). If no claim is made under above within 90 days, financial institution may pay up to $10,000 in payment of funeral expenses and expenses of last illness of deceased. Payment pursuant to 7-1-239 will operate as complete acquittal of financial institution's liability to any future claim related to decedent's deposits. (7-1-239). Upon death of depositor of building and loan association or savings and loan association, such association may pay amount of deposit or any portion thereof to executor or administrator, or other fiduciary appointed and qualified pursuant to last will of depositor or by any court of competent jurisdiction. (7-1-791). If no payment made under above within 90 days, association may pay up to $1,000 to undertaker for funeral expenses upon receipt of statement of expenses and appropriate affidavits. (7-1-792). Safe deposit box of deceased or incompetent person may be opened by court order. (7-1-356).

Multi-Party Accounts.—Regulated by 7-1-810 et seq.

Unclaimed Deposits.—Governed by Uniform Disposition of Unclaimed Property Act (Revised). (44-12-190). Unlawful to charge fee or to solicit other compensation to conduct search for document, abandoned or unclaimed deposit accounts or other abandoned properties, with certain exceptions. (7-1-359). See category Property, topic Absentees, subhead Escheat.

Deposit Collections.—Regulated by 11-4-101 et. seq. Every bank must maintain deposit insurance. Six month period of grace allowed at discretion of Department of Banking and Finance to banks which had deposit insurance withdrawn or cancelled. (7-1-244).

Stop Payment Orders.—Oral orders binding for 14 days unless confirmed in writing. Written orders binding for six months unless renewed in writing. (11-4-403).

Forged and Unauthorized Signatures and Endorsements.—Without regard to care or lack of care of customer or bank, customer who fails to report unauthorized signature or any alteration on face of item within 60 days after receiving bank statement is precluded from asserting such unauthorized signature or alteration against bank. Alterations on back of item and unauthorized endorsements must be reported within one year. (11-4-406). Bank not liable for payment of unauthorized checks to unintended payee drawn by employee, regardless of bank's negligence in cashing such checks, and loss borne by employer. (184 Ga. App. 326, 361 S.E.2d 531; 11-3-405). Checks containing only one of two required signatures are "unauthorized" checks. (228 Ga. App. 893, 495 S.E.2d 296).

Trust Companies.—May be organized only incident to transfer of trust operations from affiliated banks or trust company. (7-1-394; 7-1-320 et seq.). Many organizational requirements same as for banks. (7-1-390 et seq.).

Powers of trust company are general corporate powers (7-1-260) and certain powers also accorded banks (7-1-261). Also, power to act as fiduciary; investment advisor; custodian of property; agent or attorney-in-fact; registrar or transfer agent of securities; fiscal agent of U.S., state or public body thereof, corporation, or person; treasurer of public body or of nonprofit corporation. (7-1-310). Banks, building and loan associations and credit unions, with permission of Department of Banking and Finance, may exercise same powers. (7-1-310).

Uniform Common Trust Fund Act.—Not adopted.

Collective Investment Funds.—Provided for. (7-1-313).

Foreign Banks.—Bank holding companies located in defined region are permitted to acquire Georgia-based banks or bank holding companies under certain conditions. (7-1-620 through -626).

Banks or other institutions chartered under laws of states other than Georgia, or nationally chartered institutions located outside of Georgia, are not permitted to conduct banking business in Georgia except as provided for in 7-1-620 through -628.15 and in other limited circumstances. Out-of-state bank with lawful Georgia branch may establish de novo Georgia branch. (7-1-628.8). Various limited exceptions are available for representative offices, foreign bank agencies and certain other businesses. (7-1-241, -590, -713). Banks and bank holding companies, regardless of location, are permitted to establish limited purpose credit card banks in Georgia. (7-5-3). However, banks located in states bordering on Georgia may act as fiduciaries in Georgia merely on registration with Secretary of State, appointment of Secretary as process agent, and proof that they are authorized to act in similar fiduciary capacity in states in which they are incorporated or, if they are national banking associations, in states in which they have their principal places of business. (53-12-390 et seq.). Acting as fiduciary without more does not constitute doing business in Georgia. (53-12-392). See category Estates and Trusts, topic Executors and Administrators.

Merger and Consolidation—State Banks and Trust Companies.—One or more banks or trust companies may merge or consolidate if, among other things, parties adopt (majority of directors and two-thirds of eligible shareholders) specified plan of merger or consolidation; articles of merger or consolidation are duly executed and filed with Department of Banking and Finance; Department of Banking and Finance approves articles of merger or consolidation and any appropriate federal agency is properly notified of such merger or consolidation. (7-1-530 through -535). Institution exercising trust powers alone may merge or consolidate only with another such trust company. (7-1-530). When merger or consolidation becomes effective, each party to plan, except resulting bank or trust company, shall cease to exist as separate entity but shall continue in, and parties to plan shall be, single corporation which shall have without further act or deed, all property, rights, powers, trusts, duties and obligations of each party to plan. (7-1-536).

See note at head of Digest as to 1998 legislation covered.

See Topical Index in front part of this volume.

BANKS AND BANKING... *continued*

Conversions, Mergers and Consolidations—National Banks.—Regulated by 7-1-550 through -590.

Bank holding companies and branch banks limited. (7-1-600 through -612). Banks may establish and operate automated teller machines, cash dispensing machines and point-of-sale terminals throughout Georgia. (7-1-603).

Fiduciary Investment Company.—May be incorporated as medium for investment of funds held by trust companies in fiduciary capacity. (7-1-330 through -338).

Credit Card Banks.—Authorized and regulated. (7-5-1 et seq.).

Credit Union Deposit Insurance Corporation.—Authorized to insure deposits of participating financial institutions. (7-2-1 et seq.).

Credit Unions.—Regulated by 7-1-630 through -670.

See also category Taxation, topic Banks and Savings & Loan Association.

Interstate Acquisitions of Banks.—Bank holding companies having banking subsidiaries with offices located outside of Georgia may, subject to certain requirements, acquire bank or bank holding company with offices located in Georgia. Similarly, bank holding companies having banking subsidiaries with offices located in Georgia may, subject to certain requirements, acquire bank or bank holding company with offices located outside of Georgia. (7-1-620 through -628.15).

BILLS AND NOTES:

Uniform Commercial Code.—Adopted. (Title 11). No major variations in Georgia. See topic Commercial Code.

Days of Grace.—Governed by Commercial Code.

Special Requirements.—None.

Judgment Notes.—Not recognized.

Attorney's Fees.—Clause for, enforceable up to 15% of principal and interest provided ten days written notice is given before filing suit. (13-1-11).

BILLS OF LADING:

See topic Carriers.

BILLS OF SALE:

See topic Sales.

BLUE SKY LAW:

See topic Securities.

BROKERS:

Uniform Commercial Code adopted. (Title 11).

Real Estate Brokers.—Governed by 43-40-1 et seq. License from Real Estate Commission necessary for brokers, associate brokers, community association managers, and sales people. (43-40-30). Broker must: (1) be at least 21 years old; (2) be Georgia resident or fully comply with 43-40-9; (3) be high school graduate (or equivalent); (4) have served actively as licensee for three years; (5) have completed 60 hours in approved broker's course; and (6) pass real estate broker's examination after completion of 60 hour course and after two years of active licensure. (43-40-8[c]). Salesperson must: (1) be at least 18 years old; (2) be Georgia resident or fully comply with 43-40-9; (3) be high school graduate (or equivalent); (4) have completed 75 hours in approved salesperson's course; and (5) pass real estate examination. (43-40-8[b]). Salesperson is any person other than associate broker, who acts on behalf of broker in performing any act authorized by law to be performed by broker. (43-40-1[10]). Within one year of obtaining original license, salesperson must take 25 additional hours of approved study. (43-40-8[d]). License renewal for all persons requires completion of six hours approved continuing education course for each year of renewal period. (43-40-8[e]). Commission has power to refuse license, censure licensee or revoke or suspend license for engaging in unfair practices or for list of enumerated offenses. (43-40-14, -15, -25, -27). Licensee must immediately notify Commission of conviction of enumerated offenses. License automatically revoked unless notice is given and hearing requested within 60 days of conviction. (43-40-15[i]). Broker accepting trust funds in brokerage transaction required to maintain separate trust or escrow account in federally insured bank. (43-40-20[a]). Broker not accepting trust funds in brokerage transaction and not maintaining trust account must open trust account within one business day of receipt of any trust funds. (43-40-20[a]). Commission may require written reports concerning status of accounts and may examine during each renewal period or any time for reasonable cause. (43-40-20). Broker required to notify commission in writing within 30 days of change of business address. (43-40-19). Nonresident who is not licensed in this state may be licensed as broker in Georgia upon meeting age, education, and examination requirements in 43-40-8. (43-40-9[b]). Nonresidents who are licensed in another state may be licensed in Georgia by (1) proving current out of state licensure; (2) paying fees; (3) signing statement that nonresident has read, and will abide by statute and its rules and regulations; (4) affiliating with broker if nonresident is salesperson, community association manager or associate broker; (5) providing certification of current licensure and copies of records; (6) filing designation in writing appointing Real Estate Commissioner as agent; and (7) agreeing in writing to cooperate with any Real Estate Commission investigation. (43-40-9[c]). Licensed broker of another state may enter into written agreement with Georgia broker to conduct real estate brokerage business in Georgia without first obtaining Georgia license. (43-40-9[e]). Georgia broker shall be responsible for all real estate brokerage acts performed by out-of-state broker under such written agreement and for determining that out-of-state broker has and maintains active license in out-of-state broker's place of residence. (43-40-9[e]). Licensed Georgia broker and licensed broker of another state must enter into separate agreement for each transaction in which they become involved and Georgia broker shall maintain such agreement for at least three years. (43-40-9[e]). Each agreement shall provide (i) for procedures to be

followed in event out-of-state broker performs any acts of broker on Georgia real property; (ii) how brokers will divide commissions; (iii) that any listing or property management agreement for Georgia real property be in name of Georgia broker; (iv) that out-of-state broker shall conduct negotiations with any client of Georgia broker only with express permission of Georgia broker; (v) that any advertisement by any means of Georgia real property shall identify listing Georgia broker; (vi) that any contracts, agreements or offers on Georgia real property shall clearly identify Georgia broker and out-of-state broker with statement that out-of-state broker is not licensed by Georgia Real Estate Commission and that said contract, agreement, or offer shall be construed under Georgia Law and that Georgia superior courts shall have jurisdiction over any action brought under such contract, agreement or offer; (vii) that any trust funds obtained involving any Georgia real property shall be held in trust account of Georgia broker; and (viii) such other matters as Commission may require by rule and regulation. (43-40-9[e]). Certain enumerated groups specifically excluded from licensing requirements of statute. (43-40-29). Establishment of real estate recovery fund and procedure for aggrieved person to recover therefrom. (43-40-22). Requirement for fidelity bond by broker providing community association management services. (43-40-22.1).

Real estate brokerage activities of each firm shall be under direct management and supervision of broker or qualifying broker. (43-40-18[c]). Broker shall be responsible for establishing, implementing, and continuing procedures for certain specifically described actions. (43-40-18[c]).

Duties to Clients.—Real estate broker's relationship with and duties to client and required disclaimer are codified. (10-6A). Statutorily defined limited agency relationship created between brokers and sellers, buyers, landlords and tenants whom they represent, subject to written agreements between parties. Statute lists duties of broker to client prior to, during and after termination of relationship, as well as services broker may provide to non-clients without breaching duties to client. (10-6A-4—9). Prior to entering into brokerage relationship, broker must disclose (i) type of brokerage relationships available through broker, (ii) any known conflicts, and (iii) broker's compensation and sharing arrangements (10-6A-10). Written consent and certain disclosures required for broker to act as dual agent. (10A-6-12).

Commission earned when, during agency, agent finds purchaser ready, able and willing, and who actually offers to buy on terms stipulated by owner. (10-6-32; 27 Ga. App. 448, 108 S.E. 815). No right to maintain any action for collection of compensation without alleging and proving he was licensed broker or salesperson when cause of action arose. (43-40-24). Fact that property is placed in hands of broker to sell does not prevent owner from selling, unless otherwise agreed. (10-6-32).

Brokers' Lien.—Real estate broker who is not employee or independent contractor of another real estate broker shall have lien upon commercial real property in amount of agreed compensation between broker and landlord, seller, client or customer, in transaction arising out of any of following: Written agreement for management, sale or lease of commercial real property; written agreement signed by property owner for procurement of purchaser, tenant or other party to accept transfer of interest in real property; or written agreement with buyer or tenant provided that written notice has been provided to owner of property to be liened. Lien shall attach upon recording of notice of lien with Clerk of Court in county where property is located. Claim for lien must be filed within 90 days of date payment was due. (44-14-602).

Not unauthorized practice of law for licensee to complete listing, sales contracts or leases on form prepared by attorney. (43-40-25.1).

BULK SALES:

See topic Commercial Code.

CARRIERS:

Uniform Commercial Code adopted. (Title 11). See topic Commercial Code.

Railroads and all public service corporations or utilities subject to regulation by Public Service Commission (46-2-51, -93; 46-4-21; 46-8-22, -382), which has power to fix rates and tariffs and make regulations to prevent unjust discrimination in railroad transportation of freight and passengers. (46-8-20).

Directors.—Railroad companies must have at least three directors, each of whom must be natural person of at least 18 years, but need not be resident of Georgia or shareholder. Charter or bylaws may prescribe additional qualifications. (46-8-46).

Georgia Rail Passenger Authority created for financing construction, operation and development of public transportation projects within and without state of Georgia. (46-9-270, et seq.). Georgia Rail Passenger Authority Overview Committee created to review authority operations. (28-10-1, et seq.).

Bills of Lading.—Uniform Commercial Code adopted. (Title 11).

Lien.—Governed by Uniform Commercial Code. (11-7-307, -308). Carrier has lien on goods for freight, but it may be waived by special contract or actual delivery of goods. Lien exists pro rata where goods delivered at intermediate point with consent of consignee. (46-9-46, -191). Lien also exists on passenger's baggage for passenger's fare. (46-9-190).

Whenever carrier of passengers transports baggage to destination and it is uncalled for or refused for six months after arrival at destination, carrier may sell at public auction to highest bidder provided certain published notices given. (46-9-190).

Limiting Liability.—Common carrier may limit his liability by express contract, but not by publication on tickets or receipts. (46-9-2).

See also category Transportation, topic Motor Vehicles.

COMMERCIAL CODE:

Uniform Commercial Code.—Adopted. (Title 11). See Uniform and Model Acts section.

Following amendments and options in Permanent Editorial Board's 1966 Official Recommendations not enacted: §2-318; §2-702; §3-501; §7-209. For offices for filing

COMMERCIAL CODE . . . *continued*
and fees under Art. 9, see category Documents and Records, topic Records, subhead Filing Under Uniform Commercial Code: Place; Fees.

1972 Official Amendments.—Partially adopted.

1973 Official Amendment.—Adopted.

1977 Official Amendments.—Adopted.

1987 Official Amendments.—Adopted.

1989 Official Amendments.—Partially adopted.

1990 Official Amendments.—Adopted.

Intentional differences between Georgia Code and 1962 Official Text, 1972 Official Text of Article IX, 1977 Official Text of Article VIII and conforming amendments to Articles I, V, and IX, 1987 Official Test of Article IIA and conforming amendments to Articles I and IX, 1989 Official Text of Article IVA, and 1990 Official Text of Articles III and IV are following, typographical and technical deviations and corrections omitted. (Title No. 11 omitted before section numbers.)

§1-105(2) omits last two sentences and adds to end: "Perfection provisions of the article of this title on secured transactions (Article 9 of this title). Code Section 11-9-103. Governing law in this article on funds transfers. (Article 4A of this title). Code Section 11-4A-507."

§1-201 (4) adds to end:

"Wherever the word 'branch' is used in this title, with reference to a bank, it shall mean not only 'branch bank', but also 'bank office' and 'bank facility' as those terms are defined in Code Section 7-1-600."

§1-201(20) reads:

" 'Holder,' with respect to a negotiable instrument, means the person in possession if the instrument is payable to bearer or, in the case of an instrument payable to an identified person, if the identified person is in possession. Holder with respect to a document of title means the person in possession if the goods are deliverable to bearer or to the order of the person in possession."

§1-201(24) omits phrase "as a part of its currency" and adds to end: "and includes a monetary unit of account established by an intergovernmental organization or by agreement between two or more nations."

§1-201 omits last two sentences in subsection (27); and adds new subsection (31.1): " 'Public sale' means a sale:

(A) Held at a place reasonably available to persons who might desire to attend and submit bids; and

(B) At which those attending shall be given the opportunity to bid on a competitive basis; and

(C) At which the sale, if made, shall be made to the highest and best bidder; and

(D) Except as otherwise provided in this title for advertising or dispensing with the advertising of public sales, of which notice is given by advertisement once a week for two weeks in the newspaper in which the sheriff's advertisements are published in the county where the sale is to be held, and which notice shall state the day and hour, between 10:00 A.M. and 4:00 P.M., and the place of sale and shall briefly identify the goods to be sold. The provisions of this paragraph shall not be in derogation of any additional requirements relating to notice of and conduct of any such public sale as may be contained in other provisions of this title but shall be supplementary thereto."

§1-201(43) omits phrase "or indorsement".

§1-207 adds to beginning "(1)" and adds to end new subsection (2): "Subsection (1) of this Code section does not apply to an accord and satisfaction."

§2-107(1) includes "timber"; and reference to "timber" deleted in §2-107(2).

§2-316(3) adds new subsection (d):

"With respect to the sale of cattle, hogs and sheep by a licensed auction company or by an agent, there shall be no implied warranty by said auction company or agent that the cattle, hogs, and sheep are free from disease; provided, however, that the provisions of this paragraph shall not be applicable to brucellosis reactor cattle detected at an official state laboratory within 30 days following the date of sale."

§2-316 adds new subsection (5):

"The implied warranty of merchantability under Code Section 11-2-314 and the implied warranty of fitness for a particular purpose under Code Section 11-2-315 shall not be applicable to the procurement, processing, storage, distribution or use of whole human blood, blood plasma, blood products, blood derivatives or other human tissue or organs for the purpose of injecting, transfusing, incorporating or transplanting any of them into the human body. The injection, transfusion or other transfer of blood, blood plasma, blood products or blood derivatives and the transplanting or other transfer of any tissue, bones or organs into or unto the human body shall not be considered, for the purpose of this Article, commodities subject to sale or barter, but shall be considered as medical services."

§2-328 adds to end of subsection (2): "In sales by auction the auctioneer shall be considered agent of both parties so far as to dispense with any further memorandum in writing than his own entries."

§2A-103(1)(e) omits phrase "if the total payments to be made under the lease contract, excluding payments for options to renew, or buy, do not exceed $."

§2A-208 renumbers subsections (3) and (4) as subsections (4) and (5) and adds new subsection (3): "The requirements of the statute of frauds section of this article (Code Section 11-2A-201) must be satisfied if the contract as modified is within its provisions."

§2A-303 adds to end of subsection (3):

"For purposes of this subsection: (a) a party's 'performance' includes its rights as well as its duties; and (b) a party creating or enforcing (or seeking to create or enforce) a security interest that the lease contract prohibits or makes an event of default has the burden of proving that such a transfer does not involve an actual delegation of material performance."

§2A-303 adds to end of subsection 5(b): "For purposes of clause (b)(2), the transferor has the burden of proving that any of the damages caused by the transfer could reasonably be or have been prevented by the party not making the transfer, and of proving the extent that they could reasonably be or have been so prevented."

§2A-306 adds to end: "or (iii) with regard to the rights of a creditor of the lessor or lessee, a different priority would result by application of Code Section 11-9-310."

§2A-506(2) reads:

"A cause of action accrues when the default occurs, regardless of the aggrieved party's lack of knowledge of the default. A breach of warranty occurs when tender of delivery is made, except that where a warranty explicitly extends to future performance of the goods and discovery of the breach must await the time of such performance the cause of action accrues when the breach is or should have been discovered."

§2A-508(2)(b) reads: "In a proper case, pursue those rights contained in Code Section 11-2A-521."

§3-415(a), in opening phrase, reads: "Subject to subsections (b), (c), (d) and (e) of this Code section and to subsection (d) of Code Section 11-3-419".

§3-602 adds new subsection (c):

"Notwithstanding any other provision of this article, with respect to a note which is a negotiable instrument within the meaning of this article and which is to be paid off in installment payments or in more than one payment, the maker or drawer is authorized to pay the assignor until the assignee or its authorized agent sends a registered or certified letter to the maker or drawer at the maker's or drawer's last known address notifying the maker or drawer that the amount due or to become due has been assigned and that payment is to be made to the assignee. A notification that does not reasonably identify the rights assigned is ineffective. If requested by the drawer or maker, the assignee must furnish reasonable proof that the assignment has been made and, unless the assignee does so, the maker or drawer may pay the assignor."

§4-406(f), in its first sentence, reads: "Without regard to care or lack of care of either the customer or the bank, a customer who does not within 60 days after the statement or items are made available to the customer (subsection (a) of this Code section) discover and report the customer's unauthorized signature on or any alteration on the face of the item or who does not within one year from that time discover and report any unauthorized indorsement or alteration on the back of the item is precluded from asserting against the bank the unauthorized signature, indorsement or alteration."

§6-103 omits:

"Public notice under subsection (6) or subsection (7) may be given by publishing once a week for two consecutive weeks in a newspaper of general circulation where the transferor had its principal place of business in this state an advertisement including the names and addresses of the transferor and transferee and the effective date of the transfer." This section is not printed at last sentence of §6-103 as it appears in 1962 Official Text.

§6-104(2) omits:

"If the transferor is the obligor of an outstanding issue of bonds, debentures or the like as to which there is an indenture trustee, the list of creditors need include only the name and address of the indenture trustee and the aggregate outstanding principal amount of the issue."

§6-106 reads:

"Definition of public notice.—Public notice under Code Section 11-6-103 shall be given as follows: by advertising the transfer, giving the name of the transferor, the transferee, and the effective date thereof, once a week for two weeks in the newspaper in which sheriffs' advertisements are published in the county where the former business enterprise taken over had its principal place of business in this state."

§6-111 increases six month period to twelve months.

§7-210(2)(b) omits: "or certified."

§8-102(1)(b) adds subsection (iv): "Not a partnership interest in a limited partnership, unless the partnership interest is listed on a national securities exchange registered under the federal securities laws or quoted in the automated quotation system of a national securities association registered under the federal securities laws."

§8-106 adds:

"With respect to securities issued by a municipal corporation, county or other political subdivision, authority or other similar public corporation, governmental agency or unit of this state, the negotiability thereof is governed by the law (including the conflict of laws rules) of this state; the provisions of the following Code sections of this article shall not apply: Code Sections 11-8-104, 11-8-202(1) and (2), 11-8-203, 11-8-305, and 11-8-405, and the validity of any security issued by any such issuer and all rights arising in connection with any such issuance shall continue to be determined by the provisions for the validation of bonds by counties, municipalities or other political subdivisions in Part 1 of Article 2 of Chapter 82 of Title 36 and with respect to revenue obligations issued by any municipal corporation, county or other political subdivision, authority, governmental agency, unit or other public corporation of this state shall be determined by the provisions for validation in Article 3 of Chapter 82 of Title 36, the 'Revenue Bond Law,' as amended."

§8-320(1)(a)(ii) reads: "Is in bearer form or indorsed in blank by an appropriate person or registered in the name of the clearing corporation, another clearing corporation, a custodian bank, or a nominee of any of them; or".

§9-102(2) reads:

"This article applies to security interests created by contract including pledge, assignment, chattel mortgage, bill of sale to secure debt, chattel trust, trust deed, factor's lien, equipment trust, conditional sale, trust receipt, other lien, conveyance of title, or title retention contract and lease or consignment intended as security. This article does not apply to statutory liens except as provided in Code Section 11-9-310."

§9-103(2)(b) reads:

"Except as otherwise provided in this subsection, perfection and the effect of perfection or nonperfection of the security interest are governed by the law (including the conflict of laws rules) of the jurisdiction issuing the certificate until four months after the goods are removed from that jurisdiction and thereafter until the goods are registered in another jurisdiction, but in any event not beyond surrender of the certificate. A surrender of a certificate of title pursuant to Code Sections 40-3-

See note at head of Digest as to 1998 legislation covered.

See Topical Index in front part of this volume.

GA – 14

COMMERCIAL CODE . . . *continued*

52 and 40-3-53 for the purpose of having a lien or subsequent security interest noted thereon shall not be deemed a surrender of the certificate for purposes of this Code section. After the expiration of that period, the goods are not covered by the certificate of title within the meaning of this Code section."

§9-103(3)(c) substitutes term "chief executive office" for "major executive office."

§9-104 reads:

"This article does not apply

(a) To a security interest subject to any statute of the United States to the extent that such statute governs the rights of parties to and third parties affected by transactions in particular types of property; or

(b) To a lien given by statute or to a right represented by a judgment (other than a judgment taken on a right to payment which was collateral) except as provided in this title on priority of such lien or right; or

(c) To a transfer of a claim for wages, salary or other compensation of an employee; or

(d) To a security interest created or transferred by a government or governmental subdivision, agency, or authority in connection with any of its investment securities (Code Section 11-8-102) other than a security interest created or transferred by an authority activated under Chapter 62 of Title 36, as now or hereafter amended, or by a local authority having as its principal function the stimulation of industrial growth and the reduction of unemployment; or

(e) To a sale of accounts or chattel paper as part of a sale of the business out of which they arose, or an assignment of accounts or chattel paper which is for the purpose of collection only, or a transfer of a right to payment under a contract to an assignee who is also to do the performance under the contract or a transfer of a single account to an assignee in whole or partial satisfaction of a preexisting indebtedness; or

(f) To a transfer of an interest or claim in or under any policy of insurance, except as provided with respect to proceeds (Code Section 11-9-306) and priorities in proceeds (Code Section 11-9-312); or

(g) To any right of set-off; or

(h) Except to the extent that provision is made for fixtures in Code Section 11-9-313, to the creation or transfer of an interest in or lien on real estate, including a lease or rents thereunder, whether or not such interest, lien, lease or the like amounts to an 'estate or interest in real estate' as the same is presently defined under Georgia law; or

(i) To a transfer in whole or in part of any claim arising out of tort; or

(j) To a transfer of an interest in any deposit account (subsection (1) of Code Section 11-9-105), except as provided with respect to proceeds (Code Section 11-9-306) and priorities in proceeds (Code Section 11-9-312)."

§9-105(1)(e) reads:

"'Deposit account' means a demand, time, savings, passbook or like account maintained with a bank, savings and loan association, credit union or like organization, other than an account evidenced by a certificate of deposit that is an instrument within this article."

§9-105(1)(g): Defined term "encumbrance" includes deeds to secure debt.

§9-105(1)(h): Timber to be cut is omitted from defined term "goods". Georgia revision does not include option of real estate filing for timber to be cut.

§9-105(1)(j): Defined term "mortgage" includes deeds to secure debt.

§9-105(1)(n): Defined term "transmitting utility" omitted. See §9-302(3)(c).

§9-105(2): Defined term "commission merchant" included in §9-307.

§9-203(1)(a) omits requirements of description of real estate for security agreements covering timber to be cut.

§9-206 omits phrases referring to lessees and lessors.

§9-301(2): Reference to "ten days" changed to "fifteen days".

§9-301(4) omitted.

§9-302(1)(d) deletes suggestion that there should be filing as to motor vehicles.

§9-302(3) reads:

"The filing of a financing statement otherwise required by this article is not necessary or effective to perfect a security interest in property:

(a) Subject to a statute or treaty of the United States which provides for a national or international registration or a national or international certificate of title or which specifies a place of filing different from that specified in this Article for filing of the security interest; or

(b) Required to have a certificate of title under Chapter 3 of Title 40, as now or hereafter amended, or subject to Code Section 40-3-50 but during any period in which collateral is inventory held for sale by a person who is in the business of selling goods of that kind, the filing provisions of this article (Part 4) apply to a security interest in that collateral created by him as debtor; or

(c) Subject to certificate of title statute of another jurisdiction under the law of which indication of a security interest on the certificate is required as a condition of perfection (subsection (2) of Code Section 11-9-103)."

§9-306(3)(a) reads:

"A filed financing statement covers the original collateral and the proceeds are collateral in which a security interest may (taking into account Code Section 11-9-401(2) and (3)) be perfected by filing in the office or offices where the financing statement has been filed and, if the proceeds are acquired with cash proceeds, the description of collateral in the financing statement indicates the types of property constituting the proceeds;"

§9-307 (3) reads:

"A commission merchant who shall sell livestock or agricultural products for another for a fee or commission shall not be liable to the holder of a security interest created by the seller of such livestock or products even though the security interest is perfected where the sale is made in ordinary course of business and without knowledge of the perfected security interest."

§9-307 adds new subsection (4):

"As used in this Code section, the term "commission merchant" means any person engaged in the business of receiving any farm product for sale, on commission, or for or on behalf of another person."

§9-310 reads:

"Priority of certain liens, claims and rights

(1) Except as is expressly provided to the contrary elsewhere in this article, and in subsection (2) of this Code section, a perfected security interest in collateral takes priority over each and all of the liens, claims, and rights described in Code Section 44-14-320, relating to the establishment of certain liens, as now or hereafter amended, and Code Section 53-7-91, relating to the priority of debts against the estate of a decedent, as now or hereafter amended, provided, nevertheless, that:

(a) Year's support to the family, duly set apart in the collateral prior to the perfection of the subject security interest, takes priority over such security interest; (b) A lien for property taxes duly assessed upon the subject collateral, either prior or subsequent to the perfection of the subject security interest, takes priority over security interest; (c) A lien for all other state taxes takes priority over such security interest, except where such security interest is perfected by filing a financing statement relative thereto prior to such time as the execution for such state taxes shall be entered on the execution docket in the place and in the manner provided by law; provided, nevertheless, that, with respect to priority rights between such tax liens and security interests where under this article the same are perfected other than by filing a financing statement, the same shall be determined as provided by law prior to January 1, 1964; and (d) A lien for other unpaid taxes or a duly rendered judgment of a court having jurisdiction shall have the same priority with regard to a security interest as it would have if the tax lien or judgment were a conflicting security interest within the meaning of Code Section 11-9-312 or an encumbrance within the meaning of Code Section 11-9-313, which conflicting security interest was perfected by filing or which encumbrance arose at the time the tax lien or judgment was duly recorded in the place designated by statute applicable thereto."

(2) A mechanics' lien on farm machinery or equipment arising on or after July 1, 1985, shall have priority over any perfected security interest in such farm machinery or equipment unless a financing statement has been filed as provided in Code Section 11-9-401 and unless the financing statement describes the particular piece of farm machinery or equipment to which the perfected security interest applies. Such description may include the make, model, and serial number of the piece of farm machinery or equipment. However, such description shall be sufficient whether or not it is specific if it reasonably identifies what is described and a mistake in such description shall not invalidate the description if it provides a key to identifying the farm machinery or equipment."

§9-312(4): Reference to "ten days" changed to "fifteen days".

§9-313(4) adds new subsection (e): "The security interest is a purchase money security interest in readily removable carpeting or padding for carpeting, the interest of the encumbrancer or owner arises before the goods become fixtures, and the security interest is perfected by fixture filing before the goods become fixtures."

§9-401 reads:

"(1) The proper place to file in order to perfect a security interest is with the clerk of the superior court of any county of the state.

(2) The rules stated in Code Section 11-9-103 determine whether filing is necessary in this state." Effective date of §9-401 is Jan. 1, 1995.

§9-402(1): First sentence reads: "A financing statement is sufficient if it complies with the requirements of this Code section and gives the names of the debtor and the secured party, is signed by the debtor, gives an address of the secured party from which information concerning the security interest may be obtained, gives a mailing address of the debtor, and sets forth the social security number, or if other than a natural person, the Internal Revenue Service taxpayer identification number of the debtor, contains a statement indicating the types, or describing the items, of collateral, and, where both (i) the collateral described consists only of consumer goods as defined in Code Section 11-9-109 and (ii) the secured obligation is originally $5,000 or less, gives the maturity date of the secured obligation or specifies that such obligation is not subject to a maturity date."

Third sentence is amended to read:

"When the financing statement covers crops growing or to be grown, or minerals or accounts subject to subsection (5) of Code Section 11-9-103, or when the financing statement is filed as a fixture filing (Code Section 11-9-313) and the collateral is goods which are or are to become fixtures, the statement must also comply with subsection (5) of this Code section.

The following sentence is added to end of subsection (1): " 'Secured obligation' for purposes of this Code section and Code Section 11-9-403 shall include a loan or any series of advances of money pursuant to a loan agreement or undertaking or any forebearance to enforce a claim for the collection of money or any purchase price or any installment obligation or any other obligation."

§9-402(3) reads:

"Financing statements and all amendments to such statements must be presented for filing on forms prescribed by the Georgia Superior Court Clerks' Cooperative Authority." (See Code Section 15-6-94.)

§9-402(5) reads:

"A financing statement covering crops growing, minerals or the like (including oil and gas) or accounts subject to subsection (5) of Code Section 11-9-103, or a financing statement indexed as a fixture filing subject to Code Section 11-9-313, must show that it covers this type of collateral, must contain a reasonable description of the real estate, and must show the name of the record owner or record lessee of the real estate if the debtor does not have an interest of record in the real estate. Additionally, a notice filing for Uniform Commercial Code related real estate, on the form prescribed by the Georgia Superior Court Clerk's Cooperative Authority, must be filed in the real estate records with the filing officer in the county or counties in which the affected real estate is located as provided in subsection (7) of Code Section 11-9-403. In addition to the requirements set forth above and in subsection (1) of this Code section, a financing statement covering farm products must contain the following information:

COMMERCIAL CODE . . . *continued*

(a) The farm product name and crop year subject to the security interest, except that no crop year need be designated if the security interest applies to every crop year for the duration of the filing;

(b) The social security number or, if other than a natural person, the Internal Revenue Service taxpayer identification number of the debtor;

(c) Each county in the state in which the farm products are located; and

(d) If needed to distinguish the farm products subject to such security interest from other farm products of the debtor not subject to such security interest, further details of the farm products, including, when applicable, the amount of the farm products subject to the security interest."

§9-402(6) reads:

"In order for goods which are or are to become fixtures related to real estate to be included in the central index described in Code Section 11-9-407, a financing statement complying with this Code Section must be filed."

§11-9-403 (1) reads: "Presentation for filing of a financing statement or a notice filing pursuant to subsection (7) of this Code section, and tender of the filing fee or acceptance of the statement or notice filing by the filing officer constitutes filing under this article."

§9-403(2): First and second sentences are amended to read: "Except as provided in subsections (6) and (8) of this Code section a filed financing statement is effective for a period of five years from the date of filing or until the twentieth day following any maturity date specified in the financing statement, whichever is earlier. Except as provided in subsection (8) of this Code section, the effectiveness of a filed financing statement lapses on the earlier of the expiration of the five-year period or the twentieth day following the maturity date specified in the financing statement unless a continuation statement is filed prior to the lapse."

In addition, following sentences are added to end of said paragraph: "If a security interest perfected by filing exists at the time insolvency proceedings are commenced by or against the debtor, the security interest remains perfected until termination of the insolvency proceedings and thereafter for a period of 60 days or until the normal expiration date of the financing statement, whichever occurs later. Upon lapse the security interest becomes unperfected, unless it is perfected without filing. If the security interest becomes unperfected upon lapse, it is deemed to have been unperfected as against a person who became a purchaser or lien creditor before lapse."

§9-403(3) reads:

"A continuation statement may be filed by the secured party within six months prior to the expiration date specified in subsection (2) of this Code section. Any such continuation statement must be filed with the filing officer of the county where the original financing statement was filed or, if the original financing statement has previously been continued, with the filing officer of the county where the currently effective continuation statement was filed. The continuation statement must be presented on the form prescribed by the Georgia Superior Court Clerks' Cooperative Authority for continuation statements and must identify the file number of the original statement, state that the original statement is still effective, and contain all of the information required under Code Section 11-9-402 for an original financing statement. A continuation statement signed by a person other than the secured party of record must be accompanied by a separate written statement of assignment signed by the secured party of record and complying with subsection (2) of Code Section 11-9-405, including payment of the required fee. Upon timely filing of the continuation statement, the effectiveness of the original statement is continued for a period of five years after the date to which the filing was effective or until the twentieth day following any maturity date specified in the continuation statement, whichever is earlier, whereupon it lapses in the same manner as provided in subsection (2) of this Code section unless another continuation statement is filed prior to such lapse. Succeeding continuation statements may be filed in the same manner to continue the effectiveness of the original statement."

§9-403(4) reads: "A filing officer shall mark each financing statement, continuation statement, amendment, assignment, release or termination statement, or notice filing made pursuant to subsection (7) of this Code section, with a file number or other appropriate recording information and with the date and hour of filing and shall hold the statement or a microfilm or other photostatic, microphotographic, photographic copy, or optical image reproduction thereof for public inspection. The filing officer shall transmit, for indexing in the central indexing system, each financing statement, continuation statement, amendment, assignment, release or termination statement within 24 hours of filing to the Georgia Superior Court Clerks' Cooperative Authority or its designated agent as provided in Code Section 15-6-61. Uniform Commercial Code related real estate notice filings shall be recorded in the real estate records of the county or counties where the real estate is located, and the filing officer shall index the notice filings according to subsection (7) of this Code Section.

§9-403(5) reads:

"The uniform fee for filing and indexing and for stamping a copy furnished by the secured party to show the date and place of filing for an original financing statement, continuation statement, amendment, release, assignment or termination statement, or a notice filing made pursuant to subsection (7) of this Code section furnished by the secured party to show the date and place of filing for an original shall be as required by Article 2 of Chapter 6 of Title 15."

§9-403(6) reads: "A real estate mortgage filed prior to July 1, 1995, which is effective as a future filing under subsection (6) of Code Section 11-9-402 remains effective as a fixture filing until the mortgage is released or satisfied of record or its effectiveness otherwise terminates as to the real estate. On and after January 1, 1995, a real estate mortgage may not be filed as a fixture filing under Code Section 11-9-402."

§9-403(7) reads:

"When a financing statement covers crops growing or to be grown, or minerals or the like (including oil and gas) or accounts subject to subsection (5) of Code Section 11-9-103, or is filed as a fixture filing (Code Section 11-9-313), a notice filing for Uniform Commercial Code related real estate on the form prescribed by the Georgia Superior Court Clerks' Cooperative Authority must be filed in the real estate records in the county or counties where the real estate is located. The notice filing is

sufficient if it complies with the requirements of this Code section and gives the names of the debtor and the secured party, is signed by the debtor or the secured party, gives an address of the secured party from which information concerning the security interest may be obtained, gives a mailing address of the debtor, specifies the types or items of collateral, contains a reasonable description of the real estate, and shows the name of the record owner or record lessee of the real estate if the debtor does not have an interest of record in the real estate. The notice filing will be indexed under the name of any owner or lessee of record if any is shown thereon, or if no such name is shown, under the name of the debtor in the same fashion as if they were the mortgagors in a mortgage of the real estate described. Amendments, releases, assignments, and terminations filed with respect to original notice filings shall give the names of the debtors and current secured parties, their addresses, the names of the record owners or record lessees of the real estate if the debtors do not have an interest of record in the real estate, and the recording information (book and page numbers and filing dates) of the original notice filings, shall be signed by the current secured parties, and shall be in the same form as used for comparable instruments to amend, release, assign, or cancel mortgages in the real estate records in Georgia, except that such filings need not be attested or acknowledged, or shall be on such other forms as the Georgia Superior Court Clerks' Cooperative Authority may prescribe."

§9-403(8) reads:

"Except as provided in subsection (6) of this Code section, any financing statement or continuation statement filed on or after July 1, 1985, which described collateral not consisting only of consumer goods as defined in Code Section 11-9-109, or for which the secured obligation as defined in subsection (1) of Code Section 11-9-402 originally was greater than $5,000, is effective for a period of five years from the date of filing, in the case of financing statements, or five years from the date of the expiration of the five-year period of effectiveness of the financing statement or immediately preceding continuation statement, in the case of continuation statements, notwithstanding any maturity date specified in any such financing or continuation statement and notwithstanding any provision of prior law to the contrary, unless such financing statement or continuation statement lapsed prior to March 26, 1986."

§9-404 reads:

"(1) Whenever there is no outstanding secured obligation and no commitment to make advances, incur obligations, or otherwise give value, the secured party shall file a termination statement on a form prescribed by the Georgia Superior Court Clerks' Cooperative Authority for termination statements with each filing officer with whom the financing statement was filed to the effect that he or she no longer claims a security interest under the financing statement, which shall be identified by the file number of the original statement. A termination statement signed by a person other than the secured party of record must be accompanied by a separate written statement of assignment signed by the secured party of record and complying with subsection (2) of Code Section 11-9-405, including payment of the required fee. If the affected secured party fails to send such a termination statement within 60 days after the debt has been paid in full, he or she shall be liable to the debtor for $100, and, in addition, for any loss caused to the debtor by such failure.

(2) On presentation to the filing officer of such a termination statement he or she must mark the statement with a file number and the hour and date of filing and shall hold the statement or a microfilm or other photostatic, microphotographic, photographic copy, or optical image reproduction thereof for public inspection. In addition, the filing officer shall transmit, for indexing in the central indexing system, each statement within 24 hours of filing to the Georgia Superior Court Clerks' Cooperative Authority or its designated agent as provided by Code Section 15-6-61. If he or she has received the termination statement in duplicate, he or she shall return one copy of the termination statement to the secured party stamped to show the time of receipt thereof. If the filing officer has a microfilm or other photostatic, microphotographic, photographic record or optical image reproduction of the financing statement, and of any related continuation statement, statement of assignment, and statement of release, he or she may remove the originals from the files at any time after receipt of the termination statement, or if he or she has no such record, he or she may remove them from the files at any time after one year after receipt of the termination statement.

(3) The uniform fee for filing and indexing a termination statement of a financing statement shall be as required by Article 2 of Chapter 6 of Title 15."

§9-405 substitutes in subsections (1) "Article 2 of Chapter 6 of Title 15" for "paragraph (6) of subsection (c) of Code Section 15-6-77."

§9-405(1) reads:

"(1) A financing statement may disclose an assignment of a security interest in the collateral described in the financing statement by indication in the financing statement of the name and address of the assignee or by an assignment itself or a copy thereof on the face or back of the statement. On presentation to the filing officer of such a financing statement the filing officer shall mark the statement with a file number and the hour and date of filing and shall hold the statement or a microfilm or other photostatic, microphotographic, photographic copy, or optical image reproduction thereof for public inspection. In addition the filing officer shall transmit, for indexing in the central indexing system, each statement within 24 hours of filing to the Georgia Superior Court Clerks' Cooperative Authority or its designated agent as provided by Code Section 15-6-61. The uniform fee for filing, indexing, and stamping a copy of a financing statement so indicating an assignment shall be as required by Article 2 of Chapter 6 of Title 15."

§9-405(2) reads:

"(2) A secured party may assign of record all or part of his or her rights under a financing statement by the filing with the filing officer of the County where the original financing statement was filed of a separate written statement of assignment, on the form prescribed by the Georgia Superior Court Clerks' Cooperative Authority, signed by the secured party of record and setting forth the name of the secured party of record, the name and social security number or, if other than a natural person the Internal Revenue Service taxpayer identification number, of the debtor, the file number and the date of filing of the financing statement, and the name and address of the

COMMERCIAL CODE... *continued*
assignee and containing a description of the collateral assigned. A form which otherwise complies with the requirements of this Code section is sufficient when it is signed by the assignee instead of the secured party of record if there is filed with such form a copy of the assignment instrument containing an original or a photostatic, microphotographic, photographic copy, or optical image reproduction of the signature of the secured party of record. On presentation to the filing officer of such a separate statement of assignment, the filing officer shall mark such separate statement with a file number and the date and hour of the filing and shall hold the statement or a microfilm or other photostatic, microphotographic, photographic copy, or optical image reproduction thereof for public inspection. In addition, the filing officer shall transmit, for indexing in the central indexing system, each statement within 24 hours of filing to the Georgia Superior Court Clerks' Cooperative Authority or its designated agent as provided by Code Section 15-6-61. The uniform fee for filing, indexing, and stamping a copy of such a separate statement of assignment shall be as required by Article 2 of Chapter 6 of Title 15."

§9-406 reads:

"A secured party of record may by his signed statement release all or a part of any collateral described in a filed financing statement. The statement of release is sufficient if it contains, on the form prescribed by the Georgia Superior Court Clerks' Cooperative Authority, a description of the collateral being released, the name, address, and social security number or, if other than a natural person, the Internal Revenue Service taxpayer identification number, of the debtor, the name and address of the secured party, the file number and the filing date of the financing statement. Each statement of release shall be filed with the filing officer of the county in which the financing statement was filed. A statement of release signed by a person other than the secured party of record must be accompanied by a separate written statement of assignment and complying with subsection (2) of Code Section 11-9-405, including payment of the required fee. On presentation to the filing officer of such a statement of release, the filing officer shall mark the statement with a file number and the hour and date of filing and shall hold the statement or a microfilm or other photostatic, microphotographic, photographic copy, or optical image reproduction thereof for public inspection. In addition, the filing officer shall transmit, for indexing in the central indexing system, each statement within 24 hours of filing to the Georgia Superior Court Clerks' Cooperative Authority or its designated agent as provided by Code Section 15-6-61. The uniform fee for filing, indexing, and stamping a copy of such a statement of release shall be as required by Article 2 of Chapter 6 of Title 15."

§9-407(1) reads:

"Upon request the filing officer shall furnish a copy of any filed financing statement or statement of assignment for a uniform fee as required by Article 2 of Chapter 6 of Title 15, provided that the person requesting such copy shall furnish to the file officer the file number of the statement requested."

§9-407 adds new subsections (2) through (7):

"(2) Unless the filing officer has notice of an action pending relative thereto, he may remove from the files and destroy:

(a) A lapsed original financing statement, a lapsed continuation statement and a statement of assignment or release relating to either, immediately if he has retained a microfilm or other photostatic, microphotographic, photographic record, or optical image reproduction thereof or, in other cases, one year or more after lapse; and

(b) A termination statement, immediately if he has retained a microfilm or other photostatic, microphotographic, photographic record, or optical image reproduction thereof or in other cases, one year or more after the filing of the termination statement, but such filing officer shall not destroy any index of such statement unless he retains a microfilm or other photostatic, microphotographic, photographic record, or optical image reproduction thereof.

(3) The Georgia Superior Court Clerks' Cooperative Authority or its designated agent or agents shall develop and implement a central indexing system containing substantially the information included on financing statements, amendments to financing statements, assignments of financial statements, continuation statements, termination statements, releases of collateral, and other documents related to personal property as may be filed pursuant to this part. The Georgia Superior Court Clerks' Cooperative Authority or its designated agent shall, within 24 hours after receipt of the filing information required by Code Section 15-6-61, include such data in the central indexing system and make such information available to the public through the central index. Weekends and holidays shall not be included in the calculation of the 24 hour period.

(4) The Georgia Superior Court Clerks' Cooperative Authority or its designated agent shall provide oral confirmation regarding the existence or nonexistence of an entry in the central index within 24 hours of receipt of a request complying with the rules and regulations of the authority and the payment of such fees as may be required by the authority, which oral confirmation must be followed by a written confirmation.

(5) The Georgia Superior Court Clerks' Cooperative Authority shall issue such rules and regulations, including prescribing required forms of documents, as appropriate to develop and implement the central indexing system described in this Code section and is further authorized to set and collect fees for incidental services and information provided by the authority or its designated agent with respect to the central indexing system if such fees are not otherwise prescribed by law. Information maintained in the central index for inclusion on search reports shall consist of all currently effective original financing statements filed on or after January 1, 1995, as well as any currently effective statement of assignment, continuation, release, or amendment relating thereto. The record of the index of lapsed or terminated statements shall be maintained in accordance with subsection (7) of this Code section.

(6) The Georgia Superior Court Clerks' Cooperative Authority shall not be authorized to issue regulations to implement a notification system for farm products in conformity with the requirements of Section 1324 of the federal Food Security Act of 1985, P.L. 99-198, as now in effect or as hereafter amended, and shall not be authorized to request certification of such notification system by the Secretary of the United States Department of Agriculture.

(7) Unless the Georgia Superior Court Clerks' Cooperative Authority or its designated agent has notice of an action pending relative thereto, such authority shall be authorized to archive and store the following computerized records and thereafter remove such records from the active central indexing system database:

(a) All lapsed financing statements, lapsed continuation statements, or statements of amendment, assignment, or release, relating to either, one year or more after lapse, provided only if there is archived, stored, and retained (i) a microfilm or other photostatic, microphotographic, photographic, or optical image reproduction record of such database and index, and (ii) an electronic or computerized record of such database and index; or

(b) All financing statements which have been terminated by the secured party of record, continuation statements, or statements of amendment, assignment, or release relating thereto, and the related termination statements, one year or more after the filing of the termination statement, provided only if there is archived, stored, and retained (i) a microfilm or other photostatic, microphotographic, photographic, or optical image reproduction record of such database and index, and (ii) an electronic or computerized record of such data base and index."

§9-409 reads:

"To the extent this part requires that any financing statement, amendment, continuation statement, assignment, release, or termination statement include the social security number or, if other than a natural person, the Internal Revenue Service taxpayer identification number of the debtor, no such financing statement, amendment, continuation statement, assignment, release, or termination statement otherwise complying with the requirements of this part shall be insufficient for purposes of this article as a result of any typographical or clerical error in the social security number or Internal Revenue Service taxpayer identification number so included, or any other error in such number except where the secured party has failed to make a good faith effort to obtain an accurate number from the debtor. The secured party shall in any event be entitled to rely on the written acknowledgment of the debtor as to the accuracy of such social security number or Internal Revenue Service taxpayer identification number, or as to whether the debtor is required to have a social security number or Internal Revenue Service taxpayer identification number, and the signature by the debtor of a financing statement or amendment which includes such social security number or Internal Revenue Service taxpayer identification number or a statement as to the debtor's not being required to have a social security number or Internal Revenue taxpayer identification number, shall constitute such a written acknowledgment. The burden of establishing the failure of the secured party to make a good faith effort to obtain an accurate social security number or Internal Revenue Service taxpayer identification number from the debtor is on the person challenging the sufficiency of the financing statement, amendment, continuation statement, assignment, release, or termination statement."

§10-101 sets the effective date of Act as 12:01 A.M. on Jan. 1, 1964.

§10-102 reads:

"Provision for transition.—Transactions validly entered into before the effective date specified in Code Section 11-10-101 and the rights, duties, and interests flowing from them remain valid thereafter and may be terminated, completed, consummated or enforced as required or permitted by any statute or other law amended or repealed by this title as though such repeal or amendment had not occurred."

§10-103 is specific repealer section, §10-104 retains certain statutory remedies.

§§11-101, 11-102 adopted.

§11-103 reads as follows:

"(1) Transactions validly entered into before July 1, 1978 and the rights, duties and interests flowing from them remain valid thereafter; and, except as provided in subsection (2) of this Code section, may be terminated, completed, consummated or enforced as required or permitted by old Article 9 of this title and other statute or other law amended or repealed by this Act as though such repeal or amendment had not occurred.

(2) Continuation statements with respect to security interests perfected under the old Article 9 of this title shall, after December 31, 1977, be filed in the manner and place specified in the revised Article 9 of this title."

§11-104 amends §11-108 as follows:

"Presumption that rule of law continues unchanged.

Unless a change in law has clearly been made, the provisions of the revised Article 9 of this title shall be deemed declaratory of the meaning of the old Article 9 of this title."

§11-105 not adopted.

§11-106 not adopted.

§11-107 not adopted.

§11-108 adopted as §11-104.

Article 12 sets July 1, 1994, as effective date for amendments to Article 9 relating to filing financing statement and related documents and provides for transition to new provisions.

§12-102 reads:

"(1) A financing statement or continuation statement filed prior to January 1, 1995, which has not lapsed prior to January 1, 1995, shall remain effective for the period provided in Code Section 11-9-403 as in effect immediately prior to January 1, 1995.

"(2) The effectiveness of any financing statement or continuation statement filed prior to January 1, 1995, may be continued only by the filing of a continuation statement, in the form prescribed by the Georgia Superior Court Clerks' Cooperative Authority, signed by either the debtor or the secured party with the filing officer of the county where the original financing statement was filed or, if the financing statement has previously been continued, where the currently effective continuation statement was filed. If the original financing statement or currently effective continuation statement was filed in multiple counties, then such continuation statement may be filed in any of such multiple counties, except where the original financing statement or currently effective continuation statement covers crops growing or to be grown, or minerals or the like, including oil and gas, or accounts subject to subsection (5) of Code Section 11-9-103, or was filed as a fixture filing (Code Section 11-9-313), then such continuation statement must be filed in each of such counties where any of the related real estate is located. This continuation statement must contain the information

See note at head of Digest as to 1998 legislation covered.

See Topical Index in front part of this volume.

GA – 17

COMMERCIAL CODE . . . *continued*

required by the first sentence of subsection (1) of Code Section 1-9-402, other than a statement indicating the types, or describing the items, of collateral and the social security number or Internal Revenue Service taxpayer identification number of the debtor, and must further identify the original financing statement or currently effective continuation statement, the office where such financing statement or continuation statement was filed, and the filing number and date of filing or other recording information, and further state that the original financing statement is still effective. Except as specified in this subsection, the provisions of subsection (3) of Code Section 11-9-403 for continuation statements apply to such a statement.

"(3) Statements of amendment, assignment, release, or termination affecting original financing statements filed prior to January 1, 1995, ('transitional filings') shall be filed on the forms prescribed by the Georgia Superior Court Clerks' Cooperative Authority with the filing officer of the county where the original financing statement was filed, or if the original financing statement had previously been continued, where the currently effective continuation statement was filed. If the original financing statement or currently effective continuation statement was filed in multiple counties, then such statement of amendment, assignment, release, or termination may be filed in any one of such multiple counties, except where the original financing statement or currently effective continuation statement covers crops growing or to be grown, or minerals or the like, including oil and gas, or accounts subject to subsection (5) of Code Section 11-9-103, or was filed as a fixture filing (Code Section 11-9-313), in which event such statement of amendment, assignment, release, or termination must be filed in each of such counties where any of the related real estate is located. Each transitional filing shall identify the original financing statement or currently effective continuation statement, the office where such financing statement or continuation statement was filed, the filing number or other recording information, and identify each named debtor and secured party. Notwithstanding the requirements of subsection (2) of Code Section 11-9-405 or Code Section 11-9-406, no social security number or Internal Revenue Service taxpayer identification number of the debtor shall be required to be included in any such transitional filings. The Georgia Superior Court Clerks' Cooperative Authority shall prescribe rules and regulations, as appropriate, to govern the presentation of such transitional filings.

"(4) A filing which was made in good faith in an improper place or not in all of the places required by Code Section 11-9-401 as in effect prior to January 1, 1995, is nevertheless effective with regard to any collateral as to which the filing complied with the requirements of this article and is also effective with regard to collateral covered by the financing statement against any person who has knowledge of the contents of such financing statement.

"(5) A filing which was made in the proper place in this state pursuant to Code Section 11-9-401 as in effect prior to January 1, 1995, continues effective even though the debtor's residence or place of business or the location of the collateral or its use, whichever controlled the original filing, is thereafter changed.

"(6) A continuation statement that was timely filed pursuant to subsection (8) of Code Section 11-9-403 as in effect prior to January 1, 1995, and that remains in effect as of January 1, 1995, shall continue the effectiveness of the original financing statement for the period specified in subsection (8) of Code Section 11-9-403 as in effect on January 1, 1995, provided that such continuation statement may thereafter be further continued by the filing of a subsequent continuation statement within six months prior to the expiration of the five-year period specified in subsection (8) of Code Section 11-9-403 as in effect prior to January 1, 1995, or, if such five-year period is determined to have a different duration, within six months prior to the expiration of the five-year period specified in subsection (8) of Code Section 11-9-403 as in effect on January 1, 1995."

Following options and alternatives in 1962 Official Text, 1972 Official Text of Article IX, and 1987 Official Text of Article IIA have been exercised:

§2-107(1): Optional phrase adopted;
§2A-216: Alternative A adopted;
§3-121: Alternative B adopted;
§4-106: Optional phrase omitted;
§4-202(1)(b): Optional phrase omitted;
§4-212: Optional subsection (2) adopted;
§5-112(1): Optional phrase adopted;
§5-114: Optional subsections (4) and (5) adopted;
§6-104(1)(c) adds following optional language:

"in the office of the clerk of the superior court as follows: When the seller is a resident individual, in the county where he resides, or when the seller is a nonresident individual, or is a partnership, corporation or other business entity, in the county of the seller's principal place of business in this state."

§6-106: Optional Section omitted, see subhead Intentional Differences, supra;
§6-107(2): Optional subparagraph (e) omitted;
§6-108(3): Optional subparagraph (c) omitted;
§6-109: Optional subsection (2) omitted;
§7-204: Optional subsection (4) omitted;
§7-403(1)(b): Optional clause omitted;
§9-401: Alternative subsection (3) not adopted;
§9-407: Optional Section adopted as modified.

Supervision of Records.—Georgia Superior Court Clerks' Cooperative Authority provides for development, acquisition and distribution of records management systems. Information, services, supplies and materials for superior court clerks, etc. (15-6-94).

Forms.—See end of this Digest.

See also topics: Banks and Banking, Bills and Notes, Brokers, Carriers, Contracts, Factors, Frauds, Statute of, Sales, Securities, Warehousemen; categories Business Organizations, topic Corporations; Civil Actions and Procedure, topic Limitation of Actions; Debtor and Creditor, topics Assignments, Fraudulent Sales and Conveyances, Liens, Pledges; Documents and Records, topics Records, Seals; Mortgages, topic Chattel Mortgages; Transportation, topic Motor Vehicles.

COMMERCIAL REAL ESTATE BROKERS:

See topic Brokers.

CONDITIONAL SALES:

See topic Sales.

CONSIGNMENTS:

See topic Factors.

CONSUMER PROTECTION:

Uniform Commercial Code.—Adopted. (Title 11). See topics Interest, Sales.

Uniform Deceptive Trade Practices Act.—Adopted. (10-1-365 through -375).

Assistive Technology Warranty Act.—Approved. (10-1-350). Manufacturer that sells assistive technology device to consumer must provide consumer with express written warranty of at least one year.

Fair Business Practices.—Under Fair Business Practices Act (10-1-390 through -407), unfair or deceptive acts in conduct of consumer transactions declared unlawful. Examples of unfair or deceptive acts listed in 10-1-393 through 10-1-393.6. Governor appoints Administrator and Consumer Advisory Board. Administrator, with consent of Attorney General, may adopt regulations, and bring actions in name of State to enjoin present, past, or anticipated unfair or deceptive methods, acts, or practices. (10-1-404). Strict rules regulate farm equipment manufacturers. (13-8-11).

Actions.—Administrator may, subject to requirement of subsequent notice and opportunity for hearing, issue cease and desist order or obtain civil penalty of up to $2,000 per violation, or may obtain from superior court of competent jurisdiction varying relief, including temporary restraining order, civil penalty of up to $5,000 per violation or restitution to injured parties. (10-1-397, -398). Appeals from any order of Administrator appealable to Superior Court of Fulton County. (10-1-398.1). Administrator may, with consent of Attorney General, issue investigative demands with respect to suspected violations. (10-1-403). Administrator forwards criminal offense conduct to prosecuting attorney. (10-1-406). Private party who suffers injury or damage or whose business or property was damaged as result of violations of Fair Business Practices Act may bring action for injunctive relief and general and exemplary damages (exemplary if violation intentional). Prospective claimant must present written demand for relief identifying claimant and describing alleged violation to prospective respondent at least 30 days prior to filing action. Respondent's rejected written tender of settlement will limit recovery if court finds tender reasonable in relation to injury. Demand requirements do not apply if prospective respondent has no place of business or assets in State or in specified cases where temporary restraining orders are permitted. Respondent may make written settlement offer and pay rejected tender into court after receiving notice of suit. (10-1-399). To be subject to direct suit under Act, alleged offender must have committed volitional act to avail self of channels of consumer commerce. (145 Ga. App. 8, 244 S.E.2d 15).

Statute of Limitations.—No action may be brought under Act more than two years after claimant knew or should have known of violation, or more than two years after termination of proceeding or action by State. (10-1-401).

Penalties and Damages.—Treble damages imposed for intentional violation of Act. Attorneys' fees awarded to claimant unless incurred after rejection of reasonable written offer of settlement. If claimant continues action in bad faith or for harassment after rejection of respondent's reasonable offer of settlement, attorneys' fees may be awarded to respondent. Manufacturer or supplier whose conduct is basis for action under Act liable for damages assessed against or suffered by retailer. (10-1-399). Recovery limited to actual damages if violation is result of bona fide error notwithstanding non-negligent maintenance of procedures to avoid errors. (10-1-400).

Penalty for violation of injunction issued under Act in action brought by Administrator is fine of not more than $25,000. Each day separate violation for continuing offense. Corporate officers, directors, partners, employees, and agents with knowledge of and who authorized violative acts liable for intentional violations if judgment against corporation is not satisfied within 30 days. (10-1-405).

Exemptions.—Transactions exempt from Act include acts authorized by State or U.S. law. Publisher, owner, agent, or employee of newspaper, periodical, or radio or television station is exempt with respect to dissemination of unfair or deceptive advertisement if such person had no knowledge of false, misleading, or deceptive character of advertisement, did not prepare advertisement, and had no financial interest in sale or distribution of advertised product or service. (10-1-396).

Unsolicited Merchandise.—Offer of goods for sale employing practice of unsolicited sending of such goods prohibited. Receipt of unsolicited goods under such circumstances deemed unconditional gift. Recipient of such goods may bring action to enjoin sending of bills or requests for payment, and attorneys' fees and costs may be awarded to prevailing party. (10-1-50).

Criminal Conduct.—Deceptive business practices punishable as misdemeanor. Deceptive business practices committed by knowingly in regular course of business: Using false weights, measures, or devices for determining or recording any quality or quantity of goods; selling, offering or delivering less than represented quality or quantity of commodity; or taking more than represented quantity when furnishing weight or measure. (16-9-50). Improper solicitation of money punishable as misdemeanor, and damaged party entitled to damages of three times sum solicited. Improper solicitation of money committed by soliciting payment of money by statement or invoice, or writing so interpreted, for goods not yet ordered or services not yet performed and ordered, unless following language appears in 30-point bold face type on face of statement or invoice: "This is a solicitation for the order of goods or services and you are under no obligation to make payment unless you accept the offer contained herein." (16-9-52). Foreclosure fraud punishable as felony. Foreclosure fraud committed by knowingly or willfully representing that monies provided to or on behalf of debtor in connection with debtor's residence are loan if monies in fact used to purchase residence or debtor's interest therein. (16-9-60). Misrepresenting origin or ownership of timber valued at over $500 is felony. (16-9-61).

See note at head of Digest as to 1998 legislation covered.

See Topical Index in front part of this volume.

GA – 18

CONSUMER PROTECTION . . . *continued*

Sale of Business Opportunities.—Defined as sale or lease of products, supplies, or services with which to start business, where seller represents it will purchase products made or provide locations it does not control for certain vending operations, or make certain guarantees of income, or provide sales or marketing program; exempted from definition are sales of ongoing business and certain relationships. (10-1-410). Detailed disclosures to prospective purchaser must be made at least 48 hours before contract signed or seller receives any consideration. (10-1-411). Disclosure statement must be filed with Administrator of Fair Business Practices Act. (10-1-413). Purchaser has one year to void contract if seller has not registered with Administrator of Act. (10-1-417). Seller prohibited from making unsubstantiated claims of earning potential, using name or mark of business that neither controls seller nor accepts responsibility for seller's representations, or referring to its compliance with 10-1-410 through -416. (10-1-414). Seller may be required to obtain surety bond in amount not less than $75,000. (10-1-412). Contract must be in writing and contain required provisions. (10-1-415). Remedies for violations available to purchaser. (10-1-417).

Lemon Laws.—Motor Vehicle Warranty Rights Act sets forth duties and responsibilities of motor vehicle dealers and manufacturers and provides procedures for dispute resolution. (10-1-780). Farm Tractor Warranty Act sets forth duties and responsibilities of farm tractor dealers and manufacturers and provides procedures for dispute resolution. (10-1-810 et seq.).

Plain Language.—No "Plain Language" statute.

Transient Merchant.—Transient Merchant Act regulates merchants without permanent place of business. (43-46-1 et seq.). Must be licensed (43-46-4), meet general requirements relating to corporations, and maintain registered agent (43-46-5). Violators subject to civil and criminal penalties. (43-46-7). See also topic Licenses, Business and Professional.

Advertising.—Advertising for sale without intent to sell at price and on terms in advertisement prohibited. (10-1-420). Relevant disclaimers may not be hidden or placed in selectively deemphasized text. False or fraudulent advertising prohibited. (10-1-421). Persons using term "Doctor" or "Dr." in conjunction with name required to identify degree held. (10-1-422). Unlawful to misrepresent nature of business by use of such terms as "manufacturer", "wholesaler", or "retailer" or to use term "wholesale" unless advertiser selling items advertised at wholesale. (10-1-424). Unlawful to misrepresent or to fail to state name and address of owner in connection with liquidation sale, auction sale or going-out-of-business sale. (10-1-425). See also 10-1-392(a)(5.2) and 10-1-393(b)(24) regarding "going out of business" sales. Violations are misdemeanors. (10-1-426). Aggrieved person may sue for injunction. (10-1-423). False, misleading, or fraudulent advertising of legal services prohibited. (10-1-427). Deceptive or fraudulent telemarketing practices prohibited. (10-58-1; 10-58-4; 10-1-393.6).

Disaster Related Violations.—Whenever Administrator imposes penalty for any violation under Uniform Deceptive Trade Practices Act or Fair Business Practices Act or for false advertising and violation is disaster related violation, in addition to any other applicable penalty, additional civil penalty not to exceed $10,000 may be imposed for each transaction. Any person suffering damage or injury as result of disaster related violation has cause of action to recover actual damages, punitive damages, if appropriate, and reasonable attorneys' fees. Amounts recovered in such action have priority over civil penalty imposed under such Code section. (10-1-438).

Credit Cards.—Lender Credit Card Act repealed 1987. Credit Card and Credit Card Banking Act (7-5-1 et seq.) adopted, providing for establishment of limited credit card banks to engage in credit card account business in State. Domestic lender or credit card bank authorized to impose interest, fees, and charges as agreed upon between lender or bank and debtor, subject to requirements for fair disclosure and criminal usury. See topic Interest.

Computer Systems.—Georgia Computer Systems Protection Act makes it unlawful to knowingly transmit misleading data through computer or telephone network for purpose of setting up and operating electronic mailbox or home page, if such data uses individual name, tradename, trademark or copyrighted symbol to falsely identify person or organization transmitting data. (16-9-93.1 et seq.).

Retail Installment and Home Solicitation Sales.—Retail Installment and Home Solicitation Sales Act (10-1-1 et seq.) requires retail installment contracts to be in writing and completed before execution. Motor vehicles excluded from Act. Contracts must be in at least six-point type and carry prescribed notice and provisions. Time price differential limited to 13% per annum. Seller must give completed copy of contract to buyer upon execution and deliver, within 30 days after execution of contract, any policies or certificates of insurance purchased in connection with contract. Buyer entitled to receipt for payments upon request. Buyer may prepay balance on contract and receive refund calculated by sum-of-the-digits method. (10-1-3).

Revolving Account.—Must be in writing (printed material in at least six-point type) and completed prior to execution. Must contain prescribed notice and provisions. Time price differential restricted to 1.75% per month. (10-1-4).

Mail Order and Telephone Sales.—Retail installment contracts negotiated and entered into by mail or telephone without personal solicitation by representative of seller subject to Act. Where catalog or other printed solicitation generally available to public clearly sets forth cash price and sales terms of seller and is provided to buyer, sale may be made subject to requirements of Act, except that seller not required to deliver copy of contract to buyer and seller may complete contract by inserting appropriate price and sales terms set out in current catalog or printed solicitation. If seller inserts terms in contract, seller must deliver to buyer statement of items inserted. (10-1-5).

Right to Cancel Home Solicitation Sale.—Buyer may cancel home solicitation sale agreement by notice of cancellation given to seller at address in agreement by certified mail, return receipt requested, posted not later than midnight of third business day after buyer signs agreement. Seller must refund all deposits and downpayments and redeliver all property traded in within ten days after cancellation. Seller may charge liquidated damages of lesser of $25 or 5% of gross sales price. Buyer must return any merchandise unused and in same condition as when received. Seller must pick up

merchandise at point of sale within reasonable time after cancellation and may charge lesser of $5 or actual cost of pick up. Notice of cancellation need not be in particular form and is effective if expresses buyer's intention not to be bound by home solicitation sale. (10-1-6).

Permissible Charges.—Retail installment contract or revolving account may provide for delinquency charge not to exceed $10 on installment not paid within ten days of when due. Seller may collect court costs and reasonable attorneys' fees if referred for collection to attorney who is not salaried employee of retail seller. If buyer fails to make good on dishonored check after ten days notice, seller may charge fee not to exceed greater of $20 or 5% of dishonored check. (10-1-7).

No Security Interest in Certain Goods.—No security interest may be taken in clothing, softwares and other nondurable items. Payments on revolving account applied first to finance charge or time price differential, then to goods in order of their purchase (if goods purchased on same day, then to lowest priced goods first). Parties may agree in writing for payments to be otherwise applied. (10-1-8).

Transfer of Contracts or Accounts.—Seller may assign, pledge, hypothecate, or transfer retail installment contract or revolving account on agreed terms and price. Unless buyer has notice of assignment, payment to last known owner of contract or account is binding on all subsequent owners. Assignment does not bar action against seller or preclude defense against assignee in action for finance or other charges. (10-1-9).

Rights After Repossession.—After repossession, seller may not recover deficiency unless within ten days after repossession seller gives notice to buyer by registered or certified mail of intention to pursue deficiency claim. Notice must advise buyer of right of redemption and right to demand public sale. Buyer's demand of public sale must be given by registered or certified mail within ten days after posting of seller's notice. (10-1-10).

Penalties.—Willful and intentional violation of Act is misdemeanor. Contracting for or receiving excessive finance charge on retail installment contract bars recovery of all finance and other charges on contract. Charging or receiving excessive time price differential on revolving account bars recovery of all finance and other charges stated on or collected in connection with statement in which violation occurred. In case of willful violation, buyer may recover from seller or set-off or counterclaim lesser of (a) $100 or (b) double time price differential and delinquency charge and attorneys' fees and court costs charged and paid, but seller may recover cash price of goods or services and cost of any insurance. (10-1-15).

Statute of Limitations.—No action may be brought more than four years after claimant knew or should have known of violation. (10-1-14).

No Waiver.—Provisions of Act may not be waived. (10-1-13).

CONTRACTS:

Uniform Commercial Code.—Adopted. (Title 11). Rule for interpretation of contracts is contained in separate provision. (13-2-2). See topic Commercial Code; categories Documents and Records, topic Seals; Family, topic Infants.

In 1994, Georgia Supreme Court held that pre-litigation contractual waivers of right to trial by jury are not enforceable in cases tried under laws of Georgia. (264 Ga. 339, 444 S.E.2d 799).

FACTORS:

Factor must exercise ordinary care and diligence in keeping and protecting articles entrusted to him. (44-12-71). In absence of instructions factor may exercise discretion according to general usages of trade but greater and more skillful diligence and most active good faith are thereby required. (44-12-75). Statutory provisions do not apply to accounts receivable factor; such relationships will be governed by contract and Uniform Commercial Code. (250 Ga. 832, 301 S.E.2d 262). Factor contracting on his or her own credit has right of action on contracts made for principal. (10-6-82).

Uniform Commercial Code.—Adopted. (Title 11).

License Requirements.—See topic Licenses, Business and Professional.

Liens.—Factor's lien extends to all balances on general account and attaches to proceeds as well as goods themselves. (44-14-404). Liens satisfied by sale as established by local usage. (44-14-405). Factor's liens inferior to liens for taxes, recorded liens or ones of which factor had notice, special liens for rent, liens of laborers, judgment liens, and other general liens reduced to execution and levied upon. (44-14-400). Factor's liens regulated by 11-9-101 et seq. See topic Commercial Code.

FRANCHISES:

No statute currently exists that specifically regulates offer and sale of franchises in Georgia. However, persons engaged in franchising should be aware of Georgia Business Opportunity Sales Law, which governs offer and sale of business opportunities and multi-level distribution programs. (10-1-410 through -417). Definition of term "business opportunity" may cover certain franchise programs, subjecting them to requirements of Business Opportunity Sales Law. Such requirements include bond, trust account, escrow requirements, presale disclosure requirements, specific contractual provisions to be inserted in business opportunity agreement and certain prohibited acts in offer or sale of business opportunity. Laws also exist relating to motor vehicle franchise practices (10-1-620 through -668) and farm equipment distributorships and dealerships (13-8-12 through -45).

FRAUDS, STATUTE OF:

Following obligations not binding unless promise in writing, signed by party to be charged or some person by him lawfully authorized: (1) promise by executor, administrator, guardian, or trustee to answer damages out of his or her own estate; (2) promise to answer for debt, default or miscarriage of another; (3) agreement made on consideration of marriage, except marriage articles; (4) contract for sale of land or any interest in or concerning same; (5) agreement not to be performed within one year; (6) promise to revive debt barred by statute of limitations; (7) commitment to lend money (13-5-30); (8) contract for sale of goods for price of $500 or more (11-2-201); (9) contract

FRAUDS, STATUTE OF . . . *continued*
creating landlord-tenant relationship exceeding one year and not tenancy at will (44-7-2).

Uniform Commercial Code.—Adopted. (Title 11). See in particular: 11-1-206 (contracts for sale of personal property not otherwise covered by other U.C.C. provisions); 11-2-201 (contracts for sale of goods); 11-3-416 (guarantees written on negotiable instruments); 11-5-104 (letters of credit); 11-8-319 (contracts for sale of securities); 11-9-203 (security agreements).

Contracts of Sale.—Governed by Uniform Commercial Code. (Title 11).

Statute is inapplicable where: (1) Contract fully performed; (2) performance on one side accepted by other in accordance with contract; (3) such part performance that nonenforcement of contract would work fraud (13-5-31); contract of purchaser at judicial sale (9-13-169).

INTEREST:

Legal rate 7% per year simple interest where rate not established by written contract. (7-4-2). See, however, subhead Maximum Rate for maximum lawful rate.

Maximum Rate.—Any rate higher than 7% must be in writing; maximum is 16% per annum simple interest where principal amount involved is $3,000 or less. Subject to criminal usury limit of 5% per month (7-4-18), no limit on interest rate that may be agreed upon where principal exceeds $3,000; however, if above $3,000 but below $250,000, must be expressed in simple interest terms in written contract. No prohibition is thereby created on variable rate or other basis for interest. Foregoing is inapplicable to matters governed by specified statutes. (7-4-2).

Bar to using defense of usury is applied to endorsers of loan. (124 Ga. App. 511, 184 S.E.2d 226).

Advertisements of Interest Rates for Consumer Credit Transactions.—Must comply with Federal Truth in Lending Act, 15 U.S.C. 57(a) and 1602 et seq. (7-4-4).

Judgments bear interest at rate of 12% per annum on principal amount recovered unless rendered on written contract or obligation providing for interest at specified rate, in which case judgment bears interest at rate specified in contract or obligation. Such post-judgment interest accrues automatically, whether or not such judgment specifically reflects entitlement to such interest. (7-4-12). In actions ex delicto, claimant is entitled to receive 12% interest on claims of unliquidated damages from 30 days after statutory notice, provided judgment is for amount not less than sum claimed. (51-12-14).

Liquidated demands bear legal rate from time when due, or if payable on demand, then from date of demand. (7-4-15).

Unliquidated demands bear pre-judgment interest at legal rate in certain circumstances. (255 Ga. 117, 335 S.E.2d 547).

Commercial Accounts.—Due and payable on date statement rendered to obligor unless obligor agrees otherwise. Maximum charge of 1.5% per month interest on portion due and payable for 30 days or more. (7-4-16).

Small Industrial Loans.—On loans of $3,000 or less for period of 36½ months or less, made by lenders other than banks, savings and loan, trust companies, insurance companies, mortgage companies, etc., maximum charge is 10% annual interest computed on face amount even if repayable in installments, plus loan fee not exceeding 8% of first $600 plus 4% of excess. In addition to loan fee, maintenance charge of $2 per month may be charged for each contract. One-time late fees of 5% on any installment five days overdue permitted. (7-3-14). Statutory prepayment privilege, with proportionate refund of interest. (7-3-17). When interest charge is excessive, licensed lender shall be liable to borrower for twice interest and loan fees charged to borrower (not less than $100). (7-3-29).

Other specific statutes regulate allowable interest rates or finance charge limitations on retail installment sales, motor vehicle and manufactured home sales, loans by credit unions, insurance premium financing loans, pawnbroker loans, etc.

Revolving loan account interest restrictions repealed; replaced by provisions of Credit Card and Credit Card Bank Act. Credit card interest may be agreed upon by lender and debtor, subject to 5% per month misdemeanor provisions described below. See topic Consumer Protection.

Usury.—Any higher rate than those above specified or failure to disclose interest rates in simple interest per annum terms where principal amount of loan is greater than $3,000 but less than $250,000 (7-4-1) results in forfeiture of entire interest but no further penalty (7-4-10), except in case of small industrial loans (see subhead Small Industrial Loans, supra) or loans on which interest exceeds 5% per month, for which violations constitute misdemeanor (7-4-18). Definition of "interest" under criminal usury statute (7-4-18) is different from definition setting legal rate of interest (7-4-2; 260 Ga. 271, 392 S.E.2d 242). Usurious interest paid may be recovered by suit brought within one year of payment. (7-4-10). While plea of usury is personal, creditor cannot collect usurious interest from insolvent debtor to prejudice of other creditors. (7-4-11). Except for small industrial loans, loan not rendered usurious by brokers fees paid to persons other than lender. (7-4-8; 7-3-5). To prove usury, must show intent to charge usurious interest rate at time of making loan. (160 Ga. App. 359, 287 S.E.2d 75).

Bonds issued by housing authority may bear interest pursuant to terms of resolution, trust indenture or mortgage of such authority. (8-3-73). Bonds, notes and certificates of county, municipality, authority or public corporation (other than general obligation bonds) not governed by state usury laws. (36-82-120).

Revenue bonds and certificates may bear interest not exceeding 9% per year. (36-82-64).

See also category Mortgages, topic Mortgages of Real Property.

LICENSES, BUSINESS AND PROFESSIONAL:

Practically all businesses and occupations require licenses (Title 43); counties, municipalities are authorized to provide by local ordinance or resolution for levy, assessment, and collection of occupation tax, regulatory fees for businesses and professionals within county (48-13-5 through -28).

Occupational Licenses.—State licensing authority shall suspend or revoke licenses upon licensee's conviction of criminal offense involving controlled substance or marijuana. (16-13-110 through -114). Licenses for certain trades, businesses, professions and occupations can be suspended for failure to pay child support. (19-6-28).

Commercial Travelers.—Art. 1 of c. 13 of Title 48 shall govern municipal and county occupation taxes for following: traveling salespersons engaged in taking orders for sale of goods when no delivery of goods is made at time of taking order; merchant or dealer, site of whose business is outside taxing jurisdiction, who delivers goods previously ordered; and employees of merchant or dealer who are engaged in delivery of goods to customers. (48-5-354). See also topic Consumer Protection.

Disabled Veterans and Blind Person.—Any disabled war veteran with 10% disability, disabled peacetime veteran with 25% service-connected disability or blind person may peddle, conduct business or practice profession or semi-profession in any city or county without payment of business, occupation or professional license taxes if resident of Georgia and not liable for payment of state income taxes. (43-12-2). Proof of such disability must be established by written certification of two physicians, or by letter or other written evidence from United States Department of Veterans' Affairs, or by evidence from branch of armed forces of U.S. in which veteran served. (43-12-1, 2). Certificate from any probate judge is prima facie proof of disability. (43-12-35). Certain businesses are exempted from this law. (43-12-8). Privileges granted hereunder are not transferable. (43-12-9).

Corporation License Tax.—See category Business Organizations, topic Corporations.

Collection Agencies.—Bond required for certain agents. (10-6-100, -101).

Athlete Agents.—Registration required for agents of certain university athletes (43-4A-4), bond required (43-4A-13), and activities restricted (43-4A-16).

MONOPOLIES, RESTRAINT OF TRADE AND COMPETITION:

See subhead Contracts in Partial Restraint of Trade, infra.

Contracts in general restraint of trade are void. (13-8-2[a]). Agreements which may have effect or intended to have effect to defeat or lessen competition or to encourage monopoly are void and legislature cannot authorize such. (Const., Art. III, §VI, Paragraph V). Any person who enters into contract, combination or conspiracy in restraint of trade or in restraint of free and open competition in any transaction with state, agency thereof or political subdivision, shall, upon conviction, be punished by imprisonment of not less than one nor more than five years. (16-10-22).

Unfair Trade Practices.—Unfair or deceptive acts or practices in conduct of consumer transactions in trade or commerce are unlawful. (10-1-393[a]). Specific unfair or deceptive acts or practices, essentially identical to those set forth in Revised Uniform Deceptive Trade Practices Act §2(a) (see Uniform and Model Acts section), are listed for illustrative purposes (10-1-393[b]). Administrator may adopt as substantive rules prohibiting specific acts or practices and regulations interpreting FTC Act §5(a)(1). (10-1-394[a]). Administrator may pursue actions for equitable relief, civil penalties or restitution to adversely affected persons. (10-1-397). Person injured as result of violation of Act may, upon compliance with 30-day demand letter procedures, sue for injunctive relief, damages, reasonable attorneys' fees and expenses, but may not sue as class representative. (10-1-399). Treble damages awarded for intentional violations. (10-1-399[c]). Plaintiff's rejection of written settlement offer made within 30 days of demand letter and later found by court to have been reasonable offer may limit plaintiff's recovery to amount of offer, preclude award of attorneys' fees and expenses incurred subsequent to offer, and, if litigation pursued in bad faith, result in award of attorneys' fees and expenses to defendant. (10-1-399[d]). Act does not apply to: (1) actions specifically authorized under laws administered by or rules and regulations promulgated by any Federal or Georgia regulatory agency; and (2) acts done by media in publishing or disseminating advertisements of others if media did not prepare or did not have knowledge of deceptive nature of advertisement or did not have direct financial interest in sale or distribution of advertised product or service. (10-1-396). See category Intellectual Property, topic Trademarks and Tradenames.

Uniform Deceptive Trade Practices Act adopted. (10-1-370). See Uniform and Model Acts section.

Multilevel distribution companies (defined as persons or business entities that sell, distribute or supply for valuable consideration, goods or services through independent agents, contractors or distributors, at different levels wherein such participants may recruit other participants, and wherein commissions, cross-commissions, bonuses, refunds, discounts, dividends or other considerations in program are or may be paid as result of sale of such goods or services or recruitment, actions or performances of additional participants) (10-1-410) having any Georgia residents among their participants must abide by prohibitions and requirements of statute, which are designed to protect actual and potential participants.

Resale Price Agreements.—Fair Trade Act repealed, effective July 1, 1976.

Gasoline Marketing Practices Act.—Regulates contractual and marketing relationships between dealers and distributors, creating cause of action in favor of dealer and defenses in favor of distributor. (10-1-230 et seq.). Gasoline industry is not affected with public interest; therefore, 10-1-234 regulating prices and 10-1-254 proscribing below-cost sales are unconstitutional. (255 Ga. 480, 340 S.E.2d 16; 256 Ga. 669, 353 S.E.2d 17).

Contracts in Partial Restraint of Trade.—See topic Contracts; category Employment, topic Labor Relations.

In 1990, Georgia legislature passed Restrictive Covenant Act (13-8-2.1) to make it easier to enforce restrictive covenants, but that Act was declared unconstitutional (261 Ga. 371, 405 S.E.2d 253). Accordingly, from and after June 27, 1991, law on restrictive covenants as it existed prior to enactment of 13-8-2.1 will apply to all restrictive covenants.

See note at head of Digest as to 1998 legislation covered.

See Topical Index in front part of this volume.

NEGOTIABLE INSTRUMENTS:

See topic Bills and Notes.

RESTRAINT OF TRADE:

See topic Monopolies, Restraint of Trade and Competition.

SALES:

Uniform Commercial Code.—Adopted. (Title 11). See topic Commercial Code. See topic Consumer Protection.

Contracts of Sale.—See topic Commercial Code. (11-2). See topic Consumer Protection.

Bills of Sale.—See category Property, topic Deeds, subhead Deed to Personalty.

Conditions or Warranties.—See topic Commercial Code. (11-2).

Product Liability.—See topic Commercial Code. (11-2-318). No privity requirement in action against manufacturer by natural person. (51-1-11; 234 Ga. 868, 218 S.E.2d 580).

Transfer of Title.—See topic Commercial Code. (11-2).

Delivery.—See topic Commercial Code. (11-2).

Stoppage in Transit.—See topic Commercial Code. (11-2).

Remedies of Seller.—See topic Commercial Code. (11-2).

Remedies of Buyer.—See topic Commercial Code. (11-2).

Conditional Sales.—See topic Commercial Code. (11-2). All retail installment sales contracts and home solicitation sales subject to extremely detailed requirements as to form and content. (10-1-1 et seq.).

Retail Credit Sales.—See subhead Conditional Sales, supra, and topic Interest.

Bulk Sales.—See topic Commercial Code; category Debtor and Creditor, topic Fraudulent Sales and Conveyances, subhead Bulk Sales.

Sales of Motor Vehicles.—See category Transportation, topic Motor Vehicles, subheads Titles and Sales.

Consumer Protection.—See topic Consumer Protection.

SECURITIES:

Georgia Securities Act of 1973 (10-5-1 et seq.) regulates offer, sale and regulation of securities and registration of dealers, salespersons and investment advisers. Act has been amended to conform to federal National Securities Market Improvement Act of 1996.

Uniform Commercial Code.—Adopted. See topic Commercial Code.

Supervision.—Secretary of State (2 Martin Luther King Jr. Drive, Suite 315-West Tower, Atlanta, GA 30334) has administrative authority and is designated Commissioner of Securities. (10-5-10[a]).

Regulatory Powers of Supervising Authority.—Commissioner has power to make rules and regulations as deemed necessary. (10-5-10[d]).

Prerequisites to Sales or Offers.—It is unlawful to offer for sale or to sell any security to any person in Georgia (i) unless security is subject to effective registration statement, (ii) security or transaction is exempt under Code §10-5-8 or 10-5-9, or (iii) security is federal covered security. (10-5-5[a]). Any securities transaction subject to effective federal registration statement under Securities Act of 1933 or exempt from registration requirements may be sold in exempt transactions provided that certain notice and filing fee of $250 has been provided to commissioner. (10-5-9[5]). See subhead Exempt Transactions, infra. Four kinds of Georgia registration are: registration by qualification (10-5-5[b]), registration by notification (10-5-5[d]), small issue registration (10-5-5[e]), and nonprofit issuer registration (10-5-5[f]). Filing fee for first three types of Georgia registration is 1/20 of 1% of maximum aggregate offering price of securities to be offered in Georgia, but minimum fee is $250. (10-5-6[a]). There is no filing fee for nonprofit issuer registration. (10-5-6[a]). Registration by qualification is effective when commissioner orders (10-5-5[b][5]); registration by notification, and nonprofit issuer registration effective at 3:00 p.m. on fifth full business day after filing of registration statement, if no stop order has been entered. (10-5-5[d][3]; 10-5-5[f][6]). Small issue registrations effective at 3:00 p.m. on tenth full business day after filing of registration statement, if no stop order has been entered. (10-5-5[e][5]). All registrations effective for 12 months following effective date and may be renewed upon updating information and payment of $100 renewal fee. (10-5-6[i]). Issuer seeking registration of securities by qualification must file $25,000 bond as precondition to registration. However, issuer need not file such bond if registered securities will be sold in Georgia only through dealers and limited dealers registered under Act. No applicant need file such bond if he or she deposits with commissioner certificate of deposit with certain financial institutions or irrevocable letter of credit from certain banks or certain federal or Georgia obligations having market value of at least $25,000. (10-5-6[b][1], [2]).

Securities to Which Act Applicable.—Act applies to any note, stock, treasury stock, bond, debenture, evidence of indebtedness, certificate of indebtedness, investment certificate, certificate of interest or participation in any profit-sharing agreement, certificate of interest in oil, gas or other mineral rights, collateral trust certificate, preorganization certificate or subscription, transferable share, investment contract, voting-trust certificate, limited partnership interest, or beneficial interest in profits or earnings, or any other instrument commonly known as a security, including any certificate of interest or participation in, temporary or interim certificate for, receipt for, guaranty of or warrant or right to subscribe to or purchase, any of foregoing. (10-5-2[a][26]). For transaction to constitute securities transaction there must be investment, reasonable expectation of profits and reliance on management of another party to bring about profits. (246 Ga. 583, 272 S.E.2d 314). Investment contract shall include investment which holds possibility of return on risk capital even though investor's efforts necessary to receive such return under certain circumstances; Act is not applicable to insurance or endowment policy, or to any fixed or variable annuity contract issued by licensed insurance company, nor is it applicable to interest in residential unit and rental management arrangement relating to such unit if owner does not participate directly in income derived from rental of units owned by others. (10-5-2[a][26]).

Exempt Securities.—Following securities are exempt from registration under Act: (a) securities issued or guaranteed by U.S., any state, any political subdivision of a state, or any agency or instrumentality of foregoing; (b) securities issued or guaranteed by Canada or a province thereof or an agency or instrumentality thereof or by any government with which U.S. has diplomatic relations; (c) any security issued or guaranteed by any federal or state bank, savings institution, or trust company including any interest in any common trust fund maintained by bank exclusively for collective investment of assets contributed thereto by such bank in its capacity as trustee, executor, administrator, or guardian; (d) securities issued by and representing interest in or debt of, or guaranteed by federal savings and loan associations or by state building and loan associations or similar organizations authorized to do business in Georgia; (e) securities issued by farmers' cooperative associations as defined by §521 of Internal Revenue Code; (f) securities issued or guaranteed by federal credit unions or any other credit unions, industrial loan associations or similar associations organized and supervised under laws of Georgia; (g) securities issued or guaranteed by railroads, common carriers, public utilities or holding companies subject to certain governmental regulatory agencies and regulations; (h) securities listed or approved for listing upon notice of issuance on New York, American, Midwest, Pacific Coast, PBW Stock Exchanges or other exchanges approved by commissioner, and all securities senior or substantially equal in rank to any securities so listed, any security represented by subscription rights which have been so listed or approved or any warrant or right to purchase or subscribe to any of foregoing; (i) securities designated or approved for designation upon issuance as a national market system security by NASD, any other security of same issuer which is of senior or substantially equal rank, a security called for by subscription right or warrant so designated, or a warrant or a right to purchase or subscribe to any of the foregoing; (j) note, draft, bill of exchange, or banker's acceptance which arises out of current transaction, and which has maturity period at time of issuance not exceeding nine months; (k) notes issued to seller in connection with purchase of real or personal property or secured by all or part of such property; and (l) securities meeting following conditions: (l) if issuer not organized in U.S., has appointed duly authorized agent in U.S. for service of process and agent's name and address listed in prospectus, (2) class of issuer's securities is and has been registered under §12 of Sec. Exchange Act of 1934 for three years prior to offering date, (3) neither issuer nor significant subsidiary has had material default in last seven years or during issuer's existence if less than seven years in payment of principal, interest, dividend or sinking fund installment on preferred stock or indebtedness for borrowed money or rentals under leases with terms of three years or more, (4) issuer had consolidated net income of at least $1,000,000 in four of its last five years (including its last fiscal year) and, if interest-bearing securities offered, specified interest expense coverage, (5) if offering is of stocks or shares, other than preferred, securities have voting rights, and (6) if offering is of stocks or shares, other than preferred, securities owned within six months of offering by at least 1,200 persons with at least 750,000 such shares outstanding with aggregate market value of $3,750,000 on day of offering. (10-5-8).

Exempt Transactions.—Following transactions are exempt from registration under Act: (a) transactions by executor, administrator or guardian if not affiliate of issuer or by sheriff, marshall, conservator, receiver or trustee in bankruptcy; (b) transactions executed by bona fide pledgee provided such pledgee is not issuer or underwriter of securities or affiliate of such issuer; (c) transactions in securities not involving issuer, underwriter, or affiliate of issuer; (d) transactions in securities by affiliate of issuer, provided that affiliate does not act as underwriter, that securities are sold through registered dealer acting as affiliate's agent, that neither dealer nor affiliate solicit any orders to purchase such securities, that dealer does no more than execute orders to sell and receives no more than customary commissions and that affiliate makes no payments in connection with sale other than customary commissions; (e) transactions in securities pursuant to effective registration statement under Federal Securities Act of 1933 or pursuant to certain exemptions under §3(b) or §3(c) of such Act (principally Regulation A offering but excluding Regulation D, which is provided for under different exemption), provided that Notice of Intention to Sell containing name and address of applicant and issuer and title of securities has been filed with commissioner and that there have been filed with commissioner fee of $250, copy of initial registration statement or notification and offering circular, and copy of consent to service of process, but if transaction takes place after 14 months from date commissioner certifies availability of exemption, issuer must pay additional $100 fee and must file current prospectus for each 14-month period during which exemption will be utilized (see also Rule 590-4-5-.02); (f) issuance and delivery of securities by issuer to its security holders pursuant to dividend or other distribution (whether person distributing dividend or other distribution is issuer of securities or not), split of securities or recapitalization for which recipient pays no consideration or surrenders no right to cash or property distribution other than such securities and sale of fractional interests resulting from such dividend, split, recapitalization or distribution; (g) sales of securities to bank, savings institution, trust company, insurance company, investment company, real estate investment trust, small business investment corporation, pension or profit-sharing plan or trust, other financial institution or dealer whether purchaser acts for self or as fiduciary; (h) certain transactions pursuant to exchange offers exclusively made to existing security holders of issuer or subsidiary, if no commissions paid in connection therewith; (i) certain transactions involving employee stock purchase plans, stock bonus plans, pension or profit-sharing plans, certain retirement plans, certain individual retirement accounts, and certain stock option plans; (j) offers of securities subject to registration statement which has been filed under Federal Securities Act of 1933; (k) transactions incident to certain judicially approved reorganizations; (l) certain transactions in securities of issuer by issuer or its subsidiary to corporation or its shareholders, to business or real estate investment trust or holders of beneficial interest

---

SECURITIES . . . *continued*
thereof, or to partnership or limited partnership or partners thereof in connection with merger, share exchange, consolidation, reclassification of securities, or sale or transfer of corporate trust, or partnership assets in consideration of issuance or transfer, where transaction must be approved by holders of at least majority of voting shares or interests pursuant to articles, charter, trust instrument, partnership agreement or applicable corporation, trust or partnership statute; (m) transactions involving issuance or sale of securities of issuer by or on behalf of issuer or its affiliates to not more than 15 persons in Georgia during 12-month period ending on date of sale or issuance, provided that no advertisements are used, that certificates representing securities issued pursuant to exemption bear appropriate legend for period of one year from issuance and that purchasers represent that they are purchasing securities for investment, not for distribution (securities presumed to have been purchased for investment if held for at least one year); (n) any issuance of securities of majority-owned subsidiary to its parent or affiliated majority-owned subsidiary, or upon organization if, after such issuance, issuer is majority-owned subsidiary of such parent; (o) certain issuances of securities by certain pooled income funds qualified to receive tax-deductible charitable contributions; and (p) any limited offering transaction exempted by Rule 590-4-5-.01, version of uniform limited offering exemption (ULOE). (10-5-9). To take advantage of ULOE exemption, offering must be conducted in compliance with rules 501, 502, 503, 505, and 506 of SEC Regulation D and must meet additional conditions; commissions payable only to licensed salesmen or dealers, no exemption available if issuer or affiliates violate enumerated "bad boy" rules, and issuer must file with commissioner notice on SEC Form D prior to first sale in reliance of ULOE in Georgia, accompanied by consent to service of process, copy of written offering material (if sales to be made to any unaccredited investors), and filing fee of $250.

Registration of Securities.—Securities which are subject to effective registration statement under federal Securities Act of 1933 or which are exempt pursuant to Regulation A or certain other exemptions under §3(b) of such Act (other than Regulation D) may be sold in exempt "SEC coordinated filing" transaction if certain prerequisites are met. See subhead Exempt Transactions, supra.

There are four types of registration: registration by qualification, small issue registration, registration by notification, and nonprofit issuer registration. (10-5-5).

Qualification may be accomplished by filing registration statement signed by issuer, its chief executive, principal financial and principal accounting officers and by majority of board of directors or similar group (10-5-5[b][1]) and must be accompanied by: (a) filing fee, (b) consent to service for first-time filers (10-5-6[c]) , (c) $25,000 bond, unless exempt (see subhead Prerequisites to Sales or Offers, supra), (d) prospectus containing information similar to that required in Schedule A to federal Securities Act of 1933, (e) consent of any professional named in registration statement as having certified any part of registration statement, (f) copy of any notice or sales literature to be used in connection with registration statement, (g) specimen copy of security to be registered, (h) copies of issuer's constituent documents, (i) signed opinion of legal counsel for issuer regarding status of security when sold, (j) copy of underwriting agreement, (k) copies of all material contracts, (l) signed copies of professional opinions, reports or certifications mentioned in prospectus, (m) copies of all literature concerning issuer or offering to be distributed to persons included in sales, and (n) written consents of all directors who have not signed registration statement. (10-5-5[b] and [c]; 10-5-6). All sales of securities registered by qualification may be rescinded within 72 hours of their sale. (10-5-5[b][4]).

Notification is available if issuer or its predecessors have been in continuous operation for at least five years, have had no default during current fiscal year or within preceding three fiscal years, and, during past three fiscal years have had average net earnings equal to at least 5% of aggregate value, as determined by higher of offering or market price or, if not readily ascertainable offering or market price, book value, of all securities of issuer outstanding without fixed maturity, interest or dividend, or if issuer and its predecessors have not had any such securities for three full fiscal years, at least 5% of aggregate value, as determined by offering price, of such securities which are proposed to be outstanding. (10-5-5[d][1]). Registration statement must be signed by issuer, by person on whose behalf offering is made, by registered or limited dealer or by authorized agent and shall be accompanied by registration fee and consent to service of process. Registration statement must contain a statement demonstrating eligibility for registration by notification, issuer's name, address and form of organization, state and date of its organization, general character and location of its business, capitalization statement and description of securities which are outstanding and which are to be registered, statement of amount and kind of consideration received for securities of issuer issued within past two years, any prospectus proposed to be used in offering securities, and a copy of any underwriting agreement. (10-5-5[d][2]).

In case of offering to be made by person other than issuer, registration statement must contain name and address of person on whose behalf securities are to be sold and statement of amount of securities of issuer held by such person as of date of filing of registration statement. (Id.).

Small issue registration is available for sales of any amount of securities to no more than 50 persons in Georgia by issuer or its affiliates during any 12-month period and for sales where aggregate amount of total offering does not exceed $1 million less aggregate offering price for all securities sold within 12 months prior to and during offering of securities under small issue registration, sold in reliance on transaction (a) under subhead Exempt Transactions, or sold in violation of registration requirements. (10-5-5[e]). Issuer may not combine exempt transaction for sales to 15 persons in 12 month period with sales to 50 persons under small issue registration. Registration statement must be filed with commissioner; must be signed by issuer, chief executive, principal financial and accounting officers and by majority of board of directors or comparable group; and must contain copy of prospectus, applicable professional consents and if issuer not corporation registered with Secretary of State, copy of issuer's articles of incorporation and bylaws or their substantial equivalents and copy of any indenture relating to security. (10-5-5[e][2]). Prospectus, which must be delivered to purchasers simultaneously with or prior to earliest of payment, execution of purchase agreement, or delivery of confirmation of sale, must contain: (1) brief description of issuer and type and location of its business, (2) unaudited balance sheet as of date within 90 days of filing, unaudited profit and loss statement for each of two fiscal years preceding date of balance sheet filed and for interim between end of latest fiscal year and date of balance sheet and for corresponding period of preceding year, (3) description of securities, of any underwriting arrangements, of selling expenses and of plan of distribution, (4) estimate of net proceeds and description of use of such proceeds, (5) statements and forms regarding purchaser's right to rescind purchase within 72 hours of purchase, (6) disclosure of securities of issuer owned by directors, officers and affiliates and of any material transactions between issuer and such persons which are expected to occur or which occurred within past three years, and (7) any additional information necessary in order to make statements made not misleading. (10-5-5[e][3]). Certificates representing securities sold pursuant to this registration and subject to numerical limitation on number of investors, must be legended for period of one year to indicate such registration and that they may not be sold or transferred except in transaction which is exempt under Act, which is registered or which otherwise complies with Act and executed with statement that securities purchased for investment and for purchase account. (10-5-5[e][1][B]). Negotiations for sale of security to be registered upon small issue registration will not be offer unless consideration is given, contract is entered or security is sold before effective date. (10-5-5[e][6]).

Nonprofit issuer registration is available for any amount of securities issued by issuer which is not organized and operated for private profit and if no part of its net earnings inure to benefit of any person, private stockholder or individual. (10-5-5[f]). Registration statement to be filed with commissioner, must be signed by chief executive, financial and accounting officers and by majority of board of directors or comparable group; must be accompanied by consent to service of process, and must contain: (a) prospectus containing information described below, (b) consent of any professional named in registration statement as having certified any part of registration statement, (c) copy of any notice or sales literature to be used in connection with registration statement, (d) specimen copy of security to be registered, (e) copies of issuer's constituent documents, (f) if securities to be registered are debt securities, trust indenture containing provisions described below, (g) if securities to be registered are secured by interest in real property, opinion of counsel that such interest is as described in prospectus and has been filed of record, (h) copy of underwriting agreement, (i) copies of all material contracts, (j) copies of all literature concerning issuer or offering to be distributed to persons involved in sales, (k) signed copies of professional opinions mentioned in prospectus and (l) written consents of all directors who have not signed registration statement. (10-5-5[f][2]-[4]). Trust indenture governs disbursement of proceeds of sale, collecting and disbursing principal and interest payments, and rights and duties of trustee and holders with respect to collateral. (10-5-5[f][3][a]). Trustee must be independent attorney or corporation qualified in Georgia which has corporate trust powers and which is subject to governmental regulation. (10-5-5[f][3][B]). Prospectus must contain: (a) basic information about issuer, (b) unaudited balance sheet as of date within 90 days of filing and unaudited statement of source and application of funds for each of two fiscal years preceding balance sheet, and for interim between end of latest fiscal year and date of balance sheet and for corresponding period of previous year, (c) summary of special risk factors, (d) description of underwriter compensation, arrangements and affiliations, (e) description of material terms of security and indenture, (f) description of securities, of any underwriting arrangements, of selling expenses and of plan of distribution, (g) estimate of net proceeds and description of use thereof, (h) statement and forms regarding purchaser's right to rescind purchase within 72 hours of purchase and (i) any additional information necessary in order to make statements made not misleading. (10-5-5[f][4]).

Registration of Dealers and Salespersons.—Persons who come within Act's definitions of dealer, limited dealer, salesperson or limited salesperson must register as such to offer for sale or sell any securities within or from Georgia unless their activities as such are solely in certain exempt transactions. (10-5-3). Initial fee for dealers and limited dealers is $250. Renewal fees for both are $100. Initial fee for salespersons and limited salespersons is $50 and renewal fees for both are $40. (10-5-3[j]). Each principal of each dealer or limited dealer and each salesperson or limited salesperson must pass examinations given by commissioner or NASD. (10-5-3[c][d]). If dealer or limited dealer succeeds to and continues business of another, predecessor's registration remains effective as registration of successor for 75 days, provided successor files for registration within 30 days after succession. (10-5-3[n]). Persons who come within Act's definitions of designated dealer and designated salesperson are also extensively regulated. (10-5-1 et seq.).

Bonds.—Applicants who are to be registered as dealers and limited dealers must file $25,000 bond with commissioner and each salesperson or limited salesperson must file $2,500 bond as prerequisite to registration, unless dealer or limited dealer, by whom applicant is employed or is to be employed is not subject to bond requirements. (10-5-3[k][1]). No applicant for dealer or limited dealer is required to file bond if: (1) such applicant is registered under Securities Exchange Act of 1934; or (2) as of dates of most recent certified balance sheet and any subsequent noncertified balance sheets, such applicant had minimum net worth of not less than $250,000. (10-5-3[k][2]). No applicant for dealer or limited dealer is required to file bond if such applicant has deposited in trust with commissioner (1) certificate of deposit with certain financial institutions in amount of $25,000, (2) irrevocable letter of credit in amount of $25,000 issued by certain federal banks, and (3) obligations of U.S., or agency thereof, or of State of Georgia which mature in two years or less and which have market value of at least $25,000. (10-5-3[k][3]).

Advertisements.—It is unlawful to offer or sell any security which is registered under Act other than by those methods authorized by Act. (10-5-12). (See subhead Registration of Securities, supra.) Note: Securities registered under federal Securities Act of 1933 or exempt from such registration by virtue of Regulation A and certain other exemptions may be sold in exempt transaction and need not be registered. (See subhead Exempt Transactions, supra.) Act defines prospectus to include any advertisement or sales literature which offers any security for sale or is used in connection with any offer (10-5-2[a][23]); therefore no advertisement or sales literature may be used unless it meets requirements of prospectus or unless it comes within one of exceptions described below. Exceptions to definition of prospectus are: (a) post-effective date

See note at head of Digest as to 1998 legislation covered.

See Topical Index in front part of this volume.

GA – 22

SECURITIES . . . *continued*

confirmations of sale that are accompanied or preceded by prospectus that meets requirements of Act and (b) communications that do nothing but state from whom prospectus may be obtained, identify security and its price, state by whom orders will be executed (10-5-2[a][23][A] and [B]), and contain description of issuer's business if such description has been filed with commissioner (Ga. Comp. R. & Regs. R. 590-4-3-.02). Regulations also exempt certain communications regarding preemptive rights, exempt quarterly, annual and other periodic reports to security holders, and set forth guidelines for determining whether advertisements for products and services might be deemed prospectus. (Ga. Comp. R. & Regs. R. 590-4-3-.02).

Liabilities.—It is unlawful for any person: (1) to offer or sell security unless it is registered, exempt, or offered and sold in exempt transaction; (2) in connection with offer or sale of security, to employ any device, scheme, or artifice to defraud, to make untrue statement of material fact or omit to state material fact necessary to make statements made not misleading, or to engage in any act, practice or course of business which operates or would operate as fraud or deceit upon person; (3) to offer or sell any security registered under Act other than by notification except by means of prospectus which meets Act's requirements, but securities registered under federal Securities Act of 1933 or exempt under such Act by virtue of Regulation A (provided certain conditions are met) need not be registered and may be sold in exempt transactions; (4) in connection with sale of securities registered under Act, to make any representation of future sales of security by issuer at higher offering price or to make any representation as to future existence of public market; (5) to represent that filing or effectiveness of registration statement, registration of any security under Act or existence of any exemption means that commissioner has approved security or transaction or has passed on truth, accuracy or completeness of such registration statement or merits of security; (6) to knowingly cause to be made, in any document filed with commissioner or in any proceeding under Act, any statement which is false or misleading; or (7) to employ deceptive or fraudulent device, scheme or artifice to manipulate market in security. (10-5-12).

It is unlawful for any dealer, limited dealer, salesperson, limited salesperson, investment advisor, federal covered securities advisor or investment advisor representative, any person making notice filing or filing application for registration as one of above, issuer who has filed registration statement or notice filing or is as affiliate of any of above persons to knowingly cause any statement which is, at time it is made and in light of circumstances under which it is made, false or misleading in any material respect. (10-5-12[c]).

Basic remedy for purchaser is action for rescission. (10-5-14). Control persons, general partners, executive officers, directors and persons holding similar positions as well as each dealer, limited dealer, salesman or limited salesman who participates in any material way in sale are jointly and severally liable with person primarily liable unless person secondarily liable proves he or she did not know and, in exercise of reasonable care, could not have known of existence of facts by reason of which liability is alleged to exist. (10-5-14[c]). There is contribution among several persons so liable. (10-5-14[c]). Statute of limitations under Act is two years from contract of sale (or sale, if there is no contract). (10-5-14[d]). Suits not permitted if certain rescission offers prior to filing of suit have been refused by damaged person. (10-5-14[d]).

Persons who violate Act may also be enjoined, censured, fined or prosecuted criminally if violation is willful. (10-5-13).

Commodities.—Soliciting offers, or offering, to purchase or sell commodities under commodity contract or option, when made or accepted in state as specified, is forbidden, except in accordance with 10-5A-1 et seq. Transaction involving certain persons registered in specified capacities with CFTC or SEC or under state law are exempt, as are certain other specified transactions. (10-5A-3, -4). Commissioner of securities may issue rules or orders prescribing terms and conditions of all transactions and contracts covered by law not within exclusive jurisdiction of CFTC. (10-5A-4[b]).

Investment Advisers.—Any person who, for compensation, engages in business of advising others, either directly or through publications or writings, as to value of securities or as to advisability of investing in, purchasing, or selling securities or who, for compensation and as part of regular business issues or promulgates reports or analysis of securities, or holds self out as investment adviser or financial planner (subject to enumerated exceptions similar to Federal Investment Advisers Act of 1940) is required to register as investment adviser unless otherwise exempt. (10-5-2[a][14]; -3[a]; -3[e]). Advisers whose only clients are insurance companies or who, during last 12 months, had fewer than 15 clients, none of whom are registered investment companies, and who do not hold self out as investment advisors to public are exempt from registration as investment advisors. (10-5-3[b]). Written examination required to register. Initial registration fee is $250 and renewal fee is $100 for investment adviser and $50 and $40, respectively, for investment adviser representative. (10-5-3[i]). Contracts of investment adviser in violation of chapter void. (10-5-14[b]). Advisory client may sue to recover consideration paid under contract plus interest. (10-5-14[a]). Same statute of limitations as for other securities violations. (10-5-14[d]). Activities of certified public accountants are regulated with respect to their status as investment advisers. (10-5-2, 10-5-12, 10-5-14).

Tender Offers.—See category Business Organizations, topic Corporations.

Subdivision Offerings.—See category Property, topic Real Property, subhead Subdivided Land Sales. See also Georgia Land Sales Act of 1982. (44-3-1 et seq.).

Regulations.—Commissioner has adopted extensive regulations under Act.

Uniform Simplification of Fiduciary Security Transfers Act.—Adopted. (53-17-1 through -11). See category Business Organizations, topic Corporations, subhead Uniform Simplification of Fiduciary Security Transfers Act.

Uniform Gifts to Minors Act.—Not adopted. Georgia has adopted "The Georgia Transfer to Minors Act". See category Family, topic Infants, subhead Gifts to Minors. (44–5–110 et seq.).

STATUTE OF FRAUDS:

See topic Frauds, Statute of.

TRUST RECEIPT SECURITY:

No statute. See category Debtor and Creditor, topic Pledges.

WAREHOUSEMEN:

Uniform Commercial Code.—Adopted. (Title 11). General regulations of business are governed by 11-7 of Act. See topic Commercial Code. Caveat: 11-7 does not repeal or modify any law prescribing form or contents of documents of title or services or facilities to be afforded by bailees or regulating bailee's business in respects not dealt with specifically. (11-7-103). Fact that such laws are violated does not affect status of document of title which otherwise complies with definition of document of title. Warehouseman must insure goods stored. (10-4-25).

Agricultural warehouses are regulated under 10-4-1, -32.

Licenses.—Must be a license for each warehouse operated, issued by Commissioner of Agriculture to responsible person meeting requirements. (10-4-10). Warehousemen must be bonded. (10-4-12).

Warehouse Receipts.—Governed by Uniform Commercial Code.

Tobacco Warehousemen.—Must report weekly to Commissioner of Agriculture number of pounds of tobacco stored and sold. (10-4-108). Record of such reports to be kept open to public. Commissions on gross sales of leaf tobacco in warehouses not to exceed 3.5%. (10-4-106).

State Warehouse Department.—Established to study handling of cotton and tobacco crops. May acquire property, foster building of warehouses, receive cotton for storage and regulate grading of cotton. (10-4-50 through -60, 70-76).

Lien.—Uniform Commercial Code governs. (Title 11).

CITIZENSHIP

ALIENS:

Aliens generally enjoy all privileges of citizens of state, except right of franchise and right to hold office, and are entitled to same protection. (1-2-9, -10, -11). Aliens may not be employed by state government or any political subdivision except under limited conditions. (45-2-7). Alien corporation desiring to own real property must file annual report, pay filing fee and maintain registered office and agent in Georgia. (16-14-15).

CIVIL ACTIONS AND PROCEDURE

ACCORD AND SATISFACTION:

Accord and satisfaction is where parties to agreement, by subsequent agreement have satisfied former one and latter agreement is executed. (13-4-101). (See also category Business Regulation and Commerce, topic Commercial Code.) If payment of less than debt is agreed to, it must be actually paid or some new consideration given to constitute accord and satisfaction. (13-4-103). Endorsement of check reciting "payment in full" is accord and satisfaction notwithstanding protest of obliteration. (153 Ga.App. 383, 265 S.E.2d 325; 13-4-103[b]).

Pleading.—Defendant relying on accord and satisfaction must plead facts sufficient to put plaintiff on notice as to exact terms, and where and with whom executed. (91 S.E.2d 308).

Torts.—Claim arising out of tort may be settled but if tort is also crime, only civil wrong may be settled. (51-11-20). Certain settlements with injured persons prohibited. (51-1-35). Only those parties named in release will be discharged by release. (262 Ga. 185, 415 S.E.2d 902).

ACTIONS:

Bills in equity and all distinctions of actions into real, personal and mixed are abolished. (9-11-2).

Equity.—Jurisdiction is vested in superior courts. (23-1-1).

Federal Rules of Civil Procedure form basis of procedural statute. (Tit. 9). See topic Practice.

Commencement.—See topics Pleading, Process.

Parties.—Federal rules generally effective.

Class Actions.—Rule based on Federal Rule 23 prior to 1966 amendments. Although no provision in statute authorizes class action if common questions of law or fact and common request for relief, such actions are allowed. (229 Ga. 160, 190 S.E.2d 48). Right to be enforced by members of class must be either joint or several if adjudication may affect specific property. (9-11-23). In connection with shareholder's derivative actions, see also 14-2-831. Uniform Class Actions Act not adopted.

Intervention.—Federal rules substantially in effect, except that Georgia makes no provision for permissive intervention of governmental officer or agency. (9-11-24).

Interpleader.—Federal rule effective. (9-11-22). Also, equitable interpleader permitted. (23-3-90). Elements for equitable interpleader more stringent.

Third Party Practice.—Federal rule effective, (9-11-14); however, copies of original complaint and all prior pleadings must be attached as exhibits to third party complaint. (9-11-14). Proper venue must lie as to third party defendants or they must be sued in separate action. (248 Ga. 235, 282 S.E.2d 296). Action against third-party defendant may be tried in county where claim is pending even though third-party defendant not resident of that county. (9-10-34[b]). Venue over third-party defendant is dependent on venue over original defendant; if venue lost over original defendant, venue likewise lost over third-party defendant. (9-10-34[c]).

See note at head of Digest as to 1998 legislation covered.

See Topical Index in front part of this volume.

ACTIONS . . . *continued*

Joinder of Claims and Parties.—Federal rules effective. (9-11-18 through -19).

Consolidation and Separate Trials.—Federal Rule 42 substantially in effect except that consolidation expressly conditioned on consent of parties. (9-11-42).

Joinder and Consolidation.—Federal rules effective.

Abatement or Survival.—Action does not abate by death of either party if cause of action survives. (9-2-40). Death of party does cause immediate suspension of action as to decedent until substitute named. (236 Ga. 903, 225 S.E.2d 890). Action for death, personal injury, property injury, or any tort from which wrongdoer derived benefit survives death of either party, and if wrongdoer dies before action commenced his personal representative may be sued. (9-2-41). Action on note, bill, bond or other written obligation survives death of obligor, but if one of several obligors dies plaintiff may (but is not obliged to) join representative in action against other obligors. (9-2-27).

See also category Estates and Trusts, topic Death.

Limitation Of.—See topic Limitation of Actions.

Small Claims.—See category Courts and Legislature, topic Courts.

Termination of Actions.—Action may generally be dismissed by plaintiff, without prejudice, without order of court, by filing written notice of dismissal at any time before plaintiff rests case. (9-11-41[a]). Where defendant has counterclaimed, no voluntary dismissal over defendant's objection unless counterclaim can be independently tried. (9-11-41[a]). Although voluntary dismissal of entire complaint is allowed (208 Ga. App. 26, 430 S.E.2d 57), voluntary unilateral dismissal of party's claim against some, but not all of parties, requires court approval (208 Ga. App. 147, 430 S.E.2d 117, 223 Ga. App. 139). Action automatically dismissed after five years if no order taken. (9-11-41[e]). Continuance is deemed to be order. Announcement by trial judge of decision that will terminate civil case, though decision not formally entered in writing, precludes filing of voluntary dismissal. (238 Ga. 394, 233 S.E.2d 367). Filing of third notice of dismissal operates as adjudication of merits. (9-11-41[a]).

Administration.—See category Estates and Trusts, topic Executors and Administrators.

Direct Actions Against Insurer.—See category Transportation, topic Motor Vehicles, subhead Direct Actions.

See also topics Practice, Pleading.

APPEAL AND ERROR:

Interlocutory Appeals.—Appeal where trial judge certifies within ten days of entry of non-appealable order that immediate review should be had (5-6-34[b]), and orders granting or refusing interlocutory injunctions (5-6-34[a][4]), and from orders granting summary judgment (9-11-56[h]), and from certain other matters (5-6-34). Petition for appeal must be filed with clerk of supreme court or court of appeals, with copy served on opposing party, within ten days after trial judge's certificate granted; opposing party has ten days from date petition filed to respond; supreme court or court of appeals has 30 days thereafter to grant or deny appeal; appellant has ten days after order granting appeal to file notice of appeal and thereafter same procedure as appeal from final judgment. (5-6-34[b]). Pre-appeal demand for trial is effective post-appeal when appellate court remittitur is filed with lower court. Filing of remittitur in lower court is point in time when demand clock resumes ticking, and state shall have remainder of that term and one additional regular term of court in which to try defendant. (264 Ga. 527, 449 S.E.2d 79; 17-7-171[b]).

Appeal to Superior or State Court.—All appeals to superior court or state court shall be tried to jury unless jury trial waived by consent of both parties. (5-3-30).

Appeal from Probate Court.—Appeal lies to superior court in all cases except from appointment of temporary administrator. (5-3-2[a]). Only patient has right to appeal commitment decision of probate court, and those seeking commitment have no right to appeal. (263 Ga. 591, 436 S.E.2d 219; 37-3-150).

Appeal from Final Judgments of Superior, State or Constitutional City Courts.—Appeal lies from final judgments. (5-6-34). Application required for certain appeals. (5-6-35). Application required for appeal of zoning matters. (259 Ga. 425, 383 S.E.2d 123). Application required for appeal of superior court review of administrative agency decision. (265 Ga. 62, 453 S.E.2d 725; 5-6-35[a][1]). No appeal permitted from voluntary dismissal. (217 Ga. App. 1, 456 S.E.2d 71).

Appeal from Matters Heard in Chambers.—Either party in any civil case and defendant in any criminal proceeding may appeal from judgment or decree of superior, state, or city courts of any matter heard in chambers. Section is unclear but probably requires judgments otherwise appealable. (5-6-33).

Jurisdiction of Appellate Courts.—Supreme court has jurisdiction over cases involving: construction of Georgia or U.S. Constitutions and treaties between U.S. and foreign governments; constitutionality of any Georgia or U.S. law; election contests; title to land; equity; validity or construction of wills; habeas corpus; extraordinary remedies; divorce and alimony; certification to it by court of appeals; and death sentences. (Const., Art. VI, §VI, Paragraphs II and III). Court of appeals has jurisdiction in all cases in which jurisdiction not reserved to supreme court or conferred on other courts by law. (Const., Art. VI, §V, Paragraph III). Court of appeals has jurisdiction over appeals involving revenues of state. (265 Ga. 37, 456 S.E.2d 50). See also category Courts and Legislature, topic Courts.

Manner Taken.—Notice of appeal should be filed with clerk of court wherein case was determined. (5-6-37). All parties at trial must be served notice either personally or by mail, unless waived or acknowledged. (5-6-37). If party is represented by attorney, service must be made upon attorney unless court orders otherwise. (5-6-32). For preparation of record see 5-6-41 through -43. Appellant and cross-appellant must file enumeration of errors with clerk of appellate court under its rules, which may permit enumeration in brief. (5-6-40). Bills of exception, exceptions pendente lite, assignments of error and rules relating thereto are abolished. (5-6-49). Joint appeals permitted without regard to presence of joint interest, and parties may file separate enumeration of errors. (5-6-44).

Time Allowed.—30 days after entry of judgment; or in event that motion for new trial, in arrest of judgment, or for judgment notwithstanding verdict is filed, then 30 days after entry of order ruling on said motion; cross-appeal within 15 days of service of notice of appeal by appellant. (5-6-38). Filing with clerk of signed judgment constitutes entry of judgment. (5-6-31). Either trial or appellate judge can grant one extension for filing of notice of appeal or cross-appeal for period not greater than originally allowed. (5-6-39). Superior court's entry of order granting motion to stay judgment in order to reopen evidence will extend date for filing of notice of appeal. (248 Ga. 776, 285 S.E.2d 542 [overrules Wilson v. McQueen, 224 Ga. 420, 162 S.E.2d 313]). Application for extension must be within period originally prescribed. No extension for motions for new trial or judgment n.o.v. (5-6-39[b]) or for motions to reinstate (180 Ga. App. 732, 350 S.E.2d 317).

Stay of Proceedings, Costs and Bond.—Notice of appeal serves as supersedeas upon appellant's paying all costs in trial court or filing pauper's affidavit. (5-6-46 through -47). (See topic Costs.) $80 cost of appeal must be paid by applicant or appellant at time application for writ of certiorari or for appeal or, for direct appeals, by appellant or cross-appellant at time original brief is filed. (5-6-4). Appeal suspends but does not vacate judgment. (5-3-7). Supersedeas bond is not necessary; but on motion of appellee, trial court shall require that supersedeas bond be given with such surety and amount as prescribed in 5-5-47. Superior courts have power to grant supersedeas (15-6-9), and if trial court refuses to grant supersedeas, appellate courts may, in emergencies, do so to preserve jurisdiction or to prevent issue from becoming moot. (Ga. Ct. App. R. 40, Ga. Sup. Ct. R. 11).

Dismissal of Appeals.—Appeals can be dismissed: (1) for failure to file notice of appeal within time prescribed; (2) where decision of judgment is not appealable; or (3) where issue has become moot. Trial court may dismiss where there is unreasonable and inexcusable delay in filing of transcript or transmission of record to appellate court. Dismissal of appeal does not affect cross-appeal, if notice has been filed and appellee still stands to benefit. No dismissal because of failure to specify judgment or errors appealed, where intent apparent. Failure to perfect service of notice will not result in dismissal. (5-6-48).

Extent of Review.—Appellate courts must review all judgments or orders rendered in case raised on appeal which may affect proceedings below. (5-6-34[d]). Failure to raise claim of ineffective assistance of counsel before appeal bars raising issue on appeal. (220 Ga. App. 36, 467 S.E.2d 608).

Personal Representative.—If defeated party dies after judgment and before time for appeal expired, personal representative may take appeal within 30 days after qualifying. (5-6-16).

Character of Hearing on Appeal to Superior Court.—Appeal to superior court in any case where not otherwise provided by law is de novo investigation, and each party is entitled to be heard on merits of case. (5-3-29).

See also topic Practice.

BONDS:

Where bond required by law, undertaking in writing, without seal, sufficient. If obligor's name subscribed, though it does not appear in bond, he or she is bound. (1-3-1[d][3]). Requirement may also be discharged by depositing cash in amount of bond with appropriate person or depository. (9-10-10; 17-6-4).

Sureties.—Insurance companies may be accepted as surety upon bond of any person, company, or corporation required by law to execute bonds. (33-24-48). Surety bond may be required by court as prerequisite to issuance of temporary restraining order or interlocutory injunction. (9-11-65).

Judgment.—It is lawful to enter judgment against principal and sureties at same time, as in cases of appeal, in all cases in law or equitable proceedings when bond has been given by losing party conditioned to pay eventual condemnation money in action. Not necessary to bring action on bond. (10-7-29).

Actual damage only and not penalties may be recovered on bond; penalty is not liquidated damages. (13-6-3; 9-12-13).

CERTIORARI:

Certiorari generally available to superior courts from inferior judicatories and from court of appeals to supreme court.

Certiorari from Superior Court.—Lies for correction of errors of law committed by any inferior judiciary, or any person exercising judicial powers, including judge of probate court, except in cases touching probate of wills, granting letters testamentary and of administration. (5-4-1).

Court of appeals may certify question to supreme court for instruction, to which court of appeals will then be bound. (Art. VI, §V, Paragraph IV).

CHARITABLE IMMUNITY:

See topic Damages.

COSTS:

Party who is unsuccessful or who discontinues action is liable for costs. (9-15-1; 9-11-54).

Security for Costs.—Where party and his attorney are nonresidents, proper officers may demand full costs in advance. (9-15-6). In magistrate court plaintiff must pay filing deposit not to exceed $20. (15-10-80). In superior court cases advance costs required. (9-15-4, 15-6-77). Costs vary depending on case, court and county. In supreme court and court of appeals $80 advance costs required for all applications for writ of certiorari to supreme court, every application for appeal to supreme court or

See note at head of Digest as to 1998 legislation covered.

See Topical Index in front part of this volume.

COSTS . . . *continued*

court of appeals, and all direct appeals to courts. No additional costs when writ of certiorari or application granted. (5-6-4).

Affidavit of indigence may be taken in lieu of above deposits and costs. (9-15-2; 9-15-4; 5-6-4).

Where execution returned by levying officer "no property to be found," fi. fa. may issue against plaintiff for costs. (9-15-12).

Liability of Attorney.—Attorney liable for costs assessed against his client because of attorney's willful neglect or misconduct and for costs where client resides outside state and client's execution returned by levying officer "no property to be found". (9-15-7, -12).

Costs of Transcript.—Where trial judge requires reporting of proceedings and evidence, costs are to be borne equally by all parties. Appellant drawing in question transcript of evidence and proceedings bears cost. (5-6-41). If appellee alone designates inclusion of transcript in record, appellee bears this expense. (5-6-42). Generally, cost of transcript is expense of appeal but not a recoverable cost. (232 Ga. 92, 205 S.E.2d 293).

DAMAGES:

Common law generally prevails.

Comparative Negligence Rule.—Where negligence of plaintiff equals or exceeds that of defendant, or where plaintiff by ordinary care could have avoided consequences caused by defendant's negligence, there can be no recovery; if negligence of plaintiff is less than that of defendant, plaintiff's amount of recovery should be diminished in proportion to amount of plaintiff's negligence. (34-7-42; 46-8-291; 51-11-7). Damages may be apportioned among several defendants where plaintiff also is at fault; such liability is not joint liability and is not subject to contribution. (51-12-33).

Uniform Comparative Fault Act.—Not adopted.

Charitable Immunities.—Doctrine prevails. (51-1-20; 51-1-29.1; 118 Ga. 647, 45 S.E. 483; 27 Ga. App. 560, 109 S.E. 544).

Sovereign Immunity.—Common law sovereign immunity has constitutional status. (Const., Art. I, §II, Par. IX; 233 Ga. 487, 212 S.E.2d 627). Waived as to actions ex contractu for breach of written contract entered into by state. (Const., Art. I, §2, Par. IX[c]). Neither implied contract nor claim couched in contract but sounding in tort will support waiver of sovereign immunity. (1997 Ga. App. Lexis 556). Georgia Tort Claims Act (50-21-20 et seq.) waives state's sovereign immunity defense in specific circumstances listed therein. County's sovereign immunity defense is waived only to extent of liability insurance purchased. (33-24-51).

No-Fault Insurance.—See category Transportation, topic Motor Vehicles, subhead No-Fault Insurance.

Uniform Contribution Among Tortfeasors Act (Revised).—Not adopted.
See category Estates and Trusts, topic Death, subhead Actions for Death.

Attorney's Fees.—Expenses of litigation, including attorney's fees, are recoverable. (9-15-14; 13-1-11; 13-6-11).

Punitive Damages.—Specific prayer for punitive damages is required. (51-12-5.1). Punitive damages prohibited where entire injury is to peace, happiness or feelings of plaintiff. (51-12-6). Amount of punitive damages limited to $250,000 in cases which do not involve (1) product liability, (2) specific intent to cause harm, or (3) defendant acting under influence of drugs or alcohol. (51-12-5.1). To avoid $250,000 cap, there must be jury charge on, and separate finding by jury of, specific intent to cause harm. (269 Ga. 262, 497 S.E.2d 786). Determination of amount of punitive damages is question for jury and will only be disturbed on appeal if blatantly egregious. (166 Ga. App. 119, 303 S.E.2d 475). In product liability cases, 75% of punitive damages awarded are paid to state. (51-12-5.1).

Collateral Sources.—Evidence of compensation and benefits available to plaintiff inadmissible in tort actions. (261 Ga. 41, 402 S.E.2d 269) (holding 51-12-1[b] unconstitutional). Statute (51-12-1[b]) declared unconstitutional (261 Ga. 41, 402 S.E.2d 269).

New Trial.—Court can order new trial as to damages where they are clearly inadequate or excessive. (51-12-12). Court can condition grant of new trial on plaintiff's acceptance of decreased award if award is clearly excessive or, on defendant's acceptance of increased award, if award is clearly inadequate. (265 Ga. 861, 463 S.E.2d 108; 15-12-12[b]).

DECLARATORY JUDGMENTS:

See topic Judgments.

DEPOSITIONS AND DISCOVERY:

Deposition procedure governed by Ga. Civil Practice Act (9-11-26 et seq.), which closely follows Federal Rules. See topic Practice.

Uniform Foreign Depositions Act.—Adopted without changes. (24-10-110 through -112).

Within State for Use Within State.—Federal Rules effective, except that in Georgia, deposition can be used for any purpose if court finds: (1) witness is dead; (2) witness is out of county; (3) witness is unable to attend or testify because of age, illness, infirmity imprisonment; (4) party offering deposition has been unable to procure attendance of witness by subpoena; (5) that, because of nature of business or occupation of witness it is not possible to secure witness' personal attendance without manifest inconvenience to public or third persons; (6) witness is member of General Assembly which is in conflicting session; or (7) in discretion of trial judge, that deposition should be allowed. (9-11-32). Representative cross examination theory implicit in interpretation of Fed. R. Civ. Proc. 32, which was not adopted in Georgia. (159 Ga. App. 874, 285 S.E.2d 566).

Within State for Use Elsewhere.—Same as for use within Georgia. Uniform Foreign Depositions Act in force. (24-10-110 through -112).

Outside of State for Use Within State.—No distinction is made from depositions taken within Georgia.
See also category Estates and Trusts, topic Wills, subhead Testimony of Witnesses.

Perpetuating Testimony.—Federal Rules adopted (9-11-27), except that no provision for use of testimony perpetuated in another state, and subsequent use must involve same parties and same subject matter. (9-11-27). Also, still possible to bring equitable action to perpetuate testimony. (24-10-150).

Before Whom Taken.—
Within U.S.—Federal Rules adopted. Additionally, depositions within State may be taken before certificated court reporter or as provided by rules of Board of Court Reporting.
Also, Georgia rule substitutes term "court reporter" for "person" in §C of rule, which deals with disqualification for interest. (9-11-28).
In Foreign Countries.—Taken either on notice before secretary of embassy or legation, consul general, consul, vice-consul, or consular agent of U.S., or before someone appointed by commission or under letters rogatory. (9-11-28).

Compelling Attendance of Witnesses.—After service of notice of deposition, clerk of superior court may issue subpoena. Deponent may be required to attend examination only in county where deponent resides, is employed, transacts his business personally, or at any place not more than 30 miles from county seat of such county or in county where deponent is served with subpoena. (9-11-45; 24-10-20 through -28). However, geographic limitations in 9-11-45 do not necessarily apply to parties to lawsuits. (261 Ga. 853, 413 S.E.2d 195). Uniform Act to secure attendance of witnesses from without state adopted. (24-10-90 through -97).

Examination of Witnesses.—Federal Rules adopted. (9-11-30).

Return.—Federal Rules adopted (9-11-30), except that there is no statutory requirement that notice be given by party taking deposition of its filing in court.

Form.—No forms prescribed.

Interrogatories.—Party must limit interrogatories to total of 50. (9-11-33[a][1]; 220 Ga. App. 43, 467 S.E.2d 362).

EQUITY:

See topic Actions.

EVIDENCE:

See topic Depositions and Discovery.

Witnesses.—All persons are competent witnesses except persons who do not have use of reason, children who do not understand nature of oath, and persons so intoxicated that reason and memory are lacking. (24-9-1, 5, and 6). Persons testifying in disassociated state of split personalities held competent, admissible evidence where opportunity to cross-examine. (206 Ga. App. 709; 426 S.E.2d 224).
See also topic Depositions and Discovery; category Estates and Trusts, topic Wills.
Privileged Communications.—Attorney cannot testify as to confidential communication from client or knowledge acquired through relation. (24-9-25). Confidential communications to psychiatrists, licensed psychologists and certain other mental health care providers, ministers and accountants and between husband and wife, or attorney and client, are privileged. (24-9-21 through -24, 40; 43-3-32). Also privileged are communications in psychotherapeutic relationship between patient and patient's psychiatric specialist or licensed social worker. (24-9-21). Licensed physician, pharmacist, hospital or health care facility not required to release medical information concerning patient without authorization or waiver by patient or on appropriate court order or subpoena. (24-9-40). Veterinarian need not disclose information concerning animal care without authorization or waiver by client or appropriate court order or subpoena. (24-9-29). Nonparty engaged in gathering and disseminating news need not disclose information unless privilege is waived or information sought is material and relevant, cannot be obtained by other means and is necessary to preparation or presentation of case of party seeking information. (24-9-30).
Husbands or wives are competent to testify as to adultery of spouse and are competent to testify to his or her own innocence of adultery. (24-9-2). Husband and wife are competent but cannot be compelled to give evidence in criminal proceeding against each other. (24-9-23[a]). Husband or wife may be compelled to testify against spouse where spouse charged with crime against minor child but only with respect to specific act for which spouse is charged. (24-9-23[b]).
Communications or Transactions with Persons Since Deceased or Incompetent.—Dead Man's Statute repealed.
Expert Witnesses.—Expert opinion testimony on ultimate jury issue admissible where conclusion by expert is one which jurors would not ordinarily be able to draw unassisted for themselves. (247 Ga. 612, 277 S.E.2d 678).
Compelling Attendance.—Uniform Act to Secure the Attendance of Witnesses from Without the State in Criminal Proceedings adopted with minor variations. (24-10-90,-97). See also topic Depositions and Discovery.

INJUNCTIONS:

Remedy exists to restrain proceedings in another or in same court, a threatened or existing tort, or any other act of an individual or corporation which is illegal or contrary to equity and good conscience, and for which there is no adequate remedy at law. (9-5-1).
Injunction procedure governed by Ga. Civil Practice Act, which closely follows Federal Rules of Civil Procedure. See topic Practice.

Jurisdiction.—Superior court (15-6-8, -9) of county where one defendant resides (9-10-30).

Prerequisites.—No temporary restraining order granted without notice to adverse party unless irreparable damage will result and applicant's attorney certifies what

INJUNCTIONS . . . *continued*

efforts, if any, have been made to give notice and why no notice should be required. (9-11-65[b]). No interlocutory injunction issued without notice to adverse party. (9-11-65[a][1]). No notice required in divorce, alimony, separate maintenance or child custody suits. (9-11-65[e]).

Procedure.—Order issues on motion to judge of superior court 9-11-7[b]), and rests in discretion of court (9-5-8).

Bond.—Judge may require bond in amount court deems proper. (9-11-65[c]).

Temporary Injunction.—Temporary restraining order, for period not to exceed 30 days, will be granted without notice to adverse party if irreparable damage will result, and applicant's attorney has given proper certification. When no notice to adverse party, hearing for interlocutory injunction must be set for earliest possible time. Adverse party may move dissolution or modification of temporary restraining order on two days notice, or shorter time if court allows. (9-11-65[b]). Although hearing is adversary proceeding, it need not follow all formalities of procedure, since it is not determinative of rights. (227 Ga. 676, 182 S.E.2d 464).

JUDGMENTS:

State court procedure governed by Ga. Civil Practice Act (Title 9), which closely follows Federal Rules of Civil Procedure. See topic Practice.

All judgments of state courts are of equal dignity. (9-12-80). Judgments at same term are of equal date. (9-12-87[a]). Judgment affirmed on appeal takes date as of first rendition. (9-12-89).

Judgment may be amended (even after execution issued) to conform to verdict. (9-12-14).

Judgments by Consent.—If court had jurisdiction, binding in absence of fraud, accident or mistake. (206 Ga. 542, 57 S.E.2d 593).

Judgments on Pleadings.—Federal Rules effective. (9-11-12).

Summary Judgments.—Federal Rules effective. Motion for summary judgment permissible after 30 days from commencement of action or after service of motion for summary judgment by adverse party. Motion and supporting affidavits served at least 30 days before hearing. (9-11-56).

Declaratory Judgments.—In cases of actual controversy, respective superior courts have power, upon petition or other appropriate pleading, to declare rights and other legal relations of any interested party petitioning, whether or not further relief is or could be prayed. Declaration to have form and effect of final judgment or decree and be reviewable as such. Further relief, injunction, interlocutory extraordinary relief, etc., may be granted in same suit in order to maintain status or preserve equitable rights pending adjudication of the questions. Relief available even if plaintiff has adequate remedy at law. (9-4-2).

Default Judgments.—Any case not answered on or before time required by Civil Practice Act (9) automatically becomes in default unless time for filing answer has been extended as provided by law. Default judgment may be entered against co-defendants separately. (254 Ga. 321, 328 S.E.2d 539). Default may be opened as matter of right by filing of defensive pleadings within 15 days of day of default, upon payment of costs. If not opened within 15 days, plaintiff entitled to verdict and judgment by default except where action is ex delicto or involves unliquidated damages, in which plaintiff must establish amount of damages before court without jury, unless defendant has placed damages in issue by filing pleading raising such issue, in which event either party is entitled to jury trial as to damages upon demand. (9-11-55[a]). Judgment shall not be different in kind or exceed amount prayed for. (125 Ga. App. 707; 188 S.E.2d 908). Court may also, in its discretion, allow default to be opened for providential cause preventing filing of pleadings or for excusable neglect on terms fixed by court. Defaulting party must make showing under oath, set up defense, offer to plead instanter, and announce ready to proceed with trial. (9-11-55[b]).

Judgment Notwithstanding the Verdict.—Federal Rules effective. Party who has moved for directed verdict has 30 days after entry of judgment on verdict to have verdict set aside and judgment entered in accordance with motion for directed verdict. If no verdict returned, party has 30 days after discharge of jury to move for judgment in accordance with motion for directed verdict. (9-11-50[b]). Motion for judgment notwithstanding verdict need not be filed to preserve jurisdiction of trial court to rule on motion for directed verdict after verdict itself returned. (9-11-50[b]; 242 Ga. 419, 249 S.E.2d 224).

Docketing.—See subhead Lien, infra. Filing with a clerk of a judgment, signed by judge, constitutes entry of judgment. No judgment effective until entry. (9-11-58[b]). Decision of Supreme Court not final during term rendered until rehearing denied or remittitur transmitted. (238 Ga. 532, 233 S.E.2d 785).

Vacation or Modification.—All proceedings to set aside judgments (other than motion for new trial) must be brought within three years from entry of judgment, except that judgment void because of lack of jurisdiction of person or subject matter may be attacked at any time. (9-11-60[f]). Trial court can on its own motion modify judgment during term judgment rendered. (234 Ga. 698, 217 S.E.2d 598). Rule against modification of judgment after expiration of term, judgment entered not applicable to interlocutory rulings so long as case continues. (143 Ga. App. 715, 240 S.E.2d 100 [rev'd on other grounds]). Judgment may be attacked by motion to set aside or motion for new trial only in court of rendition. (9-11-60[b]). Use of complaint in equity to set aside judgment prohibited. (9-11-60[e]). Trial court may not modify judgment which is on appeal. (227 Ga. 485, 181 S.E.2d 495).

Motion for New Trial.—Must be predicated upon defect not appearing on face of record or pleadings. (9-11-60[c]).

Motion to Set Aside.—Judgment void for non-amendable defect on face of record. (172 Ga. App. 426, 323 S.E.2d 286). If non-amendable defect appears on face of pleadings, it is not sufficient to show that pleadings fail to state claim upon which relief can be granted; rather, pleadings must show that no claim in fact existed. Motion to set aside shall lie to attack judgment based upon lack of jurisdiction over subject

matter (9-11-60[d]) filed in court where judgment entered or by complaint in equity in county of defendant's residency (171 Ga. App. 9, 318 S.E.2d 687). Motion to set aside may be brought to set aside judgment based upon fraud, accident or mistake, or acts of adverse party unmixed with negligence or fault of movant, or non-amendable defect on face of record. (9-11-60[d]).

Clerical Mistakes.—May be corrected by court or on motion of any party. (9-11-60[g]).

Lien.—Money judgment, without entry on general execution docket, is not lien against the defendant's property with respect to third parties without notice. (9-12-81). Judgment liens rank as of date of entry if execution recorded on general execution docket, and bind all property of defendant, real and personal, in county where placed on execution docket. (9-12-80). However, liens of all judgments obtained in damage actions growing out of common disaster or occurrence are equal in rank or priority regardless of date of verdict or judgment, provided suit was filed within 12 months from date of disaster. (9-12-90). Liens from judgment where suit filed over 12 months after accident take priority as to date of judgment. (234 Ga. 186, 215 S.E.2d 240). With respect to personalty, third person not chargeable with notice of lien of money judgment except from date of entry on execution docket but with respect to real property chargeable only from entry on proper docket and indexing. (9-12-86). Judgment debtor cannot alienate his property pending appeal. (9-12-88).

Revival.—Judgment becomes dormant after seven years from date of entry on execution docket, or from date of last entry of execution by proper officer (9-12-60), but may be renewed within three years from time it becomes dormant by action or scire facias at option of plaintiff (9-12-61). Georgia provision for revival of dormant judgment is applicable to revive dormant federal judgment. (218 Ga. App. 429, 461 S.E.2d 553). Action on judgment must be brought in county of defendant's residence (9-12-66); scire facias in court of county where original judgment was obtained. (9-12-63).

Assignment.—Judgments are transferable by written assignment for valuable consideration. (9-12-21).

Forms

Partial Payment.—

A partial payment of the within judgment has been made and the clerk of said court is authorized to enter the amount of such payment upon the execution, to wit: $. . . . . . . This the . . . . . . day of . . . ., 19. . . . .

. . . .

Attorney for Plaintiff

Full Satisfaction.—

The within judgment and all interest, fees and costs have been fully paid and the clerk of said court is hereby authorized and directed to cancel the within execution and mark said judgment satisfied. This the . . . . . . day of . . . ., 19. . . . .

. . . .

Attorney for Plaintiff

Actions.—Although there is no time limitation on setting aside judgment "void on its face" due to lack of jurisdiction, all other proceedings to set aside judgments (other than motion for new trial) must be made within three years of rendering. (9-11-60[f]; 263 Ga. 280,430 S.E.2d 749). Action on judgment is action of debt. (96 Ga. App. 592, 101 S.E.2d 113).

See subhead Vacation or Modification, supra; and category Debtor and Creditor, topic Executions.

Foreign Judgments.—Action on foreign judgment, except judgments for child or spousal support, must be brought within five years after rendition. (9-3-20). Judgment conclusive as to matters at issue between parties and their privies. (9-12-40). In case of judgment of court of record, transcript duly certified under Act of Congress (28 U.S.C. 687) must be furnished, and is all the proof necessary (24-7-24). Official certificate of justice of peace of another state to any judgment and preliminary proceedings before him, with official certificate of clerk of court of record, under seal of such court, within county in which justice of peace resides, stating that he or she is justice of peace of that county, and that signature to his or her certificate is genuine, is prima facie evidence of such proceedings and judgment. (24-7-26). Where justice of peace has gone out of office, similar certificate of successor has like effect. (24-7-26).

Georgia Foreign Money Judgments Recognition Act.—Except as otherwise provided, foreign judgment that is final, conclusive, and enforceable in jurisdiction where rendered (even though appeal is pending) is conclusive between parties to extent it grants or denies recovery of sum of money. (9-12-113). Grounds for non-recognition are listed. (9-12-114). Foreign judgment is not refused recognition for lack of personal jurisdiction if certain conditions are met. (9-12-115).

Uniform Enforcement of Foreign Judgments Act.—Foreign judgment is treated in same manner as judgment of court in which it is filed. Filed foreign judgment has same effect and is subject to same procedures, defenses and proceedings as judgment of court in which it was filed and may be enforced or satisfied in like manner. (9-12-131, -132). At time foreign judgment is filed, affidavit showing name and last known address of judgment debtor and judgment creditor must be filed. (9-12-133). If judgment debtor shows court any ground on which enforcement of judgment would be stayed, court shall stay foreign judgment for appropriate period and require security for satisfaction. (9-12-134). However, Act does not permit judgment debtor to file counterclaim to foreign judgment. (203 Ga. App. 243, 416 S.E.2d 824).

LIMITATION OF ACTIONS:

Uniform Commercial Code.—Adopted. See category Business Regulation and Commerce, topic Commercial Code.

Actions must be brought within following periods:

Twenty years: on bond, note or other instrument under seal (9-3-23); or security deed (234 Ga. 297, 216 S.E.2d 79); to enforce right accruing to individual under statute

---

LIMITATION OF ACTIONS . . . *continued*
or act of incorporation or by operation of law (9-3-22). But see category Employment, topic Labor Relations, subhead Wages.

Ten years: against executors, administrators or guardians (9-3-27); from date of first sale of new personal property to active user for action against manufacturer for injury to person or property (51-1-11; 264 Ga. 540, 448 S.E.2d 347), but see subhead Two Years, infra, for product liability limitation.

Eight years: for damages and injuries resulting from deficiencies in improvements to real property including indemnification claims unless injury occurs during seventh or eighth year after substantial completion, in which case action may be brought up to two years from date of injury. (9-3-51; 215 Ga. App. 53, 449 S.E.2d 889).

Seven years: for entry of judgment on general execution document to prevent dormancy (9-12-60).

Six years: on simple contract in writing (except negotiable instruments and contracts for sale of goods) (9-3-24); but see subhead Four Years, infra for breach of contract for sale of goods; against trustee for breach of trust.

Five years: on foreign judgment except judgments for child and/or spousal support (9-3-20); however, fraudulent concealment can estop raising defense (186 Ga. App. 354; 367 S.E.2d 128). See also subhead Two Years, infra.

Four years: on open account or for breach of contract not in writing or on any implied promise or undertaking (9-3-25); for trespass on or damage to realty or injury to personalty (9-3-30, 31), including tortious interference with business (166 Ga.App. 387, 304 S.E.2d 510 and common law fraud (202 Ga. App. 770, 415 S.E.2d 510); to recover possession of personalty (9-3-32); action ex contractu for which no other period prescribed (9-3-26); on contract of sale under Uniform Commercial Code (11-2-725); for loss of consortium (9-3-33); for breach of covenant restricting land use that accrues as result of failure to pay assessments or fees (9-3-29). See also category Business Regulation and Commerce, topic Consumer Protection, subhead Retail Installment and Home Solicitation Sales.

Three Years: for shareholders to assert dissenter's rights. (14-2-1332).

Two years: on medical malpractice from date of injury or death (9-3-71), but see subhead One Year, infra, for foreign object malpractice; for injury to person and wrongful death (9-3-33), including product liability (254 Ga. 111, 327 S.E.2d 221); service of tort complaint against uninsured motorist carrier (236 Ga. 582, 224 S.E.2d 416); for medical malpractice from date injury occurred including action for foreign objects left in body (260 Ga. 502, 397 S.E.2d 117; 9-3-71); 9-3-71(a) held unconstitutional as applied to medical malpractice wrongful death (250 Ga. 470, 298 S.E.2d 484) but 9-3-71(b) five-year statute of repose is constitutional as applied to medical malpractice wrongful death (222 Ga. App. 144, 473 S.E.2d 523); for breach of covenant restricting land use, including violators of building set-back lines (except those which accrue as result of failure to pay assessments or fees) (9-3-29); for injury from unfair or deceptive acts in conduct of consumer transactions (10-1-401); for malicious prosecution action (225 Ga. App. 119, 483 S.E.2d 133); for filing claims of $500 or less against state with Claims Advisory Board or General Assembly (28-5-86); for wages and lost earning capacity (138 Ga.App. 761, 227 S.E.2d 397) (see category Employment, topic Labor Relations). Action for wrongful death of husband, wife, parent or child. (9-3-33). See also subhead Five Years, supra.

One year: for injury to reputation (9-3-33); for certain claims against counties (36-11-1) that requires that claim be "present" within 12 months, but does not require complaint to be filed within that period, for violation of bulk transfers under Uniform Commercial Code (11-6-111); for medical malpractice for foreign object left in body to run from discovery of negligence (9-3-72).

Actions Not Specifically Provided For.—No general limitation on actions not provided for.

Tolling of Limitations for Fraud of Defendant.—If defendant fraudulently defers or debars plaintiff from bringing action, action accrues upon plaintiff's discovery of fraud. (9-3-96).

Discovery Rule.—Rule confined to cases of bodily injury which develop only over extended period of time (258 Ga. 365, 368 S.E.2d 732); however, rule also applied to claims for fraud (202 Ga. App. 770, 415 S.E.2d 510). Limitations period runs from time nature of injury and causal connection between injury and negligent conduct known or should have been known. (160 Ga. App. 318; 287 S.E.2d 252). Rule not applicable to property damage claims. (258 Ga. 365; 368 S.E.2d 732). Rule not applicable to medical malpractice (674 F.2d 856) except in foreign object cases (9-3-72). Rule not applicable to contract claims. (171 Ga. App. 462, 320 S.E.2d 255).

Dismissal for Want of Prosecution.—Any suit in which no written order is taken for five years stands automatically dismissed with costs taxed against party plaintiff. (9-2-60).

New Actions.—May be brought, subject to payment of costs in original action, within statute of limitations or within six months of voluntary dismissal or discontinuance (or dismissal or discontinuance without prejudice for lack of subject matter jurisdiction), whichever is later; provided, however, that this privilege of renewal may be exercised only once if dismissal or discontinuance occurs after expiration of applicable period of limitation. (9-2-61[a]; 9-11-41[d]). This privilege of renewal shall not apply to contracts for sale of goods. (9-2-61[b]). When original action is in federal court, six-month time limit runs upon final decision of federal appeals court, not upon denial of certiorari by United Stated Supreme Court, unless stay procured. (222 Ga. App. 563, 474 S.E.2d 740).

Foreign Causes of Action.—Georgia limitation governs action brought in Georgia courts. (97 Ga. 587, 25 S.E. 335; 119 Ga. 139, 45 S.E. 979).

Disabilities of Plaintiff.—Minors and legally incompetent persons, and persons imprisoned, if disability existed when cause of action accrued, are allowed periods stated above after disability removed (9-3-90; 150 Ga. App. 234, 257 S.E.2d 209), except that in action for medical malpractice, once minor attains age of five years, two-year period of limitation applies, and after age ten, action for negligent act that occurred before fifth birthday is barred (9-3-73). If disability occurred after cause of action accrued, and was not voluntarily caused or undertaken by person claiming benefit thereof, limitation period suspended during disability. (9-3-91). In case of fraud deterring plaintiff from suing, limitation period runs from discovery of fraud. (9-3-96). For crimes designated in 17-3-2.1, infancy shall toll statute of limitations until victim is 16 years of age or until violation is reported to law enforcement authorities, whichever is sooner. (17-3-2.1; 213 Ga. App. 579, 445 S.E.2d 566).

Absence or Concealment of Defendant.—Where defendant removes from state, period of absence excluded from limitation period. (9-3-94).

Interruption of Statutory Period.—A new written promise fixes new point from which limitation runs on actions not yet barred. (9-3-110).

Revival of Barred Claim.—Debt barred by limitations may be revived by new promise, which must be in writing. (9-3-110). Any written acknowledgment sufficient. Partner or joint contractor can revive claim only against himself or herself and not against others liable with him or her. (9-3-114, -115).

Contractual Limitations.—A period shorter than the statutory period may be fixed by agreement, provided such shorter period is reasonable. (24 Ga. 97). Contract for sale may reduce to not less than one year but cannot extend period of limitation. (11-2-725).

Pleading.—Limitations must be specially pleaded (9-11-8), but may be raised at close of case in limited circumstances (154 Ga. App. 350, 268 S.E.2d 403).

See also category Business Organizations, topic Corporations, subheads Liabilities of Directors, Liabilities of Officers, and Unclaimed Distributions.

PARTITION:

At least four available methods: (1) arbitration (9-9-2, 4, 48); (2) distribution in kind by proceeding in probate court (53-4-11); (3) statutory partition (44-6-160); and (4) equitable partition (44-6-140). Where there are tenants in common and no provision is made, by will or otherwise, as to how realty is to be divided, any one of owners of undivided interest (including owner of equitable interest or holder of security deed thereto) may apply to superior court of county in which realty situated, by petition for writ of partition, stating facts of case, describing premises, and defining interest of each party. (44-6-160). Right of partition may be surrendered by contract.

Jurisdiction and Venue.—Equity has jurisdiction where remedy at law insufficient or peculiar circumstances render proceedings in equity more suitable and just; and decree passes title without conveyances by parties. (44-6-140).

Proceedings.—Twenty days notice must be given to other parties concerned. (44-6-162). Partitioners have power to select surveyor, and must give all parties, if possible, eight days notice of time of executing writ. (44-6-164). Partitioners must make just and equal division and make return to court. (44-6-164). Proceedings may be contested both before writ issued and after return of partitioners. (44-6-165).

Partition by Appraisal.—Where fair and equitable division of property cannot be made court will appoint three qualified persons to make appraisals. Average of appraisals will constitute appraisal price and each petitioner may receive his or her respective share of total value of property. (44-6-166.1).

Partition in Kind or Sale.—If lands and tenements sought to be partitioned are not sold pursuant to 44-6-166.1, court will order public sale of land. (44-6-167).

Personalty may be partitioned the same as real estate. (44-12-1).

Life tenant of undivided interest in real estate may compel partition under usual procedure where property capable of fair and equitable partition, but no sale of property allowed. (44-6-172).

Guardian ad litem can be appointed by court to represent all unborn remaindermen or reversioners as well as other interested and unrepresented minors. (44-6-173).

PLEADING:

Court procedure for courts of record governed by Ga. Civil Practice Act (9-11-1 et seq.) which closely follows Federal Rules of Civil Procedure. See topics Depositions and Discovery, Judgments, Practice, and Process.

Pleadings Permitted.—Federal Rules effective. (9-11-7[a-c]). Reply to counterclaim or cross-claim is permitted but not required since allegations in counterclaims or cross-claims are automatically deemed denied. (9-11-7[a], 9-11-12[a]).

Complaint.—Federal Rules effective. (9-11-8[a], [e], [f]). No subject matter jurisdictional allegation required: basis of venue must be stated in original complaint. (9-11-8). Demand for judgment for relief in medical malpractice actions subject to special rules. (9-11-8[a]). Professional malpractice complaint must be accompanied by expert affidavit as to alleged negligence of each individual defendant involved. (9-11-9.1). Affidavit requirement only applies to those professionals recognized under 14-7-2(2), 14-10-2(2), and 43-1-24. (218 Ga. App. 62, 460 S.E.2d 528). Expert affidavit requirement also applies to counterclaims for professional malpractice. (203 Ga. App. 519, 417 S.E.2d 338). Professional malpractice affidavit not required for strict liability claims. (223 Ga. 712, 479 S.E.2d 103). Affidavit that incorporates by reference other documents which set forth requisite averrals is not sufficient. (206 Ga. App. 108, 424 S.E.2d 54). Facsimile of original affidavit sufficient when original exists and can be acquired by plaintiff. (217 Ga. App. 156, 456 S.E.2d 718). However, pro se plaintiff failing to file requisite expert affidavit with malpractice complaint may be given leeway by court. (201 Ga. App. 480, 411 S.E.2d 322). "Professional" includes architect. (259 Ga. 435, 383 S.E.2d 867).

Sanction of Petition.—Federal Rules effective. No specific provision.

Defensive Pleadings.—Federal Rules effective. (9-11-8, -12, -13). Assumption of risk, comparative negligence and other defenses not listed in statute not pleaded separately as affirmative defenses. (9-11-8[c]). Answers to cross-claims and counterclaims are not required. (9-11-12[a]).

Answer.—Federal Rules effective. (9-11-8[b]) through [f], -12). Cross-claim or counterclaim does not require answer unless required by order of court, and stands

PLEADING . . . continued

automatically denied. *Note:* Service of motion under this section does not alter time requirement. (9-11-12). Verified petition requires verified answer. (9-10-111).

Time.—Federal Rules effective, except that filing motion under 9-11-12 does not extend time for filing answer. (9-11-6). Unless otherwise provided by statute, answer must be served within 30 days after service of summons and complaint on defendant. Filing of motion to transfer does not toll time within which to answer complaint in transfer or court. (199 Ga. App. 237, 404 S.E.2d 618). Court may order any insufficient defense or redundant, immaterial, impertinent or scandalous matter stricken from any pleading upon motion made by a party within 30 days after service of pleading upon him or her or upon court's own initiative at any time. (9-11-12[f]). If motion for definite statement is granted, order of court must be obeyed within 15 days after notice of order. (9-11-12[e]). If party elects to make motion in writing, rather than in responsive pleading, on defense of lack of jurisdiction over subject matter or person, improper venue, insufficiency of process or service of process, failure to state a claim upon which relief can be granted, or failure to join an indispensable party, motion must be made before or at time of pleading if a further pleading is permitted. (9-11-12[b]). For time requirements for motions for judgment on pleadings, summary judgment, and judgment notwithstanding verdict, see topic Judgments.

Cross actions may be filed up to and including filing date for answer or other defensive pleadings. (9-3-97).

Court order granting attorney's requested leave of absence excuses attorney from appearance at hearings or proceedings, but does not extend any filing deadlines that fall within time relating to leave of absence.

Counterclaim or Set-Off.—Federal Rules effective. (9-11-13). Counterclaims are not compulsory if: (1) at time action commenced, claim was subject of another pending action; or (2) opposing party brought action by attachment or other process by which court did not acquire personal jurisdiction and pleader does not state counterclaim; or (3) counterclaim not within jurisdiction of court. (9-11-13[a]). Unless parties agree otherwise, permissive counterclaims are separated for purposes of trial. (9-11-13[b]). Parties required for granting of complete relief in counterclaim or cross-claim, shall be brought in by order of court if subject to court's jurisdiction. (9-11-13[h]). In federal court, counterclaim for abusive litigation is permissive. (256 Ga. 92, 344 S.E.2d 414; 2 G.L.F. 25-1).

Amended or Supplemental Pleadings.—Federal Rules effective. (9-11-15). Party may amend pleading as a matter of course at any time before entry of pretrial order; thereafter, only by leave of court or consent of adverse party. Party may move in response to amended pleading and shall plead within 15 days after service of amended pleading when court requires. (9-11-15[a]).

Verification.—Federal Rules effective. Dilatory plea or plea of non est factum must be verified (15-10-89), but otherwise answer need not be verified unless petition is verified (9-10-111). *Note:* Verification is exception in Federal Rules, but failure to repeal section requiring verification of dilatory plea, despite abolition of pleas (9-11-7[c]), leaves in doubt need for verification where motion is of dilatory nature.

Verification specifically required in secondary action by shareholders (9-11-23[b]), for deposition to perpetuate testimony (9-11-27[a][1]), for temporary restraining order granted without notice to adverse party (9-11-65[b][1], 9-10-110); see topic Injunctions.

Claims against existing persons sent to this state for collection by suit should be accompanied by full name of each plaintiff. If plaintiff be partnership, full name of each partner should be given; if corporation, precise style of corporation as appearing in its charter.

No affidavit or deposition of any kind, other than as above, is necessary. Accounts and unliquidated demands should always be itemized.

See topic Judgments; category Debtor and Creditor, topic Executions.

Small Claims.—See category Courts and Legislature, topic Courts.

Frivolous Claims.—In civil action any court of record shall award reasonable and necessary attorney's fees and expenses of litigation to any party against whom is asserted claim, defense, or other position with respect to which there existed such complete absence of justifiable issue of law or fact that it could not reasonably be believed that court would accept asserted claim, defense or other position. (9-15-14[a]). Motion for attorneys' fees and expenses may be filed at any time during course of action but not later than 45 days after final disposition. (9-15-14[e]). Final disposition means entry of judgment by trial court, not disposition on appeal. (263 Ga. 792, 440 S.E.2d 464). Does not apply to claims or defenses determined by court to be asserted in good faith attempt to establish new theory of law if based on some recognized precedent or persuasive authority. (9-15-14[c]). Tort liability may arise for abusive litigation. (51-7-81; 201 Ga. App. 562, 411 S.E.2d 731). Does not authorize imposition of attorney's fees and litigation expenses for proceedings before appellate court of Georgia. (200 Ga. App. 723, 409 S.E.2d 281).

PRACTICE:

State practice governed by Ga. Civil Practice Act (9-11-1 et seq.), which closely follows Federal Rules of Civil Procedure. See topics Actions, Pleading, Judgments, Process.

No separate courts for equity causes, but superior court has both law and equity jurisdiction.

Discovery.—Federal Rules closely followed. (9-11-26 through -37). In order to utilize courts to compel discovery, parties must commence and complete discovery within six months of filing answer. (183 Ga. App. 164, 358 S.E.2d 311).

Demand for Admission of Facts.—Federal Rules closely followed. (9-11-36).

Direct Action Against Insurer.—See category Transportation, topic Motor Vehicles, subhead Direct Actions.

Small Claims.—See category Courts and Legislature, topic Courts.

Attachment.—See topic Process, subhead Service by Publication.

See also topics Actions, Appeal and Error, Depositions and Discovery, Injunctions, Judgments, Pleading, and Process. See also category Debtor and Creditor, topics Attachment, Executions, and Garnishment.

PROCESS:

Process procedure governed primarily by Ga. Civil Practice Act (9-11-1), which closely follows Federal Rules of Civil Procedure.

Suit Begun.—Suit in Magistrate Court begun by issuing statement of claim. (15-10-43). Civil action commenced by filing complaint. (9-11-3). Service, if accomplished within reasonable time, will relate back to original date of filing complaint. (239 Ga. 282, 236 S.E.2d 629).

General Requisites.—Service of process made by sheriff of county where action brought or defendant found, marshall of court, deputy, or any other U.S. citizen appointed by court for that purpose or by person over 18 and not party and who has been appointed as permanent process server by court. Outside U.S., service may be made by any U.S. citizen or resident of such country appointed by court, after order of publication. (9-11-4[c]). Rule nisi approved as process in lieu of summons where defendant is required to appear at time other than within 30 days after service. (233 Ga. 734, 213 S.E.2d 633). Process and service may be waived in writing. (9-10-73). Special requirements exist in condemnation cases. (32-3-8, -9).

Who May Serve.—See subhead General Requisites, supra.

Personal Service on Individual.—Summons and complaint may be handed to defendant, left at his or her usual place of abode with person of suitable age and discretion residing therein, or delivered to agent authorized by appointment or law to receive service. (9-11-4[d][7]). Substantial compliance insufficient; person receiving service at defendant's usual place of abode must reside there. (259 Ga. 418, 383 S.E.2d 108). Statute authorizing service by leaving copy at most notorious place of abode where principal sum under $200 (9-11-4[d][6]) unconstitutional (244 Ga. 533, 261 S.E.2d 359). In Magistrate Court, copy of verified statement of claim must be personally served, or by leaving copy at usual place of abode with person of suitable age and discretion, or by delivering copy to authorized agent for service. (15-10-43[b]). See also category Transportation, topic Motor Vehicles, subhead Actions Against Nonresidents.

Service After Complaint.—Pleadings subsequent to written complaint, written motions except those to be heard ex parte, and written notices, appearances, demands, offers of judgment and similar papers served on parties by service to party's attorney, unless ordered otherwise by court. Service on attorney or party accomplished by delivery or mail to last known address. If address unknown, to clerk of court. Service by mail complete upon mailing. Proof of service by certificate of attorney, affidavit, written admission, or other proof satisfactory to court. (9-11-5).

Personal Service on Minor.—Personal service on minor, and, unless minor is married, also on father, mother, guardian, or guardian ad litem. (9-11-4[d][3]).

Personal Service on Incompetent.—To person and appointed guardian for person judicially declared of unsound mind or on guardian ad litem if no guardian. (9-11-4[d][4]).

Personal Service on Domestic Corporation.—By delivering copy of summons and complaint to registered agent. (14-2-504[a]). If no registered agent or agent cannot be served with reasonable diligence, to secretary of corporation at its principal office by registered or certified mail, return receipt requested; service perfected at earliest of date corporation receives mail, date on return receipt if signed on behalf of corporation, or five days after postmark, if postage prepaid and correctly addressed. (14-2-504[b]). Other means may also be used (14-2-504[c]) but not service by publication (214 Ga. App. 492, 448 S.E.2d 374).

Personal Service on Unincorporated Association.—Service on any officer or official member of organization or upon any officer, or member of any branch or local of such organization or association unless association files with Secretary of State designated officer or agent for service. If designation is properly filed, service only on such person, if found within State. (9-2-25).

Personal Service on Joint Stock Company.—No special provision.

Personal Service on Foreign Corporations.—Registered agent of foreign corporation is agent for purpose of service of process or notice or demand upon corporation. (14-2-1510[a]). Process on foreign corporation cannot be perfected via service on registered agent of wholly-owned domestic subsidiary if subsidiary not otherwise agent for service of process for parent. (1998 WL 146265). If corporation has no registered agent or agent cannot be served, then by registered or certified mail, return receipt requested, address to corporate officer at principal office shown in application for certificate of authority of most recent annual registration; copy of process must also be served on Secretary of State. Service perfected at earliest of date corporation receives mail, date shown on return receipt if signed on behalf of corporation, or five days after postmark, if postage prepaid and correctly addressed. (14-2-1510[b, c]). Other means may be used to serve foreign corporations. (14-2-1510[d]). For Secretary of State as agent for service, see 45-13-26.

Proof of Service.—Proof of service of process made by affidavit or certificate of sheriff, marshal or deputy. If by other person, by affidavit only. Service other than by publication, certificate or affidavit must state date, place and manner of service. If by publication, by certificate of clerk of court certifying publication and mailing. Defendant may acknowledge service in writing. Failure to make proof of service does not affect validity of service. (9-11-4[g]).

Service by Publication.—
General.—Court may grant order for service by publication where it appears, by affidavit or verified complaint, on file, that claim exists against defendant and defendant is necessary or proper party, when fact appears by affidavit that person to be served resides outside state, or has departed state, or cannot be found within state, or conceals himself or herself to avoid service of summons. (9-11-4[e]).

PROCESS . . . *continued*

Service by publication will not support in personam judgment against defendant who does not have actual notice of suit. (Compare, 231 Ga. 246, 201 S.E.2d 150 to 242 Ga. 400, 249 S.E.2d 82.)

When affidavit is based on fact that party to be served resides outside state and present address is unknown, it is sufficient to show due diligence to state that at previous time person resided outside state in certain place; that such place is last residence of party to knowledge of affiant; that party no longer resides at such place; that affiant does not know where such party can be found; and that affiant has no reason to believe that party now resides in this state. (9-11-4[e][1][A]).

Actions Involving Property.—When action involves real or personal property in this state in which defendant claims an interest, or in which relief demanded is wholly or in part exclusion of defendant from interest therein, and defendant resides out of state or has departed state, or cannot after due diligence be found within state, or conceals himself to avoid service, judge or clerk may order service by publication. (9-11-4[e][1][B]; see also 9-10-71).

In condemnation proceedings publication is required where personal service has been perfected (32-3-8[f]) and copy of petition and declaration must be served on county or city tax collecting authority (32-3-8[e]).

Nonresident Motorist.—Service by publication not available (120 Ga. App. 307, 170 S.E.2d 318) but see subhead Long Arm Statute, infra.

Method of Publication.—Publication made in paper in which sheriff's advertisements are printed four times within ensuing 60 days, at least seven days apart. Notice contains name of plaintiff and defendant, court, character of action, name of judge, date action was filed, date of order for service by publication, and notice to party to be served commanding that answer be filed within 60 days of date of order for service by publication. Where abode of absent or nonresident is known, party obtaining order advises clerk thereof. Within 15 days after date of order, clerk must send duplicate or copy of said notice, along with copies of complaint (if any) and order, to party named in order at his or her last known address. When publication is ordered, personal service outside state of copy of summons, complaint and order of publication is equivalent to publication and mailing when proved to satisfaction of court. (9-11-4[e][1][C]).

Special additional requirements exist in condemnation cases. (32-3-8, -9).

Personal Service Outside the State.—Personal service upon natural person may be made outside state in any action where a person served is resident of this state or in any proceeding in rem without regard to residence of person served. Court may order personal service outside state where such facts are shown by affidavit and where it appears, by affidavit or verified complaint on file, that claim is asserted against person to be served and person is necessary or proper party. Service made by delivering copies of process and complaint in person to persons served. (9-11-4[e][2]).

Nonresident Motorist.—As to action arising out of motor vehicle accident, see category Transportation, topic Motor Vehicles, subhead Actions Against Nonresidents.

Long Arm Statute.—Court may exercise jurisdiction over nonresident who transacts business within state; commits tort within state; commits tortious injury in state if tortfeasor regularly does or solicits business, engages in persistent course of conduct, or derives substantial revenue from goods used or services rendered in state; owns, uses or possesses real property in state; or, for alimony, child support, division of property, in connection with divorce, or support of dependents' proceedings, maintains matrimonial domicile, in state when action commenced or resided in state preceding commencement of action. (9-10-91). Under "long arm" statute, service beyond state made same as within state by any person qualified to make service under laws of foreign jurisdiction, or by any duly-qualified attorney, solicitor, or equivalent in such jurisdiction. (9-10-94). Nonresident, to be subject to process must engage in purposeful activity with or in forum. Unclear whether Georgia's long arm statute permits assertion of jurisdiction over nonresident defendant to maximum extent permitted by U.S. Constitution. (Compare 257 Ga. 129, 356 S.E.2d 513, with 255 Ga. 505, 340 S.E.2d 597.) Georgia's statute does not apply to filing of certain classes of cases, e.g., defamation and divorce cases. (9-10-91[2, 5]). See subheads Personal Service on Foreign Corporations, Personal Service Outside the State, and Nonresident Motorist, supra.

Uniform Child Custody Jurisdiction Act.—Act permits service by certified mail and by other means reasonably calculated to give actual notice for certain child custody determinations. (19-9-40 et seq.).

REPLEVIN:

Any person holding security interest on personal property under UCC transaction may foreclose on security interest by petitioning court for writ of possession. (44-14-230). See category Mortgages, topic Chattel Mortgages. Petitioner must make statement of facts under oath to court having jurisdiction over secured property or debtor. If petitioner is not resident of county where debtor resides or secured property is located, oath may be made to any court of record in state and forwarded with petition to appropriate court. (44-14-231). Writ commands sheriff to sell secured property to satisfy debt and costs of proceedings. Petition and summons served by sheriff, deputy, or marshal through personal delivery to appropriate resident of premises, or, if necessary, by tacking copy of summons and petition on door of premises and mailing copy of same to defendant's last known address. (44-14-232). Defendant must answer either orally or in writing within seven days after service of summons (44-14-232), but may reopen default by answering within seven days after date of default (44-14-233). Defendant must provide bond for full amount of value of property or amount of alleged remaining balance if defendant desires to transfer, remove, or convey secured property after service of summons and opportunity to answer. (44-14-234, -237).

SEQUESTRATION:

No statute, but see category Debtor and Creditor, topics Attachment, Executions, Garnishment, and Receivers.

SERVICE:

See topic Process.

STAY OF EXECUTION:

See topic Appeal and Error; and category Debtor and Creditor, topic Executions.

SUBMISSION OF CONTROVERSY:

No statutory provision.

VENUE:

Unless otherwise provided, action must be brought in county where defendant resides. (Const. Art. VI, §II, Para. VI). Joint obligors may be sued in county of residence of either. (Const. Art. VI, §II, Para. IV). Department or agency of state government can be considered joint tortfeasor with other resident defendants for venue purposes. (208 Ga. App. 134, 430 S.E.2d 63). Maker and endorser of promissory note may be sued in county where maker resides. (Const. Art. VI, §II, Para. V; 9-10-32). Nonresident may be sued in any county where he or she may be found at time action brought. (9-10-33). Claim against third-party defendant may be tried in county where claim against defending party is pending. (9-10-34). Action respecting title to land must be tried in county where land lies; if single tract lies in two counties action may be tried in either (Const., Art. VI, §II, Para. II). Equity cases are tried in county where defendant against whom substantial relief is prayed resides. (Const. Art. III, §II, Para III). Petition for injunction to stay pending proceedings may be filed in county where proceedings pending. (9-10-30). Contracts may not limit intrastate venue for suit against insurers in Georgia. (209 Ga. App. 585, 434 S.E.2d 778 [citing 125 Ga. App. 829, 189 S.E.2d 130]). This rule does not apply in federal court. (Nolan v. First Commodity Corp. of Boston, No. CV586-042, 1987 U.S. Dist. LEXIS 2080 [S.D. Ga. Mar. 18, 1987]). Special venue statutes are not exclusive. (134 Ga. App. 106, 213 S.E.2d 150).

Nonresidents Doing Business in State.—May be sued in any county where business transacted, act occurred, or real property located. (9-10-93). Nonresident not subject to venue under joint obligor venue provisions in Georgia Constitution. (197 Ga. App. 718, 399 S.E.2d 241).

Unincorporated Association.—May be sued in any county where such organization does business or has a branch or local organization. (9-2-25).

Corporations.—In conjunction with above-mentioned rules, for purposes of proceedings generally, domestic corporations and foreign corporations authorized to transact business in Georgia are deemed to reside in county of registered office, and if none, in last named registered or principal office with Secretary of State. (14-2-510). Residence of foreign and domestic corporations for purposes of venue in tort action is both county in which it has its registered office and county in which tort occurred provided that corporation has office and does business in that county. (213 Ga. App. 48, 443 S.E.2d 686). In libel action against corporate publisher, venue proper in any county in which publication is circulated if defendant has office and transacts business there. (14-2-510[b][3]; 243 Ga. 760, 256 S.E.2d 443). For garnishment proceeding, venue proper in county in which is located corporate office or place of business where defendant employee is employed. (14-2-510[b][4]).

Change of Venue.—Where impartial jury cannot be obtained in county where action pending, judge must transfer cause to another county to be agreed on by parties or their counsel (9-10-50) or if they cannot agree to be selected by judge (Const., Art. VI, §II, Para. VI; 9-10-50).

COURTS AND LEGISLATURE

COURTS:

United States District Courts.—

Northern District.—Clerk's office: 75 Spring Street, Atlanta, GA 30335.

Deposit of $150 is required on filing of civil action. Habeas corpus $5.

All papers presented for filing and correspondence must have complete civil case number and three-initial suffix indicating judge, without which filing not accepted. (Loc. Rule 200-1).

Atlanta Division.—Atlanta. Counties: Cherokee, Clayton, Cobb, DeKalb, Douglas, Fulton, Gwinnett, Henry, Newton and Rockdale.

Newnan Division.—Newnan. Counties: Carroll, Coweta, Fayette, Haralson, Heard, Meriwether, Pike, Spalding and Troup.

Rome Division.—Rome. Counties: Bartow, Catoosa, Chattooga, Dade, Floyd, Gordon, Murray, Paulding, Polk, Walker and Whitfield.

Gainesville Division.—Gainesville. Counties: Banks, Barrow, Dawson, Fannin, Forsyth, Gilmer, Habersham, Hall, Jackson, Lumpkin, Pickens, Rabun, Stephens, Towns, Union and White.

Middle District.—Clerk's office: Macon.

Deposit of $120 is required on filing of action.

Macon Division.—Macon. Counties: Baldwin, Bibb, Bleckley, Butts, Crawford, Hancock, Houston, Jasper, Jones, Lamar, Monroe, Peach, Pulaski, Putnam, Twiggs, Upson, Washington and Wilkinson.

Athens Division.—Athens. Counties: Clarke, Elbert, Franklin, Greene, Hart, Madison, Morgan, Oconee, Oglethorpe and Walton.

Columbus Division.—Columbus. Counties: Chattahoochee, Clay, Harris, Marion, Muscogee, Quitman, Randolph, Stewart, Talbot and Taylor.

Albany-Americus Division.—Albany. Counties: Baker, Calhoun, Dougherty, Early, Lee, Miller, Mitchell, Schley, Sumter, Terrell, Turner, Webster and Worth.

Valdosta Division.—Valdosta. Counties: Berrien, Clinch, Cook, Echols, Irwin, Lanier, Lowndes and Tift.

Thomasville Division.—Thomasville. Counties: Brooks, Colquitt, Decatur, Grady, Seminole and Thomas.

Southern District.—Clerk's office: Savannah.

Filing fee of $120 is required on filing of action.

Savannah Division.—Savannah. Counties: Bryan, Chatham, Effingham, and Liberty.

Augusta Division.—Augusta. Counties: Burke, Columbia, Glascock, Jefferson, Lincoln, McDuffie, Richmond, Taliaferro, Warren and Wilkes.

See note at head of Digest as to 1998 legislation covered.

See Topical Index in front part of this volume.

COURTS ... *continued*

Brunswick Division.—Brunswick. Counties: Appling, Camden, Glynn, Jeff Davis, Long, McIntosh and Wayne.

Dublin Division.—Dublin. Counties: Dodge Johnson, Laurens, Montgomery, Telfair, Treutlen and Wheeler.

Waycross Division.—Waycross. Counties: Atkinson, Bacon, Brantley, Charlton, Coffee, Pierce and Ware.

Statesboro Division.—Statesboro. Counties: Bulloch, Candler, Emanuel, Evans, Jenkins, Screven, Tattnall and Toombs.

Supreme Court.—Supreme court has no original jurisdiction, but is court alone for trial and correction of errors from superior courts, juvenile courts, and other courts of original jurisdiction, in all cases that involve construction of Constitution of State of Georgia or U.S., or of treaties made by latter; in all cases in which constitutionality of any law of Georgia or of U.S. is called in question; in cases respecting titles to land, in equity cases; in cases involving validity or construction of wills; in cases of conviction of capital felony; in habeas corpus cases; in all cases involving extraordinary remedies; in divorce and alimony cases; in cases involving contested election; in cases involving validity of legislative enactment of municipalities; and in all cases certified to it by court of appeals. It may also require, by certiorari or otherwise, cases to be certified to it from court of appeals, for review and determination. (Const., Art. VI, §VI, Paragraphs II, III). Applicants may file motion for reconsideration with court of appeals but are not required to do so in order to pursue application for writ of certiorari. (Ga. Ct. App. Rule 38[a]). Notice of intention to apply for certiorari must be filed with court of appeals within ten days after judgment or order overruling motion for reconsideration, if one is filed. (Ga. Sup. Ct. Rule 38[1]). Petition must be filed with Supreme Court within 20 days after judgment or order overruling motion for reconsideration, if one is filed. (Ga. Sup. Ct. R. 38[2]). Review by certiorari is not matter of right and ordinarily will be granted only in cases involving issues of gravity and importance. (Ga. Sup. Ct. Rule 40).

Court consists of seven justices. (15-2-1.1). Sits in body. Majority constitutes quorum. (Const., Art. VI, §VI, Paragraph I).

Court sits at State Judicial Building in Atlanta, Georgia.

Court of Appeals.—This court has jurisdiction for trial and correction of errors in law from superior courts, juvenile courts, and other courts of original jurisdiction in all cases in which jurisdiction is not conferred on supreme court. (Const., Art. VI, §V, Paragraph III). It may certify to Supreme Court any question of law as to which it may desire instruction. (Const., Art. VI, §V, Paragraph IV). Court consists of ten judges who shall elect one of their number as chief judge. (15-3-1).

Court is composed of three divisions. Civil and Criminal cases heard by all three divisions. Six judges constitute quorum when entire court seated. (15-3-1).

Superior Courts.—Superior courts combine powers of courts at law and courts of equity. Under Civil Practice Act of 1966, practice is made same in both classes of causes. Superior courts have original and concurrent jurisdiction in all civil and criminal causes, with exception of certain matters relating to administration of estates and other matters of similar nature, of which probate courts have exclusive jurisdiction. (See subhead Probate Courts, infra.) They have exclusive jurisdiction in all felony criminal cases, other than certain cases involving juvenile offenders, in equity cases, divorce cases and cases involving titles to real estate. They have appellate Superior courts have exclusive jurisdiction in certain adoption cases. (See subhead Juvenile Courts, infra.) They have appellate jurisdiction as provided by law in 15-6-8. (Const., Art. VI, §IV, Paragraph I).

Judges of superior courts have authority to grant all writs, original or remedial, either in law or equity that may be necessary to exercise their jurisdiction, which are not expressly prohibited.

State is divided into 46 judicial circuits. (15-6-1).

Probate Courts.—There is popularly-elected probate judge for each county who exercises original, exclusive and general jurisdiction over, among other things, probate of wills; granting letters testamentary, or of administration, and revocation of same; controversies relating to right of executorship or administration; distribution of estates of deceased persons; appointment and removal of guardians and controversies relating to guardianship. (15-9-30). Council of Probate Court Judges of Georgia created for further improvement of probate courts. (15-9-15). Judgments of probate court are carried to superior court for correction of errors, either by certiorari or appeal, except order appointing temporary administrator. (5-3-2).

Juvenile Courts.—Juvenile court in every county. (15-11-3). Council of Juvenile Court Judges created for further improvement of court. (15-11-4.1).

Exclusive jurisdiction over juvenile matters and sole court for initiating action concerning child alleged: (1) to be delinquent, unruly or deprived; (2) to be in need of treatment or commitment as mentally ill or mentally retarded; (3) to have committed juvenile traffic offense or who has been placed under supervision of or on probation to juvenile court. (15-11-5). Sole court for initiating action involving proceedings: (1) to obtain judicial consent to marriage, employment, or enlistment of juvenile; (2) under Interstate Compact on Juveniles or other comparable laws enacted in Georgia (see category Criminal Law, topic Criminal Law, subhead Interstate Corrections Compact); (3) for termination of parent-child relationship, except that in certain adoption proceedings, Superior Courts have exclusive jurisdiction to terminate legal parent-child relationship and rights of biological father who is not legal father of child (15-11-5); (4) relating to prior notice to guardian relative to unemancipated minor's decision to seek abortion (15-11-5). As court of record, authorized to grant new trial on legal grounds. (265 Ga. 106, 454 S.E.2d 134).

Concurrent jurisdiction with superior court, over child charged with act which in superior court would be crime punishable by loss of life or life imprisonment; also jurisdiction in custody proceedings when properly transferred to juvenile court by superior court. (15-11-5).

In this title, child means under 17 years, or under 21 and having committed act of delinquency before 17 and under supervision of court, or on probation to court, or under 18 if deprived. (15-11-2).

Other Courts.—Georgia does not have uniform system of inferior courts. Each county has its own system of courts, and certain municipalities have court systems. Inferior courts may be created either by general or special act of legislature or, in some cases, by recommendation of county grand jury. Most frequently encountered categories of inferior courts are the following:

(a) State Courts.—General Assembly may create state court. (15-7-2). Where state court exists, it is trial court of most general jurisdiction other than superior court. (15-7-4). State Courts and equivalent courts have jurisdiction concurrent with that of Superior Courts over non-felony criminal cases, all civil actions except those in which superior court has exclusive jurisdiction, in matters involving issuing arrest and search warrants. (15-7-4).

(b) City, Municipal and County Courts.—City courts may be created by special act of General Assembly. (15-8-1). Jurisdiction of courts bearing these designations varies widely from county to county. Some are in effect small claims courts. Others are courts of broad original jurisdiction similar to state courts.

(c) Small Claims Courts.—These courts have been created by special legislation in many counties but vary greatly across state. In counties where small claims courts have not been specially created, other existing courts may have special small claims procedures.

(d) Magistrate's Courts. These have been created in all counties (15-10-1) with jurisdiction as provided by 15-10-2 and 15-10-150. No jury trials in magistrate court. (15-10-41). Proceedings are not subject to Georgia Civil Practice Act. (15-10-42).

LEGISLATURE:

Regular sessions are held annually in January. (Const., Art. III, §IV, Paragraph I).

Special or Extraordinary Sessions.—Governor may call extra sessions, and must do so on certification by three-fifths of members of both House and Senate that emergency exists. (Const., Art. V, §II, Paragraph VII).

Initiative and Referendum.—Not provided for with respect to State Government, except in case of Amendments to Constitution.

Lobbyists.—Defined as any natural person who, for compensation, either individually or as employee of another, promotes or opposes passage of any legislation by General Assembly or promotes or opposes approval or veto of legislation by Governor; or who promotes or opposes passage of any ordinance or resolution by public officer, or who spends more than $250 in any calendar year, not including personal travel, food, lodging expenses or informational material to promote or oppose passage, approval or veto of legislation, ordinance, or resolution; or who is employee of executive or judicial branch of state government and who promotes or opposes passage, approval or veto of any legislation, ordinance, or resolution. (21-5-70). Lobbyists must register with State Ethics Commission (21-5-71) and pay registration fee of $200, identification card fee of $5 and miscellaneous fees for filing reports, supplemental registration and late penalties (21-5-71). Registration expires Dec. 31 of each year. (21-5-71). Civil penalty of up to $2,000 per violation for failure to comply with registration, conduct or disclosure requirements of 21-5-71. (21-5-72). Any lobbyist who discusses pending measures on floor of General Assembly while General Assembly in session is guilty of misdemeanor. (28-7-4, 5). Lawyers or agents may not accept contingent compensation for aiding or opposing legislation. (28-7-3).

Ethics in Government Act applies to members of Georgia House of Representatives and Georgia Senate and certain other public officials. (21-5-1 et seq.).

REPORTS:

Supreme Court and Court of Appeals Reports are published by and at expense of state. (50-18-20 et seq.). Both Supreme Court and Court of Appeals reports numbered consecutively beginning with 1.

Unofficial Reports.—Georgia decisions are reported in Southeastern Reporter from 1887 to present.

Digests.—Georgia Digest and Southeastern Digest (both West Pub. Co.) with pocket parts cover all Georgia cases. Others are: Michie's Encyclopedia Digest of Georgia Reports with Supplements; Steven's Index-Digest of Georgia Reports; Digestive Index of Decisions of Georgia Supreme Court and Court of Appeals.

STATUTES:

Official Code of Georgia Annotated (O.C.G.A.) is current compilation. This Code includes Code of 1981, effective Nov. 1, 1982, and all subsequent statutes, codified under proper sections. Code is kept up to date by annual pocket parts, thus statute laws of each session of Georgia Legislature are codified at end of year.

The Code is cited by combined numbers referred to by the compilers of the Code as section numbers although each number actually indicates title and chapter as well as section. For example, 36-3-9, while referred to as section number, actually indicates title 36, chapter 3, section 9.

Uniform Acts adopted are: Act to Secure the Attendance of Witnesses from without State in Criminal Proceedings (1976); Alcoholism and Intoxication Treatment (1974, Revised 1978); Anatomical Gift (1969); Certification of Questions of Law (1977); Child Custody Jurisdiction (1978); †Commercial Code (effective 1964); Conservation and Easement (1976); Controlled Substances (1974); Criminal Extradition (1951); Deceptive Trade Practices (1968); Declaratory Judgments (1945); Determination of Death (1982); †Disposition of Unclaimed Property (Revised) (1990); Enforcement of Foreign Judgments (1986); †Federal Tax Lien Registration, Revised (1968); Foreign Depositions (1959); †Insurers Liquidation (1949); Interstate Family Support (1982); Juvenile Court (1971); †Land Registration (1917); Management of Institutional Funds (1984); †Motor-Vehicle Certificate of Title (1961); †Partnership (Effective 1985); †Principal and Income (1991); †Reciprocal Enforcement of Support (1956, revised 1984); Reciprocal Transfer Tax (Effective 1980); Rendition of Prisoners as Witnesses in Criminal Proceedings (1976); †Revised Limited Partnership (1988); Rules of the Road (1974); Simplification of Fiduciary Security Transfers (1991); Simultaneous Death (1966); State Administrative Procedure (Model) (1964); Statutory Rule Against Perpetuities (1990);

See note at head of Digest as to 1998 legislation covered.

See Topical Index in front part of this volume.

STATUTES...*continued*

Testamentary Additions to Trusts (1991); Transfers to Minors (1990); Unclaimed Property. (1990).

Note: Uniform Commercial Code repealed the following Uniform Acts: Negotiable Instruments; Stock Transfer; Warehouse Receipts.

Other Uniform Acts. Relocation Assistance and Land Acquisition Policy (1973).

†Adopted with significant variations or modifications. See appropriate topics as to Acts within scope of Digest volume.

For text of Uniform Acts falling within the scope of the Martindale-Hubbell Law Digests see Uniform and Model Acts section.

UNIFORM LAWS:

For list of Uniform Acts in force in this state see topic Statutes.

CRIMINAL LAW

BAIL:

See topic Criminal Law.

CRIMINAL LAW:

Crimes and criminal procedure are regulated by Titles 16 and 17 of Code, respectively.

Indictment or Information.—Felony cases may proceed by indictment or presentment of grand jury, or, in noncapital cases, by accusation preferred by prosecuting officer of superior court if accused waives indictment in writing or if felony is enumerated in statute. (223 Ga. App. 573; 17-7-70.1). In misdemeanor cases, indictment by grand jury not required, and defendant may be tried on accusation preferred by district attorney. (17-7-54, 51, 70, 71). Traffic related misdemeanors may be tried on uniform traffic citation and complaint of c. 40–13. (17-7-71). No authority for commitment hearing after indictment. (237 Ga. 112, 227 S.E.2d 20). Although no general rule that indictment can be returned wholly on hearsay evidence, testimony of law enforcement official as to statements made by criminal suspect, although hearsay, is sufficiently reliable to form basis for return of indictment. (242 Ga. 542, 250 S.E.2d 376).

Bail.—Offenses of treason, murder, rape, aggravated sodomy, armed robbery, aircraft or motor vehicle hijacking, aggravated child molestation, aggravated sexual battery, aggravated stalking, manufacturing, dealing or trafficking in Schedule I or II controlled substance, cocaine or marijuana, kidnapping, arson, aggravated assault, or burglary if previously convicted of, on probation or parole respecting or on bail regarding charges of above offenses, bailable only before judge of superior court after hearing and determination that accused poses no significant risk of fleeing jurisdiction, of failing to appear, threat or danger to any person, community or property, committing any felony pending trial, or of intimidating witnesses or otherwise obstructing justice. However, if person is charged with serious violent felony and has previously been convicted of serious violent felony, there shall be rebuttable presumption that no condition or combination of conditions will reasonably assure appearance of person as required or assure safety of any other person or community. Person charged with misdemeanor cannot be refused bail, except bail for misdemeanor DUI offense given to discretion of court. (17-6-1, 40-6-391). Superior court judge may delegate authority to set bail by written order, except in cases in which life imprisonment or death penalty may be imposed. (17-6-1). In capital cases, if defendant meets burden of production establishing no significant risk of flight, threat to community, committing another crime, or intimidating witness, burden shifts to State to prove by preponderance of evidence that defendant not entitled to pretrial release. (262 Ga. 704, 425 S.E.2d 282). Presiding judicial officer shall notify superior court in writing within 48 hours that arrested person being held without bail and superior court shall notify district attorney and set date for hearing on issue of bail within 30 days after notice. (17-6-1). Judge of court of inquiry may establish schedule of bails, bail may be increased if offense involves acts of family violence. (17-6-1). Any accused can be released upon his or her own recognizance in discretion of court having jurisdiction over him or her. (17-6-12). Driver's license may be deposited in lieu of bail for certain traffic offenses (17-6-11), and if sheriff of county wherein offense occurred so chooses, for certain misdemeanors if arrested person has been incarcerated for at least five days. (17-6-2). ABA Standards, Criminal Appeals §2.5(a) and (b) (1974) adopted as to bail pending appeal, except bail denied where appeal taken frivolously or for delay. (238 Ga. 88, 230 S.E.2d 895). No appeal bond granted to any person sentenced to more than seven years' incarceration for murder, rape, aggravated sodomy, armed robbery, aggravated child molestation, kidnapping, trafficking in cocaine or marijuana, aggravated stalking or aircraft hijacking. (17-6-1). Bail, bond or recognizance forfeited by failure to appear at arraignment. (17-6-17). Judgment may be entered at execution hearing held between 120 and 150 days from defendant's failure to appear and after notice to surety. (17-6-71).

Legal Representation.—Courts must provide legal representation for indigent persons in criminal proceedings where there is threat of incarceration (17-12-2, 4) at every stage of criminal proceedings including appeal. No constitutional right to counsel at preindictment lineup (170 Ga. App. 88, 316 S.E.2d 483) or at first appearance hearings (250 Ga. 92, 390 S.E.2d 43). Georgia Indigent Defense Act adopted to establish Georgia Indigent Defense Council to help provide counsel to all citizens in criminal actions. (17-12-30 et seq.).

Witness Immunity.—Immunity is available upon request of District Attorney or Attorney General if request is approved by Superior Court judge. (24-9-28).

Uniform Criminal Extradition Act.—In effect. (17-13-20 et seq.).

Interstate Corrections Compact adopted to provide for cooperation among contracting states with regard to sharing of correctional facilities. (42-11-1, 2).

Georgia Youthful Offender Act adopted to provide for special correctional treatment and conditions of release for offenders between 17 and 25. (42-7-1 et seq.).

Interstate Agreement on Detainers adopted to encourage expeditious and orderly disposition of detainers and charges outstanding against prisoners based on untried indictments, informations or complaints. (42-6-20).

Compensation of Victims.—Victims and other claimants sustaining economic loss because of injury to or death of such victim as result of crime occurring on or after July 1, 1995, may receive award up to $10,000 upon approval by Georgia Crime Victims Compensation Board. (17-15-8). Adult offenders convicted of offenses of theft or damage to property must make restitution to victims. (17-14-17).

Crime Victims' Bill of Rights.—Victims of crimes are accorded certain basic rights including but not limited to right of notification of accused's arrest, release, scheduled court proceedings and parole. (17-17-1 et seq.; 42-1-11 et seq.).

Parole.—

Restrictions.—Inmates convicted of misdemeanor cannot be released on parole without serving six months or one-third of sentence, whichever is greater. Inmates convicted of felony cannot be released on parole without serving nine months imprisonment or one-third of prison sentence, whichever is greater. (42-9-45). Inmates committing offense involving family violence cannot be released on parole without completing Family Violence Counseling Program. (42-9-45). Inmates convicted of voluntary manslaughter, statutory rape, incest, cruelty to children, first degree arson, vehicular homicide, aggravated battery, aggravated assault, drug trafficking or Georgia RICO Act violations cannot be released on parole without serving seven years imprisonment or one-third of prison sentence on good behavior, whichever first occurs. Inmates convicted of murder, felony murder, armed robbery, kidnapping, rape, aggravated child molestation, aggravated sodomy or aggravated sexual battery cannot be paroled without serving minimum of ten years imprisonment. (17-10-6.1). Inmates convicted of "serious violent felony" and sentenced to life imprisonment cannot be paroled without serving 14 years of sentence. Inmates convicted of "serious violent felony" who receive commuted death sentence cannot be paroled without serving 25 years of sentence. (17-10-6.1). Inmates convicted of "serious violent felony", who have previously been convicted of "serious violent felony" in any state, must be sentenced to life imprisonment without parole. (17-10-7).

Notice to Victim.—Victim of crime must receive notice of decision to parole inmate. (42-9-47).

Information on Felony Parolees.—Whereabouts of felony parolees located in Georgia available from Board of Pardons and Paroles. (42-9-20.1).

Search and Seizure.—Exclusionary rule created by statute. (17-5-30). There is no "good faith" exception to exclusionary rule. (262 Ga. 573, 422 S.E.2d 426).

DRUGS:

Persons contracting with state agency must provide drug-free workplace for employees as condition of contracting with state agency. (50-24-1, et seq.).

Possession Near School or Certain Other Facilities.—Criminal offense to manufacture, possess or distribute controlled substances or marijuana within 1,000 feet of secondary or elementary school (16-13-32.4), park, playground, recreation center or publicly operated housing project (16-13-32.5).

Destruction of Seized Property.—State may destroy all instruments, devices or objects of drug activity within 90 days after making seizure. (16-13-32).

DEBTOR AND CREDITOR

ASSIGNMENTS:

Uniform Commercial Code.—Adopted. (Title 11).

Choses in action arising on contract may be assigned, but assignee (except holder in due course of negotiable paper) takes subject to equities existing between assignor and debtor at time of assignment and until notice of assignment given to debtor. (44-12-22). But see category Business Regulation and Commerce, topic Commercial Code. (11-1-206; 11-2-210; 11-9-318). Terms of executory contract may validly preclude assignment. (133 Ga. App. 27, 209 S.E.2d 661). But see category Business Regulation and Commerce, topic Commercial Code. (11-2-210; 11-9-318). Right of action for personal torts or for injuries arising from fraud is not assignable. (44-12-24).

Fund may be assigned in writing. (44-12-23). But see category Business Regulation and Commerce, topic Commercial Code. (11-2-210; 11-3-409; 11-3-410).

Recording.—See category Business Regulation and Commerce, topic Commercial Code. (11-9-102). If significant part of accounts or contract rights assigned, financing statement must be filed in order to perfect. (11-9-302). Filing to be at office of clerk of superior court in any county of state. (11-9-401).

Effect.—Written assignment transfers legal interest and assignee may sue at law; oral assignment recognized and protected in equity. Otherwise may sue only in name of assignor for use of assignee. (156 Ga. 109, 118 S.E. 691).

ATTACHMENT:

Actions in Which Allowed.—Attachment may issue in all cases of money demands, whether contract or tort, if statutory grounds exist. (18-3-1; 18-3-2). Attachment proceedings are strictly construed. (14 Ga. 230).

In Whose Favor Writ May Issue.—Attachment may issue on behalf of any plaintiff, including a nonresident or foreign corporation. (18-3-1; 48 Ga. App. 469, 172 S.E. 847). Surety may have attachment against his or her principal, but if surety has not paid obligation, money raised on attachment must be paid to obligee. (18-3-8).

Court Which May Issue Writ.—Any court of record in county of defendant's residence if known, or in county where property is located otherwise, other than probate court, may issue writ. (18-3-9).

Against Whom Writ May Issue.—Attachment may issue against nonresident corporation transacting business in state (18-3-7); joint contractors and partners (18-3-6);

ATTACHMENT . . . *continued*

administrator or executor of estate (18-3-5); or against any person or corporation if statutory grounds exist (18-3-1; 18-3-2).

Claims on Which Writ May Issue.—Attachment may issue in all cases of money demand. (18-3-2). Attachment may issue for money not yet due, but execution is stayed until maturity of debt. (18-3-3).

Time for Issuance.—An attachment may issue at any time prior to or during pendency of suit (18-3-4) on any day of week including Sun. (18-3-16).

Grounds.—General grounds are that debtor: (1) is nonresident; (2) moves or is about to move domicile outside county; (3) absconds; (4) conceals himself or herself; (5) resists legal arrest; or (6) is causing his or her property to be removed outside state. (18-3-1).

Proceedings to Obtain.—Creditor, his or her agent, attorney, partner or joint creditors (18-3-11), must make affidavit before judge of any court of record, except probate court, in county in which defendant or property is located. (18-3-9). Judge must inquire into facts alleged. (18-3-9). Defendant must be given notice of attachment after issued. (18-3-14). Defendant entitled to post-attachment hearing. (18-3-15).

Attachment Bond.—Creditor must file bond in not less than double amount of debt conditioned to pay damages and costs if attachment not successful. (18-3-10). Agent or attorney making affidavit may sign bond for his or her principal. (18-3-11). Attorney cannot be surety, nor can nonresident unless he or she owns real estate in county. (18-3-12).

Forms.—For all cases of attachment, §18-3-19 provides forms of affidavit, bond, attachment and order authorizing issuance of attachment.

Levy.—Attachment may be levied on real or personal property of defendant anywhere in state (18-3-30), including investment securities where actually seized (11-8-317); goods covered by negotiable document of title where document is not outstanding (11-7-602); and debtor's rights in collateral (11-9-311). See category Business Regulation and Commerce, topic Commercial Code. Defendant to be notified by one of stated methods (18-3-14) and has right to post-seizure hearing (18-3-15). If plaintiff wishes to levy in different county, judge must make and certify copies of original attachment, bond and affidavit. Officer of county where property located must levy and return property to court where original attachment filed. (18-3-32).

Lien.—Between attachments, lien created by levy, not judgment. Between attachment and ordinary judgment, judgment fixes lien, not levy; but lien of attachment prior to ordinary judgment obtained on suit filed after levy has priority. Lien on real property effective from levy if recorded within five days from date of recording if recorded after five days. (18-3-74; 18-3-75).

Priorities.—Between attachments, attachment first levied has priority. (18-3-74; 18-3-75). Officer must levy attachments in order received. (18-3-31). Attachment on real property must be recorded. (18-3-31).

Indemnity.—No statutory provision.

Service and Notification to Defendant.—Notice of attachment may be given by any one of following: (1) pursuant to Civil Practice Act (9-11-4); (2) within three days of levy on attachment by written notice to defendant at last known address, by registered or certified mail, return receipt requested; return receipt must be filed with court clerk; (3) by written notice personally delivered to defendant; person making delivery must file certificate with court clerk; (4) within three days after levy upon defendant's property by written notice to defendant, if address is known, by ordinary mail; certification of same must be filed with court clerk; (5) upon defendants living outside state or who cannot be found within state, by special means provided in statute. "Written notice" consists of copy of affidavit and bond, or document naming plaintiff and defendant, amount claimed in affidavit and court where filed. (18-3-14).

Return.—Attachments returnable to court where filed and governed by same rules of procedure and practice governing all civil actions. (18-3-17).

Release of Property.—Defendant may replevy property attached by giving bond with security payable to plaintiff for not less than double amount claimed or twice value of property. (18-3-33).

Sale.—No statutory provision.

Third party claims may be asserted before or after judgment in attachment suit. (18-3-55). Officer must return claim to court issuing attachment except that claim involving land always returnable to superior court. (18-3-50). Claimant may replevy property by giving forthcoming bond to levying officer. (18-3-51). If claimant unsuccessful and property does not bring enough to satisfy judgment, plaintiff may sue claimant on bond for use and hire of property and deterioration in value, but may not recover more than enough to satisfy unpaid portion of debt. (18-3-54).

Defendant's Post Seizure Hearing.—Defendant may traverse sufficiency or veracity of affidavit any time after writ of attachment issues and hearing shall be held within ten days of filing of traverse. (18-3-15).

Vacation or Modification.—Judgment in attachment may be set aside for fraud or want of consideration. (18-3-71).

Proceedings After Attachment.—Governed by Ga. Civil Practice Act, 9-10-1 et seq. (18-3-18). See also category Civil Actions and Procedure, topic Pleading.

CREDITORS' SUITS:

Creditor petition may be filed at instance of any creditor, privilege being extended to all to appear and become parties in reasonable time. (23-2-95). Equitable assets may be reached by a creditor where he or she shows that there is danger of not being satisfied out of legal assets. (23-2-96). Equitable assets are distributed according to equitable rules; legal assets according to legal liens and priorities. (23-2-90).

See also topics Executions, Fraudulent Sales and Conveyances.

EXECUTIONS:

See also topic Practice.

Form.—Execution is by writ of fieri facias, which must follow the judgment (9-13-3); but any judge of the superior court may frame execution to carry into effect any lawful judgment or decree rendered by court (9-13-4).

Process to enforce judgment for payment of money shall be writ of execution, unless court directs otherwise. (9-11-69).

The writ is issued by the clerk of the court in which judgment was obtained, is attested in the name of the judge of such court, is directed "to all and singular sheriffs of this state and their lawful deputies" and dates from time of issuance (9-13-10).

Exemptions.—See topic Exemptions.

Time for Issuance.—Execution must be issued within seven years after judgment or entry made on execution docket every seven years, or else judgment becomes dormant; may be revived within three years from time it becomes dormant. (9-12-60, 61).

No execution issues upon judgment nor may proceedings be taken for enforcement of judgment in court of record until ten days after entry except execution may issue immediately after default judgment, or upon written agreement between all parties being filed with clerk of court. (9-11-62). Motion for new trial or for judgment notwithstanding verdict acts as supersedeas unless court orders otherwise, but court may require bond. (9-11-62).

Stay.—Execution may be stayed by party against whom judgment entered giving (within four days after adjournment of court) bond with good security for payment of amount due and costs within 60 days. (9-13-70). At expiration of 60 days, if judgment not paid execution issues against security and party without further proceedings. (9-13-70). In attachment suit on debt not due execution stayed until debt due. (18-3-3). Supersedeas stays execution. (5-6-46, 47).

Recording and Lien.—Execution must be recorded in execution docket in office of clerk of superior court in order that lien may be created; lien dates from entry on execution docket. (9-12-81). Fee for filing fieri facias, $4.50 first page, $2 per page after first. (15-6-77).

Levy.—Execution may be levied on all estate, real and personal, of defendant subject to levy and sale. (9-13-10).

Levy of execution from magistrate court, from county, city and superior courts and court of ordinary by sheriff. Defendant in fi. fa. may point out property to be levied on first. (9-13-50). Officer making levy must enter on process plain description of property levied on and amount of interest of defendant therein. (9-13-12). Constable cannot levy on real estate, unless he or she first makes entry of no personal property sufficient to satisfy judgment, or defendant points out real estate. (9-13-53). Levy on real estate by constable returned to sheriff, who proceeds as though he or she made levy himself. (9-13-53). Officer levying must within five days, give notice of levy to tenant in possession, or mail such notice to owner if address be known. (9-13-13). When levying on land, written notice must be personally delivered or sent by certified mail to possessor and to defendant (if not same person). (9-13-13[a]). Procedure for levy on stock of bank or other corporation is governed by 11-8-317. See category Business Regulation and Commerce, topic Commercial Code.

Return.—Execution is returnable to next term of court after issuance. (9-13-9).

Priorities.—No preference in case of judgments at same term of court because of first placement with levying officer. (9-12-87).

Claims of Third Persons.—Where third person claims property, enforcement of execution thereon may be postponed by making oath to claim and filing bond, payable to plaintiff in not more than double amount of execution or double value of property if property worth less than amount of execution on property, conditioned to pay plaintiff all damages assessed if claim found to be filed for delay only. (9-13-90, 91, 93). Third person may obtain possession of property by filing forthcoming bond with levying officer. (9-13-94). Claim may be made in forma pauperis. (9-13-92). Claim so interposed tried by jury in court issuing execution. (9-13-98, 100). If jury finds claim was for delay only, minimum damage award of 10% of value of property if property worth less than execution, or 10% of execution if property worth more than amount due on execution. (9-13-101, 105).

Satisfaction.—If plaintiff, for consideration, releases property subject to execution, it is satisfaction of execution to extent of value of released property. (9-13-72). If senior execution creditor allows fund in possession of sheriff to be applied to junior fi. fa., pro tanto extinguishment of senior creditor's lien as to third persons. (9-13-73). Contract not to enforce judgment or execution, supported by consideration, releases same. (9-13-74). Security or joint debtor who pays more than his or her proportion of execution, has control of execution. (9-13-77, 78). Plaintiff or his or her attorney must direct clerk of court issuing execution to mark any partial satisfactions. (9-13-79). Upon full satisfaction of judgment by judgment debtor, plaintiff or his or her attorney shall timely direct clerk to cancel execution and mark judgment satisfied. (9-13-80[a]). Judgment debtor has right of action as against plaintiff if clerk not directed timely to cancel execution and mark judgment satisfied upon satisfaction of judgment. Failure to direct cancellation and satisfaction within 60 days of judgment satisfaction is prima facie evidence of untimeliness. (9-13-80[b]).

Forthcoming Bond.—When execution levied on personal property, and claim of illegality filed, person filing claim of illegality may give bond to levying officer in double value of property, conditioned for delivery of property at time and place of sale, if legality upheld. (9-13-126).

Sale.—Under execution from superior court made by sheriff or coroner at courthouse door of county where levy was made (or elsewhere in county by general order of presiding judge of superior court; 9-13-161) on 1st Tues. in each month (1st Wed. of month if 1st Tues. of month falls on New Year's Day or Independence Day), between 10 A. M. and 4 P. M. and at public outcry. Articles difficult and expensive to transport may, by proper advertisement, be sold without exposure at courthouse door. (9-13-161). Advertisement must be once a week for four weeks preceding sale day in newspaper published in county, or if no newspaper published therein, in paper having largest general circulation in county. (9-13-140). Perishable property may be sold on quick order from judge of superior court or, in his or her absence, judge of probate court. (9-13-163).

See note at head of Digest as to 1998 legislation covered.

See Topical Index in front part of this volume.

EXECUTIONS . . . *continued*

Redemption.—Not provided for except where sale under tax execution. See category Taxation, topic Property Tax, subhead Redemption, §48-4-40 et seq.

Supplementary Proceedings.—Judgment creditor may examine any person, including judgment debtor, in manner provided for taking depositions or interrogatories. (9-11-69). See category Civil Actions and Procedure, topic Depositions and Discovery.

EXEMPTIONS:

Constitutional Homestead.—Any debtor is entitled to hold real or personal property or both, up to $5,000 in value, exempt from levy and sale except for taxes, purchase money, labor done or material furnished therefor or for removal of incumbrances thereon. (44-13-1). No exemption for cash; must be invested in personalty. (44-13-15). Application is made by petition to probate judge of county of beneficiary's residence, showing qualifications for exemption. (44-13-4). Petition must be accompanied by list of creditors and by schedule describing all real and personal property of applicant and indicating property to be exempted. (44-13-4). Notice to creditors of application and of date of hearing required. (44-13-8, 9). Property so set aside is exempt during disability of beneficiaries in whose favor exemption allowed. In order to procure levy for debt to which exemption is not applicable, affidavit must be made specifying to which of classes named above debt belongs. (44-13-60).

Statutory or Short Homestead.—There is also what is known as statutory or short homestead. (44-13-100). Individual is compelled to elect between $5,000 Constitutional exemption and Statutory homestead, and cannot supplement one with other, unless homestead and exempted property is lost by virtue of sale under outstanding claim, in which event election shall not bar application for homestead and exemption not liable to outstanding claim. (44-13-22). Statutory homestead is exempt from levy and sale except for purchase money and taxes. (44-13-107).

Waiver of statutory or short homestead and Constitutional homestead possible, except that no waiver is effective as to wearing apparel and $300 of household and kitchen furniture and provisions (44-13-40) to be selected by debtor and his family (44-13-41).

Rights of Wife and Minor Children.—Should debtor refuse to apply for exemption, debtor's spouse, or any person acting on behalf of dependents of debtor may apply for exemption. (44-13-2).

Sale for Reinvestment.—Exempted property may be sold for reinvestment on application to judge of superior court of county where debtor resides or where property located. (44-13-17).

Exemption of Wages.—See topic Garnishment.

Temporary Alternative Bankruptcy Exemption.—Georgia bankrupts may elect alternative exemptions but with smaller dollar amounts. Election of federal exemptions (11 U.S.C. §522) prohibited. Major Georgia exemptions different from federal: $5,000 real or personal property used as residence, with remainder of that amount plus $400 in any property; $1,000 in all motor vehicles; $200 in any particular item of household goods, furnishings, clothing and the like, subject to $3,500 maximum for all such household items; $500 in jewelry; $500 in implements, professional books, or tools of trade; certain alimony and pension payments; certain social security, veterans' disability and similar benefits. (44-13-100).

FORECLOSURE:

See topic Liens; category Mortgages, topics Chattel Mortgages, Mortgages of Real Property.

FRAUDULENT SALES AND CONVEYANCES:

Following transfers are fraudulent and void as to creditors: (1) assignment or transfer by insolvent debtor in trust or for benefit or on behalf of creditors where any trust or benefit reserved to assignor or any person for him or her; (2) conveyance of real or personal estate, bond, suit, judgment, execution or contract made or had with intent to delay or defraud creditors where intent known to party taking; (3) voluntary conveyance by insolvent debtor, not for valuable consideration. (18-2-22). But permission to debtor to exercise dominion over property conveyed, assigned or mortgaged to secure debt is not fraudulent as to other creditors. (18-2-24). Fraudulent conveyance under 18-2-22 will support award of damages against debtor. (257 Ga. 677, 362 S.E.2d 214).

Uniform Commercial Code adopted.(Tit. 11).

Uniform Fraudulent Conveyance Act not adopted.

Innocent purchaser from fraudulent vendee for value and without notice, before any step taken to avoid fraudulent transfer, obtains good title against creditors of fraudulent vendor. (18-2-23).

Remedies of Creditors.—Creditor may in one suit sue for recovery on debt and to set aside fraudulent conveyance. (203 Ga. 608, 48 S.E.2d 89). Creditor may levy an execution on property. (165 Ga. 694, 141 S.E. 900). Creditor may proceed by attachment against debtor. (124 Ga. 544, 52 S.E. 598). Creditor may garnish purchaser. (131 Ga. 1, 62 S.E. 82).

Bulk Sales.—Governed by Uniform Commercial Code. (11-6 et seq.). Following sections of Uniform Commercial Code not adopted: §6-106, §6-107(2)(e), §6-108(3)(c); §6-109(2). Twelve months substituted for six months in §6-111. (11-6-111). Public notice by advertising once a week for two weeks in newspaper in county where acquired business had place of business. (11-6-106). No personal liability imposed on purchaser. (125 Ga. App. 408, 187 S.E.2d 922).

GARNISHMENT:

Where money judgment obtained, judgment creditor may obtain summons of garnishment on person believed to be indebted to or to have property or effects of defendant, requiring garnishee to appear not sooner than 30 days and not later than 45 days after service to answer as to such indebtedness or property. (18-4-60; 18-4-62). Garnishment not available if based on judgment obtained in other than Georgia state court. (18-4-60). Prior to judgment, garnishment may issue only in following cases: (a) when defendant resides without state; (b) when defendant is actually removing, or about to remove, without limits of county; (c) when defendant is causing his or her property to be removed beyond limits of state; (d) when defendant has transferred, or has threatened to transfer, or is about to transfer property to defraud or delay his or her creditors; or (e) when defendant is insolvent. (18-4-40).

Property Which May Be Reached.—All debts owed by garnishee to defendant and all property, money or effects of defendant in possession or control of garnishee at date of summons or coming into possession or control of garnishee up to date of answer, except exempted property, may be garnished. (18-4-20). Partnership interests may be garnished. (14-8-28). Relation of garnishee and debtor immaterial. (154 Ga. App. 211, 267 S.E.2d 849). Salaries due officials or employees of state government and of its political subdivisions are subject to garnishment. In such cases, summons shall be issued by court located in county where warrant on government treasury drawn or check to defendant issued, and shall be directed to political entity and served upon person authorized to draw warrant or to issue check or upon chief administrative officer of political subdivision. (18-4-21).

Portions of disposable earnings of individual and pensions paid to retired employees are partially exempt (see subhead Earnings and Pensions, infra). Collateral securities in hands of creditor are exempt. (18-4-20[c]). Garnishment may not issue against receiver. (9-8-12). Creditor barred by existing, though unrecorded, set-offs and other claims in favor of garnishee. (154 Ga. App. 211, 267 S.E.2d 849). Wages of government employees exempt where liability incurred in scope of employment while responding to emergency. (18-4-21). Individual Retirement Accounts exempt from garnishment in non-bankruptcy situations. (173 Ga. App. 511, 326 S.E.2d 861; 18-4-22).

Bank Accounts.—Joint checking account not subject to garnishment for debt of one holder alone since one holder alone could not get funds from bank. (National Bank of Georgia v. 1616 Reminic Ltd. Partnership, No. C84-151, slip op. [N.D. Ga. Apr. 10, 1986]). Garnishee/bank must take whatever steps necessary to ensure that they can comply with garnishment laws of this state. Uncertainty as to what accounts are subject to garnishment should be filed as part of garnishee's answer stating such. (219 Ga. App. 299, 464 S.E.2d 903). See subhead Earnings and Pensions, infra.

Jurisdiction; Proceedings to Obtain.—Prejudgment garnishment is available where action is pending against defendant and is begun by making application under oath to judge of any court of record, other than probate courts, in county of residence of garnishee and having jurisdiction over garnishee. Application must set forth specific facts showing grounds for garnishment (see Introduction and subhead Property Which May Be Reached, supra) as well as name of court where suit pending, case number of suit, and amount claimed in suit. (18-4-41). Applicant must present bond with good security conditioned to pay defendant all costs and damages in event that amount claimed due was not due or that no lawful ground for issuance of such garnishment existed or that property sought was not subject to garnishment. Bond must be approved by clerk of court where application made and must be in twice amount claimed due (18-4-43); except that bond or deposit with court not required for action to collect fines, costs, restitution and separation ordered as condition of probation (42-8-34.2[c]). Upon approval of application, judge enters order and clerk issues summons. (18-4-42). Copy of summons must be served on defendant. (18-4-44).

Postjudgment garnishment begun by filing affidavit with clerk of any court having jurisdiction over garnishee. Affidavit must set forth existence of judgment against named defendant, amount claimed to be due, name of court which rendered judgment and case number. Plaintiff must make affidavit in one of five ways: (1) make affidavit before and obtain approval of judge of court where garnishment proceeding is filed; (2) make affidavit before and obtain approval of judge of court that rendered judgment on which garnishment based; (3) make affidavit before and obtain approval of judge of any court of record; (4) make affidavit before any officer authorized to administer oaths, including notary, submit by mail or in person to any judge described above and obtain his or her approval; or (5) make affidavit before clerk or deputy clerk of court in which garnishment filed or before any officer described above and obtain approval by clerk or deputy clerk under court rules of supervision, if provided. Filing of approved affidavit entitles plaintiff to issuance by clerk of summons of garnishment. (18-4-61). Summons of garnishment may set forth defendant's social security number if known. (18-4-20[h]). Summons of garnishment upon financial institution must state following information if reasonably available: name of defendant, all known nicknames, aliases, former or maiden names and trade names, service and current addresses, social security number or tax i.d. number and account numbers. (18-4-20[i]). If no summons issued within two years, garnishment proceeding based on that affidavit automatically dismissed. (18-4-63[b]). Posting of bond no longer required.

Notice must be given to defendant of filing of first summons, and of issuance of any additional summons where no notice given within 90 days immediately preceding issuance of additional summons. (18-4-64[a]). Notice effected by one of eight methods: (1) notice served with copy of summons as soon as reasonably practicable after filing of garnishment through office of sheriff or marshal, proceedings for such service to be initiated by plaintiff at time garnishment filed; (2) written notice sent to defendant's last known address by registered or certified mail, return receipt requested, after issuance of summons and not more than three business days after service to garnishee, return receipt or affirmed notice of failure to accept delivery to be filed with clerk of garnishment court, either to be deemed notice to defendant; (3) service by personal delivery of written notice within time period described in (2) by plaintiff or his or her attorney or agent, certificate of service to be filed with clerk; (4) when judge or clerk is satisfied by affidavit that defendant resides out of state or cannot be located by diligent search, levy and attachment of lien of garnishment is sufficient notice, except where plaintiff has actual knowledge of defendant's address, or address at which defendant was served in suit creating judgment in which case plaintiff to mail written notice to that address within period described in (2) and file certificate of mailing with clerk; (5) where defendant is not resident of state or cannot be located by diligent search, has departed state, or concealed his or her residence, two publications of written notice in paper carrying sheriff's advertisements in each county where summons served shall be sufficient notice, where publications are at least six days apart, and are not more than 21 days after service on garnishee, where certification of publications filed with clerk,

See note at head of Digest as to 1998 legislation covered.

See Topical Index in front part of this volume.

GA – 33

GARNISHMENT . . . *continued*

unless plaintiff has actual knowledge of defendant's address, in which case plaintiff to mail notice within period described in (2) and file certificate of mailing with clerk; (6) where garnishment proceeding begun within 60 days after judgment, written notice by ordinary mail to address at which defendant served in suit creating judgment is sufficient where certificate of mailing filed with clerk; (7) where defendant's address is known, notice is sufficient where plaintiff sends written notice by ordinary mail and files certificate of mailing with clerk (18-4-64[a]); or (8) receipt by defendant of actual timely notice of summons of garnishment to constitute notice (18-4-64[b]). With corporations, service upon agent in charge of office or other place of business where defendant is employed is preferred; if such service cannot be made, then service of either registered office or principal place of business of corporation is sufficient. (18-4-23). Notice consists of copy of summons or document including names of plaintiff and defendant, amount claimed in affidavit of garnishment, statement that garnishment has been or will be served on garnishee, and name of court issuing summons. (18-4-64[c]). Methods of notification cumulative, can be used in any sequence or combination. Time limit for subsequent method tolled while reasonable and diligent good faith attempt to use another method first is in progress. (18-4-64[d]). No money or other property to be distributed or judgment rendered against garnishee until after ten days from date of compliance with at least one method of notification. (18-4-64[e]).

Answer of Garnishee.—Garnishee must file answer describing property subject to garnishment not sooner than 30 days and not later than 45 days after service of summons. (18-4-62). Garnishee has common law right of set-off, but must exercise same prior to filing answer or it is forfeited. (187 Ga. App. 530, 370 S.E.2d 751). Garnishee must deliver to court any money or property admitted in answer to be subject to garnishment, and must hold contents of safe-deposit box containing property admitted in answer to be subject to garnishment. (18-4-84). If garnishee/bank is unsure as to what account is subject to garnishment, garnishee/bank must include that in its answer. (219 Ga. App. 299, 464 S.E.2d 903).Copy of answer must be served on plaintiff or attorney if name and address of plaintiff or attorney appear on face of summons. (18-4-83). Plaintiff or other claimant may traverse answer within 15 days after it is served. (18-4-85). If garnishee fails to serve answer, traverse may be filed within 15 days after actual notice of answer received. (18-4-83). Garnishee's answer may be filed in unverified form if it complies with format in 18-4-66(4). (170 Ga. App. 668, 317 S.E.2d 897). Garnishee may deduct $25 or 10% of amount paid into court, whichever is greater, not to exceed $50 as reasonable attorney's fees or expenses. (18-4-97[a]).

Release of Summons.—Clerk of court must issue release of garnishment if: (1) plaintiff or plaintiff's attorney so requests in writing; (2) amount claimed due together with costs paid into court; (3) dissolution bond filed by defendant and approved by clerk; (4) release ordered by any judge after hearing; or (5) garnishment is dismissed. (18-4-6). Release relieves garnishee of duty to file answer and authorizes delivery of property to defendant. (18-4-80).

Practice and Procedure.—Except as specifically otherwise provided, procedure, including discovery, shall be same as provided for other civil actions in Georgia Civil Practice Act. (18-4-1, -2).

Adverse Claims.—At any time before judgment rendered on garnishee's answer or before money or other property subject to garnishment distributed, defendant or other claimant may become party to garnishment. Defendant may file traverse to plaintiff's affidavit and must have hearing not more than ten days from date traverse filed. (18-4-93). Before judgment entered on garnishee's answer, other claimant may become party by filing claim under oath averring a superior claim to that of plaintiff to money or property in hands of garnishee. (18-4-95).

Judgment.—If garnishee fails to answer by 45th day after service of summons, he or she will be in default. Default may be opened as matter of right by filing answer and paying costs within 15 days of default. After 15 days following default, judgment may be entered against garnishee for amount claimed due on judgment against defendant. (18-4-90). On motion filed not later than 60 days from actual notice to garnishee of entry of judgment against him or her, he or she may have judgment modified upon payment of all accrued costs of court to reduce liability to greater of $50 or $50 plus amount garnishee was indebted to defendant from time of service of summons through last day for timely answer, less lawful exemptions. (18-4-91).

Continuing Garnishment.—Where money judgment obtained in state or federal court, plaintiff entitled to continuing garnishment against employer of defendant. (18-4-110). Debt owed at time summons served plus debts accruing through 179th day thereafter are subject. (18-4-111). Procedures generally similar to those for other garnishments. (18-4-20, -22[b]). First answer to summons must be filed no later than 45 days after service of summons; subsequent answers must be filed no later than 45 days after previous answer date; last required answer must be filed within 195 days after service of summons. (18-4-113). Filing of traverse by defendant to answer of summons does not relieve garnishee of filing additional answers or continuing to withhold funds and deliver funds to court. (18-4-116). Employer not subject to garnishment after termination of employee. (18-4-117).

Discharge of Garnished Employee.—No employer may discharge employee by reason of garnishment of earnings for any one indebtedness, even though more than one summons served with respect to such indebtedness. (18-4-7).

Earnings and Pensions.—Personal earnings of defendant not subject to garnishment prior to judgment. (18-4-46). Maximum amount of disposable earnings subject to garnishment after judgment may not exceed lesser of: (1) 25% of that week's disposable earnings; or (2) amount by which that week's disposable earnings exceeds 30 times federal minimum hourly wage. (8-4-20[d][1]). Pension or retirement payments are exempt until paid or otherwise transferred and then limited in amount as above; where garnishment of pension or retirement fund based on alimony or child support, 50% of weekly disposable earnings subject to garnishment. (18-4-22). IRA is retirement program exempt from garnishment under 18-4-22 until paid, unless based on alimony or child support. (National Bank of Georgia v. 1616 Reminic Ltd. Partnership, No. C84-151, slip op. [N.D. Ga. Apr. 10, 1986]). Where summons gives proper notice that it is based on judgment for alimony or child support, 50% of weekly disposable earnings subject to garnishment. (18-4-20; -22[b]). Wages due deceased employee of corporation doing business in state, up to $2,500 exempt from garnishment and may be paid to widow or minor children. (34-7-4). Wages owed to person involuntarily hospitalized whose wife was living with him at that time are exempt from garnishment. (29-5-12).

HOMESTEADS:

See topic Exemptions; category Taxation, topic Property Tax, subhead Exemptions from Property Taxation.

JUDGMENT NOTES:

Not recognized.

LEVY:

See topics Attachment, Executions.

LIENS:

Uniform Commercial Code.—Adopted. (11-9). See category Business Regulation and Commerce, topic Commercial Code.

Established in favor of: State of Georgia; counties and municipalities; creditors by judgment or decree; laborers; landlords; contractors, mortgagees, materialmen, subcontractors and materialmen and laborers furnishing material or labor to subcontractors, machinists and manufacturers of machinery; certain creditors against steam boats and other water craft; proprietors of saw mills, planing mills and other similar establishments; innkeepers, boarding house keepers, livery stable keepers, bailees, acceptors, carriers, pawnbrokers, factors, depositories and attorneys at law; owners of stallions, jacks, boars and bulls; railroad employees; owners of stock killed; persons furnishing supplies to railroads; jewelers (44-14-320, 361); and persons engaged in business of laundering, cleaning, tailoring, altering, repairing or dyeing clothing, goods, wearing apparel, shoes, carpets, rugs, or other similar articles (44-14-450). See also subhead Miscellaneous Liens, infra.

Artisans' Liens.—Mechanics of every sort, who have furnished labor or material in manufacturing or repairing personal property, and for storage of such property after its manufacture or repair, have a special lien thereon, which is superior to all other liens except tax liens, mechanic's liens on farm machinery or equipment arising after July 1, 1985, and liens of which mechanic had actual notice. Lien may be asserted by retaining property and mechanic not required to surrender property to holder of subordinate interests or lien. If property is surrendered, claim for lien must be filed within 90 days after completion of work (or within 180 days from repairs on aircraft or farm machinery) with clerk of superior court. (44-14-361.1, -363). If property is surrendered to debtor and lien is not filed, other personal property of debtor in possession of mechanic may be seized, if not consumer goods used for personal, family or household purposes. (44-14-363).

Depositories.—Involuntary, gratuitous or naked depositories have a lien on property in their possession for any expense incurred in caring for the property or in locating the owner thereof. (44-14-410). After two months property can be sold by depository after publishing notice, containing description of property, for two successive weeks prior thereto in newspaper of general circulation. (44-14-411). Proceeds of sale after deducting all expenses of depository are payable to owner provided he or she makes claim within one year from date of sale. (44-14-412).

Factor's Lien.—Factor's liens governed by Commercial Code. (11-9). See category Business Regulation and Commerce, topics Factors, Commercial Code.

Mechanics' Liens.—Mechanics of every sort who have taken no personal security for work done or material furnished, including architects, contractors, materialmen, registered land surveyors, registered professional engineers, registered foresters, subcontractors, laborers, machinists and manufacturers of machinery, who have done work or furnished material in building, repairing or improving real estate, have special lien on such real estate for amount of work done or materials furnished, which attaches unless owner can show that lien has been waived in writing or can produce sworn statement of contractor or other person at whose instance work was done or material furnished that agreed price has been paid. (44-14-361, 361.2). Payment defense of 44-14-361.1(a)(4) only applicable where owner can prove that payments were made to contractor and disbursed to materialmen in proper order under statute, and is not applicable where prelien payments to contractor are disbursed post-lien to interior-ranked lien claims. (267 Ga. 72; 475 S.E.2d 576). But supplier of supplier of materials not entitled to claim of lien under 44-14-360, -361. (126 Ga. App. 191; 190 S.E.2d 131). In no event may aggregate amount of liens exceed contract price. (44-14-361.1). Payee of check for merchandise delivered, or services rendered on merchandise delivered, on which payor stops payment has mechanic's lien for face amount of check where payment stopped within five days after delivery of merchandise. (44-14-516).

Contractor may file Notice of Commencement in county in which project is located, not later than 15 days after contractor commences work on property. (44-14-361.5).

In order to have and enforce such lien, lien claimant: (1) must have substantially complied with his or her contract; (2) must have filed for record his or her claim of lien, describing property, and stating amount claimed in office of clerk of superior court where property is located within three months after completion of work or furnishing of materials; (3) must, at time of filing his or her record claim of lien, send copy of lien registered or certified mail to owner of property or contractor, as agent of owner; and (4) must commence (a) his or her action against person with whom he or she contracted for recovery of his or her claim within 12 months after same became due, (b) his or her action of foreclosure against owner within same period and (c) file notice of such action with clerk of superior court of county where lien filed within 14 days after filing action. (44-14-361.1[a]). As between themselves, mechanics' liens rank according to filing dates. Mechanic's lien is inferior to: liens for taxes; general and special liens of laborers; general lien of landlord for rent when distress warrant is issued out and levied; claims for purchase money due to persons who have only given bonds for titles; and other general liens when actual notice of such liens was communicated before work was done or materials furnished. (44-14-361.1). Effective Jan. 1, 1994, any person having

See note at head of Digest as to 1998 legislation covered.

See Topical Index in front part of this volume.

GA – 34

LIENS . . . continued

right to lien (provides labor, services or materials for improvement of property) who does not have privity of contract with contractor must give Notice to Contractor to owner or agent of owner and contractor stating (a) name, address, phone number of person providing labor, services or materials, (b) name and address of each person such labor, services or materials are being furnished to, (c) name and location of project, and (d) description of labor, services or materials being provided and contract price or anticipated value. Notice to Contractor must be given within 30 days from filing of Notice of Commencement or 30 days following first delivery of labor, services or materials, whichever is later. (44-14-361.5).

If contractor or subcontractor procuring material, labor or supplies for repairing or improving real estate, buildings or structures absconds from state, dies, removes from state so personal jurisdiction cannot be obtained or is adjudicated bankrupt, persons furnishing material, labor or supplies need not file suit or obtain judgment against contractor or subcontractor as prerequisite to enforcing lien against property if suit filed within 12 months from time amount due. (44-14-361.1). Filing by materialman of claim in contractor's bankruptcy proceeding within 12 months from time amount became due satisfies requirement of commencement of action for recovery of amount of lien claim. (241 Ga. 589, 247 S.E.2d 76). In action to enforce lien, only judgment in rem may be rendered, and to avoid judgment against property, owner may either pay amount due or prove that he or she made payments to contractor which were properly applied. (44-14-361.1). Owner may discharge lien by filing bond. (44-14-364).

Preliminary notice of lien rights can be filed 30 days after potential claimant has provided materials or services. Notice should state name, address and telephone number of lien claimant, real estate owner, person who requested materials or services; and should include identifying description of materials, services and real estate against which lien can be claimed. Party filing must send copy of Notice to Contractor or property owner within seven days. (44-14-361.3). Party receiving preliminary notice may demand filing of lien claim by potential claimant within ten days of demand.

Form.—Demand statement should include all information in preliminary notice plus this statement:

"This demand was mailed to you on ___ pursuant to Code Section 44-14-361.4. You are notified that unless you file a claim of lien with respect to this claim on or before the tenth day after said date of mailing, your right to claim a lien will be dissolved." (44-14-361.4).

_____

Within ten days after claimant receives final payment for services and materials, he or she must cancel preliminary notice of lien rights or be liable to owner for all damages.

Form.—Cancellation form states:

"Clerk, Superior Court

of _____ County

You are authorized and directed to cancel of record the preliminary notice of lien rights which we filed on the property owned by (state name of owner) on (give date) and recorded by you in Book __, Page __, of preliminary notices kept by you.

This ___ day of _____, 19___.

                              _____
                              Lien Claimant or Attorney"

(44-14-362).

Form.—Substance of filing for record claim of lien shall be as follows:

"A.B., a mechanic, contractor, subcontractor, materialman, machinist, manufacturer, registered architect, registered land surveyor, registered forester, registered professional engineer, or other person (as the case may be) claims a lien in the amount of (specify the amount claimed) on the house, factory, mill, machinery, or railroad (as the case may be), and the premises or real estate on which it is erected, or built, of C. D. (describing the houses, premises, real estate, or railroad), for satisfaction of a claim which became due on (specify the date the claim was due) for building, repairing, improving, or furnishing material (or whatever the claim may be)." (44-14-361.1).

Waiver, Loss or Extinguishment.—Pawnees, factors, bailees, acceptors, and depositaries lose liens by surrendering property to debtor (44-14-401), as do persons retaining possession of articles laundered, cleaned, tailored, altered, repaired or dyed by them. (44-14-451). Lien for freight waived by contract or delivery. (46-9-191). Lien on real estate not lost by delivery of possession. (44-14-530). Supplier waives his or her lien by failing to inquire to what account payment is to be applied. (126 Ga. App. 119; 190 S.E.2d 104).

Right to claim lien or claim upon bond may not be waived prior to furnishing of labor, services or materials. For binding waiver or release of claim of lien: (1) instrument of waiver or release must be executed by claimant; (2) claimant must receive payment for claim; (3) waiver or release must follow substantially form of Unconditional Waiver and Release Upon Payment or, in event of retention, form of Interim Waiver and Release Upon Payment; and (4) will be binding against claimant, subject only to payment in full of amount specified in release or waiver. (44-14-366).

Form.—Substance of unconditional waiver and release upon final payment shall be as follows:

"STATE OF GEORGIA

COUNTY OF _____

The undersigned mechanic and/or materialman has been employed by _____ (name of contractor) to furnish _____ (describe materials and/or labor) for the construction of improvements known as _____ (title of the project or building) which is located in the City of _____, County of _____, and is owned by ____ ____ (name of owner) and more particularly described as follows: _____ (describe the property upon which the improvements were made by using either a metes and bounds description, the land lot, district, block and lot number, or street address of the project).

Upon the receipt of the sum of $_____, the mechanic and/or materialman waives and releases any and all liens or claims of liens or any right against any labor and/or material bond it has upon the foregoing described property.

Given under hand and seal this ____ day of _____, 19___.

_____   _____(SEAL)

(Witness)

Address:

_____,"

NOTICE: this document waives rights unconditionally and states that you have been paid for giving up those rights. This document is enforceable against you if you sign it, even if you have not been paid. If you have not yet been paid, use a conditional release form.

_____

Form.—Substance of interim waiver and release upon payment shall be as follows:

"STATE OF GEORGIA

COUNTY OF _____

The undersigned mechanic and/or materialman has been employed by _____ (name of contractor) to furnish _____ (describe materials and/or labor) for the construction of improvements known as _____ (title of the project or building) which is located in the City of _____, County of _____, and is owned by ____ ____ (name of owner) and more particularly described as follows: _____ (describe the property upon which the improvements were made by using either a metes and bounds description, the land lot, district, block and lot number, or street address of the project).

Upon the receipt of the sum of $_____, the mechanic and/or materialman waives and releases any and all liens or claims of liens it has upon the foregoing described property through the date of _____ (date) and excepting those rights and liens that the mechanic and/or materialman might have in any retained amounts, on account of labor or materials, or both, furnished by the undersigned to or on account of said contractor for said building or premises.

Given under hand and seal this ____ day of _____, 19___.

_____   _____(SEAL)

(Witness)

Address:

_____,"

_____

Form.—Affidavit of nonpayment under O.C.G.A. §44-14-366 shall be as follows:

"STATE OF GEORGIA

COUNTY OF _____

The undersigned mechanic and/or materialman has been employed by _____ (name of contractor) to furnish _____ (describe materials and/or labor) for the construction of improvements known as _____ (title of the project or building) which is located in the City of _____, County of _____, and is owned by ____ ____ (name of owner) and more particularly described as follows: _____ (describe the property upon which the improvements were made by using either a metes and bounds description, the land lot, district, block and lot number, or street address of the project).

Pursuant to O.C.G.A. §44-14-366 the undersigned executed a lien waiver and release with respect to this property dated _____, 19___. The amount set forth in said waiver and release ($_____) has not been paid, and the undersigned hereby gives notice of such nonpayment.

The above facts are sworn true and correct by the undersigned, this ____ day of ____ ____, 19__.

_____   _____(SEAL)
                                   Claimant's Signature

Sworn to and executed
in the presence of:

_____

Witness   _____

Address:

_____,"

Notary Public"

(44-14-366).

_____

Enforcement.—Lien on real estate foreclosed by petition to competent court within 12 months after claim became due, showing proper record of lien and notice of suit, describing property and showing compliance with statutory requirements. (44-14-360, -361, -530). Judgment against person with whom lienor contracted is prerequisite to enforcement of lien (116 Ga. App. 128, 157 S.E.2d 68) except where such person absconds, becomes bankrupt, etc. (44-14-361.1).

Statute providing for foreclosure of liens on personal property held unconstitutional. (364 F. Supp. 452). For foreclosure of security interests in personal property, see category Mortgages, topic Chattel Mortgages, subhead Foreclosure.

Redemption.—There is no right of redemption of property sold under foreclosure of any of the aforementioned liens, except lien for taxes. (48-4-40). See category Taxation, topic Property Tax, subhead Redemption.

Repairman.—Persons, firms or corporations that repair or service bicycles, motor scooters, mopeds, motorcycles, lawnmowers, garden equipment or other related equipment have possessory lien upon such items until charges have been paid. (44-14-460). Lien lost if item returned without first collecting repair charges. (44-14-461). If services or repairs are made and charges are not paid, repairman may sell item after 60 days after taking possession as long as repairman has given ten days' notice by certified mail to last known address of item's owner or person who delivered item, including in such notice (i) name of owner or person who delivered item, (ii) description of item, (iii) time and place of intended sale, (iv) amount of charges underlying sale, and (v) name of person, firm or corporation having possession of item and proposing to make sale. (44-

_____

See note at head of Digest as to 1998 legislation covered.

See Topical Index in front part of this volume.

LIENS . . . *continued*

14-463, 464). If charges are not paid within ten days after such notice is mailed, repairman may sell item. (44-14-464). If there is any residue from sale, it must be paid on demand to item owner. (44-14-465).

Satisfaction.—When lien satisfied, cancellation is by direction to clerk of superior court where lien recorded to mark same satisfied, dated and signed by lien holder. Clerk enters same of record.

Veterinarians.—Every licensed veterinarian and operator of facility for boarding animals or pets has lien on such animal or pet for payment of charges for treatment, board or care of such animal (44-14-490) and has power to dispose of animal if charges not paid within ten days of demand (44-14-491).

Assignment.—All liens may be assigned in writing. (44-14-324).

Attachment Lien.—See topic Attachment.

Attorney's Lien.—See category Legal Profession, topic Attorneys and Counselors.

Carrier's Lien.—See category Business Regulation and Commerce, topic Carriers.

Collateral Security.—See topic Pledges.

Commercial Real Estate Brokers.—See category Business Regulation and Commerce, topic Brokers.

Execution Lien.—See topic Executions.

Foreclosure on Security Interests.—See category Mortgages, topic Chattel Mortgages, subhead Foreclosure.

Judgment Lien.—See category Civil Actions and Procedure, topic Judgments.

Landlord's Lien.—See category Property, topic Landlord and Tenant.

Liens on Exempt Property.—See topic Exemptions.

Motor Vehicle Liens.—See category Transportation, topic Motor Vehicles, subhead Liens.

Real Estate Mortgage Lien.—See category Mortgages, topic Mortgages of Real Property.

Tax Lien.—See category Taxation, topic Taxes.

Miscellaneous Liens.—On boats and watercraft (44-14-510); on offspring of stallions, jacks, boars and bulls (44-14-511); for hauling lumber, stock or logs (44-14-512); in favor of planing mills (44-14-513); for articles furnished to sawmills (44-14-515); in favor of hospitals upon causes of action accruing to persons for injuries treated (44-14-470); for servicing or furnishing supplies for aircraft (44-14-518) on personal property in self storage facilities (10-4-212).

MECHANICS' LIENS:

See topic Liens.

PLEDGES:

Uniform Commercial Code.—Adopted. (Title 11). See category Business Regulation and Commerce, topic Commercial Code.

General powers of corporations include power "[t]o sell, convey, mortgage, pledge, . . . or otherwise dispose of all or any part of its property." (14-2-302[5]). Unless articles of incorporation require it, approval by shareholders of transaction described in subsection (b) of this code section is not required. (14-2-1201[c]).

Remedies of Pledgee.—See category Business Regulation and Commerce, topic Commercial Code.

RECEIVERS:

Receiver may be appointed when any fund or property in litigation and parties' rights cannot otherwise be fully protected; or when there is fund or property with no one to manage it (9-8-1); or when there is trust or joint property and danger of destruction or loss requires it (9-8-2).

Judge of Superior Court having jurisdiction may appoint receiver. (9-8-1).

Proceedings.—Petition must be verified by petitioner or supported by proof. (9-10-110). Action wherein receiver has been appointed may not be dismissed except by order of court. (9-11-66).

Qualification.—Receiver may at judge's discretion be required to give bond conditioned for faithful discharge of duties. (9-8-10).

Powers and duties are placed upon receivers by judicial order or decree; receivers are officers and servants of appointing court and are at all times subject to orders of court appointing them, and may be brought to account or removed at pleasure of court. (9-8-8). Terms on which receiver is appointed are in discretion of court. (9-8-3). Investment of funds in receivership subject to discretion and orders of judge. (9-8-7). Receiver is responsible for moneys placed in certain uninsured banks or trust companies which fail. (9-8-11).

Compensation is awarded by the court; not more than 8% of the first $1,000, 4% of the excess up to $5,000, 3% of the amount above $5,000 and not exceeding $10,000, and 2% of all sums over $10,000; provided that where receiver continues the business of an insolvent person, firm or corporation, a reasonable sum may be allowed for services in lieu of commissions; provided further that receivers and their attorneys may be allowed such compensation as their services are reasonably worth. (9-8-13[b], [c]).

REDEMPTION:

See topics Executions, Liens; categories Mortgages, topic Mortgages of Real Property; Taxation, topic Property Tax, subhead Redemption.

SUPPLEMENTARY PROCEEDINGS:

See topic Executions.

TRUSTEE PROCESS:

See topic Garnishment.

USURY:

See category Business Regulation and Commerce, topic Interest.

DISPUTE RESOLUTION

ALTERNATIVE DISPUTE RESOLUTION:

Uniform Rules for Dispute Resolution Programs.—Supreme Court of Georgia adopted in 1993 uniform rules for dispute resolution programs for state courts which have elected to use alternative dispute resolution processes of mediation, nonbinding arbitration, case evaluation or early neutral evaluation, summary jury trial, mini-trial or combinations thereof in court-annexed or court-referred program. (Georgia Supreme Court Alternative Dispute Resolution Rules, Appendix A, Uniform Rules for Dispute Resolution Programs). These uniform rules have been adopted for use by Georgia superior, state, probate, juvenile and magistrate courts. Check local court to determine if uniform rules have been implemented.

Referral To Alternative Dispute Resolution.—Any party to dispute may petition court to refer case to ADR process. (Uniform ADR Rule 2.5). Any contested civil, criminal or juvenile case may be referred to mediation by judge to whom case is assigned. Any contested civil case may be referred to nonbinding arbitration, case evaluation or early neutral evaluation or multi-door program by judge to whom case is assigned. (Uniform ADR Rule 2.1). Any party to dispute may petition court to have case removed from ADR process or to refer case to different ADR process. (Uniform ADR Rules 3.1 and 3.2).

Procedures for Alternative Dispute Resolution.—Appearance at ADR conference or hearing is required and failure to appear may subject party to citation for contempt and to impositions of sanctions. (Uniform ADR Rules 4.1 and 4.2). Attorneys are not required to attend mediation conferences. (Uniform ADR Rule 4.3). All neutrals in court-annexed or court-referred ADR program must be registered by Georgia Office of Dispute Resolution. (Uniform ADR Rule 5.1). All parties in court-annexed or court-referred ADR process are entitled to confidentiality to extent described by Georgia Supreme Court and neutrals acting in court-annexed or court-referred ADR process are entitled to immunity to extent described by Georgia Supreme Court. (Uniform ADR Rules 6.1 and 6.2). Agreements reached as result of court-connected ADR process are enforceable to same extent as any other agreements. (Uniform ADR Rule 8). Neutrals in court-annexed or court-referred ADR process will be chosen from neutrals registered by Georgia Office of Dispute Resolution. (Uniform ADR Rule 9.1). If parties referred by court to ADR process are unable to agree upon neutral within reasonable time, neutral will be selected by court. (Uniform ADR Rule 9.2). Appendix B to ADR Rules provides requirements for qualification and training of neutrals, which include requirement of at least 20 hours of classroom training for mediators and allows for grandfathering of experienced mediators. (Uniform ADR, Appendix B). Neutrals in arbitration and case evaluation or early neutral evaluation are required to be lawyers. (Uniform ADR, Appendix B).

Ethical Considerations.—Lawyer has duty to advise client as to various forms of dispute resolution and has duty to inform client of forms of dispute resolution which might constitute reasonable alternatives to litigation. (Georgia Code of Professional Responsibility, Rule 3-107, Ethical Consideration 7-5).

Education re Divorce.—Uniform superior court rule provides for establishment by any superior court circuit program designed to educate parties to domestic relations actions in regard to effects of divorce on minor children of marriage. (Uniform Superior Court Rule 24.8).

See also topic Arbitration and Award.

ARBITRATION AND AWARD:

Uniform Arbitration Act.—Not adopted.

Scope.—Georgia Arbitration Code applies to all disputes in which parties agree, after July 1, 1988, in writing to arbitrate. (9-9-2). §9-9-80 (as it existed prior to July 1, 1988) applies to construction contracts made between July 1, 1978 and July 1, 1988. (9-9-2[b]). Code does not apply to: (1) collective bargaining agreements between employers and labor unions; (2) insurance contracts; (3) other subject matters currently covered by arbitration statute; (4) loans or consumer financing for amounts of less than $25,000; (5) contracts for purchase of consumer goods or involving consumer acts or practices; (6) certain real estate sales or loan agreements unless arbitration provision initialed by parties; (7) employment agreements unless arbitration provision initialed by parties; and (8) agreement to arbitrate future claims arising out of personal injury. (9-9-2[c]).

Medical Malpractice.—Parties to medical malpractice claims may agree to submit claim for arbitration. (9-9-61 et seq.).

International Transactions.—Parties to international transactions may agree to submit claim to arbitration. (9-9-30 et seq.).

Contracts to Arbitrate Future Disputes.—Arbitration Agreement void under state law only if agreement to arbitrate all questions which may arise in execution of contract, both as to liability and loss. (193 Ga. App. 723, 389 S.E.2d 251). Unenforceable if to arbitrate all questions generally. Enforceable if provision clear and limited to certain questions. (133 Ga. App. 83, 210 S.E.2d 34).

Arbitrators.—Absent agreement by parties, arbitrators are appointed by court. (9-9-7).

Procedures.—Arbitrators appoint time and place of meeting and must give ten days notice to parties. (9-9-8). Parties are entitled to present pleadings, documents, testimony and to cross-examine witnesses. (9-9-8). Parties have right to obtain list of witnesses and to examine copy of documents relevant to arbitration. (9-9-9). Arbitrator has power to issue subpoenas. (9-9-9).

ARBITRATION AND AWARD . . . *continued*

Court Supervision.—Court has authority to stay arbitration or compel arbitration in certain circumstances. (9-9-6). Parties may seek injunctive relief or attachment to preserve rights pending arbitration. (9-9-4). Court order may be obtained to enforce subpoenas issued by arbitrator. (9-9-9).

Attorney's Fees.—There is no statutory prohibition on right to contract for recovery of attorney's fees in arbitration proceedings. (205 Ga. App. 561, 422 S.E.2d 918; 9-9-17).

Interest.—Arbitrator has inherent power to award prejudgment and post-judgment interest in absence of contrary provision in arbitration agreement. (231 Ga. App. 546, 499 S.E.2d 693).

Award.—Upon application of party within one year after award received, court must confirm arbitration award. (9-9-12). Application to vacate or modify must be made within three months of delivery of award. (9-9-13, -14). Statute provides exclusive grounds for vacating award. (266 Ga. 592, 468 S.E.2d 350; 9-9-13[b]). Award must be in writing, signed by all arbitrators and, unless parties agree or court orders otherwise, must be issued within 30 days after hearing. (9-9-10; 9-9-11).

DOCUMENTS AND RECORDS

ACKNOWLEDGMENTS:

Uniform Acknowledgments Act, Uniform Acknowledgment Act, or Uniform Recognition of Acknowledgment Act not adopted. Acknowledgments not required for real estate instruments (see topic Records, subhead Requisites for Recording), which are to be attested by two witnesses, one of whom must be attesting officer who affixes seal. When used, acknowledgments may be taken by following officers:

Within state: Judge of court of record (including municipal court), notary public, and, (within their own counties), magistrate, clerk or deputy clerk of superior court or of city court created by General Assembly. (44-2-15, -16). Statutory fee, $2. (45-17-11).

Outside state but within U.S.: Judge of court of record with genuine signature certified by clerk under seal of court, clerk of court of record under seal of court, or notary public or justice of peace with seal of office attached. If notary or justice of peace has no seal, his or her position must be certified by clerk of any court of record in county or city of his or her residence. No other authentication necessary. (44-2-21).

Outside United States: consul or vice-consul of U.S. (44-2-21).

Persons in or with U. S. Armed Forces.—As to notarial powers of officers in U. S. Armed Forces, see topic Notaries Public.

Disqualification.—Persons having personal or pecuniary interest in instrument are disqualified. (138 Ga. 258, 75 S.E. 248). However, bank employees, stockholders, directors, and officers who are notaries may sign as official witness or take acknowledgments of instruments to which bank is party if notary is not party to instrument or bank representative with respect thereto. (45-17-12).

General Requirement as to Taking: Not settled whether attesting witnesses must actually be present at time of execution. Best practice is to assure attesting witnesses' presence at time of execution. (87 Ga. 217, 13 S.E. 509; 132 Ga. 648, 64 S.E. 800).

General Requirements of Certificate.—No particular style or form required. Attestation or acknowledgment by consul or vice-consul of U.S., or judge of court of record, notary public, magistrate or clerks of court must have seal affixed. (44-2-21). Notarial seal must be affixed (by embossment or rubber or other type of stamp) showing notary's name, state and county of appointment and words "Notary Public." (45-17-6). Date of notarial act required, except for real estate instruments. (45-17-8.1). Best practice is to require seal, statement of jurisdiction and date of expiration of commission.

Effect of Acknowledgment.—Acknowledgment or attestation is required for deeds, mortgages and certain other instruments to be recorded (44-2-14; 44-2-15; see topic Records), and deed to realty must be attested by two witnesses before it can be recorded (44-5-30; 44-2-21). Instrument conclusively presumed executed in state and county where acknowledging officer is authorized to act. (44-2-17; 44-2-21). Acknowledgment or attestation not conclusive of facts certified therein. May be rebutted. (87 Ga. 217, 13 S.E. 509).

Proof by Subscribing Witnesses.—Where deed is signed by two witnesses, neither of whom is authorized officer, it may be proved for record by affidavit of either of such witnesses, before officer authorized to attest or take acknowledgment of such deed pursuant to 44-2-15. (44-2-18).

If both subscribing witnesses are dead or insane, or have moved from state, or are otherwise incapacitated to make affidavit, affidavit of third person as to such incapacity and genuineness of handwriting of subscribing witnesses is sufficient to admit deed to record. (44-2-19).

Alternative to Acknowledgment or Proof.—No statutory provision.

Authentication.—Except as indicated above, no authentication is needed with respect to acknowledgment designed for use within state. For authentication of acts, Georgia notaries public must have seal of office. (45-17-6). Acknowledgment for use outside state may be authenticated by certificate of authority from appointing clerk of superior court or Georgia Superior Court Clerk's Cooperative Authority. Fee: $2. (45-17-19[a])

Forms.—No forms are prescribed. The following may be used:

Forms

Attestation: Signed, sealed and delivered in the presence of (Official signature of officer) . . . . (L. S.)

Acknowledgment:
State of Georgia, County of . . . . ss.
I, A. B., a (state officer) residing in the county and state aforesaid, do certify that C. D., who is personally to me known, this day appeared before me personally and did

acknowledge that he or she did sign, seal and deliver the foregoing deed (or instrument) of his or her own free will and accord, for the purposes therein named and expressed.

In witness whereof, I have hereunto set my hand and official seal, this . . . . day of . . . . . 19. . . . .

Proof by Witness:
State of . . . ., County of . . . . ss.
Before me (name and title) personally came C. D., to me known to be the individual whose signature affixed to the foregoing deed as one of the witnesses thereto, who, being sworn, says that he (or she) was present at the time when said deed was executed; that he (or she) saw the same signed, sealed and delivered by A. B., whose signature is thereto affixed as grantor; that E. F., the other subscribing witness thereto, was likewise present at said time and witnessed said execution of said deed, and that he (or she), the said C. D., and the said E. F. then and there signed the same as attesting witnesses.

(Signed) C. D.

Sworn to and subscribed before me this . . . . day of . . . ., 19. . . . .
. . . . (Signature and title of officer).

Validating Acts.—If, subsequent to its execution, any recordable instrument is acknowledged before authorized officer, that fact certified on deed by such officer shall entitle it to be recorded. (44-2-16).

AFFIDAVITS:

May be made before following officers:

Within state: a notary public, magistrate, judge of court of law, or any other attesting officer of state or county where oath is made who is authorized by law to administer oaths. Official attestation of officer before whom oath or affidavit made prima facie evidence of proper authentication. (9-10-113). Oath cannot be administered telephonically. (218 Ga. App. 477, 462 S.E.2d 172).

Without state: notary public, magistrate, judge of court, or any officer authorized to administer oaths in state or county where made. Official attestation is prima facie evidence of proper authentication. (9-10-113).

Outside United States.—See topic Acknowledgments.

Persons in or with U.S. Armed Forces.—See topic Notaries Public.

Disqualification.—See topic Acknowledgments.

General Requirements of Jurat.—See topic Acknowledgments.

Authentication.—Notary's seal is sufficient authentication. (136 Ga. 241, 71 S.E. 162). Official character of other attesting officers must be authenticated by proper certificate. (121 Ga. 421, 49 S.E. 297).

Recordation of affidavit reciting facts of conveyance of land—see topic Records.

Use of Affidavit.—See category Civil Actions and Procedure, topic Pleading.

Alternative to Affidavit.—No statutory provision.

Form of Jurat.—

Form
Sworn to and subscribed before me this the . . . . . . day of . . . . ., 19. . . .
. . . ., Notary

NOTARIES PUBLIC:

Qualification.—Notaries public are appointed by clerks of the Superior Court. (45-17-1.1). Oath, but no bond required. (45-17-3). Applicant must be at least 18 and able to read and write English. (45-17-2). Except for special provisions for persons resident in bordering state with business or employment in Georgia (45-17-7), applicant must also be resident of state and county from which appointed (45-17-2). Statute specifies application information (45-17-2.1), and grounds for denial (45-17-2.3).

Authentication.— See topic Acknowledgments.

Seal.—Must provide seal for authentication of notarial acts (scrawl not sufficient). (45-17-6).

Powers and Duties.—Witness or attest signature or execution of deeds and other written instruments, take acknowledgments, administer oaths and affirmations in all matters incident to their commercial duties and other oaths and affirmations not required to be administered by other particular officers, witness affidavits upon oath or affirmation, take verifications upon oath or affirmation, make certified copies of original documents which are neither public documents nor publicly recorded documents for which certified copies are available from official source, and perform other acts authorized to perform by other laws of State of Georgia. (45-17-8).

Not lawful for notary public to issue attachments or garnishments or approve bonds for purpose of issuing attachments or garnishments or issue summons in dispossessory case, but may attest affidavit in attachment, garnishment or dispossessory action. (45-17-10).

Not obligated to perform notarial act for transaction known or suspected to be illegal, false or deceptive, for person being coerced or whose demeanor causes compelling doubts regarding person's knowledge of consequences of transaction, or in situation which compromises notary's impartiality, such as where disqualified. (45-17-8[b]). Notary disqualified when signer of document to be notarized or party to document or transaction. (45-17-8[c]). Must not execute notarial certificate containing statement known by notary to be false nor act with intent to deceive or defraud. (45-17-8[d]). Must confirm identity of signer, oath taker or affirmant based on personal knowledge or satisfactory evidence. (45-17-8[e]). Signature or certification by notary not evidence that notary had knowledge of contents of document. (45-17-8[f]).

Expiration of Commissions.—Date of expiration of commission need not be stated.

Territorial Extent of Powers.—Notary public may perform notarial acts in any county of state. (45-17-9).

Fees.—Regulated by statute. (45-17-11).

NOTARIES PUBLIC . . . *continued*

Commissioners of Deeds.—No provision.

Officers of U.S. Armed Forces are given powers to perform notarial acts for members of U.S. Armed Forces, and merchant seamen and certain other persons outside U.S. (45-17-31).

RECORDS:

Uniform Commercial Code.—Adopted. (Title 11).

Clerk of superior court has charge of all records relating to property.

Recordable Instruments and Place of Recording.—Deeds, options to purchase land (44-2-2), plats and maps (15-6-67), affidavits showing facts affecting title to land (44-2-20), mortgages, deeds to secure debt, trust deeds (44-14-35), bills of sale, conditional bills of sale, bonds for title, chattel mortgages, leases, usufructs (44-2-9), petitions in bankruptcy with schedules omitted, decrees of adjudication, orders approving trustee's bond (44-14-590), Federal tax liens (44-14-571), and all lien claims should be filed for record with clerk of superior court; in case of realty in county where land situated (see categories Mortgages, topic Mortgages of Real Property; Property, topic Deeds); in case of personalty, in county of owner's or mortgagor's residence, or in county where personalty located (see category Mortgages, topic Chattel Mortgages). *For list of Counties and County Seats see first page for this state in Volume containing Practice Profiles Section.* Clerk required to keep docket for such filing, showing day and hour instruments filed. (44-2-2).

Liens and security interests on motor vehicles governed by special rules. See category Transportation, topic Motor Vehicles, subheads Liens and Security Interests. Official records of same are maintained by Revenue Commissioner. (40-3-1 et seq.).

No judgment, decree or order or any writ of fieri facias of any court affects or becomes lien on property until recorded in office of clerk of superior court of county where property is located, and is entered in indexes of applicable records. (9-12-86).

Requisites for Recording.—Attestation or acknowledgment required for any deed to realty or personalty, or any mortgage, security deed, bond for title or other recordable instrument. (44-2-14). Instruments conveying real property interest require two witnesses. See category Property, topic Deeds, subhead Recording.

Filing Under Uniform Commercial Code: Place; Fees.—Proper place to file in order to perfect security interest under Art. 9 of Commercial Code with clerk of superior court of any county of state. (11-9-401).

Uniform fee for filing, indexing and furnishing filing data for original, amendment, partial release or continuation statement is $10 first page, $2 per page after first; filing assignment indicated on original financing statement or filing termination statement, no fee; for uncertified copy of any financing statement or assignment, 25¢ per page provided no assistance is required from clerk's office; if assistance is required then uncertified copies cost $1 per page. (11-9-401 through -408; -15-6-77). In counties having population of 350,000 or more in unincorporated areas, fee for filing and indexing original financing or continuation statement is $5 first page, 50¢ per page after first. (15-6-77.3).

Recording Fees.—Fee for recording deeds, affidavits, notices, releases and deed cancellations pertaining to real estate is usually $10 first page, $2 per page thereafter. (15-6-77; 47-14-51). In counties having population of 350,000 or more in unincorporated areas, fee is $5 per page. (15-6-77.3). Fee for recording notices of liens affecting real estate and personal property, including notice filings for Uniform Commercial Code related real estate, tax liens, writs of fieri facias, notices of lis pendens and cancellation of liens is usually $5 first page, $2 per page thereafter. (15-6-77; 47-14-51).

Foreign Conveyances or Encumbrances.—To authorize recording of deed to realty executed out of state, it must be attested by or acknowledged before one of named officials, and attested to by two witnesses. (44-2-21). Mortgages executed out of state may be acknowledged and attested in same manner as deeds. (44-14-34).

Effect of Record.—Recording of instruments mentioned is necessary to charge persons other than parties thereto with notice thereof, except that mere possession of land is notice of occupants' rights (44-5-169) other than exceptional rights not ordinarily implied from possession (30 Ga. App. 216, 117 S.E. 264).

Duration of Notice by Record.—The notice given by the filing for record of any mortgage, bill of sale to secure debt, retention of title contract or other security instrument creating a lien on, retaining title to, or conveying an interest in, personal property only, expires at the end of seven years from date of filing thereof for record. (44-14-140). Record notice of deed to realty to secure debt expires after seven years from date of last payment stated in deed or from date of instrument if no maturity date stated, except when deed establishes perpetual or indefinite security interest, then record notice expires at later of (1) seven years after last payment stated in deed or (2) 20 years after date of instruments. (44-14-80). Caveat, Uniform Commercial Code adopted.

Torrens Act.—A "Land Registration Act" for registering land titles is in force. Superior courts of counties in which land located have exclusive original jurisdiction of petitions and proceedings, which must conform to statutory requirements. (44-2-60-84).

Transfer of decedent's title to real estate to his or her devisees or heirs may be evidenced as follows:

(a) In the case of a resident testator, the original will, together with the probate proceedings thereunder, and the qualification of the executor must be filed and recorded in the office of the ordinary of the county of testator's residence, and an executor's deed assenting to the vesting of the devise must be filed and recorded in office of clerk of superior court of county where land is located.

(b) In the case of a nonresident testator, copies of the will, probate thereof and the qualification of the executor, certified according to the Acts of Congress, and an executor's deed assenting to the vesting of the devise must be filed and recorded in office of clerk of the superior court of county where land is located.

(c) In the case of an intestate resident, administration proceedings must be had in the court of ordinary in the county of said intestate's residence, and deeds only under said administration are required to be recorded in the office of the clerk of the superior court of the county where the land lies.

(d) In case of an intestate nonresident, copies of all administration proceedings, certified according to the Acts of Congress, must be filed, and recorded in the office of the clerk of the superior court in the county where the land is located, together with any deeds executed in connection with said administration.

Change of name by individuals is permitted. Procedure is by verified petition to superior court of county of residence, publication, and hearing. (19-12-1-4).

Vital Statistics.—Reports of births and deaths are filed with local registrar and state registrar of Department of Human Resources; reports of marriages, divorces and annulments are filed with State Registrar. (31-10-1 et seq.). Certified copies of certificates or records available from state registrar or local custodian of vital records. (31-10-26). Fee for each search or service and fee for each certified copy cannot exceed $10. (31-10-27).

Establishing Birth Records.—Forms and instructions for obtaining delayed birth certificates may be obtained from local registrar. No charge for filing. Order of superior or probate court required to correct delayed birth certificate, to change year of birth, or to remove name of father from birth certificate on file. (31-10-23).

SEALS:

Seal includes impression on paper itself, as well as impression on wax or wafer. With exception of official seal, scrawl or any mark intended as seal held as such. (1-3-3).

Uniform Commercial Code.—Adopted. (Title 11). See category Business Regulation and Commerce, topic Commercial Code.

Effect of Seal.—Seal imports consideration. (13 Ga. 502, 79 S.E. 374). But law with respect to sealed instruments does not apply to contract or offer relating to purchase or sale of goods. (11-2-203). Effect of corporate seal. (14-2-151).

TORRENS ACT:

See topic Records.

VITAL STATISTICS:

See topic Records.

EMPLOYMENT

EMPLOYER AND EMPLOYEE:

See topic Labor Relations.

LABOR RELATIONS:

Employment contract exempting employer from liability for negligence void as against public policy. (34-7-22).

Assumption of risk rule in force. (34-7-23). Fellow servant rule also in force (34-7-21), except that it is abolished in suits against railroad companies (34-7-21).

Employer liable for tort of employee in course of employment (51-2-2), unless employee exercises independent business judgment not subject to immediate direction and control of employer (51-2-4). Employer liable for negligence of independent contractor where: (1) work inherently wrongful or such as to cause nuisance; (2) work inherently dangerous to others; (3) wrongful act is violation of duty imposed on employer by express contract; (4) wrongful act is violation of duty imposed by statute; (5) employer retained right to direct or control work or interfered and assumed control so that injury traceable to his or her interference; (6) employer ratifies unauthorized wrong of contractor. (51-2-5).

Commissioner of Labor supervises Department of Labor. (34-2-3).

Hours of Labor.—No child under 16 years of age shall be permitted to work between 9 P.M. and 6 A.M. (or 5 A.M. in selling or delivering newspapers). (39-2-3, -5, -6). No child under 16 may be employed for more than four hours on any day in which school attended by minor is in session, or more than eight hours on non-school days or more than 40 hours in any week, and such child may not be employed at all during hours school is in session, unless he or she has been excused from attendance or completed senior high school. (39-2-4, -7). Restrictions do not apply to employment of minors in motion pictures, theatrical productions or other entertainment performances where consent of Labor Commissioner obtained. (39-2-18).

Wages.—Must be paid in lawful U.S. money or checks, or by employee-authorized credit transfer to employee's bank account. Dates of payment may be determined by employer but must be so fixed as to divide month into at least two equal periods and each payment must be of full amount due for period for which such payment is made. Statute does not apply to farming, sawmill or turpentine industries, nor does it apply to officials, superintendents or other heads or subheads of departments who may be employed by month or year at stipulated salaries. (34-7-2).

Under provisions of Georgia Minimum Wage Law, minimum wage of not less than $3.25 per hour must be paid by every employer except farm owner, sharecropper or land renter. Statute not applicable to employers with annual sales of $40,000 or less, with five employees or less or who are subject to federal minimum wage provisions, nor to employees whose compensation consists wholly or partially of gratuities, who are high school or college students, or who are domestic workers. (34-4-3).

Suit for recovery of wages, overtime, damages and/or penalties accruing under laws respecting payment of wages and overtime must be commenced within two years after accrual of cause of action. (9-3-22).

Where married employee is involuntarily hospitalized, spouse presently living with employee may demand employer pay all wages due directly to spouse and such wages paid are not subject to garnishment. (29-5-12). Wages owing deceased employee up to $2,500 must be paid surviving spouse or minor children without administration and not subject to garnishment. (34-7-4). (See also category Debtor and Creditor, topic Garnishment.) Employer must not discriminate on basis of sex by paying different wages for work requiring equal skill, effort and responsibility, and performed under similar working conditions except where payment made under: (1) seniority system; (2) merit system; (3) system based on quantity or quality of production; or (4) system creating wage differential on basis other than sex. (34-5-3). Liability for violation limited to

LABOR RELATIONS . . . *continued*
unpaid wages, reasonable attorney's fees not to exceed 25% of recovered wages, and court costs. (34-5-5). Dispute under Title 34 subject to arbitration by employer-employee agreement. (34-5-6). Civil action to recover wages must be brought within one year after cause of action arises. (34-5-5).

Lien.—Laborers have general lien on all property of employer, and special lien on products of labor. These rank higher than any other lien except tax lien and special landlords lien on yearly crops; but are not valid against bona fide purchasers for value without notice until reduced to execution and levied. (44-14-380, -382).

Discrimination.—Unlawful for private employer to discriminate on basis of sex (34-5-1 et seq.), age between 40 and 70 (34-1-2), handicap (34-6A-1 et seq.) or for attendance at judicial proceeding in response to court order or process except where employee charged with crime (34-1-3). Employer may require notice by employee of expected absence or delay. (34-1-3[c]).

Child Labor.—No child under age of 12 may be employed or permitted to work in any gainful occupation at any time, except work in agriculture, domestic service in homes or employment by parent or in any other specific category described later in Act. (39-2-9). Age restrictions do not apply to employment of minors in entertainment industry where consent of Labor Commissioner obtained. (39-2-18). Minors 14 or older may work during school vacations for lawn care if covered by accident plan or worker's compensation and if possess certificate from school administrator. (39-2-11.1).

Hazardous Work.—No child under age of 16 may be employed to work in or about any mill, factory, laundry, manufacturing establishment or workshop; in certain specified occupations designated as hazardous; or with certain machines and processes designated as hazardous. (39-2-1, 2).

Employment Certificate.—No child between 12 and 16 years of age may be employed unless certificate showing that child is not less than 12 years of age and is physically fit to follow employment sought is issued by superintendent of schools in county or city where child resides or by private school administrator. (39-2-11 through -14). Certificate shall not issue until child submits to superintendent certified copy of birth certificate and statement from employer that child could be employed immediately. Upon termination of employment of child between 12 and 16 years of age, employer, knowing of same, or if child fails to appear at work for 30 days, must, within five days, return employment certificate to authority issuing same, and thereafter new certificate must be issued prior to child's again being employed. (39-2-13).

Penalty.—It is misdemeanor for any agent of firm or corporation or parent or guardian to violate state statutes on employment of minors. (39-2-20). Superior court of any county in which violator does business may enjoin violator from employing minor. (39-2-21).

Labor Unions.—Recognized by 34-6-20 through -27.

Agency Shop, Closed Shop, Union Shop.—Prohibited. (34-6-21 through -24).

Check Off.—Employer cannot, without consent of employees, deduct from their pay fees or assessments owed by them to labor union. (34-6-25 through -26). Injured person has remedy by injunction. (34-6-27).

Labor Disputes.—

Strikes are regulated and prohibited except after certain written notices. (34-6 et seq.). Strikes by state employees prohibited. (45-19-2).

Picketing by one or more persons is illegal if accompanied by threats, obstruction of entrances, intimidation, force or interference with person, immediate family or physical property or by any threatened or actual interference with pursuit of lawful employment, in attempt to compel any person to strike or not strike. (34-6-2, -6). Also unlawful for one or more by force, intimidation or threats to prevent or attempt to prevent any employer from lawfully engaging or continuing to engage in any proper business activity, from utilizing his or her property, or from buying, selling and/or transporting goods. (34-6-4). Mass picketing prohibited. (34-6-5).

Workers' Compensation Act.—Title 34-9.

Act applies to employees of state, but does not apply to common carriers by railroad engaged in intrastate commerce, to employees whose employment is not in usual course of trade, business, occupation or profession of employer or not incidental thereto, to farm laborers or domestic servants or their employees (except employees of Department of Corrections who are engaged in farm and livestock operations [34-9-2(c)]); or to any person who buys and resells product, receiving no other compensation, under written contract of employment as independent contractor (34-9-2); or to certain independent contract carriers who transport, assemble, deliver, or distribute printed materials and maintain incidental facilities or equipment for employer who publishes or distributes printed materials (34-9-2); or to any person performing services as licensed real estate salesperson or associate broker who has written contract of employment providing that he or she shall perform all services as independent contractor, or to owner-operators of motor vehicles leased pursuant to 40-2-87 (34-9-1[2]); or to any person, firm or private corporation, including any public service corporation, that has regularly in service less than three employees in same business within this state, unless such employees and their employers voluntarily elect to be bound (34-9-2). Firefighters, law enforcement personnel, emergency medical and management personnel, civil defense agencies and rescue services covered by Act. (34-9-1). President or others in management of corporation not employee for purposes of three employee test (154 Ga. App. 742, 269 S.E.2d 890), but corporate officers must elect to be exempt to avoid being counted for purposes of three employee test (178 Ga. App. 584, 343 S.E.2d 786). Corporate officers or members of limited liability company may elect to be exempt. (34-9-1). Corporate officers or members of limited liability company who have elected exemption may revoke exemption. (34-9-2.1). Sole proprietor or partner of business whose employees are eligible may elect to be included (34-9-2.2), or may be covered by another employer (223 Ga. App. 133, 476 S.E.2d 772). Although co-employee tort immunity exists, immunity does not apply to company physicians sued for alleged tortious breach of conduct applicable to employee's profession. (34-9-11; 184 Ga. App. 560, 362 S.E.2d 97). Compensation shall not be allowed for injury or death due to willful misconduct, including acts taken under influence of controlled substances; certain exceptions may be applicable. (34-9-17). False representation defense is recognized. (259 Ga. 155, 378 S.E.2d 111).

Act provides for exclusive remedy to employees and excludes all other rights and remedies of employee, his or her personal representative, parents, dependents or next of kin on account of injury, loss of service, or death arising out of and in course of employment (34-9-11); provides exclusive remedy for medical surgical hospital care for injured covered employees (34-9-200 through -204); provides circumstances under which employer is responsible for modifications to employee's dwelling (34-9-200.1; 223 Ga. App. 751, 478 S.E.2d 139); establishes rates of compensation for specified injuries and method of insuring payment of such compensation (34-9-120 et seq.); creates and prescribes powers of State Board of Workmen's Compensation within Department of Labor for administration of law (34-9-40 et seq.) and sets forth procedures for appeal from decision of Board to superior court (34-9-105). Employer immunity provided under this code section extends to businesses using services of temporary help contracting firms or employee leasing companies when benefits required by this chapter are provided by either temporary help contracting firm, employee leasing company, or business using services of such firm or company. (34-9-11). Employee of subcontractor cannot collect workmen's compensation from general contractor and also maintain tort action against same general contractor for same injury. Two prong test applied to determine if owner of property is statutory employer entitled to tort immunity under exclusive remedy provision of Act. (183 Ga. App. 632, 359 S.E.2d 700). Where employee recovers damages in lawsuit against person other than employer, and employer has compensated employee under this statute, employer is subrogated to employee's recovery to extent of compensation paid, but only if employer has compensated employee in full. (34-9-11.1). Compensation laws of state where worker elects recovery control worker's rights against third parties. (209 Ga. App. 171, 433 S.E.2d 325). Where employee not covered by Act, statute of limitations for common law claims (9-3-33) tolled during period employee submits to worker's compensation proceedings (196 Ga. App. 98, 395 S.E.2d 277).

Notice of accident must be given in person by employee or employee's representative, or in writing, as soon after accident as practicable, to employer, employer's agent, representative, foreman or employee's immediate superior. Employee is not entitled to any physicians' fees or compensation which accrued prior to giving of notice. No compensation is payable unless such notice is given within 30 days after accident, or within 30 days after death resulting from accident, unless employee was prevented from notifying by physical or mental incapacity or by fraud or deceit, or unless employer, employer's agent, representative, foreman or immediate superior has knowledge of the accident, or unless there is some other reasonable excuse and employer has not been prejudiced by delay. (34-9-80). Actual knowledge of injury by accident arising out of and in course of employment satisfies notice requirement even though formal notice not given. (128 Ga. App. 352, 196 S.E.2d 693). Board shall publish notice of rights, benefits and obligations and distribute notice to employers and employees. (34-9-81.1).

Filing of Claim.—Right to compensation is barred unless claim is filed with State Board of Workmen's Compensation within one year after accident, or if death results, within one year after death (34-9-82), except that if proceeding is against corporation whose charter has expired, but which is still doing business, one year limit does not apply in proceeding against persons operating under corporate name. Filing complete on receipt by Board and not on deposit in mail. (34-9-86). No limitation of time for giving notice or filing claim runs against person who is mentally incompetent or minor dependent, as long as he or she has no guardian or trustee. (34-9-86). Claim based on asbestosis or asbestos exposure must be filed within one year from diagnosis or death of employee, whichever earlier. (34-9-281).

Basis of Compensation.—Compensation is computed on basis of average wage received by employee on date of accident, or if no such average wage of employee, on basis of wages of employees of same class. (34-9-260). Compensation for total incapacity is 66⅔% of average wage, not to exceed $325 nor be less than $32.50 per week. If employee's wages are less than $32.50, weekly benefit must equal average weekly wage. Period for which compensation must be paid cannot exceed 400 weeks, except in case of catastrophic injury for which compensation must be paid until there is change of condition for better. (34-9-261). For temporary partial incapacity, compensation is 66⅔% of difference between former and present wages, not to exceed $216.67 per week for maximum of 350 weeks. (34-9-262). Certain specific injuries to body members resulting in permanent partial disability, compensated additionally according to schedule. (34-9-263). For death with no dependents, compensation is reasonable expenses of last sickness and burial expenses not to exceed $5,000. For death with dependents wholly dependent on employee for support compensation is total provided for total disability under 34-9-261. (34-9-265). For death resulting from intentional act of employer with specific intent to cause such injury, 20% penalty added to weekly benefits paid to dependents with maximum of $20,000. (34-9-265[e]). All persons must show dependency to benefit under law. (246 Ga. 269, 271 S.E.2d 178). Hearing will be held for all claims for compensation for injury or death. (34-9-100). For compensation for economic change in condition, claimant must show that condition changed for worse; because of change claimant unable to locate suitable work with any employer; because of inability to work claimant has partial or total loss of income; inability to work proximately caused by injury. (141 Ga. App. 819, 234 S.E.2d 552). Upon Board ruling that claimant has had change in condition for better and resumed employment, claimant may be liable for repayment of compensation received after date of change. (146 Ga. App. 893, 247 S.E.2d 607).

Occupational Diseases.—Compensation is granted for certain occupational diseases. A medical board created to pass on medical questions pertaining to claims on account growing out of death or disability on account of such diseases. (34-9-310 et seq.). Occupational disease defined. (34-9-280 et seq.).

Attorney's Fees.—Available under certain circumstances for proceedings before Board. (34-9-108).

Group Self-Insurance Funds.—Such funds are exempt from state and local premium taxes. (34-9-171).

See note at head of Digest as to 1998 legislation covered.

See Topical Index in front part of this volume.

GA – 39

LABOR RELATIONS . . . *continued*

Rate of Insurance.—Insurer's basic rate for policies must not exceed Insurance Commissioner's approved rates. (34-9-130.1). Insured certified by State Board of Workers' Compensation to have drug-free workplace program must be granted 7.5% reduction in premium. (33-9-40.2; 34-9-410 et seq.).

Employer's Liability Insurance.—Employer who accepts compensation provisions must insure compensation payments to his or her employees (34-9-14, -120 through -134), except where employer provides proof of ability to pay employee directly (34-9-121). If employer fails to insure and is insolvent, employee may sue for value of award notwithstanding exclusive remedy provision. (247 Ga. 71, 274 S.E.2d 327).

Employer's Liability Act.—See subhead Workers' Compensation Act, supra.

Unemployment Compensation.—Employment Security is governed by 34-8 et seq.

Drug Free Public Work Force Act of 1990.—Act provides for suspension and/or termination of state employees upon conviction of drug offense. (45-23-1 et seq.).

Random Drug Testing of State Employees.—None. Statute requiring such testing unconstitutional. (749 F. Supp. 1110). Statute requires agency heads to designate positions under their supervision for which drug testing is warranted. All applicants for such positions are to be tested thereafter. (Constitutionality of statute has not been addressed by courts.) (45-20-110, -111).

Separation of State Employees.—Officers and employees covered by retirement benefits provisions of 47-2-123 may only be involuntarily separated pursuant to procedures set forth in 45-24-1 et seq.

WORKERS' COMPENSATION LAW:

See topic Labor Relations.

ENVIRONMENT

ENVIRONMENTAL REGULATION:

Supervision of environmental matters including water pollution, air pollution, solid waste management, quality of public water supplies, ground water use, management of regulated substances stored in underground tanks, oil and gas drilling, and surface mining is vested in Environmental Protection Division of Department of Natural Resources (205 Butler Street, S.E., Atlanta, GA 30334). Protection of coastal marshlands is duty of Coastal Marshlands Protection Committee of Department of Natural Resources. Commissioner of Agriculture regulates pesticide use and application. (2-7-93). Interstate Environment Compact (12-10-40), Atlantic States Marine Fisheries Compact (27-4-210) and Southeast Interstate Low-Level Radioactive Waste Management Compact (12-8-120) adopted. Coastal Marshlands Protection Act (12-5-280 et seq.), Georgia Hazardous Waste Management Authority Act (12-8-100 et seq.) and Metropolitan River Protection Act (12-5-440 et seq.) adopted. Georgia Hazardous Waste Management Act adopted concerning design, construction, operation and management of hazardous waste facilities in Georgia. (12-8-60 et seq.). Georgia Fertilizer Act of 1997 repealed Georgia Plant Food Act of 1989 and provides standards, requirements and fees for manufacturers and distributors of fertilizers and plant foods. (See 2-12-1 et seq.) Georgia Hazardous Site Response Act (12-8-90 et seq.) requiring reporting and remediation of hazardous substanee releases and requiring notations on deeds of affected properties adopted. Pollution Prevention Assistance Division created to provide voluntary guidelines for disposal and reduction of hazardous waste in Georgia. (12-8-180 et seq.). Georgia Environmental Facilities Authority assists local governments in constructing, maintaining and financing environmental facilities. (50-23-1 et seq.). Hazardous Site Reuse and Development Act limits liability of certain persons who purchase and return to usefulness property contaminated by release of hazardous substance. (12-8-200 et seq.).

Prohibited Acts of Pollution.—It is unlawful to use any state waters for disposal of sewage, industrial waste, or other waste except in compliance with rules, regulations, orders and permits issued by Environmental Protection Division. (12-5-29). Operation of public water supply system without permit is unlawful. (12-5-191). Owners or operators of combined sewer overflows must obtain permit, and, upon request, submit plan to Environmental Protection Division to meet water purity standards. (12-5-29.1 through -30.2). Unlawful to place, dump or dispose of contents of septic tank, waste water holding tank, grease trap or other such container into public storm or sanitary sewer pipeline without first obtaining written permission of owner of said storm or sewer pipeline. (12-8-2). Unlawful for operator of public water supply systems to fail to comply with regulations concerning quality of public water supply; unlawful for operator to fail to notify public health agency, Environmental Protection Division, and local media if operator: (1) does not comply with water quality standards, (2) fails to perform required monitoring of system, (3) is subject to variance issued by Division, (4) is subject to exemption, or (5) fails to comply with requirements of variance or exemption. (12-5-191, -184, -178). No person shall withdraw or use groundwater in excess of 100,000 gallons per day without permit from Division. With exception for solely agricultural water usage, permit application requires submission of water conservation plan approved by director. (12-5-96). No person shall withdraw, divert, or impound state surface water in excess of 100,000 gallons per day (monthly average) without permit from Division, subject to these exceptions: (1) diversion for construction for transportation purposes of which does not reduce flow by more than 150,000 gallons per day (monthly average); (2) withdrawal or diversion for farm use upon timely submission of permit application; (3) construction impoundment, farm ponds or farm impoundments for sole purpose of fish, wildlife, or recreation; and (4) diversion that does not reduce flow of surface water at point where watercourse leaves person's property by more than 100,000 gallons per day (monthly average). (12-5-31). Permit must be obtained for construction of dams (12-5-376) and for construction or excavation of any type within designated major stream corridors in designated metropolitan areas (12-5-444). Air Quality Control Act specifies powers and duties of Environmental Protection Division concerning regulation of air pollution. (12-9-6). Except for limited exemptions (12-8-30.10), handling of solid waste, except in conformity with all rules, regulations and orders of Environmental Protection Division is unlawful (12-8-30.8). Persons owning or having control over oil or hazardous material who have knowledge of spill or release must notify Division immediately. (12-14-3). Surface mining, except in accordance with rules, regulations, orders, and permits issued by Division of Environmental Protection, is unlawful. (12-4-70 et seq.). No person may install underground storage tank for purposes of storing regulated substance unless tank meets performing standard established by Division. (12-13-6). Certain restrictions have been imposed on transportation of waste by any person, firm, corporation, etc. pursuant to contract across county or state lines. (36-1-16).

Unlawful acts under Georgia Pesticide Use and Application Act are specified in 2-7-102; farmers, veterinarians, experimental research and persons subject to Structural Pest Control Act (43-45-1) are exempt from Georgia Pesticide Use and Application Act (2-7-112).

Enforcement.—Environmental Protection Division (12-2-2) and Coastal Marshlands Protection Committee (12-5-291) has authority to investigate any apparent violation of environmental acts under its supervision. Under Water Quality Control Act and Air Quality Control Act, Division has power to require owners of facilities discharging or emitting water or air pollutants to monitor, record and report discharge levels to authorities. (12-5-27; 12-9-5). Upon determination that any person is violating its rules, regulations, orders or permits, Division or Coastal Marshlands Protection Committee may issue order to bring about compliance; public water supply quality control (12-5-185); air quality (12-9-12); solid waste (12-8-30); surface mining (12-4-73); groundwater (12-5-99). In emergency cases, Division may, without notice or hearing, issue emergency order requiring immediate compliance: water quality (12-5-47); public water supply quality control (12-5-187); solid waste (12-8-30.1); groundwater (12-5-102). Final orders of Division unappealed from or affirmed on appeal may be filed with appropriate superior court which will render judgment in accordance therewith with same effect as any other judgment: water quality (12-5-45); public water supply quality control (12-5-189); air quality (12-9-16); solid waste (12-8-30.3); surface mining (12-4-81); groundwater (12-5-100). Division may obtain injunctive relief for: water quality violations (12-5-48); groundwater use violations (12-5-101); air quality violations (12-9-12); solid waste disposal violations (12-8-30.4); surface mining violations (12-4-79); and hazardous waste violations (12-8-72; 12-8-75). To prevent immediate public health hazard to public or community water supply, Division may obtain injunctive relief. (12-5-188). Division may issue unilateral order to parties who have contributed to release of hazardous substances requiring cleanup. (12-8-96). Division may expend funds from hazardous waste trust fund for remediation of site and seek recovery plus punitive damages against certain persons who contributed to release of substances. (12-8-95; 12-8-96.1). Expenditure by division shall constitute debt to state giving rise to lien on said property. (12-8-96). Commissioner of Agriculture may obtain injunctive relief for pesticide use or application violation. (2-7-107). To insure safe collection of ionizing radiation, Director of Division may require posting of bond. (31-13-7). Division has right to enter upon and inspect premises to determine compliance with Underground Storage Tank Act. (12-13-8). Any person who owns underground storage tank governed by Underground Storage Tank Act must notify Division of current and/or prior use of tank, as well as when tank is taken out of operation. (12-13-13). Common law rights of individuals and state to bring action under theory of nuisance are not altered by Water Quality Control Act (12-5-46), or Air Quality Control Act (226 Ga. 480, 175 S.E.2d 847).

When any area of state is suffering from emergency period of water shortage, Director of Division of Environmental Protection may, after notice and hearing, order change, restriction, or outright suspension of permit for withdrawal, diversion, or impoundment of state's surface water. (12-5-31).

Civil Penalties and Damages.—Civil penalties not to exceed $50,000 per day for each day violation continues may be imposed for violation of Water Quality Control Act (12-5-52[a]) and no more than $100,000 per day for subsequent violation within 12 months, and not to exceed $25,000 per day under Air Quality Control Act (12-9-23) and Hazardous Waste Management Act (12-8-81). Civil penalties not to exceed $1,000 per violation and $500 per day of continued violation invoked by Surface Mining Act (12-4-83), and Groundwater Use Act (12-5-106). Georgia Comprehensive Solid Waste Management Act (12-8-30.6), imposes civil penalties not to exceed $1,000 per violation and $500 per day of continued violation committed by public authority or city or county government and civil penalties not to exceed $25,000 per day of continued violation committed by any other entity. Negligent violation or violation of permit under any provision of Safe Drinking Water Act makes available penalties of $1,000 per violation (maximum) plus $500 per day if violation continues for system serving less than 10,000 individuals, and not to exceed $1,000 per day for service of 10,000 or more. Penalties for willful violation of Act may not exceed $5,000 per day. (12-5-192). Negligent or willful violation of Water Quality Control Act renders offender liable in damages to state and any political subdivision for all expenses and injuries occasioned by pollution. (12-5-51). Failure to report spill or release of oil or hazardous materials can result in civil penalty of not more than $1,000 per day. (12-14-4). Liens created pursuant to federal superfund legislation must be filed in office of clerk of superior court of county in which real property located. (44-14-517). Director of Environmental Protection Division may issue order requiring compliance with Underground Storage Tank Act. (12-13-14). Continued noncompliance with provisions of Underground Storage Tank Act can result in civil penalty of not more than $25,000 for each day of continued noncompliance. (12-13-19[a]). Any person who fails to notify or submits false information to Division shall be subject to civil penalty not to exceed $10,000 for each tank for which notification not given or false information submitted. (12-13-19[b]).

Criminal Sanctions.—Violation of Water Quality Control Act, failure to comply with court order issued thereunder, violation of requirements imposed in pre-treatment programs, or introduction into sewer systems or publicly-owned treatment works any pollutant or hazardous substance that causes or may cause personal damage or property damage or that causes such treatment works to violate any effluent limitation or permitted condition is misdemeanor punishable by fine of not less than $2,500 nor more than $25,000 per day of continued violation, or one years imprisonment, or both, or for subsequent violations fine of not more than $50,000 per day of continued violation or up

See note at head of Digest as to 1998 legislation covered.

See Topical Index in front part of this volume.

GA – 40

ENVIRONMENTAL REGULATION . . . *continued*
to two years imprisonment, or both. (12-5-53[a]). Falsification of statements and certification required by Water Quality Control Act or tampering with monitoring devices is felony punishable by fine of not more than $10,000 or imprisonment for not more than two years, or both, or for subsequent violations, fine of not more than $20,000 per day of violation or imprisonment for not more than four years or both. (12-5-53[b]). Knowing violation of Water Quality Control Act, failure to comply with court order issued thereunder, violation of requirements imposed in pre-treatment programs, or introduction into sewer system or publicly owned treatment works of any pollutant or hazardous substance which causes or may reasonably be anticipated to cause personal injury or property damage or which causes treatment works to violate any effluent limitation or permit condition is felony punishable by fine of not less than $5,000 per day, not more than $50,000 per day of violation, or by imprisonment for not more than two years, or both, or, for subsequent violations fine of not more than $100,000 per day of violation or imprisonment for not more than four years or both. (12-5-53[c]). Knowing violation of Water Quality Control Act or knowing failure to comply with court order issued thereunder, coupled with knowledge that at time another person is thereby placed in imminent danger of death or serious bodily injury is felony, punishable by fine of not more than $250,000, or imprisonment of not more than 15 years or both. Organizations, other than government entities, upon conviction of violation of this section, are subject to fine of not more than $1,000,000. (12-5-53[d]). Determination of whether individual defendant knew conduct placed another in imminent danger of death or serious bodily injury turns on defendant's actual awareness or actual belief, and knowledge of another will not be attributed to defendant but circumstantial evidence may be used. (12-5-53[d][1]). It is affirmative defense that conduct charged was consented to by person endangered and that danger and conduct charged were reasonably foreseeable hazards of occupation, business, profession, medical treatment, or medical or scientific experimentation conducted by professionally approved methods and that person endangered had been made aware of risks involved prior to giving consent. Such defense must be established by preponderance of evidence. (12-5-53[d][2]). Serious bodily injury means bodily injury which involves substantial risk of death, unconsciousness, extreme physical pain, protracted and obvious disfigurement, or protracted loss or impairment of function of bodily member, organ, or mental faculty. (12-5-53[d][4]). It is affirmative defense to subsections (a) and (c) that introduction of any pollutant or hazardous substance into sewer system or publicly-owned treatment was in compliance with all applicable federal, state, and local requirements which govern introduction of pollutant or hazardous substance into sewer or publicly-owned treatment works. (12-5-53[e]). Violations of Surface Mining Act are misdemeanors punishable by fines of not less than $100 nor more than $1,000 per offense, each day of noncompliance after notice constituting separate offense. (12-4-84). Violations of Groundwater Use Act (12-5-107), Safe Drinking Water Act (12-5-193), Air Quality Act (12-9-24), and Georgia Pesticide Use and Application Act (2-7-114), are punishable as misdemeanors. Violations of Georgia Hazardous Waste Management Act are punishable by fine of not more than $50,000 for each day of violation or imprisonment not to exceed three years or both. For second violation, punishment is doubled. (12-8-82). Knowing violation of Hazardous Waste Management Act with knowledge that another person is placed in imminent danger of death or serious bodily injury punishable by fine of not more than $250,000 or imprisonment for not less than one nor more than 15 years, or both. Organization convicted under Act is subject to fine of not more than $1,000,000. (12-8-82). Violation of Solid Waste Management Act punishable by fine of not more than $50,000 for each day in violation or imprisonment for one to two years, or both. For second violation, maximum punishment is doubled. (12-8-30.8).

Permits.—Environmental Protection Division has authority over issuance of permits for discharges into state waters (12-5-29, 30), air emissions (12-9-7), solid waste handling or disposal (12-8-24), subsurface mining (12-4-75), public water supply (12-5-179), withdrawal, diversion, or impoundment of state surface waters (12-5-31), and groundwater use (12-5-96). Commissioner of Agriculture issues pesticide contractor's licenses and certified pesticide applicator licenses for application of "restricted use pesticides." (2-7-99). Certificates for land-disturbing activity in designated major metropolitan stream corridors issued by local governing authority. (12-5-444).

ESTATES AND TRUSTS

ADMINISTRATION:

See topic Executors and Administrators.

ADVANCEMENTS:

See topic Descent and Distribution.

ALLOWANCES:

See topic Executors and Administrators.

DEATH:

Rebuttable presumption of death arises after seven years. (24-4-21, 132 Ga. 648, 64 S.E. 800). See category Property, topic Absentees.

Government Reports, etc.—Certain written findings or official written reports or records, or duly certified copies thereof by certain government officials that a person is dead, missing, missing in action, interned, captured or is alive must be received in any court or office as evidence of such. If in certain form, signature and authority of signor shall be prima facie evidence. (24-4-47).

Certificate.—Official death certificates are obtainable from Division of Vital Statistics, Dept. Public Health, 1 Hunter Street, N.W., Atlanta, Georgia 30334, or from local custodians. Fee $10 plus search fee which cannot exceed $10. Certificate to be filed with local registrar for each death which occurs in state. (31-10-15, -17, -27).

Determination of Death.—Person may be pronounced dead if it is determined that such person has suffered either irreversible cessation of circulatory and respiratory functions, or irreversible cessation of brain function. This criterion is cumulative and does not prohibit use of other medically recognized criterion for determining death. No civil or criminal liability for good faith act in accordance with this provision. (31-10-16).

Survivorship.—Uniform Simultaneous Death Act adopted. (53-10-1 et seq.). Where there is insufficient evidence that death was not simultaneous, property of each person will be disposed of as if such person had survived. (53-10-2). Beneficiary whose interest is contingent on surviving third person is deemed not to have survived where there is insufficient evidence of order of death. If there are two or more deceased persons who would have been entitled to property on surviving others, property is divided into shares. (53-10-3). Similar rules apply to property held jointly with right of survivorship. (53-10-4).

Actions for Death.—Surviving spouse or if no surviving spouse, children may recover for death of spouse or parent. (51-4-2). Recovery by surviving spouse subject to law of descents. (51-4-2). Under certain circumstances, minor child may bring wrongful death action even though there is surviving spouse, if surviving spouse abandons or otherwise leaves minor without adequate remedy at law. (207 Ga. App. 808, 429 S.E.2d 307). Parents, including those divorced, separated, or living apart, may recover for death of child leaving no spouse or child; illegitimacy does not bar recovery. (19-7-1). In case of death of person entitled to sue, action survives to others entitled. (51-4-2). Recovery measured by full value of decedent's life. (51-4-2, 3). Action may not be maintained on strict liability theory. (239 Ga. 657, 238 S.E.2d 361). If no person entitled to recover, executor or administrator may recover for benefit of next of kin. (51-4-5). In case of death of railroad employee action must be brought by executor or administrator if one appointed, for benefit of persons mentioned above. If no executor or administrator, persons mentioned above may sue. (34-7-41). Action for death of husband, wife, parent or child must be brought within two years. (9-3-33). Right of action under wrongful death statute accrues at time of victim's death, not at time injuries inflicted. (232 Ga. 747, 208 S.E.2d 838). There is no statutory limitation of amount which may be awarded.

Where death results from a crime or from criminal or other negligence, the personal representative of the deceased may recover for funeral, medical, and other necessary expenses resulting from the injury and death of the deceased. (51-4-5).

Survival of Tort Actions.—Federal Rules effective. (9-11-25, et seq.). Motion for substitution must be made within 180 days after death is suggested on record.

Uniform Anatomical Gift Act.—Adopted. (44-5-140 et seq.).

See topic Wills, subhead Living Wills.

DECEDENTS' ESTATES:

See topics Descent and Distribution, Executors and Administrators, Wills; category Debtor and Creditor, topic Exemptions.

DESCENT AND DISTRIBUTION:

See also topic Executors and Administrators.

Note: Title 53 has been amended effective Jan. 1, 1998, regardless of whether decedent dies before or after that date provided that no vested rights of title, year's support, succession or inheritance shall be impaired. This section reflects those changes. Earlier digests should be consulted regarding prior law.

Subject to rights of surviving spouse (see subhead Surviving Spouse, infra), realty descends and personalty is distributed according to same rules of inheritance, which are as follows: (1) Children stand in first degree from decedent and inherit equally, accounting for advancements. Issue of deceased children stand in place of their parents and take per stirpes; (2) parents stand next in degree and share equally; (3) siblings stand next in degree and share equally, with descendants of any deceased sibling taking per stirpes, except that if there are no siblings, nieces and nephews share equally and their descendants take per stirpes; (4) grandmothers and grandfathers stand next in degree; (5) uncles and aunts stand next in degree with children of deceased uncle or aunt inheriting in place of their parent except that if there are no aunts or uncles, first cousins share equally; (6) more remote degrees of kinship shall be determined by counting steps from claimant to closest common ancestor and from said ancestor to intestate, sum of two chains being degree of kinship. (53-2-1).

Uniform Probate Code.—Not adopted, but has influenced new Probate Code.

Year's Support.—Only award resembling dower, curtesy, or elective share in Georgia. Awarded to spouse and minor children under age 18 at time of application, who must be alive and unmarried at time of application, but separate awards may be made. If separate awards are not made, spouse has equivalent of life estate with power to include corpus for support, remainder to children, in property awarded. Tax benefits are available. (53-3-1 through -13).

Surviving spouse is sole heir if no children or descendants of children are left. Where there are surviving children or representatives of deceased children, surviving spouse shall take equally with children, with descendants of deceased child taking that child's share, per stirpes, except that spouse's portion shall not be less than one-third share. (53-2-1[b][1]).

Half-blood (on both paternal and maternal sides) inherit equally with whole blood. (53-2-1[a][2]).

Posthumous children inherit as though born in decedent's lifetime, provided they were conceived during decedent's life, were born within ten months after decedent's death and survived more than 120 hours after birth. (53-2-1[a][11]).

Illegitimates inherit from and through mother, brothers and sisters by same mother, and other maternal kin. They may also inherit from and through father or paternal kin if paternity is established by court order, certain actions of father, or genetic testing. (53-2-3). Maternal and paternal kin may inherit from and through illegitimate under similar circumstances except father and paternal kin do not inherit if father failed to support child or treat child as his own. (53-2-4).

Adopted Children.—See category Family, topic Adoption.

See note at head of Digest as to 1998 legislation covered.

See Topical Index in front part of this volume.

GA – 41

DESCENT AND DISTRIBUTION . . . *continued*

Determination of Heirship.—Any person interested in estate as distributor or possible heir may file petition in probate court or superior court of county in which administration is taking or would take place. After personal service on residents or publication on nonresidents and unknown parties, Court finds identity and quantity of interest of distributees. After time for appeal distribution in accordance with order may be made. (53-2-20 through -26).

Advancements.—Money or property advanced to child must be accounted for in distribution of estate of parent. Gift to child during parent's lifetime is not advancement unless declared to be so by transferor within 30 days or by recipient at any time. (53-1-10). See also topic Wills, subhead Legacies.

Renunciation.—Beneficiary under will may renounce succession to property or interest by filing written instrument within nine months after date of transfer or, if later, date on which renouncing person reaches age 21. Instrument also may be filed in probate court when proceedings are pending or could be commenced, or in real estate records of county where real property is located. (53-1-20).

Escheat.—On failure of heirs, property escheats with proceeds going to county educational fund. (53-2-50, -51). If no heir appears within four years, personal representative petitions for determination that escheat has occurred. Notice to heirs is given by publication and persons claiming to be heirs have opportunity to appear.

Inheritance Denial.—Where individual feloniously and intentionally kills decedent or causes decedent to be killed, such individual may not take property interest from decedent and may not serve as fiduciary of decedent's estate or any trust created by decedent. (53-1-5). Similar rule applies to life insurance proceeds. (33-25-13). Amount forfeited passes as if killer had predeceased, and anti-lapse statute does not apply unless killer's descendants are also decedent's descendants. Also, intestate share of killer's descendants cannot exceed killer's forfeited share.

ESTATES:

See category Property, topic Real Property.

EXECUTORS AND ADMINISTRATORS:

Note: Title 53 of Georgia Code has been amended effective Jan. 1, 1998, provided that no vested rights of title, year's support, succession or inheritance shall be impaired. This section reflects those changes. Earlier digests should be consulted regarding prior law.

Jurisdiction over administration is in probate court of county of decedent's residence, or of county where estate of nonresident decedent, or some portion thereof, is found. (53-5-1, 53-6-21). Uniform Probate Code not adopted.

Preferences in Right to Administer.—Letters of administration generally: surviving spouse regardless of age, unless involved in action for divorce or separate maintenance with decedent at time of death; next of kin; if several next of kin of equal degree, then person selected in writing by majority in interest. Probate judge may use discretion if no choice made by next of kin. If surviving spouse or next of kin does not apply, creditor may be appointed. Persons entitled to serve or select may select disinterested person. (53-6-24; 208 Ga. App. 411, 430 S.E.2d 794). Letters of administration with will annexed: person selected by all beneficiaries (other than spouse involved in action for divorce or separate maintenance at time of testator's death). Otherwise probate judge uses discretion, giving preference first to beneficiaries and then to those persons who could serve as administrator of intestate estate. (53-6-14).

Eligibility and Competency.—Any individual may serve, regardless of citizenship or residency, as may banks and other persons qualified to act as fiduciary in Georgia. (53-6-1). Certain foreign corporations may act, see category Business Regulation and Commerce, topic Banks and Banking, subhead Foreign Banks.

Appointment of Administrator.—Made after notice to heirs. Executor is issued letters testamentary when will has been admitted to probate. See topic Wills, subhead Probate.

No formal words in will necessary for nomination of executor, but any expression of confidence and desire that person named carry out testator's wishes sufficient. (53-6-20).

Bond is not required except for intestate administrators and temporary administrators. Heirs may consent to relieve intestate administrator from bond requirements. (53-6-50). Probate judge has discretion to require bond in any particular case. (53-6-53).

Removal.—Executor or administrator may be removed for breach of fiduciary duty (53-7-54) or other good cause (53-7-55).

Temporary Administration.—On unrepresented estate may be granted by probate judge at any time, for purpose of collecting and taking care of estate until permanent letters granted. No appeal from such order. (53-6-30). Temporary administrator may sue to collect debts or personal property, and may collect and preserve estate assets and expend funds therefore with court approval after notice (53-6-31), but may not disburse funds (82 Ga. 202, 8 S.E. 76). Temporary letters may be issued pending determination of validity of will unless letters testamentary have already been issued (i.e., because will was admitted to probate in "common form" as opposed to "solemn form"). See topic Wills, subhead Probate. (53-7-4).

Administration C. T. A. (with Will Annexed).—Granted where no executor nominated or none appears to qualify and execute will, and also temporarily where named executor is minor. (53-6-13).

County Administrator.—Appointed by probate judge in each county to take charge of estates unrepresented and not likely to be represented. (53-6-35).

Inventory and appraisal.—Inventory must be returned within six months after qualification of representative. (53-7-30). Annual returns are required. (53-7-67). Testator by will may relieve executor from making inventory or returns if creditors and other persons (other than legatees) not injured thereby. (53-7-33, 53-7-69). Heirs or beneficiaries may do same. (53-7-32, 53-7-68).

General Powers and Duties.—Broad fiduciary powers may be incorporated into wills, trusts, or other instruments in writing by reference. (53-12-232). Same powers may be granted to administrator if all heirs or beneficiaries consent, but in such case, citation and publication may not be waived. (53-7-1).

Notice of Appointment.—See subhead Appointment of Administrators, supra. See also topic Wills, subhead Probate.

Notice to Creditors.—Within 60 days from date of qualification, personal representative must give four weeks notice by advertisement in official newspaper of county where administration was granted, for creditors of estate to render account of their claims. (53-7-41).

Presentation of Claims.—Claims not presented to representative within three months from date of publication of last notice lose right to equal participation with claims of equal dignity paid before representative has notice of such unpresented claims, nor can such creditors hold administrator liable for misappropriation, but do have a claim on funds remaining with administrator, so long as no debts of higher dignity remain unpaid. (53-7-41). Unmatured claims, secured claims and claims on which actions were pending when decedent died must be presented like other claims.

Proof of Claims.—No particular form is necessary. Verification is not required, but is advisable.

Illustrative Form (not official).—

Form

STATE OF . . . .
COUNTY OF . . . .
CLAIM OF . . . . ,
A CREDITOR, AGAINST THE ESTATE OF . . . .
. . . .
(name of claimant)

The . . . . hereby files formal claim with the personal representative of the Estate of . . . . for the amount of . . . ., said amount being the amount of principal and earned interest due on a certain promissory note which was executed by (decedent) . . . ., Deceased, payable to (claimant) . . . ., dated . . . .

. . . .
By . . . .

. . . ., being duly sworn, says that he (or she) is an officer of . . . ., the Claimant in the above entitled claim, that he (or she) has read the foregoing Claim, and that the same is true of his own knowledge, except as to those matters and things herein stated upon information and belief, and as to those he (or she) verily believes them to be true.

. . . .
By . . . .

Sworn to and subscribed before me
this. . . . . day of . . . .

Notary Public

Approval or Rejection of Claims.—Personal representative may compromise doubtful claims for or against estate or may assign to creditor, heir, or beneficiary for prosecution on behalf of estate. (53-7-45).

Payment of Claims.—Debts should be paid, wholly or in part, at end of six months from appointment of representative. (53-7-41). Statutes of limitation do not run during this six-month period, or during period from death until appointment of personal representative. (9-3-93; 250 Ga. 157, 296 S.E.2d 49; 229 Ga. 771, 195 S.E.2d 15). See subhead Actions Against Representative, infra. If only partial payment made, payments required to be pro rated among all debts of equal dignity. (53-7-42). Unmatured claims are dealt with like matured claims and unliquidated, doubtful or contested claims may be compromised. (53-7-45). If secured claims exceed security, creditor shares pro rata with other creditors as to excess.

Priorities.—Debts of a decedent are paid in following order of priority: (1) year's support for decedent's family; (2) funeral expenses; (3) necessary administration expenses; (4) expenses of last illness; (5) taxes or other debts due to state or U.S.; (6) judgments, mortgages and other liens created during decedent's lifetime, according to their priority of lien, but mortgages and liens on specific property are preferred only to extent of such property; and (7) all other claims. Priority of federal claims under this statute subject to federal law.

Sales.—Personal representative has broad powers of sale but many sales require court approval. (53-8-10 through -15). Rules do not apply if private sales or sales of realty are authorized in will, including by reference to 53-12-232, or when personal representative has been granted powers described in 53-12-232 with consent of all heirs or beneficiaries. (53-7-1).

Investments Regulated.—(53-8-2 through -8). In managing property for benefit of another, personal representative must exercise judgment and care, under circumstances then prevailing, that prudent persons exercise in management of their own affairs, considering probable income as well as safety of corpus. Personal representative is authorized to acquire and retain every kind of property and investment. Within limitations of such standard, personal representative may retain property properly acquired, without limitation as to time and without regard to its suitability for original purchase. (53-8-1).

Corporate fiduciary may retain property which decedent owned at death including stock or other security of its own issue (53-8-5) and any securities held may be registered in name of nominee without mention of fiduciary relationship in instrument evidencing such securities or on books of issuer. (53-12-300).

See note at head of Digest as to 1998 legislation covered.

See Topical Index in front part of this volume.

GA – 42

EXECUTORS AND ADMINISTRATORS . . . *continued*

Actions Against Representative.—May not be brought for six months after qualification. (53-7-42). Where action against decedent was pending at time of death, representative may be substituted and proceedings suspended for the six-month period. (9-2-40). See also subhead Payment of Claims, supra.

Allowances.—See topic Descent and Distribution, subhead Year's Support.

Division of Property in Kind.—Intestate estate may distribute property in kind but if not pro rata consent of heirs or order of probate court is required. (33-2-30). Such distribution may also be authorized by will, including by reference to 53-12-232, or when administrator has been granted powers in 53-12-232 with consent of all heirs.

Accounting and Settlement.—Governed generally by 53-7-60 et seq. Any interested distributee or legatee may compel administrator or executor to submit to accounting before probate judge after six months following grant of administration, or administrator or executor may cite all distributees to be present at settlement of accounts by judge. Judge may grant additional time to settle estate. Such settlement conclusive on administrator or executor and on all distributees who receive notice of hearing. (53-7-62). Action for settlement available even if administrator or executor not required to give bond or make inventory or returns. Discharge obtainable by petition on which citation must be published one time in newspaper in which county advertisements are published. (53-7-50).

Consent Settlement.—No provision for such settlements.

Distribution.—After payment of debts and expenses, balance distributed according to law. See topics Descent and Distribution; Wills, subhead Legacies.

Distribution if Distributee Abroad.—No special provisions except for "missing persons". (53-9-10).

Compensation.—Executors and administrators allowed commissions of 2½% on money received and 2½% on money paid out. Whenever any portion of dividends, interest or rents payable to an administrator or executor are required by law of the United States or other governmental unit to be withheld by person paying same for income tax purposes, amounts so withheld are deemed to have been collected by administrator or executor. For wills executed and administration begun on or after Mar. 28, 1988, unless otherwise specifically provided by will, executor or administrator is entitled to receive commissions on debts, legacies, and distributive shares paid to himself or herself in same manner as commissions to which he or she would be entitled under terms of will or applicable law on such items paid to others. If more than one executor or administrator, division of commissions allowed them shall be according to services rendered by each. On property delivered in kind, probate judge may allow reasonable fee not exceeding 3% of value. Executors and administrators are also allowed extra compensation for extraordinary services and reasonable expenses of intercounty travel, surety bond premium, and necessary agents. (53-6-60).

Testator and executor may agree by contract in writing on executor's compensation which shall be binding upon estate and executor. (53-6-60).

Foreign and Ancillary Administration.—See topic Wills, subheads Foreign Probated Wills and Foreign Executed Wills.

See also category Documents and Records, topic Records, subhead Transfer of Decedent's Title.

When Administration Unnecessary.—When person owning real or personal property located in state dies intestate, and no administrator has been appointed, any heir may file petition in probate court of county where real property is located if decedent was nonresident, or in county of residence, if decedent was resident. Procedure not available if any creditor objects unless objection is withdrawn. (53-2-40 through -42).

Probate judge publishes notice to creditors (53-10-2), and, in absence of written objection by creditors, if probate judge finds that all heirs are sui juris and estate owes no debts, judge shall enter order of no administration necessary (53-10-2).

No administration is necessary if only asset of estate is federal tax refund. (53-1-6). Other property that may be transferred without formal probate or administration includes automobiles, bank accounts, and wages. (40-3-34, 7-1-239, 7-1-230.1, 34-7-1).

Small Estates.—See subhead When Administration Unnecessary, supra.

Uniform Fiduciaries Act.—Not adopted.

Uniform Principal and Income Act.—Adopted with substantial revision. (53-12-210 through -219).

Uniform Simplification of Fiduciary Security Transfers Act adopted. (53-12-320 through -330). See category Business Organizations, topic Corporations, subhead Uniform Simplification of Fiduciary Security Transfers Act.

Uniform Anatomical Gift Act.—Adopted. (44-5-140 through -148).

See category Business Regulation and Commerce, topic Banks and Banking.

FIDUCIARIES:

See topics Executors and Administrators, Trusts; category Family, topic Guardian and Ward.

INTESTACY:

See topic Descent and Distribution.

PROOF OF CLAIMS:

See topic Executors and Administrators; category Civil Actions and Procedure, topic Pleading.

TRUSTS:

Kinds.—Express trusts (53-12-2[2]); implied trusts (53-12-2[3]); resulting trusts (53-12-91); purchase money resulting trusts (53-12-92); constructive trusts (53-12-93); and charitable trusts (53-12-111).

Business trust may be created by owners of property in Georgia or persons desiring to acquire beneficial ownership of such property. (53-12-51).

Creation is by written instrument termed deed which must name and specify active duty for trustee or successors and provide for improvement, development and acquisition of property. Proper execution and recording of deed creates estate in such property, improvements thereon, and property to be acquired, for benefit of creators and others (whether or not sui juris) who contribute to improvement, development or acquisition, their assigns or transferees. Creation vests trustee and successors with legal title to original and subsequently acquired property and all other powers enumerated in deed, for duration of trust estate. (53-12-51).

Duration of estate created is determined by which of permissible alternative procedures provided in deed, i.e., 25 year existence with permissible option to renew for additional 25 years; or, any period specified not extending beyond any number of lives in being and 21 years. (53-12-51). Upon termination legal title to all property undisposed of vests in persons then beneficiaries in shares corresponding to their interest. (53-12-58).

Certificates of beneficial interest issued to present and future beneficiaries by trustee and such certificates transferable as personalty in same manner as corporate stock. (53-12-54). Deed may authorize trustee to repurchase or redeem outstanding certificates from corpus, income or both. (53-12-56).

Recording of deed with clerk of superior court of county in which principal office of trust located required within 30 days of execution. For recording fees, see topic Records, subhead Recording Fees. Clerk returns two certified copies which, together with $5 fee, must be delivered to Secretary of State who attaches statutory certificate. Amendments to deed recorded in same manner for same fees. Annual return such as is required of corporation must be filed with Secretary of State. (53-12-52, 57).

Business or tradename for estate may be established in deed and affairs of trust conducted under such name; may include word "trust" but not "trust company". (53-12-53).

Powers and duties of trustee include sole and exclusive management of corpus with power to lease, encumber and sell same in accordance with deed provisions. (53-12-55).

Death, resignation or removal of trustee does not terminate estate. Successor may be appointed as provided in deed and assumes full powers of original trustee over corpus. (53-12-55).

Legal investments by trustee are property, as defined in 53-12-50 through -59, and any other investment authorized to trustee under law. Deed may further limit or expand powers of trustee with regard to investments including power to invest in property outside State. (53-12-56).

Liabilities.—Trust estate subject to suit in same manner as corporation by serving trustee or, if trustee nonresident, by publication. Neither trustee nor beneficiaries personally or individually liable except insofar as officers and stockholders of private corporation can incur liability. Certificates subject to levy and sale under attachment or execution or other process as are shares of corporate stock and trustee must reveal beneficial ownership upon demand of levying officer. (53-12-54).

Merger into Corporations.—Business trust may be merged into domestic corporation. (53-12-59).

Taxation.—Net income of trusts and estates taxed. (48-7-20). In lieu of personal exemption, estate may deduct $2,700, trust may deduct $1,350. (48-7-26).

Creation.—No formal words necessary to create trust estate, only manifest intention that person other than grantee shall have benefit of property. (53-12-21). Express trusts must be in writing. (53-12-20). Implied trust is either resulting trust or constructive trust. (53-12-90). Precatory or recommendatory words may create trust if they are sufficiently imperative to show intent to create trust. (53-12-21).

Appointment of Trustee.—By grantor or by beneficiaries, if grantor confers power. (53-12-170). Trust will not fail for want of trustee. (53-12-6). Superior courts may appoint and remove trustees and successors. (53-12-176).

Eligibility and Competency.—Trustee must accept trust by acts or words before appointment effective. (53-12-171). Foreign bank or other corporation or national banking association in certain bordering states (Florida, Alabama, Tennessee, North Carolina, or South Carolina) may act as trustee (53-12-390, 391) in Georgia without qualifying to do business in Georgia.

Qualification.—If required to give bond, trustee may give bond in amount equal to value of estate (without regard to value of realty), if bond secured by licensed commercial surety authorized to do business in Ga. (53-7-34, 35). Otherwise, bond of greater amount may be required.

Removal of Trustee.—Superior court judge has power to remove on petition by interested party. (53-12-176).

General Powers and Duties of Trustees.—Trust instrument controls. (53-12-190). Principal and income allocated as provided in trust or if no provision then under 53-12-210, 219.

Sales of trust property, unless expressly authorized by trust instrument, require court order after full notice to all interested parties. (53-12-257). Where trustee transfers property improperly, purchaser takes subject to rights of beneficiary. (234 Ga. 320, 216 S.E.2d 83).

Net income of trust must be distributed at least as frequently as annually if instrument is silent as to time and frequency of distribution. (53-12-190). Whenever trust income is used for benefit of a person whose support is the legal obligation of another, the legal obligation of the other person is reduced to the extent such income is actually used for such person's support. (53-1-3).

Investments.—Certain enumerated investments are permissible even when trust instrument silent, but broader investment discretion is usually authorized in trust instrument. (53-12-280 through -286). In managing property for benefit of another, trustee must exercise judgment and care, under circumstances then prevailing, that prudent person acting in like capacity and familiar with such matters will use to attain purposes of account. In making investment decisions, trustee may consider general economic conditions, anticipated tax consequences of investment, anticipated duration of account, and needs of its beneficiaries. Trustee is authorized to acquire and retain every kind of property and investment. Propriety of investment decision is to be determined by what

See note at head of Digest as to 1998 legislation covered.

See Topical Index in front part of this volume.

GA – 43

TRUSTS . . . continued

trustee knew or should have known at time of decision about inherent nature and expected performance of investments, attributes of portfolio, general economy, and needs and objectives of beneficiaries of account as they existed at time of decision. Any determination of liability for investment performance shall consider not only performance of particular investment, but also performance of individual's portfolio as a whole. Within limitations of such standard, trustee may retain property properly acquired, without limitation as to time and without regard to its suitability for original purchase. (53-12-287).

Securities in Name of Nominee.—Fiduciaries allowed to hold securities in name of nominee. (53-12-300).

Bequests and Devises to Inter Vivos Trusts.—See topic Wills.

Accounting.—Uniform Trustees' Accounting Act not adopted. Unless trust instrument provides otherwise, trustee accounts to beneficiaries at least annually, or court may order accounting. (53-12-190).

Compensation.—Trustee entitled to receive compensation specified in trust instrument or separate fee agreement, if any, or if none, then same compensation as guardians receive for similar services. (53-12-173).

Discharge.—Trustee may resign as trustee if provided by trust instrument or allowed by court. (53-12-175).

Foreign Trustees as to Georgia Lands.—Such foreign trustees must designate Georgia agent for service concerning such trust, in absence of which designation Secretary of State is legal agent for service. (53-12-370). Venue is county where subject lands lie. (53-12-372).

Uniform Principal and Income Act.—Adopted with substantial revisions. (53-12-210 through -219).

Accumulations.—See supra subhead Net Income; and topic Perpetuities.

Perpetuities.—See category Property, topic Perpetuities.

Gifts to Minors.—See category Family, topic Infants.

Uniform Fiduciaries Act.—Not adopted.

Uniform Simplification of Fiduciary Security Transfers Act adopted. (53-12-320-330). See subhead Uniform Simplification of Fiduciary Security Transfers under topic Corporations. In case of conflict with UCC, this Act controls. (11-10-105).

Pour Over Trusts.—See topic Wills, subhead Bequests and Devises to Inter Vivos Trusts.

WILLS:

Note: Title 53 of Georgia Code has been amended effective Jan. 1, 1998, provided that no vested rights of title, year's support, succession or inheritance shall be impaired. This section reflects those changes. Earlier digests should be consulted regarding prior law.

Testamentary Capacity.—Any person age 14 or over may make will unless laboring under some legal disability arising from lack of capacity or perfect liberty of action. (53-4-10).

Intellect necessary to constitute testamentary capacity is that necessary to enable decided, rational desire as to disposition. (53-4-11).

Testamentary Dispositions.—Testator may make any disposition of his or her property not inconsistent with law or contrary to public policy. May give entire estate to strangers to exclusion of spouse and children. (53-4-1). See also topic Descent and Distribution, subhead Year's Support; category Property, topic Dower. Contracts to make will must be express, in writing, and signed by obligor, and "joint" or "mutual" wills are no exception. (53-4-30 through -33). Divorce decree may operate as contract to make will in favor of spouse. (266 Ga. 640, 648 S.E.2d 745). Cy pres doctrine applied in case of gift to charitable use. (53-4-62). Cy pres inapplicable if there is reversionary clause or valid gift over. (238 Ga. 343, 232 S.E.2d 835).

Form.—No particular form is necessary; test is intention to convey interest accruing and having effect only after death. (53-4-3).

Execution.—Will must be in writing, signed by testator or some one for him or her acting under his or her express directions and in his or her presence, and must be subscribed and attested in testator's presence by two or more competent witnesses. Testator must sign or acknowledge signature in presence of two witnesses. Witness may attest by mark provided he or she can swear to same, but one witness may not subscribe name of other, even in his or her presence and by his or her direction. (53-4-20). Testator and witnesses do not need to sign on same page for will to be properly executed. (264 Ga. 84, 441 S.E.2d 248).

Filing.—Will may be filed in probate judge's office while maker in life. Fee $5. Will docketed publicly but filed in confidence except to person making it or attorney who also may withdraw it. Filed will may be revoked without withdrawal. (15-9-37, 38, 60).

Holographic Wills.—Holographic will may constitute valid will, but not given any special consideration because of holographic nature.

Nuncupative Wills.—Not recognized. (Consult earlier digests for prior law.)

Mutual Wills.—Do not receive special treatment. Do not (without more) create contracts to make wills, and may be revoked like any other will. Revocation of one does not revoke other. (53-4-30 through -33).

Revocation.—Will is revoked in toto by subsequent marriage or birth of child unless will contains provision in contemplation of such event. (53-4-48). In case of divorce, will is not revoked but spouse is treated as predeceased, and other special rules apply. (53-4-49). Revocation by destruction accomplished only by concurrence of both intent to revoke and effective destruction. (213 Ga. 613; 100 S.E.2d 450). Obliteration or cancellation of material portion of will creates rebuttable presumption of intent to revoke. (53-4-44). Destruction of one of several executed copies of will with requisite intent revokes will. (215 Ga. 345, 110 S.E.2d 772). Original of will must be carefully safeguarded because of presumed intent to revoke by destruction if original cannot be

found. (53-4-46). Will executed pursuant to valid contract may be revoked by subsequent will, but contract remains binding upon parties. (231 Ga. 145, 200 S.E.2d 725).

Revival.—Revocation of revoking will revives earlier, revoked will under some circumstances. Earlier will may also be republished. (53-4-45).

Testamentary Gifts to Subscribing Witnesses.—Beneficiary may be competent witness to will, but devise or legacy to him or her is void unless there are at least two other subscribing witnesses who are not beneficiaries.

However, a testamentary gift to spouse of subscribing witness is valid, fact going only to credibility of witness. (53-4-23).

Bequests and Devises to Inter Vivos Trusts.—Bequest or devise may be made to trustee of trust, if identified in will and terms set forth in instrument executed before or concurrent with execution of testator's will (including will of person predeceasing testator). Not invalid because trust is amendable or revocable, or because was amended after execution of will or after death of testator. Property bequeathed or devised becomes part of trust to which given, and is administered in accordance with its terms. Devise or bequest will lapse if trust terminated or revoked before testator's death but trust instrument as in effect when will executed may be incorporated by reference to protect against disallowed pourover. (53-12-71). Trustee's duties and responsibilities limited in regard to such bequests or devises. (53-12-72).

Testamentary Guardians.—See category Family, topic Guardian and Ward.

Probate.—Will is probated in probate court of county of testator's domicile at time of death. Rebuttable presumption that person living in nursing home at time of death is resident of county in which he or she resided immediately before entering home. (53-5-1). Person having possession of will must file same with probate judge of proper county with reasonable promptness. (53-5-5). Executor has right to offer will for probate and should do so with reasonable promptness; otherwise, any interested person may offer will for probate. (53-5-2). Will must be offered within five years after petition for appointment of personal representative, order of year's support, or order of no administration necessary. (53-5-3).

Probate is in either common or solemn form.

Probate in common form is on testimony of single subscribing witness and without notice. (53-5-17). It is not immediately conclusive on any person interested in estate adversely to will, and if set aside, does not protect executor in any act except payment of debts—bona fide purchasers without notice from executor are protected if sale legally made. (53-5-18). Application must give same information required for solemn form. (53-5-17). Order to probate will in common form may be granted by probate court at any time. (53-5-18). Such probate becomes conclusive after four years (seven years for will probated before July 1, 1984, but no later than July 1, 1988) on all parties except minor heirs who interpose caveat within four years after attaining majority, and can be set aside only so far as to let in rights of such minors as in case of intestacy. (53-5-19).

Probate in solemn form is proof of will, after due notice to all heirs at law and propounders and beneficiaries under any other purported will of testator as to which probate proceedings are pending in Georgia upon testimony of all witnesses living and within state, or by proof of signatures of testator and of dead or unavailable witnesses. Only one witness required to prove will for probate in solemn form if no caveat is filed. (53-5-21). Sole issue on application for probate in solemn form is validity of paper as last will and testament. (235 Ga. 607, 221 S.E.2d 31). Parties interested and residing in state must have at least ten days notice by personal service before term of court at which probate sought, unless waived in writing, and other heirs are served by publication or mail. (53-11-1 et seq.). Such probate is conclusive on all parties notified and all devisees and legatees, and is conclusive as to heirs at law not effectively notified as if probate had been in common form. (53-5-20). Probate court has jurisdiction to vacate order probating will in solemn form if will obtained through fraud or misrepresentation. (242 Ga. 479, 249 S.E.2d 263).

Self-proved Wills.—Will may be self-proved with acknowledgment by testator and affidavits by witnesses. (53-4-24).

Contest.—Any interested person may contest by caveat at probate. (125 Ga. 122, 53 S.E. 583). No contest clause is void unless there is direction as to disposition of contesting beneficiary's share. (53-4-68).

Testimony of Witnesses.—Testimony may be taken outside Georgia or outside county of probate in person, by written interrogatories, or by deposition or any other discovery procedure available in civil cases. (53-5-23).

Legacies.—May be specific, general, demonstrative or residuary. General and demonstrative legacies receive interest at legal rate after one year, specific gifts receive income from specific property, and residuary gifts share in probate income. Residuary gifts abate first, then general legacies, then demonstrative legacies. Specific gifts are adeemed if property not owned at death. (53-4-59 through -66). See also subhead Lapses, infra. If anti-lapse statute does not apply, local gift goes to residue or to other residuary beneficiaries. (53-4-65).

Unclaimed Legacies.—See topic Executors and Administrators, subhead Distribution if Distributee Abroad. See also topic Descent and Distribution, subhead Escheat.

Lapses.—If legatee dies before testator, or is dead when will is executed, but dies leaving descendants living at time of death of testator, such legacy, if absolute, vests in descendants of deceased legatee as if inherited directly from legatee. If legatee is treated as predeceased by reason of divorce or killing, rule only applies to descendants of testator. (53-4-64).

Children.—Testator may bequeath entire estate to strangers, to exclusion of spouse and children. (53-4-1). See also subhead Revocation, supra.

Classes.—Members of class are to be ascertained as of date of testator's death unless express intent to determine class at future date or upon occurrence of subsequent event is manifested. (231 Ga. 49, 200 S.E.2d 110).

Election.—Testator may by will make provision for spouse in lieu of year's support, in which case surviving spouse must make election. (53-3-3).

Legatee having claim adverse to the will must elect whether to claim under will or against it, but legatee who is also creditor need not elect. (53-4-69).

See note at head of Digest as to 1998 legislation covered.

See Topical Index in front part of this volume.

WILLS . . . *continued*

Renunciation.—See topic Descent and Distribution, subhead Renunciation.

Inheritance Denial.—See topic Descent and Distribution, subhead Inheritance Denial.

Foreign Probated Wills.—Any foreign will, which has been admitted to probate in state of U.S. where testator resided, may be admitted to probate in Georgia in solemn form upon production of probate proceedings certified according to provisions of 24-7-24, subject to right of parties interested to resist probate on any proper grounds. (53-5-33).

Foreign Executed Wills.—Will probated in another state is effective as muniment of title for transfer of real property in Georgia and may be admitted in evidence as such muniment without being probated in Georgia when accompanied by properly certified exemplification of record admitting it to probate and when said exemplified will is recorded in office of clerk of superior court of county in which land is situated. (53-5-35).

If admitted to ancillary probate, validity and construction are governed by law of domicile. If admitted to original probate, must be valid under Georgia law. (53-5-34). No provision for recognition of will executed according to law of domicile at time of execution. See also category Documents and Records, topic Records, subhead Transfer of Decedent's Title.

Simultaneous Death.—See topic Death, subhead Survivorship.

Testamentary Trusts.—See topic Trusts.

Uniform Anatomical Gift Act.—Adopted. (44-5-140, -148, as modified by 44-5-145[b]).

Living Wills.—Georgia permits competent adult to make written directive instructing physician to withhold or withdraw life sustaining procedures in event of terminal condition, coma, or persistent vegetative state. (31-32-1). Georgia recognizes right of patients or other authorized persons to instruct physicians and other health care personnel to refrain from cardiopulmonary resuscitation. (31-39-1).

Powers of Attorney for Health Care.—Principal may appoint agent to make decisions on broad range of health-related issues, including withholding or withdrawal of life sustaining procedures. (31-36-1 through -13).

FAMILY

ADOPTION:

Any adult may petition for leave to adopt if adult is at least 25 years of age or married and living with spouse, at least ten years older than child, has been bona fide resident of Georgia for six months and is financially, physically, and morally fit and mentally able to have permanent custody. (19-8-3). If person seeking to adopt child is married, petition must be filed in name of both spouses. Adults may be adopted with written consent and shall be legally as child to parent. (19-8-21). Adoption records may be disclosed to adopted person under certain circumstances. (19-8-23).

Consent Required.—Child 14 or over must consent in writing in presence of court. (19-8-4). No adoption unless living parent(s) or guardian(s) formally consent to surrender and termination of all parental rights voluntarily and in writing, except where parent(s) or guardian(s): (1) has rights terminated by superior court of county where child resides placing child for adoption (19-8-11); (2) has abandoned child (19-8-10); (3) is incompetent (19-8-10); (4) cannot be located after diligent search (19-8-10); (5) has failed significantly (without justifiable cause) to make bona fide attempt to communicate with child in meaningful, supportive, parental manner; or (6) has failed to provide care for child as required by law for one year or longer immediately prior to filing of petition. (19-8-10). Best interests of child will govern whether adoption will occur. (160 Ga. App. 446, 287 S.E.2d 365; 19-8-10). Notice must be given to parent(s) or guardian(s) whenever nonapplicability of consent affidavit requirement is alleged. (19-8-10). If identity and location of biological father known or reasonably ascertainable or if biological father has registered with putative father registry or has performed certain acts (e.g., lived with child), notice must be given of mother's consent; biological father has 30 days to file legitimation petition or loses all rights to child. (19-8-12). Consent may be withdrawn by parent or guardian for ten days after execution. (19-8-9). Validity of surrender may be challenged after ten days on grounds of fraud, duress or other grounds which address voluntariness of consent. (224 Ga. App. 124, 479 S.E.2d 439).

Jurisdiction for adoption is in superior court, except as may be granted to juvenile court. (19-8-2). Juvenile court is not party competent to contract for disposition of child and therefore cannot be party to virtual adoption. (265 Ga. 89, 453 S.E.2d 445). Juvenile Court has jurisdiction over any matter involving termination of legal parent-child relationship brought outside adoption proceedings. (15-11-5). If termination is in connection with adoption, superior court and juvenile court have concurrent jurisdiction. (15-11-15).

Uniform Child Custody Jurisdiction Act.—Does not apply to adoption proceedings. (19-9-40; 185 Ga. App. 427, 364 S.E.2d 279).

Venue.—Petition must be brought in county of adopting parent or, on good cause being shown, may at court's discretion be brought at child's domicile or in county where child placing agency is located. (19-8-2).

Petition.—Verified petition and one conformed copy filed with clerk of superior court setting forth name, age, marital status and place of residence of petitioners; name by which child is to be known after adoption; date of birth, and sex of child; date and circumstances of placement with petitioners; description of any property of child; whether parents are alive; whether child has guardian. Attached to petition must be affidavits and applicable forms of consent from parents, guardians, or Department of Human Resources, or allegations of non-applicability of consent requirement; allegation of compliance with requirements of notice to biological father, if applicable; certificate from putative father registry (19-18-12); statement of reason for venue other than

petitioner's residence; signed and verified report of all expenses incurred in connection with adoption (19-8-13).

Proceedings.—Court must fix date not less than 60 days from filing for consideration of petition. Copy of petition and order setting date forwarded by clerk within 15 days of filing to Department of Human Resources with request for investigation and reports. (19-8-14). Department of Human Resources must investigate entire matter and make written reports to court with findings and recommendations. If one parent has voluntarily and in writing surrendered all parental rights to spouse or one parent and other parent consents to adoption, or if parents have voluntarily and in writing surrendered all parental rights to close relative, investigation is authorized, but not required. (19-8-16). Court may appoint guardian ad litem. (19-8-17).

Objections to Adoption.—Objections may be filed by any blood relative of child if parents not living. Grandparents with visitation rights have right to object. (19-8-15). Unwed father who has not abandoned his or her interest is entitled to oppose adoption of child by nonbiological parties and receive custody unless found unfit. (257 Ga. 292, 358 S.E.2d 459). Otherwise court looks to best interest of child. (257 Ga. 292, 358 S.E.2d 459).

Decree.—Where requirements are met and circumstances warrant, court shall enter decree of adoption, granting permanent custody to petitioners and declaring child to be adopted child of petitioners. (19-8-18). Upon payment of fee, clerk of court to issue certificate of adoption giving full name of adopted child. (19-8-20). Decree not subject to any judicial challenge filed more than six months after date of entry of such decree, or, as to decrees issued prior to July 1, 1995, filed more than six months after July 1, 1995, effective date of Act. (19-8-18[e] & [f]).

Effect of Adoption.—Decree relieves nonadopting natural parents of parental rights and responsibilities and terminates legal relationships between adopted child and his or her relatives, including inheritance, construction of documents, statutes, or instruments, whether executed before or after adoption, unless individual expressly included by name or other particular designation. Decree creates relationship of parent and child between petitioners and adopted individual. Adoptee inherits as natural child under laws of descent and distribution in absence of will, and takes as natural child under provisions of any instrument of testamentary gift, bequest, devise or legacy, whether executed before or after decree, unless expressly excluded. Adoptee takes by inheritance from relatives of petitioners and as "child" of petitioners under class gift in will of third person. (19-8-19). Decree terminates visitation rights of relatives. (242 Ga. 742, 251 S.E.2d 302). Adoption decree of foreign jurisdiction recognized as though issued by court of this state. (19-8-22).

Advertisements offering to adopt children or otherwise inducing parents to part with children illegal unless by licensed child-placing agency. (19-8-24).
See also topics Husband and Wife, Guardian and Ward.
For forms see 19-8-26.

ALIMONY:

See topic Divorce.

COMMUNITY PROPERTY:

System does not obtain.

DESERTION:

See topics Divorce, Husband and Wife.

DISSOLUTION OF MARRIAGE:

See topic Divorce.

DIVORCE:

Governed by 19-5-1 through -17.
Georgia has not adopted Uniform Marriage and Divorce Act but supreme court has followed its provisions in deciding divorce and alimony issues in "no-fault" divorce cases. (238 Ga. 328, 232 S.E.2d 921).

Partial Divorce.—Statutes repealed. (19-5-1).

Grounds for Total Divorce.—(1) Relationship between parties such that marriage prohibited; (2) mental incapacity at time of marriage; (3) impotency at time of marriage; (4) force, menace, duress or fraud in obtaining marriage; (5) pregnancy by man other than husband at time of marriage, unknown to husband; (6) adultery by either party; (7) willful and continued desertion by either party for one year; (8) conviction of offense involving moral turpitude where penalty two years or more in penitentiary; (9) habitual intoxication; (10) cruel treatment, consisting of willful infliction of pain, bodily or mental, upon complaining party such as reasonably justifies apprehension of danger to life, limb or health; (11) incurable mental illness determined by court of competent jurisdiction, or certified as such by two physicians, accompanied by confinement in institution and/or under continuous treatment for mentally ill for two years immediately preceding action, and statement under oath, by competent physician and chief executive officer of institution, that in his or her opinion such person evidences such incurable mental deficiencies as to prevent party from comprehending ramifications of marriage relationship; (12) habitual drug addiction; (13) irretrievably broken marriage. (19-5-3). Irreconcilable differences, while not statutory ground, is amendable defect at trial court level sufficient for divorce. (234 Ga. 836, 218 S.E.2d 619). Court may determine that marriage is irretrievably broken even though one party claims it is not. (236 Ga. 633, 255 S.E.2d 682).

Residence Requirement.—Plaintiff or defendant must have resided in the state for six months before action brought. (19-5-2).

Jurisdiction is in superior court. (19-5-1). Prior to trial, judge can refer contested petitions for divorce or permanent alimony for alternative dispute resolution, regardless of whether county has established alternative dispute resolution program pursuant to c. 23 of Title 15, Georgia Court-annexed Alternative Dispute Resolution Act. (19-5.1).

See note at head of Digest as to 1998 legislation covered.

See Topical Index in front part of this volume.

DIVORCE . . . *continued*
Trial court can grant divorce even though child custody issues are pending in another jurisdiction. (267 Ga. 841, 483 S.E.2d 577).

Venue.—County of defendant's residence if defendant is Georgia resident, or of plaintiff's residence if defendant nonresident, or in any county adjacent to army post or military reservation in which party has resided for one year next preceding filing of petition. (Ga. Const., Art. VI, §II, para. 1). Contempt application normally must be filed in county where divorce and alimony decree entered, but if superior court other than one rendering original decree acquires jurisdiction and venue to modify original decree, it also has jurisdiction and venue to entertain counterclaim alleging plaintiff is in contempt of original decree. (251 Ga. 58, 302 S.E.2d 676).

Process.—Nonresident defendant may be served by publication. See category Civil Actions and Procedure, topic Process.

Pleading.—Action for divorce must be brought by verified petition, which must show: (1) last known address of defendant; (2) that residency requirements are met; (3) dates of marriage and separation; (4) whether or not there are minor children and their ages; (5) statutory grounds for action; (6) if alimony or support or division of property is involved, property or earnings of parties, if known. (19-5-5). Respondent may ask for divorce in his or her favor without counterclaim. (19-5-6).

Practice.—Divorces triable after last day defensive pleadings required to be filed, provided parties shall be allowed reasonable discovery time. Divorce cases involving service by publication are triable 60 days after first publication. (9-11-40).

Unless a defense is filed and a jury trial is demanded in writing by either party on or before call of case for trial, judge hears and determines all issues of law and facts in petition for divorce and permanent alimony. (19-5-1).

Default judgment is not allowed, but allegations of petition must be established by evidence and court must be satisfied that legal grounds exist. (19-5-8). In uncontested divorce proceedings, court, sua sponte, or by appointment of counsel, determines legality and sufficiency of grounds alleged in petition. (19-5-10). Pleading and practice of civil actions followed in divorce. (19-5-8). In contested actions involving alimony, child support, equitable division of property, modification of alimony or attorney's fees, parties must file affidavit specifying financial circumstances. (Rule 24.2, Uniform Superior Ct. R.).

Judgment authorizing grant of total divorce annuls marriage upon rendering. (19-5-15). Judgment to pay child's support enforced under 19-6-28.

Temporary alimony for child support may be awarded to either spouse. (19-6-14).

Permanent Alimony.—May be awarded in case of divorce or voluntary separation or where spouse, against his or her will, is abandoned or driven off by other spouse (19-6-4), but adulterous spouse not precluded from obtaining equitable property division (248 Ga. 490, 283 S.E.2d 454). Where divorce is sought on ground of irretrievably broken marriage, misconduct of parties is relevant to question of amount of alimony. (243 Ga. 848, 257 S.E.2d 269). Finder of fact may grant permanent alimony to either party from corpus of estate or otherwise, and shall consider in determining amount of alimony: standard of living established during marriage; duration of marriage; age and physical and mental condition of both parties; financial resources of both parties; time necessary for either party to acquire training to enable him or her to find appropriate employment; contribution of each party to marriage; separate estate, earning capacity and fixed liabilities of parties; and other relevant factors. (19-6-5). Obligations for permanent alimony, time for performance of which has not arrived, cease upon remarriage of party to whom obligation owed unless otherwise provided. (19-6-5). Obligation to pay alimony terminates upon paying spouse's death, unless separation agreement incorporated into decree expressly states otherwise. (248 Ga. 439, 284 S.E.2d 254). Failure to pay alimony grounds for contempt proceedings. (234 Ga. 37, 214 S.E.2d 493). Parties may by contract waive right to alimony or future alimony adjustments. (234 Ga. 259, 214 S.E.2d 925). Amount of periodic payments of permanent alimony subject to revision upon petition filed by either spouse showing change in income and financial status of either spouse. (19-6-18, -19, -20). When action pending, court may allow temporary modification of prior judgment. (19-6-19). Voluntary cohabitation of former spouse in: (i) meretricious relationship (including that of having sexual intercourse or sharing living expenses) that is (ii) continuous and open is ground for modification of periodic payments. (258 Ga. 101, 365 S.E.2d 826). Former spouse's cohabitation with person of same sex is not ground for modification of payments. (262 Ga. 720, 425 S.E.2d 853). Parties to alimony agreement may obtain modification unless agreement expressly waives right of modification by referring specifically to that right. (242 Ga. 309, 248 S.E.2d 667). So long as child or children named in support order or any party action resides in state, modification of order issued by Georgia court may be obtained in Georgia court. (19-6-26[c]). Georgia court may exercise jurisdiction over foreign support order. (19-6-26[d]). Where resident's spouse obtains foreign divorce, resident may apply for alimony in superior court in county where spouse applying for alimony resides. (19-6-27). Alimony judgments not subject to dormancy or revival statutes. (9-12-60[d]). Court has power to incorporate alimony contract by parties into judgment though court could not make such agreement itself. (235 Ga. 659, 221 S.E.2d 561). Alimony is in personam issue and alimony adjudication thus requires personal service. (143 Ga. App. 709, 240 S.E.2d 119).

Division of Property of Spouses.—Property acquired by parties during marriage may be subject to equitable division. (246 Ga. 765, 273 S.E.2d 169). Property eligible for equitable division in divorce includes personal injury claim settlement for lost wages during marriage or medical expenses. (255 Ga. 461, 339 S.E.2d 591). Also eligible are interspousal gifts made during marriage. (256 Ga. 762, 353 S.E.2d 486). Obligation to pay vested retirement benefits to spouse will be considered part of division of marital property and not periodic alimony to be adjusted upon remarriage of one of parties. (265 Ga. 76, 453 S.E.2d 735 [overruling Fisher v. Frederickson, 262 Ga. 229 (1992)]).

Allowance for Support.—Where custody of children awarded to third party or to parent and decree does not set support payments, person to whom custody is given may thereafter sue parent without custody for support of children. (19-6-17). Custodial parent cannot waive child's right to seek increase in child support payments; however, noncustodial parent can waive right to seek reduction in child support payments. (265

Ga. 441, 457 S.E.2d 669). Guidelines for support obligations of noncustodial spouse are set specifically by statute and neither judge nor jury may award child support to custodial spouse inconsistent with these guidelines without explanation expressly set forth in order or judgment establishing support obligation. (19-6-15). Agreement to provide automatic increases in child support in excess of statutory guidelines enforceable. Custodial parent seeking extension of child support payments for child who has reached age of majority but who has not completed secondary education need not file modification action before child attains age 18. (267 Ga. 886, 485 S.E.2d 475). Final order of support must refer to amount, duration, and method of payment of child support, as well as gross income of parents. (19-5-12). In case of permanent alimony for support of spouse or children, judge or jury can modify previous judgment in accordance with changed income and financial status of either former spouse or in accordance with needs of children. (19-6-19, -20). Willful refusal to pay can result in civil and/or criminal contempt. (239 Ga. 860, 238 S.E.2d 920). Jury verdict attempting to set future child support at different rate than present rate illegal. (242 Ga. 598, 250 S.E.2d 465). Parent paying lump sum support for two or more children not entitled to pro rata reduction when one child no longer in custody of parent receiving support. (242 Ga. 386, 249 S.E.2d 69). Once order for award of child support is entered, court may enter immediately separate order for income deduction (garnishment) from payor's salary. (19-6-31 through -33). Garnishment to settle alimony or child support may be withheld if visitation rights denied contra to custody order. (160 Ga. App. 463, 287 S.E.2d 378). If court determines that noncustodial party has accumulated support arrears equal to or greater than current support due for 60 days and party is licensed to conduct certain trades, businesses, professions or occupations, licensed to drive motor vehicle, to hunt or to fish, owns motor vehicle registered in Georgia, or is applying for issuance or renewal of any such license or registration, court may order suspension of license or registration or deny application for such license. (19-6-28.1[b]).

Uniform Reciprocal Enforcement of Support Act.—Adopted. (19-11-40 et seq.). Applies only to proceedings pending prior to Jan. 1, 1998. (19-11-40.5).

Uniform Interstate Family Support Act.—Adopted. (19-11-100 et seq.). Applies to petitions filed or proceedings initiated on or after Jan. 1, 1998. (19-11-40.5).

Attorneys' Fees.—Grant of attorneys' fees matter for court's discretion. (19-6-2).

Property Rights.—After petition for divorce has been filed, no transfer of property by either party, except bona fide in payment of preexisting debt, passes title so as to defeat vesting according to verdict of jury in divorce action, except title to real estate not affected by filing of divorce unless notice of lis pendens is filed in clerk's office in superior court. (19-5-7). After petition for divorce is filed, court may issue standing order prohibiting parties from transferring, selling, trading, contracting to sell, or encumbering property except in ordinary course of business. (19-1-1[b][4]). Agreements in contemplation of divorce settling issues of alimony, property division, child custody, child support and visitation valid. (248 Ga. 376, 283 S.E.2d 461).

Change of Wife's Name.—Wife obtaining divorce may, by proper pleading, have her maiden name restored. (19-5-16).

Children.—Party not in default is entitled to custody of minor children unless court, in its discretion, directs otherwise. (19-9-1). Where court makes finding of family violence, court must consider safety of victim in determining custody. (19-9-1). Court can award visitation by parent who committed family violence only if adequate safeguards made for safety of child/victim of family violence. (19-9-7). After petition for divorce is filed, court may issue standing order prohibiting parties from unilaterally causing or permitting minor child to be removed from jurisdiction of court. (19-1-1[b][2]). On death of parent with custody, other parent has prima facie right to custody. (234 Ga. 145, 214 S.E.2d 882). If child has reached age of 14, child has right to select parent with whom to live unless parent determined not to be fit and proper person to have custody. Where child has reached age of 14 years, court may issue order granting temporary custody to selected parent for trial period not to exceed six months where judge hearing case determines that such temporary order is appropriate. (19-9-1). Absent change in circumstances, visitation rights subject to review and modification not more than once in each two year period. (19-9-1). Where trial court determines both parents are fit and equally capable of caring for child, court must consider joint custody but is not required to enter such order unless it specifically finds it would be in child's best interest. (265 Ga. 465, 458 S.E.2d 126). Decision as to whether there is evidence warranting modification or suspension of custody/visitation privileges is responsibility of trial court and cannot be delegated to expert. (266 Ga. 493, 467 S.E.2d 578). Adverse emotional problems caused by sudden move is factor for consideration. (19-9-1[a][1]). Change of custody determined based on change of conditions affecting child's welfare. (222 Ga. App. 301, 474 S.E.2d 12). Relocation alone not support for finding change of condition, resulting in change of custody. (217 Ga. App. 780, 459 S.E.2d 439). Sexual orientation alone should not be grounds to place undue restrictions upon visitation rights of noncustodial parent. (220 Ga. App. 861, 471 S.E.2d 6). Except where provided by court, if parent changes residence, he or she must notify other parent, and if custodial parent changes residence, he or she must notify all persons with visitation rights. Notice must be given 30 days prior to change. (19-9-1). Statute providing for grandparents visitation rights unconstitutional. (265 Ga. 189, 454 S.E.2d 769). Custody of children may be awarded to third party where conditions of 19-7-4 are found or parent found unfit. (234 Ga. 348, 216 S.E.2d 103). Parent's fitness determined by reference to that parent alone and not by comparison to third party. (247 Ga. 94, 274 S.E.2d 471). Court may enforce custody decree by contempt power even if decree contains no express injunction or prohibition (239 Ga. 244, 236 S.E.2d 599) and this power exists concurrently with provisions of Uniform Child Custody Jurisdiction Act. (19-9-40 through -64).

Remarriage.—Where divorce is granted, jury or judge, as case may be, determines rights and disabilities of parties. No person shall be placed under disability that would prevent remarriage. (19-5-17). Remarriage does not affect property settlement. (236 Ga. 318, 223 S.E.2d 697). Remarriage terminates alimony obligations unless decree provides otherwise. (19-6-5[b]). Decree must expressly exempt remarriage to prevent termination of alimony upon remarriage. (257 Ga. 71, 354 S.E.2d 828).

Annulment of Marriage.—See topic Marriage.

See note at head of Digest as to 1998 legislation covered.

See Topical Index in front part of this volume.

DIVORCE . . . *continued*

Separation Agreements.—Between husband and wife living separately or in contemplation of separation valid and enforceable as to support, payments in lieu of alimony, etc. (65 Ga. App. 222, 15 S.E.2d 626).

GUARDIAN AND WARD:

Jurisdiction and venue respecting guardianship of minors is in probate court of county of infant's domicile, or where minor is found unless interested party requests transfer to county of minor's domicile. (29-4-4). Respecting guardianship of mentally incompetent persons, jurisdiction and venue are in probate court of county where incompetent person resides. (29-5-6; language of statute limited by 247 Ga. 9, 274 S.E.2d 314). In any case involving creation of guardianship over property where proposed ward has interest in real property, judge or clerk of probate court shall file certified copy of court's order granting such petition and, upon termination of such guardianship during ward's lifetime, certified copy of order of termination of such guardianship shall be filed with clerk of superior court of each county of this state in which real property is located within 30 days of date of such order. (29-5-6[f][4]). For provisions regarding administrators and executors of estates, see category Estates and Trusts, topic Executors and Administrators.

Selection of Guardian.—Either parent, if both are alive, is natural guardian, but if one parent is dead or parents are separated or divorced, then parent in custody is natural guardian. Natural guardian must give bond unless property of child is $1,000 or less. If value of property is greater than $1,000, but less than $5,000, whether or not bond is required will be in discretion of probate court. If natural guardian does not give bond, probate judge may appoint another guardian of property. (29-4-2). Minor over 14 may select guardian subject to approval of probate judge. (29-4-4). Nearest of kin by blood preferred, but probate judge has discretion. (29-4-8). Either surviving parent may appoint testamentary guardian of person and of such property as may be inherited from that parent. (29-4-3). Probate judge may act as guardian of minor or incapacitated adult if no other guardian has been appointed. (29-8-1). Selection of guardians for incapacitated adults governed by 29-5-1 et seq. Dept. of Human Resources may be appointed guardian of insane or incompetent persons receiving or eligible for its services if no other person available. (29-5-6). If personal property due does not exceed $5,000 parent of infant or spouse or relative of incompetent may receive such property without being appointed guardian. (29-4-17; 29-1-1). Probate judge has discretionary authority to appoint successor in event of death of duly appointed guardian. (29-2-75). Appointment of temporary guardian is governed by 29-4-4.1.

Spouse as Guardian.—Spouse has preference in appointment as guardian, unless husband and wife are separated or another nominated by ward prior to incapacity. If wife is guardian of husband, her bond and all acts treated as though she were femme sole. (29-5-2).

Eligibility and Competency.—No general eligibility requirements. Certain corporations eligible for appointment as guardian of property of incapacitated adult. (29-5-2).

Appointment of Guardian.—See subhead Selection of Guardian, supra.

Qualification.—Before receiving letters of appointment, guardian must take oath or affirmation to perform duty. Probate judge may require bond of up to $1,000 for guardian of person. Guardian of estate and person must give bond payable to ordinary and his or her successors in double amount of supposed value of property of ward unless bond is secured by licensed commercial surety, in which case bond may equal value of estate. Value of estate is generally determined without regard to real property. If realty is converted to personalty, new bond is required. Bond may be reduced in judge of probate court's discretion if ward's estate is decreased. (29-4-12). Testamentary guardian need not give bond as to property from ward's parents. (29-4-3). National banks and Georgia banks and trust companies need not give bond unless capital and surplus are less than $400,000 or underlying instrument requires it. (29-4-16, 53-7-33). Judge of probate court may order guardian who is required to give bond to post such bond for period in excess of one year. (29-2-40).

Inventory.—Guardian of property must file inventory with probate judge within four months after appointment. (29-2-24). Property must be appraised if request for appraisement is filed with probate judge within 90 days after inventory is filed. (29-2-25). See category Estates and Trusts, topic Executors and Administrators.

Powers and Duties.—*Guardian of person* stands in loco parentis. (29-2-1). Powers and duties of guardian of incapacitated adult. (29-5-3).

Guardian of estate must make annual returns and final return when ward reaches majority, or when new guardian is appointed. (29-2-76, 53-7-180). Guardian allowed reasonable expenses of maintaining, supporting and educating ward and ward's dependents to extent of income and, on order of judge of probate court, may so use corpus. (29-2-2). Guardian may, on order of judge of probate court, sell, lease, encumber or exchange realty or personalty to pay ward's debts, care, etc., and for reinvestment (29-2-3), enter into contracts for labor and services, improve realty (29-2-11), continue to operate ward's farm or business (29-2-12), and borrow for such purposes. (29-2-20). See 29-2-3 through -10.1 for procedures for selling, leasing, exchanging or encumbering ward's property. On death of ward intestate during guardianship, guardian distributes estate as though administrator. (29-2-23). Guardian entitled to compensation and reimbursement for expenses. (29-2-4.1, 29-2-4.2 et seq.). May be found in contempt and imprisoned for failure to deliver property in hand to ward when so ordered by judge of probate court. (29-2-80). May employ attorney. (29-2-22). May sue. (9-11-17). May compromise contested or doubtful claims as authorized by law. (29-2-16).

Investments Regulated.—Unless fiduciary instrument provides otherwise, guardian may retain property received upon creation of guardianship, including securities issued by a corporate fiduciary. (29-2-15.1). See subhead Powers and Duties, supra. See category Estates and Trusts, topics Executors and Administrators, Trusts.

Securities in Name of Nominee.—See category Estates and Trusts, topic Trusts, subhead Securities in Name of Nominee.

Real Estate.—Probate judge may authorize sale or lease of real estate. (29-2-3, -4). See subhead Powers and Duties, supra.

Liabilities of Guardian.—Liabilities extend to failure to account with ward on coming of age. (29-2-50). See subhead Powers and Duties, supra.

Accounts.—See subhead Powers and Duties, supra.

Termination of Guardianship.—Upon investigation at regular court term of alleged misconduct, probate judge may revoke letters, require guardian to submit to settlement of accounts and/or pass such other order as in his or her judgment is expedient under circumstances of each case. If judge of probate court receives return which indicates that any guardian may have wasted property of ward or failed in any manner to comply with applicable law, in lieu of citing guardian to answer charge, court in its discretion may order return recorded without being approved or disapproved, and wait until guardianship terminated, and then allow ward or his or her successors in interest to determine whether any action should be taken against former guardian or personal representative of such former guardian for any such waste or failure. (29-2-45). Guardian ad litem for mentally ill appointed by court under 37-3 expires automatically after 90 days. (37-3-147[h]).

Mentally Ill Persons.—Guardian for person mentally incompetent may be appointed by probate judge (29-5-1) by detailed due process, including hearing, notice of hearing and right to counsel (29-5-6). Upon death intestate of ward, guardian vested with all powers of administrator of estate. (2 Ga. App. 750, 59 S.E. 15). Upon petition of any interested person, including ward, or upon motion of probate court, guardianship of adult ward may be modified or terminated and personal and property rights restored. (29-5-9). Emergency guardian may be appointed when necessary. (29-5-8). Spouse of person involuntarily hospitalized can demand any wages due to such person. (29-5-12). Rights of mentally retarded, mentally ill, or alcoholics and drug abusers detailed. (37-7-1 et seq.).

Foreign Guardians.—Georgia guardian may turn over property of nonresident ward to foreign guardian if foreign guardian files with probate judge petition showing appointment, bond in double amount value of property, and prayer for turning over, attaching to petition appropriate papers certified according to Act of Congress. (29-7-1). Order of judge in county where property is situated must be obtained in order to sell real estate for reinvestment. (29-7-9, 53-12-353).

Gifts to Minors.—See topic Infants.

Uniform Child Custody Jurisdiction Act.—Adopted. (19-9-40). Does not apply to adoption proceedings. (185 Ga. App. 427, 364 S.E.2d. 279).

Uniform Fiduciaries Act.—Not adopted.

Uniform Simplification of Fiduciary Security Transfers Act.—Adopted. (53-12-320). See category Business Organizations, topic Corporations, subhead Uniform Simplification of Fiduciary Security Transfers Act.

HUSBAND AND WIFE:

Separate Property.—Property of each spouse at time of marriage remains his or her separate property. (19-3-9).

Contracts.—Married persons may make contracts, but when transaction between husband and wife attacked as fraud on either's creditors, burden on husband and wife to show fair. (19-3-10). Discrimination in extension of credit on basis of marital status prohibited. (7-6-1). See topic Guardian and Ward, subhead Spouse as Guardian.

Either spouse may sue other on contract or in tort where action relates to property rights, but not for personal torts. (183 Ga. 766, 189 S.E. 833). However, exception to general interspousal tort immunity exists in actions for wrongful death between spouses. (259 Ga. 49, 376 S.E.2d 674).

Actions.—Statute providing parent(s) with cause of action for seduction of daughter unconstitutional. (264 Ga. 302, 444 S.E.2d 778). Fact that alleged rape victim is wife of defendant is not defense to charge of rape (16-6-1).

Agency.—Subject to aforementioned protective measures for wife, either spouse may act as attorney in fact for other (181 Ga. 787, 184 S.E. 604; 128 Ga. App. 387, 196 S.E.2d 674) and wife may engage in business with husband (98 Ga. 711, 25 S.E. 915).

Conveyance or Encumbrance of Property.—Either spouse may convey or encumber his or her real estate without joinder or consent of other (193 Ga. 758, 19 S.E.2d 919), except that wife must join in husband's conveyance of real property to which he holds record title in trust for her. However, bona fide purchaser without actual or constructive notice of wife's beneficial interest protected when taking conveyance from husband who holds record title. (149 Ga. 529, 101 S.E. 120). See also topic Infants, subhead Disabilities.

Husband and wife liable to third persons for board, support, and all necessaries furnished to or for benefit of children. (19-6-13). Party required to pay child support not liable to third persons for necessaries furnished children. (19-6-14).

Provision is made for temporary and permanent alimony to either husband or wife (19-6-1 et seq.), and is not unconstitutional (232 Ga. 352, 206 S.E.2d 458). See topic Divorce.

Domicile of married person not presumed to be domicile of spouse. (19-2-3).

Uniform Reciprocal Enforcement of Support Act (As Amended). —Adopted with modifications. (19-11-40 et seq.). Applies only to proceedings pending prior to Jan. 1, 1998. (19-11-40.5). Civil enforcement by superior courts of various counties. Differences from Uniform Act: (1) duty of support expanded to apply Georgia law to any dependents located in Georgia irrespective of residence of parent. Generally, parents severally liable for support of child under 18. (19-11-43). Common-law marriage establishes legitimacy of child and makes support mandatory. (19-11-43). Man liable to support his legally established bastard; (2) §6 of Uniform Act omitted and, in lieu thereof, provision adopted allowing obligor in Georgia to avoid extradition by voluntarily submitting to jurisdiction and order of support of superior court of county of his residence (19-11-48); (3) §12 of Uniform Act modified in that district attorney authorized to represent plaintiff-obligee on public assistance or dependent child, and may, in his or her discretion, represent plaintiff-obligee spouse or former spouse of obligor (19-11-53); (4) §14 of Uniform Act modified by addition of special provision authorizing Attorney General to declare Canadian province or territory reciprocating state (19-11-

See note at head of Digest as to 1998 legislation covered.

See Topical Index in front part of this volume.

GA – 47

HUSBAND AND WIFE . . . *continued*

44); (5) §19 of Uniform Act varied to place duty to investigate on court of responding state and local police (19-11-60, 61); and (6) §§29 and 32 and Part IV of Uniform Act omitted. Employers required to withhold wages to furnish child support where there is support order, unless court finds there is not good cause, or parties agree. (19-6-32 et seq.).

Uniform Interstate Family Support Act.—Adopted. (19-11-100 et seq.). Applies to petitions filed or proceedings initiated on or after Jan. 1, 1998 (19-11-40.5): circumstances under which Georgia court may exercise personal jurisdiction over nonresident in parentage proceeding (19-11-110) or support order (19-11-113). Circumstances in which Georgia court has exclusive jurisdiction over support order. (19-11-114). Georgia court shall enforce multiple child support orders, even if one issued in foreign jurisdiction. (19-11-117). Enforcement of support orders issued in foreign jurisdiction through income withholding. (19-11-150 et seq.).

Community Property.—System does not obtain in Georgia.

Custody of Children.—Parents of minor child may submit agreement concerning any custody issue to court which shall be ratified unless court finds agreement not in best interest of child. (19-9-5). When in dispute between parents, court will look to best interest of child. Child over 14 has right to select custodial parent unless that parent determined unfit. (19-9-3). Court may enforce custody decree by contempt power even if decree contains no express injunction or prohibition. (239 Ga. 244, 236 S.E.2d 599). In action for change of child custody, court may in its discretion change terms of custody on temporary basis pending final judgment on issue. (19-9-3). Uniform Child Custody Jurisdiction Act adopted. (19-9-40 et seq.). Statutory procedure prescribed for changing legal custody. (19-9-20-24). Court can award visitation by parent who committed family violence only if adequate provisions made for safety of child/victim of family violence. (19-9-7). Third party is permitted to become party pursuant to 19-9-50 while that party has custody of child, but third party may not petition to terminate parental rights or challenge parent's fitness. (194 Ga. App. 365, 390 S.E.2d 859). For rights of unwed father in adoption, see topic Adoption.

INFANTS:

Age of Majority.—18 both sexes. (39-1-1). Exceptions to this age of majority: Drinking age, 21 (3-3-23); capacity to commit crime, 13 (16-3-1); capacity to commit tort, 13 (51-11-6); capacity to make will, 14 (53-2-22); capacity to make or receive certain gifts, 21 (44-5-130); capacity for contributory negligence, subjective and depends on particular child's mental and physical capacity (237 Ga. 46, 226 S.E.2d 736 citing 51-1-5).

Determination of Paternity.—Upon motion by petitioner, respondent, or any other interested party, court may order mother, alleged father and child to submit to blood tests to prove parentage (19-7-45), and such tests may be used as evidence at trial (19-7-46). For purposes of establishing paternity, there is rebuttable presumption of paternity of child born out of wedlock if there has been performed scientifically credible parentage-determination genetic testing establishing 97% probability of paternity. (19-7-45 et seq.). Procedures adopted for temporary child support orders where clear and convincing evidence of paternity. (19-7-46.2).

Emancipation.—Emancipation of child is relinquishment of control and authority by parent, enabling child to earn own living and ending parents' duty to support child. Marriage, with or without parental consent, emancipates child. (237 Ga. 57, 226 S.E.2d 591).

Legitimacy.—Child born out of wedlock can be legitimized by: (i) Putative father marrying mother and recognizing child (19-7-20[c]) or (ii) petition for legitimation (19-7-22).

Custody.—See topics Husband and Wife; Divorce; Guardian and Ward.

Uniform Child Custody Jurisdiction Act.—Adopted. (19-9-40).

Adoption.—See topic Adoption.

Guardianship.—See topic Guardian and Ward.

Grandparent.—Grandparents may bring original action to seek visitation rights, or intervene in and seek visitation rights in any action concerning custody of minor child, divorce, termination of parental rights, or child visitation rights. Same rights apply with respect to children adopted by blood relative or by stepparent. Visitation rights not available where child's parents not separated and child is living with both parents. (19-7-3). Grandparent with visitation rights may file objections to adoption where father and mother have no further rights to child. (19-8-15).

Duties of Parents.—It is joint and several duty of each parent to provide maintenance, protection and education until child reaches 18, dies, marries, or becomes emancipated, whichever first occurs. (19-7-2). Same for illegitimate children. (19-7-24). Rule subject to two exceptions: (1) extent of duty may be defined by court order; and (2) in any temporary or final order for child support in proceeding for divorce, separate maintenance, legitimacy, or paternity entered after July 1, 1992, trier of fact has discretion to direct one or both parents to provide financial assistance to child enrolled in and attending secondary school and who has reached age of majority before completing secondary education provided child not previously married or emancipated, but no such support can be required after child becomes 20. (19-7-2, 19-16-15[e]). First, but not second exception same for illegitimate children. (19-7-24).

Cruelty to Children.—Parent or guardian commits crime of cruelty to children when parent willfully deprives child of necessary sustenance to extent child's well-being is jeopardized or when parent maliciously inflicts cruel or excessive mental or physical pain. (16-5-70).

Reporting Child Abuse.—Persons having cause to believe that parent or caretaker physically injured, neglected, exploited or sexually assaulted minor child must report incident to child welfare agency with immunity from liability; medical and hospital, school, daycare and law enforcement personnel must report suspected child abuse.(19-7-5).

Statutory Rape.—Person commits offense of statutory rape when he or she engages in sexual intercourse with any person under age of 16 who is not his or her spouse. If victim is 14 or 15 years of age and person convicted is no more than three years older than victim, crime may in discretion of court be punished as misdemeanor. (16-6-3).

Child Molestation.—Person commits offense of child molestation when he or she does any immoral or indecent act to, or in presence of, any child under age of 16 with intent to arouse or satisfy sexual desires of offender or child. Person commits offense of aggravated child molestation when person commits offense of child molestation that includes injury to child or sodomy. (16-6-4).

Enticing Child.—Person commits offense of enticing child when person solicits, entices, or takes child under age of 16 to any place for purpose of child molestation or indecent acts. (16-6-5).

Sexual Exploitation.—Person commits crime involving sexual exploitation when he or she knowingly employs, uses, persuades, induces, entices or coerces any person under age of 18 to engage in sexually explicit conduct for purpose of producing visual medium depicting such conduct; knowingly creates, reproduces, publishes, promotes, sells, distributes, exhibits or possesses with intent to sell any visual medium depicting minor engaged in sexually explicit conduct; knowingly advertising, selling, purchasing or exchanging any medium providing information as to where any visual medium depicting such conduct can be found or purchased; knowingly possessing or controlling any material depicting such conduct; penalties for parents and legal guardians allowing minors to engage in sexually explicit conduct for purpose of producing visual medium. (16-12-100[b]).

Uniform Reciprocal Enforcement of Support Act.—Adopted. (19-11-40 et seq.). applies only to proceedings pending prior to Jan. 1, 1998. (19-11-40.5). See topic Husband and Wife.

Uniform Interstate Family Support Act.—Adopted. (19-11-100 et seq.). Applies to petitions filed or proceedings initiated on or after Jan. 1, 1998. (19-11-40.5).

Child Support Recovery Act.—Payment of public assistance to or on behalf of child creates debt owed to State by parents; if court has ordered child support pursuant to final divorce decree or other final order for child support, debt equal to amount therein. (19-11-5).

Rights of Parents.—Court may terminate parental rights if: (1) parent has abandoned child; (2) child is deprived and that by reason thereof child is suffering serious physical, mental, moral or emotional harm; (3) parent has given written consent before court; or (4) parent has fully and wantonly failed to comply with court order to support child. (15-11-81). Order terminating parental rights of parent is without limit as to duration and terminates all parent's rights with respect to child and all child's rights and obligations to parent. (15-11-80). Parents jointly entitled to services of child and proceeds of his or her labor; but if court awards custody to one parent, only that parent entitled to child's services. This right lost by: (1) voluntary contract releasing right to third person; (2) consent to adoption by another; (3) failure to provide necessaries or abandonment of child; (4) consent that child receive proceeds of his or her own labor, which consent is revocable; (5) consent to marriage of child; or (6) cruel treatment of child. (19-7-1). Termination of parental rights does not occur if parent requests termination simply to abandon child. (180 Ga. App. 688, 350 S.E.2d 50).

Biological fathers entitled to notice of certain proceedings regarding termination of parental rights (15-11-82, -83) or adoption (19-8-12, -13), even if not child's legal father.

Child Labor.—See category Employment, topic Labor Relations.

Termination of Parental Rights.—See subhead Rights of Parents, supra.

Disabilities.—General rules of law as to contracts of and torts by and to minors are observed. Parents liable up to $10,000 plus court costs for willful or malicious acts of child under 18 resulting in reasonable medical expenses, property damage or both. (51-2-3).

Minor under 13 is immune to tort liability. (51-11-6, construed in 231 Ga. 446, 202 S.E.2d 44). Minor under 13 not subject to claim of negligence per se or contributory negligence per se but may be found contributorily negligent depending on minor's mental and physical capabilities. (218 Ga. App. 641, 462 S.E.2d 793). Due care standard for child of tender years depends upon child's mental and physical capacity as well as surrounding circumstances. (51-1-5). Whether minor has mental and physical capability to be contributorily negligent is jury question. (237 Ga. 46, 226 S.E.2d 736).

Ratification of Contracts.—Generally, contract of minor voidable. If minor retains possession or continues to enjoy benefit of property or other valuable consideration after majority, contract is ratified. Contract of minor for necessaries is binding except that party furnishing must prove parent or guardian failed or refused to supply necessaries. (13-3-20).

Consent for Medical Treatment.—Minor's consent to treatment for venereal disease is valid and binding. (31-17-7). Female minor's consent is valid and binding in connection with pregnancy or childbirth. (31-9-2). Generally, consent of person 18 or older to any recommended medical treatment is valid. (31-9-2).

Abortion.—Unemancipated minor required to notify parent or guardian prior to abortion or petition juvenile court for waiver of notification requirement (15-11-112); Georgia's notification statute withstands constitutional scrutiny (934 F.2d 1462).

Actions.—Where minor interested in litigation has no guardian or has interest adverse to guardian, court in which action pending may appoint guardian ad litem, who is responsible to such minor for his or her conduct in connection with such litigation. (29-4-7). Suit commenced and prosecuted by infant alone not void; defect of wanting guardian or next friend is amendable before verdict and cured by verdict. (9-2-28).

Gifts to Minors.—Georgia Transfer to Minors Act. (44-5-110 et seq.). Prescribed form based on that of Model Act of Association of Stock Exchange Firms. Covers gifts of securities, money, insurance policies, annuity contracts and shares in federal savings and loan associations or building and loan associations. Minor defined as person who has not attained age of 21 at time of gift.

See note at head of Digest as to 1998 legislation covered.

See Topical Index in front part of this volume.

INFANTS . . . *continued*

Juvenile Court.—Comprehensive Juvenile Justice Act of 1997 enacted. (15-11-1 et seq.). Concept to treat erring juvenile as part of family. (135 Ga. App. 234, 217 S.E.2d 470).

Uniform Securities Ownership by Minors Act.—Not adopted.

See also topics Divorce, Husband and Wife.

MARRIAGE:

Age of eligibility 16. Documentary evidence of proof of age in form of driver's license, baptismal certificate or birth certificate must be furnished at time of application for marriage license. (19-3-2, -36). Age restrictions do not apply upon proof of pregnancy, or when both applicants are parents of living child born out of wedlock. (19-3-2). Dissolution of prior marriage must be affirmatively established. (19-3-2).

Consent.—Required of parents or guardians of applicants who have not reached age 16 except when applicants are parents of living child born out of wedlock or when female applicant is pregnant. (19-3-2). Consent must be in person unless physically impossible as established by affidavit of licensed physician. (19-3-37).

Medical Tests.—Required for venereal disease for both applicants and rubella tests for fertile females. (19-3-40).

License.—Required; issued by judge of probate court (or his or her clerk) in any county in this state if both applicants reside in Georgia; or if only one person resides in state, in county in which that person resides; or if neither person resides in state, in county in which ceremony to be performed. (19-3-30). Application must be under oath (19-3-33), and license must be returned for record within 30 days of marriage, but if not recorded fact of issue can be proved by affidavit of either spouse and fact of marriage ceremony can be proved by affidavit of two witnesses (19-3-30). No license to be issued to persons of same sex. (19-3-30). Application supplement marriage report also required, prepared in connection with license. (19-3-33).

Waiting Period.—No waiting period. (19-3-35).

Ceremonial Marriage.—May be performed by judge of state or federal courts of record in Georgia, city recorder, magistrate or minister of Gospel or other religious society or sect (19-3-30), but marriage entered into in good faith and otherwise valid not invalidated by want of authority of person performing ceremony (19-3-42).

Reports of Marriage.—License returned by officer or minister solemnizing marriage to judge of probate court (19-3-30) who forwards it to parties to marriage after it has been recorded (19-3-44).

Record.—See category Documents and Records, topic Records, subhead Vital Statistics.

Common Law Marriages.—No common law marriages to be entered into subsequent to Jan. 1, 1997. Otherwise valid common law marriages entered into prior to this date shall continue to be recognized. (19-3-1.1).

Proxy Marriages.—Not authorized.

Marriages by Written Contract.—Not authorized.

Void Marriages.—Marriage is void where either party was insane or had a living spouse under a prior undissolved marriage, or entered into the marriage involuntarily or through fraud, or where parties are within certain prohibited degrees of relationship. (19-3-2, -5). Drunkenness brought about to induce consent is deemed fraud. (19-3-4). Issue of void marriage prior to annulment is legitimate. (19-3-5). Marriage is void where both persons are of same sex. (19-3-3.1).

Foreign Marriages.—Marriage contracted outside of state has same legal consequences and effect as marriage within state. (19-3-43). No recognition of foreign marriages between persons of same sex. (19-3-3.1).

Annulment.—Marriage may be annulled, by petition in equity to superior court, where party was unable to contract to marry, due to being under minimum age of eligibility to marry or where one of parties at time of marriage had previous marriage undissolved or where there existed prohibited nearness of relationship between parties. Annulment cannot be granted on ground which is also ground for divorce or where there has been ratification of marriage after disability is removed. (19-3-5; 198 Ga. 707, 32 S.E.2d 764; 195 Ga. 274, 24 S.E.2d 52; 57 Ga. App. 334, 195 S.E. 308). Annulment will not be granted where children are born or to be born as result of marriage. (19-4-1).

Divorce.—See topic Divorce.

See also topic Husband and Wife.

MARRIED WOMEN:

See topics Husband and Wife, Marriage; categories Civil Actions and Procedure, topic Evidence, subhead Witnesses; Debtor and Creditor, topic Exemptions; Documents and Records, topic Acknowledgments; Estates and Trusts, topics Executors and Administrators, Wills; Property, topic Dower.

HEALTH

DRUGS AND COSMETICS:

Manufacturing, packaging, labeling and sale of drugs and cosmetics as defined by statute are regulated. (26-3-1 et seq.). Georgia State Board of Pharmacy is empowered to grant licenses, investigate, inspect, issue regulations and conduct hearings with regard thereto. (26-4-1 et seq.). Persons possessing or using controlled substances or dangerous drugs for research, analysis, animal training or drug education must register with state unless otherwise registered. (24-4-120.2).

Pharmacist has no duty to warn customer or notify physician that drug is being prescribed in dangerous amounts, that customer is being overmedicated, or that drugs in their prescribed quantities could cause adverse reactions to customer. (209 Ga. App. 517, 434 S.E.2d 63, cert. denied Oct. 29, 1993).

NURSING:

Licensure, competency, training and discipline of registered nurses are governed by Georgia Board of Nursing and Georgia Registered Professional Nurse Practice Act. (43-26-1 et seq.). Licensure, competency, training and discipline of practical nursing are governed by Georgia Board of Examiners of Licensed Practical Nurses and Georgia Practical Nurses Practice Act. (43-26-30 et seq.).

PUBLIC HEALTH:

"Durable Power of Attorney for Health Care Act" authorizes competent adult to appoint agent to make health care decisions on his or her behalf. It further provides standards and limitations with respect to such agency, responsibilities and duties of health care providers and agents and short form durable power of attorney. (31-36-1 et seq.).

Orders not to resuscitate, including identifying bracelets and necklaces, are governed by 31-39-1 et seq.

Health care corporations, health care plans, and health maintenance organizations are subject to documentary, filing, and financial requirements set forth in 33-20-1 et seq. and 33-21-1 et seq.

"Patient Protection Act of 1996" requires managed care plans, as condition of certification, to make certain statutory disclosures regarding plan benefits and rules to prospective enrollees. (33-20A-1 et seq.).

INSURANCE

INSURANCE COMPANIES:

Supervision.—Commissioner of Insurance (7th Floor, West Tower, Floyd Building, 200 Piedmont Ave., S.E., Atlanta, GA 30303) has general supervision of insurance companies. (33-2-1).

Private Review Agents.—Statutory provisions govern certification of agents who review appropriateness and cost of health care services provided to Georgia residents. (33-45-1 et seq.).

Rates.—Regulated under c. 33-9. Commissioner of Insurance can prohibit rates found to be improperly set but cannot order refunds. (235 Ga. 141, 218 S.E.2d 754).

Annual Statements.—Must be filed with Commissioner of Insurance. (33-3-16).

Policies.—Form of all policies and application therefor must be approved by Commissioner. (33-24-9). After July 1, 1988, certain insurance policies, certificates, and coverage booklets must meet simplification standards set by Commissioner. (33-3-25). Statutes regulating types: life, 33-25-1 et seq.; annuities and pure endowment, 33-28-1 et seq.; group life, 33-27-1 et seq.; industrial life, 33-26-1 et seq.; individual accident and sickness, 33-29-1 et seq., and 33-29A-1 et seq.; group and blanket accident and sickness, 33-30-1 et seq., and 33-24-20-26; Medicare supplemental insurance, 33-43-1 et seq.; property, 33-7-6; credit life and credit accident and sickness, 33-31-1 et seq.; vehicle policy, 33-7-9; motor vehicle accident reparations, 33-34-1 et seq.; prepaid legal services, 33-35-1 et seq. Sales of variable life insurance authorized. (33-11-36). Procedures for cancellation of policy by insurer and insured specified in 33-24-44 and 33-24-44.1. Notice of nonrenewal of certain policies required. (33-24-46). Notice requirements upon issuance of life insurance policy specified in 33-24-6.

Unfair Discrimination.—Prohibited in rates. (33-9-4).

Emergency Medical Treatment.—Private insurers, HMOs and health benefit plans are obligated to pay for certain emergency medical treatment. (31-11-82).

Liens.—Life insurer may lend to policy holder with policy as security any sum not exceeding reserve on policy. (33-11-24).

Prerequisites to Issuance of Certificate of Authority.—Before Commissioner of Insurance may issue certificate of authority to insurance company (domestic or foreign) it must fully comply with all provisions of law and file statement showing specific information. (33-3-13). Foreign or alien insurers also must file annual statement. (33-3-13). Deposit and capital stock requirements must be met. (33-3-6).

Lending institutions and bank holding companies and their subsidiaries and affiliates are prohibited from obtaining license to sell insurance in any municipality having population in excess of 5,000, except underwriting for credit life insurance and credit accident and sickness insurance. (33-3-23).

Licensing or renewing of licenses or certificates of authority prohibited to companies owned or controlled by any state or foreign government or subdivision thereof unless owned and licensed before Jan. 1, 1957. (33-3-3).

Certificate of authority expires on June 30 each year unless: (1) insurer files on preceding Mar. 1 copy of annual statement as of preceding Dec. 31; (2) insurer publishes on or before preceding Mar. 1 copy of annual statement in short form in newspaper of general circulation in state, all in form approved by Commissioner. (33-3-16).

Agents and Solicitors.—All persons must procure licenses from Commissioner before soliciting business. (33-23-42[a]). Application and examination necessary for license in most instances (33-23-3, -5, -12) and Commissioner sets qualifications (33-23-3, -4). Only individuals may be licensed. (33-23-41). Applicant must be resident of state for at least six months of every year. (33-23-5). Commissioner must issue licenses to qualified persons, and upon request of licensee, must provide certificate of licensure suitable for display. (33-23-11). Each insurer must also obtain certificate of authority for each agent, renewable annually before Jan. 1. Certified list of all agents must be filed with Commission. (33-23-15, -16). Authorized issuer will be deemed to have obtained certificate of authority for its designated agent seven working days after mailing of request for such certificate (assuming use of first class mail). However, initial licensure is effective only upon granting by Commissioner. (33-23-26). License may be refused, suspended or revoked by Commissioner under certain circumstances. (33-23-21).

Process Agent.—Domestic insurers may be served in same manner as corporations generally. (33-4-2). Foreign or alien insurers must appoint resident of state as well as

INSURANCE COMPANIES . . . *continued*
Commissioner of Insurance to receive service of process. Commissioner may be served only if service cannot be effected on former. (33-4-3).

Resident agent's signature required on all policies covering Georgia risks with certain exceptions. (33-3-11).

Doing Business Without License.—Anyone issuing or delivering policy in violation of any provision of Title 33 is guilty of misdemeanor. (33-1-7). Unauthorized Insurers Process Act adopted. (33-5-50 through -59). Sale of insurance securities by insurer prior to authorization is prohibited. (33-14-10).

Investments regulated by c. 33-11. Investments in qualified investment pools permitted. (33-11A).

Deposit Requirements.—Domestic insurers must deposit $100,000 for first class of insurance and $25,000 for each additional class, total not to exceed $200,000. Foreign insurers may present in lieu of deposits required of domestic insurers, certificate from appropriate official of another state showing like deposit in such state plus amount between $10,000 and $100,000 with Commissioner of Insurance. (33-3-8, -9). Insurers in unsound financial condition may be required to make additional special deposits. (33-3-10).

Foreign Insurance Companies.—See subheads Deposit Requirements and Process Agent, supra. §14-2-293 providing for remedies against corporations after dissolution not applicable to foreign insurance companies. (235 Ga. 394, 219 S.E.2d 728). Foreign or alien insurer conducting direct response insurance must maintain Georgia office, accept collect calls from policyholders or provide toll-free telephone service to policyholders. (33-24-52). Authorization and general requirements for transaction of insurance business provided. (c. 33-3).

Retaliatory Laws.—With some exceptions, when another state imposes taxes, licenses, fees or obligations on Georgia insurers or agents in excess of those required in Georgia, same requirements will apply to insurers of such state in Georgia. (33-3-26; 33-8-2).

Health Maintenance Organizations.—Regulated by 33-21-1 et seq.

Health Plan Purchasing Cooperatives.—Regulated by 33-30A-1 et seq.

Multiple Employer Self-Insurance Health Plans.—Regulated by 33-50-1 et seq.

Obstetrics and Gynecology.—No health benefit policies issued after July 1, 1996 may limit enrollees' choice of obstetricians or gynecologists to physicians within particular health benefit network. (33-24-58).

Premium Financing.—No person shall engage in business of financing insurance premiums in State without license from Commissioner of Insurance. Requirements for obtaining license provided. (33-22-3).

Premiums.—Burden on insurer to show that it complied with its duty to act reasonably and in good faith in setting retrospective premiums. (217 Ga. 331, 457 S.E.2d 566).

Premium Tax.—All foreign and domestic insurance companies and multiple employer self-insurance health plans doing business in Georgia shall pay tax of 2¼% upon gross direct premiums upon persons, property or risks in Georgia, payable in quarterly installments, unless company's annual premium taxes for preceding calendar year were less than $500. (33-8-4 through -6). 10% penalty on amount unpaid. (33-8-6). If 25% of total assets are invested in Georgia, tax is only 1¼%; if 75% of total assets are so invested, tax is only ½ of 1%. (33-8-5). Since Jan. 1, 1966, life insurance companies may deduct from premium tax amount of all license fees and taxes paid to municipal corporations during preceding year. (33-8-8). Certain domestic insurance companies may deduct retaliatory taxes paid to other states. (33-8-7).

Other Taxes.—State license fees (33-8-1, -3). Income tax exemption for insurance companies paying premium tax (48-7-25).

Local Taxation of Insurance Companies.—Taxation for local purposes by counties, municipal corporations and other political subdivisions based on premiums received for policies insuring residents of taxing county, municipal corporation or political subdivision, maximum rate of 1% of premiums for each life insurance company (33-8-8.1) and 2.5% of premiums for each nonlife insurance company (33-8-8.2).

Direct Actions Against Insurer.—Provisions regarding actions against insurance companies, c. 33-4. See category Transportation, topic Motor Vehicles, subhead Direct Actions.

Declaratory Judgment on Coverage.—Insured may seek declaratory judgment regarding exclusion and/or amount of coverage. (258 Ga. 800). Insurer has no duty to investigate until insured apprises insurer of facts that would bring claim within policy's coverage.

Request Regarding Coverage by Claimant.—Requirements for requests by claimant of coverage information from insurer. (3-3-28). No private cause of action exists for breach of 33-3-28 (229 Ga. App. 522).

No-Fault Insurance.—See category Transportation, topic Motor Vehicles, subhead No-Fault Insurance.

Uniform Insurers Liquidation Act.—Adopted. (33-37-40 et seq.).

Insurers Insolvency Pool.—Created to provide remedy for claims under casualty and property policies (33-36-2) and life and health policies (33-38-1) to protect policy holders from insolvency of insurer or impairment of its obligations.

Unfair Trade Practice Regulations.—C. 33-6 defines, provides for determination of, and prohibits all practice in state which constitutes unfair methods of competition or unfair and deceptive practices or acts in business of insurance.

SURETY AND GUARANTY COMPANIES:

Organization and license to carry on business of surety insurance are according to statutory requirements relating to insurance companies. (See topic Insurance Companies.) Surety insurance defined. (33-7-7). May not include reinsurance. (See 316 F. Supp. 314.) Any company or corporation doing surety insurance business may, upon proof of solvency and credit, become surety on all bonds required by law to be taken, with all rights and subject to all liabilities of individual sureties. (33-24-48). Deposit with State Treasurer $100,000 to transact any one class of insurance and $25,000 for each additional class of insurance, subject to limit of $200,000 total deposit. (33-3-8). Common law, not provisions of Ga. Code, governs compensated sureties engaged in writing of surety bonds for profit (241 Ga. 460, 246 S.E.2d 316), but 10-7-24 requiring creditor to proceed against principal within three months notice by surety or surety is discharged applies to compensated and uncompensated sureties (254 Ga. 608, 331 S.E.2d 520).

INTELLECTUAL PROPERTY

TRADEMARKS AND TRADENAMES:

Registration.—Service marks and trademarks are words, names, symbols or devices adopted and used to identify services or goods (10-1-440), and may be registered by filing application and specimen or facsimile of trademark or service mark with Secretary of State (10-1-442) who issues certificate (10-1-444) effective for ten years (10-1-445). Fee for certificate is $15 (10-1-442) and certificate is renewable for successive periods of ten years upon payment of additional $15 (10-1-445).

Assignment.—Trademark or service mark assignable with goodwill. Upon payment of $15 fee new certificate issued for remainder of old term. (10-1-446).

Protection Afforded.—Registrant protected against unauthorized use, reproduction or imitation of registered trademark or service mark. (10-1-450). Rights in trademarks or service marks acquired in good faith at common law protected. (10-1-452). Unfair use of trade name enjoined in equity. (236 Ga. 30, 222 S.E.2d 322).

Infringement.—Use, reproduction or imitation of registered trademark or service mark, without registrant's consent in connection with sale of goods and services which is likely to cause confusion renders violator civilly liable to registrant. (10-1-450). Registrant may recover profits and damages. (10-1-451). Infringement of trademark or service mark may be enjoined; forged or counterfeit service marks, trademarks, copyrighted or registered designs, and goods bearing same may be destroyed or seized. (10-1-454). Forgery or counterfeiting of trademarks, service marks or copyrighted or registered designs, or sale, resale, or transportation of sale is subject to criminal penalty, including imprisonment and fines. (10-1-454). Court may enjoin subsequent use of same or similar trademark or service mark if likelihood of injury to business reputation or of dilution of distinctive quality of trademark or service mark notwithstanding absence of competition between parties or confusion of goods or services. (10-1-451). Unauthorized use with intent to deceive is misdemeanor. (10-1-453).

Use of "Georgia".—Misdemeanor to use "Georgia" in tradename, trademark, service mark or advertisement of meat not U.S. Grade "good" or better. (26-2-115).

Tradenames.—Person, persons or partnership (other than corporation doing business under corporate name; limited partnership doing business under limited partnership name or limited liability company doing business under limited liability company name properly filed for record [10-1-492]) doing business under fictitious name must file with clerk of superior court, where business conducted, or domestic corporation using name other than its corporate name must file in county of its legal domicile, verified statement of names and addresses of those owning or carrying on business and of nature of business. (10-1-490). Noncompliance is misdemeanor and noncomplying party to lawsuit may be cast with court costs but there is no other penalty. (10-1-493). Filing fee: $8. (15-6-77). In counties having population of 350,000 or more in unincorporated areas, filing fee is $25. (15-6-77.3).

TRADE SECRETS:

Georgia Trade Secrets Act, which is similar to Uniform Trade Secrets Act, defines trade secret as information, without regard to form, including, but not limited to, technical or nontechnical data, formula, pattern, compilation, program, device, method, technique, drawing, process, financial data, financial plans, product plans or list of actual or potential, customers or suppliers which is not commonly known by or available to public and which information: (1) derives economic value, actual or potential, from not being generally known to and not being readily ascertainable by proper means by, other persons who can obtain economic value from its disclosure or use; and (2) is subject of efforts that are reasonable under circumstances to maintain its secrecy. (10-1-761).

Actual or threatened misappropriation of trade secret may be enjoined. (10-1-762[a]). In exceptional circumstances, court may allow use, conditioned upon payment of reasonable royalty. (10-1-762[b]). In appropriate circumstances, affirmative acts to protect trade secret may also be compelled by court order. (10-1-762[c]). Additionally, court may order payment of damages equal to actual loss or unjust enrichment occurring as result of misappropriation. (10-1-763[a]). If willful and malicious misappropriation exist, court may award exemplary damages not exceeding twice amount of actual damages or unjust enrichment. (10-1-763[b]). In no event shall contract be required in order to maintain action for injunctive relief or payment of damages for misappropriation of trade secret. (10-1-762[d]).

If claim of misappropriation is made in bad faith, or if motion to terminate injunction is made or resisted in bad faith, or willful and malicious misappropriation exists, court may award reasonable attorney's fees to prevailing party. (10-1-764).

Court may take appropriate measures to protect secrecy of any alleged trade secret by reasonable means including use of protective orders in connection with discovery, holding in-camera hearings, sealing court records and issuing gag orders. (10-1-765).

Action for misappropriation must be brought within five years after misappropriation is discovered or by exercise of reasonable diligence should have been discovered. (10-1-766).

Trade Secrets Act does not affect contractual duties or remedies whether or not based upon misappropriation of trade secrets, provided, that contractual duty to maintain trade secret or limit use of trade secret shall not be deemed void or unenforceable solely for lack of durational or geographical limitation. (10-1-767[b][1]). Further, Trade Secrets Act does not affect civil remedies that are not based upon misappropriation of trade

See note at head of Digest as to 1998 legislation covered.

See Topical Index in front part of this volume.

TRADE SECRETS ... *continued*

secrets or definition of trade secrets contained in Code §16-18-13 regarding criminal offenses involving theft of trade secret. (10-1-767[b][2], [b][3]).

Intentional misappropriation of trade secret, value of which exceeds $100, is felony punishable by one to five years imprisonment and fine not less than $50,000. (16-8-13). Intentional misappropriation of trade secret, value of which is less than $100, is punishable as misdemeanor. (16-8-13).

LEGAL PROFESSION

ATTORNEYS AND COUNSELORS:

State Bar of Georgia is a Unified State Bar, composed of all lawyers admitted to practice in this state. (15-19-30). No person (except nonresident attorneys who may appear in isolated cases in discretion of judge) shall practice law in this state unless he or she is active member. (State Bar Rules 1-203).

Membership consists of active and inactive members who must pay annual license fees of no more than $170 and $95, respectively.

Government of State Bar is vested in Board of Governors composed of President, President-elect, immediate past President, Secretary, Treasurer, President of Younger Lawyers Section, President-elect of Younger Lawyers Section, and number of active members from each Judicial Circuit equal to number of Superior Court Judges authorized for such Circuit. (State Bar Rules 1-301, 302).

Jurisdiction over Admissions.—Superior court has jurisdiction over admissions to bar as to successful candidates passing bar examination. However, supervision of bar examination and certification of qualified candidates is responsibility of State Board of Bar Examiners and Board to Determine Fitness of Bar Applicants pursuant to Rules adopted by Supreme Court. (15-19-2, -3). In order to take examination, applicant must apply to State Board of Bar Examiners.

Eligibility.—Any person of good moral character who meets educational requirements and is certified by Board to Determine Fitness of Bar Applicants is eligible to take bar examination. No residency requirement.

Registration as Law Student.—No requirement that law students must register.

Educational Requirements.—Applicant must have three years of college and complete requirements of law school approved by American Bar Association, Association of American Law Schools or Georgia Board of Bar Examiners, requiring three years of classroom attendance (400 classroom hours each year).

Petition for Admission.—To superior court upon successful completion of examination, presentation of certificate to that effect to Clerk of Court, and taking oath provided by law. After swearing in to superior court, admission to supreme court and court of appeals is by application and proof of good private and professional character, payment of fee of $15 and taking prescribed oath. (Rule 7, Rules of Supreme Court).

Application for Admission.—To Board to Determine Fitness of Bar Applicants for certification of moral fitness with variable fee ($300 to $800). After certification, to Office of Bar Admission with $75 fee to take bar examination. Application to Board to Determine Moral Fitness should be filed not less than six months prior to examination applicant wishes to take.

Examination.—Bar examination administered by Board of Bar Examiners under supervision of Supreme Court. Held twice a year; dates determined by Supreme Court. (15-19-3). Supreme Court sets fee not above $90. (15-19-2). Multi-State Bar Examination utilized; Georgia does not accept transfer of scores from other jurisdictions. Where certain eligibility requirements are satisfied, practicing attorneys may sit for essay portion of exam. Representative subjects covered by essay questions: agency; conflict of laws; constitutional law; contracts; corporations; creditors' rights and debtor relief; criminal law; damages; equity; evidence; family law; federal jurisdiction and procedure; Georgia practice and procedure; legal ethics; partnerships; personal property; real property; taxation (state and federal); torts; trusts; Uniform Commercial Code; wills and administration of estates.

Multi-State Professional Responsibility Examination utilized; may be taken in any jurisdiction. Passing grade required within two years (before or after) passing Georgia bar examination.

Clerkship.—No requirement of clerkship prior to admission.

Admission Without Examination.—No person may be licensed to practice law in state without examination; no admission to bar by comity (Rules 15-19, 15-20, State Bar of Georgia), but court has discretionary authority to permit nonresident attorney to practice in isolated cases (234 Ga. 388, 216 S.E.2d 294).

Admission Pro Hac Vice.—No statutory provision.

Powers.—Attorney may bind client in any action or proceeding by agreement in relation to cause made in writing, and in signing judgments, entering appeals, etc., but cannot compromise client's claim without permission. (15-19-5, -6).

Disabilities.—Attorney cannot sign as surety on bail or appeal bond (Rule 28, Rules of Superior Courts) or attachment or garnishment bond (18-3-12).

Attorney Ethics.—With few exceptions, Code of Professional Responsibility adopted (Title 9 Appendix, Part III) is same as ABA Model Code (247 Ga. 406, 276 S.E.2d 607).

Liabilities.—A client is entitled to redress from his or her attorney for unskillful advice. (15-19-17).

When demand is made on attorney by client for money collected, and he or she refuses to turn over same, he or she is subject to rule and disbarment. (15-19-16).

As to liability for costs, see category Civil Actions and Procedure, topic Costs.

Compensation.—Administrator or attorney employed by estate may obtain judgment fixing attorney's fees. (53-7-10). Award of attorney's fees in eminent domain actions is not required under state constitution. (242 Ga. 707, 251 S.E.2d 243). Attorney may not recover damages under penalty clause when client exercises its right to terminate retainer contract. (264 Ga. 351, 444 S.E.2d 314).

Lien.—Attorney has lien on all money and all effects of client coming into his or her possession, on all real estate and personalty recovered, and on suits, judgments and decrees for money. Such lien is enforced as other liens and is second only to taxes and prior perfected liens. (15-19-14, -15; 44-14-550; 136 Ga. App. 268, 220 S.E.2d 716). Attorney's lien rights inapplicable to divorce, alimony and child support claims. (235 Ga. 853, 221 S.E.2d 602; 185 Ga. App. 809, 366 S.E.2d 167).

Suspension and Disbarment.—The Supreme Court, court of appeals, or superior court may disbar or suspend an attorney. The superior court of the county of attorney's residence is required to disbar any attorney for cause.

Unauthorized Practice.—No nonlicensed corporation, voluntary association, or individual may practice law for another for compensation (15-19-51), except that banks may give advice to customers incidental to banking and that title insurance companies may prepare certain documents (15-19-50, -52).

Mandatory Continuing Legal Education.—Supreme Court of Georgia has adopted program establishing minimum requirements for continuing legal education. Attorneys who are active and non-exempt must complete 12 hours per year, one hour of which must be in area of legal ethics and one hour of which must be in area of professionalism. In addition, Georgia attorneys who appear as sole or lead counsel in superior or state courts of Georgia must complete three of their 12 hours in area of trial practice. In order to educate bar about benefits of alternative dispute resolution, all attorneys must also complete one-time mandatory three-hour CLE credit in dispute resolution. ADR requirement shall be completed before 12/30/95. Lawyers admitted to bar after 12/30/95 shall complete this requirement in year of admission or year following admission.

Professional Associations.—See category Business Organizations, topics Associations, subhead Professional Associations; Corporations, subhead Professional Corporations.

MINERAL, WATER AND FISHING RIGHTS

MINES AND MINERALS:

Department of Natural Resources has general supervision over mineral resources, mining and drilling, wells and water resources. (12-4-1, 12-2-4, 12-5-70 through -73).

Operation of Mines.—Mining company (or lessee of mine) may acquire rights of way across lands of others for: building railroads; turnpikes or common roads as necessities of business require; diverting water course from usual channel when necessary for its business; cutting ditches, canals or other aqueducts to connect water power with mines; building dams necessary to control water power and cutting ditches, etc., necessary to drain mines. (44-9-70 through -76). Georgia Surface Mining Act prescribes statewide minimal regulations of surface mining but does not prevent counties from passing more stringent standards. (236 Ga. 545, 224 S.E.2d 394).

Safeguarding of Employees.—No special provisions.

Inspection of Mines.—No special provisions.

Oil and Gas.—Supervised by Board of Natural Resources. (12-4-43). Oil and Gas and Deep Drilling Act of 1975 regulates all drilling for oil and gas in state. (12-4-40 through -53).

Stream Use.—No right of public passage on stream unless "navigable", as defined in 44-8-5(a) to transport boats with freight in regular course of trade. (268 Ga. 710, 493 S.E.2d 148).

Special Permits and Licenses.—Operators of surface mines must obtain special permit, submit land use plan and file surety bond unless exempted. (12-4-75). Miners of phosphate deposits in navigable waters must obtain special license and pay $100 license fee plus $1 per ton removed. (12-4-101).

Taxes.—No severance tax.

MORTGAGES

CHATTEL MORTGAGES:

Uniform Commercial Code.—Adopted. (11-9).

What May Be Mortgaged.—Governed by Uniform Commercial Code. (11-9 et seq.). See category Business Regulation and Commerce, topic Commercial Code.

After-Acquired Property.—Governed by Uniform Commercial Code. (11-9 et seq.). See category Business Regulation and Commerce, topic Commercial Code.

Floating Stock.—Governed by Uniform Commercial Code. (11-9 et seq.). See category Business Regulation and Commerce, topic Commercial Code.

Future Advances.—Governed by Uniform Commercial Code. (11-9 et seq.). See category Business Regulation and Commerce, topic Commercial Code.

Requisites of Instrument.—Governed by Uniform Commercial Code. (11-9 et seq.). See category Business Regulation and Commerce, topic Commercial Code.

Execution of Instrument.—Governed by Uniform Commercial Code. (11-9 et seq.). See category Business Regulation and Commerce, topic Commercial Code.

Recording.—See category Documents and Records, topic Records, subhead Filing Under Uniform Commercial Code: Place; Fees.

Assignment.—Governed by Uniform Commercial Code. (11-9 et seq.). See category Business Regulation and Commerce, topic Commercial Code.

Foreclosure.—Person holding security interest in personal property may, upon statement of facts under oath, petition court for writ of possession. (44-14-231). Any owner of personal property leased or rented in consumer rental transaction may obtain writ of possession in same manner. (44-14-230). Upon such petition court will issue summons, to be served by sheriff or other specified officer, for defendant to appear at hearing to be held not less than seven days from date summons is served. (44-14-232). Defendant may answer in writing or orally at hearing. (44-14-233). If defendant answers, trial of any issue requiring trial shall be had. (44-14-233). If no determination of plaintiff's

CHATTEL MORTGAGES . . . *continued*
rights can be made at original hearing, defendant required to pay unaccelerated amounts due into registry of court. (44-14-234). Writ of possession will issue when defendant fails to answer (44-14-233) or having answered fails to comply with any provision of statute to detriment of plaintiff. (44-14-234). Whenever writ of possession is granted levy may be made by sheriff. (44-14-236). At option of plaintiff, sheriff or other specified officer may deliver property to plaintiff for retention or disposition in accordance with Uniform Commercial Code (11-9 et seq.) or may advertise and sell property (44-14-236). Defendant who desires to move property after service of summons must post bond with court. (44-14-237).

Person seeking to foreclose an interest in personal property arising out of commercial transaction (one which gives rise to obligation to pay for goods sold or leased, services rendered, or monies loaned, for use in conduct of business or profession and not for personal consumption) may seek immediate writ of possession by petition setting forth claim and sufficient grounds for issuance. (44-14-261). For immediate writ, petitioner must show that defendant has power to conceal, waste, encumber, convert, convey or remove property from jurisdiction if writ is not issued, or that petitioner's post-judgment remedy would otherwise be inadequate. (44-14-262). See category Debtor and Creditor, topic Replevin. Petitioner seeking writ of immediate possession also must either attach written waiver, signed by defendant, of right to notice prior to seizure of property or furnish bond in amount of claim. (44-14-263). Writ for immediate possession will issue if petitioner has complied with foregoing provisions (44-14-264), and petition, affidavits, waiver or bond and order will be served on defendant (44-14-265). Anytime prior to sale of property as provided under 44-14-236, but no later than 30 days after service, defendant may file any defense or counterclaim, with trial following (44-14-267), or defendant may move for dissolution of writ, which shall be granted unless petitioner proves grounds on which it was issued, or defendant may either pay full amount of petitioner's claim into court or post bond for lesser of value of property or amount of petitioner's claim. (44-14-268). If writ is dissolved, action proceeds on petitioner's claim as though no writ had originally issued. (44-14-268). Default judgment will issue against defendant for failure to appear and answer. (44-14-269).

Sale or Removal of Property by Mortgagor.—Sale or removal of mortgaged property with intent to defraud is punishable as misdemeanor. (44-14-6). There are special penalties for sale or removal of motor vehicles, including imprisonment for not less than one year nor more than three years. (44-14-7).

Satisfaction.—Governed by Uniform Commercial Code. (11-9 et seq.). See category Business Regulation and Commerce, topic Commercial Code.

Redemption.—Governed by Uniform Commercial Code. (11-9 et seq.). See category Business Regulation and Commerce, topic Commercial Code.

Forms.—No statutory forms provided. No official forms. Following may be used (For Financing Statement, Statement of Termination, and Statements of Continuation, Partial Release, Assignment, Etc. Forms, see end of this Digest):

Form
— SECURITY AGREEMENT —
(CONSUMER GOODS OR EQUIPMENT)

FOR VALUE RECEIVED, the undersigned hereby conveys to . . . . (hereafter called the "Bank"), and hereby grants to the Bank security title to, and a security interest in, the following property and all accessories, parts and equipment now or hereafter affixed thereto or used in connection therewith (hereafter collectively called "Goods"): . . . .
. . . .
. . . .
. . . . together with all proceeds thereof;

(Continued on Reverse Side Hereof)

to secure the payment of the principal of, interest on and all obligations under a promissory note (hereafter called the "Note"), dated on or about the date hereof, of the undersigned payable to the order of the Bank, in the amount of . . . . Dollars ($. . . . . . .), all obligations of the undersigned hereunder, and all other obligations of the undersigned to the Bank, its successors and assigns, however created, arising or evidenced, whether direct or indirect, absolute or contingent, or now or hereafter existing, or due or to become due. The Note and all other obligations secured hereby are herein collectively called the "Liabilities."

Until Default (as defined herein), the undersigned may have possession of the Goods and use the same in any lawful manner not inconsistent with this Agreement or with any policy of insurance on any of the Goods.

The undersigned hereby warrants and agrees that: (1) to the extent, if any, it shall have advised the Bank that any of the Goods are being acquired with the proceeds of the Note, such proceeds may be disbursed by the Bank directly to the seller of such Goods; (2) the Goods (except any thereof which prior to the execution of this Agreement the undersigned shall have advised the Bank in writing consist of equipment normally used in more than one State) will be kept at its address shown below (or if any other location is shown with respect to any such Goods in the description thereof herein, then at such other location), unless the Bank shall otherwise consent in writing; (3) if any of the Goods shall consist of equipment of a type normally used in more than one State, whether or not actually so used, it will immediately give written notice to the Bank of any change in the chief place of business of the undersigned, and of any use of any of such Goods in any jurisdiction other than a State in which the undersigned shall have previously advised the Bank such Goods will be used, and such Goods will not, unless the Bank shall otherwise consent in writing, be used outside the territorial limits of the United States; (4) it has, or forthwith will acquire, full title to the Goods, and will at all times keep the Goods free of all liens and claims whatsoever, other than the security interest hereunder; (5) no financing statement covering any of the Goods is on file in any public office and it will from time to time, on request of the Bank, execute such financing statement and other documents (and pay the cost of filing or recording the same in all public offices deemed necessary by the Bank) and do such other acts and things, all as the Bank may request to establish and maintain a valid security title and interest in the Goods (free of all other liens and claims whatsoever) to secure the payment of the Liabilities, including, without limitation, deposit with the Bank of any certificate of title issuable with respect to any of the Goods and notation thereon of the security interest hereunder; (6) it will not sell, transfer, lease or otherwise dispose of any of the Goods or any interest therein except with the prior written consent of the Bank; (7) it will at all times keep the Goods in first class order and repair, excepting any loss, damage or destruction which is fully covered by proceeds of insurance; (8) it will at all times keep the Goods insured against loss, damage, theft and other risks, in such amounts and with such companies and under such policies and in such form, all as shall be satisfactory to the Bank, which policies shall provide that loss thereunder shall be payable to the Bank as its interest may appear (and the Bank may apply any proceeds of such insurance which may be received by it toward payment of the Liabilities, whether or not due, in such order of application as the Bank may determine) and such policies or certificates thereof shall, if the Bank so requests, be deposited with the Bank; (9) the Goods, whether affixed to the realty or not, shall remain personal property; and (10) the Bank may examine and inspect the Goods or any thereof, wherever located, at any reasonable time or times. The Bank may from time to time, at its option, perform any agreement of the undersigned hereunder which the undersigned shall fail to perform and take any other action which the Bank deems necessary for the maintenance or preservation of any of the Goods or its interest therein, and the undersigned agrees to forthwith reimburse the Bank for all expenses of the Bank in connection with the foregoing, together with interest thereon at the rate of 8% per annum from the date incurred until reimbursed by the undersigned.

If the Goods or any part of them be repossessed by Bank, undersigned agrees to send notice by registered or certified mail to Bank within 24 hours thereafter if undersigned claims that any article not constituting a part of the Goods was contained therein at the time of the repossession, and agrees that failure so to do shall be a waiver of and a bar to any subsequent claim therefor.

The occurrence of any of the following events shall constitute a Default (as such term is used herein): (1) non-payment, when due, of any amount payable on any of the Liabilities or failure to perform any agreement of the undersigned contained herein; (2) any statement, representation or warranty of the undersigned herein or in any other writing at any time furnished by the undersigned to the Bank is untrue in any material respect as of the date made; (3) any Obligor (which term, as used herein, shall mean the undersigned and each other party primarily or secondarily liable on any of the Liabilities) becomes insolvent or unable to pay debts as they mature or makes an assignment for the benefit of creditors, or any proceeding is instituted by or against any Obligor alleging that such Obligor is insolvent or unable to pay debts as they mature; (4) entry of any judgment against any Obligor; (5) death of any Obligor who is a natural person, or of any partner of any Obligor which is a partnership; (6) dissolution, merger or consolidation, or transfer of a substantial part of the property of any Obligor which is a corporation or a partnership; (7) appointment of a receiver for Goods or for any property in which undersigned has an interest; (8) seizure of Goods; or (9) the Bank feels insecure for any other reason whatsoever. Whenever a Default shall be existing, the Note and all other Liabilities may (notwithstanding any provisions thereof), at the option of Bank, and without demand or notice of any kind, be declared, and thereupon immediately shall become due and payable, and the Bank may exercise from time to time any rights and remedies available to it under applicable law. The undersigned agrees, in case of Default, to assemble, at its expense, all the Goods at a convenient place acceptable to the Bank and to pay all costs of the Bank of collection of the Note and all other Liabilities, and enforcement of rights hereunder, including reasonable attorney's fees and legal expenses and expenses of any repairs to any realty or other property to which any of the Goods may be affixed or be a part. If any notification of intended disposition of any of the Goods is required by law, such notification, if mailed, shall be deemed reasonably and properly given if mailed at least five days before such disposition, postage prepaid, addressed to the undersigned either at the address shown below, or at any other address of the undersigned appearing on the records of the Bank. Any proceeds of any disposition of any of the Goods may be applied by the Bank to the payment of expenses in connection with the Goods, including reasonable attorney's fees and legal expenses, and any balance of such proceeds may be applied by the Bank toward the payment of such of the Liabilities, and in such order of application, as the Bank may from time to time elect. No delay or failure on the part of the Bank in the exercise of any right or remedy shall operate as a waiver thereof, and no single or partial exercise by the Bank of any right or remedy shall preclude other or further exercise thereof of the exercise of any other right or remedy. Time is of the essence of this Agreement. If more than one party shall execute this Agreement, the term "undersigned" shall mean all parties signing this Agreement and each of them, and all such parties shall be jointly and severally obligated hereunder. The neuter pronoun, when used herein, shall include the masculine and feminine and also the plural. If this Agreement is not dated when executed by the undersigned, the Bank is authorized, without notice to the undersigned, to date this Agreement.

The additional provisions, if any, set forth or referred to on the reverse side hereof are hereby made a part of this Agreement.

This Agreement has been delivered in the State of Georgia and shall be construed in accordance with the laws of that State. Wherever possible each provision of this Agreement shall be interpreted in such manner as to be effective and valid under applicable law, but if any provision of this Agreement shall be prohibited by or invalid under applicable law, such provision shall be ineffective to the extent of such prohibition or invalidity, without invalidating the remainder of such provision or the remaining provisions of this Agreement.

The rights and privileges of the Bank hereunder shall inure to the benefit of its successors and assigns.

IN WITNESS WHEREOF, this Agreement has been duly executed as of the . . . . . . day of . . . . . ., 19. . . . . .

Address . . . . (SEAL)
Address . . . . (SEAL)
Address . . . . (SEAL)

ADDITIONAL PROVISIONS OF AGREEMENT*
*If none, insert "None."

See note at head of Digest as to 1998 legislation covered.

See Topical Index in front part of this volume.

GA – 52

CHATTEL MORTGAGES . . . *continued*

— SECURITY AGREEMENT —
(EQUIPMENT AND INVENTORY)

FOR VALUE RECEIVED, the undersigned hereby conveys to . . . . (hereafter called the "Bank"), and hereby grants to the Bank security title to, and a security interest in, the following property and all accessories, parts and equipment now or hereafter affixed thereto or used in connection therewith (hereafter collectively called "Goods"):

. . . .
. . . .
. . . .

(Continued on Reverse Side Hereof)
and also

all other goods and property which are held by undersigned for sale or lease or are furnished or are to be furnished by the undersigned under any contract of service or are held by the undersigned as raw materials, work in process or materials used or consumed in a business, together with the products and proceeds thereof (hereafter collectively called "Inventory") ("Goods" and "Inventory" are sometimes hereafter collectively called "Collateral") to secure the payment of the principal of, interest on and all obligations under a promissory note (hereafter called the "Note"), dated on or about the date hereof, of the undersigned payable to the order of the Bank, in the amount of . . . . Dollars ($. . . . . .), all obligations of the undersigned hereunder, and all other obligations of the undersigned to the Bank, its successors and assigns, however created, arising or evidenced, whether direct or indirect, absolute or contingent, or now or hereafter existing, or due or to become due. The Note and all other obligations secured hereby are herein collectively called the "Liabilities."

Until Default (as defined herein), the undersigned may have possession of the Goods and use the same in any lawful manner not inconsistent with this Agreement or with any policy of insurance on any of the Goods, and the undersigned may have possession of the Inventory, and may sell, lease or furnish under contract any thereof that is normally held by the undersigned for such purpose, and may use or consume in the ordinary course of the undersigned's business any raw materials, work in process or materials normally held by the undersigned for that purpose.

The undersigned hereby warrants and agrees that: (1) to the extent, if any, it shall have advised the Bank that any of the Collateral are being acquired with the proceeds of the Note, such proceeds may be disbursed by the Bank directly to the seller of such Collateral; (2) the Collateral (except any thereof which prior to the execution of this Agreement the undersigned shall have advised the Bank in writing consists of equipment normally used in more than one State) will be kept at its address shown below (or if any other location is shown with respect to any such Collateral in the description thereof herein, then at such other location), unless the Bank shall otherwise consent in writing; (3) if any of the Goods shall consist of equipment of a type normally used in more than one State, whether or not actually so used, it will immediately give written notice to the Bank of any change in the chief place of business of the undersigned, and of any use of any of such Goods in any jurisdiction other than a State in which the undersigned shall have previously advised the Bank such Goods will be used, and such Goods will not, unless the Bank shall otherwise consent in writing, be used outside the territorial limits of the United States; (4) it has, or forthwith will acquire, full title to the Collateral, and will at all times keep the Collateral free of all liens and claims whatsoever, other than the security interest hereunder; (5) no financing statement covering any of the Collateral is on file in any public office and it will from time to time, on request of the Bank, execute such financing statement and other documents (and pay the cost of filing or recording the same in all public offices deemed necessary by the Bank) and do such other acts and things, all as the Bank may request to establish and maintain a valid security title and interest in the Collateral (free of all other liens and claims whatsoever) to secure the payment of the Liabilities, including, without limitation, deposit with the Bank of any certificate of title issuable with respect to any of the Goods and notation thereon of the security interest hereunder; (6) it will not sell, transfer, lease or otherwise dispose of any of the Collateral or any interest therein except as expressly permitted herein with respect to Inventory or except with the prior written consent of the Bank; (7) it will at all times keep the Collateral in first class order and repair, excepting any loss, damage or destruction which is fully covered by proceeds of insurance; (8) it will at all times keep the Collateral insured against loss, damage, theft and other risks, in such amounts and with such companies and under such policies and in such form, all as shall be satisfactory to the Bank, which policies shall provide that loss thereunder shall be payable to the Bank as its interest may appear (and the Bank may apply any proceeds of such insurance which may be received by it toward payment of the Liabilities, whether or not due, in such order of application as the Bank may determine) and such policies or certificates thereof shall, if the Bank so requests, be deposited with the Bank; (9) it will at all times keep accurate and complete records reflecting the current status of the Inventory, permit the Bank to examine and extract from the same and furnish to Bank, on request, duly verified copies of summaries thereof in form and content satisfactory to Bank; (10) the Goods, whether affixed to the realty or not, shall remain personal property; and (11) the Bank may examine and inspect the Collateral or any thereof, wherever located, at any reasonable time or times. The Bank may from time to time, at its option, perform any agreement of the undersigned hereunder which the undersigned shall fail to perform and take any other action which the Bank deems necessary for the maintenance or preservation of any of the Collateral or its interest therein, and the undersigned agrees to forthwith reimburse the Bank for all expenses of the Bank in connection with the foregoing, together with interest thereon at the rate of 8% per annum from the date incurred until reimbursed by the undersigned.

The occurrence of any of the following events shall constitute a Default (as such term is used herein): (a) nonpayment, when due, of any amount payable on any of the Liabilities or failure to perform any agreement of the undersigned contained herein; (b) any statement, representation or warranty of the undersigned herein or in any other writing at any time furnished by the undersigned to the Bank is untrue in any material respect as of the date made; (c) any Obligor (which term, as used herein, shall mean the undersigned and each other party primarily or secondarily liable on any of the Liabilities) becomes insolvent or unable to pay debts as they mature or makes an assignment for the benefit of creditors, or any proceeding is instituted by or against any Obligor alleging that such Obligor is insolvent or unable to pay debts as they mature; (d) entry of any judgment against any Obligor; (e) death of any Obligor who is a natural person, or of any partner of any Obligor which is a partnership; (f) dissolution, merger or consolidation, or transfer of a substantial part of the property of any Obligor which is a corporation or a partnership; (g) appointment of a receiver for any of Collateral or for any property in which undersigned has an interest; (h) seizure of any of Collateral; or (i) the Bank feels insecure for any other reason whatsoever. Whenever a Default shall be existing, the Note and all other Liabilities may (notwithstanding any provisions thereof), at the option of Bank, and without demand or notice of any kind, be declared, and thereupon immediately shall become, due and payable, and the Bank may exercise from time to time any rights and remedies available to it under applicable law. The undersigned agrees, in case of Default, except with written consent of Bank, to cease the sale, lease or furnishing under contract of service of any Inventory and to cease use or consumption thereof in business, and to assemble, at its expense, all the Collateral at a convenient place acceptable to the Bank and to pay all costs of the Bank of collection of the Note and all other Liabilities, and enforcement of rights hereunder, including reasonable attorney's fees and legal expenses, and expenses of any repairs to any realty or other property to which any of the Goods may be affixed or be a part. If any notification of intended disposition of any of the Collateral is required by law, such notification, if mailed, shall be deemed reasonably and properly given if mailed at least five days before such disposition, postage prepaid, addressed to the undersigned either at the address shown below, or at any other address of the undersigned appearing on the records of the Bank. Any proceeds of any disposition of any of the Collateral may be applied by the Bank to the payment of expenses in connection with the Collateral, including reasonable attorney's fees and legal expenses, and any balance of such proceeds may be applied by the Bank toward the payment of such of the Liabilities, and in such order of application, as the Bank may from time to time elect.

No delay or failure on the part of the Bank in the exercise of any right or remedy shall operate as a waiver thereof, and no single or partial exercise by the Bank of any right or remedy shall preclude other or further exercise thereof or the exercise of any other right or remedy. Time is of the essence of this Agreement. If more than one party shall execute this Agreement, the term "undersigned" shall mean all parties signing this Agreement and each of them, and all such parties shall be jointly and severally obligated hereunder. The neuter pronoun, when used herein, shall include the masculine and feminine and also the plural. If this Agreement is not dated when executed by the undersigned, the Bank is authorized, without notice to the undersigned, to date this Agreement.

The additional provisions, if any, set forth or referred to on the reverse side hereof are hereby made a part of this Agreement.

This Agreement has been delivered in the State of Georgia and shall be construed in accordance with the laws of that State. Wherever possible each provision of this Agreement shall be interpreted in such manner as to be effective and valid under applicable law, but if any provision of this Agreement shall be prohibited by or invalid under applicable law, such provision shall be ineffective to the extent of such prohibition or invalidity, without invalidating the remainder of such provision or the remaining provisions of this Agreement.

The rights and privileges of the Bank hereunder shall inure to the benefit of its successors and assigns.

IN WITNESS WHEREOF, this Agreement has been duly executed as of the . . . . day of . . . ., 19 . . . .

Address . . . . (SEAL)
Address . . . . (SEAL)
Address . . . . (SEAL)

ADDITIONAL PROVISIONS OF AGREEMENT*
*If none, insert "None."

COLLATERAL SECURITY:

See category Debtor and Creditor, topic Pledges.

Release and Collateral.—Uniform Commercial Code adopted. (Title 11). See category Business Regulation and Commerce, topic Commercial Code.

MORTGAGES OF PERSONAL PROPERTY:

See topic Chattel Mortgages.

MORTGAGES OF REAL PROPERTY:

Both mortgages and deeds to secure debt (also referred to as security deeds or loan deeds) recognized in Georgia, although latter are used almost exclusively. Mortgage creates lien only; security deed is conveyance of title. (44-14-30, -60). Persons transacting business in state as mortgage brokers or mortgage lenders must be licensed pursuant to Code §7-1-1000 et seq.

Uniform Commercial Code.—Adopted. (Title 11).

Execution.—Security deeds and mortgages of land must be executed in same form as deeds of bargain and sale, both as to validity between parties and requirements for recording. See category Property, topic Deeds, subhead Recording. (44-14-33, 44-14-61).

Recording.—Unrecorded security deed or mortgage of land is valid between parties but not against other persons without notice of unrecorded instrument. (44-14-35, 44-14-63). Same formality of execution as deed conveying real property required. (44-14-33). See category Property, topic Deeds, subhead Recording. Mailing address of grantee also required. (44-14-63).

Recording Fee.—See category Documents and Records, topic Records, subhead Recording Fees.

See note at head of Digest as to 1998 legislation covered.

See Topical Index in front part of this volume.

GA – 53

MORTGAGES OF REAL PROPERTY . . . *continued*

Trust Deeds.—Use recognized as device to secure debts by 44-14-120.

Future Advances.—Operation of "open end" clauses limited to debts arising ex contractu between original parties (44-14-1), except that security deed so providing will secure advances to pay taxes, to pay insurance premiums, to pay superior liens, to repair, maintain or preserve property or to complete improvements on property, and will secure expenses of collection and foreclosure, regardless of whether such advances made by original grantee or whether property is still owned by original grantor. (44-14-2[a]). Mortgage by person or corporation to trustee to secure issue of bonds may expressly include after acquired property of such person or corporation. (44-14-35.1).

Priorities.—Effect of recording is same as for deeds of bargain and sale. See category Property, topic Deeds, subhead Recording. (44-14-63).

Subordination Agreements.—Enforceable, whether in mortgage or security deed or separate agreement, if sufficiently specific as to amount, terms, time limitations and any other conditions. (171 Ga. 878, 156 S.E. 888; see also 233 Ga. 819, 213 S.E.2d 678).

Assignment.—Security deeds may be assigned by grantee. Rules that apply to deeds of bargain and sale as to execution, requirements for recording and effect of recording also apply to assignments. (44-14-64). No recording of transfer of deed to secure debt necessary if by certain financial institutions and lenders provided specific requirements met. (44-14-64[d], [e] and [f]). Mailing address of transferee required. (44-14-64[g]).

Releases.—Partial releases from mortgage or security deed are customarily made by quitclaim deed.

Satisfaction.—Payoff balance must be provided without charge upon written request which includes self-addressed stamped envelope. (44-14-64[h]). When debt secured by recorded mortgage is paid off, original instrument may be presented with order of grantee or holder directing that such instrument be cancelled, to clerk of superior court of county in which such instrument recorded, and clerk must index and record, in same manner as original mortgage is recorded, cancelled mortgage and cancellation order of grantee and must write words "satisfied" and "cancelled" across face of record of such instrument or page of said record, date of entry, and sign his name thereto officially. (44-14-4). Clerk must also indicate in mortgage records where cancellation order is recorded. (44-14-4). Grantee or transferee is required to furnish Clerk with sufficient satisfaction or cancellation of such instrument or other instrument within 60 days from date of payment in full of indebtedness secured by instrument and direct clerk to transmit to grantor original cancellation or satisfaction document at grantor's last known address as shown on records of grantor or holder. (44-14-3). Grantor or holder is authorized to add to pay-off amount costs of recording cancellation or satisfaction. (44-14-3). Damages for failure to transmit such satisfaction or cancellation are $500 plus any loss caused to grantor plus reasonable attorneys' fees, but grantee or holder is not liable if he demonstrates reasonable inability to comply, and no damages are due unless and until grantor makes written demand for transmittal of satisfaction or cancellation of such instrument; applies to security deeds as well as to mortgages. (44-14-3). Clerk may be authorized to cancel security deed (in same manner as cancellation of mortgage) by cancellation upon original security deed, conveyance from record holder of security deed by quitclaim deed or other deed suitable for recording which refers to original security deed, or, if original security deed has been lost, stolen, or otherwise mislaid, by cancellation instrument as follows:

Form

__________ County, Georgia

The indebtedness referred to in that certain deed to secure debt from __________ to __________, dated __________, and of record in Deed Book _____, Page _____, in the Office of the Clerk of the Superior Court of ________ County, Georgia, having been paid in full and the undersigned being the present owner of such secured interest, by virtue of being the original grantee or the heir, assign, transferee, or devisee of the original grantee, the clerk of such superior court is authorized and directed to cancel that deed of record as provided in Code Section 44-14-4 of the O.C.G.A. for other mortgage cancellations.
IN WITNESS WHEREOF, the undersigned, has set his hand and seal, this _____ day of _______, 19____.

__________________ (SEAL)
Signature

Signed, sealed and
delivered on the
date above shown

____
Unofficial Witness

____
Notary Public
(SEAL)
My Commission Expires: __________. (44-14-67).

Foreclosure.—Customarily, foreclosure is pursuant to powers of sale provided in instrument, authorizing private, nonjudicial sale. However, judicial foreclosure may be used by petition to superior court describing debt and mortgage. Rule granted requiring payment before next term of court which is published twice a month for two months or served on mortgagor 30 days before return. (44-14-180). Defenses may be filed at return term. (44-14-184). If no defense or payment, rule made absolute and judgment given for amount due and costs. Sale is as in all judicial sales by sheriff. (44-14-187).

Foreclosure may be had also in equity by petition to the superior court, which proceeds as in all other suits. (44-14-49).

There is no moratorium on mortgage foreclosures.

Nonjudicial Foreclosure Sales.—Powers of sale in deeds of trust, security deeds, mortgages, and other instruments must be strictly construed and fairly exercised. (23-2-114). Unless instrument creating such power specifically provides to contrary, personal representative, heir, legatee, devisee or successor of grantee in mortgage, deed of trust, loan, deed, bill of sale to secure debt or other like instrument, or assignee thereof, or his or her personal representative, heir, legatee, devisee or successor, may exercise any power therein contained, and such powers may be exercised by transferees. (23-2-114). Power of sale not revocable by death of grantor or donor and may be exercised after his or her death in same manner and to same extent as though such grantor or donor were in life; and it is not necessary, in exercise of such power, to advertise or sell as property of estate of deceased, nor to make any mention of or reference to such death. (23-2-114).

Under statutory procedure, sales of real estate under powers contained in mortgages, security deeds and other lien contracts must be preceded by advertisement once a week for four weeks immediately preceding day sale is to take place in newspaper in which sheriff's sales are advertised in county in which land lies. (44-14-162; 9-13-140; 9-13-141). Sale shall be made at public outcry at courthouse on first Tues. of month between 10 A.M. and 4 P.M. E.S.T. or E.D.S.T., whichever is applicable; but if first Tues. of month should fall on New Year's Day or Independence Day, such sale must take place on immediately following Wed. (9-13-160, -161). Notice must be given to debtor by certified mail at least 15 days before sale if residential property. (44-14-162.2). Actual receipt of properly addressed notice is immaterial. (261 Ga. 835, 411 S.E.2d 874). Power of sale must be created by contract. Statutory procedure merely limiting in effect and does not create power of sale by itself. Statutory procedure is constitutional, but contractual agreement containing power of sale is constitutionally enforceable only if voluntarily, intelligently and knowingly made. (230 Ga. 426, 197 S.E.2d 376). Statutory procedure does not involve necessary state action for claim of denial of due process rights. (376 F. Supp. 1379).

Deficiency Judgment.—When secured realty is sold under power of sale and does not bring amount of debt secured, no deficiency judgment can be obtained unless petition for confirmation of sale is filed with superior court judge within 30 days after sale and court confirms sale. Confirmation not necessary in judicial foreclosure. (44-14-161).

Redemption.—No statutory right of redemption exists in judicial foreclosure or power of sale foreclosure. However, power of sale foreclosure may be enjoined or set aside. (170 Ga. 75, 153 S.E. 85). If mortgagee has possession of property, mortgagor may redeem within ten years of mortgagee's last recognition of right of redemption. (44-14-42.1).

Form.—No statutory form. Usual form of loan deed with power of sale is as follows:

Form

DEED TO SECURE DEBT

STATE OF GEORGIA
COUNTY OF . . . .

THIS INDENTURE, made this . . . . day of . . . ., 19. . . . . . ., between . . . . of the State of . . . . and County of . . . ., Grantor, and . . . . of the State of . . . . and County of . . . ., whose address is . . . ., Grantee,

WITNESSETH: That, WHEREAS, Grantor is justly indebted to Grantee in the sum of . . . . Dollars ($. . . . . . .), in lawful money of the United States, and has agreed to pay the same, with interest thereon, according to the terms of a certain note (the "Note") given by Grantor to Grantee, bearing even date herewith, with final payment being due on . . . ., the Note, by reference, being made a part hereof;

NOW, THEREFORE, in consideration of the premises and of the sum hereinabove set forth, Grantor has granted, bargained, sold and conveyed, and by these presents does grant, bargain, sell and convey unto Grantee the following property, to-wit:

[insert property description]

TOGETHER WITH all the improvements now or hereafter erected on the property, and all easements, rights, appurtenances, rents, awards, royalties, mineral, oil and gas rights and profits, water, water rights, and water stock, and all fixtures now or hereafter attached to the property, all of which, including replacements and additions thereto, shall be deemed to be and remain a part of the property covered by this Deed;

TO HAVE AND TO HOLD the said premises hereby granted (all of which are collectively referred to herein as the "Premises") with all and singular the rights, members and appurtenances thereto appertaining, to the use, benefit and behoof of the Grantee, forever, in FEE SIMPLE.

Grantor warrants that Grantor has good title to the Premises, and is lawfully seized and possessed of the Premises and every part thereof, and has the right to convey same; that the Premises are unencumbered except as may be herein expressly provided; and that Grantor will forever warrant and defend the title to the Premises unto Grantee against the claims of all persons whomsoever.

This instrument is a deed passing legal title pursuant to the laws of the State of Georgia governing loan or security deeds and is not a mortgage; and is made and intended to secure the payment of the indebtedness of Grantor to Grantee evidenced by the Note in accordance with the terms thereof, together with any and all other indebtedness now owing or which may hereafter be owing by Grantor to Grantee, however incurred (including advances to pay taxes, assessments and insurance premiums on the Premises, the costs of repairing, maintaining, and preserving the Premises, and the cost of completing any improvements on the Premises), and all renewal or renewals and extension or extensions of the Note or other indebtedness, either in whole or in part (all of which are collectively referred to herein as the "Secured Indebtedness").

AND GRANTOR FURTHER COVENANTS AND AGREES WITH GRANTEE as follows:

1. Grantor shall pay to Grantee the Secured Indebtedness with interest thereon as in the Note and this deed provided.

2. Grantor shall pay, when due and payable, (a) all taxes, assessments, general or special, and other charges levied on, or assessed, placed or made against the Premises, this instrument or the Secured Indebtedness or any interest of the Grantee in the Premises or the obligations secured hereby; (b) premiums on policies of fire and other hazard insurance covering the Premises, as required in Article 3 herein; and (c) all liens or encumbrances of any kind on the Premises having priority over this instrument. Grantor shall promptly deliver to Grantee receipts showing payment in full of all of the above items.

See note at head of Digest as to 1998 legislation covered.

See Topical Index in front part of this volume.

GA – 54

MORTGAGES OF REAL PROPERTY . . . *continued*

3. (a) Grantor shall keep the Premises insured for the benefit of Grantee against loss or damage by fire, lightning, windstorm, hail, explosion, riot, riot attending a strike, civil commotion, aircraft, vehicles and smoke and such other hazards as Grantee may from time to time require, all in amounts approved by Grantee not exceeding 100% of full insurable value (in no event shall the amounts of insurance be less than the amount of the Secured Indebtedness); all insurance herein provided for shall be in form and by companies approved by Grantee; and, regardless of the types or amounts of insurance required and approved by Grantee, Grantor shall assign and deliver to Grantee, as collateral and further security for the payment of the Secured Indebtedness, all policies of insurance which insure against any loss or damage to the Premises, with loss payable to Grantee, without contribution by Grantee, pursuant to the New York Standard or other mortgagee clause satisfactory to Grantee. If Grantee, by reason of such insurance, receives any money for loss or damage, such amount may, at the option of Grantee, be retained and applied by Grantee toward payment of the Secured Indebtedness, or be paid over, wholly or in part, to Grantor for the repair or replacement of the Premises or any part thereof, or for any other purpose or object satisfactory to Grantee, but Grantee shall not be obligated to see to the proper application of any amount paid over to Grantor.

(b) Not less than 30 days prior to the expiration date of each policy of insurance required of Grantor pursuant to this Article, and of each policy of insurance held as additional collateral to secure Secured Indebtedness, Grantor shall deliver to Grantee a renewal policy or policies marked "premium paid" or accompanied by other evidence of payment satisfactory to Grantee.

(c) In the event of a foreclosure of this deed, the purchaser of the Premises shall succeed to all rights of Grantor, including any right to unearned premiums, in and to all policies of insurance assigned and delivered to Grantee, with respect to all property conveyed and to be conveyed by this deed, pursuant to the provisions of this Article.

4. Grantor shall maintain the Premises in good condition and repair, shall not commit or suffer any waste to the Premises, shall complete any improvements on the Premises and shall comply with, or cause to be complied with, all statutes, ordinances and requirements of any governmental authority relating to the Premises or any part thereof. Grantor shall promptly repair, restore, replace or rebuild any part of the Premises, now or hereafter encumbered by this deed, which may be affected by any proceeding of the character referred to in Article 6 herein. No part of the Premises, including, but not limited to, any building, structure, parking lot, driveway, landscape scheme, timber or other ground improvement, or other property, now or hereafter conveyed as security by or pursuant to this deed, shall be removed, demolished or materially altered without the prior written consent of Grantee. Grantor shall complete, within a reasonable time, and pay for any building, structure or other improvement at any time in the process of construction on the Premises. Grantee shall not initiate, join in or consent to any change in any private restrictive covenant, zoning ordinance or other public or private restrictions limiting or defining the uses which may be made of the Premises or any part thereof. Grantee and any persons authorized by Grantee shall have the right to enter and inspect the Premises at all reasonable times and access thereto shall be permitted for that purpose.

5. Grantee shall be subrogated to all right, title, lien, or equity of all persons to whom it may have paid moneys in settlement of liens, charges, or in acquisition of title of or for its benefit hereunder, or for the benefit and account of Grantor at the time of making the loan secured by this security deed, or subsequently under any of the provisions herein.

6. Notwithstanding any taking of all or any portion of the Premises by eminent domain, alteration of the grade of any street or other injury to, or decrease in value of, the Premises by any public or quasi public authority or corporation. Grantor shall continue to pay principal and interest on the Secured Indebtedness, and any reduction in the Secured Indebtedness resulting from the application by Grantee of any award or payment for such taking, alteration, injury or decrease in value of the Premises, as hereinafter set forth, shall be deemed to take effect only on the date of such receipt; and said award or payment may, at the option of Grantee, be retained and applied by Grantee toward payment of the Secured Indebtedness, or be paid over, wholly or in part, to Grantor for the purpose of altering, restoring, or rebuilding any part of the Premises which may have been altered, damaged or destroyed as a result of any such taking, alteration of grade, or other injury to the Premises, or for any other purpose or object satisfactory to Grantee, but Grantee shall not be obligated to see to the application of any amount paid over to Grantor. If, prior to the receipt by Grantee of such award or payment, the Premises shall have been sold on foreclosure of this deed, Grantee shall have the right to receive said award or payment to the extent of any deficiency found to be due upon such sale, with legal interest thereon, whether or not a deficiency judgment on this deed shall have been sought or recovered or denied, and the reasonable counsel fees, costs and disbursements incurred by Grantee in connection with the collection of such award or payment.

7. Upon the occurrence of any one of the following events (herein called an "event of default"):

(a) should Grantor fail to pay the Secured Indebtedness, or any part thereof, when and as the same shall become due and payable;

(b) should any warranty of Grantor herein contained, or contained in any instrument, transfer, conveyance, assignment or loan agreement given with respect to the Secured Indebtedness, prove untrue or misleading in any material aspect;

(c) should the Premises be subject to actual or threatened waste, or any part thereof be removed, demolished or materially altered so that the value of the Premises be diminished except as provided for in Article 6 herein;

(d) should any federal tax lien or claim of lien for labor or material be filed of record against Grantor or the Premises and not be removed by payment or bond within 30 days from date of recording;

(e) should any claim of priority to this deed by title, lien or otherwise be asserted in any legal or equitable proceeding;

(f) should Grantor make any assignment for the benefit of creditors, or should a receiver, liquidator or trustee of Grantor or of any of Grantor's property be appointed, or should any petition for the bankruptcy, reorganization or arrangement of Grantor, pursuant to the Federal Bankruptcy Code or any similar statute, be filed, or should Grantor be adjudicated a bankrupt or insolvent, or should Grantor, if a corporation, be liquidated or dissolved or its charter expire or be revoked, or, if a partnership or business association, be dissolved or partitioned, or, if a trust, be terminated or expire; or

(g) should Grantor fail to keep, observe, perform, carry out and execute in every particular the covenants, agreements, obligations and conditions set out in this deed, or in the Note, or in any instrument, transfer, conveyance, assignment or loan agreement given with respect to the Secured Indebtedness; then and thereupon Grantee may do any one or more of the following:

(i) enter upon and take possession of the Premises without the appointment of a receiver, or an application therefor, employ a managing agent of the Premises and let the same, either in its own name, or in the name of Grantor, and receive the rents, incomes, issues and profits of the Premises and apply the same after payment of all necessary charges and expenses, on account of the Secured Indebtedness, and Grantor will transfer and assign to Grantee, in form satisfactory to Grantee, Grantor's lessor interest in any lease now or hereafter affecting the whole or any part of the premises;

(ii) pay any sums in any form or manner deemed expedient by Grantee to protect the security of this instrument or to cure any event of default other than payment of interest or principal on Secured Indebtedness (specifically including the payment of taxes, assessments and insurance premiums on the Premises, the costs of maintaining, repairing, and preserving the Premises, and the costs of completing any improvements on the Premises); make any payments hereby authorized to be made according to any bill, statement, or estimate furnished or procured from the appropriate public officer or the party claiming payment without inquiry into the accuracy or validity thereof, and the receipt of any such public officer or party in the hands of Grantee shall be conclusive evidence of the validity and amount of items so paid, in which event the amounts so paid, with interest thereon from the date of such payment at the rate of ___% per annum, shall be added to and become a part of the Secured Indebtedness and be immediately due and payable to Grantee; and Grantee shall be subrogated to any encumbrance, lien, claim or demand, and to all the rights and securities for the payment thereof, paid or discharged with the principal sum secured hereby or by Grantee under the provisions hereof, and any such subrogation rights shall be additional and cumulative security to this deed;

(iii) declare the entire Secured Indebtedness immediately due, payable and collectible, without notice to Grantor, regardless of maturity, and, in that event, the entire Secured Indebtedness shall become immediately due, payable and collectible; and thereupon, Grantee may sell and dispose of the Premises at public auction, at the usual place for conducting sales at the courthouse in the county where the Premises or any part thereof may be, to the highest bidder for cash, first advertising the time, terms and place of such sale by publishing a notice thereof once a week for four consecutive weeks in a newspaper in which sheriff's advertisements are published in said county, all other notice being hereby waived by Grantor; and Grantee may thereupon execute and deliver to the purchaser at said sale a sufficient conveyance of the Premises in fee simple, which conveyance may contain recitals as to the happening of the default upon which the execution of the power of sale, herein granted, depends, and said recitals shall be presumptive evidence that all preliminary acts prerequisite to said sale and deed were in all things duly complied with; and Grantee, its agents, representatives, successors or assigns, may bid and purchase at such sale; and Grantor hereby constitutes and appoints Grantee or its assigns or agents as attorney in fact to make such recitals, sale and conveyance, and all of the acts of such attorney in fact are hereby ratified, and Grantor agrees that such recitals shall be binding and conclusive upon Grantor and that the conveyance to be made by Grantee, or its assigns, (and in the event of a deed in lieu of foreclosure, then as to such conveyance) shall be effectual to bar all right, title and interest, equity of redemption, including all statutory redemption, homestead, dower, curtesy and all other exceptions of Grantor, or its successors in interest, in and to said Premises; and

Grantee, or its assigns, shall collect the proceeds of such sale, reserving therefrom all unpaid Secured Indebtedness with interest then due thereon, and all amounts together with all costs and charges for advertising, and commissions for selling the Premises, and 15% of the aggregate amount due, as attorney's fees, and pay over any surplus to Grantor (in the event of deficiency Grantor shall immediately on demand from Grantee pay over to Grantee, or its nominee, such deficiency); and Grantor agrees that possession of the Premises during the existence of the Secured Indebtedness by Grantor, or any person claiming under Grantor, shall be that of tenant under Grantee, or its assigns, and, in case of a sale, as herein provided, Grantor or any person in possession under Grantor shall then become and be tenants holding over, shall forthwith deliver possession to the purchaser at such sale, or be summarily dispossessed in accordance with the provisions of law applicable to tenants holding over; the power and agency hereby granted are coupled with an interest and are irrevocable by death or otherwise, and are in addition to any and all other remedies which Grantor may have at law or in equity.

Grantee, in any action to foreclose this deed, or upon any event of default, shall be at liberty to apply for the appointment of a receiver of the rents and profits or of the Premises or both without notice, and shall be entitled to the appointment of such a receiver as a matter of right, without consideration of the value of the Premises as security for the amounts due the Grantee, or the solvency of any person or corporation liable for the payment of such amounts.

In case of any sale under this deed by virtue of the exercise of the power herein granted, or pursuant to any order in any judicial proceedings or otherwise, the Premises or any part thereof may be sold in one parcel and as entirety, or in such parcels, manner or order as Grantee in its sole discretion may elect, and one or more exercises of the powers herein granted shall not extinguish or exhaust the power unless the entire Premises are sold or the Secured Indebtedness paid in full.

8. Grantor, for himself and family, hereby waives and renounces all homestead and exemption rights provided for by the Constitution and Laws of the United States or the State of Georgia, in and to the Premises as against the collection of the Secured Indebtedness, or any part thereof; and Grantor agrees that where, by the terms of the conveyance or the Note secured hereby, a day is named or a time fixed for the payment

See note at head of Digest as to 1998 legislation covered.

See Topical Index in front part of this volume.

GA – 55

MORTGAGES OF REAL PROPERTY... *continued*

of any sum of money or the performance of any agreement, the time stated enters into the consideration and is of the essence of the whole contract.

9. Grantee shall have the right from time to time to sue for any sums, whether interest, principal or any installment of either or both, taxes, penalties, or any other sums required to be paid under the terms of this deed, as the same become due, without regard to whether or not all of the Secured Indebtedness shall be due on demand, and without prejudice to the right of Grantee thereafter to enforce any appropriate remedy against the Grantor, including an action of foreclosure or any other action, for a default or defaults by Grantor existing at the time such earlier action was commenced.

10. The rights of Grantee, granted and arising under the clauses and covenants contained in this deed and the Note, shall be separate, distinct and cumulative of other powers and rights herein granted and all other rights which Grantee may have in law or equity, and none of them shall be in exclusion of the others; and all of them are cumulative to the remedies for collection of indebtedness, enforcement of rights under security deeds, and preservation of security as provided at law. No act of Grantee shall be construed as an election to proceed under any one provision herein or under the Note to the exclusion of any other provision, or an election of remedies to the bar of any other remedy allowed at law or in equity, anything herein or otherwise to the contrary notwithstanding.

11. Every provision for notice and demand or request shall be deemed fulfilled by written notice and demand or request personally served on one or more of the persons who shall at the time hold the record title to the Premises, or on their heirs or successors, or mailed by depositing it in any post office station or letter box, enclosed in a postpaid envelope (a) addressed to such person or persons, or their heirs or successors, at his, their or its address last known to Grantee or (b) addressed to the street address of the Premises hereby conveyed.

12. Any indulgence or departure at any time by the Grantee from any of the provisions hereof, or of any obligation hereby secured, shall not modify the same or relate to the future or waive future compliance therewith by the Grantor. If more than one party shall execute this deed, the term "Grantor" shall mean all parties signing, and each of them, and each agreement, obligation and Secured Indebtedness of the Grantor shall be and mean the several as well as joint undertaking of each of them.

13. The words "Grantor" and "Grantee" whenever used herein shall include all individuals, corporations (and if a corporation, its officers, employees, agents or attorneys) and any and all other persons or entities, and the respective heirs, executors, administrators, legal representatives, successors and assigns of the parties hereto, and all those holding under either of them, and the pronouns used herein shall include, when appropriate, either gender and both singular and plural, and the word "Note" shall also include one or more notes and the grammatical construction of sentences shall conform thereto.

IN WITNESS WHEREOF, this deed has been duly executed and sealed by Grantor the day and year first above written.

Signed, sealed and
delivered in the
presence of:

. . . .
Unofficial Witness

. . . .(SEAL)

. . . .
Notary Public

. . . .(SEAL)

My commission expires:
[NOTARY SEAL]

Chattel Mortgages.—See topic Chattel Mortgages.

PROPERTY

ABSENTEES:

Care of Property.—Estate of person missing for one year may be administered where preponderance of evidence indicates person is dead. (53-9-1). Petition for administration of estate of person missing for four years may be filed (53-9-2), but presumption of death is rebuttable (53-9-1).

Conservator for estate of any resident of Georgia who has been missing from his or her usual place of abode for 60 days, or who has been reported missing in action as result of hostilities existing between U.S. and other nations, or has been kidnapped or otherwise detained and thus is incapable of managing estate, may be appointed on application of heir, creditor, custodian of minors or anyone having an interest in estate of such person. (53-9-10 et seq.). See also category Estates and Trusts, topic Death.

Process Agent.—No general requirement that nonresident individuals appoint agent in state for service of process. But see categories Insurance, topic Insurance Companies; Taxation, topic Income Tax, subhead Income Taxed—Individuals, catchline Nonresident Contractors; Transportation, topic Motor Vehicles.

In condemnation proceedings, where known owners or interested persons are nonresidents, notice is served on person in possession and, if nonresident's address is known, sheriff or any lawful deputy of county where petition is filed mails copy of petition and order by registered or certified mail. Where address is unknown, and so certified by condemnor and sheriff, sheriff posts notice at courthouse not less than five days before hearing and inserts notice in local newspaper in county where property is located four to seven days before hearing. Each such service is final and conclusive. (22-2-107).

Where owners or interested persons are unknown, notice is served on person in possession and another notice delivered to judge of county's probate court, who must care for absentee's interest. On reappearance of unknown owner, reassessment may be had. (22-2-24).

Service of Process.—See category Civil Actions and Procedure, topic Process.

In Partition Proceedings.—Party in interest absent from state during proceeding may object within 12 months from judgment and obtain retrial. (44-6-171).

Escheat.—See category Estates and Trusts, topic Descent and Distribution.

Uniform Disposition of Unclaimed Property Act (Revised).—Adopted. (44-12-190). Substantial variations are made from 1966 Official Revised Text. State Revenue Commissioner is substituted for State Treasurer throughout text.

ADVERSE POSSESSION:

Acquisition of title through possession of real estate inconsistent with title of another.

Character of Possession.—For possession to be foundation of prescriptive title, possession must be in right of possessor and not of another; must not have originated in fraud; must be public, continuous, exclusive, uninterrupted and peaceable; and must be accompanied by claim of right. Permissive possession cannot be basis for prescriptive title until adverse claim and actual notice to other party. (44-5-161).

Duration of Possession.—Actual adverse possession of lands for 20 years, by itself, shall give good title by prescription against everyone, except state or persons laboring under certain disabilities. (44-5-163). Under written evidence of title, adverse possession of land for seven years gives title by prescription against everyone except state, unless written title forged or fraudulent and claimant had actual notice of such forgery or fraud before or at time of commencement of possession. (44-5-164).

Personalty.—Title to personalty may be acquired by four years adverse possession in accordance with 44-5-161 unless personalty concealed or removed out of state or otherwise not subject to reclamation. (44-5-177).

Easements.—Easements may be acquired by prescription. (44-5-175). Seven years uninterrupted use of improved land, or 20 years use of wild land passes title to easement. (44-9-1).

Mineral Rights.—Mineral rights may be acquired by adverse possession by fee simple owner of property if owner of mineral rights has neither worked nor attempted to work mineral rights, nor paid any taxes due thereon, for seven years from date of conveyance and petition requesting relief. Attempting work means more than conducting research and picking up rock samples. (262 Ga. 861, 426 S.E.2d 883). To obtain absolute title to mineral rights, fee simple owner must file petition requesting relief in superior court for county where property lies. (44-5-168).

Disabilities.—Prescription does not work against minors, prisoners, or insane or retarded persons as long as disability continues (44-5-170); nor against unrepresented estates (for less than five years); nor against joint title which cannot be severally enforced or where any of joint owners under disability; nor against party who commences action in time but is dismissed with prejudice or dismisses for one time and recommences within six months (44-5-173). Period for prescription must run from removal of disability to enable previously disabled to assert claim to property (44-5-170), but tacking of prior and subsequent possession permitted (44-5-171).

CONVEYANCES:

See topic Deeds.

CURTESY:

No tenancy by curtesy. (53-1-3).

DEEDS:

Execution.—Deed to land in state must be in writing, signed by maker, attested by at least two witnesses, delivered to purchaser and be for good or valuable consideration. (44-5-30). Deed without attestation valid between parties. (213 Ga. 17, 96 S.E.2d 887). See category Family, topic Husband and Wife, subhead Conveyance or Encumbrance of Property for circumstances in which spouse must join. See also topic Real Property; category Family, topic Infants.

Form.—No prescribed form is essential to validity of deeds to lands or personalty. If sufficient in itself to make known the transaction between the parties, no want of form will invalidate it. (44-5-33). Must disclose if property used as commercial landfill. (44-5-48). Types used are general warranty, limited warranty, and quitclaim.

Deed of Infant.—See category Family, topic Infants, subhead Disabilities.

Deed to Personalty.—Needs no attesting witnesses to make it valid; in other respects principles applicable to deeds to land govern. Generally, a deed is not necessary to convey title to personalty. (44-5-31).

Title by Court Action.—Decree for specific performance or court judgment vesting title operates as a deed, effectively conveying title without action by original owner. (9-11-70). See subhead Suits to Quiet Title, infra.

Recording.—Unrecorded deed is valid between parties but not against other persons without notice of unrecorded deed. Deeds conveying land must be recorded in superior court of county where land lies. (44-2-1, -3). Deeds, deeds to secure debt, mortgages and other instruments affecting title to real property must include name and mailing address of natural person to whom instrument is to be returned at top of first page. (44-2-14).

Deed Executed in State.—To entitle deed executed in state to be recorded, it must be executed in presence of two witnesses, both of whom must sign as such, and one of whom must be attesting officer who affixes officer's seal. Such officer may be notary, judge of court of record, or if in county of their office, clerk or deputy clerk of superior court, or magistrate. (44-2-14, -15). If not witnessed by such officer such deed must be acknowledged. (44-2-16). If neither attested by, nor acknowledged before attesting officer, may be recorded upon affidavit of attesting officer as subscribing witness. (44-2-18). See category Documents and Records, topic Acknowledgments.

Deed Executed Outside State.—To authorize recording of a deed executed outside of the state it must be subscribed by two witnesses, one of whom must be U. S. consul or vice-consul, judge of court of record of place where executed with certificate of clerk of such court as to genuineness of signature of judge, clerk of court of record under seal of court, or notary who affixes seal or justice of peace with his or her seal of office

DEEDS ... *continued*

attached, or if he or she has no seal, certificate of his or her official character by clerk of any court of record in county, city or country of his or her residence. (44-2-21).

Recording Fees.—See category Documents and Records, topic Records, subhead Recording Fees.

Effect of Record.—Voluntary conveyances recorded in superior court of county in which land lies operate as notice and have priority over subsequent deeds to same land. (44-2-3). Certified copy of deed which has been properly recorded is admissible in evidence under same rule which would apply to original without having to account for original. (24-5-27). Recording of deed prima facie evidence of delivery. (236 Ga. 346, 223 S.E.2d 708). Possession of land constitutes notice of rights or title of occupant. (44-5-169).

Operation and Effect.—Grantee accepting deed but not signing it, bound by covenants in deed. (44-5-39). Acceptance of deed by grantee prevents grantee, in absence of fraud, from challenging misrepresentations relating to title not covered by covenants of deed; deed considered complete relinquishment of all conflicting claims in preceding contract of sale. (235 Ga. 87, 218 S.E.2d 828).

Taxes.—Transfer tax imposed on absolute conveyances of real property where consideration exceeds $100 (48-6-1), but not on conveyances to secure debt, leases and certain other transactions (48-6-2) (see category Taxation, topic Real Estate Conveyance Tax). Tax based on amount of consideration for or value of property conveyed (exclusive of amount of any liens or encumbrances existing prior to sale and not paid off thereby) at rate of $2 for first $1,000 and 20¢ for each additional $100 or part thereof from Jan. 1, 1999 through Dec. 31, 2002.

Suits to Quiet Title.—See topic Real Property; category Documents and Records, topic Records.

Married Women.—Wife need not join in deed by her husband unless she has interest in property conveyed. See category Family, topic Husband and Wife.

Forms.—No statutory forms provided. No official forms. Following may be used:

Forms

Return to:
[NAME]
[ADDRESS]
Quit-Claim Deed.—
STATE OF . . . .
COUNTY OF . . . .
THIS INDENTURE, made this . . . . . day of . . . ., 19 . ., between . . . . . herein called the "Grantor", and . . . . ., herein called the "Grantee";
WITNESSETH that, in consideration of Ten Dollars ($10.00) in hand paid and other valuable consideration, the receipt and sufficiency of which are hereby acknowledged, Grantor does hereby bargain, sell, remise, release, transfer, convey and forever quitclaim unto Grantee all Grantor's right, title, interest, claim, or demand in and to the land described in Exhibit "A" attached hereto and made a part hereof, and together with all rights, members and appurtenances in any manner appertaining or belonging to said property;
TO HAVE AND TO HOLD said property unto Grantee, so that neither Grantor nor any person or persons claiming under Grantor shall at any time or by any means or ways, have, claim or demand any right or title to said property or appurtenances. Where the context requires or permits, "Grantor" and "Grantee" shall include their respective heirs, successors and assigns.
IN WITNESS WHEREOF, Grantor has executed this deed under seal on the date above written.
Signed, sealed and delivered
in the presence of:
. . . . (SEAL)
Unofficial Witness

. . . .
Notary Public
My commission expires: _____
(NOTARY SEAL)
(NOTARY STAMP)

_____

Return to:
[NAME]
[ADDRESS]
Warranty Deed (General and Limited).—
STATE OF . . . .
COUNTY OF . . . .
THIS INDENTURE, made this . . . . . day of . . . ., 19 . ., between . . . . ., herein called the "Grantor", and . . . . ., herein called the "Grantee";
WITNESSETH that, in consideration of Ten Dollars ($10.00) in hand paid and other valuable consideration, the receipt and sufficiency of which are hereby acknowledged, Grantor does hereby grant, bargain, sell, alien, convey, transfer and confirm unto Grantee all that tract or parcel of land described in Exhibit "A" attached hereto and made a part hereof, together with all buildings and other improvements located thereon, and together with all rights, members and appurtenances in any manner appertaining or belonging to said property;
TO HAVE AND TO HOLD said property, together with all and singular the rights, members and appurtenances thereof, to the same being, belonging or in anywise appertaining, to the only proper use, benefit and behoof of Grantee in fee simple absolute forever. Grantor shall warrant and forever defend the right, title and interest to said property unto Grantee against the claims of all persons whomsoever [Limited Warranty Deed: all persons claiming by, through or under Grantor], except for those matters set forth in Exhibit "B" attached hereto and made a part hereof. Where the context requires or permits, "Grantor" and "Grantee" shall include their respective heirs, successors and assigns.

IN WITNESS WHEREOF, Grantor has executed this deed under seal on the date above written.
Signed, sealed and delivered
in the presence of:
. . . . (SEAL)
Unofficial Witness

. . . .
Notary Public
My commission expires: _____
(NOTARY SEAL)
(NOTARY STAMP)

_____

DEEDS OF TRUST:

See category Mortgages, topic Mortgages of Real Property.

DOWER:

Right of dower completely abolished by Georgia Laws 1969, p. 123, which repealed Title 31 of Code relating to dower. Spouse and children entitled to year's support. See category Estates and Trusts, topics Descent and Distribution, subhead Year's Support, Wills, subhead Election.

ESCHEAT:

See category Estates and Trusts, topic Descent and Distribution.

LANDLORD AND TENANT:

Landlord not liable for tenant's negligence or illegal use of premises, but liable for damages from defective construction or failure to repair. (44-7-14). Landlord is required to turn property over to tenant in condition reasonably safe and in state of repair suited for use intended by tenant and known to landlord. (99 Ga. App. 110, 107 S.E.2d 684). Implied warranty that premises in good repair at commencement of lease cannot be avoided by exculpatory provision in lease. (154 Ga. App. 217, 267 S.E.2d 811). Landlord must keep premises in repair and is liable for repair of substantial improvements placed upon premises by consent. (44-7-13). Landlord not liable in tort to third party for damages resulting from tenant's negligence after landlord parts with possession of premises. (265 Ga. 905, 463 S.E.2d 491). Landlord must give prospective residential tenant written notice of previous flooding of premises in certain circumstances. (44-7-20).

Non-waivable Lease Provisions.—Landlord or tenant may not waive, transfer or otherwise avoid in any contract, lease, or similar agreement, oral or written, for use or rental of real property as dwelling place any rights, duties or remedies contained in following provisions of law: 36-61-11 relating to local ordinances concerning habitability, health and safety; 44-7-13 relating to duties of landlord as to repairs and improvements; 44-7-14 relating to liability of landlord for failure to repair; 44-7-50 through -58 relating to proceedings against tenants holding over; 44-7-70 through -82 relating to distress warrants; and 44-7-30 through -36 relating to security deposits. (44-7-2).

Tenant's Rights and Duties.—Tenant only has right to use and enjoyment of leased premises. (44-7-11). Must surrender possession at end of term. (44-7-10). Estopped to deny landlord's title and cannot attorn to another if he or she takes any position inconsistent with position that landlord's title defective. (44-7-9). No vested interest or constitutional right to continue possession of public housing. (158 Ga. App. 734, 282 S.E.2d 141). Tenant may remove trade fixtures erected by him or her during term; after term and possession are ended, trade fixtures are regarded as abandoned to landlord. (44-7-12). Where usufruct, tenant's interest cannot be conveyed unless lease expressly so provides and is not subject to levy and sale. (44-7-1).
Special interest in real estate may be leased. (44-6-102).

Kinds of Tenancy.—Estate for years is interest in realty for definite and stated period and passes as realty. (44-6-100). Usufruct is lesser right whereby landlord has granted merely right to possess and enjoy use of real estate and no estate passes out of landlord. (44-7-1). Any tenancy for less than five years which does not purport by its own terms to create estate for years shall be held to pass only usufruct. (44-7-1).

Leases.—Parol lease for term not exceeding one year valid (44-7-2); if for longer time creates tenancy at will (151 Ga. App. 343, 259 S.E.2d 729). Transfers occasioned through leases not subject to real estate transfer tax. (48-6-2).

Disclosure of Ownership.—Landlord shall disclose to tenant in writing name and address of: (1) record owner of premises or persons to act for owner for purpose of service of process and receiving and receipting for demands and notice; and (2) person authorized to manage premises. Landlord shall advise tenants of changes of such names and addresses within 30 days after change. (44-7-3).

Security Deposits.—Security deposits regulated. (44-7-30, et seq.). Whenever security deposit is held by landlord with respect to residential lease, such deposit shall be deposited in escrow account used only for that purpose and held in trust for tenant and written notice given to tenant of account location and number. (44-7-31). Alternatively, landlord may post and maintain surety bond with clerk of superior court in which dwelling unit is located. (44-7-32). Procedures for inspection of premises and return of security deposit are provided in 44-7-33 through -35.

Recording.—Leases and usufructs may be recorded if witnessed like deeds and recorded in county where land lies. (44-2-9). Possession of land constitutes notice of rights or title of occupant. (44-5-169).

Rent.—Obligation to pay reasonable rent implied where possession under another's title. (44-7-5). Rent bears interest from time due. (44-7-16).
Destruction of premises by fire or loss of possession by casualty not caused by landlord and not resulting from defect in his or her title does not abate rent. (44-7-15). Rent may be apportioned in equity when circumstances of case render common law remedy incomplete. (23-2-72). For active duty military personnel who receive permanent change of station or temporary duty orders for period in excess of three months,

LANDLORD AND TENANT . . . *continued*

liability for residential lease limited to (1) 30 days rent after written notice and proof of assignment given to landlord and (2) cost of repairing any damage to premises caused by tenant. (44-7-37).

Residential rent control ordinances by counties and municipalities prohibited. (44-7-19).

Lien for rent inferior to liens for taxes and general and special liens of laborers. (44-14-342). Attaches from time affidavit is made in application for distress warrant but does not take precedence over pre-existing liens except as to crop raised on premises. (44-7-80). Landlord has special lien for rent on crops grown on rented land; superior to all other liens except for taxes. (44-14-341). Landlord has lien in crops for farming supplies furnished. (44-14-340).

Term.—Where no time specified for termination of tenancy, construed to be tenancy at will. (44-7-6).

Termination of Tenancy.—60 days' notice from landlord or 30 days' notice from tenant required to terminate tenancy at will. (44-7-7).

Holding Over.—Landlord may collect rent for time tenant holds over against landlord's will. Tenant at will who occupies premises after expiration of lease holds premises subject to terms of lease except as modified by parties by agreement. (147 Ga. App. 493, 249 S.E.2d 310).

Dispossession.—If rent not paid when due, owner may demand possession and if possession refused, owner may institute proceeding against such tenant without first terminating lease. (44-7-50; 247 Ga. 625, 278 S.E.2d 643). Affidavit is filed and summons is sent requiring tenant to appear on date within seven days after service. In action for nonpayment of rent, tenant may tender to landlord, within seven days of date tenant served with summons, all rents allegedly owed plus cost of dispossessory warrant and such tender shall be complete defense to action; provided landlord is required to accept such tender after issuance of dispossessory summons only once in any 12-month period. If no answer or appearance, then writ of possession issues. If answer, then civil trial is held on all issues with payments of rent into court and tenant remaining in possession until final outcome of litigation. (44-7-50 through -59). Repair receipts may not be substituted for cash rent due. (144 Ga. App. 196, 240 S.E.2d 738).

Distress.—Landlord may distrain for rent as soon as same is due if tenant is seeking to remove his or her goods from premises. Affidavit for distress warrant is filed and summons is served requiring tenant to appear on date not more than seven nor less than five days after service. Tenant may tender to landlord, within seven days of day tenant was served with summons, all rents allegedly owed plus cost of distress warrant and such tender will be complete defense to action. If no answer or appearance, then distress warrant issues. If answer, then civil trial is held on all issues with payments of rent into court and tenant remaining in possession until final outcome of litigation. (44-7-70 through -82).

Uniform Residential Landlord and Tenant Act.—Not adopted.

LEASES:

See topic Landlord and Tenant. Lease-purchase agreements are regulated as trade practice. (10-1-681 et seq.).

PERPETUITIES:

Uniform Statutory Rule Against Perpetuities, with alternative 90-year wait-and-see test, adopted. (44-6-200 through -206). Perpetual lease or perpetual right to renew lease not forbidden in perpetuity. (247 Ga. 361, 276 S.E.2d 841[2]).

Accumulations of Income.—Common law rules govern. (190 Ga. 23, 8 S.E.2d 23). Effect of Uniform Statutory Rule Against Perpetuities on accumulation of income not clear.

See also category Estates and Trusts, topic Trusts.

PERSONAL PROPERTY:

Uniform Disposition of Unclaimed Property Act (Revised).—Adopted. (44-12-190). Substantial variations are made from 1966 Official Revised Text. State Revenue Commissioner is substituted for State Treasurer throughout text.

POWERS OF ATTORNEY:

Formalities.—Where exercise or performance of agency is by written instrument, agency must be created by written instrument; provided, however that, unless contrary intent is expressed, any written instrument creating agency shall be conclusively deemed to authorize execution of instruments with formalities necessary or appropriate to accomplish purposes of agency. Corporation may appoint agent in its usual mode of transacting business, without corporate seal. Deed or other instrument executed under seal pursuant to agency created by act not under seal is binding on principal and valid as unsealed instrument if not otherwise required to be under seal for its validity. (10-6-2). Agent may not delegate authority unless specially empowered to do so. (10-6-5). Conditional powers of attorney authorized. (10-6-6).

Revocation.—Generally revocable at will of principal, unless coupled with interest. (10-6-33).

Attorneys in Fact.—A conveyance or mortgage of real estate may be executed by an attorney in fact acting under power of attorney. (25 Ga. App. 91, 102 S.E. 647; 22 Ga. App. 740, 97 S.E. 200).

Members of Armed Forces.—Agency created by power of attorney in writing given by member of the Armed Forces, or merchant seamen and certain other persons serving outside the United States, is not revoked or terminated by principal's death not known to agent or other person who acted in good faith in reliance on power. Report or listing as "missing in action" does not constitute notice of death of principal and does not operate to revoke power. (10-6-35).

Uniform Durable Power of Attorney Act.—Not enacted.

Financial Power of Attorney.—Non-exclusive form is provided for establishing financial power of attorney. (10-6-142).

REAL PROPERTY:

Word "heirs" unnecessary to create fee simple estate; every properly executed conveyance creates fee unless lesser estate mentioned. (44-6-21).

Fee tail estates abolished. (44-6-24).

Estate for life of tenant may be created by devise, deed, express agreement of parties or operation of law. (44-6-82).

Joint tenancy: Any conveyance to two or more persons must be construed to create tenancy in common without survivorship unless deed contains reference to "joint tenants", taking "jointly with survivorship" or language of like import. Any such language shall create joint tenancy estate that may be severed as to any owner's interest by recording of instrument resulting in lifetime transfer of owner's interest; provided, however, if all joint tenant owners join in same recorded lifetime transfer, no severance occurs. (44-6-190).

Tenancy by entirety not recognized. (44-6-120, -190[a]).

Covenants running with land restricting land to certain uses are of limited duration (20 years) in municipalities and areas of counties adopting zoning law. Exception to limited duration for covenants or scenic easements held for benefit of public, which covenants are perpetual, and for covenants for planned subdivisions containing no fewer than 15 individual plots, which covenants are automatically renewed for unlimited 20 year periods unless terminated, as set forth in 44-5-60. Covenants prohibiting use or ownership of subdivision property may not discriminate based on race, creed, color, age, sex or national origin. (44-5-60).

Rule in Shelley's Case.—Abolished. Deed to one and on his or her death to his or her heirs creates life estate with remainder in fee. (44-6-23; 80 Ga. 374, 377, 7 S.E. 554).

Foreign Conveyances and Encumbrances.—See category Documents and Records, topic Records.

Condominiums.—Governed by Georgia Condominium Act. (44-3-70 et seq.).

Subdivided Land Sales.—Sale and offer to sell certain subdivided lands extensively regulated. (44-3-1 et seq.).

Real Estate Appraisers.—Licensing and certification governed by statute. (43-39A-1 et seq.).

Time-Share Estates.—Governed by statute. (44-3-160 et seq.).

Discrimination.—Unlawful to discriminate in sale of housing accommodations on basis of race, color, sex, religion or national origin. (8-3-200).

See also topics Curtesy, Deeds, Dower, Landlord and Tenant; categories Civil Actions and Procedure, topic Partition; Documents and Records, topic Records; Family, topic Husband and Wife; Mortgages, topic Mortgages of Real Property.

TRUST DEEDS:

See category Mortgages, topic Mortgages of Real Property.

TAXATION

ADMINISTRATION:

Tax administration is under Department of Revenue, headed by State Revenue Commissioner ("Commissioner"). (48-2-1).

Taxes must be uniform and levied and collected under general laws. (Const., Art. VII, §I, Paragraph III).

Collection.—Suit by Commissioner. (48-2-54). Income tax refund set-off procedure for collection of certain liabilities. (48-7-160 et seq.). Nonresident who engages in acts in state giving rise to tax liability deemed to appoint Secretary of State process agent for suit to collect tax. (48-8-65). Commissioner may use garnishment to collect any tax, fee, license, penalty, interest or collection costs. (48-2-55[b][2]).

Levy and Sale.—Commissioner may levy and conduct judicial sales in same manner as provided for sales by sheriffs. (48-2-55).

Appeals.—To appeal Commissioner's decision, taxpayer must pay all taxes admittedly due within 30 days of decision and must file surety bond or other security with superior court for additional amount owed.

Penalties.—

Criminal.—See specific taxes.

Income Tax:

Late Filing or Failure to File.—If due to willful neglect, rather than reasonable cause, penalty in amount of 5% of tax per month late, to maximum of 25%. (48-7-57).

Deficiencies.—Where fraudulent, penalty in amount of 50% of deficiency. If deficiency due to negligence but not intent to defraud, 5% of deficiency collected as if it were deficiency. For other deficiencies, penalty in amount of 0.5% of deficiency per month, to maximum of 25%. (48-7-86).

Compromise.—Commissioner may compromise any penalty after verified statement has been filed with Commissioner setting forth facts and certifying that no previous settlement has been made, and that compromise is in opinion of Attorney General in best interest of state. (48-2-60). Commissioner may refund within three years of payment date any penalty paid without suit if Commissioner determines circumstances giving rise to penalty were reasonably beyond control of taxpayer. (48-2-60).

Interest.—Unless otherwise provided, interest upon deficiencies is collected at 1% per month from date prescribed for payment to date deficiency is paid. (48-7-81; 48-2-40). Commissioner may waive interest when delay in payment is attributed to action or inaction of Revenue Department. (48-2-41).

Criminal Penalties.—It is misdemeanor to assist in filing false returns (48-7-3), advise preparation of return intentionally disregarding regulations (48-7-4), or fail to pay tax, fail to make return, fail to keep records, fail to supply information or exhibit records requested by Commissioner (48-7-2).

See note at head of Digest as to 1998 legislation covered.

See Topical Index in front part of this volume.

ADMINISTRATION . . . continued

Estate Tax:

Failure to File.—If report not made within time required for filing federal returns, including extensions, estate may be appraised by Commissioner who will determine tax due. (48-12-5).

Failure to Pay.—If tax not paid on filing duplicate federal return or within 30 days after notice from Commissioner, then Commissioner shall issue execution against estate; which execution will bear interest of 1% per month until paid. Additional penalty of 10% of amount of tax for failure to file duplicate federal return or for failure to pay tax within 30 days after notice from Commissioner. (48-12-6).

Sales and Use Taxes:

Failure to File and/or Pay.—Except when providential cause shown, dealer who fails to file return and pay tax is penalized 5% of tax due or $5, whichever is greater, for each 30 days of delinquency not to exceed 25% or $25, whichever is greater, in aggregate. (48-8-66). Failure to pay tax on day due incurs interest at 1% per month until tax paid. (48-2-40).

Chronic Delinquency or Default.—Commissioner may require chronically defaulting or delinquent dealer to file surety bond not less than $1,000 nor more than $10,000. (48-8-57).

Failure to Collect.—Dealer who fails to collect sales tax is liable for it himself or herself and is guilty of misdemeanor. (48-8-7).

Fraud.—Willful falsification or failure to file return renders dealer liable for penalty of 50%, of tax due (48-8-66), and guilty of misdemeanor (48-8-8, -9).

Real and Personal Property Taxes:

Failure to Pay.—If tax willfully not paid within 90 days of due date, penalty of 10% of amount due is assessed. This penalty does not apply to taxes of $500 or less on homestead property, and, in 1986 or future years, to any homestead property if property was acquired by new owner during tax year: (1) who did not receive tax bill for that year; (2) who immediately before acquiring property resided outside State of Georgia; and (3) if taxes are paid within one year of due date.

Interest.—Taxes unpaid as of Nov. 20 (Oct. 20 in some counties) bear interest at rate of 1% per month until paid. (48-5-148). Governing authority of county may change due date to Nov. 15. (48-5-150).

Failure to Return.—Assessed unreturned property subject to penalty of 10% of tax due in addition to current assessment. (48-5-299).

BANKS AND SAVINGS & LOAN ASSOCIATIONS:

Depository financial institutions subject to all forms of state and local taxation to same extent as other business corporations in state. (48-6-90.1). Municipalities and counties may levy and collect business license tax from depository financial institutions having office located within their jurisdiction at rate not to exceed .25% of Georgia gross receipts. (48-6-93). Special state occupation tax imposed on each depository financial institution that conducts business or owns property in Georgia at rate of .25% of Georgia gross receipts. (48-6-95). Depository financial institutions get dollar-for-dollar credit against their state income tax liability equal to amount of business license and occupation tax paid. (48-7-21).

CORPORATE NET WORTH TAX:

Graduated tax imposed on Georgia corporations and corporations doing business or owning property in Georgia based on net worth; maximum tax is $5,000; returns and tax due on 15th day of third month of tax period. (48-13-70 through -79).

Corporation Tax.—See category Business Organizations, topic Corporations, subheads Taxation of Corporate Property, License Tax.

ESTATE TAX:

Representative of every deceased resident of state, whose estate must file federal estate tax return must file with Department of Revenue, Estate Tax Unit, duplicate of federal estate tax return and pay to state tax equal to maximum credit for state death taxes under §2011 of Internal Revenue Code of 1986. Credit allowed for tax paid to another state on property outside state. Return due on same date federal return is filed. (48-12-2).

Legal representative of deceased nonresident whose estate must file federal estate tax return, who owns or controls property located within state must file with Department of Revenue, Estate Tax Unit, duplicate of federal estate tax return. Tax is in proportion to amount of property in state as compared to total amount of property. (48-12-3).

Valuation Date.—Same as Federal.

Apportionment Against Inter Vivos Dispositions.—Tax apportionment statute does not exist in state.

Interstate Co-operation.—No statutory procedure available for compromise of death taxes when decedent's domicile is disputed.

Consents or Waivers.—Not necessary for transfer of corporate stock of resident or nonresident decedent. If desired, waivers may be secured by writing Department of Revenue, Property and License Tax Unit, State Office Building, Atlanta.

EXCISE TAX ON CAR RENTALS:

Counties and municipalities may impose 3% excise tax on car rentals.

FRANCHISE TAXES:

See category Business Organizations, topic Corporations. Other types of franchises defined and taxed. (48-5-420, -425).

GASOLINE AND MOTOR FUEL TAX:

Imposed by 48-9-1 through -19.

GIFT TAX:

None.

INCOME TAX:

Income tax is imposed on net income of every resident of state and on net income of nonresidents from property owned or any activity for financial gain in state. (48-7-20). Taxable net income and other terms defined. (48-7-26, -27). Taxable nonresident defined. (48-7-1). Every resident required to file federal income tax return and every nonresident who has federal gross income from within state must file return. (48-7-50). Every resident estate or trust required to file federal income tax return and every nonresident estate or trust with federal gross income from sources in state must file return unless otherwise provided in Income Tax Act of 1931. (48-7-50). Nonresident individuals whose only contact with Georgia is limited partner interest in resident investment limited partnership do not need to file return. (48-7-24). Late filing penalties of up to 25% of amount required to be shown as tax unless lateness due to reasonable cause or to extension of time to file by U.S. Internal Revenue Service. (48-7-57). Interest on late payments at 1% per month from last date prescribed for payment. (48-7-81, 48-2-40). Penalty of $500 can be imposed for frivolous position. (48-7-57.1).

Six percent income tax is imposed on corporations' Georgia taxable income. (48-721). Income tax does not apply to organizations described in §§401, 501(c), 501(d), 501(e), or 664 of Internal Revenue Code, but application for recognition of exemption must be filed with Commissioner. Also exempt are certain insurance companies, building and loan associations, cooperative banks, and bank and trust companies. Real estate investment trusts and regulated investment companies are not exempt. Exempt organizations' unrelated business income is subject to 6% tax. (48-7-25).

Returns.—Must be made by: (1) every resident individual who is required to file federal income tax return for taxable year (48-7-50); (2) every nonresident individual who has federal gross income from sources within state (48-7-50); (3) every resident estate or trust that is required to file federal income tax return (48-7-50); (4) every nonresident estate or trust that has federal gross income from sources within state (48-7-50); (5) every partnership any individual member of which is subject to state income tax (48-7-53); and (6) every corporation subject to state income tax (48-7-51). Income of two or more corporations may not be included in single return except with express consent of Commissioner. (48-7-51).

Returns for taxpayers other than corporations due by Apr. 15 or by 15th day of fourth month after close of fiscal year. (48-7-56). Returns for corporations due by Mar. 15 or by 15th day of third month after close of fiscal year. (48-7-56). Returns of DISCs, former DISCs and FSCs due by 15th day of ninth month following close of taxable year. (48-7-56). Filed with Georgia Dept. of Revenue, Income Tax Unit, Trinity-Washington Bldg., Atlanta, Georgia 30334.

Payment.—Due by Apr. 15 or by 15th day of fourth month after close of fiscal year. (48-7-80). Individuals receive credit for income tax withheld from wages (48-7-112[a]) and individuals and corporations for amounts paid as estimated income tax (48-7-121[a]).

Refunds.—State or federal income tax refunds not over $500 in favor of decedent are paid to surviving spouse without administration of decedent's estate. (53-4-7).

Declarations of Estimated Tax.—Every resident individual, every nonresident individual and fiduciary subject to Georgia income tax, must file estimated income tax for current year if his or her gross income is expected (1) to include more than $1,000 from sources other than wages subject to withholding, and (2) to exceed $1,500 if single, or $3,000 if married, living with spouse, and will claim full marital exemption. Taxpayer must show estimate of current year's income tax less tax expected to be withheld from sources subject to withholding, and any other anticipated credits against tax, result being net estimated tax. (48-7-114).

Estimated tax for individuals other than farmers or fishermen must be filed by Apr. 15 of taxable year, except that if above thresholds are met on or after Apr. 1 and before June 1 of taxable year, estimated tax must be filed by June 15 of taxable year; on or after June 1 and before Sept. 1 estimated tax must be filed by Sept. 15 of taxable year; on or after Sept. 1, estimated tax must be filed by Jan. 15 of succeeding year. (48-7115). Individual estimated tax must be paid quarterly in equal installments beginning with first quarter for which estimated tax is required to be filed. (48-7-116).

All domestic and foreign corporations subject to income tax must pay estimated tax for taxable year if net income reasonably expected to exceed $25,000. Estimated tax must be paid quarterly in equal installments beginning with quarter in which $25,000 threshold is exceeded. (48-7-117, -119).

Income Taxed—Individuals.—

Rates.—Single Person: 1% on first $750 if net income not over $750; $7.50 plus 2% of amount over $750 for net income over $750 but not over $2,250; $37.50 plus 3% of amount over $2,250 for net income over $2,250 but not over $3,750; $82.50 plus 4% of amount over $3,750 for net income over $3,750 but not over $5,250; $142.50 plus 5% of amount over $5,250 for net income over $5,250 but not over $7,000; $230 plus 6% of amount over $7,000 for net income over $7,000.

Married Person Filing Separate Return: 1% on first $500 if taxable net income not over $500; $5 plus 2% of amount over $500 for net income over $500 but not over $1,500; $25 plus 3% of amount over $1,500 for net income over $1,500 but not over $2,500; $55 plus 4% of amount over $2,500 for net income over $2,500 but not over $3,500; $95 plus 5% of amount over $3,500 for net income over $3,500 but not over $5,000; $170 plus 6% of amount over $5,000 for net income over $5,000.

Head of Household and Married Persons Filing Joint Returns: 1% of first $1,000 for net income not over $1,000; $10 plus 2% of amount over $1,000 for net income over $1,000 but not over $3,000; $50 plus 3% of amount over $3,000 for net income over $3,000 but not over $5,000; $110 plus 4% of amount over $5,000 for net income over $5,000 but not over $7,000; $190 plus 5% of amount over $7,000 for net income over $7,000 but not over $10,000; $340 plus 6% of amount over $10,000 for net income over $10,000. (48-7-20).

Capital Gains and Losses.—Separate provisions on determining basis, gain or loss, accelerated amortization repealed. Capital gains and losses taxed as reflected in federal adjusted gross income. (48-7-27).

Foreign Tax Credit.—Credit against income tax is allowed to resident individuals with business or investment in another state in amount of tax paid upon net income of such business or investment in such other state, if such state levies tax upon net income.

See note at head of Digest as to 1998 legislation covered.

See Topical Index in front part of this volume.

INCOME TAX . . . *continued*
However, credit may not exceed tax that would have been paid in Georgia upon like amount of taxable income. (48-7-28).

Deductions.—Georgia taxable net income of individual is federal adjusted gross income, as defined in Federal Internal Revenue Code of 1986, minus following deductions: (1) Standard deduction or sum of itemized nonbusiness deductions, whichever taxpayer elects in computing federal tax income; (2) exemptions outlined above; (3) income received from certain public pension and retirement funds; (4) mortgage interest eliminated from federal itemized deductions in computing federal mortgage interest credit; and (5) amount of dependent's unearned income included in parent's return; but Georgia taxable income shall include dividend or interest income on obligations of state other than Georgia and of non-Georgia political subdivisions to extent excluded from gross income under federal income tax, interest or dividends on U.S. obligations exempt from federal income tax but not exempt from state income taxes, and income taxes imposed by any jurisdiction other than Georgia to extent deducted under federal income tax. No portion of any deductions or losses, including net operating losses, which occurred in year in which taxpayer was not subject to taxation in state may be deducted in any tax year. Certain adjustments are permitted for shareholders of federal Subchapter S corporation that is not recognized for state tax purposes to avoid double taxation. Certain self-employed individuals may deduct amounts paid for medical insurance for self, spouse and dependents, not otherwise deductible on federal return. At taxpayer election, Georgia taxable net income is reduced by amount of taxpayer's capital gains, deduction or exclusion from federal adjusted gross income. (48-7-21, -27).

Exemptions and Additional Deductions (Over Itemized or Standard Deductions).—Taxpayer is allowed following exemptions from net income: $2,700 for himself or herself; $5,400 for taxpayer and spouse if joint return filed; $2,700 for each dependent. (48-7-26; -27). Additional deductions include: $1,300 if taxpayer is 65 before close of tax year; $1,300 for spouse over 65 by end of tax year if joint return filed; $1,300 if taxpayer is blind at close of tax year; $1,300 if spouse is blind before close of taxpayer's tax year and joint return is filed by taxpayer and his or her spouse. (48-7-27).

Nonresident taxpayers may deduct allowable business expenses only to extent attributable to income from state, and allowable personal deductions (charitable contributions, alimony, medical expenses, optional standard deduction, personal exemptions, credits for dependents, etc.) only in ratio that taxpayer's Georgia gross income bears to his entire gross income. (48-7-30).

Nonresident contractors performing contract in state exceeding $10,000 must register each such contract with Commissioner, appoint agent for service of process, and post bond equal to 10% of contract price for payment of all taxes due state, including unemployment insurance contributions. (48-13-32). Secretary of State is appointed agent for service in any tax proceeding arising out of contract performed or to be performed in state. (48-13-35). Violation of statute is misdemeanor and contractor denied use of state courts to recover payment for performance; also subject to injunction against further performance. (48-13-38, -33, -37). Registration fee is $10 per contract. (48-13-31).

Fiduciaries.—Tax applies to resident and nonresident fiduciaries receiving income from business done in state, having charge of funds or property in state, or having charge of funds or property for benefit of resident of state. (48-7-22). Net income of trusts and estates taxed. (48-7-20). Estate may deduct $2,700, trust $1,350, in lieu of personal exemption deduction. (48-7-26). Every resident trust or estate that is required to file federal income tax return and every nonresident trust or estate that has federal gross income from sources within this state must file return. (48-7-50).

Income Taxed—Corporations.—Domestic or foreign corporations (with certain exceptions) are taxed at rate of 6% of net income from property owned and/or business done in state. Net income generally determined by reference to federal taxable income determined under Internal Revenue Code of 1986 in effect as of Jan. 1, 1997, with adjustments to taxable income made for interest on certain government bonds, dividends on bank stock, taxes paid to jurisdictions other than Georgia, income exempt from federal tax, and certain elections made in federal returns. (48-7-21). Federal Internal Revenue Code of 1986 followed generally as to corporate reorganizations and liquidations. Subchapter S elections apply only if all stockholders are subject to tax in state on their portion of corporate income. However, election will be allowed if nonresident stockholders file with Commissioner agreement to pay tax on their portion of corporate income. (48-7-21).

Constitutional.—Income tax constitutional when applied to foreign corporation even though corporation's only contacts with state were that it maintained sales office in Atlanta with secretary who answered telephone there and salesman whose efforts were one-third directed to state and two-thirds to other states, and contracts were made in other states as to goods shipped to state pursuant to offers made by state customers. (358 U.S. 450, rev'g 213 Ga. 713, 101 S.E. 2d 197). Accord, under state constitution where foreign corporation's only contacts with state were sales office in Atlanta with seven employees and from which three salesmen regularly solicited in Georgia and ten other states, all orders from Georgia customers being accepted outside state and shipped by common carrier f.o.b. its plant or warehouses, all outside state. (216 Ga. 316, 116 S.E.2d 293). Same holding in companion case (but without opinion) where per stipulated facts foreign corporation had no office in state, all its salesmen operating from their residences in state and orders accepted and shipment made in same manner as above. (216 Ga. 389, 116 S.E.2d 299). But see Public Law 86-272, which provides some legislative protection against imposition of state taxes measured by net income on marginal activities within taxing state, if these activities constitute only activities of foreign business within state.

Allocation and Apportionment of Income.—Corporations doing business both within and without state are taxed only on net income attributable to state, determined according to Code §48-7-31, quoted below:

"(a) CORPORATIONS SUBJECT TO TAX. The tax imposed by this chapter shall apply to the entire net income, as defined in this article, received by every foreign or domestic corporation owning property or doing business within this state. A corporation shall be deemed to be doing business within this state if it engages within this state in any activities or transactions for the purpose of financial profit or gain whether or not:

(1) The corporation qualifies to do business in this state;

(2) The corporation maintains an office or place of doing business within this state; or

(3) Any such activity or transaction is connected with interstate or foreign commerce.

(b) INCOME SUBJECT TO TAX.

(1) If the entire business income of the corporation is derived from property owned or business done in this state, the tax shall be imposed on the entire business income.

(2) If the business income of the corporation is derived in part from property owned or business done in this state and in part from property owned or business done outside this state, the tax shall be imposed only on that portion of the business income which is reasonably attributable to the property owned and business done within this state, such portion to be determined as provided in subsections (c) and (d) of this Code section.

(c) ALLOCATION OF INCOME.

(1) Interest received on bonds held for investment and income received from other intangible property held for investment are not subject to apportionment. All expenses connected with such investment income shall be applied against the investment income. The net investment income from intangible property shall be allocated to this state if the situs of the corporation is in this state or if the intangible property was acquired as income from property held in this state or as a result of business done in this state.

(2) Rentals received from real estate held purely for investment purposes and not used in the operation of any business are not subject to apportionment. All expenses connected with such investment income shall be applied against the investment income. The net investment income from tangible property located in this state shall be allocated to this state.

(3) Gains from the sale of tangible or intangible property not held, owned, or used in connection with the trade or business of the corporation nor held for sale in the regular course of business shall be allocated to this state if the property sold is real or tangible personal property situated in this state or intangible property having an actual situs or a business situs within this state. Otherwise, the gains shall not be allocated to this state.

(d) APPORTIONMENT OF INCOME. Net income of the classes described in subsection (c) of this Code section having been separately allocated and deducted, the remainder of the net business income shall be apportioned as follows:

(1) For purposes of paragraphs (2) and (3) of this subsection, the Commissioner may enter into an agreement with the taxpayer establishing the allocation and apportionment of the taxpayer's income for a limited period, provided that the following conditions are met:

(A) The taxpayer is planning a new facility in the state of Georgia or an expansion of an existing facility;

(B) The taxpayer submits a proposal asking the Commissioner to enter into a contract under this paragraph requesting a different allocation and apportionment method and stating the reasons for such proposal; and

(C) Following the Commissioner's referral of the proposal to a panel composed of the commissioner of community affairs, the Commissioner of industry, trade, and tourism, and the director of the Office of Planning and Budget, said panel, after reviewing the proposal, certifies that:

(i) the new facility or expansion will have a significant beneficial economic effect on the region for which it is planned; and

(ii) the benefits to the public from the new facility or expansion exceed its cost to the public.

(2) Where the net business income of the corporation is derived principally from the manufacture, production, or sale of tangible personal property, the portion of the net income therefrom attributable to property owned or business done within this state shall be taken to be the portion arrived at by application of the following three factor formula:

(A) Property factor. The property factor is a fraction, the numerator of which is the average value of the taxpayer's real and tangible personal property owned or rented and used in this state during the tax period and the denominator of which is the average value of all the taxpayer's real and tangible personal property owned or rented and used during the tax period;

(i) Property owned by the taxpayer is valued at its original cost. Property rented by the taxpayer is valued at eight times the net annual rental rate. Net annual rental rate is the annual rental rate paid by the taxpayer less any annual rental rate received by the taxpayer from subrentals;

(ii) The average value of property shall be determined by averaging the values at the beginning and end of the tax period, except that the commissioner may require the averaging of monthly values during the tax period if such averaging is reasonably required to reflect properly the average value of the taxpayer's property;

(B) Payroll factor. The payroll factor is a fraction, the numerator of which is the total amount paid in this state during the tax period by the taxpayer for compensation and denominator of which is the total compensation paid everywhere during the tax period. The term 'compensation' means wages, salaries, commissions, and any other form of remuneration paid to employees for personal services. Payments made to an independent contractor or any other person not properly classified as an employee are excluded. Compensation is paid in this state if:

(i) The employee's service is performed entirely within this state;

(ii) The employee's service is performed both within and outside this state and the service performed outside this state is incidental to the employee's service within this state; or

(iii) Some of the service is performed in this state and either the base of operations or the place from which the service is directed or controlled is in this state or the base of operations or the place from which the service is directed or controlled is not in any state in which some part of the service is performed but the employee's residence is in this state;

See note at head of Digest as to 1998 legislation covered.

See Topical Index in front part of this volume.

GA – 60

INCOME TAX. . . *continued*

(C) Gross receipts factor. The gross receipts factor is a fraction, the numerator of which is the total gross receipts from business done within this state during the tax period and the denominator of which is the total gross receipts from business done everywhere during the tax period. For the purposes of this subparagraph, receipts shall be deemed to have been derived from business done within this state only if the receipts are received from products shipped to customers in this state or products delivered within this state to customers. In determining the gross receipts within this state, receipts from sales negotiated or effected through offices of the taxpayer outside this state and delivered from storage in this state to customers outside this state shall be excluded;

(D) Apportionment formula. The property factor, the payroll factor, and the gross receipts factor shall be separately determined and an apportionment fraction shall be calculated using the following formula:

(i) The property factor shall represent 25 percent of the fraction;

(ii) The payroll factor shall represent 25 percent of the fraction; and

(iii) The gross receipts factor shall represent 50 percent of the fraction. The net income of the corporation shall be apportioned to this state according to such average fraction.

(3) Except as otherwise provided in paragraph (3.1) or (3.2) of this subsection, where the net business income is derived principally from business other than the manufacture, production, or sale of tangible personal property, the net business income of the corporation shall be arrived at by application of the following three factor formula:

(A) Property factor. The property factor is a fraction, the numerator of which is the average value of the taxpayer's real and tangible personal property owned or rented and used in this state during the tax period and the denominator of which is the average value of all the taxpayer's real and tangible personal property owned or rented and used during the tax period;

(i) Property owned by the taxpayer is valued at its original cost. Property rented by the taxpayer is valued at eight times the net annual rental rate. Net annual rental rate is the annual rental rate paid by the taxpayer less any annual rental rate received by the taxpayer from subrentals;

(ii) The average value of property shall be determined by averaging the values at the beginning and end of the tax period, except that the commissioner may require the averaging of monthly values during the tax period if such averaging is reasonably required to reflect properly the average value of the taxpayer's property;

(B) Payroll factor. The payroll factor is a fraction, the numerator of which is the total amount paid in this state during the tax period by the taxpayer for compensation and the denominator of which is the total compensation paid everywhere during the tax period. The term 'compensation' means wages, salaries, commissions, and any other form of remuneration paid to employees for personal services. Payments made to an independent contractor or any other person not properly classified as an employee are excluded. Compensation is paid in this state if:

(i) The employee's service is performed entirely within this state;

(ii) The employee's service is performed both within and outside this state and the service performed outside this state is incidental to the employee's service within this state; or

(iii) Some of the service is performed in this state and either the base of operations or the place from which the service is directed or controlled is in this state or the base of operations or the place from which the service is directed or controlled is not in any state in which some part of the service is performed but the employee's residence is in this state;

(C) Gross receipts factor. The gross receipts factor is a fraction, the numerator of which is the total gross receipts from business done within this state during the tax period and the denominator of which is the total gross receipt from business done everywhere during the tax period. Gross receipts are in this state if the receipts are derived from customers within this state or if the receipts are otherwise attributable to this state's marketplace;

(D) The property factor, payroll factor, and the gross receipts factor shall be separately determined and an apportionment factor shall be calculated using the following formula:

(i) The property factor shall represent 25 percent of the fraction;

(ii) The payroll factor shall represent 25 percent of the fraction; and

(iii) The gross receipts factor shall represent 50 percent of the fraction.

(E) If the allocation and apportionment provisions provided for in this paragraph do not fairly represent the extent of the taxpayer's business activity in this state, the taxpayer may petition the commissioner for, with respect to all or any part of the taxpayer's business activity, if reasonable:

(i) Separate accounting;

(ii) The exclusion of any one or more of the factors;

(iii) The inclusion of one or more additional factors that will fairly represent the taxpayer's business activity within this state; or

(iv) The employment of any other method to effectuate an equitable allocation and apportionment of the taxpayer's income.

The denial of a petition under this paragraph shall be appealable pursuant to either Code Section 48-2-59 or 50-13-12;

(3.1)(A) Except as otherwise provided in this paragraph, all terms used in this paragraph shall have the same meaning as such terms are defined in 49 U.S.C. Section 1301 and the United States Department of Transportation's Uniform System of Accounts and Reports for Large Certificated Air Carriers, 14 C.F.R. Part 241, as now or hereafter amended.

(B) Where the net business income of the corporation is derived principally from transporting passengers or cargo in revenue flight, the portion of the net income therefrom attributable to property owned or business done within this state shall be taken to be the portion arrived at by application of the following three factor formula:

(i) Revenue air miles factor. The revenue air miles factor is a fraction, the numerator of which shall be equal to the total, for each flight stage which originates or terminates in this state, of revenue passenger miles by aircraft type flown in this state and revenue cargo ton miles by aircraft type flown in this state and the denominator of which shall be equal to the total, for all flight stages flown everywhere, of total revenue passenger miles by aircraft type and total revenue cargo ton miles by aircraft type;

(ii) Tons handled factor. The tons handled factor is a fraction, the numerator of which shall be equal to the total of revenue passenger tons by aircraft type handled in this state and revenue cargo tons by aircraft type handled in this state and the denominator of which shall be equal to the total of revenue passenger tons by aircraft type flown everywhere and revenue cargo tons by aircraft type flown everywhere. For purposes of this division, the term 'handled' means the product of 60 percent multiplied by the revenue passenger tons flown on each flight stage which originates in this state or 60 percent multiplied by the revenue cargo tons flown on each flight stage which originates in this state;

(iii) Originating revenue factor. The originating revenue factor is a fraction, the numerator of which shall be equal to the total of passenger and cargo revenue by aircraft type which is attributable to this state and the denominator of which shall be the total of passenger and cargo revenue by aircraft type everywhere. For purposes of this division, passenger or cargo revenue which is attributable to this state shall be equal to the product of passenger or cargo revenue everywhere by aircraft type multiplied by the ratio of revenue passenger miles or revenue cargo ton miles in this state to total revenue passenger miles everywhere or total revenue cargo ton miles everywhere for each aircraft type as separately determined in division (i) of this subparagraph. The records of total passenger revenue everywhere by aircraft type or total cargo revenue everywhere by aircraft type are not maintained, then for purposes of this division, total passenger revenue everywhere for all aircraft types or total cargo revenue everywhere for all aircraft types shall be allocated to each aircraft type based on the ratio of total revenue passenger miles everywhere for that aircraft type to all aircraft types or total revenue cargo ton miles everywhere for that aircraft type to all aircraft types;

(iv) The revenue air miles factor, the tons handled factor, and the originating revenue factor shall be separately determined and an apportionment fraction shall be calculated using the following formula:

(I) The revenue air miles factor shall represent 25 percent of the fraction;

(II) The tons handled factor shall represent 25 percent of the fraction; and

(III) The originating revenue factor shall represent 50 percent of the fraction. The net income of the corporation shall be apportioned to this state according to such average fraction;

(3.2)(A) As used in this paragraph, the term:

(i) 'Credit card data processing and related services' shall include, but not be limited to, the provision of infrastructure services for bank credit card and private label card issuers, such as new account application processing, international and domestic clearing, statement preparation, point-of-sale authorization processing, card embossing, and other related processing services for managing cardholder accounts.

(ii) 'Customer' means the banks and institutions to whom credit card data processing and related services are provided.

(iii) 'Gross receipts factor' means a fraction the numerator of which is the total gross receipts from the taxpayer's customers during the tax period, if the principal office of the customer's credit card operation is in this state or if the principal office of the taxpayer's customer is in this state, and the denominator of which is the total gross receipts from all of the taxpayer's customers during the tax period.

(B) Where more than 60% of the total gross receipts of a corporation are derived from the provision of credit card processing and related services to banks and other institutions, the portion of the net income attributable to business done in this state shall be determined by multiplying the corporation's net income by the gross receipts factor in division (iii) of subparagraph (A) of this paragraph.

(4) For the purposes of this subsection, the term 'sale' shall include, but not be limited to, an exchange, and the term 'manufacture' shall include, but not be limited to, the extraction and recovery of natural resources and all processes of fabricating and curing.

(e) DETERMINATION OF FAIR NET INCOME OF SUBSIDIARIES AND AFFILIATES. The net income of a domestic or foreign corporation which is a subsidiary of another corporation or which is closely affiliated with another corporation by stock ownership shall be determined by eliminating all payments to the parent corporation or affiliated corporation in excess of fair value and by including fair compensation to the domestic business corporation for its commodities sold to or services performed for the parent corporation or affiliated corporation. For the purposes of determining net income as provided in this subsection, the commissioner may equitably determine the net income by reasonable rules of apportionment of the combined income of the subsidiary, its parent, and affiliates, or any combination of the subsidiary, its parent, and any one or more of its affiliates."

Alternative Method.—Corporation may allocate its income based on allocation of receipts and expenditures employed in its books of account if this method of allocation reflects Georgia income more clearly than process or formulas prescribed by state law. Application to Commissioner for permission to allocate income on basis of books of account must be made at least 60 days prior to due date of state return. (48-7-34). Application may also be made to Commissioner for permission to base corporation's return on any other method which more clearly reflects Georgia income. (48-7-35).

Tax Credits.—

Jobs Credit.—Up to $2,500 credit allowed for each new full-time employee in designated less developed counties. (48-7-40). Up to $3,500 credit allowed if increase port traffic of products by certain percentage between Jan. 1, 1998 and July 1, 2002. (48-7-40.15).

Education Program Credit.—Up to one-third cost of education or $150, whichever is less, for each student-employee who successfully completes employer sponsored skills education program. (48-7-41).

See note at head of Digest as to 1998 legislation covered.

See Topical Index in front part of this volume.

GA – 61

INCOME TAX . . . *continued*

Retraining Program Credit.—Up to one-half cost of retraining or $500, whichever is less, for each student-employee who successfully completes employer sponsored retraining program. (48-7-40.5).

Child Care Credit.—Up to one-half cost of employer sponsored or employer provided child care. (48-7-40.6).

Low-Emission Vehicle Credit.—Credit of $1,500 per vehicle for purchase or lease of certain low-emission vehicles registered in specified areas; also, credit of up to $1,500 per vehicle for conversion of conventionally fueled vehicles. (48-7-40.15).

Qualified Caregiving Expenses Credit.—Lesser of $150 or up to 10% of certain health and caregiving expenses for certain qualifying family members.

Water Conservation Credit.—Credit of between 5 and 10% for persons participating in qualified water conservation investment. (48-7-4.10). Certain credits also available for taxpayers that switch from groundwater usage. (48-7-40.11).

Investment Tax Credit.—Corporation or person operating manufacturing facility or manufacturing support facility in designated less developed county is allowed tax credit equal to between 1 and 10% of cost of all qualified investment property acquired for use in construction or expansion of manufacturing facility or manufacturing support facility. (48-7-40.2, -40.3, -40.4, -40.7, -40.8, -40.9). Credit also allowed if increase port traffic of products by certain percentage between Jan. 1, 1998 and July 1, 2002. (48-7-40.15).

Rural Physician Credit.—Physicians who choose to practice in certain rural areas may be allowed income tax credit of up to $5,000. (48-7-29).

AFDC Tax Credit.—Employees who hire recipients of Aid to Families with Dependent Children receive tax credit equal to 20% to 40% of first $7,000 of wages, depending on amount by which employer's salary exceeds federal minimum wage. (48-7-42).

Withholding.—

Employer/Employee.—Every employer must withhold income tax from nonexempt wages of each employee. (48-7-101). Employer includes any person for whom state resident performs any service, within or without state, or for whom nonresident individual performs any service within state, as employee; except that if person for whom services are performed does not have control of payment of wages, then term "employer" includes person with such control, and where person pays wages on behalf of nonresident individual, foreign partnership, or foreign corporation not doing business in state, term "employer" includes person paying wages. (48-7-100[5]). Exemptions, rates and optional withholding tables set out in statute. (48-7-101). Employer whose tax withheld is $200 or less must file and remit payment to Commissioner on or before last day of month following end of quarter, however, if monthly amount withheld exceeds $200, tax must be paid on or before 15th day of following month. (48-7-103). Receipts must be given to employees by Jan. 31 of each year showing tax withheld during year (48-7-105) and annual return of employer must be filed by Feb. 28 of succeeding year or by 30th day after date on which final payment of wages is made by employer who ceased to pay wages (48-7-106). Employer failing to withhold required amount subject to penalty of $10 per quarter per employee. Employer failing to file return or pay tax liable for penalty to $25 for each failure, plus 5% of tax due for each month such failure continues, not to exceed $25 plus 25% of tax due. (48-7-126). If employer delinquent in payment of tax, Commissioner may give notice to all persons having control or possession of personal property of employer and such persons may make no disposition of such property within 30 days of receiving such notice. (48-7-108). Upon notice from Commissioner of employer's failure to withhold or pay over taxes as required, employer shall deduct and withhold tax required and employ special accounting procedures until Commissioner cancels notice requiring such procedures. (48-7-109.1).

Sales Property.—Applying to any sale or transfer of real property occurring after Jan. 1, 1994, buyer required to withhold and remit to tax commissioner 3% of purchase price in sale of real property located in Georgia by nonresident seller. If net proceeds to seller are less than 3% of purchase price, only net proceeds must be withheld. No withholding required for sale of principal residence, sale by mortgagor in foreclosure or deed in lieu thereof with no additional consideration, or if seller is agency or authority of state or federal government or government or private mortgage insurance company. (48-7-128). Resident under Code §48-7-128 must meet all of following criteria: (1) must have filed Georgia income tax returns for two preceding income tax years; (2) must continue to be in business in Georgia after sale; and (3) must report sale on Georgia income tax return for current year.

On Certain Distributions to Certain Nonresidents.—Partnerships, subchapter S corporations, and limited liability companies that own property or do business in Georgia must withhold tax from any distributions paid or credited to members who are not Georgia residents, at rate of 4%. (48-7-128, -129). Alternative to nonresident withholding is to file composite return on behalf of all nonresident members, reporting and remitting income tax due. (48-7-129). Penalties for failure to withhold amounts required, admit nonresident status of member, and furnish nonresidents with correct withholding statements set out in statute. (48-7-129).

Local Income Tax.—Although authorized by state law under certain circumstances (48-7-140 through -149), no counties or municipalities in Georgia impose local income taxes.

INHERITANCE TAX:

None.

INTANGIBLE RECORDING TAX:

Tax Imposed.—Long Term Notes Secured by Real Estate (any part of principal falling due more than three years from date of note or from date of instrument securing it) must be recorded within 90 days from date of instrument in county in which real estate conveyed or encumbered or upon which lien is created is situated. (48-6-60, -61). Prior to filing such instrument for record there must be paid to clerk of superior court of such county tax, not greater than $25,000, of $1.50 per $500 of debt as evidenced in instrument to be filed for record. (48-6-61). Collecting officer collects tax from holders of instrument. Holder may pass amount of tax to borrower or mortgagor but such amount shall not be considered part of any finance charge imposed by holder. Tax paid only once-prior to or at time instrument securing note if filed for record. Payment under protest may be made; such payment requires county official to record instrument and escrow tax paid until final determination; claim for refund must be made within 30 days of payment date. (48-6-76).

Failure to Pay.—Unless Commissioner determines that tax is not payable (48-6-71), failure to pay tax does not bar recorded instrument from constituting legal notice (48-6-62), but it does bar collection of indebtedness secured by any instrument required to be recorded, by suit, foreclosure, exercise of any power of sale, or otherwise, whether such instrument held by original party thereto or transferee. However, such instrument, subject to bar, shall continue to secure indebtedness and shall continue to encumber collateral described therein. Failure to pay tax will not affect or discharge indebtedness secured by instrument or debtor's liability on account thereof. (48-6-77). Bar may be removed by payment of tax required, plus interest from time tax due, plus penalty of 50% of amount of tax due. (48-6-77, 48-2-40). Commissioner may waive 50% penalty if he or she determines that failure to pay tax was through "ignorance of the law or inadvertence, and not in bad faith." (48-6-77). Nonresident lenders conducting lending business in state are subject to this tax. (232 Ga. 344, 206 S.E.2d 424).

Exemptions.—Tax not applicable to instruments which are extensions, transfers, assignments, modifications or renewals of, or which only add additional security for, long-term notes on which tax has already been paid or portion of new long-term note which is refinancing by original lender of unpaid principal on previous long-term note, if tax paid on previous note and amount of refinancing shown. (48-6-65).

Intangibles Personal Property Tax.—None.

LICENSES, OCCUPATIONAL AND PROFESSIONAL:

Taxes allowed under 48-13-5 et seq.

MORTGAGE TAX:

See topic Intangible Recording Tax.

MUNICIPAL TAX:

Municipality may levy tax for development not to exceed three mills per dollar on assessed property (48-5-350) and may levy tax for benefits and costs of teacher retirement system (48-5-351).

Municipal tax operating as precondition for practice of law unconstitutional regulation. (267 Ga. 571, 481 S.E.2d 818).

PROPERTY TAX:

Real and Personal Property Taxable.—All property taxable except that exempted. (48-5-3). Any estate in property is taxable, except mere usufruct. See subhead Exemptions from Property Taxation, infra.

Exemptions from Property Taxation.—Public property, with certain exceptions; places of religious worship or burial and all property owned and operated exclusively as a church or similar or related association when such entity qualifies as exempt religious organization under §501(c)(3) of Internal Revenue Code of 1986 and used in manner consistent with such exemption; institutions of purely public charity; hospitals not operated for purpose of private or corporate profit and income, with exceptions; buildings erected for and used as college, incorporated academy or other seminary of learning; all funds or property held as endowment by such colleges, nonprofit hospitals, incorporated academy or seminary of learning, provided same is not invested in real estate, and provided said institutions are open to general public and donors do not reserve right to receive or retain any part of income of property; real and personal property of public library, books, philosophical apparatus, paintings, and statuary of company or association kept in public hall; property of nonprofit home for aged or for mentally disabled used in connection with its operation, provided same has no stockholders and does not distribute income to private persons; certain property used to reduce water or air pollution; property used exclusively as headquarters, post home, or similar facility of veterans organization; property owned by historical fraternal benefit association which is used exclusively for charitable, fraternal, and benevolent purposes; provided in every case exempted property not used for profit (48-5-41); farm products grown in state and remaining in hands of producer exempt for period not longer than year next after production; certain harvested agricultural products with planting-to-harvest cycle of 12 months or less; qualified farm products remaining in hands of family owned qualified farm products producer, still in natural condition, and not held for direct retail sale by someone other than original producer. (48-5-41.1). Tax exempt status does not apply to special assessments for improvements. (235 Ga. 194, 219 S.E.2d 122).

Homestead or residence actually occupied by owner as residence is exempt from ad valorem taxation up to value of $2,000. (48-5-44). Occupant or occupants of jointly owned residence each entitled to full exemption. (48-5-44). Applications for exemption in all counties providing for collection and payment of ad valorem taxes must be filed on or before May 1 or such other date as established by local Act; in all other counties application must be filed on or before June 1. If exemption not filed in timely fashion, exemption is deemed waived for entire year. (48-5-45). Homestead of person 62 years or older with annual income of $10,000 or less exempt up to maximum value of $10,000 from ad valorem taxes for educational purposes. (48-5-52). Homestead of person 65 years or older with annual income of $10,000 or less exempt up to maximum value of $4,000 from all state and county ad valorem taxes. (48-5-47). Homestead of person 62 years or older with annual income $30,000 or less exempt up to amount equal to amount of assessed value for taxes to pay interest on and to retire bonded indebtedness. (48-547.1). Residence of disabled veteran exempt to value of $12,500. (Const., Art XI, §1, Paragraph IV).

Foreign merchandise in transit (any personal property imported into U.S. by water through any Georgia port) is exempt from property tax while stored in county in which port of original entry is located. (48-5-5). Property that is owned by non-Georgia resident who does not maintain or operate business in Georgia, but who contracts with Georgia commercial printer for printing services in Georgia and provides property to Georgia based printer is exempt from ad valorem taxation. (48-5-5). Imports not in

See note at head of Digest as to 1998 legislation covered.

See Topical Index in front part of this volume.

GA – 62

PROPERTY TAX . . . *continued*
transit but remaining in original packaging are constitutionally exempt from taxation. (233 Ga. 712, 214 S.E.2d 349, affirmed by U.S. Supreme Court, holding that nondiscriminatory property tax imposed on imported goods no longer in import transit is not prohibited by Import-Export Clause of U.S. Constitution, 423 U.S. 276).

Personal property consisting of clothing, furniture, and property used about home, etc., is exempt from all ad valorem taxation. Domestic animals and tools of trade of manual laborers are exempt to value of $300. (48-5-42). All tangible personal property except motor vehicles, trailers and mobile homes exempt to value of $500. (48-5-42.1). Dealer-owned motor vehicles held for sale or resale are exempt from ad valorem taxation. (48-5-472, 269 Ga. 202, 496 S.E.2d 727 [1998]).

In certain cases, compressed petroleum gas is exempt from motor fuel tax. (48-9-3).

Deeds in certain types of transactions exempt from tax on documents transferring real property. (48-6-2). See also topic Real Estate Conveyance Tax.

Returns.—Public utility corporations, insurance corporations, airline companies, foreign and domestic corporations holding special franchises from state must make returns to Department of Revenue on or before Mar. 1, as of Jan. 1 preceding. (48-5-422, -511, -541; 48-1-2). All other corporations and all individuals must return to tax receiver of county of residence, between Jan. 1 and Apr. 1 (Mar. 1 in certain counties), all property owned by them, except real estate in other counties, and personalty used in business therein, which is returned in counties where situated. (48-515, -16, -18). Property of nonresident must be returned in county where property is situated. (48-5-12). If owner fails to return property which he or she returned in preceding year, it is automatically returned, at valuation of preceding year, and taxpayer deemed to have claimed same homestead and personal property exemptions as in preceding year. (48-5-20). Property subject to tax must be returned at fair market value. (48-5-6). Fair market value defined. (48-5-2). Returns must be made annually for property held on Jan. 1, next preceding. (48-5-10).

Assessment.—Actual and highest and best uses of property both factors in determining fair market value of property for assessment. (236 Ga. 88, 222 S.E.2d 371). Extent of holder's interest not factor. (155 Ga. App. 591, 271 S.E.2d 727). By Apr. 11 tax receiver must present tax returns of county to board of tax assessors (48-5-301), who must inspect returns and determine value of property and equalize assessments (48-5-299, -302). Members of county board of tax assessors or county property appraisal staff may examine property (outside buildings) to appraise fair market value. (48-5-264.1). Tangible property must be assessed at 40% of fair market value. (48-5-7). Certain tangible real property devoted to bona fide agricultural purposes assessed at 75% of value which other tangible real property is assessed. (48-5-7; 7.1). Special method provided for valuing historic property. (48-5-2, -7.2, -7.3). Bona fide conservation use property and bona fide residential transitional property assessed at 40% of current use value. (4-5-2, -7). Current use value defined. (48-5-2). Bona fide conservation use defined. (48-5-7.4). Bona fide residential transitional property defined. (48-5-7.4). Different methods of valuation of real and personal property allowed. (234 Ga. 234, 214 S.E.2d 923). Uniformity of taxation does not require that only one method be used in determining fair market value of tangible property. (236 Ga. 88, 222 S.E.2d 371). Property taxes are charged against owner of property if known, and against specific property itself if owner is not known. (48-5-9). Taxing authorities are generally indifferent as to whom property actually belongs and usually proceed against property itself to collect unpaid taxes. Tax bill covering previously uncovered undervaluation of property is not reassessment or revaluation of property, but bill for default. (48-5-306; 228 Ga. 94, 491 S.E.2d 173).

Review of Assessment.—Disputed assessments must be appealed first to county board of tax assessors within 45 days (30 days for counties, municipal corporations that provide for collection and payment of taxes in installments), then to county board of equalization or to arbitrator or arbitrators within 45 days, and then to superior court within 30 days. Temporary tax bills are issued during pendency of appeal and interest may be recovered or paid by taxpayer depending on outcome of appeal. (48-5-311). Period cannot be extended. (234 Ga. 155, 215 S.E.2d 3). For certain property, including property of public utilities, airline flight property, railroad rolling stock and certain property of common carriers, assessments may be appealed to Superior Court of Fulton County within 30 days of receipt of notice of proposed assessment. (48-2-18). Notice of intent to dispute assessment required within 20 days. (48-2-18). Successful appeal by taxpayer is valid under most circumstances for two additional years unless board of assessors conducts new investigation and establishes new valuation. (48-5-299).

Payment.—Taxes are payable to county in which returns made, except as above shown, on or before Oct. 15 of year in which returns must be made (penalty ranging between 5% and 10% of unpaid tax due accrues thereafter), and are first lien on property, not divested by judicial sale under any process. (48-2-56, -57; 48-5-24). Executions on delinquent taxes issue on Dec. 20 (48-5-161) and bear interest at 12% (48-3-8; 48-2-40). See also topic Administration, subhead Penalties, catchline Real and Personal Property Taxes.

Counties and municipalities are authorized to collect ad valorem taxes on tangible personal property other than motor vehicles in installments, not to exceed two, provided such counties or municipalities have adopted resolution or ordinance by Dec. 31 of previous year (48-5-23); and to enter into prepayment agreements with certain developers (48-5-31).

Owner of any interest in property which has been returned or assessed with other property (or transferee who acquires title between lien date and payment date) may pay taxes assessed against any one or more pieces of property: (a) when listed separately by owner or assessor on return or digest, according to valuation; or (b) when not listed separately, by paying proportionate part of taxes represented by such property according to valuation. Such payment releases piece(s) of property from tax lien. Fee of 50¢ must be paid for receipt and release. (48-5-25).

For tax years beginning on or after Jan. 1, 1982, taxpayers 62 years or older may defer portion of ad valorem taxes on homestead under certain conditions. (48-5-72 et seq.). Deferred taxes constitute lien. (48-5-76).

Taxpayer may recover prejudgment interest in action for refund of wrongfully collected taxes from date of demand for refund. (183 Ga. App. 891, 360 S.E.2d 425). Taxpayer may be entitled to action for refund even if appeal procedure under 48-5-311 is not utilized. (214 Ga. App. 248, 447 S.E.2d 679).

Lien.—Attaches at time of assessment and is superior to all other liens. (48-2-56). Revised Uniform Federal Tax Lien Registration Act enacted, with modifications. (44-14-571). When legality of assessment is being litigated, Commissioner may release all or part of property subject to state tax lien if owner gives security and Attorney General approves. (48-2-58).

Tax commissioner or tax collector may commence in rem tax foreclosure to enforce lien for ad valorem taxes. (48-4-76). Prior to such foreclosure tax commissioner or collector must: file petition with superior court of county in which property is located (48-4-78); mail copies of petition by certified mail to all interested parties and occupants of property (48-4-78); advertise notice of filing of petition on two separate dates within 30 days of filing of petition (48-4-78); request that judicial hearing be held no earlier than 30 days following filing of petition (48-4-79).

Sale.—Sales of property for taxes are made by sheriff, or by tax collector or commissioner (48-5-137), and regulated by same rules governing judicial sales (48-4-1). Taxpayer must be provided with ten days written notice of sale (48-4-1), and sale must be advertised once a week for four weeks prior to sale (9-13-140, 141).

Redemption.—Real estate sold under tax execution may be redeemed by any person having interest therein within 12 months after sale, or at any time thereafter until right to redeem is foreclosed by giving defendant in tax execution notice of purchaser's intention to foreclose, by paying purchaser amount paid by him or her with 10% premium. (48-4-40, 42). Cost of redemption includes taxes paid by purchaser. (48-4-42). In cases where county, municipality, or other political subdivision purchases property at tax sale, amount required to be paid for redemption of property shall be amount paid with 20% premium. (48-4-42).

Real estate to be sold as result of in rem foreclosure may be redeemed by payment of redemption amount (48-4-77), at any point prior to moment of sale, by any interested party (48-4-80). After moment of sale, property owner has exclusive right of redemption which exists for period of 60 days from date of sale. (48-4-81).

REAL ESTATE CONVEYANCE TAX:

Tax Imposed.—Tax on deeds by which realty is transferred (48-6-1) does not apply to: (1) instruments given to secure debt; (2) deeds of gift; (3) deed to first transferee on foreclosure; certain deeds issued in lieu of foreclosure; (4) deed effecting division of real property among joint tenants or tenants in common if transaction involves no consideration other than division; (5) transfers by nonprofit public corporations; (6) transfer between husband and wife in connection with divorce; (7) leases; or (8) order for year's support under 53-5-11. (48-6-2).

Rate.—$2 for first $1,000 or part thereof, and 20¢ for each additional $100 or part thereof, exclusive of value of any lien or encumbrance. (48-6-1). On or after 1/1/2003, rate will be $1 for first $1,000 and 10¢ for each additional $100. (48-6-1). Consideration or value of conveyance must exceed $100 before tax applies. (48-6-1).

SALES AND USE TAXES:

Sales Tax.—4% state-wide sales tax is levied upon purchase or sale at retail or lease or rental within state, of tangible personal property, natural or artificial gas, oil, electricity, solid fuel, transportation, local telephone services, beverages and tobacco products when made for purposes other than resale, transient lodging furnished for less than 90 days, and admission charges to places of amusement, sports or entertainment. (48-8-2, -30). Tax is 4% of sales price or gross lease or rental charge or gross charge for services. (48-8-30). State motor fuel excise tax not elements of sales price. (121 Ga. App. 454, 174 S.E.2d 224).

Sales tax is imposed on purchaser at retail, lessee, or rentee of tangible personal property or services in state and must be collected from such person by retailer, lessor, or rentor, who must remit tax to Commissioner. (48-8-30, -32). Returns covering both sales and use taxes must be made on 20th day of each month for sales and purchases made during preceding month. (48-8-49). Dealer must remit by 20th day of month 50% of "estimated tax liability" for such month where such liability exceeds $2,500. (48-8-49). Credit on dealer's return allowed for tax collected on items returned by purchaser within 90 days. (48-8-58). Dealers permitted to retain 3% of tax due as compensation for collecting tax. (48-8-50).

Amounts charged for labor or service rendered in installing, applying or remodeling or repairing property sold, when billed separately to consumer, are not part of selling price of property for purpose of computing applicable tax. (Dept. of Revenue Reg. §560-12-2-.88).

Refunds available on purchase of solar energy equipment. (48-8-3).

Local Taxes.—Additional sales and use tax of 1% imposed by Rapid Transit Tax Act on taxable transactions occurring within MARTA area. Additional local option sales and use tax up to 2% on taxable sales and uses of property within certain joint county and municipal special districts which have adopted local option tax. (48-8-80 et seq.). Counties by referendum may otherwise impose special 1% sales and use tax for limited time period for certain purposes including to fund local homestead exemptions. (48-8-100 et seq.).

Successor Liability.—Dealer liable for sales or use tax must make final return and payment within 15 days after date of selling business or stock of goods or equipment, or quitting business. Purchaser of business is required to withhold from purchase price sufficient funds to cover any tax, interest and penalties that may be due, until former owner produces receipt from Commissioner showing that all taxes have been paid. Otherwise purchaser will be personally liable for payment of any unpaid taxes, notwithstanding compliance with Art. 6 of Uniform Commercial Code. Personal liability will not exceed purchase price, but property is subject to full amount of tax lien. (48-8-46; 233 Ga. 739, 213 S.E.2d 638). "Dealer" doesn't include any nonresident or nondomiciliary who doesn't engage in any business activity in Georgia, for printing services in Georgia simply because person distributes printed material from Georgia premises or has certain other contacts related to printing services in Georgia.

See note at head of Digest as to 1998 legislation covered.

See Topical Index in front part of this volume.

GA – 63

SALES AND USE TAXES . . . *continued*

Sales tax not applicable to certain casual and isolated sales. (Dept. of Revenue Reg. §560-12-1-.07; 89 Ga. App. 755, 81 S.E.2d 222).

Use Tax.—4% use tax is levied upon use, consumption, distribution, or storage, within state, of tangible personal property purchased at retail, leased, or rented outside state. (48-8-2, -30). 4% use tax is also imposed upon use, consumption, distribution or storage within state, of tangible personal property purchased at retail outside of state and used outside state for more than six months prior to first use in state. (48-8-30). Exemption to tangible personal property bought outside of state and brought into state for first time by new domiciliaries of state. (48-8-3). Tax is 4% of lesser of cost price or fair market value of property purchased and 4% of gross rental charge of property leased or rented. (48-8-30). Credit is given for sales or use tax paid to another state, provided that state gives reciprocal credit. For some tangible personal property credit also given even though no reciprocity. (48-8-42). Dealer who solicits or advertises or distributes catalogs and thereby sells to Georgia purchasers must collect and remit use tax. (48-8-2[3][h], -32). "Dealer" doesn't include any nonresident or non-domiciliary who does not engage in any business activity in Georgia, for printing services in Georgia simply because person distributes printed material from Georgia premises or has certain other contacts related to printing services in Georgia.

Contractor who is furnished tangible personal property for use in connection with contract must pay use tax on such property if no sales or use tax has been paid at time of purchase. (48-8-63).

Use tax not applicable to casual or isolated sale in state. (97 Ga. App. 431, 103 S.E.2d 123).

Exemptions From Sales and Use Taxes.—Exemptions include prescription drugs, hearing aids, sale of oxygen prescribed by licensed physician, prescription eyeglasses and contact lenses, federal excise tax if billed to consumer separately from selling price or from motor fuel taxes, industrial materials becoming component parts of article of tangible personal property produced for resale, labels, containers, etc., used solely for packaging articles for sale or shipment and constituting element of retail sale, insurance premiums and professional fees from service transactions which involve sale only as inconsequential elements for which no separate charges are made, services rendered by repairmen for which separate charge is made, seed, fertilizers, insecticides, etc., for growing crops, feed for livestock, fish, or poultry, sales to U.S., State of Georgia or any county or municipality of Georgia, sales of fuel and supplies for use on ocean-going ships, transportation and related charges for conveying tangible personal property, sales or exchanges of tangible personal property resulting from certain business reorganizations in which proportionate beneficial ownership interests in property remain unchanged, sales of water by political subdivisions or water associations, sales of products used to reduce water and air pollution, sales to certain educational institutions, sales to nonprofit nursing homes, general or mental hospitals and licensed in-patient hospices if tax exempt organization, sales of insulin and insulin syringes dispensed without prescription, sales of sugar used as food for honey bees, sales of cattle, hogs, sheep, horses, poultry and bees for breeding purposes, sales of food consumed on certain private school premises, sales of tangible property to certain private schools, sales of any parent-teacher organizations qualified as tax exempt, sales of certain machinery for new plant or farm or to expand productive capacity of existing plant or farm, including poultry, egg, dairy and livestock production, sales of liquified petroleum gas or other fuel used to heat structure in which broilers, pullets or other poultry are raised, property manufactured or assembled in state for export where delivery is taken outside state and for certain transportation equipment where delivery is taken in state, major components and repair parts for military craft, vehicles, and missiles, or transportation equipment used in interstate or foreign commerce. (48-8-3). Sale or use of books recognized as being Holy Scripture exempted. (48-8-3). Sales of any religious paper owned by religious institution or denomination and certain limited charitable fundraising sales by religious institutions or denominations exempted provided no profit of sales inures to benefit of private person. (48-8-3). Sale or use of certain off-road equipment and related attachments used exclusively for purpose of growing and harvesting timber exempted. (48-8-3). Certain electricity sales, manufacturing machinery sales and sales of primary material handling equipment exempted. (48-8-3). Sales of machinery and equipment incorporated into telecommunications manufacturing facility and used for improving air quality in certain advanced technology clean rooms exempt. (48-8-3). Sales of machinery and equipment incorporated into qualified water conservation facility and used for water conservation exempt. (48-8-3). Use of certain cargo containers and related chassis used in intrastate commerce exempt. (48-8-3). Sales of tangible personal property, concessions, or tickets for admission to school athletic event exempt if proceeds are used solely for benefit of school or students. (48-8-3). Transportation charges incurred before consummation of sale are included in base price upon which tax is calculated. (133 Ga. App. 665, 211 S.E.2d 916). Sales or charges in operation of public transportation by municipalities, counties and public transit authorities exempt. (48-8-3). Sale of vehicle to certain disabled veterans exempt from sales and use taxes. (48-8-3). Sale of machinery and equipment for use to combat pollution exempt under certain conditions. (48-8-3). Sale or use of certain solar energy machines exempt. (48-8-3). Sale of motor fuels generally exempt with respect to 3% of tax. (48-8-3). See also topic Gasoline and Motor Fuel Tax. Sale of motor vehicles to nonresident purchasers for use in another state exempt. (48-8-3). Contractor is consumer and must pay tax on purchase or rental of tangible property used in performing contract. Sales to certain hospital authorities exempt. (48-8-3). Sales of objects of art, etc. to public museums exempt. (48-8-3). Rentals of motion picture film exempt. (48-8-3). Sale, use, storage or consumption of paper which is manufactured in state into catalogs intended to be delivered and used outside state exempt. (48-8-3). Sales to licensed commercial fishermen of bait for taking crabs. (48-8-3). Gross revenues generated from coin-operated amusements machines which require permit under c. 16 of Title 48 exempt. (48-8-3). Sale of certain machinery and equipment used in remanufacture of aircraft engines or aircraft engine parts exempt. (48-8-3). Sale of eligible food and beverages purchased for off-premises consumption (except with respect to certain local option taxes) exempt. (48-8-3). Sales of certain tractors and attachments for farming and harvesting farm or onion crops exempt. (48-8-3). Sales of Girl Scout Cookies exempt. (48-8-3). Sales of food and beverages for fundraising by Boy Scouts exempt. (48-8-3). Sale of blood glucose measuring strips exempt. (48-8-3). Sale of grass sod in its original state of production exempt only if sold by sod producers or related entities. (48-8-3). Sale or use of funeral merchandises, burial containers, and cemetery markers bought with funds from Georgia Crime Victims Emergency Fund exempt. (48-8-3). Printed advertising inserts or advertising supplements exempt if distributed in Georgia in or as part of any newspaper for resale. (48-8-3).

STAMP TAX:

Tobacco tax payable through use of stamps. (48-11-3).

UNEMPLOYMENT COMPENSATION TAX:

Imposed in form of "contributions" on all employers who employ at least one individual for some portion of a day in each of 20 different weeks within either current or proceeding calendar year or who in any calendar quarter in either current or preceding calendar year paid wages of $1,500 or more, with certain exceptions and additions. (34-8-33 through -51, -150). Contributions are based on wages paid. (34-8-151). For period before Apr. 1, 1987, and after June 30, 2001, rate is based on actual benefit experience of employer, maximum 2.7%. (34-8-151). Beginning Apr. 1, 1987, and ending June 30, 2001, rate is based on actual benefit experience of employer, maximum 2.64%. (34-8-151). Additional .06% tax is assessed on wages of most employees. (34-8-180). Financing of benefits for employees of governmental entities and nonprofit organizations governed by different rules. (34-8-158). Contributions are payable on or before last day of month next following end of calendar quarter to Employment Security Agency, Division of Department of Labor. If authorized by regulation, certain employers may pay contributions annually rather than quarterly. (34-8-150). No contributions are required from employees. (34-8-150). Contributions are personal debt of one required to file tax return. (34-8-167). Commissioner of Labor may collect delinquent contributions by execution and levy. (34-8-168). Commissioner empowered to direct one-time unemployment Tax Amnesty Program providing for waiver of certain civil and criminal penalties upon payment of delinquent unemployment taxes. (34-8-270 et seq.). Nonresident contractor must post bond for payment of all taxes, see topic Income Tax, subhead Income Taxed—Individuals, catchline Nonresident Taxpayers.

TRANSPORTATION

MOTOR VEHICLES:

Powers and duties with respect to enforcement of motor vehicle law are vested in State Revenue Commissioner (270 Washington Street, S. W., Atlanta, Georgia 30301) and Department of Public Safety (Post Office Box 1456, Atlanta, Georgia 30301). (40-2-1, -130). Uniform Rules of Road Act adopted. (40-6-1 et seq.). Motor Vehicle Safety Responsibility Act enacted, prescribing financial and civil responsibilities of drivers. (40-9-1 et seq.).

Vehicle Registration.—Required annually. (40-2-20). Issued by county tax collector, county tax commissioner or other agent of State Revenue Commissioner. (40-2-22, -23). Vehicle must be registered within 30 days of purchase. Violators subject to fine of not more than $100. (40-2-20). Numbered license plate must be displayed in rear. (40-2-41). Current revalidation sticker must be affixed to license plate. (40-2-8). New plates issued every fifth year; revalidation stickers issued in all other years. (40-2-31). Special license plates available for certain political figures, sheriffs, diplomats, emergency medical technicians, amateur radio operators, members of National Guard, members of active reserve components of Armed Forces, commanders of certain veterans' organizations, disabled and retired veterans, Medal of Honor winners, former P.O.W.s, spouses of deceased former P.O.W.s, firefighters, owners of historic vehicles, dealers and owners of alternative fuel vehicles. (40-2-60 et seq.). Special tags for disabled individuals. (40-2-74). Personalized license tags available upon payment of additional fee. (40-2-60). License tags commemorating certain colleges and universities available if certain conditions are met and additional fee paid. (40-2-32). License tags available for veterans awarded Purple Heart (40-2-84), veterans of Pearl Harbor (40-2-85), and veterans of WWI and WWII, Korea, Vietnam and Operation Desert Storm (40-2-85.1). No special provisions for other members of Armed Forces. License tags commemorating 1996 Olympic Games and 1996 Paralympic Games may be used until date owner required to register vehicle in 1997. (40-2-46, -48). Other commemorative tags available. (40-2-86 et seq.).

No vehicle shall be licensed unless proof of minimum insurance or approved self-insurance plan is provided. Misdemeanor to misrepresent insurance. (33-34-10).

Operator's License.—Required and issued by Department of Public Safety. Licenses must be renewed every four years. (40-5-32). Special tests are required for operating motorcycles, buses and other carriers, trucks over 26,000 lbs. and tractor-trailers. (40-5-23, -147). No person under 16 years of age may be licensed, except instruction permits are issued to those 15 years of age. Those 14 years of age with parent or guardian medically incapable of being licensed due to visual impairment may be issued instruction permit. (40-5-22). License to be suspended for any driver not in compliance with order for child support. (40-5-54.1). Drivers under 18 years of age must, as prerequisite to obtaining license, present certificate or other evidence satisfactory to highway department evidencing applicant's successful completion of alcohol and drug course. (40-5-22). This requirement shall not be applicable to driver who becomes resident and has valid license obtained while he/she was resident in another state or county. (40-5-22). Persons under age 18 cannot obtain instruction permit without proof of enrollment in postsecondary school, high school diploma, GED, certificate of high school completion, special diploma, permission of parent or legal guardian to withdraw from school or record of enrollment, not under suspension, from public or private school. (40-5-22). Licenses issued to applicants under 21 years of age shall be so designed as to be readily distinguishable from all other licenses. After having obtained 21 years of age, holder of distinctive license may obtain new license which is not distinctive. (40-5-26). Visual acuity of at least 20/60 in one eye (corrected) required. (40-5-27).

See note at head of Digest as to 1998 legislation covered.

See Topical Index in front part of this volume.

GA – 64

MOTOR VEHICLES . . . *continued*

Various exemptions from requirement of driver's license, including certain nonresident members of armed forces, federal government employees operating government vehicles, nonresidents with out of state licenses, certain agricultural workers and others. (40-5-21).

Veterans, spouses of permanently disabled veterans who are unable to drive, surviving unmarried spouses of veterans and 20 year members of National Guard and reserve forces entitled to veteran's, honorary or distinctive licenses. (40-5-36, -148.1).

Titles.—Uniform Motor-Vehicle Certificate of Title and Anti-Theft Act with legislative modifications became effective Mar. 1, 1962. (40-3-1 et seq.). Certificate of title required for all 1963 and subsequent model vehicles. Direct inquiries to: Motor Vehicle License Unit, State Office Building, Atlanta, Georgia 30303. No certificate of title issued to motor vehicle not manufactured to comply with federal safety standards. (40-3-30).

Sales.—Sale and financing of motor vehicles extensively regulated. (10-1-30, -37). Used car dealerships also regulated. (43-47-1 et seq.).

Security Interests.—In motor vehicles perfected by delivery to commissioner or county tag agent of county in which seller is located, in which sale took place, in which vehicle is delivered, or in which vehicle owner resides of existing certificate of title, if any, and application containing name and address of holder of security interest and fee. Security interest perfected at time of creation if delivery completed within 20 days thereafter; otherwise as of date of delivery to commissioner or tag agent. (40-3-50, -52, -53).

Liens.—Lienholder, to perfect lien against vehicle, on form prescribed by Revenue Commissioner, executes title application and notice of lien stating type of lien and specific vehicle against which lien is claimed and forwards notice and title application, with applicable fee, either personally or by certified mail, return receipt requested, to person with current certificate of title at address shown on certificate of title. If that person not owner, copy of notice should also be sent to owner. Lien claimant should keep mail receipt to prove compliance. (40-3-53).

After receipt of notice, ten days are given for lien satisfaction. If claimed lien contested, such to be noted on lien form and other interested parties notified. If lien not satisfied or if contested, certificate of title to be sent to commissioner so new certificate of title can be issued, reflecting lien on vehicle. Lien is perfected at time lien notice, application for title, fee, and current certificate of title received by commissioner.

If person who has current certificate of title fails to forward same to commissioner, new certificate of title can be issued and old one cancelled. (40-3-53).

Mechanic's Liens.—Mechanics have special lien for work performed on motor vehicles which is superior to all liens except for taxes and other liens and security interests of which mechanic had actual or constructive knowledge before work was done or material furnished. Lien may be asserted by retention of vehicle or by surrendering vehicle and foreclosing lien claim. Mechanic who surrenders vehicle must record his or her claim of lien. Lien may be foreclosed by filing affidavit with court of competent jurisdiction, after which clerk gives owner notice of right to hearing. Owner must seek hearing within five days of receipt of notice. If no hearing is sought, lien may be foreclosed. Proceeding to foreclose a mechanic's lien must be instituted within one year from time lien is recorded or asserted by retention. (40-3-54).

Identification Numbers.—Required on new vehicles and components. (40-4-3, -4). Sale or offer of sale, or shipment or manufacture for sale in Georgia of car, engine or transmission without required identification number is misdemeanor. (40-4-7). If identification number removed or altered, such action is misdemeanor. If done with intent to convert or defraud, is felony. (40-4-21).

Odometer.—Unlawful to alter in any fashion true and correct reading of odometer to reflect lower than actual mileage or sell or install any device which causes odometer to register less than actual mileage driven. Violation is misdemeanor. (40-8-5).

Off-road vehicles defined and regulated. (40-7-1 through 6).

Operation Prohibited.—No person (except certain persons having valid licenses issued by other governments) may drive any motor vehicle upon highway in state unless he or she has valid drivers license issued by state for type or class of vehicle being driven. (40-5-20). Driver may not possess open container of alcoholic beverage while operating motor vehicle. (40-6-253). Operation prohibited by anyone under influence of alcohol, or of any drug, or of any combination of the two, to extent that it is less safe for person to drive, whether or not he or she is legally entitled to use such drug. (40-6-391). Operation prohibited if alcohol concentration is .10 grams (or .04 grams if under 18) or more within three hours after driving from alcohol consumed before or while driving. (40-6-391). Operation prohibited if there is any amount of marijuana or controlled substance in blood or urine, unless legally entitled to use such substance and capable of driving safely. Any person charged with violation of 40-6-391 shall surrender driver's license. (40-5-67). Persons who are under influence of alcohol or drugs while operating motor vehicle or who have blood alcohol concentration of 0.10 grams or more within three hours after operating or who have any controlled substance, without prescription, in their blood or urine shall be deemed to have given consent to chemical test or test of blood, breath, urine or other bodily substances. (40-5-55). Before administering chemical test, arresting officer must read person specified implied consent notice. (40-5-67.1). If chemical test is refused, person's driver's license or right to drive is suspended for at least one year. (40-5-67.1). If implied consent notice is read to person, results of any chemical test, or refusal to submit to test, shall be admitted into evidence at trial. (40-5-67.1). If breath test is administered, two sequential breath tests must be performed. (40-6-392). No person shall operate motor vehicle while wearing headset or headphones, unless for communication purposes while operating motorcycle. (40-6-250).

Accidents.—Driver must stop, and if other vehicle driven or attended, must give name, address, automobile registration and operator's license; and if any person injured must give reasonable assistance; if vehicle unattended must locate owner and give such information or leave in a conspicuous place a notice of name and address of the driver and owner of vehicle. (40-6-270 through -272). If accident results in injury, death, or property damage of more than $500, driver must immediately report it to local police, sheriff, or state patrol. (40-6-273).

Size and Weight Limits.—Regulated by 40-8-3 and 32-6-20 through -31.

Equipment.—Regulated by 40-8-1 et seq. Each truck operated in Georgia of at least 43,000 lbs. must have name and principal domicile of registered owner or lessor clearly displayed on each side of truck or trailer. (40-8-9). New passenger automobiles sold to general public must be equipped with two sets of safety belts for front seat. (40-8-76). Front seat passengers must be restrained by approved safety belt, with exceptions. (40-8-76.1). New private passenger automobiles to be warranted to meet Federal impact absorption guidelines. (40-8-77). Parking brake requirements limited to 1966 and subsequent models. (40-8-50 through -54). Every driver transporting children four years of age or younger must provide child-passenger restraining system approved by U.S. Department of Transportation. (40-8-76). Violators punished by fine of not more than $50 for first conviction. Each subsequent violation punished by fine of not more than $100. (40-8-76). Minors over four years of age must wear seat safety belt. It is unlawful for any person under 18 to ride in uncovered bed of pickup truck on interstate highway. (40-8-79).

Lighted lamps required 1/2 hour after sunset and 1/2hour before sunrise, when it is raining in driving zone, and when visibility is not clear for 500 feet ahead. (40-8-20).

Lights.—Regulated by 40-8-20 through -34. Flashing blue lights restricted to law enforcement vehicles. (40-8-90).

Traffic Regulations.—Uniform Rules of Road Act. (40-6-1 et seq.). Provisions refer to operation of vehicles on highways, as well as private property and under certain circumstances to privately-owned residential and parking areas. (40-6-3).

Liability of Owner.—Owner of car is liable for negligent operation of vehicle being used in prosecution of his business or for his or her benefit. (51-2-2). Family car doctrine followed. (144 Ga. 275, 87 S.E. 10).

Guests.—Driver of car owes duty of ordinary care to passengers. (51-1-36; 46 Ga. App. 248, 167 S.E. 533). Persons providing volunteer transportation for senior citizens, under certain circumstances, not liable for damages for injuries to such guests as result of transporting them, unless conduct amounts to willful and wanton misconduct. (51-1-42).

Proof of Financial Responsibility.—No motor vehicle to be licensed by state until proof furnished showing minimum liability coverage as required in 33-34-1 et seq. or approved self-insurance plan in effect and coverage initially issued for minimum of six months (time period required of private passenger vehicles only). (33-34-10). 30 days after accident report filed, Department of Public Safety must determine amount of security sufficient to satisfy any judgments which may be awarded against owner or operator. Unless security deposited within 30 days and owner or operator gives proof of financial responsibility for future, owner's and operator's licenses and vehicle registration will be suspended. (40-9-32). No security required if, at time of accident, owner of vehicle had in effect automobile liability policy covering that vehicle, except operator will not be exempted if at time of accident owner had not given permission, express or implied, for vehicle to be driven. (40-9-34). Public policy concerned with providing adequate resources to compensate accident victims. Liability policy other than owner's may cover accident. Public policy and "rule of election" do not conflict if vehicle operator covered under liability policy even if he expressly elects not to be covered by owner's policy. If operator has access to only one source of coverage, he or she cannot refuse coverage so as to defeat public policy. (260 Ga. 235, 392 S.E.2d 3). Policy must provide minimum liability coverage of $15,000 per person, $30,000 per accident for personal injury or death of two or more persons and $10,000 per accident for property damage. (40-9-2). If person is applying for, or operating motor vehicle with, probationary driver's license under 40-5-58 (habitual violators), proof of liability coverage must be provided in amounts of $25,000 per person, $50,000 per accident for personal injury or death of two or more persons and $25,000 per accident for property damage. (40-9-2). Security may be furnished by surety bonds and real property bonds. (40-9-38). One year suspension of license may occur upon failure to deposit security when required. (40-9-33).

Insurance.—No owner of motor vehicle required to be registered in state or other person, other than persons having approved self-insurance plans, shall operate or authorize another to operate such vehicle unless owner has insurance on such vehicle providing minimum liability coverage of $15,000 per person, $30,000 per accident for personal injury or death of two or more persons and $10,000 per accident for property damage. (33-34-4; 40-9-2). For newly acquired motor vehicles purchased within last 20 days, proof of insurance for previous vehicle which effectively covers newly acquired motor vehicle suffices if owner has proof that new vehicle was acquired within past 20 days. (40-6-10). Owner or operator of motor vehicle will keep evidence of required minimum insurance coverage in vehicle at all times during operation of vehicle. Rental agreements are satisfactory proof. (40-6-10). Same requirement applies to motorcycles. (40-6-11). Requirements for approval as self-insurer set forth at 40-9-101.

Cancellation or nonrenewal of insurance policies extensively regulated at 33-24-45. If insured feels cancellation or nonrenewal violates Code, hearing may be requested before Commissioner, with penalties available if cancellation or nonrenewal deemed abusive. (33-24-45). If insured does not give insurer required notice within 30 days of accident, injured third party with claim against insured as a result of accident can give notice via mail to insurer. (33-34-3). Insurance Commissioner may approve assigned risk plan that all insurance companies subscribe to. (40-9-100). Reduced premiums to be offered to drivers meeting certain requirements and completing certain courses. (33-9-42). Reduced premiums offered to good students. (33-9-43).

No-fault Insurance.—No longer in effect in Georgia, as of Oct. 1, 1991. Repeal of provision precluding tort damages for amount of basic no-fault benefits received is not retroactive in effect. (210 Ga. App. 139, 435 S.E.2d 621).

Vehicle owned by nonresident registered in home state or territory and displaying license plates required by laws of home state may be operated without license or registration for 30 days or such lesser period as home state extends to Georgia vehicles, unless hauling passengers. (40-2-90 through -95). Vehicles owned by visitors may be

---

See note at head of Digest as to 1998 legislation covered.

See Topical Index in front part of this volume.

GA – 65

MOTOR VEHICLES . . . *continued*

operated for pleasure purposes only for period of 90 days without registration. (40-2-90). Reciprocal agreements with other states are authorized. (40-2-91).

Nonresident Operators.—Nonresidents, at least 16 years of age, or on active duty in Armed Forces or whose spouse or parent is on active duty in Armed Forces, and who has in his immediate possession valid license from home state or country, may operate vehicle on highways of this state. (40-5-21).

Actions Against Nonresidents.—In action growing out of accident in which nonresident (at time of accident—199 Ga. App. 602, 405 S.E.2d 579) user of motor vehicle or his or her personal representative is involved by reason of operation of vehicle by or for him or her, or under his or her control or direction, within territorial limits of state, summons or other process may be served on Secretary of State with same effect as though personally served on defendant. Plaintiff or Secretary of State must, if defendant's address be known, send him or her, by registered mail, notice of such service and copy of process, and defendant's return receipt and plaintiff's affidavit of compliance must be appended to summons and filed in court. (40-12-1, -2, -8). Court must continue action for sufficient time to afford defendant reasonable opportunity to defend. (40-12-6).

Nonresident includes nonresident aliens as well as citizens of U.S. (131 Ga. App. 41, 205 S.E.2d 83).

Action against nonresident (at time of accident) must be brought in county in which accident occurred or cause of action originated, or in county of residence of plaintiff. (40-12-3).

Direct Actions.—No provision for direct actions against insurer.

Separability of Actions.—Physical injury and property damage resulting from same motor vehicle collision give rise to separate and distinct causes of action. (51-1-32).

Motor Vehicle Carriers.—Public Service Commission has power to regulate business of motor common carriers and motor contract carriers and must prescribe rates and time schedules and make other regulations in regard to service. (46-7-2; 46-1). Certificate of convenience and necessity not issued unless applicant shows financial ability to respond for damages resulting from operation, by maintaining bond with adequate security or policy of insurance with company authorized to do business in state or acting as self-insurer where financial ability warrants. (46-7-12). Fee for up to five carriers $75; six to 15 carriers $150; and 16 or more $200; for transfer, $75. (46-7-9). Each vehicle must be registered annually. Fee $5, late registration fee, $25. (46-7-15). Solely interstate motor common carriers and motor carriers or any motor common carrier engaged in exempt commodity intrastate commerce not required to secure certificate, but must secure registration permit (filing fee, $25) and annual license fee for each vehicle, $5. (46-7-16, -36). No subdivision of state may levy any excise, license or occupation tax on equipment of or right to operate motor common carrier. (46-7-15). Private carriers not required to hold certificates of public convenience and necessity or registration permits; Commission is authorized to promulgate safety requirements. (46-

7-26). Commission is vested with police power and authority to designate, deputize and delegate to employees of Commission powers to stop, inspect and arrest. (46-7-28).

Nonresident carrier must file in office of Public Service Commission designation of an agent to receive service of process in state before a certificate of authority is issued, failing in which Secretary of State is agent for this purpose and process fee is $10. (46-7-17). Commission is authorized to enforce this provision through institution of mandamus action or proceeding for injunctive relief. (46-7-30).

Secretary of State is process agent for nonresident for all actions and proceedings arising under Road Tax Act. (48-9-42).

Registration card and identification marker must be obtained from State Revenue Commission for each vehicle to be operated in this state. Fee is $3 for each card. Temporary ten day permits may be obtained. (48-9-38).

Load and Size Limitations.—Vehicles may not exceed following limits: Maximum width, 96 inches; maximum height, 13½ feet; maximum length, 60 feet; maximum total gross weight, 80,000 lbs. or 56,000 lbs. (23,000 lbs. per axle) on rural roads unless making pickup or delivery on such roads. (32-6-22, -26). Automobile carrier may not exceed 14 feet in height or 65 feet in length. (32-6-22, -24). Vehicles transporting motor vehicles may not exceed 65 feet in length. (32-6-24). Certain loads of wood products may exceed 60 feet in length. (32-6-24). Annual permits to exceed weight, length, width, or height limits obtainable for fee. Vehicles may not exceed by more than 13% following limits: Maximum load, 16,000 lbs. axle load if high pressure tires or 18,000 lbs. if low pressure. Maximum load 34,000 lbs. per set of tandem axles for vehicles exceeding 55 ft. Driver not in violation if weight can be shifted to conform. Special single trip permit available for emergencies and loads in excess of 16 feet wide. (32-6-28). Special single trip permit as well as annual permit for transport of poles and pilings may be obtained for movements where dimensional limits exceeded and load cannot be readily separated. Exemption from weight limitations for hauling forest products, live poultry, feed or granite from point of origin to processing plant in same or adjacent county. Farming and forest management vehicles may exceed limits in local, daytime travel. (32-6-20 through -29). Vehicles transporting such loads at night must be equipped with lights visible from not less than 300 feet from front and rear of vehicle. (32-6-26). Commissioner of Transportation or official of Department of Transportation designated by him or her may issue, upon written request, permit to certain vehicles allowing deviation from load and size limitations. (32-6-28).

Reciprocal Agreements.—Governor and, to limited extent, Public Service Commission, are authorized to negotiate reciprocal agreements with other states concerning operation and licensing of motor vehicles whereby residents of each state enjoy same privileges or exemptions. (40-5-5; 46-7-90, -91).

Gasoline Tax.—See category Taxation, topic Gasoline and Motor Fuel Tax.

Motor Fuel Tax.—See category Taxation, topic Gasoline and Motor Fuel Tax.

RAILROADS:

See category Business Regulation and Commerce, topic Carriers.

UNIFORM COMMERCIAL CODE FORMS
See also categories Business Regulation and Commerce, topic Commercial Code; Mortgages, topic Chattel Mortgages.

STATE OF GEORGIA

THIS FINANCING STATEMENT IS PRESENTED TO A FILING OFFICER FOR FILING PURSUANT TO THE UNIFORM COMMERCIAL CODE, STATE OF GEORGIA.

1A. Debtor Name and Mailing Address:
☐ Individual (Last, First, Middle Name)
☐ Business (Legal Business Name)

1B. Enter Social Security/Tax ID #_____ 1C. ☐ Check if exempt under Item 6

2A. Debtor Name and Mailing Address:
☐ Individual (Last, First, Middle Name)
☐ Business (Legal Business Name)

2B. Enter Social Security/Tax ID #_____ 2C. ☐ Check if exempt under Item 6

3A. Debtor Name and Mailing Address:
☐ Individual (Last, First, Middle Name)
☐ Business (Legal Business Name)

3B. Enter Social Security/Tax ID #_____ 3C. ☐ Check if exempt under Item 6

4. Secured Party Name and Mailing Address:
☐ Individual (Last, First, Middle Name)
☐ Business (Legal Business Name)

ABOVE SPACE FOR RECORDING INFORMATION ONLY

5. Assignee Name and Mailing Address
☐ Individual (Last, First, Middle Name)
☐ Business (Legal Business Name)

6. Exceptions for Social Security/Tax ID# ____ O.C.G.A. 11-9-402(9): Financing Statement filed to perfect a security interest in collateral already subject to a security interest in another jurisdiction when it is brought into this state or when the debtor's location is changed to this state, or the debtor is not required to have such a number.

7. ☐ Check Only if BOTH: (i) Collateral is consumer goods as defined in O.C.G.A. 11-9-109 and (ii) the secured obligation is originally $5,000 or less, and give maturity date (MONTH/DAY/YEAR) or state "None" _____.

8. Check ONLY if applicable.
A. ☐ Collateral on Consignment.
B. ☐ Collateral on Lease.

9A. This financing statement covers the following types or items of collateral:

9C. Enter collateral code(s) from back of form that best describes collateral covered by this filing:

_____ _____
_____ _____
_____ _____
_____ _____
_____ _____

9B. ☐ Products of collateral are also covered.

9D. Number of additional sheets presented: _____

10. Check if applicable and include reasonable description of the real estate in Item 9A:
A. ☐ Crops growing or to be grown. B. ☐ Minerals or the like (including oil and gas) or accounts subject to O.C.G.A. 11-9-103(5). C. ☐ Fixture filing pursuant to O.C.G.A. 11-9-313.

11. Name of the Record Owner(s) or Record Lessee(s) (if debtor does not have an interest of record in the real estate):

12. County or Counties in which the affected real estate is located (Must be identified if filing covers crops, mineral or fixtures):

13. This statement is filed without the debtor's signature to perfect a security interest in collateral (check only if applicable):
A. ☐ already subject to a security interest in another jurisdiction when it was brought into this state or debtor's location changed to this state;
B. ☐ which is proceeds of the original collateral described above in which a security interest was perfected;
C. ☐ as to which the filing has lapsed;
D. ☐ acquired after a change of debtor's name, identify or corporate structure; or
E. ☐ described in a security agreement/real estate mortgage attached hereto in accordance with O.C.G.A. 11-9-402(1).

14. Signature(s) of Debtor(s)

15. Signature(s) of Secured Party(ies)

16. Return Copy To: Name and Address

STATE OF GEORGIA—FINANCING STATEMENT
UCC-1 (REVISED 1/1/1995)
FORM MUST BE TYPED.
READ INSTRUCTIONS ON BACK
BEFORE FILLING OUT FORM.

STANDARD FORM UCC-1—APPROVED 1/1/1995 BY GEORGIA SUPERIOR COURT CLERKS' COOPERATIVE AUTHORITY
FILING OFFICER COPY

See note at head of Digest as to 1998 legislation covered.

See Topical Index in front part of this volume.

HAWAII LAW DIGEST REVISER

Carlsmith Ball
1001 Bishop Street
Pacific Tower, Suite 2200
Post Office Box 656
Honolulu, Hawaii 96809-3402
Telephone: 808-523-2500
Fax: 808-523-0842
Email: execdirector@carlsmith.com
Website: www.carlsmith.com

Reviser Profile

The law firm of Carlsmith Ball was established in 1857 in Hawaii. The firm currently has 115 attorneys in ten offices located throughout Hawaii, in Guam, Saipan, Los Angeles, Washington, D.C. and Mexico City, Mexico.

We practice in the areas of Admiralty & Maritime, Banking & Finance, Corporate and Business, Civil & Commercial Litigation, Energy, Environmental, Hospitality, Real Property, Tax & Estate Planning, and Labor & Employment Law.

Our firm assists businesses in solving problems or concerns that arise in the course of business operations. The attorneys in this firm concentrate exclusively in business law and have extensive experience with commercial activities in the Pacific Region. In addition, our Washington, D.C. office provides essential representation when our clients have needs at the federal level. Our clientele includes businesses from the construction, health care, retail, real estate, transportation, maritime, media, agricultural, education, tourism, hospitality, insurance, entertainment, and finance industries, among others. Our understanding of the Pacific Region, including extensive foreign language capabilities, allows us to offer a unique combination of technical skills and practical experience to serve legal and business needs.

Our extensive experience and long-established working relationships with regulators in our jurisdictions allows us to provide cost-effective representation for our clients.

HAWAII LAW DIGEST

(The following is a list of all Categories and Topics, including cross-references, covered in this Digest.)

HAWAII LAW DIGEST

Revised for 1999 edition by

CARLSMITH BALL, of the Honolulu Bar.

(Citations, unless otherwise indicated, refer to chapters and sections of Hawaii Revised Statutes. SS indicates Special Session. For abbreviations of various court rules, see category Civil Actions and Procedure, topic Practice, subhead Rules. Parallel citations to the Pacific Reporter begin with 44 Haw. Act 111 enacted in 1979 established Intermediate Appellate Court. See category Courts and Legislature, topic Courts.)

Uniform Probate Code, Arts. I through IV of 1993 adopted with modifications. (c. 560).

Note: 1998 legislation includes session laws through Act 311.

INTRODUCTION

GOVERNMENT AND LEGAL SYSTEM:

Common Law.—The Common law of England, as ascertained by English and American decisions, is the common law of Hawaii, except as modified by U.S. Constitution or laws, the Hawaiian Constitution, Hawaii laws, judicial precedent and usage. (1-1).

The State of Hawaii is a constituent state of the United States of America. For further discussion of the U.S. federal system, see Introduction to the Federal Government of the United States at the beginning of this volume. A great many laws are promulgated by the federal government of the United States and are not reflected in the topics below. See the Introduction to this volume for references to the federal law topics covered.

Like all but one of the United States, Hawaii has a common law legal system, with roots in English common law. For information on the courts and legislature of Hawaii, see category Courts and Legislature.

HOLIDAYS:

Jan. 1, 3d Mon. in Jan., 3d Mon. in Feb., Mar. 26, Good Friday, last Mon. in May, June 11, July 4, 3d Fri. in Aug., 1st Mon. in Sept., all election days except primary election day, Nov. 11, 4th Thurs. in Nov., Dec. 25, any day so proclaimed by Governor or President. (8-1). If holiday falls on Sun., it should be observed on following Mon.; if holiday falls on Sat., it is observed on preceding Fri. (8-2). Special and primary election days are not holidays. (8-1).

Banking holidays may be proclaimed by Governor when public emergency exists. (8-3).

OFFICE HOURS AND TIME ZONE:

Hawaii is in the Hawaiian (GMT −10:00) Time Zone. Hawaii does not switch to "daylight savings time" in the summer. Rather, Hawaii maintains "standard time" all year round. Office hours are generally from 8 a.m. to 4:30 p.m.

BUSINESS ORGANIZATIONS

AGENCY:

Common law rules apply generally. See also Uniform Probate Code. (c. 560).

ASSOCIATIONS:

No general statute relating to duties and liabilities of unincorporated associations. Service of process on associations, as well as effect of judgments involving associations, discussed in 634-30.

Agricultural Associations.—Authorized under c. 421. Agricultural association has authority to perform only such acts necessary or proper to accomplish purposes set forth in its activity and which are not repugnant to law. (421-9[a]). Voluntary dissolution must be approved by at least two-thirds of voting power at duly called meeting held for purpose of dissolution. (421-21). General corporation law no longer applicable to merger and consolidation of agricultural associations. Replaced by procedures for adopting plan of merger and consolidation of agricultural associations in 1993. (421-21.6).

Condominium Associations.—See category Property, topic Real Property, subhead Condominium.

Consumer Cooperative Associations.—Authorized under c. 421C. Voluntary dissolution under 421-21 applies to consumer cooperative associations. (421C-30).

Cooperative Housing Corporations.—Authorized under c. 421I. The Hawaii Business Corporation Act (c. 415) applies except to extent that its provisions are inconsistent with c. 421I. (421I-11).

Building and Loan Associations and Savings and Loan Associations.—Savings and loan associations are regulated under Art. 7 of Code of Financial Institutions. (412:7-100 to 408).

Insurance Guaranty Association.—See category Insurance, topic Insurance Companies.

Professional Corporations.—See c. 415A. See topic Corporations.

CORPORATIONS:

Note.—Model Business Corporation Act, prepared by Committee on Corporate Laws (Section of Corporation, Banking & Business Law) of American Bar Association, adopted, with certain amendments. (c. 415). Revised Model Business Corporation Act of 1984 not adopted. (See Uniform and Model Acts section.) Hawaii law (c. 415) known as "Hawaii Business Corporations Act". Provisions apply to all existing private corporations organized under any general act of Hawaii providing for organization of corporations for purpose(s) for which corporation might be organized under c. 415. (415-147). C. 415 enacted to replace existing state statutes which regulate operation of profit corporations with amended version of Model Business Corporation Act.

Under c. 415, validity of any provision of articles of incorporation or bylaws adopted by any Hawaii corporation, prior to effective date of Act, will not be impaired or affected. Any provision of articles of incorporation or bylaws, whether or not adopted prior to July 1, 1987, shall be ineffective to extent that it attempts to vary requirements for informational content, execution, delivery, filing and effectiveness of any document required to be delivered to Director of Department of Commerce and Consumer Affairs of Hawaii under c. 415. C. 415 does not affect validity of any action taken by any corporation prior to July 1, 1987. If articles of incorporation and bylaws, adopted prior to July 1, 1987 and still effective at time of particular action or transaction, do not provide for means of effectuating that action or transaction which would be valid but for c. 415 and repeal of former c. 416, then to extent not in conflict with articles of incorporation and bylaws, c. 415 shall apply to that action or transaction. (415-162).

Applicability of certain provisions depends upon incorporation status prior to July 1, 1987.

Financial institutions are regulated by Code of Financial Institutions (c. 412) and are subject to separate standards. See category Business Regulation and Commerce, topic Banks and Banking.

Hawaii Business Corporations Act.—See c. 415.

General Supervision.—Director of Department of Commerce and Consumer Affairs of Hawaii, hereafter called "Director", 1010 Richards St., Hon., HI 96813.

Purposes.—Any corporation incorporated under c. 415 must have purpose of engaging in any lawful business, other than banking, insurance or carrying on any profession (except pursuant to cc. 412, 431, 415A), unless more limited purpose is set forth in articles of incorporation. (415-3). Purposes of nonprofit corporation discussed in 415B-4.

Name.—Similar to §8 of Model Business Corporation Act (as amended through Oct. 1981), hereafter called "MBCA". Name must contain word "corporation", "incorporated", or "limited", or abbreviation thereof. Name must not be same as, or substantially identical to: (1) Name of any domestic corporation, partnership, or limited liability company existing under laws of Hawaii, (2) any foreign corporation, partnership, or limited liability company authorized to transact business in Hawaii, (3) any registered trade name, (4) any name exclusive right to which is, at time, reserved under 415-9, or (5) any corporate name which has in effect registration under c. 415. (415-8). Exceptions are discussed in 415-8(A) and 415-8(B).

Reserved Name.—Very similar to MBCA §9, except reservation to be made by applying to Director. (415-9).

Term of corporate existence may be perpetual unless limited period of duration stated in its articles of incorporation. (415-4).

Incorporators.—One or more individual(s) may act as incorporator(s) by signing and filing, with Director, articles of incorporation. (415-53).

Articles of Incorporation, hereafter "articles", must set forth: (1) Corporation's name; (2) number of authorized shares and, if more than one class of shares, number of shares of each class; (3) mailing address of corporation's initial or principal office; (4) number, names and residence addresses of initial directors; (5) name, title and residence address of each officer. Note: If no specific street address available, then rural route post office number or post office box designation must be given. No other provision is required. See 415-54(c) for additional, optional provisions. (415-54).

Filing of Articles.—Articles must be certified and executed by: (a) Individual intending to organize corporation or incorporator, if corporation has not been organized; (b) two individuals who are officers if corporation has been organized and has more than one individual as officer, or one individual who is all of officers if corporation has only one individual as officer; (c) majority of incorporators or initial board of directors with respect to articles of dissolution delivered pursuant to 415-82 or, (d) any person or persons as court shall designate or appoint in reorganization or bankruptcy proceeding or other court proceeding. (415-55[a][1]). Articles must be delivered to Director and if Director finds articles conform to law, Director will: (1) Stamp word "Filed" and date, and (2) file articles in Director's office. Director will not file articles unless all required fees have been paid. Upon filing of articles, they will become effective as of delivery. (415-55).

Incorporation Tax or Fee.—No tax or fee other than filing fees (415-128) and miscellaneous charges (415-129).

Filing Fees.—Following fees and charges are collected by Director: (1) Fees for filing documents and issuing certificates; (2) miscellaneous charges; and (3) license fees. (415-127). Upon filing of corporate documents, following fees are to be paid to Director: (1) Articles of incorporation, $100; (2) articles of amendment, $50; (3)

See note at head of Digest as to 1998 legislation covered.

See Topical Index in front part of this volume.

CORPORATIONS ... *continued*

restated articles of incorporation, $50; (4) articles of merger or consolidation, $200; (5) articles of merger (subsidiary corporation), $100; (6) articles of dissolution, $50; (7) annual report of domestic and foreign corporations organized for profit, $25; (8) filing any other statement or report, except annual report, of domestic or foreign corporation, $50; (9) application for certificate of authority, $100; (10) application for certificate of withdrawal, $50; (11) reservation of corporate name, $20; (12) transfer of reservation of corporate name, $20; (13) good standing certificate, $25; (14) special handling fee for review of corporation documents, excluding articles of merger or consolidation, $50; (15) special handling fee for review of articles of merger or consolidation, $150; (16) special handling fee for certificates issued by Department of Commerce and Consumer Affairs of Hawaii, hereafter "DCCA", $20 per certificate; (17) special handling fee for certification of documents, $1 per page. All special handling will be credited to special fund for use by DCCA in expediting processing of documents. (415-128). Miscellaneous charges: Director will charge and collect: (1) For furnishing certified copy of any document, instrument or paper relating to corporation, 25¢ per page and $10 for certificate and affixing seal thereto; (2) at time of any service of process on Director as agent for service of process of corporation, $25, which amount may be recovered as taxable costs by party to suit or action causing such service to be made if such party prevails in suit or action. (415-129). Also, Director will charge following fees: (1) For administering any oath, $1; (2) photostat copy or typewritten copy of any document on record, 50¢ per page; (3) certificate of compliance, $5 for original certificate, and $1 each additional copy; (4) comparing any document for certification, 15¢ per page; (5) certifying any document on record, 25¢ for each certification; (6) all other acts and duties, where fees not provided for, such charges as Director may prescribe. (92-24).

Filing Requirements.—Any document must contain information required by c. 415, and must be in prescribed form if Director has prescribed mandatory form. Director's duty to file documents is ministerial and does not affect validity or invalidity of document. (415-55.5).

Correcting Filed Document.—Procedure for correcting filed document set forth. Articles of corrections are effective on effective date of document they correct, except as to persons relying on uncorrected document and adversely affected by correction. As to these persons, articles of corrections are effective when filed. (415-55.6).

License to do Business.—On filing articles, persons who signed articles are deemed body corporate; have succession and corporate existence for duration set forth, which may be perpetual; have all powers and subject to all liabilities provided by law; and subject to all general laws regarding corporations. Articles of incorporation are prima facie evidence that all conditions precedent required to be performed by incorporators have been complied with and that corporation has been incorporated under c. 415. (415-4; 415-56).

No other document evidencing right to do business required for domestic corporations by c. 415. Gross income tax license required as condition precedent to doing business if corporation has gross income on which tax imposed. (237-9). See category Taxation, topic Sales and Use Taxes, subhead General Excise Tax.

All foreign corporations must obtain license annually from Department in order to do or carry on business in state of Hawaii. Annual license fee $100 and is assessed on basis of fiscal year from July 1 to June 30. First license fee prorated according to month of qualification. (415-131).

Organization.—No statutory requirement for incorporators' meeting. See subhead Bylaws, infra. Organizational meeting of directors required as set forth under MBCA §57. (415-57).

Paid in Capital Requirements.—No provision as to minimum of capital which must be paid in on organization or before commencing business.

Amendment of Certificates or Articles.—Similar to MBCA §§58, 59. (415-58, 415-59). However, with respect to corporations incorporated on or after July 1, 1987, any amendment to articles must be adopted at meeting where vote of shareholders entitled to vote on proposed amendment taken. Proposed amendment will be adopted upon receiving affirmative vote of holders of majority of shares entitled to vote, unless any class of shares entitled to vote as class, in which event proposed amendment will be adopted upon receiving affirmative vote of majority of shareholders of each class of shares entitled to vote as class and of total shares entitled to vote. (415-59[3]),

With respect to corporations incorporated before July 1, 1987, at meeting vote of shareholders entitled to vote on proposed amendment will be taken. Proposed amendment will be adopted upon receiving affirmative vote of holders of ²/₃ of shares having voting power. Articles of incorporation may be amended by such vote to provide for lesser proportion of shares, or any class or series thereof, than provided in preceding sentence, in which case articles of incorporation shall control, provided that lesser proportion shall not be less than that required for corporations incorporated on or after July 1, 1987. (415-59[4]).

Class voting on amendments same as §60 MBCA. (415-60).

Articles of amendment to be delivered to and filed by Director pursuant to 415-55 and such articles must set forth information required under 415-55.7.

Effect of Articles of Amendment.—Same as MBCA §63 except delete first paragraph, "The amendment . . . articles of amendment." (415-63).

Increase or Decrease of Authorized Capital Stock.—See supra, subhead Amendment of Certificates or Articles.

Bylaws.—§27 of MBCA adopted. (415-27).

Stock.—§15 of MBCA adopted. (415-15). §16 of MBCA adopted, except insert word, "Director" for "Secretary of State" and delete paragraph which provides: "Such statement shall be executed in duplicate . . . (3) return the other duplicate original to the corporation or its representative." (415-16). §20 of MBCA adopted, except delete last sentence which provides: "The price or prices to be . . . than the par value thereof." (415-20).

Stock Certificates.—§23 of MBCA adopted, with additional provision providing that corporation's board of directors may resolve that some or all of any classes and series of shares shall be uncertified, unless articles provide otherwise. (415-23).

Issuance of Stock.—§17 of MBCA adopted. (415-17). See 415-18 for consideration for shares. See 415-19 for payment for shares. §24 of MBCA adopted. (415-24).

Transfer of Stock.—§30 of MBCA adopted, except that 50 day limit for closing of stock transfers books and 50 day limit for record date for determination of shareholders entitled to notice of or to vote at meeting both increased to 70 days. (415-30).

Uniform Simplification of Fiduciary Security Transfers Act.—Adopted in 1945. (c. 556) Uniform Commercial Code also adopted. See category Business Regulation and Commerce, topic Commercial Code.

Stock Transfer Tax.—None adopted.

Stockholders.—Shareholder has preemptive rights except as limited or denied in articles of incorporation. Any amendment of articles of incorporation must be made in accordance with c. 415. (415-26).

Shareholder's Right to Elect Directors.—§36 of MBCA adopted. (415-36).

Voting.—§33 of MBCA substantially adopted, except paragraph providing "[Either of the following . . . among any of a number of candidates," deleted and replaced by following: "If, not less than forty-eight hours prior to time fixed for any annual or special meeting, any shareholder or shareholders delivers to any officer of corporation, request that election of directors to be elected at meeting be by cumulative voting, then directors to be elected at meeting shall be chosen as follows: each shareholder present in person or represented by proxy at meeting shall have number of votes equal to number of shares of capital stock owned by shareholder multiplied by number of directors to be elected at meeting; each shareholder shall be entitled to cumulate votes of said shareholder and give all thereof to one nominee or to distribute votes of said shareholder in such manner as shareholder determines among any or all of nominees; and nominees receiving highest number of votes on foregoing basis, up to total number of directors to be elected at meeting, shall be successful nominees. Right to have directors elected by cumulative voting as aforesaid shall exist notwithstanding that provision therefor is not included in articles of incorporation or bylaws, and this right shall not be restricted or qualified by any provisions of articles of incorporation or bylaws; provided that this right may be restricted, qualified, or eliminated by provision of articles of incorporation or bylaws of any corporation having class of equity securities registered pursuant to Securities Exchange Act of 1934, as amended, which are either listed on national securities exchange or traded over-the-counter on National Market of National Association of Securities Dealers, Inc. Automated Quotation System. This section shall not prevent filling of vacancies in board of directors, which vacancies may be filled in such manner as may be provided in articles of incorporation or bylaws." (415-33).

Voting Agreements and Trusts.—§34 of MBCA adopted, except deposits to be made at corporation's principal, not registered, office. (415-34).

Inspection of Books and Records.—Corporations required to keep accurate and complete books and records. Corporation also must keep and maintain at its principal offices, minutes of shareholders' and directors' meetings. Such books and records must include accounts of corporation's assets, liabilities, receipts, disbursements, gains, and losses. Minutes of aforementioned meetings must reflect time and place of each meeting, whether it is special or regular, whether notice was given, and if so, how, names of those present at directors' meetings, number of shares present at each shareholders' meeting, and proceedings at each meeting. Board of directors of each corporation required to keep book for registering names of persons who are or will become shareholders, showing number of shares held by them, and time they became shareholders. Such book must be open at all reasonable times for inspection by shareholders. Person having charge of such book must provide certified transcript of anything contained in that book to any shareholder, provided shareholder pays reasonable charge. (415-52).

Stockholders' Actions.—§49 of MBCA substantially adopted. (415-49). Provides that in any action pending or instituted or maintained in right of any domestic or foreign corporation by holder(s) of record of less than 5% of outstanding shares of any class or of voting trust certificates, unless such shares or voting trust certificates have market value in excess of $25,000, corporation entitled before judgment to require plaintiff(s) to give security for expenses that may be incurred in connection with action. Market value is to be determined as of date plaintiff institutes action or becomes party to action. Amount of security required may be increased or decreased in discretion of court. (415-49).

Shareholders' Meetings.—§28 of MBCA adopted, except if no place is stated or fixed, meetings shall be held at corporation's principal (not registered) office. (415-28). §29 of MBCA adopted, except written notice must be delivered not more than 70 days before meeting date. (415-29). See subhead Transfer of Stock, supra for description of changes made to §30 of MBCA which has been adopted. (415-30). §§31, 32 of MBCA adopted. (415-31 and 415-32). See subhead Stockholders, supra for description of changes made to §33 of MBCA which has been adopted. (415-33). 415-145 authorizes action by shareholders without meeting.

Voting Trusts.—See subhead Stockholders, supra for description of changes to §34 of MBCA which has been adopted. (415-34).

Directors.—§§35-39 of MBCA substantially adopted, except that under §35 as amended, at least one member of every board of directors must be resident of Hawaii. If there is no such director who is member of board, board may not function except to elect new director who is resident of Hawaii. (415-35). §36 of MBCA adopted, except that if corporation has only one shareholder, corporation shall have at least one director; if two shareholders, at least two directors required; if three or more shareholders, at least three directors required. Number of directors to be fixed by articles of incorporation or bylaws, except number constituting initial board is required to be set by articles of incorporation. (415-36). Parallel provisions to §§37, 38 of MBCA adopted. (415-37 and 415-38). See specific rules for classification of directors. (415-37). See specific rule for vacancies in board of directors. (415-38). §39 of MBCA adopted, except that resignation of directors addressed. (415-39).

CORPORATIONS . . . *continued*

Directors' Meetings.—

Quorum.—§40 of MBCA adopted. (415-40).

Committees.—§42 of MBCA adopted. (415-42). §43 adopted. (415-43).

Meetings.—§44 substantially adopted, except Hawaii version includes reference to members of committee of directors. Written consent to allow actions without meeting must be filed with minutes of directors' meetings or committee meetings. (415-44).

Powers and Duties of Directors.—See subhead Directors, supra.

Liabilities of Directors.—Generally same as §48 of MBCA adopted with additional provision providing that nothing in c. 415 shall prohibit distribution of assets to shareholders permitted or authorized by Federal Housing Commissioner by any corporation organized for purpose of providing housing for rent pursuant to regulations of Federal Housing Commissioner, where principal assets of corporation consist of real property belonging to U.S. and leased to corporation pursuant to Tit. VIII of National Housing Act. (415-48). Director must exercise such care as ordinary prudent person in like position under similar circumstances. (415-35). §46 of MBCA not adopted. Directors present at meeting where action taken presumed to have assented to same unless written dissent filed or entered in minutes. (415-35). Corporation has power to eliminate or limit its directors' personal liability in breach of fiduciary duty actions brought by shareholders as long as it is authorized by articles of incorporation or shareholder-approved amendment to articles of incorporation. (415-48.5). Bylaws eliminating or limiting personal liabilities of directors enacted prior to July 1, 1996 still valid. (415-48.5).

Officers.—§50 of MBCA substantially adopted except no restriction on individual holding both office of president and secretary. (415-50). Every corporation which has two or more directors must have at least two persons as officers. (415-50). §51 of MBCA adopted. (415-51).

Liabilities of Officers.—See subhead Indemnification of Directors and Officers, infra.

Indemnification of Directors and Officers.—§5 of MBCA adopted with substantial changes. (415-5).

Principal Office.—No statutory provision, except that it must be provided for in articles. (415-54[a][3]). §§12, 13 of MBCA not adopted.

Resident Agent.—§§12, 13 of MBCA not adopted. No provision.

General Powers of Corporation.—§4 of MBCA adopted. (415-4). §7 of MBCA adopted except provisions dealing with proceedings by Attorney General deleted. (415-7).

Dividends.—Board of directors may authorize and corporation may make distributions, unless: (1) Articles restrict distributions; (2) distribution would render corporation unable to pay its debts in usual course of business; and (3) distribution would render corporation's total assets less than total liabilities plus, unless articles permit otherwise, maximum amount then payable in any liquidation and in respect of all outstanding shares having preferential rights in liquidation. (415-45).

Unclaimed Dividends.—See category Property, topic Absentees, subhead Escheat.

Sale or Transfer of Corporate Assets.—§78 of Model Act adopted. (415-78). §79 of MBCA not adopted, except with respect to corporations incorporated on or after July 1, 1987, at meeting of shareholders, they may authorize disposition of property and fix or authorize board to fix terms and conditions of such disposition and consideration to be received. Such authorization requires affirmative vote of majority of shares of corporation entitled to vote or affirmative vote of holders of majority of shares of each class and of total shares entitled to vote, if class voting allowed. (415-79[a][3]). With respect to corporations incorporated before July 1, 1987, at meeting of shareholders, they may authorize disposition of corporate property as described supra, however, such authorization requires affirmative vote of holders of 3/4 of shares of corporation entitled to vote or affirmative vote of holders of 3/4 of shares of each class and of total shares entitled to vote, if class voting allowed. Articles of incorporation may provide for lesser proportion of shares, as long as it is not less than majority. (415-79[a][4]). If corporation retains sufficient property and assets to continue at least one significant business line after disposition, then such disposition is not disposition of all or substantially all of corporation's property and assets. (415-79[b]).

Books and Records.—Corporation required to keep accurate and complete books and records of account. Minutes of shareholders' and board of directors' meetings are to be maintained at its principal offices. Books of account must include accounts of assets, liabilities, receipts, disbursements, gains and losses. Minutes of meetings must show time and place of each meeting, whether regular or special, if notice was given and how, names of directors and shareholders present, and proceedings. Board of directors must maintain register of all shareholders, showing number of shares owned and when they became owners of shares. Book must be available for inspection by shareholders. Certified transcript is to be provided to shareholder who pays for its preparation. (415-52).

Reports.—§125 of MBCA adopted, except wording from subsection (g) and on, has been deleted. (415-125). §126 of MBCA substantially adopted, except that annual report is to be delivered to Director (not Secretary of State) between Jan. 1 and Mar. 31 in case of domestic corporation, or between Jan. 1 and June 30 in case of foreign corporation, except that for domestic corporation, first annual report is to be filed between Jan. 1 and Mar. 31, and in case of foreign corporation, between Jan. 1 and June 30, of year next succeeding calendar year in which its certificate of incorporation was filed by Director. (415-126[a]).

Corporate Bonds or Mortgages.—§4 of MBCA adopted. (415-4). Authorized under 415-4(8).

Merger and Consolidation.—§§71, 72, 72-A of MBCA adopted. (415-71, 415-72, 415-72A). §73 of MBCA substantially adopted except under subsection (b), distinction drawn between corporations incorporated before July 1, 1987 and those incorporated on or after July 1, 1987. For corporations incorporated on or after July 1, 1985, affirmative vote of holders of majority of each class and of total shares entitled to vote required. (415-73[b]). For corporations incorporated before July 1, 1985, affirmative vote of holders of 3/4 of stock having voting power required. Articles may provide for lesser proportion, so long as it is not lower than majority. (415-73[c]). Approved merger or consolidation or share exchange may be abandoned by board, subject to others' contractual rights thereto, without further shareholder action or approval. (415-73[d]). See 415-73(e) for instances when merger plan not required to be submitted to shareholder vote. §74 of MBCA substantially adopted, except subsection (d) deleted and articles of merger or consolidation are to be delivered to Director for filing. (415-74). §75 of MBCA substantially adopted except articles of merger to be delivered to Director for filing. On and after 30th day after mailing of copy of plan of merger to shareholders of subsidiary corporation or upon waiver by holders of all outstanding shares, articles of merger shall be delivered to Director for filing. (415-75). §76 of MBCA substantially adopted, except word "exchange" deleted, and merger or consolidation becomes effective upon effective time and date of filing articles of merger or consolidation. (415-76). §77 of MBCA adopted, except any reference to "Secretary of State". Filings must be with Director. (415-77).

Control Share Acquisitions.—Governed by 415-171 and 415-172. Applies to Hawaii corporation with at least 100 shareholders. "Control share acquisition" means acquisition of shares resulting in beneficial ownership by acquiring person of new range of voting power of 10% or more. Person proposing control share acquisition must provide information required in 415-172(c). Within five days of receiving statement, special meeting of shareholders must be called to vote on proposed acquisition. (415-172[d]). Control share acquisition may be consummated only if (1) holders of majority of voting power of all shares not beneficially owned by acquiring party approve acquisition, and (2) acquisition is carried out within 180 days of shareholder approval. (415-172[e]). If control shares are acquired without shareholder approval, acquiring person is denied voting rights for one year after acquisition, and company has option to redeem stock. (415-172[b]).

Tender Offers.—Governed by c. 417E. Applies only to target companies organized under Hawaii law or with at least 20% of equity securities beneficially held by Hawaii residents. (417E-1). Tender (take-over) offer defined as offer to acquire equity security of target company where offeror would be beneficial owner of more than 10% of any class of outstanding equity securities of target company, or beneficial ownership of equity securities by offeror would increase by more than 5%. (417E-1). No person shall make tender offer or acquire equity securities unless registration statement is filed with securities commissioner. (417E-2). Filing fee: $250. (417E-7). Defines fraudulent and deceptive practices (417E-4), and imposes limitations on offerors (417E-5). Acquisitions made within two years of tender offer must be made on terms substantially equivalent to earlier offer. (417E-5).

See also 343D-3: Persons beneficially owning more than 10% of voting securities shall not purchase more than additional 5% of any such security in any 12-month period without complying with environmental disclosure requirements of c. 343D. See category Environment, topic Environmental Regulation, subhead Environmental Disclosure.

Dissolution.—§§80-105, inclusive, of MBCA substantially generally adopted except §§95 and 96 not adopted. (415-80 to 105). Significant variations include: Corporate action from which shareholder may dissent includes any amendment of articles which materially and adversely affects rights appurtenant to shares of dissenting shareholder. (415-80). Corporation which has not commenced business or has not issued any shares may be voluntarily dissolved by its incorporators or initial directors at any time. (415-82). Unlike §84 of MBCA, distinction drawn between corporation incorporated on or after July 1, 1987 and those incorporated before July 1, 1987. For corporations incorporated on or after July 1, 1987, adoption of resolution requires affirmative vote of holders of majority of shares entitled to vote, or affirmative vote of holders of majority of shares of each class and of total shares entitled to vote (if class voting allowed). For corporations incorporated before July 1, 1987, adoption of resolution requires affirmative vote of holders of 3/4 of shares entitled to vote, or affirmative vote of holders of 3/4 of shares of each class and of total shares entitled to vote (if class voting allowed). (415-84). §85 of MBCA amended to provide that statement of intent to dissolve is to be delivered to and filed by Director. (415-85). In §86 of MBCA, replace "Secretary of State" with "Director". (415-86). Same for §87 of MBCA. Additionally, corporation must publish," once in each of four successive weeks (four publications) in newspaper of general circulation published in the State, notice thereof to all creditors of the corporation. The corporation, with the approval of the director, may omit the publication of the notice if the corporation has insufficient assets to pay for the publication." (415-87). Unlike §88 of MBCA, articles of dissolution to be filed by Director, and statement of revocation of voluntary dissolution must set forth residence addresses of officers and directors. (415-88). Similar amendments to §89 of MBCA. (415-89). §90 of MBCA amended to provide that statement of revocation of voluntary dissolution proceedings is to be delivered to and filed by Director. (415-90). In §91 of MBCA, replace "Secretary of State" with "Director". (415-91). Similar amendments to §92 of MBCA. Plus, articles of dissolution must also set forth dates that notice of filing of statement of intent to dissolve was published, once in each of four successive weeks (four publications) in newspaper of general circulation published in Hawaii, or state that publication of notice had been waived by Director. (415-92). Unlike §93 of MBCA, articles of dissolution must be delivered to Director for filing. (415-93). Upon filing or upon date subsequent to filing as set forth in articles, but not more than 30 days after filing, existence of corporation ceases. (415-93). §94 of MBCA amended as follows: (1) Delete portion of subsection (a) that discusses failure to pay franchise taxes; (2) delete subsections (d) and (e); and (3) corporation may also be dissolved involuntarily when it is established that corporation has failed to complete voluntary dissolution within two years. (415-94). §95 of MBCA not adopted, instead, following provision in force: if there is cause for dissolution under 415-94, Director may declare corporation dissolved. Director must first: (1) Give notice of ground or grounds for dissolution as provided in 415-94, by mailing notice to corporation at its last known address appearing in records of director; and (2) give notice of intention to dissolve corporation by publishing notice once in each of three successive weeks (three publications) in newspaper of general circulation published in state.

See note at head of Digest as to 1998 legislation covered.

See Topical Index in front part of this volume.

HI – 3

CORPORATIONS . . . *continued*

Trustee may be appointed to settle affairs of any corporation so dissolved. Trustee of that corporation required to pay state any penalty imposed by 415-135. Director required to deliver copy of decree of dissolution to director of taxation and finance officer of each county. Corporation that is being involuntarily dissolved under 415-94 because it processed its articles through fraud may petition for administrative hearing under c. 91. Reinstatement of corporation dissolved under 415-95 may occur within 90 days after dissolution. Corporation whose articles have expired shall cease to exist by operation of law. Any party of interest may petition for liquidation of corporation pursuant to 415-98 when it appears liquidation should precede dissolution. (415-95). §96 of MBCA not adopted; replaced by provision providing for appointment of provisional director when corporation has even number of directors who are equally divided and cannot agree as to management of its affairs, so that its business can no longer be conducted advantageously, or there is danger that its property will be impaired or lost. Action for such appointment may be brought by any director or shareholder holding not less than 33$^1/_3$% of voting power. Provisional director must be impartial and be neither shareholder nor creditor nor officer, and cannot be related to any other director or any judge of court by which provisional director is appointed, by consanguinity or affinity within third degree. Provisional director has all rights and powers of director until deadlock broken or he is removed by court order or shareholder vote. Provisional director entitled to compensation set by court, unless otherwise agreed with corporation. (415-96). §97 of MBCA substantially adopted except substitute word "Director" for "Attorney General". (415-97). Under §103 of MBCA, substitute word "Director" for "Secretary of State". (415-103). Under §104 of MBCA, delete words, "the State Treasurer . . . his right thereto" and add following, "director of finance for disposition in accordance with the state Uniform Unclaimed Property Act". (415-104).

Insolvency and Receivers.—See subhead Dissolution, supra.

Close Corporations.—No special statutory provisions. However, those owner-employees of family-owned private corporations owning 50% of stock shares issued by corporation, or more, may exempt themselves from unemployment compensation payments and benefits. (383-7).

Appraisal.—See subhead Dissolution, supra for discussion of adoption of §80 of MBCA. §81 of MBCA adopted. (415-81). See 415-81 for discussion of rights of dissenting shareholder to obtain payment of fair value for shares. §80 of Model Act adopted, except reference to §81 should be deleted and 415-31 inserted. (415-80). §81 of Model Act adopted. (415-81).

Foreign Corporations.—§§106 to 124, inclusive, of MBCA substantially adopted. (415-106 to 124). Significant variations include: Any reference to "Secretary of State" should be deleted, with "Director" inserted. Unlike §108 of MBCA, no requirement that foreign corporation's name contain any particular key words (e.g. "corporation" or "incorporated"). Plus, foreign corporation's board not allowed to adopt fictitious name to avoid application of 415-108(1) as in §108 of MBCA. (415-108). Unlike §108 of MCBA, foreign corporation can submit certificate of registration of trade name. (415-108). If foreign corporation is unable to change its name to name which is available to it under laws of this state, it may deliver to Director copy of certificate of registration of trade name for foreign corporation's file and thereafter become authorized to transact business in state under that name. (415-109). Delete subsections (b), (h), (i) and (j) of §110 of MBCA which deals with required information in application for certificate of authority. (415-110). Instead of articles and amendments thereto accompanying application for certificate of authority, certificate of good standing not dated earlier than 30 days prior to filing application required. (415-111). Service of process on foreign corporation may be made in manner provided in 415-14. (415-115). §117 of MBCA substantially amended. If foreign corporation authorized to transact business in Hawaii is party to statutory merger and shall not be surviving corporation, surviving corporation must deliver, within 30 days after merger becomes effective, to Director certificate evidencing merger and application for withdrawal of merged foreign corporation. If foreign corporation is surviving corporation, only certificate evidencing merger is necessary. If surviving corporation to be governed by laws of another state, it must comply with c. 415 to transact business in Hawaii. (415-117). §118 of MBCA no longer adopted (i.e., 415-118 repealed). Subsections (f), (g) and (h) of §119 of MBCA not adopted. In their place, application for withdrawal must set forth dates that notice of intent to withdraw was published, one in each of four successive weeks (four publications) in newspaper of general circulation published in Hawaii, and that all taxes, debts, obligations, and liabilities have been discharged. Application of withdrawal must be made on forms prescribed by Director and must be filed by Director. (415-119). §120 of MBCA has been amended to provide that after filing of application of withdrawal, Director will issue certificate of withdrawal to be effective as of date of filing of application of withdrawal, and authority of corporation to transact business in Hawaii shall cease. (415-120). §121(d) of MBCA not adopted. (415-121). See 415-125 and 415-126 for discussion of annual report of domestic and foreign corporations. See 415-131 for license requirements and fees for foreign corporations.

Taxation of Corporate Property.—See category Taxation, topic Property Taxes, subhead Real and Personal Property Taxable.

Taxation of Corporate Stock.—No special tax.

Franchise Tax.—Numerous references to "Franchise Tax" contained in various sections of MBCA deleted. §§132 to 134 of MBCA have not been adopted.

Professional Corporations.—Model Professional Corporation Act with certain amendments has been adopted effective July 1, 1987. (c. 415A). Hawaii Revised Statutes (HRS) amended by adding new chapter entitled, "Hawaii Professional Corporation Act". Provisions of Hawaii Business Corporation Act, c. 415 of HRS apply to professional corporations, domestic or foreign, except to extent such provisions inconsistent with c. 415A. (415A-27). C. 416 repealed in its entirety. Under prior law, professional corporations governed by and subject to c. 416 of HRS, except where such provisions were in conflict with or inconsistent with provisions found specifically in part VIII of c. 416. Significant variations from Model Professional Corporation Supplement (1984), hereafter "MPCS", include: (1) Any reference to "Secretary of State" to be changed to refer to Director of Department of Commerce and Consumer Affairs, hereafter called, "Director"; (2) all references to Business Corporation Act should be read to refer to Hawaii Business Corporation Act, c. 415, effective July 1, 1987; (3) in §20 of MPCS, delete subsections (a)(2) and (a)(3). (415A-9); (4) add provision to §22 of MPCS to effect that nothing (contained herein) prohibits transfer of shares of professional corporation by operation of law or court decree. Plus, add conditions under which shareholder may transfer shares to revocable living or inter vivos trust. (415A-9); (5) unlike §10(b) of MPCS, offer to personal representative must be accompanied by balance sheet of not more than 12 months prior to making of offer; (6) in §11 of MPCS, alternative (d) adopted. Also, minimum amount of professional responsibility security for professional corporation may be established for each profession by appropriate licensing authority (415A-11); (7) §13 of MPCS adopted, except for bracketed material (415A-13); (8) §14 of MPCS adopted. Plus, at least one director must be Hawaii resident (415A-14); (9) add 415A-14.5 to 14.8; (10) 415A-18 replaced §42 of MPCS regarding involuntary dissolution and reinstatement; (11) 415A-19 to 21 which corresponds to §§50 to 52 of MPCS repealed; (12) 415A-23 which corresponds to §61 of MPCS repealed; (13) add provision to §65 of MPCS to effect that failure or refusal to answer interrogatories is class C felony; plus delete reference to fines being imposed. (415A-25); (14) 415A-26 which corresponds to §§60, 63, 64 of MPCS repealed; (15) in §28 of MPCS, add to subsection (c) that nothing in c. 415A affects validity of any professional corporation's action or validity of any provision of articles of incorporation or bylaws adopted prior to July 1, 1987 (415A-28); (16) §74 of MPCS not adopted.

Model Nonprofit Corporation Act (2d edition) with certain amendments adopted, effective July 1, 1987. (c. 415B). Following sections of Model Nonprofit Corporation Act (2d ed.) deleted in adopting "Hawaii Nonprofit Corporation Act": §§8, 9, 24A, 72, 97-100. 415B-132 which corresponds to §75 of Model Nonprofit Corporation Act (2d ed.) repealed. (c. 415B).

Conversion of Nonprofit Organization to For-Profit Corporation.—Covered by S.B. 2575 (1998).

JOINT STOCK COMPANIES:

See topic Corporations.

Professional Associations (or Corporations).—See topics Associations, subhead Professional Corporations; Corporations, subhead Professional Corporations.

LIMITED LIABILITY COMPANY:

Limited liability companies are governed by c. 428.

General Supervision.—Director of Department of Commerce and Consumer Affairs of Hawaii, hereinafter referred to as "Director", 101 Richards St., Honolulu, HI 96813.

Formation.—One or more persons may organize limited liability company consisting of one or more members by delivering articles of organization to office of director. (428-202[a]).

Purposes.—Limited liability company may be organized for any lawful purpose other than acting as trust organization, financial institution or insurance company, or engaging in practice of dentistry, medicine, naturopathy, optometry, osteopathy, pharmacy, podiatry, psychology, public accounting, veterinary medicine, or law. (428-111).

Powers.—Limited liability company has same powers as individual to carry on its business. (428-111).

Name must contain words "limited liability company" or abbreviation "L.L.C.", "LLC". (428-105). "Limited" may be abbreviated as "Ltd." and "company" may be abbreviated as "Co." (428-105). Name must not be identical or substantially similar to name of any Hawaii partnership, corporation, or limited liability company. (428-105). Person may reserve name through filing application with director. (428-106).

Articles of Organization.—Required information of articles are set out in 428-203.

Filing Articles of Organization.—Articles must be filed in medium permitted by director and delivered to office of director. (428-206).

Registered Office and Registered Agent.—Limited liability companies authorized to do business in Hawaii must designate and continuously maintain in Hawaii office and agent for service of process. (428-107). Agent must be individual resident of Hawaii, domestic corporation, or another limited liability company. (428-107).

Management.—In member-managed limited liability company each member has equal rights in management of business and most matters relating to company's business will be decided by majority of members. (428-404). In manager-managed limited liability company, manager or managers have exclusive rights to manage and conduct company's business and any matter relating to business shall be decided by majority of managers. (428-404).

Dissolution and winding up of limited liability company's business occurs when event specified in operating agreement occurs, when specified number of members consent, or disassociation of member manager, event that makes it unlawful for company to carry on business, or upon judicial decree set out in 428-801(5), or judicial determination that it is equitable to wind up company's business. (428-801).

Filing fees are specified in 428-1301.

LIMITED LIABILITY PARTNERSHIP:

See topic Partnerships.

PARTNERSHIPS:

Uniform Partnership Act has been adopted, amended in part. (425-101 to 143).

Formation.—Partnership is association of two or more people carrying on as co-owners business for profit. (425-106).

See note at head of Digest as to 1998 legislation covered.

See Topical Index in front part of this volume.

HI – 4

PARTNERSHIPS . . . *continued*

Name.—Partnerships must register and file annual statement with director. (425-1). Registration statement must contain partnership's name. (425-1). Partnership's name shall not be substantially identical to another partnership, corporation, or limited liability company registered to do business in Hawaii. (425-6).

Rights and Liabilities of Partners Amongst Themselves.—Every partner is agent of partnership, and act of every partner within apparent scope of partnership business binds partnership. (425-109). All partners are jointly and severally liable for all debts and obligations incurred by partnership. (425-115). Every partner is bound by another partner's wrongful act or breach of trust, or both. (425-114).

Dissolution is change in relation of partners caused by any partner ceasing to be associated with carrying on of business. (425-129). Causes of dissolution enumerated at 425-131. Partnership is not terminated by dissolution. (425-131). Dissolution terminates all authority of partner to act for partnership. (425-133). Dissolution does not discharge existing liability of any partner. (425-136).

Administration of Partnership Property.—Absent agreement to contrary, partners share equally in profits of partnership, even if they contribute unequally to capital or services. (80 Haw. 274, 909 P.2d 602).

Limited Partnership.—Uniform Limited Partnership Act has been adopted, amended in part. (425D-101 to 1109). Hawaii version of Act is substantially similar to Uniform Act, with following material differences: (1) 425D-203(b) provides for extension of term of expired partnership if partners take action to amend certificate to reflect extension within two years of such expiration; (2) 425D-203.5 requires every limited partnership to file annual statement, or face cancellation of partnership's registration under 425D-203.6; (3) 425D-906.5 requires every foreign limited partnership to file annual statement, or face cancellation of partnership's registration under 425D-906.6; and (4) 425D-1108 provides for personal liability, jointly and severally, of all general partners who fail to comply with provisions of Act. Conversion or merger of domestic limited partnership with domestic limited liability company allowed. (425D-1109).

Excise tax on partnerships, see category Taxation, topic Sales and Use Taxes, subhead General Excise Tax. See also category Intellectual Property, topic Trademarks and Tradenames.

Fees for Recording.—Director of Commerce and Consumer Affairs shall collect following fees: (1) Each change of partnership name, statement of dissolution, $25; (2) each annual statement, $10; and (3) each general partnership registration, $25. Special handling fees are as follows: Certification of documents, $1 per page; certificate of good standing, $25; registration statement of foreign general partnership, $25; withdrawal application, $10; certificate of good standing, $25. (425-12).

Limited Liability Partnerships.—Hawaii Limited Liability Partnership Act (425-151 to 180) effective beginning Apr. 1, 1997. LLPs must register by filing prescribed form with director of Department of Commerce and Consumer Affairs ("DCCA") (425-153) and paying fee (425-169). Partner of LLP not liable for partnership liabilities arising (through tort, contract, or otherwise) from negligence, wrongful acts, omissions, misconduct, or malpractice committed by another partner or by employee or agent of partnership, but law does not affect liability for partner's own acts or those of persons under partner's direct supervision and control. (425-175). Last words or letters of name must be "limited liability partnership", "L.L.P.", or "LLP". (425-164). All LLPs required to maintain liability insurance. (425-178).

Foreign LLPs must register with DCCA before conducting business in Hawaii. (425-155). Organization, internal affairs and liability of foreign LLPs governed by laws of respective home state. (425-162).

Out-of-State Partnerships.—Upon filing registration statement as required in 425-1, partnership formed pursuant to laws of any other jurisdiction shall be subject to same privilege and disabilities as Hawaii partnership, provided that partnership's purpose is not repugnant to Hawaii law. (425-4).

BUSINESS REGULATION AND COMMERCE

BANKS AND BANKING:

No corporation, partnership, or individual may transact banking business except by means of corporation duly authorized for such purpose. (412:5-100, 101).

Commissioner.—Supervision of all financial institutions is by Commissioner of Financial Institutions. Commissioner is appointed by Director of Commerce and Consumer Affairs, and approved by Governor. (412:2-100). Commissioner shall examine each financial institution in state at least once every two years. (412:2-200).

Classification of Financial Institutions.—Code recognizes and regulates following types of financial institutions: (1) banks, (2) savings banks, (3) savings and loan associations, (4) trust companies, (5) depository and non-depository financial services loan companies, (6) credit unions, (7) foreign and intra-Pacific financial institutions, and (8) financial institution holding companies.

Organization of banks, savings banks, savings and loan associations, trust companies, and depository financial services loan companies is regulated by Art. 3, Part II of Code. (412:3-200 to 213). Application for Commissioner's preliminary approval to organize such institutions is required. Applicants must be three or more individuals (three of whom must be Hawaii residents) or company that seeks to be financial institution holding company. (412:3-201). Financial institutions organized by holding companies subject to different requirements than individuals. (412:3-202). After receiving preliminary approval, "applicant in organization" takes all steps necessary to complete organization and file application for charter or license. (412:3-206). Articles of incorporation and bylaws must be filed within 60 days of receiving preliminary approval. (412:3-208).

Every existing bank, savings bank, savings and loan association, trust company, and depository financial services loan company, and all applicants seeking to organize such institutions prior to filing application for charter, shall have paid-in capital and surplus of not less than $5,000,000 for banks, $3,000,000 for savings banks, $2,000,000 for savings and loan associations, $1,500,000 for trust companies, and $1,000,000 for depository financial services loan companies. (412:3-209).

Commissioner must give written approval before applicant solicits subscriptions for capital stock of financial institution. (412:3-210). Proposed financial institution has one year from date of incorporation to complete organization and obtain charter or license from Commissioner. (412:3-211).

Organization of non-depository financial services loan companies regulated by Art. 3, Part III (412:3-300 to 306) of Code. Application to Commissioner required to form non-depository financial services loan company. (412:3-301). Except to extent that provisions of Code are inconsistent, all other procedures for organization of non-depository financial services loan company are same as those under general corporation law. (412:3-401). Every non-depository financial services loan company organized under Hawaii law shall at all times have paid-in capital and surplus of not less than $500,000. (412:3-306). All financial services loan companies licensed and actively engaged in business in state as of July 1, 1993, may continue to maintain minimum capital and surplus required before effective date of Code. However, new minimum amounts will be required should there be subsequent acquisition. (412:1-103).

Management and directors of financial institutions are regulated by Art. 3, Part I of Code. (412:3-100 to 115). With exception of non-depository financial services loan companies board of directors of every financial institution shall at all times consist of at least five directors, of whom at least three shall be residents of state at time of their election, and at all times while holding office. With exception of non-depository financial services loan companies, board of directors of financial institution that is wholly-owned subsidiary of holding company incorporated in another state shall consist of at least five directors, of whom at least one shall be Hawaii resident at time of election and while on board. (412:3-104). No residency requirements for directors of non-depository financial services loan companies.

Chief executive officer of every Hawaii financial institution, with exception of non-depository financial services loan companies, shall be resident of state. (412:3-106).

Management of Stock Institutions.—Management of stock financial institutions is regulated by Art. 3, Part IV (412:3-400 to 403) and, to extent that provisions are not inconsistent, general corporation law under c. 415 (412:3-401). Mutual savings and loan associations cannot issue capital stock. (412:7-401).

Banks are regulated by Art. 5 of Code. (412:5-100 to 407). General and traditional powers of banks, such as power to make loans, and extend credit, and engage in those aspects of commerce traditional to banking are set forth in Part II. (412:5 to 200-206). Investment and lending standards are described in Part III. (412:5-300 to 306). Loans to insiders have certain restrictions, mirroring Federal Deposit Insurance Act, and Federal Reserve Act. (412:5-303). Intra-Pacific banks are regulated by Part IV. (412:5-400 to 407).

Banks organized in Hawaii may transact business of insurance upon receiving written approval from Commissioner. (412:5-205.5). New bank insurance powers will be phased in between 1996 and 2003. Prior to June 1, 2000, bank cannot underwrite insurance nor directly sell insurance except through subsidiary or affiliate. From June 1, 2000, banks may begin selling insurance at 25% of their Hawaii branches. This percentage will increase by 25% per year. After May 31, 2003, banks will be allowed to sell insurance at all their Hawaii branches. (1996, Act 225, §7).

Commissioner directed to adopt rules to prevent bank engaged in insurance activities from draining assets to detriment of insurance operations, and adopt rules to obtain diverted assets from bank in case of insolvency of insurance operations. (431:13-104).

Savings banks are regulated by Art. 6 of Code. (412:6-100 to 307). Savings banks are recognized as entities that are distinguishable from commercial banks and savings and loans. (412:6-100, 101). General powers of savings bank are set forth in Part II. (412:6-200 to 204). Lending and investments are subject to requirements in Part III (412:6-300 to 307).

Savings and loan associations are regulated by Art. 7 of Code. (412:7-100 to 408). Powers exercised by savings and loans are described in Part II. (412:7-200 to 204). Powers granted by Federal law are recognized, as well as membership in federal home loan bank. (412:7-201, 202). Lending and investments are subject to requirements in Part III. (412:7-300 to 307). Mutual savings and loan associations are recognized, and are regulated by Part IV. (412:7-400 to 408). Mutual savings and loan associations cannot issue capital stock. (412:7-401).

Unclaimed Deposits.—See category Property, topic Absentees, subhead Escheat.

Collections.—Uniform Commercial Code adopted. See topic Commercial Code.

Trust companies are regulated by Art. 8 of Code. (412:8-100 to 403). One cannot engage in business of trust company unless incorporated in state and chartered under Art. 8 specifically for that purpose, or through trust division of bank pursuant to Art. 5. (412:8-102).

General powers of trust company are described in Part II. (412:8-200 to 204). In addition to its general powers trust company also has fiduciary powers (412:8-201), and agency powers (412:8-202).

Investment of trust company assets are subject to standards set forth in Part III. (412:8-300 to 302). Generally, investment standards from banks have been adopted. (412:8-301).

Investment of fiduciary assets are subject to standards set forth in Part IV. (412:8-400 to 403).

Financial services loan companies both depository and non-depository, are regulated by Art. 9. (412:9-100 to 500). Depository financial services loan company is loan company that is authorized to accept deposits under Code, and is insured by Federal Deposit Insurance Corporation (FDIC). (412:9-100). Non-depository financial services loan company is loan company that is not authorized to accept deposits. (412:9-100).

General powers of financial services loan company are set forth in Part II. (412:9-200 to 202).

See note at head of Digest as to 1998 legislation covered.

See Topical Index in front part of this volume.

HI – 5

BANKS AND BANKING . . . *continued*

Loans and extensions of credit are subject to standards in Part III. (412:9-300 to 309). Financial services loan company may charge interest on loans on precomputed basis or simple interest basis. (412:9-301). Interest rates charged for loans are subject to limitations. (412:9-302). Open-end consumer loans are allowed subject to special restrictions. (412:9-305). Penalties are set forth for charging excessive interest. (412:9-303).

General rules regulating depository financial services loan companies are set forth in Part IV. (412:9-400 to 410). Non-depository financial services loan companies are subject to restrictions. (412:9-500).

Non-depository financial services loan companies are not required to be incorporated in state. (412:9-101). Non-depository financial services loan companies not incorporated in Hawaii required to maintain books and records of Hawaii business at principal office in state. (412:3-111). Commissioner may approve certain records to be maintained outside state. Failure to provide Commissioner books and records upon request may lead to fine. (412:3-111).

Credit unions are regulated by Art. 10 of Code. (412:10-100 to 808). Defined as cooperative, nonprofit organization, chartered under Code for purpose of promoting thrift among its members, creating source of credit at fair and reasonable rate of interest, and providing opportunity for its members to use and control their own money to improve their economic and social conditions. (412:10-100). Credit union membership is subject to certain standards. (412:10-109). Any proposed change to credit union's field of membership requires prior written approval of Commissioner. (412:10-109).

Powers of credit unions are set forth in Part II. (412:10-200 to 204). Powers granted credit union by federal law are recognized. (412:10-201). Credit union may invest its funds up to 1% of its own capital in service organizations which provide services supporting routine operations of credit union. (412:10-202). Credit union may also purchase or sell eligible obligations of its members. (412:10-203).

All credit union accounts are governed by Part III. (412:10-300 to 310). Loans, including interest rates, are subject to standards in Part IV. (412:10-400 to 413). Requirements for investments and permissible investments are generally treated under Part V. (412:10-500 to 503).

Corporate credit unions are regulated by Part VIII. (412:10-800 to 808).

Foreign Banks.—Defined as person (a) organized and authorized to conduct business under laws of its jurisdiction of origin but not Hawaii law, (b) whose operations are not principally in Hawaii, (c) in business of accepting deposits or making loans or engaging in trust business. (412:1-109). Foreign financial institutions are allowed to conduct business only as allowed under Hawaii law except nothing shall restrict foreign institution's distribution of cash through automatic teller machines (ATMs), operation as mortgage broker in state, or operation as real estate collection servicing agent. (412:3-502).

Intra-pacific banks may engage in business in Hawaii and are regulated by Art. 5, Part IV (412:5-400 to 407) of Code. Intra-pacific banks allowed to engage in business in Hawaii include banks from Guam, American Samoa, Federated States of Micronesia, Republic of Palau, Commonwealth of Northern Marianas, and Republic of Marshall Islands, as long as local economy is based on U.S. dollar. (412:5-400).

Interstate Branching and Bank Mergers.—Interstate branching by both Hawaii state banks and out-of-state banks allowed. (412:12-100 to 110). Prior interstate and international banking section of Art. 5A (412:5A, Part III) repealed. With prior approval of Commissioner, Hawaii state banks may establish and operate branches in states other than Hawaii. Interstate branches of Hawaii banks in other states will be able to conduct all activities authorized by host state except to extent activities are expressly prohibited by laws of Hawaii.

Out-of-state banks may establish interstate branches through merger, provided that acquired Hawaii state bank must have been in continuous operation for at least five years on date of acquisition. Out-of-state bank that will be resulting bank following interstate merger with Hawaii state bank must file with Commissioner copy of interstate merger application submitted to responsible federal bank supervisory agency along with nonrefundable filing fee of $9,000 or greater amount to be established by Commissioner pursuant to c. 91. (412:12-104). Out-of-state banks that do not operate branches in Hawaii are prohibited from establishing and operating de novo branch in Hawaii or branch in Hawaii through acquisition of branch. (412:12-105). Commissioner may waive federal statewide concentration limits. (412:12-106). Hawaii branches of out-of-state state banks will be able to conduct any activities that are authorized for Hawaii state chartered banks under c. 412, Art. 5.

Hawaii International Banking Act.—Foreign banks will be permitted to establish branches and agencies in Hawaii under Hawaii International Banking Act. (412:13-100 to 301). Act authorizes banking activity and operations under state licenses issued by Commissioner, consistent with federal International Banking Act, Banking Holding Company Act, Federal Deposit Insurance Act, and Interstate Banking and Branching Efficiency Act. (412:13-100).

Commissioner will approve, examine, and regulate foreign banking operations in Hawaii. (412:13-100, 200). Foreign banks must procure license to establish and operate Hawaii state branch or Hawaii state agency. Application for license must be submitted to Commissioner and include same information required by Board of Governors of Federal Reserve System for application to establish branch or agency in U.S., nonrefundable application fee of $9,000 or greater amount to be established by Commissioner by rule pursuant to c. 91, identification of agent for purpose of receipt of service of process, and other information required by Commissioner. (412:13-202).

Each foreign bank licensed to establish and maintain Hawaii state branch or Hawaii state agency shall keep on deposit $500,000 or any greater amount, as determined by Commissioner, with unaffiliated Hawaii banks selected by foreign bank and approved in writing by Commissioner. (412:13-213).

Financial institution holding companies are generally regulated by Art. 11 of Code. (412:11-100 to 106). Defined as holding company which controls Hawaii financial institution or which controls another financial institution holding company. (412:1-109). Following persons do not constitute holding company: (1) registered dealer that acts as underwriter in public offering of voting securities of financial institution or financial institution holding company, (2) person who acts as proxy for sole purpose of voting at meeting of security holders of financial institution or holding company, (3) person who gains control of financial institution by devise or descent, and (4) pledgee of voting security of financial institution or holding company who does not have right to vote such security. (412:1-109).

Registration of financial institution holding company with Commissioner, and annual reporting is required. (412:11-101). Commissioner has power to make periodic examinations of financial institution holding companies. (412:11-102).

Branch banks may be opened or closed subject to certain restrictions. (412:3-503 to 509). Hawaii financial institutions may maintain branch outside of state subject to certain restrictions. (412:3-509). Branch bank is separate office for purpose of stop payment orders. (490:4-107). Opening new branch, or relocating is subject to approval of Commissioner. (412:3-503).

Acquisitions and Other Transactions.—Uniform standards for acquisitions, conversions, mergers, consolidations, assumptions, and voluntary dissolutions of financial institutions are regulated by Art. 3, Part VI. (412:3-600 to 618). All of above transactions are subject to approval of Commissioner. (412:3-601, 603). Certain transactions require coordination with Department of Commerce and Consumer Affairs under c. 415. (412:3-606 to 609).

Deposits in financial institutions are regulated by Art. 4 (412:4-100 to 112) of Code. No bank, savings bank, savings and loan association, and depository financial services loan company which is Hawaii financial institution shall accept deposits unless deposits are insured by Federal Deposit Insurance Corporation (FDIC), or if credit union, insured by National Credit Union Administration. (412:4-104). Minors may withdraw deposits in their own name. (412:4-107). Financial institution may refuse to pay any check if, in good faith, it has reason to believe that person indorsing instrument was intoxicated at time of signing it. (412:4-110).

Financial institutions required to provide written statements on check holding policies when checking account is opened or there is change in bank policy. (490:4-215).

Subject to restrictions, financial institution may open accounts in name of person as trustee or representative for one or more persons. (412:4-106).

Uniform Common Trust Fund Act not adopted. Trust companies are regulated by Art. 8 of Code. (412:8-100 to 403).

Financial Institutions—Enforcement Actions.—Commissioner of Financial Institutions is granted power to implement enforcement actions if necessary to discontinue any violation of law or any unsafe or unsound practice. (412:2-300). Enforcement actions include: (1) cease and desist orders, (412:2-302 to 305), (2) removal of any institution-affiliated party (412:2-306, 307), (3) suspension of institution-affiliated party (412:2-308), (4) suspension or revocation of financial institution's charter or license (412:2-311, 312). Commissioner shall notify financial institution to correct capital and surplus impairment when appropriate. (412:2-314).

Commissioner may also assess administrative penalties against financial institution or any institution-affiliated party. Penalties of not more than $1,000 per day assessed for material violation of (1) statute or rule that provides for penalty, (2) order issued by Commissioner, (3) condition imposed by Commissioner in connection with grant of any application or other request, and (4) any written agreement between financial institution and Commissioner. Penalties of not more than $5,000 per day assessed for financial institution that violates any of above acts, or engages in unsafe or unsound practice, or breaches any fiduciary duty to financial institution, and such violation(s) are part of pattern of misconduct, causes or will likely cause loss to institution, or result in pecuniary gain to any one individual. Financial institution or institution-affiliated party may be fined not more than $100,000 for each day of violation if institution or individual knowingly violates (1) to (4), supra, knowingly engages in any unsound practice, knowingly breaches fiduciary duty to institution, or knowingly or recklessly causes substantial loss to institution or substantial pecuniary gain by reason of violation of Code to such party or third person. Maximum administrative fine for person other than financial institution is $500,000. Maximum fine for financial institution is lesser of $1,000,000 or 1% of institution's total assets. (412:2-609). Commissioner may modify, compromise, or suspend any administrative penalty. When assessing administrative fine, Commissioner may consider financial resources and good faith of institution or individual charged, gravity of violation, history of previous violations, imposition of federal penalties, and other matters as justice may require. (412:2-610).

Insolvency.—Commissioner may appoint conservator or receiver to take control of financial institution if it is insolvent, or has failed to correct capital deficiency, not able to meet demands of its depositors, is in any unsafe or unsound condition, has or is likely to incur losses significantly affecting capital which is not likely to be replaced except by federal assistance, or has violated laws, rules or regulations or cease and desist order of Commissioner. (412:2-400). Commissioner, and with Commissioner's approval, any duly appointed conservator may, subject to limitations, reorganize Hawaii financial institution. (412:2-410). Commissioner has power to determine that financial institution is failing one. If Commissioner's determination is contested, matter is put before circuit court for closed hearing. (412:2-501). Once financial institution is deemed to be failing financial institution, Commissioner has power to solicit applications to merge with failing financial institution or with its holding company, to purchase all or part of assets, assume all or part of liabilities of failing financial institution, or purchase all of capital stock of failing financial institution. (412:2-502). Commissioner has power to waive statewide concentration limits if waiver is deemed necessary to institution. (412:2-505).

Uniform Commercial Code adopted. See topic Commercial Code.

Stop Payment Orders.—See 490:4-303, 403.

Forged or Altered Instruments.—See 490:4-207, 401, 406.

Agreements to Extend Credit.—See topic Frauds, Statute of.

Stale Checks.—Bank not obligated to customer having checking account to pay check, other than certified check, presented more than six months after date. (490:4-404).

See note at head of Digest as to 1998 legislation covered.

See Topical Index in front part of this volume.

BANKS AND BANKING ... *continued*

Escheat of Inactive Accounts.—Uniform Unclaimed Property Act. (c. 523A).

Bank Tax.—Franchise tax is imposed on all banks, building and loan associations and other financial corporations, measured by their taxable income with various changes and adjustments, at rate of 7.92%. (241-2 to 4). Special provisions apply for computation of taxes due from financial institution for initial and subsequent year of doing business and for taxes due upon merger, acquisition, consolidation, or termination of business. (241-1.5). In general, franchise tax applies in lieu of corporate income tax (c. 235) and general excise tax (c. 237); however, certain provisions of income tax laws not inconsistent with franchise tax also apply (241-6). Limited general excise tax exemption for financial institutions. (237-24.8). Capital goods excise credit is available with respect to franchise tax as well as income tax after Dec. 31, 1987. (241-4.5). Energy conservation tax credit available to banks. (241-4.6). Low-income housing tax credit is available with respect to franchise tax. (241-4.7).

BILLS AND NOTES:

Uniform Commercial Code adopted. See topic Commercial Code (Alternative B adopted in 490:4-106[b]).

Judgment notes are not recognized.

Attorneys' Fees.—Except for planned community associations, attorney fee clauses are enforceable up to 25% of judgment amount. (607-14). No limitation for planned community associations. (607-14). Maximum of 25% of unpaid principal is allowed to collection agencies. (443B-9).

Usury.—See topic Interest.

Bills of Lading.—See topic Carriers.

BILLS OF SALE:

See category Debtor and Creditor, topic Fraudulent Sales and Conveyances.

Blue Sky Law.—See topic Securities.

BROKERS:

Mortgage Brokers.—Person who for compensation makes, negotiates, or acquires or offers to make, negotiate or acquire mortgage loan is required to be licensed as mortgage broker. (454-1, 3). In general, financial institutions, trust companies and pension trusts are exempted as well as person acting for own investment without intent to resell, institutional investor purchasing for its portfolio, for subsequent resale to other institutional investors, or for placement into pools or packaging these into mortgage-backed securities, and lawyer or real estate broker rendering such services incidentally to his practice. (454-2).

Mortgage brokers regulated by Mortgage Commissioner, presently Director of Department of Commerce and Consumer Affairs. (454-1). To be licensed, individual must be at least 18 years of age, and legal entity must be licensed to do business in State. Broker must post bond of $50,000 with State unless broker does not engage in mortgage servicing or collection, in which case bond requirement is $15,000. Application is made to Commissioner on forms provided to show experience, integrity and competency. Denial of license is subject to administrative review. Annual license fee is $100 for broker and $25 for solicitor. Licensed mortgage broker must maintain principal place of business in State. (454-3).

License may be suspended for making false promises, misrepresentation, failing to deliver money in accordance with agreement or to account for property of others coming to broker or to place funds of others in trust or escrow account within reasonable time. License may be revoked by Commissioner for material misstatement in application, negligence or incompetence in performing act for which license is required, or more than one suspension. (454-4).

Commissioner has power to investigate licensees, inspect their books and records and initiate actions enjoining violations or acts in furtherance of violation of statute. (454-5). Commissioner may adopt regulations, including maximum fees, commissions and charges. (454-6, -7). Mortgage broker and mortgage solicitors (unlicensed individuals who perform any of functions of mortgage broker) must comply with all of provisions of Real Estate Settlement Procedures Act, Truth in Lending Act and Equal Credit Opportunity Act in any transaction with borrower. Written mortgage loan commitment letters issued by mortgage brokers or mortgage solicitors and accepted by borrower must be honored if borrower satisfies all of commitment conditions in timely manner. (454-3.1).

Licenses.—Following persons require real estate broker's license: Any person who for compensation sells, offers to sell, buys, offers to buy, negotiates purchase, sale or exchange of real estate or lists or solicits for prospective purchasers or who leases or offers to lease or rents or offers to rent any real estate or improvements thereon or who secures, receives, takes or accepts or sells, offers to sell any option on real estate without exercise by him of option for purpose of evading licensing statute (467-1); managing agents of condominium projects (514A-95); sales or acquisition agents for time share project (514E-2.5).

Real Estate Brokers.—Real Estate Commission has authority to grant licenses to real estate brokers and real estate salesmen and to make, amend and repeal rules and regulations which, when approved by Governor and published, have force and effect of law. Commission is also authorized to revoke or suspend any license pursuant to such rules and regulations. (467-4). Notice and hearing required prior to refusal to grant license for causes enumerated in 467-14. (467-15). Denial or refusal of license subject to appeal to Real Estate Commission within 60 days of date of denial or refusal. Appeal to circuit court may only be taken from Real Estate Commission's final order (91-13.1). Minimum education requirements in real estate principles must be met to obtain salesman's license and broker's license. (467-8). Written examination on real property law and law of agency must also be passed. (467-8). Must possess reputation for competency, honesty, truthfulness, financial integrity, and fair dealing. (467-8). Prerequisites to take written exam: over age of majority; completion of accredited real estate course; U.S. citizen or alien authorized to work in U.S. (467-

9.5). Ten hours of continuing education required during two year period prior to renewal. (437-11.5). If not satisfied, license put on inactive status until requirement is met. (467-11.5). Real estate brokers subject to discriminatory financial practices law. (515-5).

Recovery fund set up by Commission from which person who is damaged by an act, representation, transaction or conduct of licensed broker may be compensated. Action upon grounds of fraud, misrepresentation or deceit must be brought within two years from time cause of action accrued, and Commission must be notified of action in writing. Maximum recovery $25,000; maximum liability to fund of any one licensee, $50,000. (467-16 to 25). "Damages sustained" does not include punitive damages but is limited to compensatory damages. (76 Haw. 39, 868 P.2d 457).

Uniform Land Sales Practices Act enacted. (c. 484).

Uniform Commercial Code adopted. (c. 490). See topic Commercial Code. 5

BULK SALES:

See topic Commercial Code; category Debtor and Creditor, topic Fraudulent Sales and Conveyances.

CARRIERS:

Public Utilities Commission has charge of general supervision. (c. 269, 271, 271G). Commission approval required for public utilities rules which govern independent power producers and rules regarding recovery of costs and profits from nonutility generators by public utility. (269-16.2).

Uniform Commercial Code adopted. (c. 490). See topic Commercial Code.

Rates.—Rates of common carriers must be just and reasonable and must not be unjustly discriminatory. (269-16; 271-20, 271G-16).

Limiting Liability.—Any limitation of liability by common carriers transporting property between points in Hawaii is unlawful and void, except with regard to water carriers, baggage carried on passenger trains or boats, and property subject to rate schedule established by carriers expressly authorized by public utilities commission. Carriers may not require claims to be filed in less than four months, and actions in less than two years. (269-23).

Bills of Lading.—See topic Commercial Code.

Liens.—U.C.C. provision governs. (490:7-307).

Nonresident Shipping Lines.—Process may be served by personal service, certified or registered mail or if defendant cannot be found in state then by publication as provided in 634-36. (634-34).

Surcharge Assessment in Emergency Situations.—Statewide rate increase surcharge may be applied for by any affected utility, (i) that sustains damage to its facilities due to state-declared emergency, (ii) that incurs costs for restoration and repair of facilities and (iii) that as result of damage and repairs, may need rate increase of more than 15% in damaged service territory. Surcharge outside damaged service territory is limited to 15% increase. (269-16.3).

Telephone Service.—Existing telecommunications provider must show PUC cause why alternative provider should not be granted license in area state has determined has less than adequate service. (269-16.9). PUC may consider transferring subsidies to alternative provider. (269-16.91).

Each telecommunications carrier upon request must provide services or information to entities seeking to provide intrastate telecommunications. (269-34).

Interisland Air Carrier Regulation.—Statutory scheme established to regulate interisland air carriers to extent permissible under Constitution and laws of U.S. (261C-1). State agency authorized to guarantee loans for interisland carriers under certain circumstances. (1993, Act 382, §4).

COMMERCIAL CODE:

Uniform Commercial Code has been adopted in Hawaii effective Jan. 1, 1967. (c. 490). (Code reproduced infra, Uniform and Model Acts section.)

Variations not reported in other topics:

Article 1.—§1-209: 1966 Official Optional Amendment not enacted. §1-201 to 207 conforming amendments (to revised Art. 3) adopted.

Article 2.—Right of action or defense arising out of a retail installment sale which buyer has against seller may not be cut off by assignment, and seller's assignee has recourse against seller, (476-19). §2-318: 1966 Official Optional Amendment Alternative C enacted. §2-702: 1966 Official Amendment not enacted.

Article 2A.—Leases of Goods. Adopted effective Jan. 1, 1992. (490:2A-101 to 532).

Article 3.—Revised Art. 3 adopted, effective Jan. 1, 1992. (490:3-101 to 605). Action for treble damages for dishonored checks reenacted July 1, 1992. (490:3-506). Procedures for claims involving lost, destroyed or stolen cashier's checks, teller's checks, and certified checks enacted. (490:3-312).

Article 4.—Conforming amendments (to revised Art. 3) adopted, effective Jan. 1, 1992. (490:4-101 to 504).

Article 4A.—Funds Transfers. Adopted, effective Jan. 1, 1992. (490:4A-101 to 507).

Article 5.—Letters of Credit. 1995 Revisions to Art. 5 adopted, effective July 1, 1996. (1996, Act 39). Revised Art. 5 applies only to letters of credit issued on or after July 1, 1996. Letters of credit issued prior to July 1, 1996, are governed by statutes in force at time of issuance, including repealed Art. 5. (1996, Act 39, §11).

Article 6.—Repealed. (SB 3018 (1998).

Article 7.—§7-209: 1966 Official Amendment not enacted.

Article 8.—Adopts 1994 revisions proposed by National Conference of Commissioners on Uniform State Laws. (1997, Act 33, §2).

See note at head of Digest as to 1998 legislation covered.

See Topical Index in front part of this volume.

COMMERCIAL CODE . . . *continued*

Article 9.—Deviations are stated from 1966 Official Act, 1972 Official Amendments. 9-104: Conforming amendments, due to revision of Art. 5, adopted. 9-105(1): Subsection (e) adds "negotiable" preceding "certificate of deposit." Subsection (h) added, "Filing means recording." 9-106: Conforming amendments, due to revision of Art. 5, adopted. 9-203: Blank filled in subsection (4): is "article 9 of chapter 412 and chapter 476 (credit sales act)" 9-301: Twenty-day time period for secured party to record security interest in purchase money security to determine priority over rights of transferee in bulk or lien creditor that arises between attachment and filing. 9-302: Paragraph (h) is added to subsection (1) to read, "A security interest in a deposit account. Such a security interest is perfected: (i) As to a deposit account maintained with the secured party, when the security agreement is executed; (ii) As to a deposit account maintained with any organization other than the secured party, when notice thereof is given in writing to the organization with whom the deposit account is maintained." Subsection (5) is added to read "A security interest in a vehicle required to be registered under chapter 286 which is not inventory may be perfected only by registration thereunder." 9-312: Purchase money security interest in collateral other than inventory has priority over conflicting security interest in same collateral or its proceeds if purchase money security interest is perfected at time debtor receives possession of collateral or within 20 days thereafter. 9-313: Subsection (1), paragraph (b) reads: "A 'fixture filing' is the filing in accordance with the provisions of section 490:9-401(1) of a financing statement covering goods which are or are to become fixtures and which conforms to the requirements of subsection (5) of section 490:9-402." 9-401: Subsection (1) amended to read: "The proper place to file in order to perfect a security interest is with the registrar of conveyances, bureau of conveyances." Subsections (2) and (3) are omitted. 9-402: in subsection (1), "and the name of the record owner or record lessee thereof." is added to end of third sentence; in subsection (3), form modified to allow parties to enter record owner or record lessee. 9-402.5 was added: "A consignor or lessor of goods may file a financing statement using the terms 'consignor,' 'consignees,' 'lessor,' 'lessee' or the like instead of the terms specified in section 490:9-402. The provisions of this part shall apply as appropriate to such financing statement but its filing shall not of itself be a factor in determining whether or not the consignment or lease is intended as security. (section 490:1-201[37]). However, if it is determined for other reasons that the consignment or lease is so intended, a security interest of the consignor or lessor which attaches to the consigned or leased goods is perfected by such filing. 119-403: To be filled in subsection (5): $10; in subsection (3), "book and page or document number" is substituted for "file number."; subsection (4) reads: "A filing officer shall record and index each statement in the manner provided in chapter 502. For the purpose of such indexing, each of the debtor (or assignor) and the record owner or record lessee of any real estate described in the financing statement (where the collateral is crops or goods which are or are to become fixtures) shall be considered a grantor with respect to the financing statement and the secured party (or assignee) shall be considered a grantee with respect to the financing statement."; in subsection (5) "uniform" is omitted. 9-404: in subsection (1), "book and page or document number" is substituted for "file number"; subsection (2) reads: "The filing officer, on presentation of such a termination statement, must record and index it in the manner provided in chapter 502." Subsection (3) is modified as follows: "Unless otherwise provided by rules established by the department of land and natural resources, pursuant to chapter 91, the fee for filing and indexing a termination statement shall be $10." 9-405: In subsection (1), last two sentences amended to read: "On presentation to the filing officer of such financing statement the filing officer shall process the same as provided in section 490:9-403(4). Unless otherwise provided by rules established by the department of land and natural resources, pursuant to chapter 91, the fee for filing, indexing and furnishing filing data for a financing statement so indicating an assignment shall be $10." Subsection (2) reads: "A secured party may assign of record all or a part of the secured party's rights under a financing statement by the filing of a separate written statement of assignment signed by the secured party of record. Such statement shall set forth the name of the secured party of record and the debtor, the name and address of the assignee, the date of filing of the financing statement and the book and page or document number and shall contain a description of the collateral assigned. A copy of the assignment is sufficient as a separate statement if it complies with the preceding sentence. The filing officer, upon presentation of such a separate statement, shall record and index such separate statement in the manner provided in chapter 502. Unless otherwise provided by rules established by the department of land and natural resources, pursuant to chapter 91, the fee for filing, indexing and furnishing filing data about such a separate statement of assignment shall be $10." 9-406: "book and page or document number" is substituted for "file number"; and last two sentences read: "The filing officer, upon representation of such statement of release shall record and index such statement in the manner provided in chapter 502. Unless otherwise provided by rules established by the department of land and natural resources, pursuant to chapter 91, the fee for filing and noting such a statement of release shall be $10." 9-407: Optional section adopted; "as specified in section 502-25 or by rules adopted by the department of land and natural resources, pursuant to chapter 91." to be filled in in subsection (2); and in subsection (1) "book and page or document number" is substituted for "file number." Hawaii adds section 9-408, entitled "Combined real estate and fixture mortgage," as follows: "Provision for a security interest in goods which are or are to become fixtures may be included in a mortgage or other like instrument transferring an interest in the real estate concerned. If such instrument contains a designation: 'Mortgage (or other appropriate designation) and Financing Statement', complies with the requirements for a financing statement specified in section 490:9-402, with the exception of the requirement of the secured party's signature, is recorded as an instrument affecting real estate in the manner provided in chapter 502 and has the appropriate recording fee paid for it, such recording and payment of fee shall be effective filing under this part without the necessity of any separate filing or payment of any separate fee under this part."

Hawaii adds section 490:9-409, entitled "Liability of filing officers," as follows: "No officer or employee of the department of land and natural resources, including the registrar of conveyances and any deputy registrar, and no officer or employee of the land court, including the registrar of the land court and any assistant registrar, shall be subject to personal liability by reason of any error or omission in the performance of any duty under this article 9 of the Uniform Commercial Code except in case of wilful negligence."

Article 10.—Article 10 adopted, effective Jan. 1, 1967.

Article 11.—Article 11 adopted, effective July 1, 1979. 11-105(4) substitutes reference to 490:9-408 instead of 490:9-402(6).

1972 Official Amendments.—Adopted.

1973 Official Amendment.—Not adopted.

1977 Official Amendments.—Adopted.

Uniform Simplification of Fiduciary Security Transfers Act was adopted in 1965, but was superseded by adoption of Uniform Commercial Code.

Filing Fees.—See category Documents and Records, topic Records, subhead Filing Under Uniform Commercial Code.

Forms.—See end of this Digest.

See also topics: Banks and Banking, Bills and Notes, Brokers, Carriers, Contracts, Factors, Frauds, Statute of, Sales, Securities, Warehousemen; categories Business Organizations, topic Corporations; Civil Actions and Procedure, topic Limitation of Actions; Debtor and Creditor, topics Assignments, Fraudulent Sales and Conveyances, Liens, Pledges; Documents and Records, topics Records, Seals; Mortgages, topic Chattel Mortgages.

CONDITIONAL SALES:

See topic Sales.

CONSIGNMENTS:

Uniform Commercial Code adopted. See topic Commercial Code, Arts. 7 and 9.

CONSUMER PROTECTION:

Office of Consumer Protection created to coordinate consumer laws, promote consumer education, recommend new legislation, promulgate rules defining unfair or deceptive trade practices, investigate violations of consumer laws and rules, and bring civil actions against violators. (487-5).

Automobiles.—Dealers and salesmen licensed and practices regulated. (c. 437). Motor vehicle repairmen regulated. (c. 437B). Used motor vehicle sales regulated. (c. 481J).

Collection agencies must be registered (443B-3) and are prohibited from using harassing, abusive, threatening, or coercive collection techniques (443B-15, 16). Collecting without registration and furnishing of deceptive forms that could create belief in debtor that person who furnished forms is collection agency is prohibited. (c. 443B).

Credit Cards.—Regulated in 478-11.5.

Credit Sales.—Assignment shall not cut off any rights of action or defense arising out of credit sale which buyer has against seller. Any assignee shall be subject to buyer's defenses as if assignee is seller. (476-19).

Credit Service (Repair) Organizations.—Regulated in 481B-12.

Discrimination in Public Accommodations.—Regulated in c. 489.

Door-to-Door Sales.—Regulated in c. 481C. Buyer may cancel any door-to-door sale during period of three business days from date of sale; failure to inform buyer of right of cancellation, at time of sale, or failure to supply buyer with prescribed "Notice of Cancellation" form (see topic Sales), constitutes deceptive trade practice and subjects seller to fine of at least $500 and not more than $2,500. (481C-2, 481C-4). Other deceptive trade practices in door-to-door sales (defined in 481C-2) are subject to same fine. Door-to-door sales of hearing aids prohibited. (451A-14).

Enforcement.—Attorney General has jurisdiction to enforce criminal provisions and Attorney General and Director of Office have power to enforce civil provisions. Director may secure restitution to complainants.

Gasoline Dealers.—Regulated in c. 486H. Director of Department of Agriculture must promulgate rules requiring that if gasoline is sold by liter then price per U.S. gallon must also be posted. (486-52.5).

Gift Certificates.—Regulated in 481B-13. Issuer must honor gift certificate for at least two years from date of issuance. Expiration date, if any, must be printed on face of certificate.

Going Out of Business Sales.—Regulated in c. 481D.

Hawaii Made Products.—No product may be labelled "Made in Hawaii" unless 51% of its wholesale value has been added by manufacture, assembly, or fabrication within state. (486-119). No milk product shall be labeled "Island Fresh" unless 90% produced in Hawaii. If 90% produced in Hawaii, it must be so labeled. (486-120). Labeling and packaging requirements including, but not limited to, Kona coffee and Hawaii-grown macadamia nuts restricted by 486-101 to 123.

Hotels.—Regulated in c. 486K.

Health Clubs.—Regulated in c. 486N. Every health club contract may be cancelled by buyer within five business days after date buyer signs contract. (486N-6). No contract shall exceed 36 months. No contract shall contain automatic renewal provision. (486N-8). Payment of contracts in excess of one year shall be by installment. (486N-8.5).

Inter-Island Air Carriers.—Regulated in c. 261C.

Labeling and Packaging.—All labels of consumer goods must conform to Federal Fair Packaging and Labeling Act. (328-19.1). No commodity may be packaged to conceal quantity. (486-113). Nor may words that exaggerate quantity such as "giant" or "jumbo" be used. (486-111). Agricultural products must be packaged so that unexposed portion as good as exposed. (147-5).

Landlord-tenant relationship covered by Residential Landlord-Tenant Code. (c. 521). Security deposits must be returned, or itemized notice of retention furnished,

See note at head of Digest as to 1998 legislation covered.

See Topical Index in front part of this volume.

CONSUMER PROTECTION . . . *continued*
within 14 days after termination of rental agreement. Treble damages may be awarded for wrongful and willful retention of security deposit. (521-44).

Lemon Law.—Manufacturer or authorized dealer of motor vehicles must make any repairs as are necessary to conform vehicle to express warranties, notwithstanding fact that such repairs are made after expiration of term of such warranty. If vehicle cannot be made to conform to such warranties, manufacturer must replace vehicle or refund purchase price. Consumer must report defects, in writing, within term of express warranty, two years of delivery, or first 24,000 miles of operation, whichever occurs first. Law applies to "demonstrator" models but not to mopeds, motorcycles, scooters, or off-road vehicles. (481I-2, 3). Remedies for failure to correct defects or replacement of vehicle or refund of purchase price. (481I-3).

Mail order buying clubs may not send goods without first providing an order form. Goods sent other than as specifically ordered by purchaser deemed unconditional gifts. (481B-1.5).

Motor Vehicle Rental Industry.—Regulated in c. 437D. Each rental agreement shall disclose, in plain language, that collision damage waiver is optional and that lessee's personal insurance may provide sufficient coverage. (437D-5). Lessors of rented vehicles are prohibited from paying or receiving commissions for selling collision damage waivers. (437D-8.5). Rental motor vehicles must display decal informing lessee of seat belt, child passenger restraint, and drunk driving laws. (437D-13). Taxes and license and registration fees may be passed on to lessee. (1997, Act 140).

Plain language required in all written agreements entered into on or after July 1, 1981, for: (1) Consumer transactions where sales agreement is for personal, family or household purposes in amount less than $25,000 or (2) residential lease agreements for term not exceeding five years. Creditor, seller or lessor in violation is liable for actual damages sustained by suing party, plus $50 penalty. Liability limited to $10,000 in class action. Right to sue in class action suspended on any written agreement executed before July 1, 1986. (487A-1).

Exempted from plain language requirements are: (1) Wills or trusts other than land trusts created under Land Trust Act, (2) any document, not itself written agreement subject to this law, by virtue of document being referred to or incorporated within written agreement subject to this chapter, provided that document has independent purpose, (3) legal description of real property, or (4) words or phrases or form of agreement required, authorized, or approved by state or federal law, rule, regulation, governmental agency, or instrumentality. (487A-1).

Precious Metals.—Sale, manufacture, importation, or exportation of falsely marked gold or silver articles is prohibited. (482D-2).

Promotions by "endless chain" schemes prohibited. (480-3.3).

Retail Installment Sales.—Regulated by c. 476. Form and content of every credit sale contract specified in 476-3 and 476-4. Buyer has right to refinance "balloon payment" without penalty, with terms of such refinancing no less favorable to buyer than terms of original sale, if principal balance of original loan less than $10,000. (476-5). Buyer who has not received good ordered has right to cancel contract and receive immediate refund until copy of signed contract delivered to buyer (476-7), except in case of catalog mail order sale (476-11). Provision in contract by which seller may arbitrarily accelerate payments unenforceable. (476-14). Finance charges regulated by 476-28. Advertising credit sales regulated by 476-29.

Travel Agencies.—Regulated in c. 468K.

Unsolicited Goods.—Sending unsolicited goods prohibited, and goods so sent deemed unconditional gifts. (481B-1).

Usury.—See topic Interest.

Uniform Commercial Code adopted (c. 490); see topic Commercial Code.

Uniform Deceptive Trade Practices Act adopted. (c. 481A). See topic Sales.

CONTRACTS:

Married person may make contracts, oral and written, sealed and unsealed, with his or her spouse, or any other person, in same manner as if he or she were sole. (572-22). Common law applies.

See also topic Consumer Protection; categories Documents and Records, topic Seals; Family, topic Infants.

Uniform Commercial Code adopted. (c. 490). See topic Commercial Code.

FACTORS:

Goods or effects of a defendant in the hands of agent or factor may be attached by garnishment proceedings. No other statutory provision.

License Requirements.—Goods or effects if defendant in hands of agent or factor may be attached by garnishment proceedings. No other statutory provisions.

Uniform Commercial Code adopted. (c. 490). See topic Commercial Code.

FRANCHISES:

Seller of franchise must present prospective franchisee with offering circular at least seven days prior to sale of franchise as well as comply with other notice and related provisions. (482E-3). See also generally Franchise Investment Law. (c. 482E).

$250 fee for filing or amending offering circular. (482E-11). Circular must be renewed annually. (482E-3[d]). Fee for renewal: $250. (482E-11).

FRAUDS, STATUTE OF:

No action shall be brought: (1) To charge personal representative upon special promise to answer damages out of his own estate; (2) to charge any person upon any special promise to answer for debt, default or misdoings of another; (3) to charge any person upon any agreement made in consideration of marriage; (4) upon any contract for sale of lands or any interest therein; (5) upon any agreement not to be performed within one year; (6) to charge any person on any agreement authorizing or employing agent to purchase or sell real estate for compensation or commission; (7) to charge estate of deceased person upon agreement which by its terms is not to be performed during lifetime of promisor, or, in case of agreements made prior to July 1, 1977, agreement to devise or bequeath any property, or to make provision for person by will; (8) to charge financial institution upon agreement to lend money or extend credit of more than $50,000, unless promise, contract or agreement, or some memorandum thereof shall be in writing, and signed by person to be charged, or by some person thereunto by him in writing lawfully authorized. (656-1). Consideration need not be in writing, but may be proved by any other legal evidence. (656-2). No action may be brought for representations as to another's credit or character unless such representations are in writing and signed by party to be charged or by someone authorized to sign. (656-3).

Contracts of Sale.—Notwithstanding statute, contract for sale of land executed by agent of owner in his own name as vendor and by vendee in person may be enforced by specific performance by owner against vendee. (34 Haw. 651).

Part performance of an oral contract to convey real property has been held enforceable notwithstanding statute of frauds. (4 Haw. 593). Where plaintiff's reliance was such that injustice could only be avoided by enforcement of oral contract, contract enforceable notwithstanding statute of frauds. (66 Haw. 451, 666 P.2d 582). Oral contract to make will and its part performance must be established by clear and convincing evidence to take contract out of ambit of statute of frauds. (58 Haw. 4, 563 P.2d 391).

Uniform Commercial Code adopted. See topic Commercial Code.

INTEREST:

If no express written contract fixing different rate of interest, legal rate is 10% per year for following non-state obligations: (a) Money due on bonds, bills, promissory notes, or other instruments in writing, or money lent, after it becomes due; (b) money due on settlement of accounts, from day on which balance is ascertained; (c) money received to use of another, from date of demand made; and (d) money upon open account after 60 days from date of last item or transaction. (478-2). For state obligations, interest is allowed at prime rate each quarter up to 10% per year. (478-2).

Judgments.—Interest at 10% a year allowed on any judgment in civil suit. (478-3).

Credit Unions.—State chartered credit unions may charge on loans interest rate not exceeding 18% per year on unpaid balance of loan. State commissioner of financial institutions may raise interest rate ceiling to exceed 18% per year for periods restricted to 18 months, when determined necessary for safety and soundness of credit unions. (412:10-403).

Financial services loan companies may collect advance on loans at maximum rate of advance interest of 14% a year for first 18 months, plus 10$^{1}/_{2}$% for next 12 months, plus 7% a year for next 12 months, and 4% a year for next six months. (412:9-302[b][1]).

Maximum term of precomputed loan where preceding rates are charged will be 48 months. If term of precomputed loan exceeds 48 months, financial services loan company may charge, contract for, and receive "finance charge" in any form or forms at "annual percentage rate" not to exceed 24% a year, together with any other charges that are excluded or excludable from determination of finance charge under Truth in Lending Act. (412:9-302[b][1]).

As alternative to advance interest, financial services loan company may receive simple interest computed at rate not exceeding 24% a year on principal balance remaining unpaid under contract whether interest rate under contract is fixed or variable rate. (412:9-302[b][2]). Upon maturity of loan, rate of interest on unpaid principal balance of loan shall be 24% a year, unless lesser rate is specified in contract as after-maturity interest rate. (412:9-302[c]).

If greater rate of interest than permitted by c. 412 is contracted for, contract not void. If interest has been paid, judgment on such contract will be for principal less interest paid. (412:9-303).

Late charges on consumer loans cannot exceed 5% of delinquent installment. Late charges cannot be assessed on consumer loan after acceleration of maturity of contract or be collected more than once for same delinquent installment. (412:9-304[1]).

Insurance companies may not charge interest in excess of 8% per annum on life insurance policy loans. (431:10D-102).

Usury.—Rate of 1% per month or 12% per annum permitted with respect to any "consumer credit" transaction (credit extended to natural person primarily for personal, family, or household purpose, in which principal amount does not exceed $250,000 or is secured by borrower's principal residence) except credit card agreement, and any "home business loan" (credit transaction in which principal amount does not exceed $250,000, which is not consumer credit transaction, and which is secured by mortgagor's principal dwelling), unless creditor is financial institution regulated under c. 412 (other than trust company or credit union), in which case rate of 2% per month or 24% per annum permitted. Rate of 1$^{1}/_{2}$% per month or 18% per annum permitted with respect to credit card agreement. (478-4). Compound interest prohibited on consumer credit transactions and on credit card agreements. (478-7). Usury laws applicable only to consumer credit transactions, home business loans, and credit card agreements. (478-5). Mortgages secured by FHA, VA, Small Business Act, or Small Business Investment Act are exempt. (478-8[a]). Also exempt are indebtedness secured by first mortgage lien on real property, consumer credit agreements of sale made after May 30, 1980, indebtedness secured by purchase-money junior mortgage lien on real property incurred after June 18, 1982, any transaction for sale of goods or services by seller in business of selling such goods or services, if transaction is subject to c. 476 or maximum interest rate does not exceed 18% per year, and loans made by employee benefit plan. (478-8[b], [c]).

Upon extension at maturity or renegotiation of any consumer credit agreement of sale made after July 1, 1985, maximum rate of interest charged thereafter shall not be more than greater rate of interest payable under agreement of sale immediately prior to such maturity or renegotiation or four percentage points above highest weekly average yield on U.S. Treasury Securities adjusted to constant maturity of three years. (478-8).

See note at head of Digest as to 1998 legislation covered.

See Topical Index in front part of this volume.

HI – 9

INTEREST . . . *continued*

Penalty for violation of usury laws: creditor shall recover principal only; debtor shall recover costs; creditor fined not more than $250, or imprisoned not more than one year, or both. (478-5, 6).

12 U.S.C. §§3501(a)(1), 3521-24 (1982) (Title V, Part A, §501[a][1] and Part B of Depository Institutions Deregulation and Monetary Control Act of 1980) declared inapplicable in Hawaii. (478-9).

LICENSES, BUSINESS AND PROFESSIONAL:

About 50 occupations are licensed, with varying fees. (c. 436B). Any person engaging in business regulated under Professional and Vocational Licensing Act (c. 436B) without necessary license may receive citation and be subject to civil and criminal sanctions (436B-27).

Travel industry is heavily regulated. (c. 468L).

Even after granting license, state may exercise police powers and place additional regulations on license holder. (82 Haw. 329, 922 P.2d 942).

Liquor Licenses.—Granting, renewal or transfer of liquor licenses is prohibited unless applicant or both parties to transfer certify that they owe no delinquent taxes, penalties or interest. (281-45).

Counties may restrict or deny liquor licenses to establishments Within 500 feet of school or playground. (281-39.5).

Licenses and restrictions for brewpubs and tour and cruise vessels. (281-31).

Transfer of licenses. (281-41).

Public hearing notices for liquor license applications must be sent to at least two-thirds of residential units located within 500 feet of prospective licensee. (281-57).

Motor Vehicle Licenses.—See category Transportation, topic Motor Vehicles.

Collection Agencies.—Governed by c. 443B. C. 443A repealed. Each collection agency must file and maintain with Director of Department of Commerce and Consumer Affairs ("Director") $25,000 bond for first office and $15,000 for each additional office. Bond must be conditioned that collection agency must faithfully account and pay within 30 days after calendar month net proceeds due on all collections made during calendar month. Bond must also be conditioned that collection agency will comply with c. 443B and any other applicable laws. (443B-5).

MONOPOLIES, RESTRAINT OF TRADE AND COMPETITION:

Federal statutes substantially incorporated into Hawaii law: Sherman Act §1 (480-4[a]), §2 (480-9); Clayton Act §3 (480-5), §7 (480-7), §§8, 10 (480-8); FTC Act §5(a)(1) (480-2). Construction of statutes according to judicial interpretation of similar federal statutes. (480-3). Statutes construed liberally. (80 Haw. 54; 905 P.2d 29). Protection provided by antitrust statutes is intended for individual consumers rather than businesses. (480-2). Contracts in restraint of trade, price fixing of commodities, and monopolies are prohibited. (480-4). Exclusive dealing, tying agreements, mergers, acquisitions, and holdings of stock of other corporations illegal if they may substantially lessen competition or tend to create monopoly. (480-5, 7). No person may refuse to deal with another to induce acts prohibited by c. 480. (480-6). No person may be director of two or more competing corporations if elimination of competition by agreement between them would violate c. 480. (480-8[a]). No person may be director of two or more corporations if any has net worth of more than $100,000 or if all have total net worth of more than $300,000, where effect of merger might substantially lessen competition or tend to create monopoly. (480-8[b]). Labor organizations are exempt from c. 480 under 480-10. Certain cooperative organizations, insurance transactions and approved mergers of federally regulated companies are also exempt from c. 480 under 480-11. Antitrust exemptions for newspapers repealed. (1986, Act 51).

Remedies.—State and private party may sue for injunctive relief (480-15, 480-13), or for treble damages (480-14, 480-13). Awards in private actions are trebled by law, and include reasonable attorneys' fees. (480-13). Attorney general has broad investigative powers. (480-18). Certain violations are felonies; fine up to $100,000 and up to three years in prison or both for individuals; fine up to $1,000,000 for firms. (480-16). Violations of cease and desist orders punishable by maximum fine of $10,000. (480-15.1).

Unfair Trade Practices.—FTC Act §5(a)(1) enacted as 480-2 (violation can bring private suits for treble damages). Practice is "unfair" when it is immoral, unethical, oppressive, unscrupulous, or substantially injurious to consumers. (84 Haw. 162, 931 P.2d 604). Unlawful for any person, with intent to destroy competition of any regular dealer in commodity, to discriminate between different sections or communities, by selling such commodity at lower rate in one section or community than in another. Schemes of special rebates, collateral contracts or devices whereby discrimination is effected are forbidden. (481-1). Sales at less than cost are forbidden, except: (1) Closing out sales; (2) sales of damaged goods after public notice; (3) sales by officer of court; (4) sales in endeavor in good faith to meet legal prices of competitor in same trade area; (5) sales by government agency, post exchange or ships' service store. (481-3, 6). Injunctive relief may be obtained and treble damages may be recovered. (481-10). Civil penalties under 480-2 up to $10,000 per violation. Each day counted as separate violation and penalties hereunder cumulative to all other remedies or penalties. (480-3.1).

Contracts in violation of c. 480 and 481-1 to 481-7 are void. (480-12; 481-9).

Revised Uniform Deceptive Trade Practices Act adopted. (c. 481A). See Part III of this volume; see also topic Consumer Protection.

Resale Price Agreements.—See category Intellectual Property, topic Trademarks and Tradenames.

NEGOTIABLE INSTRUMENTS:

See topic Bills and Notes.

RESTRAINT OF TRADE:

See topic Monopolies, Restraint of Trade and Competition.

SALES:

Uniform Vendor and Purchaser Risk Act has been adopted. (c. 508).

Uniform Commercial Code adopted. (c. 490). See topic Commercial Code.

Conditional Sales.—Uniform Act was repealed and new provisions entitled Retail Installment Sales Act were adopted, effective Jan. 1, 1962, name later changed to Credit Sales Act in 1984. (c. 476). Applies to any agreement for payment of purchase price of goods other than primarily for business, commercial or agricultural purpose, in four or more installments, not including down payment. (476-1). Every such contract must be in writing with certain information, signed by parties, and copy must be immediately delivered to buyer. (476-3, 7). Credit seller in credit sale contract which provides for extension of closed credit primarily for personal, family, or household purposes is required to disclose following: amount financed, which is principal less any prepaid finance charge; written itemization of amount financed or statement on buyer's right to receive such written itemization together with space for buyer to indicate if such is desired; finance charge; total payments; and total sale price. (476-4). Prior to delivery of such copy or delivery of goods, buyer may cancel contract. (476-7). Contract is unenforceable if incomplete in any necessary respect when signed. When contract is completed after signing, it is enforceable. (476-10). If sale is "door-to-door" buyer must be supplied with prescribed "Notice of Cancellation" form which buyer may use to cancel sale within three business days of date contract was signed. (481C-2). Failure to furnish completed form to buyer in door-to-door sale constitutes deceptive trade practice (481C-2) and subjects seller to fine of at least $500 and not more than $2,500. (481C-4). Other deceptive trade practices in door-to-door sales (defined 481C-2) are subject to same fine. Insurance charges and attorney's or collector's charges are regulated. Delinquency and collection charge may not exceed $50 or 5% of each delinquent installment plus certain costs and fees. (476-9). Where additional sales have been consolidated into one contract, payments are to be applied to purchases first made, and security interests terminate as each purchase becomes paid in full. (476-24). If any balloon payment for personal purchases is more than two times average of earlier payments, buyer has right to refinance without penalty, and if principal balance of original loan is less than $10,000, refinancing terms must be no less favorable to buyer than original terms except that: (1) Payment schedule can be modified to amortize total amount refinanced over period of refinancing, which cannot be less than original term; and (2) no scheduled payment can be greater than amount of average scheduled payment under original contract. (476-5). Provisions are made for deferral payments and interest. (476-6). Catalog mail order sales regulated in 476-11. Body of contract of credit sale must be at least 8 point in size and headings must be boldface and at least 10 point in size. Contract must contain title "CREDIT SALE CONTRACT" and term substantially similar to: "NOTICE TO THE BUYER: Do not sign this contract before you read it. When you sign this contract, you are entitled to a copy of it that is filled in, in every necessary respect. You should keep it. This contract is covered by Hawaii's credit sale law, and you have the rights of a buyer under that law. You also may have rights under other state and federal laws." (476-3). Buyer's rights may not be cut off by assignment. (476-19). Casual sales are excluded from coverage. (476-1).

Consumer Protection.—See topic Consumer Protection.

Bulk Sales.—See topic Commercial Code.

Product Liability.—Borrower from buyer may recover from retail seller (198 F.Supp. 78 which discusses Hawaii law on privity. Aff'd, 304 F.2d 149). Manufacturer liable for dangerous defective product. (52 Haw. 71, 470 P.2d 240). Discussions of strict products liability, proximate cause, precautions and safeguards, and occasional seller exception. (66 Haw. 237, 659 P.2d 734; 65 Haw. 447; 654 P.2d 343).

Retail Credit Sales.—See subhead Conditional Sales, supra.

Sales of franchises must be reported and are substantially regulated. (482E-1 to 12).

Sales of Motor Vehicles.—See category Transportation, topic Motor Vehicles.

Sale of Surplus Goods.—Governed by c. 481, Part II.

Contracts of Sales.—See topics Frauds, Statute of, Commercial Code, Consumer Protection.

International Sale of Goods.—See Part VI this volume, Selected Conventions.

SECURITIES:

Uniform Securities Act (modified) adopted. (c. 485).

Supervision.—Administration of c. 485 is vested in Commissioner of Securities ("Commissioner") to be appointed by Director of Commerce and Consumer Affairs ("Director"). Commissioner shall hold office at will of Director. (485-2). Commissioner may adopt, amend, or repeal rules necessary to carry out purposes of this chapter. (485-2).

Regulatory Powers of Supervising Authority.—Commissioner has broad powers similar to those set forth in Uniform Securities Act (pre-1985 version), hereafter "USA", including power to: (1) Issue stop orders against any registration under certain circumstances (485-13); (2) refuse or revoke registration of any applicant or registrant under certain circumstances (485-15); (3) inspect dealers' and investment advisers' records (485-16); (4) require escrow arrangements for certain securities (485-18); (5) issue cease and desist orders to enforce compliance with c. 485 (485-18.7); and (6) bring suit for injunctive relief (485-19). Commissioner's powers expanded to (1) suspend, complete, or rescind all securities contracts; (2) assess administrative penalty up to $100,000; and (3) seek civil penalty of $100,000 per violation. Enforcement tools for securities violations and fraud strengthened. (485-18.7; 485-20.5).

Prerequisites to Sales or Offerings.—It is unlawful for any person to sell or offer to sell any security except of a class exempt under 485-4 or unless sold or offered in a transaction exempt under 485-6 unless such security has been registered by notification or qualification in accordance with c. 485. (485-8).

See note at head of Digest as to 1998 legislation covered.

See Topical Index in front part of this volume.

HI – 10

SECURITIES ... continued

Securities to Which Act Applicable.—Substantially similar to USA; definition of security includes variable annuity contracts. (485-1). However, under certain circumstances, no issuer, dealer or salesman shall be required to be registered in order to qualify to sell variable annuities. (485-14.5).

Exempt Securities.—§402(a) of USA adopted via 485-4 with following significant differences: (1) §402(a)(7)(D) of USA includes Canada or any Canadian province; (2) §402(a)(8) of USA names specific exchanges while 485-4(8) refers to "any exchange registered or exempted under the Securities Exchange Act of 1934, as amended"; (3) 485-4(12) exempts any option on commodity futures contract subject to regulation under Commodity Exchange Act; (4) 485-4(13) exempts any security issued by "investment company" as defined by and registered under "Investment Company Act of 1940" (15 U.S.C. §80a) and subject to limitations of 485(13)(A). (5) 485-4(14) exempts any cooperative association membership stock, membership certificates or shares, or membership capital, pursuant to 421C-36 or c. 421; (6) 485-4(15) exempts any security, except securities issued by open-end management companies or unit investment trusts, for which registration statement has been filed under Securities Act of 1933, provided that no sale shall be made until registration statement becomes effective; and (7) 485-4(16) exempts any variable annuity contract which is investment contract prepared by life insurance company designed to offer continuous income through participation in mutual fund portfolio or variable annuity contract based upon separate account which is registered as management investment company with Securities and Exchange Commission ("SEC"). (SB 2469 [1998]).

Furthermore, 15 securities are exempt from §§485-A, 485-8 and 485-25(a)(7). These include: (1) any isolated nonissuer transaction, whether through dealer or not; (2) any nonissuer distribution of outstanding security if manual of Hawaiian securities or any other recognized securities manual contains names of issuer's officers and directors, balance sheet of issuer, and profit and loss statement for either fiscal year preceding that date or most recent year of fiscal operations; (3) any nonissuer transaction effected by or through registered dealer pursuant to unsolicited order or offer to buy.

Exempt Transactions.—§402(b) of USA adopted via 485-6. Significant variations include: (1) 485-6(9) designates 25 people as ceiling, not ten people as in §402(b)(9) of USA, and does not grant power to withdraw or further condition this exemption or to alter number of offerees permitted; (2) 485-6(10) designates 25 people as ceiling, not ten people as in §402(b)(10) of USA, and does not include §402(b)(10)(C) of USA; (3) 485-6(11) does not include §402(b)(11)(B); (4) 485-6(13) exempts any offer or sale by or through licensed real estate broker or salesman of security issued on or before July 1, 1961 by Hawaii corporation, holder of which is entitled to occupy house or apartment owned or leased by corporation, but subject to 485-7; (5) 485-6(14) exempts any offer or sale by or through licensed real estate broker or salesman of apartment in condominium project and rental management contract relating to such apartment; and (6) 485-6(15) exempts any transaction not involving public offering and any categories of transactions effected under rules of Commissioner under c. 91 with view to uniformity with federal law.

Uniform Transfer-On-Death Security Registration Act provides that individuals may designate non-testamentary beneficiary for transfer of registered securities. (SB 2611 [1998]).

Registration of Offerers.—Offerers must be registered in Hawaii. (See category Business Organizations, topic Corporations.)

Registration of Securities.—Securities may be registered by notification or by qualification. Manifold differences between c. 485 and USA. Hawaii statutes should be consulted. See: 425-8 as to general registration requirements, 485-9 as to registration by notification, and 485-10 as to registration by qualification. No registration by coordination discussed; 485-11 repealed.

Registration of Dealers.—Dealers, salesmen, investment advisors and investment advisor representatives must register with Commissioner under 485-14. Commissioner may require minimum capital not less than $5,000 and prescribe ratio between net capital and aggregate indebtedness, for registered dealers. For investment advisors, Commissioner may require net worth of at least $5,000. (485-14[q]).

Brokers and Agents.—Same as subhead Registration of Dealers, supra.

Bonds.—Upon approval of registration as dealer by Commissioner, $5,000 bond must be filed running to State. (485-14[f]). $50,000 bond required for investment advisors who have custody of or discretionary authority over client assets. (485-14[g]).

Advertisements.—All advertising matter must be filed with Commissioner's office unless previously exempted by Commissioner's rule or order. (485-25[a][7]).

Liabilities.—Violator of any provision of c. 485 shall be guilty of felony and shall forfeit to State any property acquired or enterprise operated in violation of c. 485. (485-21). Violators of c. 485 are also subject to civil penalties. (485-20.5).

Tender Offers.—See category Business Organizations, topic Corporations, subhead Tender Offers.

Subdivision Offerings.—Uniform Land Sales Practices Act adopted. (c. 484).

Franchising.—See topic Franchises.

Pyramid Sales, Etc.—Operation of endless chain scheme unlawful (480-3.3), and punishable by fine of not less than $500 nor more than $10,000 per violation. Penalties provided in this section are cumulative to remedies or penalties available under all other laws of this state. Each day that violation of 480-2 occurs shall be separate violation. (480-3.1).

Uniform Simplification of Fiduciary Security Transfers Act adopted in 1945. Uniform Commercial Code effective Jan. 1, 1967, also adopted.

Uniform Securities Ownership by Minors Act has not been adopted.

Uniform Commercial Code adopted. (c. 490). See topic Commercial Code.

STATUTE OF FRAUDS:

See topic Frauds, Statute of.

TRUST RECEIPT SECURITY:

See category Debtor and Creditor, topic Pledges.

Uniform Commercial Code adopted. See topic Commercial Code.

WAREHOUSEMEN:

Uniform Commercial Code adopted. (c. 490). See topic Commercial Code. See category Debtor and Creditor, topic Liens.

CITIZENSHIP

ALIENS:

Property.—Aliens not eligible for residential leases of public land. (171-74). Aliens may acquire and hold land when deraigned through private persons. Declarant aliens with five years residence in state may acquire land from Board of Land and Natural Resources. (206-9).

Occupational Restrictions.—All persons employed upon public work must be citizens of U.S. and Hawaii, or eligible for citizenship, unless citizens unavailable. (103-57; see 78-1). Aliens disqualified from service in Hawaii State Guard. (122-7). Aliens cannot be commissioned or warrant officers of Militia or National Guard. (121-14). See also category Employment, topic Labor Relations, subhead Public Employees.

State, County and Municipal Officers and Employees.—Elective officers must be U.S. citizens and Hawaii residents for three years preceding assumption of office. (78-1[a]). Appointed officers, if second deputies to department heads or higher level, must be U.S. citizens and Hawaii residents for one year preceding appointment; if lower level must be citizens, nationals or permanent residents of U.S. and residents of Hawaii at time of appointment (if nationals or permanent residents, must diligently seek citizenship upon becoming eligible). (78-1[b]). Other employees (except certain persons recruited by University of Hawaii) must be citizens, nationals or permanent residents of U.S. and residents of Hawaii at time of application for employment. (U.S. citizenship required for positions involving national security.) (78-1[c], [f], [g]).

Other Restrictions.—Aliens may not vote. (11-15[a][6]). Aliens disqualified from jury service. (612-4[1]). Aliens may not incorporate fraternal benefit insurance societies. (434-5[1]). Aliens not eligible for real estate broker examination unless authorized to work in U.S. (467-9.5[1]). Aliens, except permanent residents or aliens otherwise lawfully present at time services performed not eligible for benefits under Employment Security Law. (383-29[d]).

Firearms, Hunting and Fishing.—Accredited foreign officials and aliens commissioned as State law enforcement officers may obtain permit for firearms from chiefs of police. (134-3[g]). Other aliens may obtain 60 day permits for rifles and shotguns after procuring hunting license. (134-3[g]). Aliens employed by U.S. or State may carry firearms when performance of duty requires. (134-11). Aliens not lawfully admitted to U.S. may not engage in taking marine life for commercial purposes in waters of State. (189-5).

Miscellaneous.—Aliens whose government accords similar right to Hawaii citizens may bring claim against state. (661-4). Aliens who resided in state for five years eligible for farm loans. (155-10[2]). In order to obtain workmen's compensation benefits, alien dependents not residing in U.S. must maintain annual proof of dependency. (386-42[c]). Official in charge of institutions confining alien may release him for return to his native land conditioned upon his remaining away from state. (336-5). Directors of institutions will arrange for deportation of public charges in state hospitals. (336-1). Property forfeiture provisions of antiracketeering statute apply to nonresident aliens. (842-3). Alien may serve as personal representative of probate estate if alien submits to jurisdiction of Hawaii courts. (560:3-601[a][1]). Personal tax cannot be assessed against nonresident. Nonresident's property cannot be taxed unless it has actual situs within jurisdiction. However, any tangible personal property situated within jurisdiction may be taxed irrespective of owner's residence. (4 Haw. 172)".

CIVIL ACTIONS AND PROCEDURE

ACCORD AND SATISFACTION:

Generally, common law rules govern. Uniform Commercial Code adopted. See category Business Regulation and Commerce, topic Commercial Code.

Compromise.—
Apprenticeship disputes may be settled by Director of Labor and Industrial Relations. (372-5[7]).
Attorney must have client's written authority to compromise. (605-7).
Marriage settlements valid. (572-29).
Paternity proceedings may be compromised upon pretrial recommendation. (584-13).
Probate claims may be compromised by personal representative of estate (560:3-813) or by appointed guardian of property (560:5-424).
Tax claims may be compromised by director of taxation with governor's consent. (231-3[10]).
Tort claims against state may be compromised by attorney general. Compromise of claims exceeding $10,000 will be paid only after funds are specifically appropriated by legislature. (662-11).
Unemployment compensation disputes may be compromised by Department of Labor and Industrial Relations, but if referred to attorney general, then only with his consent. (383-75).

ACCORD AND SATISFACTION ... *continued*

Workmens' compensation claims may be compromised by Director of Labor and Industrial Relations. (386-78).

Pleading.—Accord and satisfaction must be pleaded affirmatively. (HRCP 8[c]).

ACTIONS:

Civil actions in circuit courts, Hawaii's courts of general jurisdiction, closely follow federal rules as am'd, and rule numbers generally correspond. See topic Practice. Comments in this topic refer to civil actions in circuit courts to which Hawaii Rules of Civil Procedure (HRCP) apply, unless otherwise indicated. HRCP do not apply to probate (c. 560); guardianship (c. 551); ex parte re: accounts of guardians and trustees (c. 554); family court; applications to circuit court re: arbitration; writ to inferior court (603-21.7[b]). Consult relevant statute for instances when rules do not apply in following: land court (c. 501); eminent domain (c. 101); quiet title (c. 669); quo warranto (c. 659); escheat (c. 665); forfeiture of property for violation of statute; quarantine (c. 325); commitment hearings (cc. 333, 334); tax collection; voter registration, elections; collective bargaining (cc. 89, 380); land/water rights (c. 664). Abuse of discretion to dismiss case for want of prosecution when plaintiff failed to institute selection of trial date under RCCH 12(c); HRCP. (10 Haw. App. 388, 876 P.2d 1335). See topic Practice.

Equity.—See subhead Forms of Action, infra.

Forms of Action.—There is one form of action, "civil action." (HRCP 1). There is no action in equity as distinguished from law, but equitable relief (injunction, specific performance, etc.) is granted in proper cases.

Conditions Precedent.—All tort cases are automatically in arbitration program unless plaintiff certifies case value exceeds $150,000. Sanctions for attempting to remove case from program without good cause. Judicial Arbitration Commission has discretion to accept. (Hawaii Arbitration Rules, 1/9/90).

Circuit judge from each circuit is appointed by Chief Justice to be Arbitration Judge. Arbitration Judge may impose sanctions, including costs, expert fees, and reasonable attorney's fees, for failure to participate in arbitration hearing in meaningful manner. (Hawaii Arbitration Rules, Rule 28, RCCH, Exhibit A). (a) Design Professional Conciliation Panel (c. 672). Professional negligence actions against professional engineer, architect, surveyor, or landscape architect must be preceded by filing of claim before panel. (672-2). May file motion with circuit court for determination case is unsuitable for panel review (i.e., broad public concern; need for discovery). (672-2.1). (b) Medical Claims Conciliation Panel. Submission of medical torts claims to panel is mandatory prior to bringing case in court. Statute is tolled until 60 days after decision. (671-18). Panel issues advisory opinion of liability and damages. (671-15). Settlement is voluntary; nothing from panel hearings or findings may be used in subsequent litigation. (671-16). Parties may elect to bypass court annexed arbitration program. (671-16.5).

Commencement is by filing complaint. (HRCP 3).

Parties.—(HRCP 17-25).

Necessary Parties.—(HRCP 19).

Permissive Parties.—(HRCP 20).

Class Actions.—(HRCP 23).

Misjoinder is not ground for dismissal. (HRCP 21).

Intervention.—(HRCP 24).

Interpleader.—(HRCP 22).

Third Party Practice.—(HRCP 14).

Joinder of Causes of Action.—(HRCP 18). Joinder of claims is permissive.

Splitting Causes of Action.—Common law governs res judicata.

Consolidation of Actions.—(HRCP 42[a]).

Severance of Actions.—(HRCP 42[b]).

Stay of Proceedings.—No statute governs pending actions before judgment.

Joinder of Causes of Action.—(HRCP 18).

Abatement and Revival.—(1) Tort: Right of action survives death of tortfeasor. (663-4). Cause of action in tort arising out of wrongful act, neglect, or default survives death of person injured except in actions for defamation and malicious prosecution. (663-7). (2) Other: common law applies. (3) Criminal injury compensation awards expire with death of claimant. (351-67).

Abatement.—Death of plaintiff or defendant does not cause an action to abate. Dissolution of a corporation does not cause an action to abate. (634-61). Hawaii Rules of Civil Procedure do not limit time within which court may order substitution but motion must be submitted within 120 days of date death is suggested upon record. (HRCP 25[a]).

Limitation of.—See topic Limitation of Actions.

Small Claims.—See category Courts and Legislature, topic Courts.

Termination of Actions.—No specific statute.

Prohibited Actions.—No specific statute. Statutory remedies are merely cumulative and do not abolish common law remedies unless so declared in express terms or by necessary remedy. (67 Haw. 252, 686 P.2d 12).

Administration.—See category Estates and Trusts, topic Executors and Administrators.

Against State.—Based on express or implied contracts (661-1); see topic Damages.

Direct Actions Against Insurer.—See category Transportation, topic Motor Vehicles, subhead Direct Actions Against Insurer.

APPEAL AND ERROR:

Hawaii Rules of Appellate Procedure (HRAP) adopted effective June 1, 1984. Govern procedures in appeals to Supreme Court and Intermediate Court of Appeals from circuit, district, family, land, and tax appeal courts, and from orders of administrative agencies. (HRAP 1). HRAP have force of law (Constitution Art. VI, §7; 602-11) and supersede prior rules. HRAP generally parallel Federal Rules of Appellate Procedure and Rule numbers generally correspond. In an extension for time to file notice of appeal, if cause of delay is beyond movant's control, motion may be granted on showing of good cause. If cause is within control of movant, motion may be granted only on showing of excusable neglect. (80 Haw. 345, 910 P.2d 116.)

Hawaii's Supreme Court and Intermediate Court of Appeals share concurrent jurisdiction over appeals from circuit and district courts. See category Courts and Legislature, topic Courts.

Supreme Court has adopted Hawaii Appellate Conference Program Rules (eff. 3/15/95) to provide alternative means of resolving civil appeals by providing neutral place and process to resolve issues in pending cases or to resolve in toto. All civil appeals are included except (1) petitions for extraordinary relief, (2) habeas corpus petitions, (3) petitions of incarcerated petitioner, (4) post-conviction proceedings of criminals under Rule 40, (5) pro se appeals, and (6) questions of law reserved to Hawaii Supreme Court. Participation mandatory for cases selected by court. Conferences will be conducted by neutral mediator selected by parties or appointed by court from among retired or semi-retired judges and counsel. Mediators will attempt to achieve consensus on each issue.

Appeal Bond.—Any court may require bond to ensure payment of costs on appeal. (HRAP 7).

Appeals.—

District Courts.—Appeals in all matters, civil (641-1) or criminal (641-12) made to Supreme Court or intermediate appellate court, subject to reassignment provisions set out in subsections 602-5(8) and 602-6, by filing notice of appeal and paying accrued costs within 30 days, and in civil cases, depositing costs of appeal as provided for in 607-6. (641-1). No appeal from small claims division. (633-28).

Circuit Courts.—Appeals in all matters, civil (641-1) and criminal (641-11), made from decisions, judgments, orders or decrees of circuit judges to Supreme Court or intermediate appellate court, subject to reassignment provisions set out in subsections 602-5(8) and 602-6 (except where appellant is entitled to appeal to jury), whenever appellant shall file notice of his appeal (HRAP 3) within 30 days after filing of decision, judgment, order or decree appealed from (HRAP 4). Bond for costs in civil matters may be required. (HRAP 7).

Appeals may be allowed upon like terms by circuit judge from interlocutory judgments, orders, or decrees, wherever he deems same advisable for speedy termination of litigation, both civil (641-1) and criminal (641-17).

Intermediate Appellate Court.—Appeals had after issuance of decision only upon application to Supreme Court for writ of certiorari, acceptance or rejection of which is discretionary upon Supreme Court. Application must be made within ten days after filing of decision appealed from. (602-59). See also topic Certiorari.

Administrative Agencies.—Person aggrieved may have judicial review of final decision in contested case or of preliminary ruling where necessary for adequate relief (91-14[a]; HRAP 1) by instituting proceedings in circuit court within 30 days after ruling or service of decision, in accordance with HRCP (91-14[b]; HRCP 72) except where direct appeal to Supreme Court authorized by statute (91-14[b]). Written notice of hearing of employment security appeal must be sent first class, non-registered, noncertified mail to claimant's last known address. (1997, Act 22). See also, topic Judgments, subhead Declaratory Judgments.

Stay of Proceedings.—In civil matters no execution shall issue upon judgment nor shall proceedings be taken for enforcement until expiration of ten days after entry. Upon good cause shown, court may allow execution or other appropriate action within ten day period. Stay of proceedings may be obtained in discretion of court or where appeal is taken, appellant may give supersedeas bond. (641-3). Circuit judge's order for counsel's fee, suit money, temporary alimony, or similar provisional remedy will not be stayed from execution if appellee deposits sufficient indemnity bond (641-3), upon approval by court (HRAP 8; HRCP 62[d]). In criminal matters filing notice of appeal or giving oral notice of intent to appeal at time of sentence may operate as stay, in court's discretion, subject to conditions stated by court. (641-14).

Extent of Review.—

By Circuit Court.—Where review or redetermination in circuit court is allowed by statute, person adversely affected by decision of district or government agency may appeal in accordance with HRCP 72.

Review of contested cases from administrative agencies is confined to record unless trial de novo allowed by law (91-14[f]), but review under 91-14 does not preclude other lawful modes of judicial review (91-14[a]). Circuit court may only modify, correct, or vacate arbitration award on grounds specified in arbitration statute, c. 658. (77 Haw. 187, 881 P.2d 255). Court review of awards is limited by provisions of rules implementing arbitration program. (77 Haw. 422, 886 P.2d 759). Court lacks authority to postpone arbitration actions since court has jurisdiction to review only after award is issued. Court lacks jurisdiction to consolidate multiple arbitrations between parties where several contracts each provided for separate arbitration. (77 Haw. 481, 889 P.2d 58).

By Supreme Court and Intermediate Appellate Court.—

(a) *From District Courts.*—Review of questions of law or of mixed law and fact (602-5) confined to record (641-2). Findings of fact may not be set aside unless clearly erroneous. (HRCP 52[a]; 59 Haw. 491, 583 P.2d 971).

(b) *From Circuit Court.*—Review of questions of law or mixed law and fact (602-5) confined to record (641-2). Findings of fact by circuit court may not be set aside unless clearly erroneous. (HRCP 52[a]).

Character of Hearing.—

In Circuit Court.—Where law permits trial by jury, trial is by court unless jury demanded in accordance with HRCP 38. (HRCP 72[g]).

See note at head of Digest as to 1998 legislation covered.

See Topical Index in front part of this volume.

APPEAL AND ERROR . . . continued

In Supreme Court and Intermediate Appellate Court.—Limited to record. (641-2). Full court must hear oral argument unless dispensed with in court's discretion. (602-10).

Judgment or Order on Appeal.—Supreme Court (602-5[7]), intermediate appellate court (602-57), and circuit courts (603-21.9) may render all judgments or orders and do all acts necessary to carry their powers into effect.

Lower courts may not vacate, amend, and later reenter their own judgments merely to render late-filed appeal timely. (79 Haw. 26, 897 P.2d 953).

Appeals from Family Courts are provided for by 571-54 and governed by c. 602. Legal records regarding certain juvenile offenders are open to public inspection unless otherwise decreed by family court judge. (1997, HB 107).

Appeals from Land Court provided for by 501-63 and governed by c. 602.

BONDS:

Hawaii closely follows Federal Rules of Civil Procedure on bonds submitted in civil actions.

Sureties.—Personal sureties required to justify, but not corporations organized and authorized as sureties. (78-20). Compensation is limited to one-time only fee of 5% to 15%, but not less than $50. (804-62).

Enforcement.—Surety liability enforceable on motion without necessity of independent action. (HRCP 65.1).

CERTIORARI:

Jurisdiction.—Generally, HRAP 31(e). Supreme Court may accept appeal from intermediate appellate court decision by application for writ (602-59[a]) filed within ten days after filing of decision (602-59[c]).

Grounds.—Grave errors of law or fact or obvious inconsistencies with decisions by Supreme Court, federal courts or intermediate appellate court. (602-59[b]). Court will accept no motion for reconsideration of acceptance or rejection. (HRAP 31[d][8]).

Proceedings.—Deadline for filing petition is 30 days after filing of intermediate appellate court decision. (1997, Act 24). If not accepted within ten days after filing, petition rejected. (602-59[c]). If writ issued, case transmitted to Supreme Court, supplemental briefs and oral argument allowed only upon request by Supreme Court. (602-59[d]; HRAP 31[e]).

Review.—No statute covers scope of review.

CHARITABLE IMMUNITY:

See topic Damages.

COMMISSIONS TO TAKE TESTIMONY:

See topic Depositions and Discovery.

COSTS:

Costs and fees are prescribed by statute. (607). Increased court fees are effective July 1, 1998, as described below. (1998, Act 128).

Civil court costs are $200 for civil complaints; $100 for probate cases, guardianship cases, and trust actions; and other fees are prescribed by schedule. (607-5b). Family court costs are $100. (607-5b). District court costs are $75 for regular claims (607-4) and $35 for small claims (607-29). Supreme Court costs are $75 for filing appeal, other fees prescribed by schedule. (607-6). Appeals to intermediate appellate court shall be filed with Supreme Court at same cost. (607-6). U.S. District Court costs are $60, other fees prescribed by schedule.

Court may charge additional Indigent Legal Services Surcharge. (607-Act 305, 1996).

Judges have discretionary power to waive prepayment of costs or remit costs, where in special or extraordinary cases cost of suit is onerous. (607-3).

Courts have power to require either party, upon application, to give security for costs. (607-3.5).

Judgment creditors may recover attorney's fees, costs and expenses from judgment debtors. (607-14.7).

$50 fee assessed when cases remanded from circuit court back to district court after demand for jury trial requiring case's transfer to circuit court waived. (607.5[22]). $200 fee for demand for jury trial. (607-5[c]21).

Frivolous Claims.—Vexatious litigant (as defined in statute) may be required to post security or obtain permission of court prior to filing new litigation. (c. 634J).

DAMAGES:

Counsel may make formula arguments for damages in personal injury cases. (635-52). Ad damnum clauses prohibited in personal injury or wrongful death pleadings and amendment to such pleadings. (663-1.3). Statute affects amount of recovery for lost earnings and noneconomic damages (663-8.3, 8.5, 8.7); and abolishes claims for serious infliction of emotional distress arising solely from property damage unless distress results in physical injury or mental illness. (663-8.9). Hawaii recognizes (1) parents' right to recover for wrongful death of viable fetus (745 F.Supp. 1573); (2) cause of action for child's loss of consortium due to parent's nonfatal injury (781 F.Supp. 1487); (3) dependents' claims for pecuniary injuries (867 P.2d 220). Hawaii does not require family members to be present or sustain physical injury as prerequisite to bringing cause of action for negligent infliction of severe emotional distress. (77 Haw. 2, 881 P.2d 489).

See also category Estates and Trusts, topic Death, subhead Action for Death.

Charitable immunity is uncertain. (31 Haw. 740). No immunity in favor of municipal corporations. (41 Haw. 527). Health care providers who provide free medical care to indigents in connection with project sponsored by nonprofit corporations are exempt

from civil liability. (663-1.57, 663-10.6). Volunteers to nonprofit or governmental entities have qualified immunity. (662D-2).

Immunity is granted to charitable, religious or nonprofit organizations that donate pharmaceuticals or supplies to needy. (328-2).

Immunity is granted to health care providers who report blood test results to police. (663-1.9).

Immunity is granted to insurance commissioner and employees. (431:3-414).

Persons injured on school grounds using school facilities assume risk of liability. (302A-1148.5).

See also topic Actions, subhead Conditions Precedent.

Comparative Negligence Rule.—Contributory negligence does not bar recovery if such negligence was not greater than negligence of person, (or in case of more than one person, aggregate negligence of such persons), against whom recovery sought; damages are diminished in proportion attributable to injured claimant. (663-31). Uniform Comparative Fault Act not adopted.

Uniform Contribution Among Tortfeasors Act adopted by statute (663-11 to 17) except that joint and several liability not abolished in some circumstances. Exceptions listed at 663-10.9.

Civil Defense.—State, political subdivisions, and persons engaged in civil defense per c. 128 are not liable, except for willful misconduct, for death, injury, or damages. Although recovery may not be had against State for damage sustained from operation of vehicle during civil defense emergency, injured persons may seek recovery against insurers if policies under 41D-8 cover such risks. (128-18). Recovery of fair market value or fair rental value is allowed for requisitioned property, but prospective profits and punitive or other damages are not. (128-23). Persons voluntarily and without compensation permitting their property to be used to shelter others during actual, impending, or practice attack are not liable for negligent death, injury, or damage. (128-19).

Recreational Activities.—Owners/operators of recreational activities are not liable for injuries to patrons from inherent risks if patrons voluntarily sign written waiver. (663-1.54).

Hotel keepers liable for personal property losses of guests under certain circumstances and up to certain limits. (c. 486K). Hotel keepers may be held liable to guests for injury or loss on account of hazardous beach conditions only when caused by hotel keeper's failure to warn and when hazardous condition not known to or would not have been known to reasonably prudent guest. Hotel keeper owes no duty to non-guest for beach conditions not created by hotel. (486K-5.5). Signs warning of dangerous current are presumed to be legally adequate warning of dangerous condition. (c. 663).

Aircraft.—Uniform Aeronautics Act adopted (as modified). (c. 263). Owners and lessees of aircraft operated for commercial purposes are absolutely liable, jointly and severally, for injuries caused on land or water by ascent, descent, or flights, or objects falling therefrom unless injury caused in whole or part by negligence of person injured. Injured person has lien on aircraft causing damage. (263-5).

Condemnation.—Const. Art. I, §20 on just compensation includes property damaged as well as property taken for public use. In fixing value of compensation, property will be assessed with improvements unless separately owned, in which case assessment and compensation will be separate. Severance damages accrue to portion of parcel not condemned, but only to extent in excess of special benefit of proposed improvement. In condemnation for widening or realigning existing roads, special benefits will be considered only as offset against severance damages and not against value of portion taken. (101-23).

No-Fault Insurance.—See category Transportation, topic Motor Vehicles.

Attorneys' Fees.—May be recoverable as damages where wrongful act of defendant has involved plaintiff in litigation with others or placed him in such relation with others as to make it necessary to incur expenses to protect his interest. (57 Haw. 102, 551 P.2d 171). May be recoverable as sanction against opposing party for abusive litigation practices upon showing of bad faith. (85 Haw. 238, 942 P.2d 502). Assumpsit statute (607-14); civil actions (607-14.5); tort actions (607-15); taxing costs on appeal (607-16); promissory notes (607-17).

Drug Dealers.—Providing civil remedies for damages to persons in community injured as result of illegal drug use. Parents, employers, insurers, persons in utero at time of drug use, and government entities have standing to sue. Recovered drug users also have standing but are subject to Hawaii's comparative negligence regime (to recover, users responsibility may not be greater than dealers). Drug dealers are liable under Hawaii's modified market theory of product liability, which holds that plaintiff must prove dealer provided at least one product to plaintiff's area during period when plaintiff obtained product. Dealers are presumed to have provided 100% of product supplied to plaintiff's area unless they can prove otherwise. Dealers may implead additional dealers. (663D-1 to 14). Hawaii has adopted Model Drug Dealer Liability Act (modified).

Sovereign Immunity.—State has waived immunity from torts of its employees and is liable therefor to the same extent as a private individual but is not liable for interest prior to judgment nor for punitive damages. (662-2). Attorney General may compromise or settle claims cognizable under c. 662. (662-11). Attorney General may also defend civil actions brought against health care providers under contract with Department of Public Safety for acts or omissions within contract's scope of work. (662-16). Comptroller may compromise or settle tort claims involving State owned vehicles. (41D-3). District and circuits courts have jurisdiction and actions must be commenced within two years. (662-3, -4). Court may, with consent of all parties, order jury trial. (662-5). Court costs and attorneys' fees may be allowed to prevailing party. (662-9, 12).

State has also waived immunity for breach of trust or fiduciary duty relating to management and disposition of funds of Hawaiian home lands trust and native Hawaiian public trust. Two-year statute of limitation tolled until July 1, 1990. Court costs and attorneys' fees may be awarded to prevailing party. (673-5). Whenever state is

See note at head of Digest as to 1998 legislation covered.

See Topical Index in front part of this volume.

DAMAGES ... *continued*
liable party under joint and several liability, state shall be liable for no more than that percentage share of damages attributable to state. (663-10.5).

DECLARATORY JUDGMENTS:

See topic Judgments.

DEPOSITIONS AND DISCOVERY:

Hawaii closely follows the Federal Rules. See topic Practice.

Within State for Use Within State.—Generally, HRCP 30. Perpetuation of testimony of witness before action may be obtained by verified petition to Circuit Court or by civil action. (624-41; HRCP 27 [a][1]; HRCP 27 [a][4] and [c]). Peer review activities of Health Maintenance Organizations, Preferred Provider Organizations and Preferred Provider Networks are protected from discovery. (624-25.5).

Outside of State for Use Within State.—Evidence of witnesses living in another state may be obtained on application to any court of record. (624-24.5). Commission issues to officer (usually notary public) who is to take deposition, under oath, either on oral deposition or written interrogatories as set forth in commission. Hawaii Rules of Civ. Proc. 26-37 are same as pre-July 1970 Fed. Rules 26-37 except for omission of F.R.C.P. 37(e) relating to federal subpoena for failure to respond to letters rogatory.

Compelling Attendance of Witnesses Within State.—Resident of state may be compelled to give his deposition only in county wherein he resides or is employed or transacts his business in person. Nonresident subpoenaed within state may be compelled to give his deposition only in county wherein he is served with subpoena. Residents and nonresidents may be compelled to give depositions at such other convenient place as fixed by order of court. (HRCP Rule 45[d]). Circuit court may also compel witness within state to give his deposition upon commission to take testimony within state which has been issued by court of another state. (624-27).

Depositions to Be Used in Foreign Jurisdictions.—Testimony of a witness and production of books and papers within the state to be used in an action outside of the state may be taken when a commission to take such testimony has been issued from the foreign court, and a notice has been given to take such testimony pursuant to laws of the foreign jurisdiction. On presentation of the verified petition, the local court orders the issuance of a subpoena to the witness to appear before the commissioner named in the commission at a time and place specified in the subpoena. If such witness fails to obey the subpoena or refuses to testify, or to produce books or papers pursuant to a subpoena or to subscribe to his deposition, the court shall, if it is determined that a contempt has been committed, prescribe the punishment as in the case of a recalcitrant witness in a court of record in the territory and make other additional orders as would be proper in such case. (624-27). Officer or commissioner before whom witness appears, takes down his testimony in writing and annexes thereto copies of all books and papers produced and then certifies to correctness of statements and testimony and transmits it to court in which action is pending. (624-28).

Uniform Foreign Depositions Act has not been adopted.

Examination of Witnesses.—Rules of Court allow broad use prior to trial under rules relating to discovery. See topic Practice.

EQUITY:

See topic Actions.

EVIDENCE:

Hawaii Rules of Evidence parallel Federal Rules of Evidence with some distinctions. See topic Depositions and Discovery; and subhead Witnesses, infra.

Witnesses.—See Hawaii Rules of Evidence, Art. VI, Rules 601-616. (626). Parties and interested persons may testify. Every person generally competent to be witness where he has personal knowledge of matter. Hawaii Rules of Evidence modeled after Federal Rules of Evidence. Impeachment by evidence of conviction of crime differs markedly from Fed. R. Evid. 609. (HRE 609). Conviction of crime does not disqualify. (HRE 609).

Privileged Communications.—See Hawaii Rules of Evidence, Art. V, Rules 501-513. (c. 626). Hawaii Rules of Evidence recognize lawyer-client privilege, physician-patient privilege, psychologist-client privilege, spousal privilege, political vote privilege, clergyman privilege, trade secret privilege, privilege against self-incrimination, informer privilege and victim-counselor privilege (defined, 505.5).

Husband and wife may testify against each other, but cannot be compelled to testify against each other in criminal case.

Communications or Transactions with Persons Since Deceased or Incompetent.—Everybody is competent to be witness. (HRE 601). In wrongful death actions, statement by deceased, offered against plaintiff in action for wrongful death of that deceased, is not excluded by hearsay rule. (HRE 803[a][3]). Statement made by declarant under belief of impending death is not excluded by hearsay rule if declarant is unavailable as witness. (HRE 804[b][2]).

Self-incrimination.—Privilege recognized against self-incrimination to extent granted by state (Haw. Const., Art. 1, §10) or federal constitution (U.S. Const. amend. V; HRE 509).

Compelling Attendance.—See topic Depositions and Discovery.

Victim/Witness Bill of Rights.—Relating to rights of victims and witnesses in criminal proceedings. (c. 801D).

INJUNCTIONS:

Hawaii closely follows the Federal Rules. See topic Practice.

Many statutes provide their own injunctive remedies. Check individual topic or statute consulted.

Jurisdiction.—Circuit courts have jurisdiction to issue temporary and permanent injunctions. (603-21.5; 128-29). Injunction pending appeal is writ that appellate court

may issue as necessary or appropriate in aid of its appellate jurisdiction. (602-5; HRCP Rule 62[g]).

Prerequisites.—No temporary restraining order granted without written or oral notice to adverse party or that party's attorney unless irreparable damage will result and applicant's attorney certifies what efforts, if any, have been made to give notice and why no notice should be required. (HRCP Rule 65[b]). No preliminary injunction issued without notice to adverse party. (HRCP Rule 65[a]).

Procedure.—Every temporary restraining order granted without notice shall be indorsed with date and hour of issuance; shall be filed forthwith in clerk's office and entered of record; shall define injury and state why it is irreparable and why order was granted without notice; and shall expire by its terms within such time after entry, not to exceed ten days, as court fixes, unless within time so fixed order, for good cause shown, is extended for like period or unless party against whom order is directed consents that it may be extended for longer period. Reasons for extension shall be entered of record. In case temporary restraining order is granted without notice, motion for preliminary injunction shall be set down for hearing at earliest possible time and shall take precedence over all matters except older matters of same character; when motion comes on for hearing, party who obtained temporary restraining order shall proceed with application for preliminary injunction and, if that party does not do so, court shall dissolve temporary restraining order. On two days' notice to party who obtained temporary restraining order, without notice or on such shorter notice to that party as court may prescribe, adverse party may appear and move its dissolution or modification and, in that event, court shall proceed to hear and determine such motion as expeditiously as ends of justice require. (HRCP Rule 65[b]).

Bond.—Court, on granting temporary restraining order or preliminary injunction or at any time thereafter, may require security or impose such other equitable terms as it deems proper. No such security shall be required of State or county, or officer or agency of State or county. (HRCP Rule 65[c]; Rule 65.1).

Temporary Injunction.—Test for temporary injunctive relief is three-fold: (1) whether plaintiff is likely to prevail on merits; (2) whether balance of irreparable damage favors issuance of temporary injunction, and (3) whether public interest supports granting injunction. (59 Haw. 156, 577 P.2d 1116).

JUDGMENTS:

Hawaii closely follows the Federal Rules. See topic Practice.

Judgments by Confession.—Confession of judgment prohibited in certain instances. 373-11(9), relating to employment agencies; 425-109(3)(d), relating to powers of general partners; 476-13, relating to credit sales; 481C-2, relating to door-to-door sales; 521-34, relating to residential rental agreements.

Judgment by Consent.—Final judgment entered before complaint has been filed in monopoly/restraint of trade action is prima facie evidence in any action brought by another party under c. 480; excepted are consent judgments entered into before State files complaint. (480-22; see HRCP 81[b][12]).

Judgment on Pleadings.—HRCP 12(c).

Child Support Judgments.—There is presumption that child support judgments are discharged on child's 33rd birthday. (1997, Act 294).

Summary Judgments.—HRCP 56.

Declaratory Judgments.—In case of actual controversy or imminent and inevitable litigation, antagonistic claims may be adjudicated by circuit court even though general common law remedy or equitable, extraordinary legal, or other such remedy may be available. Exception to this where statute provides special form of remedy for specific type of case such that statutory remedy must be followed. Declaratory judgment will not be permitted in tax controversies or in cases of divorce or annulment. (632-1). Interested person may obtain judicial declaration of validity of administrative agency rule by action against agency in circuit court in which petitioner resides or has principal place of business. (91-7).

Default Judgments.—When party fails to plead or defend, clerk may enter default judgment for sum certain and costs; court may enter in all other instances. (HRCP Rule 55). Upon application for judgment by default: (1) If taking of evidence is required or ordered and matter is one which would have been tried before jury had there been no default, court in its discretion may order trial without jury; (2) if defendant served by publication has not appeared, court shall require proof to be made of allegations in complaint. (636-15).

Offer of Judgment.—At any time more than ten days before trial begins, party defending against claim may serve upon adverse party offer to allow judgment to be taken against him with costs then accrued. If offer is accepted within ten days after service, either party may then file offer and notice of acceptance together with proof of service thereof and thereupon clerk will enter judgment. If final judgment obtained by offeree is not more favorable than offer, offeree must pay costs incurred after making of offer. (HRCP Rule 68).

Docketing.—Filing with clerk of judgment, signed by judge, constitutes entry of judgment. No judgment effective until entry. (HRCP Rule 58[b]).

Vacation or Modification.—
Motion for new trial must be served within ten days after entry of judgment. (HRCP Rule 59[b]). Affidavits must be served if motion is based on affidavits. (HRCP Rule 59[c]). Court may order new trial on its own initiative within ten days after entry of judgment. (HRCP Rule 59[d]). Both grant or denial of motion is within court's discretion. (57 Haw. 378, 557 P.2d 788). New trial proper where issue not answered (4 Haw. 81), or where successful party tampered with jury (24 Haw. 193). Misconduct of opposing counsel is not ground for new trial unless party had objected to that conduct and brought it to court's attention. (69 Haw. 678). New trial based on newly discovered evidence can be granted if evidence (1) is previously undiscovered even with due diligence, (2) is admissible and credible, and (3) is of such nature as will probably change outcome. (5 Haw. App. 628).

JUDGMENTS . . . *continued*

Motion to alter or amend judgment must be served within ten days after entry of judgment. (HRCP Rule 59[e]).

Grounds for relief from judgment or order: (1) mistake, inadvertence, surprise, or excusable neglect; (2) newly discovered evidence which by due diligence could not have been discovered in time to move for new trial; (3) fraud, misrepresentation or other misconduct of adverse party; (4) judgment is void; (5) judgment has been satisfied, released, or discharged; (6) any other reason justifying relief. (HRCP Rule 60[b]).

Judgment Liens.—Any money judgment or decree of a state court or U.S. District Court for District of Hawaii shall be a lien upon real property when certified copy thereof is recorded in bureau of conveyances. (636-3). Circuit court judgments quieting title to real property to be recorded. (669-8). When obligor for child support becomes delinquent through judicial or administrative process, lien arises on his/her real and personal property. (1997, Act 293).

Revival.—Death of plaintiff or defendant or dissolution of corporate plaintiff or defendant shall not cause action to abate, but it may be continued upon substitution of proper parties. (634-61). Motion for substitution may be made by any party or by successors or representatives of deceased party. (HRCP Rule 25[a]). Defamation action does not survive death of defendant. (1 Haw. App. 517).

Assignment.—Judgments are transferable by written assignment. (634-1). Partial assignment of judgment not allowed unless with assent from judgment debtor and such partial assignment does not change legal title to judgment. (27 Haw. 642).

Satisfaction.—When judgment is fully paid, creditor or his attorney shall execute, acknowledge, and deliver to debtor satisfaction thereof. Every satisfaction shall contain reference to book and page or document number of registration of original judgment. (636-3).

Form: Satisfaction of Judgment.—See end of this Digest.

Actions.—In any action brought on prior judgment, if complaint fails to credit prior payments on judgment, defendant entitled to offset against true balance due on judgment amount double amount of any such credit in addition to any other penalties by law unless plaintiff shows existence or amount of bona fide dispute or good faith mistake. (636-5).

Foreign Judgments.—Valid judgments of another state are entitled to full faith and credit in Hawaii. (7 Haw. App. 238, 752 P.2d 106). Copy of any exemplified foreign judgment may be filed in office of court clerk. Clerk shall treat foreign judgment in same manner as judgment of court of this State. Judgment so filed has same effect and is subject to same effect and is subject to same procedures, defenses, and proceedings for reopening, vacating, or staying as judgment of court of this State. (636C-3).

Uniform Enforcement of Foreign Judgments Act adopted in Hawaii. (c. 636C). Copy of exemplified foreign judgment filed in office of clerk of appropriate court with $30 filing fee and affidavit setting forth name and last known post office address of judgment debtor and judgment creditor will have same effect as judgment of court of this state.

LIMITATION OF ACTIONS:

Actions must be brought within the following periods after the respective causes of action accrue:

No Time Limit.—Prosecution for murder. (701-108[1]).

Twenty Years.—To recover possession of real property. (657-31).

Ten Years.—To recover on judgment of court of record. (657-5).

Six Years.—For recovery of debt founded on contract, obligation, or liability, except on judgment of domestic court of record; excepting further that actions for recovery of any debt founded upon any contract, obligation, or liability made pursuant to c. 577A shall be governed by c. 577A governed by c. 577A relating to legal capacity of minors regarding medical care; on judgments or decrees of foreign courts of record and domestic nonrecord courts; for taking, detaining, or injuring any goods or chattels, including replevin; personal actions of any nature whatsoever not specifically covered by laws of state (657-1) (judicially construed to include legal malpractice); on contract for compensation for loss, damage, deprivation of land, estate, or interest therein caused by fraud, error, omission, mistake, or misdescription in certificate of title to registered land or entry of memorandum covering registered land (501-217); prosecution for Class A felony (701-108[2][b]).

Five Years.—To prove will, computed from testator's death. (560:3-108).

Four Years.—For breach of contract for sale of goods (490:2-275); for recovery of debt founded on a contract, obligation, or liability arising in a foreign jurisdiction, or on judgments or decrees rendered in foreign nonrecord courts (657-6); to collect delinquent contribution to unemployment compensation fund, computed from last day of last month of quarter when due (383-71); actions under antitrust act (480-24); actions under Drug Dealer Liability Act (tolled during pendency of criminal investigation).

Three Years.—Determination of paternity, computed from birth of child (584-7); prosecution for any felony other than Class A (701-108[c]). Offenses involving fraud or breach of fiduciary within three years after discovery of offense, but no more than six years from expiration of normal limitation period. (708[3][a]).

Two Years.—For libel or slander (657-4); for compensation of damages to person or property (657-7); for personal injury or damage to property resulting from improvements to real property (657-8); for wrongful death (663-3); to annul marriage for physical incapacity (580-28); for tort action against State of Hawaii (662-4) (judicially construed to include tort action against counties); for action against state founded on contract, state statute, regulation of state executive department, or any contract and all claims referred to courts by legislature (661-5); for parking tickets or misdemeanor (701-108[2][d]); for action under horizontal property regime statute (514A-50); recover gifts received by legislator or legislative employee in violation of state code of ethics (84-19).

Causes of action for negligent injury to person or property accrue when injured party knew or in exercise of reasonable care should have discovered that an actionable wrong has been committed. (50 Haw. 150, 433 P.2d 220; 50 Haw. 397, 441 P.2d 636).

Medical Malpractice.—Suits must be brought within two years after injured discovers injury or through reasonable diligence should have discovered injury, but not more than six years after date of alleged act. (657-7.3). Filing claim with medical claim conciliation panel tolls statute of limitations until 60 days after decision by panel is mailed, but tolling cannot exceed 18 months.

One Year.—To contest land registration decree (501-71); for recoveries authorized by federal statute which does not specify period in which suit must be brought (657-11); prosecution for petty misdemeanor (701-108[e]); to contest bulk sale (490:6-110).

Four Months.—Claims against decedent's estate which arose before death of decedent (statute of limitations is three years if notice to creditor not given) (560:3-803); claims against decedent's estate which arose at or after death of decedent (including claims which are absolute, contingent, liquidated, or unliquidated, founded in tort or contract) (560:3-803).

Ninety Days.—Claims against employer under Whistle Blowers' Protection Act.

Uniform Commercial Code adopted. See category Business Regulation and Commerce, topic Commercial Code.

New Actions.—Claim asserted after statute of limitations has run will not be barred if it arose out of timely pleaded factual situation. (HRCP Rule 15[c], 52 Haw. 563, 481 P.2d 310).

Foreign Causes of Action.—Action barred by laws of place where cause of action arose cannot be maintained, except in favor of a resident of Hawaii who has held the claim since it accrued. (657-9).

Disabilities of Plaintiff.—Persons who are insane, imprisoned under a sentence less than life, or minors when a cause of action accrued to them may, after disability is removed, bring an action within period specified for such action under c. 657 pertaining to limitation of actions.

Death of Plaintiff.—Statute of limitation which was running on cause of action belonging to decedent, which was not barred as of date of death, will not bar action less than four months after death. (560:3-109).

Actions by or on Behalf of State.—No statute of limitations can bar any action by or on behalf of state and its agencies, unless state is specifically designated in those statutes as subject to limitation period. (657-1.5).

Absence, Concealment or Disability of Defendant.—If a cause of action accrues against a person who is absent from state or leaves after its accrual (657-18), or if suit on an accrued cause of action is stayed by injunction (657-19), period of absence or time injunction is effective is not deemed any part of time limited for commencement of an action.

If a wrongdoer fraudulently conceals a cause of action from knowledge of person entitled to it, action may be commenced within six years after cause of action is discovered. (657-20).

Death of Defendant.—If wrongdoer dies before wrongful death or survival action is brought against him, suit against his legal representative must be brought within two years after date of plaintiff's injury or death. (663-6).

Interruption of Statutory Period.—No statutory provision allows for circumstance, occurring before statutory period has run, to change date from which statute runs.

Revival of Barred Claims.—To remove bar of statute for debt, it is necessary to show either unconditional promise to pay debt, clear and unqualified acknowledgment of debt from which promise to pay is to be implied, or conditional promise to pay and fulfillment of condition. (23 Haw. 696). Effect of new promise is to revive remedy upon original obligation and to start statute of limitations anew. (57 Haw. 429, 558 P.2d 479). Burden is on plaintiff to prove, by preponderance of evidence, promise sufficient to revive debt otherwise barred by statute of limitations. (11 Haw. 706).

Contractual Limitations.—Parties to contract of sale may prescribe limitation period not less than one year but may not extend it beyond four years. (490:2-725). Parties to other contracts may stipulate time for action if reasonable. (23 Haw. 160).

Pleading.—Statute of limitations must be specially pleaded. (22 Haw. 655). Defense of statute of limitation is personal privilege which party may exercise or waive; court cannot exercise privilege for party. (22 Haw. 721).

PARTITION:

Jurisdiction and Venue.—Circuit courts have jurisdiction. (603-21.7).

Proceedings.—All persons interested must be made parties to suit. (668-2).

Partition in Kind or Sale.—Where partition in kind impracticable or greatly prejudicial, judge may order sale of premises and divide proceeds. (668-7).

PLEADING:

Hawaii Rules of Civil Procedure, substantially identical to Federal Rules of Civil Procedure, took effect on June 14, 1954. Rules have force and effect of law. (Const. Art. V, §6). Hawaii Rules govern only the procedure in the circuit courts in all suits of civil nature, whether at law or in equity, except those set forth in Haw. R. Civ. P. 81. (HRCP 1). Distinction between law and equity has been abolished and the common law system of pleading no longer prevails. See topic Practice. Hawaii Probate Rules adopted Mar. 1, 1995 give procedure before Circuit Courts in all probate, guardianship of property, trust, legal representation for no fault benefits, and determination of death proceedings.

Proof of Claims.—Treated under Uniform Enforcement of Foreign Judgments Act, c. 636C. "Foreign judgment" includes any judgment, decree, or order of court of U.S.

See note at head of Digest as to 1998 legislation covered.

See Topical Index in front part of this volume.

HI – 15

PLEADING . . . *continued*
or of other court entitled to full faith and credit. Copy of exemplified foreign judgment must be filed in office of clerk of appropriate Hawaii court. Judgment will have same effect and is subject to same procedures, defenses, and proceedings as judgment of court of Hawaii. (636C-3). At time of filing, judgment creditor or creditor's lawyer must file with clerk of court affidavit including name and last known addresses of judgment debtor and judgment creditor. Clerk must mail notice of filing to debtor and must note mailing in docket. Judgment creditor may mail notice of filing to debtor and may file proof of mailing with clerk. Failure by clerk to mail notice of filing will not affect enforcement if proof of mailing by creditor has been filed. (636C-4). Cost of filing foreign judgment is $30. Fees for docketing, transcription, or other enforcement proceedings will be provided by law for judgments of court of Hawaii. (636C-6). Right of judgment creditor to bring action to enforce judgment is independent of this chapter.

Note: New Hawaii Probate Rules took effect on Mar. 1, 1995. Hawaii Probate Rules govern procedure in State circuit courts for all Probate, Guardianship of Property, Trust, Determination of Death, and No Fault Legal Representative Proceedings. As of Mar. 1, 1995, Rules of Circuit Courts no longer apply to cases within categories mentioned above, unless Rules of Circuit Courts are specifically incorporated by reference in Hawaii Probate Rules.

Small Claims.—See category Courts and Legislature, topic Courts.

PRACTICE:

Rules.—Hawaii Court Rules cited herein as follows: Hawaii Rules of Civil Procedure (HRCP); Hawaii Rules of Penal Procedure (HRPP); Hawaii Rules of Evidence (c. 626) (HRE); Hawaii Rules of Appellate Procedure (HRAP); Rules of the Supreme Court of the State of Hawaii (RSCH); Rules of the Intermediate Court of Appeals of the State of Hawaii (RICAH); Rules of the Tax Appeals Court of the State of Hawaii (RTACH); Rules of the Circuit Courts of the State of Hawaii (RCCH); Hawaii Probate Rules (HPR); District Court Rules of Civil Procedure (DCRCP); Rules of the District Courts of the State of Hawaii (RDCH); Hawaii Family Court Rules (HFCR); Rules of the Land Court (HLCR).

Common law system in force, except as altered by statute, Hawaiian judicial precedent or Hawaiian usage. (1-1). Distinction between law and equity abolished. Rules of court closely follow Federal Rules of Civil Procedure as amended. Note that rule making power of Supreme Court is constitutionally derived (Art. V, §6); any legislation in area of process, practice, procedure and appeals may be superseded by new court rules or by amendments to existing rules. (See, e.g., category Legal Profession, topic Attorneys and Counselors.) Right to jury trial attaches if (1) maximum authorized term of imprisonment exceeds six months, or (2) for individuals, maximum authorized monetary penalty exceeds $5,000. When organization is charged, maximum authorized penalty may be higher before jury trial right attaches. (77 Haw. 162, 883 P.2d 83).

Jury Verdicts.—Verdict sufficient if at least 5/6 of jurors agree. (635-20). Parties may stipulate that jury shall consist of any number less than 12 or that verdict or finding of stated majority of jurors shall be taken as verdict or finding of jury. (HRCP 48).

Direct Actions Against Insurer.—See category Transportation, topic Motor Vehicles, subhead Direct Actions Against Insurer.

Small Claims.—See category Courts and Legislature, topic Courts.

See also topics Actions, Appeal and Error, Depositions and Discovery, Injunctions, Judgments, Pleading, Process; category Debtor and Creditor, topics Attachment, Executions, Garnishment.

PROCESS:

Civil action commenced by filing complaint with court. Hawaii closely follows Federal Rules, HRCP 3, 4. See topic Practice.

General Requisites.—HRCP 7-10 set out general requisites of complaint.

By Whom Issued.—Upon filing of complaint, clerk of court will issue summons and deliver it for service to person authorized to serve process. At request of plaintiff, separate or additional summons will be issued against any defendants. (HRCP 4[a]).

Who May Serve.—Within state, service of process issued by court of record must be made by sheriff or deputy, by other person specially appointed by court, investigator appointed by director of Commerce and Consumer Affairs, or by any person at least 18 years old who is not party to suit. Within particular county, chief of police or chief's authorized subordinate may serve. (634-21; HRCP 4). Service of process may be made by parties themselves in small claims matters. (633-28[a][1]). Service of process outside of state, see subhead Long Arm Statute, infra.

Personal Service on Individual.—Summons and complaint served together. Service may be made by delivering copy of summons and complaint to individual personally, or if party cannot be found, by leaving copies at home with some person of suitable age and discretion who resides there, or by delivering copies to agent authorized by appointment or law to receive service of process. (HRCP 4[d][1]).

Personal Service on Infant.—Service of process made by delivering copy of summons and complaint personally to: (A) Guardian of infant's property, or if service cannot be made to guardian, then as provided by court order, or (B) infant, if infant is at least 16 years old. (HRCP 4[d][2]).

Personal Service on Incompetent Person.—Service of process made by delivering copy of summons and complaint to: (A) Guardian of person's property, or if living in institution, then to director, or if service cannot be made to either, then as provided by court order, and (B) unless court otherwise orders, also to incompetent person. (HRCP 4[d][2]).

Personal Service on Partnership.—Service made by delivery of copy of summons and complaint to officer, managing or general agent, or to any other agent authorized by appointment or law to receive service of process and, when appropriate by statute, by mailing copy to defendant. (HRCP 4[d][4]). No statutory provision expressly addressing service of process upon partnership. See subhead Personal Service on Association, infra.

Personal Service on Domestic Corporation.—Service of process may be made upon registered agent, officer, or director of corporation found within jurisdiction of court, officer, or board; or if none listed above can be found, then upon manager or superintendent of corporation or any person found in charge of property, business, or office of corporation within jurisdiction. If no officer, director, manager, superintendent, or other person in charge of property, business, or office or corporation can be found within Hawaii, service may be made upon corporation by registered or certified mail, return receipt requested, addressed to secretary of corporation at its principal office. (415-14). See subhead Personal Service on Partnership, supra.

Personal Service on Association.—When two or more persons associate and act under common name, including labor or employer organizations, they may sue or be sued in common name and service of process may be made on officer, trustee, or agent of association, or if none can be found, upon one or more members. (634-30; HRCP 4[d][3]). Where association or its members are nonresidents, transaction of business within state subjects nonresident association and its members to state jurisdiction. Service may be made by registered mail to association at last known address and by filing affidavit with court or state agency where action is pending. Filing deemed service 20 days after filing. (634-35 to 36). See subheads Personal Service on Partnership, supra and Personal Service Outside State, infra.

Personal Service on Joint Stock Company.—No statutory provision expressly addressing service of process on joint stock company. See subhead Personal Service on Partnership, supra.

Personal Service on Foreign Corporation.—Generally same statutory provision governing service on domestic corporations controls foreign corporations. Where foreign corporation has not complied with law relating to registration, service may be made by registered or certified mail, return receipt requested, addressed to secretary of corporation at principal office. (415-4). See subhead Personal Service on Domestic Corporation, supra.

Personal Service Outside State.—Any person who personally, or through agent transacts any business within Hawaii or commits any tortious act within state (judicially construed as injury occurring within state as proximate consequence of tortious conduct in another state) (56 Haw. 306, 536 P.2d 568) or owns, uses, or possesses real property in Hawaii or contracts to insure any person, property, or risk within state may be personally served by service of certified copy of complaint out of Hawaii by authorized process server in state where service is made. (634-35, 36).

Service by Mail.—See subheads Personal Service on Domestic Corporation, Personal Service on Association, Personal Service on Foreign Corporation, supra and Long Arm Statute, infra.

Substituted Service.—In cases where writ of attachment is issued, if it appears by affidavit or otherwise to judge's satisfaction that defendant in attachment was never resident of state, or has left state, or that defendant has secreted so that process cannot be personally served, judge may order service by publication or by registered or certified mail, return receipt requested. If defendant does not appear at trial, court may proceed to hearing and judgment, and may issue execution upon attached property. (634-27).

Service by publication may be made if defendant is unknown or does not reside within Hawaii or, after due diligence, service cannot be made within Hawaii. Above facts must appear by affidavit to satisfaction of court that service cannot be provided as specified in subheads Personal Service Outside of State, supra and Long Arm Statute, infra. Publication must be made in at least one newspaper published in Hawaii and having general circulation in circuit in which action or proceeding has been instituted for period of not less than once each week for four successive weeks. Last publication must not be less than 21 days before date fixed for trial. (634-23).

Long Arm Statute.—See subhead Personal Service Outside State, supra. Statute also allows for service of summons sent by certified, registered, or express mail, postage prepaid, return receipt requested. If defendant cannot be found to serve or mail summons, and facts appear by affidavit or otherwise to satisfaction of court, service by publication is permitted. (634-36). See subhead Service by Publication, supra.

Proof of Service.—In cases where service is made by officer of court, police, sheriff, or appointed investigator, record of service must be endorsed upon back of process in form specified by statute. When service is made by any person specially appointed by court, person must make affidavit of service. (634-22). Proof of service must be made to court promptly. (HRCP 4[g]). When service is made by mail, service must be evidenced by affidavit showing that required papers were sent by registered or certified mail, and by receipt signed by defendant. (634-24). When personal service is made out of state, return of court officer, or affidavit of any other person authorized or appointed by court will evidence service. (634-24).

Nonresident Motorist.—See category Transportation, topic Motor Vehicles.

REPLEVIN:

Proceedings.—Plaintiff in replevin may procure immediate delivery of property by filing with complaint affidavit alleging that he is entitled to possession of property, that property is unlawfully detained, that it has not been taken for taxes or under execution (or if so seized that it is exempt) and giving value and description. (654-1). Plaintiff must furnish bond to defendant in amount and with sureties approved by court. (654-2). Property will then be seized by sheriff and delivered to plaintiff pending trial. (654-3).

Repossession.—On filing redelivery bond by defendant property will be returned to him pending trial. (654-5).

Claims by Third Persons.—Person not plaintiff or defendant may procure delivery of property by complying with provisions applicable to plaintiff. (654-5).

Judgment or Order.—Judgment determines party entitled to possession and damages may be awarded for detention of property. (654-7).

See note at head of Digest as to 1998 legislation covered.

See Topical Index in front part of this volume.

HI – 16

REPLEVIN ... *continued*

Interpleader.—See category Debtor and Creditor, topic Executions.

SEQUESTRATION:

No general statutory provision. Circuit judge may sequester property of spouse against whom decree of divorce or annulment has been rendered to provide maintenance for wife and children. (580-12; HFCR 70[b]).

For seizure of person or property to secure satisfaction of judgment, see HRCP 64. Hawaii law provides for sequestration of real property. Notice must be given in newspaper suitable for advertising judicial proceedings, and premise must be posted by officer serving writ. (634-29).

In actions of desertion and willful neglect, court may order sequestration from third parties of money for support of spouse or child. (575-2).

SERVICE:

See topic Process.

STAY OF EXECUTION:

See topic Appeal and Error; also category Debtor and Creditor, topic Executions.

SUBMISSION OF CONTROVERSY:

Any bona fide controversy may be submitted to the Supreme Court for decision upon agreed statement of facts. Case may be assigned to either Supreme Court or Intermediate Court of Appeals; or assigning judge may require submission to lower court, subject to subsequent appeal. (HRAP 14). See topic Appeal and Error.

VENUE:

Except as noted, actions involving title or possession of real property must be brought in judicial circuit in which property is located, and other actions must be brought in judicial circuit in which claim for relief arose or where majority of defendants reside. (603-36; 666-6).

Against Insurer Under Policy.—Venue is in judicial circuit in which aggrieved person resides or has his principal place of business if purchaser purchased policy within state. (431:10-241).

Change of Venue.—In circuit court, if court, after hearing, determines that fair and impartial trial cannot be had, or it is more fair and equitable to parties to change venue or all parties consent, venue may be changed as court orders. Court must, if venue is improper, either transfer it to court with proper venue or dismiss case. (603-37, 37.5).

Changes of venue in District Court may be ordered if, upon hearing, court determines that it will be more fair and equitable to parties to change venue or if all parties consent. (604-7.3). If venue is improper, court must transfer case or dismiss it. (604-7.4).

District Court.—Venue is in district in which majority of defendants reside or claim for relief arose or in which all defendants can be served. (604-7).

Paternity.—Venue is in county in which child, mother or putative father resides or is found or in which child is born, of if father is deceased, where his estate was or may be probated. (584-8).

Penalty or Forfeiture.—Venue is in judicial circuit in which penalty or forfeiture occurred. (603-36).

Probate.—Venue is in judicial circuit in which decedent had his domicile or owned real property at his death, or, if nondomicillary, in judicial circuit in which any property was located at death. (560:3-201). If proceedings are commenced in more than one court, court where proceedings were first brought hears matter of venue. Other courts hold in abeyance until question of venue is decided. (560:1-303).

Restraint of Trade, Monopolies.—Venue is in circuit in which defendant resides or engages in business or has agent. (480-21).

Small Claims.—Venue is in circuit in which claim arises or majority of defendants reside or in which all defendants may be served. (633-27[b]).

State Ferry System.—Venue is in first judicial circuit or circuit in which aggrieved person resides. (268-15).

Trusts.—Venue is in place of registration for registered trusts; for unregistered trusts venue is in any place trust could have been registered (principal place of administration, or if only land is in trust, place where land is located). (560:7-202, 7-101).

Unauthorized Practice of Law.—Venue is in circuit in which alleged violation occurred. (605-15).

Writs to Courts, Quo Warranto.—Venue is in circuit in which occasion for relief arose. (603-36).

See also category Courts and Legislature, topic Courts.

WITNESSES:

See topic Evidence, subhead Witnesses.

COURTS AND LEGISLATURE

COURTS:

United States District Court.—Clerk's office: 300 Ala Moana Blvd., Rm C-304, Honolulu 96850; mailing address: P.O. Box 50129, Honolulu, Hawaii 96850.

Fee of $120 for costs is required when action is commenced.

Court sits at Honolulu.

Supreme Court of Hawaii.—Supreme Court of Hawaii consists of five judges appointed by Governor for a term of ten years and confirmed by State Senate. (Const. Art. VI, §3).

Jurisdiction.—Supreme Court has appellate jurisdiction of all cases from inferior courts in state, and it has original jurisdiction to issue prerogative writs, and such other writs as may be necessary for execution of its appellate jurisdiction.

Court sits at Honolulu.

Intermediate Appellate Court.—Intermediate appellate court panel shall consist of at least three of four IAC judges. IAC judges appointed by Governor for term of ten years and confirmed by State Senate. (Const. Art. VI, §3).

Jurisdiction.—Intermediate appellate court has concurrent jurisdiction with Supreme Court on all matters, subject to assignment of cases by Supreme Court as set out in subsection 602-5(8). (602-57).

All cases addressed to jurisdiction of Supreme Court or intermediate appellate court shall be filed with Supreme Court as provided by rule of court. (602-5[8]; 607-6).

Court sits at Honolulu.

Circuit Courts.—There are four circuit courts, numbered respectively 1st, 2d, 3d and 5th. 3d Circuit covers entire island of Hawaii and there are three judges. (603-4). In first circuit (covers Oahu and all other islands not mentioned), there are 17 judges. (c. 603.3). 2d Circuit covers Maui County (Islands of Maui, Molokai, Lanai, Kahoolawe and Molokini) and there are three judges. In 5th Circuit (Islands of Kauai and Niihau) there is one. Judges are appointed by Governor for term of ten years and confirmed by State Senate. (Const. Art VI, §3).

Jurisdiction.—Circuit courts have jurisdiction over state law criminal offenses committed within their respective circuits; actions for penalties and forfeitures; civil actions; probate; nonjury cases listed at 603-21.7; appeals from district court where allowed by statute and from agencies. $5,000 minimum amount necessary for jury trial of civil controversy. (604-5). Violations of municipal ordinances tried without jury. (51 Haw. 612, 466 P.2d 422). Circuit and district courts share jurisdiction over misdemeanors. They also share jurisdiction over civil cases involving less than $20,000 but greater than $10,000 when tried without jury. Family courts, district courts and circuit courts share concurrent jurisdiction for certain criminal offenses involving family members.

One of judges of 1st circuit court is annually assigned as judge of Land Court, which has jurisdiction to register title to land anywhere in state.

Each of judicial circuits has district family court. Each circuit has family court division. (Senior Judge of family court of circuit may appoint referees in matters of neglected minors, adoptions, custody, crimes, medical treatment, consent to marriage, employment, enlistment, termination of parental rights, etc., over which family court has exclusive original jurisdiction.) (c.571).

Night Court.—First Circuit has night court that handles nonjury domestic abuse cases and prostitution related cases.

Tax Appeals Court has powers of a circuit court. Court has jurisdiction to hear all matters relating to assessment, levying and collection of property taxes. (c. 232).

District Courts.—District court is established in each of judicial circuits of State with at least one full-time district judge appointed for each circuit; sessions are held as deemed necessary by respective district judges (604-1); civil jurisdiction extends to claims of up to $20,000 and is exclusive up to $10,000 for actions triable without jury or where right to jury trial is waived. (604-5[a]). Transfer to circuit court may be had if party has right to jury trial and makes timely demand and amount in controversy exceeds $5,000. (604-5[b]). District courts have power to enjoin and temporarily restrain harassment (604-10.5) and are accorded equity powers (604-5[a]). District courts share concurrent jurisdiction with circuit courts over violations of ordinances and misdemeanors under state law. However district courts may not try real actions, nor actions wherein title to real property is in question, nor actions for libel, slander, defamation of character, malicious prosecution, false imprisonment, breach of promise of marriage, or seduction, nor may they appoint referees in any cause (604-5[d]); jurisdiction may be had in ejectment proceedings where title to real estate is not in question (604-6); 604-7 sets out specific powers of district courts, including power to subpoena witnesses from any part of state and compel production of books, papers, documents or tangible things and issue garnishee summons throughout State; proper venue is generally determined according to residence of majority of defendants or where claim for relief arose (604-7[d]); but venue may be changed as provided in 604-7.3 and 604-7.4; district courts are courts of record (604-17) from which appeal may be had to Supreme Court or intermediate appellate court, subject to reassignment provisions set out in subsections 602-5(8) and 602-5(9) (641-1[a]). District court judges are appointed by Chief Justice of Supreme Court with approval of Senate.

Small Claims Division of District Court.—Small claims procedure may be elected where matter in controversy does not exceed $2,500 as well as cases involving landlord-tenant disagreements where equitable relief can be granted for orders to repair, replace, refund, reform and rescind. (633-27). Class actions are prohibited. (633-27[d]). Actions in small claims division must be brought in circuit where majority of defendants reside or claim arose or may be brought in any circuit in which all defendants can be served if service on all cannot be made where venue would normally be proper. (633-27[b]). Service is by registered mail, certified mail with return receipt showing delivery within circuit, or as otherwise provided by law or rule of district court; with approval of court, any person may appear on behalf of another; there is no appeal from small claims division. (633-28). Service may be made by parties themselves. (1997, Act 138). Fee for issuing summons, and copies, trial, judgment and satisfaction, as prescribed by statute or rule of court; court may waive costs upon suitable showing; but if costs not paid despite ability to do so, court may deny right to file new case while costs unpaid and deny right to proceed in pending case. (633-29). If counterclaim exceeds $2,500 but is under district court limit ($20,000), jurisdiction is retained. (604-5). Where jury trial is of right and demand is made, case shall be transferred to circuit court and tried under procedure for jury trials. (633-31). Trials may be conducted as justice requires and judge is not bound by rules of evidence, whether statutory or not, except provisions relating to privileged communications. (633-32). Award of costs in discretion of court. (633-34).

Small Claims Courts.—See subhead District Courts, catchline Small Claims Division of District Court, supra.

See note at head of Digest as to 1998 legislation covered.

See Topical Index in front part of this volume.

LEGISLATURE:

Meets annually on third Wed. each Jan. limited to a period of 60 working days, which may be extended for not more than 15 days if approved by two-thirds of membership of each House or if extended by Governor. Special sessions, not to exceed 30 working days, may be called on vote of two-thirds of members of each House. Governor may call special sessions of both Houses or of Senate alone. Each regular session shall be recessed for not less than five days at some period between 20th and 40th days of regular session, as determined by concurrent resolution. (Const., Art. III, §10).

Initiative and referendum not adopted.

Lobbying and lobbyists defined. (97-1).

Lobbyists must register with state ethics commission within five days of becoming lobbyist. (97-2). Renewal of registration required biennially within ten days of opening of each odd-numbered year's legislative regular session. (97-2.5).

REPORTS:

Reports of decisions of Supreme Court and Intermediate Court of Appeals of State are published biennially. Decisions beginning with 44 Hawaii also appear in Pacific Reporter. Reports of Intermediate Court of Appeals' decisions begin May 1980 and also appear in Pacific Reporter. Four volumes of reports of U.S. District Court of Hawaii have been published; but none since 1918. Current decisions appear in Federal Supplement.

Digest of all Hawaii cases (state and federal) from 1846-date is published.

Unofficial Reports.—There is Shepard's Citator of Hawaii Reports and Hawaii Appellate Reports.

STATUTES:

Latest official compilation is Hawaii Revised Statutes, 1993 Replacement Volume. Subsequent statutes and amendments will be published in cumulative pocket part supplements.

Uniform Acts promulgated by National Conference of Commissioners on Uniform State Laws which have been adopted are: Aeronautics (c. 263) (1923); Acknowledgment (502-41 to 101) (1909); Anatomical Gift (327-1 to 14) (1987); Child Custody Jurisdiction (c. 583) (1973); Commercial Code (c. 490) (1967); Common Trust Fund (412:8-402) (1947); Contribution among Tortfeasors (663-11 to 17) (1941); Controlled Substances (c. 329) (1990); Criminal Extradition (c. 832) (1941); Custodial Trust (c. 554B) (1989); Deceptive Trade Practices (c. 481A) (1966); Disclaimer of Transfers by Will, Intestacy or Appointment (560:2-801) (1978); Disposition of Community Property Rights at Death (510-21 to 30) (1973); Division of Income for Tax Purposes (235-21 to 39) (1967); Durable Power of Attorney (c. 551D) (1989); Enforcement of Foreign Judgments (c. 636C) (1964); Estate Tax Apportionment (c. 236A) (1964); Fiduciaries (c. 556) (1945); Foreign-Money Claims (c. 658B) (1990); Fraudulent Transfer (c. 651C) (1985); Guardianship and Protective Proceedings (560:5-101 to 432) (1982); Information Practices (c. 92F) (1988); Interstate Family Support (1997, Act 295); Joint Obligations (c. 483) (1941); Jury Selection and Service (612-1 to 27) (1970); Land Sales Practices (c. 484) (1967); Limited Liability Company (c. 415) (1995); Management of Institutional Funds (c. 517D) (1972); Parentage (c. 584) (1973); Partnership (425-101 to 143) (1914); Premarital Agreement (c. 572D) (1987); Principal and Income Act Revised (c. 557) (1962); Probate Code (c. 560) (1977); Prudent Investor (Act 26) (1997); Rendition of Accused Persons (c. 833) (1971); Residential Landlord and Tenant (c. 521) (1972); Rules of Evidence (626-1 to 3) (1974); Securities (c. 485) (1956); Simultaneous Death (c. 534A) (1993); State Administrative Procedure (c. 91) (1961); Status of Convicted Persons (c. 831) (1969); Statutory Rule Against Perpetuities (c. 525) (1992); Testamentary Additions to Trusts (560:2-511) (1991; repealed effective Jan. 1, 1997); To Secure Attendance of Witnesses From Without a State in Criminal Proceedings (c. 836) (1936); Trade Secrets (c. 482B) (1989); Transfer-On-Death Security Registration (Act 63) (1998); Transfers to Minors (c. 553A) (1985); Trustees Powers (c. 554A) (1985); Unclaimed Property (c. 523A) (1981); Vendor and Purchaser Risk (508-1) (1941).

Uniform Commercial Code enacted, effective Jan. 1, 1967. See category Business Regulation and Commerce, topic Commercial Code.

For text of Uniform Acts falling within the scope of the Martindale-Hubbell Law Digests see Uniform and Model Acts section.

UNIFORM LAWS:

For list of Uniform Acts in force in this state see topic Statutes. For text of Uniform Acts within the scope of the Martindale-Hubbell Law Digests see Uniform and Model Acts section.

CRIMINAL LAW

BAIL:

See topic Criminal Law.

CRIMINAL LAW:

There are no common law crimes in Hawaii. All punishable offenses are defined by statute. (1-1). New penal code enacted in 1972. (cc. 701-712).

Hawaii Rules of Evidence are codified. (c. 62).

Hawaii Rules of Criminal Procedure are codified. (cc. 801-853).

Death Penalty.—None.

Indictment and Information.—Felony charges initiated by indictment of grand jury or information filed by prosecuting attorney. (806-6, 7).

Complaint.—Accused person can be arraigned and prosecuted upon complaint alone. Any defendant in felony case must be furnished copy of complaint before arraignment. (806-6).

Bail.—All criminal offenses bailable except where specifically precluded by statute. (804-3, 11). Amount and conditions of bail discretionary with judge. (804-5, 7.1, 9). Certain mandatory conditions for bail exist. (804-4, 7.1-7.4). Bail is matter of right. Any person charged with criminal offense bailable except where there is serious risk of flight, obstruction of justice, or danger to any person or community. Serious risk presumed where defendant is (1) charged with crime punishable by life imprisonment, (2) has been convicted of violent crime within last ten years, or (3) is on bail, probation, or parole from felony charge for violent crime. (804-3). Probable cause determination made by district court judge within 48 hours of arrest based on affidavits of arresting officer. Defendant provided copy of affidavits and attachments at commencement of hearing. (Hawaii Rules of Penal Procedure, Rule 5[a]).

Interstate Compact for Supervision of Parolees and Probationers in effect. (353-81, 82).

Uniform Act on Status of Convicted Persons in effect. (831-1 to 7).

Uniform Act to Secure the Attendance of Witnesses from Without a State in Criminal Proceedings in effect. (836-1 to 6).

Uniform Criminal Extradition Act, Revised in effect. (832-1 to 27).

Uniform Rendition of Accused Persons Act in effect. (833-1 to 6).

Compensation for victims of criminal acts may be paid by state upon application by injured person or his personal representative to Criminal Injuries Compensation Commission within 18 months after date of injury, death or property damage. Victims eligible for compensation are: (a) persons who are injured or killed by act or omission within state; (b) residents of state who are injured or killed by act or omission in another state; or (c) residents of state who are injured or killed by act of terrorism outside U.S. (1998, Act 239). 18-month period may be extended upon showing of good cause. (351-62[a]). Maximum award limited to $10,000. (351-62[b]). Compensation extends to pecuniary losses or expenses sustained of relatives or persons responsible for victim; eligible expenses are those incurred during treatment for injury sustained. (351-62).

Criminal Injuries Compensation Commission will be funded in part by fees imposed by court on every convicted defendant who is able to pay. (1998, Act 206).

Victims of crime may request court to enforce criminal restitution against convicted defendant in same manner as in civil judgment. (c. 706; 1998, Act 269).

Organized Crime.—C. 842.

Victim/Witness Bill of Rights.—Relating to rights of victims and witnesses in criminal proceedings. (c. 801D). Upon request of sexually assaulted victim, defendant is required to be tested for human immunodeficiency virus (HIV). (1998, Act 238).

Criminal Forfeitures.—Relating to forfeiture of property used in commission of crimes. Law enforcement officer may seize (1) personal property on probable cause; (2) real property pursuant to warrant following pre-seizure hearing in circuit court. Property forfeited to State may, among other things, be sold at public sale. (c. 712A). State has burden of showing that property is subject to forfeiture. Court is allowed to limit scope of forfeiture where it is grossly disproportionate to owner's conduct. (712A-5.5). Holder of immediate reversionary interest has first opportunity to acquire remaining leasehold interest and improvements on property before sale to public. (712A-16).

Registration of Sex Offenders.—Convicted Sex Offenders are required to register with law enforcement agencies. Relevant information will be released upon request to public, law enforcement, and government agencies conducting background checks. (c. 846E-3). Sex offenders who are not registered with designated law enforcement agency must respond to address verification form by mail every 90 days. (c. 846E-6).

Tort Liability of Criminals.—See category Civil Actions and Procedure, topic Damages, subhead Drug Dealers.

Death Penalty.—None.

DEBTOR AND CREDITOR

ACCOUNTS RECEIVABLE:

See topic Assignments.
Uniform Commercial Code adopted.

ASSIGNMENTS:

Uniform Commercial Code adopted. (c. 490). See category Business Regulation and Commerce, topic Commercial Code. Otherwise, common law applies except as noted below.

Assignability.—Following are not assignable under state law: Rights under state and county employees' retirement system (pensions, annuities, returns of contributions, optional and death benefits, etc.) (88-91); public assistance payments and compensation to blind and disabled persons (346-33); workmen's compensation claims (386-57[a]). Employees may assign wage and hour claims (387-12[c], 388-11[b]) to Director of Labor and Industrial Relations for any action necessary for collection, including suit.

Insurance.—Assignability of insurance policies is governed by policy terms. If beneficiary of insurance policy may be changed by sole request of insured, assignment by insured alone may be delivered to insurer, whether pledgee or assignee, and insurer may deal with assignee as owner or pledgee according to terms of assignment until it has received contrary notice in writing at its home office. (431:10-228). Every insurer must pay dividends to assignee of record under written assignment (431:10-229), but that provision does not apply to group life insurance, group annuities, group disability insurance, or any policy specifying to whom dividend is to be paid. (Ibid.). Insured party may assign all or part of incidents of ownership conferred by policy. (431:10D-25).

ASSIGNMENTS . . . continued

Debts of state may be assigned if first approved by comptroller (or, in case of University of Hawaii and department of education, by their respective chief financial officers) who shall draw warrant payable to assignee. (40-58).

Debts to State.—Contractors who contract with state or its subdivision and who have outstanding taxes due to either State or Internal Revenue Service will have their progress payments assigned to either State or Internal Revenue Service to settle tax liability. (103-53). Any officer or employee of any governmental agency who intentionally or knowingly violates this provision shall be fined, imprisoned, or both. (Ibid).

Limited Partnership.—See category Business Organizations, topic Partnerships, subhead Limited Partnership.

Instruments Transferring Title.—Commercial Code or common law governs.

Filing.—See category Business Regulation and Commerce, topic Commercial Code.

Recording.—See categories Business Regulation and Commerce, topic Commercial Code; Documents and Records, topic Records.

Notice.—Commercial Code or common law governs.

Effect.—Commercial Code or common law governs.

Assignment of Wages.—Not valid unless in writing. (388-6, 11). See generally subhead Assignability, supra. Employment agencies may not receive assignment of wages unless approved by Director of Labor and Industrial Relations. (373-11[9]).

Credit Sales.—Assignment shall not cut off any rights of action or defense arising out of credit sale which buyer has against seller. Any assignee shall be subject to buyer's defenses as if assignee is seller. (476-19).

ATTACHMENT:

Actions in Which Allowed.—Attachment of either real or personal property not exempt from execution may issue in any action on an express or implied contract, including actions by nonresident or foreign corporation except in action against State or when garnishment is authorized under c. 652. (651-2).

Courts Which May Issue Writ.—Circuit and district courts may issue writ, except that district judge may not have writ served in circuit outside one in which that district is situated nor may judge issue writ for attachment of real property. (651-1).

In Whose Favor Writ May Issue.—Plaintiff in action, including nonresident or foreign corporation, may have property attached. (651-2).

Against Whom Writ May Issue.—Property of defendant, or any one or more of several defendants, may be attached, but not that of state or political subdivision. (651-2).

Claims on Which Writ May Issue.—Before writ will issue, plaintiff, or someone on plaintiff's behalf, must file affidavit with clerk that defendant is indebted to plaintiff, specifying amount of debt over and above just credits and offsets, and that action is not prosecuted to defraud, hinder, or delay any of defendant's creditors. (651-3). No statute or case in Hawaii as to whether creditor may attach on unmatured or contingent claim.

Grounds.—No statutory restriction.

Proceedings to Obtain.—At time of commencing action or any time afterward but before judgment, plaintiff may have defendant's property attached by applying to court in which action pending, upon filing required affidavit (see subhead Claims on Which Writ May Issue, supra), filing bond and additional security as required (see subhead Attachment Bond, infra) (651-4, 5), and upon approval of court (651-7). Writ is directed to any police officer. (Ibid.)

Attachment Bond.—Plaintiff must file bond in double amount of claim, but not less than $50 in district court or $300 in any other court, together with affidavit of sureties (see category Civil Actions and Procedure, topic Bonds). Bond is not required of state, municipalities, their officers or agents. (651-4). On plaintiff's motion, court may reduce bond to one and one-half times value of property of defendant proposed to be attached for claims exceeding $50,000 (651-4); or on defendant's motion require additional security (651-5).

Levy.—Police officer is to levy on sufficient property, giving preference to clearer title (651-7, 8), 20% greater in value than plaintiff's claim (651-8).

Real property attached by filing in bureau of conveyances true copy of writ with officer's certificate that officer has attached real estate or defendant's interest in it, and describing land with convenient certainty. (651-9[1]).

Personal property capable of manual delivery is attached by taking it into custody. (651-9[2]).

A security (see category Business Regulation and Commerce, topic Commercial Code) is attached by actual seizure thereof. (651-9[3]).

Court may allow compensation to police officer. (651-8). Court may appoint receiver (compensation to be out of that of police officer). (651-14).

Indemnity.—Police officer may require indemnification. (651-10).

Requirements of 651-9 are strictly construed. (81 Haw. 257, 916 P.2d 680).

Lien.—No statutory provision.

Priorities.—Several attachments are executed in order received by police officer. (651-11). Leases, mortgages, sales, devises, etc. after attachment are void in law as against plaintiff in such cases. (51 Haw. 164, 454 P.2d 116).

Release of Property.—Writ is discharged if action is discontinued, dismissed, or if judgment is for defendant (651-16), by defendant filing a bond approved by officer having attachment or by clerk after return (651-17), or upon defendant's motion if writ improperly issued (651-18). Order of discharge on real property is to be recorded in same manner as writ and expenses of attachment must be paid by plaintiff. (651-19).

Sale.—Police officer may sell perishable property. If in interest of parties, court may, after hearing, order sale of property. Sales are in same manner as execution. (651-13).

Return.—Return is to be within same time as is allowed for return of summons. Return is to be accompanied with full inventory of property attached and certificate of proceedings indorsed on writ. (651-15).

Examination.—If on plaintiff's affidavit or on return of writ it appears that attachable property cannot be found, court may require attendance of defendant to give relevant information on oath. (651-12).

Third Party Claims.—No statutory provision.

Vacation or Modification.—See subhead Release of Property, supra.

CONSUMER CREDIT:

Uniform Commercial Credit Code provisions adopted with modifications regarding option to accelerate at will, unconscionability, and limitation on power of parties to choose applicable law. (490:2A-109, 490:2A-108 and 490:2A-106, respectively).

CREDITORS' SUITS:

No special statutes. They may be maintained as civil actions following general rules of pleading.

Creditor who has obtained judgment may apply to court for order that judgment debtor or anyone having knowledge be examined and for production of documents concerning property of debtor and debts owing to him. (636-4).

EXECUTIONS:

Hawaii closely follows Federal Rules of Civil Procedure. See topic Garnishment; category Civil Actions and Procedure, topic Practice.

Kinds of Execution.—Execution and alias executions upon any judgment or decree of court of record, or judge thereof may be issued for payment of money. (651-31). Circuit court out of which execution was issued and is returned wholly or partially unsatisfied may issue alias execution to same circuit or some other circuit. (651-38). Writ of execution or other writ to enforce final order, judgment, or decree of circuit court is available against property of person writ was issued against in whatever circuit property is situated. (651-39).

Exemptions.—See topic Exemptions.

Time for Issuance.—Executions issue at any time during life of judgment. (651-31).

Stay.—Where there is no appeal, judge of court of record may stay execution for equitable reasons upon defendant giving bond and security for payment with costs up to stay. (651-40).

Lien.—No statutory provision for lien of execution before levy.

Levy.—Levy is made by officer taking property into possession. (651-42). Officer shall make inventory of property levied thereon. (651-42). Security (see category Business Regulation and Commerce, topic Commercial Code) is levied on by actual seizure thereof. (651-47).

Return.—All executions and alias executions are returnable within 60 days from date. (651-34). Officer is to pay proceeds sufficient to satisfy judgment, if possible after deducting his costs, expenses, and commissions, to plaintiff or his attorney. (651-44).

Priorities.—Officer is to give priority according to order of time writs were received by him. (651-41).

Claims of Third Persons.—Only defendant's interest is sold. Sale of property not belonging to defendant subjects officer to suit by purchaser deprived by real owner. (651-49). Pledged stock is sold subject to obligations secured. (651-47). Interpleader is provided for where conflicting claims are asserted to personal property seized on execution. (634-12).

Sale.—Officer must advertise sale for 30 days by posting notice in three conspicuous places in district where property is situated, and if on Oahu, by publication in Honolulu newspaper at least three times. (651-43). Unless judgment, interests and costs, and fees and disbursements of officer are paid, officer will, on appointed day sell to highest bidder. (651-44). For cause, he may postpone sale, giving notice of adjournment. (651-45). Officer shall execute and deliver to purchaser whatever certificates of purchase or conveyance are necessary. (651-46). Officer may decline to levy or sell unless person beneficially interested tenders sufficient bond of indemnity. (651-51).

Supplementary Proceedings.—Judgment creditor may apply to court rendering judgment for order that judgment debtor, or anyone having knowledge, be examined and for production of documents concerning property of debtor and debts owing to him. (636-4). Such then may be executed upon in due course.

EXEMPTIONS:

Exemptions.—Real property owned by person with fair market value of $20,000 or less, real property owned by head of family or by individual 65 years of age or older with fair market value of $30,000 or less (651-92), and large number of specified articles of personal property, in some instances limited as to value (651-121) are exempt from attachment, execution, distress and forced sale of every nature and description (c. 651).

Proceeds of sale of exempt property are exempt to same extent allowed in 651-92 for six months from date of their receipt. (651-96).

Debts Against Which Real Property Exemptions Not Allowed.—Mechanic's liens, mortgage or other security instrument liens, tax or improvement district liens, and liens recorded prior to acquisition of interest in and commencement of residence. (651-92).

Debts Against Which Personal Property Exemptions Not Allowed.—Judgments for price of property, security instrument liens, taxes, fines or debts due state. (651-122).

See note at head of Digest as to 1998 legislation covered.

See Topical Index in front part of this volume.

EXEMPTIONS . . . continued

Waiver of Exemption.—If judgment debtors were fully aware of their exemption right in circuit court, then subsequent failure to assert such right in court amounts to waiver. (61 Haw. 590, 607 P.2d 411 [1980]).

Necessity and Manner of Claiming Exemption.—Claimant has right to select such property as is exempt and to advise levying officer. Levying officer shall demand in writing that defendant make such selection and failing such selection by defendant, officer's selection on defendant's behalf is conclusive. (651-61).

Earnings.—Wages and other compensation for personal services due debtor for personal services rendered during 31 days before date of proceeding exempt. (651-121). See topic Garnishment.

Homestead Exemption.—See topic Homesteads.

Surviving spouse or reciprocal beneficiary of decedent domiciled in this state entitled to value in kind from estate not exceeding $5,000 in excess of any security interests therein in household furniture, automobiles, furnishings, appliances, and personal effects. If no surviving spouse or reciprocal beneficiary, children jointly entitled to such property. (560:2-402).

Life insurance, endowment and annuity proceeds and cash values are exempt, except as to premiums paid in fraud of creditors. (431-440).

State pensions, retirement system benefits and unemployment relief benefits are exempt. (653-3, 88-91 and 383-163, respectively).

Other pensions, annuities, retirement or disability allowance, or other benefits accruing under retirement plans qualified under Internal Revenue Code shall be exempt, except as to claims arising under qualified domestic relations orders and as to contributions to plans made within three years before filing of bankruptcy or initiation of civil action against debtor. (651-24).

FORECLOSURE:

See category Mortgages, topic Mortgages of Real Property.

FRAUDULENT SALES AND CONVEYANCES:

Uniform Fraudulent Transfer Act adopted. (c. 651C).

Fraudulent Conveyance.—Due process provides transferee from judgment debtor opportunity to contest claim of fraudulent conveyance. (76 Haw. 32, 868 P.2d 450).

Uniform Commercial Code adopted. See category Business Regulation and Commerce, topic Commercial Code.

Fraud in sale of U.S. surplus goods declared unfair trade practice. (481-21).

Seller must report sale to Tax Commissioner within ten days, and purchaser must withhold payment of price until he receives certificate that taxes are fully paid. (237-43).

The law imposes no duty on the purchaser to see to the application of the purchase price to payment of the seller's debts.

Revised Uniform Deceptive Trade Practices Act adopted. (c. 481A). See category Business Regulation and Commerce, topic Consumer Protection.

Remedies.—Subject to 651C-8, creditors may obtain following: avoidance of transfer or obligation to extent necessary to satisfy creditor's claim, attachment or other provisional remedy against asset transferred or other property of transferee in accordance with c. 651, with injunction against further disposition by either or both debtor or transferee of asset transferred or of other property, appointment of receiver to take charge of asset transferred or of other property of transferee, and/or any other relief circumstances require.

If creditor obtains judgment against debtor, creditor may levy execution on asset transferred or its proceeds. (651C-7).

Bulk Sales.—Uniform Commercial Code Bulk Sales provisions repealed in 1998. (SB 3108 [1998]).

GARNISHMENT:

Creditor, in action against his debtor, may include attorneys, agents, factors, or trustees possessing property of debtor, persons indebted to debtor, and persons holding debtor's money for safekeeping as garnishee. Employers can be reached in certain cases. (652-1). Employee may not be suspended or discharged solely on ground employer was summoned as garnishee for employee's debt. (378-32).

Property Which May Be Reached.—(a) Before judgment: (1) goods and effects of debtor in possession of garnishee; (2) debts due to debtor by garnishee; (3) moneys of debtor in garnishee's possession for safekeeping. (b) After judgment: wages in amount of 5% of first $100 per month, 10% of next $100, and 20% of excess is to be withheld from debtor until judgment is paid. Wages may be garnished before judgment on order of court. (652-1).

Security in lieu of garnishment may be posted by debtor before judgment. (652-1).

Jurisdiction.—Circuit courts and district courts may order garnishment in actions between persons in debtor-creditor relationship. Summons and direction are sufficient notice to enable plaintiff to bring action to trial unless defendant is inhabitant, has office, or was at some time resident of state, in which case copy must be personally served on him or left at his last usual abode. If defendant lives outside district where process is issued, service may also be made by certified or registered mail. (652-1).

Proceedings to Obtain.—Before judgment, creditor may apply for garnishee process to issue. Court may grant application, after hearing with notice to debtor, if probable validity of creditor's claim shown and it appears that property in possession of garnishee not exempt from execution. Garnishee process may issue on verified ex parte motion if reasonable likelihood exists that debtor is not resident, is about to leave jurisdiction or has fraudulently concealed or disposed of property. (652-1.5). After judgment, creditor may summon garnishee to make full disclosure or, if action brought in district court, may, ten days after judgment, file certified copy of judgment and affidavit of amount due with employer. (652-1).

Answer of Garnishee.—Garnishee, on or before return day, may file return under oath containing full disclosure. Copy must be served on plaintiff or his attorney on or before return day. (652-1).

Practice.—After being served, garnishee must secure money or property concerned in his hands to pay whatever judgment plaintiff recovers. (652-1). Garnishee may defend principal. (652-2). After judgment in favor of plaintiff, garnishee fund is liable. Plaintiff is entitled to an order including garnishee fund in execution. If garnishee does not pay officer's demand, garnishee is liable for judgment. However, garnishee may deduct all his demands against defendant, whether or not due. (652-2). As to debts not due until some time in future, judgment is a lien on debt until due and payable. (652-10). Court, on consent of plaintiff or motion of defendant or garnishee, may release that portion of garnishee fund which is excessive. (652-1). Garnishee will not be liable to anyone for nonpayment where in good faith he believes garnishment is involved. (652-2).

Adverse Claims.—Property or moneys may be paid into court on its order, less reasonable attorneys' fees and costs allowed by court, and garnishee will be discharged. Or, garnishee may apply for an interpleader order. (652-9).

Judgment.—See subhead Practice, supra.

Earnings.—See subhead Property Which May Be Reached, supra.

State, county and municipal wages, etc. may be garnished as provided in c. 653 and c. 78.

Exempt from garnishment are: unemployment relief benefits (383-163), state pensions (653-3) and retirement system benefits (88-91), and proceeds and cash values of life insurance, endowment and annuity contracts (431:10-232).

HOMESTEADS:

Limitation of Value.—Real property consisting of one piece of land not to exceed one acre and dwellings thereon are exempt from levy and sale on execution as follows: (1) Such property of value not exceeding $30,000 owned by head of family or person 65 or older; (2) such property of value not exceeding $20,000 owned by any other person. (651-92).

Limitation on Area.—None.

Debts or Liabilities Against Which Exemption Not Available.—No exemption for prior existing lien of property, mechanic's lien, lien created by security instrument, federal or state tax lien, county or state district improvement lien. (651-92[b]).

Proceeds of Sale.—Priority of distribution of sale proceeds: Exemption amount to property owners, attorneys' fees and costs of sale, satisfaction of underlying lien, and subsequent liens, remainder to property owner. (651-95). Exempt proceeds protected for six months. (651-96).

Rights of Surviving Spouse and Family.—Surviving spouse of decedent domiciled in this state entitled to homestead allowance of $5,000. If no surviving spouse, minor and dependant children are entitled to equal shares of allowance. (560:2-401).

See also categories Family, topic Husband and Wife; Property, topics Curtesy, Deeds, Dower, Real Property.

JUDGMENT NOTES:

Not recognized.

LEVY:

See topics Attachment, Executions.

LIENS:

Persons who have liens on property entrusted to their care for value of their services include: Warehousemen (507-62); common carriers (271-18); laundrymen (507-13); adjusters (507-1); innkeepers (486K-2); auto repairmen (437B-20).

Foreclosure in each case is by sale after publication of notice. (c. 507). Uniform Commercial Code adopted in Hawaii. (c. 490). See category Business Regulation and Commerce, topic Commercial Code.

Physicians, surgeons, dentists and hospitals rendering services to injured persons have a lien for their charges on judgment recovered for such injuries. (507-4).

Persons making improvements, repairs or alterations upon personal property have a lien thereon for their work, labor and material. Foreclosure is by suit as in case of mechanics' liens. (507-18, 19). But if lien does not exceed $150, lienholder may sell personal property under certain conditions. (507-23).

Bailees may sell personal property when a lien has attached for 60 days and is unsatisfied. Four weeks notice by publication necessary. (507-5).

Department of Social Services may require lien on real property interests (346-29.5) or estate of recipient of public assistance (346-37).

Enforcement is by proceeding in pertinent circuit court by service of summons as in other cases. There is no priority among lienors who have properly filed; all intervene or are consolidated for trial and share pro rata, except laborers' claims up to $300 which have priority to that extent. (507-46, 47).

Equitable Liens.—Equitable lien not judicially recognized until judgment rendered declaring existence. (76 Haw. 396, 866 P.2d 951).

Mechanics' Liens.—Mechanics or material men have a lien, for agreed price of labor or material furnished, on both building and land. (c. 507, Part II).

Unreasonable extension of credit to contractor by supplier is defense to lien. (507-49).

Application for lien and notice of claim of lien must be filed with clerk of circuit court within 45 days after completion, and suit to perfect and foreclose lien must be begun within three months after lien attaches. Notice of completion must be published by owner or contractor twice, seven days apart, and date of filing of affidavit of publication by newspaper with clerk of pertinent circuit court constitutes "date of completion." In absence of such publication and filing of affidavit, "date of completion" is one year after substantial physical completion. Mortgages recorded prior to

LIENS . . . continued

commencement of construction operations enjoy priority. Subsequent mortgages enjoy priority to extent that proceeds are used for construction, if mortgage recites that loan has been made in whole or in part to pay for improvements. (507-43).

Where the improvement is to property under lease or agreement of sale, the interest of the fee owner is subject to the lien if the lease, contract of sale, etc., requires the construction of the improvements. (507-42).

Discharge of Lien.—Owner, lessee, principal contractor or intermediate subcontractor may discharge lien by filing with circuit court of county in which property is located or with land court (if registered land is affected) cash or bond for twice amount of claim under lien. (507-45).

Attachment Lien.—See topic Attachment.

Attorney's Lien.—See category Legal Profession, topic Attorneys and Counselors.

Collateral Security.—See topic Pledges.

Execution Lien.—See topic Executions.

Judgment Lien.—See category Civil Actions and Procedure, topic Judgments.

Landlord's Lien.—See category Property, topic Landlord and Tenant.

Liens on Exempt Property.—See topic Exemptions.

Liens on Homestead.—See topic Homesteads.

Real Estate Mortgage Lien.—See category Mortgages, topic Mortgages of Real Property.

Tax Lien.—See category Taxation, topic Property Taxes, subhead Lien.

Public Works.—Contractor must give satisfactory bond conditioned for faithful performance of contract and prompt payment for all labor and materials furnished to him and used in the work. Such bond must be for 50% of contract price or of cost as previously estimated by the Government, whichever is higher. Bond inures to the benefit of any person entitled to file a claim for labor or materials, and all such persons have a right of action on such bond. (103-34). Action must be filed within four months of "final settlement as determined by the public body involved." (507-17).

Redemption.—There is no right of redemption of property sold under foreclosure of a lien, except in case of a tax lien. See category Taxation, topic Property Taxes, subhead Redemption.

Condominiums.—Rights of persons holding liens involving condominiums are regulated in detail. (514A-90). See category Civil Actions and Procedure, topic Judgments, subhead Judgment Liens.

MECHANICS' LIENS:

See topic Liens.

PLEDGES:

Governed by c. 486M (pawnbrokers and secondhand dealers). Minimum retention 15 calendar days in counties with population of less than 300,000 and 30 calendar days in counties with population of 300,000 or more. (486M-4). Pawnbrokers may not accept motor vehicles, boats, homes or goods worth over $5,000. (445-134.13).

Any goods not redeemed within last holding period may be forfeited and become property of pawnbroker. (445-134.15). Holding period means time period not less than 30-days after maturity date. (445-131).

Uniform Commercial Code adopted. (c. 490). See category Business Regulation and Commerce, topic Commercial Code.

RECEIVERS:

Receivers may be appointed under certain circumstances in attachment (651-14) and divorce (580-13) cases.

REDEMPTION:

See topic Liens; categories Mortgages, topic Mortgages of Real Property; Taxation, topic Taxes.

SUPPLEMENTARY PROCEEDINGS:

See topic Executions.

TRUSTEE PROCESS:

See topic Garnishment.

USURY:

See category Business Regulation and Commerce, topic Interest.

DISPUTE RESOLUTION

ALTERNATIVE DISPUTE RESOLUTION:

See topic Arbitration and Award.

ARBITRATION AND AWARD:

Provision in written contract to arbitrate future controversy arising from contract or written agreement to arbitrate existing controversy is enforceable. (658-1). Agreement may provide that judgment of circuit court be entered upon award and judicial circuit in which judgment may be served. (658-2). In contract containing arbitration clause, where dispute arises from general allegations of fraud in inducement, contract still subject to arbitration. Unless there is claim made that there was fraud in inducement of arbitration clause, clause is valid and binding as remedy for general claim of fraud in inducement of contract as a whole. (81 Haw. 1, 911 P.2d 721). If any issue in action or proceeding is referable to arbitration, trial of entire action or proceeding must be

stayed until arbitration is complete on issue or parties have waived rights to arbitration. (658-5; 81 Haw. 193, 914 P.2d 1386).

Uniform Arbitration Act has not been adopted.

Form and Requisites of Submission.—Generally, agreement governs. (658-1-2).
Naming Arbitrators.—If no method provided or there is lapse in naming arbitrator, then on application by either party, circuit court will name arbitrator or arbitrators. (658-4). Arbitration is by one arbitrator unless otherwise provided. (658-4).
Compelling Compliance.—Party aggrieved may apply to circuit court for order that arbitration proceed according to agreement. (658-3). Jury trial may be demanded (658-3), but hearing shall be held in summary manner provided for hearing motions (658-3, 6). Hawaii Rules of Civil Procedure do not apply to applications to compel compliance. (HRCP 81[5]).

Contracts to Arbitrate Future Disputes.—See introductory paragraph, supra.

Rescission.—Neither contract nor submission is revocable except on grounds at law or in equity for revocation of any contract. (658-1).

Powers of Arbitrators.—Arbitrator or majority of arbitrators may summon witnesses to attendance and, in proper case, to bring documents; enforcement may be had by petition to circuit court. (658-7).

Stay of Other Suit.—If applicant is not in default, circuit court will, on application, stay trial of any action on issue referable to arbitration until after arbitration. (658-5).

Award and Enforcement Thereof.—
Award must be in writing and acknowledged or proved in like manner as deed and delivered to one of parties or his attorney, and copy served personally or by certified or registered mail on each of other parties. (658-8).
Motion to vacate, modify, or correct must be served on adverse party within ten days after award is served. (658-11; 72 Haw. 41, 805 P.2d 445). Arbitrator's authority terminates once award is issued unless such authority is reinstated in writing by all parties or matter is returned to arbitrator by appropriate court. (73 Haw. 201, 830 P.2d 503).
Confirming Award.—Within one year from award, party may apply for order from circuit court confirming award. Unless court vacates, modifies, or corrects award, it must grant order. (658-8).
Vacating Award.—Upon application, court may vacate award if it was procured by corruption, fraud or undue means; if arbitrator was partial or corrupt; if arbitrator wrongfully refused to hear material evidence, postpone hearings upon sufficient cause shown, or other misconduct prejudicial to party; or arbitrator exceeds his powers or imperfectly executes them. (658-9).
Modifying or Correcting Award.—To effect intent of award and promote justice, court may modify or correct award if miscalculation of figures or misdescription of person, thing, or property is evident, if award is on matter not submitted unless merits not affected, or where imperfect in form not affecting merits. (658-10).

Judgment on Award.—
Entry.—Order confirming, modifying or correcting award, upon filing with clerk, constitutes entry of judgment. (658-12).
Effect is same as in civil action and may be enforced accordingly. (658-14).
Appeal may be taken unless precluded by agreement. (658-15). Review of award is restricted to seven specific grounds included in §§658-9, 658-10. (74 Haw. 210, 847 P.2d 652).

Mandatory Arbitration.—
Lease Rents—Mining Lease.—Person in possession of land for which mining lease is auctioned by Board of Land and Natural Resources may require that damage and lease rent be determined by arbitration. Proceedings are governed by c. 658. (182-3[b]).
Residential Leases.—Rents to be renegotiated under lease of two acres or less and having term of at least 20 years must be submitted to Housing and Community Development Corporation of Hawaii (per Act 350) for arbitration if parties cannot agree on renegotiated rent. (519-2). Rents being renegotiated under subleases issued by housing corporation (cooperative) must be submitted to arbitration by Housing and Community Development Corporation of Hawaii (per Act 350) if parties fail to reach agreement. (519-3).
Motor Vehicle Insurance.—Dispute relating to motor vehicle (per Act 251) insurance policy may be submitted to arbitration by claimant or insurer by written request filed with clerk of circuit court. Arbitrator is appointed by administrative judge of circuit court. Proceedings are governed by c. 658. Award may be appealed to circuit court. (431:10C-213).
Condominiums.—Dispute between condominium apartment owners or between owners and condominium association, its board of directors or managing agent may be submitted to arbitration by either party. Award is enforceable by circuit court but is subject to trial de novo. Subject matter must relate to interpretation, application or enforcement of c. 514A or project declaration, bylaws or house rules. Following matters are excluded from mandatory arbitration: Dispute involving real estate commissioner, mortgagee, developer, contractor or subcontractor of project, actions seeking equitable injunctive relief involving threatened property damage or health or safety of persons, collection of assessments, personal injury claims, claims in excess of $2,500 if insurance coverage would be invalidated, or claims determined by court to be unsuitable for arbitration. See also category Civil Actions and Procedure, topic Actions, subhead Conditions Precedent.

Tort Cases.—All tort cases with probable jury award value of below $150,000 filed in circuit court are subject to determination under court-annexed mandatory arbitration program. (601-20, Hawaii Arbitration Rule 6). Hawaii Arbitration Rules govern procedures and requirements for exemption and inclusion in program.

International Business.—Hawaii International Arbitration, Mediation, and Conciliation Act adopted to encourage use of arbitration to resolve disputes arising out of international relationships and to maximize private autonomy over such proceedings. (658D).

See note at head of Digest as to 1998 legislation covered.

See Topical Index in front part of this volume.

ARBITRATION AND AWARD... *continued*

Alternative Dispute Resolution.—

Mandatory ADR.—At court's discretion, or upon motion, parties may be ordered to participate in ADR process subject to conditions imposed by court. (Circuit Ct. R. 12.2, effective 1/1/97). Court is not authorized to order binding arbitration or deprive party of right to trial. Parties must confer in person regarding ADR options, and must state in pretrial statement ADR process to which they have agreed or identify objecting party and reasons for objection. (R. 12[b][6], [7]). Pretrial statement must be filed within eight months after filing of complaint if no extension granted by court. (R. 12[b]). Additionally, ADR options will be discussed at status conference conducted by Civil Admin. Judge. (R. 12[c]). In complex cases, Judge may establish meeting deadlines for meeting with Judiciary Center for ADR. (R. 12[K][3][i]).

Judiciary Center for ADR.—Center established within judiciary to facilitate mediation, neutral fact-finding and negotiated consensus-building. Focus is on reducing costs of litigation over public issues, allocation of resources. (c. 613). Evidence relating to mediation is inadmissible except as it pertains to criminal acts or fraud. (626-1, HRE 408).

DOCUMENTS AND RECORDS

ACKNOWLEDGMENTS:

To entitle any conveyance or other instrument to be recorded, it must be acknowledged. (502-41).

Within State.—Acknowledgments may be taken before registrar of conveyances, his deputy, judge of court of record, or notaries public. (502-50).

Outside State But Within U.S.—Acknowledgment of instrument executed in another jurisdiction of U. S. for recording or to be read in evidence in Hawaii may be made before any officer of such jurisdiction who is there authorized to take acknowledgments, and certificate is sufficient if in form which would entitle instrument to be recorded in jurisdiction where acknowledged or in form provided by Hawaii statutes (see subhead Forms, infra). For reading into evidence, burden of proving due execution of instrument is on person relying thereon. (502-45). Burden can be met by attaching to acknowledgment certificate of Secretary of State where acknowledging officer resides, under seal of, or certificate of clerk of court of record where officer resides or where he took acknowledgment or certificate of executive officer or clerk of court of record of dependency of U. S., stating that officer who took acknowledgment was, at time of taking, duly authorized to take acknowledgments in jurisdiction, that certifying officer is well acquainted with handwriting of officer taking acknowledgment and that he believes signature to acknowledgment is genuine. (502-46).

Outside U.S.—Acknowledgment of instrument executed outside U. S. may be made by: (a) Any officer now authorized by laws of Hawaii; (b) any officer of U. S. diplomatic service, certified under his seal of office; (c) any person authorized by law of his country to take acknowledgments, when accompanied by certificate of his authority and that acknowledgment complies with laws of his country. Such certificate may be made by diplomatic or consular officer of U. S. or by diplomatic or consular officer of such foreign country resident in Hawaii. (502-47).

Officers of U. S. Armed Forces.—Acknowledgments of persons outside U. S. or in Armed Forces may be taken by officers of U. S. Armed Forces so authorized by Congress to exercise powers of notary public. (502-47).

General Requirements as to Taking.—See subhead Forms, infra. (502-48).

Fee for taking acknowledgment is $4 for each party and $2.50 per signature for each duplicate original. (456-17).

General Requirements of Certificate.—Notary's signature, typed or printed name of notary, and date of expiration of notary's commission must be noted. Seal of notary must be affixed by engraved seal of office or rubber stamp facsimile. (456-3).

Changes, erasures or interlineations in the instrument acknowledged must be initialed by the notary. Such initialing is prima facie evidence of extent of the interlineations, etc., and of fact that they were made prior to acknowledgment of the instrument, but does not preclude proof to the contrary. (502-61).

Married women acknowledge in the same manner as other persons. (502-44).

Attorneys in Fact.—See subhead Forms, infra.

Corporations.—See subhead Forms, infra.

Foreign Acknowledgments.—See subheads Within Another U. S. Jurisdiction; Outside U. S., supra.

Effect of Acknowledgment.—Duly acknowledged instrument is entitled to be recorded (502-41, 47, 50) and is admissible in evidence without further proof (502-47, 81).

Proof by Subscribing Witness.—As substitute for acknowledgment, instrument may be recorded on proof of execution by subscribing witness (e.g., notary public) or of handwriting of execution person and subscribing witness before judge of circuit court. (502-50).

Alternative to Acknowledgment or Proof.—When any instrument required to be acknowledged or proved has been executed by person then permanently or temporarily resident at some place where acknowledgment or proof cannot be made, such instrument may be declared acceptable for recordation by order of judge issued upon such testimony and evidence as are sufficient in judgment of judge to establish genuineness and authenticity. (502-47).

Authentication of certificate of notary in Hawaii for use elsewhere is by certificate of clerk of circuit court of judicial circuit in which he is commissioned (456-4). Fee $1. (456-9). As to authentication of certificate taken elsewhere for use in Hawaii, see subhead Within Another U. S. Jurisdiction, supra.

Forms.—Acknowledgments must be in substantially following forms:

Forms

(1) *Natural person* acting in own right. State of Hawaii, County of . . . . . ., ss. On this . . . . . . day of . . . . . ., 19. . . ., before me personally appeared A B (or A B and C D) to me known to be the person (or persons) described in and who executed the foregoing instrument, and acknowledged that he (or they) executed the same as his (or their) free act and deed. (Signature, title and seal of officer).

(2) *Person not known to officer.* Use same form up to "A B" and continue as follows: "Satisfactorily proved to me to be the person described in and who executed the within instrument, by the oath of C D, a credible witness for that purpose, to me known and by me duly sworn, and he, A B, acknowledged that he executed the same freely and voluntarily for the uses and purposes therein set forth" (502-43).

(3) *Acknowledgment by attorney in fact.* Use same form up to "foregoing instrument" and continue as follows: "In behalf of C D, and acknowledged that he executed the same as the free act and deed of said C D."

(4) *Corporation or partnership.* "(Caption) On . . . . day of . . . . . ., 19. . . ., before me appeared A B, to me personally known, who, being by me duly sworn (or affirmed), did say that he is the president (or other officer or agent of the corporation or partnership) of (describing the corporation or partnership) and that the instrument was signed and sealed in behalf of the corporation (or partnership) by authority of its board of directors (or trustees), and said A B acknowledged the instrument to be the free act and deed of the corporation (or partnership)."

(5) *Corporation acknowledging by individual as its attorney.* "(Caption) On this . . . . . . day of . . . . . ., 19. . . ., before me personally appeared A B, to me personally known, who being by me duly sworn (or affirmed) did say that he is the attorney in fact of C D (here name the corporation) duly appointed under power of attorney dated the . . . . . day of . . . . . ., 19. . . ., recorded in book . . . . . ., at page . . . . . as document no . . . . .; and that the foregoing instrument was executed in the name and behalf of said C D by said A B as its attorney in fact; and said A B acknowledged said instrument to be the free act and deed of C D."

In case enabling power of attorney has not been recorded, omit reference to its place of record and insert in lieu thereof the words "which said power of attorney is now in full force and effect."

(6) *Corporation acknowledging by another corporation as its attorney.* "(Caption) On this . . . . . . day of . . . . . ., 19. . . ., before me personally appeared A B to me personally known, who, being by me duly sworn (or affirmed), did say that he is the president (or other officer or agent of the corporation or joint stock company acting as attorney) of C D (here name the corporation or joint stock company acting as attorney) and that said C D is the attorney in fact of E F (here name the corporation or joint stock company in whose behalf the attorney is acting) duly appointed under power of attorney dated the . . . . . . day of . . . . . ., 19. . . ., recorded in book . . . . . . at page . . . . . . as document no . . . . .; that the foregoing instrument was executed in the name and behalf of E F by the C D as its attorney in fact; that the said instrument was so executed by C D by authority of its board of directors; and A B acknowledged the instrument to be the free act and deed of said E F."

In case the enabling power of attorney has not been recorded, omit reference to its place of record and insert in lieu thereof the words "which power of attorney is now in full force and effect." (502-41).

AFFIDAVITS:

Generally, notaries public may administer oaths. (456-13). Fee is $4 for administration of oath, including certificate of oath; $2.50 for affixing certificate of oath. No statute governs affidavits, as such, executed outside state. See topic Acknowledgments.

General Requirements as to Administration.—No statute governs affidavits as such. As matter of practice, they can be recorded (see topic Acknowledgments), but will not be read in evidence if objected to.

General Requirements of Jurat.—Every notary public has seal of office which includes name, words, "notary public" and "State of Hawaii". (456-3).

Form

State of Hawaii   )

)

City and County of Honolulu   )   ss:

(or County of . . . .)

Comes now . . . ., being duly sworn, on oath deposes and says:

. . . .

Further, affiant says not.   . . . .

Subscribed and sworn to before me

this . . . . day of . . . . . ., 19. . .

(seal) . . . .

Notary Public, ... Judicial Circuit,

State of Hawaii.

My commission expires: . . . .

Alternatives to Sworn Affidavits.—No statute governs alternatives to sworn affidavits, as such. Declaration of counsel may substitute for affidavits of counsel "in support or opposition of motions filed in Circuit Court" (HRCP 7) and must conclude with substantially the following statement: "I declare (or certify, verify, or state) under penalty of law that the foregoing is true and correct. Executed on (date)," (followed by signature of counsel).

NOTARIES PUBLIC:

Qualification.—Appointee must be resident of state, possess qualifications required of public officers, and be at least 18 years old. Oath for faithful discharge of duties must

---

See note at head of Digest as to 1998 legislation covered.

See Topical Index in front part of this volume.

NOTARIES PUBLIC . . . *continued*

be taken; oath must be filed in department of attorney general. (456-2). Each notary public must execute at own expense official surety bond in sum of $1,000 in Circuit Court. (456-5).

Authentication.—All appointed and commissioned notaries public must file literal or photostatic copy of person's commission, impression of person's seal, and specimen of person's official signature with clerk of Circuit Court in which notary resides. Notary may file above documents with clerk of any other Circuit Court. (456-4). Notary public must authenticate all official acts with seal, signature, typed or printed name, and declaration of date of expiration of commission. (456-3). See topic Acknowledgments.

Seal.—Notary must constantly keep engraved seal of office or rubber stamp facsimile with notary's name, words "notary public" and "State of Hawaii". Notary public must authenticate all official acts, attestations, certificates, and instruments with seal. Upon resignation, death, expiration of term without reappointment, or removal from or abandonment to office, notary public must immediately deliver seal to attorney general. (456-3).

Powers and duties of notaries are those usually appertaining to office. Notary shall record at length all acts, protests, depositions, and other things noted or done in official capacity. (456-15). Notary may sign for person physically unable to sign document, under certain conditions. (c. 456; 456-19). Powers and duties of notaries in government service are provided for in 456-18.

Territorial Extent of Powers.—Official character and acts of any notary will be certified by clerk of any court in which such notary has filed commission, seal, and signature. (456-4).

Expiration of Commission.—Notaries public serve four year terms from date of commission, unless sooner removed by attorney general for cause after hearing. (456-1). Notary must add to stamped, embossed, or impressed seal notary's official signature, typed or printed name of notary and statement showing date of expiration of commission. (456-3).

Fees for notarial acts vary from $2.50 to $5. (456-17).

Commissioners of Deeds.—No statutory provision.

Officers of U.S. Armed Forces.—No statutory provision.

RECORDS:

Registrar of Bureau of Conveyances in Department of Land and Natural Resources of State of Hawaii at Honolulu, Hawaii, has charge of records related to property. (502-1, 11). Registrar of Conveyances is assistant registrar of Land Court of State of Hawaii for land registered under Torrens system. (501-9). Department of land and natural resources may adopt rules pursuant to c. 91 relating to bureau of conveyances and to repeal and establish fees. (c. 502).

Judgments filed and recorded in land court or bureau of conveyances must contain social security number, general excise taxpayer identification number, or federal employer identification number of person against whom judgment is rendered. (501-151).

Deeds, mortgages, bills of sale, chattel mortgages, leases for more than one year, and the like must be recorded in office of Registrar of Conveyances in Honolulu, in order to constitute notice to bona fide purchasers. They must be acknowledged or proved to be entitled to record. (c. 502). See category Property, topic Deeds.

Uniform Commercial Code adopted. (c. 490). See category Business Regulation and Commerce, topic Commercial Code.

Uniform Information Practices Act adopted with significant variations. (c. 92F).

Recordable Instruments.—Every conveyance or instrument acknowledged or proved or certified may be recorded (502-81), including deeds, mortgages, leases, powers of attorney, bills of sale, assignments, grants of easements, maps or plats (if special requirements of 502-17 are met), financing statements, affidavits, judgments, lien notices, notice of lis pendens, etc.

Effect of Not Recording.—All deeds, leases for more than one year, mortgages of any interest in real estate, or of other conveyances of real estate within the state not recorded are void as against any subsequent purchaser, lessee, or mortgagee, in good faith and for a valuable consideration, not having actual notice of the conveyance of the same real estate or any portion thereof or interest therein, whose conveyance is first duly recorded. (502-83).

Place of Recording.—Recording of instruments affecting real property, including filing of instruments affecting land registered under Torrens Act, are recorded or filed at Office of the Assistant Registrar of the Land Court of the State of Hawaii, 1151 Punchbowl Street, Rm. 122, Honolulu, Hawaii 96813; mailing address: P.O. Box 2867, Honolulu, Hawaii 96803.

Requisites of Recording.—Recording of document larger than 8¹/₂ × 11 inches may be refused. Top 3¹/₂ inches of first page of each document must be reserved for recording information. Following 1 inch shall be reserved for information showing to whom document should be returned beginning 1¹/₂ inches from left margin, and not exceeding 3¹/₂ inches per line. First page shall include, if possible, all names of grantors and all names and addresses of grantees, type of document, and tax map key number. When grantee is corporation or partnership, document must contain state where entity is registered and entity's address. (502-31). Marital status and address of grantee must be shown. (502-34). All names in instrument shall be typewritten, stamped or printed beneath all signatures. (501-108). Any instrument affecting mortgage, lien or lease must refer to book and page or document number where original mortgage, lien or lease is recorded. Instruments affecting real property must be acknowledged or proved, or in case of judgments, certified, unless grantor is State of Hawaii or U.S. agency. (502-41).

Fees.—Fixed by 502-25 unless otherwise provided by rules adopted by Department of Land and Natural Resources, pursuant to c. 91. Fees for Torrens documents are fixed by 501-218 unless otherwise provided by rules adopted by Department of Land and Natural Resources, pursuant to c. 91.

Tax Lien.—Recordation by Department of Taxation with Bureau of Conveyances of certificate setting forth taxpayer's name, address, and taxes due shall be sufficient to create lien on land registered in land court. (231-33).

Torrens Act.—Land Court registration is provided for by c. 501. Documents purporting to convey or affect land registered with Land Court are not effective as conveyance and do not bind land until registered in Office of Assistant Registrar of Land Court in Honolulu. (501-101). See category Property, topic Deeds.

Transfer of Decedent's Title.—Uniform Probate Code, but not 1975 or 1977 Official Amendments, adopted (c. 560), effective July 1, 1977. Certified copy of order of distribution must be recorded in bureau of conveyances or for registered land, filed with office and Assistant Registrar of Land Court.

Filing Under Uniform Commercial Code is with Office of the Registrar of Conveyances, Bureau of Conveyances, 1151 Punchbowl Street, Honolulu, Hawaii 96813. (c. 490:9-401). Filing fees are listed in 502-25 unless provided for by rules adopted by Department of Land and Natural Resources, pursuant to c. 91.

Requisites of Filing Under Uniform Commercial Code.—Financing statement under Uniform Commercial Code must contain names and addresses of debtor and secured party, statement indicating types of or describing items of collateral, and be signed by debtor. If financing statement covers crops, timber to be cut, minerals or is fixture filing, it must contain description of real estate and record owner or lessee. (490:9-402). Any instrument relating to security investments filed under Uniform Commercial Code must refer to book and page or document number (effective Dec. 31, 1989) where original financing statement is filed or state that original instrument is unrecorded. (502-33). See category Business Regulation and Commerce, topic Commercial Code.

Vital Statistics.—Report of births, deaths, and marriages must be filed with Office of Health Statistics Monitoring, Dept. of Health, State of Hawaii, P.O. Box 3378, Honolulu, Hawaii 96801, Attn. Vital Records. (c. 881). Fee of $10 is charged for first certified copy of each document requested, additional reports of same document requested at same time are $4.

SEALS:

Seals in Hawaii are mere matters of form which never partake of essence and substance of agreement and are not necessary to validity of mortgages, deeds or bonds. (40 Haw. 92).

Notary public shall constantly keep engraved seal of office or rubber stamp facsimile seal. Notary public shall authenticate notary's official acts, attestations, certificates and instruments therewith. (456-3).

Uniform Commercial Code adopted. (c. 490). See category Business Regulation and Commerce, topic Commercial Code.

Corporate Seals.—Regulated by 415-4(3).

Effect of Seal.—Seal on writing evidencing contract for sale of goods or offer to buy or sell goods does not constitute sealed instrument. (490:2-203). Sealed instruments remain negotiable under Uniform Commercial Code. (490:3-113).

TORRENS ACT:

See topic Records; category Property, topic Deeds.

VITAL STATISTICS:

See topic Records.

EMPLOYMENT

EMPLOYER AND EMPLOYEE:

See topic Labor Relations.

LABOR RELATIONS:

Department of Labor and Industrial Relations administers all matters relating to employment law enforcement (c. 371), including unemployment compensation (cc. 383 and 385), wages and hours of labor (c. 387), payment of wages and other compensation (c. 388), child labor (c. 390), occupational safety and health (c. 396), workers' compensation (c. 386), temporary disability insurance (c. 392), prepaid health care (c. 393), manpower development and training (c. 394), receipt of funds from self-insured employers, and determination of amount of special compensation fund assessment (386-154); and apprenticeship system (c. 372). Department authorized to enter into reciprocal agreements with other states re collection of wage claims. (388-12).

Act relating to occupational safety and health adopted. (c. 396).

Wages and Hours of Labor.—Minimum wages and maximum hour provisions in effect since 1941; minimum wage in effect since Jan. 1, 1988 at $3.85 per hour. (387-2). Minimum wage increased to $4.75 per hour beginning Apr. 1, 1992, and to $5.25 per hour beginning Jan. 1, 1993. (387-2). Upon Director's certification, full-time students, student-learners and disabled persons may be paid below minimum wage. (387-9). Overtime at 1¹/₂ times employer's regular rate must be paid after 40 hours. (387-3[a]). Wage and hour law does not apply to employees with guaranteed compensation of $1,250 per month or more; other exemptions similar to federal law. (387-1). Wage and hour law does not apply to employees of air carriers, provided that any overtime hours are result of voluntary agreement between employees to exchange work time or days off. (1998, Act 158). Employer prohibited from making certain deductions from compensation. (388-6). Wages and hours of persons employed by contractors on public works regulated. (c. 104).

Occupational Safety and Health (c. 396).—Administered by Department of Occupational Safety and Health. (396-4). Penalties. (396-10). Definition of serious and willful violations. (396-3).

Prohibits retaliation for filing complaints. (396-8). Fees to be established for issuance of permits, licenses, certificates. (396-5.1).

See note at head of Digest as to 1998 legislation covered.

See Topical Index in front part of this volume.

LABOR RELATIONS . . . . *continued*

Employment-at-will is rule unless employment contract specifies definite period of time or employment relationship is covered by collective bargaining agreement. (703 F.Supp. 863). Public policy exception. (65 Haw. 370, 652 P.2d 625). Implied-in-fact contract exception. (68 Haw. 594).

Child Labor.—Employment of children ages 14-18 outside school hours permitted in any gainful occupation with certain exceptions; employment of children under 14 very limited; hours of work for children under 16 restricted. (390-2). Certificates of employment and age required from Department. (390-3).

Employment Practices.—Employers who, in good faith, provide candid information about former employees to prospective employers, have qualified immunity from civil liability for disclosure. (1998, Act 182). Employer may make post-offer inquiries about applicant's conviction record (provided conviction is less than ten years old) if inquiry is substantially related to job. (1998, Act 175). Schools may consider criminal convictions in evaluating applicant's suitability to working near children. (378-3[8]). Health care facilities may consider criminal conviction records in determining suitability of employees or applicants to work with or in proximity of vulnerable patients. (378-3). Financial institution may discharge or refuse to hire person convicted of crime involving dishonesty. (378-3[9]). Body fluid or tissue testing for HIV infection may not be done without prior written consent of subject to be tested. Exceptions for anatomical gifts and research when anonymity is ensured. Also exceptions for purposes of diagnosis or treatment, or for protection of health care workers, when person is unable to give consent. (325-16).

Unemployment Compensation.—Provisions adopted to conform to federal law. (c. 383). Almost all employees covered, exceptions enumerated in 383-7; companies which only employ family members who own at least 50% of corporation shares exempt (383-7); master and servant relationship not required, see statutory test for coverage (383-6). After one week waiting period, eligible for benefits if able to and available for work. (383-29). Individual eligible for benefits based on prior benefit year must have received wages equal to five times weekly benefit amount. (383-29). Alien receiving benefits must have been lawfully present for purposes of performing work in U.S. (383-29). Disqualification from eligibility if terminated voluntarily, discharged for misconduct, failed to apply for work, participated in labor dispute and unemployment is due to stoppage of work, and other reasons. (383-30). Employee seeking unemployment benefits for constructive discharge has burden of showing voluntary termination of employment was with "good cause", as defined in statute. (81 Haw. 84, 912 P.2d 581; 383-30[3][A]). Benefits paid weekly in amount calculated by formula up to maximum of $2/3$ of statewide average weekly wage determined annually by department. (383-22). Beginning Jan. 1, 1992, maximum amount increases to 70% of average weekly wage. (383-22). Benefits limited to 26 weeks (383-24); may be extended 13 weeks by Governor upon occurrence of disaster (c. 385). Maximum benefit period extended to 52 weeks for those who are unemployed due to plant closure or layoff. (383-29). Experience record of predecessor employer may be transferred to successor company, even when only portion of predecessor employer's business has been acquired. (383-66). Extension of benefits for long term unemployed. (383-29). System of worker profiling has been adopted. (383-92.5).

Public Employees.—U.S. citizen and state residency requirements for elected (three years) and appointed (one year) officers of state government or municipal subdivisions thereof; all other employees must be U.S. citizens, nationals or permanent resident aliens and state residents at time of application for employment. (78-1). Employment preference granted to state residents who have filed resident returns and their dependents. (78-1). Exceptions for University of Hawaii and positions requiring highly specialized technical and scientific skill or knowledge. (78-1). Public employees permitted by Const. art. XIII, §2 to organize for collective bargaining as prescribed by law. C. 87 establishes Public Employees Health Fund. C. 88 establishes State Pension and Retirement Systems. Reciprocal beneficiaries eligible for many of same benefits as spouses. (431:10A-601). Reciprocal beneficiary family coverage available to reciprocal beneficiaries to same extent family coverage available to non-reciprocal beneficiaries. (431:10A-601). C. 89 prescribes methods of organizing and collective bargaining for state, county and municipal employees, including those employed by Board of Education and University of Hawaii. Negotiations may not include proposals which violate merit principles. (85 Haw. 61, 937 P.2d 397). Hawaii Labor Relations Board created. (89-5). Provision made for grievance procedures, impasse procedures, mediation, fact-finding and arbitration (89-11), compulsory arbitration required for institutional, health, and correctional workers (89-11), firemen and police officers (89-11), and strikes by public employees permitted after all such channels exhausted, but not if disputes submitted for binding arbitration (89-12). Exclusive representative must be given access to employee's personal records which are relevant to investigation or processing of grievance. Exclusive representative cannot share or disclose specific information contained in personal records and must notify employee that access has been obtained. (89-16.5). Governor and county mayors have discretion to establish leave sharing programs in their jurisdiction which permit employees to donate sick leave credits to another employee under certain conditions. (c. 79). Post-employment restrictions. (84-18). Furloughed state and county employees retain benefits and privileges. (121-43).

Labor Disputes.—Unlawful to picket residence or dwelling place. (379A-1). Use of strikebreakers comprehensively regulated. (c. 379). Little Norris-La Guardia Act in effect. (380-4). Stringent law passed in 1949 to curb and control strikes, lockouts, stoppages and slowdowns in stevedoring industry. (c. 382). Labor disputes involving public utilities regulated in c. 381. Employers not covered by NLRA prohibited from permanently replacing strikers or giving preference to applicants willing to work during strike. (377-6).

Labor Unions are recognized. Hawaii has no "right to work" law, and Employment Relations Act has been adopted, defining relative rights of employers and employees, providing for election and certification of collective bargaining representative, specifying what are unfair labor practices and how they should be prevented and controlled; little National Labor Relations Act in effect. (c. 377).

Discrimination in Employment.—Civil Rights Commission established to enforce employment and housing antidiscrimination laws, and to be fully effective as of Jan. 1991. (c. 368). Discrimination in employment based on race, sex, age, religion, color, ancestry, disability, known relationship with disabled person, marital status, sexual orientation, arrest or court record not having substantial relationship to job prohibited (378-2); discrimination in compensation and other terms and conditions of employment also prohibited (378-2, 387-4). Employee may file civil action for sexual harassment or sexual assault in employment. (378-3). Employee may bring civil action for intentional infliction of emotional distress in addition to claim for employment discrimination under c. 378-2. (87 Haw. 57, 951 P.2d 507). Compensatory and punitive damages are available remedies in employment discrimination cases. (85 Haw. 7, 936 P.2d 643). Laws placing age limits on state and county employees have been repealed. (88-7, 378-3). Employee may not be suspended or discharged solely on ground employer was summoned as garnishee for employee's debt or because of work injury compensable under workers' compensation law. (378-32). Unlawful to require lie detector test as condition of employment and to discriminate against persons who refuse to submit thereto. (378-26.5).

Prepaid Health Care Law enacted requiring employer to provide coverage for every employee paid monthly wages of 86.67 times minimum hourly wage or more (393-11) under qualified prepaid health care plan (393-7); see statute for exemptions (393-3, -4, -5, -17, -22). Coverage must commence after four weeks employment and continue three months after employee not able to work due to disability. (393-14 & 15). Employer must pay one-half of premium, with balance paid by employee to extent not greater than 1.5% of wages. (393-13). Different prepaid health care plan and cost allocation may be established through collective bargaining. (393-13). Policies must provide mammogram screening for women. (431:10A-116). New criteria for use by Legislative Auditor to assess impact of proposed changes to mandatory health insurance coverage. (23-51).

Temporary Disability Law enacted entitling employee to weekly benefits for disability resulting from accident, sickness, pregnancy, or termination of pregnancy not connected with or resulting from employment (392-21, -22); exemptions enumerated at 392-5. After seven day waiting period (392-23, -24) in amount computed by formula based on wages up to maximum under workers' compensation law (392-22); with certain exceptions, disabled employee not eligible if not under care of physician or other licensed practitioner who certifies disability (392-26). Employer required to provide for benefits through insurance or other methods specified by statute. (392-41). Penalties for employers who fail to comply with these laws. (392-92). Each insurer must maintain complete claims service office or engage independent claims adjusting service in Hawaii. (392-42.5).

Substance Abuse Testing.—All substance abuse testing must be done in state licensed laboratory. Individual tested must receive written statement of specific substances to be tested for and medication disclosure form. Test results to be confidential. Third parties covered by federal drug testing regulation exempt. (c. 329B).

Workers' Compensation.—Uniform Workmen's Compensation Act adopted with amendments. (c. 386). Worker's Compensation Benefits Facilitator established to assist workers, employers, insurers and providers with filing and processing claims. (386-71.6). With exception of civil actions for sexual harassment or sexual assault (378-3), 386-5 provides exclusive remedy for injuries arising out of and in course of employment, including alleged emotional distress injuries arising from termination (9 Haw. App. 21, 821 P.2d 937; 899 F.2d 845). Claims for mental stress resulting solely from disciplinary action taken in good faith by employer are prohibited; provided that if collective bargaining agreement or other employment agreement specifies different standard for disciplinary actions, standards set in such agreements shall be applied in lieu of good faith standard. Exclusive remedy for participants working for private employers under Dept. of Education vocational student internship program. (300-52). Injuries covered (386-3) include psychogenic disabilities (714 F.Supp. 1108). Employer may determine benefits and coverage through collective bargaining with appropriate bargaining unit. (386-3.5). Employer disclosure of premium information to employees mandated. (431:14-110.5). Ceiling on death or disability benefits is 312 times maximum weekly benefit. (386-43[b]). Ceiling on disfigurement is $30,000. (386-32). Ceiling for weekly benefit is 66 2/3% of state's annually determined average weekly wage. (386-31, -32). (Duration depends on nature of injury, or identity of dependent in case of death.). Director of Labor and Industrial Relations must approve claims for services. (386-94). Statutory presumption that claim is for covered work injury. (386-85). Adopted temporary disability insurance for many nonoccupational accidents and sickness. (c. 392). "Odd-lot" factors such as age, limited education, and limited transferable skills cannot be considered impairments for purposes of rating preexisting permanent partial disability. (892 P.2d 468). Vocational rehabilitation unit established within Department, which allows injured employee under workers' compensation to select certified provider of rehabilitation services. (386-25; 1998, Act 256). Filing requirements for out-of-state employers. (386-10). Director of labor and industrial relations has original jurisdiction over controversies and disputes over employment and coverage under Workers' Compensation law. (386-73.5). Penalties for employers who fail to comply with these laws. (386-95, -97.5, 392-92, 393-33,-34; 386-92). Director decisions may be enforced by circuit court. (386-91). Fraudulent insurance acts subject to criminal penalties. (386-98). Hawaii Employer's Mutual Insurance Company established to provide workers' compensation coverage to employers; starting Jan. 1, 1997, applicable to Hawaii employers otherwise entitled to coverage but not able to or not electing to purchase in voluntary insurance market. (c. 431:14A). Injuries occurring on employer's premises are covered by workers' compensation only insofar as they arise out of employment-related risk. (881 P.2d 1246). Disclosure of workers' compensation evidence may be appropriate where purpose relevant to trial. (897 P.2d 941).

Business Closing or Relocation.—Dislocated Workers Act adopted. (c. 394B). Employers with 50 or more employees must provide employees and Department of Labor and Industrial Relations with 45-day written notice of business closing, partial closing or relocation of operations and must pay supplemental unemployment benefits for approximately four weeks. (394B-9, B-10). Maximum unemployment benefits period is 52 weeks for those unemployed because of layoffs or plant closures. (383-29).

See note at head of Digest as to 1998 legislation covered.

See Topical Index in front part of this volume.

LABOR RELATIONS . . . *continued*

Whistleblower Protection.—Public and private employees who report suspected violations of law can invoke judicial recourse if retaliated against for such reports by employer. (378-63).

Smoking in Workplace.—Written smoking policy required for any state or county agency or any private corporation, firm, or association which receives state funds. (328K-13).

Family Leave.—Employees employed not less than six months by employer who employs more than 100 workers may take four weeks family leave upon birth of child, adoption, or to care for child, spouse or parent with serious health condition. (c. 398). Applicable to private employers. (79-32).

Reciprocal beneficiaries receive identical benefits as spouses in many circumstances. (HB 118, 1997).

WORKERS' COMPENSATION LAW:

See topic Labor Relations.

ENVIRONMENT

ENVIRONMENTAL REGULATION:

General Supervision.—Department of Health generally responsible for prevention, control and abatement of air, noise, water, solid waste pollution and other forms of pollution.

State Emergency Response Commission established to carry out requirements of Hawaii Emergency Planning and Community Right-to-Know Act (HEPCRA). (c. 300).

State Office of Environmental Quality Control created to implement environmental quality control regulations and to advise governor on matters concerning environmental quality. (341-3).

State Board of Land and Natural Resources has specific and primary authority to prevent waste or deterioration of ground water resources (177-5) and has authority to control landscaping and architecture of commercial or industrial enterprises on leased property to prevent pollution or spread of harmful wastes (171-41), and is authorized to issue citations under Hawaii Penal Code for unauthorized activities on unencumbered public lands (171-6.5).

Prohibited acts of pollution are specifically designated covering all forms of pollution.

Penalties.—Varying civil, criminal and administrative penalties are provided for specific prohibited acts of pollution. Greater penalties are imposed for repeated violations.

Air Pollution Control.—Ambient air quality standards, emission control regulations and episode criteria promulgated by State Department of Health. Air pollution law (c. 342B) meets requirements of federal Clean Air Act Amendments of 1990, 48 U.S.C. §7608(g). Odors emanating from agricultural operations exempt from hydrogen sulfide standard of c. 342B. Permit required for construction or modification of any new source. New source must be built in accordance with best practicable control technology and may not endanger maintenance or attainment of ambient air quality standards. Permit to operate source not transferable. Permit issued for any term not to exceed five years. Open fires restricted. Permit required for agricultural burning. Storage of volatile organic compounds restricted. Smoking prohibited in certain public places. (c. 328K). Establishes ozone protection standards for motor vehicle air conditioning equipment repair. (c. 437B).

Noise Pollution.—"Excessive noise" in volume, quantity, or duration that endangers health, safety or property or unreasonably interferes with comfortable enjoyment of life and property; regulated by c. 342F.

Water Quality Control.—Water quality standards and criteria, effluent standards, treatment and pretreatment standards, and standards of performance for specific areas and types of discharges promulgated by State Department of Health. Permit required for effluent in excess of Department of Health Standards. Any person who unlawfully pollutes state waters must report discharge within 24 hours. Non-point Source Pollution Control program to mitigate non-point source pollution. (c. 345). Director of Environmental Quality Control authorized to act as certifying agency for water quality standards on dredge and fill projects conducted by U.S. Army Corps of Engineers. Director also authorized to test aquatic and other life in polluted waters and if it is determined hazardous if consumed, shall notify public. Groundwater protection program implemented. (174C-31). Any new lease or renewal of any existing lease of water rights from state requires joint development and implementation of watershed management plan by lessee and Board of Land and Natural Resources. (171-58). Counties authorized to implement Gray Water Recycling Program. (c. 342D). Department of agriculture is charged with construction and maintenance of state irrigation water systems. (1998, Act 067).

Integrated Solid Waste Management.—Standards for solid waste disposal facilities promulgated by Department of Health. (c. 342G and 342H). Impermissible dumping of solid waste is punishable by one or more of: (a) criminal penalties up to $25,000; (b) up to 30 days imprisonment; and/or (c) revocation or suspension of contractor's license or similar authorization from public utilities commission. (342H-30; 1998, Act 226). Composting and recycling encouraged. Permit required to transport petroleum-contaminated soil, unless destination is soil remediation site, whereby 48 hour notice required. (c. 342H). Permit required to establish, modify or operate any solid waste disposal facility. Disposal on single family or duplex residential property exempted from permit requirement. Responsibility for private sewage and wastewater treatment systems upon counties. Counties authorized to assess surcharge of 35¢ per ton of solid waste to support waste reduction, recovery, and diversion programs. (342G-62). All plastic containers must have labels indicating type of plastic resin used to produce container. (c. 292H). Removal of recyclable materials from designated collection sites prohibited. (c. 342H). Requires use of recycled glass for pavement construction when glassphalt is less

expensive than aggregate. (c. 264). Prohibits disposal of used tires at landfills or solid waste incinerators. Used tires must be delivered to authorized waste collection facility. (c. 342I). Litter control. (c. 339).

Hazardous Materials.—Transportation of hazardous materials, hazardous waste, infectious substances, and medical waste governed by c. 286. Transporters must notify Dept. of Health annually of disposition of hazardous waste. (c. 267). Lead abatement activities are regulated by c. 342P. (1998, Act 242).

Enforcement.—Department of Health empowered to control pollution with specific duties and powers. With regard to ground water resources, Board of Land and Natural Resources has primary power. (177-5).

Enforcement procedures for various forms of pollution are outlined in specific sections relating to respective forms (see subhead General Supervision, supra). Generally, investigations may be conducted and hearings must be held from which orders to cease acts of pollution may issue. Enforcement authorities may also institute legal proceedings in name of State to secure injunctive relief or recover penalties for violations. Judicial appeals may be had by those against whom orders have been issued.

Environmental assessments required for all proposed actions involving public lands or funds, and for all projects in designated areas. (343-5). Environmental impact statement required if proposed action may have significant effect on environment. Environmental Impact Statement must set forth sufficient information to enable decision-making body to consider fully environmental impacts of proposed action. (81 Haw. 171, 914 P.2d 1364). Draft environmental assessments made available for public review and comments before final judicial determination that environmental impact statement not required. (c. 343). Acceptance of statement by governor, when state lands or funds involved, or by mayor, when county lands or funds involved, is condition precedent to implementation of proposed action. Responsibility for making recommendations on acceptability of impact statements belongs with Office of Environmental Control, not Environmental Council. (343-5).

Historic Preservation.—Department of Land and Natural Resources given authority to acquire, preserve, restore and maintain any building, structure, object, district, area or site deemed significant in history, architecture, archaeology or culture of state. (c. 6E).

All historic property located on lands or under waters controlled by State is property of State. Control and management of all State historic property vested in Department of Land and Natural Resources. (6E-7). Determinations by Department of Land and Natural Resources regarding effects of proposed state projects may be appealed to Hawaii Historic Places Review Board. (6E-8).

Conservation.—Hawaii Statewide Trail and Access Program manages and maintains development of trails and accesses. (198D-2). Natural Area Reserve System protects and preserves geological and volcanological feature and marine and terrestrial plants and animals in natural reserve area. (c. 195D). Conservation easements recognized in c. 198. Endangered Species Recovery Act which also encourages habitat conservation and provides safe harbor provisions enacted. (195D-21; 1998, Act 237).

Marine and Aquatic Resources.—Release of nonnative aquarium fish into State waters prohibited and punishable by administrative and civil fines. (187A; 1998, Act 243).

Gill Net Fishing.—Gill nets must be inspected every two hours to remove undersized, unwanted or illegal catch, and may be left in water for only four hours in any 24-hour period. (188-30.2). Drift gill net possession and use prohibited in State waters. (188-30.5). Size of gill nets stipulated. (188-29).

Environmental Disclosure.—No person owning 10% or more of voting securities in Hawaii corporation may purchase more than additional 5% of such security or 5% or more of assets of such corporation during 12-month period without first filing detailed statement of compliance with all applicable environmental laws and regulations. (343D-3).

Permits required for: Groundwater use in designated areas (177-19); strip mining in forest reserve access (183-42); mining exploration (182-6); geothermal development (205-5.1); taking aquatic life for scientific, educational or propagation purposes (187A-6); use of restricted pesticides (149A[11][7]); transporting, marketing or recycling oil (342N-31); installation of underground storage tank (342L-31); and practices relating to sewage sludge and reclaimed water (342D-4, 6).

Pesticides are regulated under c. 149A by Board of Agriculture. Various sections describe prohibited acts, enforcement procedures, penalties and registration requirements for pesticides. Nothing in c. 149A alters functions, duties and powers of Department of Health. (c. 149A).

Use of pesticides deemed to have unreasonable adverse effects on environment will be suspended, cancelled or restricted by Board of Agriculture. (c. 149A). Determination whether unreasonable adverse effects exist will be made, in addition to other circumstances, when residues of pesticide detected in drinking water or when use of pesticide has been suspended or cancelled by U.S. Environmental Protection Agency. Unreasonable adverse effects on environment defined in 149-2(35).

Solar Energy and Heat Pumps.—Tax credit allowed for installation of approved solar energy system and/or heat pump in buildings used primarily for residential purposes. (235-12).

Coastal Zone Management.—Hawaii Coastal Zone Management Law and special management area guidelines and development procedures set forth in c. 205A. Definition of "coastal zone management area" expanded. (205A-1). Office of state planning is responsible for management of Hawaii coastal zone. (255M-2[b][8]). Public advisory board provides policy advice and assistance. Hazards from hurricane, wind and storm surge included under policies and guidelines of Coastal Zone Management program. (205A-2[C][6][8]; 205A-26[I][D]).

Underground Storage Tanks regulated under c. 342L by Department of Health. Various sections describe tank standards, notification requirements, prohibited acts, enforcement procedures, emergency procedures, petroleum releases, penalties, and permit requirements. Owner of underground storage tank that has release responsible for restoring environment to condition acceptable to Department of Health. (342L-35).

ENVIRONMENTAL REGULATION ... *continued*

Used Oil Transport, Recycling and Disposal regulated under c. 342N and 342J by Department of Health. No oil shall be discharged or allowed to enter into sewers, drainage systems, surface or ground waters, watercourses, marine waters, or into ground, with certain exceptions. (342N-30). Permit required to transport, market, or recycle used oil or used oil fuel. (342N-31). Director of Health may establish rules governing recycling, transport, and disposal of used oil and used oil fuel. (342J-52).

Asbestos emissions prohibited by c. 342P. Criminal penalties for knowing violations of c. 342P.

Lead Acid Batteries.—Disposal of lead acid batteries restricted and provisions for recycling enacted under c. 342. Advertisements required to state price of new batteries, including disposal costs for old batteries. (c. 267).

Environmental Response Law.—State "superfund" or Environmental Response Law adopted. (c. 128D). Patterned after Federal Comprehensive Environmental Response, Compensation and Liability Act (CERCLA), "hazardous substance" includes oil and trichloropropane. Limits liability for acts or omissions related to release of hazardous substance, if in accordance with c. 128D or at direction of on-scene coordinator. Does not preclude liability for costs, damages, or penalties as result of negligence, gross negligence, or intentional misconduct. (c. 324). Liability of person under 128D-6 limited to $700,000,000 for release of heavy fuel oil from interisland tank barge. Voluntary response program also in effect. (128D-6.5).

Restricting Passage Over Rights-Of-Way.—Passage over public right-of-way may be restricted by resolution or ordinance, provided resolution or ordinance contains criteria for determining restriction is in public interest. (115-3.5).

ESTATES AND TRUSTS

ADMINISTRATION:

See topic Executors and Administrators.

ADVANCEMENTS:

See topic Descent and Distribution.

ALLOWANCES:

See topic Executors and Administrators.

CLAIMS:

See topic Executors and Administrators.

DEATH:

Presumption of death from absence of five year continuous period. (560:1-107[5]).

Certificate.—Obtained from Vital Records Section, Department of Health, State of Hawaii, Honolulu, Hawaii 96813. Fee $2.

Survivorship.—Uniform Simultaneous Death Act (c. 534A) repealed effective Jan. 1, 1997. (1996 Haw. Sess. Laws 288, §9). Arts. I through IV of 1993 Uniform Probate Code adopted as 560:1-101 to 560:4-401, with modifications (existing 560:1-101 to 560:4-401 repealed). See topic Descent and Distribution.

See category Civil Actions and Procedure, topic Actions, subhead Abatement and Revival.

Action for Death.—Legal representative, surviving spouse, reciprocal beneficiary, children, father, mother, or dependent of one whose death was caused by wrongful act of another may maintain action for damages against person causing or responsible for death. Action must be brought within two years. No limitation of recovery. Damages may include loss of society, companionship, comfort, consortium, protection, marital care, attention, advice, counsel, loss of filial care, loss of parental care, training, guidance, education. (663-3).

Living Will.—Adult granted statutory right to make written declaration instructing his or her physician to provide, withhold, or withdraw life-sustaining procedures and/or food and fluids in event of terminal condition or permanent loss of ability to communicate these desires. Forms. (c. 327D). See also topic Wills. For form, see topic Wills, subhead Living Wills.

Death Certificate.—See category Documents and Records, topic Records, subhead Vital Statistics.

Uniform Anatomical Gift Act adopted. (c. 327, Part I). Modified by allowing reciprocal beneficiary to have same right as spouse to make, revoke, or object to anatomical gifts; and same right as spouse to gift request consultation. (327-3, 5).

Determination of Death.—Death occurs when irreversible cessation of spontaneous respiratory and circulatory functions first coincide, or, when artificial life support systems utilized, when there is irreversible cessation of all brain and brain stem functions. (327C-1).

DECEDENTS ESTATES:

See topics Executors and Administrators, Descent and Distribution, and Wills.

DESCENT AND DISTRIBUTION:

Uniform Probate Code.—Arts. I through IV of 1993 Uniform Probate Code adopted as 560:1-101 to 560:4-401, with following modifications: Validity of letters testamentary and letters of administration limited to three years. (560:1-201). Excepting from jurisdiction family court's exclusive jurisdiction over guardianship of person. (560:1-302). No change from 1992 law (formerly 560:2-109); adopted child has right to inherit from natural parents if child adopted within extended family; definition of natural parent expanded to include prior adoptive parents. (560:2-114). Parent of minor decedent will be treated as if parent predeceased minor if parent abandoned or failed to support minor

as defined in §560:2-103. Surviving spouse or reciprocal beneficiary may choose partial elective share. (560:2-202). Raises to $20,000 aggregate amount of pre-death transfers by decedent to donee other than spouse or reciprocal beneficiary that are exempt from augmented estate. (560:2-205). Augmented estate property gifted to or held in trust for decedent when neither decedent nor surviving spouse or reciprocal beneficiary was responsible for creating property (continuing special status of this property under Hawaii family law); property must have been held segregated from other augmented estate assets. (560:2-208). Additional protection provided to descendants of first spouse or reciprocal beneficiary to die against election by guardian of incapacitated surviving spouse or reciprocal beneficiary. (560:2-212). Increased sanctions on person who knowingly and willfully "hides" will of decedent. (560:2-516). Instances where property can be substituted for specifically devised property are restricted. (560:2-606). Hawaii rules of evidence govern Hawaii probate disputes. (560:2-703). Substitutes prior Hawaii law five year limit to submit will for probate. (560:3-108, 560:3-30[a][1][vi]). Requires prior notice of application for informal probate of will to heirs and devisees if person making application is not professional fiduciary or close family member. (560:3-302, 560:3-306). Beneficiaries and heirs must be notified that court is available to resolve disputes about attorney's fees. (560:3-302, 560:3-306). Burden of proof in contested probate cases may shift as prescribed by rules of evidence. (560:3-407). Bonds in probate do not lapse because of personal representative's errors. (560:3-606). UPC scheme generally abandoning court confirmation of sales of realty retained, except that interested party may still request judicial intervention under 531-28.5 and 531-29. (560:3-715). Personal representatives have option to publish notice to creditors and provide vehicle for trustees of decedent's trust to publish notice compelling creditors to timely present their claims or have them time barred (if no publication, creditor's claims would be barred if not presented within 18 months after death). (560:3-801, 560:3-803). New law also affects estates open before Jan. 1, 1997 (560:8-103) but rules of construction relating to "per stirpes" and "right of representation" apply only to testamentary instruments executed after Jan. 1, 1997 (560:2-709). Consult 560:8-103 for other effective dates.

Afterborn heirs must survive at least 120 hours after birth. (560:2-108).

Half Blood.—Relatives of half blood inherit same as relatives of whole blood. (560:2-107).

Children Born to Parents Not Married to Each Other.—Individual is child of natural parents regardless of their marital status. (560:2-114). Parent-child relationship may be established under c. 584-2.

Adopted Children.—See category Family, topic Adoption.

Determination of Heirship.—Judges of circuit court determines. (560:3-405).

Election.—Uniform Probate Code applies (560:2-201, et seq.), with modifications discussed supra.

Escheat.—Uniform Unclaimed Property Act. (523A). See category Property, topic Absentees, subhead Escheat.

See also topic Executors and Administrators.

ELECTION:

See topic Wills.

ESTATES:

See category Property, topic Real Property.

EXECUTORS AND ADMINISTRATORS:

Uniform Probate Code.—Effective Jan. 1, 1997, Arts. I through IV of 1993 Uniform Probate Code adopted as 560:1-101 to 560:4-401 with following modifications. Uniform Probate Code procedure applies, unless court decides, in interest of fairness, that it does not or former rules are applicable. (1996. Act 288, §5[b][2], amending UPC, Art. III). All rights and priorities of spouse also apply to reciprocal beneficiary. (431:103A-601).

Exemption From Bond.—No bond is required of personal representative unless: special administrator appointed; will requires bond; bond is requested by interested party and court is satisfied it is desirable; court determines it is needed. (560:3-603[1]).

Notice of Appointment.—State limits "no notice" ability to certain relations to decedent and corporate personal representatives. All others must give notice. (560:3-302 to 306).

Uniform Simplification of Fiduciary Security Transfers Act superseded by Uniform Commercial Code. See category Business Regulation and Commerce, topic Commercial Code.

Uniform Fiduciaries Act adopted in 1945. (c. 556). Uniform Act §3 repealed by adoption of Uniform Commercial Code. (490:10-102[1]).

Uniform Principal and Income Act (Revised) has been adopted (c. 557).

Uniform Transfer-On-Death (TOD) Security Registration Act adopted, enabling individuals to designate non-testamentary beneficiary for transfer of registered securities. (1998, Act 063).

FIDUCIARIES:

See topics Executors and Administrators, Trusts; category Family, topic Guardian and Ward.

INTESTACY:

See topic Descent and Distribution.

LIVING WILLS:

See topic Wills.

See note at head of Digest as to 1998 legislation covered.

See Topical Index in front part of this volume.

PROOF OF CLAIMS:

See topic Executors and Administrators; category Civil Actions and Procedure, topic Pleading.

TRUSTS:

Uniform Custodial Trust Act adopted (c. 554B) with following modifications: Beneficiary treated as incapacitated where required by transferor in trust instrument; or custodial trustee makes such determination. (554B-10). Custodial trust terminates when trustee receives signed instruction from beneficiary, if not incapacitated, or beneficiary's guardian; or upon beneficiary's death. (554B-17).

Uniform Probate Code.—Arts. I through IV of 1993 Uniform Probate Code adopted as 560:1-101 to 560:4-401 with modifications. See topic Descent and Distribution. Art. VII of 1969 Uniform Probate Code (c. 560), but not 1975 or 1977 Official Amendments, still applies with following modifications: Trustee personally liable on contracts entered into in fiduciary capacity in course of administration of trust estate unless otherwise provided in contract; trustee also personally liable for obligations arising from ownership or control of property of trust estate and for torts committed in course of its administration without regard to whether he is personally at fault (560:7-306). Qualification of Foreign Trustees omitted from Hawaii statute. Claim against trustee for breach of trust may be brought by beneficiary within two years after receipt of final account or statement. (560:7-307).

Uniform Prudent Investor Act adopted. (554C-1 to 554C-12).

Uniform Trustees' Powers Act adopted. (c. 554A). Applies to any trust with Hawaii situs. (554A:8). Revised to permit non-pro rata distribution. (1998, Act 024).

Generally, common law governs creation, administration, and termination. Statues should be consulted regarding vesting of title of trust estate (554-1); nomination of trustees by beneficiaries (554-2); power of circuit court to authorize or direct trustee to lease or invest (554-3); annual accounts (554-4); restriction on investments (554-6); assignees for creditors (554-7); charitable trusts (554-8, 9, 10); land trusts (c. 558). Parol trusts have been held valid.

Investments by trustees are restricted. (554-6). See category Business Regulation and Commerce, topic Banks and Banking, subhead Trust Companies.

Trustee must comply with Prudent Investor Rule. (1997, Act 26, §1).

Compensation.—Of all money and property received as trust income, trustee is allowed 7% commission for first $5,000 and 5% commission for all over $5,000 payable as income is received, but not more often than once a year. On principal, commissions are as follows: 1% on value at inception of trust, payable at such inception out of principal: 5/10 of 1% on value at end of each year, except to extent trustee employs outside clerical and bookkeeping services at expense of estate; 1% on value of all or any part of estate on final distribution thereof, payable at termination of trust out of principal; 2½% on cash principal received after inception of trust, payable at time of receipt out of principal; 2½% on final payment of any cash principal prior to termination of trust, payable at time of such final payment out of principal. Value of estate is determined in such manner as court may approve. Court approval is not required where trustees authorized to employ others for bookkeeping and clerical services at expense of estate. (607-18[b]). Further allowance may be made by court for special services, but contract for higher compensation between trustee and beneficiary is void. (607-18). Trustees of charitable trusts will receive reasonable compensation. (1998, Act 310).

Common Trust Funds.—See category Business Regulation and Commerce, topic Banks and Banking.

Employees trusts as part of plan for exclusive benefit of employees are lawful. (c. 555).

Gifts to Minors.—See category Family, topic Infants.

Eligibility and Competency.—No corporation may act as trustee in Hawaii except a trust company, or a bank authorized to engage in a trust business. (406-4). See category Business Regulation and Commerce, topic Banks and Banking.

Accounting.—Required unless statute, trust document or will provides to contrary. (554-4). Accounts usually filed annually but court can permit biennial or triennial filing. (554-4). Accounts may be referred to master (usually disinterested). Accounts of charitable trusts are referred to attorney general.

Uniform Simplification of Fiduciary Security Transfers Act superseded by Uniform Commercial Code.

Uniform Fiduciaries Act adopted in 1945. (c. 556). §189-3, Revised Laws of Hawaii 1955, pertaining to Uniform Fiduciaries Act repealed by adoption of Uniform Commercial Code. (490-10-102[1]).

Uniform Trustees' Accounting Act has not been adopted.

Uniform Common Trust Fund Act has been adopted. (406-25-34).

Uniform Principal and Income Act (Revised) adopted. (c. 557).

Securities in Name of Nominee.—Statute permits any trust company acting as fiduciary, and any fiduciary acting as co-fiduciary with a trust company to hold securities in the name of a nominee or nominees unless expressly otherwise provided by the instrument, decree or order creating the fiduciary relationship. (406-23).

Accumulations.—No statutory rule.

Perpetuities.—See category Property, topic Perpetuities.

WILLS:

Uniform Probate Code.—Effective Jan. 1, 1997, Arts. I through IV of 1993 Uniform Probate Code adopted as 560:1-101 to 560:4-401 with modifications. See topic Descent and Distribution.

Simultaneous Death.—See topic Death, subhead Survivorship.

Testamentary Trusts.—See topic Trusts.

Unclaimed Legacies.—Uniform Unclaimed Property Act adopted in amended form. (c. 523A:17). See category Property, topic Absentees, subhead Escheat.

Living wills recognized. (c. 327D). Living will allowed to take effect not only when person is terminally ill, but also in situations where person has permanently lost ability to communicate these desires. Person is allowed to draft living will that sets forth whether food and fluids should be continued, withheld or withdrawn. (c. 327D). Declaration shall: (1) Be in writing; (2) be signed by person making declaration or by another person in declarant's presence and at declarant's expressed direction; (3) be dated; (4) be signed in presence of two or more witnesses who are: (a) at least 18 years of age, (b) not related to declarant by blood, marriage or adoption, and (c) at time that declaration is executed, not attending physician, nor employee of physician or medical facility in which declarant is patient; and (5) have all signatures notarized at same time. Sample declaration form provided containing checklist to document whether or not person wishes to be sustained by feeding tubes; any living will executed after July 1, 1991 required to include checklist. (c. 327D). Durable power of attorney authorizes agent to make health care decisions. Presumption: no authority to prolong life through medical procedures unless explicitly stated. (c. 551D). For form of health care power of attorney see subhead Form of Durable Power of Attorney, infra. See also topic Death.

Form of Durable Power of Attorney.—Power of attorney authorizing health care decisions. Durable power of attorney authorizes agent to make lawful health care decisions that would have been made by principal at time of election. Requires presumption that power of attorney does not grant authority to prolong life through medical procedures unless explicitly stated. (c. 551D). See also topic Death.

DURABLE POWER OF ATTORNEY FOR HEALTH CARE DECISIONS

A. Statement of Principal

Declaration made this ____ day of _____ (month, year). I, _____, being of sound mind, and understanding that I have the right to request that my life be prolonged to the greatest extent possible, wilfully and voluntarily make known my desire that my attorney-in-fact ("agent") shall be authorized as set forth below and do hereby declare:

My instructions shall prevail even if they create a conflict with the desires of my relatives, hospital policies, or the principles of those providing my care.

CHECKLIST

I have considered the extent of the authority I want my agent to have with respect to health care decisions if I should develop a terminal condition or permanent loss of the ability to communicate concerning medical treatment decisions with no reasonable chance of regaining this ability. I want my agent to request care, including medicine and procedures, for the purpose of providing comfort and pain relief. I have also considered whether my agent should have the authority to decide whether or not my life should be prolonged, and have selected one of the following provisions by putting a mark in the space provided:

(_____) My agent is authorized to decide whether my life should be prolonged through surgery, resuscitation, life sustaining medicine or procedures, and tube or other artificial feeding or provisions of fluids by a tube.

(_____) My agent is authorized to decide whether my life should be prolonged through tube or other artificial feeding or provisions of fluids by a tube.

If neither provision is selected, it shall be presumed that my agent shall have only the power to request care, including medicine and procedures, for the purpose of providing comfort and pain relief.

This durable power of attorney shall control in all circumstances. I understand that my physician may not act as my agent under this durable power of attorney.

I understand the full meaning of this durable power of attorney and I am emotionally and mentally competent to make this declaration.

Signed _____

Address _____

B. Statement of Witnesses

I am at least 18 years of age and
—not related to the principal by blood, marriage, or adoption; and
—not currently the attending physician, an employee of the attending physician, or an employee of the health care facility in which the principal is a patient.
The principal is personally known to me and I believe the principal to be of sound mind.

Witness _____

Address _____

Witness _____

Address _____

C. Statement of Agent

I am at least 18 years of age, I accept the appointment under this durable power of attorney as the attorney-in-fact ("agent") of the principal, and I am not the physician of the principal. The principal is personally known to me and I believe the principal to be of sound mind.

Agent _____

Address _____

See note at head of Digest as to 1998 legislation covered.

See Topical Index in front part of this volume.

WILLS . . . *continued*

D. Notarization

Subscribed, sworn to and acknowledged before me by _____________, the principal, and subscribed and sworn to before me by _____________ and _________________, witnesses, this ___ day of _____________, 19__.

(Seal) Signed _______________

____

(Official capacity of officer)

FAMILY

ADOPTION:

Any proper adult person, not married, or married to legal parent of minor, or husband and wife jointly, may petition family court of circuit wherein they reside, or individual to be adopted resides or was born, for leave to adopt, and for change of name of individual. (578-1). Decree may be set aside or modified within one year, for good cause. After one year, decree may be set aside only for fraud. (578-12).

Written consent must be given by: (1) Mother of child; (2) legal father of child born of parents married to each other; (3) natural father adjudicated by court; (4) natural father as presumed by statute; (5) natural father who demonstrates concern and responsibility for child; (6) person or agency having legal custody; (7) court having jurisdiction if guardian or custodian not empowered to consent to adoption; (8) child if over ten years old. (578-2[1]-[8]). Petition to adopt adult niece, nephew or stepchild may be granted if written consent to adoption has been executed by adult and spouse, if adult is married. (578-2[8][b]). Consent not required of: (1) Parent who has deserted for 90 days without affording means of identification, or who voluntarily surrendered child to care and custody of another for over two years; (2) parent who has not communicated with child or provided support for one year; (3) natural father whose relationship has not been adjudicated, who is not entitled to presumption of paternity (578-2[d]), or who has not demonstrated reasonable degree of interest, concern or responsibility for welfare of child; (4) parent whose rights have been judicially terminated, or who is judicially declared mentally ill or retarded and has been found by court to be incapacitated from giving consent; (5) legal guardian or custodian who fails to respond to request for consent for 60 days, or who unreasonably withholds consent; (6) parent of child who has been in custody of petitioner for at least one year and who entered U.S. as consequence of extraordinary circumstances in country of origin by reason of which existence, identity or whereabouts of child's parents is not reasonably ascertainable, or there is no reasonable means of obtaining suitable evidence of child's identity or availability for adoption (578-2[c][1]). Court may dispense with consent of concerned father who has not filed petition to adopt, or whose petition to adopt has been denied, or of adjudicated, presumed, or concerned father who is not fit to give child proper home, or whose child has lived with his legal mother and petitioning stepfather for one year. (578-2[c][2]). Due notice, actual or constructive, must be given each parent who has not consented unless consent or notice waived by court as permitted by 578-2. (578-2[e]). Parental rights may be terminated for purposes of making available for adoption. (571-61[b]). Parental consent valid and binding even though does not designate any specific adoptive parent(s), if it clearly authorizes department of human services licensed child placing organization (346-17), or some proper person not forbidden by law to place child for adoption, to select and approve adoptive parent(s) for child.

Effect of Adoption.—Adopted child becomes in all respects child of adoptive parents, and inherits from and through them; loses all rights incident to former status. (578-16). If adopted before age of majority by natural relation or spouse of natural relation, then under any will, trust, or other lifetime instrument, rights of adopted individual's natural family not affected by adoption; adopted individuals included in determination of heirs or class members, unless specifically excluded. Adopted individual designated in two or more classes, both by adoption or natural relation, entitled to benefit in class with largest share. Adopting parents by earlier adoptions included in definition of "natural parent". (560:2-114).

Jurisdiction; Venue.—Family court of circuit in which adoptive parents reside or in which adoptee resides or was born or in which approved child placing organization is located. (578-1).

Petition shall be in such form and shall include such information and exhibits as may be required by family court. (578-1).

Proceedings.—Any person authorized by court may serve summons containing notice of time and place for adoption hearing. (578-4). Hearing must be held at which petitioner(s), any legal parent married to petitioner, any subject of adoption whose consent is required personally appear before court, unless expressly excused by court. Where child is adopted from foreign country, court has discretion to dispense with hearing if issues have received full consideration by foreign country and U.S. Immigration and Naturalization Service. (578-8). Investigation will be made by Director of Human Services or nearest county administrator of Department of Human Services as to fitness of petitioners to adopt individual and as to whether best interests of individual to be adopted will be served by adoption; provided that court may waive investigation. (578-8).

Decree.—Court may enter decree of adoption if it is satisfied that individual is adoptable and physically, mentally and otherwise suitable for adoption by petitioners, that petitioners are fit and proper persons and financially able to provide proper home and education, and that adoption will be for best interests of individual. (578-8).

Name.—First and last names of adopted child changed to any name stipulated by parents or in best interests of child (578-13) and birth certificate so amended (568-14). New birth certificate must include names of natural parents if requested by adoptive parents and consented to by natural parents. (578-14).

Miscellaneous.—Provision is made for confidentiality of proceedings and records. (578.15). Medical information concerning natural parents of adopted child must be filed. Adoptive parents or adult adopted child entitled to access to medical information. (578-14.5). Provision is made for petition by adopted children for access to adoption records sealed by court; court may release records based upon express or implied consent of natural parents; natural parents may file request that records remain sealed. (578-15). Provision is made for insurance coverage for newborn adopted children. (431:10A-116).

Hawaii is member of Interstate Compact on Placement of Children, effective 1985.

ALIMONY:

See topic Divorce.

COMMUNITY PROPERTY:

See topic Husband and Wife.

DISSOLUTION OF MARRIAGE:

See topic Divorce.

DIVORCE:

Generally, this subject is governed by HRS 580.

Grounds for Absolute Divorce.—Marriage is irretrievably broken; expiration of term in decree of separate bed and board without reconciliation having been effected; living separate and apart under decree of separate maintenance for period of two years or more and no reconciliation has been effected; voluntarily living separate and apart continuously for two years or more and there is no reasonable likelihood that cohabitation will be resumed, and court satisfied divorce would not be harsh or oppressive to defendant or contrary to public interest. (580-41).

Grounds for Legal Separation.—Family court may decree separation from bed and board for period not to exceed two years upon petition for separation when court finds marriage is temporarily disrupted. (580-71). Separation decree is not bar to divorce. (580-71.5). Upon decree of separation, court may further decree for support and maintenance of either spouse and minor children. (580-74).

Residence.—One party must be domiciled or physically present in state for continuous period of six months immediately before filing of complaint. Persons residing on military bases or present in state under military orders not prohibited from meeting residence requirement. (580-1).

Venue.—Action must be brought in circuit in which plaintiff has been domiciled or physically present for three months next preceding his or her application. (580-1).

Jurisdiction.—No divorce shall be granted unless either party to marriage has been domiciled or physically present in state for six months next preceding his or her application.

Process.—Action commenced by filing complaint with circuit court and issuance of summons. (580-2). Personal service required if defendant is within state unless defendant enters appearance in person or in writing. Actual receipt by defendant or service by registered or certified mail is equivalent to personal service if defendant is outside circuit. If service is not feasible, inconvenient, or defendant is outside state, personal notice through court authorized person permissible and hearing held not less than 20 days thereafter. If defendant cannot be found after 15 days reasonable search either before or after filing complaint, published notice at least once a week for three successive weeks may be authorized by court and case heard at time specified, not less than 20 days after last publication. (580-3).

Pleading.—Action commenced by filing complaint and must allege (in general terms): Residency and domicile (see subhead Residence, supra), parties are lawfully married, number of children below 18 or above 18 but still dependent on parties, best interests re custody, awards of property, payment of debts, orders for child and spousal support and grounds. In actions involving minor children, plaintiff must attach exhibit pertaining to conciliation, child care and child custody proceedings. (583-9; HFCR.90). In all actions, matrimonial action information form must accompany complaint. (HFCR.90). Defendant may file cross-complaint. (580-4).

Practice.—Decree of divorce may be entered by default. (HFCR.93). Family Court has two calendars, contested and uncontested. Contested matters are placed on calendar by filing motion to set case for trial. (HFCR.94). Motion to set must be accompanied by asset and debt, income and expense statements of movant as well as position statement re all issues of divorce. Temporary orders re restraining orders (580-10), child custody or support (580-11) or alimony (580-9) may be issued.

Decree becomes final on date fixed therein but in no event later than one month from date of decree. (580-45).

Final decree not entered because of mistake, negligence or inadvertence may be entered subsequently and divorce is deemed to have become final at date decree could have been first entered. (580-46).

Personal Judgment.—Court may render personal judgment against party outside state and over whom jurisdiction is acquired by service of process (see above) and if party was domiciliary of state: (1) At time cause of action arose, or (2) at time of commencement of proceeding, or (3) at time of service. (580-3.5).

Alimony.—Both temporary (580-9; 44 Haw. 491, 355 P.2d 188) and permanent (580-47) may be awarded. Amount is in sound discretion of court; factors considered are financial resources of parties, ability of party seeking support to meet his or her needs independently, duration of marriage, standard of living established during marriage, age of parties, physical and emotional condition of parties, usual occupation of parties during marriage, vocational skills and employability of party seeking support, needs of parties, custodial and child support responsibilities, ability of paying party to meet his or her own needs, financial condition under which parties may be left, probable duration of need (580-47; 41 Haw. 345); and may be modified upward (39 Haw. 245) or downward (34 Haw. 237), even in cases where parties stipulated that support payments

See note at head of Digest as to 1998 legislation covered.

See Topical Index in front part of this volume.

HI – 28

DIVORCE . . . *continued*
may not be modified (8 Haw. App. 391; 804 P.2d 891). May be granted to husband or wife. (1974, Act 65).

Change of husband or wife's surname may be granted in decree.

Custody and visitation of children is matter for discretion of court. (580-47). Each parent has equal right to award of custody of minor child; neither parent has any preferred status for award of custody. Criteria and procedures in awarding custody are best interests of child, may be awarded to one or both parents or other parties, wishes of child of sufficient age, social study and investigation by court personnel, expert testimony; visitation may be awarded to parents and grandparents or any person interested in welfare of child. (571-46; 56 Haw. 51, 527 P.2d 1275). Court can award joint custody upon application of either parent. Court may order any party to attend counseling. (571-46.2). Uniform Child Custody Jurisdiction Act governs interjurisdictional custody concerns. (583).

Division of Property of Spouses.—Court has discretion to divide and distribute real, personal or mixed estate of spouses, whether community, joint or separate. (580-47). Following entry of decree of divorce, spouses' rights in property are governed by H.R.S. cc. 533 and 560 until entry of order dividing property. (580-56).

Support of Children.—Complies with federal Personal Responsibility and Work Opportunity Reconciliation Act of 1996 ("Welfare Reform Act"). (1997, Act 293). All support orders accompanied by wage assignment. (571-5a). Child Support Enforcement Act (576D); Administrative Process for Child Support Enforcement (576E).

Remarriage.—There are no restrictions on remarriage of divorced persons, but on remarriage of party decree for alimony may be modified or terminated. (580-51).

Separation for period of not to exceed two years may be decreed in any matrimonial action upon petition for separation when court finds marriage is temporarily disrupted. (580-71). Decree of separation is not bar to petition for divorce; however, fact that parties have lived separate and apart under decree of separation may not be used as ground in support of such petition. (580-71.5).

Registration of divorces and annulments required. (338-29).

Annulment of Marriage.—See topic Marriage.

Effect of Divorce.—See category Estates and Trusts, topic Wills.

GUARDIAN AND WARD:

Uniform Probate Code.—Arts. I through IV of 1993 Uniform Probate Code adopted as 560:1-101 to 560:4-401 with modifications. See category Estates and Trusts, topic Descent and Distribution. Art V of 1969 Uniform Probate Code (c. 560), but not 1975 or 1977 Official Amendments, still applies with following modifications: Family court has jurisdiction over guardianship proceedings (560:5-102). Guardian may be compensated in such amount as family court deems appropriate and reasonable. (560:5-105). In appointment of guardian, preference given to testamentary nominees. (560:5-204). Jurisdiction over protective proceedings is in circuit court. (560:5-102). Guardian must file report on status of ward at least annually. (560:5-308A).

Selection of Guardian.—Any person whose appointment would be in best interests of minor may be guardian. Minor 14 years or older may nominate guardian for court approval. (560:5-206). Any competent person or any nonprofit agency or corporation, public or private, may be guardian of incapacitated person. Priority of selection is spouse or reciprocal beneficiary, adult child, parent or person nominated by will of deceased parent, relative with whom incapacitated person resided more than six months, and nominee of person caring for or paying benefits to incapacitated person. (560:5-311). Guardian of property may be individual or corporation, with general power to serve as trustee. Priority of consideration is guardian of property or other fiduciary appointed by court where protected person resides, nominee of protected person if latter is 14 years and has sufficient mental capacity, spouse or reciprocal beneficiary, adult child, parent or person nominated by will of deceased parent, relative with whom protected person resided more than six months and nominee of person caring for or paying benefits to protected person. (560:5-410). Notice of petition for guardianship need not be served upon person whose parental rights have been terminated.

Eligibility and Competency.—Any competent person may be appointed guardian of person of minor. (560:5-206). Any competent person or any nonprofit agency or corporation, public or private, may be appointed guardian of person of incapacitated person. (560:5-311).

Qualification.—Court may require guardian of property to furnish bond. (560:5-411).

Powers and Duties.—Guardian of person of minor has powers and responsibilities of parent, except not obligated to provide from own funds and not liable to others, solely by reason of guardianship, for acts of minor ward. State law mandates that each child placed in foster care must be covered by comprehensive health care plan. Other powers and duties are enumerated. (560:5-209). Guardian of person of incapacitated person has powers, rights and duties of parent, except not liable to others, solely by reason of guardianship, for acts of ward. Where guardian of property also appointed, guardian controls custody and care of ward and is entitled to reasonable compensation for services rendered. (560:5-312). Guardian of property has general duty to act as fiduciary, observing standard of care prescribed by statute for trustees. Other powers and duties include inventory, record keeping, accounting, holding title to all of protected person's property and enumerated statutory powers of administration, distribution, estate planning and claims payment. (560:5-417-420, 424-428).

Investments.—Guardian of property has power, without court authorization or confirmation, to invest and reinvest funds of estate as would trustee. (560:5-424).

Securities in Name of Nominee.—See category Estates and Trusts, topic Trusts, subhead Securities in Name of Nominee.

Real Estate.—Guardian of property has power, without court authorization, to collect, hold and retain assets, including land in another state, until he judges disposition should be made; to acquire and dispose of assets, including land in another state, for cash or on credit, at public or private sales; to repair, alter, improve or demolish buildings and other structures; to subdivide, develop or dedicate land; to enter into leases; to grant and take options; and has other powers. (560:5-424). Power to sell, lease or mortgage Hawaii real property is subject to court confirmation. (531-28.5 and 531-29).

Caveat.—For disclosure requirements in conveyance of real property made or taken in representative capacity, see category Property, topic Deeds.

Liabilities of Guardian.—Guardian of property not personally liable on contract entered in his fiduciary capacity in course of administration unless otherwise provided in contract. Is personally liable for obligations arising from ownership or control of property of estate and for torts committed in course of administration. (560:5-429).

Accounts.—Every guardian of property must account to court periodically as court may direct. (560:5-419).

Termination of Guardianship.—Guardianship of minor ward terminates on death, resignation or removal of guardian, on minor's death, adoption, marriage or attainment of majority, or on formal denial of probate where testamentary appointment under informally probated will, but guardianship cannot be terminated by resignation until approved by family court. (560:5-210). Guardianship of incapacitated person terminates on death of guardian or ward, on determination of incapacity of guardian, on removal or resignation of guardian or on formal denial of probate where testamentary appointment under informally probated will. (560:5-306). Guardian of property terminated on death, resignation or removal of guardian of property for good cause, or on determination that minority or disability of protected person has ceased. (560:5-415, 430).

Insane Persons.—Persons impaired because of mental illness, mental deficiency or mental disorder are included in definition of incapacitated persons. (560:5-101).

Gifts to Minors.—See topic Infants.

Uniform Fiduciaries Act adopted in 1945. (c. 556). Uniform Act §3 repealed by adoption of Uniform Commercial Code. (490-10-102[1]).

Uniform Simplification of Fiduciary Security Transfers Act was adopted in 1965 and superseded by Uniform Commercial Code.

HUSBAND AND WIFE:

Governed generally by HRS chapters 321, 510, 572, 573 and 560.

Married person may make contracts, oral and written, with persons other than her or his spouse, in same manner as if sole. Spouses may contract with each other: (1) By deed or assignment; (2) by agreement setting respective rights in property owned by them, or either of them, when agreement made in contemplation of divorce or judicial separation; (3) by agreement providing for periodic payments for support and maintenance of one spouse by other or for children when made in contemplation of divorce or judicial separation provided that agreement will be subject to court approval; (4) by partnership agreements (572-22); and (5) may waive rights to election as surviving spouse, before or after marriage, of deceased spouse's homestead allowance, exempt property and family allowance (560:2-204). Prospective spouses may enter into premarital agreements. (c. 321).

Upon marriage both spouses shall declare their married middle and last names. Names may be his or her own, that of spouse, or combined and hyphenated with spouse's but names must have been legally used at some time by either spouse. (574-1).

Actions.—Spouses or reciprocal beneficiaries may sue other partner in tort. (572-28; 663-1). Either spouse may maintain action in Family Court for nonfelonious offense by other spouse. Domestic violence laws define "family or household members" to include persons having child in common. Married person not liable for debts of spouse; nor is married person's property liable to be taken on execution or other process against that person's spouse. (572-23). Spouses bound to maintain, provide for, and support one another during marriage and shall be liable for all debts contracted by one another for necessaries of family during marriage. (572-24).

Agency.—Custom permits either spouse to act as attorney in fact for the other, although there is no statutory authority therefor. (See 7 Haw. 216; 17 Haw. 481.)

Desertion.—Uniform Desertion and Non-Support Act has been adopted with modifications. (c. 575).

Community Property.—Provisions establishing community property were effective from June, 1945 through June, 1949. Provisions controlling management and disposition of existing community property are in c. 510.

Uniform Premarital Agreement Act adopted. (c. 572D).

Uniform Disposition of Community Property Rights at Death Act adopted. (c. 510).

Uniform Interstate Family Support Act replaces and repeals c. 576, Uniform Reciprocal Enforcement of Support Act. (1997, Act 295).

INFANTS:

Age of majority is 18 for both sexes. Parents are liable for support of their minor unmarried children, and have equal powers and duties with respect to them: they are jointly their natural guardians, are jointly and severally liable for their torts and are jointly and severally entitled to prosecute and defend suits in which they or their property are concerned. (c. 577). Parents may sue children (51 Haw. 74, 450 P.2d 998) and vice versa (51 Haw. 484, 462 P.2d 1007). Uniform Parentage Act adopted. (c. 584). Parents and guardian also accountable for child's compliance with student code of conduct. (§302A).

Administrative Enforcement for Child Support.—See generally c. 576E. Office of Child Support Hearings established within Department of Attorney General. (1994, Act 105).

Child Support Enforcement.—If child support payments are made through agency, agency must enforce support orders. (576D-3[b]). Parent locator services extend to both custodial and absent parent. (576D-6). Child support order shall be recorded in bureau of conveyances or land court. (576D-10.5). Child support payments withheld from

See note at head of Digest as to 1998 legislation covered.

See Topical Index in front part of this volume.

INFANTS . . . *continued*

obligor's income are not to exceed maximum limits set under Consumer Credit Protection Act. (576-E16).

Emancipation.—Minor who has legally married (572) is treated as having attained age of majority and has all rights, duties, privileges and responsibilities thereunder, with certain enumerated exceptions (577-25).

Disability.—Infants may bring personal actions within respective statutes of limitation after disability of infancy is removed, or at any time while it exists. (657-13). Infants or any one claiming under them may bring real action at any time within five years after disability is removed notwithstanding that 20 year statute of limitations has expired. (657-34). But if infant dies without recovering premises, no further time is permitted by reason of disability of his successor in claim. (657-36).

Disaffirmance of contract of minor must be made within reasonable time after reaching age of majority. (19 Haw. 474).

Actions.—Guardians ad litem may be appointed to represent minors whose interests are affected by litigation. (551-2).

Involuntary Termination of Parental Rights.—Family courts may terminate parental rights only when verified petition has been filed by some responsible adult on behalf of child in family court of circuit in which child resides or was born and court has conducted hearing of petition unless hearing waived if waiver permitted by statute. (571-61). In custody proceedings, past family violence committed by parent creates rebuttable presumption that it is not in best interest of child to be placed with that parent. (571-46[9]).

Parental Responsibility.—Parents liable for torts of unmarried minor children. (577-3, 663-1).

Paternity/Parentage.—Voluntary admission of paternity admissible as evidence of parentage in any family court proceeding. (338-12). Must treat paternity determination in any state or U.S. territory as adjudication in this State. (c. 584). Sets standard for genetic testing. (584-11). Presumed to be natural father if genetic testing results do not exclude possibility of paternity. Acknowledgment of paternity filed with department of health may establish support obligation. (584-4).

Support of Minor.—Family court has continuing jurisdiction to compel parents to provide for support, maintenance and education of minor children and adult children is some cases. (580-47).

Uniform Gifts to Minors Act repealed and replaced by Uniform Transfers to Minors Act. (553). Age of majority under Act is 21 years. (553-1).

Uniform Securities Ownership by Minors Act has not been adopted.

Interstate Compact on Juveniles enacted. (c. 582).

Child Protective Act.—(c. 587).

Children's Advocacy Program.—(c. 588).

Adoption.—See topic Adoption.

MARRIAGE:

In order to make valid the marriage contract, it is necessary: (1) That respective parties do not stand in relation to each other of ancestor and descendant of any degree whatsoever, brother and sister of whole or half blood, uncle and niece or aunt and nephew, whether relationship is result of issue of parents married, or not married, to each other, (2) that each of parties be at least 16 (or 15 with written approval of family court, but in no case less than 15); (3) that neither party has any lawful spouse living; (4) that consent of neither party has been obtained by force, duress or fraud; (5) that neither party be afflicted with any loathsome disease concealed from, and unknown to, other party; (6) that marriage shall only be between a man and a woman. (572-1).

License.—It is not lawful for any persons to marry in the state without a license for that purpose duly obtained from the agent appointed to grant marriage licenses. Both applicants for a license must appear in person before the agent and file an application in writing, accompanied by a statement signed and sworn to by each applicant setting forth full name, age, race, residence, relationship of applicants if any, full names of parents and date of death of last prior spouse or date and jurisdiction of dissolution of last prior marriage, if any. (572-6).

Marriage ceremony must be performed by validly licensed person or society. (572-1). License to solemnize marriage revoked for failure to comply with rules of department of health. (c. 572). Ceremony may be performed any place in state provided man, woman and marriage officiant are all physically present at same place and time for ceremony. (572-1). Any person under 18 must have consent of parent, guardian or other person having care and government of such party. (572-2). Special licenses to solemnize marriages are required, and persons so licensed must deliver copy of certificate of marriage to all persons married by them (572-13) and report such marriage within three business days to department of health. (572-15).

Record.—Names, ages, number times married, residence, birthplace, parents' names, date and place of marriage, name of officiant required. See also category Documents and Records, topic Records, subhead Vital Statistics.

Proxy marriages and marriage by written contract are not recognized.

Common law marriages are not recognized in Hawaii. (27 F.2d 582).

Local Recognition of out of State.—Marriages legal in the country where contracted are legal in the courts of Hawaii (572-3), unless odious by common consent of civilized nations (3 Haw. 489; 12 Haw. 329). There is a presumption of validity. (29 Haw. 716).

Annulment of marriage may be granted for the following causes: (1) That the parties stood in such relation to each other that they could not lawfully marry; (2) that one or both of the parties had not attained the legal age of marriage; (3) that either party had an undivorced spouse living; (4) that one of parties lacked mental capacity to consent to marriage; (5) that consent to marriage of party applying for annulment was obtained by force, duress or fraud, and there has been no subsequent cohabitation; (6) that one of parties was suffering from leprosy or afflicted with any loathsome disease and said fact was concealed from, and unknown to, party applying for annulment. (580-21).

Same-Sex Marriage.—Only male-female marriages are recognized. (572-1; Contra Baehr v. Miike, 1996 WL 69423 [Haw.Cir.Ct., Dec. 3, 1996] [No.Civ. 91-1394]). *Note:* Pending Hawaii constitutional amendment giving state legislature authority to decide who can marry.

Foreign Marriages.—Marriages legal in country where contracted are legal in Hawaii. (572-3).

Uniform Premarital Agreement Act, adopted. (c. 572D).

MARRIED WOMEN:

See topics Husband and Wife, Marriage; categories Civil Actions and Procedure, topic Evidence, subhead Witnesses; Debtor and Creditor, topic Homesteads; Documents and Records, topic Acknowledgments; Estates and Trusts, topics Executors and Administrators, Wills; Property, topic Dower.

NAMES:

Procedure for change of names is handled by Lieutenant Governor, unless change ordered in adoption or divorce decree. (574-5).

See also topic Husband and Wife.

RECIPROCAL BENEFICIARY:

Reciprocal beneficiary status extends certain rights to couples comprised of two adult individuals who are ineligible for marriage under c. 572. (1997, H.B. 118, §1). Benefit areas include, but are not limited to, survivorship, inheritance, insurance and real property rights. Unless expressly provided, reciprocal beneficiaries shall not have same rights and obligations conferred through marriage under c. 572. (§6). *Caveat:* Provisions of Act are severable (§21), and are subject to federal preemption and pending legislative and judicial decisions.

Qualification requirements for each applicant: minimum 18 years of age; sign Declaration of Reciprocal Beneficiary Relationship form issued by Director of Health; consent to relationship not obtained by force, duress, or fraud; prohibited from marrying one another under c. 572; neither party be married nor party to another reciprocal beneficiary relationship. (§§3, 4).

Declaration fee $8, payable to Director. (§5).

Termination.—Either party may terminate relationship by filing declaration of termination with Director. (§7). Termination automatic upon obtaining marriage license in Hawaii by either party, or upon legal marriage of either party. (§7).

HEALTH

FOOD, DRUG AND COSMETICS:

Regulated generally by c. 328. Chapter covers following acts in regard to food, drug, medical device, or cosmetic: misbranding, adulteration, false advertising, misrepresentation, improper labeling, trademark infringement, and improper substitutions. (328-6).

HEALTH INSURANCE BENEFITS:

Prepaid Health Care Act.—Hawaii Prepaid Health Care Act (c. 393) requires local employers to provide coverage for employees by prepaid group health care plan. Required health care benefits addressed in 393-7. Mandatory coverage regulated by c. 393, Part II. Administration and enforcement, including penalties, provided in c. 393, Part III. Part IV of c. 393 provides for governmental subsidies to cover certain health insurance premium costs.

State Health Insurance Program Act.—Regulated by c. 431N. Establishes program within Department of Health to ensure basic health insurance coverage to Hawaii residents who are medically uninsured and who are defined as "gap group individuals". (431N-1).

Medicaid-Related Mandates.—Regulated by c. 431L. Prohibition against employers taking Medicaid status into account when making payments for benefits. (431L-1). Provides for state's right to third party payments. (431L-2). Provides for coverage of children under Medicaid. (431L-3, 5, 6). Specifies employer obligations to provide health insurance coverage for certain children of employees if such coverage is pursuant to court or administrative order. (431L-4).

Health Maintenance Organization Act.—Regulates establishment and operation of Health Maintenance Organizations. (c. 432D).

SMOKING REGULATION:

Smoking in Public Places.—Regulated by 328K-1 to 7. Smoking prohibited in certain enumerated private and publicly owned facilities and areas as specified in 328K-2. Exceptions stated in 328K-3. Posting signs required in 328K-4. Generally, no cigarette sales from vending machines and lunch wagons. (328K-7). Penalties and procedures set forth in 328K-5.

Smoking in Workplace.—(328K-11 to 14). Each employer in Hawaii must maintain written smoking policy which must contain, at minimum, statements that: (A) if nonsmoking employee objects to employer about smoke in workplace, employer will attempt to reach reasonable accommodation between preferences of smoking and nonsmoking employees, and (B) smoking policy shall be announced within two weeks of vote of preferences of employees in each respective work area and posted conspicuously in all affected workplaces. (328K-13). Smoking in property owned or leased by federal government entities is not regulated by this chapter. This chapter also does not regulate private enclosed office workplaces occupied exclusively by smokers (except where smoking is prohibited by county fire department or other ordinance). (328K-14). Penalties include fine not to exceed $500, as provided in 328K-15.

See note at head of Digest as to 1998 legislation covered.

See Topical Index in front part of this volume.

INSURANCE

INSURANCE COMPANIES:

Regulated by complete and comprehensive code, adopted in 1955, and revised effective as of July 1, 1988, as in force and governs Hawaii insurance law. (c. 431).

Supervision by Insurance Commissioner (hereafter "Commissioner") (1010 Richards Street, Honolulu, HI 96813) who serves at will of Director of Department of Commerce and Consumer Affairs. (431:2-102).

Rates must not be excessive, inadequate or unfairly discriminatory. 431:14-103[a][1]. Every insurer shall file in triplicate with Commissioner, except as to specific marine risks, every manual of classifications, rules and rates, every rating plan, every other rating rule, and modification of any of foregoing it proposes to use. (431:14-104[a]). Each filing must be accompanied by $20 fee payable to Commissioner. (431:14-104[b]). Willfully withholding information from or knowingly giving false or misleading information which will affect rates or premiums chargeable under Art. 14 of c. 431 is subject to penalties under 431:14-117. (431:14-115). Insurance Rating Organization regulations contained in c. 431:14-107 et seq. Commissioner may reduce or adjust rates annually for all types of insurance. (1998, Act 117; SB 3105).

Annual Statements.—Authorized insurance companies must file annual audit of company's financial condition by independent CPA or accounting firm. (431:3-302.5). Risk based capital formula for life and health insurers. Insurers must file annual and quarterly financial statements with National Association of Insurance Commissioners (NAIC). (431:3-302).

Policies.—Accident and Sickness Insurance Contracts. (431:10A). Insurance coverage for newborn adopted children provided. (431:10A-116). Insurers must generally provide coverage for reciprocal beneficiaries to same extent that they provide coverage for spouses and families. (1997, Act 383; HB 118). Reciprocal beneficiary couples comprised of two adult individuals who are ineligible for marriage under c. 572. (1997, Act 383, HB 118). See also category Family, topic Reciprocal Beneficiary. Code promotes availability of long term care insurance, sets policy standards and provides for coverage comparison. (431:10A-521, 531). Discrimination based on genetic information is prohibited. (1997, Act 91; SB 1565). Credit Life Insurance and Credit Disability Insurance. (431:10B). Motor Vehicle Insurance. (431:10C). Personal injury protection benefits insurance required. (431:10C-104). Life Insurance and Annuities. (431:10D). Qualifying nonprofit organizations which enter into charitable gift annuity agreements with donors are excluded from regulation under Insurance Code. (431:1-204). Property Insurance. (431:10E). Surety Insurance. (431:10F). Motorcycle and Motor Scooter Insurance. (431:10G). Liability and medical payment coverage consistent with motor vehicle insurance laws amounts. (431:10G-301). Insurance Holding Company System. (431:11). Limits acquisition of insurer authorized to do business in Hawaii. (431:11-104). Business Transacted with Producer Controlled Property/Casualty Insurer. (431:11A).

Insurance contracts generally regulated by Art. 10.

Right to Return Policy.—Purchasers of individual life or disability insurance policies have right to return policies without obligation within ten days of receipt. This does not apply to single premium nonrenewable policies or travel accident policies. (431:10-214).

Disclosure of health care coverage and benefits required. (431:10-109).

Pooled insurance allowed. (431:10-222.5; 1998, Act 268; HB 2762).

Discrimination prohibited as to terms or conditions of any insurance contract, or in rate or amount of premiums charged therefor, or in benefits payable or in any other right or privilege accruing thereunder, in favor of particular individuals or persons, or between insureds or subjects of insurance having substantially like insuring, risk, and exposure factors, or expense elements. (431:13-103[7][B]).

Rebates are prohibited except as otherwise expressly provided by law. (431:13-103[8]). Commissioner is authorized to investigate claims of unfair or deceptive acts or practices prohibited by 431:13-102 and defined by 431:13-103. (431:13-105). However, following practices will not be considered prohibited rebate: (1) Payment of bonuses (in case of any contract of life insurance or life annuity) out of surplus accumulated from nonparticipating insurance if payment is fair, equitable and in best interests of insurer and policyholders; (2) allowance to policyholders (in case of life insurance policies issued on industrial debit plan) who have continuously, for specified period, made premium payments directly to office of insurer in amount fairly representing saving in collection expense; (3) readjustment of premium rate for group insurance policy based on loss or expense thereunder, and (4) distribution of savings, earnings or surplus equitably among class of policyholders in case of any insurance contract. (431:13-103[9]).

Liens.—None.

Agents and Brokers.—All persons (general agent, subagent, solicitor, or adjuster) must procure licenses from Commissioner before soliciting business. (431:9-201). Subject to exceptions, application and examination necessary for license. (431:9-206). 431:8 provides instances allowing insurance business transactions by unauthorized insurers. 431:9A regulates licensing, duties, examination and liabilities of managing general agents. Any title insurer or insurer that operates as escrow depository must be licensed pursuant to c. 449. (431:20-106.5).

Process Agent.—Captive insurance companies required to appoint resident agent to accept service of process. (431:19-102[b][4][k]). Attorney-in-fact for reciprocal insurer empowered to accept service of process and can authorize Commissioner to receive service of process in actions upon contracts exchanged. (431:4-406[b][2]). Every fraternal benefit society authorized to do business in Hawaii shall appoint in writing Commissioner and each successor to be its true and lawful attorney upon whom all lawful process in any action against it shall be served. (432:2-701[a]). Each authorized foreign or alien insurer shall appoint Commissioner as its attorney to receive service of, and upon whom may be served, all legal process issued against it in Hawaii upon claims arising within Hawaii. (431:2-205[a]). Any act of transacting insurance business in Hawaii by unauthorized insurer constitutes irrevocable appointment of Commissioner or

successor to be true and lawful attorney of insurer upon whom may be served any notice, order, pleading or process in any proceeding before Commissioner and arising out of transacting insurance business in Hawaii. (431:8-207[a]). Each licensed nonresident agent or broker shall appoint Commissioner as agent's or broker's attorney to receive service of legal process upon claims arising within Hawaii. (431:9-220[a]).

Investments, as well as prohibitions and limitations thereon, discussed in Art. 6 of c. 431. Investments of foreign or alien insurers as permitted by laws of domicile, but must be of quality substantially as high as those required for domestic insurers. (431:6-501). Related insurers allowed to acquire investments in investment pools. (1997, Act 233; HB 1899).

Foreign Insurance Companies.—Foreign insurance company must qualify for and can transact insurance in Hawaii only through certificate of authority from Commissioner. Foreign and alien insurers must either be licensed under laws of not less than three states designated by Commissioner from among states accredited by NAIC (431:3-201; 431:3-203; 431:3-203.5) or satisfy following criteria: (1) Be stock, mutual or reciprocal insurer or same general type as may be formed as domestic insurer under Art. 4 of c. 431; (2) have capital funds as required by c. 431; (3) transact or propose to transact insurances in Hawaii which are authorized by its charter and meet standards of c. 431; (4) fully comply with provisions of c. 431; (5) appoint general agent who qualifies under Art. 9 of c. 431 (this requirement does not apply to foreign and alien reinsurers licensed to transact business in Hawaii that assume any portion of risk of another insurer); and (6) have continuously, actively and successfully transacted insurance business for at least five years immediately prior. Each foreign insurer must prepare annual statement in accordance with NAIC Practices and Procedures Manual. (431:3-301).

Insurer must notify Insurance Commissioner within three days if it believes that its financial condition is hazardous to policyholder or public. (1993, Act 50). Insurer who wishes to withdraw from State must do so in compliance with 431:3-215.

See category Business Organizations, topic Corporations, subhead Foreign Corporations.

Captive Insurance Companies.—Insurance Code applies to certain captive insurance companies. (431:19-115). Insurance Commissioner appoints advisor to review captive insurance company applications. (431:19-102). Commissioner has authority to approve service providers to captive insurance companies. (1998, Act 150; HB 2672). Each pure captive insurance company licensed to do business in Hawaii must pay Director of Finance through Commissioner 0.25% tax on gross premiums received from all risks or property resident, situated, or located in Hawaii and on risks and property situated elsewhere upon which no premium tax is otherwise paid during year ending on preceding Dec. 31, less return premiums and less any reinsurance accepted. Each association captive insurance company licensed to do business in Hawaii and each risk retention captive insurance company chartered in Hawaii must pay 1% tax instead. These taxes are due and payable on Mar. 15 of each year. When paid, these taxes shall be in settlement of and in lieu of all demands for all taxes except: (1) Taxes on real property and (2) taxes on purchase, use or ownership of tangible personal property. (431:19-116). All such taxes and fees are credited to captive insurance administration fund from which Commissioner may compensate captive insurance administrator who is responsible for implementation of rules concerning captive insurance companies. (1997, Act 261; HB 2202).

Redomestication of authorized insurance companies addressed. (c. 431, Arts. 3, 19). Requirements for foreign or alien captive insurance company to become Hawaii domestic captive insurance company. (431:19-102.3).

Requirements for domestic captive insurance company to transfer to new domicile. (431:19-102.4).

Association and risk retention captives must file NAIC annual statement blank and audit with Insurance Division and NAIC. (431:19-107; 1998, Act 072; SB 2840).

Retaliatory Laws.—None.

Premium Tax.—Insurers pay 2.75% on gross life insurance premiums, 0.8775% on gross underwriting profit of marine insurance, and 4.265% on all other gross premiums. (431:7-202). Taxes shall be paid quarterly with quarterly tax statement, failure to do so subjects insurer to fine. (1998, SB 2835).

Privilege Tax.—Annual license is $400 for first year, thereafter companies pay annual license fee of $200. Agents pay annual license fee of $50 each year. Solicitors and adjusters pay license fee of $40 first year and $20 to $30 annually thereafter. (431:7-101).

Uniform Insurers Liquidation Act.—Repealed HRS §§431-661 to 431-668, which constituted substantial adoption of major provisions of Uniform Insurers Liquidation Act, and enacted in lieu thereof HRS Art. 15 (§§431:15-101 to 431:15-411) entitled "Insurers Supervision, Rehabilitation and Liquidation". New provisions cannot be considered substantial adoption of major provisions of Uniform Act, although they contain some similar provisions and have same general purpose.

Benefit societies addressed in c. 432; mutual benefit societies (Art. 1) and fraternal benefit societies (431:2; 1998, SB 2037). Domestic mutual benefit societies required to file annual audits. (432:1-405). Separate chapter adopted in 1992 providing for stricter disclosure, review, reporting and financial examination requirements, consistent with National Association of Insurance Commissioners (NAIC) standards. Separate chapter adopted in 1976 to cover medical torts; includes provisions for establishment of medical claim conciliation panel. (c. 671). Hawaii Medical Malpractice Underwriting Plan provides contingency plan to be instituted by Commissioner upon availability of medical malpractice insurance in Hawaii. (c. 435C).

Insurer, self-insured employer or Special Fund can recover temporary disability benefits overpaid employee. (392-78).

Courts enforce objectively reasonable expectations of parties claiming coverage under insurance contracts, which are construed in accord with reasonable expectations of layperson. (72 Haw. 80, 807 P.2d 1256).

Credit for Reinsurance.—No credit allowed for reinsurance ceded to alien insurer. (431:3-211). Domestic ceding insurer can credit on its financial statements, as asset or

---

See note at head of Digest as to 1998 legislation covered.

See Topical Index in front part of this volume.

INSURANCE COMPANIES . . . *continued*
deduction from liability, risks ceded to group of incorporated underwriters and individual unincorporated underwriters. (431:4A-101).

Unfair Trade Practice Regulations.—Art. 13 entitled Unfair Methods of Competition and Unfair or Deceptive Acts and Practices in Business of Insurance. Following defined as unfair methods of competition and unfair or deceptive acts or practices in insurance business: Misrepresentation and false advertising of insurance policies; false information and advertising generally; defamation; boycott, coercion and intimidation; false financial statements; stock operations and advisory board contracts; unfair discrimination; rebates except as otherwise expressly provided by law; unfair claim settlement practices; failure to maintain compliant handling procedures; and misrepresentation in insurance applications to obtain fee. (431:13-103).

Duty to Defend.—Duty rests on possibility, however remote, that coverage exists. (78 Haw. 174, 891 P.2d 261).

Breach of duty to defend does not result in irrebuttable presumption that insurer is obligated to indemnify insured; however, presumption is appropriate where coverage was first admitted and then later denied. (81 Haw. 235, 915 P.2d 1336).

Defense costs incurred before tender of notice to insurer are not covered. (76 Haw. 346, 876 P.2d 1314).

Direct Actions Against Insurers.—See category Transportation, topic Motor Vehicles, subhead Direct Action.

Hurricane Relief Fund.—Relief fund established to monitor availability of property insurance and to offer hurricane property insurance when such insurance is unavailable in private market. Special mortgage recording fee of 0.1% of mortgage is imposed to create hurricane trust fund. Use graduated percentages to determine post-hurricane assessment on servicing facilities. (1998, HB 3437). Other provisions of fund are discussed in c. 431P, 1996, Acts 307, 445, 1998, SB 2336, and 1998, Act 106).

Worker's Compensation.—See category Employment, topic Labor Relations.

Guaranty Associations.—Guarantee payment on policies where insurer is unable to make payment. (431:16).

Hawaii Property Insurance Association.—Established to provide basic property insurance to owners and occupants of property in areas of high risk to natural disasters. (431:21-101).

Insurance Information Protection Act.—See 431:17.

SURETY AND GUARANTY COMPANIES:

Such companies must register with Director of Department of Commerce and Consumer Affairs of the State, and foreign corporations must comply with laws relating to such corporations. (78-20). See category Business Organizations, topic Corporations.

If bond executed by a principal and by corporation authorized to do surety business, corporation may be accepted as sole surety on bond. (78-20).

INTELLECTUAL PROPERTY

TRADEMARKS AND TRADENAMES:

Application to acquire trademark may be submitted by any person. Before registrant may receive certificate of registration for trademark, registrant must submit application stating: (A) That applicant is sole and original proprietor (or assignee of sole proprietor) of mark, (B) manner in which mark is to be used, and (C) description of goods for which mark is to be used. Declaration must be certified by applicant. (482-2).

What May Be Used.—As trademark or service mark purely geographical names such as "Honolulu" may not be registered. Coined words may be restricted to one registrant unless consent is granted by first registrant. Identical pronunciation of mark with registered mark, for example "Beach Days" versus "Beach Daze", will not be registered. Consideration will be given to root word of mark, for example "Island" versus "Islander". Deceptive words, symbols, or phrases will not be registered. (Hawaii Administrative Rules [HAR] 16-35-15). Department of Commerce and Consumer Affairs (DCCA) does not have explicit list of words or terms that are restricted. (482-4).

Registration.—DCCA requires that all trademark registration applications be made on its appropriate forms. Forms and filing at: Department of Commerce and Consumer Affairs, Business Registration Division, 1010 Richards Street, Honolulu, Hawaii 96813. (HAR 16-36-4[4]). Filing fee is $50 for term of one year from date of filing. (482-2, 3). Registrations may be renewed for additional periods of ten years from date of renewal by filing application for renewal and $50 fee. (482-2, 3). Two exact copies of mark must be filed with application. (482-2[b]).

Assignment.—Assignee of sole proprietor of trademark may register mark. (482-2). DCCA requires assignor to submit appropriate form, original and one true copy of mark, and $5 filing fee.

Protection Afforded.—Unlawful to adopt or use trademark or service mark identical or confusingly similar with one previously registered. Counterfeiting of mark is class C felony for which forfeiture of property is authorized. (708-875). As civil penalty, infringement of validly registered mark gives rise to: (A) Injunctive relief that may be imposed by courts (no express statutory injunctive relief provision), (B) any damages caused by infringement, (C) fine of not more that $1,000. (482-5). For violation of labor union's or association of employees' mark, attorney's fees and costs incurred in enforcement of statute and damages may be imposed. (482-4). Revised Uniform Deceptive Trade Practices Act adopted. (c. 481A).

Tradenames.—See subheads What May Be Used, Registration, Assignment, Protection Afforded supra; same basic rules apply to trademarks, service marks, and tradenames. Fictitious firm names may be registered with DCCA by single proprietor, partnership, or corporation upon payment of fee of $50 provided name is not substantially identical to previously registered name. (482-2, 3). No statutory requirement that individual, partnership, or corporation file tradename; no civil or criminal penalties for failure to file. Limited partnerships are not required to file tradenames in Hawaii, although it is common practice to do so if limited partnership operates under assumed name. Forms available at: Department of Commerce and Consumer Affairs, Business Registration Division, 1010 Richards Street, Honolulu, Hawaii 96813.

TRADE SECRETS:

Uniform Trade Secrets Act adopted, amended in part. (482B et seq.). Section provides relief for actual or threatened misappropriation of trade secret. Relief may include injunction, damages, attorneys' fee, or other affirmative acts as compelled by court order.

LEGAL PROFESSION

ATTORNEYS AND COUNSELORS:

State Bar is integrated.

Jurisdiction over Admissions.—Supreme Court is given power to regulate practice in state by Art. VI, §7 of Constitution. (See also 50 Haw. 107, 432 P.2d 887.) Supreme Court Rules prescribe procedures for admission to bar and for discipline. (Rules 1 and 2, respectively).

Model Rules of Professional Conduct are adopted with slight modifications to govern members of bar. (RSCH 2.2). Disciplinary Board of Hawaii Supreme Court and Disciplinary Counsel consider and investigate any alleged grounds for discipline of attorneys. (RSCH 2.4).

Eligibility.—Prior to any admission to bar, Supreme Court shall be satisfied of good moral character of applicant. Burden of proving good moral character is on applicant. (RSCH 1.3[c]). No applicant shall be allowed to sit for Hawaii Bar Examination or be admitted to Hawaii Bar during any period in which Hawaii's Child Support Enforcement Agency or like body in another jurisdiction has certified applicant is not in compliance with order of child support or is not in compliance with subpoena or warrant relating to paternity or child support proceeding. (RSCH 1.3[g]).

Registration as Law Student.—No requirement exists. See Supreme Court Rule 7 for rules governing supervised student practice of law. Students must make application to court clerk to become law student intern.

Educational Requirements.—Applicant must be graduate of law school approved by Council of American Bar Association on Legal Education and Admissions to Bar. Attorney who is not such graduate, but who has actively practiced law for five of six years immediately prior to application (service as judge of court of record being considered equivalent to active practice); or who is admitted in foreign country where English is language used in courts and English common law forms basis of jurisprudence and is permanent resident of U.S. under federal immigration laws; or who is admitted in state, territory or D.C. Latest information available from prerecorded message at Supreme Court; telephone (808) 539-4907.

Petition for Admission.—Applicants for bar must submit verified application on form provided by clerk of Supreme Court. Application must be accompanied by letters of recommendation from at least two attorneys licensed to practice in State which shall state circumstances under which attorney has known applicant and appraisal of applicant's moral character. Applicants for bar must submit verified application at least 90 days prior to exam date on form provided by clerk of Supreme Court. Fee for examination is $300 plus $175-$300 character report fee, and successful applicant must pay additional $10 for admission. Examinations begin on Mon. preceding last Wed. of Feb. and July each year.

Examination.—Multi-State Bar Examination used. Transfer of multi-state scores from other jurisdictions not accepted. Subjects tested on essay portion include business organizations, wills and trusts, civil procedure, Uniform Commercial Code (Arts. 2, 3 and 9), legal ethics and all of multi-state subjects.

Clerkship.—No requirement of clerkship prior to admission.

Admission without Examination.—A full-time member of faculty of University of Hawaii Law School who meets citizenship and educational requirements and is admitted to practice in another American jurisdiction may be admitted to bar without examination for a three-year period. After satisfactory completion of three-year period, said faculty member may be granted admission without limitation of time. (RSCH 1.8).

Full-time active duty military officer serving Staff Judge Advocate who meets other requirements may apply for limited admission for four years; may be extended once. JA may receive no client fees in addition to ordinary military pay.

Admission Pro Hac Vice.—Attorneys from other states, on special order, may be associated with local counsel on specific cases. For each year order is effective, attorney allowed to appear pro hac vice shall pay annual Disciplinary Board fee to State Bar Association. Only one fee is required even if attorney appears in more than one case. (RSCH 1.9). Eligibility to appear pro hac vice in U.S. District Court of Hawaii and application process therefore are regulated by Local Rules of Practice for the United States District Court for the District of Hawaii. (LR 83.1[e]).

Licenses.—License issued by Supreme Court.

Membership in Bar Assn. mandatory. Annual fee structured in three classes: Active, less than five years in profession; $275; more than five years, $430; inactive, $65.

Privileges.—Lawyer-client privilege recognized. (H.R.E. 503).

Disabilities.—Attorney cannot act as surety on any bond or undertaking in any action or proceeding unless authorized by court. (Circuit Court Rule 26).

Liabilities.—See topic Costs.

Compensation.—Fees governed by Rule 1.5 of Hawaii Rules of Professional Conduct. Fee must be reasonable. Contingent fee agreement must be in writing and must state method by which fee is to be determined. (Rule 1.5[c]). Contingent fees not permitted in criminal cases, divorce, alimony or support, or property settlement proceedings. (Rule 1.5[d][1]&[2]).

Lien.—Hawaii recognizes right of discharged attorney to assert charging lien for costs advanced and reasonable attorney fees against former client's recovery in case. (6

ATTORNEYS AND COUNSELORS . . . *continued*

Haw. App. 296, 719 P.2d 1107). Attorney who has been discharged by client but is entitled to some fees may file lien where there is fund sub judice. (1 Haw. App. 560, 623 P.2d 450). Attorney who did not prove specific amount due on asserted fee lien acquired by assignment from former employer was not entitled to enforce lien. (6 Haw. App. 296, 719 P.2d 1107).

Disbarment or Suspension.—Supreme Court may publicly censure, suspend for up to five years, or disbar and may order restitution or payment of costs (except attorney's fees). Disciplinary Board may publicly or privately reprimand or informally admonish. Practicing law during period of suspension of license may result in disbarment. See 79 Haw. 201, 900 P.2d 777.

Unauthorized Practice.—Individuals, associations or corporations not admitted to bar prohibited from practice of law. (605-14 and Supreme Court rules). Attorney General or Bar Association (605-15.1) may prosecute violators in Circuit Court (605-15).

Mandatory Continuing Legal Education.—None.

Specialty Certification Requirements.—Lawyer not permitted to publicly represent or imply that (s)he is recognized, designated, or certified specialist, except: (1) lawyer admitted to engage in patent practice before U. S. Patent and Trademark Office may use designation "Patents", "Patent Attorney", or "Patent Lawyer"; (2) lawyer engaged in trademark practice may use designation "Trademarks", "Trademark Attorney", or "Trademark Lawyer"; and (3) lawyer engaged in admiralty practice may use designation "Admiralty", "Proctor in Admiralty", or "Admiralty Lawyer". (Rule 7.4[a]&[b]). However, lawyer may communicate that (s)he is certified as specialist in field of law by named organization. (Rule 7.4[c]).

Professional Association (or Corporation).—Attorneys may associate to practice law as partners. Statute (415A, 1-31) permits professionals (including attorneys) to incorporate in restricted form. Attorneys may form professional corporations, but attorneys of such corporations retain unlimited liability as though association were partnership. (RSCH 6[g]). Attorneys may not form limited liability partnerships. (425-180). See also category Business Organizations, topic Corporations.

Powers.—Attorneys have control of an action to judgment and execution, but have no power to compromise, arbitrate, or settle without written authority. (605-7).

Rules of Professional Conduct.—Hawaii has adopted Hawaii Rules of Professional Conduct, fashioned after uniform model rules. See 81 Haw. 410, 917 P.2d 1284.

MINERAL, WATER AND FISHING RIGHTS

FISHING:

Fishing Rights.—All fishing grounds appertaining to any government land or otherwise belonging to government, except ponds, are open for free and equal use by all persons; provided that for protection of these fishing grounds, Department of Land and Natural Resources may manage and regulate taking of aquatic life. (187A-21). Act 243, 1998 establishes administrative or civil penalties for violation of statutes regulating aquatic resources and wildlife.

Konohikis.—Private vested fishing right giving tenants ability to either (1) set aside right to take one type of aquatic species for exclusive use of konohiki; or (2) prohibit all taking of aquatic life during certain months of year; provided that during fishing season within private fishery, konohiki may exact up to one-third of aquatic life taken within private fishery from each fisher among tenants. (187A-23).

MINES AND MINERALS:

Strip Mining.—Regulated and controlled by State Board of Land and Natural Resources. (c. 181). Permit required to engage in strip mining. (181-3). Permit application procedure governed by 181-4; bond required. (181-5).

State Mineral Rights.—Reservation and disposition governed by c. 182.

Geothermal Resources.—Production and utilization statutorily encouraged. State authorized to waive royalty payments from geothermal mining lessees to encourage initial or continued production of geothermal resources. (182-18). Surface owner has first right of refusal for mining lease. (182-5). Only areas designated as geothermal resource subzones may be utilized for geothermal development activities (development, or production of electrical energy from geothermal resources). (205-5.1[a]). Exploratory drilling is permitted outside of geothermal resource subzones. (c. 205). State Board of Land and Natural Resources responsible for designation of geothermal resource subzones. (205-5.2). Use of area for geothermal development activities within geothermal resource subzone governed by county planning commissions, except where conservation district affected. (205-5.1[c]). Activities within conservation district subject to state regulation. (205-5.1[d]). Naturally heated fluids below 150 degrees Fahrenheit are not geothermal resources. (c. 182-1). Thirty percent of all royalties received by state shall be paid to county in which mining operations are situated. (182-7).

Mining of sand, dead coral, coral rubble, rocks, soil or other beach or marine deposits from shoreline area is prohibited (with exceptions). (205A-44).

WATER:

Water Use.—Use of surface and ground waters governed by State Water Code and Commission on Water Resource Management. (c. 174C). Commission has jurisdiction to hear any dispute regarding water resource protection, water permits, constitutionally protected water interests, or competing needs for water. (174C-10). Coastal waters governed by Hawaii Coastal Zone Management Law and special management area guidelines. (c. 205A). Office of State Planning is responsible for management of coastal waters. (c. 205A).

Declaration of Water Use.—Any person making use of water from well or stream diversion works in any area of state must file declaration containing, among other things: information regarding quantity of water used, purpose or manner of use, time of

taking water, and point of withdrawal or diversion of water. (174C-26). Upon determination by Water Commission that use is "reasonable-beneficial use", certificate describing use shall be issued. (174C-27). "Reasonable-beneficial use" means use of water in such quantity as is necessary for economic and efficient utilization, for purpose, and in manner which is both reasonable and consistent with state and county land use plans and public interest. (174C-3).

Designated Water Management Areas.—When Water Commission determines that water resources of area are being threatened by existing or proposed withdrawals of water, Commission may, after public hearing, designate water management areas. (174C-41). Except for domestic consumption of water by individual users and uses of catchment systems to gather water, no person may make any withdrawal, diversion, impoundment or consumptive use of water in any designated water management area without first obtaining permit from Commission. (174C-48). To obtain permit, user must prove "reasonable-beneficial use", consistency with public interest, and other criteria listed in 174C-49. Permits are generally valid until designation of water management area is rescinded unless revoked or modified. (174C-55). Every 20 years, Commission is to conduct comprehensive study of all permits issued under Code to determine whether conditions of such permits are being complied with. (174C-56). Permits may be transferred in whole or in part if conditions of use of permit remain same and Commission is informed of transfer within 90 days. (174C-59). Water Code does not modify Native Hawaiian Water Rights. (174C-101).

MORTGAGES

CHATTEL MORTGAGES:

Uniform Commercial Code adopted. See category Business Regulation and Commerce, topic Commercial Code, especially for variations in connection with filing. Uniform Commercial Code has made use of chattel mortgages unnecessary.

Forms.—For UCC Forms, see end of this Digest.

MORTGAGES OF PERSONAL PROPERTY:

See topic Chattel Mortgages.

MORTGAGES OF REAL PROPERTY:

Transfers of interests in real property or fixtures made as security for performance of another act or subject to defeasance on payment of an obligation, whether such transfers are in trust or otherwise, are deemed mortgages and create liens, but do not pass title. (506-1).

Property.—If mortgage so provides, its lien may attach to additions, improvements, and purchases or substitutions made to supply place of any real property or fixtures disposed of and to all other after-acquired real property or fixtures referred to in mortgage when mortgagor acquires interest therein to extent of such interest, but subject to existing liens and lien of purchase money mortgage given by mortgagor of any such after-acquired real property or fixtures. (506-2). Further, lien does not attach to after-acquired real property and fixtures not described in mortgage until, after acquisition, instrument or affidavit is recorded referring to book and page number of mortgage and containing description of real property, fixtures, and real property to which fixtures attach. (506-3).

Execution.—The same formalities as to execution of mortgages are required as in the case of deeds. (q. v.).

Recording.—In order to constitute notice as against subsequent bona fide purchasers or encumbrancers, mortgage must be recorded in Bureau of Conveyances of State of Hawai'i, or if Torrens Act land, in Office of Assistant Registrar of Land Court of State of Hawai'i. For all recorded mortgages, copies must be single-sided, consecutively paginated, and not exceed 8½ × 11 inches. Top 3½ inches of first page of all documents must be left blank for use of recording officer. Following 1 inch space shall be reserved for information showing to whom document should be returned, beginning 1½ inches from left margin and not exceeding 3½ inches per line. First page shall include, if possible, all names of grantors and all names and addresses of grantees, type of document, and tax map key number (see example Commercial Code Form at end of this Digest). When grantee is corporation or partnership, document must contain state where entity is registered and entity's address. If more than one page, document should be stapled once in upper left corner. (502-31).

See category Property, topic Deeds.

Recording Schedule of Fees set forth in 501-218, as amended by Bureau of Conveyances, and 502-25. Special mortgage recording fee for hurricane reserve trust fund set forth in 431P-16.

Priorities.—Covered by 560-1.

Taxes.—See category Taxation, topic Property Taxes, subhead Mortgage Recording Fee.

Release.—Covered by 506-8. See subhead Satisfaction, infra.

Trust deeds are not commonly used, except to secure bond issues.

Future Advances.—Mortgage may secure past debts or future advances even though mortgagee is under no contractual duty to make such advances (506-1), but debts or advances must relate to same transaction or series of transactions for which mortgage is given or mortgage must specifically refer to it for advance to be secured (50 Haw. 304, 440 P.2d 262). Advances up to maximum amount of mortgage shall be superior to any subsequently recorded mortgage, lien or encumbrance other than liens for taxes and for public improvements. (506-1[b]).

Satisfaction.—Mortgagee shall provide mortgagor with recordable release of mortgage upon full satisfaction of mortgage and discharge of any debt secured thereby. Title insurers and underwritten title companies authorized to execute release of mortgages of real property or fixtures on behalf of mortgagee under certain circumstances. (506-8).

Discharge.—See subhead Satisfaction, supra.

MORTGAGES OF REAL PROPERTY . . . *continued*

Foreclosure.—Mortgages may be foreclosed: (1) By usual action in court; (2) by sale under power contained in mortgage, after publication of notice in English language once in each of three successive weeks, last publication not less than 14 days before sale, affidavit showing all details of notice and sale to be recorded within 30 days after sale. (c. 667). Any person who forecloses on condominium or apartment in cooperative housing project must notify board of directors by registered or certified notice. (667-5.5). Mailed notice of senior mortgagee's intent to foreclose under power of sale may be obtained by junior mortgagees of premises from foreclosing mortgagee by submitting written request to him any time after junior mortgage is filed but before period of published notice of foreclosure has run. (667-6). Recording fee is $25 per document, and $1 per page after 20 pages. Alternate, nonjudicial, power of sale foreclosure process established. (667-A through 667-V).

Sale.—See subhead Foreclosure, supra.

Redemption rights have been abolished.

Trust deeds are not commonly used, except to secure bond issues.

There are no statutory forms. The following forms may be used but not for loans under $25,000 (see category Business Regulation and Commerce, topic Consumer Protection):

Forms

Mortgage.—

KNOW ALL MEN BY THESE PRESENTS:

That (name, marital status and address of mortgagor), Mortgagor, in consideration of . . . . . . DOLLARS ($. . . . . .) to . . . . . . loaned and advanced by (name and address of mortgagee), Mortgagee, the receipt of which is hereby acknowledged, and in order to secure the repayment thereof according to the promissory note . . . . hereinafter mentioned, and also the repayment of any and all other indebtedness now or as may hereinafter be or become owing by the Mortgagor to the Mortgagee, do . . . . hereby grant . . . . . unto said (name of mortgagee—and if two or more, specify whether as joint tenants, tenants in common, or as tenants by the entirety):

(description of property)

TOGETHER with all improvements now or hereafter constructed or placed thereon and all fixtures now or hereafter attached to or used in connection with the property hereinabove described, including, without limiting the generality of the foregoing, the following described household appliances, together with any replacements thereof or additions thereto, which are, and shall be deemed to be, fixtures, a part of the interest in said property and a portion of the security for the indebtedness secured hereby:

TO HAVE AND TO HOLD the same, with all improvements now or hereafter placed or constructed being thereon, and all rights, easements, privileges and appurtenances thereto belonging, and the rents, issues and profits thereof, unto the Mortgagee and the (successors, heirs) and assigns of said Mortgagee forever.

AND the Mortgagor hereby covenants with the Mortgagee as follows:

The Mortgagor is lawfully seised in fee simple (as joint tenants, etc.) of the granted property and ha . . . . good right to grant and convey the same as aforesaid; that said property is free from all encumbrances (except as aforesaid); that the Mortgagee shall quietly enjoy and possess the same; and that the Mortgagor will and (its successors—or the executors and administrators of the survivor of them, etc.) shall warrant and defend the same unto the Mortgagee and the . . . . . . and assigns of the Mortgagee forever against the lawful claims and demands of all persons . . . . . .;

. . . . . . will pay unto the Mortgagee said sum of . . . . . . Dollars ($. . . . . .) with interest thereon, all according to the terms of the . . . . . . promissory note . . . . therefor of even date, made by the Mortgagor . . . . . . hereby secured; and will also pay all other indebtedness now or as may hereafter be or become owing by the Mortgagor to the Mortgagee on any and every account, together with interest thereon as may be specified with respect thereto;

Until such payment the Mortgagor will also pay all taxes, assessments and charges of every kind, to whomsoever assessed or chargeable, whether on the mortgaged property or any interest therein, or with respect to any improvements thereon, benefits thereto, income therefrom, or the indebtedness secured hereby, without any allowance or deduction whatsoever on account thereof from any indebtedness due under or secured by this mortgage; and will, upon request, deposit the receipts therefor with the Mortgagee;

The Mortgagor will, in the name and for the benefit of the Mortgagee, during the term of this mortgage, keep all improvements now or hereafter erected upon the mortgaged property insured against hazards of such type or types and in such amount or amounts and form of policy as the Mortgagee may from time to time require, and deposit the policy or policies with the Mortgagee (it being agreed and conditioned that in event of loss or damage the proceeds of insurance shall be applied by the Mortgagee, at the option of the Mortgagee, either to rebuilding or repair of damage or in reduction of any indebtedness secured hereby unless otherwise required by law); and if the Mortgagor shall procure any other insurance thereon, all such insurance shall likewise be made payable to and be claimable only by the Mortgagee, and whether so made payable or not it may be recovered by the Mortgagee by any appropriate proceeding and be similarly applied;

The Mortgagor will punctually pay the rent at all times and in the manner in said lease required, and otherwise observe and perform all of the covenants and conditions thereof on the part of the Lessee, and in all other respects keep the same in good standing and free from all liens and other encumbrances; (for leasehold only)

The Mortgagor will keep the mortgaged property in good condition and repair, and will permit the Mortgagee to enter and inspect the mortgaged property, and will comply with all laws, rules and regulations made by governmental authority and applicable thereto, and will not commit or suffer any strip, waste or any unlawful, improper or offensive use of said property, or any other act of negligence by which the same or any interest therein shall become liable under any lien or to seizure or attachment on mesne or final process of law, in bankruptcy or otherwise, or by which the security hereof shall be impaired or threatened;

Upon any failure of the Mortgagor to observe or perform any covenant or condition of this mortgage, or if any suit, proceeding or other contingency shall arise or be threatened relating to any of the mortgaged property, the Mortgagee may at the option of the Mortgagee, without notice or demand, make any advances or incur such expenses or otherwise act as may in the judgment of the Mortgagee seem advisable to protect the security of the Mortgagee hereunder or carry out the covenants of the Mortgagor herein, even though any tax, assessment, rate, encumbrance or charge paid in such behalf by the Mortgagee shall be invalid;

All advances, costs, expenses and attorney's fees which the Mortgagee may make, pay or incur under any provision of this instrument, for the protection of the security of the Mortgagee or any of the rights of the Mortgagee in connection with the mortgaged property, or in foreclosure proceedings commenced and subsequently abandoned, or in any dispute or litigation in which the Mortgagee or the holder of said note may become involved by reason of or arising out of this mortgage shall be paid by the Mortgagor to the Mortgagee upon demand and bear interest until paid at the rate of ten per cent per annum, all of which obligations shall be additional charges upon the mortgaged property and be equally secured hereby;

In case of condemnation of the mortgaged property or any part thereof by paramount authority, whether or not the mortgagor shall be in default hereunder at the time, any portion or all of any condemnation award to which the Mortgagor shall be entitled is hereby assigned to the Mortgagee and the Mortgagee is hereby irrevocably authorized to demand, sue for, collect, receive and receipt for the same and apply the net proceeds of the same toward the payment of the indebtedness secured hereby;

The Mortgagee shall have the right and is hereby expressly authorized to apply any payments received and any rents, issues and profits collected upon any indebtedness of the Mortgagor to the Mortgagee hereby secured and any such application shall in all respects be binding upon the Mortgagor;

PROVIDED, HOWEVER, that if the Mortgagor shall pay all indebtedness hereby secured, whether or not the same is mature, of which indebtedness the records of the Mortgagee shall be prima facie evidence, and otherwise well and faithfully perform and observe all of the covenants and conditions aforesaid, and pay the cost of release hereof, this mortgage shall become void; but all indebtedness hereafter owing by the Mortgagor to the Mortgagee shall be secured by this mortgage, whether or not at the time such indebtedness shall accrue there shall be then outstanding indebtedness owing by the Mortgagor to the Mortgagee, unless a release of this mortgage shall have been executed by the Mortgagee prior to the time such indebtedness shall accrue;

BUT UPON ANY DEFAULT in the performance or observance of any covenant or condition herein or in any promissory note contained or of the terms of any other indebtedness hereby secured, or if the Mortgagor (or any of them, if there be more than one) is adjudicated a bankrupt or insolvent, or shall file any petition or answer seeking relief as a debtor under any law for the relief or aid of debtors, or shall enter into any arrangement or composition with creditors, or if a receiver is appointed with respect to the property herein described, or if the mortgaged property, or any part thereof, shall be seized or levied upon under any legal process or under any claim of legal right, then, in each such event, the whole amount of all indebtedness owing by or chargeable to the Mortgagor under any provision of this mortgage, or intended to be secured hereby, on any and every account, shall at the option of the Mortgagee become at once due and payable without notice or demand, and with or without foreclosure the Mortgagee shall have the immediate right to receive and collect all rents and profits due or accrued or to become due, and said rents and profits are hereby assigned to the Mortgagee, and said Mortgagee is hereby irrevocably appointed the attorney in fact of the Mortgagor with power in the name of the Mortgagor or the Mortgagee to demand, sue for, collect, recover and receive all such rents and profits, to compromise and settle claims for rents or profits upon such terms and conditions as may seem proper, and to enter into, renew or terminate leases or tenancies, and the Mortgagee may foreclose this mortgage, by court proceeding (with the immediate right to a receivership with the aforesaid powers on ex parte order and without bond pending foreclosure), or, as now or then provided by law, either by entry and possession, or (with or without entry and possession) by advertisement and sale of the mortgaged property or any part or parts thereof at public auction in . . . . . ., State of Hawaii, and may in the name of the Mortgagee or as the attorney in fact of the Mortgagor, for such purpose hereby irrevocably appointed, effectually convey the property so sold to the purchaser or purchasers absolutely and forever; and any foreclosure shall forever bar the Mortgagor and all persons claiming under the Mortgagor from all right and interest in said property; and out of the proceeds of any foreclosure sale the Mortgagee may deduct all costs and expenses of foreclosure and/or suit, and retain or be awarded all sums then payable by or chargeable to the Mortgagor, rendering to the Mortgagor the surplus, if any. If such proceeds shall be insufficient to discharge the same in full, the Mortgagee may have any other legal recourse against the Mortgagor for the deficiency. The Mortgagee shall have the right to enforce one or more remedies hereunder or any other remedy the Mortgagee may have, successively or concurrently, including the right to foreclose this mortgage with respect to any portion of the mortgaged property without thereby impairing the lien of this mortgage on the remainder of the mortgaged property or affecting the remedies of the Mortgagee available with respect thereto.

If the property includes, or is under, covered, or affected by any leases, and the Mortgagor or anyone else with right to and/or obligations under any property leases, including, but not limited to lessors, lessees, sublessors, and sublessees, become a debtor in a voluntary or involuntary bankruptcy case, and an order for relief is issued pursuant to the bankruptcy laws, then Mortgagor will take the actions necessary to prevent the property lease(s) from being rejected by Mortgagor, any bankruptcy trustee or any other person pursuant to the bankruptcy laws, or from being terminated in any manner. Mortgagor will take such actions within five days from the date of filing of the order of relief. The bankruptcy laws include, but are not limited to, §365 of Title 11 of the provisions of the United States Code, as it may be amended; (for leasehold only).

IT IS ALSO AGREED:

Upon the happening of any event entitling the Mortgagee to foreclose this mortgage, or if the Mortgagee shall be served with garnishee process in which the Mortgagor (or any of them, if there be more than one) shall be named as defendant, whether or not the Mortgagor shall be in default hereunder at the time, the Mortgagee may, but shall not be required to, set off any indebtedness owing by the Mortgagee to the Mortgagor (or any of them, if there be more than one) against any indebtedness secured hereby, without

MORTGAGES OF REAL PROPERTY . . . *continued*
first resorting to the mortgaged property and without prejudice to any other rights or remedies of the Mortgagee or the lien of the Mortgagee on the mortgaged property;

In the event of a sale of said premises or any part or parts thereof under and by virtue of the provisions of this mortgage the purchaser or purchasers thereof shall have immediate and peaceable possession of the same and that if the Mortgagor shall remain in possession after the effective date of such sale such possession shall be construed as a tenancy at sufferance only, giving unto the purchaser all remedies, by way of summary possession or otherwise, conferred by law in such case.

The Mortgagor (and each of them, if there be more than one), and any successor in interest to the whole or any part of the mortgaged property, hereby waive diligence, presentment, demand and notice of dishonor, and consent to extensions of time, surrender or substitution of security, failure to apply deposit or other forbearance, without notice, with respect to any indebtedness hereby secured;

The Mortgagor will pay to Mortgagee, to the extent requested by the Mortgagee, on dates upon which interest payable, such amounts as the Mortgagee may from time to time estimate as necessary to create and maintain a reserve fund from which to pay before the same become due, all ground rentals (if any), taxes, assessments, liens and charges on or against the property hereby mortgaged, and premiums for insurance held or required by the Mortgagee. Payments from said reserve fund for said purposes may be made by the Mortgagee at its discretion even though subsequent owners of the property described herein may benefit thereby. In the event of any default under the terms of this mortgage, any part or all of said reserve fund may be applied to any part of the indebtedness hereby secured and in refunding any part of said reserve fund the Mortgagee may deal with whomever is represented to be the owner of said property at that time;

The Mortgagee or any person in behalf of the Mortgagee may purchase at any foreclosure sale, and no other purchaser shall be answerable for the application of the purchase money; and that until any default the Mortgagor may hold and enjoy the mortgaged property and receive the rents and profits thereof; that the terms "advances," "costs" and "expenses" wherever herein used, shall include reasonable attorney's fees whenever incurred; that the term "Mortgagor" shall include the plural and in such case shall bind the Mortgagors jointly and severally; that the term "indebtedness" shall mean and include, but shall not be limited to, all claims, demands, obligations and liabilities whatsoever, however, arising and whether owing by the Mortgagor (or any of them, if there be more than one) individually, or as partners, or as a partner or jointly or in common with any other or others, and whether absolute or contingent, as principal debtor or as accommodation maker or as endorser, liquidated or unliquidated, and whenever contracted, accrued or payable; and that these presents shall be equally binding upon and inure to the benefit of the legal representatives and successors in interest of the parties hereto respectively.

In the event of the existence at the date of this instrument or the adoption or amendment, after the date of this instrument, of any law of the United States, of the State of Hawaii, or any foreign country, or of any other taxing jurisdiction, which in any way shall impose a tax on mortgages or debts secured by mortgages to the end that directly or indirectly Mortgagee shall be required to pay on account of this mortgage, said promissory note or any other indebtedness secured hereby any tax other than a tax on, according to, or measured by net income, or any existing franchise tax applicable to Mortgagee, the holder of this mortgage may give at any time written notice to Mortgagor that the said holder elects to have the indebtedness secured by this mortgage become due and payable six months from the giving of such notice unless Mortgagor, within the said six months' period, shall agree in writing to pay the amount of such taxes; and in the event Mortgagor within such six months' period so agrees to pay the amount of such taxes, such agreement of Mortgagor shall be deemed to be a covenant and obligation of Mortgagor under this mortgage for all purposes and in the event Mortgagor fails within said six months' period to so agree to pay such taxes, the indebtedness secured by this mortgage shall become due and payable upon the last day of the six months' period. If at any time Mortgagor's agreement to pay the amount of such taxes shall be prohibited by law or the payment of the same by Mortgagor would make the transaction usurious, then the indebtedness secured hereby shall become due and payable six months after the giving of written notice by the holder of this mortgage and the promissory note secured hereby that it elects to have the indebtedness secured hereby become due and payable.

If without prior written consent of the Mortgagee any of the property subject to this mortgage shall be conveyed, assigned, sold, encumbered, leased or transferred, including transfer by way of agreement of sale or as security, by the Mortgagor to any other party, other than by will or intestate succession, then and in any such event all of the indebtedness hereby secured shall at once become due and payable at the option of the Mortgagee (any provision or term thereof to the contrary notwithstanding), and delay or failure on the part of the Mortgagee to demand such payment shall not prejudice the Mortgagee's rights thereto. If the Mortgagor then holding title to all or any part of the mortgaged property (or any of them if there be more than one) shall be a corporation, then as to such Mortgagor, any sale, assignment, transfer (other than by will or intestate succession) or exchange of any of the shares of the capital or common stock of the Mortgagor, or any issuance of any new shares of stock of any class of the Mortgagor, or any merger or consolidation of the Mortgagor with or into any other corporation whereby in any such event the shareholders of such Mortgagor immediately prior to such event (or their heirs or legatees) shall fail to own and control one hundred per cent (100%) of the voting stock of the Mortgagor shall be deemed a conveyance or assignment of the Mortgagor's interest in the mortgaged property for purposes of this paragraph and shall require the prior written consent of the Mortgagee. The Provisions of this paragraph shall constitute a continuing covenant or condition, and any failure on the part of the Mortgagee to exercise its option to declare all indebtedness due and payable on the occurrence of any one event hereinabove mentioned shall not prejudice the right of the Mortgagee to declare the indebtedness hereby secured at once due and payable on the occurrence of any other event hereinabove mentioned.

Mortgagee and Mortgagor intend and agree that, although the Leasehold and the Fee, which is the reversionary interest in the Property upon termination of the Leasehold, are both owned by mortgagor, for purposes of this and any other mortgages of the Fee and/or the Leasehold, the Leasehold and Fee shall be treated as separate interests and shall not be deemed to have merged, the Leasehold having been mortgaged by mortgagor, and if applicable, the Fee also having been mortgaged by mortgagor under a mortgage or mortgages prior in lien to this Mortgage; (if applicable).

This mortgage is governed by and shall be construed in accordance with the laws of the State of Hawaii. In the event that the interest rate provided herein, or in said promissory note, or in any other instrument of indebtedness hereby secured, or the interest rate applicable to any other indebtedness hereby secured, together with any late charge, fees or other charges applicable thereto, shall be in excess of the permissible rate under any applicable usury statute or similar law governing maximum rates of interest, fees or charges, then such rate of interest and/or said late charges, fees or other charges shall be reduced to the maximum rate permitted by law, anything herein or in said promissory note or other instrument to the contrary notwithstanding.

(Signatures, acknowledgment, etc.)

Partial Release of Mortgage.—
KNOW ALL MEN BY THESE PRESENTS:

That JOHN DOE and JANE DOE, husband and wife, of . . . . . ., State of . . . . . ., the Mortgagees named in that certain mortgage made by RICHARD ROE, husband of Ruth Roe, of Honolulu, City and County of Honolulu, State of Hawaii, Mortgagor, dated . . . . . ., and recorded in the Bureau of Conveyances of Hawaii in Liber . . . . . ., page . . . . . . (or "and filed in the Office of the Assistant Registrar of the Land Court of the State of Hawaii as Document No. . . . . . and noted on Transfer Certificate of Title No. . . . . issued to said Mortgagor," if Torrens Act land), in consideration of One Dollar ($1) to them paid by the Mortgagor, the receipt of which is hereby acknowledged, do hereby release and discharge from said mortgage:

(insert description)

PROVIDED, HOWEVER, that this release shall not affect or impair the security of said mortgage with respect to the remaining premises therein described and not hereby or heretofore released.

IN WITNESS WHEREOF, said Joe Doe and Jane Doe have hereunto set their hands this . . . . . day of . . . . . ., 19. . . . .

. . . .
. . . .

(Acknowledgment)

Chattel Mortgages.—See topic Chattel Mortgages.

PROPERTY

ABSENTEES:

Care of Property.—Where heirs or legatees cannot be found, personal property to which they would be entitled may be deposited with clerk of court. (531-34).

Other.—No other statutory provision.

Process Agent.—For nonresident motorists, see category Transportation, topic Motor Vehicles. For nonresident shipping lines see category Business Regulation and Commerce, topic Carriers. Otherwise see category Civil Actions and Procedure, topic Process.

Escheat.—Uniform Unclaimed Property Act. (523A). All unclaimed property subject to delivery to state if last known address of owner is in state. (523A-53). All unclaimed, intangible property, presumed abandoned after three years. Interest in Kuleana lands shall pass to state if owner of such lands dies without heirs. (560:2-105.5). See also category Business Regulation and Commerce, topic Banks and Banking (523A-2.5), subhead Escheat of Inactive Accounts.

Nonsupport by Husband or Parents.—Absence for three continuous months without support of spouse or children is prima facie evidence of desertion. (575-2, modifying Uniform Desertion and Non-Support Act).

ADVERSE POSSESSION:

Acquisition of title through possession of real estate inconsistent with title of another.

Character of Possession.—Subject real property must be five acres or less, and claim may be asserted in good faith not more than once in 20 years. (657-31.5). However, does not include similar claims made before Nov. 7, 1978. (657-31.5). Adverse possession claim allowable for real property exceeding five acres, as long as person adversely possessed for not less than 20 years prior to Nov. 7, 1978, or for not less than earlier applicable time periods. (669-1[b]).

Must be in actual, open, hostile, notorious, continuous and exclusive possession of property for statutory period. (48 Haw. 17, 395 P.2d 273). Good faith must be shown, i.e. that reasonable person would believe that person has interest in title to property, and belief based upon inheritance, written instrument of conveyance or judgment of court of competent jurisdiction. (669-1[b]). No requirement taxes be paid throughout adverse period. (50 Haw. 125, 432 P.2d 890).

Plaintiff does not need to have perfect title to establish prima facie case, but must at least prove that he has substantial interest in property and that his title is superior to that of defendant. (76 Haw. 402, 879 P.2d 507).

Duration of Possession.—Adversely possess for 20 years or more unless one has possessed for ten years prior to May 1973. (657-31). There is no adverse possession against titles registered under Torrens Act (see category Documents and Records, topic Records). An action may be brought in circuit court in which circuit property situated by any person against another person who claims or may claim adversely to plaintiff. Adverse possessor must have been in possession for period of 20 years to initiate action establishing title. (669-1).

Easements.—No different requirements.

Disabilities.—Persons under disability (minority, imprisonment, incompetency) have a further period of five years after removal of disability. (657-34). Death within 20 year

ADVERSE POSSESSION . . . *continued*

period extends time to heirs, devisees, etc., for an additional five years after death. (657-35).

CONDOMINIUMS:

See topic Real Property, subhead Condominium.

CONVEYANCES:

See topic Deeds.

CURTESY:

Uniform Probate Code, but not 1975 or 1977 Official Amendments, adopted (c. 560), effective July 1, 1977 U.P.C. section abolishing curtesy not adopted. For rights accruing prior to July 1, 1977, following is applicable:

Husband has life interest in one-third of lands owned by his wife in fee simple, freehold or in leasehold at date of her death, and absolute property in one-third of her remaining property after payment of her debts. During her life, he has no curtesy right, inchoate or otherwise. (533-16).

Bar.—Curtesy right is barred by one year's desertion or nonsupport. (533-16).

DEEDS:

Execution.—Deeds must be acknowledged in order to be recorded unless executed on behalf of U.S. or State of Hawaii. If acknowledgment cannot be obtained, proof of execution must be made before judge of Land Court or Circuit Court; no witnesses are necessary; seal not required. If executed by attorney-in-fact, power of attorney must be recorded. (502-84). If grantor is married man, wife may be required to join in order to bar her dower, see topic Dower. If grantor is married woman, no release of curtesy by husband is necessary (unless land was acquired by wife during 1945-1949 period of Community Property Law and deed of acquisition was not acknowledged by husband as wife's separate property or if property was not acquired from her separate funds or by inheritance). If grantors are husband and wife as joint tenants or as tenants by the entirety, no dower release is necessary. Husband may sign as attorney-in-fact for wife except as to release of dower in which case power must name some third party as attorney and must specifically refer to and cover her dower rights as being a subject of the power. Doctrine of merger of underlying contract for conveyance and deed applied. (76 Haw. 396, 866 P.2d 951).

See also topics Real Property, Curtesy, Dower; category Debtor and Creditor, topic Homesteads; Family, topic Husband and Wife.

Recording.—All deeds, leases for term of more than one year, mortgages of any interest in real estate, or other conveyances must be recorded in office of registrar of conveyances in Honolulu; otherwise they are void as against any subsequent purchaser, lessee or mortgagee, in good faith and for valuable consideration, not having actual notice of such conveyance of same real estate, or any portion thereof, whose conveyance shall be first duly recorded. (502-83). Deeds must contain address of grantee. All names of all natural persons signing in their individual capacity shall be typewritten, stamped, or printed by some other mechanical or electrical printing method beneath all signatures. Top 3 1/2 inches of first page must be left blank for use of recording officer. Following 1 inch space shall be reserved for information showing to whom document should be returned beginning 1 1/2 inches from left margin and not exceeding 3 1/2 inches per line. First page shall include, if possible, all names of grantors and all names and addresses of grantees, type of document, and tax map key number. When grantee is corporation or partnership, document must contain state where entity is registered and entity's address. (502-31). If more than one page, deed must be stapled once in upper left corner. Assistant registrar may refuse to record document longer than 8 1/2 inches by 11 inches.

Recording Fees.—Recording fee for deeds is $25 and $1 per page for each page over 20 pages unless otherwise provided by rules adopted by Department of Land and Natural Resources pursuant to c. 91. See category Documents and Records, topic Records.

See category Taxation, topic Real Estate Conveyance Tax. See also category Documents and Records, topic Records.

Operation and Effect.—Doctrine of merger disallows any recovery on covenant contracts once grantee accepts deed, so that deed's covenant control, rather than terms of prior sales contract. (76 Haw. 396, 879 P.2d 501).

Torrens Act.—Land Court registration is provided for by c. 501. Deed purporting to convey or affect land registered with Land Court is not effective as conveyance and does not bind land until registered in Office of Assistant Registrar of Land Court in Honolulu. (501-101). Deed must contain full name, or names, address and marital status of grantee and, if married, full name of spouse. Deed conveying (1) one or more (but not all) lots, or (2) all interests in lot appurtenant to apartments in condominium property regime shall disclose easements, rights-of-way, and all other liens and encumbrances affecting lots or interests. (501-105). Deed must refer to number of certificate of title affected. (501-108). Top 3 1/2 inches of all instruments to be filed and recorded shall be reserved for recording information. Following 1 inch space shall be reserved for information showing to whom document should be returned beginning 1 1/2 inches from left margin and not exceeding 3 1/2 inches per line. First page shall include, if possible, all names of grantors and all names and addresses of grantees, type of document, and tax map key number. When grantee is corporation or partnership, document must contain state where entity is registered and entity's address. (502-31). Each instrument shall be stapled once in upper left corner and shall not have cover or backer. All names of all natural persons signing in their individual capacity shall be typewritten, stamped, or printed by some other mechanical or electrical printing method beneath all signatures. There shall be no discrepancy in any name as it appears in body, beneath signature or in notary acknowledgment. No instrument will be filed that will not reproduce legibly or which is larger than 8 1/2 inches by 11 inches in size. (501-108). For most Torrens documents, filing fee is $25 and $1 per page for each page over 20 pages. If document is deed, fee of $25 for new certificate of title is also charged unless

otherwise provided by rules adopted by Department of Land and Natural Resources, pursuant to c. 91. (501-218). Knowledge of unregistered encumbrance does not disqualify holder of certificate of title from protection under 501-82. (75 Haw. 370, 862 P.2d 1048). Registered land subject to encumbrances noted on certificate of title; sufficiency of notation specified. (501-82).

There is no statutory form. The following may be used:

Taxes.—See category Taxation, topic Real Estate Conveyance Tax.

Form

KNOW ALL MEN BY THESE PRESENTS:

That JOHN DOE, husband of Jane Doe, of . . . . . . State of . . . . . ., Grantor, in consideration of the sum of Ten Dollars ($10) and other good and valuable consideration to him paid by RICHARD ROE and RUTH ROE, husband and wife, whose address is . . . . . Street, Honolulu, City and County of Honolulu, State of Hawaii, Grantees, the receipt of which is hereby acknowledged, does hereby grant, bargain, sell and convey unto the Grantees, as tenants by the entirety with full rights of survivorship, and their assigns, and the heirs and assigns of the survivor of them: (insert description)

SUBJECT, HOWEVER, to the following: (insert encumbrances, if any)

TO HAVE AND TO HOLD the same, together with the improvements thereon and the rights, easements, privileges and appurtenances thereunto belonging or appertaining, unto the Grantees, as tenants by the entirety, and the survivor of them and their assigns and the heirs and assigns of the survivor of them, forever.

(Insert warranty clause and provision for pro-rating of current realty taxes, if desired.)

AND, for the consideration aforesaid, JANE DOE, wife of the Grantor, does hereby release and forever quitclaim unto the Grantees, as tenants by the entirety aforesaid, all her right, title and interest in and to the premises hereinabove granted, whether by way of dower, community property, elective share or otherwise.

IN WITNESS WHEREOF, the Grantor and said Jane Doe have hereunto set their hands this . . . . . . day of . . . . . . 19. . . . .

. . . .
John Doe

. . . .   Grantor

Jane Doe

                                                                Dower

Note.—Refer to subhead Execution, supra for requirements for execution.

DEEDS OF TRUST:

See category Mortgages, topic Mortgages of Real Property.

DOWER:

Note: 533-1, dealing with dower rights, was repealed by 1997 Legislature (c. 244), effective June 17, 1997. However, dower releases for conveyances of real property may still be required by title insurance companies in connection with dower rights that have vested prior to effective date of repeal.

ESCHEAT:

See topic Absentees, subhead Escheat; categories Business Regulation and Commerce, topic Banks and Banking, subhead Unclaimed Deposits; Estates and Trusts, topics Descent and Distribution, subhead Escheat, Wills, subhead Unclaimed Legacies.

HORIZONTAL PROPERTY REGIME:

See topic Real Property, subhead Condominium.

LANDLORD AND TENANT:

Generally, common law governs rights and liabilities arising out of landlord-tenant relationship. Dwelling unit rentals also governed by comprehensive residential landlord-tenant code. (c. 521)

Uniform Commercial Code Art. 2A adopted.

Discrimination in Real Property Transactions.—Conforms to federal Fair Housing Amendments Act of 1988. Prohibits steering persons toward and away from real estate transaction and adds age as protected group. (515-2, 3). Age is exception to discrimination in real estate transaction law as it pertains to housing for elderly. (515-4).

Kinds of Tenancy.—No specific statute.

Leases.—Contract for lease or sublease is within statute of frauds. (See 656-1[4].) Lease must be acknowledged to be recorded. (502-50). Oral leases for period not exceeding one year are valid and enforceable as if in writing. (666-4).

Dwelling Unit Leases.—Leases of dwelling units are governed by Residential Landlord Tenant Code. (c. 521). "Dwelling unit" is structure or part of structure used as home, residence or sleeping place by one person or two or more persons maintaining common household to exclusion of all others. (521-8). Code does not apply to: Residence at institutions, student and faculty housing of University of Hawaii, including fraternity houses; occupancy under contract of sale with tenant as purchaser; day-to-day occupancy in hotel or motel; occupancy by employee of landlord, which occupancy is conditional on such employment or occupancy for period of up to four years subsequent thereto, pursuant to plan for transfer of dwelling unit or property of which it is part to occupant; lease of improved residential land for term of 15 years or more; occupancy by prospective purchaser after offer to purchase has been accepted and before owner's rights have been transferred; occupancy in project for temporary or transitional housing for homeless persons if operated by nonprofit corporation that has filed copy of its rules and regulations with Director of Commerce and Consumer Affairs (521-7); or residence or occupancy in public housing complex or shelter directly controlled, owned, or managed by Housing and Community Development Corporation of Hawaii (521-7).

Residential Leases.—Leases with terms in excess of 35 years, if in existence on June 24, 1976, or with terms exceeding 20 years after June 24, 1967, including options for renewal or extension of term, of parcel of land two acres in size or less and intended or

LANDLORD AND TENANT . . . *continued*
permitted to be used or occupied as principal place of residence for single family are subject to regulation under cc. 516 and 519.

State may exercise power of eminent domain to condemn underlying fee for resale to qualified holders of residential leases. (516-22 to 27). Resale restricted to lessee purchasers who do not own other lands in fee simple (including fee simple lands under trust agreement, whether as trustee, co-trustee or beneficiary) and who are both domiciled in State of Hawaii and intending to reside on lot within five years of purchase. (516-1).

Lease agreement for space to be occupied for residential purposes for term not exceeding five years, or lease for which aggregate rent over term is less than $25,000 must be written in plain language using words with common and everyday meanings. Lessor is subject to amount for actual damages plus $50 penalty for violation. Lease is not void or voidable for violation. (487A-1). See also category Business Regulation and Commerce, topic Consumer Protection, subhead Plain Language.

Security Deposits.—In lease of dwelling unit, landlord may not receive from tenant more than one month's rent as security deposit and first month's rent. If tenant is not in default, landlord must refund unearned rent and security deposit within 14 days after tenancy ends or notify tenant of any amount being retained for repairing damages, cleaning unit or as compensation for damages for wrongful quitting of unit, along with estimates of costs of remedying tenant defaults. Return of deposit is presumptively proven if mailed to tenant with acceptable proof of mailing within 14 days after termination or if there is acknowledgment of receipt by tenant within 14-day limit. Security deposit is not to be construed as last month's rent unless landlord and tenant agree in writing. (521-44).

Recording.—Leases of more than one year not recorded are void as against subsequent purchaser, in good faith and for valuable consideration, not having actual notice, whose conveyance is first duly recorded. (503-83). Leases of more than one year affecting land registered under Torrens system are only contract to lease until filed and noted on Certificate of Title. (501-102). Leases are filed or recorded in Office of Registrar of Conveyances in Honolulu, Hawaii. See category Documents and Records, topic Records. Actual possession of tenant constitutes notice. (See 26 Haw. 342.)

Rent.—Counties have power to regulate renting, subletting, and rental conditions of residential property by ordinance. (46-20). Renegotiation of rents for residential leases (defined above) or cooperative housing leases, if not agreed upon by parties, are subject to mandatory arbitration by Housing and Community Development Corporation of Hawaii (per HB 14-3) and statutory procedures for valuation and limit on rate of return. (519-2). Person must be certified or licensed to practice as appraiser and must comply with uniform standards of professional appraisal practice. (1998, Act 180). During first 20 years of residential lease, lessee may extend term for 55 years for purpose of obtaining mortgage financing if remaining term is less than 50 years. Annual rent during term is set by statute and pursuant to mandatory arbitration. (516-65, 66).

In leases of dwelling units, rents are payable monthly unless otherwise agreed and apportioned on daily basis. When tenancy is month-to-month, rent may be increased only on notice given 45 days prior to effective date of increase. (521-21). Tenancy for indefinite term with periodic rent reserved is deemed tenancy from period to period. (666-2). Tenant may withhold up to $500 in rent if landlord has been notified by state or county agency of health or safety violation on premises and repairs are not commenced within 12 days, or tenant has notified landlord that dwelling is not in compliance with applicable laws and ordinances, common areas are not in clean, sanitary and safe condition, premises are not habitable, electrical, plumbing or other facilities supplied by landlord are not in good working order, appropriate trash receptacles for normal use are not available, or running water is not provided and landlord fails to commence repairs within 12 days and provide tenant with reasonable tentative completion date, provided funds withheld are used to provide necessary repairs or facilities. (521-64).

Lien.—Landlord's lien not available. See category Business Regulation and Commerce, topic Commercial Code.

Termination of Tenancy.—Periodic tenancy is subject to forfeiture for act or creation of nuisance under 727-1 if, after warning to abate of 24 hours, nuisance is not abated and five day notice of termination is given. (666-3). However, if lease is of dwelling unit, 15 days notice is required. (521-69). Periodic tenancy may be terminated by ten days notice, if parol lease (666-1) or by notice given 25 days prior to end of period otherwise (666-2). But if lease is of dwelling unit, 45 days written notice is required for month-to-month or longer term and ten days notice written for lease less than month to month. (521-71). If landlord provides notice of termination, tenant may vacate at any time within last 28 days of period between notification and termination date provided tenant notifies landlord of date tenant will vacate and pays prorated rent for period occupied. If landlord contemplates voluntary demolition of dwelling or conversion to condominium property regime or to transient vacation rental, tenant must receive at least 120 days notice to terminate. Tenant may vacate at any time between notification and termination date, but tenant shall notify landlord of date tenant will vacate and pay prorated rent for that period of occupation. (521-38, 71).

Holding Over.—If tenant from month to month or period to period holds over, a valid, enforceable tenancy is created for additional period; if tenant fails to pay rent as agreed, landlord may terminate on five days notice. (666-2). If tenant holds over under lease of dwelling unit after expiration or termination without landlord's consent, during first month of holdover tenant may be liable, in court's discretion, to pay landlord twice monthly rent for preceding month; and monthly rent for second month of holdover, prorated on daily basis. Landlord may initiate summary possession action against tenant any time within first 60 days of holdover, except acceptance of rent during this period, in absence of agreement to contrary, creates month-to-month tenancy. Landlord's failure to commence possession action within first 60 days of holdover, in absence of rental agreement, creates month-to-month tenancy at previous rental rate beginning at end of first 60 days of holdover. (521-71).

Dispossession.—Landlord may have summary possession against tenant holding without right or holding by parol lease after ten days notice to quit. (666-1). Landlord may have summary possession against tenant for failure to pay rent by giving notice to vacate of five days. (666-2). But if lease is of dwelling unit, demand for payment within five business days must be made. Summary possession or other proceeding may be brought if tenant remains in default. (521-68). In any action for summary possession, plaintiff may join actions for rent, profits, damages and waste where these arise out of and refer to land or premises whose possession is sought. (666-7). Landlord who interrupts essential services to take possession engaged in unfair trade practice and is subject to penalties under 480-2; minimum penalty of $1,000 or three times monthly rent, whichever is greater. (521-74.5). Tenant's failure to comply with record keeping requirements of percentage lease due to gross negligence or persistent or wilful misconduct on tenant's part grounds for dispossession under c. 666. (10 Haw. App. 162, 862 P.2d 282).

Distress or Other Remedies.—Distress for payment of rent under common law is not available. Residential Landlord-Tenant Code provides landlord with right to bring action for summary possession to collect unpaid rent at any time after notice of intention to do so has been given (521-68), to terminate lease or remedy tenant's failure to comply with applicable laws or maintain premises in clean and safe condition or keep all appliances and furnishing supplied by landlord in good condition or to comply with restrictions necessary for preservation of property or protection of persons; or landlord may bring action for waste or breach of contract for tenant's willful or negligent failure to perform foregoing (521-70). Tenant is liable to landlord for unpaid future rents or damages if he wrongfully quits premises. (521-70).

Retaliatory eviction and rent increases are prohibited under lease of dwelling unit. (521-74).

Tenant under lease of dwelling unit may terminate lease on notice during first week if landlord fails to comply with rental agreement or fails to comply with applicable laws affecting premises. (521-62). Tenant may, if not at fault, terminate lease on one week's notice if landlord deprives tenant of substantial part of his benefit of his bargain under rental agreement. No notice is required if condition renders unit uninhabitable or poses imminent threat to health or safety. (521-63). Landlord is liable to tenant for $100 plus reasonable attorney's fees for failure to make required statutory disclosures. (521-67). Rental agreement may provide that reasonable attorney's fees and costs be awarded to prevailing party in suit relating to matters other than unpaid rent. (521-35).

Collection of Rent.—Landlord may, in action for summary possession, join actions for rent, lodging, board, profits, damages, and waste which arise out of land possession of which is sought. (666-7). Tenant may be required in any legal dispute over rent, to pay rent to special trust fund as it becomes due unless rent already paid to landowner or written agreement states otherwise. (521-78; 666-21).

Residential Leases.—Fee interest under residential leaseholds (defined above), is subject to condemnation by State for benefit of lessees in development tract. (c. 516). Person may not be denied right to become lessee of residential lot because of his race, religion, sex, ancestry or physical handicap. (516-62). Residential leases may be assigned without lessor's consent provided true or executed copy of assignment is provided to lessor and assignee undertakes to perform all obligations of lessee under lease. No such assignment shall release assignor from liability under lease unless lessor consents in writing to assignment. (516-63). Lessee's interest cannot be forfeited for failure to pay rent or perform his obligations without notice and at least 30 days to cure default. (516-64).

Seller of residential leasehold property must provide buyer copy of original lease and any amendments no later than ten calendar days from seller's acceptance of buyer's offer. Seller must disclose that there are no current provisions nor assurances for future laws for mandatory conversion of leasehold condominiums, cooperatives, and residential leases. Buyer has five calendar days from receipt of lease documents to review, accept or reject terms of lease. Within five calendar days of acknowledged receipt of contract, buyer may cancel offer to purchase without loss of deposit. Seller and buyer may, on standardized form, agree to reduce or extend periods for production and review of lease documents. (515 D-11, 516-71). Civil penalty of $1,000 for violation. Violator also liable for actual damages. (516-72).

Uniform Residential Landlord and Tenant Act adopted with substantial modifications. (c. 521).

Partition.—Any one or more joint tenants or tenants in common, where one or more of them have estate in fee, or life estate in possession, may bring action in circuit court of circuit in which property or some part thereof is situated. (668-1). Notwithstanding nondiscretionary nature of partition action, right to partition may be waived by express or implied contracts. (3 Haw. App. 555, 655 P.2d 881).

See category Civil Actions and Procedure, topic Partition.

PERPETUITIES:

Uniform Statutory Rule Against Perpetuities.—Adopted, with 1990 amendments. Common law rules superseded by workable wait-and-see element. Generally allows vesting no later than 21 years after life in being or 90 years after it was created. (c. 525).

Accumulations.—Governing board of institution or institutional fund may accumulate so much of annual net income of endowment fund as is prudent under standard established by §517D-8, and may hold any or all of accumulated income in income reserve for subsequent expenditure for uses and purposes for which endowment fund is established or may add any or all of accumulated income to principle of endowment fund, as is prudent under this standard. (517D-4[b]). Restriction upon accumulation of income or addition to principal of income may not be implied from designation of gift as endowment, or from direction or authorization in applicable gift instrument to apply to uses and purposes of fund "income", "interest", "dividends", "currently expendable income", or "rent, issues, or profits" or direction which contains other words of similar import. (517D-5).

See category Estates and Trusts, topic Trusts, subhead Accumulations.

PERSONAL PROPERTY:

Common law rules prevail. Personal property may be held in tenancy by entirety, including leaseholds, shares of corporate stock and automobiles. Tenancy continues in proceeds of sale of property held in tenancy by entirety.

PERSONAL PROPERTY . . . *continued*

Motor vehicle registered in two or more names presumed owned in joint tenancy. (286-49).

POWERS OF ATTORNEY:

Attorneys in Fact.—Agent lacks authority to make gift of principle's property, unless authority is expressly given in power of attorney. Fundamental rule in construing power of attorney is that intent of parties governs, as gleaned from entire context of instrument. (83 Haw. 65, 924 P.2d 559).

Recording.—If power of attorney is recorded, following requirements must be met: Top 3½ inches of first page of all documents must be left blank for use of recording officer. Following 1 inch space shall be reserved for information showing to whom document should be returned, beginning 1½ inches from left margin and not exceeding 3½ inches per line. First page shall include, if possible, all names of grantors and all names and addresses of grantees and type of document. When grantee is corporation or partnership, document must contain state where entity is registered and entity's address. (502-31). If more than one page, document should be stamped once in upper left corner.

Power of attorney authorizing transactions concerning real property must be recorded in Bureau of Conveyances. (502-84).

Form of General Power of Attorney.—There is no statutory form of General Power of Attorney. The following may be used:

KNOW ALL MEN BY THESE PRESENTS:

That I, [John Doe], a resident of [address], have made, constituted and appointed and by these presents do make, constitute and appoint [Richard Doe], of [address], my true and lawful attorney to act in, manage and conduct all my estate and all my affairs, and for that purpose for me and in my name, place and stead, and for my use and benefit, and as my act and deed, to do and execute or to concur with persons jointly interested with myself therein in the doing or executing of, all or any of the following acts, deeds and things, that is to say:

(1) To buy, receive, lease, accept or otherwise acquire; to sell, convey, mortgage, hypothecate, pledge, quitclaim, lease or otherwise encumber or dispose of; or to contract or agree for the acquisition, disposal or encumbrance of; any property whatsoever, real or personal, or any custody, possession, interest or right therein, upon such terms as my said attorney shall think proper;

(2) To take, hold, possess, invest, lease, let or otherwise manage any or all of my property, real or personal, or any interest therein; to eject, remove or relieve tenants or other persons from and recover possession of, such property by all lawful means; and to maintain, protect, preserve, insure, remove, store, transport, repair, rebuild, modify or improve the same or any part thereof;

(3) To make, do and transact all and every kind of business of whatever kind or nature, including the receipt, recovery, collection, payment, compromise, settlement and adjustment of all accounts, legacies, bequests, interest, dividends, annuities, demands, debts, taxes and obligations which may now or hereafter be due, owing or payable by me or to me;

(4) To make, indorse, accept, receive, sign, seal, execute, acknowledge and deliver deeds, leases, assignments, agreements, certificates, mortgages, releases of mortgages, hypothecations, checks, notes, bonds, vouchers, dividend warrants, receipts and such other instruments in writing of whatever kind and nature as may be necessary, convenient or proper in the premises;

(5) To deposit and withdraw for the purposes hereof or any other purpose, in either the name of my attorney or in my name, in or from any banking institution, or any account therein, any funds, negotiable paper or moneys which may come into my said attorney's hands as such attorney or which I now or hereafter may have on deposit or be entitled to;

(6) To institute, prosecute, defend, compromise, arbitrate and dispose of legal, equitable or administrative hearings, actions, suits, attachments, arrests, distresses or other proceedings, or otherwise engage in litigation in connection with the premises;

(7) To act as my attorney or proxy with respect to any stocks, shares, bonds or other investments, rights or interests I may now or hereafter hold; and to appoint any other person or persons as my proxy or proxies;

(8) To engage and dismiss agents, counsel and employees, and to appoint and remove at pleasure any substitute for, or agent of my attorney, with respect to all or any of the matters or things herein mentioned and upon such terms as my attorney shall think fit;

(9) To execute vouchers in my behalf for any and all allowances and reimbursements payable to me by the United States, including but not restricted to allowances and reimbursement for transportation of dependents or for shipment of household effects as authorized by law or Army or Navy regulations, and to receive, indorse and collect the proceeds of checks payable to the order of the undersigned drawn on the Treasurer of the United States;

(10) To prepare, execute and file income and other tax returns, claims for refunds and other governmental reports, applications, requests and documents; and to appear for me and represent me before the Treasury Department of the United States and the Tax Commissioner of any state or territory in connection with any matter involving federal, state, or territorial taxes for any year to which I am a party, giving my said attorney full power to do everything whatsoever requisite and necessary to be done in the premises, and to receive refund checks, to execute waivers of the statute of limitations and to execute closing agreements;

(11) To have access to, take possession and order the removal and shipment of any of my property from any post, warehouse, depot, dock, safety deposit box or other place of storage or safekeeping, governmental or private; and to execute and deliver any release, voucher, receipt, shipping ticket, certificate or other instrument necessary or convenient for such purpose;

(12) To borrow money and to obtain credit by letters of credit, overdrafts, notes or otherwise on such terms as my said attorney shall think proper and to execute any instruments binding me to the repayment thereof.

GIVING AND GRANTING unto my said attorney full power and authority to do and perform all and every act, deed, matter and thing whatsoever in and about my estate, property and affairs as fully and effectually to all intents and purposes as I might or could do in my own proper person if personally present, the above specially enumerated powers being in aid and exemplification of the full, complete and general power herein granted and not in limitation or definition thereof, hereby ratifying all that my said attorney shall lawfully do or cause to be done by virtue of these presents.

IN WITNESS WHEREOF I have hereunto set my hand this ____ day of ________, 19__ .

____

Revocation.—To constitute revocation of power of attorney there must be something besides mere appointment of another attorney. (13 Haw. 471). Affidavit executed by attorney-in-fact under power of attorney stating that attorney-in-fact did not have at time of exercise of power actual knowledge of termination of power by revocation or of principal's death, disability, or incapacity is conclusive proof of non-revocation or nontermination of power at that time. If exercise of power of attorney requires execution and delivery of any instrument that is recordable, affidavit when authenticated for record is likewise recordable. This section does not affect any provision in power of attorney for its termination by expiration of time or occurrence of event other than express revocation or change in principal's capacity. (551D-5).

Uniform Durable Power of Attorney Act adopted. (c. 551D).

REAL PROPERTY:

Estates in fee tail are not recognized, and will be held to create fee simple or life estate in grantee depending on construction of grant. (12 Haw. 375). Conveyances and devises to two or more persons are construed to create tenancies in common unless it shall "manifestly appear from the tenor of the instrument" that it was intended to create joint tenancy or tenancy by entirety. This does not apply to conveyances or devises to executors or trustees. (509-1).

Conveyance tax adopted. (c. 247). See category Taxation, topic Real Estate Conveyance Tax.

See also topics Curtesy, Deeds, Dower; categories Debtor and Creditor, topic Homesteads; Documents and Records, topic Records; Family, topic Husband and Wife.

Rule in Shelley's Case is not recognized. (12 Haw. 375).

Discrimination in Real Property Transactions.—Conforms to federal Fair Housing Amendments Act of 1988. Prohibits steering persons toward and away from real estate transaction and adds age as protected group. (515-2, 3). Age is exception to discrimination in real estate transaction law as it pertains to housing for elderly. (515-4).

Recording decrees quieting title to real property provided in 669-8.

Mandatory Disclosures in Residential Real Estate Transactions.—Sellers of residential real property must disclose any material fact, defect, or condition past or present, relating to real property being sold. Seller must provide buyer with requisite disclosure statement no later than ten calendar days from acceptance of purchase offer. Buyer has 15 calendar days to rescind purchase offer. Any action to rescission must be commenced prior to recorded sale of real property (closing). Certain limited exemptions apply. (c. 508D).

Foreign Conveyances.—If instrument would be valid and entitled to be recorded in state where executed, generally it may be recorded in Hawaii. But see category Documents and Records, topic Acknowledgments, subhead Changes, Erasures or Interlineations.

Condominium.—FHA model act, modified, has been adopted. (c. 514A). Ownership of single units of property intended for any type of independent use and which include all or part of building, with common elements, and located on property within "condominium property regime," can be created and recorded. To subject property to condominium property regime all holders of interest in property must execute and record declaration setting forth owner's desire to subject property to regime established by statute. Contents of declaration, master deed, apartment deeds, floor plans, and bylaws are regulated by c. 514A. For mixed use condominiums, by vote of apartment owners, bylaws of association of apartment owners may be amended to provide that composition of board of directors be proportional with number of apartments for residential, commercial or other use. (1998, Act 215). Each condominium project association must prepare and adopt annual operating budget and have adequate funding of maintenance replacement reserves. Emergency situation includes extraordinary expense necessary to respond to any legal or administrative proceeding brought against association not reasonably foreseen by board when preparing annual operating budget. (514a-83.6). Exemption provided for two-apartment condominium projects. (c. 514A-Part III). Statute and bylaws govern operation, maintenance charges, etc. Each apartment owner must comply with bylaws and house rules. (514A-88). Directors may use condominium funds for reasonable educational purposes. (514A-82). No apartment owner may withhold assessment claimed by condominium association. Disputes may be submitted to arbitration. (514A-121). Other disputes between owners, boards of directors and managing agents also subject to arbitration. (514A-121). Purchasers have statutory rescission rights. (514A-69).

Sales to Individual Lessees.—Right of First Refusal for Condominiums and Cooperative Housing Corporations provided for in c. 514C. Seller of residential leasehold property must provide buyer no later than ten calendar days from seller's acceptance of buyer's offer one of following documents which contains major provisions of lease: Current master lease, current apartment lease or, for initial buyers of condominiums, unexpired preliminary, final or supplemental condominium public report. Buyer has five calendar days from receipt of contract to review, accept or reject terms of lease. Seller and buyer may, on standardized form, agree to extend or reduce time periods for production and review of lease documents. Buyer of leasehold property may cancel offer to purchase with no loss of deposit within five calendar days of acknowledged receipt of contract. Every residential lease shall contain provision for mandatory arbitration of any rent renegotiation. (c. 516D). Liens against common elements (514A-16) and blanket mortgages (514A-18) prohibited. Partition severely regulated. (514A-21). Home exemption laws are applicable to each apartment, and property taxes are assessed

See note at head of Digest as to 1998 legislation covered.

See Topical Index in front part of this volume.

REAL PROPERTY . . . *continued*

and collected with respect to apartments taken individually (514A-6). In general, Hawaii Condominium statute is patterned after FHA model act and New York modifications. Condominium developer must publish announcement of its intent to sell project. (514A-102). Full details of such proposed structure must first be approved by State Real Estate Commission and copy of Commission's report submitted to every prospective purchaser. Commission has broad powers of investigation, imposition of penalties, injunction, etc. Owner of condominium unit may make improvements to his unit upon certain conditions. (514A-89). Any person who violates any provision of c. 514A, or rules of real estate commission adopted pursuant thereto shall be subject to civil penalty not to exceed $2,500.

If one or more existing buildings are being converted to condominium status, each residential unit must first be offered for sale to owner-occupant. (514A-105).

Time sharing plans law enacted. (c. 514E). Time-share owners association: budgets and reserves. Time-share owner's associations required to adopt annual budget, to require annual independent audit of association's financial accounts, and to extend regulation of time-sharing plans. (c. 514E). Time-share owner's association may levy assessments which shall be lien on owner's time share interest. (1996, Act 165). Director of Department of Commerce and Consumer Affairs authorized to investigate, enjoin, disapprove applications, impose fines up to $10,000 and suspend or revoke licenses. (c. 514E). Prohibited practices provided for in 514E-11. Maintenance fees paid to time share owner's associations are subject to State general excise tax. (1990, Act 181). Condominium apartments providing transient lodging for periods of less than 30 days must register with Commission on annual basis as "condominium hotel" subject to licensing and bonding requirements of 467-30. Initial sale of time share interests duly registered under current effective disclosure statement pursuant to c. 514E exempt from Mandatory Seller Disclosures in Real Estate Transactions (c. 508D) (see subhead Mandatory Disclosures in Residential Real Estate Transactions, supra). Leasehold time share interests must be registered with Bureau of Conveyances, and need not be recorded by Land Court. (1998, Act 219). See topics Curtesy, Deeds, Dower, Landlord and Tenant, subhead Partition; categories Debtor and Creditor, topic Homesteads; Family, topic Husband and Wife; Mortgages, topic Mortgages of Real Property; and Business Regulation and Commerce, topic Securities.

Uniform Simplification of Land Transfers Act not adopted.

Cooperative Housing Corporations.—The Hawaii Business Corporation Act (c. 415) applies except to extent that its provisions are inconsistent with 1993, Act 282, HB 690.

Uniform Land Sales Practices Act enacted. (c. 484).

Boundaries Along Sea.—Previously established rule that private ownership of land along sea generally runs to highwater mark as defined by U.S. Coast and Geodetic Survey has been judicially overruled by Hawaii Supreme Court decisions in 50 Haw. 314, 440 P.2d 76 and 55 Haw. 176, 517 P.2d 57, which held that boundary of unregistered land and registered land altered by accretion or erosion was upper reaches of wash of waves as marked by line of vegetation, or in its absence by line of debris.

Nonresident Owners.—See category Taxation, topic Income Tax, subhead Withholding of Tax on Disposition of Real Estate, for Hawaii Real Property Tax Act (HARPTA).

Condemnation in Fee Simple of Lands Subject to Residential Leaseholds.—Hawaii Finance and Development Corporation may acquire by condemnation contiguous parcels of land which are in excess of five acres and which are or will be subdivided into residential lots of one acre or less if land is under lease for term of 35 years or more on June 24, 1967, or for term of 20 years or more thereafter. Lessee of residential lot in condemned tract has option to purchase his lot from Authority under certain conditions. Lessee purchasers must not own other lands in fee simple (including fee simple lands under trust agreement, whether as trustee, co-trustee or beneficiary) and must be both domiciled in State of Hawaii and intending to reside on lot within five years of purchase. (516-1). Financing up to 90% of purchase price is available in certain cases from Corporation. (c. 516). Constitutionality of c. 516 upheld. (467 U.S. 229). County ordinance allowing condemnation of lessor's leased fee interest in leasehold condominium developments, cooperative housing corporation developments, and planned unit developments upheld. (76 Haw. 46, 868 P.2d 1193).

Displaced Person Compensation.—Persons lawfully occupying real property displaced by state or county action entitled to compensation under certain circumstances and, if displaced from commercial or industrial lease, right of first refusal of lease on other appropriate State land. (c. 101). (111-1). State can recover from person responsible for code violation that results in displacement costs of compensation. (111-2).

Developer Impact Fees.—Enactment of development impact fees (for public facility capital improvement costs) by counties authorized. Guidelines for assessing need for impact fees, imposition and collection, and refunding in event impact fee ordinance is repealed. Sets out specific requirements to ensure (1) fees are reasonably related to benefits accruing to development or its geographically limited benefit zone and (2) do not exceed proportionate share of costs incurred by county in accommodating development. (46-141 to 148).

Time Required to Grant Permits.—State agencies and counties to enact ordinances to limit time required to review and grant plan and permit approvals and zoning changes for housing development. (1992, Act 227).

Hawaii Hurricane Relief Fund.—Establishes Hawaii Reinsurance Assistance Corporation as mechanism for providing homeowners' and hurricane reinsurance coverage to insurers, including county insurance trusts. Mortgage recording fee is imposed on each mortgage and certain amendments to mortgage. Fees collected are deposited into hurricane reserve trust fund. (431P-16).

Covenants.—Restrictive covenants strictly construed in favor of grantee and against grantor. Party seeking enforcement of restrictive covenant has burden to prove parties clear intention to create covenant running with land. In order to provide holder of transfer certificate of title full notice of encumbrance from face of certificate, encumbrance must be separately and clearly noted therein. (75 Haw. 370, 862 P.2d 1048).

Enterprise Zones.—Upon county application, Department of Business, Economic Development and Tourism can declare area to be "enterprise zone". Enterprise zones are intended to stimulate business and industrial growth in areas which would result in neighborhood revitalization of those areas by means of regulatory flexibility and tax incentives. Enterprise zones must meet specific criteria. Certain businesses located within enterprise zones receive certain tax incentives. (c. 209E).

Seizure.—Property subject to forfeiture can only be seized pursuant to court order issued after pre-seizure hearing. (712A-1, et seq.).

See topics Curtesy, Deeds, Dower, Landlord and Tenant; categories Civil Actions and Procedure, topic Partition; Debtor and Creditor, topic Homesteads; Documents and Records, topic Records; Family, topic Husband and Wife; Mortgages, topic Mortgages of Real Property; Taxation, topic Taxes.

TRUST DEEDS:

See category Mortgages, topic Mortgages of Real Property.

TAXATION

ADMINISTRATION:

Hawaii Department of Taxation, headed by Director of Taxation, is charged with administration and enforcement of State tax revenue laws and collection of State taxes. (26-10; 231-3). Department has power to construe revenue laws, prescribe forms, make rules and regulations, compromise tax claims with approval of Governor, remit delinquency penalties and interest except in fraud or willful violation cases, enter into final closing agreements relating to liability of taxpayer, conduct investigations, hold hearings, subpoena witnesses, and require production of documents and records pertinent to such inquiries. (231-3, 7). Tax returns and return information are confidential. (235-116, 237-34, 237D-13). Written opinions of Department are open to public inspection and copying. (231-19.5). For purposes of taxation, State is divided into four tax districts: (1) City and County of Honolulu; (2) Counties of Maui and Kalawao; (3) County of Hawaii; and (4) County of Kauai. (231-2). Taxes imposed by counties are administered by county officials (for City and County of Honolulu, Director of Finance).

Penalties and interest may be assessed with respect to any taxpayer for: (a) failure to file; (b) failure to pay; or (c) failure to pay within 60 days of filing timely return. (231-39). Criminal penalties may be imposed under §§231-34, 231-35, and 231-36 on (a) any person who willfully attempts to evade or defeat tax imposed under title 14; (b) any person who willfully fails to file, supply information, or secure license; or (c) any person who willfully makes false and fraudulent statements, or willfully aids or assists in preparation of document required to be filed under title 14 which contains false or fraudulent statements. "Person" includes certain individuals of taxable entities under duty to perform and who are principally responsible for performing act in question. (1996, Act 054). Prosecutions under §§231-34, 231-35, or 231-36 must be commenced within seven years after commission of crime. (231-41). Computation of interest is not affected by subsequent reduction in tax due because of net operating loss carry back until period following taxable year in which loss arises. (231-39). Interest does not accrue on additional fees imposed for costs or expense incurred by Department as result of any action taken to enforce collection of taxes administered under title 14. (231-25.5[b]). No taxpayer is exempt from any penalty or interest by reason of having contested tax except to extent tax is adjudged excessive or contrary to law. (231-39). Additional penalty provisions exist as to specific taxes. See topics detailing particular taxes.

ALCOHOLIC BEVERAGE TAXES:

Liquor Tax.—Provides tax rates per gallon on beer, wine and other liquor. (244D-4).

BUSINESS TAXES:

Bank Tax.—See category Business Regulation and Commerce, topic Banks and Banking.

Franchise Tax.—See category Business Regulation and Commerce, topic Banks and Banking, subhead Bank Tax.

Hotel Room Tax.—6% tax on transient accommodations, including leases for less than 180 days. (237D-2).

Insurance Company Tax.—See category Insurance, topic Insurance Companies.

Nursing Facility Tax.—Quarterly tax of 6% shall be assessed and collected on all nursing facility income. (346E-2). Nursing facility income means total compensation received from furnishing nursing facility services, including all receipts from "ancillary services" to provision of nursing facility services, and receipts from items supplied in connection with these services. (346E-1). Tax assessment excepted where individual facility determined to be financially distressed. (346E-2). Director, at his discretion, may allow semiannual or annual returns in lieu of quarterly returns. (346E-3). Operator may opt to have taxes owing withheld from Medicaid payments owed by Department to operator. (345E-4). Appeals governed by 235-114. (346E-8). Taxes paid pursuant to this chapter are reimbursable costs for federal Medicaid reimbursement purposes. (346E-14). Penalties for failure to file return or filing fraudulent return include assessment of taxes plus interest, and injunctive relief. (346E-6, 11).

CIGARETTE AND TOBACCO TAX:

Cigarette and tobacco tax imposed on wholesaler or dealer. (245-3). Excise tax of 5¢ for each cigarette sold, used, or possessed by wholesaler or dealer. (245-3). Excise tax of 40% of wholesale price of each article or item of tobacco products sold by wholesaler or dealer, whether or not sold at wholesale or used by wholesaler or dealer. (245-3).

ESTATE TAX:

State death tax imposed is credit for State death taxes on federal return under IRC §2011. Estates of resident decedents receive credit for death taxes paid to another state.

See note at head of Digest as to 1998 legislation covered.

See Topical Index in front part of this volume.

ESTATE TAX... *continued*
(236D-15). Estates of nonresident decedents are subject to tax on Hawaii situs real property, including trust property and beneficial interests in land trusts, and tangible personal property located in Hawaii. For nonresident's estate, State death tax is state death tax credit under IRC §2011 times ratio of total property in Hawaii to decedent's gross estate. (236D-4). Hawaii estate tax return is due on or before date federal estate tax return is filed, including any extension of time if copy of grant of extension is filed with Department within 30 days of issuance. (236D-5). If no estate tax is due, request for release should be filed with Department. (236D-5[e]). For appeals of estate and transfer tax see 236D-15.

Apportionment Against Inter Vivos Dispositions.—Apportionment controlled by Uniform Probate Code. (560:3-916).

Interstate Cooperation.—No statutory procedure available for compromise of death taxes where decedent's domicile is disputed.

GASOLINE TAX:

Imposed by 243-4. Gasoline tax of 16¢ per gallon, to which county tax added as set from time to time by counties, except fuel used in or for airplanes which is 1¢ per gallon. Diesel oil 1¢ per gallon, unless used for operating vehicles on public highways, then tax is additional 15¢ (243-4) per gallon plus county tax. Liquified petroleum used in internal combustion engines 1¢ per gallon, and if used in vehicles operating on public highways additional tax equal to two-thirds rate on diesel oil for vehicles operating on public highways. (243-4).

GENERATION SKIPPING TRANSFER TAX:

Tax imposed on generation skipping transfers equal to federal credit on transfers of property located in state and property from resident trusts. (236D-3.5).

GIFT TAX:

None.

INCOME TAX:

State income tax provisions generally conform to Federal income tax provisions of Internal Revenue Code. (235-2.3). In general, subtitle A, c. 1 of Federal IRC, as amended through Dec. 31, 1997, has been adopted as state law; consult in particular 235-2.2, 235-2.3, 235-2.4, 235-2.5, 235-3 and 235-7 for conforming and nonconforming provisions.

Persons Subject to Tax.—Tax is imposed on: (1) Resident Individuals: Tax applies to entire income computed without regard to source in State; (2) Nonresident Individuals: For nonresident individuals, tax applies to income received or derived from property owned, personal services performed, trade or business carried on, and any and every other source in State. Tax shall be calculated as though resident, then adjusted for percentage of Hawaii gross income. For nonresident spouse filing joint return with resident spouse, tax applies to entire income of nonresident spouse computed without regard to source in State. (235-4[b]). Credit is given with certain restrictions for income tax paid to another jurisdiction on income derived or received therefrom (235-55); (3) Corporations: Foreign and domestic (Hawaii) corporations are taxed on income received or derived from property owned, trade or business carried on, and any and every other source in State. Domestic (Hawaii) corporations also taxed on income from sources outside State unless subject to income tax in another jurisdiction (235-4[d]); (4) Estates and Trusts: Income of resident estate or trust is computed without regard to source in State, except nonresident beneficiaries of resident trusts or estates are not subject to tax on their share of intangible income of trust. (235-4[e]; 235-4.5[a]). Each estate or trust must include in its return all information necessary to determine taxability of income regardless of source. (235-4). Partnership as such is not taxable under c. 235. Partners are liable for income tax only in their separate or individual capacities. (c. 235). S Corporation tax conforms to Model S Corporation State Income Act. (235-121). Valid election under IRC is effective for Hawaii law purposes. (235-122). Qualified S Corporations are exempt from State corporations tax, except to extent they are subject to federal tax. (235-122). Income of S Corporation attributable to State that is subject to federal tax is taxed at highest marginal rate of tax imposed on net income of corporations. (235-122). S Corporations are required to obtain agreements from nonresident shareholders that they shall file and pay State tax on share of S Corporation's Hawaii income. (235-128). Tax-exempt organizations are subject to tax on unrelated business taxable income if subject to tax on such income under IRC. (235-2.4[h]).

Persons Exempt.—Persons and organizations not taxable under c. 235 include: banks, building and loan associations, financial services loan companies, financial corporations, small business investment companies, trust companies, mortgage loan companies, financial holding companies, subsidiaries of financial holding companies as defined in c. 241, development companies taxable under c. 241, insurance companies, agricultural cooperative associations, fish marketing associations exclusively taxable under other laws and persons engaged in business of motion picture and television film production. (235-9).

Personal exemptions available: (1) to individuals, $1,040 for each exemption allowable under IRC, provided exemption is zero if individual's exemption is allowable to another taxpayer; (2) to estate, $400; (3) to trust, $200 if trust is required to distribute all income currently, for all other trusts, deduction is $80; and (4) to blind, deaf, or totally disabled person, $7,000 in lieu of all other exemptions. (235-54).

Rates.—For individuals, estates and trusts, rates on taxable income range from 2% to 10%. (235-51). Top rate reduced to 8.25% by 2002. (235-51). For specific rates for individuals filing joint returns and for surviving spouses, see 235-51(a); for heads of households, see 235-51(b); for unmarried individuals (other than surviving spouse and head of household), and for married individual who does not make single return jointly with individual's spouse, see 235-51(c); for estates and trusts, see 235-51(d); for individuals who do not itemize deductions or reach ceiling amount, see 235-53. For net capital gains of individuals, trusts, and estates, maximum tax rate is 7.25%. (235-51[f]). Net unearned income of child who has not reached age 14 at close of taxable year is taxed as if earned by parent where resulting tax is higher than if taxed at child's rate. (235-7.5).

Corporations are subject to tax on taxable income (other than capital gains) at rates ranging from 4.4% to 6.4%. (235-71). For corporations, regulated investment companies, and REITs with net capital gains, alternative tax under IRC §1201 may be operative if alternative tax is less than regular corporation tax. Alternative tax is sum of regular tax computed on taxable income reduced by net capital gains plus 4% of net capital gain. (235-71.5).

Withholding of Tax on Disposition of Real Estate.—Under HARPTA (Hawaii Real Property Tax Act), transferee of real property located within State must withhold 5% of amount realized on transfer. (235-68[b]). Withholding tax is applied against underlying income tax liability of transferor; excess withholding is refundable. (235-68). Withholding tax must be remitted to State within 20 days following transfer. (235-68[c]). Transferor may apply for exemption certification from Department if no gain will be recognized from transfer, or if there are insufficient proceeds to pay withholding after payment of transaction costs and mortgage liens on property. (235-68[e]). Exception provided if seller used property as principal residence for year preceding transfer and gross proceeds do not exceed $300,000. (235-68[f]). Definition of resident includes Hawaii resident individuals, trusts, estates, Hawaii corporations, partnerships, limited liability companies and limited liability partnerships and non-Hawaii corporations, partnerships, limited liability companies and limited liability partnerships registered to do business in Hawaii. (235-68[a]). Department may enter into withholding agreements with taxpayers who engage in more than one real estate transaction a year. (235-68[g]).

Wage Withholding.—Every employer is required to deduct and withhold taxes on wages paid to employees. (235-61). Maximum withholding rate is 8%. For provisions on withholding taxes see 235-61 to 235-68. Employers are required to make return with Department on or before 15th day of calendar month following month for which taxes have been withheld. (235-62). Employers with withholding tax liability in excess of $100,000 are required to make return on or before tenth day of calendar month following month for which taxes have been withheld. (235-62). Employer is required to make statement to employee of taxes withheld from employee's wages by Jan. 31 of year following tax year for which taxes have been withheld. (235-63). Taxes withheld must be held in trust. (235-64).

Returns are required by every individual doing business in State or having taxable gross income therefrom. (235-92). Return is required for estates with taxable income of $400 or more. Return is required for trust which, under its governing instrument, is required to distribute all of its income currently, and has taxable income of $200 or more. Return is required for all other trusts with taxable income of $80 or more. (235-54, 235-92[3]). Affiliated groups of Hawaii corporations may file consolidated returns in manner consistent with IRC §§1501-1505 and 1552. (235-92). Returns for taxable year must be filed by 20th day of fourth month thereafter. (235-97[b]). Informational returns may be required by regulations. (235-96). Pay-as-you-go provisions requiring declarations of estimated tax and periodic estimated tax payments are similar to IRC. (235-97). Taxpayer must report (by filing amended return) any change in federal tax or return to Department of Taxation within 90 days thereof; Department may inspect or require filing of federal return. (235-101). Partnerships are required to file returns. (235-95). Declarations of estimated taxes are filed with Department. (235-97). Returns are confidential. (235-116). Department may exchange or provide information to IRS. (235-117).

Tax Credits.—For various tax credits available, see 235-55 to 235-55.91 and H.B. 2749 (1998).

Special Provisions.—Uniform Division of Income for Tax Purposes Act has been adopted. (c. 235, Part II). Under Uniform Act, special rules apply to allocation of gain or loss from sale of partnership interest based on ratio of original cost of partnership's tangible property in state to original cost of all partnership tangible property. Special rules apply if more than 50% of partnership's assets are intangibles. (235-26). Other allocation rules apply to income not subject to Uniform Act. (235-5). Multistate Tax Compact has been adopted. (c. 255).

Penalties and interest prescribed by 231-39 and are added to tax. (235-104). Failure to make timely return subjects taxpayer to assessment by Department. (235-107). Failure to pay tax within 60 days of filing return subject to 20% penalty. (231-39[b][3]). For calculation of interest charges see 231-23. Interest may be charged with respect to underpayment or nonpayment of tax due. (231-39[b][4]). Criminal penalties may be imposed under §§231-34, 231-35, and 231-36. Interest imposed for underpayment of estimated tax owed is computed monthly. (235-97).

Audit and Assessment.—Director may audit taxpayers and employers with respect to wages and assess taxes not paid. Director must give taxpayer or employer notice of proposed assessment and taxpayer or employer has 30 days to confer with Department with respect thereto. After such 30 days, Department is to assess income it believes not theretofore assessed and give notice of tax, interest, and penalties. These must be paid within 20 days after date notice was mailed, properly addressed to taxpayer or employer at last known address or place of business. (235-108).

Appeal.—Any person aggrieved by assessment or liability imposed may appeal to board of review or tax appeal court. (235-114). For procedures for appeal to board of review or tax appeal court see topic Property Taxes, subhead Review of Assessment.

Credits and Refunds.—Overpayments of installments are to be credited against unpaid installments, if any. (235-110). Overpayments of taxes are to be refunded. (235-110). Refund procedure does not apply to payments pursuant to assessments under 235-107 or 235-108(b). No refund or credit unless payment was due to tax being interpreted differently than with respect to taxpayers generally. With respect to all tax payments for which refund is not authorized, remedies under appeal or protest procedures are exclusive. (235-110). Refunds shall be made in accordance with 231-23(c). (235-110).

Statute of limitations for assessing deficiencies, except in cases of violations under §§231-34, 231-35, and 231-36, is three years, commencing from date of filing or due date whichever is later. (235-111[a]). Prosecutions under §§231-34, 231-35, and 231-36, must commence within seven years after commission of crime. (231-41). Claim for

See note at head of Digest as to 1998 legislation covered.

See Topical Index in front part of this volume.

HI – 40

INCOME TAX . . . *continued*

credit or refund must be filed within later of three years from filing date or due date, or two years from date tax was paid. (235-111[b]). Statutory period for assessment of any deficiency or determination of refund attributable to amendment made to federal income tax return shall be one year from date Department is notified in writing of such amendment. (235-101[b]). Payments made before due date are deemed to have been paid on due date. (235-111). Limitation for assessing deficiencies respecting gains realized on conversions subject to election under IRC §1033(a)(3)(A) does not expire until three years after Department is notified of replacement or intended not to replace. (235-112).

INHERITANCE TAX:

None.

PROPERTY TAXES:

Real and Personal Property Taxable.—No tax on personal property. All real property tax functions are exercised by respective counties, except for county of Kalawao. (246A-2). County ordinances should be consulted with respect to real property tax laws, including exemptions, assessment, appeals, payment, penalties, rates, and liens, in particular county.

Exemptions.—For real property tax exemptions, see county ordinances. For income tax exemptions, see topic Income Tax, subheads Persons Exempt, Personal Exemptions Available.

Assessment of real property tax is made by county in which property is located, on annual basis. Tax year with respect to real property is July 1 to June 30. Tax is assessed as of specified date (Oct. 1 for City and County of Honolulu) preceding tax year. With certain exceptions, real property is assessed at 100% of fair market value. See specific county ordinances for details. Counties determine tax rates for land and for buildings in various classifications on each of following classes. For counties other than Kauai County, property classes are as follows: (1) improved residential; (2) apartment; (3) commercial; (4) industrial; (5) agricultural; (6) conservation; (7) hotel and resort; (8) unimproved residential; and (9) homeowner (Maui and Hawaii counties only). For Kauai County, property classes are (1) single family residential; (2) apartment; (3) commercial; (4) industrial; (5) agricultural; (6) conservation; (7) hotel and resort; and (8) homestead. Assessment of taxes administered by Department is made by Director of Taxation.

Review of Assessment.—In general, dispute between taxpayer and assessor may be appealed by filing notice of appeal with board of review or tax appeal court. (232-15, 16). Other than for real property tax, payment of assessment must be made prior to appeal. (235-114, 237-42). Taxes may be paid under protest in writing signed by person making payment, setting forth grounds for protest. (40-35, c. 232). Appeals of assessments of fuel tax (c. 243), conveyance tax (c. 247), or estate and transfer tax (c. 236D), handled in same manner as income tax appeals (235-114; 243-14.5, 247-4.5, 236D-15).

Appeals from Board of Review.—May be made to tax appeal court by filing written notice of appeal in tax appeal court within 30 days after filing of decision of board of review and payment of costs fixed by 232-22. (232-17).

Appeals from Tax Appeal Court.—May be made to Supreme Court from tax appeal court by filing written notice of appeal with tax appeal court and depositing costs of appeal within 30 days after filing of decision. (232-19).

Payment.—For real property tax, payment of tax for tax year July 1 to June 30 is due in two equal installments on Aug. 20 and Feb. 20. Fuel, tobacco and use taxes are due on last day of following month. (238-5, 243-8, 245-5). Withholding taxes are due on 15th day of following month unless withholding amount exceeds $100,000. Then, withholding taxes are due on tenth day of following month. (235-62). If due date falls on Sat., Sun., or holiday, payment may be made on next day which is not one of such days. (231-21). For other taxes, see applicable headings.

Collection.—For real property tax, county official designated by ordinance is responsible for collection (Director of Finance for City and County of Honolulu). See ordinances as to specific collection proceedings. For other taxes, see applicable topics/subheads. Department of Taxation responsible for collection of taxes imposed under title 14 (c. 231-235), except those which by law are to be collected by county treasurers. Department may charge added fee for costs or expenses incurred as result of any action taken to enforce collection of taxes administered under title 14. (231-25.5). Director is authorized to require every person whose tax liability for one taxable year exceeds $100,000 to remit payment via electronic funds transfer. (231-9.9). Action in assumpsit may be brought in courts of State or by levy on property or rights to property not otherwise exempt under 231-25(b)(5), which belongs to taxpayer or on which there is lien. (231-25). Execution may issue upon judgment and be satisfied out of any real or personal property of defendant. (231-25).

Credits and Refunds.—Except with respect to conveyance taxes (c. 247) and taxes collected under chapter containing special provision for refund and credit of tax paid in excess of tax imposed, credit or refund may be claimed under procedures set forth in 231-23. Taxpayer entitled to refund may elect to apply amount of refund as to overpayment credit to taxes subsequently accruing under same chapter. (231-23). Department is authorized to retain refunds due to overpayment of tax due for persons who owe debt to State; are delinquent in child support payment; who default on educational loans held by United Student Aid Funds; or who owe federal income tax. (231-51). Refunds or credits for reasons other than overpayment for estate and transfer taxes, general excise taxes, fuel taxes, conveyance taxes, and rental motor vehicle and tour vehicle surcharge taxes, may only be sought by appeal or by payment under protest pursuant to §40-35. (231-23[a]).

Lien.—As provided by ordinance, real property taxes are paramount liens upon property assessed. Any State tax due and unpaid is debt due to State and constitutes lien in favor of State on all real and personal property belonging to any person liable for tax. (231-33). Lien for tax, including penalties and interest arises at earlier of: (1) time of assessment; (2) time return is filed; or (3) certificate provided for under 231-33(f) is filed. (231-33). Except as provided in 231-33(c), (d), and (e), from time State tax lien arises, it is paramount lien on property and rights to property against all parties. (231-33[b]). Liens on tangible personal property held for purpose of sale to public in ordinary course of business are extinguished upon such sale for valuable consideration. (231-33[d]). Liens on securities, negotiable instruments, and money are extinguished upon transfer to person without notice for valuable consideration in money or money's worth, and lien is not valid against mortgagee or pledgee for adequate and full consideration in money or money's worth who is located outside State and takes possession of property if he is without notice or knowledge of existence of lien. (231-33[d]). Mere filing of certificates by Department does not constitute notice for this purpose. (231-33[d]). Lien does not apply if statute imposing particular tax contains specific provision for lien. (231-33[i]). If co-tenancy exists with respect to property subject to lien, co-tenant may pay noncontributing co-tenant's outstanding tax debt due to State for whom lien is imposed. (231-61). Upon proper recordation co-tenant shall acquire lien on nonpaying co-tenant's property interest. (231-61). Lien may be enforced by action in equity and has same priority as tax lien of State. (231-61). Notices of liens for State and federal taxes are kept by Director of Finance. (286-46). Liens are enforced by state tax collector in circuit court where property is located.

Sale.—In cases where Director has levied on property or rights to property of taxpayer, Director may seize and sell such property to satisfy taxes due and unpaid. (231-25). State tax collector may sell via foreclosure any property encumbered by state tax lien, and if any lien has existed thereon for three years, may sell at public auction to highest bidder after proper notice has been given. (231-63). Sale of property takes place within 30 days after seizure but may be postponed no later than 45 days after seizure. (231-5[b][6][c]). Director of taxation issues bill of sale to purchaser. (231-25). In addition, State may procure lien and enforce it by sale. (231-33[h]). Certain property is exempt from levy. (231-25).

Redemption.—As provided by ordinance, taxpayer may redeem real property sold in satisfaction of real property taxes by payment to purchaser at sale, within one year from date thereof, or if purchaser's deed is not recorded within 60 days of sale, within one year from such recordation. Taxpayer must reimburse expenses including 12% interest to purchaser.

Mortgage Recording Fee.—See categories Insurance, topic Insurance Companies, subhead Hurricane Relief Fund; Mortgages, topic Mortgages of Real Property, subhead Recording Schedule of Fees.

REAL ESTATE CONVEYANCE TAX:

Any real property or interest therein, transferred or conveyed by deed, lease, sublease, assignment, transfer, or conveyance, or any other document not otherwise exempt under 247-3, is subject to conveyance tax. (247-1). Tax imposed is 10¢ per $100 of actual and full consideration paid or to be paid. (247-2). In case of lease or sublease whose full unexpired term is for period of five years or more, tax imposed is based on cash value of lease rentals discounted to present day value, and capitalized at rate of 6% plus actual and full consideration paid or to be paid for any and all improvements. (247-2). Tax imposed for each transaction shall not be less than $1. (247-2). Certificate of conveyance declaring actual and full consideration of property transferred is required to be filed and recorded. (247-6). Exemptions from tax imposed under this section are found in 247-3. Assessments, levies, or credits for overpayment must be made within three years from filing date. (247-6.5). Refund for taxes erroneously or unjustly paid is made in accordance with 231-23. (247-8).

Tax Liability.—Party conveying real property (seller, lessor, etc.) is liable for tax imposed, except when U.S., state, or any agency thereof is conveyor, or tax liability is on purchaser (buyer, lessee, etc.). (247-4). Tax is to be paid not later than 90 days after transaction and in any event prior to imprinting of seals. (247-4).

Imprinting of Seals.—On document as evidence of tax payment, seal will be imprinted upon payment of tax and any penalties or interest and prior to recordation. (247-5).

SALES AND USE TAXES:

Sales Tax.—None, but see subhead General Excise Tax, infra.

General excise tax also known as "gross excise" tax, is assessed and collected against persons and entities on account of their business and other activities conducted in State. (237-13). Businesses are classified and taxed based on following categories: (1) manufacturers; (2) business of selling tangible personal property, producing; (3) contractors; (4) theaters, amusements, radio broadcasting stations, etc.; (5) sales representatives, etc.; (6) service business; (7) insurance solicitors and agents; (8) professions; (9) receipts of sugar benefit payments; (10) business of leasing real property; and (11) other business. Tax is measured by application of rates against values, gross proceeds of sales or gross income from engaging in business. (237-13). Tax is imposed on persons engaging in retailing activities within State. (237-16). Business includes all activities (personal, professional, or corporate), engaged in or caused to be engaged in with object of gain or economic benefit either direct or indirect, but does not include casual sales. (237-2). Tax imposed at entity level, except for certain revocable trusts. Includes tax on interstate and foreign common carrier telecommunications services. (237-13). Tax on gross proceeds from sale of electric power to public utility company for resale to public is taxed at same rate as tax on "producer" under 237-13(2)(A). (237-13.5). As condition precedent to engaging in business in state, license must be obtained. One-time fee of $20 is assessed for license. (237-9).

Application.—See 237-3 for definition of gross income. Transactions between entity and shareholder or partner are generally taxable. For treatment of expense reimbursements, see 237-20. When gross income is divided between provider of services and travel agency or tour packager, tax imposed on each person's respective portion of proceeds only. (237-18[f]). When gross income is divided between hotel and travel agency for hotel accommodations, tax imposed on respective portion of proceeds only. (237-18[g]). Partnerships are taxed at entity level.

Persons Exempt.—§§237-23 and 237-23.5 provide exemptions from tax imposed under c. 237 for certain persons. Persons exempted generally include: public service companies (as defined in 239-2), civic organizations, public utilities, fraternal benefit

---

See note at head of Digest as to 1998 legislation covered.

See Topical Index in front part of this volume.

SALES AND USE TAXES . . . *continued*
societies, religious, charitable, scientific or educational organizations or trusts, hospitals, cooperative associations (including farmers coops exempt under IRC §531), and others exempted for special purposes. (237-23). Limited excise tax imposed on persons blind, deaf or totally disabled. (237-17).

Transactions Exempt.—§§237-24, 237-24.3, 237-24.5, 237-24.7 and 237-24.9 enumerate certain amounts not taxable. Exempt transactions include wages, insurance proceeds, small business innovation grants received pursuant to 206M-15, gross proceeds arising from sale of tangible personal property imported to Hawaii from foreign or domestic source to licensed taxpayer for subsequent resale for purpose of wholesale (S.B. 2065, 1998), certain amounts received by management company from related entities engaged in business of selling interstate or foreign common carrier telecommunication services, receipts (other than rental income) by employee benefit plans, under certain circumstances, interest received by person domiciled outside State from trust company acting as payment agent on behalf of issuer of interest bearing instrument or obligation (237-24.7), amounts received from servicing or maintenance of aircraft or from construction of aircraft service and maintenance facility (237-24.9) and amounts subject to federal excise tax or other taxes (e.g., liquor, tobacco, liquid fuel), others exempted for special purposes. Specific exemptions are given to sales to federal government. (237-25). For other exemptions and exclusions see 237-23 through 237-29.7.

Rates depend on class of business engaged in. Most transactions taxed at 4%. Wholesalers, manufacturers, sugar processors, sales from disabled persons or their corporations and sellers of electric power generated from nonfossil fuels to public utilities for sale to public pay 0.5%; insurance solicitors pay 0.15%; and retailers, service businesses, professions and all others pay 4%. (237-13 to 237-17).

Payment.—Tax is payable in monthly installments on or before last day of month following month in which it accrues, but approval for quarterly payment can be obtained where total tax liability for calendar year will not exceed $2,000, or semiannual payments where total tax liability for calendar year will not exceed $1,000. (237-30). Director may permit filing of fiscal year returns. (237-30).

Returns.—Each taxpayer must make out monthly return, showing estimated tax liability and transmit same, with remittance of amount of tax, to appropriate tax official. (237-30). Quarterly or semiannual filings permitted depending on total tax liability for year. Annual reconciliation return under oath must also be made on or before 20th day of fourth month following close of taxable year, showing gross proceeds of sales or gross income for previous year. On this annual return amount of tax chargeable against taxpayer must be computed. Amount of monthly payments already made deducted and remittance of residue of tax made with return. (237-33). Amendment to federal tax return is required to be reported to Department pursuant to procedures in 235-101. (237-33.5).

Collection.—Department may collect taxes due and unpaid together with penalties and interest by action in assumpsit or other appropriate proceedings, injunction restraining further conduct of business in State may be obtained until payment of delinquent taxes, penalties and interest have been paid. (237-46). Contractor's license may be suspended for failure to pay delinquent general excise tax or to honor payment installment plan.

Penalties and interest shall be added to and become part of tax where Department determines that general excise tax on any gross income or gross proceeds of sale have not been assessed. (237-32, 39). Penalties and interest may be assessed for refusing to file return required under 237-33. Criminal penalties may also be imposed under §§231-34, 231-35, and 231-36. Advertisement that tax imposed under c. 237 is not considered as element in price to purchaser is prohibited. (237-49).

Appeal from assessment of tax is available to board of review or tax appeal court pursuant to procedure in 235-114 and 231-23. (237-42).

Credits and Refund.—Credit or refund for overpayment of tax available in manner provided in 231-23(c). (237-37).

Statute of Limitations.—Taxes imposed under c. 237 shall be assessed or levied within three years after annual return is filed or within three years of due date prescribed for filing, payment of tax. (237-40). Claims for credit or refund must be made within three years of filing, payment of tax or due date. (237-40). Amendments to federal tax return required to be reported to Department under 235-101 extend statutory period for assessment of deficiency or determination of refund for one year beginning date Department is notified in writing of such amendment. (237-33.5). Prosecution for violations under §§231-34, 231-35 and 231-36 must commence within seven years of commission of crime.

Bulk Sales.—Bulk sale or transfer of merchandise, fixtures or other assets of business, not in ordinary course of business, must be reported by seller not less than ten days after possession, title or control of property, or any part thereof, passes to purchaser. (237-43). Purchaser must withhold payment of purchase price until he receives tax clearance certificate from Department to effect that all seller's State taxes have been paid. (237-43). If purchaser does not obtain tax clearance certificate, purchaser becomes liable for seller's unpaid taxes and also for any other unpaid taxes, that are lien against items sold. (237-43). Certificate will not be issued while Department investigates (including by audit) whether taxes have been levied or accrued against seller. (237-43).

Use Tax.—Compensating Use Tax Law (c. 238) imposes tax on tangible personal property imported or purchased from unlicensed operator for use in Hawaii. No tax imposed if importer or purchaser is licensed under general excise tax and is wholesaler purchasing for resale or manufacturer incorporating imported item, which remains perceptible to senses, in his finished product, and it is sold at wholesale. (238-2). Tax of 0.5% is imposed on retailers importing for resale, or manufacturers or contractors importing material to be incorporated into their finished product which is sold at retail. (238-2[2]). In all other cases, tax is 4%. (238-2[3]). Credit given for sales or use taxes paid by purchaser or importer to other states or its subdivisions on same transaction, but not to exceed amount of use tax which would be paid in Hawaii. (238-3[i]). Tax is not applied to certain property listed in 237-3(e) to (h), (j), and (k).

STAMP TAX:

None.

UNEMPLOYMENT COMPENSATION TAX:

For purpose of providing unemployment benefits every employer is required to pay into unemployment compensation fund, percentage of payroll based upon employer's benefit experience. (383-62, 383-68).

See also category Business Organizations, topic Corporations, subheads Franchise Tax and Taxation of Corporate Stock.

UNIFORM FEDERAL TAX LIEN REGISTRATION ACT:

Adopted, with modifications. (c. 505).

TRANSPORTATION

MOTOR VEHICLES:

County finance directors have supervision over registration of vehicles, county examination of drivers over licensing of operators. (c. 286). County of Hawaii, Finance Department, 26 Aupuni Street, Hilo, Hawaii 96720; City and County of Honolulu, Motor Vehicle Licensing Division, 530 S. King Street, Rm. 208, Honolulu, Hawaii 96813, mailing address: P.O. Box 30330, Honolulu, Hawaii 96820-0330; County of Kauai, Finance Department, 44 Rice Street, Lihue, Kauai, Hawaii 96766; County of Maui, Motor Vehicle Registration, 200 S. High Street, Wailuku, Maui, Hawaii 96793.

Vehicle License.—Numbered plates on front and rear, renewed annually for all vehicles except those publicly owned or owned by certain disabled veterans. (249-4, 6,7). No exemption to vehicles owned by members of armed forces. Penalty for nonpayment includes seizure and sale. (249-10).

Operator's License.—Required of all drivers unless specifically excluded by statute. (286-102, 105, 110, 236, 239). Parents or guardian of minor under 18 liable for minor's negligence. (286-112). Exemptions granted to certain federal and state employees. (286-105). Driver License Compact provides reciprocal recognition of driver's licenses from other states, District of Columbia and Commonwealth of Puerto Rico. (c. 286C). Operation of mopeds. (291C-191 to 207).

Renewals.—License expires on licensee's 6th birthday after issuance of license except that license expires on licensee's 2nd birthday after issuance where licensee is 72 years of age or older, 24 years of age or younger, has received nine points or more for traffic violations under previous point system within two years, or has physical disabilities not overcome by doctor's certificate or special equipment on vehicle. (286-106). Driver licensing point system repealed. (c. 286).

Titles.—Issued upon initial registration. (286-47, 48, 52, 55). Vehicles may be junked by surrendering title to Director of Finance. (Act 3, 1998). All non-repairable vehicles junked under Act 3, 1998 will never be titled or registered again.

Sales.—Vehicle must be registered by new owner, old certificate of ownership must be surrendered within 30 days of transfer, and new certificate of ownership must be issued or transfer deemed incomplete. (286-52). Notice to Dept. of Finance prior to issuance of new certificate of ownership relieves transferee of civil and criminal liability incurred after Notice, by transferor, because of his ownership of vehicle. (286-52). Where vehicle is deemed abandoned and certificate of ownership or registration is unavailable, bill of sale executed by authorized seller is satisfactory evidence authorizing transfer of title or interest by operation of law. (Act 139, 1998).

Upon transfer by sale or otherwise of moped, person whose interest is to be transferred and transferee must write their signatures with ink upon certificate of registration issued for moped, together with address of transferee. Within 30 days, transferee must forward endorsed certificate of registration to Director of Finance. (Act 188, 1998).

Liens.—For unpaid taxes. (231-33). Mechanics' lien for reasonable charges for work done and materials furnished, excluding storage charges, and may retain possession of property until charges are paid. (507-18, 19). See category Business Regulation and Commerce, topic Commercial Code, subhead Article 9.

Identification Marks.—Penalty for altering, fine up to $1,000, imprisonment up to one year, or both. (286-43, 61).

Odometer systems regulated by 486-71, 75, 77-84, 87. No vehicle may be introduced into Hawaii unless odometer complies with regulations.

Operation Prohibited.—By persons whose term of suspension or revocation of operator's license has not expired, has been convicted within two years of driving while under influence of alcohol or drugs and unlicensed, has not passed examination, has not provided proof of financial responsibility, or has physical or mental disability which prevents safe operation. (286-104).

Size and Weight Limits.—Regulated by 291-34 to 37 inclusive.

Equipment Required.—Regulated by 70-63, §18 of Traffic Code of City and County of Honolulu and similar ordinances of other counties; General Safety Code of the State; regulations of State Public Utilities Commission.

Certain equipment may not be sold for use or actually used in vehicles without approval of highway safety coordinator. (286-83). Such approval may be revoked by highway safety coordinator after conducting appropriate hearings and determinating that equipment does not comply with requirements of 286-83. (286-84).

Power output for mopeds regulated by 291C-202.

Lights Required.—Regulated by 291-25 to 32 inclusive.

Inspection.—Safety inspection required every 12 months except for certain vehicles which must be inspected every six months. (286-26).

Traffic Regulations.—Generally c. 291 and c. 291C.

Accidents.—Good Samaritan Act adopted. (663-1.5). Duty to give information and render aid. (291C-14). Duty to report accidents when apparent extent of damages exceeds $3,000. (287-4). Police are required to disclose traffic accident reports to anyone directly involved in accident or having proper interest. (291C-20).

Liability of Owner.—No statutes covering liability of owner for negligence of others.

See note at head of Digest as to 1998 legislation covered.

See Topical Index in front part of this volume.

MOTOR VEHICLES . . . *continued*

Guests.—No statutes covering liability for injury to guests.

Proof of Financial Responsibility.—Regulated by c. 287.

Insurance.—Tort liability abolished with respect to accidental harm arising from accidents except where death, permanent disfigurement, or significant loss of body part or body function occurs, or where as result of injury, personal injury protection benefits incurred equal or exceed $5,000. (431:10C-306). Bodily injury and property damage insurance are mandatory for all registered vehicles. (431:10C). Minimum policy coverage of $20,000 for personal injury and $10,000 for property damage required. (431:10C-301). Insurer must offer insured opportunity to purchase coverage for damage by owners and operators of uninsured and underinsured vehicles and make available specified additional optional insurance coverage. (431:10C-301, 302). Insurer has burden of proving legally sufficient offer was made. (72 Haw. 314, 816 P.2d 968). Motor vehicle insurance requirement may be satisfied if vehicle owner provides bond and proof of qualification as self-insurer. (431:10C-105). Claimant or defendant will have option to elect arbitration to resolve claim in tort covered by motor vehicle liability insurance. (Act 275, 1998).

No-Fault Insurance.—Personal injury protection benefits replace no-fault benefits. (431:10C-303.5).

Foreign Vehicles.—Nonresidents must register vehicle within 30 days after commencing to operate vehicle or causing or permitting it to be operated within state. (286-54).

Nonresident Operators.—No statutes restricting operation by validly licensed nonresident operators.

Actions against Nonresidents.—Operation of motor vehicle by resident or nonresident on public highway in state subjects person to state's jurisdiction whether he is nonresident at time of or subsequent to accident. Service of process is of same legal force as upon resident. See category Civil Actions and Procedure, topic Process, subhead Nonresidents Generally.

Other matters governed by ordinances of the several islands, differing in their requirements.

Direct Action.—No statutory provisions regarding direct actions against insurers.

Motor Vehicle Carriers.—Economic regulation, safety, equipment, and inspection of commercial motor vehicles regulated by Public Utilities Commission. (c. 271). Certificate or permit required before transporting persons or property for compensation (271-8, 13), and must carry such insurance protection as Commission requires (271-17). Motor carrier vehicles must exhibit identification and informational markings. (286, XI).

Commercial motor vehicles, their economic regulation, safety, equipment and inspection are regulated by Public Utilities Commission. (c. 271). Certificate or permit required before transporting persons or property for compensation (271-8, 13), and must carry such insurance protection as Commission requires (271-17).

Motor Vehicle Lease Disclosure Act establishes mandatory disclosures by retail lessor to consumer. (c. 481L).

Seat Belt Requirements.—U.S. Dept. of Transportation approved child passenger restraint system required whenever transporting child under three years old. If child is three years or older, but less than four years of age, child must be restrained either by approved child passenger restraint system or seat belt assembly. For child three years or older, requirements do not apply if number of persons in vehicle exceeds greatest number of seat belt assemblies, all seat belts are in use, and unrestrained child is in back seat. (291-11.5). First conviction will result in fine of $100, required attendance at safety class, and $50 driver education assessment. Subsequent convictions result in increased fines to $500. (Act 81, 1998).

Motor Vehicle Taxes.—All motor vehicles are subject to annual tax according to net weight of each vehicle, except as otherwise provided. (c. 249).

Gasoline Tax.—See category Taxation, topic Gasoline Tax.

Lemon Law.—See category Business Regulation and Commerce, topic Consumer Protection.

COMMERCIAL CODE FORMS

See also categories Business Regulation and Commerce, topic Commercial Code and Mortgages, topic Chattel Mortgages.

[Coversheet for documents filed at Bureau of Conveyances]

LAND COURT SYSTEM	REGULAR SYSTEM

Return by Mail ( )   Pickup ( )   To:

TITLE OF DOCUMENT:

PARTIES TO DOCUMENT:

MORTGAGOR:

MORTGAGEE:

TAX MAP KEY(S): Oahu

See note at head of Digest as to 1998 legislation covered.

See Topical Index in front part of this volume.

Financing Statement.—Form UCC-1.

```
┌──────────────────────────────────────────────────────────────────┐
│  Return by Mail (  )  Pickup (  )              To:                 │
│                                                                    │
│                                                                    │
│                                                                    │
│  This STATEMENT is presented for recordation pursuant to the       │
│  Hawaii Uniform Commercial Code.                                   │
│  No. of Additional Sheets Presented:      │ 1. Maturity Date, if   │
│                                           │    any (optional):      │
│  2. Debtor (Last Name First) and Address:                          │
│  3. Secured Party: Name and Address:                               │
│  4. Assignee of Secured Party, if any, and Address:                │
│  5. This Financing Statement covers the following types or items   │
│     of property:                                                   │
│                                                                    │
│  6. Check (x) if applicable:                                       │
│     (  ) (If collateral is crops) The above described crops are    │
│         growing or are to be grown on:                             │
│     (  ) (If collateral is goods which are or are to become        │
│  fixtures) The above described goods are affixed or to be          │
│  affixed to:                                                       │
│     Describe real estate:                                          │
│  Record Owner: _____    │
│       or                                                           │
│  Record Lessee: _____    │
│  7. Check (x) if applicable: (  ) Proceeds of collateral are also  │
│     covered.                                                       │
│                              (  ) Products of collateral are also  │
│     covered.                                                       │
│  8. This statement is filed without the debtor's signature to      │
│     perfect a security interest in collateral (check appropriate   │
│     box):                                                          │
│     (  ) which is already subject to a security interest in        │
│         another jurisdiction when it was brought into this state or│
│     (  ) which is proceeds of the original collateral described    │
│         above in which a security interest was perfected.          │
│                                                                    │
│  By _____   By _____ │
│     Signature(s) of Debtor(s)         Signature(s) of Secured      │
│                                       Party(ies)                   │
└──────────────────────────────────────────────────────────────────┘
```

Directions on reverse side of Form UCC-1 are as follows:

Instructions—UCC-1

1. Please type this form in black.
2. Send original to Bureau of Conveyances, P.O. Box 2867, Honolulu, Hawaii 96803. It will be returned after recordation.
3. Filing fee for this form is $20.00, effective July 1, 1991. If the space provided for any item on the form is inadequate, the item should be continued on additional sheets preferably 8½ x 11, and in any event not exceeding 8½ x 11 inches.
4. If collateral is crops or goods which are to become fixtures, check the appropriate box in Item 6. Describe in Item 6 the real estate by street and number, if any, or if none, by another description sufficient to identify it such as tax key number, or such as "real property described in Liber ____ Page ____".
5. If there is a record lessee, give his name; otherwise give name of record owner.
6. If a copy of a security agreement is used as a financing statement the filing is $20.00 per document, effective July 1, 1991.
7. The completion of Item 1 is optional.
8. This form should be preceded by a coversheet as specified in 502-31. (see coversheet form)

See note at head of Digest as to 1998 legislation covered.

See Topical Index in front part of this volume.

Statement of Continuation, Termination, Partial Release, Assignment, Etc.—Form UCC-2.

Return by Mail ( ) Pickup ( )   To:

This STATEMENT is presented for recordation pursuant to the Hawaii Uniform Commercial Code.   (FORM UCC-2)

No. of Additional Sheets Presented: | 1. Maturity Date, if any (optional):

2. Debtor (Last Name First) and Address:

3. Secured Party: Name and Address:

4. Assignee of Secured Party, if any, and Address:

5. This Statement refers to the original financing statement recorded in book _____ page _____; or document number _____ on date _____ _____.

6. Check (X) if applicable:
  ( ) A. Continuation   The original Financing Statement above indicated is still effective and is continued.
  ( ) B. Termination   The Secured Party of record no longer claims a security interest under the above-indicated Financing Statement.
  ( ) C. Release   From the Collateral described in the above-indicated Financing Statement, the Secured Party releases the collateral described in Item 7 below.
  ( ) D. Assignment   The Secured Party of record has assigned to the above-named Assignee the Secured Party's rights under the above-indicated Financing Statement in the collateral described in Item 7 below.
  ( ) E. Amendment   The above-indicated Financing Statement is amended as set forth in Item 7 below. (Signature of Debtor is required.)

7.

(Fee $20.00 per document. Effective July 1, 1991)

By _____   By _____
  Signature(s) of Debtor(s) (only on amendment)   Signature(s) of Secured Party(ies)

Directions on reverse side of Form UCC-2 are as follows:

Instructions—UCC-2

1. Please type this form in black.
2. Send original to Bureau of Conveyances, P.O. Box 2867, Honolulu, Hawaii 96803. It will be returned after recordation. However, if property is Land Court registered, and the collateral is crops or goods which are or are to become fixtures, send original and duplicate.
3. Include filing fee of $20.00 per document, effective July 1, 1991.
4. If the space provided for any item on the form is inadequate, the item should be continued on additional sheets preferably 8½ x 14, but in any event, not exceeding 8½ x 11 inches.
5. This form should be preceded by a coversheet as specified in 502-31. (see coversheet form)

————————

Request for Information or Copies.—Form UCC-3.

STATE OF HAWAII
BUREAU OF CONVEYANCES
P.O. BOX 2867
HONOLULU, HAWAII 96803

TO: Registrar, Bureau of Conveyances

(FORM UCC-3)

Party Requesting Information or Copies Name and Address	(Must be filed in duplicate)

Debtor (Last Name First) and Address	(One name per request)

☐ INFORMATION REQUEST

Please furnish certificate showing whether there is on record as of _____, 19____ at _____M., any presently effective financing statement naming the above named debtor and any statement of assignment thereof, and if there is, giving the date and hour of filing of each such statement and the name and address of each secured party therein. Enclosed is the fee of $25.00 for the certificate plus $5.00 for each financing statement and for each statement of assignment reported therein.

☐ COPY REQUEST

Please furnish copies of presently effective financing statements and statements of assignment listed below which are on record with your office, at the rate of $1.00 per page.

Book & Page No.	Date & Hour of Recordation	Name & Addresses of Secured Parties & Assignees

_____   _____
Date   Signature of Requesting Party

CERTIFICATE: The undersigned hereby certifies that the above listing is a record of all presently effective financing statements and statements of assignment which name the above debtor and which are on record in my office as of _____ 19 ___ at _____M.

_____   _____
Date   Registrar of Conveyances

Instructions: This form should be preceded by a coversheet as specified in 502-31. (see coversheet form)

SATISFACTION OF JUDGMENT;

☐ **RELEASE OF GARNISHEE(S)**

Form #1DC48

IN THE DISTRICT COURT OF THE FIRST CIRCUIT
_____ DIVISION
STATE OF HAWAI'I

Plaintiff(s)

Reserved for Court Use

Civil No.

Filing Party(ies)/Filing Party(ies)' Attorney (Name, Attorney Number, Firm Name (if applicable), Address, Telephone and Facsimile Numbers)

Defendant(s)

Name of Garnishee(s) to be released:

Date Garnishee Summons Order Granted:
(If none, date of Garnishee Summons)

SATISFACTION OF JUDGMENT

☐ **RELEASE OF GARNISHEE**

The undersigned acknowledges full satisfaction and payment of the **JUDGMENT** in the above-entitled case.

☐ Release of Garnishee(s) as stated above.

CERTIFICATE OF SERVICE

I certify that a copy of this Satisfaction was served at the last known address(es) of Judgment Debtor(s) or Judgment Debtor(s)' attorney/☐ Garnishee(s) on _____
_____ by ☐ Hand-delivery or ☐ Mail, Postage Prepaid, at the following address(es):

Signature of Filing Party(ies)/Filing Party(ies)' Attorney:

Date:

Print/Type Name:

In accordance with the **Americans with Disabilities Act** if you require an accommodation for your disability, please contact the District Court Administration Office at PHONE NO. 538-5121, FAX 538-5233, or TTY 539-4853 at least ten (10) working days in advance of your hearing or appointment date. For Civil related matters, please call 538-5151.

SATISRLS.X (Amended 4/18/97)v

I certify that this is a full, true, and correct copy of the original on file in this office.

_____
Clerk, District Court of the above Circuit, State of Hawai'i

_____
See note at head of Digest as to 1998 legislation covered.

See Topical Index in front part of this volume.

IDAHO LAW DIGEST REVISER

Merrill & Merrill, Chartered
109 North Arthur, 5th Floor
P.O. Box 991
Pocatello, Idaho 83204-0991
Telephone: 208-232-2286
Fax: 208-232-2499

Reviser Profile

History: The firm was originally organized under the name of Deitrich & Clark, and operated until Frank S. Deitrich was appointed U.S. District Judge for the District of Idaho in 1907, whereupon the firm became Clark & Budge. This firm was reorganized in 1916 as Budge & Merrill, when A.L. Merrill became a member. R.D. Merrill became associated in 1921 and in 1923 the firm became Merrill & Merrill. Wesley F. Merrill joined the firm in 1948. Upon the death of A.L. Merrill (1961) and subsequently R.D. Merrill (1970), Wesley F. Merrill became senior partner.

Growth and Emphasis: Thereafter, the firm expanded to include Dave R. Gallafent (1975), Stephen S. Dunn (1977), D. Russell Wight (1980), David C. Nye (1987), and Kent L. Hawkins (1988), Thomas W. Clark (1995). The firm presently includes the above named attorneys each of whom are currently partners and two associates, Thomas J. Lyons (1996) and Gary L. Longmore (1998). Wesley F. Merrill retired from the firm and the practice of law in 1996. The firm is engaged in General Practice with emphasis on Litigation (primarily defense and insurance litigation), Commercial, Corporate, Banking, Insurance and Utility Law areas.

Client Base: A large majority of the clients represented by Merrill & Merrill are among the leading companies in their field. They consist of a wide variety of insurance companies, major utility, medical and health care organizations, banking interests, locally oriented corporations in water and water resources, farming, etc. The firm is attuned to the legal needs of the area and the society, and is associated with programs to provide legal services.

Firm Activities: Merrill & Merrill encourages and expects involvement of its members in professional organizations, civic groups, and local area improvement endeavors. All partners are members of the American Bar Association, the Idaho Bar Association and the local Sixth District Bar Association. Wesley F. Merrill is a past President of the Idaho State Bar Association, and a member of the American College of Trial Lawyers and International Association of Defense Counsel. Three partners are members of the Idaho Association of Defense Counsel with Wesley F. Merrill being President in 1967-1968.

Management: While the firm is a professional corporation, it is generally under the management of the senior partner. Various committees within the firm continuously monitor attorneys' performance, case assignment and disposition, office technology and advancement, finances, and the firm's rapport and attitudes.

Significant Distinctions: Major distinctions of firm members include: A.L. Merrill, Commissioner Idaho State Bar, 1925-1928; President Idaho State Bar, 1927-1928; State Delegate from Idaho to the American Bar Association, 1943-1952; American Bar Association Board of Governors, 1952-1955; Member National Conference of Commissioners on Uniform State Laws commencing 1948; Special Deputy Attorney General for Idaho for Organization of the Bear River Compact. R.D. Merrill, Commissioner Idaho State Bar, 1946-1949 and President 1948-1949. Wesley F. Merrill, Commissioner Idaho State Bar, 1961-1964 (President 1963-1964); Dave R. Gallafent, 6th District Bar Association President, 1986-1987; Stephen S. Dunn, U.S. Magistrate Judge, 1990-1992; Thomas W. Clark, 6th District Bar Association President, 1996-1997.

IDAHO LAW DIGEST

(The following is a list of all Categories and Topics, including cross-references, covered in this Digest.)

IDAHO LAW DIGEST

Revised for 1999 edition by

MERRILL & MERRILL, CHARTERED of the Pocatello Bar.

(All references, unless otherwise indicated, are to Idaho Code, 1947, of which Volume 4 has been expanded to Volumes 4 and 4A, Volume 5 has been expanded to Volumes 5 part one, part two, 5A and 5B, Volume 6 has been expanded to Volumes 6 and 6A, Volume 7 has been expanded to Volumes 7, 7A, and 7B, Volume 8 has been expanded to Volumes 8 and 8A, Volume 9 has been expanded to Volumes 9 and 9A, Volume 10 has been expanded to Volumes 10 and 10A, Volume 11 has been expanded to 11 and 11A, and Volume 12 has been expanded to Volumes 12 and 13. For mode of citation of statutes see category Courts and Legislature, topic Statutes. I.R.C.P. indicates Idaho Rules of Civil Procedure. I.R.E. indicates Idaho Rules of Evidence. Session laws are cited by year and chapter number. Parallel citations to the Pacific Reporter begin with 2 Idaho).

Uniform Probate Code adopted, with modifications (15-1-101 to 15-7-401), and in effect. 1975 and 1977 Amendments not adopted. 1979 Amendments adopted.

Note: Legislature in recess at time of going to press. This Revision incorporates the 1998 Acts passed by the Legislature during its regular session concluding on March 23, 1998.

INTRODUCTION

GOVERNMENT AND LEGAL SYSTEM:

The State of Idaho is a constituent state of the United States of America. For further discussion of the U.S. federal system, see Introduction to the Federal Government of the United States at the beginning of this volume. A great many laws are promulgated by the federal government of the United States and are not reflected in the topics below. See the Introduction to this volume for references to the federal law topics covered.

Like all but one of the United States, Idaho has a common law legal system, with roots in English common law. For information on the courts and legislature of Idaho, see category Courts and Legislature.

HOLIDAYS:

Legal holidays are Sundays, Jan. 1, 3d Mon. in Jan., 3d Mon. in Feb., last Mon. in May, July 4, 1st Mon. in Sept., 2d Mon. in Oct., Nov. 11, 4th Thurs. in Nov., Dec. 25. (73-108).

Sept. 17 designated Constitutional Commemorative Day. (73-108B).

Holiday Falling on Sunday.—Where day fixed by law or contract for doing an act falls on holiday, performance on next business day is sufficient. When any legal holiday falls on Sun. following Mon. shall be holiday. (73-108 to 73-110).

Holiday Falling on Saturday.—When any legal holiday falls on Sat. preceding Fri. shall be holiday. (73-108).

Legality of Transaction on Saturday, Sunday or Holiday.—No statutory prohibition against making contracts or enforcing.

OFFICE HOURS AND TIME ZONE:

Idaho is in the Mountain Standard (GMT −07:00) time zone. Office hours are generally from 9 a.m. to 5 p.m.

BUSINESS ORGANIZATIONS

AGENCY:

In general, rules of common law apply to principals and agents, in absence of legislation. An agent fraudulently making false statements to a principal as to price, quantity or quality of property entrusted to him for sale is guilty of misdemeanor. (18-3105).

ASSOCIATIONS:

Associations having or exercising any powers or privileges of corporations not possessed by individuals or partnerships are governed by Idaho Business Corporation Act. (30-1-101). Subject to provisions of anti-trust (48-101 to 48-119) and blue sky (30-1401) laws. Insurance Guaranty Association Act adopted to pay covered claims and avoid delay and financial loss due to insolvency of insurers. (41-3601 to 41-3621). See category Insurance, topic Insurance Companies, subhead Supervision.

Professional Associations or Corporations.—See topic Corporations, subhead Professional Associations or Corporations.

CORPORATIONS:

For unincorporated organizations, see topic Associations; see also topic Joint Stock Companies.

Model Business Corporation Act adopted, effective July 1, 1979. (30-1-1 to 30-1-152). Amendments proposed subsequent to Aug., 1977 not adopted, except as noted herein. Dec., 1979 amendments not adopted. Revised Model Business Corporation Act of 1984 adopted, effective July 1, 1997. (30-1-101 to 30-1-1704). Following are changes and omissions from Revised Model Act:

Idaho Business Corporation Act uses numbers for subsections instead of letters. Also replaces "Act" with "Chapter" throughout.

§1.02 In subsection (d) add "or, if electronically transmitted, it must be in a format that can be retrieved or reproduced in typewritten or printed form." In subsection (g) delete: "(1) the corporate seal, (2) an attestation by the secretary or an assistant secretary, (3) an acknowledgment, verification, or proof." and add "a corporate seal, attestation, acknowledgment or verification." In subsection (i) delete "and must be accompanied by one exact or conformed copy (except as provided in sections 5.03 and 15.09), the correct filing fee, and any franchise tax, license fee, or penalty required by the Act or other law", add "Delivery may be made by electronic transmission if and to the extent permitted by the Secretary of State. If it is filed in typewritten or printed form and transmitted electronically, the Secretary of State may require one (1) exact or conformed copy to be delivered with the document, except as provided in sections 30-1-503 and 30-1-1509, Idaho Code." Add paragraph (10) which reads: "When the document is delivered to the office of the Secretary of State for filing, the correct filing fee, and any other fee or penalty required to be paid therewith by this chapter or other law must be paid or provision for payment made in a manner permitted by the Secretary of State."

§1.21 In subsection (a) delete "may" and add "shall". Delete subsections (a)(1) and (a)(2) and add "(a) A foreign corporations application for a certificate of authority, amended certificate, to transact business in this state;". In subsection (b) delete "may".

§1.22 After "Article of incorporation" insert "$100.00", after "Application for use of deceptively similar name" insert "$20.00", after "Application for reserved name" insert "$20.00", after "Notice of transfer of reserved name" insert "$20.00", after "Application for registered name" insert "$60.00", after "Application for renewal of registered name" insert "$60.00", after "Corporation's statement of change of registered agent or registered office of both" insert "No fee", after "Agent's statement of change of registered office for each affected corporation" delete "not to exceed a total of" and insert "No fee", after "Amendment of articles of incorporation" insert "$30.00", after "Restatement of articles of incorporation with amendment of articles" insert "$30.00", after "Articles of merger or share exchange" insert "$30.00", after "Articles of dissolution" insert "$30.00", after "Articles of revocation of dissolution" insert "$30.00", after "Application for reinstatement following administrative dissolution" insert "$30.00", after "Application for certificate of authority" insert "$100.00", after "Application for amended certificate of authority" insert "$30.00", after "Application for certificate of withdrawal" insert "$20.00", after "Annual report" insert "No fee", after "Articles of correction" insert "$30.00", delete "Application for" in subsection (25), after "certificate of existence or authorization" insert "$10.00", after "Any other document required or permitted to be filed by this Act" insert "$20.00", add "(aa) Any document when the filing party requires the certificate therefor to be returned within eight (8) working hours, a surcharge of $20.00; (bb) Any non-typed document which required a fee, a surcharge of $20.00", after "(b) The Secretary of State shall collect a fee of" insert "ten dollars ($10.00)", insert "twenty-five cents (25¢)" in subsection (c)(1), insert "ten dollars ($10.00)" in subsection (c)(2).

§1.23 delete subsection (1), add; "(a) At the date and time of filing, as evidenced by such means as the Secretary of State may use for the purpose of recording the date and time of filing; or".

§1.24 Replace "incorrect statement" with "inaccuracy" throughout section. Add: "(1)(c) The electronic transmission was defective," delete "specify the incorrect statement and the reason it is incorrect or the manner in which the execution was defective", add "specify the inaccuracy or defect to be corrected".

§1.25 Delete subsection (b), add "(2) The Secretary of State files a document by recording it as filed on the date and time of receipt. After filing a document, except as provided in section 30-1-503 and 30-1-1509, Idaho Code, the Secretary of State shall deliver to the domestic or foreign corporation or its representative a copy of the document with an acknowledgment of the date and time of filing".

§1.26 After "may appeal the refusal within 30 days after the return of the document," add "to the Fourth Judicial District Court of the County of Ada, State of Idaho".

§1.27 Delete this section, add "A certificate from the Secretary of State delivered with a copy of a document filed by the Secretary of State is prima facie evidence that the original document is on file with the Secretary of State."

§1.28 Delete "and the period of its duration if less than perpetual", delete subsections (3) through (5), replace "conclusive evidence" with "prima facie evidence".

§1.29 Insert "punishable by a fine of not to exceed five hundred dollars ($500)."

§1.40 After "(5) Deliver" add "or 'delivery' means any method of delivery used in conventional commercial practice, including delivery by hand, mail, commercial delivery and electronic transmission", in subsection (10) after "not-for-profit corporation" insert "limited liability company", in subsection (11) delete "for profit" after "." and ", but does not include 'federally chartered corporations' which are incorporated under the laws of the United States" add "(20) Receipt of a document sent by first class mail, in the absence of evidence of earlier actual receipt by the addressee, means five (5) days after the document is mailed postpaid and correctly addressed." Add "(25) 'Sign' or 'Signature' includes any manual, facsimile, conformed or electronic signature." Add "(28) 'Treasury shares' means shares of a corporation which have been issued, have been subsequently acquired by and belong to the corporation and have not, either by reason of the acquisition or thereafter, been canceled or restored to the status of authorized by unissued shares. Treasury shares shall be deemed to be 'issued' shares, but not 'outstanding' shares."

§1.41 At end of subsection (a) add "Notice by electronic transmission is written notice." After "Notice may be communicated in person:" delete rest of sentence, add

See note at head of Digest as to 1998 legislation covered.

See Topical Index in front part of this volume.

CORPORATIONS . . . *continued*

"by mail or other method of delivery; or by telephone, voice mail or other electronic means." After "is effective" in (c) delete rest of subsection and add "(a) Upon deposit in the United States mail, if mailed postpaid and correctly addressed to the shareholder's address shown in the corporation's current record of shareholders; or (b) When electronically transmitted to the shareholders in a manner authorized by the shareholders." In subsection (d), replace "principal office" with "correspondence address." Delete "as evidenced by the postmark" in subsection (e)(2).

Delete §1.42.

§2.03 Replace "conclusive proof" with "prima facie proof".

§2.04 Delete "knowing, there was no incorporation" and add "when there was no corporation".

§4.01 After "in another language;" add "provided however that if the word 'company' or its abbreviation is used it shall not be immediately preceded by the word 'and' or by an abbreviation of or symbol representing the word 'and:', after subsection (b)(4) add "(e) the name of any limited partnership, limited liability partnership or limited liability company which is organized under the laws of this state or registered to do business in this state." Delete subsection (e) and add: "(5) This chapter does not control the use of assumed business names, governed by 'The Assumed Business Names Act of 1997.' Chapter 5, title 53, Idaho Code. (6) Nothing in this section shall abrogate or limit the law as to unfair competition or unfair practice in the use of trade names, nor derogate from common law, the principles of equity, or the statutes of this state or of the United States with respect to the right to acquire and protect trade name. (7) The assumption of a name in violation of this section shall not affect or vitiate the corporate existence, but the courts of this state, or of any person, unincorporated association, or corporation interested or affected, enjoin such corporation in violation from doing business under any name assumed in violation of this section."

§5.01 Add "or a domestic limited liability company" after "not-for-profit domestic corporation" in subsection (2)(11), add "or a foreign limited liability company" after "not-for-profit foreign corporation" in subsection (2)(iii).

§5.02 Add "(3) A corporation may also change its registered office or its registered agent, or both, by indicating such change in the appropriate space on the annual report required by section 30-1-1622, Idaho Code."

§6.20 Add "(6) A subscription for stock of a corporation, whether made before or after the formation of a corporation, shall not be enforceable against the subscriber or the corporation, unless in writing and signed by the party to be bound."

§6.21 Delete "or benefit to the corporation," and "contracts for services to be performed," in subsection (a), delete "a contract for future services or benefits" and "the services are performed,", "or the benefits are not received", "the services are not performed", "or the benefits are not received" from subsection (e).

§6.24 After "for which the shares are to be issued" add ", unless the power to make such determination is reserved to the shareholders by the articles of incorporation."

§6.31 Add "(4) A corporation has authority to use, hold, acquire, cancel and dispose of treasury shares. (5) Unless the board of directors adopts an amendment to the corporation's articles of incorporation to reduce the number of authorized shares, treasury shares of the corporation that are canceled shall be treated as authorized by unissued shares."

§7.03 Delete "within the earlier of 6 months after the end of the corporation's fiscal year or" in subsection (a)(1).

§7.20 Delete "beginning two business days after notice of the meeting is given" and add "at least ten (10) days before the meeting" in section (b).

Delete §7.21.

§7.28 Delete subsection (d).

Delete §7.29.

Delete §§7.40 through 7.47. Governed by IRCP 23(f).

§8.05 Delete "(d)" and add "(4) A director elected to fill a vacancy shall be elected for the unexpired term of his predecessor in office."

§8.09 After "The" add "Idaho district court" in subsection (a).

§8.20 Delete "the board of directors may permit" in subsection (b).

§8.33 Delete "within two years" add "within three (3) years" in subsection (c).

§8.57 Add "provided that banks, savings and loan associations and credit unions chartered under the laws of the state of Idaho may provide indemnification only by insurance."

§10.02 After "if the change is on file" add "or if an annual report has been filed" in subsection (3).

§11.01 After "One or more corporations may merge into another corporation" add "or, subject to any law applicable to limited liability companies, into a limited liability company" in subsection (a), after "each corporation" add "or limited liability company" in section (b)(1), after "shares of each corporation" add "or rights or securities of or interests in each limited liability company" in subsection (b)(3).

§11.06 After "corporation" add "or limited liability company", after "shares of each corporation" add "or rights or securities of or interests in each limited liability company".

§11.07 After "foreign corporations" add "or limited liability companies" in subsections (a), (a)(1) and (b).

§13.02 Add "(3) This section does not apply to the holders of shares of any class or series if the shares of the class or series are redeemable securities issued by a registered investment company as defined pursuant to the investment company act of 1940 (15 U.S.C. 80a-15 U.S.C. 80a-64). (4) Unless the articles of incorporation of the corporation provide otherwise, this section does not apply to the holders of shares of a class or series if the shares of the class or series were registered on a national securities exchange, were listed on the national market systems of the national association of securities dealers automated quotation system or were held of record by at least two thousand (2,000) shareholders on the date fixed to determine the shareholders entitled to vote on the proposed corporate action."

§13.23 After "section 13.22(b)(3)," add "Idaho Code, and with respect to any certificated shares," in subsection (a), after "who demands payment and" add ", with respect to any certified shares, deposits his share certificates."

§14.07 After "commenced within" delete "five years" add "two (2) years" in subsections (b)(3) and (c).

§14.20 After "The secretary of state may" delete "commence a proceeding under section 14.21 to" after "corporation" add "under section 30-1-1421, Idaho Code," , delete (1), after "secretary of state" delete "within 60 days after it is due" and add "by the date on which it is due;", delete (4) and add "(3) The secretary of state has credible information that the corporation has failed to notify the secretary of state within sixty (60) days after the occurrence that its registered agent or registered office has been changed, that its registered agent has resigned, or that its registered office has been discontinued;".

§14.21 After "he shall" delete "serve the corporation with written notice of his determination under section 5.04" add "give notice of his determination to the corporation by first class mail addressed to its mailing address as indicated on its most recent annual report or, if the corporation has not yet filed an annual report, to its registered office." Delete "after service of the notice is perfected under section 5.04" and add "after receipt of the notice of determination", delete "by signing a certificate of dissolution that recites the ground or grounds for dissolution and its effective date. The secretary of state shall file the original of the certificate and serve a copy on the corporation under section 5.04." Replace with "by noting the fact of dissolution and the effective date thereof in his records. The secretary of state shall give notice of dissolution to the corporation by first class mail addressed to its mailing address as indicated on its most recent annual report or, if the corporation has not yet filed an annual report, to its registered office."

§14.22 Delete "within two years", add "within ten (10) years", delete (1)-(4), add "(a) Recite the name of the corporation and the date of its incorporation; (b) State that the corporation applies for reinstatement; (c) If the corporation's name or one deceptively similar thereto has been appropriated by another entity whose organizational documents are filed with the secretary of state, be accompanied either by consent to the use of a deceptively similar name executed by the other entity or by articles of amendment by which the corporation adopts a new name which complies with the requirements of section 30-1-4-1, Idaho Code; and (d) Be accompanied by a current annual report, appointment of registered agent or articles of amendment to extend the corporate existence, as appropriate to the reason for administrative dissolution." Delete "certificate of", delete "his determination and the effective date of reinstatement, file the original of the certificate, and serve a copy on the corporation under Section 5.04.", add "the first and effective date of the reinstatement, file a copy thereof and return original to the corporation."

§14.23 Delete "shall serve the corporation under section 5.04", add "shall give the corporation written notice by first class mail."

§14.30 Delete "or the business affairs of the corporation can no longer be conducted to the advantage of the shareholders generally", after (2)(ii), add "and irreparable injury to the corporation is threatened or being suffered by reason thereof;", delete "(iv) the corporate assets are being misapplied or wasted;".

§14.34 After first sentence in subsection (a) add "In a proceeding under section 30-1-1430(2), Idaho Code, to dissolve a corporation that has shares listed on a national securities, exchange or regularly traded in a market maintained by one (1) or more members of a national or affiliated securities association, the corporation may elect to purchase all shares owned by the petitioning shareholder at the fair value of the shares."

§14.40 Delete "treasure or other appropriate state official for safekeeping. When the creditor, claimant, or shareholder furnishes satisfactory proof of entitlement to the amount deposited, the state treasurer or other appropriate state official shall pay him or his representative that amount."

§15.02 Delete "(d)" and add "(4) A foreign corporation which transacts business in this state without a certificate of authority shall be liable to this state, for the years or parts thereof during which it transacted business in this state without a certificate of authority, in an amount equal to all fees which would have been imposed under this chapter upon such corporation had it duly applied for and received a certificate of authority to transact business in this state as required by this chapter and thereafter filed all reports required by this chapter, plus all penalties imposed under this chapter for failure to pay such fees. The attorney general may collect all penalties due under this section."

§15.03 Delete "and period of incorporation".

§15.04 Delete "(2) the period of its duration;".

§15.06 Delete "(b)(1)" and "(b)(2)" add "(a) The name of any corporation, limited liability company, limited partnership or limited liability partnership organized under the laws of this state or authorized to transact business in this state; (b) A reserved or registered name for a corporation, limited liability company or limited partnership;", delete "the name of another corporation (incorporated or authorized to transact business in this state) that is not distinguishable upon his records from the name applied for." Add "a name which is deceptively similar to the name of another corporation, limited liability company, limited partnership or limited liability partnership which is organized under the laws of this state or which is authorized to transact business in this state." Delete "and submits an undertaking in form satisfactory to the secretary of state to change its name to a name that is distinguishable upon the records of the secretary of state from the name of the applying corporation"; after "domestic or foreign corporation" add "or limited liability company", delete "(d)(1)", delete "corporation" in (d)(2), and add "entity".

§15.06 Add "domestic limited liability company" after "domestic corporation" in subsection (2)(ii), add "foreign limited liability company" after "not-for-profit foreign corporation" in subsection (2)(iii).

§15.08 After "(either on statement or attached to it)" add "or in the corporation's next annual report filed with the secretary of state,".

§15.10 After "application for a certificate of authority or" add "the correspondence address indicated".

§15.20 Delete "and appoints the secretary of state as its agent for service of process in any proceeding based on a cause of action arising during the time it was authorized to transact business in this state;" and add "agrees that service may be made on it by mailing copies of any process, notice or demand by registered or certified mail to the

---

See note at head of Digest as to 1998 legislation covered.

See Topical Index in front part of this volume.

CORPORATIONS . . . *continued*

corporation and its officers at the addresses shown on the most current annual report filed with the secretary of state or as shown on any application for withdrawal of a corporation that has withdrawn from Idaho;", delete "(4)" and add "(d) A mailing address at which the service may be made under paragraph (c) of this subsection;", delete "on the secretary of state" in subsection (c), delete sentence beginning "Upon receipt of process" in subsection (c).

§15.30 Delete "within 60 days after its due" in subsection (1), add "by the date on which it is due;" delete "(2)", add "The secretary of state has credible information that" at beginning of (3) and (4).

§15.31 After "he shall" delete "serve the foreign corporation with written notice of his determination under section 15.10", add "give notice of his determination to the foreign corporation by first class mail addressed to its mailing address as indicated on its most recent annual report, or, if the foreign corporation has not yet filed an annual report, to its registered office." Delete "within 60 days after service of the notice is perfected under section 15.10," and add "within sixty (60) days after receipt of notice of determination,", delete "by signing a certificate of revocation that recites the ground or grounds for revocation and its effective date." Delete sentence beginning "The secretary of state shall file", add "by noting the fact of revocation and the effective date thereof in his records. The secretary of state shall give notice of the revocation to the foreign corporation by first class mail addressed to its mailing address as indicated on its most recent annual report, or if the foreign corporation has not yet filed an annual report, to its registered office." Delete "certificate revoking" and add "notice of revocation", delete "(d)", add "(4) Service of process on a foreign corporation whose certificate of authority has been revoked may be made upon its registered agent, if any, or pursuant to section 30-1-1510, Idaho Code."

§16.01 Delete "(7)".

§16.02 After "A shareholder may inspect and copy the records described in subsection (b) only if" add "(a) He has been a holder of record of shares or of voting trust certificates for at least six (6) months immediately preceding his demand or shall be the holder of record of, or the holder of record of voting trust certificates for, at least five percent (5%) of all the outstanding shares of the corporation;".

§16.20 After "A corporation" add "upon written shareholder request", after "annual financial statements" add "or, if annual financial statements are not available, other appropriate accounting records", delete "(c)".

§16.22 Delete subsection "(3)", add "(c) The address to which correspondence to the corporation's officers may be mailed;" delete subsections "(6)" and "(7)". Delete subsection "(c)", add "(3) The first annual report must be delivered to the secretary of state between July 1 and November 30 of the state fiscal year (July 1—June 30) following the state fiscal year in which a domestic corporation was incorporated or a foreign corporation was authorized to transact business. Subsequent annual reports must be delivered to the secretary of state between July 1 and November 30 of succeeding state fiscal years."

Income Tax.—See category Taxation, topic Income Tax.

Investment Trusts.—No statutory provision.

Professional Associations or Corporations.—One or more individuals licensed or otherwise legally authorized to render same professional services within state may organize and own stock in professional service corporation. Professions limited to practices of architecture, chiropractic, dentistry, engineering, landscape architecture, law, medicine, nursing, occupational therapy, optometry, physical therapy, podiatry, professional geology, psychology, certified or licensed accountancy, social work, surveying, and veterinary medicine. (30-1303). May be simultaneously officer, etc., of only one professional corporation. (30-1315). Business Corporation Act applies except as otherwise specifically provided. (30-1301 to -1314).

Deeds.—See category Property, topic Deeds.

Model Non-Profit Corporation Act not adopted. Idaho Nonprofit Corporation Act allows nonprofit groups to incorporate for "any lawful purposes". (30-3-1 to 30-3-145).

Uniform Simplification of Fiduciary Security Transfers Act adopted. (68-901 to 68-911).

Uniform Commercial Code adopted. (28-1-101 to 28-10-104). See category Business Regulation and Commerce, topic Commercial Code.

Nonprofit Corporation Act.—Extensive filing requirements, regulations, powers and limitations. (30-3-1 to 30-3-145).

Limited Liability Companies.—See topic Limited Liability Companies.

Uniform Unincorporated Nonprofit Association Act adopted. (53-701 to 53-717).

JOINT STOCK COMPANIES:

They are subject to provisions of state anti-trust and blue sky laws and to 53-501 to 53-507, relating to companies conducting business under name other than true name of person interested. See topic Associations.

Professional Associations or Corporations.—See topic Corporations, subhead Professional Associations or Corporations.

LIMITED LIABILITY COMPANIES:

Limited Liability Company Act.—(53-601 to 53-672, see also 63-3006A).

PARTNERSHIPS:

Uniform Partnership Act adopted. (53-301 to 343). Repealed effective July 1, 2001.
Uniform Partnership Act (1996) adopted, effective Jan. 1, 2001. Act governs partnerships that elect to be governed by this act and partnerships formed on or after July 1, 2001.

Registered Limited Liability Partnership.—Application to be filed with Secretary of State with $100 fee, if typed, $120 if not typed or if attachments used. (53-343A).

Name shall contain L.L.P. or LLP as last letters of name. (53-343B). Policy is for other states and countries to recognize Idaho limited liability partnerships. (53-343C).

Actions.—Partnership may be sued by partnership name, and summons may be served on any one of partners. (I.R.C.P. 4[d][4]).

Limited Partnership.—Uniform Limited Partnership Act (1976) has been adopted (53-201 to 53-267) with some variations.

§104. Subsection (1) is omitted.

§201(1). Add "or restated" at end.

§202. Subsection (b)(1) add: "; provided, however, that a change consisting exclusively of a gift of a limited partnership interest between existing limited partners shall be excluded from the requirement to file an amendment to the certificate of limited partnership." Add new subsection (b)(5) to read: "A change of the name or address of the registered agent." Delete subsection (e).

§204. Delete subsection (c).

§205. Modified to read: "RECORDS TO BE KEPT. (a) Each limited partnership shall keep the following:

(1) A current list of the full name and last known business address of each partner separately identifying the general partners in alphabetical order, and the limited partners in alphabetical order;

(2) A copy of the certificate of limited partnership and all certificates of amended thereto, together with executed copies of any powers of attorney pursuant to which any certificate has been executed;

(3) Copies of the limited partnership's federal, state and local income tax returns and reports, if any, for the three (3) most recent years;

(4) Copies of any then effective written partnership agreements and of any financial statements of the limited partnership for the three (3) most recent years; and

(5) Unless contained in a written partnership agreement, a writing setting out:

(i) The amount of cash and a description and statement of the agreed value of the other property or services contributed by each partner and which each partner has agreed to contribute;

(ii) The times at which or events on the happening of which any additional contributions agreed to be made by each partner are to be made;

(iii) Any right of a partner to receive, or of a general partner to make, distributions to a partner which include a return of all or any part of the partner's contribution; and

(iv) Any events upon the happening of which the limited partnership is to be dissolved and its affairs wound up.

Records kept under this section are subject to inspection and copying at the reasonable request, and at the expense, of any partner during ordinary business hours."

§208. Modified to read: "CERTIFICATE OF LIMITED PARTNERSHIP. (a) In order to form a limited partnership, a certificate of limited partnership must be executed and filed in the office of the secretary of state. The certificate shall be on a form prescribed by the secretary of state and shall set forth:

(1) The name of the limited partnership;

(2) The name and address of the registered agent for service of process required to be maintained by section 53-204, Idaho Code;

(3) The name and the business address of each general partner; and

(4) Any other matters the general partners determine to include therein.

(b) A limited partnership is formed at the time of the filing of the certificate of limited partnership in the office of the secretary of state or any later time specified in the certificate of limited partnership if, in either case, there has been substantial compliance with the requirements of this section."

§209(a). Add at end of first sentence: "on a form prescribed by the secretary of state."

§209(b). Delete all of subparagraph (1) and add "general" before "partner" in new subparagraphs 1 and 2.

§209(c). Delete language after "amend the certificate."

§209(e). New paragraph reads: "(e) A restated certificate of limited partnership may be executed and filed in the same manner as a certificate of amendment."

§212. Modified to read "EXECUTION BY JUDICIAL ACT. If a person is required by the provisions of section 53-211, Idaho Code, to execute any certificate fails or refuses to do so, any other person who is adversely affected by the failure or refusal may petition the district court to direct the execution of the certificate. If the court finds that it is proper for the certificate to be executed and that any person so designated has failed or refused to execute the certificate, the court may order that the certificate shall be filed by the secretary of state without such person's signature."

§215. Replace "limited" with "general."

§217. New paragraph reads: "ADMISSION OF LIMITED PARTNERS. (a) A person becomes a limited partner:

(1) At the time the limited partnership is formed; or

(2) At any later time specified in the records of the limited partnership for becoming a limited partner.

(b) After the filing of a limited partnership's original certificate of limited partnership, a person may be admitted as an additional limited partner:

(1) In the case of a person acquiring a partnership interest directly from the limited partnership, upon the compliance with the partnership agreement or, if the partnership agreement does not so provide, upon the written consent of all partners; and

(2) In the case of an assignee of a partnership interest of a partner who has the power, as provided in section 53-242, Idaho Code, to grant the assignee the right to become a limited partner, upon the exercise of that power and compliance with any conditions limiting the grant or exercise of the power."

Old "(a)" renumbered as "b."

§219. Modified to read: "LIABILITY TO THIRD PARTIES. (a) Except as provided in subsection (d) of this section, a limited partner is not liable for the obligations of a limited partnership unless he is also a general partner or, in addition to the exercise of his rights and powers as a limited partner, participates in the control of the business.

PARTNERSHIPS . . . *continued*
However, if the limited partner participates in the control of the business, he is liable only to persons who transact business with the limited partnership reasonably believing, based upon the limited partner's conduct, that the limited partner is a general partner.

(b) A limited partner does not participate in the control of the business within the meaning of subsection (a) hereof solely by doing one or more of the following:

(1) Being a contractor for or an agent or employee of the limited partnership or of a general partner or being an officer, director, or shareholder of a general partner that is a corporation;

(2) Consulting with and advising a general partner with respect to the business of the limited partnership;

(3) Acting as surety for the limited partnership or guaranteeing or assuming one (1) or more specific obligations of the limited partnership;

(4) Taking any action required or permitted by law to bring or pursue a derivative action in the right of the limited partnership;

(5) Requesting or attending a meeting of partners;

(6) Proposing, approving or disapproving, by voting or otherwise, one (1) or more of the following matters:

(i) the dissolution and winding up of the limited partnership;

(ii) the sale, exchange, lease, mortgage, pledge or other transfer of all or substantially all of the assets of the limited partnership;

(iii) the incurrence of indebtedness by the limited partnership other than in the ordinary course of its business;

(iv) a change in the nature of the business;

(v) the admission or removal of a general partner;

(vi) the admission or removal of a limited partner;

(vii) a transaction involving an actual or potential conflict of interest between a general partner and the limited partnership or the limited partners;

(viii) an amendment to the partnership agreement or certificate of limited partnership; or

(ix) matters related to the business of the limited partnership not otherwise enumerated in subsection (b) of this section, which the partnership agreement states in writing may be subject to the approval or disapproval of limited partners;

(7) Winding up the limited partnership pursuant to section 53-246, Idaho Code; or

(8) Exercising any right or power permitted to limited partners under this chapter and not specifically enumerated in subsection (b) of this section.

(c) the enumeration in subsection (b) hereof does not mean that the possession or exercise of any other powers by a limited partner constitutes participation by him in the business of the limited partnership.

(d) A limited partner who knowingly permits his name to be used in the name of the limited partnership, except under circumstances permitted by section 53-202(2)(i), Idaho Code, is liable to creditors who extend credit to the limited partnership without actual knowledge that the limited partner is not a general partner."

§220(b)(ii). Changed to read: "(ii) before an appropriate certificate is filed to show that he is not a general partner, but in either case only if the third party actually believed in good faith that the person was a general partner at the time of the transaction."

§222. Modified to read: "ADMISSION OF ADDITIONAL GENERAL PARTNERS. After the filing of a limited partnership's original certificate of limited partnership, additional general partners may be admitted as provided in writing in the partnership agreement or if the partnership agreement does not provide in writing for the admission of additional general partners, with the written consent of all partners."

§222(4). Change introduction to read: "Unless otherwise provided in writing in the partnership agreement, the general partner:"

§222(5). Modify first clause to read: "Unless otherwise provided in writing in the partnership agreement,".

§229. Modified to read: "SHARING OF PROFITS AND LOSSES. The profits and losses of a limited partnership shall be allocated among the partners, and among classes of partners, in the manner provided in writing in the partnership agreement. If the partnership agreement does not so provide in writing, profits and losses shall be allocated on the basis of the value, as stated in the records required to be kept pursuant to section 53-205, Idaho Code, of the contributions made by each partner to the extent they have been received by the partnership and have not been returned."

§230. Modified to read: "SHARING OF DISTRIBUTION. Distributions of cash or other assets of a limited partnership shall be allocated among the partners, and among classes of partners, in the manner provided in writing in the partnership agreement. If the partnership agreement does not so provide in writing, distributions shall be made on the basis of the value as stated in the records required to be kept pursuant to section 53-205, Idaho Code, of the contributions made by each partner to the extent they have been received by the partnership and have not been returned."

§231. Delete all of subparagraph (2).

§233. In first sentence, replace "the certificate of limited partnership and in accordance with" with "writing in". In second sentence replace "certificate" with "agreement" and add "in writing" after "does not specify."

§235. Change first clause to "Except as provided in writing in the partnership agreement," and add "in writing" after "Except as provided" in second sentence.

§238. Modified to read: "LIABILITY UPON RETURN OF CONTRIBUTION. (a) If a partner has received the return of any part of his contribution without violation of the partnership agreement or this chapter, he is liable to the limited partnership for a period of one (1) year thereafter for the amount of the returned contribution, but only to the extent necessary to discharge the limited partnership's liabilities to creditors who extended credit to the limited partnership during the period the contribution was held by the partnership.

(b) If a partner has received the return of any part of his contribution in violation of the partnership agreement or this chapter, he is liable to the limited partnership for a period of six (6) years thereafter for the amount of the contribution wrongfully returned.

(c) A partner receives a return of his contribution to the extent that a distribution to him reduces his share of the fair value of the net assets of the limited partnership below the value as set forth in the records required to be kept pursuant to section 23-205, Idaho Code, of his contribution which has not be distributed to him."

§242(a)(1). Delete "certificate of limited" after "described in the" and add "agreement" after "described in the partnership."

§242(b). Change "55-231 through 55-238" to "53-227 through 53-238" and delete language after "a limited partner" in last sentence.

§244. Modified to read: "NONJUDICIAL DISSOLUTION. A limited partnership is dissolved and its affairs shall be wound up upon the happening of the first to occur of the following:

(1) At the time specified in the certificate of limited partnership;

(2) Upon the happening of events specified in writing in the partnership agreement;

(3) Written consent of all partners;

(4) An event of withdrawal of a general partner unless at the time there is at least one (1) other general partner and the written provisions of the partnership agreement permit the business of the limited partnership to be carried on by the remaining general partner and that partner does so, but the limited partnership is not dissolved and is not required to be wound up by reason of any event of withdrawal, if, within ninety (90) days after the withdrawal, all partners agree in writing to continue the business of the limited partnership and to the appointment of one or more additional general partners if necessary or desired; or

(5) Entry of a decree of judicial dissolution under section 53-245, Idaho Code."

§249. Delete subparagraph (3), renumber remaining paragraphs, delete "and of each limited partner whose contribution is equal to or greater than five percent (5%) of the total contributions of all partners." and add "(6) The address of the office at which is kept a list of the names and addresses of the limited partners and their capital contributions, together with an undertaking by the foreign limited partnership to keep those records until the foreign limited partnership's registration in this state is canceled or withdrawn."

§259. Add "must have been a partner" at beginning of subparagraph (1) and replace "had" with "must have" in subparagraph (2).

§262(b). Add "or a restated certificate of limited partnership" after "certificate of amendment."

§268. New section reads: "SAVING CLAUSE. The repeal of any statutory provision by this chapter does not impair, or otherwise affect, the organization or the continued existence of a limited partnership existing at the effective date of this chapter, nor does the repeal of any existing statutory provision by this chapter impair any contract or affect any right accrued before the effective date of this chapter."

§501. Modified to read: **"Form of Contribution.**—The contribution of a partner may be in cash, other tangible property, intangible property, or labor or services actually performed."

§502. Not adopted.

§804. Modified to read: **"Distribution of Assets.**—Upon the winding up of a limited partnership, the assets shall be distributed as follows:

(1) To creditors other than partners;

(2) To limited partners who are creditors, in satisfaction of liabilities of the limited partnership other than liabilities for distributions to partners under section 53-231 or 53-234, Idaho Code;

(3) To general partners who are creditors, in satisfaction of liabilities of the limited partnership other than liabilities for distributions to partners under section 53-231 or 53-234, Idaho Code;

(4) Except as provided in the partnership agreement, to partners and former partners in satisfaction of liabilities for distributions under section 53-231 or 53-234, Idaho Code;

(5) Except as provided in the partnership agreement, to limited partners for the return of their contributions;

(6) Except as provided in the partnership agreement, to general partners for the return of their contributions;

(7) Except as provided in the partnership agreement, to limited partners respecting their partnership interests, in the proportions in which the limited partners share in distributions; and

(8) Except as provided in the partnership agreement, to general partners respecting their partnership interests, in the proportions in which the general partners share in distributions."

§902. Delete subsections (5) and (7), renumber subsection (6) to (5), add new subsection: "(6) The name and address of each general partner and of each limited partner whose contribution is equal to or greater than five percent (5%) of the total contribution of all partners."

Add at end of section: "The application will be accompanied by a certificate certifying to the lawful existence of the limited partnership, issued by the proper officer of the jurisdiction in which the certificate of limited partnership is filed or recorded."

Add new section to read: **"Change of Registered Agent of Foreign Limited Partnership or its Address.**—A foreign limited partnership authorized to transact business in this state may change its registered agent or its address upon filing in the office of the secretary of state a statement setting forth:

(a) The name of the limited partnership;

(b) The name and address of its then registered agent;

(c) If its registered agent be changed, the name of its successor registered agent;

(d) If the registered agent's address is to be changed, the address to which it is to be changed.

Such statement shall be executed by the limited partnership by a general partner, and verified by him, and delivered to the secretary of state. If the secretary of state finds that such statement conforms to the provisions of this act, he shall file such statement in his office.

Any registered agent of a foreign limited partnership may resign as such agent upon filing a written notice thereof, executed in duplicate, with the secretary of state, who

PARTNERSHIPS . . . *continued*

shall forthwith mail a copy thereof to the limited partnership at its principal office in the state or country under the laws of which it is organized. The appointment of such agent shall terminate upon the expiration of thirty (30) days after receipt of such notice by the secretary of state."

Add new section to read: **"Service of Process on Foreign Limited Partnerships.**—The registered agent so appointed by a foreign limited partnership authorized to transact business in this state shall be an agent of such limited partnership upon whom any process, notice or demand required or permitted by law to be served upon the limited partnership may be served.

Whenever a foreign limited partnership authorized to transact business in this state shall fail to appoint or maintain a registered agent in this state, or whenever any such registered agent cannot with reasonable diligence be found, or whenever the certificate of registration of a foreign limited partnership shall be cancelled or withdrawn, then any process, notice or demand required or permitted by law to be served upon the limited partnership may be served by mailing copies of the process, notice or demand by registered or certified mail to the limited partnership addressed to its principal office in its state of organization as shown on its application for registration or as shown on any application for withdrawal of a limited partnership that has withdrawn from Idaho.

Nothing herein contained shall limit or affect the right to serve any process, notice or demand required or permitted by law to be served upon a foreign limited partnership in any other manner now or hereafter permitted by law."

§906. Modified to read: **"Withdrawal From State of Foreign Limited Partnerships.**—A foreign limited partnership may withdraw from this state by filing with the secretary of state an application for withdrawal signed and verified by a general partner. The application shall set forth:

(a) The name of the limited partnership and the state or country under the laws of which it is organized;

(b) That the limited partnership is not transacting business in this state;

(c) That the limited partnership surrenders its authority to transact business in this state;

(d) That the limited partnership revokes the authority of its registered agent in this state to accept service of process and consents that service of process in any action, suit or proceeding based upon any cause of action arising in this state during the time the limited partnership was registered in this state may thereafter be made on such limited partnership by service thereon in the manner provided in section 53-252, Idaho Code;

(e) A post-office address to which a copy of any process against the limited partnership may be served on it pursuant to the provisions of section 53-252, Idaho Code.

The application for withdrawal shall be made on forms prescribed and furnished by the secretary of state and shall be executed by the limited partnership by a general partner, and verified by him."

§907. Delete subsection (d).

§908. Words "Attorney General" should be inserted in bracketed portions.

Add new section to read: **"Filing Fees.**—The secretary of state shall charge and collect for:

(a) Filing a certificate of limited partnership, sixty dollars ($60.00);

(b) Filing a certificate of amendment, twenty dollars ($20.00);

(c) Filing a certificate of cancellation, twenty dollars ($20.00);

(d) Filing a judicial decree of amendment or cancellation, twenty dollars ($20.00);

(e) Filing an application for registration as a foreign limited partnership, sixty dollars ($60.00);

(f) Filing a certificate of change or correction of an application for registration of a foreign limited partnership, twenty dollars ($20.00);

(g) Filing a statement of change of registered agent of a foreign limited partnership or its address, ten dollars ($10.00);

(h) Filing an application for withdrawal of a foreign limited partnership from the state, ten dollars ($10.00);

(i) Filing an application for a name reservation, or transfer thereof, ten dollars ($10.00);

(j) Filing any other statement, ten dollars ($10.00);

(k) Filing any document relating to a limited partnership, when the filing party requires the evidence thereof to be returned within eight (8) working hours, a surcharge of ten dollars ($10.00)." (53-262).

§1104. Modified to read: **"Transition.**—(a) Each limited partnership which was in existence on January 1, 1982, shall within two (2) years thereafter file in the office of the secretary of state a copy of its certificate of limited partnership with all amendments, certified by the recorder of the county in which the original is filed, or alternatively, it shall file a restated certificate of limited partnership incorporating all amendments which have been made to the certificate, executed in the same manner as provided for an original certificate of limited partnership in section 53-211, Idaho Code. If the limited partnership elects to file a restated certificate, it shall include therein a statement identifying the county in which the original certificate of limited partnership was filed and stating the date of the original filing.

(b) Each limited partnership which has not refiled pursuant to subsection (a) by January 1, 1984, may not maintain any action, suit, or proceeding in any court of this state until it does refile. The failure to refile shall not impair the validity of any contract or act of the limited partnership nor prevent the limited partnership from defending any action, suit, or proceeding in any court in this state. A limited partner is not liable as a general partner solely by reason of the failure of the limited partnership to refile.

(c) Each foreign limited partnership which has filed a certified copy of its certificate of limited partnership in any county of this state prior to January 1, 1982, shall within two (2) years thereafter file in the office of the secretary of state a copy of its certificate of limited partnership and all amendments thereto, certified by the official with which the original is filed in the state in which the limited partnership is

organized. The certificate shall be accompanied by a statement setting forth the name of the county in this state in which the foreign limited partnership first filed a certified copy of its certificate of limited partnership and the date of such filing, which statement shall be executed and verified by a general partner. Failure to refile as provided herein shall result in the loss of the foreign limited partnership's right to conduct business in this state.

(d) The secretary of state shall charge and collect for refilings pursuant to subsections (a) and (c) of this section, twenty dollars ($20.00)."

Mining partnerships are provided for and regulated. (53-401 to 53-412).

Out-of-State Partnerships.—Must register with secretary of state. Registration requires submission of application, signed and sworn by general partner setting forth name of foreign limited partnership, state and date of formation, general character of business, name and address of registered agent, principal office of foreign limited partnership, and list of names and addresses of partners. Application to be accompanied by copy of certificate of limited partnership certified by official where original is filed. (53-249).

BUSINESS REGULATION AND COMMERCE

BANKS AND BANKING:

Governing statute is Title 26, cc. 1-16. (26-101 to 26-2613).

Uniform Commercial Code adopted. (28-1-101 to 28-10-104). See topic Commercial Code.

Uniform Consumer Credit Code adopted 1971, repealed Mar. 31, 1983. Idaho Credit Code adopted Apr. 1, 1983. (28-41-101 to 28-49-107). See topic Consumer Credit.

Stockholders' Liability.—No special provision for.

Lien.—A banker has a general lien on all property in his hands belonging to a customer for the balance due from such customer in the course of the business. (45-808).

Collections.—See topic Commercial Code.

Deposits.—Whenever minor, or other person under disability becomes depositer in his name, bank may pay on check or order of said individual without liability. (26-718). Deposit in name of two or more payable to any of such persons or survivor, may be paid to any of said persons whether other be living or not. (15-6-109). Deposits in trust for another, in absence of further notice, may be paid to beneficiary upon proof of death of trustee. (15-6-111). Multi-party accounts designated as joint account, trust account, or P.O.D. account are authorized. P.O.D. account is account payable on request to one or more persons during his lifetime and on his death to one or more P.O.D. (pay on death) payees. (15-6-101). P.O.D. account belongs to original payee(s) during his lifetime and not to P.O.D. payee(s). Upon death of original payee(s) amounts on deposit belong to P.O.D. payee(s) or survivor of them. (15-6-104). Transfers resulting are nontestamentary for joint accounts, P.O.D. accounts and trust accounts. (15-6-106). Payment by bank upon authorized signature or to P.O.D. payee(s) upon proof of death of original payee(s) relieves bank of responsibility. (15-6-108 to 15-6-112).

Deposit of Trust Funds.—Funds held by any bank or trust company as trustee may be deposited in such bank or trust company in its name as trustee, in savings account or in time certificates of deposit provided that payment of deposit is insured by Federal Deposit Insurance Corporation. (26-1312).

Uniform Common Trust Fund Act adopted (68-701), without provision for court accounting.

Uniform Probate Code adopted, effective July 1, 1972, (15-1-101 to 15-7-401). See category Estates and Trusts, topics Executors and Administrators, Trusts, Wills.

Unclaimed Deposits.—Uniform Unclaimed Property Act (1981) adopted effective July 1, 1983. (14-501 to 14-542). See category Property, topic Absentees, subhead Escheat.

Trust companies have authority to act as fiduciary, which means personal representative of decedent's estate, guardian or conservator of estate, receiver, trustee under appointment of any court or under authority of any law or one acting as trustee for any purpose permitted by law. Fiduciary responsibilities may be transferred to affiliated banks or trust companies unless prohibited by I.C. §68-107. (I.C. §§26-1401 to 26-1404). Federal Home Loan Bank securities and mutual fund investments are permitted. (68-404 and 68-404A).

Guaranty title and trust companies organized under Tit. 30, c. 9 may furnish abstracts of title to real estate, guarantee title and make insurance pertaining thereto, act as assignee, receiver, guardian, executor, administrator, with president or secretary empowered to take necessary oaths, to act as fiscal or transfer agent of state, municipality, body politic or corporation, to take and hold real property as may have been or may hereafter be subject of insurance made by such company, and dispose of same, to act as escrow agent, to become security on writ of error, appeal or court proceedings. (30-901 to -908). Any company organized under Tit. 30, c. 9, prior to 1951 amendment may retain old powers, which included banking and general trust business. (30-901[8]). Capital deemed security. (30-904). Securities and other valuables may be deposited in company by court, guardians, executors, administrators, trustees. (30-906 to 30-907).

Foreign Banks.—No special provision for. See categories Estates and Trusts, topic Executors and Administrators; Family, topic Guardian and Ward.

Confidential communications between financial institutions and department of finance are privileged from disclosure. (26-1111 to 26-1112).

See note at head of Digest as to 1998 legislation covered.

See Topical Index in front part of this volume.

BILLS AND NOTES:

Uniform Commercial Code adopted. (28-1-101 to 28-10-104). See topic Commercial Code.

Uniform Consumer Credit Code adopted 1971, repealed Mar. 31, 1983. Idaho Credit Code adopted Apr. 1, 1983. (28-41-101 to 28-49-107). See topic Consumer Credit.

Drawing checks without funds or without sufficient funds with intent to defraud is punishable: (a) Not to exceed three years in jail or $5,000 fine, or both if no funds whatsoever in bank; (b) if check is less than $50 and insufficient funds, county jail up to six months and/or $300 fine; for second conviction, county jail up to one year and/ or fine up to $1,000; for subsequent conviction, up to three years and/or up to $5,000 fine; (c) if check is $50 or over and insufficient funds, up to three years and/or up to $5,000. Making, drawing, or delivering such check is prima facie evidence of intent and knowledge of no funds or insufficient funds. (18-3106).

Checks dishonored and not paid 15 days after notice sent, drawer liable for 12% interest from date of dishonor, cost of collection up to $20 or amount of check, whichever is less, and, if court action, may secure attorney fee. (28-3-510A.B.C.). See topic Commercial Code for section discussion. Dishonored checks for lack of funds, credit, or no account, plaintiff may recover greater of $100 or triple amount of check but recovery cannot exceed value of check by more than $500, provided written demand for check amount has been made not less than ten days prior to action. (1-2301A).

Judgment Notes.—No statutory provision.

Attorney fee clause, if judgment granted, allowable. (48 Idaho 419, 282 P. 862; 78 Idaho 298, 301 P.2d 1111). Attorney fees in collection action allowed by statute. (12-120).

See also topic Monopolies, Restraint of Trade and Competition.

Special Defenses.—See topic Consumer Credit.

BILLS OF LADING:

See topic Commercial Code.

BILLS OF SALE:

See topic Sales.

BLUE SKY LAW:

See topic Securities.

BROKERS:

Uniform Commercial Code adopted. (28-1-101 to 28-10-104). See topic Commercial Code.

Licenses.—$100 license fee and application required by person acting as commission merchant, dealer, broker, and $25 if agent dealing in farm produce. (22-1303).

Bond.—Application for license to act as broker, dealer, or commission merchant dealing in farm produce must be accompanied by bond or certificate of deposit payable to director in approved form and in amount of $10,000. (22-1304).

Real estate brokers must be licensed. (54-2021). Real Estate Commission, appointed by governor (54-2026), must examine applicants (54-2027). Applicant for broker's license and salesman's license, in addition to other requirements, must take examination and pay examination fee. For salesman's license applicant must have 30 classroom or correspondence hours of real estate course; but after Dec. 31, 1988, 90 such hours will be required. Brokers license applicant must have 90 advanced classroom or correspondence hours and in addition must have been actively engaged as real estate salesman for two years. (54-2029). Annual license fee is $100. (54-2029). Partnerships and corporations may hold license providing requirements of 54-2028 complied with. Errors and omissions insurance required for all real estate licenses. (54-2029A).

Nonresidents may be licensed as nonresident brokers and nonresident salesmen by written reciprocal agreement between this state and state of place of business of applying nonresident. (54-2031). Nonresident must file irrevocable consent to be sued with service on secretary of state and one copy mailed to applicant by registered mail. (54-2032).

Splitting fee with nonlicensed person is unlawful. (54-2039). Contracts for commissions for procuring purchasers for real property must be in writing setting out fixed amount to be paid (89 Idaho 107, 403 P.2d 585), signed by owner or his authorized agent (9-508). No statutory provision for lien.

See topic Securities.

BULK SALES:

See topic Commercial Code; category Debtor and Creditor, topic Fraudulent Sales and Conveyances.

CARRIERS:

Intra-state carriers are subject to jurisdiction of Idaho Public Utilities Commission. Annual fees required, apportioned on gross operating revenue, to defray cost of regulating. (61-1001 to -1009). Such carriers must file schedules of rates, make reports, carry liability and property damage insurance, etc. Commission may fix rates and assess fee for registrations of authority consistent with federal law. (61-801 to 61-817). Commission may enter into reciprocal agreements with other states for regulation of carriers. (61-815A).

Discrimination and preferences prohibited.

Uniform Commercial Code adopted. (28-1-101 to 28-10-104). See topic Commercial Code.

Limiting Liability.—Uniform Commercial Code adopted (28-1-101 to 28-10-104), effective Dec. 31, 1967, midnight. See topic Commercial Code.

Bills of Lading.—Uniform Commercial Code adopted (28-1-101 to 28-10-104), effective Dec. 31, 1967, midnight. See topic Commercial Code.

Liens.—Uniform Commercial Code adopted (28-1-101 to 28-10-104), effective Dec. 31, 1967, midnight. See topic Commercial Code.

Motor Vehicle Carriers.—See category Transportation, topic Motor Vehicles.

COMMERCIAL CODE:

Uniform Commercial Code adopted, effective Dec. 31, 1967, midnight. (28-1-101 to 28-10-104). Sections are identical with 1962 text of Uniform Commercial Code (see Uniform and Model Acts section).

Variations and alternate provisions adopted are:

§1-105—1972 Official Amendment not adopted.

§1-109—Not enacted.

§1-201—1972 Official Amendment adopted. Add expanded definition of "bank" effective July 1, 1984 as follows: ". . . including any insured bank, whether chartered by federal or state law, any insured savings and loan association, whether insured by federal or state law, and any insured credit union, whether chartered by federal or state law, offering deposit or other accounts on which the depositor or account holder is permitted to make withdrawals by negotiable or transferable instrument, payment orders of withdrawal, telephone transfers, or other similar items for the purpose of making payments or transfers to third persons or others, including demand deposits, negotiable order of withdrawal accounts, savings deposits subject to automatic transfers, and share draft accounts."

Add expanded definition of "Holder" as follows: (20) "Holder" with respect to negotiable instrument, means person in possession if instrument is payable to bearer or, in case of instrument payable to identified person, if identified person is in possession. "Holder" with respect to document of title, means person in possession if goods are deliverable to bearer or to order of person in possession.

Add expanded definition of "money" as follows: (24) "Money" means medium of exchange authorized or adopted by domestic or foreign government and includes monetary unit of account established by intergovernmental organization or by agreement between two or more nations.

Add expanded definition of "Security interest" which is summarized as follows: (37) "Security interest" means an interest in personal property or fixtures which secures payment or performance of an obligation. . . . The definition of security interest also includes details concerning consignments, element for determining security interests from nonsecurity interests, and rules for determining whether options are security interests. (§1-201[37]).

§1-209—1966 Official Optional Amendment not enacted.

§2-107—1972 Official Amendment adopted.

§2-318—1966 Official Amendment Alternative A enacted. Use of blood declared not a sale but a service and excluded from implied warranties of merchantability and fitness. (1971, c. 24).

§2-329—New section added: **"Voluntary and Unsolicited Sending of Goods.**—No person, firm, partnership, association or corporation, or agent or employee thereof, shall, in any manner, or by any means, offer for sale goods, wares, or merchandise, where the offer includes the voluntary and unsolicited sending of goods, wares, or merchandise not actually ordered or requested by the recipient, either orally or in writing. The receipt of any such unsolicited goods, wares, or merchandise shall for all purposes be deemed an unconditional gift to the recipient who may use or dispose of the same in any manner he sees fit without any obligation on his part to the sender."

§2-702—1966 Official Amendment not enacted.

§2-716—Word "Replevin" changed to "Claim and Delivery."

§3-121—Alternative B adopted.

§§3-101 to 3-501G repealed and replaced with new §§3-101 to 3-605. See topic Bills and Notes, subhead Drawing Checks without Funds.

§§4-101 to 4-504. Extensive technical corrections to language and citations.

§4-202(1)(b)—Optional language adopted.

§§404A, B, C—New sections added: Requires notice (and form) to customer after honoring photocopy of lost or mutilated check, unless customer has elected to have bank hold checks.

§§4-601 to 4-638—New section added governing funds transfers. Provides that time of receipt of time payment is same as under 28-1-201(27). (28-4-606). Procedure for issue and acceptance of payment orders. (28-4-609 to 28-4-620). Regulations concerning execution of sender's payment order by receiving bank. (28-4-621 to 28-4-625). Establishment of payment, orders, senders' obligation to pay receiving bank, method of payment, obligation of notice from beneficiary's bank to beneficiary, payment by beneficiary's bank to beneficiary, payment by originator to beneficiary and discharge of underlying obligation. (28-4-626 to 28-4-631). Variations by agreement permitted and funds-transfer systems permitted even if in conflict with statute. (28-4-632). Effect of levy, attachment, garnishment, notice of lien, etc., on payment order. (28-4-633). Injunctions and restraining orders regarding payment orders. (28-4-634). Order in which payment orders may be changed, order of withdrawals. (28-4-634). Preclusion of objection to debit of customer's account. (28-4-636). Rate of interest on payment orders. (28-4-637). Choice of law. (28-4-638).

§4-212(2)—Optional subsection adopted.

§§5-10 to 5-119—New section added governing "letters of credit" defined. (28-5-102[j]). Formal requirements. (28-5-104). Consideration not required. (28-5-105). Issuance, amendment, cancellation, and duration. (28-5-106). Confirmer, nominated person, and adviser. (28-5-107). Issuer's rights and obligations. (28-5-108). Fraud and forgery. (28-5-109). Warranties. (28-5-110). Remedies. (28-5-111). Transfer of Letter of Credit. (28-5-112). One year statute of limitations. (28-5-115).

§6-102(1)—Altered to read: "A 'bulk transfer' is any transfer in bulk and not in the ordinary course of the transferor's business of a major part in value of the materials, supplies, merchandise or other inventory (Section 9-109) of an enterprise subject to this Article."

COMMERCIAL CODE . . . *continued*

§6-102(3)—Coverage enlarged to "include, but not limited to the hotel, restaurant, barber shop or beauty salon business, whether or not said business is the sale of merchandise from stock."

§6-104(1)(c)—Public office is designated as "County Recorder in the County wherein the property to be transferred is located."

§6-106—Adopted, with subsection (4) omitted.

§6-107(2)(e)—Optional subsection adopted.

§6-108(3)(c)—Optional subsection adopted.

§6-109(2)—Optional subsection adopted.

§7-202(4)—New subsection added requiring name and genuine signature of every person authorized to sign warehouse receipts for warehouses be filed with Department of Agriculture and be kept current.

§7-204(4)—Section 7-204 does not impair or repeal Bonded Warehouse Law, Title 69, Chapter 2.

§7-209—1966 Official Amendment adopted with slight variation. To subsection (3)(b) is added following language beginning after word, "deposit": "any other provision of this uniform commercial code to the contrary notwithstanding."

§7-209A—New section creating lien for agricultural commodity warehousemen.

§7-403(l)(b)—Optional language adopted which states: "but the burden of establishing negligence in the case of a fire in a warehouse not licensed under Chapter 2, Title 69, Idaho Code, is on the person entitled under the document."

Article 8—1977 Official Amendment repealed, 1995. New Section adopted as 28-8-101 to 28-8-511.

§9-102(l)(a) and (b)—Application to "contract rights" deleted.

§9-103—1972 and 1977 Official Amendments adopted, additional amendments adopted 1995.

§9-104—1972 Official Amendment adopted, except that reference to "Ship Mortgage Act, 1920" in 9-104(a) has been retained. §9-104 amended to remove "deposit accounts".

§§9-105, 106—1972 and 1977 Official Amendments adopted. §9-105 adds definition of "Photographic record": images of documents stored in digital form on medium which will not permit alteration of image, as well as images of documents produced by photochemical process on film.

§9-109—"supplies" deleted from definition of "farm products"; "feed used in farming operations" included in "inventory" definition.

§9-110—Enlarged to require descriptions of real property to be legal descriptions.

§9-111—1972 Official Amendment adopted.

§9-203—1972 and 1977 Official Amendments adopted. §9-203(4) makes reference to "Uniform Consumer Credit Code, and the credit unions statute, Chapter 21, title 26, Idaho Code, and usury provisions (Sections 28-22-105; 28-22-106 and 28-22-107). . . . . ." Note: Uniform Consumer Credit Code and usury provisions repealed effective Apr., 1983. (1983, c. 119). See topic Consumer Credit.

§§9-204, 205—1972 Official Amendments adopted.

§9-301—1972 Official Amendment adopted. Purchase Money Security Interest must be filed within 21 days after debtor receives possession of collateral.

§9-302—1972 and 1977 Official Amendments adopted except new language added. §9-302(1)(h) reads: "A security interest in timber retained by the State of Idaho. §9-302(5), added stating this Article does not apply to security interest in personal property or fixtures of any utility company, as defined, which security interest is created by mortgage, trust deed, or other security agreement covering real property in Idaho, and recorded in Idaho. Provision set out for perfecting and filing such security interests.

§9-304 through §9-306—1972 and 1977 Official Amendments adopted.

§9-307—1972 and 1977 Official Amendments adopted but after Dec. 22, 1986 add at end of subsection (1) following: "A buyer who, in the ordinary course of business, buys farm products from a person engaged in farming operations, or a commission merchant or selling agent who in the ordinary course of business sells farm products for a person engaged in farming operations, shall take and sell free of a security interest created by his seller, even though the security interest is perfected and the buyer or commission merchant or selling agent knows of the existence of such interest, if he has registered with the secretary of state pursuant to section 28-9-407(4) and the security interest is not listed on the most recent master list or cumulative supplement distributed by the secretary of state pursuant to section 28-9-407(5), unless he has received written notification (as that term is used in applicable federal law and regulation) of the security interest from the secretary of state, his seller, or the secured party."

§§9-308, 309—1972 and 1977 Official Amendments adopted.

§§9-312, 313—1972 and 1977 Official Amendments adopted. §9-312 changes time period for perfection of Purchase Money Security Interest from 10 to 21 days to have priority over conflicting security interest.

§9-318—1972 Official Amendment adopted.

§9-401—1972 Official Amendment adopted; second alternative subsection (1) adopted with office of county recorder designation in subsection (a); §9-401(c) designates office of secretary of state; first alternative subsection (3) adopted.

Effective Dec. 22, 1986 second alternative repealed; 1972 official amendment first alternative subsection (1) adopted with office of county recorder designation in new subsection (a); other filings made with office of secretary of state. Subsection (2) exception added for financing statements for farm products provided in §28-9-307.

§9-401A—New section added which sets forth conditions for continuation of financing statements filed prior to amendments effective Dec. 22, 1986. See this subhead §9-307 and §9-401.

§9-402—1972 Official Amendment adopted, with variation. Subsection (1) add exception as provided in subsection (9) and delete requirement of real property legal description in crops financing statement. Subsection (3) delete provision 2. Subsection (4) modified as follows:

"(4) A financing statement may be amended as follows:

(a) A financing statement may be amended by filing a writing signed by both the debtor and the secured party, except as provided in paragraph (b) of this subsection. . . . .

(b) A financing statement other than a financing statement for farm products may be amended by filing a writing signed only by the secured party of record if the amendment consists of no more than a change of the secured party's name or address, a change of the debtor's address, a subordination of the secured party's interest in the collateral to the interest of a junior secured party, or a combination of the foregoing functions."

Add §9-402(4)(c) which reads: "(c) The secretary of state may prescribe a form or electronic equivalent whereby a secured party may amend its name or address or both on multiple financing statements by (1) writing signed by the secured party. The fee for such global amendments shall be twenty dollars ($20.00), plus one dollar ($1.00) per financing statement which is amended. Only one (1) name, address, or combination thereof, may be included on a form or electronic equivalent. If the secured party name to be amended has different endings on some financing statements, the criterion name may be a partial name, provided it does not cause the selection of names other than the secured party's name. This paragraph shall not apply to financing statements for farm products, fixtures, timber to be cut or minerals."

Add §9-402(6)(e) which reads: "the mortgage: (i) indicates conspicuously on its face either that it is intended also to be a fixture filing or that it is to be indexed not only as a mortgage but as a fixture filing: or (ii) is incorporated by reference in a recorded fixture filing financing statement or recorded amendment thereto, by written reference in such financing statement or amendment to the mortgage's book and page numbers or to its instrument recording number." Delete last sentence in Subsection 6 which in Official Text reads: "No fee with reference to the financing statement is required, other than regular recording and satisfaction fees with respect to the mortgage." Add subsection (9) and (10) as follows:

"(9) A financing statement for farm products is sufficient if it contains the following information:

(a) The name and address of the debtor;

(b) The debtor's signature;

(c) The name, address, and signature of the secured party;

(d) The social security number of the debtor, or in the case of a debtor doing business other than as an individual, the debtor's Internal Revenue Service taxpayer identification number;

(e) A description by category of the farm products subject to the security interest and the amount of such products (where applicable).

(f) A reasonable description of the real estate where the farm products are produced or located. This provision may be satisfied by a description of the county(ies), and legal description is not required.

(10) A financing statement described in subsection (9) must be amended in writing within three (3) months, and similarly signed and filed, to reflect any material changes. In the event such form is not incorporated within the financing statement, the effectiveness and continuation of that form is to be treated as if it were a part of the financing statement with which it is filed."

§9-403—1972 Official Amendment adopted with following changes:

(4) changed to delete second sentence.

(5) changed as follows: "Except for financing statements described in subsection (7) the uniform fee for filing and indexing and for stamping a copy furnished by the secured party to show the date and place for filing for an original financing statement or for a continuation statement shall be six dollars ($6.00) if the statement is typed or machine printed on the standard form prescribed by the secretary of state and otherwise shall be ten dollars ($10.00). A uniform fee of one dollar ($1.00) shall be charged for each page attached to the financing statement. The uniform fee for recording and indexing a financing statement and related instruments described in subsection (7) shall be the regular recording fee charged for recording a mortgage.

The secretary of state shall, by duly adopted administrative rule, establish a fee schedule for filing and indexing and other matters relating to filing as are described in this subsection (5) for financing statements for farm products and for public access to the secretary of state's files which are open to public inspection as required by subsection (4) of this section. A secured party shall provide an itemization of fees paid by that secured party for filing, searches or other matters relating to filing of financing statements for farm products security interests relating to that debtor."

(7) Changed to add: "Recording of a financing statement described in this subsection in the real property records shall constitute filing for all purposes under this chapter, and the financing statement need not be separately filed outside the real estate records; . . ." Only applies to financing statements filed after July 1, 1990. On or after July 1, 1990, all documents to be filed relating to financing statements covered by §9-403(7) must be filed by recording in real estate records.

§9-404—1972 Official Amendment adopted. §9-404(1) modified to delete requirement for written demand before obligation to file termination statement arises. Termination statement to be filed within one month after debtor's obligations end. §9-404(3) no fee if standard form; otherwise $1.

§9-405—1972 Official Amendment adopted. §9-405(1). Delete "or a copy thereof on the face or back of the statement" at the end of final sentence and delete last sentence. §9-405(2). Delete "He shall note the assignment on the index of the financing statement, or". Filing fee is $6 if standard form used, otherwise $10 with no additional fee for additional names.

§9-406—1972 Official Amendment adopted. Fee is $2 if standard form; otherwise $3, plus $2 additional name indexing fee.

§9-407—1972 Official Amendment adopted. New subsection (7) added which states: "Upon request of any person, the filing officer shall furnish copies of particular filed financing statements or statements of assignment at a uniform cost of one dollar ($1.00) per page if the requestor (sic) provides the filing officer with the file numbers of the statement to be copied." By administrative rule, Secretary of State is to set fee schedule for services under this section.

See note at head of Digest as to 1998 legislation covered.

See Topical Index in front part of this volume.

COMMERCIAL CODE . . . *continued*

New subsections (3) to (6), effective Dec. 22, 1986, providing central filing system at office of secretary of state for recording security documents regarding farm products. Provides master list of farm product security interests. Master list distributed to registered farm product buyers, commission merchants and selling agents. Provides for registration and fees for farm product, buyers, commission merchants and selling agents. Such registered persons may take free of known lien unless shown on master list. See §9-307. Secretary of state authorized to require separate search request for farm products. (9-407[3]).

§9-407A—New section added which states: "*Financing Statements Covering Consigned or Leased Goods.* A consignor, or lessor of goods may file a financing statement using the terms 'consignor,' 'consignee,' 'lessor,' 'lessee' or the like instead of the terms specified in section 28-9-402. The provisions of this part shall apply as appropriate to such a financing statement but its filing shall not of itself be a factor in determining whether or not the consignment or lease is intended as security, section 28-1-201(37). However, if it is determined for other reasons that the consignment or lease is so intended, a security interest of the consignor or lessor which attaches to the consigned or leased goods is perfected by such filing."

§9-408A—New section added: **"Approval of Standard Forms by Secretary of State—Effect.**—(1) Notwithstanding subsection (3) of section 38-9-402, for the purpose of standardization, the Secretary of State shall approve for general use such forms of financing statements, continuation statements, statements of assignments, statements of partial release, statements of release, termination statements and requests for information for filing with any officer pursuant to the Uniform Commercial Code, as shall conform to the provisions thereof. When the Secretary of State approves any form as a standard form, any filing officer may require payment of an additional filing fee or a certificate fee, not exceeding one dollar ($1.00) for the filing and indexing of any nonstandard form serving only the same purpose.

(2) Upon payment of the fees payable pursuant to sections 28-9-403 through 28-9-407, financing statements, continuation statements, statements of assignment, statements of partial release, statements of release, termination statements and requests for information may be filed and filing officers shall accept, file and index the same and make certificates with respect thereto at any time after the effective date of this act."

§9-502—1972 Official Amendment adopted.

§10-104—Reads:

"(1) The Article on Documents of Title (Article 7) does not repeal or modify any laws prescribing the form or contents of documents of title or the services or facilities to be afforded by bailees, or otherwise regulating bailees' businesses in respects not specifically dealt with herein; but the fact that such laws are violated does not affect the status of a document of title which otherwise complies with the definition of a document of title. (Section 1-201).

"(2) This Act does not repeal Chapter 9 of Title 68, Idaho Code, cited as the Uniform Act for the Simplification of Fiduciary Security Transfers, and if in any respect there is any inconsistency between that Act and the Article of this Act on investment securities (Article 8) the provisions of the former act shall control.

"(3) This Act does not repeal Section 38-911, Idaho Code (sales and mortgages of logs to be recorded)."

§§28-11-101 to 28-11-106—Added; defines consignment relationship between artist and "fine arts" dealer and exempts relationship from U.C.C. provisions.

§§28-12-101 to 28-12-531—Added: adopting Uniform Commercial Code—Leases.

1972 Official Amendments.—Adopted in part, see subhead Variations, supra.

1977 Official Amendments adopted.

Forms.—See end of this Digest.

See also topics Banks and Banking, Bills and Notes, Brokers, Carriers, Contracts, Factors, Frauds, Statute of, Sales, Securities, Warehousemen; categories Business Organizations, topic Corporations; Civil Actions and Procedure, topic Limitation of Actions; Debtor and Creditor, topics Assignments, Fraudulent Sales and Conveyances, Liens, Pledges; Documents and Records, topics Records, Seals; Mortgages, topic Chattel Mortgages.

CONSIGNMENTS:

Consignment relationship between artist and dealer defined by statute. (28-11-101 to 28-11-106). See topic Factors.

CONSUMER CREDIT:

Uniform Consumer Credit Code adopted 1971, repealed Mar. 31, 1983. Idaho Credit Code adopted Apr. 1, 1983. (28-41-101 to 28-49-107).

Idaho Credit Code adopted effective Apr., 1983. (28-41-101 to 28-49-107). Act applicable to Idaho credit transactions primarily for personal, family or household purposes. (28-41-204). Transaction may be subject to Act by agreement. (28-41-108). Excluded for most purposes, transactions involving credit to government entities, sale of insurance by insurer, transactions by public utility or common carrier if regulated by state or federal agency, licensed pawn brokers (28-41-202), or transactions for business purposes including agricultural, investment, debtor not natural person, and debts secured by first mortgage or deed of trust (28-41-301[7]).

Maximum finance charge is that agreed to between parties. (28-42-201). Charges on amounts within specified range when applied to lowest amount within range must not exceed by more than 8% disclosed rate. (28-42-204[4]).

Delinquency or Deferral Charge.—On precomputed credit transactions, parties may agree to charge of 5% of unpaid amount of installment overdue more than ten days. (28-42-301[1]). Non-precomputed loan secured by residence of debtor delinquency charge not more than 5% of amount overdue 15 days. (28-42-301[2]). Delinquency charge collected only once on installment. (28-42-301). Precomputed transaction may agree in writing to charge for deferral of unpaid installments. Delinquency charge may not be made if deferral charge collected. (28-42-302).

Refinancing, consolidation and conversion to open-end account allowed subject to qualification. (28-42-305).

Right to Prepay.—Debtor may prepay balance at any time without penalty. (28-42-306). Parties may agree to prepayment penalty during first three years. (28-42-306[2]). Prepayment penalty not to exceed amount equal to six months interest. (28-42-306[2][a], [6]). Creditor upon prepayment must rebate unearned finance charge calculated pursuant to Act. Minimum charge allowed not to exceed finance charge contracted for or $5 if principal $75 or less, or $7.50 if principal more than $75. (28-42-307).

Disclosures.—Made pursuant to Federal Consumer Credit Protection Act. (28-43-201). Civil liability created by Federal Act adopted in state Act. (28-45-203).

Receipt or periodic statement of account must be provided debtor for each payment made but not less than annually. (28-43-204).

Collateral and Security.—Security may be taken in property sold, in goods upon which service has been performed or in which goods have been installed, or in land to which goods are affixed or which has been improved by sale of goods or services if debt secured by land is $1,000 or more or debt secured by goods is $100 or more. (28-43-302, 28-43-309).

Cross-collateral allowed subject to release of property as debt paid and when consolidated terms are within statutory limitations. (28-43-302, 28-43-303).

Assignment of Earnings.—No assignment of earnings may be taken for payment or security. (28-43-304).

Limitations of Conditions.—Debtors cannot authorize any person to confess judgment on claim arising from regulated consumer credit transaction. (28-43-305).

Negotiable Instrument.—Creditor may not take negotiable instrument other than ten day postdated check as evidence of obligation. (28-43-306).

Balloon Payment.—Debtor may refinance any balloon payment twice as large as average scheduled payments at terms no less favorable than terms of original transaction, unless open-end credit, schedule payments adjusted to seasonal or irregular income, exempt under administrative rule, or debt secured by second deed of trust or mortgage on debtor occupied one to four family dwelling. (28-43-307).

Aiding in Sale to Another.—No value may be given to induce sale for debtor giving names of prospective buyers, or otherwise aiding in sale to another, if contingent upon occurrence of event after time of agreement. (28-43-308).

Maximum loan term if principal is $300 to $1,000 is 37 months; if principal is $300 or less term is not more than 25 months, unless adjusted to seasonal or irregular debtor income. (28-43-310).

Attorney Fee.—Agreement may provide for debtor to pay reasonable attorney fee unless transaction is regulated consumer loan with principal $1,000 or less. (28-43-311, 312).

Home Solicitation.—Upon written notice buyer may cancel home solicitation sale until midnight of third business day after agreement. (28-43-402). Home solicitation form of agreement must include buyer's signature, date of transaction, name and address of seller, and statement of buyer's rights conforming with Federal Trade Commission regulation or include under conspicuous caption: "BUYER'S RIGHT TO CANCEL", following: "If you decide you do not want the goods or services, you may cancel this agreement by mailing a notice to the seller. The notice must say that you do not want the goods or services and must be mailed before midnight of the third business day after you sign this agreement. The notice must be mailed to: __________ _____. (insert name and mailing address of seller)". (28-43-403). Buyer may cancel at any time until proper form of agreement has been given buyer. (28-43-403[3]).

Insurance.—When creditor agrees to provide insurance it must be evidenced by individual policy, certificate, application or notice disclosed to debtor, and creditor shall promptly notify debtor of delay or failure to provide. (28-44-105). Amount creditor receives for insurance may not exceed premium charged by insurer. (28-44-107). Debtor may provide required insurance. (28-44-109). Terms, amount and conditions of credit insurance defined. (28-44-201 to 28-44-304). Liability or property insurance cannot be canceled without ten day (13 if mailed) notice to debtor. (28-44-304). Cancellation of insurance pursuant to premium finance loan only allowed after compliance with statute. (28-44-401).

Remedies and penalties are applicable to all credit transactions made before or after passage of Act. (28-49-101).

Collateral Repossessed.—If collateral repossessed after sale for $1,000 or less, buyer is not personally liable for unpaid balance and seller is not obligated to resell collateral. (28-45-103). Buyer liable for wrongful damage to collateral and for failure to make collateral available to seller. (28-45-103). Seller may abandon collateral by direct action, but may not thereafter repossess or execute judgment against collateral. (28-45-103). Self help repossession after default allowed if done without entry into dwelling and without use of force or breach of peace. (28-45-108).

Garnishment limited to lesser of 25% of disposable weekly income or amount of disposable income which exceeds 40 times federal minimum wage. (28-45-104). Employee may not be dismissed for garnishment. (28-45-105).

Unconscionable agreements or parts of agreements are unenforceable. (28-45-106).

Debtor default only enforceable when debtor fails to make payment or when prospect of payment, performance or realization of collateral is significantly impaired. (28-45-107).

Debtor Remedies.—For creditor violation of debtor rights, debtor may recover actual damages and penalty of $100 to $1,000. Credit sales, loans or open-end credit actions must be brought within two years of violation. Other regulated transaction causes must be brought within one year after maturity. Debtors not obligated to pay excess charges and may recover any excess charge paid from creditor or creditor's assignee. Failure to refund amount owing to debtor within reasonable time (30 day presumption) after demand, creditor liable for penalty of $100 to $1,000. Creditor violation of Act does not impair rights on debt. Debtor may recover against creditor. (28-45-201).

Assignment of Creditors.—Subject to debtor's claims and defenses. (28-45-302).

Criminal Penalties.—Creditor willfully and knowingly making excess charges guilty of misdemeanor subject to not more than $500 fine or one year imprisonment or

CONSUMER CREDIT . . . continued

both. (28-45-401). Person willfully or knowingly engaged in regulated credit transactions without license or proper statutory qualification guilty of misdemeanor and subject to same penalty. (28-45-401). Person guilty of disclosure violations guilty of misdemeanor and subject to fine not more than $5,000 or one year imprisonment or both; penalty in lieu of criminal penalties under Federal Consumer Credit Protection Act. (28-45-402).

Administration.—Director of Department of Finance administers Act, assures compliance, and promulgates rules and regulations. (28-46-104). Administrator has power to supervise and investigate person engaged in conduct regulated by Act. (28-46-105 to 28-46-106). Administrator may hold hearings and issue orders concerning violations of Act (28-46-107 to 28-46-109), and may seek civil relief in courts (28-46-110 to 28-46-116).

Notification and Fees.—Within 30 days of commencing business and before Jan. 31 each year thereafter, each person conducting business under Act must file notification with administrator stating name of person, business name, address of principal office, address of offices and stores where transactions will be entered in Idaho, address of agent for service in state, and whether consumer loans are made. Persons must pay annual fee not to exceed $10 for each $100,000 or part thereof of unpaid consumer credit transactions outstanding Dec. 31 of preceding year. (28-46-203).

License.—Persons making or taking assignments of consumer regulated loans must obtain license. (28-46-301). License applicants must notify licensee in community to be served by newspaper publication. Application granted if financial responsibility, character, and fitness of applicant (officers and directors if corporation) such as to warrant honest and fair conduct of business under Act, and has at least $30,000 available for making loans. (28-46-302). Administrator shall review applications, hold hearings and revoke or suspend licenses. (28-46-302 and 303). All licensees will maintain adequate records with free access to administrator to show compliance with Act, and file annual composite report with director. (28-46-304). Administrator may conduct periodic examination of records at licensee expense. (28-46-305).

Idaho Administrative Procedure Act 67-5201 et seq. is applicable to administrator action under Act. (28-46-306).

Federal Preemption Override.—Act specifically exempts Idaho pursuant to federal option from application of Title V, Part A—Mortgage Usury Laws, Mortgages, §502(a)(1) of Depository Institutions Deregulation and Monetary Control Act of 1980 (Public Law 96-221, 94 Stat. 132). (28-49-105).

CONSUMER PROTECTION:

Assistive Technology Warranty Act adopted. (48-1401 to 48-1407).

Uniform Consumer Credit Code adopted 1971, repealed Mar. 31, 1983. Idaho Credit Code adopted Apr. 1, 1983. (28-41-101 to 28-49-107). See topic Consumer Credit.

Consumer Protection Act adopted. (48-601 to 48-619).

Chain or pyramid schemes, i.e., plan whereby person gives consideration for opportunity to receive consideration primarily for introduction of other persons into plan, are prohibited. Wilful or knowing promotion, etc., of such schemes felony. (18-3101).

Lease Purchase Agreement Act adopted. (28-36-101 to 28-36-111).

Uniform Deceptive Trade Practices Act adopted with modification. 48-601 adds this purpose for Consumer Protection Act: "The purpose of this act is to protect both consumers and business against unfair methods of competition and unfair or deceptive acts or practices in the conduct of trade or commerce, and to provide efficient and economical procedures to secure such protection. It is the intention of the legislature that this chapter be remedial and be so construed."

New section, 48-603C, added to define "unconscionable methods, acts or practices." New subsection, 48-603(18) added to make unlawful any use of unconscionable methods, acts or practices in conduct of trade or commerce.

"Unsolicited goods" statute adopted. (28-2-329).

Unfair Sales Act.—Any retailer or direct seller who sells or offers for sale merchandise subject to the act at less than cost or who buys from wholesaler at less than wholesaler's cost, or any wholesaler who sells or offers for sale at less than cost, as costs are defined in the act, including any scheme of special rebates, collateral contracts or similar arrangements, is guilty of misdemeanor for each single offense. So too, a misdemeanor, limiting quantity of article or product sold or offered for sale to any one customer short of entire supply. Any person, municipal or other public corporation, or state may secure injunctive relief. Act does not apply to sales: Of perishable merchandise to forestall loss; of imperfect or damaged merchandise; on final liquidation; for charitable purposes; on contract to departments of government; by officers acting under order or direction of court. (48-401 to -409).

Plain Language.—No "plain language" statute.

Telephone Solicitation Act.—Regulates telephone solicitation; requires registration with attorney general ten days before conducting business in Idaho; allows private cause of action; three day cancellation rule, criminal penalties. (48-1001 to 48-1010).

Pay-Per-Telephone Call Act.—Requires preamble message; $2 exemption; private and criminal actions, two year limitation. (48-1101 to 48-1107).

CONTRACTS:

Distinction between sealed and unsealed instruments abolished. (29-108). Written instrument presumptive evidence of consideration (29-103) which is construed to mean that one asserting want of consideration has burden of proof (17 Idaho 364, 106 P. 299; 101 Idaho 530, 617 P.2d 834).

Any agreement concerning compensation for personal injury entered into within 15 days of injury may be disavowed by injured person within one year after making agreement. (29-113).

Any agreement in connection with a contract for construction of buildings, highways, etc., purporting to indemnify promisee against liability for damages arising from injury to person or property caused from sole negligence of promisee is void. (29-114).

Uniform Commercial Code adopted. (28-1-101 to 28-10-104).

See also topics Commercial Code, Consumer Credit; category Family, topics Husband and Wife, Infants.

FACTORS:

Uniform Commercial Code adopted. (28-1-101 to 28-10-104). See topic Commercial Code.

It is a misdemeanor for an agent, broker, factor or consignee to make a false statement as to price obtained, quality or quantity of goods entrusted to his custody for sale. (18-3105).

Liens.—Factor has a general lien, dependent on possession, for all that is due to him as such, and upon all articles of commercial value that are entrusted to him by same principal. (45-807).

License Requirements—Commodity Dealers.—Persons receiving on consignment, soliciting for sale on commission, accepting from producer or warehouseman for resale, selling or offering for sale on commission, or buying, loading or receiving loaded for shipment for sale, resale, storage, processing or reconditioning during any calendar year, at least $10,000 worth of any grain, dry peas, dry beans, leguminous or other small seeds are defined as "commodity dealers". To engage in business of commodity dealer, person must obtain annual license from Department of Agriculture (69-503), give surety bond in form and amount as Director of Department of Agriculture may prescribe (69-506), provide financial statement prepared by independent certified public accountant or licensed public accountant, statement of current assets and liabilities, and statement of net worth to Department (69-521), post license in conspicuous location at place of business (69-509). License fee on original application $200 for class 1 license, $100 for class 2 license. Fee on renewal of license $40 for class 1, $20 for class 2. (69-508). Commodity dealers who purchase agricultural products on contract pursuant to which sale price is to be paid at date subsequent to delivery of product to buyer must make provision in contract for: (1) Seller's name and address; (2) conditions of delivery; (3) amount and kind of agricultural products delivered; (4) price per unit or basis of value; (5) date payments to be made. Contract must be signed by all parties and executed in duplicate; one copy retained by commodity dealer, one delivered to seller. (69-514). Licenses subject to suspension or revocation for failure to comply with statute. (69-507).

Other Farm Produce Dealers.—Brokers, commission merchants, and other persons dealing in farm products other than products specified in Commodity Dealer Law (see subhead License Requirements—Commodity Dealers, supra) and other than livestock and dairy products, must obtain annual license from Department of Agriculture. (22-1303). Bond or certificate of deposit for not less than $10,000 must accompany application. (22-1304). Dealer must keep complete record of all transactions (22-1312), must when required by consignor furnish complete report of all sales before close of next business day and must make remittance within ten days from sale (22-1313). Violation is misdemeanor and makes license subject to revocation. (22-1315). Law does not apply to cooperative organizations except to extent they handle or deal in farm products of non-members, nor to persons buying farm products for purpose of reselling in dried, canned or other preserved form, nor to cash buyers, but latter must register with Department of Agriculture. (22-1302). Director of Department of Agriculture may refuse to grant license or suspend or revoke license for cause shown (22-1310), subject to court review (22-1311). License fee, $100 for commission merchant, dealer or broker, $25 for each agent. (22-1303).

FRAUDS, STATUTE OF:

Uniform Commercial Code adopted. (28-1-101 to 28-10-104). See topic Commercial Code.

No estate or interest in real property, other than leases for a term of not exceeding one year, nor any trust or power over or concerning it, or in any manner relating thereto, can be created, granted, assigned, surrendered, or declared, otherwise than by operation of law, or a conveyance or other instrument in writing, subscribed by party creating, granting, assigning, surrendering or declaring same, or by his lawful agent thereunto authorized by writing. (9-503).

The preceding section must not be construed to affect the power of a testator in the disposition of his real property by a last will and testament, nor to prevent any trust from arising or being extinguished by implication or operation of law, nor to abridge the power of any court to compel the specific performance of an agreement, in case of part performance thereof. (9-504).

Agreements Which Must Be in Writing.—In the following cases, the agreement is invalid, unless the same or some note or memorandum thereof be in writing and subscribed by the party charged, or his agent: (1) Agreement that by its terms is not to be performed within a year from making thereof: (2) special promise to answer for debt, default or miscarriage of another, except in cases provided for in next section; (3) agreement made on consideration of marriage, other than mutual promise to marry; (4) agreement for leasing for longer than one year, or for sale of real property, or of an interest therein, and such agreement, if made by an agent of party sought to be charged, is invalid, unless authority of agent be in writing, subscribed by party sought to be charged. (5) agreement for sale of real estate on commission. (9-505; 9-508; Commercial Code §2-201). Loans of $50,000 or more must be in writing after June 30, 1995. (29-116).

Signatures.—The decisions require signature of both parties to agreements within the statute. (22 Idaho 735, 127 P. 997).

Agreements Which Need Not Be in Writing.—A promise to answer for the obligation of another, in any of the following cases, is deemed an original obligation of promisor, and need not be in writing: (1) Where promise is made by one who has received property of another on an undertaking to apply it pursuant to such promise, or

---

See note at head of Digest as to 1998 legislation covered.

See Topical Index in front part of this volume.

FRAUDS, STATUTE OF . . . *continued*

by one who has received a discharge from an obligation in whole or in part, in consideration of such promise; (2) where creditor parts with value, or enters into an obligation, in consideration of obligations in respect to which promise is made, in terms or under circumstances such as to render party making promise the principal debtor, and person in whose behalf it is made his surety; (3) where promise, being for an antecedent obligation of another, is made on consideration that party receiving it cancels the antecedent obligation, accepting new promise as substitute therefor, or on consideration that party receiving it releases property of another from a levy, or his person from imprisonment under execution on judgment obtained on the antecedent obligation, or on consideration beneficial to promisor, whether moving from either party to the antecedent obligation, or from another person; (4) where factor undertakes, for commission, to sell merchandise and guarantee sale; (5) where holder of instrument for payment of money, on which a third person is or may become liable to him, transfers it in payment of a precedent debt of his own, or for a new consideration and in connection with such transfer, enters into a promise respecting such instrument. (9-506).

INTEREST:

Where no express contract, interest allowed at legal rate, which is adjusted annually on July 1. (28-22-104).

Judgments.—Interest runs at legal rate of 5% plus base rate in effect at time of entry of judgment, determined by annual average yield on U.S. treasury securities as determined by Idaho State Treasurer. (28-22-104).

Open Accounts.—Interest runs on accounts settled from date of settlement and on open accounts from three months after last item. (28-22-104).

Uniform Consumer Credit Code adopted 1971, repealed Mar. 31, 1983. Idaho Credit Code adopted Apr. 1, 1983. (28-41-101 to 28-49-107). See topic Consumer Credit.

Securities brokers exemption on customer accounts granted, Mar. 31, 1975, repealed Mar. 31, 1987. (1987, c. 120, §6).

Usury.—See topic Consumer Credit, subhead Maximum Finance Charge.

LICENSES, BUSINESS AND PROFESSIONAL:

Licenses are required for a large number of occupations and businesses. Most licenses are issued by Department of Law Enforcement and fees vary.

Day Care Centers.—Licenses issued by Department of Health and Welfare. (39-1103). Regulated to establish minimum statewide system for protection of children. (39-1101 to 1118).

Collection agencies are governed by comprehensive regulations for examination, licensing, setting up qualifications, bond or certificate of deposit requirements, all administered by board. License renewable yearly. Act does not apply to attorneys authorized to practice in this state, regulated lender or trust companies authorized to do business in Idaho, any realtor licensed and engaged in regular practice of real estate business, abstract and title companies doing escrow business, or any court appointed trustee, receiver or conservator. Agents of permit holders licensed; fee not more than $20 annually. (26-2222 to 26-2240).

Licensed Professional Counselors.—Governed by extensive licensing requirements. (54-3401 et seq.).

Public Works Construction Managers.—Licenses issued by public works contractors state license board. (54-4501-54-4514).

MONOPOLIES, RESTRAINT OF TRADE AND COMPETITION:

Contracts, combinations or conspiracies in restraint of trade or monopolizing, or attempting to monopolize, or combining or conspiring to monopolize any part of the trade or commerce of the state are illegal. Violation a misdemeanor. Person, firm or corporation in business of selling or distributing magazines, books, comic books, to retailers, who require retailers to take all or certain groups of publications at sole discretion of distributor deemed guilty under above. Property owned under any contract by any combination or pursuant to any conspiracy within prohibition and being subject thereof, forfeited to state. Unfair competition also illegal and subject to like penalty; and is defined as contracts, combinations, conspiracy, or actions for purpose of driving out of business any other person engaged therein or selling articles or products at less than their fair market value or usual price or upon condition that they shall not be sold again by purchaser. Officers, directors and agents participating in such illegal acts liable to penalties prescribed and also personally liable civilly for all debts of offending corporation or association. Giving, soliciting or accepting rebates also unlawful and a misdemeanor. Where any corporation, joint stock company or other association, has been twice adjudged guilty of violation of these provisions, it can on a third violation be enjoined from doing business in state on information filed by Attorney-General. Any person injured in his business or property by unlawful acts above specified may recover triple damages. (48-101 to 48-119).

Price discriminations between different purchasers of commodities of like grade and quality, between different sections or cities or between different locations in sections or cities are forbidden where effect would be to prevent or lessen competition or create monopoly. But this does not forbid price differentials allowing only for difference in cost of manufacture, sale or delivery resulting from different methods or quantities in which commodities are sold or price changes in response to changing conditions affecting market; nor does it prevent persons engaged in commerce from selecting customers in bona fide transactions not in restraint of trade. Devices for evading the law are specifically prohibited. Violation may be restrained at suit of anyone injured and, either in connection with injunction or without injunctive relief, triple damages and costs, including attorneys' fees, may be recovered. (48-202 to 48-205).

Resale price agreements with respect to trademarked commodities, see category Intellectual Property, topic Trademarks and Tradenames.

Fair Trade Act adopted. (48-301 to 48-312). *Caveat:* See, however, P.L. 94-145, repealing exemption of state fair trade laws from Federal anti-trust law.

See also topic Consumer Protection and category Transportation, topic Motor Vehicles, subhead Motor Vehicle Carriers.

NEGOTIABLE INSTRUMENTS:

See topics Bills and Notes, Commercial Code.

RESTRAINT OF TRADE:

See topic Monopolies, Restraint of Trade and Competition.

SALES:

Uniform Commercial Code adopted. (28-1-101 to 28-10-104). See topic Commercial Code.

Uniform Consumer Credit Code adopted, 1971, repealed Mar. 31, 1983. Idaho Credit Code adopted Apr. 1, 1983. (28-41-101 to 28-49-107). See topic Consumer Credit.

Consumer Protection.—See topic Consumer Protection.

Contracts of Sale.—Uniform Commercial Code governs.

Bills of Sale.—Uniform Commercial Code governs.

Product Liability.—Doctrine of strict liability in tort, as set forth in Restatement of Torts, 2d, §402A, adopted in Idaho. (95 Idaho 674, 518 P.2d 857). Product Liability Reform Act adopted; provides length of time certain sellers are subject to liability, provides for comparative responsibility, sets forth individual rights and responsibilities of sellers other than manufacturers and provides guidelines for contents of complaint. (6-1401 to 6-1410). Product liability for motor vehicles limited as between dealer and manufacturer. (49-2423). Motor vehicle manufacturer required to indemnify dealer's losses arising from product related actions based on manufacturer's functions. (49-2424).

Transfer of Title.—Uniform Commercial Code governs.

Conditional Sales.—Uniform Commercial Code governs.

Retail Credit Sales.—See topic Consumer Credit.

Bulk Sales.—Uniform Commercial Code governs.

Deceptive Trade Practices.—See topic Monopolies, Restraint of Trade and Competition.

See also category Transportation, topic Motor Vehicles, subhead Titles, Sales and Liens.

Chain or pyramid schemes, i.e., plan whereby person gives consideration for opportunity to receive consideration primarily for introduction of other persons into plan, are prohibited. Wilful or knowing promotion, etc., of such schemes felony. (18-3101).

Telephone Solicitation Act.—Regulates telephone solicitation; requires registration with attorney general ten days before conducting business in Idaho; allows private cause of action; three day cancellation rule, criminal penalties. (48-1001 to 48-1010).

SECURITIES:

Comprehensive act, entitled "Idaho Securities Act" adopted. (30-1401 to 30-1462). This Act is substantially same as Uniform Securities Act. Amended (c. 381,1997), conform with National Securities Markets Improvement Act of 1996. (See Uniform and Model Acts section for text.)

Uniform Commercial Code adopted. (28-1-101 to 28-10-104). See topic Commercial Code.

Supervision.—Director of Department of Finance has general supervision and control. (30-1402).

Regulatory Powers of Supervising Authority.—Registration of securities is mandatory, unless exempt. Commissioner may issue stop order denying effectiveness to or suspending or revoking effectiveness of any registration if requirements of Act are not met. (30-1431).

Prerequisites to Sales or Offering.—Unlawful for any person to sell or to offer to sell any security in Idaho, except securities exempt under this act or except securities sold in transactions exempt under this act, unless such security is registered. (30-1416). Unlawful for any person to transact business in Idaho as broker-dealer or salesman, investment adviser, or investment adviser representative, except in transactions exempt under Act, unless he is registered under this Act. (30-1406).

Securities to Which Act Applicable.—Means any note, stock, treasury stock, bond, debenture, evidence of indebtedness, certificate of interest or participation in any profit-sharing agreement, collateral-trust certificate, preorganization certificate or subscription, transferable share, investment contract, voting-trust certificate, certificate of deposit for a security, certificate of interest or participation in an oil, gas or mining title or lease or in payments out of production under such a title or lease, or, in general, any interest or instrument commonly known as a "security" or any certificate of interest or participation in, temporary or interim certificate for, receipt for, guarantee of, or warrant or right to subscribe to or purchase, any of the foregoing. (30-1402[12]).

Exempt Securities.—For exempt securities, see §402(a) of Uniform Securities Act in Uniform and Model Acts section. This is identical to §33 of Idaho Securities Act except: Subsection 5 of Idaho Act reads: "any insurance or endowment policy or annuity contract or optional annuity contract, issued by a corporation subject to the supervision of the director of the department of insurance"; Subsection 11 of Idaho Act reads: "any investment contract issued in connection with an employee's stock purchase, savings, pension, profit-sharing or similar benefit plan"; Subsection 13

See note at head of Digest as to 1998 legislation covered.

See Topical Index in front part of this volume.

SECURITIES . . . continued

created which exempts security issued by domestic or foreign corporation, partnership, trust or association engaged in actual mining operations or exploration and development of mining properties in state. Sets out specific conditions which must be met. (30-1434[13]). Provided, to avail himself of exemption in subsections (4), (5), (6), (9), (11), (12), or (13), person must give notice 30 days after effective date of this Act prior to first sale. Commissioner may revoke exemption. (30-1434).

Exempt Transactions.—For exempt transactions, see §402(b) of Uniform Securities Act in Uniform and Model Acts section. This is identical to §34 of Idaho Securities Act except: Subsection 5 of Uniform Act is omitted; Subsection 12 of Idaho Act is added, reading; "any issuance of any stock dividend * * * if nothing of value is given by stockholders * * * other than the surrender of the right to a cash dividend where the stockholder can elect to take a dividend in cash or stock"; Subsection 13 is added, as follows: "any transaction incident to a right of conversion or a statutory or judicially approved reclassification, recapitalization, reorganization, quasi-reorganization, stock split, reverse stock split, merger, consolidation or sale of assets, if (a) no commission or other remuneration other than a standby commission is paid or given directly or indirectly for soliciting any security holder in this state or (b) the issuer files a notice in the form specified by the commissioner not less than 30 days before making the offer." Subsection 14 is added as follows: "any transaction in a bond or other evidence of indebtedness secured by a real or chattel mortgage or deed of trust, or by an agreement for the sale of real estate or chattels, if the entire mortgage, deed of trust, or agreement, together with all the bonds or other evidences of indebtedness secured thereby, is offered and sold as a unit."

Commissioner may revoke the exemptions set out in Subsections (2), (3), (10), or (13) above. (30-1435).

Sale of certain securities can be exempted from registration requirements if director approves exemption after fairness hearing. (30-1435A).

Registration of Securities.—Provisions made for registration by notification, registration by coordination and registration by qualification, under various circumstances, following closely Uniform Securities Act. Space does not permit showing all variations in application forms. Act itself should be consulted. (30-1407 to 30-1430). Fee for initial registration shall be $500.

Registration of Brokers.—Unlawful to transact business as broker-dealer or salesman, or investment adviser unless registered. (30-1406). Provisions made for qualification, forms, etc. similar to Uniform Securities Act. Consult Idaho Act. Registration effective for one year, Mar. 1 to Mar. 1. Renewable yearly by filing. Fees shall not exceed: Registration, $100 for original and $100 per renewal for broker-dealer and investment adviser and $20 for original and $20 per renewal for salesman. (30-1437).

Bonds.—Bond, unless waived by director, for investment adviser in sum of $25,000; for salesman, $10,000. (30-1407).

Liabilities.—Criminal penalties and civil liabilities provided for. Three year statute of limitations. (30-1442 to 30-1446).

Tender Offers.—Governed by Control Share Acquisition Act (30-1601 to 30-1614) and by Business Combination Act (30-1701 to 30-1710). Corporate directors must consider both long-term and short-term interests of corporation and shareholders. (30-1602; 30-1702). Under Control Acquisition Act, acquiring person must provide information statement to target company's principal executive officer. (30-1604).

Mining.—Small mining issues exempt from registration. (30-1434[13]).

Uniform Simplification of Fiduciary Security Transfers Act adopted (68-901 to 68-911) and not repealed by Uniform Commercial Code (28-10-104).

Uniform Security Ownership by Minors Act not adopted.

Chain or Pyramid Schemes.—See topic Consumer Protection.

STATUTE OF FRAUDS:

See topic Frauds, Statute of.

TRUST RECEIPT SECURITY:

See topic Commercial Code.

WAREHOUSEMEN:

Uniform Commercial Code adopted. (28-1-101 to 28-10-104). See category Business Regulation and Commerce, topic Commercial Code. Regulation of public warehouses provided for. (69-201 to 69-250).

Bonds.—Before obtaining license, warehouseman must execute and file bond, or in discretion of director annuity or irrevocable letter of credit with state department of agriculture to secure performance of obligations. (69-208).

Licenses.—Must be procured from state department of agriculture. Any person who misrepresents, forges, alters or falsely represents license is guilty of felony.

Liens.—Creates lien benefiting agricultural commodity warehouseman. (28-7-209A).

CITIZENSHIP

ALIENS:

No person is disqualified to take as heir because he or person through whom he claims is or has been an alien. (15-2-112).

Property.—Any person, whether citizen or alien, may take, hold and dispose of property, real or personal. (55-103).

CIVIL ACTIONS AND PROCEDURE

ACCORD AND SATISFACTION:

No statute. Common law governs.

Release for personal injury entered within 15 days of injury may be disavowed by injured party within one year of making. (29-113).

Uniform Commercial Code adopted. (28-1-101 to 28-10-104). See category Business Regulation and Commerce, topic Commercial Code.

Pleading.—Accord and satisfaction must be affirmatively pleaded. (I.R.C.P. 8[c]).

ACTIONS:

Governed by Idaho Rules of Civil Procedure (I.R.C.P.), patterned after Federal Rules. See topic Practice.

Equity.—Distinction between law and equity abolished. (Const. V, §1).

Forms of Action.—One form of action known as civil action. (I.R.C.P. 2).

Commencement.—Action is commenced by filing written complaint (I.R.C.P. 3) and summons may issue within reasonable time (I.R.C.P. 4). See topics Pleading, Process. Service of process in child support matters may be made by certified mail. (5-518).

Parties.—Every action must be prosecuted in name of the real party in interests (I.R.C.P. 17), but executor, administrator, guardian, trustee of express trust, party with whom or in whose name a contract has been made for benefit of another, or party authorized by statute may sue without joining beneficiary (I.R.C.P. 17).

Persons to be Joined if Feasible.—Person subject to service of process shall be joined as party in action if: (1) In his absence complete relief cannot be accorded among those already parties; or (2) he claims interest relating to subject of action and is so situated that disposition of action in his absence may (i) jeopardize ability to protect interest or (ii) leave any of other parties subject to substantial risk of multiple or inconsistent obligations by reason of his interest. (I.R.C.P. 19[a][1]).

Permissive Joinder.—All persons may join as plaintiffs if they assert right to relief, or as defendants if there is asserted against them a right to relief, jointly, severally, or in the alternative in respect of or arising out of the same transaction, occurrence, or series of transactions or occurrences and if any question of law or fact common to all will arise in the action. (I.R.C.P. 20).

Intervention.—As of right, intervention may be had upon timely application: (1) When statute confers an unconditional right to intervene, or (2) when applicant claims interest relating to property or transaction which is subject of action and he is so situated that disposition of action may impede his ability to protect that interest, unless applicant's interest adequately represented by existing parties. (I.R.C.P. 24a).

Permissive intervention may be had upon timely application (1) when statute confers a conditional right to intervene; or (2) when applicant's claim or defense and the main action have a question of law or fact in common. (I.R.C.P. 24b).

Interpleader.—Persons having claims against plaintiff may be joined as defendants and required to interplead when plaintiff may be exposed to double liability. Defendant exposed to similar liability may obtain interpleader by cross-claim or counterclaim. On motion of person possessing property claimed by two or more individuals, court may, on notice of claimants, order discharge of person possessing property from liability on condition property or its value delivered to court. Court may award attorney fees to person so delivering property. (I.R.C.P. 22; 5-321).

Class Actions.—One or more members of class may sue or be sued on behalf of entire class if: (1) Class is so numerous that joinder of all members is impracticable, (2) there are questions of law or fact common to class, (3) claims or defenses of representative parties are typical of claims or defenses of class, and (4) representative parties will adequately protect interests of class. (I.R.C.P. 23a). Requirements of I.R.C.P. 23b must also be met. Court will determine soon after commencement of action whether class action is maintainable. (I.R.C.P. 23c).

Third Party Practice.—Any time after commencement of action, defendant as third party plaintiff may bring action against person not party to action who is or may be liable to such third party plaintiff for all or part of plaintiff's claim against him. Leave of court required if defendant does not file third party complaint within ten days after serving his original answer. (I.R.C.P. 14a).

Joinder of Causes of Action.—Party asserting claim to relief as original claim, counterclaim, cross-claim, or third party claim, may join, either as independent or as alternate claims, as many claims, legal, equitable, or maritime, as he has against opposing party. (I.R.C.P. 18a).

Joinder of Remedies.—Whenever a claim is one heretofore cognizable only after another claim has been prosecuted to a conclusion, the two claims may be joined. (I.R.C.P. 18b).

Consolidation.—When actions involving a common question of law or fact are pending court may order (1) a joint hearing on any or all matters in issue; or (2) consolidation of all actions; or (3) may make such order as may tend to avoid unnecessary costs or delays. (I.R.C.P. 42a).

Severance of Actions.—The court in furtherance of convenience or to avoid prejudice may order a separate trial of any claims, cross-claims, counterclaims or third-party claims, or of any separate issue or of any number of claims, cross-claims, counterclaims, third party claims or issues. (I.R.C.P. 42b).

Substitution of Parties.—If party dies and claim is not thereby extinguished, court, upon application made within a reasonable time, may order substitution of the proper parties. If party becomes incompetent, the court, upon motion, may allow action to be continued by or against his representative. If there is a transfer of interest, action may continue against original parties, unless court, on motion, directs substitution or joinder with original party. (I.R.C.P. 25).

See note at head of Digest as to 1998 legislation covered.

See Topical Index in front part of this volume.

ACTIONS . . . *continued*

Abatement.—Actions do not abate by death, disability or transfer of interest if cause of action survives. (5-319). In case of death, resignation, retirement or removal from office of officer sued in official capacity successor in office may be substituted. (5-319).

Causes of action arising out of injury to a person or property, or death caused by wrongful act or negligence of another, except for libel and slander, do not abate upon death of wrongdoer, and each injured person or personal representative of each one meeting death as above stated, have a cause of action against personal representatives of wrongdoer; provided no punitive damages or penalties shall be awarded; provided that a judgment must be on satisfactory evidence corroborating testimony of said injured person regarding negligence and proximate cause. (5-327). See also category Estates and Trusts, topic Death, subhead Actions for Death.

Cause of action for personal injuries to spouse survives death of that spouse from unrelated causes, with damages to surviving spouse limited to loss of earnings and pain and suffering to date of death and medical, surgical, and special damages. (93 Idaho 888, 477 P.2d 511).

Revival.—In case of death or disability, the court may allow an action to continue by or against the representative or successor in interest of the party. In case of other transfers of interest, the action may continue in the name of the original party, or the person to whom the transfer is made may be substituted. (5-319).

Termination of Actions.—Voluntary dismissal may be had by plaintiff without order of court (1) by filing notice of dismissal before service by adverse party of answer or motion for summary judgment, or (2) filing stipulation of dismissal signed by all parties who have appeared. Unless otherwise stated in notice of dismissal or stipulation, dismissal is without prejudice, except notice of dismissal filed by plaintiff who has once dismissed an action on or including same claim. (I.R.C.P. 41a). Involuntary dismissal may be had (1) on motion of defendant for failure to prosecute; (2) after plaintiff has completed his evidence, defendant may, without waiving his right to present evidence, move for dismissal on ground that upon facts and laws plaintiff has shown no right to relief (I.R.C.P. 41b); or if no action taken for one year period (I.R.C.P. 40c).

Limitation of.—See topic Limitation of Actions.

Small Claims.—See category Courts and Legislature, topic Courts.

Administration.—See category Estates and Trusts, topic Executors and Administrators.

Direct Actions Against Insurer.—See category Transportation, topic Motor Vehicles, subhead Direct Actions.

APPEAL AND ERROR:

Federal Rules of Civil Procedure are basis for Idaho Rules of Civil Procedure. See topic Practice.

From District Courts.—Appeals may be taken from district courts to supreme court in civil actions in time and manner prescribed by rules of supreme court. (13-201).

Appeal Bond.—No undertaking on appeal for costs required. (Rule 16, Idaho Appellate Rules).

Appeals from magistrate division of district court taken to district court, as prescribed by rule. Unless otherwise provided by law or rule, district court shall review on record and affirm, reverse, remand or modify; may remand for new trial or order case tried de novo before him. (1-2213).

Stay of Proceedings.—On appeal of judgment or order of district court, supreme court may stay such order or judgment as provided by rule of supreme court. (13-202; Rule 13 Idaho Appellate Rules).

Judgment or Order on Appeal.—Supreme court may reverse, affirm, or modify any order or judgment appealed from, and may direct proper judgment or order to be entered, or direct new trial or further proceedings to be had.

From Industrial Commission.—Appeals may be taken from Industrial Commission decisions in time and manner provided by rule of supreme court. (72-724 to 725).

BONDS:

Sureties must justify by affidavit that they are residents and householders or freeholders within the state and that each is worth the sum specified in the undertaking over and above all just debts and liabilities, exclusive of property exempt from execution. (12-614). The state and municipalities or subdivisions and their officers, when parties to an action are exempt from giving bond. (12-615). Any bond required may be executed by surety company qualified to do business in state. (41-2604).

Enforcement.—By action prosecuted by one for whose protection bond is given.

CERTIORARI:

Writ of review may be granted by any court, except magistrate's division of district court, when inferior tribunal, board or officer has exceeded its jurisdiction, and there is no appeal or other adequate remedy. (7-202). Review upon this writ cannot be extended further than to determine whether inferior tribunal, board or officer has regularly pursued its authority. (7-208).

CHARITABLE IMMUNITY:

See topic Damages.

Charitable Solicitation Act.—Defines charitable organization and makes it unlawful to misrepresent charitable status. (48-1201 to 48-1206).

COMMISSIONS TO TAKE TESTIMONY:

See topic Depositions and Discovery.

COSTS:

Prevailing party recovers costs as of course unless court otherwise directs. (I.R.C.P. 54[d]).

DAMAGES:

Common law generally prevails as to compensatory damages. As to damages in tort against personal representative of deceased wrongdoer, see topic Actions; as to damages in actions for imputed negligence of automobile owner, see category Transportation, topic Motor Vehicles.

Amounts sought for general damages shall not be disclosed in complaint or to jury. (5-335, 10-111).

Noneconomic damages in personal injury or death action limited to maximum $400,000 (adjusted annually by industrial commission). (6-1603).

Exemplary damages are only to be given in case of wanton or outrageous conduct, fraud, malice, gross negligence, or oppression. (6-1604; 104 Idaho 897, 665 P.2d 661). Exemplary damages may be recovered under claim for damages generally. (69 Idaho 22, 202 P.2d 236). Claim for relief cannot include claim for punitive damages without leave of court. (6-1604).

Contribution between joint-tortfeasors exists, but no money judgment available until joint-tortfeasor has discharged common liability or paid more than his pro-rata share. (6-803). See subhead Joint and Several Liability, infra.

Parents of minor under 18 living at home liable for malicious or wilful destruction of property, up to $1,500. (6-210).

Double recovery prohibited by limiting judgment to amount exceeding recoveries from collateral sources. Collateral sources defined. (6-1606).

Charitable Immunity.—Nonprofit organization and its unpaid volunteers immune from liability except in situations set forth by 6-1605.

Joint and Several Liability.—Limited to actions involving: (1) Parties acting in concert or as agents; (2) violations of toxic waste laws; or (3) manufacture of medical devices or pharmaceutical products. In all other actions judgment entered only to amount of party's proportionate share of damages determined by percentage of liability. (6-803).

Comparative Negligence Rule.—Adopted. (6-801 to 6-806).

Sovereign Immunity.—Abolished to extent of insurance or statutory amount of $500,000 per occurrence after Oct. 1, 1984.

No-Fault Insurance.—See category Transportation, topic Motor Vehicles, subhead No-Fault Insurance.

Uniform Contribution Among Tortfeasors Act.—Adopted. (6-803 to 6-806).

Death.—See also category Estates and Trusts, topic Death, subhead Actions for Death.

DECLARATORY JUDGMENTS:

See topic Judgments.

DEPOSITIONS AND DISCOVERY:

Governed by I.R.C.P. 26, patterned after Federal Rules. 1970 amendments to Federal Rules not adopted. See topic Practice.

Any party may take the testimony of any person, including a party, by deposition upon oral examination or written interrogatories for purposes of discovery or use as evidence. (I.R.C.P. 26).

Uniform Foreign Deposition Act not adopted.

Within State for Use Within State.—After commencement of action and service of process on any defendant, leave of court is not necessary but must be obtained if notice of taking is served by plaintiff within 30 days after such service of process. (I.R.C.P. 30[a]).

Within State for Use Elsewhere.—Any party may take deposition of any person within this state as if such action were pending within this state.

Outside of State for Use Within State.—Within U.S. and its territories or possessions, may be taken before person authorized to administer oaths by laws of Idaho, U.S., or place where taken. (I.R.C.P. 28[a]). In foreign countries, may be taken before (1) secretary of embassy or legation, consul, vice consul, or consular agent of U.S. or any officer authorized to administer oaths under laws of Idaho or U.S., or (2) before person appointed by Court. (I.R.C.P. 28[b]).

Perpetuating Testimony.—One who desires to perpetuate his testimony or that of another in any matter that may be cognizable in any district court may file a verified petition in district court in county of resident of expected adverse party. Petition must show (1) petitioner expects to be party but is presently unable to bring action; (2) subject matter of expected action and his interest therein; (3) facts he desires to establish and his reasons for desiring to perpetuate it; (4) names or description and addresses of persons he expects will be adverse party; (5) names and addresses of persons to be examined and substance of expected testimony; (6) request for order authorizing taking of deposition. Notice and copy of petition must be served on expected adverse party at least 20 days before hearing, which notice must state that petitioner will apply at stated time and place for order sought. (I.R.C.P. 27).

Pending Appeal.—If appeal has been taken, or if time has not expired, from judgment of district court, district court may allow perpetuation of testimony for use in event of further proceedings in the district court. Motion and notice as if action was pending in district court, except motion must show (1) names and addresses of persons to be examined and substance of testimony; (2) reasons for perpetuating testimony. (I.R.C.P. 27).

DEPOSITIONS AND DISCOVERY . . . *continued*

Before Whom Taken.—Within Idaho before person authorized by laws of Idaho to administer oaths or persons appointed by Court in which action is pending. (I.R.C.P. 28).

Within United States or territories, before person authorized to administer oaths by laws of Idaho, United States, or place where examination held or person appointed by court in which action is pending. (I.R.C.P. 28).

In foreign countries, on notice before (1) secretary of embassy or legation, consul, vice consul or consular agent of the United States, or any officer authorized to administer oaths under laws of Idaho or United States; or (2) before a person appointed by the court by commission. (I.R.C.P. 28).

Stipulation.—If parties so stipulate in writing, deposition may be taken before any person, any time, at any place or in any manner.

On Oral Examination.—Party desiring to take deposition must give reasonable notice to every other party stating time and place and names and addresses of persons to be examined. The court may on motion and for good cause shown, enlarge or shorten the time, may order that deposition be not taken, specify other time or place, limit examination to written interrogatories, exclude certain matters, limit the scope of examination, provide that examination must be held with no one present except parties and officers or counsel, that after being sealed, the deposition must be opened only on order of court, that secret process need not be disclosed, that parties must simultaneously file specified documents or information enclosed in sealed envelope to be opened as directed by court, and court may make other orders which justice requires to protect a party from annoyance, undue expense, embarrassment or oppression. (I.R.C.P. 30).

Compelling Attendance of Witnesses.—Proof of service of notice authorizes clerk to issue subpoena. Resident may be required to attend only in county wherein he resides, is employed, or transacts his business in person; nonresident may be required to attend in any county in the state wherein he is served with subpoena. (I.R.C.P. 45). Where deposition is taken in Idaho pursuant to laws of another state or country to be used in proceedings there, district court or probate court of county where witness is to be served, upon proof of notice duly served, may issue subpoena. (I.R.C.P. 28).

Examination of Witnesses.—Unless otherwise ordered by the court, witness may be examined regarding any matter, not privileged, which is relevant to the subject matter involved in the action, including existence, description, nature, custody, condition, and location of any books, documents or other tangible things, and the identity and location of persons having knowledge of relevant facts. (I.R.C.P. 26).

Written Interrogatories.—A party desiring to take deposition on written interrogatories must serve them on every party with notice of name and address of person to answer, and name or description title of officer. Within ten days party served may serve cross interrogatories; within five days thereafter, re-direct interrogatories may be served; within three days thereafter re-cross interrogatories may be served. Copies of notice and all interrogatories must be delivered by party taking deposition to the officer who must promptly proceed as in case of oral examination to take deposition, prepare, certify, file or mail deposition to clerk for filing. Notice of filing must be given promptly to all parties by one taking deposition. After service of interrogatories and before taking deposition, the court where the action is pending, on prompt motion by a party or deponent, may order as in other cases which may be appropriate and just, or that deposition must not be taken before officer designated or that it must not be taken except upon oral examination. (I.R.C.P. 31).

Record of Examination.—The officer must put the witness on oath, testimony must be taken stenographically and transcribed unless the parties agree otherwise. All objections made at the time of the examination to qualifications of officer, manner of taking, evidence presented, conduct of any party, and any other objections to the proceedings must be noted by the officer. Objections to competency of witness, or competency, relevancy, or materiality of testimony, are not waived by failure to make them before or during the taking of deposition, unless ground of objection might have been obviated if presented at that time. Evidence objected to must be taken subject to objection. Parties served with notice may transmit written interrogatories to the officer who must propound them to the witness and record answers verbatim. (I.R.C.P. 30, 32).

Termination and Limiting Examination.—At any time during the taking, on motion of any party or deponent and upon showing that the examination is being conducted in bad faith or unreasonably annoys, embarrasses, or oppresses deponent or a party, the court where action is pending or if in action pending in another state, a district court in county where deposition is being taken, may order officer to cease forthwith or may limit scope and manner as stated above in case of oral examination. If so terminated, examination must be resumed only on order of court in which action is pending. (I.R.C.P. 30).

Signing and Certification.—Deposition must be read by or to witness (unless waived by witness and parties). Changes made must be entered with reasons therefor. Witness must sign before officer authorized to administer oaths, unless waived, or unless witness is ill, cannot be found or refuses to sign. If not signed by witness, officer must sign and state on the record the reason. Officer must certify on deposition that witness was duly sworn, and that deposition is true record of testimony. He must securely seal deposition, endorse with title of action, and mark thereon "Deposition of . . . . . ." and file or send it registered mail to clerk of court. (I.R.C.P. 30).

Use of Deposition.—At trial or hearing, any part or all of deposition, so far as is admissible under the rules of evidence, may be used against any party who was present or represented at the taking of the deposition, for (1) contradictory or impeaching testimony of deponent as witness, or other purpose under Idaho Rules of Evidence; (2) if deposition is of party or of an officer, director, or managing agent of corporation, association or partnership which is a party, for any purpose; (3) if court finds witness is dead or at greater distance than one hundred miles, or out of state, or unable to attend because of age, sickness, infirmity or imprisonment, or party offering has been unable to procure attendance by subpoena or in exceptional circumstances in interests of justice. (I.R.C.P. 32; I.R.E. 801-03).

Interrogatories to Parties.—May be served, without leave of court, on plaintiff after commencement of action and upon any other party with or after service of summons and complaint upon that party. Party upon whom served must serve copies of answers and objections within 15 days. (I.R.C.P. 33).

Discovery.—Upon motion, notice and good cause, court may order any party to produce and permit inspection or copies of designated documents, papers, books, accounts, letters, photographs, objects, tangible things constituting or containing evidence, or may order any party to permit entry upon land for inspection, etc. (I.R.C.P. 34).

Physical and Mental Examination.—If physical or mental condition of party is in controversy, court may order him to submit to examination by disinterested and impartial physician. (I.R.C.P. 35).

Forms.—The following may be used:

Forms

IN THE DISTRICT COURT OF THE . . . . . . JUDICIAL DISTRICT OF THE STATE OF IDAHO, IN AND FOR THE COUNTY OF . . . . . .

JOHN DOE,
Plaintiff
vs.
RICHARD ROE,
Defendant

DEPOSITION OF . . . .

This cause came regularly on for hearing, pursuant to Notice of Taking Deposition, a copy of which is hereto annexed and made a part hereof, at . . . . . ., City of . . . . . ., State of Idaho, on . . . . . . day of . . . . . ., 19. . . ., at the hour of . . . . . .o'clock . . . .M., for the taking of the deposition of . . . . . . by the . . . . . .; . . . . . . appearing for and on behalf of the plaintiff and . . . . . . appearing for and on behalf of the defendant; said deposition being taken before . . . . . ., a Notary Public for the State of Idaho, residing at . . . . . ., and an Official Reporter of the District Court of the . . . . . . Judicial District of the State of Idaho,

Whereupon, the following proceedings were had, to wit:

Certificate attached is usually as follows:

STATE OF IDAHO . . . . }
County of . . . . } ss.

I, ..., a duly appointed and commissioned Notary Public for the State of Idaho, and also a duly appointed and qualified and acting Official Reporter of the District Court of the . . . . . . Judicial District of the State of Idaho, Do Hereby Certify that on the . . . . . . day of . . . . . ., 19. . . . ., pursuant to Notice To Take Deposition hereto annexed and made a part hereof, said witness . . . . . . personally appeared at the hour of . . . . . . o'clock . . . .M., on . . . . . . day of . . . . . ., 19. . . . ., at my office in . . . . . .; the plaintiff appeared by counsel, ..., of . . . . . ., Idaho, and the defendant appeared by counsel, ..., of . . . . . ., Idaho;

The said witness . . . . . ., being by me first duly sworn to testify to the truth, the whole truth, and nothing but the truth, and being orally examined and cross-examined by counsel for the respective parties, deposed and testified as in the foregoing annexed deposition set out; and the said deposition is a true record of the testimony given by the said witness:

I further certify that the deposition was then and there taken stenographically, and later, the same day, by me reduced into longhand typewriting, and that the above and foregoing constitutes and is a full, true and correct transcript of said deposition, consisting of . . . . . . pages; that thereupon said deposition was read and corrected by said witness in every particular and thereupon subscribed by him in my presence (or reading examination and signing of said deposition by said deponent was waived by counsel for the respective parties by stipulation herein contained):

I further certify that I am not related to any of the parties to this action, or to any of their attorneys or counsel; that I am not employed by any of the parties, or by any of their attorneys or counsel, and that I have no financial interest in this action:

In WITNESS WHEREOF, I have hereunto set my hand, and affixed my Official Seal as Notary Public for the State of Idaho, this . . . . . . day of . . . . . ., 19. . . . . .

. . . .
Notary Public for Idaho
Residing at . . . . . therein.

(Seal)

EQUITY:

See topic Actions.

EVIDENCE:

Idaho Rules of Evidence effective July 1, 1985 patterned with some modifications on Federal Rules of Evidence and control all evidentiary questions. (I.R.E. 1102).

Evidence of proceedings of or statements made before medical malpractice screening panels inadmissible in civil action. (I.R.E. 413).

Privileged communications specifically defined in rules are not subject to compulsory disclosure.

See topic Depositions and Discovery.

Witnesses.—Evidentiary matters governed by Idaho Rules of Evidence, effective July 1, 1985, patterned after Federal Rules of Evidence with some modifications. See topic Depositions and Discovery.

All persons competent as witness except: (1) Persons incapable of receiving just impressions of facts or relating them truly; (2) parties prosecuting action against decedent's estate as to non-written communication or agreement occurring before decedent's death; (3) presiding judge; (4) juror before jury on which he sits; or (5) others as precluded by Rules of Evidence. (I.R.E. 601).

Criminal penalties for intimidating, influencing, impeding, deterring, threatening, harassing, obstructing or preventing witnesses. (18-2604).

See note at head of Digest as to 1998 legislation covered.

See Topical Index in front part of this volume.

EVIDENCE . . . *continued*

Privileged communications as defined within following relationships not subject to compulsory disclosure: Lawyer-client (I.R.E. 502); physician, psychotherapist-patient (I.R.E. 503); husband-wife (I.R.E. 504); clergyman-communicant (I.R.E. 505); political vote (I.R.E. 506); governmental secrets (I.R.E. 508); identity of informer (I.R.E. 509); parent-child or guardian-ward (I.R.E. 514); accountant-client (I.R.E. 515); school counselor-student (I.R.E. 516); licensed counselor or social worker-client (I.R.E. 518); hospital, medical staff or society confidential opinion or conclusions re: proceeding for research, discipline, or medical study (I.R.E. 519); medical malpractice screening panel (I.R.E. 520). Also governed by 9-203.

Husband and Wife.—Private spousal communications not intended for disclosure to others if made during marriage subject to testimonial exclusion at other spouse's request. Exceptions: (1) Issues concerning well-being of child including issues of abuse, abandonment or neglect; (2) crime against (a) spouse, (b) person in household, or (c) third person if committed with crimes against (2)(a) or (2)(b); (3) proceedings under Reciprocal Enforcement of Support Act; (4) proceedings concerning spousal desertion or nonsupport; (5) commitment proceedings; (6) civil actions between spouses. (I.R.E. 504).

Child witness called in criminal matter supportive person (parent, counselor, friend, other) may remain in courtroom at court discretion. (19-3023). Statements made by child under ten years describing sexual or physical abuse or crime committed with or upon child admissible under specific circumstances.

Self-Incrimination.—In criminal proceedings, if person refuses to testify on grounds it may incriminate him, he may then enter into agreement to testify voluntarily, with county prosecutor, who must request court approval. Court shall approve unless clearly contrary to public policy. Person shall not be prosecuted for evidence given accordingly, except for perjury. If evidence not given as agreed, witness may be compelled to appear and testify. If after testifying the evidence is privileged, he shall not be prosecuted. (19-1114, 1115, 1601).

Compelling Attendance.—See topic Depositions and Discovery.

INJUNCTIONS:

Procedure patterned after Federal Rules. (I.R.C.P. 65).

Injunctions may be granted at the time of issuing the summons upon the complaint, and at any time before judgment on affidavits. (I.R.C.P. 65).

An injunction cannot be allowed after the defendant has answered, except upon notice or an order to show cause. (I.R.C.P. 65).

When Injunction Proper.—An injunction may be granted (1) when it appears by the complaint that plaintiff is entitled to the relief demanded and such relief, or a part thereof, consists in restraining the commission or continuance of the act complained of; (2) when it appears that the commission or continuance of some act during the litigation would produce waste or great and irreparable injury to plaintiff; (3) when it appears during the litigation that defendant is doing or threatening, or is about to do, or is procuring or suffering to be done some act in violation of plaintiff's rights respecting the subject of the action and tending to render the judgment ineffectual; (4) when it appears from the affidavit that defendant pending the action threatens, or is about to remove or dispose of his property with intent to defraud plaintiff. Injunction may also be granted on motion of defendant upon filing counterclaim upon any of grounds mentioned above. (I.R.C.P. 65).

In suits for divorce, annulment, alimony, child custody the court may make prohibitive or mandatory orders, with or without notice or bond, as may be just. (I.R.C.P. 65g).

Bond.—On granting an injunction the court must require a written undertaking to pay defendant all costs, damages and reasonable counsel fees, not exceeding a specified amount, that he may sustain if the court finally decides that plaintiff is not entitled to an injunction. This requirement is mandatory and applies also to temporary restraining orders. (29 Idaho 803, 162 P. 671; 95 Idaho 360, 509 P.2d 579). However, maintenance of liquor nuisance may be enjoined without bond under certain circumstances. (23-706).

See also topic Practice.

Labor Disputes.—Courts may not restrain peaceful and lawful pursuit of strike activities. (44-701 to 44-712).

JUDGMENTS:

Procedure patterned after Federal Rules, and statute. See topic Practice.

Court judgments are docketed forthwith upon rendition. (I.R.C.P. 58[a]). Certified abstract of judgment of any court of this state or federal district court, if rendered in this state, shall be recorded and from such recording becomes lien for five years upon all real property of judgment debtor in county where recorded, not exempt from execution, owned at time or afterwards acquired. (10-1110). If decree of divorce or separation wherein periodic payments required for support or alimony, lien is only in amount of delinquent payments. (10-1110).

Confession of Judgment.—No claim, controversy or dispute may be submitted to any court in state for determination or judgment without filing complaint or petition; and no judgment shall be entered by any court without service of process upon all parties affected by such judgment or decree. (I.R.C.P. 3[a]).

Default Judgment.—When party against whom affirmative relief is sought fails to plead or otherwise defend as provided by rules and that fact is made to appear by affidavit, court, or clerk thereof, will enter default. If plaintiff's claim is not for sum certain or sum which cannot by computation be made certain, plaintiff must apply to court for default judgment. Otherwise, court or clerk thereof, upon plaintiff's request, and upon filing of affidavit showing method of computation, together with original instrument evidencing claim, will enter judgment for amount due plus costs. (I.R.C.P. 55).

No judgment by default shall be entered against infant or incompetent person unless represented in action by general guardian. If person against whom default is sought has appeared in action, then such person must be given three days written notice of application for default judgment.

Default judgment may not exceed amount prayed for in demand for judgment. (5-336). Hearing or reference required after entry of default in personal injury or death case to determine amount of damages.

Judgment on Pleadings.—Federal rule adopted.

Summary Judgment.—Federal rule adopted. (I.R.C.P. 56).

Declaratory Judgments.—Uniform Act adopted with construction of oral, as well as written, contracts authorized. §11 of Uniform Act modified to allow attorney general right of intervention but need not serve as original party. (10-1201 to 10-1216).

Offer of Judgment.—Federal rule adopted with slight modification.

Vacation or Modification.—Court may relieve party from final judgment, order, or proceeding for same reasons enumerated in Federal Rule 60(b). Motion for relief must be made within reasonable time and for reasons 1, 2, 3, and 6 not more than six months after judgment, order, or proceeding was entered or taken.

Lien.—Judgment will not operate as lien on property until abstract of judgment recorded. After recording it operates as lien on real property for five years. (10-1110).

Enforcement.—In all cases other than for the recovery of money, a judgment may be enforced or carried into execution after the lapse of five years from the date of its entry, by leave of court, upon motion, or by judgment for that purpose founded upon supplemental proceedings. (11-105; 20 Idaho 592, 119 P. 55). On death of judgment creditor after judgment, execution may be issued and en-forced on application of his personal representative or successor in interest. In case of death of debtor after judgment, execution will issue if judgment was for recovery of real or personal property or for enforcement of lien thereon. (11-106). Action on judgment may be commenced within six years. (5-215).

Action may be maintained to quiet title against a judgment the enforcement of which is barred by Statute of Limitations, without requiring proof said judgment has been paid. (6-412).

Satisfaction.—Upon full payment of judgment, party in whose favor judgment was rendered is required to record satisfaction of judgment in every county where judgment or abstract of judgment is recorded and to file it in court of entry. Satisfaction of judgment may be signed by attorney of party in whose favor judgment was entered. (I.R.C.P. 58b). Satisfaction also accomplished by paying amount due to clerk of court who must thereupon release and satisfy judgment, amount to be paid over to judgment creditor. (10-1115).

The following form of satisfaction may be used:

Form

Know all men by these presents: That in consideration of the sum of $. . . . to the undersigned in hand paid, the receipt of which is hereby acknowledged, a certain judgment in the (name court) in favor of . . . . and against . . . . for the sum of $. . . ., which judgment was docketed in . . . . county on the . . . . day of . . . ., . 19. . ., in judgment docket book . . . . at page . . . ., be, and the same is hereby, fully satisfied, released and discharged, and the clerk of the district court of the . . . . district of the state of Idaho in and for the county of . . . . is hereby authorized and directed to enter the satisfaction thereof upon his records. In witness whereof I have hereunto set my hand this . . . . day of . . . ., 19. . .

. . . .

(Acknowledgment).

Revised Uniform Enforcement of Foreign Judgments Act.—Adopted 1974. (10-1301 to 10-1308).

Uniform Foreign Money-Judgments Recognition Act.—Adopted 1990. (10-1401 to 10-1409).

LIMITATION OF ACTIONS:

Actions must be brought within the following periods (5-202 to 5-224):

Six years: On judgment or decree of court of U. S. or any state or territory within U. S.; for mesne profits of real property. (5-215).

Five years: To recover real estate (5-203 to 5-213); to recover upon written obligation, sealed or unsealed, time running from maturity. Limitation as to written contracts does not apply to action in name of or for benefit of state. (5-216). Foreclosure of real estate mortgage must be commenced within five years from date of maturity, as disclosed by public record, of obligation secured. Extension of time of maturity may be filed before expiration of this period. If public record does not disclose date of maturity, then date of execution of mortgage is deemed date of maturity. Extension may be made by affidavit or agreement filed in county where mortgage is recorded. (5-214A). If five years expired before Sept. 1, 1951, mortgagee had until Sept. 1, 1951, within which to file extension. (5-214A). Tort action in child abuse case must be commenced within five years from date child reaches 18 years of age. (19-402). Overflow easement by dam owners. (5-246).

Four years: On an obligation not in writing; on open account; on mutual accounts, time running from date of last item on either side; on judgment of a foreign court; actions on which no other limitation prescribed; breach of contract for sale. (5-217, 222, 224; UCC §2-725).

Three years: On statutory liability other than penalty or forfeiture; for injury to real or personal property; to recover possession of personal property; for relief on ground of fraud or mistake, time running from discovery thereof. (5-218). All claims arising before death of decedent barred unless presented to estate within three years after death, whether or not notice to creditors published. (15-3-803[2][b]). To contest any tax assessment or proceeding upon which tax deed issued after property sold by taxing agency and purchaser has paid taxes for three years. (63-1143). See category Business Regulation and Commerce, topic Securities, subhead Liabilities.

Two years: (1) Against ministerial officer for damages for breach of official duty; (2) action upon statute for penalty or forfeiture, unless otherwise provided; (3) damages for professional malpractice, or for personal injury, or wrongful death, including any such

See note at head of Digest as to 1998 legislation covered.

See Topical Index in front part of this volume.

ID – 14

LIMITATION OF ACTIONS . . . *continued*
action arising from breach of implied warranty or implied covenant; provided that when action is for damages arising out of placement and accidental leaving of any foreign object in body of any person by reason of professional malpractice of hospital or physician or when fact of damage has been fraudulently concealed from injured party by alleged wrongdoer who at time of alleged act was in professional relationship with injured party then action accrues when injured party knows or is put on notice regarding condition complained of; but in all other actions, whether arising from professional malpractice or otherwise, action accrued as of time of act or omission complained of, provided further that action within foregoing foreign object or fraudulent concealment exceptions must be commenced within one year following accrual as aforesaid or two years following act or omission, whichever is later. Professional malpractice refers to wrongful acts or omissions in performance of professional services by any person, association, or corporation licensed by state to perform such service; (4) for libel, slander, assault, battery, false imprisonment, or seduction; (5) against officer for escape of prisoner arrested or imprisoned on civil process (5-219); (6) against governmental entity, in tort actions two years after date claim arose or should have been discovered (6-901 to 6-928); (7) for private actions under Consumer Protection Act (48-619).

After two years from date of issue of policy of insurance no misstatements, except fraud, shall be used to deny claim. (41-2106).

One year: Against tax collector to recover property seized or damages for seizure. (5-220).

Six months: On claim against county, time running from date of rejection thereof but likely tort claims excluded from this statute by 6-901 to -928; under bulk sale provisions of Uniform Commercial Code. (5-221; 28-6-111).

One hundred eighty days: Tort claims against governmental agencies or employees for tort must be filed. (6-905 to 6-911). Minors not required to present claim until 120 days after majority or six years from time claim arose or should have been discovered. (6-906A).

Sixty days: To recover tax paid under protest.

Action for ionizing radiation injury cannot be brought more than three years after injured person had knowledge or reasonably ought to have knowledge of injury and cause, but in no event more than 30 years from date of last occurrence to which injury is attributable. (5-243).

Action for performing or furnishing design, plan, supervision or construction of improvements on real property, if action in tort, if not previously accrued, shall accrue and begin to run six years after completion, and if action in contract, action shall accrue and period begin to run at time of final completion. Times fixed shall not be asserted by way of defense by any person in actual possession or control at time of any deficiency which caused injury. (5-241).

Criminal.—Murder, no limit (19-401); crimes against children, five years after child reaches 18 (19-402); felonies, five years (19-402); misdemeanors, one year (19-403).

Foreign Causes of Action.—Where cause of action which arose outside state is barred by law of the jurisdiction where it arose, action cannot be maintained in this state except in favor of citizen of this state who has held cause of action ever since it accrued. (5-239; 15 Idaho 167, 96 P. 932).

Disabilities.—If, when cause of action accrues, other than for recovery of real property person entitled to sue is infant, insane, or imprisoned on criminal charge for term less than life, statutory period does not run until disability is removed, provided, however, that six years is maximum that time limit for commencement of action is tolled for any disability or reason except as provided in 5-213 in connection with recovery of real property. (5-230).

In connection with recovery of real property disabilities include minority; insanity; imprisonment on criminal charge for term less than life; and married woman, where husband is necessary party with her in commencing action. Action must be commenced within five years after such disability ceases. (5-213). Contract by minor may be disaffirmed by minor himself either before majority or within reasonable time after. (32-103).

Absence of defendant from state prevents running of statute during continuance of such absence (5-229), unless service of process could be obtained on defendant by reasonably diligent efforts under terms of long arm statute (96 Idaho 723, 536 P.2d 291).

Renewal or Revival.—Payment of principal or interest or an acknowledgment or new promise in writing signed by the party to be charged will continue or renew the obligation. (5-238).

Contractual Limitations.—A provision of a contract limiting the time for action thereon is void. (29-110).

Pleading.—The defense of the statute of limitations must be pleaded. (I.R.C.P. 8c).

Uniform Commercial Code adopted. (28-1-101 to 28-10-104). See category Business Regulation and Commerce, topic Commercial Code.

Tax Limitations.—Taxes must be collected within three years of return or six years of assessment. No limitation for fraudulent return or failure to file. Miscellaneous minor limitations. (63-6068). No limitation on assessment and collection of sales tax by retailer, seller or other person who was to pay over such taxes. (63-3633[d]).

PARTITION:

When several co-tenants hold and are in possession of real property as parceners, joint tenants or tenants in common, an action may be brought by one or more, for a partition thereof, according to the respective rights of the persons interested therein, and for a sale of such property, or a part thereof, if it appear that a partition cannot be made without great prejudice to the owners. (6-501).

PLEADING:

Governed by I.R.C.P. 7, et seq., patterned after Federal Rules. 1970 amendments to Federal Rules not adopted. See also topics Actions, Practice.

All pleadings typed or printed letter quality on 8½ x 11 inch paper.

Pleadings Permitted.—There must be a complaint and answer; a reply to counterclaim denominated as such; an answer to cross claim, if applicable; third party claim, if leave is given; third party answer. (I.R.C.P. 7).

Complaint.—Pleadings seeking relief, whether original claim, counterclaim, cross claim, or third party claim, shall contain (if court be of limited jurisdiction), (1) a statement of grounds of court's jurisdiction; (2) short and plain statement of the claim showing pleader is entitled to relief; (3) demand for judgment to which deemed entitled. Alternative relief may be demanded. (I.R.C.P. 8). Claim for relief may not specify amount of damages sought in personal injury or death action. (5-335). Cannot claim punitive damages without leave of court. (6-1604).

Answer.—Parties shall state in short and plain terms, defenses to each claim and admit or deny the averments upon which adverse party relies. Denial on lack of information and knowledge upon which to form a belief has effect of a denial. In pleading to a preceding pleading, party must set forth affirmatively accord and satisfaction, arbitration and award, assumption of risk, contributory negligence, discharge in bankruptcy, duress, estoppel, failure of consideration, fraud, illegality, injury by fellow servant, laches, license, payment, release, res judicata, statute of frauds, statute of limitations, waiver, and any other matter of avoidance or affirmative defense. (I.R.C.P. 8).

Frivolous claims are penalized. (I.R.C.P. 11).

Every defense to a claim for relief must be asserted in a responsive pleading if one is required, except that the following may, at pleader's option, be made by motion: (1) lack of jurisdiction over subject matter; (2) lack of jurisdiction over person; (3) improper venue; (4) insufficiency of process; (5) insufficiency of service of process; (6) failure to state a claim upon which relief can be granted; (7) failure to join an indispensable party; (8) another action pending between same parties for same cause. (I.R.C.P. 12).

Counterclaim.—Pleading shall state as counterclaim any claim which at time of serving the pleading, pleader has against any opposing party if it arises out of transaction or occurrence that is subject of opposing parties claim and does not require presence of third parties of whom court cannot acquire jurisdiction, except such claim need not be stated if it is subject of another pending action. (I.R.C.P. 13). A pleading may state as counterclaim any claim against opposing party not arising out of the same transaction or occurrence. (I.R.C.P. 13).

Cross Claim.—A pleading may state as a cross claim any claim by one party against a co-party arising out of transaction or occurrence that is subject of original action or of a counterclaim, or relating to any property that is subject matter of original action. (I.R.C.P. 13).

Verification.—Unless specifically provided by rule or statute, pleadings need not be verified. Every pleading motion or other paper of party represented by attorney must be signed by at least one resident attorney of Idaho in his individual name. Signature of attorney constitutes certificate by him that he has read document, that after reasonable inquiry it is well grounded in fact and warranted by law or good faith argument for modification of law and not interposed for improper purpose. Sanctions against party or signing attorney available for violation of rule. (I.R.C.P. 11).

Amendment.—Any pleading may be amended once as of course before time for responsive pleading has expired. Further amendment allowed in discretion of court. (I.R.C.P. 15).

Service.—All pleadings are served on adverse party or attorney and filed with clerk of court. (I.R.C.P. 5).

Filing.—Made by filing with clerk of court, if such court has a clerk, otherwise with judge. (I.R.C.P. 5).

Time.—Defendant shall serve his answer, or motions, within 20 days after service of summons upon him. Answer to cross claim must be served within 20 days, reply to counterclaim within 20 days. Service of motion permitted under rules alters above time limits. If court denies motion, responsive pleading shall be served within ten days after notice of the court's action; if court grants motion for more definite statement, the responsive pleading must be served within 10 days after service of the more definite statement. (I.R.C.P. 12).

Accounts and Claims.—No proof of accounts required in first instance to maintain suit. (I.R.C.P. 12[e]). Upon trial, account or claim must be sustained by competent evidence, given orally or by deposition. Verified account will support default.

Small Claims.—See category Courts and Legislature, topic Courts.

PRACTICE:

Governed by provisions of code taken largely from California code, and Idaho Rules of Civil Procedure, effective Nov. 1, 1958, patterned after Federal Rules for procedure in district courts, except where changed by particular rule. 1970 amendments to Federal Rules not adopted.

Evidentiary matters governed by Idaho Rules of Evidence, effective July 1, 1985, patterned after Federal Rules of Evidence with some modifications. See topic Evidence, subhead Witnesses.

Special procedure before magistrate's division, district courts, is provided for collection of claims under $2,000. (1-2208).

Supreme Court has power to make rules governing procedure in all courts. (1-212).

Discovery.—Patterned after Federal Rules. See topic Depositions and Discovery.

Demand for Admission of Facts.—Patterned after Federal Rules. Any party may serve on another party written request for admission of genuineness of any relevant documents described in and exhibited with request, or of truth of any relevant matters of fact set forth. Matter is admitted unless within 15 days party to whom service is directed serves written answer or objection thereto. (I.R.C.P. 36).

Direct Actions Against Insurer.—See category Transportation, topic Motor Vehicles, subhead Direct Actions.

See note at head of Digest as to 1998 legislation covered.

See Topical Index in front part of this volume.

ID – 15

PRACTICE ... *continued*

Small Claims.—See category Courts and Legislature, topic Courts.

See also topics Actions, Appeal and Error, Depositions and Discovery, Injunctions, Judgments, Pleading, Process; category Debtor and Creditor, topics Attachment, Executions, Garnishment.

PROCESS:

Rules of procedure patterned after Federal Rules.

Civil action is commenced by filing complaint with court. (I.R.C.P. 3). See also topic Actions.

Summons.—Any time within one year after filing complaint, at request of plaintiff, clerk of court must issue summons and deliver it for service to an officer authorized by law to serve processes. (I.R.C.P. 4).

Who May Serve.—Made by officer authorized by law to serve processes (sheriff, deputy, constable, etc.) or any person over 18 years not party to action. (I.R.C.P. 4).

Personal Service on Individual.—By delivering copy of summons and complaint to him personally, within the state, or by leaving copy thereof at his home or usual place of abode within the state with some person over 18. (I.R.C.P. 4).

Personal Service on Infant.—Upon a minor less than 14 years, service within the state on guardian, if one is appointed, or if none, then upon father or mother, or if none, on person having care and custody of minor. (I.R.C.P. 4).

Personal Service on Incompetent Person.—Service within the state upon guardian, if appointed, or if none, then upon competent adult member of his family with whom he resides. If living in an institution, then upon the chief executive officer. If service cannot be had upon any of the above, then as provided by order of court. (I.R.C.P. 4).

Personal Service on Partnership.—Service on partnership or other unincorporated association, by delivering within the state, a copy of summons and complaint to a member or an officer or managing or general agent, or to other agent authorized by appointment or by statute. (I.R.C.P. 4).

Personal Service on Domestic or Foreign Corporation.—Service by delivering within state, copy of summons and complaint, to officer, managing or general agent, or agent authorized by appointment or by statute. (I.R.C.P. 4).

Personal Service Outside State.—Any person, firm or corporation who in person or by agent transacts business, commits tortious act or owns, uses or possesses real property in state, or contracts to insure person, property or risk within state at time of contracting, or maintaining matrimonial domicile in state, or engages in sexual intercourse giving rise to paternity cause of action, submits to jurisdiction of courts for any cause of action arising therefrom. Personal service outside state authorized. (5-514 to 517).

See also category Family, topic Divorce, subhead Jurisdiction.

Child Support Matters.—Service may be by usual manner for civil actions or by certified mail with return receipt requested. Service must be by uninterested party over 18 years. Service by mail completed upon obligor's receipt, but attorney or party making service must file return certificate showing that statute was followed and attach obligor's signed receipt. (5-518).

Nonresident Motorist.—See category Transportation, topic Motor Vehicles.

Long Arm Statute.—See subhead Personal Service Outside State, supra.

Proof of Service.—Service of process, if made by private party, must be proved by affidavit of the party serving same, stating the time, place, and manner of service. If by an officer, proof is made by his official certificate. (I.R.C.P. 5[f]).

Publication.—Service of summons may be made on nonresident, or person who has departed from state, or cannot with due diligence be found within state, by publication of summons at least once a week for four consecutive weeks. Where residence of nonresident is known, copy of summons and complaint must be deposited in Post Office within ten days after making of order of publication, directed to person to be served, at his place of residence. Service of summons is complete at expiration of period of publication. Order of publication is made by the clerk, and must be based on affidavit showing necessary facts requiring service by publication or service outside state. If address of defendant is known, clerk may order that personal service of summons may be made outside state, in lieu of publication. When personal service is made outside state, service is complete at time of service. (5-508, 509).

Notices Affecting Real Property.—Published notices affecting real property must contain legal description and street address or information to locate property or name and phone number which may supply information regarding location. (60-113).

Where summons has not been personally served on nonresident, court may, on such terms as may be just, allow him to answer to merits within one year from rendition of judgment. (I.R.C.P. 60[b]).

See also topic Practice.

Sheriff's Fees.—Service of summons and complaint, $10; attachment, $10; keeper's receipt, $5; bond, $10; return of writ, $10; service of notice, writ or order, $10; posting notice, $3; subpoena, $10; commission on sales, 2% on first $1,000 plus 1% on amount over $1,000 but not to exceed $100 and only ½ of commission allowed if no money transferred because sale credited to debt; sheriff's deed, $10; certificate of sale, $5; criminal arrest, $5; commission on execution without levy or where levied goods are not sold, 1½% on first $1,000 and ½% on amounts over $1,000 but not to exceed $75; travel at 40¢ per mile on mileage over 25 miles for one way only and no charge for miles less than 25 traveled.

REPLEVIN:

Designated as claim and delivery.

Action must be brought within three years from the time that the cause accrues. (5-218).

Proceedings.—Plaintiff may claim delivery of property at time of issuance of summons or at any time before trial as provided in statute. (8-301). Plaintiff by verified complaint or affidavit shall show: (a) Plaintiff is owner or entitled to possession and

evidence of claim of title; (b) property is wrongfully detained and how defendant secured possession; (c) description of property and its location; (d) that property has not been seized pursuant to statute or execution. (8-302[1]). Court shall issue order to show cause why property shall not be taken and shall set date of hearing, no sooner than five days. Defendant may file affidavits and appear or file an undertaking to stay delivery. (8-302[2]). Court may issue writ of possession prior to hearing if probable cause appears that: (a) Defendant gained possession by larceny; (b) property consists of negotiable instruments or credit card; (c) perishable property, in danger of destruction or concealment. Defendant may request court to shorten time of hearing by notice to plaintiff of not less than 48 hours. (8-302[3]). Court may issue temporary restraining orders in lieu of writ of possession, and upon hearing, court may make preliminary determination as to possession pending final adjudication.

Undertaking.—Plaintiff shall file written undertaking executed by two or more sureties in double amount of value. (8-303).

Contents of Writ.—Direct to sheriff, describe contents, location, with copy of undertaking attached. Defendant may file exceptions to sureties or file written undertaking for redelivery. (8-304 to 8-306). Claim and delivery action has precedence over other actions. (8-312).

Claims of Third Persons.—If claimed by third party, he must file written, verified claim, stating grounds, title, and if claimed by reason of security interest, dollar amount. (11-203; 8-309).

SEQUESTRATION:

No statutory provisions.

SERVICE:

See topic Process.

STAY OF EXECUTION:

See topic Appeal and Error; category Debtor and Creditor, topic Executions.

SUBMISSION OF CONTROVERSY:

No claim, controversy or dispute may be submitted to any court in state for determination or judgment without filing complaint or petition as provided in rules of civil procedure. (I.R.C.P. 3[a]).

VENUE:

Actions for recovery or partition of real property, for injury to real property, to determine any interest therein, or to foreclose a mortgage thereon must be brought in the county where the property is situated. (5-401). Actions to recover penalties or forfeitures imposed by statute, and against public officers for acts done in virtue of their office, must be brought in county where cause of action arose. (5-402). In all other cases action must be brought in county in which defendants or some of them reside. (5-404). If none of them reside in state, or their residence is unknown, action may be brought in any county. All actions against life or fire insurance companies may be commenced and tried in county where death occurred or loss was sustained. Actions against domestic and foreign corporations (89 Idaho 506, 406 P.2d 802) shall be commenced and tried in any county of state where defendant has its principal place of business or in county in which cause of action arose (5-401 to 5-404). Venue of action against newspaper for libel is in county in which newspaper was published. (60 Idaho 326, 91 P.2d 357).

Change of venue may be had on usual grounds. (I.R.C.P. 40[e]).

Contract Provisions.—Common law applies.

Criminal matters may be removed from court before which pending if fair and impartial trial cannot be had in original court or in alternative court may order impaneling of jury from county where venue would have been transferred and thereafter transporting jury to place of trial. (19-1801 to 19-1816).

COURTS AND LEGISLATURE

COURTS:

United States District Court.—Clerk's office: Box 039, 550 West Fort Street, Boise, ID 83274.

State of Idaho constitutes a single judicial district. Regular trial terms are held at Coeur d'Alene, Moscow, Boise, and Pocatello.

Supreme Court.—Supreme Court has jurisdiction to review on appeal any decision of district courts or judges thereof. It has original jurisdiction to issue writs of mandamus, certiorari, prohibition and habeas corpus and all writs necessary to exercise of its appellate jurisdiction. It may hear claims against the state, but its decision is advisory only. Place of hearing an appeal depends upon county from which appeal is taken. (1-202 to 1-209).

Court sits at Boise, at Pocatello, at Twin Falls, at Lewiston, and at Coeur d'Alene.

Court of Appeals has jurisdiction to hear and decide all cases assigned it by Idaho Supreme Court, but not cases involving Supreme Court's original jurisdiction nor appeals from imposition of sentences of capital punishment, nor appeals from industrial commission nor appeals from public utilities commission. Court of Appeals will sit in Boise, but also may sit in such other places as it considers convenient for conduct of its business. (1-2401 to 1-2411).

District Courts.—District court has original jurisdiction in all cases, both at law and in equity. It has jurisdiction to review on appeal proceedings of magistrate division and boards of county commissioners.

Magistrate's Division.—All reference to probate courts and justice courts removed, with former duties assumed by magistrates. Proceeding to be assigned to magistrate by senior district judge. Magistrate jurisdiction, not to exceed $3,000 in civil proceeding, including action on contract, tort, damage to personal property, a reputation, taking or detaining personal property, fraud, rents, claims and delivery, proceedings in attachment

COURTS . . . continued

and garnishment, actions arising under laws of incorporation of cities or counties, collection of taxes, proceedings in forcible entry and detainer, action to foreclose liens up to $3,000 on real or personal property. Criminal proceedings where fine does not exceed $1,000 or one year in county jail or both. Probate proceeding for probate of wills, administration of estates of decedents, minors and incompetents. Supreme Court by rule, I.R.C.P. 82, has specified additional matters assignable to magistrates, including domestic affairs and matters not in excess of $10,000 in controversy. (1-2201 to 1-2219).

Small claims are in small claims department within magistrate's division of district court. Jurisdiction limited to claims for recovery of money not to exceed $3,000. Action commenced by plaintiff appearing and verifying claim, giving names, addresses, and nature and amount of claim. (1-2303). Action must be brought in county where defendant resides or where cause of action arose. (1-2301). Fee of $18. No attorney may appear. (1-2308). No attachment or garnishment may issue (1-2309), but after certificate of judgment is filed execution available (1-2313). Either party may appeal within 30 days to lawyer magistrate, different from one rendering judgment, from county in which court is located (1-2311), and prevailing party entitled to $25 attorney fee (1-2311).

Districts.—State is divided into seven judicial districts, counties of which are as follows:

First District.—Boundary, Bonner, Kootenai, Benewah and Shoshone Counties.
Second District.—Latah, Nez Perce, Lewis, Clearwater and Idaho Counties.
Third District.—Adams, Washington, Payette, Gem, Canyon, and Owyhee Counties.
Fourth District.—Valley, Boise, Ada and Elmore Counties.
Fifth District.—Blaine, Camas, Gooding, Lincoln, Minidoka, Jerome, Twin Falls and Cassia Counties.
Sixth District.—Power, Bannock, Caribou, Oneida, Franklin and Bear Lake Counties.
Seventh District.—Lemhi, Custer, Butte, Clark, Fremont, Jefferson, Madison, Teton, Bingham and Bonneville Counties.

Counties, districts and places of holding court are as follows:

Ada County: Fourth District; court sits at Boise.
Adams County: Third District; court sits at Council.
Bannock County: Sixth District; court sits at Pocatello.
Bear Lake County: Sixth District; court sits at Paris.
Benewah County: First District; court sits at St. Maries.
Bingham County: Seventh District; court sits at Blackfoot.
Blaine County: Fifth District; court sits at Hailey.
Boise County: Fourth District; court sits at Idaho City.
Bonner County: First District; court sits at Sandpoint.
Bonneville County: Seventh District; court sits at Idaho Falls.
Boundary County: First District; court sits at Bonners Ferry.
Butte County: Seventh District; court sits at Arco.
Camas County: Fifth District; court sits at Fairfield.
Canyon County: Third District; court sits at Caldwell.
Caribou County: Sixth District; court sits at Soda Springs.
Cassia County: Fifth District; court sits at Burley.
Clark County: Seventh District; court sits at Dubois.
Clearwater County: Second District; court sits at Orofino.
Custer County: Seventh District; court sits at Challis.
Elmore County: Fourth District; court sits at Mountain Home.
Franklin County: Sixth District; court sits at Preston.
Fremont County: Seventh District; court sits at St. Anthony.
Gem County: Third District; court sits at Emmett.
Gooding County: Fifth District; court sits at Gooding.
Idaho County: Second District; court sits at Grangeville.
Jefferson County: Seventh District; court sits at Rigby.
Jerome County: Fifth District; court sits at Jerome.
Kootenai County: First District; court sits at Coeur d'Alene.
Latah County: Second District; court sits at Moscow.
Lemhi County: Seventh District; court sits at Salmon.
Lewis County: Second District; court sits at Nez Perce.
Lincoln County: Fifth District; court sits at Shoshone.
Madison County: Seventh District; court sits at Rexburg.
Minidoka County: Fifth District; court sits at Rupert.
Nez Perce County: Second District; court sits at Lewiston.
Oneida County: Sixth District; court sits at Malad.
Owyhee County: Third District; court sits at Murphy.
Payette County: Third District; court sits at Payette.
Power County: Sixth District; court sits at American Falls.
Shoshone County: First District; court sits at Wallace.
Teton County: Seventh District; court sits at Driggs.
Twin Falls County: Fifth District; court sits at Twin Falls.
Valley County: Fourth District; court sits at Cascade.
Washington County: Third District; court sits at Weiser.

Small Claims Courts.—See subhead District Courts, catchline Small Claims, supra.

Indigents.—District or magistrate courts may waive payment of fees, costs or appropriate security therefor upon party's affidavit that he is unable to pay. (31-3220).

LEGISLATURE:

Meets annually, commencing on second Mon. of Jan. of each year. Governor may call special sessions. (Const., art. III, §8).

Initiative and Referendum.—Both provided for in Idaho Constitution, Art. III, §1.

Lobbyists.—Activities regulated through Secretary of State. (67-6617 to 67-6628).

REPORTS:

Decisions of Supreme Court and Court of Appeals are contained in Idaho Reports and Pacific Reporter.

Unofficial reports of Supreme Court decisions published in Idaho Supreme Court Reports (ISCR). Reports of Court of Appeals decisions published in Idaho Court of Appeals Reports (ICAR).

Digests are Idaho Digest and Pacific Digest.

STATUTES:

Latest compilation is Idaho Code, 1947, adopted 1949, of which Volume 4 has been expanded to Volumes 4 and 4A, Volume 5 has been expanded to Volumes 5 (Part 1), 5 (Part 2), 5A and 5B, Volume 6 has been expanded to Volumes 6 and 6A, Volume 7 has been expanded to Volumes 7, 7A and 7B, Volume 8 has been expanded to Volumes 8 and 8A, Volume 9 has been expanded to Volumes 9 and 9A, Volume 10 has been expanded to Volumes 10 and 10A, Volume 11 has been expanded to Volumes 11 and 11A, and Volume 12 has been expanded to Volumes 12 and 13. Code is cited in this digest as follows: Number preceding hyphen indicates title; number following hyphen indicates chapter or, if it contains more than two digits, chapter and section. Thus: 7-1 indicates Title 7, Chapter 1; 7-101 indicates Title 7, Chapter 1, Section 1; 7-1011 indicates Title 7, Chapter 10, Section 11; 7-1101 indicates Title 7, Chapter 11, Section 1. I.R.C.P. indicates Idaho Rules of Civil Procedure.

Uniform Acts which have been adopted are: Agreement on Detainers (1971); Alcohol and Intoxication Treatment (1976); 1987 Anatomical Gift (1989); Arbitration (1975); †Business Corporation Act (1979); Business Records as Evidence (1939); Child Custody Jurisdiction (1977); Commercial Code (1967); †Common Trust Fund (1949); Contribution Among Tortfeasors (1971); Controlled Substances (1971); Criminal Extradition (as am'd 1979); †Deceptive Trade Practices (1971); Declaratory Judgments (1933); Division of Income for Tax Purposes (1967); Durable Power of Attorney (1982); Revised Enforcement of Foreign Judgments (1974); Facsimile Signatures of Public Officials (1959); Federal Lien Registration (1967, 1979); Fiduciaries (1925); Foreign Money-Judgments Recognition (1990); Fraudulent Transfer (1987); Jury Selection and Service (1971); Limited Partnership, 1976 version (1982); Motor-Vehicle Registration (1927); Official Reports as Evidence (1939); Partnership (1919); Photographic Copies of Business and Public Records as Evidence (1951); Post-Conviction Procedure, as Revised (1979); Principal and Income, Revised (1963); †Probate Code (1972); Prudent Investor (1997); Reciprocal Enforcement of Support (1951), with uniform amendments (1953; 1959) Revised (1969); Reciprocal Transfer Tax (1929); Rendition of Accused Persons (1969); Rendition of Prisoners as Witnesses in Criminal Proceedings (1959); Simplification of Fiduciary Security Transfers (1959); Simultaneous Death (1971); Single Publication (1953); Transfers to Minors Act (1984); Trustees' Powers Act (1965); Unclaimed Property Act 1981 version (1983).

†Adopted with significant variations.
See also category Business Regulation and Commerce, topic Securities.
For text of Uniform Acts falling within the scope of the Martindale-Hubbell Law Digests see Uniform and Model Acts section.

UNIFORM LAWS:

For list of Uniform Acts in force in this state see topic Statutes. For text of Uniform Acts within the scope of the Martindale-Hubbell Law Digests see Uniform and Model Acts section.

CRIMINAL LAW

BAIL:

See topic Criminal Law.

CRIMINAL LAW:

Crimes and criminal procedure are covered by 18-100 to 18-8105 and 19-101 to 19-5306. Crime victims compensation program established in 72-1001 to 72-1019. Idaho Telephone Solicitation Act regulates telephone solicitation and requires registration with attorney general; applies to out-of-state solicitors. (48-1001 to 48-1010).

Indictment or Information.—An accused person is brought before court by indictment of grand jury or information filed by prosecuting attorney.

Bail.—Bail not permitted in capital cases where proof of guilt is evident or presumption thereof is great. (19-2903). Bail unavailable during appeal when defendant sentenced to death, imprisonment greater than five years, or enhanced penalty for use of firearm. (19-2905). In all other cases it is matter of right before conviction and matter of discretion thereafter. (19-2901 to 19-2923).

Uniform Criminal Extradition Act adopted. (19-4501 to 19-4527). Amended 1979. (1979, c. 228).

Uniform Rendition of Accused Persons Act adopted. (19-4530 to 19-4534).

Uniform Disposition of Detainers Act adopted. (19-5001 to 19-5008).

Interstate Compact for Supervision of Parolees and Probationers.—In effect, with Out-of-State Incarceration Amendment. (20-301 and 20-302).

Uniform Post-Conviction Procedure Act, as Revised, adopted. (19-4901 to 19-4911, am'd 1979, c. 143). Appeal must be within 42 days of judgment.

Uniform Rendition of Prisoners as Witnesses in Criminal Proceedings Act adopted. (19-3013 to 19-3022).

DEBTOR AND CREDITOR

ASSIGNMENTS:

Choses in action may be assigned like other personal property. No particular form required. Acknowledgment not necessary. No requirement of or authority for recording. (55-402).

See note at head of Digest as to 1998 legislation covered.

See Topical Index in front part of this volume.

ASSIGNMENTS . . . *continued*

Uniform Commercial Code adopted. (28-1-101 to 28-10-104). See category Business Regulation and Commerce, topic Commercial Code.

Idaho Consumer Credit Code adopted Apr. 1, 1983. (28-41-101 to 28-49-107). See category Business Regulation and Commerce, topic Consumer Credit.

Assignment of Accounts Receivable.—See category Business Regulation and Commerce, topic Commercial Code.

Assignment of Wages.—Seller, lessor, or lender in consumer credit transaction may not take assignment of earnings as payment or as security for debt. Any such assignment is revocable by buyer, lessee, or borrower, although employee is not prohibited from authorizing deductions from earnings if authorization is revocable. (28-43-304).

ATTACHMENT:

Attachment is ancillary to action and in accord with statute. (8-501 to 8-540).

Actions in Which Allowed.—Attachment can issue only in action on judgment or express or implied contract for direct payment of money not secured by mortgage, deed of trust, lien, or security interest. (8-501).

Courts Which May Issue Writ.—All district courts.

Claims on Which Writ May Issue.—Debt must be due, but it need not be payable in this state. (8-501).

In Whose Favor Writ May Issue.—In proper case, any plaintiff, including nonresident or foreign corporation may obtain attachment.

Grounds for attachment are: (1) That contract or debt sued for arose on contract, express or implied, for direct payment of money, and has not been secured by mortgage, deed of trust, security interest, or lien, on real or personal property; or if so secured, that such security has become valueless, without any act of plaintiff or person to whom such security was originally given; or (2) if defendant is nonresident, then in action upon judgment, or upon contract, express or implied, or for collection of any penalty provided by any statute of this state. (8-501). Foreign corporation is nonresident within latter provision. (26 Idaho 703, 146 P. 101).

Proceedings to Obtain.—Plaintiff shall file application for writ supported by affidavit. (8-502). Court shall issue order to show cause why writ should not issue and for hearing date, no sooner than five days, and direct time within which service on defendant be made. (8-502[b]).

Prior to hearing, court may, nevertheless, issue writ if (1) jurisdiction depends on attachment of defendant's property in state; (2) property is a negotiable instrument; (3) property is bank account subject to threat of immediate withdrawal, property is perishable, in danger of destruction, concealment or removal from state, or sale to innocent third person. (8-502[c]).

On order to show cause hearing court makes preliminary determination, and if a reasonable probability that plaintiff's claim would prevail, requires undertaking for value of property and may issue writ which may be levied upon in amount adequate to secure judgment which may be obtained. (8-502[e]).

If writ issued prior to hearing, defendant may request shortened time, with notice to plaintiff, of not less than 48 hours. (8-502[c]).

If no appearance by defendant after service, writ may issue.

Court may, in addition, issue temporary restraining order, in lieu of writ of attachment. (8-502[d]).

Affidavit for Attachment.—Plaintiff, or his agent or attorney must make and file an affidavit stating ground of attachment, that debt is due, amount due, and that attachment is not sought, or the action prosecuted, to hinder, delay, or defraud any creditor of defendant. (8-502).

Attachment Bond.—No writ shall issue except by filing a written undertaking by plaintiff in amount set by court. (8-503[a]).

Notice of Attachment.—Two days after issuing writ clerk of court must post at door of courthouse for ten days, and cause to be published in a newspaper (if a weekly, in three issues; if any other, six issues) a notice setting out title of case and fact of attachment. (8-503[b]). Published notices affecting real property must contain legal description and (a) street address or other information to assist public to locate property or (b) name of person from whom additional information can be obtained. (60-113).

Levy made on real property by filing notice of attachment describing property and copy of writ with county recorder; personal property incapable of manual delivery, by serving similar notice and copy of writ on party in possession; other personal property, by taking into custody. (8-506). Securities must be attached by actual seizing by officer making levy or by legal process pursuant to §28-8-317. Personal property subject to security interest, defendant's equity of redemption in personal property and defendant's interest in real estate mortgage or deed of trust or as secured party under security agreement may also be attached but only by methods listed in statute. (8-506A). See category Civil Actions and Procedure, topic Replevin.

Indemnity.—Officer may not demand indemnity bond before making levy, but may do so after, if defendant claims exemption or third party claims property. (11-203).

Lien of attachment merges in judgment for plaintiff when obtained. (8-528). See subhead Vacation or Modification, infra.

Priorities.—Attaching creditor has priority over subsequent attachments and judgments, except that other creditors who file suit within 30 days after first publication and posting of notice of attachment and diligently pursue to judgment, are entitled to prorate. (8-503[b]).

Sale after judgment is made as in case of execution, but perishable property may be sold before judgment and other property may also be sold before judgment under court order. (8-525-6, 528).

Release of Property.—Attachment may be discharged by judgment for defendant in action, by defendant giving bond in an amount fixed by court for redelivery or payment of value, or may be vacated for irregularity on motion. (8-531 to -538).

Claims of third persons to ownership of property levied on, or of debtor that such property is exempt, are governed by same rules as in case of execution. (8-527). Third party claim by way of security interest must set forth dollar amount of claim. (11-203). See topic Executions.

Vacation or Modification.—Where lien on real estate has in any manner been lost or destroyed, issuing court, on application, may discharge lien. (8-538). Levy is lien on real property for two years, unless sooner released, discharged, or discharged by dismissal of the action. Lien ceases after two years, unless on motion made not less than five or more than 60 days before expiration, court extends time, not to exceed two years. Lien may be so extended from time to time. (8-539).

Debtor's Personal Property.—Attachment by possession (1) if parties with UCC perfected security interest consent in writing, then subject to their rights; (2) payment of perfected security interest holder, and obtaining possession by payment is subrogated to interest of such perfected security holder; (3) attachment of defendant's equity of redemption without possession, by sheriff serving and filing writ and notice. (8-506A).

Mortgage and Trust Deed.—Interest of mortgagee and beneficiary to trust deed may be attached by sheriff recording and serving copy of writ and notice. (8-506A).

Defendant's Security Interest.—Attached by sheriff filing and serving copy of writ and notice. (8-506A).

CREDITORS' SUITS:

No statutory provisions. Doctrines of equity control. (7 Idaho 677, 65 P. 444). See topics Executions, Fraudulent Sales and Conveyances.

EXECUTIONS:

While rules patterned after Federal Rules have been adopted, executions still governed by statute. (I.R.C.P. 69).

May issue at any time after rendition and recording of appealable final judgment, within five years from entry of judgment. If five years have elapsed, and judgment is for recovery of specific property, court may, on motion, or judgment based on supplemental pleadings, grant leave to carry judgment into execution. Executions issue in name of state, under seal of court subscribed by clerk, are directed to sheriff of county to which they issue, and must briefly describe judgment, and state court in which judgment was rendered. (11-101 to -105; I.R.C.P. 62).

Exemptions.—See topic Exemptions.

Levy is made in case of real estate by filing notice of levy describing property and copy of writ with county recorder, in case of personal property incapable of manual delivery by serving similar notice and copy of writ on party in possession, and in case of other personal property by taking into custody. Property levied on is sold, except things in action collected, gold dust and money. (8-506, 11-201, 11-301).

Indemnity.—If defendant serves a verified written statement setting forth his claim that property levied on is exempt, the sheriff is not bound to keep the property unless plaintiff gives an indemnity bond. (11-203).

Lien.—Execution creates no lien until actual levy.

Return.—Execution is returnable within 60 days. (11-103).

Sale under execution must be at public auction to highest bidder, between 9 A. M. and 5 P. M. When estate sold is less than leasehold of two years unexpired term, sale is absolute. In all other cases property is subject to redemption. (11-302 to 11-310).

Redemption.—Real estate may be redeemed within one year after sale if real property consists of more than 20 acres, and within six months if 20 acres or less, by paying amount paid on sale with interest at 12% per annum from date of sale to date of redemption, together with amount of any assessments or taxes paid by purchaser since commencement of action and not included in judgment and interest at 12% on such amount, and if purchaser also holds prior lien to redemptioner other than judgment on which property was sold, amount of such prior lien with 12% interest thereon. Property may be redeemed by successive redemptioners within 60 days from last redemption and within one year from sale, by paying amount of last redemption with interest at 12% per annum from date of such last redemption, any taxes or assessments paid by last redemptioner and any prior lien held by him, together with interest at 12% per annum on each of said amounts. (11-310, 11-401 to 11-407).

Claims of Third Persons.—Third person may serve on sheriff written claim to property levied on, verified under oath, showing their title, in which event sheriff is not bound to keep property unless plaintiff gives him indemnity bond. (11-203).

Stay of Execution.—Court may stay execution of, or any proceeding to enforce, judgment pending disposition of motion for new trial or for relief from default judgment. (11-101). As to stay pending appeal, see category Civil Actions and Procedure, topic Appeal and Error.

Supplementary Proceedings.—After return of execution unsatisfied in whole or in part, the defendant or any one of several joint defendants, may be required to attend before the judge of the court in which the judgment has been recovered, and compelled to testify concerning his estate and effects. Any debtor of the defendant may satisfy an execution against the defendant, and the receipt of the sheriff is a discharge of his obligation to the defendant to the extent of the amount so paid by him. The court may order the application of any property not exempt from execution, choses in action or effects that may appear to be in his hands or in the hands of any one for him, to the satisfaction of the judgment. (11-501 to 11-508).

EXEMPTIONS:

Any actual resident of state may hold, exempt from attachment, execution or other process of law, large number of articles specifically enumerated in statutes, exemption being limited as to value in some cases. (11-601 to 11-609). Some exemptions not applicable against child or spousal support claims. (11-607[c]).

Substitution.—There is no provision authorizing a debtor who does not possess articles specifically exempted to hold money or other property exempt in lieu thereof.

See note at head of Digest as to 1998 legislation covered.

See Topical Index in front part of this volume.

EXEMPTIONS . . . continued

Earnings subject to garnishment shall not exceed lesser of 25% of disposable earnings or amount disposable earnings exceed 30 times federal minimum hourly wages. Does not apply to court orders for support, bankruptcy court orders, debts for federal or state taxes. (11-206 to 11-207). Garnishment on debt subject to Consumer Credit Code not more than amount disposable earnings exceed 40 times federal minimum wage. (28-45-104). See category Business Regulation and Commerce, topic Consumer Credit.

Necessity of Claiming Exemption.—Must be claimed by verified claim. (11-203).

Insurance.—All benefits accrued or accruing under life insurance policies, to extent reasonably necessary for support (11-604), and proceeds from group insurance policies (41-1835) are exempt.

Homestead Exemption.—See topic Homesteads. See also topic Garnishment.

FORECLOSURE:

See topic Liens; category Mortgages, topic Mortgages of Real Property.

FRAUDULENT SALES AND CONVEYANCES:

Uniform Commercial Code adopted. (28-1-101 to 28-10-104). See category Business Regulation and Commerce, topic Commercial Code.

Bulk Sales.—See category Business Regulation and Commerce, topic Commercial Code.

Uniform Fraudulent Transfer Act adopted. (55-910 to 55-921).

GARNISHMENT:

Property Which May Be Reached.—Credits or other personal property belonging to defendant and debts owing to him may be garnished, where writ of attachment has issued. (8-507). See topic Attachment; category Business Regulation and Commerce, topic Consumer Credit.

By proper pleading filed in garnishment, defendant may show property or debt is subject to exemption. (8-519). See topic Exemptions.

Jurisdiction.—Same as for attachments.

Proceedings to Obtain.—Same as for attachments.

Service of Writ and Notice.—The sheriff must serve upon the person or corporation, public or private, owing defendant or having his property, a copy of the writ of attachment, notice that such credits or other personal property are attached, notice of exemption, instructions to debtor and third parties for asserting claim of exemption. Forms are in 8-507C. (8-507). Sheriff shall serve writ and other documents within two days but for banks within one day. (8-507A). If garnishment on bank, garnishee shall mail or hand deliver copy to defendant and any co-owner within one day after service on bank. (8-507B). Sheriff can serve by mail or in person. (8-507D). Claims of exemption must be within 14 days of service and motion to determine must be brought within five days after claim of exemption served. (11-203).

Liability of Garnishee.—The person or corporation so served is liable for the amount of such credits, property or debt until the attachment is discharged or any judgment recovered by the plaintiff is satisfied, unless the property be delivered up or transferred or such debt, or a portion thereof equal to the amount of plaintiff's claim, is paid to the sheriff. (8-508).

Answer of Garnishee.—Garnishee must answer within five days from service and default judgment may be taken for failure to answer. (8-512).

Plaintiff may except to answer for insufficiency or file denial within three days and if denied trial may be had on the issues so framed. If garnishee admits liability he may be allowed a reasonable sum for his expenses and trouble in answering. (8-513 to 8-516).

Examination of Garnishee.—The garnishee may be required to attend before the court or judge or a referee for examination under oath. (8-509). Written interrogatories may be served on the garnishee as to personal property of the defendant in his hands or debts owing from him to such defendant. (8-511).

Judgment.—No final judgment can be rendered against garnishee until final judgment in the action. (8-512).

Earnings.—Continuing garnishment for future moneys coming due may be had against employer of judgment debtor. (8-509). If additional garnishments are issued, they cannot be effected until existing garnishment is satisfied or until amount taken by existing garnishment is less than maximum allowed. Additional garnishments must be executed in order presented. (8-509). See topic Exemptions, subhead Earnings.

Debts, moneys and credits due or owing by State of Idaho to any person except an elective state officer are subject to execution and garnishment after final judgment. (11-202).

HOMESTEADS:

A homestead consisting of the family dwelling and the land on which it is situated may be selected and claimed by any person residing thereon and held exempt from execution or forced sale. (55-1001).

Limitation of value which may be held exempt is $50,000, in excess of mortgage, trust deed or recorded liens, including improvements. (55-1201).

Limitation of Area.—None other than confined to dwelling house and land on which situated.

Debts or Liabilities Against Which Exemption Not Available.—The exemption is not available against judgments: (a) which became liens before the homestead declaration was recorded or were rendered in actions in which attachments were levied on the premises before that time; (b) based on debts secured by mechanics', materialmen's, laborers' or vendors' liens; (c) based on debts secured by mortgages or deeds of trust executed and acknowledged by husband and wife or by unmarried claimant; (d) based on mortgages or deeds of trust executed and recorded before homestead declaration was recorded or properly executed thereafter. (55-1004, 55-1005).

Designation of Homestead.—In order to secure the exemption, the claimant must execute, acknowledge and record in the office of the county recorder of the county where the land is situated a written declaration of homestead. (55-1203 to 55-1205). Under certain conditions may presumably apply to mobile home, if connected to utilities, or leasehold interest, etc.

Waiver or Release.—The homestead right may be waived or released by an instrument which conveys no property. (55-1007, 55-1008).

Abandonment.—The homestead can be abandoned only by a declaration of abandonment or a grant thereof duly executed and acknowledged. (55-1007, 55-1008).

Alienation or Encumbrance.—A conveyance or mortgage of the homestead must be joined in and acknowledged by the husband or wife of the owner. (55-1006).

Proceeds of Sale or Insurance.—Proceeds of voluntary sale and proceeds of insurance in event of loss are exempt. (55-1001).

Rights of Surviving Spouse and Family.—If the selection was made by a married person from community property, the land vests in the survivor on the death of either spouse subject to no other liability than it would be in the event there had been no death. In other cases it passes to the heirs or devisees, subject to the power of court to assign same for limited period to family of decedent. (55-1206).

See category Estates and Trusts, topics Descent and Distribution, Executors and Administrators. (15-2-401).

JUDGMENT NOTES:

See category Business Regulation and Commerce, topic Bills and Notes.

LEVY:

See topics Attachment, Executions.

LIENS:

Persons performing labor upon saw-logs, cord wood or other timber, or in making same into lumber or furnishing supplies to parties engaged in such work, have lien on same, the claim for which must be filed within 90 days from the close of the rendition of the services or furnishing supplies. (45-401 to 45-417). Farm laborers and any person furnishing seed have similar lien on crops which must be filed within 90 days. (45-301 to 45-317). Suit must be brought in either case within six months. There is no right of redemption of personal property after foreclosure sale. (45-301 to 45-417).

Uniform Commercial Code adopted. (28-1-101 to 28-10-104). See category Business Regulation and Commerce, topic Commercial Code.

Agricultural Commodities.—Producers and dealers in grains, legumes, seeds and other agricultural commodities have lien on product or proceeds until sale price is paid in full. (45-1802). Attaches later of day of sale to purchaser or delivery. Effective for 90 days may be extended for six months by filing with county recorder signed notice of lien, including statement of amount owing, minus credits and offsets, name of purchaser, description of product, statement that amount claimed is bona fide existing debt, and other information required by recorder, and by mailing (certified) copy of notice to persons who have filed liens on inventory and accounts of purchaser. Second six month extension available. (45-1804). Lien has priority over other creditor liens of purchaser regardless of date of attachment. (45-1805). Purchaser has right to have discharge filed after payment. (45-1806, 07).

Federal Liens.—Federal tax or other federal liens are to be recorded in county where property is situated. (45-202).

Hospital has lien for charges for care, treatment and maintenance of injured person, on cause of action for such injuries. To perfect lien, hospital must, within 90 days after discharge of patient, file with county recorder verified statement setting forth name of patient, amount of claim and name of person or corporation claimed to be liable for injury. No release of cause of action is effectual unless lienholder joins therein or executes release of lien. (45-701 to 45-705).

Mechanics' Liens.—Every person, otherwise unsecured in whole or in part, performing labor upon or furnishing materials to be used in construction, alteration or repair of any mining claim, building, ditch, railroad, or other structure, or who improves any land by grading, leveling, etc., or improving any lot in incorporated city or town, or professional engineer who renders professional services, has lien thereon for work done or material furnished. (45-501).

The land upon which any building, improvement, or structure is constructed, together with a convenient space about the same, is also subject to the lien, if at the time of the commencement of the work or of the furnishing of the materials it belonged to the person who caused the construction, alteration or repair to be done; but if such person has less than a fee simple estate in such land, then only his interest therein is subject to such lien. (45-505).

The term labor includes cost of Workmen's Compensation and occupational disease compensation security required by law, payment for which security has not been made. (45-517).

Filing.—Every original contractor must within 90 days from completion of work or furnishing of last item of materials, file for record with county recorder verified claim of lien, containing statement of his demand after deducting all just credits and offsets, with name of owner or reputed owner, name of person employing him, and description of property to be charged sufficient for identification. Within 24 hours of filing, copy of claim must be served upon or mailed (certified) to property owner. (45-507). Debtor may obtain release of lien by posting surety bond. (45-518 to 45-524).

Enforcement.—Lien must be enforced by suit within six months unless credit is given. Lien of final judgment obtained on mechanics' lien expires five years from date of final judgment. (45-510). Property subject to redemption as in cases of sales under execution (6-101) which generally is within six months if property is less than 20 acres; and within one year if property is greater than 20 acres (11-402). Subsequent redemption also available to other redemptioners. (11-403).

See note at head of Digest as to 1998 legislation covered.

See Topical Index in front part of this volume.

LIENS . . . continued

Medical Assistance Liens.—Medical assistance paid on behalf of individual 55 years of age or older when assistance received results in lien on estate of such individual, provided lien shall not attach while there is surviving spouse or child under age 21. (56-216). Lien may also attach to real property of individual in nursing facility, during his lifetime, if such individual is not expected to return home. (56-218A).

Motor Vehicles.—Lien is perfected at time of creation if filed with department within 20 days.

Physicians and nurses licensed in Idaho have lien for care of injured person on cause of action for injuries. Perfected, recorded and enforced as Hospital Lien, above. Court may allow attorney fee. (45-704A; 45-704B).

Attachment Liens.—See topic Attachment.

Attorney's Liens.—See category Legal Profession, topic Attorneys and Counselors.

Carrier's Liens.—See category Business Regulation and Commerce, topic Carriers.

Chattel Mortgage Lien.—See category Business Regulation and Commerce, topic Commercial Code.

Collateral Security.—See category Business Regulation and Commerce, topic Commercial Code.

Factor's Lien.—See category Business Regulation and Commerce, topic Commercial Code.

Judgment Lien.—See category Civil Actions and Procedure, topic Judgments.

Liens on Homestead.—See topic Homesteads.

Real Estate Mortgage Lien.—See category Mortgages, topic Mortgages of Real Property.

Tax Lien.—See category Taxation, topic Property (Ad Valorem) Taxes, subhead Lien.

MECHANICS' LIENS:

See topic Liens.

PLEDGES:

Uniform Commercial Code adopted. (28-1-101 to 28-10-104). See category Business Regulation and Commerce, topic Commercial Code.

RECEIVERS:

A receiver may be appointed by the court in which an action is pending or has passed to judgment or by the judge thereof in the following cases: (1) In action by vendor to vacate fraudulent purchase, by creditor to subject property or fund to his claim, or by partners or other joint owners in property or fund, where it is shown that property or fund is in danger of being lost, removed or materially injured; (2) in mortgage foreclosures where it appears that mortgaged property is in danger of being lost, removed or materially injured, or that condition of mortgage has not been performed and that property probably is insufficient to discharge mortgage debt; (3) after judgment to carry judgment into effect; (4) after judgment to dispose of property according thereto or to preserve it pending an appeal or in proceedings in aid of execution; (5) where corporation has been dissolved or is insolvent or in imminent danger of insolvency, or has forfeited its corporate rights; (6) for irrigation district where there are no officers, or district has ceased to function, has been abandoned, is insolvent, or is grossly mismanaged; (7) in other cases where receivers are appointed by the usages of courts of equity. (8-601). Additionally, trustee or beneficiary of deed of trust may request receiver if property is in jeopardy or if it is insufficient security for debt it secures. (8-601A).

Party, attorney or person interested in an action cannot be appointed receiver therein, without the written consent of the parties, filed with the clerk. (8-603).

Bonds.—If appointed on an ex parte application, the court may require the applicant to give an undertaking in an amount fixed by the court to pay defendant all damages he may sustain by reason of the appointment in case it was procured wrongfully, maliciously, or without sufficient cause. Receiver must also give oath that he will faithfully discharge his duties and obey orders of court therein. (8-603 and 8-604).

Powers.—Receiver can bring and defend actions in his own name, take and keep possession of property, receive rents, collect debts, compound or compromise debts, make transfers, or any other act authorized by court. (8-605).

REDEMPTION:

See topics Executions, Liens; categories Mortgages, topic Mortgages of Real Property; Taxation, topic Property (Ad Valorem) Taxes, subhead Redemption.

TRUSTEE PROCESS:

See topic Garnishment.

USURY:

See category Business Regulation and Commerce, topic Interest.

DISPUTE RESOLUTION

ALTERNATIVE DISPUTE RESOLUTION:

Mandatory Dispute Resolution.—Uniform Arbitration Act adopted. (7-901 to 7-922).

Arbitration is mandatory when any buyer claims to have been damaged by failure of tuber, plant, or plant part to perform as represented, or for failure of any seed to perform as represented by label. (22.436).

ARBITRATION AND AWARD:

Uniform Arbitration Act adopted. (7-901 to 7-922).

DOCUMENTS AND RECORDS

ACKNOWLEDGMENTS:

May be taken by following officers:

Within state: Justice or clerk of Supreme Court; Secretary of State; U. S. Commissioner; judge or clerk of court of record; county recorder; notary public; justice of peace. (55-701 and 55-702). Fee not to exceed $2. (51-110).

Outside State but within United States: Justice, judge or clerk of court of record of United States or state or territory; commissioner appointed by Governor of Idaho for that purpose; notary public; any other officer of state or territory where taken authorized by its laws to take acknowledgments. (55-703).

Outside United States: Minister, commissioner or chargé d'affaires of United States resident in and accredited to country where taken; consul or vice-consul of United States resident there; judge of court of record; commissioner appointed for such purpose by Governor of Idaho; notary public. (55-704).

Deputies.—When any of the aforementioned officers is authorized to appoint a deputy, acknowledgments may be taken by deputy in name of principal. (55-706).

Officers of U. S. Armed Forces.—As to notarial powers of officers in U. S. Armed Forces, see topic Notaries Public.

Requirements.—Notary must require personal appearance of one whose acknowledgment is taken; administer oath when required; disqualify self if has beneficial interest. (51-117). Officer must know identity of person acknowledging and if acknowledger acts in representative capacity, such capacity, or have it proved by credible source and state facts in his certificate; must affix his signature, his official seal, if required by law to have one, and if notary public in Idaho, designate his place of residence, and date of expiration of commission. (51-106, 51-109, 55-707, 55-716).

Foreign Acknowledgments.—Acknowledgments taken outside state and in accordance with Idaho requirements or those of state or country where taken are sufficient. (55-805).

Married women acknowledge in same manner as other persons. (55-708).

Authentication.—No certificate authenticating signature and official character of officer is required, whether acknowledgment taken outside state or not, unless acknowledgment taken before justice of the peace for use outside county where taken, in which event it must be authenticated by certificate of recorder of county where justice resides. (55-717). If required, district judge certifies clerk's authority and clerk certifies judge's signature.

Proof of unacknowledged instrument may be made by a subscribing witness or by proof of handwriting in certain cases before an officer or by action in district court, but judgment in such action is necessary to entitle unacknowledged instrument to record. (55-718 to 55-727).

Effect.—Acknowledgment entitles instrument affecting title to or possession of real property to record. (55-805).

Forms

Individual (55-710): State of . . . ., County of . . . ., ss. On this . . . . day of . . . . in the year . . . ., before me (here insert name and quality of officer), personally appeared . . . . known or identified to me (or proved to me on the oath of . . . .) to be the person whose name is subscribed to the within instrument, and acknowledged to me that he (or they) executed the same. In witness whereof I have hereunto set my hand and affixed my official seal the day and year in this certificate first above written.

. . . .
Notary Public, residing at . . . .
My commission expires on . . . . ,
19 . . .

Corporation (55-711): State of . . . ., County of . . . ., ss. On this . . . . day of . . . . in the year . . . ., before me (here insert name and quality of officer), personally appeared . . . . known or identified to me (or proved to me on the oath of . . . .) to be the president, or vice-president, or secretary or assistant secretary of the corporation that executed the above instrument or the person who executed the instrument on behalf of said corporation and acknowledged to me that such corporation executed the same. (Continue as in above form).

Attorney in fact: First portion and conclusion same as in above forms, balance as follows: "to be the person whose name is subscribed to the within instrument as attorney-in-fact of . . . . and acknowledged to me that he subscribed the name of . . . . thereto as principal and his own name as attorney-in-fact." (55-712).

Oath or affirmation: State of . . . . . , ss, County of . . . . . ; Subscribed and sworn (or affirmed) before me this . . . . . day of . . . . , 19. . .

Additional forms are prescribed for acknowledgment by persons in official or representative capacities and acknowledgments in partnership names (55-713 to 55-715), verbal oath or affirmation (51-109[3]), verification of instrument (51-109[4]), certify copy of public document (51-109[5]).

Alternative to Acknowledgment or Proof.—No statutory provision.

AFFIDAVITS:

There is no statute or rule which sets out affidavit requirements to be applied generally in all situations, nor is there any specific rule or statute which lists all permissible uses of affidavits.

Oaths.—Every court, every judge or clerk of any court, every justice and every notary public, secretary of state, and every officer or person authorized to take testimony in any action or proceeding or to decide upon evidence, has power to administer oaths or affirmations. (9-1401).

See note at head of Digest as to 1998 legislation covered.

See Topical Index in front part of this volume.

AFFIDAVITS . . . continued
Form
No statutory form. Usual heading is:

State of . . . ., County of . . . ., ss. May be in first or third person. Usual jurat: Subscribed and sworn to before me this . . . . day of . . . ., 19. . . . .

. . . .

(Title of officer).

Notary public must state date of expiration of his commission. (51-109[6]).

Alternative to Affidavit.—No statutory provision.

NOTARIES PUBLIC:

Qualification.—Must be 18 years, U.S. citizen, Idaho resident, able to read and write English, and not have been convicted of serious crime or in jail. (51-104, 105). May be removed for misconduct, or incapacity. (51-112 to 115). Must take and file oath, and bond in sum of $10,000 in office of Secretary of State. (51-104, -105).

Authentication and Forms.—See topic Acknowledgments.

Seal.—Required to keep official seal (embosser or rubber stamp with serrated edge) with words "Notary Public", notary's name, and "State of Idaho", to authenticate all official acts with such seal. (51-106).

Powers.—Take acknowledgments; administer oaths and affirmations; certify true copy of original document; certify affidavits, verifications or depositions; and other acts as permitted by law. Powers may be exercised anywhere in Idaho or outside state if to be admitted for record in Idaho. (51-107). Must not have disqualifying interest. (51-108). Misconduct is misdemeanor. (51-119).

Fees.—Not to exceed $2 per act plus travel expense. (51-110). Notary liable for damages resulting from official misconduct or neglect. (51-118).

Officers of U. S. Armed Forces.—Officers of any component of any branch of armed forces of U. S. have general powers of notaries public as to all notarial acts on behalf of persons in U. S. armed forces or subject to military or naval law, anywhere. (55-705).

RECORDS:

Uniform Commercial Code adopted. (28-1-101 to 28-10-104). See category Business Regulation and Commerce, topic Commercial Code.

Recordable Instruments.—Any conveyance or other instrument or judgment affecting title to or possession of real property may be recorded. (55-801). An instrument is deemed to be recorded when, being duly acknowledged, or proved and certified it is deposited in recorder's office with proper officer for record. (55-809). Every conveyance of real property acknowledged or proved, and certified, and recorded as prescribed by law, from time it is filed with recorder for record, is constructive notice of contents thereof to subsequent purchasers and mortgagees. (55-811). Term "conveyance" embraces every instrument in writing by which any estate or interest in real property is created, alienated, mortgaged or encumbered, or by which title to any real property may be affected, except wills. (55-813). Summary of instrument affecting title may be recorded. (55-818). See categories Mortgages, topic Mortgages of Real Property, subhead Execution and Recording; Property, topic Deeds.

Place of Recording.—County recorder in county where real property is situated. (55-808). *For list of Counties and County Seats see first page for this state in Volume containing Practice Profiles Section.*

Requisites for Recording.—Before instrument may be recorded it must be acknowledged by person executing it, or appropriate corporate officer, etc.; if executed in any other state or foreign country according to laws of that state or country, prima facie sufficient for recording. (55-805).

Fees.—For recording every instrument, paper or notice, $3 per page; copies of any record, $1 per page; certificates under seal, $1; recording town plat $11 for first 100 lots or less, 5¢ for each additional lot; taking acknowledgments, including seal, $1; recording location notice or amended location notice of mining claim, or for recording and indexing each notice, $3 per page, 50¢ each additional claim; filing survey, $5; making copy of survey, $4; marriage license, $10; administering oath, including jurat, $1; certifying same, $1; comparing and certifying prepared copy of record, 50¢ per page; making and certifying search for lien against personal property, excluding U.C.C., $5; add $1 for each certificate under seal. Page not to exceed 8½" x 14". If larger, additional fee of 2¢ per square inch. (31-3205).

Foreign Conveyances or Encumbrances.—See subhead Requisites for Recording, supra.

Filing Under Commercial Code.—See category Business Regulation and Commerce, topic Commercial Code. Place to file for timber to be cut, minerals, accounts, fixtures is county recorder's office. (28-9-401). Special rules established for farm product filings. (See category Business Regulation and Commerce, topic Commercial Code, subhead Variations, §9-307.) All other filings made with Secretary of State, Room 205, Statehouse, Boise, ID 83720. (28-9-401). Fee for filing original financing statement, if in form prescribed by secretary of state, $2; otherwise, $3. Fee for filing continuation statement, $3. Indexing fee for each name more than one, $2. Uniform fee of $1 for each page attached to financing statement. (28-9-403[5]). No fee for filing termination statement if in form prescribed by secretary of state; otherwise, $1. (28-9-404[3]). Fee for filing statement indicating assignment is $3 if in standard form; otherwise $4, plus $2 additional name indexing fee. (28-9-405[1]). Fee for filing separate assignment is $2 if in standard form; otherwise $3, plus $2 additional name indexing fee. (28-9-405[2]). Fee for filing statement of release, $2 if in standard form; otherwise $3, plus $2 additional name indexing fee. (28-9-406). Fee for certificate from officer set by Secretary of State. (28-9-407[2]). Copies of particular filed financing statements or statements of assignment, $1 per page. (28-9-407[3]).

Public Records.—Every person has right to inspect and copy public record, except records exempt from disclosure. (9-303 to 9-350). State agencies are to adopt guidelines that identify subject matter of public records maintained by each state agency. (9-347).

Torrens Act has not been adopted.

Transfer of Decedent's Title.—See category Estates and Trusts, topic Executors and Administrators. (15-1-305A).

Vital Statistics.—Reports of births and deaths, certificates of adoption and certified copies of marriage registers and of decrees of divorce must be filed with register of local registration district, consisting of incorporated city or town or unincorporated portions of counties as designated by Department of Health and Welfare. (39-241 to 39-272). Copies for $6 (subject to change by regulation) obtainable from Vital Statistics Unit, Capitol Building, Boise, Idaho 83700. (39-252).

Establishing Birth Records.—Certificate of birth must be recorded within 15 days of birth by person in charge of institution, attending person, father, mother or owner of premises. (39-255). If that time has expired record shall be filed in accordance with minimum standards prescribed by national agency in charge of vital statistics. (39-167).

SEALS:

All distinctions between sealed and unsealed instruments are abolished. (29-108).

A private seal may be made by a stamp or impression on the paper or upon any substance attached to the paper which is capable of receiving a visible impression or by the scroll of a pen, or by writing the word "seal" opposite the signature of the writer. A scroll or other sign made in another state or territory or foreign country, and there recognized as a seal, must be so regarded in this state. (9-401). A corporate or official seal may be affixed to an instrument by a mere impression upon the paper or other material on which said instrument is written. (29-107).

Uniform Commercial Code adopted. (28-1-101 to 28-10-104). See category Business Regulation and Commerce, topic Commercial Code.

TORRENS ACT:

See topic Records.

VITAL STATISTICS:

See topic Records.

EMPLOYMENT

EMPLOYER AND EMPLOYEE:

See topic Labor Relations.

LABOR RELATIONS:

Health insurance availability for small employers is promoted and regulated. (41-4701 to 41-4716).

Department of Labor and Industrial Services has general supervisory powers. (44-101 to 44-109).

It is unlawful for employers to exact agreements from employees not to become or continue members of labor unions. (44-901).

Right to Work.—No person shall be required as condition of employment to join or resign membership in labor organizations. (44-2001 to 44-2011).

Agricultural Labor Act defines terms, creates agricultural labor board separate from Department of Labor and Industrial Services, grants employees right to self-organization, to join labor organizations; grants employer right to manage own operations and hire from any source; lists unfair labor practices, allows collective bargaining; provides for petitions to board, hearings, orders, injunctive relief and damages. (22-4101 to 22-4113).

Public works contractors to employ Idaho residents. (44-1001 to 44-1002).

Statement To Be Recorded and Published by Employers.—Persons and corporations engaged in working mines or the development of mining claims, running tunnels, or building or repairing other structures, or constructing canals, railroads, wagon roads, or aqueducts, where mechanics or laborers are employed must make, record and publish a statement under oath, setting forth following data: (1) Name or names of owner or owners of mine, mines, mining claim or premises, tunnel, building, canal, ditch, railroad, wagon road, aqueduct or other structure upon which work is being done or upon which it is intended to begin work; (2) name or names of person, persons, company or corporations engaged in, or who contemplate engaging in, work on any properties or structures mentioned; (3) conditions under which said person, persons, company or corporation is prosecuting said work, whether as owner, agent, lessee, contractor, subcontractor, contemplative purchaser or lien holder; (4) principal office of said person, persons, company or corporation, and, if a corporation, state or country where incorporated and agent in this state on whom service may be had; (5) day of week or month when payment of laborer, mechanics and material men will be made, and place where said payments will be made; (6) statement of all mortgages and liens against the property on which work is being done, with the amount of each of said encumbrances and whether or not same is due. Such statement must be filed for record in office of county recorder of county where labor is being performed and posted in conspicuous place in office or place where payment of wages is to be made. Failure to comply with Act is misdemeanor punishable by fine or imprisonment. (44-501 to 44-503).

Children.—Employment of children under 14 in underground mines is prohibited. (Const., art. XIII, §4). No child under 14 may be employed or permitted to work in connection with any mine, factory, work shop, mercantile establishment, store, telegraph or telephone office, laundry, restaurant, hotel, apartment house, or in the distribution or transmission of merchandise or messages, or in any employment before 6 a.m. or after 9 p.m., or during school hours, except that children over 12 may be employed in any such occupations during school vacations of two weeks or more. (44-1301).

LABOR RELATIONS . . . *continued*

Hours of Labor.—Eight hour day prescribed for both men and women in mines and in smelters. (44-1104 to 44-1105).

Portal to Portal Act, modeled on U. S. Act, adopted. (44-1201 to 44-1203).

Wages and Liens.—Wages of miners, mechanics, salesmen, servants, clerks or laborers for services rendered within 60 days are prior claims to the extent of $150 for each person in case of assignment for benefit of creditors or death of employer; also in cases of execution and attachment without limitation on amount of laborer's claim if work is done upon property levied upon. (45-601 to 45-604). Employee discharged without payment has lien for wages and may charge and collect from employer wages for each day employer is in default up to 30 days. (45-606 and 45-607). Minimum wage $4.75 per hour commencing Apr. 1, 1997 and $5.15 per hour commencing Sept. 1, 1997. (44-1501 to 44-1509).

Secondary boycotts are illegal. (44-801 to 44-802).

Discrimination.—Wage rates based upon sex prohibited. (44-1701 to 44-1704). Generally, it is prohibited act to discriminate against person because of, or on basis of, race, color, religion, sex, national origin, age or handicap. (67-5909).

Labor Unions.—Public policy is established favoring collective bargaining. (44-701). Contracts between individual employee and employer for or against union membership are declared contrary to public policy and barred. (44-702).

Worker's Compensation Act.—This act (72-101 to 72-1434), applies to public employments generally and to all private employment for pecuniary gain, except domestic service, casual employment, aviation, employment by charitable organizations, employment of outworkers and employment of members of employer's family dwelling in his home (72-201 to 72-212), working member of partnership, associate real estate brokers and real estate salesmen, volunteer ski patrollers, officials of athletic contests involving secondary schools, and pilots of agricultural spraying planes when operating such planes if employer files proof of insurance coverage of $25,000 accidental death, $10,000 medical and $500 per month disability for 48 months. (72-212). Government hospitals also exempted. (72-928). As to excepted cases, employer may elect to come within act by carrying insurance and may revoke such election by cancellation of insurance or by notice filed with Industrial Commission (72-213 to 72-214); or employer and employees may agree, in writing filed with Board, that act shall apply to such cases. Surety shall not plead that worker was independent contractor. (72-229).

No proceedings under this law, except in cases of occupational diseases specially provided, can be maintained unless written notice of accident or of manifestation of occupational disease be given employer not later than 60 days after happening thereof, and unless compensation claim with respect thereto was made within one year after accident or manifestation date, or if death, then one year after death, whether or not compensation claim has been made by employee. (72-701). Notice must describe time, place, nature and cause of injury or disease and be signed by employee, or representative, or in event of death, by dependent or his representative. (72-702).

Right to compensation covers personal injuries from any accident arising out of and in course of employment, except those proximately caused by employee's willful intention to injure himself or another or by his intoxication. (72-208). Rights and remedies under act are exclusive. (72-211). Graduated scale of benefits for death, total disability and partial disability is provided. (72-301 to 72-324). If death results from injury or occupational disease, income benefits are payable to dependent spouse and children. (72-413; 1974, c. 30). Industrial Commission of three members is appointed by Governor. It requires reports, hears cases and makes awards. Appeals from awards, on questions of law, may be taken to Supreme Court within such times and manner prescribed by rule of Supreme Court. Modification due to change in condition within five years. (72-719). Employers must secure compensation to their employees by insurance in state insurance fund or by depositing with Commission security satisfactory to Commission which may consist of surety bond or guaranty contract with any company authorized to do surety and guaranty business in state. (72-301).

Occupational Diseases.—The act applies to occupational diseases. (72-437 to 72-449).

Unemployment Compensation.—Covered employment includes work performed for wages, except for domestic service in private homes or college clubs, employment by U.S., other states or for public tax supported institutions, religious or charitable institutions, together with other technical or minor exemptions. (72-1316; 72-1316A). Benefit formula listed. (72-1367, 72-1367A). Provision to collect overpayment of benefits by civil action. (72-1369).

WORKERS' COMPENSATION LAW:

See topic Labor Relations.

ENVIRONMENT

ENVIRONMENTAL REGULATION:

General Supervision.—Director of Department of Health and Welfare and Board of Health and Welfare formulate rules and regulations and otherwise administer and supervise enforcement of Idaho Environmental Protection Act to safeguard state environment. (39-101 to 39-130).

Director of Department of Health and Welfare and Board of Health and Welfare administers authorized grants and loans of financial assistance to municipalities for sewer treatment works. (39-3602 to 39-3604). Grant may not exceed 90% of estimated cost of project. (39-3604). Loan may equal 100% of estimated cost of eligible project. (39-3604). Concerned primarily with sewage disposal.

Director and board also formulate rules and regulations consistent with Federal Resource Conservation and Recovery Act of 1976 (as am'd) pursuant to Idaho Hazardous Waste Management Act for monitoring and controlling identification, transportation, storage and disposal of hazardous wastes. (39-4401 to 39-4422).

Prohibited Acts of Pollution.—Provisions for hazardous waste spills and notice requirements. (39-7101 to 39-7115).

Provisions for disposal of waste tires. (39-6501 to 39-6507).

Solid Waste Facilities Act.—Sets standards for operation of all solid waste facilities. (39-7401 to 39-7420).

Smoking prohibited in indoor public areas except in designated areas. (39-5501 to 5510). 39-5510 prohibits smoking on any bus except charter bus.

Enforcement.—Environmental quality enforcement is duty of Director of Department of Health and Welfare. Required to adopt rules and regulations. Has independent power of investigation, initiate complaints, hold hearings and enter orders of abatement (39-108); may secure injunctions in district court (39-108).

Water pollution enforcement by hearing before Board of Health and Welfare. Director may commence civil action and attorney general may commence criminal action in courts. (39-108, 39-109).

Director of Department of Health and Welfare may conduct investigations concerning hazardous waste management and upon finding noncompliance may commence administrative action against violator including post-hearing permit suspension or civil action in district court. (39-4413).

Appeals from Board of Health and Welfare, after administrative remedies, to district court in county where hearing held. Appeal filed within 30 days of final agency order; appeal to Supreme Court from district court within 42 days of final district court order. (39-107; 67-5215, 67-5216).

Penalties.—Violators subject to civil penalty not to exceed greater of $10,000 per violation or $1,000 per day for continuing violations, together with all expenses incurred by State enforcing Act. (39-108[5][6]). Injunction obtainable for pollution of air or water. (39-108[8]). For violation of public health laws, penalty is fine of not more than $300 or by six months imprisonment, or both. (39-419). Violator of firework law guilty of misdemeanor. (39-2630). Violator of radiation law guilty of misdemeanor and injunction may issue. (39-3012, 3017).

Violators of Hazardous Waste Management Act subject to civil penalties not to exceed $10,000 per violation or per day of continuing violation, may also be liable for costs of enforcement and clean-up, for compensation of private damages, and be subject to other injunctive relief. (39-4414). Hazardous waste violations also misdemeanor subject to $10,000 fine or one year imprisonment or both for each violation or day of continuing violation. (39-4415). Actions for hazardous waste violations may be brought by any injured party in derogation of Director action. (39-4416).

Permits.—Pollution source permits may be issued and permit fees charged by Director of Department of Health and Welfare. (39-115, 39-4413[A][2]). Hazardous waste transportation permit and manifest required. (49-2202). Department in compliance with statutory and regulatory requirements may issue and revoke permits to persons handling, transporting, storing, or disposing hazardous wastes. (39-4409, 39-4413).

Pesticides.—Any pesticide distributed within state must be registered and re-registered annually. Pesticide applicator, operators, and dealers shall be licensed. (22-3401 to 3425).

Petroleum.—Idaho Petroleum Clean Water Fund established to investigate and remedy any storage tank leak or release. (41-4901 to 41-4948).

Water Law.—Department of Health and Welfare is primary agency for enforcement of Ground Water Quality Protection Act. (39-120 to 39-127). Department of Agriculture is responsible for formulating rules and regulations pertaining to chemigation. (22-1401 to 22-1411). Clean Lakes Act adopted. (39-6401 to 39-6413).

See also category Mineral, Water and Fishing Rights, topic Mines and Minerals.

ESTATES AND TRUSTS

ADMINISTRATION:

See topic Executors and Administrators.

ADVANCEMENTS:

See topic Descent and Distribution.

ALLOWANCES:

See topic Executors and Administrators.

CLAIMS:

See topic Executors and Administrators; category Civil Actions and Procedure, topic Pleading.

DEATH:

Presumed dead at end of continuous absence of five years without explanation and after search. (15-1-107[c]). District Court has authority, based on clear and convincing evidence to determine if absent person is or is not legally dead. (10-1217).

Survivorship.—Person who fails to survive decedent by 120 hours is deemed to have predeceased decedent for purposes of homestead allowance, exempt property, and intestate succession. If time of death cannot be determined, person is deemed to have failed to survive. (15-2-104). Uniform Simultaneous Death Act (as am'd in 1953) adopted. (15-2-613).

Actions for Death.—Heirs or personal representatives may bring action within two years for death caused by wrongful act or negligence of another. Damages, no statutory limit, may be awarded as under circumstances may be just. Heirs—those defined in Uniform Probate Code (see topic Executors and Administrators, subhead Material Variations from Official Text, §1-201), and spouse, goodfaith "putative spouse", children, stepchildren, parents, dependent blood relatives, dependent adoptive brothers and sisters, and illegitimate child of father who has recognized responsibility for support. (5-219, 5-311). Action also available for injury or death or viable unborn fetus. (103 Idaho 570, 651 P.2d 11). See also category Civil Actions and Procedure, topic Actions, subhead Abatement.

See note at head of Digest as to 1998 legislation covered.

See Topical Index in front part of this volume.

DEATH . . . *continued*

Certificate.—See category Documents and Records, topic Records, subhead Vital Statistics.

Effect of Death on Written Instrument.—Any written instrument effective as contract, gift, or trust at death, or agreement between spouses to pass property to survivor at death, shall be deemed nontestamentary and money shall be paid or property shall pass in event of death. (15-6-201).

Uniform Anatomical Gift Act (1987) adopted 1989. (39-3401 to 39-3417). If gift is eye, qualified eye enucleator required. (39-3404). No transplantation unless there is medical certification that gift is from person tested for HIV antibodies or antigens. (39-3402, -3407).

Right to Die.—See topic Wills, subhead Living Wills.

DECEDENTS' ESTATES:

See topics Descent and Distribution, Executors and Administrators, Wills; category Debtor and Creditor, topic Homesteads.

DESCENT AND DISTRIBUTION:

See also topic Executors and Administrators.

Uniform Probate Code adopted, effective July 1, 1972. (15-1-101 to 15-7-401). 1975 and 1977 Amendments not adopted. 1979 Amendments adopted.

Material Variations from Official Text.—Material modification of 2-102 through 2-404 of code (sections pertaining to intestate succession, elective share of surviving spouse, spouse and children unprovided for in will and exempt property and allowances) are:

§2-102. Alternative provision for Community Property States (15-2-102A) adopted as Idaho Code 15-2-102.

§2-103. Substitute "a" for "1", "b" for "2", "c" for "3", and "d" for "4".

§2-105. After words "to the" add following: "state of Idaho, subject to administration by the public administrator. After deducting the expenses of administration and causing these to be paid to the county in which such administration occurred, the public administrator shall file the report of abandoned property required by section 14-517, Idaho Code, and proceed to dispose of the property in the manner set forth in the 'unclaimed property act', provided, however, that if such money is not claimed within eighteen hundred and twenty-seven (1827) days (approximately five (5) years) from the day upon which such property is paid to the state tax commission, it shall escheat to the state and be apportioned to the public school fund without regard to the provisions of said act."

§2-109. Substitute "a" for "1", "b" for "2", "1" for "i", and "2" for "ii". After words "natural parent" add: "and adoption by spouse of natural parent has no effect on the relationship between child and a deceased, undivorced natural parent."

§2-110. Add after word "otherwise" sentence, "If an advancement exceeds the share of the heir, no refund is required."

§2-114. Person related to decedent through two lines of relationship is entitled to only single share based on relationship which would entitle him to larger share.

§§2-201 through 2-207. Delete in entirety and substitute following:

15-2-201. Quasi-community property.—(a) Upon death of a married person domiciled in this state, one-half (1/2) of the quasi-community property shall belong to the surviving spouse and the other one-half (1/2) of such property shall be subject to the testamentary disposition of the decedent and, if not devised by the decedent, goes to the surviving spouse.

(b) Quasi-community property is all personal property, wherever situated, and all real property situated in this state which has heretofore been acquired or is hereafter acquired by the decedent while domiciled elsewhere and which would have been the community property of the decedent and the surviving spouse had the decedent been domiciled in this state at the time of its acquisition plus all personal property, wherever situated, and all real property situated in this state, which has heretofore been acquired or is hereafter acquired in exchange for real or personal property, wherever situated, which would have been the community property of the decedent and the surviving spouse if the decedent had been domiciled in this state at the time the property so exchanged was acquired, provided that real property does not and personal property does include leasehold interests in real property, provided that quasi-community property shall include real property situated in another state and owned by a domiciliary of this state if the laws of such state permit descent and distribution of such property to be governed by the laws of this state.

(c) All quasi-community property is subject to the debts of decedent.

15-2-202. Augmented estate.—Whenever a married person domiciled in the state has made a transfer of quasi-community property to a person other than the surviving spouse without adequate consideration and without the consent of the surviving spouse, the surviving spouse may require the transferee to restore to the decedent's estate one-half (1/2) of such property, if the transferee retains such property and, if not, one-half (1/2) of its proceeds or, if none, one-half (1/2) of its value at the time of transfer, if:

(a) The decedent retained, at the time of his death, the possession or enjoyment of or the right to income from the property;

(b) The decedent retained, at the time of his death, a power, either alone or in conjunction with any other person, to revoke or to consume, invade or dispose of the principal for his own benefit;

(c) The decedent held the property at the time of his death with another with the right of survivorship; or

(d) The decedent had transferred such property within two (2) years of his death to the extent that the aggregate transfers to any one (1) donee in either of the years exceeded three thousand dollars ($3,000).

15-2-203. Elective right to quasi-community property and augmented estate.—(a) The right of the surviving spouse in the augmented quasi-community property estate shall be elective and shall be limited to one-half (1/2) of the total augmented quasi-community property estate which will include, as a part of the property described in section 15-2-201 and section 15-2-202, of this code, property received from the decedent and owned by the surviving spouse at the decedent's death, plus the value of such property transferred by the surviving spouse at any time during marriage to any person other than the decedent which would have been in the surviving spouse's quasi-community property augmented estate if that spouse had predeceased the decedent to the extent that the owner's transferred property is derived from the decedent by any means other than testate or intestate succession without a full consideration in money or moneys worth. This shall not include any benefits derived from the federal social security system by reason of service performed or disability incurred by the decedent, and shall include property transferred from the decedent to the surviving spouse by virtue of joint ownership and through the exercise of a power of appointment also exercisable in favor of others than the surviving spouse and appointed to the surviving spouse.

(b) The elective share to the quasi-community estate thus computed shall be reduced by an allocable portion of general administration expenses, homestead allowance, family allowance, exempt property and enforceable claims.

(c) Property owned by the surviving spouse at the time of the decedent's death and property transferred by the surviving spouse is presumed to have been derived from the decedent except to the extent that the surviving spouse establishes that it was derived from another source.

15-2-204. Right of election personal.—The right of election of the surviving spouse may be exercised only during his lifetime by him. In the case of a protected person, the right of election may be exercised only by order of the court in which protective proceedings as to his property are pending, after finding that exercise is necessary to provide adequate support for the protected person during his probable life expectancy.

15-2-205. Proceeding for elective share—Time limit.—(a) The surviving spouse may elect to take his elective share in the augmented net estate by filing in the court and mailing or delivering to the personal representative a petition for the elective share within six (6) months after the publication of the first notice to creditors for filing claims which arose before the death of the decedent. The court may extend the time for election as it sees fit for cause shown by the surviving spouse before the time for election has expired.

(b) The surviving spouse shall give notice of the time and place set for hearing to persons interested in the estate and to the distributees and recipients of portions of the augmented net estate whose interests will be adversely affected by the taking of the elective share.

(c) The surviving spouse may withdraw his demand for an elective share at any time before entry of a final determination by the court.

(d) After notice and hearing, the court shall determine the amount of the elective share and shall order its payment from the assets of the augmented net estate or by contribution as appears appropriate under section 15-2-207 of this code. If it appears that a fund or property included in the augmented net estate has not come into the possession of the personal representative, or has been distributed by the personal representative, the court nevertheless shall fix the liability of any person who has any interest in the fund or property or who has possession thereof, whether as trustee or otherwise. The proceeding may be maintained against fewer than all persons against whom relief could be sought, but no person is subject to contribution in any greater amount than he would have been if relief had been secured against all persons subject to contribution.

(e) The order or judgment of the court may be enforced as necessary in suit for contribution or payment in other courts of this state or other jurisdictions.

15-2-206. Effect of election on benefits by will or statute.—(a) The surviving spouse's election of his elective share does not affect the share of the surviving spouse under the provisions of the decedent's will or intestate succession unless the surviving spouse also expressly renounces in the petition for an elective share the benefit of all or any of the provisions. If any provision is so renounced, the property or other benefit which would otherwise have passed to the surviving spouse thereunder is treated, subject to contribution under subsection 15-2-207(b), as if the surviving spouse had predeceased the testator.

(b) A surviving spouse is entitled to homestead allowance, exempt property and family allowance whether or not he elects to take an elective share and whether or not he renounces the benefits conferred upon him by the will except that, if it clearly appears from the will that a provision therein made for the surviving spouse was intended to be in lieu of these rights, he is not so entitled if he does not renounce the provision so made for him in the will.

15-2-207. Liability of others.—(a) In a proceeding for an elective share, property which passes or has passed to the surviving spouse by testate or intestate succession and property included in the augmented estate which has not been renounced is applied first to satisfy the elective share and to reduce the amount due from other recipients of portions of the augmented estate.

(b) The remaining amount of the elective share is equitably apportioned among beneficiaries of the will and transferees of the augmented estate in proportion to the value of their interest therein.

(c) Only original transferees from, or appointees of, the decedent and their donees, to the extent the donees have the property or its proceeds, are subject to the contribution to make up the elective share of the surviving spouse. A person liable to contribution may choose to give up the property transferred to him or to pay its value as of the time it is considered in computing the augmented estate.

15-2-208. Waiver.—The right of election of a surviving spouse and the rights of the surviving spouse to homestead allowance, exempt property and family allowance, or any of them, may be waived, wholly or partially, before or after marriage, by a written contract, agreement or waiver signed by the party waiving after fair disclosure. Unless it provides to the contrary, a waiver of "all rights" (or equivalent language) in the property or estate of a present or prospective spouse or a complete property settlement entered into after or in anticipation of separation or divorce is a waiver of all rights to elective share, homestead allowance, exempt property and family allowance by each spouse in the property of the other and a renunciation by each of all benefits which would otherwise pass to him from the other by intestate succession or by virtue of the provisions of any will executed before the waiver or property settlement.

See note at head of Digest as to 1998 legislation covered.

See Topical Index in front part of this volume.

ID – 23

DESCENT AND DISTRIBUTION . . . continued

15-2-209. Election of nondomiciliary.—Upon the death of any married person not domiciled in this state who dies leaving a valid will disposing of real property in this state which is not the community property of the decedent and the surviving spouse, the surviving spouse has the same right to elect to take a portion of or interest in such property against the will of the decedent as though the property was situated in the decedent's domicile at death.

§15-2-401. Add at beginning of sentence words, "If no homestead has been selected during life and set aside," and delete "$5,000" and substitute "$4,000" and add words, "or ten thousand dollars ($10,000) if there are dependent issue living with the surviving spouse." In second sentence substitute, "$10,000" for "$5,000" and after word "decedent" add "if the same condition exists".

§15-2-401A. Not adopted.

Adopted Children.—See category Family, topic Adoption.

Determination of Heirship.—See topic Executors and Administrators.

Advancements.—If person dies intestate, property given during lifetime to heir is advancement only if so declared in contemporaneous writing or so acknowledged in writing by heir. (15-2-110).

Escheat.—If heir cannot be found, personal representative shall distribute share to that heir's trustee, if any, otherwise file report and dispose of property as in Unclaimed Property Act. (14-501 to 14-541). If not claimed within 1,827 days thereafter, property accrues to state general account. (15-3-914).

See also topic Executors and Administrators; category Property, topic Absentees, subhead Escheat.

ELECTION:

See topic Wills.

ESTATES:

See category Property, topic Real Property.

EXECUTORS AND ADMINISTRATORS:

See also topics Descent and Distribution, Trusts, Wills.

Uniform Probate Code adopted, effective July 1, 1972. (15-1-101 to 15-7-401). 1975 and 1977 Amendments not adopted. 1979 Amendments adopted.

Code is given Idaho Code Annotated Title number 15, and section numbers contain said title citation followed by numerical part of Uniform Probate Code citation, e.g., 15-1-101.

Evidence of Death.—See topic Death.

Jurisdiction and Venue.—District Court, Magistrate's Division pursuant to rules of that court, has jurisdiction. (1-2208). Code applies to any proceedings commenced after July 1, 1972, regardless of date of death. Estate presently being probated may continue under former procedures upon leave of court. (See official comment to 15-1-101.)

Material Variations from Official Text.—Material Modifications of Article 1, definitional article, and articles 3 and 4, pertaining to administration of estates of decedents are:

§1-107. Substitute, "(a)" for "(1)"; "(b)" for "(2)"; "(c)" for "(3)".

§1-201. Substitute "Chapters" for "Articles". (As enacted by 1971, c. 111, Uniform Probate Code was divided into Articles and Chapters. In order to compile this law so as to make it compatible with remainder of Idaho Code, compiler, with approval of Idaho Commission, has changed designation of "Article" to "Chapter" and has changed designation "Chapter" to "Part".) Add: "(2) 'Augmented estate' means the estate described in section 15-2-202 of this code." (2) Substitute "3" for "2". (3) Substitute "4" for "3". (4) Substitute "5" for "4". (5) Substitute "6" for "5". After "decedent's" delete "." and add ", minors, incapacitated and disabled persons." Within brackets add "the district court." (6) Substitute "7" for "6". After "protected person" delete "." and add "and includes limited conservators as described by section 15-5-420, Idaho Code." Add: "(8) 'Determination of heirship of community property' shall mean that determination required by the provisions of section 15-3-303 of this code upon an application for informal probate not accompanied by presentation of a will." Add: "(9) 'Determination of heirship' required by section 15-3-409 of this code upon a finding of intestacy." (7) Substitute "10" for "7". (8) Substitute "11" for "8". (9) Substitute "12" for "9". Add after word "by" words "subsection (b)(1) of". (10) Substitute "13" for "10". At end of paragraph add words "For the purpose of this provision 'Testamentary Trustee' includes a trustee to whom assets are transferred by will, to the extent of the devised assets." Add: "(14) 'Emancipated minor' shall mean any male or female who has been married." (11) Delete all of (11) and substitute "(15) 'Estate' means all property of the decedent, including community property of the surviving spouse subject to administration, property of trusts, and property of any other person whose affairs are subject to this code as it exists from time to time during administration." (12) Substitute "16" for "12". Add after "402" words "of this code." (13) Substitute "17" for "13". (14) Substitute "18" for "14". (15) Substitute "19" for "15". Delete "s" on "means". (16) Substitute "20" for "16". After "appointment" delete "," and add "and includes limited guardians as described by section 15-5-304, Idaho Code,". (17) Substitute "21" for "17". (18) Substitute "22" for "18". Add after "101", words "of this code." (19) Substitute "23" for "19". (20) Substitute "24" for "20". (21) Substitute "25" for "21". (22) Substitute "26" for "22". (23) Substitute "27" for "23". (24) Substitute "28" for "24". Substitute "eighteen (18)" for "[21]". (25) Substitute "29" for "25". (26) Substitute "30" for "26". (27) Substitute "31" for "27". (28) Substitute "32" for "28". (29) Substitute "33" for "29". (30) Substitute "34" for "30". (31) Substitute "35" for "31". (32) Substitute "36" for "32". (33) Substitute "37" for "33". (34) Substitute "38" for "34". (35) Substitute "39" for "35". Add after "101", words "of this code." Insert "(39A) 'Quasi-community property' is the property defined by section 15-2-201 of this code." (36) Substitute "40" for "36". Substitute "magistrates or judges of the district" for "official of" and add after "307" words "of this code." (37) Substitute "41" for "37". (38) Substitute "42" for "38". (39) Substitute "43" for

"39". Add after "618" words "of this code." (40) Substitute "44" for "40". (41) Substitute "45" for "41". (42) Substitute "46" for "42". (43) Substitute "47" for "43". (44) Substitute "48" for "44". (45) Substitute "49" for "45". Add within brackets following "pursuant to", words "chapter 8, title 68, Idaho Code,". (46) Substitute "50" for "46". (47) Substitute "51" for "47". Add after "101", words "of this code." (48) Substitute "52" for "48". Add after "will", words "is a testamentary instrument and". (49) Substitute "53" for "49". Add after "Separate property", following: "includes all property of either the husband or the wife owned by him or her before marriage, and that acquired afterward either by gift, bequest, devise or descent, or that which either he or she acquires with proceeds of his or her separate property, by way of moneys or other property." (50) Substitute "54" for "50". Add after "Community property", following: "includes all other property acquired after marriage by either husband or wife, including the rents and profits of the separate property of the husband or wife, unless, by the instrument by which any such property is acquired by the wife, it is provided that the rents and profits thereof be applied to her sole and separate use. Real property conveyed by one (1) spouse to the other shall be presumed to be the sole and separate estate of the grantee."

§1-302. Not adopted.

§1-304. Not adopted.

§1-305. In first sentence delete word "record" and substitute words "single file". Add:

§15-1-305A. "Recording permitted—Effect.—Letters of personal representatives (foreign or domestic), a statement of informal probate, probated will, determination of heirship, order made in a testacy proceeding, or will otherwise admissible in evidence as provided in section 15-3-102 of this code; any deed, assignment, release or other instrument executed by an appointed personal representative of the decedent; an affidavit of a successor in interest to property of a decedent; and a decree in any testacy proceeding in another state, any of which affect title to real property, may be recorded in the office of the county recorder of the county in which the real property affected by any such letters, statement, determination, order, document or decree is located. From the time of filing the same for record, notice is imparted to all persons of the contents thereof."

§1-306. Delete "(a)". Delete all of paragraph "(b)".

§1-307. After word "registrar", delete remainder of sentence and substitute "will be performed by the magistrate or district judge."

§1-308. Not adopted.

§1-309. Not adopted.

Add new section as follows:

"§1-311. Exercise of powers.—Powers under this act may be exercised by the court at any time, in chambers or in open court, as may be appropriate. Powers conferred upon the registrar of wills by this act may be exercised at any time."

Add new section as follows:

"§1-312. Execution of deed.—Should any persons be entitled to a deed from a personal representative and such personal representative be discharged or disqualified or refuse to execute the same, such deed may be executed by the court authorizing such sale or distribution or the clerk of such court and shall entitle the buyer or distributee to his property."

§1-402. After first sentence, add new sentence as follows: "The appearance in court of an interested party is a waiver of notice."

§1-403. Substitute "a" for "1", "b" for "2", "1" for "i", "2" for "ii", "3" for "iii", "c" for "3", and "d" for "4".

Add:

§2-616. "No estate, real or personal, shall be bequeathed or devised, either directly or indirectly, to any person who owns, operates or is employed at a nursing home or residential care home, whether or not licensed, in which the testator was a resident within one year of his death if the will was executed while the testator was a resident of the facility, except the same be done by will duly executed at least one year before the death of the testator. This section shall apply to all property passing by testate succession after July 1, 1983, regardless of when the will was written; provided, this section shall in no way limit or affect the rights of a beneficiary who is related to the testator, or who is a charitable or benevolent society or corporation; provided further that the foregoing limitation shall not apply to wills of persons whose death is caused by accidental means and whose wills are executed prior to the accident which results in death."

§3-105. Delete entire third sentence.

§3-106. Delete entire article and substitute following:

"§3-106. Civil litigation—Notice.—Subject to general rules concerning the proper location of civil litigation and jurisdiction of persons, the court may herein determine any other controversy concerning a succession or to which an estate, through a personal representative, may be a party. Persons notified are bound though less than all interested persons may have been given notice."

Add new section as follows:

"§3-111. Joint probate on death of survivor of marriage dissolved by death.—In cases in which a marital community has been dissolved by the death of either spouse at any time, the survivor was then entitled to all of the property of the decedent by will, law, or both, and the survivor died before any proceeding had been commenced for the probate of the estate of the spouse whose death occurred first, the estates of both decedents may be joined for probate in a single proceeding in any court having jurisdiction of the estate of the spouse whose death occurred last. The initial application or petition filed in any such joint proceedings shall contain a statement of the facts upon which such joint proceeding is based, in addition to all other statements required by this code to be made therein."

§3-203. Add new subsection:

"(7) if a petition for appointment of a personal representative has been filed and sixty (60) days have elapsed during which no consent to act has been filed by any proper person, the public administrator shall act as personal representative unless and until a proper person consents to act.

Also in subpart (f)(1) delete "21" and substitute "18". Also add new subsection: "(i) a married woman shall have the right to serve as personal representative."

EXECUTORS AND ADMINISTRATORS... *continued*

§3-301. (All outline letters and numbering follows (a)(1) et seq. instead of (1)(i) et seq. Add subsection (g), which reads: "By verifying an application for informal probate, or informal appointment, the applicant submits personally to the jurisdiction of the court in any proceeding for relief from fraud relating to the application, or for perjury, that may be instituted against him."

Add subsection (h), which reads: "Any statement entered upon an application for informal statement of intestacy where the estate is community and there is a surviving spouse shall contain a statement of heirship setting out the heirs of the decedent and shall have the same effect as entry of a statement of informal probate of a will and be subject to the limitation periods set out in section 15-3-108, Idaho Code, notwithstanding the exception provided in that section for determining heirs of an intestate."

§3-303. After word "will" in first sentence insert "or informal statement of intestacy where the estate is community and there is a surviving spouse."

Also add new subsection:

"(8) if the application is for a statement of intestacy of a community estate with a surviving spouse, on the basis of statements in the application and affidavit: 1. the decedent left no will, 2. the decedent's estate consists solely of community property of the decedent and the surviving spouse, and 3. the decedent left a surviving spouse. In addition to this, the registrar shall set out the name of the surviving spouse."

Add new section as follows:

"§3-303A. Notice required.—Upon issuance of a statement of informal probate if no letters are issued to a personal representative or determination of heirship of community property, the applicant must give notice to all heirs and devisees of the admission of the will to probate or the determination of heirship of community property. This information shall be sent by ordinary mail to each of the heirs and devisees whose address is reasonably available to the applicant. The applicant shall be responsible to any heir or devisee damaged by failure of the applicant to give proper notice under this section."

§3-308(a)(3). Delete "20" and substitute "24".

§3-401. At end of section add following sentence:

"By submitting a petition for formal probate the petitioner subjects himself to jurisdiction of the court in which such instrument is filed. Any action by a person damaged by him, including a creditor of the estate, shall be limited in amount to the assets of the estate less the obligations of the estate paid by him. Notice of any proceedings sought to be maintained against the petitioner pursuant to his submission to jurisdiction shall be delivered to him or mailed to him by ordinary first class mail at his address as it is known to the petitioner, or is listed on any application or petition in probate proceedings previously instituted in the court where the proceeding is brought."

Qualification.—See topic Wills, subhead Material Variations from Official Text.

Exemption From Bond.—See topic Wills, subhead Material Variations from Official Text.

Removal.—See topic Wills, subhead Material Variations from Official Text.

Special Kinds of Administration.—See topic Wills, subhead Material Variations from Official Text.

Public Administrators.—County treasurers of various counties declared ex officio public administrators. (14-101 to 14-119).

Inventory and Appraisal.—See topic Wills, subhead Material Variations from Official Text.

General Powers and Duties.—See topic Wills, subhead Material Variations from Official Text.

Notice to Creditors.—See topic Wills, subhead Material Variations from Official Text.

Presentation of Claims.—See topic Wills, subhead Material Variations from Official Text.

Proof of Claims.—See topic Wills, subhead Material Variations from Official Text.

Approval or Rejection of Claims.—See topic Wills, subhead Material Variations from Official Text.

Payment of Claims.—See topic Wills, subhead Material Variations from Official Text.

Priorities.—See topic Wills, subhead Material Variations from Official Text.

Sales.—See topic Wills, subhead Material Variations from Official Text.

Actions by Representative.—See topic Wills, subhead Material Variations from Official Text.

Actions Against Representative.—See topic Wills, subhead Material Variations from Official Text.

Allowances.—See topic Descent and Distribution, subhead Material Variations from Official Text.

Final Accounting and Settlement.—See topic Wills, subhead Material Variations from Official Text.

Consent Settlement.—See topic Wills, subhead Material Variations from Official Text.

Distribution.—See topic Wills, subhead Material Variations from Official Text.

Liabilities.—See topic Wills, subhead Material Variations from Official Text.

Compensation of Representatives.—See topic Wills, subhead Material Variations from Official Text.

Small Estates.—See topic Wills, subhead Material Variations from Official Text.

Foreign Executors or Administrators.—See topic Wills, subhead Material Variations from Official Text.

Summary proceedings with reference to community property on death of either spouse (15-2-102; 15-3-1205). See category Family, topic Husband and Wife.

Revised Uniform Principal and Income Act adopted. (68-1001 to 68-1016).

Uniform Fiduciaries Act adopted. (68-301 to 68-315). See topic Trusts.

Uniform Simplification of Fiduciary Security Transfers Act adopted (68-901 to 68-911) and not repealed by Uniform Commercial Code.

Uniform Anatomical Gift Act.—See topic Death.

FIDUCIARIES:

See topics Executors and Administrators, Trusts; category Family, topic Guardian and Ward.

INTESTACY:

See topic Descent and Distribution.

TRUSTS:

See also category Business Regulation and Commerce, topic Banks and Banking.

Uniform Probate Code adopted, effective July 1, 1972. 1975 and 1977 Amendments not adopted. See topics Executors and Administrators, Descent and Distribution, and Wills.

Trustee's Powers.—Powers of trustees are set forth in Uniform Trustees' Powers Act. (15-7-401; 68-104 to 119).

Uniform Fiduciaries Act adopted. (68-301 to 315).

Investments by fiduciaries are regulated by Uniform Trustees' Powers Act. (68-104 to 113; 15-7-401).

Gift to Minors.—Uniform Transfers to Minors Act adopted. (68-801 to 825).

Securities in Name of Nominee.—Fiduciaries allowed to hold securities in name of a nominee. (68-601 to 602).

Uniform Common Trust Fund Act adopted (68-701, 702), without provision for court accounting. Expressly authorizes investment in common trust fund administered by investing bank or trust company.

Uniform Simplification of Fiduciary Security Transfers Act adopted (68-901 to 911) and not repealed by Uniform Commercial Code or Uniform Probate Code.

Uniform Principal and Income Act adopted. (68-1001 to 1016).

Uniform Prudent Investor Act adopted. (68-501 to 68-514).

Uniform Testamentary Additions to Trusts Act repealed.

Accumulations.—See category Property, topic Perpetuities, subhead Accumulations.

Perpetuities.—See category Property, topic Perpetuities.

Pour Over Trusts.—See Testamentary Additions to Trusts statute under Uniform Probate Code.

Hospital Liability Trust.—Hospital trusts permitted to accumulate funds to insure against general public liability claims. (41-3701 to 3729).

WILLS:

Uniform Probate Code adopted, effective July 1, 1972. (15-1-101 to 15-7-401). 1975 and 1977 Amendments not adopted. 1979 Amendments adopted. See topics Descent and Distribution, Executors and Administrators, and Trusts.

Material Variations from Official Text.—

§15-2-501. To first sentence add words, "Any emancipated minor or", add to second sentence, "A married woman may dispose of her property whether separate or community, in the same manner as any other person subject to the restrictions imposed by this Code".

Add new section:

§15-2-504. Self-Proved Will.—(a) Any will may be simultaneously executed, attested, and made self-proved, by the acknowledgment thereof by the testator and the affidavits of the witnesses, each made before an officer authorized to administer oaths under the laws of the state where execution occurs and evidenced by the officer's certificate, under official seal, in form and content substantially as follows:

I, ..., the testator, sign my name to this instrument this ...... day of ...., 19...., and being first duly sworn, do hereby declare to the undersigned authority that I sign and execute this instrument as my last will and that I sign it willingly (or willingly direct another to sign for me), that I execute it as my free and voluntary act for the purposes therein expressed and that I am eighteen (18) years of age or older, of sound mind, and under no constraint or undue influence.

....
Testator

We, ..., the witnesses, sign our names to this instrument, being first duly sworn, and do hereby declare to the undersigned authority that the testator signs and executes this instrument as his last will and that he signs it willingly (or willingly directs another to sign for him), and that each of us, in the presence and hearing of the testator, hereby signs this will as witness to the testator's signing, and that to the best of his knowledge the testator is eighteen (18) years of age or older, of sound mind, and under no constraint or undue influence.

....
Witness

....
Witness

The State of ....
County of ....

Subscribed, sworn to and acknowledged before me by ...., the testator and subscribed and sworn to before me by ...., and ...., witnesses, this .... day of ....
(Seal)   (Signed)

....
(Official capacity of officer)

(b) An attested will may at any time subsequent to its execution be made self-proved by the acknowledgment thereof by the testator and the affidavits of the witnesses, each

WILLS . . . *continued*

made before an officer authorized to administer oaths under the laws of the state where the acknowledgment occurs and evidenced by the officer's certificate, under the official seal, attached or annexed to the will in form and content substantially as follows:

The State of . . . .

County of . . . .

We, ..., ..., and . . . .,
the testator and the witnesses, respectively, whose names are signed to the attached or foregoing instrument, being first duly sworn do hereby declare to the undersigned authority that the testator signed and executed the instrument as his last will and that he had signed willingly (or willingly directed another to sign for him), and that he executed it as his free and voluntary act for the purposes therein expressed, and that each of the witnesses, in the presence and hearing of the testator, signed the will as witness and that to the best of his knowledge the testator was at that time eighteen (18) years of age or older, of sound mind and under no constraint or undue influence.

. . . .
Testator

. . . .
Witness

. . . .
Witness

Subscribed, sworn to and acknowledged before me by . . . ., the testator, and subscribed and sworn to before me by . . . ., and . . . ., witnesses, this . . . . day of . . . .

(SEAL)

(Signed) . . . .

. . . .
(Official capacity of officer)

(15-2-504).

§15-2-505. Insert after "person" words "eighteen (18) or more years of age."

§15-2-507. Substitute "a" for "1", "b" for "2", and add new section: "(c) The revocation of a will executed in duplicate may be accomplished by revoking one (1) of the duplicates."

§15-2-509. Add new section: "(c) Republication of a revoked will revives such will".

§15-2-602. Insert following "contrary to the", words "provisions relating to the elective share described in 15-2-201 through 15-2-209, the provisions relating to exempt property and allowances described in 15-2-401 through 15-2-404 or any other."

Add new sections:

§15-2-608. Nonademption of specific devises in certain cases—unpaid proceeds of sale, condemnation or insurance—sale by conservator.—(a) A specified devisee has the right to the remaining specifically devised property and:

(1) any balance of the purchase price (together with any security interest) owing from a purchaser to the testator at death by reason of sale of the property;

(2) any amount of a condemnation award for the taking of the property unpaid at death;

(3) any proceeds unpaid at death on fire or casualty insurance on the property; and

(4) property owned by testator at his death as a result of foreclosure, or obtained in lieu of foreclosure, of the security for a specifically devised obligation.

(b) If specifically devised property is sold by a conservator, or if a condemnation award or insurance proceeds are paid to a conservator as a result of condemnation, fire, or casualty, the specific devisee has the right to a general pecuniary devise equal to the net sale price, the condemnation award, or the insurance proceeds. This subsection does not apply if subsequent to the sale, condemnation or casualty, it is adjudicated that the disability of the testator has ceased and the testator survives the adjudication by one (1) year. The right of the specific devisee, under this subsection is reduced by any right he has under subsection (a) of this section. (1978, c. 350).

§15-2-613. Simultaneous death—Disposition of property.—Subject to extension by the provisions of section 15-2-104 and section 15-2-601 of this code, where the title to property or the devolution thereof depends upon priority of death and there is no sufficient evidence that the persons have died otherwise than simultaneously, the property of each person shall be distributed as if he had survived, except as otherwise provided in this section.

(a) Where two (2) or more beneficiaries are designated to take successively by reason of survivorship under another person's distribution of property and there is no sufficient evidence that these beneficiaries have died otherwise than simultaneously, the property thus disposed of shall be divided into as many equal portions as there are successive beneficiaries and these portions shall be distributed respectively to those who would have taken in the event that each designated beneficiary had survived.

(b) Where there is no sufficient evidence that two (2) joint tenants have died otherwise than simultaneously, the property so held shall be distributed one-half ($^1/_2$) as if one had survived and one-half ($^1/_2$) as if the other had survived. If there are more than two (2) joint tenants and all of them have so died, the property thus distributed shall be in the proportion that one bears to the whole number of joint tenants.

(c) Where the insured and the beneficiary in a policy of life or accident insurance have died and there is no sufficient evidence that they have died otherwise than simultaneously, the proceeds of the policy shall be distributed as if the insured had survived the beneficiary.

(d) This section shall not apply in the case of wills, living trusts, deeds, or contracts of insurance, wherein provision has been made for distribution of property different from the provisions of the section.

(e) This section shall be so construed and interpreted as to effectuate its general purpose to make uniform the law in those states which enact it.

(f) This section may be cited as the "uniform simultaneous death act."

§15-2-614. Effect of devise.—Every devise in any will conveys all of the estate of the devisor therein which he could lawfully devise, unless it clearly appears by the will that he intended to convey a lesser estate.

§15-2-615. Restriction on charitable devises.—(a) No estate, real or personal, shall be bequeathed or devised to any charitable or benevolent society or corporation, or to any person or persons in trust for charitable uses, except the same be done by will duly executed at least one hundred twenty (120) days before the death of the testator; and if so made at least one hundred twenty (120) days prior to such death, such devise or legacy, and each of them, shall be valid; provided, however, that the foregoing limitation shall not apply to wills of persons whose death is caused by accidental means and whose wills are executed prior to the accident which results in death.

(b) This section shall in no way limit or affect the surviving spouse's election provided by sections 15-2-201 through 15-2-207 of this code.

§15-2-616. Restriction on devises to nursing home or shelter home operators. No estate, real or personal, shall be bequeathed or devised, either directly or indirectly, to any person who owns, operates or is employed at a nursing home or shelter home, whether or not licensed, in which the testator was a resident within one (1) year of his death if the will was executed while the testator was a resident of the facility, except the same be done by will duly executed at least one (1) year before the death of the testator. This section shall apply to all property passing by testate succession after the effective date of this section regardless of when the will was written; provided, this section shall in no way limit or affect the rights of a beneficiary who is related to the testator, or who is a charitable or benevolent society or corporation; provided further that the foregoing limitations shall not apply to wills of persons whose death is caused by accidental means and whose wills are executed prior to the accident which results in death.

§15-2-801. Repealed and new section adopted as follows:

"15-2-801. Renunciation. (a) (1) A person or the representative of an incapacitated or unascertained person who is an heir, devisee, person succeeding to a renounced interest, donee, beneficiary under a testamentary or nontestamentary instrument, donee of a power of appointment, grantee, surviving joint owner or surviving joint tenant, beneficiary of an insurance contract, person designated to take pursuant to a power of appointment exercised by a testamentary or nontestamentary instrument, or otherwise the recipient of any benefit under a testamentary or nontestamentary instrument, may renounce in whole or in part, powers, future interests, specific parts, fractional shares or assets thereof by filing a written instrument within the time and at the place hereinafter provided.

(2) The instrument shall (i) describe the property or interest renounced; (ii) be signed by the person renouncing; and (iii) declare the renunciation and the extent thereof.

(3) The appropriate court may direct or permit a trustee under a testamentary or nontestamentary instrument to renounce or to deviate from any power of administration, management or allocation of benefit upon finding that exercise of such power may defeat or impair the accomplishment of the purposes of the trust whether by the imposition of tax or the allocation of beneficial interest inconsistent with such purposes. Such authority shall be exercised after hearing and upon notice to all known persons beneficially interested in such trust or estate, in the manner provided by this act.

(b) The writing specified in (a) must be filed within nine (9) months after the transfer or the death of the decedent, or donee of the power, (whichever is the later) or, if the taker of the property is not then finally ascertained, not later than nine (9) months after the event that determines that the taker of the property or interest is finally ascertained or his interest indefeasibly vested. The writing must be filed in the court of the county where proceedings concerning the decedent's estate are pending, or where they would be pending if commenced. If an interest in real estate is renounced, a copy of the writing may also be recorded in the office of the recorder in the county in which said real estate lies. A copy of the writing also shall be delivered in person or mailed by registered or certified mail to the personal representative of the decedent, the trustee of any trust in which the interest renounced exists, and no such personal representative, trustee, or person shall be liable for any otherwise proper distribution or other disposition made without actual notice of the renunciation.

(c) Unless the decedent or donee of the power has otherwise indicated, the property or interest renounced passes as if the person renouncing had predeceased the decedent, or if the person renouncing is designated to take under a power of appointment as if the person renouncing had predeceased the donee of the power. A future interest that takes effect in possession or enjoyment after the termination of the estate or interest renounced takes effect as if the person renouncing had predeceased the decedent or the donee of the power. In every case the renunciation relates back for all purposes to the date of death of the decedent or the donee, as the case may be.

(d) The right to renounce property or an interest therein is barred by: (1) assignment, conveyance, encumbrance, pledge or transfer of property therein or any contract therefor; (2) written waiver of the right to renounce; or (3) sale or other disposition of property pursuant to judicial process, made before the renunciation is effective.

(e) The right to renounce granted by this section exists irrespective of any limitation on the interest of the person renouncing in the nature of a spendthrift provision or similar restriction.

(f) The renunciation or the written waiver of the right to renounce is binding upon the person renouncing or person waiving and all persons claiming through or under him.

(g) This section does not abridge the right of any person to assign, convey, release, or renounce any property or an interest therein arising under any other statute.

(h) An interest in property existing on the effective date of this act as to which, if a present interest, the time for filing a renunciation has not expired, or, if a future interest, the interest has not become indefeasibly vested or the taker finally ascertained may be renounced within nine (9) months after the effective date of this act.

§15-2-803. Not adopted. Substituted therefor are provisions defining a slayer; prohibiting such from acquiring property from person whose life was taken by slayer; and directing that decedent's property pass as though slayer predeceased decedent.

§15-2-901. Not adopted.

§15-3-101. After words "testamentary disposition," delete words "to his heirs" and add "to the surviving spouse."

§15-3-105. Delete last sentence of section.

§15-3-106. New section: "15-3-106. Civil litigation—Notice.—Subject to general rules concerning the proper location of civil litigation and jurisdiction of persons, the court may herein determine any other controversy concerning a succession or to which an estate, through a personal representative, may be a party. Persons notified are bound though less than all interested persons may have been given notice."

§15-3-111. New Section: "15-3-111. Joint probate on death of survivor of marriage dissolved by death.—In cases in which a marital community has been dissolved by the

---

See note at head of Digest as to 1998 legislation covered.

See Topical Index in front part of this volume.

WILLS . . . *continued*
death of either spouse at any time, the survivor was then entitled to all of the property of the decedent by will, law, or both, and the survivor died before any proceeding had been commenced for the probate of the estate of the spouse whose death occurred first, the estates of both decedents may be joined for probate in a single proceeding in any court having jurisdiction of the estate of the spouse whose death occurred last. The initial application or petition filed in any such joint proceeding shall contain a statement of the facts upon which such joint proceeding is based, in addition to all other statements required by this code to be made therein."

§15-3-203. Add (7) to subsection (a), "(7) if a petition for appointment of a personal representative has been filed and sixty (60) days have elapsed during which no consent to act has been filed by any proper person, the public administrator shall act as personal representative unless and until a proper person consents to act." In subsection (f), change 21 to 18. Add subsection (i) as follows: "(i) A married woman shall have the right to serve as personal representative."

§15-3-301. In first paragraph, after words "informal probate" add ", informal statement of intestacy where the estate is community and there is a surviving spouse,". Substitute "a" for "1", "b" for "2", etc. In (a) after words "of a will" add "informal statement of intestacy where the estate is community and there is a surviving spouse,". Add to (a) "(6) a statement that an estimate of total assets of the estate has been sent to the state tax commission;". Add to (a) "(7) If the application is for an informal statement of intestacy of a community estate where there is a surviving spouse, an affidavit of the surviving spouse or someone acting on behalf of the surviving spouse that there is no will, that the decedent's estate consists solely of community property of the decedent and surviving spouse, that he or she is the surviving spouse, and a request for a statement that there is no will, that all assets are community and that the surviving spouse is the sole heir;". Add to (a) "(8) that the time limit for informal probate or appointment as provided in this article has not expired either because three (3) years or less have passed since the decedent's death, or, if more than three (3) years from death have passed, that the circumstances as described by section 15-3-108 of this code authorizing tardy probate appointment have occurred." (1978, c. 350). Delete (4) of subsection (b). Add new subsection (g) as follows: "(g) By verifying an application for informal probate, or informal appointment, the applicant submits personally to the jurisdiction of the court in any proceeding for relief from fraud relating to the application, or for perjury, that may be instituted against him." Add new subsection (h) as follows: "(h) Any statement entered upon an application for informal statement of intestacy where the estate is community and there is a surviving spouse shall contain a statement of heirship setting out the heirs of the decedent and shall have the same effect as entry of a statement of informal probate of a will and be subject to the limitation periods set out in section 15-3-108, Idaho Code, notwithstanding the exception provided in that section for determining heirs of an intestate."

§15-3-303. After words "probate of a will" in subsection (a), add "or informal statement of intestacy where the estate is community and there is a surviving spouse." Add (8) to subsection (a) as follows: "(8) if the application is for a statement of intestacy of a community estate with a surviving spouse, on the basis of statements in the application and affidavit: 1. the decedent left no will, 2. the decedent's estate consists solely of community property of the decedent and the surviving spouse, and 3. the decedent left a surviving spouse. In addition to this, the registrar shall set out the name of the surviving spouse."

§15-3-303A. New section: "15-3-303A. Notice required.—Upon issuance of a statement of informal probate if no letters are issued to a personal representative or determination of heirship of community property, the applicant must give notice to all heirs and devisees of the admission of the will to probate or the determination of heirship of community property. This information shall be sent by ordinary mail to each of the heirs and devisees whose address is reasonably available to the applicant. The applicant shall be responsible to any heir or devisee damaged by failure of the applicant to give proper notice under this section."

§15-3-401. Add a new paragraph at the end of section as follows: "By submitting a petition for formal probate the petitioner subjects himself to jurisdiction of the court in which such instrument is filed. Any action by a person damaged by him, including a creditor of the estate, shall be limited in amount to the assets of the estate less the obligations of the estate paid by him. Notice of any proceedings sought to be maintained against the petitioner pursuant to his submission to jurisdiction shall be delivered to him or mailed to him by ordinary first class mail at his address as it is known to the petitioner, or is listed on any application or petition in probate proceedings previously instituted in the court where the proceeding is brought."

§15-3-409. Add new sentence to end of section as follows. "When a lost will is established, the provisions thereof must be found by the court and the findings filed and recorded as other wills are filed and recorded."

§15-3-412. Substitute "a" for "1", "b" for "2", etc.

§15-3-601. After first sentence add "In his statement of acceptance, the personal representative shall subscribe an oath to the effect that he will perform the duties of his office according to the law."

§15-3-603. After last sentence add, "No bond will be required of any domestic bank or trust company."

§15-3-607. Add new subsection:

"(c). If any person is suspected of having concealed, embezzled, or smuggled, laid away or disposed of any money, goods, or chattels of the decedent or to have in his possession or subject to his knowledge, any deeds, conveyances, bonds, contracts, or other writings, or any personal estate, or any other claim or demand or any last will of the decedent, such person may be ordered to appear, examined on oath and held to account upon such matters.

§15-3-706. After words "inventory to" in second paragraph, add "heirs, devisees, the state tax commission, and to".

§15-3-708. After words "was filed" delete rest of language and add ", or send copies thereof to the state tax commission and to all interested persons to whom copies of the original inventory were sent pursuant to §15-3-706."

§15-3-710. After last sentence add: "The personal representative is not required to institute such an action unless requested by creditors who must pay or secure the cost and expenses of litigation."

§15-3-714. After words "Section 3-504" add ", and without regard to the constructive notice provisions of §15-1-305(A) of this Code,".

§15-3-715(3). Delete first sentence and substitute: "Exercise the same power as the decedent in performance, compromise or refusal to perform the decedent's contracts which continue as obligations of the decedent's estate."

§15-3-717. After words "concurrence of" add "a majority" and delete word "all."

§15-3-801. Add: "(b) A personal representative may give written notice by mail or other delivery to any creditor, notifying the creditor to present his claim within four (4) months after the published notice if given as provided in subsection (a) of this section or within sixty (60) days after the mailing or delivery of the notice, whichever is later, or be forever barred. Written notice must be the notice described in subsection (a) of this section or a similar notice.

(c) The personal representative is not liable to any creditor or to any successor of the decedent for giving or failing to give notice under this section.

§15-3-802(b). Changed as follows: "The running of statute of limitations measured from an event other than death or the giving of notice to creditors is suspended during the four (4) months following the decedent's death but resumes thereafter as to claims not barred pursuant to the sections which follow."

§15-3-803. "LIMITATIONS ON PRESENTATION OF CLAIMS. (a) All claims against a decedent's estate which arose before the death of the decedent, including claims of the state and any subdivision thereof, whether due or to become due, absolute or contingent, liquidated or unliquidated, founded on contract, tort, or other legal basis, if not barred earlier by another statute of limitations or nonclaim statute, are barred against the estate, the personal representative, and the heirs and devisees of the decedent, unless presented within the earlier of the following dates:

(1) two (2) years after the decedent's death; or

(2) within the time provided in section 15-3-801(b), Idaho Code, for creditors who are given actual notice, and within the time provided in section 15-3-801(a), Idaho Code, for all creditors barred by publication.

(b) All claims described in subsection (a) of this section barred by the nonclaim statute of the decedent's domicile before the giving of notice to creditors in this state are also barred in this state.

(c) All claims against a decedent's estate which arise at or after the death of the decedent, including claims of the state and any subdivision thereof, whether due or to become due, absolute or contingent, liquidated or unliquidated, founded on contract, tort, or other legal basis, are barred against the estate, the personal representative, and the heirs and devisees of the decedent, unless presented as follows:

(1) a claim based on a contract with the personal representative, within four (4) months after performance by the personal representative is due;

(2) any other claim, within the later of four (4) months after it arises, or the time specified in subsection (a)(1) of this section.

(d) Nothing in this section affects or prevents:

(1) any proceeding to enforce any mortgage, pledge, or other lien upon property of the estate;

(2) to the limits of the insurance protection only, any proceeding to establish liability of the decedent or the personal representative for which he is protected by liability insurance; or

(3) collection of compensation for services rendered and reimbursement for expenses advanced by the personal representative or by the attorney or accountant for the personal representative of the estate."

§15-3-804(a). Delete "may" and insert "shall" and delete "or may" and insert "and" in first sentence.

§15-3-805(2). Delete after "funeral expenses" remainder of subsection.

(3). Delete after "federal law" remainder of subsection. (4). Delete "all other claims" and substitute, "reasonable and necessary medical and hospital expenses of the last illness of the decedent, including compensation of persons attending him:" Add: "(5) Debts and taxes with preference under other laws of this state; (6) All other claims."

§15-807(a). Changed as follows: "PAYMENT OF CLAIMS. Upon the expiration of the earlier of the time limitations provided in section 15-3-803, Idaho Code, for the presentation of claims, the personal representative shall proceed to pay the claims allowed against the estate in the order of priority prescribed, after making provision for homestead, family and support allowances, for claims already presented that have not yet been allowed or whose allowance has been appealed, and for unbarred claims that may yet be presented, included costs and expenses of administration. By petition to the court in a proceeding for the purpose, or by appropriate motion if the administration is supervised, a claimant whose claim has been duly allowed but not paid may secure an order directing the personal representative to pay the claim to the extent funds of the estate are available to pay it."

§15-3-809. Substitute "a" for "1" and "b" for "2".

Add new section:

"§15-3-817. Community estates.—If a community estate is administered as if each decedent survived the other because of application of the simultaneous death act, section 15-2-104 and section 15-2-601 of this code, or the provisions of a will, community debts will be charged ratably to each half of the community estate and separate debts to the estate of the decedent by whom they were incurred."

§15-3-902(c). Designated "(d)".

Add new section (c):

"If an estate of a decedent consists partly of separate property and partly of community property, community debts shall be charged to community property and separate debts to separate property. Expenses of administration shall be apportioned and charged against the different kinds of property in proportion to the relative value thereof, except that none of such expenses shall be apportioned or charged to the survivor's share of the community property."

§15-3-906. Substitute "A" for "i", "B" for "ii", and "C" for "iii".

Add new section as follows:

See note at head of Digest as to 1998 legislation covered.

See Topical Index in front part of this volume.

WILLS . . . *continued*

"§15-3-907A. Deceased beneficiary as heir.—(a) If the decedent has left a surviving child or children or issue of children among the persons who are by law entitled to succeed to his estate, and any of them, before the close of administration, has died before reaching the age of eighteen (18) and not having married, no administration of such deceased issue's estate is necessary, but all the estate which such deceased issue is entitled to receive by inheritance must, without administration, be distributed to the heirs at law of the deceased issue.

"(b) If any other heir, legatee, or devisee shall die after the decedent's death and before distribution, property to which he might be entitled shall be distributed to the representative of his estate or directly to his heirs, legatees or devisees or the persons entitled thereto."

§15-3-914. After words "missing person" delete remainder of section and substitute, "to his trustee if one has been appointed; or, if no trustee has been appointed, shall file the report of abandoned property required by section 14-517, Idaho Code, and proceed to dispose of the property in the manner set forth in the 'unclaimed property act', provided, however, that in the event no person appears to claim such property within eighteen hundred and twenty seven (1827) days (approximately five [5] years) of the time such moneys or property is deposited with the state tax commission, the moneys or property so deposited shall accrue and be set over to the state building fund." Delete subsection (b).

§15-3-916(a)(1). Delete after "estate tax;" remainder of sentence. (5). After "estate tax" delete "and the additional inheritance tax imposed by . . . . ".

§15-3-1003(a)(1). Replace with: "(1) determined that the time limitation for presentation of creditors' claims has expired."

§15-3-1004. After words "claimants for amounts" add words "received as exempt property, homestead or family allowances, or for amounts".

§15-3-1006. After words "time of distribution thereof" add ", except if the claim is by a creditor of the decedent, it is forever barred two (2) years after the decedent's death."

Add new section:

"§15-3-1009. Decree of distribution to attorney general.—Whenever any estate involves, or may involve a charitable trust, the court shall at the time of distribution of said estate forward to the attorney general of the state of Idaho a certified copy of said decree of distribution of the estate which involves or may involve said charitable trust."

§15-3-1102. Substitute "a" for "1", "b" for "2", and "c" for "3".

Add new section:

"§15-3-1205. Summary administration of estates in which a surviving spouse is the sole beneficiary.—(a) Upon the testate or intestate death of a person leaving a surviving spouse as the sole devisee or beneficiary, the surviving spouse (or any person claiming title to any property through or under such surviving spouse) may file a verified petition setting out marriage and the death of a person leaving a surviving spouse as the sole devisee or heir. If the decedent died testate, the petition must be accompanied by the original of the last will and testament of the decedent. Notice of hearing shall be given pursuant to the provisions of section 15-1-401, Idaho Code.

"(b) If it shall appear at such hearing that the decedent and the person claimed to be the surviving spouse were duly married and that the surviving spouse is the sole heir or devisee, a decree shall be made to that effect. This decree shall thereafter have the same effect as a formal decree approving or determining distribution.

"(c) In the event that the surviving spouse (or person claiming through or under the surviving spouse) shall elect to proceed under this section, the surviving spouse shall assume and be liable for any and all indebtedness that might be a claim against the estate of the decedent and there will be no administration of the estate of the decedent."

§15-4-101. Substitute "a" for "1", "b" for "2", and "c" for "3".

§15-4-201. Substitute "a" for "1", "b" for "2", and "c" for "3".

§15-4-301. Substitute "a" for "1", "b" for "2", and "c" for "3".

Living Wills.—Person at least 18 years of age and of sound mind may issue directive in form of living will or durable power of attorney to attending physician to withdraw artificial life sustaining procedures or equipment. (39-4501 to 39-4509).

Simultaneous Death.—See topic Death.

Testamentary Guardian.—See category Family, topic Guardian and Ward.

Testamentary Trusts.—See topic Trusts.

Uniform Anatomical Gift Act adopted. (39-3401 to 39-3411).

FAMILY

ADOPTION:

Interstate compact on adoption and medical assistance enacted Mar. 7, 1994. (39-7501).

Any minor child may be adopted by any adult residing in and having residence in Idaho, and who is either 15 years older than child or who is 25 years of age or older; spouse of natural parent may adopt without above age restriction. (16-1501 and 16-1502). Persons not minors may be adopted by resident adult where person adopting has had relationship as parent for over one year. (16-1501 and 16-1502). No married person can adopt without consent of spouse. (16-1503).

Consent Required.—Consent of parents, if living, is necessary. Father of illegitimate child may assert parental rights by registering notice with vital statistics unit; failure to register and assume responsibilities prima facie abandonment. In adoption action putative father must be notified of need to register. (16-1513). If guardian legally appointed, his consent required. If no guardian or living parents, then nearest relative; if none, then appointee of court to act as next friend of child. No consent necessary of any person whose relationship terminated or custody removed by proceeding under 16-1601 to 16-1629 and 16-2001 to 16-2015, for abandonment or abuse of child, or from like proceedings by court of competent jurisdiction in other states. (16-1504). If voluntary child placement agency licensed by state in which it does business is authorized to place child for adoption and to give consent to adoption under laws of such state, such consent when given in adoption proceeding within this state is sufficient. (16-1504). Consent of parent who is minor not voidable because of minority. (16-1504). Consent of child, if over age of 12, is necessary. (16-1505).

Jurisdiction and Venue.—District court of the county where the person adopting resides. (16-1506). Person adopting must reside and maintain dwelling within Idaho for six consecutive months prior to initiating proceedings. (16-1506).

Proceedings.—Commenced by filing petition together with copy thereof, initiated by person proposing to adopt, in district court of county in which person adopting resides and has residence. Petition must include name and address of petitioner, name of child to be adopted and name by which it will be known if adopted, degree of relationship of child, if any, names of any person or agency whose consent to adoption is necessary, and information as to alleged date and place of birth and parentage of child, along with source of all information. (16-1506). Person adopting and child adopted, and spouse of adopting parent, if natural parent must appear; necessary consent is signed, and agreement executed by person adopting to effect that child shall be adopted and treated as his own lawful child should be treated. Any person required to consent shall execute consent in writing and shall acknowledge before officer authorized to acknowledge deeds. Acknowledged, written consent filed in court where application made shall be sufficient appearance for such person. Proceedings for termination of parent relation or custody and proceeding for adoption may be consolidated if compliance with 16-1501 to 16-1512 and 16-2001 to 16-2015. (16-1506, 16-1513). If petition is by person unrelated to child or unmarried to natural parent of child, and at discretion of court upon filing of any other petition for adoption, copy of petition with statement of full names and permanent address of child and petitioners, shall be served by court, within five days, on Director of Department of Health and Welfare. (16-1506). If adopting parent is member of armed forces and unable to attend, deposition constitutes appearance and testimony. (16-1506).

Director must verify allegations of petition and make thorough investigation within 30 days and report to court. Department of Health & Welfare may require petitioner to pay all or part of costs of investigation. If report disapproves of adoption, motion may be made to court to dismiss petition. (16-1506). But father may adopt his illegitimate child by public acknowledgment and receiving it into his family with consent of his wife and thereupon child is deemed legitimate from time of its birth. (16-1510). Father of illegitimate child may assert parental rights by registering notice with vital statistics unit. (16-1513). This provision is deemed enlargement not limitation of rights of illegitimate child. (16-1510). Records of proceedings may be sealed by motion of petitioner or court, to be broken only upon motion of petitioner or person adopted. (16-1511).

Order.—Court makes order declaring the child shall thenceforth be regarded and treated in all respects as child of person adopting. (16-1507). If adopted person is foreign born, court makes finding of facts as to probable date and place of birth and parentage. (16-1507).

Name.—Adopted child may take name of person adopting. (16-1508).

Appeal.—To district court from order granting or refusing adoption or from any other intermediate order within 30 days. (16-1512).

Effect of Adoption.—Person adopting and adopted child sustain legal relation of parent and child with all its rights and duties. (16-1508). Natural parents of adopted child are relieved of all parental duties and responsibilities; rights of child through natural parent terminated except such parent may provide for adopted child by will. (16-1509). Adopted child inherits from adopted parents and has all rights of child of whole blood to inherit from any person. (16-1508).

Access to Adoption Records.—Adopted persons older than 18, natural birthparents, birth siblings, or relatives of deceased birthparents or adult adoptees may register with vital statistics unit and upon match limited disclosure of original birth record will be made. (39-259A). Paternity decrees and lists of adoptees who have consented to release of records are confidential. (39-257, 39-259A, 39-270).

ALIMONY:

See topic Divorce.

COMMUNITY PROPERTY:

See topic Husband and Wife.

DESERTION:

See topics Divorce, Husband and Wife.

DISSOLUTION OF MARRIAGE:

See topic Divorce.

DIVORCE:

Grounds for divorce are: (1) Adultery; (2) extreme cruelty; (3) wilful desertion; (4) wilful neglect; (5) habitual intemperance; (6) conviction of felony; (7) permanent insanity, provided insane spouse has been confined in an insane asylum in any state or foreign country for at least three years prior to commencement of action and it appears to the court that such insanity is permanent (32-603 to 32-608; 32-801 to 32-805); (8) that parties have continuously lived separate and apart without cohabitation for five years or more (32-610; 69 Idaho 513, 210 P.2d 934; 76 Idaho 95, 278 P.2d 200; 89 Idaho 834, 403 P.2d 593); (9) irreconcilable differences, being determined by court as substantial reasons to dissolve marriage (32-603[8]; 32-616).

Grounds for legal separation are not recited but suit may be maintained for separate maintenance under §32-901. (32-901; 33 Idaho 255, 193 P. 386; 49 Idaho 468, 289 P. 86; 61 Idaho 261, 100 P.2d 955).

Residence Requirements.—Plaintiff must have been a resident of the state for six full weeks before commencement of the action. (32-701).

See note at head of Digest as to 1998 legislation covered.

See Topical Index in front part of this volume.

DIVORCE . . . *continued*

Jurisdiction.—Submitted to by maintenance of matrimonial domicile within state when conduct in state gives rise to cause of action for divorce or separate maintenance. (5-514).

Permanent maintenance may be allowed for either spouse. (32-705).

I.C.A. §32-909, declaring earnings from wife's separate property after separation not to be community is unconstitutional inasmuch as husband's earnings from separate property after separation were community property and this statute denies equal protection. (97 Idaho 461, 546 P.2d 1169).

Caveat: Orr v. Orr held Alabama statutory scheme providing husbands, but not wives, may be required to pay alimony upon divorce, violative of equal protection. (440 U.S. 268, 59 L.Ed.2d 306, 99 S.Ct. 1102).

Final decree is entered immediately upon determination of issues; no interlocutory decree.

Temporary maintenance may be ordered by Court in amounts and on terms just and proper under circumstances.

Allowance for prosecution of suit may be ordered by Court after consideration of financial resources of both parties and other relevant factors.

Division of Property of Spouses.—See subhead Division of Community Property, infra.

Military Retirement Benefits.—New section added, 32-713A to allow modification of any community property settlement, judgment or decree that became final between June 25, 1981, and Feb. 1, 1983, to include division of military retirement benefits. Remains effective only until July 1, 1988.

Custody of children subject to control of court, both during suit and thereafter, and either spouse may be required to pay for their support and education, payment to be made to clerk of court. (32-717; 32-717B; 32-706). All child support decrees shall contain provision to collect arrearages by income withholding, obligor's social security number, statutory notice of right. (32-1205). See category Civil Actions and Procedure, topic Process, subhead Child Support Matters.

Uniform Child Custody Jurisdiction Act adopted. (32-1101 to 1126).

Uniform Interstate Family Support Act adopted. (7-1001 to 7-1052) Amended 1997. (c. 198, 1997).

Child Support.—Court may require assignment of wages to clerk in decree for child support. (8-704). Provision made for collection without notice of child support via continuing income withholding. (32-1201 to 32-1214). Forms for income withholding order. (32-1207). Provisions for enforcement of orders requiring health insurance for dependant children. (32-1216). Action to collect child support arrearages must be commenced within five years of date child reaches majority or date child dies, whichever occurs first. (5-245). Child support guidelines adopted by Idaho Supreme Court are given presumptive effect. (32-706A). See also subhead Custody of Children, supra.

Division of Community Property.—In case of divorce court divides community property as may be just. (32-712). Agreements to pass property at death of surviving spouse are revoked by divorce. (15-6-201[c]). See also subhead Military Retirement Benefits, supra.

Reconciliation.—Upon application of one party, court may require conference, and if there are minor children, may stay proceedings for 90 days to determine practicability of reconciliation. (32-716).

Remarriage.—No restriction on remarriage after divorce.

Annulment of Marriage.—See topic Marriage.

GUARDIAN AND WARD:

Uniform Probate Code adopted, effective July 1, 1972. (15-1-101 to 15-7-401; §§1, 2, 3, and 4). Code is given Idaho Code Annotated Title Number 15, and section numbers contain said title citation followed by numerical part of Uniform Probate Code Citation, e.g., 15-1-101. 1975 and 1977 Amendments not adopted. 1979 Amendments adopted.

Material Variations from Official Text are:

§15-5-101. Substitute "a" for "1", "b" for "2", "c" for "3", and "d" for "4". In subsection (a) delete "advanced age," and delete ";" and add ", provided, that the term shall not refer to a developmentally disabled person as defined in section 66-402(4), Idaho Code, and provided further that (1) 'Incapacity' means a legal, not a medical disability and shall be measured by function limitations and it shall be construed to mean or refer to any person who has suffered, is suffering, or is likely to suffer, substantial harm due to an inability to provide for his personal needs for food, clothing, shelter, health care, or safety, or an inability to manage his or her property or financial affairs;

(2) Inability to provide for personal needs or to manage property shall be evidenced by acts or occurrences, or statements which strongly indicate imminent acts or occurrences; material evidence of inability must have occurred within twelve (12) months prior to the filing of the petition for guardianship or conservatorship;

(3) Isolated instances of simple negligence or improvidence, lack of resources, or any act, occurrence, or statement, if that act, occurrence, or statement is the product of an informed judgment, shall not constitute evidence of inability to provide for personal needs or to manage property;

(4) 'Informed judgment' means a choice made by a person who has the ability to make such a choice, and who makes it voluntarily after all relevant information necessary to making the decision has been provided, and who understands that he is free to choose or refuse any alternative available and who clearly indicates or expresses the outcome of his choice;".

§15-5-102. Delete subsection (a).

§15-5-103. Amount payable by person under duty to pay or deliver money or personal property to minor is $10,000 per annum.

§15-5-104. Changed as follows: "A parent or a guardian of a minor or incapacitated person, by a properly executed power of attorney, may delegate to another person, for a period not exceeding six (6) months, or in the case of military personnel serving beyond

the territorial limits of the United States for a period not exceeding twelve (12) months, any of his powers regarding care, custody, or property of the minor child or ward, except his power to consent to marriage or adoption of a minor ward."

Add new sections:

"§15-5-105. Evidence in proceedings involving veteran's benefits.—If benefits derived from the United States through the veteran's administration are involved in any proceeding under this chapter, a certificate of the administrator or his authorized representative shall be prima facie evidence of the necessity of appointment of a guardian or conservator or both if:

(a) It sets forth the age of the minor involved in the proceeding as shown by the records of the veterans administration and the fact that appointment is a condition precedent to payment of any moneys:

(b) It sets forth the fact that a purportedly incapacitated person involved in the proceeding has been rated incompetent by the veterans administration upon examination pursuant to the laws governing such administration and that appointment of a guardian is a condition precedent to payment of any moneys due such incapacitated person.

"§15-5-106. Copies of public records to be furnished.—When a copy of any public record is required by the veterans administration to be used in determining the eligibility of any persons to participate in benefits made available by the veterans administration, the official custodian of such public records shall without charge provide the applicant for such benefits or any person acting on his behalf or the authorized representative of the veterans administration with a certified copy of such record.

"§15-5-107. Wrongful appropriation.—Upon the petition of anyone interested in the welfare of the ward, anyone suspected of having concealed, embezzled or conveyed away any of the moneys, goods or effects belonging to the ward or his estate may be ordered by the court to appear and be examined on oath and held to account upon such matters and for such property."

§15-5-202. Add after last sentence: "Written notice of acceptance of the appointment must be given by the guardian to the minor and to the person having his care or to his nearest adult relative immediately upon acceptance of appointment."

§15-5-207. Prior to (a), insert: "Proceedings for the appointment of a guardian may be initiated by any relative of the minor, the minor if he is fourteen (14) years of age, or any person interested in the welfare of the minor."

Add new subsection:

"(e) Letters of guardianship must indicate whether the guardian was appointed by will or by court order."

§15-5-208. Delete last sentence.

§15-5-303. Alter section to read: "Procedure for court appointment of guardian of an incapacitated person.—(a) The incapacitated person or any person interested in his welfare may petition for a finding of incapacity and appointment of a guardian, limited or general.

(b) Upon the filing of a petition, the court shall set a date for hearing on the issues of incapacity and unless the allegedly incapacitated person has counsel of his own choice, it shall appoint an attorney to represent him in the proceeding, who shall have the powers and duties of a guardian ad litem. The person alleged to be incapacitated shall be examined by a physician or other qualified person appointed by the court who shall submit his report in writing to the court. The person alleged to be incapacitated also shall be interviewed by a visitor sent by the court. The visitor shall also interview the person who appears to have caused the petition to be filed and any person who is nominated to serve as guardian, and visit the present place of abode of the person alleged to be incapacitated and the place it is proposed that he will be detained or reside if the requested appointment is made and submit his report in writing to the court. Where possible without undue delay and expenses beyond the ability to pay of the allegedly incapacitated person, the court, in formulating the judgment, may utilize the service of any public or charitable agency that offers or is willing to evaluate the condition of the allegedly incapacitated person and make recommendations to the court regarding the most appropriate form of state intervention in his affairs.

(c) The person alleged to be incapacitated is entitled to be present at the hearing in person, and to see or hear all evidence bearing upon his condition. He is entitled to be present by counsel, to present evidence, to cross-examine witnesses, including the court-appointed physician or other qualified person and the visitor. The issue may be determined at a closed hearing if the person alleged to be incapacitated or his counsel so requests."

§15-5-304. Alter section to read: "Findings—Order of Appointment.—(a) The court shall exercise the authority conferred in this part so as to encourage the development of maximum self-reliance and independence of the incapacitated person and make appointive and other orders only to the extent necessitated by the incapacitated person's actual mental and adaptive limitations or other conditions warranting the procedure.

(b) The court may appoint a guardian as requested if it is satisfied that the person for whom a guardian is sought is incapacitated and that the appointment is necessary or desirable as a means of providing continuing care and supervision of the person of the incapacitated person. The court, on appropriate findings may

(1) Treat the petition as one for a protective order under section 15-5-401, Idaho Code, and proceed accordingly;

(2) Enter any other appropriate order; or

(3) Dismiss the proceedings.

(c) The court may, at the time of appointment or later, on its own motion or on appropriate petition or motion of the incapacitated person or other interested person, limit the powers of a guardian otherwise conferred by this section and thereby create a limited guardianship. Any limitations on the statutory power of a guardian of an incapacitated person shall be endorsed on the guardian's letters, or in the case of a guardian by testamentary appointment, shall be reflected in letters that shall be issued at the time any limitation is imposed. Following the same procedure, a limitation may be removed and appropriate letters issued."

§15-5-306. Add new sentence to end of section: "Termination does not affect his liability for prior acts nor his obligation to account for funds and assets of his ward."

§15-5-307. Add new subsection:

"(d) Upon request, a jury may be summoned to hear factual issues as in other civil cases.

See note at head of Digest as to 1998 legislation covered.

See Topical Index in front part of this volume.

GUARDIAN AND WARD . . . *continued*

§15-5-308. After words "social work" add "or has other qualifications that make him suitable to perform the function". Add new section: "(2) Any person appointed as a visitor shall be personally immune from any liability for acts, omissions or errors in the same manner as if such person were a volunteer or director under the provisions of section 6-1605, Idaho Code."

§15-5-309. Alter section to read: "Notices in guardianship proceedings.—(a) In a proceeding for the appointment or removal of a guardian of an incapacitated person and, if notice is required in a proceeding for appointment of a temporary guardian, notice of hearing shall be given to each of the following:

(1) the ward or the person alleged to be incapacitated and his spouse, or, if none, his adult children or if none, his parents;

(2) any person who is serving as his guardian, conservator or who has his care and custody;

(3) in case no other person is notified under subsection (a)(1) of this section, at least one (1) of his closest adult relatives, if any can be found; and

(4) any person who has filed a request for notice under this section.

(b) Notice shall be served personally on the alleged incapacitated person. Notices to other persons as required by this section shall be served personally if the person to be notified can be found within the state. In all other cases, required notices shall be given as provided in section 15-1-401 of this code. Waiver of notice by the person alleged to be incapacitated is not effective unless he attends the hearing or his waiver of notice is confirmed in an interview with the visitor. Representation of the alleged incapacitated person by a guardian ad litem is not necessary.

(c) Any person desiring notice of any order or filing in a proceeding involving an alleged incapacitated person in whom he is interested may file a request for notice with the court stating his name, the name of the incapacitated person, the nature of the requesting person's interest, and address or that of his attorney. Upon payment of any fee required by statute or court rule, the clerk shall mail a copy of the request to the guardian if one has been appointed or to the petitioner if there is no guardian. A request is effective only as to matters occurring after its filing. Any governmental agency paying or planning to pay benefits to the alleged incapacitated person, or any public or charitable agency that regularly concerns itself with methods for preventing unnecessary and overly-intrusive court intervention in the affairs of persons for whom guardians may be sought and that seeks to participate in the proceedings, is an interested person in a guardianship proceeding."

§15-5-310. Alter section to read: "Temporary guardians.—(a) If an incapacitated person has no guardian, an emergency exists, and no other person appears to have authority to act in the circumstances, the court may exercise the power of a general guardian pending notice and hearing on the petition.

(b) If an appointed guardian is not effectively performing his duties and the court further finds that the welfare of the incapacitated person requires immediate action, it may, with or without notice, appoint a temporary guardian for the incapacitated person having the powers specified in the order for a specified period not to exceed six (6) months. The authority of any permanent guardian previously appointed by the court is suspended so long as a temporary guardian has authority. A temporary guardian may be removed at any time. A temporary guardian shall make any report the court requires. In other respects the provisions of this code concerning guardians apply to temporary guardians."

§15-5-312. Alter first two sentences of subsection (a) to read: "A guardian of an incapacitated person has the powers and responsibilities of a parent who has not been deprived of custody of his unemancipated minor child except that a guardian is not legally obligated to provide from his own funds for the ward and is not liable to third persons for acts of the ward. In particular, and without qualifying the foregoing, a guardian has the following powers and duties, except as modified by order of the court when the guardianship is limited:". In subsection (a)(4) substitute "(A)" for "(i)" and "(B)" for "(ii)". Alter subsection (a)(5) to read: "A guardian shall be required to report as provided in section 15-5-419, Idaho Code." Add new subsection: "(c) A guardian may delegate certain of his responsibilities for decisions affecting the ward's well-being to the ward when reasonable under all of the circumstances."

§15-5-313. At end of subsection (a) delete "." and add ", including proceedings to limit the authority previously conferred on a guardian, or to remove limitations previously imposed." After word "resignation" in subsection (b) add ", altering his authority".

§15-5-401. Substitute "a" for "1" and "b" for "2". Delete from subsection (b)(1) term "advanced age,".

§15-5-402. Substitute "a" for "1", "b" for "2", and "c" for "3".

§15-5-403. Substitute "a" for "1" and "b" for "2".

§15-5-406. Alter section to read: "Protective proceedings—Request for notice—Interested person.—Any person desiring notice of any order or filing in a protective proceeding described in this part involving a person in whom he is interested may file a request for notice with the court stating his name, the name of the alleged disabled person, the nature of the requesting person's interest, and his address or that of his attorney. Upon payment of any fee required by statute or court rule, the clerk shall mail a copy of the request to the conservator if one has been appointed, or to the petitioner if there is no conservator. A request is effective only as to matters occurring after its filing. Any governmental agency paying or planning to pay benefits to the alleged disabled person, and any public or charitable agency that regularly concerns itself with methods for preventing unnecessary or overly-intrusive court intervention in the affairs of persons for whom protective orders may be sought and that seeks to participate in the proceedings, is an interested person in a protective proceeding under this part."

§15-5-407. In Subsection (c), change word "for" to "of". Delete word "protective" after word "appropriate."

§15-5-408. Alter section to read: "Permissible court orders.—(a) The court shall exercise the authority conferred in the part so as to encourage the development of maximum self-reliance and independence of the protected person and make protective orders only to the extent necessitated by the protected person's actual mental and adaptive limitations and other conditions warranting the procedure.

(b) The court has the following powers which may be exercised directly or through a conservator in respect to the estate and affairs of protected persons:". Subsections 1 through 5 remain the same.

Add new section:

"§15-5-409a. Compromise of disputed claim of minor—Procedure.—When a minor shall have a disputed claim for money against a third person, the father or mother or both with whom the minor resides and who has the care and custody of such minor shall have the right to compromise such claim, but before the compromise shall be valid or of any effect the same shall be approved by the court of the county where the minor resides upon a verified petition in writing, regularly filed with said court. If the court approves such compromise he may direct the money paid to the father or mother of said minor subject to the provisions of section 15-5-103, Idaho Code, or he, or any other court of competent jurisdiction, may direct the money be paid subject to the provisions of an appropriate protective order which he, or any other court of competent jurisdiction, may issue, or he may require that the money be paid to a conservator appointed pursuant to chapter 5, part 4, of this code. No filing fee shall be charged for the filing of any petition for leave to compromise as provided herein."

§15-5-410. Subsection (1) is (4) with the following words inserted after "fiduciary", "(but not a fiduciary serving only as a trustee)"; Subsection (2) is (1); (3) is (2); (4) is (3). In subsection (b) delete "1" and substitute "2".

§15-5-419. Add in front of first sentence: "Every conservator or guardian shall submit a written annual report to the court concerning the status of the ward and of the ward's estate that has been under the guardian's or conservator's control. The guardian or conservator shall also be required to provide copies of the report to all persons listed by the court as having an interest in receiving copies of the report. The court may order more frequent reports by its own ruling or pursuant to a petition of any person interested in the ward's welfare." Change "to the court for his administration of the trust" to "annually, or as otherwise directed by the court, and". Delete ", and at other times as the court may direct." Change "may" to "shall" and change "or he may" to "and shall".

§15-5-420. Alter section to read: "Conservators—Title by appointment.—(a) The appointment of a conservator vests in him title as trustee to all property of the protected person, presently held or thereafter acquired, including title to any property theretofore held for the protected person by custodians or attorneys in fact, or to the part thereof specified in the order. An order specifying that only a part of the property of the protected person vests in the conservator creates a limited conservatorship.

(b) The appointment of a conservator is not a transfer or alienation within the meaning of general provisions of any federal or state statute or regulation, insurance policy, pension plan, contract, will or trust instrument, imposing restrictions upon or penalties for transfer or alienation by the protected person of his rights or interest, but this section does not restrict the ability of persons to make specific provision by contract or dispositive instrument relating to a conservator."

§15-5-421. Alter section to read: "Recording of conservator's letters.—Letters of conservatorship are evidence of transfer of all assets, or the part thereof specified in the letters, of a protected person to the conservator. An order terminating a conservatorship is evidence of transfer of all assets of the estate subjected to the conservatorship from the conservator to the protected person, or his successors. Letters of conservatorship and orders terminating conservatorship may be recorded in the office of the county recorder in any county in which property affected by such letters or orders is located and, from the time of filing the same for record, notice is imparted to all persons of the contents of such letters or orders."

§15-5-425. Add new subsection (a)(5) to read: "(5) A conservator, in discharging the responsibilities conferred by court order and this part, shall implement the principles described in section 15-5-408(a) of this code."

§15-5-430. After words "has ceased" add following, "or that it would be in the best interests of the protected person to establish the conservatorship in another jurisdiction may terminate the conservatorship and, where appropriate, order initiation of proceedings in another jurisdiction or delivery of the assets to a foreign conservator."

§15-5-431. Substitute "a" for "1" and "b" for "2".

Add new section:

"§15-5-432. Powers of foreign conservator.—If no local conservator or guardian has been appointed and no petition for such appointment is pending in this state, a domiciliary foreign conservator may file with a court in this state in a county in which property belonging to the protected person is located authenticated copies of his appointment and of any official bond he has given. A domiciliary foreign conservator may then exercise as to assets in this state all powers of a local conservator and may maintain actions and proceedings in this state subject to any conditions imposed upon nonresident parties generally."

§15-5-501 through 15-5-502 repealed as of July 1, 1982. Uniform Durable Power of Attorney Act adopted and designated as 15-5-501 through 15-5-507.

Add new section:

"15-5-601. Designation of boards of community guardian.—(a) After making a determination that there exists a need within a county for a guardian for those persons in need of guardianship and for whom there is no person or corporation qualified and willing to act in such capacity, the board of county commissioners may create, within the county, a board of community guardian. The board of county commissioners of one or more counties within a judicial district may jointly create within a judicial district a board of community guardian."

Add new section:

"15-5-602. Board structure—Powers and duties.—(a) Any board of community guardian which is created within a county or counties in a judicial district shall operate under the laws of the state of Idaho, including the Idaho guardianship, conservatorship and trust laws.

(b) A board of community guardian shall consist of not fewer than seven (7) nor more than eleven (11) members who are representatives of community interests involving persons needing guardians or conservators as defined by chapter 5, title 15, Idaho Code.

(1) The terms of the members of the board shall be for two (2) years and shall be staggered. A number of members equaling or most closely exceeding one-half ($^{1}/_{2}$)

See note at head of Digest as to 1998 legislation covered.

See Topical Index in front part of this volume.

GUARDIAN AND WARD . . . *continued*

shall initially be appointed for one (1) year. Any vacancy created by resignation or expiration of term shall be filled in the same manner as the original appointment;

(2) No person shall be appointed for more than four (4) successive terms or eight (8) successive years on the board;

(3) The board shall meet not less than once each quarter;

(4) No person shall be a member of a board who is also an employee of: the district court or the clerk of the district court;

(5) A board member having previously provided or currently providing services to a ward shall disclose such to the board and abstain from any decision or action taken concerning that particular ward;

(6) Board members and officers shall serve without pay;

(7) Each board shall elect its own chairman and other officers.

(c) A board, in those instances when a guardian and/or conservator is required and no qualified family member or other qualified person has volunteered to serve, may:

(1) Locate a qualified person to serve as guardian and/or conservator; or

(2) Petition the court to be appointed guardian and/or conservator.

(d) The board shall have all the powers and duties where applicable by court order, as provided under section 15-5-312 of this code and/or sections 15-5-408 and 15-5-424 of this code and in addition thereto shall:

(1) Locate and recommend to the court, where necessary, that a visitor be appointed as provided in section 15-5-503 of this code;

(2) Have access to all confidential records, including abuse registry reports that may be maintained by state or private agencies or institutions, which records concern a person for whom the board acts as guardian and/or conservator. The name of the person reporting the alleged abuse shall be subject to disclosure according to chapter 3, title 9, Idaho Code;

(3) Review and monitor the services provided by public and private agencies to any incapacitated person for whom the board acts as guardian and/or conservator and determine the continued need for those services;

(4) Assess a fee for services developed pursuant to this part;

(5) Have the power, subject to the approval of the board of county commissioners, to adopt such rules as are necessary to carry out the duties and responsibilities of the board.

(e) When a board serves as guardian or conservator, it shall be compensated as other guardians or conservators pursuant to Idaho law. If, at the time the board is appointed as guardian and/or conservator, the incapacitated person for whom the board is to act has no funds, the court may waive the payment of fees.

(f) When a board serves as guardian and/or conservator there is created, at the time of filing of the order of appointment, a lien in favor of the board against any real property owned by the ward or protected person, enforceable only upon the termination of the guardianship and/or conservatorship, for all fees which were incurred throughout the duration of the services and which were not paid prior to termination. All fees incurred throughout the duration of the services and which were not paid prior to the termination of services shall relate back to the effective date of the lien. The board must record a notice of said lien within thirty (30) days of filing of the order of appointment. Such liens shall be recorded in every county where property subject to the lien is located. The notice shall contain at least the following information: full court heading of the action in which the appointment was made; the effective date of the lien; the name and address of the board; and any limitations or terms regarding the fees covered by the lien contained in the order of appointment. The court may postpone or arrange for gradual repayment of the fees if the court finds that the immediate repayment would create a hardship on the person.

(g) No member of a board of community guardian, any employees, or any visitor appointed at the request of such board pursuant to section 15-5-303 of this code, shall be liable for civil damages by reason of authorizing medical treatment or surgery for the person for whom the board is appointed, if the board member, employee or visitor, after medical consultation with the person's physician, acts in good faith, is not negligent, and acts within the limits established for the guardian and/or conservator by the court. No such person shall be liable, by reason of his authorization, for injury to the person for whom the guardian and/or conservator has been appointed which injury results from the negligence or other acts of a third person, if the court has authorized the giving of medical consent by the board or the individual members of the board. No such person shall be liable in the performance of acts done in good faith within the scope of his authority as long as the act is not of a wanton or grossly negligent nature. The board of community guardian shall be deemed to be a governmental entity for the purposes of application of the Idaho tort claims act."

Add new section:

"§15-5-603. Annual report—(a) Each board shall report annually in writing to the board of county commissioners and, in the case of a multi-county board, to each participating county, its activities for the preceding year, which report shall contain:

(1) A fiscal report which adequately reflects the financial operation of the board;

(2) The number of volunteer guardians obtained by the board;

(3) The number of incapacitated persons for whom the board is acting as guardian;

(4) Recommendations for improving guardianship services in the circuit;

(5) Such other matters as may be determined advisable by the board, or the board of county commissioners.

The report shall be filed no later than April 1 of each year and shall cover the preceding calendar year.

(b) The board of county commissioners shall review each report and shall determine whether to dissolve or continue the board of community guardian in the county. Where there is a multi-county board of community guardian, the boards of county commissioners of all concerned counties must concur in a decision to dissolve the board of community guardian."

Securities in Name of Nominee.—See category Estates and Trusts, topic Trusts, subhead Securities in Name of Nominee.

Gifts to Minors.—See topic Infants.

Uniform Fiduciaries Act adopted. (68-301 to 68-315).

Uniform Simplification of Fiduciary Security Transfers Act adopted (68-901 to 68-911) and not repealed by Uniform Commercial Code.

Revised Uniform Principal and Income Act adopted. (68-1001 to 68-1016).

HUSBAND AND WIFE:

Married woman may contract with her husband as with a third person. She may sue with reference to her separate property or for her own personal injuries, without joining her husband, but in actions for her personal injuries he is a proper party and may be brought in on motion. She may be sued alone only with reference to her separate property. No statutory prohibition against either spouse suing other. She is liable on her contracts and may bind community property. (32-912). Any community obligation incurred by husband or wife without consent in writing of other spouse shall not obligate separate property of nonconsenting spouse. (32-912).

Separate Property.—All money or other property owned by either spouse before marriage or acquired afterwards by gift, devise, bequest or descent is separate property of such spouse, as is also anything acquired with the proceeds of separate property. (32-903).

Spouses may by written agreement specifically provide that all or specified property shall be separate property of one of spouses.

Real property conveyed by one spouse to the other is presumed to be separate estate of grantee, and grantor spouse only need execute and acknowledge conveyance. (32-906).

Quasi-Community Property.—All personal property, wherever situated, and all real property in Idaho which is acquired while domiciled elsewhere but which would have been community property if decedent and surviving spouse had been domiciled in Idaho at time of acquisition, plus personal and real property acquired in exchange for such property; shall also include real property in another state owned by domiciliary of Idaho if laws of such other state permit descent and distribution of such property to be governed by laws of this state. (15-2-201). This category of property presumably effective only upon death of a spouse for property succession.

Community Property.—All property acquired after marriage, including the rents and profits of the separate property of either spouse is community property, unless in the instrument by which such property is acquired by spouse it is provided that rents and profits thereof be applied to that spouse's sole and separate use. (32-906). Husband and wife have joint management and control of community property. (32-912). Real property conveyed to revocable trust retains its community property character. (32-906A).

Disposition of Community or Quasi-Community Property on Death of Spouse.—See category Estates and Trusts, topics Descent and Distribution, Executors and Administrators.

Antenuptial Contracts.—See subhead Marriage Settlements, infra.

Right of Election.—See category Estates and Trusts, topics Executors and Administrators, Descent and Distribution.

Conveyance or Encumbrance of Property.—Neither husband nor wife may sell, convey, or encumber community real property unless other joins in executing and acknowledging deed or other instrument of conveyance. (32-912).

Agency.—Husband or wife may by express power of attorney give to the other the complete power to sell, convey or encumber, community property, either real or personal. (32-912).

Marriage settlements may be entered into prior to or during marriage. (32-916). When properly executed and recorded, marriage settlements may vary property rights of husband and wife from those given by statute. Minors may execute valid marriage settlements. (32-916 to 32-929).

Desertion and Nonsupport.—A parent deserting a child under 16, or a husband deserting or failing to support his wife when able to do so, is guilty of felony. In addition to fine, which may be paid to wife or guardian of child, court may order guilty party to pay certain amount weekly to wife or guardian of child, releasing defendant on probation on his giving bond. (18-401 to 18-405).

Uniform Reciprocal Enforcement of Support Act (as Revised) adopted. (7-1048 to 7-1089). Amended to conform with requirements of Title IV-D of federal social security act. All sections dealing with foreign support orders repealed.

INFANTS:

Age of majority: males 18; females 18. (32-101).

Emancipation.—Any male or female who has been married is competent to enter into contract, mortgage, bill of sale or conveyance, and can sue and be sued thereon. (32-101).

Contracts for Necessaries.—Minor cannot disaffirm contract, otherwise valid, to pay reasonable value of things necessary for support of himself or his family, entered into when not under care of parent or guardian able to provide for him. (32-101, 32-104 to 05). Infant 15 years or over may enter into insurance contract and cannot disaffirm by reason of minority. (41-1807). Infant 14 years or over may consent to treatment of infectious, contagious, or communicable disease without consent of parent or guardian. (39-3801).

Actions.—If infant has guardian, conservator or like fiduciary, representative may sue or defend; if not, infant may sue by next friend or guardian ad litem, appointed by court. (I.R.C.P. 17). A guardian ad litem may be appointed on the application of an infant if he is above the age of 14, or if under 14 on application of relative or friend or party to action. (15-5-206 to 15-5-207). Statutory tort action in child abuse cases. (6-1701 to 6-1705).

Parental Responsibility.—Parent is civilly liable for retail value of merchandise, plus damages of $100 but not more than $250, costs, and attorney fees, for minor who knowingly removes merchandise from merchant's premises without paying. (48-701 to 48-705). Parent responsible for wilful destruction of property up to $2,500, caused by child under 18, living with parents. (6-210). Any payment of public assistance money to

INFANTS . . . *continued*
or for benefit of dependent child creates debt due Department of Health and Welfare by parents who are responsible for child's support in amount equal to public assistance money so paid subject to modification by District Court Order. (56-203B). Owner of motor vehicle knowingly permitting minor to drive is liable for negligence of minor under 16. (49-2416). Failure to supervise is made crime; penalties and restitution imposed. (32-1301).

Adoption.—See topic Adoption.

Revised Uniform Gifts to Minors Act adopted with 1966 amendments, repealed effective July 1, 1984, replaced by Uniform Transfers to Minors Act. (1984 c. 152, 68-801 to 68-825). Minor is any person who has not attained age 18. (68-801).

Termination of Parental Rights.—Parental rights may be terminated upon specified grounds. (16-2005). Act provides extensive criteria and procedures for termination of rights by court order following petition and investigation. (16-2001 to 16-2015).

Uniform Securities Ownership by Minors Act not adopted. Uniform Transfers to Minors Act coverage includes securities. (68-809).

Uniform Transfers to Minors Act applies to transfers if transferor, minor, or custodian is resident or property in state at time of transfer and transfer refers to act by conveying property to qualified custodian "as custodian for (minor's name) under the Idaho Uniform Transfers to Minors Act" or by instrument in following form (68-809):

TRANSFER UNDER THE IDAHO UNIFORM
TRANSFERS TO MINORS ACT

I (transferor's name) hereby transfer to (custodian), as custodian for (minor) under the Idaho Uniform Transfers to Minors Act, the following: (describe property).
Dated:
(Signature)
(Name of custodian) acknowledges receipt of the property described above as custodian for the minor named above under the Idaho Uniform Transfers to Minors Act.
Dated:
(Signature Custodian)

Act also applies to transfers purportedly made under Uniform Gift Act to minors. (68-820).

Nomination of custodian may be by will, trust, deed, instrument of appointment, or contractual designation of beneficiary forwarded to obligor. (68-803). Transfer made for only one minor and to one custodian. (68-810). Transfer irrevocable and vests property in minor with statutory control in custodian. (68-811[2]). Third person without knowledge exempt from liability for transactions with custodian. (68-818). Resignation, removal and substitution of custodian procedures set forth. (68-818). Custodian must transfer property to minor or his estate when: (1) Minor is 21 years for transfers established by gift, appointment, will or trust, or (2) when minor is 18 years for all other custodial properties, or (3) at minor's death. (68-820).

MARRIAGE:

Any unmarried male and female of 18 or older is capable of consenting to marriage. (32-202).

License to marry may not be issued to a male or female under 16 except on written consent of parent and order of probate court after hearing. (32-202).

Consent Required.—Male or female between 16 and 18 may not obtain license to marry except upon written consent, duly acknowledged, of his or her father, mother or guardian. Original or certified birth certificate or proof acceptable to county recorder required. (32-202).

License is required; issued by county recorder of any county. (32-401 to 32-411). Female applicants shall file certificate from licensed physician which reports results of approved rubella test; certain exceptions included. (32-412). District judge may, however, waive medical examination on proof that emergency exists. (32-414). Each applicant must receive AIDS educational pamphlet from county recorder and certify that he or she has read pamphlet before license can be issued. (32-412A).

Record.—See category Documents and Records, topic Records, subhead Vital Statistics.

Ceremony.—No particular form of ceremony is necessary. Consent to and subsequent consummation of marriage may be manifested in any form, and may be proved under the same general rules of evidence as facts in other cases. (32-201 to 32-203). No marriage otherwise valid, will be voided because solemnizing official did not have authority he professed as long as marriage is consummated while one or both of parties believes marriage to have been validly performed. (32-308).

Common law marriages will no longer be authorized after Jan. 1, 1996. (32-201). All marriages after that date shall be solemnized, authenticated and recorded as set forth in 32-301 to 32-302.

Foreign Marriages.—All marriages contracted outside this state, if valid where contracted, are valid here, unless they violate public policy of this state. (32-209).

Proxy marriages are not authorized by any statute.

Prohibited Marriages.—Marriages between ancestors and descendants of every degree, brother and sister of the whole or half blood, uncle and niece, aunt and nephew or first cousins are incestuous and void. (32-205, 32-206).

Annulment.—Marriage may be annulled for any of the following causes, existing at time of marriage:

(1) Person when married was not of age of legal consent, and such marriage was contracted without consent of his or her parents, or of person having charge of him or her, unless after attaining age of consent such party for any time freely lives and cohabits with other as husband or wife; (2) that former husband or wife of either party was living, and marriage with such former husband or wife was then in force; (3) that either party was of unsound mind, unless such party, after coming to reason, freely cohabits with other as husband or wife; (4) that consent of either party was obtained by fraud, unless such party afterward, with full knowledge of facts constituting fraud, freely cohabits with other as husband or wife; (5) that consent of either party was obtained by force, unless such party afterwards freely cohabits with other as husband or wife; (6) that either party was, at time of marriage, physically incapable of entering into married state, and such incapacity continues, and appears to be incurable. (32-501).

Time for Commencing Action.—Time within which action for annulment may be commenced varies according to ground on which annulment is sought, as follows: On ground (1), by party to marriage, within four years after attaining majority, by parent or guardian any time prior to majority of minor; on grounds (2) and (3), at any time during the life of parties; on ground (4), within four years after discovery of fraud; on grounds (5) and (6), within four years after marriage. (32-502).

Legitimacy of children not affected by annulment, except where annulment on grounds of fraud in that wife is pregnant with child of man other than husband. (32-503).

Effect of Judgment.—A judgment of nullity of marriage is conclusive only as against the parties to the action, and those claiming under them. (32-505).

Premarital Agreements.—See topic Husband and Wife, subhead Marriage Settlements.

MARRIED WOMEN:

See topics Husband and Wife, Marriage; categories Debtor and Creditor, topic Homesteads; Documents and Records, topic Acknowledgments; Civil Actions and Procedure, topic Evidence, subhead Witnesses; Estates and Trusts, topics Executors and Administrators, Wills; Property, topic Dower.

INSURANCE

INSURANCE COMPANIES:

Comprehensive Insurance Code adopted. (41-101 thru 41-4409).

Kinds of insurance defined. (41-501 to 41-513).

Supervision.—Insurance companies are placed under supervision of Department of Insurance, headed by Director of Insurance. (41-201 to 41-252). Idaho insurance guaranty association created to help prevent loss to policyholders of insolvent insurers and to detect and avoid insolvency of insurers. (41-3601 to 3621; 41-4301 to 4319). Association is nonprofit unincorporated entity and all insurers must be members in order to transact business in state. (41-3601).

Rates and rating organizations relating to property, inland marine, marine and transportation, casualty, surety, workmen's comp. are regulated. Appeal from Director's orders taken to district court, Ada County, within 30 days of service of order. (41-1401 to 41-1435).

Annual statements required to be filed with Director by July 1, covering prior calendar year. Filing to be in accordance with National Association of Insurance Commissioners procedure manual. (41-335 to 41-336B).

Policies.—Standard provisions and prohibited provisions are fixed for policies of life and annuity, group life, disability, group disability, credit life and credit disability, property, casualty, surety, and title insurance. Coverage of new born shall be effective from moment of birth. (41-1801 to 41-2613). Policy must contain provision requiring insurer to give insured 30 days prior written notice of cancellation, nonrenewal or premium rate increase. (41-1842). Policy may not require insured to purchase prescription drugs from any particular mail order company or pharmacy. (49-1844). Insurance contracts of any type which provide coverage for mastectomies must provide mammography examinations. (41-2144, 41-2218, 41-3441, 41-3936, 41-4025). Mandatory coverage for newborns adopted within 60 days of birth. (41-2140).

Agents, brokers and consultants must be licensed by Director. (41-1020 to 41-1079). They must meet continuing education requirements established by Director. (41-1046). Agents or brokers must be 18 years of age, citizen of U.S., bona fide resident of Idaho for not less than six months preceding license application, except that director may waive residency requirement under certain circumstances, of good character and reputation, and must pass written examination unless one of exceptions listed in §41-1039 applies. Nonresident may obtain residents' license as agent or broker if he has nonresident's license pursuant to 41-1065 and maintains office in Idaho that is his principal place of business. For broker's license, must also have had special experience or training as deemed by director to be reasonably necessary for competence as broker. (41-1034). Consultant must be 25 years of age. If individual, or if firm or corporation, license powers must be exercised only by individuals qualified for individual license as consultants. Must have special experience, education or training of sufficient content and duration and possess thorough knowledge of field of insurance covered by license, meet highest fiduciary standards, file $10,000 bond in favor of State of Idaho, and pass all written examinations required for license. (41-1035). Special license available to nonresident agents and brokers. (41-1065). Director of Insurance authorized to bring actions to enjoin violations of insurance code. (41-213). One who collects charges or premiums or adjusts or settles claims on life and health insurance coverage or annuities is insurance administrator. (41-901). Administrators must be licensed and have written agreement with insurer. (41-901 to 41-915). Insurers required to have licensed managing general agent. (41-1501 to 41-1507).

Broker Controlled Insurers.—Minimum standards for business transacted with. (41-1701 to 41-1706).

Resident Agent Countersignature Required.—Resident agent or his full time salaried employee who is over 21 years and is grantee of agent's acknowledged power of attorney must process, sign and place facsimile of agent's signature on policies for indemnity, general or floating policy covering property located in state, liability in state, or undertakings to be performed in state. (41-337). However, resident agent's countersignature is not required if nonresident agent resides in state that allows Idaho resident agent to sign policy in that state without countersignature. (41-338).

Insurance Holding Companies.—Insurance holding company system shall consist of two or more affiliated persons. (41-3801). No person other than an issuer shall tender an offer to exchange securities which would result in acquiring control unless (1)

See note at head of Digest as to 1998 legislation covered.

See Topical Index in front part of this volume.

ID – 32

INSURANCE COMPANIES . . . *continued*
statement filed with Director setting forth background and identity, source of funds, fully audited financial information of acquiring party, plan to liquidate insurer, classes of stock, and (2) approval given by Director. (41-3802). Registration required. (41-3806).

Service of Process.—Director must be appointed agent for service of process on any qualified, foreign or alien insurer and domestic reciprocal insurer. (41-333). Insurer granted 30 days from service on Director to plead. Service of duplicate required and copy forwarded by registered or certified mail by Director to insurer, along with fee not over $30. (41-334). Unauthorized insurers subject to service of process. (41-1204 to 41-1210). Contracts as to credit life insurance are subject to Consumer Credit Code. (28-44-101 to 28-44-401). See category Business Regulation and Commerce, topic Consumer Credit.

Investments and allowable assets defined and regulated. (41-601 to 41-813). Reduced tax rates on Idaho investments. (41-403).

Consumer Credit Transactions.—Insurance provided in relation to consumer credit transactions governed by Consumer Credit Code. (28-44-101 to 28-44-401). See category Business Regulation and Commerce, topic Consumer Credit.

Certificates of Authority.—Before any insurer may transact insurance business, it must obtain a certificate of authority from Director. (41-305 to 41-308). To qualify, must be an incorporated stock insurer, mutual insurer, or reciprocal insurer; maintain required paid-in capital stock or unimpaired surplus from $100,000 to $650,000 depending on type, together with additional surplus of $100,000 to $650,000 depending on type; maintain required reserves depending on type. Special provision for presently qualified insurers. (41-313).

Application for certificate together with fee must be filed in accordance with detailed requirements. (41-319 to 41-320). Director may grant, deny, suspend or revoke certificate for violations, after hearing. Appeal rights available to district court. (41-322 to 41-330).

New domestic insurers regulated as to articles of incorporation, organization, sale of securities, qualifications. (41-2801 to 41-2871).

Hospital Insurance Trusts.—See category Estates and Trusts, topic Trusts.

Foreign insurance companies must secure certificate of authority from Director, but may make investments in state without certificate. (41-307). Requirements of capital fund, additional surplus, reserves are same as for new domestic insurers. (41-313). Exempt from compliance with foreign corporation laws of business corporations. (41-332). Foreign insurer admitted to do business in Idaho may become domestic insurer by complying with requirements for organization and licensing of domestic insurer and by designating place in Idaho as its principal place of business. (41-342 to 41-344).

Reporting Material Acquisitions and Dispositions.—Every insurer domiciled in Idaho shall file report with director disclosing material acquisitions and dispositions of assets or material nonrenewals, cancelations or revisions of ceded insurance agreements. (41-345). Transaction is material if it involves 5% of reporting insurer's total admitted assets. (41-346). Nonmaterial nonrenewals, cancelations or revisions of ceded reinsurance agreements defined. (41-347).

Retaliatory Laws.—Obligations, prohibitions or restrictions placed on Idaho insurers or agents, doing business in other states, which are in excess of those imposed on similar insurers, are imposed on insurers of such other states doing business in Idaho. (41-340).

Premium Tax.—If preceding year's premium tax more than $400 current year's tax must be prepaid based on preceding year's business and current year's rate as follows: 60% by June 15, 20% by Sept. 15, 15% by Dec. 15, balance due by Mar. 1. Rate: 3.0% of gross premiums in excess of premiums and cancellations returned, and premium credits or dividends paid to policyholders. Special provisions for life and annuity contracts. Title insurance rate is 1.5%. Any insurer having 25% or more of its assets or 75% gross direct premiums on in-state policies in listed investments and meeting notice requirements of 41-403A granted rate of 1.1%. (41-402 to 41-406). Director may refund any overpayment of taxes, fines or penalties if written claim is filed within one year of overpayment. (41-402A).

Refunds.—Refund of premium for canceled insurance must be paid to insured. (41-1333).

Complaint Procedures.—Every authorized insurer required to maintain complete record of all complaints. (41-1330).

Direct Actions Against Insurer.—See category Transportation, topic Motor Vehicles, subhead Direct Actions.

Unclaimed Funds.—Uniform Unclaimed Property Act (1981) adopted effective July 1, 1983. (14-501 to 14-541). See category Property, topic Absentees, subhead Escheat.

Uniform Claims Processing.—Beginning July 1, 1995, all providers of health insurance in Idaho shall use uniform form claim form/format and uniform billing and claim codes promulgated by director of insurance. Beginning July 1, 1996, all insurers shall offer compatible systems of electronic billing approved by director.

Uniform Insurers Liquidation Act adopted. (41-3301; 41-3304; 41-3305; 41-3312 to 41-3320).

No-Fault Insurance.—Not adopted. See category Transportation, topic Motor Vehicles, subhead No-Fault Insurance.

Mutual Benefit Associations.—Chapter regulating mutual benefit associations repealed. (1987, c. 78).

Risk Retention Groups.—Chapter regulating Idaho risk retention groups formed pursuant to Federal Liability Risk Retention Act of 1986. (41-4801 to 4816). Such groups must be chartered and licensed as liability insurance companies. (41-4804 to 4805). No counter signatures required. (41-4807). Risk retention group's agent or broker must be licensed by director. (41-4813). Director may promulgate rules and regulations governing such groups. (41-4815).

Reinsurance Intermediary Act.—Regulates reinsurers and insurers utilizing reinsurance intermediaries and brokers. (41-5101 to 41-5111).

Life Insurance Twenty Day Free Examination.—Life insurance and annuities contracts must include separate rider stating insured may return policy within 20 days for refund. (41-1935).

National Association of Insurance Commissioners.—Regulations, rules, directives and standards may not be enforced against insurers unless authorized by statute.

SURETY AND GUARANTY COMPANIES:

See topic Insurance Companies, generally. Also 41-2601.

Capital and Surplus Requirements.—Must have at least $550,000 in paid-up capital stock or basic surplus and additional surplus of $550,000 whether company is domestic or foreign. (41-313).

Rights and Powers.—Bond, undertaking, obligation or guaranty when required or permitted by law to be made may be executed by surety insurer.

Foreign Companies.—See topic Insurance Companies.

INTELLECTUAL PROPERTY

TRADEMARKS AND TRADENAMES:

What May Be Used.—Trademark means any word, name, symbol, or device, or combination thereof, adopted and used by person to identify goods made or sold by him and to distinguish them from others. Service mark means mark used in sale or advertising of services to identify services of a person and distinguish them from services of others. Tradename means a word, name, symbol, device or any combination thereof, used by person to identify his business, vocation or occupation and distinguish it from others. Person means any individual, firm, partnership, corporation, association, union or other organization. Trademark or service mark shall not be registered if it is immoral, deceptive or scandalous; disparages or falsely suggests a connection with persons, living or dead, institutions, beliefs or national symbol, or brings them into contempt or disrepute; comprises the flag, coat of arms or other insignia of any government entity; comprises name, signature or portrait of any living individual, except with his written consent; consists of a mark which is merely descriptive or deceptively misdescriptive, geographically descriptive or deceptively misdescriptive, or merely surname; however, a distinctive mark may be used (mark considered distinctive if used continuously for five years in Idaho or elsewhere); resembles mark registered in Idaho or mark or trade name previously used in Idaho and not abandoned. Terms of Act defined in accord with U.S. trademark law. (48-501 to 48-518 and 44-603).

Registration.—Application is filed with Secretary of State on forms furnished, and must contain name, business address, and if applicable, state of incorporation; goods or services in connection with which mark is used and manner used; date first used anywhere and date first used in Idaho; statement of ownership and that no other has right to use. Application is to be signed and verified and contain specimen or facsimile of mark in triplicate. Filing fee is $30. (48-503).

Assignment.—Registered mark is assignable by written instrument executed and recorded on form provided by Secretary of State who shall issue new certificate for remainder of registration term; assignment is void as to subsequent purchaser without notice, unless filed within three months, or prior to subsequent purchase. Filing fee $30. (48-507).

Protections Afforded.—Certificate of registration is issued and this certificate, or certified copy thereof, is admissible in evidence as competent and sufficient proof of registration in any action or judicial proceeding in Idaho. (48-505).

Duration of Registration.—Registration effective for ten years. Registration renewable for mark still used in Idaho for additional ten years upon application filed within six months prior to expiration. $30 renewal fee. Registration may be renewed for successive periods of ten years in like manner. Secretary of State required to notify registrants of necessity of renewal within year next preceding expiration date. Registrations cancelled on voluntary request of registrant or assignee; upon failure to renew; upon finding by court of competent jurisdiction that registered mark has been abandoned, improperly or fraudulently obtained, that registrant is not true owner of registered mark, that registered mark is similar to or likely to cause confusion with mark previously registered by another with U.S. Patent Office and never abandoned. (48-506; 48-509).

Infringement.—Infringement renders one liable for any or all of following: injunctive relief; suit to enjoin manufacture, use, display or sale of any counterfeit or imitation with order requiring defendant to pay all profit derived from infringement and/or all damages suffered. Registrant may prosecute under penal law. All common law rights preserved. (48-512; 48-514).

Resale Price Agreements.—Owners of trademarks, tradenames and brands are permitted to establish minimum resale prices for their products. (48-301 to 48-312). Any person, public corporation, or state may seek injunctive relief and triple damages, if any damages accrue. Any person, whether as principal or as agent, who violates act is guilty of misdemeanor for each single violation. Governor of State of Idaho has responsibility for supervision and administration of Act. (48-310). *Caveat:* See, however, P.L. 94-145, repealing exemption of state fair trade laws from Federal anti-trust law.

Tradenames.—All persons, partnerships, associations, etc., transacting business in state under assumed or fictitious name or designation other than true name or names of such person or persons, must file in office of county recorder of county or counties in which business is conducted a certificate setting forth business name and true full name of party or parties conducting business, together with their postoffice addresses, which certificate must be acknowledged as a deed. In case of failure to file such certificate, such person or persons may not maintain any suit in any state court, and such failure is prima facie evidence of fraud in securing credit. Conducting business without certificate is misdemeanor. Filing fee for certificate $2 per page. Act does not apply to corporations. (53-501 to 53-507). But see category Business Organizations, topic Corporations.

See note at head of Digest as to 1998 legislation covered.

See Topical Index in front part of this volume.

TRADEMARKS AND TRADENAMES . . . *continued*
  Deceptive Trade Practices.—See category Business Regulation and Commerce, topic Monopolies, Restraint of Trade and Competition.

LEGAL PROFESSION

ATTORNEYS AND COUNSELORS:

Idaho has an integrated bar and all persons admitted to practice before Supreme Court, who have not been disbarred or suspended, and who have paid their annual license fee, are members and entitled to practice law.

Attorney Ethics.—Idaho has adopted American Bar Association Model Rules of Professional Conduct. (3-301).

Jurisdiction over Admissions.—Board of Commissioners of Idaho State Bar, consisting of five members, has power to determine by rules, subject to approval of Supreme Court, requirements for admission, to conduct examinations, and to certify to Supreme Court names of qualified applicants. Board has formulated rules which have been approved by Supreme Court. (3-402, 3-408). Approval by court of persons whose names are so certified entitles them to practice law. Board formulates rules governing conduct of all persons admitted, passes upon all complaints concerning professional conduct and is empowered to take disciplinary measures, subject to review by Supreme Court. (3-408). For 1999, annual license fee of $100, if admitted prior to July 1, or $60, if admitted after July 1, for calendar year of admission; $205 for next three calendar years; $275 a year thereafter until calendar year following 72d birthday when annual fee reduced to $50. (3-409). Affiliate members pay annual fee of $105. (3-409). For 2000 and thereafter, annual license fee of $115, if admitted prior to July 1, or $65, if admitted after July 1, for calendar year of admission; $230 for next three years; $315 a year thereafter until calendar year following 72d birthday when annual fee reduced to $55. (3-409). Affiliate members pay annual fee of $120. (3-409).

Eligibility.—Any individual age of majority, of good moral character, and who possesses necessary qualifications of learning and ability may, under such rules as Supreme Court may prescribe, be admitted as attorney and counselor in all state courts. (3-101).

Registration As Law Student.—None.

Educational Requirements.—Applicant must show graduation from law school approved by American Bar Association. Attorney applicant meets requirements if admitted to highest court of another state and has actively practiced as principal occupation at least five out of last seven years before application.

Examinations.—Conducted by Board of Commissioners of Idaho State Bar, usually in Feb. and July of each year. Application must be filed 120 days for student applicants and 150 days for attorney applicants preceding examination. Examinations usually given in Boise and Moscow.

Idaho uses multi-state bar exam. Dates are correlated with other states giving multi-state exam.

Other subjects tested include civil procedure, conflicts of laws, constitutional law, contracts, business organizations, ethics, Arts. 1, 2, and 9, of U.C.C., domestic relations, criminal law, equitable remedies, real property and water law, torts, community property, wills, succession and trusts. Idaho accepts transfer of multi-state bar exam scores from another jurisdiction. All applicants must take essay portion. Attorney applicants licensed in other jurisdictions for more than five years need not take multi-state portion of exam.

Appearance by Nonresident Attorney.—Nonresident attorney permitted to appear only if he has associated with him attorney practicing law in Idaho and who is personally present at all stages of any proceeding.

Suretyship.—Disability of attorneys as sureties on bonds in proceedings in which they are professionally engaged is regulated by local court rules.

Liens.—From commencement of action or service of answer containing counterclaim, an attorney has a lien upon his client's cause of action or counterclaim which attaches to a verdict, report, decision or judgment in his client's favor and the proceeds thereof in whosoever hands they may come. This lien is not affected by any settlement between the parties before or after judgment. (3-205).

Disbarment or Suspension.—Supreme Court or District Court may remove, suspend or disbar for stated causes. (3-301).

Unauthorized Practice.—Practice of law by persons not admitted or by attorney whose right to practice terminated by disbarment, suspension, failure to pay license or otherwise, is illegal and punishable by fine and imprisonment. (3-420).

Mandatory Continuing Legal Education.—All attorneys engaged in active practice must complete minimum of 30 credit hours of legal education accredited by Board of Commissioners every three years and must make written report of participation to Board.

Specialty Certification Requirements.—None.

Professional Associations or Corporations.—See category Business Organizations, topic Corporations, subhead Professional Associations or Corporations.

MINERAL, WATER AND FISHING RIGHTS

MINES AND MINERALS:

Principal regulations, under U.S. laws. For all mining claims, monuments must be established at all exterior angles of claim, and copy of location notice must be posted at discovery point at time of making of location. (47-602). Must record notice of location within 90 days after location with county recorder of county where claim is located. Failure to record in 90 days constitutes abandonment. (47-604). Location notice must contain name of locator, name of claim, date of discovery, dimensions, distance from some prominent natural or artificial object, name of mining district, county, and state.

(47-602). Revegetation required with penalties for failure. (47-1510). Dredge mining prohibited in National Wild and Scenic Rivers System of federal government. (47-1323).

Operation of Mines.—Dredge mining operators must secure permit and bond (47-1317); operations supervised by State Board of Land Commissioners. Injunctive relief available for dredge or placer mining without permit or bond. Civil and criminal penalties provided for violations of Dredge and Placer Mining Act, 47-1301 to 1324. (47-1324).

Oil and Gas.—Oil and gas conservation commission to prevent waste and to make investigations as it deems proper. (47-306 to 47-330).

Mining partnerships are provided for and regulated by 53-401 through 53-412.

Mining Tax.—For privilege of mining and extracting ores there is imposed, in addition to all other taxes, license tax of 2% of net value of ores mined or extracted. (47-1201 to 47-1208).

Small Mining Securities.—See category Business Regulation and Commerce, topic Securities.

MORTGAGES

CHATTEL MORTGAGES:

Uniform Commercial Code adopted. (28-1-101 to 28-10-104).

Uniform Consumer Credit Code adopted 1971, repealed Mar. 31, 1983. Idaho Credit Code adopted Apr. 1, 1983. (28-41-101 to 28-49-107). See category Business Regulation and Commerce, topic Consumer Credit.

What May Be Mortgaged.—Uniform Commercial Code governs.

After-acquired Property.—Uniform Commercial Code governs.

Future Advances.—Uniform Commercial Code governs.

Requisites of Instruments.—Uniform Commercial Code governs. §9-110, Sufficiency of Description, enlarged to require real property to be described by legal description. (28-9-110).

Execution of Instruments.—Uniform Commercial Code governs.

Filing.—Uniform Commercial Code governs. §9-302—1972 official amendment adopted with §9-302(2)(f) amended to exclude filing as to security interests in securities, and §9-302(5) added as new section, changing filing requirements for security interests in personal property or fixtures of utility companies when included with real property security agreements. (28-9-302). §9-401(1)(a) designates Office of County Recorder; §9-401(1)(b) designates Office of Secretary of State; §9-401(2) excepts financing statements for farm products. (28-9-401). See category Business Regulation and Commerce, topic Commercial Code, subhead Variations, §9-401.

Fees.—See category Business Regulation and Commerce, topic Commercial Code.

Refiling or Extension.—Uniform Commercial Code governs. See category Business Regulation and Commerce, topic Commercial Code, subhead Variations, §9-401A.

Removal of Property by Mortgagor.—Uniform Commercial Code governs.

Satisfaction or Release.—Uniform Commercial Code governs.

Foreclosure.—Uniform Commercial Code governs.

Redemption.—Uniform Commercial Code governs.

Foreign Mortgages.—Uniform Commercial Code governs.

Forms.—Following, may be used. For Financing Statement, Statements of Continuation, Release, Assignment, Termination, etc., and Request for Information and Copies forms, see end of this Digest.

Security Agreement.—
SECURITY AGREEMENT COVERING CONSUMER GOODS, FIXTURES, OR EQUIPMENT INCLUDING FARM EQUIPMENT
(MAY BE USED FOR MOTOR VEHICLES)

. . . .
(DATE)
1. . . . .
(NAME)
. . . .
(NO. AND STREET)   (CITY)
. . . .
(COUNTY)   (STATE)
(hereinafter called "Debtor") hereby grants to . . . .
(hereinafter called "Secured Party"), ... successors and assigns, a security interest in the following goods together with all replacements thereof and accessories, parts, additions and accessions now or hereafter affixed or used in connection therewith (hereinafter called the "Collateral"):
(Insert full description of Collateral, including identifying data such as year, make, model, serial and identification numbers.)
or as described on exhibits attached hereto.
2. The security interest granted hereby is to secure payment and performance of the liabilities and obligations of Debtor to Secured Party of every kind and description, direct or indirect, absolute or contingent, due or to become due, now existing or hereafter arising (all hereinafter called "Obligations").
3. DEBTOR HEREBY WARRANTS AND COVENANTS:
3. 01 TITLE. Debtor is now or, by using the proceeds of loans by the Secured Party, will become the owner of the Collateral free from any adverse lien, security interest or encumbrance.
3. 02 USE. The Collateral is bought or used primarily for
☐ Personal, family or household purposes
(Check one)   ☐ Farming operations
☐ Business use

See note at head of Digest as to 1998 legislation covered.

See Topical Index in front part of this volume.

CHATTEL MORTGAGES . . . *continued*
and if checked here ☐, is being acquired with the proceeds of loans by Secured Party to Debtor.
3. 03 LOCATION OF COLLATERAL: The Collateral will be located in . . . . County, Idaho. Debtor will not remove the Collateral from said state without written consent of Secured Party.
3. 04 RESIDENCY. Debtor resides in the county set forth above, unless some other county is indicated here:
. . . . County, Idaho.
3. 05 FIXTURES. If checked here ☐, the Collateral is to be or has been attached to real estate. Except as otherwise indicated, the parties intend that said Collateral shall always remain personal property. A legal description of the real estate is as follows:
or as described on exhibits attached hereto, and the name of the record owner is . . . . . .
. . . .

THE TERMS AND CONDITIONS APPEARING ON THE BACK HEREOF ARE PART OF THIS SECURITY AGREEMENT
Signed and delivered to Secured Party on the day and year first above written.
. . . .
. . . .
. . . .
(SIGNATURE OF DEBTOR)
CERTIFICATE OF TRUE COPY
STATE OF . . . . }
COUNTY OF . . . . }ss
I hereby certify that this is a true and correct copy of the original instrument.
. . . . Residing at . . . .
Notary Public
County, State of . . . .
Debtor will on demand of Secured Party furnish the latter with a disclaimer or disclaimers, signed by all persons having an interest in the real estate, of any interest in the Collateral which is prior to Secured Party's interest.
3. 06 PERFECTION OF SECURITY INTEREST. The Debtor agrees to execute and file financing statements and do whatever may be necessary under applicable law to perfect and continue the Secured Party's interest in the Collateral, all at Debtor's expense.
3. 07 SALE PROHIBITED. Debtor will not sell or offer to sell or otherwise transfer the Collateral or any interest therein without the written consent of Secured Party. By claiming proceeds or products of the collateral in any financing statement prepared in conjunction with this security agreement, the Secured Party shall not be deemed to have given Debtor an implied power to sell or otherwise transfer the Collateral or any interest therein.
3. 08 INSURANCE. Debtor will keep the Collateral continuously insured by an insurer approved by Secured Party against fire, theft and other hazards designated at any time by Secured Party, in an amount equal to the full insurable value thereof or to all sum secured hereby, with such form of loss payable clause as designated by and in favor of Secured Party, and will deliver the policies and receipts showing payment of premiums to the Secured Party. In the event of loss, Secured Party shall have full power to collect any and all insurance upon the Collateral and to apply the same at its option to any obligation secured hereby, whether or not matured, or to the restoration or repair of the property. Secured Party shall have no liability whatsoever for any loss that may occur by reason of the omission or lack of coverage of any such insurance.
3. 09 ADVERSE LIENS AND USE. Debtor will keep the Collateral free from any adverse lien, security interest or encumbrance. Debtor will not create nor permit the existence of any adverse lien, security interest or encumbrance other than that created hereby on the property without the written consent of Secured Party. Any certificate of title now or hereafter existing on any of the property will be delivered to Secured Party and will recite the interest of Secured Party. Debtor will keep the Collateral in good order and repair and will not waste or destroy the Collateral or any part thereof. Debtor will not use or permit anyone to use, the Collateral in violation of any statute, ordinance, or state or federal regulation; and Secured Party may examine and inspect the Collateral at any reasonable time, wherever located.
3. 10 TAXES AND ASSESSMENTS. Debtor will pay promptly when due all taxes and assessments upon the Collateral or for its use or operation or upon this agreement or upon any note or notes evidencing the obligations.
4. PURCHASE MONEY. To the extent the proceeds of any note shall be used to acquire said collateral, Secured Party shall have a purchase money security interest therein. Debtor hereby authorizes Secured Party to disburse said proceeds to the seller of the Collateral and/or to the insurance agent or broker, as shown on the records of the Secured Party.
5. SECURED PARTY'S RIGHT TO PAY TAXES, ETC.; DEBTOR'S RIGHT TO POSSESSION. The Secured Party is not required to, but may, at its option discharge taxes, liens or security interests or other encumbrances at any time levied or placed on the Collateral, pay for insurance on the Collateral, pay for the maintenance and preservation of the Collateral, pay any filing or recording fees, or any other charges payable by Debtor and any amount so paid, with interest thereon at the maximum rate permitted by law from date of payment until repaid shall be secured hereby and shall be repayable by Debtor on demand. The rights granted by this paragraph are not a waiver of any other rights of Secured Party arising from breach of any of the covenants hereof by Debtor.
5. 1 Until default Debtor may have possession of the Collateral and use it in any lawful manner not inconsistent with this agreement and not inconsistent with any policy of insurance thereon.
6. DEFAULT. Time is of the essence of this Security Agreement, and Debtor shall be in default under this agreement upon the happening of any of the following events or conditions:
6. 01 Default in the payment or performance of any obligation, covenant or liability contained or referred to herein or in any note evidencing the same;
6. 02 Any warranty, representation or statement made or furnished to Secured Party by or on behalf of Debtor proves to have been false in any material respect when made or furnished;
6. 03 Any event which results in the acceleration of the maturity of the indebtedness of Debtor to others under any indenture agreement or undertaking;
6. 04 Loss, theft, damage, destruction, sale or encumbrance to or of any of the Collateral, or the making of any levy, seizure or attachment thereof or thereon;
6. 05 Death, dissolution, termination of existence, insolvency, business failure, appointment of a receiver of any part of the property of, assignment for the benefit of creditors by, or the commencement of any proceeding under any bankruptcy or insolvency laws by or against, Debtor or any guarantor or surety for Debtor, or entry of any judgment against them, or failure of any guarantor or surety for Debtor to provide Secured Party with financial information promptly when requested by Secured Party.
6. 06 The Secured Party deems itself insecure.
7. REMEDIES. Upon the occurrence of any default hereunder and at any time thereafter, the Secured Party may without notice or demand declare immediately due and payable all amounts secured hereby and shall have the remedies of a Secured Party under the Idaho Uniform Commercial Code or other applicable law; and without limiting the generality of the foregoing:
7. 01 Debtor agrees to put Secured Party in possession of the Collateral on demand; and
7. 02 Secured Party is authorized to enter any premises where the Collateral is situated and take possession of said property without notice or demand and without legal proceedings; and
7. 03 At the request of Secured Party, Debtor will assemble the Collateral and make it available to Secured Party at a place designated by Secured Party which is reasonably convenient to both parties; and
7. 04 Debtor agrees that a period of five (5) days from the time notice is sent, by first class mail or otherwise, shall be a reasonable period of notification of a sale or other disposition of the Collateral; and
7. 05 Debtor agrees that any notice or other communication by Secured Party to Debtor shall be sent to the mailing address of the Debtor stated herein; and
7. 06 Debtor agrees to pay on demand the amount of all expenses reasonably incurred by Secured Party in protecting or realizing on the property. In the event that this Security Agreement or any obligation secured by it is referred to an attorney for protecting or defending the priority of Secured Party's interest or for collection or realization procedures, Debtor agrees to pay a reasonable attorney's fee, including fees incurred in both trial and appellate courts, or fees incurred without suit, and expenses of title search and all court costs and costs of public officials. The sums agreed to be paid in this subparagraph shall be secured hereby; and
7. 07 If Secured Party disposes of the property, Debtor agrees to pay any deficiency remaining after application of the net proceeds to any indebtedness secured hereby.
7. 08 Secured Party shall have the right immediately and without further action by it, to set off against the obligations of Debtor all money owed by Secured Party in any capacity to Debtor, whether or not due, and Secured Party shall be deemed to have exercised such right of setoff and to have made a charge against any such money immediately upon occurrence of such default even though such charge is made or entered on the books of Secured Party subsequent thereto.
8. GENERAL. This agreement constitutes the entire agreement between the parties and may not be altered or amended except by a writing signed by the Debtor, accepted by Secured Party and attached hereto. Any provision found to be invalid shall not invalidate the remainder hereof. Waiver of any default shall not constitute a waiver of any subsequent default. All Secured Party's rights and remedies, whether evidenced hereby or by any other writing shall be cumulative and may be exercised singularly or concurrently. Any demand upon or notice to Debtor that Secured Party may give shall be effective when addressed and mailed to Debtor's address at which Secured Party customarily communicates with Debtor. This agreement and all rights and liabilities hereunder and in and to any and all obligations secured hereby, and in and to all collateral described above, shall inure to the benefit of the Secured Party and its successors and assigns, and shall be binding upon the Debtor and its successors and assigns. Whenever there is no outstanding obligation and no commitment on the part of Secured Party under any agreement which might give rise to an obligation, Debtor may terminate this agreement upon written notice to Secured Party. Prior to such termination, this shall be a continuing agreement in every respect. This instrument is to be governed by the laws of the State of Idaho. If this instrument is signed by more than one Debtor, the obligations of Debtor shall be joint and several. All words used herein shall be construed to be of such gender and number as the circumstances require and all references to Debtor shall include all other persons primarily or secondarily liable hereunder. This agreement is intended to take effect when signed by Debtor and delivered to Secured Party. This agreement shall be binding upon the heirs, personal representatives, successors and assigns of the Debtor and shall inure to the benefit of the Secured Party, its successors and assigns.

MORTGAGES OF PERSONAL PROPERTY:

See topic Chattel Mortgages; category Business Regulation and Commerce, topic Commercial Code.

MORTGAGES OF REAL PROPERTY:

Character of Mortgages.—Mortgage is a lien (45-901, 45-906) and shall not be deemed conveyance whatever its terms, so as to allow owner of mortgage to recover possession without foreclosure sale (6-104).

Every transfer of an interest in real property, other than in trust to secure performance of any obligation of trustor made only as security for the performance of another act is deemed to be a mortgage. (45-904).

A deed absolute on its face may be shown to be a mortgage by parol, except as against subsequent purchasers without notice or trustee under trust deed. (45-905).

Parties may make mortgage loan subject to Consumer Credit Code by agreement. (28-41-108).

Execution and Recording.—Mortgages or deeds of trust must be in writing, and may be acknowledged and recorded in the same manner and with the same effect as deeds. (45-902).

See note at head of Digest as to 1998 legislation covered.

See Topical Index in front part of this volume.

ID – 35

MORTGAGES OF REAL PROPERTY ... *continued*

Recording of instruments providing master forms of mortgages and trust deeds allowed. (45-1004).

Record of mortgage prior to July 1, 1945, does not constitute notice to subsequent purchasers or encumbrancers for more than ten years from date of maturity, except as date of maturity may be changed by extension agreement recorded before expiration of the ten-year period, or before Sept. 1, 1951, if the ten-year period from maturity expired before that date. (55-817).

Summary instrument allowed to be recorded to create any interest in real property, if it contains parties' names, complete mailing address of grantee, title and date of instrument, description of interest, legal description of real property and acknowledgment of all parties. (55-818).

Recording Fees.—See category Documents and Records, topic Records, subhead Fees.

Lien exists until debt secured by it is barred by limitations. Action may be maintained to quiet title against a mortgage, the collection and enforcement of which is barred by the Statute of Limitations, without proof that amount secured has been paid. (6-411 to 6-413).

After-acquired title of mortgagor or grantor in trust deed inures to benefit of mortgagee. (45-907).

Assignment of mortgage debt carries the security of mortgage with it. (45-911). Assignment of mortgage may be recorded and is notice to subsequent purchasers (45-909), but actual notice to mortgagor is necessary to invalidate payment made by him to mortgagee (45-910; 10 Idaho 618, 81 P. 55).

Release.—A recorded mortgage or chattel mortgage may be discharged by an entry in the margin of the record thereof, signed by the mortgagee, or his personal representative or assignee, acknowledging the satisfaction of the mortgage, in the presence of the recorder who must certify to the acknowledgment. (45-912). If not discharged by marginal release the same may be discharged by a certificate filed with the County Recorder for record and signed by the mortgagee, his personal representative, or assigns stating that the mortgage has been paid, satisfied or discharged. (45-913). Such certificate must be acknowledged as in the case of a mortgage or deed to real estate and must be recorded at length and a minute of the discharge made by the recorder on the record of the mortgage. (45-914). When any mortgage has been paid or satisfied the mortgagee or his assignee must immediately, on demand of the mortgagor, discharge the same as provided above, or deliver to the mortgagor such certificate of discharge. Refusal to do so renders the offending party liable to the mortgagor, his grantees or heirs for all damages, and also to a forfeit of the sum of $100. (45-915).

Deed of Trust.—Use of deed of trust of estates in real property located in incorporated cities or not exceeding 20 acres regardless of location authorized to secure performance of obligation, with power of sale in trustee upon breach. (45-1502[5]). Foreclosure by advertisement and sale or, as mortgage. (45-1503). Beneficiary cannot initiate judicial action to enforce obligation against grantor or his successor unless trust deed has been foreclosed by advertisement and sale or beneficiary's interest in property is substantially valueless as defined in 45-1503(2). (45-1503). Trustees must be member of bar, bank or savings and loan association, or corporation authorized to conduct trust business, licensed title insurance agent or title insurance company. (45-1504). Foreclosure by advertisement and sale if trust deed recorded in mortgage records of county and grantor is in default and notice of default containing nature of breach and election to sell is filed for record in county with copy to anyone requesting such notice. (45-1505). One hundred and twenty days notice of time, place, and basis for sale required to be given to grantor or successor in interest of record, lessee or occupant and lien holder of record, and also published in county where property situated once a week for four successive weeks, last publication at least 30 days prior to sale. If property be vacant, notice to be posted on premises. Affidavit of compliance to be recorded at least 20 days before sale. Any person, including beneficiary may bid. Trustee to execute trustee's deed conveying interest of grantor. Purchaser entitled to possession on tenth day following sale. (45-1506). Sale may be postponed if notice periods are interrupted by court order or bankruptcy stay. (45-1506A, 45-1507B). 30 days notice of rescheduled sale must be given by registered or certified mail to all persons entitled to notice of original sale and to all persons properly requesting notice. (45-1506A). Published notices affecting real property must contain legal description and street address or information to locate property or name and telephone number which may supply information regarding location. (60-113).

Grantor or junior encumbrancer, within 115 days of recording of notice of default if power of sale exercised, or any time prior to entry of decree of foreclosure, may pay amount due plus costs, trustee's fee incurred, not exceeding $115 in case default is cured prior to last newspaper publication of sale and attorney's fees as provided in promissory note, whereupon all proceedings must be discontinued and deed of trust reinstated. (45-1506).

Sale may be postponed at beneficiary's request by trustee announcing at time and place originally scheduled postponement to subsequent date and hour not more than 30 days after original date. Postponed sales may also be postponed in like manner. (45-1506[8]).

Proceeds of sale applied to expense of sale including charge of trustee and reasonable attorney's fees, obligation, any person having inferior recorded lien, and surplus to grantor. Sale forecloses all interest of all persons to whom notice is given such persons have no right of redemption. (45-1507, 1508).

Recorded trustee's deed prima facie evidence of truth of its recitals and of recorded affidavits regarding notice. These are conclusive in favor of purchasers in good faith for value. (45-1510). Additional notification of notice of default and notice of sale required as to person making recorded request therefor before recording of notice of default. (45-1511).

Money judgment may be sought within three months after sale for balance due, for amount that entire indebtedness exceeds fair market value at time of sale, with interest, as determined by court, but in no event for amount exceeding difference between amount for which property sold and entire amount of debt. (45-1512).

Time limits for advertisement and sale or foreclosure governed by law for foreclosure of mortgage. (45-1515).

Future Advances.—Mortgage may cover future advances. (45-108).

Foreclosure.—Foreclosure can only be by decree of the district court, which directs the sale of the property by the sheriff. Practice is similar to that in other civil actions. (See category Civil Actions and Procedure, topic Actions.) Proceeds of sale are applied first to costs and expenses of sale and then to amount due plaintiff. If balance still remains due deficiency judgment may be docketed against the defendants personally liable. Mortgagee cannot obtain property without foreclosure sale. Unrecorded lien holder or mortgagee need not be made party but sale is conclusive against such person. (6-101 to 6-107).

Redemption.—Property sold under mortgage foreclosure may be redeemed within one year from date of sale if land is more than 20 acres and six months if 20 acres or less, as in case of sale on execution. (11-401, 11-402). Amount necessary to redeem does not include any sum for attorney's fees greater than fee actually paid by creditor, or which he has by written instrument become unconditionally obligated to pay, within six months after sheriff's certificate of sale. (11-402).

Deficiency judgment may not be entered for any amount greater than the difference between the mortgage indebtedness as determined by the decree, plus costs of foreclosure and sale, and the reasonable value of the mortgaged property to be determined by the court in the decree. (6-108).

The following is a form of mortgage in use.

Forms

This indenture, made this . . . . day of . . . . in the year of our Lord one thousand nine hundred and . . . . between . . . . of . . . ., County of . . . ., State of . . . ., the part . . . . of the first part, and . . . . of . . . ., County of . . . ., State of . . . ., the part . . . . of the second part.

Witnesseth, that the said part . . . . of the first part, for and in consideration of the sum of . . . . dollars, ... of the United States of America, to . . . . h. . . . in hand paid by the said part . . . . of the second part, the receipt whereof is hereby acknowledged, have granted, bargained, sold and conveyed, and by these presents do . . . . grant, bargain, sell and convey, unto the said part . . . . of the second part, and to . . . . h . . . . heirs and assigns forever, all . . . . certain lot . . . ., piece . . . ., or parcel . . . . of land situate, lying and being in . . . ., County of . . . . and State of Idaho, and particularly described as follows: . . . ., together with all and singular the tenements, hereditaments, and appurtenances thereto belonging or in any wise appertaining.

This grant is intended as a mortgage to secure the payment of . . . . certain promissory note . . . . of even date herewith, executed and delivered by the said . . . . to the said part . . . . of the second part, which note . . . . in words and figures following, to wit: (note may be set forth in full or substance briefly stated).

And these presents shall be void if such payment . . . be made; but in case default shall be made in the payment of said principal sum . . . . of money or any part thereof as provided in said note . . . . or if the interest be not paid as therein specified, then and from thenceforth, it shall be optional with the said part . . . . of the second part, ... h . . . . executors, administrators or assigns to consider the whole of said principal sum . . . . expressed in said note . . . . as immediately due and payable, although the time expressed in said note . . . . for the payment thereof shall not have arrived and immediately to enter into and upon all and singular the above described premises, and to sell and dispose of the same according to law, and out of the money arising from such sale, to retain the principal and interest which shall then be due on said promissory note . . . . together with the costs and charges of foreclosure suit, including reasonable counsel fees, and also the amounts of all such payments of taxes, assessments, incumbrances, or insurance as may have been made by said part . . . . of the second part, ... h . . . . heirs, executors, administrators or assigns by reason of the permission hereinafter given, with the interest on the same hereinafter allowed, rendering the overplus of the purchase money (if any there shall be), unto the said . . . . part . . . . of the first part . . . . h . . . . heirs, executors, administrators, or assigns. And the said part . . . . of the first part . . . ., do . . . . hereby further covenant, promise and agree, to and with the said part . . . . of the second part to pay and discharge at maturity, all such taxes or assessments, liens or other incumbrances, now subsisting or hereafter to be laid or imposed upon said premises, or which may be in effect a prior charge thereupon to these presents during the continuance hereof and in default thereof the said part . . . . of the second part may pay and discharge the same, and may, at his option, keep fully insured against all risks by fire the buildings which now or may be hereafter erected thereon, at the expense of the said part . . . . of the first part, and the sums so paid shall bear interest at the rate of . . . . per cent per . . . . until paid, and shall be considered as secured by these presents and be a lien upon said from the proceeds of the sale thereof, above mentioned, with interest as herein provided.

In witness whereof, the said part . . . . of the first part ha. . . . hereunto set . . . . h . . . . hand . . . . and seal . . . . the day and year first above written.

Signed, Sealed and Delivered in the presence of: (Acknowledgment).

Assignment: Know all men by these presents: That . . . ., the part . . . . of the first part, for and in consideration of the sum of $. . . ., lawful money of the United States of America, to . . . . in hand paid by . . . ., the part . . . . of the second part, the receipt whereof is hereby acknowledged, do . . . . by these presents grant, bargain, sell, assign, transfer and set over unto the said part . . . . of the second part a certain indenture of mortgage bearing date the . . . . day of . . . . 19. . . . made and executed by . . . . mortgagor . . . ., to . . . . mortgagee . . . ., recorded in Book . . . . of Mortgages, page . . . . in the records of the office of the County Recorder of the County of . . . ., together with the note . . . . therein described and the money due and to grow due thereon with interest.

(Witness clause and acknowledgment as in above form).

Satisfaction: Know all men by these presents: That . . . . do . . . . hereby certify and declare that a certain mortgage bearing date the . . . . day of . . . . A.D. 19. . . ., made and executed by . . . . the part . . . . of the first part therein to . . . . the part . . . . of the second part therein, recorded in the office of the County Recorder of the County of . . . ., State

MORTGAGES OF REAL PROPERTY . . . *continued*
of Idaho, in Book . . . of Mortgages at page . . . ., on the . . . . day of . . . . A.D. 19. . . .,
together with the debt thereby secured, is fully paid, satisfied and discharged.
(Witness clause and acknowledgment as in mortgage form above).

Form for partial release same except that it is usual to describe the property released
and state that as to the remaining property included in the mortgage the same remains in
full force and effect.

Mortgage Guaranty Insurance.—Mortgage Guaranty Insurance Act (41-2650 to
41-2656) authorizes insurer of paid-in capital stock of not less than $1,000,000, and
surplus of $1,000,000 to insure against loss by reason of nonpayment of indebtedness
secured by mortgage or trust deed on real estate consisting of residences, industrial or
commercial buildings. (41-2653).

Chattel Mortgages.—See topic Chattel Mortgages.

PROPERTY

ABSENTEES:

Process Agent.—No statutory provision. See, however, category Civil Actions and
Procedure, topic Process, subhead Publication, and category Business Organizations,
topic Corporations.

Escheat.—Uniform Unclaimed Property Act (1981) adopted effective July 1, 1983.
(14-501 to 14-541). Following are changes or omissions from 1981 draft: Intangible
property defined to include judgment interest in favor of members of class. (14-
501[10][f]). Seven years must pass before presumption of abandonment arises under
general rule (14-502), for checks (14-505), deposit accounts (14-506), property held by
fiduciaries (14-512) and safe deposit boxes (14-516). 14-542 allows county to assume
responsibility for administration of unclaimed property in county hands.
Act enforced pursuant to Idaho Income Tax Act procedures and penalties. (14-523,
14-533). §34 of Uniform Act deleted.

ADVERSE POSSESSION:

To bar entry on or action to recover real property, adverse possession must be based
on a claim of title exclusive of any other right and must be actual, continuous, visible
and notorious for a period of five years prior to the commencement of the action and all
taxes legally assessed against said land during such period must have been paid by
claimant or his predecessors in interest. Where the claim of right is not founded on a
written instrument, judgment or decree, the land must have been protected by a substantial inclosure or must have been cultivated or improved. (5-210). If the claim of right is
founded upon a written instrument, judgment or decree substantial inclosure, usual
cultivation or improvement of all or a portion of the land or actual and ordinary use are
necessary. (5-208).

Easements.—Prescriptive easement must be established by open, notorious use of
servient property with actual or imputed knowledge thereof by owner of servient
tenement; use must be continuous for prescriptive period of five years and done under
claim of right. (98 Idaho 326, 563 P.2d 50). Statutory provisions pertaining to acquisition of title to realty by adverse possession do not apply to action to establish easement
by prescription. (83 Idaho 514, 365 P.2d 952).

Disabilities.—Persons under disability include those within age of majority, insane,
imprisoned upon conviction of criminal offense for term less than life, or married
woman where her husband is necessary party with her. During time of disability statute
of limitations for recovery of real property and period of time available to person under
disability to make entry or defense founded on title to real property is tolled. Person
under disability may make such entry or defense at any time within five years after
disability ceases. (5-213).

CONVEYANCES:

See topic Deeds.

CURTESY:

Abolished. (32-914). See category Estates and Trusts, topics Executors and Administrators, Descent and Distribution.

DEEDS:

See topic Real Property for types of estates.

Execution.—Conveyance of community real estate must be executed and acknowledged by husband and wife. (32-912). Either may, by express power of attorney, give to
the other complete power to sell or convey said community property. (32-912). See
also categories Debtor and Creditor, topic Homesteads, subhead Alienation or Encumbrance; Family, topic Husband and Wife.
Real estate is conveyed by instrument in writing subscribed by party or his authorized
agent in writing. Name of grantee and his complete mailing address must appear. (55-
601). Seals and attesting witnesses are unnecessary, though often used. Deed must be
acknowledged in order to be entitled to record. (55-805). For circumstances in which
spouses must join, see categories Debtor and Creditor, topic Homesteads, subhead
Alienation or Encumbrance; Family, topic Husband and Wife.

Recording in county where land is situated is necessary to afford protection against
third persons; unrecorded deed is void against subsequent purchaser or encumbrancer
for value without notice whose conveyance is first recorded. (55-812). (See also category Documents and Records, topic Records.)

Recording Fees.—See category Documents and Records, topic Records, subhead
Fees.

Summary Instrument.—55-818 allows recording of summary of any instrument
creating interest in real derperty. Must contain parties' names, grantee's complete

---

mailing address, title and date of instrument, description of interest, legal description of
real property, signature and acknowledgment of all parties.

Taxes.—There is no recording tax.

Conveyance by Attorney.—See topic Powers of Attorney.

Operation and Effect.—If the word "grant" is used in a conveyance of a fee simple
or an inheritance, the following covenants, and none others, are implied, unless changed
by express terms, on part of grantor (a) that grantor has not conveyed, previously, the
same estate or any right, title, or interest therein, to any person other than grantee and
(b) that such estate is free from encumbrances done, made or suffered by grantor or any
person under him. Such covenants may be sued upon as if expressly inserted. (55-612).
An instrument purporting to grant real property to take effect upon condition precedent
is merely an executory contract and does not pass the estate on performance of condition. (55-609). After-acquired interest in property passes by bargain and sale, grant and
warranty deeds. (55-605). Every grant is conclusive against grantor and all who claim
under him, except good faith purchaser or encumbrancer who acquires title or lien by
instrument or valid judgment lien that is first duly recorded. (55-606).
Forms in common use are as follows:

Forms

Warranty Deed: For Value Received . . . . . . the grantor . . . ., do . . . . hereby grant,
bargain, sell and convey unto . . . . . ., whose current address is . . . . . ., the grantee . . . .,
the following described premises, in . . . . . . County, Idaho, to wit: . . . . . . To have and
to hold the said premises, with their appurtenances unto the said Grantee . . . ., ...
heirs and assigns forever. And the said Grantor . . . . do . . . . hereby covenant to and
with the said Grantee . . . ., that . . . . he . . . . . . the owner . . . in fee simple of said
premises; that they are free from all encumbrances . . . . . . and that . . . . he . . . . will
warrant and defend the same from all lawful claims whatsoever. Dated: . . . . . .
[Signature lines][Acknowledgment]

Quitclaim Deed: For Value Received . . . . . . do hereby convey, release, remise and
forever quit claim unto . . . . . ., whose current address is . . . . . ., the following
described premises, to-wit: . . . . ., together with their appurtenances. Dated: . . . . . .,
[Signature lines][Acknowledgment]

DEEDS OF TRUST:

See category Mortgages, topic Mortgages of Real Property.

DOWER:

Does not exist. (32-914). See category Estates and Trusts, topics Executors and
Administrators, Descent and Distribution.

ESCHEAT:

See topic Absentees, subhead Escheat; category Estates and Trusts, topic Descent and
Distribution, subhead Escheat.

LANDLORD AND TENANT:

Leases for more than one year must be in writing and acknowledged and recorded
like deeds (9-503), but tenant's possession under unrecorded lease is generally considered sufficient notice to put third persons on inquiry as to his rights although there is no
statute or decision on the point.
Husband and wife must join in lease of community property. (32-912; 35 Idaho 359,
206 P. 692).

Recording.—Void as against subsequent purchasers or mortgagees unless recorded.
Recorded in recorder's office of county where land situated. (55-812).

Termination of Tenancy.—A tenancy or other estate at will, however created, may
be terminated by the landlord giving notice in writing to the tenant to remove from the
premises within a period of not less than one month, to be specified in the notice. (55-
208).
After such notice has been served and the period specified by such notice has expired,
but not before, the landlord may reenter or proceed according to law to recover
possession. (55-209).

Holding Over.—Where tenant continues in possession of tract five acres or less, in
person or by subtenant, after default in payment of rent, landlord, after a three days
notice in writing requiring payment of rent or delivery of possession of premises served
upon tenant, may bring an action in district court to recover possession. (6-303). If
included in notice attorney fees available in action. (6-324).

Dispossession.—Failure to perform any of the conditions or covenants of the lease
and three days notice served upon the tenant requiring the performance of such conditions or covenants or the delivery of possession of the premises entitles the landlord to
maintain an action for the restitution of the leased premises. (6-303).
In an action exclusively for possession of five acres or less for nonpayment of rent,
complaint must state description, possession with defendant, and defendant in default of
rent, all notices have been served on defendant, and plaintiff is entitled to possession.
Court shall issue summons and schedule trial 12 days from filing complaint, but not less
than five days from service on defendant. No continuance shall be granted without
defendant giving an undertaking. After hearing court may grant judgment against
defendant for restitution and costs. Plaintiff may still bring action for damages. Execution directed to sheriff directs defendant and goods to be removed and levy may be
made for costs and disbursements on goods of defendant. Plaintiff may file action for
restitution and damages but no hearing may be set for early trial. Damages occasioned
by forcible entry shall be assessed, judgment shall be three times damages and rent
found due. If tract of land is larger than five acres and lease has not expired, tenant may
pay amount found due as rent, interest, damages and costs within five days and be
restored to his estate. If payment not made in five days judgment may be enforced and

---

See note at head of Digest as to 1998 legislation covered.

See Topical Index in front part of this volume.

LANDLORD AND TENANT . . . *continued*

possession returned to landlord. In all other cases judgment may be enforced immediately. (6-310 to 6-316). If included in notice attorney fees available in action. (6-324). Treble damages available. (6-317).

Action by Tenant.—Tenant may file action for specific performance of lease or for damages for stated causes. If action for specific performance only, trial may be had within 12 days of filing complaint but not less than five days after service. Complaint must set forth relevant facts, description and any additional circumstances. Landlord must have three days written notice before filing. (6-320). Treble damages available. (6-317).

Security Deposits.—Any deposit other than rent is security deposit. Upon termination and surrender security deposit must be refunded except as per agreement. Landlord cannot retain deposit to cover normal wear and tear. (6-321).

Fixtures.—A tenant may remove from the premises, during the continuance of his term, anything affixed thereto for the purpose of trade, manufacture, ornament or domestic use, if the removal can be effected without injury to the premises, unless the thing has by manner in which affixed become an integral part of premises. (55-308).

Lien.—No statutory provision.

Uniform Residential Landlord and Tenant Act.—Not adopted.

LEASES:

Leases of more than ten head of livestock must be in writing, acknowledged like real property grants and recorded. (25-2001).
See topic Landlord and Tenant.

PERPETUITIES:

The absolute power of alienation of real property cannot be suspended by any limitation or condition for a longer period than during the continuance of the lives of persons in being at the creation of the limitation or condition and 25 years thereafter, except that a contingent remainder in fee may be created on a prior remainder in fee to take effect in the event that the persons to whom the first remainder is limited die under 21 years, or upon any other contingency by which the estate of such persons may be determined before majority. (55-111, 55-202).

No rule against perpetuities on real or personal property; no prohibition of restraints on alienation of personal property; trusts, past or future, to be construed as to eliminate parts violating statute, and not to be declared void, no presumption that person capable of having children at any stage of adult life. (55-111).

Common law rule against perpetuities not in force. (69 Idaho 84, 203 P.2d 380).

Accumulations.—No statutory restrictions. Common law rules presumably prevail. See also category Estates and Trusts, topic Trusts.

PERSONAL PROPERTY:

Presumption that all property acquired during marriage is community property. Tenancy by entirety nonexistent concept.

POWERS OF ATTORNEY:

Attorneys in Fact.—Real property may be conveyed or mortgaged by an attorney in fact under power of attorney, who must subscribe the name of his principal as well as his own name. (55-602).

An instrument so executed may not be recorded until the power of attorney, duly acknowledged, is filed for record in the same county office. (55-806).

Revocation.—Power of attorney may not be revoked by instrument unless revoking instrument is recorded in same office original power was recorded. (55-814).

Uniform Durable Power of Attorney Act adopted effective July 1, 1982. (15-5-501 to 15-5-507).

If power of attorney contains words "This power of attorney shall not be affected by the disability of the principal," power is exercisable regardless of disability of principal or uncertainty as to whether principal is dead or alive. (15-5-501). Acts undertaken in good faith by agent prior to actual knowledge of death of principal are valid and binding. (15-5-504).

REAL PROPERTY:

Conveyance is presumed to pass fee simple estate. (55-604). Grant or devise to two or more persons creates tenancy in common, unless expressly declared to create joint tenancy or unless property is acquired as partnership or community property. (55-104, 508). Remainders and life estates are recognized. (55-201). No tenancy by entirety recognized by case or statute.

Instruments affecting real estate in Idaho are not valid unless executed in substantial conformity with Idaho laws.

Rule in Shelley's Case has been abrogated. (55-206).

Foreign Conveyances or Encumbrances.—See category Documents and Records, topic Records.

Condominiums permitted. (55-1501 to 55-1527).

See also topics Curtesy, Deeds, Dower, Landlord and Tenant; categories Business Regulation and Commerce, topic Consumer Credit; Civil Actions and Procedure, topic Partition; Debtor and Creditor, topic Homesteads; Family, topic Husband and Wife; Mortgages, topic Mortgages of Real Property.

TRUST DEEDS:

See category Mortgages, topic Mortgages of Real Property.

TAXATION

ADMINISTRATION:

State Taxes.—State Tax Commission has general supervision over administration of tax laws. (63-105).

County, School and Municipal Taxes.—See topic Property (Ad Valorem) Taxes.
Resort Tax.—Resort cities with population under 20,000 authorized to impose certain non-property resort taxes. (1978, c. 261). Resort counties authorized to impose sales or use tax. (63-2603). Resort county defined. (63-2602).

Assessment of Taxes.—See topic Property (Ad Valorem) Taxes, subhead Assessment.

Board of tax appeals established to provide appeal from final determination tax liability, including that from 63-501 (real and personal property assessment), 63-511, appeal may be concurrently to district court (property valuation by Board of Equalization), 63-3049 (income tax deficiency) and 63-3632 (sales tax liability). (63-3811). See topics Property (Ad Valorem) Taxes, subhead Review of Assessment; Income Tax.

Exemptions.—See topics Income Tax, subhead Income Taxed—Individuals and Property (Ad Valorem) Taxes, subhead Exemptions.

Penalties.—
Real and Personal Property Tax.—Real property tax delinquents are assessed 2% penalty and interest at 1% from Jan. 1 of following year, if on first instalment and Jan. 1 of same year if on second installment. (63-903). Delinquency entry made one year after first Mon. in Jan.; and if property not redeemed by taxpayer within three years of delinquency entry, county treasurer makes tax deed to county. (63-1005;-1007). Personal property tax becomes delinquent on 20th day of Dec. of taxing year, 2% penalty plus 1% interest assessed. If one-half instalment paid on tax by Dec. 20, remaining instalment becomes delinquent on June 20 of following year, 2% penalty plus 1% interest assessment. (63-904). Delinquent taxes collectible by warrant of distraint. (63-904;-1012).
Inheritance and Estate Tax.—Estate and transfer tax due on same date as federal estate tax. Interest upon deficiency is at 12% per year. (14-406; 63-3045).
Income tax returns filed late bear 12% interest and any deficiency bears 12% interest. (63-3045). Any deficiency due to negligence without fraud is assessed 5%; if due to fraud 50%. If no required return is filed or in event return is filed but tax shown thereon to be due is not paid, penalty assessed of 5% of tax due for each month until penalty amounts to 25% of tax due. Additional 10% imposed on underpayment resulting from substantial understatement (as defined) of tax required. (63-3046). Failure to pay tax or make return is misdemeanor with fine of not more than $300 or imprisonment for not more than six months or both; failure to collect, account for or pay over tax money is felony and subject to fine of not more than $10,000 or imprisonment for not more than five years or both; willful assisting, counseling or advising in preparation of false and fraudulent return is felony with fine of not more than $10,000 or imprisonment for not more than five years or both. (63-3075).
Sales and Use Tax.—Engaging in retail business without permit is misdemeanor subject to fine of $100 per day; giving false resale exemption certificate for purpose of evading tax is misdemeanor subject to fine not to exceed $1,000 or imprisonment not to exceed one year or both. 12% interest charged on late payment. (63-3621, 63-3622). Collector may require retailer to provide security for payment in amount of three times estimated average monthly payment or $10,000 whichever is less. (63-3625). Penalties in case of deficiencies, failure to make return, failure to remit tax collected are same as under catchline Income Tax, supra, for similar offenses. (63-3634). Use tax violation is misdemeanor, with fine not to exceed $100; each violation is separate offense. (63-3621).
Motor Fuels (Gasoline Tax).—Violation is misdemeanor. (63-2411, 63-2433).

Interstate Co-operation.—No procedure provided.

Taxpayer Bill of Rights.—Governs location of information, communications by tax officials, harassment or abuse, false or misleading representations, unfair practices, multiple tax obligations, civil liability against revenue officers, etc. (63-4001 to 63-4011).

CARAVANING TAX:

See category Transportation, topic Motor Vehicles, subhead Caravaning Tax.

CIGARETTE TAXES:

Cigarette tax imposed by 63-2506.

CORPORATE LICENSE TAXES:

See topic Income Tax, subhead Income Taxed—Corporations.

ESTATE TAX:

See topic Inheritance Tax.

GASOLINE AND SPECIAL FUELS TAXES:

Motor Fuels Tax.—Imposed by 63-2402, 63-2405, 63-2416, 63-2417.

Special Fuels Tax.—Imposed by 49-1231.

GENERATION SKIPPING TAX:

None.

GIFT TAX:

None; but inheritance tax applies to gifts in contemplation of donor's death, or to take effect after his death. See topic Inheritance Tax.

See note at head of Digest as to 1998 legislation covered.

See Topical Index in front part of this volume.

INCOME TAX:

Provisions are identical, so far as possible, with Internal Revenue Code of 1986, as in effect on Jan. 1, 1997. (63-3002, 63-3004).

Returns required by resident individual required to file federal return under §6012(a)(1) of Internal Revenue Code (63-3030[a][1]); corporations; estates if $600 gross income; trust with $100 gross income; partnerships; fiduciaries. Husband and wife, if both residents, may make joint return. Return due Apr. 15 following close of taxable year or 15th day of fourth month after close of fiscal year. (63-3032). Tax payable in full. Employers, except farmers, required to withhold amount substantially equivalent to tax to be due from employee (pursuant to tables prepared by state tax commission), unless employee's wages are less than $1,000 a year. Payment and reporting to be monthly. (63-3035, 36). Employers must register with State Tax Commission if they are required to withhold wages. (63-3035). Farmer-employer to withhold 1% if wages paid exceed $150 a year. Corporations must pay estimated taxes if tax liability will exceed $500. (63-3036A).

Income Taxed—Individuals.—Any taxpayer having income taxable both within and without state must allocate and apportion such income in accordance with rule set forth in §63-3027. Business income apportioned to Idaho according to formula. Rents and royalties from real or tangible personal property, capital gains, interest, dividends, or patents or copyrights, to extent that they constitute nonbusiness income, are allocable to this state if they were derived from sources within state. (63-3027). Net operating losses of corporation in year corporation had no business situs may not be subtracted. (63-3022[d]).

Rate.—Graduated tax is imposed on taxable income of individuals, estates and trusts, at following rate:

When taxable income is:	Rate is:
Less than $1,000	2%
$1,000 to $1,999	$20 plus 4% of amount over $1,000
$2,000 to $2,999	$60 plus 4.5% of amount over $2,000
$3,000 to $3,999	$105 plus 5.5% of amount over $3,000
$4,000 to $4,999	$160 plus 6.5% of amount over $4,000
$5,000 to $7,499	$225 plus 7.5% of amount over $5,000
$7,500 to $19,999	$412.50 plus 7.8% of amount over $7,500
Over $20,000	$1,387.50 plus 8.2% of amount over $20,000

(63-3024). Additional tax of $10 levied on every person—husband and wife filing joint return considered as single person—required to file income tax return. Tax payable at time of filing income tax return. (63-3082).

Exemptions.—Taxable income, gross income, adjusted gross income are defined same as in Internal Revenue Code. Idaho taxable income means income as modified in 63-3001 to 63-3068. Also include state income taxes paid or assessed during taxable years plus net operating loss deduction used in arriving at taxable income as defined in IRC. (63-3022). Special definition for corporations and no deduction allowed for federal income tax paid. (63-3027, 63-3021[a]). Compensation paid active servicemen by armed forces for services performed outside state is deducted. (63-3022). Special individual deductions for certain retirement benefits (63-3022[o], 63-3022A), insulation of residences (63-3022B), alternative energy devices at residences (63-3022C), household and dependent care services (63-3022D), dependents 65 years of age or older living with taxpayer and developmentally disabled (63-3022E), certain capital gains (63-3022H), and amounts resulting from participation in residential energy conservation and weatherization programs (63-3022F). Deduction for interest earned on farm operating loans repealed effective Jan. 1, 1987. (1987, c. 290).

Tax Credits.—Resident individual allowed credit or refund equal to $15 or balance of his unused credit, whichever is greater, per personal exemption. (63-3024A). Credit to individual taxpayers given for income taxes paid to another state in respect to income included in taxable income in Idaho, subject to qualifications. (63-3029). Certain payments to retired civil service employees exempt. (63-3022A).

Nonresidents.—Resident is individual who resided or domiciled in Idaho for full taxable year. Specific exceptions provided for absences from state (63-3013); part-year resident is individual who is absent from state at least 445 days in first 15 months after leaving state, except for stated exceptions (63-3013[b]). Nonresident defined as any individual who is not resident or part-year resident. (63-3014). Special provisions for part-year residents and nonresidents. (63-3027A).

Appeals.—Provision for redetermination or deficiency notice, with 63 days thereafter for taxpayer to protest to Tax Commission or seek review by complaint in District Court of Ada County or county of taxpayer's residence, upon payment of deficiency or posting bond. Redetermination by State Tax Commission may be reviewed in District Court for Ada County or in District Court in taxpayer's county by complaint filed within 91 days of receipt of decision of State Tax Commission, or within same 91 days, by filing appeal with Board of Tax Appeals. (63-3045 to 63-3049). Final order of District Court subject to appeal to Supreme Court as provided under rules of appeal. See category Civil Actions and Procedure, topic Appeal and Error. Enforcement of collection by suit, certificate of lien, writ of distraint, jeopardy assessment as appropriate. (63-3050 to 63-3065). Taxes to be assessed within three years, or if taxable income increased by federal audit and no adjustment reported to state, then within one year from notice of final determination to tax collector: assessments barred thereafter: if fraud, taxes to be assessed within three years after discovery of fraud, otherwise barred. (63-3068, 63-3070).

Election Campaign Fund.—Every individual whose income tax liability is $1 or more may designate that $1 be paid into political party of his choice as designated on form or into general election campaign fund to be distributed according to statute. (63-3088).

Income Taxed—Corporations.—Corporate rate 8% of all taxable income derived from sources within Idaho, but minimum tax is $20. (63-3025). Franchise tax equal to 8% of all taxable income derived from sources within Idaho imposed on corporation exercising corporate franchise within Idaho; minimum franchise tax is $20. (63-3025A). Corporation taxed under 63-3025A not taxed under 63-3025. (63-3025).

Exemptions.—Exempt organizations are those in §501 IRC plus (unless specifically denied by §§502, 503, 504 IRC) fraternal beneficiary societies of lodge type; farmers' or other mutual hail, cyclone, casualty or fire insurance companies or associations income of which is used or held only for payment of losses; certain cooperative farmers for fruit growers associations; federal land banks; national farm loan associations. (63-3025B).

Forms, etc., may be obtained from State Tax Commissioner, Boise.

INHERITANCE TAX:

Governed by 14-401 to 14-412.

Taxable Estate.—Idaho uses definition found in §§2032A and 2051 of U.S. Internal Revenue Code, as amended. (14-402[13], 14-402A).

Rates of Tax and Exemptions.—For residents, tax is in amount equal to federal credit and is imposed on transfer of taxable estate. Different tax imposed if resident's property is subject to death tax imposed by another state. (14-403). Tax on nonresident's Idaho estate is computed by multiplying federal credit by fraction, numerator of which is Idaho property's value and denominator is decedent's gross estate's value. (14-404).

Administration and Enforcement.—Subject to administration of State Tax Commission. (14-412).

When Due.—Tax due and payable by personal representative on or before date return is required to be filed under 14-405. (14-406).

Returns and Reports.—Personal representative of estate subject to Idaho Estate and Transfer Tax and who is required by U.S. law to file federal estate tax return must file state tax return and copy of federal tax return with commission on or before date that federal tax return must be filed. (14-405).

Liability.—Any personal representative who fails to pay any required tax prior to distributing any portion of property is personally liable for tax and applicable interest and penalties. (14-410).

Apportionment Against Inter Vivos Dispositions.—None.

INSURANCE PREMIUM TAX:

See category Insurance, topic Insurance Companies.

MINING TAX:

See category Mineral, Water and Fishing Rights, topic Mines and Minerals.

MOTOR CARRIER FUELS TAX:

See topic Gasoline and Special Fuels Taxes.

PROPERTY (AD VALOREM) TAXES:

All property not exempt is subject to assessment and taxation. (63-203).

Exemptions.—Following property is exempt: Public property of U.S. (except where taxation authorized by Congress), state, county, city or school district (63-602A); property of religious, fraternal, benevolent or charitable corporations or societies, or World War veteran organization buildings and memorials, to extent used for purposes of society or organization only, portion used for commercial purposes not being exempt (63-602B, C); capital stock, bonds and other intangible personal property; deposits in banks and shares and accounts of savings and loan associations and credit unions (63-602L); household goods and furniture, and wearing apparel, in actual use in private home or on person of owner (63-602I); possessory right to public lands (63-602F); mining claims not patented (63-602F); irrigation canals, ditches with essential operating personal property of nonprofit canal company, and water rights (63-602N); property used for generating and delivering electric power and natural gas energy to extent such property is used for furnishing power for pumping water for irrigation or drainage on Idaho land (63-602O); hospitals and refuge homes and their furniture and equipment owned and operated by religious or benevolent society from which no gain or profit can be derived (63-602D); property used exclusively for school or educational purposes from which no profit is derived (63-602E); public cemeteries (63-602F); cooperative telephone lines of 25 or fewer subscribers from which no profit is derived (63-602Q); public libraries (63-602F); motor vehicles properly registered and licensed under Idaho laws, including pleasure boats (not to include mobile homes [63-603]) (63-602L); dues and credits secured by mortgage trust deeds or other liens (63-602M); facilities, installations, machinery, installed and utilized in water or air pollution control (63-602P); assessment on fruits and vegetables held for sale for human consumption, and any processed product thereof, or seed, in hands of farmers, producers or processors, or such items being held, transported, or held in storage in public or private warehouses (63-602S), and assessments on personal property, manufactured or processed in state by persons having domicile or place of business in Idaho, being stored in public or private warehouses are canceled upon proof that goods were actually sold or shipped out of Idaho on or before Dec. 1 of current year of assessment (63-602T); also exempt is personal property in transit, including personal property shipped into state and stored in public or private warehouse, not offered for sale in state and designated for reshipment outside of state, and exemption not lost if, while in storage, property is labeled, packaged, disassembled, divided, broken in bulk, repackaged, or held for reshipment for customers outside state (63-602U, V); agricultural crops, while title remains with producer, fruit and nut bearing trees and grape vines, except as they enhance value of land, provided that this exemption does not include timber, forest land or forest products (63-602R); business inventory (63-602K); upon application lesser of first $50,000 or 50% of market value for assessment purposes of residential improvements on primary dwelling is exempt from ad valorem taxation (63-602G); qualified equipment utilizing post-consumer waste or postindustrial wasted (63-602cc); real or personal property owned or leased by nonprofit organization deferred (63-202DD).

All property defined as business inventory is exempt from taxation. (63-602W). Leased business inventory not exempt but shall return to its exempt status after any lease expires. (63-602Y).

Hardship Situations.—Real and personal property exempt when payment of tax would create undue hardship on owner of property. Exemption exists for current tax year only. Two types of exemptions. (63-602AA, 63-711).

See note at head of Digest as to 1998 legislation covered.

See Topical Index in front part of this volume.

PROPERTY (AD VALOREM) TAXES . . . *continued*

Partial, Graduated Exemption.—Allowed person 65 or older; fatherless child under age 18; widow; blind person; service-connected disabled veteran of any war engaged in by U.S.; disabled person receiving disability benefits pursuant to 42 USCA 423, 45 USCA 228, 45 USCA 231 or 5 USCA 8337; prisoners of war. Claimant must have been domiciled in Idaho with family income from all sources not exceeding $8,750 and own homestead as defined in statute, evidenced by proof of taxes levied in Idaho during calendar year immediately preceding year of claim. (63-701 to 63-710). Must claim between Jan. 1 and Apr. 15 of each year. (63-706).

Members of Armed Forces.—No exemption for members of armed services presently in service, except they are exempt from occupational or professional licenses while in service. (63-2620A).

Assessment.—Property must be assessed as of 12:01 a.m. of first day of year in year in which taxes are levied. (63-205, 63-206[1]). All property is assessed by county assessor of county where located. (63-219). Exceptions include operating property of public utilities and car companies which are assessed by State Tax Commission. (63-401). Assessor may require resident property owner to furnish by Mar. 15, list of all taxable personal property owned by him or in his possession and situate in county from which list assessor will determine assessed valuation. (63-302[1]).

Nonresident Property Owners.—Must forward to assessor by Mar. 15 list of all taxable real and personal property. Failure may result in penalty of $100 plus 2% of assessed value. (63-302).

Transient Personal Property.—Subject to assessment and taxation in each of counties in which it is moved or kept during same year on pro rata basis. (63-201[24] and 63-313).

Review of Assessment.—Board of County Commissioners meets as Board of Equalization at least once each month up to fourth Mon. of June for purpose of equalizing assessment for real and personal property, and on fourth Mon. of June and from day to day thereafter as needed, to complete equalization. Equalization must be completed by second Mon. in July. (63-501). Appeal to Board of Tax Appeals must be taken within 30 days after mailing of notice of decision, or oral pronouncement at hearing by Board of County Commissioners. (63-511). Appeal from Board of Tax Appeals is to District Court in county of residence, or county in which property affected is located. Notice specifying grounds is filed with clerk of Board of Tax Appeals within 30 days after deposit in mail of decision by Board of Tax Appeals. Any record made and record of procedure filed by clerk with District Court heard by District Court without jury, de novo. Final order of District Court is subject to appeal to Supreme Court as provided by law. (63-38 12). Decision of State Tax Commission assessing value of operating property may be appealed to District Court in which property located. (63-409). See category Civil Actions and Procedure, topic Appeal and Error.

Payment.—All real property taxes payable on or before Dec. 20 without penalty and may be paid in two equal installments, Dec. 20 and June 20 of following year. No payments received between Dec. 21 and fourth Mon. in Jan. or June 21 and fourth Mon. in July. If Dec. 20 or June 20 falls on Sat., Sun., or holiday, payment required payable on next regular workday following Dec. 20 or June 20. Not less than two nor more than five months before period of redemption expires county tax collector must give notice of pending issuance of tax deed. (63-1005).

Except as hereinafter provided, all personal property taxes are payable to tax collector on demand and become delinquent if not paid on or before due date specified on demand notice. If no demand is made, taxes must be paid in two instalments; one-half becomes delinquent if not paid by Dec. 20 and second half becomes delinquent if not paid by June 20, together with penalty of 2% of instalment plus 1% per month dating back to Jan. 1. If first instalment not paid by Dec. 20, entire tax is due and payable together with penalty of 2% of tax plus 1% per month dating back to Jan. 1. Taxpayer may appeal to board of county commissioners for extension not to exceed four months. (63-904).

All taxes and all other fees and amounts in excess of $100,000 must be paid by electronic funds transfer. (67-2026, 67-2026A).

Migratory Property.—Personal property coming into state from without state after first day of Jan. and before Apr. 1 is assessed at full cash value; from Apr. 1 to July 1, three-fourths; from July 1 to Oct. 1, one-half; thereafter one-fourth. (63-205[1], [2] and 63-311[3]).

Lien.—Taxes are lien from and after property becomes subject to assessment. (63-205 and 63-206[21]).

Sales.—All property acquired by counties by tax deed must be offered for sale at least biennially. Notice is published for 30 days and property sold to highest bidder, and any property not sold can be sold later without further notice. (31-808, 834-5).

Where purchaser from county has peaceably possessed property and paid taxes thereon for six years, no action can thereafter be maintained to contest tax deed or tax proceedings. (63-1011[1], [2]). County may exchange real property not needed for other real property.

If any person refuses to pay tax levied on personal property, sheriff shall seize and sell enough personal property to satisfy tax. (63-1101). Tax collector may purchase personal property in name of county if sum sufficient to defray tax and costs of sale has not been bid. (63-1108).

Redemption.—May be made within three years from date of delinquency entry, and thereafter up to time contract of sale of property is entered into by county or property has been transferred by county deed, by paying all taxes with penalties and interest to date of redemption. (63-1004, -1005 and -1007). Right to redemption expires five years after issuance of tax deed to county even if county never contracts for sale of property. (63-1007).

Public Service Corporation Property Tax.—Operating property of any utility for transportation of commodities, wholly or partly within state, and operating in more than one county shall be assessed for state, county, city, town, village, school district and other purposes by State Tax Commission. Statement showing all taxable property to be submitted by owner. (63-701).

REAL ESTATE CONVEYANCE TAX:

None.

SALES AND USE TAXES:

Sales tax on retail sales is 5% (63-3619), including rentals, hotels, instalment and credit sales. Auditorium district may levy 5% sales tax on hotel-motel receipts. (67-4917A, 46-4917B). Retailer must collect tax from purchaser, keeping records. Presumption is that all sales of personal property are taxable and retailer has burden of proof giving rise to claim for exemption from tax unless purchaser provides resale certificate to retailer. (63-3620 to 63-3626). It is duty of purchaser to provide certificate of exemption for resale. Sale or purchase of prefabricated building is sale or purchase of real estate, not tangible personal property. (63-3606A). Vending machine sales are presumed to be at price 117% of cost. Resort cities authorized to impose certain sales taxes related to dominant trade. (1978, c. 261). No time limitation on assessment and collection of sales tax from retailer, seller or other person who has failed to pay over such taxes to commission. (63-3633[d]).

Use Tax.—Excise tax at rate of 4% on storage, use or consumption in Idaho of tangible personal property, unless retailer pays Idaho sales tax on transaction and collects tax from customer. Certain exemptions detailed in statutes. (63-3622A thru DD). Reciprocity granted for sales tax paid to other states which allow similar credit against use tax for purchases made in Idaho. (63-3601 to 63-3638).

Exemptions from Sales and Use Taxes.—Exemptions include, among other things, sale for resale and personal property used or consumed primarily in production process. (63-3622A thru DD). Specific exemption for property donated to nonprofit organization or to state or its subdivisions. (63-3621).

Returns.—Retailers to remit on monthly basis; accounting procedures detailed in statutes. (63-3601 to 63-3638).

Utility Taxes.—Special license tax of one-half mill per kilowatt hour is imposed on individuals, firms, partnerships, common law trusts, corporations, associations or other organizations manufacturing or producing electricity and electrical energy in state except that generated or sold for use in manufacturing, mining, milling, smelting, refining or processing. Persons liable for tax must file monthly statements with State Tax Commissioner on or before last of each month and pay tax at same time. (63-2701).

SPECIAL FUELS TAX:

See topic Gasoline and Special Fuels Taxes.

STAMP TAX:

No requirement of documentary stamps.

UNEMPLOYMENT COMPENSATION TAX:

Unemployment compensation tax (in guise of "contributions") is imposed on every employer who, in any calendar quarter, becomes liable for wages of $300 or more, except for following exempt services: Those to U. S. government when exempted by constitution; services with respect to which unemployment compensation is payable under system established by Act of Congress; contractual services where free from control or direction and where contractor is customarily engaged in independently established trade, occupation, profession or business same as involved in contract; agricultural labor, unless employer pays at least $20,000 for agricultural labor in any one year or employs ten agricultural laborers at least one day during 20 different weeks of year; services in employ of spouse and services performed by person under age of 18 in employ of father or mother; service performed by individual under 22 enrolled as full time student at accredited nonprofit or public education institution for which credit is earned in program combining academic instruction with work experience; services of individual under 18 in delivery or distribution of newspapers or shopping news; domestic services in private home, local college club or local chapter of college fraternity or sorority unless person is paid wages exceeding $1,000; services as student nurse in employ of hospital or nurses' training school where regularly enrolled and approved by state law, and services performed as hospital intern by individual having completed medical course in medical school chartered or approved pursuant to law of Idaho; services in employ of convention or association organized and operated primarily for religious activities; services performed by elected official, member of legislative body or judiciary; member of national guard, employee serving on temporary basis during emergency; employee in position designated as major nontenured policy making or advisory, or policy making or advisory position performance of duties of which ordinarily does not require more than eight hours per week; inmate of custodial or penal institution; employee of educational institution devoted to preparing ministers; duly ordained or licensed minister; facilities conducted to provide remunerative work for physically or mentally handicapped; service performed by individual as part of unemployment work relief or work training program financed by any federal or state agency or political subdivision thereof; insurance agents or real estate brokers whose sole remuneration is commission; service performed by student at school where he is regularly enrolled; service performed at hospital by patient.

Employers' contributions, levied as excise tax, are payable at rates set forth on table in 72-1350. Contribution rate based upon experience factor, set out in detail in statute. (72-1351). No contributions required from employees. Tax payable to Director for Employment Security Fund. (72-1301 to 72-1380).

UNIFORM FEDERAL LIEN REGISTRATION ACT AMENDED:

Adopted. (45-201 to 45-207 am'd 1979, c. 226).

USE TAX:

See topic Sales and Use Taxes.

See note at head of Digest as to 1998 legislation covered.

See Topical Index in front part of this volume.

TRANSPORTATION

MOTOR VEHICLES:

Uniform Acts Adopted.—Motor Vehicle Anti-theft; Motor-Vehicle Registration with changes. (49-441 to 49-456). Regulating Traffic on Highways, with changes. (49-206 to -223; 49-601 to -673; 49-701 to -724; 49-801 to -810; 49-901 to -965; 49-1001 to -1013; 49-1301 to -1315; 49-1401 to -1430). Motor Vehicle Nonresident Violator Compact. (49-2501).

Department of Transportation supervises registration and licensing of motor vehicles and motor vehicle manufacturers, dealers and chauffeurs. Department of Law Enforcement has general supervision over all penal and regulatory laws relating to motor vehicles, address Motor Vehicle Division Department of Law Enforcement, P.O. Box 34, Boise, Idaho 83731. (49-201; 67-2901).

Vehicle registration required annually excepting nonpay passenger vehicles, then by 12 month periods with plates issued no less than every five years with annual registration stickers. (49-441; 49-443). Number plates must be displayed front and rear. Properly registered vehicles exempt from taxation. (49-401). Applicant must display to county assessor current certificate of liability insurance before vehicle can be registered. (49-1229).

Driver's license is required; expires on birthday of operator in fourth year following date of issuance. (49-319). May be extended under certain conditions for up to 12 months. (49-319). No person may receive license until he surrenders all valid operator's licenses issued to him and in his possession from other states or executes affidavit that he does not possess driver's license. (49-301). License required after 90 days continuous residence in Idaho. (49-119[11]). Applicant for license must be examined by sheriff or deputy in any county most convenient to applicant. (49-313). Minimum age limit for license is 16 years (limited license available if 15 and successfully completed approved driver training course [49-305]). (49-303). Following are exempt: operators of vehicles in service of Armed Forces, operators of special mobile equipment and farm tractors, nonresidents at least 15 years old licensed in home state, nonresidents over 18 years whose home state does not require license, may operate for 90 days in each calendar year as operator. (49-302). Issued by Department of Transportation.

Titles, Sales and Liens.—Every sale or transfer of a motor vehicle must be registered with Department of Transportation on forms provided by it and certificate of title issued, which must evidence all liens on vehicle. (49-503 to 49-510). Electronic (paperless) record of title is authorized. (49-505).

Lien or encumbrance on a motor vehicle is not valid against creditors or subsequent purchasers or encumbrancers without notice until holder has filed with Department copy of conveyance documentation and application signed by purchaser (49-510, 49-504), which must be accompanied by properly endorsed certificate of title. Fee is $1. Thereupon new certificate will be issued upon which facts concerning lien or encumbrance will be endorsed. (49-510).

Conditional Sales Act does not apply to motor vehicles.

Express Warranties.—Manufacturer of motor vehicle making express warranty must maintain service and repair facility reasonably close to all areas in which its motor vehicles are sold. (48-901 to 48-909). Manufacturer's duty to repair. (48-902). Manufacturer's duty to refund or replace. (48-903).

Possessory Liens.—Persons performing labor upon, repairing, storing or caring for motor vehicles have lien thereon dependent on possession for their compensation. If not paid within two months, lienor may sell on ten days' published notice, paying any surplus over amount of lien and costs to owner. (45-805).

Weight Limitations.—Regulated by 49-1001 to 49-1012.

Equipment Required.—Regulated by 49-619 and 49-901 to 49-965. Car safety seat required of resident parents when transporting child under four years or less than 40 lbs. Failure to comply infraction but not evidence of contributory negligence. (49-672). Seat belts must be worn by all occupants in front seat of vehicle. (49-673). Failure to comply is infraction but not evidence of contributory negligence.

Lights Required.—Regulated by 49-901 through 49-920.

Inspection.—State inspection not required.

Accidents.—Driver or another occupant if driver is unable, must stop, give reasonable assistance, and give name, address, name of insurance agent or company and registration number. (18-8007, 49-1301 to 49-1315). Must also report accident to city police department, county sheriff's office or state police department in other cases where damage to person or property exceeds $750. (49-1305). Failure to report is cause for suspension of license. Every investigating officer must make report. (49-1306).

Owner's Liability.—Owner is responsible for negligent operation of motor vehicle by person using same with permission, expressed or implied, and negligence of such operator is imputed to owner for all purposes of civil damages. Liability for imputed negligence of owner, not arising through relationship of principal and agent or master and servant, is limited to amount of $25,000 for death or injury to one person in one accident, $50,000 with respect to death or injury to more than one person, and $15,000 for damage to property. Chattel mortgagee is not deemed owner. (49-2417).

Injury to Guest.—Idaho statute declaring owner not liable for injury or loss to guest transported without payment, except in cases of intentional injury, intoxication or gross negligence (49-2415) held unconstitutional (Thompson v. Hagen, 96 Idaho 19, 523 P.2d 1365).

Financial Responsibility.—A Motor-Vehicle Safety Responsibility Act has been adopted. Owners and operators, resident and nonresident, of motor vehicles involved in motor vehicle accident in state, in which death, personal injury, or damage in excess of $100, result, must, within 60 days of report of such accident to Department of Transportation, provide security within defined limits for payment of any claims or damages arising from said accident. Failure so to do may result in suspension of driver's license and subject owner or operator to penalties provided in said act. Insurance policy of $25,000 for bodily injury to or death of one person, $50,000 for bodily injury to or death of two or more persons, and $15,000 for property damage, or proof of financial responsibility by deposit of $25,000 in cash or securities, may be submitted to Department. Operation of motor vehicle on highway by one having been involved in motor vehicle accident without compliance with said Act is infraction. (49-1201 to 49-1232). Applicant must display to county assessor current certificate of liability insurance before vehicle can be registered. (49-1230). No exemption granted for members of armed forces. (49-441).

Insurance.—See subhead Financial Responsibility, supra.
Uninsured motorist coverage, $10,000/$20,000, mandatory in every policy, unless insured rejects it in writing. (41-2502).

No-Fault Insurance.—Not adopted.

Foreign Vehicles.—All vehicles, trailers and semitrailers of nonresidents must pay same fee as resident, unless exempt by provisions of reciprocity. If nonresident's state grants temporary permit privileges to like vehicles from Idaho, nonresident vehicle may obtain temporary trip permit for not to exceed 96 hours for $12 per trip permit plus 24.75 mills per mile for vehicles between 16,001 and 26,000 pounds gross; 35.80 mills per mile for vehicles between 26,001 and 40,000 pounds gross; 44.20 mills per mile for vehicles between 40,001 and 50,000 pounds gross; 54.25 mills per mile for vehicles between 50,001 and 60,000 pounds gross; 78.95 mills per mile for vehicles between 60,001 and 80,000 pounds gross and 116.65 mills per mile for vehicles between 80,001 and 105,500 pounds gross. (49-432).

Nonresident operators duly licensed in their home states or whose home states do not require driver's licenses may operate in Idaho without local license if over 15. (49-302). Adoption of Nonresident Violator Compact to allow jurisdiction of proceeding in motorists' home state rather than detention in Idaho. (49-2501). Also requires reporting of violations among participating states. (49-2501).

Actions Against Nonresidents.—Operation of motor vehicle by any person, either as principal or agent on any public way in state shall be deemed appointment of secretary of state to be person's lawful attorney for receipt of process in any action growing out of any accident in which he is involved while driving in Idaho. (49-1602). Such service has same legal force and validity as personal service within the state, provided plaintiff serves a copy of the summons and complaint on defendant by registered mail and obtains registry return receipt, or personal service outside the state is made in accordance with general laws relating to service of process on nonresidents. (49-2421).

Direct Actions.—Not authorized by injured person against insurer of other party.

Motor vehicle carriers must obtain permit from Public Utilities Commission. Must procure and maintain on file insurance or surety bond for each vehicle covering liability for personal injury and property damage as Commission sets by general order, except those which qualify as self-insurer with U. S. I.C.C. are exempt. Commission may fix rates. (61-801 to 61-817). Multi-carrier agreements allowed and exempted from state anti-trust law. (61-335). Foregoing does not apply to: school buses; taxicabs of not more than seven passengers; vehicles operated by or on behalf of hotels for patrons; farm trucks; newspaper distribution vehicles; transportation incidental to aircraft transportation; carriers operating exclusively within corporate limits or territory contiguous thereto as part of such service; vehicles of U.S. mail; transportation of agricultural products or livestock, products of forest or of mines to market; carriers engaged in transportation of sand, gravel and aggregate thereof; and carriers transporting household goods as defined by Interstate Commerce Commission. (61-801).

Caravaning Tax.—License tax for use of highways of $12 per vehicle is imposed for transportation within, into, across or out of state of any motor vehicle operating on its own wheels, in tow, or in saddlemount fashion of another vehicle for purpose of selling or offering for sale such vehicle either within or without this state, unless said vehicle is licensed in Idaho or owned by duly licensed Idaho auto dealer. (49-1101 to 49-1105).

Gasoline Tax.—See category Taxation, topic Gasoline and Special Fuels Taxes.

Service contracts for motor vehicles regulated. Required provisions for contracts. Reimbursement policy. Record keeping. Licensing. (49-2801 to 49-2810).

See note at head of Digest as to 1998 legislation covered.

See Topical Index in front part of this volume.

UNIFORM COMMERCIAL CODE FORMS

Financing Statement.—Form UCC-1. File three copies, one of which is acknowledgment.

This FINANCING STATEMENT is presented to filing officer for filing pursuant to the Uniform Commercial Code.	No. of additional sheets presented:	3. FOR FILING OFFICER ONLY (Date, time, number and filing office)
1. Debtor(s): (last name first, and mailing address(es)	2. Secured Party(ies) and address(es):	

4. This Financing Statement covers the following types (or items) of property: (Use this space for Real Property legal description and name of record owner, if required.)	5. Assignee(s) of Secured Party(ies) and address(es)

CHECK ☒ IF COVERED ☐ Products of collateral are also covered.

Filed with: ☐ Secretary of State ☐ County Recorder of   County.

If one of the following boxes is checked, the secured party may sign the financing statement. The collateral described herein is:
☐ Brought into this state already subject to a security interest in another jurisdiction.
☐ Subject to a security interest in another jurisdiction, and the debtor's location has changed to this state.
☐ Proceeds of the original collateral described above in which a security interest was perfected.
☐ The subject of a financing statement which has lapsed.
☐ Subject to a security interest perfected under a prior name or identity of the debtor.

BY: _____   BY: _____
    Signature(s) of Debtor(s)   SIGNATURE(S) OF SECURED PARTY(IES)
                                                 OR ASSIGNEE OF RECORD
1—FILING OFFICER—ALPHABETICAL

Idaho Form UCC-1 Rev. 79

FORM APPROVED BY PETER T. CENARRUSA,
SECRETARY OF STATE

Statements of Continuation, Release, Assignment, Termination, etc.—Form UCC-3. File three copies, one of which is acknowledgment.

This STATEMENT is presented to filing officer for filing pursuant to the Uniform Commercial Code.	No. of additional sheets presented:	
1. Debtor(s): (last name first, and mailing address(es)	2. Secured Party(ies) and address(es)	3. FOR FILING OFFICER ONLY (Date, time, number and filing office)

4. This Statement refers to original Financing Statement No. . . . .

. . . .

Filed with . . . . .Date filed. . . . . .19 . .

☐ CONTINUATION. The original financing statement between the foregoing Debtor and Secured Party, bearing file number shown above, is still effective.
☐ TERMINATION. Secured party no longer claims a security interest under the financing statement bearing file number shown above.
☐ ASSIGNMENT. The secured party's right under the financing statement bearing file number shown above to the property described below has been assigned to the assignee whose name and address appears below.
☐ AMENDMENT. Financing Statement bearing file number shown above is amended as set forth below.
☐ RELEASE. Secured Party releases the collateral described below from the financing statement bearing file number shown above.

Assignee(s) of secured party(ies)
and address(es):

BY: _____   BY: _____
    Signature(s) of Debtor(s)   Signature(s) of Secured Party(ies) or Assignee
    (Required only on some amendments)   of Record
1—FILING OFFICER—ALPHABETICAL

Idaho Form UCC-3 Rev. 79

FORM APPROVED BY PETER T. CENARRUSA,
SECRETARY OF STATE

See note at head of Digest as to 1998 legislation covered.

See Topical Index in front part of this volume.

Request for Information and Copies.—Form UCC-4.

REQUEST FOR INFORMATION OR INFORMATION AND COPIES—Present in triplicate to filing officer.

1. Debtor: (last name first, and mailing address)	2. Party requesting information or copies (name and address)	3. FOR FILING OFFICER ONLY (Date, time, number and filing office)

4. ☐ INFORMATION REQUEST Filing officer: Please furnish certificate showing whether there are on file in your office any presently effective financing statements and statements of assignment relating thereto naming the above debtor;

Signature of Requesting Party _____

FILE NO.	DATE AND HOUR OF FILING	NAME(S) AND ADDRESS(ES) OF SECURED PARTY(IES)

The undersigned hereby certifies that the above listing shows all presently effective financing statements and statements of assignment naming the above debtor which are on file in my office as of this date and hour.

Dated _____ 19 ____, _____, ___M.   Signature of Filing Officer _____

5. ☐ COPY REQUEST Filing officer: If you find any financing statements and statements of assignment described in the foregoing Information Request, please provide a copy of each statement and of each assignment which consists of only one page; if any such statement or assignment consists of more than one page, please provide a copy of the first page thereof and of each page of description of collateral attached thereto.

Signature of Requesting Party _____

The undersigned hereby certifies that the attached _____ copies are true and exact copies of all presently effective financing statements and statements of assignment consisting of one page only and excerpts of others as requested above on file in my office as of this date and hour.

Dated _____ 19 ____, _____, ___M.   Signature of Filing Officer _____

1—TO BE RETURNED WITH COPIES
  OR INFORMATION

Idaho Form UCC-4 Rev. 79

FORM APPROVED BY PETE T. CENARRUSA,
SECRETARY OF STATE

See note at head of Digest as to 1998 legislation covered.

See Topical Index in front part of this volume.

ILLINOIS LAW DIGEST REVISER

Professor Celeste M. Hammond
The John Marshall Law School
321 S. Plymouth Court
Chicago, IL 60604
Telephone: 312-987-2366
Fax: 312-427-5280
Email: 7hammond@jmls.edu

Research Assistant:
Therese Clarke

Reviser Profile

Celeste M. Hammond is a Professor at the John Marshall Law School and Director of the Center for Real Estate Law and the LLM in Real Estate Law Program. Before joining the faculty in 1976, she practiced law for seven years in Chicago after admittance to the Illinois Bar. She is a graduate of the University of Chicago Law School where she served in the Mandel Legal Aid Clinic and was a Research Assistant to Professor Kenneth Culp Davis in Administrative Law. She lectures and writes on real estate law, real estate finance law and alternative dispute resolution in the real estate context. She is a leader in the American Bar Association's Section on Real Property Law, the Chicago Bar Association and the International Bar Association where she recently was appointed Vice-Chair of the Academic Forum. Professor Hammond has been elected to membership in Lambda Alpha International Honorary Land Economics Society and the American College of Real Estate Lawyers.

Research Assistant: Therese Clarke earned her JD at the John Marshall Law School and her MLS in Library Sciences from Dominican University.

The John Marshall Law School: The John Marshall Law School, in the heart of downtown Chicago, is celebrating its 100th anniversary of educating lawyers in the theory and practice of the law. Its programs continue to build upon the law school's tradition of diversity, innovation and opportunity. The law school's 1,300 students are enrolled in the traditional JD program and seven LLM programs offered through John Marshall's seven Centers of Excellence.

ILLINOIS LAW DIGEST

(The following is a list of all Categories and Topics, including cross-references, covered in this Digest.)

ILLINOIS LAW DIGEST

Revised for 1999 edition by

CELESTE M. HAMMOND, Professor, The John Marshall Law School and member of Illinois Bar.

(Citations, unless otherwise indicated, are to chapters and paragraphs of Illinois Complied Statutes (ILCS) and Illinois Revised Statutes, 1991. Parallel citations to the North Eastern Reporter begin with 114 Ill., and 284 Ill. App.)

Note: This revision covers all legislation within the scope of the Digest topics approved by the Governor through May 1, 1998.

INTRODUCTION

GOVERNMENT AND LEGAL SYSTEM:

The State of Illinois is a constituent state of the United States of America. For further discussion of the U.S. federal system, see Introduction to the Federal Government of the United States at the beginning of this volume. A great many laws are promulgated by the federal government of the United States and are not reflected in the topics below. See the Introduction to this volume for references to the federal law topics covered.

Like all but one of the United States, Illinois has a common law legal system, with roots in English common law. For information on the courts and legislature of Illinois, see category Courts and Legislature.

HOLIDAYS:

Legal holidays upon which bank may, but is not required to remain closed, are Jan. 1, 3d Mon. in Jan., Feb. 12, third Mon. in Feb., Good Friday, 1st Mon. in Mar., May 30, July 4, first Mon. in Sept., 2d Mon. in Oct., Nov. 11, Dec. 25, any day of fast or thanksgiving recommended by Governor or President, and any day proclaimed by Governor. Legal holidays also include days of general elections for members of State House of Representatives. (10-5/17-25, 205-630/17). 12 noon to 12 midnight on Sat. is half holiday in cities of 200,000 or more. (205-630/17). Commemorative holidays are at 105-5/24-2.

Holiday Falling on Sunday.—When holiday falls on Sun., following day is holiday. (205-630/17).

Holiday Falling on Sat.—No postponement of holiday falling on Sat. (205-630/17).

Legality of Transactions on Saturday, Sunday or Holiday.—When last day on which act provided by law must be performed is holiday or Sat. or Sun., such act may be performed on next business day. (5-70/1.11).

A **contract** requiring performance on Sun. will be enforced according to its terms, and contract is not void because executed on that day. (107 Ill. 429). Payment, certification or acceptance of check or other negotiable instrument or any other transaction by bank is not void or voidable even if done on Sat., Sun., holiday or day selected by bank to remain closed. (205-630/17).

With respect to presenting for payment or acceptance, maturity and protesting and giving notice of dishonor of bills of exchange, bank checks, promissory notes and other negotiable or commercial paper or instruments, each holiday, half-holiday and any day selected by bank to remain closed, as authorized, shall be deemed Sun. (205-630/17).

All notes, bills, drafts, checks, or other evidences of indebtedness falling due on any holiday are deemed as due or maturing on following business day. (205-630/17).

Teachers or other school employees are not required to teach on Sats. or legal school holidays, which are Jan. 1, 3d Mon. in Jan., Feb. 12, 1st Mon. in Mar., Good Friday, Federal Memorial Day, July 4, 1st Mon. in Sept., 2d Mon. in Oct., Nov. 11, Dec. 25, any day of fast or thanksgiving appointed by Governor or President. School boards may grant commemorative or special holidays whenever in their judgment such action is advisable. Commemorative holidays are regular school days devoted to commemoration of specified persons or occasions. (105-5/24-2).

OFFICE HOURS AND TIME ZONE:

Illinois is in the Central (GMT −06:00) time zone. Office hours are generally from 9 a.m. to 5 p.m.

BUSINESS ORGANIZATIONS

AGENCY:

See category Property, topic Powers of Attorney.

ASSOCIATIONS:

Unincorporated association has been judicially defined as body of persons acting together without charter by methods and forms used by incorporated bodies for prosecution of some common enterprise. (389 Ill. 102, 58 N.E.2d 906). Specific forms of unincorporated associations (e.g., building and loan associations) are regulated by statute.

Formation.—Unincorporated associations are formed by agreement between (and among) parties thereto.

Rights and Powers.—Unincorporated association has power to adopt constitution and to enact by-laws, rules and regulations that are not illegal or contrary to public policy. Constitution, by-laws, rules and regulations of association become, in effect, contract between members governing their mutual rights and liabilities. (140 Ill. App.3d 127, 488 N.E.2d 623).

In absence of statutory authority unincorporated association cannot make contracts or take or hold title to property in its own name. However, where association contracts as legal entity, it may be estopped to deny its right to contract. (389 Ill. 102, 58 N.E.2d

906). Statutory provisions expressly authorize unincorporated association to take, hold, convey and defend interests in real property. (765-115/1 to 115/3).

Liabilities.—In order to bind association or its members, acts of officer or agent of association must be done pursuant to authority duly vested in such officer or agent. (99 Ill. App. 290). There is no limited liability as to third persons but there is contribution among members. (65 Ill. 532).

Actions.—Voluntary unincorporated association may sue or be sued in own name. (735-5/2-209).

Dissolution.—Meeting to dissolve unincorporated association must be preceded by reasonable notice of time, place and object of meeting to members. (318 Ill. App. 605, 48 N.E.2d 760).

Professional Associations.—Persons rendering any type of personal service to public requiring license permitted under specified conditions (805-305/1 et seq.) to form professional association, including practice of law (805-305/1 et seq.; Ill. S. Ct. 721).

Professional Corporations.—See topic Corporations, subhead Professional Service Corporations.

Unit Owners' Association.—See category Property, topic Real Property, subhead Condominium Property Act.

CORPORATIONS:

Business Corporation Act of 1983, which became effective July 1, 1984 ("Act") (805-5/1.01-5/17.05) governs generally. References in this topic are to sections of Act (c. 32), unless otherwise indicated.

Provisions of Act apply to all existing corporations, including public utility corporations, organized under any general law of Illinois providing for organization of corporations for purpose or purposes for which corporation might be organized under Act. (805-5/1.70). Act does not generally apply to corporations organized for purpose of banking or insurance (805-5/3.05) and only applies to corporations organized for purpose of operation of railroads to extent provided in 805-5/1.70. Certain of provisions of Act may not be applicable to corporations formed prior to July 1, 1971. (See Roanoke Agency, Inc. v. Jim Edgar, 101 Ill.2d 315, 461 N.E.2d 1365.) Limited Liability Company Act (805-180/1-180/60) effective Jan. 1, 1994 (see topic Limited Liability Companies).

General Supervision.—Secretary of State has supervision of administration of Act.

Definitions.—"Paid-in capital" means sum of cash and other consideration received, less expenses, including commissions, paid or incurred by corporation in connection with issuance of shares, plus any cash and other consideration contributed to corporation by or on behalf of its shareholders or transferred to paid-in capital by action of board of directors or shareholders, plus amounts added pursuant to share dividend, share split, or otherwise, minus reductions as provided elsewhere in Act. Irrespective of manner of designation thereof by laws under which foreign corporation is or may be organized, paid-in capital of foreign corporation shall be determined on same basis and in same manner as paid-in capital of domestic corporation, for purpose of computing license fees, franchise taxes and other charges imposed by Act. (805-5/1.80[j]). "Net assets", for purpose of determining right of corporation to purchase its own shares and of determining right of corporation to declare and pay dividends and make other distributions to shareholders is equal to difference between assets of corporation and liabilities of corporation. (805-5/1.80[k]). "Insolvent" means that corporation is unable to pay debts as they become due in usual course of business. (805-5/1.80[m]). "Common shares" means shares which have no preference over any other shares with respect to distribution of assets on liquidation or payment dividends. (805-5/1.80[q]). *Note:* Concept of treasury shares has been abolished (at least prospectively) under Act. Shares of corporation held prior to July 1, 1984 as treasury shares shall: (1) Remain treasury shares unless and until such shares are sold, used to pay share dividend, restored to status of authorized and unissued shares, or cancelled; (2) not be voted, directly or indirectly, at any meeting and shall not be counted in determining total number of outstanding shares entitled to vote at any time; and (3) if restored to status of authorized and unissued shares, be reported to Secretary of State on cumulative report of changes in paid-in capital. (805-5/1.70[i]).

Purposes.—Corporations for profit may be organized under Act for any lawful purpose or purposes, except banking or insurance; corporations may be organized for buying, selling, or otherwise dealing in notes (not including discounting bills and notes or buying and selling bills of exchange), open accounts, and other similar evidences of debt, or for purpose of carrying on business of syndicate or limited syndicate permitted under Art. V 1/2 of Illinois Insurance Code. (805-5/3.05). Corporation may have corporate seal but seal will not give instruments additional force or effect and use of corporate seal is not mandatory. Corporations may make contracts of guaranty and suretyship provided that corporation may not be organized for purposes of insurance. (805-5/3.10). Articles may provide for general purpose clause stating that corporation is organized to transact any and all lawful business for which corporations may be organized under Act. (805-5/2.10). Organization of corporation for such excepted purposes or of corporations not for pecuniary profit may be effected under other general statutes. Certain sections of Act relate to railroads, chiefly those sections relating to dissolution, annual reports and fees. (805-5/1.70).

See note at head of Digest as to 1998 legislation covered.

See Topical Index in front part of this volume.

CORPORATIONS . . . *continued*

Name.—Corporate name: (a) Must contain, separate and apart from any other word or abbreviation in such name, word "corporation," "company," "incorporated," or "limited," or abbreviation of one of such words; (b) must not contain any word or phrase which indicates or implies that corporation (i) is authorized to conduct business of insurance, indemnity or acceptance of savings deposits or (ii) is authorized to conduct business of banking unless otherwise permitted by Commissioner of Banks and Real Estate; (c) must be distinguishable upon records in office of Secretary of State from corporate name or assumed name, of any domestic corporation existing under any Act of Illinois, or any foreign corporation authorized to transact business in Illinois, or name exclusive right to which is, at time, reserved in manner provided in Act; (d) must contain word "trust," if it be corporation organized for purpose of accepting and executing trusts, must contain word "pawners," if it be corporation organized as pawners' society, and must contain word "co-operative," if it be corporation organized as co-operative association for pecuniary profit; (e) must be name under which corporation shall transact business in Illinois unless corporation shall also elect to adopt one or more assumed names as provided in Act, but corporation may use divisional designation or trade name along with its corporate name or assumed name as long as it clearly discloses its corporate name or assumed name; provided that identification by corporation of its business with trademark or service mark of which it is owner or licensed user shall not constitute use of assumed name. (805-5/4.05, 5/4.15). Exclusive right to use of corporate name may be reserved for 90 days upon filing of application for name reservation. $25 fee. $25 fee to assign reserved name to another party. (805-5/4.10, 5/15.10). Corporation may elect to adopt assumed name that is not same as or deceptively similar to corporate name or assumed name of any other domestic corporation existing under laws of Illinois or of any foreign corporation authorized to transact business in this State, or same as or deceptively similar to any name registered or reserved under provisions of Act. Such election must be made by filing with Secretary of State application executed by officer of corporation, pursuant to resolution adopted by corporation, setting forth such assumed name and paying to Secretary of State filing fee ($20 + $2.50 for each month or part thereof between date of filing such application and date of renewal of assumed corporate name). Corporation may change assumed name for period remaining until renewal date of original assumed name, $25 fee. Right to assumed corporate name shall be effective from date of filing by Secretary of State until first day of anniversary month of corporation that falls within next calendar year evenly divisible by five, however, if application is filed within two months immediately preceding anniversary month of corporation that falls within calendar year evenly divisible by five, right to use assumed corporate name shall be effective until first day of anniversary month of corporation that falls within next succeeding calendar year evenly divisible by five. Renewal fee must be paid ($150). (805-5/4.15, 5/15.10). Multiple assumed corporate names are allowed. If such assumed name complies with provisions of Act, Secretary of State shall issue certificate authorizing use of that name, but such certificate shall not confer any right to use of that name as against any person having any prior right to use thereof. (805-5/4.05).

Corporation Division of Office of Secretary of State in Springfield will informally answer inquiries by telephone or mail as to whether corporate name is available. No fee.

Term of Corporate Existence.—Duration of corporation is perpetual unless otherwise specified in articles of incorporation. (805-5/2.10).

Incorporators.—Corporation may be organized by one or more incorporators who need not be subscribers. Each incorporator must be corporation or natural person of 18 years or more. (805-5/2.05).

Articles of Incorporation.—Incorporators must sign and file in duplicate articles of incorporation (805-5/2.10) setting forth: (a) Name of corporation; (b) purpose or purposes for which corporation is organized, which may be stated to be, or to include, transaction of any or all lawful businesses for which corporations may be incorporated under Act; (c) address of corporation's initial registered office in Illinois and name of its initial registered agent at that office; (d) name and address of each incorporator; (e) number of shares of each class corporation is authorized to issue; (f) number and class of shares which corporation proposes to issue without further report to Secretary of State, and consideration to be received, less expenses, including commissions, paid or incurred in connection with issuance of shares, by corporation therefor. If shares of more than one class are to be issued, consideration for shares of each class shall be separately stated; (g) if shares are divided into classes, designation of each class and statement of designations, preferences, qualifications, limitations, restrictions, and special or relative rights with respect to shares of each class; and (h) if corporation may issue shares of any preferred or special class and series, then designation of each series and statement of variations and relative rights and preferences of different series, if same are fixed in articles of incorporation, or statement of authority vested in board of directors to establish series and determine variations and relative rights and preferences of different series. (805-5/2.10[a]). Other specified information may, but it is not necessary to, be set forth in articles of incorporation. (805-5/2.10[b]). It is not necessary to set forth in articles of incorporation any of corporate powers enumerated in Act. Corporation may adopt special voting provisions in articles of incorporation for certain business combinations. (805-5/7.85). See subhead Vote Required for Certain Business Combinations, infra. If no optional information is given in articles of incorporation with respect to amount of property owned by corporation to be located within Illinois, then franchise tax shall be computed on basis of entire paid-in capital as set forth in articles of incorporation. (805-5/2.10[e]).

License Fees of Domestic Corporation.—Domestic corporation must pay initial license fee and, in some cases, additional license fee. In each case fee is 1/20 of 1%. Basis for initial license fee is dollar value of entire consideration received by corporation for, or on account of, its issued shares reported to Secretary of State in its first report of issuance of shares. Basis for each additional license fee, except in case of statutory merger or consolidation, is dollar value of increase in paid-in capital over amount thereof last reported in any document, other than annual report, required by Act to be filed in Office of Secretary of State. (805-5/15.20-5/15.30).

License fees are payable to Secretary of State.

As to license fees of foreign corporations, see infra, subhead Foreign Corporations.

Filing fees charged by Secretary of State for filing various papers are: (a) Articles of incorporation, $75; (b) articles of amendment, $25, unless amendment is restatement of articles of incorporation, in which case $100; (c) articles of merger or consolidation, $100, but if merger or consolidation involves more than two corporations, $50 for each additional corporation; (d) filing articles of share exchange and issuing certificate of exchange, $100; (e) articles of dissolution, $5; (f) application to reserve corporate name, $25; (g) notice of transfer of reserved corporate name, $25; (h) statement of change of address of registered office or change of registered agent, or both, $5; (i) statement of establishment of series of shares, $25; (j) application of foreign corporation for certificate of authority to transact business in State and issuing certificate of authority, $75; (k) application of foreign corporation for amended certificate of authority to transact business in State and issuing certificate of authority, $25; (l) copy of amendment to articles of incorporation of foreign corporation holding certificate of authority to transact business in State, $25 (unless amendment is restatement of certificate of authority, in which case fee shall be $100); (m) copy of articles of merger of foreign corporation holding certificate of authority to transact business in State, $100, but if merger involves more than two corporations, $50 for each additional corporation; (n) application for withdrawal and final report of foreign corporation and issuing certificate of withdrawal, $25; (o) annual report of domestic or foreign corporation, $25; (p) application for reinstatement, and issuing certificate of reinstatement, $100; (q) filing application for use or change of assumed corporate name, $20 + $2.50 for each month or part thereof between date of filing such application and date of renewal of assumed corporate name; and renewal fee for each assumed corporate name, $150; (r) filing application for cancellation of assumed corporate name, $5; (s) filing application to register corporate name of foreign corporation, $50; and annual renewal fee for such registered name, $50; (t) application for cancellation of registered name of foreign corporation, $25; (u) statement of correction, $25; (v) petition for reduction or refund, $5; (w) filing any other statement or report, $5. (805-5/15.10).

Certificate of Incorporation and Filing Thereof.—Secretary of State issues certificate of incorporation, which must be filed for record within 15 days in office of recorder of county in which registered office of corporation in Illinois is situated. (805-5/2.10, 5/1.10).

Organization.—If no preincorporation subscribers and if initial directors not named in articles of incorporation, meeting of incorporators shall be held at call of majority of incorporators for purpose of naming initial directors. If preincorporation subscribers and if initial directors not named in articles of incorporation, first meeting of shareholders shall be held after issuance of certificate of incorporation at call of majority of incorporators for purpose of electing initial directors, adopting by-laws if articles of incorporation so require or shareholders so determine, and such other matters as shall be stated in notice of meeting. It is possible for shareholder action to be taken by consent, in lieu of meeting, in writing pursuant to Act. First meeting of initial directors shall be held at call of majority of them for purpose of adopting by-laws if shareholders have not adopted them, electing officers, and transacting other business. At least three days written notice of organizational meeting shall be given unless persons entitled to such notice waive same in writing, either before or after such meeting. Organizational meeting may be held either within or without Illinois. (805-5/2.20). Unless otherwise provided in articles of incorporation, any action by incorporators to organize corporation, amend articles of incorporation before issuance of shares and voluntarily dissolve corporation may be taken without meeting upon unanimous written consent of incorporators. (805-5/2.05).

Paid-In Capital Requirement.—There is no paid-in capital requirement. (805-5/2.10, 5/2.15).

List of Corporations.—Secretary of State is required to publish daily list of all newly formed corporations, business and not for profit, chartered by him on that day, which will be available for inspection or copying. (805-5/1.25).

Amendments to Articles.—Corporation may amend its articles of incorporation to add new provision or change or remove existing provision, provided that articles as amended contain only such provisions as are required or permitted in original articles of incorporation at time of amendment. Articles as amended must contain all provisions required by Act except that names and addresses of initial directors may be removed and names of initial registered agent or address of initial registered office may be removed if statement of change is filed. Corporation whose period of duration as provided in articles of corporation has expired may amend articles to revive its articles and extend period of corporation duration, including making duration perpetual, at any time within five years after date of expiration. (805-5/10.05).

If corporation has not issued shares, amendment to articles may be adopted by majority of incorporators if initial directors not named in articles or have not been elected, or if initial directors named in articles or have been elected, amendment to articles may be adopted by majority of directors. (805-5/10.10). Majority of whole board of directors of corporation may adopt one or more amendments to its articles without shareholder action if it is to: (a) Remove names and addresses of initial directors if such directors named in original articles; (b) remove name and address of initial registered agent or address of initial registered office, if statement of change is filed with Secretary of State; (c) split issued whole shares and unissued authorized shares by multiplying them by whole number, so long as no class or series of shares is adversely affected thereby; (d) to change corporate name by substituting word "corporation", "incorporated", "company", "limited", or abbreviation "corp.", "inc.", "co.", "ltd.", for similar word or abbreviation in name, or by adding geographical attribution to name; (e) to reduce authorized shares of any class pursuant to cancellation statement filed with respect to such shares after acquisition by corporation in circumstances in which articles prohibit reissuance of such shares after acquisition by corporation; or (f) to restate articles as currently amended; such restated articles supersede original articles and all amendments thereto. (805-5/10.15). If it is necessary to secure shareholder approval for amendment, board of directors shall adopt resolution setting forth proposed amendment and directing that it be submitted to vote at meeting of shareholders, which may be either annual or special meeting. Written notice setting forth proposed amendment or summary of changes to be effected

See note at head of Digest as to 1998 legislation covered.

See Topical Index in front part of this volume.

IL – 2

CORPORATIONS . . . *continued*
thereby shall be given to each shareholder of record within time and manner provided in Act for giving of notice of meetings of shareholders. If such meeting is annual meeting, proposed amendment or such summary may be included in notice of such annual meeting. If adoption of amendment would give any class or series of shares right to dissent, notice shall also enclose copy of relevant section of Act or otherwise provide adequate notice of right to dissent and procedures therefor. At such meeting vote of shareholders entitled to vote on proposed amendment shall be taken. Proposed amendment shall be adopted upon receiving affirmative vote of holders of at least two-thirds of votes of shares entitled to vote on such amendment, unless any class or series of shares is entitled to vote as class in respect thereof, in which event proposed amendment shall be adopted upon receiving affirmative votes of at least two-thirds of votes of shares of each class or series of shares entitled to vote as class in respect thereof and of total votes of shares entitled to vote on such amendment. Articles of incorporation may supersede two-thirds vote requirements by specifying any smaller or larger vote requirement not less than majority of outstanding shares entitled to vote on amendment and not less than majority of outstanding shares of each class or series of shares entitled to vote as class on amendment. Any number of amendments may be submitted to shareholders and voted upon by them at one meeting. (805-5/10.20). Holders of outstanding shares of class are entitled to vote as class on proposed amendments in number of cases specified in Act. (805-5/10.25). Corporation which adopts provision for higher voting requirements for certain business combinations requires higher vote to amend such provision. (805-5/7.85). Articles of amendment shall be signed and filed in duplicate (805-5/10.30), and amendment becomes effective upon issuance of certificate of amendment by Secretary of State, or time established under articles of amendment, not to exceed 30 days after issuance of certificate of amendment by Secretary of State (805-5/10.35). If amendment restates articles of incorporation, such restated articles of incorporation shall, upon such amendment becoming effective, supersede and stand in lieu of corporation's preexisting articles of incorporation. If amendment revised articles of incorporation and extends period of corporate duration, amendment becomes effective upon issuance of certificate of amendment by Secretary of State and corporate existence deemed to have continued without interruption from date of expiration of original period of duration. (805-5/10.35).

By-laws.—Unless power to make, alter, amend or repeal by-laws is reserved to shareholders by articles of incorporation, by-laws of corporation may be made, altered, amended or repealed by shareholders or board of directors, but no by-law adopted by shareholders may be altered, amended or repealed by board of directors if by-laws so provide. By-laws may contain any provisions for regulation and management of affairs of corporation not inconsistent with law or articles of incorporation. (805-5/2.25).

Stock Certificates.—Corporation has power to create and issue number of shares stated in its articles. Such shares may be divided into one or more classes, including classes of common shares, any or all of which classes may consist of shares with such designations, preferences, qualifications, limitations, restrictions, and such special or relative rights as shall be stated in articles, provided that common shares may not have preference with respect to distribution of assets upon liquidation or payment of dividends. Subject to voting restrictions in Act, articles may limit or deny voting rights of or provide special voting rights for shares of any and all classes or of any series of class. If authorized in articles, corporation may issue shares of preferred or special classes subject to one or more of following conditions: (a) Subject to right of corporation to redeem any of such shares at not exceeding price fixed by articles for redemption thereof; (b) entitling holders thereof to dividends which are cumulative or partially cumulative, or which are noncumulative; (c) having preference over any other class or classes of shares as to payment of dividends; (d) having preference as to assets of corporation over any other class or classes of shares upon voluntary or involuntary liquidation of corporation; (e) convertible into shares of any other class, or into shares of any series of same or any other class. (805-5/6.05).

If articles provide, shares of any preferred or special class may be divided and issued in series. If shares of any such class are to be issued in series, then each series shall be so designated to distinguish shares thereof from shares of all other series in classes. Any or all of series of any such class and variations in relative rights and preferences as between different series may be determined by articles or by resolution of board of directors pursuant to authority granted in articles, subject to voting requirements of Act, provided all shares of same class shall be identical except as to following relative rights and preferences, in respect of any or all of which there may be variations between different series: (1) Rate of dividend; (2) price at and terms and conditions on which shares may be redeemed; (3) amount payable upon shares in event of involuntary liquidation; (4) amount payable upon shares in event of voluntary liquidation; (5) sinking fund provisions for redemption or purchase of shares; (6) terms and conditions on which shares may be converted, if shares of any series are issued with privilege of conversion; (7) limitation or denial of voting rights, or grant of special voting rights. Corporation must file statement with Secretary of State. (805-5/6.10). Corporation may issue fractional shares. (805-5/6.15).

Issued shares of corporation shall be represented by certificates or shall be uncertificated shares. Every certificate representing shares issued by corporation which is authorized to issue shares of more than one class shall set forth upon face or back of certificate full summary or statement of all designations, preferences, qualifications, limitations, restrictions, and special or relative rights of each class authorized to be issued, and, if corporation is authorized to issue any preferred or special class in series, variations in relative rights and preferences between shares of each such series so far as same have been fixed and determined and authority of board of directors to fix and determine relative rights and preferences of subsequent series. Such statement may be omitted from certificate if it shall be set forth upon face or back of certificate that such statement, in full, will be furnished by corporation to any shareholder upon request and without charge. Each certificate representing shares shall also state that corporation is organized under laws of Illinois, name of person to whom issued, and number and class of shares, and designation of series, if any, which such certificate represents. Unless articles or by-laws provide otherwise, board of directors of corporation may provide by resolution that some or all of any or all classes and series of its shares shall be uncertificated shares, providing that such resolution shall not apply to shares represented by certificate until such certificate is surrendered to corporation. After issuance or transfer of uncertificated shares, corporation must send to registered owner thereof written notice containing information required to be set forth or stated on certificates pursuant to Act. Except as otherwise expressly provided by law, rights and obligations of holders of uncertificated shares and rights and obligations of holders of certificates representing shares of same class and series shall be identical. (805-5/6.35).

Issuance of Stock.—Shares may be issued for such consideration as shall be authorized from time to time by board of directors through action which establishes price in cash or other consideration, or both, or minimum price or general formula or method by which price can be determined. Upon authorization by board of directors, corporation may issue its own shares in exchange for or in conversion of its outstanding shares, or may distribute its own shares pro rata to its shareholders or shareholders of one or more classes or series to effectuate dividends or splits, provided that value fixed by board of directors in connection with such dividend or split shall be transferred to paid-in capital of corporation, and provided, no such issuance of shares of any class or series shall be made to holders of shares of any other class or series unless it is either expressly provided for in articles or authorized by affirmative vote of holders of at least majority of outstanding shares of class or series in which distribution is to be made. (805-5/6.25). Higher vote is required for certain issuance or transfer of securities of corporation which has class of registered equity securities or which adopts such voting requirement. (805-5/7.85). See subhead Vote Required for Certain Business Combinations, infra.

Consideration for issuance of shares may be paid, in whole or in part, in money, and other property, tangible or intangible, or in labor or services actually performed for corporation. When payment of consideration for which shares are to be issued shall have been received by corporation, such shares shall be deemed to be full paid and nonassessable. In absence of actual fraud in transaction, and subject to provisions in Act regarding director conflict of interest, judgment of board of directors or shareholders, as case may be, as to value of consideration received for shares shall be conclusive. (805-5/6.30). No certificate shall be issued for any share until such share is fully paid. (805-5/6.35). Shareholders of corporation organized under Act on or after Jan. 1, 1982, shall have no preemptive rights to acquire unissued shares of corporation, or securities of corporation convertible into or carrying right to subscribe to or acquire shares, except if provided for in articles of incorporation. Preemptive right of shareholder to acquire additional shares, whether then or thereafter authorized, of corporation organized prior to Jan. 1, 1982 may be limited or denied to extent provided in articles of incorporation. Unless otherwise provided in articles, any such corporation may issue and sell its shares to its employees or to employees of any subsidiary corporation, without first offering same to its shareholders, for such consideration and upon such terms and conditions as shall be approved by holders of two-thirds of its shares entitled to vote with respect thereto or by its board of directors pursuant to like approval of shareholders. (805-5/6.50).

Transfer of Stock.—Uniform Simplification of Fiduciary Security Transfers Act not adopted. See Illinois Fiduciary Security Transfer Simplification Act. (760-70/1 to 70/9). Art. 8 of Uniform Commercial Code governs transfers, except to extent of any inconsistency between it and Illinois Fiduciary Security Transfer Simplification Act.

Stock Transfer Tax.—No state stock transfer tax is imposed.

Redemption of Stock.—No redemption of shares may be made which will reduce remaining assets of corporation so that corporation would be insolvent, or which will reduce net assets below aggregate amount payable to holders of shares having prior or equal rights to assets on dissolution. (805-5/9.10). If corporation acquires own shares, except when shares pledged for payment of purchase price, shares are cancelled and constitute authorized but unissued shares, and, if articles provide such shares shall not be reissued, number of authorized shares is reduced by number of shares acquired. If corporation acquires own shares, corporation shall file cumulative report of changes in paid-in capital with Secretary of State. Shares of corporation acquired by it may be pledged as security for payment of purchase price of shares and, until purchase price paid, such shares are not cancelled and do not constitute authorized, but unissued shares. (805-5/9.05). Until cumulative report of changes in paid-in capital shall have been filed with Secretary of State, basis of annual franchise tax payable by corporation shall not be reduced, provided, however, in no event shall annual franchise tax for any taxable year be reduced if such report is not filed prior to first day of anniversary month of that taxable year and before payment of its annual franchise tax. (805-5/9.05).

Shareholders Actions.—No action shall be brought in Illinois by shareholder in right of domestic or foreign corporation unless plaintiff was shareholder of record at time of complained of transaction or his shares or voting trust certificates thereafter devolved upon him by operation of law from person who was holder at such time; provided, however, that shareholder who does not meet such requirement may nevertheless be allowed in discretion of court to bring such action on preliminary showing to and determination by court, upon motion and after hearing at which court may consider such evidence by affidavit or testimony as it deems material, that plaintiff acquired shares before there was disclosure to public or to plaintiff of wrongdoing of which plaintiff complains. (805-5/7.80[a]).

Shareholders Liabilities.—Holder of or subscriber to shares of corporation is under no obligation to corporation or its creditors with respect to such shares other than to pay full consideration for such shares. No person holding shares as executor, administrator, conservator, guardian, trustee, assignee for benefit of creditors, or receiver is personally liable as shareholder; but beneficial owner thereof and estate and funds in such person's hands are liable. No pledgee or other holder of shares as collateral security is personally liable as shareholder. Any person becoming assignee or transferee of shares or of subscription in good faith and without knowledge or notice that full consideration therefor has not been paid is not personally liable to corporation or

See note at head of Digest as to 1998 legislation covered.

See Topical Index in front part of this volume.

IL – 3

CORPORATIONS . . . *continued*
its creditors for any unpaid portion of such consideration. (805-5/6.40). Shareholder may be liable to injured creditors if shareholder sells his stock to corporation at time when corporation is insolvent. (31 Ill.2d 297, 201 N.E.2d 444).

Meetings of shareholders may be held either within or without Illinois, as provided in by-laws. Special meetings may be called by president, directors, holders of not less than one-fifth of shares or by such officers or persons as may be provided in articles or by-laws. (805-5/7.05). Written or printed notice stating place, day and hour of meeting and, in case of special meeting, purpose or purposes, must be delivered to each shareholder, either personally or by mail, not less than ten nor more than 60 days, or in case of merger or consolidation not less than 20 nor more than 60 days, before date of meeting. (805-5/7.15). Unless otherwise provided in articles, majority of votes of shares constitutes quorum; provided that in no event may quorum consist of less than one-third of votes of shares. If quorum is present, affirmative vote of majority of votes of shares represented is act of shareholders unless greater vote or voting by classes is required by Act, articles of incorporation or by-laws. (805-5/7.60). Higher vote is required for certain business combinations by domestic corporation which has class of registered equity securities or which adopts such higher voting requirements. (805-5/7.85). See subhead Vote Required for Certain Business Combinations, infra. Articles of incorporation may require any number or percent greater than majority of votes up to and including requirement of unanimity to constitute quorum. (805-5/7.60).

Officer or agent having charge of transfer book must make, within 20 days after record date for meeting of shareholders or ten days before such meeting, whichever is earlier, complete list of shareholders in alphabetical order, with address of each and number of shares held by each, which list must be kept at registered office for ten days prior to meeting and kept open at meeting, for inspection by any shareholder. (805-5/7.30).

Voting.—Each outstanding share, regardless of class, is entitled to one vote on each matter submitted. Shareholder may vote either in person or by written proxy, but no proxy is valid after 11 months from date of execution, unless otherwise provided in proxy. (805-5/7.50). In election for directors every shareholder has right to cumulate his votes, provided that articles of incorporation for corporations organized after Dec. 31, 1981 may limit or eliminate cumulative voting rights as to any or all classes or series of stock. Corporation organized prior to Jan. 1, 1982 may amend its articles to eliminate cumulative voting. If articles of incorporation provide for more or less than one vote for any share on any matter, reference in statute to majority or other proportion greater than majority of shares shall refer to that majority or other proportion greater than majority of votes of shares. (805-5/7.40). Shares held by corporation in fiduciary capacity may be voted. (805-5/7.45). Shares standing in name of deceased person, minor ward or person under legal disability may be voted by administrator, executor, or court appointed guardian without transfer into name of such person. (805-5/7.45).

Vote Required for Certain Business Combinations.—Higher votes are required for certain business combinations by domestic corporation which has class of equity securities registered under Securities Exchange Act of 1934 or which adopts this provision in articles of incorporation.

These enumerated business combinations require affirmative vote of 80% of outstanding voting shares and majority of outstanding voting shares held by disinterested shareholders. Business combinations subject to higher voting requirement include: (a) Merger, consolidation or share exchange involving interested shareholder, or other corporation which is or would become affiliate or associate of interested shareholder; (b) sale, lease, exchange, mortgage, pledge, transfer or other disposition of assets representing 10% or more of consolidated net worth to or with interested shareholder or affiliate or associate of interested shareholder; (c) issuance or transfer of securities of corporation or subsidiary to interested shareholder or affiliate or associate; (d) adoption of plan or proposal for liquidation or dissolution proposed by, or in which anything other than cash will be received by, interested shareholder, affiliate or associate; and (e) reclassification of securities, recapitalization or merger, consolidation, or share exchange involving subsidiary which has effect of increasing proportionate share of equity or convertible securities of corporation or subsidiary owned directly or indirectly by interested shareholder, affiliate or associate. Higher vote is also required when corporation adopting this provision amends, repeals, or adopts provision inconsistent with, provision in articles of incorporation which specifically adopts this section. Interested shareholder is defined as: (a) Beneficial owner of 10% or more of combined voting power of outstanding voting shares, or (b) affiliate or associate, as defined in Rule 12b-2 under Securities Exchange Act of 1934, of corporation who was beneficial owner of 10% or more of combined voting power of then outstanding voting shares at any time within two-year period.

Higher vote is not required for such business combinations if either: (a) Business combination is approved by two-thirds vote of disinterested directors, or (b) following conditions are met: (1) business combination must provide for consideration to all holders of all classes of shares, in exchange for shares, subject to certain price requirements; (2) consideration received by shareholders must be cash or same form interested shareholder or affiliate or associate previously paid to acquire shares of such class; (3) certain requirements regarding declaration, payment and rate of dividends must be met during specified period; (4) interested shareholder must not receive benefit of loans, advances, guarantees, pledges, other financial assistance, tax credits or tax advantages during specified period; and (5) proxy or information statement must be mailed to public shareholders at least 30 days prior to consummation of business combination. This section shall not relieve interested shareholder from fiduciary obligation imposed by law. Note statutory definitions of beneficial ownership, disinterested director and disinterested shareholder. (805-5/7.85).

Inspectors.—At any meeting of shareholders, chairman of meeting may, or upon request of any shareholder must, appoint one or more persons as inspectors for such meeting, unless inspector has or inspectors have been previously appointed pursuant to by-laws of corporation. Inspector or inspectors must determine validity and effect of proxies and conduct election and voting at meeting and file written reports on results of voting thereat. (805-5/7.35).

Action by Consent of Shareholders Without Meeting.—Unless otherwise provided in articles of incorporation and except for voluntary dissolution of corporation any action required by Act to be taken at any annual or special meeting of shareholders of corporation, or any other action which may be taken at meeting of shareholders, may be taken without meeting and without vote, if consent in writing, setting forth action so taken, shall be signed: (i) By holders of outstanding shares having no less than minimum number of votes that would be necessary to authorize or take such action at meeting at which all shares entitled to vote thereon were present and voting or (ii) by all shareholders entitled to vote with respect to subject matter thereof. If such consent is signed by less than all shareholders entitled to vote, then such consent shall become effective only if at least five days prior to execution of consent notice in writing is delivered to all shareholders entitled to vote with respect to subject matter thereof and, after effective date of consent, prompt notice of taking corporate action without meeting by less than unanimous written consent shall be delivered in writing to shareholders who have not consented in writing. (805-5/7.10).

Voting Trusts and Voting Agreements.—Any number of shareholders may create voting trusts for periods up to ten years by entering into written voting trust agreement and by transferring their shares to trustee or trustees. Such trust agreement does not become effective until counterpart of agreement is deposited with corporation. Such counterpart subject to same right of examination by shareholder or holder of voting trust certificate of corporation as are books and records of corporation. (805-5/7.65). Shareholders may provide for voting their shares by signing agreement for that purpose. Voting agreement so created not subject to rules regarding voting trust agreements. Voting agreement so created is specifically enforceable in accordance with principles of equity. (805-5/7.70).

Directors.—Except as provided in Art. 2A of this Act, business and affairs are managed by or under direction of board of directors, who need not be residents or shareholders unless articles of incorporation or by-laws so provide. (805-5/8.05). No judge of any Illinois court may be director of any business corporation or other for-profit corporation. Unless otherwise provided in articles of incorporation or by-laws, board of directors, by affirmative majority vote, irrespective of personal interest, have authority to set reasonable compensation of all directors for services to corporation in any capacity. (805-5/8.05). Board of directors of corporation shall consist of one or more members. Number of directors shall be fixed by by-laws, except number of initial directors shall be fixed by incorporators in articles or at organizational meeting. In absence of by-law fixing number of directors, number shall be same as that fixed in articles or at organizational meeting. Number may be changed by amendment to by-laws. Terms of all directors expire at next annual shareholders' meeting following their election unless their terms are staggered. If board of directors consists of six or more members, in lieu of electing membership of whole board of directors annually, articles or by-laws may provide that directors shall be divided into either two or three classes, each class to be as nearly equal in number as is possible. Term of office of directors of first class shall expire at first annual meeting of shareholders after their election, second class shall expire at second annual meeting after their election, and third class, if any, shall expire at third annual meeting after their election. At each annual meeting after such classification, number of directors equal to number of class whose terms expire at time of such meeting shall be elected to hold office until second succeeding annual meeting, if there be two classes, or until third succeeding annual meeting, if there be three classes. (805-5/8.10). Variable range board of directors authorized. If articles authorized dividing shares into classes or series, articles may also authorize election of all or specified number or percentage of directors by holders of one or more authorized classes or series of shares. (805-5/8.10). Vacancy among directors may be filled by election at annual meeting or at special meeting of shareholders called for that purpose; provided, however, by-laws may provide method for filling vacancies arising between meetings of shareholders by reason of increase in number of directors or otherwise, by director or shareholder action, and in absence of such provision, board of directors may fill vacancy. Director elected by shareholders to fill vacancy shall hold office for balance of term for which he or she was elected. Director appointed to fill vacancy shall serve until next meeting of shareholders at which directors are to be elected. (805-5/8.30). One or more of directors may be removed, with or without cause, at meeting of shareholders by affirmative vote of holders of majority of outstanding shares then entitled to vote at election of directors, except that no director shall be removed at meeting of shareholders unless notice of such meeting shall state that purpose of meeting is to vote upon removal of one or more directors named in notice. Only named director or directors may be removed at such meeting. In case of corporation having cumulative voting, if less than entire board is to be removed, no director may be removed, with or without cause, if votes cast against his or her removal will be sufficient to elect him or her if then cumulatively voted at election of entire board of directors. If director is elected by class or series of shares, he or she may be removed only by shareholders of that class or series. Corporation whose board is classified may provide in its articles of incorporation that directors may be removed only for cause. (805-5/8.35). Circuit Court of county in which corporation's registered office is located may remove director for cause. (805-5/8.35).

Directors may remove officers or agents, but without prejudice to contract rights, if any, of person removed. Election or appointment of officer or agent does not of itself create contract rights. (805-5/8.55).

In considering best interests of corporation, board of directors may consider effects of action on employees, suppliers and customers of corporation, communities in which establishments of corporation are located and all other pertinent factors. (805-5/8.85).

Executive Committee.—If articles or by-laws so provide, majority of directors may create one or more committees and appoint members of board to serve on committee or committees. Each committee shall have two or more members, who serve at pleasure of board. Unless appointment by board of directors requires greater number, majority of any committee shall constitute quorum and majority of quorum is necessary for committee action. Committee may act by unanimous consent and writing without meeting and, subject to provisions of by-laws or action by board of directors, committee by majority vote of its members shall determine time and place of meetings

See note at head of Digest as to 1998 legislation covered.

See Topical Index in front part of this volume.

CORPORATIONS . . . *continued*
and notice required therefor. There are certain restrictions on committees' powers. (805-5/8.40).

In considering best interests of corporation, committees of board may consider effects of action on employees, suppliers and customers of corporation, communities in which establishments of corporation are located and all other pertinent factors. (805-5/8.85).

Directors' meetings, regular or special, may be held within or without Illinois. (805-5/8.20). Majority of number of directors fixed by by-laws or, if not fixed in by-laws, stated in articles constitutes quorum, unless greater number is required by articles or by-laws. Majority of quorum of board may transact corporate business unless greater number required by articles or by-laws. Unless prohibited by articles or by-laws, directors may participate in and act at any meeting through use of conference telephone or other communication equipment by means of which all persons participating can hear each other. (805-5/8.15). Attendance at any meeting constitutes waiver of notice except where director attends for express purpose of objecting to transaction of any business because meeting not lawfully called or convened. Notice or waiver need not specify business to be transacted at, or purpose of, meeting. (805-5/8.25).

Action by Consent of Directors and Committees Without Meeting.—Any action required or allowed by Act to be taken at meeting of board of directors or committees thereof, unless otherwise provided in articles or by-laws, may be taken without meeting if all directors, or members of committees, entitled to vote with respect to subject matter thereof consent in writing to such action. Consent has same force and effect as unanimous vote of directors or committees. (805-5/8.45).

Liability of Directors.—Act imposes severe penalties on directors for improperly paying dividends or distributing assets, or not taking reasonable steps to cause notice of dissolution to be mailed to known creditors or carrying on active business after filing articles of dissolution in violation of Act. Directors may rely on balance sheet and profit and loss statement, under certain specified conditions, and may in good faith consider assets to be of their book value in authorizing dividends or distributions of assets. (805-5/8.65). If transaction is fair to corporation at time it is authorized, approved, or ratified, fact that director of corporation is directly or indirectly party to transaction is not grounds for invalidating transaction or director's vote regarding transaction; however, in proceeding contesting validity of transaction, person asserting validity has burden of proving fairness with some exceptions. (805-5/8.60).

Any corporate director or officer who commits commercial bribery or commercial bribe receiving as defined in Art. 29 of "Criminal Code of 1961" is liable to corporation for treble damages, based on aggregate amount given or received, plus attorneys' fees. Conviction in criminal proceeding is deemed prima facie evidence of convicted director's or officer's liability under Act. (805-5/8.70).

Indemnification of Directors and Officers.—Corporation may indemnify any person who was or is party, or is threatened to be made party to any threatened, pending or completed action, suit or proceeding, whether civil, criminal, administrative or investigative (other than action by or in right of corporation) by reason of fact that he is or was director, officer, employee or agent of corporation, or serving at request of corporation as director, officer, employee or agent of another corporation, partnership, joint venture, trust or other enterprise, against expenses (including attorneys' fees), judgments, fines and amounts paid in settlement actually and reasonably incurred by him, if he acted in good faith and in manner he reasonably believed to be in or not opposed to best interests of corporation and, with respect to criminal action or proceeding, had no reasonable cause to believe his conduct unlawful. Lack of good faith not presumed from settlement or nolo contendere plea. Indemnification of expenses (including attorneys' fees) allowed in derivative actions except no indemnification in respect of any claim, issue or matter as to which any such person shall have been adjudged to be liable for negligence or misconduct in performance of duty to corporation unless court decides indemnification is proper. To extent any such person succeeds on merits or otherwise, he shall be indemnified against expenses (including attorneys' fees). Determination that person to be indemnified met applicable standard of conduct, if not made by court, is made by board of directors by majority vote of quorum consisting of directors not party to such action, suit or proceeding, or if quorum not obtainable or disinterested quorum so directs, by independent legal counsel or by stockholders. Expenses may be paid in advance upon receipt of undertaking to repay. Such indemnification not deemed exclusive and continues as to person who has ceased to be director, officer, employee or agent, and inures to benefit of heirs, executors and administrators of such person. Corporation may purchase indemnity insurance. (805-5/8.75). Similar provisions are also contained in Not for Profit Corporation Act. (805-405/101.01).

Loans.—Corporation has power to lend money to its directors, officers, employees and agents. (805-5/3.10[f]).

Officers.—Corporation shall have such officers as shall be provided in by-laws, each of whom shall be elected by board of directors at such time and in such manner as may be prescribed by by-laws. Officers and assistant officers and agents as may be deemed necessary may be elected or appointed by board of directors or chosen in such other manner as may be prescribed by by-laws. If by-laws so provide, any two or more offices may be held by same person. One officer, in Act generally referred to as secretary, shall have authority to certify by-laws, resolutions of shareholders and board of directors and committees thereof, and other documents of corporation as true and correct copies thereof. (805-5/8.50). No judge of any Illinois court may be officer of any business corporation or other for-profit corporation. (705–60/1).

In considering best interest of corporation, officers may consider effects of action on employees, suppliers and customers of corporation, communities in which establishments of corporation are located and all other pertinent factors. (805-5/8.85).

Penalties Imposed on Officers and Directors.—Officer or director of corporation who fails or refuses to answer truthfully and fully interrogatories propounded to him by Secretary of State, or who signs any report or statement filed with Secretary of State which is known to such officer or director to be false in any material statement or representation, commits Class C misdemeanor. (805-5/16.10).

Waiver of Notice.—Any notice required to be given under Act, or articles of incorporation or by-laws of corporation may be waived by written waiver signed by person or persons entitled to such notice, whether before or after time stated therein; such waiver shall be deemed equivalent to giving of such notice. (805-5/7.20).

Registered Office and Agent.—Each corporation must have registered office in Illinois and registered agent, whose business office is identical with such registered office. (805-5/5.05). Registered agent may resign (805-5/5.15) or corporation may change registered agent or address of registered office by following statutory procedure (805-5/5.10). Registered agent is agent of corporation for receipt of any process, notice, or demand required to be served upon corporation. (805-5/5.25).

General Powers.—In order to carry out purposes for which organized, corporation has general power, among others, to: acquire and otherwise deal in and with real or personal property or any interest therein; sell, mortgage and dispose of all or any part of its property and assets; acquire real property improved or unimproved, and lend money to its employees, acquire, sell, and otherwise use and deal in and with, shares or other interests in, or obligations of, other corporations, associations, partnerships, or individuals, and, subject to §§9.05 and 9.10 of Act, purchase, take, receive or otherwise acquire, hold, own, pledge, transfer or otherwise dispose of own shares. If corporation shall comply with applicable provisions of Illinois Bank Holding Company Act of 1957; borrow money for its corporate purposes without regard to any state usury law; invest surplus funds from time to time; lend money for corporate purposes and take and hold real and personal property as security for payment of funds so invested or lent; make donations for charitable, scientific, religious or educational purposes; establish deferred compensation plans, pension plans, profit sharing plans, share bonus plans, share option plans and other incentive plans for directors, officers and employees; indemnify directors, officers, employees or agents in accordance with 8.75. (805-5/3.10). Unless otherwise provided by articles, corporation may sell its shares to its employees or to employees of any subsidiary, without first offering same to its shareholders, on terms approved by holders of two-thirds of its shares or by its directors pursuant to like approval of shareholders. (805-5/6.50).

Except in specified instances, no limitation on business, purposes or powers expressed or implied in articles or implied by law may be asserted to defeat any action between corporation and third person or between shareholder and third person involving any contract to which corporation is party, or any right of property or any alleged liability of whatsoever nature. (805-5/3.15).

Dividends.—Act sets forth in detail circumstances under which dividends may be declared by directors. (805-5/9.10).

Unclaimed Dividends.—See category Property, topic Absentees, subhead Escheat.

Disposition of Assets.—Sale, lease, exchange, mortgage, pledge, or other disposition of all, or substantially all, property and assets, when made in usual and regular course of business, may be made by directors; no authorization or consent of shareholders is required. (805-5/11.55). Sale, lease, exchange, mortgage, pledge, or other disposition of all, or substantially all, property and assets, with or without good will, if not made in usual and regular course of business, may be made by following statutory procedure, which includes securing approval of holders of two-thirds of outstanding shares, by classes of shares, where applicable. (805-5/11.60). Higher vote is required for certain sales, leases, exchanges, mortgages, pledges, transfers or other dispositions of assets representing 10% or more of consolidated net worth by domestic corporation which has class of registered securities or which adopts such higher voting requirements. (805-5/7.85). See subhead Vote Required for Certain Business Combinations, supra. Dissenting shareholder has right to be paid fair value of his shares by following statutory procedure. (805-5/11.65; 5/11.70).

Books and Records.—Corporation must keep at its registered office or principal place of business in Illinois, or at office of transfer agent or registrar in Illinois, record of its shareholders, giving names and addresses of all shareholders and number and class of shares held by each. Any person who is shareholder of record, has right to examine, for any proper purpose, its books and records of account, minutes, and record of shareholders, and to make extracts therefrom. In order to exercise this right, shareholder must make written demand upon corporation, stating with particularity records sought to be examined and purpose therefor. If corporation refuses examination, shareholder may file suit in Circuit Court of county in which either registered agent or principal office of corporation is located to compel by mandamus or otherwise such examination as may be proper. If shareholder seeks to examine books or records of accounts, burden of proof is upon shareholder to establish proper purpose. If purpose is to examine minutes or records of shareholders or voting trust agreement, burden of proof is upon corporation to establish that shareholder does not have proper purpose. Any officer or agent, or corporation, which refuses to allow any such shareholder, or such holder of voting trust certificate, or his agent or attorney, so to examine and make extracts, is liable to such shareholder, or holder of voting trust certificate, for penalty of up to 10% of value of his shares, in addition to any other damages or remedy afforded him by law. It shall be defense to any action for such penalties that person suing therefor within two years sold or offered for sale any list of shareholders of such corporation or any other corporation or aided or abetted any person in procuring any list of shareholders for any such purpose or has improperly used any information secured through any prior examination of books and records of account, or minutes, or records of shareholders of any corporation. (805-5/7.75). Upon written request of shareholder, corporation must mail to such shareholder within 14 days after receipt of request balance sheet as of close of latest fiscal year and profit and loss statement for such fiscal year. (805-5/7.75).

Reports of Domestic Corporations.—Each domestic corporation organized under any general law or special act of Illinois authorizing such corporation to issue shares, other than homestead associations, building and loan associations, banks and insurance companies, must file annual report on forms prescribed and furnished by Secretary of State (805-5/14.05) within 60 days before first day of corporation's anniversary month (805-5/14.10). Articles of incorporation are deemed to be first report of issuance of shares and, for purpose of determining initial license fee, initial franchise tax and assessment of annual franchise tax thereafter until basis therefor is changed, shares

See note at head of Digest as to 1998 legislation covered.

See Topical Index in front part of this volume.

IL – 5

CORPORATIONS . . . *continued*
which articles state corporation proposes to issue without further report to Secretary of State are deemed to be issued at date of filing of such articles, and for such purpose only, consideration which such articles state is to be received by corporation therefor is deemed to have been received by corporation. (805-5/14.15). Each domestic corporation must file with Secretary of State, cumulative report of changes in paid-in capital regarding following: (a) issuance of any shares not previously reported to Secretary of State as having been issued, or (b) increase in amount of its paid-in capital without issuance of shares, or (c) exchange or reclassification of shares resulting in increase in amount of its paid-in capital. Cumulative report must be filed (a) within 60 days for issuances or increases prior to either Jan. 1, 1991 or last day of third month immediately preceding corporation's anniversary month in 1991, or (b) at time of filing of corporation's annual report for issuances or increases after both Dec. 31, 1990 and last day of third month immediately preceding corporation's anniversary month in 1991. (805-5/14.20).

As to reports of foreign corporations, see infra, subhead Foreign Corporations.

Penalties Imposed on Corporations.—Corporation which fails to file any annual report or report of cumulative changes in paid-in capital and pay any franchise tax within time prescribed shall pay penalty of 10% of any delinquent franchise tax due for such report. Corporation which fails to file report of issuance of shares or increase in stated capital and paid-in surplus subject to penalty, for each month or part of month that same is delinquent, of 1% of amount of license fees and franchise taxes. (805-5/16.05).

Corporation which fails or refuses: (a) To file in office of recorder of deeds within time prescribed by Act any document required to be so filed, (b) to answer truthfully and fully interrogatories propounded by Secretary of State, or (c) to perform any other act required by Act to be performed by corporation, is guilty of Class C misdemeanor. (805-5/16.05).

Corporation which fails or refuses to file articles of revocation of dissolution within time prescribed by Act is subject to penalty for each calender month or part of month that it is delinquent in amount of $50. (805-5/16.05).

No corporation required to pay franchise tax, license fee or penalty under Act may maintain any civil action until all such franchise taxes, license fees and penalties are paid in full. (805-5/15.85).

Merger or Consolidation.—Any two or more corporations may merge into one of such corporations or consolidate into new corporation. (805-5/11.05).

Statutory procedure for merger or consolidation includes requirement of approval by each corporation by affirmative vote of at least two-thirds of votes of shares entitled to vote on plan at meeting held to obtain such approval. Where classes of shares are entitled to vote as class with respect to merger or consolidation, approval requires, in addition to approval by two-thirds of votes of shares entitled to vote, approval by two-thirds of votes of such class. Articles of corporation may supersede two-thirds vote requirement as to that corporation by specifying any smaller or larger vote requirement not less than majority of votes of shares entitled to vote on issue and not less than majority of votes of shares of each class or series of shares entitled to vote as class on issue. (805-5/11.20). Higher vote is required for certain mergers, consolidations or share exchanges by corporation which has class of registered securities or which adopts such higher voting requirements. (805-5/7.85). See subhead Vote Required for Certain Business Combinations, supra.

Dissenting shareholder has right to be paid fair value of his shares, by following statutory procedure. (805-5/11.65; 11.70).

Any "parent" corporation owning at least 90% of outstanding shares of each class of shares of any other corporation may merge such subsidiary corporation into itself or another subsidiary if merged corporation is solvent without approval by vote of shareholders of either of corporations. Dissenting shareholder has right to be paid for his shares on following statutory procedure. (805-5/11.30).

After effective date of merger or consolidation of corporations, surviving or new corporation must file with Secretary of State cumulative report of changes in paid-in capital. (805-5/14.25).

Taxes and Fees.—See supra, subhead License Fees of Domestic Corporation and infra, subheads Franchise Taxes on Domestic Corporations; Franchise Taxes on Foreign Corporations.

Tender Offers.—Effective Aug. 2, 1989, takeover of any Illinois corporation which (A) has any equity securities registered under §12 of Securities Exchange Act of 1934 or is subject to §15(d) of that Act; and (B) either (i) has its principal place of business or its principal executive office located in Illinois, or (ii) owns or controls assets located within Illinois that have fair market value of at least $1,000,000; and (C) either (i) has more than 10% of its shareholders resident in Illinois, (ii) has more than 10% of its shares owned by Illinois, or (iii) has 2,000 shareholders resident in Illinois shall, with certain exceptions, be subject to Act. (805-5/11.75).

Dissolution.—Corporation which has not commenced business and has not issued any shares may be voluntarily dissolved by its incorporators. (805-5/12.05). Corporation may elect to dissolve voluntarily and wind up its affairs by written consent of holders of record of all outstanding shares (805-5/12.10) or by act of corporation, with affirmative vote of holders of two-thirds of outstanding shares entitled to vote at meeting held to obtain such approval. Where classes of shares are entitled to vote as class with respect to dissolution, approval requires approval by two-thirds of class entitled to vote as well as by two-thirds of shares entitled to vote at meeting. Articles of incorporation may supersede two-thirds vote requirement as to that corporation by specifying any smaller or larger vote requirement not less than majority of votes of shares entitled to vote on dissolution and not less than majority of votes of shares or any class entitled to vote as class on dissolution. (805-5/12.15). Higher vote is required for certain plans or proposals of dissolution or liquidation by corporation which has class of registered equity securities or which adopts such higher voting requirement. (805-5/7.85). See subhead Vote Required for Certain Business Combinations, supra. Act sets forth in detail procedure to be followed, which includes cessation of active business upon effectiveness of dissolution and notice of such dissolution to each known creditor. (805-5/12.30). By following statutory procedure, voluntary dissolution may be revoked within 60 days of its effective date if corporation has not begun to distribute its assets or has not commenced proceeding for court supervision of its winding up. (805-5/12.25).

Corporation may be dissolved involuntarily by order of circuit court on complaint filed by Attorney General in certain cases. (805-5/12.50). Corporation may be dissolved involuntarily in certain cases by act of Secretary of State. Corporation so dissolved shall be reinstated within five years following date of issuance of certificate of dissolution upon delivery of application for reinstatement containing prescribed information, and payment of all fees and filing of all reports then due. Certificate of reinstatement, and application therefor, are then returned to corporation and must be filed within 15 days of mailing thereof in office of recorder of county in which corporation's registered office is situated. (805-5/12.45).

See also infra, subhead Liquidation.

Liquidation.—Circuit courts have full power to liquidate assets and business of corporation, in certain cases, on suit of shareholder or creditor, or on application by corporation or where action has been filed by Attorney General to dissolve corporation. (805-5/12.50). Corporation may revoke dissolution within 60 days of its effective date if certain procedures followed under Act. (805-5/12.25).

Dissolution or liquidation does not impair claims if suit thereon is commenced within five years. (805-5/12.80).

Time for filing documents for record in county office of recorder is within 15 days after mailing thereof by Secretary of State to person or corporation charged with duty of filing, unless document cannot with reasonable diligence be filed within such time, in which case shall be filed as soon thereafter as is reasonably possible. (805-5/1.10).

Forms for Corporate Documents.—All reports required by Act to be filed in Office of Secretary of State must be made on forms prescribed and furnished by Secretary of State. Forms for all other documents furnished on request, but use thereof, unless otherwise specifically prescribed in Act, not mandatory. (805-5/1.10).

Verification of Documents.—Whenever any document must be verified, such requirement is satisfied by either: (1) Formal acknowledgment by person or one of persons signing instrument that it is his act and deed or act and deed of corporation, as case may be, and that facts stated therein are true. Such acknowledgment shall be made before person who is authorized by law of place of execution to take acknowledgments of deeds and who, if he has seal of office, shall affix it to instrument; or (2) signature, without more, of person or persons signing instrument, in which case such signature or signatures shall constitute affirmation or acknowledgment of signatory, under penalties of perjury, that instrument is his act and deed or act and deed of corporation, as case may be, and that facts stated therein are true. (805-5/1.10).

Papers from Secretary of State's Office as Evidence.—Certificates issued by Secretary of State and copies of documents filed in his office when certified by him must be taken and received in all courts, public offices, and official bodies as prima facie evidence of facts therein stated. (805-5/1.20).

Unauthorized Assumption of Corporate Powers.—Persons who assume to exercise corporate powers without authority so to do are jointly and severally liable for all debts and liabilities incurred or arising as result thereof. (805-5/3.20).

Appraisal.—Shareholders dissenting from merger, consolidation or sale of all or substantially all assets not in usual course of business (805-5/11.65) are entitled to fair value for shares upon proper objection. Court appraisal procedure is available in event parties fail to agree on value.

Close corporations regulated by Close Corporation Act. (805-5/2A.05 to 2A.60). Provisions of Business Corporation Act applicable to all close corporations, except insofar as Close Corporation Act otherwise provides, and to close corporation that has voluntarily or involuntarily terminated close corporation status, except insofar as Close Corporation Act otherwise provides. Corporation not electing to become close corporation subject to Business Corporation Act.

Close corporation defined as corporation organized under or electing to be subject to Close Corporation Act and articles of incorporation of which contain provisions required by 32-1.01 through 17.05, inclusive, of Business Corporation Act of 1983 and provide that all issued shares of each class be subject to one or more restrictions on transfer permitted by 6.55, such restrictions to be uniform within each class. Articles of incorporation may set forth qualification of shareholders. Close corporation formed in accordance with provisions of Business Corporation Act, except that articles to contain provisions required by 2A.05 and heading stating name of corporation and that being organized as close corporation.

Corporation organized under Business Corporation Act may become close corporation by amending articles of incorporation to comply with 2A.05. Heading of amendment must state it is reorganized as close corporation. Amendment must be approved unanimously in writing or by vote of holders of record of all outstanding shares of each class.

Corporation may voluntarily terminate status as close corporation by amending articles of incorporation to delete provisions required by 2A.05. Amendment must be approved in writing or by vote of holders of record of two-thirds of outstanding shares of each class, unless articles provide for vote greater than two-thirds. Corporation's status as close corporation involuntarily terminated if any event occurs as result of which one or more of provisions or conditions required or permitted by 1.80(s) are breached and neither corporation nor any of its shareholders proceeds under 2A.30 to prevent such loss of status or to remedy such breach.

Following sections of Close Corporation Act govern certain aspects of close corporations, as indicated: 2A.25 (issuance or transfer of shares in breach of qualifying conditions), 2A.31 (corporate option where restriction on transfer held invalid), 2A.40 (shareholders' agreement), 2A.45 (management by shareholders), 2A.50 (shareholders' option to dissolve corporation).

Foreign Corporations.—Foreign corporation organized for profit, before it transacts business in Illinois, must procure certificate of authority to do so from Secretary of State; but no foreign corporation may obtain certificate of authority under Act to act as trustee, executor, administrator to collect, guardian, or in any other like fiduciary capacity in Illinois or to transact in Illinois business of banking, insurance, suretyship,

See note at head of Digest as to 1998 legislation covered.

See Topical Index in front part of this volume.

IL – 6

CORPORATIONS . . . *continued*
or business of character of building and loan corporation. Foreign professional service corporation may secure certificate of authority to transact business upon (1) demonstrating compliance with act regulating professional services and (2) complying with requirement of Professional Services Corporation Act 805-10/1, et seq. concerning ownership and control by specified licensed professionals who must be licensed in state of domicile or Illinois. (805-5/13.05).

Except corporation, person or entity required to be chartered, licensed, certified, registered, regulated or supervised under state law other than Business Corporation Act of 1983, foreign corporation authorized by its charter to invest or loan money may without qualifying to transact business in Illinois, invest or loan money, purchase or contract to purchase notes or other evidences of indebtedness or interests therein, secured by any security instrument, including mortgages or trust deeds in nature of mortgages conveying real or personal property in Illinois. Such foreign corporation shall have same rights and powers for recovery, servicing, protection and enforcement, by foreclosure or otherwise, of such notes or other evidences of indebtedness subject to same penalties for usury, as private persons, citizens of Illinois and shall have power to acquire, hold, lease, mortgage, sell, contract with respect to, or otherwise protect or convey property in Illinois heretofore or hereafter assigned, transferred, mortgaged or conveyed to it as security for, or in whole or part satisfaction of indebtedness purchased or owned by it. When sale is made under any judgment, decree or power in mortgage or deed, such foreign corporation may purchase, in its corporate name, property offered for sale, and become vested with title wherever natural person might do so in like cases; provided, however, that in case such corporation shall not, within period of five years after acquiring such title, sell any real estate so acquired it is duty of State's Attorney to proceed by information, in name of People of Illinois, against such corporation, in Circuit Court of county within which such land is situated, and such court has jurisdiction to hear and determine fact, and to order sale of such land or real estate, at such time and place, subject to such rules as court shall establish. Any such acts by foreign corporation are not deemed as "doing business" in state. (815-125/1).

Qualification.—Foreign corporation, in order to procure certificate of authority, must make application to Secretary of State, executed and filed in duplicate, on forms prescribed and furnished by Secretary of State and also deliver to Secretary of State copy of its articles of incorporation and all amendments thereto, duly authenticated by proper officer of state or country wherein it is incorporated. Thereupon certificate of authority to transact business in Illinois will be issued, which must be recorded in office of recorder of county where registered office of corporation is located within time prescribed by Act. (805-5/13.15, 5/1.10).

If articles of incorporation are amended, corporation must forthwith file in Office of Secretary of State copy of such amendment duly authenticated by proper officer of state or country under laws of which such corporation is organized. (805-5/13.30).

License Fees of Foreign Corporations.—Foreign corporation must pay initial license fee and, in some cases, additional license fee. In each case fee is 1/20 of 1%. Basis for initial license fee is amount represented in Illinois of its paid-in capital. Basis for additional license fee, except in case of statutory merger, is increased amount represented in Illinois of sum of its paid-in capital as disclosed by annual report, by any report of issuance of additional shares, or of increase in paid-in capital, without issuance of shares, or of exchange or reclassification of shares. Amount represented in Illinois is that portion of sum of its paid-in capital which sum of: (1) Value of its property located in Illinois and (2) gross amount of business transacted by it at or from places of business in Illinois bears to sum of (1) value of all of its property, wherever located, and (2) gross amount of its business, wherever transacted. License fees are payable to Secretary of State. (805-5/15.50, 15.55, 15.60).

Reports.—Foreign corporation must file with Secretary of State annual report on forms prescribed and furnished by Secretary of State within 60 days before first day of corporation's anniversary month. (805-5/14.05, 5/14.10). Foreign corporation, within 60 days after: (a) Issuance of any shares not previously reported to Secretary of State as having been issued, (b) increase in paid-in capital, without issuance of shares or (c) exchange or reclassification of shares resulting in increase in paid-in capital , or (d) issuance of any shares of acquiring corporation in share exchange, must file report of such issuance or increase. (805-5/14.20). Whenever foreign corporation: (a) Is party to statutory merger and is surviving corporation, or (b) effects acquisition and cancellation of its shares, or (c) effects reduction in its paid-in capital in connection with acquisition and cancellation of its shares, as permitted by Act, and such change is not reported to Secretary of State by any other report required by Act, it must, within 60 days after effective date of such change, file report of changes in paid-in capital. (805-5/14.25).

Effect of Failure to Obtain Certificate of Authority.—No foreign corporation transacting business in Illinois without certificate of authority may maintain civil action in any court of Illinois, until it has obtained such certificate. However, failure to obtain certificate of authority does not impair validity of any contract or act of such corporation, nor prevent it from defending any action at law or suit in equity in any court of Illinois. Foreign corporation which transacts business in Illinois without obtaining certificate of authority within 60 days after it commences business in Illinois is liable, for years or parts thereof during which it so transacted business, in amount equal to all fees, franchise taxes, penalties and other charges which would have been imposed by Act on it if it had been duly qualified and had filed all required reports, plus penalty of either 10% of such filing fee, license fee and franchise taxes or $200 plus $5 for each month or fraction thereof in which it has continued to transact business in Illinois without certificate of authority therefor, whichever penalty is greater. (805-5/13.70).

Revocation of Certificate.—Certificate of authority of foreign corporation may be revoked by Secretary of State for number of specified acts. (805–5/13.50).

Withdrawal.—Foreign corporation may withdraw from qualification in Illinois by following statutory procedure. (805-5/13.45).

Foreign Insurance Companies.—See category Insurance, topic Insurance Companies.

Franchise Taxes on Domestic Corporations.—Basis for initial franchise tax payable by domestic corporation is amount represented in Illinois of sum of its paid-in capital as disclosed by its first report of issuance of shares. Basis for additional franchise tax, except in case of statutory merger or consolidation, is increased amount represented in Illinois of sum of its paid-in capital as disclosed by any report of issuance of additional shares, or of increase in paid-in capital without issuance of shares, or of exchange or reclassification of shares. Basis for annual franchise tax is amount represented in Illinois of sum of its paid-in capital on last day of third month preceding anniversary month of corporation. Amount represented in Illinois is that proportion of sum of paid-in capital which sum of: (a) Value of its property located in Illinois and (b) gross amount of business transacted by it at or from places of business in Illinois bears to sum of (a) value of all of its property, wherever located, and (b) gross amount of business, wherever transacted, with certain exceptions prescribed by Act relating to election to pay on entire paid-in capital, failure to file annual report, and in case of statutory merger and consolidation. (805-5/15.40). Additional franchise tax in case of statutory merger or consolidation. (805-5/15.35).

Franchise taxes are payable to Secretary of State. (805-5/15.35).

Franchise Taxes on Foreign Corporations.—Foreign corporations are subject to initial, additional in some cases, and annual franchise taxes, at same rate and computed on same bases as franchise tax on domestic corporations. Initial tax based on amount represented in Illinois of paid-in capital as disclosed in application for certificate of authority. (805-5/15.70).

Franchise taxes payable to Secretary of State. (805-5/15.65).

Minimum Annual Franchise Taxes.—Minimum annual franchise tax payable by each domestic corporation is $25. (805-5/15.45). Maximum annual franchise tax for domestic and foreign corporations. (805-5/15.45, 805-5/15.75). Minimum annual franchise tax payable by each foreign corporation. (805-5/15.75).

Income Tax.—For taxable years beginning after June 30, 1989, all corporations are subject to 4.8% state income tax. (35-5/201). Personal Property Replacement Income Tax, effective July 1, 1979, imposes additional tax on corporations (except S corporations) of 2.85% of net income, reduced to 2.5% of net income Jan. 1, 1981. See category Taxation, topic Income Tax.

Professional Service Corporations.—Illinois has adopted Act authorizing formation of professional service corporations. (805-10/1 to 10/17). Medical Practice Act allows two or more corporations authorized under Medical Corporation Act to form partnership or joint venture.

Professional Associations.—See topic Associations, subhead Professional Associations.

Deeds.—See category Property, topic Deeds.

Political Contributions.—Campaign or other political contributions may not be made by organizations licensed to conduct horse race meeting or any concessionaire or officer, director or holder or controller of 5% or more legal or beneficial interest in any such organization or concession. (230-5/24).

General Not For Profit Corporation Act of 1986 enacted at 32-101.01 et seq. This Act, which takes effect Jan. 1, 1987, repeals General Not For Profit Corporation Act, approved July 17, 1943, as amended.

Illinois Administrative Procedure Act.—This Act is incorporated into Business Corporation Act (805-5/1.50) and Not for Profit Corporation Act (805-105/101.01).

Limited Liability Company Act.—See topic Limited Liability Companies.

JOINT STOCK COMPANIES:

There is no specific legislation dealing with joint stock companies or business trusts other than 765-1025/1 to 1025/30, relating to disposition of unclaimed property by joint stock companies and business trusts; and 240-5/8, relating to licensing business trusts to engage in business of renting safety deposit boxes). State income tax defined to include joint stock companies. (35-5/1501[4]). Purposes for which they may be formed, their rights, powers and liabilities, how they sue or are sued, when and how they may be dissolved, and rights and liabilities of members thereof are governed by case law. See topics Associations and Corporations.

LIMITED LIABILITY COMPANIES:

Limited Liability Company Act.—
Generally (805-180/1-180/60). Effective Jan. 1, 1994.

Name.—Shall contain terms "Limited Liability Company", "L.L.C." or "LLC". Shall not contain "corporation", "Corp.", "Incorporated", "Inc.", "Ltd.", "Co.", "Partnership" or "L.P." (805-180/1-10). Shall not contain any word or phrase indicating authorized or empowered to be in business of corporate fiduciary unless permitted by Commissioner of Office of Banks and Real Estate. May use word "trust", "trustee" or "fiduciary" if complied with Corporate Fiduciary Act. Shall contain word "trust" if organized for purpose of accepting and executing trusts. (805-180/1-10).

Nature of Business.—Any lawful purpose except banking exclusive of fiduciary organized for purpose of accepting and executing trusts; business of syndicate or limited syndicate under Insurance Code; or practice of dentistry unless all dentists and managers are licensed under Illinois Dental Practice Act or practice of medicine unless all members and managers are licensed under Medical Practice Act of 1987. (805-180/1-25).

Articles.—Shall include: Name and address of LLC, purpose, name of registered agent, name(s) of manager(s) where applicable, latest date if any of dissolution where applicable, name and address of each organizer and any other lawful provision members elect to include for regulation of internal affairs. (805-180/5-5[a]).

LLC is organized at time articles are filed with Secretary of State or any later stated date but not more than 60 days after filing. (805-180/5-5[b]).

Member and Manager Liability.—Member or manager is not personally liable for debt, obligation or liability of company solely by reason of being or acting as member or manager. (805-180/10-10).

See note at head of Digest as to 1998 legislation covered.

See Topical Index in front part of this volume.

IL – 7

LIMITED LIABILITY COMPANIES . . . *continued*

Management.—By member(s) or manager(s) elected by members in manner prescribed by operating agreement or articles. (805-180/15-1). Only certain matters require consent of all members. (805-180/15-1[C]).

Contribution.—May be cash, property, services rendered, promissory note or other obligation to contribute cash or property, or agreement to perform services. (805-180/20-1).

Liability for Contribution.—Member's obligation to contribute money, property or other benefit or to perform services is not excused by member's death, disability or other inability to perform personally. Creditor of limited liability company who extends credit without notice of compromise under §15-1(c) may enforce original obligation. (805-180/20-5[a]).

Interest.—Member's interest is personal property. (805-180/30-1). Interest transferable but no management or member status is given transferee unless in accordance with authority in operating agreement; unanimous consent of all other members required. (805-180/30-10).

Dissolution.—(1) Time or events specified in operating agreement; (2) upon agreement of members in writing; (3) death, retirement, resignation, bankruptcy unless otherwise provided; (4) upon entry of decree of judicial dissolution (805-180/35-5); (5) upon administrative dissolution (805-180/35-1, 180/35-25).

Suit by Member.—Derivative suit, similar to corporation. (805-180/40-1). Where member is successful court may award reasonable expenses to plaintiff and direct plaintiff to remit remainder of proceeds to LLC. (805-180/40-15).

Fees.—Various fees charged and collected by Secretary of State: (a) filing articles: $500; (b) amendments: $100; (c) articles of dissolution: $100; (d) application to reserve name: $300; (e) registration of name: $300. (805-180/50-1).

Foreign limited liability companies authorized to transact business within Illinois by application to Secretary of State (805-180/45-5) and registration (805-180/45-20). Provisions as to transaction of business without admission. (805-180/45-45).

PARTNERSHIPS:

Uniform Partnership Act (805-205/1 to 205/43), Uniform Limited Partnership Act prospectively repealed, generally effective Jan. 1, 1990, by Revised Uniform Limited Partnership Act (805-210/110 to 210/1205). Professional Associations Act (805-305/1 to 305/10) adopted.

Revised Uniform Limited Partnership Act (805-210/110 to 210/1205) ("Revised Act") shall govern all limited partnerships formed on or after July 1, 1987 (805-210/1205). In addition, all foreign limited partnerships shall be governed by Revised Act from and after July 1, 1987. Except as otherwise provided in §1205 of Revised Act, all limited partnerships formed prior to July 1, 1987, under Uniform Limited Partnerships Act, shall continue to be governed by provisions of Uniform Act until Jan. 1, 1990, at which time such limited partnerships shall be governed by Revised Act, subject to certain exceptions. (805-210/1205).

Actions.—A partnership may be sued in names of partners as individuals doing business as partnership, or in firm name, or both. Unsatisfied judgment against partnership in firm name does not bar action to enforce individual liability of partner. (735-5/2-111).

Name.—If persons conduct partnership business under assumed name, certificate setting forth assumed name, names of persons conducting business and business addresses must be filed with county clerk of county in which partnership transacts business and notice of filing published. (805-405/1).

BUSINESS REGULATION AND COMMERCE

BANKS AND BANKING:

Regulated By.—Banks and Banking are regulated by 17 and Commercial Code.

Uniform Commercial Code has been adopted in Illinois. (c. 810). See topic Commercial Code.

Formation Of.—Banks may be formed for purpose of discount and deposit, buying and selling exchange, and doing general banking business, except issuing of bills to circulate as money. (205-5/8 to 5/12). Charter must be obtained from state commissioner. (205-5/6.1 to 5/12). Bank chartered pursuant to Act subsequent to Nov. 1, 1985 and out of state bank that merges with state bank and establishes or maintains branch in Illinois after May 31, 1997, shall obtain and maintain with Federal Deposit Insurance Corporation, or such other instrumentality or corporation chartered by U.S., deposit insurance as authorized under federal law. (205-5/13).

Reports.—All state banks shall make and publish a full statement of their affairs at least one time during each calendar quarter according to directions from state commissioner. (205-5/47).

Stockholder's Liability.—No provision for assessment of liability against stockholders.

Liabilities of Directors and Officers.—Directors or officers of any state bank violating or participating in, or assenting to, or permitting any officer or agent of bank to violate loan, marketable investment securities limitations, affiliate transactions and lease limitations set out in Illinois Banking Act (205-5/32, 5/33, 5/34, 5/35.1 and 5/35.2) are personally and individually liable for all damages which bank, its stockholders or any other person sustains in consequence of violation (205-5/39). Any state bank, and after May 31, 1997, branch of out of state bank subject to examination by Commissioner or officer, director or employee thereof who makes loan or grants gratuity to bank examiner is guilty of Class A misdemeanor. (205-5/40). Any bank or officer shall not condition granting of any loan on borrower contracting with specific person or organization for insurance, legal or real estate services. Violation is business offense punishable by fine of up to $1,000. (205-5/48.2). Directors, officers or agents are subject to civil penalties up to $10,000 for violating provision of Act, any order of Commissioner, or any other action which is Commission's discretion, is detriment or impediment to banking. Bank's quarterly statement required to be published within time specified by Commissioner and penalty of $100 per day for first instance of noncompliance may be imposed for noncompliance. (205-5/48). See also subhead Confidential Financial Records, infra.

Deposits and Collections.—Deposits in trust by one person (as trustee) for another person (as beneficiary) are permitted, and upon death of depositor/trustee, beneficiary will be sole holder of account. (205-625/3). Payable on Death accounts are permitted, and upon death of holder of account, person designated shall be sole owner of account. (205-625/4). When deposit is made in names of two or more persons payable to them, such deposit may be paid to any one of said persons whether other or others be living or not, and when agreement permitting such payment is signed by all said persons, receipt or acquittance of person so paid shall be valid and sufficient discharge from all parties to bank for any payments so made. (765-1005/2). Bank is liable for deposits made in outside depository from time deposit is made unless notice is provided to depositor in manner provided for in Act that bank's liability begins when deposit is recorded. "Outside depository" defined not to include automatic teller machine or point of sale terminal. (205-5/5b). Deposits and collections governed by Art. 4 of Commercial Code.

Unclaimed Deposits.—Illinois has adopted Uniform Disposition of Unclaimed Property Act. (765-1025/1 to 1025/30). Deposits presumed abandoned unless owner has, within five years, increased or decreased amount of deposit or presented passbook for crediting of interest, corresponded in writing with banking organization concerning deposit, or otherwise indicated interest in deposit as evidenced by memorandum on file with bank. See category Property, topic Absentees, subhead Escheat. Deposits with definite maturity date not presumed abandoned less than five years after final maturity date and property in individual retirement account not presumed abandoned earlier than five years after owner attains age at which distributions are mandatory. (765-1025/2[e]).

Confidential Financial Records.—No bank may disclose to any person, except customer or his agent, customer's financial records unless customer has authorized such disclosure or in response to lawful subpoena, summons, warrant or court order which has also been served upon customer. Service upon customer may be waived by court for good cause. Willful violation by bank officer or employee or inducement of violation is business offense punishable by fine up to $1,000. Financial records may be examined by CPA during audit, by agent of specified governmental entities, by other enterprises or consumer reporting agency during regular exchange of credit information. Financial information may be used in tax returns and in published data (where information cannot be identified to particular customer or account), and information concerning dishonor of negotiable instrument permitted to be disclosed under Commercial Code may be furnished. Financial information may be furnished to law enforcement authorities if bank believes it has been victim of crime, and pursuant to Uniform Disposition of Unclaimed Property Act, Illinois Income Tax Act, Illinois Currency Reporting Act (205-685/1 et seq.), Federal Currency and Foreign Transactions Reporting Act, Federal Personal Responsibility and Work Opportunity Reconciliation Act or any other statute which requires disclosure of financial records (205-5/48.1). Bank may furnish information about existence of account of person to judgment creditor of that person who has made written request for such information.

Trust companies are governed by provisions of Corporate Fiduciary Act. (205-620/1/1 et seq.). Corporation organized to accept and execute trusts shall contain word "trust" in corporate name. No corporation that is not corporate fiduciary shall be allowed to use word "trust", "trustee" or "fiduciary". (805-5/4.05).

Foreign corporations, including banks, savings and loan associations, and national banking associations domiciled in other states also allowed to act in fiduciary capacity under stated conditions. All such trust companies and authorized foreign corporations empowered absent contractual prohibition to register securities held in fiduciary capacity in name of nominee without disclosing fiduciary capacity, may hold such securities in bulk, and deposit same with a clearing corporation, as defined in Commercial Code Art. 8-102. (810-5/8-102; 760-75/1 to 75/4).

Bank holding companies include corporations, trusts, associations, partnerships, joint ventures, or like (205-10/2), which directly or indirectly own or control, or have power to vote 25% or more of voting shares of any class of voting securities of bank or bank holding company; control in any manner election of majority of directors or trustees of bank or bank holding company; for benefit of whose shareholders, members or employees 25% or more of voting shares of bank or bank holding company is held by trustees; or directly or indirectly exercise controlling influence over management or policies of bank or bank holding company as determined by Board of Governors of Federal Reserve System (205-10/2).

Change in control and becoming bank holding company restricted. (205-10/3.02, 10/3.07). Bank holding company restricted in certain circumstances from acquiring ownership or control of any Illinois bank(s). (205-10/3.02). Out-of-state bank holding company may acquire Illinois bank(s) or Illinois bank holding companies provided certain conditions are met. (205-10/3.071 to 10/3.074).

Prohibition against acquiring directly or indirectly any voting shares of Illinois bank if, after such acquisition, acquiror will own or control more than 5% of voting securities of such bank. (205-10/3.02). Under certain circumstances (including reciprocity), bank holding company which is "Out-of-state bank holding company" may acquire control of Illinois bank, and Illinois bank holding company may acquire control of "Out-of-state bank". (205-10/3.07).

Credit Unions are organized under 17-4401 through 17-4473.

Credit service organizations are regulated under Credit Services Organization Act. (815-605/5 to 605/16).

Common Trust Funds.—Illinois has adopted Uniform Common Trust Act. (760-45/1 to 45/7).

See note at head of Digest as to 1998 legislation covered.

See Topical Index in front part of this volume.

IL – 8

BANKS AND BANKING. . . *continued*

Currency exchanges and ambulatory currency exchanges may be organized to cash checks, drafts, etc., to pay utility and other bills, to issue money orders and travelers cheques and engage in distribution of food stamps. Director of Financial Institutions may authorize currency exchange to render additional services consistent with provisions of Act. License must be obtained from Director of Financial Institutions and bond must be posted. Maximum rate charged for check cashing and writing of money orders not to exceed schedule formulated by Director of Financial Institutions. (205-405/19.3 [*Note*: predecessor statute 17-4838 held unconstitutional, 74 Ill.2d 404, 385 N.E.2d 699]). No deposits may be accepted, exchanges may not act as bailee or agent to hold funds and exchanges may not issue tokens to be used in lieu of money. (205-405/1 to 405/30).

Private Banking Prohibited.—No person, firm, partnership, or corporation that is not bank may transact business in manner that has substantial likelihood of misleading public by implying that it is bank or use word "bank," "banking," or "banker" in connection with his or its business. (205-5/46). Violations are Class A misdemeanor and also subject to Commissioner's cease and desist order plus civil penalty of up to $10,000 for each violation. (205-5/46[b]).

Branch Banking.—Banks may establish and maintain branches offering any services permitted at main premises subject to certain limitations as to number of branches (205-5/5) and after May 31, 1997, establish and maintain branches in another state that may conduct any activity in that state that is authorized or permitted for any bank that has banking charter issued by that state (205-5/15[b]). 1968 amendment to Banking Act deleted prohibition on branches in foreign countries. Bank may establish temporary service facility at any International Fair held in State which is approved by U.S. Dept. of Commerce for sole purpose of exchanging foreign currency. (205-5/5). Special statutory procedure for adoption of branch banking prescribed by Constitution of 1970. (Art. XIII, §8). Foreign banking corporations permitted to establish single banking office in central business district of Chicago. (205-645/1 to 645/19). Automatic teller machines and point of sale terminals, if established and maintained in accordance with Act, do not come under definitions of branch bank or branch office. (205-5/5). Location of automatic teller machines is regulated by 205-5/5.

Savings and loan associations are regulated by Illinois Savings and Loan Act (205-105/1-1 et seq.) and Illinois Financial Institutions Banking Act (205-110/1 to 205-110/76). Commissioner has power to issue orders requiring correction of harmful conditions and suspending persons when necessary to protect savings and loan association or depositors.

Savings banks are regulated by Savings Bank Act. (205-205/1001 to 205/11011, 205/8017).

Remittance agents, as defined, must obtain license from Secretary of State. As of July 1, 1970, subject matter is covered by Vehicle Code of 1969. (625-5/2-122).

Financial planning and management services, with designated exceptions, must obtain license from Director of Financial Institutions who receives recommendation from Board of Financial Planning and Management Service Advisors. (205-665/1 to 665/22).

Electronic Transfer of Funds.—Electronic Fund Transfer Act in effect to provide ability to complete certain financial transactions through electronic means. (205-616/1 et seq.).

Merger.—State bank may, by vote of its board of directors and without vote of its stockholders, merge with another bank (within ten miles distance) in same or contiguous county if Commissioner of Banks, with concurrence of regional director of Federal Deposit Insurance Corporation, agrees that such merger is absolutely necessary for protection of depositors and creditors. (205-5/31).

Foreign bank representative officers are authorized and regulated under Foreign Bank Representative Act. (205-650/1 to 650/6). Nonresident financial institutions must provide information on nature and extent of activities and income earned in Illinois pursuant to Financial Institution Activity Reporting Act. (205-680/1 et seq.).

Credit Agreements.—Nonconsumer debtor may not maintain action on or in any way related to agreement or commitment to lend money or extend credit unless such agreement or commitment is in writing, sets forth relevant terms and conditions, and is signed by creditor and debtor. (815-160/2). 815-160/3 lists specific actions of creditors that do not give rise to claims or defenses by debtor unless they comply with 815-160/2.

BILLS AND NOTES:

Uniform Commercial Code became effective July 2, 1962; 1972 Official Text became effective July 1, 1973. See topic Commercial Code. Article 3 of Code has replaced Uniform Negotiable Instruments Law. Local governments and school districts may issue interest-bearing commercial paper. (30-365/1).

Attorney fee clauses are enforceable. (142 Ill. 589, 32 N.E. 495).

Judgment notes recognized (735-5/2-1301) and under such note judgment may be entered at any time after its due date, without process, provided that after Sept. 24, 1979, power to confess judgment in any instrument used in "consumer transaction" is null and void. Circuit Court of Cook County (includes Chicago) will not accept affidavit for non-wage garnishment and will not issue summons in such proceeding based on judgment by confession unless judgment is confirmed after service of process, Gen. Order 6.4(b) of that Court. Execution of non-wage garnishment based on judgment by confession without such confirmation is unconstitutional. (343 F.Supp. 1272). Cannot seek deduction order in wage garnishment based upon judgment by confession without service of process unless such judgment confirmed after service of process by trial de novo. (See category Debtor and Creditor, topic Garnishment, subhead Garnishment of Wages, and category Civil Actions and Procedure, topic Judgments, subhead Judgment by Confession. See also Prefatory Note to category Debtor and Creditor, topic Garnishment.) Confession clause does not affect negotiability. (810-5/3-112).

Form of judgment note which is commonly used is as follows:

Form

. . . ., 19. . . . .

$. . . . .

. . . . after date, for value received . . . . promise to pay to the order of . . . . dollars, at . . . . with interest at . . . . .% per annum.

And to secure the payment of said sum . . . . authorize, irrevocably, any attorney of any court of record to appear for . . . . in said court, in term time or in vacation, at any time hereafter, and confess a judgment without process in favor of the holder of this note, for such amount as may appear to be unpaid thereon, with costs and 5% attorney's fees, and to waive and release all errors in any such proceedings and consent to immediate execution upon such judgment, hereby ratifying and confirming all that said attorney may do by virtue hereof.

. . . . (Signature).

BILLS OF LADING:

See topic Carriers.

BILLS OF SALE:

See topic Sales.

BLUE SKY LAW:

See topic Securities.

BROKERS:

Real Estate Brokers.—Real estate broker means individual, partnership, limited liability company or corporation other than real estate salesperson who for another and for compensation sells, exchanges, purchases, rents or leases real estate, or offers to perform any of these acts, or who negotiates, offers, attempts or agrees to negotiate any of these acts, or who lists, offers, attempts or agrees to list real estate for sale, lease or exchange, or who buys, sells, offers to buy or sell or otherwise deals in options on real estate or improvements thereon, or who collects, offers, attempts or agrees to collect rent for use of real estate, or who advertises or represents himself as being engaged in business of buying, selling, exchanging, renting or leasing real estate, or who assists or directs in procuring prospects intended to result in sale, exchange, lease or rental of real estate, or who assists or directs in negotiation of any transaction intended to result in sale, exchange, lease or rental of real estate or employs or supervises leasing agent. Salesperson means individual, other than broker or associate broker, who is employed by broker or associated by written agreement with broker as independent contractor and participates in activity requiring broker's license. (225-455/4). However, Real Estate License Act of 1983 does not apply to persons, limited liability companies, partnerships or corporations who as owners or lessors or through regular employees perform any of these acts with reference to property owned or leased by them, where such acts are performed in regular course of or as incident to management, sale or other disposition of such property and investment therein, provided said employees shall not perform any acts requiring broker's license in connection with vocation of selling or leasing any estate or improvements thereon not so owned or leased. (225-455/6). Act also does not apply to attorney in fact acting under duly executed, recorded power of attorney to convey real estate from owner or lessor, or attorney at law in rendering services as attorney at law, or receiver, trustee in bankruptcy, administrator, executor or guardian, or person acting under court order or authority of will or trust instrument, or resident manager for owner or any employee acting as resident manager for broker managing apartment building, duplex, apartment complex or court, when said manager resides on premises and is engaged in leasing property in connection with such employment, or officer or employee of federal agency, state government or political subdivision performing official duties, or any multiple listing service wholly owned by not-for-profit organization or association of brokers, or not-for-profit referral system or organization of brokers formed for purpose of referrals of prospects for sale or listing of real estate. (225-455/6).

Leasing agent license is limited scope license and is required for those persons who engage in activities relating to leasing of residential real property, and only those activities. [225-455/6.1].

Brokerage Relationships in Real Estate Transaction Law.—Governed by 225 ILCS 455/38.1 et seq.

Licensee considered to be representing consumer as designated agent for consumer unless (1) there is written agreement between broker and consumer stating different relationship or (2) licensee is performing only ministerial acts. (225-455/38.15).

Licensee shall (1) Perform terms of brokerage agreement, (2) promote best interest of client, (3) exercise reasonable skill and care in performing brokerage services, (4) keep confidential all confidential information received from client, (5) comply with all requirements of this Art. and all applicable statutes and regulations. (225-455/38.20).

Licensee shall also treat all customers honestly and shall not negligently or knowingly give them false information. When engaged by seller client shall timely disclose to customers all material adverse facts pertaining to physical condition of property that are actually known by licensee and could not be discovered by customer through reasonable inspection of property. (225-455/38.25[a]). Licensees are not responsible for providing false information to customer when such information was provided by client and licensee had no actual knowledge of falsity. (225-455/38.25[a]). Broker can perform ministerial acts for customer. (225-455/38.25[b]).

No later than entering into brokerage agreement with consumer broker shall: (1) advise of agency relationship that will exist unless written agreement provides otherwise, (2) advise of any other agency relationships available, advise consumer in writing of name(s) of designated agent(s), (3) advise consumer in writing of designated agents and (4) advise as to broker's compensation and whether that will be shared with other parties to transaction. (225-455/38.40[a]). Licensee shall disclose in writing to customer that licensee is not acting as agent for customer at time intended to prevent disclosure of confidential information. Disclosure shall take place no later than offer to purchase or lease real property. (225-455/38.35[b]).

See note at head of Digest as to 1998 legislation covered.

See Topical Index in front part of this volume.

IL – 9

BROKERS . . . *continued*

Licensee may act as dual agent only with informed written consent of all clients. (225-455/38.45[a]). Disclosure form must be presented by licensee to client at time brokerage agreement is entered. (225-455/38.45[b]). No cause of action shall arise on behalf of any person against dual agent for making disclosures allowed or required by this Art. Dual agent does not terminate any agency relationship by making allowed or required disclosures. (225-455/38.45[d]). There shall be no imputation of knowledge or information among or between clients, brokers, or their affiliated licensees. (225-455/38.45[e]). Broker is not considered subagent of client of another broker solely by reason of membership or other affiliation by broker in multiple listing service or other similar information source. (225-455/38.55).

Consumer shall not be vicariously liable for acts or omissions of licensee in providing brokerage services for or on behalf of consumer. (225-455/38.65).

Licensing.—Persons, corporations, limited liability companies or partnerships to whom Act applies may not act as brokers or salespersons or advertise or assume to act as such without properly issued sponsor card certifying employment with real estate broker or license issued by Office of Banks and Real Estate. No partnership, corporation, or limited liability company shall be granted license unless every partner in partnership, every officer of corporation, or every managing member of limited liability company who actively participates in brokerage business holds broker's license and unless every employee who acts as salesperson for such partnership, corporation, or limited liability company holds salesperson's license. No partnership, corporation, or limited liability company will be licensed if salesperson(s) control(s) more than 49% of stock or interest. (225-455/3). All applicants for licenses must be at least 21 years of age and have graduated from high school or equivalent. However, minimum age of 21 years shall be waived for person seeking license as real estate salesperson who has attained age 18 and can provide evidence of successful completion of at least four semesters past secondary school study as full-time student or equivalent, with major emphasis on real estate courses approved by Real Estate Advisory Council. (225-455/11). Applicants for broker's license, except applicants admitted to practice law by Supreme Court of Illinois, shall have first served actively for one of previous three years as salesperson, must give satisfactory evidence of having completed at least 90 classroom hours in real estate courses approved by Real Estate Education Advisory Council or correspondence course approved by Real Estate Education Advisory Council, or have baccalaureate degree including at least minor courses involving real estate or related materials from college or university approved by Real Estate Education Advisory Council, and must pass written examination. Applicants for salesperson's license, except those admitted to practice law by Supreme Court of Illinois, must give satisfactory evidence of completion of at least 30 hours real estate courses approved by Real Estate Education Advisory Council, or correspondence course approved by Real Estate Education Advisory Council, or have baccalaureate degree including at least minor courses involving real estate or related materials from college or university approved by Real Estate Education Advisory Council, and all applicants must pass written examination. (225-455/11). Expiration date and renewal period for license set by rule. (225-455/13). Broker shall maintain definite office or place of business for real estate business within State and shall conspicuously display therein license and licenses of all associate brokers and salespersons employed by or associated at that location. (225-455/13). Completion of six hours of real estate continuing education courses required for renewal of broker or salesperson license. (225-455/37.1).

Independent Contractor Relationship.—Broker and salesperson may establish independent contractor rather than employment relationship, but this does not relieve broker of liability for salesperson's unlawful act of which broker has knowledge. (225-455/4, 455/20).

Refusal to Issue, Renew.—Office of Banks and Real Estate may refuse to issue or renew, may suspend or may revoke any license, or may censure, reprimand or impose civil penalty up to $10,000 upon any licensee for numerous specified causes including misrepresentation, untruthful advertising, failure to account for or to remit monies or documents, failure to maintain separate accounts for monies held for others, various acts constituting "block busting", "racial steering", racial, color, religious, national, sex or physical or mental handicap discrimination and requiring party to transaction who is not client of licensee to allow licensee to retain portion of escrow monies for payment of licensee's commission or expenses as condition for release of escrow monies to that party. (225-455/18). Office of Banks and Real Estate conducts hearings on proceedings to suspend, revoke or refuse to issue or renew licenses on notice and subject to Administrative Review Law. (225-455/20, 455/21). Criminal penalties are provided for certain conduct. (225-455/22). Office of Banks and Real Estate has duty and any States Attorney or resident citizen may act to enjoin such conduct. (225-455/22, 455/23).

Nonresident registered in state that has reciprocal agreement may be granted broker's license without examination and without having to maintain office or place of business in Illinois provided he maintains office or place of business in home state and has been actively practicing as broker in home state for at least two years prior to application. Nonresident salesperson employed by or associated with broker holding broker's license may be granted nonresident salesperson's license without examination provided he/she resides in same state as broker with whom he/she is associated, (which state has reciprocal agreement), and maintains active license there. Nonresident corporate broker, to be eligible, must be qualified to do business in Illinois for such registration. (225-455/14). Nonresident broker from any state may cooperate and divide commissions with broker registered in Illinois. (225-455/3).

Compensation If Not Licensed.—No recovery for real estate broker or salesperson service unless claimant registered as broker or salesperson prior to time of offer to perform such act or service or procuring any promise or contract for payment of compensation for such act or service. (225-455/7). "Isolated transaction" principle not applicable as commission of single act prohibited by Act constitutes violation. (225-455/5). Finder's fees may be recoverable. (162 F.Supp. 486).

Statute of Frauds.—There is no provision in Act or in Statute of Frauds (see topic Frauds, Statute of) prohibiting recovery on oral listing agreement. However, General Rule VII of rules and regulations adopted by Department provides that all exclusive listing agreements should be written.

Preparation of Documents.—Real estate brokers may fill in blanks of forms of contracts customarily used in community and make appropriate deletions from such contracts to conform to facts. But subsequent preparation of deeds, mortgages and other legal instruments constitutes practice of law. (34 Ill.2d 116, 214 N.E.2d 771).

Real Estate Recovery Fund.—Persons aggrieved by act or omission, representation, transaction or conduct of real estate broker or salesperson who was at time of act or omission apparently acting in such capacity in violation of Act or Office of Banks and Real Estate regulations, or which constitute embezzlement, false pretenses, artifice, trickery or forgery, fraud, misrepresentation, discrimination or deceit and which result in actual cash loss (not merely market value loss) may receive by order of circuit court amounts up to $10,000, plus costs of suit and attorneys' fees not to exceed 15% of actual damages. However, no person aggrieved by any act, representation or transaction which is in violation of Illinois Real Estate Time-Share Act (765-100/1), Land Sales Act of 1989 or Real Estate Appraiser Licensing Act may recover from Real Estate Recovery Fund (225-455/23). Failure to name as parties defendant to any action that may result in recovery from Fund any and all individual real estate brokers, real estate salespersons or real estate associate brokers, or their employees, alleged to have committed or be responsible for acts or omissions giving rise to right of recovery from Fund shall preclude recovery from Fund of any portion of judgment received in such action. (225-455/25). No private right of action for damages exists under Act. (225-455/32). Maximum liability of Fund arising from activities of any single broker may not exceed $50,000. (225-455/23). Two year statute of limitations on recovery from Fund. (225-455/25). License of broker involved is automatically terminated on court order authorizing payment from Fund and broker is not eligible for new license until he has repaid in full, plus interest at 9% per annum. (225-455/25, 735-5/2-1303). Fund is maintained at minimum amount of $1,500,000 by mandatory contributions of brokers and salespersons. (225-455/15, 455/24).

Attorney-Brokers.—Licensee who is also attorney may not act as attorney for buyer or seller in same transaction in which he/she has acted as broker or salesperson. (225-455/18).

Listing Contracts.—Any written listing contract not providing for automatic expiration within definite period of time is void. (225-455/19).

Security Brokers.—See topic Securities.

Insurance Brokers.—See category Insurance, topic Insurance Companies.

Warehouse Brokers.—No person is to hold himself out as warehouse broker or to do business as such without first being listed on license application of duly licensed personal property warehouseman; his services as broker are limited to those warehousemen who so list his name and address. (240-10/2).

Real Estate Time-Share Brokers.—See 765-100/1 et seq.

Commercial Code.—Uniform Commercial Code adopted. (c. 810).

BULK SALES:

See Commercial Code Art. 6, 26-6-101 to 6-110. §6-106 of 1972 Official Text, requiring application of proceeds, is not in force in Illinois. Remaining sections of 1972 Official Text are advanced one number. See also category Debtor and Creditor, topic Fraudulent Sales and Conveyances, subhead Bulk Sales.

Article 6 (Bulk Sales) of Uniform Commercial Code repealed effective 1992.

CARRIERS:

Illinois Commerce Commission has general supervision over common carriers of household goods (625-5/18c-1104, 5/18c-1201, 5/18-1202), with power to regulate carriers' services, rates, and practices; establish systems of accounting, and reporting and record-keeping requirements; establish systems for classification of carriers, commodities, and services; regulate leasing and interchange of equipment among carriers; establish safety and insurance standards; regulate brokers; adjudicate disputes, complaints, or petitions for relief; and issue certificates (625-5/18c-1202). Provision made for proceedings before Commission. (625-5/18c-2102 et seq.).

Inquiries may be addressed to Illinois Commerce Commission, 527 East Capital Avenue, Springfield, Illinois 62756.

Local Transit Commission.—Local city transit is governed by local transit commissions, instead of Illinois Commerce Commission. (220-5/14-101). One or more municipalities or one or more counties or combinations or portions thereof may also form Mass Transit Districts to operate public transportation systems as municipal corporations; Districts have power to issue revenue bonds, to annex contiguous territory and of eminent domain. (70-3610/1 et seq.). Regional Transportation Authority created to provide coordinated mass transportation to six northeastern Illinois counties. (70-3615/1.01 et seq.). Authority has power to issue revenue bonds, tax, regulate rates, exercise power of eminent domain and generally operate all modes of mass transit within its jurisdictional area.

Mass transportation in nonurbanized areas also governed by statute, e.g., Downstate Public Transportation Act (30-740/1-1 to 740/2-18) and Nonurbanized Area Public Transportation Act (30-740/3-1).

Uniform Commercial Code adopted. (810-5/1-101 et seq.). See topic Commercial Code.

Rates.—See supra, subhead Illinois Commerce Commission.

Discrimination.—Discrimination in rates is prohibited (220-5/9-241) and, in certain circumstances, unjust discrimination and extortion is punishable by fine (625-5/18c-1101 et seq.).

Limitation of Liability.—Common carrier may not limit its common law liability safely to deliver property received for transportation by stipulation or limitation in receipt given by it for such property (740-25/1) or by any condition in its bill of lading (810-5/7-309).

Bills of Lading.—Art. 7 of Uniform Commercial Code governs. (810-5/7-101 to 5/7-603).

See note at head of Digest as to 1998 legislation covered.

See Topical Index in front part of this volume.

IL – 10

CARRIERS . . . *continued*

Liens.—Carrier may sell unclaimed articles when charges are unpaid for six months after arrival and owner or consignee cannot be found or when owner or consignee refuses to pay three months charges. Notice of time and place of sale must be given owner or consignee 15 days before sale by mail or publication. Carrier may retain sale proceeds sufficient to pay his charges. Other carriers' liens are covered by Uniform Commercial Code. (770-90/1).

Hazardous Materials.—Transportation of hazardous materials is regulated for rail (625-5/18c-7404) and motor carriers (430-50/1 et seq., 430-30/1 to 30/16).

Air Carriers.—Illinois Air Carriers Act repealed. (15¹/₂-501-502).

Motor Vehicle Carriers.—See category Transportation, topic Motor Vehicles.

COMMERCIAL CODE:

Uniform Commercial Code adopted by Act effective 1962. Art. 2A adopted by Act effective 1992. Art. 6 and 9-111 have been repealed effective 1992. 1977 Official Text, subject to several amendments, in effect with following exceptions and additions:

(1) addition of 20-205/40.23 (§1-104a) which provides that if any provision of Commercial Code conflicts with 127-40.23 (statute granting priority lien on "grain assets" of warehouseman or grain dealer for benefit of persons holding written evidence of ownership indicating storage obligation), latter statute prevails;

(2) amendment to §2-316(3) to add (d), that implied warranties of merchantability and fitness for particular purpose do not apply to sale of livestock of their unborn offspring;

(3) addition of §3-806 that makes person liable for all costs and expenses, including reasonable attorney's fees, incurred in connection with collection of amount of check where drawer has no account with drawee or insufficient funds; however, no fee or charge may be assessed against anyone other than drawer because drawer does not have account with drawee or because there were insufficient funds at time of presentment unless party charged knew or should have known for reasons such a past history that instrument would not be honored; in addition, a fee or charge may be assessed against any bank or other depository institution or to any noncommercial checking account or other similar noncommercial account;

(4) §4-213(5) redesignated §4-312(6); new §4-213(5) added, specifying time periods after which credit given by bank on certain enumerated items becomes available for withdrawal as of right, subject to right of bank to apply credit to obligation of its customer or to withhold credit for reasonable time beyond stated time periods, if bank has good faith belief that item may be dishonored upon presentment and gives notice to customer of decision to withhold this credit;

(5) amendments repealing 5/8-8-308 to 8-320;

(6) amendment of §9-103(2)(d) to delete words "who is in the business of selling goods of that kind;" addition of §9-103(6) to cover investment property [810-5/9-103(6)];

(7) amendment of 9-105(n) so that transmitting utility includes person primarily engaged in distribution of electricity, steam, gas or water or provision of sewer service;

(8) addition of §9-205.1, which allows secured party to require that debtor include as part of security agreement list of persons to whom debtor wishes to convey collateral. Conveyances to persons not on list require at least 7 days prior notice to secured party;

(9) time periods mentioned in §§9-301(2), 9-306(3), 9-306(4)(d)(ii), 9-312(4) are changed from 10 to 20 days;

(10) amendment to §9-306.01 which makes debtor's failure to pay to secured party proceeds of unlawful sale or disposition, within 10 days after sale, prima facie evidence of willful and wanton failure to pay;

(11) addition of §9-306.02 which imposes criminal penalties on debtors who violate §9-205.1 and which creates affirmative defense for debtors who pay to secured party proceeds of unlawful sale within 10 days after sale;

(12) amendment to §9-307 which provides that person buying farm products in ordinary course of business from person engaged in farming operations takes subject to any security interest created by seller if within 1 year prior to purchase, secured party has sent written notice of his interest to buyer by certified or registered mail;

(13) addition of §9-307.1 and addition of §9-307.2; §9-307.1 provides that commission merchant or selling agent who sells farm products is subject to any security interest created by seller of such products if within 1 year prior to purchase, secured party sent written notice of his interest to commission merchant or selling agent by certified or registered mail; §9-307.2 requires commission merchant or selling agent who sells farm products, and persons buying farm products in ordinary course of business, to post statutory notice relating to security interests in such farm products at their place or places of business;

(14) amendment of §§9-403(5), 9-404(3), 9-405(2) and 9-406 to provide that additional filing fee applies for each name listed at same address;

(15) amendment to §9-403(5) to provide that filing fee is also applicable to amended statement;

(16) amendment to §9-402(1) which provides that legal description in financing statement covering growing crops, giving quarter section, section, township, range, and name of record owner, if other than debtor, satisfies requirement of legal description; and

(17) addition of §4-403(d) requiring bank customer to examine account statements and notify bank within one year of any items improperly paid by bank over customer's properly lodged stop payment order.

Code appears as Chapter 26 of Illinois Revised Statutes, State Bar Association edition. Section numbers of Illinois Code correspond to those of 1977 Official Text with nine exceptions:

(1) inclusion of §8-403(3)(d);

(2) inclusion of §8-407;

(3) inclusion of §9-306.01.

(4) inclusion of §1-104a;

(5) inclusion of §3-806;

(6) inclusion of §8-320(6), (7);

(7) inclusion of §9-205.1;

(8) inclusion of §306.22i;

(9) inclusion of §3-505A.

None of last nine sections has counterpart in 1977 Official Text.

Following options and alternatives in Official Text have been exercised:

§2-318, Alternative A adopted;

§4-106, Optional phrase omitted;

Alternative A used for clause (b);

§4-212, Optional subsection (2) adopted;

§7-204, Option to refer to local statutes not exercised and optional subsection (4) omitted;

§7-403(1)(b) Optional clause omitted;

§9-203(4), Option to refer to local statutes exercised and following statutes referred to: Consumer Finance Act (17-5601-5637), Retail Installment Sales Act (815-405/1 et seq.), Motor Vehicle Retail Installment Sales Act (815-375/1 et seq.), Article II of Chapter 3, The Illinois Vehicle Code (625-5/3-201), Act for regulation of pawnbrokers (205-510/1 to 510/11), Article III B of the Boat Registration and Safety Act (625-45/3B-1 et seq.);

§9-302(3)(b), The Illinois Vehicle Code (625-5/1-100 et seq.) and Boat Registration and Safety Act (625-45/1-1);

§9-401(1), Second alternative version of subsection (1) adopted, with "Recorder of Deeds" inserted into 3 blank spaces in paragraph (a) and "Secretary of State" in blank space of paragraph (c);

§9-401(3), Optional text omitted;

§9-401(5), Reference to "Secretary of State" added;

§9-401(6), Adopted;

§9-402(3) and (5), Optional language omitted;

§9-403(5), Uniform fee of $20 added: "Secretary of State" added:

§9-403(7), Optional language omitted;

§9-404, Effective date and Uniform fee of $20 added;

§9-405, Uniform fee of $20 added;

§9-406, Uniform fee of $20 added;

§9-407, Uniform fee of $20 added; section adopted;

§§10-101 through 11-108, Statutory references and effective dates inserted.

For offices for filing and fees under Article 9, see category Documents and Records, topic Records, subhead Filing Under Commercial Code—Place; Fees.

Forms.—See end of this Digest.

See also topics: Banks and Banking, Bills and Notes, Brokers, Carriers, Contracts, Factors, Frauds, Statute of, Sales, Securities, Warehousemen; categories Business Organizations, topic Corporations; Civil Actions and Procedure, topics Accord and Satisfaction, Limitation of Actions; Debtor and Creditor, topics Assignments, Fraudulent Sales and Conveyances, Liens, Pledges; Documents and Records, topics Records, Seals; Mortgages, topic Chattel Mortgages.

COMMISSION MERCHANTS:

See topic Factors.

CONDITIONAL SALES:

See topics Sales and Commercial Code.

CONSIGNMENTS:

See topics Factors and Commercial Code.

CONSUMER CREDIT:

Not enacted.

CONSUMER PROTECTION:

Advertising.—

Deceptive Advertising Generally.—Any entity that, with intent to acquire or dispose of property or services, places before public advertisement which is untrue, misleading or deceptive, is guilty of Class A misdemeanor. (720-295/1a). Any entity that advertises for sale goods or services with intent not to sell goods or services or not to sell them as advertised is guilty of Class A misdemeanor and may be enjoined from so advertising by state's attorney or attorney general. (720-295/1b). Any entity that advertises sale, lease, or use of real estate located outside Illinois may be enjoined from so advertising and is guilty of Class A misdemeanor unless advertisement states proximity of real estate to public schools, public highways, fresh water supply, public sewers, electric power, stores and shops, and telephone service. (720-295/1c).

Advertising specifically regulated in following areas: Going out of business and other special sales (815-350/3); bankruptcy sales (815-350/7); sale of second hand watches (815-410/4); claims of availability of periodic payments (815-505/2J); coupon sales of merchandise at less than regular price (815-505/2J.1); use of automatic price look-up system (815-505/2J.2); use of term "bank rates" or "bank financing" in credit advertising (815-505/2K); advertising factory authorized services (815-505/2M); ophthalmic materials (815-385/1 to 385/8); promotion of consumer credit (815-405/29.1); retail installment sales of motor vehicles (815-375/21 to 375/22.1); sale of franchises (815-705/30); gasoline prices (720-305/1 to 305/2); cemeteries: advertising of perpetual care (760-100/5); eye exams and glasses (815-355/1); food products: eggs (410-615/6 & 7), food and drugs (225-2/2.11), kosher food (410-645/1), meat and poultry (225-650/13), refrigerated food (240-35/9); free prizes, gifts, and gratuities (815-505/2P); insurance (215-5/148); loans: advertising regulations in connection with bankrupt

CONSUMER PROTECTION . . . *continued*
borrowers (720-330/1); mutual benefit associations (215-5/335); retailers: prohibition of advertising Illinois sales and use tax discounts (35-105/7); schools: advertising prohibitions for private schools (105-425/4); serviced items: advertising provisions for items requiring service (720-350/1 et seq.); union labeled items: unauthorized advertisement (815-425/5); union workers on strike or locked out: advertising restrictions for replacements (820-25/1); warehousemen (240-10/12). Advertising of consumer loans under $10,000 (205-670/18) also are specifically regulated to prevent deception.

Assignment of Wages.—See category Debtor and Creditor, topic Assignments.

Barber, Cosmetology and Esthetic Act.—No barber, cosmetology or esthetic school shall make false and misleading statements to influence persons to enroll in school. No such school shall fail to make disclosures, refund fees and unearned tuition to student who cancels enrollment agreement or employ certified instructors as required by Act. Violation of these provisions of Act constitutes unlawful practice under Consumer Fraud and Deceptive Business Practice Act. (225-410/3B-3).

Chain Referral Sales.—Sales unlawful wherein buyer receives promise of reduced price for supplying seller with names of other prospective buyers, with reduction in price contingent on seller's ability to sell like merchandise to named prospective buyers. (815-505/2A).

Consumer Credit Reporting.—No local statutory regulation.

Consumer Finance Act.—Repealed. (P.A. 84-1004).

Consumer Fraud and Deceptive Business Practices Act (815-505/1 et seq.).—Unfair methods of competition and unfair or deceptive acts including deception, fraud, misrepresentation, concealment, suppression or omission of material fact in conduct of any trade or commerce with intent that others rely thereon, is deemed unlawful practice, regardless of actual reliance or damage. (815-505/2). Sale or attempted sale of right to participate in pyramid scheme expressly made unlawful. (815-505/2A). When seller physically present at customer's residence sells merchandise involving $25 or more, consumer can avoid transaction by notifying person within three business days following sale and returning merchandise. Three day period does not begin to run until buyer furnished with written "Notice of Cancellation" in statutory form. (815-505/2, 505/2B).

Note: P.A. 85-869 amends c. 815-505/2 et seq. to provide protection against fraudulent real estate loans.

If furnishing of merchandise is conditioned upon consumer's providing credit references acceptable to seller, and seller rejects credit application of buyer, seller must return to customer any down payment customer has made. (815-505/2C).

If consumer in retail installment sales transaction gives seller negotiable instrument as payment, assignment or transfer of that negotiable instrument does not bar customer from asserting against assignee or transferee any defense he may have against seller unless contract contains notice in statutory form. (815-505/2D).

Any person who is regularly engaged in business of providing or furnishing merchandise to consumers or making loans to consumers and who in any calendar year has committed three or more violations of Consumer Finance Act, Consumer Installment Loan Act, Retail Installment Sales Act, or certain other Acts, is guilty of unlawful practice. (815-505/2E).

Any person who is held to have wilfully and materially violated any Illinois statute regulating extension of credit to borrowers is guilty of unlawful practice. (815-505/2F).

Installment seller who willfully and materially resells goods he has repossessed from buyer in default to person who is not good faith purchaser for value, or with whom seller is in collusion or at price intended to increase amount of deficiency recoverable from defaulting buyer is guilty of unlawful practice. (815-505/2G).

No person may make any attempt to collect obligation from spouse of obligor unless spouse cosigned instrument evidencing obligation, or unless obligation is in default at least 30 days, or unless goods or services furnished to obligor are necessities for which spouse would be liable under statute or common law. Person who violates section is guilty of Class C misdemeanor. (815-505/2H).

No person may attempt to collect obligation by communicating in any way with employer unless there has been default of payment for at least 30 days and at least five days prior notice of intention to communicate with employer has been given to employee. Violation of section constitutes unlawful practice and violator liable for damages resulting from wrongful communication. (815-505/2I).

Any retailer or motor vehicle dealer that issues coupons for purchase of merchandise at less than its regular price must state discount or fact that coupon featured price is "sale" price. (815-505/2J.1).

Any retailer using automatic look-up system shall display price information in close proximity to any item which is not individually marked with selling price. (815-505/2J.2).

No seller may include in any advertisement statement that goods may be purchased by periodic payments unless statement includes cash sale price (in immediate conjunction with total amount of periodic payments); down payment (if any); number, amount, and due dates or periods of scheduled payments; and rate of charge for credit expressed as annual percentage rate. Violation constitutes unlawful practice. Compliance with Federal Truth in Lending Act is deemed compliance with this section. (815-505/2J).

No person engaged in making of loans to consumers or furnishing goods or services to consumers in credit transaction may advertise by using such terms as "bank rates," "bank financing" or words of like import unless it is bank, banking association or trust company. (815-505/2K). It is unlawful to promote or advertise business, product or utility service through use of prizes, gifts, or gratuities unless all material terms and conditions relating to offer are clearly and conspicuously disclosed at outset. (815-505/2P).

Automobile dealers are liable to purchasing consumer for specified portions of cost of repair or replacement of power train components of automobiles for period of 30 days after date of delivery, unless such repairs have become necessary by abuse, negligence, or collision or unless vehicle is specifically sold with no warranty as to mechanical condition and statutory notice thereof is given. Executive's and officials' cars when so advertised must be used exclusively by executives and must not have been sold to public. (815-505/2L). No person engaged in performing services on merchandise may advertise such services as factory authorized unless such services are performed by factory authorized personnel. (815-505/2M).

Unlawful practice to negotiate or conduct retail transaction in language other than English unless buyer given unexecuted copy of contract in other language prior to entering into such transaction. Section not applicable to transaction made pursuant to credit card issued to buyer by seller or any third person. (815-505/2N). Immigration assistance service is now regulated, including type of service, charging fees, advertising, and registering with Attorney General with proof of malpractice insurance surety bond violation constitutes misdemeanor for first offense and Attorney General has broad power to enforce. (815-505/24). Attorney General and State's Attorney are given special powers to enforce Act (815-505/3 to 505/7), including acceptance of assurances of voluntary compliance (815-505/6.1) and consumer has private right of action (131 Ill.App.2d 434, 266 N.E.2d 183). In interpreting Act consideration should be given to Federal Trade Commission rulings and cases interpreting same. (815-505/2). Attorney General and State's Attorney are empowered to investigate and to seek injunctive and other relief prohibiting such practices, restoring property and, in case of substantial and willful violations of consumer protection statutes, receivership, license revocation, and civil penalties up to $50,000 per violation. In case of receivership persons suffering damage may prove such, in which event they may participate with general creditors in distribution of assets to extent of out-of-pocket losses. Claims against persons acquiring property by means of unlawful practice may be filed, subject to court order, in cases of receivership. (815-505/3 to 505/9).

Person is not obligated to return or pay for unsolicited goods except where they were misdirected. (815-430/1).

Any person damaged by violation of Act can bring action for actual damages or injunctive relief. Proof of public injury, pattern, or effect on consumers is not required. (815-505/10a). Court can award attorneys fees and costs to prevailing party. (815-505/10a[c]). If party seeking relief against new or used car dealer rejects offer of settlement and court judgment is less than amount offered, court may not award court costs and attorney fees incurred after date of offer. (815-505/10a[f]). Action must be filed within three years after cause of action accrued. (815-505/10a[e]).

Person who issues check in violation of Criminal Code (720-5/17-1) is liable for treble damages between $100-$500 and costs and attorneys' fees.

Consumer Installment Loan Act.—Regulates and licenses lenders of from $800 to $10,000. (205-670/1 et seq.).

Credit Cards.—In deciding whether to grant application for credit card, issuer must not base decision solely on race, color, religion, national origin, ancestry, age, sex, marital status, handicap or unfavorable discharge from military service. (815-140/1b). Credit card issuer must consider financial status either of individual married person, or of couple, as applicant requests (815-140/4); and must furnish, on applicant's request, reasons for any rejection of application (815-140/3). Maximum liability for unauthorized use of credit card is $25 if card has signature panel, and $50 if card does not have signature panel for property or services obtained prior to notification of card issuer. (815-145/2). Criminal penalties are provided for various misuses of credit cards. (Unsolicited Credit Card Act [New], [815-150/1]). Credit card issuer must disclose annual interest rate, annual membership fees, grace period for payments and transaction fees and must advise cardholders that Illinois Commissioner of Banks and Trust Companies has comparative information on rates, charges, fees and grace periods. (815-140/6). Credit card issuer must file with Commissioner statement containing its rates, charges, fees, grace periods and any transaction fee. (815-140/7). Violation of Act is Class A misdemeanor. (815-140/8).

Credit Life Insurance.—Credit life insurance for loans of less than ten years must be limited to amount of indebtedness (215-5/155.54) and to duration of loan plus an additional 15 days (215-5/155.55); requires detailed disclosure to debtor (215-5/155.56). Debtor must be allowed to substitute his own life insurance in lieu of credit policy suggested by creditor. (215-5/155.61).

Debt Collection.—See topic Licenses, Business and Professional, subhead Collection Agencies.

Door-to-Door Sales.—When merchandise having cash price of more than $25 is sold to consumer in connection with salesman's direct contact with or call on consumer without consumer's soliciting contact, consumer may avoid sale by notifying salesman and returning merchandise within three business days after receiving notice of right to cancel. (815-505/2B). Salesman must provide consumer with contract stating in large letters that consumer has right to cancel contract within three days. Contract must include detachable notice of cancellation. (815-505/2B).

Garnishments/Wage Deduction Orders.—See category Debtor and Creditor, topic Garnishment.

Hearing Instrument Consumer Protection Act.—Hearing instrument sales regulated by Department of Public Health. Hearing instrument dispensers must be licensed by Department. Consumer has 45 days to cancel sale of hearing instrument sold by mail. Sales by mail must inform consumer in large letters of right to cancel and must include detachable notice of cancellation. Hearing instrument dispensers must conduct consumer education programs recommended by Board. (225-50/1, 50/4, 50/7, 50/11-50/34). Anyone who knowingly violates provision of this act commits unlawful practice under Consumer Fraud and Deceptive Business Practices Act. (815-505/20).

Job Referral and Job Listing Services Consumer Protection Act.—Attorney General is empowered to enforce provisions of this Act which regulate job referrals and job listing services. (815-630/5). Every service shall be required to make available to Attorney General various records pertaining to their services. (815-630/5). Prior to acceptance of fee, service must provide job seeker with written contract (815-630/6) and other documents listed in Act. Contract must contain refund provision in bold face type stating that job seeker is entitled to full refund if service fails to supply at least three employment opportunities within ten calendar days following payment of fee. (815-630/8).

See note at head of Digest as to 1998 legislation covered.

See Topical Index in front part of this volume.

IL – 12

CONSUMER PROTECTION . . . *continued*

Act prohibits false and misleading advertising, representations or dissemination of information as well as listing of jobs requiring illegal acts. (815-630/9[2][b]). Violation of any provision under Act constitutes unlawful practice under Consumer Fraud and Deceptive Business Practice Act. (815-505/2Z).

Motor Vehicle Installment Sales.—See topic Sales.

New Car Buyer Protection Act.—If seller unable to conform new car to express warranties after reasonable number of attempts, manufacturer must provide consumer with comparable car or refund full purchase price. Provision not applicable unless consumer first resorted to manufacturer's informal settlement procedure. Consumer includes one who leases new vehicle for period of at least one year for purpose of transporting self and others, as well as their personal property, for primarily personal, household or family purposes. (815-380/1 et seq.). Person who converts, modifies, or alters warranty parts inconsistent with original design is liable for defective parts.

Plain Language.—No "Plain Language" statute.

Pre-Need Cemetery Sales Act.—Sale of pre-need cemetery merchandise, services, and interment is regulated by Pre-Need Cemetery Sales Act. (815-390/1 to 390/27).

Real Estate Time-Share Act.—See 765-100/1 et seq.

Rental-Purchase Agreements.—Agreements for lease of consumer merchandise which permit consumer to become owner of merchandise are regulated by "AN ACT relating to rental-purchase agreements". (815-655/1 et seq.). Agreements must be written in plain English and may not contain provisions which: Require confession of judgment; authorize breach of peace in repossession of merchandise; waive rights of consumer; require insurance from merchant; assess certain late charges; or require excessive end-charges for ownership. (815-655/2). Agreements must disclose: Whether merchandise is new or used; amount and timing of payments; number of payments and total amount to acquire ownership; amount and purpose of any payment, charge or fee in addition to periodic payments; extent of consumer's liability for loss or damage to merchandise; that consumer does not acquire ownership unless terms of agreement are met; and cash price of merchandise. (815-655/2). Advertising of agreements subject to regulated disclosures. (815-655/3). Enhanced damages and attorney's fees awarded to consumer for violation of Act. (815-655/4). Intentional violation of Act is petty offense. (815-655/5).

Replevin.—See category Civil Actions and Procedure, topic Replevin.

Retail Installment Sales.—See topic Sales.

Travel Promotion Consumer Protection Act.—(815-420/1 et seq.). Travel promoter may not advertise air or sea transportation prior to contracting with carrier for same. (815-420/3). Certain disclosures must be made upon receipt of payment for transportation services. (815-420/4). If transportation is cancelled through no fault of passenger, all money paid shall be refunded. (815-420/5). Promoter must deposit 90% of funds received into insured trust account. (815-420/6). Violation of Act is unlawful practice under Consumer Fraud and Deceptive Business Practices Act. See subhead Consumer Fraud and Deceptive Business Practices Act, supra. (815-420/7).

Uniform Deceptive Trade Practices Act.—Adopted. (815-510/1 et seq.). See topic Monopolies, Restraint of Trade and Competition.

Unsolicited Goods.—Recipient of unsolicited goods has right to refuse delivery and is not bound to return goods to sender. If goods are addressed to or intended for recipient they are deemed gift to recipient; recipient may dispose of goods in any manner without obligation to sender. (815-430/1).

Usury.—See topic Interest.

Additional Relevant Consumer Protection Provisions.—Electronic fund provisions (720-250/2.14); Fairness in Lending Act provisions (815-120/1 to 120/5); fraudulent sale of gold, silver, or coins (720-290/1 et seq.); Home Repair Fraud Act (815-515/1 et seq.); Motor Fuel Sales Act (815-365/0.1 et seq.); ticket scalping (720-375/1 et seq.); transient merchants (new) (225-465/1 et seq.); Video Movie Sales & Rental Act (720-395/1 et seq.); Pay-Per-Call Services Consumer Protection Act (815-520/1).

CONTRACTS:

Uniform Commercial Code (c. 810) and Uniform Vendor and Purchaser Risk Act (765-65/1) adopted. See topics Commercial Code, Frauds, Statute of; categories Documents and Records, topic Seals; Family, topic Infants.

With respect to contracts made after Sept. 23, 1971 dealing with construction, agreements to indemnify person for that person's own negligence are void. (740-35/1, 35/2). No contract made or sought to be enforced in Illinois is valid if it contains any provision which discriminates against any person on basis of race, color, creed, national ancestry, sex, ethnic or religious grounds or connection with any entity; such provisions are void. (775-15/5). Contracts to represent persons in personal injury claims or fire damage claims are subject to provisions of 815-640/1, 625/1.

FACTORS:

The Factor's Lien Act, 82-102 to 112 was repealed by Uniform Commercial Code. Factor's liens are now regulated by UCC—Secured Transactions (810-5/9-101 to 5/907). See especially 810-5/9-109, 5/9-108, 5/9-114, 5/9-201, 5/9-203, 5/9-207(2)(a), 5/9-301, 5/9-302(1), 5/9-303(1), 5/9-110, 5/9-401, 5/9-403, 5/9-408, 5/9-307, 5/9-310, 5/9-317, 5/9-205, 5/9-306(5), and 5/9-111. 1972 Official Text of Uniform Commercial Code became effective July 1, 1973. See topic Commercial Code.

Liens.—Necessity of filing or recording notice of factor's liens covered by 26-9-301 to 9-305. (Proper place to file and proper form, see 810-5/9-401 to 9-407.)

Consignment Agreements.—Provisions for filing or recording to protect rights of consignor. (810-5/2-403, 5/9-114, 5/9-408). Consignments of works of fine art. (815-320/1 to 320/8).

Criminal Misrepresentation of Factoring Act, 38-40-1 to 3, was repealed by P.A. 84-1047.

Prohibition.—Factors prohibited from forming nonprofit consumer credit corporation. (805-140/7).

Excluded.—For excluded transactions see 810-5/9-104.

FRAUDS, STATUTE OF:

No action may be brought to charge any executor or administrator to answer any debt or damages out of his own estate, to charge one for the debt or default of another, or on any agreement made on consideration of marriage or not to be performed within one year from the making thereof, unless promise or agreement, or some memorandum thereof, is in writing and signed by person to be charged therewith, or by some authorized person. (740-80/1). Consideration need not be expressed in writing, but may be proved by parol or other legal evidence. (740-80/3). All express trusts must be in writing. Resulting trusts or other trusts created by operation of law or implication need not be in writing and may be proved by parol. (740-80/9).

Contracts for Sale of Lands.—No action may be brought on any contract for sale of any lands or any interest therein for a longer term than one year, unless such contract or some memorandum thereof is in writing and signed by the party to be charged therewith, or by some other person authorized in writing signed by such party. This does not apply to judicial sales. (740-80/2). Contract for sale of land must include names of vendor and vendee, identification of property, price, and terms and conditions of sale, and be signed by parties to be charged, to be specifically enforceable. (404 Ill. 362, 89 N.E.2d 51).

Part performance may remove realty from Statute of Frauds. (119 Ill.App.2d 390, 256 N.E.2d 44).

Sales of or Contracts to Sell Personalty.—See Uniform Commercial Code. (810-5/2-201, 810-5/1-206, 810-5/8-319).

See also topic Banks and Banking, subhead Credit Agreements.

INTEREST:

Rate.—In absence of written contract on loan of money, goods, or things in action legal rate is 5% per annum. (815-205/1; 76 Ill.2d 427, 394 N.E.2d 380). Statute provides that creditors may receive interest at rate of 5% per annum: (a) On any sum after due date on any bond, bill, promissory note or other instrument of writing, (b) on money lent or advanced for use of another, (c) on money due on settlement of account from day of liquidating accounts between parties and ascertaining of balance, (d) on money received to use of another and retained without owner's knowledge, and (e) on money withheld by unreasonable and vexatious delay of payment. In general, rate of 9% per annum is lawful. (815-205/4).

No contract for installment purchase of residential real estate or note evidencing loan secured by residential real estate may provide for any change in contract rate of interest during its term, unless Congress or federal agency authorizes lenders to make such contracts or notes in which rate of interest may be changed during their term. (815-205/4). Greater rates may be specified under terms of Consumer Installment Loan Act (205-670/1 to 670/27); revolving credit rate is 1 1/2% per month or less except banks, branch of out-of-state bank as defined in 205-5/2, savings and loans, credit unions and lenders licensed under Consumer Finance Act, Consumer Installment Loan Act or Sales Finance Agency Act (205-660/1 to 660/17) may contract for and receive any rate agreed by parties to revolving credit arrangement (815-205/4, 205-670/1 to 670/27, 815-205/4.1, 205/4.2); certain short-term loans (six months or less) may bear maximum charge of $15 in lieu of interest and certain other charges not deemed to be interest (815-205/4.la). Any rate is permitted with respect to following: Written contracts, agreements or bonds for deed providing for installment purchase of real estate; loans secured by mortgage on real estate; where corporation is debtor; in case of demand loan of not less than $5,000 secured by warehouse receipts, bills of lading, certificates of stock, certificates of deposits, bills of exchange, bonds, or other negotiable instruments pledged as collateral for repayment; on any credit transaction between merchandise wholesaler and retailer; on certain business loans to business associations or to persons owning and operating businesses (with some limitations on collateral); on any loan made under 12 U.S.C. §1702 et seq.; on any mortgage loan guaranteed under 38 U.S.C. §1810 et seq.; on any loan insured under 12 U.S.C. §1701; for interest charged by registered broker or dealer of investment securities on debit balance in account for customer if such balance is payable at will without penalty and is secured by securities; loan by employee pension benefit plan, as defined by Employee Retirement Income Security Act of 1974; any loan made by participating bank as part of any loan guarantee program which provides for loans and for refinancing of such loans to medical students, interns, and residents and which are guaranteed by American Medical Association Education and Research Foundation; and any loan made, guaranteed, or insured in accordance with provisions of Housing Act of 1949 and Consolidated Farm and Rural Development Act. (815-205/4). Except in case of loans described in third, fifth, sixth, seventh, eighth, and 12th phrases of preceding sentence, it is unlawful to provide for repayment penalty wherever rate of interest exceeds 8% per annum on any written contract for installment purchase of residential real estate or on any loan secured by mortgage on residential real estate. State bank may charge interest at any rate or rates agreed upon by bank and borrower. (815-205/4).

On money loaned to or owing from any person (except for purchase of real estate which is secured by lien or retention of title) to amount not more than $25,000 (excluding interest) which is evidenced by written instrument providing for payment in two or more periodic installments over period of not more than 181 months from date of execution, it is lawful to contract to receive: (i) Interest in amount equivalent to interest computed at rate not exceeding 9% per annum on entire principal amount and to add that amount to principal, except no limit on rate of interest which may be received or contracted to be received by banks, after May 31, 1997, branch of bank, savings and loans or lenders licensed under Consumer Finance Act, Consumer Installment Loan Act or Sales Finance Agency Act, but debtor may satisfy such debt in full at any time before maturity in which case debtor is entitled to receive pro rata refund credit against total amount of interest added to principal, or (ii) interest accrued on principal balance from time to time unpaid at rate not exceeding annual percentage rate equivalent of rate permitted to be charged under clause (i) above, but debtor may

See note at head of Digest as to 1998 legislation covered.

See Topical Index in front part of this volume.

IL – 13

INTEREST . . . *continued*
at any time prepay principal balance in full or in part in which case interest shall cease to accrue on amount prepaid. (815-205/4a).

On retail installment charge agreements executed after Sept. 25, 1991, there is no limit on finance charges which may be charged or received. Annual notification of finance charges is required. (815-405/28.1). On contracts executed after Sept. 25, 1981 there is no limit on finance charges which may be charged or received on motor vehicle installment retail contracts. (815-375/21). Other credit sales are not subject to interest regulation (111 Ill. App.3d 953; 444 N.E.2d 818) unless considered disguised loans (273 Ill. 332, 112 N.E. 988).

Disclosure Requirements.—Compliance with Federal Truth in Lending Act deemed compliance with disclosure requirements of general interest Act (815-205/4.2), Consumer Installment Loan Act (17-5420), Motor Vehicle Retail Installment Sales Act (815-375/5, 375/22.1), Consumer Fraud and Deceptive Business Practices Act (815-505/2J), An Act relating to the issuance and use of credit cards (815-140/6), Financial Services Development Act (205-675/1).

Judgments.—Interest rate of 9% per annum recoverable on every judgment from date of recovery of judgment to date of payment or 6% when judgment debtor is unit of local government or school district or community college district. However, judgment debtor, by tender of payment of judgment, costs and accrued interest to date of tender, can stop further accrual of interest on same notwithstanding prosecution of appeal or other action to reverse, vacate or modify judgment. (735-5/2-1303).

Computation of Time.—Interest treated as per annum if no other time period is mentioned. (815-205/9). Month is calendar month, and year consists of 12 calendar months. In computations for any number of days less than month, day is one thirtieth of month. (815-205/10).

Pawnbrokers may charge 3% per month. (205-510/2).

Consumer Installment Loans.—On loans not exceeding $25,000, licensees of Department of Financial Institutions may charge interest at any rate or rates agreed upon by licensee and borrower, subject to provisions of Act. (205-670/15; 205-670/21).

Farm Development Loans.—Loans to farmers guaranteed pursuant to Illinois Farm Development Act must carry interest charge which Authority determines to be below market rate of interest generally available to borrower. (20-3605/5 to 3605/12).

Home Improvement Loans.—No disbursement of funds pursuant to loan for improvement or repair of residential construction shall be made without receipt of completion certificate (815-135/1). No funds may be disbursed in excess of amount of labor performed and materials delivered as certified in completion certificate (815-135/4). Violation of act carries fine not to exceed $1,000. (815-135/6). Home improvement retail installment contracts are subject to Retail Installment Sales Act rates. (815-405/21 & 405/2.2).

Reverse Mortgage Loans.—Bank, association or credit union, in making reverse mortgage loan, may add deferred interest to principal or otherwise provide for charging of interest or premium on such deferred interest except extensions of credit secured by residential real estate subject to laws applicable thereto. (205-105/1-6a; 205-305/46).

Usury subjects recipient to suit for twice the total of all interest, discount, and charges determined by the loan contract or paid by obligor, whichever is greater, plus attorneys fees and court costs. (815-205/6). To constitute defense or partial defense to action for money loaned, usury must be pleaded. (815-205/7). Savings and loan associations are not subject to usury claim or defense. (205-105/6-10).

Statute on usury applies, on its face, to any written contract, wherever payable, made in Illinois or to which citizen or corporation of Illinois is a party or which is secured by mortgage or trust deed on land in Illinois and interest applied must not exceed lawful rate. (815-205/8). Supreme Court of Illinois has held that foregoing provision cannot be constitutionally applied to contracts made outside Illinois unless foreign legal rate is less than Illinois rate. (250 Ill. 543, 95 N.E. 631).

LICENSES, BUSINESS AND PROFESSIONAL:

State licenses are required for numerous occupations, professions and activities. Corporate authorities of cities, villages and incorporated towns are empowered by statute to license numerous occupations and activities. (65-5/11-42-1). No license is required of commercial travelers. Conduct of bingo games by certain nonprofit organizations is lawful, subject to licensing. (230-25/1). Hospital Licensing Act at 210-85/1 to 210-85/16. Riverboat gambling operations authorized subject to licensing. (230-10/1).

Collection Agencies.—

Note: P.A. 85-894 repealed c. 111-2001-2040 relating to collection agencies, effective 12/31/95.

Activities of collection agencies governed by Collection Agency Act. (225-425/1 to 425/15). No collection agency may in any way do business in Illinois without first obtaining certificate of registration from Director of Department of Registration and Education unless agency's activities in this State limited to collecting debts from debtors by interstate communication including telephone, mail or facsimile from agency's location in another State if licensed in that State and reciprocal arrangement for Illinois agencies in that State. (225-425/4). Engaging in collection of debts without valid certificate is Class A misdemeanor. (225-425/14). Collection agency may qualify to obtain certificate or renewal certificate if officers are citizens of U.S. or lawfully admitted aliens over age of 18 years, have had at least one year experience working in credit field or related area, have not been convicted of crime involving moral turpitude, have acceptable credit rating, have no unsatisfied judgments, and have not been officers of former registrant under Act whose certificates were suspended or revoked without subsequent reinstatement. (225-425/7). Registered collection agency must file surety bond in amount of $25,000. No action on bond may be commenced more than one year from date creditor obtains judgment against collection agency. (225-425/8).

Collection agency may assign account for collection provided assignment is by written agreement specifically stating effective date of assignment and consideration for assignment, and consideration must be given prior to effective date of assignment and not be contingent upon settlement or outcome of litigation. Each licensed agency office shall maintain separate bank account in which all monies received on assigned claims must be deposited, referred to as "Trust Account". (225-425/8b-8c).

It is unlawful under Act, while collecting or attempting to collect debt, to communicate with debtor or any member of his or her family, without prior consent of debtor given directly to debt collector or express permission of court of competent jurisdiction, at any unusual time or place or time or place known or which should be known to be inconvenient to debtor. In absence of knowledge of circumstances to contrary, debt collector shall assume that convenient time for communicating with consumer is after eight o'clock a.m. and before nine o'clock p.m. local time at consumer's location. Also unlawful is threat of publication or publication of list of consumers who allegedly refuse to pay debts, except to consumer reporting agency, threat of advertisement or advertisement for sale of any debt to coerce payment of debt, and causing telephone to ring or engaging any person in telephone conversation repeatedly or continuously with intent to annoy, abuse, or harass any person at called number. Private right of action for damages may be founded upon violation of unlawful collection practices enumerated in Act. (74 Ill. App.3d 21, 392 N.E.2d 154).

Director may revoke or suspend for period of which he shall find proper, any certificate issued under Act if registrant fails to produce books and records requested by Director, acts in manner in violation of Act, fails to appear at hearing when directed by Director or by hearing officer appointed by Director, or is subject of complaint or other allegation which is proved at hearing. Director must revoke certificate of registrant upon finding of four violations of Act by registrant within one year. Repealed see now 225-425/9.

Act creates Collection Agency Advising Board composed of five members employed in collection agency registered under Act and two members representing general public. Board members receive no compensation, and shall be constituted in order to make suggestions to Director on matters affecting collection agencies. (225-425/13.1).

Collection agency or employee who knowingly, while attempting to collect debt, makes telephone call to debtor designed to harass, annoy or intimidate commits business offense of disorderly conduct punishable by fine not to exceed $3,000. (720-5/26-1). In addition to fine, court shall order person convicted to perform community service of not less than 30 and not more than 120 hours if community service is available and funded by county board where offense committed. (720-5/26-1[c]).

Collection agency or employee who while attempting to collect debt represents he is person authorized by statute to enforce law or court order; threatens to adversely affect debtor's credit rating without disclosing right to inspect credit rating; misrepresents to debtor or family business name under which engaging in debt collection or adds illegal fees or charges to existing debt; or accepts payment knowing it is not owed, commits business offense of deceptive collection practice punishable by fine not to exceed $3,000. (720-5/17-5).

MONOPOLIES, RESTRAINT OF TRADE AND COMPETITION:

Antitrust Act.—Illinois Antitrust Act has been adopted, effective July 21, 1965. (740-10/1 to 740-10/11).

Violations.—Persons violate Act who:

(1) Make any contract or engage in any combination or conspiracy with any other person who is or except for prior agreement would be competitor of such person: (a) fixing prices or rates charged for any commodity sold or bought, or any service performed or received by parties; (b) controlling, limiting, or discontinuing production, manufacture, mining, sale or supply or any commodity, or sale of any service, having effect of price-fixing; (c) allocating or dividing customers, territories, markets, either functionally or geographically, relating to any commodity or service; or

(2) By contract, combination, or conspiracy unreasonably restrain trade or commerce; or

(3) Establish, maintain, use or attempt to acquire monopoly power over any substantial part of trade of this State for purpose of excluding competition or controlling, fixing, or maintaining prices; or

(4) Lease or sell goods or services upon condition that purchaser not deal with competitor of seller where effect of such lease or sale may substantially lessen competition or tend to create monopoly; or

(5) Enforce, attempt to enforce, or further, while employee, officer or agent of foreign government or of company doing business with foreign government or instrumentality thereof, any discriminatory practice of foreign government based on race, color, creed, national ancestry, sex, ethnic or religious grounds when conduct or agreement takes place in U.S. and affects business in state. (740-10/3).

An exclusive dealing contract does not violate this Act absent proof of a substantial lessening of competition in relevant competitive market. (302 N.E.2d 79).

Definitions.—"Trade or commerce" includes all economic activity involving any commodity or service. "Commodity" means any kind of real or personal property. "Service" means any activity not covered by definition of "commodity," performed in whole or in part for purpose of financial gain including master or cable television services. "Service" does not include labor performed by natural persons as employees. (38-60-4).

Exceptions.—The Act excepts the following: (1) legitimate activities of labor organizations; (2) activities of agricultural or horticultural co-operative organizations; (3) activities of public utilities or telecommunication carriers subject to jurisdiction of Illinois Commerce Commission, or activities of telephone mutual concerns; (4) regulated activities of insurers, subject to regulation by Director of Insurance; (5) religious and charitable activities of not-for-profit corporations and organizations, established exclusively for religious or charitable purposes; (6) activities of telephone or electrical service co-operatives, operating not-for-profit; (7) activities of securities dealers who are licensed by State or are members of National Association of Securities Dealers or members of any National Securities Exchange registered with the Securities and Exchange Commission, in business of offering, selling securities as agent, broker, or

See note at head of Digest as to 1998 legislation covered.

See Topical Index in front part of this volume.

IL – 14

MONOPOLIES, RESTRAINT OF TRADE AND COMPETITION . . . *continued*
principal, including establishment of commission rates and schedules of charges; (8) activities of any board of trade designated as "contract market" by Secretary of Agriculture; (9) activities of motor carriers regulated by Illinois Commerce Commission; (10) activities of state or national banks to extent that activities are regulated under banking laws of this state or United States; (11) regulated activities of state or federal savings and loan associations; (12) fee schedules, to be used solely as guidelines by enumerated professions; (13) certain conduct involving trade or commerce (other than import trade or commerce) with foreign nations; (14) activities of units of local governments and their employees and of school districts and their employees. (740-10/5).

Prosecutions.—Persons knowingly doing any act prohibited by (1)(a), (b) and (c) and (4) under catchline Violations, supra, commits Class 4 felony and may be fined up to $100,000 or $1,000,000 if corporation. Prosecution must be commenced within four years of commission of offense. No prosecution may be commenced against any defendant who, at that time, is defendant in action filed by U.S. for violation of Federal Antitrust laws. (740-10/6).

Investigations.—Attorney General may subpoena documents and witnesses (740-10/7.2 to 10/7.6), and may appear before grand jury (49 Ill.2d 403, 273 N.E.2d 835), in investigating violations. Privilege against self-incrimination may not be invoked, and actions brought by Attorney General based on compelled testimony are prohibited. (740-10/7.7). But testimony to grand jury convened by court, even if at request of Attorney General, is admissible in prosecution under Act. (28 Ill. App.3d 622, 329 N.E.2d 28).

Civil Actions.—Civil remedies are provided by Act:

(1) Attorney General may sue to prevent and restrain acts prohibited under catchline Violations, supra. Court may exercise all equitable powers necessary, including injunction, divestiture, dissolution, and suspension or termination of foreign corporation's right to do business in state.

(2) Attorney General may sue on behalf of people of state in lieu of penalty otherwise prescribed by Act, but in addition to suit under (1) above, against any person, foreign or domestic corporation, trustee, director, manager or officer or agent of corporation for penalty up to $50,000 for individual and up to $100,000 for corporation, for acts committed in violation of any provision of Act.

(3) Any person who suffers or may suffer injury by acts prohibited under sections (1), (4) and (5) of catchline Violations, supra, may sue for treble damages, injunction, or both and costs and reasonable attorney's fees.

(4) Any person who suffers or may suffer injury by acts prohibited under sections (2) and (3) of catchline Violations, supra, may sue for actual damages, injunction, or both and costs and reasonable attorney's fees, and if violation found willful, court has discretion to award up to three times amount of actual damages.

(5) For purposes of (3) and (4) above, "person" includes state, counties, municipalities, townships and other political subdivisions. Attorney General also may sue on their behalf to recover damages provided under (3) and (4) above or any comparable Federal Law. (740-10/7). Actions by indirect purchasers are not barred.

(6) Judgment in defendant's favor in suit brought by Attorney General under (2) above bars subsequent private suit for same cause. (18 Ill. App.3d 884, 310 N.E.2d 710). Judgment for defendant in damage actions gives court discretion to avoid attorneys fees if action commenced in bad faith.

Per Se Violations.—Conduct described under (1) of catchline Violations constitutes per se violation of Act. All other conduct judged by federal "reasonableness" test, irrespective of federal common law characterizations. (36 Ill. App.3d 730, 345 N.E.2d 18).

Prima Facie Evidence.—Final judgment or order rendered in any civil or criminal proceeding brought by Attorney General under Act to effect that defendant has violated Act is prima facie evidence in action brought by other person against that defendant under (3)-(5) of catchline Civil Actions, supra, as to matters that judgment or order would be estoppel between parties thereto. Section does not apply to civil consent judgments or orders entered before taking of testimony. (740-10/8).

Limitations.—Four-year limitation on criminal prosecutions. (740-10/6). Four year limitation on actions brought under (2)-(5) of catchline Civil Actions, supra, but suit by Attorney General for violation of Act tolls statute with respect to every private right of action for damages based in whole or part on matter in Attorney General's suit during pendency thereof and for one year thereafter. (740-10/7).

Common Law Conspiracies.—Conduct which violates Act not actionable as conspiracy at common law. (740-10/9).

Fair Trade Laws.—Illinois Fair Trade Act and §10 of Illinois Antitrust Act (Savings Clause) have been repealed. (P.A.80-233). Federal enabling legislation previously repealed. (89 Stat. 801). See category Intellectual Property, topic Trademarks and Tradenames, subhead Fair Trade Act.

Federal Antitrust Law.—When language of Act is similar to federal antitrust law, state courts to follow construction given to federal law in federal courts (740-10/11), but not compelled to do so (21 Ill. App.3d 97, 315 N.E.2d 124). State exemption from Federal Antitrust Laws available to municipalities and their agents, officers and employees acting within authority. (65-5/1-1-10).

Repeals.—Act repeals Illinois Antitrust Act of 1891, and Antitrust Act of 1893 (Laws 1893, p. 182).

See also topics: Banks and Banking, Brokers, Carriers, Consumer Protection, Securities; categories Business Organizations, topics Associations, Corporations; Civil Actions and Procedure, topics Injunctions, Limitation of Actions; Employment, topic Labor Relations; Intellectual Property, topic Trademarks and Tradenames.

Deceptive Trade Practices.—The Uniform Deceptive Trade Practices Act has been adopted. (815-510/1 to 510/7).

Acts Prohibited.—A person engages in a deceptive trade practice when, in course of his business, vocation or occupation, he: passes off goods or services as those of another; causes likelihood of confusion or of misunderstanding as to source, sponsorship, approval or certification of goods or services or as to affiliation, connection or association with or certification by another, except when any trade identification was used in good faith and not abandoned prior to January 1, 1966; uses deceptive representations or designations of geographic origin in connection with goods or services; represents that goods or services have sponsorship, approval, characteristics, ingredients, uses, benefits or quantities that they do not have or that a person has a sponsorship, approval, status, affiliation or connection that he does not have; represents that goods are original or new if they are deteriorated, altered, reconditioned, reclaimed, used or secondhand; represents that goods or services are a particular standard, quality or grade or that goods are a particular style or model, if they are of another; disparages goods, services or business of another by false or misleading representation of face; advertises goods or services with intent not to sell them as advertised; advertises goods or services with intent not to supply reasonably expectable public demand, unless advertisement discloses a limitation of quantity; make false misleading statements of fact concerning reasons for, existence of or amounts of price reductions; engages in any other conduct which similarly creates likelihood of confusion or of misunderstanding. A complainant need not prove competition between parties or actual confusion or misunderstanding. (815-510/2 to 510/4). Conduct creating likelihood of confusion is not limited to practices used to effect sale but also reaches practices used in financing of sale. (340 F.Supp. 1095).

Injunctive Relief.—In addition to remedies provided under the common law or other Illinois statutes, injunctive relief is available to a person likely to be damaged by a deceptive trade practice without proof of monetary damage, loss of profits or intent to deceive. (815-510/3). Where allegations of complaint based on deceptive trade practice are denied in answer preliminary injunction may not be issued without hearing. (129 Ill. App.2d 181, 262 N.E.2d 713). Injunction not proper where alleged confusing names are composed of generic terms, unless secondary meaning is shown. (39 Ill.App.3d 73, 350 N.E.2d 109). Costs and attorneys' fees may be assessed against a defendant whose deceptive trade practices are wilfull. (815-510/3).

Inapplicability of Act.—The act does not apply to conduct in compliance with orders, rules or statutes administered by any governmental agency; or persons engaged in the dissemination of information or reproduction of printed or pictorial matter without knowledge of its deceptive character. (815-510/4).

Scope of Protection.—Act does not provide relief from past conduct or sales. (47 Ill. App.3d 266, 361 N.E.2d 815). Protection against false representations extends only to non-functional aspects of goods (46 Ill. App.3d 145, 360 N.E.2d 798) and injunction not proper, where alleged confusing names are composed of generic terms, unless secondary meaning is shown (39 Ill. App.3d 73, 350 N.E.2d 109).

Class Actions.—Consumer class action alleging only past and not future injury is improper under Act. (47 Ill. App. 3d 266, 361 N.E.2d 815). Class representative may not act as attorney in same suit. (45 Ill. App.3d 494, 359 N.E.2d 886).

Consumer Buying Clubs.—Misrepresentations by consumer buying clubs or club membership salesmen that mislead purchaser violate Act (46 Ill. App.3d 252, 361 N.E.2d 1370) irrespective of intent of seller (46 Ill. App.3d 270, 361 N.E.2d 1383).

Damages.—No private right of action for damages is created by this Act (47 Ill. App.3d 266, 361 N.E.2d 815) but damages or other relief may be available under other statutes and common law. See topic Consumer Protection.

Fraudulent Advertising and Consumer Fraud.—See topic Consumer Protection.

Instructional Materials.—Person offering instructional materials for adoption, sale or exchange in State shall not enter into any understanding, agreement or combination to control prices or restrict competition in sale of such materials. (105-5/28-1).

Resale Price Agreements.—Illinois Fair Trade Act repealed Aug. 4, 1977. (P.A.80-233).

NEGOTIABLE INSTRUMENTS:

Article 3, Uniform Commercial Code became effective on July 2, 1962. (810-5/3-101 to 5/3-806). 1972 Official Text became effective July 1, 1973. See topic Commercial Code.

RESTRAINT OF TRADE:

See topic Monopolies, Restraint of Trade and Competition.

SALES:

Art. 2, Uniform Commercial Code governs. See topic Commercial Code.

Bills of sale need not be witnessed, acknowledged or recorded, except between husband and wife living together, in which case to be valid against third persons they must be in writing and filed in same manner as security interests are required to be filed in cases where person giving security retains possession of property. (705-65/9).

Product Liability.—Manufacturer of any product which, when it is sold by manufacturer, is in defective condition, unreasonably dangerous to user or to consumer or to his property, is liable to ultimate user or consumer for personal injury or property damage, resulting from such defective condition, regardless of existence of privity or negligence. (32 Ill.2d 612, 210 N.E.2d 182). Assumption of risk, but not contributory negligence, is a bar to recovery in strict liability tort action. (45 Ill.2d 418, 261 N.E.2d 305). Specific limitations period for products liability claims is imposed by statute. (735-5/13-213).

Retail Installment Sales.—Act of 1967 (815-405/1 to 405/33) covers retail installment contracts entered into in Illinois for goods or services purchased primarily for personal, family or household purposes (excludes "motor vehicle" as defined in The Illinois Motor Vehicle Code (815-405/2 to 405/2.14) but includes bicycles, motorcycles, motor scooters, snowmobiles and trailers when purchased primarily for personal, family or household purposes). (815-405/2 to 405/2.14). Every retail installment contract must be in writing, dated, signed by buyer and seller, and must contain certain notices printed in at least ten point bold type. (815-405/3). Printed or typed portion of contract must be at least eight point type. (815-405/3). Contract must contain names of seller, buyer, their addresses, description of goods or services and all other information required in such transactions by Federal Truth-in-Lending Act. There is no obligation to disclose to obligor (1) any agreement to sell, transfer or assign contract to third party for amount equal to, in excess of or less than amount financed or (2) that assignee may pay seller of contract all or portion of prepaid finance charges and other

See note at head of Digest as to 1998 legislation covered.

See Topical Index in front part of this volume.

IL – 15

SALES . . . *continued*
fees. (815-405/4, 405/5). Installment payments must be periodic and may provide for balloon-note financing. (815-405/6). Retail installment contract is unenforceable by seller when it contains blank spaces to be filled in with essential terms after it has been signed by buyer unless delivery of goods is not made at time of execution of contract, in which case certain information identifying goods and date first payment is due may be inserted after execution by buyer. (815-405/3, 405/15).

Buyer's written acknowledgment of delivery of copy of contract in accordance with this Act protects assignee who buys contract without knowledge that seller has failed to comply with Act. (815-405/14).

Buyer may cancel contract at any time before seller delivers copy if buyer not yet received goods or furnished services. (815-405/14).

Provision in contract providing for arbitrary acceleration in absence of buyer default is unenforceable. Provision for acceleration when buyer in default unenforceable unless prior to acceleration buyer in default for at least 30 days or has abandoned or destroyed property or holder has reasonable cause to believe buyer is about to leave state. (815-405/13).

Provisions in contracts waiving buyer's legal rights against seller are unenforceable. (815-405/13). All defenses available against holder in due course under Uniform Commercial Code (810-5/3-305[2]) may be asserted by buyer notwithstanding any agreement to contrary (815-405/18). Rights of assignee under waiver of defense clause as holder in due course are valid unless he is affiliated with seller or on notice of repeated statutory breaches by seller or buyer fails to receive required notice. (815-505/2D). Cosigner agreements require explanation in statutory form. (815-405/19).

Refund credit for prepayment is mandatory. (815-405/7). Credit insurance may be required by seller subject to limitations. (815-405/8 to 405/11). Delinquency charges are limited. (815-405/12). Notwithstanding other statutes on retail installment contracts executed after Sept. 25, 1987 there shall be no limit on finance charges charged, collected and received. (815-405/27). Upon account holder's request total finance charges charged to or paid by account holder shall be provided within 60 days after end of year or within 60 days after termination of account. (815-405/28.1).

Seller or holder must give buyer written receipt for payment in cash and, upon request, written statement of amounts of payments and total amount unpaid covering transactions during period not to exceed 18 months from request. One statement every six months must be furnished without charge; seller or holder may charge up to $10 for each additional statement. (815-405/16).

Parties shall have rights and remedies provided in Art. 9 of The Uniform Commercial Code (810-5/9-101 et seq.) with respect to default and disposition of collateral. If buyer has paid 60% or more of deferred price at time of default, holder may elect to: (1) Receive and retain goods and release buyer from further obligation, or (2) allow buyer to retain goods and be limited to an action to recover unpaid balance. (815-405/26). If buyer has paid 30% or more of deferred payment price at time of repossession, buyer may, within 15 days, redeem collateral from holder by tendering all unpaid amounts, including delinquency and deferred charges, and performance necessary to cure default and any reasonable costs incurred by holder in retaking goods. (815-405/26).

One who knowingly violates Act is guilty of Class A misdemeanor. Attorney General or States Attorney may bring action to restrain violations. Violators may not recover finance charges. (815-405/30, 405/31). Violation does not render entire contract unenforceable. (53 Ill.2d 396, 292 N.E.2d 726).

Seller may waive right to insist upon prompt installment payments if he repeatedly accepts late payments. (132 Ill.App.2d 527, 270 N.E.2d 140).

Rental Purchase Agreement.—Merchant who leases goods to consumer for non-business uses for four months or more with automatic renewal and option to buy must disclose facets of deal in rental agreement. Agreement cannot include confession of judgment clause, waiver of defense clause or required insurance clause. Agreement must disclose total number of payments, amount, timing of payments, explanation of fees, liability, notice of right to reinstate agreement and cash price. (815-655/2).

"Going Out of Business" Sales.—All sales which will be represented to the public as "going out of business sales," regardless of how described, are licensed and regulated under the provisions of 815-350/1 to 350/12. Failure to comply with act constitutes Class B misdemeanor. (815-350/11). Attorney General may enjoin sale conducted without license. (815-350/10.5). See also Motor Vehicle Retail Installment Sales Act. (815-375/1).

Type Size.—See subhead Retail Installment Sales, supra.

Bulk Sales.—See topic Bulk Sales.

Sales of Motor Vehicles.—See category Transportation, topic Motor Vehicles.

Sales of Real Estate.—See topic Brokers; category Property, topic Real Property.

Resale Price Maintenance.—See category Intellectual Property, topic Trademarks and Tradenames, subhead Fair Trade Act.

Fraudulent Advertising.—See topic Consumer Protection, subhead Advertising.

Deceptive Trade Practices.—See topic Monopolies, Restraint of Trade and Competition.

Consumer Fraud and Deceptive Business Practice Act.—See topic Consumer Protection.

Consumer Protection.—See topic Consumer Protection.

Illinois Franchise Disclosure Act.—See topic Securities, subhead Franchise Disclosure Act.

SECURITIES:

Blue Sky Law known as Illinois Securities Law of 1953 ("Act"). (815-5/1 to 5/19). Uniform Securities Act not adopted. Uniform Commercial Code adopted. See topic Commercial Code.

Supervision.—Secretary of State, Securities Division. (815-5/11).

Regulatory Powers of Supervising Authority.—Secretary has broad regulatory powers including power to: Make rules and regulations; conduct investigations; prohibit or suspend sale of securities or prohibit or suspend person from selling securities or from acting as investment adviser; deny or revoke registration of securities or of dealer, salesperson or investment adviser; and raise or lower any fee imposed by, and which he is authorized by law to collect under, Act. (815-5/11 and 5/11a).

Prerequisites to Sales or Offerings.—All securities except those set forth in 815-5/2a, those exempt (815-5/3) or sold in transactions exempt (815-5/4) must be registered prior to sale.

Securities to Which Act Applicable.—"Security" means any note, stock, treasury stock, bond, debenture, evidence of indebtedness, certificate of interest or participation in any profit-sharing agreement, collateral-trust certificate, preorganization certificate or subscription, transferable share, investment contract, investment fund share, face-amount certificate, voting-trust certificate, certificate of deposit for security, fractional undivided interest in oil, gas, or other mineral lease, right, or royalty, any put, call, straddle, option or privilege on any security, certificate of deposit, or group or index of securities (including any interest therein or based on value thereof), or any put, call, straddle, option or privilege entered into on national securities exchange relating to foreign currency, or, in general, any interest or instrument commonly known as "security", or any certificate of interest or participation in, temporary or interim certificate for, receipt for, guarantee of, or warrant or right to subscribe to or purchase, any of foregoing. (815-5/2.1).

Exempt Securities.—Provisions of 815-5/2a, 5/5, 5/6, 5/7 do not apply to any of following securities: (A) Any security (including revenue obligation) issued or guaranteed by U.S., any state, any political subdivision of state, or any agency or corporation or other instrumentality of any one or more of foregoing, or any certificate of deposit for any such security; (B) any security issued or guaranteed by Canada, any Canadian province, any political subdivision of any such province, any agency or corporation or other instrumentality of one or more of foregoing, or any other foreign government with which U.S. then maintains diplomatic relations, if security is recognized as valid obligation by issuer or guarantor; (C) any security issued by and representing interest in or debt of, or guaranteed by any bank or savings bank organized under laws of U.S., or any bank, savings bank, savings institution, or trust company organized and supervised under laws of any state; or any security issued or guaranteed as to both principal and interest by international bank of which U.S. is member, or any interest or participation in any common trust fund or similar fund maintained by any such bank, savings bank, savings institution or trust company exclusively for collective investment and reinvestment of assets contributed thereto by such bank, savings bank, savings institution or trust company or any affiliate thereof, in its capacity as fiduciary, trustee, executor, administrator or guardian; (D) any security issued by and representing interest in or debt of, or guaranteed by, any federal savings and loan association, or any savings and loan association or building and loan association organized and supervised under laws of any state; or any security issued or guaranteed by any federal credit union or any credit union, industrial loan association, or similar organization organized and supervised under laws of any state; (E) any security issued or guaranteed by any railroad, other common carrier, public utility or holding company where such issues or guarantor is subject to jurisdiction of Interstate Commerce Commission or is registered holding company under Public Utility Holding Company Act of 1935 or subsidiary of such company within meaning of that Act or is regulated in respect of its rates and charges by governmental authority of U.S. or any state or is regulated in respect of issuance or guarantee of security by governmental authority of U.S., any state, Canada, or any Canadian province; (F) equipment trust certificates in respect of equipment leased or conditionally sold to person, if securities issued by such person would be exempt under 815-5/3; (G) any security which at time of sale is listed, or approved for listing upon notice of issuance on New York Stock Exchange, Inc., American Stock Exchange, Inc., Pacific Coast Stock Exchange, Inc., Midwest Stock Exchange,Inc., Chicago Board of Trade, Philadelphia Stock Exchange, Inc., Chicago Board of Options Exchange, Incorporated, National Market System of Nasdaq Stock Market, or any other exchange, automated quotation system or board of trade which Secretary of State, by rule or regulations, deems to have substantially equivalent standards for listing or designation as required by any such exchange, automated quotation system or board of trade; and securities senior or of substantially equal rank, both as to dividends or interest and upon liquidation, to securities so listed or designated; and warrants and rights to purchase any of foregoing; provided that exemption does not apply to investment fund shares or securities of like character, which are being continually offered at price or prices determined in accordance with prescribed formula; (H) any security issued by person organized and operated not for pecuniary profit and exclusively for religious, educational, benevolent, fraternal, agricultural, charitable, athletic, professional, trade, social or reformatory purposes, or as chamber of commerce or local industrial development corporation, or for more than one of said purposes and no part of net earnings of which inures to benefit of any private stockholder or member; (I) instruments evidencing indebtedness under agreement for acquisition of property under contract of conditional sale; (J) note secured by first mortgage upon tangible personal or real property when such mortgage is made, assigned, sold, transferred and delivered with such note or other written obligation secured by such mortgage, either to or for benefit of purchaser or lender; or bonds or notes not more than ten in number secured by first mortgage upon title in fee simple to real property if aggregate principal amount secured by such mortgage does not exceed $500,000 and also does not exceed 75% of fair market value of such real property; (K) note or notes not more than ten in number secured by junior mortgage lien if aggregate principal amount of indebtedness represented thereby does not exceed 50% of amount of then outstanding prior lien indebtedness and provided that total amount of indebtedness (including indebtedness represented by subject junior mortgage note or notes), does not exceed 90% of fair market value of property securing such indebtedness; provided each such note or notes bears across face thereof required legend; (L) any negotiable promissory note or draft, bill of exchange or bankers' acceptance which arises out of current transaction or proceeds of which have been or are to be used for current transactions, and which evidences obligation to pay cash within nine months of

See note at head of Digest as to 1998 legislation covered.

See Topical Index in front part of this volume.

IL – 16

SECURITIES . . . *continued*
date of issuance exclusive of days of grace, or any renewal of such note, draft, bill or acceptance which is likewise limited, or any guarantee of such note, draft, bill or acceptance or of any such renewal; (M) any security issued by and representing interest in or debt of, or guaranteed by, any insurance company organized under laws of any state; (N) any security issued pursuant to employee stock option or other security-purchase plans, if securities which are subject of such plans would be exempt, pursuant to any other subsection of 815-5/3, from registration under 815-5/5, or, if securities which are subject of employee stock option or other security-purchase plans are registered under provisions of 815-5/7; (O) any security issued by or pursuant to employee profit-sharing trusts or plans or employee pension trusts or plans (interpreted by regulation to mean trusts or plans exempt under §3[a][2] of Federal Securities Act of 1933 or trusts or plans that meet requirements for qualification under §401(a) of Internal Revenue Code); (P) any option, put, call, spread or straddle issued by clearing agency registered as such under Federal Securities Exchange Act of 1934, if security, currency, commodity, or other interest underlying option, put, call, spread or straddle is not required to be registered under 815-5/5; (Q) any security which meets all of following conditions: (1) if issuer is not organized under laws of U.S. or state, it has appointed duly authorized agent in U.S. for service of process and has set forth name and address of agent in its prospectus; (2) class of issuer's securities is required to be and is registered under §12 of Federal Securities Exchange Act of 1934, and has been so registered for three years immediately preceding offering date; (3) neither issuer nor significant subsidiary has had material default during last seven years, or for period of issuer's existence if less than seven years, in payment of (i) principal, interest, dividend, or sinking fund installment on preferred stock or indebtedness for borrowed money, or (ii) rentals under leases with terms of three years or more; (4) issuer has had consolidated net income, before extraordinary items and cumulative effect of accounting changes, of at least $1,000,000 in four of its last five fiscal years including its last fiscal year; and if offering is of interest bearing securities, has had for its last fiscal year, net income, before deduction for income taxes and depreciation, of at least 1½ times issuer's annual interest expense, giving effect to proposed offering and intended use of proceeds. (For purposes of this clause "last fiscal year" means most recent year for which audited financial statements are available, provided that such statements cover fiscal period ended not more than 15 months from commencement of offering); (5) if offering is of stock or shares other than preferred stock or shares, securities have voting rights and rights include: (i) right to have at least as many votes per share, and (ii) right to vote on at least as many general corporate decisions, as each of issuer's outstanding classes of stock or shares, except as otherwise required by law; (6) if offering is of stock or shares, other than preferred stock or shares, securities are owned beneficially or of record, on any date within six months prior to commencement of offering, by at least 1,200 persons, and on that date there are at least 750,000 such shares outstanding with aggregate market value, based on average bid price for that day, of at least $3,750,000. (In connection with determination of number of persons who are beneficial owners of stock or shares of issuer, issuer or dealer may rely in good faith for purposes of clause upon written information furnished by record owners); and (7) issuer meets conditions specified in 815-5/3(Q)(2)(4) if either issuer or issuer and issuer's predecessor, taken together, meet such conditions and if: (a) succession was primarily for purpose of changing state of incorporation of predecessor or forming holding company and assets and liabilities of successor at time of succession were substantially same as those of predecessor; or (b) all predecessors met such conditions at time of succession and issuer has continued to do so since succession; (R) any security appearing on List of OTC Margin Stock published by Board of Governors of Federal Reserve System; any other securities of same issuer which are of senior or substantially equal rank; any securities called for by subscription rights or warrants so listed or approved; or any warrants or rights to purchase or subscribe to any of foregoing; (S) any security issued by bona fide agricultural cooperative operation in Illinois that is organized under laws of Illinois or as foreign cooperative association organized under law of another state that has been duly qualified to transact business in Illinois. (815-5/3).

Exempt Transactions.—Provisions of 815-5/5 to 5/7 do not apply to any of following transactions, except where otherwise specified in 815-5/4: (A) Any offer or sale in good faith, whether through dealer or otherwise, of securities by person who is not issuer, underwriter, dealer or controlling person in respect of such securities, and who, being bona fide owner of such securities, disposes thereof for his own account; provided, that such offer or sale not made directly or indirectly for benefit of issuer, underwriter or controlling person; (B) any offer, sale, issuance or exchange of securities of issuer to or with security holders of issuer except to or with persons who are security holders solely by reason of holding transferable warrants, transferable options, or similar transferable rights of issuer, if no commission or other remuneration paid or given directly or indirectly for or on account of procuring or soliciting of such sale or exchange (other than fee paid to underwriters based on their undertaking to purchase any securities not purchased by security holders in connection with such sale or exchange); (C) any offer, sale or issuance of securities, other than fractional undivided interests in oil, gas or other mineral lease, right or royalty, to any corporation, bank, savings bank, savings institution, Savings and Loan Association, trust company, insurance company, building and loan association, dealer, pension fund or pension trust, employees' profit sharing trust, other financial institution or institutional investor, any government or political subdivision or instrumentality thereof, whether purchaser is acting for itself or in some fiduciary capacity, or to any partnership or other association engaged as substantial part of its business or operations in purchasing or holding securities, or to any trust in respect of which bank or trust company is trustee or co-trustee or to any entity which at least 90% of equity is owned by persons described under 815-5/4(c), (d), (h) or (s); or to any employee benefit plan within meaning of Title I of Federal ERISA Act if (i) investment decision is made by plan fiduciary as defined in §3(21) of Federal ERISA Act and such plan fiduciary is either bank, insurance company, registered investment adviser or investment adviser registered under Federal 1940 Investment Advisers Act, or (ii) plan has total assets in excess of $5,000,000, or (iii) in case of self-directed plan, investment decisions are made solely by persons described under 815-5/4(c), (d), (h) or (s); or to any plan established and maintained by, and for benefit of employees of, any state or political subdivision or agency or instrumentality thereof if such plan has total assets in excess of $5,000,000; or to any organization described in §501(c)(3) of Internal Revenue Code of 1986, any Massachusetts or similar business trust, or any partnership, if such organization, trust, or partnership has total assets in excess of $5,000,000; (D) any offer, sale or issuance of fractional undivided interests in any oil, gas or other mineral lease, right, or royalty to any bank, corporation, savings bank, savings institution, Savings and Loan Association, trust company, insurance company, building and loan association, dealer, pension fund, pension trust, employees' profit sharing trust, other financial institution or institutional investor or to any partnership or other association or trader buying or selling fractional undivided interests in oil, gas or other mineral rights, in frequent operations, for its or his own account rather than for account of customers, to such extent that it or he may be said to be engaged in such activities as trade or business; or to any trust in respect of which bank or trust company is trustee or co-trustee; or any entity which at least 90% of equity is owned by persons described under 815-5/4(c), (d), (h) or (s); or to any employee benefit plan within meaning of Title I of Federal ERISA Act if (i) investment decision is made by plan fiduciary as defined in §3(21) of Federal ERISA Act and such plan fiduciary is either bank, insurance company, registered investment adviser or investment adviser registered under Federal 1940 Investment Advisers Act, or (ii) plan has total assets in excess of $5,000,000, or (iii) in case of self-directed plan, investment decisions made solely by persons described under 815-5/4(c), (d), (h) or (s); or to any plan established and maintained by, and for benefit of employees of, any state or political subdivision or agency or instrumentality thereof if such plan has total assets in excess of $5,000,000; or to any organization described in §501(c)(3) of Internal Revenue Code of 1986, any Massachusetts or similar business trust, or any partnership, if such organization, trust, or partnership has total assets in excess of $5,000,000; (E) any offer or sale of securities by executor, administrator, guardian, receiver or trustee in insolvency or bankruptcy, or at any judicial sale, or at public sale by auction held at advertised time and place, or offer or sale of securities in good faith and not for purpose of avoiding provisions of Act by pledgee of securities pledged for bona fide debt; (F) any offer or sale by registered dealer, either as principal or agent, of any securities (except face amount certificate contracts and investment fund shares) at price reasonably related to current market price of such securities, provided: (1)(a) securities are issued and outstanding; (b) issuer required to file reports pursuant to §13 or §15(d) of Federal 1934 Act and has been subject to requirements during 90 day period immediately preceding date of offer or sale, or is issuer of security covered by §12(g)(2)(B) or (G) of Federal 1934 Act; (c) dealer has reasonable basis for believing that issuer is current in filing reports required to be filed at regular intervals pursuant to provisions of §13 or §15(d), as case may be, of Federal 1934 Act, or in case of insurance companies exempted from §12(g) of Federal 1934 Act by subparagraph 12(g)(2)(G) thereof, annual statement referred to in §12(g)(2)(G)(i) of Federal 1934 Act; and (d) dealer has in its records, and makes reasonably available upon request to any person expressing interest in proposed transaction in securities, issuer's most recent annual report filed pursuant to §13 or §15(d), as case may be, of Federal 1934 Act or annual statement in case of insurance company exempted from §12(g) of Federal 1934 Act by subparagraph 12(g)(2)(G) thereof, together with any other reports required to be filed at regular intervals under Federal 1934 Act by issuer after such annual report or annual statement; provided that making available of such reports pursuant to 815-5/4(F), unless otherwise represented, will not constitute representation by dealer that information is true and correct, but constitute representation by dealer that information is reasonably current; or (2)(a) prior to any offer or sale, application for authorization thereof and report set forth under subparagraph (d) of this paragraph (2) has been filed by any registered dealer with and approved by Secretary of State pursuant to such rules and regulations as Secretary of State may prescribe; (b) Secretary of State has power to refuse to approve any application or report filed pursuant to clause (2) if (i) application or report does not comply with provisions of clause, or (ii) offer or sale would work or tend to work fraud or deceit, or (iii) issuer or applicant have violated any of provisions of Act; (c) each application and report filed pursuant to clause shall be accompanied by filing and examination fee in amount established pursuant to 815-5/11(a), which shall not be returnable in any event; (d) there is submitted to Secretary of State certain information no later than 120 days following end of issuer's fiscal year, each year during period of authorization; (e) prior to any offer or sale of securities under provisions of this paragraph (2), each registered dealer participating in offer or sale of such securities shall provide upon request of prospective purchasers of such securities copy of most recent report required under provisions of sub-paragraph (d) of this paragraph (2); (f) approval of application filed pursuant to clause expires five years after date of granting of approval, unless approval is sooner terminated by (1) suspension or revocation by Secretary of State in same manner as is provided for in 815-5/11 in (E), (F) or (G) or (2) applicant filing with Secretary of State affidavit evidencing either that (i) subject securities have become exempt under 815-5/3 or (ii) applicant no longer is capable of acting as applicant and reasons therefor or (iii) applicant no longer desires to act as applicant. In event of filing of affidavit under either of subclauses (ii) or (iii) Secretary of State may authorize substitution of applicant upon new applicant executing application as originally filed. Substituted execution shall have no effect upon date of expiration of approval of application. Notwithstanding provisions of 815-5/4(F)(2)(f) approvals granted under 815-5/4(F)(2) prior to effective date of Act are governed by provisions of Act in effect on such date of approval; (g) no person shall be considered to have violated 815-5/5 by reason of any offer or sale effected after termination under 815-5/4(F)(2)(f) if official notice of such termination has not been circulated generally to dealers by Secretary of State and if such person sustains burden of proof that he did not know, and in exercise of reasonable care, could not have known, of termination; or (3) securities or securities of same class, are subject of existing registration under 815-5/5; exemption provided by 815-5/4(F) applies only if offer or sale is made in good faith and not for purpose of avoiding any provisions of Act and only if offer or sale is not made for direct or indirect benefit of issuer of securities, or controlling person in respect of such issuer; (G)(1) any offer, sale or issuance of security, whether to residents or to nonresidents of Illinois, where: (a) all sales of such security to residents of Illinois (including most recent such sale) within immediately preceding 12-month

SECURITIES . . . *continued*
period have been made to not more than 35 persons or have involved aggregate sales price of not more than $1,000,000; (b) such security has not been sold by means of any general advertising or general solicitation in Illinois; and (c) no commission, discount, or other remuneration exceeding 20% of sale price of such security, if sold to Illinois resident, is paid or given directly or indirectly for or on account of such sales; (2) in computing number of resident purchasers or aggregate sales price under 815-5/4(G)(1)(a), there is excluded any purchaser or dollar amount of sales price, as case may be, with respect to any security which at time of its sale was exempt under 815-5/3 or was registered under 815-5/5 to 5/7 or was sold in transaction exempt under other subsections of 815-5/4; (3) prospectus or preliminary prospectus with respect to security for which registration statement is pending or effective under Federal Securities Act of 1933 shall not be deemed to constitute general advertising or general solicitation in Illinois as such terms are used in 815-5/4(G)(1)(b) provided such prospectus or preliminary prospectus has not been sent or otherwise delivered to more than 150 residents of Illinois; (4) Secretary of State by rule or regulation requires and prescribes form of report containing certain information to be filed in connection with all sales made in reliance upon exemption provided by 815-5/4(G), but failure to file any such report does not affect availability of such exemption; provided that failure to file any such report will constitute violation of 815-5/12(D), subject to penalties enumerated in 815-5/14, and provided further that civil remedies of rescission and appointment of receiver, conservator, ancillary receiver or ancillary conservator provided for in 815-5/13(F) will not be available against any person by reason of failure to file any such report or on account of contents of any such report. Such report must set forth name and address of issuer and of controlling person, if sale was for direct or indirect benefit of such person, total amount of securities sold under 815-5/4(G) to Illinois residents, names and addresses of resident purchasers, representation that sales of such securities were not made to Illinois residents in excess of those permitted by 815-5/4(G) and any other information deemed necessary by Secretary of State to enforce compliance with 815-5/4(G). Filing fee is prescribed by rule or regulation of Secretary of State, but will not be less than minimum amount nor more than maximum amount established pursuant to 815-5/11(a), and is not returnable in any event. Secretary of State may impose, in such cases as he may deem appropriate, penalty for failure to file any such report in timely manner, but no such penalty shall exceed amount equal to five times filing fee. Any such report shall be deemed confidential and shall not be disclosed to public except by order of court or in court proceedings; (H) any offer, sale or issuance of security to (1) any natural person who has, or is reasonably believed by person relying on 815-5/4(h) to have, net worth, or joint net worth with that person's spouse, at time of offer, sale or issuance in excess of $1,000,000 or (2) natural person who had, or is reasonably believed by person relying on 815-5/4(h) to have had income or joint income with that person's spouse in excess of $200,000 in each of two most recent years and who reasonably expects or is reasonably expected to have, income in excess of $200,000 in current year, or (3) any person that is not natural person and in which at least 90% of equity interest is owned by persons who meet either of tests set forth in 815-5/4(h)(1) or (2); provided that such security is not offered or sold by means of any general advertising or general solicitation in Illinois; (I) any offer, sale or issuance of securities to or for benefit of security holders incident to vote by such security holders pursuant to such person's organizational document or applicable statute of jurisdiction of such person's organization, on merger, consolidation, reclassification of securities, or sale or transfer of assets in consideration of issuance of securities of same or another issuer; (J) any offer, sale or issuance of securities in exchange for one or more outstanding securities, claims or property interests, or partly in such exchange and partly for cash, where such offer, sale or issuance is incident to reorganization, recapitalization, readjustment, or composition or settlement of claim, as approved by court of competent jurisdiction of U.S., or any state; (K) any offer, sale or issuance of securities for patronage, or as patronage refunds, or in connection with marketing agreements by cooperative associations organized exclusively for agricultural, producer, marketing, purchasing, or consumer purposes; and sale of subscriptions for or shares of stock of cooperative associations organized exclusively for agricultural, producer, marketing, purchasing, or consumer purposes, if no commission or other remuneration is paid or given directly or indirectly for or on account of such subscription, sale or resale, and if any person does not own beneficially more than 5% of aggregate amount of issued and outstanding capital stock of such cooperative association; (L) offers for sale or solicitations of offers to buy (but not acceptance thereof), of securities which are subject of pending registration statement filed under Federal Securities Act of 1933 and: (1) which are subject of pending application for registration under Act, or (2) sale of which would be exempt under 815-5/3(B) if registration under Federal Securities Act of 1933 were then in effect; (M) any offer or sale of preorganization subscriptions for any securities prior to incorporation, organization or formation of any issuer under laws of U.S., or any state, or issuance by such issuer, after its incorporation, organization or formation, of securities pursuant to such preorganization subscriptions, provided number of subscribers does not exceed 25 and either (1) no commission or other remuneration is paid or given directly or indirectly for or on account of such sale or sales or issuance, or (2), if any commission or other remuneration is paid or given directly or indirectly for or on account of such sale or sales or issuance, securities are not offered or sold by any means of general advertising or general solicitation in Illinois; (N) execution of orders for purchase of securities by registered dealer, provided such dealer acts as agent for purchaser, has made no solicitation of order to purchase securities, has no direct interest in sale or distribution of securities ordered, receives no commission, profit, or other compensation other than commission involved in purchase and sale of securities and delivers to purchaser written confirmation of order which clearly identifies commission paid to registered dealer; (O) any offer, sale or issuance of securities, other than fractional undivided interests in oil, gas or other mineral lease, right or royalty, for direct or indirect benefit of issuer thereof, or of controlling person, whether through dealer (acting either as principal or agent) or otherwise, if securities sold, immediately following sale or sales, together with securities already owned by purchaser, would constitute 50% or more of equity interest of any one issuer provided that number of purchasers is not more than five and provided further that no commission, discount or other remuneration exceeding 15% of aggregate sale price of securities is paid or given directly or indirectly for or on account of sale or sales; (P) any offer, sale or issuance of securities (except face amount certificate contracts and investment fund shares) issued by and representing interest in issuer which is business corporation incorporated under laws of Illinois purposes of which are to provide capital and supervision solely for redevelopment of blighted urban areas located in municipality in Illinois and whose assets are located entirely within that municipality, provided: (1) no commission, discount or other remuneration is paid or given directly or indirectly for or on account of sale or sales of such securities; (2) aggregate amount of any securities of issuer owned of record or beneficially by any one person will not exceed lesser of $5,000 or 4% of equity capitalization of issuer; (3) population of municipality within which area that is to be redeveloped is located does not exceed 50,000 population as based on last U.S. Census; (4) officers and directors of corporation have been bona fide residents of municipality not less than three years immediately preceding effectiveness of offering sheet for securities under 815-5/4(P); and (5) issuer files with Secretary of State offering sheet descriptive of securities that sets forth certain information. Secretary of State will within reasonable time examine offering sheet so filed and, unless Secretary of State makes determination that offering sheet so filed does not conform to requirements of 815-5/4(P), will declare offering sheet to be effective, which offering sheet shall continue effective for period of 12 months from date it becomes effective. Fee for examining offering sheet shall be as established pursuant to 815-5/11(a), and shall not be returnable in any event. Secretary of State may by rule or regulation require and prescribe form of report to be filed and time within which such report shall be filed in connection with all sales made in reliance upon 815-5/4(P) and every six months after first such sale unless report due upon conclusion of all such sales has been filed, but failure to file any such report shall not affect availability of such exemption; provided that failure to file any such report will constitute violation of 815-5/12(D), subject to penalties enumerated in 815-5/14, and provided further that civil remedies provided for in 815-5/3(A) and civil remedies of rescission and appointment of receiver, conservator, ancillary receiver or ancillary conservator provided for in 815-5/13(F) will not be available against any person by reason of failure to file any such report or on account of contents of any such report. Filing fee is prescribed by rule re regulation of Secretary of State, but such fee shall not be less than minimum amount nor more than maximum amount specified in 815-5/11a, and will not be returnable in any event. Secretary of State may impose, in such cases as he may deem appropriate, penalty for failure to file any such report in timely manner. Any such report shall be deemed confidential and shall not be disclosed to public except by order of court or in court proceedings. (This exemption not available for sale of face amount certificate contracts or investment fund shares); (Q) any isolated transaction whether effected by dealer or not provided that such security is not offered or sold by means of any general advertising or general solicitation in Illinois; (R) any offer, sale or issuance of security to any person who purchases at least $150,000 of securities being offered, where purchaser's total purchase price does not, or it is reasonably believed by person relying on 815-5/4(r) that such purchase price does not, exceed 20% of purchaser's net worth at time of sale, or if natural person joint net worth with that person's spouse, for one or any combination of following: (i) cash, (ii) securities for which market quotations are readily available, (iii) unconditional obligation to pay cash or securities for which quotations are readily available which obligation is to be discharged within five years of sale of securities to purchaser, or (iv) cancellation of any indebtedness owed by issuer to purchaser; (S) any offer, sale or issuance of security to any person who is, or is reasonably believed by person relying on 815-5/4(s) to be, director, executive officer, or general partner of issuer of securities being offered or sold, or any director, executive officer, or general partner of general partner of that issuer. For purposes of 815-5/4(S), "executive officer" means president, any vice president in charge of principal business unit, division or function [such as sales, administration or finance], any other officer who performs policy making function, or any other person who performs similar policy making functions for issuer. Executive officers of subsidiaries may be deemed executive officers of subsidiaries may be deemed executive officers of issuer if they perform such policy making functions for issuer.); (T) any offer, sale or issuance of security pursuant to limited offering transactional exemption pursuant to rule or regulation of Secretary of State. (815-5/4).

Registration of Securities.—All securities except those set forth in 815-5/2a, those exempt under 815-5/3 or offered or sold in transactions exempt under 815-5/4, or face amount certificate contracts if required to be registered under 815-5/6, or investment fund shares if required to be registered under 815-5/7 must be registered prior to their offer or sale in Illinois either by coordination or qualification. (815-5/5). Fee for registration is established by rule or regulation, and in no case shall such fee be returnable, plus examination fees, if any. (815-5/5(C). Registration effective for one year from date of registration or renewal of registration unless sooner terminated. (815-5/5[D]).

Registration by Coordination.—Securities which have been or are being registered under Federal 1933 Act may be registered by coordination by filing with Secretary of State following: (a) One copy of the registration statement (without exhibits) descriptive of securities on file with Securities and Exchange Commission in its most recent form as of date of initial filing under 815-5/5(A); (b) consent to service of process executed by issuer or controlling person conforming to requirements of 815-5/10, provided that such consent need not be filed if: (i) applicant is registered dealer and securities are being offered and sold in Illinois by one or more registered dealers as principal and not as agent, or (ii) issuer or controlling person is corporation organized or authorized to transact business under laws of Illinois; (c) application, in such form and executed by such person as Secretary of State shall by rule or regulation prescribe, setting forth title and total amount of securities to be offered, amount of securities, and proposed maximum aggregate price thereof to be offered in Illinois under 815-5/5(A) and, if applicant is electing date of effectiveness of post-effective amendment as its effective date as provided in 815-5/2.13, specifying such date as effective date for purposes of registration under 815-5/5(A); (d) undertaking to forward to Secretary of State, in writing (which may be by electronic transmission), any and all subsequent amendments of and supplements to registration statement not later than seventh day

See note at head of Digest as to 1998 legislation covered.

See Topical Index in front part of this volume.

IL – 18

SECURITIES . . . *continued*
after forwarding thereof to Securities and Exchange Commission, or such longer period as Secretary of State may permit by rule, regulation or order; (e) if applicant is not registered dealer, name of at least one registered dealer for securities being registered under this subsection A (except that, in case of securities being offered and sold on delayed or continuous basis pursuant to Rule 415 under Securities Act of 1933, or any similar or successor rule thereto as may be designated by Secretary of State by rule or regulation, name of registered dealers may be furnished no later than close of business on second business day following commencement of sales of registered securities in this state) or written statement setting forth method of offer and sale in this state of securities being registered in compliance with 815-5/8. Registration of securities by coordination takes effect automatically as of effective date of registration statement (or post-effective amendment) filed under Federal 1933 Act, provided that on effective date, required information has been on file with Secretary of State for at least ten business days, or such shorter period as Secretary of State may permit by rule, regulation or order. If, however, time period referred to in preceding sentences shall not have expired on effective date of registration statement (or post-effective amendment) filed under Federal 1933 Act, registration of such securities by coordination, upon expiration of such time period, takes effect automatically as of effective date of registration statement (or post-effective amendment) filed under Federal 1933 Act. If required information is not filed with Secretary of State prior to effective date of registration statement (or post-effective amendment) filed under Federal 1933 Act, any registration of securities by coordination under 815-5/5(A) takes effect automatically as soon as all of following conditions have been satisfied: (a) Required information has been on file with Secretary of State for ten business days, or for such shorter period as Secretary of State may permit by rule, regulation or order; (b) registration statement filed under Federal 1933 Act is then in effect; and (c) prospectus then on file with Secretary of State satisfies requirements of §10(a)(3) of Federal 1933 Act.

Registration by Qualification.—Any security may be registered by qualification by filing with Secretary of State application, certain documents and prospectus. Required documents waived or supplemented by Secretary of State. Unless within reasonable time Secretary of State finds that filing does not conform to requirements of 815-5/5(B) or there is proceeding pending under 815-5/11, upon receipt of registration fee Secretary of State will register securities. Additional information may be required if all securities not sold within six months of registration date. Amendments or supplements to prospectus after registration must be filed with Secretary of State forthwith. (815-5/5[B]).

Registration of Face Amount Certificate Contracts and Investment Fund Shares.—Unless set forth in 815-5/2a, all face amount certificate contracts and investment fund shares not exempt under 815-5/3 or offered or sold in transaction exempt under 815-5/4 must be registered either by coordination or qualification prior to offer or sale in Illinois by filing with Secretary of State application and certain documents. Unless within reasonable time Secretary of State finds that filing does not conform to requirements of 815-5/6 with regard to face amount certificate contracts, or 815-5/7, with regard to investment fund shares, or there is proceeding pending under 815-5/11, upon receipt of registration fee and, in case of face amount certificate contracts, deposit, Secretary of State will register face amount certificate contracts and investment fund shares. (815-5/6[B] and 815-5/7[B]). Registration effective for one year from date of registration or renewal of registration unless sooner terminated, provided certain statements and reports filed on issuance and throughout year. (815-5/6[D] and 815-5/7[F]).

"Face amount certificate contract" means any form of "face amount certificate" or "periodic payment plan certificate" (as so designated and defined under Federal Investment Company Act of 1940) and also means any form of annuity contract (other than annuity contract issued by life insurance company authorized to transact business in Illinois), or installment face amount certificate contract, or installment face amount certificate, or installment participation certificate, or installment face amount certificate bond, or similar security evidencing obligation on part of issuer to pay stated or determinable sum or sums at fixed or determinable date or dates more than 24 months after date of issuance, or to pay proceeds of liquidation of interest in certain specified securities or in unit or fund, upon payment of single lump sum at date of issuance, or in consideration of payment of periodic installments of stated or determinable amount. (815-5/2.14). Issuer must establish and maintain with Secretary of State deposit of debt obligations of kind in which life insurance companies organized under laws of Illinois permitted to invest their funds, in amount having fair market value of not less than $100,000 and at no time less than current contract liability on all such face amount certificate contracts held by Illinois residents. (815-5/6[G]).

"Investment fund shares" means securities issued by persons known as "investment funds" or "investment companies" or "investment trusts" but not including securities issued by persons not within intent of this definition as Secretary of State may designate by rules and regulations or order. (815-5/2.15). Investment fund shares will not be registered unless underlying securities or cash are and are to be deposited and held under appropriate agreement for holders with and by trustee or custodian which is clearing corporation, bank, trust company or member of national securities exchange registered under Securities Exchange Act of 1934, provided any such bank, trust company or member has aggregate capital, surplus and undivided profits of at least $2,000,000 and any such member complies with provisions of Investment Company Act of 1940 and rules and regulations of Securities and Exchange Commission promulgated thereunder relating to custody of underlying securities of investment funds. (815-5/7[B]).

Registration of Dealers, Salespersons and Investment Advisers.—Every dealer, salesperson and investment adviser must be registered as such with Secretary of State; provided that no dealer or salesperson need be registered when offering or selling securities in transactions believed in good faith to be exempted by subsections A, B, C, D, E, G, H, I, J, K, M, O, P, Q, R or S of 815-5/4, provided that such dealer or salesperson is not regularly engaged in business of offering or selling securities in reliance on exemption set forth in 815-5/4(g) or 815-5/4(m). No dealer, issuer or controlling person shall employ salesperson unless such salesperson is registered as such with Secretary of State or is employed for purpose of offering or selling securities solely in transactions believed in good faith to be exempted by subsections A, B, C, D, E, G, H, I, J, K, L, M, O, P, Q, R or S of 815-5/4. Registration as dealer, salesperson or investment adviser effectuated by filing with Secretary of State application and certain documents and by applicant passing examination. Registration may be denied, suspended or revoked by Secretary of State upon certain occurrences. (815-5/8).

Advertising.—Secretary of State may by rule or regulation require filing of any prospective, pamphlet, circulars, form letter, advertisement or other sales literature or advertising communication addressed or intended for distribution or dissemination in this state to prospective investors, including clients or prospective clients of and investment adviser; provided that no such filing may be required with respect to: (1) Securities exempt from registration pursuant to 815-5/3 or sold solely in transactions set forth in 815-5/4, (2) securities registered under both Federal Securities Act of 1933 and 815-5/5(A) or 815-5/6(A) or 814-5/7(A), or (3) advertisements appearing in newspapers, magazines and periodicals of regular publication and established paid circulation, other than any such advertisement which constitutes offer of securities which is not covered by any of exemptions set forth in 815-5/4, and which securities are not exempt from registration pursuant to provisions of 815-5/3.

Violations of Act specifically enumerated (815-5/12), and severe criminal penalties provided therefor (815-5/14) along with injunctive relief (815-5/13). Sales in violation voidable at election of purchaser within six months after purchaser has knowledge that sale is voidable provided purchaser serves written notice of election by registered letter or personal service within said six months. Sale is not voidable if purchaser failed, within 15 days from receipt thereof, to accept offer to repurchase at full price plus interest less income received. Limitation period of three years from date of sale. (815-5/13).

Uniform Simplification of Fiduciary Security Transfers Act.—Not adopted. See Illinois Fiduciary Security Transfer Simplification Act. (760-70/1 to 70/9). Art. 8 of Uniform Commercial Code governs transfers, except to extent of any inconsistency between it and Illinois Fiduciary Security Transfer Simplification Act. (810-5/8-407).

Uniform Securities Ownership by Minors Act.—Not adopted.

Franchise Disclosure Act.—Offer and sale of franchises regulated by Franchise Disclosure Act of 1987. (815-705/1-705/44). Act requires registration of franchise by filing disclosure statement. Registration effective on 20th business day after date of filing unless prior thereto Administrator takes certain action. (815-705/10). Act also requires registration of franchise brokers and salespersons. (815-705/13). Civil (815-705/24) and criminal (815-705/25) penalties for noncompliance and private right of action (815-705/26). Administered by Office of Attorney General. (815-705/3[19]).

STATUTE OF FRAUDS:

See topic Frauds, Statute of.

TRUST RECEIPT SECURITY:

Uniform Trust Receipts Act has been replaced by Art. 9 of Uniform Commercial Code. (810-5/9-101). 1972 Official Text became effective July 1, 1973. See topic Commercial Code.

WAREHOUSEMEN:

Uniform Commercial Code adopted. (810-5/7-101 to 5/7-603). See topic Commercial Code.

Bonds.—Required for public warehouses (240-10/6) and grain warehouses (240-10/6).

Regulation and Licenses.—There are other statutory provisions in respect to regulation and licensing of public warehouses, including governmental fairs, which store personal property for compensation or hold themselves out as offering storage facilities (240-10/1 to 10/22), cold storage locker plants (225-650/3), refrigerated warehouses (240-35/1 to 35/13), unclaimed property (770-90/1 to 90/3), salvage warehouses and stores for food, alcoholic liquors, drugs, medical devices and cosmetics (240-30/1 to 30/14), and warehouses receiving, holding, storing or delivering alcoholic liquors (235-5/7A-1 to 5/7A-6).

Lien.—See topic Commercial Code. See also special rule granting priority lien on "grain assets" of warehousemen for benefit of persons holding written evidence of ownership indicating storage obligation. (20-205/40.23).

CITIZENSHIP

ALIENS:

Personal Property.—Alien may acquire and hold personal property same as citizen. Personal estate of alien dying intestate is distributed same as estate of citizen, and alien can share therein. (765-60/7).

Personal and Real Property.—Alien may acquire, hold and dispose of real and personal property same as natural born citizens. (765-60/7).

Report to Director of Agriculture must be filed by alien individual, corporation or entities controlled by or benefitting alien individuals upon acquisition or transfer of agricultural land. (765-50/3).

Dower Rights.—See category Property, topic Dower.

CIVIL ACTIONS AND PROCEDURE

ACCORD AND SATISFACTION:

Common law rules govern. Must be unliquidated claim, over which bona fide dispute exists as to which settlement is reached and executed. (103 Ill.App.3d 380, 431 N.E.2d 445). General release by insured-subrogor does not bar insurer-subrogee's claim against tortfeasor, if tortfeasor or his insurance carrier had knowledge of insurer-

See note at head of Digest as to 1998 legislation covered.

See Topical Index in front part of this volume.

IL – 19

ACCORD AND SATISFACTION . . . *continued*
subrogee's interest prior to release. (71 Ill.2d 210, 375 N.E.2d 115). See category Business Regulation and Commerce, topic Commercial Code. See Illinois Contribution Among Joint Tortfeasors Act. (740-100/1-100/5).

Pleading.—(735-5/2-613, 735-5/2-619).

ACTIONS:

Under amended Civil Practice Law, effective July 1, 1982, neither names theretofore used to distinguish ordinary actions at law nor any prior formal requisites of pleading are necessary or appropriate, and there are no distinctions in manner of pleading between actions at law and suits in equity except as specified in Civil Practice Law and rules adopted under it. Fact averments necessary to state any cause of action either at law or in equity, are in no way affected by Civil Practice Law. (735-5/2-601).

Particular Actions or Proceedings.—Provisions of Civil Practice Law apply to all civil proceedings except as otherwise provided in cases of administrative review (735-5/3-101), attachment (735-5/4-101), ejectment (735-5/6-101), eminent domain (735-5/7-101), forcible entry and detainer (735-5/9-101), habeas corpus (735-5/10-101), injunctions (735-5/11-101), enforcement of judgments (735-5/12-101), mandamus (735-5/14-101), foreclosure of mortgages (735-5/15-101), ne exeat (735-5/16-101), partition (735-5/17-101), quo warranto (735-5/18-101), replevin (735-5/19-101), or other proceedings in which, and to extent, that separate statutes regulate matters of procedure (735-5/1-108).

Immunity.—Except as General Assembly may provide, sovereign immunity has been abolished. (Const., Art. 13, §4). Smaller government units are granted only such immunity as provided in Local Governmental and Governmental Employees Tort Immunity Act. (c. 85).

Actions Against the State.—Except for actions arising under Workers' Compensation Act or Workers' Occupational Diseases Act, State has consented to be sued in Court of Claims only. State may be sued on claims founded upon any law of State, on contract, for time unjustly served in prisons, and in tort. Claims are also heard for Law Enforcement Officers, Firemen's and National Guardsmen's compensation and for compensation of victims of crime. (705-505/8). Except for infants, incompetents, and persons under other disability, contract claims are barred unless filed with clerk of court within five years after they first accrue. However, claims by vendors of goods or services under Illinois Public Aid Code shall have one year after accrual of cause of action. (705-505/22). Actions under Law Enforcement Officers, Firemen's and National Guardsmen's Compensation Acts must commence within a year of on-duty death. All other claims are barred unless filed with clerk of court within two years after they first accrue. (705-505/22). Actions for personal injuries or death will be barred unless, within one year from date of injury or accrual of cause of action, signed written statement is served on Attorney General and clerk of court of claims, giving name of person to whom cause of action has accrued, name and residence of person injured, date, hour, and place or location of accident, and general nature thereof, and name and address of attending physician and hospital unless claimant files claim within one year of accrual. (705-505/22-1, 505/22-2). Notice under Crime Victims Compensation Act must be served on Attorney General within six months of date of injury, or within such further extension as Court of Claims, for good cause shown, allows. (740-45/6.1).

Immunity of Local Public Entities and their Employees.—A local public entity includes any county, township, municipality, municipal corporation, school district or board, forest preserve or park district, fire protection district, sanitary district, museum district and all other local governmental bodies. (745-10/1-206).

Punitive Damages.—A local public entity is not liable for punitive damages. (745-10/2-102).

General Immunity.—A local public entity and its employees are not liable for injury caused by: adoption or failure to adopt or enforce any law; any authorized issuance, denial, suspension or revocation of a permit or license; or failure to inspect or negligent inspection of any property not its own. (745-10/2-103 to 2-105; 745-10/2-205 to 2-207).

A local public entity is not liable for injury caused by: its employees' oral promises or misrepresentations, whether negligent or intentional; its employees' libelous or slanderous actions; or for provision of information either orally, in writing by computer or other electronic transmission; granting or failure to grant public welfare goods or monies; or for injury resulting from employee's act or omission, where employee is not liable. (745-10/2-106 to 2-109).

A public employee in position involving determination of policy or exercise of discretion is not liable for injury resulting from act or omission in determining policy, even if discretion is abused. (745-10/2-201). Public employee is not liable for injury caused by: act or omission in executing or enforcing law unless willfully and wantonly negligent; good faith acts under unconstitutional, invalid or inapplicable enactment except to extent of liability had enactment been constitutional, valid and applicable; acts or omissions of another person; instituting or prosecuting any judicial or administrative proceeding within scope of employment, unless employee acts maliciously and without probable cause; entry upon any property where entry is expressly or impliedly authorized by law; negligent misrepresentation within scope of employee's employment. (745-10/2-202 to 2-204, 10/2-208 to 2-210).

Immunity from Liability for Injury Occurring in Use of Public Property.—A local public entity must use ordinary care to maintain its property in reasonably safe condition but is not liable for injury unless it has actual or constructive notice of unsafe condition in sufficient time prior to injury to have remedied or protected against such condition. (745-10/3-102).

Special Provisions.—Special provisions provide, under certain circumstances, immunity to local public entities and their employees for police and correctional activities (745-10/4-101 to 107), fire protection activities (745-10/5-101 to 103), and medical, hospital and public health activities (745-10/6-101 to 109).

Limitation of Actions and Notice.—Civil actions against local public entity must be commenced within one year from date of injury or accrual of action. (745-10/8-101). Special one year limitation and six month notice provisions of School Tort Liability Act (745-25/2, 25/3) invalid as to both public and nonprofit private schools (57 Ill.2d 384, 312 N.E.2d 635).

Payment of Judgments by Local Government.—Local governments have specific authority to settle and compromise tort claims and law suits and pay judgment arising therefrom. (745-10/9-102). Local government may pay tort claim or judgment through insurance (745-10/9-103), installments over ten years plus interest (745-10/9-104), bond issue (745-10/9-105), rate or fee increases (745-10/9-106), or special tax levy (745-10/9-107) at discretion of local government.

Charitable Immunity.—Doctrine of charitable immunity has been abolished in Illinois as to causes of action accruing after Nov. 18, 1965. (33 Ill.2d 326, 211 N.E.2d 253).

Immunity from Liability.—Special provisions provide, under certain circumstances, immunity to licensed dentists for free dental clinic services unless willful or wanton misconduct (225-25/54), and immunity to mental health or developmental disability facilities and their employees for disclosure to State Police information necessary to disqualify patient from retaining Firearm Owner's Identification Card or where peace officers or prosecuting authority who is conducting bona fide investigation of criminal offense or attempting apprehension of fugitive, disclosing whether person is present. (740-110/12).

See also category Family, topics Marriage, subhead Action for Breach of Promise; Dissolution of Marriage.

Commencement of every civil action, unless otherwise expressly provided by statute, is by filing of complaint. (735-5/2-2011[a]). Duplicate original summons may be issued to facilitate service. (735-5/2-2011[b]). Copy of complaint must be attached to each copy of summons. (ILCS S.Ct. Rule 104[a]). See also topic Process.

Jury Trial.—Plaintiff waives jury trial unless demand made when complaint filed. Defendant waives jury trial unless demand filed not later than date answer filed. Unless either party expressly demands jury trial by 12 jurors in cases involving $15,000 or less, trial shall be before jury of six. (735-5/2-1105).

Lis Pendens.—If a plaintiff in a suit in equity or in the nature of equity affecting real property files a statutory notice of pendency of the proceeding in office of recorder of deeds in county where real estate is located, this statutory notice operates from time it is filed as constructive notice to every person subsequently acquiring an interest in the property (including persons with a prior interest who are not in possession and whose interest is not shown of record at the time of filing of the notice). If plaintiff fails to complete service within six months the statutory notice ceases to be constructive notice until service is accomplished. (735-5/2-1901). If property is registered in torrens (765-35/1), no constructive notice is created unless procedure specified in statutes relating to property in torrens (765-35/84) is first followed (735-5/2-1901). For constructive notice to be created in foreclosure action, requirements with respect to notice of foreclosure must also be met. (735-5/15-1503).

Certified copy of petition or adjudication in bankruptcy proceeding may be filed in office of recorder of deeds in county where real estate is located. Recorder shall record such certified copy in same manner and for same fee as recording deeds. (735-5/2-1702).

Parties.—Party commencing an action shall be called plaintiff; the adverse party defendant. (735-5/2-401). On appeal the relative position of parties and their designation is same as in trial court, but they are further designated appellant and appellee (ILCS S.Ct. Rule 341[b]). For good cause shown, parties may appear under fictitious names. (735-5/2-401).

Misnomer of parties is not ground for dismissal, but name of any party may be corrected at any time before or after judgment on motion on any terms and proof as court requires. (735-5/2-401[b]).

Medical Malpractice-Respondents in Discovery.—Plaintiff in action based on allegation of negligence in performance of health care services may designate as respondents in discovery those individuals, other than defendants, believed to have information essential to determination of who should be named as additional defendants. Those persons so named shall be required to respond to discovery in same manner as are defendants, and may on motion be added as defendants if evidence discloses probable cause for such action. Plaintiff must serve copy of complaint on each individual named as respondent in discovery. Person named as respondent in discovery may on his own motion be made defendant, in which case this section of statute is no longer applicable to that person. Each respondent in discovery shall be paid expenses and fees as provided for witnesses. Respondent in discovery may be made defendant in same action within six months after he is named as respondent in discovery, even though time during which action may otherwise be initiated against him may have expired during such six month period. (735-5/2-402).

Who may be Plaintiff.—Assignee of nonnegotiable chose in action may sue thereon in his own name, but must in his pleading on oath allege that he is the actual bona fide owner, and set forth how and when he acquired title. Such action is subject to any defense or set-off existing before notice of assignment. (735-5/2-403[a]). Where chose in action consists of wages, at least five days written notice of the pendency of such action must be served on assignor before trial; and he may, on application, intervene, and he or defendant may set up any set-off or defense to the assignment or the indebtedness, and judgment against defendant may not exceed the amount found due and unpaid from assignor to assignee, judgment for any balance remaining due from defendant being rendered in favor of assignor. (735-5/2-403[b]). Suit brought by virtue of subrogation (by contract or operation of law) must be brought either in name or for use of subrogee, who must, in his pleading on oath, allege that he is the actual bona fide subrogee, and set forth how and when he became such. (735-5/2-403[c]).

Joinder of Plaintiffs.—Subject to rules of court, all persons in whom any right to relief arising out of same transaction or series of transactions is alleged to exist, whether jointly, severally, or in the alternative, may join in one action as plaintiffs whenever, and separate actions been brought, any common question of law or fact would arise, provided that if on application of any party it appears that such joinder may embarrass or delay trial, court may order separate trials or make such order as may be expedient, and judgment may be given for one or more of the plaintiffs for the relief to which he or they may be found entitled. A necessary plaintiff, counterclaimant

See note at head of Digest as to 1998 legislation covered.

See Topical Index in front part of this volume.

IL – 20

ACTIONS . . . *continued*
or third party plaintiff, declining to join may be made a defendant, cross defendant or third party defendant, the reason therefor being stated in the complaint, counterclaim or third party complaint. (735-5/2-403).

Joinder of Defendants.—Any person may be made defendant who, jointly, severally, or in alternative, is alleged to have or claim interest in controversy or in any part thereof or in transaction or series of transactions out of which same arose, or whom it is necessary to make party for complete determination or settlement of any question involved, or against whom liability is asserted jointly, severally, or in alternative, arising out of same transaction or series of transactions, regardless of number of causes of action joined. It is not necessary that each defendant be interested as to all relief prayed or as to every cause of action included in any proceeding, but court may make any order that may be just to prevent any defendant from being embarrassed or put to expense by being required to attend proceeding in which he may have no interest. Where plaintiff is in doubt as to person from whom he is entitled to redress, he may join two or more defendants and state his claim against them in alternative, in same count, or plead separate counts in alternative against different defendants, so that question which, if any, of defendants is liable and to what extent, may be determined. (735-5/2-405).

Bringing in New Parties.—If complete determination of controversy cannot be had without presence of other parties, court may direct them to be brought in. If person not party has interest or title which judgment may affect, court, on application, may direct him to be made party. (735-5/2-406[a]).

Third Party Proceedings.—Within time for filing answer or thereafter by leave of court, defendant may by third party complaint bring in as defendant a person not a party to the action who is or may be liable to defendant for all or a part of the plaintiff's claim. Third party defendant may assert any defense he has against third party complaint or which third party plaintiff has against plaintiff's claim. Third party defendant has same right to file counterclaim or third party complaint as any other defendant. Plaintiff may assert any claim against third party defendant which might have been asserted had third party defendant been originally joined as a defendant. When a counterclaim is filed against a party, he may likewise proceed against third parties. Nothing herein applies to liability insurers or creates any substantive right to contribution among tort feasors or against any insurer or other person which has not heretofore existed. (735-5/2-406[b]). Action is commenced against new party by filing of appropriate pleading or entry of order naming him party. Process is had upon new party in like manner as is provided for service on defendants. (735-5/2-406[c]).

Contribution and Indemnity.—In causes of action arising out of occurrences on or after Mar. 1, 1978, one tortfeasor may seek contribution from other tortfeasors. (740-100/2[a]). Right of contribution exists only in favor of tortfeasor who pays more than his pro rata share of common liability; recovery limited to excess paid. Liability of tortfeasor for contribution limited to pro rata share of common liability. (740-100/2[b]). Release or covenant not to sue or not to enforce judgment given in good faith does not discharge other tortfeasors but reduces amount recoverable against other tortfeasors to extent of greater amount stated or consideration actually paid. (740-100/2[c]). Tortfeasor who settles with claimant pursuant to above is discharged from all liability for any contribution to any tortfeasor (740-100/2[d]), and is not entitled to recover contribution from another tortfeasor whose liability is not extinguished by settlement (740-100/2[e]). One who discharges tortfeasor's obligation is subrogated to right of contribution. (740-100/2[f]). Pro rata share of each tortfeasor determined by relative culpability. (740-100/13). Where no underlying action for recovery for injury or death to person or damage to property has been filed, no action for contribution or indemnity may be commenced more than two years after party seeking contribution or indemnity has made payment to claimant. Where underlying action has been filed by claimant, no action for contribution or indemnity may be commenced more than two years after party seeking contribution or indemnity has been served with process in underlying action or more than two years from time party, or his privy, knew or reasonably should have known of act or omission giving rise to action for contribution or indemnity whichever is later. Effect of these limitation periods on application of other statutes of repose and limitation is noted in certain instances. These limitation periods do not apply to action for damages in which contribution or indemnification is sought from party alleged to have been negligent where negligence has been alleged to have resulted in injuries or death by reason of medical or healing art malpractice. (735-5/13-204). Counterclaims and third-party claims for contribution must be asserted in pending action. (105 Ill.2d 191, 473 N.E.2d 939). If tortfeasor brings action against plaintiff's employer, employer's liability shall not exceed employer's liability to plaintiff under Worker's Compensation Act or Worker's Occupational Diseases Act and tortfeasor not entitled to recover money from employer only credit against liability of tortfeasor in amount equal to amount of contribution, if any, for which employer is found liable to that tortfeasor even if amount exceeds employer's liability under Worker's Compensation Act and Worker's Occupational Diseases Act. (740-100/3.5).

Several Liability.—In any action brought on account of death, bodily injury to person or physical damage to property where recovery based on fault, defendant is severally liable only and is liable only for that proportion of recoverable economic and noneconomic damages, if any, that amount of that defendant's fault, if any, bears to aggregate amount of fault of all other tortfeasors in all actions filed after 3/5/95. (735-5/2-1117).

Nonjoinder or Misjoinder.—No action will be dismissed for misjoinder of parties, or dismissed for nonjoinder of necessary parties without reasonable opportunity to add them as parties. New parties may be added and parties misjoined dropped by order of court before or after judgment, as ends of justice require. (735-5/2-407).

Joint Debtors or Partners.—All parties to joint obligation, including partnership obligation, may be sued jointly or separate actions may be brought against one or more of them. Judgment against fewer than all of parties to joint or partnership obligation does not bar action against those not included in judgment or not sued. Statute does not permit more than one satisfaction. (735-5/2-410).

Actions Against Partnerships.—Partnership may be sued in names of partners as individuals doing business as partnership, or in firm name, or both. (735-5/2-411[a]). Unsatisfied judgment against partnership in its firm name does not bar action to enforce individual liability of any partner. (735-5/2-411[b]).

Actions Against Voluntary Unincorporated Associations.—Voluntary unincorporated association may sue or be sued in own name. (735-5/2-209.1).

Change in Parties.—No change in parties impairs any previous attachment of estate or body of any person remaining defendant, or bonds or recognizances of any person remaining party as against himself or sureties, or receipts to officers for property attached. When parties are changed, court may order new bonds if deemed necessary. (735-5/2-412).

Class Actions.—Action may be maintained as class action either by or against representative party only if court determines that: (1) Class is so numerous that joinder of all members is impracticable; (2) there are questions of fact or law common to class, which predominate over any questions affecting only individual members; (3) representative parties will fairly and adequately protect interest of class; and (4) class action is appropriate method for fair and efficient adjudication of controversy. (735-5/2-801). Court shall determine by order whether suit may be maintained as class action and may divide class into sub-classes. (735-5/2-802). Court may in its discretion order notice to protect interests of class and parties and may condition class certification upon giving of such notice. (735-5/2-803). Intervention by any class member is to be liberally granted except where such intervention is found to be disruptive or prejudicial. (735-5/2-804[a]). Any class member may be excluded from class upon request. (735-5/2-804[b]). Any judgment entered in class action shall be binding on all class members who have not been excluded. (735-5/2-805). Class action may not be dismissed except with court approval. (735-5/2-806).

Unknown Parties.—If persons whose names are unknown are interested in any action, they may be made parties by description as unknown owners or unknown heirs or devisees of any deceased person who may have been interested in subject matter previous to death, or as unknown heirs or devisees of person not known to be living or dead. On filing of affidavit stating that names of such persons are unknown, process may issue and publication be had against such persons by the names and description so given, and judgments rendered in respect to such parties are of same effect as though they had been designated by their proper names. Affidavit as to unknown parties may be combined with affidavit for service by publication. (735-5/2-413). Persons required to register under assumed business name who fail to do so may be sued as unknown owners and are bound by judgment against business under its assumed name. (805-405/6).

Joinder.—Subject to rules of court, plaintiffs may join any causes of action against any defendant or defendants; and defendant may set up by answer any and all cross-demands whatever, whether recoupment, set-off, or otherwise, which are designated as counter claims. Court may order separate trials of causes of action or counterclaims which cannot be conveniently disposed of with other issues. Legal and equitable issues may be tried together if no jury is employed. (735-5/2-614).

Consolidation and Severance.—An action may be severed and actions pending in the same court may be consolidated whenever it can be done without prejudice to a substantial right. (735-5/2-1006).

Intervention.—Upon timely application anyone shall be permitted to intervene as of right when statute confers unconditional right to do so, when representation by existing parties of applicant's interest is or may be inadequate and applicant will or may be bound by order or judgment, or when applicant will be adversely affected by disposition of property subject to control or disposition of court or officer thereof. (735-5/2-408[a]). Upon timely application anyone may in court's discretion be permitted to intervene when statute confers conditional right or when applicant's claim or defense and main claim have common question of law or fact. (735-5/2-408[b]).

In all cases involving validity of constitutional provision, statute or regulation of state, ordinance or regulation of municipality or governmental subdivision of state and affecting public interest, state, municipality or government subdivision involved upon timely application may, in discretion of court, be permitted to intervene. (735-5/2-408[c]-[d]).

Petition setting forth grounds for intervention shall accompany applicant's proposed initial pleading or motion. In cases in which intervention is discretionary, court shall consider whether it will unduly delay or prejudice adjudication of rights of original parties. (735-5/2-408[e]). Intervenor shall have all rights of original party, except court may in its order allowing intervention provide that intervenor shall be bound by orders or judgments theretofore entered or evidence theretofore received, that intervenor shall not raise issues more properly raised at earlier stage of proceeding, that intervenor shall not raise new issues or add new parties, or that in other respects intervenor shall not interfere with control of litigation, as justice and avoidance of undue delay may require. (735-5/2-408[f]).

Interpleader.—Persons having claims against plaintiff arising out of same or related subject matter may be joined as defendants and required to interplead when their claims may expose plaintiff to double or multiple liability. It is not a ground for objection to interpleader that claims of the several claimants or titles upon which their claims depend do not have a common origin or are not identical or are adverse to or independent of one another or that plaintiff avers that he is not liable in whole or in part to any of or all claimants. Defendant under similar circumstances may obtain like relief by counterclaim. Provisions are not a limitation upon joinder of parties or causes of action. (735-5/2-409).

Abatement and Revival.—If by reason of marriage, bankruptcy, assignment or other event occurring after commencement of action, either before or after judgment, causing change or transmission of interest or liability, or by reason of any person interested coming into existence after commencement of action, it becomes necessary or desirable that any person not already party should be before court, or that any person already party should be made party in another capacity, action does not abate but on motion order may be entered that proper parties be substituted or added and cause be carried on with remaining parties and new parties with or without change in title of cause. (735-5/2-1008[a]).

Death.—If a party dies and the action is one which survives, the proper party or parties may be substituted by order of court upon motion. If motion to substitute is not

See note at head of Digest as to 1998 legislation covered.

See Topical Index in front part of this volume.

ACTIONS . . . *continued*
filed within 90 days after death is suggested of record, the action may be dismissed as to the deceased party. If a party dies and the action is one in which the right sought to be enforced survives only as to the remaining parties to the action, action does not abate. Death is suggested of record and action proceeds in favor of or against remaining parties. No action brought for use of another abates by reason of death of plaintiff whose name is used but may be maintained by party for whose use it was brought in his own name upon suggesting death of record and entry of order of substitution. If death of party to personal action is suggested of record and no petition for letters of office for his estate has been filed, court, upon motion, may appoint special administrator for deceased party for purpose of prosecuting action of any party who appears entitled to participate in decedent's estate and reciting names and last known addresses of all known heirs and legatees and name of executor named in any will that has been filed. Within 90 days special representative shall mail certain information to heirs and legatees. If estate subsequently opened with representative other than special representative, such person shall substitute, and disbursements and fees of special representative and attorney will be allowed as claim against proceeds. If person against whom action has been brought dies, and cause of action survives, personal representative of decedent's estate shall be substituted. If no petition has been filed for letters of office, court may, upon motion of plaintiff, appoint special representative; recovery limited to any liability insurance protecting estate but estate not barred from enforcing any claims available to it as counterclaims. (735-5/2-1008[b]).

Suit instituted by administrator to collect does not abate by the revocation of his letters, but may be prosecuted by permanent executor or administrator. (755-5/10-4). On death of garnishee procedure is same as that when defendant dies in other civil cases. (735-5/12-711; 735-5/2-1008[b]). Interested person may file petition to contest validity of will within six months after admission of will to probate. Right to institute or continue such proceeding survives and descends to heir, legatee, devisee, executor, administrator, grantee, or assignee of person entitled to institute proceeding. (755-5/8-1).

In addition to actions which survive by common law, the following survive: replevin, actions for damages for injury to the person (except slander and libel); actions for damages for injuries to real or personal property or for detention or conversion of personal property; actions against officers for misfeasance, malfeasance or non-feasance, actions for fraud or deceit, and Dram shop actions. (755-5/27-6).

Legal Disability.—If party is declared to be person under legal disability, that fact is suggested of record and prosecution or defense maintained by his representative, guardian ad litem or next friend, as may be appropriate. (735-5/2-1008[c]).

Trustees and Public Officers.—If any trustee or public officer ceases to hold the trust or office and that fact is suggested of record the action shall proceed in favor of or against his successor. (735-5/2-1008[d]).

Service of Process.—Parties against whom relief is sought, substituted under 735-5/2-1008(a), must be brought in by service of process. Service of process on parties substituted under 735-5/2-1008, is not required, but notice must be given as court may direct. (735-5/2-1008[e]).

Use or operation of motor vehicle by any person or his agent or employee shall be deemed appointment of Secretary of State as agent for service of all legal process in action growing out of such use and operation if person is nonresident or is resident at time cause arises but subsequently becomes nonresident. Service made by serving Secretary with copy and affidavit from plaintiff stating that all service requirements have been met is sufficient if notice of service and copy of process are sent registered mail by plaintiff to defendant at defendant's last known address within ten days. (625-5/10-301). See topic Process.

Sanctions may now be imposed against both client and counsel for unfounded or frivolous pleadings, or filings made for other improper purposes. (735-5/2-611).

Single Action for Libel, Slander, etc.—Uniform Single Publication Act is in effect. (740-165/1 to 165/5).

Small Claims.—See category Courts and Legislature, topic Courts.

Limitation of.—See topic Limitation of Actions.

Direct Actions Against Insurer.—See category Insurance, topic Insurance Companies.

APPEAL AND ERROR:

To seek review of final appealable order of circuit court, party generally must file notice of appeal in manner set out in Supreme Court Rules, which contain verbatim forms and precise instructions for civil (Ill. S. Ct. 303) and criminal (Ill. S. Ct. 606) cases. Appeals to Appellate Court matter of right except with respect to acquittal on merits in criminal cases. (Const. Art. VI, §6). When death sentence imposed, appeal is automatically perfected. (Ill. S. Ct. 606[a]). Appeals by State in criminal cases are limited by Rules. (Ill. S. Ct. 604[a][1],[e]).

Appeal Bond.—No cost or other bond required as condition of appeal, except under circumstances discussed infra subheads Security for Costs, Stay Pending Appeal.

Civil Appeals.—Procedure for civil appeals made uniform. (P.A. 81-262).

Certification of State Law Questions.—U.S. Supreme Court or U.S. Court of Appeals for Seventh Circuit may certify state law questions to Illinois Supreme Court in absence of controlling Illinois Supreme Court precedents. Briefs and oral argument allowed pursuant to Rules. (Ill. S. Ct. 20).

Direct Appeals to Supreme Court.—Direct appeals as matter of right to Supreme Court from final judgments of circuit courts are limited to: (a) Cases in which statute of U.S. or Illinois has been held invalid, (b) criminal cases in which death sentence has been imposed and (c) proceedings commenced under Ill. S. Ct. 21(c). (Const. Art. VI, §4; Ill. S. Ct. 302[a], 603). In other cases Supreme Court may permit direct appeal if public interest requires prompt adjudication. (Ill. S. Ct. 302[b]).

Appeals from Appellate Court to Supreme Court.—Appeals from Appellate to Supreme Court lie as matter of right only in cases in which (a) Federal or state constitutional question arises for first time in and as result of action of Appellate Court, or (b) Appellate Court issues certificate of importance. (Const. Art. VI, §4; Ill. S. Ct. 316, 317). Otherwise all appeals from Appellate to Supreme Court permitted only if petition for leave to appeal granted. (Ill. S. Ct. 315). Form for and grounds for granting such petition prescribed in Rules. (Ill. S. Ct. 315). Forms for and grounds for granting appeals from orders of Industrial Commission division of Appellate Court are prescribed in Rules. (Ill. S. Ct. 315).

Final judgment as to less than all parties or claims appealable upon express finding that there is no just reason for delaying enforcement or appeal (Ill. S. Ct. 304[a]) and in certain situations described in Rules (Ill. S. Ct. 304[b]) primarily concerning administration of estates, receiverships, etc., and proceedings under 735-5/2-1401, 1402.

Appeals from interlocutory orders may be taken as of right within 30 days if order respects injunction, receiver, parental rights, temporary commitment in adoption case, custody of assets of financial institution, mortgagee's right to possess mortgaged premises, §2.2(b) of Eminent Domain Act, or parental notice of abortion (c. 38, §81-61 et seq.) and meets Rule requirements which include expedited schedule for filing record and briefs (Ill. S. Ct. 307). To appeal interlocutory order entered on ex parte application, party intending to appeal must first present motion to trial court to vacate order. Appeal may be taken if motion denied or if court does not act within seven days of its presentation. (Ill. S. Ct. 307[b]).

Appeal of temporary restraining order is by petition filed with Appellate Court, with proof of service, within two days of entry or denial of order in question. Petitioner and respondent may each file memoranda, but no replies are permitted and no oral argument will be heard. Appellate Court shall consider and decide petition within two days of receiving memoranda. (Ill. S. Ct. 307[d]).

Appellate Court may permit appeal from any interlocutory order if the trial court has certified that there is substantial ground for difference of opinion and that immediate appeal may materially advance the litigation. (Ill. S. Ct. 308). Application for leave to appeal to Appellate Court must thereafter be filed within 14 days and must contain statement of facts, question presented, and reason why substantial question exists. Party opposing appeal may answer within 14 days of due date of application. (Ill. S. Ct. 308).

Appeal from order awarding new trial, denying motion to transfer or dismiss on grounds of forum non conveniens, denying motion to dismiss for lack of jurisdiction, granting or denying transfer of venue or from interlocutory order affecting care and custody of unemancipated minor allowed only if petition for leave to appeal filed within 30 days and granted by Appellate Court. Record must be filed with petition. Answer may be filed within 21 days of petition due date. If petition granted, all rulings on post-trial motions may be reviewed without filing cross-appeal. (Ill. S. Ct. 306[a]).

Transfer of Cases Appealed to Wrong Court.—A case appealed to the wrong court must be transferred to proper court and then proceeds as though properly appealed in the first instance. Any bond theretofore given remains binding. (Ill. S. Ct. 365[b]). Taking of an appeal to either Supreme Court or Appellate Court does not waive right to present any issue in the appropriate court. Matter decided by either court not subject to collateral attack on ground the other should have decided it. (Ill. S. Ct. 365[a]).

Time for Appealing—Perfecting Appeal.—Except for local improvement cases and Illinois Drainage Code cases, no appeal may be taken to Supreme or Appellate Court after expiration of 30 days from entry of order, decree, judgment or other determination complained of or from entry of order disposing of timely post-trial motion. (Ill. S. Ct. 303[a], [b], 307[a], 606[b]). Extension of time for filing notice of appeal may be granted by reviewing court under circumstances discussed infra under subhead Notice of Appeal. In civil cases, other parties may join in appeal or file separate or cross-appeals within later of 30 days from judgment or ten days from service of notice of appeal. (Ill. S. Ct. 303[a]).

Appeal is initiated when notice of appeal is filed in trial court. No other step is deemed jurisdictional. (Ill. S. Ct. 301). If death sentence is imposed, appeal is automatically perfected. (Ill. S. Ct. 301, 606[a]).

Case placed on appellate docket by clerk once notice of appeal filed. (Ill. S. Ct. 303[f]). Within 14 days of filing notice of appeal, appellant must file docketing statement, proof of service, and filing fee. (Ill. S. Ct. 303[g]). Appellant must thereafter file record or certificate in reviewing court within 63 days after filing of last notice of appeal, or within 14 days after expiration of any trial court extension (up to 42 days) of 49-day period for filing report of proceedings. (Ill. S. Ct. 326, 323).

Notice of Appeal.—Rules specify forms verbatim and manner of service. (Ill. S. Ct. 303[c], [d], 606[d], [e]). Filing required within 30 days of judgment or within 30 days after entry of order disposing of last pending post-trial motion. (Ill. S. Ct. 303[a], 606). May be extended if motion filed in reviewing court within 30 days after due date, supported by affidavit showing reasonable excuse for tardiness, and accompanied by proposed notice of appeal and filing fee. (Ill. S. Ct. 303[e]). Criminal rules permit motion within six months of due date if showing made that appeal has merit and not due to appellant's culpable negligence. (Ill S. Ct. 606). Failure to file timely notice of appeal properly identifying order appealed from may result in dismissal of appeal with prejudice. (24 Ill. App.3d 751, 320 N.E.2d 576).

As to notice of separate appeal or cross appeal, see Ill. S. Ct. 303(a)(3).

Motions in Reviewing Court.—If record has not been filed, all motions made to reviewing court (e.g., for stay or for extension of time for filing notice of appeal or record) must be accompanied by supporting record (authenticated by clerk's certificate or by affidavit of filing party or attorney) containing appealable order, timely notice of appeal, and other necessary matter. (Ill. S. Ct. 361[a]). Motions must be in writing. Written objections may be filed within three days of personal service, five days of mailing, or such further time as court may allow. No further replies or oral argument without leave of court. (Ill. S. Ct. 361).

Record, Procedure, Etc., on Appeal.—As to contents and filing of record, see Ill. S. Ct. 321 to 331; abstracts and briefs, Ill. S. Ct. 341 to 345, oral argument, Ill. S. Ct. 351-352, rehearings, Ill. S. Ct. 367.

See note at head of Digest as to 1998 legislation covered.

See Topical Index in front part of this volume.

APPEAL AND ERROR . . . *continued*

Security for Costs.—Where appellant is shown by affidavit to be nonresident or insolvent, and no bond for costs has been filed, rule must be entered against appellant to show cause why appeal should not be dismissed. (Ill. S. Ct. 364). See also topic Costs.

Stay Pending Appeal.—Appeal stays enforcement of judgment for money if notice of appeal filed within 30 days of entry of judgment and bond presented, approved and filed within same 30 days. Trial court may grant extension of not more than 45 days unless agreement of parties to contrary. (Ill. S. Ct. 305[a]).

Trial court or reviewing court may stay, pending appeal, enforcement of judgment for money not otherwise stayed, or enforcement of any other final or interlocutory judgment or judicial or administrative order. (Ill. S. Ct. 305[b]).

Application for stay of enforcement ordinarily made first to trial court. Motion for stay may be made to reviewing court only on showing that application to trial court is impracticable or trial court denied application or failed to afford requested relief. (Ill. S. Ct. 305[b]).

Bond may be required in any case and is mandatory in case of money judgment or protection of property interests. (Ill. S. Ct. 305[b]).

Where stay is not perfected within 30 days after entry of judgment (or such extended time up to 45 days as trial court allows on motion made within such 30 days), reversal or modification of judgment does not affect right, title, or interest of any person not party to such action in any real or personal property acquired after judgment becomes final but before judgment stayed. Reversal or modification does not affect rights of any person not party to such action by virtue of any certificate of sale issued before judgment is stayed. (Ill. S. Ct. 305[i]).

Extent of Review.—Reviewing courts have original jurisdiction as may be necessary to complete determination of any cause on review. (Const. Art. VI, §§4, 6). Reviewing court may exercise all powers of amendment of trial court, allow substitution of parties, allow new parties to be added or parties to be dropped or allow parties to be rearranged as appellants or appellees on reasonable notice; order or permit record to be amended by correcting errors or adding matters which should have been included; draw inferences of fact; give any judgment and make any order which ought to have been given or made, and make such further orders and grant such relief, including remandment, partial reversal, partial new trial, entry of remittitur or issuance of execution, as case may require. (Ill. S. Ct. 366[a]).

Disposition of Cause.—Clerk of reviewing court must transmit mandate to trial court, with notice to parties, not earlier than 21 days after entry of judgment unless petition for rehearing or affidavit of intent to petition Supreme Court is filed within such 21 day period. (Ill. S. Ct. 368[a], [b]). Appellate Court or Supreme Court or judge of either may stay or recall mandate from Appellate Court until time for appeal to Supreme Court has expired. (Ill. S. Ct. 368[c]). On dismissal of appeal or affirmance, execution may issue and other proceedings be had as if no appeal had been taken, on filing of mandate of reviewing court with clerk of lower court. When cause is remanded for new trial or hearing, upon filing of mandate, cause is reinstated on ten days notice served on adverse party. (Ill. S. Ct. 369).

On dismissal of appeal for want of prosecution, reviewing court upon motion may enter judgment against appellant for amount between minimum of $50 and maximum of 10% of judgment. (Ill. S. Ct. 371).

Review of Decisions of Administrative Agencies.—Administrative Review Act provides for uniform method of review by circuit courts, or by appellate court in case of Illinois Educational Labor Relations Board, of final decisions of administrative agencies, where act creating or conferring power on such agency, by express reference, adopts Administrative Review Act as method of review. (735-5/3-102, 3-104). Illinois Constitution permits legislature to authorize direct review by appellate court (Art. VI, §6). Procedure for statutory direct review to appellate court at 735-5/3-113, which it has done in Pollution Control Board cases (415-5/41; Ill. S. Ct. 335). In other cases, review is pursuant to statute creating agency (220-5/10-201 et seq.); held unconstitutional in part in 144 Ill. App. 3d 229, 493 N.E.2d 1148) or common law (see, e.g. topic Certiorari). In all cases, especially local tax cases, essential to consult statutes, rules and common law respecting exhaustion and election of remedies, need for seeking preliminary relief or for posting bond, timing of review and similar technical matters because such doctrines are complex, variegated and strictly applied.

Action for review is commenced by filing, within 35 days from service by summons of copy of decision, complaint containing statement of decision or part thereof to be reviewed and specifying whether agency should file transcript of evidence. (735-5/3-103, 5/3-108). Unless a particular venue is prescribed by statute under authority of which the decision sought to be reviewed is rendered, actions to review decisions of administrative agencies may be commenced in the circuit court of any county in which: (1) any part of hearing or proceeding was held; (2) any part of subject matter involved is situated; (3) any part of the transaction which gave rise to the proceedings before the agency occurred. (735-5/3-104). Summons is served by clerk by registered mail on the agency and other defendants. (735-5/3-105). If pertinent statute requires plaintiff to pay to agency costs of preparing record of proceedings, failure to make such payment relieves agency from answering and authorizes dismissal of complaint and entry of judgment for amount shown to be due plus costs. (735-5/3-109).

Review covers all questions of law and fact presented by the entire record. Additional evidence is not admissible. Findings of agency are prima facie correct. (735-5/3-110). Circuit court may stay decision upon notice to agency and good cause shown; amend record; allow substitution of, dismiss or realign parties; affirm, reverse, remand in whole or in part; enter money judgment where agency decision requires that; and take proofs and enter appropriate orders in cases of failure to comply with statutory provisions requiring bond to be filed by plaintiff. (735-5/3-111). Final decisions of circuit court are appealable as in ordinary civil cases. (735-5/3-112).

Special Appeal Rules exist for certain proceedings, including local improvement, Illinois Drainage Code, and pollution cases.

Failure to comply with rules or frivolous appeals may result in appropriate sanctions being imposed on offending party. (Ill. S. Ct. 375).

BONDS:

See topics Appeal and Error, Costs, Injunctions, Replevin; categories Business Organizations, topic Corporations; Business Regulation and Commerce, topics Brokers, Securities; Debtor and Creditor, topics Attachment, Execution; Estates and Trusts, topic Executors and Administrators; Family, topic Guardian and Ward; Legal Profession, topic Attorneys and Counselors; Mortgages, topic Mortgages of Real Property.

By statute, many public officials, e.g. sanitary district trustees, must be bonded. Some types of businesses, e.g. importing distributors, must post bond as condition of doing business. State, counties, districts, regional authorities and municipalities authorized by statute to issue variety of revenue bonds, e.g. "Capital Development Bond Act of 1972", (30-420/3). Local government units and school districts authorized to issue bonds may issue interest-bearing commercial paper instead. Authority to issue such paper shall not be construed to permit issuing unit of local government or school district to increase or otherwise alter its debt limits. (30-365/3).

Surety.—Surety on official bond may be released on petition. (5-260/10). Surety may compel creditor to sue within reasonable time or face discharge of surety's obligations (740-155/1), but surety may not confess judgment if principal intervenes with counter-security (740-155/4).

Surety company may execute bond whenever bond required or authorized. (215-5/390). Surety company estopped to deny liability on executed bond. (215-5/392).

False swearing in application to become surety for another on bail bond as to ownership or value of property, willfully done to secure approval of bond, constitutes crime of perjury or subornation of perjury. (720-540/1).

Enforcement.—Requirements vary with type of bond. Ordinarily action on bond must be between parties to it, but assignees of bond owner may bring suit. (735-5/2-403). Official bond may be enforced through suit against surety. (5-260/13). In action on penal bond, number of breaches which may be alleged not limited. Damages assessed on breaches proved. Judgment for penalty stands as security for all subsequent breaches. (735-5/2-901).

CERTIORARI:

Though largely supplanted by statute, common law writs of certiorari may be issued by Supreme Court (705-5/8), appellate courts (705-25/11), and circuit courts (705-35/26). Common law review extends only to determination from record whether inferior tribunal has exceeded jurisdiction or proceeded illegally and writ is available if no other remedy. (18 Ill. App.3d 412, 305 N.E.2d 404).

Administrative Review Act (735-5/3-101) has replaced certiorari for review of administrative decisions where state statute so provides. Numerous forms of statutory certiorari have expanded scope of review to questions of both law and fact. (See e.g. Revenue [35-120/12, 35-620/12]; Industrial Commission [820-225/7.09 et seq.]; Workmen's Compensation [820-305/19]). Review of municipal administrative agency decisions may be by writ of certiorari. (62 Ill.2d 11, 338 N.E.2d 186). See topic Appeal and Error.

CHARITABLE IMMUNITY:

See topic Actions, subhead Immunity.

COMMISSIONS TO TAKE TESTIMONY:

See topic Depositions and Discovery.

COSTS:

Costs statutory, taxed against losing (judgment, dismissal or nonsuit) party (735-5/5-108, 5/5-109, 5/5-110, 5/5-113, 5/5-116, 5/5-118, 5/5-119), but not against State (735-5/5-117) or executors (735-5/5-109). Discretionary where decision not on all issues. (735-5/5-111, 5/5-112). Includes fees for filing, service of process, jury, court officer charges, and two witnesses. Court also may tax fees for additional witnesses (735-5/5-115) and costs of depositions (Ill. S. Ct. 208[d]). Cost of preparing abstract of record for appeal is recoverable, except for unnecessary matter incorporated therein (Ill. S. Ct. 342[e]), as is stenographer's fee in supplementary proceedings to enforce judgment (Ill. S. Ct. 277[i]). Cost of incorporating unnecessary matter in report of proceedings may be taxed by reviewing court against party designating matter, even if he prevails. (Ill. S. Ct. 330). Attorneys' fees and other expenses not recoverable unless parties agree or statute allows, e.g., as discovery sanctions (Ill. S. Ct. 201[k], 209, 219), or in suits to recover wages (705-225/1). Defendant who tenders sufficient amends for injury, or pays unliquidated damages or demands, including costs of suit if commenced up to time of tender, not liable to pay costs of suit after tender if tender sufficient. (735-5/5-126). Defendant may recover costs after sufficient tender. (735-5/5-126).

Security for Costs.—Nonresident plaintiff (735-5/5-101) or appellant (Ill. S. Ct. 364) must furnish cost bonds or action may be dismissed (735-5/5-101 to 5/5-104). Bonds also necessary for qui tam actions and actions on bonds of executors, administrators, guardians, or officials. (735-5/5-101).

Liability of Attorney.—Where bond required but not filed, plaintiff's attorney liable for costs. (735-5/5-103).

Indigents.—Indigents may sue or defend without paying costs as incurred (735-5/5-105), but unsuccessful indigent plaintiff must later pay his costs, unless excused by court (735-5/5-107). If action is settled, lien for costs attaches to any property received by indigent. (735-5/5-106).

See also topic Bonds.

DAMAGES:

Common law generally prevails as to compensatory damages, except where specific statute grants cause of action. See e.g., Wrongful Death Statute (740-180/1, 180/2); Dram Shop Act (235-5/6-21). Contribution among joint tortfeasors provided. (740-100/2).

DAMAGES . . . *continued*

Comparative Negligence Rule.—Modified Comparative Negligence Rule adopted. (735-5/2-1116).

Sovereign Immunity.—State immunity statute adopted. (745-5/1).

No-Fault Insurance.—Statute creating no-fault insurance held unconstitutional. (51 Ill.2d 478, 283 N.E.2d 474). See category Transportation, topic Motor Vehicles, subhead No-Fault Auto Insurance.

Limitations on Recovery.—Recovery in wrongful death action is without dollar limitation if death occurred on or after Aug. 18, 1967. Jury determines amount of damages without regard to and with no special instructions as to statutory limit on recovery for deaths after 1967 (740-180/2) except recovery of noneconomic damages only as allowed by 735-5/2-1115.1. Amount of damages shall be reduced or barred because of contributory fault of decedent or beneficiary as to actions accruing on or after 3/9/95. (740-180/2). In its application to nonprofit private schools and school districts, previous $10,000 limitation provision of 122-825 was held to violate Art. 4, §22 of Old Illinois Constitution. (41 Ill.2d 336, 243 N.E.2d 203). Recovery in tort actions other than those involving operation of State vehicle against State is limited to $100,000. (705-505/8[d]). Recovery against State for time unjustly served in prison is limited to various amounts up to $35,000 plus cost of living adjustment, depending on length of imprisonment, except court of claims shall make adjustment in maximum award to reflect increase in cost of living after Dec. 31, 1996 but no annual increase greater than 5%, and attorney's fees not to exceed 25% of award granted. (705-505/8[c]). Recovery under Law Enforcement Officers, Civil Defense Workers, Civil Air Patrol Members, Paramedics and Firemen Compensation Act limited to $10,000 if death occurred prior to Jan. 1, 1974, to $20,000 if death occurred after Dec. 31, 1973 and before July 1, 1983, to $50,000 if death occurred on or after July 1, 1983 and before effect of amendatory act of 1995 and to $100,000 if death occurred on or after this effective date. (820-315/3). Under National Guardsman's and Naval Militiaman's Compensation Act recovery is limited to $10,000, but effective Jan. 1, 1994 limit is $50,000. (20-1825/3). Punitive damages are not recoverable in legal and/or medical malpractice actions. (735-5/2-1115). Maximum attorney's contingent fee recoverable in medical malpractice actions is set by statute. (735-5/2-1114).

In all actions on account of bodily injury or death or physical damage to property, in which recovery is predicated on fault, plaintiff is barred from recovering damages if contributory fault of plaintiff is more than 50% of proximate cause of injury or damage for which recovery is sought. If contributory fault of plaintiff is less than 50%, any damages allowed shall be diminished in proportion to amount of fault attributable to plaintiff. (735-5/2-1116).

In all actions that seek damages on account of death, bodily injury or physical damage to property based on negligence or product liability based on any theory, recovery of noneconomic damages shall be limited to $500,000 per plaintiff. No recovery for hedonic damages is allowed. Courts shall utilize liability limits at time at which damages subject to such limits are awarded by final judgment or settlement. (735-5/2-1115.1).

In product liability action, product presumed safe if aspect of product or product component that allegedly caused harm was specified or required by state or federal statute or regulation promulgated by agency responsible for safety or use of product before product is distributed into stream of commerce. (735-5/2-2103). Presumption that design of product or product component is reasonably safe unless, at time product left control of manufacturer, practical and technically feasible alternative design was available that would have prevented harm without significantly impairing usefulness, desirability or marketing of product. (735-5/2-2104). Manufacturer or product seller not liable for harm caused by failure to warn anticipated users if warnings, instructions or labelling were adequate under statute and where, at time product left control of manufacturer, knowledge of danger that allegedly caused harm was not reasonably available in light of existing scientific, technical or medical information. (735-5/2-2106). No liability for harm caused by inherent characteristic of product that is generic aspect of product that cannot be eliminated without substantially compromising product's usefulness and which is recognized by ordinary person. (735-5/2-2106.5).

No punitive damages in product liability action if conduct of manufacturer, seller or reseller that allegedly caused harm was in compliance with state or federal statutes or regulations promulgated by agency responsible for safety or use of product which regulation was in effect at time of alleged misconduct unless plaintiff proves by clear and convincing evidence that manufacturer or product seller intentionally withheld from or misrepresented to Congress, state legislature or agency material information regarding safety or use of product that would have or could have changed rule created. (735-5/2-2107).

In specified instances, recoveries may be reduced to reflect certain collateral payments. (735-5/2-1205, 2-1205.1).

Exemplary damages will not be awarded unless conduct complained of includes willfulness, wantonness, reckless malice or such willful or reckless action as to imply malice. (90 Ill. App.2d 60, 234 N.E.2d 45). There can be no award of punitive damages where actual damages are not recoverable. (6 Ill. App.3d 827, 286 N.E.2d 827). Exemplary damages generally not recoverable in breach of contract actions. (100 Ill. App.2d 6, 241 N.E.2d 697). Certain statutes prohibit award of exemplary damages (e.g., Alienation of Affections [740-5/3]); others prescribe fixed and treble damages. See e.g. Anti-trust (740-10/7).

Trial court may, in its discretion, determine whether jury award of punitive damages is excessive, and, if so, enter remittitur and conditional new trial. Trial court may also apportion the punitive damage award among plaintiff, plaintiff's attorney, and Illinois Department of Human Services. (735-5/2-1207).

Claim for punitive damages may be pled in negligence cases only where permitted by court upon filing of motion not later than 30 days after close of discovery and at conclusion of appropriate hearing. (735-5/2-604.1).

For causes of action accruing after 3/5/95 punitive damages may only be awarded if actual damages are awarded, shall not exceed three times economic damages and requires showing by clear and convincing evidence that defendant's conduct was with evil motive or with reckless and outrageous indifference to highly unreasonable risk of harm and with conscious indifference to rights and safety of others except where defendant charged and convicted of criminal act for which incarceration is or may be part of sentence. (735-5/2-1115.05).

See also topic Actions, subhead Immunity; category Estates and Trusts, topic Death, subhead Actions for Death.

DECLARATORY JUDGMENTS:

See topic Judgments.

DEPOSITIONS AND DISCOVERY:

Depositions are to be taken pursuant to Supreme Court Rules 201 to 212 (Ill. S. Ct. 201 to Ill. S. Ct. 212).

See topic Actions, subhead Parties, for medical malpractice discovery.

Uniform Foreign Depositions Act not adopted.

Outside of State for Use Within State.—See subhead Persons Before Whom Taken infra.

Within State for Use Elsewhere.—See subhead Compelling Appearance of Deponent, infra.

Commissions.—See subhead Persons Before Whom Taken, infra.

Return.—See subhead Errors, Irregularities and Objections, infra.

Depositions in Pending Action—Purposes and Time of Taking.—Any party may take deposition of any other party or person, orally or on written questions, for discovery or for use in evidence. Notice, order or stipulation to take deposition must specify whether deposition is for discovery or evidence, and in absence of specification deposition is for discovery only. Discovery and evidence depositions of same witness must be taken separately unless parties stipulate or court orders otherwise. (Ill. S. Ct. 202).

Deposition may be taken without leave of court any time after commencement of action, except that leave must be obtained if deposition is to be taken before all defendants have appeared or are required to appear. (Ill. S. Ct. 201[d]). On special appearance, discovery is allowed only on issue of personal jurisdiction. (Ill. S. Ct. 201[1]). Except by leave of court, depositions may not be taken in small claims cases, i.e., civil actions for money not in excess of $2,500, exclusive of interest and costs. (Ill. S. Ct. 281, 287). Trial of case will not be delayed for taking of depositions unless due diligence is shown. (Ill. S. Ct. 201[f]).

Persons Before Whom Taken.—Depositions within United States or territory or insular possession thereof are to be taken before officer authorized to administer oaths by laws of Illinois or United States or place where examination is held, or before person appointed by court. Depositions in foreign state or country are to be taken before secretary of embassy or legation, consul general, consul, vice consul, or consular agent of United States, or any officer authorized to administer oaths under laws of Illinois, United States, or place where examination is held, or before person appointed by court. A dedimus potestatem or commission is not required but if desired will be issued by clerk upon application without notice and may designate officer either by name or descriptive title. No deposition can be taken before person who is relative of or attorney for any party or is relative of attorney or is financially interested in action. (Ill. S. Ct. 205).

Scope and Manner of Examination.—On discovery depositions deponent may be examined regarding any matter not privileged relating to subject matter of pending litigation, including existence, location, etc., of documents or tangible things, and identity and location of persons having knowledge of relevant facts, and deponent may be questioned by any party. (Ill. S. Ct. 206[c][1]). Examination on evidence deposition is same as though deponent were testifying at trial. (Ill. S. Ct. 206[c][2]).

Matters Privileged Against Discovery.—All matters privileged against disclosure on trial are privileged against disclosure on discovery. Disclosure will not be required of memoranda, reports or documents made by or for a party in preparation for trial or any privileged communications between party or his agent and his attorney. Material prepared by or for a party is subject to discovery only if it does not disclose theories, mental impressions, or litigation plans of party's attorney. (Ill. S. Ct. 201[b][2]). Court may enter orders for protection of parties and deponents. (Ill. S. Ct. 201[c][1]). If communication is otherwise privileged, privilege is not waived by presence of interpreter aiding party with hearing or speaking impairment or language difficulty. (735-5/8-911[b]). See topic Evidence, subhead Witnesses, catchline Privileged Communications.

Method of Taking Deposition on Oral Examination.—Party desiring to take deposition serves notice in writing reasonable time in advance on other parties, time and place of taking deposition, names and addresses of deponents, if known, or, if not known, information sufficient to identify them or class or group to which they belong, and whether deposition is for discovery or evidence. Notice of intent to record deposition by audio-visual device required. (Ill. S. Ct. 206[a]). If deposition is taken pursuant to subpoena, copy of subpoena must be attached to notice. Court may extend or shorten time on motion. (Ill. S. Ct. 206[a]).

Officer before whom deposition is taken must swear deponent and personally, or by someone acting under his direction and in his presence, record testimony of deponent. Deposition taken stenographically by sound recording device, by audio-visual recording device, or any combination thereof. Testimony will be transcribed at request of any party. Objections made at time of examination to qualifications of officer taking depositions, manner of taking it, evidence presented, conduct of any person, and any other objection to proceedings, are included in deposition. Evidence objected to is taken subject to objection. Parties served with notice of taking deposition may transmit written questions to officer in lieu of oral examination, and officer shall propound questions to deponent and record answers verbatim. (Ill. S. Ct. 206[e]).

During taking of deposition, on motion of any party or deponent, upon showing that examination is being conducted in bad faith or so as to unreasonably annoy, embarrass, or oppress deponent or party, court may order deposition to cease or may limit scope and manner of taking deposition. Deposition terminated by order shall resume

See note at head of Digest as to 1998 legislation covered.

See Topical Index in front part of this volume.

DEPOSITIONS AND DISCOVERY . . . *continued*
only on further order of court. On demand of objecting party or deponent, taking of deposition will be suspended for time necessary to present motion for order. Court may require either party or deponent to pay costs or expenses, including reasonable attorney's fees. (Ill. S. Ct. 206[d]).

If testimony is transcribed, deponent must provide officer with address to which notice may be sent when transcript is available for examination and signing. Any changes in form or substance which deponent desires to make are entered on deposition by officer along with reasons given by deponent for making them. Deponent has 28 days after notice to appear or within that time to make other arrangements for examination. If neither is done and if transcript remains unsigned at end of 28 day period, officer must state in his certificate reason therefor, and deposition may then be used as though signed, unless court determines on motion to suppress that deposition should be rejected. (Ill. S. Ct. 207[a]).

Certification and Filing.—If testimony is transcribed, officer shall certify on deposition that deponent was duly sworn and that deposition is true record of testimony given by deponent. Certified deposition requires no further proof of authenticity. At request of party, officer shall securely seal deposition together with all exhibits or copies thereof in envelope bearing title and number of action and marked "Deposition(s) of (here insert names of deponent[s])" and promptly file it or send it by registered or certified mail to clerk of court for filing. Party causing deposition to be filed shall promptly serve notice thereof on other parties. (Ill. S. Ct. 207[b]).

Fees and Charges.—Physician or surgeon deposed as witness in professional capacity (other than as expert witness) shall be paid reasonable professional fee. (Ill. S. Ct. 204[c]). Party at whose instance deposition is taken pays witness and officer fees and charges of recorder and stenographer. Party at whose request deposition is transcribed and filed pays cost of transcription and filing. Party requesting filing of tape recorded deposition pays cost of filing, but if later transcribed, party requesting transcription shall pay for cost of transcription. However, if scope of examination by any other party exceeds scope of examination by party at whose instance deposition is taken, fees and charges, due to excess, must be summarily taxed by court and paid by other party. Upon payment of reasonable charges therefor, officer must furnish copy of deposition to any party or to deponent. (Ill. S. Ct. 208[a]).

Failure to Attend or Serve Subpoena.—Court may order payment of expenses, including reasonable attorney's fee, occasioned by failure of party serving notice of taking deposition to attend or proceed therewith or to serve subpoena or notice on deponent whose deposition is to be taken. (Ill. S. Ct. 209).

Deposition on Written Questions.—Depositions may be taken on written questions, which shall be served on other parties with notice stating name and address of deponent, or if unknown, general description sufficient to identify him, and name or descriptive title and address of officer before whom deposition is to be taken. Cross questions may be served within 14 days thereafter. Redirect and recross questions may be served at seven day intervals after that. Party at whose instance deposition is taken shall transmit copy of notice and copy of initial and subsequent questions served to officer designated in notice, who shall proceed, in manner provided with respect to oral depositions (Ill. S. Ct. 206[e]; Ill. S. Ct. 207), to take testimony of deponent and prepare, certify and file or mail deposition, attaching thereto copy of notice and questions received by him. No other party, attorney, or person interested in event of action may be present during taking of deposition or dictate, write, or draw up any answers to questions. Party causing deposition to be filed shall promptly serve notice thereof on other parties. (Ill. S. Ct. 210).

Compelling Appearance of Deponent.—When action is pending in Illinois, clerk of trial court shall issue subpoena on request except that subpoena for discovery deposition of physician or surgeon in professional capacity (other than as expert witness) may only be issued on order of court. When deponent is to be party or currently officer or agent of party, service on party of notice of taking of deposition is sufficient to require appearance of deponent. Subpoena or notice may command person to whom it is directed to produce documents or tangible things which constitute or contain evidence relating to any matters within scope of permitted examination. (Ill. S. Ct. 204[a][1],[3]).

Deponent must respond to any lawful subpoena of which he has actual knowledge, if fee and mileage are tendered. Service by mail may be proved prima facie by return receipt, certified or registered mail, dated at least seven days before appearance date together with mailing affidavit including statement of fee tender. (Ill. S. Ct. 204[a][2]).

When action is pending in another state, territory, or country, any officer or person authorized by laws of that jurisdiction to take deposition in Illinois, with or without commission, may petition circuit court in county in which deponent resides or is employed or transacts his business in person or is found for subpoena to compel appearance of deponent or for order to compel giving of testimony by him. Court may hear and act upon petition, with or without notice as court directs. (Ill. S. Ct. 204[b]).

Place of Examination.—Unless otherwise agreed upon, deponent may be required to attend examination only in county in which he resides, is employed or transacts his business in person, or in case of plaintiff—deponent, in county in which action is pending. However, court may order party or officer, director or employee of party to appear at designated place in Illinois or elsewhere for purpose of having deposition taken upon just terms and conditions including payment of reasonable expenses. (Ill. S. Ct. 203).

Errors, Irregularities and Objections.—Errors and irregularities in notice for taking deposition are waived unless written objection is promptly served upon party giving notice. Objection to qualification of person before whom deposition is to be taken is waived unless made before deposition begins or as soon as disqualification is known or could have been discovered with reasonable diligence. Grounds of objection to competency of deponent or admissibility of testimony which might have been corrected if presented during taking of deposition are waived unless then made; otherwise they may be made when testimony is offered in evidence. Objections to form of question or answer and errors and irregularities which might be corrected if promptly presented are waived unless seasonably objected thereto at taking of deposition. Objections to form of written question are waived unless served in writing on party propounding them within time allowed for serving succeeding questions, and in case of last questions authorized, within seven days after service thereof. Objection seasonably made is preserved without motion to suppress, but any party may obtain ruling on objections in advance of trial. Errors and irregularities in manner in which testimony is transcribed or deposition is dealt with by officer are waived unless motion to suppress is made with reasonable promptness after defect is or with due diligence might have been ascertained. (Ill. S. Ct. 211). If parties so stipulate, depositions may be taken before any person, at any time or place, for any purpose and in any manner. (Ill. S. Ct. 201[i]).

Use of Depositions.—Discovery depositions may be used to impeach deponent as witness like any inconsistent statement, as admission, if otherwise admissible as exception to hearsay rule, or for any purpose for which an affidavit may be used. Evidence depositions may be used for any purpose for which discovery depositions may be used and for any purpose if court finds at time of trial that deponent is dead, out of county (unless party offering deposition procured his absence) or unable to attend or testify because of age, sickness, infirmity, or imprisonment; or if party offering deposition has exercised due diligence but has been unable to procure attendance of deponent by subpoena. Party who is nonresident of Illinois may introduce his own deposition if he is absent from county. Evidence deposition may also be used for any purpose if court finds in advance of trial that exceptional circumstances exist which make it desirable in interest of justice to allow deposition to be so used. (Ill. S. Ct. 212). Substitution of parties does not affect right to use depositions previously taken. In any action in which same matter and parties (or successors) involved and which was previously dismissed or remanded, all depositions previously taken and filed in former action or before remand may be used. (Ill. S. Ct. 212[d]).

Refusal to Comply with Rules or Order as to Depositions.—Refusal of deponent to answer any question without substantial justification subjects him or party responsible to liability to aggrieved party for expenses incurred in requiring answer, including reasonable attorney's fee. If refusal to answer question was justified court may require party moving to compel answer to pay opposing party or deponent reasonable expenses incurred in opposing motion, including reasonable attorney's fee. Failure to comply with rules or order relating to depositions subjects offender to contempt proceedings and, if party, dismissal of all or part of his pleadings, on issue to which refusal or failure relates, prevention of his witnesses from testifying on that issue, dismissal of suit or default judgment on claims or defenses to which issue is material, or stay of proceedings pending compliance. (Ill. S. Ct. 219). Parties must personally confer and reasonably attempt to resolve differences before seeking order of court. (Ill. S. Ct. 201[K]).

Perpetuating Testimony.—Any person who desires to perpetuate his own testimony or that of another person regarding any matter that is or may be cognizable in any court or proceeding may file verified petition for that purpose and proceed after notice and service, as required by rule, to take deposition by substantially same procedure prescribed for taking of other depositions. (Ill. S. Ct. 217[a]).

Depositions Pending Appeal.—If appeal is taken or before appeal is taken if time therefor has not yet run, trial court may, on motion and for good cause, allow taking of depositions of witnesses to perpetuate their testimony in event of further proceedings in that court. (Ill. S. Ct. 217[b]).

De Bene Esse.—Other than the statute and rule regulating the matter of perpetuating testimony there is no statute with respect to depositions de bene esse. The common law and general equity rules obtain, and the circuit courts will entertain applications to take testimony de bene esse.

The following form may be used:

Forms

STATE OF ILLINOIS }
COUNTY OF COOK } SS.

IN THE CIRCUIT COURT OF COOK COUNTY, ILLINOIS

JOHN DOE,
Plaintiff,
vs. } No. . . . . . .
RICHARD ROE,
Defendant.

The deposition of Robert Smith, 1 N. State Street, Chicago, Illinois, called by the (plaintiff) (defendant) for examination, pursuant to (notice) (notice and subpoena) (agreement of counsel for the respective parties), and pursuant to the provisions of the Illinois Code of Civil Procedure of the State of Illinois and the rules of the Supreme Court thereof pertaining to the taking of depositions, for the purpose of (evidence) (discovery), taken before Mary Jones, a notary public in and for the County of Cook and State of Illinois, at 135 S. LaSalle Street, Chicago, Illinois, on the 5th day of November, 19. . . . ., at the hour of 2 P.M.

Certificate attached is usually in the following form:

STATE OF ILLINOIS }
COUNTY OF COOK } ss.

I, Mary Jones, a notary public in and for the County of Cook, State of Illinois, do hereby certify that Robert Smith was by me first duly sworn to testify to the truth, the whole truth, and nothing but the truth in the cause aforesaid; that the deposition of the said Robert Smith was taken before me commencing at the hour of 2 o'clock P.M. on Tuesday, the 5th day of November, 19. . . . ., and was concluded on that date: that the testimony given at said deposition by said witness was taken down by me in shorthand, in the presence of said witness, and was thereafter (by me) (under my direct personal supervision) transcribed into typewriting; I further certify that the foregoing transcript of said deposition is a complete and correct transcript of my shorthand notes so made as aforesaid and is a complete and correct report of the entire testimony so given by said witness, together with such other matters and things as counsel for the parties present at the taking of said deposition desire to have appear of record, including Exhibits 1 to 10, marked by me for identification at said deposition and

DEPOSITIONS AND DISCOVERY . . . *continued*

attached hereto; that William White appeared on behalf of plaintiff and Harold Green appeared on behalf of defendant during the taking of said deposition; that I am not of counsel for, nor attorney for any of the parties to the aforesaid cause, nor am I related to any of the parties to said cause, nor am I interested in any manner in the said cause or in its outcome: (I further certify that the reading and signing of said deposition was waived by the witness and counsel for the respective parties;)

In witness whereof I have hereunto set my hand and affixed my seal of office, at Chicago, Illinois, this 10th day of November, 19. . . . .

Notary Public in and for the
County of Cook, State of Illinois

My commission expires:
. . . ., 19. . . .

EQUITY:

See topic Actions.

EVIDENCE:

See topic Depositions and Discovery.

Witnesses.—No person is disqualified in a civil action solely by reason of interest in the event or by reason of conviction of crime; interest or conviction only affect credibility. (735-5/8-101). Test of competency is not age or religious belief, but intelligence, understanding, and moral obligation to speak the truth. (17 Ill.2d 502, 162 N.E.2d 381; 22 Ill.2d 513, 177 N.E.2d 224; 2 Ill.2d 311, 118 N.E.2d 1; 317 Ill.App. 538, 46 N.E.2d 857, abst.). No witness may be compelled to testify if his testimony is to be broadcast or televised, or if motion pictures are to be taken of him while testifying (735-5/8-701) but see, Ill. S. Ct. 206(f) regarding videotape depositions. Provision is made for appointment of interpreters in cases in which deaf persons are parties or witnesses. (735-5/8-1402).

See also topic Depositions and Discovery.

Book Account.—Any writing or record, in form of a book entry or otherwise, made as a memorandum or record of any act, transaction, occurrence, or event, is admissible as evidence of the act, transaction, occurrence or event, if made in regular course of business, and if it was regular course of the business to make such a memorandum or record at time of such an act, transaction, occurrence, or event or within a reasonable time thereafter. All other circumstances of making of record, including lack of personal knowledge by entrant or maker, may affect its weight, but not its admissibility. Term "business" includes business, profession, occupation, and calling of every kind, but rule does not sanction admissibility of police accident reports. (Ill. S. Ct. 236). Books of account not admissible to show loan or payment of money. (108 Ill. App.2d 264, 247 N.E.2d 631). Account books and documents photographed or microfilmed in usual course of business or pursuant to statute authorizing reproduction of public documents and meeting certain standards of quality are deemed original records for evidence purposes. (735-5/8-401).

Privileged Communications.—Attorney is not allowed to disclose anything communicated by his client to him in his professional capacity. (See 219 Ill. App. 230.) Client can waive this privilege. (See 265 Ill. 448, 107 N.E. 165.) Statements of client to attorney in presence of third parties or opposing party are not within rule of exclusion. (211 Ill. 612, 71 N.E. 1112).

No physician or surgeon may disclose any information he acquires in attending patients in a professional character necessary to enable him to serve the patient except in certain enumerated cases. (735-5/8-802). Both recipient of mental health services and therapist (defined to include psychiatrist, physician, psychologist, social worker, and nurse under appropriate circumstances) may refuse to disclose or prevent disclosure of recipient's records or communications except in certain enumerated cases. (740-110/10). Psychologist may not disclose any information acquired from patient consulting him in his professional capacity or necessary to enable him to render services in his professional capacity except in enumerated case. 740-110/1 controls in case of conflict. (715-70/6). However, therapist has right to communicate with his counsel or professional liability insurance company concerning treatment provided by recipient or disclose record or communication to therapist's supervisor and others on team providing services; persons conducting peer review of therapist; Institutes for Juvenile Research and Study of Developmental Disability; Inspector General of Dept. of Family and Children Services when investigation pending under 20-505/35.5. (740-110/9).

Rape crises personnel may not disclose statements made by victim unless victim consents in writing. (735-5/8-802.1).

Trial court shall determine reasonable fee for expert witness if fee dispute arises between parties. (735-5/8-1101).

A clergyman or religious practitioner cannot be required to disclose a confession or admission made to him in his professional capacity in a court proceeding, before an administrative board or to a public officer. (735-5/8-802.2).

Public accountant cannot be required by court to divulge information or evidence obtained by him in his confidential capacity. (225-450/27).

News reporter may not be compelled to disclose source of information unless court finds that other sources of information have been exhausted, disclosure is essential to public interest and information does not concern secret information under laws of State or U.S. or, in libel and slander cases, need for information outweighs public interest in confidentiality of sources under facts of each case. (735-5/8-901 to 5/8-909).

Husband and wife may testify for or against each other in civil or criminal actions, except as to communications or admissions made by either to the other or conversations between them during marriage. Exception does not apply in civil cases in actions between husband and wife, or where custody or support of children is directly in issue, or where either has acted as agent for other. (735-5/8-801).

Where husband is disqualified by reason of interest, wife is also incompetent; and that incompetency continues after the marriage relation is dissolved, whether by death or divorce. (331 Ill. App. 535, 73 N.E.2d 624).

Communications or Transactions with Persons Since Deceased or Incompetent.—No party to any civil proceeding or person directly interested may testify on own behalf to any conversation with deceased or incompetent person or any event that took place in presence of deceased or incompetent person when any adverse party sues or defends as representative of deceased or incompetent person with following exceptions: (a) If any person testifies on behalf of representative to conversation or event occurring in presence of deceased or incompetent person, adverse party or interested person may testify to same; (b) if deposition of deceased or incompetent person is admitted in evidence at trial, any adverse party may testify concerning same matters; (c) any testimony competent under account books exception (735-5/8-401) is not affected by this act; (d) no person is barred from testifying to heirship of decedent (735-5/8-201).

Partners, Joint Contractors, Agents, etc.—In suit by or against surviving partner or partners, joint contractor or joint contractors, no adverse party or person adversely interested is a competent witness to testify to any admission or conversation by any deceased partner or joint contractor, unless some one or more of the surviving partners or joint contractors were also present at the time of such admission or conversation; nor is the adverse party who has contracted with an agent, since deceased, of the opposite party, a competent witness as to conversation with that agent unless that conversation took place in the presence of a surviving agent or agents, and then only if he would be permitted to testify by 735-5/8-201 & 735-5/8-401 had deceased been principal rather than agent. (735-5/8-301).

Incompetency cannot be removed by an assignment or release of claim made in suit for purpose of enabling witness to testify. (735-5/8-501).

Self-incrimination.—No person may be compelled in any criminal case to give evidence against himself. (Const. Art. 1, §10).

INJUNCTIONS:

Jurisdiction.—Circuit courts have jurisdiction to grant injunctions. (705-35/25 & 35/26; Const. Art. 6, §9).

Procedure.—Code of Civil Procedure (735) and Supreme Court Rules (Ill. S. Ct.) apply, except as provided herein. Exhaustion of administrative remedies is not condition precedent to issuance of injunction. (86 Ill.2d 274, 427 N.E.2d 550).

Temporary restraining order may be issued without notice only if it clearly appears from specific facts shown by verified complaint or affidavit accompanying same that immediate and irreparable injury will result to applicant before notice can be served and hearing had thereon. (735-5/11-101). Every temporary restraining order granted without notice shall expire by its terms within such time after signing of order as fixed by court, not to exceed ten days, subject to extension for like period for good cause shown. (735-5/11-101). Party restrained without notice may, on two days' notice to party who obtained restraining order, appear and contest restraining order. (735-5/11-101). If temporary restraining order is granted without notice, motion for preliminary injunction shall be set for hearing at earliest possible time, and if party obtaining such temporary restraining order does not proceed with application for preliminary injunction, temporary restraining order shall be dissolved.

Preliminary Injunction.—No preliminary injunction shall be granted without previous notice of time and place of application having been given adverse party. (735-5/11-102).

Bond.—In all cases before issuance of restraining order or preliminary injunction, bond may be required in such sum with such security and upon such conditions as deemed proper by court. (735-5/11-103). Damage provision of Injunction Act applies only to wrongful issuance of temporary injunction. (42 Ill.2d 45, 245 N.E. 2d 468). No bonds required of any governmental office or agency. (735-5/11-103). Party wrongfully enjoined may sue on injunction bond or for damages. (735-5/11-110).

Dissolution.—Motion to dissolve injunction may be made at any time before or after answer. If motion to dissolve filed after answer, court will rule on motion upon weight of evidence. (735-5/11-108). Affidavits may be filed by either party on motion to dissolve and may be read in evidence at hearing (735-5/11-109), but only if answer to petition for injunction on file (39 Ill. App. 2d 289, 188 N.E.2d 893). If temporary restraining order or preliminary injunction is dissolved as having been wrongfully issued, court shall, prior to final disposition of matter, upon filing of petition under oath from party claiming damages by reason of such temporary restraining order or preliminary injunction, determine and enter judgment in favor of party injured by such temporary restraining order or preliminary injunction for damages suffered by reason thereof. (735-5/11-110).

Supreme Court Rules on appeals supersede statutory provisions inconsistent with rules and govern all appeals. (Ill. S. Ct. 1). Orders granting, modifying, refusing, dissolving, or refusing to dissolve or modify injunction or temporary restraining order are appealable as of right. Appeal from granting or denial of temporary restraining order must be perfected within two days of entry of order; otherwise, appeal must be perfected within 30 days of entry of order. If such order granted ex parte, party intending to appeal must first present, on notice, motion to trial court to vacate order; if such motion is denied or not acted upon within seven days, 30 days for appeal begins to run on day such motion is denied or from last day for action thereon. (Ill. S. Ct. 307).

Persons Bound.—Injunction is binding only upon parties to action, their officers, agents, servants, employees and attorneys, and persons in concert with parties who receive actual notice. (735-5/11-101).

Liability on bond may be enforced on motion. No new action required. (735-5/11-103). In all cases where restraining order or injunction is dissolved, circuit court will grant damages on petition by aggrieved party. (735-5/11-110).

Amended pleadings may be permitted on motion to pleadings or summary judgment or at trial if wrong remedy sought, court to consider effect on defendant as well. (735-5/11-107).

See also specific statutes authorizing injunctive relief.

See note at head of Digest as to 1998 legislation covered.

See Topical Index in front part of this volume.

JUDGMENTS:

Court must determine rights and grant relief to which party is entitled based on pleadings and proofs. More than one judgment may be rendered. If satisfaction of judgment creates reimbursement rights against another party, court may render later judgment accordingly, upon motion and notice. (735-5/2-1301). If judgment is entered as to less than all parties or claims, it is generally not enforceable or appealable, and is subject to revision, until adjudication of all claims is completed, unless trial court expressly finds no just reason for delaying enforcement or appeal. There are exceptions to this rule for probate, receivership, and certain post-judgment proceedings. (Ill. S. Ct. 304).

Copy of judgment order, certified by clerk of court, performs function of writ of execution and other writs. (735-5/2-1501).

Determination in favor of plaintiff on defense of abatement shall be that defendant answer or otherwise plead.

Judgments by Default or Dismissal for Want of Prosecution.—May be entered, but court may require proof of allegations upon which relief is based. (735-5/2-1301[d]). Court may determine damages without jury (735-5/2-1206); relief is limited to that originally demanded unless notice of amended relief is given to defaulted party, who has 30 days to answer or appear with respect to new or additional relief (Ill. S. Ct. 105). Notice of entry of default shall be given by attorney for moving party to each party who has appeared, against whom order was entered, or to such party's attorney of record; notice of dismissal for want of prosecution is required if plaintiff had been notified that court was considering entry of such order, unless required by local rule. (735-5/2-1302).

Setting Aside Defaults.—Default may be set aside by court before final order or judgment and thereafter, upon motion filed within 30 days after entry of default, set aside any final order or judgment upon any reasonable terms and conditions (735-5/2-1301[3]); joint judgment or order may be set aside as to fewer than all parties (735-5/2-1301[P]). Motion is addressed to court's discretion, and is treated liberally with view toward doing substantial justice. (20 Ill. App.3d 253, 313 N.E.2d 613). Judgment entered against defendant served only by publication, who did not appear, may be set aside or amended upon motion made within 90 days if he received written notice of judgment, and within one year if no notice was received. (735-5/2-1301[g]). If there has been sale pursuant to such judgment, court may permit it to stand, but redemption must be permitted if debtor was entitled to it.

Sureties may not confess judgment or default if principal enters as defendant and tenders counter-security. (740-155/4).

Judgment by confession, without service of defendant, may be entered on any bona fide debt except consumer transaction in county where defendant resides or owns property, or where instrument executed. (735-5/2-1301[c]). Statute constitutional on its face (424 F.Supp. 1200), but enforcement of confessed judgment through garnishment statute providing no procedure for determining "knowing and voluntary" waiver of due process rights is unconstitutional (343 F.Supp. 1272). General Order 6.4(b), Circuit Court of Cook County, now prohibits non-wage garnishments based on confessed judgments unless debtor has been served. For form of judgment note see category Business Regulation and Commerce, topic Bills and Notes.

Consumer Transactions.—No power to confess judgment will be required or given after Sept. 24, 1979, in any instrument used in consumer transaction; any power to confess given in violation of Act is null and void, and any judgment entered by court based upon such power is unenforceable. Consumer transaction means sale, lease, assignment, loan, or other disposition of item of goods, consumer service, or intangible to individual for purposes that are primarily personal, family, or household. (735-5/2-1301).

Opening Judgments by Confession.—Upon motion diligently filed, accompanied by verified answer and affidavit, which shows complete or partial prima facie defense, court must open judgment to extent defense is stated, and proceed to additional pleading and trial. Unopened parts of judgment may be executed. If defendant presents counterclaim, court may permit its filing and stay execution of judgment. (Ill. S. Ct. 276). Determination of defendant's diligence in moving to open judgment is within court's discretion. (10 Ill. App.3d 322, 293 N.E.2d 719).

Judgment by Consent.—No applicable statute. Consent decree treated as contract binding on parties. (30 Ill. App.3d 880, 334 N.E.2d 825).

Judgment on pleadings may be granted upon seasonable motion (735-5/2–615[e]), if no issues of material fact are presented (30 Ill. App.3d 423, 331 N.E.2d 832).

Summary judgment may be granted upon motion, with or without supporting affidavits, filed after opposite party has appeared. (735-5/2-1005[a-b]). Opposing party may present counter-affidavits before or at hearing. Record must show no issue of material fact. (735-5/2-1005[c]).

Affidavits must be made on personal knowledge and set forth material evidentiary facts with particularity; if material facts are known only to opposing parties, affidavits may state facts as believed, and court may proceed to grant summary judgment or order discovery. (Ill. S. Ct. 191). Affidavits made in bad faith or for delay may cause imposition of resulting expenses, and contempt citations. (735-5/2-1005[e]).

Declaratory Judgments.—Illinois declaratory judgment statute (735-5/2-701) not based on Uniform Act, but follows similar format. In cases of actual controversy, court may make binding declaration of rights, including construction of statutes, ordinances, regulations, wills and other private written instruments. Such declaration must terminate part or all of controversy. Political questions may not be considered if defendant is constitutional officer. Declaratory relief may be sought alone or in addition to other relief. Supplementary declaratory relief may be granted after initial declaration, upon petition. Issues of fact must be tried as in other civil cases, to jury if required. Actual controversy exists if there is substantial dispute, between parties with adverse interests, of sufficient immediacy and reality. (18 Ill. App.3d 33, 309 N.E.2d 408). In general, existence of another remedy does not preclude declaratory judgment action, except in revenue cases (86 Ill.2d 479, 427 N.E.2d 1226), but administrative remedies must be exhausted (83 Ill. App.3d 1034, 404 N.E.2d 1050).

Offer of Judgment.—Offer can be made before or after suit filed. If sufficient to make amends for injury, and to pay costs if suit commenced, plaintiff cannot recover costs incurred after such tender, and is liable for defendant's costs. Offer of judgment is admissible as admission of liability (30 Ill. App.578), but offer to compromise claim is not admissible (37 Ill. App.3d 848, 346 N.E.2d 475).

Docketing.—Judgments are rendered or entered by court and docketed or registered by clerk. (705-105/14, 105/15). Interest accrues at 9% rate from date of rendering. (735-5/2-1303).

Relief from Judgments and Decrees.—

Within 30 days after entry of order of judgment, court may on motion set aside order of judgment on such terms as are reasonable. (735-5/2-1301[e]).

After 30 days and before two years, relief may be sought by petition under 735-5/2-1401, general statute abolishing and supplanting writs of error coram nobis and coram vobis, writs of audita querela, and bills of review. Petition is filed in proceeding which produced judgment, but is not continuation of that proceeding, and does not affect or stay judgment automatically. Matters not of record must be shown by affidavit or other appropriate means. Notice must be given by service, by registered mail, or by publication in appropriate cases. (Ill. S. Ct. Rule 105). Relief from judgment under 735-5/2-1401 does not affect property rights of nonparties acquired after judgment, unless lack of jurisdiction to enter judgment appears in record. Procedure does not affect relief from void judgments.

Note: Except as provided in 750-50/206 (adoption) or in petition based upon 725-5/116-3 (criminal procedure), computation of two year period excludes time during which petitioner under legal disability or duress or where ground for relief is concealed.

Lien.—Legislation enacted in 1963 substantially revised law concerning liens arising from judgments entered subsequent to Dec. 31, 1963. Prior statute should be consulted for treatment of prior judgments.

Land.—As to land registered under Land Titles ("Torrens") Act (765-35/1), judgment is lien when properly filed with registrar of titles and memorial is entered upon register, under 765-35/85, 35/86. As to land not registered under Land Titles Act, judgment is lien on debtor's real estate only from time when transcript, certified copy or memorandum of judgment is filed with recorder of deeds in county in which land is located. (735-5/12-101). In either case, lien runs for seven years from rendering of judgment. (735-5/12-101 to 12-104). Lien may be extended for additional seven years by revival of judgment (735-5/12-101) and filing of revival order with recorder of deeds. Foreign judgments registered pursuant to 110-12-601 et seq. are liens: (a) As to land not registered under Land Titles Act, only when petition for registration of foreign judgment, or judgment of domestic court on that petition, is filed with recorder of deeds in county where land located and (b) as to land registered under Land Titles Act, only when foreign judgment is filed under 765-35/85. Final judgment entered by appellate court is lien when filed in manner described above. (Ill. S. Ct. Rule 366.)

Personalty.—Judgments become liens against personal property only on delivery of certified copy of execution to proper officer to be executed (735-5/12-111); but party placing execution with proper officer may lose lien by failure to enforce it promptly by levy and sale (19 Ill. App.2d 165, 153 N.E.2d 298).

Chancery.—Chancery decrees for money are liens like judgments. Chancery decrees respecting realty are liens on such realty; court may order acts other than payment of money to be lien on realty or personalty.

Federal Courts.—Judgments of federal courts held in state may be recorded in public offices of state. (735-5/12-501). Upon filing under procedures for registered and unregistered land described above, judgment of federal court is lien upon real estate in same manner as state judgment. (735/5-12-502).

Scope.—All nonexempt property of judgment debtor is subject to execution. (735-5/12-112). Judgment rendered against partnership in firm name is enforceable only against firm property and is lien only upon realty held in firm name. (735-5/12-102). Judgment rendered against person solely because he is holder of title to property in fiduciary capacity will support execution only against property held in particular representative capacity. (735-5/12-103).

Judgment rendered against unregistered business operating under assumed name in action against business and known and unknown owners, is personal judgment against all named known owners, immediately enforceable against property of business, and is lien upon real estate held in name of business. If identity of previously unknown owner is discovered, that person is to be named as party defendant by motion to court upon proper notice supported by affidavit; and, within ten days after service, previously unknown owner may appear and defend, which defense will not affect any personal judgment previously entered. If previously unknown owner does not appear or is found liable, judgment theretofore entered may be amended to include him personally. (805-405/6).

Arrest of Judgment.—When judgment is arrested pursuant to post trial motion, plaintiff is not compelled to recommence. If appropriate, the court must order new pleadings. (735-5/2-1204).

Revival of judgment of court may be had by action brought within 20 years after its date. (735-5/13-218).

Assignment.—Judgments are assignable. (388 Ill. 392, 58 N.E.2d 545). Assignee may enforce judgment. (735-5/2-403).

Satisfaction.—Judgment creditor who has received full payment on judgment is required, at request of judgment debtor, to execute and deliver to judgment debtor or his legal representative a written release of judgment. Clerk of Court which rendered judgment required to record satisfaction of judgment and release of liens (no fee), or record assignment of judgment ($2 fee), and make appropriate notations on judgment and execution docket of book and page where release or assignment of judgment recorded. (735-5/12-183). If judgment creditor willfully refuses to execute satisfaction on tender by debtor of full amount due, court, on petition and tender, may satisfy judgment of record. (735-5/12-183). Upon filing of release or satisfaction of judgment,

See note at head of Digest as to 1998 legislation covered.

See Topical Index in front part of this volume.

JUDGMENTS . . . *continued*

signed by party in whose favor judgment was entered or by his attorney, court shall vacate judgment and dismiss action. (735-5/12-183).

Form

Form of Satisfaction.—

. . . ., the . . . .
                                        (judgment creditor)

(assignee of record)   (legal representative)
having received full satisfaction and payment, releases the judgment entered on . . . . . .
. . . . ., 19. . . ., against defendant . . . . for $. . . . . . . and costs.

Actions.—See topic Limitation of Actions.

Foreign Judgment.—Uniform Enforcement of Foreign Judgments Act, with certain modifications, has been adopted. (735-5/12-627 to 12-629 repealed see now 735-5/12-651 to 12-653).

Uniform Foreign Money-Judgments Recognition Act has been adopted. (735-5/12-618 to 12-626).

LIMITATION OF ACTIONS:

This section describes in general terms limitation periods for Illinois civil actions. It summarizes time requirements for actions commonly filed in Illinois courts. It does not purport to present limitation periods for every action recognized under Illinois law, nor to present every exception to limitation periods that are described.

Actions must be brought within the following periods after the respective causes of action accrue:

No Limitation.—Action for damages against person for conduct which resulted in conviction for first degree murder, Class X felony, or Class 1 felony. (735-5/13-202.1).

Seventy-five Years.—No deed, will, plat, affidavit, or other proof of ownership, including court judgment, etc., dated, entered into or recorded more than 75 years prior to effective date of Act (1872) or more than 75 years prior to date claim of interest or ownership, etc. is asserted can constitute cloud on title or be used as evidence in any proceeding affecting title. (735-5/13-114). Limitation is deferred for ten more years by written claim describing real estate filed with Recorder of Deeds of county where land is located if filed within three years prior to 75 year limit, within three years after effective date of Act or, after 75 year limit in case of infant or otherwise incompetent claimant, within two years after competency disability has been removed or guardian has been appointed. (735-5/13-114).

Forty Years.—Actions to recover or establish interest in real estate against record title holder and his grantors who have held chain of title for 40 years prior to action; unless:(1) Claimant has filed verified statement with county recorder describing real estate and setting forth interest in and basis of his claim within 40 years after action accrued or (2) real estate is in adverse possession of one other than record title holder. (735-5/13-118).

Thirty Years.—Lien of mortgage, trust deed in nature of mortgage, and vendor's lien, where no due date is stated on face or is ascertainable from its written terms, unless, within 30 year period, owner of lien files for record affidavit showing amount due or files for record extension agreement. Affidavit or extension agreement can extend lien only ten years. (735-5/13-116[b]).

Twenty years: Actions for recovery of or entry upon lands (735-5/13-101), except that period is seven years from time action accrues:(a) When action is based upon breach of condition subsequent (continuing or recurring breaches do not extend time) or upon termination of estate upon limitation or upon estate upon conditional limitation (735-5/13-102, 5/13-103); (b) when land is possessed by actual residence thereon for seven successive years by persons with connected record title (as defined in statute) (735-5/13-107); (c) with exceptions, when there is actual possession under claim and color of title for seven years and payment of taxes is made for those seven years (735-5/13-109); or, (d) with exceptions, when in case of vacant land, there is payment of taxes for seven years by person with color of title (735-5/13-110); see exceptions (735-5/13-108, 5/13-111, 13-112, 13-113). Proceedings to revive circuit court judgments under 735-5/2-1601. (735-5/13-218). Mortgage, trust deed in nature of mortgage, or vendor's lien on both registered and unregistered land, due date of which is stated on its face, ceases to be lien if more than 20 years have lapsed after last payment on indebtedness is due upon its face and according to its written terms, unless owner of such lien within prescribed time files extension agreement for record or files affidavit showing amount due. (735-5/13-116). Affidavit or extension agreement can extend lien only ten years. (735-5/13-116[b]).

Ten years: Except as provided in §2-725 of Uniform Commercial Code (c. 810), actions on bonds, notes, bills of exchange, written leases and written contracts and other evidences of indebtedness in writing—part payment or new promise to pay in writing within or after initial ten year period extends time to ten years after such payment or promise. With regard to promissory note dated on or after amendatory Act of 1997, cause of action on promissory note payable at definite date accrues on due date or date stated in note or date upon which note is accelerated. With respect to demand promissory note dated on or after Jan. 1, 1998 if demand is made to maker, action to enforce obligation must be commenced within ten years after demand. Action to enforce demand promissory note is barred if neither principal nor interest on such note has been paid for continuous period of ten years and no demand for payment has been made to maker during that period. (735-5/13-206). Foreclosure of mortgages (735-5/13-115); but see subhead Twenty Years, supra as to cessation of lien of mortgage or trust deed in nature of mortgage. Actions under Registered Titles Act for loss or damage as result of omission, mistake, misfeasance in registering, or recording land titles must be brought within ten years. (765-35/103).

Murder or Class X Felony.—Actions for damages for injuries described in 735-5/13-202 or 203 (for personal injury, loss of consortium, or other injury to another person derived from victim's injury) arising out of murder or Class X felony must be filed

within ten years after perpetrator has completed sentence. (735-5/13-214.1). Actions for loss of means of support or loss of parental or in loco parentis relationship sustained by minor from injury described in 735-5/13-214.1 must be filed within ten years after person who inflicted injury has completed sentence. (735-5/13-203.1).

Seven years: Actions for recovery of or entry upon lands (see exceptions to 20-year limitation above). Actions to enforce judgments (with exceptions, including revival of judgment under 735-5/2-1601, see subhead Twenty Years, supra and judgments recovered for injuries specified in 735-5/13-214.1, see subhead Ten Years, supra) but real estate, levied upon within the seven years, may be sold to enforce judgment within one year after expiration of seven years. Child support judgments, including those arising by operation of law, may be enforced at any time. (735-5/12-108).

Six years: Actions or claims against bank in dissolution, from date of publication of dissolution, unless this time would extend limitation period on action otherwise earlier barred. (205-5/73).

Five years: Actions against state founded upon contract. (705-505/22). Actions by or against dissolved corporation, from date of dissolution, if action existed prior to dissolution (805-5/12.80), except if action based on written instruments and falls within ten year limitation period of 735-5/13-206 (142 Ill. App.3d 948, 492 N.E. 2d 528). Except as provided in §2-725 of Uniform Commercial Code (c. 810) and in §§11-13 of Illinois Public Aid Code 305-5/11-1 to 5/13-5 (c. 305) actions on unwritten contracts, express or implied, part oral and part written contracts (53 Ill. App. 3d 344, 368 N.E. 2d 767) and awards of arbitration; actions for injuries to real or personal property; actions to recover possession of or damages for detention or conversion of personal property; and all civil actions not otherwise expressly provided for (735-5/13-205). Last category named includes judgments of courts of another state. (735-5/13-205; 139 Ill. 311, 28 N.E. 841). It also includes, inter alia, statutory causes of action for which limitation period is not otherwise provided. (446 F.Supp. 1048; 90 Ill. App.2d 61, 234 N.E. 2d 109). Five year period also applies to fraudulently concealed causes of action (735-5/13-215) (see subhead Concealment of Cause of Action, infra).

Trade Secrets Act.—Actions for misappropriation as defined in Trade Secrets Act must be brought within five years after misappropriation is discovered or by exercise of reasonable diligence should have been discovered. (765-1065/7).

Four years: Action for breach of any contract for sale of goods must be commenced within four years unless by original agreement parties reduce period of limitations to not less than one year. (810-5/2-725). No action may be brought against registered land surveyor for negligence more than four years after the person claiming damages actually knows or should have known of such negligence. (735-5/13-222). Action for violation of state antitrust laws barred unless commenced within four years after cause of action arose. (740-10/7[2]). See category Business Regulation and Commerce, topic Monopolies, Restraint of Trade and Competition, subhead Antitrust Act.

Improvements to Real Property.—With exceptions, any actions arising from design planning, supervision, observation, management or construction of improvements to real property, including negligence and Structural Work Act claims of worker injured at contract site (149 Ill.2d 190 [1992]), must be commenced within four years from date plaintiff knew or should have known of action, but in no event more than ten years after improvements made unless defendant expressly warranted or promised improvements for longer period (735-5/13-214).

Three years: Suits against sheriff or other officers for damages in replevin (735-5/13-115); and actions by or against carriers to collect or recover transportation charges for property moved wholly in Illinois (735-5/13-219); action to recover on accident or health insurance policy, measured from time proof of loss required to be submitted (215-5/357.12); actions under Consumer Fraud Act (815-505/11a).

Franchise Disclosure Act.—Actions for violations of Franchise Disclosure Act of 1988 must be brought within three years of violation except that: (a) If plaintiff becomes aware of facts or circumstances reasonably indicating that plaintiff may have claim for relief under this Act, then action must be brought within one year from date of discovery; and (b) if plaintiff was given written notice disclosing violation, then action must be brought within 90 days of delivery of written notice. (815-705/27).

State Securities Act.—Actions for violations of state securities laws must be brought within three years of date of sale of securities except that if violation involves 815-5/12(E)-(J), and purchaser did not and would not with reasonable diligence have known of violation, three year period commences at earlier of: (1) Date of actual knowledge; (2) notice of facts that should lead to knowledge, but in no event can limitation period be extended more than two years beyond initial three year period. (815-5/13[D]).

Two years: Actions for injury to person, or for abduction, seduction, criminal conversation, false imprisonment, malicious prosecution, or for statutory penalty, except actions against defendant arising from Structural Work Act, see subhead Four Years supra; and from first degree murder or Class X felony, and perpetrator is convicted of crime, must be brought within two years after cause of action accrued. However, such action against defendant under Crime Victim's Escrow Account Act must be brought within two years of establishment of account and, victim must register notice of intent to file claim with Treasurer within one year of establishment of account (735-5/13-202, 725-145/4); but see subhead Ten Years supra as to actions for damages, loss of means of support, or loss of parental or in loco parentis relationship arising out of first degree murder or Class X felony; and actions arising under "The Illinois Public Aid Code," "Law Enforcement Officers and Firemen Compensation Act," or "Illinois National Guardsman's and Naval Militiaman's Compensation Act," against State in Claims Court, including personal injury or wrongful death actions (705-505/22). Wrongful death actions (740-180/2); actions to recover for unlawful interest rates, discounts or charges in connection with loans of money from earlier of: (1) Date of last scheduled payment; or (2) date total amount is fully paid (815-205/6); with several exceptions and varying accrual provisions, action brought by party alleging s(he) is child's natural parent must be commenced within two years after child reaches age of majority (18 years) (750-45/8). Effective Jan. 1, 1991, actions by non-minor for damages based on childhood sexual abuse must be brought within two years of date claimant discovers or should have discovered that abuse occurred and injury was caused by abuse. (735-5/13-202.2). Mechanics' lien action must be filed within two years after completion of

LIMITATION OF ACTIONS . . . *continued*

contract or additional work. (770-60/9). Actions to enforce contracts to make will must be commenced within two years after death or, if letters are applied for within two years after death, within time for claims against estate. (735-5/13-221).

Professional Treatment.—Actions for injury or death against physician, dentist, registered nurse or hospital must be brought within two years of date claimant knew or should have known of existence of injury, but no action may be commenced after four years after date act or omission causing injury occurred except as provided in 735-5/13-215 (see subhead Concealment of Cause of Action, infra). (735-5/13-212). Minority of plaintiff: Effective 7/20/87, where action for injury or death from patient care, and person entitled to bring action is under 18 years of age at time action accrues, action must be brought within eight years after date of act or omission causing injury, and in no event may action be brought after person's 22nd birthday, except as provided in 735-5/13-215 (see subhead Concealment of Cause of Action, infra). (PA 85-18, eff. 7/20/87; to be codified at 735-5/13-212[b]). If this statutory revision bars action or there remains less than three years to bring action, person may bring action within three years from effective date of Act (i.e., 7/20/90). (Id.).

Attorney Malpractice.—Effective Jan. 1, 1991, actions for damages against attorney or attorney's employee must be brought within two years of date claimant knew or should have known of injury, but not more than six years after date of act or omission causing injury. (735-5/13-214.3).

Contribution.—Action for contribution among joint tortfeasors may be commenced within two years after payment only where no lawsuit initiated by injured party. Where underlying action has been filed by claimant, no action for contribution or indemnity may be commenced more than two years after party seeking contribution or indemnity has been served with process in underlying action or more than two years from time party, or his privy, knew or reasonably should have known of act or omission giving rise to action for contribution or indemnity whichever is later. However, these rules shall not apply where contribution or indemnification sought from party whose alleged negligence has caused injuries or death by reason of medical malpractice. (735-5/13-204; 105 Ill.2d 191, 473 N.E.2d 939 [1984]; 135 Ill. App.3d 794, 482 N.E.2d 382 [1985]).

Improvements to realty superceded by subsequent enactment, see subhead Four Years, supra.

One year: Actions for slander, libel or publication of matter which violates right of privacy (735-5/13-201); actions for personal injuries against Chicago Transit Authority (70-3605/41); as to actions accruing after Jan. 1, 1996, actions for wrongful death or personal injury against Regional Transportation Authority (70-3615/5.03); actions against local public entity or its employees under Local Governmental Tort Immunity Act (745-10/8-101); actions against school districts (745-25/2) (questioned or invalidated 57 Ill.2d 384, 312 N.E.2d 635); and actions against State arising under "The Illinois Public Aid Code," "Law Enforcement Officers and Firemen Compensation Act," "Crime Victims Compensation Act," or "Illinois National Guardsman's and Naval Militiaman's Compensation Act" (705-505/22); actions under Liquor Control Act ("Dram Shop Act") (235-5/6-21); actions for violation of Sale of Fine Prints Act must be brought within one year of discovery of violation, but no more than three years after sale of print (815-345/8); action to void or revoke consent to adoption must be brought within 12 months of date of consent or surrender (705-50/11); breach of promise or agreement to marry (740-15/6). See topic Actions, subhead Immunity; category Employment, topic Labor Relations, subhead Worker's Compensation Act.

Six Months.—Actions or levies with respect to bulk transfers under Commercial Code must be effected within six months after transferee took possession of goods unless transfer was concealed. If transfer was concealed, action or levy must be within six months of discovery of transfer. (810-5/6-110). Six months limitation applicable only to transferee. (4 Ill. App.3d 881, 280 N.E.2d 266). Actions for violation of Female Employment Act must be brought within six months of alleged violation. (820-110/2). See subhead, Notice of Claims, infra.

See also category Estates and Trusts, topic Wills, subhead Contest.

Three Months (90 days).—Motion to substitute party, after death of party to action that survives, must be filed within 90 days after death is suggested of record or action may be dismissed as to deceased party. (735-5/2-1008).

Notice of Claims.—In certain cases notice of claims prior to expiration of applicable limitation period, must be filed as prerequisite to commencing actions. Although such notice provisions apply to several of actions described in this section, they are not set forth. See topic Actions.

Accrual of Action.—Date action is considered to have accrued, for limitation purposes, depends upon common law or statutes applying to particular action. This section does not, in all instances, describe manner in which accrual date is determined.

New Actions.—Where an action is brought within the time limit and judgment is given for the plaintiff but reversed on appeal, or there is a verdict for the plaintiff and, upon matter alleged in arrest of judgment, the judgment is given against plaintiff, or by U.S. District Court for lack of jurisdiction, or for improper venue plaintiff may bring new action within one year after such termination or reversal or within remaining period of limitation, whichever is greater. No action voluntarily dismissed by plaintiff or for want of prosecution may be filed where time for commencing action has expired. (735-5/13-217).

Actions Unknown at Common Law.—Provision in statute creating a right unknown at common law and limiting the time in which an action thereon may be brought is not a statute of limitation and is not in pari materia with the statute of limitations; bringing suit within the designated time is a condition precedent to assertion of the right (404 Ill. 307, 89 N.E.2d 22; 20 Ill. App.2d 401, 156 N.E.2d 241), e.g., wrongful death, two years unless person entitled to recover is under 18 years, then within two years of such person attaining 18 (740-180/2); action under Dram Shop Act, one year (235-5/6-21); products liability, various limitations (735-5/13-213). Provisions in general statutes of limitation extending time for bringing action in case of death or disability do not apply; however, particular statute creating right of action may expressly provide for extension of limitation period. (92 Ill.2d 1, 440 N.E.2d 42; 20 Ill. App.2d 401, 156 N.E.2d 241). These statutes may make specific provision for extensions of time and should be consulted. However, 735-5/13-217 (see subhead New Actions supra) applies equally to these actions. (51 Ill. App.3d 523, 366 N.E.2d 1068).

Foreign Causes of Action.—Action may not be brought in this state if barred by statute of limitations of state, territory or foreign country where it arose. (735-5/13-210).

Derivative Actions.—Actions for loss of consortium or other actions including actions for medical expenses if minors or persons under legal disability deriving from injury to person of another, except for damages for first degree murder or commission of Class X felony, must be commenced within same period of time as any action that person might have for injury to himself. (735-5/13-203).

Disabilities of Plaintiff.—In case of disability (generally minority, incompetency, imprisonment or other legal disability), unless otherwise provided, time is extended for two years after disability removed. (735-5/13-112, 5/13-211). However, effective 7/20/87, actions against health care professionals subject to statutorily specified tolling provisions where disability involves minority of person at time cause of action accrued. (735-5/13-212[b]; see subhead Two Years, catchline Professional Treatment, supra). Although not otherwise identified in this section, different extension times, after disability is removed, apply to certain of actions described in this section. Particular statutes or rules should be consulted to determine effect of disability upon applicable limitation period. See supra, subhead Actions Unknown at Common Law.

Death of Party.—In case of death of person entitled to bring action, if cause survives, action may be brought by representative within limitations period or within one year from death, whichever is later. If person against whom action may be brought dies within limitations period and cause survives and is not otherwise barred, action may be commenced against his representatives after expiration of limitations period and within six months after letters of office are issued. (735-5/13-209). (See supra, subhead Three Months where party dies after he has previously commenced action on his own behalf.) See supra, subhead Actions Unknown at Common Law.

Defective Products.—In general product liability actions based on any theory or doctrine to recover for injuries or death must be commenced within applicable limitation period for type of injury, but no action may be brought more than 12 years of first sale by seller or within ten years of delivery to initial user whichever occurs first; provided that if injury or death occurs within above 12 or ten year periods, action may be commenced within two years from date claimant knew or should have known of injury, death or property damage but in no event later than eight years after injury, death or property damage. (735-5/13-213).

Absence or Concealment of Defendant.—In general statutes of limitation do not run during absence of potential defendant from state even if both parties were nonresidents (76 Ill.2d 439, 394 N.E.2d 385 [1979]) when cause of action accrued. Limitations period also tolled for time that, after cause of action accrues, potential defendant departs from and resides out of state. (735-5/13-208). By amendment of Oct. 1, 1973 party is not absent from state and statute of limitations runs if he is subject to long-arm jurisdiction statutes (735-5/13-208, 5/13-209, 625-5/10-301) or any other service of process statute. If service of process attempted pursuant to certain specified statutes but not obtained, statute of limitation does not run. (735-5/13-208). Amendment applies only to actions commenced after Oct. 1, 1973. (735-5/13-208).

Concealment of Cause of Action.—If person fraudulently conceals action against himself from person entitled to assert that action then action may be commenced within five years from time potential plaintiff discovered cause of action. (735-5/13-215).

Interruption of Statutory Period.—Statute does not run while action stayed by injunction or statutory prohibition. (735-5/13-216). See supra, subhead Ten Years.

Revival of Barred Claims.—Any payment or new written promise to pay made after full statutory period has run will revive certain barred claims. (735-5/13-206). See supra, subhead Ten Years.

Set-off or Counterclaim.—Defendant may plead set-off or counterclaim otherwise barred by statute of limitations to cause of action owned by plaintiff before defendant's claim was barred. (735-5/13-207).

Contractual Limitations.—Permitted subject to UCC. (810-5/2-718, 5/2-719).

Pleading.—Statute of limitations is an affirmative defense and should be pleaded by one who relies thereon. (735-5/2-613).

Actions Not Specifically Provided For.—See supra, subhead Five Years.

Uniform Commercial Code.—See category Business Regulation and Commerce, topic Commercial Code.

Other Actions.—Limitation periods for actions not addressed in this section may be located in category sections addressing those specific areas of law, e.g., Business Regulation and Commerce, topics Banks and Banking, Bills and Notes, Commercial Code, Sales; Estates and Trusts, topics Trusts, Wills; Mortgages, topics Mortgages of Personal Property, Mortgages of Real Property; Property, topic Real Property; Taxation, topic Taxes, etc.

PARTITION:

Lands, tenements or hereditaments, held in joint tenancy or tenancy in common, whether right or title is derived by purchase, devise or descent, irrespective of claimant's age, may, by one or more of such claimants, be partitioned. (735-5/17-101). Common elements in condominium units may not be partitioned (765-605/8), except in limited circumstances relating to damage or destruction (765-605/14).

Upon complaint for partition, court may determine all questions of conflict over title and may remove all clouds on title. (735-5/17-124).

Jurisdiction and Venue.—Suit must be commenced in circuit court of county in which land or some part thereof is situated. Where premises are situated in two or more counties, the venue may be in either circuit court, but the one first acquiring jurisdiction shall retain sole and exclusive jurisdiction. (735-5/17-101).

See note at head of Digest as to 1998 legislation covered.

See Topical Index in front part of this volume.

IL – 29

PARTITION . . . *continued*

Proceedings.—Action is commenced by verified complaint, and proceedings and practice are same as in other civil cases. (735-5/17-102). Complaint must describe premises and set forth interests of all parties, including tenants for years and life tenants, and all persons entitled to any beneficial interest in premises, and must pray for partition, or if partition would result in manifest prejudice to owners, for sale and distribution of proceeds. (735-5/17-102). Every person having any interest, possessory, contingent or otherwise, who is not plaintiff, must be made defendant. (735-5/17-103). Appropriate allegations regarding unknown persons having interests in property must be stated in complaint. (735-5/17-104). Upon entry of decree of partition declaring right, title and interest of all parties, court must appoint one or three, at its discretion, entirely disinterested commissioners to make partition according to decree. If property is susceptible of division without manifest prejudice to rights of parties, they must make partition thereof. (735-5/17-105 to 5/17-108). Court may decree pecuniary sum or easement to equalize shares in kind. (301 Ill. 191, 133 N.E. 658; 6 Ill.2d 577, 129 N.E.2d 673). If commissioners determine that property cannot be apportioned in kind without manifest prejudice to owners, they must value each individual parcel. (735-5/17-108). Commissioners must report finding to court. (735-5/17-109). Parties in interest may, after decree of partition and before division or sale, voluntarily settle their respective rights and interests so that division or sale becomes unnecessary, whereupon court must discontinue further proceedings, although decree remains in full force and effect respecting rights and interests adjudicated therein. (735-5/17-126). Costs, including reasonable attorney's fee to plaintiff's attorney, must be apportioned so that each party pays his equitable portion thereof; except where good defense to complaint is interposed, in which event parties so defending will recover their costs against plaintiff. (735-5/17-125).

Partition in Kind or Sale.—Property may be sold at public vendue rather than partitioned in kind only when whole or any of premises cannot be divided without manifest prejudice to owners and commissioners so report (735-5/17-116); but no property may be sold except for at least two-thirds of value thereof as fixed by commissioners, although court may order revaluation by other commissioners of those parcels which will not sell for two-thirds or more of value (735-5/17-117).

Report of sale must be filed within ten days by person making such sale pursuant to directions of court, to which exceptions may be filed. Upon confirmation of report person making sale must execute and deliver proper conveyances to purchasers and distribute proceeds of sale to those entitled thereto according to their interests. (735-5/17-118, 17-119).

When appropriate, payment shall be made in accordance with applicable sections of Probate Act relating to small estates. (735-5/17-119). See category Estates and Trusts, topic Executors and Administrators, subhead When Administration Unnecessary. Shares payable to unknown parties are deposited with county treasurer, to be paid out upon order of court. (735-5/17-122).

Homestead.—Homestead in premises may be set off in suit to partition. (735-5/17-112). However, right of homestead cannot be asserted between joint tenants or tenants in common. (735-5/12-901; 74 Ill.2d 27, 383 N.E.2d 973).

Effect on Lien.—Mortgage, attachment, or other liens on the share of a part owner remain in effect only on the part assigned to said part owner. (735-5/17-114).

PLEADING:

Pleading is governed by Civil Practice Law (c. 735) and Supreme Court Rules (Ill. S. Ct.). See topics Actions, Practice, Process; category Debtor and Creditor, topic Garnishment. First pleading by plaintiff is complaint, first pleading by defendant is answer. When answer pleads new matter by defense or counterclaim, plaintiff files reply and further pleadings may be permitted by court. (735-5/2-602, 5/2-608[d]).

General Form of Pleadings.—Pleadings must contain plain, concise statement of cause of action, counterclaim, defense or reply. (735-5/2-603[a]. Notice pleading, which prevails under federal rules, is not sufficient. Pleader must state facts essential to his cause of action. (18 Ill. App.2d 273, 151 N.E.2d 819; 108 Ill. App.2d 251, 247 N.E.2d 434). Each separate claim or cause of action on which separate recovery might be had must be stated in separate count or counterclaim. (735-5/2-603[b], 2-613[a]).

Each count, counterclaim, defense or reply must be separately pleaded, designated and numbered and divided into paragraphs numbered consecutively containing separate allegations. (735-5/2-613[a]).

A pleading must set forth names of all parties for and against whom it seeks relief. (735-5/2-401[c]).

Every pleading, motion or other paper must contain signature and address of attorney or of party if not represented by counsel. No verification or affidavit required unless by rule or statute. Signature constitutes certification of knowledge of contents and good faith assertion of law and facts. If pleading, motion or other paper is signed in violation of this section, court shall impose upon signer appropriate sanction. (Ill. S. Ct. 137).

General issues are not permitted. Every answer and subsequent pleading must contain explicit admissions or denials. Allegations, except of damages, not explicitly denied, are admitted unless pleader states on affidavit that he has no knowledge sufficient to form a belief, or unless he has had no opportunity to deny. An issue as to amount of damages only may be raised by so stating. (735-5/2-610).

Parties may plead as many causes of action, counterclaims, defenses, and matters in reply or rejoinder as they may have, each separately designated and numbered. When in doubt as to which of two or more statements of fact is true, parties may state them in the alternative or hypothetically in same or different counts or defenses. A bad alternative does not affect a good one. (735-5/2-613[a], [b]).

All defenses, whether to jurisdiction of subject matter, in abatement, or in bar, may be pleaded together, without waiving any defense so pleaded, but court may order defenses to subject matter jurisdiction or in abatement to be tried first. (735-5/2-613[c]). However, to contest personal jurisdiction, special appearance must be used. See topic Practice, subhead Appearance. Answer containing only defenses to subject matter jurisdiction or in abatement does not constitute admission of facts alleged in complaint, counterclaim or third party complaint. (735-5/2-613[c]). Facts constituting affirmative defense or defense which if not expressly stated would be likely to take opposite party by surprise, must be plainly set forth. (735-5/2-613[d]).

Subject to rules, plaintiff may join any cause of action against any defendant; defendant may answer with any cross demand whatever, designated as counterclaim. Court may, in its discretion, order separate trial of any action, counterclaim or third-party claim. Legal and equitable issues may be tried together if no jury is used. (735-5/2-614).

Medical Malpractice.—Special provisions for pleading medical malpractice actions. (735-5/2-622).

Frivolous Claims.—All pleadings and claims may be brought only after reasonable inquiry shows claim is well grounded in fact and is warranted by existing law or good-faith argument for extension, modification, or reversal of existing law. Claims cannot be brought for any improper purpose such as harassment, delay or to needlessly increase cost of litigation. (Ill. S. Ct. 137). Signature of attorney or party on any pleading filed with court serves as certification that above is true. (Ill. S. Ct. 137). If pleading is signed in violation of this section, court may impose sanctions on attorney and/or client. Sanctions may include, but are not limited to, reasonable attorneys' fees as result of filing pleading. (Ill. S. Ct. 137).

Counterclaim or Set-off.—Any demand by one or more defendants against one or more plaintiffs, or one or more co-defendants, whether set-off, recoupment or otherwise, in tort or contract, for liquidated or unliquidated damages, or for other relief, may be pleaded in separate part of answer as counterclaim in same manner and with same particularity as complaint. (735-5/2-608). Counterclaims under Illinois law are permissive and not compulsory. However, counterclaims seeking relief under Illinois Contribution Act (740-100/5) must be asserted in injured party's action or will be barred (Lane v. Leifheit, 105 Ill.2d 191 [1984]).

Prayers for Relief.—Every complaint and counterclaim must contain specific prayer for relief which, whether based on one or more counts, may be asked in alternative. In personal injury actions, no ad damnum may be pleaded except to minimum extent necessary to comply with circuit rules of assignment. Relief demanded but not sustained by pleading may be objected to by motion or by answering pleading. Except in case of default, prayer for relief does not limit relief obtainable, but where other relief is sought court must by proper orders on just terms protect adverse party from prejudice by surprise. In case of default, if relief beyond that prayed is sought, notice must be given to defaulted party as provided by rule. (735-5/2-604).

Punitive Damages.—For causes of action accruing after Nov. 25, 1986, no complaint shall contain prayer seeking punitive damages in bodily injury or property damage actions based on negligence or product liability based on any theory or doctrine. Plaintiff may amend complaint to add punitive damage prayer only upon pretrial motion and hearing establishing reasonable likelihood of proof of facts at trial supporting punitive damages award. (735-5/2-604.1). No punitive or exemplary damages are allowed in cases alleging medical or legal malpractice (735-5/2-1115) or malicious prosecution of medical malpractice claims (735-5/2-109). See also topic Damages, subhead Limitations on Recovery.

Pleadings must be liberally construed to do substantial justice. (735-5/2-603[c]).

Demurrer.—Not in use. (735-5/2-615).

Amendments.—At any time before final judgment, amendments may be allowed on just and reasonable terms, introducing any party who ought to have been joined, discontinuing as to any plaintiff or defendant, changing cause of action or defense, or adding new causes of action or defenses, and in any matter either of form or substance in any process, pleading, bill of particulars, or proceedings, which may enable plaintiff to sustain claim or defendant to make defense or establish cross-demand. (735-5/2-616[a]).

On motion directed to pleadings or for summary judgment or upon trial, amendments may be allowed on just and reasonable terms to change remedy sought. (735-5/2-617).

For causes of action accruing after Nov. 25, 1986, complaints for bodily injury or property damage, or based on negligence or product liability based on any theory or doctrine, can be amended to seek punitive damages only upon motion and after hearing where plaintiff establishes reasonable likelihood of proving facts at trial sufficient to support award of punitive damages. (735-5/2-604.1).

For further particulars regarding amendment see 735-5/2-616(b)(d), 5/2-617.

Supplemental pleadings setting up matters arising after original pleadings were filed, may be filed within a reasonable time by leave of court. (735-5/2-609).

Bills of Particulars.—Where allegations are wanting in details, pleader must file and serve copy of bill of particulars on being served with notice demanding same and pointing out specifically defects complained of or details desired. A copy of notice must be filed. Pleader shall have 28 days to file and serve bill of particulars, and party who requested bill shall have 28 days to plead after being served with bill. On unreasonable neglect to furnish, or if bill of particulars furnished is insufficient, court may strike pleading, allow further time or require more particular bill. Items of indebtedness in an action on a contract stated in bill of particulars and verified by oath are admitted except insofar as opposite party files affidavit specifically denying same and stating facts as to each item denied, unless such affidavit is excused by court. Party may move court to deny or modify demand for bill of particulars. (735-5/2-607).

Verification.—Any pleading, although not required to be sworn to, may be verified by any person having knowledge, in which event all subsequent pleadings must be verified unless verification is excused by court. Verified allegations do not constitute evidence except by way of admission. An allegation of the execution or assignment of any written instrument is deemed admitted unless denied by verified pleading or unless latter is excused by court. (735-5/2-605). Verification by certification under penalty of perjury has same effect as verification under oath. (735-5/1-109).

Exhibits.—If claim or defense is founded upon written instrument, a copy thereof, or so much of same as is relevant, must be attached to pleading as exhibit or recited therein unless pleader attaches to his pleading affidavit stating facts showing that instrument is not accessible to him. In either case exhibit constitutes part of pleading for all purposes. (735-5/2-606).

See note at head of Digest as to 1998 legislation covered.

See Topical Index in front part of this volume.

IL – 30

PLEADING . . . *continued*

Motions are used in place of demurrers and must point out specifically defects complained of and ask for appropriate relief. Court may make appropriate orders as to pleading over or amending. Any party may seasonably move for judgment on the pleadings. (735-5/2-615). Motions for involuntary dismissal based on certain defects or defenses also are governed by 735-5/2-619 and may require support by affidavit if defects or defenses do not appear on face of pleading attached.

Service.—Plaintiff must furnish copies of the complaint, which must be attached to every copy of a summons used in making service. (Ill. S. Ct. 104[a]). Proper service of process is governed by 735-5/2-201 through 735-5/2-213.

Pleadings subsequent to the complaint, written motions and other papers must be filed with a certificate of counsel or other proof that copies thereof have been served on all parties who have appeared. (Ill. S. Ct. 104[b]).

Failure to comply with the foregoing in no way impairs the jurisdiction of the court but the aggrieved party may obtain a copy of any pleading from the clerk and the court must order the offending party to reimburse the aggrieved party for the expense thereof. (Ill. S. Ct. 104[d]).

Time for Filing.—Filing complaint commences action. (735-5/2-201[a]). Answer (or motion to dismiss) must be filed 30 days after service of summons except in forcible detainer actions, actions for recovery of personal property, and actions for money not in excess of $15,000. (Ill. S. Ct. 101 [b, d]). In latter case, defendant must appear at a date specified in summons, not less than 21 or more than 40 days after issuance of summons (Ill. S. Ct. 101 [b][1]); if appearance is not by answer or motion, defendant has ten days after date of appearance to file answer or motion (Ill. S. Ct. 181[b][1]). In forcible detainer actions and actions for recovery of personal property, defendant must appear at date specified in summons, not less than seven or more than 40 days after issuance of summons (Ill. S. Ct. 101[b][2]); defendant, unless required by court, need not appear by filing answer and, when he does not, plaintiff's allegations are deemed denied and any defense may be proved as though specifically pleaded (Ill. S. Ct. 181[b][2]).

Replies to answers, responses to counterclaims and motions attacking pleadings other than complaints must be filed within 21 days after last day allowed for filing of answer, counterclaim or pleading. (Ill. S. Ct. 182). Subsequent pleadings shall be filed as court may order. (Ill. S. Ct. 182[a]).

Special provision is made for small claims (actions for money not in excess of $2,500). (Ill. S. Ct. 281 et seq.).

See also topic Practice, subhead Appearance.

Small Claims.—See category Courts and Legislature, topic Courts.

PRACTICE:

New Illinois Code of Civil Procedure has been adopted effective July 1, 1982. (c. 110). Practice is governed by The Code and Supreme Court Rules (Ill. S. Ct.) which specify trial and appellate practice.

See also topics Actions, Appeal and Error, Depositions and Discovery, Injunctions, Judgments, Pleading, Process, Venue; category Debtor and Creditor, topics Attachment, Executions, Garnishment.

Appearance.—Special appearance may be made prior to filing any other pleading or motion, for purpose of objecting to jurisdiction of court over person of defendant, as to entire proceeding or any cause of action involved therein. Every other appearance prior to judgment is a general appearance. (735-5/2-301[a]).

If objection to jurisdiction is overruled and defendant takes part in further proceedings he waives the objection unless it is on ground that he is not amenable to process issued by a court of Illinois. (735-5/2-301[c]).

In actions for forcible detainer or for recovery of possession of tangible personal property, defendant must appear at date specified in summons not less than seven or more than 40 days after issuance of summons. (Ill. S. Ct. 101[b][2]). In actions for money not in excess of $15,000 answer must be filed at date specified in summons not less than 21 or more than 40 days after issuance of summons. (Ill. S. Ct. 101[b][1]). In other actions for money, appearance must be filed within 30 days after service of summons, exclusive of day of service. (Ill. S. Ct. 101[d]). 30 day period is computed from day copy of summons is left with person designated by law and not from day copy is mailed, in case mailing is also required. (Ill. S. Ct. 181[a]).

Special provision is made for small claims (actions for money not in excess of $2,500). (Ill. S. Ct. 281 et seq.).

Discovery.—May be had by deposition, interrogatories to parties, inspection of documents, tangible things or premises, physical examination, or mental examination or by admissions of facts obtained from opposite party. (Ill. S. Ct. 201 to 219). Request procedure permits discovery of documents or tangible things and entry on real estate, in control of party, without court order. (Ill. S. Ct. 214). Except by leave of court, no discovery proceedings are permitted in small claims actions (not in excess of $2,500) (Ill. S. Ct. 287) or in suits for violations of municipal ordinances where penalty is fine only (Ill. S. Ct. 201). In all cases, plaintiff may initiate discovery upon nonparty who is believed to have information essential to determine who should be named as additional defendants. Fictitious defendants may not be named in complaint in order to designate respondents in discovery. (735-5/2-402). See topic Depositions and Discovery.

Demand for Admission of Facts or Genuineness of Documents.—Each matter of which admission is requested is admitted unless opposing party, within 28 days after service of notice to admit, files sworn statement denying specifically matters of which admission is requested or setting forth reasons he cannot admit or deny those matters or files written objections on ground that matter is privileged or irrelevant or that request is otherwise improper. (Ill. S. Ct. 216).

Direct Actions Against Insurer.—See category Insurance, topic Insurance Companies.

Interrogatories to Parties.—A party may direct written interrogatories to any other party. The attorney directing interrogatories has the duty to restrict them to the subject matter of the particular case, avoid undue detail and avoid imposing unnecessary burdens and expenses on the answering party. The party to whom the interrogatory is directed has 28 days after service to file a sworn answer or an objection. Where an answer may be obtained from documents in possession or control of party on whom interrogatory was served, affording opportunity for inspection and copying of pertinent documents is sufficient answer. If a party makes an answer that is complete when made, he has no duty to supplement answer to include information thereafter received, unless requested to do so by a timely supplemental interrogatory. (Ill. S. Ct. 213). Except by leave of court, interrogatories are not permitted in small claims actions (not in excess of $2,500) (Ill. S. Ct. 287) or in suits for violations of municipal ordinances where penalty is fine only (Ill. S. Ct. 201).

Trial by Jury in Civil Actions.—A plaintiff desirous of a trial by jury must file demand with clerk at time action is commenced. Defendant must file demand no later than date of filing of answer. (735-5/2-1105[a]). If court determines, in equitable action, that party is entitled to jury, plaintiff within three days from entry of order or defendant within six days may file demand for jury. If plaintiff or co-defendant files jury demand and thereafter waives jury any defendant may promptly demand jury. (735-5/2-1105[a]). All jury cases where claim for damages does not exceed $15,000 shall be tried by jury of six, unless either party demands jury of 12. (735-5/2-1105[b]).

Default Judgment.—Additional relief may be sought against defaulted party by serving notice of amended relief by personal service, certified or registered mail or by publication where provided for. (Ill. S. Ct. 105).

Small Claims.—See category Courts and Legislature, topic Courts.

PROCESS:

General Requisites.—Summons is issued by clerk of court under seal of court, attested and signed in name of clerk of court, dated on day issued. Its caption must contain names of all parties plaintiff and defendant, together with number of cause. It must be directed to each defendant, in most cases advising that he is summoned to answer complaint or otherwise file appearance within 30 days after service, exclusive of day of service. In action for money judgment not in excess of $15,000, exclusive of interest and costs, summons shall require each defendant to appear on day specified in summons not less than 21 nor more than 40 days after issuance. In any action for forcible detainer or recovery of possession of tangible personal property, summons shall require each defendant to appear on day specified in summons not less than seven or more than 40 days after issuance. Summons must bear address and telephone number of plaintiff or his attorney and if service or notices of motion or filings by facsimile transmission will be accepted, telephone number of facsimile machine of plaintiff or his attorney. [735-5/13-101 to 13-224] (Ill. S. Ct. 101; 110-13). Copy of complaint must be attached to copy of summons used in making service. (Ill. S. Ct. 104). Person making service must indorse date of service on copy served. (Ill. S. Ct. 102[c]). See topics Actions; Pleading.

Who May Serve.—Summons is served by sheriff, or if he be disqualified, by coroner. In counties with fewer than 1,000,000 people, any licensed private detective may serve process. Sheriff of county with population less than 1,000,000 may employ civilian personnel to serve process. Court may, upon motion, permit service by some private person over age of 18 if not party to action. It is not necessary that service be made by sheriff or coroner of county in which service is made. If served or sought to be served by sheriff or coroner he must endorse his return thereon and if by private person return shall be by affidavit. Any person who refuses or neglects to make return may be held for contempt. (735-5/2-202). In countries with population of 3,000,000 or more members of housing authority police force may serve process for forcible entry and detainer actions by housing authority and may execute orders of possession for that housing authority. (735-5/2-202[e]).

Summons returnable on a day certain may not be served later than three days before day for appearance. (Ill. S. Ct. 102[b]).

Summons requiring defendant to appear within 30 days after service may not be served later than 30 days after its date. (Ill. S. Ct. 102[b]).

Waiver of Service.—Plaintiff may request that defendant waive service by providing notice of action. Notice and request must be: (1) addressed to defendant or representative of defendant; (2) sent via first class mail or other equally reliable means; (3) contain copy of complaint; (4) identify consequences of compliance and failure to comply; (5) allow at least 30 days, if mailed in U.S., or 60 days if mailed outside of U.S., in which to respond to request for waiver; and (6) provide prepaid means of compliance in writing. (735-5/2-213).

Defendant who waives service is not required to appear or answer complaint until 60 days from date on which request was sent (notices and requests sent outside U.S. are granted 90 days from date request was sent). (735-5/2-213). Upon filing waiver of service, action shall then proceed as if summons and complaint had been served. If defendant does not return waiver, plaintiff must serve summons and complaint as otherwise provided. (735-5/2-213).

Personal Service on Individual.—Except as otherwise expressly provided, service of summons upon individual defendant must be made: (a) By leaving copy thereof with defendant personally, or (b) by leaving copy at his usual place of abode with some person of family of age of 13 years or upwards or person residing there and informing that person of contents thereof, provided officer or other person making service shall also send copy of summons in sealed envelope with postage fully prepaid addressed to defendant at his usual place of abode. Certificate of officer or affidavit of person that he has sent copy is evidence he has done so. (735-5/2-203).

Service in Small Claims Cases.—Special provision is made for service by certified or registered mail in small claims (civil actions based on tort or contract for money not in excess of $2,500, exclusive of interest and costs) unless otherwise provided by circuit court rule. (Ill. S. Ct. 284).

Service on Partnership.—Partnership sued in its firm name may be served by leaving copy of the process with any partner personally or with any agent of partnership found anywhere in state. A partnership sued in its firm name may also be notified by publication and mail and with like manner and like effect as individuals. (735-5/2-205[a]). When personal judgment is sought against partner for partnership liability partner may be served: (1) In any manner provided for service on individuals, or (2) by leaving copy of summons for him with any other partner and mailing copy of summons

---

See note at head of Digest as to 1998 legislation covered.

See Topical Index in front part of this volume.

PROCESS . . . *continued*
in sealed envelope with postage prepaid addressed to partner against whom judgment is sought at his usual place of abode as shown by affidavit filed in cause. Service on nonresident partner against whom personal judgment is sought may be made by leaving copy with any other partner and mailing copy as provided herein only if cause of action sued on is partnership liability arising out of transaction of business within state. (735-5/2-205[b]).

Service on Private Corporations.—Private corporation may be served by leaving copy of process with its registered agent or any officer or agent of corporation found anywhere in state or in any other manner now or hereafter permitted by law. Private corporation may also be notified by publication and mail in like manner and in like effect as for individuals. (735-5/2-204).

A corporation must have registered agent on whom process may be served. (805-5/5.05). If corporation does not have registered agent, or if agent cannot be found, service can be made upon Secretary of State. (805-5/5.25).

Service on Voluntary Unincorporated Associations.—Voluntary unincorporated association sued in own name may be sued by leaving copy of process with any officer of association or at office of association with any agent of association. (735-5/2-205.1). Voluntary unincorporated association, sued in its own name may also be notified by publication and mail in like manner, and with like effect as individuals. (735-5/2-205.1).

Service on Persons Doing Business Under Assumed Name.—Persons doing business under an assumed name who have failed to register names of true owners as required under Assumed Name Act (805-405/1) may be served by leaving copy of summons with any agent of business and thereafter publishing notice as provided (735-5/2-205[c]). See also topic Judgments, subhead Lien.

Personal Service on Public, Municipal, Governmental and Quasi-municipal Corporation.—May be served by leaving copy of summons with chairman of board or clerk of a county, mayor or clerk of a city, president of board or clerk of village, supervisor or clerk of a town, and president or clerk or other officer corresponding thereto in case of other such corporations. (735-5/2-211).

Personal Service on Trustee of Corporation or Any Receiver.—Such party may be served in any manner provided for service on individuals or corporations as is appropriate or by leaving a copy with an agent in employ of trustee or receiver anywhere in state. (735-5/2-212).

Personal Service Outside of State.—Personal service of summons may be made upon any party outside Illinois. If upon a citizen or resident of Illinois or upon person who has submitted to jurisdiction of the courts of Illinois it has force and effect of personal service of summons within Illinois; otherwise it has force and effect of service by publication. (735-5/2-208[a]). Service of summons must be made in like manner as service within Illinois by any person over 18 years of age not party to action. No court order is required. Affidavit of service must be filed stating time, manner and place of service and court may consider affidavit or other competent proof in determining if service has been properly made. (735-5/2-208[b]). No default may be entered until expiration of at least 30 days after service. Default judgment rendered on such service may be set aside only on showing which would be timely and sufficient to set aside a default judgment rendered on personal service within Illinois. (735-5/2-208[c]).

Service of Process on Nonresidents for Collection of State Taxes.—Any nonresident acting as a supplier, retailer or serviceman and maintaining a place of business in Illinois as defined in statutes, and any resident who incurs use tax liability and then leaves Illinois, may be served for purposes of Illinois Revenue Act by leaving certified copy of process or notice, at least 15 days before return day, with Secretary of State and by sending nonresident at his last known address a like certified copy by registered or certified mail. (35-105/12a, 110/13, 115/13).

Service on Unauthorized Insurance Companies.—See category Insurance, topic Insurance Companies.

Service by Mail.—Such service is made only in addition to whatever mode of service is used when defendant is not served personally except in small claims and actions to review final administrative decisions under the Administrative Review Law. (735-5/3-105).

Substituted Service.—This is covered under the above personal service classifications.

Actions Arising from Motor Vehicle Accidents.—See category Transportation, topic Motor Vehicles.

Long Arm Statute.—Any person whether or not a citizen or resident of Illinois, who, in person or through an agent does any of acts hereinafter enumerated, thereby submits such person, and, if an individual, his or her personal representative, to jurisdiction of the courts of this state as to any cause of action arising from doing of any of such acts: (1) Transaction of any business within Illinois; (2) commission of tortious act within Illinois; (3) ownership, use or possession of any real estate situated in Illinois; (4) contracting to insure any person, property or risk located within Illinois at time of contracting; (5) with respect to actions of dissolution of marriage, declaration of invalidity of marriage, and legal separation, maintenance in Illinois of matrimonial domicile at time this cause of action arose or commission in Illinois of any acts giving rise to cause of action; (6) with respect to actions brought under Illinois Parentage Act of 1984, as now of hereinafter amended, performance of act of sexual intercourse within Illinois during possible period of conception; (7) making or performance of any contract or promise substantially connected with Illinois; (8) performance of sexual intercourse within Illinois which is claimed to have resulted in conception of child who resides in Illinois; (9) failure to support child, spouse or former spouse who continued to reside in Illinois since person either formally resided with them in Illinois or directed them to reside in Illinois; (10) acquisition of ownership, possession or control of any asset or thing of value present within Illinois when ownership, possession or control was acquired; (11) breach of any fiduciary duty within Illinois; (12) performance of duties as director or officer of corporation organized under laws of Illinois or having principal place of business within Illinois; (13) ownership of interest in any trust administrated within Illinois; or (14) exercise of powers granted under authority of Illinois as fiduciary. (735-5/2-209[a]). Court may exercise jurisdiction in any action arising within or without Illinois against any person who: (1) Is natural person present within Illinois when served; (2) is natural person domiciled or resident within Illinois when cause of action arose, action was commenced, or process was served; (3) is corporation organized under laws of Illinois; or (4) is natural person or corporation doing business within Illinois. (735-5/2-209[b]). Court may also exercise jurisdiction on any other basis now or hereinafter provided by Illinois Constitution and Constitution of U.S. (735-5/2-209[c]). Service of process upon any person who is subject to jurisdiction of courts of Illinois, as above provided, may be made by personally serving summons upon defendant outside Illinois, with same force and effect as though summons had been personally served within Illinois. (735-5/2-209[d]). Service of process on nonresident in action based on product liability may be made by service of summons upon Secretary of State. Said summons shall be accompanied by copy of complaint, $5 fee, affidavit stating defendant's last known address and certificate verifying that copy of summons and complaint was mailed to defendant at such address. (735-5/2-209[e]). However, only causes of action arising from acts enumerated above may be asserted against defendant in action in which jurisdiction over him is based upon these provisions. (735-5/2-209[f]). Above in no way limits or affects right to serve process in any other manner now or hereafter provided by law. (735-5/2-209[g]). If person is engaged in Illinois in conduct which violates Illinois Antitrust Act, he is deemed to have submitted to jurisdiction of Illinois courts and may be personally served outside Illinois. (740-10/7.1).

Service by Publication.—Whenever, in any action affecting property or status within jurisdiction of court, including actions for specific performance, reformation or rescission of a contract for conveyance of land, or in action to revive judgment or decree, plaintiff or his attorney shall file, at office of clerk of court where action is pending, affidavit showing that defendant resides or has gone out of state, or on due inquiry cannot be found or is concealed within this state, so that process cannot be served on him, and stating residence, if known, or that on diligent inquiry his place of residence cannot be ascertained, clerk must cause publication to be made in newspaper published in county where suit is pending, or if there be none in newspaper in adjoining county having circulation in county where suit is pending, containing notice of pendency of suit, title of court, title of case showing first named plaintiff and defendant, number of case, names of parties to be served by publication, date on or after which default may be entered, and clerk must also within ten days of first publication mail copies to defendants whose residences are stated in affidavit. (735-5/2-206[a]). In any action brought by government for demolition, repair or enclosure of dangerous or unsafe, uncompleted, or abandoned building, notice by publication may be started while attempts are being made to locate defendant for personal service. (735-5/2-206[b]). Such published notice may be given any time after commencement of action, and must be published at least once a week for three successive weeks. No default or other proceeding may be taken against defendant not served with summons or copy of complaint unless first publication is at least 30 days prior to time when such default is sought to be taken. (735-5/2-207).

Affidavit in support of service by publication may be combined with that for unknown parties. (735-5/2-414).

In Cook County, such publication must be made in a newspaper published in a township in said county where it appears by affidavit that (1) none of defendants reside in City of Chicago, (2) one or more defendants reside in a township or townships of Cook County, and (3) a newspaper is published in said township or townships.

Proof of Service.—Where officer has sent a copy of summons by mail, his certificate that he has complied with statute is evidence that he did so. (735-5-5/2-203[b], 5/2-206). In other cases of service, affidavit of server filed with court stating manner of service constitutes evidence thereof. (735-5/2-208). Person making service must make return by filing proof of service immediately after service on all defendants has been had, and in any event: (a) Not less than three days before specific return day specified in summons, or (b) in other cases, immediately after last day fixed for service. Failure of server to return summons or file proof of service does not invalidate summons or service thereof, if accomplished. (Ill. S. Ct. 102[d]). Mail service of subpoena on witness or deponent proved prima facie by return receipt showing delivery by certified or registered mail at least seven days before date appearance required and affidavit showing mailing prepaid, addressed to witness or deponent, restricted delivery, return receipt requested, with check or money order for fee and mileage enclosed. (Ill. S. Ct. 204, 237).

Nonresident Motorist.—See category Transportation, topic Motor Vehicles.

Dismissal for Lack of Diligence.—Defendant may move for, or court on own motion may order, dismissal if plaintiff fails to exercise reasonable diligence to obtain service. If dismissal is prior to applicable statute of limitations, it is without prejudice. If after running of applicable statute, dismissal is with prejudice. (Ill. S. Ct. 103[b]).

REPLEVIN:

Right to Maintain.—Person entitled to possession or owner of chattels may bring replevin for wrongful taking or detaining, but not to recover chattels taken under execution or attachment, unless such goods are exempt from seizure. (735-5/19-101 to 5/19-102).

Cook County.—By local rule Cook County court clerk may not issue orders for replevin except upon court order. (General Order 6.4).

Venue provisions as to other civil cases (see topic Venue) apply, but action also may be brought in county where goods, or a part thereof, are found. (735-5/19-103). Order for replevin may also be directed to other counties, upon request of plaintiff. (735-5/19-110).

Commencement of Action.—Action is commenced by filing a verified complaint describing property, stating that plaintiff is owner or entitled to possession of such property, that property has been wrongfully detained by defendant, and that property has not been taken for any tax, assessment, or fine levied by law of this state against property or against plaintiff individually, nor seized under any lawful process, nor held

See note at head of Digest as to 1998 legislation covered.

See Topical Index in front part of this volume.

IL – 32

REPLEVIN . . . *continued*
under any order for replevin against plaintiff. (735-5/19-104). Answer or appearance must be made as in other civil cases. (735-5/19-119).

Notice and Waiver.—Defendant shall be given five days written notice of hearing in manner required by Supreme Court Rule 72 to contest entry of order for replevin. No order may issue nor property be seized prior to such notice and hearing, except as provided in 735-5/19-106 (see subhead Hearing, infra). Right to notice and hearing as to any particular property may not be waived by any consumer. Consumer is defined as individual who obtained possession of property for personal, family, household, or agricultural purposes. Any waiver of notice and hearing must be in writing and must be given voluntarily, intelligently, and knowingly. (735-5/19-105). Notice to defendant is not required if plaintiff establishes and court finds as matter of record and supported by evidence that summary seizure of property is necessary to protect plaintiff from immediate impending harm resulting from imminent destruction or concealment of disputed property, imminent removal from state of property (taking into consideration availability of judicial remedies in event of such removal), perishable nature of property, imminent sale, transfer or assignment to extent such is fraudulent or in derogation of plaintiff's rights in property, or to recover property from defendant who has obtained possession by theft. If court determines at ex parte hearing that notice is not required or waiver is in accordance with law, it shall order hearing as soon as practicable on issuance of order for replevin. (735-5/19-106).

Hearing.—Court shall review plaintiff's claim to possession at hearing on issuance of order for replevin, which may be pursuant to notice under 735-5/19-105 or ex parte pursuant to finding under 735-5/19-106. Court shall issue order for replevin if plaintiff establishes prima facie case of superior right to possession and also demonstrates probability that he will ultimately prevail on underlying claim to possession. (735-5/19-107).

Bond.—Prior to service of order for replevin, plaintiff must give secured bond, to sheriff or other officer, for double value of property to be replevied. (735-5/19-112). Officer serving order must deliver property replevied to plaintiff immediately, unless, before actual delivery to plaintiff, defendant gives forthcoming bond and security approved by such officer in amount double value of property. (735-5/19-116).

Proceedings.—If the property, or any part, is not found by or delivered to officer, and defendant is summoned or enters his appearance, plaintiff may proceed as in action for wrongful taking and detention of such unfound or undelivered property. If his action is sustained, he is entitled to judgment for value of his interest therein and damages for wrongful taking and detention. (735-5/19-120).

Claims of Third Persons.—Any person other than defendant claiming property replevied, may intervene, verifying petition by affidavit; and if judgment is rendered for such claimant he must receive his costs, and if he is found entitled to immediate possession, the property must be ordered delivered to him. If judgment is for plaintiff, he recovers costs from claimant. Nonresident claimant must file security for costs. (735-5/19-124).

Judgment or Order.—If judgment is for plaintiff he recovers damages for wrongful detention. (735-5/19-125). If judgment is for defendant, he recovers damages for use of property from time it was taken until its return, less any time in which plaintiff was entitled to possession; if property was held by defendant for payment of money, defendant recovers either amount for which such property was rightfully held, with proper damages, or property itself, if it was delivered to plaintiff. (735-5/19-123).

Amendment of Pleadings.—Where relief is sought under this Act and court determines that plaintiff has pleaded or established facts entitling him to relief but that he has sought wrong remedy, it shall permit pleadings to be amended and grant relief to which plaintiff is entitled on amended pleadings or upon evidence. In considering whether a proposed amendment is just and reasonable, court shall consider right of defendant to assert additional defenses, to demand a trial by jury, to plead a counter-claim or third party complaint, and to order plaintiff to take additional steps which were not required under pleadings as previously filed. (735-5/19-122).

SEQUESTRATION:

See category Debtor and Creditor, topics Attachment, Executions, Garnishment, and Receivers.

Insurance holding companies, sequestration of voting securities for wrongful acquisition. (215-5/131.23).

SERVICE:

See topic Process.

STAY OF EXECUTION:

See topic Appeal and Error; category Debtor and Creditor, topic Executions.

SUBMISSION OF CONTROVERSY:

No statutory provision for submission directly to court. As to submission to arbitrators, see category Dispute Resolution, topic Arbitration and Award.

VENUE:

Every civil action must be commenced (a) in county or residence of any defendant who is joined in good faith and with probable cause for purpose of obtaining judgment against him and not solely to fix venue in that county, or (b) in county in which transaction or some part thereof occurred out of which cause of action arose, with certain exceptions. If all defendants are nonresidents of State, action may be commenced in any county. If corporate limits of city, village or town extend into more than one county, venue of action or proceeding by such municipality to enforce any fine, imprisonment, penalty or forfeiture for violation of any law of municipality regardless of county in which violation occurred may be venued in appropriate court in county where municipal clerk's office is located, or in any county in which at least 35% of territory within municipality's corporate limits is located. (735-5/2-101).

Actions Against Private Corporations and Partnerships.—Residence for venue purposes of private corporation, railroad or bridge corporation or foreign corporation authorized to do business in Illinois is county in which corporation has registered office or other office or is doing business. Partnership sued in firm name is resident of county in which any partner resides or firm has office or is doing business; if no partners are residents, partnership is nonresident. (735-5/2-102). Action may be brought against insurance company incorporated under law of this state or doing business in this state in any county where plaintiff or one of plaintiffs resides. (735-5/2-103).

Actions Against Voluntary Unincorporated Associations.—Residence for venue purposes of voluntary unincorporated association is any county in which association has office, or, if on due inquiry no office found, in which any officer resides. If association has no member or office within state, it is deemed nonresident of state. (735-5/2-102).

Actions Against Public or Quasi-Public Corporations.—Action against public, municipal, governmental or quasi-municipal corporation must be brought in county in which its principal office is located, or in county in which transaction or some part thereof occurred out of which cause of action arose. Action to recover damages to real estate overflowed or otherwise damaged by reason of act of such corporation may be brought in county where such real estate is situated or in county where corporation is located, at option of plaintiff. (735-5/2-103).

Actions By or Against Counties.—Action, local or transitory, against a county may be brought in circuit court in said county; action, local or transitory, by a county may be brought in county where defendant resides. (55-5/1-6001).

Actions for Libel.—Action against owner, publisher, editor, author or printer of a newspaper or magazine of general circulation for libel contained therein must be commenced in county in which defendant resides or has his principal office or in which article was composed or printed, except that when defendant resides or article was printed outside of state, action may be commenced in any county in which libel was circulated or published. (735-5/2-103).

Administrative Agency Review.—Except where prescribed expressly by administrative procedure statute, action to review final administrative decisions may be brought in circuit court in county in which administrative proceeding was held, or subject matter situated, or transaction giving rise to proceeding occurred. (735-5/3-104).

Real Actions.—Action to quiet title to real estate, to partition or recover possession thereof or to foreclose mortgage or other lien must be brought in county where real estate or some part of it is situated. (735-5/2-103).

Confession of Judgment.—See topic Judgments.

Local Actions.—Any action made local by statute must be brought in county designated in such statute. (735-5/2-103).

Defendants in Different Counties.—When defendants reside in different counties and venue is based on residence, overruling of nonresident defendant's motion to transfer is not ground for reversal, if after it is overruled moving defendant proceeds to trial on merits, unless motion is renewed at close of all evidence and it then appears from record that defendant was joined in bad faith solely for purpose of fixing venue. (735-5/2-105).

Place of Trial.—All actions must be tried in county in which instituted except as otherwise provided by law. (735-5/2-108).

Effect of Wrong Venue.—No order, judgment or decree is deemed void for want of jurisdiction because rendered in the wrong venue (735-5/2-104), except judgment by confession rendered in county in which obligation was not executed, no defendant resides and no property of any defendant is located (735-5/2-1301[c]).

Substitution of judge in civil cases as matter of right once without cause upon motion before trial or hearing begins and before ruling on any substantial issue (735-5/2-1001[a][2]); and when judge is party, interested in action, material witness or is counsel to party, or related to such counsel (735-5/2-1001) for cause by verified petition setting forth specific cause for substitution and upon hearing by judge other than judge named in petition (735-5/2-1001[a][3]); and in contempt proceedings by defendant who fears he will not receive fair trial because defendant attacked character or conduct of judge otherwise than in open court, on verified petition filed before trial of contempt proceeding (735-5/2-1001[a][4]).

Change of venue in any civil action when court determines any party may not receive fair trial in court where action is pending because inhabitants of that county are prejudiced against party, party's attorney or adverse party has undue influence over minds of inhabitants. (735-5/1001.5). Application for change of venue shall be by verified petition setting forth facts and supported by affidavits of at least two other reputable persons residing in county. Adverse party may controvert petition by counter-affidavits. Petition must be presented before trial or hearing begins and before judge has ruled on any substantial matter. However, if ground for change of venue occurs thereafter, petition may be presented based upon that ground (735-5/2-1001.5[c]). When change of venue is granted, it shall be to convenient county to which there is no valid objection (735-5/2-1001.5[e]). Upon entry of judgment when venue has been changed, transcript of judgment may be filed with clerk of court in which action was instituted and shall have same effect as if judgment was originally recovered in such court. (735-5/2-1001.5[m]).

Forum Non Conveniens.—Even where venue is proper, if original forum causes unnecessary hardship to defendant and interested parties, circuit court may in its discretion transfer cause to circuit court of another county in state. (98 Ill.2d 338, 456 N.E.2d 601).

Waiver of Objections.—Objections to improper venue waived unless motion to transfer is made on or before date defendant must appear or within further time that is granted him to answer or move with respect to complaint except that if defendant upon whom venue depends is dismissed upon motion of plaintiff, remaining party may promptly move for transfer. (735-5/2-104). Objections to change of venue waived after verdict. (735-5/2-1001).

Waiver of service by defendant does not waive any objection to venue or jurisdiction. (735-5/2-213).

See note at head of Digest as to 1998 legislation covered.

See Topical Index in front part of this volume.

IL – 33

VENUE . . . *continued*

Proceedings to Compel or Stay Arbitration.—See category Dispute Resolution, topic Arbitration and Award.

COURTS AND LEGISLATURE

COURTS:

United States District Courts.—

Fees.—Filing fee is $120. (28 U.S.C. §1914).

Northern District (Clerk's office: Chicago 60604) divided into Eastern and Western Divisions. Eastern Division comprises counties of Cook, DeKalb, DuPage, Grundy, Kane, Kendall, Lake, LaSalle, McHenry and Will, and sits in Chicago; Western Division comprises counties of Boone, Carroll, Jo Daviess, Lee, Ogle, Stephenson, Whiteside and Winnebago, and sits in Rockford.

Costs.—Court may order filing of security bond in amount sufficient to pay costs and fees. (Local Civil Rule 2). Removal petitions must be accompanied by $500 bond to pay costs and disbursements if removal was improper. (Local Civil Rule 3).

Southern District (Clerk's office East St. Louis 62202) comprises counties of Alexander, Bond, Calhoun, Clark, Clay, Clinton, Crawford, Cumberland, Edwards, Effingham, Fayette, Franklin, Gallatin, Hamilton, Hardin, Jackson, Jasper, Jefferson, Jersey, Johnson, Lawrence, Madison, Marion, Massac, Monroe, Perry, Pope, Pulaski, Randolph, Richland, St. Clair, Saline, Union, Wabash, Washington, Wayne, White and Williamson, and sits at Alton, Benton and East St. Louis.

Costs.—Nonresident plaintiffs must file $200 bond as security with complaint. Removal petitions must be accompanied by $500 bond to pay costs and disbursements if removal was improper. (General Rule 2).

Central District (Clerk's office Springfield 62705) comprises counties of Adams, Brown, Bureau, Cass, Champaign, Christian, Coles, DeWitt, Douglas, Edgar, Ford, Fulton, Greene, Hancock, Henderson, Henry, Iroquois, Kankakee, Knox, Livingston, Logan, McDonough, McLean, Macoupin, Macon, Marshall, Mason, Menard, Mercer, Montgomery, Morgan, Moultrie, Peoria, Piatt, Pike, Putnam, Rock Island, Sangamon, Schuyler, Scott, Shelby, Stark, Tazewell, Vermilion, Warren and Woodford, and sits at Champaign-Urbana, Danville, Peoria, Quincy, Rock Island and Springfield.

Costs.—Nonresident plaintiff must file with complaint security bond for costs of $200. Petitions for removal must be accompanied by $500 bond to pay costs and disbursements if removal was improper. (General Rule 2).

State Courts Generally.—As of July 1, 1970, new constitution abolished various courts of limited jurisdiction (e.g., Superior Court of Cook County; probate courts; county, city, municipal and village courts, justices of peace, police magistrates), and consolidated their functions in Circuit Courts, which are ranged into five judicial districts. (Art. VI, §2; 37-1.1 et seq.).

First District.—Cook County.

Second District.—Counties of Boone, Carroll, DeKalb, Du Page, Jo Daviess, Kane, Kendall, Lake, Lee, McHenry, Ogle, Stephenson and Winnebago.

Third District.—Counties of Bureau, Fulton, Grundy, Hancock, Henderson, Henry, Iroquois, Kankakee, Knox, LaSalle, Marshall, McDonough, Mercer, Peoria, Putnam, Rock Island, Stark, Tazewell, Warren, Whiteside and Will.

Fourth District.—Counties of Adams, Brown, Calhoun, Cass, Champaign, Clark, Coles, Cumberland, DeWitt, Douglas, Edgar, Ford, Greene, Jersey, Livingston, Logan, Macon, Macoupin, Mason, McLean, Menard, Morgan, Moultrie, Piatt, Pike, Sangamon, Schuyler, Scott, Vermilion and Woodford.

Fifth District.—All counties south of Fourth District.

Supreme Court sits at Springfield, consists of seven judges: three from first district and one from each remaining district. (Art. VI, §3; 37-6) They are nominated by primary election or petition and elected at general or judicial elections (Art. VI, §12), for terms of ten years (Art. VI, §10). Court elects chief justice from their number for three year term. Four judges quorum; four necessary for decision. (Act VI, §3). Court has original and exclusive jurisdiction over cases relating to redistricting of General Assembly (Art. IV, §3) and ability of Governor to serve or resume office (Art. V, §6), and may exercise original jurisdiction over revenue, habeas corpus, prohibition and mandamus cases; appellate jurisdiction over all other cases. (Art. VI, §4). Appeal is of right only in special cases (Art. VI, §4; 37-32.2) or where Appellate Court certifies importance of question (Ill. S. Ct. 316). Direct appeal from circuit court to Supreme Court may be taken when statute held unconstitutional, or in cases commenced to compel person or agency to comply with administration order of chief circuit judge. (Ill. S. Ct. 302; Ill. S. Ct. 21). If notice of appeal from circuit court to Appellate Court has been filed in case in which public interest requires prompt adjudication, Supreme Court or justice thereof may order that appeal be taken directly to it. (Ill. S. Ct. 302).

Appellate Court sits in five branches, one in each judicial district. Each district constitutes single division unless Supreme Court orders otherwise. Supreme Court assigns judges to divisions, and presiding judge of division designates three-judge panels. (Art. VI, §35; 37-25; Ill. S. Ct.22) Selection and terms of judges same as for Supreme Court. (Art. VI, §§10 & 12). Appeal from circuit courts within district is of right. (Art. VI, §6; 37-32.1).

Circuit Court sits in 21 judicial circuits (705-35/1; Art. VI, §7), each with numbers of circuit and associate judges prescribed by statute (705-35/2). Circuit judges elected from within circuits at general elections (705-35/2) for six year terms (Art. VI, §10). Associate judges appointed by judge of circuit (Art. VI, §8; Ill. S. Ct. 39) for terms of four years (Art. VI, §10), and may be assigned to any matter except trial of felony (Ill. S. Ct. 295). Circuit courts have jurisdiction of all justiciable matters except where Supreme Court has exclusive and original jurisdiction relating to redistricting of general assembly and ability of Governor to serve or resume office (Art. VI, §9), and of appeals from decisions of administrative bodies (735-5/3-104). Circuits are:

Circuit Court of Cook County consists of Municipal Department and County Department. Municipal Department divided into six geographical districts, which determine proper venue, and has jurisdiction over actions for less than $15,000, criminal actions based on complaint or information, and certain other proceedings. County Department divided into seven divisions: Law (general jurisdiction of money claims over $15,000), Chancery, Domestic Relations, County (civil commitment, adoption, and other actions), Probate, Juvenile, and Criminal (prosecutions commenced by indictment). (Gen. Orders, Cir. Court of Cook County, 1-2).

First Circuit.—Counties of Alexander, Jackson, Johnson, Massac, Pope, Pulaski, Saline, Union and Williamson.

Second Circuit.—Counties of Crawford, Edwards, Franklin, Gallatin, Hamilton, Hardin, Jefferson, Lawrence, Richland, Wabash, Wayne and White.

Third Circuit.—Counties of Bond and Madison.

Fourth Circuit.—Counties of Christian, Clay, Clinton, Effingham, Fayette, Jasper, Marion, Montgomery and Shelby.

Fifth Circuit.—Counties of Clark, Coles, Cumberland, Edgar and Vermilion.

Sixth Circuit.—Counties of Champaign, DeWitt, Douglas, Macon, Moultrie and Piatt.

Seventh Circuit.—Counties of Greene, Jersey, Macoupin, Morgan, Sangamon and Scott.

Eighth Circuit.—Counties of Adams, Brown, Calhoun, Cass, Mason, Menard, Pike and Schuyler.

Ninth Circuit.—Counties of Fulton, Hancock, Henderson, Knox, McDonough and Warren.

Tenth Circuit.—Counties of Marshall, Peoria, Putnam, Stark and Tazewell.

Eleventh Circuit.—Counties of Ford, Livingston, Logan, McLean and Woodford.

Twelfth Circuit.—Counties of Iroquois, Kankakee and Will.

Thirteenth Circuit.—Counties of Bureau, Grundy and LaSalle.

Fourteenth Circuit.—Counties of Henry, Mercer, Rock Island and Whiteside.

Fifteenth Circuit.—Counties of Carroll, Jo Daviess, Lee, Ogle and Stephenson.

Sixteenth Circuit.—Counties of DeKalb, Kane and Kendall.

Seventeenth Circuit.—Counties of Boone and Winnebago.

Eighteenth Circuit.—County of DuPage.

Nineteenth Circuit.—Counties of Lake and McHenry.

Twentieth Circuit.—Counties of Monroe, Perry, Randolph, St. Clair and Washington.

Twenty-first Circuit.—Counties of Iroquois and Kankakee.

Court of Claims (705-505/1 et seq.) has exclusive jurisdiction of all claims against state founded on any law, regulation, contract, or tort (tort damages limited to $100,000 except in cases involving operation of motor vehicle by state employee), claims for time unjustly served in state prisons (subject to limits), claims made under certain statutes (crime victims compensation, national guardsman compensation, police and fireman compensation), claims in tort (subject to $100,000 limitation) against certain state agencies (Medical Center Commission, governing boards of state colleges and universities) and all claims for recipient made by state against any claimant. Excepted are Workers' Compensation and Workers' Occupational Disease claims and claims for expenses in civil litigation. Actions based on personal injury are barred unless notice given within one year of injury. Court consists of seven judges appointed by governor and sits at Springfield, but may take evidence elsewhere. Court may direct immediate enforcement of judgments. See category Civil Actions and Procedure, topic Limitation of Actions for special period applicable.

Small Claims actions may be brought in circuit courts for tort or contract claims of $2,500 or less, exclusive of interest and costs, or tax collections of like amount. (Ill. S. Ct. 281-88).

In any small claims case, on motion by either party or by court, dispute may be adjudicated by court at informal hearing during which court may relax rules of procedure and rules of evidence. (Ill. S. Ct. 286).

Service of simplified complaint in many circuit courts may be made by certified mail, handled by court.

Appearance is all that is required of defendant; he need not plead unless ordered to.

Jury of six or 12 may be demanded by plaintiff upon filing, or by defendant upon appearance, subject to payment of fees.

Discovery, including depositions, available only by leave of court.

Judgments may be paid by installments over period of up to three years.

See category Civil Actions and Procedure, topics Pleading, subhead Time for Filing; Practice, subheads Appearance and Discovery.

JUSTICES OF THE PEACE:

Justices of the Peace were abolished effective January 1, 1964.

LEGISLATURE:

General Assembly consisting of Senate and House of Representatives convenes annually on second Wed. in Jan. Governor may call special sessions for stated purposes. (Const. Art. IV, §5). Presiding officers of both houses may call special sessions by joint proclamation stating purpose. (Const. Art. IV, §5; [25-15/1]). State is divided into 59 legislative districts. (Const. Art. IV, §§1,3; [10-90/1]). One senator elected from each Legislative District. Each Legislative District divided into two Representative Districts, with one Representative elected from each Representative District (Const. Art. IV, §2); senators' terms two or four years according to system of staggering (10-85/1 et seq.); representatives' terms are two years. Legislators elected at general elections in even-numbered years. (Const. Art. IV, §4).

Effective Dates of Laws.—Bill passed prior to June 1 of calendar year with no effective date provided in terms of bill becomes effective on Jan. 1 of following year, or on becoming law, whichever is later. Bill passed prior to June 1 of calendar year that provides for effective date in terms of bill becomes effective on that date, if it is same as or subsequent to date bill becomes law. If effective date provided in terms of bill is prior to date bill becomes law, then date bill becomes law shall be effective date. Bill passed after May 31 shall become effective on June 1 of following year unless later date if provided in bill or unless earlier effective date is approved by three-fifths vote of both houses of General Assembly. (Const. Art. IV, §10; [5-75/2]). If Jan. 1 of following year precedes date bill becomes law, then bill becomes effective on date it becomes law. (Const. Art. IV, §10; [5-75/1]).

See note at head of Digest as to 1998 legislation covered.

See Topical Index in front part of this volume.

IL – 34

LEGISLATURE . . . *continued*

Initiative and Referendum.—While many statutes provide for local initiative and referendum on specific matters, there is no general provision covering legislative enactments.

Lobbying.—Lobbyist Registration Act (25-170/1 to 170/12) requires registration with Secretary of State of all persons individually or employed by others who by communication with official of executive or legislative branch of government seek to influence executive, legislative or administrative action. Exceptions to broad definition include government employees and uncompensated persons appearing only before legislative committees, bona fide news media and persons drafting legislation as professional service (25-170/4). Detailed reports under oath need to be filed under four categories: travel and lodging; meals, beverages and entertainment; gifts; honorarium. Also, individual expenditures over $100 shall be itemized. Registrant shall preserve receipts and records used in preparing reports for two years and within 30 days notify each official on whose behalf expenditure has been reported. (25-170/6). Violators barred from lobbying for three years, subject to $10,000 fine. (25-170/10).

REPORTS:

Decisions are contained in Illinois Reports, Illinois Appellate Reports, and Illinois Court of Claims Reports. Series are numbered consecutively. First ten volumes of Supreme Court and first 20 of Appellate Court are cited by name of reporter and volume number.

Reporter of Decisions.—Preparation of official reports of Supreme Court and Appellate Court decisions is duty of reporter of decisions, a salaried employee of State appointed by Supreme Court who receives no remuneration for services other than salary. (705-65/1).

Publication and Distribution.—Reporter, subject to prior approval of Supreme Court, contracts with publisher for sale of official reports on terms most advantageous to public and state. Reporter shall supervise publication. (705-65/2).

Style, Quality and Format.—Supreme Court determines style, manner, size, quality and general format in which official reports are published. (705-65/4). Volumes containing official reports are copyrighted in name of Supreme Court and reporter of decision. (705-65/5). Reporter of decisions may license use.

Clerk of Supreme and Appellate Courts.—Clerks of Supreme and Appellate Courts furnish, without cost, opinions of court to reporter within ten days. Clerk furnishes opinions to other persons at price fixed by Supreme Court. (705-65/7). (Currently 25¢ per page with $1 minimum for Supreme Court opinions.)

Unofficial Reports.—Decisions of both Supreme and Appellate Courts, commencing with volumes 114 Ill. and 284 Ill. App., respectively, are also reported in the Northeastern Reporter and Illinois Decisions.

Digests and Encyclopedia: Callaghan's Ill. Digest, West's Ill. Digest, Ill. Law and Practice and Ill. Law Reporter, all Ill., Ill. App. and federal cases to date; older digests primarily of historical importance.

Legislative Reference Bureau.—Reviews Federal and Illinois appellate court decisions that affect interpretation of Illinois Constitution or statutes, indicates problem areas, reports annually to legislature. (23-135/5.05).

STATUTES:

See topic Legislature.

On Jan. 1, 1993 new official compilation of Illinois Statutes became effective. New statutes are known as "Illinois Compiled Statutes". The session laws are printed at close of each session. Accurate but unofficial compilations are also published and are known as "Illinois Compiled Statutes (19—)."

Legislative Reference Bureau has authority to make computerized text of statutes and administrative rules and regulations available to public and governmental agencies. (25-140/2).

Uniform Acts adopted and presently in force are Anatomical Gift (1969); †Arbitration (1961); Child Custody Jurisdiction (1979); †Commercial Code (1972 Official Text); †Common Trust Fund (1943); Controlled Substances (1971); †Criminal Extradition (1955); Deceptive Trade Practices (1965); †Declaratory Judgments (1945); Disclaimer of Property Interests (1983); Disposition of Unclaimed Property (1961); †Enforcement of Foreign Judgments (1951); Extradition of Persons of Unsound Mind (1917); Facsimile Signature of Public Officials (1959); Federal Tax Lien Registration (1967); †Fiduciaries (1931); Foreign Money-Judgments Recognition (1963); Fraudulent Transfer (1990); Judicial Notice of Foreign Law (1939); ††Limited Partnership (1917 & 1976); Limited Partnership, Revised (1981); Management of Institutional Funds (1973); †Marriage and Divorce (1977); †Parentage (1984); ††Partnership (1917); Premarital Agreement (1990); Preservation of Private Business Records (1957); †Principal and Income (1981); Proof of Statutes (1939); Reciprocal Enforcement of Support, Revised (1969); Reciprocal Liquidation (1941); Recognition of Acknowledgements (1969); Rendition of Accused Persons (1969); †Rendition of Prisoners as Witnesses in Criminal Proceedings (1963); Simultaneous Death (1941); Single Publication (1959); State Administrative Procedure (1975); †Supervision of Trustees for Charitable Purposes Act (1961); Testamentary Additions To Trusts (1955); To Secure Attendance of Witnesses from Within or Without a State in Criminal Proceedings (1959); Trade Secrets (1988); Transfers to Minors Act (1986); Vendor and Purchaser Risk (1963).

†Adopted with significant variations or modifications.

††Prospectively repealed effective Jan. 1, 1990.

Fiduciary Security Transfers Simplification Act is patterned after Uniform Simplification of Fiduciary Security Transfers Act, but differences are so substantial as not to make Uniform Act usable as a reference.

For text of Uniform Acts falling within the scope of the Martindale-Hubbell Law Digests see Uniform and Model Acts section.

Effective Dates of Laws.—Bill passed prior to June 1 of calendar year with no effective date provided in terms of bill becomes effective on Jan. 1 of following year, or on becoming law, whichever is later. Bill passed prior to June 1 of calendar year that provides for effective date in terms of bill becomes effective on that date, if it is same as or subsequent to date bill becomes law. If effective date provided in terms of bill is prior to date bill becomes law, then date bill becomes law shall be effective date. Bill passed after May 31 shall become effective on June 1 of following year unless later date is provided in bill or unless earlier effective date is approved by three-fifths vote of both houses of General Assembly. (Const. Art. IV, §10; 1-1202). If Jan. 1 of following year precedes date bill becomes law, then bill becomes effective on date it becomes law. (Const. Art. IV, §10; 1-1201).

UNIFORM LAWS:

For list of Uniform Acts in force in this state, see topic Statutes. For text of Uniform Acts within the scope of the Martindale-Hubbell Digests see Uniform and Model Acts section.

CRIMINAL LAW

BAIL:

See topic Criminal Law.

CRIMINAL LAW:

Criminal Code defines crimes, Code of Criminal Procedure and Supreme Court Rules govern procedure, and Unified Code of Corrections governs penalties and sentences. (c. 720). Miscellaneous procedural rules and definitions of crimes are found in other portions of Illinois Statutes. Rules of Evidence applicable to civil proceedings are applied in criminal proceedings unless expressly provided otherwise or unless such application would be inconsistent with intention of rule read in context. (735-5/8-2401). Portion of Criminal Code defining substantive crimes was completely revised effective Jan. 1, 1962. Code of Criminal Procedure, revising and reorganizing older laws, became effective Jan. 1, 1964.

Uniform Acts.—Illinois has adopted, with some modifications, Uniform Criminal Extradition Act (725-225/1 to 225/32), Revised Uniform Reciprocal Enforcement of Support Act (750-20/1 to 20/42), Uniform Act to Secure the Attendance of Witnesses from Within or Without a State in Criminal Proceedings (725-220/1 to 220/6), Uniform Rendition of Accused Persons Act (725-230/1 to 230/6), Uniform Extradition of Persons of Unsound Mind Act (405-10/1 to 10/6) and Uniform Rendition of Prisoners as Witnesses in Criminal Proceedings Act (725-235/1 to 235/11), Uniform Controlled Substances Act 720-570/101 et seq. and Interstate Corrections Compact (730-5/3-4-4).

Other Acts.—Crime Victims Compensation Act extends to spouses, parents, children, or siblings of persons killed as result of felony and affords such persons opportunity to be heard at sentencing (740-45/1 et seq.); Rape Victims Emergency Treatment Act (410-70/1 et seq.); Rights of Crime Victims and Witnesses Act (725-120/1).

Criminal Victims' Asset Discovery Act provides victim or victim's representative right to depose person convicted of first degree murder, Class X felony or aggravated kidnapping or person found not guilty by reason of insanity or guilty but mentally ill of first degree murder, Class X felony, or aggravated kidnapping; right to seek attachment against property of such person. (725-145/3, 735-5/4-101).

Narcotics Profit Forfeiture Act (725-175/1 to 175/11) creates separate offense, Class I felony, for narcotics racketeering and mandates forfeiture of assets obtained by or used in narcotics racketeering or obtained through any act which violates §3 of Drug Paraphernalia Control Act (720-600/3).

Unlawful Use of Computer.—Criminal violators also subject to civil remedies including $5,000 in damages, reasonable attorneys' fees, other litigation expenses, or other relief. (720-5/160-3).

Child Abduction.—Intentional violation of court order awarding custody of child under age of 18 is Class 4 felony. (720-5/10-5).

Indictment or Information.—Prosecution may be begun by complaint, information or indictment when authorized by law. (725-5/111-1). Felony prosecutions must be commenced by indictment or information. If begun by information, accused must be given preliminary hearing unless informed waiver is made in open court. (725-5/111-2). Accused is entitled to speedy trial. (725-5/103-5; Const., Art. I, §8). Failure to provide accused with speedy trial is grounds for dismissal of charges. (725-5/114-1). Dismissal authorized where State fails to use due diligence to bring to trial. (725-5/114-4[e]). For contents of a charge, see 725-5/111-3. Uniform Traffic Ticket or Uniform Conservation Ticket filed with circuit court is complaint, unless defendant requests filing of verified complaint. (725-5/111-3).

Bail is governed by Art. 110, Code of Criminal Procedure, which initiates nonbondsmen system (725-5/110-1 to 5/110-17 and 725-195/1 to 195/5), which regulates bail in quasi-criminal offenses and misdemeanors.

All persons bailable before conviction except for following offenses where proof is evident and presumption great: Capital offenses; offenses for which life imprisonment may be imposed; felony offenses for which sentence of imprisonment, without conditional and revocable release, shall be imposed by law or consequence of conviction; and stalking or aggravated stalking, when court, after hearing, determines that release would pose real and present threat to physical safety of any person. (Const., I-9). Person charged with capital offense or offense for which life imprisonment may be imposed shall not be bailable until hearing is held wherein such person has burden to demonstrate that guilt is not evident and presumption is not great. (725-5/110-4). Court may release defendant on own recognizance under certain circumstances. (725-5/110-2).

Person for whom bail has been set must execute bail bond and deposit with clerk of court before which proceeding is pending sum of money equal to 10% of bail, but in no event less than $25. Where person is charged with offense under Controlled Substances Act that is Class X felony, court may require deposit equal to 100% of bail. (725-5/110-7). 90% of sum deposited returned to accused when discharged from all obligations in cause unless court enters order that bail bond deposited by or on behalf of accused be used to satisfy financial obligations of same accused in different case. In no event shall amount retained be less than $5. (725-5/110-7). In lieu of bail deposit, bond may be

---

See note at head of Digest as to 1998 legislation covered.

See Topical Index in front part of this volume.

CRIMINAL LAW . . . *continued*
secured by deposit with clerk of court, in amount equal to required bail, of cash, or stocks and bonds in which trustees are authorized to invest trust funds or by real estate situated in this state with unencumbered equity not exempt owned by accused or by sureties worth double amount of bail set in bond. (725-5/110-8). Judge is to endorse required bail on warrant issued after filing of information or charge. (725-5/111-2).

When bail has been set by a judicial officer for a particular offense or offender, any sheriff or other peace officer may take bail in accordance with 725-5/110-7 or 725-5/110-8 and release offender to appear in accordance with conditions of bail bond, Notice to Appear or Summons. (725-5/110-9). Other provisions apply in cases involving traffic, quasi-criminal, and certain misdemeanor offenses (725-5/110-10[d]) and domestic violence (725-5/110-15).

Violation of Bail Bond.—If bail is given in connection with felony charge, pending appeal or certiorari after conviction, person who incurs forfeiture of bail and willfully fails to surrender within 30 days following date of forfeiture commits felony of next lower class or Class A misdemeanor if underlying offense was Class 4 felony. If bail is given in connection with misdemeanor charge or for appearance as witness, person who incurs forfeiture of bail and willfully fails to surrender within 30 days following date of forfeiture commits misdemeanor of next lower class but not less than Class C misdemeanor. Person who violates condition of bail by possessing firearm commits Class 4 felony for first violation and Class 3 felony for second violation. Statute does not affect court's power to punish for contempt. (720-5/32-10). Bail bondsman may not seize or transport person found in Illinois who is allegedly in violation of bail bond posted in another state. (725-5/103-9).

Pretrial service agencies provide courts with background data regarding pretrial release of persons charged with felonies and supervise compliance with terms and conditions of release. (725-185/3 to 185/33).

DEBTOR AND CREDITOR

ASSIGNMENTS:

Uniform Commercial Code adopted. (c. 810). See categories Business Regulation and Commerce, topic Commercial Code; Documents and Records, topic Records; Property, topic Deeds.

Assignee and bona fide owner of any nonnegotiable chose in action may sue thereon in his own name. (735-5/2-403).

Voluntary assignment in trust for benefit of creditors is valid, if in writing. (15 Ill. App.2d 207, 145 N.E.2d 797).

Partner's right in specific partnership property is not assignable except in connection with assignment of rights of all partners in same property. (805-205/25[2][b]).

Assignment of wages earned or to be earned is invalid unless: (1) In writing signed by assignor, bearing date of execution, and stating name of employer at time of execution, consideration given, rate of interest or time-price differential, if any, and date payments due; (2) given to secure existing debt of assignor or one contracted by assignor simultaneously with execution; (3) exact copy furnished to assignor at time of execution; (4) words "Wage Assignment" in bold face letters one-quarter inch or more in height appear at head of instrument and one inch above or below signature line; (5) written as separate instrument complete in itself. Wage assignments made after Jan. 1, 1966 must include assignor's social security number. (740-170/1). Demands served on employer have no legal effect unless: (1) There is continuing default which has existed in excess of 40 days in payment of indebtedness secured by assignment; (2) demand contains correct statement of amount in default; (3) original or photostatic copy of assignment is exhibited to employer; (4) notice of intention to make demand is served upon employee by registered or certified mail and copy sent to employer not less than 20 days prior to service of demand. (740-170/2). Demand applies only to wages due at time of service of demand and to subsequent wages until amount due under assignment is paid or until expiration of payroll period ending immediately prior to 84 days after service of such demand, whichever first occurs. (740-170/2). Assignor may file with his employer affidavit of existence of defense within 20 days after receipt of notice of intention to make demand or within five days after service of demand. If copy of affidavit is served upon creditor by registered or certified mail before service of demand, creditor may not serve demand. (740-170/4.1). If affidavit of defense is filed with employer within five days after service of demand, no wages are subject to demand unless employer receives copy of subsequent written agreement between assignor and creditor authorizing payments; and creditor must then proceed by filing action on claim against assignor. In this action creditor may serve summons by registered or certified mail. If no affidavit of defense is filed with employer within five days after service of demand, employer is to pay to creditor wages subject to demand. (740-170/4.2). Provision is made for collection of statutory damages for wrongful service of demand, service of notice, or failure to release demand. Service of demand when no assignment was in fact executed or under assignment known to be invalid is petty offense. (740-170/6). Statute contains forms for demand, notice to employee, and affidavit of defense. (740-170/2.1, 170/2.2, 170/4.1). Assignment is valid against employer of assignor at time assignment is made only for three years from date of execution and against future employers of assignor only for two years from date of execution. (740-170/3, 170/5). Amount subject to collection by any and all assignees for any work week shall not exceed lesser of: (1) 15% of gross amount payable for that week or (2) amount by which disposable earnings for that week exceeds 45 times Federal minimum hourly wage; order of service of demand on employer determines priorities. (740-170/4). Employer must withhold fee of greater of $12 for each wage assignment or 2% of amount required to be withheld by employer, to be credited against assignor's outstanding debt. (740-170/4). Wages of state and municipal government employees are not subject to collection under wage assignment. (740-170/9). Any employer who discharges or suspends employee on account of wage assignment is guilty of Class A misdemeanor. (740-170/10).

For special procedures and defenses involving wage assignments see 735-5/2-403(b). Special provisions exist regarding assignment of wages in connection with support payments. (705-405/6-9, 750-5/706.1, 750-15/2.1, 15/3).

Benefits due under Unemployment Compensation Act may not be assigned but individual may voluntarily elect to have federal and state income tax deducted and withheld from unemployment benefit payments. (820-405/1300). Annuities and other benefits payable pursuant to State Employees' Retirement System of Illinois and State Universities Retirement System are not assignable. (40-5/14-147). Compensation due under Viet Nam Veterans Compensation Act may not be assigned. (330-30/4).

Interest in common trust fund under Common Trust Fund Act not assignable. (760-45/6). Payment, claim, award, or decision under Illinois Workmen's Occupational Diseases Act or Illinois Workmen's Compensation Act not assignable. (820-310/21, 820-305/21).

ATTACHMENT:

Constitutionality.—§§735-5/4-101, 4-104, 4-105, 4-112, 4-114 and 4-119 held unconstitutional by three judge federal district court. (405 F.Supp. 757; 471 F.Supp. 516). Reversed and remanded on grounds of equitable restraint. (97 S.Ct. 1911). §§735-5/4-104, 4-105, 4-107, 4-110, 4-114 and 4-132, §735-5/4-137 added, to cure defects.

Actions in Which Allowed.—May be used in all actions whether contract or tort or based upon statutory cause of action created by law in favor of State of Illinois or any agency thereof. (735-5/4-101). But re prejudgment attachment, see 407 U.S. 67.

Courts Which May Issue Order.—Any court having competent jurisdiction may issue order. (735-5/4-101).

In Whose Favor Order May Issue.—Any person, including a nonresident or foreign corporation, may obtain an attachment.

Against Whom Order May Issue.—Order may issue against resident or nonresident. (735-5/4-101).

Claims on Which Order May Issue.—An attachment may issue on any money claim exceeding $20, whether liquidated or unliquidated. (735-5/4-101).

Property Subject to Attachment.—Attachment may issue against both real and personal property. For property exempt from attachment, see topic Exemptions.

Water Craft.—Special provision is made for attachment of water craft used in state or having home port therein to enforce certain liens or claims, and also for attachment to enforce lien for freight on goods shipped by water craft. (735-5/4-201 to 5/4-228).

Time for Issuing Attachment.—Attachment may issue either at time of instituting suit or thereafter. (735-5/4-101). Order may issue prior to filing of complaint upon affidavit of creditor, provided that complaint shall be filed ten days before return day of order, in which event defendant is required to appear or answer on or before return day. If complaint is not so filed, defendant is not required to appear or to answer until 15 days after return day; and if complaint is not filed five days after return day, defendant may, at court's discretion, have suit dismissed. (735-5/4-130).

Attachment may issue in aid of a pending case. Notice of pendency of suit and of issue and levy of order is given as in cases of original attachments, unless defendant has previously been served with process in original cause. (735-5/4-138).

Grounds.—Attachment may issue where: (1) Debtor is nonresident; (2) debtor conceals himself or defies officer so that process cannot be served on him; (3) debtor has departed from state with intention of having his effects removed from state; (4) debtor is about to depart from state with intention of having his effects removed therefrom; (5) debtor is about to remove his property from state to injury of creditor; (6) debtor has within two years preceding filing of affidavit, fraudulently conveyed or assigned all or part of his effects, or (7) fraudulently concealed or disposed of his property so as to hinder or delay his creditors; (8) debtor is fraudulently about to conceal, assign or otherwise dispose of his property or effects so as to hinder or delay creditors; or (9) debt was fraudulently contracted by debtor, provided fraudulent statement was in writing and debtor's signature attached thereto by himself, his agent or attorney; (10) debtor convicted of first degree murder, Class X felony or aggravated kidnapping or found not guilty by reason of insanity or guilty but mentally ill of those crimes against creditor so that creditor is "victim" under Criminal Victims Asset Discovery Act or debtor is defendant in suit brought by Attorney General to cover debtor's incarceration expense. (735-5/4-101). Provisions for attachment are to be construed in most liberal manner for detection of fraud. (735-5/4-102).

Affidavit must be filed with court by plaintiff, stating: Amount of claim, after allowing just credits and set-offs; facts establishing at least one of above causes; place of residence of defendant or that on diligent inquiry plaintiff could not ascertain it; facts establishing cause of action. Judgment will be set aside if affiant has not complied with requirement of diligent inquiry to ascertain address of defendant. (13 Ill. App.2d 76, 141 N.E.2d 63). In addition, written statement showing whether action sounds in tort and designation of return day for summons shall be filed. Where action sounds in tort, plaintiff, his agent or attorney must apply to judge and be examined under oath concerning cause of action. Such judge endorses on affidavit amount of damages for which order will issue and no greater amount may be claimed. (735-5/4-104).

Form of affidavit may be substantially as follows (735-5/4-105):

Form

STATE OF ILLINOIS, }
. . . . County } ss.

A B, being duly sworn, says: That (here state if affiant is agent or attorney of the creditor; if suit is by an individual or corporation, the name of the individual or corporation, and if the suit is by a firm, the name of the partners) has a just demand against (name of debtor), on account of (here state facts giving rise to cause of action and amount of the claim), and the affiant believes (the name of the creditor) is entitled to recover of said (name of debtor), after allowing all just credits and set-offs . . . . dollars and . . . . cents, which is now due, and that he has good reason to believe and does believe that (name of debtor) (here state facts which give rise to one or more of the causes which authorize an attachment). (Name of debtor) resides at (here state the residence of the debtor if known, or if not, that the affiant has made diligent inquiry and cannot ascertain his place of residence).

Affiant has personal knowledge that the foregoing statements are true.

. . . .

See note at head of Digest as to 1998 legislation covered.

See Topical Index in front part of this volume.

IL – 36

ATTACHMENT ... *continued*

Subscribed and sworn to before me on this . . . . . . day of . . . . . ., ..., A.D.
. . . .

My commission expires . . . . . ., ..., A.D.

(If action sounds in tort here include the endorsement of judge as to amount of damages for which writ shall issue.)

Bond must be taken by court with sufficient security, payable to People of State of Illinois, for use of person interested in property attached, in double sum sworn to be due, conditioned for satisfying all costs awarded to defendant or any others interested in proceedings, and all damages and costs recovered against plaintiff for wrongfully suing out attachment. All attachments issued without bond and affidavit taken (except where State is plaintiff) are void. (735-5/4-107). Court may, on ex parte motion, without notice, supported by affidavit of plaintiff describing specific property to be attached and value thereof, fix bond at double value of property to be attached instead of double sum sworn to be due. (735-5/4-108).

If no property found or a designated garnishee is not served, and where property seized is of insufficient value, alias and pluries orders may issue without additional bond, except where additional specific property is desired to be attached, in which case additional bond at least double value of additional property is furnished as stated above. (735-5/4-115).

Form of Order for Attachment.—Order commands sheriff to attach property described, summon debtor to appear at hearing or prior thereto, and summon any garnishee to hearing. (735-5/4-110).

Issuance on Sunday.—If debtor is actually absconding or concealed, or stands in defiance of officer, or has left state with intention of having his effects removed, or intends to depart with such intention, order may issue and be served on Sun. (735-5/4-117).

Property Outside County.—Order may be levied only in county to which issued (735-5/4-112) unless defendant, or person acting for defendant, is in act of removing personal property (735-5/4-116). Orders may issue to other counties in state. (735-5/4-118).

Execution of Order.—In case of joint debtors order issues against property of those brought within Act; and others are summoned to answer action. (735-5/4-111). Order may be executed upon property described in order, or in absence of such description, upon debtor's real and personal property, or upon lands or tenements in which debtor has equitable interest or title. (735-5/4-112).

Service of Order.—Order must be served on defendant within five days of execution; if later, defendant may have order quashed at any time absent showing of good cause for delay. (735-5/14-114). Defendant may move for hearing on order any time after issuance. Order will be quashed unless plaintiff shows cause for issuance and probability of success on merits. (735-5/4-137).

Indemnity.—In practice, officer executing order demands indemnity bond in double the amount alleged due where personal property is seized. (735-5/4-107).

Sale of perishable property is provided for. (735-5/4-125). Provision also made for sale of live stock. (735-5/4-145).

Lien.—Attachment becomes lien on real estate after officer making levy files a certificate of said fact with recorder (735-5/4-113) unless land is registered under Torrens system, in which event attachment becomes lien on real estate only upon (a) filing of certificate with registrar of titles and (b) entry in registry of a memorial thereof (765-35/86).

Priorities.—Judgments in attachments against same defendant returnable on same day, and judgments in suits by summons, capias or attachment against such defendant recovered within 30 days from day when judgment in first attachment on which judgment is recovered is rendered, share pro rata in proceeds of attached property. Court may allow priority to creditors through whose diligence property being removed was secured. (735-5/4-142).

Proceedings in Action.—Where defendant is a nonresident, or has left state, or cannot be found, or is concealed so process cannot be served, and where property has been attached or garnishees summoned, clerk must give notice by publication, and by mailing copy of such notice to defendant, if his place of residence is stated. (735-5/4-127). At any time after issuance of order, upon motion of defendant, court shall set hearing on order or affidavit to be held not more than five days after service on plaintiff. At hearing, either party may introduce affidavits or oral testimony. Order shall be quashed unless plaintiff shows by preponderance of evidence that cause for issuance exists, and demonstrates probability that he will ultimately prevail on his cause of action. If defendant is personally served or appears, judgment is of same force as in suit commenced by summons. (735-5/4-139). Where defendant is notified by publication but not served and does not appear, judgment is in rem against property attached and special execution issues. (735-5/4-140). Defendant may traverse facts stated in affidavit by verified answer. If, on trial, that issue is found for plaintiff, defendant may answer or move as in other cases; if found for defendant, attachment is quashed. Where personal jurisdiction of defendant has been obtained, suit proceeds to final judgment as if commenced by summons. (735-5/4-131). Any defendant may file any counterclaim pleadable by laws of Illinois. (735-5/4-135). Original affidavit or attachment bond may be amended by filing legally sufficient affidavit or bond; and order itself may also be amended, in such time and manner as court may direct. (735-5/4-132).

Third Party Claims.—Person other than defendant may intervene by verified petition, without giving bond, but property is not thereby replevied. Jury is impaneled to inquire into right of property. If jury finds for claimant, he is given judgment for his costs, and if it further finds he is then entitled to possession of property, it is ordered delivered to him. If jury finds for plaintiff, he is given judgment against claimant for his costs. Nonresident claimant must file security for costs as in case of nonresident plaintiffs. (735-5/4-134).

Release of Property.—Person from whose possession property is taken may obtain same by entering into bond to officer, approved by him, in double value of property,

conditioned that property will be forthcoming to answer judgment. (735-5/4-119). In lieu of said bond defendant desiring return of attached property may give like bond and security in sum sufficient to cover debt and damages sworn to, with interest, damages and costs, conditioned that defendant will pay plaintiff amount of judgment and costs rendered on final trial within 90 days after judgment; or recognizance in same substance may be taken in open court, entered of record, and approved by court, on forfeiture of which judgment may be rendered and execution issued. In either case attachment is dissolved, property restored, and cause proceeds as if commenced by summons. (735-5/4-120).

Amendment of pleadings may be permitted on motion directed to pleadings or for summary judgment or upon trial, if wrong remedy sought; court to consider effect on defendant in considering amendment. (735-5/4-133).

CREDITORS' SUITS:

Creditors' suits have been abolished. However, supplementary proceedings are available. See subhead Supplementary Proceedings under topic Executions.

EXECUTIONS:

After judgment, execution against all nonexempt real and personal property of judgment debtor (735-5/12-112) may be issued to any county (735-5/12-106).

Kinds of Execution.—Execution may be issued against person or property. (735-5/12-106).

Exemptions.—See topic Exemptions.

Special Limitation.—Special rule is applicable when judgment to be enforced is against police officer employed by municipality which allows judgment creditor in certain circumstances to enforce judgment against municipality. (735-5/12-108[b]).

Time for Issuance.—Execution may issue at once or at any time within seven years (735-5/12-108), not counting period of injunction, appeal, stay or delay due to defendant's death (735-5/12-104). Execution may issue after seven years on judgment pursuant to Illinois Civil Practice Act and real estate levied on within seven years may be sold within one year after expiration of said seven years. (735-5/12-108). Judgment in action for damages for injuries described in 735-5/13-214(a) and child support judgments may be enforced at any time. (735-5/12-108).

Stay of execution for cause is within inherent power of courts. There is no automatic stay in court of record when no appeal is taken. On motion for retrial, rehearing or new trial, judgment in arrest or judgment notwithstanding verdict, made before judgment is entered or within 30 days thereafter, final judgment and execution thereon are stayed until such motion can be heard. (735-5/2-1202, 5/2-1203). Statute is silent as to security for issuance of execution and in practice none is required.

Lien.—See category Civil Actions and Procedure, topic Judgments, subhead Lien.

Interest.—Every execution issued upon judgment will direct collection of interest thereon as provided in 735-5/2-1303. (735-5/12-109).

Death of Judgment Creditor.—If judgment creditor dies, personal representative may record his letters in court which entered judgment, proceed with execution in his own name (735-5/12-155) and if necessary to secure collection, must purchase real estate at sale thereof (735-5/12-156).

Death of Judgment Debtor.—When judgment debtor dies, execution may be issued against real estate and sale made without reviving judgment against heirs or legal representatives; but no execution may issue or sale be made until 12 months after death, and no sale may be made except on three months' notice of existence of judgment to representative, or if there is none, to heirs. (735-5/12-157).

Set Off of Judgments.—Judgments between same parties may be set off (735-5/12-176, 5/12-177) except: (1) When parties are not in same capacity and trust, (2) when sum due has been assigned bona fide, (3) when there are several creditors in one execution and sum due on other is from part of them, and (4) when there are several debtors in one judgment and sum due on other is owing to part of them. Also, setoff is not allowed as to so much of judgment as is due attorney for fees and disbursements. (735-5/12-178).

Return.—Certified copies of judgments delivered to appropriate officer for enforcement are returnable in 90 days. (735-5/12-110).

Priorities.—See infra, subheads Levy, Sale, Redemption.

Orders granting equitable relief may be enforced by sequestration of real and personal estate, attachment against person, fine, imprisonment by causing possession of property to be delivered and may be carried into effect by execution or other final process having same operation and force as similar writ issued on judgment at law. (735-5/2-1402). General execution may issue on attachment judgment when defendant appeared or was served. (735-5/4-139). Special execution issues against only property attached when defendant defaults. (735-5/4-140). Judgment or order of execution may serve as writ if specific conditions are met. (735-5/2-1501).

Claims of Third Persons.—See infra, subhead Trial of Right of Property.

Levy.—Judgment creditor may elect on what property to levy provided personalty be last taken, except that municipalities, at their option, may levy against either personalty or real property with no restrictions as to priority. (735-5/12-113).

Satisfaction.—See infra subheads Release of Judgment, Supplementary Proceedings and Body Execution and topic Judgments, subhead Satisfaction.

Sale.—Real estate is sold at public sale between 9 A.M. and sundown, after three weeks published and posted notice. (735-5/12-115). Party who gives notice of public sale shall also give notice to all parties in action who have appeared and not previously been found in default for failure to plead. (735-5/15-1507).

Redemption.—On such sale by judgment, or enforcement of lien, purchaser obtains certificate of sale (735-5/12-119), and any defendant or his privies may redeem within six months of sale by paying sum for which premises sold with interest at 10% from date of sale unless right of redemption is waived or sale is had upon consent to waiver

EXECUTIONS . . . *continued*
of deficiency judgment (735-5/12-122). For liens arising on or after Aug. 7, 1961, redemption period is six months after foreclosure sale. (735-5/15-1101 et seq.). Where premises are abandoned, redemption period may be shortened. (735-5/15-1101 et seq.). Misrepresentation or wrongful inducement of abandonment is Class B misdemeanor. (735-5/15-1101 et seq.). If any defendant or his privies fails to redeem after three months and within six months after sale (except as provided in 735-5/15-1101 et seq.), judgment creditor or his successor may redeem within remaining time by getting execution on his judgment, levying, and paying sum for which premises were sold with interest at 10%, whereupon property is sold under this execution. (735-5/12-132). If no greater amount is bid at that sale than amount of redemption money with interest at 6% from date of redemption, such creditor is entitled to deed forthwith, and no further redemption is allowed. (735-5/12-133). If greater amount is bid, excess is applied on execution under which redemption was made, and certificate of purchase given to new purchaser for deed in 60 days unless redemption is made within said time by other judgment creditors or by defendants. (735-5/12-134).

Successive redemptions may be made any time within 60 days of last sale for more than redemption money, interest and costs, on like procedure. (735-5/12-135). Creditor having senior judgment or decree has preference to redeem during first two days after commencement of period in which creditors may redeem, and others respectively have preference during like time in order of seniority. Where judgments bear equal date creditor first paying redemption money has preference. (735-5/12-136). Defendant or privies may redeem after redemption by creditor within six months after original sale and thereby terminate right to further redemptions by creditors. (735-5/12-137). Redemption of parcels as sold is allowed. (735-5/12-138).

A joint owner or a judgment creditor of a joint owner may redeem his interest on payment of his proportionate amount. (735-5/12-139). Certified copy of order allowing probated claim issued by court permits redemption of decedent's real estate by claimant as judgment creditor on probated claim. (735-5/12-140). Upon redemption, redeeming party must reimburse sums paid by certificate holder for taxes and assessments, plus 10% interest. (735-5/12-141). Certificates of purchase are assignable. (735-5/12-144). When not redeemed, holder is entitled to deed from officer at any time within five years from expiration of time of redemption; and if deed is not taken, certificate is void, unless purchaser has gone into possession relying on certificate. Refusal of officer to deliver deed or pendency of injunction restraining delivery does not weigh against five year period. (735-5/12-145). Suggested form of deed is prescribed by statute. (735-5/12-147):

Form

Whereas, A.B. . . . . . in the . . . . . Court of . . . . . County recovered a judgment against C.D. for the sum of . . . . . and costs on . . . . . 19 . . . . . and a certified copy of the judgment, issued on . . . . . 19 . . . . ., by virtue of which . . . . . levied upon the premises hereinafter described, and the time and place of the sale thereof having been duly advertised according to law, the same were struck off and sold to . . . . , he or she being the highest and best bidder therefor. (If the certificate has been transferred, recite the fact.)

Now, therefore, I, ..., of the county of . . . . ., in consideration of the premises, hereby convey to . . . . ., his or her heirs and assigns, the following described lot or parcel of land (here describe the premises), to have and to hold the same with all the appurtenances thereto belonging, forever.

Witness my hand and seal this . . . . . 19 . . . . .

Title of purchaser or assignee of sale who was not party to proceeding resulting in such sale is not divested by action or proceeding to review judgment, unless at time of sale appeal was pending which operated as supersedeas, or petition under 735-5/2-1401 had been filed. (735-5/12-149).

When levy is made on real estate in any county, it is ineffective against creditors and bona fide purchasers without notice until certificate of levy is recorded. (735-5/12-152). Levy of attachment on real estate is effective as to such creditors and purchasers after the filing of certificate of levy with recorder of county where land situated. (735-5/4-113). In case of land registered under Land Titles Act no lien arises from levy on attachment or execution until memorial is entered on register. (765-35/86).

Where the state, as real party in interest, holds a judgment which is a lien on land junior to a lien which is foreclosed, the state's right to redeem terminates 12 months (except under enumerated circumstances) after filing for record or registering in county where land is situated of a copy of certificate of sale endorsed by state's attorney for such county, showing service of such copy on him. (735-5/12-401, 5/12-404).

Mortgage Foreclosures.—For special provisions applicable to mortgage foreclosure proceedings see category Mortgages, topic Mortgages of Real Property, subheads Foreclosure and Sale, Deficiency Judgment, Redemption.

Sale of Personalty.—Ten days notice of sale of personalty must be given by posting notice. (735-5/12-166). Postponements not to exceed ten days at one time may be made, on notice at time fixed for sale, or by posting if postponed for more than a day. (735-5/12-167). Compensation to officer for sustenance of live stock or care of personalty levied upon is collectible as part of costs. (735-5/12-158). Levying officer may require indemnity for taking property. (735-5/12-161). Defendant may retain property levied on by giving delivery bond to officer in double amount of judgment. (735-5/12-162). Where property has been attached or seized on other writs, proceeds of sale are applied in order in which writs became liens. (735-5/12-169). If goods are perishable, and in danger of immediate waste or decay, officer shall demand in writing that plaintiff obtain order for sale within 24 hours after levy; failure or refusal by plaintiff absolves officer from liability for failure to sell. (735-5/12-158).

Provision is made for levy on and sale of corporate stock by delivery of attested copy of execution and return to an officer of the company without actual seizure of the shares (735-5/12-170 to 5/12-175), but Uniform Commercial Code provides that no attachment or levy on shares of stock for which certificate is outstanding shall be valid until such certificate is actually seized or surrendered to corporation (810-5/8-317).

Trial of right of property may be had whenever execution or attachment is levied on personalty claimed by person other than defendant, or claimed by defendant as exempt. On notice in writing to officer of such claim, officer notifies judge, who causes a court proceeding to be entered, claimant being plaintiff therein, and plaintiff in execution or attachment being defendant. Clerk issues notice to said defendant of the time and place of trial not more than ten nor less than five days from date of notice. In apt cases notice is by publication. Trial is had without written pleadings, and either party may demand a jury, which may be of six jurors. If property is found exempt or claimant found entitled to it, it is released and costs awarded; and if claimant is entitled to immediate possession, delivery to him is ordered. Otherwise, costs are awarded the plaintiff in the execution or attachment and the officer directed to sell. (735-5/12-201 to 51/12-205).

Release of Judgment.—Judgment creditor, his assigns or legal representative having received full payment of sums due from judgment debtor on any judgment rendered shall, at request of judgment debtor or his legal representative, execute and deliver to judgment debtor or his legal representative written release of judgment. (735-5/12-183[a]). If judgment creditor, his assigns or other legal representative to whom tender has been made of money due from judgment debtor, including interest, on any judgment rendered in court, willfully fails or refuses, at request of judgment debtor or his legal representative, to execute and deliver to judgment debtor or his legal representative written release of judgment, judgment debtor may petition court in which such judgment is of record making tender therewith to court of principal sums plus interest on such judgment, for use of judgment creditor, his executors, administrators and assigns, whereupon court shall enter judgment satisfying judgment and releasing all liens based on such judgment. (735-5/12-183[b]). After Jan. 1, 1952, no judgment shall be released of record except by instrument in writing recorded in court in which such judgment is of record; however, nothing contained in statute shall affect validity of any release of judgment made, prior to Jan. 1, 1952, in judgment and execution dockets by judgment creditor, his attorney, assignee or other legal representative. (735-5/12-183[f]).

Supplementary Proceedings.—A judgment creditor or his successor in interest, when that interest is made to appear of record, may prosecute supplementary proceedings for the purposes of examining the judgment debtor or any other person to discover nonexempt assets or income of the debtor and compel the application of such assets or income toward the payment of the amount due under judgment. Supplementary proceeding is commenced by the service of a citation issued by the clerk. Procedure for conducting supplementary proceedings is prescribed by rules, including statutory language for citation and citation notice and it is not prerequisite to commencement of proceeding that execution be returned wholly or partly unsatisfied. (735-5/2-1402[a]). When nonexempt assets or income of judgment debtor are discovered, court may by appropriate order or judgment: (a) Compel judgment debtor to deliver up money, property or effects in his possession or control capable of delivery and to which his title or right of possession is not substantially disputed; (b) compel judgment debtor to pay judgment creditor in installments portion of his income having due regard for reasonable requirements of judgment debtor and his family, provided that court may modify order for installment payments from time to time upon application of either party upon notice to other; (c) compel any person cited other than judgment debtor to deliver up assets so discovered to be applied in satisfaction of judgment when assets are held under circumstances that in action by judgment debtor he could recover them in specie or obtain judgment for proceeds or value thereof; (d) enter any order upon or judgment against person cited that could be entered in garnishment proceeding; (e) compel any person cited to execute assignment of any chose in action or conveyance of title to real or personal property in same manner and extent as court of chancery could do in any proceeding by judgment creditor to enforce payment of judgment or in aid of execution; (f) authorize judgment creditor to maintain action against any person or corporation that is indebted to judgment debtor for recovery of debt, forbid transfer or other disposition of debt until action can be commenced and prosecuted to judgment, direct that papers or proof in possession or control of judgment debtor and necessary in prosecution of action be delivered to judgment creditor or impounded in court and provide for disposition of any monies in excess of sum required and judgment creditor's judgment and by costs allowed by court. (735-5/2-1402[c]).

All property ordered delivered up, except as otherwise provided, shall be delivered to sheriff to be collected or sold by him at public sale, and proceeds of such sale will be applied to satisfaction of judgment. (735-5/2-1402[e]). Citation may prohibit party to whom it is directed from making or suffering any transfer or other disposition of, or interfering with, any nonexempt property belonging to judgment debtor or to which he may be entitled or which may thereafter be acquired by or become due to him, and from paying off or otherwise disposing of any nonexempt monies which are due or to become due judgment debtor; provided that third party shall not be obliged to withhold payment of any monies beyond double amount of balance due to be enforced by judgment creditor. Court may punish any party who violates restraining provision of citation as and for contempt, or if third party may enter judgment against him in amount of unpaid portion of judgment and costs allowable under this section or in amount of value of property transferred, whichever is lesser. (735-5/2-1402[f][1]).

The court may enjoin any person, whether or not a party to the supplementary proceedings, from making or allowing any transfer, disposition of or interference with property of judgment debtor or property or debt concerning which any person is required to attend and be examined until further direction in premises. (735-5/2-1402[f][2]). If any property, chose in action, credit or effect discovered, or any interest therein, is claimed by any person other than judgment debtor, court shall, as in garnishment proceedings, permit or require claimant to appear and maintain his right. Rights of person cited (other than judgment debtor) and rights of any adverse claimant shall be asserted and determined pursuant to law relating to garnishment proceedings. (735-5/2-1402[g]). Costs in proceedings authorized by this section shall be allowed, assessed and paid in accordance with rules. (735-5/2-1402[h]). This section is in addition to and does not affect enforcement of judgments or proceedings supplementary thereto, by any other methods now or hereafter provided by law. (735-5/2-1402[i]). This section does not grant power to any court to order installment or other payments from, or compel sale, delivery, surrender, assignment or conveyance of any property exempt by statute from exemption, garnishment, attachment, sequestration, process or other levy or seizure. (735-5/2-1402[j]).

See note at head of Digest as to 1998 legislation covered.

See Topical Index in front part of this volume.

IL – 38

EXECUTIONS . . . *continued*

See also Ill. S. Ct. 277 for rules as to conduct of supplementary proceedings. Use of supplementary proceedings to reach wages is limited by wage deduction procedure. See topic Garnishment, subhead Garnishment of Wages.

Citation of Behalf of Decedent's Estate.—Upon filing of petition, court shall order citation for appearance of any person believed to have concealed, converted, embezzled or possessed property of estate or having information regarding same. (755-5/16-1).

Body Execution.—No order shall be rendered for incarceration of defendant to satisfy money judgment except when judgment is obtained for tort committed by him, it appears from special finding that malice is gist of action and defendant refuses to deliver up estate for benefit of creditors. (735-5/12-107).

EXEMPTIONS:

Following personal property is exempt from execution, writ of attachment and distress for rent: Necessary wearing apparel, bible, school books, and family pictures of debtor and debtor's dependents; debtor's equity interest, not to exceed $2,000 in value, in any other property; debtor's interest, not to exceed $1,200 in value, in any motor vehicle; debtor's equity interest, not to exceed $750 in value, in any implements, professional books or tools of trade of debtor; professionally prescribed health aids for debtor and debtor's dependents; benefits and net cash value of life insurance, endowment policies and annuity contracts payable to spouse or dependent of insured; debtor's right to receive social security, unemployment compensation, public assistance, veteran's benefit, disability, illness or unemployment benefits, certain pension benefits to extent reasonably necessary for support, alimony and support benefits to extent reasonably necessary for support; debtor's right to receive property traceable to award under crime victim's reparation law, wrongful death payment for person of whom debtor was dependent, payment under life insurance contract on individual of whom debtor was dependent (to extent reasonably necessary for support), or payment (not to exceed $7,500) on account of personal bodily injury of debtor or individual of whom debtor was dependent for certain limited period as listed; debtor's right to receive award relating to crime victim's awards. Exempt property purchased with intent of converting nonexempt property into exempt property is not exempt. (735-5/12-1001). Money from sale of exempt property remains exempt. Debtor cannot convert nonexempt property to exempt property within six months of Petition for Bankruptcy. (735-5/12-1001).

Federal exemptions provided in Bankruptcy Code, 11 U.S.C. §522(d), are not available to residents of Illinois. (735-5/12-1201).

Statutory provisions also exempt from attachment, garnishment, judgment, levy, execution and other process, all pensions, annuities and disability benefit funds, received by employees (735-5/12-803, 5/12-804), see also Ill. Pension Code (40-5/2-154). Exemption also extends to payments, claims and awards under Worker's Compensation Act (820-305/21); and to proceeds and aggregate net cash value of life and endowment policies and annuity contracts payable to wife, husband, child, parent or other person dependent upon insured except as to premiums paid in fraud of creditors (215-5/238). See individual statutes for exceptions.

Maximum amounts subject to deduction order for any week not to exceed lesser of: (1) 15% of gross weekly wages or, (2) amount by which disposable income for week exceeds 30 times amount of current Federal Minimum Wage. (29 U.S.C. 206[a][1]). All amounts so deducted are exclusive of deductions required by law. (735-5/12-803).

Debts for Which Exemption Not Allowed.—Claim for wages of laborer or servant, provided court finds demand sued on is for such wages and such finding is expressed in record and endorsed on execution when issued. (735-5/12-1004). Term "laborer or servant" has been strictly construed to include only one performing manual or menial labor requiring no special knowledge or skill. (98 Ill. App. 245).

Waiver of Exemption.—Exemption rights may not be waived by contract if debtor is head of family, but may be waived by individual where his rights are purely personal. (163 Ill. 646, 45 N.E. 414).

Improper Seizure of Exempt Property.—Officer seizing exempt property is liable for double its value plus costs. (735-5/12-1005).

Trial of right of property is provided as to property levied upon if owner claims it is exempt. (735-5/12-201 to 12-205). Debtor cannot both recover exempt property and sue for double its value. (217 Ill. App. 234).

Necessity of Claiming Exemption.—The debtor need not make a schedule of his personal property to secure exemption of his equity interest in any other personal property not to exceed $2,000. In order to select certain household furniture for exemption or to select other personal property instead of household furniture or to select part household furniture and part other personal property, debtor must give schedule, under oath, of all his personal property, including money on hand and debts due him, to officer having judgment, or attachment or distress warrant within ten days after service of judgment, or attachment or distress warrant. Anything not in schedule will not be exempt. Three householders, appointed by court, value each article on schedule, and debtor may select articles at appraised values, but not exceeding aggregate amount of exemptions; balance being subject to judgment, or attachment or distress warrant. If no schedule is filed and value of household furniture exceeds debtor's exemption, appraisal is made in same manner and officer selects and disregards household furniture of aggregate value equal to debtor's exemption. If debtor presents sufficient schedule, return of execution unsatisfied and issuance of alias or subsequent execution will not require him to file additional schedule in order to retain exemption, unless debtor acquires additional property before 90 days from certified judgment. (735-5/12-1002).

Rights of Debtor's Family.—When head of family dies, deserts or does not reside with the same, family is entitled to same exemptions. (735-5/12-1003).

Attempts to Evade Exemption Law.—It is petty offense punishable by fine not less than $10 nor more than $50 to send claim to another state for collection from wages of debtor by garnishment, or other process, in order to avoid exemptions provided by laws of Illinois where all parties are within jurisdiction of Illinois courts. (735-5/12-1101). It is petty offense to assign or transfer claim for same purpose. (735-5/12-1102).

Exemption of Compensation.—See topic Garnishment.

Homestead Exemption.—See topic Homesteads.

FORECLOSURE:

See topic Liens; category Mortgages, topic Mortgages of Real Property.

FRAUDULENT SALES AND CONVEYANCES:

Uniform Fraudulent Transfer Act adopted. (740-160/1 et seq.).

Every gift, grant, conveyance, assignment or transfer of, or charge upon any estate, real or personal, or right or thing in action, or any rent or profit thereof, made with intent to disturb, delay, hinder or defraud creditors or other persons, and every bond or other evidence of debt given, suit commenced, decree or judgment suffered, with like intent, shall be void as against such creditors, purchasers or other persons. (740-160/1 et seq.).

Conveyance of goods and chattels on consideration not deemed valuable at law is fraudulent, unless it is by will proved and recorded or by written deed acknowledged or proved, and recorded, or unless actual bona fide possession remains with donee. (740-160/1 et seq.).

Delivery of goods on pretended loan or reservation of interest, followed by five years' possession, is fraudulent as to creditors of and purchasers from the person in possession, unless the loan, etc., is declared by will or deed in writing, proved and recorded. (810-5/2-403, 5/9-114, 5/9-408).

Uniform Fraudulent Conveyance Act.—Not adopted.

Attachment.—Creditor may have an attachment against property of debtor where debtor is about to fraudulently convey or has conveyed his effects so as to hinder or delay his creditors. (735-5/4-116). Illinois Attachment Act held violative of due process. (405 F. Supp. 757, rev'd on other grounds).

Penalty.—Criminal penalties are provided for debtor when under terms of security agreement: (i) without right of sale of collateral, or (ii) with right of sale of collateral but under duty to account to secured party for proceeds of sale thereof, debtor sells collateral and willfully and wrongfully fails to pay secured party amount due under security agreement. (810-5/9-306.01). Criminal penalties are provided for when, under terms of security agreement, debtor is required to disclose to secured party persons to whom he desires to sell or otherwise dispose of collateral, and debtor fails to do so. (810-5/9-306.02).

Consumer Fraud.—See category Business Regulation and Commerce, topics Consumer Protection, Sales.

Bulk Sales.—Article 6 of Uniform Commercial Code repealed and replaced by Uniform Fraudulent Transfer Act (UFTA) effective for transfer on or after Jan. 1, 1990.

Director of Illinois Department of Employment Security must be informed at least seven days before sale by any person of substantially all of: (a) Business, or (b) stock or goods, or (c) furniture or fixtures, or (d) machinery and equipment, or (e) good will of any employing unit. Failure to do so makes such person personally responsible for all loss of Illinois Unemployment Compensation Act contributions, etc., thereby suffered. Any employing unit which, outside of usual course of its business, makes any of above sales and ceases to do business must, within ten days thereafter, pay all contributions, etc., due under Illinois Unemployment Compensation Act. Purchaser must withhold sufficient of purchase money to pay all such contributions, etc., in event seller fails to pay. Failure to withhold sufficient of purchase money makes purchaser personally liable to Director for payment of such contributions, etc., up to amount of reasonable value of property acquired by such purchaser. (820-405/2600). Any person who acquires any property subject to valid lien in favor of Director of Illinois Department of Employment Security shall be personally liable to Director for sum equal to amount of contributions secured by such lien but not to exceed reasonable value of such property. (820-405/2600). In event taxpayer, outside usual course of business, sells or transfers major part of any one or more of: (i) Stock of goods which he is engaged in business of selling, (ii) furniture or fixtures, or (iii) machinery and equipment or (iv) real property, of any business subject to Retailer's Occupation Tax Act (35-120/1 et seq.), seller or buyer must within ten days after such sale or transfer, submit report to Illinois Director of Revenue setting forth names and addresses of each of seller and buyer, description of assets conveyed and purchase price thereof. Buyer or transferee are personally liable to Director for amounts owing by seller to Director under Act at date of sale up to reasonable value of assets conveyed by seller. (35-120/1h). Buyer is to withhold from purchase price amount of all unpaid taxes, etc. owing by seller under Act at date of sale and may request at least 30 days prior to sale that Director audit books and records of seller to determine amount owing by seller to Director. (35-120/5j).

GARNISHMENT:

Prefatory Note.—In 1961, laws relating to garnishment in Illinois were altered to provide two separate sets of garnishment proceedings, one relating to garnishment of wages, the other relating to all other garnishments. (735-5/12-701 to 12-819). Illinois garnishment statute, 735-5/12-701, unconstitutional when invoked to satisfy judgment by confession. (343 F.Supp. 1272).

Garnishment of Property Other Than Wages.—

Commencement.—Clerk of court in which judgment was entered will issue summons upon filing by judgment creditor, its attorney or other designee of (1) affidavit that affiant believes any person is indebted to judgment debtor, other than for wages, or has possession of property of debtor, or property in which debtor has an interest, and (2) written interrogatories to be answered by garnishee respecting said indebtedness or other property. (735-5/12-701).

Practice.—Summons is issued by clerk following filing of affidavit and written interrogatories, as set forth above, returnable not less than 21 days nor more than 30 days after date of issuance. Where summons is served less than 10 days prior to return date, case is continued to new return date 14 days later. In counties of less than 1,000,000 population, service by certified or registered mail, return receipt requested, is permitted instead of personal service. In such instance, Clerk shall mail by first class copy of garnishment notice and summons to judgment debtor no sooner than two business days nor later than four business days after date of mailing. (735-5/12-705).

See note at head of Digest as to 1998 legislation covered.

See Topical Index in front part of this volume.

IL – 39

GARNISHMENT . . . *continued*

Judgment creditor or judgment debtor may contest answer, and trial is conducted as in other civil cases. Answer shall be considered denied without further pleading. If findings are against garnishee, judgment is entered against garnishee and in favor of judgment debtor for use of judgment creditor. (735-5/12-711). If garnishee fails to answer, then conditional judgment is entered against garnishee for amount due upon judgment against debtor, and a summons to confirm conditional judgment then issues against garnishee returnable in same manner as original garnishment summons. If garnishee fails to answer summons to confirm conditional judgment, a final judgment is then entered. (735-5/12-706). Judgment against garnishee is enforceable as in other civil cases and acquits garnishee of all claims by judgment debtor for the indebtedness or other property paid, delivered or accounted for by virtue of judgment. (735-5/12-712, 735-5/2-1402). As to procedural matters not specifically provided for in 735-5/12-701 to 12-819; Code of Civil Procedure, 735-5/1-108, controls. (735-5/12-711[b], 735-5/12-811[b]; 52 Ill. App.2d 394, 202 N.E.2d 73).

Property Subject to Garnishment.—Any nonexempt indebtedness or nonexempt property of judgment debtor, or in which debtor has an interest, which garnishee has in his possession, custody, or control, other than wages, is subject to garnishment. Answer to written interrogatories filed by garnishee speaks in all cases as of date of service of garnishment summons. Answer must list any indebtedness due or to become due to judgment debtor, as well as any other property in garnishee's possession, custody, or control (a) belonging to debtor or (b) in which debtor has an interest. Judgment or balance due becomes lien on indebtedness and other property held by garnishee at time of service and remains lien pending garnishment suit. (735-5/12-707).

Adverse Claims.—Adverse claimant to property in garnishee's hands may become party to garnishment proceeding by appearing and filing his claim within time allowed by court and by serving copy of claim on judgment creditor, judgment debtor and garnishee. This claim is tried with other issues in garnishment proceeding. Claimant not voluntarily appearing must be served with notice as court shall direct. If claimant fails to appear after notice, he is concluded by judgment entered in garnishment proceeding. (735-5/12-710). Garnishee has duty to notify court of any conflicting claim to property. Notice to claimant mandatory. (3 Ill. App.3d 299, 278 N.E.2d 526).

Negotiable Paper.—No one is liable as garnishee on negotiable paper in hands of judgment debtor at time of service of garnishment summons or of rendition of judgment when instrument not yet due. (735-5/12-709). However, installment interest due on negotiable instrument is subject to garnishment. (48 Ill. App.3d 915, 363 N.E.2d 619).

Assignment of Claims Against Garnishee.—Notice to garnishee, given before filing of his answer but after commencement of garnishment proceeding, of assignment of claim of his creditor, made prior to garnishment proceedings, is sufficient to protect rights of assignee; and assignee is entitled to prosecute garnishment proceedings. (161 Ill. 85, 43 N.E. 727). Assignment by judgment debtor prior to commencement of garnishment proceedings, absent fraud, precludes garnishor from prevailing against garnishee. (19 Ill. App.3d 27, 311 N.E.2d 250).

Set-off by Garnishee.—Garnishee is entitled to set-off against judgment creditor and judgment debtor. (735-5/12-708).

Sale of Pledged Property.—Garnishee's power to sell pledged property is not disturbed by service of summons, if sale would be authorized as between garnishee and judgment debtor. (735-5/12-714[c]).

Release of Property.—Creditor may pay debt or perform condition for which pledge was made and have property released by court order. (735-5/12-714[b]).

Executors and administrators may be garnisheed, but no judgment may be had against them until after order of distribution. (735-5/12-703). No assignment or transfer by heir or distributee defeats garnishment, unless it be in writing and filed with clerk of court issuing letters before service of garnishment. (735-5/12-719).

Attachment Suits.—Persons named as garnishees in attachment writs and all other persons whom creditor shall designate as having property belonging to defendant or as being indebted to defendant, although not named in such attachment writ, may be summoned as garnishees and thereafter must hold said property or indebtedness subject to the order of court. Said property is treated as attached pending disposition of plaintiff's claim. (735-5/4-126).

Attachment proceedings (including garnishment in attachment, or before judgment) are regulated by 735-5/4-101 to 5/4-145. Straight garnishment proceedings after judgment are regulated by 735-5/12-701 to 5/12-819.

Costs and Fees.—Costs of obtaining garnishment order to be charged to judgment debtor unless court determines costs incurred by judgment creditor were improperly incurred, in which case costs to be paid by judgment creditor. (735-5/12-716[a]). No appearance fee for garnishee. (735-5/12-716[c]). No fee due garnishee unless called as witness. (735-5/12-716[d]).

Garnishment of Wages.—

Prefatory Note.—In Chicago and environs clerk of court no longer accepts any type of garnishment summons based on confessed judgments unless judgment has been confirmed after service of process. Provisions of 735-5/12-801 do not apply to orders for withholding of income entered under Illinois Public Aid Code or under several domestic relations Acts. (735-5/12-819).

Commencement.—Upon filing by judgment creditor, its attorney or other designee, defined as recipient of any judgment except judgment by confession which has not been confirmed, of (a) affidavit that affiant believes any person is indebted to judgment debtor for wages due or to become due and last known address of judgment debtor known to affiant, and (b) written interrogatories to person named with respect to indebtedness, clerk of court in which its judgment was entered will issue summons against employer named. Summons shall command federal agency employers to pay over deducted wages in accordance with 735-5/12-808(b). Summons must be accompanied by copy of judgment relied on or statement of amount of judgment, name of court issuing it, and case number, and copy of Title III of Federal Consumer Credit Protection Act, certified to by judgment creditor's attorney or clerk of court issuing judgment. (735-5/12-805).

Practice.—Summons returnable not less than 98 nor more than 112 days after issuance. If employer is served less than 84 days prior to return date, case is continued to new date not less than 84 days after service. Requirements for service and return are same as in other civil cases. (735-5/12-806). In counties of less than 1,000,000 population, at request of judgment creditor or attorney Clerk shall mail to employer copy of judgment, summons, interrogatories and wage deduction notice by certified or registered mail, return receipt requested at address shown in affidavit instead of personal service. Return receipt must be attached to original summons and, if delivery at least 84 days before return date, constitutes proof of service. (755-5/12-805[b]).

Upon service of summons amount due on underlying judgment becomes lien on wages due at time of service plus all subsequent earnings up to end of payroll period ending immediately prior to 84 days after service, or until balance of underlying judgment and costs is paid, whichever is sooner. Lien on subsequent earnings terminates sooner if underlying judgment vacated or modified or employment ends. Lien for support of spouse or dependent children has priority. Subsequent summonses are effective for successive 84 day periods in order in which they are served. (735-5/12-808).

When summons served, employer must pay employee all exempt wages due and hold all nonexempt wages to extent of balance due on underlying judgment. (735-5/12-808).

On or before return date, but no sooner than 84 days from service, employer files sworn answer to interrogatories. (735-5/12-808). Illinois Supreme Court may by rule allow employer to file answers to interrogatories by facsimile. (735-5/12-808[d]).

Judgment creditor may contest answer without further pleading, and case will proceed to trial, conducted as in other civil cases. If finding is against employer, "deduction order" is rendered against employer, in favor of judgment debtor. (735-5/12-811). "Deduction order" has same force and effect as judgment. (735-5/12-802). Deduction orders are enforceable in same manner as judgment in other civil cases and acquit employer of all claims by judgment debtor for indebtedness paid or accounted for under deduction order. (735-5/12-812, 5/2-1402).

If employer fails to appear and answer, conditional judgment may be entered against employer for amount due on underlying judgment against judgment debtor. Summons to confirm conditional judgment then issues against employer returnable not less than ten nor more than 20 days after issuance. If employer fails to answer summons to confirm, final judgment is entered for balance of underlying judgment and costs. If summons to confirm cannot be served on employer by reason of his leaving state or concealing himself within state, he may be notified in same manner as nonresident defendants in attachments. Plaintiff may then proceed as though summons to confirm had been personally served. If employer appears and answers summons to confirm, same proceedings are had as in other cases. (735-5/12-807).

Plaintiff who wrongfully causes issuance of summons is liable to employer and employee for damages, including attorneys' fees. (735-5/12-817).

Maximum Amounts Collectible.—Maximum wages, salary, commissions and bonuses subject to collection under deduction order for any work week shall not exceed lesser of: (1) 15% of gross amount paid for that week, or, (2) amount of disposable earnings in excess of 45 times Federal minimum hourly wage. (29 U.S.C. 206[a][1]). "Disposable earnings" means earnings remaining after deduction of amounts required by law to be withheld. Applies regardless of place where wages earned or state where employee resides. No payroll deductions of any kind required by law may be taken from amount collected by creditor. (735-5/12-803). Benefits and refunds payable by pension or retirement funds or systems and any assets of employees held by such funds or systems, and any moneys employee is required to pay or contribute to such funds or systems, are exempt and not subject to garnishment. (735-5/12-704, 735-5/12-804).

Penalty for Employer.—Any employer discharging or suspending employee because earnings are subject to deduction order for any one indebtedness may be fined not to exceed $1,000 or imprisoned for less than a year or both (Class A misdemeanor). (735-5/12-818).

Judgments by Confession.—Judgment by confession without process will not support deduction order unless judgment is confirmed, by trial de novo after service of process. (735-5/12-813; 6 Ill. App.3d 956, 286 N.E.2d 83). If employee is not found, alias summons to confirm judgment by confession may be served by leaving copy with employee's employer, or at employer's place of business with employer's superintendent, manager, cashier, general agent or clerk, upon filing by creditor of affidavit that employee-debtor is in fact employed by named employer at time alias is sought. If notice of defense to wage assignment has been filed under 48-39.4a summons to confirm judgment by confession may be served by registered or certified mail to address shown on notice of defense within six months after filing such defense. (735-5/12-813).

Adverse Claims.—Same rules apply as in garnishment of property other than wages, except notice to claimant not appearing served in person or by certified or registered mail. (735-5/12-810).

Set-Off by Garnishee.—Same rules apply as in ordinary garnishment. (735-5/12-809).

Costs and Fees.—Court shall order costs of obtaining deduction order paid by judgment debtor unless costs incurred by judgment creditor improper, in which case those costs paid by judgment creditor. No appearance fee for employer. Employer entitled to fee greater of $12 or 2% of amount deducted off judgment debt but no other fee unless called as witness. (735-5/12-814).

Supplementary Proceedings.—See 735-5/12-1402.

HOMESTEADS:

Every individual has estate of homestead in land and buildings thereon, in condominium or in personal property, owned or possessed by lease or otherwise and occupied as residence, or in cooperative that owns property that individual uses as residence, which estate is exempt from attachment, judgment, levy or sale for payment of debts or other purposes, and from laws of conveyance, descent and devise, except as otherwise provided or as provided in §20-6 of Probate Act. This provision is not applicable between joint tenants or tenants in common, but applies as to creditors of those persons. (735-5/12-901).

Limitation of value of homestead which is exempt is $7,500. If two or more persons own property exempt as homestead, value of exemption for each person may not exceed proportionate share of $15,000 based upon percentage of ownership. (735-5/12-901).

If creditors believe homestead premises are worth more than $7,500, officer holding execution must summon three individuals, as commissioners, to appraise property, and if in their opinion property may be divided without injury they must set off to debtor so

HOMESTEADS . . . *continued*
much of said premises, including dwelling house, as shall be worth $7,500 and residue may be sold. (735-5/12-910). When premises cannot be divided, and in opinion of commissioners value is more than $7,500, unless execution debtor pays to officer the excess value within 60 days, premises may be sold and out of proceeds $7,500 must be paid to debtor and balance applied on execution. (735-5/12-911, 735-5/12-912). If court of equity orders sale to enforce a lien, bid must exceed $7,500. (735-5/12-908, 735-5/12-909).

Proceeds of sale of homestead property to extent of $7,500 exempt from execution for one year and may be reinvested in new homestead. (735-5/12-906). Same is true of proceeds of insurance on homestead property. (735-5/12-907).

Limitation of Area.—There is no statutory provision limiting extent of area of homestead.

Debts or Liabilities Against Which Exemption Not Available.—Homestead is not exempt as against taxes or assessments or debts or liabilities incurred for purchase or improvement thereof or from lien for nonpayment of common expenses pursuant to Condominium Property Act. (735-5/12-903).

Designation of Homestead.—There is no statutory provision for filing or recording homestead claim.

Waiver of Exemptions.—Release or waiver of right of homestead by husband or wife does not bind other spouse unless other spouse joins in release or waiver. No deed or other instrument waives right of homestead unless it contains clause expressly releasing or waiving such right. (765-5/27). It must be acknowledged. (413 Ill. 204, 108 N.E.2d 438).

Conveyance of homestead must be in writing signed by individual and his or her spouse. (735-5/12-904).

Rights of Surviving Spouse and Family.—Exemption continues after death of individual for benefit of surviving husband or wife so long as he or she occupies homestead, and for benefit of children until youngest child becomes 18 years of age; and in case husband or wife deserts family, exemption continues in favor of the one occupying premises as resident. (735-5/12-902). If exception is continued to minor, court order is necessary to release homestead. (735-5/12-904). Guardian of minor or conservator of incompetent may assent in writing pursuant to court order to sale free of his ward's homestead interest. (755-5/20-22).

In case of divorce, court may dispose of homestead estate according to equities. (735-5/12-905).

In case of partition, see category Civil Actions and Procedure, topic Partition.

JUDGMENT NOTES:

See categories Business Regulation and Commerce, topic Bills and Notes; Civil Actions and Procedure, topic Judgments, subhead Judgment by Confession.

LEVY:

See topics Attachment, Executions.

LIENS:

Uniform Commercial Code is in force. (c. 810). See category Business Regulation and Commerce, topic Commercial Code.

Statutes provide liens in favor of: State on real property of welfare recipients (305-5/3-10); credit union on shares of member for debts owing by member to credit union; horse shoers on animals shod (770-30/1); landlord for growing crops; contractors, subcontractors, laborers and material men on oil and gas wells and pipelines (770-70/1); miners for value of their labor (770-65/1); hotel, boarding house and inn keepers on baggage and other valuables of guests or boarders on the premises (770-40/48) (section held unconstitutional, 338 F.Supp. 390); stable keepers and others on horses, carriages and harnesses kept by them (770-40/49); agisters and persons keeping, yarding, feeding or pasturing domestic animals (770-40/50); contractors, subcontractors, laborers and material men on railroad property (770-40/50); owner or lessee of threshing machine, clover huller, corn sheller or hay baler for work done for others (770-40/50a); laborers or servants for wages (770-85/1); every hospital on claims of injured persons (770-35/1); physicians on claims of injured persons (770-80/1); dentists on claims of injured persons (770-80/1); psychologists on claims of injured persons (770-20/1); agent on property for which he has paid assessments on behalf of his principal (35-205/219); township supplying water on real estate for which it is supplied (60-65/14.1); sanitary districts for delinquent user charges on real property to which service supplied (70-2605/7); physical therapists on claims of injured persons (770-75/1); commercial real estate brokers on commercial real estate (770-15/1); plastic or metal processors on tools, dies, molds, jigs, fixtures, forms or patterns (770-105/1).

Court may order lien on nonmarital property for contributions made by spouse. (750-5/503).

Provision is made for recording of notices of lien by United States for internal revenue taxes. (770-110/1).

There is a statutory lien on water craft navigated in state, used between ports within state, or having its home port here, for debts contracted and liabilities incurred in use of such craft (735-5/4-201); also lien on goods shipped by water for freight, advanced charges and demurrage (735-5/4-202).

Waiver, Loss and Extinguishment.—See individual subheads.

Chattel liens exist in favor of persons expending labor, skill or materials on any chattel or furnishing storage therefor at request of owner, his agent, reputed owner, or lawful possessor thereof. Lien attaches as of date of commencement of expenditure of labor, skill and/or materials, or of storage; it continues for one year after completion of expenditure of labor, skill or materials or of such storage notwithstanding surrender of possession of chattel (770-45/1); it ceases 60 days from date of surrender unless lien claimant within said 60 days files with recorder of local county notice of claim for lien (770-45/2). It is subject to lien of bona fide security interest as defined by Uniform Commercial Code (810-5 et seq.) recorded prior to time chattel lien attaches; it is subject to prior liens and is not exclusive of liens afforded by common law (770-45/4); it may be enforced through foreclosure in equity or through advertisement and sale by sheriff (770-45/6).

Inexpensive means of enforcing liens for $2,000 or less is provided by permitting public sale after 30 days notice unless chattel is redeemed within 90 days after completion of work or date agreed upon for redemption. (770-50/1 to 50/6).

Mechanics' Liens.—Any person who by any contract, express or implied, with owner of land, or with one whom owner has authorized or knowingly permitted to contract to improve same, furnishes material, fixtures, apparatus, or machinery, forms or form work used in process of construction where cement, concrete or like material is used, for purpose of, or in building, altering, repairing or ornamenting any house or other building, walk, driveway, fence or improvement or appurtenance thereto on such lot, or connected therewith and upon, over or under sidewalk, street or alley adjoining, or fills, sods or excavates such lot, or does landscape work, or raises or lowers any house thereon, or removes any house thereto, or removes any house or other structure therefrom, or drills any water well thereon, or performs services as architect, superintendent, structural engineer, professional engineer, surveyor, property manager, timekeeper, mechanic, laborer or otherwise, is contractor, and has lien on such premises for amount due to him for such material, fixtures, apparatus, machinery, services or labor and interest at rate of 10% per annum from date same is due. (770-60/1).

Lien extends to estates in fee, for life, for years, or any other interest which owner may have in premises at time of contract or may subsequently acquire. (770-60/1). Labor and materials furnished with consent of particular condominium unit owner is lien only against that unit. (765-605/9.1). Taking of security does not waive lien in absence of agreement or if prohibited by this Act. Agreement to waive lien in anticipation of and in consideration for awarding contract unenforceable. (770-60/1.1). As against owner, contractor must file proper lien claim and bring suit not more than two years after completion of work. As against third person, contractor must file lien claim or bring suit within four months after last work. (770-60/7). In all cases, suit to enforce lien must be commenced within two years after completion of work. (770-60/9). Lien claim, verified by affidavit, consists of brief statement of contract, balance due after allowing all credits, and sufficient description of land so that it can be identified. Lien claim is filed with recorder of deeds of county where work was performed. (770-60/7).

Subcontractor has lien on the real estate co-extensive with contractor's and, in addition, on material, fixtures, apparatus or machinery furnished and on moneys or other considerations due or to become due from owner under original contract. Agreement to waive any right to enforce or claim lien, where agreement is in anticipation of and in consideration for awarding of contract or subcontract, is against public policy and unenforceable. (770-60/1). Provision in contract, agreement or understanding conditioning payment to subcontractor or supplier by contractor on receipt by contractor of payment from any other party, whether private or public owner, is not defense to claim under §21, 22, 23, or 28. (770-60/21). Where subcontractor furnishes materials or labor with respect to existing owner-occupied single family residency, to preserve lien he must give occupant personal or certified notice in statutory form within 60 days from first furnishing labor or materials (770-60/5, 60/21); provided that notice given after 14 day period is effective to extent owner not prejudiced by payments made prior to receipt of such notice. Any contractor who, with intent to defraud, induces subcontractor to waive his lien for the purpose of enabling contractor to obtain final payment and upon representation that contractor will pay subcontractor from final payment, and who then wilfully fails to pay subcontractor within 30 days of final payment, is guilty of class A misdemeanor. (770-60/21.01).

Subcontractor must within 90 days of completion of his contract cause written notice of his claim to be personally served, or sent registered mail return receipt requested, on owner or his agent, architect or superintendent, unless contractor's statement to owner sets forth subcontractor's name and amount due him. If land in question is registered pursuant to 765-35/1, then notice must be filed with register of titles in county wherein land is situated. (770-60/24).

It shall be duty of contractor to give to owner, and of owner to require of contractor, before any consideration is paid on behalf of owner to contractor, statement in writing under oath or verified by affidavit of names and addresses of all parties furnishing materials and labor, and of amounts due or to become due each. (770-60/5). Each subcontractor shall, as often as requested by owner or contractor in writing, furnish to such owner or contractor statement under oath listing names of all persons furnishing material and labor and amounts due or to become due each. Penalty for failure to furnish within five days of demand such statement is forfeiture of $50 for each offense to such owner or contractor, subordination of lien to all other creditors, and such contractor shall have no right of action against either owner or contractor until statement is furnished. (770-60/22).

Payment by owner to contractor is not rightful as against subcontractor, laborer, or party furnishing labor or materials, if owner has not exercised and enforced rights and powers conferred upon owner by §§5, 21 and 22 of this Act. (770-60/32). Subcontractor must file his petition or suit to enforce lien within same period as given to contractor or may sue owner and contractor jointly. (770-60/28).

Liens are assignable. Pleading and practice are the same as in other civil actions. All persons having any interest in the premises must be made parties. (770-60/8, 60/11).

Public Works.—Contractor and subcontractor have lien for value of material, apparatus, fixtures, machinery or labor furnished on money due contractor on public improvement with state or political subdivision provided notice is given to government unit by registered or certified mail, return receipt requested and delivery limited to addressee only, or by delivery to public officials responsible for paying contractor. Notice must be given clerk or secretary of public entity and contractor prior to payment. Subcontractor must notify state or political subdivision of lien within 30 days after written demand by contractor to do so or forfeit lien. (770-60/23). Accounting suit against contractor must be commenced within 90 days after filing such notice and certified copy of complaint must be delivered to political subdivision or lien is forfeited. In addition, contractor must furnish bond to state or political subdivision thereof, conditioned on payment for all materials and labor but county or municipality may not require cash bond to guarantee completion of project improvement when builder or developer has filed

LIENS . . . continued

current irrevocable line of credit in amount equal to greater than 110% of amount bid. (30-550/3; 30-550/1). Upon notice of lien, public unit must withhold sufficient sums to satisfy claim and upon notice of suit, these funds shall be withheld until final adjudication, unless court orders substitution of contractor's surety bond as adequate security. (770-60/23). To sue on said bond subcontractor, materialman or laborer must file verified notice of claim setting forth certain requisite facts with officer or body awarding such contract within 180 days after date of furnishing last item of material or labor and shall furnish copy of such verified notice to contractor within ten days of filing notice with public body or officer. Such action cannot be brought until 120 days after date of furnishing of last item of material or labor, except that when final settlement is made between contractor and officer or body awarding such contract action may be brought immediately after final settlement. No action may be brought after six months from date when state or political subdivision thereof accepted building, project or work. Such action must be brought in circuit court of district in which contract was performed. (30-550/2).

Liens Upon Public Nuisances.—Any building used in commission of an offense defined as a public nuisance in 720-5/37-1 (including, inter alia, murder, kidnapping, prostitution, theft, abortion, gambling, and violations of Uniform Narcotics Drug Act) with intentional, knowing, reckless or negligent permission of owner thereof, or agent of owner managing building, is, together with underlying real estate and all fixtures, subject to lien and may be sold to pay any fine imposed for maintaining nuisance or to pay to any person any unsatisfied judgment for damages sustained as consequence of nuisance. Action to enforce lien may be commenced by State's Attorney or by person suffering damages or both, except that person seeking to recover damages must pursue his remedy within six months after damages are sustained. This lien does not affect rights of any subsequent purchaser, mortgagee, judgment creditor or other lien holder unless filed in office of recorder where real estate is located. Notice shall include description of real estate, nature and extent of lien, and facts upon which it is based. (720-5/37-2).

Commercial Vehicle Relocation Lien.—Relocation of trespassing vehicles may establish lien on vehicles for reasonable charges for removal and storage. (770-50/1, 625-5/4-203, 625-5/18a-501).

Redemption of sales made in enforcement of mechanics' lien may be made in same manner as provided for redemptions of real estate from sales under judgments and executions at law. (770-60/20).

Attachment Lien.—See topic Attachment.

Attorney's Lien.—See category Legal Profession, topic Attorneys and Counselors.

Chattel Mortgage Lien.—See Uniform Commercial Code, Article 9.

Collateral Security.—See Uniform Commercial Code, Article 9.

Condominium Owners Lien.—See category Property, topic Real Property, subhead Condominium Property Act.

Execution Lien.—See topic Executions.

Factor's Lien.—See category Business Regulation and Commerce, topics Factors and Commercial Code, Article 9.

Judgment Lien.—See category Civil Actions and Procedure, topic Judgments.

Landlord's Lien.—See category Property, topic Landlord and Tenant.

Miner's Lien.—See category Mineral, Water and Fishing Rights, topic Mines and Minerals.

Liens on Homestead.—See topic Homesteads.

Real Estate Mortgage Lien.—See category Mortgages, topic Mortgages of Real Property.

Tax Lien.—See category Taxation, topics Estate Tax, subhead Lien of Tax, Property Taxes, subheads Real Property Taxes, Liability, Lien, and Personal Property Taxes, Liability, Lien.

MECHANICS' LIENS:

See topic Liens.

PLEDGES:

Pledgee of corporate stock not liable as stockholder. (805-5/6.40).

Uniform Trust Receipts Act has been replaced by Article 9 of the Uniform Commercial Code. (810-5/9-101 et seq.). 1972 Official Text became effective July 1, 1973. See category Business Regulation and Commerce, topic Commercial Code.

See also category Business Organizations, topic Corporations, subhead Disposition of Assets.

RECEIVERS:

Specific provisions are made for receivers in foreclosing mechanics' liens (770-60/12), winding up community currency exchanges, banks, savings and loan associations (205-105/1-3), corporations (805-5/12.60), not-for-profit corporations (805-105/101.25), development credit corporations (805-35/28), insurance companies, cemetery authorities (760-100/15a), credit unions (205-305/62), publicly run airports in counties under 500,000 population. Court may appoint receiver to take possession and to dispose of property of debtor in hands of garnishee (735-5/12-718), to cause building or structure to conform to municipal regulations (65-5/11-31-2), to administer and operate health facility project for protection of rights of bondholders and others (20-3705/16), to take possession of and operate housing project where housing authority is in default (310-10/23), and to prevent use of advertising fraudulent as consumers (815-505/7, 505/8), to administer and deal with problem of improperly tapped utility line service (765-735/2), administration of certain municipal toll bridges where bond default occurs (605-5/10-711) and in other instances of bond defaults such as, pollution control facility related bonds (20-3515/10), defaults on bonds for roads and bridges over rivers forming state boundaries (605-10/807) and river conservancy districts (70-2105/15.4). Interlocutory

appeal from order appointing or refusing to appoint receiver may be perfected to Appellate Court by filing notice of appeal in trial court and record in Appellate Court within 30 days of order. (Ill. S. Ct. 307).

Court may appoint trust company as receiver. (205-620/3-1 to 620/3-3). Sale of securities by receiver is exempt transaction under Securities Act of 1953. (815-5/4[E]).

Mortgage Foreclosures.—In lieu of appointing receiver (735-5/15-1704), court may place mortgagee in possession of premises (735-5/15-1701 to 5/15-1702). In foreclosure mortgagee may use form complaint (suggested form set forth in statute) to apply for receiver. (735-5/15-1504).

Bonds.—Party applying for receiver shall give bond covering all damages and attorney's fees resulting from appointment and acts of receiver, unless court for good cause, on notice and hearing, is of opinion that a receiver ought to be appointed without bond. (735-5/2-415[a]). Court may, in lieu of appointing receiver, permit party to retain possession upon court-approved bond. (735-5/2-415[b]).

Actions Against Receivers.—Receiver of any property, appointed by any Illinois court, may be sued in respect of any act or transaction of his in carrying on business connected with such property, without previous leave of the court appointing him; but such suit is subject to general equity jurisdiction of appointing court so far as necessary to ends of justice. (735-5/2-415[c]). Service on receiver can be made as provided for individual or corporation, as is appropriate, or by serving agent employed within state. (735-5/2-212).

REDEMPTION:

See topics Executions, Liens; categories Mortgages, topic Mortgages of Real Property; Taxation, topic Property Taxes, subhead Redemption.

SUPPLEMENTARY PROCEEDINGS:

See topic Executions.

TRUSTEE PROCESS:

See topic Garnishment.

USURY:

See category Business Regulation and Commerce, topic Interest.

DISPUTE RESOLUTION

ALTERNATIVE DISPUTE RESOLUTION:

Arbitration.—See topic Arbitration and Award.

Mandatory Dispute Resolution.—Governed by Mandatory Arbitration System (735-5/2-1001A to 1009A) and Illinois Supreme Court Rules 86 to 95. Supreme Court of Illinois may provide for mandatory arbitration of civil action in order to expedite in less costly manner any litigation with claim not exceeding $50,000. (735-5/2-1001A).

Arbitrators.—Qualifications and method of appointment are proscribed by rule. (S.Ct. rule 87). Arbitrators are entitled to reasonable compensation, $200 per day or $100 if only one-half day is served. (S.Ct. rule 87[e]). Hearings will be conducted before panel of three arbitrators or lesser number agreed to by parties. (735-5/2-1003A).

Decisions.—Following hearing arbitrator's decision shall be filed with circuit court together with proof of service on parties. (735-5/2-1004A). Parties to proceeding may file with clerk written rejection within 30 days of filing of award and upon payment of $200 fee. (735-5/2-1004A, S.Ct. rule 93). In case of such rejection parties may proceed to trial before judge or jury. (735-5/2-1004A). Filing of single rejection will enable all parties, not debarred from rejecting, to proceed to trial without filing separate rejections. (S.Ct. rule 93).

Award and Judgment.—Panel shall make award promptly upon termination of hearing and dispose of all claims for relief. (S.Ct. rule 92). Award shall be signed by arbitrators or majority of them. (S.Ct. rule 92). Where no rejection is filed, judge may enter award as judgment of court. (735-5/2-1006A).

Expenses including arbitrator fees shall be determined by Illinois Supreme Court and paid from State Treasury. (735-5/2-1007A). Arbitration fee will be charged at time of filing first pleading, paper or other appearance. (735-5/2-1009A).

Circuit Court of Cook County.—Mandatory arbitration program is governed by Supreme Court rules for Conduct of Mandatory Arbitration Proceedings. (Circuit Ct. Cook Cty. [Cook] rule 18.2). All actions filed in First Municipal District after Jan. 16, 1990 involving injury to person in whole or in part, seeking money damages only, not in excess of $30,000, shall be assigned to arbitration calendar. Small claims actions are excluded. (Cook rule 18.3).

Appointment of Arbitrator-Cook County.—Applicants shall be eligible for appointment to serve as members of panel by filing application with Arbitration Administrator certifying that applicant has (1) attended mandatory arbitration seminar, (2) has read and is informed of rules of Supreme Court, (3) is presently licensed to practice law in Illinois and (4) has engaged in practice of law in Illinois for minimum of three years or is retired judge. (Cook rule 18.4).

Scheduling.—Cases filed after effective date of these rules will be given hearing date and time 270 days from filing date, or next available hearing date. (Cook rule 18.5).

Conduct and Award.—Stenographic records are not provided unless party does so at his or her own expense. Witness fees and costs are paid in same manner as provided for at trial. (Cook rule 18.6). Panel shall render its award same day hearing is completed. Arbitration panel will file its decision with Clerk of Court, who will serve notice of award. (Cook rule 18.7).

Defective Hearing Dates.—If defective hearing date is received litigants should request new date within seven days of receiving defective date and not later than 20 days prior to defective date. (Cook rule 18.11).

See note at head of Digest as to 1998 legislation covered.

See Topical Index in front part of this volume.

ALTERNATIVE DISPUTE RESOLUTION . . . *continued*

19th Circuit Arbitration (Lake and McHenry Counties).—Generally, Rules of Circuit Court-19th Circuit Part 17.00. All civil actions are subject to mandatory arbitration if each claim is exclusively for money in amount exceeding $2,500 but not exceeding $30,000, interest, costs and attorneys fees not included. (19th Circuit rule 17.01[c]). Every complaint or counterclaim filed shall contain specific prayers for relief, except in actions for injury to person, no ad damnum may be pleaded except to state amount of damages sought. (19th Circuit rule 17.01[d]).

Cases not assigned to arbitration may be ordered to arbitration at status call, pretrial conference or upon receipt from another jurisdiction where claim is greater than $2,500 but does not exceed $30,000. (19th Circuit rule 17.01[e]).

Appointment, Qualification and Compensation of Arbitrators.—Retired judges licensed to practice in Illinois and residing in 19th Judicial Circuit and all attorneys licensed in Illinois who reside in, maintain offices in or practice in counties of Lake and McHenry may be eligible as arbitrators in their respective counties, upon filling out appropriate forms. (19th Circuit rule 17.02).

Motions.—All motions shall be addressed to supervising Judge of Arbitration of respective county. (19th Circuit rule 17.04).

Hearings.—Cases are to be heard in one-half day where possible, but shall not exceed one full day. (19th Circuit rule 17.04). Hearings shall be conducted in conformity with procedures followed in civil trials. (19th Circuit rule 17.06[a]). Failure of party to be present either in person or through counsel will be governed by S.Ct. rule 91a. (19th Circuit rule 17.06[d]).

Awards.—Panel shall make award promptly on termination of hearing. Award shall not be greater than $15,000 or $30,000, depending upon amount pled, exclusive of interest costs and attorney's fees. Award will be filed immediately with Clerk of Court, who shall serve notice of award, to all parties, including any in default. (19th Circuit rule 17.07).

18th Circuit Mandatory Arbitration (DuPage County).—Generally Rules of Circuit Court-18th Circuit Art. 13. All civil actions are subject to mandatory arbitration on all claims exclusively for money in amount exceeding $2,500 but not to exceed limit authorized by Illinois Supreme Court. Cases not originally assigned to arbitration calendar may be ordered to arbitration on motion of either party, by agreement of parties or by order of court, when it appears case is within prescribed monetary limits. (18th Circuit rule 13.01).

Arbitrators.—Must complete required Arbitrator Training Seminar. All arbitrator applicants must maintain law office or residence in 18th Judicial Circuit. (18th Circuit rule 13.02).

Hearings.—Upon return date of all summons court shall assign hearing date on earliest date thereafter, provided that not less than 60 days notice be given to parties or their attorneys of record. Consolidated cases are heard on dates date assigned. (18th Circuit rule 13.03[c], [e]). Upon settlement plaintiff shall immediately notify Arbitration Administrator in writing. Presentation and decision is expected to take maximum of two hours. Plaintiff's counsel is to confer with all other counsel to determine approximate time required for presentation. Administrator is to be notified of length at least 21 days in advance of hearing date. (18th Circuit rule 13.03[f], [g]).

ARBITRATION AND AWARD:

The Uniform Arbitration Act, modified in certain respects, is in effect. (710-5/1 to 5/23).

Health Care arbitration is also governed by "Health Care Arbitration Act" effective Sept. 19, 1976, as am'd Sept. 22, 1977. (710-15/1). Disputed questions are subject to arbitration under "Workmen's Compensation Act". (820-305/19).

Illinois Supreme Court has authorized circuit courts to adopt procedures requiring mandatory arbitration for civil actions if each claim therein is exclusively for money in amount or value of $50,000 or any lesser amount as authorized by Supreme Court for any circuit or if judge of circuit court determines at pretrial conference that no greater amount appears genuinely to be in controversy, exclusive of costs and interest. (735-5/2-1001A to 2-1009A). Steps are currently being taken by some of circuits to implement system for mandatory arbitration of such claims. Provisions of Uniform Arbitration Act summarized below will not be applicable to claims within scope of mandatory arbitration rules. (735-5/2-1006A).

Form and Requisites of Submission.—See infra, subheads Validity of Arbitration Agreement; Hearing.

Contracts to Arbitrate Future Disputes.—See infra, subhead Validity of Arbitration Agreement.

Rescission.—See infra, subhead Validity of Arbitration Agreement.

Powers of Arbitrators.—See infra, subheads Appointment of Arbitrators; Hearing; Witnesses, Subpoenas, Depositions; Awards; Change of Award by Arbitrators; Vacating an Award.

Enforcement.—See, infra, subhead Judgment or Decree of Award.

Validity of Arbitration Agreement.—Written agreement to submit either existing or future controversies to arbitration is valid, enforceable, and irrevocable except upon such grounds as any contract may be subject to revocation. (710-5/1). Agreements to arbitrate claims arising out of providing of health care services are also subject to "Health Care Arbitration Act". (710-15/3).

Proceedings to Compel or Stay.—Any circuit court may compel or stay arbitration. If existence of agreement to arbitrate is challenged, that issue is to be summarily determined. If issue referable to arbitration is involved in pending litigation, party seeking arbitration is to apply to court wherein litigation is pending; otherwise application is to be made as set forth under subhead Venue, infra. If issue in any pending action is subject to arbitration, application to stay may be made in that proceeding; if issue is severable, stay may be entered with respect to that issue only. Arbitration order will not be refused merely because claim in issue lacks merit, bona fides, or because any fault or grounds for claim sought to be arbitrated have not been shown. (710-5/2[a]-[e]). In proceeding to stay or compel arbitration, court will decide whether parties have agreed to arbitrate items on which arbitration is sought. (13 Ill. App.3d 485, 300 N.E.2d 795).

Appointment of Arbitrators.—If agreement provides method, that method is to be followed; in absence thereof, any method upon which parties agree is to be followed. When arbitrator fails or is unable to act, his successor is to be appointed in same manner as original arbitrator. If no method of appointing arbitrator is set forth in agreement and parties cannot agree upon method, arbitration agreement is terminated. (710-5/3).

Majority Action by Arbitrators.—Arbitrators may act by majority vote unless agreement provides otherwise. (710-5/4).

Hearing.—Unless agreement provides otherwise, arbitrators are to set time and place for hearing and notify parties personally or by registered mail not less than five days before hearing. Appearance constitutes waiver of notice. Arbitrators may adjourn hearings from time to time when necessary or upon request of party for good cause. Arbitrators may determine controversy notwithstanding failure of duly notified party to appear. Upon application court may direct arbitrators to promptly hear and determine controversy. All parties are entitled to be heard, present evidence, and cross-examine witnesses. Hearings are to be conducted by all arbitrators, but majority may determine any question and render final award. If during hearing arbitrator ceases to act, remaining arbitrators or arbitrators appointed to act as neutrals may continue hearings and determine controversy unless otherwise provided in agreement. (710-5/5[a] to [c]).

Representation by Attorney.—Party has right to be represented by attorney, and waiver of such right prior to hearing is ineffective. (710-5/6).

Witnesses, Subpoenas, Depositions.—Arbitrators may issue subpoenas for attendance of witnesses and production of documents, etc., and are to have power to administer oaths. Subpoenas are to be served and are, upon proper application to court by either party or arbitrator, to be enforced as provided by law for subpoenas in civil cases.

Arbitrators may permit use of depositions to be taken in manner and upon terms designated by arbitrators of witnesses who cannot be subpoenaed or are unable to attend hearings.

All provisions of law compelling persons under subpoena to testify are to be applicable. Fees for attendance of witnesses are to be same as witnesses in Circuit Court. (710-5/7[a] to [d]).

Awards.—Award must be in writing, signed and served upon parties personally or by registered mail. Award must be within time fixed by agreement or within such time as court may order upon application by party. Parties may extend time for award either before or after expiration thereof, and party waives any objection that award is not made within required time unless he objects before it has been delivered to him. (710-5/8).

Change of Award by Arbitrators.—Arbitrators may upon application or upon order of court modify or correct award where there has been evident miscalculation of figures or mistake in description of any person, thing or property, or where award is imperfect as matter of form or to clarify award. Application is to be made within 20 days after delivery of award. Written notice is to be given opposing party, who must serve his objections thereto within ten days of notice. (710-5/9).

Fees and Expenses of Arbitration.—All fees other than attorney's fees are to be paid as provided in award unless agreement provides otherwise. (710-5/10).

Confirmation of Award.—Upon application court is to confirm award unless timely, valid application is made to vacate, modify or correct award. (710-5/11).

Vacating an Award.—Upon application court is to vacate award where (1) it was procured by corruption, fraud or other undue means; (2) neutral arbitrator showed evident partiality, or any arbitrator showed corruption or misconduct; (3) arbitrators exceeded their powers; (4) arbitrators refused to postpone hearings even though sufficient cause was shown or refused to hear material evidence or acted in some other way prejudicial to substantial rights of any party; or (5) if there was no arbitration agreement and issue was not adversely determined in any proceeding to compel or stay arbitration. (710-5/12[a]). In vacating award court may order rehearing under certain circumstances. (710-5/12[c]).

Application for vacation must be made within 90 days of delivery of copy of award to applicant or corruption, fraud or other undue means was known or should have been known. (710-5/12[b]).

If an application to vacate is denied and there is no motion pending to modify or correct award, court is to confirm award. (710-5/12[d]).

Labor Controversies.—Nothing in Act is to apply to vacating, modifying or correcting award under arbitration agreement which is part of a collective bargaining agreement; grounds for vacating, modifying or correcting such an award are those which existed prior to enactment of Act. (710-5/12[e]). See also category Employment, topic Labor Relations, subhead Labor Disputes.

Agricultural Controversies.—Nothing in Act is to apply to arbitration of seed purchaser's claim under Seed Arbitration Act. (710-25/1 through 25/80). See also subhead Seed Arbitration Act, infra.

Modification or Correction of Awards.—Upon application within 90 days after service of copy of award, court may modify or correct award when there has been evident miscalculation of figures or mistake in description of any person, thing or property; where arbitrators have acted upon matter not submitted to them; or, where award is imperfect as matter of form. If modification application is granted, court is to correct award so as to effect proper intent and then confirm award as corrected. Application to modify or correct may be joined in alternative with application to vacate award. (710-5/13).

Judgment or Decree of Award.—Upon court confirmation or modification of award, judgment or decree is to be entered in conformity therewith and have same force and effect as any judgment or decree. Court may enter judgment for costs as it sees just. (710-5/14).

Applications to Court.—Except as otherwise provided, applications are to be by motion and to be heard in same manner and upon same notice as provided for motions in civil cases. Unless parties have otherwise agreed, notice of initial application for order is to be served in manner provided for service of summons in civil cases. (710-5/15).

See note at head of Digest as to 1998 legislation covered.

See Topical Index in front part of this volume.

IL – 43

ARBITRATION AND AWARD . . . *continued*

Court, Jurisdiction.—Term "court" as used in Act means any circuit court. Making of agreement for arbitration in Illinois confers jurisdiction upon court to enforce agreement and to enter judgment upon award thereunder. (710-5/16).

Venue.—Initial application is to be made to court of county in which arbitration agreement provides for hearing or where hearing is actually held. Otherwise application may be made in any county where adverse party resides or has place of business or, if neither applies, in any county. All subsequent applications are to be made in court hearing initial application unless that court otherwise directs. (710-5/17).

Appeals.—Appeals may be taken in same manner and with same effect as in civil cases. (710-5/18). See category Civil Actions and Procedure, topic Appeal and Error.

Act not Retroactive.—Act applies only to agreements made subsequent to effective date of Act (Aug. 24, 1961). (710-5/19).

Construction of Act.—Act is to be construed in same manner as Uniform Act is construed in other states where it has been adopted. (710-5/20).

Severability.—Act contains severability clause. (710-5/21).

Repeal.—Act of June 11, 1917, as amended, is repealed. However, any agreement entered into under prior Act, and any proceedings under prior Act which were commenced prior to effective date of Uniform Act (Aug. 24, 1961) remain unaffected. (710-5/23).

Health Care Arbitration Act.—

Applicability.—Act applies to and governs all agreements to arbitrate claims arising out of providing health care services. Uniform Arbitration Act (710-5/1 to 5/23) governs health care arbitration agreements except where inconsistent with this Act (710-15/3). "Health care arbitration agreement" or "agreement" defined as written agreement between patient and hospital or health care provider to submit to binding arbitration claims for damages or death of patient due to provider's or hospital's negligence or wrongful act, but not included intentional torts. "Health care provider" is person or entity in practice of medicine, surgery, chiropractics, dentistry, podiatry, optometry, physical therapy or nursing. "Hospital" is person or entity operating or administering hospital, clinic, nursing home or sanitarium. (710-15/2). Act does not apply to arbitration claims arising out of Seed Arbitration Act. (710-25/1 through 25/80). See subhead Seed Arbitration Act, infra.

Conditions of Agreement.—Every health care arbitration agreement must be separate, independent instrument; be clearly captioned "Health Care Arbitration Agreement"; state date of commencement of hospitalization or specify cause for which services are provided; must contain specified notice to patient printed in letters at least 3/16" high; and copy must be delivered to and be reaffirmed by patient at time of discharge. Failure to so deliver voids agreement. Such agreements may not be required as condition to rendering health care services, limit, nor impair or waive substantive rights or defenses (including statute of limitations) or procedural due process rights. (710-15/8, 15/9). Employees of hospitals or health care providers are deemed parties to every agreement signed by their employers. Agreements may bar action at law against such employers based on respondeat superior for negligent or wrongful act of employee. (710-15/6).

Parent may bind minor child to health care arbitration agreement. Parent may be minor and agreement will not be voidable for this reason. (710-15/7).

Cancellation of Agreement.—Health care arbitration agreements may be cancelled within 60 days of execution, discharge from hospital or last treatment, whichever is later and become invalid one year after execution. Nonsignatory employees may cancel (as to themselves) until 30 days following notification that they are parties to disputes on which arbitration is demanded under agreement. Personal representatives may cancel agreements of decedents who die during period of cancellation up to 60 days from appointment. (710-15/9[c]). If no legal representative is appointed within six months, next of kin may cancel agreement within eight months of death.

Proceedings.—(a) Demand and Claim: Arbitration is commenced by serving notice of demand for arbitration and statement of claim and cause of action on all parties from whom damages are sought. Statement is to be in form of complaint and it and demand are to be served in accordance with Civil Practice Act. Service of notice of demand tolls statute of limitations for parties named in notice. (710-15/10). (b) Parties: Necessary parties include hospital, health care provider, employee of either, or supplier (defined as person or entity that manufactured, designed, distributed, sold or otherwise provided medication, device, equipment, service or other product used in diagnosis or treatment (710-15/2) reasonably alleged to be joint tortfeasor. Arbitration may be stayed on basis that necessary party is not signatory or party to agreement. (710-15/5). By consent of all parties, person or entity which did not sign agreement may participate upon execution of written undertaking to be bound by award. (710-15/4). (c) Discovery and admissibility of evidence governed by rules applicable to civil cases. (710-15/11, 15/12; 710-5/7).

Arbitrators.—Parties may agree to single arbitrator. Otherwise there is to be panel of three, one to be appointed by each side (multiple parties to resolve differences by lot) and third to be appointed by other two. Upon affidavit that agreement cannot be reached, court shall submit list of five practicing attorneys (including retired Supreme, Appellate or Circuit judges), each party shall strike two names and remaining person shall be single or neutral arbitrator. (710-15/13). Court appointed arbitrators are to receive $100 per day compensation (others maximum of $100 per day) and reimbursement for expenses to be apportioned equally among parties selecting arbitrator or all parties when arbitrator is appointed by court or agreement of parties. (710-15/14).

Seed Arbitration Act.—Act requires seed purchasers to submit claim to arbitration prior to civil action. Arbitration results are nonbinding. (710-25/10).

DOCUMENTS AND RECORDS

ACKNOWLEDGMENTS:

Uniform Recognition of Acknowledgments Act adopted. (765-30/1 to 30/10).

Short Form Acknowledgments valid whether executed in Illinois or any other state. (765-30/7).

Within State.—May be taken before notary public, United States commissioner, county clerk, or any court, or any judge, clerk or deputy clerk of any such court. When taken before notary public or United States commissioner, official seal must be affixed. When taken before court or clerk or deputy clerk thereof, seal of court must be affixed. (765-5/20).

Outside State but Within United States.—May be taken before justice of peace, notary public, master in chancery, United States commissioner, commissioner to take acknowledgments of deeds, mayor of city, clerk of county, or any judge, justice, clerk or deputy clerk of Supreme, circuit or district court of United States, or any judge, justice, clerk, deputy clerk, prothonotary, surrogate or registrar of supreme, circuit, superior, district, county, common pleas, probate, orhpan's or surrogate's court of any state, territory or dependency of United States. In dependency may also be taken before any commissioned officer in military service of United States. Acknowledgment before notary public or United States commissioner or commissioner of deeds must be under seal of office; if before mayor, under seal of city; if before clerk, deputy clerk, prothonotary, registrar or surrogate, under seal of court; if before justice of peace or master in chancery, certificate of proper clerk under his seal of office stating that person was such justice of peace or master in chancery must be supplied. If clerk of any court of record within state, territory, dependency or district shall, under signature and seal of court, certify acknowledgment was made in conformity within its laws or it appears by laws of such state, territory, dependency or district, instrument or duly proved or certified copy of record of deed, mortgage or other instrument relating to real estate made and recorded in proper county may be admitted in evidence as in other cases involving admission of certified copies. (765-5/20).

Outside United States.—May be taken before any court of any republic, dominion, state, kingdom, empire, colony, territory or dependency having a seal, or any judge, justice or clerk thereof, any major or chief officer of any city or town having a seal, notary public, commissioner of deeds, ambassador, minister or secretary of legation, or consul of United States, vice consul, deputy consul, commercial agent or consular agent of United States, attested by his official seal, or any officer authorized by laws of place where taken to take acknowledgments of conveyances of real estate or to administer oaths in proof of conveyances of real estate. Such acknowledgment must be attested by official seal of court or officer; or if no official seal, then certificate by ambassador, minister, secretary of legation, consul, vice consul, deputy consul, commercial agent or consular agent of United States residing in such place, under his official seal, showing court or officer was duly elected, appointed or created and acting at time of acknowledgment must be added. (765-5/20).

Persons Serving in or with U.S. Armed Forces within or without the U.S., and the spouse or former spouse of any such person, may acknowledge the instrument wherever located before any commissioned officer in active service of armed forces of the U.S. with rank of second lieutenant or higher in army, air force or marine corps or ensign or higher in navy or U.S. Coast Guard. Instrument is not invalid for failure to state therein place of execution or acknowledgment; nor is authentication of officers' certificate of acknowledgment required and such certificate need not be under seal but certificate in form substantially same as that prescribed by statute must be endorsed on acknowledgment or attached thereto. (765-5/20).

General Requirements as to Taking.—Judge or other officer before whom acknowledgment is taken must personally know person acknowledging or identity of person acknowledging must be established by credible witness. Foregoing must be affirmatively recited in instrument. (765-5/24, 5/26). No general statutory provision disqualifying acknowledging officer from acting in certain cases.

General Requirements of Certificate.—Seal of acknowledging officer must be affixed. (765-5/20).

Married woman may acknowledge as though unmarried. (765-5/19).

Attorneys in Fact.—When power of attorney relating to real estate executed by person in service or employment of Federal Government and reported missing, missing in action, or being held incommunicado or imprisoned in foreign country is recorded in county where real estate is located along with affidavit of attorney-in-fact or agent declaring absence of actual knowledge or notice of revocation or termination of power by death or otherwise, or facts indicating same, persons dealing with attorney-in-fact in good faith are not required to ascertain whether person he represents is living, and are protected against claims against real estate interests acquired in dealings with such attorneys-in-fact unless prior to acquisition revocation of power or affidavit of death of person who executed power has been filed in office of recorder of deeds where power recorded. Military report of "missing" does not constitute actual notice of death of principal nor shall it operate to revoke agency. (725-5/28b).

Corporations.—All documents required to be filed with Secretary of State which must be verified may be acknowledged and sworn to before officer competent to take acknowledgments of deeds, or by signature, without more, of person signing instrument. (805-5/1.10 & 805-105/101.01). Acknowledgment of corporation or person signing on its behalf may be taken by notary public who is officer, director or employee of corporation provided notary public does not sign instrument acknowledged on behalf of corporation. (765-25/1.1).

Foreign Acknowledgments.—Uniform Recognition of Acknowledgments Act adopted. (765-30/1 to 30/10). Where any deed, conveyance or power of attorney has been acknowledged in foreign state, certificate, under seal, of any consul or minister of U.S. in said country that deed, etc. was executed in conformity with such foreign law shall be prima facie evidence of that fact and all deeds, etc. acknowledged in conformity with foreign law shall be deemed as good and valid as though acknowledged in conformity with Illinois law. (765-5/22, 5/23).

Effect of Acknowledgment.—Acknowledgment is not necessary to validity of conveyance or recordation thereof. Unacknowledged document may not be read as evidence unless execution is proved in accordance with rules of evidence. (765-5/31). Deeds, mortgages, powers of attorney, conveyances or other writings concerning lands, tenements or hereditaments required or entitled to be recorded, being acknowledged or proved by subscribing witness, may be read in evidence without further proof of

See note at head of Digest as to 1998 legislation covered.

See Topical Index in front part of this volume.

IL-44

ACKNOWLEDGMENTS . . . *continued*

execution. (765-5/35). Certified copy of lost original, or of original not in personal power of person wishing to use it, may be read in evidence without further proof of execution if original was acknowledged or proved by subscribing witness. (765-5/35, 5/36). All deeds which may be executed by any administrator, executor, guardian, commissioner, sheriff, or other officer, of any real estate sold in pursuance of any judgment upon being acknowledged or proved by subscribing witness before any officer authorized to take acknowledgments or proof of deeds, and certified as other deeds, shall be admitted to record in county where real estate is situated. (765-5/32).

Proof by Subscribing Witness.—A deed or instrument not duly acknowledged may be proved by testimony of subscribing witness, or in case of death of grantor and subscribing witnesses, or when subscribing witnesses cannot be had, by proof of handwriting of grantor and of at least one subscribing witness, such proof to consist of testimony of two or more disinterested persons swearing to each signature. (765-5/25).

Authentication—Certificate of Conformity.—Acknowledgment taken in conformity with laws of state, territory, dependency or district of United States where taken is sufficient if certified to be such by clerk of court of record under court seal. (765-5/20).

Certificate of any consul or minister of the United States in any foreign state, kingdom, empire or country, under his official seal, that execution or acknowledgment is in conformity with such foreign law is deemed prima facie evidence thereof. (765-5/22).

An acknowledgment made before a justice of peace or master in chancery in another state, territory, dependency or district of United States must have added a certificate of proper clerk under seal of his office that person was such justice of peace or master in chancery at time of acknowledgment. (765-5/20).

Fraudulent Acknowledgments.—A person, knowing that his acknowledgment is not authorized by law and who acknowledges the execution of any document which by law may be recorded, may be fined not to exceed $25,000 or imprisoned from one to three years or both. (720-5/32-6, 730-5/5-9-1). Statute provides that any officer authorized to take proof and acknowledgment of any conveyance of real or personal property, or other instrument, who wilfully certifies that such was duly proven or acknowledged when none such was made, or when such was not made at time it was certified to have been made, with intent to injure or defraud or to enable another to injure or defraud, shall be fined not to exceed $25,000 or imprisoned from one to three years or both. (720-260/128, 730-5/5-9-1).

Forms.—By statute the following are sufficient:

Forms

State of (name of state) County of (name of county) ss. I (here give name of officer and his official title) do hereby certify that (name of grantor and, if acknowledged by wife, her name and add 'his wife') personally known to me to be the same person whose name is (are) subscribed to the foregoing instrument, appeared before me this day in person, and acknowledged that he (she or they) signed and delivered the said instrument as his (her or their) free and voluntary act, for the uses and purposes therein set forth. Given under my hand and official seal, this (day of the month) day of (month) A. D. (year). (Signature of officer) (Seal). (765-5/26).

Acknowledgment by Persons Serving in or with U.S. Armed Forces and spouse or former spouse of any such person:
On this . . . . . day of . . . . ., 19. . . . ., before me, ..., the undersigned officer, personally appeared . . . . ., known to me (or satisfactorily proven) to be serving in or with the armed forces of the United States (and/or the spouse or former spouse of a person so serving) and to be the person whose name is subscribed to the within instrument and acknowledged that, he . . . . executed the same as . . . . . free and voluntary act for the purposes therein contained. And the undersigned does further certify that he is at the date of this certificate a commissioned officer of the rank stated below and is in the active service of the armed forces of the United States. (Signature of Officer, Rank of Officer and Command to which attached.) (765-5/20).

Acknowledgment on Behalf of Corporation on Document filed with Secretary of State:
State of . . . . . County of . . . . . ss.
I (insert name and official capacity of official) do hereby certify that on the . . . . . day of . . . . . 19. . . ., (insert names of persons signing document), personally appeared before me and being first duly sworn by me severally acknowledged that they signed the foregoing document in the respective capacities therein set forth and declared that the statements therein contained are true.
In Witness Whereof, I have hereunto set my hand and seal the day and year before written. (insert official capacity of official). (805-105/101.01).

Short Form for Individual Acting in Own Right:
State of . . . County of . . .
The foregoing instrument was acknowledged before me this (date) by (name of person acknowledged).
(Signature of person taking acknowledgment)
(Title)

Short Form for Corporation:
State of . . . County of . . .
The foregoing instrument was acknowledged before me this (date) by (name of officer or agent, title of officer or agent) of (name of corporation acknowledging) a (state or place of incorporation) corporation, on behalf of the corporation.
(Signature of person taking acknowledgment)
(Title)

Short Form for Partnership:
State of . . . County of . . .
The foregoing instrument was acknowledged before me this (date) by (name of acknowledging partner or agent), partner (or agent) on behalf of (name of partnership), a partnership.

(Signature of person taking acknowledgment)
(Title)

Short Form for Individual Acting as Principal by Attorney in Fact:
State of . . . County of . . .
The foregoing instrument was acknowledged before me this (date) by (name of attorney in fact) as attorney in fact on behalf of (name of principal).
(Signature of person taking acknowledgment)
(Title)

Short Form for any Public Officer, Trustee, or Personal Representative:
State of . . . County of . . .
The foregoing instrument was acknowledged before me this (date) by (name and title of position).
(Signature of person taking acknowledgment)
(Title)

The following forms are in common use, but are not specifically sanctioned by statute.
Acknowledgment on Behalf of Corporation:
State of . . . . County of . . . . ss.
I (name and official title) do hereby certify that (name of President or other authorized officer) personally known to me to be the (official capacity) of (name of corporation), a (state) corporation, and (name of Secretary or other authorized officer) personally known to me to be the (official capacity) of said corporation, and personally known to me to be the same persons whose names are subscribed to the foregoing instrument, appeared before me this day in person and severally acknowledged that as such (official capacities of both officers), they signed and delivered the said instrument as (official capacities of both officers) of said corporation, and caused the corporate seal of said corporation to be affixed thereto, pursuant to authority, given by the Board of . . . . of said corporation as their free and voluntary act, and as the free and voluntary act and deed of said corporation, for the uses and purposes therein set forth. Given under my hand and (private or official, as the case may be) seal, this (date). Commission expires (date). (Signature of officer). (Seal).

Proof by a subscribing witness:
State of . . . . County of . . . . ss.
I (here give name of officer and his official title), hereto duly appointed and commissioned, do hereby certify that on this . . . . day of . . . . 19. . . . before me personally appeared A. B., personally known to me (or proved to me by C. D., a credible witness under oath) to be the person whose name appears subscribed to the foregoing deed as a witness of the execution thereof, who on oath testified that E. F., whose name appears subscribed to said deed as grantor, is the real person who executed the same as grantor, and that he, A. B., subscribed his name as a witness thereto in the presence and at the request of said E. F.; which is satisfactory proof to me of the due execution of said deed.
In witness whereof I have hereunto set my hand and seal this . . . . day of . . . . 19. . . . .

(Signature, title, and seal).

Proof where subscribing witnesses are dead or unavailable:
State of . . . . County of . . . . ss.
I (here give name of officer and his official title), hereto duly appointed and commissioned, do hereby certify that on this . . . . day of . . . . 19. . . . before me personally appeared C. D., a competent and credible witness, who stated on oath that he personally knew E. F., and A. B., both now deceased, whose names appear subscribed to the foregoing deed as grantor and witness respectively, and well knew their signatures (here state means of knowledge), and that he believes the names of said E. F. and A. B. to said deed were subscribed thereto by said E. F. as grantor and said A. B. as witness respectively; which is satisfactory proof to me of the due execution of said deed.
In witness whereof I have hereunto set my hand and seal this . . . . day of . . . . 19. . . . .

(Signature, title, and seal).

Alternative to Acknowledgment or Proof.—Unless Supreme Court Rules provide otherwise, whenever any complaint, petition, answer, reply, bill or particulars, answer to interrogatories, affidavit, return or proof of service, or other document or pleading filed in Illinois state court is required or permitted to be verified or sworn to under oath, this includes certification of pleading, affidavit or other document. One having knowledge of matter stated in pleading, affidavit or other document shall certify in following form:
"Under penalties as provided by law pursuant to Section 1-109 of the Code of Civil Procedure, the undersigned certifies that the statements set forth in this instrument are true and correct, except as to matters therein stated to be on information and belief and as to such matters the undersigned certifies as aforesaid that he verily believes the same to be true."
Any pleading, affidavit, or other document so certified may be used as affidavit. False statements, not believed to be true, are subject to penalty as Class III felony. (735-5/1-109).

Validating Acts.—All deeds or other instruments duly certified or proven which have been acknowledged or proven prior to Aug. 30, 1963, in manner provided in 765-5/20 shall be deemed to be good and effectual in law and may be read in evidence without further proof of their execution. (765-5/20).
All deeds or mortgages heretofore irregularly executed by omission of seal are validated and made effective as though seal affixed (adopted 1941). (765-5/35b).

AFFIDAVITS:

All courts and each judge, and clerk thereof, county clerks, deputy county clerks, Secretary of State, notaries public, commissioned officers in active service of U.S. Armed Forces and persons certified under 255-415/1 have power to administer oaths and take affidavits and depositions in Illinois in respective counties or jurisdictions. (5-

See note at head of Digest as to 1998 legislation covered.

See Topical Index in front part of this volume.

AFFIDAVITS . . . *continued*
255/1.2). Persons having conscientious scruples against oaths may affirm. (5-255/4). See topic Acknowledgments.

Outside Illinois, oaths may be administered by any officer there authorized, and his certificate, under his official seal, stating that he is authorized, is prima facie evidence of authority. (5-255/6).

Commissioned officer in U. S. Armed Forces may administer oaths within or without U.S. Oaths, affidavits and depositions need not be authenticated nor attested by any seal and jurat need not state venue. (5-255/2).

Forms.—No form of affidavit is prescribed. In common practice the venue is followed by the statement of facts and the affiant's signature. Affidavit is completed with the usual jurat:

Form

"Subscribed and sworn to before me this . . . . day of . . . . A. D., 19. . . ., (name and title of officer)" and official seal.

If officer has no official seal, certificate of magistracy should be supplied.

In case of oath administered outside Illinois, jurat may read:

Form

"Subscribed and sworn to this . . . . day of . . . . A. D., 19. . . ., before me, a (here state official title), who hereby certifies under my official seal that I am duly authorized by the laws of the State of . . . . to administer oaths in the county and state (or whatever the venue may be) aforesaid." (Add signature, official seal, and date of expiration of commission).

Certification is fully effective alternative to verification under oath from notary public. (735-5/1-109). Person having knowledge of matters shall subscribe to certification in substantially following form:

Form

Under penalties as provided by law pursuant to Section 1-109 of the Code of Civil Procedure, the undersigned certifies that the statements set forth in this instrument are true and correct, except as to matters therein stated to be on information and belief and as to such matters the undersigned certifies as aforesaid that he verily believes the same to be true. (735-5/1-109).

Use of Affidavits.—When used in opposition to or in support of summary judgment or motion to dismiss, affidavit made on personal knowledge of affiant and shall set forth with particularity facts upon which claim is based. (Ill. S. Ct. R. 191).

Alternative to Affidavit.—See topic Acknowledgments.

NOTARIES PUBLIC:

Note: The Illinois Notary Public Act has been adopted, effective July 1, 1986.

Qualification.—Secretary of State appoints and commissions all notaries. (5-312/2-101). Notary must be at least 18 years old, citizen of U.S. or alien lawfully admitted for permanent residence in U.S., resident in Illinois for at least 30 days preceding notary application, able to read and write English, never convicted of felony, and must not have had commission as notary, if any, revoked within past ten years. (5-312/2-102). Notaries must post bond with surety of $5,000 and take oath prescribed by statute. Fee for commission is $25. (5-312/2-103). Recording fee is $5 if done in person or $10 if done by mail. (5-312/2-106).

Seal.—Notaries must provide themselves with official rubber stamp seal conforming to specified design and containing specified information. (5-312/2-301). Seal must be used to authenticate their official acts. (5-312/3-102).

Powers and Duties.—Notaries public may do anything authorized by law, including taking acknowledgment, administering oath or affirmation, taking verification upon oath or affirmation, and witnessing or attesting signature. (5-312/6-101). Notary may not acknowledge any instrument in which notary's name appears as party to transaction. (5-312/6-104).

Civil and criminal penalties imposed for violation of notarial responsibilities. These can extend to employers if notary was acting within course or scope of employment, with employer's consent. (5-312/7-101 to 7-109).

Territorial Extent of Powers.—Notaries public may act anywhere in state so long as they reside in county of appointment. (5-312/3-105).

Expiration of Commission.—Term of office is four years. (5-312/2-101). No statutory duty to state date of expiration of commission in connection with official signature.

Fees.—Maximum fee for any notarial act is $1. (5-312/3-104).

Acknowledgment by Corporation Employee.—No specific provision.

Authentication.—See topic Acknowledgments.

RECORDS:

Recorder is elected in each county having population of 60,000 or more; in counties having less population county clerk is recorder. (55-5/3-5001).

Recordable Instruments.—Deeds, mortgages and other instruments relating to real estate must be recorded in county in which real estate is situated and take effect as to creditors and subsequent purchasers without notice from time of filing same for record, but otherwise are not required to be filed for record within any certain time. (765-5/28, 5/30).

For list of Counties and County Seats see first page for this state in Volume containing Practice Profiles Section.

No deed, mortgage assignment of mortgage or other instrument relating to or affecting title to real estate may prohibit recording of instrument and any such provision in instrument signed after July 19, 1995 is void and of no force.

Effective Jan. 1, 1968, all contracts for sale of dwelling structure may be recorded in same manner as deed or other instrument relating to real estate. Any provision in contract for sale of dwelling structure which forbids contract buyer to record contract or provides that recording shall not constitute notice or provides for any penalty for recording is void. (765-70/2). Possession of real property is notice of unrecorded deed. (118 Ill. 619, 8 N.E. 808). Tax deeds must be recorded within one year after time of redemption expires. (35-205/271). County board of counties having population of 250,000 or more may require recording of diagrams indicating location and size of drain tiles within 30 days after installation. (70-605-2-13).

Requisites for Recording.—County recorder may require that prior to recording any conveyance containing metes and bounds description for unsubdivided land, affidavit be attached as to facts which exempt conveyance from provisions of Plat Act. (765-205/5a). Plat Act requires that whenever owner of land subdivides it into two or more parts, any of which is less than five acres, he must first have survey and plat (no smaller than 8 1/2" by 14" and no larger than 30" by 36") made by Registered Land Surveyor, signed and approved by specified parties, and recorded. (765-205/1 to 205/2). Act contains following specific exemptions from its application: (1) Division or subdivision of land into parcels or tracts of five acres or more in size which does not involve any new streets or easements of access; (2) division of lots on blocks of less than one acre in any recorded subdivision which does not involve any new streets or easements of access; (3) sale or exchange of parcels of land between owners of adjoining and contiguous land; (4) conveyance of parcels of land of interests therein for use as right of way for railroads or other public utility facilities and other pipelines which does not involve any new streets or easements of access; (5) conveyance of land owned by railroad or other public utility which does not involve any new streets or easements of access; (6) conveyance of land for highway or other public purposes or grants or conveyances relating to dedication of land for public use or instruments relating to vacation of land impressed with public use; (7) conveyances made to correct descriptions in prior conveyances; (8) sale or exchange of parcels or tracts of land following division into no more than two parts of particular parcel or tract of land existing on July 17, 1959 and not involving any new streets or easements of access; (9) sale of single lot of less than five acres from larger tract when survey is made by registered surveyor; provided that this exemption shall not apply to sale of any subsequent lots from same larger tract of land, as determined by dimensions and configuration of larger tract on Oct. 1, 1973, and provided also that this exemption does not invalidate any local requirements applicable to subdivision of land. (765-205/1[b]). If plat made of parcel otherwise exempt, such plat must be recorded. (765-205/1[c]).

No instrument affecting title to real estate shall be recorded without name and address of preparer on face thereof. Failure to comply does not impair validity and effect of recorded instrument. (55-5/3-5022). Several counties, including Cook County, require instrument to indicate permanent tax identification number of parcel. Recorder cannot record plat unless plat states current mailing address of person submitting plat for recording. (765-205/2).

Recording Fees.—For recording deeds or other instruments: $12 for first four pages, $1 for each additional page plus $1 for each additional document number therein noted; minimum fee $12. If premises affected by instrument to be recorded is referred to by document number and not legal description, additional $1 for each document number noted. For recording maps or plats of additions or subdivision approved by county or municipality or plats of condominiums, $50 for first page, plus $1 for each additional page except, if single page, 8 1/2 x 14 plat of survey in which there are no more than two lots or parcels, $12. Maps or plats must be accompanied by such number of exact, true, legible copies as recorder deems necessary. For certified copies, same fee as for recording except $10 fee maximum for map or plat of addition, subdivision or other. After Jan. 1, 1995, recorder shall charge additional fee equal to fee otherwise charged for documents that do not conform to certain standards of page size (8.5 by 11 inches); except graphic displays accompanying document up to 11 inches x 17 inches recorded without additional fee; legibly printed in black ink by hand, type or computer; signatures and dates may be in contrasting colors if reproducible; white paper of at least 20 lb. and 1/2 inch margin on top, bottom and sides; blank space of at least 3 in. by 5 in. in upper right corner of first page; no attachment stapled or affixed to any page. Unless additional fee is paid, recorder will not record such nonconforming document. No filing fee charged for informational copies of financing statements pursuant to §9-403 of UCC. (55-5/3-5018).

In third class counties (population exceeding 1,000,000) for recording deeds or other instruments: requirements as to page size, paper, printing etc. are same as for counties that are not third class counties except: $20 for first two pages, $2 for each additional page, any page over 8.5 by 11 inches equals two pages; minimum fee $20. If referred to by document number and not legal description, additional $4 for each document number noted. If instrument describes more than one tract or parcel and such are in separate subdivision, addition, or quarter-section, $4 for each subdivision or addition referred to. For recording maps or plats of additions or subdivisions, $100 plus $2 for each tract, parcel or lot therein. Filing release of chattel mortgage or trust deed, $10. For certified copies, same fee as for recording except $200 fee maximum for map or plat of addition, subdivision or other. (55-5/4-12002).

For processing sworn statement required for filing deed or assignment of beneficial interest in land trust, $2. Recorder shall charge additional fee equal to fee otherwise provided by law for documents that do not conform to paper size (8.5 x 11 inches), not permanently bound and not continuous form; black ink, typewritten or computer generated in 10 point type or higher; white paper of at least 20 lb. and 1/2 inch margin on top, bottom and sides; blank space of at least 3 in. by 5 in. in upper right corner of first page; no attachment stapled or affixed to any page. Unless additional fee is paid, recorder will not record such nonconforming document.

Real Estate Transfer Tax.—See category Property, topic Real Property, subheads State Stamp Tax, County Stamp Tax, and Local Stamp Tax.

Filing Under Commercial Code—Place; Fees.—Uniform Commercial Code was adopted by Act approved July 31, 1961 and became effective July 2, 1962. 1972 amendments became effective July 1, 1973. See category Business Regulation and Commerce, topic Commercial Code.

See note at head of Digest as to 1998 legislation covered.

See Topical Index in front part of this volume.

RECORDS . . . *continued*

Proper place to file to perfect security interest under 1972 revisions of Art. 9 of Commercial Code is as follows: (a) When collateral is consumer goods, in office of Recorder in county of debtor's residence or, if debtor nonresident, in office of Recorder in county where goods are kept; (b) when collateral is timber to be cut, minerals, or like (including oil and gas) or accounts subject to 810-5/9-103(5), when collateral is investment property subject to 810-5/9-103(6), or when financing statement filed as fixture filing (810-5/9-313) and collateral is goods which are or are to become fixtures, then in office where mortgage on real estate would be filed or recorded; and (c) in all other cases, in office of Secretary of State, but with respect to filings to perfect security interest in collateral, including fixtures, of transmitting utility, proper place of filing is in office of Secretary of State (810-5/9-401). Neither Secretary of State nor Recorder, nor any of their respective employees or agents, incurs personal liability by reason of any error or omission in performance of duties under Art. 9 of Uniform Commercial Code, except for willful negligence. (810-10/1; 55-5/3-5045).

Residence of organization is place of business or, if more than one, chief executive office. (810-5/9-401).

See Art. 11 of Uniform Commercial Code for transition provisions on changes in requirements of filings and required refilings and priorities. (810-5/11-101 to 5/11-108).

Prior to July 1, 1973 proper place of filing in order to perfect security interest under Art. 9 of Commercial Code was as follows: (a) When collateral is equipment used in farming operations, farm products, or accounts, contract rights or general intangibles arising from or relating to sale of farm products by farmer, or consumer goods, then in office of Recorder in county of debtor's residence; or, if debtor is nonresident, then in office of Recorder in county where goods are kept; in addition, when collateral is crops, in office of Recorder in county where land on which crops are growing or are to be grown is located; (b) when collateral is goods, which at time security interest attaches are or are to become fixtures, then in office where mortgage on real estate concerned would be filed or recorded; and (c) in all other cases, in office of Secretary of State. (810-5/9-401).

Fees are: (a) for filing, indexing and stamping furnished copy of original financing statement or continuation statement, $20 if in Secretary of State's prescribed form; (c) for filing, indexing and furnishing filing data for financing statement disclosing assignment, $20 if in Secretary of State's prescribed form, otherwise $8, plus $4 for each additional name or address against which such statement required to be indexed (810-5/9-405); (d) for filing, indexing and furnishing filing data for separate statement of assignment, $20 if in Secretary of State's prescribed form, otherwise $8, plus $4 for each additional name or address against which statement of assignment required to be indexed (810-5/9-405); (e) for filing of statement releasing all or part of collateral described in filed financing statement, and noting same, $20 if in Secretary of State's prescribed form, otherwise $8, plus $4 for each additional name or address against which statement of release must be indexed (810-5/9-406). Certificate obtainable from filing officer showing whether any presently effective financing statement naming particular debtor or statement of assignment exists; fee is $10 per name searched. Copies furnished on request at $1 per page. (810-5/9-407).

Federal Tax Lien Notices.—Notices of liens for internal revenue taxes and certificates discharging such liens must be filed in office of Recorder of county within which property subject to lien is situated. (770-110/2).

Torrens Repeal Law.—Effective Jan. 1, 1991, all property registered under Torrens Registration System which is transferred will be converted to regular title system. No additional land may be registered under Registered Titles (Torrens) Act. Effective July 1, 1997, all converted to regular title system. Effective July 1, 2037, Torrens Act repealed. Torrens Act had only been adopted in Cook County and only as to certain limited lands. (765-35/1 to 35/110.3).

Transfer of Decedent's Title.—If decedent was a resident of Illinois, probate proceedings are sufficient evidence of transfer to his devisees or heirs of his real estate in the county where such proceedings were had. (335 Ill. 184, 166 N.E. 538). With respect to other real estate, a certified transcript of the probate proceedings should be filed with the recorder of deeds or registrar of titles of county in which such real estate is situated. (765-5/33).

If decedent was nonresident, probate of his will, whether originally proved in state of his residence (or elsewhere) or not, is necessary to transfer title to his devisees. (755-5/7-1 to 5/7-5). Record of foreign will probated in other state but not in Illinois, exemplified according to Act of Congress, may be recorded with recorder of deeds or registrar of titles in county where real estate is located (765-5/33); but such recording only provides notice of existence of will. (328 Ill. 431, 159 N.E. 780). If probate of will already proved in another state is had in one county in Illinois, filing of transcript of said probate proceedings in another Illinois county where decedent's real estate is located has effect of transferring title to that real estate. (765-5/33). Probate proceedings are also necessary to bar claims of decedent's creditors against real estate except all claims other than expenses of administrator and surviving spouse's or child's award are barred two years after decedent's death whether or not letters of office are issued. (755-5/18-12). Transfer of title of real estate of nonresident decedent is accomplished by ancillary probate proceedings in Illinois.

Vital Statistics.—Office of Vital Records of Department of Public Health operates system of maintaining vital records. (410-535/2). State Registrar of Vital Records supervises such office and establishes registration districts throughout State. (410-535/5 to 535/6).

Births and Deaths.—Births and deaths must be registered within seven days with local registrar of district in which birth or death occurs. (410-535/12, 535/18). Local Registrar transmits monthly copy of registration to State Registrar and to County Clerk of his county. (410-535/8). State Registrar, local registrars and county clerks are official custodians of birth and death records. (410-535/23). Upon request to State Registrar, and payment of $10 search fee, certification of birth and death records will be furnished if available and if other statutory requisites are satisfied. Certified copies require additional $5 fee for first copy and $2 for each additional copy. (410-535/25). Birth and death records from 1916 to present available by request to State Registrar, Division of Vital Records, 535 W. Jefferson, Springfield, Illinois 62761. In case of resident of Chicago deceased less than three months from date of request, request for death certificate must be directed to Chicago Board of Health, Daley Center, Chicago, Illinois 60602 which also has record of all deaths occurring in Chicago from 1947 to present date. After three month period request may also be made to County Clerk of Cook County, Bureau of Vital Statistics, 130 N. Wells St., Chicago, Illinois 60606 which has record of all deaths occurring in Cook County from 1871 to present date.

Establishing Birth Records.—Delayed registration of birth will be made upon submission of satisfactory documentary proof and payment of $15 fee. (410-535/14).

Marriages, Divorces and Annulments.—System of central registration of marriages, divorces or annulments occurring after Jan. 1, 1962 is maintained by Department of Public Health. (410-530/1 et seq.). Forms relating to divorce must, among other things, show age of individuals at time of marriage and at time of divorce. (410-530/1). Department may reproduce on microfilm records subject to Act. Such microfilm deemed original record for all purposes including as evidence in all courts and administrative agencies. (410-530/2). Requests for copies of records of marriages, divorces or annulments occurring after Jan. 1, 1962 may be made to Department of Public Health in Springfield, Illinois, by parties to marriage, their children or their parents. Fee of $5 should accompany request. If record is found, Department will verify fact of marriage, divorce or annulment in writing and notify applicant of place where original record is maintained. (Clerk of county in which marriage, divorce or annulment occurred.) Certified copies may be obtained only from such local office, except upon court order or request of court clerk. (410-530/3).

Records of marriages, divorces and annulments occurring prior to Jan. 1, 1962 are maintained by clerk of county in which such marriages, divorces or annulments occurred. Copies of such records should be requested from such county clerks.

Private Business Records.—Uniform Preservation of Private Business Records Act has been adopted. (805-410/1 to 410/6). Records required by law to be preserved may be destroyed after three years unless express contrary provision. (805-410/2). Durable reproductions of original business records constitute compliance if made in the regular course of business and if certain conditions are met. (805-410/3). Reproductions are admissible in evidence when satisfactorily identified if original would be admissible. (805-410/3[b]).

State Records.—Art. 5, §19 of Ill. Constitution requires all officers of executive branch to keep accounts, to make such reports as may be required by law and to provide Governor with information relating to their offices as Governor may require.

Art. 8, §1(c) of Ill. Constitution provides that reports and records of obligation, receipt and use of public funds of State, units of local government and school districts are available for public inspection according to law. There is also statutory provision to this effect. (5-160/3).

Public has access to these public records for purpose of copying. (5-160/4). Custodian may charge fee for supervising inspection equal to fee for providing certified copy of documents or record. Where fees not otherwise fixed by law, may charge for providing photocopy as follows: 35¢ per page less than legal sized; $1 per page equal to or exceeding legal sized. (5-160/4).

SEALS:

Use of private seals on written contracts, deeds, mortgages, or any other written instruments heretofore required by law to be sealed is abolished, but addition of a private seal to any such instrument does not in any manner affect its force, validity or character, or in any way change construction thereof. (815-650/1).

Use of corporate seals is authorized. (805-5/3.10[c]).

Uniform Commercial Code has been adopted, effective July 2, 1962. (c. 810). See category Business Regulation and Commerce, topic Commercial Code.

TORRENS ACT:

See topic Records.

VITAL STATISTICS:

See topic Records.

EMPLOYMENT

EMPLOYER AND EMPLOYEE:

See topic Labor Relations.

LABOR RELATIONS:

Statutes cover labor disputes, hiring of strike breakers, length of workweek, child labor, payment of wages, minimum wages and overtime, assignment of wages, workmen's compensation, unemployment compensation, discrimination in employment, employment agencies and regulation and inspection of factories, mills, and workshops with regard to health, safety and comfort of employees. (c. 820).

Hours of Labor.—Eight hour day, except for farm occupations, or where parties agree otherwise. (820-145/1, 145/2). Illinois Female Employment Act, setting maximum hours for females employed in mechanical or mercantile establishments or other enumerated occupations held unconstitutional in 1977 and repealed. (317 F.Supp. 1304).

Employer must allow one day of rest in seven, and a 20-minute meal period within five hours after start of $7^1/_2$ continuous hours of work, with exceptions. (820-140/1 to 140/8). Employer must post schedule of employees for Sun. work and alternative day of rest and keep time book. (820-140/4 to 140/5).

Jury Duty.—Employer must allow employee giving reasonable notice unpaid leave for petit or grand jury duty pursuant to summons regardless of employee's shift. (705-305/4.1, 705-310/10.1).

Child labor laws provide no minor under 16 may be employed in enumerated occupations except for minors 14 and 15 in certain federal programs; but minors between 14 and 16 may work outside school hours except in dangerous or hazardous factory work. (820-205/1 to 205/7). Minors under 12, except members of farmer's

See note at head of Digest as to 1998 legislation covered.

See Topical Index in front part of this volume.

IL – 47

LABOR RELATIONS . . . *continued*

family, may not work in agriculture; minors ten or older, however, may work in agriculture outside school hours. (820-205/1). Otherwise, law does not apply to agricultural work. Law also does not apply to work around home outside school hours and not in connection with business, or to distribution or sale of newspapers or magazines during school hours; or caddies 13 years old or over. (820-205/2). During summer hours minors under 16 in enumerated occupations limited to eight in one day, 48 in one week, six consecutive days in one week; with time of day regulated; may not exceed three in one day when school is in session or total of eight workhours in one day outside and in school with special rules for employees of park district or municipal park and recreation department. (820-205/3). Minors under 16 must receive 30-minute meal period in five continuous hours of work. (820-205/4). Employer must post abstract of law and hours of work and meals and Department's toll free telephone number conspicuously and keep time records (820-205/5, 820-205/6), and must obtain and keep on file employment certificate for minors under 16 (820-205/9, 820-205/10). On termination of employment, certificate must be returned to issuing officer. (820-205/13). Violations are subject to civil penalties and wilful violations are Class A misdemeanor; each day wilful violation continues and each minor affected, is separate offense. (820-205/17, 205/19). Minors under 16 may appear in theatrical productions on authorization of school superintendent, with some limitations. (820-205/8[a]). Minors under 16 may appear as model or in movie, radio, or television on authorization of school superintendent, with some limitations. (820-205/8[b]). Employment of minors in certain street trades (e.g., shoe shining, advertising, distribution) requires employer to obtain certificate from Department of Labor and issue permit to minor to be carried while working. (820-215/1 to 215/10). Violators are subject to criminal penalties. (820-215/9). No person under 18 may be employed at manual labor in mines. (225-705/9.01).

Wages.—Employer of six or more persons in the manufacture of any article must pay women equally with men for equal work, except due to seniority, skill, training, experience or where otherwise provided by contract with recognized bargaining agent. (820-110/1). (See also, catchline General Minimum Wage Law and Overtime, infra.) Every employer shall, at least semi-monthly, pay every employee all wages earned during that semi-monthly period, except that period for professional, executive and administrative employees may be monthly. At request of person employed by employment or labor placement agency which ordinarily makes daily wage payments, agency shall hold daily wages and make weekly or semiweekly payments. Such agencies shall provide written notification to all such employees. (820-115/3). Absent contrary collective bargaining agreement, wages must be paid within 13 days after end of semi-monthly pay period, within seven days after end of weekly pay period, within 24 hours after day worked by day laborer, and for professional, executive and administrative employees within 21 days after relevant pay period ends. Employee absent on payday must be paid within five days of payday or, if that expired, on five days demand. (820-115/4). Wages of separated employees shall be paid in full at time of separation but in no case later than next scheduled payday. Unless otherwise provided in collective bargaining agreement, employer must pay all earned vacation to employee on resignation or termination as final compensation in accordance with contract or employment policy; no forfeiture of earned vacation time. (820-115/5). All commissions due at termination of contract with sales representative shall be paid within 13 days of termination. Contracts to contrary are void. Treble damages for violation. (820-120/1 to 120/3). Deductions by employer from wages prohibited unless required by law, to benefit of employee, in response to valid wage assignment or deduction order or pursuant to employee's voluntary written consent given at time of deduction. Employer must timely pay undisputed portion. Employee's acceptance does not release disputed amount and employer efforts to obtain such release are void. (820-115/9). Contributions to employee benefit, trust or fund treated like wages for purposes of collection. (820-115/8). "Wages" defined broadly to include monetary equivalent of earned vacations and holidays. (820-115/2). Willful failure to pay "wages" is class C misdemeanor; each day constitutes separate offense. (820-115/14). State's Attorney may enforce, and Department of Labor, upon assignment by employee, or employee, may also institute civil suit for wages and costs. (820-115/11). Employer must maintain records of employees and wages, furnish employees with itemized statement of deductions and post notices of payday and place for payment. Employer must notify employees, whenever possible in writing and acknowledged by both parties, of rate of pay and time and place of payment and changes therein prior to implementation. (820-115/10). Officer or agent of employer knowingly permitting violation of Act deemed employer of employee. (820-115/13). Employer or agent who discharges or discriminates against employee for complaint concerning payment of wages or for testifying in wage proceeding is guilty of Class C misdemeanor. (820-115/14).

Enumerated employee benefit trusts are exempt from rules against perpetuities or suspension of power of alienation, with exceptions. (760-40/1 to 40/3). Employers obligated in writing to make payments to certain employee benefit plans may under certain circumstances be held criminally liable for failure to do so. (820-160/1).

Employer operating leased mine, quarry, oil or gas well or leased plant manufacturing certain designated products must file with Circuit Court Clerk surety bond in double semi-monthly or weekly payroll to secure payment of wages, unless employer owns property worth that amount. (820-155/1). Where business is suspended by action of creditors, or put in hands of receiver or trustee, wage and pension fund claims have preference. (770-851). Employee who agreed to permit deductions from wages for payments to certain medical service plans must be permitted to continue such payments to employer for six months where wages do not exceed deductions but employee status continues. (820-150/1 & 150/2). Employers must pay cost of medical examination or of furnishing records of such examination where required by employer. (820-235/1, 235/4).

General prevailing wage rates, determined in accordance with statute, must be paid employees on public works. Statute provides for injunctive relief and two year debarment of employer who disregards statutory obligations. State will not approve project until certificate of compliance is filed. (820-130/1 to 130/12). Public Works employees paid less than prevailing wage rates may request Department of Labor to take assignment of wage claim in trust and bring legal action to collect claim. (820-130/11).

Discharge or discipline or discrimination against employee or representative of employees because employee or representative has filed action under Prevailing Wage Act is prohibited. (820-130/11[b]).

A minimum wage for women and minors in any occupation may be fixed by Department of Labor, after public hearing on report of wage board, in a directory order which, after nine months, may be made mandatory after public hearing. Name of employer violating directory order may be published. Violation of mandatory order subjects employer to Class B misdemeanor each week of continued violation constituting separate offense. Employee receiving less than minimum wage under mandatory order, even under agreement, may recover difference and attorney's fee. Contract as to employment of woman or minor at oppressive or unreasonable wage is void. (820-125/1 to 125/17). General minimum wages and overtime rates are now set by statute. (820-105/1 to 105/15). See, catchline General Minimum Wage Law and Overtime, infra.

Where collective bargaining agreement sets minimum wages, it is illegal and punishable by fine to require employee to pay back any part of such wages (820-165/2); but contributions for hospitalization, union dues and other designated purposes are allowed (820-165/3).

In action for wages, attorney's fees may be allowed in favor of plaintiff where demand for sum not exceeding amount recovered was made in writing at least three days prior to suit. (705-225/1).

Assignments of wages are regulated. (740-170/.01 to 170/11). See also category Debtor and Creditor, topic Assignments, subhead Assignment of Wages.

See also category Debtor and Creditor, topic Garnishment, subhead Garnishment of Wages. Employer subject to Class "A" misdemeanor for discharging or suspending employee whose wages are garnished for any one indebtedness. (735-5/12-818).

See also category Family, topic Dissolution of Marriage, subhead Support of Children.

General Minimum Wage Law and Overtime.—All employers must pay wages of not less than federal minimum wage prescribed by 29 U.S.C. §206(a)(1) ($5.15 per hour as of Sept. 1, 1997) and for employees under 18 not less than 50¢ less than federal minimum wage for employees 18 and over. (820-105/4[a]). No employer shall employ any of employees for more than 40 hour week unless wage for time over 40 hours is not less than 1½ times regular rate. (820-105/4[a]). No employer may discriminate on basis of sex or handicap by paying less for same or substantially similar work, except where payment is pursuant to: (a) Seniority system; (2) merit system; (3) quality or quantity of production; (4) factor other than sex or mental or physical handicap. (820-105/4[b]). In occupations where gratuities customarily form part of wages, employer may recognize to extent of actual receipt up to 40% of applicable minimum, but employer must provide substantial evidence that exempt amount claimed was received. (820-105/4[c]). Camp counselors residing on premises of seasonal camp of not-for-profit corporation not subject to adult minimum wage if working 40 hours or more per week and receiving weekly salary equal to adult minimum wage for 40 hour week. Employers of camp counselors entitled to 25% of minimum wage rate for meals and lodging allowance. (820-105/4[d]). Exemptions may be promulgated by Department of Labor for learners, those of impaired capacity, and handicapped. (820-105/5, 105/6, 105/10). Pay records must be kept for three years. (820-105/8). Act and regulations must be posted (820-105/9), and actions for wages due, with attorneys' fees and costs, may be brought by employee within three years of date of underpayment. Employer is liable to employee for punitive damages equal to 2% of amount of underpayment per month that amount remains unpaid. (820-105/12[a]). Director of Labor may bring legal action for unpaid wages and punitive damages, and employer must pay costs and 20% of amount of underpayment. (820-105/12[b]). Employer paying or agreeing to pay wages at rate less than provided for by law subject to Class B misdemeanor, and each week in which on one day such minimum wage provided for by law was not paid is separate offense. (820-105/11[b]). Employees excludes certain categories of farm laborers, domestics, outside salesmen, members of religious orders and certain students covered by Fair Labor Standards Act employed by accredited Illinois college or university. (820-105/3). Commissioned salesman covered by §7(i) of Fair Labor Standards Act, salesmen or mechanics primarily engaged in selling, servicing automobiles, trucks or farm implements employed by non-manufacturers if sales are to ultimate purchaser, and salesmen of trailers, boats or aircraft employed by non-manufacturers if sales are to ultimate purchaser, agricultural employees, governmental employees, bona fide executive, administrative and professional employees, including any radio or television announcer, news editor or chief engineer, certain child care employees and employees in worktime exchange agreements are excluded from overtime requirements. (820-105/4a[2]). Act does not amend more favorable standards under other acts. (820-105/13).

Labor Unions.—Contracts whereby either party promises not to join or remain a member of a labor or employers' organization, or to terminate employment relation in case he joins or remains a member of such organization, are wholly void. (820-15/1). Illinois has no "right to work" law.

The president or executive officer of every labor organization must report to Department of Labor concerning any strike or lockout, actual or threatened, involving members of his organization. (820-35/6[a]).

Discrimination.—

Human Rights Act (755-5/101 to 5/9-102).—"Employer" includes all persons, including labor organization, labor union or association, employing 15 or more persons within state during 20 or more calendar weeks within calendar year of or preceding alleged violation. Additionally, party to public contract and joint apprenticeship or training committee included regardless of number of employees, and all persons with one or more employees are covered regarding alleged handicap discrimination. (755-5/2-101[B][1]). Excluded is any religious corporation, association, educational institution (except, for purposes of sexual harassment, institution offering degree beyond secondary school level), society, and certain nonprofit nursing institutions regarding employment of individuals of particular religion to perform work connected with carrying on by entity of its activities. (755-5/2-101[B][2]). State, its subdivisions and other governmental units included as "employer" regardless of number of employees (755-5/2-101[B][1][c]), but excluded from "employee" are elected officials, members of their

LABOR RELATIONS . . . *continued*
immediate personal staffs, and principal administrative officers, as well as domestics, and certain clients in certified vocational rehabilitation facilities (755-5/2-101[A]).

It is civil rights violation for employer to discriminate because of race, color, religion, national origin, ancestry, age (40 to 70), marital status, sex, physical or mental handicap (present, past or perceived and including physical characteristics which necessitate use of guide, support or hearing dog) unrelated to ability to perform particular job, unfavorable discharge from military service (except for dishonorable discharge or when authorized by federal law or regulation or position requires exercise of fiduciary responsibility) or citizenship status in hiring, segregating, recruiting, selecting, disciplining, promoting, renewing employment or tenure, terms or conditions of employment; for employment agency to discriminate in aiding and referring individuals; for labor organization to discriminate in membership or providing training and employment terms and opportunities; for employer, employment agency, or labor organization to inquire regarding arrest record that has been ordered expunged, sealed or impounded on written application except unit of local government or school district may utilize conviction information when evaluating employee qualifications and private employer providing services for children may require statement from employee/applicant regarding convictions for injury, abuse or abduction of children; for employer, employee, agent of employer, employment agency, labor organization or higher education representative to engage in sexual harassment; or for any person(s) to retaliate against individual for opposing action individual reasonably and in good faith believes to be unlawful discrimination or sexual harassment in employment or higher education or for participating in proceeding under Act; to aid, abet, compel or coerce any violation; or to wilfully interfere with performance of duty or exercise of power by Commission, Department or agents thereof. (755-5/2-102, 5/2-103, 5/5A-102, 5/6-101). Public employers must permit public employees who take time off for religious purposes to make up work and receive same rate of pay they would have received. Public employer may require up to five days notice of intention to be absent. (755-5/2-102[E]). Act exempts action based on certain professionally developed ability tests; action based on certain merit and retirement systems; action based on bona fide occupational qualification; preferential treatment of veterans and relatives as required by law; and use of age in certain apprenticeship programs, or in effecting compulsory retirement of certain executives at age 65 and certain firefighters/paramedics and law enforcement officers at age set by state or local law. (755-5/2-104).

Act enforced by Department of Human Rights and Human Rights Commission. Sworn charge to be filed with or issued by Department within 180 days after alleged violation. (775-5/7A-102[A][1]). Department must serve copy of charge on respondent within ten days (non-jurisdictional) of receipt and investigate (775-5/7A-102[B], [C]), and may hold fact-finding conference, on reasonable notice, within 365 days of filing of charge unless time is waived (775-5/7A-102[C][4]). Absent finding of substantial evidence, charge is dismissed subject to complainant's right to request review by Chief Legal Counsel of Department within 30 days from receipt of dismissal notice. (775-5/7A-102[D][2][a]).

If there is substantial evidence of violation, designated Department attorney must attempt to eliminate effects and prevent repetition by conference and conciliation. (775-5/7A-102[D][2][b]). Parties must be given ten days written notice of formal conference, if called, to be within 35 miles of place of alleged violation. (775-5/7A-102[e]). Department and Commission have authority to approve settlement. Department may dismiss charge if respondent has eliminated effects of violation and has taken steps to prevent its repetition or if complainant refuses to accept terms of settlement which Department deems sufficient, subject to complainant's right to request review of dismissal. (775-5/7A-103, 755-5/8-105). Absent settlement or dismissal, Department must file sworn complaint with Commission or order that no complaint issue, within 365 days of filing of charge or written extension agreed to by all parties. (775-5/7A-102[F]). Within 30 days of expiration of 300-day period or such longer period agreed to by parties, aggrieved party may file complaint with Commission if Department has not done so. Department then stops processing charge. (775-5/7A-102[G][2]). Any time after charge is filed, Department may petition court for temporary interim relief, or at Commission request, to enforce Commission order. (775-5/7A-104).

Within five days after Department or aggrieved party files complaint, Commission must serve it upon respondent with notice of hearing before Commission hearing officer to be held within 100 miles of alleged violation at stated time not less than 30 nor more than 90 days after service of complaint. (775-5/8A-102[A], [B]). Respondent must file sworn answer within 30 days after service of complaint or within 15 days of denial of motion to dismiss. (775-5/8A-102[D][1], [2]). Hearing officer may, for good cause shown, extend date of hearing or grant further time for filing of answer.). Complainant and respondent have right of cross-examination and transcript of hearing, and rules of evidence applicable in state courts apply. Attendance of parties or their employees at hearing may be compelled by serving notice. (775-5/8A-102[H]).

Hearing officer's determination sustaining complaint must be based upon preponderance of evidence. (775-5/8A-102[I][1]). He must make findings of fact and either issue recommended order dismissing complaint, which may include award of reasonable attorneys fees in favor of respondent if complaint was frivolous, unreasonable, or groundless or complainant continued to litigate after it became clearly so (775-5/8A-102[I][3], [5]), or, if finding against respondent, issue recommended order for appropriate relief, which may include cease and desist order, payment of actual damages, hiring, reinstatement, back pay, interest (from date of violation), restoration of fringe benefits, award of reasonable attorney and expert witness fees, compliance reports and posting of notices (775-5/8A-102[I][2], 775-5/8A-104), and, regarding party to public contract, termination of contract, (three year maximum) debarment, and penalty of sum no greater than profit acquired as direct result of violation (775-5/8-109).

Parties may file written exceptions with argument within 30 days of receipt of service of recommended order. (775-5/8A-103[A]). Non-excepting party may file response within 21 days of receipt of service of exceptions (775-5/8A-103[B]), and either party may request oral argument (775-5/8A-103[C]). Commission may, on own motion or written request, remand case to hearing officer for rehearing or for taking additional evidence (775-5/8A-103[D]), and may adopt, modify or reverse in whole or in part hearing officer's findings and recommendations, but must adopt hearing officer's findings of fact unless contrary to manifest weight of evidence (775-5/8A-103[E]). Commission may modify or set aside in whole or in part any finding or order any time prior to final order by reviewing court. (775-5/8A-103[G]). Decisions of Commission or panels thereof shall be published within 120 days of completion of service of written decision upon parties. (775-5/8-110). Subpoenas available to Department and party to aid investigation and hearing, respectively. (775-5/8-104). Commission order is judicially reviewable in appellate court under Administrative Review Act but finding of fact at administrative level must be sustained unless contrary to manifest weight of evidence. (775-5/8-111[A]). Commission must enforce its order by proceeding in circuit court if violation of order and effects thereof not promptly corrected. (775-5/8-111[A]).

All parties to public contract must refrain from violations, undertake affirmative action to assure equal employment opportunity, eliminate effects of past discrimination, comply with Department regulations, provide Department with certain information and have written sexual harassment policies with minimum amounts of prescribed information. (775-5/2-105[A]).

Human Rights Act repeals, with savings provisions, following statutes, among others: (1) certain provisions of Criminal Code of 1961; (2) Equal Opportunities for the Handicapped Act; (3) Fair Employment Practices Act; and (4) age discrimination prohibitions.

Right to Privacy in the Workplace Act prohibits employer from refusing to hire, discharge or otherwise disadvantage individual with respect to terms or conditions of employment because individual uses lawful products off premises of employer during nonworking hours. (820-55/1).

Not violation of Act for employer to have health, disability or life insurance policy that makes distinctions among employees with regard to coverage based upon employees' use of lawful products if certain requirements are met. (820-55/5). Act administered, enforced by Director of Labor. (820-55/15).

Constitution.—Art. 1, §17 of 1970 Illinois Constitution authorizes civil action for compensatory and punitive damages to remedy employment discrimination based on sex. (60 Ill. App.3d 616, 377 N.E.2d 242). That section also forbids discrimination in employment or in sale or rental of property based on race, color, creed, and national ancestry. Employment protection limited to hiring and promotion practices. (107 Ill.App.3d 748, 438 N.E.2d 245). Former employee cannot sue directly under Constitution without exhausting administrative remedies of Human Rights Act. (120 Ill.App.3d 878, 58 N.E.2d 985). Art. 1, §18 of 1970 Illinois Constitution prohibits denial or abridgement of equal protection of laws on account of sex by State or its units of local government and school districts. Art. 1, §19 of 1970 Illinois Constitution protects persons with physical and mental handicaps from discrimination unrelated to ability in hiring and promotion practices of any employer.

Employee Patent Act prohibits employment agreements from requiring employee to assign rights to employer for invention when no equipment, supplies, facilities, or trade secret information of employer was used and invention developed on employee's own time unless it relates to business of employer, anticipated research and development, or results from any work performed for employer. Employer to provide written notification to employee of requirements of Act. (765-1060/2).

Access to personnel records granted to current employees, those on layoff or leave and employees terminated within preceding year (820-40/1); right to inspect and obtain copies of documents used by employer to determine qualifications for employment, promotion, transfer, compensation, discharge or discipline, with certain exceptions (820-40/2, 40/10). Employer to grant two inspection requests per year within seven working days of request with seven additional days if cannot reasonably meet deadline. Employer may require written requests on its own forms. (820-40/2). Employees may submit written position statement on documents contained in file. Employer must serve written notice to employee before divulging disciplinary reports to third parties; disciplinary records more than four years old must be deleted unless disclosure required pursuant to legal proceeding. (820-40/7 & 40/8). Employees may file complaint with Department of Labor, which can subpoena employer's files and sue in circuit court. Employee can also file suit if Department does not. Willful violation or retaliation against employee is petty offense. (820-40/12).

Labor Disputes.—Controversies between employer employing not less than twenty-five persons and employees not involving questions which may be the subject of civil actions may be submitted to Department of Labor for arbitration. (820-35/2). Statute provides procedure to be followed. (820-35/3). Decision is binding for six months, unless terminated by either party on 60 days notice to other party. (820-35/5). Failure to abide by decision subjects party to court proceedings for contempt. (820-35/5a). Uniform Arbitration Act, modified in certain respects is in effect. (710-5/1 to 5/23). Written agreements to arbitrate enforceable at law or equity. (710-5/1). Arbitration may be compelled (710-5/2[a]) or stayed (710-5/2[b]), confirmed (710-5/11), vacated (710-5/12) or modified (710-5/13). Any controversy between employer and its employees or bargaining representative may, if all parties request, be submitted to Department of Labor, which shall provide arbitration services in accordance with Uniform Arbitration Act. (710-10/1 to 10/3). See also category Dispute Resolution, topic Arbitration and Award, subhead Labor Controversies.

It is a punishable offense for employer to advertise for employees during a strike unless advertisement states that a strike is in progress. (820-25/1). This section of statute held unconstitutional. (62 Ill.2d 549, 344 N.E.2d 1). Except for purposes of maintenance and protection, employment of professional strikebreakers prohibited. (820-30/1 to 30/4).

As to duties of Department of Labor in case of strike or threatened strike, see 820-35/6 to 35/6b.

Exception to ban on picketing residence used as place of employment and involved in labor dispute repealed. (720-5/21.1-2).

Injunction may not be granted against peaceful picketing by striking employees. (820-5/1).

Public Employees.—Collective bargaining procedures established for public employees, except employees of school districts, higher education institutions (not including state university firefighters), and legislative branch of State government. (5-315/1 to

See note at head of Digest as to 1998 legislation covered.

See Topical Index in front part of this volume.

IL – 49

LABOR RELATIONS . . . *continued*
315/27). Given right to organize, bargain and strike, except security employees, State police, State firefighters, and State legislative branch employees may not strike. Separate statute grants collective bargaining rights to State educational employees. (115-5/1 to 5/21).

Worker's Compensation Act is compulsory as to State and its political subdivisions and as to following extra-hazardous businesses: erection, maintaining, removing, remodeling, altering or demolishing of any structure; construction, excavating or electrical work; carriage by land, water or aerial service; warehouse operations; mining or quarrying; any enterprise in which explosive materials are manufactured, handled or used; any enterprise where molten metal or explosive or injurious gases, dusts, or vapors, or inflammable vapors, dusts or fluids, or corrosive acids or atomic radiation are manufactured, used, generated, stored or conveyed; any enterprise in which sharp edged cutting tools are used; any enterprise in which statutory or municipal ordinance regulations are imposed on use of machinery; any enterprise in connection with laying out or improvement of subdivisions of tracts of land; any enterprise for treatment of cross-ties, timber or other wood with creosote or other preservatives; establishments open to general public, where alcoholic beverages are sold to general public for consumption on premises; any public beauty shop; any enterprise serving food to public for consumption on premises, where any employee uses cutting instruments or where any employee is in hazard of being scalded or burned; businesses using electric, gasoline or power driven equipment; businesses in which goods, merchandise or wares are produced; businesses with annual payroll of $1,000 or more in which goods, merchandise or wares are sold or services are rendered to public at large; on and after July 1, 1980, households where domestics are employed 40 or more hours per week in 13 or more weeks per calendar year; and certain agricultural enterprises. (820-305/3). All other employers including sole proprietors and partners, may elect to submit voluntarily to Act. (820-305/1 to 305/2).

Employers engaged in erection, maintaining, removing, altering or demolishing any structure or construction, excavating, or electrical work are liable to pay compensation to employees of uninsured contractors or subcontractors they engage. (820-305/1[a][3]). Liability of borrowing and loaning employers is joint and several. (820-305/1). Act applies to employees if contract of hire made within Illinois, injury occurs in Illinois, or employment is principally localized in State. (820-305/1[b][2]). Also applies to aliens and minors. Excluded from coverage are real estate brokers and salespersons paid by commission only. (820-305/1[b][3]).

Employer who has submitted to Act voluntarily may withdraw by giving written notice at least 60 days prior to end of calendar year. Employee of voluntarily submitting employer may reject coverage by written notice within 30 days of hiring, or of employer's election to submit, and can withdraw from coverage by written notice at least ten days prior to end of calendar year. (820-305/3). Act provides exclusive remedy for employee and his representatives against covered employer or employer's insurer or broker or service organization hired to provide safety services, except that an illegally employed minor or his representative has right to reject his rights under Act and to pursue his common law remedies by filing rejection within later of six months after injury, death, or appointment of legal representative. (820-305/5). Also, fact that employee's action for damages against his employer is barred by Act does not preclude manufacturer, which is sued by employee on strict product liability theory, from filing third-party action against employer for indemnification or for contribution. (70 Ill.2d 1, 374 N.E.2d 437). Employer must self-insure, with or without security, indemnity or bond, or acquire insurance. (820-305/4). Self-insured employers must reapply to Commission for approval annually. (820-305/4[a]). Self-insurers advisory board provides continuation of benefits due to inability of insolvent self-insured employer to meet obligations. (820-305/4a-1 to 4a-9). Insurer must notify employer of compensable claims each month, and employer may challenge certain payments in proceeding before Commission. (820-305/19[o]). Two or more employers with similar risks can pool their liabilities to qualify as group self-insurers. (820-305/4a). Agreements requiring employee to pay for covered insurance are null and void; withholding wages to pay for insurance is Class B misdemeanor. Discrimination because of exercise of rights or remedies under Act is unlawful. (820-305/4). Civil action for compensatory and punitive damages allowed for discharge in retaliation for asserting compensation claim. (74 Ill.2d 172, 384 N.E.2d 353).

Employee may bring action against third parties responsible for injury or death despite acceptance of benefits from employer under Act, but employer is subrogated to employee's claim to the extent of his payments to employee, and may institute action against third party if employee has failed to do so prior to three months before the statute of limitations would run against employee. (820-305/5). Employer is bound by statute of limitations applicable to employee in action against third party for recovery of payments under the Act. (25 Ill.2d 241, 184 N.E.2d 882). Injuries resulting from participation in recreational programs are not compensable unless employer orders employee to participate, and injuries occurring while participating in drug or alcohol rehabilitation program are not compensable. (820-305/11).

Amount of compensation is fixed by 820-305/7 to 305/10. Compensation for injury resulting in death payable to surviving spouse and children and under some circumstances to collateral heirs. (820-305/7). Employer may elect to apply life insurance benefits to satisfy portion or all of death benefit due. (820-305/4[i]).

Notice of injury must be given to employer within 45 days and application for compensation filed with Commission within three years of injury, death, or within two years of last payment of compensation, with certain exceptions, particularly regarding radiation and incompetents. Any agreement between employer and employee or beneficiary made within seven days after injury is presumed to be fraudulent. Employer is obligated to post notices regarding Act, and insurance status, and to make timely reports and to maintain records regarding certain work-related deaths, injuries and illnesses. Commission is to compile and distribute aggregate statistics based on employers' reports. Injured employee granted compensation under Act must be notified of rights to and location of rehabilitation services. (820-305/6). Employer's liability to pay for medical services chosen by employee is limited to emergency treatment plus medical services provided by two doctors or hospitals and any subsequent services in chain of referral. (820-305/8[a]).

Industrial Commission is composed of seven members appointed by Governor, two representing employer class, two representing employee class, and three not identified with either class. (820-305/13). Commission determines questions not settled by parties. (820-305/18). Complaints about conduct of commissioners and arbitrators may be filed with seven-member Commission Review Board which is led by Chairman of Industrial Commission and which can recommend to Governor that arbitrator be dismissed or commissioner not be reappointed. (820-305/14.1).

Arbitrators conduct initial hearings and render decisions containing findings of fact and conclusions of law. Employees not receiving medical, surgical, or hospital services or compensation may petition for emergency hearing on issue whether they are entitled to such services or compensation. Such petitions have priority over all others. Petition for review by Commission may be filed by either party within 30 days. Either party may request oral argument before panel of three commissioners and decision containing findings of fact and conclusions. Except for claims against State, final award can be presented to circuit court where accident occurred or where either party resides for judgment to be rendered thereon. (820-305/19).

Except in cases of claims against the State, which are not subject to review, certiorari lies to circuit court of county where defendant may be found or, if no defendant may be found in State, county where accident occurred, to review all questions of law and fact in decision of Commission. Absent such review or fraud, decision of Commission within its powers is conclusive. Suit by writ of certiorari must be sought within 20 days of receipt of notice of Commission's decision and be supported by bond to secure payment of award and costs of court proceedings.

Commission may review agreement or award within 30 months after entered on ground disability recurred, increased, diminished or ended. Act provides penalties in form of additional compensation for unreasonable or vexatious delay of payment, intentional underpayment, institution or carrying on of proceedings without real controversy which are frivolous or for delay, and wilful violation of health and safety standard in 820-225/1 to 820-225/23. (820-305/19).

Losing party in circuit court may appeal to Industrial Commission Division of Appellate Court. (Ill. S. Ct. 22[g]).

Payment, claim, award or decision under Act is not assignable or subject to lien or attachment except beneficiaries of deceased annuitants under Illinois Pension Code may assign benefits to State Employee's Retirement System. Compensation allowed is entitled to preference over unsecured debts of employer contracted after date of injury apart from wages. (820-305/21). Employee, personal representative and beneficiary, in effect, may not waive Act regarding compensation amount or compromise or settle compensation rights without prior approval of Commission. (820-305/23). Wilful neglect, refusal or failure to do things required by Act is punishable by fine up to $500 per day. (820-305/26). Commission may seek enforcement in civil action. (820-305/4).

See also Workers' Occupational Diseases Act (820-310/1 to 310/27), Health and Safety Act (820-225/1 to 225/23), and Safety Inspection and Education Act (820-220/1 to 220/11) which are administered by Industrial Commission and Department of Labor.

It is petty offense to fail to provide shield and hood on automobiles or auto trucks to protect chauffeurs (625-20/1, 20/2), and suitable and sanitary washroom and soap in certain businesses where working conditions warrant such facilities (820-230/1 to 230/5).

Employer must furnish to each employee whose duties may reasonably be expected to involve entering underground sewer information concerning prevention of injury and disease by contact with poisonous or deleterious materials, vapors, gases or fumes. Employer must also have certain safety information and equipment available at such work site. (820-250/2 to 250/3).

See also Work Under Compressed Air Act. (820-245/1 to 245/8).

Statute regulating poisonous fumes and dust unconstitutional and repealed. (365 Ill. 384, 6 N.E.2d 623).

See also Vehicle Code provision which renders employer not liable for passenger injuries in ride-sharing arrangements when employer does not own or lease vehicle or pay driver. (625-5/10-202).

Toxic Substances Disclosure to Employees Act (820-255/1 to 255/20) requires employers to obtain material safety data sheet for toxic substances used, produced or stored in workplace to which employees are exposed (820-255/9[a]). Material safety data sheet describes properties and methods of safe handling toxic substances. (820-255/3[j]). Employees, their representatives, treating health care professionals, emergency service agencies and Director of Labor are entitled to material safety data sheets within ten days of written request. (820-255/9[d]). Employee may refuse to work if employer does not provide requested information it possesses. (820-255/14[a]). Toxic substance means any substance mixture, or compound containing substance which is determined as hazardous as defined in 29 C.F.R. 1910.1200. (820-255/3[m]). Department of Labor enforces provisions of Act with right of judicial review. (820-255/17). Act does not apply to use of toxic substances intended for personal consumption by employees in workplace, certain consumer goods, substances with less than 1% toxicity, certain laboratories, and various retail trade establishments. (820-255/6).

Unemployment Insurance.—Illinois has compulsory unemployment insurance program. (805-405/100 to 405/3200). "Employer" (defined 820-405/205) includes with respect to years 1972 and thereafter, any employing unit (any individual or type of organization, including State, its political subdivisions and municipal corporations and instrumentality of foregoing entities) which pays or paid, for services in employment, wages of at least $1,500 within calendar quarter of current or preceding calendar year or which has or had in employment one individual within each of 20 or more calendar weeks within current or preceding calendar year, certain nonprofit organizations, State of Illinois; and, with respect to years 1978 and thereafter, certain governmental entities, certain agricultural employers, employers of domestics, successor employers, and employers electing to become "employer." "Employer" pays contributions to state to be held as unemployment trust fund. Benefits are payable upon involuntary unemployment of individual who received from "employer" during base period (first four consecutive of last five calendar quarters before benefit year [820-405/237]) for "insured work", at least $1,600 in wages with respect to benefit year beginning on or after Jan. 3, 1982. At least $440 of wages during base period must have been paid outside of calendar quarter

LABOR RELATIONS . . . *continued*
in which wages paid were highest. (820-405/500). "Benefit year" normally begins on first day of week with respect to which valid benefit claim is filed (820-405/242). Amount of benefits depends on amount of wages received and number of dependents. (820-405/401 to 405/403). Certain employees working fewer hours because of employer's work sharing plan to reduce unemployment are entitled to shared work benefits. (820-405/407.1). Employee is ineligible if, among other reasons, loss of work is due to discharge for felony, he fails to actively seek work or is unable to or unavailable for work, unemployment is from stoppage of work caused by labor dispute, he seeks benefits to which he is entitled from another state, he is receiving workers' compensation, he receives full weekly benefits for certain period of time, he is employed in connection with educational institution and is unemployed between academic years or terms, he is athlete unemployed between sport seasons, or, with limitations he is nonresident alien. Employee may be ineligible, or amount of benefits may be reduced, because of vacation pay, holiday pay, social security benefits, or retirement pay. (820-405/402, 820-405/500 to 405/614). Employees who leave work voluntarily without good cause attributable to employing unit, with exceptions, are discharged for misconduct, or refuse to accept suitable work are ineligible for benefits until reemployed and earn amount equal to benefit amount in each of four weeks. (820-405/601 to 405/603). However, lockouts or failures to cross picket line do not automatically disqualify employee from benefits. (820-405/604). Act excludes certain agricultural labor and enumerated other occupations (820-405/214 to 405/232) but noncovered employing units may elect coverage (820-405/302). Employer's tax is based upon wages paid up to $9,000 per employee per year for calendar years 1988 through 1999 and up to $10,000 per employee per year for calendar year 2001. (820-405/235). Rate of tax varies from minimum of .2% to maximum of approximately 6.4% plus emergency rate. (820-405/1500 to 405/1506.1).

Insurance Code provides employees with continuation privilege for group hospital, surgical and major medical coverage and group Health Maintenance Organization (HMO) coverage (215-125/4-9.2) after termination from employment (215-5/364) except persons covered by Medicare or other group plan or persons who exercise conversion privilege; dental, vision care, drug benefits, disability income and other supplementary benefits need not be included. Continuation only available to employees insured under group policy for three months prior to termination. Employer to provide written notice of continuation to employee upon termination; employee must pay premium. Continuation effective for up to six months. (215-5/367e[i][6]). Retired or disabled police officers and deputies have continuation privileges under group accident and health insurance policies (215-5/367g-h), as do employees' spouses and dependent children after divorce or death of employee (215-5/367.2). Employees discharged for committing felony or theft in connection with work are not entitled to continuation if they admit guilt or are convicted. (215-5/367e[8]). HMO continued coverage similarly unavailable. (215-125/4-9.2).

Employers agreeing to make payments to employee health insurance plan must notify employees of failure to make payments if loss of insurance may result. Employer guilty of Class B misdemeanor if fails to provide timely notice of prospective termination of health insurance plan. (820-160/2).

Farm Labor Contractor Certification Act (225-505/1 to 505/14).—No person may act as "farm labor contractor" without possessing non-assignable certificate of registration issued by Director of Department of Labor. (225-505/3). "Farm labor contractor" includes with exceptions anyone who for valuable consideration recruits, supplies or hires, or transports in such connection, into or within State any farmworker (anyone who moves seasonally to obtain employment relating to agricultural or horticultural commodities) not of his immediate family to work for third person or for farm labor contractor. (225-505/2). Full-time and regular employees of contractor must carry identification of such employment. (225-505/5). Contractor may not require farmworkers to purchase goods or services from him or other person (225-505/10), is required to post certain notices (225-505/8), and is regulated regarding payroll, security bond, records, and recruiting (225-505/6 to 505/9). Act provides for civil actions, administrative regulation with judicial review and criminal penalties. (225-505/8, 505/7, 505/12, 505/13, 505/14).

Private Employment Agencies (225-515/1 to 515/15).—Any person engaged for gain or profit in business of attempting to secure employment for persons seeking employment or employees for employers, except person who is compensated solely by employer to identify, appraise or recommend individual at least 18 years old or holds high school diploma and no fee directly or indirectly charged to that individual (exception for theatrical and domestic service employment agencies), must procure license from Department of Labor, file bond, schedule of intended fees, charges and commissions, and all intended forms and contracts and changes therein. (225-515/1, 515/2, 515/11). Licensing requirements include among other things furnishing affidavit to establish business integrity and financial responsibility, good moral character and lack of ever having been party to fraud, and lack of jail or prison record or membership in subversive societies. License fees vary with number of "employment counselors" or "placement counselors" (employees of agency who interview, counsel or advise applicants or employers or both on employment or allied problems, or who arrange contracts or contacts between employers and employees or who solicit orders for employees from employers [225-515/11]). (225-515/1). Employment counselors are individually licensed. (225-515/4).

Agency must keep records including among others record of job orders, advertisement register, applicant's records, fee transaction record, record of all registration fees charged pursuant to permit, separate record of receipts for additional fees charged to applicants and referral slip record. (225-515/3, 515/5). Licensee may not solicit, persuade or induce employee to leave employment in which placed or induce employer to discharge such employee; divide or offer to share fee received from employee with person connected with employer; or give or promise anything of value to employer or applicant if contingent upon use of licensee's services except licensee may incur reasonable business entertainment expenses or distribute items for promotional or advertisement purposes. (225-515/6). Licensee must file and give person sent to work as contract or railroad workers, outside licensee's city statement of name and nature of work, wages offered, destination, and terms of transportation and probable employment duration. Licensee must first notify applicant and record on referral slip given to applicant any facts regarding strike, lock-out or other labor trouble existing at place applicant is sent. (225-515/7). See under subhead Labor Disputes, supra, holding regarding 48-2c.

Additional records are required of theatrical employment agency (225-515/8), nurses' registry (225-515/9.1), and farmworker recruiters (225-515/10.1, 515/10.2). Licensee must file with Department of Labor annual statement showing number and character of placements. (225-515/5). Licensee may not send females to certain questionable places; permit certain questionable characters to frequent agency; accept applications from or place children in violation of Child Labor Law; publish or print misleading or anonymous notice, advertisement or sign or excerpt of Act. (225-515/10). Licensee providing employees for domestic service must require all such employees receive annual physical examination. (225-515/9.1).

Agency deriving no placement fees from applicants may act with same rights and powers as persons not "employment agency" with regard to contacting applicants and identifying selves and advertising to public so long as advertisement states agency is acting as agency or representative of employer. Such licensee placing individual and accepting fee for such placement which recontacts individual for replacement is subject to hearing and revocation of license. (225-515/5.1).

Illinois Laborers on Public Work Projects.—If Illinois unemployment exceeds 5% for two consecutive months, public works projects shall employ only Illinois laborers (skilled, semi-skilled, or unskilled), if available or capable. Contractors may use no more than three nonresident executives or experts. Willful violation is Class C misdemeanor, but statute not enforced if it conflicts with federal law when federal funds expended. (30-570/1 to 570/7).

WORKERS' COMPENSATION LAW:

See topic Labor Relations.

ENVIRONMENT

ENVIRONMENTAL REGULATION:

Constitution.—1970, Article XI: Each person has right to healthful environment and may enforce right against any party, governmental or private, through appropriate legal proceedings.

State Bodies.—State pollution control is administered by: (1) Environmental Protection Agency (surveillance, investigation of facilities, presentation of enforcement cases to Board, administration of permit and certification system, collection and dissemination of information, recommendation of regulations) (415-5/4), (2) Pollution Control Board (regulations defining, controlling and eliminating pollution, with quasi-judicial authority to implement and enforce Act and regulations (415-5/5), (3) Department of Commerce and Community Affairs (research, provide assistance, and preparation of economic impact studies) (20-1105/1), (4) Department of Nuclear Safety (regulation of transporting and disposal of radioactive materials and registration, licensing, and inspection of radiation sources) (20-2005/71), (5) Illinois Coal Development Board (20-1105/8), and (6) Illinois Emergency Management Agency (20-3305/5). Hazardous Waste Advisory Council prepares annual report to Governor and General Assembly. (415-5/5.1). Department of Public Health is mandated by Environmental Toxicology Act to establish program to study threats to public health from exposure to hazardous substances and to assess health effects of such exposure. (415-75/1-75/8).

Records.—All records of above bodies available to anyone except (1) trade secrets, (2) judicially privileged information, (3) internal communication, (4) secret manufacturing processes or confidential data submitted under Act. (415-5/7, 5/7.1). All documents submitted with application to Environmental Protection Agency, except trade secrets, must be made available to public at office of county Board or governing body of municipality. (415-5/39, 5/39.2, 5/39.3).

Prohibitions.—Cause, threaten, or allow discharge of any contaminant so as to cause air or water pollution or so as to violate regulations. (415-5/9[a], 5/12[a], [b]). Open dumping of garbage or refuse. (415/5-21). Open burning of refuse or burning in unapproved chambers except in certain circumstances. (415-5/9[c]). Burning of landscape waste is permitted except in specified instances. (415-5/9[c]). Sale or use of fuel or other articles prohibited by Board because of air or water pollution. (415-5-9[d], 415-5/12[e]). Sale of used oil for burning. (415-5/9[f]). Land contaminant dumping creating water pollution hazards. (415-5/12[d]). Unsafe public water supply. (415-5/18). Open dumping on public land except where approved by Agency and under regulations. (415-5/21[b]). Disposing of refuse or transporting refuse into state for disposal except at a site in compliance with Act and regulations. (415-5/21[e], [g]). Disposal by land application of untreated grease trap sludge. (415-5/22.27). Disposal of any "potentially infectious medical waste". (415-5/56). Abandonment of autos in violation of Illinois Vehicle Code. (415-5/21[c]). Beginning July 1, 1994, offer for collection or collection of "white goods" for disposal in landfill unless "white good components" are moved. (415-5/22.28). Noise which unreasonably interferes with enjoyment of life or business and violates a Board standard including nighttime noise emission standards for some organized amateur and professional sporting events. (415-5/24, 415-5/25). Actions in violation of terms of permits required by Act. (415-5/9[b], 5/12[b])). Breaking or removing seal affixed on pollution source by Agency. (415-5/34[c]). Use, cause, or allow spraying of loose asbestos or to otherwise permit asbestos fibers to pollute air. (415-5/9[e]). Operating private sewage disposal system in violation of regulations or without license except that homeowner may service his own sewer system without license. (225-225/4). Violating provisions of §§111 and 112 of federal Clean Air Act (42 USC 7411-12) relating to emissions from new stationary sources and emissions of hazardous air pollutants (415-5/9.1). Conducting refuse collection or disposal operations without permit. (415-5/21[e]). Depositing liquid or hazardous hospital wastes in landfill. (415-5/21[g], 415-5/22.6). Unauthorized use, delivery or disposal, or concealment of disposal, of hazardous waste. (415-5/44). To expose ionizing radiation in amounts which are or may be detrimental to health. (420-40/2). Act to be repealed Dec. 12, 2000.

See note at head of Digest as to 1998 legislation covered.

See Topical Index in front part of this volume.

IL – 51

ENVIRONMENTAL REGULATION . . . *continued*
(420-40/1). Dispose of, store, or accept spent nuclear fuel used in facility outside State unless other State has disposal or storage facilities like those in Illinois and grants reciprocity. (420-15/2). Failure to pay hazardous waste disposal fees. (415-5/21.2). Liability for all costs of removal or remedial action taken by state as result of release or substantial threat of release of hazardous substance. (415-5/22.2). Failure to provide and record disclosure document when transferring certain real property as required by Responsible Property Transfer Act. (765-90/7). Failure to disclose test results within 45 days. Releasing genetically engineered organism into environment without complying with 430-95/1, et seq. (430-95/1). No person shall smoke in public place except where posted as smoking area. (410-80/4). Does not apply where public room or hall used for private social function or to factories, warehouses or places of work not frequented by general public. Beginning July 1, 1994, no product or packaging may be sold if it contains any ink, dye, pigment, adhesive, stabilizer or other additive containing lead, cadmium, mercury or hexavalent chromium intentionally introduced or exceeds certain limits. (415-5/21.5). Beginning July 1, 1996, no knowing mix of liquid used oil with municipal waste intended for collection and disposal at landfill. (415-5/21.6).

Transfer of Property.—After Jan. 1, 1990, in order to sell property containing facility subject to reporting under 42 U.S.C. §11022 or containing underground storage tanks, seller must deliver disclosure statement to both buyer and lender, if any. If statement discloses environmental defects then transfer may be voided or commitment to finance may be revoked. (765-90/4). Disclosure statement must include information on Illinois Environmental Protection Act and other environmental data set forth in 765-90/5. Statement must also be recorded in county records and with Environmental Protection Agency within 30 days of transfer. (765-90/6).

Hazardous Waste.—Regulations and guidelines. (415-5/4[r], 5/22[g], 5/22.4). Responsibility for 20 years after site closure. (415-5/22.3). Funding of "Hazardous Waste Fund" and "Hazardous Waste Research Fund". (415-5/22.2). Bond shall be required for hazardous waste disposal site permit. (415-5/39[a]). County Boards and Municipal Boards have veto power over location of landfills and disposal sites within their jurisdictions. (415-5/39[c]). Deposit of waste streams at disposal sites prohibited unless specifically authorized by agency. (415-5/39). Labeling requirements and uniform response system. (430-50/.01 et seq.). Local approval of regional pollution control facility. (415-5/39.2). Once State expends funds for certain cleanups of property, environmental reclamation lien in favor of State attaches to real property. (415-5/21.3). Act authorizes Agency to acquire fee, or any lesser interest, in real property where, among other things, it is necessary to respond to hazardous substance release. (415-5/21.4).

Solid Waste Management Regulations and Guidelines.—Conducting certain landscape waste composting operations without permit unlawful. (415-5/21[q]). Permit not required in certain situations. (415-5/21[q][1-3]). Accepting landscape waste at sanitary landfill unless certain conditions met. (415-5/22.19[c]). Knowingly mixing landscape waste with municipal waste (415-5/22.9[a]), or knowingly putting landscape waste into non-biodegradable container if container is bound for landfill (415-5/22.9[b]). State should consider using compost in maintenance of public lands. (415-20/3). State shall begin program to separate and collect office wastepaper for recycling and implement aluminum can recycling program in State buildings (415-20/3), and shall, except in certain circumstances, purchase only recyclable paper (415-20/3). Disposing of lead-acid batteries in municipal waste sanitary landfills. (415-5/22.23). Failure to accept used lead-acid battery turned in by customer when purchasing new battery. (415-5/22.23). Failure to provide method at sanitary landfill, in county over 275,000, for cleaning mud and debris from vehicles entering upon property (415-5/22.4). Any person violating act or regulating determination or order of board shall be liable for civil penalty. (415-5/42[h]). Institutions of higher learning shall develop comprehensive waste reduction plan addressing management of solid waste generated by academic, administrative, student housing and other institutional functions. (415-20/3.1). Sanitation Code violations dealing with any municipal ordinance that pertains to or regulates sanitation practices, forestry practices, attachment of bills or notices to public property, abatement of public nuisances, accumulation, disposal, and transportation of garbage, refuse and other forms of solid waste in municipality. (65-5/11-19.2-1). Corporate authorities of municipality having population of 100,000 or more may establish code hearing unit. (65-5/11-19.2-2). Hearing procedures and administrative review. (65-5/11-19.2-3[13]). Used Motor Oil Recycling Act and Recycled Newsprint Use Act governed by (20-1140/1001, 415-110/2001). Landfill and incinerator operators must report quarterly volume and state of origination of nonhazardous solid waste. (415-5/22.27).

Water Pollution.—Discharge of oil or other pollutants into any waters used for water supply, recreation or navigation is prohibited. (415-25/1). Any governmental body having polluted such waters, from violation of 415-25/3, within its territory is authorized to remove oil or other pollutants. (415-25/4). Owner or operator of facility discharging oil or pollutant into waters is liable to governmental body for actual costs of removal, attorneys fees, court costs and other expenses of litigation. (415-25/5). Stormwater and Floodplain Management governed by 55-5/5-1012.

Soil Erosion.—Department of Agriculture shall adopt guidelines for erosion and sediment control. (70-405/36). Soil and water conservation districts shall adopt technically feasible, economically reasonable control programs. (70-405/38). Any person engaged in land disturbing activities (except those subject to Pollution Control Board regulations) shall comply with standards established by district. (70-405/39). Department shall hold hearings following complaint by unit of government or aggrieved party. (70-405/41). All final administrative decisions of any district or department are subject to judicial review under Administrative Review Law. (70-405/42).

Toxic Substances.—Certain businesses must prepare emergency response plans and publish inventory of toxic chemicals, including any petroleum, stored on site. (430-45/4). Agency must review these plans and prepare written findings and recommendations; these must then be acted upon by business which submitted plan. (430-45/8). Agency Toxic Pollution Prevention program to identify all federal and state laws or regulations pertaining to waste disposal and release of toxic substances into environment. (415-85/4). Every pesticide distributed, sold, offered for sale within state, delivered for transportation or transported in interstate commerce between points within state through any point outside state, shall be registered and renewed annually. Registration not required if pesticide is shipped from one plant or warehouse to another plant or warehouse by same person and used solely at such plant or warehouse as constituent part to make pesticide which is registered under provisions of Illinois Act and FIFRA. (415-60/6[1]). Registration fees. (415-60/6[6]). Commercial applicators of pesticides must obtain license. (415-60/10). Pesticide dealers shall be registered. (415-60/13). Department of Agriculture shall develop procedures, methods and guidelines for addressing agrichemical pesticide contamination at agrichemical facilities in Illinois. (415-60/19[8]).

Groundwater Contamination.—No new noncommunity, semiprivate or private water supply well may be located within prescribed distance from potential source of groundwater contamination. (415-30/6a). Minimum setback zones for new community water supplies (415-5/14.1) and for new sources of groundwater contamination (415-5/14.2). Counties and municipalities may increase setback zones for particular community water supplies upon petition and approval by EPA. (415-5/14.3). EPA to propose standards and requirements for activities which could cause groundwater contamination. (415-5/14.4). Certification system for sites which represent minimal groundwater contamination hazard. (415-5/14.5). Any county or municipality served by community water supply may prepare groundwater protection needs assessment. (415-5/17.1). EPA to establish regional groundwater protection planning program. (415-5/17.2).

Underground Storage Tanks.—Underground Storage Tank Fund monies deposited are received and may be used by Agency and Office of State Fire Marshall. (415-5/57.11). Where notice was provided, Agency has authority to require owner, operator or both to undertake preventive or corrective action whenever there is release or substantial threat of release. (415-5/57.12). Failure to respond to release or substantial threat of release of petroleum may subject owner or operator of tank to treble damages for state response. (415-5/57.12). Owner or operator is eligible for fund reimbursement of specified corrective action or indemnification if costs were incurred from release of designated petroleum products and owner or operator meets specified requirements. (415-5/57.13).

Agency Permits Required.—To construct, install or operate facility Board determines to be capable of causing or contributing to air or water pollution. (415-5/9[b], 5/9.1, 5/12[b], 5/39.1). Agency may deny application for issuance or renewal of air pollution operating permit if site fee not paid within 60 days of due date. Denial of fee subject to Board review. (415-5/9.6[f]). Amounts of fees with regard to water pollution. (415-5/12.2[c]). Agency shall approve or disapprove application for construction permit within 45 days of receipt of permit application and fee. (415-5/12.2[g]). Fees not required from state or local governments. (415-5/12.2[e]). To conduct refuse collection or disposal operations. (415-5/21[d]) or landscape waste composting operations. Fee required to operate hazardous disposal site. (415-5/22 et seq.). Fee and registration of radiation machines. (420-30/2.1).

Board Required Permits.—Section granting Board power to adopt standards to protect citizens from radiation hazard where not preempted (415-5/25b).

Regulations.—Board may adopt regulations related to air pollution (415-5/10), water pollution (415-5/13), public water supplies (415-5/17), groundwater contamination (415-5/14), land pollution (415-5/22), hazardous waste disposal (415-5/4[r], 5/22[g]), noise pollution (415-5/25), nuclear facility construction (415-5/25b). Board shall adopt hazardous waste regulations identical to federal regulations promulgated under §§3001 to 3005 of Resource Conservation and Recovery Act. (415-5/22.4). Board must adopt rules in substantially same form as final federal regulations promulgated by U.S. EPA under Federal Clean Air Act. (415-5/28.4) (automatic repeal 12/31/97). Board shall adopt regulations identical, if necessary and appropriate, to federal regulations promulgated under §§111-12 of Federal Clean Air Act (415-5/7.2, 415-5/9.1) and federal regulations implementing §105 of Comprehensive Environmental Response, Compensation and Liability Act (415-5/7.2, 415-5/22.1). Board may adopt regulations relating to state contingency plan not identical to federal regulations implementing §105 of Comprehensive Environmental Response, Compensation and Liability Act. (415-5/22.1). Agency shall adopt specific limitations on emission of mercury, chromium, cadmium and lead and good combustion practices from municipal waste incinerators. (415-5/22.16b[c]). Agency shall establish household hazardous waste collection centers and shall ensure that wastes collected are properly disposed of. Such centers shall not be regulated as hazardous waste facilities under RCRA. (415-5/22.16b[d]). Department of Nuclear Safety shall promulgate rules to establish standards applicable to facilities for storage, treatment or disposal of low-level radioactive wastes away from point of generation. (420-20/6[a], 420-20/10.1). Board regulations may be procedural (415-5/26) and substantive (415-5/27[a]). Substantive regulations may apply to sources outside Illinois causing, contributing to, or threatening environmental damage in Illinois (415-5/27[a]). Regulation by imposition of monetary charges for emission of air or water contaminants is prohibited. (415-5/27([a]). Board shall consider economic impact of proposed regulations. (415-5/27). Board may establish alternative requirements in adjusted standard proceeding for direct discharge of waste solids to Mississippi or Ohio Rivers. (415-5/28.3). Board may grant variances beyond limitations of Act and individual adjusted standards from regulations of general applicability if consistent with federal Water Pollution Control Act Amendments of 1972, Safe Drinking Water Act, Clean Water Act of 1977, Clean Air Act as am'd in 1977 and Resource Conservation and Recovery Act of 1976. (415-5/28.1, 415-5/35).

Public may propose adoption, repeal or change of regulations and compel prescribed hearings thereon if nonfrivolous petition with 200 signatures is presented and Board has not dealt with matter in hearing within six months. (415-5/28). Petitioner must submit recommendation as to whether economic impact study is advisable and describe reasons for recommendation. (415-5/27). When Agency proposes rule that it believes to be required, Agency shall certify in proposal identifying federal law which proposed rule will respond and rationale upon which certification is based. (415-5/28.2[b]). In addition, within 21 days of Board's acceptance of proposal for hearing, any person may request Board to determine that economic impact study be prepared or not be prepared and submit reasons therefor. (415-5/27, 415-5/28.2). If Board determines that economic impact study is necessary for required rule, Department shall prepare study within six months. (415-5/28.2). If Board determines that economic study is not necessary, it shall consider economic impact of proposed rule to extent possible. (415-5/28.2[d]). Whether

See note at head of Digest as to 1998 legislation covered.

See Topical Index in front part of this volume.

ENVIRONMENTAL REGULATION . . . *continued*
or not study is submitted within six months, Board may proceed to adopt required rule. (415-5/28.2). Prior to initiating any hearing on regulatory proposal, Board may schedule prehearing conference before qualified hearing officer. (415-5/27). Notice requirements of §28 do not apply and record need not be kept. (415-5/27). Prescribed hearings must always be held on Agency or Department proposals. (415-5/28). Anyone adversely affected or threatened by any regulation may obtain determination of its validity or application by petition for review (415-5/29), except in any subsequent proceeding under Title VIII, Title IX or §40 of this Act (415-5/29). See subhead Judicial Review, infra.

Complaints.—Within 180 days of becoming aware of alleged violation of Act, rule adopted or permit granted by Agency, Agency shall issue and serve by certified mail written notice of alleged violation. Written response shall be submitted to Agency within 45 days of receipt of notice of violations unless extended by Agency. If person complained against fails to respond, failure considered waiver of requirements on Agency in §31(a) and Agency may proceed to pursue legal action. If person complained against requests meeting with Agency personnel, it shall be held within 60 days of notice by person complained against unless Agency agrees to postpone. If meeting occurs, person complained against has 21 days to submit written response or if none Agency may pursue legal action. (415 ILCS 5/31[a][1]). Upon prescribed notice public hearings are held. (415-5/31). Complainant has burden of showing actual or threatened: (1) Air or water pollution or (2) violation of Act or Board regulations or permit conditions. Upon such showing, respondent has burden of showing compliance would impose arbitrary or unreasonable hardship. (415-5/31). Any party may be represented by counsel, present evidence, and cross-examine. Record of hearing is kept. (415-5/32).

When complaint is filed by Agency or State, parties may file with Board stipulation and proposal for settlement accompanied by request for relief from requirement of hearing before Board. Unless Board in its discretion determines that hearing will be held, Board must publish proposed settlement and request relief from hearing. If any person requests hearing, Board must deny settlement request. (415-5/31).

Specific considerations for decision are (1) character and degree of injury to health, welfare and property, (2) social and economic value of pollution source, (3) suitability of pollution source to its area, including priority of location, and (4) technical practicality and economic reasonableness of reducing or eliminating pollution source. (415-5/33[c]). Compliance with regulations under this Act prima facie defense in proceedings on complaints. (415-5/49[e]). Subsequent compliance with regulations is not defense to violation of those regulations. (415-5/33[a]).

Out of State Service.—C. 110, §§2-208 and 2-209, apply to service of complaints based on actual or threatened acts outside Illinois contributing to environmental damage in Illinois. See category Civil Actions and Procedure, topic Process, subhead Long Arm Statute.

Orders.—Board may enter cease and desist orders, assess money penalties not to exceed $50,000 plus $10,000 for each day violation continues, assess money penalties of up to $10,000 per day for National Pollutant Discharge Elimination System violations, assess money penalties of at least $10,000 per day for violation of underground injection control program and assess civil penalties of $25,000 per day for violation of hazardous waste control program regulations, require in addition payment for destroyed aquatic life, and revoke permits. (415-5/33[b], 5/42). Summary powers granted to Agency if it determines violation of Board regulations creates emergency, including power to seal pollution source. Owner or operator may secure hearing or injunctive relief from sealing. (415-5/34). Final order or determination of Board must be based solely on evidence in record and must not be against manifest weight of evidence. (415-5/41).

Variances.—Persons seeking variances may petition Agency on grounds of arbitrary or unreasonable hardship. Upon investigation, Agency recommends action to Board, which may hold hearings and must if objection is made. In granting variance, Board may impose conditions, including posting of performance bond where request is solely for reasonable delay in which to correct violation. Board upon granting or denying variance must publish opinion. If Board fails to take final action within 120 days variance is deemed granted. Filing petition within 20 days after effective date of complained-of regulation stays effectiveness of regulations as to petitioner. (415-5/35 to 5/38). Board may grant provisional variances for period not to exceed 45 days. (415-5/35, 5/36[c]).

Individual Adjusted Standards.—Board may grant individual adjusted standards from regulations of general applicability. (415-5/28.1). If Board has not specified level of justification required for adjusted standard, one may be sought by showing that factors relating to petitioner are substantially and significantly different than factors relied on by Board in adopting general regulation, that these factors justify adjusted standard, that adjusted standard will not adversely affect health or environment, and that adjusted standard is consistent with federal law. (415-5/28.1). If petition is filed within 20 days of effective date of regulation, operation of regulation shall be stayed as to that petitioner pending resolution of petition providing such action is consistent with federal law. (415-5/28.1).

Permits.—Permits for individual sewerage disposal systems. (55-5/5-15010). Any well for which permit is required under Illinois Oil and Gas Act, other than plugged well, drilled prior to Aug. 15, 1990 and for which no permit has been issued, is required to be permitted. (225-725/12). Agency permits for development or operation of new municipal waste incinerator conditions. (415-5/22.16b[b]). Agency authorized to grant experimental permits which include provision for disposal of wastes from combustion of coal and other materials. (415-5/21[r]). Agency shall issue development or construction permit for composting facility if applicant gives adequate notice. (415-5/22.26). Agency must issue Board-required permits upon applicant's proof of nonviolation of Act and regulations. In granting permits, Agency may impose such conditions as may be necessary to accomplish purpose of this Act. From Sept. 4, 1990 to Dec. 31, 1993, Agency shall not issue permit for development or construction of new facility for incineration of any hazardous waste unless intended for use as part of state or federally designated clean-up action. (415-5/39[o]). Refusal of permit reviewable by petition to Board within 35 days which may be extended to no more than 90 days by applicant giving written notice to Board and Agency within initial appeal period. (415-5/40). Generally if Agency or Board fails to take final action within 90 days of application or review, application deemed granted, except extended to 120 days where review requires public hearing. (415-5/39, 5/40[a]). Contestant of hazardous waste disposal site permit may petition Board within 35 days for hearing. (415/40[b]). If Agency issues NPDES permit that imposes limits which are based upon criterion or denies permit based upon application of criterion, then Agency shall have burden of going forward with basis for derivation of limits of criterion which were derived under Board's rules. (415-5/40[a][1]). Review procedure, including direct review to appellate court of final order of Department of Nuclear Safety under Low Level Radioactive Waste Management Act. (420-20/18). No sewerage system which is planned or designed to discharge into any waters, sewage, industrial wastes, or other wastes which may cause pollution of waters within sanitary district may be installed unless written permit for such sewerage system has been granted by sanitary district. (70-2605/7bb).

Judicial Review.—(1) Party to Board hearing or (2) any person who was denied a hearing, variance or permit or (3) any party adversely affected by a final order or determination of Board or (4) any person adversely affected or threatened by any Board regulation, may obtain judicial review by filing petition for review within 35 days from date copy of order or other final action was served upon affected part, under Administrative Review Law, in Appellate Court of District in which cause of action arose (415-5/41). Any person affected by final order or determination of Department of Nuclear Safety may obtain judicial review, under Administrative Review Law except that review will be directly in Appellate Court. (420-20/18[a]).

Actions.—Existing civil and criminal actions not affected by Act. (415-5/45[a]). Authorization of E.P.A. to prosecute cases before Pollution Control Board held unconstitutional (65 Ill.2d 485, 359 N.E.2d 149) and statute amended (415-5/4[e]).

By State.—Violations of Act or regulations, or submitting false information, are misdemeanors. Certain violations, particularly those relating to delivery and disposal of hazardous wastes, are felonies. (415-5/44). If State brings action to compel waste removal or clean-up against person with real interest in property for allowing open dumping or burning by third party, defendant may bring in third-party defendant. (415-5/45[d]). State may sue to recover penalties and to compel compliance with Responsible Property Transfer Act. (765-90/7). State may prosecute corporation for any offense defined in §44 of Act (720-5/5-4), and if convicted, corporation may be fined up to $50,000 or amount stated in offense, whichever is greater, for offense (730-5/5-9-1).

By Private Person.—Any person adversely affected in fact by a violation of Act or regulations may sue for injunctive relief. (415-5/45). Regardless of whether landfill operation for disposal of hazardous substances has been licensed, it must still be operated in way that does not constitute nuisance. Otherwise, court may order shutdown of landfill and removal of hazardous substances buried there. (86 Ill.2d 1, 426 N.E.2d 824). Plaintiff must complain to Board first and wait 30 days after denial of relief before instituting suit. Prevailing party awarded costs and attorney's fees. (415-5/45[b]). Any person who suffers damage by reason of violation of Responsible Property Transfer Act by any other person may bring action against such person. (765-90/7). Any person in county may bring action against seller of beverages packaged in unapproved plastic containers. (415-15/10.1[d]). Penalty for knowing violation not to exceed $5,000, and may include attorney fees. (415-15/10.1[d]).

State of Illinois has no liability to person or entity by reason of failure, delay or cessation in operation of disposal facility. (420-20/6[f]).

Defenses.—Compliance with Act or regulation prima facie defense to any action by any person. (415-5/49[e]).

Financing.—Agrichemical Incident Response Fund created for payment of costs of response action incurred by owners of agrichemical facilities to take emergency action in response to release of agricultural pesticides from agrichemical facility and for costs of administering activities. (415-60/22.2, 60/22.3). Environmental Facilities Financing Authority may construct or finance environmental facilities within state. Special consideration to small business. (20-3515/1). Special consideration to projects reducing volume of hazardous waste products or recycling hazardous waste. Environmental Protection Trust Fund receives and administers funds for environmental protection. (30-125/1). Sanitary districts under order to abate violations. (415-5/46). Environmental Protection Agency receives and administers funds for waste disposal. (415-5/4). Hazardous Waste Fund receives funds to prevent or correct immediate or long-term danger caused by hazardous waste disposal sites. (415-5/22.2[d]). Low-Level Radioactive Waste Development and Operation Fund is created from fees assessed against generators of low-level radioactive waste. (420-20/13). Underground Storage Tank Fund created from fees for underground storage tanks and used for payment of costs of corrective action and indemnification, as well as other costs relating to tanks. (415-5/57.11). Beginning Jan. 1, 1991, Agency shall assess and collect fee from owner or operator of new municipal waste incinerator. (415-22.16b[a]). Toxic pollution prevention assistance program fund used for consulting, for developing plans to prevent toxic pollution and for sponsoring projects to develop innovative technologies. (415-85/5). Financial incentives provided to encourage recycling of lead-acid batteries. (415-5/22.23).

ESTATES AND TRUSTS

ADMINISTRATION:

See topic Executors and Administrators.

ADVANCEMENTS:

See topic Descent and Distribution.

ALLOWANCES:

See topic Executors and Administrators.

CLAIMS:

See topic Executors and Administrators; category Civil Actions and Procedure, topic Pleading.

See note at head of Digest as to 1998 legislation covered.

See Topical Index in front part of this volume.

IL – 53

DEATH:

Death defined under Uniform Anatomical Gift Act as irreversible cessation of total brain function, according to usual and customary standards of medical practice. (755-50/2[b]).

Unexplained and unaccounted for absence for seven years raises presumption of death at end of period. (92 Ill.2d 207, 441 N.E.2d 71).

Administration of estate may be sought on presumption of death. (755-5/9-6). In such case costs of administration and claims are paid in usual course, but distributees must furnish bond for double value of their distributive shares or have their distributive shares on deposit with county treasurer for period of 20 years. (755-5/24-5).

Special death certificate available for presumed-dead missing persons, pursuant to court order. (410-535/18).

Letters of administration to collect may be issued on estate of missing person. (755-5/10-1). Upon issuance of letters testamentary or of administration or location of missing person, power of administration to collect ceases. (755-5/10-5).

Living Wills.—See topic Wills, subhead Living Wills.

Survivorship.—Illinois has adopted Uniform Simultaneous Death Act. (755-5/3-1).

Coroners.—Every coroner informed that body of dead person is within county shall take charge of body and investigate circumstances of death when death is suspected of being (a) sudden or violent; (b) due to abortion, sex crime, or crime against nature; (c) suspicious or mysterious or where attending physician indicates in writing that cause of death is unknown; (d) death where addiction to alcohol or any drug may have been contributory cause; or (e) death where decedent was not attended by licensed physician. (55-5/3-3013).

Actions for Death.—Action for wrongful death may be brought by and in names of personal representatives of decedent for exclusive benefit of spouse and next of kin; must be brought within two years after death; unless person entitled to recover benefits is under 18 at time cause of action accrued, then suit must be brought within two years after attainment of age of 18; there is no numerical limitation on damages recoverable. (740-180/1, 180/2). Where no spouse or next of kin survive decedent, action may be brought by personal representatives for benefit of persons furnishing hospital and medical services to decedent in connection with last illness or injury; to personal representative for expenses and costs of administering estate. Recoveries in such case are limited to: (a) $450 to persons providing hospital services, (b) $450 to persons providing medical or surgical services, and (c) $900 plus reasonable attorney's fee to personal representatives for hospital, medical, funeral, litigation, and estate administration expenses. (740-180/2).

Child, including unborn child, is "person" within meaning of Wrongful Death Act, upon determination of viability. (55 Ill.2d 368, 304 N.E.2d 88). Statutory cause of action available for death of unborn child. Physicians performing lawful abortion under valid consent exempted. (740-180/2.2).

Certificate.—See category Documents and Records, topic Records, subhead Vital Statistics.

DECEDENTS' ESTATES:

See topics Descent and Distribution, Executors and Administrators, Wills; category Debtor and Creditor, topic Homesteads.

DESCENT AND DISTRIBUTION:

Entire estate, both real and personal, of deceased resident, and real estate of deceased nonresident, where there is no surviving spouse (see subhead Surviving Spouse, infra), descends and is distributed as follows, each class of which a member is living taking to exclusion of subsequent classes: (1) descendants per stirpes; (2) parents, brothers and sisters equally, descendants of deceased brothers and sisters taking by representation and, if one parent be dead, surviving parent taking a double portion; (3) one-half to paternal grandparents or to survivor of them or to their descendants per stirpes and one-half to maternal grandparents in like fashion or, if only one set of grandparents or descendants survive, entire estate to those grandparents or descendants; (4) one-half to paternal great grandparents or to survivor of them or to their descendants per stirpes and one-half to maternal great grandparents in like fashion or, if only one set of great grandparents or descendants survive, entire estate to those great grandparents or descendants; and (5) nearest kindred of equal degree according to civil law rules, without representation. (755-5/2-1).

Surviving Spouse.—If there is surviving spouse and also descendant of decedent, one-half of entire estate to surviving spouse; if there is surviving spouse but no descendant of decedent, entire estate to surviving spouse. (755-5/2-1). If surviving spouse renounces will, surviving spouse takes one-third of entire estate if testator leaves descendant or one-half of entire estate if testator leaves no descendant. (755-5/2-8).

Election.—Dower and curtesy are abolished in Illinois. See category Property, topic Dower.

Half Blood.—No distinction is made between relatives of the whole blood and those of the half blood. (755-5/2-1).

Posthumous child receives same share of ancestor's estate as though born in decedent's lifetime. (755-5/2-3).

Adopted Child.—See category Family, topic Adoption, subhead Effect of Adoption.

Illegitimate child, or his or her lawful issue, inherits from and through mother and from any person from whom mother might have inherited if living. Surviving spouse of illegitimate who left descendants has same rights as any other surviving spouse; if illegitimate left no descendants, surviving spouse takes entire estate. Where there is no descendant or surviving spouse, estate goes one-half to mother and other half to her descendants per stirpes, or failing such heirs, to maternal grandparents in equal parts or to survivor of them, or to their descendants per stirpes or, failing such, to maternal great-grandparents or their descendants per stirpes or, failing such, to next of kin of mother according to civil law rules. Illegitimate is legitimized by intermarriage of parents and acknowledgment by father. If decedent acknowledges illegitimate or if prior to or after death decedent is adjudged father of illegitimate, illegitimate is heir of father and any paternal ancestor. Descendants of illegitimate represent him and take through him on descent. Paternity proved by copy of judgment where adjudged; by clear and convincing evidence in all other cases. After illegitimate is adopted, that person's relationship to adopting and natural parents governed by 755-5/2/4 as to decedents who die on or after Jan. 1, 1998 and as to property rights of person under any instrument executed on or after Jan. 1, 1998. (755-5/2-2).

Person Causing Descendent's Death.—See topic Wills, subhead Person Causing Decedent's Death.

Determination of Heirship.—All courts having probate jurisdiction are given power to make determinations of heirship. (755-5/5-3). On absence of contrary evidence, court may presume that decedent and any person through whom heirship is traced was not parent of any child born out of wedlock, and, if decedent or person was male, that no child born out of wedlock was filiated or acknowledged or legitimated by decedent or person. (755-5/5-3).

Advancements must be so expressed by decedent or so acknowledged by recipient in writing and are regarded as part of estate and included in share of person by whom received, but refund not required although share exceeded. (755-5/2-5).

Disclaimer.—See topic Wills, subhead Disclaimer.

Liabilities of Heirs for Debts.—Under certain limitations, heirs are liable for ancestor's debts to the extent of assets received. (740-80/11, 80/12).

Escheat.—If decedent left no surviving spouse or kindred, property escheats as follows: Real estate to county where located; personal estate, within state and personal estate outside state but subject to ancillary administration of Illinois estate, to county where decedent resided, or if decedent was a nonresident, to county where located; all other personal estate wherever situated to state. (755-5/2-1, 5/2-2).

See also topic Executors and Administrators.

ESTATES:

See category Property, topic Real Property.

EXECUTORS AND ADMINISTRATORS:

Probate jurisdiction is exercised by branches of the circuit court. (Art. VI, §9). See category Courts and Legislature, topic Courts.

Probate venue is (1) in the county where decedent had a known place of residence, or (2) if he had no known place of residence, in the county wherein the greater portion of his real estate is located, or (3) if none of the above, in the county where the greater part of his personal estate is located at death. (755-5/5-1).

Preferences in Right to Administer.—Right to administration is in following order: (1) Surviving spouse; (2) legatees with preference to legatees who are children; (3) children; (4) grandchildren; (5) parents; (6) brothers and sisters; (7) next of kin; (8) representative of estate of deceased ward; (9) Public Administrator; (10) creditor of estate. Nominee of person in classes 1 to 7 inclusive, has same precedence as person making nomination. Only persons who can qualify as administrators have right to nominate; but residents of U.S. not qualified to act solely because of nonresidence in Illinois may nominate. Person removed as representative loses right to name successor. (755-5/9-3).

Eligibility and Competency.—Person not qualified to act as executor or administrator if less than 18 years of age or of unsound mind or disabled person or convicted of felony or not resident of U.S. (755-5/6-13, 755-5/9-1). Any corporation qualified to accept and execute trusts in Illinois is qualified to act as executor or administrator. (755-5/1-3). Person who is not resident of Illinois can act as administrator (755-5/9-1), and can act as executor and must file in court where estate is pending designation of resident agent to accept service of process, notice or demand, and failing such designation, clerk of court is constituted executor's agent and must mail copy of process, notice or demand to executor at last known address and to his attorney of record (755-5/1-11, 755-5/6-13). Foreign corporation may act as such only if: (1) It is authorized by laws of state of its organization or domicile to act in such fiduciary capacity in that state and (2) corporation organized under law of Illinois may act in similar fiduciary capacity in coterminous state under conditions and qualifications which commissioner finds not unduly restrictive when compared to Illinois requirements. (205-620/4-2). Before acting as executor or as administrator in Illinois, foreign corporation must obtain certificate of authority from Commissioner of Banks and Real Estate. (205-620/4-5).

Qualification.—Individual representatives must execute oath of faithful performance of duties. (755-5/12-2). To qualify, every individual representative must file bond in double value of personalty if individuals act as sureties or if security on bond is excused, or one and one-half times such value if surety company acts as surety. (755-5/12-2, 5/12-4, 5/12-5). Cause of action for wrongful death initially valued at $500 for this purpose but must be adjusted to amount likely to be received as proceeds of judgment or settlement. (755-5/12-5). Additional bond related to income required if representative takes possession of real estate. (755-5/12-5).

Exemption from Surety.—Where will excuses representative from giving security no surety is required unless court has cause to suspect fraud or incompetence or believes estate insufficient to discharge claims, and amount of bond required from time to time is in effect without writing, unless required by court. (755-5/12-2, 5/12-4). If will specifies security, no greater security can be required than is so specified unless same grounds exist. (755-5/12-4). But court may in its discretion require bond and surety of nonresident executor despite contrary provision of will. (755-5/6-13). Except for appeal bonds, corporations qualified to act as representative need not furnish bond. (755-5/12-1). Office of State Guardian not required to have sureties. (755-5/12-4[c]).

Issuance of Petition for Letters.—Admission of will or issuance of letters testamentary requires verified petition stating, if known: (1) Name and residence of decedent at death; (2) date and place of death; (3) date of will and petitioner's belief that will is valid last will of testator; (4) approximate value of real and personal estate in Illinois; (5) names and addresses of all heirs and legatees and whether any are minors or

See note at head of Digest as to 1998 legislation covered.

See Topical Index in front part of this volume.

IL – 54

EXECUTORS AND ADMINISTRATORS . . . *continued*

disabled persons; (6) name and address of executor; (7) unless supervised administration is requested, name and address of personal fiduciary acting or designated under (755-5/28-3). When will creates or adds to trust, trustee's name and address is sufficient and beneficiary's name and address not necessary unless beneficiary is also legatee or heir. For letters of administration with will annexed, petition must also state, if known: (1) Reason for issuance; (2) facts showing right to act as administrator or to nominate; (3) name and address of person nominated and of each person entitled to administer or nominate in equal or greater preference to petitioner; (4) date of admission where will previously admitted. (755-5/6-2).

Issuance of letters of administration for intestate estate requires petition stating, if known: (1) Name and residence of decedent at death; (2) date and place of death; (3) approximate value of real and personal estate in Illinois; (4) names and address of all heirs and whether any are minors or disabled persons and whether any are entitled either to administer or to nominate person to administer equally with or in preference to petitioner; (5) name and post office address of person nominated administrator; (6) facts showing right to act as administrator or to nominate; (7) when de bonis non, reason for issuance; (8) unless supervised administration is requested, name and address of personal fiduciary acting or designated under 755-5/28-3. (755-5/9-4).

When letters sought on presumption of death, petition must include items 3 through 8 above, and: (1) Facts and circumstances raising presumption; (2) name and last known address of decedent; (3) name and address of each person in possession or control of decedent's property, if known. (755-5/9-6). Special notice provisions for presumption of death cases. (755-5/6-20[b]).

When any person entitled to administer or nominate equally with or in preference to petitioner, petitioner must mail copy of petition to such persons and give such persons 30 days notice by mail of hearing on petition. Petitioner must file proof of mailing with clerk of court. (755-5/9-5). Within 14 days after letters have issued, administrator must give notice of petition and order by mail, or by publication if necessary, to each heir not entitled to prior notice. Administrator must file proof of mailing and of publication, if required, with clerk of court. (755-5/9-5). Copy of petition and order need not be sent to, nor notice published for any person not under disability or minor who personally appears at hearing or who files waiver of notice. (755-5/9-5). Letters may be revoked for failure to give notice if petition is filed within three months of issuance of letters. (755-5/9-7).

Removal.—On petition of interested person or on court's own motion, representative may be removed when: (1) Letters were secured by false pretenses; (2) adjudged incompetent or in need of mental treatment under Mental Health Code; (3) convicted of felony; (4) wastes or mismanages estate; (5) endangers co-representative or surety on his bond; (6) fails to give sufficient bond or security pursuant to court order; (7) fails to file inventory or accounting pursuant to court order; (8) conceals himself to avoid process or notice; (9) becomes incapable of or unsuitable for discharge of his duties; (10) other good cause; (11) becomes nonresident of U.S. (755-5/23-2). Procedure for citation for removal, notice, answer and hearing are prescribed. (755-5/23-3).

Special Kinds of Administration.—General statutory provisions apply to administrator de bonis non, administrator with will annexed, and administrator de bonis non with will annexed. (755-5/1-2). Executor or administrator with will annexed administers all testate and intestate estate. (755-5/6-15). Administrator to collect may be appointed by court on its own motion or upon petition of any interested person when: (a) Delay occurs in issuance of letters and it appears estate is liable to waste, loss or embezzlement or, (b) person is missing from his usual place of residence and cannot be located, or when in military service is reported missing. Court may appoint any person who is qualified to act as administrator. (755-5/10-1). On issuance of letters testamentary or of administration powers of administrator to collect cease. (755-5/10-5).

Public Administrator.—When person dies and no person in this state has prior right to administer, public administrator of proper county may take steps to protect property until issuance of letters or until demand for removal of property is made by nonresident representative. (755-5/13-4).

Inventory and Appraisal.—Inventory to be filed within 60 days from date of letters. (755-5/14-1). If representative believes that appraisal of goods and chattels is necessary for proper administration, he may appraise them or appoint one or more competent, disinterested appraisers with compensation. (755-5/14-2). Additional inventories and appraisals may be made from time to time as new assets are discovered and must be filed within 60 days after discovery of property. (755-5/14-1).

Collection of Assets.—Court, upon filing of petition by representative or person interested in estate, by citation proceedings, may compel persons to produce and deliver to personal representatives any personal property, books of account, evidences of debt or title to lands belonging to decedent or any information relating to any of these matters. In such proceedings, court may decide questions of title and rights of property. Court enforces its decisions by imprisonment for contempt or by execution against respondent's property. (755-5/16-1).

Access to Safe Deposit Box.—Effective for decedents dying after Dec. 31, 1982, lessor of safe deposit box permitted to open deceased lessee's box in presence of person who presents affidavit stating he is interested in filing decedent's will or in decedent's burial arrangements, believes safe deposit box contains decedent's will or burial instructions, and is interested person. Interested person includes anyone who had right of access to box prior to decedent's death, presents copy of decedent's will naming him or her as executor, or is decedent's surviving spouse, adult descendant, parent, brother or sister, or otherwise has legitimate interest in filing of will or in burial arrangements. Only will and burial instructions can be removed. Lessor must deliver burial instructions to interested person and will to Circuit Court Clerk in county of decedent's residence, or if unknown, in county where safe deposit box is located. Delivery may be made by registered mail. Lessor must not open box if he has received copy of letters of office or other applicable court order. Box need not be opened if it has previously been opened, key or combination is not available, or lessor has reason to believe someone would object. (755-5/15-1).

Operation of Decedent's Business.—Unless provided otherwise in decedent's will or by law, representative may continue to operate decedent's unincorporated business, during one month next following date of issuance of letters and for further time as court may authorize under court supervision without personal liability except for malfeasance or misfeasance. Obligations incurred or contracts entered into are entitled to priority of payment out of assets of business. (755-5/19-6).

Filing of Tax Return and Payment of Taxes.—For decedents dying after Dec. 31, 1982, no inheritance tax due; estate tax due in amount equal to maximum federal credit for state death taxes. Executor, administrator or, if no legal representative appointed, person in possession of property must file copy of Illinois return and of federal estate tax return with Attorney General. Must also file Illinois return with county treasurer of county in which decedent resided and any tax due payable at same time federal estate tax return due.(35-405/6).

Executor or administrator is personally liable for payment of estate tax and interest. (35-405/10).

Illinois Income Tax applies to trusts and estates. (35-5/201). See category Taxation, topic Income Tax. Representative may file, with surviving spouse, joint federal or state income tax return. (755-5/27-7).

Notice to Creditors.—Representative must publish once each week for three successive weeks and mail or deliver to each known or reasonably ascertainable creditor whose claim has not been disallowed under §18-11, notice of decedent's death which notice shall include name and address of representative and attorney of record, that claim must be filed on or before six months from date of publication or three months from date of mailing or delivery of notice, whichever is later, or claim is barred. (755-5/18-3). Publication must be in newspaper published in county where estate is being administered. (755-5/18-3). If no newspaper is published in county, such notice must be published in such newspaper as court directs. (755-5/27-8). Representative must file proof of publication with court. (755-5/18-3).

Presentation of Claims.—Representative may at any time pay or consent in writing to all or any part of any claim filed within date stated in original notice or notice of disallowance, as applicable, if not disallowed by court and representative determines claim is valid. Representative's payment or consent constitutes allowance and binds estate. Representative must file notice of allowance with court, but failure does not affect allowance. Any interested person can compel representative to establish propriety of allowance. (755-5/18-11[a]).

Representative may at any time disallow all or any part of any claim not filed with court by mailing notice to claimant and his attorney, if known stating that claim not filed with court on or before date stated in notice, which date shall not be less than two months from date of notice, will be barred. Claim thus disallowed is barred as if not timely filed.

Every claim against estate, except administration expenses and spouse or child award, is barred if proper notice is given by representative and claimant fails to file claim with representative or court, as appropriate, on or before required date stated in applicable notice. (755-5/18-12[a]). Execution of judgment is not barred against estate assets after six months if suit was pending at decedent's death and executor is properly substituted defendant. (77 Ill.2d 452, 397 N.E.2d 842). All claims except those under Illinois Public Aid Code §§3-9 and 5-13, which could otherwise have been barred are barred two years after descendent's death whether or not Letters of Office are issued. (755-5/18-12[b]). Actions to establish decedent's liability are not barred to extent estate is protected by liability insurance. (755-5/18-12[c]). Except with respect to claims known to representative and not paid or otherwise barred, representative acting in good faith to give proper notice to creditors is not personally liable to creditors. Any claim not barred may be asserted against estate or distributee except distributee's share shall not be diminished below that which he or she would have received had claim been paid by representative. (755-5/18-12[d]).

Unmatured claims may be presented. (755-5/18-4).

Contingent claims may not be presented. (288 Ill. 142, 123 N.E. 300). But see 321 Ill. 612, 152 N.E. 539 regarding certain types of guarantees treated as unmatured claims.

As to secured claims, see subhead Secured Claims, infra.

Proof of Claims.—Every claim filed must be in writing and state sufficient information to notify representative of nature of claim or other relief sought. (755-5/18-2). Following is approved, though not required, form of affidavit of claim: State of Illinois, County of Cook, ss. In the Circuit Court of Cook County. In the matter of the estate of . . . ., deceased . . . ., being duly sworn, says that the annexed claim against the estate of . . . . deceased is just and unpaid, after allowing all just credits, and that (name of claimant) has no other claim against said estate. (Signature and jurat).

Prosecution of Claims.—Every claim against decedent's or ward's estate may be filed with representative or court or both. If filed only with representative, representative may file with court but is under no duty. (755-5/18-1[a]). Claimant must, within ten days after filing claim, mail or deliver copy of claim to each representative to whom letters of office have been issued and not revoked, including guardian of person of ward and his attorney of record, unless either consents to claim or waives delivery, and must file with court proof of any required mailing or delivery. (755-5/18-1[b]). Any interested party may demand jury trial. (755-5/18-6). When claim is called, if consented to or no pleading filed, court may allow claim or require proof. (755-5/18-7). Contested claims are set for trial and tried as in other civil cases. (755-5/1-6). Appeals lie from final orders, judgments or decrees of circuit court to Appellate or Supreme Courts as in other civil cases. (755-5/26-1).

Payment of Claims.—Representative is required to pay from estate all claims entitled to be paid therefrom, in order of their classification; and when estate is insufficient to pay claims in any one class, claims in that class are paid pro rata. (755-5/18-13).

Where unmatured claim is allowed, interest included in the principal obligation from date of allowance to time when debt would have become due is deducted. (755-5/18-4).

As to secured claims, see subhead Secured Claims, infra.

Priorities.—Claims against estates are classified as follows and paid in that order: (1) funeral expenses and costs of administration; (2) surviving spouse's or children's awards; (3) debts due U.S. Government; (4) (a) money due employees for services

EXECUTORS AND ADMINISTRATORS . . . *continued*

within four months of death but not more than $800 for each claimant, and (b) expense of last illness; (5) money and property received or held in trust by decedent which cannot be traced or identified; (6) debts due State of Illinois and any county, township, city, town, village or school district within state; (7) all other claims. (755-5/18-10).

Secured claims need not be presented to protect security (162 Ill. 410, 44 N.E. 742), but must be filed in order to participate as to excess over security. In insolvent estates, if claimant first realizes on security and then files claim, he may file and participate only to the extent of the excess. If claim is first allowed for entire debt, security may then be liquidated; and if claimant realizes from security less than amount of claim, he is entitled to receive dividend on the basis of entire debt, amount realized from security being taken into account only to prevent dividend in excess of complete satisfaction. (147 Ill. 570, 35 N.E. 624).

Nonresident creditors have no special rights.

Sale of Personalty.—Where necessary for proper administration, court may authorize representative to sell personal property at public or private sale or at public auction or to mortgage or to pledge personal property. (755-5/19-1, 5/19-5). Where will gives executor power to sell, mortgage or pledge personal property, no order of court is necessary. (755-5/19-1).

Lease, sale, mortgage or pledge of any personal estate by representative under power given in will is valid regardless of subsequent setting aside of will or any other action which might limit or restrain right of representative to transfer title or to lease, sell, mortgage, or pledge such personal estate. (755-5/19-1). Personal property specifically bequeathed or directed by testator not to be sold may not be sold, mortgaged or pledged unless necessary for payment of claims, expenses, taxes or proper administration of estate. (755-5/19-1). If sale of personal estate is not necessary for payment of claims or expenses of administration, court may order personal estate to be distributed in kind. (755-5/19-1).

Sale or Mortgage of Real Estate.—In absence of power in will, court may grant representative power to sell or mortgage real estate for proper administration of estate. (755-5/20-4).

Representative selling or mortgaging real estate, whether pursuant to court order or power in will, must file bond for one and one-half times value thereof if surety on bond is corporate, or for double value thereof if surety on bond is individual. Bond must identify real estate or interest therein being sold or mortgaged. No security required where will so provides, and no greater security required than specified in will. (755-5/12-9). If will excuses written bond, then amount of bond without writing increases, unless court requires written bond. (755-5/12-9[d]).

Foreign representative, acting pursuant to validly admitted will in foreign domiciliary jurisdiction, may give deed to real property in Illinois upon admission of foreign will in Illinois without issuance of letters of office in Illinois. (755-5/22-6, 755-5/7-1 through 5/7-5).

If representative with power under will to lease, sell or mortgage any real estate or interest therein leases, sells, or mortgages such real estate, such lease, sale or mortgage is valid regardless of subsequent setting aside of will or any other action limiting right of representative to alienate realty involved. (755-5/20-15).

Upon petition of representative or other interested party, court may, with or without notice, order representative to perform contract of decedent or incompetent legally subsisting at time of death or adjudication to convey real estate or interest therein and to execute all necessary documents. Petition must contain description of real estate and factual basis for right to convey. Court may authorize representative to waive defaults or compound or compromise any balance due. If contract requires warranties, instrument given, whether pursuant to court order or power in will, shall contain required warranties which shall bind estate but not representative personally. (755-5/20-17).

All real and personal property and the income therefrom are chargeable with claims, expenses, taxes and legacies without distinction, except if the will otherwise provides. (755-5/18-14).

Possession of Real Estate.—Representative must take possession of real estate, except where provided otherwise in will or real estate is occupied by heir or legatee as his residence, and must collect rents and pay various expenses. (755-5/20-1).

Actions by Representative.—If no letters have been issued in Illinois upon estate of nonresident decedent, representative to whom letters have been issued by court of competent jurisdiction of another state may sue in Illinois in any case in which resident representative could sue. (755-5/22-3). If letters are subsequently issued in Illinois, resident representative shall be substituted on motion. (755-5/22-5). Concerning survival of cause of action, see 755-5/8-1.

If party to action dies, court on motion may substitute proper parties if action survives. If motion to substitute is not filed within 90 days after death suggested of record, action may be dismissed as to deceased party. If no letters have been issued, court may appoint special administrator to prosecute or defend action. If legal representative later appointed for estate, he is substituted for special administrator. (735-5/2-1008[b]).

Actions against Representatives.—Right to sue on claims is not suspended and action may be brought within period of statute of limitations without first presenting claim, but judgment in suit filed after expiration of period for filing claims can be satisfied only from property other than that inventoried. (162 Ill. 410, 44 N.E. 742). Service of process on personal representative must be made within claims period in order for tort claimant to share in inventoried assets, unless claim is filed in probate proceedings. (28 Ill. App.2d 110, 170 N.E.2d 640).

Action pending at time of decedent's death may be continued against representative. (735-5/2-1008).

It is the duty of the executor or administrator with will annexed to defend suits contesting validity of will. (755-5/8-1[e]).

Personal Property Claimed by Third Parties.—On petition, court may hear and determine rights of third parties to personal property in possession or control of representative. (755-5/16-2).

Allowances.—Surviving spouse of resident decedent whose estate is being administered in state, whether spouse died testate or intestate, must, to exclusion of all debts except funeral and administration expenses, be allowed as such spouse's sole exclusive property, such sum of money as court deems reasonable for proper support of such spouse and minor and adult dependent children residing with spouse for nine months after death of decedent in manner suited to such spouse's condition in life, taking into account condition of estate. Non-probate assets received by spouse may be considered. (120 Ill. App.3d 917, 458 N.E.2d 1147). Award shall in no case be less than $10,000 together with additional sum not less than $5,000 for each minor child and adult dependent child of decedent. That part of award to be paid in cash must be paid in not more than three installments, as court directs. If surviving spouse dies before award for his support is paid in full, amount unpaid shall be paid to his estate. If spouse dies or abandons child, amount allowed for that child remaining unpaid shall be paid for benefit of child. Spouse entitled to award unless will provides that bequest is in lieu of award and spouse does not renounce will. (755-5/15-1).

Surviving spouse may receive award in money or at his election, in whole or in part, in personal property not specifically bequeathed at appraised value, selection to be made within 30 days after written notice of allowance of award. (755-5/15-4).

Each minor child of decedent and each adult dependent child must be allowed at least $5,000 plus, if there is no surviving spouse, share of at least $10,000 divided among all such children, with same right of selection of chattels. Such award may be apportioned as court may direct. (755-5/15-2, 755-5/15-4).

Representative shall apply to court to make award when allowable. (755-5/15-3).

Where assets, after payment of first class claims, do not exceed surviving spouse's or child's award or both, court shall discharge representative and order personal estate delivered to person entitled to award without such person being liable for any of decedent's debts except first class claims to extent of personal estate so received. (755-5/24-7).

Investments.—In addition to investments authorized in will, representative may invest funds of estate during period of administration in obligations of U.S. or obligations principal and interest of which is unconditionally guaranteed by U.S., maturity of which is no longer than five years from date of purchase; in certain obligations of public housing agency secured by Public Housing Administration and which mature within 18 months; in savings accounts or certificates of deposit in state or national bank doing business in Illinois to extent insured by U.S. Government; withdrawable capital accounts, deposits, investment certificates and certificates of deposit of savings and loan associations doing business in Illinois, to extent they are insured by U.S. Government or Government Agency; common trust fund as provided in Common Trust Fund Act; mutual funds and money market funds investing solely in securities authorized by statute for investment by representatives; and any other investments authorized by court or legislature. (755-5/21-1 to 5/21-2.15).

Intermediate Accountings.—Representative must present accounts to court within 60 days after expiration of 12 months from date of letters and thereafter whenever required by court until estate has been fully administered. Court may excuse accountings if all interested persons file written consents. (755-5/24-1).

Final Accounting and Settlement.—Representative's final account will not be approved until allowance or rejection of all claims filed, or if allowed claims are unsatisfied and there are assets applicable thereto. If representative fails to make settlement of estate within 30 days after expiration of the time provided in statute he may be brought before court by citation and ordered to do so. Failure to appear authorizes issuance of body attachment against representative, and failure to make settlement after such attachment may be dealt with as for contempt. If representative fails or refuses to pay any money or deliver any property to any person entitled thereto, pursuant to court order, within 30 days after demand, court may on verified petition of any interested party or on its own motion attach delinquent representative and imprison him until he complies or is discharged by due course of law and may remove him as representative. (755/24-16). Also, such failure or refusal is deemed to amount to devastavit, and action on representative's bond or against sureties may be maintained. (755-5/24-17).

Representative must give notice of final settlement to unpaid creditors and to every person entitled to share of estate who has not received that share in full, or waived notice, and account as approved at hearing is binding on all persons to whom notice was given or who waived notice, in absence of fraud, accident or mistake. (755-5/24-2). For procedure in reopening closed estate to permit administration of newly discovered asset see 755-5/24-9.

Notice.—Must be given, as court directs, to unpaid creditors and persons who have not received their full share, to bind them. In Cook County notice and copy of account must be given ten days before hearing. Other counties have similar provisions. Trust beneficiaries may be entitled to notice although not named in will. (143 Ill. App.3d 741, 493 N.E.2d 121).

Distribution.—On settlement, when assets are sufficient to pay claims, court may order distribution of estate to persons entitled thereto. Unless otherwise provided by will, if estate is insufficient to pay all legacies under will, specific legacies shall be satisfied pro rata before general legacies and general legacies shall be paid pro rata without priority in either case between realty and personalty. (755-5/24-3). If assets are sufficient to pay claims, court may order distribution before expiration of period when claims are barred, if distributee gives bond. (755-5/24-4). Distributee of estate of person presumed to be dead must give bond. (755-5/24-5). Suit for accounting may be maintained by distributee against representative. (755-5/24-8). There is no statute or well settled statewide practice regarding distribution to legatee residing abroad.

Liabilities.—Representatives and sureties on bond are liable to successor representatives, to co-representatives, and to any person aggrieved thereby for any mismanagement of the estate committed to their care. (755-5/24-18).

Compensation.—Representatives and their attorneys allowed reasonable compensation. (755-5/27-1, 5/27-2).

Independent Administration.—Independent administration with minimal court filings, available as of Jan. 1, 1980, for estates not then under administration and those

EXECUTORS AND ADMINISTRATORS . . . *continued*

under administration but not yet closed. Independent administration is available regardless of monetary value of estate. (755-5/28-1).

Independent administration is granted unless petition for letters requests supervised administration, or at any time on petition during supervised administration. When independent administration is granted, independent representative must explain rights of heirs and legatees and provide petition for termination of independent administration in notice to heirs and legatees. (755-5/28-2). Independent representative must file proof of mailing, and, when required, proof of publication, with clerk of court. (755-5/28-2).

Court must grant supervised administration on objection of interested person (as defined in 755-5/1-2.11), unless objector is creditor or legatee other than residuary, then only if court finds supervision necessary to protect objector's interest; or, if will directs independent administration, only upon good cause shown (755-5/28-2[b]).

Special notice provisions applicable. (755-5/28-2[a]).

Any interested person may petition court at any time during independent administration for hearing and order on matters germane to estate. (755-5/28-5).

Independent administrator must mail or deliver copy of inventory to all interested persons at least 30 days before closing estate, but need not file with court. (755-5/28-6). Independent administrator must provide surety with inventory by certified mail within 90 days after issuance of letters, and thereafter when he receives notice of additional property. Failure to do so may result in termination of independent administration. (755-5/28-6).

Special powers and limitations provided for independent administrators. (755-5/28-8).

Independent administrator may distribute estate to persons entitled at any time he finds sufficient assets to pay all claims. Administrator may require bond and must require it if distribution is before expiration of period when claims are barred. (755-5/28-10[a]).

Independent administrator is accountable to all interested persons for administration and distribution, but need not present account to court unless interested person requests accounting. Separate procedures for closing independent administration. (755-5/28-11).

When Administration Unnecessary.—Where heirs (and legatees, if will) are residents of Illinois and under no disability, no Illinois inheritance or federal estate tax is due and all claims are paid, estate may be settled without issuance of letters if all interested parties agree (755-5/6-8, 755-5/9-2); order directing specified holders of property to distribute directly to heirs or legatees is issued in lieu of letters. Distribution on summary administration available upon petition of interested person after ascertainment of heirship and admission of will to probate. Requirements are: (1) Gross value of probate assets not in excess of $50,000; (2) no unpaid claims, or all claimants and amounts of claims known and listed in petition; (3) no state or Federal death taxes due or all such taxes paid or obligation of another fiduciary; (4) no person entitled to surviving spouse or child's award, or, if allowable, name and age of each person so entitled and amount already paid is listed in petition; (5) all heirs and legatees consent in writing; and (6) each distributee gives bond to extent of distributive share and conditioned to refund due proportion of any valid claim or prior right of distribution, along with costs of recovery and reasonable attorneys fees. (755-5/9-8).

Where aggregate personal estate does not exceed $25,000, no probate is required; and any person or corporation must turn over assets of decedent on filing of required affidavit by heirs or persons entitled thereto. (755-5/25-1).

Small Estates.—See subhead When Administration Unnecessary, supra.

Foreign Executors or Administrators.—Representative to whom letters are issued on estate of nonresident by court of competent jurisdiction of state or territory of U.S. may collect any personal estate of decedent in Illinois and remove it to jurisdiction in which his letters are issued upon delivering to person or corporation indebted to or holding personal estate, following: (1) affidavit by representative that no letters have been issued or no application for letters is pending in Illinois, and there are no creditors in Illinois; (2) copy of letters must be certified within 60 days before date of presentation. No delivery may be made until 30 days after decedent's death. (755-5/22-1). Such representative may sue, when no letters are issued in this state, in any case in which resident representative may sue (755-5/22-3) and may petition circuit court of county where greater part of personal or real estate is located for sale, lease or mortgage of estate for any purposes for which resident representative may sell, lease or mortgage (755-5/22-4). Deed executed pursuant to power vested in foreign executor is evidence of title in grantee to same extent as was vested in testator if will is admitted to probate in circuit court of proper county in Illinois before delivery of deed unless letters have been issued in Illinois and remain unrevoked. (755-5/22-6).

See also topic Wills, subhead Foreign Wills.

Uniform Fiduciaries Act.—See topic Trusts.

Uniform Principal and Income Act.—See topic Trusts.

Uniform Simplification of Fiduciary Security Transfers Act.—Not adopted. But see Illinois Act for Fiduciary Security Transfers. (760-70/1 to 70/9).

See also topic Wills, subhead Contest.

FIDUCIARIES:

See topics Executors and Administrators, Trusts; category Family, topic Guardian and Ward.

INTESTACY:

See topic Descent and Distribution.

PROOF OF CLAIMS:

See topic Executors and Administrators; category Civil Actions and Procedure, topic Pleading.

TRUSTS:

Equitable principles applicable to trusts under the common law are generally followed by the courts except where specific statutes govern.

Creation.—All declarations or creations of trusts in lands, tenements, or hereditaments must be manifested and proved by some writing signed by party who is by law enabled to declare such a trust, or by his last will in writing, provided that resulting or constructive trusts may be proved by parol. (740-80/9).

Revocation.—Unless instrument or dissolution decree provides otherwise, judicial termination of marriage of grantor or settlor of trust revokes every provision which is revocable by settlor or grantor pertaining to former spouse, for all trusts and amendments executed before entry of dissolution decree. Former spouse is treated as having been deceased on date of entry of dissolution decree. Land trusts, totten trusts, and other special trusts are exempt. Effective for trusts executed after effective date of Jan. 1, 1982. (760-35/1).

Appointment of Trustee.—Any corporation incorporated in Illinois or any state bank or state savings and loan authorized by law to accept or execute trusts may be appointed trustee. (205-620/2-1). Grantor can designate trustee and provide for successor in trust instrument (116 Ill. 83, 4 N.E.773) and can authorize trustee to choose own successor (209 Ill. 222, 70 N.E.731) or court in default can appoint trustee (300 Ill. 302, 133 N.E.335).

Eligibility and Competency.—Corporations must comply with Corporate Fiduciary Act in order to serve as trustees. (205-620/1-2). Foreign corporations, including banks, and national banking associations domiciled in other states, may also serve as trustees under stated conditions. (205-620/4-2).

Qualification of Trustee.—No statutory requirement of bond.

Removal of Trustee.—Commissioner of Banks and Trust Companies has power to remove corporate trustee for violation of law for unsafe or unsound practice in conduct of business. Commissioner may issue order prohibiting former director, officer, employee or agent of corporate fiduciary from further service with corporate fiduciary if Commissioner is of opinion that such person violated law, rule or order relating to corporate fiduciary or engaged in unsafe or unsound practice prior to termination of service with corporate fiduciary. (205-620/5-6). Court has power to remove trustee for breach of trust or misconduct. (368 Ill. 146, 13 N.E.2d 153).

Discharge.—Beneficiaries receiving final accounting and such beneficiaries' heirs and assigns are bound by final accounting unless action against trustee instituted within three years of final accounting or trustee guilty of fraud in which case 725-5/13-215 controls time within which action may be brought. Effective for trusts terminating Jan. 1, 1988 and thereafter. (760-5/11).

Virtual Representation.—Except as to agreement that accelerates termination of trust in whole or in part, if all primary beneficiaries are adults and not incapacitated, any written agreement (including one construing provision of trust or any duty, power, responsibility or action of trustee) between trustee and all of primary beneficiaries shall be final and binding as to trustee and all beneficiaries, current and future, as if ordered by court with competent jurisdiction over all parties. Effective Aug. 16, 1993 as to all existing and future trusts but only as to agreements entered into after effective date. (760-5/4.25).

General Powers and Duties of Trustees Under Express Trusts.—As to all trusts created after Sept. 30, 1973, powers and duties of trustees, unless otherwise specified in instrument creating express trust or by order of court, are defined by statute. (760-5/4). Previous statutory provisions (148-31-37) are repealed. Trustee has power to lease, borrow, mortgage and pledge, grant easements, appoint trustee in another jurisdiction, enter into deposit, investment and agency agreements, exercise powers of individual owner over securities, pay taxes and expenses, appoint attorneys and other agents, delegate powers to co-trustee, compromise or abandon claims, execute contracts which may contain warranties binding upon trust estate and excluding personal liability, receive additional property in trust (and for trusts created and action is taken before, on or after Jan. 1, 1994, to administer additional property as part of trust estate or as separate trust having terms identical to existing trust), invest in undivided interests, deal with other fiduciaries, distribute in cash or in kind, rely upon affidavit, certificate, etc., for distribution, exercise rights pending distribution and during litigation and purchase insurance for protection of trust estate (760-5/4.02); for trusts created and actions taken before, on or after Jan. 1, 1994, to sever any trust on fractional basis into two or more separate trusts for any reason; to segregate amount to reflect partial disclaimer; to reflect differences in federal tax treatment including generation-skipping transfer tax liability (760-5/4.25). Bank operated by or affiliated with trustee may provide certain services to trust. (760-5/4.06). If beneficiary under legal disability trustee may distribute income and principal to beneficiary or others or expend for beneficiary's benefit. (760-5/4.20). Trustee may cause stocks, bonds and other property belonging to trust to be registered and held in name of nominee. (760-5/6). Majority of trustees are competent to act after notice or waiver. (760-5/10). Trustee may resign by written notice to settlor, if living, to co-trustee, if any, and to income beneficiaries. (760-5/12). During vacancy of trusteeship, where more than one trustee is provided for, remaining trustees have all rights, powers and duties of original trustees, and beneficiaries may appoint successor trustee if there is no remaining trustee. (760-5/13). Representative of estate of beneficiary under legal disability, if any, otherwise relative of such beneficiary may act for beneficiary in approving accounts, executing receipt and receiving notice from trustee. (760-5/15). See also category Business Regulation and Commerce, topic Banks and Banking, subhead Trust Companies. Trust and Trustees Powers Act expanded to include special farm powers, oil and gas powers, specific provision for one or more trustees to act as manager or to continue unincorporated business and provision for trustee or trustee's agent to continue partnership, act as partner, limited partner, employee of partnership or enter into partnership and incorporate existing partnership. Effective Sept. 2, 1981. (760-5/1 to 5/20). Regarding powers over partnerships, trustees or trustees' agent are not personally liable for actions not sounding in tort, unless they have failed to identify trust estate or that they were acting in representative capacity. Effective Jan. 1, 1986. (760-5/4.24).

Accounting.—Trustee must furnish at least annually to beneficiaries then entitled to receive or receiving income from trust estate, or if none, then those beneficiaries eligible to have benefit of income from trust estate current account of receipts, disbursements and inventory of trust. Upon termination of trust, trustee must furnish to beneficiaries

---

TRUSTS . . . *continued*
final account for period from date of last current account to date of distribution showing inventory, receipts, disbursements and distributions of trust and must make available to beneficiaries copies of prior accounts not theretofore furnished. (760-5/11).

Compensation.—Trustee must be reimbursed for proper expenses incurred in management and protection of trust and is entitled to reasonable compensation for services rendered. (760-5/7).

Uniform Principal and Income Act previously in effect as modified is repealed effective Jan. 1, 1982. New Principal and Income Act effective for all receipts and disbursements after 12/31/81 in any trust, decedent's estate, or legal life estate, notwithstanding date of establishment or date of acquisition of assets. Act follows Uniform Principal and Income Act with substantial revision. Absent trust provisions or statutory provisions to contrary, trustee may now allocate in accordance with what is "reasonable and equitable." Income and expenses of estates are now credited and charged in accordance with identical rules applicable to trusts, with minor exceptions. (760-15/1). Act allows accrued but undistributed income to be paid to income beneficiary at termination of income interest where necessary to qualify for marital deduction under Federal Estate and Gift Tax. Any pecuniary bequest to sur-viving spouse under either will or trust entitled to proportionate part of income of estate or trust. (760-15/1 to 15/17).

Gifts to Minors.—See category Family, topic Infants.

Uniform Fiduciaries Act adopted (760-65/1, 65/2, 65/4 to 65/12) except as to transfers of securities, governed by Fiduciary Security Transfer Simplification Act (760-70/1 to 70/9).

Investments.—When not otherwise provided by will, agreement, court order or other instrument creating or defining trustee's duties and powers, trustees, including trustees of common trust funds, shall, in acquiring, investing, reinvesting, exchanging, retaining, selling, and managing trust property, exercise judgment and care under circumstances then prevailing which men of prudence, discretion and intelligence exercise in management of their own affairs, not in regard to speculation but in regard to permanent disposition of their funds, considering probable income as well as probable safety of their capital. Within limitations of foregoing standard, trustees are authorized to acquire and retain every kind of property, real, personal or mixed, and every kind of investment which men of prudence, discretion and intelligence acquire or retain for their own account; and to retain property properly acquired without limitation as to time and without regard to its suitability for original purchase. (760-5/5.1). Although still subject to duty of using reasonable care, trustee may invest in certain obligations of state of Illinois or subdivisions thereof (30-335/1, 335/2) and in unit investment trust funds, including mutual funds for which trustee or its affiliate acts as manager or advisor (760-5/5.1; 760-5/5.2). When entering into contract with State or local government affecting ownership or use of real property to which he has title, trustee is required to disclose in writing and under oath identity of every owner and beneficiary having any interest in property. (50-105/3.1). Trustees may not delegate performance of acts involving exercise of judgment and discretion. (760-5/5.1).

The terms "legal investment" or "authorized investment" or words of similar import as used in any such instrument shall be taken to mean any investment which is permitted by the foregoing standard. (760-5/5.2).

Sales.—Trustee is empowered to sell, contract to sell and grant options to purchase any part or all of trust estate at public or private sale, for cash or on credit, and to exchange any part or all of trust estate for other property. (760-5/4.01).

Securities in Name of Nominee.—A trustee may register securities in name of a nominee without mention of trust, and trustee shall be liable for acts of nominee with respect to any investment so registered. (760-5/6). See also category Business Regulation and Commerce, topic Banks and Banking, subhead Trust Companies.

Bequests and Devises to Inter Vivos Trusts.—See topic Wills, subhead Bequests and Devises to Inter Vivos Trusts.

Disclaimers under nontestamentary instruments may be made as provided in Probate Act. See topic Wills, subhead Disclaimers. (760-25/1).

Uniform Common Trust Fund Act.—Uniform Common Trust Fund Act has been adopted with significant changes and additions and is known as Common Trust Fund Act. (760-45/1 to 45/7). See category Business Regulation and Commerce, topic Banks and Banking.

Charitable Trusts.—Uniform Supervision of Trustees for Charitable Purposes Act, with significant changes, adopted. (760-55/1 to 55/4). Act is known as Charitable Trust Act (760-55/1) and applies to trustees who hold property, whether under a written instrument or not, corpus of which exceeds $4,000 (760-55/2). "Trustee" means any individual, group of individuals, corporation, not for profit corporation, estate representative or other legal entity holding property for any charitable purpose. (760-55/3). Excluded legal entities include U.S., any state, territory or possession of U.S., District of Columbia, Puerto Rico and their agencies or governmental subdivisions, corporation sole, or other religious, charitable, educational and hospital organizations and those organizations operating cemeteries and homes for aged. (760-55/4). Attorney General is required to establish and maintain register of trustees subject to Act. (760-55/5). Trustee must file copies of trust instruments, or if there is no written instrument, then statement of title, powers and duties, and, except for Illinois banks and trust companies, periodic reports in accordance with rules and regulations of Attorney General. (760-55/6 to 55/8). Attorney General is empowered to conduct investigations and issue subpoenas. (760-55/9, 55/10). Register, copies of instruments and reports filed with Attorney General are open to public inspection. (760-55/11). Trustees of trusts that fall within §509 or §4947 of Internal Revenue Code, subject to governing instrument provisions, may amend terms of trust instrument to conform to requirements of Federal Tax Reform Act of 1969. (760-60/1).

Uniform Act for Simplification of Fiduciary Security Transfers.—Not adopted. See Fiduciary Transfer of Securities Act. (760-70/1 to 70/9).

Accumulations.—See category Property, topic Perpetuities.

Perpetuities.—See category Property, topic Perpetuities.

Testamentary Trustee as Beneficiary of Insurance.—See topic Wills, subhead Insurance Payable to Testamentary Trustee.

Pour Over Trusts.—See topic Wills, subhead Bequests and Devises to Inter Vivos Trusts.

Illusory Trust.—See topic Wills, subhead Renunciation of Will.

Real Estate Investment Trusts ("REIT").—Shareholders or beneficiaries of "real estate investment trust" (defined by reference to Federal Internal Revenue Code) not, as such, personally liable for obligations of REIT arising after July 1, 1963 and persons who become shareholders or beneficiaries of REIT after July 1, 1963, not personally liable, as such, for obligations of REIT. Effective registration with Secretary of State of securities issued or issuable by such unincorporated trust or association under §5 of Illinois Securities Law of 1953 is conclusive evidence that unincorporated trust or association is REIT as to all persons who become shareholders or beneficiaries after such effective registration and as to all REIT'S obligations arising after July 1, 1963, whether they arose before or after such effective registration.

Land Trusts.—See category Property, topic Real Property, subhead Land Trust.

WILLS:

Every person, of age of 18, who is of sound mind and memory, may make a will. (755-5/4-1).

Testamentary Disposition.—There is no limitation on charitable gifts, except that right of surviving spouse to renounce cannot be defeated thereby.

Execution.—Will must be in writing, signed by testator or by another in his presence and at his direction and attested in his presence (but not necessarily in each other's presence) by two or more credible witnesses. (755-5/4-3).

Form of Attestation Clause.—

Form

We, the undersigned, certify that the foregoing instrument was, on the date thereof, signed and declared by . . . . . . as . . . . . . last will in the presence of us, who in . . . . . . presence and in presence of each other have, at . . . . . . request, hereunto signed our names as witnesses of the execution thereof this . . . . . . day of . . . . . ., 19. . . ; and we hereby certify that we believe said . . . . . . to be of sound mind and memory. (Signatures of witnesses, together with their addresses.)

Holographic wills as such are not valid.

Nuncupative wills are not valid.

Living Wills.—Living will is written declaration, executed by same persons eligible to make, and with same formalities required for, valid will, instructing declarant's attending physician to withhold or withdraw life-sustaining procedures in event declarant is diagnosed as having terminal condition. Physician who certifies declarant terminally ill is immune from civil or criminal liability. No health care professional or medical care facility or employee who in good faith and pursuant to reasonable medical standards withholds or withdraws life sustaining procedures pursuant to declaration is subject to criminal or civil liability. Living will may be revoked in same manner as will; also may be revoked by oral expression in presence of witness who signs and dates writing confirming oral expression of intention to revoke. (755-35/1). Statutorily prescribed form follows:

DECLARATION

Declaration made this . . . . day of . . . . (month, year). I, ..., being of sound mind, willfully and voluntarily make known my desires that my moment of death shall not be artificially postponed under the circumstances set forth below, do hereby declare:

If at any time I should have an incurable injury, disease, or illness judged to be a terminal condition by my attending physician who has personally examined me, and has determined that my death is imminent except for life-sustaining procedures, I direct that such procedures be withheld or withdrawn, and that I be permitted to die naturally with only the administration of medication, sustenance, or the performance of any medical procedure deemed necessary to provide me with comfort care.

In the absence of my ability to give directions regarding the use of such life-sustaining procedures, it is my intention that this declaration shall be honored by my family and physician as the final expression of my legal right to refuse medical or surgical treatment and accept the consequences from such refusal.

I understand the full import of this declaration and I am emotionally and mentally competent to make this declaration.

Signed . . . .

City, County and State of Residence . . . .

The declarant has been personally known to me and I believe him or her to be of sound mind. I did not sign the declarant's signature above for or at the direction of the declarant. I am not related to the declarant by blood or marriage, entitled to any portion of the estate of the declarant according to the laws of intestate succession or under any will of declarant or codicil thereto, or directly financially responsible for declarant's medical care.

Witness . . . .
Witness . . . .

Durable Powers of Attorney for Property and Health Care.—See subhead Durable Powers of Attorney under category Property, topic Powers of Attorney—includes statutory forms.

Revocation is effected only (a) by burning, tearing, cancelling or obliterating by testator or by some person in his presence and at his direction, (b) by execution of some later will declaring same, (c) by later will to extent it is inconsistent with prior will or (d) by execution of instrument in writing declaring revocation and signed and attested as will. (755-5/4-7[a]).

See note at head of Digest as to 1998 legislation covered.

See Topical Index in front part of this volume.

IL – 58

WILLS . . . *continued*

Will may not be revoked by any change in circumstances of or marital status of testator, except that divorce or annulment revokes every devise, legacy, or interest or power of appointment or nomination to fiduciary office made to or for former spouse before entry of decree, and will takes effect as if former spouse died before testator. (755-5/4-7[b]).

Revival.—No will in any manner revoked is revived otherwise than by (1) re-execution thereof or (2) an instrument in writing declaring revival and signed and attested in manner prescribed for will. If will is partially revoked by an instrument which is itself revoked, revoked part of will is revived. (755-5/4-7[c]).

Testamentary Gifts to Subscribing Witnesses.—Persons, or spouses of persons, incompetent as attesting witnesses because of interest are by statute rendered competent and may be compelled to testify, but such persons are deprived of any interest under will, except so must as does not exceed amount witness would be entitled to were will not established. Such persons are not so deprived if there is statutorily sufficient number of other attesting and testifying witnesses. Fact that employee or partner of individual or employee or shareholder of corporation attests execution of will or testifies thereto does not disqualify said individual or corporation from acting or from receiving compensation for acting in any fiduciary capacity with respect to will of decedent. No attorney is disqualified to act or to receive compensation by reason of fact that such attorney is attesting or testifying witness or is employee or partner of attesting or testifying witness. (755-5/4-6).

Bequests and Devises to Inter Vivos Trusts.—Pour-over wills to existing and identified revocable trusts, and to testamentary trust of predeceased person where will in existence and identified by pouring testator's will, are valid. Unless will provides otherwise, gifts are governed by instrument creating trust, including written amendments or modifications made at any time before death of testator, or after if testator's will directs, and if trust revoked prior to testator's death, gift takes effect as trust existed at revocation. (755-5/4-4).

Testamentary Guardians.—See category Family, topic Guardian and Ward.

Simultaneous Death.—See topic Death, subhead Survivorship.

Probate of will is in first of following counties applicable: (a) where testator has a known place of residence, (b) if no known place of residence, wherein greater portion of his real estate is located, (c) if no known place of residence and no real estate, wherein greater portion of his personal estate is located. (755-5/5-1). On application for probate, two witnesses must recount facts of execution, each stating that in his belief testator was then of sound mind and memory. Other competent evidence to establish will may be introduced. If proponent establishes will by sufficient evidence it will be admitted to probate unless there is proof of fraud, forgery, compulsion or other improper conduct. (755-5/6-4[a]). Above statements to prove will may be by: (1) Testimony before court; (2) attestation clause signed by witnesses and forming part of or attached to will; (3) affidavit signed at or after attestation which forms part of will or is attached to will or to accurate facsimile of will. (755-5/6-4[b]).

Self-proved Wills.—Statements required to prove will may also be made by: (1) Attestation clause signed by witness and forming part of or attached to will; (2) attestation clause signed by witnesses and forming part of or attached to will; (3) affidavit signed at or after attestation which forms part of will or is attached to will or to accurate facsimile of will. (755-5/6-4[b]).

If will is admitted to probate before notice given under 755-5/6-10, any person so entitled may file petition within 42 days after effective date of order admitting will to require formal proof of will. Court must set hearing at which will may be proved by testimony of witnesses and other evidence allowable under Probate Act, but not by attestation clause or affidavit under 755-5/6-4(b). If will established by sufficient evidence, original order is confirmed and effective against all persons. This petition does not extend time for filing contest under 755-5/8-1 unless original order is vacated, at which point time begins to run. (755-5/6-21).

Form Of Affidavit.—

Form

Each of the undersigned, attesting witnesses to the will of . . . . ., dated . . . . ., 19. . . ., of which this affidavit is a part, first having been sworn on oath states that said testator stated to us that the above and foregoing instrument was . . . . . last will and requested each of us to witness . . . . . signing of said will, that each of us was present and saw the said testator sign said will in the presence of each of us, that said will was attested by each of us in the presence of the said testator and each other and that each of us believed said testator to be of sound mind and memory at the time of signing said will. (Signature and address of each witness; signatures must be acknowledged. See category Documents and Records, topic Acknowledgments, subhead Forms.)

Contest.—Petition for contest of domestic or foreign will may be filed within six months of admission to probate either in administration proceeding or, if none, in court which admitted will. Petitioner shall mail or deliver copy of petition to representative, representative's attorney of record, and to each heir and legatee named in petition to admit will. Failure to so mail or deliver does not extend time to file contest or affect validity of judgment entered. (755-5/8-1[b]).

Process served as in other civil proceedings.

Any proponent or contestant may demand jury. Contestant has burden of proving invalidity. Witness affidavits admissible. (755-5/8-1[c]).

Right to institute or continue proceeding survives and descends to heir, etc. of person so entitled. (755-5/8-1[d]).

It is duty of representative to defend contest and prosecute appeal from judgment, and court may appoint special administrator for that purpose if he fails or refuses to do so or if there is no representative then acting. (755-5/8-1[e]).

Similar provision for contest of denial of will to probate. (755-5/8-2).

Legacies need not be paid until period of administration has expired. When it appears that estate is solvent, court may order payment of all legacies, specific legacies being first satisfied. (755-5/24-3). Executor or administrator is chargeable with interest at rate of 10% per annum on fair market value of all personal estate which has come into his possession or control and has not been properly distributed; interest runs for period in excess of two years from issuance of letters testamentary or of administration, with certain exceptions. (755-5/24-10).

Ademption.—Gift of specifically bequeathed or devised property where subject property is transferred or disposed of or destroyed during decedent's lifetime is forever adeemed, notwithstanding reacquisition. (167 Ill. 129, 47 N.E.376).

Unclaimed Legacies.—See category Property, topic Absentees, subhead Escheat.

Lapse.—A legacy or devise lapses in case of death of legatee or devisee before testator unless will provides otherwise, except (1) in case of legacy or bequest to descendant of testator, in which case his descendants take per stirpes, and (2) in case of legacy or bequest to class and member of class predeceases testator, in which case surviving members of class take share of deceased member unless deceased member is descendant of testator, in which case his descendants take per stirpes. Otherwise lapsed legacy or devise passes as residue under will. (755-5/4-11).

Person Causing Decedent's Death.—Effective for decedents dying on or after Sept. 8, 1983, any person intentionally and unjustifiably causing decedent's death will not receive any interest of decedent, by reason of death, as heir, legatee, beneficiary, joint tenant, survivor, appointee or in any other capacity. Interest will pass as if person causing death died before decedent. Any interest in joint tenancy property possessed prior to death by person causing death will not be affected by this statute. Any person convicted of first or second degree murder, or otherwise determined by any court apart from criminal proceeding to have intentionally and unjustifiably caused decedent's death, will be barred from taking pursuant to this provision. Holder of property covered by this statute who knows or has reason to know that potential beneficiary caused death of decedent shall cooperate fully in investigation of decedent's death. (755-5/2-6).

Children may be disinherited, and mere failure to mention children living when will is executed is sufficient to disinherit them; but child born after making of will and not provided for therein takes share of estate to which entitled under law of descent unless will shows intention to disinherit. (755-5/4-10).

Disclaimer.—Person receiving property by any means may disclaim in whole or in part. Power with respect to property also can be disclaimed. Disclaimer may be made at any time before acceptance of property or interest. Legal representative of decedent, minor, or disabled person may disclaim with leave of court, or without leave of court if will or designation of guardian so authorizes. Place of delivery or filing disclaimer and its effect are set forth. (755-5/2-7).

Renunciation of Will.—Renunciation is effected by filing in court where will was admitted to probate a written declaration of renunciation within seven months after admission of will to probate or within such further time as court allows upon filing verified petition within such seven months or any extension, setting forth pendency of litigation which affects spouse's share. Filing of instrument is complete bar to any claim of surviving spouse under will. (755-5/2-8[b]).

In case of renunciation, surviving spouse takes, after payment of claims, one-third of entire estate if testator leaves descendant, or one-half of entire estate if testator leaves no descendant. (755-5/2-8[a]). Payment of claims include federal estate tax. (83 Ill.2d 379, 415 N.E.2d 416).

If no intent to defraud by colorable or sham transaction, valid lifetime transfer in trust or otherwise by decedent is not invalid on ground that it is illusory because decedent retained right regarding property. (755-25/1, 25/2; 73 Ill.2d 342, 383 N.E.2d 185).

When will is renounced by testator's surviving spouse, any future interest to take effect in possession or enjoyment at or after termination of estate given by will to surviving spouse takes effect as if surviving spouse had predeceased testator, unless will expressly provides against acceleration in case of renunciation. (755-5/2-8[c]).

Contribution.—Court must increase or decrease proportionately other legacies when spouse renounces. (755-5/2-8[d]). Discriminatory abatement required. (26 Ill. App.3d 780, 326 N.E.2d 167). All devises and bequests abate proportionately for afterborn child. (755-5/4-10). When real or personal estate specifically devised is sold by executor, other devisees or legatees will be ordered by court to contribute to devisee or legatee whose part of estate was sold, to accomplish abatement and equalization. (755-5/24-3).

Executory contract for sale of property specifically devised or bequeathed by testator does not revoke legacy, but property passes to legatee subject to contract. (755-5/4-8).

Foreign Wills.—A written will admitted to probate outside Illinois or executed outside Illinois in accordance with law of Illinois, of place where executed, or of testator's domicile may be admitted to probate in Illinois. (755-5/7-1). Procedure for admission is same as for domestic will except for manner of proof. (755-5/7-2). Where foreign will has been admitted to probate outside Illinois, duly authenticated copy of will and order admitting it to probate is sufficient proof; or if other state or country does not require probate, then authenticated copy of will and certificate of legal custodian thereof that will has become operative is sufficient proof; or if other state or country requires will to remain in custody of notary, then copy of will authenticated by notary is sufficient proof. (755-5/7-3). When foreign will has not been admitted to probate outside Illinois, it may be admitted to probate in Illinois by proof sufficient for domestic will or by proof in manner provided by law of place where executed or by law of testator's domicile. (755-5/7-4).

Order admitting will to probate makes will effective to transfer title to real and personal property devised or bequeathed therein. (755-5/4-13, 5/7-5). (See also topic Executors and Administrators, subhead Foreign Executors or Administrators.)

Testamentary Trusts.—See topic Trusts.

Uniform Anatomical Gift Act adopted in Illinois. (755-50/1 to 755-50/11). Act defines death as irreversible cessation of total brain function, according to customary standards of medical practice. (755-50/1 to 755-50/11).

See note at head of Digest as to 1998 legislation covered.

See Topical Index in front part of this volume.

IL – 59

WILLS . . . *continued*

Insurance Payable to Testamentary Trustee.—Person having right to designate beneficiary under any insurance, annuity or endowment contract or any pension, retirement, or other employee benefit plan or trust may designate trustee named or to be named in will. Will need not be in existence when designation made. Proceeds are held as part of trust estate under will terms. Unless otherwise provided in policy or beneficiary designation, if within 18 months no trustee qualifies or it is shown no trustee can qualify, executor or administrator takes proceeds. Proceeds subject to claims, estate and inheritance taxes only to same extent that named beneficiary other than estate would be. (755-5/4-5).

FAMILY

ADOPTION:

Adoption Act of 1959 became effective Jan. 1, 1960. Terms appearing in quotes herein are defined in Act as amended.

Any reputable person of legal age who has resided continually in Illinois for at least six months, or, if member of U.S. armed forces has been domiciled in Illinois for 90 days, may initiate proceeding to adopt. There is no residence requirement if adoption is of "related child" or child placed by "agency." If petitioner is married, husband or wife must join in petition; and adoption must be by both spouses jointly. Minor may also petition by leave of court upon good cause shown. (750-50/2).

Any minor child may be adopted. An adult may be adopted under certain circumstances. (750-50/4).

Definitions.—Unfit person means person court finds unfit to have child without regard to whether that child will be placed for adoption. Grounds include: abandonment of child; failure to maintain interest, concern or responsibility as to child's welfare; substantial, repeated neglect; continuous or repeated neglect of any child residing in household which resulted in death of that child; open and notorious adultery or fornication; drunkenness or drug addiction for one year; conviction of first degree murder creates presumption of unfitness; failure to show interest, concern or responsibility in welfare of newborn during first 30 days after birth; inability to discharge parental responsibilities supported by competent evidence from psychiatrist, licensed clinical social worker, or clinical psychologist; two or more findings of physical abuse to any children supported by clear and convincing evidence or criminal conviction or finding of not guilty by reason of insanity resulting from death of any child or finding of physical abuse resulting from death of any child; failure to protect child from injurious conditions within child's environment; other neglect or misconduct toward child; desertion of child for more than three months next preceding adoption proceeding; failure of parent to make reasonable efforts to correct conditions that were basis for removal of child from parent or to make reasonable progress toward return of child within 12 months after adjudication of neglected, abused or dependent minor; repeated or continuous failure by parents, though physically and financially able, to provide adequate food, clothing or shelter; finding at birth of certain controlled substances in infant's blood, urine or meconium where biological mother is biological mother of at least one other child who was adjudicated neglected minor; and evidence of interest to forego parental rights including burden on alleged father to take affirmative action in some cases to establish parental rights. (750-50/1).

Consent Required.—Consent of parents, including father of illegitimate, required except where parent found by court by clear and convincing evidence to be "unfit person" or in case of adoption of adult. Other party with legal custody of child, such as legal guardian or "agency," may consent and in certain circumstances consent is not required. For consent parent does not include man who is child's father as result of criminal sexual abuse or assault. (750-50/8, 750-50/15.1). Notice may be served on putative father who may affirm or deny paternity. (750-50/12a). If party adopted is 14 years or over, his written consent is required. (750-50/12).

Consent to adoption by parent, including a minor, is irrevocable unless it has been obtained by fraud or duress and court so finds. (750-50/11).

No consent or surrender may be made by mother until 72 hours after birth of child. Consent or surrender may be made by father prior to birth, but such consent or surrender is revocable by written notification within 72 hours after birth. (750-50/9).

Consent of mother or father must be acknowledged before appropriate authority including presiding judge of court where petition is brought, designated judge or licensed child welfare agency. (750-50/10). Surrender or consent occurring in another jurisdiction is valid if it conforms to law of that jurisdiction. Certificate of magistry or other comparable proof of office of notary public satisfactory to court shall be attached to consent acknowledged in another state. If person signing consent or surrender is in military, execution may be made before commissioned officer.

Consents or surrenders to agency for purposes of adoption must be executed in substantial conformance with specified forms. (750-50/12). Consent to adoption by specified person or persons in whose physical custody child resided at least one year or in whose physical custody at least one sibling of child has resided for at least one year or in whose physical custody child under one year of age has resided at least three months and where petition under Juvenile Court Act is pending (705-405/2-13) may be given by parent(s) with approval of Department of Children and Family Services (750-50/10[o]).

Actions to revoke consent or surrender for adoption must be commenced within one year from execution. (750-50/11).

Jurisdiction and Venue.—Petition may be filed in circuit court of county in which (a) petitioner resides, (b) person to be adopted resides or was born, or (c) parents of child reside. Petition may be filed in any county (a) if an "agency" has acquired custody and control of child and is authorized to consent to adoption or (b) if guardian of person of child has been appointed by court of competent jurisdiction. (750-50/4).

Petition.—Petition to adopt an adult or a "related child" may be filed at any time. Petition to adopt a child other than a "related child" must be filed within 30 days from time child has become "available for adoption" (or at later date under certain conditions). (750-50/5). In case of child born outside U.S., if prospective adoptive parents

have been appointed guardians by court in foreign country, such parents shall file petition to adopt child within 30 days of child's entry into U.S. (750-50/5).

Verified petition must state petitioners' names, place and length of residence in Illinois, when and from whom custody acquired; child's name, sex, place and date of birth, and relationship to petitioners; parents' names, place of residence, and any legal incapacity, or if no parent, name of guardian and appointing court, or if none, name of near relative. Parents' names and addresses shall be omitted and they shall not be made parties defendant if: (a) Their rights have been judicially terminated, or (b) child has been surrendered to an agency, or (c) parents deny or fail to declare paternity. Must state name to be given child and consent of authorized person or agency, and any prior orders affecting parties or proceedings. (750-50/5).

Person over 18 who has cared for child for continuous period of one year or more in licensed foster home may petition guardian for consent to adopt and petition will be given preference over other applications subject to final judicial approval. (750-50/15.1).

Guardian's final decision shall be based on welfare and best interest of child. Guardian shall consider all relevant factors including child's wishes, relationship with applicant, need for stable and continuous relationship with parent figures, adjustment to present home, school and community, and family ties with applicant and relatives, and wishes of child's parent (if expressed in writing prior to consent for adoption), mental and physical health of all involved and background, race, age, and criminal background check report required by 750-5/6. (750-50/15.1).

Proceedings.—All persons (except petitioners) named in petition are made parties defendant and notified in same manner as in other civil proceedings. (750-50/7).

Notice of proceeding shall be given to following for sole purpose of enabling such persons to present evidence relevant to best interests of child: person adjudicated in Illinois or other state to be father of child; person registered in Putative Father Registry; person recorded on child's birth certificate as father; person openly living with child or child's mother and openly holding self out as father; person identified as child's father by mother in written sworn statement including Affidavit of Identification under §11; person married to child's mother on date of child's birth or within 300 days prior to child's birth.

Adoption records shall be impounded in accordance with Illinois Supreme Court's Administrative Order of Record Keeping.

Investigation.—Within ten days after filing of petition for adoption of child other than "related child," court must appoint an agency, a licensed child placement agency, a probation officer of the court, or in Cook County, Court Services Division of Cook County Department of Public Aid, to investigate (a) allegations of petition, (b) character, reputation and general standing in community of petitioners, (c) religious faith of petitioners and of child, (d) whether petitioners are proper persons to adopt child, (e) health of petitioners, (f) whether child is proper subject of adoption. Written report on such investigation shall remain confidential and shall not become part of record or be considered at hearing of such proceeding unless established by competent evidence and (g) criminal background check not more than two years old including list of when, where and by whom criminal background check was prepared with review of fingerprints by state and federal authorities. (750-50/6).

Counsel.—If petition alleges person to be unfit because of inability to discharge parental responsibilities that person shall be represented by counsel. If that person has failed to appear or does not have sufficient funds for attorney court shall appoint counsel. (750-50/13).

Interim Order.—After appointing licensed attorney other than State's Attorney acting in official capacity as guardian ad litem to represent child to be adopted (and any other incompetent defendants), court will hold hearing to determine validity of consent and temporary custody of child. An interim order terminating parental rights, and awarding temporary custody may be entered after service of summons or reasonable notice on parents whose rights not terminated and opportunity to be heard. Interim custody order without notice possible upon presentation of written petition accompanied by affidavit that there is immediate danger to child and irreparable harm if notice given to parents or legal guardian. (750-50/13). In case of child born outside U.S., if court of foreign country has previously appointed petitioners as guardians of child, court may order that petitioners continue as guardians of such child. (750-50/13).

Death of Adoptive Child.—After a court has acquired jurisdiction over child in adoption proceeding, if such child dies before entry of final decree, upon petition by intended adoptive parents, the court may proceed to hearing and final decree to enable child to have intended name by adoption. (750-50/14a). In case of adoption proceeding commenced after death of child sought to be adopted, intended adoptive parents shall not, by reason of such adoption, acquire any interest in estate of such child, or incur any other right or obligation with respect to such child. (750-50/14a).

Decree.—In any case other than adoption of related child or of adult, each petitioner, person, or agency consenting to adoption must execute affidavit setting forth any monetary cost given, promised, or received. If total of money or things of value given, promised or received is less than $3,500, affidavit to that effect is sufficient. No affidavit need be filed by non-consenting parent, judge or clerk. After expiration of six months from entry of interim order, unless waiver of six month waiting period is found to be for welfare of child (750-50/16), petitioners may apply to court for decree of adoption. Petitioners must serve notice of such application upon investigating agency or person and guardian ad litem. Decree for adoption of: (a) "Related child," (b) adult or (c) child to whose adoption "agency" or person has authority to consent, may be entered at any time after service of process and return day designated therein. (750-50/14).

Final propriety of adoption shall be within sole discretion of court, which shall base its decision on welfare and best interest of child. Court shall consider all relevant factors including those to be considered by guardian when determining whether to consent to child's adoption by foster parent. If court finds that guardian abused discretion in consenting to adoption, court may grant or deny adoption without guardian's consent. (750-50/15.1).

Prohibition of Compensation for Placing Children.—No compensation is allowed any person, agency, etc., for placing out a child for adoption, except a statutorily

ADOPTION . . . *continued*
defined child welfare agency. (750-50/21, 720-525/1 to 525/5). Any person who gives or receives compensation for placing child out for adoption is guilty of Class 4 felony, if first conviction, or Class 3 felony, if subsequent conviction. (720-525/5).

Payment of Certain Expenses.—Person who has filed or intends to file petition to adopt with prior court approval may pay reasonable expenses of biological parents during biological mother's pregnancy and for no more than 30 days after birth of child. Payments will only be permitted where there is demonstrated need to protect heath of biological parents or child. Within 14 days after completion of permitted payments, petitioners shall present final accounting to court with verified statements of petitioners, attorneys of record and biological parent(s) attesting to accuracy of accounting. Petitioners also permitted to pay reasonable attorneys fees of biological parents with leave of court. (720-525/4.1).

Effect of Adoption.—Adopted child is deemed a descendant of adopting parent for purposes of inheritance from adopting parent and lineal or collateral kindred of adopting parent. (755-5/2-4). For purposes of inheritance from or through natural parent and for determining property rights under any instrument, adopted child is not child of natural parent, nor descendant of natural parent or lineal or collateral kin of natural parent unless (1) child is adopted by descendant or spouse of descendant of greatgrandparent of child in which case adoptee is child of both natural parents, (2) natural parent died before child was adopted in which case adoptee is child of deceased parent and heir of lineal and collateral kin of that parent, (3) contrary clear and convincing evidence by terms of instrument effective Jan. 1, 1998 for purposes of inheritance and for purposes of determining property rights as to all instruments executed on or after that date. Heir of adopted child, who is not child of natural parent under 755-5/2-4(d) is not heir of that natural parent or of lineal or collateral kin of that natural parent. (755-5/2-4[d]). Adopting parent is deemed parent for purposes of inheritance from adopted child, but not as to property which child has taken by gift, will or intestate succession from natural parent or lineal or collateral kindred of natural parent. For purposes of determining property rights under agreement executed after Aug. 31, 1955, adopted child deemed child born to adopting parent unless contrary intent is demonstrated by terms of instrument by clear and convincing evidence. After Sept. 30, 1989 adopted child is deemed child born to adopting parent for purposes of determining property rights of any person under instrument executed before Sept. 1, 1955 unless contrary intent is demonstrated by instrument by clear and convincing evidence or unless adopting parent's belief that instrument executed prior to Sept. 1, 1955 would not benefit adopted child is demonstrated by adopting parent's acts to substantially benefit adopted child. (755-5/2-4[f]).

Natural parents of child are deprived of all legal rights with respect to child, and child is free from all obligations of maintenance or obedience with respect to natural parents. (750-50/17). But natural parents have ultimate liability to support their child. (48 Ill.2d 16, 268 N.E.2d 11).

Registry.—Child surrendered for adoption, adoptee, biological parent, and biological sibling may register to obtain identifying information, and information will be exchanged if child surrendered for adoption, adoptee, biological parent, and biological sibling authorize exchange through Illinois Department of Health, but not before adoptee reaches age 18 or 21, depending upon statutory factors. (750-50/18.1 to 50/18.6). Confidential intermediary may be appointed to obtain medical background of adoptee from biological parent or sibling where statutory criteria met. (750-50/18.3a).

ALIMONY:

See topic Dissolution of Marriage.

ANNULMENT:

See topic Marriage.

COMMUNITY PROPERTY:

This system does not prevail in Illinois.

DESERTION:

See topics Dissolution of Marriage, Husband and Wife.

DISSOLUTION OF MARRIAGE:

Grounds.—One of following grounds for dissolution must be proved: Without fault by petitioner respondent is impotent, or has another spouse living at time of marriage or has committed adultery or has deserted himself or herself from petitioner for one year which includes any time in which parties were involved in proceedings for dissolution or separation; habitual drunkenness for two years; attempt on life of spouse by poisoning or other means showing malice; extreme and repeated mental or physical cruelty; conviction of felony or infamous crime; infection of spouse with sexually transmitted disease; or excessive use of addictive drugs for two years. Additionally, marriage may be dissolved if spouses have been separated for two years and irreconcilable differences have caused breakdown in marriage and reconciliation has failed or would be impracticable; if separation has been for six months two year requirement may be waived upon written stipulation. (750–5/401). At any time after parties cease to cohabit, following periods shall be included in period of separation: (1) Any period of cohabitation during which parties in good faith attempt to reconcile and seek marriage counseling as defined by statute, and (2) any period of cohabitation under written agreement of parties to attempt to reconcile. (750-5/401[a][2]).

Residence Requirements.—One of spouses must be resident of Illinois or stationed here and residence had been maintained for 90 days before commencement of action or finding. (750-5/401).

Jurisdiction of proceeding for dissolution of marriage, legal separation or declaration of invalidity of marriage is exclusively in Circuit Courts. (Const. Art. VI, §9). Court may enter judgment for dissolution which reserves any issue, including custody, child support, maintenance and disposition of property upon agreement of both parties or motion of either party and court's finding that appropriate circumstances exist. If party dies after entry of judgment but before resolution of reserved issues proceedings shall continue. (750-5/401).

Commencement of Action.—By filing verified petition, containing required allegations (750-5/403), as in other civil actions, or, at petitioner's option, by filing praecipe for summons with clerk. Where action is commenced by filing precipe for summons, petition shall be filed within six months thereafter or action shall be dismissed. (750-5/411[d]). Until petition is filed or unless respondent voluntarily files appearance precipe for summons filed without petition shall be served on respondent within 30 days of issuance and upon failure to obtain service action shall be dismissed. (750-5/411[c]). Identification of party's street address in proceedings not required if court finds that physical, mental or emotional health of party or minor child would be seriously endangered by such disclosure. (750-5/708).

Venue.—Must be had in county where plaintiff or defendant resides. Objection to venue is barred if not made by time defendant's response is due. (750-5/104).

Process.—May be directed to any county in state. (750-5/104).

Practice.—When respondent appears and files response in contested action, trial may be on bifurcated basis with grounds being tried first. If court finds grounds exist, it may allow parties additional time to settle remaining issues or it may proceed to trial immediately. (750-5/403). Parties may waive 48 hour waiting period and proceed immediately to trial on remaining issues or settle remaining issues. In cases where grounds are uncontested and proved as in cases of default, trial on all other remaining issues shall proceed immediately by court order or by stipulation of parties. No trial by jury available. (750-5/103). Conciliation may be ordered on court's own motion or at request of either party. (750-5/404). In case of default, cause is heard by examination of petitioner in open court. (750-5/405). No confession of respondent shall be taken as evidence unless court is satisfied it was made in sincerity and without fraud or collusion to enable petitioner to obtain relief sought. (750-5/407). Fault or conduct of petitioner not bar to action unless raised in pleadings. (750-5/406). If court is satisfied that injury complained of was occasioned by collusion of parties, relief sought shall not be granted. (750-5/408). Defenses of recrimination and condonation abolished. (750-5/403).

Temporary Custody of Children.—Pending suit court may make orders concerning custody, support and visitation of minor children and provisions for their education and maintenance by either or both spouses. (750-5/501).

Temporary Alimony and Suit Expenses.—Court may require any party to pay temporary maintenance (formerly known as temporary alimony) and expenses to other, including attorney's fees and including interim fees to achieve substantial parity in parties' access to funds for litigation costs. (750-5/501, 5/508). For cases pending on or after June 1, 1997, after proofs have closed in final hearing and before judgment entered, Court shall decide party's petition for contribution to fees and costs incurred. (750-5/503[j]). Court also has power to restrain any party from transferring, concealing or disposing of any property; to enjoin party from removing child from jurisdiction of court or from striking or interfering with personal liberty of other party or any child; or to grant any other proper injunctive relief. (750-5/501).

Division of Property of Spouses.—Marital property distribution system used. See subhead Disposition of Property, infra.

Disposition of Property.—Marital property means all property acquired by either spouse subsequent to marriage, except certain described non-marital property, regardless of whether title is held individually or in some form of co-ownership. Non-marital property does not become marital where increase in its value arose from contribution of material property, non-marital property or personal effort of spouse. Right to reimbursement does exist. Where marital and non-marital property have been commingled contributing property is classified as receiving property unless both classes are commingled into newly acquired property which will be marital. Right to reimbursement exists, but no reimbursement for contribution which is not traceable by clear and convincing evidence, or which was gift, or which was result of personal effort which was not both significant and resulted in substantial appreciation. In proceeding for dissolution of marriage or declaration of invalidity of marriage, court shall assign each spouse's non-marital property to that spouse and divide marital property, without regard to marital misconduct, in just proportions, considering relevant factors, including: (1) Contribution of each party to acquisition of property, (2) dissipation by each party of marital or nonmarital property, (3) value of property, (4) duration of marriage, (5) economic circumstances of each spouse, (6) obligations and rights arising from prior marriages, (7) any antenuptial agreement, (8) age, health, occupation, needs, etc. of parties, (9) custodial provisions for children, (10) whether apportionment is in lieu of or in addition to maintenance, (11) reasonable opportunity of each spouse to acquire future assets and income, and (12) tax consequences of property division. Each spouse has species of common ownership in marital property during dissolution proceedings. Such interests shall not restrict property unless specifically enjoined. (750-5/503). In determining value of marital and nonmarital property, court shall value property as close to date of trial as practicable. (750-5/503).

Unless otherwise provided in trust instrument, judicial termination of marriage revokes all revocable provisions which pertain to settlor's spouse in trust. (760-35/1).

Transfer of marital property between spouses per agreement or by court order is not considered taxable event. Court may set aside portion of each spouse's property in separate fund or trust for support, maintenance and welfare of child. (750-5/503).

Court may enforce judgments affecting marital property by ordering sale of marital property with proceeds to be applied as determined by court. (750-5/503).

Possession of Marital Residence.—Court may, during pendency of proceedings, enter order granting exclusive possession of marital residence to either spouse until final determination of proceeding, where physical or mental well-being of either spouse or children is jeopardized by occupancy of marital residence by both spouses. Order does not affect estate of homestead of either party. (750-5/701).

Custody.—Illinois has adopted Uniform Child Custody Jurisdiction Act. (750-5/601). Court has jurisdiction to make child custody determination if: (1) Illinois is home state of child or was within six months prior to commencement of action, or (2) it is in best interest of child that Illinois court assume jurisdiction because child or other

See note at head of Digest as to 1998 legislation covered.

See Topical Index in front part of this volume.

IL – 61

DISSOLUTION OF MARRIAGE . . . *continued*

contestant has significant connection with Illinois or there is available in this state substantial evidence concerning child's present or future care, or (3) child is physically present in Illinois and has been abandoned or abused, or (4) another state has declined jurisdiction and it is in child's interest that Illinois assume jurisdiction. (750-5/601). Court retains such jurisdiction over child until it concedes jurisdiction to foreign state or no party, including child, remains in Illinois. (750-35/4). Child custody proceeding is commenced by: (1) Parent filing petition for dissolution of marriage or legal separation or declaration of invalidity of marriage or for custody of child, or (2) by person other than parent by filing petition for custody, if child not in physical custody of one of his parents. (750-5/601).

Notice Provisions for Custody Proceedings.—Before making judgment, reasonable notice must be given to contestants, any parent whose rights have not been terminated, and any person who has physical custody of child. Process and notice governed by Civil Practice Law. Where person is out of state, notice must be served, mailed or delivered at least ten days before any hearing either by personal delivery outside state as with service inside state, under laws of service of process where notice given, or mail, return receipt requested, or pursuant to court order. (750-5/601, 750-35/6). In action for modification of previous custody order, written notice and copy of modification petition must be served on child's parent, guardian and custodian at least 30 days prior to hearing. (750–5/601).

Simultaneous Custody Proceedings in Other States.—Court shall not exercise jurisdiction if at time of filing of custody petition, custody proceeding was pending in another state exercising jurisdiction in substantial conformity with Act unless such proceeding is stayed. Court which has jurisdiction under this Act may decline to exercise jurisdiction if it finds it is inconvenient forum. (750-35/7[a], 750-35/9). Court may decline to exercise jurisdiction if petitioner has wrongfully taken child from another state or engaged in similar reprehensible conduct.

Res Judicata Custody Judgment.—Custody judgment binds all parties who have been served, or who have submitted to jurisdiction of court or notified in accordance with Act and who have been given opportunity to be heard. (750-35/13).

Recognition of Foreign Judgment and Registration.—Illinois courts shall recognize and enforce initial or modification judgment of court of another state which assumed jurisdiction under statutes substantially in accordance with Act, and shall not modify foreign judgment unless foreign court does not have jurisdiction under jurisdictional requisites of this Act or has declined to assume jurisdiction and Illinois has jurisdiction. Certified copy of custody judgment of another state may be filed in office of any circuit clerk and shall be treated as judgment of this State. Registry of out-of-state custody judgments and proceedings maintained by clerk of each circuit. (750-35/14, 35/15, 35/16, 35/17).

Deposition in Another State.—Any party to proceeding or guardian ad litem or other representative of child may adduce testimony of witnesses by evidence or discovery deposition or otherwise in another state. Court on own motion may direct that testimony of person be taken in another state. Illinois court may request appropriate court of another state to hold hearing to adduce evidence, to order party to produce or give evidence, or to have social studies made. (750-35/19, 35/20, 35/21).

Practice.—Court shall determine custody in accordance with best interests of child and shall consider: (1) Wishes of parents, (2) wishes of child, (3) relationship of child with parents and siblings, (4) child's adjustment to home, school and community, (5) mental and physical health of all persons involved, (6) physical violence or threat of physical violence by child's potential custodian, whether directed against child or another person but witnessed by child, (7) occurrence of ongoing abuse in household whether directed at child or another person and (8) willingness and ability to encourage continuing close relationship between other parent and child. (750-5/602). Court shall not consider conduct of present or proposed custodian that does not affect relationship with child and shall presume that both parents' maximum involvement regarding physical, mental, moral and emotional well-being of their child is in child's best interest. There shall be no presumption in favor or against joint custody. (750-5/602).

Upon application of either parent, both parents or upon court's own motion, court shall consider award of "joint custody". (750-5/602.1). Court shall initially request parents to produce joint parenting agreement specifying each parent's powers, rights and responsibilities for personal care of child and for major decisions and procedure for mediating future disputes. If parents fail to produce joint parenting agreement, court may enter joint parenting order containing same elements. (750-5/602.1). Before ordering joint custody, court must find it is in best interests of child after taking into account parents' ability to cooperate, parents' residential circumstances and all other relevant factors. (750-5/602.1).

Court may interview child in chambers, seek professional advice, or order investigation of custodial arrangements. (750-5/604, 750-5/605). Counsel shall be present at child's interview in chambers, unless otherwise agreed upon by parties. Attendance of court reporter during child's interview mandatory and cannot be waived by parties. (62 Ill. App.3d 837, 379 N.E.2d 396). Temporary custody orders may be entered. (750-5/603). Court may grant leave to remove child from Illinois. Party seeking removal has burden of proving removal is in child's best interest. (750-5/609). Court may appoint attorney to represent best interests of minor or dependent child with respect to support, custody, visitation and property. Same attorney may be appointed child's guardian ad litem. (750-5/506). Except for certain circumstances, no motion can be made to modify custody within two years of its date. (750-5/610).

Adult Education Program.—In divorce or post-judgment proceeding involving minor children, if it is determined to be in best interests of child, court may order parties to attend education program not to exceed four hours in duration focusing on effects of divorce on minor children. Unless stipulated in writing, facts adduced at program shall not be considered in adjudication of any action and resulting report shall not become part of record of case. (750-5/404.1).

Expedited Procedure for Enforcement of Visitation Orders.—Where one party wilfully and without justification denies other party visitation or exercises his or her visitation rights in harmful way, complaining party may commence action stating (a) name and address of both parties; (b) nature of abuse; (c) that reasonable attempt was made to resolve dispute; and (d) relief sought. Court may order one or more of following: (1) Modification of visitation order; (2) supervised visitation; (3) makeup visitation; (4) counseling or mediation, except where there is evidence of domestic violence; (5) other appropriate relief. (750-5/607.1).

Investigation and Report.—In contested cases, upon request of parent or custodian, court may order report of custodial arrangements for child. Such support may be considered by court in determining custody. (750-5/605).

Cost and Attorneys Fees.—In every proceeding for enforcement of order or judgment where court finds failure of party to comply with order or judgment is without compelling cause, that party must pay other party's costs and reasonable attorneys fees. (750-5/508[b]). Court may order any party to pay reasonable amount for own or other party's costs and attorney fees including interim attorney fees and costs from opposing party under 750-5/501(c-1) in wide variety of proceedings, including prosecution of claim on appeal if prosecuting party substantially prevailed. (750-5/508[a]).

Maintenance.—In proceeding for dissolution of marriage or legal separation or declaration of invalidity of marriage court may grant temporary or permanent maintenance order for either spouse in such amounts and for such periods of time, as court deems just, without regard to marital misconduct, considering: (1) income and property of each party including marital and nonmarital property assigned to party seeking maintenance, (2) needs of each party, (3) present and future earning capacity of each party, (4) any impairment of present and future earning capacity of party seeking maintenance due to party's commitment to domestic duties or delayed education, training, employment, or career opportunities due to marriage, (5) time needed to acquire education or training and employment of party seeking maintenance and whether that party is able to support self through employment or is custodian of child so that it is appropriate that custodian not seek employment, (6) standard of living established during marriage, (7) duration of marriage, (8) age and physicial, emotional condition of parties, (9) tax consequences of property division upon parties, (10) contributions and services by party seeking maintenance to education, training, career, career potential or license of other party, (11) any valid agreement of parties, (12) other factors court considers just and equitable. (750-5/504).

Modification.—Judgment for maintenance or support may be modified only as to installments accruing after proper notice of filing of motion for modification with notice and only upon showing of substantial change in circumstances unless party is receiving child and spouse support services from Illinois Department of Public Aid and if certain other conditions exist. Property dispositions may not be revoked or modified unless Court finds conditions justifying reopening of judgment under Illinois law. (750-5/510).

Termination.—Unless otherwise agreed by parties in written separation agreement approved by court, obligation to pay future maintenance terminates upon death of either party, or remarriage of party receiving maintenance, or if person receiving maintenance cohabits with another person on resident, continuing conjugal basis. (750-5/510).

Support of Children.—In proceeding for dissolution of marriage, legal separation, declaration of invalidity of marriage, or subsequent proceedings for child support, court may order either or both parents to pay reasonable and necessary child support, without regard to marital misconduct. Court shall determine minimum amount of support in accordance with guidelines in statute, which establish amount as minimum percent of supporting party's "net income" based upon number of children. These guidelines are to be applied in each case, unless court, after considering evidence presented on all relevant factors as to best interests of child, finds reason for deviating from guidelines. (750-5/505). If necessary best interest of child, court may set aside portion of joint or separate estate of parties in separate trust or fund for support, maintenance, education and general welfare of minor, dependent or incompetent child. Court may consider special needs for child's care, healing and counselling if child is victim of crime perpetrated by one of parties. (750-5/503). All child support payments shall commence with date summons is served and level of support under order shall not be reduced in accordance with level of payments made prior to entry of support order. (750-45/15[b]). Net income shall include funds available from federal, state and local government programs. Regardless of non-custodial parent's net income, court shall order such non-custodial parent to pay not less than $10 per month as child support. (750-45/15[a]).

As of Jan. 1, 1982, child support payment orders entered in any county with population of 2,000,000 or more (or any other county desiring to be included within mandatory child support payment program) must direct that such payments be made to clerk of court if person entitled to payment receives public assistance; otherwise court may direct payments to clerk. (750-5/709 to 5/712). Support is terminated by emancipation of child except as otherwise provided, but not by death of parent obligated to support child. In event of death of such parent, amount of support may be modified, revoked or commuted to lump sum payment as appropriate, which may be determined at time of dissolution of marriage or later. (750-5/510). In counties covered by this program support shall be enforced by clerk of circuit court and state's attorney. (750-5/710).

Upon entry of support order on or after Jan. 1, 1989, court shall enter order for withholding of income to take effect immediately unless agreement is reached between parties and approved by court, in which case withholding to take effect if support payments delinquent. (P.A. 85-1156).

With respect to orders entered on or after Jan. 1, 1990, if obligor is not U.S. citizen, obligor is required to provide court with certain identification which shall become part of record of case. (750-20/26.1[B][1]).

Note: Expedited Child Support Act of 1990 providing for creation, by counties, of system for expeditious determination of parentage and for establishment, modification and enforcement of child support obligations beginning July 1, 1991, became effective Sept. 1, 1990.

Failure to Pay Support.—Effective Oct. 1, 1985, Illinois Department of Public Aid may direct Comptroller to withhold from state income tax refunds amounts for past due child support. (305-5/10-17.5). Failure of either party to comply with order to pay support shall be punishable as in other cases of contempt. Lien arises against real and personal property of non-custodial parent for each installment of overdue support. Order shall require obligor to report to obligee and clerk of court within ten days each time obligor obtains new employment and each time obligor's employment is terminated for any reason. Failure to report is indirect criminal contempt. Order shall include provisions requiring obligor/ee parents to advise each other of change of residence except

See note at head of Digest as to 1998 legislation covered.

See Topical Index in front part of this volume.

IL – 62

DISSOLUTION OF MARRIAGE...*continued*

where court finds disclosure would seriously endanger child. Where parent is 90 days or more delinquent in payment of support, court may order that parent's Illinois driving privileges be suspended. (750-5/505).

Spousal Health Insurance Rights.—Effective Dec. 1, 1985, no group accident or health insurance policy shall be issued, renewed, amended or extended unless it provides for continuation of existing insurance benefits for employee's spouse and dependent children who are insured thereunder notwithstanding that marriage is dissolved by judgment or terminated by death of employee spouse without any other eligibility requirements. (215-5/367.2).

Social Security Requirements.—Parent or custodian of child who fails or refuses to comply with federal Social Security requirements and regulations regarding child or spousal support obligations may be ineligible for medical assistance. (305-5/5-2.2).

Unemployed.—Court may order unemployed person owing duty of support or maintenance obligation to seek employment and report periodically to court on efforts. (305-5/5-2.2).

Visitation.—Parent not granted child custody is entitled to reasonable visitation rights, unless after hearing, court finds that visitation would seriously endanger child's physical, mental, moral or emotional health. Court may grant visitation to grandparents, great-grandparents or siblings of child upon petition if court finds it is in best interests of child. If both natural parents of grandchild have died and grandchild was subsequently adopted, however, grandparents shall not be granted visitation rights unless adoption is by "close relative". (755-5/11-7.1). If custodian's street address is not identified pursuant to court order, court shall require parties to identify reasonable alternative arrangements for visitation. (750-5/607).

Change of Wife's Name.—Court may allow wife to resume maiden name or any former name. (750-5/413).

Change of Minor Child's Name.—Minor child's name may be changed upon petition to court by parent only if court finds by clear and convincing evidence that change is necessary to serve best interest of child. Court shall consider all relevant factors including wishes of child, parents, and custodian, relationship of child with parents, custodian, stepparents, siblings and step-siblings and child's adjustment to home, school and community. (735-5/21-101).

Remarriage.—No restrictions on remarriage of persons whose marriage was dissolved.

Legal Separation.—Party may choose to pursue action for legal separation rather than dissolution of marriage and obtain maintenance during legal separation if, without fault of that party, he or she is living separately and apart from other spouse. (750-5/402). Pendency of action or judgment for legal separation does not bar either party from moving for dissolution of marriage. (750-5/402).

Separation agreements may be entered into to provide for disposition of property, maintenance of either spouse, and support, custody and visitation of children. Terms of separation agreement, except those providing for support, custody and visitation of children, are binding on court, unless it finds that terms are unconscionable. Separation agreement shall be set forth in judgment or shall be identified in judgment with statement that court has approved its terms. Except for terms concerning support, custody or visitation of children, separation agreement may preclude or limit modification of its terms. (750-5/502).

Annulment of Marriage.—See topic Marriage.

DIVORCE:

See topic Dissolution of Marriage.

GUARDIAN AND WARD:

Estate of minors and disabled adults are administered in Circuit Courts. (755-5/11-1 to 5/11a-22). See category Courts and Legislature, topic Courts.

Appointment of Guardian.—Guardian may be appointed by court in county wherein minor resides or, if minor is nonresident, in county where he has real estate, or personal estate as court finds to be in best interest of child. (755-5/11-6). No guardian need be appointed if personal estate of minor does not exceed $10,000, in which case any person or corporation holding personal estate of minor may deliver same to parent or person standing in loco parentis upon receiving affidavit setting forth certain facts and said person or corporation is thereby released. (755-5/25-2). Court lacks jurisdiction to appoint guardian for minor if minor has living parent, adoptive parent or adjudicated parent whose rights have not been terminated, whose whereabouts are known and who is willing and able to carry out day to day child care. Rebuttable presumption that parent is willing and able to carry out day to day child care that can be rebutted by preponderance of evidence. (755-5/11-5[b]). Guardian for disabled adult may be appointed by court in county where he resides, or, if nonresident, in county where his real or personal estate is located. (755-5/11a-7). Petition for appointment filed by any interested person or by disabled person. Minor age 14 or over may nominate guardian of person and estate subject to court approval. (755-5/11a-3). Disabled adult is defined in 755-5/11a-2. Power to appoint guardian of estate of disabled adult limited to finding of inability to manage estate or financial affairs. Power to appoint guardian of person for disabled adult limited to finding of inability to communicate responsible decisions regarding self-care. (755-5/11a-3).

Selection of Guardian.—Parent, adoptive parent or adjudicated parent whose parental rights have not been terminated may designate in any writing, including will, guardian or standby guardian to become effective at later date (755-5/1-2.23, 5/11-5.3) of person or estate or both of unmarried minor or of child likely to be born. Writing must be witnessed by two or more credible persons over 18 years and not designated guardian. (755-5/11-5). Minor over 14 years old may nominate with court's approval. (755-5/11-5). Court, however, shall not appoint as guardian someone who either has caused or has substantially contributed to minor becoming abused or neglected (755-5/

11-5[d]) and previous statements by minor as to abuse and neglect of minor is admissible at hearing on appointment (755-5/11-5[e]). In all other cases, court may nominate upon petition of reputable citizen or on its own motion. (755-5/11-5). Person of sound mind and memory may designate in writing person, qualified not-for-profit corporation, department or agency to become guardian of his person or estate if later adjudged disabled. Corporation qualified to accept and execute trusts in state may be designated guardian of estate. Designation does not bind court, but is prima facia valid if executed and attested as will. (755-5/11a-6).

Eligibility and Competency.—Resident of U.S. who has attained 18 years of age, is not of unsound mind, is not ward, has not been convicted of felony, and who court finds is capable of providing active and suitable guardianship may be guardian of person and estate of minor. (755-5/11-3).

Nonresident guardian, when no guardian has been appointed in this state, may bring suit (755-5/22-3) or sell minor's personal estate (755-5/22-4) or lease, sell or mortgage real estate (755-5/22-4). Petition of nonresident guardian to sell personal estate or lease, sell or mortgage real estate must have attached authenticated copies of: (1) His authority to act; (2) order of court issuing letters authorizing application in court of this state for leave to lease, sell or mortgage; (3) bond required by court which issued letters; and (4) order of that court approving bond. (755-5/22-4).

Parents are entitled to custody of person of minor, even though minor has guardian of estate. (755-5/11-7).

Grandparents and close relatives have certain visitation rights after death of both parents of minor, unless minor has subsequently been adopted by persons other than close relative. (755-5/11-7.1).

Requirements for guardians for disabled adults same as for minors, plus court must find guardian capable of providing active and suitable program of guardianship for disabled, and potential guardian must not be directly providing residential services for ward. (755-5/11a-5).

Qualification.—Guardian of minor or disabled adult must file bond unless bond is waived by court or by will or if guardian is Office of State Guardian; or by person designating in event of becoming disabled. (755-5/12-4). He must also file acceptance of office and oath that he will faithfully perform his duties. (755-5/12-1, 5/12-2).

Appointment of Guardian Unnecessary.—When personal estate of ward does not exceed $10,000, property may be transferred or indebtedness paid on affidavit of one standing in loco parentis to minor or spouse of ward, or if no spouse, relative having responsibility to support ward, stating that no representative has been appointed for estate. Transferor or debtor is protected as though transfer has been made to legally qualified representative. (755-5/25-2).

Inventory.—Guardian must file inventory within 60 days after appointment. (755-5/14-1).

Powers and Duties.—Guardian of minor shall have custody, responsibility for nurturing and providing education, and must care for, manage frugally and invest estate under direction of court. (755-5/11-13). Guardian may, with approval of court, operate ward's business. (755-5/19-7). Guardian must keep ward's funds invested, character of investments being regulated by statute. (755-5/21-2, 5/24-21). Guardian shall also represent ward in all legal proceedings. (755-5/11-13).

Guardian of disabled adult by court order must have custody of ward and children, make provision for care, comfort, maintenance, education and professional services, and provide for ward's self-reliance. Ward's spouse not to be deprived of child custody without consent unless adjudged unfit by court. If court directs, guardian must file annual or more frequent report stating ward's mental, physical and social condition, present living arrangement, professional services rendered, and resume of guardian's visit with recommendations regarding continued need for guardianship. (755-5/11a-17).

Guardian of ward other than minor, with authority of probate court, may take action not required for ward's current and future maintenance and support so long as they are in keeping with ward's wishes so far as ascertainable whether or not tax savings are involved. These actions include making gifts of income or principal either outright or in trust; conveying, releasing or disclaiming contingent and expectant interests including marital property rights; exercising options regarding securities; exercising rights to elect benefits, terminate, assign, borrow or receive cash for life insurance, annuities, mutual fund investment plan, retirement and employee welfare plans; changing ward's residence or domicile; modifying terms of ward's will or trust in light of tax law changes. If ward's intentions cannot be ascertained, presumption ward favors reduction in taxes. (755-5/11a-5).

Adjudication of disability does not revoke or terminate trust revocable by ward. Guardian of ward's estate has no authority to revoke or amend trust revocable or amendable by ward, except that court may authorize guardian to revoke Totten trust or similar deposit or withdrawable capital account in trust to extent necessary to provide for authorized expenditures. If trustee of any trust for benefit of ward has discretionary power to apply trust's income or principal for ward's benefit, trustee is not required to distribute any income or principal to guardian of ward's estate. (755-5/11a-18).

Securities in Name of Nominee.—See category Estates and Trusts, topic Trusts, subhead Securities in Name of Nominee.

Real Estate.—Guardian, by leave of court, may sell, at private sale if interest in estate is less than $2,500, or mortgage ward's real estate when court deems it necessary for support and education of persons entitled thereto, for payment of ward's debts or for reinvestment (755-5/20-3, 755-5/25-4) and by leave of court may lease real estate (755-5/20-2), including leasing for mineral development (755-5/20-20).

Liabilities of Guardian.—Guardian and surety are liable for mismanagement to ward, successor guardian or conservator, co-guardian or co-conservator, or to any aggrieved person. Any of these persons may maintain action against guardian and surety for all money and property withheld, wasted, embezzled or misapplied and no satisfaction made therefor. (755-5/24-18).

Personal property may be sold, leased, mortgaged or pledged by leave of court if it is for best interest of ward or his estate. (755-5/19-2).

GUARDIAN AND WARD . . . *continued*

Accounts.—At end of first year and at termination of guardianship and whenever required by court, guardians must file verified accounts. Accounts shall list receipts and disbursements and personal estate on hand. (755-5/24-11).

Termination of Guardianship.—Office of guardian terminates (1) when ward dies (except that certain authority continues until personal representative is appointed [755-5/24-19]) or attains majority, (2) when guardian dies or his letters are revoked (755-5/24-12), or (3) if estate consists only of cash by leave of court under special statutory provision (755-5/24-21). Marriage of minor ward terminates right of guardian to custody and education of ward but not to control of estate. (755-5/24-12).

Upon written notice and hearing, court will discharge conservator (appointed under prior law) or guardian of disabled person or his estate, or modify his duties, when ward's capacity for self-care and management has been demonstrated by clear and convincing evidence. Petition may be made by ward or any person on ward's behalf. (755-5/11a-20).

Gifts to Minors.—See topic Infants.

Compensation.—Guardians and their attorneys are allowed reasonable compensation for their services. (755-5/27-1, 5/27-2). Guardian may be authorized by court order to make conditional gifts from estate of disabled to spouse, brother, sister or child of disabled who lives with and personally cares for disabled for at least three years but gift not distributed to donee until disabled person's death. All potential heirs and legatees of disabled person entitled to notice on hearing of conditional gifts. Gifts may be revoked or modified in order to release funds for care of disabled. (755-5/11a-18.1). Potential recipient of conditional gift is entitled to claim against estate of disabled person based in part on nature and extent of person's disability. (755-5/18-1.1).

Insane Persons.—Conservatorships and findings of incompetency are eliminated. (755-5/11-2, 5/11-4 repealed). Guardians now appointed for disabled adults, as defined by statute. (755-5/11a-1, 5/11a-2, 5/11a-3).

Uniform Fiduciaries Act.—See category Estates and Trusts, topic Trusts.

Uniform Simplification of Fiduciary Security Transfers Act.—Not adopted. See Illinois Act for Simplification of Fiduciary Transfers. (760-70/1 to 70/7).

HUSBAND AND WIFE:

Abortion.—Provision of Illinois Abortion Act of 1975 requiring spousal consent to abortion held unconstitutional. (Wynn v. Scott, 449 F. Supp. 1302 [1978]).

Disabilities of Married Women.—All disabilities have been removed.

Separate Property.—A married woman may hold real and personal property, and dispose of the same in same manner and to same extent that husband may deal with his property. However, transfers of personal property between husband and wife living together, to be valid as against third parties, are required to be in writing, acknowledged and recorded in same manner as chattel mortgages (750-65/9). If either husband or wife unlawfully retains possession or control of property belonging to other, either before or after marriage, owner may maintain action therefor, or for any right growing out of same in same manner as if they were not married. (750-65/10).

Uniform Premarital Agreement Act adopted, effective Jan. 1, 1990. Agreement must be in writing, signed by both parties and is enforceable without consideration. Agreement can cover any matter not in violation of public policy or criminal statute. (750-10/1 to 10/11).

Earnings of Married Person.—Married person is entitled to his or her own earnings, and may sue for same in his or her own name, free from interference of his or her spouse or his or her creditors. (750-65/7).

Contracts may be made and liabilities incurred by married person and same may be enforced against him or her to same extent, and in same manner, as if he or she were unmarried. (750-65/6). Husband and wife may contract with each other as with third person (750-65/6; 195 Ill. 378, 63 N.E. 269), and may become bound as surety for other.

Actions.—Married person may, in all cases, sue and be sued, without joining his or her spouse, to same extent as if he or she were unmarried. (750-65/1). Attachment or judgment may be enforced against him or her as if he or she were single. (750-65/1). If husband and wife are sued together, wife and husband may defend for his or her own right, and if either neglect to defend, they may defend for such one also. (750-65/2). Husband and wife may sue each other on all contracts (106 Ill. 36), or for tort committed during marriage. Testimony and judgment in dissolution proceedings are barred as prima facie evidence of tort. (750-65/1).

When husband has deserted his family, wife may prosecute or defend, in his name, any action which he might have prosecuted or defended, and under like circumstances, same right applies to husband upon desertion of wife. (750-65/3). For all civil injuries committed by married woman, damages may be recovered from her alone, and husband is not responsible therefor because of marital relation. (750-65/4).

With some exceptions, husband and wife competent to testify for or against each other. (735-5/8-801).

Agency.—Husband or wife may constitute other as his or her attorney in fact, to control or dispose of his or her property for their mutual benefit or otherwise, and may remove such attorney at will. (750-65/14).

Conveyance or Encumbrance of Property.—Homestead must be expressly waived. (765-5/27). Dower and curtesy are abolished. See category Property, topic Dower.

Liability for Debts of Spouse.—Neither husband nor wife is responsible for debts or liabilities of other before or after marriage, except for expenses of family, and education of children, which are chargeable upon property of both husband and wife, or either of them, and for which they are jointly and severally liable. (750-65/5, 65/15).

Liability for Support.—Husband is liable for support of his wife, and wife for support of her husband if he is in need of support and is, or is likely to become, public charge. Husband and wife are severally liable for support of any child under age 21 except that parent is not liable for child age 18 or over if child is not living with such parent or parents. (305-5/10-2).

Consumer Fraud Act-Penalty.—No person may make any attempt to collect an obligation from spouse of obligor unless spouse cosigned instrument evidencing obligation or unless obligation is in default at least 30 days or unless goods or services furnished to obligor and giving rise to obligation were necessaries for which spouse would be liable to pay under statute or common law. Person who commits an unlawful practice within meaning of this act is guilty of a Class C misdemeanor. (815-505/2H).

Criminal Acts of Wife.—Married woman not entitled, by reason of presence of husband, to any presumption of compulsion, or to any defense of compulsion against liability for criminal offense unless such defense exists by reason of other provisions in Criminal Code. (720-5/7-11).

Desertion and Nonsupport.—Husband or wife who neglects or refuses to provide for other and children under 18 years in need of support is guilty of Class A misdemeanor. (750-15/1). Offending party liable in civil action under Public Aid Code. (305-5/10-1 et seq.; 750-15/1). Where husband or wife abandons other, and leaves state for a year without providing for family maintenance, or is imprisoned in penitentiary, any court of record in county where remaining spouse resides may authorize remaining party to manage, sell or encumber property of other to support family and pay debts of other. (750-65/11).

Domestic Violence.—Action for order of protection commenced by filing petition in any civil court unless specific courts are designated by local rule or order, or if in conjunction with other civil proceedings involving same parties, or in conjunction with delinquency petition or criminal prosecution under same case number. (750-60/102). Civil Practice Law applies and standard of proof is by preponderance of evidence. (750-60/205). No right to trial by jury. (750-60/206). Upon finding of abuse, court may issue order of protection granting certain specified remedies. (750-60/214). Order to be filed with clerk of court, copy to be served on sheriff, and respondent to be served personally. (750-60/222). Violation may be enforced by contempt procedures and court permitted to award additional penalties. (750-60/223).

Insurance.—Spouse of employee may choose to continue coverage under group policy at previous combined charge to employee and employer for period of two years. After two years, if spouse is age 55 or older and if spouse wishes to continue coverage, insurer may add additional 20%. (215-5/367.2).

Revised Uniform Reciprocal Enforcement of Support Act adopted as amended where court has no requirement of immediate withholding. (750-20/26.1[B]). Civil enforcement is by verified petition filed in court. Periodic support payments treated as separate, enforceable judgments. (750-20/1 to 20/42).

Alienation of Affections and Criminal Conversation.—Recovery is limited to actual damages; no punitive, exemplary, vindictive or aggravated damages allowed. (740-5/1, 5/2, 5/3, 5/4, 50/1, 50/2, 50/3, 50/4).

Separate Maintenance.—See topic Dissolution of Marriage, subhead Legal Separation.

Community Property.—This system does not prevail in Illinois.

INFANTS:

Age of Majority.—Males 18 and females 18 years of age are of legal age for all purposes, except that it is unlawful to sell, give or deliver alcoholic liquor to any male or female under age of 21 years or for any parent or guardian to permit residence to be used by invitee of parents' child who is under age of 21 in manner that constitutes violation (235-5/6-16); and except as provided in Illinois Uniform Transfers to Minors Act (755-5/11-1). For purpose of Uniform Act all persons under 21 years of age are minors. (760-20/2).

Emancipation.—Minors between ages of 16 and 18 may apply for court ordered emancipation if parents or guardian do not object. Court order may partially or completely emancipate minor regarding ability to contract or other rights not inconsistent with federal or state law. (750-30/1).

Power of appointment under testamentary or non-testamentary instruments may be exercised by a holder who has attained age of 18 years, unless instrument contains express contrary provision. (755-5/4-2, 765-320/1).

Contracts of infants are voidable, except contract for "necessaries," even when executed or partially executed. (20 Ill. App.2d 528, 156 N.E.2d 597). Executory contract is binding only if it is ratified after attainment of majority. (345 Ill. 219, 177 N.E. 730). Executed contract is binding unless it is disaffirmed within reasonable time after attainment of majority. (288 Ill. 64, 122 N.E. 808). Ratification of contract after attainment of majority may be express or implied. Upon disaffirmance, consideration remaining in possession or control of minor must be returned, but if lost or expended minor not obligated to make restitution. (241 Ill. 398, 89 N.E. 796).

A minor student accepted for admission to an approved institution of higher education in Illinois may execute a legally binding promissory note for a loan necessary to attend or continue in attendance at that institution, subject to approval by institution. (815-155/0.01).

Married or pregnant minors, parent who is minor or anyone 18 years of age or older, can consent to performance of medical or surgical procedure by licensed physician. (410-210/1). Provision of Illinois Abortion Act of 1977 providing that no abortion may be performed if unmarried woman under age 18, unless such woman consents within 48 hours prior thereto and written consent of parents or guardian is obtained or judge of circuit court so orders after hearing held unconstitutional. (599 F.2d 193). Similar provision in Illinois Abortion Law of 1975 (38-81-23[4]) also held unconstitutional. (449 F.Supp. 1302, appeal dismissed, 439 U.S. 8, 99 S.Ct. 49). Anyone 12 years old or older who might have had contact with sexually transmitted disease, or suffers from use of stimulant, depressant or narcotic drugs may give consent to medical care or counseling related to treatment of disease. (410-210/4). Parental notification may, however, be required. (410-210/5). Anyone 17 years of age or older can consent to give blood. (210-15/1). Minor child is bound by health care malpractice arbitration agreement executed by parent, even if parent is minor. (710-15/7).

Duty to Support.—Child's mother or person found to be father of child pursuant to Illinois Parentage Act of 1984 is not relieved of support and maintenance obligations to

---

INFANTS . . . *continued*
child because he or she is minor. (750-45/3.1). See topics Husband and Wife, subhead Liability for Debts of Spouse, catchline Liability for Support; Dissolution of Marriage, subhead Support of Children.

Artificial Insemination.—Illinois Parentage Act, effective July 1, 1984, provides that sperm donor is not considered father of child conceived by artificial insemination unless he is husband of child's mother. Where mother's husband is not donor, he will be treated as child's natural father if both he and mother consent in writing to artificial insemination. Records regarding insemination are open to inspection only upon court order for good cause shown. (750-40/1 to 40/3).

Actions.—Representative of ward's estate shall represent ward in all actions unless another appointed for that purpose. (755-5/11-13). In civil action by or against infant, guardian ad litem must be appointed. (28 Ill. App.3d 670, 329 N.E.2d 365).

Parental Responsibility.—Parent or guardian liable for willful or malicious acts of unemancipated minor who resides with such parent or guardian. (740-115/1 to 115/7). Act held constitutional. (69 Ill. App.3d 193, 387 N.E.2d 341).

Disabilities.—See categories Employment, topic Labor Relations, subhead Child Labor Laws; Transportation, topic Motor Vehicles, subhead Operator's License.

Sexual Abuse Counseling Programs.—Juvenile Division shall establish and offer sexual abuse counseling to both victims of sexual abuse and sexual offenders in as many facilities as necessary to insure sexual abuse counseling throughout State. (730-5/3-9-7).

Revised Uniform Gifts to Minors Act.—Repealed and replaced with Uniform Transfers to Minors Act (760-20/1 to 20/24) effective July 1, 1986, with following differences: (1) In §2 definition of "benefit plan" expanded and several definitions added; (2) in §4, custodian may be nominated by court order; (3) in §6 transfers permitted by court order; (4) in §10 mechanism for transfer of beneficial interests in Illinois land trusts provided; (5) in §12 appointment of ineligible transferor as custodian does not void creation of custodianship; (6) in §13 custodian may invest custodial property in common trust funds; (7) in §16 custodian not compensated for his services liable only for losses due to bad faith, gross negligence, intentional wrongdoing or failure to maintain standard of prudence required by Act; and (8) in §19 transferor may designate successor custodian.

Uniform Securities Ownership by Minors Act not adopted.

Adoption.—See topic Adoption.

Uniform Child Custody Jurisdiction Act adopted. See topic Dissolution of Marriage, subhead Custody.

MARRIAGE:

Persons of age 18 or over may marry without consent of parent or guardian. (750-5/203).

Consent Required.—Where person is of age 16 but under age 18, parent or guardian must consent. (750-5/203).

License issued by county clerk of county where marriage is to take place is required. Both applicants must appear in person with satisfactory proof each party will have attained age 18 at time license is to be effective or have attained age 16 and obtained proper consent and proof that marriage is not prohibited. (750-5/203). All persons applying for marriage license shall be provided with brochure concerning sexually transmitted diseases and inherited metabolic diseases. (750-5/204). Any judge of circuit court in county in which license is to be issued may waive medical examination and tests if satisfied that same will offend applicants' religious tenets or practices. (750-5/205). Court has power to order issuance of license to underaged applicant aged 16 or 17 who has no parent capable of consenting to marriage or whose parent has not consented. (750-5/208). Any person who violates Part II of Act (dealing with licensing and solemnization of marriages) is guilty of Class B misdemeanor. (750-5/215).

Waiting Period.—License to marry becomes effective one day after date issued (unless court orders it effective when issued) and expires 60 days after it becomes effective. (750-5/207).

Ceremony may be performed by judge of court of record, county clerk in counties having 2,000,000 or more inhabitants, public official with power to marry, or in accordance with prescriptions of any religious denomination or Indian Nation or Tribe. (750-5/209).

Reports of Marriages.—Person performing marriage, or if no individual acting alone performed marriage, both parties to marriage must complete marriage certificate form and forward same to county clerk within ten days after marriage. (750-5/209[a]).

Record.—See category Documents and Records, topic Records, subhead Marriages, Divorces and Annulments.

Common law marriages contracted in Illinois after June 30, 1905 are invalid. (750-5/214).

Prohibited Marriages.—Marriages between parent and child, grandparent and grandchild, brother and sister (half blood included), uncle and niece, aunt and nephew, and first cousins (half blood included) under 50 years of age, marriages entered into prior to dissolution of earlier marriage of one of parties, and marriage between two individuals of same sex are prohibited. (750-5/212). Parties to marriage prohibited because marriage entered into prior to dissolution of earlier marriage of one of parties, who cohabit after impediment is removed are lawfully married as of date of removal of impediment. Children born or adopted of prohibited or common law marriage are legitimate. (750-5/212). If resident of Illinois contracts in another state marriage prohibited in Illinois, such marriage shall be null and void in Illinois. (750-5/216).

Annulment.—Court may enter judgment declaring invalidity of marriage (formerly known as annulment) on grounds of lack of capacity to consent to marriage, incapability to consummate marriage by sexual intercourse, underaged party lacking parental consent, or marriage prohibited by this statute. (750-5/301). Children born of marriage declared invalid are legitimate. (750-5/303).

Action for Breach of Promise.—Actual damages only are recoverable; no punitive, exemplary, vindictive or aggravated damages allowed. (740-15/1, 15/2, 15/3). Such actions must be brought within one year after cause accrued (740-15/6) and will be dismissed unless notice of intent to sue was given within three months after breach (740-15/5).

Court Ordered Marriages.—Persons of age 16 and 17 may receive license and marry on presentation of court order. (750-5/208).

Injunction Against Abortion.—Court may issue injunction against performing abortion upon finding that interests of husband in preventing abortion outweigh those of wife in having abortion performed after unborn child is viable, but only where court makes finding that mother's life or physical health are not in danger. (735-5/11-107.1).

MARRIED WOMEN:

See topics Husband and Wife, Marriage; categories Civil Actions and Procedure, topic Evidence, subhead Witnesses; Debtor and Creditor, topic Homesteads; Documents and Records, topic Acknowledgments; Estates and Trusts, topics Executors and Administrators, Wills; Property, topic Dower.

SEPARATE MAINTENANCE:

See topic Dissolution of Marriage.

INSURANCE

INSURANCE COMPANIES:

Regulated generally by Illinois Insurance Code (215-5/1 to 140/1) and regulations. Following provisions are repealed effective Dec. 31, 1992 (5-80/4.13): domestic stock companies (215-5/6 to 5/35.1); domestic mutual companies (215-5/36 to 5/60); reciprocals (215-5/61 to 5/85); Lloyds (215-5/86 to 5/107); unauthorized companies (215-5/121-1 to 5/121-19); advisory organizations (215-5/123A-1-123A-15); fraternal benefit societies (215-5/245.21 to 5/245.62). Specific provisions of Illinois Insurance Code should be consulted in connection with holding companies and certain acquisitions (215-5/131.1 to 5/131.28), not-for-profit organizations (215-5/245.2), cancellation, nonrenewal, or refusal to issue insurance policies (215-5/141.01, 5/143.10 to 5/143.26 & 5/155.22), uninsured motor vehicle policies (215-5/143a), motor vehicle theft and insurance fraud (215-5/155.24), limitation of risk (215-5/144, 5/144.1), improper claims practice procedures (215-5/154.5 to 5/155), claims for excessive charges (720-325/1), merger, consolidation or plans of exchange (215-5/156 to 5/172), reinsurance (215-5/173 to 5/179), rehabilitation, liquidation, conservation and dissolution (215-5/180 to 5/221.13), credit life and credit accident and health insurance (215-5/155.51 to 5/155.65), legal reserve life insurance (215-5/222 to 5/245.1, 215-5/245.21 to 5/245.62), group life insurance (215-5/230.1 to 5/231.1), assessment legal reserve life companies (215-5/274 to 5/281.1), fraternal benefit societies (215-5/282.1 to 5/314.1, 215-5/245.21 to 5/245.62), mutual benefit associations (215-5/316 to 5/337), burial societies (215-5/338 to 5/351), accident and health insurance (215-5/351A1 to 5/370d), fibrocystic breast conditions coverage (215-5/356m, 215-125/4-16), infertility coverage (215-5/356m), family life insurance coverage of newborn children (215-5/356c), breast implant removal coverage (215-5/356p), group accident and health insurance (215-5/367), continuation of existing group accident and health coverage after involuntary termination of employment (215-5/367.1), municipal group accident and health insurance (40-5/7-199.1), continuance of insurance for municipal employees (215-5/367i), casualty insurance, fidelity bonds and surety companies (215-5/378 to 5/392.1), fire and marine insurance (215-5/393 to 5/400.1), cancellation of fire and marine insurance (215-5/143.20a), unfair methods of competition (215-5/423 to 5/431), premium finance companies (215-5/513al to 5/513a12), urban property insurance (215-5/522 to 5/530), legal expense insurance (215-5/900 to 5/906), insurance guaranty fund (215-5/532 to 5/553), group vehicle insurance (215-5/388a to 5/388g), group professional liability insurance (215-5/393a to 5/393g), life and health insurance guaranty association (215-5/531.01 to 5/531.19), patients' compensation fund (215-5/700 to 5/715), property line loss information (215-145/0.1 to 140/1), earthquake coverage (215-5/143.21c), Insurance Exchange (215-5/107.01 to 5/107.27), mine subsidence insurance (215-5/801.1 to 803.1), comprehensive health insurance plan (215-105/1 to 105/14), registration of policies and deposit of reserves (215-5/246 to 5/253), separate accounts (215-5/245.21 to 5/245.62), risk retention for banking associations (215-5/531.01), condominium risk-pooling (765-605/12.1), municipal insurance availability program (65-5/11-152-1). Statutes other than Illinois Insurance Code govern district, township and county mutual companies (215-120/1 et seq.), insurance of titles to real estate (215-155/3), health maintenance organizations (215-125/1-1 to 125/5-9), including continuation of Group HMO coverage after termination of employment (215-125/4-9.2), property subject to bailment contract (765-1015/1 to 1015/4), voluntary health service plans (215-165/1 to 165/30), long term care (320–35/1), HIV coverage (305-5/5-17), vision service plans (215-165/21 to 160/31), dental service plans (215-165/10, 215-110/1 to 110/46), State Employees Group Insurance (5-375/1 to 375/17), and pharmaceutical service plans (215-135/1 to 135/45).

Supervision by Director of Insurance.—Director is charged with enforcement and execution of insurance laws. He has power to make rules and regulations, to conduct investigations and examinations (215-5/132.1 to 5/132.7), to hold hearings and to issue subpoenas and orders. His orders and decisions are subject to judicial review. (215-5/401 to 5/407.2). Jurisdiction of Insurance Department over entities supplying insurance coverage in Illinois presumed unless otherwise shown. (215-5/122-1).

Rates.—Workers' compensation and employer's liability rates. (215-5/454 to 5/471). (See category Employment, topic Labor Relations.) Property and casualty rates. (215-5/472.1 to 5/488.1).

Annual Statements.—Insurance companies must file annual statement with Director of Insurance. (215-5/136, 5/155.25, 5/223[1a], 140/1).

Claims Reporting.—Director of Insurance can issue rules requiring insurance companies to report information concerning casualty and property claims. (215-5/155.23).

See note at head of Digest as to 1998 legislation covered.

See Topical Index in front part of this volume.

IL – 65

INSURANCE COMPANIES ... *continued*
Director of Insurance shall issue rules requiring medical liability insurers to report information concerning experience in this state. (215-5/155.25).

Policies.—Policy forms regulated generally by 215-5/143 to 5/143.11 and, in some instances, by certain sections cited under subhead Regulated Generally By, supra.

Discrimination is prohibited by 215-5/236, 5/364, 5/356g, 5/368h, 5/424. See also various cancellation provisions, supra.

Privacy Protection.—Collection of information from insured and disclosure of information regulated. Insured allowed access to information collected for purposes of correction. (215-5/1001 to 5/1024).

Rebates.—Payment or acceptance prohibited except nothing prevents company from offering child passenger restraint system or discount on restraint system purchase price to policyholders. (215-5/151). Penalties. (215-5/152).

Agents and Brokers.—Now regulated as "insurance producers, limited insurance representatives and registered firms" article of Code. (215-5/490.1 through 5/511.1 and 215-5/141 to 5/141.1).

Process Agent.—Nonresident agents and brokers and foreign and alien insurance companies must appoint Director as attorney to accept service of process and service upon any such agent, broker or foreign or alien insurance company may be made upon Director. (215-5/497.1, 5/112). Principal place of business of domestic stock companies and domestic mutual companies must be located within Illinois, unless Director approves otherwise. (215-5/8, 5/38). Principal office of attorney-in-fact of domestic reciprocal and domestic Lloyds must be maintained in Illinois. (215-5/64, 5/89). Attorney-in-fact of each domestic, foreign and alien reciprocal and Lloyds transacting business in Illinois must appoint Director of Insurance as attorney to accept service of process and service of process may be made on any reciprocal or Lloyds by service upon its attorney-in-fact or by service upon Director. (215-5/77, 5/105). Domestic, foreign and alien fraternal benefit societies and mutual benefit societies transacting business in Illinois must appoint Director as attorney to accept service of process and service upon any such fraternal benefit society or mutual benefit society may be made upon Director. (215-5/315.2, 5/321). Service of process on company not authorized to do business in Illinois may be made, under certain circumstances, by serving Director or by serving persons acting for company within Illinois. Act subjects to jurisdiction of Director of Insurance and to jurisdiction of courts of Illinois insurers not authorized to transact business in Illinois which place or send into Illinois false advertising designed to induce Illinois residents to purchase insurance from such insurers. (215-5/123, 215-5/123.1). Filing of statement required for acquisition of control or merger with domestic company subjects filer to jurisdiction of Illinois courts and constitutes appointment of Director as attorney to accept service. (215-5/131.12).

Investments.—Regulated by 5/131.2 & 5/131.3.

Insurance Exchange.—Regulated by 215-5/107.01 to 5/107.27.

Foreign Insurance Companies.—Regulated by 215-5/118 to 5/120. Foreign or alien insurance company applying for certificate of authority to transact business in Illinois must file application with Director. (215-5/109). Supporting documents, including articles of incorporation or power of attorney of attorney-in-fact (reciprocal or Lloyds), appointment of U.S. manager (alien companies), by-laws, appointment of Director as agent for service of process, financial statements in compliance with requirements for annual statement, report of examination and certificate of authority from official of state of incorporation, must be delivered to Director with application. (215-5/110). Applicant must satisfy Director that its funds invested in accordance with laws of its domicile and in securities or property which afford degree of financial security equal to that required of domestic companies and that it meets capital, surplus and/or contingent liability requirements of domestic companies. (215-5/111). Applicant must deposit with Director securities in amount required to be deposited by domestic companies or certificate of deposit from official of another state certifying that such company has deposited like amount of securities with such official. (215-5/111). Director shall renew annually certificate of authority of foreign or alien company if he is satisfied that grounds for revoking such certificate of authority do not exist (215-5/119) and that company is complying with conditions for admission (215-5/114). Unauthorized foreign and alien companies regulated by 215-5/121 to 5/123.1. Any foreign or alien company admitted to do business in Illinois may withdraw from Illinois by filing statement of withdrawal with Director. (215-5/118).

Retaliatory Laws.—Whenever laws of foreign state or country require, as condition precedent to qualification of Illinois insurance companies to do business in such jurisdiction, compliance with laws which are more burdensome than those imposed by Illinois on foreign and alien companies or require larger deposit of securities than required by Illinois or otherwise require of Illinois insurance companies or their agents or brokers higher penalties, fees, charges or taxes than imposed by Illinois on foreign or alien companies and their agents and brokers, then such more burdensome laws, requirement of larger deposit and higher penalties, fees, charges or taxes shall apply to foreign or alien companies incorporated in such jurisdiction and doing business in Illinois and their agents and brokers. (215-5/444).

Premium or Privilege Taxes.—Fees, charges and taxes regulated by 215-5/408 to 5/415. Every foreign and alien company, and every domestic company unless it maintains in Illinois its principal place of business and officers and personnel knowledgeable of and responsible for its operations, books, records, administration and annual statement and conducts in Illinois substantially all of its underwriting, policy issuing and serving operations relating to Illinois business is required to pay privilege tax equal to 2% of its net taxable premium income on direct business covering risks in Illinois. (215-5/409).

Direct Actions Against Insurer.—Liability policies must contain provision that injured party or his representative may maintain action against insured's insurance company if execution against insured is returned unsatisfied. (215-5/388). Limitation period tolled from date proof of loss filed until date claim denied. (215-5/143.1).

No-Fault Auto Insurance.—None. Statute repealed.

Insurance Holding Company Systems regulated by 215-5/131.1 to 5/131.28.

Political Contributions.—See category Business Organizations, topic Corporations, subhead Political Contributions.

SURETY AND GUARANTY COMPANIES:

Director of Insurance has jurisdiction over surety and guaranty companies and they are governed generally by Insurance Code. For specific provisions, see 215-5/378 through 5/392.1. See topic Insurance Companies.

Rights and Powers.—Unearned premium and loss reserve must be maintained. (215-5/378, 5/379.1). Bonds and guaranties of surety and guaranty company satisfy legal requirement of bond and guaranty. Two or more companies may execute bond and guaranty assuming pro rata liability. (215-5/390). Trustee may have corporate surety. (215-5/391). Surety bond may be deposited with court in lieu of appeal bond to stay execution pending appeal. (215-5/392.1).

INTELLECTUAL PROPERTY
TRADEMARKS AND TRADENAMES:

Acquired by prior, exclusive appropriation and continuing use by person or entity of distinctive name, word, character, device, label, brand, seal, or like identifying source of origin.

What May be Used.—Mark may not be registered if immoral, scandalous or deceptive, disparaging of or falsely suggesting connection with persons or beliefs, consisting of flag of country or state, consisting of name, signature or portrait of nonconsenting living individual, or confusingly similar to another's mark. (765-1036/10). Merely descriptive, deceptively misdescriptive, primarily geographically descriptive or misdescriptive marks or primarily merely surnames not registrable unless mark has become distinctive of applicant's goods or services. (765-1036/10).

Registration.—Trademarks adopted and used to identify goods made, sold, produced or distributed and service marks adopted and used to identify services rendered may be registered with Secretary of State. Filing fee of $10. Application must set forth description of mark, goods and services to which mark applies, mode or manner in which mark is being used, classes of goods or services (765-1036/50), date applicant first used mark in Illinois and elsewhere, and owner's statement he believes he owns mark. Application must be accompanied by specimen or facsimile of mark in triplicate. (765-1036/15). Upon compliance with Act certificate of registration is issued. (765-1036/25). Secretary's decisions on registration are subject to judicial review. (765-1035/5).

Duration and Renewal.—Registration of mark is effective for five-year term subject to renewal for successive five-year periods 60 days prior to end of term. Renewal application must have affidavit by registrant that mark is still used in Illinois or excusing nonuse in Illinois. Notice before expiration is furnished by Secretary of State. Renewal fee is $5. (765-1036/30).

Assignment of marks must be in writing and recorded with Secretary of State for $5 fee, and new certificate of registration will issue. Assignment void as to subsequent purchaser for valuable consideration without notice unless recorded with Secretary of State within three months or prior to such subsequent purchase. (765-1036/35).

Protection Afforded.—Certificate of registration admissible as evidence of registration of mark. (765-1036/15). Registrant may proceed by suit to seek injunction and to acquire profits and/or damages suffered by reason of acts enumerated in 765-1036/60 and to compel destruction of reproductions, counterfeits, copies, etc. under control of defendant. (765-1036/70). Common law rights preserved. (765-1036/80).

Cancellation of Registration.—Secretary of State may cancel a registration (a) for failure to renew ten-year old marks registered under prior acts, (b) upon request of registrant, (c) failure to renew and (d) pursuant to a judgment of a court of competent jurisdiction.

Action to cancel mark may be brought in circuit court on grounds that (1) mark has been abandoned, (2) registrant is not owner of mark, (3) registration was granted contrary to Act, (4) registration was obtained fraudulently, (5) mark is so similar to a mark registered in U.S. Patent Office or in Illinois as to be likely to cause confusion or mistake or to deceive, and (6) mark is generic name for goods or services for which it has been registered. (765-1036/45).

Infringement.—Civil action available to registrant for injunction and recovery of profits and damages for another's use of copy or colorable imitation of registered mark in sale, offering for sale, or advertising goods or services if likely to cause confusion or mistake or to deceive as to source of origin; if copy or colorable imitation applied to labels, signs, prints, etc. intended to be used on goods, injunctive relief available, but registrant may recover profits and damages only if use is knowing and intended to cause confusion, mistake or to deceive. (765-1035/12, 1035/13).

Person adopting and using trademark, tradename or service mark may sue to enjoin subsequent use by another of same or similar mark or name if there is likelihood of injury to business reputation or dilution of distinctive quality of mark or name, even in absence of competition or confusion as to source of goods or services. (765-1036/65).

Fair use of famous mark by another person in comparative commercial advertising or promotion to identify competing goods or services; noncommercial use of mark and all forms of news reporting and news commentary are not actionable. (765-1036/65[b]).

Fair Trade Act.—Illinois Fair Trade Act repealed Aug. 4, 1977. (P.A. 80-233).

Deceptive Trade Practices.—The Uniform Deceptive Trade Practices Act has been adopted. (815-510/1 to 510/7). See category Business Regulation and Commerce, topic Monopolies, Restraint of Trade and Competition. Consumer Fraud and Deceptive Business Practices Act (815-505/1 to 505/12) grants damaged consumers relief for damage suffered through unfair methods of competition and unfair or deceptive acts, including violations of Uniform Deceptive Trade Practices Act. See category Business Regulation and Commerce, topics Monopolies Restraint of Trade and Competition, Consumer Protection, and Sales.

Tradenames.—Assumed business names or designations, if other than real names of individuals owning or conducting such business, must be registered before commencing

See note at head of Digest as to 1998 legislation covered.

See Topical Index in front part of this volume.

TRADEMARKS AND TRADENAMES . . . *continued*

business. Certificate must be filed with County Clerk of county in which business is to be conducted and county of each new or additional place of business setting forth assumed name, business address, true names and post office addresses of all proprietors, and must be duly acknowledged by persons intending to conduct such business. Notice of certificate filing must be published in newspaper of general circulation in filing county once a week for three consecutive weeks commencing within ten days of filing. Certificate void unless proof of publication filed with clerk within 50 days of certificate filing. (805-405/1). Indexing and filing fee $2.50. (805-405/3). Filing requirement inapplicable to corporations, limited liability companies, limited partnerships, and limited liability partnerships, trusts created by written instruments or partnerships using names of all partners. (805-405/4). Use of words Army, Navy, etc. in name of mercantile establishment prohibited. (720-230/1). Persons not complying with Act are subject to fine and imprisonment (805-405/5, 720-230/2) and may be sued under assumed name (805-405/6). For corporate name regulations, see category Business Organizations, topic Corporations.

TRADE SECRETS:

Uniform Trade Secrets Act adopted, with slight variations, effective Jan. 1, 1988. (765-1065/1 to 1065/9). "Trade secret" includes financial data and lists of actual or potential suppliers or customers. (765-1065/2[d]). Limitations is five years. (765-1065/7).

LEGAL PROFESSION

ATTORNEYS AND COUNSELORS:

The bar of Illinois is not integrated.

Jurisdiction over Admission.—By statute licenses to practice may be obtained from Supreme Court. (705-205/1). By Supreme Court Rule, jurisdiction over admission to bar is vested in Board of Law Examiners. (Ill. S. Ct. 701). Supreme Court has held that power to prescribe qualifications for admission to Bar is judicial and not legislative. (66 Ill.2d 398, 362 N.E.2d 1047).

Eligibility.—Persons may be admitted to practice if they are U. S. citizens, have declared intention to become citizens or have applied for naturalization within 30 days after becoming eligible to do so (705-205/2), are 21 years of age, of good moral character, have satisfactorily passed examination before Board of Law Examiners and, effective July 1, 1981, have satisfactorily passed professional responsibility examination—all subject, however, to certain conditions and requirements hereinafter described. (Ill. S. Ct. 701).

Registration as Law Student.—No registration requirement.

Educational Requirements.—Applicant must have graduated from four-year high school or preparatory school and must have satisfactorily completed at least 90 semester hours at college or university approved by Board of Law Examiners. In lieu of such college or preliminary work, Board may accept satisfactory completion of program or curriculum of particular college or university. (Ill. S. Ct. 703). Applicant must have pursued course of law studies and received first degree in law from A.B.A. approved school. (Ill. S. Ct. 703).

Petition for Admission.—Any person who meets educational requirements and pays required fee may make application for admission on examination provided, however, that following must first receive certification from Committee on Character and Fitness: Individuals who (1) have been convicted of felonies or misdemeanors involving moral turpitude or have indictments or complaints charging same pending against them; (2) were rejected in another jurisdiction on character and fitness grounds; or (3) have been reprimanded, censured, disciplined, suspended or disbarred in another jurisdiction or have such charges or proceedings pending against them. (Ill. S. Ct. 704, 706).

Examination.—Form of application prescribed by Board; must be accompanied by proof of educational qualifications and proof applicant meets other statutory requirements. (Ill. S. Ct. 704).

Academic and professional responsibility examinations are held separately. Academic examination held semiannually at times determined by Board, generally Feb. and late July; professional responsibility examination held tri-annually in Mar., Aug., and Oct. Both examinations conducted under supervision of Board, academic by uniform printed questions on subjects listed below, professional responsibility either by uniform printed questions on Ill. Code of Prof. Resp. or by Multistate Professional Responsibility Examination, as Board designates. Academic examinations may cover subjects of administrative law, agency, business organizations, commercial paper, conflict of laws, contracts, criminal law and procedure, domestic relations, equity jurisprudence including trusts and mortgages, evidence, federal and state constitutional law, federal jurisdiction and procedure, federal taxation, Illinois procedure, personal property including sales and bailments, real property, suretyship, torts, and wills and administration of estates. (Ill. S. Ct. 704).

Applicant failing to pass first examination may take successive examinations provided he furnishes Board satisfactory evidence of diligent study of law subsequent to prior examination. After fifth examination failure, permission of Board or Supreme Court is required before admission to another examination. (Ill. S. Ct. 704).

Clerkship.—No requirement that applicant serve clerkship before admission.

Admission Without Examination.—Attorney licensed to practice in highest court of any other state, U.S. territory or District of Columbia, may apply for admission to Illinois bar without taking written examination provided that certain criteria are met. One of requirements is that jurisdiction from which applicant is applying grants reciprocal admission to Illinois attorneys. (Ill. S. Ct. 705).

Fees Required of Applicants for Admission.—$150 on application for examination for admission; $400 on application for admission on foreign license. (Ill. S. Ct. 706).

Character and Fitness Requirements.—Before admission, applicant must be passed on by Character and Fitness Committee in his District as to his character and moral fitness. Applicant must furnish Committee with affidavit, in form prescribed by Board, concerning applicant's history. Applicant must appear before Committee of his District or member thereof. (Ill. S. Ct. 708).

Admission Pro Hac Vice.—Under statute (705-205/12) attorney residing in another state may practice in courts of this state on same terms that attorneys residing in this state may practice in such other state; and Supreme Court Rule provides that attorney from another jurisdiction in U.S. or foreign country may, in discretion of any court of record, be permitted to participate before such court in trial or argument of particular cause (Ill. S. Ct. 707).

Group Legal Services.—No attorney shall participate in plan that provides group legal services unless plan is registered with Administration of Attorney Registration and Disciplinary Commission. (Ill. S. Ct. 730).

Licenses.—No one may practice law without obtaining license from Supreme Court. No person shall be granted license or renewal who has defaulted on educational loan guaranteed by Illinois Student Assistance Commission or who is more than 30 days delinquent in child support order unless person has established satisfactory repayment record. (705-205/1). Annual fees are required (Ill. S. Ct. 756), but see subhead Disbarment or Suspension, infra.

Lien.—Attorney has lien on claim or cause of action placed in his hands for collection or suit, or upon which suit instituted, for agreed fee or, in absence of agreement, for reasonable fee, provided he serves written notice of his claim of lien. Service by registered or certified mail is sufficient. (770-5/1).

Privileges.—Attorneys are privileged from arrest while attending, going to or returning from court. (705-205/9).

Disabilities.—No attorney shall post bail or act as surety in any criminal action or proceeding. (725-5/110-13).

Liabilities.—See category Civil Actions and Procedure, topic Costs.

Attorney Ethics.—American Bar Association Rules of Professional conduct modified in certain respects, is in effect. (Ill. S. Ct. Art. VIII).

Disbarment or Suspension.—Conduct which violates Illinois Code of Professional Responsibility, defeats administration of justice or brings courts or profession into disrepute is ground for discipline by Supreme Court including disbarment, disbarment on consent, suspension for specified time or censure. (Ill. S. Ct. 771; Ill. S. Ct. 1-101 to 9-102). Procedures for investigation, hearing, review, and reinstatement set forth in Rules of Attorney Registration and Disciplinary Commission.

Disciplinary proceedings affecting members of Illinois Bar are under administrative supervision of Attorney Registration & Disciplinary Commission (Ill. S. Ct. 751) and Administrator (Ill. S. Ct. 752). Commission appoints members of subordinate Inquiry and Hearing Boards pursuant to statute. (Ill. S. Ct. 752, 753). Inquiry and Hearing Boards empowered to take and transcribe evidence of witnesses and cause issuance of subpoenas. (Ill. S. Ct. 754). Burden of proving misconduct is on accusers. (64 Ill.2d 407, 356 N.E.2d 333).

If attorney licensed in Illinois and another state is disciplined in foreign state, he may upon proof of order be subjected to concurrent discipline in Illinois after specified notice and hearing. (Ill. S. Ct. 763).

With certain exceptions, every attorney admitted to practice law in Illinois must pay annual registration fee to Disciplinary Commission. No fee required of members of Bar for less than one year; $70 annual fee required of members of Bar for more than one but less than three years; $140 annual fee is required of members of Bar for more than three years. (Ill. S. Ct. 756).

Justices of Supreme Court may at their discretion strike name of any attorney from roll of attorneys for misconduct. Any judge of Circuit Court may for like cause suspend any attorney from practice in court over which he presides for such time as he deems proper. (705-205/6). If person's name is stricken from roll of attorneys, he may petition for reinstatement by filing with Clerk of Supreme Court and depositing $500 against costs of investigation. Petition may not be made sooner than five years after order of disbarment, three years after disbarment on consent, two years after denial of prior petition, or one year after order allowing withdrawal of prior petition. (Ill. S. Ct. 767). Burden of proving rehabilitation is on petitioner (64 Ill.2d 407, 356 N.E.2d 333), who must establish rehabilitation by clear and convincing evidence (77 Ill.2d 155, 395 N.E.2d 571).

When attorney refuses or neglects on demand and tender of reasonable fees and expenses to pay over or deliver client's money or property to client, any person interested may apply to Supreme Court for rule on attorney to show cause why name should not be stricken from roll. (705-205/7).

Solicitation.—Contract of employment of attorney is void if obtained as result of solicitation by non-attorney of claim for personal injuries or death. (705-210/3).

Unauthorized Practice.—Only licensed attorneys may receive fees for legal services. Violation subjects offender to contempt of court proceeding. (705-205/1). Unauthorized practice may be enjoined. (59 Ill. App.3d 560, 375 N.E.2d 871).

No coroner, sheriff or deputy sheriff may practice law in the county in which he is commissioned. No clerk or deputy clerk of a court may practice before that court. (705-205/10).

Law students and recent graduates may, under certain circumstances, perform certain specified tasks. (Ill. S. Ct. 711).

Professional Associations.—See category Business Organizations, topic Associations, subhead Professional Associations.

Professional Corporations.—See category Business Organizations, topic Corporations, subhead Professional Service Corporations.

See note at head of Digest as to 1998 legislation covered.

See Topical Index in front part of this volume.

IL – 67

MINERAL, WATER AND FISHING RIGHTS

MINES AND MINERALS:

Mining Board of Department of Natural Resources administers Coal Mining Act. (225-705/2.01). Mineral mining regulated by Mines-inspection Act. (225-110/1). Surface mining regulated by Surface Coal Mining Land Conservation and Reclamation Act. (225-720/1.01).

Operation of Mines.—Coal Mining Act is comprehensive and deals with mine safety, including regulation and inspection, operation, employment requirements, standards for construction and equipment, and use of explosives. Mining Board of Department of Natural Resources adopts rules to promote health and safety of mine workers. (225-705/2.12). Director of Office of Mines and Minerals appoints inspectors under Mines-inspection Act, and each mine operator must make monthly reports. (225-710/2.01 to 710/6.01).

Mine operators and workers must observe detailed rules governing mine operations, and failure is misdemeanor. (225-705/36.01). Serious violations are subject to criminal prosecution. (225-710/16).

Miners and laborers in coal mines have lien on real and personal property of owner used in operating coal mine. (770-65/1).

Safeguarding of Employees.—Coal Mining Act and Mines-inspection Act contain detailed safety rules applicable to mine work.

Inspection of Mines.—Certified mine examiner is required at each mine, and examiner must conduct inspections required by statute. (225-705/6.01 to 705/6.16).

Taxes.—Statute governs valuation of real property on which coal mine is located. (35-205/20).

Oil and Gas.—Oil and gas drilling regulated by Oil and Gas Act (225-725/1), and Department of Natural Resources adopts rules (225-725/3). Act also establishes rules for leases of public lands for exploration and extraction (5-615/22) and plugging and restoration (225-730/1). Other statutes involving oil and gas pertain to abandonment (765-515/1) and administration of decedents' estates (755-5/20-20). Contractor or subcontractor furnishing labor or materials for drilling operations for oil or gas has lien on land, leaseholds, machinery and oil or gas products. (770-70/2).

MORTGAGES

CHATTEL MORTGAGES:

Uniform Commercial Code, Article 9, replaced chattel mortgage statutes effective July 2, 1962. 1972 Official Text was enacted, effective July 1, 1973. See category Business Regulation and Commerce, topic Commercial Code.

For forms see end of this Digest.

COLLATERAL SECURITY:

This subject is covered comprehensively by Art. 9 of Uniform Commercial Code.

MORTGAGES OF PERSONAL PROPERTY:

See topic Chattel Mortgages; category Business Regulation and Commerce, topic Commercial Code.

MORTGAGES OF REAL PROPERTY:

Mortgages and trust deeds are made and acknowledged like deeds, and requirements concerning release of homestead are same.

Execution.—Execution may be proved by secondary evidence without producing or accounting for the absence of subscribing witnesses. (735-5/8-1601).

Trust deeds are extensively used in the place of mortgages.

Reverse Mortgages.—Bank, savings and loan association or credit union may make "reverse mortgages" on basis of existing equity in homestead property. Mortgagee may add deferred interest to principal or provide for interest on interest. (205-5/5a, 105/1-6a, 305/46). Additional provisions made for nonrecourse reverse mortgage loans available only to homeowners who are at least 62 years of age. (205-5/5b).

Revolving Credit Loans.—Banks, savings and loan associations or credit unions may make revolving credit loans secured by mortgages or deeds of trust on real property or by security assignments of beneficial interest in land trusts. Lien arising thereunder includes existing indebtedness and such future advances as are made within 20 years from date thereof. (205-5/5d, 105/1-6a, 305/46, 205/4.1).

Recording.—In order to be effective against creditors of mortgagor and subsequent purchasers from him without notice, mortgage must be recorded in office of recorder of deeds of county where real estate is situated. No deed, mortgage, assignment of mortgage, or other instrument affecting title to real estate may include provision prohibiting recording and any such provision in instrument signed after July 19, 1995 is void and of no effect. (765-5/28, 5/30).

Recording Fees.—Fees of recorder of deeds (which must be paid in advance) for recording real estate mortgages and trust deeds are same as those for deeds. See category Documents and Records, topic Records.

Taxes on realty are normally paid into escrow by mortgagor. Absent agreement, no interest is due to mortgagor on such funds. (1 Ill.App.3d 621, 275 N.E.2d 300).

Future Advances.—The lien includes all moneys thereafter advanced or applied on account of the principal indebtedness or authorized to be advanced by the provisions of the mortgage or by law; but as to subsequent purchasers and judgment creditors the mortgage is, as to moneys advanced or applied on account of the principal indebtedness, a lien only from the time such moneys are advanced or applied, unless such advancement or application occurs within 18 months of the date of recordation, or unless the mortgagee is required by contract to make it. (765-5/39). Future advances clauses must set upward limit to be advanced or lose protection. (48 Ill.App.3d 82, 365 N.E.2d 382).

Rights of Junior Mortgagee.—Mortgagee of land against which prior mortgage exists may pay prior mortgage defaults of principal or interest, and such payments become part of debt secured by his junior mortgage and bear interest from date of payment at same rate as prior mortgage indebtedness, and are collectible with, as a part of, and in the same manner as the amount secured by the junior mortgage. (765-905/13).

Assignment.—Mortgagee may assign his interest.

Release and satisfaction of mortgage or trust deed in nature of mortgage may be made by release deed, executed by mortgagee, trustee or his executor, administrator, heirs or assignee of record and acknowledged, and delivering same to mortgagor or grantor, his heirs, legal representatives or assigns. If delivered to mortgagor or grantor, it must have imprinted on its face in bold letters at least 1/4 inch in height following:

"FOR THE PROTECTION OF THE OWNER, THIS RELEASE SHALL BE FILED WITH THE RECORDER OR THE REGISTRAR OF TITLES IN WHOSE OFFICE THE MORTGAGE OR DEED OF TRUST WAS FILED." (765-905/2).

If any mortgagee or trustee, in deed in nature of mortgage, of real property, or his executor or administrator, heirs or assigns, knowing same to be paid, shall not, within one month after payment of debt secured by such mortgage or trust deed, comply with requirements of 905/2, he shall, for every such offense, be liable to pay to party aggrieved sum of $200 which may be recovered by party aggrieved in a civil action, together with reasonable attorney's fees. In any such action, introduction of loan payment book or receipt which indicates that obligation has been paid shall be sufficient evidence to raise presumption that obligation has been paid. Upon finding for party aggrieved, court shall order mortgagee or trustee, or his executor or administrator, heirs or assigns, to make, execute and deliver release as provided in 905/2. Successor in interest to mortgagee or trustee in deed in nature of mortgage shall not be liable for penalty prescribed in this section if he complies with requirements of 905/2 within one month after succeeding to interest. (765-905/4).

Note: New mortgage foreclosure law took effect July 1, 1987. (735-5/15-1101 to 5/15-1706).

New mortgage foreclosure law applies to: (1) Any mortgage created prior to or after July 1, 1987; (2) any real estate installment contract for residential real estate entered into on or after July 1, 1987 and under which (i) purchase price is to be paid in installments over period in excess of five years and (ii) amount unpaid under terms of contract at time of filing of foreclosure complaint is less than 80% of original purchase price of real estate as stated in contract; (3) any collateral assignment of beneficial interest made on or after July 1, 1987 (i) which is made with respect to land trust which was created contemporaneously with collateral assignment of beneficial interest, (ii) which is made pursuant to requirement of holder of obligation to secure payment of money or performance of other obligations and (iii) as to which security agreement or other writing creating collateral assignment permits real estate which is subject of land trust to be sold to satisfy obligations. (735-5/15-1106[a]). Contract seller may elect to enforce in foreclosure under new law under any other real estate installment contract entered into on or after July 1, 1987. (735-5/15-1106[c]).

Curing Default on Accelerated Maturity.—In case of mortgage executed after July 21, 1959, where entire principal sum has become due prior to fixed maturity date through acceleration because of default, mortgagor may, at any time prior to expiration of 90 days from date court obtains jurisdiction over mortgagor cure all existing defaults by paying principal amount due, including costs, expenses, attorneys' fees and other fees, excluding portion of principal which would not have been due in absence of acceleration. This relief may be granted only once every five years under any particular mortgage if court has made express written finding that mortgagor has exercised its right to reinstate. Judgment of foreclosure prior to expiration of reinstatement period is subject to mortgagor's right to reinstate mortgage. (735-5/15-1602; 765-905/7).

Foreclosure and Sale.—Power of sale is ineffective, and mortgages must be foreclosed in accordance with Mortgage Foreclosure Law. (735-5/15-1405). Common law remedy of strict foreclosure is still available in Illinois. (14 Ill. App.3d 68, 302 N.E.2d 248; 735-5/15-1403). Due on sale clauses are enforceable. (61 Ill.2d 119, 333 N.E.2d 1).

After default, mortgagor may agree with mortgagee to provide deed in lieu of foreclosure to terminate mortgagor's interest and relieve all personal liability by its acceptance. (735-5/15-1401).

Shortened redemption period ends at later of expiration of 90-day reinstatement period (735-5/15-1602) or 60 days after judgment entered if court: (i) Finds value of mortgaged real estate is less than 90% of specified amount and mortgagee waives right to deficiency judgment; or (ii) enters consent foreclosure judgment (735-5/15-1603[b]). If mortgaged real property was abandoned, redemption and reinstatement periods end 30 days after judgment. (735-5/15-1603).

A form of complaint is provided by statute (735-5/15-1504) and optional procedure for barring redemption rights of non-record claimants is also detailed (735-5/15-1502[c]). Under certain circumstances, court may empower mortgagee to take possession of property during foreclosure. (735-5/15-1701 to 5/15-1706).

Trial of foreclosure action must be in open court. No evidence is required in support of facts stated in verified complaint or if separate affidavit verifies allegations which are not controverted by verified answer or verified counterclaim or if response states no knowledge of allegations in complaint pursuant to 735-5/2-610. If none of such facts are controverted, plaintiff may have judgment on motion supported by affidavit stating amount due. (735-5/15-1506[a]).

Court may enter judgment satisfying mortgage indebtedness by vesting absolute title to mortgaged property in mortgagee, free of all claims of mortgagor, if owner of mortgaged property expressly consents thereto and if other conditions are met. (735-5/15-1402). In such event, mortgagor has later of 90-day reinstatement period (735-5/15-1602) or 60 days after judgment entered to redeem by paying judgment creditors amount due on mortgage with interest and costs (735-5/15-1603[b]). Subject to redemption rights of mortgagor, non-mortgagor party objecting to consent foreclosure may redeem within 30 days after judgment entered. (735-5/15-1402[b]).

Deficiency Judgment.—Personal judgment for deficiency against any party shall be entered if: (i) Otherwise authorized and (ii) to extent requested in complaint and proven. Entering and enforcement of deficiency judgment permitted only when personal service

MORTGAGES OF REAL PROPERTY . . . *continued*
made upon persons personally liable for mortgage indebtedness, unless appearance entered in foreclosure action. (735-5/15-1508[e]).

Redemption.—Except for consent foreclosures, only owner of redemption (i.e. mortgagor, other owner or co-owner of mortgaged premises) may redeem. (735-5/15-1603[a]). Residential real estate redemption period ends on later of: (i) Date seven months from date mortgagor served with summons or by publication or otherwise submitted to jurisdiction or (ii) date three months from date of entry of judgment. Redemption period for all other foreclosures ends on later of: (i) Date six months from date mortgagor served with summons or by publication or otherwise submitted to jurisdiction or (ii) date three months from date of judgment. (735-5/15-1603[b]). Shortened redemption period procedure described supra. Redemption period may be extended only by proper court stay order or by statute of U.S., as provided in 735-5/15-1603(c)(2). Amount required to redeem and procedure involved described in 735-5/15-1603(d-q).

Waiver.—Mortgagor of residential real estate or agricultural real estate may not waive mortgagor's rights of reinstatement and redemption. Domestic or licensed foreign corporation or any corporate trustee of any express trust when waiver is authorized by trust instrument or person having power of direction, who is mortgagor of agricultural real estate may waive redemption rights. Unless otherwise prohibited, mortgagors of nonresidential real estate may waive redemption rights. (735-5/15-1601).

Fairness in Lending.—Financial institution may not deny or vary loan terms without considering all regular and dependable income of each person liable for repayment of debt or because real estate offered as security is located in specific geographical area or by utilizing lending standards having no economic basis and which are discriminatory in effect. (815-120/1 to 815-120/5).

Statutory form is as follows (765-5/11):

Form

The mortgagor (here insert name or names), mortgages and warrants to (here name or names of mortgagee or mortgagees), to secure the payment of (here recite the nature and amount of indebtedness, showing when due and the rate of interest, and whether secured by note or otherwise), the following described real estate (here insert description thereof), situated in the County of . . . . in the State of Illinois.

Dated this . . . . day of . . . ., A.D., 19. . . . .

A.B. [L.S.]

Names of parties signing shall be typed or printed below signatures, and instrument shall have blank space 3 1/2 x 3 1/2 inches for recorder's use. Omission of these requirements will not affect validity of instrument.

PROPERTY

ABSENTEES:

There is no general provision affecting rights or liabilities of absentees or nonresidents. Particular provisions are digested under following categories/topics: categories Business Organizations, topic Corporations; Civil Actions and Procedure, topics Costs, Limitation of Actions, Process; Debtor and Creditor, topic Attachment; Estates and Trusts, topics Death, Executors and Administrators; Family, topic Husband and Wife; Transportation, topic Motor Vehicles.

Missing Persons in Armed Forces and Other Missing Persons.—The Circuit Court has jurisdiction to administer the estates of persons missing from their usual place of residence or reported missing while in military service. Upon issuance of letters testamentary or discovery of the missing person, the administrator's power ceases. (755-5/5-2, 5/10-1 through 5/10-5).

Escheat.—Uniform Disposition of Unclaimed Property Act is in effect. (765-1025/1 to 30). Act held unconstitutional in part but has since been amended. See category Business Regulation and Commerce, topic Banks and Banking, subhead Unclaimed Deposits.

Voting.—A qualified elector expecting to be absent from county of his residence on election day may, within statutorily prescribed time periods, apply for an absentee ballot. (10-5/19-1 through 5/20-15).

ADVERSE POSSESSION:

Duration and Character of Possession.—In general, open, adverse and uninterrupted possession for 20 years defeats legal title to real estate. (735-5/13-101). Right of entry accrues from date of wrongful ouster, death of prior owner where title derived as heir or devisee, or upon termination of prior estate where title derived from remainder interest. (735-5/13-106). Action to recover lands or entry thereon for breach of condition subsequent must occur within seven years of first breach. (735-5/13-102). Seven year limitation applies to actions by reason of termination of estates upon limitation or conditional limitation. (735-5/13-103). Limitations on actions for recovery of or entry on lands do not affect time for enforcement of any right under mortgage or lease. (735-5/13-104). Possession by actual residence for seven years under grant from public authority, such as sale for nonpayment of taxes or on execution, is sufficient; but if possessor gets color of title after possession, seven year period runs from date of title. (735-5/13-107). Bona fide claim and color of title, with possession and payment of taxes for seven successive years, gives legal title to extent of paper title. (735-5/13-109). Bona fide color of title to vacant land with payment of taxes for seven successive years gives legal title to extent of paper title except as to person having better paper title who during any one or more of such seven years pays taxes. (735-5/13-110). Adverse possession does not defeat title to real estate registered in Torrens system. (765-35/41).

Easement by prescription arises only if there is adverse, uninterrupted, exclusive, open, continuous use of land under claim of right for 20 years. (129 Ill. App.2d 45, 263 N.E.2d 356). No easement by prescription arises if owner posts notice that use permitted and subject to owner's control. (735-5/13-122).

Disabilities, etc.—Such payment of taxes (735-5/13-109, 110) of no aid in strengthening title against U.S. or State, or on lands held for religious or public use, or where adverse title is held by minor or person under legal disability, imprisoned, or out of limits of U.S. in employment of U.S. or State, provided person under such disability brings action within three years after termination of disability, or in case of vacant and unoccupied land pays to adverse possessor all taxes paid during disability with 12% interest (735-5/13-111). Adverse possession does not operate against minor or person under legal disability, or imprisoned or absent from U.S. in service of U.S. or Illinois, if action is brought within two years after removal of disability. (735-5/13-111, 112). Death of disabled person first entitled to bring action tolls statute for two years. (735-5/13-113).

Tacking.—Heirs, devisees, and assigns of adverse possessor have same benefits as person from whom they take title or possession. (735-5/13-108).

CONVEYANCES:

Livery of seizin unnecessary, but every conveyance must be signed and in writing. (765-5/1). Grantees may disclaim interests conveyed to them by delivering and recording written disclaimer within time set by statute. (760-25/1 et seq.). See topic Deeds.

CURTESY:

Abolished. (755-5/2-9). See topic Dower.

DEEDS:

See topic Real Property for types of estates.

Execution.—Deed must be signed by grantor. Grantor's marital status should appear in deed. It must be delivered and accepted. It should be properly acknowledged before notary public or other officer. Witness to execution is not required. Corporate seal should be affixed to corporate deed even if by-laws do not so require.

Curtesy and dower have been extinguished. (755-5/2-9).

To waive homestead, deed must expressly contain clause releasing or waiving such right. It must be acknowledged. (413 Ill. 204, 108 N.E.2d 438). No release or waiver of right of homestead unless spouse joins in execution of said deed. (765-5/27).

Names of parties signing conveyance, including witnesses, if any, and name of person taking acknowledgment, must be typed or printed below their signatures. There shall be 3 1/2" square blank space on each document for recorder's use. Name and address of owner to receive tax bills must be stated on conveyance. Metes and bounds description in conveyance must contain section, township and range with identifiable point of beginning. Subsequent courses must contain linear distances and direction values either by angular description or by bearing of one course relative to bearing of previous course, another described course or known point. Failure to comply with these requirements does not invalidate instrument. (765-5/35c). However, it may furnish basis for refusal by county recorder to record.

See topic Real Property, subheads Foreign Conveyances or Encumbrances, and Land Trust; categories Debtor and Creditor, topic Homesteads, subhead Conveyance; Family, topic Husband and Wife, subhead Conveyance or Encumbrance of Property.

Risk of Loss.—Uniform Vendor and Purchaser Risk Act adopted. Unless contract provides otherwise, risk of loss is on vendor until either legal title or possession is transferred. (765-65/1).

Recording.—Deeds, mortgages and other instruments of writing relating to real estate shall be deemed, from time of being filed for record, notice to subsequent purchasers and creditors, though not acknowledged or proven according to law; but same shall not be read as evidence, unless their execution be proved in manner required by rules of evidence applicable to such writings, so as to supply defects of such acknowledgment or proof. (765-5/31).

No deed transferring title to real estate may be recorded unless and until name and address of grantee appears on its face. (55-5/3-5026). In counties with 3,000,000 or more inhabitants, no deed or assignment of beneficial interest in land trust transferring title to real estate in transaction which is exempt from filing real estate transfer declaration may be recorded unless deed or assignment of beneficial interest is accompanied by: (1) sworn statement executed by grantor or his agent stating that name of grantee shown on deed or assignment of beneficial interest is either natural person, Illinois corporation or foreign corporation authorized to do business or acquire and hold title to real estate in Illinois, partnership authorized to do business or acquire and hold title to real estate in Illinois, or other entity recognized as person and authorized to do business or acquire and hold title to real estate under laws of State of Illinois; and (2) sworn statement executed by grantee or his agent verifying that name of grantee shown on deed or assignment of beneficial interest is either natural person, Illinois corporation or foreign corporation authorized to do business or acquire and hold title to real estate in Illinois, partnership authorized to do business or acquire and hold title to real estate in Illinois, or other entity recognized to do business or acquire and hold title to real estate under laws of State of Illinois. If conveyance is due to resignation of Land Trustee, sworn statement to that effect with name of beneficiary is required. (55-5/3-5020 & 3-5020[c]). See also category Documents and Records, topic Records.

Recording Fees.—See category Documents and Records, topic Records, subhead Recording Fees.

Real Estate Transfer Tax.—See topic Real Property, subheads State Stamp Tax, County Stamp Tax, and Local Stamp Tax.

Abutting Street or Alley.—Deed deemed to convey grantor's existing or subsequently acquired rights in abutting street or alley for continued use in manner of grantor's use unless such rights expressly excluded in description of property. Grantor's covenants do not apply to such rights. (765-5/7a).

Form.—The following form may be used:

Form for Warranty Deed.—"The grantor, A, of . . . ., for and in consideration of . . . . dollars in hand paid, conveys and warrants to B the following described real estate . . . . situated in the county of . . . ., in the State of Illinois. Dated this . . . . day of . . . ., A. D. 19. . . . . A. B." (765-5/9).

See note at head of Digest as to 1998 legislation covered.

See Topical Index in front part of this volume.

IL – 69

DEEDS . . . *continued*

Words "convey and warrant" include all covenants of general warranty (765-5/9); a deed in above form conveys fee simple title, with covenants: (1) That grantor was, at execution of deed, seized with an indefeasible estate in fee simple, with full power to convey; (2) that property was then free from all incumbrances; (3) that grantor warrants to grantee, his heirs and assigns, quiet and peaceable possession, and will defend title against all persons who may lawfully claim same (765-5/9). Such covenants are as obligatory on grantor, his heirs and personal representatives, as if written at length in deed (765-5/9), and after-acquired interest inures to grantee (765-5/7).

A deed in which the words "grants, bargains and sells" are used in place of "conveys and warrants" conveys fee simple title, with covenants: (1) That grantor was seized with an indefeasible estate in fee simple, free from encumbrances done or suffered by grantor, except rents or services reserved; (2) quiet enjoyment against the grantor, his heirs and assigns. (765-5/8).

Form for quitclaim deed is the same except "conveys and quitclaims to . . . . all interest in" is substituted for "conveys and warrants to . . . . ." Deed in such form conveys in fee all existing legal or equitable rights of the grantor. (765-5/10).

Contracts for Sale of Dwelling Structure.—See topic Real Property.

DEEDS OF TRUST:

See category Mortgages, topic Mortgages of Real Property.

DOWER:

Dower abolished. All inchoate rights to elect to take dower existing on Jan. 1, 1972 are extinguished. (755-5/2-9).

ESCHEAT:

See topic Absentees, subhead Escheat; categories Business Regulation and Commerce, topic Banks and Banking, subhead Unclaimed Deposits; Estates and Trusts, topic Descent and Distribution, subhead Escheat.

LANDLORD AND TENANT:

Leases.—"Lease" includes every letting, whether verbal or written. (735-5/9-214). Municipal ordinances—regarding landlord-tenant relationship supercedes state law when municipality has "home rule" powers under 1970 Ill. Const. art. VII §6(a), 95 Ill.2d 101, 421 N.E.2d 196. See e.g., Residential Landlord and Tenant Ordinance (Municipal Code of Chicago 5-12). Rental for over 30 days of land for mobile home or of mobile home and land is lease of real property but does not affect classification of mobile home for purposes of taxation. (735-5/9-103). Mobile Home Landlord and Tenant Rights Act sets forth comprehensive list of rights and duties of parties to leases of mobile homes or mobile home lots in mobile home parks containing five or more units. (765-745/1 et seq.). Lessor covered by Act must offer written 12-month lease to prospective tenant. (765-745/6). Lease of condominium must be delivered to Board within ten days of execution prior to occupancy. (765-605/18). Leasehold estate, when unexpired term exceeds five years, is "real estate" under Judgments Act. (735-5/12-105). See category Civil Actions and Procedure, topic Judgments.

Leases must be definite as to property leased, term, amount of rent and time and method of payment to be valid. (53 Ill. App.3d 145, 368 N.E.2d 196).

Lease provision permitting landlord to terminate or refuse to renew residential lease because tenant complained to governmental authority of bona fide building code violation, health ordinance or similar regulation is void; landlord's termination or refusal to renew lease for such reason is against public policy. (765-720/1).

Agreement exempting landlord from liability for damages for injuries to person or property as result of landlord's negligence void as against public policy and wholly unenforceable. (765-705/1).

Waiver of provisions in Mobile Home Landlord and Tenant Act is void. (765-745/10).

Limitations.—No action can be brought on lease for more than year which is not in writing and signed by parties to be charged or their agents authorized in writing. (740-80/2).

Recording.—Unacknowledged lease may be recorded but execution thereof must be proved in accordance with rules of evidence. (765-5/31). Leases take effect as to creditors and subsequent purchasers, without notice, from date of recordation. (765-5/30). However, actual and open possession by tenant under unrecorded lease constitutes notice of his rights. (106 Ill.App.2d 16, 245 N.E.2d 539).

Recovery of rent or a reasonable charge for use and occupation may be had by civil action: (1) When rent is due and in arrears on lease for life or lives; (2) when lands are held and occupied without special agreement for rent; (3) when possession is obtained under agreement for purchase, and before deed, agreement is terminated by fault of purchaser and possession is wrongfully refused on written demand by party entitled thereto, but payments made by vendee may be set off against such rent; (4) when land has been sold under judgment or decree, and party to such judgment or person holding under him refuses to surrender possession after demand in writing by person entitled thereto; (5) when lands have been sold upon mortgage and mortgagor, or person holding under him, refuses to surrender possession after written demand by person entitled thereto. (735-5/9-201).

Rent Concession.—Where rent concession is given in any lease, except of farm property, lessor must place across face and text thereof, plainly legible and in letters not less than one-half inch in height, words: "Concession Granted," with notation on margin stating nature of concession. Failure to do so constitutes Class A misdemeanor. (765-730/2, 730/3, 730/5a, 730/6). Agreement by lessor to waive condition or terms of lease other than those relating to rent payment is not rent concession. (765-730/2).

Termination of Tenancy.—When tenancy is for certain period and term expires by terms of lease, tenant must surrender possession; no notice to quit or demand of possession necessary. (735-5/9-213).

Year to year tenancies (except farm leases) may be terminated by 60 days written notice given within four months preceding last 60 days of year. (735-5/9-205). Year to year farm leases require four months written notice to terminate. (735-5/9-206). Tenancies for less than year, except week to week, may be terminated by 30 days written notice. (735-5/9-207). Week to week tenancies may be terminated by seven days written notice. (735-5/9-207). Tenant at will not entitled to notice. (14 Ill. App.3d 652, 303 N.E.2d 251). Where tenancy is terminated by notice, no further demand is necessary before bringing forcible detainer or ejectment suit. (735-5/9-208).

Any time after rent due, landlord may demand payment and serve written notice that unless payment made within time stated in notice, not less than five days after service thereof, lease terminated. If rent not paid within time stated, landlord may consider lease ended and sue for possession. Partial payment of past due rent demanded in notice does not waive landlord's right to terminate lease where notice demands payment in full and states that only full payment will waive right to terminate, unless landlord agrees in writing to continue lease for partial payment. (735-5/9-209). When default is made in any lease term, landlord may give ten days notice to quit or of termination of tenancy. (735-5/9-210). Notices may be served by delivering copy to tenant, or by leaving with person above age 12 residing on or in possession of premises, or by sending copy to tenant by certified or registered mail with return receipt from addressee; in case no one in actual possession of premises, notice may be served by posting on premises. (735-5/9-211). Parties to lease may waive statutory notices (397 Ill. 497, 74 N.E.2d 699) or provide for method of service other than statutory methods (3 Ill. App.2d 368, 122 N.E.2d 292).

Dispossession.—When year to year tenancy of farmland, or tenancy for less than year where tenant holds over without special agreement, terminated by written notice, no further demand necessary before bringing forcible detainer or ejectment suit. (735-5/9-208). When tenancy terminated by written demand for rent ("five day notice"), landlord may consider lease ended and sue for possession by forcible entry and detainer or maintain ejectment; claim for rent may be joined in complaint. (735-5/9-209). After ten days notice to quit for default in lease term, no other notice, demand of possession or termination of tenancy necessary. (735-5/9-210). See subhead Termination of Tenancy, supra.

Forcible entry and detainer may be maintained, inter alia, when lessee or person holding under him holds possession without right after termination of lease by its own terms, by notice to quit or otherwise or when lessor-owner of condominium unit fails to comply with leasing requirements of Condominium Property Act 765-605/18, declaration, bylaws and regulations of condominium or if lessee of condominium unit owner is in breach of same and Board of Managers have served demand under 765-5/9-104.2. (735-5/9-102). Forcible entry and detainer summons requires defendant to appear on day specified in summons not less than seven or more than 40 days after issuance. (Ill. S. Ct. Rule 101). If defendant appears, no answer need be filed unless ordered by court; complaint is deemed denied and any defense may be proved as if specifically pleaded. (Ill. S. Ct. Rule 181). Either party may demand jury, notwithstanding jury waiver in lease only if property is used for residential purposes. (735-5/9-108). Dispossession of tenant without process of law, even if such right provided for in lease, may be enjoined and may create liabilities for landlord. (11 Ill. App.3d 791, 298 N.E.2d 262). Judgment for possession normally enforceable only for 90 days after entry. (735-5/9-117).

Holding Over.—If tenant wilfully holds over, and after written demand by landlord, he is liable for holdover period at double rent while possession withheld. (735-5/9-202). If tenant pursuant to lease gives notice of intention to quit and fails to do so, he is liable for double rent. (735-5/9-203). Statutory double rent remedy excludes right to recover other damages in tort by reason of wilful holdover. (19 Ill. App.2d 459, 154 N.E.2d 327). It does not, however, affect enforceability of liquidated damages provisions in lease. (3 Ill. App.3d 165, 278 N.E.2d 188).

Mitigation of Damages.—Landlord must take reasonable measures to mitigate damages recoverable against defaulting tenant. (735-5/9-213.1). If former tenant tenders "suitable tenant," landlord must either consent or credit former tenant with amount which would have been paid by new tenant had he been accepted. (67 Ill. App.2d 8, 214 N.E.2d 506).

Lien.—Landlord has lien on crops grown or growing on land, for rent thereof, whether payable in money or property, and for performance of terms of lease. Such lien is good for six months after expiration of term and may be enforced by distraint. (735-5/9-316). Lessor may enforce lien rights against sub-lessee or assignee. (735-5/9-317). No liens other than those expressed in statute exist. (112 Ill. 247; 138 Ill. 483, 28 N.E. 955).

Distress.—Landlord may seize for rent any personal property of tenant found in county where tenant resides. (735-5/9-301). However, statutory right of distress may not be exercised without resort to judicial proceedings; due process rights of notice and hearing must also be observed. (11 Ill. App.3d 791, 298 N.E.2d 262). Person making distress must immediately file with clerk of circuit court copy of distress warrant, together with inventory of property levied on, whereupon clerk will issue summons against party against whom distress shall have been issued, returnable as other summons. (735-5/9-302, 5/9-303). When by proper affidavit it appears that defendant is a nonresident or has departed from state or cannot be found, notice may be given by publication, as in case of attachment. (735-5/9-304). Case proceeds as in attachment, but plaintiff need file no complaint, as distress warrant stands for complaint and is amendable, like other complaints. (735-5/9-305). Defendant may counterclaim or assert any defense which would have been proper in suit for rent. (735-5/9-306). If defendant is served or appears and plaintiff prevails, judgment is in personam and not in rem; but execution is first applied to property distrained. (735-5/9-308). If defendant is not served and does not appear, judgment is in rem; and execution applies only to distrained property. (735-5/9-309). Defendant may release property distrained by giving bond in double amount of rent claimed, with sufficient sureties. (735-5/9-311). If property distrained is perishable, lessor may, on giving notice to defendant or his attorney, or without notice if they cannot be found, apply to judge for order for immediate sale. (735-5/9-312). Right of distress continues for six months after termination of tenancy. (735-5/9-313). Personal property which by law is exempt from execution is also exempt from distress, except crops grown or growing on premises. (735-5/9-315). Subject to right to distrain for rent, tenant may remove removable fixtures erected by him during tenancy. (735-5/9-319).

See note at head of Digest as to 1998 legislation covered.

See Topical Index in front part of this volume.

IL – 70

LANDLORD AND TENANT ... *continued*

Exculpatory Clause.—Agreement in or collateral to lease exempting lessor from liability for own negligence is void. (765-705/1).

Rent Withholding and Implied Warranty of Habitability.—With respect to single-family and multiple dwelling structures there is implied warranty of habitability fulfilled by substantial compliance with pertinent provisions of local building codes. In forcible entry and detainer action (see subhead Dispossession, supra) brought because of non-payment of rent, tenant may establish that damages suffered as result of landlord's breach of implied warranty equal or exceed rent claimed to be due, no rent is owed and action fails. (50 Ill.2d 351, 280 N.E.2d 208; 84 Ill.2d 178, 417 N.E.2d 1297). County department or local government unit may withhold rent payments from grant of financial aid to public aid recipient or directly from lessor or owner renting to public aid recipient, if, within ten days of notice of violation of any law or ordinance establishing construction, plumbing, heating, electrical, fire prevention or any other health and safety standards which causes premises to be dangerous, hazardous or detrimental to life or health, such violation is not corrected. Act applies only to recipients of public aid, and no recipient is subject to eviction as result of withholding of rent under Act. There is 90 day grace period and all rents shall be paid if correction is made within it. (305-5/11-23). It is unlawful for any landlord to terminate or cause termination of utility service to any building containing housing accommodations occupied by public aid applicants or recipients whose rent allowances or payments have been withheld under Act. Doing so is Class B misdemeanor. (305-5/11-23.1).

Owner may also, under specified conditions, be liable, to tenant or governmental unit making vendor payments, for up to three times amount of rent collected while number of apartments in building exceeds that permitted by ordinance, plus costs and attorney's fees. (65-5/11-31.1-1 to 5/11-31.1-12).

Rent Credit.—Where lessor is required to pay for water, gas, or electricity and fails to pay, lessee may pay. Utility must restore service and lessee may deduct amount paid from rent. (765-735/1).

Security Deposits.—Lessor of residential real property, containing five or more units, who has received security deposit from lessee to secure payment of rent or to compensate for damage to leased property may not withhold any part of deposit for property damage unless he has within 30 days of lessee's vacation of premises, personally delivered or mailed to said lessee itemized statement of damage allegedly caused and actual or estimated cost to repair or replace each item on statement, attaching paid receipts or copies thereof for repair or replacement. If lessor utilizes own labor to repair any damage caused by lessee, lessor may include reasonable cost of labor to repair such damage. If estimated cost is given, lessor must furnish lessee paid receipts or copies thereof within 30 days after above statement of estimated cost was furnished. If no such statement and receipts, or copies thereof, are furnished to lessee as required by this Act, lessor must return security deposit in full within 45 days after lessee vacated premises. Upon circuit court's finding that lessor refused to supply itemized statement, or supplied statement in bad faith, and failed to return security deposit within time permitted, lessor is liable for twice amount of deposit plus court costs and reasonable attorneys' fees. (765-710/1). Where property is transferred by lessor who has collected security deposit, transferee is jointly and severally liable to lessee for security deposit. (765-710/2).

When security deposit delivered as security only and not as advance rent, landlord's obligation is personal as pledgee and landlord's assignment of benefits of lease and conveyance of reversion does not result in release of duty to act as pledgee. (28 Ill. App.3d 732, 328 N.E.2d 897). If, on other hand, security deposit is clearly intended to be applied to last rent installments, deposit becomes lessor's property immediately upon receipt and is not held in trust for tenant. (12 Ill. App.2d 479, 139 N.E.2d 865).

Lessor of mobile home park, where security deposit is required, must send lessee itemized list of damages and cost of repair within 15 days after tenancy expires. If tenant fails to object in 15 days, amount of damages is deducted from deposit and balance returned to tenant. If no list furnished, deposit must be returned in full. (765-745/18).

Interest on Security Deposits by Lessees.—Lessor of residential real estate with 25 or more units, in either single building or complex of buildings located on contiguous parcels of real property, must pay at end of each 12-month term interest on any security deposit by lessee at rate equal to interest paid by largest commercial bank in state on minimum passbook savings account as of Dec. 31 of calendar year immediately preceding inception of rental agreement on any security deposit held for more than six months, and if security deposit not with respect to public housing. Penalty for lessor's wilful failure to pay interest is amount equal to security deposit plus attorneys fees and court costs. (765-715/1 to 3).

Management and Insurance.—Owner of residential real property, containing more than four living units, who does not reside or maintain office on premises and does not employ manager or agent who resides or maintains office on premises, is required to notify residents of person responsible for managing building, companies insuring building and cancellation of insurance. (735-5/9-320).

Utilities.—Agreements dealing with payment for and termination of utilities are restricted. (765-735/1, 735/2).

LEASES:

See topic Landlord and Tenant.

PERPETUITIES:

Common law rule is modified in Illinois by statute for instruments becoming effective after Sept. 22, 1969.

Application of Rule.—Rule does not apply to disposition of property expressly exempted by statute; to powers of trustee to sell, lease, or mortgage property or to administer or manage trust assets; to mandatory powers of trustee to distribute income or to discretionary powers to distribute principal prior to termination of trust, to a beneficiary having a vested interest in principal; to discretionary powers of a trustee to allocate income and principal among beneficiaries, but such power may not be exercised after expiration of period of rule; to leases commencing in future, provided lease

commences in possession 40 years from date of execution; to commitments by a lessor to enter into a lease with a subtenant or holder of leasehold mortgage, or by a lessee or sublessee to enter into a lease with holder of mortgage; to options in gross or rights of first refusal, but no option in gross is valid for more than 40 years from its creation; or to qualified perpetual trusts created by will or inter vivos agreement executed or amended after Jan. 1, 1998. (765-305/4[a]).

Rule does not commence to run as long as, by terms of instrument, maker of instrument has power to revoke instrument or transfer or direct to himself entire legal and equitable ownership of property. (765-305/4[b]).

There is a presumption that interest was intended to be valid; that will was to be probated or any administrative contingencies occur within period of rule; and that "widow," "widower," or "spouse" of another person mentioned in instrument was living at date period of rule commenced to run. (765-305/4[c][1]).

Where interest would be invalid because it is made to depend upon a person attaining or failing to attain an age in excess of 21 years, age specified is to be reduced to 21 years. (765-305/4[c][2]). Furthermore, no person is deemed capable of having child before he has attained 13 years or after he has attained age 65; evidence is admissible to show incapacity of having child by living person who has not attained 65; and possibility of having child or more remote descendant by adoption is disregarded. (765-305/4[c][3]).

Trusts.—New statutory section states various rules as to when a trust which would violate rule against perpetuities actually terminates and how principal is to be distributed. (765-305/5).

Accumulations.—Accumulations must be limited to 21 years after end of life or lives in being at effective date of settlement or disposition. (765-315/1). Exceptions are trusts to which §5 of statute concerning perpetuities (765-305/5) applies, cemetery trusts, qualified perpetual trusts as defined, and trusts created by employers as part of stock bonus, pension or profit-sharing plan, etc. (765-315/1). No disposition is effective as long as, by terms of instrument, maker of instrument has power to revoke instrument or have entire legal and equitable ownership of property transferred to himself. (765-315/1).

PERSONAL PROPERTY:

Tenancy by entirety in personal property does not exist in Illinois. (392 Ill. 477, 64 N.E.2d 729). Expressed intent is necessary to create joint tenancy with right of survivorship in personal property. (765-1005/2).

POWERS OF ATTORNEY:

Power of Attorney.—Principal who appoints agent by written instrument while competent deemed competent for purposes of agency and agent's dealings until principal is adjudged to be legally disabled. Absent actual knowledge to contrary, third party may presume valid execution of agency instrument and competence of principal at time of execution. (755-5/11a-23).

Durable Powers of Attorney.—Under Illinois Power of Attorney Act (755-45/1-1 to 45/4-12), principal in writing may authorize agent to make financial and health care decisions for principal throughout principal's lifetime including periods of disability; health care personnel and other third parties who rely in good faith will be protected. Statutory form power of attorney for property (755-45/3-3); statutory form power of attorney for health care (755-45/4-10[a]).

REAL PROPERTY:

Estates recognized are as follows: fee simple; life estate; estate for years; estate from year to year; homestead; joint tenancy with right of survivorship; tenancy in common; and tenancy by entireties. Tenancy by entirety is created with conveyance assignment or other transfer of property (including beneficial interest in land trust) maintained or intended for maintenance as homestead by both husband and wife together during coverture to husband and wife not as joint tenants or tenants in common but as tenants by entirety. (765-1005/1c). Joint tenancy with right of survivorship can be created only by express declaration that estate must pass in joint tenancy and not as tenancy in common. (765-1005/1). Grantor can create joint tenancy with right of survivorship notwithstanding fact that he is also grantee. (765-1005/1b).

Conservation right is created by statute as interest in real property, which may be conveyed to governmental body or to nonprofit trust or corporation whose primary purpose is conservation. Conservation rights are enforceable by certain parties other than grantee and his privies. (765-120/1).

See also topics Curtesy, Deeds, Dower; category Family, topic Husband and Wife.

Rule in Shelley's Case is recognized in Illinois, but only in connection with documents executed and delivered prior to July 15, 1953, and wills of decedents dying before that date. (765-345/1, 2).

Doctrine of worthier title is recognized in Illinois only in connection with instruments and wills which became effective on or before July 1, 1955. (765-350/1, 2). However, statute does not require trust to be construed in such a way as to override expressed intent of maker. (3 Ill. App.3d 337, 278 N.E.2d 10).

Rule Against Perpetuities.—Rule against perpetuities has been modified by statute. (765-305/1 to 305/6). See topic Perpetuities.

Foreign Conveyances or Encumbrances.—Deeds, conveyances, and powers of attorney for the conveyance of Illinois land, acknowledged, proved, or authenticated pursuant to law of any foreign state, are deemed good and valid as though acknowledged or proved pursuant to Illinois law. (765-5/22, 5/23). Illinois has adopted Uniform Recognition of Acknowledgments Act. (765-30/1 to 30/10).

Land Trust.—"Land Trust" is Illinois institution and is widely used. Land trust is trust in which corpus consists of real estate and in which deed to trustee appears to confer upon him full powers to deal with real estate and complete legal and equitable title to trust property. So far as public records are concerned, trustee's powers are complete. Such powers, however, are in fact restricted by trust agreement mentioned in

---

REAL PROPERTY . . . *continued*

deed in trust. Such trust agreements typically vest in beneficiary full powers of management and control. While not specifically authorized by statute, land trusts have been defined as any arrangement under which title, both legal and equitable, to real property, is held by trustee and interest of beneficiary is personal property and under which beneficiary or any person designated in writing by beneficiary, has exclusive power to direct or control trustee in dealing with title, and exclusive control of management, operation, renting and selling of trust property together with exclusive right to earnings, avails, and proceeds of said property is in beneficiary of trust. (765-430/1, 765-405/1). However, beneficiary cannot deal with property as if no trust existed. (18 Ill.App.3d 1, 309 N.E.2d 368). Unless appointed as agent for trustee, beneficiary cannot purport to act as trustee's "agent" (131 Ill.App.2d 1087, 266 N.E.2d 401) and generally, when he contracts without authority with third parties, his contract is void (18 Ill.App.3d 1, 309 N.E.2d 368). Under appropriate circumstances, beneficiary may contract to sell trust property. (9 Ill.App.3d 419, 292 N.E.2d 71; 9 Ill.App.3d 361, 292 N.E.2d 177). Beneficiary's interest is personal property, not real property. (11 Ill.2d 178, 142 N.E.2d 94). Beneficiary, and not trustee, of land trust is liable for injuries sustained on trust property. (132 Ill.App.2d 307, 270 N.E.2d 254; rev'd on other grounds, 54 Ill.2d 504, 301 N.E.2d 296). Trust agreement may provide that trustee, when directed by beneficiaries, may convey trust property directly to another trustee on behalf of beneficiaries or others named by beneficiaries. (765-410/2).

Recent legislation provides that secured creditor trustee has same rights as any other secured creditor, including right to purchase trust property at judicial sale, and such dealings are not breach of fiduciary duty. (765-415/1). Illinois Supreme Court upheld retroactive application of legislation. (108 Ill.2d 1, 483 N.E.2d 226).

Trustee or managing agent of real property must disclose to enforcement agency, within ten days after receipt of notice or complaint, identity of owners and beneficiaries of trust holding property against which complaint has been filed alleging violation of ordinance, regulation or resolution enacted by political subdivision relating to condition or operation of property affecting health or safety. For residential buildings, if violation charged is not cured within 180 days of notice, enforcing agency shall make public disclosure of owners' or beneficiaries' identity. If violation is subsequently corrected, information will be removed from register where such information is kept. (765-425/1). Where trust property is damaged or destroyed by fire, inspector may require prompt disclosure by trustee of identities of beneficiaries of land trust and may require any named beneficiary to: (1) Disclose identity of those having direct or indirect interest in trust or deriving any direct or indirect benefit therefrom; and (2) provide list of properties located in same county as damaged or destroyed property and with respect to which any claim has been made, directly or indirectly, by or for such beneficiary's benefit under any fire insurance policy for loss or damage by fire within previous five years, together with identity of insurer and policy number. (765-425/1.1). Violation is petty offense, penalty for which is fine of $100 per day. (765-425/2).

Residential property (single family residence or multiple dwelling structure of six or less family units) subject to a land trust may not be sold under a real estate installment contract (purchase price to be paid over period in excess of five years with title conveyed upon payment of purchase price or a specified portion thereof) unless, when contract is executed, names of trustee and beneficiaries and designation of trust are disclosed to buyer and beneficiaries having power of direction sign contract. Contract deemed to include provision that beneficiaries will convey or cause to be conveyed the property in accordance with contract. Violation of act makes contract voidable at purchaser's option. (765-430/1 to 430/2).

A cause of action against a beneficiary of a land trust not originally named as a defendant is not barred by any limitation period if, among other statutory conditions, service of summons was had within the limitation period upon a land trustee who had title but no power of management or control over the real estate. (735-5/2-616).

Condominium Property Act (765-605/1) became effective July 1, 1963 Act applies to all condominiums. Provisions in condominium instrument inconsistent with Act are void and against public policy and ineffective. (765-605/2.1). Terms appearing in quotes are defined in Act.

Owner may submit "parcel" to provisions of Act by recording "declaration" and "plat" in accordance with Act. (765-605/3, 605/4, 605/5).

Each "unit owner" is entitled to percentage of ownership in "common elements" appertaining to his or her "unit" as set forth in "declaration". (765-605/6). "Condominium instruments" may contain provisions for adjustment and reallocation of percentage ownership in limited circumstances by recording amended "plat". (765-605/6). "Unit owners" may, unless prohibited by "condominium instruments" subdivide or combine "units" in manner provided by Act, and may, in certain situations, transfer use of "limited common elements". (765-605/26, 605/31). "Unit owner" owning two or more "units" may, subject to reasonable limitations contained in "condominium instruments" remove or alter intervening partitions upon notice to board of managers, unless removal or alteration would weaken, impair or endanger another "unit" or any "common element". (765-605/29). See also category Civil Actions and Procedure, topic Partition.

Deed, leases, mortgages or other instruments may describe "unit" by its identifying number or symbol as shown on "plat" and as set forth in "declaration". (765-605/7).

Each "unit owner" must pay proportionate share of "common expenses". "Developer" must pay proportionate share of "common expenses" prior to first conveyance of unit. (765-605/9). Foreclosure purchaser, mortgagee in possession, or mortgagee-owner must pay proportionate share. (765-605/9[3]). Unit which is individually owned and includes right to use common area is assessed for real estate tax purposes at value which includes proportional share of value of common area. (35-205/20c-2).

Amount of unpaid "common expenses" together with interest, late charges, reasonable attorneys' fees and costs of collection only for services actually incurred or amount of any unpaid fine, constitutes lien on defaulting "unit owner's" interest in his or her "unit". Lien is in favor of board of managers for benefit of all other "unit owners" and, upon recording of notice by board of managers or if developer is manager or has majority of seats on board of managers and manager or board of managers fails to record notice, upon recording of notice by any unit owner, may be foreclosed in like manner as mortgage. (765-605/9). Such lien shall be prior to all other liens and

encumbrances except: (i) Taxes, special assessments and special taxes or Federal taxes which are lien prior to preexisting recorded encumbrance, and (ii) encumbrances recorded prior to unit owner's refusal to pay "common expenses". With respect to encumbrances executed prior to Sept., 1984 and encumbrances which are neither bona fide first mortgages or trust deeds and contain mailing address in Illinois, upon notice to encumbrancer by manager or board of managers of unpaid common expense, prior recorded encumbrance may be subject to lien of unpaid common expenses becoming due in 90-day period following mailing of notice. (765-605/9). In event of default by unit owner, tenant, invitee or guest, board of managers may file action for possession against defaulting unit owner, among other remedies. (765-605/9.2, 735-5/9-102).

Declaration or bylaws may require mediation or arbitration of disputes where value of controversy less than $10,000, other than levying and collection of assessments, or that arises out of violation of declaration, bylaws, or rules and regulations of association. Disputes not required to be mediated or arbitrated may be submitted by disputants. Illinois Uniform Arbitration Act (710-5/1 et seq.) applies. Association may require disputants to bear costs. (765-605/32).

Board of managers has standing to act in representative capacity on behalf of "unit owners" or in relation to matters involving "common elements" or more than one "unit". (765-605/9.1). Statute of limitations for actions brought by condominium association does not run until unit owners have elected majority of board of managers. (765-605/18.2). Actions requiring vote of majority of board of managers require vote of more than 50% of total number of persons constituting such board. (765-605/2). Board of managers in condominium of 30 or more units required to obtain fidelity bond and directors' and officers' liability coverage and to have management company furnish fidelity bond as provided in Act. (765-605/8).

Except as provided in 765-605/12.1, board of managers has duty to obtain comprehensive public liability insurance and to obtain insurance for full insurable replacement cost covering "common elements" and "units", including improvements made by unit owner if so provided in "declaration" against loss or damage by fire or other hazards covered by standard extended coverage provisions. (765-605/12[a][1]). Issuer of fire or other hazard insurance policy must include statutorily prescribed notice with policy advising that policy may not satisfy Act requirements for insurance to be obtained by condominium association. (765-605/12). In case of fire or other damage, building must be reconstructed if insurance proceeds are sufficient. (765-605/13). If insurance proceeds are not sufficient, board of managers may, in certain circumstances, record notice whereby "property" shall be owned in common by "unit owners", or, if "condominium instruments" make provision, assessments may be voted for reconstruction if fewer than one-half of units are rendered uninhabitable or portion of "property" may be withdrawn. (765-605/14).

"Property" may be sold in manner provided in Act. (765-605/15). "Property" may be removed from provisions of Act by all "unit owners", provided that all lienholders consent, by recorded instrument, to that effect. (765-605/16).

Unless "condominium instrument" provides for greater percentage, 2/3 majority of unit owners at meeting may elect to dedicate portion of common elements to public body for street or utility (765-605/14.2) and greater than 50% majority of unit owners at meeting may authorize granting of easement for television cable (765-605/14.3).

"Condominium instruments" may be amended by vote of 2/3 of those voting or upon majority specified by condominium instruments, together with approval of any mortgagees required by condominium instruments, unless Act provides otherwise. For property subject to declaration recorded on or after July 1, 1984, no condominium instruments shall require more than 3/4 vote of unit owners to amend bylaws. (765-605/27). Amendments to declaration or bylaws are effective upon recordation unless amendment states otherwise. (765-605/17).

Administration of "property" is governed by by-laws which may either be in "declaration" or in separate instrument recorded with "declaration". (765-605/17). Bylaws must contain certain provisions as required by Act. In event of conflict between declaration and bylaws or other condominium instruments, unless otherwise specifically provided in Act, provisions of Act are applicable. Any condominium instruments to contrary are void as against public policy and ineffective. (765-605/18).

Board of managers must provide to each "unit owner" copy of proposed annual budget indicating which portions are intended for reasonable reserves for capital expenditures or repairs or payment of real estate taxes, and other financial information concerning condominium. (765-605/18).

Owners or board of managers may form not-for-profit corporation to facilitate administration and operation of "property". (765-605/18.1).

"Developer" may manage "property" prior to election of first unit owner board of managers. First unit owner board must be elected within 60 days after conveyance of 75% of "units" or three years after "declaration" is recorded, whichever is earlier. "Developer" must give at least 21 days notice of meeting to elect first unit owner board of managers and must provide to any unit owner, within three working days of request, names, addresses, phone numbers, and weighted vote of each "unit owner" entitled to vote at meeting. Any unit owner must be provided same information within same time period with respect to each subsequent meeting to elect members of Board of Managers. If developer does not call meeting to elect board managers within above-referenced time period, unit holders holding 20% interest in association may call meeting. After election of first unit owner board of managers, "developer" must turn over certain funds, documents and personal property. Any contract made by "developer" for term longer than two years may be cancelled as provided in Act. (765-605/18.2).

Buyer or prospective buyer of "unit" at initial sale or offering is entitled to disclosures by seller prior to executing contract of sale. (765-605/22). Earnest money deposited with "developer" under sale contract or option where conveyance is to be made within one year must be held in escrow account. Deposits, payments or advances towards purchase price for initial sale of unit, received by developer, must be held in escrow account until title is conveyed to purchaser. Developer shall deposit all payments in interest bearing account at federally insured bank or savings and loan institution and such interest credited to purchaser toward purchase price of unit. Interest accrues from time of deposit, payment or advance. No interest where transfer of title occurs 45 days from time contract to purchase is entered. In event of refund or default, interest follows disposition of deposit, payment or advance. (765-605/24). In event of

REAL PROPERTY . . . *continued*

any resale of condominium unit, owner, if other than developer, must make disclosures to prospective buyer upon demand. (765-605/22.1).

"Add-on Condominiums" are authorized by Act. (765-605/25).

"Conversion Condominiums" are permitted under Act, but tenants are given certain rights with respect thereto and specific disclosures are required. Notice of intent to convert must include schedule of prices for units in conversion project. (765-605/30).

Act permits formation of unit owners' association which shall have responsibility for overall administration of condominium property, shall consist of each "unit owner" and shall have powers specified in General Not for Profit Corporation Act of 1986 not inconsistent with Act or condominium instruments, whether or not association is incorporated. (765-605/18.3). Powers of unit owners' association may be exercised by "master association," provided certain requirements are met. (765-605/18.5).

"Condominium and Common Interest Community Risk Pooling Act" permits formation of trust fund for insurance purposes by two or more "condominium associations". Trust fund to be funded by unit owner assessments and is authorized to indemnify unit owners, as beneficiaries of trust fund, against risk of loss due to damage, destruction or loss of property or imposition of legal liability as required or authorized by Act or declaration. Act prescribes procedure for formation and administration of trust fund. (765-605/12.1).

Local Condominium Ordinances.—Number of municipalities, including Chicago, have enacted ordinances with respect to condominiums.

Chicago ordinance, which became effective Jan. 1, 1978, requires that developer prepare property report for distribution to prospective purchasers which must disclose information concerning condominium. (13-72-020 and 13-72-050 Chicago Municipal Code). Ordinance, in addition, requires developer to give notice of intent to tenants in buildings undergoing conversion to condominium no less than 120 days prior to recording declaration. During 120 day period after notice has been given (180 days if tenant is over 65, blind, deaf or handicapped) tenant may continue to occupy unit, with right of first refusal to purchase. (13-72-060).

Real Estate Time–Share Act.—See 765-100/1.

Dormant Mineral Interests.—Surface owner may gain title to severed mineral interests owned by unknown or missing owners by instituting proceeding in circuit court of county where such interest is located, seeking judgment that surface owner and his or her privies are exercising presumptive adverse possession of severed interests from date of judgment. If: (1) Owners of severed interests remain unknown or missing for seven years thereafter, or (2) owners of severed interests remain unknown or missing for one year thereafter and severance occurred over 20 years prior to date of filing original petition, court shall enter judgment vesting title to severed interests in surface owner, provided that notice requirements have been met and surface owner has paid all taxes assessed on severed interests. (765-515/11). Prior statute held unconstitutional. (82 Ill.2d 364, 412 N.E.2d 522).

State Stamp Tax.—Tax is imposed on privilege of transferring title to real estate, as represented by deed filed for recordation, and on privilege of transferring beneficial interest in real property which is subject of land trust as represented by trust document filed for recordation, at rate of 50¢ for each $500 of value or fraction thereof. If real estate is transferred subject to mortgage, amount of mortgage outstanding at time of transfer is not included in basis for computing the tax. Tax is collected by Recorder of Deeds or Registrar of Titles through sale of revenue stamps. (35-200/31-10, 31-15, 31-20, 31-25, 31-30, 31-35).

Deeds exempt from tax include: transfers made before Jan. 1, 1968; property acquired from, by or between governmental or tax exempt corporations; which secure debt or other obligation; correction or supplementary deeds; actual consideration under $100; tax deeds; release deeds; partition deeds; pursuant to mergers, consolidation, or sales pursuant to plans of reorganization; or by subsidiary to parent corporation in exchange for cancellation or surrender of subsidiary's stock; exchange deeds except to extent of money difference; deeds issued to holder of mortgage pursuant to mortgage foreclosure proceeding or pursuant to transfer in lieu of foreclosure; deed or trust document related to purchase of principal residence under Home Ownership Made Easy Act. (35-200/31-45).

When a deed or trust document transferring title to real estate is presented for recordation, declaration of value must also be presented. (35-200/31-10, 31-15, 31-20, 31-25, 31-30, 31-35). No declaration is required for deeds or trust documents exempt from tax; except that declaration must be presented for deeds or trust documents conveying property from, by or between governmental bodies or tax exempt corporations. (35-200/31-45). Declaration must state full consideration for property, must include complete description of property and transaction value of personal property sold with real estate, sales finance charges (points), sales price, type of financing (conventional, VA, FHA, seller-financed), down payment, term, interest rate, type and description of interest rate (fixed, adjustable, or renegotiable), monthly principal and interest, year contract initiated if contract of sale name, address, and telephone number of person filling out declaration, and must be signed by seller and buyer or their attorneys or agents, must state type of improvement, if any, whether transfer is between relatives or compulsory, and that parties are advised State of Illinois has enacted Smoke Detector Act. (35-200/31-10, 31-15, 31-20, 31-25, 31-30, 31-35). Any person who willfully falsifies value of real estate or willfully omits any other required information on declaration is guilty of Class B misdemeanor. All declarations of value made pursuant to this Real Estate Transfer Tax Act are public records, available for inspection. (35-200/31-50, 31-55).

County Stamp Tax.—County board may impose transfer tax upon privilege of transferring title to real estate and upon privilege of transferring beneficial interest in land trust holding legal title to real estate at rate of 25¢ for each $500 of value or fraction thereof as stated in declaration of value for State transfer tax purposes. If real estate is transferred subject to mortgage, amount of mortgage outstanding at time of transfer is excluded from determination of value. Tax is collected prior to recording deed or registering title. Real estate exempt from State transfer tax is also exempt from county tax. (55-5/5-1031). Cook County imposes tax on assignment of beneficial interest in land trust. (85-033 Cook County Code). In counties with 3,000,000 or more

inhabitants deed or assignment of beneficial interest in land trust will not be recorded unless accompanied by sworn or affirmed statement of grantor and grantee that grantee is either natural person, Illinois corporation or foreign corporation, partnership or other entity which is authorized to do business or acquire and hold title to real estate in Illinois. (55-5/3-5020).

Local Stamp Tax.—Number of home-rule municipalities impose local tax on transfer of real property. Check with municipality for information. After ordinance has been of record 30 days instruments transferring title to real estate in municipality which imposes tax may not be accepted for recording or registration without proof of payment of local transfer tax. (55-5/3-5021).

Chicago imposes local transfer tax of $3.75 per $500 of transfer price or fraction thereof on transfer of title or assignment of beneficial interest in land trust. (3-32-030 Chicago Municipal Code). Tax is collected by City Department of Revenue through sale of revenue stamps. Declaration which states full consideration for property must be presented together with certificate from Commissioner of Water certifying that water and sewer assessments have been paid in full at time stamps are purchased. (3-32-030 and 3-32-060 Chicago Municipal Code). Certain transactions are exempt. (3-32-030 and 3-32-050 Chicago Municipal Code).

Contracts for Sale of Dwelling Structure.—After Aug. 20, 1968 installment contracts voidable at buyer's election unless there is attached to or incorporated in contract (a) certificate of compliance or (b) (i) express written warranty that owner has not received notice of any dwelling code violations which existed before contract was executed within ten years of date of execution or (ii) if such notice received, a list of all such notices with detailed statement of all violations referred to in notices. Requirements of section cannot be waived by buyer or seller. (765-75/2).

Any provision in a contract for the sale of a dwelling structure which forbids the buyer to record the contract or provides any penalty for recording is void. (765-70/2).

Fraudulent Transfers.—See category Debtor and Creditor, topic Fraudulent Sales and Conveyances.

Fair Housing.—Corporate authorities of municipalities may enact ordinances prescribing fair housing practices in accordance with Fair Housing Act (65-5/11-11.1-1) and Human Rights Act (775-5/7-108).

Demolition and Repair of Unsafe Buildings.—Corporate authorities of each municipality may demolish or repair dangerous and unsafe buildings or uncompleted and abandoned buildings within territory, except that in counties having county health departments, county board may demolish or repair such buildings. (65-5/11-31-1[a]). Any owner or tenant of real property within 1,200 feet of such buildings within municipality with population of 500,000 or more may file with municipal authority request that municipality apply to circuit court of county for order permitting demolition or repair of building. (65-5/11-31-1[b]). Corporate authorities may remove or environmentally remediate hazardous substances on, in or under any abandoned and unsafe property and cost incurred is lien on real estate superior to all prior or existing liens and encumbrances except taxes and other liens created under 65-4/11-31-1(a) or (e). (65-5/11-31-1[f]).

TRUST DEEDS:

See category Mortgages, topic Mortgages of Real Property.

TAXATION

ADMINISTRATION:

Interstate Co-operation.—Illinois does not have a procedure for determining disputed domiciles in inheritance tax matters, but Attorney General does have authority to enter into agreements with taxing authorities of other states in case of disputed domicile of a decedent under certain circumstances. (120-405.11).

Penalties.—As to taxes not listed below, see particular subhead, supra.

Sales (Retailers' Occupation), Use, Service Occupation, Service Use and Hotel Occupancy Taxes.—Any person who fails to file return, fails to keep books and records as required, files fraudulent return, or willfully violates any rule or regulation of Department of Revenue for administration and enforcement of taxes, or any accountant or other agent who knowingly enters false information on return, may be fined not in excess of $1,000 or imprisoned for not more than one year, or both. Any purchaser who either obtains registration number or resale number through misrepresentation, or knowingly represents he has number when he does not, or knowingly misrepresents that he is buying for resale may be fined up to $1,000 or imprisoned for not more than one year, or both (inapplicable to hotel operators). Any person who engages in business without appropriate certificate of registration may be fined not in excess of $1,000 or imprisoned for not more than one year, or both; each day of operation without certificate constitutes separate offense. Any person who accepts money that is due to Department and fails to remit such payment or collects or attempts to collect tax which he knows is not properly collectible may be fined not in excess of $1,000 or imprisoned for not more than one year, or both. (35-120/13, 105/14, 115/15, 110/15, 145/8). *(Above penalties are applicable for Use, Service Occupation, Service Use and Hotel Occupancy Taxes. Penalties for Sales [Retailers' Occupation] tax are higher.)* Any person who fails to file annual information return for Service Occupation and Retail Occupation Taxes subject to penalty of 1/6 of 1% of tax due per month until filed until Jan. 1, 1993. (35-115/9, 120/3). After Jan. 1, 1993, see Uniform Penalty and Interest Act. (35-115/9, 120/3).

In event of late filing or late payment penalty determined in accordance with Uniform Penalty and Interest Act, see 35-115/9, 120/3 will be added. If return is not filed, Department may determine tax and assess such amount, together with penalty of 30% thereof. In addition, any amount of tax not paid when due bears interest at rate of 1.25% per month or fraction thereof from date when such tax becomes past due. However, if failure to file sales tax return is unintentional, nonfraudulent and has not occurred in previous two years, or is due to other reasonable cause, penalties will not be imposed. Failure to pay tax may result in revocation or no reissuance of certain occupational licenses. (35-120/5, 105/12, 115/12, 110/12, 145/7).

ADMINISTRATION . . . *continued*

Liability of Corporate Officers or Employees for Sales Tax.—Officer or employee who has control, supervision or responsibility for filing returns and paying tax who wilfully fails to do so will be personally liable for such amounts including interest and penalties if corporation is unable to pay; liability survives dissolution of corporation. Liability expires three years after latest date all proceedings in court for review of any final assessments have terminated, or proceedings could have been instituted but were not, or date return was filed. (35-120/13.5). Repealed as of Jan. 1, 1994.

Motor Fuel Tax.—Any person who knowingly acts as distributor of motor fuel without license or who knowingly fails to pay taxes to Department shall be guilty of Class 3 felony. Any person who fails or refuses to make required monthly or quarterly returns or to keep required books and records is guilty of Class 4 felony and for each subsequent offense is guilty of Class 3 felony. Any person who makes false return or report to Department as to facts required by designated sections of statute imposing tax is guilty of Class 3 felony. Violations other than those above are Class 4 felonies.

Gas Revenue Tax.—Any taxpayer who willfully violates Act or fails to make or makes fraudulent return may be fined not less than $750 nor more than $7,500. (35-615/13).

Cigarette Tax and Cigarette Use Tax.—Any person who makes, files, signs, verifies, etc. fraudulent return or fails to file required return and any person who fails to keep, or falsifies, required records may be fined not to exceed $10,000 or imprisoned for any term greater than one year but less than three years, or both. (35-135/14, 130/25, 135/22, 135/31). Any person who fails to preserve required records for three years may be fined not more than $5,000. (35-130/15, 135/23). Anyone participating in counterfeiting of required stamps, or who sells packages containing such stamps, may be fined not to exceed $10,000 or imprisoned for in excess of three but not to exceed seven years, or both. (35-130/22, 130/23, 135/29). Any person acting as distributor without required license or violating provisions of Act regarding transporting may be fined not more than $10,000 or imprisoned for any term greater than one year but less than three years, or both. (35-130/26, 130/9c). Any person other than licensed distributor who sells, offers for sale, or possesses with intent to sell, unstamped original cigarette packages may be fined not more than $10,000 or imprisoned for any term greater than one year but less than three years, or both. (35-130/24, 135/30). Any distributor who illegally sells original package of unstamped cigarettes may be fined not more than $10,000 or imprisoned for in excess of two but not to exceed five years, or both. (35-130/24, 135/30). Anyone other than distributor possessing unstamped cigarettes in original packages may be fined $15 for each such package of cigarettes in excess of 100 packages. (35-135/25a).

Unemployment Compensation Tax.—Any employing unit or person willfully violating any provision of Unemployment Compensation Act may be fined not in excess of $500 or imprisoned for not to exceed six months, or both. Each violation is separate offense. (820-405/2800).

Messages Tax.—Any taxpayer who fails to make or makes fraudulent return or willfully violates Act may be fined not less than $750 nor more than $7,500. (35-610/13).

Public Utilities Revenue Act.—Any taxpayer who fails to make or makes fraudulent return or willfully violates Act may be fined not less than $750 nor more than $7,500. (35-620/13).

Alcoholic Beverage Tax.—Transporters who fail to file required reports may be fined not more than $500 or imprisoned for any term less than 30 days, or both. For continuing violations each day's continuance is a separate offense. (235-5/8-12). In general, other violations of Liquor Control Act, which includes Alcoholic Beverage Tax, may be fined not more than $500 for first offense and for second and subsequent offenses may be fined not more than $500 or imprisoned for not more than six months, or both. (235-5/10-1). Underpayment of tax on sale or use of alcoholic liquors results in penalty of 37.5% of deficiency. In general, penalty of 7% plus 1.5% per month is assessed for late payment of any taxes under Act. (235-5/8-5).

Coin-in-slot Amusement Devices.—Any person displaying or operating any device such that it could be played by public without paying tax may be fined not more than $500 or imprisoned for any term less than 30 days, or both. Tax on every device found to be displayed without tax having been paid shall be increased by 30%. (35-510/5, 510/8).

Bingo Tax.—Any person violating any provision of law or filing fraudulent return or violating rule or regulation of Department of Revenue may be fined $1,000 or imprisoned for not more than one year, or both. (230-25/1 et seq.).

Income Tax.—Interest imposed on amount of tax not paid when due at rate established under §6621(b) of Internal Revenue Code. (35-5/1003). In event of failure to file tax return without reasonable cause, penalty of 7.5% per month, not to exceed 37.5%, on amount of tax required to be shown on return. (35-5/1001). Prior to Jan. 1, 1986, in event of failure to pay tax without reasonable cause, penalty of 7.5% per month, not to exceed 37.5% on amount of tax required to be shown on return. If penalty for failure to file equals or exceeds penalty imposed for failure to pay tax, latter penalty shall not apply. (35-5/1001). Effective Jan. 1, 1986, in event of underpayment of tax without reasonable cause, penalty of 6% per annum on amount of underpayment. (35-5/1005). If any part of deficiency is due to negligence or intentional disregard for rules (without intent to defraud) penalty imposed amount prescribed by §3-5 of Uniform Penalty and Interest Act (35-735/3-5); if due to fraud, 75%; 7.5% penalty plus interest for nonwillful failure to file return or pay over withholding tax; penalty imposed by Uniform Penalty and Interest Act (35-735/3-7) for willful failure to collect, account for or pay over any taxes assessed under Act (35-5/1002). Any person who files frivolous return, in addition to any other penalty, may be fined $500. (35-5/1006). Any person who willfully fails to file return, keep books or records as required, files fraudulent return, attempts to evade or defeat tax, or fails to pay any tax, in addition to any other penalty, shall be guilty of Class A misdemeanor for first offense and Class 4 felony for each subsequent offense. (35-5/1301, 5/1302). Any person required to file information report in connection with payment of rents and royalties, personal service contracts, prizes or awards (35-5/1405.1, 5/1405.2, 5/1405.3) who fails to do so is subject to penalty prescribed by §3-4 of Uniform Penalty and Interest Act (35-735/3-4) (35-5/1405.2[d]/1405.3[d]). Any person required to file certain withholding returns who fails to do so is subject to penalties ranging from $75 to $300. (35-5/1004).

Chicago Transaction Tax.—Upon finding, after hearing by Mayor of Chicago, that person wilfully evaded payment of tax, all City licenses held by that person may be revoked. Additionally, anyone convicted of violating provisions of Act shall be fined not less than $50 nor more than $300 for first offense within 180 day period. Fine for any subsequent offense within 180 day period shall be not less than $200 nor more than $500. If more than three offenses are committed within 180 day period, violator may be incarcerated for up to six months. (Municipal Code of Chicago, c. 200.1-9.-200.1-10).

Water Company Invested Capital Tax Act.—Any taxpayer who fails to make or makes fraudulent return or willfully violates Act may be fined not less than $500 nor more than $5,000. (35-625/15).

General.—Taxpayer Bill of Rights. (20-2520/4). Uniform Penalties and Interest Act may apply in addition to any of foregoing penalties. (35-735/3-1). Tax statutes imposing licenses commonly provide, in addition to other penalties, that violations of all, or stated, provisions are grounds for revoking license. Individual statutes should be checked.

ALCOHOLIC BEVERAGES TAX:

Alcoholic beverages tax imposed on manufacturers, importing distributors and certain retailers. (235-5/8-1). Credit of 75% of tax for each gallon of beer up to 4.9 million gallons produced and sold in Illinois applies to calendar years 1982 through 1986.

BINGO TAX ACT:

Tax of 5% of gross proceeds of any game of bingo is imposed. Quarterly reports and payments are due before 20th day of Apr., July, Oct. and Jan. Insofar as practicable, administrative provisions of Retailers' Occupation Tax Act are applicable. (230-25/1 to 25/7).

CHICAGO TAXES:

Chicago Employers' Expense Tax.—Employers doing business in Chicago who have 15 or more full-time employees are subject to a tax of $5 per employee per month ($4 per employee per month for period Jan. 1, 1986 to June 10, 1986). Taxes to be paid to Chicago Dept. of Revenue on or before last day of month following close of each calendar quarter. Governmental agencies and federally tax-exempt organizations are, in general, exempt. (Municipal Code of Chicago, 3-20-030). Illinois Supreme Court has held ordinance valid exercise of home rule powers not violating constitutional prohibition against imposition of taxes upon or measured by earnings or upon occupations. (57 Ill.2d 553, 317 N.E.2d 3).

Chicago Service Tax.—Tax held unconstitutional by Ill. Sup. Ct. (89 Ill.2d 45, 432 N.E.2d 227).

Chicago Transaction Tax.—Tax imposed on two types of transaction, rentals of personal property and transfers of interests in real property.

Rental or Lease of Personal Property.—Tax of 6% of lease price is imposed on all leases and rentals of personal property delivered or used in City of Chicago unless lease is consummated outside City and at least 50% of use occurs outside City. Personal property is defined as all property other than real property, including leased time on equipment, such as computer, not otherwise rented. Specifically excluded is medical equipment leased by consumers for their own use. Ultimate liability for tax is on lessee. However, lessor is required to collect and remit to Chicago Department of Revenue on monthly basis tax due on all such leases. Exemptions from tax include leases which involve, as lessee, governmental entity or international, charitable, religious or educational organization; and certain fiduciary transfers.

Transfers of Interest in Real Property.—Tax of $3.75 for each $500 of transfer price or fraction thereof is imposed on all transfers of title to and transfers of beneficial interest in real property located within City of Chicago. Beneficial interests in Illinois land trusts are expressly included. Tax is paid through purchase of tax stamps which must be affixed to face of deeds. Ultimate liability for tax is on grantee or purchaser. However, person making or effectuating transfer is responsible for payment of tax. Exemptions from tax include transfers involving governmental bodies or charitable, religious or education organizations; transfers where consideration is less than $500; and certain fiduciary transfers. (Municipal Code of Chicago, 3-32-010—3-32-120).

Chicago Vehicle Fuel Tax.—Vehicle fuel tax of 5¢ per gallon imposed on privilege of purchasing or using, in City of Chicago, vehicle fuel purchased in sale at retail, effective Oct. 6, 1986. (Municipal Code of Chicago, 3-52-020). Tax held valid as to all taxpayers by Ill. Sup. Ct. (116 Ill.2d 311, 507 N.E.2d 858).

CIGARETTE AND TOBACCO TAXES:

Cigarette Tax.—Tax at rate of ten mills per cigarette (20¢ per pack of 20; 25¢ per pack of 25) prior to Jan. 1, 1994 and 22 mills per cigarette (44¢ per pack of 20) sold or otherwise disposed of imposed on retailers, prepaid by distributors and passed on to consumers. Complementary use tax (not payable where retailers' tax has been paid) imposed at same rate. (35-130/2, 135/2, 135/3). Municipalities are authorized to tax retail vendors of cigarettes. (65-5/8-11-3).

Tobacco Products Tax.—Repealed.

COIN-IN-SLOT AMUSEMENT DEVICES:

License and annual $15 privilege tax requirement exists. (35-510/1 to 510/16). Counties and municipalities may license, control and tax such devices. (35-510/7).

ESTATE TAX:

Note.—New Estate and Generation-Skipping Transfer Tax Act approved Sept. 1, 1989, effective with respect to taxable transfers occurring on or after Jan. 1, 1990. Effective for decedents dying after Dec. 31, 1982, only estate tax imposed equal to greater of: (1) State death tax credit for federal estate tax purposes reduced by state death taxes actually paid to other states and eligible for credit and (2) maximum state death tax credit provided on federal return with respect to property having taxable situs

See note at head of Digest as to 1998 legislation covered.

See Topical Index in front part of this volume.

ESTATE TAX . . . *continued*

in Illinois. (120-405.1) For decedents dying before Jan. 1, 1983, estate tax imposed on difference between maximum tax credit allowable for state death taxes against federal estate tax on that portion of estate having taxable situs in Illinois and Illinois inheritance taxes. (120-403a). For residents, all property subject to federal estate tax has taxable situs in Illinois, except real property and tangible personal property physically situated in another state. For nonresidents, only real property and tangible personal property physically situated in Illinois has taxable situs in Illinois. (120-405.1). All Illinois real property, whether or not held in trust, has taxable situs in Illinois. (120-405.1).

Return and Appraisement.—Effective for decedents dying after Dec. 31, 1982, return must be filed with treasurer of county in which decedent resided and with Attorney General. Copy of federal estate tax return must be filed with Attorney General. Return due at same time federal return due. (120-405.3).

Lien of Tax.—Same as under Inheritance Tax Act—see subhead Inheritance Tax, supra. (120-405.6).

Payment.—Effective for decedents dying after Dec. 31, 1982, tax due same time federal estate tax due, and payable to county treasurer. Interest charged at rate of 10% per annum from due date of tax to date tax paid. (120-405.3). Penalty of 5% of tax due is charged each month return is not filed after due date, not to exceed 25% of tax due. Penalty of .5% of tax due charged for each month tax is past due, not to exceed 25% of tax due. (120-405.3).

Original Proceedings.—Same as under Inheritance Tax Act—see topic Inheritance Tax. (120-405.7).

Valuation Date.—Effective for decedents dying after Dec. 31, 1982, assets valued same as for federal estate tax return. (120-405.1).

Application for Transfer of Assets.—For decedents dying after Dec. 31, 1982, executor, survivor, or heirs not required to apply to Attorney General for inheritance tax consent to transfer assets owned by decedent.

Apportionment.—No statute. Federal estate tax and administration expenses apportioned between probate and non-probate assets under doctrine of equitable apportionment in intestate estate (69 Ill.2d 525, 372 N.E.2d 662) and testate estate (82 Ill.2d 15, 411 N.E.2d 266); surviving spouse's share of probate or nonprobate property which qualifies for federal estate tax marital deduction not charged with federal estate tax (82 Ill.2d 15, 411 N.E.2d 266), except that surviving spouse's statutory renunciatory or intestate share computed after payment of federal estate tax (83 Ill.2d 379, 415 N.E.2d 416); doctrine of equitable apportionment not applicable to estates consisting exclusively of probate assets, rather Illinois follows burden on residue rule (383 Ill. 489, 50 N.E.2d 461; 109 Ill.App.3d 57, 440 N.E.2d 222).

FRANCHISE TAXES:

See category Business Organizations, topic Corporations.

GIFT TAX:

None; but, for decedents dying before Jan. 1, 1983, inheritance tax applies to gifts in contemplation of death made within two years of death. (120-375).

HOTEL OCCUPANCY TAX:

Hotel occupancy tax is imposed at rate of 5% of 94% (plus 1% of 94% for Tourism Fund) of gross rental receipts from hotel rooms (other than from "permanent residents"). (35-145/1 to 145/10). Chicago Municipal Tax is additional 3%. (Municipal Code of Chicago, 3-24-030).

INCOME TAX:

Income tax imposed on every individual, corporation, trust, estate and partnership on privilege of earning or receiving income in or as resident of state. (35-5/201[a], 5/201[c]). Tax is administered by Illinois Department of Revenue. Unless expressly provided otherwise or clearly appearing from context, any term used in income tax act has same meaning as when used in comparable context in U.S. Internal Revenue Code and other statutes of U.S. relating to federal income tax as are in effect for that taxable year. (35-5/102, 5/103).

Base of tax is "net income," which is "base income" allocated and apportioned to Illinois, less standard exemption. (35-5/202). "Base income" is computed by making adjustments to federal adjusted gross income of individuals and to federal taxable income of corporations, estates, trusts and partnerships. (35-5/203). Standard exemption of $1,000 (or portion thereof representing base income allocable to Illinois) is allowed every taxpayer, with additional exemptions of $1,000 (or portion thereof) allowed individuals 65 years of age or older or blind. For taxable year ending on or after Dec. 31, 1992, taxpayer whose Illinois base income exceeds $1,000 and who is claimed as dependent on another person's federal income tax return shall not be allowed basic amount. (35-5/204).

Basic tax for individuals, trusts and estates is as follows: Taxable years ending prior to July 1, 1989, basic tax is 2½% of net income. Taxable years beginning prior to July 1, 1989 and ending after June 30, 1989, basic tax is sum of (i) 2½% net of income for period prior to July 1, 1989 and (ii) 3% of net income for period after June 30, 1989. Taxable years beginning after June 30, 1989 and ending prior to July 1, 1991, basic tax is 3% of net income. Taxable years beginning prior to July 1, 1991 and ending after June 30, 1991, basic tax is sum of (i) 3% of net income for period prior to July 1, 1991 and (ii) 2½% of net income for period after June 30, 1991. Taxable years beginning after June 30, 1991, basic tax is 2½% of net income. Basic tax for corporations is as follows: Taxable years ending prior to July 1, 1989, basic rate is 4% of net income. Taxable years beginning prior to July 1, 1989 and ending after June 30, 1989, basic rate is sum of (i) 4% of net income for period prior to July 1, 1989 and (ii) 4.8% of net income for period after June 30, 1989. Taxable years beginning after June 30, 1989, and ending prior to July 1, 1991, basic rate is 4.8% of net income. Taxable years beginning prior to July 1, 1991, and ending after June 30, 1991, basic tax is sum of (i) 4.8% of net income for period prior to July 1, 1991 and (ii) 4% of net income for period after June 30, 1991. Taxable years beginning after June 30, 1991, basic tax is 4% of net income. (35-5/201[b]). Special provisions applicable for taxable years beginning before Jan. 1, 1983 and ending after June 30, 1984. (35-5/202.1, 5/202.2). Effective for taxable years ending after June 30, 1979, Personal Property Tax Replacement Income Tax imposes additional income tax of 2.85% on corporations except subchapter S corporations, reduced to 2.5% after 1980, additional income tax of 1.5% on trusts, partnerships and subchapter S corporations. (35-5/201[c], [d], [f]). Special provisions applicable for taxable years beginning before July 1, 1979 and ending after June 30, 1979. (35-5/201[e]). Personal Property Replacement Income Tax determined constitutionally valid. (78 Ill.2d 387, 401 N.E.2d 491). See topic Property Taxes, subhead Personal Property Taxes, Liability, Lien. Special rules for certain insurance companies, regulated investment companies, real estate investment trusts, financial organizations, (including bank-holding companies), international banking facilities, consolidated corporations, Western Hemisphere trade corporations, China Trade Act corporations, possessions corporations, transportation service companies, cooperatives, exempt organizations, subchapter S corporations, certain trusts, combat zone deaths, military pay, and government civilian employee pay earned while prisoners of war or missing in action. (35-5/203, 5/205, 5/304).

Credits.—Taxpayers allowed investment tax credit against personal property tax replacement income tax of .5% of basis of property used in manufacturing, mining, or retailing placed in service after June 30, 1984, additional .5% credit for property placed in service after June 30, 1986, provided taxpayer's base employment increased by 1% over preceding year. Credit limited to taxpayers replacement tax liability and credit not allowed for any year other than year in which property was placed in service. For tax years ending on or after Dec. 31, 1985, excess investment tax credits may be carried forward five years if taxpayer meets certain conditions. (35-5/201[e]). Credit terminates after Dec. 31, 2003. (35-5/201[e]). Tax credit against income taxes of .5% of basis of qualified property placed in service by taxpayer in High Impact Business or Enterprise Zone. (35-5/201[h][j]). For tax years ending on or after Dec. 31, 1985, excess investment credits for enterprise zone property may be carried forward five years. (35-5/201[h]). Taxpayers conducting trade or business in enterprise zone or qualifying as high impact business in foreign trade zone are allowed jobs credit of $500 per eligible employee, effective for employees hired on or after Jan. 1, 1986. For tax years ending on or after Dec. 31, 1988, credit allowed in year following year employees hired. Excess jobs credits may be carried forward five years. (35-5/201[i]). Training expense credit against income tax of 1.6% of amounts paid or accrued by taxpayer for educational or vocational training for tax years beginning on or after Dec. 31, 1986. Excess training expense credits may be carried forward five years. (35-5/201[j]). For tax years beginning July 1, 1990, taxpayer given credit equal to 6½% of qualifying expenditures for increased research in state. (35-5/201[k]). For tax years ending after Dec. 31, 1997 and on or before Dec. 31, 2001 taxpayer allowed credit for certain unreimbursed eligible environmental mediation costs. (35-5/201[l]). Excess may be carried forward five years if taxpayer meets certain conditions. (35-5/201[l]).

Residents receive tax credit for taxes paid to another state on income which is also subject to Illinois basic income tax (no credit against replacement income tax). Credit provided, however, shall not exceed amount which bears same ratio to tax otherwise due as amount of taxpayer's base income subject to tax by other taxing jurisdiction bears to his total base income for taxable year, and provided further that such credit shall not be allowed if any creditable tax has been deducted in determining base income for taxable year. (35-5/601[b][3]). Income up to $2,000 annually per account, derived by individuals from investments in accordance with College Savings Programs are exempt from state and political subdivision taxes, except estate, transfer and inheritance taxes.

Tax Credit for Residential Property Taxes.—Beginning tax years ending Dec. 31, 1991, individual income taxpayers entitled 5% tax credit of real property taxes paid on principal residence. (35-5/208).

Resident individuals, estates, trusts, and partners: entire base income allocated to Illinois. (35-5/301).

Nonresident individuals, estates, trusts, and partners are taxed on net income from business transactions or property located within state and from performance of personal services within state. (35-5/302 to 5/307). Nonresident shareholders of Subchapter S corporation are taxed on their share of income allocated or apportioned to Illinois. (35-5/308[a]).

Part-year residents are taxed in same manner as residents for part of year they reside in state, and as nonresidents for part of year they reside outside state. (35-5/301[b]).

Corporations and others deriving business income from within and without state must determine that apportionable to state on three-factor basis consisting of property, payroll, and sales. (35-5/304). Effective Aug. 29, 1975, Illinois repealed Act adopting Multistate Tax Compact. Effective for tax years ending on or after Dec. 31, 1982, members of "unitary business group" must use combined method to apportion domestic corporate income. (35-5/1501, 35-5/304). "Unitary business group" excludes members which conduct 80% or more of their total business activity outside U.S. (35-5/1501). Worldwide combined reporting may be used for years prior to 1982. (84 Ill.2d 102, 417 N.E.2d 1343, appeal dismissed, 457 U.S. 1103).

Partnerships are taxed and must determine income allocable and apportionable to state in same manner as corporations; partners are taxed on shares of partnership profits, whether or not distributed. (35-5/205[b], 35-5/305).

Returns.—Return shall be made by every person for any taxable year for which person is liable for tax or where person is resident or corporation qualified to do business in Illinois and required to file federal tax return whether or not liable for Illinois income tax. No return needed if person has Illinois income less than $1,000 and is claimed as dependent on another person's federal or Illinois income tax return. (35-5/502). Returns of individuals, partnerships and fiduciaries are due on or before 15th day of fourth month following close of taxable year. Two month extension available for certain individuals traveling abroad. (35-5/505[c]). Corporate returns due by 15th day of third month following close of taxable year. Exempt organizations returns due by 15th day of fifth month following close of taxable year. (35-5/505[a]). Director of Revenue

See note at head of Digest as to 1998 legislation covered.

See Topical Index in front part of this volume.

INCOME TAX . . . *continued*

may grant extensions of time to file return, not to exceed six months in aggregate. (35-5/505[a]). If extension granted, tentative return must be filed on or before due date of return (without regard to extension period) and payment made of tax estimated to be due for such taxable year. (35-5/602). When taxpayer has been granted extension of time to file federal return, filing of copy of federal extension with Department will automatically extend due date of Illinois return for same taxable year, provided tentative return is filed on time and proper amount of tax estimated is paid. (35-5/505[b]; 35-5/602); Effective for tax years ending on or after Dec. 31, 1985, corporate members of unitary group may elect to be treated as one taxpayer and file single return. (35-5/505[f]). No penalty or interest applicable for taxable year ending on or after Dec. 31, 1990 following filing extension granted by presidential proclamation under ARC §7508 for member or spouse, if filing joint return, of armed forces serving in combat zone. (35-5/602)

Payment in full required with return. Credit given for tax withheld, estimated payments previously made, foreign tax paid and overpayments made in previous years. (35-5/601, 35-5/909).

Limitations on Assessment.—None if fraud, if no return filed, if supplemental return is required but is not filed, if taxpayer fails to notify Department of change in his federal return, or if taxpayer fails to report change or correction that is treated in same manner as if it were a deficiency for federal income tax purposes; six years from date return was filed if more than 25% of base income stated in return is omitted; otherwise, three years from date return (or supplemental return) was filed. (35-5/905). Period of assessment and collection against transferee is two years after expiration of period of limitation against transferor. (35-5/905[m], 35-5/1405).

Sales Outside Usual Course of Business.—Transferee of assets outside usual course of transferor's business must file disclosure report with Illinois Department of Revenue within ten days of transfer. Transferee may be personally liable for transferor's unpaid taxes up to reasonable value of property transferred if transferee fails to file disclosure report. (35-5/902[d]).

Where Returns Filed and Taxes Paid.—Returns are filed with and taxes paid to Illinois Department of Revenue, Springfield, Illinois.

Appeal and Refund.—Taxpayer may protest a proposed assessment of tax by filing a written protest with Department within 60 days after issuance of a notice of deficiency (150 days if taxpayer is outside U.S.) and may request hearing. (35-5/908[a]). After hearing, if any, Department will mail to taxpayer notice of its decision, briefly setting forth its findings of fact and basis of decision in each case decided adversely to taxpayer. (35-5/908[b].) Taxpayer may then, within 30 days, file written request for rehearing. (35-5/908[c]). Department's action on taxpayer's protest request becomes final 30 days after issuance of notice of decision or, if timely request for rehearing is filed, upon issuance of denial of request or issuance of notice of final decision. (35-5/908[d]). If no protest filed, taxes covered by notice of deficiency deemed assessed upon expiration of 45 days following issuance of such notice (150 days if taxpayer is outside U.S.). (35-5/904[d]). Provisions of Administrative Review Law apply to and govern all proceedings for judicial review of final action of Department. Circuit court of county wherein taxpayer has his residence or commercial domicile, or Cook County in those cases where taxpayer does not have his residence or commercial domicile in state, shall have power to review all final administrative decisions of Department in administering provisions of Act. (35-5/1201, 1202).

Claims for refund must be filed with Department within three years after date return was filed or one year after date tax was paid, whichever is later. (35-5/911). If denied, or if no notice of denial is issued before expiration of six months from date claim was filed, taxpayer may file written protest with Department within 60 days and may request hearing. (35-5/909[e], [f], 910[a]). After hearing, if any, Department will mail to taxpayer notice of its decision, briefly setting forth its findings of fact and basis of decision for each case decided adversely to taxpayer. (35-5/910[b]). Taxpayer may within 30 days file written request for rehearing. (35-5/910[c]). Department's action on taxpayer's protest becomes final 30 days after issuance of notice of decision or, if timely request for rehearing is filed, upon issuance of denial of request or issuance of notice of final decision. (35-5/910[d]). Rules for judicial review of such denial of request, or issuance of notice of final decision same as under catchline Appeal and Refund, supra.

Withholding.—Every employer maintaining office or transacting any business in state and required to withhold federal income tax on compensation paid in state to an individual must deduct and withhold, from such compensation amount equal to applicable tax rate for individuals as provided in 35-5/201(b) after deducting appropriate withholding exemption attributable to payroll period. (35-5/701). Each individual entitled to withholding exemption in amount equal to $1,000 times number of such exemptions permitted him under Internal Revenue Code (other than those permitted under IRC §3402m), or lesser amount claimed by him. (35-5/702). Any person maintaining office or transacting business in Illinois must deduct and withhold amount equal to applicable tax rate for individuals from any payment for certain personal service contracts, prizes or awards in excess of $1,000. (Repealed eff. Jan. 1, 1989.) Any person making payment of lottery winnings in excess of $1,000 must deduct and withhold amount equal to applicable tax rate for individuals. (35-5/710). No withholding is required for payments of interest, dividends, pensions, annuities or certain other deferred income. (35-5/701[f]). Withheld taxes are required to be paid to Department, or to designated depositary, on or before third banking day following close of quarter monthly period whenever aggregate amounts withheld (together with amounts previously withheld and not paid to Department) exceed $1,000. Withheld taxes are required to be paid to Department, or to designated depositary, on or before 15th day of second and third months of each calendar quarter, and on or before last day of month following last month of each calendar quarter, whenever aggregate amount withheld (together with amounts previously withheld and not paid to Department) exceeds $500 but does not exceed $1,000. Quarterly returns required, due on or before last day of first month following close of calendar quarter. Annual return reconciling quarterly and monthly returns required on or before Feb. 28 of following calendar year. (Form IL-700). If

amount of compensation paid by employer is not sufficient to require withholding tax for any employees, or if aggregate amount withheld, is less than $500 for calendar year, employer may request permission from Department to file only annual return and to pay taxes required to be withheld at time of filing annual return. On and after Jan. 1, 1998 employer who deducts and withholds from person engaged in domestic service employment may file annual return and pay tax on or before 15th day of fourth month following close of employer's taxable year and return may be submitted with employer's individual tax return. Permission for annual filing must be renewed on or before Apr. 30 of each year. (35-5/704; Form IL-700).

Estimated Tax.—Every taxpayer, other than estate, trust, partnership or subchapter S corporation, must file declaration of estimated tax for taxable year if amount payable as estimated tax can reasonably be expected to be more than $250. Due dates, rules and procedures parallel federal. (35-5/803). Effective for taxable years ending after Jan. 1, 1986, estimates must be paid in four equal installments. (35-5/803[d]). Penalty for underpayment of estimated tax is 24% per annum on amount of underpayment, but not applicable if underpayment results solely because of increased tax rate in effect July 1, 1989 through Dec. 1989. (35-5/804).

Electronic Payments.—Beginning Oct. 1, 1993, taxpayer, other than individual, having average monthly tax liability of $150,000 or more shall make all payments by electronic funds transfer. Beginning Oct. 1, 1994 tax liability amount requiring electronic funds transfer is $100,000 per month; beginning Oct. 1, 1995, minimum amount is $50,000. Any taxpayer, other than individual, is allowed to make payment by electronic funds transfer. (35-5/601.1).

Information Statements.—Every employer shall furnish two copies of statement with respect to compensation paid in calendar year to each employee by Jan. 31 of succeeding year and to each former employee on date of last payment of compensation. (35-5/703). Effective Jan. 1, 1989, any person maintaining office or transacting business in Illinois who makes payments with respect to certain personal service contracts, prizes and awards in excess of $1,000 shall maintain record in format in which record is available to review by Department of all payments made under contract for personal services. (35-5/1405.2; 35-5/1405.3). Any person maintaining office or transacting business in Illinois and required under §6041 and §6050N of Internal Revenue Code to report to U.S. Secretary of Treasury payments made to another person shall not also be required to file with Department copies of those reports. Person shall maintain, in format available for review by Department, copies of reports that include payments for rents or royalties of $1,000 or more from real or tangible personal property located in Illinois, or royalties on patent or copyright used in Illinois. (35-5/1405.1).

Reciprocal Agreements for Exemption of Compensation of Nonresidents.—Agreements with Indiana, Iowa, Kentucky, Michigan, and Wisconsin providing for exemption of compensation paid to residents of one state for performance of services in other state and for similar exemption from withholding are in effect.

INHERITANCE TAX:

Effective for decedents dying after Dec. 31, 1982, inheritance tax repealed, leaving in place estate tax equal to greater of: (1) State death tax credit for federal estate tax purposes reduced by state death taxes actually paid to other states and eligible for credit and (2) maximum state death tax credit provided on federal return with respect to property having taxable situs in Illinois. (120-405 et seq.).

For decedents dying before Jan. 1, 1983, inheritance tax applies. (35 ILCS 405/1 et seq.).

Valuation Date.—Assets are valued as of date of decedent's death. (See, 120-375; 192 Ill. 106, 61 N.E. 489.)

Valuation.—Special use valuation of farms and closely held business real estate determined in accordance with §2032A of Internal Revenue Code available for estates of decedents dying on or after Jan. 1, 1977.

MOBILE HOME LOCAL SERVICES TAX:

Annual local services tax imposed payable, at rates between 15¢-7.5¢ per square foot, depending on model year of mobile home, in county in which home located. 20% reduction is provided for owners who are disabled or age 65 or older who live in mobile home. (35-515/1). Taxpayers have six months from receipt of tax bill to claim error in tax. (35-515/6.1).

MOTOR FUEL TAX:

Tax at rate of 16¢ per gallon from Aug. 1, 1989, until Jan. 1, 1990 and 19¢ per gallon after Jan. 1, 1990 imposed on privilege of operating motor vehicles. Additional tax of 2$\frac{1}{2}$¢ per gallon is imposed on diesel fuel. Aircraft fuel is exempt. Tax usually collected by distributors or suppliers. (35-505/1 to 505/20). Penalty of at least $1,000 will be imposed on operators of commercial motor vehicles who fail to secure license or display decals for vehicles. (35-505/13a.6).

Tax at rate of 3/10th% per gallon on motor fuel owned or possessed on Aug. 1, 1990 and before Jan. 1, 2013 and 3/10th% per gallon on motor fuel owned or possessed on Jan. 1, 1990 and before Jan. 1, 2013 as imposed upon privilege of engaging in business of selling motor fuel as retailer or reseller on all motor fuel used in motor vehicles operating on public highways and recreational type watercraft operating in waters in State with exceptions for specified aviation fuels and kerosenes at certain airports and no tax on diesel fuel used in operation of ships, barges, or vessels transporting property in interstate commerce on rivers bordering on Illinois. (35-505/2a).

MOTOR VEHICLE TAXES:

Flat Weight or Mileage Tax on Motor Vehicles.—See category Transportation, topic Motor Vehicles, subhead Motor Vehicle Carriers.

PROPERTY TAXES:

Real Property Taxes, Liability, Lien.—Owner of real property on Jan. 1 is liable for taxes for that year. (35-205/27a). Leasehold on tax exempt property is taxed as real

PROPERTY TAXES . . . *continued*
estate. (35-205/20, 205/26). Real estate taxes first lien, superior to all other liens and encumbrances, on or from Jan. 1. (35-205/216).

Personal Property Taxes, Liability, Lien.—Illinois Constitution mandated legislature to adopt substitute for personal property tax by Jan. 1, 1979. (Const. Art. IX, §5c). Repeal by constitutional amendment of individual personal property tax effective Jan. 1, 1971 held valid. (410 U.S. 356). Illinois passed Personal Property Tax Replacement Income Tax to substitute for ad valorem personal property tax on corporations, partnerships and trusts. No property taxed as personal property shall be classified as real property subject to taxation. [35-200/24-5]. Personal Property Replacement Income Tax determined constitutionally valid. (78 Ill.2d 387, 401 N.E.2d 491). See topic Income Tax.

Exemptions.—Property used for educational, religious, governmental, charitable and certain other such purposes exempt from taxation. (35-205/19 to 205/19.23). Duty of owner of any property which is exempt from taxation to file certificate, on or before Jan. 31 of each year, stating facts that qualify property for exemption or continued exemption, and owner that qualifies for homestead must file by May 1 of each year. (35-200/15-10, 15-15, 15-20, 15-30). Also exempt are certain city and village harbor facilities. (35-200/15-55). Taxpayer may appeal exemption denial to Circuit Court under Administrative Review Act only after Department of Revenue has acted on hearing application. (35-200/8-35). Judicial determination of tax exempt status of property must be made pursuant to Administrative Review Law, except that governmental agency may seek judicial determination of exempt status for years during which eminent domain proceedings were pending, judicial determination of exemption for disabled veterans and homestead exemptions is permitted, and court proceedings for exemption for 1985 and preceding assessment years are permitted. (35-205/194.1). If exemption approved by Department of Revenue or circuit court, then certification of error issued for: (a) Prior period of eligibility of up to three assessment years immediately preceding assessment year for which exemption approved, or (b) subsequent erroneous assessment of property as nonexempt, or (c) subsequent assessment year for which property remains eligible for exemption but owner fails to file application for exemption or certificate of status. (35-205/194.2).

State-owned property leased to Illinois Prairie Path Corporation and used for conservation and certain other specified purposes is exempt from property taxes. (35-200/15-55).

Exempt from state and municipal taxes are: Municipal retirement fund benefits (40-5/7-217), park and retirement board employees' annuity and benefit fund in cities over 500,000 (40-5/12-190), teacher pension and retirement funds in cities over 500,000 (40-5/17-151), and teacher's retirement system (40-5/16-190). Exemption for tangible personal property for farming purposes held invalid. (55 Ill.2d 393, 304 N.E.2d 65). Retirement trust exempt from personal property tax. (Helson v. Rosewell, Cook Co. Doc. No. 78CH-5168).

Assessment.—Except in counties with population of more than 200,000 which classify and except for "farms" that qualify for farm value assessment and except for real property constituting coal, real property valued for tax assessment purposes at 33¹/₃% of its fair cash value. (35-205/20, 205-20e, 205/20k). Counties, with population of more than 200,000, by ordinance of county board, may classify real property for purpose of fixing assessed valuation at percentage other than 33¹/₃% of its fair cash value. (35-205/20a). Farm is eligible for farm value assessment. (35-205/20e, 205-20f-1). Farm dwelling, appurtenant structures and tract upon which they are immediately situated are assessed at 33¹/₃% of fair cash value except that in counties with population of more than 200,000, county board by ordinance may fix assessed valuation at percentage other than 33¹/₃% of fair market value. (35-205/20g). Department of Revenue has power to lower or raise total assessed value of property in any county so that assessments in county will be uniform with assessments in all counties by applying equalization factor to all property (except farm that has qualified for farm value assessment and except for property qualified for coal assessment) in county. (35-205/146-205/152). No tax may be assessed against property with equalized assessed value under $150 for particular year. (35-205/161).

Taxing districts may abate portion of taxes for period not to exceed ten years and in aggregate amount not to exceed $1,000,000 where industrial firm locates within taxing district from another state, territory, or country, was newly created within Illinois, or expands existing facility. (35-205/162).

Pollution control facilities given special consideration in determining fair cash value for purposes of fixing assessed valuation for tax purposes. (35-205/21a-1 to 205/21a-8). $2,000 maximum reduction from value of real property, as equalized, given owner of residence if owner is 65 or over, is liable for payment of tax, and occupies residence. (35-205/19.23-1). Similar exemption (35-205/19.24) under prior constitution held invalid (48 Ill.2d 323, 269 N.E.2d 465). New provisions provide for annual maximum exemption of $30,000 in actual value for any new improvements on property owned and used exclusively for residential purposes. (35-200/10-15). Cooperatives and condominiums assessed on same basis as single family residence in counties with population of over 200,000 which classify real property. (35-200/10-15). Residential property which is individually owned and includes right to use common area is assessed at value which includes proportional share of value of common area. (35-200/10-35).

Repairs and maintenance to residential real estate owned and used exclusively for residential purposes shall not increase assessed value of real property if such work does not increase area of improvements, materially alter character or condition of structures, is performed to keep property in good condition, and materials used are not of value greater than replacement value of materials removed. (35-205/20h-1, 205/20i).

As of Jan. 1, 1981 single family residential property constructed before July 1, 1939 located in National Historic District or Municipal Landmark Area may be entitled to continuing assessment at 1979 valuation until such time as classification, use, lot changes or substantial non-preservation improvements are made. (35-205/44.1). Application for assessment under 35-205/44.1 must be made prior to Jan. 1, 1983. This section is repealed as of Dec. 31, 1989. (35-205/44.1).

Owner-occupied single-family residence or building owned and operated as cooperative and listed on National or Illinois Register of Historic Places or designated historic building by municipal ordinance entitled to special valuation if Director of Historic Preservation issues certificate of rehabilitation to owner who has restored or preserved residence in accordance with standards set by Secretary of Interior. Valuation is as follows: For eight year period following rehabilitation, fair cash value of residence in year in which rehabilitation begins (base year); ninth year, base year valuation plus 25% of adjustment in value; tenth year, base year plus 50% of adjustment; 11th year, base year plus 75% of adjustment; following years, current fair market value. Any taxing district by majority vote may elect to bar application of this section to taxes levied by it. (35-200/10-40, 10-45, 10-50, 10-55, 10-60, 10-65, 10-70, 10-75, 10-80, 10-85).

Tax Credit for Residential Property Taxes.—Beginning tax years ending Dec. 31, 1991, individual income taxpayers entitled 5% tax credit of real property taxes paid on principal residence. (35-5/208).

Homestead Exemption.—Persons over 65 who are liable for real estate taxes on their residence may claim $2,000 through 1990 levy year in all counties maximum reduction in equalized valuation. Beginning with 1991 levy year maximum reduction of $2,500 in counties with 2,000,000 population or more and $2,000 in all other counties. (35-205/19.23-1). In case of land improved by apartment building owned and operated as cooperative or life care facility that qualifies as cooperative (210-40/2), maximum reduction from value of such real property shall be multiplied by number of apartments or units occupied by each person 65 years or older who is liable for paying real estate taxes and is owner of record of interest in cooperative, other than leasehold interest. If such person becomes resident of licensed facility after exemption granted, exemption shall continue so long as former residence is occupied by qualifying person's spouse and spouse is 65 years or older, or if residence remains unoccupied but is still owned by person qualified for homestead exemption. (35-200/15-170). Assessor shall notify person who qualifies for exemption that person may qualify for deferral of taxes under Senior Citizen Real Estate Tax Deferral Act (320-30/1 et seq.).

Owners of residential property used by owner as principal dwelling place may claim annual homestead exemption of maximum reduction of $3,000 for levy years 1979-1982; $3,500 levy years 1983-1990; beginning 1991 $4,500 in counties of 2,000,000 or more and $3,500 in all other counties. (35-200/15-175). Married persons residing in separate residences qualifying for exemption may each claim 50% of authorized reduction. (35-200/15-175). Statute as applied by Cook County Assessor declared invalid. (84 Ill.2d 229, 417 N.E.2d 1290).

Cooperative association must credit savings resulting from homestead exemptions to apportioned tax liability of owner eligible for exemption. (35-200/15-175).

Homestead improvement exemption of up to $30,000 in actual value of improvements available to residential buildings upon demonstration that increased assessment is attributable solely to new improvements or rebuilding of residential structure following catastrophic event. Exemption lasts until later of four years from date improvement is completed and occupied or next general assessment. (35-200/15-180).

Cash Grant to Elderly and Disabled.—Persons over 65 or who will become 65 years old during calendar year in which claim is filed, and any surviving spouse of such claimant who at time of death received or was entitled to receive grant pursuant to this Section, which surviving spouse will become 65 years of age within 24 months immediately following death of such claimant and which surviving spouse but for his or her age is otherwise qualified to receive grant pursuant to this Section and disabled persons whose annual household income is less than $14,000 and whose household is liable for property taxes may claim cash grant from state under Property Tax Relief Act. (350-25/1 to 25/12). If claimant dies after filing claim, amount disbursed to surviving spouse, or dependent minor children if no surviving spouse, provided same resided with claimant at time claim filed. (350-25/1 et seq.).

Review of Assessment.—If values placed on real property are deemed excessive, taxpayer should file complaint with Board of Appeals on or before date specified by Board which shall be at least 20 days from date of publication of notice in counties over 3,000,000 population (35-200/16-110) and with Board of Review on or before Aug. 10 in counties with fewer than 150,000 inhabitants, and on or before Sept. 10 in counties with 150,000 or more but fewer than 3,000,000 inhabitants (35-200/12-40, 16-20, 16-50, 16-55, 16-60, 16-70, 16-75, 16-80). These boards have power to revise entire assessment of any taxpayer or any part thereof. (35-200/12-40, 16-20, 16-50, 16-55, 16-60, 16-70, 16-75, 16-80). Taxpayer may appeal decision of Board of Review to Property Tax Appeal Board and then to Circuit Court under Administrative Review Act. (35-200/1-5, 16-160). If Board of Review or Property Tax Appeal Board lowers assessment of owner-occupied residence, reduced assessment shall remain in effect for remainder of general assessment period, unless that parcel is subsequently sold in arm's length transaction establishing fair market value that is different from fair market value on which Board's assessment is based, or unless reversed or modified upon review. (35-200/16-185, 16-190, 16-195). Taxpayer may contest decision of Board of Appeals in Circuit Court by paying total tax under protest except that payment under protest not required if basis for objection is that property exempt and proceeding to determine tax exempt status is pending before board of review, board of appeals or Department of Revenue. (35-205/194, 205/235).

Payment.—Real estate taxes are due and payable in two equal installments in year following year tax becomes lien, first normally becoming delinquent on, and bearing interest after, June 1 at rate of 1 1/2% per month; for all real property other than farmland, 1% per month for farmland; and second becoming delinquent on, and bearing interest at same rate after, Sept. 1. In counties with accelerated method of billing, first installment is due on Mar. 1 and second installment on Aug. 1. (35-200/21-15). In counties of less than 2,000,000 population in which unemployment rate equals or exceeds 10% county board may defer payment of 50% of each installment of taxes for 60 days. (35-205/224.1b). No taxes on homestead real property due in 1991 and 1992 deemed delinquent and no interest or penalty assessed until one year after owner who is member of National Guard or armed forces reserves returns to civilian status after active duty. (35-200/21-15). Interest on unpaid taxes shall be charged to mortgage lender in certain circumstances and duty on mortgage lender to redeem property and take steps to remove liens accruing because of delinquency where mortgage lender received all payments due under written terms of mortgage or promissory note secured by mortgage. (35-200/21-15).

See note at head of Digest as to 1998 legislation covered.

See Topical Index in front part of this volume.

PROPERTY TAXES . . . *continued*

Collection and Sale.—After Sept. 1 next after delinquent taxes become due real estate may be advertised for sale for nonpayment of taxes and judgment applied for to circuit court and sale made at later date to be designated, except that in counties over 3,000,000 population time for advertisement and application for judgment has been extended. (35-200/21-110, 21-115, 21-120). Payment may be made at any time before sale. (35-204/233). Collector or deputy must, on day of sale, attend at court house, and between 9 A.M. and 4 P.M. (between 8 A.M. and 8 P.M. in counties having population of 3,000,000 or more) offer for sale separately and in consecutive order each tract of land or lot. (35-200/21-205). Person offering to pay amount due on each tract or lot for least percentage thereon as penalty is considered purchaser thereof, provided, that no bid may be accepted for penalty exceeding 18% of amount of tax or special assessment. (35-205/245). Person offering to pay amount due must provide, not less than ten days prior to making offer, letter of credit or unconditional bond for not less than one and one-half times amount of tax or special assessment owed. (35-200/21-210). Every tract or lot so offered at public sale and not sold is forfeited to state. (35-200/21-225).

Collector may conduct special "scavenger" sale of tracts for which all or part of general taxes for two or more years are delinquent. Such tracts are sold at public sale to highest bidder for cash, notwithstanding fact that bid less than amount of taxes, assessments, and penalties due. Sale extinguishes in rem lien of taxes; redemption does not revive lien. Confirmation of sale neither affects owner's personal liability for taxes, interest and penalties nor prevents institution of in personam suit under 35-205/275 to collect amount remaining due after sale. (35-200/21-145, 21-180, 21-185). No certificate of purchase for scavenger sales held after Jan 1, 1980 shall issue to bidder unless bidder provides affidavit that bid is not made by party or agent for party who is responsible for delinquent taxes. (35-200/21-145, 21-180, 21-185).

Redemption may be made by owners of property or those having interest in property, other than undisclosed beneficiary of Illinois land trust, even if interest is not recorded or filed; this does not apply to undisclosed beneficiaries of Illinois land trusts. (35-200/21-345, 21-350, 21-355, 21-360, 21-365, 21-380). Redemption may be made at any time before expiration of two years from date of sale, subject to certain exceptions, by payment in money or in other specified form, to county clerk, of amount for which property was sold, together with following amounts: If redemption within first six months after sale, amount of penalty bid at sale; if within second six months, double amount of penalty; if within third six months, treble amount of penalty; if within fourth six months, four times amount of penalty; if between 24 and 30 months, five times amount of penalty; and if between 30 and 36 months, six times amount of penalty. Person redeeming must also pay amount of all taxes and special assessments accruing after such sale, and paid by purchaser or his assignee, with 12% penalty thereon for each year or portion thereof between time of payment and redemption. Additional amounts including redemption of forfeitures occurring after tax sale with 12% penalty for each year between date of forfeiture redemption and redemption from sale; and certain fees paid by certificate holder, to county clerk, registrar of titles, circuit clerk, sheriff, owner, city, village or town and for publication of notice of tax sale and receivership. Period of redemption may be extended by purchaser or his assignee and redemption may be made during extended period by payment of amount for which property was sold, 6% interest, penalties, taxes, special assessments and miscellaneous fees and costs. For scavenger sales after Jan. 1, 1980, excepting owner-occupied condominium units, cooperative units or dwellings, single family residential units, amount required to be paid for redemption must also include amount equal to all delinquent taxes on property at time of sale. (35-205/253, 205/263, 205/235a). Purchaser or assignee shall not be entitled to tax deed to property sold unless he delivers, within five months after sale, notice of sale and date that redemption period expires to County Clerk. Clerk is required to mail notice to party last shown on Collector's warrant books as taxpayer for property. (35-205/241a). Further, purchaser or assignee must give notice of sale and date of expiration of redemption period to owners and other interested parties, through Sheriff, not less than three nor more than five months prior to expiration of redemption period. Any notice by publication where allowed under Act shall be given three times any time after filing petition for tax deed, but not less than three months nor more than five months prior to expiration of redemption period. (35-205/263).

Redemption after scavenger sale under same time conditions as judgment sale except time period is six months from date of sale for commercial, industrial, vacant nonfarm real estate, or real estate improved with structure containing seven or more residential units, and in lieu of penalty, person redeeming pays interest as follows: 3% per month on amount for which property sold if redeemed within two months of sale; if redeemed between two and six months of sale, 12% of amount for which property sold; if between six and 12 months, 24%; if between 12 and 18 months, 36%; if between 18 and 24 months, 48%; if after 24 months, 48% for 24 months and 6% per annum thereafter. (35-205/235a, 205/253).

Effect of Forfeiture.—In counties of 3,000,000 persons or less, when land has been forfeited for nonpayment of taxes in any year, there is added to tax thereafter assessed upon it all back taxes, costs, penalty and 12% per year interest on previous forfeitures, and the total is collected in the usual way. In counties of more than 3,000,000 persons, same procedure is followed except that previous forfeitures are not added, but remain a lien on the land and bear same interest as if forfeited annually. In counties of more than 3,000,000 county clerk in 1995 through 2000 shall make examination of collector's warrant books and Tax Judgment, Sale, Redemption and Forfeiture record for tax years previous to 1993 and note all taxes due or forfeited that have not been subject to Uncollectable Tax Act and clerk shall enter such taxes upon collector's books of following year in same manner as taxes remaining due or forfeited for 1993. After Jan. 1, 2000, any taxes remaining due or forfeited against real property in such county not entered in warrant books for 1994 through 1999 shall be deemed uncollectable and void and not subject to posting or other requirement of Uncollectable Tax Act. (35-200/18-250).

Reimbursement.—Beginning July 1, 1992, taxing districts determining surplus funds from any source must disburse surplus proportionally among owners of taxable homestead property based on most recent ad valorem property tax bill on homestead property.

REAL ESTATE CONVEYANCE TAX:

See topics Stamp Tax, and Real Property, subheads State Stamp Tax, County Stamp Tax, and Local Stamp Tax.

RIVERBOAT GAMBLING ACT:

License fee $25,000 first year and $5,000 for each succeeding year. (230-10/7[a]). Tax imposed for admission to gambling excursions at $2 per person. (230-10/12[a]). Tax imposed for wagering at 20% of gross receipts. (230-10/13[a]).

SALES AND USE TAXES:

Sales Tax.—*Note:* Effective Jan. 1, 1990, sales tax rate is 6.25% of gross receipts from sales and 1% of sales of food, medicine and drugs, medical appliances, modifications to motor vehicle rendering it usable by disabled person, insulin and certain equipment used by diabetics. Certain cities, counties and villages may impose additional sales tax. Certain municipalities may impose additional 1/2% sales tax for public infrastructure. Regional Transportation Authority may impose in Cook County additional sales tax of 3/4% and on food, drugs and medicine sales tax of 1%; in DuPage, Kane, Lake, McHenry and Will Counties additional sales tax of 1/4%. Also alters sales tax on gasohol. Corresponding charges made to use tax, service occupation tax and service use tax. (P.A. 85-1135).

Sales tax (called "retailers' occupation tax") is imposed on persons engaged in business of selling tangible personal property at retail in Illinois at rate of 6.25% of gross receipts from sales in Illinois. (35-120/2-10). Sales of food which is to be consumed off premises where sold (excluding alcoholic beverages, soft drinks and food prepared for immediate consumption) and sales of prescription and nonprescription medicines, drugs and certain medical related materials are taxed at rate of 0%. However, units of local government, Regional Transportation Authority, and any Metro East Mass Transit District are authorized to impose 1% sales tax on sales of food, drugs, medical supplies, and insulin. (35-120/2). Exemptions include among others: Sales for resale; newspapers and magazines; newsprint and ink used in newspapers and magazines; meals served under Federal Nutrition Program for the Elderly; occasional sales; sales through bulk vending machines; pollution control facilities; low sulfur dioxide emission coal fuel devices, including coal gasification equipment; coal exploration, mining, offhighway hauling, processing, maintenance and reclamation equipment costing $250 or more, including replacement parts and equipment costing $250 or more purchased for lease, and excluding motor vehicles required to be registered pursuant to Illinois Vehicle Code; graphic arts machinery and equipment; certain motor vehicles to be used in automobile renting; farm machinery and equipment; farm chemicals; personal property sold by teacher-sponsored student organization affiliated with Illinois elementary or secondary school; sales to federal, state and local governments; sales to Illinois county fair associations for use in operating or promoting county fair; sales to charitable religious or educational institutions; sales in interstate commerce; tangible personal property used by interstate carriers for hire for use as rolling stock in interstate commerce; machinery and equipment used in manufacturing or assembling, and machinery and equipment used in general maintenance or repair of exempt machinery and equipment; photo processing machinery and equipment and repair and replacement parts; transactions with out-of-state florists; proceeds from sale of motor vehicles subject to Replacement Vehicle Tax; fuel for certain river vessels; motor vehicles sold to nonresidents for out-of-state use; sales to nonprofit organizations operated exclusively for persons 55 years of age or older; sales of oil field exploration drilling and production equipment costing $250 or more, including replacement parts costing in excess of $250 and equipment purchased for lease and excluding motor vehicles required to be registered pursuant to Illinois Vehicle Code; sales of building materials by any retailer located in county or municipality which has established enterprise zone so long as sales meet certain conditions; subject to county or municipal limitation after Feb. 18, 1992 (35-120/5K); sales of property used or consumed in manufacturing or assembling of property for wholesale or retail conducted within enterprise zone; purchase of machinery and equipment by aircraft maintenance facility in enterprise zone provided certain conditions are met; semen used for artificial insemination of livestock for direct agricultural production; horses, or interests in horses meeting requirements of certain registries as appropriate to be used for purposes of breeding or racing for prizes. Sales of building materials to high impact business may qualify for credit or refund of state, municipal and county retailers' occupation tax; effective July 1, 1987, charities, religious or educational institutions must provide exemption identification number to make tax-free purchases (35-120/2-5). Taxes imposed on sale of gasohol (in which ethanol has been distilled in Illinois or certain other states with reciprocal exemption) at rate of 1% from Jan. 1, 1984 through Aug. 31, 1985, 2% from Sept. 1, 1985 through May 31, 1986, plus additional 1% per gallon for each cent of reduction in Federal excise tax on gasohol occurring on or after Sept. 1, 1985, 3% from June 1, 1986 through Dec. 31, 1992, plus additional 1% per gallon for each cent of reduction in federal excise tax on gasohol occurring on or after Sept. 1, 1985, and 5% beginning Jan. 1, 1993, and thereafter. (35-120/2). Base for tax on gasohol 70% of proceeds of sale for Jan. 1, 1990—July 1, 1999 and 100% thereafter subject to adjustment for certain sales in Illinois July 1, 1996—July 1, 1999. (35-120/2-10). Returns and payment of tax liability for each month required on or before last day of following month, but Department may authorize quarterly or annual returns where average monthly tax liability does not exceed $200 or $50 respectively, or taxpayer can prove to satisfaction of Department that substantial change has occurred. Department may request annual information return for specific tax years to be filed within 60 days after receipt of notice. (35-120/3). Transient merchants and certain retail concessionaires (county fairs, art shows, etc.) may be required to make daily reports and payments. (35-120/3). Retailers granted credit against remittance of tax of 2.1% of tax liability or $5 per calendar year (whichever is greater) to cover remittance and recordkeeping expenses incident to tax collection. (35-120/3). Beginning Oct. 1, 1993 and thereafter taxpayer, who has average monthly tax liability of $150,000 shall

See note at head of Digest as to 1998 legislation covered.

See Topical Index in front part of this volume.

IL – 78

SALES AND USE TAXES . . . *continued*
make all payments by electronic funds transfer; beginning Oct. 1, 1994, amount requiring electronic funds transfer is $100,000; beginning Oct. 1, 1995, amount is $50,000. Any taxpayer may make electronic funds transfer. (35-120/3). Penalty on tax due will be added in accordance with §3-3 of Uniform Penalty and Interest Act. (35-735/3-3). Responsible corporate officer or employee personally liable for tax, interest and penalties if corporation unable to pay same. (35-735/3-7). Counties, cities and villages have power to impose additional sales tax of 1% without referendum. (65-5/8-11-1). Effective Jan. 1, 1986, by order or resolution, counties of less than 3,000,000 inhabitants have power to impose supplementary retailers' occupation tax of 1/4%. In addition, effective Jan. 1, 1987, municipalities with more than 130,000 but fewer than 2,000,000 inhabitants may impose additional municipal retailers' occupation tax of 1/2 of 1% for expenditure on public infrastructure if approved by referendum. (65-5/8-11-1, 65-5/8-11-1.1, 65-5/8-11-1.2). City of Chicago imposes additional 1% sales tax under home rule powers (Municipal Code of Chicago, 3-28-030), on basis similar to state sales tax. Regional Transportation Authority imposes additional sales tax of 1% in Cook County and 1/4% in five counties (DuPage, Kane, Lake, McHenry and Will). (70-3615/4.03[e]). RTA tax determined constitutionally valid. (81 Ill.2d 221, 407 N.E.2d 28). Metro East Mass Transit Districts may impose additional sales tax of 1/4% within such districts. (70-3610/5.1[b]). Retailers may pass on to consumers municipal, county, Metro East Mass Transit Districts and regional transportation authority retailer's occupation taxes. (70-3615/4.03[e]; 70-3610/5.1[b]; 65-5/8-11-1; 57 Ill.2d 272, 312 N.E.2d 271). Transferee of assets outside usual course of transferor's business must file disclosure report with Illinois Department of Revenue within ten days of transfer. Transferee may be personally liable for transferor's unpaid taxes up to reasonable value of property transferred if transferee fails to file disclosure report. (35-120/5j).

Use Tax.—See Note under subhead Sales Tax, supra. Tax complements sales tax and is imposed at same rates. (35-105/3). Use Tax is computed on selling price (or lower of fair market value or selling price for by-products or waste products used in Illinois and refined, manufactured and produced from property purchased at retail). (35-105/3). Cities and villages may impose additional use tax of 1% of selling price of tangible personal property purchased from out-of-state retailer which is titled or registered with Illinois. (65-5/8-11-6). City of Chicago imposes additional 1% use tax under home rule powers (Municipal Code of Chicago, 3-28-030), on basis similar to state use tax. Regional Transportation Authority imposes additional use tax of 1% in Cook County and 1/4% in five counties (DuPage, Kane, Lake, McHenry and Will) of selling price of tangible personal property purchased from out-of-county retailer which is titled or registered with Illinois. (70-3615/4.03[g]). Certain vehicles or trailers not otherwise subject to use tax are subject to motor vehicle tax equal to 5% of selling price, or fair market value, for vehicles acquired by gift, transfer, or purchase for use in Illinois prior to Jan. 1, 1988; thereafter tax varies depending on whether selling price is less than $15,000 and model year of vehicle. Statute includes table of tax owed. (625-5/3-1001).

Service Occupation Tax.—See Note under subhead Sales Tax, supra. Tax is imposed on servicemen at rate of 6.25% on cost of all tangible personal property transferred as incident to sale of service and is collected by supplier. Sales of food which is to be consumed off premises where sold (excluding alcoholic beverages, soft drinks and food prepared for immediate consumption) and sales of prescription and nonprescription medicines, drugs and medical related materials to certain residents of long-term care facilities are exempt. However, units of local government, Regional Transportation Authority, and any Metro East Mass Transit District are authorized to impose 1% service occupation tax on sales of food, drugs, medical supplies, and insulin. (35-115/3). Returns and payment of tax liability for each month required on or before last day of following month but Department may authorize quarterly or annual returns where average monthly tax liability does not exceed $100 or $20 respectively. Supplier granted credit against remittance of tax of 2.1% of tax liability or $5 per calendar year (whichever is greater) to cover remittance and recordkeeping expenses incident to tax collection. Beginning Oct. 1, 1993 taxpayer with average tax liability of $150,000 shall make payment by electronic funds transfer; beginning Oct. 1, 1994 amount requiring electronic funds transfer is $100,000; beginning Oct. 1, 1995, amount is $50,000. Any taxpayer may make payment by electronic funds transfer (35-115/9). Department shall adopt rules to effectuate program of electronic funds transfer. (35-115/9). Counties, cities and villages have power to impose additional service occupation tax of 1% without referendum. (65-5/8-11-5). In addition, effective Jan. 1, 1987, municipalities with more than 130,000 but less than 2,000,000 inhabitants may impose additional service occupation tax of 1/2 of 1% for expenditure on public infrastructure if approved by referendum. (65-5/8-11-5; 65-5/8-11-1.1; 65-5/8-11-1.2). Regional Transportation Authority imposes additional service occupation tax of 1% in Cook County and 1/4% in five counties (DuPage, Kane, Lake, McHenry and Will). (70-3615/4.03[F]).

Service Use Tax.—See Note under subhead Sales Tax, supra. Tax complements service occupation tax, is imposed at same rates, and is collected from user by serviceman. (35-110/1-110/21).

For purposes of use, service occupation and service use taxes, "retailer (supplier, serviceman) maintaining a place of business in this state" (defined to include any representative operating within state and any retailer (supplier, serviceman) engaged in soliciting orders within state from users by means of catalogues or other advertising, whether orders received or accepted within or without state) is required to collect use tax and service use and occupation taxes. (35-105/2; 35-115/2; 35-110/2). Requirement that sellers who solicit orders only by means of catalogues or other advertising must collect use tax was declared unconstitutional. (386 U.S. 753). See category Civil Actions and Procedure, topic Process.

If property acquired and used outside Illinois before brought to Illinois, selling price reduced by reasonable allowance for depreciation. (35-110/3).

For purposes of use, service occupation and service use taxes, "tangible personal property" includes computer software.

Automobile renting occupation and use tax is imposed at rate of 5% on rental of automobile for period of one year or less (35-155/2-155/4) effective 1/1/82. Additional tax of 1% each may be imposed by municipalities (65-5/8-11-7), Metro East Transit Districts (70-3610/5.02) and Regional Transportation Authority (70-3615/4.03.1). Additional municipal tax of $2.75 per rental may be imposed by municipalities through Jan. 17, 1987, and $1 per rental thereafter. (65-5/8-11-11).

Replacement Vehicle Tax of $200 is imposed on any motor vehicle purchased by or on behalf of insurance company to replace vehicle of insured person in settlement of total loss claim. (625-5/3-2001). Tax is paid by purchaser insurance company or broker. (625-5/3-2002). Motor vehicles subject to Motor Vehicle Replacement Tax are exempt from Use Tax (35-105/3) and Sales Tax (35-120/2). Counties, cities and villages have authority to impose additional replacement vehicle tax of $50. (65-5/8-11-9, 55-5/5-1035). Regional Transportation Authority may impose additional replacement vehicle tax of $50. (70-3615/4.03[h]).

Leasing occupation tax repealed.

Leasing use tax repealed.

STAMP TAX:

No requirement of documentary stamps on corporate stock or other instruments exists, except on privilege of transferring title to real estate at rate of 25¢ for each $500 of value or fraction thereof. (35-305/3). See category Property, topic Real Property.

TELECOMMUNICATIONS EXCISE TAX ACT:

Tax is imposed at rate of 5% of gross charge on interstate and intrastate telecommunications. Additional tax of 5% of gross charge may be imposed by municipality. Monthly returns are due by 15th day of following month and estimated quarter monthly payments are due on seventh, 15th, 22nd and last day of month. (35-630/1 to 630/21). Application of every exemption, credit and deduction against this tax is limited by any reasonable and appropriate sunset date specified in public act creating exemption, credit or deduction and if none specified, then taxpayer shall not be entitled to exemption, credit or deduction beginning five years after effective date of public act creating it. (35-630/4.5).

UNEMPLOYMENT COMPENSATION TAX:

Unemployment compensation tax (termed "contributions") is imposed by 48-300-820, which is administered by Director of Department of Employment Security.

Act applies to all employers who pay wages of at least $1,500 in a calendar quarter of current or preceding calendar year or employ at least one individual on at least part of one day within each of 20 or more weeks during current or preceding calendar year, any nonprofit organization employing four or more individuals within each of 20 or more calendar weeks, State of Illinois, and other employers who elect to come within Act. (820-405/205).

Following employees not within Act: Agricultural workers unless work in unit which either paid wages of $20,000 or more per calendar quarter or employed ten or more individuals for 20 weeks; domestic servants, unless wages paid by employer for domestic service equaled or exceeded $1,000 in calendar quarter; certain governmental workers; members of crews of foreign vessels or aircraft (if such services are performed while aircraft is outside U.S.) and crews of U.S. vessels if operating office is outside Illinois; commissioned real estate salesmen and insurance agents; U.S. government employees; those working for certain nonprofit organizations' workers covered under unemployment compensation plan created by Congress; students and spouses of students who work at same school student is attending; those under 18 who deliver newspapers; those engaged in illegal recording or making of bets; students participating in work experience program; those engaged in services performed entirely outside State of Illinois pursuant to reciprocal arrangements with other states; patients, student nurses or interns performing services to hospital; workers covered by unemployment compensation law of another state; directors of corporations while performing their services as directors; children under 18 employed by their parents or persons employed by their children or spouse; certain direct sellers of consumer products. (820-405/214-405/232).

Contributions by employers are required only with respect to wages not in excess of $7,000 per annum to any individual; $8,000 for last three calendar quarters of 1983 and calendar year 1984; $8,500 for calendar years 1985 and 1986 and 1987. For 1984, 1985, 1986 and 1987 new employers pay greater of 2.7%, 2.7% multiplied by current adjusted state experience factor or average contribution rate for employer's major classification in Standard Industrial Code. Contribution rate for employers who were liable for contributions during three (two for 1984, 1985 and 1986) preceding calendar years is determined under experience-rating provisions. (820-405/1500). Implementation of emergency contribution rates determined by fund balance on preceding June 30 computation date may raise total rates for following calendar year from .04% to .06%. (820-405/1506.2). For calendar years 1991 through 1995, employer's minimum contribution shall be greater of .2% or product obtained by multiplying .2% by adjusted state experience factor for applicable calendar year. For calendar year 1996 minimum contribution rate is .1%. Maximum contribution rate is greater of 6.4% or product of 6.4% and adjusted state experience factor for applicable calendar year. If quarterly payroll is less than $50,000, rate may not exceed 3.7% for 1985, 4.1% for 1986, 4.5% for 1987, 5.0% for 1988, or 5.4% for 1989 and subsequent years. (820-405/1506.1).

Contributions are not exacted from employees, and agreement by employees to pay part of employer's contributions is void. (820-405/1600). Deduction from wages by employer to pay contributions is misdemeanor. (820-405/2800).

Contributions are payable quarterly on or before last day of month next following calendar quarters for which such contributions have accrued, calendar quarters being three-month periods ending Mar. 31, June 30, Sept. 30 and Dec. 31. (820-405/238, 405/1400). Delinquent employer may be required to pay on calendar month basis. (820-405/1400). Late contributions subject to interest of 2% per month. Returns must be made and contributions paid to Director of Department of Employment Security.

UTILITIES TAXES:

Public Utilities Revenue Act.—Tax imposed at rate of 5% of gross receipts upon persons (other than municipal corporations owning and operating public transportation

See note at head of Digest as to 1998 legislation covered.

See Topical Index in front part of this volume.

IL – 79

UTILITIES TAXES . . . *continued*

systems) engaged in intra-state distribution, supplying, furnishing or selling of electricity for use or consumption. For electric bills having meter reading date on or after Jan. 1, 1986, rate of tax is lesser of above rate or 0.32¢ per kilowatt hour of electricity. Additional tax is imposed at rate of 0.8% on amount of "invested capital" allocated and apportioned to Illinois and additional tax at variable rate on taxpayer who distributes electricity. Exemption for persons not regulated by Illinois Commerce Commission and electric cooperatives not subject to Rural Electrification Administration filing requirements. (35-620/2a.1). Annual returns are due by 15th day of second month following close of taxable year. Estimated quarterly tax payments are due on first day of third, sixth and ninth months of each taxable period. (35-620/1 to 620/14a).

Water Companies Tax Act.—In addition to income taxes, tax of 0.8% is imposed on "invested capital" of water companies allocable or apportionable to Illinois. Annual returns and payments are due by 15th day of second month following close of taxable year. Estimated quarterly payments are due on first day of third, sixth, and ninth months of each taxable period. (35-625/1 to 625/15). Application of every exemption, credit and deduction against this tax is limited by any reasonable and appropriate sunset date specified in public act creating exemption credit or deduction and if none specified, then taxpayer shall not be entitled to exemption, credit or deduction beginning five years after effective date of public act creating it. (35-625/4.5).

TRANSPORTATION

MOTOR VEHICLES:

Illinois Vehicle Code adopted in 1969 became effective July 1, 1970. (625-5/1-101 to 5/20-402).

Secretary of State is responsible for administration of Illinois Vehicle Title and Registration Law (625-5/2-101 to 5/5-801), Illinois Drivers Licensing Law (625-5/6-101 to 5/6-708), Illinois Safety Responsibility Law (625-5/7-101 to 5/7-503), Registration of Motor Vehicles Used for Transportation of Passengers Law (625-5/8-101 to 5/8-116), Regulation of Owners of For Rent Vehicles For-Hire Law (625-5/9-101 to 5/9-110), Boat Registration and Safety Act (625-45/3-13 to 45/10-2), Snowmobile Registration and Safety Act (625-40/1-1 to 40/11-1), and Hazardous Materials Transportation Act (430-30/1 to 30/16). Correspondence may be addressed to Secretary of State, Statehouse, Springfield, IL 62756.

Other aspects of motor vehicle regulation, including motor common carriers, are under jurisdiction of Illinois Commerce Commission, 527 East Capitol Avenue, Springfield, IL 62706.

Vehicle License.—Registration plates have indefinite term of at least one year, providing that current annual registration stickers are attached to rear registration plates. Registration stickers shall designate year number for which they are issued and such other letters or numbers as Secretary of State may prescribe and shall be of contrasting color with registration plates and previous year's registration sticker. Illinois has adopted system of staggered registration. (625-5/3-414 to 5/3-802). It is unlawful to drive unregistered motor vehicle or vehicle without evidence of registration displayed. (625-5/3-401, 5/3-701). New residents need not secure registration until 30 days after establishing residency provided vehicle is properly registered in another jurisdiction. (625-5/3-801). Effective Oct. 1, 1984 no vehicle required to pay Federal Highway Users Tax will be registered without proof of payment. (625-5/3-401). Registration plates for motorcycle, trailer, semitrailer, apportioned bus shall be securely fastened to rear of vehicle. Registration for truck-tractor or apportioned truck shall be fastened to rear of vehicle. Registration for truck-tractor or apportioned truck shall be fastened to the front. All other motor vehicles must have plates securely fastened to front and rear in position to be clearly visible and in condition to be clearly legible. (625-5/3-413). Loss of registration plate(s) requires $7, $11, or $12 replacement fee. (625-5/3-820). Registration of motor vehicle expires upon sale. (625-5/3-501). Registration is subject to suspension or revocation. (625-5/3-704). *Note:* Effective Jan. 1, 1990 through Dec. 31, 1993, applicant for motor vehicle registration shall affirm that vehicle is insured as required by Motor Vehicle Code. (625-5/3-405[5]). No person shall operate motor vehicle unless operator and motor vehicle are covered by insurance policy in accordance with §7-601 of Motor Vehicle Code, regardless of state or jurisdiction in which licensed or registered. (625-5/3-707). All motorboats must now be equipped with muffler or underwater exhaust system.

Secretary of State will make title or registration search of records of his office and a written report on same for any person upon application accompanied by fee of $4 for each registration or title search. (625-5/2-123).

Operator's license is required (625-5/6-101) except for (1) Employees of U.S. Government or members of Armed Forces when operating on official business a vehicle owned or leased by U.S. Government; (2) persons operating road machines temporarily on a highway or farm machines or tractors in farming operations; (3) residents of Illinois for period of 45 days following return to continental limits of U.S. after service as member of Armed Forces outside said continental limits; (4) nonresidents who hold valid licenses in their home state, generally, for 90 days, or for duration of attendance at Illinois college or university or active military duty; (5) new residents who hold valid licenses from their original home state, for 90 days. (625-5/6-102). License is not issued to person under 18 except for instruction purposes, or unless applicant is at least 16 and has passed an approved driver's education course. Graduated Licensing Program for applicants under 18 years of age with special rules. (625-5/6-103, 5/6-107). Licenses issued to persons under 21 to be distinct from those issued to persons over 21. (625-5/6-110). Licenses are subject to cancellation, revocation or suspension (625-5/6-201, 5/6-202), including summary suspension for refusal to submit to chemical, blood, breath or urine tests for presence of alcohol concentration of 0.08% or more or drugs (625-5/11-501.1). Secretary of State must examine every licensed driver at least every eight years. (625-5/6-109). Driver's license compact requiring interstate reporting of motor vehicle violations has been adopted. (625-5/6-700 to 5/6-708). Revocation of operator's license

or permit mandatory in certain cases. (625-5/6-205). License contains space for operator's picture and approved stickers concerning Uniform Anatomical Gift Act and operator's blood type and Rh factor. Anyone rendering emergency aid and relying in good faith upon such stickers is free from civil liability. (625-5/6-110). See infra, subhead Nonresident Operators.

Restricted driving permit available for drivers whose privileges have been suspended, revoked, or cancelled. Restricted permit is immediately invalidated upon issuance of citation for certain offenses. (625-5/6-113[e]).

Short term permit may be issued to operate nonregistered first or second division vehicle for not more than 48 hours.

Motorized pedalcycle, which produces no more than two horse power and is capable of propelling vehicle at maximum speed of no more than 30 m.p.h., and which, if driven by internal combustion engine, has displacement of no more than 50 cubic centimeters and requires no gear shifting authorized. Any person may operate motorized pedalcycles, if such person has valid, current Illinois drivers' license, regardless of classification. (625-5/1-148.2).

Driver's Training School.—Commercial driver training schools and teachers must register with, and be licensed by, Secretary of State. (625-5/6-401, 6-411).

Auto Towing.—Commercial vehicle relocators in counties over 1,000,000 population, and in any other county by county request, must register with, be licensed by, and file indemnity bond, insurance bond, or certificates or bonds of insurance with Illinois Commerce Commission. Methods of regulation, amount of fees, and collection of fees regulated by statute. (625-5/18a-100 to 5/18a-700).

Special Restrictions for Vehicle Operators.—No person under age of 21 years or who has had less than one year of driving experience shall drive school, day camp, summer camp or nursery school vehicle for transportation of children or any motor vehicle of second division when used for transportation of persons for compensation; no person under age of 18 years shall be licensed to transport property for hire or for purpose of transporting persons for compensation in motor vehicle of first division; school bus drivers shall have school bus driver permit issued by Illinois Office of Education; religious organization bus drivers shall have school bus driver permit or specially classified license. (625-5/6-104 to 5/6-406.2). Any individual or business entity that contracts with school district to transport students and whose drivers have not met requirements to drive bus is guilty of business offense and will be fined. (625-5/6-106.11). Driver of school bus involved in accident is deemed as matter of law to have given consent to submit to test of driver's breath, blood or urine for purpose of determining presence of alcohol, or other drugs in person's system. (625-5/6-516). Any school bus driver who is found guilty of transporting children while under influence of drugs or alcohol is guilty of Class A misdemeanor for first conviction with more serious classification and penalties for subsequent convictions and under certain circumstances. (625-5/11-501). Minimum driving requirements for persons driving vehicle for transportation of elderly in connection with organization activities. (625-5/6-106.3).

Certificate of title is issued by Secretary of State on registration or renewal of registration by owner of motor vehicle and must be obtained before any person may operate motor vehicle. (625-5/3-103). Certificate must include odometer certification. Certificate of title unnecessary for husbandry vehicles. (625-5/3-102). Proof of payment of use tax or of nonliability therefor condition precedent to issuance of certificate of title. (625-5/3-104). Scrapping, junking or destroying vehicle permissible only upon application to Secretary of State for appropriate certificate and surrender of certificate of title; additional provision applicable to insurance companies. (625-5/3-117.1). When certificate of title is made out to two or more persons, it is presumed that title is held as joint tenants with right of survivorship. (625-5/3-107.1).

Liens and encumbrances are required to be shown on certificate of title in order of priority and dates of security agreements. (625-5/3-107).

Sales.—Except as between parties to sale, no sale of motor vehicle is effective without owner's having obtained certificate of title and without an endorsement and assignment of certificate of title, showing all interests, liens, or incumbrances thereon, and delivering same to purchaser with warranty of title in seller. Transferee must thereupon apply for new certificate of title, surrendering endorsed and assigned certificate. (625-5/2-112). Vendor must remove license plates when sale is made. (625-5/3-501). Retail installment sales of motor vehicles are regulated by 815-375/1 to 375/8. Sunday closing Law for motor vehicle establishments declared constitutional. (102 Ill.2d 3, 464 N.E.2d 275).

Consumer Protection.—See category Business Regulation and Commerce, topic Consumer Protection, subhead New Car Buyer Protection Act.

Identification Marks.—Altering engine number or other distinguishing mark or giving wrong description in application for registration is Class 4 felony. (625-5/4-103, 5/4-105, 5/4-108[b]). If vehicle uses liquified petroleum or compressed natural gas, marking in accordance with National Fire Protection Association (NFPA) standards for storage and handling of Liquified Petroleum Gases and Compressed Natural Gas Vehicular Fuel System and published as NFPA 58 and NFPA 52 dated 2/10/92 and 8/14/92 is required. (625-5/12-704.3).

Operation Prohibited.—The following persons may not be issued operator's licenses: Persons who use alcohol or any other drug to degree which renders such person incapable of safely driving motor vehicle; persons convicted within 12 months of license application of sex offenses enumerated in 625-5/6-205; persons adjudged afflicted with physical or mental disease; persons who are required to take an examination including drug and alcohol evaluation or to prove financial responsibility but have not done so. (625-5/6-103).

Vehicle Classification.—Vehicles designed and used for carrying not more than ten persons are vehicles of first division. Vehicles designed and used for pulling or carrying freight or for carrying of more than ten persons, or for living quarters, are vehicles of second division. (625-5/1-146). Motorized wheelchairs are not deemed motor vehicles. (625-5/1-146).

Motorboat Operators.—No person less than ten years of age may operate motorboat. Persons at least ten years of age, but less than 12 years of age, may operate

MOTOR VEHICLES . . . *continued*

motorboat, if accompanied and controlled by parent or guardian or designee of parent or guardian at least 18 years of age. Persons at least 12 years of age but less than 18 years of age may operate motorboat only if accompanied and controlled by parent or guardian or person at least 18 years of age designated by parent or guardian, or if such motorboat operator possesses Boating Safety Certificate issued by Department of Natural Resources authorizing holder to operate motorboats. (625-45/5-18). Each boat shall carry one flotation device per person as well as one emergency flotation device of approved type. (625-45/4-1).

Snowmobile Operators.—Persons less than ten years of age may not operate snowmobiles. Snowmobiles may be operated on public highway, where permitted, only with valid driver's license or snowmobile safety instruction certificate. Persons ten years but less than 12 years of age may operate snowmobile if accompanied and controlled by parent or guardian or designee of parent or guardian at least 18 years of age. Persons 12 years but less than 16 years of age may operate snowmobile only if accompanied and controlled by parent or guardian or designee of parent or guardian at least 16 years of age, or such operator possesses operation certificate issued by Department of Conservation. (625-40/5-3). Snowmobiles must be registered and display registration number. (625-40/3-1). Registration valid for three years, expires Sept. 30 of second year following registration. (625-40/3-8). Snowmobiles must have one white headlamp, one red taillamp, reflective side markings, brakes and adequate sound suppression. (625-40/4-1).

Annual Fees.—Generally, registration fee for vehicles of first division varies with taxable horsepower, e.g., $48 for vehicle of more than 35 taxable horsepower; $36 for vehicles of 35 or less taxable horsepower. (625-5/3-806). Beginning in 1986, fees are reduced 50% for all vehicle owners eligible under Senior Citizens and Disabled Persons Property Tax Relief Act. Exceptions to this general fee are made for particular vehicles, e.g., electric or antique vehicles. (625-5/3-804, 5/3-805). Municipality where owner resides may charge license fee. (625-5/2-121).

Owners of most vehicles of second division must pay registration fee of $10 for each such vehicle. (625-5/3-813). Fees other than this general fee are specified for particular vehicles, e.g., not-for-profit organization vehicles, busses, farm machinery, etc. (625-5/3-807 to 5/3-809). Also such owners are required to pay either flat-weight tax or mileage-weight tax, depending upon written election made at time of application for or renewal of registration, which election is binding until end of calendar year and applies only to particular vehicle for which made. Failure to file election subjects owner to payment of flat-weight tax.

Flat-weight tax (which includes $10 registration fee) is graduated in amount by brackets according to gross weight, including weight of vehicle and maximum load, it varies from $48 on vehicles having gross weight of 8,000 lbs. or less to $2,232 on vehicles having gross weight of between 77,001 and 80,000 lbs. (625-5/3-815). Two-axle vehicles used as busses in public system for transporting more than ten passengers entirely within territorial limits of single or contiguous municipalities and whose rates for transportation are subject to regulation of Illinois Commerce Commission, must pay registration fee of $10 per two-year registration period, but are exempt from either flat-weight tax or mileage-weight tax. (625-5/3-807).

Owners electing mileage-weight tax must pay minimum guaranteed mileage-weight tax, which permits operation for a specified number of miles in Illinois. An additional tax must be paid at rates depending upon gross weight of vehicle for each mile traveled in Illinois in excess of maximum mileage provided under minimum guaranteed basis. Daily record of mileage and monthly returns thereof, including payment of appropriate tax for excess mileage, is required; and failure so to act prohibits further operation without first paying applicable flat-weight tax. Owner electing to pay a mileage weight tax must file a bond in the amount of $500, conditioned upon his paying all moneys due by reason of his operation of second-division vehicles in Illinois. (625-5/3-818).

Aforesaid annual fees do not apply to nonresident owner, if (1) he has complied with registration laws in force at his place of residence and (2) like exemptions and privileges are granted to motor vehicles owned by residents of Illinois when operated at place of his residence. Nonresidents operating places of business in Illinois and using motor vehicles in connection with such business must comply with aforesaid annual fees. (625-5/3-402[B]).

Owner of vehicle fleet operating vehicles in Illinois and one or more other states may make proportional registration in Illinois in lieu of registration under general provisions of 625-5/3-402, 5/3-815, 5/3-819. Apportionment factor based on ratio of Illinois miles to total fleet miles used to determine portion of fleet license fee payable. (625-5/3-402.1).

Size and Weight Limits.—Regulated by 625-5/15-101 to 5/15-319.

Equipment.—Regulated by 625-5/12-100 to 5/12-710.

Lights Required.—Regulated by 625-5/12-101 to 5/12-216.

Inspection.—Second class vehicles and limousines, with numerous exceptions, must submit to state safety test and secure safety certificate before operation on state highways. Department of Transportation is authorized to promulgate inspection rule. (625-5/13-101 to 5/13-114). Municipalities with over 40,000 population may require their residents to submit vehicles to inspections not more frequent than semi-annually. (65-5/11-40-2). Secretary of State may decline to register vehicle subject to safety inspection unless registration application accompanied by valid certificate of safety. (625-5/3-825).

Emissions Inspection.—With certain exceptions, after Jan. 1, 1986, owner of every motor vehicle must display valid unexpired emission inspection sticker. Initial inspection sticker for each vehicle is obtained from Illinois Environmental Protection Agency and specifies date by which owner must have vehicle inspected and obtain renewal emission inspection sticker. Inspection consists of test of exhaust gas sample to determine if pollutants emitted exceed standards set for vehicles of that type. Exempt vehicles include motorcycles, farm vehicles, antique vehicles, diesel powered vehicles, parade or ceremonial vehicles, vehicles for which junking certificate has been issued, vehicles with model year before 1967, and vehicles used exclusively in amateur or professional sports.

Traffic Regulations.—Illinois traffic regulations are set out in 11 ("Rules of the Road") of Illinois Vehicle Code. (625-5/11-100 to 5/11-1425). Traffic rules provide regulation of traffic signs (625-5/11-301 to 5/11-313), driving while intoxicated, transporting alcoholic beverages and reckless driving (625-5/11-501 to 5/11-504), speeding (625-5/11-601 to 5/11-610), passing (625-5/11-701 to 5/11-711), turning and starting (625-5/11-801 to 5/11-806), right-of-way (625-5/11-901 to 5/11-907), pedestrians (625-5/11-1001 to 5/11-1011), street cars and safety zones (625-5/11-110 to 5/11-1104), special stops (625-5/11-1201 to 5/11-1205), stopping, standing and parking (625-5/11-1301 to 5/11-1305), and miscellaneous (625-5/11-1401 to 5/11-1425). Court proceedings in traffic offense cases now governed by uniform practice rules (Ill. St. Ct. 501 to 556); parents of minors charged with traffic offenses may be required to appear in court (625-5/16-107).

Accidents.—Any driver involved in motor vehicle accident causing injury, death or vehicle damage must stop, give his name, address, identity of vehicle's owner if known, vehicle registration number, and chauffeur's number, if any, to injured persons, driver or occupant(s) of other vehicle, or, if no such persons are capable of receiving and understanding such information, to nearest police officer or police station. If any person is injured, driver must render reasonable assistance or make arrangements for such assistance, including carrying person to medical assistance, if such assistance is requested or is apparently necessary. Failure to comply with foregoing provisions is Class A misdemeanor. (625-5/16-107).

Driver, or passenger if driver is unable, involved in accident resulting in personal injury or death or property damage amounting to more than $250 must give notice of accident to police immediately. (625-5/11-406, 5/11-407). Driver must also submit written report to Administrator, Dept. of Transportation within ten days. (625-5/11-406). Municipal ordinance may also require driver or owner of vehicle involved in accident to file with designated municipal office written report of accident. (625-5/11-415).

Any person failing to stop at scene of an accident in which he is a party must within three hours after accident, or, if hospitalized and incapacitated, within 48 hours after being discharged from hospital, report accident at police station or sheriff's office near place where accident occurred. (625-5/11-401).

Driving while under influence of alcohol or drugs, or driving with blood or breath alcohol concentration of 0.08% or more, are prohibited. (625-5/11-501). Person is presumed not under influence if alcohol concentration is .05% or less; if between .05% and 0.08%, no presumption arises; if 0.08% or more, person presumed under influence. (625-5/11-501.2). First conviction is Class A misdemeanor. Variety of mandatory punishments including fines, community service or imprisonment under circumstances where offense committed while transporting person under age 16 or second conviction within five years or prior conviction of this section or similar provision of law of another state or local ordinance or during period where driving privileges already revoked, suspended or restricted. (625-5/11-501[c]). Driving under influence of alcohol or drugs (1) if driving school bus with children on board, (2) if involved in accident causing great bodily harm, (3) by person who committed violation for third or subsequent time or (4) by person who committed violation second time and prior conviction of reckless homicide while under influence of alcohol or drugs is Class 4 felony. (625-5/11-501[d]).

Any person driving in state impliedly consents to chemical test of breath, blood or urine, following lawful arrest, to determine alcohol or drug content of blood. (625-5/11-501.1). Illinois law enforcement officer, who is investigating person for 625-5/11-501 offense, may travel to adjoining state to complete investigation and request tests where person has been transported to adjoining state for medical care. Instead of arrest, officer shall issue Uniform Traffic Ticket notifying person of probable cause for arrest in county where offense was committed (625-5/11-501.1[a]). Refusal to submit to such test will result in summary suspension of drivers license for period of six months on first arrest and one year on each subsequent arrest. (625-5/6-208.1, 5/11-501.1). Refusal to submit to test is admissible in any civil or criminal action arising out of acts allegedly committed while person was driving while under influence of alcohol or drugs. (625-5/11-501.2). Results of chemical tests of blood performed during medical treatment in hospital emergency room are admissible in evidence as business record exception to hearsay rule only in prosecutions for violation of §11-501 or prosecutions for reckless homicide and only if certain testing criteria are met. (625-5/11-501.4). If person submits to test which reveals alcohol concentration of 0.08% or more, drivers license will be summarily suspended for three months for first offense and one year for each subsequent offense. (625-5/6-208.1). Subsequent to notification of statutory summary suspension, person may apply for limited Judicial Driving Permit to relieve undue hardship with persons under age of 18 years excepted. (625-5/6-206.1).

Department of Law Enforcement or other law enforcement agencies may furnish copy of Illinois State Police Accident Report for fee of $5, or $20 for accident investigated by Accident Reconstruction Officer or Team. (625-5/11-416).

Safety Belts.—Drivers and passengers required to use safety belts. (625-5/12-603.1).

Child Passengers.—Parents and legal guardians of children under four years are required to provide child restraint system to any person who transports such child. Any person who transports child under four years shall secure child in such system if it is provided by parent or guardian. Any person who transports child between four and six years shall secure such child in either child restraint system or seat belt. Failure to secure child not contributory negligence and not admissible in civil action. (625-25/1 to 25/9).

Liability of owner for negligence of another is dependent on relationship of principal and agent or master and servant and has not been extended by statute. But proof of ownership is prima facie proof of agency. (8 Ill.2d 468, 134 N.E.2d 311). Family purpose doctrine has not been adopted. Mere relationship of parent and child does not fix liability on parent even though car is family car, but fact of agency must be present. (342 Ill. 266, 174 N.E. 371).

Liability to Guests.—Nonpaying guest passenger who has solicited a ride in violation of 625-5/1006(a) or his representatives may not recover damages from owner or operator for injury or death caused by any accident unless attributable to willful and wanton misconduct. (625-5/10-201).

See note at head of Digest as to 1998 legislation covered.

See Topical Index in front part of this volume.

MOTOR VEHICLES . . . *continued*

Proof of Financial Responsibility.—Secretary of State must suspend all registration certificates and license plates issued for vehicle registered in name of owner whose operator's license has been revoked unless such owner immediately gives and thereafter maintains for three years proof of ability to respond in damages for any liability arising out of operation of motor vehicle to extent of $15,000 for injury to or death of one person or $30,000 for injury to or death of two or more persons in same accident, and $10,000 for damage to property. (625-5/7-304). Such proof must be furnished for each vehicle registered by such person and may be given either by policy of liability insurance or deposit of bond or securities. (625-5/7-314). Similar proof of financial responsibility is required in order to prevent suspension of operator's license issued to any person failing to satisfy within 30 days final judgment in action arising from operation of vehicle. (625-5/7-303).

Administrator, Department of Transportation, as soon as practicable after receipt of report of motor vehicle accident resulting in bodily injury or death to any person or in which damage to property of any one person exceeds $250, determines (1) whether provisions of Act require deposit of security and filing of proof of financial responsibility for future by person who was operator or owner of motor vehicle in any manner involved in accident, (2) what amount of security will be sufficient to satisfy any judgment for damages resulting from said accident, and certifies his determination to Secretary of State. (625-5/7-201).

Secretary of State is authorized to suspend drivers' licenses and registration unless (1) security is deposited or (2) a liability insurance policy (with company meeting specified requirements) in effect at time of accident is exhibited showing coverage of not less than (a) $15,000 in event of injury to or death of one person, (b) $30,000 in event of death of or injury to two or more persons arising out of accident, and (c) $10,000 in event of property damage only. (625-5/7-205, 5/7-201, 5/7-202, 5/7-203).

An owner or operator of a motor vehicle is relieved from foregoing requirements if he files (1) proof of financial responsibility for future and (2) satisfactory evidence of (a) a release from liability, (b) a covenant not to sue or (c) a final adjudication of nonliability. (625-5/7-206, 5/7-207).

Secretary of State may also suspend or revoke registration or certificate of title when he determines that owner of a for-hire motor vehicle has failed to give proof of financial responsibility.

See 625-5/7-101 to 5/7-329 for detailed provisions relative to security following accident and proof of financial responsibility for future.

Insurance.—All persons who operate motor vehicles and all motor vehicles subject to registration under Motor Vehicle Code shall be covered by liability insurance policy or bond in amounts as set forth in §7-203 of Code. (625-5/7-601). Every operator of motor vehicle subject to this section shall carry proper evidence of insurance within vehicle. (625-5/7-602).

No-Fault Auto Insurance.—None. Statute creating same held unconstitutional. (51 Ill.2d 478, 283 N.E.2d 474).

Foreign vehicle registered in home state or country and displaying license plates (including dealer's plates) required by laws of home state may operate without license to extent that such state or country allows reciprocal privileges. (625-5/3-402[B]).

Nonresident Operators.—See subhead Operator's License, supra. If nonresident has been convicted of offense which would require revocation of operator's license of resident, such nonresident must give proof of financial responsibility in order to cause registration of or to operate within this state any vehicle owned by him. (625-5/7-306).

Actions Against Nonresidents.—Service of process on nonresident or those who were residents of state at time cause of action arose but who subsequently became nonresidents or, if motor vehicle or motorcycle is owned by nonresident and operated on highways, with owner's permission, may be had by serving upon or filing copy of process in office of Secretary of State, paying fee of $5, sending notice and copy of process within ten days by registered mail to defendant at last known address and appending to summons an affidavit of compliance with statute. If such notice and process are not received and judgment is entered against nonresident defendant, he may, within one year of notice of judgment, if notice thereof is given him, or within five years of entry of judgment, if notice thereof is not given, appear and open judgment and proceed to trial. (625-5/10-301).

Direct Actions.—See category Insurance, topic Insurance Companies.

Soliciting rides from driver of vehicle by standing on roadway prohibited except local government may expressly permit soliciting of charitable contributions from vehicle occupants if certain criteria met. (625-5/11-1006).

Motor vehicle carriers of passengers cannot operate any motor vehicle for any purpose without approval of Illinois Commerce Commission. (625-5/18c-6103). Operators must file proof of continuous insurance or surety coverage in accordance with regulations, minimum amounts, and maximum deductible limits established by Commission. (625-5/18c-4902, 15/18c-6503). Commission may exempt carrier from filing proof of insurance or surety coverage if Commission determines that carrier has financial ability to pay for all damages for which proof of insurance or surety coverage would otherwise be required. (625-5/18c-4905). When operating in incorporated cities, towns or villages, operator must file with Secretary of State either: (a) Approved bond of surety company authorized to do business in state; (b) approved personal bond with surety owning Illinois real estate valued at minimum of $250,000 over-encumbrances; (c) approved policy of insurance covering personal and property damage with designated types of insurers; or (d) if person operates more than 25 registered motor vehicles, certificate of self insurance issued by Secretary of State. (625-5/7-502, 5/8-101 to 8-103, 5/8-108). Surety bond or real estate bond shall be in sum of $250,000 for each motor vehicle operated, conditioned to pay each final judgment for injury, death or damage to property through negligence of owner or agent in operation of vehicle. (625-5/8-103, 5/8-104). Policy of insurance shall insure owner for liability for injury, death or property damage to property through negligence of owner or agent in operation of vehicle to sum of $300,000 on each vehicle. (625-5/8-109). Bonds and insurance policies expire June 30 or Dec. 31 annually for vehicles registered on fiscal and calendar years respectively, but expiration does not terminate liabilities arising during period for which bond or policy filed. (625-5/8-112).

Business of transportation of property for hire by motor vehicles is regulated by statute under administration of Illinois Commerce Commission. (625-5/18c-1101). No such service may be furnished by household goods common carrier without first obtaining from Commission certificate of public convenience and necessity (625-5/18c-4202), as well as license, for intrastate carriers, or registration, for interstate carriers (625-5/18c-4104). Before furnishing service in Illinois, household goods contract carrier must first obtain permit from Commission, which issues after hearing upon finding that applicant is able to perform proposed service and that said service will be in public interest. (625-5/18c-4203). Transportation of property between points which are both within ten mile radius of corporate limits of municipality is exempt from statutory provisions respecting tariffs and rate schedules. (625-5/18c-4503). Before terminating authorized services, household goods common carrier must obtain Commission approval. (625-5/18c-4207). Interstate carrier may not operate over public highways without first obtaining from Commission registration, issuance of which depends upon payment of any registration fee or tax due to state. (625-5/18c-4104[1][a], 5/18c-4401 to 5/18c-4402).

Dual operation as household goods common and household goods contract carrier is prohibited, except where authorized by Commission. (625-5/18c-4206). Commission to provide for approval of certain agreements between carriers. (625-5/18c-4502). Provision is made for temporary authority to operate as common or contract carrier and for amendment, suspension, cancellation, or revocation of authority upon complaint, or upon Commission's own initiative, after notice and hearing, for wilful failure to comply with statute. (625-5/18c-2017). Security approved by Commission and executed by surety, indemnity or insurance company authorized to transact business in Illinois is required for both common and contract carriers, in amounts set by Commission. (625-5/18c-4901 to 5/18c-4905).

Exemptions from statute include vehicles operated: (1) For U.S. Postal Service, (2) by agricultural co-operative association, (3) for transportation of farm or dairy products or livestock when incident to principal business of farming or livestock raising, or for shipment of such products to or from farm, market, warehouse, dairy or shipping terminal, (4) for transportation of farm machinery, (5) for towing pursuant to legal order or pursuant to towing license issued by Secretary of State, (6) by commercial relocators of trespassing vehicles, (7) by owner for incidental purpose of delivering newspapers, (8) for transportation of nonhazardous waste of no commercial value, and (9) incidentally to person's primary business other than transportation of persons or property for hire. (625-5/18c-4102).

Before operating in Illinois, motor carrier must also obtain motor fuel use tax license and decals from Department of Revenue and file bond to secure payment of motor fuel taxes. Identification cards and decals issued by Department must be carried in cab of commercial motor vehicle. (35-505/13a4). Beginning with membership of State of Illinois in International Fuel Tax Agreement, decals shall be placed on both exterior sides of cab. (35-505/13a4).

Rented Vehicles.—Renters of motor vehicles required to have insurance policy, bond, or, if person has more than 25 registered motor vehicles, a certificate of self-insurance. (625-5/9-101, 5/9-102). Bond shall be in sum of $50,000, executed by surety company qualified to do business in state or by person and surety owning Illinois real estate of value of at least $50,000 in excess of encumbrances, and shall be conditioned to pay trial judgment against customer and owner, or against person operating vehicle with customer and owner's express or implied consent, for injury, death or damage to property arising out of operation of vehicle. (625-5/9-103). Insurance policy shall cover same liabilities as bond, in minimum amount of $50,000. (625-5/9-105). Approval of Secretary of State required. (625-5/9-108). Sureties may withdraw on appropriate notice, and must be replaced. (625-5/9-104). Insurance policies may be cancelled on notice, and expire June 30 or Dec. 31 annually for vehicles registered on fiscal and calendar years, respectively. (625-5/9-105). No lessor of motor vehicle will be liable for parking tickets incurred by lessee provided lessor provides name and address of lessee to authorities upon request. (625-5/11-1306).

Motor Fuel Tax.—See category Taxation, topics Motor Fuel Tax; Administration, subhead Penalties.

Traffic and Parking Violations.—Secretary of State shall suspend without hearing license of person having warrant outstanding for arrest on ten or more parking violations or two or more traffic violations in any one county. Suspension may not be removed until outstanding warrant satisfied. (See 625-5/6-306.1.)

Replacement Vehicle Tax.—$200 tax imposed on passenger car purchased by or on behalf of insurance company to replace passenger car of insured in settlement of total loss claim. (625-5/3-2001). Municipalities and counties may impose replacement vehicle tax of $50 on any passenger car to be collected by Department of Revenue. (65-5/8-11-9).

RAILROADS:

See category Business Regulation and Commerce, topic Carriers.

See note at head of Digest as to 1998 legislation covered.

See Topical Index in front part of this volume.

IL – 82

COMMERCIAL CODE FORMS

See also categories Business Regulation and Commerce, topic Commercial Code and Mortgages, topic Chattel Mortgages. Following forms have been approved by Secretary of State.

Financing Statement (UCC-1).—

This STATEMENT is presented to a filing officer for filing pursuant to the Uniform Commercial Code.

For Filing Officer
(Date, Time, Number, and Filing Office)

Debtor(s) (Last Name First) and address(es)

Secured Party(ies) and address(es)

1. This financing statement covers the following types (or items) of property:

ASSIGNEE OF SECURED PARTY

2. ☐ Products of Collateral are also covered.

_____Additional sheets presented.
_____Filed with Office of Secretary of State of Illinois.
_____Secured Party is a transmitting utility as defined in UCC §9-105.

By: _____
Signature of (Debtor)
(Secured Party)*
*Signature of Debtor Required in Most Cases: Signature of Secured Party in Cases Covered By UCC §9-402(2)

(1) Filing Officer Copy—Alphabetical
This form of financing statement is approved by the Secretary of State.
STANDARD FORM—UNIFORM COMMERCIAL CODE—FORM UCC-1—REV. 4-73

*Termination Statement.—*Addendum to page 3 of Form UCC-1.

TERMINATION STATEMENT: This Statement of Termination of Financing is presented to a Filing Officer for filing pursuant to the Uniform Commercial Code. The Secured Party certifies that the Secured Party no longer claims a security interest under the financing statement bearing the file number shown above.

Date_____ 19____

By:_____
(Signature of Secured Party or Assignee of Record. Not Valid Until Signed.)

(3) Filing Officer Copy—Acknowledgment
This form of financing statement is approved by the Secretary of State.
STANDARD FORM—UNIFORM COMMERCIAL CODE—FORM UCC-1—REV. 4-73

Financing Statement (UCC-2), with Real Estate Description.—

This STATEMENT is presented to a filing officer for filing pursuant to the Uniform Commercial Code.

For Filing Officer
(Date, Time, Number, and Filing Office)

Debtor(s) (Last Name First) and address(es)

Secured Party(ies) and address(es)

1. This financing statement covers the following types (or items) of property:

2. (If collateral is crops) The above described crops are growing or are to be grown on: (Describe Real Estate)

ASSIGNEE OF SECURED PARTY

3. (If applicable) The above goods are to become fixtures on (The above timber is standing on . . .) (The above minerals or the like (including oil and gas) or accounts will be financed at the wellhead or minehead of the well or mine located on . . .) (Strike what is inapplicable) (Describe Real Estate)

and this financing statement is to be filed in the real estate records. (If the debtor does not have an interest of record) The name of a record owner is

4. ☐ Products of Collateral are also covered.

_____Additional sheets presented.
_____Filed with Recorder's Office of _____
County, Illinois.

By: _____
Signature of (Debtor)
(Secured Party)*
*Signature of Debtor Required in Most Cases: Signature of Secured Party in Cases Covered By UCC §9-402(2)

(1) Filing Officer Copy—Alphabetical
This form of financing statement is approved by the Secretary of State.
STANDARD FORM—UNIFORM COMMERCIAL CODE—FORM UCC-2—REV. 4-73

See note at head of Digest as to 1998 legislation covered.

See Topical Index in front part of this volume.

Statement of Continuation, Partial Release, Assignment, etc. (UCC-3).—

This STATEMENT is presented to THE FILING OFFICER for filing pursuant to the Uniform Commercial Code:

Debtor(s) (Last Name First) and address(es)	Secured Party(ies) and address(es)	For Filing Officer (Date, Time, Number, and Filing Office)

This Statement refers to original Financing Statement No. _____

Date filed: _____, 19_____
Filed with _____

A. ☐ **CONTINUATION** . . . . The original financing statement between the foregoing Debtor and Secured Party, bearing the file number shown above, is still effective.

B. ☐ **PARTIAL RELEASE** . . . . . From the collateral described in the financing statement bearing the file number shown above, the Secured Party releases the property indicated below.

C. ☐ **ASSIGNMENT** . . . . The Secured Party certifies that the Secured Party has assigned to the Assignee whose name and address is shown below. Secured Party's rights under the financing statement bearing the file number shown above in the property indicated below.

D. ☐ **TERMINATION** . . . . The Secured Party certifies that the Secured Party no longer claims a security interest under the financing statement bearing the file number shown above.

E. ☐ **AMENDMENT** . . . . The financing statement bearing the above file number is amended.
☐ To show the Secured Party's new address as indicated below;
☐ To show the Debtor's new address as indicated below;
☐ As set forth below:

_____(Debtor)   _____(Secured Party)
(Signature of Debtor, if required)   By: _____
Dated _____, 19_____   (Signature of Secured Party)
(1) Filing Officer Copy—Alphabetical
This form of Financing Statement is approved by the Secretary of State.
STANDARD FORM—UNIFORM COMMERCIAL CODE—FORM UCC-3 REV. 4-73

Request for Copies or Information (UCC 11.7).—

REQUEST FOR COPIES OR INFORMATION Present to Secretary of State, U.C.C. DIVISION, Springfield, Illinois

Debtor(s) (Last Name First) and address(es)	Party Requesting Copies or Information	For Filing Officer Use

☐ COPY REQUEST: Filing officer please furnish exact copies of all financing statements and statements of assignment listed below, which are on file with your office. Upon receipt of these copies, the undersigned party agrees to pay to the Office of the Secretary of State $.50 for each page of each financing statement or statement of assignment furnished by the Office of the Secretary of State.

☐ INFORMATION REQUEST: Filing officer please furnish certificate showing whether there is on file as of _____19__, at __M, any presently effective financing statement, or any statement of assignment thereof, naming the above debtor, give the date and hour of filing of each such statement, and the names and addresses of each party named therein. Enclosed is the statutory fee.

_____
(SIGNATURE OF REQUESTING PARTY)

FILE NO.	DATE AND HOUR OF FILING	NAME AND ADDRESS OF SECURED PARTY

The undersigned filing officer hereby certifies that the attached _____copies are true and exact copies of all available financing statements or statements of assignment listed in the above request.
Additional fee required $_____. Dated this _____, day of _____, A.D., 19___.

_____
(SIGNATURE OF FILING OFFICER)

The undersigned filing officer hereby certifies that the above listing is a record of all presently effective financing statements and statements of assignment which name the above debtor, and which are on file in my office as of ____, 19___ at __ M.

_____
(SIGNATURE OF FILING OFFICER)

UNIFORM COMMERCIAL CODE—FORM U.C.C. 11.7 *(Revised for use in the State of Illinois)*
TO BE RETURNED WITH COPIES OR INFORMATION

See note at head of Digest as to 1998 legislation covered.

See Topical Index in front part of this volume.

INDIANA LAW DIGEST REVISER

Ice Miller Donadio & Ryan
One American Square
Box 82001
Indianapolis, Indiana 46282-0002

Telephone: 317-236-2100

Fax: 317-236-2219

Email: hurston@imdr.com

Reviser Profile

History: The firm was founded in Indianapolis on April 28, 1910, when three general practitioners formed a partnership under the name of Henley, Matson & Gates. Based in Indianapolis and with offices in South Bend and Chicago, the firm experienced modest growth until 1945, when Harry T. Ice returned to the firm after having served a tour of duty with the United States Navy. Under his leadership, the firm experienced continuous growth until the time of his death in 1982 by which time the firm had grown to 90 lawyers and had acquired a national reputation and a national practice. The firm has continued to grow and presently consists of over 180 lawyers and over 25 paraprofessionals.

Core and Growth Areas: A full service law firm, Ice Miller's core departments are Business, Litigation, Labor and Employment, Real Estate Development, and Public Finance. From these core disciplines, Ice Miller lawyers have developed in-depth expertise in a variety of highly refined areas of concentration (see below) which allows the firm to put together teams of attorneys to satisfy the increasingly sophisticated and multi-faceted needs of its clients. Most notable growth areas include: Antitrust, Drug and Device, Employee Benefits (including public employee plans), Employment Litigation, Dispute Resolution, Entrepreneurial Services, Gaming, Governmental Services, Healthcare, Intellectual Property, International, Mergers and Acquisitions; Professional Liability, and Federal and State Tax.

Client and Referral Base: Ice Miller clients cover the full spectrum—from Fortune 500 publicly owned companies with multiple legal requirements to sole proprietorships; from clients located in rural Indiana to clients with national and worldwide facilities. Ice Miller has established close and continuing relationships with attorneys in virtually every community in the state, and highly values these relationships both as a source of new business and as a referral network. This philosophy, as well as a studied determination to control growth, has led Ice Miller to a measured approach to practice development that relies primarily on developing growth from within, thereby building upon known quality.

Governance: The management of the firm is entrusted to three managing partners who have responsibility both for strategic planning and the day-to-day operations of the firm. The managing partners report to and serve at the pleasure of a nine member policy board which in turn is elected by the partnership. Assisting the managing partners in the administration of the firm is a chief operating officer, a partner-equivalent position with responsibility for managing and implementing firm-wide operational policies established by the managing partners and the policy board.

Significant Distinctions: Ice Miller is structured in such a way as to provide in-depth expertise in a number of highly refined areas of concentration, including the following: Architects and Engineers Consulting and Dispute Resolution, Banking, Coal Industry, Commercial and Business Litigation (including Antitrust), Computer, Construction, Corporation, Corporate Finance, Creditors' Rights, Drug and Device, Employee Benefits, Environmental, Gift and Estate Tax, Governmental Services, Health, Housing and Securitization, Federal Tax, Gaming, Indiana State Tax, Intellectual Property (including Patent), Immigration, Information Services, International, Medical Malpractice, Mergers and Acquisitions, Municipal Finance, Occupational Hazards (black lung, asbestosis, etc.), Personal Services, Product Liability, Real Estate Development, Regulation and Risk and Claims Management, Securities, Sports and Entertainment, Tort, Utilities, Venture Capital Financing and White Collar Crime.

The firm is nationally recognized as the premier public finance firm in Indiana and one of the national leaders in that practice area. It has drafted most of the legislation in the state relating to issuance of tax-exempt debt, has given its opinion on most of the major bond issues done in Indiana over the past seventy years, and represents hundreds of governmental entities of all sizes.

Ice Miller also has the largest litigation practice in the state, representing national, regional and locally domiciled clients for which it has obtained numerous "landmark" decisions in areas which include corporate, product, professional, drug and device and contractual liability.

INDIANA LAW DIGEST

(The following is a list of all Categories and Topics, including cross-references, covered in this Digest.)

INDIANA LAW DIGEST

Revised for 1999 edition by

ICE MILLER DONADIO & RYAN, of the Indiana Bar.

(Citations unless otherwise indicated are to the Indiana Code. For mode of citation, see topic Statutes. "IC" refers to the Indiana Code. "I.A.C." refers to Indiana Administrative Code. "PL" refers to a Public Law passed during sessions of the Legislature. "TR" refers to Rules of Trial Procedure. "AP" refers to Rules of Appellate Procedure. "AD" refers to Admission and Discipline Rules. Parallel citations to the North Eastern Reporter begin with 102 Ind. and 1 Ind. App.)

Note: Revision includes legislation adopted through the 1998 session of the Indiana General Assembly.

INTRODUCTION

GOVERNMENT AND LEGAL SYSTEM:

The State of Indiana is a constituent state of the United States of America. For further discussion of the U.S. federal system, see Introduction to the Federal Government of the United States at the beginning of this volume. A great many laws are promulgated by the federal government of the United States and are not reflected in the topics below. See the Introduction to this volume for references to the federal law topics covered.

Like all but one of the United States, Indiana has a common law legal system, with roots in English common law. For information on the courts and legislature of Indiana, see category Courts and Legislature.

HOLIDAYS:

Legal Holidays.—Legal holidays are: Sun.; Jan. 1; 3d Mon. in Jan.; Feb. 12; 3d Mon. in Feb.; Good Friday; last Mon. in May; July 4; 1st Mon. in Sept.; 2d Mon. in Oct.; Nov. 11; 4th Thurs. in Nov.; Dec. 25; day of any general, municipal or primary election (IC1-1-9-1).

In computing time prescribed by Trial Rules, if last day falls on Sat., Sun., legal holiday, or day office in which act is to be done is closed during regular business hours, it is not counted in computation. (Rule TR 6).

Holiday Falling on Sunday.—When legal holiday falls on Sun., following Mon. is holiday. (IC1-1-9-1).

Holiday Falling on Saturday.—When legal holiday falls on Sat., preceding Fri. is holiday. (IC1-1-9-1).

Legality of Transactions on Saturday, Sunday or Holiday.—Some transactions are prohibited by penal statute on Sun. Bank transactions done or performed other than at regular banking hours are valid. (IC28-2-2-1). Any action taken by General Assembly on any holiday shall be valid for all purposes. (IC1-1-9-1).

OFFICE HOURS AND TIME ZONE:

Indiana is in the Eastern (GMT −05:00) time zone. State generally does not observe daylight saving time, although certain individual border counties observe daylight saving time in conjunction with metropolitan areas in neighboring states. Office hours are generally from 9 a.m. to 5 p.m.

BUSINESS ORGANIZATIONS

AGENCY:

Common law rules govern.

ASSOCIATIONS:

Unincorporated associations governed by rules of common law but certain associations also governed by statute.

Formation.—Veterans may form associations for educational and charitable purposes. (IC10-7-11-1 to 6).

Persons engaged in production of agricultural products may form nonprofit cooperative association with or without capital stock to engage in any activity in connection with producing, marketing or selling agricultural products of its members and others, provided that business with and services provided for nonmembers do not amount to greater value than to members. (IC15-7-1-1 to 29). Nonprofit associations organized under agricultural cooperative laws of other states, before doing business in Indiana, must apply for admission to do business in Indiana. (IC15-7-1-30 to 32).

Fraternal benefit societies may incorporate and engage in social, benevolent and insurance activities subject to law. (IC27-11-1-1 to 9-4). Such societies may engage in land acquisition and construction of buildings for benevolent purposes subject to law. (IC23-10-2-1 to 22).

Rights and Powers.—No special provisions.

Liabilities.—No special provisions.

Actions.—Unincorporated association may sue or be sued in its common name. Judgment by or against unincorporated association will bind organization as if it were an entity. Money judgment against unincorporated association not binding on individual member unless he is named as party or is bound as class member under TR 23 or 23.2. (Rule TR 17[E]).

Dissolution.—No special provisions.

Professional Associations.—See topic Corporations, subhead Professional Corporation.

Partnerships.—Governed by Uniform Partnership Act. (IC23-1-4-1 et seq.). See topic Partnerships.

Limited Liability Companies.—Governed by Indiana Business Flexibility Act. (IC23-18-1-1 et seq.). See topic Limited Liability Companies.

Limited Liability Partnerships.—Governed by IC23-1-4-44 et seq. See topic Partnerships, subhead Limited Liability Partnership.

CORPORATIONS:

Indiana Business Corporation Law.—In 1986 Indiana adopted modified version of Official Text of Revised Model Business Corporation Act (1984) ("Model Act"), known as "Indiana Business Corporation Law" ("IBCL"), which automatically applies to all domestic corporations in existence on July 31, 1987 (regardless of law under which such corporation was incorporated) or incorporated thereafter, and to all foreign corporations. Foreign corporations qualified to do business in Indiana on July 31, 1987, are governed by IBCL, but need not obtain new certificate of authority. (IC23-1-17-3). IBCL repealed The Indiana General Corporation Act effective Aug. 1, 1987. Official comments to IBCL (which incorporate, with exceptions, Model Act official comments) approved by General Assembly available from Secretary of State's office.

IBCL is based on Model Act (IC23-1-17-1 to 23-1-54-3), although there are number of significant variations: (1) All references to "mail" mean first class certified or registered U.S. mail, postage prepaid, or private carrier service, fees prepaid or billed to sender (IC23-1-20-15); (2) all notices must be in writing, unless articles or bylaws authorize oral notice (IC23-1-20-29); (3) "emergency", for purposes of emergency powers and bylaws, exists if extraordinary event prevents quorum of directors from assembling in time to deal with business (IC23-1-21-7[d]); (4) corporation may establish in articles or bylaws procedures regulating transactions that would result in changes of control as defined in IC23-1-22-4; (5) corporate name must be distinguishable from names already on Secretary of State's records, although name that is not distinguishable may be used if written consent filed by other corporation (IC23-1-23-1[b] and [c]); reservation of corporate name renewable (IC23-1-23-2); (6) preemptive rights created under prior law remain in effect until articles of incorporation are amended with respect to preemptive rights (IC23-1-54-2); (7) if corporation acquires its own shares, those shares are authorized, but unissued, unless resolution of board of directors or articles provide otherwise (IC23-1-27-2[a]) and corporation has authority to use, hold, acquire, cancel and dispose of treasury shares (as defined by prior law) (IC23-1-27-2[d]); (8) cancelled treasury shares are authorized, but unissued (IC23-1-27-2[e]); (9) IBCL has not adopted 1986 amendments to Model Act §§6.40(f) and (g) which relate to distributions to shareholders; (10) if bylaws so provide, shareholders may participate in annual or special meetings through telephonic communications where all may simultaneously hear (IC23-1-29-1[d] and 2[e]); (11) for corporations with more than 50 shareholders, if articles require special meeting on demand of shareholders but do not specify percentage of votes entitled to be cast at shareholders meeting required for valid shareholder demand for special meeting, board of directors may establish percentage in bylaws; if no bylaw provision, percentage is 100% (IC23-1-29-2[a]); for corporations with 50 or fewer shareholders, at least 25% of votes entitled to be cast at shareholders meeting required for valid shareholder demand for special meeting (IC23-1-29-2[b][2]); (12) notice of special meeting must be given within 60 days of shareholder demand or court may order meeting to be held (IC23-1-29-3); (13) court may only order that meeting be held and time and place of meeting, otherwise meeting conducted in accordance with articles and bylaws (Id.); (14) action taken by consent of shareholders is effective when last shareholder signs, unless prior or subsequent effective date is stated (IC23-1-29-4[c]); (15) shareholder access to shareholders list limited to shareholders entitled to vote at meeting, and availability of list only required five days before date of meeting through meeting (IC23-1-30-1[b]); other revisions exist regarding access to shareholders list (IC23-1-30-1); (16) appointment of proxy valid for 11 months unless shorter or longer period provided in appointment form (IC23-1-30-3[d]); (17) procedure authorized for recognition by and disclosure to corporation of beneficial owners of shares (IC23-1-30-4[b]); (18) IBCL deletes §§7.25(d) and 7.27(b) of Model Act regarding amendment of articles changing quorum or voting requirements for voting group; (19) IBCL revises provisions relating to voting trusts (IC23-1-31-1); (20) derivative proceedings may not be maintained if it appears person commencing proceeding not fairly and adequately representing shareholders' interests (IC23-1-32-1); IBCL provides for establishment of disinterested committee to consider derivative action (IC23-1-32-4); (21) IBCL deletes §8.03(b) of Model Act regarding limits on increasing or decreasing number of directors, and part of §8.03(c); (22) term of directors elected to fill vacancy expires at end of term for which director's predecessor was elected (IC23-1-33-5[d]); (23) regardless of number of directors, board may be staggered (IC23-1-33-6[a]); (24) articles or bylaws may designate additional officer to whom resignations from board may be delivered (IC23-1-33-7[a][2]); (25) articles may set forth provision regarding manner of removal of directors (IC23-1-33-8); (26) IBCL deletes §8.09 of Model Act regarding removal of director by judicial proceedings; (27) unless articles provide otherwise, only directors can fill vacancy on board of directors (IC23-1-33-9[a]); (28) committees of board may consist of one or more members (IC23-1-34-6[a]); (29) committees not prohibited from authorizing issuance of shares or determination of relative rights, preferences or limitations of class or series of shares within limits prescribed by board, or from authorizing distributions within formula, method or range set by board (IC23-1-34-6[e]); (30) IBCL has not adopted §§8.61-8.63 of Model Act but is based on original provisions of §§6.31 through 6.33 of Model Act; (31) in considering best interests of

CORPORATIONS . . . *continued*
corporation, director may consider effects of action on shareholders, employees, suppliers and customers and on community, among other factors (IC23-1-35-1[d]); (32) director not liable for action taken as director, or failure to take action, unless director breached or failed to perform duties, and breach or failure to perform constitutes willful misconduct or recklessness (IC23-1-35-1[e]); this standard also applicable for distributions (IC23-1-35-4); (33) in exercising business judgment, directors may consider effects of proposed corporate action on any particular corporate constituent group or interest as they deem appropriate (IC23-1-35-1[f]). Directors not required to consider any constituency as predominant or controlling. (Id.). Both directors and validity of corporate action taken by them in good faith exercise of their business judgment after reasonable investigation are protected under statute. (Id.); (34) in exercising business judgment, directors may also consider any other factors they deem pertinent, assigning whatever weight they deem appropriate to various competing factors. (IC23-1-35-1[g]). If director action is approved by majority of disinterested directors, defined in IC23-1-35-1(h) and (i), it will be conclusively presumed valid unless not made in good faith after reasonable investigation (IC23-1-35-1[g]); (35) IBCL deletes §8.51(d) of Model Act which prohibits indemnifying director liable to corporation or in proceeding charging director with improper personal benefit; (36) indemnification under IBCL not exclusive of other rights to indemnification or advance for expenses (IC23-1-37-15); (37) amendment to articles without shareholder vote permitted for reduction in authorized shares upon cancellation of treasury shares (IC23-1-38-2[6]); (38) unless articles of incorporation provide otherwise, only board of directors may amend or repeal bylaws (IC23-1-39-1); (39) short form merger procedure added for merger of parent into 90%-owned subsidiary (IC23-1-40-4); (40) provisions of plan of merger or share exchange not included in articles create only contract rights (IC23-1-40-6); (41) IBCL contains two new chapters regulating "control share acquisitions" (IC23-1-42) and "business combinations" (IC23-1-43). Former chapter applies to corporation with 100 or more shareholders and designated contacts with State of Indiana. Constitutionally upheld in CTS Corporation v. Dynamics Corporation of America, 481 U.S. 69, 95 L.Ed.2d 67, 107 S.Ct. 1637 (1987). Latter chapter applies to corporations with 100 or more shareholders and class of shares registered under §12 of Securities Exchange Act of 1934 (unless articles provide otherwise), and limits for period of five years certain business combinations with acquirer of 10% or more voting shares unless specified approval obtained and otherwise in accordance with specified mechanism; (42) provisions on dissenting shareholders rights not applicable to holders of shares traded on registered U.S. securities exchange or traded on NASDAQ or similar market (IC23-1-44-8[b]). Dissenting shareholders or those who would be entitled to dissent but for IC23-1-44-8(b) may not challenge corporate action creating shareholders' entitlement (IC23-1-44-8[c]); (43) requirement that corporation pay accrued interest on fair value of dissenters' shares partially deleted (IC23-1-44-15[a]); (44) court may assess cost in appraisal proceedings on value of dissenters' shares against such parties in such amount as court finds equitable (IC23-1-44-20[a]); (45) procedure expanded concerning claims against dissolved corporations (IC23-1-45-6[b] through [e]). Claims barred unless proceeding to enforce commenced within two years of publication of notice of dissolution (IC23-1-45-7[b] and [c]); (46) IBCL deletes §14.30(2)(ii) and (iv) of Model Act regarding grounds for dissolution; (47) qualification requirements for foreign corporations do not apply to foreign banking, surety, trust, safe deposit, railroad, insurance and building and loan corporations (IC23-1-49-1[a]); exemptions from qualification for transaction of business apply for purposes of Financial Institutions Act and Indiana Insurance Law; (48) use and distribution of information or records obtained from corporation by shareholder restricted solely to proper purpose (IC23-1-52-5); (49) Exchange Act reports satisfy certain state requirements (IC23-1-53-2[b]).

Filing Fees.—Articles of incorporation—$90; application for certificate of authority—$90. Filing fees may be paid by credit card, debit card, charge card or similar method.

Paid in Capital Requirements.—None.

Reports.—(1) Corporation must provide annual financial statements to shareholder upon written request (IC23-1-53-1); (2) corporation must report to shareholders indemnification of or advancement of expenses to directors and issuance of shares for promissory notes or for promises to render services in future (IC23-1-53-2); and (3) domestic corporations and foreign corporations authorized to transact business in state must file biennial report with Secretary of State (IC23-1-53-3).

Transfer of Stock.—Uniform Commercial Code in effect since July 1, 1964. (IC26-1-1-101 to IC26-1-10-105).

Uniform Simplification of Fiduciary Security Transfers Act adopted. (IC30-2-5-1 to 11).

Stock Transfer Tax.—See category Taxation.

Unclaimed dividends or other distributions neglected for seven years are presumed abandoned where there have been at least seven dividends or other distributions paid during such period, none of which has been claimed by owner. (IC32-9-1-7.1). Uniform Disposition of Unclaimed Property Act adopted. (IC32-9-1-1 to IC32-9-10-16).

Business Take-Over Act.—See category Business Regulation and Commerce, topic Securities.

Close Corporations.—Corporations with 50 or fewer shareholders may dispense with board of directors (IC23-1-33-1[c]), requirements for special meetings (IC23-1-29-2[b]) otherwise no special statutory provisions. Common law fiduciary duty officers, director and shareholders of closely held corporations, W & W Equipment Co., Inc. v. Mink, 568 N.E.2d 564 (Ind.App. Ct. 1991).

Taxation of Corporate Property.—See category Taxation, topic Property Tax.

Tax Administration.—Unless exempt, corporations that carry on any business activity or own or maintain property in Indiana for taxable year must file business activity report with Indiana Department of Revenue for each taxable year in order to pursue certain claims in Indiana courts. (IC6-8.1-6-6).

Franchise Tax.—No franchise tax is imposed on foreign or domestic corporations.

Continuing Care Contracts.—Special provisions dealing with continuing care contracts entered into in Indiana, providing for care at home in Indiana or executed by Indiana residents. (IC23-2-4-1 to 24).

Deceptive Franchise Practices.—Special provisions dealing with deceptive practices as to franchisee who is resident of Indiana. (IC23-2-2.7-1 to 7).

Gross income tax, applicable to corporations, see category Taxation, topic Income Tax.

Professional Corporation.—Professional corporations are governed by Indiana Business Corporation Law (IC23-1-17-1 to IC23-1-54-3) and special provisions pertaining to various professions (IC23-1.5-1-1 to IC23-1.5-5-2). In event of conflict between provisions of IBCL and special provisions, special provisions are controlling. (IC23-1.5-2-1). Professional corporation may be formed by individual or group of individuals, at least one shareholder of whom holds unlimited license to practice profession in state, only to render professional accounting, architectural or engineering, legal, health care, veterinary or real estate professional services. (IC23-1.5-2-3). Name of professional corporation must include words "Professional Services Corporation" or "Professional Corporation", or abbreviation thereof. (IC23-1.5-2-8).

Deeds.—See category Property, topic Deeds.

Model Non-Profit Corporation Act, adopted with variations, is effective immediately for all not-for-profit corporations formed after July 31, 1991 (IC23-17-1-1 to IC23-17-30-4) ("Model Non-Profit Act"). Model Non-Profit Act applies to all domestic not-for-profit corporations effective July 1, 1993 or such earlier time as they shall elect.

Limited Liability Companies.—See topic Limited Liability Companies.

JOINT STOCK COMPANIES:

Business trusts are authorized by statute. (IC23-5-1-1 to 11). Business trust is unincorporated association including Massachusetts trusts and real estate investment trusts under §856 of Internal Revenue Code, but excluding certain land trusts. Statute does not invalidate any such associations formed prior to effective date. (IC23-5-1-3).

Purposes and Powers.—Business trust may engage in such business or professional activities as are stated in trust instrument, with certain stated exceptions. Subject to these exceptions, persons dealing with business trusts are bound by terms of trust instrument. (IC23-5-1-8).

Formation.—Business trust created after effective date of act must be formed in compliance with provisions of the act. (IC23-5-1-3 to 6). Every business trust transacting or authorized to transact business in Indiana must file biennial report with Secretary of State by end of anniversary month of creation or authorization to transact business of each year. (IC23-5-1-10.1).

Actions.—Business trust may sue or be sued (IC23-5-1-8), and is subject to law applicable to corporations as to service of process (IC23-5-1-9). Business trust may adopt provision of law related to domestic and foreign corporations not listed in statute by filing notice of adoption with Secretary of State and recording same with county recorder where principal office is located. (IC23-5-1-9.1).

Certificates of Beneficial Interest.—Trust instrument may provide for limited liability of holders of certificates of beneficial interest, and may restrict their transferability. (IC23-5-1-8).

Dissolution.—Statute provides method and requirements for dissolving. (IC23-5-1-11).

Professional Corporations.—See topic Corporations, subhead Professional Corporation.

LIMITED LIABILITY COMPANIES:

The Indiana Business Flexibility Act (referred to in this subsection as "Act"), which provides for creation and operation of limited liability companies, became effective July 1, 1993. Following summarizes principal provisions of Act.

Purpose.—Limited liability companies may be formed and may conduct business for any lawful purpose unless restricted by articles of organization, and must comply with other applicable statutes. (IC23-18-2-1).

Powers.—Unless restricted by articles of organization, every limited liability company has same powers as individual to do all things necessary or convenient to carry out its business and affairs. (IC23-18-2-2).

Other Authorities.—Act does not affect, restrict or limit licensing authority or authority to regulate provision of professional services or engaging in practice of profession. (IC23-18-2-3).

Formation.—At least one person, who need not be member, may form limited liability company by causing articles of organization to be executed and filed with secretary of state. (IC23-18-2-4 [a]).

Articles of Organization.—Shall contain name of limited liability company, street address of limited liability company's registered office, name of limited liability company's registered agent, and latest date for dissolution or statement that duration shall be perpetual; articles of organization may contain statement as to whether limited liability company will have manager and any other matters not inconsistent with Act. (IC23-18-2-4). Articles of organization may be amended (IC23-18-2-5) or restated (IC23-18-2-6) in accordance with prescribed procedures.

Name of limited liability company must contain words "limited liability company" or either of following abbreviations: "L.L.C." or "LLC". Provisions with respect to registering or reserving name are similar to Indiana Business Corporation Law ("IBCL").

Registered Office and Agent.—Must be continuously maintained by limited liability company (IC23-18-2-10); these may be changed in accordance with prescribed procedures (IC23-18-2-11).

See note at head of Digest as to 1998 legislation covered.

See Topical Index in front part of this volume.

IN – 2

LIMITED LIABILITY COMPANIES... *continued*

Powers, Rights, and Duties of Members and Managers.—Members generally will have authority to bind limited liability company if act is for carrying on of usual business of limited liability company, unless articles of organization provide for manager and limit power of members, or member does not have authority and other party is aware of lack of authority. (IC23-18-3-1). Notice to member, or to manager if provided for in articles of organization, constitutes notice to limited liability company. (IC23-18-3-2). Member, manager, agent, or employee is not personally liable for debts of limited liability company (IC23-18-3-3), but Act does not alter or affect any law with respect to professional liability (IC23-18-3-4). Members shall manage affairs of limited liability company unless manager is provided for in articles of organization and duly elected according to prescribed procedures or in accordance with operating agreement. (IC23-18-4-1). Members and managers will not be liable for damages caused to limited liability company by their acts except due to willful misconduct or recklessness. (IC23-18-4-2). Approval or consent of majority of members or managers is generally required to conduct business, but approval of all members is required to adopt or amend operating agreement. (IC23-18-4-3, 6). Members may enter into operating agreement to regulate or establish any aspect of affairs of limited liability company. (IC23-18-4-5). Copies of governing documents must be kept at principal office of limited liability company and members shall have access to such documents. (IC23-18-4-8).

Contributions and Distributions.—Unless otherwise provided in operating agreement, profits and losses must be allocated on basis of agreed value, as stated in records of limited liability company, of contributions made by each member to extent contributions have been received by limited liability company and not previously returned. (IC23-18-5-3). Unless otherwise set forth in operating agreement, distributions must be allocated on basis of agreed value of contributions made by each member to extent such contributions have been received and not returned and except upon event of dissociation that does not cause dissolution. (IC23-18-5-4). Distributions may not be made if such would render limited liability company insolvent. (IC23-18-5-6).

Membership.—May have at least one member. (IC23-18-6-0.5). Person may become member in accordance with articles of organization and operating agreement. (IC23-18-6-1). Interest in limited liability company is assignable (IC23-18-6-3), but assignee may only become member upon unanimous consent of remaining members or in accordance with articles of organization and operating agreement (IC23-18-6-4). Person ceases to be member upon event of disassociation, such as withdrawal, removal, death and other specified circumstances, or in accordance with operating agreement. (IC23-18-6-5).

Merger.—Limited liability company may merge into another limited liability company in accordance with prescribed procedures similar to those in IBCL. (IC23-18-7).

Dissolution.—May occur voluntarily (IC23-18-9) or administratively by proceedings instituted by secretary of state (IC23-18-10). Upon event of disassociation, limited liability company will be dissolved unless all members consent to continuation of business within 90 days. (IC23-18-9-1[3]). Provisions with respect to winding up of business of limited liability company upon dissolution and distribution of assets are similar to corresponding provisions respecting partnerships. Secretary of state may commence dissolution proceedings for failure to deliver annual reports, lack of registered agent or office, and expiration of period of duration specified in articles of organization (IC23-18-10-1), and proceedings for dissolution and reinstatement are prescribed (IC23-18-10-2, 4, 5).

Foreign Limited Liability Companies.—Certificate of authority is required for foreign limited liability company to transact business. Procedures to obtain certificate of authority, ongoing requirements for foreign limited liability companies and penalties for failure to comply with these provisions are set forth at IC23-18-11.

Filing Fees and Reports.—Filing of articles of organization must be accompanied by $90 fee, and amendments thereto or restatement thereof require $30 fee; application for certificate of authority must be accompanied by $90 fee; biennial report required by IC23-18-12-11 must include $15 filing fee; other fees are set forth. (IC23-18-12-3). Biennial reports, setting forth name of limited liability company, address of registered office, name and address of registered agent, and address of principal office, must be filed with secretary of state by both domestic and qualified foreign limited liability companies. Filing fees may be paid by credit card, debit card, charge card or similar method.

PARTNERSHIPS:

Uniform Partnership Act adopted. (IC23-4-1-1 to 43).

Limited Liability Partnership.—IC23-4-1-45 to 52, added to Uniform Partnership Act effective Oct. 1, 1995, permits formation of limited liability partnerships.

Limited Partnership.—Revised Uniform Limited Partnership Act (1976) adopted. (IC23-16-1 to 12). Uniform Limited Partnership Act adopted (IC23-4-2-1 to 31) repealed effective July 1, 1993, which repeal does not impair or affect organization or existence of limited partnership existing before July 1, 1988, nor impair any contract or affect any right accrued before July 1, 1988.

Partnership Name.—For foreign limited partnership, must file name with Secretary of State and must contain words "limited partnership" or abbreviation "L.P." (IC23-16-10-4). For limited liability partnership, exclusive right to use may be reserved by filing with Secretary of State (IC23-4-1-45.3) and must contain words "Limited Liability Partnership" or abbreviation "L.L.P." or "LLP".

Out-of-State Partnership.—Foreign limited partnership (IC23-16-10-2) and foreign limited liability partnership (IC23-4-1-45) must register with Secretary of State.

Actions.—Partnership may sue or be sued in its common name. Judgment by or against partnership will bind organization as if it were entity. Money judgment against partnership is not binding on individual partner unless he is named as party or is bound as class member under TR 23 or 23.2. (Rule TR 17[E]).

BUSINESS REGULATION AND COMMERCE

BANKS AND BANKING:

Uniform Commercial Code in effect since July 1, 1964. 1972 amendments in effect since Jan. 1, 1986. 1977 Amendments in effect since Sept. 1, 1987. 1990 amendments in effect since July 1, 1994. 1994 and 1995 amendments in effect since July 1, 1996. (IC26-1-1-101 et seq.). Uniform Consumer Credit Code in effect since Oct. 1, 1971. (IC24-4.5-1-101 et seq.).

All financial institutions organized under Indiana law are controlled by "Indiana Financial Institutions Act." (IC28-1-1-1 et seq.).

Supervision is by the Department of Financial Institutions, which has rule-making power. (IC28-11-1-12). Department is required to make periodic examinations of all financial institutions. (IC28-11-3-1).

Stock.—Articles of Incorporation must prescribe number of shares that corporation organized under Act is authorized to issue. If more than one class of shares authorized by articles, articles must prescribe number of shares in each class and distinguishing designation for each class. Before issuance of shares of class, preferences, limitations, and relative rights of class must be described in articles. (IC28-13-1-1). Act requires that articles authorize at least one class of shares that together have unlimited voting rights and at least one class of shares (which may be same class or classes of shares with voting rights) that together are entitled to receive net assets of corporation upon dissolution. (IC28-13-1-2). Shareholders of corporation do not have preemptive rights, except to extent such rights are provided in articles of incorporation. (IC28-13-3-1). Bank or trust company may not purchase or make loans secured by its own stock, except when stock is taken to prevent loss on previous debt, in which case it must be resold within six months. (IC28-1-13-8).

Bank Holding Companies.—Multi-bank holding companies are permitted. Out-of-state bank holding companies may acquire existing Indiana banks. (IC28-2-16-17; IC28-2-17-1 et seq.).

Deposits.—Joint accounts, P.O.D. accounts and trust accounts are controlled by Non-Probate Transfer Act. (IC32-4-1.5).

At death of party to joint account sums remaining on deposit belong to surviving party or parties as against estate of decedent unless there is clear and convincing evidence of different intention when account is created. (IC32-4-1.5-4).

Right of survivorship arising from express terms of account or under this section, beneficiary designation in trust account or P.O.D. payee designation cannot be changed by will, but only by signed order of request to change form of account or to stop or vary payment under terms of account which is received by financial institution during party's lifetime. (IC32-4-1.5-5).

Unclaimed Deposits.—Uniform Unclaimed Property Act adopted, effective July 1, 1996. (IC32-9-1.5).

Branch Banking.—Interstate branching, de novo and by acquisition, is authorized. However, out-of-state banks may not establish de novo branches or branches through branch acquisitions unless laws of home state of out-of-state bank permit Indiana state banks reciprocal privileges. Indiana banks may establish new branches and may acquire existing branches in any location with approval of Department of Financial Institutions and subject to certain other statutory requirements. (IC28-2-13-19; IC28-18-1 et seq.). Establishment of automated teller machines (ATMs) is unrestricted. (IC28-2-13-22).

Trust Department.—Every bank or trust company exercising fiduciary powers must maintain a trust department, keeping separate books of account and maintaining all trust property segregated from other property. (IC28-1-12-3). Every bank or trust company holding securities as fiduciary is authorized to deposit securities in clearing corporation as defined by IC26-1-8.1-102(a)(5). (IC28-1-12-3). Trust departments may establish or invest in common trust funds. (IC30-1-8-2). No profit or commission, other than interest at legal rate on loan, may be received by any bank, trust company or corporate fiduciary, directly or indirectly, out of sale to or purchase from any estate, guardianship, or trust of which it is fiduciary, unless specifically authorized by creator or court. (IC28-1-12-4). Money awaiting investment or distribution may be kept on deposit in its commercial banking department provided sufficient book entries show true ownership of such money in both bank and trust departments. On liquidation of any bank, trust company or corporate fiduciary, all persons beneficially entitled to receive property or proceeds held by it in trust have preference and priority in all assets over general creditors for all uninvested funds, to extent that such money is commingled with general assets and is not duly accounted for. (IC28-1-12-6). Bank holding company, in some circumstances, may by resolution filed with Department cause Indiana affiliate to succeed to trust business of another Indiana affiliate. (IC28-2-14-18).

Common trust funds provided for. (IC30-1-8-1 et seq.).

Institutions Other Than Banks or Trust Companies.—Department of Financial Institutions also regulates formation, management, etc., of various financial institutions other than banks and trust companies, such as corporate fiduciaries (IC28-14-1-1 et seq.), savings associations (IC28-15-1-1, et seq.) credit unions (IC28-7-1-0.5 et seq.), pawn brokers (IC28-7-5-1 et seq.). C. 21 of Financial Institutions Act was repealed effective July 1, 1997 and replaced by IC28-15 et seq. Industrial loan and investment companies are regulated by IC28-5-1-1 et seq. and may offer negotiable order of withdrawal (NOW) accounts. (IC28-5-1-12). Currency Exchange Act (IC28-8-3-1) was repealed effective Jan. 1, 1994, and replaced with chapter governing money transmitters (IC28-8-4-1 et seq.). Check cashing businesses are also regulated, effective Jan. 1, 1994. (IC28-8-5-1 et seq.).

Foreign Corporations.—Before transacting business in Indiana, bank, savings bank, trust company, corporate fiduciary, credit union, industrial loan and investment company or savings association organized under laws of any other state or U.S., other

BANKS AND BANKING . . . *continued*
than those domiciled in Indiana, must procure certificate of admission from Department, which must be filed with Secretary of State.

The application submitted to the Department must include copy of articles of incorporation or association, state names of certain officers, identify resident agent of corporation and contain such other information as Department may require. (IC28-1-22-4).

Filing and Recording Certificate.—Within ten days of issuance of certificate, there must be filed with county recorder of county wherein principal office in state is to be located, duplicate certificate of admission and notify Secretary of State of recording. (IC28-1-22-9).

If any foreign corporation transacts business in this state, after it has received, but before it has recorded its certificate of admission and notified Secretary of State, officers and directors participating therein are severally liable for debts of corporation arising out of such business and certificate shall be revocable. (IC28-1-22-10).

Supervision.—Department and Secretary of State have power to interrogate applicant corporation in matters pertaining to its proposed business or other matters stated in admission application. Interrogatories and answers filed with application operate as limitation upon corporation to transact business in State. (IC28-1-22-11). Department's power of examination (IC28-1-2-29) is same as for domestic corporations. (IC28-1-22-2).

Permissible Business.—No foreign corporation may be admitted for the purpose of transacting any kind of business in this state which a domestic corporation is not permitted by the laws of state to transact. (IC28-1-22-2).

Name.—No foreign corporation admitted to do business in this state may have a name which a domestic corporation with like powers could not have. (IC28-1-22-3).

Certificate of admission may be revoked at any time by the Department or by the Secretary of State with approval of the Department: (a) on failure for 30 days to maintain resident agent; (b) on failure to keep authenticated copies of instruments amending charter of corporation on file with Secretary of State within 30 days after amending; (c) on failure for 30 days to file certificate of admission or amendments thereof with county recorder; (d) on failure for 30 days to pay fees required; (e) for willful misrepresentation of material matters in application, affidavits or other papers. (IC28-1-22-24).

Foreign corporation transacting business without procuring certificate of admission may not maintain any suit or action in any courts of the state and such corporation is subject to injunctive action and penalty not exceeding $10,000 to be recovered in suit brought by Attorney General. (IC28-1-22-28).

Application for withdrawal from the state by any corporation must be filed with and approved by Department. (IC28-1-22-22).

Franchise Tax.—Tax on corporation transacting business of financial institutions in Indiana at rate of 8½% on remainder of adjusted gross income or apportioned income, minus deductible Indiana net operating losses and minus apportioned net capital losses multiplied by apportionment percentage applicable to taxpayer. Replaces other taxes on financial institutions. (IC6-5.5).

Bank Share and Deposit Tax.—To extent taxpayer is not subject to franchise tax, tax at rate of .25% of value is imposed on: (a) Taxable shares; (b) taxable deposits; and (c) taxable surplus and profits. (IC6-5-10-3). This tax is in lieu of all other taxes, except inheritance tax or gross income tax, on shares of stock, surplus, undivided profits, reserves, deposits and owners of such items. (IC6-5-10-17). Where bank or trust company is subject to Indiana gross income tax and is not national banking association, it is entitled to credit against this excise tax for amount of gross income tax paid. (IC6-5-10-7).

Savings and Loan Association Tax.—To extent taxpayer is not subject to franchise tax, excise tax is imposed on building and loan associations (IC6-5-11-2), in lieu of all other taxes on mortgages, notes and contracts for sale of real estate (IC6-5-11-11).

Tax is at rate of .14% multiplied by total of paid-in value of association's shares of capital stock and surplus, after deducting therefrom assessed value of all taxable real estate owned, amount of any loan secured by pledge of capital stock, value of shares of association held by certain entities, amount of mortgage loan on which foreclosure proceedings filed, investments and deposits in any home loan bank, and, within size limitations, amount of Federal debt and Indiana state and local debt. (IC6-5-11-2). Where association is subject to Indiana gross income tax or tangible personal property tax, it is entitled to credit against this excise tax for amount of gross income tax or tangible personal property tax paid. (IC6-5-11-3).

See also topics Commercial Code, Consumer Credit.

BILLS AND NOTES:

Uniform Commercial Code in effect since July 1, 1964. 1990 Amendments in effect commencing July 1, 1994. (IC26-1-1-101 et seq.).

Judgment notes or cognovit notes are expressly prohibited and any agreement or authority to confess judgment made before action accrues, is void, and procurement of execution of such note or attempt to recover upon or enforce such note is Class B misdemeanor. (IC34-54-3, 24-4.5 and 26-1). But see category Civil Actions and Procedure, topic Judgments, subhead Foreign Judgments.

See also topic Commercial Code.

BILLS OF LADING:

See topic Carriers.

BILLS OF SALE:

No statutory provisions.

BLUE SKY LAW:

See topic Securities.

BROKERS:

Uniform Commercial Code in effect since July 1, 1964. (See IC26-1-8-303, 306, 313, 314.)

Real estate brokers and salespersons are under supervision of Indiana Real Estate Commission and required to be licensed thereby. (IC25-34.1-2 et seq.). To obtain salesperson's license, one must be 18, and not have conviction for act or crime which would constitute ground for disciplinary sanction under IC25-1-11 or which has direct bearing on applicant's ability to practice competently or that indicates that person has propensity to endanger public, complete eight semester credit hours in principles, practices and laws of real estate at accredited college or university or have completed approved salesperson course, pass written exam and submit $25 for license within 120 days after passing exam. Salespersons must be associated with and act under auspices of broker. (IC25-34.1-3-3.1). To obtain broker's license, one must be 18 and not have conviction for act or crime which would constitute ground for disciplinary sanction under IC25-1-11 or which has direct bearing on applicant's ability to practice competently or that indicates that person has propensity to endanger public, have completed educational requirements for salesperson's license and have continuous active experience as licensed salesperson in Indiana for one year immediately preceding application (which experience requirement may be waived upon Commission finding of equivalent experience) and have successfully completed approved broker course, submit application and fee, pass written exam and submit $50 for license within 120 days after passing exam. (IC25-34.1-3-4.1). Commission may issue license to nonresidents meeting requirements as long as one files written consent for suit or service of process arising from conduct. (IC25-34.1-3-5). Commission may waive requirements if jurisdiction of nonresident grants same privilege to licensee of Indiana, nonresident is licensed in his jurisdiction, licensing requirements of that jurisdiction are substantially similar to requirements of Indiana, and nonresident states that he has studied, is familiar with and will abide by statutes and rules of Indiana. (IC25-34.1-3-5). Broker's licenses granted to corporations, limited liability companies and partnerships. (IC25-34.1-3-4.1). Brokers and salespersons may form professional corporation. (IC25-1.5-2-3). Lapsed license reinstated if within 120 days, one pays back fees and $20 or, if after 120 days but within 18 months, one pays back fees and $100. (IC25-34.1-3-3.1, 4.1). Commission has authority to revoke or suspend license for misconduct, censure, issue reprimand, put licensee on probation or assess civil penalty up to $1,000. (IC25-1-11-12). Statute provides for granting of inactive license to salespersons or brokers. (IC25-34.1-3-10). Statute establishes guidelines for real estate courses and for school's acquiring Commission's approval. (IC25-34.1-5-1 to 11). Except for those with inactive licenses, statute imposes continuing education requirements on individuals who are licensed brokers or salespersons including special requirements regarding Indiana attorneys in good standing who are also licensed brokers or salespersons. (IC25-34.1-9-10 & -11). Statute establishes Real Estate Recovery Fund to provide pool of funds from which recovery may be obtained for any act by licensee of embezzlement, unlawfully obtaining property or money by false pretenses, use of device, trickery or forgery, to extent such act results in actual cash loss to aggrieved person and aggrieved person is unable to obtain recovery directly from licensee. (IC25-34.1-7 et seq.). Recovery limited to $20,000 per judgment and aggregate lifetime limit of $50,000 against any one licensee. (IC25-34.1-7-4). Statute provides funding of Real Estate Recovery Fund through license fee surcharge. (IC25-34.1-7-2). Recovery available only if act occurred after Dec. 31, 1987, when licensee was licensed, and is act for which license was required under IC25-34.1 et seq. (IC25-34.1-7-4).

Relationship between broker, broker's client and other parties to real estate transaction is regulated under IC25-34.1-10, which, inter alia, specifies duties and obligations of broker with respect to client and other parties to transaction. Broker may act as limited agent representing both seller and buyer or both landlord and tenant with written consent (containing certain requirements) of all parties to real estate transaction. (IC25-34.1-10-12). Principal broker must develop and enforce among its salespersons written office policy on brokerage relationships which specifically permits or rejects practice of disclosed limited agency. (IC25-34.1-10-13[a]). Broker must advise parties to transaction whether it will share broker's compensation with other brokers who may represent other parties whose interests are different or even adverse. (IC25-34.1-10-13[c]). Duties and responsibilities of broker set forth in IC25-34.1-10 supersede any fiduciary duties of broker based on common law principles of agency to extent of any inconsistency. (IC25-34.1-10-15). With certain exceptions, client is not liable for misrepresentations made by broker and broker is not liable for misrepresentations of another broker he retains to provide brokerage services to client. (IC25-34.1-10-16).

Contract for commission on sale of real estate must be in writing, signed by the owner of the real estate or his legally appointed and qualified representative. (IC32-2-2-1).

Commission Sales Representatives.—Payment of commissions by principal to sales representative, upon termination of contract, is due within 14 days after payment would have been due under contract if contract had not been terminated. (IC24-4-7-5). Sales representatives are persons who contract with principal to solicit wholesale orders in Indiana and are compensated, in whole or in part, by commission. (IC24-4-7-4).

See also topic Commercial Code.

BULK SALES:

Governed by Art. 6.1 of Uniform Commercial Code, in effect since July 1, 1964. (IC26-1-1-101 et seq.). See topic Commercial Code.

CARRIERS:

Department of State Revenue supervises and regulates motor carriers that transport property (IC8-2.1-18-1 et seq.) and passengers or household goods (IC8-2.1-22-1 et seq.). Certificates or permits required for common carriers (IC8-2.1-18-8 and 9), contract carriers (IC8-2.1-18-14 and 15), carriers that transport passengers (IC8-2.1-

See note at head of Digest as to 1998 legislation covered.

See Topical Index in front part of this volume.

IN – 4

CARRIERS . . . *continued*

22-11), carriers that transport household goods (IC8-2.1-22-12.5), and special or charter carrier (IC8-2.1-22-28). Certification and annual renewal of motor carrier required. (IC8-2.1-24 et seq.). Annual registration of vehicles required. (IC8-2.1-18-29 and 38; IC8-2.1-22-33). Additional rules required for registration of vehicles to transport passengers or household goods. Annual registration of certificate or permit required. (IC8-2.1-20-5 and 7; IC8-2.1-22-12.5). Surety bonds, insurance or other proof of financial responsibility required. (IC8-2.1-18-13 and 16; IC8-2.1-22-46). Brokerage licenses required. (IC8-2.1-18-22; IC8-2.1-22-27). Annual fuel permit required. (IC6-6-4.1-12). All other carriers are under supervision of Indiana Department of Transportation. (IC8-23-2-4.1). Rules of transportation coordinating board, planning office, department of highways and department of transportation treated as adopted by Department of Transportation. (IC8-23-2-10).

Certain Federal Regulations incorporated into State law effective Jan. 1, 1996. (IC8-2.1-24-18). Federal requirements regulating hours of service of drivers, including requirements for maintenance of logs, do not apply to vehicles used as farm trucks. (IC8-2.1-24-18). Notwithstanding incorporated federal requirements, persons between ages 18 and 21 may operate commercial motor vehicles intrastate. (IC8-2.1-24-18).

Discrimination defined and prohibited. (IC8-2.1-18-17 and 34; IC8-2.1-22-18 and 38; IC8-3-1-12). Railroads may be both civilly and criminally liable for discrimination. (IC8-3-1-13 to 15).

Rates.—Department of State Revenue has power to prescribe just and reasonable rates, fares and charges of motor carriers. (IC8-2.1-18-17; IC8-2.1-22-21). Contract carriers must establish and observe reasonable minimum rates, fares and charges (IC8-2.1-18-21; IC8-2.1-22-24) and common carriers must file tariffs showing all rates, fares and charges (IC8-2.1-18-20; IC8-2.1-22-23). Indiana Department of Transportation has authority to hold hearings and pass on reasonableness of railroad rate schedules. (IC8-2-19-1).

Sale to Enforce Lien.—Baggage or freight unclaimed for period of three months at place to which it is consigned or checked may be sold at public auction by common carrier. (IC8-2-6-1). Perishable freight or livestock may be sold after expiration of five days at public auction. (IC8-2-6-4).

No liability for stock injured when railroad is securely fenced in and properly maintained. (IC8-4-32-1 to 7). Railroads are obligated to construct and maintain fencing along right-of-way. (IC8-4-33-1 to 4).

Statute of Limitations.—All actions for recovery of charges shall commence within two years. (IC8-2.1-18-18; IC8-2.1-22-22).

Express companies are subject to regulation. (IC8-2.1-21-1 et seq.).

Motor Vehicle Carriers.—See category Transportation, topic Motor Vehicles. See topics Brokers, Commercial Code.

COMMERCIAL CODE:

Uniform Commercial Code (as reproduced in Uniform and Model Acts section) was enacted by the 1963 Legislature, and became effective on July 1, 1964. (IC26-1-1-101 et seq.). 1972 Official Amendments, with variations discussed below, adopted in 1985. Indiana's version differs from 1972 Official Amendments in three major subject areas: Farm products, grace period for purchase money security interest, and requirements for filing financing statement. 1977 Official Amendments adopted in 1987, with some provisions effective retroactively to Jan. 1, 1986; no variations from official text. 1991 Legislature adopted (i) 1987 Official Text of Art. 2A with 1990 Official Amendments, including conforming amendments to §§1-105, 1-201(37) and 9-113, and (ii) 1989 Official Text of Art. 4A. 1993 Legislature adopted 1990 Official Text of Art. 3 and Art. 4, effective July 1, 1994. 1995 Legislature adopted (i) 1994 Official Text of Art. 8 and (ii) conforming amendments to §§9-103, 9-105, 9-106, 9-115, 9-116, 9-203, 9-301-305, 9-309, 9-312, effective July 1, 1996. 1996 Legislature adopted 1995 Official Text of Art. 5, effective July 1, 1996. 1997 Legislature adopted 1989 Official Text of Revised Art. 6, effective Jan. 1, 1998.

The U.C.C. Sections below are numbered identically under Title 26, Burns' Indiana Statutes and under Title 26, Article 1 of Indiana Code with exception of Art. 2A, Revised Art. 3, Art. 4A, Revised Art. 5, Revised Art. 6, and Revised Art. 8 which are numbered as 2.1, 3.1, 4.1, 5.1, 6.1 and 8.1, respectively.

Intentional Deviations from 1962 Official Text are as follows (Tit. 26, Art. 1 omitted before section numbers):

§1-109, U. C. C.—Omitted.

§1-108.1. New nonuniform section added governing acceptance of payment of U.C.C. filing fees by Secretary of State.

§1-201(9), U.C.C.—After phrase "does not include a pawnbroker." there is inserted "All persons who sell minerals or the like (including oil and gas) at a wellhead or minehead shall be deemed to be persons in the business of selling goods of that kind."

§1-201(37), U.C.C.—Omits phrase "buyer of accounts, chattel paper, or contract rights" and inserts "buyer of accounts or chattel paper."

§2-102, U.C.C.—Adds sentence which reads: "IC 26-1-2 does not impair or repeal IC 9-14, IC 9-17 or IC 9-22-5."

§2-107(1), U.C.C.—Omits phrase "A contract for the sale of timber, minerals or the like or a structure" and inserts "A contract for the sale of minerals or the like (including oil and gas) or a structure or its materials to be removed from realty."

§2-207(2), U.C.C.—After phrase "but not described in subsection (1)" there is inserted "or of timber to be cut."

§2-316(3), U. C. C.—Adds subparagraphs (d) and (e), providing: No implied warranty that cattle, hogs or sheep are free from disease if seller shows that all federal and state regulations concerning animal health have been met; and, with respect to audio or visual entertainment products solicited through mail order catalogue, all implied warranties may be excluded if contract is in writing and conspicuously states product is sold "as is" or "with all faults" and that "the entire risk as to the quality and performance of the product is with the buyer."

§2-702(3), U.C.C.—Omits phrase "or lien creditor."

§2-721, U. C. C.—Also provides for recovery of attorneys fees in fraud cases.

§7-403(1)(b), U. C. C.—After optional clause, there is inserted, "whenever the claimed loss or destruction resulted from fire, and the amount of the claimed loss or destruction under the document exceeds the sum of ten thousand dollars ($10,000)."

§7-503(3), U. C. C.—Words "a bill issued by the freight forwarder covering such goods has been duly negotiated" substituted for "a bill issued by the freight forwarder is duly negotiated."

Optional Provisions from 1962 Oficial Text.—

§3-121, U. C. C.—Alternative B is adopted.

§4-106, U. C. C.—Optional Language omitted.

§4-202, U. C. C.—Optional clause adopted.

§4-212, U. C. C.—Optional subsection adopted.

§5-112, U. C. C.—Optional clause omitted.

§5-114, U. C. C.—Optional subsections omitted.

§7-204, U. C. C.—Optional subsection (4) omitted.

§7-403, U. C. C.—Optional clause adopted.

§10-104(2), U. C. C.—Saving Uniform Simplification of Fiduciary Security Transfers Act from repeal, enacted.

Intentional Deviations from 1972 Official Text are as follows (Tit. 26, Art. 1 omitted before section numbers):

§9-102, U. C. C.—adds paragraph (2)(a)(ii) making IC26-1-9 applicable to "a transfer of an interest or a claim in a contractual right of a person to receive commissions or other compensation payable by an insurer."

§9-104, U. C. C.—amends paragraph (d) to provide that IC26-1-9 does not apply to transfer of claim for commissions, to extent such transfers are subject to IC22-2-7 (governing assignment of wages). Amends paragraph (g) to provide IC26-1-9 does not apply to transfers of interests or claims in or under insurance policies except claims under §9-102(2)(a)(ii).

§9-204, U.C.C. adds paragraph (4) excepting application of after-acquired property clause to crops which become such more than one year after security agreement is executed, with exceptions for lease, land purchase or improvement transaction under certain circumstances (same as text of paragraph [4][a] of 1962 Official Text).

§9-301(1)(c), U.C.C. deletes special priority given to ordinary course buyer of farm products over unperfected security interest.

§9-301(2), U.C.C.—changes "ten (10)" to "twenty (20)." (i.e. extends from 10 to 20 days time period within which purchase money secured party may file after debtor receives possession of collateral and thereby takes priority over other rights arising during that period.)

§9-307(1), U.C.C. deletes "farm products exception," and adds subsections (a)-(c) which govern priority between farm products purchasers and secured parties holding perfected or unperfected interests in farm products. Generally, it requires that secured party who desires to have priority over farm products purchasers must request list of all potential buyers from debtor and send written notice of security interest to everyone listed.

§9-312(4), U.C.C. extends grace period within which purchase money secured party may subordinate rights of competing security interests in same collateral to 20 days.

§9-313(4)(a), U.C.C.—Words and figures "ten (10)" changed to "twenty (20)".

§9-401(1)(a), U.C.C.—deletes Secretary of State filing requirement for certain collateral when debtor is corporation.

§9-401(1)(c), U.C.C. requires dual filing if debtor is corporation and collateral consists of farm products, equipment and like. Filing is required in both county of corporate debtor's residence and in office of Secretary of State. Third filing would be required if crops are grown on land in county other than that of debtor's residence.

§9-401(6), U.C.C. adds requirement that State of Indiana pay for judgments recovered against its filing officers.

§9-401(7)-(12), U.C.C. contain filing fee provisions which are scattered throughout part 4 of Art. 9 in Uniform Act.

§9-402(1), U.C.C.—amended to state that financing statement is sufficient if it is on form prescribed by Secretary of State.

§9-402(2)(e), U.C.C. adds that financing statement is valid even without debtor's signature if filed in accordance with security agreement.

§9-402(3), U.C.C.—adds that financing statement may be amended by filing form referencing original financing statement number and date of filing and further provides that amendment that changes only secured party information must be signed by secured party; all other amendments must be signed by debtor and secured party.

§9-402(9), U. C. C.—Subsection added, reading "(9) The provisions of IC36-2-11-15 requiring the identification of draftsmen of instruments transferring interests in real estate do not apply to filings under IC26-1."

§9-403(3), U.C.C.—adds that when filing officer has noted filing in mortgage records, if filing officer has microfilm or other photographic record of filing, filing officer may remove notation from mortgage records at any time after statement lapses, otherwise notation may be removed any time after one year from when statement lapses.

§9-403(4), U.C.C.—deletes requirement that filing officer mark hour of filing on financing statements.

§9-404(2), U.C.C.—adds language for termination statements similar to language added to §9-403(3).

§9-407(2), U.C.C.—deletes requirement that filing officer disclose hour of filing of financing statements.

§9-408, U.C.C.—adds nonuniform section covering maintenance of records by secretary of state, filing by mail, and administrative powers and duties.

§9-409, U.C.C.—adds nonuniform section covering maintenance of records by county recorder, statement or security agreement covering both real and personal property, filing by mail, and administrative powers and duties.

§9-410, U.C.C.—adds nonuniform section covering certified copies of documents as prima facie evidence.

§9-411, U.C.C.—adds nonuniform section covering certified copies of foreign documents as prima facie evidence.

See note at head of Digest as to 1998 legislation covered.

See Topical Index in front part of this volume.

COMMERCIAL CODE . . . *continued*

§9-508, U.C.C.—adds nonuniform section covering correction statements that may be filed if person believes in good faith that financing statement indexed under his or her name is inaccurate or wrongfully filed; this section further prescribes rights of secured party upon filing of correction statement and provides criminal penalties (Class A misdemeanor) for fraudulent filings.

Optional Provisions from 1972 Official Text.—

§9-401, U. C. C.—adopted second alternative to subsection (1) with changes noted under subhead Intentional Variations from 1972 Official Text. Alternative subsection (3) not adopted.

§9-402, U. C. C.—adopted optional language requiring full legal description of real estate.

Blanks filled in 1972 Official Text.—

§9-302(3)(b) "IC9-17 concerning motor vehicles, including IC9-17-6 concerning manufactured homes, or IC9-31-2-24 concerning watercraft" precedes "but during any period . . . "

§9-401(1)(a) "county recorder" in all blanks.

§9-401(1)(c)—"secretary of state."

§9-404(1)—"Jan. 1, 1986."

1972 Official Amendments.—Adopted.

1973 Official Amendments.—Adopted.

1977 Official Amendments.—Adopted.

Optional Provisions from 1987 Official Text.—

§2.1-216, U.C.C.—adopted alternative A.

Intentional Deviations from 1989 Official Text are as follows (Tit. 26, Art. 1 omitted before section numbers): Indiana adopted official text of Revised Art. 6, effective Jan. 1, 1998. Indiana variations to Revised Art. 6 are as follows:

§6.1-108(3), U.C.C.—Words "[End of Notice]" omitted.

§6.1-109, U.C.C.—Term "filing officer" replaced with "Secretary of State".

§6.1-109(4), U.C.C.—Referenced to fee for indexing each name more than two is deleted; cross reference is made to IC26-1-9-401 for filing fees.

§6.1-109(5), U.C.C.—Cross-reference is made to IC26-1-9-401 for fees.

Intentional Deviations from 1990 Official Text are as follows (Tit.26, Art. 1 omitted before section numbers): Indiana adopted Official Text of Art. 2A, effective July 1, 1991. Art. 2A is codified at 26-1-2.1. Indiana variations to Revised Art. 2A are as follows:

§2.1-507(1), U.C.C.—Words "at the times specified in sections 2A-519 and 2A-528" replaced with "at the time of default."

Indiana adopted 1990 Official Text of U. C. C. Arts. 3 and 4 effective July 1, 1994. Revised Art. 3 is codified at new Art. 26-1-3.1; Revised Art. 4 is codified at 26-1-4 as amendments to existing Art. 4. Indiana variations to Revised Arts. 3 and 4 are as follows:

§3.1-307(b)(2) and (b)(4), U.C.C. reads: "(2) In the case of an instrument payable to the represented person or the fiduciary as such, the taker has notice of the breach of fiduciary duty if the instrument is '(A) taken in payment of or as security for a debt known by the taker to be the personal debt of the fiduciary; (B) taken in a transaction known by the taker to be for the personal benefit of the fiduciary; or (C) deposited to an account other than an account of the fiduciary, as such, or an account of the represented person and the bank receiving the deposit has:' (i) actual knowledge that the fiduciary is committing a breach of its obligation as fiduciary in making the deposit; or (ii) knowledge of other facts that the bank's action in receiving the deposit constitutes bad faith" Subsection (b)(4) reads: "(4) If an instrument is issued by the represented person or the fiduciary as such, to the taker as payee, the taker has notice of the breach of fiduciary duty if the instrument is: (A) taken in payment of or as security for a debt known by the taker to be the personal debt of the fiduciary; (B) taken in a transaction known by the taker to be for the personal benefit of the fiduciary; or (C) deposited to an account other than an account of the fiduciary, as such, or an account of the represented person and the bank receiving the deposit has: (i) actual knowledge that the fiduciary is committing a breach of its obligation as fiduciary in making the deposit; or (ii) knowledge of other facts that the bank's action in receiving the deposit constitutes bad faith."

§3.1-404(d), U.C.C.—adds after "the failure to exercise ordinary care" the word "substantially."

§3.1-405(b) U.C.C.—adds a provision allocating loss in instances where party has failed to exercise ordinary care.

§3.1-420, U.C.C.—provides that measure of liability for conversion is presumed to be amount payable on instrument, notwithstanding IC34-4-30-1 which allows awards of treble damages, attorneys fees and costs.

§3.1-502.5 adds new section: "A person to whom a check, a draft, an order, or like instrument is tendered may, if the instrument is dishonored or returned unpaid for any reason, charge and collect from the maker or drawer, or the person for whose benefit the instrument was given, an amount not to exceed twenty dollars ($20) plus an amount equal to the actual charge by the depository institution for each returned or dishonored instrument. The charge shall not be considered an interest charge, a finance charge, a time price differential, or any charge of a similar nature."

§4-104(a)(3), U.C.C.—specifies that "Banking Day" does not include Sat., Sun. or legal holiday.

§4-107(1) and (2), U.C.C.—Eliminated; replaced with: "A branch or separate office of a bank is a separate bank for the purpose of computing the time within which and determining the place at or to which action may be taken or notices or orders must be given under IC26-1-4 and IC26-1-3.1."

§4-405(1), U.C.C.—Adds "mental" before "incompetence."

1994 Official Amendments.—Adopted.

1995 Official Amendments.—Adopted.

Permanent Editorial Board's Recommendations for Amendments.—

§2-702—1996 Official Amendment adopted 1985, effective Jan. 1, 1986.

§3-501—1966 Official Amendment not enacted.

§7-209—1966 Official Amendment not enacted.

Permanent Editorial Board's Recommendations for Optional Amendments.—

§1-209—1966 Official Optional Amendment not enacted.

§2-318—1966 Official Optional Amendment Alternative A enacted.

For filing offices and fees under Art. 9, see category Documents and Records, topic Records, subhead Filing Under Commercial Code.

See also topics: Banks and Banking, Bills and Notes, Brokers, Carriers, Contracts, Factors, Frauds, Statute of, Sales, Securities, Warehousemen; categories Business Organizations, topic Corporations; Civil Actions and Procedure, topic Limitation of Actions; Debtor and Creditor, topics Assignments, Fraudulent Sales and Conveyances, Liens, Pledges; Documents and Records, topics Records, Seals; Mortgages, topics Chattel Mortgages, Mortgages of Real Property.

CONDITIONAL SALES:

See topic Sales.

CONSIGNMENTS:

See topic Factors.

CONSUMER CREDIT:

Effective 12.01 a. m. Oct. 1, 1971, consumer loans and credit sales are controlled by Consumer Credit Code. (IC24-4.5-1-101 to IC24-4.5-6-203). Provisions of Code setting maximum charges for revolving charge accounts and revolving loan accounts and establishing debtor's remedies and criminal penalties for violations thereof and also provisions dealing with regulated and supervised lenders and with administration became effective Mar. 5, 1971. 1968 final draft of Uniform Law with 1970 amendments was enacted into law with certain minor changes.

Principal Changes.—

Deleted from Indiana law were §§1.106(6), 1.203(2), 1.301(1)-(2), 2.104(3), 2.106(3), 2.203, 2.207(5), 2.302-2.313, 2.403, 2.416, 2.503-2.505, 2.602(4), 3.104(2), 3.203, 3.301(3), 3.302-3.312, 3.408, 3.409, 3.501(1) and (2), 3.514, 3.602(1)(b), 3.602(3), 5.302(2) and (3), 6.104(2), 6.104(3), 6.202(e)-(g), and 6.301 to end of Uniform law.

Deleted from Indiana law was all language with respect to "agricultural" purpose in §§2.106, 2.403-2.407, 2.409, 3.104, 3.402 and 4.202 of Uniform law.

Alternative B was used in §§2.404, 2.413 and 3.404 of Indiana law.

Deviations from Uniform Law.—§1.102 paragraph (4) added stating that reference to federal law is reference to law in effect Dec. 31, 1997; §1.106(1), substitute "October, 1971" for "December, 1967" as reference base index; §1.201(1) includes receipt by persons acting on behalf of seller/lessor/lender, as applicable, in paragraphs (a), (b) and (c); §1.202 exempts from Consumer Credit Code (i) extension of credit primarily for business, commercial, or agricultural purpose, (ii) installment agreement for purchase of home fuels in which finance charge is not imposed, (iii) loans made, insured or guaranteed under a program authorized by Title IV of Higher Education Act of 1965 (20 U.S.C. 1070 et seq.), and (iv) transactions in securities or commodities accounts in which credit is extended by broker-dealers registered with Securities and Exchange Commission or Commodity Futures Trading Commission; §1.301(2) which previously defined "Administrator" has been deleted and replaced by definition of "Department" (§6.103); §1.301(6) defines "Consumer Credit"; §1.301(8) defines "Creditor" in manner consistent with Federal Truth-in-Lending Act (Reg. Z); §1.301(9) defines "Earnings" in manner consistent with Federal Truth-in-Lending Act (Reg. Z); §1.301(12) includes limited liability companies within definition of "Organization"; §1.301(13) defines "Payable in installments" in manner consistent with Federal Truth-in-Lending Act (Reg. Z); §1.301(18) defines "Regularly engaged" in manner consistent with Federal Truth-in-Lending Act (Reg. Z); §1.301(19) defines "Seller credit card" replacing "or others licensed or franchised to do business under his business or trade name or designation." with "or from that person and any other person. The term includes a card that is issued by a person, that is in the name of the seller, and that can be used by the buyer or lessee only for purchases or leases at locations of the named seller."; §1.303 adds definition of "Director", which means director of department of financial institutions (§6.103.5); §1.309(20) (a) and (b) expands definition of "supervised financial organization" by replacing references to "this state" with "a state"; §§2.104(1)(e) and 3.104(1)(d) include personal property used or expected to be used as principal dwelling of debtor and change dollar amount to $50,000; §2.106(1)(b) change dollar amount to $50,000; §2.109 deletes requirement of seller to include charges/fees of loan broker/arranger in finance charge and excludes from meaning of "credit service charge" certain charges paid to third parties not required by seller as a condition to extension of credit except for borrower paid mortgage broker fees; §2.201(2)(b), 21% replaces 18%; §2.201(4) thirty (30) days replaces ten (10) days; §2.201(4)(a) adds exceptions to delay in commencement date of sale agreement where delays are attributable to customer or partial deliveries are made within thirty days; §2.201(6) permits minimum credit service charge of $30 (subject to change) regardless of amount financed; §2.201(7) $840 replaces $300, $2,800 replaces $1,000; §2.202(1)(c) notwithstanding provisions of Federal Consumer Protection Act concerning disclosure, allows lenders and sellers to assess additional charges provided that such charges are determined by Department of Financial Institutions to be reasonable and of benefit to borrower or buyer; §2.202(1)(e) allows participation fees assessed in connection with revolving charge account; §2.202(2)(b) includes insurance providing coverage for unemployment or other loss of income; §2.202(3) includes as additional charges in transactions where debt is secured by interest in land reasonable closing costs such as title and recording fees, fees for credit reports, amounts required to be paid into escrow or trust account, and appraisal fees; §2.203.5 provides for delinquency charges on consumer credit sales, refinancings or consolidations that are not precomputed and permits creditor to convert precomputed consumer credit sale to sale with service credit charge on unpaid balance if all or part of two installments are in default for ten days or more; §2.205(1) deletes exception for not allowing minimum credit service charge; §2.207(3) limited to 1³/₄% charge on all

CONSUMER CREDIT . . . *continued*

balances; §2.210(3) delete references regarding sale of interest in land or consumer credit sale secured by interest in land; §2.210(5)(c) expands from four (4) to five (5) the additional number of days that will be considered a computation period. §2.210(9) applies whether or not credit sale is precomputed; §2.210(10) added to require that unearned part of credit service charge on prepayment of precomputed consumer loan be calculated by applying disclosed annual percentage rate that would yield credit service charge originally contracted for to unpaid balances for period following prepayment whenever transaction with term of more than 61 months is prepaid in full; §2.301(2) adds disclosure by lessor to lessee in consumer lease; §2.301(3) excuses disclosure requirement on consumer credit sales exempt from Federal Consumer Credit Protection Act; §2.405(1) includes sales on which only credit service charges are payable before time final payment is due; §§2.405(2) and 3.402(2) added to define "terms of refinancing" to include fixed and variable rate consumer credit sales and loans; §2.406 three times replaces twice; §2.407(4) $840 replaces $300, $2,800 replaces $1,000; §2.413 15% limit deleted; §2.501 includes telephone solicitations and solicitations through mailing, advertisements or telephone where seller has no permanent business establishment in city or town and buyer is required to meet seller at location other than seller's permanent business establishment; §2.502 revised to be consistent with Federal Truth-in-Lending Act (Reg. Z), and specifically references compliance with 16 CFR 429; §2.602(1) dollar amount changed to $50,000; §§2.602(2) and 2.604(1)(b) 21% replaces 18%; §3.104(1)(d) dollar amount changed to $50,000; §3.105 exempts home mortgage transactions from certain requirements; §3.109 deletes requirement of lender to include charges/fees of loan broker/arranger in finance charge and excludes from meaning of "loan finance charge" certain charges paid to third parties not required by seller as a condition to extension of credit except certain borrower paid mortgage broker fees; §3.201(1) 21% replaces 18%; §3.201(4) substitute maximum annual percentage rate for 18% per year, substitute 1¾% for 1 ½% and substitute "1/12th the maximum annual percentage rate" for "1½%"; §3.201(6) permits minimum loan finance charge of $30 (subject to change); §3.201(8) for consumer loan secured by interest in land, lender may contract for loan origination fee of not more than 2% of loan amount or, if revolving loan account, of line of credit contracted for; §3.201(9) loan origination fee under §3.201(8) not subject to refund or rebate, not permitted if lender makes specified settlement charge; §3.201 fees for preparing deeds, mortgages, reconveyances and similar documents are permitted in addition to charges under §3.201(8); §3.202(1) added four new additional charges for which lender may contract and receive with loan finance charges on consumer loan; §3.202(1) allows creditors to assess additional charges provided that such charges are determined by Department of Financial Institutions to be reasonable and of benefit to debtor and establishes maximum limits on some fees; §3.202(1)(c) revised to apply to annual or periodic participation fees assessed in connection with revolving loan account; §3.202.1(1)(e) adds notwithstanding provisions of Federal Consumer Credit Protection Act concerning disclosure; §3.203.5 provides for delinquency charges on consumer loans, refinancings or consolidations provides that delinquency charge on consumer loan made under revolving loan account may be applied each month that payment is less than minimum required payment on account, prohibits delinquency charge on deferred installments if deferral fee has been paid, and permits lender to convert precomputed loan to loan with finance charges on unpaid balance if all or part of two installments are in default for ten days or more; §3.209 allows lenders 2% charge for prepayment in full of loan that is secured by interest in land, subject to three limitations; §3.210(2) mirrors §2.210(2); §3.210(3) delete last sentence and first clause regarding exception with respect to a loan primarily secured by an interest in land; §3.210(9) applies whether or not precomputed; §3.210(10) added to require lenders to compute unearned finance charge by applying disclosed annual percentage rate that would yield loan finance charge originally contracted for to unpaid balances for periods following prepayment on loans with term of more than 61 months; §3.301(3) mirrors §2.301(3); §3.404 deletes introductory exception and 15% maximum; §3.501 loan finance charge changed from 18% to 21%; §3.502 deletes requirement that supervised financial organization have a place of business in this state; §3.503(2) allows director to request evidence of compliance; §3.503(3) cross-references IC4-21.5; §3.503(4) requires annual licensing; §3.503(5) permits deduction of fees (other than delinquent renewal fees) under §3.503(4) from filing fees paid under §6.203; add §3.503.9 providing for license revocation for at least two years if person fails to file renewal form or pay license renewal fee; §3.504(2) provides exception for revocation of licenses under §3.503.5; §3.504(8) adds ability of director to proceed with revocation of license under IC4-21.5-3-6 if director (1) has just cause to believe emergency exists from which it is necessary to protect public or (2) determines person for whom license was obtained does not qualify; §3.505(2), replaces Apr. 15 with "as required by the department, but not more frequently than annually" and permits $5 fee for each day that licensee fails to file required report; §3.505.5 added to define "automated loan machine"; §3.508(2)(b), 21% replaces 18%; §3.508(6) $840 replaces $300, $2,800 replaces $1,000; §3.508(7) permits minimum loan finance charge up to $30 (subject to change); §3.510(2) $2,800 replaces $1,000; §3.511(2) $840 replaces $300, $2,800 replaces $1,000; §3.602(1) dollar amount changed to $50,000; §3.604(1)(b) 21% substituted for 18%; §4.103 deletes exclusion for insurance provided in credit transaction with payment ten years after credit extended; §4.108(5) added to provide for interest at contract rate on amounts of refunds and credits not made to debtor within 60 days after insurance terminates; §4.301(4) $840 replaces $300; add §4.305 unearned premium for property insurance with respect to which creditor or credit account of consumer is beneficiary refunded by creditor or creditor's assignee on payment in full of consumer credit sale or consumer loan; §5.102 part also applies to garnishments of individual's earnings; §5.103(7) $2,800 replaces $1,000; §5.104 no attachment of debtor's earnings by garnishment prior to entry of judgment; §5.105 adds health and child support as part of withholding and authorizing employer to collect $2 fee for each withholding; §5.105(2)(b) substitutes 30 for 40 times; §5.105(4) limits wages subject to garnishment for purpose of support to 50% if such person is supporting spouse or child, and to 60% if supporting any other person, increased to 55% and 65% respectively, if support is at least 12 weeks overdue; §5.105(5) allows employer to impose fee for garnishment, equal to greater of 3% or $12, to be borne equally by

creditor and employee; §5.202(9) added to enable department to enforce debtor's requests against creditor's licensed/registered or required to be licensed/registered; §5.203 provides for creditor's liability in class action as well as in individual action, provides for one recovery of damages if multiple obligors, and provides for one recovery for multiple failures to disclose to any person; §5.203(2) replace 15 days with 60 days; §5.204 right to rescind per §125 of Federal Consumer Credit Protection Act, no interest accrued during period when loan may be rescinded; §5.302 modified so that only offense is Class A misdemeanor for supplying false information or failing to provide information as required in §§2.301 and 3.301; §6.106(1) records of any transaction must be retained for two years; §6.106(2) examination fee may be charged if examination exceeds three days; §6.117 defines "civil court" as any court of Indiana having civil jurisdiction except justices of peace; §6.201 applies to persons, including a supervised financial organization, placing consumer credit insurance, receiving commissions or acting as agent in sale of same, not applicable if seller's entire credit sales are made pursuant to seller credit card issued by lender in name of seller which can be used only at locations of named seller, provided conditions of §§6.202 and 6.203 are met; §6.203 provides that Department of Financial Institutions is to fix uniform fee per $100,000; §6.203(3) added to require credit sellers to pay volume fees when they assign consumer credit transactions to institutions which are not filed with or refuse to file with Department of Financial Institutions; §6.203(4) added to allow licensees/registrants that pay fee under §3.503 to deduct such fees from §6.203(3); §6.203(5) added to require fee for notification filed under §6.202; add §6.204 which provides that c. 6, part 2, is not applicable to payment of attorneys' fees. For details of all variations see U.L.A. Master Edition.

Blanks filled by Indiana law.—§6.103, administrator refers to Department of Financial Institutions; §6.104(5), Dec. 1, and Governor; and §6.203, fee is fixed by Department of Financial Institutions based on unpaid balances amounts.

CONSUMER PROTECTION:

Residential Real Estate Sales Disclosure.—(IC24-4.6-2-1 to IC24-4.6-2-13). Disclosure form required for sales and exchanges of, installment sales contracts for, and leases with options to buy residential real estate containing four or less dwelling units, other than first sales of new homes. Applies to all such offers accepted on or after July 1, 1994. (IC24-4.6-2-1). Form prescribed by Indiana real estate commission provides for disclosure regarding foundation, mechanical systems, roof, structure, water, sewer system and airports located within geographical distance as determined by Indiana real estate commission. (IC24-4.6-2-7). Owner to complete disclosure form and submit to buyer before accepting offer. (IC24-4.6-2-10). If disclosure form disclosing defect received after acceptance of offer, buyer has two business days to send owner written rescission of contract. (IC24-4.6-2-13). At closing, owner must disclose any material change or recertify condition of property as already disclosed. (IC24-4.6-2-12).

Deceptive Consumer Sales Act.—(IC24-5-0.5-1 to IC24-5-0.5-10). Deceptive act defined by IC24-5-0.5-3. Consumer or consumer class may recover actual damages and prevailing party may be awarded attorneys fees. Attorney general may seek injunction, litigation costs, and civil penalty of up to $15,000 can be levied on person violating injunction against deceptive act. Civil penalties of up to $500 fine may be imposed on any person who commits incurable deceptive act. Actual damages awarded to class have priority over civil penalties. Persons at least 65 years of age may seek treble damages. (IC24-5-0.5-4 and 8). Any supplier organized to offer benefits to persons from cooperative purchase of goods which offers contract for that purpose which is to be effective for more than five years is subject to $500 civil fine. (IC24-5-0.5-8, 9). Certain unconscionable acts constitute deceptive acts. There is rebuttable presumption that person has knowledge of terms of contract or agreement if person signs written contract. (IC24-5-0.5-10). Two year statute of limitations governs all actions brought under this Act, including actions brought by attorney general to enjoin deceptive acts. (IC24-5-0.5-5).

Retail Installment Sales.—(IC24-5-2-21 to 24, IC24-5-3-1 to 10). Agreements to lessen competition prohibited. Licenses subject to revocation and injunction available to prohibit such acts. (IC24-5-3-7 to 9).

Health Spa Services.—(IC24-5-7-1 to IC24-5-7-18). Contracts for health spa services must be in writing and contract and payment term may not exceed three years. (IC24-5-7-2 and 3). Services at health spa facility within 45 days for existing facility and within 12 months for planned facility, from date contract executed. (IC24-5-7-4). Contracts must provide in 10 point bold face type for cancellation within three days contract executed, and for cancellation by buyer or buyer's estate if buyer dies, becomes physically disabled, facility moves over five miles without transferring contract to facility within five miles, or seller discontinues operation. (IC24-5-7-6 to 8). Money must be refunded within 30 days of notice of cancellation. Contracts voidable by buyer if not in compliance with this chapter and contract void if based on willfully or fraudulently disseminated false or misleading information. (IC24-5-7-10 and 11). Waiver by buyer of rights under chapter void. (IC24-5-7-12). Health spa selling contracts prior to commencing services must file and maintain surety bond with secretary of state of Indiana in amount not less than $25,000 until services commence. (IC24-5-7-13 to 15). Violation of chapter is deceptive act under IC24-6-0.5-1 et. seq. (IC24-5-7-17).

Business Opportunity Transactions.—(IC24-5-8-1 to IC24-5-8-21). Business Opportunity Transactions defined as solicitation of investors, wherein representation of earnings are made, involving sale or lease or offer to sell or lease any goods or services to be used in beginning or operating business and requiring payments greater than $500 but less than $50,000 within first six months of business. (IC24-5-8-1). Detailed written disclosures, including express language in ten point type, must be made to prospective investors at least 72 hours before contract is signed or seller receives any consideration. (IC24-5-8-2). Seller must obtain surety bond, or issue irrevocable letter of credit to state upon approval of attorney general in amount not less than $75,000. (IC24-5-8-3). Prior to any advertisement or representation, seller must file disclosure statement and bond with consumer protection division of office of attorney general, pay $50 initial filing fee, $10 annual fees, and $10 fee for any amendments to such filings (which are necessary when material changes occur); all

CONSUMER PROTECTION... *continued*
advertisements must contain registration number issued by division. (IC24-5-8-4). Seller must provide investors detailed substantiation for all claims of earnings potential. (IC24-5-8-5). Contract must be in writing with detailed provisions, including express language in specified size type. (IC24-5-8-6). Seller must keep detailed records. (IC24-5-8-7). No waiver or attempt of waiver of rights by investors is allowed, and no note can cut off rights or defenses of investor or third party. (IC24-5-8-8 to 10). Limits placed on investor's payments prior to receipt of goods or services. (IC24-5-8-11 and 12). Seller prohibited from referring to compliance with these provisions and from using mark or name of business that neither controls seller nor accepts responsibility for seller's representations. (IC24-5-8-13 and 14). Investor may cancel any contract where seller fails to comply with these provisions. (IC24-5-8-15). Investor may recover all consideration paid if seller uses any untrue or deceptive statement, fails to deliver promised goods or services within 45 days or fails to provide written contract pursuant to IC24-5-8-6. (IC24-5-8-16). If seller fails to comply with any of these provisions or breaches contract, investor may recover actual damages and attorney fees to extent of amount of seller's bond and obtain injunction. (IC24-5-8-17 and 18). Seller who fails to file as required with consumer protection division commits Class D felony (up to four years imprisonment and $10,000 fine). (IC24-5-8-19). Substantial sellers of business opportunities, those with net worth of at least $5,000,000 or at least $1,000,000 if seller is at least 80% owned by corporation with net worth of at least $5,000,000 are exempted from many of above requirements. (IC24-5-8-1 to 6). Attorney general may bring action under Deceptive Consumer Sales Act for failure to comply with any of these provisions. (IC24-5-8-20). Compliance with these provisions does not relieve seller from compliance with IC23-2-1 (securities regulations), IC23-2-2.5 (franchises) or IC23-2-2.7 (deceptive franchise practices). (IC24-5-8-21).

Time Share and Camping Club Projects.—(IC24-5-9-1 to IC24-5-9-36). Requires developer of time share project or camping club project, involving sale of more than 12 real property units, to register with consumer protection division of attorney general, and file detailed disclosure statements, prior to sale of any unit or membership, subject to Class D felony. (IC24-5-9-22). Time share includes right to use and occupy unit on periodic basis pursuant to arrangement allocating such right among various participants. (IC24-5-9-17). Camping club membership includes right, title or interest in use of camping or outdoor recreation facilities for more than 30 days under agreement not expiring within three years. (IC24-5-9-3). Developer must pay initial $250 registration fee; with annual renewal registration and fee of $50 required each July 1. (IC25-5-9-24). Each project must be created pursuant to instrument containing detailed mandatory provisions controlling project. (IC24-5-9-26). Each transfer of interest must be pursuant to written contract containing detailed description of rights and obligations. (IC24-5-9-27). Purchaser has right to cancel contract within 72 hours following execution. Right to cancel contract not waivable by purchaser and must be set forth in contract as specified in IC24-5-9-28. Division may require developer to file performance bond until project is substantially completed and ready for occupancy. (IC24-5-9-29). Action may be maintained for judicial sale of time-share or camping club site, but not for partition. (IC24-5-9-32). Special rules for exchange programs. (IC24-5-9-23). Violation of chapter constitutes deceptive act under IC24-5-0.5-1 et seq. (IC24-5-9-35).

Uniform Deceptive Trade Practices Act not adopted.

Home Solicitation Sales.—Buyer's right to cancel is governed by IC24-5-10, IC24-4.5-2-501 to 505.

Home Improvement Contracts.—Regulates residential home improvement contracts (IC24-5-11) and imposes criminal penalties for fraud (IC35-43-6).

Automatic Dialing Machines.—Regulates use of automatic dialing/announcing devices in commercial telephone solicitation. (IC24-5-14).

Motor Vehicle Protection.—(IC24-5-13-1 to IC24-5-13-24 and IC24-5-13.5-1 to IC24-5-13.5-14). IC24-5-13-5 now includes in its definition of "motor vehicle" or "vehicle" any self-propelled vehicle that is sold to buyer in Indiana who is not Indiana resident. If motor vehicle suffers from defect that substantially impairs its use, value or safety or renders it nonconforming to terms of applicable manufacturer's warranty, and buyer reports same within 18 months or 18,000 miles to manufacturer or authorized dealer, then manufacturer or dealer must make necessary repairs to correct defect. (IC24-5-13-8). If vehicle has been subject to repair at least four times and defect continues to exist, or if vehicle is out of service by reason of repair for cumulative total of at least 30 business days and defect continues to exist, then manufacturer must accept return of vehicle and must, at buyer's option, either, within 30 days, refund amount paid by buyer or provide replacement vehicle of comparable value. (IC24-5-13-10). IC24-5-13.5 imposes requirements on resale of motor vehicle that has been replaced or repurchased by manufacturer, or nonresident manufacturer's agent, or authorized dealer.

Unsolicited Merchandise.—Intended receiver may refuse delivery or may deem it a gift. (IC24-5-5-1).

Plain Language.—See topic Contracts.

Interest.—See topic Interest.

Sales.—See topic Sales.

CONTRACTS:

Uniform Commercial Code in effect since July 1, 1964. (IC26-1-1-101 et seq.).

Plain Language.—No "plain language" statute. However, Indiana Constitution does require every act and joint resolution to be plainly worded. (Ind. Const. Art. 4, §20).

Where one of following provisions applies, contrary agreement is effective only to extent permitted by law specified: IC26-1-2-402, rights of creditors against sold goods; IC26-1-2.1-105, IC26-1-2.1-106, IC26-1-5.1-116, letters of credit; leases; IC26-1-4-102, bank deposits and collections; IC26-1-4.1-507, fund transfers; IC26-1-6-102, bulk transfers; IC26-1-8.1-110, investment securities; IC26-1-9-103, perfection of secured transactions. (IC26-1-1-105).

See also topic Commercial Code.

FACTORS:

Relation of principal and factor gives factor possession of property and power to sell it, and factor may do anything not inconsistent with such general power of sale. (207 Ind. 374, 192 N.E. 887).

Uniform Commercial Code in effect since July 1, 1964. (IC26-1-1-101 et seq.). See topic Commercial Code.

Consignment Agreements.—See IC26-1-2-326; IC26-1-9-114.

See topic Commercial Code.

Liens.—See IC26-1-9-301; IC26-1-9-310 to 312.

FRANCHISES:

Franchises may not be sold in Indiana unless properly registered or exempt from registration. (IC23-2-2.5-9). Exemptions from registration are provided for in IC23-2-2.5-3 through IC23-2-2.5-5.

Application for registration must contain disclosure statement. (IC23-2-2.5-10). Disclosure statement may be in form of Uniform Franchise Offering Circular. Applicants must file irrevocable consent to receive service of process through Secretary of State. (IC23-2-2.5-24). Advertisements offering franchise subject to registration must be filed with Commissioner five days prior to publication. (IC23-2-2.5-25). If no stop order issued by Commissioner, registration becomes effective 30 days after filing application. (IC23-2-2.5-17). Franchisor must provide to prospective franchisee disclosure statement and copy of all proposed contracts at least ten days prior to execution of binding franchise agreement or receipt of consideration, whichever is earlier. (IC23-2-2.5-9[2]).

Franchisor must promptly notify Commissioner in writing of material changes of information in effective registration by filing application to amend registration. (IC23-2-2.5-20). Amendment becomes effective five days after filing date. (IC23-2-2.5-20[b]).

Registration is effective for one year. (IC23-2-2.5-17). Renewal application must be filed 30 days prior to expiration of registration, unless waived. (IC23-2-2.5-18). Unless stop order in effect, renewal registration is effective at time registration would otherwise expire and is effective for one year, unless shorter period specified by Commissioner. (IC23-2-2.5-18).

Unlawful franchise agreement provisions, acts and practices governed by Indiana Deceptive Franchise Practices Law, IC23-2-2.7 et seq.

Business opportunity transactions governed by IC24-5-8-1 et seq.

FRAUDS, STATUTE OF:

Uniform Commercial Code in effect since July 1, 1964. (IC26-1-1-101 et seq.).

Unless there is some note or memorandum thereof in writing, signed by party to be charged, or some person lawfully authorized by him, no action may be maintained: (1) To charge executor or administrator to answer damages out of his own estate upon special promise (IC32-2-1-1); or (2) to charge any person upon special promise to answer for debt, default or miscarriage of another (IC32-2-1-1); or (3) on contract made in consideration of marriage (IC32-2-1-1); or (4) on contract for sale of lands (IC32-2-1-1); or (5) on contract not to be performed within one year (IC32-2-1-1); or (6) upon any representation made concerning character, conduct, credit, ability, trade or dealings of any other person (IC32-2-1-6); or (7) on lease for term longer than three years (IC32-2-1-1); or (8) upon agreement, promise, contract or warranty of cure relating to medical care or treatment; provided, however, that this does not affect right to sue for malpractice or negligence (IC32-2-1-1); or (9) on contract to pay commission for sale of lands (IC32-2-2-1); or (10) on conveyance of existing trust in lands, goods or things in action (IC32-2-1-3); or (11) on contract for sale of goods for price of $500 or more, except between merchants if confirmation of contract is received by party to be charged and no written objection to confirmation is given within ten days, or except for goods received and accepted or for which payment has been made and accepted, or unless goods are to be specially manufactured for buyer, are not suitable for sale to others in ordinary course of seller's business, and seller, before receipt of notice of repudiation, has substantially begun manufacture or commitments for procurement, or unless party to be charged has admitted in court that contract for sale was made (IC26-1-2-201); or (12) upon contract for sale of standing trees or standing timber (IC32-9-5-13); or (13) upon contract between teachers and school corporations (IC20-6.1-4-3); or (14) on contract for sale of securities except to extent of payment made or securities delivered, or unless delivery of certificated security or transfer instruction has been accepted, or transfer of uncertificated security has been registered and transferee has failed to send written objection within ten days after confirmation of registration has been received, or unless writing in confirmation of sale is received by party to be charged and he has failed to send written objection to confirmation within ten days, or unless party to be charged has admitted in court that contract for sale was made (IC26-1-8-319); or (15) on contract for sale of personal property in excess of $5,000, except for contract for sale of goods or securities and security agreements (IC26-1-1-206). Contract for sale of goods is not enforceable beyond quantity of goods shown in writing. (IC26-1-2-201). Contract for sale of securities is enforceable only if writing states specific quantity of described securities at defined or stated price. (IC26-1-8-319).

The consideration for any promise required by the statute of frauds to be in writing does not have to be stated in writing. (IC32-2-1-2).

The rules of common law apply as to cases taken out of the statute.

INTEREST:

See topic Consumer Credit.

Judgments.—Effective Jan. 1, 1994, interest runs at contract or agreed upon rate up to 8% or if no agreement at 8%. (IC24-4.6-1-101). Governmental entities are liable for

See note at head of Digest as to 1998 legislation covered.

See Topical Index in front part of this volume.

IN – 8

INTEREST... *continued*
6% interest from date of judgment or settlement if not paid within 180 days, unless structured settlement, even if case appealed, provided original judgment upheld. (IC34-13-3-18).

Prejudgment.—Court may award prejudgment interest in tort action of 6%-10% per year for period not exceeding 48 months and beginning to accrue no earlier than 15 months after action accrued and six months after claim filed if party filing makes written offer to settle within one year after filing for amount exceeding $1^1/_3$ of judgment and party against whom claim is filed fails to make written offer to settle within nine months after filing for at least $^2/_3$ of judgment. (IC34-51-4).

Pawnbrokers.—Interest charged by pawnbrokers is controlled by law and cannot exceed maximum loan finance charge for supervised lenders under IC24-4.5-3-508. Additionally, pawnbroker may impose storage charge for each article held which cannot exceed $1 per month or any fractional part of month on principals not exceeding $50 or $1.50 per month or any fractional part of month on principals from $50 to $1,000. (IC28-7-5-28).

Maximum annual rate for unsupervised consumer loan is 21%. (IC24-4.5-3-201). Class A misdemeanor for lender to knowingly charge in excess of amount specified in IC24-4.5-3-508 for consumer loan. (IC24-4.5-5-301). Consumer who pays in excess of statutorily determined amount has right to refund of excess. (IC24-4.5-5-202).

Usury.—Most business loans are not subject to limitation. At time of publication, Indiana had not acted to reimpose state limits as allowed by federal Depository Institutions Deregulation Act of 1980.

LICENSES, BUSINESS AND PROFESSIONAL:

License, registration or certification is required for large number of businesses and occupations, including following: Accountant (IC25-2.1-12), architect (IC25-4-1-6, -26), attorney (IC33-1-5-1), auctioneer (IC25-6.1-3-1), barber, barber instructor, barber school, barber shop (IC25-7-1-1), cosmetologist, cosmetology salon, master cosmetologist (IC25-8-4-9, IC25-8-7 through IC25-8-9, IC25-8-14-5), electrologist, electrology salon (IC25-8-10, IC25-8-7.2), manicurist, manicurist salon (IC25-8-11; IC25-8-7.1), shampoo operator (IC25-8-12), esthetician, esthetician shop (IC25-8-12.5 to 25-8-12.6), cosmetology school (IC25-8-5), cosmetology instructor (IC25-8-6), esthetics instructor (IC25-8-6.1), electrology instructor (IC25-8-6.2), cosmetology educator (IC25-8-15-7), boxing, sparring and wrestling (IC25-9-1), money transmission (IC28-8-4-20), chiropractor (IC25-10-1-11), collection agency (IC25-11-1-3, 7), dental hygienist (IC25-13-1-3), dentist (IC25-14-1-1), embalmer and funeral director (IC25-15-4-4, IC25-15-8-21 to 24), employment services (IC25-16-1-1), electrical contractor (regulated by local ordinance), geologist (IC25-17.6-4), going out of business, removal of business, fire, or other altered goods sales (IC25-18-1-2), health facility administrator (IC25-19-1-11), hearing aid dealer (IC25-20-1-2), physician, osteopath (IC25-22.5-8-1), dietician (IC25-14.5-4), midwife (IC25-23-1-13.1), nurse (IC25-23-1-27), occupational therapist (IC25-23.5-3-1), marriage and family therapist (IC25-23.6-3-1), social worker (IC25-23.6-4-1), optometrist (IC25-24-1-17), pharmacist and pharmacies (IC25-26-13-1 to 25-26-13-29), wholesale legend drug distributors (IC25-26-14-14), physical therapist (IC25-27-1-1), physician's assistant (IC25-27.5-4-1); boat pilot (IC25-28-1-1; IC14-22-15-1), plumber (IC25-28.5-1-11), podiatrist (IC25-29), private detective (IC25-30-1-3), engineer (IC25-31-1-13), land surveyor (IC25-21.5-13-2), environmental health specialist (IC25-32-1-16), psychologist (IC25-33-1-14 and IC20-1-1.9), real estate broker, real estate salesperson (IC25-34.1-3-2), real estate appraiser (IC25-34.1-8-12), respiratory care practitioners (IC25-34.5-3-1), speech pathologist and audiologist (IC25-35.6-1-3), television and radio serviceman (IC25-36-1-3), timber buyer (IC25-36.5-1-10), retail merchant (IC6-2.5-8), transient merchant (IC25-37-1-3), water well drilling (IC25-39-3-1, IC25-39-5), alcoholic beverages (IC7.1-3), aircraft pilot (IC8-21-2-3), dry cleaning (IC25-1-2-2.1), fireworks display (regulated by Fire Prevention and Building Safety Commission pursuant to IC22-11-14-2), bail agent (IC27-10-3-1), surety (IC27-10-2-4), bedding manufacturer (IC16-41-32-21), locker plant (IC16-42-7-2), egg wholesalers and retailers (IC16-42-11-9), hospital and ambulatory outpatient surgical center (IC16-21-2), nursing home and other health facilities (IC16-28-2-1), home health agencies (IC16-27-1-8); emergency medical services (IC16-31-3), advanced life support (IC16-31-3-22), radioactive material (IC16-41-35-26), tanning facility (IC25-8-15.4-5); milk products (IC15-6-1-8 to -11; IC15-2.1-22-5; IC15-2.1-23-2), budget service company (IC28-1-29-3), pawnbroker (IC28-7-5-3), livestock dealer (IC15-2.1-14-2), feeder pig dealer (IC15-2.1-12-1), nursery dealer (IC14-24-7-1), veterinarian (IC15-5-1.1-9), child care (IC12-17.2-4-1, IC12-17.4-3-1), driver training schools and instructors (IC9-27-4), ferries operating to and from points outside Indiana (IC8-2-15-1 and IC8-2-17-1), mobile home park (IC16-41-27-18); handguns: dealer (IC35-47-2-14), individual (IC35-47-2-1), hunting, fishing, trapping wild animals (IC14-2-2), fur buyer (IC14-22-19-1), game breeders (IC14-2-2-20-1), insurance agent, representative, consultant (IC27-1-15.5-3), strip mining (IC14-34-3-1, IC14-36-1-13), mining (IC14-35-1-1), oil and gas well drilling (IC14-37-41, IC14-38), boat racing, water ski events (IC14-15-5-1), motor fuel distributor (IC6-6-1.1-401), securities broker, dealer, agent, investment advisor (IC23-2-1-8), taxidermist (IC14-22-21-2), teacher (IC20-6.1-3-1 to 10), polygraph examiner (IC25-30-2-5), professional fund raiser consultant or professional solicitor for charitable organization (IC23-7-8-2), warehouseman, grain dealer (IC26-3-7-4, 34), motor vehicle buying and selling (IC9-23-2-1), hazardous waste facilities, disposal, emissions, and transportation of contaminants (IC13-22 and IC13-15), manufacturer, distributor, dispenser of controlled substances (IC35-48-3-3), pari-mutuel wagering (IC4-31), games of chance (IC4-32), riverboat gambling (IC4-33), tobacco (IC6-7-2-8, IC6-7-2-15), public utility (IC8-1-2-91), transportation brokerage (IC8-2.1-18-22), vending stands in public buildings (IC12-12-5-1), private mental health institution (IC12-25-1-3), supervised group living facility (IC12-28-5), disposal of dead animals (IC15-2.1-16-2), commercial lawn care—fertilizer and pesticide (IC15-3-3, IC15-3-3.3, IC15-3-3.6), pest inspector (IC15-3-3.6-3), certain contractors in Lake and Porter counties (IC22-11-3.1-2), boiler and pressure vessel inspector (IC22-15-6-5), consumer loans (IC24-4.5-3-502), agriculture commodities warehouse (IC26-3-7-4). Other activities, occupations and professionals regulated by statute and related ordinances.

Collection Agency Licenses.—Any person desiring to conduct collection agency or renew collection agency license must accompany application for license or renewal thereof with fee of $100 plus additional $30 for each office. Renewal applications must be accompanied by renewal fee and fee of $30 for each office. Issuance of licenses is staggered and licenses are effective for two years. (IC25-11-1-9). Renewal and original must be accompanied by $5,000 surety bond for each office. (IC25-11-1-3). All bonds and applications filed with Secretary of State. Nonresident applicant must appoint resident service agent and stipulate validity of service on himself by service on agent. (IC25-11-1-3). Nonresident collection agency having only incidental contact with debtor is not required to be licensed. (IC25-11-1-5). Applicants must be U.S. citizens, 18 or older, of good moral character, not defaulted in payment of money collected or received for another, and not be former licensee under act whose license was suspended or revoked and not subsequently reinstated. (IC25-11-1-4). Foregoing does not apply to attorneys, persons regularly employed as credit men, banks, fiduciaries and financial institutions, licensed real estate brokers, employees of licensees under act, any person or business whose primary object is not collection of claims, or any public utility or any express company subject to motor carrier or railroad regulation under IC8-2.1 or 8-3. (IC25-11-1-2).

Powers of Collection Agent.—Licensed collection agent may receive or be assignee of another person's accounts, bills or other evidence of indebtedness, and, at direction of assignor(s), may file action to collect debt in county of preferred venue. Assignee may consolidate claims against individual or joint debtors in county of preferred venue. Court upon motion shall order assignee to pay attorneys' fees necessitated by transfer of action to preferred venue county. (IC25-11-1-13).

MONOPOLIES, RESTRAINT OF TRADE AND COMPETITION:

Monopolies of and attempts to monopolize any part of trade or commerce within state, and combinations which are in restraint of trade or which limit production or control prices are Class A misdemeanors. (IC24-1-2-1 to 3). Private party may recover treble damages, costs and attorneys' fees. (IC24-1-2-7).

Agricultural co-operative association is not a combination in restraint of trade. (IC15-7-1-27).

Contracts Controlling Output or Prices.—Arrangement, contract, combination, etc., between persons or corporations controlling output of article of merchandise made with view or tending to lessen competition in importation or sale of articles, or designed or tending to advance, reduce or control price or cost to producer or consumer is unlawful and void. Penalty: domestic corporation forfeits charter, foreign corporation may not do business in state, individual subject to fine and imprisonment. Person or corporation injured may recover full consideration paid for articles controlled. Violation committed knowingly is Class C felony. (IC24-1-1-1 to 6).

Refusing Sales to Dealer or Mechanic.—Contract or combination to prevent sales to dealer or mechanic of merchandise or articles intended for trade or used by mechanic, etc., in business is void, and party thereto who refuses to sell because intending purchaser is not member of combination, etc., is guilty of Class A misdemeanor. Violation punishable by forfeiture of $50 for each day of continuation after notice. Person injured may recover damages, with costs and attorneys' fees. (IC24-1-3-1 to 5).

Forcing Manufacturers Out of Business.—Arrangement or agreement to refuse to furnish articles required in manufacture of merchandise, to charge more than usual price therefor, or to do or omit any act to prevent or hinder manufacturing, and arrangement or act to compel manufacturer to cease manufacturing article or close down or go out of business is unlawful and void. Penalty: domestic corporation forfeits charter, foreign corporation may not do business in state, individual subject to fine and imprisonment. Person injured may recover consideration paid for controlled goods. Violation committed knowingly is Class C felony. (IC24-1-4-1 to 4).

Collusive Bidding.—Scheme or agreement restricting bidding on public or private work illegal and punishable by fine and imprisonment. Person injured may recover treble damages with costs and attorneys' fees. Person letting contract secured by collusive bidding may recover all amounts paid with interest and attorneys' fees, and contract cannot be enforced. (IC24-1-2-3 to 12).

Retail installment sales licensees are prohibited from entering into any contract or agreement which would tend to lessen competition in such business field. (IC24-5-3-1 to 10).

Insurance unfair trade practices policed by Insurance Commission through cease and desist orders, imposition of civil penalties, and suspension or revocation of licenses. (IC27-4-1-1 to 19).

Discrimination in price of milk and milk products to destroy competition prohibited, and contracts in violation are void. Penalty: corporation forfeits right to do business in state, individual subject to fine and imprisonment. (IC24-4-1-1 to 6).

Cigarette retailers and distributors prohibited from selling cigarettes below cost with intent to injure competitors or destroy or substantially lessen competition. (IC24-3-2-1 to 13).

Motion picture distributors subject to legislation prohibiting blind selling, requiring notice of trade screening and regulating bid procedure. (IC24-1-5-1 to 7). Plaintiff in civil action may recover damages and attorney fees.

Unfair Trade Practices.—Common law tort of unfair competition recognized. (676 F.Supp. 1421; 554 F.Supp. 1088; 501 N.E.2d 458). Common law tort of trade libel recognized. (411 N.E.2d 653). See also topic Consumer Protection.

NEGOTIABLE INSTRUMENTS:

See topic Bills and Notes.

RESTRAINT OF TRADE:

See topic Monopolies, Restraint of Trade and Competition.

SALES:

Uniform Commercial Code in effect since July 1, 1964. (IC26-1-1-101 et seq.).

Uniform Consumer Credit Code in effect with respect to revolving charge accounts and revolving loan accounts since Mar. 5, 1971, and in other respects since Oct.1, 1971.

No statutory limitation on type size in printed contracts for either contracts of sales or conditional sales contracts. However, implied warranty disclaimers or modifications must be conspicuous. (IC26-1-2-316).

See topic Commercial Code.

Bills of Sale.—No statutory provisions.

Product Liability.—Privity of contract no longer necessary for injured party to maintain an action against manufacturer. All product liability actions are governed by IC34-20-1-1 et seq. and IC34-6-2 to 10, which restates law of strict liability in tort, defines defective products, establishes three defenses to strict liability in tort, establishes new statute of limitations for product liability actions, creates rebuttable presumption that certain products are not defective, and imposes several liability on defendants.

Statute of Limitations.—Regardless of minority or legal disability and notwithstanding IC34-11-6-1, any product liability action, excepting certain asbestos-related actions, in which theory of liability is negligence or strict liability in tort must be commenced within two years after cause of action accrues or within ten years after delivery of product to initial user or consumer. However, if cause of action accrues at least eight years but less than ten years after that initial delivery, action may be commenced within two years after cause of action accrues. (IC34-20-3-1).

Product liability action based on property damage, personal injury, disability, disease, in death resulting from exposure to asbestos must be commenced within two years of date when injured person knows that he has asbestos related disease, injury, or property damage. This section applies only to product liability actions against persons who mined and sold commercial asbestos, and against funds which have been created for payment of asbestos related claims. (IC34-20-3-2).

See also category Civil Actions and Procedure, topic Limitation of Actions.

Conditional Sales.—Governed by Uniform Commercial Code. See topic Commercial Code.

Retail Installment Sales.—See topic Consumer Credit.

Consumer Protection.—See topic Consumer Protection.

Bulk Sales.—Governed by Uniform Commercial Code, see topic Commercial Code.

Sales of Motor Vehicles.—See category Transportation, topic Motor Vehicles.

SECURITIES:

Uniform Commercial Code in effect since July 1, 1964. (IC26-1-1-101 et seq.). See topic Commercial Code.

The Indiana Securities Law is based to certain extent on 1956 version of Uniform Securities Act, as amended in 1958, promulgated by National Conference of Commissioners on Uniform State Laws. Uniform Securities Act (1956) was superseded by Uniform Securities Act (1985). Indiana has not adopted 1985 version of Act and Indiana statute contains many variations from that uniform law.

Supervision.—Chapter administered by Office of Secretary of State of Indiana. Secretary of State appoints Securities Commissioner, 302 W. Washington Street, Room E-111, Indianapolis, Indiana 46204. (IC23-2-1-15).

Regulatory Powers of Supervisory Authority.—Commissioner may issue stop order denying, suspending or revoking registration statement or may censure registrant or its officers, directors, partners, person performing similar functions, or other persons who offered or sold securities in Indiana, or bar such person from employment with registered broker dealer or investment advisor if he finds that such order is in public interest and finds present violation of any of numerous statutory provisions relating to contents of statement, or application, method of issuance or operation, or activities of persons identified with issuer, broker-dealer, agent, investment adviser, or investment adviser representative. (IC23-2-1-7; IC23-2-1-11). Commissioner may deny or revoke exemption for certain securities and all transactions exemptions as described below if he finds securities would not qualify for registration. (IC23-2-1-2). Commissioner may require investment advisers to disseminate information necessary to protect investors or clients. (IC23-2-1-12.1; IC23-2-1-11). Commissioner may issue subpoena if requested by another state administrator if concerns alleged violation of Indiana law. (IC23-2-1-16.5). Commissioner may issue cease and desist orders, orders to show cause, and notices with or without hearing and after notice and hearing may issue order of rescission, restitution or disgorgement, including interest at rate of 8% per year. (IC23-2-1-17.1).

Prerequisites to Sales or Offerings.—Unlawful for any person to offer or sell security in Indiana unless security is registered under Act, security or transaction exempted under Act or exempt from registration or security is covered in §18(b) of Securities Act of 1933. (IC23-2-1-3). No person may transact business in Indiana as broker-dealer, agent, investment adviser or investment adviser representative unless registered under Act or exempt from registration. (IC23-2-1-8). No person required to be registered as investment advisor under §203 of Investment Advisors Act of 1940 may employ, supervise, or associate with investment advisor representative having place of business in Indiana, unless investment advisor representative is registered under Act or exempt from registration. (IC23-2-1-8).

Securities Defined.—Statute uses language of §101(16) of 1985 Uniform Act, except limited partnership interests and various option securities not specifically mentioned and interests in limited liability companies and limited liability partnerships are expressly included in definition; and commodity futures contract, option, put, call, privilege or other right to purchase or sell commodity futures contract, margin accounts for purchase of commodities or commodity futures contracts and automatic extension or rollover of existing security are specifically included. "Security" does not include any insurance or endowment policy or annuity contract under which insurance company promises to pay money either in lump sum or periodically for life or some other specified period or any contract or trust agreement under which money is paid pursuant to charitable remainder annuity trust or charitable remainder unitrust (described in §664 of Internal Revenue Code), or pooled income fund (described in §642 [c][5] of Internal Revenue Code), or any annuity contract under which purchaser receives charitable contribution deduction under §170 of Internal Revenue Code or interest in limited liability company if person claiming that interest is not security can prove that all members of limited liability company are actively engaged in management of limited liability company. (IC23-2-1-1).

Exempt Securities.—The following securities are exempted from registration: (1) Security (including revenue obligation) issued or guaranteed by U.S., any state, any political subdivision of state, or any agency or corporate or other instrumentality of foregoing; or any certificate of deposit for any of foregoing; (2) security issued or guaranteed by Canada, any Canadian province, any political subdivision of any Canadian province, any agency or corporate or other instrumentality of foregoing, or any other foreign government with which U.S. currently maintains diplomatic relations, if security recognized as valid obligation by issuer or guarantor; (3) security issued by and representing interest in or debt of, or guaranteed by bank organized under laws of U.S., bank, savings institution or trust company organized and supervised under laws of any state, any federal savings association, savings association organized under laws of any state and authorized to do business in Indiana, federal credit union or any credit union, industrial loan association or similar association organized and supervised under laws of Indiana, or corporation or organization whose securities, as to issuance thereof, are required by any other law to be passed upon and authorized by Indiana Department of Financial Institutions or by any federal agency or authority; (4) security issued or guaranteed by railroad or other common or contract carrier, public utility, or common or contract carrier or public utility holding company if issuer or guarantor subject to regulation or supervision as to issuance of its own securities by public commission, board, or officer of government of U.S., of any state, territory, or insular possession thereof, of any municipality located therein, of District of Columbia, or of Dominion of Canada or any province of Canada; (5) security listed or approved for listing upon notice of issuance on New York Stock Exchange, American Stock Exchange, Chicago Stock Exchange, or on any other exchange approved and designated by Commissioner; or designated for trading in National Association of Securities Dealers Automatic Quotation National Market System or other national market system approved and designated by Commissioner; other security of same issuer which is of senior or substantially equal rank; security called for by subscription rights or warrants so listed or approved; or warrant or right to purchase or subscribe to any of foregoing; (6) promissory note, draft, bill of exchange or banker's acceptance evidencing obligation, guarantee, renewal or guarantee of renewal of obligation to pay cash within nine months of date of issuance, exclusive of grace days, if in denominations of at least $50,000 and rated in one of three highest categories by nationally recognized statistical rating organization; (7) security issued in connection with employee stock purchase, savings, pension, profit-sharing, or similar benefit plan; (8) security issued by association incorporated under IC15-7-1; (9) industrial development bonds as defined in Internal Revenue Code of 1954, if §103(b)(1) of such Code does not apply to such security by reason of application of paragraph (4) or (6) of §103(b); (10) security issued by not-for-profit corporation that meets requirements of §103(e) of Internal Revenue Code of 1954 and is designated by governor as secondary market for guaranteed student loans under IC20-12-21.2; and (11) qualified bonds under §141(e) of Internal Revenue Code. (IC23-2-1-2).

Exempt Transactions.—Subject to Commissioner's power to revoke or deny exemption with respect to specific security or transaction, following are exempted from registration: (1) isolated nonissuer offer or sale; (2) nonissuer sale effected by or through registered broker-dealer pursuant to unsolicited order or offer to buy; (3) nonissuer offer or sale by registered broker-dealer, acting as principal or agent, if: (a) Securities sold at prices reasonably related to current market price at time of sale, and, commission collected by registered broker-dealer acting as agent is not in excess of usual and customary commissions collected with respect to comparable securities and transactions; (b) securities do not constitute unsold allotment to or subscription by broker-dealer as participant in distribution of securities by issuer or by or through underwriter; (c) either (i) names of issuer's officers and directors, balance sheet as of date not more than 18 months prior to date of sale, and profit and loss statement for either fiscal year preceding that date or most recent year of operations published in securities manual approved by Commissioner; (ii) issuer is required to file reports with Securities and Exchange Commission pursuant to §§13 and 15 of Securities Exchange Act of 1934 and is not delinquent in filing such reports at date of sale; or (iii) names of issuer's officers and directors, balance sheet as of date not more than 16 months prior to date of sale, and profit and loss statement for either fiscal year preceding that date or most recent year of operations on prescribed form is on file with Commissioner ($25 filing fee charged for initial filings; $15 for subsequent annual renewals); and (d) if share is transferable, issuer appoints qualified transfer agent to handle all transfers; and (e) unless issuer is registered under Investment Company Act of 1940, following are true at time of transaction: (i) security belongs to class publicly held for at least 90 days, (ii) issuer of security is going concern, engaged in business and not in bankruptcy or receivership, and (iii) except as permitted by order of commissioner, issuer and predecessors in continuous operation (as defined in statute) for five years. (Commissioner may revoke exemption with respect to any securities by order if he finds that: (i) further sale of such securities in Indiana would work or tend to work fraud on purchasers thereof; (ii) financial condition of issuer makes it in public interest and necessary for protection of investors to revoke or restrict exemption; or (iii) due to limited number of shares in hands of public or limited number of broker-dealers making market in securities, there is not sufficient market for securities so that there is not current market price therefor); (4) transactions between issuer or other person on whose behalf offering is made and underwriter, or among underwriters; (5) transaction in bond or other evidence of indebtedness secured by real or chattel mortgage or deed of trust, or by agreement for sale of real estate or chattels, if entire mortgage, deed of trust, or agreement, together with all bonds or other evidences of indebtedness secured thereby, is offered and sold as unit; (6) transaction by executor, administrator, personal

See note at head of Digest as to 1998 legislation covered.

See Topical Index in front part of this volume.

IN – 10

SECURITIES . . . *continued*
representative, sheriff, marshall, receiver, trustee in bankruptcy, guardian, conservator, or anyone acting in trust or fiduciary capacity if transaction effected pursuant to authority of or subject to approval by any court of competent jurisdiction; (7) transaction executed by bona fide pledgee without purpose of evading statute; (8) offer or sale to bank, savings institution, trust company, insurance company, investment company as defined in Investment Company Act of 1940, pension or profit-sharing trust, or other financial institution or institutional buyer, or to broker-dealer whether purchaser is acting for itself or in some fiduciary capacity; (9) offer or sale of securities of issuer: (i) to person who is: (A) director, executive officer, general partner, administrator or person who performs similar functions for or who is similarly situated with respect to issuer; (B) director, executive officer or general partner of general partner of issuer; or (C) any other natural person employed on full-time basis by issuer as attorney or accountant, if person has acted in that capacity for at least one year immediately prior to offer or sale; (ii) to entity affiliated with issuer; or (iii) if issuer is corporation, to person owning shares representing and possessing 10% or more of total combined voting power of all classes of stock of such corporation or affiliated corporation issued and outstanding and who is entitled to vote; (iv) if issuer is limited liability company, to person who is owner of interest in limited liability company representing and possessing at least 10% of total combined voting power of all classes of such interests issued and outstanding; (10) offer or sale of any security by issuer thereof if all of following conditions are satisfied: (A) issuer reasonably believes either: (i) there are no more than 35 purchasers of securities from issuer, including purchasers outside Indiana; or (ii) there are no more than 20 purchasers in Indiana. Purchaser whom issuer reasonably believes to be accredited investor or who purchases securities after they are registered under statute excluded from number of purchasers; (B) issuer does not offer or sell securities by means of any form of general advertisement or general solicitation; (C) issuer reasonably believes each purchaser is acquiring securities for own investment and is aware of restrictions imposed on transferability and resale of securities. Basis for reasonable belief may include: (i) written representation signed by purchaser; and (ii) placement of legend on certificate or other document evidencing securities stating securities have not been registered under §3 of Indiana law, and setting forth or referring to restrictions on transferability and sale; (D) issuer: (i) files with Commissioner and provides each purchaser in state offering statement that sets forth all material facts with respect to securities ($100 filing fee, consent to service of process and notice of sales required); and (ii) reasonably believes immediately before making sale that each purchaser who is not accredited investor either alone or with purchaser representative has knowledge and experience in financial and business matters to extent that purchaser is capable of evaluating merits and risks of prospective investment; (E) if aggregate offering price of securities in offering (including securities sold outside of Indiana) does not exceed $500,000, issuer need not comply with clause (D) if issuer files with Commissioner and provides each purchaser in Indiana: (i) copies of all written materials, if any, concerning securities provided by issuer to any purchaser; and (ii) unless clearly presented in written materials, written notification setting forth name, address, form of organization and nature of business of issuer and specified information ($100 filing fee, consent to service of process and notice of sales required); (F) Commissioner does not disallow exemption within ten full business days after receipt of clause (D) or (E) filing. Issuer may make offers (but not sales) before and during ten-day period if: (i) each prospective purchaser is advised in writing that offer is preliminary and subject to material change; and (ii) no enforceable offer to purchase securities may be made by prospective purchaser, and no consideration in any form may be accepted or received (directly or indirectly) from prospective purchaser, before expiration of ten-day period and vacation of any order disallowing exemption; (G) issuer need not comply with clause (D), (E) or (F) if: (i) each purchaser has access to all material facts with respect to securities by reason of such purchaser's active involvement in organization or management of issuer or such purchaser's family relationship with person actively involved in organization or management of issuer; (ii) there are not more than 15 purchasers in Indiana and each Indiana purchaser is accredited investor or purchaser described in item (i) of this clause; or (iii) aggregate offering price of securities, including securities sold outside Indiana, does not exceed $500,000; total number of purchasers, including purchasers outside Indiana, does not exceed 25; and each purchaser either receives all material facts with respect to security or is accredited investor or purchaser described in item (i) of this clause; (H) Commissioner may by rule deny exemption to particular class of issuers, or may make exemption available to such issuers upon compliance with additional conditions and requirements, if appropriate in furtherance of intent of Act; (11) offer or sale of securities to existing security holders of issuer, including holders of convertible securities, nontransferable warrants, or transferable warrants exercisable within not more than 90 days of their issuance if no commission or other remuneration (other than standby commission) is paid or given for soliciting security holder in Indiana; (12) any offer (but not sale) of security for which registration statements or applications have been filed under Act and Securities Act of 1933 if no stop order or refusal order in effect and no public proceeding or examination looking toward such order pending under either law; (13) deposit of shares under any voting trust agreement and issue of voting trust certificates therefor; (14) offer or sale of commodity futures contract; (15) offer or sale of securities to or for benefit of security holders incident to vote of security holders pursuant to articles of incorporation or applicable instrument on merger or share exchange under IC23-1-40 or laws of another state, reclassification of securities, exchange of securities under IC28-1-7.5, or sale of assets of issuer in consideration of issuance of securities of same or another issuer; or (16) Commissioner authorized to create limited offering transactional exemption for compatibility with federal exemptions and uniformity among states. (IC23-2-1-2).

Exemption rulings may be granted by the Commissioner at his discretion upon proper application. Requests for exemption rulings must be accompanied by $100 filing fee. (IC23-2-1-2[c]).

ULOE.—Indiana Securities Commission has adopted Uniform Limited Offering Exemption effective Mar. 21, 1996.

Registration of Offerers.—No requirements other than in connection with registration of securities and dealers and agents. See subheads Registration of Securities, Registration of Dealers, etc. infra.

Registration of Securities.—All securities except those specifically exempted and those offered or sold in exempt transactions must be registered under Act. (IC23-2-1-3). Application for registration may be filed by issuer, other person on whose behalf offering is made or registered broker-dealer. Sealed and acknowledged consent appointing Secretary of State as agent to receive service of process required. (IC23-2-1-16). Filing fee of $^{1}/_{20}$ of 1% of maximum aggregate offering price of registered securities offered in Indiana. Minimum fee is $250 and maximum fee is $1,000. Fee of $25 for filing amendment to effective registration requiring order of Commissioner. (IC23-2-1-6). Registration effective for two years from effective date or shorter period security being offered or distributed in nonexempted transaction by or for account of issuer or other person making distribution. Post-effective amendment to increase registered shares permitted if offer price and discount unchanged. Periodic reports required so long as registration is effective. (IC23-2-1-6).

Registration by coordination is available for any security for which a registration statement has been filed under the Securities Act of 1933 in connection with same offering. Application for registration by coordination automatically effective when federal registration effective if no stop order in effect, application containing prescribed information and documents on file with Commissioner for ten days, statement of maximum and minimum proposed offering prices and maximum underwriting discount on file for two full business days, Commissioner promptly notified by telephone or telegram of date and time of effectiveness of federal registration and pricing amendment promptly filed as post-effective amendment. (IC23-2-1-4).

Registration by qualification is available for all securities. Registration statement must be filed with Commissioner and must contain documents enumerated by statute including a prospectus containing information specified in Act. Registration by qualification effective on 30th day after filing. (IC23-2-1-5).

Federal Covered Services.—Commissioner may by rule require filing of following with respect to federal covered securities described in §18(b)(2) of Securities Act of 1933: (1) before being offered in Indiana, all documents that are part of current federal regulation statement, consent to service of process and fee of no more than $1,000; (2) after initial offer in Indiana, all documents that are part of amendment to current federal registration statement; and (3) annual or periodic report of value of federal covered securities offered or sold in Indiana, a fee. (IC23-2-1-6.1[a]). Commissioner may by rule require filing of following with respect to federal covered securities described in §18(b)(4)(D) of Securities Act of 1933: (1) Form D; (2) consent to service of process. (IC23-2-1-6.1[b]). With respect to federal covered security described in §18(b)(3) or §18(b)(4) of Securities Act of 1933, Commissioner may, by rule or otherwise, require issuer to file any document filed with Securities and Exchange Commission. (IC23-2-1-6.1[c]). IC23-2-1-6.1 does not apply to federal covered securities described in §18(b)(1) of Securities Act of 1933. (IC23-2-1-6.1[d]). Commissioner may issue stop order suspending offer and sale of federal covered security if certain conditions are met. Commissioner may waive provisions of IC23-2-1-6.1. (IC23-2-1-6.1[e]). Until Oct. 11, 1999, if Commissioner provides written notice to issuer of federal covered security that fees have not been fully paid and fees are not promptly paid after notice, commissioner may require federal covered security to be registered. (IC23-1-1-6.1[f]).

Fraudulent and Prohibited Practices.—Indiana has adopted language of §§101, 102, 404 and 405 of 1956 Uniform Securities Act. Investment advisers and representatives must accurately disclose all material facts when soliciting clients; may not sell to or purchase from client unless disclose and obtain consent. Persons required to be registered under §203 of Investment Advisors Act of 1940 must accurately disclose all material facts when dealing with client.

Registration of Dealers, etc.—Unlawful for any person to transact business in state as broker-dealer or agent unless registered. Unlawful to transact business as investment adviser or investment adviser representative unless: (i) Registered, (ii) only clients are certain types of institutional investors, or (iii) during preceding 12 months had less than six clients who are Indiana residents. (IC23-2-1-8). Unlawful for person required to be registered as investment advisor under §203 of Investment Advisors Act of 1940 to employ, supervise or associate with investment advisor representative having place of business in Indiana, unless investment advisor's representative is registered or exempt from registration. (IC23-2-1-8). Broker-dealer, agent, investment adviser or investment adviser representative may apply for registration by filing application with Commissioner (IC23-2-1-9), together with consent to service of process (IC23-2-1-16) and payment of $250 initial registration and $125 renewal fee for broker-dealer; $100 initial registration and $50 renewal fee for investment adviser; and $25 initial registration and renewal fee for agent or investment adviser representative (IC23-2-1-9). Applicant for registration as broker-dealer or agent must pass examination in form approved by Commissioner. If partnership, corporation or similar association at least two partners, officers, directors or similar persons must pass examination, unless have no branch officers and no more than ten agents then only one person required. (IC23-2-1-11[b] and accompanying regulations). Registration effective at noon on 30th day after filing application and expires on following Dec. 31. Commissioner retains entire amount of broker-dealer or investment adviser registration fee if initial or renewal application for registration is denied or withdrawn. (IC23-2-1-9). Broker-dealers required to keep accounts and records required by Commissioner which requirements may not exceed limitations provided in §15 of Securities and Exchange Act of 1934. Investment advisor required to keep accounts required by Commissioner, which requirements may not exceed limitations provided in §222 of Investment Advisors Act of 1940. Commissioner may prescribe period that investment advisor must retain records. (IC23-2-1-10). Broker-dealers and investment advisors required to file financial and other reports with Commissioner which requirements cannot exceed limitations provided for in §15 of Securities and Exchange Act of 1934, for broker-dealers, and in §222 of Investment Advisors Act of 1940, for investment advisors. Selected broker-dealers required to file annual compliance report. (IC23-2-1-10). All loan brokers are required to register with Commissioner and pay fee. See infra,

See note at head of Digest as to 1998 legislation covered.

See Topical Index in front part of this volume.

IN – 11

SECURITIES . . . *continued*

subhead Loan Brokers. Commissioner may deny, revoke or suspend registration, censure registrant or its officers, directors, partners, person performing similar functions or any other person who offered or sold securities in Indiana, or bar such person from employment with registered broker dealer or investment advisor. See subhead Regulatory Powers of Supervisory Authority, supra. (IC23-2-1-11).

Bonds.—Commissioner may by order require registered broker-dealer, agent or investment adviser with custody of or discretionary authority over client funds to maintain bond and establish amount of bond. Deposit of cash and securities may be accepted instead of bond. No bond required if broker-dealer or investment registrant whose net capital or minimum financial requirements, respectively, exceed amount required by commissioner. Bond shall provide for action or bond if (1) person has cause of action under IC23-2-1-19 or (2) commissioner by rule or order requires that such action be brought on bond. Bond shall provide that action may not be maintained unless action is included within time specified in IC23-2-1-19. (IC23-2-1-9.1).

Liabilities.—Provisions are made for criminal penalties (class C felony) for persons violating provisions of Act (IC23-2-1-18.1), and for civil liability to other parties to transaction of persons who offer, purchase or sell in violation of Act and those who control sellers or purchasers and certain affiliates liable to others unless purchaser or seller did not know and through exercise of reasonable care could not have known of violation. May rescind transaction or recover amount paid plus interest at rate provided in security or 8% interest per year for non-interest-bearing securities, costs and reasonable attorney's fees. Statute of limitations is three years after discovery of violation. Suit precluded if offer to refund consideration plus interest at rate provided in security or 8% interest for non-interest-bearing securities less income received on security and offer not accepted within 30 days. (IC23-2-1-19). Commissioner may, after hearing, impose civil penalty not exceeding $10,000 for each violation. (IC23-2-1-19.5). Investment advisers who violate Act liable to clients for consideration paid for advice, loss due to advice, 8% interest per year from date consideration paid, costs and reasonable attorneys fees less value of cash received due to advice. (IC23-2-1-19).

Franchise agreements are regulated pursuant to statute. (IC23-2-2.5-1, et seq.). No person may offer or sell any franchise unless franchise is registered or is exempt from registration. (IC23-2-2.5-9).

Commodity contracts and commodity options are regulated pursuant to statute. (IC23-2-6). No person may sell, purchase or offer to sell or purchase commodity under commodity contract or commodity option or offer to enter into as seller or purchaser any commodity contract or commodity option unless exempt transaction. (IC23-2-6-17).

Business Take-Over.—"Tender Offers" are regulated pursuant to Take-Over Offers Act (IC23-2-3.1) requiring filing with Commissioner of disclosure statement prior to offer to acquire equity security of "target company," if after acquisition, offeror is directly or indirectly record or beneficial owner of more than 10% of any class of outstanding equity securities of target company. "Target company" means issuer of securities organized under laws of Indiana, with principal place of business in state, and with substantial assets in state. Does not include certain domestic corporations, regulated by Utility Regulatory Commission, financial institutions, public utilities, public utility holding companies, bank holding companies or savings and loan associations if takeover offer subject to regulation of entity's primary regulatory agency. Acquisitions of less than 2% of class of shares, issuers of class of equity securities held of record by 75 or fewer persons at time of offer and acquisitions Commissioner determines to be not for purpose and without effect of changing or influencing control are exempt from regulation. (IC23-2-3.1-8.6). Before making takeover offer, offeror must file statement with Commissioner and deliver copy to president of target company at principal office no later than filing date. Consent of offeror to service of process specified in IC23-2-1-16 and filing fee of $750 must accompany statement. If takeover offer subject to any federal law including Securities Exchange Act of 1934, statement must include copy of all documents filed with Securities and Exchange Commission or other proper federal agency. If takeover offer not subject to federal law, statement must be filed on forms prescribed by Commissioner and must include: (1) Identity and material facts concerning offeror; (2) source and amount of funds used to acquire any equity security; (3) if purpose of offer is to gain control over target company, statement of any plans to liquidate, sell assets, effect merger or consolidation or other major changes in business, structure, management or personnel of target company; (4) number of shares or units of equity security of target company of which offeror is record or beneficial owner or has right to acquire; (5) information as to any contracts, arrangements, understandings or negotiations with any person concerning any equity security of target company; (6) information as to any contracts, arrangements or understandings with any person who is officer, director, administrator, manager or executive employee, or owner of any equity securities of target company, with respect to tender of equity securities of target company, purchase of any equity security from such person otherwise than pursuant to tender offer and retention of any person in his present or any other management position or giving or withholding of favorable recommendation regarding offer; (7) description of provisions for providing material information of takeover offer to offerees and any other information Commissioner prescribes by regulation. Must describe contract or subsidy received by offeror during three years prior to filing or office or appointment held by offeror, directors or officers from or with foreign (non-U.S.) government. If offeror incorporated in or citizen of non-U.S. country must disclose financial sources and proposed consummation date. Hearing must be held within 20 business days after statement filed. Following hearing and within 20 business days after statement filed, Commissioner may prohibit or condition purchase if Commissioner finds by preponderance of evidence that takeover statement fails to provide full and fair disclosure to offerees of all material information concerning takeover offer or if takeover offer is not made to all offerees of same class of equity securities of target company on substantially equivalent terms. No shares may be purchased or paid for pursuant to takeover offer within 20 business days after it is made. Offeror may not acquire equity security of target company for two years after conclusion of takeover offer unless seller offered terms substantially equivalent to takeover offer. Commissioner may investigate, issue ex

parte cease and desist orders without notice, or bring suit if he believes any person is violating or about to violate any provision or regulation of Takeover Offers Act. Offeror, target company, or any beneficial owner of equity security subject to offer may bring court action to enforce Act or enjoin violation. Any party to proceeding may appeal to Indiana Court of Appeals from final order of Commissioner.

For discussion of provisions relating to consequences of acquisition of controlling interest in and business combinations with certain Indiana corporations see category Business Organizations, topic Corporations.

Uniform Simplification of Fiduciary Security Transfers Act adopted. (IC30-2-5-1 to 11).

Uniform Securities Ownership by Minors Act not adopted.
See topic Commercial Code.

Continuing care contracts are regulated pursuant to statute. (IC23-2-4-1, et seq.). Persons who agree to furnish living accommodations in home and meals, nursing care, medical or other health related services, or any combination thereof, to five or more individuals for life of individual or for more than one month in exchange for payment of entrance fee and periodic charges must register each such home with Commissioner. Form of application for registration is prescribed by Commissioner, and must be accompanied by $250 application fee. Application must contain initial disclosure statement whose contents are mandated by statute. (IC23-2-4-4). Provider must file annual disclosure statement within four months of end of Provider's fiscal year containing specified financial information, together with $100 filing fee. (IC23-2-4-5). Obligation to amend disclosure statements to prevent material misstatement or omission of fact and to reflect sale of home. Copies of initial and latest annual disclosure statements must be delivered to prospective resident prior to execution of continuing care agreement. Commissioner after notice and hearing may deny, revoke or not renew registration or prohibit execution of continuing care agreements if finds failure to file annual statement or to deliver disclosure statements to prospective resident, use of misleading disclosure statement, failure to comply with cease and desist order of Commissioner or willful violation of statute, or provider insolvent and financial condition may jeopardize care of residents. Failure to comply with registration or disclosure requirements is class A infraction. (IC23-2-4-9). Commissioner must act upon application within 60 days of filing. If application insufficient, Provider has 60 days to correct deficiencies. Provider must establish interest-bearing escrow account to hold entrance fees received prior to occupancy of living unit by prospective resident. Conditions for release of funds from escrow established by statute. (IC23-2-4-10). Provider may post letter of credit, negotiable securities or bond in favor of Commissioner in lieu of escrow account. Statute establishes Indiana Retirement Home Guaranty Fund to protect financial interests of residents from bankruptcy of Provider. $100 fee levied on each person who enters into continuing care agreement after Aug. 31, 1982, to be collected by Provider and forwarded to Commissioner within 30 days of occupancy.

Loan brokers must register with Commissioner. (IC23-2-5-4). Loan broker is any person who, for consideration, promises to procure or assist in procuring loan from any third party or who promises to consider whether or not to make loan to any person. Banks or other regulated financial institutions (other than person who is financial institution solely because licensed to make consumer loans under IC24-4.5-3-503 or similar license from another state), attorneys rendering services in practice of law, accountants performing practice of accountancy (as defined by IC25-2.1-1-10), licensed real estate brokers, persons authorized to make, issue, sell and service loans or securities for, or guaranteed or insured by, certain federal agencies, insurance companies, registered broker-dealers, agents or investment advisors, any person that procures, promises to procure or assists in procuring loan that is not subject to Truth in Lending Act, any person who arranges financing for sale of that person's product and persons who are or propose to be creditors for loan are not loan brokers. (IC23-2-5-3 and IC23-2-5-19). Information to be contained in application for registration specified by statute. (IC23-2-5-5). Filing fee of $250, consent to service of process and $25,000 bond required. Registration effective on 30th day after filing and expires Jan. 1 of year following effective date. Renewal application to be filed annually together with $100 filing fee. Contracts for services of loan broker must be in writing and signed by all contracting parties with copy retained by borrowing party. Loan brokers required to keep records specified in statute for two years. Antifraud provisions adopted for loan brokers. (IC23-2-5-20). Commissioner authorized to enforce statute through notices and orders, investigations and hearings. Commissioner may issue certificate of compliance or noncompliance with statute admissible in criminal or civil action arising under loan broker provisions and may impose civil penalty not to exceed $5,000 per violation. Knowing violation of loan broker provisions is class D felony. Provisions for civil liabilities to other parties for violation of statute. May recover damages, interest at legal rate and attorneys' fees. If loan broker violates statute, contract void and prospective borrower entitled to recover funds paid to loan broker. (IC23-2-5-15).

STATUTE OF FRAUDS:

See topic Frauds, Statute of.

TRUST RECEIPT SECURITY:

Uniform Commercial Code in effect since July 1, 1964. (IC26-1-1-101 et seq.).

WAREHOUSEMEN:

Uniform Commercial Code in effect since July 1, 1964. (IC26-1-1-101 et seq.). See topic Commercial Code.

Lien.—Governed by Uniform Commercial Code. (IC26-1-7-209, 210). See topic Commercial Code.

Warehouses for Grain Storage—Governed by IC26-3-7-1 et seq.

Cold Storage Warehouses.—Governed by IC16-18-2-57, 58.

Bonds.—Required for grain storage warehouses. (IC26-3-7-9 to 16.6).

Licenses.—Required for grain storage warehouses. (IC26-3-7-4 et seq.).

CITIZENSHIP

ALIENS:

Aliens residing in foreign countries or U.S. may acquire by purchase, devise, or descent, and may hold, convey, devise, transmit, mortgage, or otherwise encumber lands in this state, with equal privilege of citizens of state or U.S., except that holdings in excess of 320 acres are subject to escheat to state unless conveyed within five years after acquired or from reaching age 18, or unless owner shall have become citizen of U.S. within such time. (IC32-1-8-1, 2).

Aliens are not permitted to serve as grand jurors. (IC35-34-2-3[c]), It shall be good cause for challenge to any person called as juror in criminal trial if that person is alien. (IC35-37-1-5).

No unemployment benefits may be paid on basis of services performed by alien unless alien is lawfully admitted for permanent residence or to perform such services or otherwise permanently residing in U.S. under color of law at time services were performed. (IC22-4-14-9).

Failure of attorney to advise noncitizen defendant that consequences of guilty plea may be deportation constitutes ineffective assistance of counsel. (In. Const. Art. 1, §13; 641 N.E.2d 44).

Aliens may not hold permits for the sale of beer. (IC7.1-3-4-2).

CIVIL ACTIONS AND PROCEDURE

ACCORD AND SATISFACTION:

Accord is agreement to compose or settle, and satisfaction is execution of agreement. (29 N.E.2d 560, 629 N.E.2d 1280). Where amount of debt is uncontroverted, payment of less than amount due will not amount to satisfaction, unless it is supported by some new or independent consideration. (116 Ind. 370, 19 N.E. 159). If amount is unliquidated and disputed, compromise will be binding. (49 Ind. App. 109, 96 N.E. 791). Where goods are received in full satisfaction of debt, it amounts to accord and satisfaction. (59 Ind. 27). Accord and satisfaction is affirmative defense which must be pled in responsive pleading, upon which pleader carries burden of proof. (Rule TR 8[C]; 554 N.E.2d 1180). Offer in satisfaction must be accompanied by express condition that acceptance is in full satisfaction of claim or circumstances must clearly indicate such condition. (629 N.E.2d 1280). Accord and satisfaction requires meeting of minds or evidence that parties intended to agree to accord and satisfaction. (629 N.E.2d 1280). Satisfaction is shown as matter of law when judgment for damages is lower than funds received in settlement. (597 N.E.2d 337). Creditor's approval of bankruptcy reorganization plan cannot constitute accord and satisfaction. (629 N.E.2d 1246).

See also category Business Regulation and Commerce, topic Commercial Code.

ACTIONS:

Indiana Rules of Trial Procedure to some extent are based on Federal Rules of Civil Procedure.

There is one form of action to be known as "civil action." Right of a civil action is not merged in a public offense or a public remedy, but may be sought independently of and in addition to punishment given or relief granted for public offense. (Rule TR 2).

Equity.—The distinction between actions at law and suits in equity, and the forms of each, are abolished. (Rule TR 2).

Conditions Precedent.—Tort actions against state are banned unless notice is filed with attorney general or state agency involved within 270 days after loss occurs. (IC34-13-3-6). Tort action against political subdivision is barred unless notice is filed with governing body of political subdivision and Indiana political subdivision risk management commission within 180 days after loss occurs. (IC34-13-3-8). Actions pertaining to assessment of contributions; penalties and interest; which accounts should be charged for benefits to be paid or ordered to be paid; successorship; and claims for refunds of contributions under Employment Security Act shall be preceded by notice of intent to institute judicial review, served on adverse party at any time before decision of administrative law judge becomes final. (IC22-4-32-8). Actions for refund of virtually all taxes administered by state department of revenue must be filed with department within three years of due date of return or date of payment, whichever is later. (IC6-8.1-9-1). For list of taxes see IC6-8.1-1-1. Actions for slander or libel against news service requires four days' notice prior to suit and, in case of newspaper, six days for daily publication and 11 days for weekly. (IC34-15-4-2). In action for wrongful death, personal representative must file suit within two years of date of death. (IC34-23-1-1).

Commencement.—See topic Process; also category Transportation, topic Motor Vehicles, subhead Action Against Nonresident.

Parties.—Every action must be prosecuted in name of real party in interest. Executor, administrator, guardian, bailee, trustee of an express trust, party with whom or in whose name contract has been made for benefit of another, or state, when authorized by statute to sue on relation of another, may sue in his own name on behalf of benefiting party. No action will be dismissed that is not prosecuted in name of real party in interest until reasonable time after objection. Ratification, joinder, or substitution has same effect as action commenced originally in name of real party in interest. (Rule TR 17[A]).

Partnership or unincorporated association may sue or be sued in its common name. (Rule TR 17[E]).

State may be made a party defendant to an action involving real estate. (Rule TR 17.1).

There is no distinction for purposes of suing or being sued between men and women because of marital or parental status; however, this does not apply to actions in tort. (Rule TR 17[D]).

Infant or incompetent person may sue or be sued in any action: (1) In his own name, (2) in his own name by his guardian ad litem or a next friend, or (3) in name of his court-appointed representative. (Rule TR 17[C]).

One or more members of a class may be sued or sue as representative parties on behalf of all if statutory prerequisites are met. (Rule TR 23).

All persons may be joined in one action as plaintiffs or defendants if they assert or if there is asserted against them any right of relief jointly, severally, or in alternative, they arise out of same transaction or occurrence, or series of transactions or occurrences and if any question of law or fact common to all these persons will arise in action. (Rule TR 20).

Person who is subject to service of process can be joined by court as party in action if person is needed for just adjudication. (Rule TR 19).

Joinder of assignor or transferor of a claim will not be required in a suit by assignee who establishes his title by appropriate pleading and proof, but such assignor or transferor shall be subject to permissive joinder as provided in Rule TR 20. (Rule TR 19[E]).

Court may order substitution of proper parties upon death, incompetency, or transfer of interest. (Rule TR 25).

Intervention is allowed, as of right or by permission, on application in certain statutory instances, or where applicant's ability to protect property may be affected, or where applicant's claim or defense and main action have common question of law or fact. (Rule TR 24).

Interpleader of other parties by either defendant or plaintiff is permitted when other parties have, or are asserting, claims which may expose plaintiff or defendant to double or multiple liability. (Rule TR 22).

Third Party Practice.—Defendant may implead person not party to action who is or may be liable to him for all or part of plaintiff's claim against him. When counterclaim or other claim is asserted against plaintiff, he may bring in third party under circumstances that would entitle defendant to do so. (Rule TR 14).

Joinder of Causes of Action.—Party asserting a claim for relief may join as many claims as he has against opposing party. Whenever claim is one heretofore cognizable only after another claim has been prosecuted to a conclusion, two claims may be joined in a single action; but court can grant relief in that action only in accordance with relative substantive rights of parties. (Rule TR 18).

Consolidation of Actions.—Courts have broad discretion to consolidate actions which involve common questions of law or fact, and to order joint hearings or trials of any or all of matters in issue. (Rule TR 42[A]).

Severance of Actions.—Court may order parties dropped or added at any stage of action and on such terms as are just and will avoid delay. Any claim against a party may be severed and proceeded with separately. (Rule TR 21[A]). Incorrect names and misnomers may be corrected by amendment. (Rule TR 21 [A]; Rule TR 15). Courts have broad discretion to order separate trials of claims, cross-claims, counterclaims, third-party claims, or any separate issue when convenient or to avoid prejudice. (Rule TR 42[B]).

Stay of Proceedings.—Appeals in eminent domain actions do not stay proceedings. (IC32-11-1-5).

Survival of Action.—If individual who is entitled or liable in cause of action dies, action survives by or against decedent's representative, except actions for libel, slander, malicious prosecution, false imprisonment and invasion of privacy. (IC34-9-3-1). In actions for personal injuries which were reduced to judgment, and were thereafter reversed on appeal for new trial, such actions survive death of plaintiff. (IC34-9-3-5). If person receives personal injuries caused by wrongful act or omission of another, and subsequently dies from causes other than those personal injuries, decedent's personal representative may maintain action against wrongdoer to recover all damages resulting before date of death from those injuries to which decedent would have been entitled had decedent lived. Damages inure to exclusive benefit of decedent's estate. (IC34-9-3-4).

Prohibited Actions.—All civil causes of action for breach of promise to marry, alienation of affections, criminal conversation or seduction of female over 18 years old are abolished (IC34-12-2-1) and contracts and instruments executed after June 10, 1935 which are in settlement or compromise of such causes of action are void (IC34-9-3-7).

There are criminal penalties for knowingly filing suit on such causes of action. (IC34-12-2-3).

Limitation of.—See topic Limitation of Actions.

Direct Actions Against Insurer.—See category Transportation, topic Motor Vehicles, subhead Direct Actions.

Small Claims.—See category Courts and Legislature, topic Courts.

APPEAL AND ERROR:

Appeals (except application to Supreme Court for writs) are generally covered by Rule TR 59 and Rules of Appellate Procedure. Motion to correct errors addressed to trial court is prerequisite to appeal only when party seeks to address: (1) Newly discovered material capable of production within 30 days of final judgment but which in exercise of reasonable diligence could not have been discovered and produced at trial; or (2) claim that monetary award is excessive or inadequate. (Rule TR59[A]). Motion to correct error must be filed not later than 30 days after final judgment or appealable final order. (Rule TR59[C]). Motions to correct error not timely set for hearing or ruled upon may be deemed denied by procedure specified in Rule TR 53.3.

Appeal is initiated by filing with clerk of trial court within 30 days after: (1) Court's ruling on motion to correct errors, (2) motion to correct error is deemed denied under TR53.3, (3) entry of final judgment, or (4) entry of appealable final order, praecipe designating what is to be included in record of proceedings; otherwise, right to appeal forfeited. (Rule AP 2).

Within 14 days after filing praecipe or, in case of interlocutory appeal under Appellate Rule 4(B)(6), with petition to Court of Appeals requesting permission to file

APPEAL AND ERROR . . . *continued*
interlocutory appeal, notice of appeal shall be filed. (Rule AP 2[C]). Notice of appeal shall include party information, trial information, record information, and appeal information. (Rule AP 2[C][1]). Following documents must be attached to notice of appeal: (a) in civil cases, copy of judgment or order appealed from, to include findings of fact and conclusions, where made; (b) in criminal cases, copy of judgment or order appealed from, to include any sentencing order; (c) copy of any motion to correct errors filed in trial courts; and (d) copy of praecipe. (Rule AP 2[C][1]). Copy of notice of appeal format is found in Indiana Appellate Rules. (Rule AP 2[C]). No record, motion or other documents of proceedings can be filed with Clerk until notice of appeal has been filed. (Rule AP 2[C][1]).

Appearances.—Party initiating appeal to Supreme Court, Court of Appeals or Tax Court must file appearance form with clerk of respective court contemporaneously with first document filed. Other parties participating in appeal must file appearance form within 30 days of filing of initiating party's appearance or contemporaneously with first document filed, whichever comes first. Suggested form is set out in Rule AP 2.1. (Rule AP 2.1). Notice of Appeal filed pursuant to Rule AP 2(C) will satisfy requirement to file appearance pursuant to Rule AP 2.1. (Rule AP 2[C]).

Pre-Appeal Conference.—Court of Appeals may direct, or parties may request, pre-appeal conference to consider simplification of issues, stipulations of fact, designation of what record is necessary, scheduling, settlement and other matters which may aid in disposition of appeal. Failure to participate in pre-appeal conference, gross unpreparedness for conference or unreasonable refusal to stipulate to relevant record or facts can result in sanctions. (Rule AP 2[D]).

From Courts of General Jurisdiction.—Final judgments of circuit, superior, probate, criminal, juvenile, county, and municipal courts, or ruling or order by trial court granting or denying motion to correct errors will be deemed to be final judgment from which appeal may be taken. (Rule AP 4[A]). Supreme Court has exclusive jurisdiction of admission to practice law; discipline of attorneys and judges; unauthorized practice of law; supervision of exercise of jurisdiction; writs necessary to aid its jurisdiction; appeals in criminal cases where sentence is death, life imprisonment or minimum sentence greater than 50 years for single offense, and appeal from denial of post-conviction relief where sentence was death or life imprisonment; cases where federal or state statute has been declared unconstitutional; transfers of cases of great public importance and urgency. (Rule AP 4[A]). In all other cases, appeal must be taken to Court of Appeals. (Rule AP 4[B]).

On appeal, records of proceedings must be filed in office of Clerk of Supreme Court and Court of Appeals within 90 days from date praecipe is filed, except that if statute under which appeal or review is taken fixes shorter time it shall control. (Rule AP 3[B]). In appeals from interlocutory orders (as limited by Rule AP 4[B]), record must be filed within 30 days of order. (Rule AP 3[B]). Appellant's brief and eight copies must be filed within 30 days of filing of record of proceedings and appellee's brief shall be filed within 30 days after filing of appellant's brief; appellant shall file reply brief within next 15 days; times are altered for interlocutory appeals to ten days from filing of record for appellant's brief, and ten days therefrom for appellee's brief and five days therefrom for appellant's reply brief. (Rules AP 9[B]; AP 8.1).

Court to which Appeal is Taken.—Appellate Rules of Procedure specify jurisdiction of Supreme Court and of Court of Appeals. (Rule AP 4).

Petitions for extension of time to file record are subjected to technical requirements and must be filed at least five days before expiration of time. Separate notice to opposing party or his counsel is required in all instances. No extensions as to briefs are granted in appeals from Industrial Board, and no extensions are granted or allowed as to briefs on or petitions for rehearing or transfer. (Rule AP 14, 11[B][8]).

Petitions for rehearing before either court must be filed within 30 days of decision along with any optional brief. Opposing party has 15 days to file brief. After ruling on rehearing, losing party may seek transfer to Supreme Court by petition and optional briefs to be filed within 30 days of said ruling and opposed by optional brief within 15 days. There are very technical requirements as to such petition, and grounds are limited to: (a) Decision contravenes ruling precedent of Supreme Court; (b) decision erroneously decides new question of law; (c) conflict between decision and prior opinion of Court of Appeals; (d) decision correctly follows precedent of Supreme Court but precedent should be overruled; (e) decision fails to give opinion in writing on question properly raised; (f) decision erroneously and materially misstates record. (Rule AP 11).

Mandate and Prohibition Writs.—Separate rules apply to procedure for seeking writs of mandate and prohibition from Supreme Court. (See Rules of Procedure for Original Actions.)

Certification of Questions from Federal Courts.—Rule AP 15(O) allows Supreme Court of U.S. and circuit courts of appeals to certify questions under Indiana law where there is no clear controlling precedent of Supreme Court of Indiana on questions or propositions of Indiana law.

Bonds.—No bond necessary to perfect appeal from any judgment or appealable interlocutory order; however, bond generally required to stay enforcement during appeal. Trial court can fix and approve bond and order stay prior to and pending appeal. At any time after trial court denial of stay, appellate court can grant or deny stay and fix bond. (Rule TR62[D], AP 6[B]).

Appeals prosecuted by nonresident without bond sufficient to secure payment of costs may be dismissed unless bond sufficient to cover costs is filed within time fixed by court. (Rule AP 6[A]).

Bonds on appeal from the appointment of a receiver are governed by a special statute which requires them to be given within ten days from the appointment of receiver and to be for amount required of receiver as bond. Filing of such bond with perfecting of appeal suspends authority of receiver until final termination of appeal. (IC34-1-12-10).

But government organizations, executors, administrators, guardians, and other court appointed representatives may have stay on appeal without filing bond. (Rule TR 62[E]; AP6[B]).

Appeal bonds in criminal cases are governed by criminal code which prohibits them in certain serious cases, sets qualifications for sureties, requires certain terms in bonds, and sets penalties for noncompliance. (IC35-33-9-1 to 4).

Stay of Proceedings.—Enforcement of judgment or appealable interlocutory order generally will be suspended during appeal upon giving of adequate bond with approved sureties. Appellate court may reconsider trial court denial of stay. (Rule TR62[D], AP 6[B]).

In its discretion court may suspend enforcement of judgment during pendency of motion to correct errors, for judgment on evidence, for new trial, or judgment for relief from judgment. (Rule TR62[B]). In its discretion court may modify order for specific relief during appeal. (Rule TR62[C]). Certified appeal from interlocutory order does not stay proceedings except by court order. (Rule AP 4[B][6][c]).

Court rules preserve prior case law which exempts certain judgments from stay pending appeal. (Rule TR62[D][3]).

In criminal cases appeal from conviction stays execution only if sentence is death or if court orders stay of judgment for fine and costs. State appeal does not affect judgment until reversal. (IC35-38-4-4 to 6). If criminal defendant is released on bail during appeal, conviction is stayed until disposition of appeal. (IC35-33-9-5).

BONDS:

Bond must be filed before relief is granted in following classes of civil cases: (1) Attachment; (2) arrest; (3) injunction, where injunction or restraining order demanded before final hearing; (4) ne exeat; (5) replevin suits in which possession of property is demanded before final hearing; (6) will contests; and (7) ejectment. See also topic Appeal and Error, subhead Bonds.

Bail Agents.—Must be approved by insurance commissioner and appointed by insurer qualified to transact surety business in Indiana. (IC27-10-1-4). If defendant fails to appear, bail agent must produce defendant or prove, within 365 days, that defendant could not appear (1) by reason of defendant's illness or death; (2) because defendant was in custody of U.S., state, or political subdivision; or (3) because required notice was not given; and that defendant's absence was without consent or connivance of surety. (IC27-10-2-12). If bail agent fails to comply with these requirements within 120 days after mailing of notice, late surrender fee is charged according to statutory schedule. (IC27-10-2-12). Licensure and regulation of bail agents and runners are controlled by IC27-10-3-1 to -3-18 and 760 IAC 1-6.2-1 to 6.2-10.

Defective Official Bonds.—Official bonds entered into by any officer in discharge of duties of his office that contain certain defects are cured by statute. (IC34-1-64-1).

Fixed Sum.—If not provided by statute, judge fixes amount of bond as he deems adequate but not less than $100. (IC34-2-33-1).

Foreign Bonds.—Domiciliary foreign personal representative may file authenticated copies of official bond with court. (IC29-2-1-5; IC29-1-11-1).

Personal Representative.—Personal representative of estate not required to file bond unless will or court so provides. (IC29-1-11-1).

Public Officials.—Bonding of public officials provided for. (IC5-4-1 to 5-4-5).

Public Welfare Directors.—Official bonds of county directors of public welfare upon appointment are $5,000 for counties having population less than 100,000 according to last U.S. Census, and $10,000 for counties having population of 100,000 or more according to last U.S. Census. (470 IAC 1-2-8).

CERTIORARI:

Application to Court on appeal for certiorari requires a clear designation of part of record asserted to be defective, improperly omitted, or improperly incorporated in transcript. Affidavits are permitted to be filed in support of application. Respective parties may file briefs but oral argument will not be heard. (Rule AP 15[D]). See also Rule AP 7.2(C); Rule AP 11(B).

CHARITABLE IMMUNITY:

See topic Damages.

COMMISSIONS TO TAKE TESTIMONY:

See topic Depositions and Discovery.

COSTS:

In all civil actions, the party recovering judgment shall recover costs, except in those cases in which different provision is made by law. Prevailing party may recover attorneys' fees if suit was frivolous or litigated in bad faith. (IC34-1-32-1). Costs allowed to prevailing party as matter of course unless court otherwise directs. Costs may be computed and taxed by clerk on one day's notice. On motion served within five days thereafter, action of clerk may be reviewed by court. (Rule TR54[D]).

DAMAGES:

Common law prevails as to compensatory damages.

Indiana follows "impact rule" and damages for mental suffering may be awarded only if such condition arises from physical injury or certain torts likely to invade legal rights and cause emotional trauma. (621 F. Supp. 244, 331 F.2d 241). Physical impact must occur prior to or simultaneously with infliction of emotional distress. (587 N.E.2d 118).

"Impact rule" does not apply to prohibit recovery for emotional distress when sustained in course of tortious trespass (570 N.E.2d 27) or when conduct causing injury inspired by fraud, malice, or like motives and conduct was intentional (545 N.E.2d 572), or when plaintiff sustains direct impact and sustains emotional trauma serious in nature and of kind normally expected to occur in reasonable person (579 N.E.2d 452). Even where defendant's conduct is extreme and outrageous, plaintiff must show defendant intentionally or recklessly caused plaintiff's emotional problems to recover for intentional infliction of emotional distress. (587 N.E.2d 118).

See note at head of Digest as to 1998 legislation covered.

See Topical Index in front part of this volume.

DAMAGES . . . *continued*

Punitive damages must be proven by clear and convincing evidence (IC34-51-3-2) and may not exceed greater of three times amount of compensatory damages or $50,000. Seventy-five percent of punitive damages award is deposited in State's Violent Crime Victim's Compensation Fund. (IC34-51-3-5 and 6). Immunity from damages in civil actions extends to all persons who gratuitously render care at scene of an accident or emergency, except acts or omissions amounting to gross negligence or willful or wanton misconduct. (IC34-6-2-51).

Similar rule exists for persons who make gifts of food to charitable entities unless damages result from that person's intentional, knowing or reckless misconduct (IC34-30-12-1) and for persons who, without compensation, attempt to prevent harm from discharge of hazardous substance at scene of emergency (IC34-6-2-55, 34-30-13-1 et seq.).

Immunity is available to "mental health service providers" under some circumstances for failing to warn or protect persons from violent patient. (IC34-30-16-1 et seq.).

Charitable Immunity.—Doctrine of charitable immunity has been abolished. (250 Ind. 491, 237 N.E.2d 242).

Sovereign Immunity.—Immunity is available to governmental entities in some situations (IC34-13-3-1 et seq.), and political subdivisions may enter structured settlements (IC34-13-3-23). Notice requirement for claims against State and local governments. (IC34-13-3-6 and 8). Immunity exists in other unique circumstances.

Immunity from damages in civil actions extends to certain volunteer directors for liability arising from negligent performance of volunteer directors' duties. (IC34-30-4-1 et seq.).

Damages are available to persons suffering pecuniary loss from certain crimes (theft, conversion, criminal confinement, interference with custody, etc.) in amount not to exceed three times actual loss in addition to costs of action, reasonable attorney's fees, certain travel expenses, and compensation for time lost to file papers and attend proceedings and all other reasonable costs of collection. (IC34-24-3-1).

Prejudgment interest in tort actions shall be computed by court at simple rate between 6% and 10% per year. (IC34-51-4-9). Prejudgment interest is not available if certain conditions are either satisfied by defendant or not satisfied by plaintiff. (IC34-51-4-5).

Punitive damages are recoverable in actions where there is clear and convincing evidence that defendant acted with malice, gross fraud, oppressive conduct or heedless disregard of consequences. (622 N.E.2d 515). Punitive damages are not recoverable in breach of contract action absent pleading and proof of independent tort. (608 N.E.2d 975). Without compensatory damages, there can be no punitive damages. (622 N.E.2d 515). Rapidly developing case law in area of punitive damages must be consulted for specifics. Punitive damages may be no more than greater of: (1) three times amount of compensatory damages awarded in action; or (2) $50,000. (IC34-51-3-4). If trier of fact awards more than these amounts, court shall reduce punitive damage award within foregoing limits. Party against whom punitive damages are awarded shall pay amount of punitive damages to court. Upon receiving payment, court shall (1) pay person to whom punitive damages were awarded 25% of punitive damage award; and (2) pay remaining 75% of punitive damage award to treasurer of state, who shall deposit funds into violent crime victims compensation fund. (IC34-51-3-6). Jury shall not be advised of limitation on punitive damages or distribution of punitive damages.

Comparative Fault Rule has been adopted providing that plaintiffs may not recover if fault attributed to them is 51% or more. (IC34-51-2-1 et seq.). Defendant may assert as defense that damages of claimant were caused in full or in part by nonparty. (IC34-51-2-14).

Medical Malpractice Act.—(IC34-18-1-1 et seq.). If action qualifies under IC34-18-1-1 et seq., then total amount recoverable for any injury or death of patient may not exceed $500,000. That limit was increased to $750,000 for malpractice occurring after Jan. 1, 1990. (IC34-18-14-3). Act applies to all "qualified" health care providers, and maximum recovery from health care provider is $250,000. (IC34-18-14-3).

No-Fault Insurance.—Not adopted.

Uniform Contribution Among Tortfeasors Act.—Not adopted.

See also category Estates and Trusts, topic Death, subhead Actions for Death.

DECLARATORY JUDGMENTS:

See topic Judgments.

DEPOSITIONS AND DISCOVERY:

After commencement of action, any party may take testimony of any person, including a party, by oral or written deposition. (Rules TR 30-31). Leave of court, granted with or without notice, must be obtained only if plaintiff seeks to take oral deposition prior to expiration of 20 days after service of summons and complaint upon any defendant except that leave is not required: (1) If defendant has served notice of taking deposition or otherwise sought discovery, or (2) if special notice is given as provided in subdivision (B)(2) of Trial Rule 30. (Rule TR 30[A]).

Uniform Foreign Depositions Act not adopted.

Outside of State for Use within State.—See subhead Before Whom Taken, infra.

Within State for Use Elsewhere.—Court of this state may order a person domiciled or found within this state to give his testimony or statement, to produce documents or other things, to allow inspections and copies, or to permit physical and mental examination for use in proceeding in tribunal outside this state. (Rule TR 28[E]).

Perpetuating Testimony.—Person who desires to perpetuate his own testimony or that of another person regarding any matter that may be cognizable in any such court in which action may be commenced, may file verified petition in any court of this state. Deposition may be used in any action involving same subject matter subsequently brought in court of this state in accordance with provision of Rule 32. (Rule TR 27).

Before Whom Taken.—Depositions may be taken within U.S., territory or insular possession of U.S. before officer authorized to administer oaths or before person appointed for that purpose by court in which action is pending. Depositions may be taken in foreign countries before person authorized to administer oaths in place in which examination is held; before person commissioned by court; or pursuant to interrogatory. No deposition can be taken before person who is relative or employee or attorney or counsel of any of parties, or is relative or employee of such attorney or counsel, or is financially interested in action. (Rule TR 28).

Unless court orders otherwise, parties may by written stipulation provide that depositions may be taken before any person, at any time or place, upon any notice and in any manner and may by written stipulation modify procedures provided by these rules for other methods of discovery. (Rule TR 29).

Compelling Attendance of Witnesses.—Attendance of witnesses may be compelled by use of subpoena as provided in Rule 45. (Rule TR 30[A]). Failure to obey subpoena without adequate excuse may be deemed contempt. (Rule TR 45[F]). See Rule TR 45(D).

Witnesses.—Depositions of person confined in prison may be taken only by leave of court on such terms as court prescribes. (Rule TR 30[A]). Organization may be named as deponent and matter on which examination is requested designated with reasonable particularity. Organization must designate appropriate individual to testify on its behalf. (Rule TR 30[B]).

Notice.—Party desiring to take deposition of any person upon oral examination must give reasonable notice in writing to every other party to action. (Rule TR 30[B]). Notice shall state time and place for taking deposition and name and address of each person to be examined, if known, and if name is not known, general description sufficient to identify him or particular class or group to which he belongs. If subpoena duces tecum is to be served on person to be examined, designation of material to be produced thereunder shall be attached to or included in notice. (Rule TR 30 [B]).

Party desiring to take deposition upon written questions must serve them upon every party with notice stating name and address of deponent and officer before whom deposition is to be taken. (Rule TR 31).

When Used.—Any deposition may be used by any party for purpose of contradicting or impeaching testimony of deponent as witness. (Rule TR 32[A]).

Deposition of party, agent, or anyone who at time of deposition is officer, director, managing agent, executive officer, or person designated under Rule 30(B)(6) or 31(A) to testify on behalf of organization may be used by adverse party for any purpose. (Rule TR 32[A]).

Any part or all of a deposition may be used against any party who was present or represented at taking of deposition, by or against any party who had reasonable notice thereof or by any party in whose favor it was given in accordance with provisions of Rule 32(A)(1)-(4). (Rule TR 32[A]).

Deposition of a witness may be used by any party for any purpose, so far as admissible under rules of evidence applied as though witness were then present and testifying, if court finds: (1) That witness is dead; or (2) that witness is outside state; or (3) that witness is unable to attend because of age, sickness, infirmity, or imprisonment; or (4) that party offering deposition has been unable to procure attendance of witness by subpoena; or (5) exceptional circumstances exist; or (6) by agreement of parties. (Rule TR 32[A]).

Examination of Witness.—Examination and cross-examination of witness may proceed as permitted at trial under provisions of Rule 43(B). Officer before whom deposition is to be taken must put witness on oath and must record testimony of witness. All objections made at time of examination must be noted by officer upon deposition. (Rule TR 30[C]).

When testimony is fully transcribed, deposition must be submitted to witness for reading and signing unless waived by witness and by each party. Deposition should then be signed by witness or upon refusal to sign within 30 days of its submission to him, officer must execute certificate and cause certificate to be delivered to party taking it. (Rule TR 30[E]).

Court may, for cause shown, enlarge or shorten time for taking deposition or grant any protective relief requested. (Rule TR 30[B] and Rule TR 26[C]).

Certificate and Filing.—Officer must certify on deposition that witness was duly sworn by him and that deposition is a true record of testimony given by witness. He must then securely seal deposition in envelope indorsed with title of action and marked "Deposition of (here insert name of witness)" and must promptly deliver it to party taking deposition. Officer must give prompt notice to all parties of its delivery to party taking deposition. (Rule TR 30[F]).

Form

The following form may be used:

Deposition of . . . ., a witness produced before and sworn by me, a notary public of . . . ., at . . . ., in the county of . . . ., and state of . . . ., on the . . . ., day of . . . ., 19. . . ., in pursuance to the notice hereto attached (and commission, if any), in a cause now pending in the . . . . court, of . . . . county, in the State of Indiana, wherein . . . . is plaintiff, and . . . . is defendant, on the part of said . . . . .

Appearances for the plaintiff: . . . . .

Appearances for the defendant: . . . . .

The said . . . ., having been first duly sworn by me, to testify the truth, the whole truth, and nothing but the truth, relating to the said cause, deposes and says as follows:

Questions by . . . . .

Question 1. . . . . .

Answer. . . . . .

(And so on, all questions being numbered consecutively.)

State of . . . ., county of . . . ., ss.:

I, ..., a . . . ., in and for the said county, do hereby certify that . . . ., the above named witness, was first by me duly sworn according to law, to testify the truth, the whole truth, and nothing but the truth, relating to the above named cause; that the foregoing deposition was reduced to writing by me (by said deponent, [or by . . . ., a

DEPOSITIONS AND DISCOVERY . . . *continued*

disinterested person], in my presence, and under my direction); that the said . . . ., (adverse party) attended the taking of the said deposition in person (by . . . ., his attorney), (was not present or represented at the taking of the said deposition); and that the said deposition was taken at . . . ., in the county of . . . ., and state of . . . ., on the . . . . day of . . . ., 19. . . ., between the hours of . . . . A. M., and . . . . P. M.

In witness whereof I have hereunto set my hand and my official seal this . . . . day of . . . ., 19. . . . . (Signature). County of Residence . . . .

EQUITY:

See topic Actions.

EVIDENCE:

Rules of Evidence.—Indiana courts follow Indiana Rules of Evidence which are modeled on Federal Rules of Evidence.

Witnesses.—All persons, including parties, are competent except insane persons insane at time they are offered as witnesses, whether they have been so adjudged or not. (IC34-1-14-4, 5).

See also topic Depositions and Discovery.

Privileged Communications.—The following communications are privileged: (a) to attorneys as to confidential communications made to them in course of their professional business and as to advice given professionally; (b) to physicians as to matters told them by patients, in course of their professional business, or advice given by them professionally; (c) to clergymen as to confessions and admissions made to them in the course of discipline enjoined by their respective churches; and (d) between husband and wife as to communications made to each other subject to limitations noted below. (IC34-1-14-5).

Husband and Wife.—A spouse may testify as to communications made in the presence of third persons and business transactions, or in dissolution proceedings.

Accountant and Client.—Information derived from or as result of provision of professional accounting services is confidential and privileged. (IC25-2-1-23).

Subpoena.—Upon application of any party to an action, witness may be served with subpoena on trial anywhere in state and thereby require his attendance. Attorney admitted to practice law in Indiana, may also issue subpoena on behalf of (a) court in which attorney has approval on behalf of party or (b) court in which deposition or production is compelled by subpoena, if deposition or production pertains to action pending in court where attorney has approval for party in that case. (Rule TR45[A]). When permitted by laws of U.S., this or another state or foreign country, court may authorize service of subpoena outside state. (Rule TR 45[E]).

Communications or Transactions with Persons Since Deceased or Incompetent.—Where a judgment may be rendered for or against an estate involving matters occurring during the lifetime of the decedent, a necessary party to proceedings with interest adverse to the estate is not a competent witness except as to matters testified to by the decedent in a deposition or otherwise prior to his death. (IC34-1-14-6). In suits by or against heirs or devisees founded on contract with or against ancestor concerning property, neither party to such suit shall be competent witness as to any matter which occurred prior to death of ancestor. (IC34-1-14-7). Agent contracting with decedent shall be competent witness in suit on such contract only if called by representatives of decedent and only to extent that he is interrogated by them. In suits for conversion or damage to personalty, defense that acts were done as excecutor, administrator, guardian, or heir, as such, renders incompetent any person who would not be competent if person so defending were complainant. When, on behalf of estate, decedent's agent testifies as to his transactions as agent with party to suit or his privy and in absence of decedent, party against whom this evidence is introduced is competent to testify. If any witness testifies on behalf of estate as to any conversations or admissions of party to suit, or his privies, as having been had or made in absence of deceased, party against whom such evidence is introduced becomes competent. (IC34-1-14-8). Assignors of parties incompetent under preceding sections are likewise incompetent in suits involving estates except that they be called by adverse party in its discretion. (IC34-1-14-10). Adversely interested parties are incompetent in suits by or against insane persons in actions on contract or affecting property, unless insane person is adjudged competent to testify. This section is inapplicable when party is called by adverse party. (IC34-2-20-1).

Experts may be compelled to testify in any court in county of residence of witness or any court in adjoining county on normal per diem and mileage allowed other witnesses. (IC34-1-14-12).

Self-incrimination.—No person in any criminal proceeding may be compelled to testify against himself. (Const., Art. 1, §14).

INJUNCTIONS:

Jurisdiction.—Injunctions and restraining orders may be granted (a) by Supreme Court, or justice thereof when necessary and proper for exercise of jurisdiction and powers of court or (b) by circuit courts, or by judges thereof in vacations, and temporary injunctions and restraining orders only, by judges of adjoining circuits when regular judge is unavailable. (IC34-26-1-2). Other courts are in specific cases given concurrent jurisdiction with circuit courts. (See category Courts and Legislature, topic Courts.) Appellate Court has in practice issued injunctions. (28 Ind. App. 185, 62 N.E. 520).

Prerequisites.—Plaintiff must show by his complaint that he is entitled to some relief consisting in restraining commission or continuance of some act, commission or continuance of which during litigation would produce great injury to plaintiff. During litigation plaintiff is entitled to injunctive relief if it appears that defendant is doing, or threatens, or is about to do, or is procuring or suffering some act to be done, in violation of plaintiff's rights, respecting subject of action, and tending to render judgment ineffectual, or when such relief consists in restraining proceedings upon any final order or judgment. Temporary injunction may be granted to restrain removal or disposition of property which defendant threatens or is about to move or dispose of with intent to defraud his creditors. (IC34-26-1-5 and 6). Remedies in addition to use of injunctions are provided for Securities Commission. (IC23-2-1-17.1).

Bond.—No restraining order or preliminary injunction will be issued except upon giving of security by applicant, as court deems proper, for payment of such costs and damages as may be incurred or suffered by any party who is found to have been wrongfully enjoined or restrained. (Rule TR 65[C]). If a bond is given upon a temporary injunction or upon a restraining order, no second bond is required upon granting of permanent injunction unless first bond is deemed insufficient. (IC34-26-1-10).

Procedure.—Applications for injunctions must be verified by affidavit. (IC34-26-1-7). Notice to opposing parties is necessary before injunction can issue. (Rule TR 65[A]). However, temporary restraining order may be issued in emergencies until notice can be given. (Rule TR 65[B]). In hearing on application for temporary restraining order or injunction it is proper to read affidavits or documentary or record evidence. (IC34-26-1-8). Court may impose conditions upon granting or continuing of injunction. (IC34-26-1-9). Writs of injunctions are not issued but instead order of court certified by clerk is served upon adverse party. (IC34-26-1-11). Injunctions may be enforced by contempt proceedings when it appears there has been willful disobedience of order. (IC34-26-1-14, 15 and 16).

Motion to Dissolve or Modify.—Upon court's own motion or motion of any party, orders granting or denying temporary restraining order or preliminary injunction may be dissolved, modified, granted, or reinstated. (Rule TR 65[A]).

When appeal is taken from interlocutory or final judgment granting, dissolving, or denying injunction, court may suspend, modify, restore, or grant injunction as it considers proper for security of rights of adverse party. (Rule TR 62[C]). See Rule TR 65.1.

Labor Disputes.—Issuance of injunctions in labor disputes is limited to cases prescribed in statute. (IC22-6-1-1, IC22-6-1-12, IC22-6-2-14).

Nuisance Actions.—Issuance of injunctions or restraining orders in nuisance actions is further governed by IC34-19-1.

Indecent Nuisance.—Issuance of injunctions or restraining orders in actions for indecent nuisance is further governed by IC34-19-2.

Racketeering Activities.—Issuance of injunctions or restraining orders with respect to civil remedies for racketeering activities is further governed by IC34-24-2.

JUDGMENTS:

Appeals may be taken by either party from all final judgments including ruling or order by trial court granting or denying Motion to Correct Error. (Rule AP 4[A]). Upon verdict or decision announced, court must promptly prepare and sign judgment and clerk must thereupon enter it. Judgment must be set forth on separate document, except judgment may appear on same document with court's findings, conclusions, or opinion upon issues. (Rule TR 58).

Default Judgment.—When party against whom judgment for affirmative relief is sought has failed to plead or otherwise defend party may be defaulted. In all cases party entitled to judgment by default can apply to court therefor. Judgment by default may be entered against governmental organization. (Rule TR 55). Default judgment can be set aside by court for reasons including mistake, excusable neglect, newly discovered evidence, fraud or fact that default judgment was entered against party who was served only by publication and who was without actual knowledge of action and judgment. (Rule TR 60[B]).

Confession of Judgment.—Authority to confess judgment, made before cause of action accrues on any negotiable instrument or other written contract to pay money, is void. (IC34-54-3-1 to 3). Whenever confession of judgment is made by power of attorney or otherwise, party confessing must make affidavit that debt is just and owing and that confession will not defraud creditors, and affidavit must be filed with court. (IC34-54-2-3).

Declaratory Judgments.—Uniform Declaratory Judgments Act adopted. (IC34-14-1-1 to 16).

Declaratory relief may be allowed even though property right is not involved. Affirmative relief may be allowed under such remedy when right thereto is established. (Rule TR 57).

Summary Judgments.—Claimant may move for summary judgment after expiration of 20 days from commencement of action. Motion may be filed by defending party at any time. Court shall hold hearing not less than ten days from filing of motion by defending party. Partial summary judgment expressly permitted. (Rule TR 56).

Offer of Judgment.—At any time more than ten days before trial begins, a party defending against a claim may serve upon adverse party an offer to allow judgment to be taken against him with costs then accrued. If offer is accepted within ten days after service, either party may then file offer and notice of acceptance together with proof of service thereof and thereupon clerk will enter judgment. If final judgment obtained by offeree is not more favorable than offer, offeree must pay costs incurred after making of offer. (Rule TR 68).

Support Judgments.—Any payment delinquent under child support order is judgment against individual obligated to make payment under order, and is lien against real and personal property of that individual. (IC31-16-16-2 to 3). Upon application to court for enforcement of support order, court may enforce judgment created under IC31-16-16-2, or may issue or activate income withholding order. (IC31-16-12-4). When court finds that person is delinquent court shall issue order to bureau of motor vehicles, board regulating practice of person's profession or occupation, Indiana horse racing commission, Indiana gaming commission, commissioner of department of insurance as appropriate. (IC31-16-12-6 to 10).

Lien.—Judgment of court of record is a lien on all defendant's real estate within county where rendered and becomes a lien on real estate in any other county on filing of transcript in such county. Lien continues for ten years. (IC34-55-9-2; IC33-17-2-3).

See note at head of Digest as to 1998 legislation covered.

See Topical Index in front part of this volume.

IN – 16

JUDGMENTS . . . continued

Limitation.—After lapse of ten years from entry, judgment can be enforced only on leave of court upon proof that judgment remains unsatisfied, and only after ten days notice to adverse party. (IC34-55-1-2).

Relief from Judgment.—Clerical mistakes in judgments and orders may be corrected by court at any time before record is filed on appeal of its own initiative or on motion of any party. On motion and upon such terms as are just, court may relieve party from final judgment, order, default, or proceeding for reasons that include mistake, excusable neglect, newly discovered evidence, and fraud. (Rule TR 60). Order denying or granting relief is final judgment from which appeal may be taken. (Rule TR 60).

Revivor of Judgments.—Claim based upon judgment against party who dies before or after judgment is entered must be allowed by court administering his estate. Judgments upon an action against party who dies must be satisfied from assets of his estate by decedent's representative. (Rule TR 25[E]).

Assignment.—Judgments of courts of record for the recovery of money may be assigned by plaintiff or complainant. Assignees successively on or attached to entry of judgment and assignment, and when attested by clerk of court vests title to judgment in each assignee successively. (IC34-54-7-1 to 4). There may be equitable assignment of judgment without complying with statute. (20 Ind. App. 169, 49 N.E. 856).

Satisfaction.—Every endorsement of payment, satisfaction or release in whole or in part upon the record or margin thereof of any judgment or decree, or upon any execution or order of sale issued thereon, signed by the judgment plaintiff or his attorney of record or attorney in fact or by the assignee of such judgment plaintiff (whose assignment is upon or annexed to the record of such judgment and attested by the clerk), upon the record of such judgment or decree or by the sheriff upon such execution or order of sale, operates as a satisfaction or release of such judgment or decree, or of such part thereof so endorsed thereon as paid, satisfied or released, in favor of subsequent purchasers or lienholders in good faith, and when such satisfaction, payment or release is entered by an attorney in fact, such fact must be noted on the margin of the record or the execution, as the case may be, but such power of attorney must be recorded in miscellaneous records of the recorder's office. (IC34-54-6-1).

Unless court directs otherwise, payment of money owing under judgment may be made to judgment creditor or his attorney, to sheriff holding writ of execution, or to clerk of court where judgment is rendered. Person receiving payment or satisfaction of judgment must furnish sheriff, clerk, or person making payment signed statement of total or partial satisfaction and any necessary assignment identifying judgment by cause number and acknowledged as is deed. When delivered to clerk, statement of satisfaction must be entered in records with judgment. (Rule TR 67[B]).

Judgment on Evidence.—Where issues tried before a jury are not supported by sufficient evidence or a verdict thereon is clearly erroneous, court must withdraw such issues from jury and enter judgment thereon or must enter judgment thereon notwithstanding verdict. (Rule TR 50).

Foreign Judgments.—Where it appears that court of general jurisdiction of sister state has entered judgment, rebuttable presumption exists that judgment is valid. (160 Ind. App. 244, 311 N.E. 2d 640). In pleading judgment or decision of domestic or foreign court, it is sufficient to aver judgment or decision without setting forth matter showing jurisdiction to render it. (Rule TR 9[E]). Cognovit judgment obtained in another state may be enforced in this state. (223 Ind. 570, 63 N.E.2d 417).

Revised Uniform Enforcement of Foreign Judgments Act not adopted.

LIMITATION OF ACTIONS:

General.—

Fifteen years: Action arising before Sept. 1, 1982, and not limited by any other statute. (IC34-11-1-2).

Ten years: Action arising on or after Sept. 1, 1982, and not limited by any other statute. (IC34-11-1-2).

Specific.—

Fifty years: To rectify certain defects in record title. (IC32-1-5-1 to 10).

Twenty years: On contracts in writing, other than for payment of money if contract entered into before Sept. 1, 1982 (IC34-11-2-11); on real estate mortgages or vendors' liens on real estate created before Sept. 1, 1982, time running from date when last installment became due, or if mortgage does not show when debt became due, from date of mortgage or, if that date be not shown, from time of recording (IC32-8-4-1 to 3).

Twelve years: From date of completion of real estate improvement and submission of plans and specifications to owner for action based on deficiency of design (IC34-15-1-2); with additional two year period for personal injury or wrongful death occurring during ninth and tenth years following completion of improvements (IC34-15-1-3).

Ten years: On judgment of courts of record; on deeds of trust; on action for recovery of possession of real estate (IC34-11-2-11); on promissory notes, bills of exchange and other written contracts, for payment of money executed before Sept. 1, 1982 (IC34-11-2-9); for recovery of real property sold under execution by debtor, or any person claiming under him, by title subsequent to date of judgment, if sale of property occurred before Sept. 1, 1982 (IC34-11-2-8); to foreclose lien of series mortgage (IC32-8-19-2); from date of substantial completion of improvement, action based on any deficiency, or alleged deficiency, in design, planning, supervision, construction or observation of construction of improvement to real property, and for injury or death to person or property arising therefrom, with certain exceptions for injuries occurring during ninth and tenth years following substantial improvements (IC34-15-1-2 to 3); on real estate mortgages or vendors' liens on real estate created after Aug. 31, 1982, time running from when last installment becomes due (IC32-8-4-1); on written contracts other than for payment of money entered into after Aug. 31, 1982 (IC34-11-2-11).

Six years: On accounts and contracts not in writing; for use, rent, or profits of real property; for injuries to real property; damages for detention and for recovery of

personal property; for relief on ground of fraud (except private actions under securities law) (IC34-11-2-7); for moneys collected by public officer (IC34-11-2-6); for recovery of real property sold on execution by debtor or any person claiming under him by title acquired after date of judgment, effective Sept. 1, 1982 (IC34-11-2-8); upon promissory notes, bills of exchange, or other written contracts for payment of money executed after Aug. 31, 1982 (IC34-11-2-9).

Five years: Against a public officer or his sureties (IC34-11-2-6); for recovery of real property sold by fiduciaries under judgment directing sale, by party to judgment or any person claiming under him by title subsequent to date of judgment, time running from confirmation of sale (IC34-11-2-5).

Four Years: On actions for breach of any contract for sale of goods. Cause of action accrues when breach occurs under Commercial Code, regardless of aggrieved party's lack of knowledge of breach. Breach of warranty occurs with tender of delivery except where warranty explicitly extends to future performance and discovery must await performance, with cause of action then accruing when breach is, or should have been discovered. Law on tolling of statute of limitations not altered by these provisions. (IC26-1-2-725).

Three years: On action for railroad transportation charges (IC8-2-21-1); employer's subrogation rights under Workmen's Compensation (IC22-3-2-13); wages under minimum wage law (IC22-2-2-9); private actions under securities laws (IC23-2-1-19[g]).

Two years: For injuries to person or character; for injuries to personal property; for forfeitures of statutory penalties (IC34-11-2-4); for malpractice, two years from act or omission, subject to certain exceptions (IC34-11-2-3; IC34-18-7-1 to 3 but see Martin v. Richey, 674 N.E.2d 1015 [Ind. App. 1997], holding occurrence statute of limitations for medical malpractice unconstitutional); for original claims or modifications arising under Workmen's Compensation (IC22-3-3-3; IC22-3-3-27) and occupational diseases (IC22-3-7-32); in death caused by radiation or asbestos-related diseases two year period starts from date of knowledge of injury (IC22-3-3-3; IC34-20-3-2); for violation of Deceptive Franchise Practices Act (IC23-2-2.7-7); for violation of Deceptive Consumer Sales Act (IC24-5-0.5-5); wrongful death (IC34-23-1-1); actions relating to terms, conditions and privileges of employment not based on written contract (IC34-11-2-1 and 2); paternity actions by mother or father (IC31-14-5-3).

One year: Actions to reopen judgments or invalidate deeds involving foreclosure of public improvement liens (IC32-8-9-1); application for increased permanent partial impairment (IC22-3-3-27); actions to foreclose mechanics' liens (IC32-8-7-1); claims against decedent's estate, following date of decedent's death, subject to certain requirements (IC29-1-14-1).

Five months: Action to contest or resist probate of will in court having jurisdiction over probate of will must be brought within five months after date of order admitting will to probate. (IC29-1-7-17).

30 days for state employee to initiate complaint for change in status of employment. (IC4-15-2-34).

Product Liability Actions.—Any negligence or strict liability product action must be commenced within two years after cause accrues or within ten years after delivery of product to initial user or consumer; except that if cause of action accrues more than eight years but not more then ten years after initial delivery, action may be commenced at any time within two years after action accrues; but this does not affect right of indemnification. (IC34-20-3-1).

Disabilities.—Persons who are under legal disabilities at time cause of action accrued may bring action at any time within two years after removal of disability, though period of limitation has expired. (IC34-11-6-1). Case law defines disabilities, and must be carefully reviewed.

Absence.—The statute will not run during the time of defendant's nonresidence except where there is within the state a person who may be served with process as agent for the defendant. (IC34-11-4-1).

New Actions.—If action fails from any cause except negligence in prosecution, or action abates or is defeated by death, or judgment is arrested or reversed on appeal, new action may be brought within later of: (1) three years after action fails, or (2) last date action could have been commenced under statute of limitations governing original action. (IC34-11-8-1).

Mutual Accounts.—In actions on mutual, open, and current accounts the cause is deemed to have accrued on the date of the last item on either side. (IC34-11-3-1).

Acknowledgment, New Promise, and Partial Payment.—New promise or acknowledgment will not toll statute unless in writing, and signed by party to be charged. Acknowledgment or promise of one joint party does not make other joint party liable. Endorsement or memorandum of payment made upon instrument of writing and by or on behalf of party to whom payment is purported to be made is not sufficient to exempt action from statute of limitations. (IC34-11-9-1 to 4).

Death.—In case of death of person entitled to sue or liable to be sued on any cause of action, before expiration of prescribed period of limitation, cause will survive for or against his representatives or successors, and may be brought within 18 months after date of death, though time limited has expired. (IC34-11-7-1).

Nonresidence.—When cause has been fully barred by laws of place where defendant resides and where cause of action arose, such bar is same defense as though it had arisen in this state. (IC34-11-4-2). See also subhead Absence, supra.

Emergencies.—Where war, insurrection, pestilence or act of God prevents performance of an act essential to conserve substantial rights, proper court official may declare emergency and period of such emergency is excluded from time within which such act must be done. (IC34-7-6-1 to 3).

Counterclaims.—Statute of limitations will not bar a counterclaim to extent that it arises out of subject matter of opposing party's claim. (TR 13[J]).

Pleading.—Statutes of limitations are affirmative defenses and must be affirmatively pleaded. (TR 8[C]).

See also category Business Regulation and Commerce, topics Commercial Code, Sales.

LIMITATION OF ACTIONS...*continued*

Child Support.—Action to enforce child support obligation must be commenced not later than ten years after (1) 18th birthday of child; or (2) emancipation of child; whichever occurs first. (IC34-11-2-10).

Judgment of any court of record considered satisfied after expiration of 20 years. (IC34-11-2-12).

Paternity Action by Child.—Child may file paternity action any time before child reaches 20 years of age. If incompetent at age 18, may file action within two years after becoming competent. (IC31-14-5-2).

PARTITION:

Any person holding lands as joint tenant or tenant in common, whether in his own right or as executor or trustee, may compel partition thereof. Trustees, administrators and executors may also be made defendants in actions for the partition of real estate to answer as to any interest they may have in the same. Any person owning an undivided interest in fee simple in lands and at the same time owning a life estate in the remaining portion of such lands, or any part thereof, may compel partition thereof. Such action is commenced by petition in circuit court or court having probate jurisdiction of county in which such lands are situated, and proceedings, practice and pleadings shall be same as in civil suits, and interlocutory judgment may be entered ordering such partition and appointing commissioners to make such partition, or if land can not be divided without damage to owners, sale may be ordered, with division of proceeds according to respective interests of owners. (IC32-4-5-1 to 23; IC32-4-6-1).

Where one or more persons is or are entitled to an estate in real estate for life or years, or to estate tail, to fee-simple conditional, base or qualified fee, or any particular limited or conditional estate in real estate or any interest in personal property, and any person or persons, whether in being or not, is or are entitled to remainder or remainders, vested or contingent or executory devise or any other interest vested or contingent in the same real estate or personal property, decree may be entered by proceedings in circuit court authorizing sale, exchange or lease of real estate, or sale or exchange of personal property. (IC32-4-8-1 to 3).

PLEADING:

Indiana Rules of Trial Procedure to some extent are based on Federal Rules of Civil Procedure.

Every pleading must contain a caption setting forth name of court, title of action, file number, and designation. In complaint, title of action must include names of all parties, but in other pleadings it is sufficient to state name of first party with appropriate indication of other parties. All averments of claim or defense must be made in numbered paragraphs. (Rule TR 10).

Every pleading of party represented by attorney must be signed by at least one attorney of record in his individual name, whose address, telephone number and attorney number must be stated, except pleadings and motions made and transcribed at trial or hearing before judge and received by him in such form. As in Federal Rule, attorney's signature certifies pleading, and attorney may be subject to sanctions for willfully violating rule. (Rule TR 11).

Pleadings Permitted.—Only pleadings allowed are: complaint, answer, reply to denominated counterclaim, answer to cross-claim, third-party complaint, and third party answer. (Rule TR 7).

Complaint.—Action is commenced when complaint is filed. (Rule TR 3). No technical forms of pleading are required. To state a claim for relief, pleading must contain a short and plain statement of claim showing that pleader is entitled to relief and a demand for relief to which he deems himself entitled. Relief in alternative or of several different types may be demanded. In complaint seeking damages for personal injury or death, or seeking punitive damages, no dollar amount shall be included in demand, which may pray only for reasonable damages. (Rule TR 8).

Answer.—Responsive pleading must state in short and plain terms pleader's defenses to each claim asserted and must admit or controvert averments set forth in complaint. If in good faith pleader intends to deny all averments in complaint, he may do so by general denial. Denials must fairly meet substance of averments denied. Pleader without sufficient knowledge to form opinion regarding averments shall so state, and statement will be considered denial. Averments to which responsive pleading is required, except as to amount of damages, are admitted when not denied. (Rule TR 8).

Affirmative Defenses.—Responsive pleading shall set forth affirmatively and carry burden of proving: Accord and satisfaction, arbitration and award, discharge in bankruptcy, duress, estoppel, failure of consideration, fraud, illegality, injury by fellow servant, laches, license, payment, release, res judicata, statute of frauds, statute of limitations, waiver, lack of jurisdiction, improper venue, insufficiency of process or service of process, same action pending in another state court, and any other affirmative defense. (Rule TR 8).

Counterclaim or Set-Off.—Pleading must state as a counterclaim any claim pleader has against opposing party, if it arises out of transaction or occurrence that is subject matter of opposing party's claim and if court has jurisdiction over all necessary third parties. Pleading may state as a counterclaim: (a) Any claim against an opposing party not arising out of transaction or occurrence that is subject matter of opposing party's claim; (b) any claim owned by person against whom he has recourse who has notice of suit, is a party, is insolvent, has assigned his claim to party asserting it or surety or cannot be found. As to (b), counterclaim must diminish or defeat recovery sought by opposing party, or claim or opposing claim must relate to payment or security for other. This is necessary unless person against whom there is recourse is party, or counterclaim has been assigned to party asserting it. If counterclaim recovery exceeds opposing party's claim, excess is held in trust for person against whom there is recourse. (Rule TR 13).

Frivolous Claims.—Court may award attorney fees as part of costs to prevailing party if it finds that either party brought action or defense that was frivolous, unreasonable, or groundless or continued to litigate action or defense after party's claim or defense clearly became frivolous, unreasonable, or groundless. (IC34-1-32-1[b][1] and [2]). Claim or defense is "frivolous" for purpose of determining whether attorney fees should be imposed if it is taken primarily for purpose of harassment, if attorney is unable to make good faith and rational arguments on merits of action, or if attorney is unable to support action taken by good faith and rational argument for extension, modification, or reversal of existing law. Claim or defense is "unreasonable" for purpose of determining whether attorney fees should be awarded if, based on totality of circumstances, including law and facts known at time of filing, no reasonable attorney would consider claim or defense worthy of litigation or justified. Claim or defense is "groundless" for purpose of determining whether attorney fees should be awarded if no facts exist which support legal claim presented by losing party. (611 N.E.2d 135; 581 N.E.2d 1279; 577 N.E.2d 588; 569 N.E.2d 748; 543 N.E.2d 627).

Reply.—Any reply, other than a counterclaim, may be filed only upon order of court. Court may in its discretion order a reply to an answer or third-party answer. Matters formerly required to be pleaded by a reply or other subsequent pleading may be proved even though they are not pleaded. (Rule TR 7).

Demurrer.—Demurrers and exceptions for insufficiency of a pleading or improper service cannot be used. (Rule TR 7). All fictions in pleadings are abolished. (Rule TR 8 [E]).

Abatement.—Pleas in abatement are abolished. (Rule TR 7).

Amended or Supplemental Pleadings.—Party may amend his pleading once as a matter of course at any time before a responsive pleading is served, or if pleading is one to which no responsive pleading is permitted, and action has not been placed upon trial calendar, he may amend it at any time within 30 days after it is served. Otherwise, leave of court or written consent of adverse party is necessary. Upon motion of a party, court may permit him to serve a supplemental pleading setting forth transactions or occurrences or events which have happened since date of pleading sought to be supplemented. (Rule TR 15).

Bills of Particulars.—If pleading is so vague or ambiguous that party cannot reasonably be required to frame a responsive pleading, he may move for a more definite statement. (Rule TR 12 [E]).

Verification.—When in connection with any civil or special statutory proceeding it is required that all pleadings be verified, it is sufficient if subscriber simply affirms truth of matter to be verified by affirmation in substantially following language (Rule TR 11):

Form

I affirm, under the penalties for perjury, that the foregoing representation is true.

(Signed) . . . .

Service.—Every party must be served with every pleading subsequent to original complaint, as well as with any other paper described in Rule 5. Whenever party is represented by attorney of record, service must be made upon such attorney. Service upon attorney or party must be made by delivering or mailing copy of papers to him at his last known address. (Rule TR 5).

Time.—Responsive pleading must be served within 20 days after service of prior pleading. Three days are added to this period for response to pleading or paper served by mail. Reply must be served within 20 days after entry of order requiring it. In computing any period of time, day of act is not included whereas last day of period so computed is included. This is subject to some exceptions. (Rule TR 6).

Proof of Claims.—Party required to affirmatively plead any matter has burden of proving such matters. Burden of proof is subject to rules of evidence. (Rule TR 8).

Small Claims.—See category Courts and Legislature, topic Courts.

PRACTICE:

Indiana's Rules of Trial Procedure became effective Jan. 1, 1970. Rules are basically patterned after Federal Rules of Procedure. General summaries of procedural matters can be found under appropriate digest topics.

Discovery.—Parties may obtain discovery regarding any matter, not privileged, which is relevant to subject-matter involved in pending action. Discovery can be obtained by one or more of following methods: (1) Depositions upon oral examination or written questions; (2) written interrogatories; (3) production of documents or things or permission to enter upon land or other property; (4) physical and mental examinations; (5) requests for admission. Court may make an order to protect party or person from annoyance, embarrassment, oppression, or undue burden or expense. (Rule TR 26). Party under duty to seasonably supplement discovery relating to identity and location of persons with knowledge of discoverable matters and expert witnesses expected to be called at trial. Before filing any discovery motion or request, party must make reasonable effort to resolve discovery dispute with opposing party.

Request for Admissions.—Party may serve upon any other party a written request for admission, for purposes of pending action only, of truth of any matters subject to discovery. Matter is admitted unless matter is answered or objection is addressed to matter. Any matter admitted is conclusively established unless court permits withdrawal or amendment of admission. (Rule TR 36).

Jurisdiction.—Court acquires jurisdiction over a party or person who is served with a summons or enters an appearance, or who is subjected to power of court under any other law. (Rule TR 4). Broad basis of jurisdiction is asserted which includes almost any action arising from acts which have sufficient nexus between person or thing and state to permit court's power to be asserted over it, including marital relationship within state despite later departure of one party. Court has power to order litigation to be held at more convenient forum. (Rule TR 4.4).

Local Courts.—Each local court may make and amend rules governing its practice not inconsistent with Indiana Rules of Trial Procedure. (Rule TR 81).

See note at head of Digest as to 1998 legislation covered.

See Topical Index in front part of this volume.

PRACTICE . . . *continued*

Direct Actions Against Insurer.—See category Transportation, topic Motor Vehicles, subhead Direct Actions.

Small Claims.—See category Courts and Legislature, topic Courts.

See also topics Actions, Appeal and Error, Depositions and Discovery, Injunctions, Judgments, Pleading, Process; category Debtor and Creditor, topics Attachment, Executions, Garnishment.

PROCESS:

Indiana Rules of Trial Procedure to some extent are based on Federal Rules of Civil Procedure.

Civil actions are commenced by filing complaint with court or such equivalent pleading or document as may be specified by statute. (Rule TR 3).

General Requisites.—Contemporaneously with filing of complaint or equivalent pleading, as many copies of complaint and summons as are necessary shall be furnished to clerk. Summons must contain name and address of person on whom service is to be effected; name of court and cause number; title of case; name, address, and telephone number of attorney for person seeking service; and time required for person being served to respond and penalty for not responding (i.e., possible default judgment). (Rule TR 4).

Issuance.—After service is effectuated and summons returned to clerk, he will enter filing date and issuance date on summons. Such filing or issuance dates are evidence of date of filing or issuance without further authentication when entered in court records, or when paper is admitted into evidence. (Rule TR 4.15).

Who May Serve.—Clerk of court will cause service to be made by mail. (Rule TR 4.11). Whenever service is made by delivering copy to person personally or at his dwelling or place of employment, summons will be issued to and served by sheriff, his deputy, or some person appointed by court. (Rule TR 4.12). Upon application of any party court may make appropriate order for service in manner not provided by these rules or statutes when such service is reasonably calculated to give defendant actual knowledge of proceeding and opportunity to be heard. (Rule TR 4.14). Summons can be served in any county of state. (Rule TR 4.12).

Personal Service on Individuals.—Service may be made upon individual or individual acting in representative capacity by (1) Sending copy of summons and complaint by registered or certified mail to his residence, place of business, or employment, with return receipt requested and returned showing receipt; (2) delivering copy of summons and complaint to him personally; (3) leaving copy of summons and complaint at his dwelling house or usual place of abode; or (4) serving his agent. Whenever service made under (3) or (4), must also send copy of summons by first class mail to last known address of person being served, and this fact shall be shown upon return. (Rule TR 4.1).

Personal Service on Infants.—Service shall be made upon his next friend or guardian ad litem if infant is so represented in case; if there is no next friend or guardian ad litem service shall be made upon his court-appointed representative; if there is no court-appointed representative, service shall be made upon parent known to have custody of infant or if no parent, then person standing in position of custodian or parent. If infant is 14 years of age or older, he must also be served. (Rule TR 4.2).

Personal Service on Incompetent Persons.—Service shall be made upon his next friend or guardian ad litem if incompetent is so represented in case, or his court appointed representative, or upon named party and person known to be standing in position of custodian of his person. (Rule TR 4.2).

Service Upon Institutionalized Persons.—Service must be made by delivering or mailing a copy of summons and complaint to official in charge of institution. Official must then immediately deliver it to person being served. (Rule TR 4.3).

Service upon a partnership may be made upon a general partner thereof. (Rule TR 4.6).

Service on Domestic Organization.—Service may be made upon executive officer thereof, or if there is an agent appointed or deemed by law to have been appointed to receive service, then upon such agent, in same manner as service on individuals. (Rule TR 4.6). Under certain circumstances, Secretary of State can be deemed to be such agent. (Rule TR 4.7). When service upon individual cannot be made, service may be made by leaving copy of summons and complaint at any office of such organization located within this state with person in charge of such office. (Rule TR 4.6).

Personal Service on Domestic Corporation.—See subhead Service on Domestic Organization, supra.

Service on Governmental Organizations.—State governmental organization may be served by service made upon executive officer thereof and also upon Attorney General. Service on a local governmental organization may be made upon executive thereof and attorney who represents government organization. (Rule TR 4.6[A]).

Personal Service on Associations.—No specific statutory provisions.

Personal Service on Joint Stock Companies.—No specific statutory provisions.

Service on Foreign Organizations.—Foreign corporations admitted to do business in state are reached by service upon resident agent, which may be a corporation, or, if he cannot be found, then, upon Secretary of State. (Rules TR 4.6, 4.7 and 4.10). Service may also be made as on domestic organizations.

Foreign banks doing business within the state may be served by process upon the agent named in the application for permission to do business within the state. (IC28-1-22-12).

Foreign insurance companies must appoint Commissioner of Insurance or his successor as agent for the service of process in order to be admitted to do business. (IC27-1-17-4[h]). Unauthorized foreign insurers who are transacting insurance business within state impliedly appoint secretary of state as agent for service of process. (IC27-4-5-4[a]).

Personal Service Outside the State.—Personal service, when permitted to be made outside state (see Rule TR 4.4), may be made there by any disinterested person or by attorney representing person seeking such service (Rule TR 4.12).

Service by Mail.—If service made by mail, papers shall be deposited in U.S. mail addressed to person on whom being served, with postage prepaid. Service shall be deemed complete upon mailing. Proof of service of all papers permitted to be mailed may be made by written acknowledgment of service, by affidavit of person who mailed papers, or by certificate of attorney. (Rule TR 5[B][2]). Personal service may be effected in or out of state by mailing summons and complaint by clerk to person to be served, unless attorney designates different method of service. (Rule TR 4). If address of person served is not included on summons or cannot be determined, or if service by mail is returned without acceptance, complaint and summons will be delivered to sheriff or his deputy for service. (Rule TR 4).

Service by Registered or Certified Mail.—When service by registered or certified mail is requested, clerk must send summons and complaint to person being served, and make notation of date, place of mailing, and on return, file receipt and return with pleadings as part of record. (Rule TR 4.11).

Substituted Service.—Service by leaving a copy of summons and complaint at individual's dwelling house or usual place of abode is permitted. If this mode of service is employed, copy of summons without complaint shall be sent by first-class mail to last known address of person being served and this fact shall be shown upon return. (Rule TR 4.1).

Service by Publication.—Service of summons by publication shall be made and procured by clerk, by person appointed by court for that purpose, or by clerk or sheriff of another county where publication is to be made. Person seeking such service must submit his request therefor upon praecipe for summons along with supporting affidavits that diligent search has been made and that defendant cannot be found, has concealed his whereabouts, or has left state, and must prepare contents of summons to be published. Summons shall be signed by clerk or sheriff. Summons must be published three times, first publication promptly and each two succeeding publications at least seven and not more than 14 days after prior publication, in newspaper authorized by law to publish notices, and published in county where complaint or action is filed, where res is located, or where defendant resides or where he was known last to reside. (Rule TR 4.13).

Unknown husband, wife, widow, widower, heir or devisee may be made party to suit to quiet title and brought into court by publication. (IC32-6-4-1).

Long Arm Statute.—See topic Practice, subhead Jurisdiction.

Proof of Service.—Person making service must make his return upon or attach it to a copy of summons. When delivered to clerk, return becomes part of record and will have evidentiary effect. Written admission stating date and place of service, signed by person being served, will constitute evidence of proper service. Filing and issuance date made by clerk of court will constitute evidence of date of filing and issuance. (Rule TR 4.15).

Nonresident Motor Vehicle Operators.—See category Transportation, topic Motor Vehicles.

Process Against State Employees.—When suit is filed against state employee in his official capacity and attorney general is required or authorized to represent state or is entitled to be heard then copies of complaint, cross-complaint, petition, bill or pleading must be served on attorney general before proceedings will begin. (IC4-6-4-1).

REPLEVIN:

When any personal goods are wrongfully taken, or unlawfully detained, from the owner or person claiming the possession thereof, or when goods taken on execution or attachment are claimed by any person other than the defendant, the owner or claimant may bring an action in replevin for them. (IC34-21-1-1). Property seized by law enforcement officer subject to lawful arrest, search or administrative inspection is not subject to replevin. (IC34-24-1-2[c]).

Proceedings.—At time of issuing summons or at any time before final judgment plaintiff may apply for immediate delivery of property in question by filing affidavit describing property and stating that he is owner or is lawfully entitled to possession of property and stating that property has been wrongfully taken or wrongfully detained, that estimated value is in stated amount, that property is believed to be detained in specific county and that property has not been taken for tax assessment or fine pursuant to statute or seized under execution or attachment against property of plaintiff or if so seized that property is exempt from such seizure. (IC34-21-2-1 to IC34-21-2-3). Upon filing of such affidavit, (as practical matter, court) clerk issues order directing defendant to appear to contest plaintiff's affidavit, or show cause why prejudgment order for possession and delivery to plaintiff should not issue. Hearing on replevin must be set for no earlier than five days after service of order on defendant (exclusive of Sundays and holidays. (IC34-21-3-1 to IC34-21-3-2). Order to show cause must inform defendant that it may file affidavits, appear and present testimony at hearing, and file undertaking with court to stay delivery of property. If defendant fails to appear, plaintiff may be granted judgment of possession. (IC34-21-3-3).

Upon examination of complaint, affidavits, and other evidence, court may give order of possession prior to hearing on probable cause when: (1) Defendant gained possession by theft or criminal conversion; (2) property consists of negotiable instruments or credit cards; or (3) property is perishable or is in immediate danger of destruction, harm, concealment, sale or removal from state. (IC34-21-4-2). Order of possession issued without notice shall direct sheriff or other executing officer to hold property until order of court. (IC34-21-4-5). Affidavit or certificate showing efforts to give notice and reasons why notice cannot be given is prerequisite to order issuing without notice. (IC34-21-4-3). Where order of possession is issued prior to hearing, defendant may apply for order shortening time for hearing to not less than 48 hours after providing notice of such hearing to plaintiff. In lieu of ordering immediate possession prior to hearing, court may issue temporary restraining order directed to defendant prohibiting such acts with respect to property as may appear to be necessary for preservation of rights of parties and status of property. (IC34-21-4-4; IC34-21-4-6).

Repossession by Defendant.—At any time prior to preliminary hearing or final judgment, defendant may recover or retain possession by posting bond in amount fixed by court. If posted prior to preliminary hearing, that proceeding terminates unless there is objection to surety. (IC34-21-5-2 to IC34-21-5-4).

See note at head of Digest as to 1998 legislation covered.

See Topical Index in front part of this volume.

IN – 19

REPLEVIN . . . *continued*

Possession by Plaintiff.—Court may order possession given to plaintiff, if he has a reasonable probability of entitlement or defendant defaults by failure to appear at preliminary hearing. If defendant defaults, judgment of possession is final. (IC34-21-3-3).

Order of possession for plaintiff cannot be issued unless he posts bond in amount fixed by court, not less than value of property, except for order upon default. If defendant fails to appear and final judgment is entered, no bond is required. (IC34-21-5-1).

Unique Property.—If property claimed by plaintiff is unique and of such a nature that its loss cannot be compensated for by damages, court may, in lieu of possession order, appoint a receiver to hold property pending further order of court. (IC34-21-4-9).

Issuance and Execution of Order of Possession.—Order of possession shall describe property to be seized and shall direct executing officer to take property into custody, and, unless issued without notice, deliver it to plaintiff if defendant does not file written undertaking within time fixed by court to show why delivery to plaintiff should not be made. (IC34-21-4-11). If order is final judgment, delivery to plaintiff should be immediate. (IC34-21-4-12). If property is being used as principal dwelling of defendant, executing officer may not take possession of property prior to 48 hours after issuance of order of possession. (IC34-21-8-1). If property is in building or enclosure and property is not voluntarily relinquished, executing officer may cause building or enclosure to be broken open to retrieve property. (IC34-21-8-2). Executing officer must return order of possession to court, with his proceedings indorsed thereon, within five days after taking property. (IC34-21-8-4). Executing officer may receive reasonable fees for keeping property until delivered to plaintiff. (IC34-21-8-3).

Concealment of Property.—See subhead Proceedings, supra.

Claims of Third Persons.—No specific statutory provision.

Judgment or Order.—If judgment is for plaintiff it entitles him to delivery of property or value thereof, and damages for unlawful detention. When property has been delivered to plaintiff prior to final judgment, and defendant claims return thereof, judgment for defendant may be for return of property, or its value, in case return cannot be had, and damages for taking and withholding of property. (IC34-21-9-1 to IC34-21-9-2). If possession is not surrendered judgment is for full value of property and damages for taking or unlawful detention. (IC34-21-10-1).

SEQUESTRATION:

On application of party entitled to performance, clerk shall issue writ of attachment, writ of assistance, or sequestration against property of disobedient party to compel obedience to judgment. (Rule TR 70). See Rule TR 64(A).

SERVICE:

See topic Process.

STAY OF EXECUTION:

See topic Appeal and Error; category Debtor and Creditor, topic Executions.

SUBMISSION OF CONTROVERSY:

Parties have the right, with or without process, by agreement to that effect, to submit any matter of controversy between them, to any court that would otherwise have jurisdiction of such cause, upon agreed statement of facts made out and signed by parties, but it must appear by affidavit that controversy is real and proceedings in good faith. Thereupon court proceeds to try cause and render judgment as in other cases. (IC34-54-5-1).

VENUE:

Preferred Venue.—Any case may be filed in any county in any court, subject to transfer to preferred venue. (Rule TR 75[A]). Cases will not be dismissed or abated for failure to select proper venue but will, upon filing of pleading or motion to dismiss under Rule TR 12(B)(3), be transferred to preferred venue if court determines that court or county where action is filed does not meet preferred venue requirements, and that court or county selected by party first filing motion to transfer meets preferred venue requirements. When case is transferred to preferred venue plaintiff must pay cost incidental to transfer. These costs include filing costs or refiling in proper court and mileage reasonably incurred by parties and their attorneys in resisting venue. They shall also include reasonable attorney's fees incurred in resisting venue if action was commenced in wrong county by sham pleading, in bad faith, or without cause. (Rule TR 75[C]). Where proper objection has been made, court shall order case transferred to proper court, and papers and records shall be certified to court of transfer in like manner as upon change of venue. (Rule TR 75[B]). Preferred venue lies in: (1) County where greater percentage of individual defendants reside or if no greater percentage, place where any defendant resides; or (2) county where land or chattels are regularly located if claim includes interests in or injuries thereto; or (3) county where accident or collision occurred if relating to vehicle; or (4) county where principal office or agency of defendant organization is located; or (5) county where either one or more individual plaintiffs reside or office of governmental organization is located, if one or more governmental organizations are included as defendants; or (6) county fixed by written stipulation signed by all parties and filed with court; or (7) county where individual is held in custody if action pertains to that custody; or (8) county where claim may be commenced under any statute recognizing or creating special or general remedy or proceeding; or (9) county where property is located if case seeks only judgment in rem against property of defendant being served by publication; or (10) county where either one or more individual plaintiffs reside or office of governmental organization is located, if case is one not subject to above nine requirements or if defendants are nonresident individuals or nonresident organizations without principal office in state. (Rule TR 75[A]).

Appeal.—Order transferring or refusing to transfer case pursuant to preferred venue requirements is interlocutory order appealable pursuant to Ind. Appellate Rule 4(B)(5). However, interlocutory appeal does not stay proceedings in trial court unless trial court or Court of Appeals so orders. (Rule TR 75[E]).

Change of Venue from County or Judge.—In civil actions, change of venue from county may be had only upon filing of verified motion stating grounds for requested change of venue. Party shall be entitled to only one change in venue from county. Motion shall be granted only upon showing that county where suit is pending is party, or that party seeking change of venue will be unlikely to receive fair trial due to local prejudice or bias regarding party, claim, or defense. Specifically, causes justifying change of venue include: (1) judge has been engaged as counsel in cause prior to becoming judge or is in some other way interested in outcome of case; or (2) judge is related to either party; or (3) opposite party has undue influence over citizens of county; or (4) county is party; or (5) convenience of witnesses and ends of justice would be promoted by change; or (6) judge is material witness; or (7) judge is otherwise biased or prejudiced. (IC34-35-1-1; IC34-35-3-3). Party is entitled to only one change of venue. For purposes of changing venue from county, all plaintiffs are considered one party, and all defendants are considered one party. (IC34-35-3-1). Denial of motion for change of venue is reviewable only for abuse of discretion. (Rule TR 76[A]).

In civil actions in which change may be taken from judge, motion shall be granted upon filing of unverified application or motion without stating specific grounds for change. Party is entitled to only one change of judge. (Rule TR 76[B]).

Except in criminal cases, application for change of venue or change of judge must be filed not later than ten days after issues are first closed on merits, except: (1) in cases where no pleading or answer is required by defending party to close issues or no responsive pleading is required, each party has 30 days from date action is placed and entered on issue and trial docket of court; (2) in cases of claims in probate, receivership, remonstrances, and like, parties have 30 days from date matter is placed and entered on issue and trial docket of court; (3) when new trial is granted, parties have ten days from date order granting new trial is entered on record of trial court. (Rule TR 76[C]).

In event change of judge or county is granted within prescribed period, request for change of judge or county may be made by party still entitled thereto within ten days after qualification of special judge or after moving party has knowledge cause has reached receiving county or there has been failure to perfect change. Provided, however, that this provision will only operate to enlarge time allowed for such requests. (Rule TR 76[C][4]).

Where party has appeared at or received advance notice of hearing prior to expiration of time within which to move for change of venue or change of judge, and where at such hearing trial date is set and is entered on court's Chronological Case Summary, that party will be deemed to have waived request for change of judge or change of venue unless within three days such party files written objection to trial setting and motion for change of venue from judge or county. (Rule TR 76[C][5]).

If moving party first obtains knowledge of grounds from change of venue from judge or county after expiration of time limits described above, that party may file application for change of venue or change of judge. Such application must be personally verified by party, and must allege when cause was first discovered, how cause was discovered, facts showing grounds for change, and reason why such cause could not have been discovered before through exercise of due diligence. Opposing party may file counter-affidavits on issue within ten days. Ruling of court is reviewable only for abuse of discretion. If review is sought, it must be sought pursuant to interlocutory appeal under Ind. Appellate Rule 4(B)(5). (Rule TR 76[C][6]).

Selection of New Venue After Change.—When change of venue is granted, cause is transferred to county agreed on by parties if they agree in open court within three days. In absence of agreement, court shall, within two days thereafter, submit list of all adjacent counties. Moving party strikes one, then nonmoving party strikes one, and so on until only one county remains. Cause is venued to such county. If moving party fails to strike within seven days or within time set by court, not to exceed 14 days, court resumes general jurisdiction of case. If nonmoving party fails to strike within that time limit, clerk of court shall strike for that party. (Rule TR 76[D]; IC34-35-2).

In event moving party seeks change of judge, judge shall call judge of any circuit, superior or other court of general jurisdiction, or any judge of supreme court, to preside in such case, and try same. (IC34-35-1-3).

Jurisdiction Pending Change of Venue.—Whenever court has granted change of venue and costs have been paid, either party may file certified copy of order making such change in new court, and thereafter new court has full jurisdiction, even though transcript has not been filed. This rule does not divest original court's jurisdiction to hear and determine emergency matters between filing and granting of motion. (Rule TR 78).

Other Rules.—See Ind. Crim. Rule 12 (change of venue in criminal cases); Ind. Tax Court Rule 13 (Venue of tax appeals lies with Tax Court); and Ind. Small Claims Rule 12.

Statutes.—See Ind. Code §34 (civil procedure) and §35 (criminal procedure). See also Burn's Indiana Statutes Annotated, General Index and West's Annotated Indiana Code, General Index.

Waiver.—Defense of improper venue must be set forth affirmatively in responsive pleading, or may be made by motion. (Rule TR 8[C]; Rule TR 12[B][3]). Defense is waived if it is omitted from motion made under Rule 12 or from responsive pleading or amendment thereto. (Rule TR 12[H]). Also, if party appears at or receives advanced notice of hearing held before expiration of date within which that party may ask for change of venue, and at that hearing trial date is set and reduced to order book, that party waives right to change venue unless party files written objection and written notice for change of venue within three days. (Rule TR 76[C][5]).

See note at head of Digest as to 1998 legislation covered.

See Topical Index in front part of this volume.

COURTS AND LEGISLATURE

COURTS:

United States District Courts.—

Northern District is divided into four divisions and clerk maintains office in city from which each division takes its name. (Hammond 46325, Lafayette 47902, Fort Wayne 46802, South Bend 46601).

Fort Wayne Division is composed of following counties: Adams, Allen, Blackford, DeKalb, Grant, Huntington, Jay, Lagrange, Noble, Steuben, Wells and Whitley.

South Bend Division is composed of following counties: Cass, Elkhart, Fulton, Kosciusko, LaPorte, Marshall, Miami, Pulaski, St. Joseph, Starke and Wabash.

Hammond Division is composed of following counties: Lake and Porter.

Lafayette Division is composed of following counties: Benton, Carroll, Jasper, Newton, Porter, Tippecanoe, Warren and White.

Southern District.—Southern District is divided into four divisions and clerk maintains an office in city from which each division takes its name (Indianapolis 46204, Terre Haute 47808, Evansville 47708, New Albany 47150).

Indianapolis Division is composed of following counties: Bartholomew, Boone, Brown, Clinton, Decatur, Delaware, Fayette, Fountain, Franklin, Hamilton, Hancock, Hendricks, Henry, Howard, Johnson, Madison, Marion, Monroe, Montgomery, Morgan, Randolph, Rush, Shelby, Tipton, Union and Wayne. Court is held in Indianapolis and Richmond.

Terre Haute Division is composed of following counties: Clay, Greene, Knox, Owen, Parke, Putnam, Sullivan, Vermillion and Vigo.

Evansville Division is composed of following counties: Daviess, Dubois, Gibson, Martin, Perry, Pike, Posey, Spencer, Vanderburgh and Warrick.

New Albany Division is composed of following counties: Clark, Crawford, Dearborn, Floyd, Harrison, Jackson, Jefferson, Jennings, Lawrence, Ohio, Orange, Ripley, Scott, Switzerland and Washington.

For filing fees in U.S. District Courts, see 28 U.S.C. §1914.

United States Bankruptcy Courts.—

Northern District is divided into four for filing (Fort Wayne Division, South Bend Division, and Hammond Division at Gary).

Fort Wayne Division is comprised of counties of Adams, Allen, Blackford, DeKalb, Grant, Huntington, Jay, LaGrange, Noble, Steuben, Wells and Whitley.

South Bend Division is comprised of counties of Cass, Elkhart, Fulton, Kosciusko, LaPorte, Marshall, Miami, Pulaski, St. Joseph, Starke and Wabash.

Hammond Division at Gary is comprised of counties of Lake and Porter.

Hammond Division at Lafayette is comprised of counties of Benton, Carroll, Jasper, Newton, Tippecanoe, Warren and White.

Southern District is divided into four Divisions (Indianapolis, Terre Haute, Evansville and New Albany).

Indianapolis Division is comprised of counties of Bartholomew, Boone, Brown, Clinton, Decatur, Delaware, Fayette, Fountain, Franklin, Hamilton, Hancock, Hendricks, Henry, Howard, Johnson, Madison, Marion, Monroe, Montgomery, Morgan, Randolph, Rush, Shelby, Tipton, Union and Wayne.

Terre Haute Division is comprised of counties of Clay, Greene, Knox, Owen, Parke, Putnam, Sullivan, Vermillion and Vigo.

Evansville Division is comprised of counties of Daviess, Dubois, Gibson, Martin, Perry, Pike, Posey, Spencer, Vanderburgh and Warrick.

New Albany Division is comprised of counties of Clark, Crawford, Dearborn, Floyd, Harrison, Jackson, Jefferson, Jennings, Lawrence, Ohio, Orange, Ripley, Scott, Switzerland and Washington.

For filing fees in bankruptcy cases, see 28 U.S.C. §1930.

Supreme Court and Court of Appeals.—

Selection of Justices.—When a vacancy occurs on Supreme Court or Court of Appeals, Judicial Nominating Commission presents to Governor a list of three attorneys. Governor fills vacancy with a person from list without regard to political affiliation. (Const., art. 7, §10). Judicial Nominating Commission consists of seven members. Chairman is Chief Justice of Supreme Court or Justice of Supreme Court whom he designates. Three attorney-members are elected by attorneys of state, and three non-attorney members are appointed by Governor. (Const., art. 7, §9).

A justice of the Supreme Court or a judge of the Court of Appeals serves initially until next general election following expiration of two years from date of appointment, at which time he is subject to referendum by voters. Electorate of entire state votes on question of approval of Supreme Court Justices, while electorate of particular Court of Appeals District (infra) votes on Court of Appeals judge. Approval by voters means retention in office for ten year term. At end of ten year term, justice or judge is again subject to referendum. (Const., art. 7, §11). There is no limitation on number of terms of office that may be served. (Const., art. 7, §15).

Supreme Court consists of a chief justice and four justices, any three of whom constitute quorum. (Const., art. 7, §2; IC33-2.1-2-1).

Chief Justice is selected by Judicial Nominating Commission from members of Supreme Court. He serves five-year term of office. (Const., art. 7, §3).

Jurisdiction.—This Court has exclusive jurisdiction in admission to practice of law; discipline and disbarment of those admitted; unauthorized practice of law; discipline, removal and retirement of justices and judges; supervision of exercise of jurisdiction by other courts of state; issuance of writs necessary or appropriate in aid of its jurisdiction; appeals in criminal cases from a judgment imposing a sentence of death, life imprisonment, or imprisonment for a term greater than 50 years for single offense, appeal from denial of post-conviction relief in which sentence was death; appealable cases involving constitutionality of statutes; and appeals, upon granting of petition to transfer, involving substantial question of law of great public importance and where need exists for speedy determination. (Const., art. 7, §4; Rule AP4[A]).

Court of Appeals is composed of 15 judges sitting in five geographic districts. (Const. art. 7, §5; IC33-2.1-2-2[a]).

First District.—Counties: Bartholomew, Boone, Brown, Clark, Clay, Crawford, Daviess, Dearborn, Decatur, Dubois, Fayette, Floyd, Fountain, Franklin, Gibson, Greene, Hancock, Harrison, Hendricks, Henry, Jackson, Jefferson, Jennings, Johnson, Knox, Lawrence, Martin, Monroe, Montgomery, Morgan, Ohio, Orange, Owen, Parke, Perry, Pike, Posey, Putnam, Randolph, Ripley, Rush, Scott, Shelby, Spencer, Sullivan, Switzerland, Union, Vanderburgh, Vermillion, Vigo, Warrick, Washington, and Wayne.

Second District.—Counties: Adams, Blackford, Carroll, Cass, Clinton, Delaware, Grant, Hamilton, Howard, Huntington, Jay, Madison, Marion, Miami, Tippecanoe, Tipton, Wabash, Wells, and White.

Third District.—Counties: Allen, Benton, DeKalb, Elkhart, Fulton, Jasper, Kosciusko, LaGrange, Lake, LaPorte, Marshall, Newton, Noble, Porter, Pulaski, St. Joseph, Starke, Steuben, Warren, and Whitley. (IC33-2.1-2-2[b]).

Fourth District.—Entire State constitutes Fourth District.

Fifth District.—Entire State constitutes Fifth District.

All cases appealed to Court of Appeals are placed upon the docket of district from which appeals originated. To prevent congestion, Court may order transfer from one district to another. (IC33-2.1-2-2[d]).

Chief Judge.—The judges of the Court of Appeals elect one of their number to serve as chief judge for a three year period. (IC33-2.1-2-4[a]).

Presiding Judges.—Each district, other than district from which chief judge was chosen, selects one of their number as presiding judge of their respective district. (IC33-2.1-2-4[b]).

Jurisdiction.—Court has jurisdiction of appeals of all cases other than those in which Supreme Court has exclusive jurisdiction, including interlocutory orders for payment of money or to compel execution of any instrument of writing, or delivery or assignment of any securities, evidence of debt, documents or things in action; delivery of possession of real property or sale thereof; granting or refusing to grant, or dissolving or overruling motions to dissolve preliminary injunctions; or appointment of receivers; habeas corpus actions not authorized to be taken directly to Supreme Court; transferring or refusing to transfer case pursuant to Trial Rule 75; any other interlocutory order, if trial court certifies and court of appeal or judge thereof finds on petition that appellant will suffer substantial damage if order is erroneous and appeal delayed or there is substantial question of law, early determination of which will promote more orderly disposition of case or remedy by appeal after judgment is otherwise inadequate. (Rule AP4[B]). Court has jurisdiction to review final decisions of various administrative agencies. (Rule AP4[C]).

Superior Courts.—In 64 counties, Superior Courts have been statutorily authorized. (IC33-5-4.5 to 50). Each court is individually created and authorized.

Small Claims and Misdemeanor Division of Superior Courts (IC33-5-2-2 et seq.).—Superior courts may have standard small claims and misdemeanor division established by statute. This division has small claims docket and minor offenses and violations docket. Small claims docket has jurisdiction over civil actions where amount in controversy is $3,000 or less and possessory actions between landlord and tenant where rent due does not exceed $3,000. Trials within small claims docket are to be conducted informally and are not bound by statutes or rules governing practice, procedure, pleadings or evidence except for provisions relating to privileged communications and offers of compromise. Minor offenses and violations docket has jurisdiction over all class D felony, misdemeanor, infraction and ordinance violation cases. Court shall also establish traffic violations bureau. Standard small claims and misdemeanor divisions have been established by statute in Adams, Allen, Boone, Carroll, Cass, Clay, Clinton, Daviess, Decatur, DeKalb, Delaware, Dubois, Fayette, Fulton, Gibson, Grant, Greene, Hamilton, Hancock, Harrison, Hendricks, Henry, Howard, Huntington, Jackson, Jasper, Jay, Jefferson, Johnson, Knox, LaGrange, LaPorte, Marshall, Miami, Newton, Ohio and Switzerland, Porter, Pulaski, Randolph, Scott, Shelby, St. Joseph, Steuben, Sullivan, Vanderburgh, Warrick, Washington, Wayne, Wells, White and Whitley. (IC33-5-4.5 to 50).

Courts, Creating Statute, Location and Jurisdiction.—

Adams Superior Court (IC33-5-4.5-1 et seq.) Decatur.—Jurisdiction concurrent with Adams Circuit Court excluding juvenile matters.

Allen Superior Court (IC33-5.5.1-1 et seq.) Fort Wayne.—Jurisdiction concurrent with Allen Circuit Court including family relations, civil, and criminal. Juvenile cases shall be assigned to family relations division.

Bartholomew Superior Court (IC33-5-8-1 et seq.) Columbus.—Jurisdiction concurrent with Bartholomew Circuit Court excluding juvenile matters.

Boone Superior Court No. 1 (IC33-5-9-1 et seq.) Lebanon.—Jurisdiction same as Boone Circuit Court excluding juvenile matters; specially including probate matters.

Boone Superior Court No. 2 (IC33-5-9-1 et seq.) Lebanon.—Jurisdiction same as Boone Superior Court No. 1 excluding probate matters.

Carroll Superior Court (IC33-5-9.5 et seq.) Delphi.—Jurisdiction same as Carroll Circuit Court.

Cass Superior Court (IC33-5-9.7-1 et seq.) Logansport.—Jurisdiction same as Cass Circuit Court excluding juvenile matters.

Clark Superior Court No. 1 (IC33-5-10-2.5 et seq.) Jeffersonville.—Jurisdiction same as Clark Circuit.

Clark Superior Court No. 2 (IC33-5-10-1.5 et seq.) Jeffersonville.—Jurisdiction same as Clark Superior Court No. 1.

Clark Superior Court No. 3 (IC33-5-10-1.5 et seq.) Jeffersonville.—Jurisdiction same as Clark Superior Court No. 1. Clark Superior Court No. 3 has small claims and misdemeanor docket.

Clay Superior Court (IC33-5-10.5-1 et seq.) Brazil.—Jurisdiction same as Clay Circuit Court, excluding juvenile and probate matters.

Clinton Superior Court (IC33-5-10.3-1 et seq.) Frankfort.—Jurisdiction same as Clinton Circuit excluding juvenile matters.

Daviess Superior Court (IC33-5-10.6 et seq.) Washington.—Jurisdiction same as Daviess Circuit Court.

Decatur Superior Court (IC33-5-10.7 et seq.) Greensburg.—Jurisdiction same as Decatur Circuit Court.

DeKalb Superior Court (IC33-5-10.8-1 et seq.) Auburn.—Same jurisdiction as DeKalb Circuit Court excluding juvenile and probate matters.

See note at head of Digest as to 1998 legislation covered.

See Topical Index in front part of this volume.

COURTS . . . continued

Delaware Superior Court No. 1 (IC33-5-12.1-1 et seq.) Muncie.—Jurisdiction same as Delaware Circuit Court.

Delaware Superior Court No. 2 (IC33-5-12.1-1 et seq.) Muncie.—Jurisdiction same as Delaware Circuit Court.

Delaware Superior Court No. 3 (IC33-5-12.1-1 et seq.) Muncie.—Jurisdiction same as Delaware Circuit Court excluding Class A, B, C felonies, juvenile and probate matters.

Delaware Superior Court No. 4 (IC33-5-12.1-1 et seq.) Muncie.—Jurisdiction same as Delaware Superior Court No. 3.

Dubois Superior Court (IC33-5-12.5-1 et seq.) Jasper.—Jurisdiction same as Dubois Circuit Court.

Elkhart Superior Courts (IC33-5-13.1-1 et seq.) Elkhart and Goshen.—Jurisdiction same as Elkhart Circuit Court. Five courts. Three shall hold sessions in Elkhart. Two shall hold sessions in Goshen. Superior Court has standard small claims and misdemeanor division.

Fayette Superior Court (IC33-5-17.1-1 et seq.) Connersville.—Jurisdiction same as circuit court excluding juvenile matters.

Floyd Superior Court (IC33-5-18.1-1 et seq.) New Albany.—Jurisdiction same as Floyd Circuit Court excluding juvenile jurisdiction.

Fulton Superior Court (IC33-5-10.9-1 et seq.) Rochester.—Jurisdiction same as Fulton Circuit Court excluding juvenile matters.

Gibson Superior Court (IC33-5-18.3-1 et seq.) Princeton.—Jurisdiction same as Gibson Circuit Court excluding juvenile and probate matters.

Grant Superior Court No. 1 (IC33-5-11-1 et seq.) Marion.—Jurisdiction same as Grant Circuit Court.

Grant Superior Court No. 2 (IC33-5-19-1 et seq.) Marion.—Jurisdiction same as Grant Circuit Court.

Grant Superior Court No. 3 (IC33-5-9.3-1 et seq.) Marion.—Jurisdiction same as Grant Circuit Court; dollar amounts in small claims docket raised to $6,000.

Greene Superior Court (IC33-5-19.5-1 et seq.) Bloomfield.—Jurisdiction same as Greene Circuit Court.

Hamilton Superior Court No. 1 (IC33-5-22-1 et seq.) Noblesville.—Court of record and general jurisdiction.

Hamilton Superior Court No. 2 (IC33-5-22-1 et seq.) Noblesville.—Court of record and general jurisdiction.

Hamilton Superior Court No. 3 (IC33-5-22 et seq.) Noblesville.—Court of record and general jurisdiction.

Hamilton Superior Court No. 4 (IC33-5-22-2 et seq.) Noblesville.—Court of record and general jurisdiction. Hamilton Superior Court No. 4 has standard small claims and misdemeanor division.

Hamilton Superior Court No. 5 (IC33-5-22-2 et seq.) Noblesville.—Court of record and general jurisdiction. Hamilton Superior Court No. 5 has standard small claims and misdemeanor division.

Hancock Superior Court No. 1 (IC33-5-23-1 et seq.) Greenfield.—Jurisdiction same as Hancock Circuit Court.

Hancock Superior Court No. 2 (IC33-5-23-1 et seq.) Greenfield.—Jurisdiction same as Hancock Circuit Court.

Harrison Superior Court (IC33-5-19.8-1 et seq.) Corydon.—Jurisdiction same as Harrison Circuit Court.

Hendricks Superior Court No. 1 (IC33-5-25-1 et seq.) Danville.—Original and exclusive jurisdiction in all probate, guardianship, estate administrations, trusts, adoptions, surviving partnerships and concurrent jurisdiction with other superior court(s) excluding juvenile matters.

Hendricks Superior Court No. 2 (IC33-5-25-1 et seq.) Danville.—Jurisdiction same as Hendricks Superior Court No. 1. Hendricks Superior Court No. 2 shall have standard small claims and misdemeanor division.

Hendricks Superior Court No 3. (IC33-5-25-1 et seq.) Danville.—Jurisdiction same as Hendricks County Superior Court No. 1 excluding juvenile matters. Hendricks Superior Court No. 3 shall have standard small claims and misdemeanor division.

Henry Superior Court No. 1 (IC33-5-21-1 et seq.) New Castle.—Jurisdiction same as Henry Circuit Court.

Henry Superior Court No. 2 (IC33-5-21-1 et seq.) New Castle.—Jurisdiction same as Henry Circuit Court.

Howard Superior Court No. 1 (IC33-5-20.1-1 et seq.) Kokomo.—Jurisdiction same as Howard Circuit Court excluding juvenile matters.

Howard Superior Court No. 3 (IC33-5-20.2-1 et seq.) Kokomo.—Jurisdiction same as Howard Circuit Court.

Huntington Superior Court (IC33-5-25.3-1 et seq.) Huntington.—Jurisdiction same as Huntington Circuit Court excluding juvenile matters.

Jackson Superior Court (IC33-5-25.4-1 et seq.) Seymour.—Jurisdiction same as Jackson Circuit Court.

Jasper Superior Court (IC33-5-25.5-1 et seq.) Rensselaer.—Jurisdiction same as Jasper Circuit Court except that only circuit court has jurisdiction over juvenile matters. Jasper Superior Court has standard small claims and misdemeanor division.

Jay Superior Court (IC33-5-25.7-1 et seq.) Portland.—Jurisdiction same as Jay Circuit Court, excluding juvenile matters.

Jefferson Superior Court (IC33-5-25.8-1 et seq.) Madison.—Jurisdiction same as Jefferson Circuit Court.

Jennings Superior Court (IC33-5-25.9-1 et seq.) Vernon.—Jurisdiction same as Jennings Circuit Court.

Johnson Superior Court No. 1 (IC33-5-24-1 et seq.) Franklin.—Court of record and general jurisdiction. Johnson Superior Court has standard small claims and misdemeanor division.

Johnson Superior Court No. 2 (IC33-5-24-1 et seq.) Franklin.—Court of record and general jurisdiction. Johnson Superior Court has standard small claims and misdemeanor division.

Johnson Superior Court No. 3 (IC33-5-24-1 et seq.) Franklin.—Court of record and general jurisdiction. Johnson Superior Court has standard small claims and misdemeanor division.

Knox Superior Court No. 1 (IC33-5-26-1 et seq.) Vincennes.—Jurisdiction same as Knox Circuit Court, except exclusive jurisdiction over juvenile matters.

Knox Superior Court No. 2 (IC33-5-26-1 et seq.) Vincennes.—Jurisdiction same as Knox Circuit Court, except exclusive jurisdiction over juvenile matters.

Kosciusko Superior Court No. 1 (IC33-5-27-1 et seq.) Warsaw.—Jurisdiction same as Kosciusko Circuit Court.

Kosciusko Superior Court No. 2 (IC33-5-27-1 et seq.) Warsaw.—Jurisdiction same as Kosciusko Superior Court No. 1 plus small claims and misdemeanors.

Kosciusko Superior Court No. 3 (IC33-5-27-1 et seq.) Warsaw.—Jursidiction same as Kosciusko Circuit Court No. 2.

LaGrange Superior Court (IC33-5-27.5-1 et seq.) LaGrange.—Jurisdiction same as LaGrange Circuit Court.

Lake Superior Court (IC33-5-29.5-1 et seq.) Places in Lake County as court determines.—Jurisdiction same as Lake Circuit Court in all civil and probate cases and matters whether original or appellate, has original exclusive jurisdiction of all felony cases, has original concurrent jurisdiction of all misdemeanor cases, infraction cases and ordinance violation cases, has such appellate jurisdiction in criminal cases as is rested in circuit court, and has original exclusive juvenile jurisdiction.

LaPorte Superior Court No. 1 (IC33-5-31.1-1 et seq.) Michigan City.—Jurisdiction same as LaPorte Circuit Court.

LaPorte Superior Court No. 2 (IC33-5-31.1-1 et seq.) Michigan City.—Jurisdiction same as LaPorte Circuit Court.

LaPorte Superior Court No. 3 (IC33-5-31.1-1 et seq.) Michigan City.—Jurisdiction same as LaPorte Circuit Court.

LaPorte Superior Court No. 4 (IC33-5-31.1-1 et seq.) Michigan City.—Jurisdiction same as LaPorte Circuit Court.

Lawrence Superior Court (IC33-5-32.5-1 et seq.) Bedford.—Original and concurrent jurisdiction with Lawrence Circuit Court in all civil and criminal cases, excluding juvenile and probate matters. Court has standard small claims and misdemeanor division.

Madison Superior Court (IC33-5-33.1-1 et seq.) Anderson.—Jurisdiction same as Madison Circuit Court and exclusive juvenile jurisdiction.

Marion Superior Court (IC33-5-35.1-1 et seq.) Indianapolis.—Concurrent and coextensive jurisdiction with circuit court in civil, criminal, probate, juvenile, and statutory cases and matters, whether original or appellate.

Marshall Superior Court No. 1 (IC33-5-35.5-1 et seq.) Plymouth.—Jurisdiction same as Marshall Circuit Court.

Marshall Superior Court No. 2 (IC33-5-35.5-1 et seq.) Plymouth.—Jurisdiction same as Marshall Circuit Court.

Miami Superior Court (IC33-5-35.8-1 et seq.) Peru.—Jurisdiction same as Miami Circuit Court.

Montgomery Superior Court (IC33-5-36.6-1 et seq.) Crawfordsville.—Jurisdiction same as Montgomery Circuit Court.

Morgan Superior Court No. 1 (IC33-5-37-1 et seq.) Martinsville.—Jurisdiction same as Morgan Circuit Court.

Morgan Superior Court No. 2 (IC33-5-37.1-1 et seq.) Martinsville.—Jurisdiction same as Morgan Circuit Court.

Along with Morgan Circuit Court, one judge in Morgan Superior Court has exclusive jurisdiction in all juvenile matters. Morgan Superior Court has standard small claims and misdemeanor division.

Newton Superior Court (IC33-5-37.2-1 et seq.) Kentland.—Jurisdiction same as Newton Circuit Court excluding juvenile matters.

Noble Superior Court (IC33-5-37.5-1 et seq.) Albion.—Jurisdiction same as Noble Circuit Court.

Ohio and Switzerland Superior Court (IC33-5-37.7-1 et seq.) Rising Sun and Vevay.—Same jurisdiction as circuit court under IC33-4-3 and 4.

Porter Superior Court (IC33-5-38-1 et seq.) Valparaiso and Portage Township.—Jurisdiction same as Porter Circuit Court excluding matters concerning delinquent children or children in need of services.

Posey Superior Court (IC33-5-38-1 et seq.) Mount Vernon.—Jurisdiction same as Posey Circuit Court. Court has standard small claims and misdemeanor division.

Pulaski Superior Court (IC33-5-38.2-1 et seq.) Winamac.—Jurisdiction same as Pulaski Circuit Court excluding juvenile matters.

Putnam Superior Court (IC33-5-38.3-1 et seq.) Greencastle.—Jurisdiction same as Putnam Circuit Court. Court has standard small claims and misdemeanor division.

Randolph Superior Court (IC33-5-38.5-1 et seq.) Winchester.—Jurisdiction same as Randolph Circuit Court, excluding juvenile matters.

Ripley Superior Court (IC33-5-38-7-1 et seq.) Versailles.—Jurisdiction same as Ripley Circuit Court. Court has standard small claims and misdemeanor division.

St. Joseph Superior Court (IC33-5-40-1 et seq.) South Bend and Mishawaka.—Exclusive original jurisdiction of traffic violations within cities of county and violation of ordinances of cities in county. Original and appellate jurisdiction concurrent with circuit court of county traffic violations, civil, criminal and probate matters.

Scott Superior Court (IC33-5-38.91 et seq.) Scottsburg.—Jurisdiction same as Scott Circuit Court.

Shelby Superior Court No. 1 (IC33-5-39-1 et seq.) Shelbyville.—Jurisdiction same as Shelby Circuit Court and exclusive juvenile jurisdiction.

Shelby Superior Court No. 2 (IC33-5-39-1 et seq.) Shelbyville.—Jurisdiction same as Shelby Circuit Court.

Steuben Superior Court (IC33-5-40.1-1 et seq.) Angola.—Jurisdiction same as Steuben Circuit Court.

Sullivan Superior Court (IC33-5-40.5-1 et seq.) Sullivan.—Jurisdiction same as Sullivan Circuit Court.

Switzerland Superior Court.—See Ohio and Switzerland Superior Court.

Tippecanoe Superior Court (IC33-5-41-1 et seq.) Lafayette.—Jurisdiction same as Tippecanoe circuit excluding probate and juvenile matters.

See note at head of Digest as to 1998 legislation covered.

See Topical Index in front part of this volume.

COURTS . . . *continued*

Tippecanoe Superior Court No. 2 (IC33-5-42-1 et seq.) Lafayette.—Jurisdiction same as Tippecanoe circuit excluding probate and juvenile matters.

Tippecanoe Superior Court No. 3 (IC33-5-42.1-1 et seq.) Lafayette.—Jurisdiction same as Tippecanoe circuit excluding probate and juvenile matters.

Vanderburg Superior Court (IC33-5-43-1 et seq.) Evansville.—Original and exclusive jurisdiction of probate matters, estate administrations, juvenile matters, trust assignments, adoptions and surviving partnerships. Original and appellate jurisdiction concurrent with circuit court of civil and criminal matters.

Vigo Superior Court (IC33-5-44.1-1 et seq.) Terre Haute.—Jurisdiction same as Vigo Circuit Court.

Wabash Superior Court (IC33-5-45.1-1 et seq.) Wabash.—Jurisdiction same as Wabash Circuit Court. Court has standard small claims and misdemeanor division.

Warrick Superior Court No. 1 (IC33-5-45.5-1 et seq.) Boonville.—Jurisdiction same as Warrick Circuit Court.

Warrick Superior Court No. 2 (IC33-5-45.5-1 et seq.) Boonville.—Jurisdiction same as Warrick Circuit Court.

Washington Superior Court (IC33-5-45.8-1 et seq.) Salem.—Jurisdiction same as Washington Circuit Court excluding juvenile matters.

Wayne Superior Court No. 1 (IC33-5-46-1 et seq.) Richmond.—Jurisdiction same as Wayne Circuit Court.

Wayne Superior Court No. 2 (IC33-5-47-1 et seq.) Richmond.—Jurisdiction same as Wayne Circuit Court.

Wayne Superior Court No. 3 (IC33-5-48-1 et seq.) Richmond.—Jurisdiction same as Wayne Circuit Court.

Wells Superior Court (IC33-5-48.5-1 et seq.) Bluffton.—Jurisdiction concurrent with Wells Circuit Court excluding juvenile matters.

White Superior Court (IC33-5-49-1 et seq.) Monticello.—Jurisdiction same as White Circuit Court.

Whitley Superior Court (IC33-5-50-1 et seq.) Columbia City.—Jurisidiction same as Whitley Circuit Court excluding juvenile matters.

Probate Courts.—In St. Joseph county there is probate court. Excluding civil matters, St. Joseph Probate Court exercises concurrent jurisdiction with superior court over all probate matters and exclusiver jurisdiction of juvenile matters. (IC33-8-2-1).

Circuit and/or superior courts have probate jurisdiction in other counties.

Circuit courts have general, civil and criminal jurisdiction over cases, except where exclusive jurisdiction is conferred upon some other court, board, or officer. See subheads dealing with superior, probate, county, municipal, city, criminal, magistrate, town and juvenile courts.

Adams County: Twenty-sixth Circuit; court sits at Decatur.

Allen County: Thirty-eighth Circuit; court sits at Fort Wayne.

Bartholomew County: Ninth Circuit; court sits at Columbus.

Benton County: Seventy-sixth Circuit; court sits at Fowler.

Blackford County: Seventy-first Circuit; court sits at Hartford City.

Boone County: Twentieth Circuit; court sits at Lebanon.

Brown County: Eighty-eighth Circuit; court sits at Nashville.

Carroll County: Seventy-fourth Circuit; court sits at Delphi.

Cass County: Twenty-ninth Circuit; court sits at Logansport.

Clark County: Fourth Circuit; court sits at Jeffersonville.

Clay County: Thirteenth Circuit; court sits at Brazil.

Clinton County: Forty-fifth Circuit; court sits at Frankfort.

Crawford County: Seventy-seventh Circuit; court sits at English.

Daviess County: Forty-ninth Circuit, court sits at Washington.

Dearborn County: Seventh Circuit; court sits at Lawrenceburg.

Decatur County: Sixty-ninth Circuit; court sits at Greensburg.

DeKalb County: Seventy-fifth Circuit; court sits at Auburn.

Delaware County: Forty-sixth Circuit; court sits at Muncie.

Dubois County: Fifty-seventh Circuit; court sits at Jasper.

Elkhart County: Thirty-fourth Circuit; court sits at Goshen.

Fayette County: Seventy-third Circuit; court sits at Connersville.

Floyd County: Fifty-second Circuit; court sits at New Albany.

Fountain County: Sixty-first Circuit; court sits at Covington.

Franklin County: Thirty-seventh Circuit; court sits at Brookville.

Fulton County: Forty-first Circuit; court sits at Rochester.

Gibson County: Sixty-sixth Circuit; court sits at Princeton.

Grant County: Forty-eighth Circuit; court sits at Marion.

Greene County: Sixty-third Circuit; court sits at Bloomfield.

Hamilton County: Twenty-fourth Circuit; court sits at Noblesville.

Hancock County: Eighteenth Circuit; court sits at Greenfield.

Harrison County: Third Circuit; court sits at Corydon.

Hendricks County: Fifty-fifth Circuit; court sits at Danville.

Henry County: Fifty-third Circuit; court sits at New Castle.

Howard County: Sixty-second Circuit; court sits at Kokomo.

Huntington County: Fifty-sixth Circuit; court sits at Huntington.

Jackson County: Fortieth Circuit; court sits at Brownstown.

Jasper County: Thirtieth Circuit; court sits at Rensselaer.

Jay County: Fifty-eighth Circuit; court sits at Portland.

Jefferson County: Fifth Circuit; court sits at Madison.

Jennings County: Eighty-sixth Circuit; court sits at Vernon.

Johnson County: Eighth Circuit; court sits at Franklin.

Knox County: Twelfth Circuit; court sits at Vincennes.

Kosciusko County: Fifty-fourth Circuit; court sits at Warsaw.

Lagrange County: Thirty-fifth Circuit; court sits at Lagrange.

Lake County: Thirty-first Circuit; court sits at Crown Point.

LaPorte County: Thirty-second Circuit; court sits at LaPorte.

Lawrence County: Eighty-first Circuit; court sits at Bedford.

Madison County: Fiftieth Circuit; court sits at Anderson.

Marion County: Nineteenth Circuit; court sits at Indianapolis.

Marshall County: Seventy-second Circuit; court sits at Plymouth.

Martin County: Ninetieth Circuit; court sits at West Shoals.

Miami County: Fifty-first Circuit; court sits at Peru.

Monroe County: Tenth Circuit; court sits at Bloomington.

Montgomery County: Twenty-second Circuit; court sits at Crawfordsville.

Morgan County: Fifteenth Circuit; court sits at Martinsville.

Newton County: Seventy-ninth Circuit; court sits at Kentland.

Noble County: Thirty-third Circuit; court sits at Albion.

Ohio County: Seventh Circuit; court sits at Lawrenceburg.

Orange County: Eighty-seventh Circuit; court sits at Paoli.

Owen County: Seventy-eighth Circuit; court sits at Spencer.

Parke County: Sixty-eighth Circuit; court sits at Rockville.

Perry County: Seventieth Circuit; court sits at Cannelton.

Pike County: Eighty-third Circuit; court sits at Petersburg.

Porter County: Sixty-seventh Circuit; court sits at Valparaiso.

Posey County: Eleventh Circuit; court sits at Mt. Vernon.

Pulaski County: Fifty-ninth Circuit; court sits at Winamac.

Putnam County: Sixty-fourth Circuit; court sits at Greencastle.

Randolph County: Twenty-fifth Circuit; court sits at Winchester.

Ripley County: Eightieth Circuit; court sits at Versailles.

Rush County: Sixty-fifth Circuit; court sits at Rushville.

Scott County: Sixth Circuit; court sits at Scottsburg.

Shelby County: Sixteenth Circuit; court sits at Shelbyville.

Spencer County: Eighty-fourth Circuit; court sits at Rockport.

Starke County: Forty-fourth Circuit; court sits at Knox.

Steuben County: Eighty-fifth Circuit; court sits at Angola.

St. Joseph: Sixtieth Circuit; court sits at South Bend.

Sullivan County: Fourteenth Circuit; court sits at Sullivan.

Switzerland County: Fifth Circuit; court sits at Vevay.

Tippecanoe County: Twenty-third Circuit; court sits at Lafayette.

Tipton County: Thirty-sixth Circuit; court sits at Tipton.

Union County: Eighty-ninth Circuit; court sits at Liberty.

Vanderburgh County: First Circuit; court sits at Evansville.

Vermillion County: Forty-seventh Circuit; courts sits at Newport.

Vigo County: Forty-third Circuit; court sits at Terre Haute.

Wabash County: Twenty-seventh Circuit; court sits at Wabash.

Warren County: Twenty-first Circuit; court sits at Williamsport.

Warrick County: Second Circuit; court sits at Boonville.

Washington County: Forty-second Circuit; court sits at Salem.

Wayne County: Seventeenth Circuit; court sits at Richmond.

Wells County: Twenty-eighth Circuit; court sits at Bluffton.

White County: Thirty-ninth Circuit; court sits at Monticello.

Whitley County: Eighty-second Circuit; court sits at Columbia City.

Small Claims and Misdemeanor Division of Circuit Courts.—Following circuit courts are to maintain standard small claims and misdemeanor division for civil actions in which amount sought is not more than $3,000, and for all possessory actions between landlord and tenant in which rent reserved is not more than $3000 per month (IC33-4-3-5 et seq.); and for all Class D felonies, misdemeanors, infractions and ordinance violations (IC33-4-3-5): Benton, Brown, Carroll, Crawford, Fountain, Franklin, Jennings, Martin, Newton, Owen, Parke, Perry, Pike, Ripley, Spencer, Starke, Tipton, Union, Vermillion, Warren, and Washington.

City and Town Courts.—IC33-10.1-1-3 provides for city or town courts in second or third class cities or towns. Judges elected under IC33-10-6 or 7. Jurisdiction of all violations of city ordinances and all infractions and misdemeanors. Original concurrent jurisdiction with circuit courts in all civil cases where amount in controversy does not exceed $3,000. During 1986 and every fourth year thereafter, second or third class cities or towns by ordinance may create or abolish city or town court. (IC33-10.1-1-3).

Juvenile Court.—Circuit courts have juvenile jurisdiction unless it is given exclusively to another court in that county. Other courts have juvenile jurisdiction only when provided by statute. (IC33-12-3-1). See also IC33-5-29.5-4.

Justices of the Peace.—Justice courts abolished Jan. 1, 1976. Replaced by county court system.

County Courts have original and concurrent jurisdiction in: all civil cases founded in contract or tort where amount at issue is $10,000 or less; all cases involving violation of city, town, or municipal ordinances; all possessory actions between landlord and tenant; all actions involving violations of traffic ordinances; and all class D felony, misdemeanor, and infraction cases. Original exclusive jurisdiction in actions for possession of property where value of property sought does not exceed $10,000. (IC33-10.5-3-1). Judgments shall be liens on real estate when entered in county court judgment docket in same manner as judgments in court of general jurisdiction become liens on real estate under IC34-55-9. (IC33-10.5-7-9). County courts are located in following counties: Adams, Bartholomew, Boone, Cass, Clay, Clinton, Daviess, Dearborn, Delaware, Fayette, Floyd, Gibson, Hancock, Hendricks, Henry, Howard, Huntington, Jackson, Jasper, Jay, Johnson, Knox, Kosciusko (abolished as of Jan. 1, 1997), Lagrange, Lake, LaPorte, Madison (two judges), Marshall, Miami, Monroe, Montgomery, Noble, Porter, Putnam, Randolph, Rush, Shelby, Steuben, Tippecanoe (two judges), Vigo (two judges), Wells, White and Whitley; and following with one court serving both counties: Fulton and Pulaski, Harrison and Crawford.

Other special statutes as to jurisdiction for particular county courts above should be consulted.

Small Claims Courts.—There shall be small claims court in each county containing consolidated city of first class (Marion County). County-wide jurisdiction with original and concurrent jurisdiction with circuit and superior in all civil cases founded in contract or tort where amount in controversy is $6,000 or less (excluding attorney fees and interest); in possessory actions between landlord and tenant where rent due at time of filing does not exceed $6,000. Trial shall be informal and not bound by statutory provisions or rules of practice, procedure, pleadings and evidence except provisions

See note at head of Digest as to 1998 legislation covered.

See Topical Index in front part of this volume.

COURTS . . . *continued*

relating to privileged communications and offers of compromise. All judgments rendered in civil actions may be recorded in judgment docket book of proper division of small claims court. Such judgment shall be lien on real estate when entered in circuit court judgment docket in same manner as judgment in court of general jurisdiction becomes lien on real estate under IC34-55-9. Appeals shall be taken to superior court and tried de novo. (IC33-11.6-1 to 9; IC33-11.6-4-3).

See subheads County Courts; Municipal Court; Circuit Courts; Superior Courts.

Tax Court.—Indiana has tax court with exclusive jurisdiction over any case that arises under tax laws of state and that constitutes initial appeal of final determination made by Department of State Revenue or State Board of Tax Commissioners. Tax court decisions may be appealed directly to Indiana Supreme Court. (IC33-3-5-1 et seq.).

LEGISLATURE:

Reorganizes biannually with annual sessions. Convenes in Nov. in even-numbered years and may extend through Apr. 29 of following year. Convenes in Nov. in odd-numbered years and may extend through Mar. 14 of following year. (IC 2-2.1-1 to 3). Governor may call special session. (Const. art. 4, §9).

Legislation must be confined to one subject matter. (Const. art. 4, §19).

Initiative and referendum do not exist in Indiana.

Lobbyists.—Regulated by Indiana Lobby Registration Commission. (IC 2-7-1).

REPORTS:

Decisions of Supreme Court: Blackford's Reports, 8 vols., and Indiana Reports beginning with vol. 1 and ending with vol. 275 (1984). Decisions of appellate court, Indiana Appellate Court Reports ends with vol. 182 (1984). Indiana decisions are also reported in Northeastern Reporter.

Citation Form in State Courts.—Citation to cases should follow format put forth in current edition of Uniform System of Citation (Bluebook). Thus, cases decided prior to May 5, 1981, in Indiana Supreme Court and Nov. 7, 1979, in Indiana Court of Appeals shall be cited by giving title of case followed by volume and page of state report, volume and page of regional reporter, and year of final disposition. (E.g., Warren v. Indiana Tel. Co., 217 Ind. 93, 26 N.E.2d 399 [1940].) Cases decided after above noted dates shall be cited by giving title of case, followed by volume and page of regional reporter, Court of disposition, and year of final disposition. (E.g., Condon v. Patel, 459 N.E.2d 1205 [Ind. Ct. App. 1984].)

Digests.—West's Indiana Digest and supplements; Callaghan's Indiana Digest; Burns' Indiana Digest and supplement; Ripley's Digest; Black's Digest; Woolworth's Digest; Remy's Digest. The four last named cover only earlier reports.

STATUTES:

The 1975 Legislature officially revised and codified statutes of this State into Indiana Code. Code is divided into 36 titles and each title is then subdivided into articles, chapters, and sections. Thus, citation, IC29-1-5-1 would be found under Title 29, Article 1, Chapter 5, and Section 1 of Indiana Code. Note: Public Laws (PL) of Legislature are not included in official publication of Indiana Code, but are added in separate volumes of sessions. Latest unofficial compilations are Burns' Indiana Statutes, with pocket supplement covering all current legislation, and West's Annotated Indiana Code, also with pocket parts.

Uniform Acts adopted by National Conference of Commissioners enacted in state are: †Anatomical Gift (1969, 1987, 1995); Arbitration (1969); †Attendance of Witnesses from Without the State in Criminal Cases (1983); Certification of Questions of Law (1971); Child Custody Jurisdiction (1977); †Commercial Code (1963, 1985, 1995, 1996); Conservation Easement (1984); Consumer Credit Code, 1968 edition (1971, 1988); Controlled Substances (1977, 1988); †Criminal Extradition (1935, 1984); Declaratory Judgments (1927); Determination of Death (1986); Durable Power of Attorney (1985); †Fiduciaries (1927); †Fraudulent Transfer (1994); Gifts to Minors, 1966 edition (1969, 1985); Health-Care Consent (1987); Interstate Family Support (1996); Jury Selection and Service, 1971 edition (1974); †Limited Partnership, 1976 edition (1988); †Management of Institutional Funds (1989); Partnership (1949); Premarital Agreement (1995); †Principal and Income, 1962 edition (1969); Reciprocal Transfer Tax (1953); †Securities Act (1961, 1988); †Simplification of Fiduciary Security Transfers (1961); Simultaneous Death, 1940 edition (1941); Statutory Rule Against Perpetuities (1991); Testamentary Additions to Trusts (1954); Trade Secrets (1982, 1983); Unclaimed Property (1996); Veterans' Guardianship, 1942 edition (1953, 1971).

†Adopted with significant variations or modifications. See appropriate topics.

Uniform Commercial Code enacted by 1963 Legislature and in effect since July 1, 1964. (IC26-1-1-101 et seq.).

See category Business Regulation and Commerce, topic Commercial Code.

For text of Uniform Acts falling within the scope of the Martindale-Hubbell Law Digests see Uniform and Model Acts section.

UNIFORM LAWS:

For list of Uniform Acts in force in this state see topic Statutes. For text of Uniform Acts within the scope of the Martindale-Hubbell Law Digests see Uniform and Model Acts section.

CRIMINAL LAW

BAIL:

See topic Criminal Law.

CRIMINAL LAW:

Generally, IC Tit. 35, Arts. 41-49 define crimes, IC Tit. 35, Art. 50 governs sentences and IC Tit. 35, Arts. 1-9, 32-38 govern procedure.

Criminal liability for omission can only result when one has statutory, common law or contractual duty to act. (IC35-41-2-1[a]).

Guidelines for use of deadly force are those approved by U.S. Supreme Court in Tennessee v. Garner, 471 U.S. 1, 105 S.Ct. 1694, 85 L.E. 2d 1 (1985).

Indictment or Information.—Prosecutions of crimes shall be instituted by prosecuting attorney in court with jurisdiction over offense. (IC35-34-1-1 et seq.).

Bail.—Offenses other than murder and treason are bailable. Murder and treason are not bailable where proof is evident or presumption strong. (Const., art. I, §17; IC35-33-8-1 et seq.).

Violent Crime Victims' Compensation Fund.—Persons injured as result of violent crimes or terrorist act may receive assistance. (IC5-2-6.1 et seq.). Victims of crimes entitled to certain information and services under Victim Assistance Programs. (IC33-14-10-1 et seq.).

Interstate Compact for Supervision of Parolees and Probationers.—Out-of-State Probationer or Parolee. (IC11-13-4). Interstate Parole and Probation Hearings. (IC11-13-5).

Uniform Act to Secure Attendance of Witnesses from Without a State in Criminal Proceedings.—Adopted. (IC35-37-5-1).

Uniform Criminal Extradition Act.—Adopted, but is original act of 1926 not 1936 version. (IC35-33-10-3).

Agreement in Detainers.—Adopted. (IC35-33-10-4).

Child Abuse Registry.—Established with tracking system and automated child protection system. (IC31-33-17-1 et seq.).

Sex Offender Registry.—Established. (IC5-2-12).

DEBTOR AND CREDITOR

ASSIGNMENTS:

Uniform Commercial Code in effect since July 1, 1964. (IC26-1-1-101 et seq.).

Action may be continued by or against original party, unless court upon motion directs that person to whom interest is transferred be substituted in action or be joined with original party. (Rule TR 25[C]).

Wages.—Any direction given by employee to his or her employer to make deduction from wages to be earned constitutes assignment of wages. (IC22-2-6-1).

An assignment of wages is valid only if: (1) It is in writing and signed by employee, by its terms revocable at any time by employee upon written notice, and agreed to in writing by employer; (2) executed copy is delivered to employer within ten days of date of its execution; and (3) it is made for purpose of paying any of 12 specified obligations, including dues to become owing by employee to labor organization of which he or she is member. (IC22-2-6-2).

No assignment of wages or salary by any employee or wage earner to any wage broker as defined in IC22-2-7-1 is valid unless it is for fixed and definite part of wages or salary earned as to be earned during period not to exceed 30 days immediately following date of assignment. (IC22-2-7-2).

No assignment of wages by married person who is living with person's spouse residing in Indiana to any wage broker is valid without consent of spouse evidenced by spouse's signature to assignment executed and acknowledged before notary public except for deductions applied to credit union account or nonprofit organizations of employees. (IC22-2-7-4).

No assignment of wage is valid unless notice in writing of same, accompanied by copy of assignment, is given to employer within ten days from date of its execution. (IC22-2-7-5).

Court may require support payments be made through clerk of court. Clerk of court shall forward payments to Title IV-D agency if child receives assistance under federal Aid to Families with Dependent Children Program (42 U.S.C. 601 et seq.) and assignment in effect against person obligated to make payments. Clerk obligated to maintain specified records.

See also category Business Regulation and Commerce, topic Commercial Code.

ATTACHMENT:

New Rules of Civil Procedure extend prior remedies of attachment. (IC34-1-11-1; Rule TR 64 [B]).

Actions in Which Allowed.—Attachment is allowed upon any claim of creditor if plaintiff's complaint is for money or to determine rights in property or obligation attached. (IC-34-1-11-1; Rule TR 64[B]). See subhead Grounds, infra.

Courts Which May Issue Writ.—Any court of first instance having civil jurisdiction.

In Whose Favor Writ May Issue.—Any plaintiff, whether resident or nonresident.

Claims on Which Writ May Issue.—Attachment may issue on a claim which is not payable in the state. (96 Ind. App. 325, 183 N.E. 699, reh'g denied, 96 Ind. App. 341, 185 N.E. 169). As to unmatured claims, see infra, subhead Grounds.

Time for Issuance.—Attachment may issue any time, or during pendency of action after filing of complaint, even though summons has not been served (183 N.E. 699), and on Sundays in emergencies (IC34-1-11-8).

Grounds.—An attachment may be issued when defendant is a foreign corporation or a nonresident, or being a resident, if he secretes himself so that summons may not be served upon him, or is secretly about to leave state, or has departed therefrom, or is removing his property therefrom or has sold or is about to sell or to dispose of his property subject to execution with intent to defraud or delay his creditors, or is a person whose residence and whereabouts are unknown and cannot be determined after reasonable investigation before commencement of action. (IC34-1-11-1, 2; Rule TR 64[B]).

Unmatured Claims.—Attachment may not issue on unmatured claim, except on ground that defendant is removing or has removed his person, has sold or is about to

---

See note at head of Digest as to 1998 legislation covered.

See Topical Index in front part of this volume.

ATTACHMENT . . . *continued*
sell or convey his property with intent to defraud or is removing or about to remove property subject to execution leaving an insufficient excess subject to execution. (IC34-1-11-1).

Proceedings to Obtain.—Plaintiff must file an affidavit showing the nature and amount of his claim and existence of one or more of the statutory grounds for attachments. (IC34-1-11-4.1). Writ of attachment against defendant's real estate or his interest is effectively served by recordation of action in appropriate lis pendens record, and, unless vacant, by serving writ of attachment or notice thereof upon person in possession of land. (Rule TR 64[B][6]). Exception: No attachment shall issue against any debtor whose spouse and family remain in county of debtor's usual residence prior to his absence, until debtor has been absent from state for more than one year, unless attempt has been made to conceal his absence. Exception does not apply when debtor is removing, selling or otherwise disposing or about to dispose of his property. (IC34-1-11-2).

Attachment Bond.—Any plaintiff except the State, must file a written undertaking with security to the approval of the county clerk conditioned that plaintiff will prosecute the attachment (IC34-1-11-5, 39) and pay defendant all damages he may sustain if proceedings prove to be wrongful or oppressive (IC34-1-11-38).

Levy and Lien.—Attachment must be levied first on personalty and may be levied on realty if sufficient personalty is not found. (IC34-1-11-11).

Indemnity.—There is no statutory authority for the officer to demand indemnity before making a levy.

Lien attaches from time of delivery of order of attachment to sheriff. (IC34-1-11-10).

Release of Property.—Defendant or any other person having had possession may secure release of property by giving bond for the appraised value of the goods attached or for payment of any judgment which plaintiff may secure. (IC34-1-11-13).

Sale.—Perishable goods held under attachment may be ordered sold at public auction by the court upon reasonable notice. (IC34-1-11-18).

Third Party Claims.—Where personal property is in the possession of officer by virtue of writ of attachment and third person brings action to replevy same, such officer may demand of attachment plaintiff indemnifying bond against loss for attorney's fees or judgment for damages and costs, and after five days in default thereof may deliver property to replevin plaintiff. (IC34-2-4-1).

Consigned goods are attached subject to lien of consignee. (IC-34-1-11-16).

Adverse claimants to attached property may be examined under oath. (IC34-1-11-15).

Intervention of Other Creditors.—Any other creditors of defendant may enter complaint and file their affidavits and bonds and prove their claims as parties to the original action at any time before final judgment. The money realized from sale and garnishees after paying costs and expenses is shared pro rata on the amount of all claims filed. The original attaching creditor has no preference. (IC34-1-11-31, 37).

Dismissal by original creditor does not affect intervening creditors. (IC34-1-11-32).

Appeals.—After judgment for the defendant, attached property is released unless plaintiff files notice of appeal within 72 hours. (IC34-1-11-34).

CREDITORS' SUITS:

There is but one form of action in Indiana, but suits in the nature of creditors' bills may be brought by a creditor to reach assets fraudulently concealed. If receiver has been appointed, right to bring such action or right to bring suit is exclusively in receiver. (128 Ind. 222, 27 N.E. 494).

Procedure for filing, consideration, allowance or trial of claims in receiverships and assignments for benefit of creditors must, insofar as is practical, conform with procedure relating to claims in decedents' estates. (Rule TR 66[D]).

EXECUTIONS:

Process to enforce a judgment or a decree for payment of money must be by writ of execution, unless court directs otherwise or a particular statute provides otherwise. (Rule TR 69).

Time for Issuance.—Execution from court of record may issue at any time within ten years after rendition of judgment, but thereafter may be issued only on leave of court obtained on notice and motion. (IC34-1-34-2). Execution may issue to sheriff of any county in state, but if it requires delivery of real or personal property, it must be issued to sheriff of county where property is situated. (IC34-1-34-6; 835 F.2d 1215). Execution is lien on personal property within jurisdiction of officer from time of delivery, but if there are several executions in hands of different officers, first levied has preference, and divests all liens created by prior delivery. (IC34-1-34-9). Execution to another county from that in which judgment is rendered is lien against real estate of judgment debtor in such other county only from time of levy. (IC34-1-45-5). Executions are returnable in 90 days unless judgment creditor designates shorter time in praecipe. (IC34-1-34-8). On judgment rendered on delivery bonds no stay is permitted, and execution is returnable in 30 days. (IC34-1-38-6).

Exemptions.—See topic Exemptions.

Stay of Execution.—Execution upon judgment for recovery of money or sale of property may be stayed. However, party has right to protection of surety bond or security. (Rule TR 62[F]). Stays are not allowed on judgments on delivery bonds, for money received in fiduciary capacity or for breach of official duty. (IC34-1-35-11, IC34-1-38-6). Extraordinary relief is allowed by parties furnishing bonds, subject to furnishing of counterbonds under special statutes such as injunction proceedings, replevin, ejectment, and attachment. (Rule TR 62[F]).

Sale.—Before property may be sold, it must be appraised by two disinterested householders of neighborhood where levy is, one of whom shall be selected by plaintiff and other by defendant, and sale cannot be effected for less than two-thirds of appraised value, unless judgment orders that it is to be executed without relief from appraisement laws. Except for requirements of appraisal and that land must sell for two-thirds of its appraised value, sale of real estate must be conducted under same rule and same procedures applicable to foreclosure of mortgages. Real estate cannot be sold until elapse of six months from time judgment or execution thereon becomes lien on property. (Rule TR 69[A]; IC34-1-37-1 to 7; IC34-1-27-4).

Unless otherwise ordered by court, sheriff or person conducting sale of any property upon execution is not required to offer it for sale in any particular order, in parcels, or first offer rents and profits and is required to sell real and personal property separately pursuant to applicable law. (Rule TR 69[A]). Court may order judgment creditor, person seeking sale, or officer conducting sale to procure qualified title opinion or title insurance policy with respect to interest of person whose land is being sold. (Rule TR 69[F]).

Supplementary Proceedings.—Proceedings supplemental to execution may be enforced by verified motion or with affidavits in court where judgment is rendered. If court determines that motion meets statutory requirements as to supplementary proceedings it will, ex parte and without notice, order judgment debtor and other named party defendants to appear for hearing thereon or to answer interrogatories attached to motion. Date fixed for appearance and hearing cannot be less than 20 days after service. Judgment creditor or debtor may utilize discovery provisions. Witnesses may be required to appear and testify in supplementary proceedings. Court shall issue order directing depositary financial institution to place hold on deposit account in which judgment debtor has interest, either individually or jointly, when certain conditions are met. Such order is subject to limitations of IC34-1-44-7. (IC34-1-44-2 to 8; Rule TR 69[E]). Proceedings supplemental to execution are applicable to debt that is or will be due from garnishee to judgment debtor, even though amount of debt is not presently discernible. Thus, third party who has property or will be indebted to judgment debtor at any time, in undetermined amount, is subject to proceedings supplemental. (627 N.E.2d 1323; IC34-1-44-5).

See also topic Garnishment.

EXEMPTIONS:

On judgments obtained after Sept. 30, 1977, every debtor domiciled in state may exempt from levy or sale on execution or other final process, for judgment founded upon express or implied contract or tort claim, following: Up to $7,500 of real estate or personal property constituting personal or family residence of debtor, $4,000 other real estate or tangible personal property, $100 intangible personal property, including choses in action (provided total of above does not exceed $10,000), plus professionally prescribed health aids, real estate held as tenants by entireties and interests, whether vested or not, that judgment debtor has in retirement plan to extent that contributions were made by or on behalf of debtor and contributions were not subject to federal income tax at time of contribution or earnings on contributions that are not subject to federal income taxation at time of judgment, and money that is in medical care savings account established under IC6-8-11. (IC34-2-28-1). Creditor of one spouse may not seize, sell or attach entireties property. (172 Ind. App. 279).

Right to exempt property may be claimed by spouse of execution defendant if latter is absent. (IC34-2-28-12).

Municipal property is exempt from execution except where judgment arises from action against another municipality or state. (IC34-4-16.4-2).

There is no exemption for real estate from mechanic's or purchase money liens, nor any exemption from sale for taxes. (IC34-2-28-14).

Claim of Exemption.—The debtor must file with the officer a schedule of all of his property, and claim property he desires to exempt, which shall be appraised under direction of officer. (IC34-2-28-2 to -11).

Sale of Property.—Provision is made for sale of property claimed under exemption law, but whose value exceeds exemption. (IC34-2-28-8).

Voluntary Liens.—On judgments obtained after June 30, 1989, real estate or personal property upon which debtor has voluntarily granted lien is not, to extent of balance due on debt secured by lien: (1) Subject to IC34-2-28; or (2) exempt from levy or sale on execution or any other final process from court. (IC34-2-28-1[d]).

FORECLOSURE:

See topic Liens; category Mortgages, topic Mortgages of Real Property.

FRAUDULENT SALES AND CONVEYANCES:

Uniform Commercial Code in effect since July 1, 1964; revised to conform with 1972 version. (IC26-1-1-101 et seq.).

Uniform Fraudulent Transfer Act adopted. (IC32-2-7-1 et seq.).

Bulk Sales.—Governed by Uniform Commercial Code. See category Business Regulation and Commerce, topic Commercial Code.

GARNISHMENT:

Uniform Consumer Credit Code, in effect since Oct. 1, 1971, prescribes maximum earnings which may be garnished. (IC24-4.5-5-105). All other assets of debtor in possession of third persons may be reached by garnishment (IC34-25-3-2 to 13; IC34-25-2-19 to 24; and IC34-25-1-4) or by proceedings supplementary to execution (IC34-55-8-1 to 8). Garnishment will be allowed in favor of plaintiff suing upon claim for money, whether founded on contract, tort, equity, child support, or any other theory and whether it is liquidated, contingent or unliquidated; or upon claim to determine rights in property or obligation garnished. (Rule TR 64[B][3]). Proceedings supplementary may be had after return of execution on any type of judgment. (IC34-55-8-1). See Rule TR 69(E).

Property Which May Be Reached.—On proceedings supplementary, property in excess of statutory exemptions may be reached. (IC34-55-8-7). Any interest in tangible or intangible property owned by defendant can be subject to garnishment if it is subject to execution, proceedings supplementary to execution or any creditor process allowed by law. Wages or salaries shall not be subject to attachment and garnishment under IC34-25. (TR 64[B][2]; Rule TR 64[B]).

Money judgment creditors who wish to garnish deposit account in financial institution must comply with notice procedures, including notice to be sent by financial

See note at head of Digest as to 1998 legislation covered.

See Topical Index in front part of this volume.

IN – 25

GARNISHMENT . . . *continued*
institution to debtor concerning legal exemptions from judgment and right to prompt hearing. (IC28-9-3-4). Restriction on withdrawal from deposit account may not exceed 90 days pending court's determination or rights. (IC28-9-4-2).

It is not objectionable that property or obligation garnished is in possession of plaintiff or is owing by plaintiff to defendant or by defendant to plaintiff. (TR 64[B][4]; Rule TR 64[B]).

Jurisdiction.—Proceedings supplementary are within jurisdiction of any circuit, superior, municipal or city court. (IC34-55-8-1). Garnishment proceedings are within jurisdiction of any court of general jurisdiction. (IC34-25-3-2). Jurisdiction is denied any court if plaintiff-creditor and principal debtor are both nonresidents and garnishee doing business within state owes debtor for wages or personal earnings. (IC34-25-1-2).

Proceedings to Obtain.—Upon plaintiff's filing an affidavit and bond to protect garnishee, clerk issues summons making garnishee a party. (IC34-25-3-2). No garnishment of earnings is allowed prior to entry of judgment against debtor. (IC24-4.5-5-104). After return of execution and upon affidavit, but without requirement of bond, plaintiff may reach his debtor's debtor on proceedings supplementary. (IC34-55-8-5). See Rule TR 69(E).

Answer of Garnishee.—A garnishee must make a statement to the sheriff within five days of the service of the writ, listing a schedule of the debtor's property which he holds. (IC34-25-3-4). Garnishee failing to answer may be defaulted and judgment rendered against him as against other defendants. (IC34-25-3-5). Third parties in proceedings supplementary need appear only if specially ordered to do so by court. Normal practice provides only for answering interrogatories by mail. (IC34-55-8-5).

Practice.—A garnishee expected to abscond may be held under bail. (IC34-25-3-6). Garnishee defendants may be examined under oath as to property in their possession and are liable for disbursements from time of service of writ. (IC34-25-3-3, 4). Garnishees may discharge themselves from liability by delivery of defendant's property to sheriff or court. (IC34-25-3-11).

Governmental organization, or a representative, including guardian, receiver, assignee for benefit of creditors, trustee or representative of decedent's estate may be named as garnishee and bound by duties of garnishee. (Rule TR 64[B][5]).

Adverse Claims.—Other creditors of the defendant debtor may join in a garnishment proceeding by filing affidavits and bond. (IC34-25-3-13). Thereafter dismissal by original plaintiff does not dismiss as to such creditors. (IC34-25-2-19). No statutory provision is made for other creditors of judgment debtor joining in proceeding supplementary.

Judgment.—After hearing with notice to debtor, court may order application of property, income or profits to judgment. (IC34-55-8-7). Final judgment cannot be rendered against garnishee until action against defendant debtor is determined. (IC34-25-3-7).

Earnings.—Amount to be garnished is 25% of disposable earnings or amount by which disposable earnings exceed 30 times Federal minimum wage, whichever is less. Amount to be garnished for support orders is not to exceed 50% of disposable earnings where individual is supporting spouse or child, or 60% where he is not. These increase to 55% and 65% if withholding is to enforce support order for period more than 12 weeks prior to withholding. This limitation applies to cumulative total of all liens and not merely lien of one creditor on proceedings supplementary. Employer required to make deductions is entitled to greater of $12 or 3% of total deducted as fee for services; 1/2 of fee is to be borne by debtor, and that amount may be deducted from disposable earnings. 1/2 of fee is chargeable to creditor and may be deducted from amount due. Judgment debt is not increased by amount of collection fee. Child support withholding orders take priority over garnishment orders. If person is subject to both, garnishment is allowed only to extent that disposable income withheld under support order does not exceed statutory maximum amount subject to garnishment. (IC24-4.5-5-105).

HOMESTEADS:

Urban homesteading is allowed in any city, town or county adopting ordinance to administer program in accord with IC36-7-17-1 to 12.

For exempt real property, see topic Exemptions.

JUDGMENT NOTES:

See category Business Regulation and Commerce, topic Bills and Notes.

LIENS:

Uniform Commercial Code in effect since July 1, 1964. (IC26-1-1-101 et seq.).

Mortgagor, or other person with right to demand, may cause forfeiture and recover up to $500 with costs and attorney's fees for failure, by neglect or refusal, to release, discharge, and satisfy of record any mortgage, mechanic's lien, judgment or other lien when obligation secured, including interest, has been fully paid. Cause arises after 15 days from written demand by registered or certified mail, return receipt requested. (IC32-8-1-2).

Laborers and employees of individuals or corporations have preferred claims to amount of $600 against assets for wages earned during the three months preceding seizure of property of employer on any mesne or final process, suspension of business by action of creditors, or appointment of trustee or receiver. (IC22-2-10-1). Corporate employees have special priority lien upon corporate property and earnings for work performed from date of employment. Corporate employee lien arising out of sale of real estate is limited to lien upon real estate. Lien acquired by filing notice with county recorder and enforced by filing complaint within six months of acquiring lien. (IC32-8-24-1 to 6).

Boats and water craft are subject to liens for supplies, wages, repairs, equipment, etc. (IC32-8-22-1). Lien is dischargeable before judgment by filing bond with sureties for amount of lien. (IC32-8-22-7).

Keepers of hotels, motels, boarding houses, restaurants and the like have a lien upon baggage or other articles of value belonging to the boarder or lodger being in house to extent of bill for food, lodging, entertainment, and other accommodation. Keeper may sell such articles after 60 days by giving ten days notice. (IC32-8-27-2).

Hospital has a lien for reasonable service fees on judgment for personal injuries if recorded on judgment docket, except in cases under state or federal workmen's compensation acts, or federal liability act. (IC32-8-26-1).

Providers of emergency ambulance services have lien for reasonable and necessary service fees on patient's cause of action, suit, or claim arising from illness or injury. Lienholder perfects lien by filing verified statement with county recorder within 60 days after providing services. Lien does not apply to cases under federal workmen's compensation acts or federal employers' liability act. (IC32-8-38-1 to 7).

Bailees.—All entities engaged in storing, warehousing and forwarding merchandise have lien upon such merchandise to extent of value of their services. All such merchandise that has remained in their possession for six months or more may, with ten days notice, be sold at public auction to pay amount of lien. (IC32-8-35-1 to 3).

Persons repairing, storing, servicing, or furnishing supplies for motor vehicles, airplanes, construction or farm machinery have lien if filed in recorder's office of county where repairs, storage or servicing was performed or supplies were furnished within 60 days after performance which may be foreclosed in circuit or superior court within one year from time lien is recorded. (IC32-8-31-1 to 7).

Transfer men and draymen have a lien upon goods, merchandise, etc., for charges for hauling, packing, transferring, conveying or erecting the same and for money paid for freight, storage or demurrage on the same. Notice of lien must be filed within 60 days after performing such labor or payment of money. No redemption after sale. Lien may be foreclosed within one year from time lien is recorded. (IC32-8-32-1 to 6).

Mechanics and tradesmen have a lien upon goods left for alteration or repair, liverymen and feeders on stock left with them, blacksmiths on animals shod, forwarding men and commission merchants on goods in storage, watch, clock or jewelry workers on articles worked on, all regulated by statute. (IC32-8-30-1 to 9, IC32-8-29-1, IC32-8-21-1 to 6, IC32-8-35-1 to 3, IC32-8-34-1).

Owner or operator of threshing machine or other farm machinery has a lien upon grain threshed or crops produced to secure payment of services. Notice of lien must be filed within 30 days after work for plowing, disking or cultivating and ten days after work for combining, bailing or picking. (IC32-8-33-1 to 2).

Board of Public Works has lien against any lot, parcel of real estate, or building connected with and using works by or through sewage system of city or town for payment of rates or charges assessed by board for said sewage service. (IC36-9-23-32).

Electronic home entertainment repairmen have possessory lien on equipment repaired to extent of reasonable value of labor performed and materials used. Lienholder may sell equipment in his possession at public auction if payment not made within 60 days of due date after giving owner 30 days notice of intent to sell. (IC32-8-36-1 to 4).

Dry cleaners, launderers and servicers of household goods have liens for services which have not been paid for 90 days or more. (IC32-8-23-1 to 5).

Engineers, Surveyors and Architects.—Registered professional engineers, registered land surveyors and registered architects may have same lien for services rendered as is provided for in mechanics' lien statute. (IC32-8-25-1).

Fabricators have possessory lien on dies, molds, jig forms or patterns to extent of amount due for work performed. Lienholder may sell items at auction if payment not made within 60 days of due date after giving owner and perfected secured parties 30 days' notice of intent to sell. (IC32-8-37-1 to 8).

Landlords have lien for payment of rent upon crops raised on leased premises. Lien acquired by filing with recorder 30 days prior to maturity of crop notice specifying amount claimed and substantial description of real estate. Landlord may sell crop subject to lien when rent becomes overdue, but tenant has right to remove his portion of crop not subject to lien after notifying landlord. (IC32-7-1-18).

Federal Liens.—In order to perfect any federal lien on real property or any federal tax lien on personal property (including liens for federal taxes and superfund liability), agency must file notice of lien in recorder's office of county where subject real or personal property is located. (IC36-2-11-25).

Mechanics' Liens.—All persons performing labor or furnishing material or machinery for erecting, repairing or removing any structure have lien on said structure and upon real estate upon which structure is situated, for their pay, by filing in recorder's office within 60 days after time labor was performed or material furnished, sworn statement in duplicate of their intention to hold lien upon such property, specifically setting forth amount claimed, and giving substantial description of lot or land upon which structure stands. Suppliers to materialmen, however, are not entitled to hold liens. (IC32-8-3-1 to 15).

Such lien may be enforced by suit in the circuit or superior court, and if no action is brought within one year from time notice of lien is filed to enforce same, lien becomes null and void. (IC32-8-3-6). Mechanics' liens have priority over all liens suffered or created after date when mechanic or other person began to perform labor or furnish materials or machinery (this is limited by fact that notice of lien must be recorded within 60 days after labor has been performed or materials have been furnished, except liens of other mechanics and materialmen, as to which there is no priority). (IC32-8-3-5). Notice of intention to hold lien, otherwise valid and enforceable, but filed prior to Mar. 10, 1967, is valid and enforceable. (IC32-8-3-4).

Railroad laborers and mechanics have a lien on right of way and franchises and appurtenances of railways on filing notice with recorder. Person who, in doing business with railroad company, has constructed building on portion of right of way adjacent to such person's place of business may have lien on right of way in event of sale or abandonment by railroad company. (IC32-8-3-12).

Contract between property owner and contractor, providing that there shall be no lien on the premises, is not valid against subcontractors, laborers, etc., unless in writing, containing specific references by legal description of real estate to be improved, acknowledged in same manner as deeds, and recorded within five days of execution.

See note at head of Digest as to 1998 legislation covered.

See Topical Index in front part of this volume.

LIENS . . . *continued*
(IC32-8-3-1). No-lien contract need not be posted on premises, and is not valid against any work or material supplied prior to recording of such contract. (IC32-8-3-1).

Owner may give notice to lienholder to sue within 30 days, and if he does not do so lien is discharged. (IC32-8-3-10).

Mechanics' liens are released by the recorder after 13 months from filing, on application of owner supported by a filed affidavit alleging no suit is pending to enforce lien. (IC32-8-6-1 to 2). Liquidated damages provided if lienholder fails to cause lien to be released after it has been satisfied. (IC32-8-6-1).

Lien may be released by filing bond with sureties before judgment. (IC32-8-3-11).

No redemption after sale.

Criminal penalty provided for certain acts. (IC32-8-3-15).

When owner-occupied dwelling is involved, if work was done or delivery made to other than owner or his representative, then written notice of work or delivery and existence of lien rights must be given to owner within 30 days from date of first work or delivery. When original construction is done for intended occupancy of owner upon whose land construction is performed, then as to all work and materials furnished to other than owner or his representative, written notice of such work and material and existence of lien rights must be given to owner within 60 days from date of first work or delivery. In all cases involving original construction, mechanic's lien is not valid against innocent purchaser for value without notice unless notice of intent to hold lien is properly recorded prior to recording of deed by which such purchaser takes title. This paragraph applies only to single or double family dwelling. (IC32-8-3-1).

Public Works.—Contractor must execute good and sufficient bond, in amount equal to contract price, conditioned on payment for all labor and materials. Materialmen and laborers may also claim against funds due contractor from the public agency. Claim is made by filing duplicate verified statements of amount due with public agency within 60 days of last services or materials furnished. (IC5-16-5-1 to 2).

Common Law Liens.—Common law lien is lien against real or personal property that is not statutory lien, security interest created by agreement, or judicial lien obtained by legal or equitable proceeding. (IC32-8-39-1). Person asserting common law lien must prove existence of lien as prescribed by common law of Indiana. (IC32-8-39-2.7). No common law lien exists against property of public official for performance or nonperformance of public official's official duty. (IC32-8-39-2.7[b]). Party may record common law lien by recording statement of intent to hold lien in county where property is located, including statement of amount claimed, full description of property and legal basis upon which right to hold common law lien is asserted. (IC32-8-39-3). Property owner may give notice to lienholder to sue within 30 days after notice is given; if suit is not commenced, lien is void. (IC32-8-39-4). Upon recording of affidavit from property owner that suit was not commenced, lien is released. (IC32-8-39-5). Lienholder must file certificate of satisfaction when lien is satisfied. (IC32-8-39-5.5).

For other liens, see categories Business Regulation and Commerce, topic Warehousemen; Employment, topic Labor Relations; Legal Profession, topic Attorneys and Counselors; Mineral, Water and Fishing Rights, topic Mines and Minerals. See also category Business Regulation and Commerce, topic Commercial Code.

MECHANICS' LIENS:

See topic Liens.

PLEDGES:

Uniform Commercial Code in effect since July 1, 1964. (IC26-1-1-101 et seq.).

See also category Business Regulation and Commerce, topic Commercial Code.

RECEIVERS:

Receiver may be appointed by court in following cases: (1) In action by vendor to vacate fraudulent purchase of property, or by creditor to subject any property or fund to his claim; (2) in actions between partners, or persons jointly interested in any property or fund; (3) in all actions when it is shown that property, fund or rent, and profits in controversy, is in danger of being lost, removed or materially injured; (4) in actions in which mortgagee seeks to foreclose mortgage, except that upon motion by mortgagee court shall appoint receiver if at time motion is filed property is not occupied by owner as owner's principal residence and: it appears that such property is in danger of being lost, removed or materially injured, it appears that such property may not be sufficient to discharge mortgaged debt, either mortgagor or owner of property has agreed in mortgage or in some other writing to appointment of receiver, person not personally liable for debt secured by mortgage has, or is entitled to, possession of all or portion of property, owner of property is not personally liable for debt secured by mortgage, or all or any portion of property is being, or is intended to be, leased for any purpose; (5) when corporation has been dissolved, or is insolvent, or is in imminent danger of insolvency, or has forfeited its corporate rights; (6) to protect or preserve, during time allowed for redemption, any real estate or interest therein sold on execution or order of sale, and to secure to person entitled thereto rents and profits thereof; (7) in such other cases as may be provided by law, or where, in discretion of court, it may be necessary to secure ample justice to parties. (IC34-48-1-1).

Jurisdiction.—Receivers may be appointed by courts of general jurisdiction under circumstances listed above. (119 Ind. App. 63, 78 N.E.2d 881).

Proceedings.—An adverse party must appear or have had reasonable notice to appear before a receiver can be appointed, except upon sufficient cause shown by affidavit. (IC34-48-1-9). There is right of appeal within ten days from order appointing or refusing receiver without waiting for final determination of entire case. (IC34-48-1-10). Proper bond on appeal suspends authority of receiver pending appeal. (IC34-48-1-10). When receiver is appointed to take over business or assets of any person, organization, or partnership, appropriate person representing that person, organization, or partnership may be required to file with clerk full, complete, itemized statement in affidavit form, setting forth in detail all assets and liabilities including all known creditors. (Rule TR 66[B]). There is same right as in any civil action to change of judge and right to change of venue from county except as to trial of certain specified issues enumerated in act. (IC34-2-7-3).

Eligibility and Competency.—No party, attorney, or other interested party may be a receiver. (IC34-48-1-2).

Qualification and Bond.—Receiver before entering upon his duties must be sworn to perform them faithfully, and must, with one or more sureties approved by court, execute written undertaking, payable to such person as court shall direct, to effect that he will faithfully discharge duties of receiver in action and obey orders of court or judge thereof. (IC34-48-1-3).

Powers and Duties.—Receiver must give reasonable notice of his appointment by publication as ordered by court and must mail copy of notice to all creditors listed on sworn statement of assets and liabilities of organization in receivership. This notice must fix time, not less than six months from date of appointment, in which creditors may file claim. (Rule TR 66[C]). Procedure for filing, consideration and allowance or trial of claims, must, insofar as is practicable, conform with procedure relating to claims in decedent's estate. (Rule TR 66[D]). Receiver has power, under control of court, to bring and defend actions, to take and keep possession of property, to receive rents, to collect debts, and generally to do such acts respecting property as court may authorize. (IC34-48-1-7). He is obligated to file report of receipts and disbursements and other appropriate information. (IC34-48-4-1 through 6). Receiver must pay or make distributions according to priorities as required by law upon all claims if claim is liquidated in amount, owing, and shown to be unpaid. (Rule TR 66[E]). Receiver has no discretion in application of funds in his hands but holds them strictly subject to order of court to be disposed of as court directs. (199 Ind. 311, 157 N.E. 441).

Compensation.—No statutory provisions generally applicable to all receivers appointed by court; however Indiana statutory law in certain particular circumstances expressly authorizes reasonable compensation for receivers.

Discharge.—All objections to a receiver's report must be filed within time set by clerk of court (not less than 30 days after report has been filed) or be forever barred. Hearing on all objections filed is set by court without delay following 30-day period. (IC34-48-4-6). Discharge of receiver and his surety follows court's approval of receiver's final report and upon receiver duly complying with court's order made on final report. (IC34-48-5-1 and 2).

REDEMPTION:

See topics Executions, Liens; categories Mortgages, topic Mortgages of Real Property; Taxation, topic Property Tax, subhead Redemption.

SUPPLEMENTARY PROCEEDINGS:

See topic Executions.

TRUSTEE PROCESS:

See topic Garnishment.

USURY:

See category Business Regulation and Commerce, topic Consumer Credit.

DISPUTE RESOLUTION

ALTERNATIVE DISPUTE RESOLUTION:

Mandatory Dispute Resolution.—With limited exceptions, medical malpractice claims must be submitted for evaluation by independent medical review panel. (IC27-12-8-4 et seq., IC27-12-9-1 et seq., IC27-12-10-1 et seq.). By statute, action against health care provider may not be commenced in Indiana court before claim is submitted to medical review panel and panel issues opinion unless specific conditions are met. (IC27-12-8-7). Statutes govern selection of, and proceedings before, medical review panel. (IC27-12-10-4, 9, 10, 21 and 22).

Arbitration is precondition to maintaining certain legal actions, claims, or defenses against seller of agricultural or vegetable seed products. (IC15-4-11-1 et seq.).

Indiana courts may not issue restraining order or grant injunctive relief in labor dispute until complainant makes every reasonable effort to settle dispute by negotiation through governmental mediation or voluntary arbitration. (IC22-6-1-7).

Collective bargaining impasse between administration and public school employees subject to mandatory mediation. (IC20-7.5-1-12).

Voluntary Dispute Resolution.—Specific alternative dispute resolution rules adopted. (ADR Rules 1.1 to 7.7). Settlement negotiations, arbitration, mediation, conciliation, facilitation, mini-trials, mini-hearings, summary jury trials, private judges and judging, convening or conflict assessment, neutral evaluation and fact-finding, multi-door case allocation and negotiated rulemaking are recognized but not exclusive forms of alternative dispute resolution. (ADR Rule 1.1). ADR Rules do not apply in following cases and proceedings: criminal, actions to enforce infractions or ordinance violations, juvenile, forfeitures of seized properties, habeas corpus or other extraordinary writs, matters in which there is very great public interest and which must receive immediate court decision, small claims proceedings. (ADR Rule 1.4). Any claim involving estate in fee or for life to any real estate may not be submitted for arbitration, but any claim to interest in term, in term for years, or for one year or less, in real estate, and controversies respecting partition of land may be submitted for arbitration. (IC34-57-1-2). Presiding judge may order case referred to mediation or mini-hearing, but may not order arbitration or summary jury trial without consent of parties. (ADR Rule 1.6).

Program to subsidize private community dispute resolution centers established. (IC34-57-3-2 et seq.). Program and funding administered by chief justice of Indiana Supreme Court. (IC34-57-3-2 et seq.). Civil action submitted to dispute resolution center is suspended until court receives decision from dispute resolution center. (IC34-57-4-3).

Uniform Arbitration Act adopted. (IC34-57-2-1 et seq.).

See note at head of Digest as to 1998 legislation covered.

See Topical Index in front part of this volume.

ALTERNATIVE DISPUTE RESOLUTION . . . *continued*

Shareholder disputes relating to stock value arising out of sale or lease of railroad property may be submitted to arbitration. Railroad company may seek arbitration without consent of dissenting shareholder. (IC8-4-21-2, IC8-4-21-3).

Administrative agencies may elect to use mediation procedures and statutes govern use of mediation within administrative proceedings. (IC4-21.5-3.5 et seq.).

Indiana Natural Resources Commission may mediate disputes between users of surface water in watershed areas. (IC14-25-1-8).

Boards of trade, exchanges, and chambers of commerce may adopt rules, by-laws, and regulations relating to arbitration and settlement of business controversies. (IC23-5-2-7).

See also topic Arbitration and Award.

ARBITRATION AND AWARD:

Uniform Arbitration Act adopted. (IC34-57-2-1 to 22).

Inclusions.—Consumer leases, sales, and loan contracts are specifically excluded from coverage. (IC34-57-2-1[b]). Arbitration is initiated by written notice delivered to other party stating claim, grounds for claim, and amount of claim. Issues are joined upon written notice of admissions, denials, counterclaims, or set-offs. (IC34-57-2-2). Court will stay arbitration if other proceedings by parties make arbitration unnecessary or upon showing method of appointment has resulted in majority of biased arbitrators. (IC34-57-2-3[f], [g]). In arbitration between labor and management, neither party may subpoena financial records of other. (IC34-57-2-8).

Deviations from Uniform Act.—§5a of Uniform Act, unless parties otherwise agree, 30 days notice of hearing time and place is required. (IC34-57-2-6[a]).

§15 of Uniform Act was excluded and has no effect.

§17 of Uniform Act, term court means any circuit or superior court. (IC34-57-2-17).

§18 of Uniform Act, initial application is made to court in county where adverse party resides or has place of business; if nonresident or no place of business in state, court in any county. (IC34-57-2-18).

Chapter on Community Dispute Resolution adopted and becomes effective July 1, 1998. (IC34-57-3-1 et seq.).

Purpose.—Establishes community dispute resolution centers program and gives Chief Justice of Indiana power to supervise program, select centers to receive funding, distribute funds for establishment and continuance of centers, adopt rules for program, and hire personnel necessary to administer program. (IC34-57-3-2).

Inclusion.—Applies to (1) criminal offense referred to community dispute resolution center under diversion program; (2) civil action referred by court to community dispute resolution center after court action has been filed; and (3) civil disputes that do not involve insurance claim where parties voluntarily submit to community dispute resolution. (IC34-57-3-1).

Centers are not state agencies, but are nonprofit corporations or organizations and are required to submit applications for funding. (IC34-57-3-3; IC34-57-3-9).

Party who has been referred to community dispute resolution center after court action has been filed can file motion for trial de novo. (IC34-57-3-14).

Chapter on Alternative Dispute Resolution adopted and becomes effective July 1, 1998. (IC34-57-4-1 et seq.).

Purpose.—Applies to any civil action referred by court to dispute resolution center under IC34-57-3-1 et seq. (IC34-57-4-1).

Suspension.—Court shall suspend action on case until written agreement or decision from dispute resolution center is submitted to court. (IC34-57-4-3).

Funding.—Effective June 30, 1993, Indiana Supreme Court can collect voluntary contributions of $25 from each attorney admitted to practice before it. (IC34-57-3-2).

DOCUMENTS AND RECORDS

ACKNOWLEDGMENTS:

Within the State.—Acknowledgments may be taken within state by clerks of circuit courts and master commissioners within their respective counties; mayors, clerks and clerk-treasurers of cities and towns in their respective cities and towns, judges of state courts and U.S. District Courts and U.S. Commissioners appointed for any U.S. District Court of Indiana within their respective jurisdictions; State Election Commission members and employees; precinct election officials; Secretary of State, notaries public and members of General Assembly of Indiana anywhere in state (IC33-16-4-1); probate commissioners (IC29-2-2-3); Attorney-General and his deputies and assistants (IC4-6-1-5); prosecuting attorneys and their deputies (IC33-14-5-1); official court reporters (IC33-15-24-1); and township trustees (IC33-16-8-1). When any instrument required to be recorded is acknowledged in any county in this state other than one in in which same is required to be recorded, acknowledgment must be certified by clerk of circuit court of county in which such acknowledging officer resides and attested by seal of said court; but acknowledgment before officer having official seal, if attested by such official seal, is sufficient without such certificate. (IC32-1-2-19). Acknowledgments by Attorney-General and his or her deputies shall be attested by official seal. (IC4-6-1-5).

Head of any state department, division, board, bureau or commission may appoint special deputies to take free acknowledgments in connection with matters pertaining to said office. (IC4-2-4-1).

Within the United States.—Acknowledgments may be made in other states in the United States in the same manner as they may be made in this state, and in addition they may be made before any commissioner appointed in any other state by the Governor of this state. To entitle the instrument so acknowledged to record in this state, the same must be certified by the clerk of any court of record of the county in which the officer receiving the acknowledgment resides, and attested by the seal of said court, but an acknowledgment before an officer having an official seal, attested by his official seal, is sufficient without such certificate. (IC32-1-2-18, 20).

Outside of the United States.—To entitle instruments made in foreign countries to record in this state, they must be acknowledged by the grantor or person executing the same and proved before diplomatic or consular official of the United States duly accredited or before any officers of such countries who by the law thereof, are authorized to take acknowledgments or proof of conveyances, and if such acknowledgment or proof is in English language and attested by official seal of such officer, it shall be sufficient to admit such instrument to record, but if in some other language or not attested by such official seal, then such instrument must be accompanied by a certificate of officer of U.S., as aforesaid, to effect that it is duly executed according to laws of such foreign countries, that officer certifying to acknowledgement or proof had legal authority to do so, and giving meaning of certificate if same is made in foreign language. (IC32-2-4-1).

Members of U. S. Armed Forces or any person who is serving as merchant seaman outside limits of U.S., wherever located, may acknowledge instruments before commissioned officers of Army, Navy, Marine Corps or Coast Guard. (IC32-2-3-1).

Persons engaged in the prosecution of a war on behalf of the United States Government and outside of the United States by consent of the Government may make acknowledgments under the same terms as members of the United States Armed Forces. (IC32-2-3-1).

Authentication.—Clerks of circuit courts authenticate acknowledgments for use outside of state, and fee is usually 50¢ to $1, according to kind of authentication required.

Proof by Subscribing Witness.—There is no express statutory provision for proof by a subscribing witness instead of acknowledgment by the grantor; but it is provided that deeds may be proved according to the common law before any officer authorized to take acknowledgments and, when so proved, are entitled to record. (IC32-1-2-21).

Necessity and Effect.—Acknowledgment or proof in due form is necessary to entitle an instrument to be recorded (32-1-2-18) but is not essential to its validity.

Acknowledgments before officers of the Armed Forces are prima facie evidence of identity, authority, agency and free volition of persons making them. (IC32-2-3-2).

Forms.—The statutory form of an acknowledgment for an individual is as follows:

Form

"Before me, A. B. (title of officer), this . . . . day of . . . ., Y. Z acknowledged the execution of the annexed deed (mortgage, etc.)."

No statutory form is given for corporations, but the following form is suggested:

Before me, A. B. (name of corporation), this . . . . day of . . . . personally appeared by C. D. and X. Y. (name of officers), its President and Secretary respectively, and acknowledged the execution of the foregoing instrument.

Form for member of U. S. Armed Forces:

With the Armed Forces of the United States . . . . } ss.
At . . . .

The foregoing instrument was acknowledged this . . . . day of . . . ., 19. . . ., by . . . . serving (in) . . . . (with) the Armed Forces of the United States, before me, a commissioned officer in the active service of the (United States Army, Navy, Marine Corps or Coast Guard as the case may be).

Signature of officer
Rank and branch of service.

Place where acknowledgment is taken before officer in Armed Forces need not be stated (IC32-2-3-3) or it may be stated to be taken at "an undisclosed place" (IC32-2-3-1). If Indiana notary public takes acknowledgment, he must state his county of residence. (IC33-16-2-9).

Alternative to Acknowledgment or Proof.—No statutory provision.

Legalizing Acts.—No statutory provision.

See also topic Notaries Public.

AFFIDAVITS:

Affidavit is written statement of fact sworn to as truth before authorized officer. (609 N.E.2d 1104). Affidavit may not be certified by notary public unless affiant appears before notary public and acknowledges truth of statements therein. (IC33-16-2-2).

Official court reporters are authorized to administer oaths generally and to take and certify affidavits, examinations and depositions. (IC33-15-24-1).

Generally, no arrest or search warrant shall be issued until there is filed with judge affidavit particularly describing house or place to be searched and things to be searched for or particularly describing person to be arrested alleging substantially offense in relation thereto and that affiant believes and has good cause to believe that things to be searched for are there concealed or person to be arrested committed offense. When based on hearsay, affidavit must contain, among other things, reliable information establishing credibility of source or information establishing that totality of circumstances corroborates hearsay. (IC35-33-5-2).

Alternative to Affidavit.—When in connection with any civil or special statutory proceeding it is required that any pleading, motion, petition, supporting affidavit, or other document of any kind, be verified, or that oath be taken, it is sufficient if subscriber simply affirms truth of matter to be verified by affirmation or representation in substantially following language: "I (we) affirm, under the penalties for perjury, that the foregoing representation(s) is (are) true." (Rule TR 11[B]).

NOTARIES PUBLIC:

The jurisdiction of any notary public is coextensive with limits of the state but he cannot be forced to act outside of the county in which he resides. (IC33-16-1-1). Every notary must attest all notarial acts with seal which will stamp distinct impression on paper so as to indicate his official character (IC33-16-2-4) and must append to all acknowledgments and jurats true statement of date of expiration of his commission (IC33-16-3-1). Each notary in addition to affixing his name, expiration date, and seal, shall print or type his name below his signature on all acknowledgments, jurats, or other official documents unless his name appears in printed form on document or as part of his stamp and also shall indicate his county of residence on document. (IC33-16-2-9).

See note at head of Digest as to 1998 legislation covered.

See Topical Index in front part of this volume.

NOTARIES PUBLIC . . . *continued*

Every notary public has power to administer oaths and to take and certify affidavits and depositions, and to take and certify all acknowledgments of deeds or other instruments of writing required or authorized by law to be acknowledged. (IC33-16-2-5).

Certificate of Authority.—See topic Acknowledgments, subhead Authentication.

Notary public may not acknowledge execution of affidavit unless affiant acknowledges truth of statements therein. (IC33-16-2-2).

Notary public may not acknowledge execution of instrument unless person who executed instrument signs instrument before notary or affirms to notary that it is his signature on instrument. (IC33-16-2-2).

Notary public may not acknowledge execution of instrument in which his name appears as party. (IC33-16-2-2).

Township trustee has power to perform any act notary public may perform. (IC33-16-8-1).

RECORDS:

Uniform Commercial Code in effect since July 1, 1964. (IC26-1-1-101 et seq.).

To entitle any conveyance, mortgage or instrument in writing to be recorded it must be acknowledged by the grantor or proved in due form. (IC32-1-2-18). To be eligible for recording, all instruments executed on or after July 1, 1959, which convey, create, encumber, assign or otherwise dispose of interest in or lien upon any real or personal property (except court orders, wills, death certificates, and instruments executed or acknowledged outside state) must contain, at conclusion thereof, name of person who, and governmental agency, if any, which prepared instrument. All instruments recorded prior to July 26, 1967, not complying with these requirements, but in all other respects correct and in proper form, are deemed legally recorded. (IC36-2-11-15). Subject to few exceptions, to be eligible for recording, instrument or photocopy of it must contain legibly printed, typewritten or stamped names of all persons executing, witnessing and acknowledging instrument immediately beneath their respective signatures, and names of all persons executing instrument must appear identically in body of instrument, in acknowledgment or jurat, in signature and beneath signature. (IC36-2-11-16).

Form

This instrument was prepared by (name).

To be eligible for recording, certain "conveyance documents" must be accompanied by sales disclosure form. (IC6-1.1-5.5). See category Property, topic Deeds.

Every conveyance or mortgage of land or of any interest therein and every lease for more than three years must be recorded in the recorder's office of the county where such land is situated, and every conveyance, mortgage or lease takes priority according to the time of filing thereof. (IC32-1-2-16). Memorandum of lease may be recorded in lieu of lease. (IC36-2-11-20). *For list of Counties and County Seats see first page for this state in Volume containing Practice Profiles Section.*

IC32-1-2-16.3 provides that assignment, mortgage, or pledge of rents and profits arising from real estate that is intended as security, whether contained in separate interest or otherwise, shall be recorded under IC32-1-2-16. Upon recording, security interest is immediately perfected. §16.3 does not apply to security interests in: (1) farm products; (2) accounts or general intangibles relating to sale of farm products by farmer, (3) timber to be cut, (4) minerals or the like (including oil and gas); or (5) accounts subject to interest in minerals before extraction or sale thereof at wellhead or minehead as set forth in IC26-1-9-103(5) that may be perfected under IC26-1-9. §16.3 applies to instrument regardless of when such was recorded except that §16.3 does not divest rights that vested before May 1, 1993.

Before any conveyance of interest in real estate by corporation may be recorded, gross income tax due on transfer must be paid and stamp evidencing payment affixed to deed or, in alternative, signed affidavit by seller or grantor certifying certificate that no tax is due must accompany deed. (IC6-2.1-8-6).

Recording Fees.—For recording most documents not larger than 8½" by 14", cost is $6 for first page and $2 for each additional page. There is additional $1 fee for recording of deed. For documents larger than 8½" by 14", cost is $15 for first page and $5 for each additional page.

Typewritten copies of records are $3 per page; photographic copies are $1 per page for documents 8½" x 14" or smaller, $2 per page for documents larger than 8½" x 14"; certification of document costs $5 plus 50¢ per page for proofreading any copy presented for certification. By ordinance, county legislative body may authorize fee for duplicating computer tape, computer disk, optical disk, microfilm, or similar media. (IC36-2-7-10).

Filing Under Commercial Code.—Fees for filing Uniform Commercial Code documents are as follows: UCC-1 costs $4 ($8 if filed with county recorder); UCC-2 (fixture) additional costs $1; UCC-3 costs $4; UCC-4 additional costs $1; $1 for each additional name on UCC-1, UCC-2 and UCC-4; UCC-3 (as partial release) - no additional fee; pink copy (as termination) - no fee; other copy (used as termination copy) costs $4. All of UCC fees quoted herein are for exhibits not larger than 5" x 8". Filing fees are increased for any UCC document with exhibit larger than 5" x 8" and $4 for terminations larger than 5" x 8". (Information provided by Office of Secretary of State, U.C.C. Division: (317) 232-6393). Address of Secretary of State— U.C.C. Division: 300 West Washington St., Room E111, Indianapolis, Indiana 46204.

Transfer of Decedent's Title.—The clerk of the circuit court of each county, who is also clerk of the superior and probate courts, is required to record all proceedings in relation to decedent and guardianship estates in separate books kept for that purpose and, in addition, to keep final record book on which must be spread complete record of all matters and proceedings in administration of estates. (IC29-1-1-23).

Vital Statistics.—Information on certificates of birth and death and stillborn registrations may be obtained from State Department of Health at 1330 West Michigan, Indianapolis, Indiana 46204. (Phone [317]383-6400.)

Establishing Birth Records.—Provision is made for judicial determination by circuit or superior court of time and place of birth of residents (IC34-28-1-1) in absence of recorded birth certificate, and also of nonresidents who were born in Indiana (IC34-28-1-2). Proceedings are instituted by filing of verified application (IC34-28-1-1, 2) and publication of notice (IC34-28-1-4). Certified copies of decrees are prima facie evidence of time and place of birth. (IC34-28-1-8).

Bankruptcy Records.—Certified copy of matter relating to bankruptcy must be recorded where federal law requires that copy be filed in county in which bankrupt's lands are located in order to give notice of bankruptcy. Recorder must index such records in same manner as deeds under names of both bankrupt and trustee. (IC36-2-11-22).

See category Business Regulation and Commerce, topic Commercial Code.

SEALS:

Uniform Commercial Code in effect since July 1, 1964. (IC26-1-1-101 et seq.). See category Business Regulation and Commerce, topic Commercial Code.

No seal or scroll is necessary on deeds or other instruments of natural persons, business trusts, or corporations. (IC32-2-5-1; IC23-17-22-6). Authenticating officers must use seal when law so requires. (IC32-2-5-1). There is no difference in evidence between sealed and unsealed writings. (IC34-37-1-1).

TORRENS ACT:

Not adopted.

VITAL STATISTICS:

See topic Records.

EMPLOYMENT

EMPLOYER AND EMPLOYEE:

See topic Labor Relations.

LABOR RELATIONS:

Cognizance of labor matters lies with Department of Labor. (IC22-1-1-1). Created within Department of Labor are: (a) Bureau of Mines and Mine Safety and (b) Bureau of Child Labor. (IC22-1-1-4).

Alien Labor.—Importing or assisting or encouraging the importation of alien labor on contract to work in the state of Indiana, such contract being made prior to their arrival in Indiana, is made a misdemeanor and contracts are void. (IC22-5-1-1, 2).

Service Letters.—Employer must give to employee who quits or is discharged a "service letter" on written request of employee, unless employer is one who does not require written recommendations or written applications showing qualifications or experience for employment. (IC22-6-3-1).

Armed Forces.—Reserve members of armed forces are entitled to temporary leave of absence not exceeding 15 days a year. Such leaves may be granted with or without pay within discretion of employer. (IC10-5-9-1). Employer subject to suit in damages for violation. (IC10-5-9-2).

Wages must be paid semi-monthly or bi-weekly, except for salaried employees eligible for overtime compensation under federal Fair Labor Standards Act. (IC22-2-5-1; IC22-2-5-1.1). However, in certain industries mutual agreement and/or contract may provide payment on weekly basis. (IC22-2-4-1). Farmers are specifically exempt. (IC22-2-5-3). Payment must be made in money or negotiable checks, drafts or money orders, or by electronic transfer to financial institution designated by employee (IC22-2-5-1, IC22-2-4-2), and failure to make payments in accordance with statute subjects employer to penalties and attorney's fees of employee (IC22-2-5-2, IC22-2-4-4).

Minimum wage of $3.35 per hour until Oct. 1, 1998. Between Oct. 1, 1998 and Mar. 1, 1999 minimum wage is $4.25 per hour. After Mar. 1, 1999, minimum wage is $5.15 per hour. (IC22-2-2-4). Act provides for certain exceptions including minors under 16, commission-paid employees, farm labor and students performing jobs for schools. (IC22-2-2-3). Effective July 1, 1998, employers must pay overtime to nonexempt employees for time worked in excess of 40 hours in work week at rate not less than one and one-half (1.5) times employee's regular rate. (IC22-2-2-4). Failure to comply with this law may result in suit by employees for double wages (IC22-2-2-9) and class A infraction or class B misdemeanor for repeat violations (IC22-2-2-11). When employer separates any employee from payroll, unpaid wages or compensation become due and payable at regular payday for pay period in which separation occurred; such provision does not apply to railroads. If work is suspended due to industrial dispute, wages and compensation earned and unpaid at time of suspension become due and payable at next regular payday including all amounts due all employees whose work has been suspended due to such dispute. (IC22-2-9-2).

Operator leasing mine, quarry or manufacturing plant to engage in business must file with clerk of circuit court bond equal to twice such lessee's weekly payroll to insure payment of wages unless lease is from U.S. or one of its subsidiary agencies or value of physical property owned by lessee in conducting such business is at least double amount of weekly payroll of such lessee. (IC22-2-11-1).

Wage claims of laborers or employees not exceeding $600 may be preferred debts against failing employer. (IC22-2-10-1).

Employer may not assess fine against any employee and deduct it from wages due. (IC22-2-8-1). Sale of merchandise or supplies to employees at higher prices than such is sold to others is prohibited. (IC22-2-4-3).

Authorization for deductions from wages for payment of union dues and other purposes is governed by statute. (IC22-2-6-2).

Child Labor.—Certificate issued by guidance counselor, school social worker, or licensed attendance officer necessary for employment of minor between 14 and 18 years of age. (IC20-8.1-4-1). Minor between ages of 14 and 16 years may withdraw from school if bureau of child labor issues employment certificate and parent or guardian agrees. (IC20-8.1-4-3). Employment certificates issued in form approved by, and under rules adopted by department of labor and state board of education. (IC20-8.1-4-14).

See note at head of Digest as to 1998 legislation covered.

See Topical Index in front part of this volume.

IN – 29

LABOR RELATIONS . . . *continued*

No minor between ages of 14 and 16 years may be employed before 7:00 a.m. nor after 7:00 p.m., nor more than eight hours in any one day, nor more than 40 hours in any one week, nor more than three hours on any day followed by school day, nor more than 18 hours in any week in which school is in session. Minors between ages of 14 and 16 years may work until 9:00 p.m. from June 1 through Labor Day. No minor between ages of 16 and 18 years may be employed more than eight hours in any one day, nor more than 40 hours in any one week, nor more than six days in any one week, nor before 6:00 a.m., except that such minor may be employed up to nine hours in any one day and up to 48 hours in any one week when schools are closed for summer vacation if employer obtains written permission from minor's parent. Children who are 16 years of age may be employed until 10:00 p.m. on nights followed by school day except in occupations determined to be physically dangerous or injurious to health or morals; it is also lawful for minors 16 years of age to work until midnight at such times as schools are closed for summer vacation and on nights not followed by school day if written permission is obtained from minor's parent. Children who are 17 years of age and are students in grades 9 through 12 may work until 11:30 p.m. on two nonconsecutive nights followed by school days if employer has obtained written permission from child's parent. Children between ages of 16 and 18 may be employed same hours and times as adults if they: (1) are high school graduates, (2) have completed approved vocational or special education program, or (3) are not enrolled in regular school term. (IC20-8.1-4-20).

Employment in designated hazardous occupation prohibited to any person under 18 years of age. (IC20-8.1-4-25).

No minor under age of 14 years may be employed or allowed to work in any occupation other than farm labor or domestic services, or as carrier of newspapers or as golf caddie. No minor under 12 years of age may work at farm labor except on farm operated by minor's parents. (IC20-8.1-4-21). Any child, regardless of age, may appear in various enumerated theatrical or musical performances under conditions set by statute. (IC20-8.1-4-21.5).

Emancipated minors are subject to statutory provisions regulating employment of minors. (Opinion of Attorney General, 1968, No. 3, p. 16).

Labor Unions.—Contracts between an employer and a current or prospective employee whereby either party agrees to resign from or not join a labor organization are unenforceable. (IC22-6-1-3).

Right to work law repealed in 1965.

Labor Disputes.—No Indiana court has jurisdiction to issue a restraining order or injunction, in any case involving or growing out of a labor dispute, prohibiting strikes and other specified lawful activities. (IC22-6-1-4). In such cases unlawful activities may be prohibited by injunction after hearing of testimony in open court and specific findings of facts as set forth in statute. (IC22-6-1-6).

A special act governs public utilities and requires compulsory arbitration. (IC22-6-2-1 to 15). (Indiana act was held unconstitutional in Marshall v. Schricker [1951] Cir. Ct. of Vanderburg County, 28 LRRM 2167.)

Employee Benefit Plans.—Employer who has contracted in writing to make payments to any type of employee benefit plan must give written notice to employees of failure to make payment to plan. Employee may recover double damages plus costs and attorney fees from employer who fails to give notice or make payments. (IC22-2-12-4).

Public Employee Bargaining.—Public Employee Bargaining Act was enacted by 1975 Legislature. (IC22-6-4-1 to 13). This Act was subsequently held to be unconstitutional by Supreme Court of Indiana. See: 266 Ind. 491, 365 N.E.2d 752. Act was repealed by 1982 Legislature. (Acts 1982, P.L. 3).

Executive order establishing terms, conditions, and procedures for recognition of employee organizations representing employees of executive branch of State government became effective May 22, 1990. (E.O. 90-6).

School teacher collective bargaining is governed by statute which sets out duty to bargain collectively on certain subjects, recognizes right of teachers to form and join unions, and proscribes strikes and certain defined unfair practices. (IC20-7.5-1-1 et seq.).

Discrimination.—It is unlawful for employer or union to discriminate on basis of race, religion, color, sex, handicap, national origin, ancestry, and age (where individual is between 40 and 70) except that institutions of learning that traditionally limit admission to students of one sex need not remodel to accommodate both sexes. (IC22-9-1-1 et seq.; IC22-9-2-1 et seq.). It is unlawful for employer to discriminate on basis of sex as to wage payments, except where such payment is made pursuant to seniority system, merit system, system which measures earnings by quantity or quality of production, or differential based on any other factor other than sex. (IC22-2-2-4). The Employment Discrimination Against Disabled Persons Act mirrors requirements of Title I of Americans With Disabilities Act. (IC22-9-5-1 et seq.).

If, after investigating complaint of unlawful discrimination, Indiana Civil Rights Commission issues finding of probable cause, parties have option of proceeding to full hearing before Commission or, upon consent of both complainant and respondent before Commission has begun hearing with regard to finding of probable cause, may elect to file civil action in circuit or superior court in county in which discriminatory practice allegedly occurred. Such civil action must be tried by court without benefit of jury. (IC22-9-1-16, IC22-9-1-17).

Worker's Compensation Act applies to all employees except railroaders and certain municipal workers. (IC22-3-2-2). It does not apply to casual or farm workers or to domestics unless employer so chooses. (IC22-3-2-9). Volunteer workers at state institutions (as defined by IC12-7-2-184) are subject to medical benefits described under IC22-3-2 through IC22-3-6. (IC22-3-2-2.3).

Compliance with act is required. (IC22-3-2-2). Remedy of employee against his employer under act is exclusive (IC22-3-2-6), except for remedies available under Compensation for Victims of Violent Crimes Act (IC16-7-3.6-1 et seq.).

Employers must carry insurance or obtain permission to be self-insured. (IC22-3-2-5).

Employers subject to act must post notice in their places of business informing employees of worker's compensation coverage and name, address, and telephone number of employer's administrator or insurance carrier. (IC22-3-2-22).

Rights against third parties are alternative to compensation for same accident but acceptance of compensation by employee or his dependents does not bar action against third parties. If employee proceeds against third party employer has lien upon any amount paid by third party to employee in amount of employer's liability to employee, subject to employer paying its pro rata share of costs, expenses, and attorney's fees. If employee does not proceed against third party, within two years after cause of action accrues, or if such proceeding is commenced but later dismissed, employer is subrogated against third party in amount of his liability to employee and may maintain action within one year from date of two years from when cause of action accrued or date when employee's action was dismissed. (IC22-3-2-13).

Contractors who fail to demand of subcontractors a certificate that the subcontractors have accepted the provisions of the Act are liable for injuries to the employees of the subcontractors in accordance with the terms of Act. Employers can not relieve themselves from terms of this Act by contract. (IC22-3-2-14, IC22-3-2-15).

Claims under the terms of the act must be filed within two years from the date of accident or death, except for claims resulting from exposure to radiation, which must be filed within two years from date on which employee knew or should have known of existence of such injury and its causal relationship to his employment. (IC22-3-3-3). Act contains complicated schedule of injuries for which recovery may be had and of persons who are conclusively presumed to be dependents. (IC22-3-3-10, IC22-3-3-19).

Compensation, average weekly wages, and maximum recovery determined and restricted by date of injury. In addition to temporary total disability benefits limited to 78 weeks, one receives weekly compensation of 60% of average weekly wages limited to $166 if injury between July 1, 1988 and June 30, 1989; between July 1, 1989 and June 30, 1990, 60% limited to $183; if after July 1, 1990, 60% limited to $200. If injury occurs on or after July 1, 1991, temporary total benefits shall not exceed 125 weeks and employee shall receive weekly compensation at rate of 66⅔% with limits of $492 for injuries before July 1, 1992; $540 for injuries on or after July 1, 1992 and before July 1, 1993; $591 for injuries on or after July 1, 1993 and before July 1, 1994; $642 for injuries on or after July 1, 1994. Lower levels and less weeks of compensation for injuries occurring prior to these dates, as set forth in statute. Weekly compensation may not exceed average weekly wages of employee at time of injury. Average weekly wage figure to be determined without regard to any salary reduction agreement under §125 of Internal Revenue Code. Average weekly wage figure varies from minimum of $30, maximum of $70 if injury before Apr. 1, 1965 to minimum of $75, maximum of $441 on or after July 1, 1990. Maximum compensation varies similarly but in no case may exceed, exclusive of medical benefits, $128,000 for injuries occurring between July 1, 1988 and June 30, 1989; $137,000 for injuries occurring between July 1, 1989 and June 30, 1990; and $147,000 for injuries occurring between July 1, 1990 and June 30, 1991; $164,000 for injuries occurring between July 1, 1991 and June 30, 1992; $180,000 for injuries occurring between July 1, 1992 and June 30, 1993; $197,000 for injuries occurring between July 1, 1993 and June 30, 1994; and $214,000 for injuries occurring on or after July 1, 1994. (IC22-3-3-10, IC22-3-3-22). For purposes of computing average weekly wage of minor student employee who has been permanently impaired employed part-time as part of approved training program, such student's hourly wage rate is multiplied by 40 hours. (IC22-3-6-1). Employer must furnish medical service during period of temporary total disability until adjudication of permanent partial impairment, and may be ordered by Workers Compensation Board to furnish services for longer period. (IC22-3-3-4). Burial expenses are limited to $6,000. (IC22-3-3-21).

Workers Compensation Board composed of seven members, one or more of whom hears cases and awards compensation in case employer and employee or employee's dependents do not agree upon compensation to be received as early as practicable after time of accident. (IC22-3-1-1, IC22-3-4-5, IC22-3-4-6). Any party dissatisfied with award may file petition for review, and case is reviewed by full board, which files finding of facts and conclusions of law. Within 30 days from the date of award by full board, either party may appeal on questions of law to Court of Appeals, subject to discretionary transfer to Supreme Court. (IC22-3-4-5, 8).

Employer's Liability Act applies to employers in business, trade or commerce employing five or more persons. Act is of little importance being largely succeeded in fact by compensation law, although sections are not repealed and affect persons not operating under compensation law. (IC22-3-9-1 to 11).

Unemployment Compensation.—Unemployed are required to register and report in manner and at places, times, and with frequency prescribed by rule. (IC22-4-14-2). Unemployed are eligible only if able to work, available, making effort to obtain full-time work and participating in reemployment services. (IC22-4-14-3). Ineligible unemployed include, generally: Students; certain governmental employees; those in full-time military service or civilian service as conscientious objectors; those suspended due to misconduct at work (IC22-4-14-3); those unemployed due to labor dispute in which they or members of class or grade of workers to which they belong participate or are directly interested or which they finance (IC22-4-15-3); and persons employed in educational institutions and who cease working at beginning of normal vacation period with reasonable expectations of resuming work when vacation period ends (IC22-4-14-7). Persons retired under compulsory provisions of collective bargaining agreements are eligible for benefits if they otherwise qualify. (IC22.4-14-1). See IC22-4-11-1; IC22-4-12-2 for benefit rates.

Workmen's Occupational Diseases Act provides for compensation for death or disablement by occupational disease arising out of and in course of employment. Provisions of this Act follow closely corresponding provisions of Workmen's Compensation Act and compensation payments are substantially same. (IC22-3-7-1 to 38).

Employees' Off-Duty Use of Tobacco.—Employer may not require employee or prospective employee to refrain from using tobacco outside of course of employment, nor may employer discriminate against employees who use tobacco in terms of compensation, benefits, or working conditions. (IC22-5-4).

Indiana Occupational Safety and Health Act has established agencies of Department of Labor to regulate and promote health and safety standards. These agencies have

See note at head of Digest as to 1998 legislation covered.

See Topical Index in front part of this volume.

IN – 30

LABOR RELATIONS... *continued*

power to tax and enforce penalties. (IC22-8-1.1-1 et seq.). No state standard may be more stringent than corresponding federal standards. (IC22-8-1.1-17.5).

WORKERS' COMPENSATION LAW:

See topic Labor Relations.

WORKMEN'S OCCUPATIONAL DISEASES ACT:

See topic Labor Relations.

ENVIRONMENT

ENVIRONMENTAL REGULATION:

General Supervision.—Indiana Department of Environmental Management provides for comprehensive environmental development and control on statewide basis. (IC13-12-3-1; IC13-13). Specific areas of responsibility are vested in Indiana State Department of Health (IC16-41-27) (mobile home parks); Water Pollution Control Board (IC13-18); Air Pollution Control Board (IC13-17); Department of Natural Resources (IC14-9); Natural Resources Commission (IC14-10); Solid Waste Management Board (IC13-19); Hazardous Waste Facility Site Approval Authority (IC13-22-10-6); State Chemist for control of pesticides (IC15-3-3.5); Institute on Recycling (IC13-20-18); Groundwater Task Force (IC13-18-17); Indiana Energy Development Board (IC4-23-5.5); and Solid Waste Management Districts created under IC13-21-3. Local units of government may also regulate generation of sound or emissions into air. (IC36-8-2-8; IC13-14-1-10; IC13-14-3-1).

Prohibited Acts.—Pollution of air or water, disposal or dumping solid waste, surface mining activities, and transportation, treatment, storage or disposal of hazardous waste in violation of statutes, standards and regulations of appropriate state agency or local government are prohibited. (IC13-7-5-3; IC13-18-4; IC13-30-2-1; IC14-34-3-1; Indiana Administrative Code, Titles 310 [Department of Natural Resources], 323 [Indiana Hazardous Waste Facility Site Approval Authority], 326 [Air Pollution Control Board], 327 [Water Pollution Control Board], 329 [Solid Waste Management Board], 355 [State Chemist]). Certain activities with regard to use and labeling of pesticides prohibited. (IC15-3-3.5, -3.6).

It is unlawful to use or sell any nondegradable detergent containing alkyl benzine sulfonate. It is unlawful to use or sell detergent with any phosphorus, except for those amounts not exceeding 1/2 of 1% by weight incidental to manufacturing in accordance with Indiana Water Pollution Control Board regulations. These standards do not apply to detergents for cleaning in place food processing and dairy equipment, phosphoric acid products including sanitizers, brighteners, acid cleaners and metal conditioners; detergents for use in dish washing equipment including household and commercial dishwashers; detergents for use in hospitals, health care facilities; institutional laundry detergents for use in dairy, beverage, food processing and other industrial cleaning equipment; and any other use of detergent in which phosphorous contents are not emptied into public or private sewer or disposed into natural environment. (IC13-18-9-1 to -3).

Person may not act as waste tire transporter without being registered with Indiana Department of Environmental Management. Tire retailers must post notices regarding tire recycling and disposal and must accept used tires from customers. (IC13-20-14).

Person may not create or maintain certain waste tire processing operations without obtaining certificate of registration from Indiana Department of Environmental Management. (IC13-20-13-2).

Person may not incinerate PCB in incinerator without permit from IDEM and approval of county executive of county in which incinerator is located. (IC13-17-10-1).

Person shall not sell or manufacture for sale in this state compound polychlorinated biphenyls or terphenyls (PCB). There are also various restrictions as to amounts of PCB that may be in products or materials sold or manufactured in Indiana. (IC13-20-15).

Person may not engage in lead-based paint activities such as inspection or abatement and must obtain license after undergoing training in approved program. (IC13-17-14).

Certain plastic bottles may not be sold in Indiana unless bottles are coded for recycling. (IC13-20-19-1).

Disposal of vegetative matter in landfills prohibited after (IC13-20-9). Composting operations require registration. (IC13-20-10).

Water quality standards and rights to public use do not apply to off-stream privately-owned bodies of water used to reduce pollutants or cool water before discharge into public waters. (IC14-26-2-14).

Vehicle that has been used to transport more than 4,000 pounds of solid waste to landfill, incinerator or transfer station may not be used to transport food for at least 15 days unless vehicle has been sanitized in accordance with State Board of Health rules. (IC16-42-18-3).

Disposal of lead-acid batteries is restricted, and retailers must accept used lead-acid batteries from purchasers of new batteries. (IC13-20-16).

No person may install, test, retrofit, or remove underground storage tank unless person has been certified by State Fire Marshall. (IC13-23-3-3).

No person may inspect, manage, or abate asbestos-containing materials without being accredited or licensed. (IC13-17-6-1).

Registration or license required for certain pesticide activities and certain of these activities may be restricted. (IC15-3-3.5,-3.6).

No person may engage in waste transfer activities without submitting disclosure statement to IDEM. (IC13-20-6).

Enforcement.—Agencies regulating environmental matters have control over enforcement of their regulations. However, under specified conditions and procedures, any person, corporation, association, or governmental unit may maintain action for declaratory and equitable relief for protection of environment from significant pollution, impairment, or destruction. (IC13-30-1-1; IC13-30-3).

For surface mining activities, special enforcement provisions conducted by Director of Dept. of Natural Resources provide for inspection, written notice of violations, and

opportunity for public hearing. Civil actions by any person with interest which may be adversely affected to remedy violation also permitted. (IC14-34-15-12).

Department employees authorized to enter premises to inspect and obtain samples of hazardous substances but must give owner report. (IC13-14-2-2; IC13-14-5-2). Department authorized to issue order mandating corrective action and to seek court order to permit entrance on private land to carry out corrective action, including order requiring removal of hazardous substances released from containment or other appropriate action. (IC13-14-2-1; IC13-14-2-6; IC13-30-3-11).

Asbestos project may be enjoined if it is not performed in accordance with state rules, and asbestos contractors and workers may be reprimanded or their licenses may be suspended or revoked under certain circumstances. (IC13-17-6-10 to -11).

Judicial Review.—To obtain judicial review of final order of department, board or agency, proceed under IC4-21.5-5.

Emergency Orders.—Whenever contamination of air, water or land constitutes a clear and present danger to health and safety of persons, Governor may proclaim existence of an emergency and order all persons causing contamination to reduce or discontinue immediately emission and/or discharge of contaminants. (IC13-14-10-1).

Penalties.—Persons who violate statutes, regulations or standards adopted by agency or board are liable for civil penalty not to exceed $25,000 per day of violation. (IC13-30-4-1). Department enforcement action must commence by issuing notice of violation within three years after date department first discovers event or last of series of events that serves as basis for enforcement action. (IC13-14-6-2). Persons who fail to pay annual fees for underground storage tanks subject to penalty of $50 per day per tank. (IC13-23-12-7). Violation of surface mining statutes or regulations only, civil penalty not to exceed $5,000 per violation, plus $750 per day of continuing violation. (IC14-34-16-1). Penalties not to exceed $1,000 per day of violation of flood control laws, regulations, or permits. (IC14-28-1-36). Penalty of up to $1,000 for violation of pesticide laws or regulations. (IC15-3-3.5-18.3, IC15-3-3.6-14.5).

Violation of Emergency Order.—Penalty not to exceed $500 per hour of violation. (IC13-30-4-2).

Criminal Penalties.—Fine of $2,500 to $25,000 per day of violation and imprisonment for two years; hazardous waste violations only, fine not to exceed $25,000 per day plus imprisonment. Penalty for second and subsequent convictions is fine not to exceed $50,000 per day and imprisonment. For falsification of documents or monitoring, fine not to exceed $10,000 and imprisonment not to exceed six months. (IC13-30-6-1 to -2). Class C infraction for person to obstruct, delay, resist, prevent, or interfere with inspection or investigation of department. Each day of violation constitutes separate infraction. (IC13-30-5-1). Responsible corporate officers may be prosecuted. (IC13-30-6-4). Class C Misdemeanor for violation of certain pesticide rules. (IC15-3-3.5-21). Class B infraction for failure to deliver disclosure document under Indiana Responsible Transfer Law; Class A infraction for false statement or failure to record disclosure document. (IC13-25-3-10 to -12). Failure of final disposal facility to pay to state fee collection for disposal of solid waste in Indiana constitutes Class D felony. (IC13-20-22-19).

Permits or certificates are required for various activities affecting environment (IC13-15-2-2); for certain air pollutant emitting facilities (IC13-15-1-1); certain discharges into navigable waters (IC13-15-1-2); solid and hazardous waste activities (IC13-15-1-3); surface mining activities (IC14-34-3-1); chemical munitions destruction or treatment facilities (IC13-11-3-10); hazardous waste facility sites (IC13-22-3-1). Applicants for permits involving management of solid waste, hazardous waste, or atomic radiation must disclose history of past violations, actions, and other "good character" matters. (IC13-19-4). Owner or operator of final disposal facility in Indiana must register with IDEM. (IC13-20-22-4). Applicants for construction or operation of landfill or transfer station also must satisfy financial responsibility requirements. (IC13-20-2-1; IC13-22-9-1). Municipal waste collection and transportation vehicles must be licensed. (IC13-20-4). Underground storage tanks must be registered. (IC13-23-12-1). Permits are required for construction in floodways. (IC14-28-1-22). Registration required for composting operations (IC13-20-10-2), and for waste tire storage site (IC13-20-13).

Fees.—Owners or operators of underground storage tanks must pay annual fees. (IC13-23-12-1). Annual fees are assessed against facilities required to submit emergency and hazardous chemical inventory form. (IC6-6-10-6). Fees required for various permits, registrations, licenses, authorizations, and certificates. (See subhead Permits or Certificates, supra.) Fees established by statute are charged for disposal or incineration of solid waste in Indiana; additional fees established by rule may be assessed against solid waste generated outside Indiana. (IC13-20-22-1). Fee required for registration of final disposal facility in Indiana. (IC13-20-22-4). Fees are charged for mandatory inspection of solid waste transfer stations. (IC13-20-6-7).

Reports.—Department of Environmental Management responsible for collection of information and copying of records concerning hazardous substances. Operations producing at least 100 kilograms of hazardous waste transported for disposal or storage must file report with Department. Manifest prepared by and purchased from department is required for transportation of hazardous waste. (IC13-22-4). Specified information concerning generation of hazardous waste must be reported. (IC13-22-11). Spills of pollutants into waters of Indiana must be reported within 24 hours. (327 IAC 2-6-2). Notification required for asbestos demolition or renovation activities. (326 IAC 14-10-3; see also local government rules).

Interstate Compacts.—Indiana belongs to several interstate compacts and commissions: Ohio River Valley Water Sanitation Compact Commission (1939) (IC13-29-2); and Midwest Interstate Low-Level Radioactive Waste Compact (1983) (IC13-29-1).

Responsible Property Transfer Law.—Transferor of certain real property must furnish disclosure document to other parties to transfer which discloses prior uses of property. Disclosure document must include criteria set forth in statute and must be recorded in county where property is located. (IC13-25-3).

State Cleanup Laws.—Persons who are liable under 42 U.S.C. 9607(a) are liable, in same manner and to same extent, to State of Indiana, subject to additional defenses for creditors and fiduciaries. (IC13-25-4-8). State may impose lien on property with respect to which state has incurred environmental response costs. (IC13-25-4-11; IC13-24-1-4).

See note at head of Digest as to 1998 legislation covered.

See Topical Index in front part of this volume.

ENVIRONMENTAL REGULATION . . . *continued*
Owners and operators of underground storage tanks are liable to state for costs of corrective action with respect to release of hazardous substances or petroleum from tanks; private parties who have incurred corrective action costs have right of contribution. (IC13-23-13-8). Owners or operators of petroleum facilities, or other responsible persons, are liable to state for reasonable costs of response or remedial actions taken with respect to facility; owner, operator, or responsible person is entitled to all rights of state to recover such costs from responsible person. (IC13-24-1-4). State or private person may bring action to recover reasonable costs of removal or remedial action against persons who caused or contributed to certain releases of hazardous substances or petroleum. (IC13-30-9). Voluntary remediation can result in contribution protection, covenant not to sue, and certificate of completion. (IC13-25-5).

ESTATES AND TRUSTS

ADMINISTRATION:

See topic Executors and Administrators.

ADVANCEMENTS:

See topic Descent and Distribution.

ALLOWANCES:

See topic Executors and Administrators.

CLAIMS:

See topic Executors and Administrators; category Civil Actions and Procedure, topic Pleading.

DEATH:

Presumption of Death.—Where a resident of the state is absent for five years without tidings, presumption of death arises and his will may be probated or administration had on his estate. (IC29-2-5-1 and IC29-2-6-1). Before court may determine that individual should be presumed dead, notice to individual must be published for 30 days in newspaper of general circulation in county where individual last resided or where individual's property is located and state capital. (IC29-2-5-1).

In case of life insurance, absence of the insured for five years is not sufficient to raise a presumption of death, but the common law presumption of death after seven years prevails. (197 Ind. 50, 149 N.E. 718, 410 N.E.2d 1377).

Where a nonresident of state who, if alive, would be entitled to real estate in state by descent or devise, has been absent from his place of residence for seven years and not heard from by his or her spouse, parents, children, brothers or sisters he or she is presumed to be dead. In such case his real estate or that which he would have inherited vests in his heirs after complaint and notice filed in circuit or superior court of county in which real estate is situated to quiet title to real estate as against him. Judgment becomes absolute at end of three years unless, within that time, he appears and moves to have it vacated. (IC32-6-6-1 to 2).

Uniform Determination of Death Act adopted. (IC1-1-4-3).

Definition of Death.—At least for purposes of homicide law, death legally occurs when all brain functions irreversibly cease or when circulatory and respiratory functions irreversibly cease. (421 N.E. 2d 596).

Proof of Death.—Official findings and records or certified copies of the same issued by authorized officer or employee of U.S. concerning death, presumed death or other status of missing persons, upon receipt in any court, is evidence of death or status of any missing person. (IC34-37-4-1 to 2).

Local health officers maintain permanent record of deaths occurring in their jurisdiction. These records are open to public inspection. (IC16-37-3-9).

Survivorship.—Uniform Simultaneous Death Act has been adopted. (IC29-2-14-1 et seq.).

Actions for Death.—Personal representative of deceased may bring action against one causing death of his decedent by wrongful act or omission, if decedent might have brought action had he lived. Such action must be brought within two years after death. Damages in death actions shall be in such amount as may be determined by court or jury to compensate for pecuniary loss. (400 N.E.2d 778). Pecuniary loss for which damages are recoverable in wrongful death action pursuant to IC34-23-1-1 may include loss to children of their parents' care, reasonable value of loss of care, love and affection sustained by decedent's spouse, and loss of parental training and guidance sustained by children during their minority. (489 N.E.2d 78). Punitive damages are not allowed. (609 F.2d 286, 489 N.E.2d 78). Damages recovered for medical and burial expenses inure to exclusive benefit of decedent's estate for payment thereof. Remaining damages must inure to exclusive benefit of widow or widower and dependent children, if any, or dependent next of kin, to be distributed as personal property. If there is no surviving spouse, dependent children, or dependent next of kin, damages inure to benefit of those who provided hospital and medical services and for burial expenses, administrator's expenses and attorney's fees. (IC34-23-1-1).

Father or mother, or in case of divorce or dissolution of marriage, person to whom custody of child was awarded, may maintain action for death of child, and guardian may maintain such action for death of protected person. "Child" defined as unmarried individual without dependents who is: (1) Less than 20 years of age; or (2) less than 23 years of age and enrolled in institution of higher education or vocational school or program. Damages may be recovered: (1) For loss of child's services; (2) for loss of child's love and companionship; and (3) to pay expenses for deceased child's medical care necessitated by wrongful act which caused child's death, child's funeral expenses and counseling for surviving parent or minor sibling, uninsured debts of child, including debtors for which parent is obligated on behalf of child, and administration of child's estate, including reasonable attorney's fees. In addition, uninsured debts of child may be recovered as well as expenses related to administration of child's estate. (IC34-23-2-1).

Court having probate jurisdiction may appoint administrator for estate of a nonresident for sole purpose of bringing action to recover damages for wrongful death of such nonresident. (IC29-1-10-18). See also category Transportation, topic Motor Vehicles, subhead Action Against Nonresident.

In action against personal representative of wrongdoer brought after death of wrongdoer, cause must be prosecuted in same manner as claims against estate. (IC34-9-3-3). See also topic Executors and Administrators, subhead Time for Filing.

For survival of tort actions see IC34-9-3-1 et seq.

Medical Malpractice Act.—(IC34-18-1-1 et seq.). If action qualifies under IC34-18-1-1, then total amount recoverable for any injury or death of patient may not exceed $500,000. That limit was increased to $750,000 for malpractice occurring on or after Jan. 1, 1990. (IC34-18-14-3[a]). That limit will be increased to $1,250,000 for malpractice occurring on or after July 1, 1999. (IC34-18-14-3[a]). Act applies to all "qualified" health care providers, and maximum recovery from health care provider is $100,000. (IC34-18-14-3[b]). That limit will be increased to $250,000 for malpractice occurring on or after July 1, 1999. (IC34-18-14-3[b]).

Death Certificate.—See category Documents and Records, topic Records, subhead Vital Statistics.

Uniform Anatomical Gift Act adopted with modifications. (IC29-2-16-1 to 9).

Living Wills.—See topic Wills.

DECEDENTS' ESTATES:

See topics Descent and Distribution, Executors and Administrators, Wills; category Debtor and Creditor, topic Homesteads.

DESCENT AND DISTRIBUTION:

See also topic Executors and Administrators.

The share of the net estate not distributable to the surviving spouse, or the entire net estate if there is no surviving spouse, will descend as follows: (a) to the issue of the intestate; if they are all in the same degree of kinship to the intestate, they will take equally, otherwise, to those of more remote degrees, by representation; (b) if there is surviving spouse but no surviving issue of intestate, then to intestate's surviving parents; (c) if there is no surviving spouse or issue of intestate, then to surviving parents, brothers and sisters and issue of deceased brothers and sisters of intestate, provided that each parent will get no less than one-fourth of net estate and issue of deceased brothers and sisters take by representation; (d) if there is no surviving parent or brother or sister of intestate, then to issue of brothers and sisters, equally if all of same degree of kinship to intestate, otherwise, to those of more remote degrees by representation; (e) if no surviving issue, or parent of intestate, or issue of parent, then to surviving grandparents of intestate equally; (f) if there is no surviving issue, or parent, or issue of parent, or grandparent, then estate shall be divided into number of shares equal to sum of: (1) number of brothers and sisters of decedent's parents surviving decedent, plus (2) number of deceased brothers and sisters of decedent's parents leaving issue surviving both them and decedent; such shares shall pass per stirpes to each of said brothers and sisters of decedent's parents or their issue per stirpes; (g) if interest in real estate go to husband and wife under this section, aggregate interests shall be owned by them as tenants by entireties, while personal property shall be owned as tenants in common; if there is no person mentioned in (a) through (g), then to state. (IC29-1-2-1).

Surviving Spouse.—Common law dower and curtesy are abolished and a surviving spouse takes as a statutory heir. (IC29-1-2-11).

If the decedent left a surviving child or children or other descendants by a prior marriage, and no issue by the surviving spouse, the surviving spouse will take only a life estate in one-third of real property of decedent with fee vesting in such surviving issue. Surviving spouse will receive regular statutory share in personal property of decedent. (IC29-1-2-1).

Subject to the exceptions above, the surviving spouse will receive the following share of the net estate: (1) One-half, if intestate is survived by at least one child or by issue of at least one deceased child; (2) three-fourths, if there is no surviving issue, but intestate is survived by one or both of intestate's parents; (3) all, if there is no surviving issue or parent. (IC29-1-2-1).

Widow.—Any interest acquired by widow in the decedent's real estate, not exceeding one-third of the real estate, is received by her free from all demands of creditors; provided, that if value of real estate is over $10,000 widow shall have only one-fourth and if it is over $20,000 she shall have only one-fifth free from creditors. Widow's share is subject to purchase money mortgages, mortgages executed prior to marriage or in which she was joined. (IC29-1-2-2).

Surviving spouse of decedent domiciled in Indiana at his death is entitled to receive allowance of $15,000 in personal property from estate, or residence of surviving spouse, or combination of both. If no surviving spouse, decedent's children who are under 18 years of age at time of decedent's death are entitled to same allowance to be divided equally among them. If less than $15,000 in personal property in estate and residence of surviving spouse, spouse or decedent's children who are under 18 years of age at time of decedent's death are entitled to any real estate in estate to extent necessary to make up difference. Amount of difference is lien on remaining real estate. Allowance under this section is not chargeable against distributive share of either surviving spouse or children, and is deductible for inheritance tax purposes from value of property interests transferred by resident decedent under his will or under laws of intestate succession. (IC6-4.1-3-13[b]10; IC29-1-4-1).

Circumstances Barring Participation in Estate of Deceased Spouse.—Surviving spouse who is living apart in adultery at time of death of other spouse is barred from any participation in estate of deceased spouse. (IC29-1-2-14). Individual who abandons spouse, without just cause, shall take no part of estate of deceased spouse. (IC29-1-2-15).

Half Blood.—Kindred of half blood inherit the same share which they would have inherited if they had been of the whole blood. (IC29-1-2-5).

See note at head of Digest as to 1998 legislation covered.

See Topical Index in front part of this volume.

DESCENT AND DISTRIBUTION . . . continued

Posthumous Children or Other Issue.—Descendants of intestate begotten before but born after his death inherit as if they had been born during his lifetime and survived him. (IC29-1-2-6).

Children born out of wedlock inherit from and through mother and she and her relatives from them. Children born out of wedlock inherit from and through father if: (1) Paternity has been established by law during father's lifetime or within five months after father's death; or (2) putative father marries mother of child and acknowledges child to be his own. If either of above occurs father and his relatives inherit from child born out of wedlock. (IC29-1-2-7).

Adopted Children.—See category Family, topic Adoption.

Forfeiture of Rights.—Person is constructive trustee of property to which he is otherwise entitled to receive as result of decedent's death if person found guilty or guilty but mentally ill, of murder, causing suicide, or voluntary manslaughter, because of decedent's death. Beneficiaries of constructive trust include those who are legally entitled to property other than constructive trustee. However, if any property under constructive trust is sold to innocent purchaser, that property is no longer subject to constructive trust, but property received in transaction becomes subject to constructive trust. (IC29-1-2-12.1).

Determination of Heirship.—With exception of treatment of posthumous issue, descent and distribution of intestate estate is determined by relationship to intestate at date of death. (IC29-1-2-6). At any time during administration of estate, personal representative or any interested person may petition court to determine heirs of decedent and their respective interests in estate. (IC29-1-6-6). When no administration has been commenced, nor any will offered for probate, within five months after decedent's death, any person claiming interest in decedent's property as heir or through heir may petition to determine heirs of said decedent and their respective interests as heirs in estate. (IC29-1-17-15.1).

Advancements.—Advancements may be made to any heir, including spouse. Gifts are deemed not to be advancements unless contrary is proved by written declaration of decedent or acknowledgment by heir. Advancements are counted toward intestate share of the advancee to extent of value of the advancement at time the advancee came into possession or enjoyment or at death of intestate, whichever occurs first. If advancee dies before the intestates, leaving lineal heir who takes from intestate, advancement is taken into account as if it had been made directly to heir. But if heir is entitled to lesser share than advancee would have been, heir is charged only with that part of advancement as amount he would have inherited bears to amount advancee would have received had there been no advancement and had advancee survived intestate. (IC29-1-2-10).

Disclaimer.—See topic Wills, subhead Disclaimer.

Escheat.—Estate of person dying intestate without heirs escheats to the state. (IC29-1-2-1, IC29-1-17-12).

ESTATES:

See category Property, topic Real Property.

EXECUTORS AND ADMINISTRATORS:

Jurisdiction and Venue.—Jurisdiction over administration of estate of a decedent (including probate of will and issuance of letters testamentary or of administration) is in the court exercising probate jurisdiction (see category Courts and Legislature, topic Courts) in the county where decedent had his domicile at the time of his death or, in the case of a decedent not domiciled in this state, (1) in any county wherein he left assets or (2) in any county into which assets subsequently come. Where jurisdiction may be in courts in more than one county, court first assuming jurisdiction has exclusive jurisdiction extending to all counties unless and until proper venue is determined to be elsewhere. (IC29-1-7-1).

Preferences in Right to Administer.—Letters testamentary or of administration will be granted to persons in the following order: (1) the executor or executors designated in will that has been admitted to probate; (2) surviving spouse who is devisee in will admitted to probate; (3) devisee in will admitted to probate; (4) surviving spouse and/or surviving spouse's nominee; (5) heir and/or his/her nominee; (6) any other qualified person. (IC29-1-10-1).

Eligibility and Competency.—No person is qualified to serve as a personal representative who is: (1) under 18 years of age; (2) incapacitated (unless incapacity is caused by physical illness, physical impairment or physical infirmity); (3) convicted felon; (4) resident corporation not authorized to act as fiduciary in this state; or (5) person whom court finds unsuitable. (IC29-1-10-1).

Nonresident individual or corporate fiduciary may serve as joint personal representative with resident personal representative by filing bond with court that has jurisdiction of administration, if otherwise qualified. Nonresident individual who otherwise qualifies may serve as personal representative by filing notice of acceptance of appointment, notice of appointment of resident agent, and bond. (IC29-1-10-1).

Exemption from Bond.—Personal representative is not required to execute and file bond unless: (1) Will provides for filing of bond; or (2) court finds on its own motion or petition by interested person bond is necessary to protect creditors, heirs, legatees or devisees. (IC29-1-11-1).

Special Administration.—Unsupervised administration: If decedent dies intestate, heirs at law of estate, or, if testate, legatees and devisees under will, or personal representative may file petition for administration without court supervision. Court may grant petition if: (1) All heirs or devisees and legatees have joined in petition; (2) estate is solvent; (3) personal representative is qualified to administer estate without court supervision; (4) heirs or legatees and devisees, or parent (as defined in IC29-3-1-11), or if none, guardian (as defined in IC29-3-1-6), of heir, legatee, or devisee, as case may be, freely consent to and understand significance of administration without supervision; and (5) will does not request supervised administration. (IC29-1-7.5-1, 2). In addition, court may grant petition without (1) and (4) above, if decedent in will authorized unsupervised administration and if all other requirements met. (IC29-1-7.5-2). If granted,

personal representative may then perform any act necessary or appropriate to administer estate and follow procedures of statute. (IC29-1-7.5-3, 4).

Representative not required to file bond unless will provides for it or court finds bond is necessary. (IC29-1-7.5-2.5). Within two months of being appointed, representative shall prepare verified inventory of estate's assets. (IC29-1-7.3-3.2). Distribution of real property by representative in unsupervised administration is sufficient to distribute all title therein if conveyance includes certain language. (IC29-1-7.5-3.4, 3.6). Representative must close estate administered without supervision as promptly as possible. (IC29-1-7.5-3.8). Unless barred by adjudication and except as provided in closing statement, claims against personal representative are barred, including claims by person under disability, unless proceeding to assert claims is commenced within three months after filing of closing statement. Rights barred do not include rights to recover from personal representative for fraud, misrepresentation, or inadequate disclosure. (IC29-1-7.5-6).

Special administrators may be appointed for a specified time to perform duties respecting specific property or to perform particular acts. (IC29-1-10-15).

Inventory.—Executor or administrator must prepare inventory showing fair market value of decedent's property which he has received or of which he has knowledge, including statement of all known liens and other charges on any item. Fair market value of each item may be established by appraisals. Personal representative or administrator may employ disinterested appraiser to assist him in valuing asset whose value may be subject to doubt. (IC29-1-12-1).

Extension of Time for Payment of Debt to Estate.—When it appears to be in best interest of estate, personal representative may, on order of court, extend time for payment of any debt due estate or make any fair and reasonable compromise with any debtor. (IC29-1-13-5).

Notice of Appointment.—Executor or administrator must give notice of appointment by publication and by mail to heirs, devisees, legatees and known creditor. (IC29-1-7-7).

Notice to Creditors.—Executor or administrator must give notice of appointment by publication and by mail to each known creditor of decedent upon issuance of letters testamentary. Actual notice must be given to all creditors known or reasonably ascertainable within three months of published notice of appointment and whose claims have not been paid or settled by personal representative. (IC29-1-7-7). Executor or administrator must exercise reasonable diligence in discovering reasonably ascertainable creditors within three months of first publication of notice. (IC29-1-7-7.5).

Filing of Claims.—The holder of any claim against the decedent, whether such claim be due or not, must file a succinct and definite statement thereof in the office of the clerk of the court in which the estate is pending. (IC29-1-14-2). Certain negligence claims are subject to special rules. (IC29-1-14-1). See subhead Time for Filing, infra.

If the claim is secured by lien on any real or personal property such lien must be particularly set forth in such statement and a reference given to where the lien, if of record, will be found. (IC29-1-14-2).

Time for Filing.—Unless executor or administrator fails to give actual notice to known or reasonably ascertainable creditors, all claims other than expenses of administration and claims of governmental body, whether due or to become due, absolute or contingent, are barred unless filed within five months after first published notice to creditors or three months after court has revoked probate of will if claimant was named as beneficiary in will, whichever is later. (IC29-1-14-1). If executor or administrator fails to give actual notice to known or reasonably ascertainable creditors, creditor may submit claim against estate during time period above specified plus additional two months after date actual notice is given to creditor but no later than one year after decedent's death. (IC29-1-7-7). Claims arising out of negligence for injury to person or damages to property against estate are not so limited if recovery does not affect any interest in assets of estate. Such negligence claims may be filed within regular period of limitations. (IC29-1-14-1).

Proof of Claims.—If claim is on a written instrument, the original or a complete copy thereof must be filed with the statement which must set forth all credits and deductions to which the estate is entitled. (IC29-1-14-2).

There must be an affidavit attached that the claim, after deducting all credits, set-offs and deductions to which the estate is entitled, is justly due and wholly unpaid or if not yet due, when it will or may become due. (IC29-1-14-2).

Form for proof of claim may be obtained from clerk of court exercising probate jurisdiction.

Contest of Claims.—Any interested person may contest a claim upon petition to the court and at his own expense. (IC29-1-14-14).

Allowance or Disallowance of Claims.—Claims which have been filed are immediately entered on the claim docket, and all claims must be allowed or disallowed within five months and 15 days after first published notice to creditors. Any claim disallowed is set for trial in probate court. Trial of such claims is conducted as ordinary civil case. (IC29-1-14-10, 13). Claims by personal representative cannot be acted upon unless all interested parties consent. If interested parties do not consent, special personal representative appointed by court to examine and allow or disallow claim. (IC29-1-14-17).

Payment of Claims.—Claims are paid prior to final report on estate. Prior to expiration of five months after first published notice to creditors, personal representative, if estate clearly is solvent, may pay any claims which he believes are just and correct, whether or not such claims have been filed, and must pay claims ordered by court at any time so long as such claims were filed within five months after date of publication of notice to creditors. (IC29-1-14-19).

Insolvent Estates.—If applicable assets of estate are insufficient to pay all claims and allowances in full, personal representative must make payment in following order: (1) costs and expenses of administration; (2) reasonable funeral expenses; (3) allowance made to surviving spouse or children; (4) all debts and taxes having preference under law of U.S.; (5) reasonable and necessary medical expenses of last sickness including compensation of persons attending him; (6) all debts and taxes having preference under laws of this state; (7) all other claims allowed. (IC29-1-14-9).

EXECUTORS AND ADMINISTRATORS ... *continued*

Actions Against Representative.—No action by a summons or complaint may be brought against an executor or administrator for recovery of any claim against the decedent, but the sole remedy is filing and prosecuting a claim. (IC29-1-14-2). Enforcement of claims arising out of certain negligence actions is excepted. (IC29-1-14-1). Action against decedent, started before his death, may be continued by substitution of executor or administrator as party. (IC34-1-1-1).

Liens on real estate by judgment or otherwise cannot be enforced until five months from death of decedent unless earlier date is authorized by judge of court with jurisdiction of estate. (IC29-1-14-16). See Rule TR 69(C).

Sales.—In determining what portion of the estate will be sold, there is no priority as between real and personal property except as provided by will, court order, or IC29-1-17-3. (IC29-1-15-1). If will gives personal representative power to sell, mortgage, lease, or exchange any estate property then he may do so without obtaining court order. When will does not authorize sale, executor must get court order. (IC29-1-15-2). No sale of real estate by unsupervised personal representative is voided by irregularity or defect if he acted in substantial conformity with power given in will and premises are held by or under one who purchased in good faith. (IC29-1-15-19).

An executor appointed in another state for the estate of one not an inhabitant of Indiana at the time of his death may be authorized to sell real estate in this state by a court having probate jurisdiction in county in which real estate of deceased is located subject to conditions imposed on nonresidents generally. (IC29-2-1-6). Court in which appointment was first filed has jurisdiction over all sales of real estate in this state. (IC29-2-1-8 to 10).

Liability of Beneficiaries.—If distribution made with contingent claim pending, distributees are liable to holder of claim when it becomes absolute, but not in excess of the amount distributed. Action must be brought within five months of time when claim becomes absolute. (IC29-1-14-8).

Allowances.—See topic Descent and Distribution, subhead Surviving Spouse.

Final Account and Settlement.—Estate must be closed as promptly as possible. Unless for good cause shown, final account must be filed within one year after appointment of personal representative. (IC29-1-16-2). Upon filing final account, clerk of court must set deadline for filing written objections at least 14 days prior to hearing and must give notice to all interested persons by publication at least 14 days prior to deadline for objections and by mail to those entitled to share in residue of estate if their addresses are known. (IC29-1-16-6). If any person entitled to part of estate cannot be found after reasonable search, that part will be paid into court. Upon sufficient proof clerk will pay person share to which he is entitled as distributee, heir, or claimant. No payment will be made seven years after court has received proceeds. (IC29-1-17-12).

Consent Settlement.—There are provisions for the settling of disputes over the estate and for the appointment of a guardian ad litem to represent minors, incapacitated and absent parties whose consent will make agreement binding upon all interested persons. (IC29-1-9-1 to 3).

After-Discovered Property.—When other property is discovered after estate is closed, the discharged personal representative or any interested person may petition to have estate reopened and the property administered. If estate was solvent, court may order the property distributed without reopening estate. (IC29-1-17-14).

Compensation of Representatives.—Personal representative receives compensation which court considers just and reasonable in absence of provision for compensation in will. Executors may renounce all claims for compensation provided for by the will before qualification and have their compensation determined by court. (IC29-1-10-13).

Distribution if Abroad.—No specific provision.

When Administration is Unnecessary.—If value of gross estate less liens and encumbrances does not exceed $25,000, costs and expenses of administration, and reasonable funeral expenses, personal representative or person acting on behalf of distributees, if not supervised personal representative or prohibited by court order from distributing assets, may immediately distribute estate to persons entitled to it without any administration and may file closing statement with court. (IC29-1-8-3, 4). Person claiming right to payment or delivery of personal property of decedent is entitled thereto provided: (1) 45 days have elapsed since decedent's death; (2) value of gross probate estate less liens and encumbrances does not exceed $25,000; (3) no petition for appointment of personal representative is pending or has been granted; (4) claimant is entitled to payment or delivery of property; and (5) affidavit showing above conditions is given to anyone owing debts to estate or in custody of any assets of estate. (IC29-1-8-1). Person paying or delivering personal property is discharged and released as if he dealt with personal representative of decedent. (IC29-1-8-2).

Small Estates.—See subhead When Administration is Unnecessary, supra.

Foreign executors or administrators have generally all rights of executors and administrators under wills duly executed and admitted to probate in state. (IC29-2-1-6). However, petition for appointment of local personal representative terminates power of foreign executor or administrator. (IC29-2-1-7). Objection by resident creditor to payment to foreign personal representative by debtor of nonresident decedent prevents payment or delivery without court authorization. (IC29-2-1-4).

Uniform Fiduciaries Act.—See topic Trusts.

Revised Uniform Principal and Income Act adopted with modifications. (IC30-4-5-1 et seq.).

Uniform Simplification of Fiduciary Security Transfers Act adopted. (IC30-2-5-1 to 11).

Uniform Anatomical Gift Act adopted with modifications. (IC29-2-16-1 to 12).

FIDUCIARIES:

See topics Executors and Administrators, Trusts; category Family, topic Guardian and Ward.

INTESTACY:

See topic Descent and Distribution.

PROOF OF CLAIMS:

See topic Executors and Administrators; category Civil Actions and Procedure, topic Pleading.

TRUSTS:

Uniform Fiduciaries Act has been adopted (IC30-2-4-1 to 14), but §3 (IC30-2-4-3) was repealed on effective date of Uniform Commercial Code, July 1, 1964, to extent that §3 is inconsistent with Code.

Creation.—Trust in real or personal property enforceable only if there is written evidence of terms signed by settlor or by authorized agent. No formal language required except terms must be definite as to property, trustee, trustee's interest, beneficiary, beneficiary's interest, and purpose of trust. If same person is sole trustee and sole beneficiary trust terminates. (IC30-4-2-1, 8).

Trustee's Eligibility and Competency.—Natural person must have capacity to take, hold and deal with property for his own benefit, be 18 years old, and be of sound mind and good moral character. Natural person from another state can act as trustee of property located in Indiana. Corporation must have power to take, hold, and deal with property for its own benefit and act as trustee. (IC30-4-2-11). Person may be both trustee and beneficiary. (IC30-4-1-1).

Qualifications.—Trustees need not post bonds unless specified by terms of trust or required by judicial discretion. (IC30-4-6-8).

Removal of Trustee.—Trustees may be removed by court or person authorized by terms of trust. Court in its discretion may permit resignation, upon petition of trustee, if not detrimental to trust. Successors are named by terms of trust or by court if trust terms do not provide for a successor. (IC30-4-3-29).

General Powers and Duties of Trustees.—Powers and duties of trustees specified by statute. Standard of care required by a trustee is prudent man rule. (IC30-4-3-3).

Sales.—Trustee has power to sell or convey all real, personal, or mixed property. (IC30-4-3-3).

Investments.—Governed by IC30-4-3-3. Self dealing by trustee governed by IC30-4-3-7 and IC30-4-3-5.

Securities in Name of Nominee.—Statute allows fiduciary to hold securities in name of a nominee. (IC28-2-6-1).

Bequests and Devises to Inter Vivos Trusts.—See topic Wills.

Uniform Common Trust Fund Act not adopted. Common trust funds provided for. (IC30-1-8-1 to 7).

Accounting.—Annual written report must be sent to each income beneficiary containing all receipts, disbursements, and items of property. Report may be waived by terms of trust or in writing by an adult beneficiary. (IC30-4-5-12).

Compensation.—Unless terms of trust provide otherwise, trustees are entitled to reasonable compensation subject to reduction in discretion of court in event of breach. (IC30-4-5-16, 17).

Discharge.—Upon petition, court may terminate trust that has been fulfilled or becomes illegal or impossible of fulfillment, or would impair accomplishment of purpose owing to unforeseen circumstances. (IC30-4-3-24).

Compromise.—If controversies exist with respect to construction, validity or effect of trust instrument, identity, rights or interests of beneficiary, or trust administration, parties may execute compromise. (IC30-4-1 to 10).

Revised Uniform Principal and Income Act adopted with modifications. (IC30-4-5-1 to 23).

Gifts to Minors.—See category Family, topic Infants.

Uniform Simplification of Fiduciary Security Transfers Act adopted. (IC30-2-5-1 to 11).

Accumulations.—Limited to lives in being plus 21 years after effective date of the instrument. (IC32-1-4.1-1 et seq.). Employee trusts excepted. (IC30-2-6-2).

Perpetuities.—See category Property, topic Perpetuities.

Pour Over Trusts.—See topic Wills, subhead Bequests and Devises to Inter Vivos Trusts.

Renunciation.—Beneficiary may disclaim interest in trust, in whole or in part, as provided in IC32-3-2-1 to 15.

WILLS:

A will may be executed by any person of sound mind, who is 18 years of age or older or who is member of armed forces or merchant marine even though under 18. (IC29-1-5-1).

Testamentary Disposition.—A testator may not limit a gift by a noncontesting provision nor devise to his wife with a condition in restraint of remarriage. (IC29-1-6-2, 3).

Execution.—Will, unless nuncupative, must contain signatures of testator and at least two witnesses. Testator, in presence of two or more attesting witnesses, shall signify to them that instrument is his will and then sign will, or at his direction and in his presence have someone else sign his name for him, or acknowledge his signature as already made. Attesting witnesses must sign will in presence of testator and presence of each other. If will is to be self-proved, acknowledgment by testator and verifications of witnesses must be attached or annexed to will. (IC29-1-5-3). Subject to rules of trial procedure, videotape may be admissible evidence of proper execution of will. (IC29-1-5-3[c]).

Attestation Clause.—No formal attestation clause required unless self-proved will. See subhead Self-Proved Will, infra.

See note at head of Digest as to 1998 legislation covered.

See Topical Index in front part of this volume.

WILLS ... *continued*

Holographic Wills.—There are no statutory provisions governing holographic wills.

Nuncupative Wills.—Valid only if made in imminent peril of death and testator died from such peril. Must be declared by testator as his will before two disinterested witnesses, reduced to writing by or under direction of one of witnesses within 30 days after declaration and submitted to probate within six months after death. May only dispose of personal property not exceeding $1,000 in value, person in active military service in time of war may dispose of personal property not exceeding $10,000 in value. Does not revoke existing written will, but does modify to extent necessary to give effect to nuncupative will. (IC29-1-5-4).

Revocation.—Written will may be revoked by testator or another in his presence and at his direction mutilating or destroying will with intent to revoke same. Will may also be revoked by writing signed and subscribed and attested as required for making of will. Partial revocation may be only by written instrument properly executed. (IC29-1-5-6).

If testator is divorced or his marriage annulled, all provisions in will in favor of his former spouse are revoked. Otherwise, no written will can be revoked by any change in circumstances or conditions of testator. (IC29-1-5-8).

A nuncupative will or any part of it can be revoked by another nuncupative will. (IC29-1-5-7).

Revival.—Revoked will may be revived only by republication or when revocation of second will shows clearly that testator intended to revive prior will. (IC29-1-5-6).

Testamentary Gifts to Subscribing Witnesses.—A subscribing witness may not take under a will where his testimony is necessary to prove will, except that if he is otherwise entitled to distributive share of testator's estate, he shall take amount of estate equal to lesser of: (i) Such distributive share, or (ii) amount provided for him in will. (IC29-1-5-2).

Bequests and Devises to Inter Vivos Trusts.—Instrument creating inter vivos trust need not be executed as testamentary instrument, even though settlor reserves power to alter or amend or power to control investments, or power to consume principal. (IC29-1-5-9). Testator may devise or bequeath property to trust which is clearly described in his will and in existence at his death. Unless will provides otherwise, property shall pass subject to provisions of trust, including any amendments in writing made before or after execution of will and before or after testator's death. (IC29-1-6-1[j]).

Uniform Testamentary Additions to Trusts Act adopted. (IC29-1-5-9).

Probate.—Original jurisdiction over administration of decedent's estate and probate is vested in circuit courts (IC33-4-4-3) and in certain superior and probate courts specified by statute (IC33-5). Probate proceedings are considered in rem. (IC29-1-7-2). Venue is in county of decedent's domicile at death, and if not domiciled in this state, then in county where he left property or into which property may have come after his death. (IC29-1-7-1).

If letters testamentary or of administration are not taken out on decedent's estate within three years after decedent's death, will of decedent shall not be probated. In case of individual presumed dead, three year period commences with date individual's death has been established by appropriate legal action. (IC29-1-7-15.1[d]). Personal representative or any interested person may petition to have will probated. Such petition may be combined with petition for issuance of letters testamentary to executor or for appointment of administrator with will annexed if no executor. (IC29-1-7-4).

Unless objection is filed, will must be admitted to probate upon finding that: (i) Testator is dead, (ii) will was executed according to law (IC29-1-7-13[a]), and (iii) unless self-proved, will proved by testimony of one or more subscribing witnesses, or, if they are dead, out of state, or incapacitated, by proof of handwriting of testator or of one of subscribing witnesses. (IC29-1-7-9). Every will proved must have certificate to that effect endorsed on it giving number and page of record where it is recorded. (IC29-1-7-14).

Grounds for contest include unsound mind, undue execution of will, duress or fraud in execution, and any other valid objection. (IC29-1-7-17).

Self-Proved Will.—Attested will may be admitted to probate without testimony of any subscribing witness if self-proved. Non-self-proved will may later be made self-proved if testator and all witnesses execute self-proving clause. Language for self-proved will is as follows:

Under penalties for perjury, we, the undersigned testator and the undersigned witnesses, respectively, whose names are signed to the attached or foregoing instrument declare:

(1) that the testator executed the instrument as the testator's will;
(2) that, in the presence of both witnesses, the testator signed or acknowledged the signature already made or directed another to sign for the testator in the testator's presence;
(3) that the testator executed the will as a free and voluntary act for the purposes expressed in it;
(4) that each of the witnesses, in the presence of the testator and of each other, signed the will as witnesses;
(5) that the testator was of sound mind when the will was executed; and
(6) that to the best knowledge of each of the witnesses the testator was, at the time the will was executed, eighteen (18) or more years of age or was member of the armed forces or of the merchant marine of the United States or its allies.

. . . .
Date   Testator
                                   . . . .
                                   Witness
                                   . . . .
                                   Witness

(IC29-1-5-3).

Will is presumed self-proved if it is executed by testator and includes attestation clause signed by at least two witnesses that contains information similar to foregoing self-proof clause except that information in first clause need only contain reference that testator signified instrument is testator's will. (IC29-1-5-3[d]).

Contest.—Any interested person may, after filing proper bond, contest validity of will within five months after date of order admitting will to probate, by properly filing allegations in court having probate jurisdiction. Attack must be made by verified pleading setting forth objections to will's validity. (IC29-1-7-17, 19).

Grounds for contest include unsound mind, undue execution of will, duress or fraud in execution and any other valid objection. (IC29-1-7-17).

Legacies.—Partial distribution may be decreed after the period allowed for filing claims and before final settlement of accounts. (IC29-1-17-1). General legacies do not bear interest unless will shows contrary intent. (IC29-1-17-8). Common law rules govern questions of ademption. (See 294 N.E.2d 141.)

Unclaimed Legacies.—If any heir, distributee, devisee or claimant cannot be found, personal representative shall sell that share of estate and pay proceeds to clerk of court for benefit of persons entitled thereto according to law. If there are no known heirs proceeds escheat to common school fund. (IC29-1-17-12). See IC29-1-17-12(e) for exceptions to this section. See also topic Executors and Administrators, subhead Distribution if Abroad.

Lapse.—Where testamentary devise is made to descendant of testator, who died before testator, leaving descendant who survives testator, such devise does not lapse and the descendant will take. (IC29-1-6-1[g]).

Posthumous Children.—See topic Descent and Distribution, subhead Posthumous Children or Other Issue.

Testamentary Guardian.—See category Family, topic Guardian and Ward, subhead Eligibility and Competency.

Election.—Surviving spouse may not by will be deprived, without consent, of one-half of testator's net personal and real estate. However, if surviving spouse is second or other subsequent spouse without issue by decedent and decedent left surviving issue, surviving spouse may elect only one-third of personal property and life estate in one-third of real estate. (IC29-1-3-1[a]). When value of property given surviving spouse under will is less than elective share, spouse may elect to retain specific bequests or devises at fair market value at time of decedent's death and receive balance in cash or property. (IC29-1-3-1[b]). In electing against will, spouse is deemed to renounce all interests in property of deceased. (IC29-1-3-1[c]). Election must be in writing, signed and acknowledged by surviving spouse or guardian of his estate and must be filed in office of clerk of court in which will was probated not later than ten days after period allowed for filing claims. If there is litigation pending which will affect amount of surviving spouse's share, then he (or if incompetent, his conservator [540 N.E. 2d 74]) has 30 days after final determination of such litigation within which to elect. (IC29-1-3-2, 3).

Children.—When testator fails to provide in will for child born or adopted after making last will, such child entitled to receive share of estate equal to share if testator had died intestate, unless it appears from will that omission was intentional or testator had one or more children living when will made and devised substantially all estate to surviving spouse. (IC29-1-3-8[a]). If testator believed child was dead at time will executed and failed to provide for such child in will, such child entitled to receive share of estate equal to share if testator had died intestate, unless it appears that testator would not have provided for child had he known child was alive. (IC29-1-3-8[b]).

Contribution.—When property that has been specifically devised, or charged with legacy, must be sold to pay claims, allowance provided by IC29-1-4-1, or elective share of surviving spouse or pretermitted children, other legatees and devisees must contribute portion of respective interests so as to accomplish proper abatement as provided by statute. (IC29-1-17-4). Order of abatement, unless otherwise provided in will, is as follows: (1) Property not disposed of by will, (2) residuary devises, (3) property disposed of by will but not specifically devised and not devised to residuary devisee, (4) specific devises. (IC29-1-17-3).

Disclaimer of interest devolved from decedent is effective only if: (1) Filed in court where estate proceedings pending, or if no proceedings are pending then in court where proceedings could be pending if commenced, (2) delivered in person or by first class mail to personal representative or to holder of legal title of property, (3) recorded in each country where real property located, and (4) above requirements accomplished in case of present interest, not later than nine months after date of death, or in case of future interest, not later than nine months after later of (a) event by which final taker ascertained or (b) day disclaimant turns 21. (IC32-3-2-3).

Foreign Wills Generally.—A will is legally executed if the manner of its execution complies with Indiana law, place of execution, or domicile of testator at time of execution or at time of his death. (IC29-1-5-5).

Foreign Probated Wills.—Will proved or allowed in another state or country may be received and recorded in Indiana within three years of testator's death if: (1) Will is duly certified by seal of court or official originally probating it, or (2) copy of will and probate thereof is duly certified by clerk of court admitting it to probate and by attestation of power of clerk by presiding or sole judge of court, or (3) Indiana court having probate jurisdiction is satisfied that will should be allowed. (IC29-1-7-25 to 27). After expiration of 45 days following death of nonresident decedent and upon affidavit and proof of appointment, foreign personal representative of estate of nonresident may collect payment for debt, personal property, or instrument evidencing debt, obligation, stock, or chose in action belonging to estate of nonresident without any local administration. (IC29-2-1-2).

Simultaneous Death.—See topic Death, subhead Survivorship.

Testamentary Trusts.—See topic Trusts.

Uniform Anatomical Gift Act adopted. (IC29-2-16-1 to 16).

Living Will.—Competent adults have right to control decisions relating to their own medical care, including decision to have medical or surgical means of prolonging life provided, withheld, or withdrawn. (IC16-36-4-6). Any competent person may consent to or refuse consent for medical treatment, including life-prolonging procedures. (IC16-36-4-7). ("Life-prolonging procedure" does not include medical procedure necessary to comfort or alleviate pain.) (IC16-36-4-1). Duly appointed health care representative or

WILLS . . . *continued*
certain family members may consent, on behalf of nonterminal incompetent patient, to withholding of life prolonging procedures, including nutrition and hydration. (IC16-36-1; 579 N.E.2d 32). Health care providers are not obligated to treat patient properly refusing to consent thereto, nor are they subject to civil or criminal penalty for failure to treat such patient. (IC16-36-4-7).

Person of sound mind, and at least 18 years of age or older, may execute life-prolonging procedures will declaration or living will declaration. (IC16-36-4-8). Life-prolonging procedures will declaration (see form infra) is for person desiring use of life-prolonging procedures in event of terminal condition. (IC16-36-4-11). Life-prolonging declaration requires physician to use life-prolonging procedures as requested. (IC16-36-4-8[g]). Mentally competent person desiring that dying not be artificially prolonged may execute living will declaration (see form infra). (IC16-36-4-10). Living will declaration does not obligate physician, but is presumptive evidence of patient's desires, and must be given great weight by physician. (IC16-36-4-8[f]).

Declarations must be voluntary, written, dated and signed by declarant or by another in declarant's presence and at his express request, and signed in presence of at least two competent witnesses of at least 18 years of age. Witness may not be person signing declaration at declarant's request; parent, spouse or child of declarant; person entitled to take part of declarant's estate; or person financially responsible for medical care of declarant. (IC16-36-4-8).

Attending physician of patient with terminal condition who executed living will or life-prolonging procedures declaration must certify patient as "qualified patient" to gain protection from potential civil or criminal liability offered by statute. Certificate must state that diagnosis is terminal condition and that patient executed declaration in accordance with statute. (IC16-36-4-13). Attending physician may lawfully withhold or withdraw life-prolonging procedures from such qualified patient. Such withholding or withdrawal, if in good faith and in accordance with reasonable medical standards, will not subject health care provider or employees thereof to criminal or civil liability. (IC16-36-4-13[d]).

Statutory procedures are required of attending physician who refuses to honor qualified patient's declaration. (IC16-36-4-13). Physician must attempt to transfer patient to another physician who will honor declaration, unless reason to believe declaration invalid or patient no longer desires that it be enforced, and patient is unable to validate declaration. In latter event, procedure exists to be followed for consultation with certain designated persons, including those with knowledge of patient's intentions and any appointed guardian of person. Procedure does not require appointment of guardian. (IC16-36-4-13[g]).

Living will or life-prolonging declaration may be revoked by signed and dated writing, physical cancellation or destruction of declaration by declarant or at declarant's direction in his presence, or by oral expression of intent to revoke. Revocation is effective when communicated to attending physician. (IC16-36-4-12).

Criminal sanctions are imposed for knowingly or intentionally destroying declaration without declarant's consent or forging revocation of declaration (Class D felony), and for forging living will or concealing or withholding knowledge of revocation of living will, with intent to cause withholding or withdrawal of life-prolonging procedures (Class C felony). (IC16-36-4-15, 16).

IC16-36-4 also contains provisions to effect that: (i) Declaration of no effect during patient pregnancy; (ii) qualified patient not committing suicide; (iii) declaration does not affect sale or issuance of life insurance, nor does it modify terms of life insurance policy; (iv) life insurance not impaired; (v) declaration cannot be made as condition for issuing or receiving health care services; (vi) no presumption regarding person who does not execute declaration; (vii) affirmative or deliberate acts to end life (euthanasia) not authorized; and (viii) withholding or withdrawing life-prolonging procedures not to be considered as intervening force and not to affect proximate cause with respect to conduct that placed patient in terminal condition.

Written appointment of health care representative under IC16-36-1-7 must include language of IC30-5-5-17 if appointment authorizes withholding or withdrawing care from terminal individual. (IC16-36-1-14).

Forms

Living Will Declaration:

Declaration made this . . . day of . . . . . (month, year) I, ... being at least eighteen (18) years of age and of sound mind, willfully and voluntarily make known my desires that my dying shall not be artificially prolonged under the circumstances set forth below, and I declare:

If at any time my attending physician certifies in writing that: (1) I have an incurable injury, disease, or illness; (2) my death will occur within a short time; and (3) the use of life prolonging procedures would serve only to artificially prolong the dying process, I direct that such procedures be withheld or withdrawn, and that I be permitted to die naturally with only the performance or provision of any medical procedure or medication necessary to provide me with comfort care or to alleviate pain, and, if I have so indicated below, the provision of artificially supplied nutrition and hydration. (Indicate your choice by initialling or making your mark before signing this declaration):

I wish to receive artificially supplied nutrition and hydration, even if the effort to sustain life is futile or excessively burdensome to me.

I do not wish to receive artificially supplied nutrition and hydration, if the effort to sustain life is futile or excessively burdensome to me.

I intentionally make no decision concerning artificially supplied nutrition and hydration, leaving the decision to my health care representative appointed under IC 16-36-1-7 or my attorney in fact with health care powers under IC 30-5-5.

In the absence of my ability to give directions regarding the use of life prolonging procedures, it is my intention that this declaration be honored by my family and physician as the final expression of my legal right to refuse medical or surgical treatment and accept the consequences of the refusal.

I understand the full import of this declaration.

Signed: . . . .

City, County, and State of Residence . . . .

The declarant has been personally known to me, and I believe (him/her) to be of sound mind. I did not sign the declarant's signature above for or at the direction of the declarant. I am not a parent, spouse, or child of the declarant. I am not entitled to any part of the declarant's estate or directly financially responsible for the declarant's medical care. I am competent and at least eighteen (18) years of age.

Witness . . . . Date . . . .

Witness . . . . Date . . . .

Life-Prolonging Procedures Declaration:

Declaration made this . . . day of . . . . . (month, year) I, ..., being at least eighteen (18) years old and of sound mind, willfully and voluntarily make known my desire that if at any time I have an incurable injury, disease, or illness determined to be a terminal condition I request the use of life-prolonging procedures that would extend my life. This includes appropriate nutrition and hydration, the administration of medication, and the performance of all medical procedures necessary to extend my life, to provide comfort care, or to alleviate pain.

In the absence of my ability to give directions regarding the use of life-prolonging procedures, it is my intention that this declaration be honored by my family and physician as the final expression of my legal right to request medical or surgical treatment and accept the consequences of the request.

I understand the full import of this declaration.

Signed: . . . .

City, County, and State of Residence . . . .

The declarant has been personally known to me, and I believe (him/her) to be of sound mind. I am competent and at least eighteen (18) years old.

Witness: . . . .

Date: . . . .

Witness: . . . .

Date: . . . .

FAMILY

ADOPTION:

Both children and adults may be adopted. (IC31-3-1-1, 11). Any resident of state may by petition adopt another person but, if married, spouse of adopter must join in petition, or merely give duly acknowledged consent if such spouse is natural or adoptive parent. Interstate Compact on placement of children applies to interstate adoptions. (IC31-19-1-1, IC12-17-8).

Consent Required.—Written consent executed by: (1) Living parents of legitimate child; (2) mother of child born out of wedlock, and father established by court proceedings other than adoption proceeding or by paternity affidavit; (3) any person, agency, or county department with lawful custody; (4) court of jurisdiction, if legal guardian without consent power; (5) child over 14; and (6) spouse of child to be adopted. Consent unnecessary for: (1) Parents who abandon child for six months, fail to communicate when able to do so for one year period (not necessarily from time of petition) or fail to provide support, or make only token effort at support or communication; (2) natural father of illegitimate child whose paternity has not been established by court proceeding other than adoption proceeding nor by paternity affidavit; (3) parent who relinquishes right to consent; (4) parent whose parental rights are terminated by court order; (5) parent judicially declared incompetent or mentally defective; (6) any legal guardian who unreasonably withholds consent; (7) natural father of illegitimate child conceived as result of rape, child molesting, sexual misconduct with minor or incest. (IC31-19-9-8). Agency arranging adoption may give notice to putative father prior to birth, foreclosing any challenge to adoption made by him more than 30 days later. (IC31-19-9-15). Parent under 18 may give consent unless court requires concurrence of parent's guardian or parents. Agency arranging for adoption must receive written consent from birth parents prior to releasing identifying information. (IC31-19-21). Consent given in foreign jurisdictions is valid if valid in that jurisdiction. (IC31-19-28). Adults adopted must consent in open court. (IC31-19-2-1). Putative father of illegitimate child has 30 days after notice of adoption proceeding to contest adoption or his consent is irrevocably implied. (IC31-19-9-12). Putative father registry maintained by state to assist putative fathers in obtaining notice. (IC31-19-5).

Conditions Precedent.—A period of supervision by an approved agency of a length determined by court must precede adoption. (IC31-19-8). Written approval by approved agency is needed to place child in proposed adoptive home except where child is to be adopted by stepparent or blood relative, received from agency outside state with consent of welfare department, or court waives this requirement after a hearing. (IC31-19-7).

Proceedings require filing of extensive medical history on adopted child and natural family. Information to be retained by state registrar and released under certain conditions to qualified persons. Information also to be provided to adoptive parents at time of adoption. (IC31-19-20, 31-19-2-7).

Jurisdiction lies with any county court having probate jurisdiction and is not limited to county of residence. (IC31-19-1).

Venue lies in the county of petitioner's residence or in the county where agency has custody of children to be adopted or in county where child resides. (IC31-19-2).

Dependent Children.—Human Services Division of Family and Children has power and duty to administer and supervise care of dependent children and children placed for adoption. (IC12-13-5-1; IC31-10-2-1).

Petition.—Proceedings are begun by a verified petition stating name, if known, sex, color and age, if known, place of birth of child, name to be given child, amount of its property, if any; name, age, place of residence of adopting parent or parents, and if married, place and date of their marriage; name, place of residence, if known to adopting parent or parents, of (a) parent or parents of child; or (b) if child is orphan, guardian; or (c) if there is no guardian, name of child's nearest kin; or (d) name of court or agency of which child is ward, if he is ward; or (e) of agency sponsoring adoption;

See note at head of Digest as to 1998 legislation covered.

See Topical Index in front part of this volume.

ADOPTION . . . *continued*
period during which child has lived in home of petitioners; and additional information including whether seeking subsidy. Report of health status and medical history of adoptee and adoptee's birth parents must be filed within 60 days of petition. (IC31-19-2).

Decree.—A final decree of adoption is granted on proof of: (1) the best interest of the child; (2) suitability of adopting parents; (3) proper consents; and (4) proper investigation reports. (IC31-19-11-1). Parents whose parental rights terminated by decree must appeal within six months of decree or one year of custody. (IC31-19-14-2).

Name.—Child takes name in which it is adopted. (IC31-19-11-4).

Effect of Adoption.—Legal relations between adopted child and adoptive parent are the same as in case of natural born child of such parent. (IC31-19-15-2).

Birth parent voluntarily terminating parent-child relationship may petition for visitation rights at time decree is entered. (IC31-19-16).

There is no distinction as to inheritance rights between a person adopted as a minor and a person adopted as an adult. (IC29-1-2-8).

Provision is made for recording of decrees of adoption and issuance of birth certificates based thereon. (IC31-19-12, 31-19-13).

Health and accident insurance policies must cover adopted children on same basis as other dependents. (IC27-8-5-21).

Confidentiality.—All files and records bearing upon court, agencies, county and state departments of welfare proceedings are confidential and may only be released to adoptee, birth parent, adoptive parents and certain specified others. (IC31-19-19). Adoption history files contain medical history, identifying information, and nonidentifying information. (IC31-19-20, 31-19-21, 31-19-22, 31-19-23). Nonidentifying information is information other than medical history that does not identify birth parent, adoptive parent or adoptee. Certain persons and organization may have access to non-identifying information if petition is filed alleging that adoptive child is in need of special services. (IC31-19-23).

Adoptee, birth parent and adoptive parents and certain specified others may obtain nonidentifying information upon request (IC31-3-4-29), and may request search by guardian ad litem of other records (IC31-19-23).

Identifying information may only be released upon consent of following persons: Adoptee, birth parents (if alive). (IC31-19-22-2). Adoptees adopted after Dec. 31, 1993 may, if age 21, request identifying information by request to state registry unless birth parent has filed non-release form. (IC31-19-25). Adoptees and pre-adoptive siblings may also ask state registry to locate each other if both are 21 years of age. (IC31-19-25-6).

Subsidies For Adoption.—IC31-19-27 provides for public programs to encourage adoption of hard to place children. Division of Family and Children authorized to enter into interstate compacts on adoption assistance to aid in adoption of hard to place children. (IC31-19-29).

Adoptions in other states or countries, if valid under the law where proceedings were effected, are recognized if filed with any court clerk of this state in county within this state. (IC31-19-28).

ALIMONY:

See topic Dissolution of Marriage.

COMMUNITY PROPERTY:

System does not obtain in Indiana.

DESERTION:

See topics Dissolution of Marriage, Husband and Wife, Adoption, subhead Dependent Children.

DISSOLUTION OF MARRIAGE:

This subject is governed by IC31-15-1-1 to 31-17-7-2.

Grounds for Dissolution of Marriage.—Marriage may be dissolved by decree upon court finding of one of following grounds: (1) Irretrievable breakdown; (2) conviction of felony subsequent to marriage; (3) impotency existing at time of marriage; (4) incurable insanity for two years or more. (IC31-15-1-2).

Common Law Marriage.—Claims brought as common-law spouse under current Indiana dissolution of marriage or intestate succession statutes clearly would not be actionable; however, recovery can be based upon legally viable contractual and/or equitable grounds which parties could establish according to their own particular circumstances. (410 N.E.2d 1325).

Grounds for Legal Separation.—Court may grant decree for separation for period not to exceed one year if neither party has filed petition for dissolution of marriage and court finds conditions of marriage render it currently intolerable for both parties to live together. Marriage shall be maintained during that period. (IC31-15-3-9).

Citizenship Requirements.—None.

Residence Requirements.—At time of filing of petition, at least one party to marriage must have been resident of Indiana or stationed at U.S. military installation in Indiana for prior six months, and a resident of county or stationed at a U.S. military installation in county where filed for prior three months. These residence requirements do not apply to actions for child support; however, one of such parties must reside in state and county at time of filing of action. (IC31-15-2-6).

Jurisdiction.—Separate acts confer jurisdiction on Indiana courts, each court being subject to its own act. In general, circuit and superior courts have jurisdiction of actions.

Indiana statutes relating to recognition and enforcement of custody decrees of other states apply to other nations when legal institutions are similar in nature if rendered by appropriate authorities of other nations and reasonable notice and opportunity to be heard were given to all affected persons. However, state has jurisdiction to make child custody and support determination by modification decree if: (1) child is citizen of U.S.; (2) custody determination was made in another nation; (3) child is physically present in state; and (4) there is reasonable probability child will be moved outside U.S. if determination regarding custody made in another nation is given effect in U.S. (IC31-17-3-25).

Any person submits to jurisdiction of Courts of Indiana by living in marital relationship within state notwithstanding subsequent departure from state, as to all obligations for alimony, custody, child support, or property settlement, if other party to marital relationship continues to reside in state. (Rule TR 4.4).

Venue.—See subhead Residence Requirements, supra.

Process.—When petition filed for dissolution of marriage or child support, summons and petition must be served on other partner, or person allegedly responsible for child support. Service in same manner as in civil actions generally. (IC31-15-2-1 and 8, 31-16-2-1 and 5).

Pleadings.—Verified petition is necessary and must set forth: (1) Residence of each party and length of residence in state and county; (2) date that parties separated; (3) date of marriage; (4) names, ages, addresses of living children under 21 or over 21 and incapacitated, and whether wife is pregnant; (5) grounds for dissolution; (6) relief sought. (IC31-15-1-5). Responsive pleading may be filed but is not required. (526 N.E.2d 231).

Practice.—Proceedings for dissolution of marriage must be commenced by filing verified petition entitled: "In Re the Marriage of . . . . . and . . . . .". (IC31-15-1-4). Final hearing cannot be held until 60 days from filing of petition. (IC31-15-2-10; Rule TR 6[F]). Proceedings for legal separation must be commenced by filing of verified petition entitled "In Re the Legal Separation of . . . and . . ." (IC31-15-3-4).

Provisional orders may be granted either party for temporary maintenance, support or custody of children, counseling, or possession of property, including restraining orders if certain conditions are met. Affidavit setting forth factual basis and relief sought must accompany motion. (IC31-15-4).

Temporary restraining orders may be requested to restrain party from: (1) transferring, encumbering, concealing, selling or disposing of any joint property of parties or asset of marriage except in usual course of business or for necessities of life, without written consent of parties or permission of court; (2) abusing, harassing, disturbing peace or committing battery upon person of other party or any child or stepchild of parties; and (3) removing any child of parties then residing in State with intent to deprive court of jurisdiction over such child without prior written consent of all parties or permission of court. (IC31-15-5-6; Rule TR 65[E]).

Temporary restraining order may be issued if court finds on basis of moving party's affidavit that injury would result to moving party if no immediate order were issued. (Rule TR 65[B]).

Judgment or Decree.—Upon final hearing, court shall hear evidence and, if it finds material allegations true, enter dissolution decree or continue matter 45 days if reasonable possibility of reconciliation exists. Upon request of party after 45 day period, judge may enter dissolution. After 90 days without such request, matter automatically dismissed. (IC31-15-2-15). Summary dissolution decree may be entered on some or all issues, without hearing, if verified pleadings signed by both parties have been filed which state that: (1) Both parties waive final hearing, and (2) there are no contested issues or written agreement as to all contested issues has been reached. Hearing must be held as to remaining contested issues. (IC31-15-2-13 and 14).

Dissolution decree is final when entered, subject to appeal. Appeal from dissolution decree that does not challenge findings as to dissolution itself does not delay finality of provision dissolving marriage, so that parties can remarry pending appeal. (IC31-15-2-16).

Decree may include terms of agreement between parties as to provisions for maintenance, disposition of property, and custody and support of children. Disposition of property by agreement not subject to later modification by court except as provided in agreement itself or with consent of parties. (IC31-15-2-17). Decree may also contain orders for disposition of property in lump sum or installment payments, child support, educational support, payment of support, persons entitled to receive payments, security for payment, attorneys fees, and name change of woman. (IC31-15-7-1 through 8; IC31-15-2-18). Provisions on child support may be modified on showing of changed circumstances which make original terms unreasonable or upon showing that child support amount differs by more than 20% from Indiana Child Support Guidelines. (IC31-15-7-3; IC31-16-8-1). Provisions on property division may only be modified or revoked within six years and only for fraud. (IC31-15-7-9.1). Court may enter order for money judgment not limited to existing property for financial contribution of one spouse to other spouse's higher education. (IC31-15-7-6).

Dissolution decree may be enforced by contempt, assignment of wages, or other income, or any other remedy available for enforcement of court order. (IC31-15-7-10).

Temporary Alimony.—See subhead Practice, supra.

Allowance for Prosecution of Suit.—Court may order one party to pay costs and attorneys fees of other party. (IC31-15-10-1).

Permanent Alimony.—

Agreement.—Parties may agree in writing to maintenance, division of property, child support and custody. Agreement, if approved by court, shall be incorporated into final decree. (IC31-15-2-17). Court may order maintenance of spouse in case of: (1) Physically or mentally incapacitated spouse; (2) spouse lacks sufficient property to provide for his needs and spouse is custodian of child whose physical or mental incapacity requires custodian to forego employment; or (3) rehabilitative maintenance, not to exceed three years, is necessary after considering educational level of each spouse, interruption in education or employment of spouse due to homemaking or child care responsibilities, earning capacity of each spouse, and time and expense necessary to acquire sufficient education or training to find appropriate employment. (IC31-15-7-1 and 2).

Disposition of Property.—Court presumes equal division of marital property is just and reasonable. Presumption may be rebutted based on following factors: (1) Contribution of each spouse to acquisition; (2) extent of acquisition prior to marriage or through

See note at head of Digest as to 1998 legislation covered.

See Topical Index in front part of this volume.

DISSOLUTION OF MARRIAGE . . . *continued*
inheritance or gift; (3) economic circumstances of spouse (including desirability of custodial parent living in marital residence while raising children); (4) conduct of parties during marriage as related to disposition of property; (5) earnings or earning ability of each party. (IC31-15-7-5).

Division of Property of Spouses.—See subhead Permanent Alimony, supra.

Change of Wife's Name.—Wife's name or prior married name must be restored if requested in petition. (IC31-15-2-18).

Custody of Children.—Child custody proceedings are commenced by a parent or person seeking determination filing petition. (IC31-17-2-3).

Uniform Child Custody Jurisdiction Act adopted. (IC31-1-11.6-1 et seq.).

Custody Order.—Court must determine custody in best interests of child based on all relevant factors with no presumption favoring either parent. (IC31-1-11.5-21). Joint legal custody may be awarded if in best interests of child. Court may order investigations and reports on custodial arrangements in custody proceedings if requested by parent or custodian. (IC31-1-11.5-22). Custody proceedings have priority in being heard. (IC31-1-11.5-23). If party seeking custody intends to move party's residence at time of or after granting of final order to place outside Indiana or 100 miles from residence specified in party's pleadings, party must file notice of intent and give notice to other party. (IC31-1-11.5-20). Upon request of either party, court can review and, if warranted, modify custody, visitation and support orders. (IC31-1-11.5-17; 31-1-11.5-22).

Visitation.—Parent not granted custody entitled to reasonable visitation rights, unless court determines visitation would be harmful to child. (IC31-1-11.5-24). In action filed to enforce or modify order granting or denying visitation rights, court may award reasonable attorneys' fees, court costs and other reasonable expenses of litigation. (IC31-1-11.5-24[c]). Non-custodial parent may also obtain temporary restraining order or permanent injunction to enforce visitation rights. (IC31-1-11.5-26). If child's mother or father is deceased, marriage is dissolved, or, in some cases, if child is born out of wedlock, grandparents may be granted reasonable visitation rights when court determines that it is in best interests of child. Proceeding for grandparent's visitation must be commenced by filing of verified petition entitled "In Re The Visitation of . . . . . ." (IC31-1-11.7-1 through 8). Visitation rights survive adoption of child by stepparent, grandparent, sibling, aunt, uncle, niece or nephew. (IC31-1-11.7-2).

Allowance for support of children may be ordered of either parent or both based on all relevant factors including: (1) Financial resources of custodial parent; (2) child's standard of living within marriage; (3) child's physical, mental condition, and educational needs; (4) financial resources and needs of noncustodial parent. Support order may include sums for education, special medical, hospital, or dental expenses, basic health and hospitalization insurance coverage, and will terminate when: (a) Child becomes 21; except for order for educational needs which may continue in court's discretion; (b) child is over 18, has not attended secondary or post-secondary school for four months and is capable of supporting himself through employment, or (c) child is emancipated. Support order will continue if child is incapacitated. If under subsection (b) child is partially capable of supporting himself, order may be modified rather than terminated. (IC31-1-11.5-12 and 12.1). Upon death of parent obligated to pay support, amount of support may be modified or revoked to extent necessary on petition of representatives of deceased parent's estate. (IC31-1-11.5-17). For enforcement of child support orders, see IC31-1-11.5-13, 14, 17; IC31-6-6.1-16; IC31-7-11; IC9-25-6-20; IC12-17-2-34 and 35; IC25-1-1.2; and IC27-8-23.

Uniform Reciprocal Enforcement of Support Act adopted. (IC31-2-1-1 to 39). (Repealed effective Jan. 1, 1997).

Remarriage.—See topic Marriage, subhead License. Parties may remarry pending appeal of provisions of dissolution decree if appeal does not challenge dissolution of marriage. (IC31-1-11.5-9).

Foreign Divorce.—No provisions.

Antenuptial Contracts.—See topic Husband and Wife.

DIVORCE:

See topic Dissolution of Marriage.

GUARDIAN AND WARD:

Jurisdiction to appoint guardian for incapacitated person or minor rests in court having probate jurisdiction of county in which incapacitated person or minor resides, or if incapacitated person or minor is nonresident of state, in county in which there is property of incapacitated person or minor. Temporary guardian may be appointed for incapacitated person or minor in need of medical care in county where medical facility is located. (IC29-3-2-2). Residence determined by actual presence, not domicile. (IC29-3-2-5). Juvenile court has exclusive original jurisdiction over certain matters relating to minors under IC31-30-1-1(a). Courts with child custody jurisdiction have original and continuing jurisdiction over other custody matters relating to minors. Mental health division of superior court has concurrent jurisdiction in matters relating to guardianship in connection with mental health proceedings under IC12-26. (IC29-3-2-1). Court may appoint attorney to appear for alleged incapacitated person or minor in action to determine competency. (IC29-3-5-1).

Incapacitated person is any person who (1) cannot be located upon reasonable inquiry, (2) is incapable by reason of mental deficiency, mental or physical illness, habitual drunkenness, excessive use of drugs, insanity, duress, fraud, detention, incarceration, confinement, undue influence of others, or other incapacity of managing his personal property or caring for himself or both, or (3) has developmental disability. (IC29-3-1-7.5).

Selection of Guardian.—Court will appoint person, persons, corporate fiduciary, or any combination most suitable and willing to serve, considering: (1) Requests by one for whom guardian appointed in certain instances; (2) requests in wills, durable powers of attorney, or other written instruments; (3) requests of minors age 14 and over; (4) requests of spouses of incompetents; (5) relationship of proposed guardian to incompetent; (6) best interest of incompetent and his property. (IC29-3-5-4).

Certain persons are entitled to priority as follows: (1) Persons designated in durable power of attorney; (2) incompetent's spouse; (3) incompetent's adult child; (4) incompetent's parent or person nominated by will of deceased parent; (5) person related by blood or marriage with whom incompetent has resided for more than six months; and (6) person nominated by incompetent who is caring for or paying for care of incompetent. Court shall appoint person with lower or no priority if in best interest of incompetent. (IC29-3-5-5).

Eligibility and Competency.—Foreign guardian of estate may file if no local guardian has been appointed and no petition for Indiana guardianship proceeding is pending. (IC29-3-13-1, 2). See category Estates and Trusts, topic Executors and Administrators, subhead Eligibility and Competency.

Appointment of Guardian.—Any person may file petition for appointment of himself or another as guardian. (IC29-3-5-1).

If petition is for minor, notice must be given to: (1) Minor if at least 14 years of age; (2) living parents of minor; and (3) persons having care and custody of minor for 60 days prior to petition. If petition is for alleged incapacitated person, notice must be given to: (1) Alleged incapacitated person; (2) alleged incapacitated person's spouse; (3) alleged incapacitated person's adult child or, if none, alleged incapacitated person's parents; (4) if no spouse, child, or parent is notified, at least one person most closely related by blood or marriage; (5) person serving as guardian or having care and custody of incapacitated person; (6) person serving as alleged incapacitated person's attorney in fact under durable power of attorney. (IC29-3-6-1, 2, 3).

Alleged incapacitated person must be present at hearing unless court determines by evidence that (1) health or safety of alleged incapacitated person is threatened; (2) incapacitated person is unavailable due to disappearance or absence from state; or (3) person has knowingly and voluntarily consented to appointment of guardian. Court may appoint attorney to represent alleged incapacitated person. (IC29-3-5-1). After notice and hearing, guardian may be appointed by adjudication of disability in court proceedings. (IC29-3-5-2, -3).

Under certain circumstances court may appoint temporary guardian to deal with emergencies. Temporary guardian may be appointed for period not to exceed 60 days, and without notice and hearing only if court finds immediate and irreparable harm in delay. (IC29-3-3-4). Without appointing guardian, court may order protective order for benefit of minor or incapacitated person. (IC29-3-4-1, 2, 3). Also without appointing guardian, chief of social services, or his appointee may execute documents on behalf of minor or incapacitated person to receive public assistance or transfer patient to alternate care facility. (IC29-3-3-5).

Qualification.—Guardians must file bond procured at expense of guardianship estate and must take oath. (IC29-3-7-1-6).

Inventory.—Within 90 days of appointment (30 days in case of temporary guardian), guardian must file inventory indicating fair market value of property under guardian's control and known liens or other charges on any item. (IC29-1-12-1, IC29-3-9-5). Guardian must provide notice of filing of inventory to each party that was required to be notified of hearing on petition to establish guardianship. (IC29-3-9-5).

Powers and Duties.—Guardian of minor has responsibilities of parent and is responsible for preservation of all minor's property regardless of location. Guardian of incapacitated person is responsible for care and custody and is responsible for property to extent ordered by court. (IC29-3-8-1). Parent or guardian of incompetent, by properly executed power of attorney, may delegate for certain periods any of his powers except consent to marriage or adoption of incompetent under age 18. (IC29-3-9-1). Guardian remains liable for acts or omissions of donee of power of attorney. (IC29-3-9-1). Guardian of estate has power to take possession of all property of ward, continue business of ward, represent ward in all actions, invest property, pay debts of ward, sell, lease and mortgage property under court order to pay debts of ward, provide for care, maintenance, and education of ward and other powers as specified. (IC29-3-8). Orders binding guardian of estate bind ward. (IC29-3-2-4[b]). Temporary guardian has only court ordered powers necessary to prevent immediate and substantial injury or loss to ward or ward's property. (IC29-3-3-4).

Uniform Veterans' Guardianship Act adopted. There are special provisions concerning guardian of ward whose estate includes assets derived from Veterans Administration benefits. (IC29-1-19-1 et seq.).

Investments.—See category Estates and Trusts, topic Trusts.

Securities in Name of Nominee.—See category Estates and Trusts, topic Trusts, subhead Securities in Name of Nominee.

Real Estate.—Guardian may purchase real property for home for ward or for ward's dependent family, or protect ward's existing home, or protect ward's existing interest in any real estate, or purchase remaining fractional interest in real property of which ward owns fractional interest where court finds purchase is in best interest of ward. (IC29-3-8-2). Guardian may sell, lease, and mortgage real property to pay debts of ward and provide for his and his dependents' care, maintenance and education. (IC29-3-8-1, 4).

Liabilities of Guardian.—Guardian may be personally liable for breach of duty to protected person or acts or omissions in bad faith. (IC29-3-11-2).

Accounts.—Guardian shall file with court biennially within 30 days after anniversary date of appointment, and within 30 days after termination of appointment, written verified account of his administration and as provided by rules for accounting in decedent's estates. (IC29-3-9-6).

Termination of Guardianship.—Guardianship shall be terminated: (1) By ward's attaining his 18th birthday if sole reason for guardianship was ward's minority; (2) by adjudication of ward's competency; (3) by death of ward. (IC29-3-12-1).

Court may terminate guardianship: (1) On ward's adoption or marriage if sole reason for guardianship was ward's minority; (2) if guardianship is of estate and estate is exhausted or does not exceed $3,500; (3) if ward's residence is changed to another state and another guardian has been appointed by that state; (4) if guardianship is no longer necessary for any other reason. (IC29-3-12-1).

See note at head of Digest as to 1998 legislation covered.

See Topical Index in front part of this volume.

GUARDIAN AND WARD . . . *continued*

Insane Persons.—Court may establish guardianship for mentally ill individual or individual's property in lieu of regular commitment to facility under IC12-26-7, or at any other time, at request of individual or any other person. (IC12-26-16-1).

Removal of Guardian.—Guardian may be removed for cause as specified. (IC29-3-12-4). Guardian may be removed for cause after notice and hearing. (IC29-1-10-6, IC29-3-12-4).

Compensation.—Guardians are entitled to such compensation for their services as the court shall determine to be just and reasonable. (IC29-3-4-4, IC29-3-9-3).

Foreign Guardians.—A foreign guardian, by following the prescribed procedure, is entitled to sell real estate of his ward located in this state as if he were resident guardian, to take possession of personal property or real property and to sue to recover property of ward in courts of this state. (IC29-3-13-1, 2).

Gifts to Minors.—See topic Infants.

Uniform Fiduciaries Act.—See category Estates and Trusts, topic Trusts.

Uniform Simplification of Fiduciary Security Transfers Act adopted. (IC30-2-5-1 to 11).

HUSBAND AND WIFE:

Contracts of Married Women.—All the legal disabilities of married women to make contracts abolished, except as otherwise provided. (IC31-11-7-1). Married women have same rights concerning real and personal property as unmarried women. (IC31-11-7-2).

A married woman may contract with her husband the same as with a third person and may become bound as surety for her husband or any other person. (93 Ind. 389).

Actions.—A married woman may sue without joinder of her husband when action is on her contract, concerns her separate property or is between herself and her husband. No distinction is made between men and women because of marital status or parental status; however, this does not apply to actions in tort. (Rule TR 17[D]).

Doctrine of interspousal immunity is not applicable to actions in tort, notwithstanding allowance for such distinction in Rule TR 17(D). (259 Ind. 16, 284 N.E.2d 794).

It is Class D felony to knowingly touch spouse in rude, insolent or angry manner if it results in bodily injury and if spouse was previously convicted of battery in which victim was same spouse. (IC35-42-2-1).

Agency.—Either spouse may act as attorney in fact for other if power executed and recorded. (IC32-1-2-6).

Antenuptial Contracts.—Uniform Premarital Agreement Act in effect for agreements made on or after July 1, 1995. All such agreements must be in writing, signed by both parties. Such agreements are not enforceable if not voluntarily executed or unconscionable at time of making. Allows premarital agreement to be amended or revoked after marriage under certain circumstances. Premarital agreement may not restrict child's right to support. (IC31-11-3).

Conveyance or Encumbrance of Property.—Married woman may sell, exchange, mortgage, lease or execute any instrument of any kind affecting her property same as if she were unmarried. (IC31-11-7-2). Married man may sell, exchange, mortgage, lease or execute any instrument of any kind affecting his property without his wife's joinder, and any such act or instrument as to real property extinguishes wife's right to one third of such property and to other rights in property by reason of marriage. (IC29-1-2-3.1). See also category Property, topic Deeds, subhead Married Persons.

Liability of Husband for Debts of Wife.—Husband not liable for contracts or torts of his wife. (IC31-11-7-4).

Married Woman as Fiduciary.—A married woman may act in fiduciary capacity, e. g., as executrix or administratrix, etc. (IC29-1-10-1).

Estate by Entireties.—When husband and wife take title to real estate, it creates estate by entireties, estate in which each owns equal and unseverable interest, and upon death of either, survivor holds entire estate in severalty. (IC32-1-2-8).

Real estate purchased by husband and wife under written contract, or held as lessees with option to purchase deemed to be held by them as tenants by entireties. (IC32-4-2-1).

Custody of Children.—The father, if living, and the mother in case of his death, if fit for trust, is entitled to custody of minor children and care of their education. (IC29-3-3-3 and 29-3-3-6). See also topic Dissolution of Marriage. Uniform Child Custody Jurisdiction Act adopted. (IC31-17-3-1 to 31-17-3-25).

Desertion and Nonsupport.—Dependent spouse may obtain provision from other spouse for support and support of dependent children in his or her custody where other spouse has deserted dependent spouse or dependent children without cause, when other spouse has been convicted of felony and imprisoned, when other spouse is habitual drunkard, when other spouse renounces marriage covenant, refuses to live with spouse in conjugal relation, joins sect which prohibits cohabitation, or when other spouse is insane. Dependent spouse or children must also show there is no sufficient provision for support. (IC31-16-14).

Community property system does not obtain in Indiana. See Black's Law Dictionary 280 (6th ed. 1990).

Uniform Reciprocal Enforcement of Support Act (1958 version) is repealed effective Jan. 1, 1997 and is replaced by Uniform Interstate Family Support Act. (IC31-18-1-1 to 31-18-9-4).

Validity of Marriage.—Circuit Court may issue declaratory judgment order, upon proof by oral testimony or affidavits that any errors made by individual who solemnized marriage do not affect validity of marriage. (IC31-11-4-17).

INFANTS:

Age of majority, 18 for most purposes.

Alcohol.—Persons under age of 21 years are minors for purposes of laws relating to sale and consumption of alcohol. (IC7.1-1-3-25).

Contracts.—Males and females under age of 18 years are not competent to contract, except for necessities and borrowing of money to defray expenses of higher education. (IC20-12-21.3-1). Contracts are voidable rather than void and may be ratified upon coming of age. (IC29-3-8-5). Infants may become purchasers of certificates of investment or indebtedness issued by industrial loan and investment company organized under laws of Indiana. (IC28-5-3-1).

Conveyance or Encumbrance of Property.—Infant married to person at least age 18 may convey real estate with approval of Circuit, Superior or Probate Court of county where person resides, upon payment of required fee. (IC32-1-13-1).

Actions.—If infant is not represented, court will appoint guardian ad litem for him. Court, in its discretion, may honor infant's choice of next friend or guardian ad litem but court may deny approval or remove person who is not qualified. It is not necessary that person for whom guardianship is sought be represented by guardian ad litem in such proceeding. (Rule TR 17[C]). See category Civil Actions and Procedure, topic Actions, subhead Parties. See Rule TR 71. Infant not represented by guardian or next friend can get relief from judgment. (Rule TR 60[B]). Juvenile court has concurrent original jurisdiction with probate court in proceedings to terminate parent-child relationship. (IC31-30-1-1).

Insurance.—Minors age 16 or older are deemed competent to contract life, accident, and sickness insurance or annuities. (IC27-1-12-15). Persons above age of majority, 18, are competent to contract for any kind of insurance. (IC27-2-11.1 et seq.). Person over 18 has right to enjoy and exercise benefits of insurance contracts; to receive and give full acquittance and discharge for payments made by company under such contract, or settlement agreement on such contract. (IC27-1-12-15).

Parental Responsibility.—Parents liable up to $5,000 for damages to person or property knowingly, intentionally or recklessly caused by child under 18. (IC34-4-31-1). However, parent of child who is member of criminal gang (as defined in IC35-45-9-1), who actively encourages or knowingly benefits from child's involvement in criminal gang, liable for actual damages caused by child while engaged in gang activity if parent has custody of child, child is living with parent, and parent failed to use reasonable efforts to prevent child's involvement in criminal gang.

Paternity of Child.—Court may order, upon motion, blood test or genetic testing to determine paternity. Genetic test results are admissible as evidence of paternity unless properly objected to. (IC31-6-6.1-8). Court may enter default order against man who fails to appear at hearing related to his paternity. (IC31-6-6.1-8.5).

Revised Uniform Transfers to Minors Act adopted. Age of majority under Act is 21. (IC30-2-8.5-1 to -40).

Uniform Securities Ownership by Minors Act not adopted.

Adoption.—See topic Adoption.

Abortion.—No physician may perform abortion upon unemancipated pregnant woman under age 18 without first having obtained written consent of one of parents or legal guardian, subject to certain exceptions. (IC16-34-2-4).

See also topic Dissolution of Marriage.

MARRIAGE:

Any male or female 18 or over may marry. (IC31-11-1-4). However, consent of parent, guardian or presiding judge is required for any male or female under 18. (IC31-11-1-5, IC31-11-2). Judge of circuit, superior or juvenile court may authorize license for pregnant female, or mother, 15 or over with consent of parent or guardian. (IC31-11-1-6). Only marriages to persons of opposite sex permitted. (IC31-11-1-1).

Medical Examination.—Any unsterilized female under age 50 must submit with application for license medical report stating whether she has immunological response to rubella, or written record that rubella vaccine was administered on or after her first birthday. Circuit or superior judge may by order dispense with these requirements. Applicants may object to tests on various grounds. (IC31-11-5).

License.—Clerk of circuit court may not issue marriage license unless individuals have authority to marry each other under IC31-11-1. (IC31-11-4-2). License is issued by clerk of circuit, superior or juvenile court of county where either resides. No license may be issued except upon written and verified application containing statement of full names, birthplace, residence and ages of parties, names of dependent children and showing such other facts as may be necessary to determine whether any legal impediment to proposed marriage exists. (IC31-11-4-4). Each individual applying for marriage must provide clerk of circuit court with birth certificate or other evidence of date and place of birth and full name, last known address and place of birth of applicant's parent, if known. If written consent is required by IC31-11-2, clerk of circuit court may not receive application for marriage license unless clerk has filed consent form in clerk's office. (IC31-11-4-8).

Application for marriage license expires 60 days after issuance. (IC31-11-4-10).

Ceremony may be performed by minister of gospel, priest or rabbi, by judges within or without their respective jurisdictions, mayors within their cities, by clerks and clerk-treasurers of cities and towns within their respective cities and towns, and by clerks of circuit courts within or without their respective jurisdictions. Friends Church, German Baptists, Bahai religion, Church of Jesus Christ of Latter Day Saints and religion of Islam may solemnize according to rules of each. (IC31-11-6).

Common law marriages entered into after Jan. 1, 1958 are null and void. (IC31-11-8-5). No authority concerning local recognition of out-of-state common law marriage. See also topic Dissolution of Marriage, subhead Common Law Marriage.

Prohibited Marriages.—Declared void: between persons nearer of kin than second cousins; however, marriages entered into after 9-1-77 between first cousins 65 years of age and older shall not be void (IC31-11-8-3); where either party had husband or wife living or was of unsound mind when marriage was solemnized (IC31-11-8-2; IC31-11-8-4). Issuance of license prohibited: Where either party has been adjudged to be of

MARRIAGE . . . *continued*
unsound mind, unless that adjudication is no longer in effect, or where either party is under influence of liquor or drugs at time of application. (IC31-11-4-11).

Status of Children.—Children born of marriage void on account of consanguinity, affinity or by reason of prior marriage of one of parties, shall be treated as if they were children of valid marriage if parties reasonably believed such disability did not exist. (IC31-13-1). Petition may be made to circuit or superior court to determine status of child. (IC31-13-2).

Foreign Marriages.—If residents of state, with intent to evade provisions of law relative to license, go to another state and there have marriage soleminized with intention of returning and residing in this state, and do so return and reside in this state, such marriage is void. Does not apply to persons who in good faith become or are citizens of another state. (IC31-11-8-6).

Annulment.—Court having jurisdiction in divorce may annul marriage of party incapable of marrying because of lack of age or understanding, on application of incapable party, or may annul marriage procured through fraud of one party on application of innocent party. (IC31-11-10). Children begotten before annulment are legitimate. (IC31-13-1-3).

Record.—See category Documents and Records, topic Records, subhead Vital Statistics.

Offenses.—(IC31-7-9).

Antenuptial Contracts.—See topic Husband and Wife.

MARRIED WOMEN:

See topics Husband and Wife, Marriage; categories Civil Actions and Procedure, topic Evidence, subhead Witnesses; Debtor and Creditor, topic Homesteads; Documents and Records, topic Acknowledgments; Estates and Trusts, topics Executors and Administrators, Wills; Property, topic Deeds.

INSURANCE

INSURANCE COMPANIES:

Regulated by Indiana Code Title 27.

General supervision is by Department of Insurance (IC27-1-1-1), which is administered by Insurance Commissioner (IC27-1-1-2). Uniform Unauthorized Insurers Act regulates conduct of insurers not authorized to conduct business in Indiana. (IC27-4-5-1 to 8).

All policy forms filed with Insurance Commissioner after June 30, 1982 and all policies issued after June 30, 1985 must meet certain policy simplification standards. (IC27-1-26-1 et seq.). See category Business Regulation and Commerce, topics Consumer Protection, Contracts.

Rates.—Worker's compensation insurance regulated by IC27-7-2-1.1 to 39. Casualty (including fidelity, surety and guaranty bonds), motor vehicle, fire and inland marine insurance rates are established by insurers and rating bureaus under supervision of Department of Insurance. (IC27-1-22-1 to 26).

Annual Statements.—Each company must file annual financial statement with Department of Insurance before Mar. 1 of each year. (IC27-1-20-21).

Life insurance policies issued after Jan. 1, 1948, are required to have certain statutory clauses including provision for thirty days of grace, prepayment of premiums, inclusion of the application in the contract of insurance, an incontestability clause, a clause providing for automatic adjustment of the policy to correct for a misstatement of age, a provision that statements by the assured are representations and not warranties, provisions for extended insurance and non-forfeiture, provisions for loans on the security of the policy, and provision for determination of claim within two months after proof of death. Policies must be properly labeled on both face and back. (IC27-1-12-6). Standard policy provisions do not need to be included on substandard or impaired risks. Insurance Department may approve policy forms more favorable to assured than policies containing standard provisions. (IC27-1-12-6). Required nonforfeiture provisions are extensive and detailed. (IC27-1-12-7).

Variable life insurance providing for immediate or future life insurance benefits, must contain a statement that benefits are variable instead of stipulating dollar amount. Such policies must contain other provisions so prescribed by Insurance Commissioner. (IC27-1-12-33).

Regulation of advertisements containing guaranteed interest rates. (IC27-8-21-2).

Wholesale, franchise or employee life insurance must be issued or delivered according to statutory regulations. (IC27-1-12-34.1).

Interest on policy loans on policies issued after Aug. 31, 1983 is established at no more than 8% or at adjustable rate per certain guidelines. (IC27-1-12.3-1 et seq.).

Group Life Insurance Policies.—Employees or members may insure against loss due to death of spouse or dependent subject to certain limitations. (IC27-1-12-40). Representations by employees cannot be made warranties, and no statement by employee can support defense unless statement is in writing on application. These policies must further provide for adjustment of premium for misstatement of age and for delivery to employee of certificate of insurance. Group policies must further provide for conversion to standard policies upon cessation of employment. (IC27-1-12-41).

Annuity Contracts.—IC27-1-12.5-1 et seq.

Health and Accident Policies.—No policy of accident and sickness may be issued until a copy of the form, the classification of the risks and the premium rates have been filed with the commissioner. (IC27-8-5-1). There are special provisions relating to group accident and sickness policies. (IC27-8-5-16 to 24). Preferred provider organizations are subject to special reporting requirements. (IC27-8-11-5).

Comprehensive health insurance is made available to all residents via association established by state. (IC27-8-10-1 et seq.).

Legal insurance policies may be issued by certain insurers to insure against legal expenses incurred in connection with use of professional services of attorneys, in consideration of specified payment for interval of time, regardless of whether payment is made by beneficiaries individually or by third person for them. Certain legal expenses resulting from following are excepted and may not be insured against: (1) Retainer contracts made with single client and similar contracts made with group of clients involved in same or closely-related legal matters (class actions); (2) plans providing no benefits other than limited amount of consultation and advice on simple matters either alone or in combination with referral services; (3) plans providing limited benefits on simple legal matters on voluntary and informal basis; (4) legal services provided by unions or employee associations to its members in matters solely relating to employment or occupation; and (5) payment of fines, penalties, judgments, or assessments. Group legal services, except for (4) above, are permitted and can be provided by issuance of group legal insurance. (IC27-1-5-1, IC27-7-8-1 to 7).

Liability policies are required to have certain standard provisions including: provisions against release of liability by bankruptcy, provision that notice to any authorized agent is notice to the insurer. The statute also provides for an omnibus insuring clause protecting the owner against liability because of the negligent operation of such vehicle by another person using such vehicle in the business of the owner or otherwise with the express or implied permission of the owner. All motor vehicle liability policies must include uninsured and underinsured motor vehicle coverage unless insured specifies in writing that he does not want coverage. (IC27-7-5-2 et seq.). Failure to include these provisions in liability policy does not invalidate policy but policy is deemed amended to conform to Act. (IC27-1-13-7). "Uninsured motor vehicle" includes insured motor vehicle where liability insurer thereof is unable to make payment with respect to legal liability of its insured because of insolvency. (IC27-1-5-4). Restrictions established as to cancellation of automobile insurance policies. (IC27-7-6-1 to 12).

Garage liability policy is primary insurance for damage to motor vehicle occurring when under control of person, or his agent, in business of storing, parking, servicing, or repairing vehicles and that vehicle is owned by another person. (IC27-8-9-5 et seq.). If only motor vehicle insurance provided by owner of vehicle is garage liability policy, primary insurance for damage is that of permissive operator of vehicle. (IC27-8-9-10). In all other cases, primary insurance for damage is that of owner when vehicle is operated with permission of owner and within scope of that permission. (IC27-8-9-7).

Credit life insurance and credit accident and health insurance are controlled and regulated by statute. (IC27-8-4-1 to 14; IC24-4.5-4-101 to 203).

Prearranged funeral insurance is controlled by IC27-1-15.5-3.5.

Crop hail insurance is controlled by IC27-1-15.5-3.6.

Long term care insurance policies may be issued pursuant to specified statutory requirements. (IC27-8-12-1 to 18).

Medicare supplement insurance policies may be issued pursuant to specified statutory requirements. (IC27-8-13-1 to 20).

Discrimination.—Insurance Commissioner is empowered to regulate rates to end that they are not discriminating. (IC27-1-22-1).

Rebates are prohibited. (IC27-1-20-30).

Fair trade practices in insurance are defined in detail and regulated by cease and desist orders, monetary penalties ranging from $25,000 to $200,000, and license or certificate of authority revocation, in discretion of Insurance Commissioner. (IC27-4-1-1 to 18, IC4-21.5-5-1 to 15). Insurance company may not cancel individual or group policy between policy renewal dates because of individual's medical or physical condition. (IC27-4-1-4). Person who believes they have been subject to unfair claim settlement practice can file complaint with Commissioner, who then has duty to investigate it and forward it to insurer and report to complaining party. Insurer must respond in writing. (IC27-4-1-5.6).

Insurance agents, insurance consultants and limited insurance representatives are licensed separately after investigation and compliance with minimum requirements (IC27-1-15.5-1 to 3) and payment of nominal fee (IC27-1-15.5-4). They are required to take specified program of study and written examination except that nonresidents may be licensed without examination if Commissioner of state of applicant's residence certifies that applicant has passed similar examination. (IC27-1-15.5-4). Subject to certain limitations, provisions are made for nonresident agents. (IC27-1-15.5-4). Agent may represent one company exclusively but if he represents two companies, company cannot require or induce him to refrain from representing others. (IC27-4-3-2).

To renew license, licensee must complete at least 30 hours of credit in continuing education courses. (IC27-1-15.5-7.1 to -7.7). Licenses must be reviewed biennially. (IC27-1-15.5-3[f]; IC27-1-15.5-7.7).

Special requirements apply to surplus license agents including requirement that they keep in force bond in penal sum of not less than $20,000. (IC27-1-15.5-5). Certain individuals are exempt from licensing requirements for consultants including attorneys, duly licensed insurance agents, surplus lines insurance agents, trust officers of banks, actuaries and certified public accountants. (IC27-1-15.5-7).

Process Agent.—Insurance Commissioner is agent for service of process for foreign insurance companies. (IC27-1-17-4, IC27-4-4-3). Domestic companies are served in same fashion as other corporations.

Adjusters.—With certain exceptions, public adjusters are required to be certified. Certificates are issued by Insurance Commissioner upon payment of $50 fee and passing examination. Residency of one year is required. (IC27-1-27-1 to 11). Commissioner may issue nonresident certificate of authority only to applicant who holds resident certificate of authority from another state or any foreign country. (IC27-1-27-3).

Investments by life (IC27-1-12-2 to 4) and all other (IC27-1-13-3 to 5) insurance companies are regulated by statute.

Each life insurance company shall deposit amount equal to lesser of its reserve liabilities, net reserve value of its policies, or $1,000,000 for security and benefit of its policyholders. (IC27-1-12-11).

See note at head of Digest as to 1998 legislation covered.

See Topical Index in front part of this volume.

IN – 40

INSURANCE COMPANIES . . . *continued*

Advertising referring to the financial condition of an insurance company must set forth certain minimum information as to assets, surplus, etc. (IC27-1-20-19 to 20).

Indiana Insurance Guaranty Association protects claimants or policyholders from delay and excessive loss due to insolvency of insurer. (IC27-6-8-1 to -19). Excepted are certain types of insurance, including life, annuity, health, or disability. (IC27-6-8-3).

Life and Health Insurance Guaranty Association protects policy owners, insureds, beneficiaries, annuitants, payers, and assignees of life insurance policies, health insurance policies, annuity contracts, and supplemental contracts against failure in performance of contractual obligations because of impairment or insolvency of insurer issuing policies or contracts, and allows tax credit or premium increase to compensate member insurers for assessments paid to association. (IC27-8-8-1 to 18).

Receivership.—No insurance company may be placed in receivership except by action of a judgment creditor, proceedings supplementary to execution, or in an action brought by Department of Insurance. (IC27-1-20-23).

Title insurance companies operate under a separate act by which they are required to have not less than $100,000 fully paid in stock (IC27-7-3-5) and are required to maintain deposit with state of 10% of premiums collected until fund reaches $50,000 (IC27-7-3-9). Foreign corporations may be admitted to do title insurance business. (IC27-7-3-12). Such companies are under same supervision as other insurance companies, except that higher percentage of single risk to total capital, surplus, and reserves may be assumed, namely 50%, by title insurance company. (IC27-7-3-20).

Companies organized under prior acts still exist and those which are not subject to regulation may adopt the Act of 1935. (IC27-1-11-1).

Fraudulent insurance acts are defined in detail and specific provisions regarding reporting and civil liability therefor have been enacted. (IC27-1-3-22 and 23).

Insurers required to file annual statements with National Association of Insurance Commissioners and with Indiana State Department of Insurance. (IC27-1-20-33).

Insurance rates regulated by separate chapter. (IC27-1-22-1 to 26).

Utilization review agents must be registered with Department of Insurance. Utilization review agents review medical necessity and appropriateness of proposed health care services. (IC27-8-17).

Charitable entity may purchase, own, or be transferred ownership of life insurance policy on life of individual consents to charitable entity's purchase or ownership of policy. (IC27-8-18).

Special charter companies are regulated and must make specified reports. (IC27-2-2-1).

Partnerships or corporations issuing "Lloyd's Insurance" are subject to regulation. (IC27-7-1-1 to 12).

Model Risk Retention Act adopted. (IC27-7-10-1 to 34). Governs establishment of risk retention groups, establishes reporting and disclosure requirements and prescribes rules of conduct for purchasing groups and risk retention groups.

Insider Trading.—Directors, officers, or beneficial owners of 10% of any class of equity security of domestic insurance company must file number of such securities he owns with Indiana Insurance Commissioner. Any changes in that number must be reported within ten days after end of month of sale. (IC27-2-10-1). Any profit realized by sale of securities within period less than six months is recoverable by insurance company in either direct or derivative suit within two years after gain was realized. (IC27-2-10-2).

Qualification of foreign companies is handled through the Department of Insurance, which requires copies of the company's articles of incorporation and information as to its place of business, the names of other states in which it has been admitted or qualified to do business, the character of the business it will transact, its total authorized capital stock, the total amount of its assets and its surplus and other matters concerning its financial condition. The company must also file a certificate from the state of incorporation attesting its power to do insurance business and a power of attorney appointing the Commissioner of Insurance its agent for process. (IC27-1-17-4). In addition, company must meet financial requirements of domestic companies. (IC27-1-17-5). Company must make $100,000 deposit or prove that equivalent amount is on deposit in another state for payment of claims and creditors. (IC27-1-17-6). If its charter or articles are amended this must be filed with Commissioner. (IC27-1-18-3).

Any foreign insurance company may, upon complying with requirements for formation of domestic company, become domestic insurer. (IC27-1-6.5-1 to 6).

Powers of Foreign Insurance Companies.—Foreign insurance companies are required to be qualified before transacting business (IC27-1-17-1) and when qualified have any powers permitted by charter and available to domestic companies (IC27-1-17-2). They are permitted to reorganize under Indiana insurance law (IC27-1-19-1 to 8) and may withdraw from state (IC27-1-18-6).

Retaliatory Provisions.—If any state imposes on Indiana insurance companies doing business therein taxes, fines, penalties, obligations, prohibitions, license requirements or deposit requirements greater than are imposed by the laws of Indiana, the same obligations, prohibitions, etc., are imposed on all insurance companies incorporated under the laws of such state and on alien companies with their principal agency in such state. If any jurisdiction refuses admission to Indiana insurance companies presenting proper credentials, companies from that jurisdiction may not be permitted to do business in Indiana. (IC27-1-20-12). Specific retaliatory provisions are also provided for mutual life and accident companies (IC27-8-1-14), in connection with live stock insurance (IC27-5-9-18).

Premium Tax.—For the privilege of doing business in the state foreign insurance companies must pay a tax of 2% of gross premiums received for insurance covering Indiana risks less the following deductions: Amounts received for reinsurance of risks within the state; dividends paid or credited to resident insureds or used to reduce their current premiums; premiums returned to residents on account of applications not accepted, policies not delivered or cancellation of policies. Estimated tax payments are made on a quarterly basis, payable on or before Apr. 15, June 15, Sept. 15, and Dec. 15. Any balance of tax is due upon filing of annual report; any overpayment is an allowable credit on first installment of current year. (IC27-1-18-2).

The Political Subdivision Risk Management Fund and the Political Subdivision Catastrophic Liability Fund, administered by Indiana Political Subdivision Risk Management Committee, is available for payment of liabilities of political subdivisions of state. (IC27-1-29-1 to 17, IC27-1-29.1-1 to 22).

The Mine Subsidence Insurance Fund is available to owners of property in certain counties for damage resulting from collapse of underground coal mines. (IC27-7-9-1 to 16).

Direct Actions Against Insurer.—See category Transportation, topic Motor Vehicles, subhead Direct Actions.

No-Fault Insurance.—Not adopted.

See also category Business Regulation and Commerce, topic Securities, subhead Prerequisites to Sales or Offerings.

See also category Family, topic Infants, subhead Insurance.

SURETY AND GUARANTY COMPANIES:

Surety and guaranty companies are subject to Indiana Insurance Law, surety and guaranty contracts constituting one type of class 2 insurance (IC27-1-5-1); see topic Insurance Companies.

Mortgage guarantee company may not be incorporated or organized under any law of Indiana except that mutual savings bank may be organized with all rights and privileges under IC28-6.1 only by mutual bank conversion under IC28-1-21.7. (IC28-1-23-6).

INTELLECTUAL PROPERTY

TRADEMARKS AND TRADENAMES:

What May Not Be Used.—Cannot register mark which: (1) consists of immoral, deceptive, or scandalous matter; (2) may disparage or falsely suggest connection with persons, institutions, beliefs or national symbols; (3) resembles flag, coat of arms, or insignia of any government or nation; (4) consists of name, signature or portrait of living individual, without person's consent; (5) is not distinctive and is merely descriptive, geographically descriptive, or primarily merely surname; or (6) is confusingly similar to another mark registered in Indiana, without mark owner's consent. (IC24-2-1-3). Foreign entities are required to qualify and be admitted to do business in Indiana prior to registration of mark.

Registration.—Trademark must be registered with Secretary of State and several statutory requirements for registration met. Three specimens and filing fee of $10 are required. (IC24-2-1-4).

Assignment.—Trademark and its registration assignable with good will of businesses. Assignment must be in writing and recorded with Secretary of State for $10 fee. (IC24-2-1-8).

Protection Afforded.—Registration is effective for ten years and may be renewed for successive periods of ten years. Renewal fee is $10. (IC24-2-1-6). Registration does not grant statutory presumption of right to use or priority. Common law rights not affected by registration.

Infringement.—Remedies: all common law remedies, injunction, and destruction of counterfeits; if act is intentional damages may be obtained; criminal penalties available. (IC24-2-1-12 to 15).

Dilution.—Indiana has no statutory or common law dilution or antidilution doctrine.

Counterfeiters.—Action against counterfeiters is provided under common law for unregistered marks, under statute for registered marks. (IC24-2-1-13).

Tradenames.—Following are subject to tradename filing requirements: (1) Person conducting or transacting business in Indiana under name or title other than real name of person conducting or transacting such business; (2) corporation or limited liability company conducting business in Indiana under name or title other than name shown by its articles; (3) foreign corporation conducting business in Indiana under name or title other than name shown by its application for certificate of authority to transact business in Indiana; (4) limited partnership, limited liability company or limited liability partnership conducting business in Indiana under name or title other than name shown by its certificate of limited partnership; and (5) foreign limited partnership, limited liability company or limited liability partnership conducting business in Indiana under name or title other than name shown by its application for registration. Each must file certificate in office of recorder of each county in which place of business or office (if none, then registered office) is situated. Certificate must state assumed name to be used, in case of person full name and address of each person engaged in or transacting such business, and in case of a foreign or domestic corporation, partnership, or foreign limited partnership full name and address of principal office in Indiana (if none, then registered agent and office). Corporations, limited liability companies, and limited partnerships shall also file copy of certificate with secretary of state. Does not apply to person doing business under name that includes true surnames of person (or true surnames of individuals comprising person), or to any church, lodge, or association business of which is transacted by trustees under written instrument or declaration of trust that is recorded in recorder's office of each county in which business is conducted or transacted. Violation is Class B infraction. (IC23-15-1-1 to 5).

Federal Names.—Use of names such as Army, Navy, PX, GI, Marines, Government, Federal, etc., are prohibited in selling goods where name may mislead public to believe goods have been sold by, manufactured for, or manufactured in accordance with specifications of named agency. (IC24-2-2-1 to -4).

Certain Names.—Special requirements govern use of names which include "bank", "trust", "building and loan association", "savings and loan association", "savings bank" "savings association", "rural", "guaranty" (IC28-1-20-4, 28-12-3-3), "credit

See note at head of Digest as to 1998 legislation covered.

See Topical Index in front part of this volume.

IN – 41

TRADEMARKS AND TRADENAMES . . . *continued*
union" (IC28-7-1-8), "lottery" (IC4-30-14-7), "engineer" (IC25-4-1-15.1, 25-31-1-30, 25-31-1-34), "architect" (IC25-31-1-22.1), "land surveyor" (IC25-21.5-1-8).

Right of Publicity.—Indiana recognizes person's right of publicity to include their name, voice, signature, likeness and certain other aspects, if they have commercial values. (IC32-13-1-7). Use of any of those aspects of person for commercial purpose (such as on or in connection with products, services or commercial activities, including use in advertisements or promotions) without that person's consent violates person's right of publicity. Violators may be liable for actual damages, profits derived from unauthorized use, treble or punitive damages, attorneys' fees and costs incurred by other party, and may be subject to injunction.

Certain exceptions to this right are included for uses in material that has political or newsworthy value, in literary works, musical compositions, film, radio and television programs, and also for uses by newspapers, magazines and television stations. (IC32-13-1 et seq.).

TRADE SECRETS:
Indiana has adopted Uniform Trade Secrets Act. (IC24-2-3-1 to 8). Minor variations to uniform act were made regarding displacement of law (IC24-2-3-1[c]), circumstances permitting future use of trade secret upon payment of royalty (IC24-2-3-3[b]), and additional damages in form of royalty (IC24-2-3-4[b]). Indiana has not adopted 1985 amendments to Uniform Trade Secrets Act. Listed examples in IC24-2-3-2 do not constitute exhaustive list of protectible trade secrets. (634 N.E.2d 778, at 783). Any information that requires substantial investment of time, expense or effort to obtain may be trade secret. (622 N.E.2d 912).

LEGAL PROFESSION

ATTORNEYS AND COUNSELORS:
State bar consists of all attorneys in good standing admitted by circuit courts prior to July 1, 1931 and all attorneys in good standing admitted by state Supreme Court thereafter. (Rule AD 1).
State Bar is not integrated.

Jurisdiction over Admission.—The Supreme Court of Indiana has exclusive jurisdiction to admit attorneys to practice law in all courts of state. (IC33-2-3-1; Rule AD 3).

Eligibility.—An applicant for admission to bar must: (1) be 21 years of age or older; (2) be of good moral character; (3) have passed bar examination; and (4) certify satisfactory completion of coursework at approved law school. (Rule AD 12, 13).

Registration As Law Student.—No such requirement.

Educational Requirements.—Graduation from law school located in U.S. on approved list of Council of Legal Education and admissions to bar of American Bar Association or school approved by Indiana Supreme Court or agency thereof is required as prerequisite to taking bar examinations. (Supreme Court of Indiana reserves right to disapprove any school regardless of other approval.) (Rule AD 13).

Petition for Admission.—Application for admission upon examination is required to be made on forms prepared and furnished by State Board of Law Examiners and must be accompanied by certified transcript of applicant's law school record and affidavit of dean or faculty that nothing in record or personal knowledge indicates applicant is not of good moral character or unfit to practice law. (Rule AD 15). Application for admission should be filed with Executive Director of Board of Law Examiners by Apr. 1 for July examination and by Nov. 15 of previous year for Feb. examination. (Rule AD 15). Applicant must be at least 21 years old and of good moral character; graduate of approved law school, and have completed two cumulative semester hours of legal ethics or professional responsibility. (Rule AD 13).

Examination.—Bar examination is conducted by Board of Law Examiners in Feb. and July. (Rule AD 18). Examinations are usually held in Indianapolis. Fee is $225 for examination within one year of application; fee is $100 for reexamination. (Rule AD 15). Board must report on applications within 75 days after examination. (Rule AD 18). Does not use Multi-State Bar exam. Applicants must pass Multistate Professional Responsibility Examination. MPRE passing score is scaled score of 80 which must be achieved within two years before or after date applicant passes bar examination. (Rule AD 17).

Review of final action by Board of Law Examiners may be obtained from Supreme Court as to failure to recommend admission for failing reexamination, or for reason other than failing any examination, by filing petition with Board within 20 days of final determination. There is no review by Supreme Court on failure of first examination. (Rule AD 14).

Clerkship.—No requirement for clerkship before admission.

Admission Without Examination.—Persons admitted to practice law in highest courts of other state or territory of U.S. or District of Columbia may be conditionally admitted to bar upon proof of fact that he or she is member in good standing of bar(s) of his admission, and that he engaged in private or government practice of law, judicial position, or teaching of law for period of at least five of seven years immediately preceding application; that admission of applicant is in public interest; that applicant meets character and fitness requirements, has paid $750 fee, has not failed Indiana Bar examination within two years of application, and has filed affidavit of applicant's intent to engage actively and predominantly in practice of law in Indiana. Conditional admission continues in force for one year and may be renewed for five one-year periods. Fee for each renewal is $50. Upon fifth consecutive renewal, admission to practice shall be permanent. (Rule AD 6).

Admission Pro Hac Vice.—As matter of courtesy, any member of bar of another state in good standing may be admitted to appear in this state for any particular proceeding and for limited time. (Rule AD 3). Before trial court, attorneys from outside state must petition court to appear with local counsel who will sign all briefs, papers, and pleadings, and be jointly responsible therefor. Before Supreme Court and Court of Appeals, attorneys from outside state may appear only with member of Indiana bar by special permission. Local counsel must sign all pleadings, briefs, and other papers. (Rule AD 3).

Licenses.—None; however, registration with Clerk of Supreme Court required. (Rule AD 2).

Privileges.—No special provisions.

Authority.—Attorneys have authority to receive money claimed by a client in action and to discharge claim or acknowledge satisfaction of judgment upon payment thereof; and to bind client by actions filed with clerk or entered in court minutes. (IC34-1-60-5). Written authority is required for attorney to confess judgment in absence of notice to party or party's personal appearance. (IC34-1-60-6).

Disabilities.—No special provisions.

Liabilities.—Attorneys appearing without authorization become liable for consequent injuries. (IC34-1-60-8). Attorneys refusing to deliver money or papers to person for whom or from whom received may be held in contempt and subject to suspension and/or judgment for amount of money withheld plus 10% damages. (IC34-1-60-10, 34-1-60-11).

Lien.—Attorneys have a lien for their fees on all judgments taken by them upon entering notice upon the docket or order book within 60 days from the time such judgment was rendered. (IC33-1-3-1).

Compensation.—Fee in medical malpractice action may not exceed 15% of any recovery when claim is satisfied from patients compensation fund. (IC27-12-18-1). Attorney and client may agree to compensation on per diem basis if agreement is in writing at time of employment. (IC27-12-18-2).

Disbarment or Suspension.—Supreme Court of Indiana has exclusive jurisdiction over charges of attorney misconduct. Grounds for disbarment or suspension are: (1) violation of Rules of Professional Conduct, (2) disbarment or suspension by another state, (3) disability by reason of physical or mental illness or because of use of or addiction to alcohol or drugs. (Rule AD 23).

Unauthorized Practice.—Practice of law by persons not admitted to the bar is made a misdemeanor. (IC33-1-5-1). Supreme Court has exclusive jurisdiction to issue restraining orders and injunctions against unauthorized practice of law. (IC33-2-3-1). Corporations must appear by attorneys in most cases with exceptions for some corporations appearing in small claims courts. (IC34-1-60-1). Original actions may be brought to Supreme Court by Attorney-General, Indiana State Bar Association or committee thereof without leave, and local bar association with court's leave. (Rule AD 24).

Mandatory Continuing Legal Education.—Each attorney and judge who is not attorney shall complete at least six hours of approved continuing legal education per year and at least 36 hours of approved continuing legal education each three year educational period. Grace periods are provided based on attorney's year of admission to Bar and means of admission (i.e. on foreign license, by passing exam, etc.). (Rule AD 29).

Specialty Certification Requirements.—None.

Attorney Ethics.—ABA Model Rules of Professional Conduct have been adopted with modification. (Ind. Code Ann. Title 34, Appendix R.P.C. 1.1 et seq. [West 1995]).

Professional Association (or Corporation).—See category Business Organizations, topic Corporations, subhead Professional Corporation.

MINERAL, WATER AND FISHING RIGHTS

MINES AND MINERALS:
Mine laws are administered by Bureau of Mines and Mining Safety in Department of Labor. (IC22-1-1-5).

Statutes regulate number of miners to be employed, number of outlets and shafts, furnishing of maps, ventilation of mines, protection against gas and water, management of engines and cages, use of explosives, and types, examination and inspection of machinery. Statute also provides for examination and certification by Mining Board of any mine foreman, assistant foreman, fire-boss, shot-firer, hoisting engineer, mine electrician, and belt examiner. Certificate is required for any person employed as miner. (IC22-10-2, 3 and 7).

Miners in deep shaft (IC22-10-11-16) and strip (IC32-8-10-2) coal mines have liens on mines, machinery and fixtures for work and labor.

Surface mining and reclamation of surface mines are regulated by Department of Natural Resources and Natural Resources Commission. Power to grant, suspend, revoke, modify or release permits for surface mining is defined by I-SMCRA. (See IC14-34 et seq.) Historical properties protected. (IC14-34-4-10). Self-bonding permitted. (IC14-34-7).

Indiana has also adopted legislation to implement federal Surface Mining Control and Reclamation Act of 1977. (IC14-34).

Indiana has adopted Interstate Mining Compact. (IC14-35-4, et seq.).

Geophysical Survey.—Regulated by Natural Resources Commission. (IC14-37-2, IC14-37-3). Permit and bond required. (IC14-37-1, IC14-37-4, IC14-37-6).

Oil and gas permits are treated by IC14-37 et seq.; may be refused for pattern of willful violations of statute. (IC14-37-4-9). Department of Natural Resources Membership in Interstate Oil and Gas Compact Commission authorized. (IC14-38-3-1).

Petroleum Severance Tax.—Tax of 1% of value of petroleum and gas removed is imposed on producers and owners at time of severance from land. (IC6-8-1-1 to 28).

MORTGAGES

CHATTEL MORTGAGES:
Uniform Commercial Code in effect since July 1, 1964. (IC26-1-1-101 et seq.).

CHATTEL MORTGAGES . . . *continued*

Household goods cannot be sold except on judicial sale and mortgagor is entitled to possession unless mortgage specially provides for possession by the mortgagee and possession is taken when mortgage is executed and holds it continuously until sale. (IC26-2-2-1, 2).

Payments made under such a mortgage must be evidenced by a receipt (unless payment is made by check), which must show amount paid and unpaid balance. Failure to supply such receipt makes mortgage void. (IC26-2-2-3).

Possession.—When mortgage is silent as to possession, mortgagee is entitled to immediate possession upon execution of mortgage (81 Ind. 433), except as to household goods (IC26-2-2-2).

Perfection and filing requirements are governed by applicable UCC provisions. (See IC26-1-9-302 to 313 and IC26-1-9-401 to 403.)

Removal of Property.—Mortgagor does not commit theft against mortgagee by removing property contrary to terms of security agreement (IC35-43-4-5); however, transferring or encumbering property while failing to disclose lien, etc., with requisite intent may be felony (IC35-43-4-1 to 5).

Mortgages to Public Utilities.—See topic Mortgages of Real Property.

Levy on Mortgaged Chattels.—Goods and chattels mortgaged as security may be levied upon and sold subject to the mortgage and the purchaser is entitled to possession upon complying with the conditions of the pledge or mortgage. (IC34-55-3-4).

Motor Vehicles.—See category Transportation, topic Motor Vehicles.

Suit for possession of mortgaged chattels may be brought at any time after default. (IC26-1-9-503).

Foreclosure.—No special statutory proceedings for foreclosure are provided, but see IC26-1-9-501.

Foreign Mortgages.—If property subject to a chattel mortgage in another state is brought into the state, such mortgage will be enforced. (76 Ind. 512). It may be necessary to perfect interest in Indiana within four months of bringing property into state and before period of perfection in other jurisdiction expires to continue prior perfection uninterrupted. (IC26-1-9-103).

Forms.—No approved or recommended form for security agreements. They may be in same form as under prior law for the specific financing device. For UCC-1 and UCC-3 forms see end of this Digest.

COLLATERAL SECURITY:

See category Debtor and Creditor, topic Pledges.

MORTGAGES OF PERSONAL PROPERTY:

See topic Chattel Mortgages.

MORTGAGES OF REAL PROPERTY:

Lien theory of mortgages prevails. (117 Ind. App. 68, 66 N.E.2d 614).

A mortgagee is entitled to the possession of the property only if such an agreement is contained in the mortgage. This rule does not apply to security interests in rents and profits arising from property. (IC32-8-11-1).

Execution and Recording.—Mortgages of real property must be in writing, executed and acknowledged (IC32-1-2-4; IC32-1-2-31), and, in order to be effective as against certain third persons, recorded, as are deeds (IC32-1-2-16).

Recording fee is $6 for first page and $2 for each page thereafter unless pages are larger than 8½" by 14" in which case fee is $15 for first page and $5 for each page thereafter. Some counties charge additional $3 for each recorded document. (IC36-2-7-10).

Trust deeds are recognized. Power of sale is forbidden. (IC32-8-11-3). Sale may only be had under judicial proceeding.

Mortgages by public utilities, railroads, and pipeline companies executed and recorded in manner provided for execution and recording of mortgages on real estate may extend to cover all or any of property of mortgagor, real, personal, or mixed, chattels real and fixtures. Mortgage need not be filed in compliance with any other filing requirements to perfect security interest in collateral covered by IC26-1 (Uniform Commercial Code). Such mortgages may also include terms to cover property acquired after instrument's date. (IC8-1-5-1).

Purchase Money Mortgages.—A mortgage given to secure all or part of purchase price of property mortgaged has preference over prior judgment against purchaser. (IC32-8-11-4). Purchase money mortgage should state on its face that it is given for that purpose.

Under common law, liens of obligatory future advances, as well as extensions, renewals, and modifications made under or to existing mortgages were generally given priority relating back to that of original mortgage, so long as there was no resulting increase in principal amount of debt or interest payment secured thereunder. Mortgage liens created after June 30, 1990 may secure any future advances, up to maximum amount stated in mortgage, and modifications, extensions and renewals, if and to extent that mortgage states that same are so secured, with priority of all such future advances, modifications, extensions and renewals relating back to time and date of filing of original mortgage in county recorder's office without regard to fact that such future advances, modifications, extensions or renewals may occur thereafter. (IC32-8-11-9). Uncertainty exists as to effect of IC32-8-11-9 on existing rule as to priority between mechanic's liens and construction loan mortgages. (173 Ind. 535, 91 N.E. 7).

Deficiencies.—Unless a mortgage contains an express covenant for payment of the money intended to be secured thereby, or there is separate bond, or note, or other agreement to pay sum due, remedy of mortgagee is limited to property mortgaged. (IC32-8-11-2).

Assignments.—At county recorder's discretion, assignments of mortgages may be made by entry on margin of record, executed by assignor and attested by recorder, or

assignments may be made in writing and executed, acknowledged, and recorded in same manner as original mortgage. Facsimile (machine generated) signature allowed on assignment of mortgage. (IC32-8-11-7).

Release.—A mortgage which has been satisfied may be released by certificate of satisfaction, acknowledged and recorded, or by entry made on the margin of the record, by the mortgagee, and attested by the recording officer. (IC32-8-11-5, 6, IC32-8-13-1). President or other listed officer, attorney-in-fact or other authorized representative, of corporation may act for it in executing such release. (IC32-8-15-1). Failure to release mortgage properly within 15 days after written demand, if mortgage has actually been discharged, renders mortgagee liable to penalties. (IC32-8-1-1, 2).

Assignment and Release Fees.—Fee for attesting to each release or assignment of instrument on multiple transaction document is $6 for first page and $2 for each page thereafter, plus $1 for each cross reference of recorded document and $1 for marginal assignments or releases. Some counties charge additional $3 for each recorded document. (IC36-2-7-10). Number of releases or assignments by each county recorder to be included in single instrument, whether one or more, may vary, and if recorder permits more than one such release or assignment per instrument, recording fee for each transaction is $6 for first page and $2 for each page thereafter, plus $1 for each cross reference of recorded document and $1 for marginal assignments or releases. (IC32-8-15-1; IC32-8-11-7).

Foreclosure.—Execution may issue on any judgment three months after filing of complaint on any mortgage executed on or after July 1, 1975, provided that such period is 12 months for mortgages executed before Jan. 1, 1958, and shall be six months for mortgages executed after Dec. 31, 1957, but before July 1, 1975. However, for complaints filed on or after July 1, 1995, execution may issue on date judgment is entered, regardless of date mortgage was executed, if court finds mortgaged real estate is residential and has been abandoned. (IC32-8-16-1). Also, if owner files with clerk of court waiver of time limitation upon which judgment holder has endorsed his consent, then process shall issue immediately. Consideration for waiver, whether or not expressed by its terms, shall be waiver and release by judgment holder of any deficiency judgment against owner. (IC32-8-16-1.5). Sale can be made after publication once each week for three successive weeks in newspaper of general circulation and published in each county where real estate is located, and posting notice in at least three public places in each township where real estate is located and at door of courthouse and posting in each county where real estate is situated. First publication must be at least 30 days prior to date of sale. At time of first publication, sheriff must serve each owner of real estate with notice of sale. (IC32-8-16-1). Where real estate lies in more than one county, court of either county has jurisdiction to foreclose mortgage and sale must be in county where action is brought, unless court directs otherwise. Judgement shall be recorded in lis pendens record of each county where real estate is located, unless judgment is filed in judgment docket of clerk in county as provided in IC33-17-2-3. (IC32-8-16-2). Owner of real estate may redeem same from judgment at any time prior to sale. Part owner redeeming real estate has lien on same for respective shares due from other owners. (IC32-8-16-3). Real estate must be sold as entire body unless otherwise ordered by court. (IC32-8-16-4). Sheriff or his agent may not directly or indirectly purchase property. (IC32-8-16-5). Sheriff's deed must be given immediately after sale and conveys all right, title and interest in and to property claimed by parties to action. (IC32-8-16-6). If owner resides in dwelling upon property, he may remain in possession of mortgaged property, rent-free, until sale, provided he continues to pay all taxes, assessments, and does not commit waste, etc.; if he does not pay taxes, assessments, etc., he is entitled to occupy, rent free, portion actually occupied as dwelling, not to exceed 15 acres, so long as he does not commit waste. (IC32-8-16-7). In addition, owner of mortgaged premises or owner of crops thereon may at any time within one year from filing action enter and care for and harvest any crop growing at time action was filed. (IC32-8-16-7, 8). Mortgagee can move for appointment of receiver for mortgaged property if owner does not occupy property as his principal residence and if one of six other conditions exists. (IC34-48-1-1). No redemption from foreclosure after date of sale. (IC32-8-16-1 to 10).

See IC32-15-6-1 to 12 for procedure.

Form (With Warranty)

The following form may be used:

This indenture witnesses, That . . . . of . . . . County, in the State of . . . . mortgages and warrants to . . . . of . . . . County, in the State of . . . ., the following described real estate, in . . . . County, in the State of Indiana, to wit: (Description of real estate) to secure the repayment of (sum loaned, note or other evidence of debt, including maturity date) . . . . dollars.

And the mortgagor expressly agrees to pay the debt above secured, without any relief whatsoever from valuation or appraisement laws of the State of Indiana.

In witness whereof, the mortgagor has executed this mortgage this . . . . . day of . . . . . ., 19 . . . . .

(Signature of Mortgagor)

(Acknowledgment)

This instrument prepared by:

(See IC32-1-2-15.)

Chattel Mortgages.—See topic Chattel Mortgages.

PROPERTY

ABSENTEES:

Property of absentee may be attached. (IC34-25-2-1; Rule TR 64[B]). Where property of nonresident is sold on judgment recovered in case in which notice was provided by publication, plaintiff is required to give refunding bond. (IC34-55-7-8).

See also categories Estates and Trusts, topic Death; Transportation, topic Motor Vehicles.

See note at head of Digest as to 1998 legislation covered.

See Topical Index in front part of this volume.

ABSENTEES . . . *continued*

Guardian to act under court supervision may be appointed, under certain circumstances for property of absentee person serving with armed forces or merchant marine. (IC29-2-8-1 to -3).

Escheat.—Effective July 1, 1996, Indiana follows Uniform Unclaimed Property Act (32-9-1.5) instead of Uniform Disposition of Unclaimed Property Act. This chapter does not apply, among other things, to property held in foreign country and arising out of foreign transaction or to unclaimed overpayments of utility bills. Time for abandonment of property held in normal course of business varies greatly depending upon type of property. (IC32-9-1.5-20). Unclaimed property is subject to custody of State if it falls within IC32-9-1.5-21 requirements. Unclaimed property in safe deposit box is presumed abandoned seven years after expiration of rental or lease period on box. (IC32-9-1.5-24).

Attorney general has three years to sell abandoned property. (IC32-9-1.5-31). Under certain circumstances, another state may recover abandoned property. (IC32-9-1.5-37). If attorney general denies claim for abandoned property, aggrieved person may seek administrative hearing and then judicial review. (IC32-9-1.5-38). Holder that fails to abide by requirements of this chapter may be assessed civil penalties and/or charged with misdemeanor. (IC32-9-1.5-47).

See categories Business Organizations, topic Corporations, subhead Unclaimed Dividends; Business Regulation and Commerce, topic Banks and Banking, subhead Unclaimed Deposits; Citizenship, topic Aliens; Estates and Trusts, topics Descent and Distribution, subhead Escheat, Wills, subhead Unclaimed Legacies.

ADVERSE POSSESSION:

Adverse possession to bar entry or action to recover land requires showing that one was in possession continuously for statutory period and that possession was actual, visible, open and notorious, exclusive, under claim of ownership and hostile. (401 N.E.2d 102). Cause of action for recovery of possession of real estate must be brought within ten years or action is barred. (IC34-11-2-11).

This statute of limitation may be extended for person under legal disability, who may bring suit within two years after disability is removed. (IC34-11-6-1).

In suit to establish title by adverse possession, claimant must prove that he has paid and discharged all taxes and special assessments falling due on real estate during period he claims to have possessed same adversely (IC32-1-20-1); however, adverse possession may be established without payment of taxes when notice is not in issue, such as in cases of boundary line disputes. (386 N.E. 2d 982).

Easement may be acquired by 20 years continuous uninterrupted adverse use. (IC32-5-1-1). Owner may cause interruption by written notice served on adverse user or, if adverse user cannot be found, posted for ten days in some conspicuous place on or adjoining premises where right is disputed and recorded. (IC32-5-1-2 to -4).

Persons cannot acquire title by adverse possession of real property owned by state or political subdivisions of state. (IC32-1-20-2).

CONVEYANCES:

See topic Deeds.

CURTESY:

Common law curtesy is abolished. (IC29-1-2-11). As to right of husband in deceased wife's estate, see category Estates and Trusts, topic Descent and Distribution.

DEEDS:

See topic Real Property for types of estates.

Execution.—Conveyances of lands, or any interest therein, shall be by deed in writing, subscribed, sealed and duly acknowledged by grantor or his attorney. (IC32-1-2-4). Seal or scroll is not necessary in deed of natural person, business trust or corporation. (IC32-2-5-1). See infra subhead Married Persons, also category Family, topic Husband and Wife, subhead Conveyance or Encumbrance of Property.

Recording.—In order to be entitled to be recorded deed must be acknowledged or proved. (IC32-1-2-18). See category Documents and Records, topics Acknowledgments, Records.

In order to be effective as against third persons without notice, deed must be recorded in office of recorder of county in which land is situated. (IC32-1-2-11). Conveyances, mortgages and leases for more than three years take priority according to time of filing. (IC32-1-2-16). Every "conveyance document" transferring real property interest for valuable consideration must be accompanied by sales disclosure form, signed by all parties to transaction, for filing with county auditor. (IC6-1.1-5.5-3). County auditor may not accept conveyance document without proper sales disclosure form included. (IC6-1.1-5.5-6). County recorder shall not record conveyance document without evidence that parties have filed completed sales disclosure form with county auditor. (IC6-1.1-5.6-6). Certain transfers of interests in real estate are exempt from requirement to file sales disclosure form. (IC6-1.1-5.5-2). Preprinted forms available from county auditor.

Recording fee is $6 for first page, plus additional $1 for deed, and $2 for each page thereafter provided such page is not larger than 8½" in width and 14" in length. For any document larger, fee is $15 for first page and $5 for each page thereafter. (IC36-2-7-10). Additional fee of $1 per nonconforming page will be due if document is not typewritten or computer generated in black ink in at least 10 point type and has margins of at least 2" at top and bottom of first and last pages, at least ½" margins at top and bottom of all other pages and at least ½" margins on each side of each page, or if any page exceeds 8½" by 14". (IC36-2-11-16.5). In case of multiple transaction, e.g. blanket release of several instrument numbers, fee for attesting to each release, partial release, or assignment of instrument on record after first is $6 for first page, $2 for each additional page plus $1 for each cross reference. For marginal mortgage assignments or marginal mortgage releases, $1. Acknowledgment or certification to document, $5, plus 50¢per page for proofreading certification copy. For each cross reference of recorded document, $1. County may, by ordinance, collect supplemental fee not to exceed $3. (IC36-2-7-10). Fee of $5 is charged by county auditor for filing sales disclosure form. (IC6-1.1-5.5-4).

If auditor of county or township assessor determines it necessary, deed for less than whole of tract which will result in division of tract into two or more parcels for property tax purposes may not be recorded unless auditor or assessor is furnished with drawing or other reliable evidence of number of acres in each new tax parcel being created, existence or absence of improvements on each new tax parcel being created and location within original tract of each new tax parcel being created. (IC32-1-2-37).

Conveyance by tenant for life or years of an estate greater than he has, or could lawfully convey works no forfeiture, but passes to grantee all of estate which tenant could convey. (IC32-1-2-36).

Conveyance by Attorney in Fact.—See topic Powers of Attorney.

Married Persons.—Joint deed of a husband and wife is sufficient to convey and pass any interest described therein of either or both husband and wife in lands held by them. (IC32-1-2-6). Married man may execute deed to his separate property as if he were unmarried without his spouse's joinder. (IC29-1-2-3.1). Married women have same rights concerning real and personal property that unmarried women have. (IC31-11-7-2).

Form of Warranty Deed

Any conveyance of lands worded in substance as follows:

"A.B. conveys and warrants to C.D." [here describe premises]"for the sum of" [here insert consideration] said conveyance being dated and duly signed, sealed and acknowledged by the grantor, shall be deemed to be a conveyance in fee simple to the grantee, his heirs and assigns, with covenant from grantor that he is lawfully seized of the premises, has good right to convey the same, and guarantees quiet possession thereof; that the same are free from all encumbrances, and that he will warrant and defend the title to the same against all lawful claims. (IC32-1-2-12).

Actual consideration does not need to be recited in deed and it is customary to recite consideration as "Ten Dollars and other good and valuable consideration". (35 Ind. 170).

The words "heirs and assigns of the grantee" are not necessary to create in the grantee an estate of inheritance. (IC32-1-2-14).

The substitution of the word "quitclaims" for "conveys and warrants" makes a sufficient deed in quitclaim to the grantee, his heirs and assigns. (IC32-1-2-13).

No special statutory form for corporate deed. See, however, category Documents and Records, topic Records.

DEEDS OF TRUST:

See category Mortgages, topic Mortgages of Real Property.

DOWER:

Common law dower is abolished. (IC29-1-2-11). As to right of widow in deceased husband's estate, see category Estates and Trusts, topic Descent and Distribution.

ESCHEAT:

See categories Business Organizations, topic Corporations, subhead Unclaimed Dividends; Business Regulation and Commerce, topic Banks and Banking, subhead Unclaimed Deposits; Citizenship, topic Aliens; Estates and Trusts, topics Descent and Distribution, subhead Escheat, Wills, subhead Unclaimed Legacies.

LANDLORD AND TENANT:

All general tenancies, in which the premises are occupied by the consent, either express or constructive, of the landlord, except those covering lands used for agricultural purposes, are deemed tenancies from month to month. (IC32-7-1-2).

Tenancy at will can be created only by express contract, and may be terminated by one month's notice in writing. Tenancies from year to year require at least three months' notice; and in all tenancies from one period to another of less than three months duration, notice equal to interval between such periods is required. Where tenancy is for definite period of time, or time for termination of tenancy is expressed, or where tenant at will commits waste, or, in case of tenancy at sufferance, or where rent is agreed to be paid in advance and tenant has entered and refuses or neglects to pay rent, or where relation of landlord and tenant does not exist, no notice to quit is necessary; otherwise, ten days notice to quit is required unless otherwise provided in contract or by agreement between parties. Notice provisions apply only to landlord; tenant has no statutory obligation to give notice of intent to surrender leased premises. (431 N.E. 2d 543). Landlord may obtain lien on crop for his rent upon timely filing in County Recorder's office of notice of intention to hold such lien. (IC32-7-1-1 to 18).

Lease for more than three years must be in writing and signed by party to be charged (IC32-2-1-1, IC32-1-2-4), and recorded, being void against subsequent purchaser, lessee or mortgagee in good faith and for valuable consideration whose grant is first recorded. (IC32-1-2-16). Possession of land by person other than vendor is notice to world of rights of one in possession. (103 Ind. App. 16, 5 N.E.2d 315).

Upon termination of lease, landlord must return all of security deposit to tenant, except for amounts applied to accrued rent, actual damages, and unpaid utility charges tenant is obligated to pay under lease. (IC32-7-5-12). Landlord, however, is only entitled to deduct such amounts from security deposit if landlord provides itemized list of specific deductions claimed to tenant within 45 days of termination of lease. (IC32-7-5-15). Tenant is required to provide landlord mailing address to which to deliver notice and any refund of security deposit. Tenant is entitled to return of entire security deposit plus reasonable attorney fees if landlord fails to comply with statutory requirements regarding use of security deposits. (IC32-7-5-12).

Ejectment may be instituted to recover possession of property. (IC34-1-48-1). Plaintiff may be entitled to possession prior to judgment. To obtain possession prior to judgment, plaintiff must file affidavit stating his right to possession, defendant's unlawful possession, estimated value, and estimated rental value of property. (IC32-6-1.5-1). Clerk then orders defendant to appear to contest affidavit or show cause why he should

LANDLORD AND TENANT . . . *continued*

not be removed and plaintiff put in possession. (IC32-6-1.5-2). Court may issue order for possession prior to hearing if probable cause of immediate harm, destruction, or sale of property. (IC32-6-1.5-3). Court may also issue temporary restraining orders as deemed proper. When possession ordered prior to hearing, defendant may apply for hearing upon 48 hours' notice to plaintiff. (IC32-6-1.5-4).

On hearing, court may give prejudgment order for possession, or appoint a receiver if property has unique value. (IC32-6-1.5-5).

Bond in amount fixed by court is required before plaintiff may have order of possession. (IC32-6-1.5-6). Defendant may retain or regain possession prior to final judgment by bond in amount fixed by court. (IC32-6-1.5-8).

Upon issuance of order for plaintiff's possession, executing officer must remove occupants and take property into custody within 48 hours of service of order. (IC32-6-1.5-10).

LEASES:

See topic Landlord and Tenant.

PERPETUITIES:

Statute adopted Uniform Statutory Rule Against Perpetuities. (IC32-1-4.5). Additional exception is made to applicability of statute for accumulations of income of trust reasonably needed for upkeep, repair or proper management of subject matter of trust estate, accumulations for sinking or reserve funds, accumulations made in accordance with statutory provisions or accumulations made under directions in trust which provide for allocation wholly or in part to principal of trust of stock dividends or stock rights derived from shares held in trust. (IC32-1-4.5-2[8]).

PERSONAL PROPERTY:

Estates by entirety do not exist as to personal property except when such property is directly derived from real estate held by entirety, e.g., crops. (194 Ind. 433, 142 N.E. 117). Profits, such as rental income, derived from real property owned by entireties do not retain character of entireties' ownership. (Ind. App., 544 N.E.2d 179).

Personal property, other than account, which is owned by two or more persons is owned by them as tenants in common unless expressed otherwise in written instrument. However, household goods acquired during coverture and in possession of both husband and wife and any promissory note, bond, certificate of title to motor vehicle, or any other written or printed instrument evidencing interest in tangible or intangible personal property, other than account, in name of both husband and wife, shall upon death of either become sole property of surviving spouse unless clear contrary intention is expressed in written instrument. (IC32-4-1.5-15).

Although IC32-4-1.5-15 provides for right of survivorship in certain cases, it does not prevent joint tenant from entering contract pursuant to which she is obligated to sell what would otherwise pass to her under right of survivorship. (Ind. App., 434 N.E.2d 97).

POWERS OF ATTORNEY:

Indiana has adopted comprehensive Power of Attorney Act. (IC30-5-1 to 10).

Attorneys in Fact.—Attorney-in-fact may act under power of attorney that has not been recorded with county recorder. However, attorney-in-fact must duly record power authorizing execution of document that must be recorded before presenting such document for recording. Document presented by attorney-in-fact for recording must reference book and page or instrument number where instrument creating power is recorded. (IC30-5-3-3).

Formalities.—To be valid, power of attorney must be in writing, name attorney-in-fact, give attorney-in-fact power to act on behalf of principal and must be signed by principal in presence of notary public. (IC30-5-4-1). To be recorded, instrument creating power of attorney must comply with all recording requirements, including notary and preparation statements. County recorder may not accept document for recording if document was executed and is presented by attorney-in-fact whose power is unrecorded. (IC30-5-3-3). General power of attorney, designation of health care representative, and appointment of representative under living will declaration or life prolonging procedures declaration may be made concurrently or independently. (IC30-5-7-5). Model living will and life prolonging procedures declaration forms effective since July 1, 1993, and revised effective July 1, 1994. (IC16-36-4-10, 11). Health care powers extend to consent for mental health services effective July 1, 1996. (IC16-36-1.5) Except as otherwise provided in instrument creating power of attorney, revocation of executed power must be in writing signed by principal that identifies power being revoked. Revocation is not effective until attorney-in-fact has actual knowledge of revocation. If executed power of attorney was recorded, revocation must be recorded and refer to book and page or instrument number where instrument creating power is recorded. (IC30-5-10-1). No conveyance of land by attorney is valid unless there is a written power of attorney, subscribed and acknowledged by principal as conveyance is required to be. (IC32-1-2-5). Revocation of living will or life prolonging procedures declaration or appointment of health care representative may be oral or in writing. (IC16-36-1-7, IC16-36-4-12).

Revocation.—Except as otherwise stated in instrument creating power of attorney, power of attorney is not terminated by incapacity of principal. Generally power of attorney terminates on death of principal. However, death of principal who has executed power of attorney, does not revoke or terminate agency as to attorney-in-fact or other person, who, without actual knowledge of death, acts in good faith. Any otherwise valid or enforceable action binds principal's successors. Notice from U.S. Dept. of Defense of death of principal who has executed power of attorney constitutes actual notice of participant's death. Report or listing of principal being missing or missing in action does not constitute notice of principal's death or terminate any executed power of attorney. (IC30-5-10-4). Disability or incapacity of principal who has executed durable power of attorney has no effect at all on acts done by attorney-in-fact. Disability or

incapacity of principal who has executed power of attorney that terminates on principal's incapacity does not revoke or terminate agency as to attorney-in-fact or other person, who, without actual knowledge of disability or incapacity, acts in good faith. Any otherwise valid and enforceable action binds principal and his successors. (IC30-5-10-3).

Uniform Durable Power of Attorney Act.—Indiana has repealed statute that adopted Uniform Durable Power of Attorney Act (formerly IC30-2-11-1 to 7). (P.L. 149, 1991, §6).

REAL PROPERTY:

All the common law estates exist, except estate in tail which has been abolished. (IC32-1-2-33). Joint tenancy, tenancy in common and tenancy by entirety are recognized.

Conveyance or devise of land or interest therein to two or more persons is taken to create a tenancy in common and not a joint tenancy, unless a contrary intention is expressed in the instrument of conveyance, grant or devise. This does not apply to mortgages, conveyances in trust or conveyances to husband and wife. Estate vested in executors or trustees as such is held by them in joint tenancy. (IC32-1-2-7 to 8).

Freehold estates and less than freehold estates may be created to begin at future date. Estates for life may be created in a term of years with or without the intervention of the precedent estate, and remainder limited thereon. Remainder of freehold or less than freehold, either contingent or vested, may be created expectant on termination of term of years. (IC32-1-2-34).

A remainder may be limited on contingency which would operate to abridge or determine precedent estate. (IC32-1-2-35).

Rule in Shelley's Case is recognized by courts. (141 Ind. 170, 40 N.E. 662).

Condominiums are allowed. (IC32-1-6-1 to 31).

See also topics Curtesy, Deeds, Dower, Landlord and Tenant; categories Business Regulation and Commerce, topic Consumer Protection; Civil Actions and Procedure, topic Partition; Family, topic Husband and Wife; Mortgages, topic Mortgages of Real Property.

TRUST DEEDS:

See category Mortgages, topic Mortgages of Real Property.

TAXATION

ADMINISTRATION:

The administration of tax and revenue laws is delegated to State Board of Tax Commissioners ("State Board") in case of tax on real and personal property and to Department of State Revenue ("Department") in case of most other taxes.

Business Activity Report.—Every corporation that carries on any business activity or owns or maintains property in Indiana for taxable year shall file annual business activity report with Department by 15th day of fourth month after end of corporation's taxable year. Report is not required if tax return was filed under IC6-3 or IC6-5.5, corporation received written authority from this state to conduct business, or corporation is exempt from tax under IC6-3 and IC6-5.5. (IC6-8.1-6-6).

Penalties.—See subheads detailing particular taxes, supra; also IC6-8.1-1-1, IC6-8.1-10-1 et seq.

Revised Uniform Federal Tax Lien Registration Act.—Not adopted. See IC36-2-11-25.

Tax court, established by IC33-3-5-1, has exclusive jurisdiction over any case that arises under tax laws of state and that constitutes initial appeal of final determination made by Department or State Board, except cases that arise under any provision of Charity Gaming (IC4-32), other than Gaming Card Excise Tax provision. (IC35-3-5-2). In addition to its regular division, tax court has small claims division of limited jurisdiction (claims for refund not exceeding $5,000 and appeals of assessed property values not exceeding $45,000). (IC33-3-5-12). Tax court's principal office is in Indianapolis, but court holds trials in various county seats. (IC33-3-5-9, 2[d]). Tax court has its own rules of procedure and evidence. Taxpayers may petition Indiana Supreme Court to review tax court decisions.

ALCOHOLIC BEVERAGE EXCISE TAXES:

Imposed by IC7.1-4-1-1 et seq.

CIGARETTE TAX:

Imposed by IC6-7-1-1 et seq.

CONTROLLED SUBSTANCE EXCISE TAX:

Imposed by IC6-7-3-3.

COUNTY EMPLOYMENT TAX:

Every county with population of more than 400,000 but less than 700,000 may impose employment tax on each employer and employee. (IC6-3.5-2-2). Rate must not be in excess of 50¢ per employee per month. (IC6-3.5-2-2).

Exempted Parties and Employees.—(1) Agricultural labors; (2) domestic service solely on daily basis for private homes; (3) newspaper carrier delivery or distribution if individual under 18; (4) services in employ of one's father, mother, son, daughter or spouse; following employers only: (i) U.S.; (ii) agency of U.S.; (iii) Indiana; (iv) agency of political subdivision of Indiana; and (v) any organization operated exclusively for religious, charitable, scientific, literary, educational and/or civic purposes whose gross income is not used for private gain or benefit. (IC6-3.5-2-1, 4).

See note at head of Digest as to 1998 legislation covered.

See Topical Index in front part of this volume.

ENTERTAINMENT TAXES:

Closed Circuit Television.—5% tax is imposed on gross receipts received from closed circuit telecasts of boxing or sparring matches, semiprofessional elimination contests, or exhibitions. (IC25-9-1-22).

Charity Gaming.—Qualified organizations required to obtain license to conduct charity games; preclusion of local governments from regulating and taxing charity games. (IC4–32 et seq.).

Gaming Card Excise Tax.—10% tax imposed on gross receipts received by wholesalers. (IC4-32-15-1 et seq.).

Local Tax on Admissions to Professional Sporting Events.—If held in certain facilities located in certain counties. (IC6-9-13-1 to 5).

Local Tax on Amusement Park Attendance.—In certain counties. (IC6-9-28-1).

Local Tax on Food and Beverage.—In certain counties. (IC6-9-12, 21 and 23 to 27).

Local Tax on Hotels, Motels, and Tourist Camps.—In certain counties. (IC6-9-1-1 et seq.).

Pari-Mutuel Tax (IC4-31-9 et seq.) imposed on permit holders.

ESTATE TAX:

Indiana estate tax is greater of (i) zero or (ii) value of decedent's Indiana gross estate divided by value of decedent's total gross estate, multiplied by federal state death tax credit allowable against decedent's federal estate tax, and subtracted therefrom amount of all Indiana inheritance taxes actually paid as result of decedent's death. Nonresident decedent's Indiana gross estate equals total fair market value of tangible personal property and real estate having actual situs in Indiana at time of decedent's death which is included for federal estate tax under IRC §§2031-2044. Resident decedent's Indiana gross estate equals total fair market value of personal property and real estate having actual situs in Indiana at time of decedent's death and all intangible personal property wherever located that is included for federal estate tax.

Any personal representative, trustee, or transferee of resident or nonresident decedent's estate subject to Indiana Estate or Inheritance Tax must file with Department executed copy of federal estate tax return when same is filed. Within 30 days after receipt of final determination of federal estate tax by Internal Revenue Service or federal court same must be filed with Department. (IC6-4.1-4-8).

Tax accrues at death of decedent but does not become due until 18 months after his death, or one month after final notice of federal estate tax due is given, whichever is later. (IC6-4.1-11-3).

If tax is not paid when due, interest at 6% per annum is added. (IC6-4.1-11-4).

Apportionment Against Inter Vivos Disposition.—By statute, federal estate tax liability is allocated to property included in taxable estate unless otherwise directed by will. (IC29-2-12-2).

Interstate Co-operation.—No statutory procedure available for compromise of death taxes where decedent's domicile is disputed.

FINANCIAL INSTITUTIONS TAX:

Imposed by IC6.5.5-1-1 et seq. Tax is imposed on corporation that is transacting business of financial institution in Indiana, including: (1) Holding company (corporation registered under Bank Holding Company Act of 1956 [12 U.S.C. 1841-1849], or registered as savings and loan holding company other than diversified savings and loan holding company [as defined in §10(a)(F) of Home Owners' Loan Act of 1933 (12 U.S.C. 1467[a][1][F])]); (2) regulated financial corporation (which includes: [a] institution, deposits, shares or accounts of which are FDIC insured, [b] Federal Home Loan Bank member, [c] any other bank or thrift institution incorporated or organized under laws of state that is engaged in business of receiving deposits, [d]credit union incorporated and organized under laws of this state, [e]production credit association organized under 12 U.S.C. 2071, [f] Edge Act corporation organized under 12 U.S.C. 611 through 631, [g] federal or state agency or branch of foreign bank [as defined in 12 U.S.C. 3101] or [h] trust company formed under IC28-1-4); (3) subsidiary of holding company or regulated financial corporation; and (4) any other corporation organized under laws of U.S., this state, another taxing jurisdiction, or foreign government that is carrying on business of financial institution. Carrying on business of financial institution includes: (1) For holding company, regulated financial corporation, or subsidiary of either, activities that each is authorized to perform under federal or state law, including activities authorized by regulation or order of federal or state law, including activities authorized by regulation or order of Federal Reserve Board for such subsidiary under §4(c)(8) of Bank Holding Company Act of 1956 (12 U.S.C. 1843[c][8]); and (2) for any corporation described in (4) above, all of corporation's business activities, if 80% or more of corporation's gross income, excluding extraordinary income, is derived from: (a) making, acquiring, selling, or servicing loans or extensions of credit, (b) leasing, or acting as agent, broker, or adviser in connection with leasing real and personal property that is economic equivalent of extension of credit if transaction is not treated as lease for federal income tax purposes; and (c) operating credit card, debt card, charge card, or similar business. (IC6-5.5-1-17).

If corporation is transacting business of financial institution (as defined in IC6-5.5-1-17[d]) and is partner in partnership or grantor and beneficiary of trust transacting business in Indiana, and partnership or trust is conducting in Indiana activity that would be business of financial institution if transacted by corporation, corporation is taxpayer and shall, in calculating corporation's tax liability, include in corporation's adjusted or apportioned income on corporation's percentage of partnership or trust adjusted gross or apportioned income. (IC6-5.5-2-8[a]). Term "partnership" means association of two or more entities formed to conduct business. (IC6-5.5-1-19).

Rate of Tax.—Tax is measured by adjusted gross income or apportioned income and imposed for privilege of exercising franchise or corporate privilege of transacting business of financial institution in Indiana. Amount of tax is 8.5% of remainder of: (1) Taxpayer's adjusted gross income or apportioned income, minus (2) taxpayer's deductible Indiana net operating losses (with certain statutory restrictions), minus (3) taxpayer's net capital losses minus taxpayer's net capital gains computed under IRC for

each taxable year or part thereof after Dec. 31, 1989, multiplied by apportionment percentage applicable under IC6-5.5-2 for taxable year of loss. (IC6-5.5-2-1). Except for credit unions and investment companies for which there are separately stated provisions, "adjusted gross income" means taxable income as defined in IRC §63, adjusted as follows: (1) Subtract income that U.S. Constitution or any U.S. statute prohibits from being used to measure tax; (2) subtract income that is derived from sources outside U.S. (as defined by IRC); (3) subtract amount equal to IRC §166(a) worthless debt; (4) subtract amount equal to bad debt reserves included in federal income because of accounting method changes required by IRC §§585(c)(3)(A) or 593; (5) add amount equal to deduction allowed or allowable under IRC §§166, 585 or 593; (6) add amount equal to deduction allowed or allowable under IRC §170; (7) add amount equal to deduction or deductions allowed or allowable under IRC §63 for taxes based on or measured by income and levied at state level by state or levied at local level by any subdivision of state, or for taxes on property levied by subdivision of state; (8) add amounts of interest excluded under IRC §103 or under any other federal law, minus associated expenses disallowed in computation of taxable income under IRC §265; (9) add amount equal to deduction allowed under IRC §§172 or 1212 for net operating losses or net capital losses. (IC6-5.5-1-2); and (10) add for taxpayer that is not large bank (as defined in IRC §585[c][2]) amount equal to recovery of debt, or part of debt, that becomes worthless to extent IRC §166(a) deduction was allowed in prior taxable year.

All of adjusted gross income of resident taxpayer not filing combined return is subject to tax. (IC6-5.5-2-2). Apportioned income of nonresident taxpayer not filing combined return is subject to tax. Apportioned income is taxpayer's adjusted gross income multiplied by quotient of taxpayer's total receipts attributable to transacting business in Indiana divided by taxpayer's total receipts (as determined under IC6-5.5-4). (IC6-5.5-2-3). Combined group's income subject to tax is its adjusted gross and apportioned income determined by adding adjusted gross and apportioned income of each member and multiplying result by quotient of all receipts of resident taxpayer members of group from whatever source derived plus receipts of nonresident taxpayer members of group attributable to transacting business in Indiana, divided by receipts of all members of group from transacting business in all taxing jurisdictions. (IC6-5.5-2-4).

Apportioned Receipts.—For purposes of apportionment, receipts means gross income (as defined in IC6-5.5-1-10), plus gross income excluded under IRC §103, less gross income derived from sources outside U.S. However, upon disposition of assets such as securities and money market transactions in regular course of business receipts are limited to gain (as defined in IRC §1001) that is recognized upon disposition. (IC6-5.5-4-2). Receipts attributed to Indiana include receipts from: (1) Lease or rental of property located in Indiana (IC6-5.5-4-3); (2) loan and installment sale contracts dealing with or secured by property located in Indiana (IC6-5.5-4-4); (3) unsecured consumer loans to Indiana residents (IC6-5.5-4-5); (4) unsecured commercial loans and installment obligations (and receipts from letters of credit, acceptance of drafts and other devices for assuring or guaranteeing loans or credit) where funds applied in Indiana, or if application undeterminable, if loan applied for in Indiana (IC6-6.5-4-6, -7); (5) credit cards regularly billed in Indiana (IC6-5.5-4-8); (6) sales of property apportioned to Indiana if income from property would be apportioned to Indiana (IC6-5.5-4-6, -7); (7) performance of fiduciary and other services to extent benefits are consumed in Indiana (IC6-5.5-4-10); (8) traveler's checks, money orders or U.S. savings bonds purchased in Indiana (IC6-5.5-4-11); and (9) investments in securities of Indiana or its political subdivisions, agencies or instrumentalities (IC6-5.5-4-12).

Credits.—Resident taxpayer or resident member of unitary group is entitled to credit equal to lesser of (1) amount of creditable tax (net income, franchise or other tax measured by net income, or imposed instead of income tax, or based on deposits, investment capital or shares, net worth or capital) actually paid to another taxing jurisdiction, or (2) amount equal to amount of creditable tax that would be due at financial institution's tax rate described above on (a) taxpayer's adjusted gross income subject to taxation by other taxing jurisdiction or (b) taxpayer's adjusted gross income or apportioned income attributable to other taxing jurisdiction using rules for attributing gross receipts under IC6-5.5-4. (IC6-5.5-2-5). Credit provided in IC6-5.5-2-5 may be allowed only after taxpayer provides to Department of Revenue satisfactory evidence of payment of taxes to other taxing jurisdiction. (IC6-5.5-2-5.3). Nonresident taxpayer is entitled to credit for amount of net income tax, franchise tax, or other tax measured by net income that is due to nonresident taxpayer's domiciliary state if receipt of interest or other income from loan or loan transaction of at least $2,000,000 is attributable to both Indiana and domiciliary state under its laws. Amount of credit is lesser of: (1) Tax actually paid to domiciliary state attributable to loan or loan transaction, or (2) tax due to Indiana under IC6-5.5 attributable to loan or loan transaction. Amount determined under (1) and (2) above shall be reduced by amount of any credit for tax due from nonresident taxpayer under IC6-5.5 (calculated without credit in IC6-5.5-2-6) and that may be used by nonresident taxpayer in calculating income tax due under laws of nonresident taxpayer's domiciliary state. (IC6-5.5-2-6). Additional credits available for hiring math and science teachers during summer recess (IC6-3.1-2-1 to 7), investing in special state corporations (IC6-3.1-5-1 to 16), donating computer hardware or software to schools (IC6-3.1-3-1 to 10), qualified investments in industrial recovery sites (IC6-3.1-11-1 to 23) and lending money to entities in enterprise zones (IC6-3.1-7-1 to 6).

Exemptions.—No tax imposed on: (1) Insurance companies subject to tax under IC27-1-18-2 or IC6-2.1, (2) international banking facilities (as defined in Regulation D of Board of Governors of Federal Reserve System), (3) any corporation that is exempt from federal income tax under IRC §1363, or (4) any corporation exempt from federal income taxation under IRC, except for corporation's unrelated business income. However, exemption does not apply to corporation exempt from federal income taxation under IRC §501(c)(14). (IC6-5.5-2-7). Depositor or owner of capital stock, capital shares, share accounts, certificates of indebtedness or investment, or comparable investment or interest in taxpayer with its principal offices in Indiana is not liable for tax on such interest. (IC6-5.5-9-5).

If tax is held inapplicable or invalid with respect to taxpayer, then notwithstanding statute of limitations set forth in IC6-8.1-5-2(a), taxpayer is subject to IC6-2.1, IC6-3 and IC6-5 for such periods. Personal property is exempt from IC6-1.1 if: (1) Owned by

---

See note at head of Digest as to 1998 legislation covered.

See Topical Index in front part of this volume.

FINANCIAL INSTITUTIONS TAX . . . *continued*
financial institution, (2) financial institution is subject to bank tax (IC6-5-10), and (3) property is not leased by financial institution (IC6-5.5-9-3). Taxpayer subject to this tax is not subject to gross income tax (IC6-2.1), income taxes (IC6-3), and bank, savings and loan or production credit association taxes (IC6-5), except to extent taxpayer is acting in fiduciary capacity (IC6-5.5-9-4).

Transacting Business within Indiana.—Taxpayer is transacting business within Indiana if taxpayer: (1) Maintains office (regular, continuous and fixed place of business) in Indiana; (2) has employee, representative, or independent contractor conducting business in Indiana (regularly engaged in taxpayer's business in Indiana, or employee's activities are directed or controlled by Indiana office and majority of employee's service is not performed in another taxing jurisdiction, or contribution to Indiana employment security fund is required under IC22-4-2 with respect to employee); (3) regularly sells products or services to Indiana customers that are received in Indiana; (4) regularly solicits business from Indiana customers (subject to IC6-5.5-3-4 threshold); (5) regularly performs services outside Indiana that are consumed within Indiana; (6) regularly engages in transactions in Indiana that involve certain intangible property and result in receipts from Indiana customers; (7) owns or leases tangible personal or real property located in Indiana; or (8) regularly solicits and receives deposits from Indiana customers. (IC6-5.5-3-1 to 7). Taxpayer, except for trust company formed under IC28-1-4, is not transacting business in Indiana solely by: (1) Maintaining or defending lawsuit; (2) filing, modifying, renewing, extending, or transferring mortgage, deed of trust, or security interest; (3) acquiring, foreclosing or otherwise conveying property in Indiana as result of default under terms of any mortgage, deed of trust, or other security instrument relating to property; (4) selling tangible personal property, if taxation is precluded by 15 U.S.C. 381 through 384; (5) owning interest in (or activities related to): (a) real estate mortgage investment conduit, real estate investment trust, or regulated investment company (as defined by IRC), (b) loan backed security in pool of promissory notes or certificates of interest, (c) loan or other asset from which interest is attributed in IC6-5.5-4-4, IC6-5.5-4-5, and IC6-5.5-4-6 and originated by independent party, (d) right to service or to collect income from loan or other asset from which interest is attributed in IC6-5.5-4-4, IC6-5.5-4-5 and IC6-5.5-4-6 and originated by independent party, and (e) amount held in escrow or trust account with respect to foregoing property; or (6) acting as executor of estate, trustee of benefit plan or employees' pension, profit sharing or other retirement plan, or of testamentary or inter vivos trust or corporate indenture, or in any other fiduciary capacity, including holding title to real property in Indiana. (IC6-5.5-3-8).

Returns.—Annual return required for each taxpayer subject to tax (or subject to tax but for loss), except that only one return must be filed for unitary group. (IC6-5.5-6-1). Returns and unpaid taxes are due 15th day of fourth month following close of taxpayer's taxable year, with filing extensions available. (IC6-5.5-6-2,-4). Quarterly reports and payments of 25% of annual estimated tax due last day of month for quarter ending on last day of preceding month. This only applies to taxpayers having financial institutions tax liability in excess of $1,000. If Department determines taxpayer's (i) estimated quarterly financial institutions tax liability for current year or (ii) average quarterly financial institutions tax payment for preceding year exceeds $10,000, then taxpayer shall pay quarterly financial institutions taxes due by electronic fund transfer (as defined in IC4-8.1-2-7) or by delivering in person or by overnight courier payment by cashier's check, certified check, or money order to Department. Transfer or payment shall be made on or before date tax is due. If taxpayer pays by electronic fund transfer, taxpayer need not file quarterly financial institutions tax return. (IC6-5.5-6-3). Duty to file notice with Department of any alteration or modification of federal income tax return within 120 days. (IC6-5.5-6-6). Except as otherwise provided in IC6-5.5-5-1, unitary group consisting of at least two taxpayers shall file combined return covering all operations of unitary business and including all of members of unitary business. However, only one combined return needs to be filed, as provided in IC6-5.5-6-1. In order to fairly represent taxpayer's income within Indiana, Department may require or allow: (1) Separate accounting, (2) filing of separate return for taxpayer, or (3) reallocation of tax items between taxpayer and member of its unitary group. (IC6-5.5-5-1). Partnership or trust shall file information return in compliance with IC6-5.5-2-8(b) and (c). Partnership or trust transacting business in Indiana, which if transacted by corporation would constitute business of financial institution, shall withhold from all nonresident corporate partners or beneficiaries amount prescribed in withholding instructions issued by Department of Revenue. (IC6-5.5-2-8[b][3]).

Penalties.—Penalty prescribed by IC6-8.1-10-2.1(b) for failing to pay tax is applicable, except that no penalty shall be assessed for quarterly payment if payment is at least 20% of final tax liability or 25% of prior year's final tax liability, and penalty is only assessed to extent of shortfall. (IC6-5.5-7-1). Violation of IC6-5.5 can be class C infraction. (IC6-5.5-7-2). Failure to file or other actions taken with intent to defraud state or to withhold evidence can be class D felony. (IC6-5.5-7-3,-4).

GASOLINE AND SPECIAL FUELS TAXES:

Gasoline Tax (IC6-6-1.1-101 et seq.).—15¢ per gallon tax imposed on use of all gasoline, subject to certain exceptions. Motor Carrier Fuel Tax (IC6-6-1.1-101 et seq.). Rural transit system meeting certain requirements and submitting properly completed claim for refund is entitled to refund of tax paid on gasoline used for transporting persons by means of motor vehicle or trackless trolley. (IC6-6-1.1-902.5).

Petroleum Severance Tax.—(IC6-8-1-1 to -28). See category Mineral, Water and Fishing Rights, topic Mines and Minerals.

Special Fuel Tax (IC6-6-2.5 et seq.).—16¢ per gallon tax imposed on all special fuel sold or used in producing or generating power for propelling motor vehicles, subject to certain exceptions. Each supplier of special fuel must obtain supplier's license.

GENERATION-SKIPPING TRANSFER TAX:

Indiana generation-skipping transfer tax greater of (i) value of transferred property legally located in Indiana divided by total value of transferred property, multiplied by maximum allowable tax credit under IRC §2604, or (ii) maximum allowable tax credit under IRC §2604 minus generation-skipping transfer taxes paid to other states. (IC6-4.1-11.5-8 [a]). Value of transferred property is final value of property determined for federal generation-skipping transfer tax purposes. (IC6-4.1-11.5-8[b]).

Indiana generation-skipping transfer tax imposed on every generation-skipping transfer. (IC6-4.1-11.5-7). Indiana generation-skipping transfer includes every transfer subject to tax under IRC §§2601 et seq. if (1) original transferor is resident of Indiana on date of original transfer or (2) transferor is not resident of Indiana and transferred property is real property located in Indiana or tangible personal property legally located in Indiana. (IC6-4.1-11.5-3). Original transferor means donor, grantor, testator, or trustee who by gift, grant, will, or trust makes transfer of real or personal property that results in imposition of federal generation-skipping transfer tax. (IC6-4.1-11.5-4). Transferred property means real or personal property, whether located in Indiana or another jurisdiction, transfer of which gives rise to federal generation-skipping transfer tax. (IC6-4.1-11.5-6).

Tax due 18 months after date of death of person whose death resulted in generation-skipping transfer. (IC6-4.1-11.5-9). Tax paid to Indiana Department of Revenue. (IC6-4.1-11.5-10). Late payments subject to interest at 6% from due date of tax until date tax is paid. (IC6-4.1-11.5-12). Must file with Department of Revenue copy of federal return and schedule indicating value of transferred property and tax. (IC6-4.1-11.5-11).

GIFT TAX:

None; but inheritance tax applies to gifts in contemplation of death or to take effect after death.

HAZARDOUS WASTE LAND DISPOSAL TAX:

Imposed on disposal of hazardous waste in disposal facilities. (IC6-6-6.6-1 et seq.). $50 fee imposed on "facility" (defined in 42 U.S.C. 11049[4]) submitting emergency and hazardous chemical inventory form. (IC6-6-10-1-1.7).

INCOME TAX:

Adjusted Gross Income Tax, enacted by 1963 legislature, applies to individuals, trusts, estates and corporations. (IC6-3-1-1 to 25). Provisions are tied to Internal Revenue Code of 1986 as amended and in effect on Jan. 1, 1998 ("IRC"). (IC6-3-1-11).

Rate of Tax.—Rate is 3.4% of adjusted gross income of resident persons and nonresident persons and corporations when derived from sources within state.

Relation to Gross Income Tax.—Gross income tax does not apply to income received by individuals, estates, trusts, S corporations and corporations eligible to be S corporations which meet certain requirements. (IC6-2.1-1-16, IC6-2.1-3-24.5). Corporations, other than S corporations, are subject to both gross income tax and adjusted gross income tax and pay whichever is higher. (IC6-3-3-2).

Adjusted gross income for individuals consists of "adjusted gross income" as defined for individuals in IRC §62, modified as follows: Subtract income exempt from taxation by statutes or Constitution of U.S.; add amount equal to any deduction allowed or allowable pursuant to IRC §62 for taxes based on or measured by income and levied at state level by any state and for taxes on property levied by any subdivision of any state; subtract $1,000, or in case of joint return subtract $1,000 for each spouse, subtract $1,000 for each exemption provided by IRC §151(c) and additional amount allowable under IRC §63(f), and $1,000 for spouse of taxpayer if separate return is made by taxpayer if such spouse for taxable year has no gross income and is not dependent of another taxpayer; subtract $500 for each of exemptions allowed under IRC §151(c)(1) for taxable years beginning after Dec. 31, 1996, and before Jan. 1, 2001; subtract lesser of adjusted gross income, as defined in IRC §62, that is subject to income tax by political subdivision of another state or $2,000. (IC6-3-1-3.5). Add amount equal to total capital gain portion of lump sum distribution, as defined in IRC §402(e)(4)(D), if lump sum distribution is received during taxable year and capital gain portion is taxed as provided in IRC §402; subtract amounts included in federal adjusted gross income under IRC §111 as recovery of items previously deducted as itemized deduction from adjusted gross income, and subtract amounts received by individual as supplemental railroad retirement annuities under 45 U.S.C. 231. Subtract principal contributed by employer to medical care savings account and interest earned thereon if such amount is included in "adjusted gross income" computation. (IC6-8-11). Add amount of deduction allowed under IRC §221 for married couples filing jointly. Add amount excluded from federal gross income under All Savers Interest Exclusion of IRC §128. Subtract amount equal to amount of federal Social Security and Railroad Retirement benefits included in taxpayer's federal gross income by IRC §86 and subtract certain amounts for recipients of welfare assistance under IC12-1-5.5-1, -1.2, or IC12-1-7-21. (IC6-3-1-3.5). Adjusted gross income of corporations consists of "taxable income" as defined in IRC §63, modified as follows: Subtract income exempt from taxation by Constitution or statutes of U.S.; add deductions allowed or allowable pursuant to IRC §170; add any deduction or deductions allowed or allowable pursuant to IRC §63 for taxes based on or measured by income levied at state level by any state and for taxes on property levied by any subdivisions of any state. (IC6-3-1-3.5). Adjusted gross income for trusts and estates is "taxable income" as defined for trusts and estates in IRC §641(b) less income that is exempt from taxation under this Act by constitution and statutes of U.S. (IC6-3-1-3.5).

Adjusted Gross Income Subject to Tax.—In cases of resident individual, trusts with situs in state, or estates of deceased residents, tax is imposed on entire adjusted gross income. For corporations and nonresident individuals, trusts and estates, tax is imposed on adjusted gross income derived from sources within the state. (IC6-3-2-1, IC6-3-1-12). Income derived from sources within Indiana includes income from following sources: income from real or tangible personal property located in state; income from doing business in state; income from trade or profession conducted in state; compensation for labor or services rendered within state; income from various enumerated intangibles attributable to Indiana. (IC6-3-2-2, -2.2).

Return and Payment of Tax.—Corporations, trusts, estates, nonresident individuals having any gross income from Indiana sources except for team member (as defined in IC6-3-2-2.7) who is covered by composite return filed under IC6-3-2-2.7, and any resident individual having gross income in excess of personal exemptions must file

See note at head of Digest as to 1998 legislation covered.

See Topical Index in front part of this volume.

IN – 47

INCOME TAX . . . *continued*

annual returns on or before 15th day of fourth month following close of taxable year (IC6-3-4-1; IC6-3-4-3). Taxable year must be same as used for federal income tax purposes. (IC6-3-1-16). Any individual required to file declaration of estimated tax for federal purposes must file one for Indiana purposes at same time federal is filed. (IC6-3-4-4). In addition, if individual has gross income subject to tax and from which no withholding is made declaration of estimated tax must be filed unless estimated tax can reasonably be expected to be less than $400. Every corporation with $1,000 adjusted gross income tax liability must report and pay quarterly 25% of estimated liability, less credits in conjunction with reporting of gross income tax. 10% penalty per annum is assessed for failure to pay estimated tax. (IC6-3-4-4). Employers generally must withhold tax on wages subject to tax. (IC6-3-4-8). Partnerships and S corporations must withhold payments or credits to nonresident partners or shareholders. (IC6-3-4-12, 13). Trusts and estates must withhold payments to nonresident beneficiaries. (IC6-3-4-15). Penalties of 10% for willful negligence and 100% for fraud added to deficiencies. If taxpayer fails to make return, Department may prepare return from best information available and add to computation of tax therein penalty of 20% of such tax, together with interest on such tax at rate of 12% per annum or at adjusted rate of interest established by commissioner from date such tax was due. (IC6-8.1-10-1 to 5). In addition to above penalties, fine of not more than $10,000 or imprisonment for two years, with up to one year subtracted for mitigating circumstances and up to two years added for aggravated circumstances, or both, may be imposed for failure or refusal to file return or making false or fraudulent return with intent to defraud state or evade payment of tax. (IC6-3-6-11).

Allocation and Apportionment of Income.—Adjusted gross income includes nonbusiness income allocable to state, and business income derived from sources within state determined by using specified three factor formula which takes property, payroll and sales into account, giving extra weight to sales factor after certain periods of economic growth. Department also has discretion to vary terms of apportionment formula either on its own motion or upon taxpayer's petition. (IC6-3-2-2, -2.2).

Credits.—Credits are allowed to individuals for wages withheld (IC6-3-3-1), for 50% of donations to higher education and 21st century scholars program (IC20-12-70.1-5) in Indiana, but not to exceed $100 on single return or $200 on joint return for taxpayers other than corporations and not to exceed $1,000 for corporations (IC6-3-3-5, -5.1), and certain taxes paid to other states (IC6-3-3-3). Taxpayer entitled to credit on enterprise zone income under formula. (IC6-3-3-10). Refundable credit is allowed to individuals 65 years or over whose federal adjusted gross income is less than $10,000 for taxable year to provide relief from state adjusted gross income taxes. (IC6-3-3-9). Corporations are allowed credit against adjusted gross income tax in amount not to exceed amount of tax liability under gross income tax. (IC6-3-3-2).

Neighborhood Assistance Credit.—Any business entity authorized to do business in state and subject to gross, adjusted gross, supplemental net income, or financial institutions tax or any individual subject to adjusted gross income tax shall receive credit, not to exceed $25,000 for any year, against such tax due of 50% of amount invested or contributed to qualified neighborhood assistance program. (IC6-3.1-9-1 to 3).

Business firms or individuals desiring credit under this provision must file application with Department, and total amount of credits allowed in any state fiscal year shall not exceed $2,500,000. (IC6-3.1-9-4 and 5). Applications will be acted upon in order of submission and once $2,500,000 limit is reached no further applications will be approved. (IC6-3.1-9-5).

Energy System Credit.—Any person, corporation, or partnership subject to gross or adjusted gross or supplemental net income tax is entitled to credit against such tax in amount based on type and use of qualified energy system. (IC6-3.1-8-1 to 12).

Additional credits are provided for: Companies that qualify for Economic Development for a Growing Economy tax credit (IC6-3.1-13); investing in special state corporations formed by lieutenant governor (IC6-3.1-5-1 to 16); entering into agreement to invest in or employ inmates within correctional facilities (IC6-3.1-6-1 to 5); lending money to entities in "enterprise zones" (IC6-3.1-7-1 to 6); qualified investments in enterprise zones (IC6-3.1-10-1 to 9); industrial recovery sites (IC6-3.1-11-1 to 23); incurring certain Indiana qualified research expenses (IC6-3.1-4-1 to 6); hiring math and science teachers during summer recess (IC6-3.1-2-1 to 7); preserving or rehabilitating historic property (IC6-3.1-16); owning and operating maternity home in Indiana (IC6-3.1-14-1 to 8); incurring certain qualified costs to build or refurbish riverboat (IC6-3.1-17-1 to 8); and incurring certain qualified costs to rehabitate property within military base recovery site (IC6-3.1-11.5).

Deductions.—Deduction of up to $2,000 is provided for income, including retirement or survivor's benefits, received by individual or his surviving spouse for individual's service in armed forces of U.S. provided recipient has attained age 60. (IC6-3-2-4). Individual may also deduct difference between first $2,000 received from federal civil service annuity which is included in adjusted gross income under IRC §62, and total amount of Social Security benefits and railroad retirement benefits received. (IC6-3-2-3.7). Individual renting dwelling as principal place of residence may deduct lesser of amount of rent paid during taxable year or $1,500. Deduction not available for dwelling exempt by Indiana property tax. (IC6-3-2-6). Resident individual receives deduction limited to lesser of $1,000 or cost of installing new insulation in three year old residence. (IC6-3-2-5). Deduction available for certain export sales. (IC6-3-2-13).

Exemption is provided for: Organizations described in IRC §501 (except as to unrelated business income of most such organizations); S corporations; corporations subject to financial institutions tax; insurance companies subject to tax under state insurance law; international banking facilities, building and loan associations (IC6-3-2-2.8, IC6-5.5-9-4); all fares collected for public transportation services which qualify for gross income tax exemption (IC6-3-2-3.5). Exemption provided up to $1,000 for certain law enforcement rewards. (IC6-3-2-17). Lottery prize money is exempt. (IC6-3-2-14). Amount deposited by employer in employee's medical care savings account is exempt in taxable year of deposit and is exempt in taxable year of withdrawal if used for payment of eligible medical expenses unless taxpayer excluded or deducted amount deposited into medical care savings account from adjusted gross income under IRC §106, IRC §220 or any other section of Internal Revenue Code. (IC6-3-2-18).

Multistate Tax Compact.—Indiana's membership terminated July 1, 1977.

County Adjusted Gross Income Tax.—Unless County Option Income Tax is in effect, every county is authorized to impose tax on adjusted gross income of all county taxpayers ("county taxpayer" meaning only individuals), and on taxpayers residing in other counties not imposing County Adjusted Gross Income Tax, County Option Income Tax or County Economic Development Income Tax but working in taxing county. (IC6-3.5-1.1-1 and 2).

Rate of Tax.—County may impose a rate of .5%, .75% or 1% on adjusted gross income of resident taxpayers, and .25% on other taxpayers from counties without tax but working in taxing county. (IC6-3.5-1.1-2). County council may decrease county adjusted gross income tax rate pursuant to specified procedures. (IC6-3.5-1.1-3.1).

Credits.—Individual allowed credit for elderly and totally disabled under IRC §22 is entitled to credit equal to lesser of tax imposed or credit for elderly multiplied by county rate and divided by .15. (IC6-3.5-1.1-7). Credits allowed to: county taxpayers for tax liability to governmental entities of another state on income derived outside Indiana but subject to this tax. (IC6-3.5-1-6). Credits may be subject to certain reciprocity requirements. (IC6-3.5-1.1-17).

Collection and Administration of Tax.—Except where expressly provided, all provisions of adjusted gross income tax (IC6-3 et seq.) are applicable to imposition, collection and administration of tax. Employers must annually submit report to Department along with annual withholding report of amount of withholdings attributable to each county. (IC6-3.5-1.1-18).

County Economic Development Income Tax imposed by IC6-3.5-7-1 et seq.

County Option Income Tax.—Every county income tax council of any county in which County Adjusted Gross Income Tax will not be in effect may impose County Option Income Tax on "adjusted gross income" of county taxpayers ("county taxpayer" meaning only individuals) and on taxpayers residing in other counties not imposing County Option Income Tax, County Adjusted Gross Income Tax or County Economic Development Income Tax but working in taxing county. (IC6-3.5-6-1 and 8). Except as provided in IC6-3.5-7-1, term "adjusted gross income" has same meaning as set forth in IC6-3-1-3.5(a) for adjusted gross income tax purposes.

Rate of Tax.—County may initially impose rate of 0.2% on adjusted gross income of resident taxpayers, and 0.05% on other taxpayers from counties without tax but working in taxing county. (IC6-3.5-6-8). If tax is imposed, then rate in effect for resident county taxpayers increases by 0.1% each succeeding year until rate equals 0.6%. (IC6-3.5-6-8). By ordinance, county may then increase rate by 0.1% each year up to maximum rate of 1%. (IC6-3.5-6-9). County income tax council may decrease county option income tax rate pursuant to specified procedures. (IC6-3.5-6-12.5). Rate in effect for county taxpayers who are not resident county taxpayers is at all times one-fourth of tax rate imposed on resident country taxpayers. (IC6-3.5-6-8).

Credits.—Individual allowed credit for elderly and totally disabled under IRC §22 is entitled to credit. (IC6-3.5-6-24). Credit also available for tax liability to government entities of another state. (IC6-3.5-6-23).

Collection and Administration of Tax.—Except where expressly provided, all provisions of adjusted gross income tax (IC6-3 et seq.) are applicable to imposition, collection and administration of tax. Employers must annually submit report to Department along with annual withholding report of amount of withholdings attributable to each county. (IC6-3.5-6-22).

Gross Income Tax.—Gross income tax applies to all corporations, other than S corporations, corporations subject to Financial Institutions Tax, certain organizations of nonprofit character and small business corporations which are eligible to be, but do not elect to be, S corporations. (IC6-2.1-1-1 et seq.) However, small business corporation is not exempt from gross income if 25% or more of its gross income consists of passive investment income. (IC6-2.1-3-24.5). Gross income tax does not apply to gross income received by individuals, partnerships (however, amounts received by corporations as distributive shares of corporate partnership's income is not exempt), trusts, or estates. (IC6-2.1-1-1 et seq., IC6-2.1-1-16, IC6-2.1-3-24, 24.5, 25). See subhead Adjusted Gross Income Tax, supra. Indiana corporations are taxed on entire gross income, except on income derived from interstate transactions (304 U.S. 307), on income from business situs which is outside state, or on income from activities incident to such business (IC6-2.1-1-2[c]). Foreign corporations are taxed on gross income from sources within state. (IC6-2.1-2-2). Gross income is defined with considerable detail. (IC6-2.1-1-2).

High rate for gross income tax is 1.2% and low rate is .3%. Low rate is imposed on gross income from certain wholesale sales, display advertising, retailing, dry cleaning and laundry (excluding gross income from coin operated facilities), water conditioning, renting accommodations for less than 30 day periods and commercial printing. High rate is imposed on gross income from any other sources. (IC6-2.1-2-3, 4, 5). When taxpayer receives income taxable at different rates, whole is taxable at highest rate unless parts are segregated. (IC6-2.1-2-7).

Exemptions and Deductions.—Every taxpayer is entitled to deduct $1,000 per year from gross income, allocated to portion of year covered by return. (IC6-2.1-4-1). Also deductible is amount equal to depreciation deduction allowable for federal income tax purposes for resource recovery systems which process solid and hazardous waste. (IC6-2.1-4-3). Following items of income are exempt: Income derived from interstate commerce or commerce with foreign countries, interest and earnings paid upon bond or other securities issued by U.S., and sales to U.S. government, to extent U.S. Constitution prohibits taxing of foregoing by state; taxes received or collected as agent for state or U.S.; amounts received under life insurance policies by reason of death or personal injury of insured; amounts received under life insurance endowments or annuity contracts, not in excess of total premiums paid thereon; amounts received under health or disability insurance contracts; amounts received from property damage insurance used for replacement; certain amounts received by charitable, religious, scientific, educational, civic not for profit corporations and cemetery associations; amounts received by fraternities, sororities, or student housing organizations which are connected with educational institution; amounts received by hospitals licensed by Indiana State Board of Health and shared hospital services organizations exempt from federal income tax under IRC §501(c)(3) or (e); all amounts subject to tax on gross receipts from athletic exhibitions, under IC25-9-1; all amounts received by insurance companies which pay tax of more than 1% upon premiums; retailers' federal excise taxes; amounts received

INCOME TAX . . . *continued*
from condemnation of real estate by state; amounts represented by any encumbrance on tangible personal property received by retail merchant in reciprocal exchange for tangible personal property of like kind; gross receipts received from transportation and related charges for moving goods by truck or rail or passengers by bus or rail in initial, intermediate or final link in interstate commerce; gross receipts from sale or reciprocal exchange of new, untitled and unregistered motor vehicles between registered motor vehicle dealer, enfranchised by same motor vehicle manufacturer or distributor to sell or service motor vehicles of same make; gross receipts derived from national broadcasting networks for broadcasting national network programs; qualified increased enterprise zone gross income; gross income received by conservancy district established under IC13-3-4 (before its repeal effective July 1, 1995) or IC14-33-20, regional water, sewage or solid waste district established under IC13-3-2, and county solid waste management district or joint solid waste management district established under IC13-9.5-2; gross income received by not-for-profit corporation formed solely to supply water to public; gross income received by partnership (other than IRC §7704 publicly traded partnership); sales of lottery tickets authorized by IC4-30 are exempt; and gross receipts from gambling game conducted by entity that possesses owner's license. (IC6-2.1-3-1 to 35).

Also exempt: Certain fares collected for public transportation services (IC6-2.1-3-27), value of mortgage on receipts from sale of real estate (IC6-2.1-3-16), amounts received after Dec. 31, 1964 by state municipal corporations and political subdivisions of state, and state agencies and instrumentalities, from operation of park and recreation facilities, sale or lease of property, or performance of similar governmental services (IC6-2.1-3-29), and gross receipts of international banking facility (IC6-2.1-3-31).

Returns and Payment of Tax.—Subject to certain exceptions, taxpayer who utilizes taxable year that ends on Dec. 31 shall file taxpayer's estimated gross income tax return and pay tax on or before Apr. 20, June 20, Sept. 20, and Dec. 20. Taxpayer who utilizes taxable year which does not end on Dec. 31 shall file taxpayer's estimated gross income tax return and pay tax on or before 20th day of fourth, sixth, ninth and 12th months of taxable year. (IC6-2.1-5-1). Amount due with each estimated return shall be equal to 25% of estimated or exact amount of gross income tax due, minus gross income tax withheld pursuant to IC6-2.1-6. If taxpayer's estimated annual gross income tax liability does not exceed $1,000, then taxpayer is not required to file estimated gross income tax return. (IC6-2.1-5-1[d]). Taxpayer's annual return must be filed on or before 15th day of third month of taxable year. (IC6-2.1-5-2). Taxpayer must use same fiscal year as used for federal income tax purposes. (IC6-2.1-1-15). Parent corporation and subsidiaries may make consolidated return and are entitled to deduct with certain limitations that portion of gross income which is received from transactions between such members as are incorporated in Indiana or duly authorized to do business therein. (IC6-2.1-4-6, IC6-2.1-5-5)..

Exempt organizations must file an application for exemption with Department and must file annual information returns. (IC6-2.1-3-19 to 22).

Tax on a conveyance of an interest in real estate by a corporation must be paid before recording. (IC6-2.1-8-6).

Deficiencies in amount of tax paid, plus interest from due date or at adjusted rate established by commissioner, payable upon notice and demand by Department. (IC6-8.1-8-2, IC6-8.1-10-1).

Penalties of 100% for fraud added to deficiencies, and knowingly failing to file return is class A misdemeanor. (IC6-8.1-10-4). Failure to file return or pay tax when due may result in 10% penalty. (IC6-8.1-10-2.1). If taxpayer fails to make return within 30 days from date of notice on his original failure to file return, Department may prepare return from best information available and add penalty of 20% of tax plus interest from due date. (IC6-8.1-10-3). If any tax is not paid within 30 days after due date and within ten days after demand notice, warrant may be issued, which warrant may be recorded by circuit court clerk where taxpayer has property and will become judgment lien on such property, and which warrant will further be directed to sheriff, commanding levy on property of delinquent taxpayer for amount of tax plus damages of 10% of tax, appropriate penalties, interest, and costs of executing warrant. (IC6-8.1-8-2, 3). Court may award Department attorney's fees in valid collection action. (IC6-8.1-8-4). Warrant will authorize Department to levy against taxpayer's property held by financial institutions, garnish wages and levy upon and sell tangible property. (IC6-8.1-8-8). Delinquent taxpayer may be enjoined from engaging in business until tax is paid. (IC6-8.1-8-5). In addition to above penalties, fine of not more than $1,000, or imprisonment not exceeding six months, or both, may be imposed for failure or refusal to file return or making false or fraudulent return with intent to defraud state or evade payment of tax. (IC6-2.1-7-4).

Withholding required on all payments, including payments by any kind of governmental agency, to nonresident corporate contractors for performance within state of contracts other than contracts of sale. (IC6-2.1-6-1).

Supplemental net income tax is imposed on net income of every corporation excluding corporations subject to Financial Institutions Tax but not domestic insurance companies. (IC6-3-8-1, 2 and 5, IC6-5.5-9-4).

Rate of Tax.—Rate of supplemental net income tax is 4.5%. (IC6-3-8-4.1).

Collection and Administration of Tax.—Imposition, collection, payment, and administration are governed by IC6-3 et seq., except IC6-3-3-2 and IC6-3-3-5 providing for certain credits do not apply, and IC6-3-2-2 does not apply to allocation or apportionment of domestic insurance company net income. (IC6-3-8-5).

Neighborhood assistance tax credit (IC6-3.1-9-1 to 6) is available to every corporation subject to supplemental net income tax (IC6-3.1-9-1).

INHERITANCE TAX:

Inheritance tax is imposed and regulated by IC6-4.1-1-1 et seq.

Department is charged with enforcement of Act and will provide forms required. Department, 202 State Office Building, Indianapolis, Indiana 46204.

Taxable Transfers: (1) By will; (2) under laws of intestate succession; (3) made in contemplation of transferor's death (transfer within one year prior to death presumed to have been so made); (4) made in such manner that they are intended to take effect in possession or enjoyment at or after transferor's death; (5) made in payment of claim against transferor's estate, provided that claim is result of contract or antenuptial agreement made by transferor and payment of amount claimed is due at or after transferor's death under terms of his will or contract; (6) exercise, by surviving joint owner or owners, of rights to immediate ownership or possession and enjoyment of property held jointly by surviving joint owner or owners and decedent is taxable transfer, and total value of jointly held property is subject to tax, less value of that portion of jointly held property which surviving joint owner or owners prove belonged to him or them; (7) made by deed of trust in such manner that transferor reserves to himself any interest or reserves to himself and others powers of revocation, alteration, or amendment which if exercised would cause property to revert to transferor is taxable transfer upon death of transferor, and value of property subject to tax is equal to value of property subject to powers, and in respect to which powers remain unexercised at transferor's death; (8) made to executor or trustee in lieu of executor or trustee's fee, and value to be taxed is amount by which value of property transferred exceeds fee that would have been due if transfer had not been made. If transfer described in (1) through (5) is made for valuable consideration, value of property transferred is reduced by equivalent in money value of consideration received by transferor. "Consideration" does not include love and affection. (IC6-4.1-2-4 to 7).

Property Taxed.—Subject to conditions and limitations, tax applies to property interest transfer: made by resident decedent in real property located in state (unless real property was transferred without retained interest to irrevocable trust during decedent's lifetime and transfer was not made in contemplation of transferor's death), tangible personal property which does not have actual situs outside state, and intangible personal property wherever located; made by nonresident decedent in real property located in state (unless real property was transferred without retained interest to irrevocable trust during decedent's lifetime and transfer was not made in contemplation of transferor's death), tangible personal property having actual situs in state. (IC6-4.1-2-2 and 3). Real property located outside state is not subject to tax, regardless of whether property is held in trust or whether trustee is required to distribute property in-kind. (IC6-4.1-2-2[b][1]).

Deductions.—

Resident Decedent.—For resident decedent following items may be deducted from value of property interests transferred by will or laws of intestate succession or under trust: Decedent's debts which are lawful claims against his resident estate; taxes on decedent's real property which is located in this state and subject to inheritance tax if real property taxes were lien at time of decedent's death; taxes on decedent's personal property which is located in this state and subject to inheritance tax if personal property taxes are personal obligation of decedent or lien against property and if taxes were unpaid at time of decedent's death; taxes imposed on decedent's income to date of death if taxes were unpaid at time of his death; inheritance, estate, or transfer taxes, other than federal estate taxes, imposed by other jurisdictions with respect to intangible personal property which is subject to inheritance tax; mortgages or special assessments which, at time of decedent's death, were lien on any of decedent's real property which is located in this state and subject to inheritance tax (but only from value of real property encumbered by mortgage or special assessment); decedent's funeral expenses; amounts, up to $1,000, paid for memorial for decedent; expenses incurred in administering property subject to the inheritance tax, including but not limited to reasonable attorney fees, personal representative fees, and trustee fees; amount of any allowance provided to resident decedent's dependent children by IC29-1-4-1; value of any property actually received by resident decedent's surviving spouse in satisfaction of allowance provided by IC29-1-4-1, regardless if claim for allowance filed under IC29-1-14. (IC6-4.1-3-13).

Deductions from property interests transferred by resident decedent other than by will or laws of intestate succession or under trust are: inheritance, estate, or transfer taxes, other than federal estate taxes, imposed by other jurisdictions with respect to intangible personal property which is subject to inheritance tax; liens against property interests that are transferred; decedent's debts and funeral expenses and estate administration expenses, including reasonable attorney's fees incurred in filing inheritance tax return, and in addition, any portion of deduction for amount of allowance provided to resident decedent's children by IC29-1-4-1 which is not needed to reduce to zero value of probate property transferred by decedent may be deducted from value of nonprobate property transferred by decedent to his children who are entitled to such allowance, each such child entitled to equal share of deduction. (IC6-4.1-3-14).

Nonresident Decedents.—For nonresident decedents, deductions from value of property interests transferred are: Taxes other than federal estate taxes; expenses incurred in administering property subject to inheritance tax, including but not limited to reasonable attorney fees, personal representative fees and trustee fees; liens against property so transferred; claims against decedent's domiciliary estate which are allowed by court having jurisdiction over that estate and which will not be paid from that estate because it is exhausted. (IC6-4.1-3-15).

Exemptions and Rates of Tax.—

General Exemptions.—Transfer of property to cemetery association if property used for cemetery purposes; proceeds of life insurance which do not become subject to distribution as part of his estate and subject to claims against his estate; each property interest which decedent transfers to surviving spouse; each transfer described in IRC §2055(a); annuity or other payment to extent excluded from federal gross estate under IRC §2039. Transfers of property interests described in IRC §2056(b) that were exempt from inheritance tax will be subject to that tax at death of surviving spouse. (IC6-4.1-3-1, 1.5, 6, 6.5 to 7). Specified amounts exempt for transfers to classes of transferees. (IC6-4.1-3-9.1 to 12).

Rates of tax and exemptions based on class vary according to relationship of beneficiary and amount of transfer, as follows:

Each property interest decedent transfers to surviving spouse is exempt from inheritance tax.

Class A.—Lineal ancestor or descendant of transferor. Adopted children are treated as if they are natural children of adopting parents. If relationship of loco parentis has existed for period of ten years and if relationship began before child's 15th birthday child is considered natural child of loco parentis parent. (IC6-4.1-1-3).

See note at head of Digest as to 1998 legislation covered.

See Topical Index in front part of this volume.

INHERITANCE TAX... *continued*

Exemptions in Class A are: If transfer to child of transferor who is under 21 years at time of transferor's death, then entitled to exclude $10,000 of property interest so transferred per child. (IC6-4.1-3-9.1). If transfer to child of transferor who is at least 21 at time of transferor's death, then entitled to exclude $5,000 of property interest so transferred per child. (IC6-4.1-3-9.5). If transfer to parent, then entitled to exclude $5,000 of property interest transferred to each parent. (IC6-4.1-3-9.7). Any other member of class, $2,000. (IC6-4.1-3-10).

Rates of tax for Class A are: 1% on amount by which amount or value of transfer exceeds exemption and deductions applicable and does not exceed $25,000; 2% on next $25,000 or part thereof (excess over $25,000 up to $50,000); 3% on next $150,000 or part thereof (excess over $50,000 up to $200,000); 4% on next $100,000 or part thereof (excess over $200,000 up to $300,000); 5% on next $200,000 or part thereof (excess over $300,000 up to $500,000); 6% on next $200,000 or part thereof (excess over $500,000 up to $700,000); 7% on next $300,000 or part thereof (excess over $700,000 up to $1,000,000); 8% on next $500,000 or part thereof (excess over $1,000,000 up to $1,500,000); 10% on excess over $1,500,000. (IC6-4.1-5-1).

Class B.—Brother or sister of transferor; descendant of brother or sister of transferor; spouse, widow or widower of child of transferor. (IC6-4.1-1-3).

Exemptions in Class B are: $500 to any member of class. (IC6-4.1-3-11).

Rates of tax for Class B are: 7% on amount by which amount or value of transfer exceeds exemption and deductions applicable and does not exceed $100,000; 10% on next $400,000 or part thereof (excess over $100,000 up to $500,000); 12% on next $500,000 or part thereof (excess over $500,000 up to $1,000,000); 15% on excess over $1,000,000. (IC6-4.1-5-1).

Class C.—All others.

Exemptions in Class C are: $100 to any member of class. (IC6-4.1-3-12).

Rates of tax for Class C are: 10% on amount by which amount or value of transfer exceeds exemption and deductions applicable and does not exceed $100,000; 15% on next $900,000 or part thereof (excess over $100,000 up to $1,000,000); and 20% on excess over $1,000,000. (IC6-4.1-5-1).

Basis of Tax.—Tax is imposed on fair market value of property minus specified exemptions and deductions. (IC 6-4.1-5-1).

Tax Report and Schedule.—Executors, administrators, trustees, heirs, etc., must file inheritance tax report and schedule of property with probate court within 12 months after death of resident decedent. (IC6-4.1-4-1). Personal representative of nonresident decedent's estate or trustee or transferee of property transferred by decedent must file inheritance tax report and schedule of property with Department, Inheritance Tax Division, State Office Building, Indianapolis, Indiana 46204, within 12 months after nonresident decedent's death. (IC6-4.1-4-7). No return or statement is required if value of transferred property does not exceed exemption amounts. (IC6-4.1-4-0.5).

Value.—In general, each future, contingent, defeasible, or life interest in property and each annuity is determined by using rules, methods, standards of mortality and actuarial tables used by Internal Revenue Service on Oct. 1, 1988, for federal estate tax purposes. (IC6-4.1-6-1[a]).

Value of future interest in specific property equals remainder of: (1) Total value of property minus (2) value of all others' interest in property. (IC6-4.1-6-1[b]).

Any property interest which may be divested because of act or omission of transferee shall be appraised as if there was no possibility of divestment. (IC6-4.1-6-2).

When it is impossible to compute present value of property interest transferred or tax on transfer cannot be computed because contingency makes it impossible to determine who will take property, personal representative of estate, or trustee of trust, without approval of probate court, may enter into agreement with Department to have Department determine tax due. However, if contingency makes it impossible to determine each transferee's exact interest and no agreement is made between taxpayer and Department, then appropriate probate court shall, so far as possible, determine manner in which property will probably be distributed. Unless this court determination is appealed, it is final and binding on all parties. (IC6-4.1-6-3 and 4). If proceedings are not instituted to determine inheritance tax due by transfer of contingent or defeasible future interest in property, or inheritance tax due is postponed until enjoyment or possession of property, property interest shall be appraised at its fair market value when transferee of interest obtains beneficial enjoyment or possession of property. (IC6-4.1-6-6).

Appraisal Date.—Value of assets is determined as of date used to value property interest for federal estate tax purposes or, if no federal estate tax return filed, as of date of decedent's death. (IC6-4.1-5-1.5).

Determination of Tax.—Tax on transfer by a resident of the state is determined by the appropriate court having probate jurisdiction of the decedent's estate. After filing of the tax return, court refers return to county inheritance tax appraiser to appraise fair market value of property in estate and if it appears to court's satisfaction that no tax could be payable, it enters decree to that effect. Otherwise provision is made for notice of appraisal, hearing upon appraisal report and rehearing to persons interested or department of state revenue. Court may impose appraisal charge where no inheritance tax is due and net worth of decedent's estate is $500. (IC6-4.1-5-2 to 13). Person may obtain rehearing of probate court's determination if petition for rehearing is filed with probate court within 120 days after determination is made. (IC6-4.1-7-1). Person may petition court for reappraisal within one year after entry of order determining value of estate and tax thereon or within two years in cases where tax determination has been fraudulently or erroneously made. (IC6-4.1-7-2).

Department shall determine inheritance tax imposed as result of nonresident decedent's death. Department may appraise property transferred by decedent and determine tax due without intervention of court. (IC6-4.1-5-14). Any appeal from this determination shall be made to probate court of county in which administration of decedent's estate is pending; or, if no administration is pending, probate court of any county in which any of decedent's property was located at time of his death within 90 days after notice of department's determination of inheritance tax due. (IC6-4.1-7-5).

Resident or special administrator may be appointed by Probate Court of Marion County for nonresident decedent's estate if Department shows that property interest transferred by decedent under taxable transfer has not been properly appraised for inheritance tax purposes and that property involved is located in this state or that decedent has been dead for at least two years and inheritance tax as determined by Department has not been paid. (IC6-4.1-9-12).

Tax on Future Estates.—Inheritance tax imposed on decedent's transfer of contingent or defeasible interest in property accrues and is due when transferee of interest obtains beneficial enjoyment or possession of property if fair market value of property interest as of appraisal date cannot otherwise be ascertained. (IC6-4.1-6-6[b]).

Liability for Tax.—Trustees, executors or administrators of estates and transferees are personally liable for the tax. (IC6-4.1-8-1).

Personal representative or trustee may not transfer or deliver property to transferee unless inheritance tax imposed with respect to transfer has been paid. (IC6-4.1-8-2). Personal representative or trustee may sell property of decedent to pay inheritance tax. (IC6-4.1-8-3).

Person holding personal property of resident decedent including property held jointly shall not transfer such property without written consent of Department or county assessor of deceased's domicile at death, unless surviving joint tenant is decedent's surviving spouse or if property is money held in joint checking account. Person with possession over or control of personal property subject to inheritance or estate tax which is held in trust at time of resident decedent's death may only transfer property without written consent of department of state revenue or county assessor if (i) transferee is decedent's surviving spouse; or (ii) transferee is domiciled in Indiana and files sworn affidavit that property isn't subject to inheritance or estate tax and reasons property is not subject to tax with department of state revenue. If transfer is made without requisite consent, transferor is liable for tax and also subject to penalty of not more than $1,000. (IC6-4.1-8-4 and 7).

Tax is lien on property transferred, provided that such lien expires five years after death. (IC6-4.1-8-1).

Payment.—Inheritance tax due 18 months after date of decedent's death or within 30 days of final determination of inheritance tax redetermination. (IC6-4.1-9-1 and 1.5). Tax on transfer of property of a resident of the state is payable to treasurer of county where resident decedent was domiciled at time of death. (IC6-4.1-9-5). If one believes more tax due than determined by court, he can pay additional tax and interest without court order. Tax on transfer or property of nonresident is payable to Department. (IC6-4.1-9-4). In either case, if tax is paid within one year from date of decedent's death deduction of 5% is allowed, while if tax is not paid within 18 months from date of decedent's death interest at 10% from date is assessed, although interest rate reduced to 6% if nonpayment due to unavoidable delay. (IC6-4.1-9-1, 2 and 5).

Confidentiality of Information.—Information gained from contents of safety deposit box of decedent is confidential and it is misdemeanor for anyone required by this act to examine such box for tax purposes to disclose any information gained therefrom except for collection of taxes under this Act. (IC6-4.1-8-6, 8).

Compromise Agreements.—Department may enter into compromise agreement as to amount of inheritance tax due or interest charges on delinquent inheritance tax provided approval of attorney general is given and both department and attorney general have substantial doubt as to: (1) right to impose tax under applicable Indiana law; (2) constitutionality under either Indiana or U.S. Constitutions of tax; (3) correct value of property transferred under taxable transfer; (4) correct amount of tax due; (5) collectability of tax; or (6) whether decedent was resident or nonresident of this state. (IC6-4.1-12-5).

See also category Property, topic Personal Property.

MOTOR VEHICLE USAGE TAX:

County Motor Vehicle Excise Surtax.—In certain counties. (IC6-3.5-4-1 et seq.).

Motor Vehicle Excise Tax.—See category Transportation, topic Motor Vehicles, subhead Excise Tax and IC6-6-5-1 et seq. Trailer excise tax (IC 6-6-5-5.5). Auto Rental Excise Tax (IC6-6-9-1 to 11) which imposes upon rental of passenger motor vehicles in Indiana for period less than 30 days 4% tax on such gross retail income.

County Wheel Tax.—In certain counties. (IC6-3.5-5-1 et seq.).

Boat Excise Tax.—Imposed by IC6-6-11 et seq.

Boat may not be operated, used, docked or stored in Indiana unless boat excise tax, department of natural resources fees, and lake and river enhancement fees have been paid for that year and required decals are affixed (with certain exceptions). Boats subject to boat excise tax are not subject to Indiana personal property tax. (IC6-6-11-8). Exemption provided for boats: (1) Owned by U.S.; (2) owned by Indiana or political subdivision; (3) owned by IRS §501(c)(3) organization; (4) which are human powered vessels; (5) held by boat manufacturers, distributors, or dealers for sale in ordinary course of business and subject to personal property tax; (6) used by person for production of income and subject to personal property tax; (7) stored in Indiana for less than 22 consecutive days during year and not operated, used or docked in Indiana; (8) registered outside Indiana and operated, used or docked in Indiana for combined total of less than 22 consecutive days during year; and (9) subject to commercial vessel tonnage tax under IC6-6-6. (IC6-6-11-9).

Amount of tax is based on boat class and age. Motorized boats and sailboats are classified for excise tax purposes according to value of boat when boat was new and are taxed at statutory rates set forth in IC6-6-11-10. Tax is $12 for motorized boat or sailboat stored in Indiana for 60 consecutive days or more but not operated, used, or docked in Indiana waters, except to facilitate storage of boat. (IC6-6-11-10). Tax due under IC6-6-11-10 is reduced by 5% for each year since boat was manufactured, but not to exceed 50%. However, tax may not be reduced to less than $6. (IC6-6-11-11). In addition to excise tax, annual $5 natural resources fee and $5 lake and river enhancement fee if decals required. (IC6-6-11-12). Taxes are payable to Bureau of Motor Vehicles at same time owner pays or would pay registration fee and motor vehicle excise tax on motor vehicles under IC9-1-4 and IC6-6-5. (IC6-6-11-13). Additional provisions for situations in which boats are purchased or brought into Indiana after regular annual tax payment date. Credit is available if boat is sold and refund is available if boat is destroyed. (IC6-6-11-14 to 18). 100% delinquent fee for failure to

See note at head of Digest as to 1998 legislation covered.

See Topical Index in front part of this volume.

IN – 50

MOTOR VEHICLE USAGE TAX . . . *continued*
timely pay tax (IC6-6-11-26), and class C infraction and class C misdemeanor sanctions for certain actions in violation of these taxing provisions (IC6-6-11-25, -27).

Aircraft License Excise Tax payable upon obtaining certificate of registration. (IC6-6-6.5-1 et seq.).

Commercial Vessel Tonnage Tax is 3¢ per net ton on any vessel registered at Indiana port on May 1 of any year. (IC6-6-6-1 to -10).

MUNICIPAL BOND EXEMPTION:

Interest on Indiana bonds and similar indebtedness issued in 1959 and thereafter, and proceeds received at maturity or redemption prior to maturity are exempt from taxation except state inheritance tax. Proceeds received by holder on sale are exempt to extent of holder's cost of acquisition. Does not apply to measuring franchise tax imposed on privilege of transacting business of financial institution in Indiana under IC6-5.5. No other statute exempting interest paid on debt obligations of state or local public entity or corporation or other entity leasing real or personal property to state or local public entity applies to measuring franchise tax imposed on financial institutions under IC6-5.5. (IC6-8-5-1).

PROPERTY TAX:

For assessment dates before Mar. 1, 2001, all property not expressly exempt must be valued and assessed for taxation purposes at a uniform and equal rate on a just valuation basis at one-third of its true tax value. (IC6-1.1-1-3, IC6-1.1-2-1 and 2, IC6-1.1-4-1). For assessment dates after Feb. 28, 2001, all property not expressly exempt must be valued and assessed at uniform and equal rate on just valuation basis at true tax value of such property. Certain commercial vessels, motor vehicles and trailers, boats, and property used by certain cemetery is not subject to assessment and taxation under Art. 1.1. (IC6-1.1-2-7).

Sales Disclosure Statement.—No conveyance documents (i.e., deeds, contracts of sale, agreements, certain leases, or any other documents presented for recording) will be accepted by country recorder unless properly completed and executed sales disclosure form is included with document. (IC6-1.1-5.5).

Exemptions.—Property of U.S. (except where U.S. Constitution permits taxation thereof), this state or political subdivision of this state, and city or town used to provide municipal service. (IC6-1.1-10-1 to 6). Generally and under certain conditions, following property is exempt from taxation: Certain property used for educational, literary, scientific, religious, fraternal or charitable purposes, water and sewage systems, public airports, public libraries, cemetery property used for cemetery purposes, church parsonages, and property owned by certain organizations, and nonprofit corporations promoting or housing fine arts, operating health facility, operating residential facility for aged, Christian Science home or sanatorium. (IC6-1.1-10). Tangible property is not exempt from property taxation if it is used by exempt organization in trade or business not substantially related to exercise or performance of organization's exempt purpose. (IC6-1.1-10-36.5). If exempt real or personal property under §2 or 4 is purchased by another person (i) whose property is not exempt, and (ii) who is not engaged in exempt activity with purchased property, then purchased property shall be assessed and taxed as if property were owned by purchaser or purchaser's assignee. (IC6-1.1-10-41). Certain property used predominantly for industrial air pollution control (IC6-1.1-10-12 to 14) and as industrial waste control facility is also exempt (IC6-1.1-10-9 to 11) (including certain spare parts, property under construction or property in process of installation as long as such property will qualify for exemption when placed in service), as is property held under Urban Homestead Statute. Certain in transit property held in public or private warehouses. (IC6-1.1-10-29 to 31). Property held on assessment date in foreign trade zone which was either imported into foreign trade zone or was placed in zone exclusively for export to foreign country. (IC6-1.1-10-30.5). Certain truck chassis, certain passenger motor vehicles, and certain school bus bodies and chassis. (IC6-1.1-10-31.4-31.7). Intangible personal property is exempt (IC6-1.1-10-39). Certain commodities located or stored in warehouse, shipping plant, depositary, or other facility in Indiana that has been designated by board of trade or certain metal exchanges as regular delivery point. (IC6-1.1-10-40). No specific exemptions for members of armed forces. Failure to comply with statutory procedure to obtain exemption amounts to waiver of exemption. (IC6-1.1-11-1). See also IC6-1.1-10-38.

Personal property owned by financial institution subject to bank tax (IC6-5-10) and not leased under circumstances in which possession is transferred to lessee is exempt (IC6-5.5-9-3).

Deductions.—Certain deductions from assessed valuation allowed for disabled veterans and veteran's surviving spouse (IC6-1.1-12-13, 14, 16), blind or disabled persons (IC6-1.1-12-11), persons over 65 (IC6-1.1-12-9), real property subject to mortgage or being purchased under recorded land contract which provides that buyer is to pay property taxes (IC6-1.1-12-1), increases in assessments of certain rehabilitated real property which do not exceed certain levels of assessed valuation (IC6-1.1-12-18 to 22), of solar energy heating or cooling systems (IC6-1.1-12-26), resource recovery systems (IC6-1.1-12-28.5), wind power devices (IC6-1.1-12-29), increases in assessment of certain real property located in economic revitalization areas (IC6-1.1-12.1-1 to 12), certain coal conversion systems (IC6-1.1-12-31), certain maritime opportunity districts (IC6-1.1-40 et seq.), hydroelectric power devices and geothermal energy heating or cooling devices (IC6-1.1-12-33, 34), real property that qualifies for homestead credit (IC6-1.1-12-37) and certain contracts with respect to which buyer of property is required to pay property tax under IC6-1.1-10-41 (IC6-1.1-12-39).

"Homestead Credit".—Credit available to individuals and certain other taxpayers who on Mar. 1 of year either own or are buying homestead under contract requiring purchaser to pay taxes. Homestead means individual's principal residence in Indiana consisting of dwelling and immediately surrounding real estate not exceeding one acre. Credit may be claimed by filing statement with county auditor during 12 months before May 11 of year prior to first year of credit. (IC6-1.1-20.9-1 et seq.).

Assessment.—Personal property is listed for taxation between Mar. 1 and May 15 of each year, with reference to quantity held or owned on first day of Mar. in year for which property is required to be listed. Household goods and automobiles are excluded. Realty is listed and assessed by township assessor. Reassessment of real property must begin July 1, 1999, and each fourth year thereafter. Each reassessment must be completed by Mar. 1 of immediately following odd-numbered year and is basis for taxes payable in year following year in which assessment is completed unless consolidated returns are filed with county assessor. (IC6-1.1-4-4). Assessment returns of personal property are filed with township assessor. (IC6-1.1-3-7). From assessment of township assessor, appeal may be taken to county board of review. Appeal lies from county board to State Board, and from State Board to Indiana Tax Court. (IC6-1.1). Class action suit before any court, including Indiana Tax Court, may not be maintained on behalf of any person who has not complied with administrative requirements prior to certification of class. (IC6-1.1-15-15). Taxpayer must be informed in writing of opportunity and procedures for review at time notice of assessment is given and after each step of administrative procedure. (IC6-1.1-9-1, IC6-1.1-15-1 et seq.). When claim for refund is allowed on appeal, amount shall be equal to amount of claim plus 6% interest. (IC6-1.1-26-5[a]).

A special procedure for assessment of property of public utilities is provided. (IC6-1.1-8-1 et seq.).

There are special provisions relating to reassessments of real estate (IC6-1.1-4-5 to 12), and personal property, one of which provides for reassessment of property values and corresponding tax adjustment in areas sustaining substantial amount of damage and destruction due to disaster (IC6-1.1-4-11). Another applies to counties having populations between 140,000 and 200,000 people. IC6-1.1-4-13.5, 21.5 repealed effective Jan. 1, 1996. Another allows for percentage deduction from assessed valuation over five year period for qualifying rehabilitation of property 50 years or older. (IC6-1.1-12-22).

Return and Payment of Tax.—On or before May 15 of each year taxpayer shall file returns with assessor of each township in which taxpayer's personal property is subject to assessment or may file consolidated return with county assessor if taxpayer has personal property subject to assessment in more than one township in county and total assessed value of personal property in county is less than $1,500,000. (IC6-1.1-1-7, IC6-1.1-3-7). County assessor may refuse to accept consolidated return if there is no attached schedule listing, by township, all personal property and its assessed value. (IC6-1.1-3-7[g]). $25 penalty shall be added to next installment for failure to file return or include requisite information. In addition, 20% penalty shall be added for failure to file return within 30 days after such return is due. (IC6-1.1-37-7). Additional penalties are provided for failing to report property and for undervaluing property. (IC6-1.1-37-7, 7.5, 9, 10). Property taxes are payable in two equal installments: First half becomes delinquent if not paid on or before May 10th of year following year of assessment; second installment becomes delinquent if not paid on or before Nov. 10th of year following year of assessment. (IC6-1.1-22-9). Personal property taxes are payable to treasurer of county in which property is assessed; real property taxes are payable to treasurer of county in which realty is situated. (IC6-1.1-3-1, IC6-1.1-4-1, IC6-1.1-22-8). No discount is allowed for prompt payment but penalty of 10% is imposed on delinquent taxes and underpayments. (IC6-1.1-37-9, 10). On May 10th and Nov. 10th in each year following year of initial delinquency, additional penalty of 10% of any tax remaining unpaid shall be added, unless payment delayed by emergency. (IC6-1.1-37-10).

Collection.—Collection is made by county treasurer, who sells property and enters into contracts for collection services where necessary. (IC6-1.1-23-1 et seq.).

Lien.—Taxes attach as a lien on real estate on Mar. 1 of year for which taxes assessed. (IC6-1.1-1-2, IC6-1.1-22-13). Lien remains valid for ten years and is not divested by any sale or transfer. (IC6-1.1-22-13). After written demand has been given and 30 days have passed if total amount due is not paid county treasurer shall levy upon and sell sufficient personal property of taxpayer to pay delinquent taxes, penalties and anticipated collection expenses. (IC6-1.1-23-1, 2). Taxing unit may institute civil suit for delinquent property taxes and may collect penalties, costs and expenses if successful. (IC6-1.1-22-13[d]).

Sales of real estate for taxes take place on or after Aug. 1 and before Nov. 1, annually (IC6-1.1-24-2). If tract or item of real property is offered for sale but statutory minimum amount is not received, it may be offered for sale a second time and county treasurer and county auditor may jointly agree to expedited sale on or after Jan. 1 and before Mar. 31 of year immediately following initial offer for sale, provided such date is at least 90 days after initial offer. (IC6-1.1-24-2, 6-1.1-24-5.5). If minimum sales price is not received in second sale, county acquires lien in amount of minimum sale price which attaches on day on which tract or item was offered for sale second time. (IC6-1.1-24-6). Upon such lien, county commissioners in county having consolidated city may, after public notice and hearings, transfer such property to nonprofit corporation for use for public good. (IC6-1.1-24-6.7). No real estate may be sold until 15 months after installment is delinquent, until payment of special assessment is delinquent or until unpaid costs of prior tax sale incurred by county are due and certain notice requirements are satisfied. (IC6-1.1-24-1 et seq.). Personal property taxes that are delinquent are not to be included in sale of real estate for delinquent taxes. (IC6-1.1-24-5).

Redemption.—Property may be redeemed from private purchaser by payment of delinquent property taxes and delinquent special assessments plus penalty of 10% if within six months, 15% if within second six months, and 25% if after one year, plus amount of purchase price in excess of delinquent property tax and delinquent special assessments plus 7% interest plus annum, plus taxes and special assessments paid after sale plus 12% interest per annum, plus filing fees, plus costs of giving notice, plus costs of updating and examining title abstract, less certain amounts that must be claimed from tax sale surplus fund. (IC6-1.1-25-2). Redemption may be made within specified periods following date of sale. Upon expiration of such periods, no redemption may thereafter be made. (IC6-1.1-25-4). Notice of sale and expiration of period of redemption must be provided within specified periods to owner and any person with substantial property interest of public record. (IC6-1.1-25-4.5, 4.6). Failure to ask for tax deed within two years of sale results in loss of lien as does failure to provide notice prior to specified redemption period. (IC6-1.1-25-7). Tax deed may be set aside if any substantial provision of law has not been complied with, and redemptions are generally favored by courts, even after deed has issued. (IC6-1.1-25-16). Special procedures allow for transfer of certain environmentally hazardous property to petitioner agreeing to eliminate hazardous conditions. (IC6-1.1-25-4.1).

See note at head of Digest as to 1998 legislation covered.

See Topical Index in front part of this volume.

IN – 51

PROPERTY TAX... *continued*

Forest Lands, Windbreaks, Wildlife Habitats, or Filter Strips Property Tax may impose more favorable rates on land falling in defined classifications. (IC6-1.1-6-1 et seq.; IC6-1.1-6.2-1 et seq.; IC6-1.1-6.5-1 et seq.; IC6-1.1-6.7-1 et seq.).

Property Tax Replacement Credit.—Each year taxpayers of each county receive 20% property tax replacement credit against liability for real and personal property taxes. (IC6-1.1-21-5).

Real Estate Conveyance Tax.—None. (However, gross income tax may be due by certain corporations under certain circumstances.)

PUBLIC WELFARE TAXES:

In order to finance program of assistance to certain needy classes, a separate county tax must be levied annually by county council on all taxable property of such county in order to raise portion of fund which that county is obliged to raise subject to limit on amount of levy to be imposed. (IC12-1-11-1, IC6-1.1-18.6-2). Any county which may become indebted by reason of welfare payments may refund its debt and issue serial bonds, and in addition to other tax levies, county council may levy tax to pay interest on such bonds. (IC12-1-11-1, 3, 6, 13).

SALES AND USE TAXES:

Rate is 5% on gross income from retail sales over 90¢. (IC6-2.5-2-2). Tax is added to sales price and borne by purchasers and collected and paid by retail merchants. (IC6-2.5-2-1).

Sales Tax (State Gross Retail Tax).—

Taxable Transactions.—Tax imposed on retail transactions of retail merchants constituting selling at retail (IC6-2.5-1-1 and 2, IC6-2.5-2-1), including transfers of tangible personal property in ordinary course of regularly conducted business (IC6-2.5-4-1), wholesale sales except for certain transactions (IC6-2.5-4-2), regularly furnishing accommodations for less than 30 days (IC6-2.5-4-4), furnishing public utility services, with certain exceptions (IC6-2.5-4-5 to 6), private or proprietary activities of governmental units and agencies where taxable if by retail merchant (except activities by political subdivisions related to annual festival, carnival, fair or similar event) (IC6-2.5-4-8), sales of property for incorporation in structure constituting part of land (IC6-2.5-4-9), leasing tangible personal property (IC6-2.5-4-10), cable television service (IC6-2.5-4-11), auctions of tangible personal property (IC6-2.5-4-12), sales of prepaid telephone calling cards or authorization numbers (IC6-2.5-4-13), sales of cigarettes at retail on full amount of sales price including other taxes imposed (IC6-2.5-4-1[f]), sales of motor fuel at retail on full amount of sales price including other taxes imposed except that part of sales price which is state or federal motor fuel tax (IC6-2.5-4-1[f]), engaging in business of softening and conditioning water (IC6-2.5-4-3).

Exemptions.—(a) Tax does not apply to sales for resale nor to sales: of food for human consumption, excluding food prepared and sold at eating or carry-out establishments and certain specific consumables; of certain specific consumables used by merchant regularly furnishing accomodations for less than 30 days; to farmers of certain items used in production of food and commodities; of nonreturnable and returnable containers under certain circumstances; of newspapers; of tangible personal property or services directly used or consumed in rendering public transportation; to State, counties, townships, municipal corporations and their agencies and instrumentalities of (including county solid waste management districts and joint solid waste management districts established under IC13-9.5-2) tangible personal property, and public utility services and commodities predominantly for use in performing governmental functions; of manufacturing machinery, tools, equipment and utilities to be directly used in the direct production, manufacture, fabrication, assembly, extraction, mining, processing, refining or finishing of tangible personal property; of specific tangible personal property to certain public utilities; of agricultural machinery, tools and equipment to be directly used in agriculture or in animal waste transportation; of tangible personal property to be directly used in direct production or manufacture of exempt manufacturing or agricultural machinery, tools, and equipment; sales of tangible personal property purchased with food stamps; certain sales to and by various educational, cultural, religious, social and charitable organizations; sales of motor vehicles, watercraft, aircraft, and trailers delivered in Indiana for immediate transportation to destination outside of Indiana and to be titled or registered for use in another state; tax does not apply to 35% of gross income received from sales of manufactured homes or of structure that is both industrialized building system and one or two family private residence and sales of preowned manufactured homes; sales of drugs by registered pharmacist or licensed practitioner; sales of insulin and equipment used to administer insulin, oxygen, blood, or plasma when used for medical purposes; sale of non-legend drugs; prescribed orthopedic devices; sale of hearing aids, sales of prescribed dental devices, sales of prescribed eye glasses and contact lenses by licensed seller; rentals of medical equipment, supplies, and devices; sales of tangible personal property incorporated in school building; sales of meals to hospital patients; sales of food prescribed as medically necessary; sales of school meals; sales of tangible personal property to be incorporated as part of public street or public utility service required under approved subdivision plat; sales of tangible personal property constituting or incorporated into, or consumed in operation of environmental device, facility, or structure; sales of tangible personal property used in direct production or publication of free distribution newspaper; sales of free distribution newspaper or printing services performed in publishing free distribution newspaper; and receipts representing charges for serving or delivering food or beverages furnished, prepared or served for consumption at location or on equipment provided by retail merchant (IC6-2.5-5-1 to 33); (b) other receipts exempt from sales tax are: such receipts from interstate commerce and payments by U.S. as state is constitutionally prohibited from taxing; taxes received or collected as agent of state or U.S.; such receipts from sales to U.S. as state is constitutionally prohibited from taxing; certain excise taxes imposed by U.S.; amounts represented by incumbrance on tangible personal property received by retail merchant in reciprocal exchange for property of like kind (IC6-2.5-5-24); sales of engines and chassis that are leased, owned, or operated by professional racing teams, and all spare replacement and rebuilding parts for those items (IC6-2.5-5-37); and like-kind exchanges of vehicles in lease transactions (IC6-2.5-5-38).

Permit.—Every retail merchant must procure certificate and must list each place of business where he makes retail transactions. Manufacturers and wholesalers may apply to Department for certificates. (IC6-2.5-8-1, to -5). Person required to procure certificate if such person: makes retail transactions from outside Indiana to destination in Indiana; does not maintain place of business in Indiana; and engages in regular soliciting of retail transactions from potential customers in Indiana. (IC6-2.5-8-10). Registration fee is $25 for each place of business. (IC6-2.5-8-1). Certificate is valid so long as business is in existence and certificate not revoked by Department for cause or on account of unsatisfied tax liabilities owed by taxpayer. (IC6-2.5-8-5 and 7). Exempt organizations must obtain certificate for which there is no fee. (IC6-2.5-8-4).

Liability for Tax.—Tax must be added to purchase price of goods and purchaser is liable for tax (IC6-2.5-2-1) and retail merchant may not advertise or state to public or any customer that tax will be paid by him (IC6-2.5-9-4). Taxes collected by retail merchant constitute a trust fund owned by State, and retail merchant and officers, employees or members thereof are personally liable for payment of tax, and intentional failure to collect or remit is class D felony. (IC6-2.5-9-3). Retail merchants are entitled to deduct 1% of merchant's accrued state gross retail and use tax liability and retain it as collection allowance. (IC6-2.5-6-10, 11).

Returns and Payments.—Procedures are same as for gross income tax (IC6-8.1-1-1) except that persons collecting sales tax must file return and pay tax collected for previous month to Department 30 days after end of each month if average monthly liabilities for prior year did not exceed $1,000. Otherwise, person must file return and pay taxes collected within 20 days after end of each month. If taxpayer files combined sales and withholding (IC6-3-4-8 and 8.1) report, it must be filed within 20 days of end of preceding month. Permission may be obtained for depositing on quarterly, semiannual or annual basis. (IC6-2.5-6-1).

Penalties.—Upon failure to make a return, return may be computed by Department using best information available, and tax computed thereon. 20% penalty will be added and interest at 12% per year or adjusted rate established by commissioner will be charged, and taxpayer may also be subject to 10% negligence penalty, 100% fraud penalty, and taxpayer knowingly failing to file return commits class A misdemeanor. (IC6-8.1-10-1 to 4).

Use tax is imposed on storage, use or consumption within state of tangible personal property acquired in retail transaction regardless of location of transaction or retail merchant at same rate (5%) as gross retail tax under IC6-2.5-2-2 (IC6-2.5-3-2 and 3), including isolated sales of vehicles, aircraft and watercraft required to be titled, registered, or licensed or registered by state (IC6-2.5-3-2[b]). Storage, use or consumption does not include keeping, retaining or exercising right or power over tangible personal property delivered by, or for purchaser into state solely for processing, printing, fabricating, or manufacturing, attaching or incorporating into other tangible personal property if property is thereafter transported outside state for use solely outside state. (IC6-2.5-3-2[d]).

Exemptions.—Use tax does not apply to storage, use, or consumption within state of tangible personal property sold in state in transaction subject to sales tax or listed as exempt from sales tax under category described under subhead Sales Tax, catchline Exemptions, of this topic. (IC6-2.5-3-4). Burden of proving that property sold by retail merchant for delivery in state has not been purchased for storage, use or consumption within state is placed upon purchaser and also on retail merchant unless he receives exemption certificate from purchaser. (IC6-2.5-3-7). Purchaser of vehicle, watercraft or aircraft must prove payment of sales or use tax in respect to vehicle as prerequisite to titling or registration. Knowingly failing to remit all or part of state use tax due is class A misdemeanor. (IC6-2.5-9-6).

Liability for Tax.—Use tax is paid by purchaser either collected by retail merchant as agent for state or paid directly to Department. (IC6-2.5-3-6). Retail merchants engaged in business within state, if requested, must give receipt to purchaser for amount of tax paid. (IC6-2.5-3-8). Persons subject to use tax are personally liable for tax imposed on transactions for which no receipt or other written evidence of collection of tax was procured from registered retail merchant. (IC6-2.5-3-8).

Credit.—Persons liable for payment of use tax other than on vehicles, watercraft or aircraft that are required to be titled, registered or licensed by State are entitled to credit in amount of any sale, purchase or use tax paid to any other state or to territory or possession of U.S. with respect to acquisition of such property. (IC6-2.5-3-5).

Permit.—Retail merchants engaged in business in the state but not required to register for purposes of sales tax must prior to conducting transactions subject to use tax, apply to Department for certificate. (IC6-2.5-8-1).

Returns and Payments.—Provisions are same as for sales tax. See subhead Sales Tax (State Gross Retail Tax), supra.

UNEMPLOYMENT COMPENSATION TAX:

Unemployment Compensation Tax, in the form of "contributions," is imposed on every employing unit which, in 20 different weeks, whether or not consecutive, employs four or more individuals. Employing units owned or controlled by the same interests are treated as one unit. Exemptions of employing units extend generally to charitable, religious, educational and scientific organizations, and employment is defined to exclude work for governmental units, agricultural labor, domestic service and service by child under 21 years old in employ of parent. (IC22-4-7-1 to 22-4-8-3). Employer's contribution rate is 2.7% or as fixed by Indiana Employment Security Board on basis of statutory merit rating. (IC22-4-11-2, 3). Contributions are payable to Board in such manner as Board may prescribe. Under Board rules, reports must be made quarterly and contributions are payable on or before last day of month following quarter for which such reports and contributions are made.

TRANSPORTATION

MOTOR VEHICLES:

General administration of motor vehicle laws is under Bureau of Motor Vehicles. Commissioner of Motor Vehicles, State Office Building, Indianapolis, Indiana 46204.

See note at head of Digest as to 1998 legislation covered.

See Topical Index in front part of this volume.

IN – 52

MOTOR VEHICLES . . . *continued*

Vehicle license and registration required annually. (IC9-18-2-8). Proof of ownership and financial responsibility required to register. (IC9-18-2-10, 9-18-2-11). Owner of trailer has option to register for two consecutive years; owner of semitrailer has option to register for five consecutive years or permanently. (IC9-18-9-2[2], 9-18-10-2[2], 9-18-10-2[3]). Farm vehicles and new disabled vehicles are exempt. (IC9-18-1-1). Number plate must be displayed in rear (front for farm tractor used in transportation) (IC9-18-2-26) and registration certificate or copy must be kept in vehicle or on person of driver (IC9-18-2-21). Transport operators may secure special registration for all cars transported. (IC9-18-2-23). Members of armed forces not generally exempt, but may register in absentia. (IC9-18-5-1). If active member of armed forces assigned outside of Indiana, is exempt from registration and excise and property taxes for previously-registered vehicle for any year so assigned if vehicle not being operated. (IC9-18-2-1[e]). New residents must register within 60 days. (IC9-18-2-1). Nonresidents are exempt if resident state reciprocates with Indiana. (IC9-18-2-2). Certain dual residents exempt for limited periods of operation. (IC9-18-2-1[d]). Generally, registration in lessee's or owner's county of residence required, unless not in person at full-service branch. (IC9-18-2-13). Unless state's International Registration Plan requires otherwise, leased vehicles subject to motor vehicle excise tax must be registered in lessee's county of residence, unless not in person at full-service branch; other leased vehicles may be registered in county of residence of owner or lessee. (IC9-18-2-13, 9-18-2-15). Commissioner of Bureau of Motor Vehicles may suspend registration for various reasons, including failure to pay parking tickets (IC9-30-11-1 to 8) or to comply with any emissions control rules (IC9-18-2-39, 13-1-1-6), upon conviction for violation of motor vehicle laws (IC9-30-4-6), or for other reasonable grounds (IC9-30-4-1). See IC9-29-4-1, 9-29-5-1 for registration fees, IC9-18-3-1 for exemption of certain vehicles from registration fees.

Operator's license required to operate motor vehicle on Indiana highway or street, unless exempted under IC9-24-1-7. (IC9-24-1-1). Members of armed forces exempt if operating official vehicle of Armed Forces. (IC9-24-1-7[1]). License must be renewed every four years (IC9-24-12-1), or if applicant is 75 years or older every three years (IC9-24-12-1) and must be in immediate possession of operator of motor vehicle (IC9-24-13-3). Reissuance provided for residents temporarily residing outside state with good cause shown (IC9-24-12-6), except that person serving in armed forces has 90 days following discharge in which to obtain reissued license (IC9-24-12-6). Written examination not required for renewal unless applicant is under 21 or has accumulated six or more points on driving record. (IC9-24-12-5). Commercial drivers must have special license unless in approved training course. (IC9-24-1-6). Learner permit not issued to person under 15 years of age (IC9-24-7-1) or persons under 18 years with certain school disciplinary record (IC9-24-2-1); nor operator's license or learner's permit under 18 if person suspended, expelled, or withdrawn from school (IC9-24-2-1) or is delinquent child as determined by juvenile court (IC9-24-2-2); nor validated learner's permit under 16 (IC9-24-7-3); nor operator's license under 16 and one month (IC9-24-3-2); nor public passenger chauffeur's license under 21 (IC9-24-5-2), nor chauffeur's license to person under 18 (IC9-24-4-2); nor commercial driver's license—property—under 18 (IC9-24-6-4) or commercial driver's license—individuals—under 21 (IC9-24-6-3); public passenger chauffeur's license to drive taxicab may be issued to person age 18 and older (IC9-24-5-2[b]). License not issued to minor under 18 without guarantee of financial responsibility by parent or guardian (IC9-24-9-3), or meeting of certain requirements (IC9-24-9-1). Restricted driving permit allowed where suspension of license would result in undue family hardship or where public transportation is unavailable and travel is for certain designated purposes. (IC9-24-15-2, 9-24-15-6.7). Exceptions to restricted permit listed in IC9-24-15-9. Special motorcycle license or endorsement required for operation of motorcycle on public highways. (IC9-24-8-1). Bureau of Motor Vehicles must maintain operating record for each licensed operator, record available on request to insurance carrier. (IC9-24-3-7). State identification card also available from Bureau of Motor Vehicles. (IC9-24-16-1). For permit and license fees see IC9-29-1 to 9-29-13.

Titles and Sales.—Owner must obtain certificate of title, issued by Bureau of Motor Vehicles, and good for life of car while held by original owner. On sale, or within 21 days of sale in case of certain transfers by licensed vehicle dealer, certificate must be assigned to purchaser. (IC9-17-3-3). Unlawful to operate under Indiana registration without certificate. (IC9-17-1-1, et seq., 9-29-4-4). Certified copy of certificate of title is prima facie evidence of ownership of motor vehicle in criminal or civil proceeding. (IC34-40-4-1, IC35-37-4-9). Provision made for certificates of origin for manufacturers and dealers. (IC9-17-8-1, et seq.).

Owner who is in armed forces may authorize transfer of title by letter to Bureau of Motor Vehicles. (IC9-17-3-4).

Liens and Encumbrances.—Applicant for certificate of title must indicate on application all liens and encumbrances on vehicle. (IC9-17-2-2). Upon transfer of any certificate already issued, transferor must list all liens and encumbrances on certificate. (IC9-17-3-3). Lienholder having possession of certificate by reason of lien must surrender same to owner upon satisfaction of lien and failure to so deliver certificate is Class C infraction. (IC9-17-5-1, et seq.). Certificate may not issue to lienholder for reason of repossession except when records show person repossessed from was last registered owner, and lienholder establishes his entitlement to certificate. (IC9-17-5-2).

Identification Marks.—Class C felony to alter or remove engine serial number (IC9-18-8-12) and Class D felony to sell or offer for sale car so altered (IC9-18-8-13). Persons possessing car with altered or destroyed serial number must obtain replacement number within 20 days. (IC9-18-8-2). Vehicle may be impounded for up to 48 hours to determine internal serial numbers if external serial numbers undeterminable. (IC9-18-8-7). Class D felony to misuse identification number assigned to motor vehicle or part thereof or to misuse plate or label containing such number. (IC9-8-8-15). Class C infraction to operate motor vehicle if engine number removed. (IC9-19-8-16).

Operation Prohibited.—Persons with suspended licenses or permits; physically, mentally or legally impaired persons (i.e., illiterates, child support defaulters) cannot get license. (IC9-24-2-3). Class A misdemeanor to operate vehicle while intoxicated. (IC9-30-5-2). Class C misdemeanor to operate vehicle under influence of narcotics or with .10% blood-alcohol content (IC9-30-5-1), or with .02% if under age 21 (IC9-30-5-8.5). Class D felony if cause serious bodily injury. (IC9-30-5-4). Class C felony if prior conviction within five years or if cause death. (IC9-30-5-5.4). Class B felony if cause death and had prior conviction within five years. (IC9-30-5-5). Person who operates motor vehicle impliedly consents to submit to analysis of blood, breath, urine or other bodily substance to determine presence of alcohol or controlled substance. (IC9-30-7-2). Commissioner of Bureau of Motor Vehicles may for good cause suspend or revoke driver's right to operate. (IC9-30-4-1). Court may order driving privileges restricted to automobiles equipped with alcohol ignition interlock device during probationary period for DWI conviction. (IC9-30-5-16) Class B infraction to permit open container of alcoholic beverages in passenger compartment of vehicle if operator has 4% blood-alcohol content. (IC9-30-15). Class D felony to knowingly operate motor vehicle with suspended or revoked license. (IC9-24-18-5).

Habitual Traffic Offenders.—Regulated by IC9-30-10-1, et seq. Any person found to be "habitual violator" must surrender operator's license and may be placed on probation for up to ten years. (IC9-30-10-9).

See infra, subhead Suspension of License.

Size and Weight Limits.—Regulated by IC9-20-1-1, et seq.

Equipment Required.—Regulated by IC9-19-1-1, et seq.

Seat Belts.—(IC9-19-10-1 to 9). All post-1964 model autos bought, sold, leased or transferred must have front seat safety belts. Front seat occupants in passenger motor vehicles (excludes trucks, tractors and recreational vehicles) equipped with safety belts must wear such belts while vehicle is in forward motion. Violation is Class D infraction. Effective July 1, 1998, operator of passenger motor vehicle equipped with safety belts must properly restrain children four to 12 years of age in child passenger restraint systems or safety belts. Violation is Class D infraction. Effective July 1, 1998, vehicle must be stopped solely because of violation of this chapter. (IC9-19-10-3). Failure to comply may not be admitted in evidence in civil action to mitigate damages, except in product liability action involving motor vehicle restraint or supplemental restraint system. (IC9-19-11-1 to 8). Exceptions to seat belt requirement listed in IC9-19-10-1.

Child Restraint Systems.—Children less than four years old must be restrained in child passenger restraint system or, if it is reasonably determined that child will not fit in child passenger restraint system, seat belt. Violation is Class D infraction. (IC9-19-11-1 to 8).

Emission control equipment and testing governed by IC13-1-1-1 to 12.

Rear bumper required on vehicles of certain length and height. (IC9-19-4-1).

Odometer repair, replacement, tampering governed by IC9-19-9-1 to 7. Violation thereof with intent to defraud is Class D felony and is subject to up to $1,500 civil penalty per violation.

Window transparency standards governed by IC9-19-19-1 to 7.

Lights Required.—Regulated by IC9-19-6-1 to 24.

Inspection.—State police department may inspect vehicles used to provide transportation of six or more passengers by profit or not-for-profit corporation that receives revenue for transportation service from government (IC9-19-20-1,2) except private buses (defined in IC9-12-2-133). Vehicles not purchased or previously registered in Indiana must be inspected by police officer or other authorized person prior to obtaining Indiana certificate of title. (IC9-17-2-12).

Traffic Regulations.—Regulated by IC9-21-1-1 to 9-21-20-3. Class C misdemeanor not to stop vehicle meeting or overtaking school bus stopped on roadway when arm signal device is extended. Rebuttable presumption exists that vehicle involved in violation committed violation. (IC9-21-12-1 to 11).

Implied Consent.—Drivers of vehicles on public highways are deemed to have consented, by virtue of such driving, to submit to a chemical test for intoxication. (IC9-30-6-1).

Accidents.—Driver must stop when injury to person or property occurs and give name, residence and registration number, exhibit drivers license upon request, and give reasonable assistance when person injured. (IC9-26-1-1 to 4). Written reports by driver are required ten days thereafter. (IC9-26-1-1 to 4). Failure to stop may result in fine and/or imprisonment. (IC9-26-1-8). Failure to file written report may result in revocation or suspension of driver's license. (IC9-26-1-10).

Owner liable for negligence of others only when servant or agent operating car within scope of authority. Owner of car kept for family use probably not liable for negligence of member of family, unless owner knows at time of entrustment that driver is incompetent to drive safely. (489 N.E.2d 144 [Ind. App.]).

Suspension of License.—Any person arrested for driving under influence of intoxicants who refuses to submit to a breath analysis test when it is within his capacity to do so may have his driver's license suspended for a period not to exceed one year. (IC9-30-6-7).

Any person using motor vehicle to commit recklessness, obstruction of traffic or criminal mischief may have license suspended not less than 60 days nor more than two years. (IC9-30-13-1). Any person who commits involuntary manslaughter or reckless homicide resulting from operation of motor vehicle may have license suspended for from two to five years. (IC9-30-13-4).

Commission of Motor Vehicles must suspend for at least 90 days license or permit of person for reasons listed in IC9-17-2-16, 9-18-2-42, and 9-24-18-8.

Commissioner of Bureau of Motor Vehicles may suspend or revoke license for conviction of traffic offenses listed in IC9-30-4-6, or for traffic offenses committed in jurisdiction with whom Indiana has Nonresident Violator Agreement. (IC9-28-2-1 to 12).

Driving with suspended license is Class A misdemeanor. (IC9-24-18-5).

Suspension may be extended 90 days to two years upon conviction for driving while license or permit suspended. (IC9-24-18-5).

Person whose driving privileges suspended for intoxication and who requests early trial may have driving privileges reinstated for delay in trial or disposition of charges. (IC9-30-6-18).

See supra, subhead Operation Prohibited.

See note at head of Digest as to 1998 legislation covered.

See Topical Index in front part of this volume.

IN – 53

MOTOR VEHICLES . . . continued

Guests.—No liability for death of, injury to or loss sustained by parent, spouse, child or stepchild, brother or sister of owner, operator or responsible person, or hitchhiker, unless accident was caused by wanton or willful misconduct of operator, owner or person responsible for operation of vehicle. (IC34-30-11-1, 484 N.E.2d 967 [Ind. App.]). This does not apply to common carrier or owner or operator of vehicle being demonstrated to prospective purchaser. (IC34-30-11-2).

Proof of financial responsibility must be produced in order to obtain registration of motor vehicle and must be continuously maintained. (IC9-25-4-1 to 3). Sufficient proof may be policy of insurance, execution of bond, or obtaining certificate of self-insurance. (IC9-25-4-7 to 11). Proof by nonresidents governed by IC9-25-5-10. Bureau may suspend registration of vehicle owned by registrant who provides bureau with false indicia of financial responsibility. (IC9-25-6-19.2). Operator and/or owner of vehicle which is involved in motor vehicle accident resulting in bodily injury, death, or property damage in excess of $750 must post security (or give proof of insurance coverage in lieu thereof) for any judgment which may be rendered against him arising out of such accident, and proof of his financial responsibility in future, or receive suspension of his operator's license. (IC9-25-5-1 to 10). However, Commissioner may not revoke license of driver involved in accident resulting in bodily injury or property damage in excess of $750 solely because of failure to show financial responsibility, if his insurer has become insolvent either after or within 15 days before accident. (IC9-25-7-1). Persons convicted of any of certain offenses and crimes under and in connection with motor vehicle laws must give, and thereafter maintain for three years, proof of financial responsibility. (IC9-30-4-6, 9-30-6-12).

Such proof must be in amount of $25,000 for damages resulting from bodily injury to or death of any one person, or $50,000 for two or more persons in any one accident; and $10,000 for property damage in any one accident. (IC9-9-25-2-3).

Insurance, bond or other certain types of security is required to operate vehicle. Amount required is $25,000/$50,000 bodily injury and $10,000 property damage. (IC9-25-4-5). Motor vehicle manufacturers, factory representatives, distributors, auctioneers, dealers and brokers must maintain garage liability insurance in amounts specified in IC9-23-2-10. See also category Insurance, topic Insurance Companies, subhead Liability Policies.

No-fault insurance not adopted.

Uninsured motorist coverage must be made available by all motor vehicle insurers, though named insured may reject such coverage. (IC27-7-5-2).

Foreign vehicle registered in home state or country and conspicuously displaying license plates may be operated without registration for 60 days, to extent that home state gives reciprocal rights to Indiana cars. (IC9-18-2-1 and 9-24-1-7[6]). Nonresident transporting nonprocessed agricultural products grown in state may get 90-day permit. (IC9-18-1-6). New residents must register and title vehicles within 60 days. Violation is Class C infraction. (IC9-18-2-40). Any trailer or semitrailer properly registered and licensed in another state with no permanent base or fixed terminus in Indiana is exempt from Indiana registration and plate requirements to extent home state gives reciprocal rights. (IC9-18-2-5). Any person may obtain special registration permit for motor vehicle, semitrailer, trailer designed for use with semitrailer, or recreational vehicle, valid for 30 days, if person obtained vehicle in Indiana and will title or register in another state; or person resident of Indiana plans to leave and current registration will expire before moving; or person resident of Indiana and registration in another state will expire while waiting for Indiana title; or if person not operating as lessor both owns and operates empty vehicle which is being moved from one lessee-carrier to another. Manufacturers of trailers or semitrailers who lease same for 30 day periods may be bulk-issued special registration permits. (IC9-18-7-1). Ninety day temporary permits available for vehicles manufactured in Indiana purchased by individuals that are citizens of foreign countries if vehicles are intended to be registered in country of purchaser's citizenship. (IC9-18-7-1.5).

Nonresident operators have same operating privileges as Indiana resident has in nonresident's state. (IC9-18-2-3). See IC9-24-1-7 for license exemptions.

Action against nonresident arising out of accident or collision while operating motor vehicle on highway or street in state, may be commenced by leaving copy of process, with fee of $5, with Secretary of State, who forwards copy thereof, by registered mail, to defendant. (IC34-33-3-2). Such service also permissible for resident who becomes nonresident and executor or administrator of nonresident who died prior to commencement of action. If nonresident dies after commencement of action, action may be continued against executor or administrator. (IC34-33-3-5). See also category Civil Actions and Procedure, topic Venue.

Direct actions against insurer by injured person not allowed based on contract theory. (409 N.E.2d 1239 [Ind. App. 1980]). However, it is possible such action may be brought under third party beneficiary theory. (567 N.E.2d 838, 840 [Ind. App. 1991]).

Pedestrians are governed by IC9-21-17-1 to 24.

Motor vehicle carriers are regulated by Department of State Revenue. (IC8-2.1-24-4 et seq.). Common carriers must have certificate of convenience and necessity. Permits required for contract carriers of persons or household goods. (IC8-2.1-22-11, 12.5, 16). Carriers operating interstate vehicles into or through Indiana must register ICC permit with and obtain acknowledgment from Department of State Revenue. (IC8-2.1-20-5). Intrastate carriers must register under single state registration system. (IC8-2.1-22-33). Nonresident carriers must file name of agent for service of process. (IC8-2.1-22-34). See IC8-2.1-24-1 for rules on intrastate motor carriers. Operation of motor busses governed by IC8-2.1-25.

Vehicle Equipment Safety Compact Act has been adopted. (IC9-28-6-1 to 8).

Driver License Compact Act has been adopted. (IC9-28-1-1 to 6).

Nonresident Violator Agreement may be in force between Indiana and other jurisdictions. (IC9-28-2-1 to 12). See supra, subhead Suspension of License.

Manufacturers, Distributors and Dealers.—Persons engaged in distributing and selling motor vehicles are governed by IC9-23-1-1 to 9-23-6-9. Manufacturer or distributor may terminate new vehicle family franchise for good cause only. (IC9-23-5-1). See IC9-23-2.5 for disclosure requirements imposed on retail lessors.

Motor clubs' ability to guarantee payment of fines and costs imposed on member governed by IC9-30-2-8.

Motorboats.—Operation of all boats is regulated by special provisions. (IC14-15). Motorboats are required to be inspected, registered and titled. (IC14-15-6).

Motorcycles.—Operation and equipment of motorcycles and operators is regulated by a special act. (IC9-21-10-1 to 13). Motorcyclists and passengers less than 18 years old must wear protective headgear. (IC9-21-10-9).

Bicyclists have same rights and duties as operators of other types of vehicles. (IC9-21-11-2). Special rules governing motorized bicycles in IC9-21-11-12, 13.

Snowmobiles must be registered and are further regulated by special provisions. (IC14-16-2). Other off-road vehicles, with some exceptions, must be registered and are specially regulated. (IC14-16-1).

Mobile or "manufactured homes" governed by special provisions concerning certificate of title. (IC9-17-6-1 et seq.).

Aircraft registration governed by IC6-6-6.5 et seq.

Excise Tax.—Excise tax on passenger cars payable when license plates purchased. Certain types of vehicles and vehicles owned, operated, or leased by entities such as government or institutions of higher education are exempt from motor vehicle excise tax. (IC6-6-5-1 to 16). Registering vehicle without paying tax is Class B misdemeanor. (IC6-6-5-11). All boats are subject to boat excise tax based on boat's class and age. (IC6-6-11-1 to -36). See IC6-6-9.7 for excise tax on auto rentals.

Gasoline Tax.—Governed by IC6-6-1.1 et seq. See category Taxation, topic Gasoline and Special Fuels Tax, subhead Gasoline Tax.

Disclosure of Personal Information.—Mobile or "manufactured homes" governed by special provisions concerning certificate of title. (IC9-17-6-1 et seq.).

Lemon Law.—(IC24-5-13-1 et seq.). See category Business Regulation and Commerce, topic Consumer Protection, subhead Motor Vehicle Protection.

RAILROADS:

See category Business Regulation and Commerce, topic Carriers.

See note at head of Digest as to 1998 legislation covered.

See Topical Index in front part of this volume.

IOWA LAW DIGEST REVISER

Finley, Alt, Smith, Scharnberg, Craig, Hilmes & Gaffney, P.C.
Equitable Building, 4th Floor
604 Locust Street
Des Moines, Iowa 50309-3773
Telephone: 515-288-0145
Fax: 515-288-2724
Email: Finleylaw@AOL.com

Reviser Profile

History: This firm was founded in 1924 under the name of Carr, Cox, Evans & Riley. In the firm's 70 year history the firm name has changed a number of times. The firm is now known as FINLEY, ALT, SMITH, SCHARNBERG, CRAIG, HILMES & GAFFNEY, P.C.

Areas of Emphasis: Finley, Alt, Smith, Scharnberg, Craig, Hilmes & Gaffney, P.C., is a full service law firm with particular emphasis on Insurance Defense, Professional Negligence, Real Estate, Health Care, Workers Compensation, Employment, ERISA, Personal Injury, Corporation, Business Finance and Banking Law. The firm has 11 lawyers.

Firm Activities: The firm encourages participation in community activities and mandates CLE hours for each lawyer each year. A practice management committee supervises the assignment of work and monitors the work of younger lawyers. Monthly meetings of all lawyers and paraprofessionals are held to discuss new and revised laws and regulations. All lawyers are members of the American Bar Association, the Iowa State Bar Association and the Polk County Bar Association. In addition, firm members are encouraged to belong to specialized groups such as the American Academy of Hospital Attorneys.

Management: Finley, Alt, Smith, Scharnberg, Craig, Hilmes & Gaffney, P.C., is managed by an executive committee of three lawyers working with a professional administrator. The committee is responsible for client development, client relationships, economic and technological development and firm growth. Membership on the management committee is determined annually.

Client Base: Clients represent leaders in their industries such as insurance, mortgage lending, railroads, banking and health care institutions. Although a significant amount of work comes from corporations, the firm continues to represent individuals and small businesses.

IOWA LAW DIGEST

(The following is a list of all Categories and Topics, including cross-references, covered in this Digest.)

IOWA LAW DIGEST

Revised for 1999 edition by

FINLEY, ALT, SMITH, SCHARNBERG, CRAIG, HILMES & GAFFNEY, P.C., of the Polk County Bar.

(Citations, unless otherwise indicated, are to Code of Iowa, 1997, as amended through the 1997 regular session of the Iowa General Assembly which is numbered according to a decimal system by which figures preceding the decimal point indicate chapters and those following indicate sections. R.C.P. refers to Rules of Civil Procedure revised effective January 24, 1998. R.A.P. refers to Rules of Appellate Procedure. R. Crim. P. refers to Rules of Criminal Procedure. D.R. refers to Disciplinary Rules. Parallel citations to the North Western Reporter begin with 51 Iowa.)

Note: This revision covers legislation adopted and approved by the Governor through October, 1998.

INTRODUCTION

GOVERNMENT AND LEGAL SYSTEM:

The State of Iowa is a constituent state of the United States of America. For further discussion of the U.S. federal system, see Introduction to the Federal Government of the United States at the beginning of this volume. A great many laws are promulgated by the federal government of the United States and are not reflected in the topics below. See the Introduction to this volume for references to the federal law topics covered.

Like all but one of the United States, Iowa has a common law legal system, with roots in English common law. For information on the courts and legislature of Iowa, see category Courts and Legislature.

HOLIDAYS:

Following are legal holidays: Jan. 1, 3d Mon. in Jan., Feb. 12, 3d Mon. in Feb., last Mon. in May, July 4, 1st Mon. in Sept., Nov. 11, 4th Thurs. in Nov., Dec. 25. (4.1).

Uniform Commercial Code adopted. (554). See category Business Regulation and Commerce, topic Commercial Code.

Legality of Transactions on Holiday.—No statutory prohibition of business transactions on Sundays or holidays. Banking transactions on holiday are specifically declared to be valid. (541.202).

OFFICE HOURS AND TIME ZONE:

Iowa is in the Central (GMT −06:00) time zone. Office hours are generally from 8:30 a.m. to 5 p.m.

BUSINESS ORGANIZATIONS

AGENCY:

Common law rules govern.

ASSOCIATIONS:

No general statutory provisions governing unincorporated associations.

Method of service, R.C.P. 56.1(f), (g). See category Civil Actions and Procedure, topic Process.

Professional Associations.—See topic Corporations, subhead Professional Corporations.

CORPORATIONS:

Note: New Iowa Business Corporation Act was enacted in 1989 with effective date of Dec. 31, 1989. It appears as c. 490 of 1989 Iowa Code.

New Iowa Business Corporation Act, c. 490 (hereinafter cited as I.B.C.A.) repealed c. 496A (Senate File 502 §195). It specifically excludes various types of corporations, foreign and domestic, from its operation, as hereinafter noted. Except as specifically provided in this chapter, this chapter applies to all domestic corporations in existence on effective date of this Act that were incorporated under any general statute of this state providing for incorporation of corporations for profit or power to amend or repeal statute under which corporation was incorporated was reserved. (1701). For more specific transitional rules, see 1701 through 1704. Following is summary of this new I.B.C.A., effective Dec. 31, 1989. Citations are to sections within c. 490 of 1989 Iowa Code.

Purposes.—Corporation incorporated under I.B.C.A. has purpose of engaging in any lawful business unless more limited purpose is set forth in articles of incorporation. (301).

Name.—Names of domestic and foreign corporations must include word "corporation," "company," "incorporated," or "limited," or abbreviation thereof. (401). Such name may be registered, and a domestic or foreign corporation may also file with Secretary of State fictitious name, other than corporate name, under which it will do business. (401-403).

Secretary of State will indicate, without fee, whether corporate name available.

To reserve corporate name, file with Secretary of State application to reserve specified corporate name, executed by applicant. If available, Secretary will reserve same for exclusive use of applicant for 120 days. (403).

Term of corporate existence of domestic corporation may commence on any date, within 90 days of filing of articles, specified in articles and in certificate issued by Secretary of State, and is deemed perpetual unless otherwise specified in articles. In absence of specification of future date, existence commences on date of issuance of certificate. (123, 203, 302).

Incorporators.—Corporation need have only one incorporator. (201).

Articles of Incorporation.—Articles must contain certain items specified by statute. (202).

Filing Requirements.—To be entitled to be filed in office of Secretary of State, document must contain information required by chapter, be typewritten or printed, be in English (except corporate names), be properly executed and signed, be on prescribed form (if there is one), be delivered to office of Secretary of State for filing and be accompanied by correct filing fee.

Fees.—Filing fees $50 for filing articles of incorporation, articles of amendment and certificate of amendment, restated articles of incorporation, articles of merger or share exchange and $30 for annual report; $20 for application for renewal of registered name; $10 for filing application to reserve corporate name, notice of transfer of reserved corporate name, application for use of indistinguishable name; $5 for articles of dissolution, revocation of voluntary dissolution proceedings, application for reinstatement following administrative dissolution, articles of correction, and application of certificate of existence or authorization; $2 for application for registered name per month or part thereof. (122). Fee of $5 for any other document required to be filed.

Judicial Review.—Where Secretary of State refuses to file document delivered to Secretary of State for filing, corporation has 30 days after document's return to appeal to District Court for county in which corporation's principal office, or, if none in this state, its registered office is or will be located. (126).

Organization.—After incorporation, initial directors (if named in articles of incorporation) or incorporator(s) shall hold organizational meeting or take action without meeting if action is evidenced by written consents. (205).

Transfer of Stock.—Uniform Commercial Code adopted. See category Business Regulation and Commerce, topic Commercial Code. (554). Articles of incorporation, bylaws, agreement among shareholders, or agreement between shareholders and corporation may impose restrictions on transfer or registration of transfer of shares of corporation. (627).

Shareholders.—Articles of incorporation may specify greater or lesser vote than that statutorily required for corporate action. (1003, 1103, 1202, 1402). Preemptive right to unissued shares does not exist, unless articles provide it, except for corporations which were incorporated under, or which elected to be governed by, c. 496A prior to Dec. 31, 1989, in which case §1704 applies until Dec. 31, 1992. (630, 1704).

Shareholders' Meetings.—Corporation shall hold annually, at time stated in or fixed in accordance with bylaws, meeting of shareholders. (701). Corporation shall hold special meeting of shareholders either on call of board of directors or person(s) authorized to call special meeting by articles of incorporation or bylaws or if holders of at least 10% of all votes entitled to be cast on any issue proposed to be considered at proposed special meeting deliver signed, written demand for meeting. (702). Court may also order meeting. (703). Shareholders may vote by proxy. (722). Action required or permitted to be taken at shareholders' meetings may be by consent. (704). Number of shares establishing quorum may be varied by articles. (1021). Percentage of vote statutorily required for various corporate actions may also be varied by articles of incorporation. (1003, 1103, 1202, 1402).

Following corporate actions require majority of votes of shareholders entitled to vote thereon: Amendment of articles (1003); disposition (other than mortgage or pledge) of assets other than in ordinary course of business (1202); voluntary dissolution by act of corporation (1402).

Merger and Consolidation.—Shareholder approval of share exchange or consolidation requires majority vote of outstanding shares. (1103).

Voting Trusts—One or more shareholders may create voting trust. (730). Voting trusts are valid for not more than ten years unless extended for additional term of not more than ten years. (730).

Directors.—Corporations need have only one director. (803). Procedure for removal of directors may be contained in articles. (808). Informal action of board of directors or committee thereof can be formalized by consent in writing to such action by all entitled to vote. (821).

Articles of incorporation may contain provision eliminating or limiting personal liability of director to corporation or its shareholders for monetary damages for breach of fiduciary duty as director, provided that provision does not eliminate or limit liability of director for breach of director's duty of loyalty to corporation or its shareholders, for acts/omissions not in good faith or which involve intentional misconduct of knowing violation of law, for transaction from which director derives improper personal benefit, or under §833 (liability for unlawful distribution). (832).

Unless articles of incorporation or bylaws require different number, quorum of board of directors is majority. (824).

Officers.—Corporation has officers described in its bylaws or appointed by board in accordance with bylaws. (840). Any two or more offices may be held by same person. (840).

Dividends.—Board of directors may authorize and corporation may make distributions to shareholders subject to restriction by articles of incorporation. Also, no distribution may be made if, after giving effect, either (1) corporation would not be able to pay its debts as they become due in usual course of business or (2) corporation's total assets would be less than sum of its total liabilities plus, unless articles permit otherwise, amount that would be needed, if corporation dissolved at time of

CORPORATIONS . . . *continued*

distribution, to satisfy preferential rights of shareholders whose rights are superior to those receiving distribution. (640). Share dividends may also be issued. (623).

Unclaimed Dividends.—See category Property, topic Absentees, subhead Escheat.

Reports.—Annual report due between Jan. 1 and Apr. 1. (1622). Fee for filing annual report is $30. (122). If not filed within time allowed by notice, certificate may be cancelled. (1420).

Dissent.—Shareholder is entitled to dissent from and obtain payment of fair value of shareholder's shares in event of certain corporate actions. (1302).

Foreign corporations shall not transact business in Iowa until they obtain certificate of authority from Secretary of State. (1501). Statute outlines activities which do not constitute "transacting business" under statute. (1501).

Dissolution.—Statutes provide that incorporators, initial directors (1401), board of directors and shareholders (1402), Secretary of State (1420), or court (1430) may dissolve corporation.

Poison Pill Defense.—Terms and conditions of stock rights or options issued by corporation may include restrictions or conditions that preclude or limit exercise, transfer, or receipt of such rights or options by person or group of persons owning or offering to acquire specified number or percentage of outstanding common shares or other securities of corporation, or transferee of offeror, or that invalidate or void such stock rights or options held by offeror or transferee of offeror. (624A).

Income Tax on Corporations.—See category Taxation, topic Income Tax.

Professional Corporations.—Corporation may be formed under general corporation law (490, 496C.3) for purpose of qualifying as professional corporation to render specific professional service. Certificate of incorporation must be obtained from Secretary of State. All shareholders, directors and officers must be licensed professionals. Professions which may incorporate: certified public accountancy, architecture, chiropractic, dentistry, physical therapy, psychology, professional engineering, land surveying, landscape architecture, law, medicine and surgery, optometry, osteopathy, osteopathic medicine and surgery, accounting practitioner, podiatry, speech pathology, audiology, veterinary medicine, pharmacy and practice of nursing. (496C).

Limited Liability Companies.—See topic Limited Liability Companies.

Deeds.—See category Property, topic Deeds.

Model Non-Profit Corporation Act not adopted.

JOINT STOCK COMPANIES:

No statutory provisions.

Professional Corporations.—See topic Corporations, subhead Professional Corporations.

LIMITED LIABILITY COMPANIES:

Limited liability companies may generally be formed for any lawful purpose. (490A.201). Articles must state name of LLC, name and address of registered agent, address of principal office, period of duration, and may state other provisions. (490A.303). Entity formed under Iowa LLC Act will have limited liability unless otherwise provided in articles. (490A.601). LLC's can be dissolved under multiple conditions. (490A.1301).

PARTNERSHIPS:

Uniform Partnership Act adopted. (486). Uniform Limited Partnership Act (1976) adopted with modifications. (487).

BUSINESS REGULATION AND COMMERCE

BANKS AND BANKING:

Regulated by Iowa Banking Act of 1969 (524) and Uniform Commercial Code (554). (Revised c. 3 and 4, 1994).

Uniform Common Trust Fund Act not adopted.

Powers.—State banks may be authorized by superintendent of banking to act in a fiduciary capacity. Bank has rights which an individual has in such capacity; however, superintendent of banking may limit such authorization to such capacities as he deems appropriate. (524.1001).

Foreign Banks.—Person other than state bank which is subject to provisions of this chapter, and national bank authorized by laws of U.S. to engage in business of receiving money for deposits, shall not engage in this state in business of receiving money for deposit, transact business of banking or lawfully establish in this state place of business for such purpose. (524.107).

Fiduciary Powers.—See category Estates and Trusts, topic Executors and Administrators, subhead Eligibility.

Liability of Shareholders.—Holder of shares of state bank under no obligation to state bank or creditors with respect to such shares, except as provided in 524.521 or 524.525. Subscriber to shares same as holders except additional obligation to pay full consideration for shares prior to issuance. (524.527).

Deposits.—

Minors.—Bank may deal with minor with respect to deposits without consent of parent as though minor were an adult. Actions of minor with respect to deposits are binding as if he were an adult. (524.805).

Joint Accounts.—If deposit is made in name of two individuals, payable to either, or to either or survivor, deposit may be paid to either individual whether other is living or not. (524.806).

Pay-on-Death Account.—State bank may receive deposit with provision that upon death of depositor account shall be property of designee, subject to debts and charges of depositors and payment of Iowa inheritance tax. (524.805).

See also Uniform Commercial Code. (554).

Unclaimed Deposits.—Revised Uniform Disposition of Unclaimed Property Act adopted, with some modifications. (556).

Collections.—Uniform Commercial Code adopted. (554).

Trust Companies.—Trust company existing and operating on Jan. 1, 1970 and which was authorized to act only as trust company may continue to act only in fiduciary capacity according to terms of its articles of incorporation. Articles of incorporation of trust company may be renewed in perpetuity. See §524.1005.

BILLS AND NOTES:

Uniform Commercial Code adopted. See topic Commercial Code.

Recitals.—No special requirements as to recitals in notes given for particular purposes or based on particular considerations.

Attorney fee clauses are enforceable, with fee to be determined by court. (625.22). Affidavit showing no improper fee-sharing arrangement and that requested compensation for services actually rendered must be filed prior to any fees being taxed. (625.24). Reasonable opportunity to pay indebtedness before action brought required with some exceptions. (625.25).

BILLS OF LADING:

See topic Carriers.

BILLS OF SALE:

See topic Sales.

BLUE SKY LAW:

See topic Securities.

BROKERS:

Real estate brokers and salesmen must be licensed by Iowa Real Estate Commission. Commission may after hearing, deny, suspend or revoke license. Nonresident may be licensed if he has license issued by state of domicile and has an active place of business in such state, and consents that process against him may be served on chairman of commission. (543B).

See also topic Securities; category Insurance, topic Insurance Companies.

Uniform Commercial Code adopted. (554). See topic Commercial Code.

BULK SALES:

Art. 6 of Commercial Code (Bulk Transfers) repealed Jan. 1, 1995.

CARRIERS:

Iowa Department of Transportation has general supervision of all carriers within state.

Uniform Commercial Code adopted. (554). See topic Commercial Code.

Property Damage Claims.—Department of Transportation is to prescribe by rule, pursuant to §17A, regulations necessary for orderly disposition of claims arising from loss or damage to property tendered for transportation. (327D. 160).

Limiting Liability.—Contract may not exempt common carrier from any liability which would exist had no contract been made except as may be provided for liability for property loss by order of regulation board. (327D.186).

Bills of Lading.—Uniform Commercial Code adopted. (554). See topic Commercial Code.

Liens.—Uniform Commercial Code adopted. (554). See topic Commercial Code.

Motor Vehicle Carriers.—See category Transportation, topic Motor Vehicles.

COMMERCIAL CODE:

Uniform Commercial Code adopted. (554). Section numbers will not include dashes that appear in Uniform Code. Thus, Section 1–101 of Uniform Commercial Code will be Iowa Code Section 554.1101, etc.

Material Variations from 1962 Text.—
§1-209—1966 Official Optional Amendment enacted.
§2-318—1966 Official Optional Amendment Alternative C enacted.
§2-702—1966 Official Amendment enacted.
§2-725(1)—First sentence omitted. Ordinary statute of limitations will govern. See category Civil Actions and Procedure, topic Limitation of Actions.
§2-725(3)—Words "law or by agreement as provided in" added after words "time limited by."
§3—Revised Article 3 adopted.
§4—Amended Article 4 adopted.
§6—Repealed.
§7-209—1966 Official Amendment enacted.
§9-307 of Uniform Commercial Code states that buyer in ordinary course of business buying farm products from debtor engaged in farming operations takes subject to security interest if buyer has received written notice of security interest within one year before sale. Statute sets forth requirements for written notice. Secured party may require, in documents creating security interest, that debtor furnish secured party list of potential buyers to or through whom debtor may sell farm products. Debtor is subject to civil fine of greater of $5,000 or 15% of value or benefit received by debtor if debtor sells farm products to buyer not included on list as potential buyer. (9-307).

See note at head of Digest as to 1998 legislation covered.

See Topical Index in front part of this volume.

COMMERCIAL CODE ... *continued*

§9-401—Second alternative subsection adopted as subsection (1). Proper office in county courthouse for filing pursuant to subparagraph (a) of this subsection is office of County Recorder.

§10-102(1)—Following acts and all other acts and parts of act inconsistent herewith are hereby repealed: Bills of Lading Act; Stock Transfer Act; Negotiable Instruments Law; Warehouse Receipts Law; Conditional Sales Act; Bulk Sales Act; Chattel Mortgages and Conditional Sales of Personal Property Law; Common Carrier's Lien Law; Foreclosure of Chattel Mortgage Law; Foreclosure of Pledges Law.

§10-104(2)—This Act does not repeal sections 633.130 to 633.138 inclusive, cited as Uniform Act for the Simplification of Fiduciary Security Transfers, and if in any respect there is any inconsistency between that Act and Article of this Act on investment securities (Art. 8) provisions of former Act shall control.

Minor Variations from 1962 Text have been made in several Sections.

Blanks Filled Up.—

Section	Action Taken
554.9203(4)	chapters 322, 534, 535, 536 and 536A.
554.9401(1)(a)	Recorder; Recorder; Recorder.
554.9401(1)(c)	Secretary of State.
554.9403(5)	on a form conforming to standards prescribed by the secretary of state shall be ten dollars. If statement is not on form conforming to standards prescribed by secretary of state but otherwise conforms to requirements of law, fee shall be twelve dollars. However, if original financing statement is filed electronically in office of secretary of state, fee shall be eight dollars if statement is in standard form prescribed by secretary of state, and otherwise twelve dollars.
554.9404(1)	on a form conforming to standards prescribed by the secretary of state shall be three dollars, or if the assignment or statement thereof otherwise conforms to the requirements of this section, five dollars.
554.9404(3)	no fee for filing termination statement.
554.9405(1)	on a form conforming to standards prescribed by the secretary of state shall be five dollars, or if such statement otherwise conforms to the requirement of this section, six dollars.
554.9405(2)	on a form conforming to standards prescribed by the secretary of state shall be five dollars, or if such statement otherwise conforms to the requirements of this section, six dollars.
554.9406	on a form conforming to standards prescribed by the secretary of state shall be five dollars, or if such statement otherwise conforms to the requirements of this section six dollars.

1972 Official Amendments.—Adopted. Filing fee for release of collateral filed electronically in office of Secretary of State is $8 if statement is in standard form, and otherwise $10.

1973 Official Amendment not adopted.

1977 Official Amendments not adopted.

See Uniform and Model Acts section for 1962 Official Text of Uniform Commercial Code.

Forms.—See end of this Digest.

See also topics Banks and Banking, Bills and Notes, Brokers, Carriers, Contracts, Factors, Frauds, Statute of, Sales, Securities, Warehousemen; categories Business Organizations, topic Corporations; Civil Actions and Procedure, topic Limitation of Actions; Debtor and Creditor, topics Assignments, Fraudulent Sales and Conveyances, Liens, Pledges; Documents and Records, topics Records, Seals; Mortgages, topic Chattel Mortgages.

CONDITIONAL SALES:

See topic Sales.

CONSIGNMENTS:

See topic Factors.

CONSUMER CREDIT:

Iowa has enacted consumer credit code patterned after uniform act. (537). Major variance from uniform act is section regulating debt collection practices. Section applies to all debt collectors including attorneys who send collection letters or contact debtors.

Debt collector not to collect or attempt to collect debt by illegal threat, coercion or attempt to coerce. Following described conduct deemed illegal threat, coercion or attempt to coerce under section: Use or threat of use of force, violence or other criminal means, to cause harm to person or property; false accusation or threat to falsely accuse person of fraud or other crime; false accusations made to person, including credit reporting agency, or threat to falsely accuse, that debtor is willfully refusing to pay just debt (failure to reply to requests for payment and failure to negotiate disputes in good faith are deemed willful refusal); threat to sell or assign to another obligation of debtor with attending representation or implication that result of sale or assignment will be to subject debtor to harsh or abusive collection attempts; false threat that nonpayment of debt may result in arrest of person or seizure, garnishment, attachment or sale of property or wages; action or threat of action prohibited by consumer credit code or other law. (537.7103[1][a]-[f]).

Debt collector not to oppress, harass, or abuse person in connection with collection or attempted collection of debt. Following described conduct deemed oppressive, harassing or abusive under this section: use of profane or obscene language or language intended to abuse hearer or reader and by which its utterance would tend to incite immediate breach of peace; placement of telephone calls to debtor without disclosure of name of business or company collector represents; causing expense to person in form of long distance telephone tolls, telegram fees, or other charges incurred by medium of communication by attempting to deceive or mislead persons as to true purpose of communication; causing telephone to ring or engaging person in telephone conversation repeatedly or continuously or at unusual hours or times known to be inconvenient, with intent to annoy, harass, or threaten person. (537.7103[2][a]-[d]).

Debt collector not to disseminate information relating to debt or debtor as follows: communication or threat to communicate or imply fact of debt to person other than debtor or person who might reasonably be expected to be liable for debt, except with written permission of debtor given after default. Use of language on envelopes indicating communication relates to collection of debt considered communication of debt. However, prohibition on disseminating information does not prohibit debt collector from any of following: notifying debtor of fact he may report debt to credit bureau or engage agent or attorney for purpose of collecting debt; reporting debt to credit reporting agency or other person reasonably believed to have legitimate business need for information; engaging agent or attorney for purpose of collecting debt; attempting to locate debtor whom debt collector has reasonable grounds to believe has moved from his residence, where purpose of communication to trace debtor and content of communication restricted to requesting information on debtor's location; communicating with debtor's employer or credit union not more than once during three month period when purpose of communication to obtain employer or credit union's debt counselling services for debtor. If no response received by debt collector from communication to debtor's employer or credit union collector may make one inquiry as to whether communication was received. Debt collector may respond to communications from employer or credit union; communicating with debtor's employer once during one-month period if purpose of communication to verify with employer fact of debtor's employment and if debt collector does not disclose (except as permitted above) any information other than fact debt exists. This does not authorize debt collector to disclose to employer fact debt is in default; communicating fact of debt not more than once in three month period, with parents of minor debtor, or with trustee or conservator of debtor's property or debtor's guardian. Debt collector may respond to inquiry from parent, trustee, conservator or guardian; communicating with debtor's spouse with consent of debtor or responding to inquiry from debtor's spouse. (537.7103[3][a][1]-[8]).

Debt collector not to disseminate information relating to debt or debtor as follows: disclosure, publication or communication of information relating to person's indebtedness to another by publishing or posting list of indebted persons, commonly known as "deadbeat lists" or by advertising for sale claim to enforce payment of debt when advertisement names debtor; use of form of communication to debtor, except telegram, original notice or other court process, or envelope displaying only name and address of debtor and return address of debt collector, intended or so designed as to display or convey information about debt to another other than name, address and phone number of debt collector. 537.7103[3][b]-[c]).

Debt collector not to use fraudulent, deceptive or misleading representation or means to collect or attempt to collect debt or to obtain information concerning debtors. Following conduct deemed fraudulent, deceptive or misleading under this section: use of business, company or organization name while engaged in collection of debts, other than true name of debt collector's business, company, or organization or one he represents; failure to disclose in initial written or oral communication with debtor, that debt collector attempting to collect debt and that information obtained will be used for that purpose, and failure to disclose in subsequent communications that communication is from debt collector, except in pleading made in connection with legal action; false representation debt collector has information in his possession or something of value for debtor, which made to solicit or discover information about debtor; failure to clearly disclose name and full business address of person to whom claim has been assigned at time of making demand for money; intentional misrepresentation, or representation which tends to create false impression of character, extent or amount of debt or its status in legal proceeding; false representation, or representation which tends to create false impression debt collector vouched for, bonded by, affiliated with, or instrumentality, agency or official of state or agency of federal, state or local government; use or distribution or sale of written communication which simulates or falsely represents to be document authorized, issued or approved by court, official, or other legally constituted or authorized authority, or which tends to create false impression about source, authorization or approval; representation that existing obligation of debtor may be increased by addition of attorney's fees, investigation fees, service fees or other fees or charges, when in fact such fees or charges may not legally be added to existing obligation; false representation or representation which tends to create false impression, about status or true nature of, or services rendered by, debt collector or his business. (537.7103[4][a]-[i]).

CONSUMER CREDIT . . . *continued*

Debt collector not to engage in following conduct to collect or attempt to collect debt: seeking or obtaining written statement or acknowledgment in any form that specifies debtor's obligation are chargeable upon property of either husband or wife or both, under 597.14, when original obligation not in fact so chargeable; seeking or obtaining written statement or acknowledgment containing affirmation of obligation discharged in bankruptcy, without clearly disclosing nature and consequences of affirmation and fact debtor not legally obligated to make affirmation. This does not prohibit accepting promises to pay which are voluntarily written and offered by bankrupt debtor; collection of or attempt to collect from debtor part or all of debt collector's fee for services rendered, unless debt collector legally entitled to collect fee from debtor and fee is reasonably related to actions taken by debt collector; collection of or attempt to collect interest or other charge, fee or expense incidental to principal obligation unless interest or incidental charge, fee or expense expressly authorized by agreement creating obligation and legally chargeable to debtor or otherwise legally chargeable; communication with debtor when debt collector knows debtor represented by attorney and attorney's name and address are known or could be easily ascertained, unless attorney fails to answer correspondence, return phone calls, or discuss obligation in question, within reasonable time or prior approval is obtained from debtor's attorney or when communication response in ordinary course of business to debtor's inquiry. (537.7103[5][a]-[e]).

Debt collector not to use or distribute, sell, or prepare for use, written communication that violates or fails to conform to U.S. postal laws and regulations. (537.7103[6]).

Exclusions from Act are: (1) Extensions of credit to government agencies or instrumentalities, (2) sales of certain insurance, (3) transactions regulated by public utility or common carrier tariffs regulated by state or federal government, (4) credit extended by pawn brokers under certain circumstances and to certain extents, (5) transactions in securities and commodities with registered broker dealer. (537.1202).

Maximum annual interest rates as follows: Consumer credit sale or loan other than one pursuant to open end credit: 21%.

Consumer credit sale or loan pursuant to open end credit: For each billing cycle, charge may be made which is percentage of amount not exceeding greatest of following: (a) Average daily balance of open end account in billing cycle for which charge is made, which is sum of amount unpaid each day during that cycle, divided by number of days in that cycle. Amount unpaid on day is determined by adding to balance, if any, unpaid as of beginning of that day all purchases and other debits and deducting all payments and other credits made or received as of that day; (b) balance of open end account at beginning of first day of billing cycle, after deducting all payments and credits made in cycle except credits attributable to purchases charged to account during cycle; (c) median amount within specified range including balance of open end account not exceeding that permitted by "a" or "b". Charge may be made pursuant to this paragraph only if organization, subject to classifications and differentiations it may reasonably establish, makes same charge on all balances within specified range and if percentage when applied to median amount within range does not produce charge exceeding charge resulting from applying that percentage to lowest amount within range by more than 8% of charge on median amount.

If charge determined pursuant to preceding paragraph is less than 50¢, charge may be made which does not exceed 50¢ if billing cycle is monthly or longer, or pro rata part of 50¢ which bears same relation to 50¢ as number of days in billing cycle bears to 365 divided by 12 if billing cycle is shorter than monthly. (537.2202).

CONSUMER PROTECTION:

Consumer fraud section in Iowa Code. (714.16). Unlawful to use deception or fraud in sale or advertisement of merchandise. Unlawful to advertise or sell merchandise at price or with rebate or other consideration to purchaser contingent upon procurement of prospective customers by purchaser and any obligation incurred in such manner completely void. Unlawful to advertise sale of merchandise at reduced rate due to cessation of business operations and after such advertisement to remain in business under same or substantially same ownership or trade name or continue to offer for sale same type merchandise at same location for more than 120 days. Not permissible to offer or advertise within Iowa for sale or lease certain subdivided lands without first filing with real estate commission true and accurate copies of all road plans, plats, field notes and diagrams of water, sewage and electric power lines as they exist at time of filing. Attorney General may require sellers to file reports on facts and circumstances surrounding sales and advertisements and examine individuals and records. Special civil penalties for consumer fraud against elderly. (714.16A).

See topics Consumer Credit, Interest, Sales.

Plain Language.—No Plain Language statute.

CONTRACTS:

Uniform Commercial Code adopted. (554). See topic Commercial Code.

See topic Frauds, Statute of; categories Documents and Records, topic Seals; Family, topic Infants.

FACTORS:

Consignments of merchandise which are to be sold by the consignee as sales agent for a consignor, reserving the title in the latter, are recognized and the common law of factors and bailees applies.

Lien.—Uniform Commercial Code adopted. (554). See topic Commercial Code.

Uniform Commercial Code adopted. (554). See topic Commercial Code.

FRANCHISES:

§523H.1-523H.17 delineates duties and limitations on franchisors, providing certain exemptions, and establishing civil cause of action for violations of chapter. Franchise may be subject to statutory "business opportunity promotions" requirements. (523B). Generally, seller or solicitor of "business opportunity" must register and pay $500

initial fee and annual $250 renewal fee (523B.2), may be required to obtain surety bond or letter of credit (523B.3) and must provide prospective purchaser disclosure statement conforming to statutory requirements (523B.3). Penalties for violation of statutory requirements are provided. (523B.11). Code provides express treatment for following types of franchises: Motor vehicle (322A); farm implement and motorcycle (322D); motor fuel and special fuel (323).

FRAUDS, STATUTE OF:

No evidence of following classes of contracts is competent, unless in writing, signed by party to be charged, or his authorized agent: (1) Those in consideration of marriage; (2) when one person agrees to answer for debt, default of miscarriage of another; (3) for creation or transfer of interest in lands for a term not exceeding one year, except where purchase money, or a part thereof, has been received by vendor, or where vendee, with actual or implied consent of vendor, has taken and held possession under contract, or where there is any other circumstance, which, by law heretofore in force, would take it out of statute; (4) those not to be performed within one year from making thereof. But in any of above cases opposite party may be called as a witness and contract proven by his oral testimony. (622.32-.35).

Uniform Commercial Code adopted. (554). See topic Commercial Code.

INTEREST:

(535). See also topic Consumer Credit.

Judgments.—Variable rate tied to latest average auction price of 52 week U.S. Treasury bills plus 2% unless different rate (not exceeding maximum under 535.2) is expressed in contract on which judgment is based, in which case judgment should express such rate. (535.3, 668.13). Interest shall accrue on judgment from date action was commenced. (668.13).

Finance Charges.—2% of loan principal where loan processing fee on loan for purchase of one or two family owner occupied dwelling. (535.8).

1% of amount refinanced or assumed where loan processing fee on refinancing or assumption of existing loan on one or two family owner occupied dwelling. (535.8).

10% computed by add-on or discount method where loan from industrial loan company. (536A.23[1]).

Accounts receivable in absence of written agreement: Closed-end transaction up to $35,000, 21% with proper notice; closed-end transaction over $35,000, no maximum level with proper notice; open-end transaction, 18% on initial $500 and 15% on any excess balance with proper notice. (535.11, 537.1302).

Automobile installment sales: New autos, 21%; autos not more than two years old, 24%; autos over two years old, 27%.

Mobile and modular home sales contracts, 21% irrespective of age. (321).

Semi-tractor and travel trailer installment sales: New vehicles, 21%; vehicles not more than two years old, 24%; vehicles more than two years old, 27%. (321).

Finance charge for consumer loans or sales pursuant to open-end credit, see topic: Consumer Credit, subhead Maximum Annual Interest Rates.

Finance charge for consumer loans or sales not pursuant to open-end credit, 21%. (537-.2201[2], 2401[1]).

Usury.—Where contract sued on is usurious, plaintiff can have judgment only for principal debt without interest or costs, and judgment is entered in favor of state against defendant for 8% per annum on amount of judgment. (535.5).

LICENSES, BUSINESS AND PROFESSIONAL:

Licenses and permits from different authorities, on varying conditions and at various fees, are required for a large number of occupations and activities.

Commercial travelers need not be licensed.

Collection Agencies.—Certain prohibited debt collection practices specified by statute. (537.7103). Civil penalties and injunctive relief authorized. (537.6111, 537.6113). See topic Consumer Credit.

MONOPOLIES, RESTRAINT OF TRADE AND COMPETITION:

Combination to regulate or fix price of commodity or limit quantity to be manufactured, produced or sold prohibited. Party to such combination guilty of conspiracy. (553). Combination restraining or preventing full and free competition in trade prohibited (553.4 & .5) but labor unions excepted (553.6). Violations punishable by fine and imprisonment. (553.12-.14).

NEGOTIABLE INSTRUMENTS:

See topic Bills and Notes.

RESTRAINT OF TRADE:

See topic Monopolies, Restraint of Trade and Competition.

SALES:

Uniform Commercial Code adopted. (554). See topic Commercial Code.

Product Liability.—Common law rules prevail except as modified by Uniform Commercial Code. Privity abolished by decision at least in certain situations. (252 Ia. 1289, 110 N.W. 2d 449). Effective for claims arising on or after July 1, 1986, retailers immune from strict liability or breach of implied warranty which arise solely from alleged defect in original design or manufacture of product. (613.18). See category Civil Actions and Procedure, topic Damages.

Retail Credit Sales.—No special restrictions. See also topic Consumer Credit.

Consumer Protection.—Sale of merchandise with a rebate contingent upon procurement of prospective customers by purchaser is unlawful unless in writing and made part of sales contract. (714.16). See also topics Consumer Credit, Interest.

"Unsolicited goods" statute adopted. (556A.1).

Bulk Sales.—Art. 6 of Commercial Code repealed.

See note at head of Digest as to 1998 legislation covered.

See Topical Index in front part of this volume.

SALES . . . *continued*

Sales of Motor Vehicles.—See category Transportation, topic Motor Vehicles, subhead Sales.

SECURITIES:

Uniform Securities Act adopted, effective Jan. 1, 1976. See Uniform and Model Acts section. (502.101-.612).

Major departures from Uniform Act: Broker-dealers and agents' licenses expire on Sept. 30 of each year. Persons filing with SEC under Regulation A may become registered by coordination in Iowa. Registration of securities is perpetually effective. Registration of equity securities under qualification provisions limited to aggregate of $2,000,000. No registration by notification section. Administrator may deny securities registration if it is found to be unfair or inequitable. Limited offering exemption available if not more than 35 purchasers, exemption not available for oil, gas and mining leases or for partnerships formed in foreign jurisdictions. Mergers, reorganizations, and stock dividends treated as exempt transactions. Additional prohibitions include trading on inside information, market manipulation, use of manipulative devices by broker-dealers, misstatements in publicity, and employees of administrator using official capacity to promote security. Contains varying statutes of limitations depending upon alleged violation and its discovery. Registration by coordination automatically effective if it has been on file with administrator for 20 days.

Model State Commodity Code, adopted Apr. 16, 1990. (502A.1-22).

Uniform Simplification of Fiduciary Security Transfers Act repealed.

Uniform Commercial Code adopted (554). See topic Commercial Code.

Uniform Securities Ownership by Minors Act not adopted.
See also topic Consumer Protection.

STATUTE OF FRAUDS:

See topic Frauds, Statute of.

TRUST RECEIPT SECURITY:

See category Debtor and Creditor, topic Pledges.

Uniform Commercial Code adopted. (554). See topic Commercial Code.

WAREHOUSEMEN:

Uniform Commercial Code adopted. (554). See topic Commercial Code.

CITIZENSHIP

ALIENS:

Nonresident aliens, corporations incorporated under laws of foreign country, corporations organized in this country in which majority interest is owned directly or indirectly by nonresident aliens, or foreign governments may acquire, by grant, purchase, devise or descent, real property, except agricultural land or any interest in agricultural land as hereinafter noted, and may own, hold, devise or alienate real property. (567.1).

Agricultural Land.—Nonresident aliens, or corporations organized or owned as above-mentioned or foreign governments, may not purchase or acquire agricultural land after Jan. 1, 1980. Agricultural land owned or held on Jan. 1, 1980 may continue to be owned or held. (567.3).

Restriction set forth above does not apply to agricultural land acquired by devise or descent; bona fide encumbrance taken for purposes of security; agricultural land acquired by process of law in collection of debts, by deed in lieu of foreclosure, pursuant to forfeiture of contract for deed, or by any procedure for enforcement of lien or claim on land, however, agricultural land so acquired must be sold or otherwise disposed of within two years after title transferred and must be leased for farming purposes in interim; agricultural land acquired primarily for research or experimental purposes used for testing, development, or production of seeds, or until July 1, 2001, to develop breeding stock; or plants for sale or resale to farmers, or for incidental activities; nor to interest in agricultural land, not to exceed 320 acres, acquired for immediate or pending use other than farming. (567.3, am'd 1986, c. 1217). If more than 320 acres of agricultural land is lawfully owned on Jan. 1, 1980, additional agricultural land must not be purchased or acquired except by devise or descent from nonresident alien. (567.3).

Nonresident aliens, corporations organized or owned as above-mentioned or foreign governments which acquire agricultural land or interest in agricultural land by devise or descent after Jan. 1, 1980, must divest selves of all right, title and interest in land within two years from date of acquisition. Agricultural land acquired by nonresident alien by devise or descent from nonresident alien will not have to be divested if such land or interest in such land was acquired by any nonresident alien prior to July 1, 1979. (567.5).

Nonresident aliens, or corporations organized or owned as above-mentioned or foreign governments must not transfer title to or interest in agricultural land to nonresident aliens, corporations organized or owned as above-mentioned or foreign governments except by devise or descent. (567.3).

Certain authorized farm corporations and authorized trusts may not acquire or lease more than 1,500 acres of agricultural land, upon certain conditions. (9H).

CIVIL ACTIONS AND PROCEDURE

ACCORD AND SATISFACTION:

Common law rules govern except as modified by Uniform Commercial Code. See category Business Regulation and Commerce, topic Commercial Code. Defense must be specifically pleaded. (R.C.P. 86).

ACTIONS:

Every proceeding in court is an action either civil, special or criminal. Civil actions are of two kinds, ordinary or equitable. Cases formerly cognizable in equity are tried as equitable proceedings and all others by ordinary proceedings. (611.1-.3).

Equity.—A plaintiff may prosecute an action by equitable proceedings in all cases where courts of equity had jurisdiction before adoption of code. (611.4). Mortgages and deeds of trust are foreclosed (611.5) and mechanics' liens enforced (572.26) by equitable proceedings.

Commencement.—See topic Process.

Parties.—Every action must be prosecuted in the name of the real party in interest. (R.C.P. 2). Any person may be made a defendant who has or claims an interest in controversy adverse to plaintiff, or is a necessary party to complete determination or settlement of question involved. (R.C.P. 25).

Class Actions.—Uniform Class Actions Rules adopted. (R.C.P. 42.1-42.18).

Intervention.—Any person interested in subject-matter of the litigation, or the success of either party to the action, or against both parties, may intervene at any time before trial begins by joining with plaintiff or defendant, or claiming adversely to them. (R.C.P. 75).

Interpleader.—A person who is or may be exposed to multiple liability or vexatious litigation because of several claims for the same thing, may bring an equitable action of interpleader against all such claimants. Their claims or titles need not have a common origin nor be identical, and may be adverse to or independent of each other. Such person may dispute liability, wholly or in part. (R.C.P. 35).

Joinder.—Plaintiff may join in same petition as many causes of action, legal or equitable, independent or alternative, as he may have against a single defendant. Any number of persons claiming relief jointly, severally or alternatively, arising out of the same transaction may join as plaintiffs in a single action, presenting any question of law or fact common to all of them. Any number of defendants may be joined in one action which asserts against them, jointly, severally or in the alternative, any right to relief in respect of, or arising out of the same transaction, when any question of law or fact common to all is presented. Misjoinder is not ground for dismissal of the action, but parties may be dropped by order of court on its own motion or that of any party at any stage of the action. Actions improperly joined may be severed on motion. (R.C.P. 22-28).

Splitting Causes of Action.—Not allowed in Iowa. (158 N.W.2d 739).

Consolidation of Actions.—Unless some party shows he will be prejudiced thereby, the court may consolidate separate actions which involve common questions of law or fact, or order a single trial of any or all issues therein. In such cases it may make such orders concerning the proceedings as tend to avoid unnecessary cost or delay. (R.C.P. 185).

Severance of Actions.—In any action, the court may for convenience or to avoid prejudice, order a separate trial of any claim, counterclaim, cross-claim, or of any separate issue of fact, or any number of any of them. Any claim against a party may be thus severed and proceeded with separately. (R.C.P. 186).

Stay of Proceedings.—A continuance may be allowed for any cause not growing out of the fault or negligence of the applicant, which satisfies the court that substantial justice will be more nearly obtained. It shall be allowed if all parties so agree, and the Court approves. (R.C.P. 182-183).

Abatement.—No action abates by the transfer of any interest therein during its pendency. (R.C.P. 16). All causes of action survive death, and action may be begun or continued by or against personal representative. (611.20, .22).

Prohibited Actions.—No action may be brought to renew or extend judgment on promissory obligation secured by mortgage or in real estate foreclosure or on a claim for rent or judgment assigned by receiver of closed bank or federal governmental agency to which bank or receiver is indebted, or on credits assigned by such receiver when the assignee is not trustee for depositors or creditors. (615).

Limitation of.—See topics Limitation of Actions, Pleading, Practice.

Small Claims.—See category Courts and Legislature, topic Courts.

Direct Actions Against Insurer.—See category Transportation, topic Motor Vehicles, subhead Direct Actions.

APPEAL AND ERROR:

Supreme Court.—Appeals may be taken from district courts to Supreme Court, at any time within 30 days from rendition of judgment or order appealed from where an interest in real estate is involved or where amount in controversy exceeds $5,000 or where trial judge certifies that case is one in which appeal should be allowed. Review by Supreme Court of small claims is discretionary. Interlocutory appeals may be allowed by Supreme Court or justice thereof. When motion for new trial is filed, time is extended to 30 days after entry of ruling on such motion. (R.A.P. 1-5).

Court of Appeals.—Appeals to Supreme Court may be transferred by supreme court to court of appeals by issuing order of transfer. Party to appeal decided by court of appeals may, as matter of right, file application with supreme court for further review within 20 days of filing of decision by court of appeals upon payment of $25 fee. If application not acted upon by supreme court within 30 days after filed it is deemed denied. (602.4102[4]).

District Court.—Defendant may appeal to district court from judgment of conviction by judicial magistrate or district associate judge. Plaintiff may appeal only if ordinance or statute is found invalid. Notice of appeal may be oral at time of judgment or written within ten days of judgment. Notice of appeal must be given to magistrate. Execution of judgment is stayed upon filing of appeal bond. Case is tried anew in district court. (R. Crim. P. 54).

Stay of Proceedings.—No appeal to Supreme Court shall stay proceedings under a judgment or order unless appellant executes a bond with sureties to be filed with and

APPEAL AND ERROR... *continued*

approved by clerk of court where judgment or order was entered. If judgment or order appealed from is for money, penalty of such bond must be 125% of amount, including costs; in all other cases an amount sufficient to save appellee harmless from consequences of appeal, but in no event less than $300. (R.A.P. 7).

Appeal Cost Bond.—Appellant may be required to give bond for costs under the same circumstances and upon the same showing as plaintiffs in civil actions in the inferior court may be. See topic Costs, subhead Security for Costs. (625A.12).

Character of Hearing.—Equity cases are heard de novo in Supreme Court. In other cases, errors at law only are reviewable. (R.A.P. 4).

Discretionary Review by Supreme Court.—Civil actions tried as small claims may be appealed for discretionary review to supreme court. (631.16).

BONDS:

Executors', administrators', guardians' and receivers' bonds are fixed by judge or clerk of district court and sureties approved by clerk. (633.170). Other bonds are fixed by statute, and generally sureties must be approved by clerk of district court. However, in case of indemnifying bond given to sheriff under execution and attachment proceedings, sureties are approved by him.

Sureties.—The bond of a surety company licensed to do business in the state will be accepted in all cases where a bond is required, except in case of bail bonds. No corporate surety may qualify on any one bond for more than 10% of its paid up cash capital and surplus unless excess be reinsured in company authorized to do business in state and reinsuring company may not assume such obligations for more than 10% of its capital. (625A.11-.18). All agents for surety company licensed to do business in Iowa must be resident of Iowa for purpose of acting on behalf of surety company with respect to any bond or bail in criminal cases. (625A.11).

See also category Insurance, topic Surety and Guaranty Companies.

Enforcement.—Action on a bond given to the state, any municipal corporation or any officer for the security of the public may be brought in name of any person intended to be secured who has sustained an injury by any breach. (R.C.P. 3). Summary enforcement may be had in undistributed estates. (633.186).

CERTIORARI:

Writ is not a substitute for appeal or writ of error, but may be granted in all cases where an inferior tribunal, board or officer, exercising judicial functions is alleged to have exceeded its proper jurisdiction, or otherwise acted illegally. (R.C.P. 306-318).

Jurisdiction.—Writ may be granted only by district court acting through district judge unless it is directed to that court, district judge, district associate judge or full time magistrate appointed pursuant to 602.51 or 602.59. Stay of proceedings may issue only upon petitioner giving bond; but court granting writ may on its own motion stay original proceedings.

Proceedings.—By ordinary proceedings so far as applicable. The court may receive the transcript of the original proceedings and other evidence, but may consider only the legality of the original proceedings and the sufficiency of the evidence therein.

Review.—Appeal to Supreme Court lies from judgment of district court and is governed by rules applicable to appeals in ordinary actions. No writ may issue unless petition is filed within 30 days from time inferior tribunal exceeded its jurisdiction. (R.C.P. 307[c]; 318).

CHARITABLE IMMUNITY:

See topic Damages.

COMMISSIONS TO TAKE TESTIMONY:

See topic Depositions and Discovery.

COMPARATIVE NEGLIGENCE:

See topic Damages.

COSTS:

Costs generally are awarded in favor of prevailing party.

Security for Costs.—Where plaintiff in action in district court is nonresident or private or foreign corporation, defendant may, on motion, require plaintiff to file bond for costs, to be approved by clerk. (621).

DAMAGES:

Common law generally prevails as to compensatory damages. Multiple or exemplary damages are permitted by statute for waste or malicious or wanton injury to property (658.1); for certain deceits (602.10113); for certain violations by rail carriers (327G.7); for malicious attachment (639.14); for libel and slander (659.3); and under common law where malice, recklessness, fraud or gross negligence are proven. Where plaintiff seeks punitive damages in action filed on or after July 1, 1986, court shall instruct jury to answer following interrogatories: (1) Was defendant's conduct willful and wanton, to be proven by preponderance of clear, convincing and satisfactory evidence; (2) was defendant's conduct specifically directed at plaintiff. If (1) and (2) both affirmative, all punitive recovery goes to plaintiff. If (1) affirmative and (2) negative, plaintiff recovers 25% of punitive findings and remaining 75% goes to state fund. Plaintiff cannot discover defendant's wealth until plaintiff establishes prima facie evidence exists for affirmative finding to interrogatory (1). (668A.1).

Party may petition court to pay judgment on structured, periodic or other non-lump sum payment basis. Collectibility and equitable considerations govern. (668.3, am'd 1986, c. 1214).

Charitable immunity abrogated as to paying hospital patients. (241 Ia. 1269, 45 N.W. 2d 151).

Person not manufacturer, assembler or designer who sells product is immune from suit based on strict liability or breach of implied warranty of merchantability which arises solely from alleged defect in original design or manufacture of product, with some exceptions. (613.18).

Collateral Source Rule Partially Abolished in Personal Injury Actions.—Evidence of past or future payment, from sources other than state or federal program or claimant's immediate family, of expenses of medical, rehabilitative, and custodial care is admissible. (668.14). This rule has been abolished in medical malpractice actions. (147.136).

Comparative Negligence Rule.—Comparative fault statute enacted in 1984. Fault means one or more acts or omissions that are in any measure negligent or reckless toward person or property of actor or others, or that subject person to strict tort liability. Term also includes breach of warranty, unreasonable assumption of risk not constituting enforceable express consent, misuse of product for which defendant otherwise would be liable, and unreasonable failure to avoid injury or to mitigate damages. (668.1).

Party means any of following: (1) Claimant; (2) person named as defendant; (3) person who has been released pursuant to §668.7; (4) third-party defendant. (668.2).

Contributory fault shall not bar recovery in action by claimant to recover damages for fault resulting in death or injury to person or property or to recover damages for loss of services, companionship, society, or consortium, unless claimant bears greater percentage of fault than combined percentage of fault attributed to defendants, third-party defendants and persons who have been released pursuant to §668.7, but any damages allowed shall be diminished in proportion to amount of fault attributable to claimant. (668.3[1][a] and [b]).

Rule of joint and several liability shall not apply to defendants who are found to bear less than 50% of total fault assigned to all parties. Defendants found 50% or more at fault are jointly and severally liable only for economic damages and not for any noneconomic awards. (668.4).

For cause of action arising on or after July 1, 1986, nonuse of safety belt admissible to mitigate damages, provided substantial evidence first introduced that failure to wear safety belt contributed to injuries claimed. Maximum mitigation reduced factor of 5% of plaintiff's damages. (321.445).

Comparative fault percentage not assigned if defendant pleads and proves product conformed to state of the art. However, duty to warn still applies to subsequently acquired knowledge of defect or dangerous condition. (668.12).

Sovereign Immunity.—Suits against State of Iowa are governed by c. 669 of Iowa Code. Notice of claim must be given within two years or barred.

See also category Estates and Trusts, topic Death, subhead Action for Death.

DECLARATORY JUDGMENTS:

Uniform Act substantially adopted. (R.C.P. 261-269).

DEPOSITIONS AND DISCOVERY:

Deposition of any person may be taken on any relevant matter, not privileged, for discovery or for use as evidence. (R.C.P. 140-143). Federal R.C.P. 30(a)-(b)(5), 30(c), 30(d), 30(e), 30(f)(1)(2), 30(g), and 45(b) were substantially adopted effective July 1, 1973.

Uniform Foreign Depositions Act not adopted.

Oral depositions may be taken only in Iowa or within 100 miles from the state, except on motion and notice of hearing. Court may order such deposition taken orally if sufficiently important and written interrogatories are not desirable. Conduct of oral deposition is as follows: Deponent first sworn in by officer taking deposition, testimony then taken including any objections thereto, including objections to officer's qualifications. Any adverse party may cross-examine or submit written interrogatories which the officer will put to deponent, whose answers will be recorded. (R.C.P. 147-148). Telephonic depositions may be taken upon reasonable notice. Absent agreement of all parties, reporter must be present with witness. Any desired exhibits must be sent to deponent and parties prior to deposition. Party or counsel may be in witness' presence at time of deposition. (R.C.P. 140).

Compelling Attendance and Testimony of Witnesses.—Attendance of witnesses can be compelled by subpoena issued by clerk of court in cases pending in Iowa district court, or by officer or commissioner authorized to take deposition, if it is being taken for use in court of another state or country, pursuant to the laws of such state or country. If witness fails to attend or refuses to testify, such officer or commissioner can report same to a judge of the district court, who may enforce obedience as if such action was pending in district court or such refusal had occurred in district court. (622.84, .102). No resident of Iowa can be thus compelled to attend out of the county where he resides, or is employed, or transacts his business in person (R.C.P. 155) except that a party can normally be deposed in the county where the action is pending (R.C.P. 140[e]; 147).

Deposition on written interrogatories may be taken after all parties are served with copies thereof and with a notice stating name and address of officer taking them and names and addresses of deponents. Officer can be anyone qualified to administer an oath, except a party interested in the suit. Adverse party may elect to appear and orally cross-examine. The party taking the deposition may then waive written interrogatories and examine orally. (R.C.P. 150-153).

Outside of State for Use within State.—Depositions within U.S. or a territory or insular possession thereof may be taken before any person authorized to administer oaths, by laws of U.S. or of place where examination is held. Depositions in a foreign land may be taken before secretary of Embassy or legation or a consul, vice-consul, consul general or consular agent of U.S. When witness is in military or naval service of U.S., his deposition may be taken before any commissioned officer under whose command he is serving, or any commissioned officer in Judge Advocate General's department. (R.C.P. 153).

DEPOSITIONS AND DISCOVERY . . . *continued*

To Perpetuate Testimony.—Court's common law powers to entertain actions to perpetuate testimony are not limited by statute. (R.C.P. 159).

Application to take depositions to perpetuate testimony for use in an action not yet pending must be entitled in the name of the applicant, be supported by affidavit and show: that he expects to be a party to an action in Iowa which he is unable to bring; the subject matter of such action and his interest therein; facts to be shown by the proposed testimony and his reasons for desiring to perpetuate it; name and address of each expected adverse party; name and address of each deponent and substance of his testimony. Application must be filed with court where prospective action might be brought, and notice and copy of application served on person named in petition as expected adverse party. Deposition is taken in manner hereinbefore outlined. (R.C.P. 160-161).

The following form may be used:

Form

The deposition of . . . ., of the county of . . . ., in the state of . . . ., produced, sworn and examined on his oath on the . . . . day of . . . ., A.D. 19. . . ., at the office of . . . ., in the city of . . . ., in the county of . . . ., and state of . . . ., by . . . ., a commissioner duly appointed by a commission issued from the office of the clerk of the district court of . . . . county, in the State of Iowa, bearing the signature of . . . ., clerk, and directed to said commissioner for the examination of said witness in a certain suit and matter in controversy now pending and undetermined in the said court, wherein . . . . is plaintiff and . . . . is defendant, in behalf of the said . . . ., both upon the interrogatories of the . . . . and the cross-interrogatories of the . . . . .

Oath of Shorthand Reporter.—State of . . . ., county of . . . ., ss: I, ..., being first duly sworn upon my oath do solemnly swear that I will take down and transcribe correctly the testimony of . . . ., witness, whose deposition is hereinafter set forth.

Subscribed and sworn to before me this . . . . day of . . . ., A.D. 19. . . . .
Notary Public in and for said
county and state.
Seal.

The said . . . ., witness as aforesaid, being first duly sworn by said commissioner as a witness in said cause previous to the commencement of his examination, to testify the truth as well on the part of the plaintiff as the defendant, testified and deposed as follows: (Here set forth first interrogatory, or if upon written interrogatories state same by number; then insert answer of witness to first interrogatory and so on successively in order in which interrogatories propounded and answered. Then follow: "Cross-interrogatories of the . . . . and answers of the witness thereto." Here again insert interrogatories, or if upon written interrogatories state same by number, and answers thereto successively in order aforesaid.)

(After deposition is completed, the whole must be reduced to writing and read over by or to the witness and subscribed and sworn to by him in the usual manner. The shorthand reporter, if the testimony is taken in shorthand, and the commissioner should then append to the deposition their respective certificates as follows:)

Affidavit of Shorthand Reporter.—State of . . . ., county of . . . ., ss: I, ..., of the city of . . . ., county of . . . ., state of . . . ., being first duly sworn, upon oath state that I was called to the office of . . . ., in the city of . . . ., county of . . . ., state of . . . ., to take down and transcribe the testimony of . . . ., the witness whose name is subscribed to the foregoing deposition; that previous to the commencement of the examination of said witness, I took and subscribed the oath above set forth to take down and transcribe correctly the testimony of said witness; that pursuant thereto I correctly took down the interrogatories and answers of said witness thereto in shorthand, that I correctly transcribed said shorthand notes and that the full, true and complete translation thereof in the order in which said interrogatories were propounded and answered is as in said deposition set forth.

(Jurat) . . . .

Certificate of Commissioner.—I, ..., of the city of . . . ., county of . . . ., state of . . . ., commissioner duly appointed as aforesaid to take the deposition of said . . . ., the witness whose name is subscribed to the foregoing deposition, do hereby certify that previous to the commencement of the examination of said witness, ..., the shorthand reporter called to take the testimony of said witness, was duly sworn by me as such commissioner to take down and transcribe correctly the testimony of said witness and to correctly translate the shorthand notes thereof and reduce same to writing, and that also previous to the commencement of the examination of said witness he was duly sworn by me as such commissioner to testify the truth in relation to the matters concerning which he should be interrogated; that said deposition was taken by me at my office (or at the office of . . . .) in the city of . . . ., county of . . . ., state of . . . ., on the . . . . day of . . . ., A.D. 19. . . .; that I caused all the interrogatories and cross-interrogatories enclosed with or attached to said commission (or in the case of oral interrogatories all the interrogatories directed to be put to said witness by either party litigant) to be propounded to said witness; that the testimony of said witness in answer thereto was correctly and fully written down by me (or by . . . ., a disinterested person under my direction and in my presence) and the said interrogatories and answers were read over by me to said witness and subscribed and sworn to by him in my presence; that exhibits . . . . were offered, identified and received in evidence as a part of said deposition and said exhibits (or true copies thereof) so marked and identified as exhibits . . . . are attached to and returned with said depositions; and that said . . . ., the aforesaid shorthand reporter, made affidavit as above set forth, certifying that the testimony and answers of said witness were correctly taken down and transcribed and that the deposition as above set forth is a true, full and complete translation of said testimony as given by said witness. In witness whereof, I have hereunto set my hand and official seal this . . . . day of . . . ., A. D. 19. . . . .

. . . .
Commissioner

EQUITY:

See topic Actions.

EVIDENCE:

See topic Depositions and Discovery.

Witnesses.—No person is disqualified as a witness because he is a party to the action or interested in the result thereof. (622.3).

Depositions.—See topic Depositions and Discovery, subhead Compelling Attendance and Testimony of Witnesses.

Expert Witnesses.—In professional liability cases, plaintiff must disclose and certify to court plaintiff's expert witness within 180 days of defendant's answer. Defendant must disclose within 90 days of plaintiff's certification. Failure to follow time requirements shall bar expert's testimony, unless leave of court for good cause shown is obtained. Rule not applicable to rebuttal or court appointed experts. (668.11). Medical malpractice experts must possess medical or dental qualifications which relate directly to medical problem at issue. (147.139).

Privileged Communications.—Attorney, counselor, physician, surgeon, physician's assistant, mental health professional, confidential stenographer or clerk of such person who obtains information by reason of that employment, minister or priest shall not be allowed, in giving testimony, to disclose any confidential communication properly entrusted to person in professional capacity. Such prohibition does not apply in civil action to recover damages for personal injury or wrongful death in which condition of person in whose favor such prohibition is made is element or factor of claim or defense of such person or party claiming through or under such person. Such evidence shall be admissible upon trial of action only as it relates to condition alleged. (622.10).

Husband and Wife.—In all civil and criminal cases, husband and wife may be witnesses for each other. (622.8).

Neither husband or wife can be examined as to communications made by one to other while married, nor may either, after marriage relation ceases, reveal such communication. (622.9).

Self-incrimination.—A witness cannot be compelled to answer or produce evidence after asserting answer or evidence would tend to incriminate or violate his 5th Amendment rights unless he waives rights or is granted immunity under statutory procedure. Refusal to testify after grant of immunity is subject to punishment for contempt of court. (R. Crim. P. 19).

INJUNCTIONS:

Injunction may be obtained as an independent remedy by an action in equity or as an auxiliary remedy in any action. In either case the party applying therefor may claim damages or other relief in same action. Injunction may be granted as part of the judgment; or may be granted by order at any prior stage of the proceedings, and is then known as a temporary injunction. (R.C.P. 320).

Writs of injunction may also be obtained in many special cases mentioned in the statute.

Temporary writs of injunction may be obtained by making application to the proper court or judge and the giving of a bond to be fixed by such court or judge. (R.C.P. 321-327).

JUDGMENTS:

Judgment by confession for money due may be entered without action on a written statement by the defendant setting forth the facts out of which the indebtedness arose. (676).

Judgment by default is entered when defendant fails to appear or file pleading when due. (R.C.P. 230-236).

Declaratory Judgments.—Uniform Act substantially adopted. (R.C.P. 261-269).

Offer of Judgment.—Defendant may, either before or after action is commenced, offer to confess judgment for a stated amount. If such offer be not accepted and plaintiff fails to recover judgment in excess of the amount offered, all costs after the offer must be paid by plaintiff. If judgment exceeds offer, all costs are taxed against defendant. (677).

Real property redeemed by debtor after sale under judgment (see category Debtor and Creditor, topic Executions) is free from liability for unpaid portion of judgment under which sold. (628.3).

Lien.—District court judgment is a lien, from date judgment is entered in the judgment docket and lien index of the clerk of the court having jurisdiction, on all real estate of the judgment debtor in the county in which judgment was entered and becomes a lien on other real estate on filing of a transcript of the judgment in district court of the county in which such real estate is located. The same rule applies to a judgment of a United States district court within the state. (624.24 and 624.24A).

Lien of judgments of appellate courts shall not attach to real estate until attested copy of judgment is filed with clerk of court of county in which real estate lies. (624.25).

On filing of transcript of judgment, clerk must docket and index same as though rendered in his own county. (624.26).

Lien of judgment continues for ten years after rendition, and attaches to real estate acquired after its rendition. (624.23). Judgment liens shall not remain lien upon real estate of defendant, platted as homestead pursuant to 561.4, unless execution is levied within 30 days of time defendant or defendant's agent has served written demand on owner of judgment. Demand shall state that lien and all benefits derived therefrom as to real estate platted as homestead shall be forfeited unless owner of judgment levies execution against that real estate within 30 days from date of service of demand. Written demand shall be served in any manner authorized for service of original notice under Iowa rules of civil procedure. Copy of written demand and proof of service thereof shall be filed in office of county recorder of county where real estate platted as homestead is located. Judgment liens described in this section shall not attach to

JUDGMENTS ... *continued*

subsequently acquired real estate owned by defendant if personal liability of defendant on judgment has been discharged under bankruptcy laws of U.S. (624.23).

Revivor of Judgment.—The death of one or all of the plaintiffs shall not prevent an execution being issued. In such case, one of the plaintiffs or the personal representatives, or heirs or their attorneys, shall file an affidavit with the clerk, of the death of plaintiff, and the clerk shall then indorse on the execution, the death of plaintiff, or if all be dead the names of the representatives, and the execution shall then be proceeded with, as if the survivor or the representatives were the only plaintiffs. The death of part only of defendants does not prevent execution issuing against survivors. (626.103-.107).

Action on judgment of court of record may not be brought after 20 years, nor on judgment of court not of record after ten years. (614.1). Action may not be brought on any judgment within nine years without leave of court. (614.3).

See also topic Actions, subhead Prohibited Actions.

Assignment.—General assignments of judgments are proper and are recognized the same as any other sale of intangibles.

Where a levy is made on a judgment which is held or owned by the execution debtor, the sheriff may assign the judgment to the execution creditor, and such assignment has the same validity as if made by the execution debtor. (626.21).

Satisfaction of judgment may be by marginal entry on the record or by acknowledged instrument. (624.37). There is no statutory form of satisfaction.

Foreign Judgments.—Suit must be brought on a foreign judgment here in order to secure judgment thereon in this state. Foreign judgment may be proved by the attestation of the clerk and seal of the court annexed if there be a seal, together with a certificate of judge, chief justice or presiding magistrate, that the attestation is in due form of law, and the official certificate of a justice of the peace of any state to any judgment and the preliminary proceedings before him, supported by the official certificate of the clerk of any court of record, within the county in which said justice resides, stating said justice is an acting justice of the peace of that county, and that the signature to his certificate is genuine, is sufficient evidence of such proceeding and judgment. (622.52 et seq.).

Uniform Enforcement of Foreign Judgments Act adopted. Judgment creditor has option to proceed under this Act. (626A).

Judgment Notes.—See category Business Regulation and Commerce, topic Bills and Notes.

Interest.—See category Business Regulation and Commerce, topic Interest, subhead Judgments.

LIMITATION OF ACTIONS:

Actions must be commenced within following periods. (614):

Twenty years: On judgment of a court of record of any state of the United States or of a federal court. (614.1[6]).

Fifteen years: For injury to person or property related to unsafe or defective condition of improvement to real property, except against owner, occupant, or operator of improvement. (614.1[11]). Product liability actions must be brought within 15 years after product first purchased, leased, bailed, or installed for use unless expressly warranted for longer time. (614.1[2A]).

Eleven years: Actions in connection with transfers or obligations regarding public bonds must be brought within 11 years of cancellation, transfer, redemption, or replacement of public bonds or obligations. (614.1[13]).

Ten years: On judgment of a court not of record; to recover real property; on written contract; or to set aside decree quieting title to real estate (614.1[5]); to enforce title to real estate conveyed after July 1, 1981 by deed, mortgage, or other instrument, where spouse failed to join in conveyance (614.15[2]).

Five years: On unwritten contract; on account, time running from date of last item; for injury to real or personal property including injury suffered as result of sexual abuse by counselor or therapist; to recover possession of personal property; for fraud, time running from discovery thereof; action not otherwise provided for. (614.1[4] and [12]).

Three years: Against public officer for liability incurred in official capacity. (614.1[3]).

Two years: To enforce mechanic's lien, time running from expiration of time allowed for filing lien claim; for injuries to person or reputation, including injuries to relative rights whether based on contract or tort; for statutory penalty; action founded on claim for wages or for liability or penalty for failure to pay wages. Claims permitted against state under c. 25A barred unless within two years after claim accrued claim in writing made to State Appeal Board. Claims founded on secured interest in farm products within two years of date of sale of farm products against secured interest of creditor. (572.27, 614.1[2], [8], [10]).

One year: To enforce payment of a penalty or forfeiture under an ordinance. (614.1[1]).

Six months: Claims against governmental subdivision permitted under 613A unless claimant gives governing body of municipality written notice within 60 days of alleged wrong which gives claimant two years from date of notice to commence action. (613A.5). (Held unconstitutional in Miller v. Boone County Mem. Hosp., 394 N.W.2d 776 [Iowa 1986]. Now governed by c. 614.)

Three months: In special charter cities for claims arising from defective streets or sidewalks or from any cause originating in neglect or failure of municipal corporation or its officers to perform their duties, notice must be filed within 30 days after incident and actions must be commenced within three months. (420.45). In special charter cities, no suit against such city for unliquidated claim or demand can be brought unless within three months from time same became due or accrued and notice must be filed with clerk 30 days prior to commencement of said suit. (420.44).

Absence.—Time of nonresidence of defendant not included in computing period; but suit can not be maintained on claim barred in another county prior to defendant coming here, unless cause of action arose in this state. (614.6. .7).

Disability of Plaintiff.—In case of infancy or mental illness of the person having a right of action, except for a penalty or forfeiture, the time is extended for one year after the removal of the disability. (614.8, .19, .27).

Death of Defendant.—In all cases where by the death of the party to be charged, the bringing of an action against his estate shall have been delayed beyond the period provided for by statute, the time within which action may be brought against his estate is extended for six months from the date of the death of said decedent. (614.2).

Death of Plaintiff.—If person having a cause of action dies within one year previous to expiration of limitation, time to sue is extended to one year after death. (614.9).

Revival of Barred Claims.—Cause of action on contract barred by limitations is revived by an admission that the debt is unpaid or a new promise to pay, either of which must be in writing and be signed by the party to be charged in order to have this effect. (614.11).

Pleading.—Bar of limitations of actions is primarily affirmative defense to be specially asserted in separate division of responsive pleading to claims for relief, except where obvious from face of assailed pleading not only that claim may be barred but that necessarily barred when action commenced, then motion to dismiss is proper. (173 N.W.2d 549).

Contractual limitations are permitted.

Uniform Commercial Code adopted. (554). See category Business Regulation and Commerce, topic Commercial Code. However, §2-725(1) has been modified so as to remove four year limitation found in Uniform Commercial Code. Ordinary limitations, as outlined above, apply to contracts of sale.

PARTITION:

(651).

Real or personal property may be partitioned by equitable proceedings. Petition must describe the property and the interests of the parties therein. Court may order the abstract filed; if none is available, plaintiff may be ordered to have one prepared and filed. All owners of undivided interests and lienholders are indispensable parties. Where the entire interest in real estate was owned by a decedent of whose estate the administration is begun, action cannot be started for six months after notice of issuance of letters or at any time while an application for authority to sell is pending in probate. (651).

Partition in Kind or Sale.—Real property must be partitioned by sale and division of proceeds, unless partition in kind is prayed. Personal property subject to lien can be partitioned only by sale. (R.C.P. 284).

Service may be made by publication when an affidavit is filed that personal service cannot be made within the state. See topic Process, subhead Publication.

Costs of partition proceedings are paid eventually by all parties in proportion to their interests, except costs created by contests, which are taxed against the losing contestant unless otherwise ordered. (R.C.P. 293).

PLEADING:

(R.C.P. 68-120).

All common counts, general issues, demurrers, fictions and technical forms of pleading are abolished. The pleadings are: Petition, answer and such counter-claim, reply, amendment, cross-claim, third party petition or petition of intervention as are proper.

Petition must contain: (1) Name of court and county in which action is brought; (2) names of parties to action, with words "Petition at Law" or "Petition in Equity;" (3) statement of facts constituting plaintiff's cause of action; (4) demand of relief to which plaintiff considers himself entitled. Petition must not specify amount of damages sought, except in small claims cases and cases involving only liquidated damages, although petition must certify that amount sought satisfies applicable jurisdictional amount. (619.18, R.C.P. 69). Petitions must be separated into numbered paragraphs, and separate causes of action must be stated in separate counts. (R.C.P. 69, 70, 78, 79).

Answer must show on whose behalf it is filed and specifically admit or deny each paragraph of the petition. Denial may be for lack of information. It must state any additional facts deemed to show a defense and may raise points of law appearing on the face of the petition. It may contain as many defenses, legal or equitable, as the pleader claims, which may be inconsistent. It may contain a counterclaim, which must be in a separate division. Each separate cause of action or defense must be stated in a separately numbered division. (R.C.P. 72).

Counterclaim.—Unless prohibited by statute or rule, counterclaim may be filed on any matured cause of action against opposing party. Compulsory if arising out of same transaction. (R.C.P. 29 and 30).

Reply.—There must be a reply to a counterclaim and to new matter in an answer, but this must not be inconsistent with the petition. Points of law arising on the face of the answer may be raised by a reply. Facts asserted in a reply are denied by operation of law. (R.C.P. 68; 100[e]).

Demurrer is no longer recognized in Iowa. (R.C.P. 67).

Verification.—Pleadings need not be verified unless special statutes so require. Counsel's or party's signature to every motion or pleading deemed person's certificate that has read motion, to best of person's knowledge, information, and belief formed after reasonable inquiry it is grounded in fact, warranted by existing law or good faith argument for extension, modification, or reversal of existing law, good grounds for making claims therein, and not interposed for harrassment or delay. (R.C.P. 80). Unsigned pleading or motion may be stricken unless signed promptly after brought to

PLEADING . . . *continued*

signer's attention. If signed in violation of Rule, court must impose appropriate sanction on person signing, party, or both. (619.19).

Service on adverse parties is made by party or his attorney, by mail; copies for them must be provided if they have appeared. (R.C.P. 106).

Time.—Motions attacking pleading must be served before responding to pleading or, if no response required, within 20 days after service of pleading on such party. Answer to petition must be served on or before appearance date prescribed in R.C.P. 53. Party served with pleading stating cross-claim against party must serve answer thereto within 20 days of service of that pleading. Plaintiff must serve reply to counterclaim in answer within 20 days after service of answer, or if reply ordered by court, within 20 days after service of order unless order otherwise directs. Service of motion permitted under rules alters time periods as follows unless different time ordered by court: (1) If court denies motion or postpones disposition until trial on merits, responsive pleading must be served within ten days after notice of court's action; (2) if court grants motion for more specific statement, responsive pleading must be served within ten days after service of more specific statement; unless parties stipulate in writing otherwise, filing of motion for additional time shall delay responsive pleading for ten days after service of motion unless court orders otherwise.

Party must respond to amended pleading within time remaining in response to original pleading or ten days after service, whichever longer, unless court orders otherwise. (R.C.P. 106[d]).

Proof of Claims.—An attorney forwarding a claim for collection should forward the instrument or contract, if any, sued upon, a full statement of the facts upon which the cause of action is based, an itemized statement of the claim, together with an affidavit of one who has knowledge thereof that such statement is true and correct, that the amount stated is due and unpaid after allowing all just deductions, credits and offsets, and that the claim is the property of the claimant, and information about the parties, including addresses, whether an individual, an individual doing business under a trade name, a firm or a corporation; if a corporation, state of organization and location of principal place of business, and if a partnership, the names of the partners.

Small Claims.—See category Courts and Legislature, topic Courts.

Frivolous Claims.—If party commencing action has in preceding five year period unsuccessfully prosecuted three or more frivolous actions, proceedings may be stayed until party furnishes undertaking secured by cash or approved securities to pay all costs resulting to opposing parties to action including reasonable attorney fee. (Iowa Rule of Civil Procedure 80, Iowa Code 617.16).

PRACTICE:

Regulated by Rules of Civil Procedure.

Discovery.—Allowed liberally by various methods. (R.C.P. 121-134, 140-166).

Demand for admission of facts may be served. Failure to admit, not in good faith, may make party subject to paying other party's expenses of proving same, including reasonable attorneys fees. (R.C.P. 127, 134[c]).

Direct Action Against Insurer.—See category Transportation, topic Motor Vehicles, subhead Direct Actions.

Small Claims.—(631). See category Courts and Legislature, topic Courts.

See also topics Actions, Appeal and Error, Depositions and Discovery, Injunctions, Judgments, Pleading, Process; category Debtor and Creditor, topics Attachment, Executions, Garnishment.

PROCESS:

Original Notice.—Civil action is commenced by filing petition with court. Must also deliver to clerk original notice to be served with petition and sufficient copies of both. Original notice must contain name of court where action brought, names of parties, be directed to defendant, state name and address of plaintiff's attorney, and time within which rules require defendant to serve, and within reasonable time thereafter file, motion or answer, and must notify defendant that in case of his failure to do so, judgment by default will be entered against him for relief demanded. Original notice must be signed by clerk and be under seal of court. Clerk may require party delivering original notice to advance reasonable costs of service. Original notice and copy of petition must be served together except when service by publication. If service by publication, original notice alone shall be published and must contain general statement of cause or causes of action, relief demanded, and if for liquidated damages or for small claim, amount thereof. Defendant served by publication or publication and mailing must appear on or before date fixed in notice as published, which cannot be less than 20 days after date of last publication. Defendant served in manner prescribed by statute or court order must appear on or before date so fixed. If service by mail under R.C.P. 56.2 appearance date shall appear in original notice and must be not less than 60 days following mailing date. In all other cases defendant shall serve and within reasonable time thereafter file motion or answer within 20 days after service of original notice and petition upon such defendant. (R.C.P. 49, 53).

Who May Serve.—Notice may be served by any person not a party to the action nor an attorney therein. A party, his agent or attorney may take acknowledgment of service and deliver copy of notice in connection therewith and may mail copy of original notice when mailing is required or permitted under any rule or statute. (R.C.P. 49[e]).

Personal Service.—Original notices are served by delivering copy to proper person along with copy of petition. (R.C.P. 56.1; 56.2).

Personal service on individual aged 18 years or more, who has not been adjudged incompetent, may be made by serving him personally; or by serving, at his dwelling house or usual place of abode, any person residing therein who is at least 18 years old, but if such place is a rooming house, hotel, club, or apartment building, the copy must be delivered to such a person who is either a member of defendant's family or the manager, clerk, proprietor or custodian of such place. (R.C.P. 56.1[a]).

Personal service on minor under eighteen years old is made by serving either the guardian of his person or property unless the notice is served on behalf of such guardian, or his parent or some person aged 18 years or more who has his care and custody, or with whom he resides, or in whose service he is employed. Where the notice upon a minor is served on behalf of one who is the guardian or other fiduciary and the guardian or other fiduciary is the only person who would be available upon whom service could be made, the court must appoint, without prior notice on the ward, a guardian ad litem upon whom service shall be made. (R.C.P. 56.1[b]).

Personal service on incompetent person not confined in a state hospital for the mentally ill may be made by serving the guardian of his person or property, unless the notice is served on behalf of such guardian, or his spouse, or some person aged 18 years or more who has his care and custody or with whom he resides. Where the notice upon an incompetent is served on behalf of one who is the guardian or other fiduciary, and there is no other person upon whom service could be made, the court must appoint, without prior notice to the ward, a guardian ad litem upon whom service shall be made. (R.C.P. 56.1[c]).

Personal service on person, whether competent or not, confined to county home or state hospital for the mentally ill, university of Iowa hospital, or other institution in charge of Iowa Board of Control or of U. S. may be made by the official in charge of such institution or his assistant. (R.C.P. 56.1[d]).

Personal service on patient in hospital for the mentally ill, or person adjudged incompetent confined to county home shall be accepted, in the patient's behalf, by the official in charge of such institution or his assistant if, in the opinion of the official in charge or his assistant, direct service on the defendant would injuriously affect him, which fact must be stated in such acceptance. (R.C.P. 56.1[e]).

Personal service on a partnership or association suable under a common name may be made by serving any present or acting or last known officer thereof, or any general or managing agent or any agent or person now authorized by appointment or by law to receive service of original notice, or on the general partner of a partnership. (R.C.P. 56.1[f]).

Corporations.—If an action is against a domestic corporation organized for profit, service may be had on any trustee or officer thereof, or on any agent employed in the general management of its business, or on any of the last known or acting officers of such corporation. (617.6).

Foreign Corporations.—If foreign corporation doing business in state has made application for permit to transact business and has failed to file designation of agent for service of process (see category Business Organizations, topic Corporations), or such agent cannot be found, service on said corporation may be had by sending notice to Secretary of State. (617.3). Service may also be made on general agent of foreign corporation wherever found within state. (617.3). Statute purports to make foreign corporation making contract with Iowa resident to be performed in whole or in part in Iowa, or committing tort in Iowa, subject to suit in this state by serving notice on Secretary of State. (617.3).

Insurance Companies.—If action for loss or damage on contract of insurance or indemnity, service may be on general agent, recording agent, or agent with authority to issue policies. (617.5).

Surety Companies.—If action on bond, service may be upon any agent in this state, or if none, on Commissioner of Insurance 15 days before term. (636.20).

Foreign Insurance Companies.—Service may be on Commissioner of Insurance. (636.21).

Service on Local Agent or Clerk.—When a corporation or individual has, for the transaction of any business, an office or agency in any county other than that in which the principal resides, service may be made on any agent or clerk employed in such office or agency, in all actions growing out of or connected with the business of that office or agency. (R.C.P. 56.1[f, g]). Foregoing has been construed to afford process sufficient to give jurisdiction over nonresidents. (See 294 U.S. 623.)

Long Arm Statute.—See subhead Foreign Corporations, supra and subhead Nonresident Individuals, infra.

Nonresident defendant in criminal action, present in this state, either voluntarily or involuntarily, may be served with process, either civil or criminal. (617.1).

Nonresident Individuals.—For mode of service on nonresident motorist see category Transportation, topic Motor Vehicles, subhead Actions Against Nonresidents.

Service on nonresident who makes contract to be performed in whole or in part in Iowa or commits a tort in whole or in part in Iowa by serving notice on Secretary of State. Nonresident includes resident at time of tort but later becomes nonresident or a person who has absented himself from state at least six months from commission of tort. (617.3).

Nonresident Watercraft.—Nonresident who uses any watercraft on Iowa waters may be served by sending notice to Secretary of State under procedure similar to actions against nonresident motorists. (461B.4).

Publication.—Service may be made by publication when an affidavit is filed that personal service cannot be made on the defendant within this state. Such service is made by publishing notice, in paper selected by the plaintiff, once each week for three consecutive weeks. In every case where service is made upon a known defendant by publication, copy of the original notice must also be sent by ordinary mail addressed to defendant at last known mailing address, unless affidavit of party or his attorney if filed before entry of judgment or decree, stating that no mailing address is known and that diligent inquiry has been made to ascertain it. Such copy of notice must be mailed not less than 20 days before date set for appearance. Proof of such mailing must be by affidavit filed before entry of judgment or decree. (R.C.P. 60.1).

Service by publication may be had in the following cases: for recovery of real property or any estate or interest therein; for the partition of real or personal property in Iowa; to foreclose a mortgage, lien, encumbrance or charge on real or personal property; for specific performance of a contract for sale of real estate; to establish, set aside or construe a will, if defendant resides out of Iowa, or if his residence is

PROCESS . . . *continued*

unknown; against a nonresident of Iowa or a foreign corporation which has property, or debts owing to it in Iowa, sought to be taken by any provisional remedy, or appropriated in any way; against any defendant who, being a nonresident of Iowa, or a foreign corporation, has or claims any actual or contingent interest in or lien on real or personal property in Iowa which is the subject of such action, or to which it relates; or where the action seeks to exclude such defendant from any lien, interest or claim therein; against any resident of the state who has departed therefrom, or from the county of his residence, with intent to delay or defraud his creditors, or to avoid service, or who keeps himself concealed with like intent; for divorce or separate maintenance or to modify a decree in such action, or to annul an illegal marriage, against a defendant who is a nonresident of Iowa or whose residence is unknown; to quiet title to real estate, against a defendant who is a nonresident of Iowa, or whose residence is unknown; against a partnership, corporation or association sueable under a common name, when no person can be found on whom personal service can be made; to vacate or modify a judgment or for a new trial under Rules 252 and 253. (R.C.P. 60).

Personal judgment cannot be had against any defendant served with notice by publication. When publication is completed, proof of publication by affidavit of the publisher must be filed with the clerk. (R.C.P. 63).

REPLEVIN:

(643.)

An action of replevin may be brought in any county in which the property or some part thereof is situated. District court sitting in small claims has concurrent jurisdiction of action of replevin if value of property claimed $4,000 or less. (631.1[3]).

Petition must be verified and must state:

1. A particular description of the property claimed.

2. Its actual value and where there are several articles, the actual value of each.

3. The facts constituting the plaintiff's right to the present possession thereof, and the extent of his interest in the property, whether it be full or qualified ownership.

4. That it was neither taken on the order or judgment of a court against him, nor under an execution or attachment against him, or against the property; but if it was taken by either of these modes, then it must state the facts constituting an exemption from seizure by such process.

5. The facts constituting the alleged cause of detention thereof, according to his best belief.

6. The amount of damages which the affiant believes the plaintiff ought to recover for the detention thereof. (643.1).

District court sitting in small claims has concurrent jurisdiction of action for abandonment of mobile home or personal property pursuant to §555.B3, if no money judgment in excess of $4,000 is sought.

Bond must be filed with clerk for use of any person injured by proceeding. (643.6). When plaintiff desires immediate delivery of property, he must execute bond to defendant, with sureties approved by clerk, in double value of property conditioned upon plaintiff appearing and prosecuting action to judgment and returning property if ordered to do so. (643.7).

Writ.—Upon direction of court after notice and opportunity for such hearing as court may prescribe, clerk shall issue a writ directed to proper officer requiring him to take property described and deliver it to plaintiff. (643.5). If petition shows that property has been wrongfully removed into another county from one in which action is commenced, writ may issue from county whence property was wrongfully taken, and may be served in any county where it may be found. (643.8).

Retention by Defendant.—Before delivery to plaintiff, the defendant may stay delivery and retain possession by executing a bond with sureties to be approved by the clerk or sheriff. (643.12).

Concealment.—When it appears by affidavit that the property claimed has been disposed of or concealed so that the writ cannot be executed, the court upon verified petition therefor, may compel the attendance of the defendant or other person claiming or concealing the property, and examine him on oath as to the situation of the property, and punish a wilful obstruction or hindrance or disobedience of the order of court in this respect, as in case of contempt. (643.21).

Claims of Third Persons.—If a third person claims the property or any part thereof, the plaintiff may amend and bring him in as a co-defendant or the defendant may obtain his substitution by the proper mode, or the claimant may himself intervene by the process of intervention. (643.4).

Judgment.—The judgment must determine which party is entitled to the possession of the property and designate his right therein and, if such party has not the possession thereof, must also determine the value of the right of such party, which right shall be absolute as to an adverse party, and must also award such damages to either party as he may be entitled to for the alleged detention of the property. If the judgment be against the plaintiff for the money value of the property, it must also be against the sureties on his bond. (643.17).

SEQUESTRATION:

No statutory provision.

SERVICE:

See topic Process.

STAY OF EXECUTION:

See topic Appeal and Error; category Debtor and Creditor, topic Executions.

SUBMISSION OF CONTROVERSY:

Parties to question which might be subject of civil action may present agreed statement of facts to any court having jurisdiction of subject matter, and on showing

that controversy is real and proceeding in good faith court will hear and determine case and render judgment which is enforcible and reviewable in same manner as if rendered in action. (678).

VENUE:

Actions must be brought in the county where the defendants or some of them reside, or where the real property is situated, or where, by its terms, a written contract is to be performed; or if none of the defendants has any residence in this state, then in a county where either of them may be found. Motor vehicle damage actions may also be brought in the county in which the damage or injury is sustained. (616).

Public Utilities.—Actions against express, railroad, telegraph, telephone or electric transmission line companies may be brought in any county through which their line passes. (616.8).

Corporations.—When any corporation or person has an office or agency in any county for the transaction of business, any suits growing out of or connected with the business of that office or agency, may be brought in such county. (616.14). Foreign corporations served under "single act" statute may be sued in county of plaintiff's residence, or county where contract was to be performed or tort was committed. (617.3).

Insurance companies may be sued in the county of the principal place of business, the county of the residence of the plaintiff, the county in which the contract of insurance was made, or in which the loss occurred, or, on death or disability policy, in county of insured's domicile at time of loss. (616.10).

Actions Against Nonresident Motorists.—See category Transportation, topic Motor Vehicles, subhead Actions Against Nonresidents.

Action Brought in Wrong County.—May be transferred to proper county on motion of defendant prior to answer. (R.C.P. 175).

Change of Venue.—The place of trial may be changed on motion showing one of the following grounds: (a) if the county where the case would be tried is a party, and the motion is by the adverse party, and the issue being triable by a jury and a jury having been demanded; (b) where the trial judge is directly interested in the action or related by consanguinity or affinity within the fourth degree to any party so interested; (c) if a trial judge or the inhabitants of the county are so prejudiced against the moving party or if an adverse party has such undue influence over such inhabitants that the movant cannot obtain a fair trial; (d) pursuant to written agreement of the parties. A defendant, sued in a county where he does not reside, on a written contract expressly performable in such county, who has filed a sworn answer claiming fraud in the inception of said contract as a complete defense thereto, may have the case transferred to the county of his residence. (R.C.P. 167).

Contract Provisions.—Written agreements fixing venue are enforceable. (R.C.P. 167).

COURTS AND LEGISLATURE

COURTS:

United States District Courts.—

Northern District.—Clerk's office: 329 Federal Building, Cedar Rapids 52407.

Cedar Rapids Division is composed of following counties: Benton, Cedar, Grundy, Hardin, Iowa, Jones, Linn and Tama.

Court sits at Cedar Rapids.

Eastern Division is composed of following counties: Allamakee, Black Hawk, Bremer, Buchanan, Chickasaw, Clayton, Delaware, Dubuque, Fayette, Floyd, Howard, Jackson, Mitchell and Winneshiek.

Court sits sometimes at Dubuque and Waterloo.

Western Division is composed of following counties: Buena Vista, Cherokee, Clay, Crawford, Dickinson, Ida, Lyon, Monona, O'Brien, Osceola, Plymouth, Sac, Sioux and Woodbury.

Court sits at Sioux City.

Central Division is composed of following counties: Butler, Calhoun, Carroll, Cerro Gordo, Emmett, Franklin, Hamilton, Hancock, Humboldt, Kossuth, Palo Alto, Pocahontas, Webster, Winnebago, Worth and Wright.

Court sits sometimes at Fort Dodge and Mason City.

Deposit for fees required in all cases; plaintiff, $120.

Southern District.—Clerk's office: Federal Building, 1 E. 1st and Walnut, Des Moines 50309.

Central Division is composed of following counties: Boone, Dallas, Greene, Guthrie, Jasper, Madison, Marion, Marshall, Polk, Poweshiek, Story and Warren.

Court sits at Des Moines.

Eastern Division is composed of following counties: Des Moines, Henry, Lee, Louisa and Van Buren.

Court sits at Davenport.

Western Division is composed of following counties: Audubon, Cass, Fremont, Harrison, Mills, Montgomery, Page, Pottawattamie and Shelby.

Court sits at Council Bluffs.

Southern Division is composed of following counties: Adair, Adams, Clarke, Decatur, Lucas, Ringgold, Taylor, Union and Wayne.

Court sits at Des Moines by order of Pretermission of Judicial Council of 8th Circuit.

Davenport Division is composed of following counties: Clinton, Johnson, Muscatine, Scott and Washington.

Court sits at Davenport.

Ottumwa Division is composed of following counties: Appanoose, Davis, Jefferson, Keokuk, Mahaska, Monroe and Wapello.

Court sits at Des Moines.

Deposit for fees required in all cases; plaintiff, $120.

Supreme Court.—Sits at Des Moines.

See note at head of Digest as to 1998 legislation covered.

See Topical Index in front part of this volume.

COURTS . . . *continued*
Court of Appeals.—Sits at Des Moines.

District Courts.—State is divided into eight judicial districts, composed of several counties and judges in each district. District courts are courts of general original jurisdiction in all cases, including civil, criminal, and probate matters.
Districts.—
First District: Counties of Dubuque, Delaware, Clayton, Allamakee, Winneshiek, Chickasaw, Fayette, Buchanan, Black Hawk, Howard, and Grundy.
Second District: Counties of Mitchell, Floyd, Butler, Bremer, Worth, Winnebago, Hancock, Cerro Gordo, Franklin, Wright, Humboldt, Pocahontas, Sac, Calhoun, Webster, Hamilton, Carroll, Greene, Hardin, Marshall, Story, and Boone.
Third District: Counties of Kossuth, Emmet, Dickinson, Osceola, Lyon, O'Brien, Clay, Palo Alto, Cherokee, Buena Vista, Plymouth, Sioux, Woodbury, Ida, Monona and Crawford.
Fourth District: Counties of Harrison, Shelby, Audubon, Pottawattamie, Cass, Mills, Montgomery, Fremont, and Page.
Fifth District: Counties of Guthrie, Dallas, Polk, Jasper, Madison, Warren, Marion, Adair, Adams, Union, Clarke, Lucas, Taylor, Ringgold, Decatur, and Wayne.
Sixth District: Counties of Tama, Benton, Linn, Jones, Iowa and Johnson.
Seventh District: Counties of Jackson, Clinton, Cedar, Scott, and Muscatine.
Eighth District: Counties of Poweshiek, Mahaska, Keokuk, Washington, Monroe, Wapello, Jefferson, Appanoose, Davis, Van Buren, Louisa, Henry, Des Moines, and Lee.
Place of Sitting.—
Adair County: Fifth District; court sits at Greenfield.
Adams County: Fifth District; court sits at Corning.
Allamakee County: First District; court sits at Waukon.
Appanoose County: Eighth District; court sits at Centerville.
Audubon County: Fourth District; court sits at Audubon.
Benton County: Sixth District; court sits at Vinton.
Black Hawk County: First District; court sits at Waterloo.
Boone County: Second District; court sits at Boone.
Bremer County: Second District; court sits at Waverly.
Buchanan County: First District; court sits at Independence.
Buena Vista County: Third District; court sits at Storm Lake.
Butler County: Second District; court sits at Allison.
Calhoun County: Second District; court sits at Rockwell City.
Carroll County: Second District; court sits at Carroll.
Cass County: Fourth District; court sits at Atlantic.
Cedar County: Seventh District; court sits at Tipton.
Cerro Gordo County: Second District; court sits at Mason City.
Cherokee County: Third District; court sits at Cherokee.
Chickasaw County: First District; court sits at New Hampton.
Clarke County: Fifth District; court sits at Osceola.
Clay County: Third District; court sits at Spencer.
Clayton County: First District; court sits at Elkader.
Clinton County: Seventh District; court sits at Clinton.
Crawford County: Third District; court sits at Denison.
Dallas County: Fifth District; court sits at Adel.
Davis County: Eighth District; court sits at Bloomfield.
Decatur County: Fifth District; court sits at Leon.
Delaware County: First District; court sits at Manchester.
Des Moines County: Eighth District; court sits at Burlington.
Dickinson County: Third District; court sits at Spirit Lake.
Dubuque County: First District; court sits at Dubuque.
Emmet County: Third District; court sits at Estherville.
Fayette County: First District; court sits at West Union.
Floyd County: Second District; court sits at Charles City.
Franklin County: Second District; court sits at Hampton.
Fremont County: Fourth District; court sits at Sidney.
Greene County: Second District; court sits at Jefferson.
Grundy County: First District; court sits at Grundy Center.
Guthrie County: Fifth District; court sits at Guthrie Center.
Hamilton County: Second District; court sits at Webster City.
Hancock County: Second District; court sits at Garner.
Hardin County: Second District; court sits at Eldora.
Harrison County: Fourth District; court sits at Logan.
Henry County: Eighth District; court sits at Mt. Pleasant.
Howard County: First District; court sits at Cresco.
Humboldt County: Second District; court sits at Dakota City.
Ida County: Third District; court sits at Ida Grove.
Iowa County: Sixth District; court sits at Marengo.
Jackson County: Seventh District; court sits at Maquoketa.
Jasper County: Fifth District; court sits at Newton.
Jefferson County: Eighth District; court sits at Fairfield.
Johnson County: Sixth District; court sits at Iowa City.
Jones County: Sixth District; court sits at Anamosa.
Keokuk County: Eighth District; court sits at Sigourney.
Kossuth County: Third District; court sits at Algona.
Lee County: Eighth District; court sits at Ft. Madison and Keokuk.
Linn County: Sixth District; court sits at Cedar Rapids.
Louisa County: Eighth District; court sits at Wapello.
Lucas County: Eighth District; court sits at Chariton.
Lyon County: Third District; court sits at Rock Rapids.
Madison County: Fifth District; court sits at Winterset.
Mahaska County: Eighth District; court sits at Oskaloosa.
Marion County: Fifth District; court sits at Knoxville.
Marshall County: Second District; court sits at Marshalltown.
Mills County: Fourth District; court sits at Glenwood.

Mitchell County: Second District; court sits at Osage.
Monona County: Third District; court sits at Onawa.
Monroe County: Eighth District; court sits at Albia.
Montgomery County: Fourth District; court sits at Red Oak.
Muscatine County: Seventh District; court sits at Muscatine.
O'Brien County: Third District; court sits at Primghar.
Osceola County: Third District; court sits at Sibley.
Page County: Fourth District; court sits at Clarinda.
Palo Alto County: Third District; court sits at Emmetsburg.
Plymouth County: Third District; court sits at LeMars.
Pocahontas County: Second District; court sits at Pocahontas.
Polk County: Fifth District; court sits at Des Moines.
Pottawattamie County: Fourth District; court sits at Avoca and Council Bluffs.
Poweshiek County: Eighth District; court sits at Montezuma.
Ringgold County: Fifth District; court sits at Mt. Ayr.
Sac County: Second District; court sits at Sac City.
Scott County: Seventh District; court sits at Davenport.
Shelby County: Fourth District; court sits at Harlan.
Sioux County: Third District; court sits at Orange City.
Story County: Second District; court sits at Nevada.
Tama County: Sixth District; court sits at Toledo.
Taylor County: Fifth District; court sits at Bedford.
Union County: Fifth District; court sits at Creston.
Van Buren County: Eighth District; court sits at Keosauqua.
Wapello County: Eighth District; court sits at Ottumwa.
Warren County: Fifth District; court sits at Indianola.
Washington County: Eighth District; court sits at Washington.
Wayne County: Fifth District; court sits at Corydon.
Webster County: Second District; court sits at Ft. Dodge.
Winnebago County: Second District; court sits at Forest City.
Winneshiek County: First District; court sits at Decorah.
Woodbury County: Third District; court sits at Sioux City.
Worth County: Second District; court sits at Northwood.
Wright County: Second District; court sits at Clarion.

Probate Courts.—There are no separate probate courts. Probate jurisdiction is exercised by district courts.

Judicial Magistrates.—Judicial magistrates have jurisdiction of simple misdemeanors, including traffic and ordinance violations, preliminary hearings, search warrant proceedings, county and municipal infractions and small claims. Magistrates have jurisdiction to exercize powers specified in 556F.2 and 556F and to hear complaints or preliminary informations, issue warrants, order arrests, make commitments, and take bail. Magistrates have jurisdiction over violations of §123.49. They may conduct hearings authorized under §§809.4 and 809.10. (602.6405). They have power to act any place within district as directed, and venue is as in other district court proceedings. Judicial magistrates serving on full-time basis and district associate judges have jurisdiction of indictable misdemeanors. (Rules Crim. Pro. 1, et seq.). Plaintiff may appeal only upon finding of invalidity of ordinance or statute. Defendant may appeal upon judgment of conviction. Execution of judgment stayed by filing of appeal bond. Defendant may orally notify magistrate of appeal or deliver written notice of appeal to magistrate within ten days of judgment. Payment of fine or serving sentence of imprisonment does not waive right to appeal. Upon appeal, case is tried anew in district court. (Rule Crim. Pro. 54).

District Associate Judges.—District associate judges serve as full-time magistrates and have jurisdiction possessed by judicial magistrates (see 602.6405) and jurisdiction of civil actions to $5,000, DWI felonies, indictable misdemeanors, and juvenile proceedings. They shall hold court as directed at any place within judicial district that judicial magistrate may do so, and shall employ judicial magistrates practice and procedure. They may temporarily exercise jurisdiction of district court judge. While exercising such temporary jurisdiction they shall employ district judges' practice and procedure. Venue shall be as in other district court proceedings. Appeals from judgments of district associate judges while exercising jurisdiction possessed by judicial magistrates shall be governed by laws relating to appeals from judicial magistrates. Appeals from judgments while exercising any other jurisdiction shall be governed by laws relating to appeals from district judges. See category Civil Actions and Procedure, topic Appeal and Error. (602.6301-.6306).

Small Claims.—Small claim is civil action for $4,000 or less, and certain replevin and forcible entry and detainer actions. Small claims on file for 90 days and not determined are dismissed without prejudice by clerk with costs assessed to plaintiff. (631.8[1]). If commenced as regular action, shall be transferred to small claims docket. (631.8). Small claim action is commenced by filing of original notice with clerk. (631.3). Service is by clerk mailing by certified mail, restricted delivery of copy of original notice to defendant, or service as provided in R.C.P. (631.3). If action for money judgment, defendant required to appear not later than 20 days following date of filing of original notice. If action for forcible entry or detention original notice to be personally served, service to be at least three days prior to hearing date. (631.4[2]). If personal service cannot be made, plaintiff may post original notice on real property sought to be detained and mail copy of original notice to defendant's last known address. (631.4[2]). Both mailing and posting must be done five days before hearing date and only after three attempts to perfect personal service have been made. (631.4[2]). Service shall be deemed complete upon filing with district court clerk, affidavit indicating that copies of original notice were both mailed and posted. (631.4[2]). If defendant appears before appearance date, clerk assigns claim to magistrate for hearing at time not less than five days nor more than 20 days after defendant's appearance. Clerk notifies parties of time for hearing by ordinary mail. (631.5). Hearing is informal, to court, is conducted without regard to technicalities of procedure, and not reported unless party provides reporter at party's expense. (631.11). Judgment is entered on original notice, and court may provide for installment payments. Such judgments are liens to same extent as other judgments of district courts.

COURTS . . . *continued*

(631.12). If defendant fails to appear, clerk renders judgment if relief is readily ascertainable. If relief not readily ascertainable, magistrate determines claim. (631.5).

LEGISLATURE:

Meets in January of each year. Governor may call special sessions. (Const., art. III, §2, Legislative Dept.).

REPORTS:

The decisions of Supreme Court of Iowa are published in the Iowa Reports, namely, 1 Morris, 1 to 4 Greene and Iowa reports beginning with Vol. 1 and continuing to Vol. 261. Iowa decisions in 158 N.W. 2d and subsequent thereto are official opinions of Iowa Supreme Court.

Digests are West's Iowa Digest and Iowa and Northwestern Digest, Iowa Code Annotated, and Callaghan's Iowa Digest.

STATUTES:

Latest compilation of Iowa statutes is Code of Iowa (1995).

Uniform Acts adopted are: Alcoholism and Intoxication Treatment (1974); Anatomical Gift (1969); Arbitration (1981); Attendance of Witnesses from Without a State in Criminal Proceedings, Act to Secure (1976); †Business Corporation (ABA 1959); Certification of Questions of Law (1979); Child Custody Jurisdiction (1977); Class Actions (1980); †Commercial Code (1966); Common Trust Fund (1961); Consumer Credit Code (1974); Controlled Substances (1971); Criminal Extradition (1949); Declaratory Judgments (1943); †Disposition of Unclaimed Property, Revised (1967); Enforcement of Foreign Judgments (1979); Evidence, Rules of (1983); Federal lien Registration (1981); Foreign Money-Judgments Recognition (1989); Fraudulent Transfer (1995); Interstate Family Support (1997); Limited Partnership (1976); Management of Institutional Funds (1990); Military Justice (1965); Partnership (1971); Photographic Copies of Business and Public Records as Evidence (1951); Post-Conviction Procedure (1970); Premarital Agreement (1991); Reciprocal Enforcement of Support (1968); Reciprocal Transfer Tax (1929); Rendition of Prisoners as Witnesses in Criminal Proceedings Act (1995); †Residential Landlord and Tenant (1978); Rights of the Terminally Ill (1985); Securities (1976); Simultaneous Death (1963); State Administrative Procedure (1974); State Antitrust (1976); Statutory Construction (1971); Testamentary Additions to Trusts (1964); Trade Secrets (1990); Transfer on Death Security Registration (1997); Transfers to Minors (1986). (Some Acts are substantially similar to Uniform Act, but not identical.)

Uniform Commercial Code adopted. (554). See category Business Regulation and Commerce, topic Commercial Code.

For text of Uniform Acts falling within the scope of the Martindale-Hubbell Law Digests see Uniform and Model Acts section.

†Adopted with significant variations or modifications. See appropriate topics.

UNIFORM LAWS:

For list of Uniform Acts in force in this state see topic Statutes. For text of Uniform Acts within the scope of the Martindale-Hubbell Law Digests see Uniform and Model Acts section.

CRIMINAL LAW

BAIL:

See topic Criminal Law.

CRIMINAL LAW:

Crimes and criminal procedure governed by Titles XXXV and XXXVI of Code.

Indictment or Information.—Prosecutions unless provided otherwise are by indictment or information.

Bail.—By constitution and by statute, all persons are bailable with sufficient sureties, except for capital offenses where proof is evident or presumption great. (811).

Uniform Fresh Pursuit Law adopted. (806).

Uniform Criminal Extradition Act adopted. (820).

DEBTOR AND CREDITOR

ASSIGNMENTS:

(539).

Bonds, due bills and all non-negotiable instruments, and open accounts, are assignable, even though instrument purports to prohibit it. (539.1-.3). Where provisions of foregoing sections conflict with Uniform Commercial Code, latter governs. (539.1-.3). Includes those taking assignments in regular course of business. (539.1).

Uniform Commercial Code adopted. (554). See category Business Regulation and Commerce, topic Commercial Code.

Instrument Transferring Title.—Except as required by Uniform Commercial Code, assignment is made by indorsement on instrument, or by other writing. (539.1).

Filing and Recording.—Not required, except as provided in Uniform Commercial Code.

Notice.—Not required, except as provided in Uniform Commercial Code.

Effect.—Assignee's rights are subject to any defense or counterclaim which maker or debtor had against assignor before notice of such assignment, except as provided in Uniform Commercial Code. (539.1-.3).

Assignment of wages of head of family must be signed and acknowledged by both husband and wife. Wage assignments, other than to labor union representing employee in labor relations with employer, are not binding on employer unless agreed to by employer in writing. (539.4).

ATTACHMENT:

(639).

Attachment may be obtained in any civil action, by any plaintiff, including nonresident or foreign corporation, provided one or more of the necessary grounds exists. It may issue on a claim not payable in the state.

Grounds for attachment are that defendant is: (1) A foreign corporation or acting as such; or (2) a nonresident; (3) is about to remove property from the state without leaving sufficient to pay debts; (4) has disposed; or (5) is about to dispose of property with intent to defraud creditors; (6) has absconded so that ordinary process cannot be served on him; (7) is about to remove permanently out of the county and has property therein not exempt; or (8) is about to remove permanently out of the state, and refuses to pay or secure plaintiff's debt; (9) is about to remove property out of county with intent to defraud creditors; (10) is about to convert property into money in order to place it beyond reach of creditors; or (11) has property or rights in action which he conceals; (12) that debt is due for property obtained under false pretenses; (13) is about to dispose of property belonging to plaintiff; (14) is about to convert plaintiff's property into money for purposes of placing it beyond reach of plaintiff; or (15) is about to move permanently out of state and refuses to return property belonging to plaintiff. (639.3). Attachment may be had before debt due on grounds 4, 5, and 12, or where defendant has removed or is about to remove from state and refuses to secure payment of debt, if plaintiff did not know of removal or contemplated removal when debt contracted. (639.9).

Proceedings.—Plaintiff must file petition sworn to by him, or his agent or attorney (knowing the facts) setting out the claim and one or more grounds for attachment. (639.3).

Bond.—Plaintiff must give bond with surety approved by clerk of court in penalty at least double value of property sought to be attached, in no event less than $250. Where only real property is attached, bond must be in penalty fixed by court or clerk. (639.11, .12).

Levy.—The sheriff must, as nearly as the circumstances of the case will permit, levy upon property 50% greater in value than the amount of the claim. Any property not exempt from execution may be attached. (639.7, .19).

Indemnity.—There is no statute authorizing the officer to demand indemnity before levying.

Priorities.—In case of two or more attachments, the attaching creditors do not share pro rata, but the attachments have priority in the order of their levy. (639.20).

A valid attachment levied before a general assignment for the benefit of creditors is not affected thereby.

Release.—The defendant, or any person in possession of any attached property, or any person making affidavit that he has an interest in same, may, at any time before judgment, discharge the property attached by giving bond with security to be approved by the sheriff, or after return of the writ, by the clerk, in a penalty at least double value of property. Bond must be filed with clerk of court. (639.45).

Sale.—Where the property attached is perishable, the sheriff may summon three persons having the qualification of jurors to examine it. Defendant, if within county, must have three days notice of the hearing. If it is the opinion of those who examine the property that it should be disposed of, they must specify in writing a day beyond which the property should not be kept. If this day occurs before trial, the property must be sold as goods are sold on execution. An earlier sale may be made if the condition of the goods warrants it. Sale may be made on written consent of defendant without such finding. (639.48-.50).

Third Party Claims.—Any third party may, before sale of attached property or before payment to plaintiff of the proceeds thereof or any attached debt, present his verified petition to the court disputing the validity of the attachment or stating a claim to the attached property and setting forth the facts upon which the claim is founded. (639.60).

Uniform Commercial Code enacted, effective July 4, 1966. See category Business Regulation and Commerce, topic Commercial Code.

CREDITORS' SUITS:

No statutory provisions, except those auxiliary to execution. (630.16).

EXECUTIONS:

Judgments requiring payment of money or delivery of possession of property are enforced by execution.

Exemptions.—See topic Exemptions.

Time for Issuance.—Executions may issue at any time before judgment is barred by statute of limitations, and from district and appellate courts may issue into any county. (626).

Issuance of Writ.—The writ is issued by the clerk and delivered to the sheriff by the judgment creditor with instructions as to the property on which the officer is to levy.

Stay of Execution.—Stay must be taken within ten days from date of judgment. Time of stay under $100, three months, over $100, six months. No appeal allowed after stay. No stay allowed on judgment obtained by laboring men, or mechanics, for wages. (626). In order to obtain stay, debtor must give bond for payment of judgment, with interest and costs, with one or more freehold sureties. As to stay pending appeal, see category Civil Actions and Procedure, topic Appeal and Error.

See note at head of Digest as to 1998 legislation covered.

See Topical Index in front part of this volume.

EXECUTIONS . . . *continued*

Levy.—The officer must execute the writ by levying on the property of the judgment debtor, collecting the things in action by suit in his own name, or selling the same, and paying the proceeds, less his own costs, to the clerk. The officer must select for levy such property, in such quantities, as will be likely to bring the exact amount required to be raised as nearly as practicable, and may make other levies if necessary. If real estate is levied upon, except by special execution under foreclosure, the officer must make an entry in the Incumbrance Book in the clerk's office, showing the number and title of the case, date of levy, date of entry, amount claimed, description of the real estate, and signature of the officer. This constitutes notice to all persons of such levy. Levy upon a judgment is made by entering upon the judgment docket a memorandum thereof. Property of the defendant in the possession of another or debts due him may be reached by garnishment or attachment. When levy is made on personal property, the sheriff takes possession thereof and either retains the same or places it in the hands of a custodian until the sale.

If the creditor or his agent first so requests in writing, the officer may view the property, inventory its exact description at length, and append such inventory to the execution, with his signed statement of the number and title of the case, the amount claimed under the execution, the exact location of the property and in whose possession, and the last known address of the judgment debtor; and, if the property is consumer goods or if judgment debtor is not resident of this state, file with County Recorder of county where property is located his certified transcript of such inventory and statement; and, in all other cases, file with Secretary of State his certified transcript of such inventory and statement. Such filing shall be accepted by County Recorder or Secretary of State as financing statement and shall be marked, indexed and certified in same manner, and shall be constructive notice of levy to all persons. Whenever writ is satisfied or levy discharged officer shall file termination statement with County Recorder or Secretary of State. Fees normally charged by County Recorder or Secretary of State for filing of financing statement and filing of termination statement shall be paid by officer and shall be taxed by him as part of his costs of levy. (R.C.P. 260). Sheriff's duty to levy not applicable to garnishments. (626.50).

Sale.—The sheriff must give four weeks notice of the sale of real estate and three weeks notice of the sale of personal property, by posting notice in three public places in the county, one of which must be in place where last district court was held, and in case of real estate or personal property of the value of $200, there must be two newspaper publications in addition. In constable sales there must be two weeks notice by posting in three public places in the township, one of them at the office door of the justice. If the debtor is in actual occupancy of any part of the land levied on, the officer must, at least 20 days previous to the sale, serve him with written notice of the levy mentioning the time and place of sale. Sale must be at public auction. (626).

Return.—An officer receiving an execution must give receipt therefor, stating when it was received, and make return thereof, together with the money collected, on or before the seventieth day from the date of its issuance. (626.16).

Redemption.—Real property, or an interest therein larger than a leasehold with two years unexpired term, may be redeemed by the debtor within one year after sale, during which time he is entitled to possession. His right to redeem is exclusive except that after expiration of six months and before expiration of nine months creditors whose claims became liens before expiration of the nine months or mortgagees, whether or not debt has matured, may redeem. (628.2-.3). Mortgage on less than ten acres may provide for six months redemption period if mortgagee waives right to deficiency judgment. (628.-26).

Creditors having right of redemption may redeem from each other within the time above limited. When a senior creditor redeems from his junior, he is required to pay off only the amount of those liens which are paramount to his own; but junior creditor may redeem from senior creditor as often as the land is taken from him by virtue of a paramount lien.

Mode of redemption by a lien holder is by paying into the clerk's office the amount necessary to effect the same and filing his affidavit or that of his agent, stating as nearly as practicable the nature of his lien and the amount still due and unpaid thereon. Mode of redemption by the title holder is by paying into the clerk's office the amount of the certificate and all sums paid by the holder thereof in effecting redemptions with interest and costs.

The rights of a debtor in relation to redemption are transferrable.

Real property redeemed by the debtor is thereafter free from any liability on the judgment under which sale was made.

Chattels and leasehold interests with less than two years to run, when sold under execution, may not be redeemed. (628).

If real property is not used for agricultural purposes and is not residence of debtor, or if it is residence of debtor but not single-family or two-family dwelling, period of redemption after foreclosure is 180 days. First 90 days after sale, right of redemption is exclusive to debtor and time periods provided in §§628.5, 628.15, and 628.16 are reduced to 135 days. (628.28). If, for such property, deficiency judgment waived, then period of redemption reduced to 90 days. First 30 days after sale, debtor has exclusive right of redemption and time periods provided in §§628.5, 628.15, and 628.16 reduced to 60 days. (628.28).

Where §654.18 alternative nonjudicial voluntary foreclosure procedure used, junior lienholders have 30-day redemption period from date required notice sent. (628.29).

Supplementary Proceedings.—When execution has been returned unsatisfied, plaintiff is entitled to an order for examination of the debtor, or such order may be had on proof by affidavit that the debtor has property which he unjustly refuses to apply towards satisfaction of the judgment. If debtor refuses to appear or refuses to answer all proper interrogatories he may be arrested and imprisoned until he complies. Upon proof that defendant will leave state, or conceal himself, he may be arrested and required to give bonds to appear, or in default thereof be imprisoned for safekeeping until his examination is concluded. Other witnesses may also be required to appear and testify. If any property, rights, or credits, subject to execution, are thus ascertained, they may be levied upon accordingly. Court may also appoint receiver. (630).

EXEMPTIONS:

(627).

General Exemptions.—Debtor who is resident of this state may hold exempt from execution following property: (1) All wearing apparel of debtor and debtor's dependents kept for actual use and trunks or other receptacles necessary for wearing apparel, not to exceed in value $1,000 in aggregate; (2) one shotgun, and either one rifle or one musket; (3) private libraries, family bibles, portraits, pictures, and paintings not to exceed $200 in value and $1,000 in aggregate; (4) interment space or interest in public or private burying ground, not exceeding one acre for any defendant; (5) debtor's interest, in household furnishings, household goods, and appliances held primarily for personal, family, or household use of debtor or dependent of debtor, not to exceed in value $2,000 in aggregate; (6) certain, specific interests in life insurance policies; (7) professionally prescribed health aids for debtor or dependent of debtor; (8) debtor's rights in: (a) social security benefit, unemployment compensation, or local public assistance benefit, (b) veteran's benefit, (c) disability or illness benefit, (d) alimony, support, or separate maintenance, to extent reasonably necessary for support of debtor and dependents of debtor, (e) payment under pension, annuity, or similar plan or contract on account of illness, disability, death, age, or length of service, to extent reasonably necessary for support of debtor and any dependent of debtor; (9) any combination of following, not to exceed value of $5,000 in aggregate: (a) musical instruments, not including radios, television sets, or record or tape playing machines, held primarily for personal, family, or household use of debtor or dependent of debtor; (b) one motor vehicle; (c) in event of bankruptcy proceeding, debtor's interests in accrued wages and in state and federal tax refunds as of date of filing of petition in bankruptcy, not to exceed $1,000 in aggregate. This exemption is in addition to limitations contained in §§642.21 and 537.5105; (10) if debtor engaged in any profession or occupation other than farming, proper implements, professional books, or tools of trade of debtor or dependent of debtor, not to exceed $10,000 in aggregate; (11) if debtor engaged in farming and does not exercise delay of enforceability of deficiency judgment or general execution under §654.6 in relation to execution under which exemption claimed, any combination of following, not to exceed $10,000 in aggregate: (a) implements and equipment reasonably related to normal farming operation. This exemption in addition to motor vehicle held exempt under paragraph 9(b), (b) livestock and feed for livestock reasonably related to normal farming operation; (12) if debtor engaged in farming agricultural land upon commencement of action for foreclosure of mortgage on agricultural land or for enforcement of obligation secured by mortgage on agricultural land, if deficiency judgment issued against debtor, and if debtor does not exercise delay of enforceability of deficiency judgment or general execution under §654.6 in relation to execution under which exemption claimed, disposable earnings of debtor are exempt from garnishment to enforce deficiency judgment after two years from entry of deficiency judgment, §§642.21 and 642.22 notwithstanding. However, earnings paid to debtor directly or indirectly by debtor not exempt; (13) debtor's interests, not to exceed $100 in any cash, bank deposits, credit union share drafts or other deposits, or other personal property not otherwise specifically provided; (14) debtor's interest, not to exceed $500 in any residential rental deposit, residential utility deposit and any prepaid rent under any expired residential base. (627.6).

Purchase Money Claims.—No property is exempt from execution issued for the purchase money. (627.5).

Automobile necessary and used for purpose of earning a living is exempt, except as against purchase money mortgage or claim for damage occasioned by use on public highway in this state. (627.7).

Money received as a pension from the United States is exempt in case of a resident, whether head of a family or not. (627.8).

Workmen's compensation awards are exempt except for non-Federally protected financial support indebtedness. (627.13).

Rights of surviving widow in exempt property. See category Estates and Trusts, topic Descent and Distribution.

Proceeds of Insurance.—See 627.6(6) as amended by 1988 legislation and 627.6(8) as amended by 1992 legislation.

Earnings.—Individual earnings exempt as provided by Federal Consumer Protection Act, Title III. No judgment creditor can garnish debtor earning less than $12,000 per year for more than $250 per year. Debtor earning more than $12,000 per year can be garnished in higher amounts pursuant to 642.21. (642).

Homestead Exemption.—See topic Homesteads.

Bankruptcy Exemption.—Debtor to whom law of this state applies on date of filing of petition in bankruptcy is not entitled to elect to exempt from property of bankruptcy estate property that is specified in 11 U.S.C. §522(d) (1979). This section is enacted for purpose set forth in 11 U.S.C. §522(b)(1) (1979). (See 627.10.)

FORECLOSURE:

See topic Liens; category Mortgages, topic Mortgages of Real Property.

FRAUDULENT SALES AND CONVEYANCES:

Fraudulent conveyances may be set aside at the suit of the creditors.

Bulk Sales.—Art. 6 of Uniform Commercial Code repealed. (554).

GARNISHMENT:

Property or money belonging to a defendant in the hands of a debtor may be garnished either in attachment proceedings or upon execution. However, sheriff has no duty to levy.

Answer of Garnishee.—The lien is effected by the service of notice upon the debtor, who is then required to disclose by answer the amount of indebtedness, if any, owing defendant. (642).

See note at head of Digest as to 1998 legislation covered.

See Topical Index in front part of this volume.

GARNISHMENT . . . *continued*

Judgment.—If garnishee is indebted to defendant or is in possession of property not exempt, judgment may be entered against him for amount of his indebtedness, not exceeding amount of claim, or the property in his hands. (642).

Release.—The garnishee may be released by payment or delivery to officer of the money or property in his possession belonging to the defendant. (642).

Exemption of Earnings.—See topic Exemptions.

HOMESTEADS:

The homestead of every family, whether owned by the husband or wife, and within the limit as to value, is exempt except as to debts contracted prior to its acquisition, those created by written contract by persons having the power to convey expressly stipulating that it shall be liable, and those incurred for work done or material furnished exclusively for the improvement of the homestead. (561.16, 561.21).

Limitation of Value and Area.—A homestead must embrace the house used as a home by the owner and may contain one or more contiguous lots or tracts of land with the building and other appurtenances thereon used in good faith as part of the same. If within a city or town plat, it must not exceed one-half acre, otherwise it must not contain more than 40 acres but, if the value of such area is less than $500, the area may in either event be enlarged until it reaches the value of $500. It must not embrace more than one dwelling house, and the buildings appurtenant thereto; but may include building situated thereon used by owner in business not exceeding $300 in value. (561.1, .2, .3).

Designation of Homestead.—Owner may select homestead and record plat of it, and may change or vacate plat.

Claim of Exemption.—After levy, owner must plat and record, where statutory notice to do so is given by levying officer to owner or spouse. Owner failing, officer must plat and record. (561.5).

Conveyance or Encumbrance.—Subject to the rights of the surviving husband or wife, the homestead may be devised like other real estate of a testator, but no conveyance or encumbrance of or contract to convey or encumber the homestead is valid unless the husband and wife join in the execution of the same joint instrument. However, if one spouse specifically relinquishes homestead rights in a conveyance by the other spouse it is not necessary that the first mentioned spouse join in the granting clause. (561.13). A purchase money mortgage is valid although the purchaser's spouse did not join therein or relinquish homestead rights. (See 14 Ia. 438.)

Effective May 23, 1986, if homestead exemption waiver contained in written contract, affecting agricultural land or appurtenances on land, contract must contain statement in substantially following form, in boldface type of minimum size of ten points, signed and dated by person waiving exemption at time of contract's execution: "I understand that homestead property is in many cases protected from the claims of creditors and exempt from judicial sale; and that by signing this contract, I voluntarily give up my right to this protection for this property with respect to claims based upon this contract." (561.22).

Rights of Surviving Spouse.—In case of death of homestead owner, surviving spouse has a right to elect to retain the homestead for life in lieu of his or her distributive share of the real estate. (561.12; 633.240).

JUDGMENT NOTES:

See category Business Regulation and Commerce, topic Bills and Notes.

LEVY:

See topics Attachment, Executions.

LIENS:

Livery and feed stable keepers, herders, feeders and keepers of stock and garage keepers have liens on all property coming into their hands for charges and expenses of keeping; may be enforced by sale of said property after giving to the owner or claimant, if found within the county, ten days notice in writing of the time and place of sale and posting written notices thereof in three public places in the township where the property was kept. (579).

Artisan has a lien for services or material in making, repairing or improving personal property, while same is lawfully in his possession; may be enforced by suit in equity or in same manner as common carrier's lien. (577).

Hotel keeper has a lien on baggage of guest for accommodations, etc., furnished and money paid for or advanced to guest; may be enforced by taking and retaining possession of all baggage and by action at law aided by attachment and execution or, after 90 days, by sale of baggage. (583).

Hospital furnishing medical or other service to person injured in accident not covered by Workmen's Compensation Act has lien for its reasonable charges on any recovery by such person or his representative for such injury. Written notice of lien must be filed in office of clerk of district court of county in which hospital is located and a copy mailed to person alleged to be liable. (582).

Veterinarian.—Licensed and registered veterinarian has a lien for value of services rendered and products used in prevention or control of any contagious livestock disease. Lien has priority over any other lien on such livestock if verified statement describing livestock, services and products used, with name of person to whom rendered, is filed within 60 days in office of clerk of district court of county in which owner of livestock resides. Lien may be enforced by suit in equity. (581).

Thresherman and Sheller's Lien.—Those operating a machine for threshing or combining grain or seed, shelling or husking corn, or for baling hay, straw, or other farm product, have a first lien on any grain, seed or corn threshed, shelled or husked, for reasonable value of said services. Such lien is superior to any landlord's lien or mortgage lien on property. In order to preserve such lien, verified statement must be filed within ten days from completion of work with Secretary of State. Such verified statement must set forth services rendered, number of bushels of grain threshed or corn shelled, value of services, person for whom services rendered, and place where services rendered. Filing fee of $4 if on regular form, otherwise $5. Proceedings to enforce lien must be brought within 30 days of filing. Lienholder must immediately file stamped copy of petition with Secretary of State. Lien is foreclosed in manner provided under UCC, Art. 9, Part 5. (571).

Release of Property.—The owner of any personal property within the state where the same is held by any one claiming a common law or statutory lien upon the said property, may have the property released upon the giving of a bond in double the amount of the lien claimed, conditioned on the payment to the one claiming the lien, any sum that may be found to be due and to have been a lien on the personal property at the time the bond was given, by the judgment of any court having jurisdiction. The bond must be signed by one or more sureties and be filed with and approved by clerk of district court. After the bond is filed and written notice of such filing given, the one claiming the lien must surrender possession of the property to the owner thereof. (584).

Redemption.—There is no right of redemption as to personalty sold in the enforcement of a lien thereon.

Mechanics' Liens.—Person laboring on or furnishing material, machinery, or fixtures for any building or improvement upon land, including those engaged in the construction or repair of any work of internal improvement, or in grading any land or lot by virtue of any contract with the owner or his agent, may have for his labor done or material furnished, a lien upon said improvement and upon the land belonging to the owner on which it is situated. (572.2).

To protect lien against subsequent purchasers in good faith and without notice, party entitled to lien must file with clerk of district court verified statement of claim after allowing all credits, showing dates of performing labor or furnishing material together with correct description of property to be charged with lien and name and last known mailing address of owner, agent, or trustee of property. If principal contractor, or if subcontractor within 90 days from date on which last material or labor was furnished. Failure to file such statement does not defeat lien, but it becomes subject to rights of purchasers or encumbrancers in good faith, without notice, whose rights accrued after expiration of 90 days and before statement was filed. In case of lien upon railway, subcontractor shall have 90 days from last day in month in which last labor was done or material furnished in which to file his statement. In case of "owner-occupied dwelling" lien of subcontractor is not enforceable except to extent of amount owed to principal contractor at time subcontractor serves written notice form of claim on owner. (572.8 et seq.). Subcontractor filing his statement after lapse of 90 days must also serve notice of filing of lien on owner or his agent in order fully to protect his lien against subsequent purchasers or encumbrances. (572). Subcontractor may be awarded exemplary damages from principal contractor for failure to pay after receiving full payment from owner. (572.30).

Foreclosure.—Mechanic's lien is enforced by equitable proceeding within two years from expiration of time for filing lien. (572.26-.27). If owner serves written demand for suit, action must be commenced within 30 days or rights are lost. (572.28).

Public Improvements.—Person performing labor or furnishing materials, service, transportation, feed, provisions, fuel, lubricants, or workmens compensation insurance, in construction of any public improvement may obtain lien therefor on retained portion of contract price of improvement in hands of public corporation by filing with board or commission authorized by law to let contracts for such improvement verified, itemized statement of demand, within 30 days after completion and final acceptance of improvement. Claims for material, unless ordered by general contractor or his authorized agent, must be supported by certified statement that general contractor was notified within 30 days after materials were furnished, or by itemized invoices rendered to contractor during progress of work, of amount, kind and value of material. On improvement involving $25,000 or over, principal contractor must give bond, in amount not less than 75% of contract price, for faithful performance of contract and payment of all just claims for labor or material. If no part of contract price paid until after completion of improvement, amount of bond may be 25% of contract price. (573.16).

Public corporation, principal contractor, any claimant for labor or material who has filed his claim, or surety on any bond given for performance of contract, may after expiration of 30 days and not later than 60 days following completion and final acceptance of such improvement, bring action in equity in county where improvement is located to adjudicate all rights to said fund or to enforce liability on said bond. Court must adjudicate all claims and payments must be made in following order: Costs of action, claims for labor, claims for materials, claims of public corporation. (573).

Attachment Lien.—See topic Attachment.

Attorney's Lien.—See category Legal Profession, topic Attorneys and Counselors.

Execution Lien.—See topic Executions.

Judgment Lien.—See category Civil Actions and Procedure, topic Judgments.

Landlord's Lien.—See category Property, topic Landlord and Tenant.

Liens on Exempt Property.—See topic Exemptions.

Liens on Homestead.—See topic Homesteads.

Real Estate Mortgage Lien.—See category Mortgages, topic Mortgages of Real Property.

Tax Lien.—See category Taxation, topic Property Taxes, subhead Lien.

Uniform Commercial Code adopted. (554). See category Business Regulation and Commerce, topic Commercial Code.

MECHANICS' LIENS:

See topic Liens.

PLEDGES:

Uniform Commercial Code adopted. (554). See category Business Regulation and Commerce, topic Commercial Code.

See note at head of Digest as to 1998 legislation covered.

See Topical Index in front part of this volume.

PLEDGES . . . *continued*

Pledgee of stock of corporation under Iowa Business Corporation Act may vote. (490.724[2][d]). See category Business Organizations, topic Corporations.

RECEIVERS:

On the petition of either party to a civil action or proceeding, where he shows that he has a probable right to or interest in any property which is the subject of the controversy, and that such property or its rents and profits are in danger of being lost or materially injured or impaired, the court, or in vacation, the judge thereof, may appoint a receiver to take charge of such property during the pendency of the action. (680).

See also category Business Organizations, topic Corporations.

REDEMPTION:

See topics Executions, Liens; categories Mortgages, topic Mortgages of Real Property; Taxation, topic Taxes.

SUPPLEMENTARY PROCEEDINGS:

See topic Executions.

TRUSTEE PROCESS:

See topic Garnishment.

USURY:

See category Business Regulation and Commerce, topic Interest.

DISPUTE RESOLUTION

ALTERNATIVE DISPUTE RESOLUTION:

Mandatory Dispute Resolution.—Neither Iowa legislature nor Iowa courts have imposed any rules or regulations requiring individuals to submit to mandatory alternative dispute resolutions. In certain situations involving issues of public welfare, parties may be required to submit to mediation, arbitration or binding arbitration. (20.20-22, 275.30, 357A.21, 358.30, 697B).

Voluntary Dispute Resolution.—Locally organized dispute resolution centers have been created to make mediators and informal dispute resolution procedures available in many types of cases, including civil claims and disputes, child custody and visitation disputes, juvenile offenses and criminal complaints. (679). Mediation also is contemplated under Iowa law in several other types of matters such as farm credit disputes and warranty disputes. (654A). Arbitration is available to individuals if enforceable arbitration agreement exists, but generally application can be made to district court to confirm, modify or vacate award. (679A-679B).

ARBITRATION AND AWARD:

(c. 679A).

Uniform Arbitration Act adopted.

Controversy which might be subject of civil action may be submitted to decision of one or more arbitrators by written agreement of parties specifying demands to be submitted, names of arbitrators, and court by which judgment on award to be rendered.

Rescission.—Submission cannot be revoked except by consent of parties.

Award and Action Thereon.—Award must be delivered to court designated and is then docketed and when called for hearing may be either adopted by court, rejected for any legal and sufficient reasons, or recommitted for rehearing to same arbitrators or any others agreed on by the parties or appointed by the court if they cannot agree. (679A.8).

Judgment on Award.—When award is adopted it has same force and effect as jury verdict and judgment may be entered and execution issued accordingly and appeal may be taken to Supreme Court. (679A.14).

Labor Disputes.—A dispute arising between any employers and their employees or association of employees, except employers or employees having interstate trade relations operating through or by state or international boards of conciliation, which dispute is likely to cause a strike or lock-out involving ten or more wage earners and is likely to interfere with business, or public peace, or the welfare of the community, may be referred to a board of arbitration, on application of either of the parties, or of the mayor of the city, or the chairman of the board of supervisors of the county or on petition of twenty-five citizens. The Governor appoints two members of the board, who appoint a third. Witnesses may be subpoenaed, evidence taken and decisions made and filed with the Governor who shall publish the same. The decision is binding only if so agreed in advance by the parties. (679B.1-679B.5).

Implementation of Agreements to Arbitrate.—Validity of agreement, and procedural aspects of arbitration process including hearing, vacating award, modification and judgment or decree or award, adopted in 679A, and applies to agreements made after July 1, 1981.

DOCUMENTS AND RECORDS

ACKNOWLEDGMENTS:

May be taken by following officers:

Within state: Court having a seal, or judge or clerk thereof; county auditor within his county; judicial magistrate or district associate judge within county; notary public within state. (558.20).

Without state but within United States: Judge of a court of record or officer holding seal thereof; commissioner appointed by Governor of Iowa to take acknowledgments of deeds; notary public; or justice of peace; any officer authorized to take acknowledgments by law of state, territory or district where taken. (558.21-.23).

Without United States: Ambassador, minister, secretary of legation, consul, vice-consul, chargé d'affaires, consular agent, or any other officer of United States in the country authorized to issue certificates under seal of United States; any officer of country authorized by laws thereof to certify to acknowledgments of written instruments. (558.27-.28).

Persons in U.S. Armed Forces may acknowledge instruments before any commissioned officer in active service of U. S. Armed Forces of the rank of Second Lieutenant or higher in the Army or Marine Corps, or Ensign or higher in the Navy or Coast Guard. No authentication is required, but the officer taking the acknowledgment must endorse thereon or attach a certificate substantially in the form set forth infra. (558.26).

General Requirements as to Taking and Certificate.—Certificate must show title of court or person taking, that person making acknowledgment was known to be person named in it, and that such person acknowledged the instrument as his voluntary act and deed. (558.30).

Married women acknowledge as though sole; separate examination not required. (558.35).

Attorneys in Fact.—Execution of written instrument by attorney in fact may be acknowledged by attorney executing it. (558.36-.37).

Necessity and Effect.—Acknowledgment is not necessary to validity of any instrument except assignment of wages by head of family. (539.4). It is necessary to entitle instrument to be recorded, and instrument recorded without acknowledgment does not constitute constructive notice, except that affidavits and certified copies of petitions in bankruptcy with or without schedules appended, of decrees of adjudication in bankruptcy and of orders approving trustees' bonds in bankruptcy, and Uniform Commercial Code financing statements and financing statement changes need not be acknowledged. (558.42).

Proof by Witness.—Proof of the due and voluntary execution and delivery of a deed or other instrument may be made before any officer authorized to take acknowledgments by one competent person other than the vendee or other person to whom the instrument is executed in the following cases: (1) If the grantor dies before making the acknowledgment; (2) if his attendance cannot be procured; (3) if, having appeared, he refuses to acknowledge the execution of the instrument.

In such case the certificate of the officer must state (1) title of officer taking proof, (2) that it was satisfactorily proved that grantor was dead, or that for some other reason his attendance could not be procured in order to make acknowledgment, or that, having appeared, he refused to acknowledge same, (3) name of witness by whom proof was made, and that it was proved by him that instrument was executed and delivered by person whose name is thereunto subscribed as party. (558.31-.32).

Authentication.—To entitle instrument made and acknowledged outside state but within United States to be recorded in Iowa (except where acknowledged before notary public of jurisdiction where acknowledgment taken or before commissioner appointed by Governor of Iowa), there must be subjoined or attached a certificate of Secretary of State or clerk of court of record of state where acknowledgment taken that officer taking same was at the time duly authorized to take such acknowledgment by laws of state where taken, that conveyance and acknowledgment are in due form of law, that said Secretary of State or clerk of court is well acquainted with the handwriting of such officer, and that he verily believes that the signature attached to the certificate or acknowledgment or proof is genuine. (558.22, 558.24-.25).

Secretary of State will issue certificate stating person residing in state bordering Iowa is Notary Public in State of Iowa if such person has place of work in Iowa. (9E.3). Fee for issuance is $30. (9E.6).

When acknowledgment is made outside United States before a foreign officer, certificate must be authenticated by an authorized officer of United States, whose official written statement that full faith and credit is due to the certificate of such foreign officer is sufficient. (558.29).

Section 558.39 provides that foreign acknowledgment of instruments affecting Iowa real estate which is valid where made is valid in Iowa. *Quaere,* as to effect of this section on requirement of authentication.

Alternative to Acknowledgment or Proof.—No statutory provision.

Forms

Natural person acting in own right: State of . . . ., county of . . . ., ss. On this . . . . day of . . . ., A. D. 19. . . ., before me (insert title of acknowledging officer) personally appeared . . . ., to me known to be the person named in and who executed the foregoing instrument, and acknowledged that . . . . executed the same as . . . . voluntary act and deed. (Signature and title of officer).

Natural person acting by attorney: Same as preceding form up to words "be the person" and continues as follows: who executed the foregoing instrument in behalf of . . . ., and acknowledged that . . . . executed the same as the voluntary act and deed of said . . . . . (Signature, etc.).

Corporation or joint stock association: (Venue) On this . . . . day of . . . ., A. D. 19. . . ., before me, a (insert title of acknowledging officer) in and for said county, personally appeared . . . ., to me personally known, who being by me duly (sworn or affirmed) did say that that person is (insert title of executing officer) of said (corporation or association), (name of corporation or association), and that said instrument was signed on behalf of the said (corporation or association) by authority of its board of (directors or trustees) and the said . . . . acknowledged the execution of said instrument to be the voluntary act and deed of said (corporation or association) by it voluntarily executed. (Signature, etc.).

Partnerships:

See note at head of Digest as to 1998 legislation covered.

See Topical Index in front part of this volume.

ACKNOWLEDGMENTS . . . *continued*

On this . . . . day of . . . ., 19. . ., before me, the undersigned, a Notary Public in and for the State of Iowa, personally appeared . . . ., to me personally known, who being by me duly sworn, did say that the person is one of the partners of . . . ., a partnership, and that the instrument was signed on behalf of the partnership by authority of the partners and the partner acknowledged the execution of the instrument to be the voluntary act and deed of the partnership by it and by the partner voluntarily executed.

Individual fiduciary:

On this . . . . day of . . . ., 19. . . ., before me, the undersigned, a Notary Public in and for the State of Iowa, personally appeared . . . ., to me known to be the identical person named in and who executed the foregoing instrument, and acknowledged that the person, as the fiduciary, executed the instrument as the voluntary act and deed of the person and of the fiduciary.

Corporate fiduciary:

On this . . . . day of . . . ., 19. . . ., before me, the undersigned, a Notary Public in and for the State of Iowa, personally appeared . . . . and . . . ., to me personally known, who, being by me duly sworn, did say that they are the . . . . and . . . ., respectively, of the corporation executing the foregoing instrument; that the instrument was signed on behalf of the corporation by authority of its Board of Directors; that . . . . and . . . . acknowledged the execution of the instrument to be the voluntary act and deed of the corporation and of the fiduciary, by it, by them and as the fiduciary voluntarily executed.

Limited partnership with corporate general partner:

On this . . . . day of . . . ., 19. . ., before me, the undersigned, a Notary Public in and for the State of Iowa, personally appeared . . . ., to me personally known, who being by me duly sworn did say that the person is the . . . . of . . . ., the General Partner of . . . ., a . . . . limited partnership, executing the foregoing instrument, that the instrument was signed on behalf of the corporation as General Partner of . . . ., a . . . . limited partnership, by authority of the corporation's Board of Directors; and that . . . . as that officer acknowledged execution of the instrument to be the voluntary act and deed of the corporation and limited partnership by it and by the officer voluntarily executed.

Limited partnership with an individual general partner:

On this . . . . day of . . . ., 19. . . ., before me the undersigned, a Notary Public in and for the State of Iowa, personally appeared . . . ., to me personally known, who, being by me duly sworn, did say that the person is (a) (the) General Partner of . . . ., an Iowa limited partnership, executing the foregoing instrument, that the instrument was signed on behalf of the limited partnership by authority of the limited partnership; and the general partner acknowledged the execution of the instrument to be the voluntary act and deed of the limited partnership, by it and by the general partner voluntarily executed.

Joint Ventures:

On this . . . . day of . . . ., 19. . . ., before me, the undersigned, a Notary Public in and for the State of Iowa, personally appeared . . . . and . . . ., to me personally known, who, being by me duly sworn, did say that they are the . . . . and . . . ., respectively, of . . . ., an Iowa corporation, a joint venturer of . . . ., a joint venture, executing the foregoing instrument, that the instrument was signed on behalf of the corporation as a joint venturer of . . . ., a joint venture, by authority of its Board of Directors; and that . . . . and . . . ., as such officers, acknowledged the execution of the instrument to be the voluntary act and deed of the corporation and joint venture, by the corporation and joint venture and by them voluntarily executed.

Municipalities:

On this . . . . day of . . . ., 19. . ., before me, ..., a Notary Public in and for the State of Iowa, personally appeared . . . . and . . . ., to me personally known, and, who, being by me duly sworn, did say that they are the Mayor and City Clerk, respectively, of the City of . . . ., Iowa; that the seal affixed to the foregoing instrument is the corporate seal of the corporation, and that the instrument was signed and sealed on behalf of the corporation, by authority of its City Counsel, as contained in Ordinance No. . . . passed (the Resolution adopted) by the City Council, under Roll Call No. . . . of the City Counsel on the . . . . . . day of . . . ., 19. . . ., and that . . . . and . . . . acknowledged the execution of the instrument to be their voluntary act and deed and the voluntary act and deed of the corporation, by it voluntarily executed.

Counties:

On this . . . . day of . . . ., 19. . ., before me . . . ., a Notary Public in and for the State of Iowa, personally appeared . . . . and . . . ., to me personally known, and who, being by me duly sworn, did say that they are the Chairperson of the Board of Supervisors and County Auditor, respectively, of the County of . . . ., Iowa; that the seal affixed to the foregoing instrument is the corporate seal of the corporation, and that the instrument was signed and sealed on behalf of the corporation, by authority of its Board of Supervisors, as contained in Ordinance No. . . . passed (the Resolution adopted) by the Board of Supervisors, under Roll Call No. . . . of the Board of Supervisors on the . . . . day of . . . ., 19. . ., and . . . . and . . . . acknowledged the execution of the instrument to be their voluntary act and deed and the voluntary act and deed of the corporation, by it voluntarily executed. (558.39).

Natural persons acting as custodian pursuant to Uniform Transfers to Minors Act:

On this . . . . day of . . . ., 19. . . ., before me, the undersigned, a Notary Public in and for said State, personally appeared . . . ., to me known to be the person named in and who executed the foregoing instrument, and acknowledged that the custodian executed the instrument as custodian for . . . ., under

(name of minor)

the . . . . Uniform Transfers to Minors Act, as the voluntary act and deed of the

(State)

person and of the custodian.

Corporations or national banking associations acting as custodians pursuant to Uniform Transfers to Minors Act:

On this . . . . day of . . . ., 19. . ., before me, the undersigned, a Notary Public in and for said State, personally appeared . . . . and . . . ., to me personally known, who, by me duly sworn, did say that they are the . . . . and . . . ., respectively, of the Corporation executing the foregoing instrument; that the instrument was signed on behalf of the Corporation by authority of its Board of Directors: that . . . . and . . . . acknowledged the execution of the instrument as custodian of . . . ., under the . . . .

(name of minor)   (State)

Uniform Transfers to Minors Act, to be the voluntary act and deed of the person and of the custodian. (1987, H.F. 129).

Person in U. S. Armed Forces: On this . . . . day of . . . ., 19. . . ., before me, ... the undersigned commissioned officer, personally appeared . . . ., known to me (or satisfactorily proven) to be serving in or with the armed forces of the United States and to be the person whose name is subscribed to the within instrument and acknowledged that . . . . that person . . . . executed the same as . . . . voluntary act and deed. (Signature of officer and rank and command to which attached.) (558.26).

Validating Acts.—Any written instrument, and recording thereof, acknowledged more than ten years earlier, in proper county, is legalized and valid, although defectively acknowledged. (586.1).

AFFIDAVITS:

Affidavits should be made in writing, under oath, before any person authorized to administer oaths within or without the state. (622.85).

Affidavits may be made before: The judges, including district associate and magistrates, official reporters and clerks of courts, notaries public, certified short hand reporters. (78.1-.2). Affidavits taken out of state before any judge or clerk of court of record, before notary public, or before commissioner appointed by governor of Iowa, are of same credibility as if taken within state. (622.86).

General Requirements.—The parties making oath must appear before the officer; otherwise the officer may not lawfully attach his seal to the document sworn to. (9E.9).

Use of Affidavits.—May be used to evidence facts such as posting of notice, supporting motion or statement for attorney's fees, etc.

Alternative to Affidavit.—No statutory provision.

Form of Jurat

State of . . . ., County of . . . ., ss: Subscribed and sworn to before me this . . . . day of . . ., ... (Seal impression affixed, followed by title and signature of officer.)

NOTARIES PUBLIC:

(9E).

Secretary of state may appoint as notaries public Iowa residents and residents of bordering states whose work or business is within state of Iowa. (9E.3, 9E.6). All applicants, except members of general assembly, must pay $30 fee. Notary public term is three years for Iowa residents and one year for residents of bordering states.

Powers.—Notaries are authorized to take acknowledgments, take verifications upon oath or affirmation, witness or attest signature, certify or attest copy of document, and make or note protest to negotiable instrument. (9E.9).

Certificate of Authority.—See topic Acknowledgments, subhead Authentication.

Jurat.—Not necessary to append to jurat statement as to when commission expires.

Stamp or Seal.—No stamp or seal is required to execute notarial act.

RECORDS:

No instrument affecting real estate is valid against subsequent purchasers for value without notice unless filed and recorded in county in which real estate is located. (558.41). *For list of Counties and County Seats see first page for this state in Volume containing Practice Profiles Section.* No instrument deemed lawfully recorded unless previously acknowledged in manner prescribed. (558.42). No deeds or other instruments unconditionally conveying real estate will be recorded until entered for taxation upon transfer books in office of county auditor. (558.57).

Uniform Commercial Code adopted. (554). See category Business Regulation and Commerce, topic Commercial Code.

Filing Under Commercial Code.—In §9-401, relating to place of filing to perfect security interest, second alternative subsection has been adopted as subsection (1). Proper office for filing pursuant to this subsection is office of County Recorder or secretary of state (Secretary of State, UCC Filings, Hoover State Office Building, Des Moines, IA 50319), depending on nature of collateral. If on form conforming to standards prescribed by secretary of state, filing fee shall be $10. If statement is not on form conforming to standards prescribed by secretary of state, but otherwise conforms to requirements of law, filing fee shall be $12.

Recording Fees.—$5 for each page or fraction thereof. (331.604).

Torrens Act.—No Torrens Act or other statute for registration of land titles is in force.

See note at head of Digest as to 1998 legislation covered.

See Topical Index in front part of this volume.

RECORDS . . . *continued*

Transfer of Decedent's Title.—Probate records are sufficient to show transfer to decedent's devisees or heirs of his title to real estate in county where estate was administered. Certified transcript of probate proceedings should be filed with clerk of district court in any other county in which real estate of decedent is situated in order to show transfer of title thereto. If decedent was a nonresident, ancillary administration is usually necessary, although in some situations where the statute of limitations has run or security for claims of creditors has been given the filing of a transcript of foreign probate proceedings may be accepted as showing merchantable title, save for showing as to inheritance tax. (633.350).

Vital Statistics.—Reports of births and deaths must be made to local registrar of vital statistics; of marriages to clerk of district court of county where solemnized. (144).

Copies of birth, death or marriage certificates may be obtained from Clerk of District Court of county or from State Registrar of Vital Statistics, Iowa State Department of Health, Records Division, Lucas Building, Des Moines, Iowa 50319. Fee, $10.

Establishing Birth Records.—Department of Vital Statistics will issue a certificate on presentation of prescribed evidentiary requirements. (144.13).

SEALS:

Use of private seals on written contracts, except those of corporations, is abolished. (537A.1).

Corporate Seals.—In the execution of instruments affecting real estate a corporation may attach its seal. If none has been adopted such fact may be stated in conveyance. (558.2-.3).

Effect of Seal.—Use of seals has no legal effect.

Uniform Commercial Code adopted. (554). See category Business Regulation and Commerce, topic Commercial Code.

TORRENS ACT:

None.

VITAL STATISTICS:

See topic Records.

EMPLOYMENT

EMPLOYER AND EMPLOYEE:

See topic Labor Relations.

LABOR RELATIONS:

For regulations as to labor disputes, see category Dispute Resolution, topic Arbitration and Award. For provisions as to lien for labor, see category Debtor and Creditor, topic Liens.

Child Labor.—Child under ten may not work in street occupations of peddling, bootblacking, distribution or sale of newspapers, magazines, periodicals, or circulars. Child under 12 may not work in connection with migratory labor. Child 12 to 14 may not work in connection with migratory labor during school hours. Child under 16 may not work in any occupation during school hours except for limited exceptions. Child 14 to 15 may work in retail food and gasoline service areas, office and clerical work, cashiering, selling, modeling, art work, advertising, window trimming, comparative shopping, price marking, assembling orders, bagging and carry-out service, errand and delivery, clean-up work, kitchen work, cleaning vegetables and fruits. Child 14 to 15 may not work in any mine, manufacturing occupation, processing occupations, public messenger service, operation of any power-driven machinery, hazardous occupations, transportation of persons or property, warehousing and storage, communications and utilities, construction, including repair, certain occupations in retail food or gasoline service establishments. Child under 18 shall not work in any occupation concerning explosives, motor vehicle driver and helper, logging and sawmill occupations, power-driving wood-working machines, radioactive substances, elevators, power-driving machinery, mining, meat packing and slaughtering, manufacturing of brick and tile, shipbreaking operations, roofing operations, excavation, foundries, laundry and poisonous dyes or chemicals. (92).

Health and Safety Appliances-Labor-Occupational Safety and Health Act.—Labor commissioner authorized to set mandatory occupational safety and health standards applicable to business, and an occupational safety and health review commission created for carrying out adjudicatory functions. Each employer, a person engaged in a business who has one or more employees, including state, its agencies and political subdivisions, has duty to furnish to employees employment and a place of employment free from recognized hazards that are causing or likely to cause death or serious physical harm to his employees, and comply with standards promulgated under Act. Each employee has duty to comply with such standards applicable to him. Each employer must keep such records as prescribed by commissioner including records of deaths, injuries, illnesses, loss of consciousness, restriction of work or motion, transfer to another job, and exposures to toxic materials. (88).

Wages must be paid employee at least monthly on regular paydays. Regular payday shall not be more than 12 days, excluding Sundays and legal holidays, after end of period in which wages were earned, except upon written agreement between employer and employee. Expenses incurred by employee and authorized by employer must be reimbursed in advance or within 30 days after submission of expense claim. (91A.3). When employment suspended or terminated, employer must pay all wages earned (less deductions) up to time of suspension or termination not later than next regular payday. If vacations are due employee under agreement with employer or policy of employer establishing pro rata vacation accrued, increment shall be in proportion to fraction of year which employee was employed. (91A.4).

Priority is accorded to all wage claims for services rendered within 90 days preceding an assignment for benefit of creditors (681.13); to extent of $100 when property is seized under process or placed in the hands of a receiver (626.69).

Labor Unions.—Membership in unions recognized and protected. (731.1). "Right to work" law adopted. (732).

Workmen's Compensation Act provides compensation for injuries to employees in the course of, and arising out of, the employment. (85). Exemptions from compensation listed. (85.1 et seq.).

In said act there is a schedule by which the compensation of any injured employee is to be determined, and a provision for arbitration in the event of disagreement between the parties. All settlements are subject to the approval of the Industrial Commissioner. Action for recovery under compensation law must be begun within two years after injury. (85.26). Action for review of award or agreement for settlement must be brought within three years after last payment of compensation. (85.26). Judicial review of decisions or orders of Industrial Commissioner may be sought in accordance with c. 17A, Iowa Administrative Procedure Act, or petitions for judicial review may be filed in district court of county where hearing was held. Said reviews are given priority over other matters pending before district court. (86.26).

Each employer coming within the provisions of the act is required to insure with some responsible company against liability under said act, and all insurance is required to be carried for the benefit of employees or their dependents. Upon a showing of financial responsibility or posting security which is satisfactory to the Industrial and Insurance Commissioner, an employer may be relieved from the obligation of carrying insurance. (87).

Occupational Diseases.—Certain occupational diseases are compensable. (85A).

Unemployment Compensation.—With numerous exceptions and qualifications, payable to persons involuntarily unemployed who have worked for a covered employer. (96).

Discrimination.—Employer shall not discriminate on basis of race, religion, color, sex, national origin, or ancestry. (216).

WORKERS' COMPENSATION LAW:

See topic Labor Relations.

ENVIRONMENT

ENVIRONMENTAL REGULATION:

General Supervision.—Department of Natural Resources: Environmental Protection Commission. (455A.5-.6).

Prohibited Acts of Pollution.—

Air Pollution.—Defined as: Presence in outdoor atmosphere of one or more air contaminants in sufficient quantities and of such characteristics and duration as is or may reasonably tend to be injurious to human, plant, or animal life, or to property, or which unreasonably interfere with enjoyment of life and property (455B.131). Prohibited acts specified in statute. (455B).

Water Pollution.—Defined as: Contamination or alteration of physical, chemical, biological, or radiological integrity of any water of state by source resulting wholly or partly from activities of humans, which is harmful, detrimental, or injurious to public health, safety, or welfare, to domestic, commercial, industrial, agricultural, or recreational use or to livestock, wild animals, birds, fish, or other aquatic life. (455B.171). Prohibited acts specified in statute. (455B).

Solid, Radioactive, Hazardous Wastes.—Defined by statute. (455B.301, -.331, -.411). Prohibited acts specified in statute. (455B). Moratorium on construction and operation of certain commercial waste incinerators. (455B.151). Ownership of hazardous condition sites. (455B.171).

Enforcement.—Director of Department of Natural Resources, Environmental Protection Commission, and Attorney General may enforce. Citizens' suits permitted in certain situations. Injunctive relief, civil and criminal penalties available. (455B.111).

Penalties.—Civil and criminal penalties will be imposed for specified violations. (455B.109). Federal Air Quality regulations and civil penalties for violations. (455B.133[3]).

Permits.—Granted, modified, denied, suspended, or revoked by Director of Department of Natural Resources. (455B). Moratorium on granting permits for infectious waste treatment or disposal facilities. (455B.503).

ESTATES AND TRUSTS

ADMINISTRATION:

See topic Executors and Administrators.

ADVANCEMENTS:

See topic Descent and Distribution; category Mortgages, topic Mortgages of Real Property.

ALLOWANCES:

See topic Executors and Administrators.

CLAIMS:

See topic Executors and Administrators; category Civil Actions and Procedure, topic Pleading.

DEATH:

Five years unexplained absence of a person will raise a presumption of death, provided his relatives show that a diligent inquiry has been made. (633.510 et seq.). See category Property, topic Absentees.

Survivorship.—Uniform Simultaneous Death Act has been adopted. (633.523-.528).

Action for Death.—Action for death survives and may be maintained by administrator of decedent. (611.20, 22; 613.15). Must be commenced within two years. Parent may maintain action for wrongful death of infant child and recover for loss of services. (R.C.P. 8). No statutory limitation on amount of recovery. In case of both men and women, recovery may include value of services and support as spouse or parent. (613.15).

If decedent leaves spouse, child or parent, damages for wrongful death shall not be subject to debts and charges of decedent's estate, except for amounts repaid to Dept. of Human Services for Medical Assistance paid pursuant to c. 249A. (633.336).

Official certificate of death of a person may be obtained from the State Registrar of Vital Statistics, Iowa State Department of Health, Records Division, Lucas Building, Des Moines, Iowa 50319, or from county registrar. Fee, $10.

DECEDENTS' ESTATES:

Notice.—At any time following issuance of letters testamentary or of administration upon decedent's estate, any interested person may file written request for notice of time and place of all hearings in such estate. (633.42).

Share of Heirs.—Order intestate estate passes when not passed to surviving spouse. See 633.219.

See also topics Descent and Distribution, Executors and Administrators, Wills; category Debtor and Creditor, topic Homesteads.

DESCENT AND DISTRIBUTION:

Entire estate of intestate decedent, real and personal, or excess over share of surviving spouse, if any (as to which see subhead Share of Surviving Spouse, infra), descends and is distributed as follows, each class of which a member is living taking to the exclusion of subsequent classes: (1) children and/or issue of deceased children; (2) parents equally or all to surviving parent; (3) in case both parents are dead the portion which would have fallen to each of them must be disposed of in the same manner as if he or she had outlived the intestate and died in the possession and ownership of such portion; (4) and so on through ascending ancestors and their heirs; (5) if heirs are not thus found, uninherited portion shall go to spouse of decedent, if living, or to heirs of dead spouse, or spouses.

Share of Others than Surviving Spouse.—Part of intestate estate not passing to surviving spouse passes as follows: (1) To issue of decedent per stirpes; (2) if no surviving issue, to parents of decedent equally; (3) if not (1) or (2) of this section, estate shall be divided and set aside into two equal shares. One share shall be distributed to issue of decedent's mother per stirpes and one share shall be distributed to issue of decedent's father per stirpes. If there is no surviving issue of one deceased parent, entire estate passes to issue of other deceased parent; (4) if not (1), (2) or (3) of this section, and decedent is survived by one or more grandparents, half estate passes to paternal grandparents if both survive, or to surviving paternal grandparent if only one survives. If neither paternal grandparent survives, this half share shall be further divided into two equal sub-shares. One sub-share shall be distributed to issue of decedent's paternal grandmother per stirpes and one sub-share shall be distributed to issue of decedent's paternal grandfather per stirpes. If there are no surviving issue of one deceased paternal grandparent, entire half share passes to issue of other deceased paternal grandparent and their issue in same manner. Other half of decedent's estate passes to maternal grandparents and their issue in same manner. If there are no surviving grandparents on either paternal or maternal side, surviving grandparents or issue of grandparents on either paternal or maternal side, entire estate passes to decedent's surviving grandparents or their issue on other side; (5) if not (1), (2), (3) or (4) of this section, uninherited portion shall go to issue of deceased spouse of intestate, per stirpes. If intestate has had more than one spouse who died in lawful wedlock, it shall be equally divided between issuer, per stirpes, of those deceased spouses; (6) if not (1), (2), (3), (4) or (5) of this section, intestate property shall escheat to State of Iowa.

Share of Surviving Spouse.—If decedent dies intestate leaving surviving spouse and leaving no issue or leaving issue all of whom are issue of surviving spouse, surviving spouse shall receive following share: (1) All value of all legal or equitable estates in real property possessed by decedent at any time during marriage, which have not been sold on execution or by other judicial sale, and to which surviving spouse has made no relinquishment of right; (2) all personal property that, at time of death, was, in hands of decedent as head of family, exempt from execution; (3) all other personal property of decedent which is not necessary for payment of debts and charges. (633.211).

If decedent dies intestate leaving surviving spouse and leaving issue some of whom are not issue of surviving spouse, surviving spouse shall receive following share: (1) One-half in value of all legal or equitable estates in real property possessed by decedent at any time during marriage, which have not been sold on execution or by other judicial sale, and to which surviving spouse has made no relinquishment of right; (2) all personal property that, at time of death, was in hands of decedent as head of family, exempt from execution; (3) one-half of all other personal property of decedent which is not necessary for payment of debts and charges; (4) if property received by surviving spouse under subsections 1, 2, and 3 of this section is not equal in value to sum of $50,000, then so much additional of any remaining homestead interest and of remaining real and personal property of decedent that is subject to payment of debts and charges against decedent's estate, after payment of debts and charges, even to extent of whole of net estate, as necessary to make amount of $50,000. (633.212).

Except as provided in §§633.211 and 633.212, shares of distributees shall abate, for payment of debts and charges, federal and state estate taxes, legacies, shares of children born or adopted after making of will, or share of surviving spouse who elects to take against will, without any preference or priority as between real and personal property, in following order: (1) Property not disposed by will; (2) property devised to residuary devisee, except property to surviving spouse who takes under will; (3) property disposed of by will, but not specifically devised and not devised to residuary devisee, except property devised to surviving spouse who takes under will; (4) property specifically devised, except property devised to surviving spouse who takes under will; (5) property devised to surviving spouse who takes under will.

This Act applies to estates of decedents dying on or after effective date of Act. (July 1, 1985).

Half-blood share equally with whole blood in inheritance derived through the common parent. (172 Ia. 575, 154 N.W. 940).

Posthumous children inherit as though born in decedent's lifetime. (633.220).

Biological children inherit from mother and mother inherits from them. They inherit from father if evidence proving paternity is available during father's lifetime or they are recognized by him during his lifetime. Recognition must be general and notorious, or in writing. If recognition is mutual, father inherits from them. (633.221-.222).

Adopted Children.—See category Family, topic Adoption.

Advancements.—Property given by the intestate prior to his death to an heir, for the purpose of division and distribution of his estate, is considered to have been given toward the heir's share of the estate, but if advancement exceeds his share he cannot be required to refund any portion thereof. (633.225).

Effective Disclaimer.—Unless otherwise provided for by decedent, any disclaimed interest shall be distributed as if disclaimant had predeceased decedent. (633.704).

Election between distributive share and homestead, see category Debtor and Creditor, topic Homesteads; testamentary provision, see topic Wills.

Escheat.—Revised Uniform Disposition of Unclaimed Property Act adopted, with some modifications. (556). In default of heirs, property escheats to state, subject to reclamation of proceeds within ten years. (633.219, .543-.546).

See also topic Executors and Administrators.

ELECTION:

See topic Wills; category Debtor and Creditor, topic Homesteads.

ESTATES:

See topic Decedents' Estates; category Property, topic Real Property.

EXECUTORS AND ADMINISTRATORS:

The jurisdiction of estates of decedents is in the district courts. Venue is in the county where the decedent resided, or if decedent was a nonresident, where he owned property. If a nonresident owned property in more than one county, that court has jurisdiction in which proceedings are first commenced. (633.10-.14).

Preferences in Right to Administer.—Administration is granted in the following order of preference: (1) To surviving spouse; (2) to heirs; (3) to creditors; (4) to any other person showing good grounds therefor. Surviving spouse 20 days in which to apply for letters, after burial of decedent; other classes have ten days each; then any member of any class may file. (633.227-.228).

Eligibility.—Any person of full age, not a mental retardate, mentally ill, chronic alcoholic, spendthrift, or determined by court to be unsuitable, and any bank or trust company organized under laws of U.S. or state of Iowa when approved by superintendent of banking under 524-.1001 of Code, are authorized to act in fiduciary capacity in Iowa, and may serve as executor or administrator. (633.63). Nonresident may be appointed. (633.63, 633.64). Banks and trust companies organized under laws of U.S. or other state, and authorized to act in fiduciary capacity in other state, are permitted to act as fiduciary in Iowa if banks and trust companies of this state are permitted to act as fiduciary in state where such bank or trust company is located. (633.64). Private nonprofit corporations organized under 504 or 504A qualified to act as guardian or conservator under certain circumstances. (633.63).

Bond.—Administrators, and executors must give bonds fixed by court or clerk. (633.169-.171). Bond may be waived by will, and court may waive it if distributees consent in writing or other good cause is shown. (633.172-.175). Banks and trust companies not required to provide bond unless required by instrument creating relationship or order of court. (633.172).

Removal.—When fiduciary becomes ineligible for original appointment, has mismanaged estate, has failed to perform any duty imposed by law or by court order, or ceases to be a resident of the state, he may be removed. (633.65).

Limitations.—Probate of will, original administration of intestate estate or ancilliary administration of estate, shall not be granted after five years from death of decedent, unless petition for probate or administration is filed within five year period. (633.331).

Inventory must be filed by executor or administrator within 90 days after his qualification unless longer time is granted by court. (633.361).

Notice to Creditors.—Executors and administrators must, as soon as letters are issued, publish notice of appointment once each week for two consecutive weeks. (633.230, .304). If personal knowledge of name and address of potential, heir must give notice by ordinary mail. (633.230).

Presentation of Claims.—Claim must be filed with the clerk of court within four months after publication of notice to creditors. (633.410). This does not bar claims for which there is insurance coverage, to extent of coverage.

Unmatured claim must be presented like any other claim. (633.421).

Secured claim need not be presented in order to protect security, but must be presented in order to protect excess over security. (633.414, .422, .423).

See note at head of Digest as to 1998 legislation covered.

See Topical Index in front part of this volume.

EXECUTORS AND ADMINISTRATORS ... *continued*

Claim on which action was pending when decedent died need not be presented, but notice of substitution must be served on personal representative within time for filing claims. (633.415).

Separate action may be commenced against personal representative within four months in lieu of filing claim. (633.415).

Proof of Claims.—Claims must be entitled in the name of the claimant against the executor or administrator, naming him, and the estate, and must be correctly stated; if based on a written instrument must have a copy thereof attached; and must be sworn to. (633.418-.420).

Form

Form for proof of claim is as follows:

In the District Court of . . . . County, Iowa. . . . . vs. . . . ., administrator (or executor) of the estate of . . . ., deceased. Probate No. . . . .

. . . ., claimant, claims of . . . ., administrator (or executor) of the estate of said decedent, the sum of $. . . . and interest at the rate of . . . .% from the . . . . day of . . . ., 19. . . ., for (here set forth the nature of the claim) as now fully appears by the (statement of account or other evidence of claim) hereto attached, marked Exhibit A, and made a part hereof.

Wherefore claimant asks the allowance of said claim.

. . . .
Claimant
by . . . . Attorney

State of Iowa, County of . . . . ss.

. . . ., being first duly sworn, states that he is . . . ., and that the claim against the estate of . . . ., deceased, as above set forth, is just, true and correct and remains unpaid and that there is no legal offset to the same or any part thereof. (Jurat).

. . . .

Approval or Rejection of Claims.—In absence of fraud or collusion, claim stands allowed if admitted in writing by the personal representative. If he rejects claim, he must mail notice of disallowance to claimant and attorney of record. Claim then is barred unless claimant within 20 days, files request for hearing. (633.428, .439-.443).

Priorities.—(1) Court costs; (2) other costs of administration; (3) reasonable funeral and burial expenses; (4) debts and taxes having preference under laws of U.S.; (5) expenses of last illness; (6) taxes having preference under laws of Iowa; (7) any debt for medical assistance paid pursuant to c. 249A.5(2); (8) debts owing to employees for labor performed during the 90 days next preceding death of decedent; (9) unpaid support payments; (10) all other claims allowed. (633.425).

Claims Barred.—All claims not filed within four months after giving of notice of appointment are forever barred, unless personal representative waives such limitation, or unless peculiar circumstances entitle claimant to equitable relief. (633.410). This does not bar claims for which there is insurance coverage, to extent of coverage, or claims for certain debts relating to recovery of medical assistance payments, or claimants entitled to equitable relief under peculiar circumstances.

Sale of realty to pay debts, and charges, distribute estate, or for any other purpose in best interests of estate, may be had on petition of the representative. (633.386 et seq.).

Allowances.—Court may, set off to surviving spouse, or to decedent's minor children not living with surviving spouse, sufficient of decedent's property of such kind as is appropriate to support them for 12 months from time of his death. (633.374-.377). Right of surviving spouse in exempt property, see topic Descent and Distribution.

Actions.—There is no suspension of right to sue on claims and claimant may bring action, within four months after the giving of the notice of appointment without other presentation of claim. Action pending against decedent at time of death may be continued against the representative. (633.415).

Accounts and Final Settlement.—Representative may, and must upon order of court, file interlocutory accountings from time to time. Final settlement must be made in three years unless otherwise ordered by court. (633.469, .473). Unless notice is waived in writing, representative shall serve notice of final report at such time and in such manner as court may prescribe. (633.478).

Distribution of Estate.—Property not otherwise disposed of may be distributed in kind. (633.472). Partial distribution may be made, on court order, during the six month period for filing claims. (633.353-.354). Specific bequests must be delivered after estate has been open nine months unless court orders otherwise. (633.355). Final settlement must be made within three years unless otherwise ordered by court. (633.473).

Inability to Distribute.—Where fiduciary cannot make delivery to person entitled to funds, he may deposit same with clerk. (633.109).

Fees.—Executors and administrators are allowed reasonable fees, as determined by the court, not in excess of the following percentages upon gross assets listed for Iowa inheritance tax purposes: 6% on the first $1,000; 4% on the excess up to $5,000; 2% on the excess over $5,000. Gross assets do not include life insurance proceeds unless payable to decedent's estates. Fees of attorney for representative are determined in same manner and subject to same limitations. Further allowances may, however, be made by court to executors or administrators and their attorneys for actual, necessary and extraordinary services or expenses. (633.197-.199).

Small Estates.—See c. 635.

When total value of probate and nonprobate property of decedent subject to jurisdiction of this state does not exceed $50,000 and decedent died intestate survived by spouse, children, or does not exceed $15,000 and is survived by parent, or grandchildren, or if decedent leaves will that is admitted to probate but there is no present administration and only beneficiaries are surviving spouse, children or parent, petition may be filed with clerk for administration of small estate. Petitioner is personally liable for payment of debts of estate to extent assets of estate would be subject to

payment of those debts under regular estate administration. Clerk shall issue letters of appointment of personal representative which entitle personal representative to possession of any property of estate. Personal representative must file report and inventory. Unless interested person petitions for administration of estate on basis other than for small estate within one year after letters of administration issued, property of estate is free of debts and charges of estate, but personal representative remains liable for period of time otherwise provided by law. (635.1[2]).

When Administration Unnecessary.—As a practical matter, administration is necessary in most estates. All of property of decedent is subject to possession of personal representative of estate and control of court for purposes of administration, sale, or other disposition under law. If heirs or persons entitled to inherit property of an estate desire to avoid appointment of administrator, they or one of them shall file under oath inventories and reports and perform all of duties required under law, of administrators, including payment of taxes. (633.350, 450.22).

Ancillary Administration.—If a nonresident decedent has property within this state and an administrator has been appointed in accordance with the laws of the state or country where he resided at his death, the administrator may qualify in Iowa for the purpose of administering the property in Iowa by filing with the clerk, in the county in which the property is situated, a certified copy of the original letters or other authority making him administrator. A resident fiduciary must also be named unless otherwise ordered by court. Court may require payment of all claims filed and allowed belonging to residents of this state, and all legacies or distributive shares payable to residents of this state, before allowing the property to be removed from this state. (633.500-.504). See also topic Wills, subhead Foreign Probated Wills.

Uniform Fiduciaries Act not adopted.

Uniform Principal and Income Act not adopted.

Uniform Simplification of Fiduciary Security Transfers Act repealed.

Uniform Transfer on Death Security Registration Act adopted. (633.800).

FIDUCIARIES:

See topics Executors and Administrators, Trusts; category Family, topic Guardian and Ward.

INTESTACY:

See topic Descent and Distribution.

PROOF OF CLAIMS:

See topic Executors and Administrators; category Civil Actions and Procedure, topic Pleading.

TRUSTS:

Kinds.—Definition in probate code includes testamentary trusts and other trusts where court's jurisdiction is conferred or invoked. (633.3[35]).

Creation.—No statutory provision as to creation of testamentary trusts. Nontestamentary declarations or creations of trusts or powers in relation to real estate must be executed in same manner as deeds of conveyance, except as to trusts resulting from operation or construction of law.

Trustees, appointment, qualification, removal, general powers and duties of trustees and sales and accountings by trustees are similar to those of executors and administrators. See topic Executors and Administrators.

Eligibility and Competency.—Same as for executors and administrators. (633.63). Nonresident may be appointed.

Investments.—Model Prudent Person Investment Act applies to fiduciaries subject to Probate Code. (633.123). See also 636.

Securities in Name of Nominee.—Permissible for bank or trust company fiduciaries, but court authority is required if trust is pending in district court. (633.124, .125).

Compensation.—Fixed by Court. No statutory scale. (633.200-.204).

Uniform Common Trust Fund Act adopted. (633.126-.127).

Uniform Principal and Income Act not adopted.

Gifts to Minors.—Uniform Act repealed effective July 1, 1986. (565A).

Uniform Fiduciaries Act not adopted.

Uniform Simplification of Fiduciary Security Transfers Act repealed.

Uniform Transfers to Minors Act adopted effective July 1, 1986. (565B).

Accumulations.—No statutory restrictions.

Perpetuities.—See category Property, topic Perpetuities.

Pour Over Trusts.—See topic Wills, subhead Bequests and Devises to Inter Vivos Trusts.

WILLS:

Testamentary Capacity.—Any person of full age and sound mind may dispose of his property by will. (633.264).

Testamentary Disposition.—Testator may dispose of all his property, subject to the rights of homestead and exemption created by law, and the distributive share of surviving spouse, except sufficient to pay debts and costs of administration.

Execution.—All wills must be in writing, signed by the testator, or by some person in his presence and by his express direction, declared by him to be his will, and witnessed, at his request, by two competent witnesses. The witnesses must sign in the presence of the testator and of each other. (633.279).

Form

Form of Attestation.—The following may be used:

In witness whereof I have hereunto set my hand this . . . . day of . . . ., A. D., 19. . . ., (Signature).

WILLS . . . continued

The foregoing instrument was on the day of the date thereof signed, published, and declared by . . . . as, and for, his last will and testament in the presence of us, the undersigned, who at his request and in his sight and presence and in the sight and presence of each other have hereunto subscribed our names as witnesses. (Signatures).

Holographic will not executed as stated above is not recognized.

Nuncupative Wills.—Not authorized.

Revocation.—Will can be revoked in whole or in part only by being cancelled or destroyed by act or direction of testator with intention of revoking or by execution of subsequent will. Revocation by cancellation must be witnessed in same manner as making of new will. (633.284).

Testamentary Gifts to Subscribing Witnesses.—No will is invalidated because attested by interested witness; but any interested witness shall, unless will is also attested by two competent and disinterested witnesses, forfeit so much of provisions therein made for him as in aggregate exceeds that which he or she would have received had testator died intestate. (633.281).

Probate.—District court of county of which decedent died resident has original and exclusive jurisdiction to probate will. (633.10, .12). Any person having custody of will must, as soon as notified of death of testator, file same with clerk. (633.285).

Upon filing of a petition for probate of a will, court or clerk may hear it forthwith, or at such time and place as court may direct, with or without requiring notice. (633.293).

Self-proved Will.—Attested will may be made self-proved at time of execution, or at any subsequent date, by acknowledgment thereof by testator and affidavits of witnesses, each made before person authorized to administer oaths and take acknowledgments under laws of state, and evidenced by such person's certificate, under seal, attached or annexed to will, in form and content substantially as follows:

Affidavit

County of . . . . } ss

We, the undersigned, ..., ... and . . . ., the testator and the witnesses, respectively, whose names are signed to the attached or foregoing instrument, being first duly sworn, declare to the undersigned authority that said instrument is the testator's will and that the testator willingly signed and executed such instrument, or expressly directed another to sign the same in the presence of the witnesses, as a free and voluntary act for the purposes therein expressed; that said witnesses, and each of them, declare to the undersigned authority that such will was executed and acknowledged by the testator as the testator's will in their presence and that they, in the testator's presence, at the testator's request, and in the presence of each other, did subscribe their names thereto as attesting witnesses on the date of the date of such will; and that the testator, at the time of the execution of such instrument, was of full age and of sound mind and that the witnesses were sixteen years of age or older and otherwise competent to be witnesses.

. . . .
Testator
. . . .
Witness
. . . .
Witness

Subscribed, sworn and acknowledged before me by . . . ., the testator; and subscribed and sworn before me by . . . . and . . . ., witnesses, this . . . . day of . . . ., 19. . . .

. . . .
(Seal)   Notary Public, or other officer authorized to take and certify acknowledgments and administer oaths

Self-proved will shall constitute proof of due execution of such instrument as required by section 633.293 and may be admitted to probate without testimony of witnesses. (633.279).

Contest.—Admission of will to probate may be contested either at time of hearing on application to admit or by action to set will aside brought in district court within four months from time of second publication of notice of admission to probate or one month following mailing of notice. (633.308-.311).

Children.—Legitimate children (posthumous or otherwise) born after execution of the will and not provided for by the will or by settlement and not mentioned in the will, take the share of the estate to which they would have been entitled in case of intestacy, unless it appears from will that omission was intentional. (633.267). Children living when will is executed may be disinherited by mere disposition of entire estate otherwise than to them, without any declaration of intent to disinherit them.

Legacies may be paid during the six months period for filing claims upon court order. Specific legacies must be delivered after estate has been open nine months unless court orders otherwise. (633.353-.355; 633.410).

Unclaimed legacies must be paid to Clerk of District Court, who deposits same with State Treasurer, after filing a report to State Treasurer with respect to the property. If unclaimed for one year, such funds become part of general fund of state. (636.31; 556). Revised Uniform Disposition of Unclaimed Property Act adopted, with some modifications. (556).

See also topic Executors and Administrators, subhead Inability to Distribute.

Lapses.—A devise or bequest does not lapse if the devisee or legatee die before testator and leaves issue who survive testator. Heirs of devisee or legatee inherit property devised or bequeathed, unless from terms of will contrary intent is manifest. But devise to spouse lapses if spouse does not survive testator, unless contrary intent is manifest in will. (633.273, .274).

Election.—Surviving spouse may elect to take or refuse to take under a will within two months after date of second publication of notice of admission of will to probate. If no voluntary election is filed within that time, executor must serve notice upon such surviving spouse, reciting admission of will to probate and date thereof, stating name of court, and requiring such spouse within four months thereafter to elect either in open court or by writing filed therein. If surviving spouse does not make such election within four months after such notice, or if such surviving spouse is executor of will and fails to make such election within four months after second publication of notice, it is conclusively presumed that such survivor elects to take under will, unless within such period an affidavit is filed that such survivor is incapable of making an election, in which case court must enter an order electing for such survivor as court shall deem for best interests of such spouse. Surviving spouse who elects not to take under will may elect right to occupy homestead as set forth under category Debtor and Creditor, topic Homesteads, subhead Rights of Surviving Spouse, or may elect statutory share as set forth under topic Descent and Distribution, subhead Share of Surviving Spouse. (633.237).

Bequests and Devises to Inter Vivos Trusts.—Permitted. (633.275). Uniform Testamentary Additions to Trusts Act adopted. (633.276-.278).

Testamentary Guardian.—See category Family, topic Guardian and Ward.

Foreign Executed Wills.—Last will and testament executed without this state, in mode prescribed by the law of the place where executed or of the testator's domicile, is deemed to be legally executed, and has the same force and effect as if executed in the mode prescribed by the laws of this state, provided said last will and testament is in writing and subscribed by the testator. (633.283).

Foreign Probated Wills.—Will probated in any other state or country shall be admitted to probate in this state, without notice required in case of domestic wills, on production of a copy thereof and of original record of probate, authenticated by certificate of clerk of court in which such probation was made, or, if there be no clerk, by certificate of judge thereof, and seal of office of such officers, if they have a seal. (633.496).

Living Wills.—Living wills are governed by c. 144A of Iowa Code. Person who is competent may execute in writing declaration directing that life sustaining procedures be withdrawn if terminal illness occurs. Declaration may be revoked at any time.

Simultaneous Death.—See topic Death, subhead Survivorship.

Testamentary Trusts.—See topic Trusts.

FAMILY

ADOPTION:

Following persons may adopt: (1) Unmarried adult; (2) husband and wife together; (3) husband or wife separately if person to be adopted is not other spouse and if adopting spouse (a) is stepparent of person to be adopted or (b) has been separated from other spouse by reason of said spouse's abandonment as prescribed in §597.10 or (c) if unable to petition with other spouse because of prolonged and unexplained absence, unavailability or incapacity of other spouse or because of unreasonable withholding of joinder by other spouse as determined by court under Act. (600.5).

Consent of following persons needed, although if person required to consent refuses or cannot be located to give consent, court can determine such person's consent unnecessary: (1) Guardian of person to be adopted; (2) spouse of petitioner who is stepparent; (3) spouse of petitioner who is separately petitioning to adopt adult; (4) person to be adopted if 14 years or older.

Consent must be in writing, name person to be adopted and petitioner, and be signed by person consenting in following manner: (1) If by minor 14 or older, in presence of court in which adoption petition filed; (2) if by adult to be adopted, either in presence of court in which petition filed or before notary public; (3) if by any other person, before notary public.

Consent may be withdrawn prior to issuance of decree by filing affidavit of consent withdrawal with court. (600.7).

Condition Precedent.—Child must have lived 180 days in home of adopter before adoption unless court waives or shortens this requirement. (600.10).

Jurisdiction and Venue.—District court of county in which adopter or adoptee if adult or guardian if minor person resides has jurisdiction. (600.3).

Procedure is by petition by adopter. Upon filing of petition for adoption of minor child, State Department of Human Services or designated agency conduct investigations to determine if home of prospective adopter is suitable and if adopter suitable, although investigation may be waived by court if prospective adopter is stepparent or relative to person to be adopted within fourth degree of consanguinity. (600.8).

Name of adoptee may be changed by decree.

Decree.—If petition is granted, decree must be entered, setting forth all facts and name by which adoptee shall thereafter be known.

ALIMONY:

See topic Dissolution of Marriage.

COMMUNITY PROPERTY:

System does not obtain.

DESERTION:

See topics Dissolution of Marriage, Husband and Wife.

DISSOLUTION OF MARRIAGE:

Jurisdiction and Venue.—District court in county where either party resides has jurisdiction in all cases of dissolution of marriage. (598.2).

See note at head of Digest as to 1998 legislation covered.

See Topical Index in front part of this volume.

DISSOLUTION OF MARRIAGE... *continued*

Grounds for Absolute Divorce.—Decree dissolving marriage may issue when there has been breakdown of marriage relationship to extent that legitimate objects of matrimony have been destroyed and there remains no reasonable likelihood that relationship can be preserved. (598.17).

Grounds for Legal Separation.—May be decreed on same grounds as dissolution of marriage.

Residence Requirements.—Except where respondent is a resident of state and served by personal service, petition must show that petitioner has been for last year a resident of state, specifying town and county in which he has so resided. (598.6).

Process.—Service by publication is authorized where respondent is a nonresident of Iowa or his residency is unknown. See category Civil Actions and Procedure, topic Process, subhead Publication.

Temporary Matters.—Court may order either party to pay to clerk sum of money for separate support of adverse party and children and to enable such party to prosecute or defend action, and such order may be aided by attachment. Notwithstanding 561.15, court may order either party to vacate homestead pending entry of decree upon showing that other party or children in imminent danger of harm if order not issued. (598.36).

Trial shall be in open court on oral testimony or deposition; however, court may close hearing. No dissolution of marriage granted on testimony of petitioner alone.

Decree.—Final decree is entered on determination of issues; no interlocutory decree.

Change of Wife's Name.—Return of maiden name to wife is discretionary with court.

Division of Property of Spouses.—See subhead Property Disposition and Custody of Children, infra.

Property Disposition and Custody of Children.—When dissolution of marriage is decreed, court may make such order in relation to children, property, parties and maintenance of parties as may be just. (598.21). Court may grant joint custody of children in dissolution action. With regard to division of property of spouses, ultimate question is whether distribution of property and assets is equitable under specific facts of case (309 N.W.2d 511, 514 [Iowa 1981]); where accumulated property is not product of joint efforts of both parties, or where one party brings property into marriage, there need not necessarily be division (305 N.W.2d 448 [Iowa 1981]).

Upon finding of willful disobedience court may cite for contempt, or order assignment of periodic earnings or trust income to clerk or collection services center for use of person for whom assignment ordered. Amounts not to exceed that set forth in 15 U.S.C. §1673(b). Assignment binding on employer, trustee or other payor two weeks after receiving notice of same, and must withhold and transmit payments to clerk or collection services center. (598.22).

Waiting Period.—Dissolution of marriage will normally not be granted until 90 days after service of notice. (598.19).

Separation agreements are recognized and enforced.

Annulment of Marriage.—See topic Marriage.

DIVORCE:

See topic Dissolution of Marriage.

GUARDIAN AND WARD:

Probate court has jurisdiction to appoint a guardian of the person for one who is minor, or by reason of mental, physical or other incapacity lacks sufficient capacity to make or carry out important decisions concerning proposed ward's person or affairs, other than financial affairs. (633.556). Or guardian may be appointed for person or property of any person other than minor under 14 upon his own application. (633.557, .572, .635).

Eligibility and Competency.—Selection of guardian is within discretion of court. Guardian cannot be appointed by will but person named in will must be preferred, after parents. (633.559). No statutory prohibition or authorization of nonresident guardian for resident ward.

Bond.—Bond is required as in estates of decedents, except that guardian of the person need not give bond unless ordered by court to do so. (633.633).

Powers and Duties.—A guardian has control of the person, and a conservator has control of property, of the ward. Same person may serve in both capacities. Conservator has the authority, with approval of court, to sell property of the ward for any purpose which may be deemed conducive to his interest. (633.628, .641-.649).

Real estate may be sold or mortgaged under same conditions and subject to same procedure as in estates of decedents. (633.652).

Investments by guardians are subject to Court approval. (633.647).

Securities in Name of Nominee.—See category Estates and Trusts, topic Trusts, subhead Securities in Name of Nominee.

Reports.—Guardians and conservators must make reports as provided by 633.669 and 633.641.

Exoneration.—He can be exonerated from responsibility only upon the filing of such final report and notice to the ward of the time and place of hearing thereon. (633.677-.682).

Insane Persons.—No special provisions.

Foreign Guardians.—A foreign guardian or conservator of a nonresident ward may be appointed conservator of the property of such person in this state. Such appointment may be made by applying with clerk of district court of county where there is any such property; application shall include certified copy of original letters or other authority conferring power upon foreign conservator or guardian to act as such. Court may dispense with requirement of appointment of resident co-conservator. (633.603-.604).

Foreign conservator or guardian may be authorized to receipt for personal property by filing in office of clerk of court in county where the property is situated a certified copy of his official bond duly authenticated by court granting the letters. (633.605-.608).

See also category Estates and Trusts, topic Executors and Administrators, subheads Eligibility, and Bond.

Uniform Gifts to Minors Act repealed effective July 1, 1986.

Uniform Fiduciaries Act not adopted.

Uniform Simplification of Fiduciary Security Transfers Act repealed.

Uniform Transfers to Minors Act adopted effective July 1, 1986. (565B).

HUSBAND AND WIFE:

Husband and wife may contract with each other and transact business with each other as though unmarried, except that they may not contract for compensation for the performance of obligations incident to the marital relation (224 Ia. 109, 275 N.W. 490) or contract with each other with relation to the interest which one spouse has in the property of the other arising out of the marital relation (597.2).

Disabilities of Married Women.—All disabilities have been removed.

Separate Property.—A married woman may own in her own right real and personal property, and manage and dispose of it in the same manner as the husband can dispose of property belonging to him. But the right of either spouse to a distributive share in the realty of the other (see category Estates and Trusts, topic Descent and Distribution) cannot be affected by a conveyance or mortgage in which he or she does not join.

Antenuptial Agreements.—Antenuptial contracts are recognized under Iowa law and should be construed liberally to carry out intentions of parties. (Norris v. Norris, 174 N.W.2d 368 [Iowa 1970]). Uniform Premarital Agreement Act adopted in 1991. (596.1).

Wages.—A married person may recover and retain his or her own wages.

Actions.—A married person may sue and be sued in his or her own separate name.

Liabilities.—Neither husband nor wife is liable for the separate debts of the other. For the expenses of the family and education of the children both are liable, and they may be sued therefor either jointly or separately. (597.17).

Contracts of Married Person.—May make contracts and incur liabilities to same extent as if unmarried. Person may become surety for spouse or any other person. (597.18).

Agency.—Husband or wife may constitute the other attorney in fact to control and dispose of property for their mutual benefit. (597.5).

Negligence.—As it pertains to actions for personal injury resulting from spousal negligence or intentional torts, doctrine of inter-spousal immunity abrogated with respect to all actions in which final order, decree or judgment has not been entered as of 8-25-79. (281 N.W.2d 616).

Desertion or wilful neglect or refusal to provide for dependent adult (726.8) or children (726.5) is felony.

Support of Dependents Law has been adopted in substantially form proposed by Council of State Governments. (252A). Variations from that form follow: (1) State may institute proceedings, without consent of dependent, to obtain reimbursement for support furnished dependent. (252A.5-2). (2) Persons entitled to periodic support payments pursuant to order or judgment entered in uniform support action under this chapter, who are welfare recipients, must assign their rights to payments to department of social services. (598.34). (3) Verified petition may be filed by petitioner or petitioner's representative, in District Court, in equity, and may include such exhibits or information as may assist in identifying and locating respondent. (252A.6-1). (4) Support payments made to clerk of district court, dependent, or collection services center, as court may direct. (252A.6-5). (5) Costs incurred in Iowa shall be advanced by initiating party or agency, unless action brought by state or county, or unless court otherwise directs. (252A.10). New paternity determination procedures adopted 1994. (252A).

Uniform Interstate Family Support Act adopted. (252K).

Community property system does not apply.

INFANTS:

Age of majority 18 both sexes. Infant attains majority by marriage. Person who is convicted and sentenced as adult but who is less than 18 years old and incarcerated shall be deemed to have reached age of majority for purposes of making decisions and giving consent to medical care while incarcerated. (599.1).

Contracts.—Minor is bound by his contract for necessaries and for other contracts unless disaffirmed within a reasonable time after attaining majority and restoration made to other party of all money or property received by the minor by virtue of such contract, and remaining within his control. (599.2).

Actions.—The action of a minor must be brought by his guardian if he has one, if not, by his next friend, but the court may dismiss it if not for his benefit, or may substitute a guardian or other person as next friend. (R.C.P. 12). At or before the hearing of petitions and contest for the probate of wills, letters testamentary or of administration, for sale of real estate and confirmation thereof, settlements and distribution of estates and all other proceedings where all the parties interested in the estate are required to be notified thereof, the court may in its discretion, appoint some competent attorney at law to represent therein minors having an interest in the estate or the proceeds from the estate, who have no general guardian in the county. (633.118-.120).

Termination of Parental Rights.—Parent may petition juvenile court for termination of parental rights, if parent has signed release of custody, petitioned for termination, abandoned child, failed to contribute to support, or failed to object to termination. (600A). Guardian, Department of Human Services, juvenile court officer, or county attorney may petition juvenile court for termination of parental rights over child in need of assistance if parents have consented to termination, if child has been abandoned, physically or sexually abused, or otherwise in need of assistance. (232.109 et seq.).

See note at head of Digest as to 1998 legislation covered.

See Topical Index in front part of this volume.

INFANTS . . . *continued*

Uniform Gifts to Minors Act repealed effective July 1, 1986.

Uniform Securities Ownership by Minors Act not adopted.

Uniform Transfers to Minors Act adopted effective July 1, 1986. (565B).

Interstate Compact on Juveniles.—State of Iowa through its courts and agencies authorized to enter into with other states in form approved by Council of State Governments on Jan. 21, 1955. (232.171).

Adoption.—See topic Adoption.

MARRIAGE:

Age of consent—18. (595.2).

Consent Required.—Consent of parents or guardian necessary where either party is under 18. If parents are divorced, one having custody of minor may give consent. (595.2).

License is required and must be issued by a clerk of district court. (595.3). License must be procured in person and may be procured by either of prospective parties. Clerk must require affidavit from some competent disinterested person stating facts as to age and qualification of parties. (595.4). Clerk must wait three days after application is filed before issuing license. (595.4). Marriage must be performed within 20 days following issuance of license.

Ceremony may be performed by judicial magistrate, judge of Supreme, court of appeals or district court, or minister ordained or licensed according to usages of his denomination. Marriages solemnized in any other manner with consent of parties are valid but parties to such proceedings are liable to fine. Where marriage solemnized without services of clergyman or magistrate husband must make return to clerk. (595).

Reports of Marriages.—Officiating minister or magistrate must file return within 15 days with county registrar on form provided for that purpose. (595.13).

Record.—See category Documents and Records, topic Records, subhead Vital Statistics.

Common law marriages are recognized including those contracted out of state.

Prohibited Marriages.—Between people related by blood are void, including first cousins. Where either party has spouse living marriage is void but becomes valid if parties live and cohabit together after death or divorce of former spouse. (595.19).

Annulment.—Marriage may be annulled: (1) Where marriage between parties is prohibited by law; (2) where either party was impotent at time of marriage; (3) where either party had a husband or wife living at time of marriage, provided they have not with knowledge of such fact lived and cohabited together after death or divorce of former spouse of such party; (4) where either party was mentally ill or a mental retardate at time of marriage. (598.29). Nonage is not specific ground for annulment but marriage of party below age of consent will be nullity at option of such party made known at any time before such party reaches his or her 18th birthday. (595.2).

Children.—Children of a marriage terminated or annulled shall be legitimate. (598.31).

Alimony.—In case either party enters into the marriage in good faith supposing the other to be capable of contracting and the marriage is declared to be a nullity, the court may decree that such innocent party shall receive compensation as in case of dissolution of marriage. (598.21, .22, .32).

MARRIED WOMEN:

See topics Husband and Wife, Marriage; categories Civil Actions and Procedure, topic Evidence, subhead Witnesses; Debtor and Creditor, topic Homesteads; Documents and Records, topic Acknowledgments; Estates and Trusts, topics Executors and Administrators, Wills.

INSURANCE

INSURANCE COMPANIES:

Department of Commerce's Insurance Division has supervision of domestic insurance companies and business of foreign companies transacted in this state. (505 et seq.).

Classes of Risk Permitted.—With certain exceptions, companies may write on all classes of risks provided certain reinsurance for excess loss is in effect. (515.48-.49 as am'd 1988, H.F. 2307). Mutual life insurance companies are subject to certain special conditions. (508.9).

Annual statement of condition must be filed by all companies with Commissioner before Mar. 1 on form which Commissioner must furnish. (511.1; 515.63).

Policies.—Standard forms of fire insurance policies are required (515.138); also for sickness and accident policies (514A). Forms of all policies and of applications and endorsements must be approved by Insurance Commissioner. (508.25; 515.109). Health, life, and accident policies under group plan must comply with 509. As to assignability of life policy, see category Debtor and Creditor, topic Assignments.

Annuities may be sold by any life insurance company organized on stock or mutual plan. (508.31).

Combinations or agreements between companies as to rates, commissions or manner of doing business are forbidden; but companies may appoint same person as common agent to file forms of policies or permits required by law to be examined and approved by commissioner. (515.131).

Investments of life insurance companies are controlled by 511.8. Investments of life insurance companies in agricultural land are controlled by 511.8A. Investments of nonlife companies are controlled by 515.35.

Brokers and agents must be licensed by Commissioner of Insurance. (522).

Process Agent.—See infra, subhead Foreign Companies.

Foreign Companies.—Foreign stock company may not do non-life insurance business in state unless it has $2,500,000 paid-up capital, plus surplus in cash or authorized securities of $2,500,000, exclusive of assets deposited in state or territory for benefit of those insured therein. (515.69). Foreign life insurance companies must meet same standards as domestic life companies. (508.10).

Foreign company must file with Insurance Commissioner an agreement in writing that service of notice or process of any kind may be made on Insurance Commissioner. (511.27, 515.73).

For other requirements pertaining to foreign companies see category Business Organizations, topic Corporations, subhead Foreign Corporations.

No foreign company admitted in Iowa may write any policy or contract covering property risks located in this state or contract of indemnity or suretyship except by a duly licensed agent residing in Iowa. Such policies must be countersigned by Iowa agent paid on commission basis. When policy originates outside of Iowa, such agent is entitled to 5% of premium. This does not apply to insurance on railroad rolling stock or property in possession of railroad in transit or on marine risks or property in transportation, to life insurance, or to insurance companies which do not write insurance on commission basis. (515.52-.61).

Premium Tax.—A 2% tax on the gross amount of premiums received from business within the state during the preceding calendar year applies to both domestic and foreign companies payable on or before Mar. 1 of year following calendar year for which tax due, except if premium tax greater than $1,000, then prepayment schedule applies. Dividends, except those granted as paid-up additions, and premiums on policies issued in connection with certain pension plans are excluded. Fraternal beneficiary associations, county mutual associations and nonprofit hospital and medical service corporations are exempt. (432.1). Reinsurance premiums are exempt. (515.24).

Trade Practices.—Unfair methods of competition and discriminatory or deceptive trade practices in sale of insurance prohibited and subject to jurisdiction of Insurance Commissioner. (507B).

Direct Actions Against Insurer.—See category Transportation, topic Motor Vehicles, subhead Direct Actions.

SURETY AND GUARANTY COMPANIES:

Companies engaged in the business of becoming sureties upon bonds must file with the clerk of any county in which they do business a certificate from the Commissioner of Insurance that they have complied with the law, and are authorized to do business in the state. The filing of this certificate enables the officer or body having the approval of same to approve the sufficiency of same, but these provisions are not applicable to criminal bonds. No bond may be accepted for an amount in excess of 10% of the paid-up cash capital of such company, unless the excess be re-insured in some other company so authorized, and then not to exceed 10% of the capital of the re-insuring company. Agent for authorized surety must be Iowa resident for purposes of acting on behalf of company with respect to any bond or bail in criminal cases. (636.11-.18).

Commissioner of Insurance is process agent. (636.21).

Surety companies may be released from liability on bond, except performance bond on public works contract, or criminal appearance bond, by petitioning the approving officer or board for relief stating the grounds therefor, giving the principal at least 24 hours notice of the filing of such petition. The approving officer or board may conduct a hearing and if there appears substantial ground for apprehension may order a new bond, and upon such being given the petitioning surety may be declared discharged for future acts. (65).

INTELLECTUAL PROPERTY

TRADEMARKS AND TRADENAMES:

Person, firm, association or corporation that has adopted any label, trademark or form of advertising, may file same for record in office of Secretary of State by leaving two duplicate originals thereof. Such trademark must be of distinctive character and not of any near resemblance to any trademark previously filed. Fee: $10 for filing. Certificate is prima facie proof of adoption and right to use trademark. Its use, imitation or infringement by any other person may me enjoined by owner and damages recovered. Unlawful use is punishable by imprisonment or fine.

Registrations expire five years from date thereof, and may be renewed at any time within six months before date of termination by filing application for renewal in office of Secretary of State and payment of renewal fee. (548.106).

Assignment.—Trademarks, labels and forms of advertising registered in the office of the Secretary of State may be assigned of record by the registrant or record owner thereof by the execution of an appropriate written instrument duly executed filed in office of Secretary of State, and upon payment to Secretary of State of an appropriate fee for each filing. (548.107).

Tradenames.—It is unlawful to conduct business under tradename other than surname of each person owning business, unless verified statement showing name, post-office address and residence address of each person having interest in business, and address where business is to be conducted, is filed with county recorder of county where business is to be conducted. Fee, $5. All changes must likewise be recorded. (547). Corporations may use assumed name after filing same with Secretary of State. (490.401).

TRADE SECRETS:

Uniform Trade Secrets Act adopted 1990. (c. 550).

Injunctions.—Owner of trade secret may petition district court to enjoin actual or threatened misappropriation. (550.3).

Damages may include actual loss caused by misappropriation, plus unjust enrichment caused by misappropriation. In lieu of damages measured by any other method, damages may be measured by imposition of reasonable royalty. (550.4). Prevailing party

TRADE SECRETS . . . *continued*
may recover attorney fees if evidence of bad faith or willful or malicious conduct. (550.6).

Limitations.—Action must be brought within three years after misappropriation discovered or reasonably should have been discovered. (550.8).

LEGAL PROFESSION

ATTORNEYS AND COUNSELORS:

State bar is not integrated.

Jurisdiction over admission is in the Supreme Court. (602.10101).

Eligibility.—Applicant for admission must be (1) of good moral character, (2) inhabitant of this state, (3) graduated from reputable law school. (602.10102).

Registration as law student required.

Educational Requirements.—Applicant for admission on examination must have pursued a regular course of study of law in a reputable law school and have degree of LL.B. or J.D. However, law student in reputable law school who expects to receive degree of LL.B. or J.D. within 45 days from first day of July or Feb. examination permitted to take examination upon filing of affidavit by dean of said school stating he expects such student to receive degree within said time, affidavit being in addition to other requirements. (Ct. Rule 107; 602.10102).

Continuing Legal Education.—All attorneys required to complete minimum of 15 hours legal education accredited by continuing legal education commission during each calendar year and minimum of two ethics credits during every two-year period. (Ct. Rule 123.3).

Application for examination must be made to Supreme Court in writing and under oath on forms furnished by clerk of Supreme Court showing applicant's eligibility and compliance with educational requirements, and must be filed no later than Mar. 1 preceding July examination or Oct. 1st preceding Feb. examination next bar exam date. (Ct. Rule 104). All applicants examined in June, 1989, and thereafter are required to pass The Multistate Professional Responsibility Examination for admission to practice. (Ct. Rule 102).

Examination is conducted by Board of Law Examiners at Polk County on Mon. preceding last Wed. in July in even-numbered years and on Mon. preceding last Wed. in Feb. in odd-numbered years and at Iowa City on Mon. preceding last Wed. in July in odd-numbered years and on Mon. preceding last Wed. in Feb. in even-numbered years. Multi-State Bar Examination is now used in Iowa. (Ct. Rule 102).

Admission fee and examination fee set by Board of Examiners. (602.10108).

Admission Without Examination.—An attorney of bar of any state or any territory of United States or District of Columbia, who is a resident of Iowa, may be admitted to Iowa bar without examination and proof of study on showing, in addition to all other requirements of law, that he has practiced for five full years under license in such other jurisdiction within the seven years preceding date of application and that he still holds such license. (602.10109; Ct. Rule 111).

In order to secure admission without examination following proofs must be filed with Iowa Board of Law Examiners: (1) Certificate of admission in state of former residence; (2) certificate of clerk or judge of court of record in such state that applicant was regularly engaged in practice of law in said state for five years; (3) certificate of judge or clerk of district court where applicant intends to practice in this state that he is of good moral character; (4) affidavit of qualifications as to inhabitancy or intent to establish office for practice of law in Iowa. (Ct. Rules 111, 112).

Person applying for admission pursuant to this rule must pay to Clerk of Supreme Court at time of filing application for admission fee of $500, no part of which is refundable. (Ct. Rule 111).

The applicant must appear for admission before Supreme Court or member thereof. (Ct. Rule 112).

Admission Pro Hac Vice.—An out-of-state attorney may appear in and conduct any cause or matter pending in Iowa courts in which he is actually engaged, provided that he files with clerk of court an appointment of some attorney of the county where suit is pending, upon whom service may be had in all matters connected with action. Failing to make such appointment, his pleadings must be stricken from court files and he may not be permitted so to practice. (602.10111, Ct. Rule 113).

License.—License renewed in multi-year intervals by Supreme Court under conditions determined by Court. (602.10137).

Powers.—Attorneys may receipt for money claimed by client in an action or proceeding, during pendency thereof or afterward, unless previously discharged, and acknowledge satisfaction. (602.10114).

Liens.—An attorney has a lien for a general balance of compensation on: (1) Any and all papers or money in his hands belonging to his client; (2) any money due his client in the hands of the adverse party or attorney of said party in an action or proceeding in which the attorney claiming the lien was employed, from the time of giving notice in writing to such adverse party or his attorney; (3) after judgment in any court of record such notice may be given and the lien made effective against the judgment debtor by entering the same in the judgment or combination docket, opposite the entry of the judgment. (602.10116). Lien may be released by executing bond in sum double amount claimed or in such sum as fixed by district judge, payable to attorney, and will be released in any case unless attorney, within ten days after demand thereof, files with clerk full and complete bill of his services. (602.10117, .10118).

Grievances.—Members of grievance committee of Iowa State Bar Association are Commissioners of the Supreme Court, with authority to hear complaints against conduct of attorneys which tends to defeat the administration of justice or to bring the courts or the legal profession into disrepute, to reprimand the accused, and to file an action to revoke or suspend the license of such attorney if such action appears justified. (Ct. Rule 118.1).

Suspension or Disbarment.—Supreme Court may suspend or revoke an attorney's license to practice, upon proceedings instituted at direction of court or on petition of any individual. (602.10121-.10123).

Advertising Law Lists.—Numerous restrictions on lawyer holding out publicly as practicing in certain fields of law and explicit directions for publication of disclaimer in connection therewith. (D.R. 2-105). Must obtain written consent from all clients listed as clients regularly represented. (D.R. 2-101[B][6]).

Professional Corporations.—See category Business Organizations, topic Corporations, subhead Professional Corporations.

Attorney Ethics.—Iowa Court adopted American Bar Association Code of Professional Responsibility, Ct. R. 119. Ethical considerations mandatory.

MINERAL, WATER AND FISHING RIGHTS

MINES AND MINERALS:

Supervision.—Department of Agriculture and Land Stewardship supervises mines and mining operations. (208). Department of Agriculture and Land Stewardship may commence proceedings to suspend, revoke, or refuse to renew license for repeated or willful violation of any provisions of Act. (208.8).

Operation of Mines.—No person, firm, partnership or corporation shall engage in mining without first obtaining license from Department of Agriculture and Land Stewardship. Licenses are issued upon application, expire on Dec. 31 of each year, and are renewable upon application. (208.7).

Inspection of Mines.—Department of Agriculture and Land Stewardship may enter lands on which operator is licensed to operate mine at any time to determine compliance with Act. (208.26).

Oil and gas wells are regulated by 458A.

MORTGAGES

CHATTEL MORTGAGES:

Uniform Commercial Code adopted. (554). See category Business Regulation and Commerce, topic Commercial Code.

Motor Vehicles.—Security interests in motor vehicles are perfected by notation on certificate of title and delivery to county treasurer. (321). Except as provided in 321, Uniform Commercial Code applies to security interests in motor vehicles. (321.47-.50).

Forms.—For free samples of form of Financing Statement, and Statement of Continuation, Partial Release, Assignment, Termination or Amendment, write Iowa Secretary of State. For forms of Security Agreement and Financing Statement, see end of this Digest.

COLLATERAL SECURITY:

See category Debtor and Creditor, topic Pledges.

MORTGAGES OF PERSONAL PROPERTY:

See topic Chattel Mortgages.

MORTGAGES OF REAL PROPERTY:

Lien theory of mortgages obtains.

Execution and Recording.—Mortgages must be executed, acknowledged and recorded in the same manner as deeds. Names of signers must be typed or printed legibly beneath signatures, or an affidavit containing the typed or printed names must accompany instrument, to entitle instrument to recordation. (558). Recording fee is $5 for each page or fraction thereof. (331.604).

Husband or wife of mortgagor must join in mortgage in order to bar his or her right to a distributive share of the property. See categories Debtor and Creditor, topic Homesteads, subhead Conveyance or Encumbrance; Estates and Trusts, topic Descent and Distribution; Family, topic Husband and Wife.

Advancements made by junior lien holders for the protection of the junior lien may be made liens by filing a verified statement of said expenditures with the clerk of the district court of the county in which the land is situated and such advancements may be recovered in an action to foreclose the junior lien. (629).

Redlining and discrimination is prohibited where loans are for purchase, construction or rehabilitation of residential property (four or fewer family dwellings), where property is used for security.

Priority.—Where two or more mortgages each grant the right to subject rents and income of the real estate to payment of the debt, the respective mortgagees have priority in this respect in the same order as priority of the mortgage liens. (654.13).

Release, Satisfaction or Assignment.—Whenever the amount due on any mortgage is paid off, the mortgagee, or those legally acting for him, must acknowledge satisfaction thereof by written instrument referring to mortgage, duly acknowledged and recorded. (655.1). Where released or assigned by separate instrument, recorder must so note on original instrument. (558.45).

Foreign Fiduciaries.—Mortgage or deed of trust may be released, satisfied or assigned, in whole or in part, by foreign fiduciary officer when no resident fiduciary officer has been appointed or qualified in state. To effect this there must be recorded in office of county recorder of county in which mortgage or deed of trust is of record such release, satisfaction or assignment by such foreign officer, accompanied by certificate of judge or clerk of court by which he was appointed, showing name of court making appointment, date of appointment and that foreign officer has not been discharged at time of executing such release, satisfaction or assignment and is authorized to execute same. Release, satisfaction or assignment by foreign officer may be made in any

See note at head of Digest as to 1998 legislation covered.

See Topical Index in front part of this volume.

MORTGAGES OF REAL PROPERTY . . . *continued*
manner, or by any instrument, which would be valid and effective if made by like officer qualified under law of Iowa. (633.144-.147).

Foreclosure.—Except where §654.18 alternative nonjudicial voluntary foreclosure procedure employed, real estate mortgage can be foreclosed only by equitable proceedings (654.1) in county where property or some part thereof is located (654.3). Special moratorium provisions may apply upon Governor's declaration of economic emergency. (654.15).

Service of notice may be by publication once each week for three consecutive weeks, in some newspaper printed in the county where the petition is or will be filed, provided an affidavit is first filed that personal service cannot be made within state. See category Civil Actions and Procedure, topic Process, subhead Publication.

In foreclosure proceedings, judgment may be rendered against the mortgagor for the whole debt, and after sale of the mortgaged premises under special execution the mortgagee has a right to a general execution against the mortgagor for any deficiency, but judgment on mortgage foreclosure has no force except as a set-off or counterclaim after two years from entry thereof, and no action may be brought to renew or extend such judgment. (615).

Mediation proceedings required prior to foreclosure on agricultural land securing debt of over $20,000 and where borrower is individual operating farm, family farm corporation, or authorized farm corporation. Creditor must file, or, borrower may file, request for mediation with Farm Mediation Service. Borrower may waive mediation only after initial consultation, otherwise, notice must be given and initial meeting must be held within 42-day period following filing of request. Foreclosure proceedings may be commenced only after mediation release is issued or if, after notice and hearing, court has determined that time delay required for mediation would cause creditor irreparable harm. Mediation release can be acquired after written statement is prepared representing agreement made or showing that agreement could not be reached. (654A).

Also, prior to foreclosure proceedings, creditor must give borrower notice of alleged default and of right to cure. Borrower has right to cure unless: (a) Creditor has given borrower proper Notice of Right to Cure with respect to two prior defaults on obligation secured by deed of trusts or mortgage; (b) borrower has voluntarily surrendered possession of agricultural land and creditor has accepted it in full satisfaction of any debt owing on obligation in default; or (c) if creditor has given borrower proper Notice of Right to Cure with respect to prior default within 12 months prior to alleged default. If borrower has right to cure default creditors may not accelerate unpaid balance of obligation or take possession of land, other than by voluntary surrender, or otherwise attempt to enforce obligation until 45 days after proper Notice of Right to Cure is given. During 45-day period, running concurrently with 42-day period provided in c. 654A, borrower may cure by tendering unpaid installments due at time of tender plus delinquency charge of scheduled annual interest rate plus 5% per annum for period between giving of Notice of Right to Cure and tender or amount stated in Notice of Right to Cure, whichever is less. Borrower may always voluntarily surrender possession of land. (654.2A).

Notice of Right to Cure shall: (a) Be in writing; (b) conspicuously state name, address and telephone number of creditor to which payment is to be made; (c) give brief identification of obligation secured by mortgage and of borrower's right to cure default; (d) contain statement of nature of right to cure default; (e) contain statement of nature of alleged default; (f) contain statement of total payment including itemization of any delinquency or deferral charges or other performance necessary to cure alleged default; (g) state exact date on which amount must be paid or performance tendered; and (h) notify borrower that creditor may proceed with foreclosure. (654.2B).

If homestead exemption waiver contained in written contract, contract must contain statement in substantially following form, in boldface type of minimum size of ten points, and be signed and dated by person waiving exemption at time of execution of contract: "I understand that homestead property is in many cases protected from the claims of creditors and exempt from judicial sale; and that by signing this contract, I voluntarily give up my right to this protection for this property with respect to claims based upon this contract." (561.22).

Alternative nonjudicial voluntary foreclosure procedure available upon mutual written agreement of mortgagor and mortgagee and fulfillment of following requirements: (1) Mortgagor must convey to mortgagee all interest in mortgaged property; (2) mortgagee must accept such conveyance and waive any right to deficiency; (3) mortgagee must be given immediate access to mortgaged property to maintain and protect same; (4) mortgagor and mortgagee must file jointly executed statement of election to follow said nonjudicial voluntary foreclosure procedure with recorder in county where mortgaged property located; (5) mortgagee must send notice of election either by certified mail or by general publication to all junior lienholders as of date of paragraph 1 conveyance, notifying junior lienholders of 30 day redemption period from date of such mailing or from completion of publication, respectively; and (6) when mortgagor signs agreement to proceed under said nonjudicial voluntary foreclosure procedure, mortgagee must furnish mortgagor duplicate completed "Disclosure and Notice of Cancellation" form set forth below, which must be in 10 point type and attached to said agreement. (654.18).

DISCLOSURE AND NOTICE OF CANCELLATION

____
(enter date of transaction)

Under a forced foreclosure Iowa law requires that you have the right to reclaim your property within one year of the date of the foreclosure and that you may continue to occupy your property during that time. If you agree to a voluntary foreclosure under this procedure you will be giving up your right to reclaim or occupy your property.

Under a forced foreclosure, if your mortgage lender does not receive enough money to cover what you owe when the property is sold, you will still be required to pay the difference. If your mortgage lender receives more money than you owe, the difference must be paid to you. If you agree to a voluntary foreclosure under this procedure you will not have to pay the amount of your debt not covered by the sale of your property but you also will not be paid any extra money, if any, over the amount you owe.

NOTE: There may be other advantages and disadvantages, including an effect on your income tax liability, to you depending on whether you agree or do not agree to a voluntary foreclosure. If you have any questions or doubts, you are advised to discuss them with your mortgage lender or an attorney.

You may cancel this transaction, without penalty or obligation, within five business days from the above date.

This transaction is entirely voluntary. You cannot be required to sign the attached foreclosure agreement.

This voluntary foreclosure agreement will become final unless you sign and deliver or mail this notice of cancellation to ______ (name of mortgagee) before midnight of ______ (enter proper date).

I HEREBY CANCEL THIS TRANSACTION.

______________________ ______________________
DATE SIGNATURE

Receivers.—When receiver is appointed, preference in leasing the premises must be given to owner or person in possession and rents or income must be applied to: (1) Costs of receivership; (2) payment of taxes; (3) payment of insurance and such other benefits to real estate as court may order; (4) distribution as fixed by court. (654.14).

Redemption.—The right of redemption is the same as in case of sale under a general execution. See category Debtor and Creditor, topic Executions. Real property redeemed by debtor is free from any liability for deficiency judgment. (628.3).

Form

The usual form is:

Know all men by these presents: That . . . . of . . . . county, and state of . . . ., in consideration of the sum of . . . . dollars, in hand paid by . . . . of . . . . county, and state of . . . ., do hereby sell and convey unto the said . . . . the following described premises, situated in the county of . . . . and state of . . . ., to-wit: . . . . And . . . . hereby covenant with the said . . . . that . . . . hold . . . . said premises by title in fee simple; that . . . . ha. . . good right and lawful authority to sell and convey the same; that they are free and clear of all liens and incumbrances whatsoever; and . . . . covenant . . . . to warrant and defend the said premises against the lawful claims of all persons whomsoever; and the said . . . . hereby relinguish . . . . h. . . . right of dower in and to the above-described premises. Provided, always, and these presents are upon this express condition, that if the said . . . . heirs, executors or administrators, shall pay or cause to be paid to the said . . . . executors and administrators or assigns, the sum of (here describe payments), with interest thereon . . . . according to the tenor and effect of the . . . . promissory note . . . . of the said . . . . payable to . . . . bearing . . . . date . . . . then these presents to be void, otherwise to remain in full force. It is hereby agreed that said . . . . shall pay all taxes and assessments levied upon said real estate before the same shall become delinquent, and in case not so paid, the holder of this mortgage may pay such taxes or assessments and be entitled to interest on the same at the rate of . . . . . .% per annum, and this mortgage shall stand as security for such taxes, assessments and interest so paid. That so long as this mortgage shall remain unpaid the said . . . . shall keep the buildings thereon insured in some responsible company or companies, which shall be satisfactory to the holder of this mortgage for the use and security of said mortgagee in the sum of not less than $. . . ., and shall deliver the policies and renewal receipts therefor to said mortgagee, and if the said . . fails to effect such insurance in manner as agreed, then said mortgagee may effect such insurance, and the amount paid for such purposes by the mortgagee shall be recovered from . . . . with . . . . . .% per annum interest thereon, and shall be a lien upon the foregoing premises, under and by virtue of this mortgage. And it is further expressly agreed, that in the event of failure to pay said sums of money, or any part thereof, or the interest thereon, when due and payable, said second party, its successors or assigns, shall have, from the date of such default made, as additional security for the sums of money secured by this mortgage, a lien on all crops thereafter raised on said real estate and all rents and profits thereafter accruing thereon, and shall be, and hereby is authorized to take immediate possession of said property, and to rent the same, and shall be held liable to account to said first party only for the net profits thereof. It is also agreed that the taking possession thereof as above provided shall in no manner prevent or retard the collection of said sums by foreclosure or otherwise. It is further agreed that in the event action is brought to foreclose this mortgage, the court shall have the right and power to appoint a receiver to take possession of said premises and apply the rents and profits therefrom upon said indebtedness. That if the said . . . . allows the taxes to become delinquent upon said property, or permits the same or any part thereof to be sold for taxes, or if . . . . fail to pay the interest on said note . . . . promptly as the same becomes due, the note . . . . secured hereby shall become due and payable in . . . . days thereafter; and the mortgagee . . . . heirs, or assigns, may proceed to at once foreclose this mortgage; and in case it becomes necessary to commence proceedings to foreclose the same, then the said . . . . in addition to the amount of said debt, interest and costs, agree . . . . to pay to the mortgagee herein named, or to any assignee of the mortgagee herein, a reasonable attorney's fee for collecting the same, which fee shall be included in judgment in such foreclosure case.

Signed this . . . . day of . . . ., 19. . . . .

. . . .
. . . .

(Acknowledgment)

If waiver of homestead exemption desired, special requirements apply. See category Debtor and Creditor, topic Homesteads, subhead Conveyance or Encumbrance.

Chattel Mortgages.—See topic Chattel Mortgages.

PROPERTY

ABSENTEES:

Care of Property.—Conservator may be appointed to take charge of, preserve and control property of an adult person whose whereabouts unknown and no provision has been made for such property, when such person's property within state is liable to

See note at head of Digest as to 1998 legislation covered.

See Topical Index in front part of this volume.

IA – 24

ABSENTEES . . . *continued*

become injured, lost or damaged by reason of such absence, or dependents of such owner are likely to be deprived of means of support because of such absence. (633.580).

Administration of Absentee's Estate.—Administration may be had on the estates of persons who have absented themselves from their usual place of residence and concealed their whereabouts from their family without known cause for five years as though such persons were dead, but petition praying administration must be filed by one who would be entitled to administer upon such estate if absentee were known to be dead. Notice must be published three weeks and mailed to alleged distributees at their last known address. Proof of such service must be filed on or before day set for hearing and proof of such notice filed with petition. Written findings of presumed death under Federal Missing Persons Act are admissible as evidence of that fact. (633.510-.517).

Escheat.—Uninherited property escheats to state of Iowa. (633.219, .543-.546). Revised Uniform Disposition of Unclaimed Property Act adopted, with some modifications. (556). Unclaimed legacies or trust funds must be paid to Clerk of District Court. (682.29-.38).

If unclaimed for period of years intangible personal property is presumed abandoned, and holder of such property must then file report to State Treasurer. Within 120 days from final date for filing report State Treasurer shall publish notice of names of persons appearing to be owner of abandoned property. Notice shall state that claims must be presented by owner to holder and if owner's right to receive property is not established to holder's satisfaction within 65 days from date of second published notice, property will be placed no later than 85 days after such publication in custody of State Treasurer to whom all further claims must be directed. If no claims are timely filed or filed claims are disallowed, funds are deposited in general funds of state. (556.12). Holding periods vary according to identity of holder. (556.13).

See also category Estates and Trusts, topics Descent and Distribution, subhead Escheat, and Wills, subhead Unclaimed Legacies.

Process Agent.—Nonresident may in writing appoint resident of county in which parcel is located as agent, and file appointment with county treasurer, who shall make note of appointment, after which personal service of notice shall be made upon agent. (447.11).

ADVERSE POSSESSION:

Real Property.—Ten years hostile, actual, open, exclusive and continuous possession of real property under claim of right or color of title bars action for recovery of same from person thus in possession. (242 Ia. 692, 46 N.W.2d 72).

Easements.—When an easement is claimed by prescription, the fact of claim of right and adverse possession must be established by evidence distinct from and independent of its use and there must be a showing that party against whom easement is claimed had express notice thereof. (564.1). Notice in writing served by owner on person claiming the easement of owner's intention to dispute any right arising from the use, when recorded in county recorder's office, will prevent acquiring of any right to property by any use thereof. (564.4-.7).

Boundaries.—Ten years acquiescence by parties in any corner or boundary is sufficient to establish the same. (650.14).

CONVEYANCES:

See topic Deeds.

CURTESY:

Abolished. (636.5). As to rights of surviving spouse see category Estates and Trusts, topic Descent and Distribution.

DEEDS:

Execution.—Deeds conveying real estate (see topic Real Property for types of estates) must be in writing and subscribed by the grantor. Seal is not necessary. Acknowledgment is not necessary to validity as between parties, but is necessary to entitle instrument to be recorded. Names of signers must be typed or printed legibly under signatures or instrument must be accompanied by affidavit wherein those names are typed or printed legibly, to entitle instrument to be recorded. No witnesses are necessary. For circumstances in which spouse must join, see also categories Family, topic Husband and Wife, subhead Separate Property; Debtor and Creditor, topics Homesteads, subhead Conveyance or Encumbrance, Assignments, subhead Assignment of Wages; Civil Actions and Procedure, topic Limitation of Actions.

Recording.—To be valid against subsequent purchasers for valuable consideration without notice, or against state or any of its political subdivisions during or after condemnation proceedings against real estate, deed must be filed and recorded in county in which real estate office is located. (558.41). See also category Documents and Records, topic Records.

Recording fee is $5 for filing or recording each page or fraction thereof. (331.604). In addition, transfer fee of $5 per parcel imposed. (331.507).

Tax.—When there is consideration and actual market value of real property transferred exceeds $500, grantor, assignor, transferor, or conveyor must pay tax of 55¢ for each $500 or fractional part in excess of $500. Tax does not apply to mortgages, plats, leases, certain executory contracts for deed, satisfactions or releases of mortgages, certain corrective deeds, deeds in lieu of foreclosure, deeds without consideration, and other statutorily specified documents. (428A). Written declaration of value signed by at least one party or agent required prior to recording document of conveyance or assignment with numerous statutory exceptions. With each declaration of value submitted to County Recorder under 428A, there shall also be submitted ground water hazard statement. (558.69, adopted 1987, H.F. 631).

Form.—No particular form of deed is required. The following or equivalent form is sufficient to convey title to real estate:

Form

For the consideration of . . . . dollars I hereby convey to A.B. the following tract of real estate (describing it) and warrant the title against all persons whomsoever (or other words of warranty as the party may desire). (558.19).

Add acknowledgment. See category Documents and Records, topic Acknowledgments.

DEEDS OF TRUST:

See category Mortgages, topic Mortgages of Real Property.

DOWER:

Abolished. (633.211; 633.238). As to rights of surviving spouse see category Estates and Trusts, topic Descent and Distribution.

ESCHEAT:

See topic Absentees, subhead Escheat; categories Business Regulation and Commerce, topic Banks and Banking, subhead Unclaimed Deposits; Estates and Trusts, topics Descent and Distribution, subhead Escheat, Wills, subhead Unclaimed Legacies.

LANDLORD AND TENANT:

Kinds of Tenancy.—At will and for a fixed term.

Leases for more than one year must be in writing; no seal or witnesses required; acknowledgment necessary only for recording.

Farm Tenancy.—At termination of life estate, farm tenancy granted by life tenant continues until following Mar. 1st for that year. If life estate terminates between Sept. 1st and Mar. 1st, then tenancy will continue for that year as provided by 562.6 of Iowa Code and until proper notice under 562.7. (562.8).

Recording is not required; those dealing with property must take notice of tenants in possession.

Rent.—If tenant remains in possession without landlord's consent after expiration of term of rental agreement landlord may bring action for possession. If tenant's holdover is willful, landlord may also recover actual damages and attorneys fees. Landlord may assign right to rent.

Lien.—Lien on behalf of landlord on tenant's household goods abolished.

Mobile Homes.—Actions for abandonment under lease agreement. (555B).

Termination of Tenancy.—Thirty days notice is necessary to terminate tenancy at will, unless rent is paid at less than 30 day intervals, in which case notice must be same as such interval. (562.4). But if property is farm occupied and cultivated by tenant he cannot be dispossessed before Mar. 1 and notice of termination of tenancy must be given on or before Sept. 1 preceding in manner prescribed by statute. (562.7). Mere field tenant or cropper who does not live on land may be put off when crop is harvested. (562). Week to week tenancy may be terminated by written notice given to other at least ten days prior to termination date specified in notice. Landlord may file suit to recover possession after three days written notice of termination and to quit if tenant creates clear and present danger. Petition must state incidents giving rise to notice of termination and notice to quit. (562A.27A; 562B.25A).

Dispossession.—An action of forcible entry and detainer is allowable where tenant's lease has expired either by own provisions or notice and he holds over. (648).

Distress for rent is not recognized.

Implied Warranty of Habitability.—Landlord impliedly warrants at outset of lease that there are no latent defects in facilities and utilities vital to use of premises for residential purposes and that these essential features shall remain during entire term in such condition to maintain habitability of dwelling. Implied warranty in lease situation is a representation that there neither is nor shall be during term a violation of applicable housing law, ordinance or regulation which shall render premises unsafe, or unsanitary and unfit for living therein. (200 N.W.2d 791, codified by amendment (562A).

Residential.—Uniform Residential Landlord and Tenant Act substantially adopted. (562A).

LEASES:

See topic Landlord and Tenant.

PERPETUITIES:

Every disposition of property is void which suspends the absolute power of controlling the same for a longer period than during the lives of persons then in being and 21 years thereafter. Nonvested interest that would violate rule against perpetuities whether its period is measured by actual or by possible events will be judicially reformed to most closely approximate intention of creator of interest in order that nonvested interest will vest, even though it may not become possessory, within period of rule. Section applies to all non-vested interests created at any time. (558.68).

Accumulations.—Common law rules prevail. See also category Estates and Trusts, topic Trusts.

PERSONAL PROPERTY:

Tenancies by the entireties not permitted.

POWERS OF ATTORNEY:

Power of Attorney.—Conveyance or mortgage of real estate may be executed by an attorney in fact acting under written power of attorney executed in the same manner as conveyance (557.10), which must be recorded (558.41).

Forms of power of attorney (Official Form No. 10.2) available from Iowa State Bar Assn., Fleming Bldg., Des Moines, Iowa 50309.

See note at head of Digest as to 1998 legislation covered.

See Topical Index in front part of this volume.

POWERS OF ATTORNEY . . . *continued*

Death of principal ordinarily revokes power of attorney unconnected with an interest, even though the agent be without knowledge of the death. (39 Ia. 426). But a written power of attorney given by a principal who at the time of execution thereof is or thereafter becomes a member of the U. S. Armed Forces, a merchant seaman outside the limits of the U. S. or any person outside said limits by permission, assignment or direction of the U. S. government in connection with the prosecution of a war in which the U. S. is engaged is not revoked or terminated by the death of the principal unless the attorney has actual knowledge or actual notice of such death. (29A.74).

Undisclosed Principal.—Uniform Commercial Code adopted. (554). See category Business Regulation and Commerce, topic Commercial Code.

Uniform Commercial Code adopted. (554). See category Business Regulation and Commerce, topic Commercial Code.

REAL PROPERTY:

Among estates recognized are: fee simple, legal, equitable, tenancy in common, joint tenancy, life estate; also the various uses and remainders. (557).

Conveyances to two or more are construed as creating a tenancy in common unless intent to create joint tenancy is expressed. (557.15).

Tenancies by the entirety are not recognized. (201 Ia. 1290, 207 N.W. 369).

Rule in Shelley's Case does not apply. (557.20).

Condominiums.—Horizontal property act adopted. (499B). Co-operative apartments also provided for. (499A).

See also topics Curtesy, Deeds, Dower, Landlord and Tenant; categories Business Regulation and Commerce, topic Consumer Protection; Civil Actions and Procedure, topic Partition; Debtor and Creditor, topic Homesteads; Documents and Records, topic Records; Family, topic Husband and Wife; Mortgages, topic Mortgages of Real Property.

TRUST DEEDS:

See category Mortgages, topic Mortgages of Real Property.

TAXATION

ADMINISTRATION:

(Title XVI, Chapters 421-454).

Penalties.—
Sales Tax.—Penalties as provided by 422.58.
Use Tax.—Failure to furnish required return, or failing or refusing to furnish supplemental return or other data required by director, is fraudulent practice. (423.18[3]).
Cigarette Tax.—Penalty imposed by 453A.43.
Beer Tax.—Penalty imposed by 123.137.
As to penalties with regard to income and inheritance taxes, see subheads detailing those taxes.

ALCOHOLIC BEVERAGE TAXES:

Beer tax imposed by 123.136.

BUSINESS TAXES:

Premium tax on insurance companies, see category Insurance, topic Insurance Companies.

CIGARETTE TAX:

Cigarette tax imposed by 453A.43.

ESTATE TAX:

In addition to inheritance tax (see topic Inheritance Tax) there is estate tax not exceeding maximum credit allowed by Federal Estate Tax Law for any estate, inheritance, legacy or succession tax actually paid to any state or territory or District of Columbia. (451).
Application for information, forms, etc., should be made to director of revenue.

Valuation Date.—Date of death.

Apportionment Against Inter Vivos Dispositions.—No statute.

Interstate Co-operation.—No statutory procedure for compromise or arbitration where decedent's domicile is disputed.

EXCISE TAX:

Excise tax on grain imposed by 428.35.

GIFT TAX:

None; but inheritance tax applies to gifts in contemplation of death or to take effect after death. (450.3).

INCOME TAX:

Income tax is imposed on taxable income of individual residents of the state. "Taxable income" means "net income" less allowable deductions. "Net income" is Federal adjusted gross income less interest and dividends on Federal securities, plus interest and dividends on securities exempt from federal income tax. Credit is allowed for tax paid to other states on income of resident earned outside the state. Income tax is imposed on nonresidents with respect to income from property and business within the state. Income of nonresident not subject to Iowa income tax, if taxed where person resides and that state allows a similar exclusion for income received in that state by Iowa residents.

(422.8). Income from estates and trusts is subject to the tax. Deductions similar to federal income tax deductions, with certain exceptions, are allowed. (422).

Rates for tax years beginning on or after Jan. 1, 1998 are: (a) On all taxable income from zero through $1,000, $36/100$ of 1%; (b) taxable income exceeding $1,000 but not exceeding $2,000, $72/100$ of 1%; (c) exceeding $2,000 but not exceeding $4,000, $2^{43}/100$%; (d) exceeding $4,000 but not exceeding $9,000, $4^{1}/2$%; (e) exceeding $9,000 but not exceeding $15,000, $6^{12}/100$%; (f) exceeding $15,000 but not exceeding $20,000, $6^{48}/100$%; (g) exceeding $20,000 but not exceeding $30,000, $6^{8}/10$%; (h) exceeding $30,000 but not exceeding $45,000, $7^{92}/100$%; and (i) exceeding $45,000, $8^{98}/100$%.

Exemptions for tax year 1989 deductible from computed tax, are: estate or trust, single individual, or married person filing separate return, $20; head of household, or husband and wife filing joint return, $40; for each dependent, $40. Nonresidents are allowed full exemptions. Additional exemptions of $20 are allowed for persons over 65 or blind. (422.12). Additional deductions are allowed for parents of children for tuition and textbooks in private schools, provided certain conditions are met. (422.12 am'd 1987). Resident of Iowa who is on active duty in armed forces of U.S. for more than six months in calendar or fiscal year excludes income for such service between Jan. 1, 1969 and Jan. 1, 1977. (422.5).

Alternative Minimum Tax.—(422.5).

Corporations.—Domestic corporations and foreign corporations doing business within the state, or deriving income from sources within state, are taxed annually on basis of net income received during income year. Rates are: 6% on first $25,000 or part thereof; 8% on taxable income between $25,000 and $100,000; 10% on taxable income between $100,000 and $250,000; 12% on taxable income of $250,000 or more; capital gains and losses in accord with 422.33(2)(b)(2). (422.33). Certain corporations are entirely exempt. (422.34).

Returns on forms provided by director of revenue must be filed with director of revenue on or before last day of 4th month after expiration of tax year, except that cooperative associations must file returns before 15th day of ninth month. (422.21).
Residents and nonresidents required to file a federal income tax return who have net income from taxable source of $9,000 or more must file return. (422.13).

Payment.—Total tax due to be paid in full at time of filing return. (422.24).

Penalties.—Willful filing of false return, or willful failure to file return or to pay tax is punishable by imprisonment of up to five years and fine of up to $7,000. Variable rate of interest as set forth in 421.31 is payable on all tax delinquencies. Current interest rate, effective Jan. 1, 1983, is 14% per annum. 5% per month, with maximum of 25%, is added to tax if taxpayer has failed to file return or to pay tax due on time, for reasonable cause not involving willful neglect. If such failure is willful, 75% is added to tax. (422.25).

INHERITANCE TAX:

Estates of all deceased persons, whether decedents be inhabitants of this state or not, which estates or property are or are brought within state or subject to jurisdiction of courts of this state, or property of any decedent domiciled within this state even though situated outside of this state, except real estate, are subject to tax when passing: (a) By will or under statutes of inheritance; (b) by deed, grant, sale, gift or transfer made within three years of death of grantor or donor which is not bona fide sale for adequate and full consideration in money or money's worth and which is in excess of annual gift tax exclusion allowable for each donee under state and federal law; (c) under power of appointment exercised after adoption of inheritance tax law; (d) property held jointly or as tenants in entirety by decedent and any other person or persons; however if joint property held by decedent and surviving spouse one-half not subject to tax and any additional percentage spouse can show he or she helped to acquire then that portion also not subject to tax; and in addition such portion as may be proven to have belonged to any other joint tenant not subject to tax; (e) property disposed of by decedent in any manner to take effect at his death. (450.2-.3).
In estates of decedents dying on or after July 1, 1997, property passing to surviving spouse and all lineal ascendants and descendants is fully exempt from tax. (450.9).
There is no tax if estate is not over $10,000, or on value of annuity payments under employees' pension or retirement plan, where beneficiary pays income taxes on same, or when property passes to charitable, educational, religious, cemetery or humane societies within state, or for maintenance of burial lot, or to any veterans' organization, or to charitable organizations in other states which would not tax property passing to similar Iowa organizations. (450.4).
There is a provision for reciprocal exemption as to nonresidents. (450.91).
Property passing to surviving spouse and lineal ascendants and descendants from decedents dying on or after July 1, 1997 is not subject to tax. Rates of tax for other beneficiaries are based upon individual share and vary according to beneficiary classification and amount received. (450.10):
Brother, sister, son-in-law or daughter-in-law. No exemption. Rates: 5% on first $12,500 or part thereof; 6% on next $12,500 or part thereof; 7% on next $50,000 or part thereof; 8% on next $25,000 or part thereof; 9% on next $50,000 or part thereof; 10% on excess over $150,000.
All other persons (except those falling within subsequent classes). No exemption. Rates: 10% on first $50,000 or part thereof; 12% on next $50,000 or part thereof; 15% on excess over $100,000.
Societies, institutions or associations of other states or countries for charitable, educational, religious, cemetery or humane purposes, or resident trustees for uses without the state, 10% on entire amount.
Firm, corporation or society organized for profit, 15% on entire amount.

Payment.—Tax accrues at death of decedent owner and must be paid to director of revenue on or before last day of ninth month after death of decedent unless period is extended by director. It is lien (on property in estates of persons dying after July 4, 1951), until paid and draws interest as provided. (450.6-.7, .63).

Penalties.—$7^{1}/2$% of amount due is added to tax if less than 90% of tax paid by due date, with specified exceptions. (450.63).

See note at head of Digest as to 1998 legislation covered.

See Topical Index in front part of this volume.

PROPERTY TAXES:

Exemptions from taxation, subject to specified limitations in some cases, are accorded the following classes of property: federal property, unless taxation thereof is authorized by U. S.; state property; municipal and military property; public grounds and cemeteries; fire equipment and grounds; bonds or certificates issued by municipal subdivisions; property of associations of war veterans; certain property of nonprofit cemetery associations; libraries and art galleries for public use; real and personal property of religious, literary and charitable societies; like property of students of said institutions used for their education; real property of educational institutions; homes for soldiers; growing agricultural produce harvested within one year, including all wool shorn, all poultry, ten stands of bees, honey and beeswax produced during year and remaining in possession of producer; all livestock; obligations for rent not yet due; private libraries up to $300; all tangible personal property customarily located and used in or about residence; all wearing apparel and food to be used by owner; and all personal effects; farming utensils of farmers, team, wagon and harness of teamsters, and tools of mechanics up to $1,111 taxable value; government lands entered or purchased, for year in which made; funds of fraternal beneficiary associations; shares of stock of certain utility and manufacturing companies; public airports; all grounds and buildings used or under construction for public television stations not leased or otherwise used or under construction for pecuniary profit; grain being handled by elevator or mill; personal property in transit; personal property held in public ware-house for ultimate sale or resale; and property owned and operated by nonprofit organization providing low-rent housing for elderly and physically and mentally handicapped but only until terms of original low-rent housing development mortgage paid in full or expires and subject to filing requirements. (427). In addition to foregoing, exemptions are granted to war veterans (427.3), persons over age 65 and owners of homesteads (425).

There is no real property tax exemption for members of armed forces. However, disabled veterans have tax credit equal to entire tax levy on homestead. (425.15).

Persons receiving cash payments under Title XVI of Social Security Act and certain state supplementary assistance, or persons residing in a health care facility who are receiving payment from department of social services for their care, are deemed unable to contribute to public revenue, and collection of taxes on all property, real and personal, owned by them is suspended while they receive assistance. (427.9).

Assessment.—Property is assessed by county assessor, except that cities over 125,000 shall have city assessors; personal property annually as of Jan. 1; real property in 1981 and every two years thereafter. (428.4).

Budget requirements of taxing districts, including townships, school districts, cities, towns and counties, are certified to county auditor or board of supervisors and taxes are levied at such rate as will raise the required amount. Moneys necessary for election expense fund are part of levy for next year. (444).

Review of Assessment.—Redress in case of excessive assessment is by complaint presented to local board of review. Appeals from action of the board may be taken within 20 days after its adjournment to the district court of the county in which the board sits, by written notice of appeal served on presiding officer of the board in same manner as an original notice. The appeal is heard in equity and the court determines anew the questions raised before the board of review and fixes amount of assessment. Appeals may be taken from the decree of the district court in the usual manner. Director of revenue adjusts valuation of property in the several counties. (441).

Lien.—Lien attaches at time of levy, but sale after assessment and before levy will not defeat lien. (123 Ia. 485, 99 N.W. 133). Where buildings are erected by person other than land owner, taxes thereon are lien from date of levy until paid. (445.32). Taxes on real estate are lien on real estate against all persons except state. Taxes on real estate shall be lien on real estate against state which is liable for payment of property taxes as purchaser under certain provisions of Act. (445.28).

Payment.—Fiscal year adopted. Real estate and personal property taxes for preceding fiscal year must be paid between first Mon. in Aug. and Sept. 1, and may be paid one-half before Sept. 1 and other half before Mar. 1 without be-coming delinquent. If first half is not paid before Oct. 1, that half becomes delinquent and draws interest from Oct. 1 at 1½% per month. Second half becomes delinquent if not paid before Apr. 1. Personal property taxes draw additional 5% after first Mon. in June. (445).

Tax sales are had on third Mon. in June when all lands on which there are delinquent taxes are sold. (446.7).

Redemption.—Owner may redeem within three years by paying amount for which land sold with penalty of 4% and interest at ¾% per month on sale price plus penalty from date of sale. (447).

REAL ESTATE CONVEYANCE TAX:

88¢ for each $500 or fractional part in excess of $500, when actual market value is in excess of $500. When there is no consideration or when deed or writing is executed and recorded to correct title, and so states, there is no tax. At time of recording document of transfer declaration of value must be filed, with certain exceptions. (428A.1).

SALES AND USE TAXES:

Sales Tax.—A general tax of 5% is imposed on gross receipts from all retail sales of tangible personal property in state or taxable services, or for resale of tangible personal property in connection with taxable services, sales of gas, electricity, water and communication service, including pay television, sales of admissions to places of amusement and athletic events except those of elementary and secondary educational institutions, fairs; and like rate of tax upon that part of private club membership fees or charges paid for privilege of participating in any athletic sports provided club members and on gross receipts of commercial amusements, and services, rendered, furnished or performed, with certain exceptions, such as resale of property accepted as trade-in on articles sold at retail and other sales as defined by statute; consumer rental purchase agreements; soliciting retail sales by broadcasting within state or by mail if continuous or regular and retailer benefits in some additional way in state. (422.42-.59).

Report for each calendar quarter year must be made, and tax for such quarter paid, to director of revenue on or before last day of month following close of quarter.

Use tax of 5% is imposed to supplement and enlarge application of sales tax to cover sales and services involving interstate shipments where the subject of the sale is used in this state, with certain exceptions. (423).

UNEMPLOYMENT COMPENSATION TAX:

Unemployment compensation tax, in the form of "contributions," is imposed. (96).

Contributions are required from all employers who, for some portion of day in each of 20 different weeks in current or preceding calendar year have or had in employment one or more individuals.

Exemptions.—Act does not apply to following employments: Agricultural labor; domestic service in private home; service of federal, state, municipal or other government; service in employ of son, daughter, or spouse or service of minor in employ of parent; service in employ of religious, charitable, scientific, literary or educational enterprise, or after school or vacation employment of students. Employers operating under unemployment compensation system established by act of Congress, who have made arrangements with department providing for reciprocal treatment of unemployed, are also exempt.

Rate of contributions is based on employer's benefit experience in accordance with rules adopted by Job Division on all taxable wages paid by employer for insured work. (96.7).

Contributions are payable to Department of Employment Services' Job Services Division at such time as it may prescribe.

TRANSPORTATION

MOTOR VEHICLES:

Regulated by Revised Motor Vehicle Code. (321).

Vehicle license required annually. Issued by County Treasurer. Nonresidents may apply to Dep't. of Public Safety. No exemption for members of armed services. Number plates must be displayed front and rear.

Operator's or chauffeur's license from the Motor Vehicle Department is required to operate a motor vehicle on a highway, but there are exemptions in favor of operators of road or farm machinery, persons in the service of the United States Army, Navy or Marine corps, holders of temporary permits, and nonresident operators.

Operator's license may not be issued to any person under the age of 16, except that on written application, supported by school superintendent's affidavit, a person between the ages of 14 and 16 may have a minor's license, valid only in going to and from school. Chauffeur's license may not be issued to a person under the age of 18, except that licenses to operate certain light trucks may be issued to persons over age of 16. Chauffeur must be licensed as such and must display chauffeur's badge. Every licensee must have license in immediate possession at all times when operating a motor vehicle and must display same upon demand.

Operators' and chauffeurs' licenses expire during second or fourth year of issuance depending on age of applicant and rules of Public Safety Commissioner and are to be renewed within 60 days after operator's birthday. (321.196).

Transfer of Title.—Transfer can only be effected by assigning registration card and certificate of title. Transferee must then apply for transfer of registration and new certificate of title. Decedent's car can be transferred upon filing of affidavit by heirs, without opening estate. (321.47).

Sales.—Conditional sales must be noted on certificate of title. (321.50). Security interest in vehicle is perfected through application for certificate of title which lists security interest. (321.50). Dealer selling motor vehicle in transaction that does not include sale of liability insurance must obtain buyer's signature on statement to that effect. (321A.39).

Identification Marks.—Criminal offense to deface or alter, with fraudulent intent, any serial, engine or assembling number or knowingly to possess any vehicle, serial or engine number of which is defaced, altered or tampered with. (714.8).

Operation Prohibited.—By person without valid operator's or chauffeur's license, unless exempted; by intoxicated person. Person under the age of 16 may not drive a school bus. Person under age of 21 may not drive motor carrier of persons or of flammables.

Where final judgment for damages caused by operation of a motor vehicle has not been satisfied within 60 days after entry, license is suspended until judgment is satisfied and proof of financial responsibility is given. But payment of $15,000 for injury to or death of one person, $30,000 for two or more persons and/or $10,000 for property damage is deemed satisfaction. (321A.5).

Size and Weight Limits.—Regulated by 321.452-.466.

Equipment Required.—Regulated by 321.384-.451.

Child restraint devices must be used for children zero-six years of age in motor vehicles. Violation may result in misdemeanor conviction. (321.446).

Safety belt or harness must be worn by driver and front seat occupants. (321.445). See also category Civil Actions and Procedure, topic Damages.

Lights Required.—Regulated by 321.317.

Accidents.—Driver must stop, give reasonable aid, give his name and address and vehicle registration number to injured person or driver, occupant or person attending vehicle, and report accident at office of peace officer as near as practicable to place of accident. (321.263).

Liability of Owner.—The owner of a motor vehicle is liable for the negligence of any person operating the same with the owner's consent. Former owner who has made bona fide sale of vehicle is not liable for its negligent operation, regardless of whether certificate of title has been transferred. (321.493).

No motor vehicle is exempt from judgment for damages occasioned by use of same.

See note at head of Digest as to 1998 legislation covered.

See Topical Index in front part of this volume.

MOTOR VEHICLES . . . *continued*

Guests.—Formerly governed by 321.494, but declared unconstitutional under Iowa Constitution. (293 N.W.2d 577).

Financial Responsibility.—In case of accident involving personal injury or death or property damage exceeding $1,000, licenses or operating privileges of persons involved are suspended 60 days thereafter, unless approved security, sufficient to satisfy any possible judgment, is furnished. This provision does not apply, however, to owner where there is no injury or damage except to him or his property, to owner whose vehicle was stopped, standing or parked in legal manner and properly lighted at time of accident, or to owner whose vehicle was being operated without his permission. Neither does it apply if evidence is filed with Director that person who would otherwise have to file security has been released from liability, or adjudicated not liable, or has confessed judgment with agreement for payment satisfactory to both parties.

The security required must be in such form and in such amount as Director may require, except that where certificate of insurance is filed this must show coverage of not less than $20,000 for injury to or death of one person, $40,000 for injury to or death of two or more persons in same accident, and $15,000 for property damage. (321A).

Insurance compulsory as of Jan. 1, 1998.

Foreign vehicle registered in home state or country and displaying license plates required by laws of home state may operate without registration, provided home state or country grants similar privilege to Iowa vehicles. Such vehicle need not be registered nor are any fees required. The exemption from local registration does not extend to vehicles used in transportation for hire or other remunerative business within the state. Vehicles purchased for removal from state must purchase transit plates from county treasurer.

Actions Against Nonresidents.—A nonresident motorist is subject to suit for damages to person or property arising out of his operation of a motor vehicle in this state. Such operation is deemed: (1) An agreement by him that he is subject to the jurisdiction of the district court of this state; (2) an appointment by him of the State Commissioner of Public Safety to act as his process agent; and (3) an agreement that process served on said Commissioner shall be of the same force and validity as if personally served in this state. (321.498). Method of service is by filing copy of notice or process with said Commissioner, together with fee of $2, and mailing notice of such filing, together with copy of process or notice of suit, to each defendant by restricted registered mail (i.e., mail delivered to addressee only) within ten days after such filing. In lieu of such mailing, plaintiff may cause such notice to be personally served upon nonresident defendant.

Venue may be in county of plaintiff's residence or in county where injury occurred. If judgment is against plaintiff, it must include reasonable expenses incurred by defendant or his attorney in appearing and defending, if in the judgment of the trial court the action was commenced maliciously or without probable cause. Liability insurance policy of nonresident decedent is considered asset of estate with situs in Iowa. Person who was Iowa resident at time of accident, but who later moves out of state is deemed nonresident. (321.498; .507).

Direct Actions.—Liability insurance policies issued in this state must contain provision that in event execution on judgment against insured be returned unsatisfied, judgment creditor shall have right of action against insurer to same extent that insured could have enforced his claim against such insurer had such insured paid such judgment. Period of limitation on such action is 180 days from entry of judgment or, in case of appeal, from affirmance of judgment on appeal. (516).

Motor vehicle carriers must have special license and are subject to regulation by Iowa Department of Commerce. They must file approved liability insurance policy or bond with minimum limits as specified in chapter. (325A).

Division of Highway Safety Patrol of Department of Public Safety enforces provisions of chapter relating to traffic on public highways. (321A.2).

RAILROADS:

See category Business Regulation and Commerce, topic Carriers.

See note at head of Digest as to 1998 legislation covered.

See Topical Index in front part of this volume.

COMMERCIAL CODE FORMS
See also categories Business Regulation and Commerce, topic Commercial Code; Mortgages, topic Chattel Mortgages.

IOWA STATE BAR ASSOCIATION

Official Form No. 171

FOR THE LEGAL EFFECT OF THE USE OF

THIS FORM, CONSULT YOUR LAWYER

CAVEAT: DO NOT USE THIS FORM IF THIS TRANSACTION IS A CONSUMER CREDIT TRANSACTION

SECURITY AGREEMENT—GENERAL FORM

1. GRANT OF SECURITY INTEREST. For value received, as security for the Obligations (as defined below) the undersigned ("Debtor") hereby grants to _____ ("Secured Party")
a security interest in the property described in the paragraphs checked below:

☐ All of Debtor's inventory now owned or hereafter acquired;
☐ All of Debtor's accounts, now existing or hereafter arising, together with all interest of Debtor in any goods, the sale or lease of which give rise to any of Debtor's accounts, and all chattel paper, documents and instruments relating to accounts;
☐ All of Debtor's general intangibles, now owned or hereafter acquired;
☐ All of Debtor's equipment now owned or hereafter acquired;
☐ All of Debtor's farm products now owned or hereafter acquired;
☐ All of Debtor's fixtures on the real estate described in paragraph 3 below;

☐ Property described as _____
_____
_____;

together with the proceeds, products, increase, issue, accessions attachments, accessories, parts, additions, repairs, replacements and substitutes of, to, and for all of the foregoing. Debtor will promptly deliver to Secured Party, duly endorsed when necessary, all such chattel paper, documents and instruments and related guaranties, now on hand or hereafter received.
All such property in which a security interest is granted is herein called the "Collateral."

2. OBLIGATIONS. The aforesaid security interests secure payment and performance of the following liabilities (the "Obligations"): _____
_____
_____;

together with all other obligations of Debtor to Secured Party now existing or hereafter arising, whether direct or indirect, contingent or absolute and whether as maker or surety and including, but not limited to, future advances and amounts advanced and expenses and attorneys' fees incurred pursuant to this Security Agreement.

3. REAL ESTATE. Any collateral attached to, or grown upon, land (such as fixtures, crops, timber or minerals) will be grown upon or attached to the following described real estate: _____
_____
_____

and the name of the record owner of such real estate (if other than Debtor) is: _____
_____

4. COPY—FILING. A carbon, photocopy or other reproduction of this Security Agreement may be filed as a financing statement. IF FOR FIXTURES, TIMBER OR MINERALS, SUCH A FILING SHALL BE FILED FOR RECORDING IN THE REAL ESTATE RECORDS.

5. DEBTORS. Each of the undersigned, if more than one, execute this Security Agreement as his, her, its, their joint and several obligation and it shall be binding upon and fully enforceable against either or both, or any or all of them, and reference herein to "Debtor" shall in such case be deemed to be plural, provided however that nothing contained herein shall extend personal liability under any of the Obligations as to which such Debtor is not otherwise liable.

6. COLLATERAL. Debtor represents, warrants and agrees:

a. All Collateral is bona fide and genuine and Debtor is authorized to grant a security interest in the Collateral, free and clear of all liens and encumbrances, except the security interest created hereby and except_____
_____
_____

b. Debtor's principal place of operation is the address shown herein, and Debtor shall promptly give Secured Party written notice of any change thereof, unless prior written consent of Secured Party is obtained. All Collateral and all of the Debtor's business records are now kept, and shall continue to be kept, at such address, or if not, at _____
_____

THIS AGREEMENT SPECIFICALLY INCLUDES ALL OF THE ADDITIONAL PROVISIONS SET FORTH BELOW AND ON THE REVERSE SIDE HEREOF.
DEBTOR ACKNOWLEDGES RECEIPT OF A FULLY COMPLETED COPY OF THIS SECURITY AGREEMENT.

DATED: _____ 19 _____

_____
(Debtor)

ADDRESS OF SECURED PARTY (FROM WHICH INFORMATION
CONCERNING THE SECURITY INTEREST MAY BE OBTAINED)

_____
(Debtor)

See note at head of Digest as to 1998 legislation covered.

See Topical Index in front part of this volume.

Number and Street		Number and Street
City		City
County	State	County	State

1. REPRESENTATIONS AND AGREEMENTS. Debtor represents and warrants to Secured Party, and agrees that:

a. If a corporation or other business entity, Debtor is duly organized, existing, and is qualified and in good standing in all states in which it is doing business, and the execution, delivery and performance of this Security Agreement are within Debtor's powers, have been duly authorized, and are not in contravention of law or the terms of Debtor's charter, bylaws, if any, or any indenture, agreement, or undertaking to which Debtor is a party, or by which it is bound. If an individual, Debtor is of legal age. Debtor will not change his, her or its name, or identity unless written notice is given in advance to Secured Party.

b. Debtor shall maintain insurance upon the Collateral which is tangible property against all customarily insured risks for the full insurable value thereof (and furnish Secured Party with duplicate policies if Secured Party so requests), loss to be payable to Debtor and Secured Party as their respective interests may appear. In the event of any loss or damage to any Collateral, Debtor will give Secured Party written notice thereof forthwith, promptly file proof of loss with the appropriate insurer and take all other steps necessary or appropriate to collect such insurance. If Secured Party so elects, Secured Party shall have full authority to collect all such insurance and to apply any amount collected to amounts owed hereunder, whether or not matured. Secured Party shall have no liability for any loss which may occur by reason of the omission or the lack of coverage of any such insurance.

c. Debtor shall at all times maintain Collateral which is tangible property in good condition and repair, defend at Debtor's expense all Collateral from all adverse claims and shall not use any of the Collateral for any illegal purpose.

d. Debtor shall (i) keep such books and records pertaining to the Collateral and to Debtor's business operations as shall be satisfactory to Secured Party; (ii) permit representatives of Secured Party at any time to inspect the Collateral and inspect and make abstracts from Debtor's books and records; and (iii) furnish to Secured Party such information and reports regarding the Collateral and Debtor's business operations and its financial status, as Secured Party may from time to time reasonably require. SECURED PARTY IS HEREBY AUTHORIZED TO REQUEST CONFIRMATION OF SUCH INFORMATION OR ADDITIONAL INFORMATION OF ANY KIND WHATSOEVER DIRECTLY FROM ANY THIRD PARTY HAVING DEALINGS WITH DEBTOR. SECURED PARTY IS FURTHER IRREVOCABLY AUTHORIZED TO ENTER DEBTOR'S PREMISES TO INSPECT THE COLLATERAL.

e. Debtor shall give such notice in writing (including but not limited to notice of assignment or notice to pay Secured Party directly) as Secured Party may require at any time to any or all account debtors, with respect to accounts which are Collateral, and, if Secured Party shall so request, deliver to Secured Party copies of any and all such notices.

171 SECURITY AGREEMENT
Current December, 1985

f. Debtor shall promptly transmit to Secured Party all information that it may have or receive with respect to Collateral or with respect to any account debtor which might in any way affect the value of the Collateral or Secured Party's rights or remedies with respect thereto.

g. Unless in default under this Agreement, Debtor may sell Inventory in the ordinary course of business and consume any raw materials or supplies, the use and consumption of which are necessary to carry on Debtor's business. Debtor shall not otherwise consume, assign or transfer any Collateral without prior written consent of Secured Party. The provision of this Security Agreement granting a security interest in proceeds shall not be construed to mean that Secured Party consents to any sale or disposition of any Collateral.

h. Debtor shall pay when due all taxes, assessments, and any other governmental levy which is, or may be, levied against any Collateral, and shall otherwise maintain the Collateral free of all liens, charges, and encumbrances (except liens set forth herein and the Security Interest created hereby).

i. Debtor shall not store any Collateral with any warehouseman without Secured Party's consent.

j. Debtor shall promptly, unless Secured Party shall waive such requirement in writing, deliver to Secured Party all certificates of title, if any, (or any other documents evidencing title) to all Collateral with such proper notations, assignments or endorsements as may be necessary or appropriate to create, preserve or perfect Secured Party's security interest in the Collateral.

k. Debtor shall, at its cost and expense, execute, deliver, file or record (in such manner and form as Secured Party may require) any assignment, financing statement or other paper that may be necessary or desirable, or that Secured Party may request, in order to create, preserve or perfect any security interest granted hereby or to enable Secured Party to exercise and enforce its rights hereunder or under any Collateral. Secured Party is further granted the power, coupled with an interest, to sign on behalf of Debtor as attorney-in-fact and to file one or more financing statements under the Uniform Commercial Code naming Debtor as debtor and Secured Party as secured party and describing the Collateral herein specified.

2. EXPENSES. Debtor upon demand shall pay to Secured Party forthwith the amounts of all expenses, including reasonable attorneys' fees and legal expenses, incurred by Secured Party in seeking to collect any sums secured hereunder or to enforce any rights in the Collateral. Such amount shall be secured hereby, and if not paid on demand shall bear interest at the highest rate payable on any of the Obligations.

3. COLLECTION AUTHORITY ON ACCOUNTS. Debtor hereby irrevocably appoints Secured Party its true and lawful attorney, with full power of substitution, in Secured Party's name, Debtor's name or otherwise, for Secured Party's sole use and benefit, but at Debtor's cost and expense, to exercise, if Secured Party shall elect after an event of default has occurred (whether or not Secured Party then elects to exercise any other of its rights arising upon default) all or any of the following powers with respect to all or any accounts which are Collateral:

a. To execute on Debtor's behalf assignments of any or all accounts which are Collateral to Secured Party, and to notify account debtors thereunder to make payments directly to Secured Party;

b. To demand, sue for, collect, receive and give acquittance for any and all moneys due or to become due upon or by virtue thereof;

c. To receive, take, endorse, assign and deliver any and all checks, notes, drafts, documents and other negotiable and non-negotiable instruments and chattel paper taken or received by Secured Party in connection therewith;

d. To settle, compromise, compound, prosecute or defend any action or proceeding with respect thereto;

e. To sell, transfer, assign or otherwise deal in or with the same or the proceeds thereof or the relative goods, as fully and effectually as if Secured Party were the absolute owner thereof; and

f. To extend the time of payment of any or all thereof and to make any allowance and other adjustments with reference thereto.

Any funds collected pursuant to such powers shall be applied to the payment of the Obligations. The exercise by Secured Party of, or failure to so exercise, any of the foregoing authority, shall in no manner affect Debtor's liability to Secured Party on any of the Obligations. Secured Party shall be under no obligation or duty to exercise any of the powers hereby conferred upon it and it shall be without liability for any act or failure to act in connection with the collection of or the preservation of any rights under any such accounts. Secured Party shall not be bound to take any steps necessary to preserve rights in any instrument or chattel paper against prior parties.

4. SET OFF. In the event of default hereunder, Secured Party, at its option at any time, and without notice to Debtor, may apply against the Obligations any property of Debtor held by Secured Party. As additional security for payment of the Obligations, Debtor hereby grants to Secured Party a security interest in any funds or property of Debtor now or hereafter in possession of Secured Party and with respect thereto Secured Party will have all rights and remedies herein specified.

5. WAIVER. Debtor waives protest, notice of dishonor, and presentment of all commercial paper at any time held by Secured Party on which Debtor is in any way liable, notice of non-payment at maturity of any account or chattel paper, and notice of any action taken by Secured Party except where notice is expressly required by this Security Agreement or cannot by law be waived.

6. DEFAULT. Debtor will be in default upon the occurrence of any of the following events: (a) failure to make the payment, when due and payable, of any of the Obligations; (b) failure of the performance of any obligation or covenant contained or referred to herein; (c) any warranty, representation or statement made or furnished to Secured Party by or on behalf of Debtor proves to have been false in any material respect when made or furnished; (d) any event which results in the acceleration of the maturity of the indebtedness of Debtor or any guarantor or co-maker of any of the Obligations to others under any indenture, agreement or undertaking; (e) loss, theft, damage, destruction or encumbrance to, or of, the Collateral or the making of any levy, seizure of attachment thereof or thereon; (f) death of, dissolution of, termination of existence of, insolvency of, business failure of, appointment of a receiver of any part of the property of, assignment for the benefit of creditors by, or the commencement of any proceeding under any bankruptcy or insolvency law by or against, Debtor or any guarantor or co-maker of any of the Obligations; (g) the occurrence or nonoccurrence of any event or events which causes the Secured Party, in good faith, to deem itself insecure for any reason whatsoever.

See note at head of Digest as to 1998 legislation covered.

See Topical Index in front part of this volume.

In any such event Secured Party may at its option declare any or all of the Obligations to be due and payable and such sums shall then be due and payable immediately, without notice or demand.

7. RIGHTS AND REMEDIES ON DEFAULT. After the occurrence of any event of default, Secured Party may exercise at any time and from time to time any rights and remedies available to it under applicable law, including but not limited to the right to sell, lease or otherwise dispose of the Collateral, and the right to take possession of the Collateral. FOR THAT PURPOSE SECURED PARTY MAY ENTER UPON ANY PREMISES ON WHICH THE COLLATERAL OR ANY PART THEREOF MAY BE SITUATED AND REMOVE IT. Secured Party may require Debtor to assemble the Collateral and make it available at a place to be designated by Secured Party which is reasonably convenient to both parties. If at the time of repossession any of the Collateral contains other personal property not included in the Collateral, Secured Party may take such personal property into custody and store it at the risk and expense of Debtor. Debtor agrees to notify Secured Party within forty-eight (48) _____ hours after repossession of the Collateral of any such other personal property claimed, and failure to do so will release Secured Party and its representatives from any liability for loss or damage thereto. Any notice of intended disposition of any of the Collateral required by law shall be deemed reasonable if such notice is given at least ten (10) _____ days before the time of such disposition. Any proceeds of any disposition by Secured Party of any of the Collateral may be applied by it to the payment of expenses in connection with the Collateral, including but not limited to repossession expenses and reasonable attorneys' fees and legal expenses, and any balance of such proceeds shall be then applied against the Obligations and other amounts secured hereby in such order of application as Secured Party may elect.

8. GENERAL

a. Secured Party may, at its option, pay any tax, assessment, or other Governmental levy, or insurance premium or any other expense or charge relating to Collateral which is payable by Debtor (and not timely paid by it), and further may pay any filing or recording fees. Any amount or amounts so paid, with interest thereon at the highest rate payable on any of the Obligations (from the date of payment until repaid) shall be secured hereby and shall be payable upon demand.

b. Secured Party shall not be deemed to have waived any of its rights hereunder or under any other agreement, instrument or paper signed by Debtor unless such waiver be in writing and signed by Secured Party. No delay or omission on the part of Secured Party in exercising any right shall operate as a waiver of such right or any other right. A waiver on any one occasion shall not be construed as a bar to, or waiver of, any right or remedy on any future occasion.

c. Any notice, if mailed, shall be deemed given when mailed postage prepaid, addressed to Debtor at its address shown above, or at any other address of Debtor appearing on Secured Parties' records.

d. Covenants, representations, warranties and agreements herein set forth shall be binding upon Debtor, its legal representatives, successors and assigns. This Security Agreement may be assigned by Secured Party and all rights and privileges of Secured Party under this Security Agreement shall then inure to the benefit of its successors and assigns. (Note: Perfection requires a filing of notice of assignment.)

e. If any provision of this Security Agreement shall be for any reason held to be invalid or unenforceable, such invalidity or unenforceability shall not effect any other provision hereof, but this Security Agreement shall be construed as if such invalid or unenforceable provision had never been contained herein.

f. If Debtor is a guarantor, endorser, co-maker, or an accommodation party with respect to the Obligations, Debtor hereby waives the benefit of any and all defenses and claims of damage which are dependent upon Debtor's character as a party other than the maker. Each party to any of the Obligations hereby consents to and waives notice of (1) any and all extensions (whether or not for longer than the original period) granted as to the time of payment of any or all of the Obligations, and (2) any renewal of any or all of the Obligations.

g. This Agreement and all rights and duties hereunder, including but not limited to all matters of construction, validity, and performance, shall be governed by the law of Iowa.

h. Unless otherwise defined or the context otherwise requires, all terms used herein which are defined in the Iowa Uniform Commercial Code shall have the meanings therein stated. The rights and remedies herein conferred upon Secured Party shall be in addition to, and not in substitution or in derogation of, rights and remedies conferred by the Iowa Uniform Commercial Code and other applicable law.

i. All words and phrases used herein shall be construed as in the singular or plural number, and as masculine, feminine or neuter gender, as the context may require.

j. Captions are inserted for convenience only and shall not be taken as altering the text.

See note at head of Digest as to 1998 legislation covered.

See Topical Index in front part of this volume.

UCC-1 (Long Form)

STATE OF IOWA UNIFORM COMMERCIAL CODE—FINANCING STATEMENT—FORM UCC-1 (rev. 1/92)

Use only for County consumer goods filings and for ALL State filings

INCLUDING all transitional (County to State) filings pertaining to farm collateral.

INSTRUCTIONS

1. Please type this form.
2. Remove pages 4 and 5 (Debtor and Secured Party copies) and send the first 3 pages with interleaved carbon paper to the filing officer with $10.00 filing fee. If the space provided for any item(s) is inadequate, the item(s) should be continued on additional sheets. Use of additional sheets or a non-standard form requires an additional fee of $2.00. At the time of original filing, the filing officer will return the third copy as evidence of filing. The Secured Party may use the third copy as a termination statement by dating and signing the termination section at the bottom of the form. No fee is required for filing a termination statement.
3. If the security agreement is filed as a financing statement, include a completed set of 3 pages of this form which need not be signed, and an additional fee of $2.00.
4. If the property is crops, (crops are filed only with the Secretary of State) the description of the real estate must reasonably identify what is described (UCC 9-110).

This **FINANCING STATEMENT** is presented to THE FILING OFFICER for filing pursuant to the Uniform Commercial Code:

1. Debtor(s) (Last Name First) and address(es)

2. Secured Party(ies) and address(es)

3. For Filing Officer (Date, Time, Number, and Filing Office)

4. This Financing Statement covers the following types (or items) of property:

5. Name and Address of Assignee

6. Description of Real Estate (see instruction 4).

7.

Signature of Secured Party

Type or Print all Names (Iowa Code 335.2)

(Secured Party or other appropriate signature may be substituted for debtor(s) signature only in cases covered by UCC 9-402(2), 9-408 and must be identified as such when used.)

8. ☐ Products of Collateral are Covered.   ☐ Debtor is a transmitting utility as defined in UCC 9 105(1)

Debtor(s) acknowledge(s) receipt of a copy of this instrument.

9. _____
Signature of Debtor

_____
Signature of Debtor

_____
Type or Print all Names (Iowa Code 335.2)

Form Approved (1-2-87) by: Elaine Baxter, Secretary of State

See note at head of Digest as to 1998 legislation covered.

See Topical Index in front part of this volume.

UCC-2 (County Only)

STATE OF IOWA UNIFORM COMMERCIAL CODE—FINANCING STATEMENT—FORM UCC-2 (rev. 1-2-87)

Use ONLY for recording Fixture, Timber or Mineral security interests in County real estate records, and cross indexing in County UCC records.

INSTRUCTIONS

1. Please type this form.
2. Remove pages 4 and 5 (Debtor and Secured Party copies) and send the first 3 pages with interleaved carbon paper to the filing officer with $4.00 filing fee. If the space provided for any item is inadequate, the item(s) should be continued on additional sheets. Use of additional sheets or a non-standard form requires an additional fee of $1.00. The filing officer will return the third copy as evidence of filing as soon as it has been filed and assigned a real estate number.
3. In addition to the filing fee for fixture filings (in County Real Estate Records), there will be a fee of $5.00 per page for recording and a fee of $5.00 per page for a partial release or termination of the fixture filing.
4. If the security agreement is filed as a financing statement, it must include all information required by UCC 9-402(1) (5). Also submit a complete set of 3 pages of this form which need not be signed, and an additional fee of $1.00.
5. The real estate description must be sufficient to give constructive notice under the real estate mortgage laws of the State of Iowa (UCC 9-402(5)): The name of a record owner of the described real estate must be given.
6. This financing statement shall be filed and recorded in county real estate records under a real estate number. This statement also shall be indexed under a real estate number in the UCC files in a County Recorder's office.

This **FINANCING STATEMENT** is presented to THE FILING OFFICER for filing for record in the real estate records:

1. Debtor(s) (Last Name First) and address(es)	2. Secured Party(ies) and address(es)	3. For Filing Officer (Date, Time, Number, and Filing Office)

4. This Financing Statement covers the following types (or items) of property:

5. Name and Address of Assignee

6. Check appropriate box(s). The above goods are or are to become fixtures on ☐ The above timber is standing on ☐ The above minerals or the like (including oil and gas) or mineral accounts will be financed at the wellhead or minehead located on ☐ (Describe real estate below. See instruction #4):

The name of a record owner is . . . .

7. ☐ **Products of collateral are covered.**

By signing, the Borrower signs this form and also acknowledges receipt of a copy of the form on the date hereof.

8. _____   _____
    Signature of Debtor   Signature of Debtor

    _____   _____
    Type or Print all names (Iowa Code 335.2)   Type or Print all names (Iowa Code 335.2)

Secured party or other appropriate signature may be substituted for debtor(s) signature only in cases covered by UCC 9-402(2), 9-408 and 11105, and must be identified when substituted.

Form Approved (1-2-87) By: Elaine Baxter, Secretary of State

STATE OF IOWA
UNIFORM COMMERCIAL CODE—FINANCING STATEMENT CHANGES—FORM UCC-3 (rev. 7-1-81)
Use for ALL State filings. Use for all County filing EXCEPT those recorded in real estate records.

INSTRUCTIONS
1. Please type this form.
2. Remove pages 4 and 5 (Debtor and Secured Party copies) and send the first 3 pages with interleaved carbon paper to the filing officer with $4.00 filing fee, except termination. **NO FEE IS REQUIRED FOR FILING A TERMINATION STATEMENT.** If the space provided for any item(s) is inadequate, the item(s) should be continued on additional sheets. Use of additional sheets or a non-standard form requires an additional fee of $1.00. At the time of original filing, the filing officer will return the third copy as evidence of filing. This UCC-3 must be signed by Secured Party of record.
3. **Check ONLY one box below.**

This **STATEMENT** is presented to THE FILING OFFICER for filing pursuant to the Uniform Commercial Code:

Debtor(s) (Last Name First) and address(es)	Secured Party(ies) and address(es)	For Filing Officer (Date, Time, Number, and Filing Office)

This Statement refers to original Financing Statement No ....

Date filed: ...., 19 ..... Filed with ....

A. ☐ **CONTINUATION** .... The original financing statement bearing the file number shown above, is still effective.

B. ☐ **PARTIAL RELEASE** .... From the collateral described in the financing statement bearing the file number shown above, the Secured Party releases the property indicated below.

C. ☐ **ASSIGNMENT** .... The secured party certifies that the assignee, (name and address is shown below), has been assigned the secured parties rights under the financing statement bearing the file number shown above in the property indicated below.

D. ☐ **TERMINATION** .... The Secured Party certifies that a security interest no longer is claimed under the financing statement bearing the file number shown above.

E. ☐ **AMENDMENT** .... The financing statement bearing the above file number is changed to show ☐ Name, identity, corporate structure, or address of Secured Party as indicated below; ☐ Name, identity, corporate structure, or address of Debtor Party as indicated below; ☐ as indicated below;

CHANGES:

Debtor Signature(s) necessary only if filing an amendment:

_____ (Debtor)   By: _____ (Secured Party)
                                            (Signature of Secured Party. See instruction #2)

_____ (Debtor)

Type or Print name (Iowa Code 335.2)   Type or Print name (Iowa Code 335.2)

From Approved (7-1-81) By: Secretary of State   Dated: ...., 19 ...

See note at head of Digest as to 1998 legislation covered.

See Topical Index in front part of this volume.

STATE OF IOWA UNIFORM COMMERCIAL CODE—FINANCING STATEMENT CHANGES—FORM UCC-4

(Rev. 5/92)

Use ONLY for all County Filings Recorded in Real Estate Records and cross indexed in County UCC Records.

INSTRUCTIONS

1. Please type this form.
2. Remove pages 4 and 5 (Debtor and Secured Party copies) and send the first 3 pages with interleaved carbon paper to the filing officers with $10.00 filing fee, except in the case of termination. If the space provided for any item is inadequate, the item should be continued on additional sheets. Use of additional sheets or a non-standard form requires an additional fee of $2.00. This UCC-4 must be signed by Secured Party of record.
3. In addition to the filing fee for fixture filings (in County Real Estate Records), there will be a fee of $5.00 per page for recording and a fee of $5.00 per page for a partial release of the fixture filing.
4. This form shall be filed and recorded in county real estate records under a real estate number. This form shall also be indexed under a real estate number in the UCC files in a County Recorder's office.

This **STATEMENT** is presented to THE FILING OFFICER for filing for record in real estate records:

1 Debtor(s) (Last Name First) and address(es)	2 Secured Party(ies) and address(es)	3 For Filing Officer (Date, Time, Number and Filing Office)

4. Check one only:

☐ Original financing statement real estate record number

☐ Pre-1975 fixture filing county UCC number _____

_____ . Record owner of real estate: _____

_____ Date filed: _____ , 19____ Filed with _____

5. Check only one:

A. ☐ **CONTINUATION** . . . . The original financing statement between the foregoing Debtor and Secured Party, bearing the file number shown above, is still effective.

B. ☐ **PARTIAL RELEASE** . . . . The secured party releases the property indicated below from the collateral described in the financing statement bearing the file number shown above.

C. ☐ **ASSIGNMENT** . . . . Except to the extent otherwise specified below, the secured party certifies that the assignee, whose name and address is shown below, has been assigned all the Secured Party's rights under the financing statement bearing the file number shown above.

D. ☐ **TERMINATION** . . . . The Secured Party certifies that a security interest no longer is claimed under the financing statement bearing the file number shown above.

E. ☐ **AMENDMENT** . . . . The financing statement bearing the file number shown above is changed to show: ☐ Name, identity, corporate structure, or address of Secured Party as indicated below; ☐ Name, identity, corporate structure, or address of Debtor Party as indicated below; ☐ Other, as indicated below.

6. CHANGES:

7. Debtor Signature(s) necessary only if filing an amendment: by signing Debtor(s) also acknowledge(s) receipt of a copy of this instrument:

_____ **(Debtor)**

_____ **(Debtor)**

By: _____
(Signature of Secured Party. See Instruction #2)

. . . . **(Secured Party)**
Type or Print all names (Iowa Code 335.2)

Date: . . . . , 19 . . . . .

. . . .
Type or Print all names (Iowa Code 335.2)

Form Approved (1-2-87) By: ELAINE BAXTER—Secretary of State

UCC-11

STATE OF IOWA UNIFORM COMMERCIAL CODE—REQUEST FOR INFORMATION OR REQUEST FOR COPIES—FORM UCC-11
(REV. 5/92)

Use for Requests to the Secretary of State, County Recorders, and County Treasurers

INSTRUCTIONS

1. Please type this form.
2. Place an "X" in the appropriate box to designate whether this form is being used as a Request for Information or as a Request for Copies. It cannot be used for both at the same time.
3. If information or copies are to be requested from different filing officers, **separate requests must be submitted to each filing officer.**
4. **FEES.** Request for Information—$5.00   Copies—$1.00 Per Page
   When requesting copies, you must indicate the file numbers and number of pages of copies requested in the space provided, and accompany the request with the fee of $1.00 per page.
5. All requests submitted on other than this form are classified as Non-Standard, and an additional fee of $2.00 is required.

---

1 ☐ **REQUEST FOR INFORMATION ONLY** | PRESENT IN DUPLICATE | This REQUEST is presented to a filing officer for filing pursuant to the Uniform Commercial Code:

2 Debtor(s) (Last Name First) and address(es) | 3 Party requesting information or copies: (Name and Address) | 4 For Filing Officer use

5 Filing officer please furnish a certificate showing whether there are any presently effective financing statements, financing statement changes, or certificate of title lien notations with respect to the above-named debtor(s), and, if so, giving the date and hour of each filing or certificate of title lien notation, and the name and address of each secured party. Enclosed is the fee of $5.00.

File No.	Number of Pages	Date and Hour of Filing	Name(s) and Address(es) of Secured Party(ies)

CERTIFICATE: The undersigned filing officer certifies that, as of the time indicated, the above list contains all presently effective financing statements, financing statement changes, or certificate of title lien notations on file in my office which name the above debtor(s).

_____   _____
(date)   (Signature of Filing Officer)
                                            Request for Information

---

1 ☐ **REQUEST FOR COPIES ONLY** | PRESENT IN DUPLICATE

Filing officer please furnish exact copies of each page of the financing statements, financing statement changes, or certificate of title lien notations listed below which are on file in your office. Enclosed is the fee of $1.00 for each page requested.

2 File No.	No. of Pages	Date and Hour of Filing	File No.	No. of Pages	Date and Hour of Filing

CERTIFICATE: The undersigned filing officer hereby certifies that the attached _____ pages are true and exact copies of all the available financing statements, financing statement changes, or certificate of title lien notations listed on the above request.

_____   _____
(date)   (Signature of Filing Officer)
                                    STANDARD FORM—REQUEST FOR COPIES—FORM UCC-11

                                    ELAINE BAXTER, Secretary of State

---

See note at head of Digest as to 1998 legislation covered.

See Topical Index in front part of this volume.

KANSAS LAW DIGEST REVISER

Young, Bogle, McCausland, Wells & Blanchard, P.A.

(Formerly Gott, Young & Bogle P.A.)
First National Bank Building
106 West Douglas, Suite 923
Wichita, Kansas 67202-3392
Telephone: 316-265-7841
Fax: 316-265-3956

Reviser Profile

History: The firm is the oldest continuously operating law firm in Wichita, Kansas and one of the oldest firms in the State. It was founded in 1886 by R. R. Vermillion and William E. Stanley, who later was elected Governor of the State of Kansas. Earle Evans joined the firm in 1897. Evans possessed outstanding legal skills and obtained national recognition for the firm, serving as President of the American Bar Association in 1933. The firm has represented many national clients continuously since the turn of the century. The firm has a staff of eight lawyers.

Areas of Emphasis: Young, Bogle, McCausland, Wells & Blanchard, P.A. concentrates on state and federal civil trial and appellate practice in diverse areas, including Commercial and Corporate Litigation, Employment Law, Insurance Defense, Workers' Compensation, Products Liability and Oil and Gas Law. The firm's general practice includes counseling and litigation in the areas of Real Estate, Business, Bankruptcy and Probate Law.

Client Base: The firm's major clients include national and regional manufacturers, retailers, railroads, oil and gas producers and insurance companies, as well as national and international banking and investment companies. The firm serves many of these clients for the entire state. The firm provides general legal services for individuals and local businesses, including pro bono representation through state and local referral services.

Firm Activities: Firm members participate in local and state professional and civic activities, including active memberships on local bar committees and mediation panels.

Significant Distinctions: Major distinctions of firm members include: William E. Stanley, 15th Governor of the State of Kansas (1899 to 1903); Earle W. Evans, President of Wichita Bar Association (1920), President of the American Bar Association (1933).

KANSAS LAW DIGEST

(The following is a list of all Categories and Topics, including cross-references, covered in this Digest.)

KANSAS LAW DIGEST

Revised for 1999 edition by

YOUNG, BOGLE, McCAUSLAND, WELLS & BLANCHARD, P.A. of the Wichita Bar.

(Citations, unless otherwise indicated, are to chapters and sections of Kansas Statutes Annotated. (K.S.A.). House and Senate bill numbers are used for those 1996 bills that do not yet have statutory citation. "Rules" refers to Supreme Court rules, which are published in chapter 20, article 31 of K.S.A. Parallel citations to Pacific Reporter begin with 30 Kan. and 1 Kan. App. See also category Courts and Legislature, topic Statutes.)

Note: This revision covers all legislation enacted by the 1998 legislature.

INTRODUCTION

GOVERNMENT AND LEGAL SYSTEM:

The State of Kansas is a constituent state of the United States of America. For further discussion of the U.S. federal system, see Introduction to the Federal Government of the United States at the beginning of this volume. A great many laws are promulgated by the federal government of the United States and are not reflected in the topics below. See the Introduction to this volume for references to the federal law topics covered.

Common Law.—Like all but one of United States, Kansas has common law legal system, with roots in English common law. For information on courts and legislature of Kansas, see category Courts and Legislature.

HOLIDAYS:

Following are legal holidays: New Year's Day, Jan. 1; Lincoln's Birthday, Feb. 12; Washington's Birthday, 3d Mon. in Feb.; Memorial Day, last Mon. in May; Independence Day, July 4; Labor Day, 1st Mon. in Sept.; Columbus Day, 2d Mon. in Oct.; Veteran's Day, Nov. 11; Thanksgiving Day, 4th Thurs. in Nov.; Christmas Day, Dec. 25. (35-107).

Legality of Transactions on Sat., Sun. or Holiday.—Holidays do not affect commercial paper, making or execution of agreements or instruments in writing. (38-108).

OFFICE HOURS AND TIME ZONE:

Kansas is in the Central Standard (GMT −06:00) time zone. Office hours are generally from 9 a.m. to 5 p.m.

BUSINESS ORGANIZATIONS

AGENCY:

Common law rules govern.

ASSOCIATIONS:

Formation.—No statutes or case law.

Rights and Powers.—No statutes or case law.

Liabilities.—Member of unincorporated association is generally liable for tortious acts committed by association's agents acting within scope of employment where wrongful acts were within range of purposes for which association was formed. (206 Kan. 682, 481 P.2d 958).

Actions.—No capacity to sue or be sued. (196 Kan. 1, 408 P.2d 891). Certain members may be named as representative parties if court satisfied they will adequately represent association. (60-223b).

Dissolution.—No statutes or case law.

Massachusetts or Business Trust.—See topic Joint Stock Companies.

Partnerships.—See topic Partnerships.

Professional Associations.—See topic Corporations, subhead Professional Corporations.

CORPORATIONS:

Kansas general corporate code (17-6001 to 7513) based on Delaware code. Governs all corporations whenever organized. (17-6101[b]). For statutes applying to particular kinds of corporations, see particular categories and topics such as category Business Regulation and Commerce, topic Banks and Banking, category Insurance, topic Insurance Companies, etc.

General Supervision.—Secretary of State, State Capitol, Topeka, KS 66612, (785) 296-2564 (corporation division).

Purposes.—Corporation may engage in any lawful activity. (17-6002[a][3]). However, corporations generally prohibited from directly or indirectly owning or leasing agricultural land in Kansas. Prohibition does not apply to: (1) Encumbrance taken as security; (2) land acquired as gift by educational, religious or charitable nonprofit corporation; (3) land needed and used for nonfarming operations; (4) land acquired by process of law if divested within ten years; (5) land held in fiduciary capacity; (6) land held by family farm corporation, authorized farm corporation, limited liability agricultural company, family farm limited liability agricultural company, and certain other trusts and entities; and (7) land held for feedlots, swine, dairy or poultry production, coal mining, forestry, farming research and miscellaneous other exceptions. (17-5904).

Name, except for banks and where conflicts with special regulation, must include "association," "church," "college," "company," "corporation," "club," "foundation," "fund," "incorporated," "institute," "society," "union," "syndicate," or "limited," or one of the abbreviations "Co.," "Corp.," "Inc.," "Ltd.," or words or abbreviations of like import (17-6002[a][1]). Name may be reserved for 120 days. (17-

7402). Application to Secretary of State with $20 fee required. (17-7506[a][17]). Availability of name may be determined by contacting Secretary of State.

Term of corporate existence is perpetual unless otherwise provided in articles of incorporation. (17-6002[b][5]).

Incorporators.—Any person, partnership, association or corporation, singly or jointly may incorporate or organize a corporation. (17-6001[a]). There are no restrictions as to residence or citizenship.

Articles of Incorporation.—

Must set forth: (1) Corporate name; (2) address, including street, number, city and county of registered office in Kansas and name of registered agent at that address; (3) nature of business, which may be any lawful activity; (4) classes of stock authorized, number of authorized shares in each class, par value of each share in each class or statement that shares have no par value, and any preferences or restrictions on any class or any series of any class; (5) name(s) and mailing address(es) of incorporator(s); and (6) if powers of incorporators terminate on filing, names and mailing addresses of initial directors. (17-6002[a]).

May set forth, instead of in by-laws, any provision required or permitted in by-laws, or any provision: (1) For management of corporation; (2) defining powers of corporation, directors, stockholder, any class of stockholders or members of non-stock corporation; (3) regulating sale or disposition of stock; (4) granting stockholders preemptive right to subscribe to any or all additional issues of any or all stock; (5) requiring supermajority vote of any class or series of stock of or directors; (6) limiting duration of corporation's existence to specified date; (7) on manner of adoption, alteration and repeal of by-laws; (8) eliminating or limiting personal liability of director for breach of fiduciary duty (see subhead Liabilities of Directors, infra); and (9) provision using specified words, requiring ³/₄ shareholder approval of compromise between corporation and its creditor on application by corporation, any stockholder, any creditor, any receiver or trustees in dissolution to court of competent jurisdiction in Kansas. (17-6002[b]).

Filing of Articles.—Articles must be signed by each incorporator (17-6003[a]) and acknowledged (17-6006). Original signed instrument together with one duplicate, either signed or conformed, must be delivered to Secretary of State along with all taxes and fees. Secretary will stamp filing date on original. If duplicate is identical to original, Secretary will certify duplicate. If steps carried out, corporate existence begins on filing date unless date within 90 days specified. (17-6003[d]). Before July 1, 1998, no corporation existed until articles were filed with both Secretary and register of deeds. (6 Kan.App.2d 627, 631 P.2d 1240). From July 1, 1998, corporation exists upon filing with Secretary only.

Incorporation Tax.—None.

Filing Fees.—

Articles of Incorporation.—At time of filing each domestic corporation organized for profit must pay to Secretary of State application and recording fee of $75. Fee for domestic not for profit corporation is $20. (17-7502[a]).

Foreign Corporation Authorization to do Business.—$75 filing fee plus $20 fee for issuance of certificate of authority to do business in Kansas. (17-7502[b], 17-7506[a][12]).

Other Fees.—$20 for issuing, filing and indexing: (1) Restated articles of incorporation; (2) certificate of extension, restoration, renewal or revival of articles of incorporation; (3) certificate of amendment of articles of incorporation, either prior to or after payment of capital; (4) certificate of designation of preferences; (5) certificate of retirement of preferred stock; (6) certificate of increase or reduction of capital; (7) certificate of dissolution, either prior to or after beginning of business; (8) certificate of revocation of voluntary dissolution; (9) certificate of change of location of registered office and resident agent; (10) agreement of merger or consolidation; (11) certificate of ownership and merger; (12) certificate of authority of foreign corporation to do business in Kansas; (13) certificate of extension, restoration, renewal or revival of certificate of authority of foreign corporation to do business in Kansas; (14) change of resident agent by foreign corporation; (15) certificate of withdrawal of foreign corporation; (16) certificate of correction of any of foregoing instruments; (17) reservation of corporate name; (18) any other certificate for which filing or indexing fee is not prescribed by law. (17-7506[a]).

Secretary of State will charge following: (1) For certified copies, $7.50 for each copy certified, plus fee per page fixed by Secretary if Secretary supplies copies; (2) for certificate of good standing and certificate of fact, $7.50; (3) for written report of search, $5; (4) for photocopies of instruments not certified, fee fixed by Secretary of State. (17-7506).

License to do Business.—Duly certified copy of articles of incorporation or of any other instrument filed with Secretary of State is prima facie evidence of: (1) Due execution, acknowledgment and filing of instrument; (2) performance of all conditions precedent to instrument's effectiveness; and (3) any other facts required or permitted to be stated in instrument. (17-6005).

Organization.—The incorporators have control of the organization until directors are named or elected, with power to obtain stock subscriptions and perfect organization. (17-6007).

CORPORATIONS . . . continued

Notice of first meeting may be waived by all incorporators, and need not be given to anyone who attends meeting; otherwise person calling meeting must give other incorporators or directors two days written notice. (17-6008).

Paid-in Capital Requirement.—No minimum paid-in capital required.

Amendment of Articles.—Articles of incorporation may be amended to include any provision lawful to insert in original articles and in particular: (1) To change its corporate name; or (2) to change its corporate powers and purposes; or (3) to increase, decrease or reclassify its capital stock; or (4) to cancel or affect right of shareholders of any class to receive dividends accrued but not declared; or (5) to create new classes of stock; or (6) to change period of its duration. (17-6606[a]).

Any or all such changes may be effected by one certificate of amendment. Amendment is effected by a majority vote of voting stock entitled to vote, adopting a resolution by board of directors setting forth proposed amendment, at an annual or special stockholders' meeting held upon proper notice. Certain restrictions on open ended investment company amendments. (17-6602[b]). Certificate duly executed, setting forth amendment and certifying that such amendment has been duly adopted, must be filed with Secretary of State and register of deeds in county where original articles are recorded. If amendment would alter preferences, special rights or powers of any class of stock so as to affect such class adversely, or would increase or decrease amount of authorized stock of any class, or would increase or decrease par value of any class, affirmative vote of a majority in interest of each class so affected is necessary in addition to majority vote of all stock; provided, amount of authorized stock of any class may be increased or decreased by affirmative vote of a majority of voting stockholders only, if articles of incorporation so provide. (17-6602[c]).

Majority vote of directors or governing body of a corporation without capital stock may amend articles of incorporation. (17-6602[c][3]).

Increase or Decrease of Authorized Capital Stock.—Corporation may amend its articles of incorporation to increase or decrease its authorized capital stock or to reclassify same by changing number, par value, designations, preferences or relative, participating, optional or other special rights of shares. (17-6602[a][3]).

Corporation may reduce its capital by resolution of directors, provided assets remaining after such reduction are sufficient to pay all debts. Duly executed and acknowledged certificate of such reduction must be filed and recorded in manner of articles of incorporation. (17-6604).

By-laws.—Articles of incorporation may provide manner of and authority for adoption, alteration and repeal of by-laws, otherwise by-laws are adopted by incorporators or stockholders or, on their failure to act, by board of directors. Thereafter power to make, alter or repeal by-laws is in stockholders or members of a nonstock corporation, but corporation may confer that power concurrently on directors. For corporations in existence on July 1, 1972, right to amend, alter or repeal is in board of directors, unless otherwise provided in corporation articles and subject to power of stockholders so to act. (17-6009).

Stock.—Corporation may issue different classes of stock, with or without par value and with such full or limited voting rights, preferences, optional or special rights, qualifications, limitations or restrictions as is provided for in articles of incorporation or in resolution of board of directors authorized thereby preferred or special stock may be made redeemable, or convertible into or exchangeable for shares of other classes, and its holders be entitled to receive dividends at such rates, on such conditions, and at such times, payable in preference to, or in relation to, dividends payable on any other class, cumulative or noncumulative, and have such preferences on distribution or dissolution as are provided for in articles of incorporation or resolution of board of directors authorized thereby. (17-6401).

For purposes of title, actions, garnishment and jurisdiction of Kansas courts, situs of stock of Kansas corporation is regarded as being in Kansas. (17-6419).

Stock Certificates.—Every stockholder is entitled to a certificate, certifying number of shares owned by him. (17-6408).

Issuance of Stock.—Share having par value must be issued for at least par value. No-par shares may be issued for consideration determined by board or, if articles so provide, by stockholders. (17-6403). Consideration may be paid in whatever form and manner board determines. Absent actual fraud, judgment of directors as to value of such consideration is conclusive. Stock so issued will be fully paid and nonassessable if corporation received either: (1) Entire consideration in cash, services rendered, personal or real property, or leases of real property, or (2) par value, or stated value for no-par shares, in such consideration and binding obligation from purchaser for remainder of purchase price. (17-6402).

Transfer of Stock.—Governed by Art. 8 of Uniform Commercial Code. (84-8-101 et seq.; 17-6409).

Determining Stockholders Entitled to Notice of or to Vote at Meeting.—Board may fix record date not preceding date of resolution and between ten and 60 days before date of meeting. If no record date fixed, record date will be close of business two days before date notice of meeting is given or, if notice is waived, at close of business two days before meeting date. Directors may set new record date for adjourned meeting. (17-6503[a]).

Determining Stockholders Entitled to Consent in Writing without Meeting.—Board may fix record date within ten days after resolution. If no date fixed and no prior act of directors required, date is first date that signed, written consent is delivered to corporation. If prior action of directors is required and no date has been fixed, date is at close of business on day directors adopt resolution taking action. (17-6503[b]).

Determining Stockholders Entitled to Other Rights.—Board may fix record date within 60 days after resolution. If no date fixed, date is close of business on date of resolution affecting shares. (17-6503[c]).

Uniform Simplification of Fiduciary Security Transfers Actadopted. (17-4903-4913). Uniform Commercial Code (K.S.A. 84-1-101 et seq.) specifically provides that it does not repeal this uniform act and if any inconsistency between two, provisions of Simplification of Fiduciary Security Transfers Act control (84-10-101[2]).

Stock Transfer Tax.—None.

Stockholders Actions.—60-223a follows Federal Rule 23.1. See also subhead Liabilities of Directors, infra.

Stockholders' Liabilities.—Not personally liable for debts of corporation, absent contrary provision in articles of incorporation, except as may be liable by reason of own conduct. (17-6002[b][6]). Liable for stock not paid in full unless bona fide purchaser. (17-6412).

Stockholders' Meeting.—

When and Where Held.—Annual meeting must be held at time and date specified in by-laws. (17-6501[b]). Special meetings may be called by board or by persons so authorized by articles of incorporation or by-laws. (17-6501[e]). Meetings may be held inside or outside Kansas at place specified in by-laws or, if not designated, at registered office in Kansas. (17-6501[a]).

Right to Vote.—One vote per share unless otherwise specified in articles of incorporation. (17-6502[a]). See also subhead Share Exchanges or Acquisitions, infra.

Quorum.—Articles or by-laws may set at not less than 1/3of shares conferring voting powers. If not specified, quorum is majority of shares entitled to vote. (17-6506).

Proxies.—Effective for three years unless different period specified. (17-6502[b]). Duly executed proxy is irrevocable if stated to be irrevocable and if coupled with sufficient legal interest. Such interest may be in stock itself or in corporation generally. (17-6502[c]).

Cumulative Voting.—Articles may permit. (17-6501[f]).

Vote Required.—Absent specification in articles or by-laws, directors are elected by plurality and all other matters approved by majority of stockholders represented and entitled to vote. (17-6506). Unless otherwise provided in articles, all elections of directors must be by written ballot. (17-6501[f]).

Voting Trusts.—Stockholders may, by agreement in writing, create voting trusts for any period not exceeding ten years, and if agreement so provides it may be extended from time to time for additional periods of not more than ten years each by written agreement of one or more beneficiaries with consent of trustee. Stockholders by agreement may waive provisions of Corporation Code pertaining to voting trusts when interest of public or some third party is not involved. (175 Kan. 479, 264 P.2d 888). If copy of agreement filed in registered Kansas office it is open to inspection of any stockholder. Certificates of stock deposited under said agreement must be cancelled and new certificates issued to voting trustees, in which certificates, and on stock ledger, it must appear that they are issued under agreement. Voting trustees may vote in person or by proxy, but incur no liability as stockholders, trustees or otherwise except for individual malfeasance. Majority of voting trustees determine manner of voting unless otherwise provided in agreement; if equally divided, vote must be divided equally among trustees. (17-6508).

Directors.—Board consists of one or more directors. Number fixed by articles, by by-laws or in manner provided by by-laws. Directors need not be stockholders unless articles or by-laws provide otherwise. Articles or by-laws may prescribe other qualifications. Director serves until successor elected and qualified or until resignation or removal. (17-6301[b]). See also subhead Stockholders' Meeting, supra.

Classes.—Directors may be divided into one, two or three classes serving staggered terms by articles, initial by-law or by-law adopted by vote of stockholders. Articles may give class or series of stock right to elect one or more directors. (17-6301[d]).

Removal.—Director may be removed by majority of shares entitled to vote. If directors serve in classes, cause required unless articles provide otherwise. If less than entire board to be removed, no director may be removed without cause if votes cast against removal would be sufficient to elect director if voted cumulatively. (17-6301[k]).

Director's Meetings.—

Where Held.—Unless articles or by-laws require otherwise, board may have office(s) and hold meetings outside Kansas. (17-6301[g]). Directors may take action without meeting if all members consent in writing filed with minutes. (17-6301[f]). Directors may hold meeting using telephone conference call or similar communications equipment. (17-6301[i]).

Quorum and Required Vote.—Unless articles or by-laws require otherwise, majority vote when quorum is present is act of board. Quorum is majority of board, but articles or by-laws may require greater number or lesser number not less than 1/3. (17-6301[b]).

Powers and Duties of Directors.—Business and affairs of corporation must be managed by or under direction of board of directors. (17-6301[a]). Board may delegate powers to committee by majority vote. (17-6301[c]).

Liabilities of Directors.—

Articles of incorporation may incorporate provision eliminating or limiting personal liability of director to corporation or stockholders for monetary damages for breach of fiduciary duty, but such provision may not limit liability for: (1) Any breach of duty of loyalty; (2) acts or omissions not in good faith or which involve intentional misconduct or knowing violation of law; (3) unlawful payment of dividend or unlawful stock purchase or redemption; or (4) any transactions from which director derived improper personal benefit. Provision does not affect liability for acts committed before effective date. (17-6002[b][8]).

Nonprofit Organizations.—If nonprofit organization carries general liability coverage, liability of non-compensated director limited to insurance coverage available unless director's misconduct was willful or wanton or intentionally tortious. (60-3701[b]).

Officers.—Officers and means of choosing officers determined by by-laws or directors' resolution. (17-6302).

Liabilities of Officers.—

Nonprofit Organizations.—If nonprofit organization carries general liability coverage, liability of non-compensated officer or volunteer limited to insurance coverage available unless misconduct was willful or wanton or intentionally tortious. (60-3601[b]).

See note at head of Digest as to 1998 legislation covered.

See Topical Index in front part of this volume.

CORPORATIONS . . . *continued*

Indemnification of Directors and Officers.—

Actions Other Than in Behalf of Corporation.—Corporation may indemnify if person acted in good faith and in manner he reasonably believed to be not opposed to best interests of corporation and, in criminal actions, had no reasonable cause to believe his action was unlawful. (17-6305[a]).

Actions in Behalf of Corporation.—Corporation may indemnify if person acted in good faith and in manner he reasonably believed to be not opposed to best interest of corporation. No indemnification permitted regarding claims for which person adjudged liable to corporation unless court determines he is fairly and reasonably entitled to such expenses court deems proper. (17-6305[b]).

Insurance may be purchased on behalf of directors, officers, employees or agents of corporation against any liability arising out of person's status as such regardless of corporation's power to indemnify. (17-6305[g]).

Registered Office.—Corporation must maintain registered office in Kansas. This need not be its place of business. (17-6201[a]). Directors may change by resolution stating new location. Certificate certifying change must be executed, acknowledged and filed like articles of incorporation. (17-6203[a]). See subheads Filing of Articles and Filing Fees, supra.

Resident Agent.—Corporation must maintain resident agent in Kansas. This may be either individual Kansas resident or Kansas corporation. Kansas corporation may be its own resident agent. (17-6202[a]). Directors may change by resolution stating name and location of new agent. Certificate certifying change must be executed, acknowledged and filed like articles of incorporation. (17-6203[a]). See subheads Filing of Articles and Filing Fees, supra.

If corporation does not name new agent within 30 days after agent dies or leaves state, Secretary of State, after 30 days notice, may declare existence of Kansas corporation forfeited or, in case of foreign corporation, authority to do business in Kansas forfeited. (17-6203[b]).

General Powers.—In addition to enumerated powers every corporation may exercise all powers granted by Corporation Code so far as necessary or convenient to conduct, promotion or attainment of business as set forth in articles.

Every domestic corporation has power to: Have perpetual succession by its corporate name; sue and be sued; have a corporate seal; acquire, own and otherwise deal in and with real and personal property and mortgage or pledge any of its assets, wherever situated; appoint and pay such officers and agents as business requires; adopt, amend, and repeal by-laws; wind up and dissolve itself; conduct business and have offices within or without this state; make public welfare or charitable donations; be an incorporator, promoter, or manager of other corporations; participate with others in any corporation, partnership, limited partnership, joint venture or association of any kind; transact any lawful business directors find to be in aid of governmental authority; contract, including contracts of suretyship, incur liabilities, borrow money, issue notes, bonds and other obligations and encumber all or any of its property; lend money; pay pensions and carry out pension and profit sharing plans; provide insurance on life of any officers or employees. (17-6102).

Corporation may hold and otherwise dispose of any security of any corporation, partnership, association, individual, or governmental body. While owner corporation may exercise all incidents of ownership including right to vote. (17-6202).

May purchase and otherwise deal in and with its own shares; but it cannot do so if capital of corporation would be impaired. (17-6410).

Any corporation may lend money to or otherwise assist any officer or other employee when, in judgment of directors, it would benefit corporation. (17-6303).

Ultra Vires.—No act of corporation and no conveyance or transfer of real or personal property to or by corporation is invalid for lack of capacity or power. Lack of capacity or power may be asserted: (1) By stockholder to enjoin corporation; (2) in derivative action; or (3) by attorney general to enjoin or dissolve corporation. (17-6104).

Dividends.—Subject to restrictions in articles of incorporation, directors may declare and pay dividends out of (a) net assets in excess of capital, or (b) net profits for fiscal year then current or preceding fiscal years in case there shall be no excess as mentioned in (a). No dividends can be declared out of such net profits if capital is less than aggregate amount of capital represented by issued and outstanding stock having a preference on distribution. (17-6420). Corporations exploiting wasting assets may determine net profits from exploitation or liquidation without considering depletion of such assets. (17-6420). Dividends may be paid in cash, property, or shares of stock. (17-6423).

Unclaimed Dividends.—Uniform Unclaimed Property Act adopted. Unclaimed property presumed abandoned after five years. (58-3935).

Sale or Transfer of Corporate Assets.—Board may sell, lease or exchange all or substantially all of corporation's assets if authorized by stockholders' resolution adopted by majority vote at meeting called on 20 days' notice. (17-6801[a]).

Books and Records.—Stockholders have right to inspect by-laws, stock register, books of account and records of proceedings of stockholders and directors and to make copies thereof. Director has similar right for purposes reasonably related to his position. (17-6510).

Reports.—Every corporation must file annual report with Secretary of State on forms prescribed by Secretary. Report must show corporate name, principal office, officers and directors and their residence addresses, shares authorized and issued, stockholders owning 5% or more of capital stock and any holdings of Kansas agricultural land. (17-7503 to -7505). If report is not filed within 90 days of due date, in addition to penalties (17-7509) Secretary may forfeit articles of Kansas corporation and authorization to do business of foreign corporation (17-7510). At time of filing corporation must pay annual franchise tax. See subhead Franchise Tax, infra.

Nonprofit corporations must file report by 15th day of sixth month after end of tax year, but Secretary may grant 90 day extension. (17-7504).

Kansas For Profit Corporations.—Report must be filed at same time Kansas income tax return is due. (17-7503[a]).

Foreign for profit corporations must show date of last annual election of officers and directors, nature and kind of business, places of business both inside and outside Kansas, value of property owned and used both inside and outside Kansas, and shareholder's equity attributable to Kansas. Must be filed when Kansas income tax return is due. (17-7505[a]).

Corporate Bonds or Mortgages.—Corporation may issue notes, bonds and other obligations, and may secure any obligation by mortgage, pledge or other encumbrance of any or all of its property, franchises and income. (17-6102[13]).

Merger and Consolidation.—Domestic corporations (17-6701) or any foreign corporation and domestic corporation (17-6702) may merge or consolidate on filing with Secretary of State, duly certified written agreement to that effect which has been adopted by vote representing majority of capital stock of each corporation at meeting duly called for that purpose except that under certain conditions stockholder vote is not required, or by filing certificate of merger or consolidation. (17-6701, 17-6701[c], 17-6702[c]). Resultant corporation possesses all rights, privileges, powers, franchises and property of all kinds of each constituent corporation, subject to all restrictions, disabilities, debts, liabilities and taxes of said constituent corporations. (17-6709). Merger or consolidation does not affect rights of creditors or holders of liens, does not abate actions pending against either corporation (17-6711) and does not affect liabilities of stockholders or officers of either corporation (17-6709). Resultant corporation has power to issue bonds, mortgage its franchise and property and issue certificated or uncertificated shares of stock in exchange or payment for original shares. (17-6710).

Business Combinations.—Corporation shall not engage in any business combination with any interested stockholder for period of three years following date stockholder became interested stockholder, can opt out in articles of incorporation, or by amending articles or bylaws. (17-12,100).

Share Exchanges or Acquisitions.—New Act (17-1286 et seq.) regulates exchanges of certain Kansas corporations.

Applies to Kansas corporations having: (1) At least 100 shareholders and its principal place of business, principal office or substantial assets in Kansas; and (2) at least 10% of its shareholders reside in Kansas, at least 10% of its shares are owned by Kansans, or 2,500 shareholders reside in Kansas. Corporations may provide in articles or by-laws that this act does not apply. (17-1289).

Restrictions.—If any person acquires shares within 120 day period bringing his voting power above one of three thresholds (see catchline Thresholds, infra), his shares lose voting rights. Rights may be restored at special or next annual shareholders' meeting by: (1) Majority vote of all shares entitled to vote for directors by class; and (2) same test excluding interested shares. (17-1287).

Thresholds are: (1) $^1\!/_5$ to $^1\!/_3$; (2) $^1\!/_3$ to $^1\!/_2$; or (3) majority of all voting power. (17-1286).

Dissolution.—Before payment of capital stock or beginning business, incorporators may surrender franchise by filing certificate to that effect with Secretary of State (17-6803); otherwise, dissolution may be effected by consent in writing of all stockholders having voting power, without a meeting, or by vote of two-thirds in interest of voting stockholders at a meeting called for that purpose (17-6804).

On dissolution, corporate existence is continued for three years for winding up (17-6807), or court may appoint directors as trustees or appoint receivers (17-6808). In latter case, creditors must prove and file claims as directed by court. (17-6905). Action pending against corporation dissolved does not abate but proceeds to final judgment against trustees or receivers in name of corporation. (17-6811).

Insolvency and Receivers.—On application of any creditor or stockholder of insolvent corporation, district court may appoint receiver. (17-6901). Receiver is vested with title of all property except real estate outside Kansas. (17-6902). Receiver must file inventory of assets with court. (17-6904). Creditors must file proof of claims within six months of receiver's appointment. (17-6905). If receiver disputes claim, creditor must submit to examination. Court may approve, disprove or modify recommendations of receiver. (17-6906). If cause for liquidation no longer exists, court has discretion to dismiss proceedings on appropriate conditions. (17-6911).

Close Corporations.—Corporations may be organized as close corporations by complying with 17-7201-7216. If a corporation, which is not a close corporation, desires to become a close corporation it may amend its articles of incorporation to comply with said sections by a two-thirds vote. (17-7204). Special provisions must be included in articles of incorporation. (17-7202). Many requirements applicable to regular corporations do not apply to close corporations and there are special statutory requirements applicable to close corporations which do not apply to regular corporations. Breach of certain special requirements relating to close corporations can cause a loss of status as such. (17-7208).

Appraisal.—In corporation merging or consolidating, dissenting stockholder who, within 20 days of mailing of notice of merger, demands, in writing, payment on shares and is unable to reach agreement with corporation as to value of shares may, by petition filed in district court of county where resulting corporation has principal place of business, demand determination of value of stock by three appraisers to be appointed by court. Petition may be filed by corporation if accompanied by verified list of names and addresses of all stockholders demanding payment and with whom agreements as to value of shares have not been reached. (17-6712).

Nonprofit corporations may or may not have capital stock and have power to set forth, in by-laws or articles, rules for ascertaining membership at any given time, in absence of which only persons with dues for the current year fully paid are qualified members with right to vote. Members may vote by proxy. (17-6505). Articles of incorporation must state conditions of membership or that conditions will be fixed by by-laws. (17-6002).

Foreign Corporations.—Foreign corporation may not do business in Kansas until it files application for authority to engage in business in Kansas with Secretary of State. (17-7301[b]).

Application must set forth: (1) Certificate issued within 90 days of application by proper officer of jurisdiction of incorporation stating that corporation is in good

---

See note at head of Digest as to 1998 legislation covered.

See Topical Index in front part of this volume.

CORPORATIONS . . . *continued*

standing in that jurisdiction; (2) address of principal office of corporation; (3) address of principal office or place of business in Kansas, if known; (4) full nature of business to be conducted in Kansas; (5) name and address of each officer, trustee and director; (6) when corporate existence will expire; (7) detailed statement of assets and liabilities as of date within past 12 months; (8) location of registered office in Kansas and name of resident agent; (9) date when corporation intends to commence business in Kansas. (17-7301[b]).

Filing Requirements.—Corporation must give written, irrevocable consent to actions against it in proper court of any county having proper venue by service of process on Secretary of State. Consent and application must be subscribed and sworn to by president or vice-president and secretary or assistant secretary of corporation. Consent must be accompanied by duly certified resolution authorizing signers to execute it. (17-7301[b]). Original signed instruments must be filed with duplicate copy with Secretary of State. Filing fee is $75 plus $20 for issuance of certificate of authority. (17-7502[b], 17-7506[a][12]).

To withdraw from state, corporation must file with Secretary of State: (1) Certificate, under seal and attested by secretary, stating it surrenders authority in Kansas and withdraws therefrom, and stating address to which process may be mailed; or (2) certificate of dissolution issued by jurisdiction of incorporation and address to which to mail process; or (3) order or decree of dissolution of court of jurisdiction of incorporation and address to which to mail process. Secretary of State shall issue a certificate of withdrawal and appointment of resident agent is revoked. (17-7306). After withdrawal state courts still have jurisdiction in actions arising out of any act or transaction of corporation prior to order of withdrawal or revocation of license. (17-7306).

See other subheads throughout this topic, including Purposes, Registered Office, Resident Agent, and Reports, *supra.*

Franchise Tax.—At time of filing its annual report all corporations for profit, domestic and foreign, except banking, insurance, savings and loan corporations or associations, credit unions, or corporations organized under electric cooperative act, must pay a franchise tax in an amount equal to $1 for each $1,000 of corporation's shareholders' equity attributable to Kansas, as defined in 17-7501, except that tax can be no less than $20 and no more than $2,500. (17-7503[c], 17-7505[c]).

Every corporation organized under electric cooperative act must pay an annual franchise tax of $20. (17-4634).

Professional corporations pay same franchise tax as regular corporations for profit. Nonprofit corporations must pay an annual franchise tax of $5. Annual fee for tax periods after 12/31/92 shall be $20. (17-7504[c]).

Professional corporations permitted are: CPA; architect; attorney; chiropractor; dentist; engineer; optometrist; osteopathic physician or surgeon; physician, surgeon or doctor of medicine; veterinarian; podiatrist; pharmacist; real estate broker or salesperson; land surveyor; clinical social work specialist; physical therapist; landscape architect; RPN; and licensed psychologist. (17-2707). Generally, provisions of general corporation code control. Corporate name may be any name not contrary to law or ethics of profession, and must end with word "chartered" or "professional association" or abbreviation "P.A." (17-2711).

Taxation of Corporate Property.—See category Taxation, topic Taxes, subhead Real and Personal Property Tax.

Deeds.—See category Property, topic Deeds.

Model Non-Profit Corporation Act.—Not adopted.

Income Tax.—See category Taxation.

JOINT STOCK COMPANIES:

Massachusetts or Business Trust.—

Formation.—Must file with Secretary of State: (1) Executed copy and certified copy of trust instrument; (2) verified list of trustees' names and addresses; (3) balance sheet certified by CPA; (4) location of registered office and name of resident agent; and (5) for foreign trusts, irrevocable consent to service of process similar to that required of foreign corporations (see topic Corporations, subhead Foreign Corporations). (17-2030). Filing fee is $50. (17-2031).

Rights and Powers.—As provided in trust instrument, but may not engage in any business forbidden to for profit corporations. (17-2034). Corporation laws generally apply. (17-2035). See topic Corporations.

Liabilities.—Holders of certificates have same limitation of liability as stockholders of corporation. (17-2038[a])

Actions.—Same capacity to sue or be sued as corporation. (17-2035).

Professional Corporations.—See topic Corporations, subhead Professional Corporations.

LIMITED LIABILITY COMPANIES:

General Supervision.—Limited liability company (LLC) is authorized by Kansas limited liability company act. (K.S.A. 17-7601 to 7656). Formation, operation, reporting, and dissolution of Kansas LLC and registration of foreign LLC are supervised by Kansas Secretary of State, as for corporations.

Formation.—Any "person" may form LLC, which shall have one or more "members", by executing and filing with Secretary of State articles of organization. (17-7605). "Person" means any individual, general partnership, limited partnership, LLC, trust estate, association, corporation or other association. "Member" is any person admitted to LLC in accordance with act. (17-7602[d] and [h]). LLC is considered organized upon filing of articles of organization. (17-7609[a]). Date of existence is date of filing, except articles may specify date of subscription if articles are filed within five days of such date and specified date is not later than 90 days subsequent to filing. (17-7609[c]).

Professional LLC.—"Qualified person" may be member of LLC limited to one profession. "Qualified person" is natural person licensed to practice some type of profession as professional corporation. Professional LLC is subject to authority of licensing body and may execute all powers of professional corporation. (Ks. Sess. Laws. c. 121, §§1-5).

Purposes.—LLC may conduct or promote any lawful business or purpose, except as otherwise provided by law, which partnership or individual may conduct or promote. LLC is separate legal entity and not construed as corporation. (17-7603).

Powers.—Kansas LLC may generally do all acts necessary to transact any lawful business, within or without state, including acting as promoter or member of other legal entity, and including employment of professionals to practice profession. Specific powers are enumerated at 17-7604.

Name.—Words or abbreviations "limited company" or "L.C." or "limited liability company" or "L.L.C." shall be included. Name shall be such as to distinguish it upon records from any corporation, limited partnership, or limited liability company reserved, registered or organized under Kansas law. Omission of required words or abbreviations renders member with knowledge of omission liable for debt, damage or liability caused by omission. (17-7606).

Articles of Organization.—Information required is: (1) name of LLC; (2) period of duration; (3) purpose for which LLC is organized; (4) address of registered office and name of initial resident agent; (5) right, if given, to admit additional members and terms and conditions of admission; (6) if LLC is to be managed, statement to that effect, names and addresses of managers until successors are elected and qualified, and, if management reserved to members, names and addresses of such members; and (7) any other provision not inconsistent with law. (17-7607). Articles are signed by person forming LLC or by any member or manager. (17-7634[a][1]).

Filing Articles of Organization.—Original and duplicate signed or conformed copy are filed with filing fee. Secretary of State certifies time and date of filing, files and indexes original, and returns certified duplicate copy to person filing. Professional LLC must file certificate from licensing body. (17-7608).

Registered Office and Registered Agent.—Kansas LLC must have and continuously maintain registered office and resident agent. Office may be, but need not be, same as place of business. Agent must be individual or domestic corporation or LLC itself. (17-7611[a]). 17-7611(b) to (e) set forth provisions for change of address, resignation, death, move and appointment of successor. Service of process may be served by law as if LLC were partnership or to resident agent. (17-7632). Foreign LLC must register with Secretary by submitting fee and original and duplicate application with following: (a) name of foreign LLC; (b) state or jurisdiction of its organization and date of organization; (c) nature of business to be conducted in Kansas; (d) address of registered office and name and address of resident agent; (e) irrevocable written consent to jurisdiction, venue and service of process; (f) names and addresses of members and/or managers; and (g) date LLC first did or intends to do business in Kansas. (17-7637). Secretary files and indexes application. (17-7638). Foreign LLC has requirements similar to Kansas LLC for maintaining registered office and agent. (17-7639). Foreign LLC may not maintain any legal action in Kansas until it has registered and paid all fees and penalties for years it did business in Kansas. (17-7642).

Management is vested in members, each with one vote, unless articles provide for manager or managers, who shall be chosen by members as prescribed in articles or operating agreement. Articles or operating agreement establish responsibilities of managers. (17-7612). Operating agreement adopted and approved by members governs rights, duties and obligations of members and managers, including terms for members transacting business with LLC. Agreement also provides for location of principal office and meetings of members and managers. (17-7613).

Dissolution.—LLC shall be dissolved upon occurrence of following: (1) as specified in articles; (2) as specified in operating agreement; (3) at any time there are no members; (4) upon entry of judicial decree of dissolution; or (5) unanimous agreement of all members. (17-7622[a]). Death, retirement, resignation, expulsion, bankruptcy or other event terminating continued membership of any member does not cause dissolution unless members agree in writing to dissolve. (17-7622[b]). As soon as possible following occurrence of event of dissolution, statement of intent to dissolve must be filed with Secretary of State. (17-7622[c] and 17-7623). Effect of statement of intent to dissolve is LLC shall cease to carry on its business, except for winding up business, but separate existence continues until Secretary issues certificate of dissolution or decree is issued by court of competent jurisdiction. Provisions for winding up and distribution of assets are at 17-7624 and 7625. When all debts, liabilities and obligations are paid or discharged and remaining property has been distributed, articles of dissolution are executed and filed with Secretary. Articles are canceled by issuance of certificate of dissolution. (17-7626 to 7628). LLC may be dissolved involuntarily by court order for statutorily enumerated acts of misconduct. (17-7629).

Filing Fees.—Filing fee for articles of organization is $150. (17-7646[b]). Fee for foreign registration is $150. (17-7646[c]). Fee of $20 is specified for other filings including amendments, statement of intent to dissolve, articles of dissolution, certificate of change of location of registered office or resident agent or other certificate, affidavit or paper provided for in act. (17-7646[a]). Annual report of domestic and foreign LLC is filed by Dec. 31 with required franchise tax, calculated as $1 for each $1,000 of net capital accounts located in or used in Kansas at end of preceding year, but not less than $20 or more than $2,500. (17-7647, 7648). Any instrument required by act may be filed by facsimile for additional fee to be prescribed by Secretary. Such filing is effective upon its filing date if original instrument is filed within seven days of facsimile date. (17-7652).

PARTNERSHIPS:

Uniform Partnership Act is repealed effective July 1, 1998, and Revised Partnership Act enacted effective Jan. 1, 1999. (56-301 et seq.). Only significant deviations are that §25 (b)(4) (K.S.A. 56-325) and §37 (K.S.A. 56-337) are expressly made subject to Art. 10 of c. 59 (article on partnership estates in Kansas Probate Code).

See note at head of Digest as to 1998 legislation covered.

See Topical Index in front part of this volume.

PARTNERSHIPS . . . *continued*

Limited Partnerships.—Revised Uniform Limited Partnership Act adopted with variations. (56-1a101, et seq.).

Nature.—Limited partnership may conduct any lawful business or purpose. (56-1a106). Foreign limited partnership must register with secretary of state and submit to jurisdiction in state before doing business. (56-1a502).

Formation.—Two or more persons must execute certificate of limited partnership which is filed with secretary of state. Must establish registered office and have resident agent in state. Name must contain words "Limited Partnership" or "L.P." (56-1a102).

Dissolution.—Upon dissolution and winding up, certificate of cancellation of limited partnership must be filed with secretary of state. (56-1a451—1a454).

Fees.—For issuing, filing, indexing documents, secretary of state shall collect following fees: For certificate of amendment, restated certificate of limited partnership, certificate of cancellation of limited partnership, certificate of change of location of registered office, $20; for certified copies, $7.50 for each copy certified; providing certificate of good standing and certification of fact, $7.50; report of record search, $5; photocopies of documents not certified, fee per page in amount set by secretary of state. At time of filing certificate of domestic limited partnership or application to do business of foreign limited partnership, application and recording fee of $150 must be paid. (56-1a605).

Purposes.—Partnerships, limited partnerships, LLPs and corporate partnerships are subject to same restrictions on ownership and leasing of agricultural land in Kansas as corporations. (17-5904). See topic Corporations, subhead Purposes.

Actions.—Partnership may sue or be sued. (Ks. Sess. Laws, c. 93, §18).

Limited Liability Partnership.—1996 Revised Uniform Partnership Act enacted effective Jan. 1, 1999.

Out-of-State Partnerships.—Foreign LLP must file statement of qualification and annual report. (Ks. Sess. Laws, c. 93, §§56, 59).

BUSINESS REGULATION AND COMMERCE

BANKS AND BANKING:

Uniform Commercial Code (K.S.A. 84-1-101 et seq.) in effect. See topic Commercial Code.

Regulated by State Banking Commissioner, 700 Jackson, Topeka, KS 66603, (785) 296-2266. (74-1304 et seq.). Commissioner must examine each bank at least once every 18 months and shall provide to bank's board of directors copy of examination report. (9-1701). Commissioner must approve merger, consolidation (9-1724), or change of control (9-1720). Advised by State Banking Board. (74-3004 et seq.).

Stockholders.—If capital stock is impaired, commissioner must notify bank to restore capital within 90 days. Directors must levy assessment on common stockholders within 15 days to restore capital or, if permissible, reduce capital. (9-906). Preferred stockholders not liable for assessments. (9-909).

Deposits.—

Joint accounts may be maintained in name of two or more persons, including minors, payable to either or any of them or payable to either or any survivors or sole survivor. (9-1205).

Deposits of minors may be received and paid on order of minor until bank receives certified copy of appointment of guardian. (9-1204).

Payable on Death Contracts.—Individual adult or minor may contract in writing for balance of his account at death to be paid to designated beneficiary. (9-1215).

Adverse claim to deposit is not effective until claimant adequately indemnifies bank or bank is served with court order. (9-1207).

Unclaimed Deposits.—Uniform Unclaimed Property Act adopted. (58-3934-3978).

Collections.—Uniform Commercial Code (K.S.A. 84-1-101 et seq.) in effect. See topic Commercial Code.

Trust Companies.—May: (1) Receive for safekeeping personal property; (2) accept and execute any trust agreement and perform any trustee duties; (3) act as assignee, transfer agent, registrar or receiver; (4) accept and execute all trusts and perform any fiduciary duties; (5) act as agent or attorney in fact in any agreed capacity; (6) act as executor or trustee under last will and testament or administrator of estate of deceased; (7) be conservator for any minor, incapacitated person or trustee for any convict; (8) loan money upon real estate, chattel, collateral or personal security; (9) execute and issue notes, bonds or debentures; (10) receive money in trust; (11) act in any fiduciary capacity and perform any act Kansas state bank could under state banking laws; (12) act as originating or contracting trustee; (13) buy and sell foreign or domestic exchange, gold, silver, coin or bullion; and (14) exercise any other power expressly conferred upon trust companies by any laws of state. (9-2103). Banking code is applicable with some exceptions. (9-702).

Uniform Common Trust Fund Act.—Adopted with minor variations. (9-1609, 9-1610). 1952 Amendment not adopted.

Foreign Banks.—See categories Estates and Trusts, topics Executors and Administrators, and Trusts, subhead Eligibility and Competency; Family, topic Guardian and Ward. No financial institution insured by FDIC may conduct business in state unless it may legally accept demand deposits and make commercial loans. (9-811).

Credit unions may be organized by seven residents of state on application to Bank Commissioner. (17-2201). Membership is limited to groups having common bond of occupation or association, or residing within well defined neighborhood, community or rural district. (17-2205).

Union may lend money, provide checks, money orders, other money type instruments or transfer methods and safe deposit boxes or similar facilities to members. (17-2204). Name "Credit Union" may not be used by any company other than one organized under Act or credit union organized pursuant to federal law. (17-2203).

Savings and loan associations are under supervision of State Banking Commissioner (75-1309 et seq.), prescribing and limiting investments, loans (see also 17-5001) and management. Provision is made for conversion to federal savings and loan association.

Branch Banking.—After applying for and obtaining approval of state banking board, branch banks may be established and operated in Kansas by bank incorporated under Kansas law. (9-1111[b]).

Bank Holding Companies.—Permitted. (9-519 et seq.). No holding company and its subsidiaries may control more than 15% of total deposits in state as determined by Banking Commissioner. (9-520[a]). After July 1, 1992 bank holding company located in state contiguous to Kansas or in Arkansas or Iowa may acquire ownership or control of or power to vote shares of interest in or assets of Kansas bank or bank holding company.

BILLS AND NOTES:

Uniform Commercial Code (K.S.A. 84-1-101 et seq.) in effect. See topic Commercial Code.

Days of Grace.—Not provided for.

Judgment Notes.—Not in common use. Void in consumer credit transactions. (16a-3-306).

Attorney Fees.—Any note, mortgage or other credit agreement may provide payment of reasonable collection costs including court costs, attorney fees and collection agency fees. (58-2312).

BROKERS:

Uniform Commercial Code (K.S.A. 84-1-101 et seq.) in effect. See topic Commercial Code.

Licenses.—Generally not required. See also topic Licenses, Business and Professional.

Real Estate Brokers.—Salespersons and brokers must be licensed by Real Estate Commission. (58-3036). Applicants must pass written exam and provide proof of good reputation. (58-3039, 58-3040). Applicants for original salesperson license must also attend 30 hours of approved instruction within 12 months prior to applying for license. Six months temporary salesperson license granted on application. (58-3039[f]). Broker applicants must attend 24 hours (58-3046a) and must have been salespersons in Kansas or other state for at least two of preceding five years (58-3039[c]).

Liability.—Act does not create private cause of action and does not affect other statutory or common law causes of action. See 229 Kan. 252, 624 P.2d 420. State real estate recovery fund provides reimbursement up to $15,000 aggregate per transaction for losses caused by certain statutory violations. (58-3066 to 58-3072).

Futures Dealers.—Buying, selling or dealing in grain, stocks, bonds, securities or any other commodities upon telegraphic or telephone market reports without intent to receive or deliver prohibited. (50-121). Preempted by federal law regarding interstate grain sales (142 Kan. 426, 49 P.2d 973) and of doubtful application today.

Security Brokers.—See topic Securities.

CARRIERS:

All common carriers supervised by Kansas Corporation Commission, State Office Bldg., Topeka, KS 66612, (785) 296-3355. (66-1,216; 66-105). Exceptions listed in 66-1,109.

Uniform Commercial Code (K.S.A. 84-1-101 et seq.) in effect. See topic Commercial Code.

Licenses.—Before any carrier may engage in business, application must be made to Commission and certificate obtained that public convenience will be promoted by transaction of business and permit obtained to transact such business within state. (66-131; 66-1,114).

Rates.—Must be reasonable. (66-1,217). Carrier must file schedule of all rates affecting Kansas traffic. (66-1,218). Commission may investigate and alter rates that are unreasonable, unreasonably discriminatory or unduly preferential. (66-1,219). Formal public hearing required before rates may be altered. (66-1,220).

Discrimination.—Unreasonably discriminatory or unduly preferential rates prohibited. (66-1,217). See subhead Rates, supra.

Limiting Liability.—Common carrier transporting property from one point in Kansas to another point in Kansas may not limit liability for loss. (66-304). However UCC limits liability of connecting carrier to period goods are in its possession. (84-7-302[2]).

Bills of Lading.—Uniform Commercial Code governs. (84-7-301 et seq.). See topic Commercial Code.

Liens.—Carrier or other bailee may sell liened goods remaining in bailee's possession for six months or more. (58-208). Uniform Commercial Code governs. (84-7-301).

Motor Vehicle Carriers.—See category Transportation, topic Motor Vehicles.

COMMERCIAL CODE:

Uniform Commercial Code adopted, effective Jan. 1, 1966. Code is given Kansas Statutes Annotated (K.S.A.) chapter number 84, and running section numbers contain said chapter citation followed by numerical part of Uniform Commercial Code citation, for example, 84-1-101. A new and separate volume of K.S.A. (Vol. 7) has been printed containing Code. Code as adopted in Kansas is virtually word for word the same as 1972 Code found in Uniform and Model Acts section.

1972 Amendments.—Adopted.

1977 Amendments.—Adopted.

1986 Amendments.—Not adopted.

Articles 2a, Leases, and 4a, Fund Transfers adopted.

See note at head of Digest as to 1998 legislation covered.

See Topical Index in front part of this volume.

COMMERCIAL CODE . . . *continued*

Blanks in 1972 official version of Uniform Commercial Code are filled in as follows (Official U.C.C. section is designated first and then Kansas citation designated in parentheses):

6-104 (84-6-104)—under (1) (c) "The Clerk of the District Court."

7-204 (84-7-204)—(4) reads as follows: "This section does not repeal any part of chapter 82 of Kansas Statutes Annotated not specifically repealed by this act."

9-203 (84-9-203)—(4) reads in part as follows:

"May be subject to the Kansas Uniform Consumer Credit Code (16A-1-101, et seq.)."

9-401 (84-9-401)—second alternative subsection (1) adopted and modified. See infra subhead Material Variations.

Alternative provisions of the 1972 official Uniform Commercial Code which have been adopted in Kansas (Official U.C.C. section is designated first and then Kansas citation designated in parentheses):

1-209—1966 Official Optional Amendment enacted.

2-318 (84-2-318)—1966 Official Optional Amendment Alternative B enacted.

2-702 (84-2-702)—1966 Official Amendment enacted.

Major revisions in Arts. 3 and 4 to clarify points of ambiguity in case law and to serve as companion to Art. 4A applying to funds transfers.

6-106 (84-6-106)—adopted with modifications. See infra subhead Material Variations.

7-209 (84-7-209)—1966 Official Amendment enacted.

7-403 (84-7-403)—bracketed part of (1) (b) not adopted.

9-106 (84-9-106)—1966 Official Optional Amendment enacted.

9-302 (84-9-302)—alternative B adopted.

9-401 (84-9-401)—second alternative subsection (1) adopted with modifications. See infra subhead Material Variations. First subsection (3) adopted.

Material variations from 1972 official version of Uniform Commercial Code are as follows (Official U.C.C. section is designated first and then Kansas citation designated in parentheses):

6-106 (84-6-106) is amended in subsection (4) (a) to require a filing of a copy of scheduled property and list of creditors as required by section 6-104 and providing that notice required by subsection (4) shall fix a reasonable time by which any such interested party shall file his claim. Subsection (b) is amended to read "On motion of any interested party, after the time fixed for filing claims, the court may order the distribution of the consideration to the persons entitled to it according to the following order of priorities (i) Secured claims (ii) Taxes (iii) Non-secured claims which shall be on a pro rata basis if sufficient funds are not available to satisfy all unsecured claims."

9-307 (84-9-307)—"For purposes of this section only, 'farm products' does not include milk, cream and eggs" is added.

9-312 (84-9-312)—subsection (4) is altered to provide 20 days to perfect.

9-401 (84-9-401)—(1)(a) altered to read: "When the collateral is consumer goods, then in the office of the register of deeds in the county of the debtor's residence or if the debtor is not a resident of this state then in the office of the register of deeds in the county where the goods are kept;".

9-402 (84-9-402)—Following language in (1) ". . . shall give a mailing address of the debtor and shall contain a statement indicating the types, or describing the items, of collateral," Kansas adds: "When the financing statement is filed according to paragraph (c) of subsection (1) of K.S.A. 84-9-401, and amendments thereto, it shall contain the SSN or the FEIN of the debtor, except that when the debtor is a sole proprietorship, the financing statement shall contain only the SSN of the debtor. A statement of collateral in a financing statement is adequate if it generally identifies goods by one or more of the classifications listed in K.S.A. 84-9-109, and amendments thereto, or generally identifies other collateral by one or more of the following classifications: fixtures, documents, instruments, general intangibles, chattel paper or accounts. A statement of collateral in a financing statement shall not be deemed inadequate solely because it is broader than, or otherwise differs from, that found in the security agreement. A description of the location of the collateral is not necessary to an adequate statement except insofar as a description of location is specifically required by the uniform commercial code." Electronic filing of financing statement permitted per Secretary of State's rules and regulations. Subsection (5) altered to require legal description of real estate concerned and name of record owner. Last sentence of subsection (6) has been amended to read: "In addition to the regular recording and satisfaction fees with respect to the mortgage, there is required a filing fee of $6 plus $1 for each additional page, or amount fixed by rules and regulations adopted by secretary of state on or after effective date of this act of not to exceed $10 plus $1 for each additional page." Kansas adds sentence to subsection (7) which follows original first sentence stating: "Where married debtors are jointly engaged in business and it is unclear whether a partnership exists, the financing statement may be filed in the names of the individual debtors." Kansas adds a subsection (9), "Any financing or other statement or security agreement filed pursuant to part 4 which contains a copy, however made, of the signature of a secured party or a representative of such debtor or of a debtor or a representative is of such debtor 'signed' by the secured party or the debtor as the case may be."

9-403 (84-9-403)—(4) Altered to read: "Except as provided in subsection (7) a filing officer shall mark each statement with a file number and with the date and hour of filing and shall hold the statement on a microfilm or other photographic copy thereof for public inspection. In addition the filing officer shall index the statements according to the names of the debtors but shall not index the names of corporate officers or signatures of the debtors, shall note in the index the file number, the address of the debtor given in the statement, the date of filing, and a general description of the collateral, and shall cause the index to be accessible to the public." (5) Altered to read: "The fee for filing and indexing and for stamping a copy furnished by the secured party to show the date and place of filing for an original financing statement, any amendments thereto or for a continuation statement shall be $6 plus $1 for each additional page, or an amount fixed by rules and regulations adopted by the secretary of state on or after the effective date of this act of not to exceed $10 plus $1 for each additional page." (7) Altered to read: "or accounts subject to subsection (5) of K.S.A. 84-9-103," "or indicates that it covers goods which are or are to become fixtures and contains the information required by K.S.A. 84-9-402, the filing officer, other than the Secretary of State, shall also index the statement according to the name of the record owner of the real estate in the general real estate mortgage index."

9-404 (84-9-404)—(3) Altered to read: "Termination statements may be destroyed after such statements have been on file for five (5) years."

9-405 (84-9-405)—(1) Altered to read: "On presentation to the filing officer of such a financing statement the filing officer shall mark the same as provided in subsection (4) of K.S.A. 84-9-403, as amended. The fee for filing, indexing and furnishing filing data for a financing statement so indicating an assignment shall be the amount fixed for filing original financing statements."

(2) Following language: "The filing officer shall mark such separate statement with the date and hour of the filing." altered to read: "The filing officer shall note the assignment on the index of the financing statement or in the case of a fixture filing, or a filing covering timber to be cut, or covering minerals or the like (including oil and gas) or accounts subject to subsection (5) of K.S.A. 84-9-103, the filing officer shall index the assignment under the name of the assignor as grantor and, to the extent that the law of this state provides for indexing the assignment of a mortgage under the name of the assignee, the filing officer shall index the financing statement under the name of the assignee. The fee for filing, indexing and furnishing filing data about such a separate statement of assignment shall be the amount fixed for filing original financing statements. Notwithstanding the provisions of this subsection, an assignment of record of a security interest in a fixture contained in a mortgage effective as a fixture filing (subsection [6] of K.S.A. 84-9-402 and amendments thereto) may be made only by an assignment of the mortgage in the manner provided by the law of this state other than this act."

9-406 (84-9-406)—Altered to require SSN or FEIN of debtor when financing statement filed per 84-9-401(1)(c). Following language: "shall note the same upon the margin of the index of the filing of the financing statement." altered to read: "The fee for filing and noting such a statement of release shall be the amount fixed for filing original financing statements."

9-407 (84-9-407)—(2) Altered to read: "the names and addresses of each secured party therein. If the filing officer is the secretary of state, the SSN or FEIN of the debtor may be used to determine whether there is on file any such financing statement and any related statement but a search of filings for any number shall be considered a separate search for which an additional fee shall be charged pursuant to this subsection. The fee for providing the information shall be $8 or an amount not to exceed $10 fixed by rules and regulations adopted on or after the effective date of this act by the secretary of state of not to exceed $10. If the filing officer is other than the secretary of state, the fee for providing the information shall not exceed $3 and an additional $.25 for each financing statement and for each related statement reported. Upon request the filing officer shall furnish a copy of any filed financing statement or related statement after payment of a fee of $1 per page, except that if the filing officer is the secretary of state, the fee shall be in an amount fixed by the secretary of state and approved by the director of accounts and reports under K.S.A. 45-219 and amendments thereto. (3) Except with respect to willful misconduct, the state, counties and filing officers, and their employees and agents, are immune from liability for damages resulting from errors or omissions in information supplied pursuant to this section."

Kansas Additions to Part 4: (84-9-410) Financing statement covering farm equipment, farm products or accounts or general intangibles arising from or relating to sale of farm products and filed before Jan. 1, 1984 shall continue to be effective until effectiveness lapses or is terminated. Any amendment or statement of termination, assignment or release to be filed in office of register of deeds where original financing statement filed until continuation statement filed with secretary of state. Before Jan. 1, 1989 financing statement can be continued only by filing with secretary of state, within six months before effectiveness lapses, financing statement which complies with 84-9-402. Statement may be signed by secured party of record or debtor and must be accompanied by copy of most recent effective prior financing statement and related documents on file with register of deeds and, statement that prior financing statement is still effective. (84-9-410).

Financing statements filed in two or more counties which relate to same secured transaction may be consolidated into single filing with secretary of state by filing financing statement within six months before effectiveness of any one prior financing statement lapses. Must be accompanied by documents as outlined above from each county. Time for any future filings after consolidation of multiple filings determined by date financing statement properly filed with secretary of state. (84-9-410).

84-9-411 allows secretary of state and registers of deeds to provide access to filing information to interested parties by (1) telecopier access to secretary of state's office; (2) subscription periodic written summaries; (3) copies of microfilm; (4) data storage material; (5) access to data processing functions; or (6) any other appropriate method of disseminating information. Secretary of state sets fees.

84-9-412 allows secretary of state to provide filing information by telephone to persons who have received prior approval of secretary of state. Secretary of state sets fee.

Filing Fees.—See category Documents and Records, topic Records, subhead Filing Under Commercial Code.

Forms.—See end of this Digest.

See also topics Banks and Banking, Bills and Notes, Brokers, Carriers, Contracts, Factors, Frauds, Statute of, Sales, Securities, Warehousemen; categories Business Organizations, topic Corporations; Civil Actions and Procedure, topic Limitation of Actions; Debtor and Creditor, topics Assignments, Fraudulent Sales and Conveyances, Liens, Pledges; Documents and Records, topics Records, Seals; Mortgages, topic Chattel Mortgages.

CONSUMER CREDIT:

Uniform Consumer Credit Code adopted with numerous minor variations. Numbering generally corresponds to section number of Official Text with prefatory addition of "16a". Administrator is Kansas Consumer Credit Commissioner.

CONSUMER CREDIT . . . *continued*

Application.—Act applies to credit transactions in Kansas. Includes multistate transaction if creditor received in Kansas signed obligation or offer from consumer, or creditor solicited consumer face-to-face in Kansas. (16a-1-201[1]).

Definitions.—
Consumer means buyer, lessee or debtor to whom credit is granted in consumer credit transaction. (16a-1-301[9]).

Consumer credit transaction means consumer credit sale, consumer lease or consumer loan or modification thereof including refinancing, consolidation or deferral. (16a-1-301[11]).

Consumer credit sale is sale of goods, services or interest in land on credit in which: (1) Creditor regularly grants credit in similar transactions, except for lender credit cards; (2) buyer is person other than organization; (3) goods, services or interest in land are purchased primarily for personal, family or household purposes; (4) either debt is by written agreement payable in installments or finance charge is made; and (5) with respect to sale of goods or services, amount financed does not exceed $25,000. Consumer credit sale does not include purchases through lender credit cards or, unless made subject to act, sales of interest in land if interest rate does not exceed 12%, or sales by contract for deed of real estate if interest rate is governed by 16-207. (16a-1-301[10]). See topic Interest.

Consumer lease means lease of goods in which: (1) Lessor in business of leasing regularly makes to individual for personal use; (2) amount payable does not exceed $25,000; (3) term does not exceed four months; and (4) not made with lender credit card. (16a-1-302[12]).

Consumer loan is loan made by person regularly engaged in business of making loans in which: (1) Debtor is individual; (2) loan is for personal use; (3) either debt is payable in installments or finance charge is made; and (4) either amount financed does not exceed $25,000 or debt is secured by interest in land. However, unless loan made subject to act by agreement, "consumer loan" does not include: (1) Loan secured by first real estate mortgage; (2) second or other subordinate mortgage granted to same lender as first mortgage; or (3) loan made by qualified 401 plan to individual participant. (16a-1-301[13]).

Finance Charges.—See topic Interest.

CONSUMER PROTECTION:

Kansas Consumer Protection Act (50-623 et seq.) is substantial enactment of Uniform Consumer Sales Practices Act. Act applies to "consumer transactions", including sale, lease, assignment or other disposition for value of property or services in Kansas. (50-624[c]). "Consumer" means individual or sole proprietor who seeks or acquires property or services for personal, family, household, business or agricultural purposes. (50-624[b]). Consumer may not waive rights except in conscionable settlement of claim. (50-625).

Deceptive acts are prohibited, including knowing misrepresentations and willful omissions of material facts. (50-626).

Unconscionable acts and practices are prohibited, including unconscionable advertising techniques, contract terms and debt collection practices. (50-627).

Disclaimer or Limitation of Warranties.—Supplier in consumer transaction may not exclude, modify or limit implied warranties of merchantability and fitness for particular purpose, nor may he exclude, modify or limit any remedy provided by law, including measure of damages available, for breach of implied warranty. Government surplus is subject to notice requirements of 16 CFR 455.2, et seq. (50-639).

Door-to-Door Sales.—Consumer may cancel sale of $25 or more within three business days. Seller must make required disclosures. (50-640).

Enforcement.—Attorney general investigates and enforces. (50-628; 50-631). Attorney general or district attorney may obtain declaratory and injunctive relief in addition to actual damages on behalf of individual consumers, or enter into consent decree. (50-632).

Private Remedies.—Consumer may bring individual or class action. Attorneys' fees may be recoverable. (50-634). Civil penalties available. (50-636).

Venue is in district court of county where violation occurred or where defendant resides or has principal place of business. If defendant is nonresident with no place of business, venue is also proper in Shawnee county. (50-638).

Collision Damage Waiver Act.—Applies to all persons leasing rental motor vehicles for 60 days or less from locations in Kansas. If agreement obligates lessee to pay for any damages to vehicle, any waiver clause must use simple language, be prominently displayed and include specified language in at least 10 point type. Deceptive acts prohibited. (50-657).

Fair Credit Reporting Act (50-701 et seq.) is enactment of federal act (15 USC §1681).

Lemon Law.—Applies only to original purchaser or lessee of new vehicle. If manufacturer or authorized dealers cannot conform vehicle to applicable warranty after reasonable number of attempts, manufacturer must replace with comparable vehicle or refund purchase or lease price less allowance for use. Reasonable number of attempts presumed if: (1) Same nonconformity subject to repair four times or more during either warranty period or one year after delivery; (2) vehicle out of service because of repair for cumulative total of 30 days or more during such period; or (3) ten or more repair attempts for any nonconformities substantially impairing vehicle's use and value. (50-645).

Odometer Tampering.—See category Transportation, topic Motor Vehicles, subhead Odometer Alteration.

Receipt of Unsolicited Property.—If supplier delivers goods or services not actually ordered or requested by recipient, receipt of such unordered goods or services shall be deemed unconditional gift. (50-617).

Attempts to collect for goods or services received as unconditional gift is deceptive act or practice. (50-617[b]).

Uniform Deceptive Trade Practices Act.—Not adopted.

Plain Language.—No Plain Language statute.

CONTRACTS:

Uniform Commercial Code (K.S.A. 84-1-101 et seq.) in effect. See topic Commercial Code.

All contracts which by common law are joint only shall be construed to be joint and several. (16-101). All contracts in writing signed by party bound thereby import a consideration. (16-107). Want of consideration a defense in action on contract brought by one not a bona fide holder. (16-108). See also categories Documents and Records, topic Seals; Family, topic Infants.

Uniform Consumer Credit Code (K.S.A. 16a-1-101 et seq.) in effect.

FACTORS:

Uniform Commercial Code (K.S.A. 84-1-101 et seq.) in effect. See topic Commercial Code.

FRANCHISES:

City authorized to grant franchises to person, firm or corporation to supply certain services within city. (12-2001 et seq.).

Uniform Franchise and Business Opportunities Act not adopted.

FRAUDS, STATUTE OF:

Uniform Commercial Code (K.S.A. 84-1-101 et seq.) in effect. See topic Commercial Code.

The person to whom goods or chattels loaned becomes owner if possession thereof is retained for five years unless a written reservation of title in lender recorded in Register of Deeds office in county where one or both parties reside, within six months from date of lending the property. Exception in museum property act. (58-4001, et seq.). No leases or interest in land, for more than one year, may be made, except by deed or note in writing and signed by the person assigning or granting same or his authorized agent or by act and operation of law. (33-105). No action may be brought to charge a party on special promise, for debt of another or an executor or administrator, to answer charges out of his own estate, nor to charge on any marriage contract, or contract concerning lands, or agreement for over a year, unless the agreement or a memorandum or note thereof, be in writing, and signed by the party to be charged, or some one duly authorized by him or her. (33-106).

Credit Agreements.—Debtor or creditor may not maintain action or defense unless agreement is in writing and signed by creditor and debtor. Includes agreement to lend or delay repayment of money, goods or things in action. (16-117; 16-118).

Doctrine of part performance recognized in contracts relating to land. (187 Kan. 418, 357 P.2d 757).

INTEREST:

Legal rate, 10%. (16-201).

Maximum rate which may be contracted for is 15%, except as otherwise specifically authorized by law. (16-207). Lender may collect actual fees paid government and reasonable expenses incurred in connection with making, closing, disbursing, extending, readjusting or renewing loans subject to provisions of 16-207. (16-207[d]). Parties may contract for higher rates if they agree in writing to abide by requirements of uniform consumer credit code. (16-207; 16a-1-109).

Business or agricultural loans are not subject to interest rate limitation. (16-207[f]).

Consumer loans are covered by uniform consumer credit code. (16a-1-101 et seq.). Maximum rates for unsupervised lender is 18% for amounts less than $1,000 and 14.45% for amounts over $1,000. Supervised loans under license have maximum rates which vary according to size of loan, except that up to 18% on unpaid balance may always be charged. (16a-2-401[1]). Minimum finance charge of $5 may be assessed if amount financed does not exceed $75, and $7.50 when amount financed exceeds $75. Lender may contract for 3% nonrefundable loan origination fee on amount financed if loan secured by interest in land; otherwise lesser of 2% or $100. (16a-2-401).

Consumer sales are covered by uniform consumer credit code. (16a-1-101 et seq.). Maximum rate for closed end sale is 21% on part of unpaid balance under $1,000, and 14.45% on unpaid balance over $1,000. Minimum finance charge of $5 if amount financed does not exceed $75, and $7.50 when amount financed exceeds $75. Seller may contract for any finance charge not exceeding that agreed to by consumer. Rebate may be required upon prepayment. (16a-2-201). Rate for open end credit is finance charge contracted for in agreement governing account. Minimum finance charge of 50¢ may be assessed. (16a-2-202).

Notes secured by mortgages and contracts for deeds to real estate executed after May 17, 1980 may not charge interest in excess of 1½% above yield of 30-year fixed rate conventional home mortgages committed for delivery within 61 to 90 days accepted under federal home loan mortgage corporation's daily offerings for sale on last day when commitments for such mortgages were received in preceding month, unless otherwise specifically authorized by law. Maximum rate is computed and published by secretary of state monthly in Kansas Register. Rate of interest upon conventional loan is rate quoted in application executed by borrower on day application is made. Notes secured by mortgage or contracts for deed that permit adjustment of interest rate, term or amortization schedule are not subject to interest rate limitation. (16-207[b]).

No penalty may be assessed because of prepayment of home loan evidenced by note secured by mortgage made subject to 16-207 where prepayment is over six months after execution of note. (16-207[c]). Lender may collect actual fees paid government and reasonable expenses incurred. (16-207[d]).

Judgments, including judgments against state or political subdivision, bear interest at 8% until July 1, 1980. Judgments rendered or unpaid thereafter bear interest at 12% until July 1, 1982. Judgments rendered or unpaid thereafter and before July 1, 1986 bear interest at 15%. After July 1, 1986, post-judgment rate will be 4% above federal discount rate as of July 1 preceding date of judgment. (16-204). Where judgment founded on contract specifying different rate, contract rate controls. (16-205).

See note at head of Digest as to 1998 legislation covered.

See Topical Index in front part of this volume.

INTEREST . . . *continued*

Open accounts bear interest from the time when they are liquidated and balance ascertained. (16-201).

Small Loans.—Uniform Consumer Credit Code, 16a-1-101 et seq., applies.

Usury.—Usury statute repealed. (1973, c. 85, §158). Defense of usury not available to corporations. (17-7105).

See also topic Consumer Credit.

LICENSES, BUSINESS AND PROFESSIONAL:

State licenses are required for a large number of businesses and occupations.

Collection Agencies.—No legislation:

MONOPOLIES, RESTRAINT OF TRADE AND COMPETITION:

Trust is defined as combination of capital, skill or acts, by two or more persons, firms, corporations or associations to restrict trade or commerce, fix prices, control costs or rates of insurance, prevent competition or enter into any agreement for these purposes. (50-101). Such combination is unlawful and may not do business in state. (50-105). Corporation party to such combination forfeits charter and may be dissolved by proceedings brought for purpose. (50-103, 4). Contract violating above provisions void. (50-107). Trust agreement placing two or more businesses in hands of trustees to control prices or limit production or sale of commodities is illegal and void. (50-113).

Pooling agreements to divide earnings or fix prices are illegal. (50-136).

Discrimination in prices between different localities (except to equalize freight charges) is illegal and subjects to fine and imprisonment. (50-149).

Fair Trade Act.—See category Intellectual Property, topic Trademarks and Tradenames.

RESTRAINT OF TRADE:

See topic Monopolies, Restraint of Trade and Competition.

SALES:

Uniform Commercial Code (K.S.A. 84-1-101 et seq.) in effect. See topic Commercial Code.

Contracts of Sale.—Uniform Commercial Code governs. (84-2-101 et seq.).

Conditions or Warranties.—Uniform Commercial Code governs. (84-2-301 et seq.).

Product Liability.—Commercial Code defines warranty claims. (84-2-314 through 84-2-318). Alternative B to 2-318 adopted. Kansas Consumer Protection Act abolishes privity in all consumer warranty cases. (50-639[b]). Kansas Product Liability Act governs all product liability claims on issues of useful safe life, regulatory, compliance, duty to warn, product seller's liability. (60-3301 to 60-3307).

Retail Credit Sales.—See topic Consumer Credit.

Transfer of Title.—Uniform Commercial Code governs. (84-2-401 et seq.).

Delivery.—Uniform Commercial Code governs. (84-2-501 et seq.).

Retail Credit Sales.—No special restrictions. See topic Interest.

Bulk Sales.—Uniform Commercial Code governs. (84-6-101 et seq.). See also category Debtor and Creditor, topic Fraudulent Sales and Conveyances.

Sales of Motor Vehicles.—See category Transportation, topic Motor Vehicles.

International Sales of Goods.—See Part VI this volume, Selected International Conventions.

SECURITIES:

The Speculative Securities Act or Blue Sky Law is 17-1252 et seq. Kansas Act is substantial adoption of major provisions of Uniform Securities Act, promulgated by National Conference of Commissioners on Uniform State Laws, but there are numerous differences. Kansas statute is summarized below. For text of Uniform Act, see Uniform and Model Acts section.

Uniform Commercial Code (K.S.A. 84-1-101 et seq.) in effect. See topic Commercial Code.

Supervision.—Securities Commissioner of Kansas, 503 Kansas, Topeka, 66603, (785) 296-3307 has jurisdiction to administer Act. (17-1270).

Regulatory Powers of Supervising Authority.—Commissioner has investigatory powers; may promulgate rules, regulations and forms necessary to carry out provisions of Act; may, under certain circumstances, by order deny, suspend, or revoke any registration of a broker-dealer, investment advisor or agent; and has other discretionary powers necessary to administer Securities Act. (17-1270).

Security means any note; stock; treasury stock; bond; debenture; evidence of indebtedness; certificate of interest or participation in any profit-sharing agreement; collateral-trust certificate; preorganization certificate or subscription; transferable share; investment contract; voting-trust certificate; thrift or investment certificates or thrift notes issued by investment companies; certificate of deposit for a security; certificate of interest in oil and gas royalties, leases or mineral deeds; or, in general, any interest or instrument commonly known as a "security," or any certificate of interest or participation in, temporary or interim certificate for, guarantee of, or warrant or right to subscribe to or purchase, any of foregoing. "Security" does not include any insurance or endowment policy or annuity contract under which an insurance company promises to pay money either in a lump sum or periodically for life or some other specified period. (17-1252).

Exempt Securities.—Act exempts following securities: (1) issued or guaranteed by U.S., any state, territory, insular possession, or political subdivision of such, or by District of Columbia, or any public agency of foregoing; (2) issued or guaranteed by Canada, or province thereof, or political subdivision of such, or any agency of foregoing; or any other foreign government with which U.S. maintains diplomatic relations if security is recognized as valid obligation by issuer; (3) issued by and representing an interest in, debt of, or guarantee by, any federal bank, or any domestic bank, savings institution, credit union or trust company: provided, issuer is subject to banking, savings and loan department, or credit union administrator supervision; (4) issued by and representing an interest in, debt of, or guarantee by, any federal or domestic savings and loan association; (5) issued by and representing an interest in, debt of, or guarantee by, any insurance company authorized to do business in this state when sold by issuer (6) issued or guaranteed by any railroad or public utility which is (a) registered holding company under public utility holding company act, or (b) regulated by governmental authority; (7) any security as to which commissioner finds registration is not necessary or appropriate for protection of investors; (8) issued by any person organized exclusively for religious, educational, benevolent, charitable, fraternal, social, athletic, or reformatory purposes, or as chamber of commerce or trade or professional association; provided, no part of net earnings inure to any private stockholder (issuer must file with commissioner notice setting forth terms of proposed sale and copies of sales and advertising literature used ten days prior to sale); (9) any commercial paper arising out of current transaction and which evidences obligation to pay cash within nine months; (10) any securities issued in connection with employees' stock purchase, savings, pension, profit sharing, or similar plan; (11) issued as patronage or membership dividend by domestic cooperative conducting exclusively agricultural, dairy, livestock or produce business; (12) issue representing interest in, debt of, membership in, or patronage dividend to residents or landowners of not to exceed five contiguous counties in Kansas by cooperative association organized in Kansas exclusively to conduct agricultural, dairy, livestock or produce business, or selling, processing, storing, marketing, retailing, or otherwise handling above products or farm supplies and any incidental activities; (13) issue, which has been heretofore lawfully sold and distributed to public in this and any other state, when offered for resale in good faith, and not to benefit issuer; (14) annuity, gift annuity, charitable remainder unitrust, charitable remainder annuity trust, endowment contract, life income contract, or investment contract issued by governing body of any four year liberal arts college situated in state, except where handled by broker-dealer or agent under 17-1254; (15) any nonprofit corporation or foundation, organized under laws of state, for religious, charitable or educational purposes, or for treatment and rehabilitation of children, which corporation or foundation is licensed, if in existence for more than five years; (16) issued by bank holding company wholly or partially in exchange for capital stock of bank that is or will become subsidiary of said holding company or issued by savings and loan holding company wholly or partially in exchange for capital stock of insured institution that is or will become subsidiary of said holding company. (17-1261).

Cooperatives are exempt from Securities Act. (17-4632).

Exempt Transactions.—Act does not apply to the following transactions: (1) Any isolated transaction, whether effected through a broker-dealer or not; (2) any nonissuer distribution by a registered broker-dealer at reasonable market price, if any recognized securities manual contains issuer's officers, directors, a balance sheet, and a profit and loss statement; (3) any non-issuer transaction by a registered broker-dealer pursuant to an unsolicited offer to buy; (4) any transactions in a bond or other evidence of indebtedness secured by a real or chattel mortgage or deed of trust, or by an agreement for the sale of real estate or chattels, if such are offered and sold as a unit; (5) any transaction by an executor, administrator, sheriff, marshal, receiver, trustee in bankruptcy, guardian, or conservator; or any transaction executed by a bona fide pledgee; (6) any offer or sale to a bank, savings institution, trust, insurance, or investment company, pension or profit-sharing trust, or other financial institution, or to a broker-dealer or underwriter; (7) any offer or sale of a preorganization certificate or subscription if no commission is paid for soliciting any prospective subscriber and no advertising has been published in connection with any such sale, and no payment is made by any subscriber and such certificate or subscription is expressly voidable by subscriber until notification of final acceptance or completion of organization and until securities subscribed for have been registered; commissioner may by rule or order require reports of sales under this exemption; (8) any transaction pursuant to offer to existing security holders of issuer, including persons who at time are holders of convertible securities, nontransferable warrants, or transferable warrants exercisable within 90 days, if (a) no commission or other remuneration (other than standby commission) is paid directly or indirectly for soliciting any security holder in this state, or (b) issuer first files notice specifying terms of offer and commissioner does not disallow exemption within next five business days; (9) any offer (but not sale) of security if registration statements for such security have been filed under both this act and securities act of 1933 if no stop order or refusal order is in effect, or pending or registration statement for such security has been filed under 17-1256 or 1258, no stop order or emergency order issued is in effect and offer made is by registered broker-dealer; (10) issuance of any stock dividend, whether by issuer or not, if nothing of value is given by stockholders for distribution other than surrender of right to cash dividend; (11) transaction involving distribution of securities of issuer to security holders of another person in connection with merger, consolidation, exchange of securities, sales of assets or other reorganizations to which issuer, or its parent or subsidiary, and other person, or its parent or subsidiary, are parties, if: (a) securities to be distributed are registered under Securities Act of 1933 before consummation of transaction, or (b) securities to be distributed are not required to be registered under Securities Act of 1933, written notice of transaction and copy of materials, if any, by which approval of transaction will be solicited is given to commissioner at least ten days before consummation of transaction and commissioner does not disallow, by order, exemption within next ten days; (12) offer or sale by Kansas corporation, limited partnership or limited liability company of its securities to purchaser if aggregate number of sales by corporation in 12-month period ending on date of sale does not exceed 20 sales, if (a) seller believes purchaser is purchasing for investment, (b) no commission nor other remuneration is paid or given, directly or indirectly, for soliciting purchaser, and (c) neither issuer nor any person acting on its behalf offered or sold securities by any form of general solicitation or general advertising. Sales made in violation of Act and sales exempt from registration under exemptions (1) or

SECURITIES . . . *continued*

(12) are counted toward 20 sales limit of this exemption. Corporation, partnership, association, joint-stock company, trust, other unincorporated organization or husband and wife, is considered one purchaser for purposes of this exemption; (13) any transaction pursuant to rule or regulation of securities commissioner for limited offerings; (14) any transaction pursuant to rule or regulation of securities commissioner concerning offer or sale of oil, gas or mining lease; (15) any offer or sale by investment company, defined by 16-630, of its investment certificates; (16) offer or sale of security issued by Kansas Venture Capital, Inc. or its successor. (17-1262).

Oil and Gas.—Any offer or sale of limited partnership interest involving, or any fractional or undivided interest, or any certificate based upon fractional or undivided interest in oil or gas royalty, lease or deed, including subsurface gas storage and payments out of production, where land involved is situated in Kansas is exempt only if: (1) All sales are to persons engaged for two previous years primarily in business of drilling for, producing or refining oil or gas or whose corporate predecessor has been so engaged or in case of corporation in existence less than two years, whose officers and two-thirds of directors have been so engaged; or (2) all sales are to no more than 32 purchasers whether or not Kansas residents, seller reasonably believes all purchases are for investment and not for resale, no commissions are paid for solicitation of sales, and no public solicitation is used; or (3) all sales involve producing property in paying quantities and seller retains no ownership or control. (17-1262a).

Registration of Securities.—Securities not exempt, or not sold in an exempt transaction, cannot be sold unless registered. Intentional violation is severity level 7, nonperson felony. (17-1255).

Registration by notification (17-1256) is repealed.

Registration of federally covered securities is by rules and regulations issued by Commissioner. (17-1270a).

Registration by co-ordination of any security for which registration statement has been filed under Federal Securities Act of 1933 in connection with same offering by filing in office of Commissioner by, any other person on whose behalf securities will be offered or any registered broker-dealer following information: (1) One copy of prospectus filed under Securities Act of 1933 with all amendments; (2) amount of securities to be offered in Kansas; (3) any adverse order, judgment or decree relating to offering made by regulatory authorities in any state or by any court or Securities & Exchange Commission; (4) copy of current articles and by-laws, underwriting agreements, any indenture or other instrument governing security's issuance, and specimen copy of security; (5) payment of registration fee; (6) consent to service of process of nonresident applicant or issuer which will offer security in Kansas through agent or broker-dealer on agency basis; (7) undertaking to forward promptly all amendments to federal registration statement other than those merely delaying effective date. Registration becomes effective at moment federal registration becomes effective if: (1) No stop order by Commissioner or proceeding therefor is in effect or pending; (2) registration statement has been on file ten days; (3) statement of maximum and minimum offering prices and maximum under-writing discounts and commissions has been on file two full business days or such shorter period permitted by Commissioner. Registrant must promptly notify Commissioner by telephone or telegraph of effective date and time of federal registration and content of any federal price amendment and must file post-effective amendment of federal price amendment information and documents. Commissioner may make retroactive stop order without notice or hearing upon failure to receive notification and post-effective amendment if he promptly notifies registrant thereof by telegraph or telephone (confirmed by letter or telegraph). Commissioner may waive prior filing specified in (2) and (3). If federal registration becomes effective prior to compliance and compliance is not waived registration becomes effective when compliance is made. If registrant advises Commissioner of expected effective date of federal registration, Commissioner must promptly advise registrant by telephone or telegraph, at latter's expense, whether all conditions are satisfied and whether stop order is contemplated, but he is not precluded thereby from instituting such proceeding at any time. (17-1257).

Registration by qualification is permitted of any other securities. The statute enumerates fifteen requirements to be filed in applying for registration of such securities. (17-1258).

Registration and License of Dealers.—Act provides "dealer" shall mean "broker." (17-1252).

Registration and License of Brokers, Investment Advisors and Agents.—Broker-dealer means person engaged in purchasing, offering for sale or selling securities for account of others or his own account; but not including bank, agent, issuer, savings institution, insurance company or one effecting transactions exclusively with issuer or person to whom sale is exempt. Investment advisor means person who, for compensation, advises others, directly or through publications or writings, as to value of securities or advisability of investing in, purchasing or selling securities or who issues or promulgates analyses or reports concerning securities; but not including: (1) Investment advisor representative; (2) bank, savings and loan association, credit union or trust company; (3) lawyer, accountant, engineer, or teacher whose performance of services is incidental to practice of profession; (4) broker-dealer whose performance of services is incidental to conduct of business as broker-dealer and who receives no special compensation; (5) publisher of bona fide newspaper, news magazine or business or financial publication of general, regular and paid circulation; (6) federal covered advisor; or (7) other persons not within intent of rule as determined by commissioner. Agent means one who represents broker-dealer or issuer. Investment advisor representative means partner, officer, director or similar person employed by or associated with investment advisor who (1) recommends or advises regarding securities, (2) manages accounts or portfolios, (3) determines recommendations or advice to be given, (4) solicits, offers or negotiates for sale or sells investment advisory services, (5) supervises employees performing above acts; or, (6) federal covered advisor. Federal covered advisor is person registered or excluded under federal acts. (17-1252).

Broker-dealer, investment advisor, investment advisor representative, or agent must be registered or licensed. (17-1254). Federal covered advisor must file federal documents and consent to service of process.

Loan Brokers.—Any person who, for fee, promises to procure loan, assist in procuring loan from third party, or to consider making loan himself must register with Securities Commissioner. Act does not apply to financial institutions regulated by U.S. or other state agencies, insurance companies, or any person arranging financing of sale of his own product. (50-1001 et seq.).

Fees.—Broker-dealer, investment advisor, federal covered advisor—original or renewal registration is $300. Agent or investment advisor representative—original or renewal is $50. (17-1254[1]).

Nonresident issuer or registrant must file irrevocable consent that suit or action growing out of any violation of act may be commenced in any county in which cause of action arose or in which plaintiff resides by service of process or Secretary of State. (17-1263).

Bonds.—Registrants must post bonds and maintain minimum capital requirements as required by Commissioner. (17-1254[h][i]).

Liabilities.—No action will lie to enforce any contract for sale made in violation of Act. Person making offer or sale or contract for sale, and every director, officer or agent of or for seller who shall have participated or aided in any way in making sale, is jointly and severally liable to purchaser for the full amount paid by him (upon tender to seller of the securities sold or of contract made less any income from the securities or contract) together with interest at 15% per annum from date of purchase, court costs and reasonable attorneys' fees. (17-1268).

Uniform Simplification of Fiduciary Security Transfers Act adopted. (17-4903-4913). Uniform Commercial Code (K.S.A. 84-1-101 et seq.) specifically provides that it does not repeal this uniform act and if any inconsistency between two, provisions of Simplification of Fiduciary Security Transfers Act control. (84-10-101[2]).

Uniform Trustees' Powers Act adopted. (58–1201 et seq.).

Uniform Securities Ownership by Minors Act not adopted.

WAREHOUSEMEN:

Uniform Commercial Code (K.S.A. 84-1-101 et seq.) in effect. See topic Commercial Code. Grain warehousemen regulated by S. 34-228 et seq.

Bond is required in the sum of not less than $5,000, or more than $50,000. (82-165).

License must be procured from the Secretary of State. Fee $25. (82-163). Expires on July 1st following date of issuance if issued before July 1, 1984, otherwise expires Dec. 31 following date of issuance. (82-164).

CITIZENSHIP

ALIENS:

Property.—Aliens eligible to citizenship may transmit and inherit realty as citizens. Other aliens may transmit and inherit realty only in manner and to extent prescribed by treaty between U. S. and alien's country. When alien heir or devisee cannot take real estate, district court must order its sale and proceeds must be distributed to such alien. (59-511, 59-512).

If an alien heir has conveyed for a valuable consideration and the land has been held without claim by the state for 25 years, the right to escheat is deemed barred. (58-2238).

CIVIL ACTIONS AND PROCEDURE

ACCORD AND SATISFACTION:

The agreement that a smaller sum shall be accepted in discharge of a larger one originally claimed must have been entered into by the parties understandingly and with unity of purpose. (214 Kan. 769, 522 P.2d 959).

Pleading.—An accord and satisfaction must be pleaded. (60-208).

See also category Business Regulation and Commerce, topic Commercial Code.

ACTIONS:

Federal Rules of Civil Procedure form the basis for procedural statutes, with few minor variations. (60-101 et seq.). For rules applying to specific actions, see topics Pleading and Practice.

Equity.—No distinction in form between legal and equitable remedies. (60-202).

Forms of Action.—One form of action known as "civil action". (60-202).

Conditions Precedent.—

Claims Against Municipality.—Written notice of claim must be submitted to municipality and denied before action may be brought against municipality. (12-105b).

Punitive Damages.—See topics Damages, subhead Punitive Damages; Pleading, subhead Punitive Damages.

Commencement.—See topics Process, Pleading.

Parties.—Action must be prosecuted in name of real party in interest, but fiduciary may bring suit on behalf of another without joining that person. (60-207[a]). Representative may sue or defend on behalf of minor or incapacitated person. (60-217[a]).

Claim accruing under law of another state may be sued upon in Kansas by person authorized to bring or maintain action in state where claim arose. (60-217[b]).

Class Actions.—May be brought if: (1) Class so numerous that joinder of all members is impractical; (2) common questions of law or fact; (3) claims or defenses of representative parties are typical of class; and (4) representative parties will adequately protect interest of class. (60-223[a]). Additionally, (1) separate actions must create risk

ACTIONS . . . *continued*
of inconsistent judgments or practically dispose of claims of class members who are not parties; (2) final injunctive or declaratory relief must be appropriate to class as whole; or (3) common questions predominate over individual questions and class action is superior method of adjudication. (60-223[b]).

Court determines whether class action is maintainable. (60-223[c][1]). Judgment binds all class members except those opting out. Reasonable notice must be given to class. (60-223[c][2] and [3]). Court must approve dismissal or compromise. (60-223[e]).

Uniform Class Actions Act not adopted.

Intervention.—Anyone may intervene of right when: (1) Statute gives right to intervene or (2) applicant claims interest in property or transaction which is subject of action and disposition might affect his interest, unless interest is adequately represented by existing parties. (60-224[a]). Anyone may intervene with permission of court when: (1) Statute gives conditional right to intervene or (2) applicant's claim or defense has question of law or fact in common with main action. (60-224[b]).

Interpleader.—When plaintiff may be exposed to multiple liability, persons having claims against him may be joined as defendants. Defendant may obtain interpleader by crossclaim or counterclaim. (60-222[a]). Defendant may deposit money or property subject to multiple claims in court with notice to possible claimants. (60-222[b]).

Third Party Practice.—Defendant may issue third party summons and petition against person who is or may be liable to him for all or part of plaintiff's claim. (60-214).

Joinder of Causes of Action.—Party may join as many claims as he has against opposing party. (60-218[a]).

Splitting Causes of Action.—All grounds or theories upon which cause of action is founded must be asserted in one action or they will be barred in any subsequent action. (216 Kan. 138, 531 P.2d 435).

Consolidation of Actions.—Court may consolidate actions involving common questions of law or fact. (60-242[a]).

Severance of Actions.—Court may order separate trial of separate claims or issues for convenience, to avoid prejudice, or for judicial economy. (60-242[b]).

Stay of Proceedings.—No special provision for stay before judgment while action is pending.

Abatement and Revival.—In addition to the causes of action which survive at common law, causes of action for mesne profits, or for injury to the person, or to real or personal estate, or for any deceit or fraud, or for death by wrongful act or omission, also survive; and the action may be brought notwithstanding the death of the person entitled or liable for same. (60-1801). No action pending abates by the death of either or both the parties thereto, except an action for libel, slander, malicious prosecution, or for a nuisance. (60-1802). If a party dies and the claim is not thereby extinguished, the court must on motion by any party or by successors or representatives of the deceased party order substitution of the proper parties. If such motion is not made within a reasonable time, action must be dismissed as to the deceased party. If a party dies in an action in which the right sought to be enforced survives only to the surviving plaintiffs or against the surviving defendants, the action does not abate and the action proceeds in favor of or against the surviving parties. In case of any transfer of interest, the action may be continued by or against original party, unless court directs transferee to be substituted in the action or joined with the original party. (60-225).

Limitation of.—See topic Limitation of Actions.

Small Claims.—See category Courts and Legislature, topic Courts.

Termination of Actions.—Action may terminate by judgment (60-254); by stipulation or voluntary dismissal (with or without prejudice) (60-241[a]); by court sua sponte or on defendant's motion for lack of prosecution (60-241[a][2], [b]).

Prohibited Actions.—No statutory prohibitions.

Direct Actions Against Insurer.—See category Transportation, topic Motor Vehicles, subhead Direct Actions.

APPEAL AND ERROR:

From Administrative Agency.—All appeals are to district court unless otherwise specifically provided by statute for particular agency. Must exhaust all administrative remedies before petitioning for district court review. Petition for review may be filed by person directly affected by administrative proceedings or by party to administrative proceedings. Reconsideration not mandatory unless statutorily prerequisite for seeking judicial review. If reconsideration not requested and not prerequisite to judicial review, petition shall be filed within 30 days of administrative order. If reconsideration requested, petition for judicial review shall be filed within 30 days of service of order rendered upon reconsideration, unless further reconsideration required by 66-1186; within 30 days of order denying reconsideration; or in KCC proceeding within 30 days of date request for reconsideration is deemed denied. 30-day time does not run while administrative remedies are pursued. (77-612, 613).

Stay of Proceedings.—Agency may grant stay on appropriate terms or other temporary remedies during pendency of judicial review. (77-613).

From District Magistrate Judge.—All appeals are to district judge. Taken by notice of appeal specifying order, ruling, decision or judgment complained of and filed in district court from which appeal is taken within ten days from date of order, ruling, decision or judgment. (60-2103a).

Appeal Bond.—Security for costs must be given with notice of appeal, amount to be determined by court. (60-2103).

Stay of Proceedings.—Taking of an appeal does not stay proceedings for enforcement of final judgment unless party appealing gives bond in amount to satisfy judgment, costs, interest and damages for delay. (60-262, 61-2105).

Character of Hearing.—There is a trial de novo on appeal, except where record made in civil cases appeal tried and determined on record. (20-302b[c]).

Judgment or Order on Appeal.—Case is determined by district judge same as if originally set with that judge, except that in civil cases where record was made of original proceeding, appeal shall be determined on record. (20-302b[c]).

From District Courts.—Court of Appeals hears appeals from decisions of district judge, except where direct appeal to Supreme Court required by law. (22-3601, 60-2102). Court of Appeals may transfer appeal to Supreme Court when: it lacks jurisdiction; subject matter has significant public interest; case involves significant legal questions; or caseload is burdensome. (20-3016). Court of Appeals has jurisdiction to correct, modify, vacate or reverse any act, order or judgment of district court in order to assure that, any such act, order or judgment is just, legal and free of abuse. (60-2101[a]). Appellate jurisdiction of Court of Appeals may be invoked by appeal as matter of right from: (1) Order that discharges, vacates or modifies provisional remedy; (2) order that grants, continues, modifies, refuses or dissolves injunction, or order that grants or refuses relief in form of mandamus, quo warranto or habeas corpus; (3) order that appoints receiver, or refuses to wind up receivership or to take steps to accomplish purposes thereof; (4) final decision in any action, except in action where direct appeal to Supreme Court is required by law. Appellate jurisdiction may also be invoked where district court certifies, on order not otherwise appealable, that there is involved controlling question of law involving substantial ground for difference of opinion and immediate appeal may materially advance ultimate end of litigation. (60-2102).

Supreme Court has exclusive appellate jurisdiction of district court decisions declaring federal or state law unconstitutional. (60-2101[b], 22-3601, 22-3602). In cases appealed originally to Court of Appeals, Supreme Court may accept or reject transfer before final decision of Court of Appeals (20-3016) and after decision by Court of Appeals may accept petition for review considering following factors: (1) General importance of question; (2) existence of conflict between decision and prior law; (3) need for exercising Supreme Court supervisory authority; (4) final or interlocutory character of judgment, order or ruling sought to be reviewed. (20-3018[b]).

Appeal Bond.—Security for costs on appeal must be given in such sum and manner as may be prescribed by general rule of Supreme Court unless court makes different order applicable to particular case. (60-2103).

Stay of Proceedings.—Stay granted in district court's discretion upon presentment of supersedeas bond conditioned for satisfaction of judgment costs, interest and damages for delay. (60-262, 60-2103, 61-2105). Court of Appeals may stay pending appeal. (20-3001).

Time for Appeal.—Appeal to Court of Appeals taken within 30 days of entry by district court except, where state or officer or agency is party, time is 60 days from entry (possible extension of up to 30 days on grounds of excusable neglect). (60-2103). Petition for review from Court of Appeals to Supreme Court filed within 30 days of decision. (20-3018). Record on appeal must contain such matters and be prepared in such manner and form, as prescribed by rules of Supreme Court. (60-2104).

BONDS:

Bonds are required in a great variety of cases.

Enforcement.—Procedure varies with type of bond.

Surety Company Bonds.—Whenever a bond or undertaking conditioned for the faithful performance of any contract of duty, or for the doing or refraining from doing of anything in such bond or undertaking specified, is by the law of the State of Kansas required to be given with one surety or with two or more sureties, the execution of the same is sufficient when executed or guaranteed solely by a corporation incorporated under the laws of the United States or of any state, having power to guarantee the fidelity of persons holding positions of public or private trust and to execute and guarantee bonds and undertakings in judicial proceedings. Such corporation must be authorized to do business in the state, and the bond must be approved by the head of the department, court judge, officer, board of directors or body executive, legislative or judicial, required to approve the same. (78-102).

It is no defense on such a bond that false statements or representations were made in the application therefor by the person or party named as principal therein or giving the same. (78-102).

As to venue of action on bond, see topic Venue.

CERTIORARI:

The writ of certiorari was abolished in 1868.

CHARITABLE IMMUNITY:

See topic Damages.

COSTS:

Unless otherwise provided by statute, or by order of court, costs must be allowed to successful party. Court has discretion to award alternative dispute resolution fees. (60-2002).

Docket fee for district courts in sum of $66.50 must be paid by plaintiff before case can be filed or docketed unless plaintiff files affidavit that claim is just and he is unable to pay costs. Secretary of Corrections authorized to disburse money from inmates trust fund to satisfy costs determined by court. (60-2001). Fee for cases filed under Code of Civil Procedure for limited actions is $19.50 if amount in controversy is under $500; $39.50 if amount in controversy exceeds $500 but does not exceed $5,000; $64.50 if amount in controversy exceeds $5,000. (61-2501).

DAMAGES:

Common law generally prevails. Numerous statutes allowing punitive damages, penalties, trebling or doubling of damages, are discussed under topics relating to substantive provisions.

Collateral Source Rule.—Evidence of collateral source benefits admissible in any action for personal injury or death accruing on or after July 1, 1988, if claimant states

See note at head of Digest as to 1998 legislation covered.

See Topical Index in front part of this volume.

DAMAGES . . . *continued*
claim for more than $150,000. Exceptions are proceeds from life or disability insurance and any source where there is lien or subrogation interest. Trier of fact determines collateral benefits received and reasonably expected in future. Court reduces judgment by amount of collateral benefits less cost of those benefits, with some exceptions. (60-3403).

Medical Malpractice.—$1,000,000 cap for all claims against all defendants in actions accruing between July 1, 1986 and June 20, 1988, unconstitutional. (60-3407; 243 Kan. 333, 757 P.2d 251 [1988]).

Noneconomic Loss.—For medical malpractice actions accruing on or after July 1, 1986, and for all personal injury or wrongful death actions accruing on or after July 1, 1987, each party limited to $250,000. (60-3407, 60-19a01). Cap on noneconomic loss upheld. (244 Kan. 726, 771 P.2d 71 [1989]).

Punitive Damages.—Trier of fact determines whether to allow. Court in separate proceeding determines amount. Plaintiff must prove by clear and convincing evidence that defendant acted with willful conduct, wanton conduct, fraud or malice. Limited to lesser of $5,000,000 or defendant's highest gross annual income during five years before wrongful act, except court may award 1.5 times amount of profit defendant earned or will earn from wrongful act. Applies to all civil causes of action accruing on or after July 1, 1988, and all nonmedical malpractice causes of action accruing on or after July 1, 1987. (60-3701, et seq.).

In medical malpractice actions accruing between July 1, 1985 and June 30, 1988, punitives may not exceed lesser of $3,000,000 or 25% of defendant's highest annual gross income during five years before wrongful act. (60-3401, 3402). One-half punitive damages collected paid to health care stabilization fund and one-half to plaintiff. (60-3402[e]).

Person or entity may purchase insurance covering vicarious liability for punitive damages payable when insured lacks actual prior knowledge of tortfeasor's acts or omissions. (40-2,115). See also categories Employment, topic Labor Relations; Estates and Trusts, topic Death, subhead Action for Death; Mortgages, topics Chattel Mortgages, Mortgages of Real Property; Transportation, topic Motor Vehicles, subhead No-Fault Insurance.

Comparative Negligence Rule adopted. Joint and several liability abolished. (60-258a, 258b).

Charitable Immunity.—Abrogated. (175 Kan. 751, 267 P.2d 934).

Sovereign Immunity.—Kansas Tort Claims Act (75-6101 et seq.) imposes liability on "governmental entity", including state, any political subdivision, and any agency, authority or institution thereof, for damages caused by negligent or wrongful act or omission of government employee acting within scope of employment if private person would be liable. (75-6102, 75-6013). Members of municipal governing bodies and municipal appointive boards are immune unless they act with actual fraud or malice. (75-6119). Act not applicable to claims arising from negligence of health care provider other than charitable health care provider; municipally owned hospital and its employees; local health department; indigent health care clinic or district coroner. (75-6115[a]). Claims for damages against health care provider other than in (a) recovered same as against private health care provider. (75-6115).

Government entity and employees are immune for damages resulting from: (1) Legislative functions; (2) judicial functions; (3) enforcement of or failure to enforce law; (4) any discretionary function; and (5) assessment or collection of taxes. See statute for other exceptions. (75-6104).

Damages arising from single event limited to $500,000 unless greater amount of insurance purchased. (75-6105, 75-6111). Governmental entity not liable for punitive damages or prejudgment interest. Employee acting within scope of employment not liable for punitives or prejudgment interest unless actual fraud or malice. (75-6105[c]).

See also topic Practice, subhead Claims Against Government.

No-Fault Insurance.—See category Transportation, topic Motor Vehicles, subhead No-Fault Insurance.

Itemized Verdicts.—Trier of fact must itemize verdict in all personal injury actions, including medical malpractice and wrongful death. Except for wrongful death, verdict must show amount awarded for: (1) Noneconomic losses including pain and suffering, disability, disfigurement and accompanying mental anguish; (2) reasonable expenses of necessary medical and hospital care; and (3) other economic injuries. (60-249a, 60-19a02). Wrongful death verdicts must show amounts awarded for: (1) Nonpecuniary damages; (2) expenses for care of deceased; and (3) other pecuniary damages. In all personal injury actions, amount awarded must be itemized to reflect current and future damages. Court may instruct jury only on items of damages for which there is evidence on which to base award. (60-1903).

Hazardous Waste Cleanup.—See category Environment, topic Environmental Regulation, subhead Hazardous Waste Cleanup.

DEPOSITIONS AND DISCOVERY:

Federal Rules of Civil Procedure generally followed. (60-226 to 60-237). See topic Practice. Parties by stipulation of court upon motion may order that deposition be taken by telephone. Stenographic record shall be made while deposition being taken. Deposition may be videotaped by giving notice. (60-230[b]).

Uniform Foreign Depositions Act not adopted.

Within State for Use Within State.—Federal Rules 26 to 32 generally followed.

Within State for Use Elsewhere.—District court in county where deponent resides or is employed or transacts his business in person may, upon ex parte petition, order issuance of subpoena in aid of taking of deposition and may make any order in accordance with 60-230(d), 60-237(a) or 60-237(b), 60-228(d).

Outside of State for Use Within State.—Within U.S. must be taken before official authorized to administer oaths by law of place where examination held or before person appointed by court in which action is pending. (60-228[a]). In foreign countries may be taken: (1) Pursuant to treaty or convention; (2) pursuant to letter request; (3) on notice before person authorized to administer oaths in place where examination is held, either by U.S. or local law, or (4) before person appointed by commission. (60-228[b]).

De Bene Esse.—Rule 27 followed with variations based on Uniform Perpetuation of Testimony Act, particularly regarding wills. (60-227). Deposition taken under similar procedure of another jurisdiction admissible in Kansas to same extent as deposition taken under Kansas law. (60-227[f]).

Perpetuation of Testimony.—Court may act on equitable considerations. (60-227[d]). See also subhead De Bene Esse, supra.

Before Whom Taken.—Depositions may be taken in this state before any officer or person authorized to administer oaths. (60-228). See also this topic, various subheads.

Commissions.—Any court of record in Kansas before which action is pending may grant commission to take depositions within or without Kansas. (60-228[a]).

Compelling Attendance of Witnesses.—Subpoena compelling attendance at trial or hearing issues from district where proceeding is held. Deposition subpoena issues where deposition taken. Clerk may issue blank subpoena on request. (60-245[a]). Each subpoena must set forth statutory requirements for protection of persons subject to subpoena with provision for timely motion to quash or modify subpoena. (60-245[c]). Complicated procedure added for subpoena of records of business not party. (60-245[a]).

Examination of Witnesses.—Rule 30(c) followed. Reference to Federal Rules of Evidence replaced with reference to 60-243. (60-230[c]).

Review by Witness.—Unless waived, deponent has 30 days after receiving notice to obtain, review and correct transcript. (60-230[3]).

Form.—Officer administering must certify on deposition that witness was duly sworn by officer and that deposition is true record of testimony given by witness. (60-230[f]).

Discovery.—Modified Rule 26(b) followed. (60-226[b]).

Demand for Admission of Facts.—Rule 36 followed. (60-236). Court may hold case management conference and order disclosures of witnesses and evidence. (60-216[b]).

Interrogatories.—Rule 33 followed.

EVIDENCE:

Witnesses.—A person is disqualified as a witness if he is incapable of expressing himself concerning the matter so as to be understood by the judge and jury either directly or through interpretation by one who can understand him, or is incapable of understanding the duty of a witness to tell the truth. (60-417).

Privileged Communications.—Lawyer-client (60-426); physician-patient (60-427); penitential communications (60-429).

Husband and Wife.—Communications are privileged except: In an action by one spouse against the other; in an action for damages for alienation of affection of the other; for criminal conversation with the other; in a criminal action in which one of them is charged with a crime against the person or property of the other or of a child of either; a crime against the person or property of a third person committed in the course of committing a crime against the other; bigamy or adultery; desertion of the other or of a child of either; in a criminal action in which the accused offers evidence of a communication between him and his spouse; or if the judge finds that sufficient evidence, aside from the communication, has been introduced to warrant a finding that the communication was made, in whole or in part, to enable or aid anyone to commit or to plan to commit a crime or a tort. The privilege terminates if the judge finds that the spouse while the holder of the privilege testified or caused another to testify in any action to any communication between the spouses upon the same subject matter. (60-428).

Communications or Transactions with Persons Since Deceased or Incompetent.—No special provision. See 60-460(e) for hearsay exception for dying declarations.

Self Incrimination.—Every natural person has a privilege to refuse to disclose in an action or to a public official of this state or the United States or any other state or any governmental agency or division thereof any matter that will incriminate him. (60-425).

Compelling Attendance.—See topic Depositions and Discovery.

Medical Malpractice.—To qualify as expert witness on standard of care given by defendant, must have devoted at least 50% of professional time in two years before incident to actual clinical practice in same profession in which defendant is licensed. (60-3412).

INJUNCTIONS:

May be the final judgment in the action, and may also be allowed as a provisional remedy. (60-901).

Prerequisites and Procedure.—Party demanding relief must file affidavit or verified pleading showing that relief demanded consists in restraining the actual or threatened commission or continuance of some act which would produce injury to a party, violate a party's rights respecting the subject of the action, or which would render the judgment ineffective. (60-902). Restraining order may issue without notice or bond, except on issue growing out of labor dispute (60-904) or if it appears that order may result in damages. Application for restraining order shall also be considered as application for temporary injunction and either party may give notice of hearing thereon. (60-903).

Temporary Injunction.—Reasonable notice and an opportunity to be heard must be granted the party to be enjoined. (60-905).

Bond.—No temporary injunction may operate unless the party obtaining same gives bond in an amount fixed by the court, securing to the party injured the damages he may sustain, including attorney fees, if it be finally determined that the injunction should not have been granted. (60-905).

See note at head of Digest as to 1998 legislation covered.

See Topical Index in front part of this volume.

INJUNCTIONS . . . *continued*

Form and Scope.—Every order granting an injunction and every restraining order must set forth the reasons for its issuance; must be specific in terms; must describe in reasonable detail act or acts sought to be restrained; and is binding only upon the parties to the action, their officers, agents, servants, employees, and attorneys, and upon those persons in concert with them who receive actual notice of the order. (60-906).

JUDGMENTS:

A judgment is a final determination of rights of parties in an action. Partial judgment for fewer than all claims or parties may be directed. Before default judgment is taken where money damages exceed $75,000, party seeking relief must notify other party by certified mail at least ten days prior to date judgment is sought. (60-254). Federal Rules of Civil Procedure form basis for procedural statutes. (60-254 et seq.). See topic Practice.

Judgments by Confession.—Void in consumer credit transactions. (16a-3-306).

Judgments on Pleadings.—Federal rule 12(c) followed. (60-212[c]).

Summary Judgments.—Federal rule 56 followed. (60-256).

Declaratory Judgments.—Authorized. (60-1701 et seq.).

Default Judgments.—Federal rule 55 followed. (60-255). Default judgment rendered on service by publication may be reopened within two years. (60-309).

Satisfaction.—Judgment creditor or his assignee must file satisfaction and release of judgment within 20 days after demand therefor. (60-2803).

Form

IN THE ____(number)____ JUDICIAL DISTRICT, DISTRICT COURT,
________ COUNTY, KANSAS
________, Plaintiff.

v. Case No. ________

________, Defendant.

SATISFACTION OF JUDGMENT

The judgment in this case has been paid and satisfied and same is hereby fully released as to ________.
Done this ____ day of ________, 19 ____.

(attorney's signature)

____
Attorney for ________

Liens.—Any judgment rendered in Kansas by district court under c. 60 or U.S. court becomes lien on debtor's real estate in county where judgment rendered. Effective date of lien limited to shorter of four months before entry of judgment or date petition was filed. Attested copy of judgment together with statement of costs may be filed with clerk of court of any other county and judgment will become lien on real estate in that county from date copy is filed. (60-2202[a]). Fee if execution can be issued is $15, otherwise $5. Judgments in c. 61 limited actions do not become liens until creditor pays filing fee and clerk enters judgment on appearance docket. (60-2202[b]). Support order from another state creates lien when order is filed on this state's appearance docket. (60-2202[d]).

Revival of Judgment.—Judgment becomes lien against debtor's real property in county from date judgment revived. (60-2418[a]).

Revival.—Dormant judgment may be revived if, within two years of date on which such judgment became dormant, holder thereof files a motion and gives notice for revivor and requests the immediate issuance of an execution thereof if such motion is granted. If motion for revival filed within two years after judgment became dormant, court shall order revival and execution shall follow. In child support cases if motion for revival filed prior to child's emancipation, within two years of emancipation, or within two years after judgment became dormant, court shall order revival and execution shall follow. A judgment may also be revived by filing of a written stipulation of revivor signed by all the parties affected thereby. (60-2404). See category Debtor and Creditor, topic Executions.

Uniform Enforcement of Foreign Judgments Act in effect. (60-3001 et seq.).

LIMITATION OF ACTIONS:

Uniform Commercial Code (K.S.A. 84-1-101 et seq.) in effect. See category Business Regulation and Commerce, topic Commercial Code.

Actions must be commenced within the following periods after the respective causes of action accrue (60-501 et seq.):

Fifteen Years.—No action can be maintained for recovery of real property or for the determination of any adverse claim or interest therein after 15 years. (60-503). See category Property, topic Adverse Possession.

Five Years.—An action upon any agreement, contract or promise in writing; an action brought on any covenant of seizin contained in any deed of conveyance of land; any action brought on a covenant of warranty contained in any deed of conveyance of land, after there shall have been a final decision against the title of the covenantor in such deed; an action upon the official bond or undertaking of an executor, administrator, guardian, sheriff, or any other officer, or upon the bond or undertaking given in attachment, injunction, arrest, or in any case required by statute. (60-511). An action for recovery of real property by the execution debtor, his heirs, or any person claiming under him by title acquired after the date of judgment, from the date of the recording of the deed made in pursuance of the sale. (60-504). An action for recovery of real property sold by executors, administrators or guardians, upon an order or judgment of a court directing such sale, brought by the heirs or devisees of the deceased person, or the ward or his guardian, or any person claiming under any of them by after-acquired title, from the date of the recording of the deed made in pursuance of the sale. (60-505).

Four Years.—Action for breach of any contract for sale must be commenced within four years after cause of action has accrued, and by original agreement parties may reduce period of limitation to not less than one year but may not extend it. (84-2-725).

Three Years.—All actions upon contracts, obligations, or liabilities expressed or implied but not in writing; an action upon a liability created by a statute other than a penalty or forfeiture. (60-512).

Two Years.—Forcible entry and detention, or for forcible detention only. (60-506). An action for trespass upon real property; an action for taking, detaining or injuring personal property, including actions for specific recovery thereof; an action for relief on ground of fraud, but cause of action is not deemed to have accrued until fraud is discovered; an action for injury to rights of another, not arising on contract, and not herein enumerated; an action for wrongful death; action for malpractice against health care provider. Cause of action in this section is not deemed to have accrued until act giving rise to cause of action first causes substantial injury, or, if fact of injury is not reasonably ascertainable until some time after initial act, then period of limitation does not commence until fact of injury becomes reasonably ascertainable to injured party, but in no event may action be commenced more than ten years beyond time of act giving rise to cause of action. (60-513). Action against health care provider accrues at time of act giving rise to cause of action, unless injury not reasonably ascertainable at time of act, but in no event shall action be commenced more than four years from time of act. (60-513[c]). Negligence cause of action by corporation against officer or director does not accrue until substantial ascertainable injury but in no event more than five years from time of act. All other causes of action by corporation against officer or director do not accrue until substantial ascertainable injury and non-culpable directors are majority but in no event more than ten years from time of act. (60-513[d]).

One Year.—An action for libel or slander; for assault, battery, malicious prosecution, or false imprisonment; an action upon a statutory penalty or forfeiture. (60-514).

Six Months.—No action brought nor levy made more than six months after date on which bulk transferee took possession of goods unless transfer has been concealed, in which event date of discovery controls. (84-6-111).

Foreign Causes of Action.—Where a cause of action has arisen in another state or country in which such action cannot be maintained by reason of lapse of time, no action can be maintained thereon in this state except in favor of one who is a resident of this state and who has held cause of action from time it accrued. (60-516).

Legal Disabilities.—If any person entitled to bring an action, other than for the recovery of real property or a penalty or a forfeiture, at the time the cause of action accrued, or at any time during the period the statute of limitations is running, is under 18, or incapacitated, or imprisoned for a term less than his natural life, such person may bring an action within one year after such disability is removed. No such action can be maintained after eight years from time of act giving rise to cause of action. If the person dies during the continuance of any disability so specified and no determination is had of the title, claim, interest, or action to him accrued, any person entitled to claim from, by or under him, may commence such action within one year after his death, but in no event more than eight years after act giving rise to cause of action. Notwithstanding foregoing, person imprisoned for any term having access to court to bring action is not under legal disability. (60-515).

Absence of Concealment of Defendant.—If a cause of action accrues against a person who is out of the state, or has absconded or concealed himself, the limitation period does not begin to run until he comes into the state or while he is so absconded or concealed. If after the cause of action accrues he departs from the state, or absconds or conceals himself, the time of his absence or concealment is not computed as any part of the period within which the action must be brought. This does not extend the period of limitation as to any defendant whose whereabouts are known and upon whom service of summons can be effected. (60-517).

Interruption of Statutory Period.—In any contract case, when any part of the principal or interest has been paid, or an acknowledgment of an existing liability, debt or claim, or any promise to pay same, has been made, an action may be brought within the period prescribed for the same, after such payment, acknowledgment or promise; but such acknowledgment or promise must be in writing, signed by the party to be charged thereby. (60-520).

New Action.—If the plaintiff fails in any action commenced within due time otherwise than upon the merits, and the time limited for the same has expired, the plaintiff, or if he dies, and the cause of action survives, his representatives, may commence a new action within six months after such failure. (60-518).

PARTITION:

When the object of the action is to effect a partition of personal or real property or an estate or interest created by an oil, gas or mineral lease or an oil or gas royalty, the petition must describe the property and, with reasonable certainty, the respective interest of the owners thereof. Persons claiming a specific or general lien upon all or any portion of the property may be made parties. Allegation of ownership of an interest implies an allegation of right to possession, and it is not necessary to claim the remedy of ejectment. (60-1003).

Venue.—Action must be brought in county in which real estate situated, except if it be an entire tract situated in two or more counties and there is common ownership, the action may be brought in any county in which a part thereof is situated. (60-601).

Proceedings.—Upon all interests being determined and partition ordered, the court appoints three commissioners to partition the property among the parties according to their respective interests, but if such cannot be done without manifest injury, or is impracticable, the commissioners appraise the value of the property. Where the property is not subject to partition in kind, any one or more of the parties may elect to take the property or any separate tract at the appraised value, but if none of the parties elect to so take, or two or more so elect to take, in opposition to each other, the court must order a sheriff's sale in the manner provided for sale of property on execution, at not less than two-thirds valuation. (60-1003).

See note at head of Digest as to 1998 legislation covered.

See Topical Index in front part of this volume.

KS – 12

PARTITION . . . *continued*

Costs and Fees.—The court must tax the costs, attorney fees and expenses, including an allowance for bringing up to date an abstract of title or title insurance, and apportion same among the parties according to their respective interests. (60-1003).

PLEADING:

Federal Rules of Civil Procedure form basis for procedural statutes. (60-201 et seq., 61-1601 et seq.). See topics Actions and Practice.

Pleadings Permitted.—Federal Rule 7 followed except provision added for substituting lost, destroyed or withheld pleadings. (60-207).

Complaint.—Rule 8 followed except no need for jurisdictional statement and, except in contract, no need to specify exact amount of damages in excess of $75,000. (60-208[a]).

Answer.—Rule 8 followed. (60-208).

Counterclaim or Set-Off.—Rule 13 followed except new subsection (d) substituted on effect of death or statute of limitations. (60-213).

Reply.—Rule 12 followed except subsection (a) makes specific provision for time to respond to service by mail or publication and new subsection (i) allows answer for minor or incapacitated person. (60-212).

Demurrer.—Abolished. (60-207[c]). Substitute is Rule 12(b) defenses. (60-212[b]).

Amended or Supplemental Pleadings.—Rule 15 followed. (60-215).

Affidavits of Merits.—Not required. (60-211).

Affidavits of Defense.—Not required. (60-211).

Bills of Particulars.—Rule 12(e) followed. (60-212[e]). May be demanded in divorce actions, but will not become part of record except on appeal. (60-1604[d]).

Verification.—Not required (60-211) except for motions to vacate or modify injunction after final judgment (60-1001[b]), restraining orders (60-902), divorce actions (60-1604 et seq.), and where otherwise specifically required.

Service.—Rule 5(b) followed. (60-205[b]). Service by telefacsimile permitted. However other methods may be authorized by substantive law. (60-205).

Filings.—Rule 5(e) followed. (60-205[e]).

Time.—Federal Rules followed.

Proof of Claims.—

Sister States.—Revised Uniform Enforcement of Foreign Judgments Act adopted. (60-3001 et seq.). No material variations, except §3(c) not adopted. §5 docket fee is $55.

Foreign Countries.—No statute or case law on enforcement of judgments. Kansas has acceded to Hague Convention Abolishing the Requirement of Legalisation for Foreign Public Documents. (See Part VI, Selected International Conventions.) (53-401).

Punitive Damages.—No tort claim for punitives may be included in petition or other pleading without permission of court. Court may allow filing of amended petition seeking punitives on motion and on basis of supporting and opposing affidavits establishing probability that plaintiff will prevail. Motion must be filed before pretrial conference. (60-3703). See topic Damages, subhead Punitive Damages.

Small Claims.—See category Courts and Legislature, topic Courts.

PRACTICE:

Federal Rules of Civil Procedure form basis for procedure in civil matters.

Chapter 60 Actions.—Rules of procedure (60-201 et seq.) are identical except for minor variations. Apply to all civil actions not brought under 61-1601 et seq.

Verdicts.—Agreement of ten of 12 jurors sufficient to render verdict. Parties may stipulate that fewer jurors be used. In cases using less than 12 jurors, verdict must be unanimous unless parties have stipulated otherwise. (60-248).

Chapter 61 Actions.—Actions for $10,000 or less may be brought pursuant to 61-1601 et seq. which is abbreviated form of Federal Rules. Places limitations on certain discovery and pretrial procedures. Ch. 61 does not apply to following actions regardless of amount in controversy: (1) Against state officers or state, except as authorized by Kansas tort claims act; (2) specific performance of real estate contracts; (3) title to real estate; (4) foreclosure of real estate; (5) divorce, separate maintenance, or child custody; (6) habeas corpus; (7) receivership; (8) change of name; (9) declaratory judgments; (10) mandamus and quo warranto; (11) injunction; (12) class actions; (13) rights of majority; (14) appeal of administrative order or ruling. (61-1603).

Discovery.—Federal Rules generally followed. (60-226 to 60-237). Court may conduct case management conference and order disclosures of key documents and witnesses. (60-216[b]). Information transmitted between party to dispute and neutral person conducting mediation shall be confidential. Admissions, representations or statements not admissible as evidence or subject to discovery. (60-452a).

Demand for Admission of Facts.—Federal Rules followed. (60-236).

Direct Action Against Insurors.—Generally not permitted. See category Transportation, topic Motor Vehicles, subhead Direct Actions.

Claims Against Government.—Kansas Tort Claims Act (75-6101 et seq.) abrogates sovereign immunity for some acts. Action for less than $10,000 may be brought as limited action. (75-6103[b][1], see 61-1606 et seq.). Action may not be brought under small claims procedure act. (75-6103[b][2], see 61-2701 et seq.). Written notice of claim must be submitted to municipality and denied before action may be brought against municipality. (12-105b). Lien is created against employee's real or personal property on date of judgment, not usual date of filing. (60-2203, 2203a). Judgment against either governmental entity or employee is complete bar to action against other. (75-6107). See topic Damages, subhead Sovereign Immunity.

Medical Malpractice.—On request of any party, screening panel must be convened. (65-4901). Panel determines whether there was departure from standard practice of care and whether such departure caused claimaint's damages. (65-4903). If either party rejects panel's recommendations, plaintiff may proceed with action. (65-4905). Settlement conference with judge, attorneys and all parties mandatory within 30 days of trial. (60-3413). Attorney fees must be reasonable and approved at evidentiary hearing. (7-121b). See topics Damages, Pleading, subhead Punitive Damages, Evidence, subhead Witnesses, catchline Medical Malpractice.

Professional Malpractice.—Applies to any profession which professional corporation is licensed to practice except health care provider. (60-3501). See category Business Organizations, topic Corporations, subhead Professional Corporations. On request of any party, screening panel must be convened. (60-3502). Panel determines whether breach of standard practice caused claimant's damages. (60-3505[a]). Panel's written report is admissible in any subsequent legal proceeding and panel members may be subpoenaed to testify. (60-3505[c]). If any party rejects panel's recommendations, plaintiff may proceed with action. (60-3506).

Small Claims.—See category Courts and Legislature, topic Courts.

See also topics Actions, Appeal and Error, Depositions and Discovery, Injunctions, Judgments, Pleading, Process; category Debtor and Creditor, topics Attachment, Executions, Garnishment.

PROCESS:

Federal Rules of Civil Procedure form the basis for procedural statutes. (60-204, 301 et seq.). See topic Practice.

Civil action is commenced at time of filing petition with clerk of court if service is obtained or first publication made within 90 days. Court may extend that time additional 30 days upon showing of good cause, otherwise action is commenced at time of service or first publication. If service or first publication purports to have been made within specified time but is later found invalid due to any irregularity in form or procedure or defect in making service, action is still deemed commenced at applicable time under 60-203(a) if valid service obtained or first publication made within 90 days of that finding. Court may extend time additional 30 days upon showing of good cause. (60-203).

General Requisites.—Summons is signed by clerk under seal of court, dated, and must be in substantial conformity with forms for summons in appendix following 60-269. (60-302). Restricted mail is delivered to addressee only and requires return receipt showing address where delivered. If addressee not natural person endorsement "deliver to addressee only" not required. (60-103).

By Whom Issued.—Upon filing of petition, clerk issues summons for service upon each defendant in accordance with K.S.A 60-303. (60-301).

Methods of Service.—Unless personal or residence service requested, sheriff shall serve any process by certified mail or attorney for party requesting service may elect to serve process by certified mail. Service of process considered obtained under 60-203 upon delivery of certified mail envelope. When plaintiff files written request, service or process shall be made by personal or residence service. Personal service shall be made by delivering copy of process to person to be served. Residence service shall be made by leaving copy of process to be served at dwelling house or usual place of abode of person to be served with some person of suitable age and discretion residing therein.

If service cannot be made upon individual other than minor or disabled person by personal service, service may be made by leaving copy of process at defendant's dwelling house or usual place of abode and mailing notice by first class mail to individual. (60-303).

Service of process, making service by any method described in 60-303 shall be made as follows:

Upon Individual.—By serving individual, other than minor or disabled person, or agent authorized to receive service. Service by certified mail shall be addressed to individual's dwelling or usual place of abode and to authorized agent's usual or designated address. If service by certified mail is refused or unclaimed, service may be completed by certified mail, restricted delivery, at business address if return on service filed stating certified mail refused or unclaimed. (60-304).

Upon Minor.—By serving minor and also either minor's guardian, conservator, father, mother or other person having care or control of minor or if service cannot be had upon any of them, then as provided by judge's order. Service by certified mail shall be addressed to individual's dwelling house or usual place of abode and to corporate guardian or conservator's usual place of business. (60-304).

Upon Disabled Person (as defined by 59-3002).—By serving disabled person and such person's guardian, conservator or competent adult member of such person's family with whom person resides; if such person is living in institution then to director or chief executive officer of institution; or if service cannot be had upon them, then as provided by judge's order. Service by certified mail shall be addressed to director or chief executive officer of institution, to any individual at their dwelling or usual place of abode, and to corporate guardian or conservator at their usual place of business. (60-304).

Service on Partnership, Association or Corporation.—Service is made upon domestic or foreign corporation, partnership or other unincorporated association by serving officer, partner or resident, managing or general agent by leaving copies at any business office of defendant with person having charge thereof or serving any other agent authorized by appointment or law and if agent is authorized by law, and law requires, by mailing copy to defendant. Service by certified mail on officer, partner or agent shall be addressed to such person at their usual place of business. (60-304).

Service on Foreign Corporation.—Service upon foreign corporation or foreign limited partnership may be made on its resident agent. Whenever any foreign corporation or foreign limited partnership authorized to transact business or transacting business without authority shall fail to appoint or maintain resident agent upon whom service may be had, or whenever any such resident agent cannot with reasonable diligence be found at registered office in this state, or whenever certificate of authority of any foreign corporation or foreign limited partnership shall be forfeited, secretary of state shall be irrevocably authorized as agent and representative of such foreign corporation or foreign limited partnership to accept service. Such service shall be made by delivering to and leaving with him, or with any clerk having charge of corporation department of his office, duplicate copies, or clerk of court may send such duplicate copies directly to

PROCESS . . . *continued*
secretary of state by restricted mail. When any process is served on secretary of state, he shall immediately cause a copy to be forwarded by restricted mail, addressed to such corporation or limited partnership at its principal office as same appears in his records or to registered or principal office of such corporation or limited partnership in state of its incorporation or formation. Fee of $30 paid to Secretary of State for costs of such service. (60-304).

Where foreign corporation has been licensed to do business in state, service may be made upon secretary of state. (17-7301[b]). All methods of service upon foreign corporations, including publication service, are cumulative.

Person with cause of action against foreign corporation, whether or not corporation qualified to do business in Kansas, which cause of action arose out of corporation's doing business in Kansas, may file suit in county with venue. Service of process obtained in manner of 60-304, supra. (17-7307).

Service on Governmental Bodies.—Service upon county may be made by serving one of county commissioners or county clerk or county treasurer; upon township, by serving clerk or trustee; upon city by serving clerk or mayor; upon any other public corporation, body politic, district or authority by serving clerk or secretary or, if not to be found, to any officer, director, or manager thereof; and upon state or any governmental agency of state, when subject to suit, by serving attorney general or assistant attorney general; income withholding orders for support and orders of garnishment of earnings of state employees served on state or agency as in 60-723. (60-304).

Process against state or any board, commission, department or agency thereof, except secretary of transportation, may be served on attorney general. (60-304).

Service on Insurance Companies.—Unauthorized Insurers Process Act provides for service of process upon insurance companies authorized to do business in Kansas. Prescribes conditions upon which suit may be defended and for allowance of attorneys' fees. (40-2001-6). Service may also be made on any insurance company or association, organized under laws of Kansas by service on commissioner of insurance in same manner as that provided for service on foreign insurance companies and requirements of law relating to service on foreign insurance companies so far as applicable also apply to domestic insurance companies. (60-304).

Service Outside the State.—Service may be made upon any party outside state. If upon person domiciled in this state or upon person who has submitted to jurisdiction of courts of this state, it shall have force and effect of service of process within this state; otherwise it shall have force and effect of service by publication.

Service shall be made in like manner as service within this state, by any officer authorized to make service of process in this state or in state where defendant is served or by sending copy of process and petition to person to be served in accordance with subsection (e) of 60–308.

No default shall be entered until expiration of at least 30 days after service.

Service upon Employee.—Plaintiff, his agent or attorney may file affidavit of belief that defendant's residence unknown, or that defendant is nonresident employed in this state, and direct process server to serve process by directing officer, partner, managing or general agent having charge of defendant's place of employment to make defendant available for service. (60-304[i]).

Service by Publication.—Service may be made by publication in any of following cases: (1) In actions to obtain divorce, maintenance or annulment of contract of marriage if defendant resides out of state or if party is unable to make service of summons upon defendant within state; (2) in actions brought against nonresident or foreign corporation having in this state property or debts owing to him or her sought to be taken by any of provisional remedies or to be appropriated in any way; (3) in actions which relate to or subject of which is real or personal property in this state, if any defendant has or claims lien or interest, vested or contingent, in property, or relief demanded consists wholly or partly in excluding defendant from any interest in property, or for partition or for foreclosure of lien, and such defendant is nonresident or foreign corporation or where plaintiff is unable to make service of summons upon defendant within state; (4) in all actions where defendant, being resident of this state, has departed from this state, or from county of defendant's residence, with intent to delay or defraud his creditors or to avoid service, or hides in state or county with like intent; or in action against domestic corporation which has not been legally dissolved, where officers thereof have departed from state or cannot be found; (5) in any of actions mentioned above publication service may be had on unknown heirs, executors, administrators, devisees, trustees, creditors and assigns of any deceased defendants; unknown spouses of defendants, unknown officers, successors, trustees, creditors and assigns of such defendants as are existing, dissolved or dormant corporations; unknown executors, administrators, devisees, trustees, creditors, successors and assigns of such defendants as are or were partners or in partnership; and unknown guardians, conservators and trustees of such of defendants as are minors or are in anywise under legal disability; and unknown heirs, executors, administrators, devisees, trustees, creditors and assigns of any person alleged to be deceased.

If defendant so served does not appear, judgment may be rendered affecting said property, res or status within jurisdiction of court as to said defendant, but such service shall not warrant a personal judgment against such defendant.

Before service by publication as provided in this section can be made, one of parties or party's attorney shall file his affidavit stating such of following facts as are applicable: (1) Residences of all named defendants sought to be served, if known, and names of all such defendants whose residences are unknown after reasonable effort to ascertain same; (2) that affiant has made reasonable but unsuccessful effort to ascertain names and residences of any defendants sought to be served as unknown parties; (3) that party seeking service by publication is unable to procure service of summons on such defendants in this state; (4) that case is one of those authorizing service by publication.

Notice shall be published once a week for three consecutive weeks in newspaper published in county where petition is filed authorized by law to publish legal notices. It must name defendants to be served and notify them and all other persons who are or may be concerned that he or they have been sued in named court and must answer or plead to petition, or other pleading, filed therein, on or before date to be stated, not less than 41 days from date notice is first published, or petition or other pleading so filed will be taken as true, and judgment, nature of which shall be stated, will be rendered accordingly.

Within seven days after first publication, copy of publication notice shall be mailed by plaintiff to each defendant whose address is stated in affidavit for service by publication. (60-307).

Submitting to Jurisdiction.—Any person, whether or not citizen or resident of this state, who in person or through agent or instrumentality does any of acts hereinafter enumerated, thereby submits said person, and, if individual, his personal representative, to jurisdiction of courts of this state as to any cause of action arising from doing any of said acts: (1) Transaction of any business within this state; (2) commission of a tortious act within this state; (3) ownership, use, or possession of any real estate situated in this state; (4) contracting to insure any person, property or risk located within this state at time of contracting; (5) entering into express or implied contract, by mail or otherwise with resident, to be performed wholly or partly within state; (6) acting within state as director, manager, trustee or other officer of corporation organized under laws of state or having place of business within state, or as executor or administrator of estate within state; (7) causes injury to persons or property within this state arising out of act or omission outside of this state by defendant, provided in addition, that at time of injury either (i) defendant was engaged in solicitation or service activities within this state; or (ii) products, materials or things processed, serviced or manufactured by defendant anywhere were used or consumed within this state in ordinary course of trade or use; (8) living in marital relationship within state notwithstanding subsequent departure from state, as to all obligations arising for maintenance, child support, or property settlement, if other party to marital relationship continues to reside in state; (9) serving as insurer at time of act of insured which results in judgment being taken against him; (10) performing act of sexual intercourse within state as to paternity action or as to support action if conception of child results and other party to act remains in state; (11) entering into express or implied arrangement, whether by contract, tariff or otherwise, with corporation or general or limited partnership, residing or doing business in this state under which corporation or partnership has supplied transportation services, or communication services or equipment, including telephonic communication services, for business or commercial user where services supplied are managed, operated or monitored within this state, provided such person is put on reasonable notice that arranging or continuing such transportation or telecommunication services may result in extension of jurisdiction pursuant to this section. (60-308).

Long Arm Statute.—See subhead Methods of Service, catchlines Service Outside the State; and Service on Foreign Corporation, supra.

Proof of Service.—

Personal Service.—Officer makes statement under penalty of perjury stating time, place and manner of service. Private process server makes affidavit as to time, place and manner of service. (60-312[a]).

Service by Certified Mail.—Shall be in manner provided for in 60–303(b) or 60–308(e).

Publication Service.—Proved by affidavit showing newspaper and dates when notice was published. Copy of notice must be attached to affidavit. When mailing copies of publication notice is required, proof is by affidavit of person mailing copies. Affidavit must be filed with clerk of court. (60-312[c]).

Long Arm Statute.—Affidavit of server must be filed stating time, manner and place of service. Court may consider affidavit or any other competent proofs in determining whether service has been properly made. (60-308[a][2]).

Nonresident Motorist.—See category Transportation, topic Motor Vehicles.

Probate.—Probate Code specifies many instances in which publication service is necessary. Form of notice is prescribed by statute and must be published each week for three consecutive weeks. First publication must be had ten days after order fixing time and place of hearing. Seven days after first published notice petitioner must mail or cause to be mailed copy of notice, petition and attachments, will, accounting and settlement agreement (if applicable) to persons designated and prove mailing by affidavit. (59-2208-11).

REPLEVIN:

The plaintiff in an action to recover possession of specific personal property, may at any time before judgment is rendered claim immediate possession thereof as hereinafter set out. (60-1005).

Proceedings.—By filing a verified petition or an affidavit showing that plaintiff owns described property, or is lawfully entitled to possession thereof, and that it is wrongfully detained by defendant, or if it is held by an officer under legal process, that demand has been made and refused, and estimated value thereof. After hearing judge may order delivery of property to plaintiff. Judge may enter order ex parte if satisfied: (1) Possession by plaintiff is necessary to protect governmental or public interest; and (2) immediate danger defendant will destroy or conceal property. Plaintiff files with clerk of court a bond in not less than double amount of value of property. (60-1005).

Redelivery.—Order for delivery of the property is delivered to sheriff of any county in the state in which the property is located, commanding him to take immediate possession of the property and deliver it to plaintiff at the expiration of 24 hours unless the defendant delivers to said sheriff a redelivery bond in not less than double the amount of the value of the property in which event the sheriff shall return the property to the defendant. (60-1005).

Judgment.—Judgment may be for possession or for the recovery of possession, or the value thereof in case a delivery cannot be had, and for damages for the detention. (60-1005).

Code of Procedure for Limited Actions allows replevin up to jurisdictional amount. Affidavit in replevin fixing value of property will govern. (61-1603). Otherwise law is substantially same as in cases under 60-101 et seq. (61-2401).

SEQUESTRATION:

No statutory provisions.

See note at head of Digest as to 1998 legislation covered.

See Topical Index in front part of this volume.

SUBMISSION OF CONTROVERSY:

No statutory provision. However controversies are commonly submitted to district court on agreed statement of facts.

VENUE:

General Rules.—Unless specifically provided otherwise:

Action against resident may be brought in county where: (1) Defendant resides; (2) plaintiff resides if defendant is served therein; (3) cause of action arose; (4) where defendant has place of business or of employment if served therein; (5) estate of decedent is being probated if decedent was jointly liable with defendant and demand has been duly exhibited in probate proceeding; or (6) there is tangible personal property which is subject of action for immediate possession. (60-603).

Action against Kansas or qualified foreign corporation may be brought in county in which: (1) Registered office is located; (2) cause of action arose; (3) defendant is transacting business at time of filing of petition if plaintiff is resident of such county at time cause of action arose; (4) there is tangible personal property which is subject of action for immediate possession; or (5) equipment or facilities for use in supply of transportation services or communication services are located, where subject of action relates to transportation services or communication services supplied or rendered using such equipment or facilities. (60-604).

Action against nonresident or non-qualified corporation may be brought in county where: (1) Plaintiff resides or if plaintiff is corporation, where it has registered office or place of business; (2) defendant is served; (3) cause of action arose; (4) defendant is transacting business at time of filing of petition; (5) there is property of defendant or debts owing to defendant; (6) there is tangible personal property which is subject of action for immediate possession. (60-603).

Particular Actions.—

Real property actions must be brought in county in which real estate is situated. If tract or tracts are situated in two or more counties, action may be brought in county where any tract or part thereof is situated. Real property actions include: (1) Ejectment; (2) partition; (3) actions for sale under mortgage, lien or other encumbrance or charge; (4) actions for specific performance of contract for sale of real property; and (5) eminent domain actions. Action for specific performance may also be brought in any county where defendant resides. (60-601).

Recovery of fine, forfeiture or penalty, other than against public utilities or common carriers; venue is in county in which cause arose, except if act was committed on road or river which forms boundary of two or more counties, action may be brought in any one of bordering counties. (60-602).

Action against public official under color of office or for neglect of official duties or on official bond must be brought in county in which cause arose. (60-602).

Action against public utility, common carrier or transportation system for any liability or penalty or forfeiture may be brought in any county through which such operates regularly. But action for personal injury or death must be brought in county where plaintiff lived at time of injury or where injury occurred. (60-606).

Actions concerning marriage may be brought in county in which petitioner is actual resident at time of filing petition or in county where respondent resides or may be served or if petitioner resides or is stationed at U.S. military post within state at time of filing petition, in county adjacent to post. For venue purposes, spouse may have residence separate from residence of other spouse. (60-607).

Uniform Arbitration Act.—Initial application must be made to court of county where agreement provides that arbitration hearing will be held or, if hearing has already been held, in county where hearing was held. Otherwise application must be made in county where adverse party resides or has place of business or, if party has no residence or place of business in Kansas, to court of any county. (5-417).

Multiple Parties.—If several plaintiffs properly joined and venue is determined by residence of one of them, it is necessary that such plaintiff's claim is substantial part of action. If several defendants properly joined, venue may be determined at election of plaintiff as to any one of defendants against whom substantial claim exists. (60-608).

Change of Venue.—If it appears that a fair and impartial trial cannot be had in the district court in the county where the suit is pending, for reasons other than the disqualification of the judge, the court may upon application of either party change the place of trial to some county where the objection does not exist. On motion of any party court may transfer any civil action to county where it might have been brought upon finding that transfer will serve convenience of parties, witnesses and interests of justice. When all non-defaulting parties agree, and agreement is approved by court of original venue and supreme court, civil action may be transferred to any county. (60-609).

Contract Provisions.—No statutes or case law.

COURTS AND LEGISLATURE

COURTS:

United States District Court.—Clerk's office, 401 N. Market, Wichita, 67202, (316) 269-6491.

Record offices are maintained at Topeka, Kansas City, Wichita. Cases may be filed at any one of these offices.

Parties may file designation of city where they desire trial to be held.

Court sits at Kansas City, Topeka, Salina, Leavenworth, Wichita, Hutchison, Dodge City, Fort Scott, and at such places as may be required.

Supreme Court.—Court has original jurisdiction in quo warranto, mandamus, and habeas corpus, and appellate jurisdiction as provided by law. (Const. Art. 3. §3). Jurisdiction is coextensive with state.

Appellate jurisdiction fixed by statute extends to review of Court of Appeals decisions (20-3018) and exclusive jurisdiction over district court decisions declaring federal or state statute unconstitutional (60-2101[b]). Supreme Court is court of record.

Court sits at Topeka. Address: Kansas Judicial Center, Topeka, 66612, (785) 296-3220 (clerk).

Court of Appeals.—Court of Appeals has jurisdiction over appeals in civil and criminal cases and from administrative bodies and officers of state as prescribed by law. (20-3001, 60-2101[a]).

Principal office at Topeka. May hear oral argument in any county. (20-3013).

District Courts.—

Jurisdiction.—In each county there is district court with general original jurisdiction over all matters, civil, criminal, juvenile, and probate. (20-301). Judges divided into two classifications: district judge and district magistrate judge. Administrative judge assigns all cases to appropriate judge. (20-301a).

District judge has jurisdiction over all civil, criminal, juvenile, and probate matters, and appeals from district magistrate judge. (20-301).

District Magistrate Judge has jurisdiction in criminal misdemeanor charges and preliminary examination of felony charges. Concurrent jurisdiction exists in civil actions other than: (1) Cases exceeding $10,000 in controversy excepting certain replevin cases and actions seeking judgment for unsecured debt not sounding in tort and arising out of contract for provision of goods, services or money; (2) against state officers or state; (3) specific performance of real estate contracts; (4) real estate titles; (5) foreclosure of real property mortgages or liens; (6) divorce, separate maintenance, custody of minors, issuance of support orders, actions for care of children or under juvenile justice code; (7) habeas corpus; (8) receivership; (9) change of name; (10) declaratory judgments; (11) mandamus or quo warranto; (12) injunctions; (13) class actions; (14) rights of majority; (15) actions pursuant to protection from abuse act; and (16) actions pursuant to Sexual Predator Act. In absence, disability or disqualification of district judge other powers are specified. Orders appealed to district judge for trial de novo, except where record made of magistrate proceedings, appeal tried and determined on record. (20-302b).

Districts.—District courts sit in at least one location in each county. Administrative judge of each judicial district, with approval of Supreme Court may designate other locations within county whenever suitable facilities are available. (20-347). District courts currently sit in at least following communities (Rules of District Court #101):

Allen County: Thirty-first District; court sits at Iola.
Anderson County: Fourth District; court sits at Garnett.
Atchison County: First District; court sits at Atchison.
Barber County: Thirtieth District; court sits at Medicine Lodge.
Barton County: Twentieth District; court sits at Great Bend.
Bourbon County: Sixth District; court sits at Fort Scott.
Brown County: Twenty-second District; court sits at Hiawatha.
Butler County: Thirteenth District; court sits at El Dorado.
Chase County: Fifth District; court sits at Cottonwood Falls.
Chautauqua County: Fourteenth District; court sits at Sedan.
Cherokee County: Eleventh District; court sits at Columbus and Galena.
Cheyenne County: Fifteenth District; court sits at St. Francis.
Clark County: Sixteenth District; court sits at Ashland.
Clay County: Twenty-first District; court sits at Clay Center.
Cloud County: Twelfth District; court sits at Concordia.
Coffey County: Fourth District; court sits at Burlington.
Comanche County: Sixteenth District; court sits at Coldwater.
Cowley County: Nineteenth District; court sits at Winfield and Arkansas City.
Crawford County: Eleventh District; court sits at Girard and Pittsburg.
Decatur County: Seventeenth District; court sits at Oberlin.
Dickinson County: Eighth District; court sits at Abilene.
Doniphan County: Twenty-second District; court sits at Troy.
Douglas County: Seventh District; court sits at Lawrence.
Edwards County: Twenty-fourth District; court sits at Kinsley.
Elk County: Thirteenth District; court sits at Howard.
Ellis County: Twenty-third District; court sits at Hays.
Ellsworth County: Twentieth District; court sits at Ellsworth.
Finney County: Twenty-fifth District; court sits at Garden City.
Ford County: Sixteenth District; court sits at Dodge City.
Franklin County: Fourth District; court sits at Ottawa.
Geary County: Eighth District; court sits at Junction City.
Gove County: Twenty-third District; court sits at Gove.
Graham County: Seventeenth District; court sits at Hill City.
Grant County: Twenty-sixth District; court sits at Ulysses.
Gray County: Sixteenth District; court sits at Cimarron.
Greeley County: Twenty-fifth District; court sits at Tribune.
Greenwood County: Thirteenth District; court sits at Eureka.
Hamilton County: Twenty-fifth District; court sits at Syracuse.
Harper County: Thirtieth District; court sits at Anthony.
Harvey County: Ninth District; court sits at Newton.
Haskell County: Twenty-sixth District; court sits at Sublette.
Hodgeman County: Twenty-fourth District; court sits at Jetmore.
Jackson County: Second District; court sits at Holton.
Jefferson County: Second District; court sits at Oskaloosa.
Jewell County: Twelfth District; court sits at Mankato.
Johnson County: Tenth District; court sits at Olathe.
Kearny County: Twenty-fifth District; court sits at Lakin.
Kingman County: Thirtieth District; court sits at Kingman.
Kiowa County: Sixteenth District; court sits at Greensburg.
Labette County: Eleventh District; court sits at Oswego and Parsons.
Lane County: Twenty-fourth District; court sits at Dighton.
Leavenworth County: First District; court sits at Leavenworth.
Lincoln County: Twelfth District; court sits at Lincoln.
Linn County: Sixth District; court sits at Mound City.
Logan County: Fifteenth District; court sits at Oakley.
Lyon County: Fifth District; court sits at Emporia.
Marion County: Eighth District; court sits at Marion.
Marshall County: Twenty-second District; court sits at Marysville.
McPherson County: Ninth District; court sits at McPherson.

See note at head of Digest as to 1998 legislation covered.

See Topical Index in front part of this volume.

KS – 15

COURTS . . . continued

Meade County: Sixteenth District; court sits at Meade.

Miami County: Sixth District; court sits at Paola.

Mitchell County: Twelfth District; court sits at Beloit.

Montgomery County: Fourteenth District; court sits at Independence and Coffeyville.

Morris County: Eighth District; court sits at Council Grove.

Morton County: Twenty-sixth District; court sits at Elkhart.

Nemaha County: Twenty-second District; court sits at Seneca.

Neosho County: Thirty-first District; court sits at Erie and Chanute.

Ness County: Twenty-fourth District; court sits at Ness City.

Norton County: Seventeenth District; court sits at Norton.

Osage County: Fourth District; court sits at Lyndon.

Osborne County: Seventeenth District; court sits at Osborne.

Ottawa County: Twenty-eighth District; court sits at Minneapolis.

Pawnee County: Twenty-fourth District; court sits at Larned.

Phillips County: Seventeenth District; court sits at Phillipsburg.

Pottawatomie County: Second District; court sits at Westmoreland.

Pratt County: Thirtieth District; court sits at Pratt.

Rawlins County: Fifteenth District; court sits at Atwood.

Reno County: Twenty-seventh District; court sits at Hutchinson.

Republic County: Twelfth District; court sits at Belleville.

Rice County: Twentieth District; court sits at Lyons.

Riley County: Twenty-first District; court sits at Manhattan.

Rooks County: Twenty-third District; court sits at Stockton.

Rush County: Twenty-fourth District; court sits at LaCrosse.

Russell County: Twentieth District; court sits at Russell.

Saline County: Twenty-eighth District; court sits at Salina.

Scott County: Twenty-fifth District; court sits at Scott City.

Sedgwick County: Eighteenth District; court sits at Wichita.

Seward County: Twenty-sixth District; court sits at Liberal.

Shawnee County: Third District; court sits at Topeka.

Sheridan County: Fifteenth District; court sits at Hoxie.

Sherman County: Fifteenth District; court sits at Goodland.

Smith County: Seventeenth District; court sits at Smith Center.

Stafford County: Twentieth District; court sits at St. John.

Stanton County: Twenty-sixth District; court sits at Johnson.

Stevens County: Twenty-sixth District; court sits at Hugoton.

Sumner County: Thirtieth District; court sits at Wellington.

Thomas County: Fifteenth District; court sits at Colby.

Trego County: Twenty-third District; court sits at Wakeeney.

Wabaunsee County: Second District; court sits at Alma.

Wallace County: Fifteenth District; court sits at Sharon Springs.

Washington County: Twelfth District; court sits at Washington.

Wichita County: Twenty-fifth District; court sits at Leoti.

Wilson County: Thirty-first District; court sits at Fredonia.

Woodson County: Thirty-first District; court sits at Yates Center.

Wyandotte County: Twenty-ninth District; court sits at Kansas City.

Probate Courts.—Abolished, Jan. 10, 1977. (20-335). See subhead District Courts, supra.

City Courts.—Abolished, Jan. 10, 1977. (20-335). See subhead District Courts, supra.

County Courts.—Abolished, Jan. 10, 1977. (20-335). See subhead District Courts, supra.

Justices of the Peace.—Abolished. (61-1603).

Magistrate Courts.—Abolished, Jan. 10, 1977. (20-335). See subhead District Courts, supra.

Small Debtor's Courts.—20-1301 et seq. repealed, Jan. 10, 1977.

Small Claims Procedure Act.—Provides alternate procedure supplementing Code of Civil Procedure for Limited Actions processing small claims. (61-2701). Jurisdiction limited to $1,800. (61-2703). Action commenced by filing written statement of claim and payment of $19.50 filing fee for claims of $500 or less, and $39.50 for claims exceeding $500 unless waived. Only ten claims per person in one court per year allowed. (61-2704). No party may be represented by attorney until judgment. (61-2707). Judgment debtor must submit to clerk of court list of assets and place of employment within 30 days after receipt of court provided form. (61-2707). List mailed to judgment creditor by court, copy is not retained. (61-2707). Appeal may be taken to district court for trial and determination de novo. (61-2709).

LEGISLATURE:

General Session.—Meets annually in Jan. (Const. art. 2, §8).

Special Sessions.—Governor may call. (Const. art. 1, §5). Must call if petitioned by 2/3 of each house. (40-1401 to 1403).

Initiative and Referendum.—Not provided for.

Lobbyists.—46-265 to 280.

REPORTS:

Decisions of Supreme Court are reported in Kansas Reports. Reports of first court of appeals, now abolished, comprise ten volumes. New court of appeals created Jan. 10, 1977 and decisions published in Kansas Court of Appeals Reports, second.

Kansas decisions are also published in Pacific Reporter, covering from December 1883 (30 Kan.) to present date.

Digests.—West's Kansas and Pacific Digests.

STATUTES:

Kansas Statutes Annotated (K.S.A.) is 15 volume work, including index and state constitution, published by state. K.S.A. was first published in 1965. Individual bound volumes are updated and replaced every few years. Bound volumes are supplemented annually with cumulative supplements. Supreme Court rules are published in c. 20; art. 31 of K.S.A.

Uniform Acts of the National Conference of Commissioners on Uniform State Laws which have been adopted are: (1990) Alcoholism and Intoxication Treatment (1972); Anatomical Gift (1969); Arbitration (1973); Attendance of Witnesses from Without a State in Criminal Proceedings, Act to Secure (1951); Certification of Questions of Law (1979); Child Custody Jurisdiction (1978); Commercial Code (1965); Common Trust Fund (1951); Consumer Credit Code (1973); †Consumer Sales Practices enacted under title Consumer Protection (1974); Controlled Substances (1972); †Crime Victims Reparations (1978); Criminal Extradition (1937); Determination of Death (1984); †Disclaimer of Transfers by Will, Intestacy or Appointment, Revised (1985) and †Disclaimer of Transfers Under Nontestamentary Instruments, Revised (1985) (enacted as single act); Division of Income for Tax Purposes (1963); Durable Power of Attorney (1980); Enforcement of Foreign Judgments (1970); Facsimile Signatures of Public Officials (1963); Federal Lien Registration (1988); Fraudulent Transfer (1998); Interstate Family Support (1994); Land Sales Practices (1967); †Limited Partnership (1976 version) (1983); Management of Institutional Funds (1973); Mandatory Disposition of Detainers (1959); Motor Vehicle Operators' and Chauffeurs' License (1931); Motor Vehicle Registration (1929); Notarial Acts (1984); Revised Partnership (1998); Photographic Copies of Business and Public Records as Evidence (1963); Premarital Agreement (1988); Principal and Income Revised (1965); †Residential Landlord and Tenant (1975); Simplification of Fiduciary Security Transfers (1961); Simultaneous Death (1947); Testamentary Additions to Trusts (1968); Trade Secrets (1981); Transfers to Minors (1985); Trustees' Powers (1968); Unauthorized Insurers (1969); Unclaimed Property (1994); Vital Statistics (1951); Voting by New Residents in Presidential Elections (1972).

As to Uniform Securities Act, see topic Securities.

For text of Uniform Acts falling within the scope of the Martindale-Hubbell Law Digests see Uniform and Model Acts section.

Other Uniform Acts adopted are: Adoption and Relinquishment Act (1990).

UNIFORM LAWS:

For list of Uniform Acts in force in this state see topic Statutes. For text of Uniform Acts within the scope of the Martindale-Hubbell Law Digests see Uniform and Model Acts section.

CRIMINAL LAW

BAIL:

See topic Criminal Law.

CRIMINAL LAW:

Kansas Criminal Code (21-3101 et seq.) defines crimes and punishments therefor. There is a code of criminal procedure. (22-2101 et seq.).

All crimes punishable by death or confinement in penitentiary are felonies, as well as any crime defined as felony by law. There are separate classifications for traffic and tobacco infractions. All other offenses are misdemeanors. (21-3105).

Indictment and Information.—Offenses are prosecuted by complaint, by information filed by county attorney or (rarely) by indictment by grand jury. (22-2301, 2303).

Bail.—All offenses are bailable, unless offense charged is one shown to be punishable by death or life imprisonment under laws of state where offense committed. (22-2716).

Uniform Criminal Extradition Act.—Adopted. (22-2701 et seq.). Amended Act not adopted.

DEBTOR AND CREDITOR

ASSIGNMENTS:

Generally all choses in action, except torts, are assignable (189 Kan. 649, 371 P.2d 181) except where nature or terms of contract make it nonassignable (230 Kan. 361, 634 P.2d 1123).

Uniform Commercial Code (K.S.A. 84-1-101 et seq.) in effect. See category Business Regulation and Commerce, topic Commercial Code.

Instrument Transferring Title.—No particular form is necessary. (201 Kan. 412, 441 P.2d 815). Acknowledgment is not necessary.

Filing or recording is not necessary, except that state or municipal bonds require formal assignment before notary public, identifying bond by name of issuing municipality, number, date, and amount and acknowledged like conveyance of real property and filed with State Treasurer. Printed forms furnished on request from State Treasurer, State Capitol, Topeka, KS 66612, (785) 296-3171. (10-602).

Notice.—Debtor must have notice of assignment before he has duty to pay assignee. (183 Kan. 190, 326 P.2d 299).

Effect.—Assignment passes all assignor's title or interest to assignee and divests assignor of all right of control over subject matter of assignment. (215 Kan. 856, 528 P.2d 1198).

Assignment of Wages.—Recognized and enforced. (201 Kan. 412, 441 P.2d 815).

Assignment of Unemployment Benefits.—Not assignable, but benefits may be subject to withholding for child support obligation being enforced under plan described in §454 federal Social Security Act or overissuance of Food Stamps. (44-718).

ATTACHMENT:

Actions in Which Allowed.—At or after commencement of any civil action. (60-701).

Court Which May Issue Writ.—District court (60-701). Limitations on writ in limited actions involving $3,000 or less. (61-1601 et seq.).

In Whose Favor Writ May Issue.—Any plaintiff, resident or nonresident.

Against Whom Writ May Issue.—Any defendant or defendants, resident or nonresident.

Claims Upon Which Writ May Issue.—An action may be commenced and attachment issued on a demand not yet due in any of cases mentioned under subhead Grounds (infra), clauses (1) and (2), but no judgment may be rendered until maturity of demand. (60-702). No order of attachment shall be issued before judgment where defendant's property is in possession of third party and is in form of earnings due and owing. (60-703).

Grounds.—When defendant whose property is to be attached, (1) is a nonresident or a foreign corporation; (2) has absconded or concealed himself so that summons cannot be served upon him, or is about to move out of state with intent of changing his domicile; (3) is about to remove his property or effects out of this state; (4) is about to convert his property into money for purpose of placing it beyond reach of his creditors; (5) has concealed, removed, assigned, conveyed or otherwise disposed of his property so as to hinder or delay his creditors or is about to do so; (6) fraudulently contracted debt or incurred liability; (7) is liable for damages for injuries arising out of commission of some felony or misdemeanor, or seduction of a person; (8) has failed to pay price or value of any article or thing delivered which by contract he was bound to pay upon delivery. (60-701).

Proceedings to Obtain.—Affidavit must be filed by plaintiff stating: (1) Grounds upon which attachment sought, specifying facts with particularity, (2) that plaintiff has just claim, and (3) amount of claim, less credits and setoffs. (60-703, 60-704).

Attachment Bond.—Required except in actions instituted on behalf of State of Kansas or county thereof. (60-703). Bond is executed by plaintiff with sufficient sureties, in sum double amount of plaintiff's claim, or such lesser amount as may be approved by court order. (60-705).

Levy.—Order commands sheriff or county officer to attach property of defendant, real or personal, tangible or intangible, or so much thereof as will satisfy plaintiff's claim, or such specific property as plaintiff directs, and to summon as garnishees all persons in whose possession any personal property or money of defendant may be. (60-706).

Indemnity.—No statutory authority for levying officers to require.

Priorities.—Orders of attachment are levied on in the same order in which they were received by levying officers. If several attachments issue out of different courts, all questions arising must be determined by court out of which was issued first attachment served. (60-713).

Release of Property.—Defendant or any other person in whose hands property of defendant is found may retain or regain possession at any time before final judgment or sale of such property under court order by giving bond with sufficient sureties in an amount which is (1) Equal in amount to plaintiff's claim and probable court costs, or (2) equal to appraisal of property pursuant to 60-706, or (3) lesser amount as required by court. Person giving bond has option of clause (1) or (2). (60-707).

Sale.—When property seized is likely to perish or materially depreciate in value before probable termination of the suit, or keeping of which would be attended with unreasonable loss or expense, the property may be ordered sold. (60-710). See topic Executions.

Third Party Claims.—Any person claiming an interest in any property attached and, in discretion of the judge, any creditor of a party if creditor's claim is liquidated in amount will be permitted to intervene and court will adjudicate their respective rights. (60-713).

Vacation or Modification.—Any interested person may file a motion to dissolve attachment, verified by affidavit, putting in issue sufficiency of proceedings, defendants or other persons claim of exemption as to attached property, or truth of facts alleged in attachment affidavit. Court may permit amendments to petition or affidavit. Court shall hold hearing within five days of receipt of motion. (60-712).

Upon filing of bond, attachment is discharged and restitution of property taken is made. (60-707).

Receiver.—Receiver may be appointed in aid of attachment. (60-711).

CONSUMER CREDIT:

Uniform Consumer Credit Code enacted. (16a-1-101, et seq.).

CREDITORS' SUITS:

Creditors' bill is a proceeding in rem and used to make effective a judgment against property which cannot be reached by execution. Governed by rules of common law and successful creditors' bill conditioned on affirmative showing that indebtedness reduced to judgment. (158 Kan. 242, 146 P.2d 665).

EXECUTIONS:

An execution may be issued upon a judgment in any court of record.

Kinds of Execution.—A general execution is a direction to an officer to seize any nonexempt property of a judgment debtor and cause it to be sold in satisfaction of judgment. Special execution or order of sale is court direction to officer to effect some action as to some specified property. (60-2401).

Exemptions.—See topic Exemptions.

Time for Issuance.—No execution may issue nor proceedings be taken for enforcement until expiration of ten days after entry of judgment, with some exceptions. (60-262). May be issued any time within five years from date of judgment, revival of judgment, or last execution. (60-2403; 61-2201). See category Civil Actions and Procedure, topic Judgments.

Stay.—When a court has ordered a final judgment on some but not all multiple claims, enforcement may be stayed until the entering of subsequent judgment. (60-262). See category Civil Actions and Procedure, topic Appeal and Error.

In actions brought pursuant to Ch. 61, Code of Civil Procedure for Limited Actions, stays of execution are granted only on appeal by posting a supersedeas bond. (61-2015). See category Civil Actions and Procedure, topic Appeal and Error.

Levy.—General execution is levied upon any nonexempt real or personal property. Special executions or orders of sale are levied as court directs. (60-240).

Return.—Officer must return execution or order of sale to court from which it issued within 60 days from date thereof (60-2401) but c. 61 execution is returnable within 30 days from date of its receipt by officer to whom it is directed (61-2201).

Priorities.—Subject to any rights, liens, or preferences existing by law independently of levy of an execution, when two or more general executions are levied against property of same judgment debtor, all questions of priority must be determined by court out of which was issued first execution served. (60-2402; 60-713).

Claims of Third Persons.—An officer may refuse to proceed against property claimed by third persons until the plaintiff gives him a bond to pay all costs and damages that may be sustained by reason of the detention or sale of such property. (60-2407).

Sale.—Personal property taken on execution may not be sold until at least ten days public notice of sale is given by advertisement in some newspaper meeting qualifications of 64-101 for legal publications, or, in court's discretion, posting advertisements in five public places in county. Notice must be sent to defendant within five days of first publication or posting notice. (60-2409). Real property taken on execution may not be sold until public notice of time and place of sale be given once each week for three consecutive weeks prior to day of sale, by publication in county where judgment rendered and county where real property located, with last publication not less than seven nor more than 14 days prior to day of sale. (60-2410[a]). Interest of judgment debtor may be sold on execution subject to liens or encumbrances already existing. (60-2406). All sales of real property must be held at courthouse located in county seat of county in which judgment was rendered. Upon application, district judge whose jurisdiction includes county where judgment rendered, may, for good cause shown, order such sale on premises or other location. (60-2410[b]). Sale must be confirmed by court and officer making sale must execute to purchaser certificate of sale or deed. Court may decline to confirm sale where bid is substantially inadequate, or may fix minimum or upset price at which property must be bid in if sale is to be confirmed, or, after hearing, may require fair value of property be credited upon judgment, interest, taxes and costs. Sale for full amount of judgment, taxes, interest and costs is deemed adequate. (60-2415). Sheriff's deeds vests in purchaser as good and perfect title as was vested in person against whom execution or order of sale was issued. Title to property conveyed vests in grantee as of date of execution of sheriff's deed. (60-2416).

Redemption.—Purchaser at execution sale of real estate receives a certificate of sale stating amount paid by such purchaser, amount of costs to that date, a proper description of property and that unless redemption is made according to law, purchaser, his heirs or assigns will be entitled to deed therefor. (60-2410[e]). Owner has 12 months within which to redeem, except that if land has been abandoned or not occupied in good faith court may shorten or extinguish. Period of redemption may also be reduced to three months where mortgage or instrument giving lien is in default before 1/3 of original indebtedness secured by mortgage has been paid. Three month redemption period may be extended to six months if owner involuntarily lost primary source of income after sale and before three month period expired. During period of redemption owner is entitled to possession of property and income therefrom. For first three months after sale right of defendant owner to redeem is exclusive: thereafter, any lien creditor may redeem same within six months from date of sale. All redemption periods and rights of lien creditors under this section commence on date of judgment or date of judicial sale and expire three months thereafter, if judgment of foreclosure finds no redemption for owner by reason of valid waiver. Any creditor whose claim becomes lien prior to expiration of time allowed by law for redemption of creditors may redeem. Creditors may redeem from each other. Any corporation, general partnership or limited partnership organized under law of U.S. or any state may agree in mortgage instrument to shorter redemption period or waive same entirely as to mortgagor and its assigns. Any person may agree in mortgage instrument to shorter period or waive same entirely, excepting mortgagee of dwelling or dwellings for occupancy by not more than two families or of agricultural land. (60-2414).

Defendant owner may redeem for amount paid by current holder of certificate of purchase together with interest, costs and taxes to date of redemption. During redemption period holder of certificate of purchase or creditor who has redeemed may pay taxes on land, insurance premiums on improvements thereon, and other sums necessary to prevent waste, and interest on sums due, upon any prior lien or encumbrance thereon, and upon redemption he is entitled to repayment of all sums thus paid by him, together with interest thereon. All expenses incurred by holder of certificate or creditor who has redeemed shall be shown by receipts or vouchers filed in office of clerk of district court. (60-2414).

If defendant fails to redeem, purchaser or creditor who last redeemed prior to expiration of redemption period will hold property absolutely. If held by redeeming creditor, his lien will be extinguished, unless, redeeming creditor is unwilling to hold property and credit defendant owner therefor with full amount of his lien, he files at time of redemption statement with clerk of court of amount that he is willing to credit on his claim. If redeeming creditor files statement and defendant owner fails to redeem, creditors claim extinguished by amount in statement. Sheriff executes deed to owner of certificate of purchase. (60-2414).

Mode of redemption is by paying the proper amount to clerk of the district court and filing an affidavit, if the redemption is by other than defendant owner, stating amount still unpaid due on his claim. Any distinct portion of property sold in parcels may be

See note at head of Digest as to 1998 legislation covered.

See Topical Index in front part of this volume.

KS – 17

EXECUTIONS . . . *continued*

redeemed and undivided interests of tenants in common may be redeemed separately. Defendant owner's redemption rights may be assigned or transferred but are not subject to levy or sale on execution. Holder of the legal title has same right of redemption and possession as defendant in execution. (60-2414).

Party entitled to a deed under sale may, after the deed is made to him, assert claim for damages for any injury or waste permitted on the property after sale. (60-2414).

Real estate once sold upon proper legal process is not again liable for any balance due upon the judgment or decree under which it has been sold, nor for any judgment or lien inferior thereto including unadjudicated liens filed after petition is filed in foreclosure action. (60-2414).

Holder of certificate of purchase may get injunction or a receiver to prevent waste or destruction of premises, but income still goes to person entitled to possession during redemption, except fees and expenses of receiver and as is necessary to keep up repairs, pay taxes and insurance premiums and prevent waste. (60-2414).

Supplementary Proceedings.—When an execution is returned unsatisfied, in whole or in part, or judgment creditor lacks knowledge of debtor's assets, judgment creditor is entitled to order requiring debtor to appear and answer concerning his property and income. Debtor may be ordered to periodically appear and answer as to his property and income if it appears that debtor will have nonexempt property or income in future. Witnesses may also be subpoenaed. Out of county debtor may be ordered to appear if no undue hardship. Debtor or witness who fails to appear or answer is subject to citation for contempt. (60-2419).

If at hearing, nonexempt property is disclosed, court must order debtor to deliver to sheriff who must sell any such property that is not cash and apply proceeds to judgment and costs. (60-2419).

Executions in Special Cases.—If execution be for delivery of possession of real or personal property, it must require the officer to deliver same to party entitled thereto and may at same time require officer to satisfy any costs or damages recovered in the same judgment out of the personal property of the party against whom it was rendered; and for want of such personal property, then out of the lands and tenements, and in this respect it is deemed an execution against the property. In special cases not otherwise covered, the execution shall conform to the order of the court. (60-2417).

EXEMPTIONS:

Every person residing in Kansas, except as otherwise provided, has exempt from seizure and sale any: (1) Pension, retirement or disability benefit; (2) public assistance benefits; (3) worker's compensation; (4) unemployment benefits; (5) partnership property; (6) crime victims reparations award; (7) liquor license; (8) interest in life insurance; (9) fraternal benefit society benefit; (10) cemetery merchandise trust fund; (11) prearranged funeral account or trust; and (12) money held by court order for support of any person whether child or spousal support, alimony or maintenance. (60-2313, 60-2308). Following personal property is also exempt: (1) Furnishings, equipment and supplies, including food, fuel and clothing, for person for period of one year on hand and reasonably necessary at principal residence; (2) ornaments of debtor's person, including jewelry, not exceeding $500 in value; (3) one means of conveyance regularly used for transportation of person or for transportation to and from regular place of work; (4) burial plot, crypt or cemetery lot; (5) books, documents, furniture, instruments, tools, implements and equipment, breeding stock, seed grain or growing plants stock, or other tangible means of production regularly and reasonably necessary to carrying on profession, trade, business or occupation in aggregate value not to exceed $5,000. (60-2304).

No personal property is exempt from sale for taxes (60-2306), nor from attachment or execution for wages of any clerk, mechanic, laborer or servant (60-2307).

Earnings.—Only aggregate disposable earnings may be subjected to garnishment and maximum which may be subjected to garnishment for any work week or multiple thereof may not exceed either (1) 25% of aggregate disposable earnings for work week or multiple thereof, or (2) amount by which aggregate disposable earnings for work week or multiple thereof exceed an amount equal to 30 times federal minimum hourly wage, or equivalent multiple thereof for longer period, whichever is less. Provided, no one creditor may issue more than one garnishment against same debtor per month. Act not construed as charging plaintiff with knowledge of amount of defendant's earnings prior to commencement of garnishment action. If debtor is prevented from working due to own or family sickness for at least two weeks, provisions of this section shall not be invoked against such debtor until after two months after recovery. Collection agency taking assignment of account may not garnish wages. Restrictions on wage garnishment inapplicable to order for child support, alimony, order in bankruptcy, or on debt due for state or federal tax.

Maximum part of aggregate disposable earnings for any workweek subject to garnishment to enforce order for support of person shall not exceed: (1) 50% for individual supporting spouse or child, (2) 60% for individual not supporting spouse or child, and (3) for unpaid support for period 12 weeks prior to garnishment, as to individuals in paragraphs (1) and (2), 55% and 65% respectively. (60-2310). Garnishment to enforce order for support shall not exceed 50% unless specified in application and order. (60-718).

Pensions.—All money received for pension from the United States by the debtor, within three months next preceding the issue of execution, attachment or garnishment is exempt, if pensioner makes affidavit that it is necessary for support of debtor or family supported wholly or in part by said pension. Money, assets, interests from any qualified retirement plan are also exempt, except from qualified domestic relations order. (60-2308).

Nonprofit hospital property income and proceeds therefrom, is exempt from attachment, garnishment, execution or other forced process, except for contractual obligations and those due the state and its agencies. (17-1745).

See topic Homesteads.

FRAUDULENT SALES AND CONVEYANCES:

Uniform Commercial Code (K.S.A. 84-1-101 et seq.) in effect. See category Business Regulation and Commerce, topic Commercial Code.

Uniform Fraudulent Conveyance Act.—Not adopted.

Uniform Fraudulent Transfer Act.—Enacted (1998).

Gifts and conveyances, made in trust for the use of the person making same, are void as to past, present and future creditors, but otherwise valid. (33-101). Gifts, grants or conveyances of lands, etc., or executions made or obtained, with intent to defraud, hinder or delay creditors, or to deceive the buyers of such, are void. (33-102). See also category Estates and Trusts, topic Trusts.

Bulk Sales.—No statutory provision. UCC Art. 6 repealed.

GARNISHMENT:

Before judgment, order of garnishment may be obtained upon order of court pursuant to proceedings for attachment. Order may be in lieu of or in addition to order of attachment, except that garnishment shall not be commenced before judgment on plaintiff's claim in principal action where such garnishment proceedings affect earnings of defendant except on order for temporary support while divorce action pending. (60-715). After judgment, order of garnishment may be obtained either in connection with or independently of execution, and no bond is required. (60-716).

Property Which May Be Reached.—Order of garnishment attaches all property of defendant in or coming into possession or control of garnishee, and all credits and indebtedness due or becoming due from garnishee to defendant after service of order until answer of garnishee is signed. (60-717[c]).

Jurisdiction.—District court has jurisdiction. (60-715; 60-716).

Answer of Garnishee.—Within ten days after service of order of garnishment attaching property or funds other than earnings and within 40 days after order attaching earnings, garnishee must file his verified answer. If garnishment attaches earnings and defendant is not employed by garnishee or has terminated employment, answer not required to be verified. If garnishee fails to so answer judgment may be taken against garnishee for amount of plaintiff's judgment or claim. Garnishee's answer may not contain less than statutory form. (60-718).

Practice.—Order of garnishment is served along with two copies of statutory form for garnishee's answer, on garnishee by officer making service in same manner as an order of attachment. Order of garnishment issued to attach funds held by bank, savings and loan association, credit union or finance company shall include defendant's address and tax identification number if known and specify amount garnished at $1^1/_2$ times plaintiff's claim if prejudgment or $1^1/_2$ times judgment. Garnishee may withhold administrative fee of $10 for each order. Fee is in addition to amount withheld. Party seeking order must have good faith belief that party served has or will have assets of debtor. No more than two garnishments in any 30 day period except when judge finds (1) garnishment not to harass and (2) facts indicate garnishee has nonexempt property or credits of debtor. (60-726). If served prior to judgment on plaintiff's claim, said order must also be served on defendant, if he can be found, but failure to serve defendant will not relieve garnishee from liability under said order. (60-717). Defendant may controvert statements in answer of garnishee, defend proceedings against garnishee, and he may participate in trial of any issue between plaintiff and garnishee for protection of his interests. Garnishee in his answer may, on behalf of defendant, state any claim of exemption or other objection which defendant may have, and may defend principal action for defendant who defaults, but he is under no obligation to do so. (60-720). If any person, firm or corporation sells or assigns his account to any person or collecting agency, then such person, firm or corporation or their assignees may not garnish wages except for certain state and federal claims regarding support, taxes and restitution. (60-2310).

Adverse Claims.—When the garnishee claims that he is not indebted to the defendant for the reason that the defendant is indebted to the garnishee, or that the indebtedness due to the defendant is reduced thereby, the garnishee is not discharged unless and until he applies the amount of his indebtedness to the defendant to the liquidation of his claim against the defendant. (60-719).

Judgment.—Judgment shall be entered: (1) By determining the liability of garnishee upon default; or (2) discharging the garnishee; or (3) making available to the satisfaction of plaintiff's claim any indebtedness due from the garnishee to the defendant or any property in the hands of the garnishee belonging to the defendant, including ordering the payment of money by the garnishee into court, or the impoundment, preservation and sale of property as provided for the disposition of attached property; or (4) rendering judgment against the garnishee for the amount of his indebtedness to the defendant held by the garnishee; and (5) if the answer of a garnishee is controverted without good cause, awarding the garnishee judgment against the controverting party for the garnishee's expenses, including reasonable attorney's fees. Court may enter continuing order for garnishment to enforce order for support under specified circumstances. (60-721). Defendant may at any time after proceeding is commenced file with clerk bond in double amount of claim or such lesser amount as court may approve to effect that he will pay amount of judgment and costs that may be assessed against him and thereupon garnishee will be discharged. (60-722).

Earnings.—See topic Exemptions, subhead Earnings.

Exceptions.—No judgment shall be rendered in garnishment by reason of the garnishee: (1) Having drawn, accepted, made, endorsed, or guaranteed any negotiable bill, draft, note, or other security; or (2) holding moneys on a claim not arising out of contract and not liquidated as to amount; or (3) holding moneys or property exempt by law, or the proceeds therefrom. (60-724).

Public Officials.—Garnishment laws apply to all state, county, city, township and school district officers and employees, as well as to all officers and employees of all municipal or quasi-municipal corporations to same extent and effect as such laws apply to officers and employees of private corporations. Order of garnishment on state employee is served on director of accounts and reports. Provided, if garnishee is public

See note at head of Digest as to 1998 legislation covered.

See Topical Index in front part of this volume.

KS – 18

GARNISHMENT . . . *continued*

officer of state or instrumentality thereof and indebtedness sought by plaintiff to be withheld from defendant is an indebtedness to defendant incurred by or on behalf of state or instrumentality thereof, judgment against state or such instrumentality shall be limited to an amount for claim and costs not exceeding total amount of indebtedness of state or instrumentality thereof to defendant. (60-718[c]). Property, funds, credits and indebtedness of state or state agency are exempt from garnishment, attachment, levy and execution and sale. Judgment against state does not create charge or lien on property of state. (60-723).

Under Code of Procedure for Limited Actions, 61-1601 et seq., garnishment may be obtained before judgment only upon order of court pursuant to procedure for attachment. Garnishment shall not be commenced before judgment on plaintiff's claim in principal action where such garnishment proceedings affect earnings of defendant. (61-2003). Ten days after judgment garnishment may be obtained either in connection with execution or independently thereof and no bond is required (61-2004). Garnishee stands liable to plaintiff for all property, money and articles in his hands belonging to defendant at time of service of such summons and all such property, money and articles coming into his hands until time of signing his answer. (61-2005).

Garnishee must answer within ten days from date of service of garnishment attaching property or funds other than earnings or within 40 days of a garnishment attaching earnings or within 40 days in either case if office or principal place of business of garnishee is outside county where court situated. Answer must be verified except where garnishment attaches earnings and defendant is not employed by garnishee or has terminated employment. (61-2006).

HOMESTEADS:

Homestead occupied as residence by owner or family of owner, together with all improvements on same, is exempt from forced sale under any process of law, except as hereinafter stated. (Const., art. 15, §9; 60-2301).

Limitation of Value.—None.

Limitation of Area.—One hundred and sixty acres of farming land or one acre within the limits of an incorporated city or town. (Const., art. 15, §9; 60-2301).

Debts or Liabilities Against Which Exemption Not Available.—Taxes; obligations contracted for purchase of premises or erection of improvements thereon; liens given by consent of homestead owner and his or her wife or husband, if any. (Const., art. 15, §9; 60-2301).

Claim of Exemption.—Whenever any levy is made upon lands of a householder whose homestead has not been selected and set apart, such householder, householder's spouse, agent or attorney may notify officer in writing at time of making such levy, or at any time before sale, of what householder regards as homestead, with description thereof, and remainder alone is subject to sale under such levy. (60-2302).

Homestead Waiver.—There is no form of homestead waiver.

Alienation or Incumbrance.—A conveyance or incumbrance of the homestead of a married person is absolutely void unless the husband and wife join in the same instrument. (Const., art. 15, §9). A contract for the sale of a homestead is also void unless it is signed by both husband and wife.

Where one spouse is an incapacitated person, consent to lease for oil and gas or mortgage may be obtained by appropriate district court proceedings. (59-2314 et seq.).

Proceeds of sale of the homestead are not exempt unless debtor intends to invest in another homestead. (217 Kan. 683, 538 P.2d 655).

Rights of Surviving Spouse and Family.—The homestead, which for this purpose may be manufactured or mobile home, is exempt from distribution, and exempt from debts of decedent to same extent that it was exempt in his lifetime. Homestead descends just as other real property, but it is not divided until spouse dies or remarries or children arrive at age of majority. (59-401).

See also categories Family, topic Husband and Wife; Property, topic Dower.

LIENS:

Types of Liens Recognized.—Kansas recognizes variety of liens, including: (1) Mechanic's (58-201 et seq.) (see subhead Mechanic's Lien, infra); (2) contractor's (60-1101 et seq.) (see subhead Contractors, infra); (3) bailee's (58-208); (4) agister's for grazing of livestock (58-220); (5) on crops or grain harvested, threshed and seeded, or baled (58-203; 58-204; 58-218); (6) agricultural production input (58-241 et seq.); (7) attorney's (7-108, 7-198) (see category Legal Profession, topic Attorneys and Counselors); (8) innkeeper's (38-201); (9) carrier's (see category Business Regulation and Commerce, topic Carriers); (10) on manufactured or mobile homes for amounts due for leased space (58-227); (11) hospital on first $5,000 of patient's claim for nonworker's compensation injury (65-406 et seq.); (12) landlord's (see category Property, topic Landlord and Tenant); (13) judgment (60-2202) (see category Civil Actions and Procedure, topic Judgments); (14) tax (79-1804) (see topic Taxation); and (15) county or township bonds on all real estate in county or township (10-1001). Other miscellaneous liens exist.

Uniform Commercial Code (84-1-101) adopted. See category Business Regulation and Commerce, topic Commercial Code. See also category Transportation, topic Motor Vehicles, subhead Liens.

Mechanic's Lien.—Whenever any person, at owner's request or with owner's consent, performs work or makes repairs or improvements on owner's personal property, first and prior lien on personal property is created in his favor for reasonable amount of his services, including materials used. (58-201).

Lien is valid so long as claimant retains possession. Claimant may retain lien after parting with possession by filing statement under oath with register of deeds within 90 days. If claimant never had possession, he may file within 90 days after work was last performed or materials last furnished. Statement must include items of account, description of liened property and owner's name. Must be filed in county where work was performed and in county where owner resides, if known. (58-202).

Lien may be enforced and foreclosed like security agreement under Uniform Commercial Code. (58-202).

Contractors.—Any person furnishing labor, equipment, material or supplies, including cost of transporting same, used or consumed for improvement of real property, under a contract with owner or with trustee, agent or spouse of owner, has lien upon the property. (60-1101).

Subcontractors.—Any subcontractor or other person furnishing labor, equipment, material or supplies, used or consumed at the site of the property subject to the lien, under an agreement with the contractor, subcontractor or owner contractor may obtain lien. Notice of intent to perform must have been filed on new residential property and attached to lien statement. (60-1103).

Filing and Notice.—Contractors must file verified statement within four months after date materials, equipment or supplies used or consumed were last furnished or last labor performed. Statement filed with clerk of the district court and must contain name of owner, claimant, description of real property, and itemized statement and the amount of the claim. If claim is evidenced by written instrument or promissory note, a copy thereof may be attached in lieu of the itemized statement. (60-1102). Subcontractors must file lien statement within three months after date material or equipment was last furnished or labor performed, and statement must also include name of contractor. Subcontractor claimant must mail a copy of lien statement to owner of property and to party obligated to pay same by registered or certified mail, or must post a copy of lien statement on premises if address of owner or such party obligated to pay same is unknown. Requirements for service of lien statement are complied with if it is shown that person to be served actually received copy. Subcontractor may only claim lien for improvement of residential property if claimant has mailed warning statement to owner of property or has owners signed statement that general contractor or claimant has given such statement. Warning statement not required if claim is under $250. (60-1103; 60-1103a).

Rights and Liability of Owner.—As to a subcontractor the owner of the real property is not liable for a greater amount than he has contracted to pay the original contractor, except for any payments to the contractor made prior to the expiration of the three month period for filing lien claims if no warning statement required or subsequent to date owner received warning statement if required. Owner may discharge any lien which contractor fails to discharge and credit such payment against amount due contractor. (60-1103[d]).

Preference of Liens.—Such liens are preferred to all other liens or encumbrances which are subsequent to commencement of the furnishing of such labor, equipment, materials or supplies. (60-1101).

Assignment.—All claims for liens and rights of action to recover therefor are assignable so as to vest in the assignee all rights and remedies. (60-1104).

Enforcement.—Action to foreclose must be brought within one year from the time of filing the lien statement, but if a promissory note has been attached to the lien statement in lieu of an itemized statement, the action must be commenced within one year from the maturity of said note. (60-1105). All persons whose liens are filed, and other encumbrancers of record, shall be made parties. (60-1106). Court may stay foreclosure action on building or improvement still under construction to permit the filing of a lien statement by a party engaged in furnishing labor or materials. (60-1107). If proceeds of the sale are insufficient to pay all claimants, court must order them to be paid in proportion to the amount due each. (60-1109).

Action by Landowner for Adjudication.—If no action to foreclose has been commenced, landowner may bring an action, making lien claimants defendants, for adjudication of such liens. (60-1108).

Limitations.—If no action commenced within the time allowed, clerk of the district court enters on the mechanic's lien docket a statement that the lien is cancelled by limitation of law. (60-1108).

Bond to Prevent Liens.—Contractor or owner may execute a bond to State of Kansas for the use of all persons in whose favor liens might accrue, conditioned for payment of all claims which might be the basis of liens in a sum not less than the contract price. When approved and filed, no liens shall attach, and liens already filed are discharged. Suit may be brought on said bond by any person interested. (60-1110).

Public Buildings and Improvements.—If contract exceeds $40,000, contracting public official must take from party contracted with bond to State of Kansas in sum not less than contract price, conditioned that such contractor or subcontractor of said contractor shall pay all indebtedness incurred for labor furnished, materials, equipment, or supplies, used or consumed in connection with said construction. Any person to whom there is due any sum for labor or material furnished, or his assigns, may bring action on said bond, but no such action may be brought after six months from completion of said public improvements. In case of contract for construction or improvements for state or state agency under 75-3739 or 75-3741, certificate of deposit payable to state may be accepted in lieu of bond. (60-1111).

Oil and Gas.

Contractor.—Any person furnishing under contract, express or implied with the owner of an oil and gas leasehold or oil and gas pipe line either labor or material or machinery or oil well supplies used in making, operating or repairing any oil or gas well or constructing or putting together machinery so used has a lien upon the whole of such leasehold or oil pipe line or gas pipe line and the buildings and appurtenances and upon the material and supplies so furnished. (55-207).

Lien Statement of Contractor.—Unless a period of more than four months elapses between the dates of employing labor or furnishing material or supplies, whether labor or material, machinery or supplies are upon the same or different wells, performing such labor or furnishing material constitutes a single transaction or contract, whether done under a single contract or a series of contracts, and it is only necessary for the claimant to file one lien statement covering the transactions as a whole.

Preference of Lien.—The lien is preferred to all other liens or encumbrances, which attach subsequent to the commencement of or furnishing or putting up of any such machinery or supplies. (55-207).

Subcontractors' Lien.—A person who furnishes machinery or supplies to a subcontractor under a contractor or a laborer under a subcontractor with the contractor may

LIENS . . . *continued*

obtain a lien upon the leasehold or pipe lien in the same manner and to the same extent as the original contract for the amount due him. (55-208).

Lien statement of subcontractor must be filed in the office of the clerk of the district court of the county in which the land and leasehold is situated, setting forth the amount claimed and the items thereof as nearly as practicable, the name of the owner of the land, the name of the owner of the leasehold, the name of the contractor, the name of the lien claimant and a description of the property subject to the lien, whether personal or real or both, and it must be verified by affidavit. If a promissory note bearing a lawful rate of interest is taken, it is not necessary to file an itemized statement of labor or material furnished, but in lieu thereof, a copy of the note may be filed with a statement that the note or any part thereof was given for such labor or material furnished. The statement must be filed within four months after the date upon which the material was last furnished or labor last performed. (55-208).

Enforcement.—The lien is enforced in the same manner and notice of the same is given in the same manner, whether by contractor, subcontractor, material man or laborer, as is provided for the enforcement of liens of mechanics. After the sale of the property, there is no redemption. (55-210).

Trucker's Lien.—One who transports or hauls oil field supplies, machinery, heavy machinery, buildings, tanks, engines, etc., under express contract with owner or operator of oil and gas lease or pipe line has a lien on interests of such owner in the leasehold or pipe line, equipment, buildings and appurtenances. Lien statement must be filed, within 120 days after equipment was transported and delivered, in office of clerk of district court of county where equipment delivered. Copy of statement must be served on owner by registered mail to last known address. Owner must notify lien claimant before removing equipment and material from leasehold. If material is moved to another county, lien claimant has thirty days after receiving notice to file copy of lien statement in office of clerk of district court of county to which material moved. Action on lien must be commenced within six months. Lien is not prior to any valid and existing chattel mortgage of record. (55-212 et seq.).

Uniform Federal Lien Restoration Act.—Adopted. (79-2613 et seq.).

Attachment Lien.—See topic Attachment.

Attorney's Lien.—See category Legal Profession, topic Attorneys and Counselors.

Carrier's Lien.—See category Business Regulation and Commerce, topic Carriers.

Chattel Mortgage Lien.—See category Mortgages, topic Chattel Mortgages.

Collateral Security.—See topic Pledges.

Execution Lien.—See topic Executions.

Factor's Lien.—See category Business Regulation and Commerce, topic Factors.

Judgment Lien.—See category Civil Actions and Procedure, topic Judgments.

Landlord's Lien.—See category Property, topic Landlord and Tenant.

Liens on Exempt Property.—See topic Exemptions.

Liens on Homestead.—See topic Homesteads.

Real Estate Mortgage Lien.—See category Mortgages, topic Mortgages of Real Property.

Tax Lien.—See category Taxation.

MECHANICS' LIENS:

See topic Liens.

PLEDGES:

Uniform Commercial Code (K.S.A. 84-1-101 et seq.) in effect. See category Business Regulation and Commerce, topic Commercial Code.

Remedies of Secured Party.—Secured party may bring action in district court to reduce indebtedness to money judgment and to foreclose security interest in specific personal property given to secure such indebtedness. (60-1006).

Secured party must file either affidavit or verified petition showing: (1) Terms of indebtedness; (2) amount owed; (3) terms of security agreement; (4) description of personal property; (5) plaintiff is lawfully entitled to foreclosure of specific personal property; (6) estimated value of each piece of personal property; and (7) personal property is wrongfully detained by defendant. (60-1006[a]).

Plaintiff must apply for order for delivery of property to him. Copy of motion must be served on defendant. After hearing and presentation of evidence, if court satisfied as to probable validity of plaintiff's claim and that justice will be served, court may grant order. Expedited procedure available if immediate danger that defendant will destroy or conceal property. (60-1006[b]). Order will command sheriff to seize property. (60-1006[c]).

Judgment for plaintiff must be for money judgment and foreclosure of security interest in accord with Uniform Commercial Code. If judgment not satisfied within ten days, court directs sheriff to sell property. (60-1006[h]).

Notice of sale must be given at least ten days before sale through publication in legal newspaper each week for two consecutive weeks. Plaintiff must send copy of notice by restricted mail to defendant and to persons known to have security interest in property. (60-1007).

RECEIVERS:

May be appointed whenever deemed necessary to keep, preserve and manage all property and protect any business or business interest entrusted to him pending the determination of any proceeding in which such property or interest may be affected by the final judgment. (60-1301).

Jurisdiction.—Justice of supreme court, judge of court of appeals, district judge, or in absence of said judge, district magistrate judge, has authority to appoint receiver. (60-1301).

Proceedings.—Receiver cannot be appointed without notice and an opportunity for the interested parties to be heard unless the judge finds that immediate and irreparable injury is likely to result, and a bond may be required of the applicant conditioned on such terms as judge may direct. This does not apply where defendant is a nonresident or a foreign corporation not authorized to do business in Kansas. (60-1304).

Eligibility and Competency.—A person who has an interest in property or in the outcome of the proceeding cannot be appointed or continued as a receiver if objection is made thereto by another interested party unless the judge finds such objection is arbitrary or unreasonable. (60-1301).

Qualification.—Receiver must be sworn to perform duties faithfully and execute a bond to such persons on such conditions and in such sum as judge directs. (60-1302).

Powers.—Receiver shall perform such acts respecting the property or business as judge may authorize. (60-1303).

Appeal.—An aggrieved party may within ten days appeal from an order appointing or refusing to appoint a receiver without awaiting final determination of the proceedings. If receiver has been appointed and appellant files an appeal bond with such terms and conditions as the judge may direct, appointment is suspended and the property retained in possession of the appellant pending final determination of the appeal. (60-1305).

See category Business Organizations, topic Corporations, subhead Insolvency and Receivers.

DISPUTE RESOLUTION

ARBITRATION AND AWARD:

Uniform Arbitration Act.—Adopted. (5-401 et seq.). Existing arbitration statutes (5-201 to -213) not repealed.

Form and Requisites of Submission.—

Uniform Act.—If opposing party refuses to arbitrate, party may apply to district court to compel arbitration. If opposing party denies existence of agreement, court must summarily determine issue. (5-402).

Voluntary Arbitration.—All persons having controversy may submit it to arbitration of mutually agreed upon parties. Such submission may be made rule of any court of record. (5-201).

Contracts to Arbitrate Future Disputes.—Written agreement to arbitrate future disputes valid except in contracts between employer and employees, insurance contracts, except contracts between insurance companies, or contracts providing for arbitration of tort claim. (5-401).

Rescission.—Contract to submit disputes may be revoked if grounds exist in law or equity. (5-401).

Powers of Arbitrators.—

Uniform Act.—Arbitrators may issue subpoenas and administer oaths. (5-407).

Award and Enforcement Thereof.—

Uniform Act.—District court must confirm award unless urged to vacate, correct or modify award. (5-411).

Judgment on Award.—

Uniform Act.—Judgment entered on confirmed award. (5-414).

Voluntary Arbitration.—If no exceptions raised, district court may enter judgment and issue execution on award. (5-209).

Mandatory Arbitration.—In all medical malpractice actions filed in district court upon request of party, judge must convene medical malpractice screening panel. Where dispute is unfiled, court may convene panel on own motion. (65-4901). Findings by panel are not binding and dispute may be pursued by civil action if findings are rejected but written report of screening panel is admissable into evidence in subsequent legal action. (65-4904, 65-4905).

DOCUMENTS AND RECORDS

ACKNOWLEDGMENTS:

Uniform Law on Notarial Acts adopted July 1, 1984. (53-501 et seq.). Uniform Recognition of Acknowledgments Act repealed July 1, 1984. Uniform Acknowledgments Act and Uniform Acknowledgment Act not adopted.

Within State.—By notary public, or judge, clerk or deputy clerk of any state court. (53-504). Instruments affecting real property may also be acknowledged by county clerk, register of deeds, mayor or clerk of incorporated city. (58-2211).

Outside State but within U.S.—By notary public or judge, clerk or deputy clerk, or by any person authorized by law of that jurisdiction to perform notarial acts. (53-505).

Outside U.S.—By notary public or notary, or judge, clerk or deputy clerk of court of record, or any other person authorized by law of that jurisdiction to perform notarial acts. (53-507).

Persons in or with U.S. Armed Forces.—No special provision.

General Requirements as to Taking.—Notarial officer must determine from personal knowledge, affirmation of credible witness personally known to him, or identification documents that person appearing before him is person who signed instrument. (53-503).

General Requirements of Certificate.—Must be signed and dated by notarial officer. Must identify jurisdiction and title of notarial office. Notary public must give date appointment expires. Commissioned U.S. officer must give rank. Official stamp or seal optional. (53-508[a]). See subhead Forms, infra.

Married Women.—No special requirements.

Attorneys-in-Fact.—No special requirements.

Corporations.—Uniform Law on Notarial Acts governs (17-6003[b]), except conveyances of real property interests must be acknowledged by president, vice-president

ACKNOWLEDGMENTS . . . *continued*

or presiding member or trustee, or by authorized agent under letter of attorney (17-6003[g]).

Foreign Acknowledgments.—Same effect as if performed in Kansas if performed within jurisdiction of and under authority of foreign nation or its constituent units, or multi-national or international organization by specified persons. (53-508[a]). See also subhead Outside U.S., supra.

Instruments affecting real property valid if executed in conformity with either Kansas law or law of foreign state or country where executed. (58-2228).

Effect of Acknowledgment.—Instrument may be recorded (58-2221) and read in evidence without further proof (58-2229). Unacknowledged instrument, even though recorded, does not impart constructive notice of its contents. However latent defect in acknowledgment does not prevent constructive notice. (9 Kan.App.2d 614, 683 P.2d 1288).

Proof by Witnesses.—If the grantor dies before acknowledging the execution of a deed, or if for any other reason his attendance cannot be procured, or if, having appeared, he refuses to acknowledge, proof of the due execution and delivery of the deed may be made by any competent testimony. (58-2214). Such proof may be made before any court or officer authorized to take acknowledgments. (58-2215). Certificate endorsed upon a deed thus proved must state: (1) Title of court or officer taking proof; (2) that it was satisfactorily proved that grantor was dead or that for some other cause his attendance could not be procured, or that, having appeared, he refused to acknowledge deed; and (3) names of witnesses by whom proof was made and that it was proved by them that instrument was executed by person whose name is thereto subscribed as party. (58-2216). Proof of handwriting may only be resorted to where all subscribing witnesses are dead or cannot be had. (58-2220). Witnesses may be subpoenaed. (58-2219).

Authentication.—Signature and title of person performing notarial act are prima facie evidence that signature is genuine and person holds designated title. (53-504[c], 53-505[c], 53-506[b]). Signature and title of notary public or judge, clerk or deputy clerk outside Kansas but in U.S. conclusively establish that signature is genuine and person holds designated title. (53-505[d]). Signature and title of judge, clerk or deputy clerk or active duty commissioned U.S. officer acting under federal law also given conclusive effect. (53-506[c]). Foreign notarial acts conclusively established by "Apostille", certificate by U.S. or foreign consul, or listing in recognized source of information. (53-507[b, c, f]). Official stamp or seal is prima facie evidence. (53-507[d, e]).

Forms.—Following are acceptable statutory forms. (53-509).

Forms
Individual:
State of . . . .
County of . . . .
This instrument was acknowledged to me on (date) by (name of person).
(Signature of notarial officer)
(Seal, if any)
Title (and Rank)
My appointment expires: . . . .

Representative Capacity:
State of . . . .
County of . . . .
This instrument was acknowledged to be on (date) by (name of person) as (type of authority, e.g., officer, trustee, etc.) of (name of party on behalf of whom instrument was executed).
(Signature of notarial officer)
(Seal, if any)
Title (and Rank)
My appointment expires: . . . .

For witnessing or attesting signature:
State of . . . .
County of . . . .
Signed or attested before me on (date) by (name of person).
(Signature of notarial officer)
(Seal, if any)
My appointment expires: . . . .

For attestation of copy of document:
State of . . . .
County of . . . .
I certify that this is a true and correct copy of a document in the possession of . .
Dated: . . . .
(Signature of notarial officer)
(Seal, if any)
My appointment expires: . . . .

Validating Act.—Unacknowledged or defectively acknowledged instrument, of record ten years, is validated. (58-2237).

Alternative to Acknowledgment or Proof.—Unsworn written declarations may be permitted as support or evidence. (53-601). Exceptions noted. (53-601[b]).

Forms.—Following are acceptable statutory forms. (53-601).

Forms
If executed inside or outside this state:
I declare (or verify, certify or state) under penalty of perjury that the foregoing is true and correct. Executed on (date).

AFFIDAVITS:

An affidavit may be made in or out of the state before any person authorized to take depositions. See category Civil Actions and Procedure, topic Depositions and Discovery.

General Requirements as to Administration.—Affidavit must be sworn to before some person authorized to administer oath. Simple acknowledgment before notary not sufficient. (219 Kan. 863, 549 P.2d 1397). Affidavit must be signed in presence of notary. (5 Kan.App.2d 622, 621 P.2d 1021).

General Requirements of Jurat.—Jurat is not required. It is mere evidence that oath was duly administered. This may be proved by other evidence. (199 Kan. 652, 433 P.2d 454). Use of jurat given under subhead Forms, infra, is advisable.

Use of Affidavit.—See specific topics.

Forms
State of . . . . . ., County of . . . ., ss: . . . . . ., of lawful age, being first duly sworn, upon his oath deposes and says: (Here insert statement, followed by signature of affiant). Subscribed and sworn to before me, a . . . . . . in and for the county and state aforesaid, on this . . . . . . day of . . . . . ., 19 . . . . (Signature, seal, and if notary public, expiration date of appointment).

If the affidavit is to be filed for record, the following jurat is advisable:
Subscribed and sworn to before me, a . . . . . . in and for the county and state aforesaid, by said . . . . . ., who is personally known to me, and he duly acknowledged to me the execution of the foregoing instrument. (Signature, seal, and if notary public, expiration date of appointment).

Alternative to Affidavit.—No statutory provision.

NOTARIES PUBLIC:

Qualification.—Must file with Secretary of State an oath of office and bond in sum of $7,500. (53-102).

Authentication.—See topic Acknowledgments, subhead Authentication.

Seal.—Notary must provide seal containing name exactly as it appears on application for appointment and words "notary public" and "State of Kansas" and authenticate all official acts therewith. Seal of notary shall be either seal press, or impression thereof inked or blackened, or rubber stamp used with permanent ink. (53-105).

Powers and Duties.—Notary has authority to take acknowledgments, administer oaths and affirmations, take verification upon oath or affirmation, witness or attest signature, certify or attest copy, note protest of negotiable instrument, and perform any other act permitted by law. (53-503). Notary must determine from personal knowledge or satisfactory evidence that signature notarized is that of person appearing before notary. (53-503[c]). Satisfactory evidence of identity is personal knowledge, identification upon oath or affirmation by credible witness personally known to notary, or identification documents. (53-503[f]).

Depositions may be taken before notary. (60-228[a], 53-107).
Uniform Law on Notarial Acts adopted. (53-501 et seq.).

Territorial Extent of Powers.—Notaries may perform services throughout state.

Expiration of Appointment.—Notary must add to his official signature date thereof. (53-105).

Fees vary.

Certification of Authority.—See Acknowledgments, subhead Authentication.

Officers of U.S. Armed Forces.—Notarial act performed under authority granted by law of U.S. while on active duty has same effect as if done by notary of this state. (53-506[a]).

RECORDS:

Uniform Commercial Code (K.S.A. 84-1-101 et seq.) in effect. See category Business Regulation and Commerce, topic Commercial Code.

All books, records, deeds, mortgages, maps, instruments, microphotographs and writings authorized by law to be recorded in office of register of deeds must be recorded in books for that purpose, on computer disks, tapes or other electronically accessed media, and indexed. (19-1204). Photographic copies of instruments, bound, paged and indexed, are sufficient recordation. (58-2224). *For list of Counties and County Seats see first page for this state in Volume containing Practice Profiles Section.*

Recording Fees.—Deeds, mortgages and other instruments filed with county register of deeds: First page, $6; each additional page, $2; recording town plats, $20 per page; release or assignment of mortgage, $5; notice or release of tax liens, $5; liens for material and services, $5. (28-115).

Filing Under Commercial Code.—Local filing of financing statements made with register of deeds of appropriate county and central filing made in office of Secretary of State, Capitol Building, Topeka, 66612. (84-9-401). Filing fees: Financing statement, amendments thereto, continuation statement, assignment of security interest, release of collateral filed with Secretary of State shall be $6 plus $1 for each additional page not to exceed $10 plus $1 for each additional page. (84-9-402, 03, 05, 06).

Transfer Book.—County clerk must keep a transfer book recording all transfers of real estate in his county. (58-2239). His certificate of transfer must be upon deed before register of deeds may record it. When registrar receives instrument not entered on transfer record he shall have such instrument entered on said record immediately upon recording same in his office. (58-2241).

Necessity and Effect of Recording.—Every instrument in writing conveying or affecting real estate or any interest created by an oil and gas lease, properly acknowledged, may be recorded in the office of the register of deeds of the county in which said land is located. (58-2221). Such instrument imparts notice to all persons of the contents thereof from the date of filing. (58-2222). No such instrument in writing is valid except

RECORDS . . . *continued*
as to the parties thereto and such as have actual notice thereof until it is deposited with the recorder of deeds for record. (58-2223).

Certified copy of the record of an instrument shall be received in court as evidence, upon proof that the original cannot be produced. (58-2230).

Foreign Records.—Where instrument has been recorded for ten years in another state, a certified copy of same will be taken as prima facie evidence of the existence of the original by courts in this state and may be filed in any county in this state where the land is located with like effect as the original instrument. (58-2230).

Torrens System of land registration has not been adopted.

Transfer of Decedent's Title.—Where decedent died testate, probate of the will passes title to devisees. If real estate is in counties other than county where will is probated, authenticated copies of the will and order of probate must be admitted to record in district courts of such other counties. (59-2249).

Duly authenticated copy of a foreign will may be admitted to record in the district court of any county where real estate devised is located and when so recorded has same validity as will duly proved in this state. (59-806).

When final decree of distribution of decedent's estate includes real estate, certified copy thereof must be entered on transfer record of county clerk of county where the real estate is located. (59-2249).

Vital Statistics.—Records of births, deaths, marriages and divorces are kept by Division of Health of Department of Health and Environment, State Capitol, Topeka, Kansas 66612. (65-2419-21). Fee for certified copies of birth and death certificates is $6 for first copy and $3 for each additional copy of same certificate. (K.A.R. 28-17-6).

Establishing Birth Record.—Provision is made for delayed registration of birth of persons born in this state, upon such proof as Secretary of Health and Environment requires. (65-2410 to 2421).

SEALS:

Seals and scrolls abolished (16-106), except corporation may have seal if so desired (17-6102).

Uniform Commercial Code (K.S.A. 84-1-101 et seq.). See category Business Regulation and Commerce, topic Commercial Code.

EMPLOYMENT

LABOR RELATIONS:

Jurisdiction over industrial relations is exercised by Department of Human Resources, 401 Topeka, Topeka, 66603, (785) 296-5000 (information). (75-3404).

Safety Appliances.—Secretary of human resources has power to enter and inspect place of business to examine employee protection from dangerous and unsanitary conditions. Employers are notified of hazardous or unsanitary conditions and given up to 60 days in which to correct condition. Employers are prohibited from removing safety apparatus or devices. Secretary may order closing of business until hazardous conditions are corrected. (44-636).

Hours of Labor.—No statutory provision.

Wages.—Employer must pay time and half for hours worked in excess of 46 hours per week. (44-1204[a]). Employer must pay employees at least once per month and within 15 days of end of pay period. (44-314). Employee who has quit or been discharged must be paid wages owed not later than next regular pay period. (44-314[a]).

Employee may assign claim to Secretary of Human Resources who may maintain action pursuant to Act for fee not to exceed $25 per claim. (44-324). Except for such assignment, no provision of or right under act may be contravened, set aside or waived. (44-321).

Where employer becomes insolvent, wages due his employees for six months prior thereto are preferred to every other debt or claim. (44-312).

See category Debtor and Creditor, topic Assignments, subhead Assignment of Wages.

Child Labor.—Children under 14, with limited exceptions, may not work. (38-601). Children under 16 generally may not work more than eight hours per day or 40 hours per week and may not work between 10 p.m. and 7 a.m. on school nights. (38-603[a]). Children under 18 may not work at jobs that are dangerous or injurious to their lives, health, safety, morals or welfare. (38-602).

Female Labor.—No special provisions.

Discrimination in employment by reason of race, religion, color, sex, disability, national origin or ancestry prohibited unless valid business motive exists. (44-1009).

Age discrimination prohibited unless valid business motive exists. (44-1113). Executives may be forced to retire at 65 if they will receive at least $44,000 per year in retirement benefits. (44-1118).

Labor Unions.—Employees have right to organize and to bargain collectively. (44-803). "Right to Work" laws in effect. (Const. art. 15, §12).

Actions.—Unincorporated labor organization may sue or be sued in its commonly used name. (44-811).

Labor Disputes.—Members of collective bargaining unit may not strike unless unit approves strike by secret ballot. (44-809[3]). No person may picket beyond area of industry in which dispute arises (44-809[13]) or engage in non-peaceful picketing (44-809[14]). Secondary boycotts prohibited. (44-809a[1]). Secretary of Human Resources may investigate and make orders for welfare of public and parties. (44-607 et seq.).

Workers' Compensation Act (44-501 et seq.) is administered by Workers' Compensation Board. Covers accidental injury or death arising out of and in course of employment. Burden of proof on claimant to establish right to award of compensation by proving conditions on which rights depend. Employee not entitled recovery for aggravation of preexisting condition, except to extent injury increases disability. Employer not liable where use or consumption of alcohol or illegal drugs contributes to injury. (44-501). Subject to 44-506, Act applies to all employments wherein employers employ employees within state except Act does not apply to: (1) Agricultural pursuits and employment incident thereto; (2) any employment where total gross annual payroll for preceding calendar year and estimated gross payroll for current year are less than $20,000 for all employees; except, no wages paid to employee who is member of employer's family by marriage or consanguinity shall be included in total gross annual payroll; (3) any employment where employer had no payroll for calendar year and estimated gross payroll for current year is less than $20,000; (4) employment of fireman in firemen's relief association; or, (5) services by real estate agent as independent contractor. (44-505[a]). Employers excepted from Act by 44-505(a) may elect to come within provisions of Act by becoming member and maintaining membership in qualified group-funded workers' compensation pool or filing with Director written statement of election to accept thereunder. Election effective until employer files written statement withdrawing election with Director. Written statements of election or withdrawal to be made in such form as required by regulation of Director. (44-505[b]).

Employers must report all accidents on forms prepared by director within 28 days after receipt of knowledge and must keep liability insurance in force, or may carry own insurance subject to approval by Director. Five or more employers of same trade or profession may agree to pool their liabilities for Kansas workers' compensation benefits and employers' liability, to be known as group-funded workers' compensation pools. (44-532, 44-557, 44-581).

Notice of Accident.—To entitle injured workman to compensation, notice of accident must be given employer within ten days from date of same, but no notice is necessary where the employer or his agent has actual knowledge. Extended to 75 days for just cause. (44-520).

Written claim for compensation must be served on employer, personally, through agent or by registered mail, within 200 days from date of accident, or date of last payment of compensation, or if death results from injury within five years, then within one year from date of death. These limitations are tolled under certain conditions. (44-520a).

Procedure.—Amount of compensation due may be settled by agreement of parties. (44-521). Whenever employer, workman or insurance carrier cannot agree upon right to compensation or upon any issue regarding compensation benefits due, employer, workman, or insurance carrier may apply in writing to Director for determination of such. Application must be in form prescribed by Director's rules and must set forth substantial and material facts of claim. No proceeding maintainable under Act unless application for hearing is on file in Director's office within three years of accident date or within two years of date of last compensation date, whichever is later. (44-534). Director, administrative law judge, or court not bound by technical rules of procedure, but shall give parties reasonable opportunity to be heard and present evidence. (44-523a). Upon application for hearing under 44-534, matter shall be assigned to administrative law judge for hearing. Claimant is to submit all evidence no later than 30 days after initial hearing before administrative law judge and respondent is to submit all evidence no later than 30 days thereafter. When all parties submit case for award, administrative law judge must issue award within 30 days, unless time extended by agreement of parties, if employee receiving temporary or permanent disability, for medical examination, or other good cause. If award not entered in 30 days, any party to action may so notify Director and Director shall assign matter to Assistant Director to enter award forthwith based on record evidence. Director may also remove case on his own motion when administrative law judge fails to issue award within 30 days. Prehearing settlement conference scheduled not less than ten days before hearing. (44-523).

Review.—Workers' Compensation Board established with exclusive jurisdiction to review all decisions, findings, orders and awards of administrative law judges. Review of law and fact as shown by transcript. Action of board, other than disposition of appeals of preliminary orders or awards, is subject to review per act for judicial review and civil enforcement of agency actions by appealing directly to court of appeals. Any party may appeal from final order of board by filing with court of appeals within 30 days of final order. Review by court of appeals limited to questions of law. (44-556).

Enforcement of award is by court action as for collection of debt, except that civil penalties and attorney fees may also be awarded. (44-512a).

Rate of compensation is based upon percentage of average weekly wage of employee in accordance with schedule contained in act. Maximum weekly rate is 75% of state's average weekly wage, as determined by 44-511. (44-510c). Maximum compensation benefits payable by employer shall not exceed $125,000 for permanent total disability, $100,000 for temporary total disability and $100,000 for permanent or partial disability except that when permanent partial disability where functional impairment only is awarded limit is $50,000. (44-510f).

Rehabilitation benefits reasonably necessary to restore injured employee to work at comparable wage are provided for when agreed to by employer or insurance carrier. (44-510g).

Death benefits are payable to dependents in accordance with statutory formula, up to $200,000 including funeral expenses up to $4,300. (44-510b).

Occupational diseases are covered. (44-5a01).

Subrogation.—Where insurer or qualified group funded workers' compensation pool pays compensation of employee or employee's dependents under Act, insurer or pool is subrogated to rights, duties and immunities of employer. (44-532). Worker's Compensation Fund subrogated to rights of employer. (44-504).

See category Legal Profession, topic Attorneys and Counselors, subhead Compensation.

Employer's Liability.—Railroad company employees injured through negligence or mismanagement of its agents, employees, etc., are entitled to damages from such railroad, provided written notice, stating time and place of injury, is given railroad within eight months from date of injury. If injured person dies or commences suit during said eight months, no notice need be given. Eight months does not begin to run until injured employee is discharged from company hospital. (66-235).

Such notice may be served on any process agent, or upon local superintendent of affairs, freight agent, ticket agent or station keeper. (66-236).

Contributory negligence is no defense, but may be shown in mitigation of damages (66-238), except that neither contributory negligence nor assumption of risk may be

LABOR RELATIONS . . . *continued*
shown for any purpose where the violation by the railroad of any federal or state safety statute contributed to the injury (66-238, 9).

Unemployment Compensation.—Individual performing service for wages or under contract of hire, written or oral, express or implied, eligible for benefits if Commissioner finds that he has registered for work at an unemployment office, has made a claim for benefits, is able and available for work and is making reasonable efforts to obtain work. (44-701 et seq.). Discharge due to misconduct, gross misconduct or failure to apply for, or accept suitable work are grounds for disqualification. Terms defined by statute. (44-706). Regulations of Commissioner largely govern procedure. (44-701 et seq.).

WORKERS' COMPENSATION LAW:

See topic Labor Relations.

ENVIRONMENT

ENVIRONMENTAL REGULATION:

General Supervision.—State Board of Health, Secretary of Health and Environment and State Corporation Commission have general supervision of all pollution control acts and receive assistance under certain acts from advisory councils. Disposal of oil or gas field brines and mineralized waters supervised by Secretary of Health and Environment. (55-1003; 65-184; 65-3301; 65-3401).

Kansas Storage Tank Act.—(K.S.A. 65-34,100 et seq). Requires owners of storage tanks to notify Department of Health and Environment of tank's existence, age, size, type, location, other equipment and uses. Owner of underground storage tank taken out of service after Jan. 1, 1974 and prior to May 8, 1986 shall notify department of date, age, capacity, type, location, and type and quantity of contents on date removed from operation. Notice form provided by department. No person shall construct, modify or operate underground storage tank without permit or other approval from secretary. Petroleum storage tank release trust fund established. Owner or operator liable for all costs of corrective action taken in response to release.

Prohibited Acts of Pollution.—Plans for disposal of oil or gas field brines and mineralized waters must be submitted to State Corporation Commission. Commission determines sufficiency of plan in protecting from loss or waste of resources and determines adequacy of protection against pollution of water resources. (55-1003). No person, company, corporation, institution or municipality may dispose, discharge or allow escape of sewage, chemical or waste products into waters of state without permit issued by Secretary of Health and Environment. Not applicable to public sewer system established prior to Mar. 20, 1907, unless Secretary determines system polluting waters in manner prejudicial to health of citizenry. (65-164). Secretary authorized to designate sanitation zones surrounding certain impoundments of water and to fix standards to prevent pollution in said area. (65-184 to 189). It is unlawful to operate, construct, or alter solid waste processing facility or disposal area or allow dumping or depositing of solid wastes without permit (certain exceptions). Solid waste management committee required for each county, which committee must review management plan annually, hold public hearings and notify Secretary of Health and Environment of review or hearing. Permit for solid waste facility contingent upon surety bond. Permit revocable if facility is hazard to area or environment or public nuisance. (65-3405, 65-3407, 09). Installation, alteration or use of any machine or device found to contribute to air pollution may be prohibited by Secretary and Secretary has authority to prescribe motor vehicle emission controls, industrial emission controls and establish requirements and prohibitions relating to open burning. (65-3001 et seq.). Cities and counties authorized to provide for disposal of solid wastes and levy charges on persons receiving service. (65-3410).

Enforcement.—Primary enforcement responsibilities rest with county attorney and may be enforced by attorney general. Enforcement actions may include actions for injunction, mandamus or quo warranto. Certain acts provide for administrative hearings. (55-1007; 65-171d; 65-188; 65-3001 et seq.; 65-3412; 65-3414). Secretary may take necessary action to protect health of persons or environment when emission of air pollution presents substantial endangerment to persons or environment or imminent or actual violation of act occurs. Action includes order to owner/operator to prevent or eliminate practice; commencing injunctive action through attorney general or district attorney or seek court order directing compliance. When temporary restraining order or preliminary injunction sought not necessary to allege or prove irreparable damage. (65-3012).

Penalties.—Violation of restrictions on disposal of oil or gas filed brines and mineralized waters constitutes a misdemeanor allowing a fine of up to $500 and imprisonment of one year. Each day violation continues is a separate offense. (55-1003; 55-1007). Penalty for discharge of sewage into waters of state without permit allows minimum $2,500 and maximum $25,000 fine and further penalty of not more than $25,000 for each day violation continues. Penalty for discharge without filing report where required is minimum $1,000 and maximum $10,000 per day offense is maintained. (65-167). Failure to furnish information required by Secretary of Health and Environment relative to discharge a misdemeanor with $50 minimum fine to $500 maximum fine. Failure to comply with requirements of Secretary a misdemeanor with fine ranging from $25 to $100 for each offense and each day constitutes separate offense. (65-169). Secretary may establish regulations relating to motor vehicle emissions. (65-3017). Violation of air pollution regulations allows fine not to exceed $10,000 with each day a separate offense. Right of individual to civil action for damage maintained. (65-3018).

Permits.—Disposal of oil or gas field brines and mineralized waters subject to plan approved by State Corporation Commission. (55-1003). Permit to discharge sewage, chemical or waste products subject to approval of application accompanied by plans and specifications submitted to Secretary of Health and Environment. (65-166). Compliance with sanitation zone regulations subject to exceptions where undue hardship shown and where granting of exceptions not unduly harmful to health and welfare of area.(65-189f). Operation of solid waste processing facility or disposal area unlawful without permit. Application for permit made on forms provided by Secretary of Health and Environment. Fee established by Secretary. (65-3407). Secretary may require notice be given prior to construction, installation or establishment of air contaminant sources specified in its rules and regulations and may require application for permit prior to construction, installation or establishment of such air contaminant source. Permit may be denied if applicant fails to show other sources under applicant's control comply with applicable standards. Permit fee may be fixed by secretary. (65-3008).

Hazardous Waste Cleanup.—Any person who assists in cleaning up hazardous materials accident is not civilly liable for his acts or omissions while mitigating or attempting to mitigate damage or assisting cleanup, unless he caused accident, is compensated for assistance, or is grossly negligent. (65-3472).

ESTATES AND TRUSTS

ADMINISTRATION:

See topic Executors and Administrators.

ADVANCEMENTS:

See topic Descent and Distribution.

DEATH:

See category Property, topic Absentees.

Survivorship.—Uniform Simultaneous Death Act adopted. (58-701).

Action for death may be maintained for damages resulting from wrongful act or omission of another if decedent might have maintained action had he lived. (60-1901). May be commenced by any of the heirs at law of deceased who sustained a loss by reason of death, and is for exclusive benefit of all of heirs who have sustained loss regardless of whether they join or intervene in action. (60-1902). No limitation on amount of damages recoverable for pecuniary loss sustained by heir at law, but $250,000 limitation on amount recoverable for intangibles such as mental anguish, suffering, or bereavement; loss of society, companionship, comfort, or protection; loss of marital care, attention, advice or counsel; loss of filial care or attention; and loss of parental care, training, guidance, or education. (60-1903[a]). If no probate administration for estate of deceased has been commenced, expenses for care of deceased which resulted from wrongful act may also be recovered by any heir who paid or became liable for them, and such expenses, and funeral expenses, are not included in $250,000 limitation. (60-1904). Jury makes separate awards for pecuniary damages without instruction on limitation on nonpecuniary damages. Court enters judgment for maximum of $250,000 for nonpecuniary loss. (60-1903[b]). Net amount recovered, after allowance by court of costs and reasonable attorney's fees, must be apportioned by court upon hearing with notice to all known heirs. Apportionment must be in proportion to loss sustained by each of heirs whether or not they joined or intervened in action. In absence of fraud, no person who failed to join or intervene in action may claim any error in such apportionment after order has been entered and funds distributed. (60-1905).

See also category Civil Actions and Procedure, topic Actions, subhead Abatement and Revival.

Death Certificate.—See category Documents and Records, topic Records, subhead Vital Statistics.

Transfer on Death.—See category Property, topic Deeds, subhead Transfer on Death, and category Transportation, topic Motor Vehicles, subhead Titles and Sales.

Uniform Anatomical Gift Act.—See topic Wills.

Living Wills.—See topic Wills, subhead Living Wills.

DECEDENTS' ESTATES:

See topics Descent and Distribution, Executors and Administrators, Wills; category Debtor and Creditor, topic Homesteads.

DESCENT AND DISTRIBUTION:

In case of intestacy, real and personal estate descends and is distributed as follows: (1) where the decedent left a surviving spouse and child or children, one-half to the surviving spouse and one-half to the child or children surviving and the living issue, if any, of prior decreased children, but such issue inherit per stirpes; if no surviving spouse, then all to the children as aforesaid; (2) if the decedent left no issue, the whole of the estate goes to the surviving spouse; (3) if the decedent left no surviving spouse or issue, the whole of the estate goes to the parents. If one of the parents be dead, the whole of the estate goes to the surviving parent. If both parents be dead, the property which would have passed to the parents had both been living passes to the heirs of such parents, respectively (excluding their respective spouses), the same as it would have passed had such parents owned it in equal shares and died intestate, but if either of said parents left no such heirs, then to the living heirs of the other parent. Each generation in ascending and descending line is counted as one degree of blood relationship and no property will pass except by lineal descent to persons more than six degrees removed from decedent. (59-502-509).

See also topic Executors and Administrators.

Rights of Surviving Spouse.—See Introductory Paragraph, supra.

Half Blood.—No statutory provision. Children of half blood inherit equally with children of whole blood from common parent only. (136 Kan. 228, 14 P. 2d 722).

Stepchildren do not inherit from brother or sister of half blood, through stepparent. (68 Kan. 53. 74 Pac. 623).

Children.—"Children" means: (1) Biological children, including posthumous child; (2) children adopted as provided by law; and (3) children whose parentage is or has been determined under Kansas Parentage Act or prior law. (59-501[a]). See category Family, topic Infants, subhead Determination of Parentage.

See note at head of Digest as to 1998 legislation covered.

See Topical Index in front part of this volume.

KS – 23

DESCENT AND DISTRIBUTION . . . *continued*

"Issue" includes adopted children of deceased children or issue. (59-501[b]).

Determination of Descent.—When person has been dead for more than six months and has left property, and no petition has been filed for probate of will nor administration commenced, any person interested in estate may petition for determination of descent in county of decedent's residence or in any county where any property or any interest in property is situated. (59-2250). Where real estate is involved, notice must be by publication and mailing. Otherwise, notice is as court directs. (59-2251). Decree determines descent of property and is conclusive (59-2251), except that party served only by publication in proceeding to determine descent of real property may within one year have decree opened or set aside (59-2252).

Informal Administration Act permits one comprehensive notice of all assets to interested parties and one court appearance for court approval of plan for disposition of property. May be used for testate and intestate proceedings. (59-3301).

Advancements.—Property given by way of advancement to an heir is considered part of the estate and is taken by such heir toward his part of the estate at what it would be worth in the condition in which it was so given him. If advancement exceeds amount to which he would be entitled, he cannot be made to refund any portion thereof. If person who received advancement is deceased and property advanced has descended to his heir, advancement is considered as having been made directly to such heir. (59-510).

Election.—None.

Incapacity to Take.—Person convicted of feloniously killing or obtaining killing of another person cannot inherit or take by will, by intestate succession, as a surviving joint tenant, as a beneficiary under a trust or otherwise any portion of estate or other property in which decedent had an interest. When any person kills or causes killing of own spouse and thereafter takes own life, estates and property of both persons disposed of as if deaths were simultaneous. (59-513). See topic Death.

Renunciation.—Beneficiary may disclaim interest in whole or in part. (59-2291[a]). Written disclaimer must be filed within nine months latest of: (1) Decedent's death; (2) date taker's interest is finally ascertained both in quality and quantity; or (3) date taker becomes 21 years of age. (59-2292[a]). Disclaimer must be filed in district court in which estate is or may be administered. (59-2292[b]). Disclaimer valid to extent it does not conflict with K.S.A. 39-709 eligibility requirements for welfare assistance. (59-2292[c]).

Effect.—Disclaimer will relate back to death of decedent. Disclaimant will be treated as if he predeceased decedent. Once filed and recorded, disclaimer is irrevocable. (59-2293).

Escheat.—If an intestate decedent leaves no person entitled to receive property as an heir, then such property passes to living heirs of intestate's last spouse dying prior to death of intestate, and if there be no such heirs, then estate escheats to state. (59-514). Where no heirs are found within six months after appointment of an administrator, court must direct decedent's real and personal property to be sold for cash and estate must be closed. Net proceeds of estate are remitted to State Treasurer and become temporarily a part of escheat proceeds suspense fund. (59-901). Claimant as heir must present his claim to such money or any part thereof to district court not later than ten years after administrator was appointed. (59-903). If money is paid to such claimant, another person who thereafter establishes a claim as heir has no action against state but only against person to whom money was paid. (59-904).

EXECUTORS AND ADMINISTRATORS:

Proceedings for probate of will or administration must be in district court of county of residence at time of death if decedent owned real property in that county. If decedent did not own real property in county where he resided at death, probate proceedings allowed in county of death or any county where he owned real property. If decedent a nonresident, proceedings may be had in any county wherein he left any estate to be administered. Administration first granted extends to all property within state and is exclusive. (59-2203).

See topic Wills, subhead Probate.

Preferences in Right to Administer.—Where decedent left a will, letters testamentary are granted to executor named in will if he is legally competent and accepts the trust; otherwise letters of administration with will annexed must be granted. (59-701).

Administration of an intestate's estate must be granted, in order, to: (1) Surviving spouses or next of kin or both, or person or persons selected by them; (2) if such persons are incapable, unsuitable or do not accept, one or more creditors or their nominees; (3) if court determines that it is for the best interests of the estate, any other person. (59-705).

Eligibility and Competency.—In administration of resident's estate letters testamentary or of administration may not be granted to nonresident of this state, unless nonresident appointed agent by defendant pursuant to law, and if executor or administrator becomes a nonresident, court must revoke his letters. (59-706).

Corporate fiduciaries prohibited except for: (1) Banks and savings and loan located in Kansas or in state that would allow Kansas banks or savings and loans as fiduciaries; or (2) other corporations incorporated and having principal place of business in Kansas. (50-1701[a]).

Qualification.—Executor or administrator must take oath (oath of corporate fiduciary by duly authorized officer [59-1702]) and execute and file bond with sufficient sureties, approved by court, in such amount as court directs, not less than 125% of value of personalty and probable annual income from real estate which comes into his possession. Court may thereafter order bond increased or reduced or a new bond given. Joint executors or administrators may have separate or joint bonds. Bond may be waived by provision in will to that effect. (59-1101 et seq.).

Removal.—A fiduciary may be removed whenever he (1) becomes incapable of performing the duties of his trust, or (2) fails or refuses to perform any duties imposed upon him by law or lawful order of the court. (59-1711).

Special Kinds of Administration.—When person named as executor is a minor without rights of majority, administration with will annexed may be granted during his minority or disability unless another executor will accept the trust until the minor arrives at full age or possesses the rights of majority, when he may be admitted as joint executor, (59-702).

If authority of sole or surviving executor or administrator terminates before estate is fully administered, a new administrator with the same powers and duties as his predecessor must be appointed. (59-708). For good cause shown court may appoint special administrator to perform particular duties, either before or after appointment of general administrator, without the latter's removal. (59-710).

Inventory and Appraisal.—Within 30 days after appointment, executor or administrator must make a verified inventory of estate coming into his possession or knowledge. (59-1201). Independent appraisement not required unless requested by party in interest. Appointment subject to approval of court. No more than three allowed. Have 30 days after approval to file appraisement. (59-1202). Supplemental inventory and appraisal of properties not included in original inventory shall be filed within 30 days after discovery thereof. (59-1203). Discharge or bequest in will of debt to testator is not valid against creditors, but amount thereof must be included in inventory an if necessary applied to payment of debts. Any claim which testator had against his executor must be included in inventory. Annual crops, severed or not from land at time of his death, are deemed personal property and must be inventoried and administered as such. (59-1201 et seq.). Representative may employ advisor(s) whose compensation set by court. (59-1207).

General Powers and Duties.—Personal representative has right to possession of all properties of resident decedent except homestead and allowances for surviving spouse and minor children and to all real and personal property of nonresident within state. Representative must pay taxes, collect rents and earnings, keep in tenantable repair buildings and fixtures under his control, and may, by himself or with heirs or devisees, maintain action for possession of, or to quiet title to, real estate. (59-1401). Executor or administrator may, with court's consent, authorize representative to continue any business of decedent under such conditions, restrictions, regulations and requirements and for such periods, not exceeding six months for any one period, as court may determine. (59-1402). Executor or administrator has same right to foreclose mortgage or collect debt secured or complete any such proceedings in that regard, receive money and execute release, as decedent would have had if living. (59-1403).

Property specifically bequeathed may be delivered to legatee on his giving security for its redelivery. (59-1406). Executor or administrator may, by court order, compromise any debt or other obligation or pay encumbrances on assets if this appears to be for best interest of estate. (59-1304).

Required notice of probate proceedings must be given to all interested persons in manner and for time considered reasonable by court. Copies of petition and attachments, will (if applicable), accounting and settlement agreement must be served with notice unless excused by order. (59-2208).

Until letters testamentary are granted, executor has no power to dispose of any part of estate except to pay reasonable funeral expenses and to conserve the estate. (59-704).

Executor of executor has no authority to administer estate of first testator. (59-703).

Notice of Appointment.—Petitioner for administration, probate of will or refusal to grant letters must, within ten days after filing, commence publication of notice to creditors in county newspaper weekly for three consecutive weeks, unless petition filed nine months after decedent's death. (59-709). Notice must be to all creditors concerned, must state date of filing and must notify creditors to exhibit their demands within four months from date of first published notice or be forever barred. (59-2236).

Notice to Creditors.—See subhead Notice of Appointment, supra.

Claims against estate of decedent may be made by filing verified petition for their allowance in district court, stating nature of demand and all offsets entitled. Petitioner shall provide copy of demand to personal representative of estate. Court from time to time after proper hearing must enter its judgment allowing or disallowing such claims. Verified claim under $1,500 may be allowed by executor or administrator without filing and allowance by court. (59-2237). If action was pending against decedent at time of death, which by law survives, it is revived in court where action pending, and is considered demand legally exhibited from time of revival; if action commenced against administrator or executor after death of decedent, it is considered demand legally exhibited from time of serving process on administrator or executor; judgment creditors in such cases must file certified copy of such judgment in district court within 30 days after judgment is final. (59-2238). Demands payable at future date may be allowed at then present value thereof or court may order executor or administrator to retain sufficient funds to satisfy same at maturity, or heirs, devisees or legatees may give bond in satisfaction thereof. (59-2240).

All demands against a decedent's estate (including an action in tort or for wrongful death [157 Kan. 336, 139 P.2d 401], and any "demand" that amounts to a contest of the will [158 Kan. 345, 148 P.2d 278]), due or to become due, absolute or contingent, including demands arising out of any statutory or suretyship liability of decedent, not exhibited within four months after date of first published notice to creditors, are forever barred from payment, unless testator's will requires payment of a demand exhibited later. No creditor may have any claim against estate, other than liens existing at date of death, unless petition filed for probate of will or administration of estate within six months after death of decedent and creditor has exhibited his demand in manner and within time above described. (59-2239).

Form.—No specific form required. The following is in common use:

Form

IN THE DISTRICT COURT OF . . . .COUNTY, KANSAS IN THE MATTER OF THE ESTATE OF . . . . Deceased. PETITION PURSUANT TO CHAPTER 59 FOR ALLOWANCE OF DEMAND

. . . ., whose residence and address is . . . ., for and on behalf of . . . . does hereby represent that said estate is indebted to . . . . as herein set forth.

. . . .
Less off-sets of . . . .
Balance due, ...

EXECUTORS AND ADMINISTRATORS . . . *continued*

WHEREFORE, petitioner respectfully requests the Court to fix the time and place for the hearing of this demand and at said hearing to make allowance of said demand, and assign the same to the . . . . Class.

. . . . Petitioner

By . . . .

STATE OF KANSAS,
COUNTY OF . . . ., ss.

I do solemnly swear that I am the above claimant, or agent of said claimant, and individually, or as such agent, had the management and transaction of the business out of which the above demand originated and have had the means of knowing, personally, the facts set forth above, and same are true; that allowance has been made for all payments and set-offs, and that the amount claimed is justly due said claimant and remains unpaid. So help me God.

. . . .

Subscribed and sworn to before me, this . . . . . day of . . . ., 19 . . .

. . . . Notary Public

My Appointment expires . . . .

Payment of Claims.—All property of decedent, except homestead and allowances to spouse and minor children, is liable for payment of lawful demands against his estate. Unless will provides otherwise, or court otherwise determines, property of testator is applied to payment of debts in following order: (1) Personal property not disposed of by will; (2) real estate not disposed of by will; (3) personal property bequeathed to residuary legatee; (4) real estate devised to residuary legatee; (5) property not specifically bequeathed or devised; (6) property specifically bequeathed or devised. (59-1405).

If assets are insufficient to pay all demands allowed, payment must be made in following order: (1) reasonable funeral expenses; (2) reasonable and necessary expenses of last sickness and costs of administration; (3) judgments rendered against decedent in his lifetime; and (4) all other demands duly proved and for tombstone if approved by court. Debts having preference by laws of Kansas or U. S. must be paid according to such preference. No demand may be given preference in payment over any other demand of same class, nor may a demand due and payable be given preference over demands not due. (59-1301). If claimant holds security for his demand it must be allowed for the full amount due if security has been surrendered, or for remaining amount found due after security has been exhausted. (59-1303). If estate is solvent executor or administrator may, after four months from notice of his appointment, pay claims in order of classification. (59-1302).

Sale of Personal Property.—Executor or administrator must, as the court directs, sell the personal property or any part thereof (1) when its sale is necessary for payment of debts or legacies, (2) when division thereof cannot be made in kind to those entitled thereto, or (3) when sale is to best interests of the estate. (59-1407). Verified petition for sale of personal property may be heard with or without notice and the property may be sold at private sale for not less than three-fourths of the appraised value, determined by law or at public auction after notice by publication not less than ten days before sale in newspaper of county where sale is to be had. (59-2242, 3).

Sale or Lease of Real Property.—Executor or administrator may lease real estate in his possession for not more than one year or, together with heirs and devisees, for longer than one year; and may execute an oil and gas or other mineral lease. Income from lease must be received by executor or administrator as income from such property. (59-1409).

Executor or administrator may file a petition to sell real estate of decedent whenever necessary for payment of expenses of decedent's funeral, last sickness, servant's wages during last sickness or costs of administration, taxes, debts, legacies charged on such property or whenever court determines realty is wasting asset detrimental to estate, or otherwise determines sale in best interests of estate. Proceeds distributed as if real estate. Bona fide purchaser takes free of all liens and claims of creditors, including lien of state for inheritance taxes, and all such liens and claims are transferred to proceeds of sale. (59-1410). When such petition is filed, court must fix time and place for hearing and notice of same must be published as court directs. (59-2304). Petition for lease for three years or less may be heard with or without notice. (59-2032). On hearing of petition, court may order sale, lease or mortgage of real estate described in petition, and manner thereof, and with consent of mortgagee may order sale of real estate subject to mortgage. (59-2304). Such consent releases estate should deficit appear later. (59-2304). Lease cannot be made for less than three-fourths of appraised value of lease-hold interest, and realty cannot be sold at private sale for less than three-fourths of its appraised value. (59-2305). Appraisal in both cases is made by no more than three disinterested persons appointed by personal representative and approved by court. (59-2307). Notice of public sale must be given by weekly publication for three consecutive weeks in newspaper of county in which real estate is located, and sale may not be held earlier than seven nor later than 14 days after date of last publication of notice. (59-2308). Sale must be confirmed and execution of deed ordered. (59-2309).

Sale of any property may be made by executor or administrator with will annexed without order of district court if will authorizes executor to sell such property, unless will provides otherwise. (59-1413).

Allowances.—After inventory and appraisement have been filed, surviving spouse of Kansas decedent, on petition to court, must be allowed from personal or real property, for benefit of such spouse and decedent's minor children during minority, wearing apparel, family library, pictures and musical instruments, furniture and household goods, utensils and implements used in the home, one automobile, provisions and fuel on hand necessary for support of spouse and minor children for one year, and not more than $25,000 cash or other personal or real property at appraised value in full or part payment thereof. If no minor children, such property belongs to spouse. If there are minor children and no spouse, it belongs to minor children. Selection must be made by spouse, if living; otherwise by guardian of minor children. (59-403). Surviving spouse, by electing to take under will of decedent, or by consenting thereto, does not waive homestead right nor right to allowances unless will clearly provides otherwise. (59-404).

Widow's Quarantine.—None.

Accounting and Settlement.—Executor or administrator has nine months from date of appointment for settlement of estate. Administrator de bonis non has such time, not exceeding nine months, as court may determine. Limited period may be extended by court not exceeding nine months at a time. (59-1501). (Caution—This section was not changed, but all other time limits for probate administration were shortened to six months in 1985.) If prior to final settlement there is sufficient money to pay all demands against estate, personal representative may pay legacies and distributive shares (satisfying specific legacies first) upon court order. (59-1503). If four months have not passed since date of death, representative may not be compelled to pay partial distribution unless redelivery bond and court so orders. (59-1503). Personal representative must present verified account within time limited and make application to court to settle and allow account and assign estate to persons entitled thereto. (59-1502). If title to real property is to be assigned, notice of hearing for final account and settlement must be published weekly for three consecutive weeks in county newspaper, beginning within ten days after order fixing time and place of hearing, and copy of notice, and petition and attachments, will, accounting and settlement agreement, when applicable, must be mailed to each known heir, devisee or legatee within seven days after first published notice. (59-224, 59-2209). Otherwise notice is as court directs. (59-2247, 2208). On hearing, court must determine the heirs, devisees and legatees entitled to the estate, and if it appears that there is sufficient money to satisfy all demands against the estate, must assign and make distribution of legacies and shares by its decree. Said decree is binding as to all of decedent's estate, but no final decree may be entered until after determination and payment of inheritance taxes. If distributee is defendant of garnishment and executor or administrator is garnishee no funds may be delivered to distributee until order of court issuing garnishment. (59-2249).

If by will the use or income of personal property is given to a person for a term of years or for life, and another person has an interest in such property as remainderman, the court, unless will provides otherwise, may order such property delivered to or held for benefit of person having limited estate. (59-1506).

After executor or administrator has transferred all property of the estate to the persons entitled thereto, paid taxes required to be paid by him, and otherwise fully discharged his trust, the court must finally discharge him and his sureties. (59-1718).

Distribution if Abroad.—See subhead Unclaimed Money, infra.

Unclaimed Money.—If any part of unclaimed money has not been paid over because person entitled thereto cannot be found or refuses to accept the same, "or for any other good and sufficient reason" the court may order it paid to the County Treasurer. (59-1508).

Liabilities.—Any person who embezzles or converts any personal property of a decedent is liable for double the value thereof. (59-1704).

Compensation.—Personal representative is allowed necessary expenses and reasonable compensation for services and attorney fees of estate. (59-1717). If will makes provision for executor's compensation, this must be taken as full compensation unless executor files waiver of will's provisions. Heir or beneficiary who prosecutes or defends action for benefit of estate may receive expenses. (59-1504). If executor or administrator fails or refuses to perform any duty imposed on him by law, he may be removed and his compensation reduced or forfeited in discretion of court. (59-1711).

When Administration Unnecessary.—Where decedent has been dead more than six months and no petition has been filed for probate of a will nor administration commenced in this state, then short proceeding to determine heirs may be filed. (59-2250). See topic Descent and Distribution, subhead Determination of Descent.

When established that estate of decedent, exclusive of homestead and allowances to spouse and minor children, does not exceed amounts required for funeral expenses, expenses of last sickness, wages of servants during last sickness, costs of administration, debts having preference under laws of U.S. or this state, and taxes, executor or administrator may by order of court pay same in order named, and present his account with application for settlement and allowance. Court with or without notice, may adjust, correct, settle, allow or disallow such account, and if allowed, summarily determine heirs, legatees, and devisees, and close administration. (59-1507). Court may remit court costs where total assets of estate do not exceed $500. (59-2215). See subhead Estate of Nonresidents, infra.

Small Estates.—

Simplified Estates Act, see topic Wills, subhead Probate.

Informal Administration Act (59-3301) provides for one comprehensive notice of all assets to interested parties (59-3301) and one court appearance for approval of dispositional plan for property (59-3301). Act applies to testate and intestate proceedings. (59-3302). Required contents of petition are specified in 59-3302. Court may determine informal administration is not appropriate be-cause of contested matter, need for administration, disagreement among beneficiaries or other circumstances. (59-3305).

Estate of Nonresidents.—Administered with respect to all property within jurisdiction as original proceedings as if decedent were a resident. (59-804). To avoid hardship to creditors or others, court may order distribution to foreign personal representative or may find administration unnecessary and order distribution. If liabilities exceed assets, court must distribute pro rata to creditors here and elsewhere with regard to preferential rights. (59-806). Nonresident may be appointed executor or administrator. (59-807). In intestate estate personal property passes under laws of place of residence at death; real estate governed by laws of Kansas. (59-806). See topic Wills, subheads Foreign Executed Wills and Foreign Probated Wills.

Determination of Descent.—Where decedent has been dead more than six months, no will has been filed under 59-618a, no petition has been filed for probate of will nor administration commenced in this state, then short proceeding to determine heirs may be filed. (59-2250). See topic Descent and Distribution, subhead Determination of Descent.

See note at head of Digest as to 1998 legislation covered.

See Topical Index in front part of this volume.

KS – 25

EXECUTORS AND ADMINISTRATORS . . . *continued*

Foreign executors or administrators, on filing in proper district court proof of authority, and appointment of resident agent to receive service of process (59-1706), may assign, extend, release, satisfy or foreclose any mortgage, judgment or other lien, or collect any debt secured thereby, belonging to the estate. They must follow same proceeding as domestic representative in making sale, lease or mortgage of real property acquired on execution or judicial sale. (59-1707).

Foreign executor or administrator may sue or be sued in any Kansas court in like manner and under like circumstances as nonresident may sue or be sued. (59-1708).

Foreign Beneficiaries.—If it appears that a citizen of a foreign country is interested in estate, district court must notify consular representative of such country for Kansas, provided such consular representative has filed his credentials with probate court. Failure to give such notice does not affect validity of any proceeding. (59-1705). Whenever notice is mailed to person in foreign country, notice must be mailed by air mail. (59-2209).

See also subhead Unclaimed Money, supra.

Uniform Disclaimer of Transfers by Will, Intestacy or Appointment Act and Uniform Disclaimer of Transfers Under Nontestamentary Instruments Act, combined and adopted with modification. (59-2291).

Uniform Fiduciaries Act not adopted.

Uniform Principal and Income Act adopted. (58-901 to 913).

Uniform Simplification of Fiduciary Security Transfers Act adopted. (17-4903-4913). Uniform Commercial Code (K.S.A. 84-1-101 et seq.) specifically provides that it does not repeal this uniform act and if any inconsistency between two, provisions of Simplification of Fiduciary Security Transfers Act control. (84-10-101[2]).

Uniform Anatomical Gift Act.—See topic Wills.

TRUSTS:

Kinds.—

Testamentary Trusts.—Actions must be brought in district court under c. 59 (probate code). (59-103).

Inter Vivos Trusts.—Actions must be brought in district court under c. 60 (Code of Civil Procedure), except that trusts in favor of imprisoned convicts or persons subject to conservatorship are treated as testamentary trusts. (59-103[a][7, 8]).

Implied trusts arise by operation of law.

"Business", "Common Law" or "Massachusetts" Trust.—See category Business Organizations, topic Associations.

Creation.—

Express trust created by: (1) Explicit declaration with intent to create; (2) definite property or subject matter; and (3) acceptance of subject matter by trustee. (241 Kan. 698, 740 P.2d 571). If subject matter is real property, must be created by writing signed by settlor (59-2401) and executed like conveyance (58-2210).

Resulting Trust.—When conveyance for valuable consideration is made to one person but consideration is paid by another, title vests in grantee and no use or trust results in favor of person paying consideration. (58-2406). However conveyance is presumed fraudulent as to creditors of person paying consideration. If fraudulent intent not disproved, trust will result in favor of prior creditors to extent of just demands and, if sufficient evidence of fraudulent intent, in favor of subsequent creditors. (58-2407). Trust will also result if grantee takes conveyance in own name without consent of person paying consideration, if purchase money belonged to another and was used in violation of trust, or if party buying and party advancing money intended for trust to arise. (58-2408).

Trust Purposes.—Trusts are generally prohibited from directly or indirectly owning or leasing agricultural land in Kansas. Prohibition does not apply to: (1) Defined family and testamentary trusts; (2) certain authorized trusts; and (3) agricultural land held by charitable nonprofit corporation, held for nonfarm purposes, or acquired by process of law if divested within 10 years. (17-5904).

Trust for use of settlor void as to all creditors. (33-101).

Cy-Pres doctrine codified. (59-22a01).

Appointment of Trustee.—

Testamentary Trusts.—District court appoints. If nominee unsuitable, court may appoint another. (6 Kan.App.2d 1001, 637 P.2d 444).

Inter Vivos Trust.—Settlor appoints.

Eligibility and Competency.—Corporate fiduciaries prohibited except for: (1) Banks and savings and loans located in Kansas or in state that would allow Kansas banks or savings and loans as fiduciaries; or (2) other corporations incorporated and having principal place of business in Kansas. (59-1701[a]).

Qualification.—Trustee, before entering on duties, must take oath unless qualification with court has been excused or waived. (59-1702). Court may require bond of at least 125% of value of personal property and probable annual income from real estate which will come into trustee's possession (59-1101), unless: (1) Will or trust agreement waives bond; (2) all beneficiaries file written waiver; or (3) trustee is bank with trust authority or trust company organized and having principal place of business in Kansas (59-1104). Court may increase or decrease bond. (59-1106).

Foreign fiduciary must appoint agent residing in county of appointment and consent to service on agent. Writing must state agent's address and must be filed in district court. (59-1706).

Removal of Trustee.—District court on petition and after hearing may remove trustee for violation or attempted violation of express trust, insolvency or other good cause. (58-2412). Court may also remove trustee if incapacitated or otherwise incapable of performing trust duties or for failure or refusal to perform any duty imposed by law or court order. (59-1711).

General Powers and Duties of Trustees.—Trustee has power, without court authorization, to perform every act which prudent man would perform for purposes of trust. (58-1203[a]). Uniform Trustees' Powers Act adopted. (58-1201 et seq.).

Foreign Fiduciary.—Fiduciary appointed by court of competent jurisdiction in another state or country must file authenticated copy of fiduciary's letters or other record of authority and certificate that authority is still in force in district court of proper county. (59-1707).

Sales.—Sale of land is void if in contravention of trust (58-2405), however this will not defeat title of bona fide purchaser without notice of trust (58-2402).

Investments.—(17-5001 et seq.).

Securities in Name of Nominee.—Bank or trust company may appoint nominee. (9-1607).

Bequests and Devises to Inter Vivos Trusts.—See topic Wills.

Accounting.—

Testamentary Trust.—Within 30 days after end of each annual trust period or termination of trust, trustee must file accounting in district court of county where will was probated showing: (1) Period account covers; (2) complete statement of trust capital and income received and expended; (3) present investments and other trust property held; (4) names and addresses of beneficiaries and which, if any, are minors or incapacitated; (5) proposed distribution; (6) payment of expenses, commissions and counsel fees; and (7) such other facts as court may require. (59-1602, 59-1603, Rule 109). Distribution accounting must be filed within 30 days of distribution. (59-1604).

Accounting is required on resignation of fiduciary (59-1709) or death or disability of sole or last surviving fiduciary (59-1712).

Inter Vivos.—No specific statutory provisions.

Compensation.—

Testamentary Trust.—On application to district court fiduciary is allowed necessary expenses, reasonable compensation and reasonable attorney fees. (59-1717). Court may reduce or forfeit compensation if fiduciary is removed for failing or refusing to perform lawful duties. (59-1711).

Discharge.—Trustee of any express trust may resign by petitioning district court. Court accepts resignation and discharges trustee on terms set by court. (58-2411).

Testamentary Trust.—Court may discharge trustee upon approved intermediate distribution accounting (59-2255) or upon final distribution if trustee has otherwise fully discharged his duties (59-1718).

Uniform Common Trust Fund Act.—Adopted. (9-1609, 9-1610). Official amendment not adopted.

Revised Uniform Principal and Income Act.—Adopted. (58-901 et seq.).

Gifts to Minors.—See category Family, topic Infants.

Uniform Fiduciaries Act.—Not adopted.

Uniform Simplification of Fiduciary Security Transfers Act adopted. (17-4903-4913). Uniform Commercial Code (K.S.A. 84-1-101 et seq.) specifically provides that it does not repeal this uniform act and if any inconsistency be-tween two, provisions of Simplification of Fiduciary Security Transfers Act control. (84-10-101[2]).

Accumulations.—No statutory provisions.

Perpetuities.—See category Property, topic Perpetuities.

Pour Over Trusts.—See topic Wills, subhead Bequests and Devises to Inter Vivos Trusts.

Renunciation.—Beneficiary of testamentary or inter vivos trust may disclaim any interest in whole or in part. (59-2291[a]). Disclaimer must: (1) Describe interest subject to disclaimer; (2) contain declaration of disclaimer and extent thereof; and (3) be signed and acknowledged by disclaimant. (59-2291[b]). Disclaimer must be filed and recorded in district court within nine months after latest of: (1) Death of decedent; (2) date taker's interest becomes finally ascertained and fixed both in quality and quantity; or (3) date taker becomes 21 years of age. (59-2292). Disclaimer valid to extent it does not conflict with K.S.A. 39-709. (59-2292[c]).

WILLS:

Any person of sound mind and possessing rights of majority may dispose of property by will, subject to statutory provisions. (59-601). To be effectual, will must be admitted to probate. (59-616).

Uniform Probate Code.—Not adopted.

Testamentary Disposition.—There is no limitation as to amount or time of making of devise or bequest to religious, charitable and educational institutions.

Any devise of real estate located in Kansas and any bequest of personal property by resident of Kansas, to, or in trust for, any foreign country, subdivision or city, body politic or corporation of such foreign country, except devises and bequests to religious, charitable and educational institutions, is void. (59-602).

Execution.—Every will, except an oral will, must be in writing signed at end by testator, or someone for him in his presence and at his express direction, and must be attested and subscribed in presence of testator by two or more competent witnesses, who saw testator subscribe or heard him acknowledge same. Will may be made self-proved, at execution or during lifetime of testator and witnesses, by their affidavit acknowledged and sealed by proper officers. Codicil or election to take under will may be proved in same manner. (59-606).

Forms

Attestation Clause: In witness whereof, I have hereunto subscribed my name this . . . . . day of . . . . . ., in the presence of A. B. and C. D., whom I have requested to become attesting witnesses hereto.

(Signature of testator).

The foregoing instrument was subscribed, published and declared by (name of testator) as and for his last will and testament in our presence and in the presence of each of us, and we, at the same time, at his request, in his presence, and in the presence of each other, hereunto subscribe our names as attesting witnesses, this . . . . . . day of . . . .

(Signatures of both witnesses).

WILLS . . . *continued*

Spouse's Consent: I, A. B., wife (or husband) of C. D., do hereby consent to each and all of the terms and provisions of the foregoing last will and testament of the same C. D., and, having been fully advised of my rights under the law and being fully acquainted therewith, do hereby accept the provision made in said will for me, expressly waiving any and all rights that I have or might have as his wife (or husband) in or to his (or her) property under the law. In witness whereof, I have hereunto subscribed my name in the presence of two witnesses in the city of . . . . . ., County of . . . . . ., State of . . . ., this . . . . . . day of . . . .

(Signature of wife or husband).

Testator and Witnesses Affidavit:
State of Kansas . . . . } ss.
County of . . . . }

Before me, the undersigned authority, on this day personally appeared . . . ., ..., and . . . ., known to me to be the testator and witnesses, respectively, whose names are subscribed to the annexed or foregoing instrument in their respective capacities, and, all of said persons being by me first duly sworn, said . . . ., testator, declared to me and to the said witnesses in my presence that said instrument is his last will and testament, and that he had willingly made and executed it as his free and voluntary act and deed for the purposes therein expressed; and the said witnesses, each on his oath stated to me, in the presence and hearing of said testator that the said testator had declared to them that said instrument is his last will and testament, and that he executed same as such and wanted each of them to sign it as a witness; and upon their oaths each witness stated further that they did sign the same as witnesses in the presence of each other and in the presence of the testator and at his request, and that said testator at that time possessed the rights of majority, was of sound mind and under no restraint.

. . . .
(Testator)

. . . .
(Witness)

. . . .
(Witness)

Subscribed, acknowledged and sworn to before me by . . . ., testator, and . . . . and . . . ., witnesses, this . . . . . day of . . . . . ., A.D., ...
(Seal) (Signed) . . . .

. . . .
(Official capacity of officer)

(Certificate concerning witnesses similar to that in attestation clause of will, followed by signatures of two witnesses). (59-606).

Holographic wills are not recognized.

Nuncupative will made in last sickness is valid in respect to personal property if reduced to writing and subscribed by two disinterested witnesses within 30 days after speaking of testamentary words, when testator called on some person present to bear testimony to said disposition as his will. (59-608).

Revocation.—A will is revoked by some other will in writing; by some other writing of testator declaring such revocation, executed with formalities required for execution of a will; by burning, tearing, cancelling, obliterating or destroying such will with the intent and purpose of revoking same by testator or by another in his presence by his direction. If, after making a will, the testator marries and has a child by birth or adoption, the will is revoked. If, after making a will, the testator is divorced, all provisions in such will in favor of the testator's spouse so divorced are thereby revoked. (59-610, 11).

Revival.—Revocation of a second will does not revive the first unless it appears by the terms of the revocation that such was testator's intention or unless first will is duly republished. (59-612).

Testamentary Gifts to Subscribing Witnesses.—Void if testimony is required to prove will. But if such witness would have been entitled to share of estate in absence of will, so much of such share as does not exceed value of devise or bequest will pass to him from part of estate included in void devise or bequest. (59-604).

Bequests and Devises to Inter Vivos Trusts.—Pour over trusts valid. Trust instrument may be amended after date of will. (59-3101). Uniform Testamentary Additions to Trusts Act adopted. (59-3101 et seq.).

Testamentary Guardians.—See category Family, topic Guardian and Ward.

Probate proceedings are had in district court in county of decedent's last residence, if decedent owned real property in that county. If decedent did not own real property in county where he resided at death, probate proceedings allowed in county of death or any county where he owned real property. If decedent nonresident, proceedings in county where he left estate to be administered. (59-2203). After petition is filed, court fixes time and place for hearing and statutory notice of same must be given unless court makes order to contrary, in which case notice, unless waived, must be by per personal service on all persons interested at least ten days before hearing. All parties interested may, when petition is filed, enter their appearance in writing, waive notice required and consent to immediate hearing, which may be had. Any heir, devisee or legatee may prosecute or oppose probate of any will. (59-2219 et seq.).

Undue Influence.—If will appears to have been prepared by principal beneficiary who, at time of preparation of same occupied any relationship of confidence or trust to testator, it must be affirmatively shown that testator read or knew contents of such will and had independent advice with reference thereto. (59-605).

Time for Filing Petition.—Will is not effective to pass real or personal property unless petition is filed for probate of such will within six months after testator's death. (59-617). Person who has possession of will or knowingly withholds same from probate for more than six months forfeits all rights under will and is liable for all damages and reasonable attorney fees sustained by beneficiaries; but will may be probated as to any innocent beneficiary within 90 days after he has knowledge of will and access thereto, if within five years after testator's death, although title of innocent purchaser in good faith, without knowledge of will, is not defeated if application for probate is not filed within six months after testator's death. (59-618). If estate contains no real property and value of assets less than claims specified in 59-1301, person possessing will may file it and affidavit pursuant to 59-618a(b) to preserve will for record in case probate is necessary later. (59-618a). Oral will of testator who died while resident of Kansas is not admitted to probate unless application for probate is made within six months after testator's death except as provided by 59-2229,30. (59-619).

Simplified Estates Act provides for one comprehensive notice of all assets to interested parties and one court appearance for approval of plan for disposition of property if court finds that there are no contested matters. (59-3301 et seq.). Request for procedure made in petition. (59-2219). Notice given parties, advising of procedure, stating court will not take part in administration unless written objection filed. (59-2222). Once estate opened under act, further court supervision unnecessary until closing estate, unless executor or administrator requests court determination of proceeding or act. (59-3205). Executor or administrator may sell, liquidate or exchange personal property not specifically bequeathed or make distribution subject to bond, prior to closing. (59-3204). Court may terminate administration under act if valid objection filed or executor or administrator shows procedure disadvantageous under circumstances. (59-3206).

Informal Administration Act provides for one comprehensive notice of all assets to interested parties and one court appearance for approval of plan for disposition of property if court finds there are no contested matters. (59-3301 et seq.).

Lost will may be established if its provisions are clearly and distinctly proved. (59-2228).

Self-proved Wills.—Will may be made self-proved, at execution or during lifetime of testator and witnesses by their affidavit acknowledged and sealed by officer authorized to administer oaths. Codicil or election to take under will may be proved in same manner. Self-proved will, unless contested, shall be admitted to probate without testimony of subscribing witnesses. Form and contents of affidavits should be substantially similar to those under subhead Forms. (59-606, 2224).

Living Wills.—Any adult person may execute declaration directing withholding or withdrawal of life-sustaining procedures in terminal condition. Form must be executed like will or acknowledged before notary public. (65-28,103[a]). Statutory form provided. (65-28,103[c]).

Contest.—Will must be proved before judgment or decree may issue, verified petition sufficient absent written defenses or appearance by adverse party. (59-2213). Proof may be either by self-proof or by testimony and affidavit, but if self-proved will is contested it must be proved by testimony, affidavits or depositions. Court may waive testimony of witnesses upon showing of unavailability. (59-2224). Contest is made when will is presented for probate. (59-2225). Order admitting will to probate must be appealed within 30 days of entry. (59-2401[a]). If after will is admitted to probate another will is presented, probate proceedings will be held for second will. If second will admitted to probate, order admitting first will is revoked. (59-2226).

Legacies.—

Time for Payment.—May be paid on order of court at any time prior to final settlement if estate has sufficient money to satisfy all demands. Specific legacies must be first satisfied. (59-1503).

Ademption.—Whether inter vivos gift to legatee works ademption by satisfaction depends on intention of testator when gift was made. (222 Kan. 245, 564 P.2d 472).

Unclaimed Legacies.—Court may order unclaimed legacies paid to county treasurer and held for ten years. After ten years no recovery may be had. (59-1508).

Lapse.—Where will makes devise or bequest to spouse, relative by lineal descent or within sixth degree, whether by blood or adoption, and spouse or relative dies before testator leaving issue surviving testator, such issue shall take estate said devisee or legatee entitled to had he survived unless will otherwise provides. In will executed after July 1, 1973, unless provisions of will otherwise provide, term "issue" means offspring, progeny, or lineal descendants, by blood or adoption, in whatever degree. (59-615).

Children.—

Living Children Not Provided for in Will.—No statute or case law requires affirmative showing of intent to disinherit.

Children Born after Execution of Will.—If, after making will, testator marries and has child, will is thereby revoked. (59-610). No other statute or case law.

Election.—Surviving spouse may take elective share determined by length of marriage. (59-6a202). Election against will is made by filing written instrument within six months after probate of will with district court. If surviving spouse has consented to will consent controls. (59-2233). If surviving spouse is incapacitated, court must order election if more favorable than will to spouse. (59-2234).

Contribution.—Unless will provides otherwise or court in interest of estate otherwise determines, property subject to payment of debts or other items exhausted in following order (all of one class to contribute ratably if all property therein not required): (1) Personal property not disposed of by will; (2) real estate not disposed of by will; (3) personal property bequeathed to residuary legatee; (4) real estate devised to residuary devisee; (5) property not specifically bequeathed or devised; (6) property specifically bequeathed or devised. (59-1405).

Renunciation.—Beneficiary may disclaim in whole or in part any real or personal property or any interest therein. (59-2291[a]). Disclaimer is by written instrument filed within nine months of latest of: (1) Death of decedent; (2) date that taker's interest is ascertained and becomes indefeasibly fixed in quality and quantity; or (3) date taker becomes 21 years of age. (59-2292). Disclaimer valid to extent it does not conflict with K.S.A. 39-709. (59-2292[c]).

Foreign Executed Wills.—Will executed outside Kansas is valid if in writing and signed at end by testator and executed according to: (1) Kansas law; (2) law of place of execution; or (3) law of testator's residence either at time of execution or time of death. (59-609). This is variation of Uniform Wills Act, Foreign Executed.

See note at head of Digest as to 1998 legislation covered.

See Topical Index in front part of this volume.

WILLS . . . *continued*

Foreign Probated Wills.—Authenticated copies of a will duly executed and proved according to laws of any other state or territory, relative to any property in Kansas, may be admitted to probate or record at any time in district court of any county where any part of such property is situated. Authenticated copies so admitted to probate or record have same validity as wills made in Kansas in conformity with laws thereof. (59-806).

Procedure.—Verified petition with notice of hearing the same as in a resident decedent's estate required to admit authenticated copy of will to probate or record. Title of good faith purchaser of estate property shall not be defeated by production of will and petition to probate after expiration of six months from testator's death. (59-2229, 30).

Administration.—Same, with respect to all property within jurisdiction, as original proceedings as if decedent were a resident (59-804) and assets distributed: (1) personal property according to terms of will applicable, but if no will applicable, then according to law of decedent's residence; and (2) real property is assigned according to terms of will applicable, but if no will applicable, then according to laws of Kansas. (59-806).

See also topic Executors and Administrators, subhead Estates of Nonresidents.

Simultaneous Death.—See topic Death, subhead Survivorship.

Testamentary Trusts.—See topic Trusts.

Transfer on Death.—See categories Property, topic Deeds; and Transportation, topic Motor Vehicles.

Uniform Anatomical Gift Act.—Adopted. (65-3209 et seq.). No material variations except provision that hospitals must encourage organ donations. (65-3218).

FAMILY

ADOPTION:

Kansas Adoption and Relinquishment Act. (59-2111 et seq.).

Any adult, or husband and wife jointly may adopt minor or adult as their child, except one spouse cannot do so without consent of other.

Consent.—Must be given in writing acknowledged by: (1) Living parents of child; (2) one of parents if other failed to assume duties of parent for two consecutive years or is incapable of consenting; (3) legal guardian if both parents dead or if both failed to assume duties of parent for two consecutive years; (4) court entering order under K.S.A. 38-1584(c)(1)(B); (5) judge of court with jurisdiction over child if parental rights not terminated; (6) child if over 14 and of sound intellect. (59-2105). Minority of parent does not invalidate consent.

Consent acknowledged before judge of court of record. Court must advise consenting person of consequences. Consent is final when executed unless consenting party, prior to final decree of adoption, alleges and proves by clear and convincing evidence that consent was not freely and voluntarily given.

Consent or relinquishment may not be given by mother or accepted until 12 hours after birth.

Consent or relinquishment executed and acknowledged outside of Kansas in accordance with Kansas law or law of place where executed is valid.

See topic Infants, subhead Termination of Parental Rights.

Conditions Precedent.—None.

Jurisdiction.—District court has jurisdiction.

Venue.—In county of residence of adopting party or in county where child resides, except if child is in custody of agency authorized to place child for adoption, venue is in county where agency is located. If adopting party resides upon or is stationed at U.S. military post or reservation within Kansas and child resides with adopting party, venue is proper in county where post is located or in any immediately adjacent county.

Petition must state: (1) Medical and social history of child and parents; (2) names, addresses and telephone numbers of child's biological parents, if known; (3) any hospital records for child or properly executed release for such records; (4) child's birth verification, including date, time and place of birth and name of attending physician. See Kansas Administrative Regulations 30-45-1 thru -4 for detailed requirements.

Proceedings.—

Minor Child.—Hearing must be held between 30 and 60 days after petition is filed. Notice must be given to parents or presumed parents, unless parental rights have been terminated, and any other persons as court directs.

Except for stepparent adoption, court must require petitioner to obtain adoption advisability assessment by licensed social worker or adoption placement agency. For nonresidents, assessment must be completed in petitioner's state of residence. Assessment must be less than one year old when petition is filed. Assessment must be filed with court not less than ten days before hearing on petition.

See topic Infants, subhead Termination of Parental Rights.

Adult.—Petition may be heard forthwith, with or without notice, in court's discretion.

Decree.—Final order of adoption entered after hearing on petition. No interlocutory decree, however court may make appropriate order for care and custody of child pending hearing.

Name.—Child assumes surname of adoptive parent, but court may permit different surname upon request. Upon request, given name may be changed.

Effect of Adoption.—Adopted child entitled to same personal and property rights as natural child of adoptive parent. Adoptive parent has all rights and liabilities of natural parent.

Upon adoption natural parent's rights cease, including right to inherit from child, except for natural parent who is spouse of adopting parent.

Setting Aside Adoption.—Adoption proceeding not subject to collateral attack unless record affirmatively shows lack of jurisdiction. (215 Kan. 102, 523 P.2d 743).

Charges.—Request for, offer of, gift of or receipt of consideration in connection with adoption is prohibited except reasonable legal fees, reasonable fees of licenced child-placing agency, actual and necessary expenses incident to placement and proceeding, actual medical expenses for child and mother due to pregnancy and birth, and reasonable living expenses incurred by mother during or as result of pregnancy. Court reviews all expenditures.

Record of adoption proceeding is not open to public inspection.

Interstate Compact on Adoption and Medical Assistance.—Entered into July 1, 1985. (38-336).

DIVORCE:

This subject is governed by 60-1601 et seq.

Protection from Abuse.—Act provides emergency relief to protect household members from abusive treatment by person with whom petitioner resides or has resided or has child in common. (60-3101 et seq.). Any person on own behalf or parent or adult residing with minor on behalf of minor may seek relief by filing petition. Service of process shall be personal and not by certified mail, return receipt requested. (60-3104). Abuse defined at 60-3102. District judge may grant relief out of court when court not in session. Order issued ex parte expires at 5:00 p.m. on first day court resumes regular business. (60-3105). Hearing on petition must be held within 20 days and plaintiff must prove abuse by preponderance of evidence. Defendant must have opportunity to present evidence. (60-3106). Court may approve consent agreement or grant following relief; (1) Direct defendant to refrain from abuse; (2) grant possession of residence or household to party to exclusion of other party who is spouse; (3) require party to provide suitable, alternate housing for such party's spouse and minor children of parties; (4) award temporary custody and establish temporary visitation rights; (5) order law enforcement officer to evict party from residence or household; (6) order support payments by party for support of minor child or spouse; (7) award costs and attorneys fees; (8) make provision for possession of personal property; (9) require parties to seek counseling. (60-3107[a]). Limitations in length of support order (60-3107) and number of petitions each year (60-3111).

Grounds for Divorce or Separate Maintenance.—(1) Incompatibility; (2) failure to perform material marital duty or obligation; (3) incompatibility by reason of mental illness or incapacity (requires finding of confinement of spouse in institution by reason of mental illness for two years which need not be continuous or adjudication of mental illness or incapacity while spouse is confined in institution by reason of mental illness. In either case two or three court appointed physicians must find poor prognosis for recovery but decree granted on this ground will not relieve party from contributing to support and maintenance of mentally ill or incapacitated spouse). (60-1601).

Citizenship Requirements.—None.

Residence Requirements.—Petitioner or respondent must have been actual resident of state for 60 days next preceding filing of petition. This includes persons stationed at or resident of U.S. military base within state for 60 days preceding filing of petition. Spouse may have residence in this state separate and apart from residence of other spouse. (60-1603).

Jurisdiction.—District courts. (60-1601).

Venue.—May be brought in county in which petitioner is actual resident at time of filing petition or where respondent resides or may be served. Military residents may file in any county adjacent to base. (60-607).

Process.—A summons is issued as in other cases. See category Civil Actions and Procedure, topic Process.

Pleading.—Grounds for divorce or separate maintenance must be alleged in the general language of the statute, without detailed statement of facts. Names and dates of birth of minor children must be stated. Affidavit containing jurisdictional information concerning children required. Respondent may answer and may also file counter petition. New material set up in answer must be verified by respondent in person. Opposing party may demand bill of particulars and facts stated therein will be specific facts upon which action will be tried. Copy delivered to judge, but not filed with clerk of court or made part of record except on appeal, and then only when issue to be reviewed relates to such facts. (60-1604, 60-1605).

Practice.—An action for divorce may not be heard until 60 days after filing of petition unless court declares existence of emergency. In case of emergency, unless waived by parties, action shall not be heard until time permitted for filing answer expires. Upon request of either party or sua sponte, court shall set pretrial conference to explore possibilities of settlement and to expedite trial. After filing of responsive pleading, court may require both parties to seek marriage and parental counseling if available within judicial district of venue of action. Cost of counseling may be assessed as costs in case. (60-1608). Either party is competent to testify upon all material matters involved in controversy. Decree of divorce, separate maintenance or annulment may be granted upon uncorroborated testimony of either party or both of them. (60-1609). Attorney for prevailing party to divorce or annulment must provide certain information to court for report to state registrar of vital statistics. (65-2422b).

Decree.—Becomes final when time for appeal expires or waiver of appeal is incorporated into decree or signed by parties. (60-1610[c]).

Temporary Alimony.—After filing of petition, court may, if necessary, provide for support of either party while action is pending. (60-1607[a][3]). Support order may be enforced by garnishment. (60-1607[c]).

Allowance for Prosecution of Suit.—

Interlocutory Decree.—If necessary to ensure either party's efficient preparation for trial, court may provide for expenses of suit including reasonable attorney's fees. (60-1607[a][4]).

Final Decree.—Court may award costs and attorney fees to either party as justice and equity require. (60-1610[b][4]). Costs may include family counseling (60-1617[b]), marriage counseling (60-1608[d]) and enforcement of visitation rights (60-1616[d]; 23-701[f][4]).

See note at head of Digest as to 1998 legislation covered.

See Topical Index in front part of this volume.

KS – 28

DIVORCE . . . *continued*

Permanent Alimony.—Court may award allowance for future support, called maintenance, to either party in amount court finds fair, just and equitable under circumstances. Maintenance may be in lump sum, periodic payments, on percentage of earnings or on any other basis. (60-1610[b][2]).

Termination.—Court may not award in excess of 121 months. Decree may specify circumstances terminating, but court may reserve power to order reinstatement. (60-1610[b][2]).

Modification.—Decree may specify circumstances modifying, but court may reserve power to reinstate. At any time, on hearing with reasonable notice to affected party, court may modify maintenance payments not already due. Court may make modification of maintenance retroactive to date at least one month after date motion to modify was filed with court. (60-1610[b][2]).

Division of Property of Spouses.—Court may divide all real and personal property of parties acquired before or during marriage. Court may consider: (1) Age of parties; (2) duration of marriage; (3) property owned by parties; (4) parties' present and future earning capacities; (5) time, source and manner of acquisition; (6) family ties and obligations; (7) allowance or disallowance of maintenance; (8) dissipation of assets; and (9) other factors necessary to just and reasonable division of property. (60-1610[b][1]).

Change of Spouse's Name.—On request of spouse, court must order restoration of maiden or former name. (60-1610[c][1]).

Custody of Children.—

Interlocutory decree restraining parties and providing for child custody and support may be entered after petition is filed. (60-1607[a]).

Final Decree.—Best interests of child control. Relevant factors include: (1) Length of time someone other than parent has cared for child; (2) desires of parents; (3) desires of child; (4) relationship of child with parents, siblings and other persons; (5) child's adjustment to home, school and community; (6) ability of each parent to allow continuing relationship between child and other parent; and (7) evidence of spousal abuse. Provisions of written agreement of parties, if any, presumed in best interests of child, but presumption may be overcome on specific findings of fact. (60-1610[a][3]).

Types of Custodial Arrangements.—Court may order any arrangement that is in best interests of child, including, in order of preference, joint custody, sole custody, divided custody of two or more children, and non-parental custody. (60-1610[a][4]).

Change in Custody.—Subject to Uniform Child Custody Jurisdiction Act (38-1301 et seq.) court may change or modify any prior order upon showing of material change in circumstances, but may not enter ex parte change order absent sworn testimony showing extraordinary circumstances (60-1610[a][2]).

Visitation Rights.—Court may grant grandparents of unmarried minor child reasonable visitation rights during child's minority. (38-129). If custody is awarded to person other than parent, court may grant any person visitation rights. (38-129). If court orders non-parental custody, court will prefer to award custody first to relative of child and second to person with close emotional ties to child. (60-1610[a][4][D]). Court will award reasonable attorney's fees and costs of any proceeding to enforce visitation rights against parent who unreasonably denies or interferes with such rights. (60-1616[d]).

Allowance for Support of Children.—

Interlocutory Decree.—After filing of petition, court may, if necessary, provide for support of minor children during pendency of action. (60-1607[a][3]). Order may be enforced by garnishment. (60-1607[c]).

Final Decree.—Court must provide for support and education of minor children. Regardless of custodial arrangement, court may order expenses paid by either or both parents for any child less than 18 years of age unless: (1) Parent(s) agree in writing approved by court to pay support beyond 18 years of age; (2) child reaches 18 while still attending high school, in which case support continues, unless court orders otherwise, until June 30 of that school year; (3) if child still bona fide high school student after June 30 of school year in which child turned 18, court may order support to continue through school year during which child turns 19 provided parents jointly participated or acquiesced in delaying child's completion of high school. (60-1610[a][1]).

In determining amount of support court must consider all relevant factors without regard to marital misconduct, including: (1) Financial resources and needs of both parents; (2) financial resources and needs of child; and (3) physical and emotional condition of child. Until child reaches 18, court may set apart any portion of property of husband or wife or both that seems necessary and proper for support of child. (60-1610[a][1]).

Remarriage.—Any marriage contracted by party inside or outside Kansas before decree becomes final is voidable until decree becomes final. Agreement waiving right of appeal either incorporated in decree or signed by parties and filed will shorten time during which remarriage is voidable. (60-1610[c][2]).

Foreign Divorces.—Judgment or decree of divorce rendered in any other state or territory of U.S., in conformity with laws thereof, must be given full faith and credit in this state; except, that if respondent in action, at time of judgment or decree, was resident of this state and did not personally appear or defend action in court of that state or territory, and that court did not have jurisdiction over his person, all matters relating to maintenance and property rights of parties and to support of minor children of parties are subject to inquiry and determination in any proper action or proceeding brought in courts of this state within two years after date of foreign judgment or decree, to same extent as though foreign judgment or decree had not been rendered. Court may not enter custody decree contrary to provisions of Uniform Child Custody Jurisdiction Act. (60-1611).

Separation Agreements.—If the parties have entered into a valid, just and equitable separation agreement, it must be incorporated and confirmed in decree, except that any provisions for custody, support or education of minor children are subject to control of court. Matters so settled by separation agreement are not subject to subsequent modification by court except as agreement itself may prescribe or parties may subsequently consent. (60-1610[b][3]).

Antenuptial Contracts.—See topic Husband and Wife.

Annulment of Marriage.—See topic Marriage.

GUARDIAN AND WARD:

"Guardian" means any person who has been appointed by a court to control person of disabled person or minor. "Conservator" is same except applies to control over estate. Proceedings for appointment of guardian may be had in district court of county of proposed ward's residence or where he may be found. Proceedings for appointment of conservator may be in district court of county of proposed conservatee's residence, or, if nonresident, in any county where any of his property is situated. (59-3002). "Disabled person" means any adult person whose ability to receive and evaluate information effectively or to communicate decisions, or both, is impaired to extent person lacks capacity to manage financial resources, except for reasons of indigency, or meet essential requirements for physical health or safety, or both. Person shall not be considered disabled for sole reason such person relies on treatment by spiritual means through prayer in lieu of medical treatment in accordance with tenets and practice of recognized church or denomination of which person is member or adherent. "Manage financial resources" means actions necessary to obtain and administer property, benefits and income. "Meet essential requirements for physical health and safety" means actions necessary to provide health care, food, shelter, clothing, personal hygiene, other care without which serious injury or illness is likely to occur. (59-3002).

Selection of Guardian.—Natural guardian (father and mother of minor if rights not terminated [59-3002(e)]) may, by last will or inter vivos trust, nominate guardian or conservator of person and estate of his minor children. In other cases, district court appoints guardian or conservator upon recommendation of applicant. (59-3004).

Eligibility and Competency.—No restriction against appointment of nonresident. No corporation, other than certified nonprofit Kansas corporation (59-3037), may be appointed guardian (59-1701[c]). Corporation may not be appointed conservator except: (1) Banks and savings and loans located in Kansas or in state that would allow Kansas banks or savings and loans as fiduciaries; or (2) other corporations incorporated and having principal place of business in Kansas. (59-1701[a]).

Qualification.—Guardian must take oath (oath of corporate fiduciary by duly authorized officer [59-1702]) and give bond with sufficient sureties in such amount as court directs, but not less than 125% of value of personalty and probable annual income from real estate which comes into his possession. (59-1101). District court may thereafter order bond increased or decreased or new bond given. (59-1106; 59-1107).

Inventory.—Within 30 days after appointment, representative must make verified inventory of ward's estate coming into his possession or knowledge. Three disinterested persons will be appointed by personal representative and approved by court to appraise property if requested by party in interest. Appraisal must be filed within 30 days of appraisers' appointment and is subject to court approval. (59-1202).

Real Estate.—Conservator may, subject to court's approval, lease for three years or less ward's real estate and, if necessary, may in manner of an executor or administrator (see category Estates and Trusts, topic Executors and Administrators) sell, lease for more than three years for oil and gas or other minerals or mortgage such property. Conservator may, subject to approval of court, extend mortgage for five years or less if rate of interest is not increased. (59-3021 to -3024).

Powers and Duties.—Guardian and conservator always subject to control and direction of district court. Guardian shall have charge of person of ward and shall diligently perform duties assigned by court and assure protection of ward's civil and human rights. Ward may be placed in institution only on court approval. (59-3018). Conservator shall (1) Prosecute and defend suits; (2) sell assets of estate; (3) pay reasonable support charges; (4) pay just and lawful debts of conservatee; (5) possess and manage property; (6) possess and manage going business of conservatee; (7) invest funds; (8) acquire title to real estate. (59-3019).

Limited Guardianship or Conservatorship.—If court finds that disabled person should be permitted to make some decisions regarding his person or property, guardian or conservator may be appointed with specified, limited powers. (59-3014[d]; 59-3018[c]).

Investments by guardian are governed by 59-3019, 59-3020; 17-1502; 17-1503.

Securities in Name of Nominee.—See category Estates and Trusts, topic Trusts, subhead Securities in Name of Nominee.

Liabilities of Guardian or Conservator.—Any person who embezzles or converts any personal property of a ward is liable for double the value of such property. (59-1704). Conservator is not personally liable on any mortgage note or by reason of covenants in any instrument of conveyance duly executed in representative capacity. (59-3025).

Accounting.—

Guardian.—Unless expressly waived by court, must file annual report with court on condition of ward. Supreme Court prescribes form. (59-3029[a]).

Conservator.—Must file verified annual account. Upon termination of conservatorship, or removal or resignation, must file verified final account with petition for settlement and allowance thereof. Supreme Court prescribes forms. (59-3029[b]).

Gifts to Minors.—See topic Infants.

Termination of Guardianship.—Guardianship or conservatorship of a minor terminates upon (1) Death, (2) attainment of legal age, or (3) marriage, except as to conservatorship of his estate unless rights of majority be conferred by such marriage. Other guardianships and conservatorships terminate upon death or restoration to capacity of ward. Whenever there is no further need for guardianship or conservatorship court may terminate it. (59-3028).

Insane Persons.—There are provisions for hearing by court, or trial by jury if demanded, prior to appointment of guardian or conservator for disabled person. (59-3013).

Foreign Guardian.—Must appoint resident agent for service of process (59-1706) and file authenticated copy of letters of authority and certificate that letters are still in force with district court (59-1707).

See note at head of Digest as to 1998 legislation covered.

See Topical Index in front part of this volume.

GUARDIAN AND WARD . . . continued

Foreign guardian may sue or be sued in Kansas courts in like manner and under like circumstances as nonresident may sue or be sued. (59-1708).

Uniform Fiduciaries Act not adopted.

Uniform Simplification of Fiduciary Security Transfers Act adopted. (17-4903-4913). Uniform Commercial Code (K.S.A. 84-1-101 et seq.) specifically provides that it does not repeal this uniform act and if any inconsistency between two, provisions of Simplification of Fiduciary Security Transfers Act control. (84-10-101[2]).

HUSBAND AND WIFE:

Disabilities of Married Women.—None.

Separate Property.—All property: (1) Owned by spouse before marriage, and rents, issues and profits thereof; (2) acquired by descent, devise or bequest, and rents, issues and profits thereof; or (3) acquired by gift except from other spouse remains spouse's sole and separate property. (23-203[a]). Spouse's earnings also separate property. (23-204). At time divorce action is filed, however, all property becomes marital property for purposes of divorce action. (23-203[b]). See topic Divorce, subhead Division of Property of Spouses.

Contracts.—Married person may buy, sell and contract with respect to such person's separate property. (23-202).

Antenuptial Contracts.—

Uniform Premarital Agreement Act adopted 1988. Applies to agreements executed on or after effective date. (23-801 et seq.).

Common Law.—Applies to agreements executed before effective date of Uniform Premarital Agreement Act. Contracts made either before or after marriage that fix property rights between husband and wife are not against public policy unless terms encourage separation of parties. Such contracts are liberally interpreted to carry out maker's intentions when contract was fairly made and its terms are equitable. (223 Kan. 679, 576 P.2d 629). Homestead rights cannot be waived. (202 Kan. 684, 452 P.2d 286).

Actions.—Married person may sue and be sued as if unmarried. (23-206).

Agency.—Neither husband or wife has power to act as agent of other merely by virtue of marital relation. (195 Kan. 626, 408 P.2d 697).

Conveyances.—It is not necessary that either husband or wife join in a conveyance by other except to bar inchoate statutory interest (see category Property, topic Dower) or where the property conveyed is a homestead (see category Debtor and Creditor, topic Homesteads).

Loss of Spouse's Services.—Right of action for loss or impairment of married person's ability to perform household and domestic services is in such person for benefit of such person's spouse so far as spouse is entitled thereto. (23-205).

Children.—Husband and wife have equal rights in the possession of their children. (Const., art. 15, §6). See topic Divorce, subhead Custody of Children.

Desertion or Nonsupport.—Any individual who, without just cause, fails to provide for support and maintenance of his or her spouse, if in necessitous circumstances, or any parent who, without lawful excuse, deserts, neglects or refuses to provide for support and maintenance of his or her child or children under age of 18 years, if in necessitous circumstances, is guilty of a crime. Court may make orders providing for support. (21-3605).

Uniform Interstate Family Support Act.—Adopted effective 1-1-95.

Community property system does not obtain in Kansas.

INFANTS:

Age of majority, 18 for both sexes; except married persons 16 years of age have majority in matters relating to contracts, property rights, liabilities, and capacity to sue and be sued. (38-101). Minimum age to consume cereal malt beverages (41-2701) and alcoholic beverages (41-102; 41-175) is 21.

Emancipation.—Rights of majority may be conferred on minors by proceedings in district court. (38-109).

Contracts.—A minor is bound by contracts for necessaries and for other contracts unless he disaffirms within a reasonable time after reaching majority and restores all of the money or property received and then remaining within his control (38-102), unless the minor obtained the contract by misrepresentations as to his age and the other party had good reasons to believe the minor was capable (38-103). Where a minor is paid for his personal services under a contract made with him alone this is a complete satisfaction. (38-104).

Minors may be shareholders in building and loan associations (17-1048), and may carry a deposit in a bank. Payment by the bank, on order of the minor, releases it from liability. (9-1204).

Minors may consummate contracts respecting insurance same as adults, and any policy, certificate or other evidence of such contract and any promissory note or installment contract for premium payment is as binding upon minor as though he were of legal age, but all such contracts made by a minor must have written consent of a parent, guardian, or conservator, and contract or note must be cosigned by person over 18 years. (40-237).

Actions.—Infant's representative may sue and defend on behalf of infant, and if no representative, infant may sue by his next friend or by a guardian ad litem. Court must appoint a guardian ad litem for an infant not otherwise represented in an action. (60-217; 59-2205). In any probate proceeding the court may appoint a guardian ad litem to defend any minor who is a party, and unborn beneficiaries may be represented by living competent members of class to which they would belong or by a guardian ad litem. (59-2205).

Support of Minor.—Parent's failure to support minor in necessitous circumstances is severity level 10, nonperson felony. (21-3605[7]).

Parental Responsibility.—Any person may bring action against parents for bodily injury or property damage caused by willful or malicious act of child living with parents. Damages limited to lesser of actual damages or $1,000. If child's act resulted from parental neglect, $1,000 limitation does not apply. (38-120). Resulting injury must be intended. (240 Kan. 30, 726 P.2d 1319).

Determination of Parentage.—Kansas Parentage Act adopted. (38-1110 et seq.).

Artificial Insemination.—Child treated as natural child of husband and wife if both consented to use of technique. (23-129).

Termination of Parental Rights.—

Procedure.—Any interested party may petition district court to terminate rights of either or both parents. Pleading must include statement of specific facts. (38-1581). Court must order hearing. Before hearing court must determine due diligence was used in determining identity of interested parties and in serving process. Attorney must be appointed for any parent who fails to appear. (38-1582).

Criteria.—If child is in need of care, court may terminate parent's rights on clear and convincing evidence that parent is unfit to care for child or parent has been convicted of certain offenses listed in 38-1585. (38-1583[a]). Court may also terminate if parent abandoned child or if parent's identity cannot be ascertained. (38-1583[d]).

Procedure after Termination.—Court may authorize adoption if viable, or long-term foster care. (38-1584[b]). See topic Adoption.

Kansas Parentage Act.—(38-1110).

Adoption.—After father or possible fathers are identified, each must be given notice as court directs. If any fail to appear, their rights are terminated. Father's rights may also be terminated if he cannot be identified and does not appear to assert rights. When father or alleged father appears, court may order parental rights be terminated upon finding by clear and convincing evidence that father: (1) Abandoned or neglected child after learning of birth; (2) is unfit parent; (3) made no reasonable effort to communicate with child after learning of birth; (4) failed without cause to support mother during six months prior to birth; (5) abandoned mother after learning of pregnancy; (6) birth resulted from rape; or (7) failed or refused to assume duties of parent for two consecutive years.

Uniform Transfers to Minors Act adopted. (38-1702). Age of majority under Act is 21. (38-1702). Optional subsection (c) to §22 of Act not adopted.

Uniform Securities Ownership by Minors Act not adopted.

MARRIAGE:

Age of consent for common law marriage: Males 14; females 12. (216 Kan. 445, 532 P.2d 1325).

Consent of parent or guardian required where person is under 18. Where no legal guardian judge of district court may give required consent. (23-106).

Medical Examination.—None.

License is required; issued by clerk or judge of district court of any county. One of applicants must personally apply for license. (23-106).

Waiting period of three calendar days after application is filed must elapse before license is issued, unless judge of district court orders immediate issuance. (23-106).

Ceremony may be performed by ordained, licensed or appointed clergyman or judge or retired judge of court of record or municipal. (23-104a).

Reports of Marriage.—Person performing marriage must endorse certificate of marriage on license and return same within ten days to judge or clerk issuing same. Judge or clerk must thereupon make record of same and forward license and certificate of marriage to secretary of health and environment. (23-109).

Record.—See category Documents and Records, topic Records, subhead Vital Statistics.

Common law marriage recognized. (220 Kan. 225, 552 P.2d 629). No decision concerning local recognition of purported marriage in another state where such would be void.

Proxy marriages are neither authorized nor prohibited by statute and are sometimes performed.

Prohibited Marriages.—Between: parent and child, grandparent and grandchild, brother and sister (half blood included), uncle and niece, nephew and aunt, first cousins. Such marriages absolutely void. (23-102).

Foreign Marriages.—Marriages between parties of opposite sex valid under law of place where contracted are valid in this state. (23-115).

Annulment.—District court shall grant decree of annulment for either of following grounds: (1) Marriage is void for any reason; or (2) contract of marriage is voidable because induced by fraud. District court may grant annulment if contract of marriage was induced by mistake of fact, lack of knowledge of material fact or other reason justifying rescission of contract of marriage. (60-1602).

Antenuptial Contracts.—See topic Husband and Wife.

HEALTH

Secretary of Health and Environment supervises and regulates sickness, disease and sanitation.

FOOD, DRUGS AND COSMETICS:

Governed by Kansas Food, Drug and Cosmetic Act. (65-655, et seq.).

HEALTH INSURANCE BENEFITS:

Health care benefits are governed by general provisions of Kansas insurance code (40-201 to 40-2, 162), Kansas uniform policy provisions (40-4601, et seq.), and special provisions for life and health insurance guaranty associations (40-3001, et seq.), health maintenance organizations (40-3201, et seq.) and managed care (40-4601, et seq.).

SMOKING REGULATION:

Smoking in public places or public meetings is prohibited except in designated areas pursuant to Kansas Criminal Code. (21-4009, et seq.). Local regulations may be more stringent. (21-4013).

INSURANCE

INSURANCE COMPANIES:

Commissioner of Insurance through Insurance Department supervises, regulates and controls organization of insurance companies and conduct of insurance business.

Copy of Insurance Code may be obtained by writing Commissioner of Insurance, 420 S.W. 9th, Topeka, KS 66612 (1-800-432-2484). Code does not apply to certain fraternal benefit societies. (40-202).

Rates.—Ks. Sess. L. c. 154, §§1-17, effective July 1, 1997.

Cancellation.—Property or casualty policy, except accident or sickness, used primarily for business or professional needs, in effect for 90 days or more, cannot be canceled except for: (1) Nonpayment of premium; (2) policy issued under material misrepresentation; (3) insured violated material term or condition of policy; (4) unfavorable underwriting factors, specific to insured, not present when policy written; (5) Commissioner determines that continuation of coverage could place insurer in hazardous financial condition or in violation of state laws; (6) insurer no longer has adequate reinsurance to meet its needs. Insurer to cancel for valid reason, must give 60 days written notice and written explanation. (40-2,120).

Reports.—All insurance companies must file with the Commissioner annual statements of their condition as of Dec. 31. (40-225).

Discrimination.—Excessive and discriminatory rates are prohibited. (44-2404).

Mental or Physical Handicap.—Rate discrimination prohibited unless based on sound actuarial principles or related to actual or reasonably anticipated experience. (40-2,109).

Rebates.—Prohibited. (40-242[a][3], 40-956).

Limits of Risk.—No company, other than title insurance company, may insure single risk for amount exceeding 10% of company's capital or surplus unless excess is reinsured with authorized insurer. (40-1107).

Title Insurance.—No insurer may insure single risk exceeding 50% of capital and surplus unless reinsured by authorized insurer or nonauthorized company meeting Kansas requirements. (40-1107a).

Agents and Brokers.—

Agent.—May be individual or legal entity. Must have license from Commissioner. Application fee $30; Commissioner prescribes forms. (40-240). Individual applicant must pass examination. (40-241). Commissioner collects annual fee from insurer. (40-242j; 40-252). Continuing education required. (40-240f).

Broker.—Must be individual (40-3702[a]) and have license from Commissioner (40-3703). Application fee $50; Commissioner prescribes forms. (40-3704). Must have been licensed agent in U.S. or Canada for preceding five years. (40-3706[a]). Must be citizen of U.S. (40-3706[c]). Annual fee $20. (40-3708). Continuing education required. (40-3707).

Process Agent.—

Authorized Insurer.—Insurance Commissioner deemed process agent. (40-3304[g]).

Unauthorized Insurer.—Secretary of State acts as process agent. (40-2704).

Investments.—17-5002, 40-2a01 et seq.; 40-2b01 et seq.

Foreign Insurance Companies.—Must obtain certificates before selling stock in state and may not do business in state until authorized by Commissioner. When certificate is issued, company is not subject to general corporation code relating to foreign corporations. (40-209, 40-214).

Commissioner of Insurance may only issue license to write policies of insurance to legal residents of this state. Commissioner may issue license to nonresident agents who are licensed in state where they reside, on payment of annual fee of $25. (40-246).

Retaliatory Laws.—Whenever another state or country requires Kansas insurer to pay greater taxes or fees than Kansas requires of foreign insurers, insurers from that state or country must pay increased amount equal to that required by their state or country. (40-253).

Premium Tax.—Imposed by 40-252.

Privilege Tax.—Repealed for calendar year 1998 and thereafter. (40-2801).

Uniform Unauthorized Insurers Act adopted. (40-2701).

Uniform Insurers Liquidation Act.—Not adopted.

Direct Actions Against Insurer.—See category Transportation, topic Motor Vehicles, subhead Direct Actions.

No-Fault Insurance.—See category Transportation, topic Motor Vehicles, subhead No-Fault Insurance.

Plain Language.—See category Business Regulation and Commerce, topic Consumer Protection.

SURETY AND GUARANTY COMPANIES:

Surety companies are under control of Commissioner of Insurance. (40-103). See topic Insurance Companies.

Reports.—Must file annual reports same as life insurance companies. (40-225).

Surety Company Bonds.—See category Civil Actions and Procedure, topic Bonds.

Venue of action on surety company bond, see category Civil Actions and Procedure, topic Venue.

Foreign companies admitted to do business in Kansas must have the same capital and surplus as a domestic company. Foreign company organized under laws of country other than United States must show that it has on deposit with proper state officials somewhere in United States securities equal to capital and surplus required of domestic companies. Such companies must also file with Commissioner of Insurance a copy of charter and by-laws, and verified, detailed statement of all matters required to be included in annual report of domestic company. (40-1104).

INTELLECTUAL PROPERTY

TRADEMARKS AND TRADENAMES:

Any person may register trademark he adopts and uses in Kansas. (81-113).

What May Be Used.—Any word, name, symbol, device or combination thereof used to identify and distinguish goods made or sold and services (81-111), unless it: is immoral, deceptive, or scandalous; disparages or falsely suggests connection with persons, living or dead, institutions, beliefs, or national symbols; simulates flag or other insignia of any governing body; is the signature or portrait of any living person, except with written consent; is merely descriptive or misdescriptive of goods or geographical location; is merely a surname; or so resembles trademark registered in Kansas or United States Patent Office by another that it is likely to cause confusion or mistake (except that registration in United States Patent Office justifies registration in Kansas) (81-112).

Labor unions, veterans' organizations, fraternal or benefit associations and societies may register names and insignia with Secretary of State. (75-421 et seq.).

Registration.—Verified application filed with Secretary of State on form furnished by him, accompanied by specimen of trademark in triplicate. Filing fee, $25. (81-113). Certificate of registration is issued. (81-114). Must be renewed every ten years. (81-115). Fraudulent registration renders party liable for any damages caused thereby. (81-120).

Assignment.—Trademark may be assigned with good will of business, but such assignment is void as to subsequent purchaser unless instrument is duly executed and recorded with Secretary of State within three months or prior to subsequent purchase. Fee is $5. (81-116).

Protection Afforded and Infringement.—Use of registered trademark or counterfeit or imitations thereof without consent can be enjoined and all damages caused thereby can be recovered. (81-122). Common law trademark rights not affected. (81-123).

Resale Price Agreements.—Fair Trade Act repealed. (1963, c. 291).

Tradenames.—No statutory provisions for registration.

TRADE SECRETS:

Uniform Trade Secrets Act adopted. (60-3320, et seq.). Provides for injunctive relief of actual or threatened misappropriation of trade secret upon application to court. Except when inequitable recovery of damages for misappropriation allowed and includes actual loss and unjust enrichment caused by misappropriation or by imposing liability for reasonable royalty for unauthorized disclosure or use of trade secret. Punitive damages and attorney fees may be awarded in cases involving willful and malicious misappropriation, bad faith claims or motions to terminate injunction. (60-3321-3). Court shall preserve secrecy of trade secret by reasonable means. (60-3324). Action must be brought within three years of discovery of misappropriation. (60-3325).

LEGAL PROFESSION

ATTORNEYS AND COUNSELORS:

The state bar is not integrated.

Admission to the bar of the Supreme Court entitles one to practice in any court in the state.

Jurisdiction Over Admission.—For admission to bar one must comply with rules adopted by Supreme Court. (Rule 701 et seq.). Supreme Court has jurisdiction of admission. (7-103).

Eligibility.—Applicants for admission to bar must be of good moral character and have requisite education. (Rule 702[a]). See subhead Educational Requirements, infra.

Registration as Law Student.—Not required.

Educational Requirements.—Applicant must hold degree from accredited college and law school. (Rule 702[a]).

Petition for admission is made on forms which may be procured from clerk of Appellate Courts, and must be verified by applicant and filed with clerk of Appellate Courts 90 days prior to examination.

Examination.—Board of Law Examiners conducts written examinations each year in Feb. and July using essay questions on local law and Multistate Bar Examination. (Rule 704[e]). Applicant may transfer MBE scores from another jurisdiction if taken within 13 months of current examination and if applicant passed entire bar examination of other jurisdiction. (Rule 704[f]). Applicant must pass Multistate Professional Responsibility Examination not later than 180 days after taking Kansas Bar Examination. (Rule 704[h]). Current fee is $175. (Rule 707[a][3]).

Clerkship not required for admission.

Admission without Examination.—Not permitted. However attorney may be granted special temporary permit to practice law if: (1) Attorney passed written bar exam in some other jurisdiction more than five years ago; (2) has or intends to become Kansas resident to accept employment other than practice of law; (3) will perform legal services for single employer only; and (4) is of good moral character. (Rule 706[a]). Forms available from Clerk of Appellate Courts. (Rule 706[b]). Current fee is $400 plus current charge for investigation and report. (Rule 707[a][4]).

Admission Pro Hac Vice.—Non-Kansas attorney may be admitted for purposes of particular case upon taking oath, upon filing showing local counsel and on personal appearance of local counsel. All service may be had on local counsel. Non-Kansas attorney is subject to Kansas disciplinary rules. (7-104, Rule 116).

See note at head of Digest as to 1998 legislation covered.

See Topical Index in front part of this volume.

ATTORNEYS AND COUNSELORS . . . *continued*

Licenses.—All attorneys must register on or before July 1 each year with Clerk of Appellate Courts. Supreme Court sets annual fee. (Rule 208[a], [c]). Current fee is $60. Attorneys subject to mandatory continuing legal education pay annual fee set by CLE Commission. (CLE Rule 11.01). Current fee is $20. Attorneys must also register and pay fees to clerk of local district court.

In larger counties attorneys must pay registration fee for county law library. Fee varies from $10 to $25 depending on county population and assessed valuation. (19-1308). Registered attorneys are exempt from all municipal license fees or occupation taxes. (19-1310).

Privileges.—No special provisions.

Disabilities.—Attorney may not be surety on any official bond or bond in any legal proceeding in district in which he resides. (78-101[a]).

Liabilities.—See category Civil Actions and Procedure, topic Costs.

Compensation.—Generally no requirement for filing fee agreements. Fee must be reasonable. Basis for fee must be communicated to client. All fee contracts are subject to review by appropriate court. (M.R.P.C. 1.5).

Insurance Actions.—Insurer liable for reasonable attorney's fees if it lacked just cause for refusing to pay and judgment exceeds any settlement offer. (40-256). In action on policy against loss by fire, tornado, lightning or hail, insurer liable for reasonable attorney's fees if judgment exceeds settlement offer. (40-908).

Kansas Consumer Protection Act.—Consumer recovers reasonable attorney's fees if supplier violated act. Supplier recovers if consumer knowingly brought groundless action. (50-634[e]).

Medical Malpractice Actions.—Attorney's fees must be reasonable and approved at evidentiary hearing. (7-121b).

Negligent Operation of Motor Vehicle.—Prevailing party allowed reasonable attorney fees for property damages less than $7,500 unless prevailing party recovers no damages or adverse party tendered amount equal to or greater than judgment. Written demand must be made within 30 days of commencing action or within 30 days of answer. (60-2006).

Unemployment Benefits.—Fees must be approved by Secretary of Human Resources. (44-718[b]).

Uniform Consumer Credit Code.—If creditor violates, court must award reasonable attorney's fees to consumer's attorneys. (16a-5-201[8]).

Worker's Compensation.—Written contract must be filed and approved. (44-536[b]). Generally fee limited to total of 25% of compensation recovered and paid. (44-536[a]).

Wrongful Death Actions.—Court determines reasonable attorney's fees. If more than one attorney, court apportions fees in accordance with services rendered. Fees are paid out of net recovery. (60-1905).

Lien.—An attorney has a lien for a general balance of compensation upon any papers of his client which have come into his possession in the course of his professional employment, upon moneys in his hands belonging to his client, and upon money due to his client and in the hands of the adverse party, in any action or proceeding in which the attorney was employed, from the time of giving notice of the lien to the party. Such notice must be in writing and may be served in the same manner as a summons, and upon any person, officer or agent upon whom a summons may be served, and it may also be served upon a regularly employed salaried attorney of the party. (7-108). When a judgment upon which a lien is claimed has been collected and paid, the clerk in term time or the judge at chambers on application may determine the amount due on the lien and make an order for distribution. Notice of the application and the time and place of the hearing must be served on the opposite party at least five days prior to the time named in the notice. (7-109).

Disbarment.—An attorney may be disbarred or suspended by the Supreme Court for collusion, deceit, bringing an action without authority, willful disobedience of a court order, willful violation of oath, neglecting or refusing to pay over money due a client, or destroying, secreting or altering court papers or records (7-106, 111), or for violation of disciplinary rules (Rule 202).

Sanctions may be imposed if any motion or other paper signed without first making reasonable inquiry to support position taken. Abuse of procedural devices also subject to sanctions. (60-211).

Unauthorized Practice.—Prohibited.

Mandatory Continuing Legal Education.—All attorneys must earn minimum of 12 hours per year including two hours of professional responsibility, except: (1) Attorneys newly admitted during first year of practice; (2) retired or inactive attorneys; (3) federal and state judges; and (4) others exempted for good cause. (Rule 802).

Specialty Certification Requirements.—Specialties are not recognized in Kansas.

Professional Corporations.—See category Business Organizations, topic Corporations, subhead Professional Corporations.

Prepaid Legal Service Plans.—Authorized. (40-4201 et seq.).

MINERAL, WATER AND FISHING RIGHTS

MINES AND MINERALS:

Secretary of Human Resources has supervision of operation of mines, and provisions for safety and inspection which are required. (49-201 et seq.).

Oil and Gas.—The State Corporation Commission has supervision of provisions pertaining to regulation of oil and gas wells (55-101 et seq.), production and sale of crude oil or petroleum (55-601 et seq.), and production and conservation of natural gas (55-701 et seq.).

Mineral Deeds.—Estates in oil and gas in place may be created in the same quantity and quality as estates in land. They may be created by reservations in a deed or by a separate conveyance which is commonly but erroneously called a royalty deed. (79-420).

Recording Mineral Deed.—A deed conveying or reserving title to minerals in place must be recorded within ninety days after execution or it is void (fees, see category Property, topic Deeds), but if listed for taxation within such period it is valid as between parties without recording. (79-420). Time for recording may be extended under some circumstances. (145 Kan. 88, 64 P.2d 56).

Oil and gas lease is a mere privilege to go on the land and explore and if production is obtained to appropriate the working interest (generally seven-eighths of the oil and gas produced) provided for in the lease. It is not a conveyance of the minerals in place, and passes no title thereto. (214 Kan. 415, 521 P.2d 454). Law implies covenant to explore and develop. (55-223).

Execution and Recording of Lease.—Leases should be executed the same as deeds and may be recorded in the same manner. If executed prior to Jan. 1, 1925, a lease is void unless recorded prior to Jan. 1, 1952, and after Jan. 1, 1952, no assignment of such an unrecorded lease, or any interest therein, can be recorded. (55-216-8). Husband and wife should join in the execution of lease but it is not necessary for husband or wife of an assignor to join in an assignment.

Recording and Extending Lease.—The recording of an oil and gas lease in the office of the register of deeds imparts notice to the public of the validity and continuance of the lease for the definite term therein expressed but no longer. If the lease contains a statement of any contingency upon the happening of which the term of such lease may be extended (such as "and as long thereafter as oil and gas or either of them are produced in paying quantities") the owner of the lease may at any time before the expiration of the definite term thereof file with the register of deeds an affidavit setting forth the description of the lease, that the affiant is the owner thereof and the facts showing that the required contingency has happened. The affidavit is notice to the public of the existence and continuing validity of the lease. (55-205).

Royalty interest refers to right to share in production of oil and gas at severance and is personal property, concerning proceeds from oil and gas leases if and when there is production. (204 Kan. 658, 465 P.2d 938).

Forfeiture of Lease.—It is the duty of a lessee of a forfeited oil and gas lease to release the same of record within 60 days after the date of forfeiture and if the lessee, his successors or assigns fail or neglect to execute and record such surrender within the time provided for, the owner of the land may serve upon the lessee, his successors or assigns, by registered mail at his last known address, or by publication for three consecutive weeks in a newspaper of general circulation in the county where the land is situated, a statutory notice, and the owner of the land may after twenty days from the date of service registration or first publication of the notice file with the register of deeds of the county where said land is situated an affidavit setting forth that the affiant is the owner of the land, that the lessee, his successors or assigns have failed to comply with the terms of the lease, reciting the facts constituting such failure, and that the lease has been forfeited and is void. A copy of the notice served should be attached to the affidavit. The lessee, within 30 days after the filing of such affidavit, may give notice in writing to the register of deeds of the county where the land is located that the lease has not been forfeited and that he still claims that the lease is in full force and effect. If the lessee does not so notify the register of deeds then the register of deeds must record the affidavit and thereafter the record of the lease is not notice to the public of the existence of the lease or any interest therein or rights thereunder and the record thereof can not be received in evidence in any court of this state on behalf of the lessee, his successors or assigns. (55-201).

If the owner of the lease refuses to execute a release as provided for, the land owner may sue to obtain such release and may recover the sum of $100 as damages and costs, together with a reasonable attorney's fee, and he may also recover any additional damages that the evidence in the case may warrant. (55-202).

Taxation.—Estates in oil and gas in place are taxed separately from the land. Excise tax upon severance and production of oil, gas and coal for profit or commercial use. (79-4216 et seq.).

Reclamation of Surface-Mined Real Property.—See category Taxation.

MORTGAGES

CHATTEL MORTGAGES:

Uniform Commercial Code (K.S.A. 84-1-101 et seq.) in effect. See category Business Regulation and Commerce, topic Commercial Code.

Filing.—

Consumer Goods.—Office of register of deeds in county of debtor's residence or, if debtor is not Kansas resident, in county where goods are kept. (84-9-401[1][a], Kansas variation).

Land Related Transactions.—In office where mortgage on real estate would be filed or recorded (84-9-401[1][b]; UCC 9-401[1][b] 2d alternative), i.e., register of deeds (58-2308). Note that legal description and name, SSN and FEIN of record owner of real estate must always be given on financing statement for security interest in timber, minerals or fixtures located on that realty. (84-9-402[3], Kansas variation).

Transmitting Utility.—Office of secretary of state. (84-9-401[5]; UCC 9-401[5]).

In All Other Cases.—In office of secretary of state. (84-9-401[1][c]; UCC 9-401[1][c] 2d alternative).

Filing Fees.—Fee is $6 plus $1 for each additional page (see subhead Forms infra and Commercial Code Forms at end of Kansas Digest). (84-9-403[5]). Last sentence of UCC 9-403(5) allowing secured party to index under debtor's trade name for extra fee is deleted. See also category Documents and Records, topic Records, subhead Filing Under Commercial Code.

Taxation.—Unless otherwise agreed, when collateral is in secured party's possession, taxes incurred are chargeable to debtor. (84-9-207[2][a]).

Forms.—Security agreement is illustrative. Secretary of State has approved forms of Financing Statement, Statement of Continuation, Termination, Release, Assignment, etc., and Request for Information, printed infra. Latter forms are available from printing companies, names of which Secretary will provide on request, and which may also be

See note at head of Digest as to 1998 legislation covered.

See Topical Index in front part of this volume.

CHATTEL MORTGAGES ... *continued*

used for local filings. Various security agreement forms are also available from these printing companies.

For forms for Financing Statement, Statement of Continuation, Termination, Release, Assignment, etc. and Request for Information or Copies see end of this Digest.

Forms

Security Agreement.—Form UCC SA-1.

Date . . . . , 19 . . . . .

. . . .
                    (Name)   (Street Address)

. . . .
           (City)   (County)   (State)

hereinafter called "Debtor," hereby grants to . . . .
. . . ., hereinafter called "Secured Party," a security interest in the following described property:

. . . .
. . . .

together with all additions, accessions and substitutions thereto or therefor, and all similar property hereafter acquired, hereinafter called "Collateral." Proceeds of Collateral are also covered but this shall not be construed to mean that Secured Party consents to any sale of such Collateral.

If Collateral includes livestock, Debtor hereby grants a security interest in all increase thereof, all feed, both hay and grain, owned by Debtor, all water privileges, all equipment used in feeding and handling said livestock, and all of Debtor's right, title, and interest in and to all contracts and leases covering lands for pasture and grazing purposes.

If any of the collateral has been attached to or is to be attached to real estate, or if the Collateral includes crops or oil, gas or minerals to be extracted or timber to be cut, a description of the real estate is as follows:

and the name of the record owner of the real estate is . . . .

This security interest is given to secure: (1) Payment of a note dated . . . .
. . . ., executed and delivered by Debtor to Secured Party in the principal sum of
$. . . . ., payable as to principal and interest as therein provided; (2) future advances to be evidenced by like notes to be made by Secured Party to Debtor at Secured Party's option; (3) all expenditures by Secured Party for taxes, insurance, repairs to and maintenance of the Collateral and all costs and expenses incurred by Secured Party in the collection and enforcement of the note and other indebtedness of Debtor; and (4) all liabilities of Debtor to Secured Party now existing or hereafter incurred, matured or unmatured, direct or contingent, and any renewals and extensions thereof and substitutions therefor.

DEBTOR EXPRESSLY WARRANTS AND COVENANTS:

OWNERSHIP FREE OF ENCUMBRANCES. Except for the security interest granted hereby, Debtor now owns or will use the proceeds of the advances hereunder to become the owner of the Collateral free from any other prior lien, security interest or encumbrance, and Debtor will defend the Collateral against all claims and demands of all persons at any time claiming the same or any interest therein.

FINANCING STATEMENTS. No financing statement covering the Collateral or any proceeds thereof is on file in any public office and Debtor will join with Secured Party in executing one or more financing statements in form satisfactory to Secured Party.

INSURANCE. Debtor will insure the Collateral with companies acceptable to Secured Party against such casualties and in such amount as Secured Party shall require. All insurance policies shall be written for the benefit of Debtor and Secured Party as their interests may appear, and such policies or certificates evidencing the same shall be furnished to Secured Party. All policies of insurance shall provide at least ten (10) days prior written notice of cancellation to Secured Party.

MAINTENANCE. Debtor will keep the Collateral in good condition and free from liens and other security interests, will pay promptly all taxes and assessments with respect thereto, will not use the Collateral illegally or encumber the same and will not permit the Collateral to be affixed to real or personal property without the prior written consent of Secured Party. Secured Party may examine and inspect the Collateral at any time, wherever located.

REIMBURSEMENT FOR EXPENSES. At its option, Secured Party may discharge taxes, liens, security interests, or other encumbrances on the Collateral and may pay for the repair of any damage to the Collateral, the maintenance and preservation thereof and for insurance thereon. Debtor agrees to reimburse Secured Party on demand for any payments so made and until such reimbursement, the amount of any such payment, with interest at ten (10%) per cent per annum from date of payment until reimbursement, shall be added to the indebtedness owed by Debtor and shall be secured by this security agreement.

CHANGE OF RESIDENCE OR LOCATION OF COLLATERAL. Debtor will immediately notify Secured Party in writing of any change in Debtor's residence, and Debtor will not permit any of the Collateral to be removed from the location specified herein without the written consent of Secured Party.

DEBTOR FURTHER WARRANTS AND COVENANTS:

1. The Collateral covered by this agreement is to be used by Debtor primarily for
   ☐ Personal, family or household purposes
   ☐ Farming operations
   ☐ Business other than farming operations.
2. The Collateral is
   ☐ Now owned by the Debtor
   ☐ Being acquired with the proceeds of the advance evidenced by this agreement.
3. Debtor's residence is
   ☐ At the address shown above
   ☐ At . . . .
      (Street Number)   (City)   (State)
4. The Collateral will be kept at

☐ Debtor's residence as shown above
☐ At . . . .
   (Street Number)   (City)   (State)
5. Debtor's chief place of business is
   ☐ In the county of Debtor's residence
   ☐ At . . . .
      (Street Number)   (City)   (State)

EVENTS OF DEFAULT. Debtor shall be in default under this agreement upon the happening of any of the following events or conditions:

1. Default in the payment or performance of any obligation, covenant or liability contained or referred to herein;
2. Any warranty, representation or statement made or furnished to Secured Party by or in behalf of Debtor proves to have been false in any material respect when made or furnished;
3. Any event which results in the acceleration of the maturity of the indebtedness of Debtor to others under any indenture, agreement or undertaking;
4. Loss, theft substantial damage, destruction, sale or encumbrance to or of any of the Collateral, or the making of any levy, seizure or attachment thereof or thereon;
5. Any time the Secured Party believes that the prospect of payment of any indebtedness secured hereby or the performance of this agreement is impaired;
6. Death, dissolution, termination of existence, insolvency, business failure, appointment of a receiver for any part of the Collateral, assignment for the benefit of creditors or the commencement of any proceeding under any bankruptcy or insolvency law by or against Debtor or any guarantor or surety for Debtor.

REMEDIES. Upon such default and at any time thereafter Secured Party may declare all obligations secured hereby immediately due and payable and may proceed to enforce payment of the same and exercise any and all of the rights and remedies provided by the Uniform Commercial Code as well as all other rights and remedies possessed by Secured Party. Secured Party may require Debtor to assemble the Collateral and make it available to Secured Party at any place to be designated by Secured Party which is reasonably convenient to both parties. Unless the Collateral is perishable or threatens to decline speedily in value or is of a type customarily sold on a recognized market, Secured Party will give Debtor reasonable notice of the time and place of any public sale thereof or of the time after which any private sale or any other intended disposition thereof is to be made. The requirements of reasonable notice shall be met if such notice is mailed, postage prepaid, to the address of the Debtor shown at the beginning of this agreement at least ten days before the time of sale or disposition.

No waiver by Secured Party of any default shall operate as a waiver of any other default and the terms of this agreement shall be binding upon the heirs, executors, administrators, successors, and assigns of the parties hereto.

Signed and delivered the day and year first above written.

SECURED PARTY:

By . . . .
           (Name)   (Title)

DEBTOR:

. . . .
           (Name)

. . . .
           (Name)

. . . .
      (Corporate or partnership name)

By . . . .
           (Name)   (Title)

MORTGAGES OF PERSONAL PROPERTY:

See topic Chattel Mortgages.

MORTGAGES OF REAL PROPERTY:

A mortgage of real property must be executed, acknowledged and recorded like a deed. (See category Property, topic Deeds.) Lien theory obtains.

Recording Fees.—See category Documents and Records, topic Records, subhead Recording Fees.

Mortgage Registration Tax.—All mortgages on real estate or renewals or extensions of same filed for record are in addition to recording fee subject to a registration fee of .26% of "principal debt or obligation". "Principal debt or obligation" does not include finance charge or interest. "Mortgages" are defined by law to include every instrument by which lien is created or imposed on real property and executory contracts for sale on real estate which are not to be completed within 90 days and by which grantee is entitled to possession but grantor holds legal title to secure payment of unpaid purchase money. (79-3101). No mortgage subject to registration fee shall be filed for record by any register of deeds or received in evidence in any suit or proceeding, and no judgment, decree or order of enforcement shall be rendered, unless registration fee has been paid. (79-3107). Where mortgaged land is partly within and partly without state, register of deeds requires affidavit of fair market or appraisal value. Registration fee collected by applying relative values of property in and out of state to indebtedness secured by mortgage. (79-3106).

No registration fee is required on any mortgage (1) solely for correcting previous instrument, (2) given for additional security where fee was paid on original instrument, (3) upon that portion verified by affidavit to be principal in previous instrument with same lender upon which fee has been paid, (4) instruments incident to migration to Kansas of corporation by merger or consolidation with domestic corporation where original instrument for which fee has been paid is continued or otherwise acknowledged or validated, (5) given in form of affidavit of equitable interest solely for purpose of providing notification by purchaser of real property of his interest therein, (6) participated in by certified development corporation certified by U.S. small business administration pursuant to community economic development program, (7) given for purpose of

MORTGAGES OF REAL PROPERTY . . . *continued*

changing trustee; or (8) for which registration fee is otherwise not required by law. (79-3102).

Possession of Mortgaged Premises.—A mortgagor of real property is entitled to possession thereof in the absence of any stipulation to the contrary. (58-2301).

Reasonable costs of collection, including attorney fees, permitted in mortgage. (58-2312).

Trust deeds are infrequently used. They must be foreclosed in same manner as regular mortgages. Trustee cannot obtain judgment for fees or compensation. (136 Kan. 247, 14 P.2d 659).

Future Advances.—Mortgage may secure future advances. Lien of such mortgage attaches upon execution and has priority from time of recording as to all advances made thereunder until mortgage is released. However lien of such mortgage may not at any one time exceed maximum amount stated in mortgage. (58-2236).

Priorities.—A mortgage for purchase money has preference over a prior judgment against the purchaser. (58-2305).

Rents and Profits.—Where a real estate mortgage covers rents and profits or an assignment of rents and profits to take effect either before or after default, the provision is valid but is effective only until sheriff's sale. Before mortgagee is entitled to benefit of such stipulation rents and profits must be subjected to possession of mortgagee by appropriate legal proceedings. (136 Kan. 247, 14 P.2d 659).

If mortgagor fails to pay taxes on mortgaged land, mortgagee may pay them and have amount thereof, with interest prescribed by law from date of payment, included in mortgage. (79-2901; 79-2004).

Removal of Buildings.—No buildings may be removed from real property covered by properly recorded, unsatisfied mortgage without written permission of mortgagee. (58-2315).

Assignment of mortgage must set forth clearly the full name and post office address of the assignee (58-2319) and must be acknowledged and recorded like a deed. Unless the assignment is recorded all payments made to the original mortgagee, or to a known assignee without knowledge of a subsequent unrecorded assignment, are effectual as proper payments. (58-2321).

Discharge or Release.—Any mortgage more than 32 years old is void by operation of law unless within that time holder or assignee either commences suit or files affidavit identifying mortgagee. (58-2333[b]).

Mortgage shall be assigned or discharged by instrument acknowledging assignment or satisfaction of such mortgage, signed by mortgagee, attorney in fact, assignee of record, personal representative, or by lender or closing agent in sale, financing or refinancing of real estate subject to mortgage who has caused indebtedness to be paid in full and duly acknowledged and certified as other instruments affecting real estate. Mortgages released prior to July 1, 1977 by notation on original instrument and duly signed by mortgagee may be filed with register of deeds. (58-2306, 58-2307).

Where mortgage has been foreclosed but no execution or order of sale issued within five years and no proceedings to revive or appeal taken within seven years, clerk of district court must, on application file separate instrument releasing said mortgage on record. (58-2314).

A duly executed release of a mortgage by last recorded assignee is effectual both as a release of the land and as a release of the debt secured by the mortgage, unless specifically stated to be only a partial release of property covered.

See also category Documents and Records, topic Records, subhead Recording Fees.

Satisfaction.—When any recorded mortgage is paid, mortgagee or his assignee must record satisfaction and pay recording fees. (58-2309a). If mortgagee or his assignee fails to enter satisfaction within 20 days of demand, lender or closing agent may pay indebtedness and enter satisfaction. If mortgagee not paid lender or closing agent liable to mortgagee. Mortgagee's failure to enter satisfaction within 20 days makes mortgagee liable for $500 plus reasonable attorney's fees and any additional damages evidence warrants. (58-2309a[a], [d]).

Foreclosure and Sale.—In actions to enforce mortgages a judgment for sale of the property must be rendered. Sale is the same as in executions. See category Debtor and Creditor, topic Executions.

Stay on Foreclosure of Agricultural Land.—Family Farm Rehabilitation Act (2-3401 et seq.) unconstitutional (240 Kan. 624, 732 P.2d 710).

Deficiency Judgments.—Judgment is for amount due and proceeds of sale are applied thereon. Deficiency judgments are not uncommon. However, court, in its power of confirmation of sale, may refuse to confirm where sale price is not equivalent to or more than amount of judgment. See category Debtor and Creditor, topic Executions.

Redemption from foreclosure sale is governed by the same rules as apply to execution sales (see category Debtor and Creditor, topic Executions).

Forms.—Statutory form is as follows:

Form

"A. B. mortgages and warrants to C. D. (here describe the premises) to secure the payment of (insert the sum for which the mortgage is granted or the notes or other evidences of debt sought to be secured; also date of payment)."

A mortgage so drawn, being dated, signed, and acknowledged by the grantor is deemed a sufficient mortgage with warranty and if the words "and warrants" be omitted, the mortgage is good without warranty. (58-2303).

The following forms are in general usage:

Forms

Assignment: A, in consideration of the sum of . . . . . . dollars, the receipt whereof is hereby acknowledged, does hereby sell, assign, transfer, set over and convey unto B, heirs and assigns, one certain mortgage, dated the . . . . . . day of . . . . . ., 19. . . ., executed by . . . . . . to . . . . . . covering the following described property, to-wit: . . . . . . given to secure the payment of $. . . . . . and the interest thereon, and duly filed for

record in the office of the Register of Deeds of . . . . . . County, Kansas, and recorded in book . . . . . . on page . . . . . . together with the note, debt and claim secured by said mortgage, and the covenants contained in said mortgage. Dated this . . . . . . day of . . . . . ., 19. . . .

(Signed) . . . . "

Acknowledgment is necessary.

Satisfaction: "In consideration of full payment of the debt secured by a mortgage made by . . . . . . in favor of . . . . . . and assigned to . . . . . . given to secure the payment of . . . . dollars, dated the . . . . . day of . . . . . ., 19. . . ., which is recorded in book . . . . . . of mortgages, at page . . . . . ., of the records of . . . . . . County, Kansas, satisfaction of said mortgage is acknowledged and the same is hereby released. Dated this . . . . . . day of . . . . . ., 19. . . .

(Signed) . . . . "

Acknowledgment is necessary.

Partial release: A, mortgagee in (or assignee of) that certain mortgage hereinafter described, does hereby certify that said mortgage, dated the . . . . . . day of . . . . . ., 19. . ., executed by . . . . . . to . . . . . ., and recorded in the office of the Register of Deeds of . . . . . . County, Kansas, in book . . . . . . at page . . . . . ., is, as to the property herein described, to-wit: . . . . . ., released and discharged. This release is given on the express terms and condition that it shall in no way affect the lien of the above mentioned mortgage on the remaining land described in said mortgage, but shall only be construed as a release from the lien of said mortgage of the land herein described. Dated this . . . . . . day of . . . . . ., 19. . . .

(Signed) . . . . "

Acknowledgment is necessary.

Chattel Mortgages.—See topic Chattel Mortgages.

PROPERTY

ABSENTEES:

Absentee refers to any person who has disappeared and remains unheard from by persons most likely to hear from him or any person who is reported by U.S. Department of Defense to be a prisoner of war or missing in action. (59-2701).

Care of Property.—District court has jurisdiction to appoint trustee to manage and conserve property within state of any absentee. (59-2702). If absentee remains unheard from for five years and diligent search has been conducted, death is presumed. (59-2704). Upon petition by absentee or his attorney-in-fact court must direct termination of trust estate and transfer of property to absentee or attorney-in-fact. (59-2705[a]). Upon filing of petition by person interested in estate, district court administers estate as if absentee was known to have died on date of said filing. (59-2705[a]). Upon petition of person interested in estate of absentee declared by U.S. to be missing in action for three years, district courts shall terminate trust estate and administer it as if person deceased on date of filing, except, court shall not declare absentee to be deceased. (59-2705[c]). Title under order of final settlement does not pass until distributees file bond conditioned for return of property or value thereof if absentee returns and sets aside order of final settlement upon application filed within three months after he learned or should have learned of such order. Action on bond may be brought only within one year after absentee learned of distribution and in no event more than six years after such distribution. (59-2705[d]).

Escheat.—See category Estates and Trusts, topics Executors and Administrators, subhead Unclaimed Money, Descent and Distribution, subhead Escheat.

Uniform Unclaimed Property Act adopted. (58-3934-3978). Act does not apply to estates of absentees administered (59-2701 et seq.), estates passing by intestate succession (59-514, 59-901 to 905), salvage property (70-101 et seq.), or abandoned motor vehicles (8-1101 et seq.).

ADVERSE POSSESSION:

Fee simple title to real property may be acquired by possession inconsistent with title of another.

Character and Duration of Possession.—No action may be maintained against any person for recovery of real property who has been in open, exclusive and continuous possession of such, either under a claim knowingly adverse or under a belief of ownership, for a period of 15 years. (60-503).

Easements may be acquired by adverse use.

Disabilities.—Person entitled to bring action must do so within two years after disability removed. If person dies during disability period, his heirs, or any person entitled to claim from, by or under him, may commence such action after time specified as a limitation, and within two years after his death, but not after that period. (60-508).

CURTESY:

Estate by curtesy is abolished. Husband has same interest in deceased wife's property as widow has in deceased husband's property. (59-505). See topic Dower.

DEEDS:

The term "heirs" or other words of inheritance are not necessary to create or convey an estate in fee simple. Every conveyance of real estate passes all of the estate of the grantor therein unless the intent to pass a less estate expressly appears or is necessarily implied in the terms of the grant. (58-2202). See topic Real Property for types of estates.

Execution.—Seals are abolished. (16-106). The grantor may sign by mark and no witnesses are necessary in any case. It is not necessary that a spouse join in a conveyance by the other except as to homestead (see category Debtor and Creditor, topic Homesteads, subhead Alienation or Incumbrance) and to bar the inchoate statutory interest (see topic Dower).

See note at head of Digest as to 1998 legislation covered.

See Topical Index in front part of this volume.

DEEDS . . . *continued*

See also category Family, topic Husband and Wife.

Recording.—Conveyances and instruments affecting lands are not valid except as between the parties thereto and such as have actual notice, until they are deposited for record with the register of deeds of the county where the land is situated. (58-2223). No deed or instrument providing for transfer of title to real estate or affidavit of equitable interest in real estate shall be recorded unless such deed, instrument or affidavit shall be accompanied by completed real estate sales validation questionnaire, available from Register of Deeds office. Real estate validation questionnaire shall not apply to transfers of title: (1) solely for security; (2) to modify or supplement prior recorded instrument without new consideration; (3) as gifts; (4) for cemetery lots; (5) by leases and transfers of severed mineral interests; (6) to trust and without consideration; (7) resulting from divorce settlement; (8) made for purpose of creating joint tenancy or tenancy in common; (9) by way of sheriff's deed; (10) by way of deed escrowed for more than five years; (11) by way of quit claim deed for purpose of clearing title encumbrances; (12) when title transfers right of way or pursuant to eminent domain; (13) made by guardian, executor, administrator, conservator, or trustee of estate pursuant to judicial order; or (14) when title transferred due to repossession. (79-1437[e]). See subhead Forms, infra. Failure to acknowledge does not impair validity (except statutory short form deeds, which must be acknowledged); but unacknowledged or defectively acknowledged instrument is not entitled to record, even though spread of record gives no notice of its contents. (169 Kan. 342, 219 P.2d 345). Filing of conveyance for record is deemed to impart notice to all persons of contents thereof. (58-2222). See also category Documents and Records, topic Records.

Recording Fees.—See category Documents and Records, topic Records, subhead Recording Fees.

Corporation.—Corporate deed must be executed by president, vice-president, chairman, or vice chairman of board, and attested by secretary. (17-6003[g]).

Conveyance by Attorney.—See topic Powers of Attorney.

Foreign Executed Deeds.—Conveyances of real estate, executed and acknowledged or proved in any other state, territory or country in conformity with the laws thereof or in conformity with the laws of Kansas, are as valid as if properly executed within this state. (58-2228).

After-acquired title passes under a warranty deed but not under a quitclaim deed. (58-2207).

Transfer on Death.—Interest in real estate may be titled in transfer-on-death. (59-3501, et seq.). Statutory deed is recorded in county where real estate is located. (59-3502). Transfer on death deed may not be revoked by will. (59-3503). Alternative beneficiaries may be designated.

Forms.—The following forms are contained in the statute:

Form

Any conveyance of lands, worded in substance as follows: "A. B. conveys and warrants to C. D. (here describe the premises), for the sum of (here insert the consideration), the said conveyance being dated, duly signed and acknowledged by the grantor, shall be deemed and held a conveyance in fee simple to the grantee, his or her heirs and assigns, with covenants from the grantor, for himself or herself and his or her heirs and personal representatives, that the grantor is lawfully seized of the premises, has good right to convey the same and guarantees the quiet possession thereof, that the same are free from all encumbrances, and the grantor will warrant and defend the same against all lawful claims" (58-2203).

If word "quitclaims" is substituted for words "conveys and warrants" in above form, conveyance will be a good and sufficient quitclaim deed to grantee, his or her heirs and assigns. (58-2204).

The following forms are in general usage:

Form

Warranty Deed: This Indenture, Made this . . . . . . day of . . . . . ., A. D., 19. . . ., Between . . . . . . of . . . . . . County, in the State of . . . . . ., of the first part and . . . . . . of . . . . . . County, in the State of . . . . . . of the second part. Witnesseth, That the said part. . . . of the first part, in consideration of the sum of . . . . . . Dollars, the receipt whereof is hereby acknowledged, do . . . . by these presents grant, bargain, sell and convey unto the said part . . . . of the second part . . . . . . heirs and assigns all the following described real estate, situated in the County of . . . . . . and State of . . . . . . to-wit: . . . . . . To Have and to Hold the Same, Together with all and singular the tenements, hereditaments and appurtenances thereunto belonging or in anywise appertaining forever. And said . . . . . . for . . . . . . and for . . . . . . heirs, executors, or administrators, do . . . . hereby covenant, promise and agree to and with said part. . . . of the second part, that at the delivery of these presents . . . . . . lawfully seized in . . . . . . own right, of an absolute and indefeasible estate of inheritance, in fee simple, of and in all and singular the above granted and described premises, with the appurtenances; that the same are free, clear, discharged and unincumbered of and from all former and other grants, titles, charges, estates, judgments, taxes, assessments and incumbrances of what nature and kind soever: . . . . . . and that . . . . . . will Warrant and Forever Defend the same unto said part . . . . of the second part, ... heirs and assigns, against said part . . . . of the first part . . . . heirs, and all and every person or persons whomsoever, lawfully claiming or to claim the same. In Witness whereof, the said part . . . . of the first part . . . . hereunto set . . . . . . hand . . . . the day and year first above written. (Signature and acknowledgment.)

Quitclaim Deed: Same as warranty deed except: (1) Substitute "remise, release and quitclaim" for "grant, bargain, sell and convey"; and (2) eliminate warranty sentence beginning "And said . . . . . . for . . . . . . and for . . . . . . heirs," and ending "or to claim the same."

Transfer on Death: (Name of Owner), as owner, transfers on death to (Name of Beneficiary), as grantee beneficiary, the following described interest in real estate (here insert description of interest in real estate). THIS TRANSFER ON DEATH DEED IS REVOCABLE. IT DOES NOT TRANSFER ANY OWNERSHIP UNTIL THE DEATH OF THE OWNER. IT REVOKES ALL PRIOR BENEFICIARY DESIGNATIONS BY THIS OWNER FOR THIS INTEREST IN REAL ESTATE.

DOWER:

Common law dower is abolished. In lieu thereof, a surviving spouse is given the right to receive an undivided one-half interest in all of the real estate in which the deceased spouse at any time during the marriage had a legal or equitable interest. (59-505).

Release, Election, Bar.—A conveyance by the spouse alone in whom the title is vested does not defeat the inchoate interest of the other spouse unless: (1) Other spouse has consented in writing (usually by joining as grantor) or by election to take under grantor's will (see category Estates and Trusts, topic Wills); (2) real estate has been sold on execution or judicial sale or taken by other legal proceeding; or (3) non-joining spouse was not resident of Kansas at time of conveyance and was never such resident during existence of marriage relation. (59-505).

Effect of Sale by One Spouse Alone.—Purchaser from spouse in whom title is vested takes the entire fee simple, subject to the inchoate right of the non-joining spouse. Until the death of such grantor the other spouse is not entitled to profits and has no right of possession. (59-505).

ESCHEAT:

See categories Business Regulation and Commerce, topic Banks and Banking, subhead Unclaimed Deposits; Estates and Trusts, topics Descent and Distribution, subhead Escheat, Executors and Administrators, subhead Unclaimed Money.

LANDLORD AND TENANT:

Uniform Commercial Code Art. 2A.—Adopted.

Kinds of Tenancy.—Tenancy at will presumed unless shown otherwise. (58-2501). If premises are let for one or more years and tenant, with assent of landlord, continues to occupy after expiration of term, tenant deemed to be tenant from year-to-year. (58-2502). If rent is payable at intervals of three months or less, tenant holds for period equal to interval unless express contract to contrary. (58-2503).

Uniform Residential Landlord and Tenant Act.—Unless rental agreement fixes definite term, tenancy of roomer paying weekly rent is week-to-week and all others hold month-to-month. (58-2546).

Leases.—Statute of Frauds is applicable to leases. (33-105). See category Business Regulation and Commerce, topic Frauds, Statute of.

Security Deposits.—

Residential Dwellings.—Limited to one month's rent for unfurnished apartments and 1.5 month's rent for furnished apartments. Landlord may collect additional 1/2 month's rent if rental agreement permits tenant to keep pets. (58-2250[a]).

Recording.—Leases may be recorded same as deeds. (58-2221). See topic Deeds and category Documents and Records, topic Records. Public has notice of rights of tenant actually in possession of property.

Term.—Any person in possession of real property with the assent of the owner is presumed to be a tenant at will, unless contrary is shown. (58-2501). Where tenant continues to occupy land, with the assent of the owner, after the expiration of a term for one or more years, he is a tenant from year to year. (58-2502). Where rent is payable at intervals of three months or less, tenant holds from one payment date to next, except where there is an express contract. (58-2503).

Occupant of land without special contract is liable for rent to the person entitled thereto. (58-2520).

Rent.—

Residential Dwellings.—Duty to pay rent must be conditioned on landlord's performance of duties. (58-2549; 58-2553; 58-2559).

Assignment of Lease.—A tenant at will, by sufferance or for a term of less than two years cannot assign his lease or interest without consent of the landlord. (58-2511).

Attornment of tenant to a stranger is void, unless with consent of the landlord or pursuant to a judgment or court order. (58-2514).

Conveyance by landlord of leased real estate is valid without attornment of tenant, but payment of rent to grantor before tenant receives notice of sale is good as against grantee. (58-2513).

Waiver of Exemption.—A tenant may waive, in writing, the benefit of exemption laws with respect to all debts contracted for rent. (58-2530).

Attachment for Rent.—Where a tenant liable for rent, which may either be due or to become due within a year, intends to remove, is removing, or has within 30 days removed his property or crops from the leased premises, landlord may sue for such rent, and may, upon filing affidavit stating amount due and setting out one or more of above grounds, and giving bond as in other cases of attachment, have an attachment issued. (58-2527).

Lien.—Rent due for farming land is a lien on the crop grown on the premises. (58-2524). Purchaser of crop, with notice of lien, takes subject thereto. (58-2526). Lien may be enforced by attachment. (58-2528). This is the only statutory lien for rent, although a lien may be reserved by contract in the lease.

Residential Dwellings.—Lien or security interest in tenant's personal property unenforceable. (58-2567[a]).

Termination of Tenancy.—Thirty days notice in writing required by either party to terminate tenancy at will, or tenancy for a period of three months or less. If rent is payable at intervals of less than 30 days, notice equaling such interval must be given. Where tenant is employee of landlord, ten days written notice to vacate is sufficient. Where tenant in military, 15 days written notice by tenant sufficient if termination necessitated by government ordered move. (58-2504).

LANDLORD AND TENANT . . . *continued*

Tenancies from year to year, except farm tenancies, are terminated by 30 days notice in writing, given prior to expiration of year. (58-2505).

Notice of termination of farm tenancies must be given 30 days before Mar. 1 and must fix date of termination as Mar. 1, or for fall seeded crops day following end of harvest or Aug. 1, except, where tenant becomes tenant from year to year by holding over after written lease, date of termination is same day of same month as fixed in written lease. 30 days notice required. If notice given after Mar. 30 and prior to planting of fall seeded crops, but cropland prepared for fall seeded crop, termination is last day of harvest or Aug. 1 of succeeding year, whichever comes first. (58-2506).

The above periods apply where there has been no breach of lease. If, however, tenant fails to pay rent when due, notice in writing for following period shall be sufficient (unless rent is paid during such notice period): tenancies for three months or longer, ten days (58-2507); tenancies for less than three months, three days (58-2508).

Notices may be served on tenant, or if he cannot be found, by leaving a copy at his usual place of residence, or by delivering a copy to some person over 12 years of age residing on premises, or if no person is found thereon, by posting a copy of said notice in a conspicuous place thereon, or by registered mail or registered or certified mail, return receipt requested, addressed to tenant at usual place of residence. (58-2510).

No notice to quit is necessary where the time for termination is specified in contract, or where a tenant at will commits waste, or in the case of a tenant by sufferance, or where the relation of landlord and tenant does not exist. (58-2509).

Residential Dwellings.—Landlord may terminate for material noncompliance by tenant upon 30 days notice to tenant, during which tenant has 14 days to remedy breach (58-2264), or if tenant abandons dwelling (58-2565).

Tenant may terminate for material noncompliance by landlord on 30 days notice. If landlord begins good faith effort to remedy within 14 days, lease will not terminate, unless landlord has previously failed to remedy same condition. (58-2259).

Landlord or tenant may terminate week-to-week tenancy by seven days written notice. Month-to-month tenancy may be terminated on 30 days notice, except tenant may terminate on 15 days notice if tenant is in military and termination is necessary due to military orders. (58-2570).

Holding Over.—Landlord may bring limited action in nature of forcible entry and detainer for recovery of possession. (61-2301 et seq.). In residential leases landlord may bring action for possession and, if holdover is not in good faith, may recover damages or rent. (58-2570).

Dispossession.—If tenant for term of less than two years assigns interest to another without written consent of landlord, landlord, on ten days notice, has right to reenter and dispossess tenant. (58-2511; 58-2512).

Distress.—

Residential Dwellings.—Distraint for rent abolished (58-2567[b]) unless tenant abandons dwelling and property (58-2565).

Uniform Residential Landlord and Tenant Act adopted. (58-2540, et seq.). Following sections omitted: §§1.102 to 1.106, 1.201, 1.302, 1.304, 2.104(b), 4.103, 4.104, 4.202. Jurisdiction is in district court and actions may be commenced under 61-1601 et seq. regardless of amount in controversy. (58-2542).

Following provisions are in addition to Uniform Act: Paragraph 58-2548 requires inventory of premises by landlord and tenant within five days of occupancy. Paragraphs 58-2565(d), (e), (f) provide for seizure and sale by landlord of tenant's personal possessions where tenant abandons lease. Paragraph 58-2570(d) provides for immediate possession by landlord upon motion, notice, and hearing in district court.

LEASES:

See topic Landlord and Tenant; category Mineral, Water and Fishing Rights, topic Mines and Minerals.

PERPETUITIES:

Common law rule as to perpetuities in force. (215 Kan. 472, 524 P.2d 1187).

PERSONAL PROPERTY:

Tenancy by the entirety does not exist. (58-501).

POWERS OF ATTORNEY:

Power of Attorney.—Power of attorney and revocation thereof may be acknowledged and recorded in same manner as deeds. (58-601; 58-602).

For Health Care Decisions.—Power of attorney by which principal designates another as his agent. Must be in writing containing words indicating principal's intent that authority conferred shall be exercisable notwithstanding principal's subsequent disability or incapacity. (58-625).

Uniform Durable Power of Attorney Act.—Adopted. (58-610 et seq.).

Members of Armed Forces.—No special provisions.

REAL PROPERTY:

Fee simple estates and life estates exist. The word "heirs" or other words of inheritance are not necessary to create an estate in fee simple. (58-2202). Marketable record title act in force. (58-3401).

Joint tenancies and estates by entirety were abolished May 20, 1891. Those existing prior that date were not affected (78 Kan. 215, 96 Pac. 140), and it was held that a joint tenancy may be created by specific contract in spite of the statute (95 Kan. 798, 149 Pac. 691). Under a law passed in 1939, an estate which would have been at common law a joint tenancy or estate by entirety is a tenancy in common, unless the language used in the grant or devise makes it clear that a joint tenancy was intended to be created. (58-501). However, a grant or devise to executors or trustees as such creates a joint tenancy unless there is an express declaration to the contrary. Joint tenancy may be created by grant from owner to himself and another. (58-501).

Estates tail are abolished after July 1, 1939. (58-502). Prior to that date such estates existed and could be barred by conveyance of tenant in tail. (88 Kan. 708, 129 Pac. 1131).

Rule in Shelley's Case is abolished as to all instruments taking effect after July 1, 1939. Under a devise or conveyance, after that date, to "A for life and then to his heirs," or "heirs of his body," "issue" or the like, A takes a life estate and his heirs, issue, etc., take a fee simple in remainder. (58-503).

Construction of Instruments.—In instruments disposing of property such as "to B and his heirs, but if B dies without issue then to C and his heirs," death of B without having issue living at the time of his death is indicated, and B's death without living issue need not occur in lifetime of maker of instrument. These rules apply when limitation is on death without "heirs," "heirs of the body," "issue," "children," "offspring," "descendants" or any such relatives, however described. (58-504).

A conveyance "to B and his children," or "issue" or words of similar import creates a life estate in B and remainder in the children, etc.(58-505).

A devisee who is also heir or next of kin of testator takes under the will and not by descent. (58-506).

Foreign Conveyances or Encumbrances.—Instruments executed and acknowledged or proved in any other state, territory or country in conformity with the laws of such state, territory or country, or in conformity with the laws of Kansas, are as valid as if executed within this state. (58-2228).

Death of a life or joint tenant, and fact of devolution of title of real or personal property may be judicially determined in probate court. (59-2286).

Condominiums permitted. (58-3101 et seq.). Uniform Condominium Act not adopted.

See also topics Curtesy, Deeds, Dower, Landlord and Tenant; categories Civil Actions and Procedure, topic Partition; Debtor and Creditor, topic Homesteads; Family, topic Husband and Wife; Mortgages, topic Mortgages of Real Property.

TAXATION

ADMINISTRATION:

State Taxes.—General supervision of tax matters is in division of taxation of Department of Revenue. (75-5102). Forms, waivers, etc. can be obtained from Division of Taxation, State Office Building, Topeka 66625; (785) 296-3044.

County, School and Municipal Taxes.—Local government agencies impose and collect various taxes, including property (ad valorem) taxes, occupational license taxes, economic and industrial development taxes. School financing is equalized and provided by state income tax and local mill levy.

Assessment of Taxes.—All property, except that appraised by state, is listed and appraised annually as of Jan. 1 by county or district appraiser. (79-301, 79-1412a). Property sold after Jan. 1 is taxed to owner of record as of that date. (79-306). Every person who owns tangible personal property must list it for assessment. (79-303). Individuals file between Jan. 1 and Mar. 1, corporations by Apr. 1, and merchants listing inventory by Apr. 15. (79-306). Appraiser notifies taxpayer of appraised value for real property by Mar. 1 and for personal property by May 1. (79-1460).

Appeal of Assessed Value.—

Informal Meeting.—Taxpayer files notice of appeal within 30 days of mailing of notice for real property and by May 15 for personal property. Appraiser must hold informal meeting regarding real property by May 15 and make determination before May 20. (79-1448).

Hearing Panel.—Taxpayer may appeal final determination to hearing officer or panel. (79-1448). Officer or panel appointed by county commissioners. (79-1602). Orders uniformly changing assessment to all property of any class must be approved by board upon written application and hearing, with Director of Property Valuation party thereto. (79-1481).

County Board of Equalization.—Taxpayer may appeal final determination to state board of tax appeals. (79-1448). Appeal must be made within 18 days of final determination by officer or panel. County clerk furnishes forms. Hearing must be held before July 1. (79-1606).

State Board of Tax Appeals.—Taxpayer aggrieved by any order of hearing officer or panel may appeal to state board by written notice within 30 days. County appraiser may appeal also. (79-1609). State board may change value (79-1409) or order reappraisal of all or part of property in tax district (79-1413a). Board must make written findings of fact in final order. (74-2426).

Small Claims.—Division may hear appeals of decision under certain amounts made by director of taxation or for taxes paid in protest where tax does not exceed $15,000 or valuation is less than $2,000,000. (Ks. Sess. Laws, c. 146, §§7-9).

Judicial Review.—Final order of state board may be reviewed pursuant to Act for Judicial Review and Civil Enforcement of Agency Actions. (77-601 et seq.). Motion for rehearing with state board is condition precedent for judicial review. (74-2426[b]). Court of Appeals has jurisdiction to review any property appraisal. (74-2426[c][3]).

Exemptions.—

Government Property.—All property of U.S. is exempt unless Congress declares otherwise. Property used exclusively by state, municipality or political subdivision or Kansas Turnpike Authority is exempt. (79-201a).

Property used for religious, educational or other benevolent purposes is exempt. (79-201).

Property used for nonprofit hospitals and housing is exempt. (79-201b).

Household goods not used for production of income and wearing apparel are exempt. (79-201c).

Personal property in interstate commerce is exempt including certain goods stored in flow of commerce. (79-201g).

Farm Related.—Exemptions include: (1) Certain livestock and all hay and silage (79-201d); (2) all grain before milling or processing (79-201n); (3) most farm or ranch

ADMINISTRATION . . . *continued*

machinery and equipment (79-201j); and (4) all farm machinery and equipment in merchant's inventory after taxation preceding year (79-217).

Intangibles.—Money, notes and other evidence of debt are exempt from tax by State. (79-3109c). Counties, cities and townships may tax intangibles. (12-1,101 et seq.).

Aircraft actually and regularly used to earn income in conduct of owner's business is exempt. (79-201k).

Miscellaneous exemptions exist at 79-201 et seq.

Penalties.—

Uniform Civil Penalty Act.—Not adopted.

Real and Personal Property Tax.—Taxable property not listed or underreported is subject to 50% penalty, unless underappraisal was appraiser's mistake. Decedent's estate is liable for two calendar years preceding death. (79-1427a). Owner removing residence or building from real property without paying taxes due and delinquent thereon is guilty of misdemeanor and subject to fine up to $500. (79-319a). Giving false or fraudulent list of oil and gas property is misdemeanor subject to fine of $50 to $5,000. (79-333). Giving knowingly false answer to questions submitted by Director of Property Valuation is perjury with sentence of one to five years; willfully refusing to answer questions is misdemeanor with fine of $100 to $1,000 and imprisonment of six to 12 months. (79-1420). Knowingly giving false list, schedule or statement to assessor, or temporarily converting property to evade taxes is misdemeanor with fine of not less than $1,000 or more than $5,000. (79-1420).

Inheritance and Estate Tax.—Inheritance tax is abolished. Estate tax must be paid before final accounting is approved in probate estate. Tax, with interest, is lien on all property of estate. Interest is charged at legal rate from nine months after date of death.

Income Tax.—10% penalty and 1¹/₂% monthly interest for failure to file or pay taxes without intent to evade if return or payment is made within six months after due date. 25% penalty and interest for voluntary failure to file or pay taxes within six months of due date. 50% penalty and interest for failure to file return within 20 days of notice of failure to file from Director of Revenue. Penalty equal to amount of unpaid tax plus interest for fraudulent failure to pay tax, make return or provide required information. Tax fraud is misdemeanor with fine up to $1,000 and imprisonment of 30 days to one year. Willfully signing fraudulent return is felony punishable by imprisonment of not more than five years. (79-3228).

Interstate Co-operation.—No statutory provision for compromise of death taxes where decedent's domicile disputed.

Taxpayer Bill of Rights.—No specific provisions. All taxing authority derives from Kansas Constitution, Art. 11.

ALCOHOLIC BEVERAGES TAXES:

Cereal malt beverage tax on beverages containing 3.2% or less alcohol by weight. (41-501[2]). Liquor tax imposed. (41-501 et seq.).

CIGARETTE TAX:

Imposed by 79-3310, 11.

COAL SEVERANCE TAX:

Excise tax upon severance and production of coal. (79-4216 et seq.).

CORPORATE STOCK TAX:

Financial Institutions State Franchise Tax.—None. See category Business Organizations, topic Corporations, subhead Franchise Tax.

Tax on Corporate Stock.—See category Business Organizations, topic Corporations, subhead Franchise Tax.

CORPORATION LICENSE TAXES:

None.

ESTATE TAX:

For estates of decedents dying after June 30, 1998, new "pickup" tax is amount equal to maximum credit allowed by §2011 of Internal Revenue Code against tax that otherwise would be imposed on transfer of taxable estate of decedent, multiplied by fraction, numerator of which is Kansas gross estate value and denominator of which is total gross estate value.

GASOLINE AND SPECIAL FUELS TAXES:

Gasoline and Fuel Tax.—Imposed by 79-3408.

GENERATION SKIPPING TAX:

No provision.

GIFT TAX:

None.

INCOME TAX:

Imposed by 79-3201 et seq. which closely parallels federal code.

Returns and Payment.—Returns must be filed by individual filing federal return or whose gross income exceeds Kansas exemption and standard deduction. (79-3220). Return due on 15th day of 4th month following close of tax year. (79-3221). Extensions for payment up to six months, or longer for taxpayer who is abroad, with 1¹/₂% monthly interest. (79-3225). Extension granted by IRS will extend state return date if agreement filed with state within 30 days. (79-3230). Withholding and declaration of estimated tax act adopted. (79-3294). Any entity doing business in Kansas which makes payments to Kansas residents or entities subject to Kansas income tax and which files information returns to IRS must file copy with state at same time. (79-3222).

Individuals in Military or in Support of Armed Services.—Excluded from time computation in respect to any tax liability for time served in designated combat zone and periods of hospitalization outside U.S. resulting from injury incident to service, with 180 day grace period. (79-3221).

Income Taxed—Individual.—Resident taxed on entire federal adjusted gross income with certain statutory modifications. (79-32,117).

Rate.—For married couples filing joint return rate is 3.5% of first $30,000; $1,050 plus 6.25% of excess over $30,000; and $2,925 plus 6.45% of excess over $60,000. For all others, rate is 3.5% of first $15,000; $525 plus 6.25% of excess over $15,000; and $1,462.50 plus 6.45% of excess over $30,000. (79-32,110).

Exemptions.—$2,250 for each federal exemption and additional exemption for head of household. (79-32,121).

Optional Tax Table.—Provided for taxable income less than $50,000 in tax booklet.

Nonresidents.—Taxed on Kansas taxable income based on ratio of income derived from sources in Kansas to Kansas adjusted gross income. (79-32,110).

Income Taxed—Corporations.—Corporations doing business within or deriving income from within Kansas are taxed at rate of 4% on Kansas taxable income. Surtax at 3.35% of Kansas taxable income in excess of $50,000. (79-32,110).

INHERITANCE TAX:

Kansas inheritance tax repealed for estates of decedents dying after June 30, 1998. For decedents dying on or before repeal date, act was at 79-1537 et seq.

MARIJUANA AND CONTROLLED SUBSTANCES TAX:

Taxed pursuant to 79-5201, et seq.

MOTOR CARRIER FUELS TAX:

No separate tax. See topic Gasoline and Special Fuels Taxes.

POLLUTION ABATEMENT AUTHORITY TAX:

Use of tax increment finance districts allows municipalities to use bonds to abate blighted areas. (12-..., et seq.). Abatement by state is paid by cost recovery actions against responsible party. See category Environment.

PROPERTY (AD VALOREM) TAXES:

All property not exempt is taxable. See topic Administration, subheads Assessment of Taxes and Exemptions.

State Tax Rates.—None.

Local Tax Rates.—Levied on or before Aug. 25 by local, school and county taxing authorities. (79-1801, et seq.).

Payment and Collection.—All taxes due on Nov. 1, payable to county treasurer. (79-1804). County treasurer must mail tax information form by Dec. 15. (79-2001). One-half may be paid on Dec. 20 and second half on June 20, without penalty or interest. (79-2004; 79-2004a).

Protesting Payment.—Taxpayer must file written statement on form provided by county treasurer stating ground of protest. Protest must be made at time of payment or by Dec. 20 or for taxes paid by escrow or tax service no later than Jan. 31 of next year. (79-2005[a]). Within 30 days of result, taxpayer may appeal to state board of tax appeals. (79-2005[g]).

PROVIDER TAX:

No special tax.

RACE TRACKS:

No special tax.

REAL ESTATE CONVEYANCE TAX:

No special tax.

SALES AND USE TAXES:

Sales Tax.—4.9% tax imposed on all sales of tangible personal property at retail; sales of motor vehicles; repair and servicing of tangible personal property; and many services, including food, entertainment and temporary lodging. (79-3603).

Exemptions are numerous, including purchases by many nonprofit organizations; isolated and occasional sales; custom computer software; motor fuel; motor vehicles and aircraft sold to nonresidents and registered in another state; all farm machinery; and manufacturing machinery and equipment sold. (79-3606).

Collection by retailer at time of sale. Tax on motor vehicles paid to county treasurer at time of registration. Tax on various other transactions paid to director of taxation. (79-3604).

Retailer returns and payment made to director of taxation. Deadlines vary from annually to bimonthly depending upon annual tax liability. (79-3607).

Use Tax.—Rate of 4.9% of purchase price imposed for privilege of using, storing or consuming within state any article of tangible personal property, except such articles as: (a) property brought into state by nonresident within state not to exceed 60 days for personal use or enjoyment or by railroad or public utility for use in interstate commerce; (b) purchase otherwise than at retail; (c) property which has been subject to tax of 4.9% under Kansas or other state law; (d) which would not have been subject to sales tax if purchased in this state. Where tax of sale or use of article has been imposed at lesser rate in Kansas or other state, tax is difference between tax imposed and 4.9%. (79-3702-13, 79-3603).

STAMP TAX:

No documentary stamp tax, but cigarette, cereal malt beverage and liquor taxes are payable by affixing stamps. See applicable topics.

See note at head of Digest as to 1998 legislation covered.

See Topical Index in front part of this volume.

UNEMPLOYMENT COMPENSATION TAX:

Imposed as contributions from employers by 44-701 et seq. Contributions payable by each contributing employer to Employment Security Fund. (44-710). Amount payable is based upon category of employer and wages paid during calendar year. (44-710-11). Contributions for each employee are subject to statutory maximum. (44-703[o]). Returns are made and paid to Secretary of Human Resources at times prescribed with penalty and interest charges for unpaid contributions. (44-717).

UNIFORM FEDERAL LIEN REGISTRATION ACT AMENDED:

Act adopted with 1982 amendments. (79-2613 et seq.). Filing fee for all liens or certificate of discharge or subordination is $5; for other notices except certificate of release or nonattachment is $2. (79-2617).

USE TAX:

See topic Sales and Use Taxes.

TRANSPORTATION

MOTOR VEHICLES:

General supervision is by the Department of Revenue, Division of Vehicles, State Office Building, Topeka, 66626, (785-296-3601) headed by Vehicle Commissioner, and under jurisdiction of State Highway Commission. Kansas Highway Patrol functions as enforcement agency.

Vehicle license plates are required. Special vehicle plates available for antique vehicles. (8-172). Issued from officer of county treasurer in county where owner resides or has principal place of business if such vehicle is garaged in such county for period exceeding 90 days. (8-129). Number plates must be attached to rear, except plates must be displayed in front on truck tractors. Personalized plates may also be attached to front. Special plates for person with disability. (8-1, 124 et seq.).

Members of Armed Forces.—No specific exemption. However, in their case application for registration may be signed by member's spouse, parent, eldest brother or sister, in order named. (8-129).

Operator's License.—An operator's or chauffeur's license, issued by state division of vehicles (8-243), is required (8-235), except for those exempted (8-236), and must be in immediate possession of person to whom issued when operating motor vehicle (8-244). For persons at least 21 years old but less than 65 years old, licenses expire on sixth anniversary of date of birth of licensee nearest date of application. Licenses issued to persons under 21 or over 65 and commercial licenses expire every four years. (8-247). Licenses may be suspended or canceled. (8-250 et seq.). Examination may be required. (8-235[d], 8-241, 8-245). Restricted licenses (8-245) and temporary instruction permits (8-239) may be issued. Age limit: 16 and 18 for operators' and chauffeurs' licenses, respectively, except that restricted operators' licenses may be issued at 15 upon completion of driver training course and written application of parent or guardian. (8-237).

Members of Armed Forces.—No specific exemption.

Titles and Sales.—Certificate of title, good for life of vehicle, is issued on each motor vehicle required to be registered in Kansas. Certificate contains form for assignment of title, and blank spaces so that abstract of mileage as to each owner will be available. It is unlawful to buy or sell such vehicle unless at time of delivery or within 30 days of delivery if parties agree such certificate is given to buyer with assignment duly executed. Sale without such assignment and exchange of certificate of title is fraudulent and void unless title is in possession of seller at time of delivery and parties on form prescribed by department agree that title and assignment pass within 30 days of delivery and assigned title thereafter mailed by registered or restricted mail to purchaser within 30 days. Sale may be reaffirmed in writing when title is not timely delivered. (8-135).

Manufacturers and Dealers.—Regulation and licensure pursuant to 8-2401 et seq.

Members of Armed Forces.—In case of members of Armed Forces while U.S. is engaged in war and for period of six months next following cessation of hostilities, application for certificate of title may be signed by member's spouse, parents, eldest brother or sister, in order named. (8-135[c][1]).

Transfer on Death.—Motor vehicle may be registered in transfer-on-death form by designating on certificate of title names of tenant in common or joint tenant followed by words "transfer on death to (Name of Beneficiary)" or by abbreviation "TOD".

Liens.—Assignment of certificate of title contains statement of no more than two liens or encumbrances on vehicle at time of assignment. (8-135[c][2]).

Identification Marks.—Sale or possession of motor vehicle, original engine number of which has been defaced, altered or removed, is punishable by fine and imprisonment. (8-113). Unlawful to knowingly own or have custody or possession of motor vehicle, original identification number of which has been destroyed, removed, altered or defaced. (8-116[b]).

Odometer Alteration.—Prohibitions based on federal odometer law. (15 USC §1981 et seq.). Injured consumer may void sale and recover civil penalties and attorney's fees. Attorney General may act on behalf of injured consumers. Criminal penalties provided. (21-3757).

Operation prohibited, by persons not having valid licenses (8-235): licenses may not be issued to habitual violators, habitual drunkards or drug addicts who are incapable of safely driving vehicle, or to persons adjudged as affected with or suffering mental disability or disease and who have not been rehabilitated. (8-237). Operation prohibited if opened container of alcoholic beverage accessible to driver. Second or subsequent violation results in restriction or suspension of driver's license. (41-804).

Size and Weight Limits.—Regulated by Uniform Act to Regulate Traffic on Highways. (8-1401, et seq.; 8-1901 et seq.).

Equipment Required.—Regulated by 8-1701 et seq.

Seat Belts.—Use required (8-2503), but evidence of nonuse not admissible in any action for purpose of determining comparative negligence or mitigation of damages (8-2504[c]).

Lights Required.—Regulated by 8-1701 et seq.

Inspection.—Any police officer or properly designated department of revenue agent or employee may, upon reasonable cause, stop vehicles for inspection and test. If vehicle found with unlawful weight, it cannot be operated until placed in proper condition. (8-1910).

Accidents.—Driver involved must give name, address and vehicle registration number to other party and render reasonable assistance to injured persons. If other vehicle unattended must either locate owner or leave name and address. If injury or property damage of $200 or more, must forward report to Vehicle Department within ten days. (8-1607).

Liability of Owner.—Owner is liable for operation of his car by himself or a person acting in his service or under his direction. An owner who causes or knowingly permits a minor under age of 16 to drive his vehicle upon a highway, or any person who gives or furnishes a motor vehicle to such minor, is jointly and severally liable with minor for any damages caused by minor's negligence in driving such vehicle. (8-222). Otherwise, "family car doctrine" not recognized.

Liability to Guest.—Guest Statute repealed. (1974, c. 32 §1).

Proof of Financial Responsibility.—Driver must carry proof of insurance card issued by insurer. Card must show both effective date and expiration date. Police must ticket any driver who fails to show proof upon demand. Ticket may be cancelled within ten days upon showing that insurance was in effect. (40-3104).

Insurance.—See subhead No-Fault Insurance, infra.

No-Fault Insurance.—"No-fault" insurance legislation embodied in 40-3101, et seq. Purpose is to compensate persons promptly for accidental bodily injury arising out of ownership, operation, maintenance or use of motor vehicles in lieu of liability for damages to extent provided in act. (40-3102).

Requires every owner to provide motor vehicle liability insurance coverage in accordance with provisions of act for every motor vehicle owned by him unless such motor vehicle is included under an approved self-insurance plan or is expressly exempted by act. (40-3104[a]). Liability insurance coverage required by act includes $25,000/$50,000 liability for bodily injury or death and $10,000 liability for property damage. (40-3107[e]). Liability coverage for passengers' bodily injuries shall be included in policy unless insured rejects in writing. (40-3107). Coverage also includes personal injury protection benefits to named insured, relatives residing in same household, persons operating insured motor vehicle, passengers in such motor vehicle and pedestrians. (40-3107[f]).

Plaintiff in action for tort may recover damages for pain, suffering, mental anguish, inconvenience and other non-pecuniary loss only if injury requires medical treatment of kind described in Act as medical benefits, reasonably valued at $2,000 or more, or injury consists in whole or part of permanent disfigurement, fracture to weightbearing bone, compound, comminuted, displaced or compressed fracture, loss of a body member, permanent injury with reasonable medical probability, permanent loss of a bodily function or death. (40-3117). No motor vehicle shall be registered or reregistered in state unless owner at time of registration has in effect policy of liability insurance covering such motor vehicle as provided by Act, or is self-insurer thereof. (40-3118[a]). Personal injury protection benefits may be rejected by insured in policies covering motorcycles and motor-driven cycles. (40-3107[f]).

Any person who knowingly drives or permits operation of an uninsured motor vehicle is guilty of a class B misdemeanor or class A misdemeanor for second conviction within three years. (40-3104[g]). Additional penalties for violation include suspension of operator's and owner's licenses, vehicle registration, and operating privileges in state. (40-3104[h]). These penalties can be avoided by presenting evidence of coverage in court or before arresting officer within ten days. (8-1604[c], 40-3104[e]).

Foreign Vehicles.—Director of vehicles is empowered to enter into interstate compacts regulating use of vehicles owned or operated by citizens of other states provided that other state grants reciprocal rights to Kansas citizens. (74-4302).

Nonresident Operator.—A nonresident over the age of 16, possessing valid home state operator's license may operate a motor vehicle in Kansas only as operator. If home state does not require license, nonresident over 18 may operate vehicle in Kansas for 90 days in any calendar year, if vehicle operated is registered in home state or country of nonresident. (8-236). These privileges may be suspended in like manner as residents' licenses. (8-251).

Actions Against Nonresidents.—Operation by a nonresident or his authorized chauffeur or agent of a motor vehicle on the public highways is deemed equivalent to an appointment of the Secretary of State as his agent on whom may be served all lawful processes in any action against the nonresident growing out of any accident or collision in which said motor vehicle may be involved while it is operated in Kansas. (8-401).

Direct Actions.—Action may be brought directly against insurance company on its liability policy to recover for personal injuries or property damage caused by the negligent operation of a licensed motor carrier. (66-1,128; 185 Kan. 50, 341 P.2d 90).

Motor vehicle carriers regulated by State Corporation Commission. (66-1,108 et seq.). Must have a certificate of convenience and necessity if operated over a regular route. Must pay a special license fee and carry liability insurance. Public motor carriers who have more than 25 registered vehicles may be approved as self-insurers. (66-1,128).

Motor carrier inspection stations authorized under authority and control of superintendent of Kansas highway patrol. Superintendent enforces laws of state concerning operation and registration of motor carriers. (66-1318 et seq.).

Gasoline Tax.—See category Taxation, topic Gasoline and Special Fuels Taxes.

Lemon Law.—See category Business Regulation and Commerce, topic Consumer Protection.

See note at head of Digest as to 1998 legislation covered.

See Topical Index in front part of this volume.

COMMERCIAL CODE FORMS

See also categories Business Regulation and Commerce, topic Commercial Code; Mortgages, topic Chattel Mortgages.
Following are standard forms currently in use.

Financing Statement.—Form UCC-1.

This FINANCING STATEMENT is presented to a filing officer for filing pursuant to the Uniform Commercial Code:

3. Maturity date (if any):

1. Debtor(s) (Last Name First) and address(es)

2. Secured Party(ies) and address(es)

For Filing Officer (Date, Time, Number and Filing Office)

4. This financing statement covers the following types (or items) of property:

Assignee of Secured Party

Check [X] if covered: ☐ Proceeds of Collateral are also covered. ☐ Products of Collateral are also covered. Number of Additional Sheets, if any _____

Filed with:

By:_____
Signature(s) of Debtor(s)

By:_____
Signature(s) of Secured Party(ies)

Statement of Continuation, Termination, Release, Assignment, etc.—Form UCC-2

This STATEMENT is presented to a Filing Officer for filing pursuant to the Uniform Commercial Code:

No. of Additional Sheets Presented:

Maturity Date
3. (Optional):

1. Debtor(s) (Last Name First) and Address(es)

2. Secured Party(ies) Name(s) and Address(es)

4. For Filing Officer: Date, Time, No., Filing Office

5. This Statement Refers to Original Financing Statement No. _____ Filed (date) _____ with _____

6. ☐ A. Continuation — The original Financing Statement bearing the above file number is still effective.

☐ B. Termination — The Secured Party of record no longer claims a security interest under the Financing Statement bearing the above file number.

☐ C. Release — From the Collateral described in the Financing Statement bearing the above file number, the Secured Party of record releases the collateral below.

☐ D. Assignment — The Secured Party of record has assigned the Secured Party's rights in the property described below under the Financing Statement bearing the above file number to the Assignee whose name and address are shown below.

☐ E. Amendment — The Financing Statement bearing the above file number is amended as set forth below: (Signature of Debtor is required if Collateral is added.)

7. This area for description of Collateral, Release, Collateral if assigned, or description of Real Estate if necessary.

Number of Additional Sheets, if any _____

By:_____
Signature(s) of Debtor(s)

By:_____
Signature(s) of Secured Party(ies)

See note at head of Digest as to 1998 legislation covered.

See Topical Index in front part of this volume.

Request for Information or Copies.—Form UCC-3

		For Filing Officer Use
Debtor(s) (Last Name First) and address(es):	Party requesting information or copies: (Name and Address)	

INFORMATION REQUEST: ☐

Filing officer please furnish certificate showing whether there is on file as of .... 19 .... at .... M., any presently effective financing statement naming the above named debtor(s) and any statement of assignment thereof, and if there is giving the date and hour of filing of each such statement and the name(s) and address(es) of each secured party(ies) therein. Enclosed is uniform fee of $5.00.

COPY REQUEST: ☐

The undersigned party further agrees to pay to the filing officer, upon receipt of this certificate, the sum of $.25 for each financing statement and each statement of assignment reported on the certificate. Filing officer please furnish exact copies of each page of financing statements and statements of assignment listed below, at the rate of $1.00 each, which are on file with your office. Enclosed is $_____ fee for copies requested. In case any of said statements contain more than one page the undersigned agrees to pay the sum of $1.00 for each additional page.

Date _____   (Signature of Requesting Party) _____

File No.	Date and Hour of Filing	Name(s) and Address(es) of Secured Party(ies)

CERTIFICATE: The undersigned filing officer hereby certifies that:

☐ the above listing is a record of all presently effective financing statements and statements of assignment which name the above debtor(s) and which are on file in my office as of _____ _____, 19 ____ at _____ _____M.

☐ the attached .... pages are true and exact copies of all available financing statements or statements of assignment listed in above request.

Additional fee requested $_____ _____   _____

Date   Signature of Filing Officer

KENTUCKY LAW DIGEST REVISER

Stites & Harbison
Suite 1800 Aegon Center
400 West Market Street
Louisville, Kentucky 40202-3352
Telephone: 502-587-3400
Fax: 502-587-6391
Website: www.stites.com

Frankfort, Kentucky Office: 421 West Main Street 40601. Telephone: 502-223-3477. Fax: 502-223-4124.
Hyden, Kentucky Office: 23211 U.S. Highway 421, P.O. Box 1927, 41749.
Lexington, Kentucky Office: 250 West Main Street, Suite 2300 40507.
Telephone: 606-226-2300. Fax: 606-253-9144.
Jeffersonville, Indiana Office: Court House Plaza, 323 East Court Avenue, P.O. Box 946, 47131.
Telephone: 812-282-7566. Fax: 812-284-5519.
Washington, D.C. Office: 1200 G. Street N.W., Suite 800, 20005.
Telephone: 202-434-8968. Fax: 202-737-5822.

Reviser Profile

History: Stites & Harbison is successor to one of the oldest continuous law practices in the nation and is one of the largest firms in Kentucky. It traces its origins in Louisville to 1832. Its current 132 attorney cadre includes two past presidents of the Kentucky Bar Association, four fellows of the American College of Trial Lawyers including the National 1994-95 President, three fellows of the American College of Probate Counsel and one fellow of the American College of Real Estate Lawyers.

Nature of Practice: Stites & Harbison is a full service firm practicing through departmental groupings with specialty and industry teams. Its Litigation Section handles general business and insurance defense litigation; antitrust, securities and environmental matters, admiralty cases, medical malpractice, attorney malpractice and product liability cases; toxic tort, asbestos and disaster class action litigation. Its Business Section handles mergers and acquisitions, bank and bank holding company formation, federal and state securities registration and regulation, equine law matters, health care law, municipal bond financing, utilities regulation, natural resources regulation, employment discrimination, bankruptcy and reorganization, ERISA matters, and tax planning for individuals and business organizations on both federal and state tax matters. The Real Estate group represents a number of bank, mortgage, leasing and insurance company lenders on a regional basis in real estate financing transactions as well as real estate developers and agricultural interests. During the past five years, the fastest areas of firm practice growth have been in product liability litigation, general commercial litigation, bank holding company formation mergers and acquisitions, commercial and real estate lending, employment law and insurance company regulation.

Client Base: Representative clients of the firm include Aegon USA; A. H. Belo Corporation; Alcan Aluminum Corporation; Ambrake Corporation; American Electric Power Service Corporation (Kentucky Power Co.); American Institute of Steel Construction; Anthem Inc.; Ashland Oil, Inc.; Bank One, Kentucky, N.A.; BellSouth Corporation; Brown-Forman Corporation; Brown & Williamsom Tobacco Corporation; Goodyear Tire and Rubber Company; James N. Gray Construction Co., Inc.; Kentucky Commissioner of Insurance as Rehabilitator for Kentucky Central Life Insurance Company; Modis Professional Services, Inc.; National City Bank of Kentucky; NBD Bank, N.A.; Ohi-Automotive of America, Inc.; PNC Bank, Kentucky; Pyramid Mining Co., Inc.; Regional Airport Authority of Louisville & Jefferson County; Steel Technologies, Inc.; Stock Yards Bank & Trust Co.; Thermo View Industries, Inc. and Zurich American Insurance Companies.

Firm Activities: Partners and associates of the firm participate actively in the affairs of the organized bar and serve as members of its governing bodies and its continuing legal education programs. Most attorneys are also actively engaged in civic and charitable work and have served in such positions as Chairman of the Louisville School Board, Chairman of the Louisville and Lexington Chapters of the American Red Cross, President of Habitat for Humanity and President of the Louisville Chamber of Commerce.

Management: The Firm is managed by a Managing Partner elected by the Partnership and a Management Committee of six other partners elected for two year staggered terms by and from the partners at large. Reporting to the Management Committee are an Executive Director, and committees of partners and associates for Recruiting, Marketing, Investments and Ethics.

Significant Distinctions: Former or deceased partners include persons who served as a United States Attorney General, a Chief Judge of the Kentucky Court of Appeals (now Supreme Court), a Kentucky Court of Appeals Judge, numerous federal and state trial court and appellate judges, and a Master Commissioner of the United States Supreme Court.

KENTUCKY LAW DIGEST

(The following is a list of all Categories and Topics, including cross-references, covered in this Digest.)

KENTUCKY LAW DIGEST

Revised for the 1999 edition by

STITES & HARBISON, of the Louisville, Frankfort, Lexington and Hyden Bars.

(KRS indicates Kentucky Revised Statutes; CR indicates Kentucky Rules of Civil Procedure; SCR indicates Rules of Supreme Court; RCr. indicates Rules of Criminal Procedure; KRE indicates Kentucky Rules of Evidence; KAR indicates Kentucky Administrative Regulations. Session Laws are cited by year and chapter number. O.A.G. indicates Opinions of Attorney General. Parallel citations to the South Western Reporter begin with 85 Ky. and 12 K.L.R. Official reports end with 314 Ky. [1951]).

This revision reflects all Acts passed through the 1998 Regular Session of General Assembly.

INTRODUCTION

GOVERNMENT AND LEGAL SYSTEM:

The Commonwealth of Kentucky is a constituent state of the United States of America. For further discussion of the U.S. federal system, see Introduction to the Federal Government of the United States at the beginning of this volume. A great many laws are promulgated by the federal government of the United States and are not reflected in the topics below. See the Introduction to this volume for references to the federal law topics covered.

Like all but one of the United States, Kentucky has a common law legal system, with roots in English common law. For information on the courts and legislature of Kentucky, see category Courts and Legislature.

HOLIDAYS:

Following are legal holidays: Jan. 1; 3d Mon. in Jan.; Jan. 19; Jan. 30; Feb. 12; 3d Mon. in Feb.; last Mon. in May; June 3; July 4; first Mon. in Sept.; 2d Mon. in Oct.; Nov. 11; Dec. 25; and all days appointed by President or Governor as days of thanksgiving. (KRS 2.110). Presidential election days are state holidays. (KRS 2.190).

Holiday Falling on Sunday.—No statutory provision.

Holiday Falling on Sat.—No statutory provision.

Legality of Transactions on Holiday.—No objection may be taken to any process, writ, summons, affidavit, order for provisional remedy or bond in any action because issued, made or dated on holiday (KRS 454.125), but distinction has been taken between holiday and Sun. (63 Ky. [2 Duv.] 37).

OFFICE HOURS AND TIME ZONE:

The eastern half of Kentucky, including cities of Louisville, Lexington, Somerset, Campbellsville, Elizabethtown and Brandenburg, are in Eastern (GMT −05:00) time zone; the western half, including cities of Owensboro, Bowling Green, Paducah, Jamestown, Leitchfield and Hardinsburg, are in the Central (GMT −06:00) time zone. Daylight saving time is observed from first Sun. in Apr. to last Sat. in Oct. Office hours for state government offices are from 8 a.m. to 4:30 p.m.; for other offices, generally from 9 a.m. to 5 p.m.

BUSINESS ORGANIZATIONS

AGENCY:

Common law principles prevail generally. As to agent's authority to sign negotiable instrument under Uniform Commercial Code, see KRS 382.110.

ASSOCIATIONS:

Common law principles apply to voluntary, unincorporated associations. No special statutes for joint stock companies. Agricultural marketing associations regulated by KRS c. 272. Burial Associations regulated by KRS c. 303. Fraternal benefit societies regulated by subtitle 29 of KRS c. 304. Labor unions recognized and locals required by KRS 336.170. KRS 273.070-273.140 set forth rules governing rights and property of unincorporated religious, charitable and educational societies. Business trusts defined and governed by KRS 386.370.

Ky. Const. §208 defines corporation "as used in the Constitution" to include joint stock companies and associations, but this definition does not apply in construing common or statute law. (123 Ky. 720, 97 S.W. 386). As used in statutes, words "corporation" and "company" may extend and be applied to any corporation, company, partnership, joint stock company or association unless context requires otherwise. (KRS 446.010).

Formation.—Members of association may adopt reasonable constitutions, articles, by-laws or rules for governance of membership and enforce compliance with them. (211 Ky. 638, 277 S.W. 500; 126 F.2d 254). Unincorporated associations not required to file statements required of corporations by KRS 271B.16-220. (123 Ky. 720, 97 S.W. 386).

Rights and Powers.—Association may determine property rights and interests of its members and rights to funds and property accumulated by association. (211 Ky. 638, 277 S.W. 500).

Liabilities.—Individual members of unincorporated associations organized for gain or profit, such as joint stock companies, are liable for contracts, torts, and undertakings of association (172 Ky. 693, 189 S.W. 914), but individual members of unincorporated associations, such as mutual benefit associations, organized for moral, social, political or like nonprofit purposes are not liable for contracts or undertakings of association unless they have authorized or ratified transactions out of which obligation or contract arose (215 Ky. 177, 284 S.W. 1045; 126 F.2d 254).

Actions.—Generally, voluntary associations and partnerships may not sue or be sued in common name (CR 4.04[4]; 375 S.W.2d 389; 153 Ky. 329, 155 S.W. 729). If individual members of association actually appoint agent for service of process, service upon agent is valid service upon individual members. (CR 4.04[4]). Joint stock company may sue or be sued in common name if it has large number of members. (111 Ky. 832, 64 S.W. 903; 218 Ky. 172, 291 S.W. 21). Labor unions may sue or be sued in class action proceeding under CR 23. (307 Ky. 485, 211 S.W.2d 138). Service upon business agent has been held service on union and its members. (240 S.W.2d 49).

Professional Associations.—See topic Corporations, subhead Professional Corporations.

CORPORATIONS:

Revised Model Business Corporation Act (1984), printed in Uniform and Model Acts section and referred to in this topic as "Act," adopted effective Jan. 1, 1989 as basis for Kentucky Business Corporation Act. Kentucky Business Corporation Act is codified as KRS c. 271B. Prior to 1989, Kentucky statutes, which were codified as KRS c. 271A, were based on Model Business Corporation Act (1969 revision).

Codification of sections of Act begins with KRS 271B.1-200 and continues by tens through 271B.17-050, with numbering following sections of Act. For example, §3.01 of Act is codified as KRS 271B.3-010; §10.22 of Act is codified as KRS 271B.10-220; §15.31 of Act is codified as KRS 271B.15-310; etc. Principal subdivisions of Act codified numerically and then alphabetically in Kentucky statutes rather than alphabetically and then numerically in Act, e.g., §1.20(f)(2) of Act is codified as KRS 271B.1-200(6)(b). All sections of Act are adopted with exception of §§1.01, 1.02, 8.09, 10.21 and 17.06. Minor substitutions in text made to conform to statutory style, such as replacing "must" in Act with "shall". Material additions to and other deviations from Act are noted under following substantive subheads. Unless otherwise indicated, section numbers appearing in text refer to Act. 1986 technical corrections to Act noted in Uniform and Model Acts section adopted. Amendments proposed to §§7.40 to 7.47 by ABA Committee on Corporate Laws in Dec. 1989 not adopted.

General supervision of Kentucky corporations and Act placed with Secretary of State, New Capitol Building, Frankfort, Kentucky 40601. Information concerning availability of corporate names, corporate status, registered offices and registered agents, etc. may be obtained by telephone from Corporate Records Office (502) 564-7330.

Purposes.—Every corporation has purpose of engaging in any lawful business unless more limited purposes set forth in articles of incorporation. (KRS 271B.3-010).

Name.—§4.01 of Act substantially adopted with following variation: Corporate name must be distinguishable from name of domestic limited partnership, name of foreign limited partnership registered to do business in Kentucky, and assumed name filed with secretary of state pursuant to KRS 365.015. (KRS 271B.4-010). Name availability may be determined by telephone from Corporate Records Office of Secretary of State, (502) 564-7330. Name may be reserved for 120 days. Application fee to reserve name—$15. (KRS 271.B.1-220).

Term of Corporate Existence.—Every corporation has perpetual duration unless its articles of incorporation provide otherwise. (KRS 271B.3-020).

Incorporators.—KRS 271B.2-010 is identical to §2.01 of Act.

Articles of Incorporation.—KRS 271B.2-020 substantially similar to §2.02 of Act but, as addition, articles must set forth mailing address of corporation's principal office and of each incorporator or initial director. Permissive provisions of articles authorize incorporators or shareholders to adopt nonuniform provisions, allow eliminating or limiting personal liability of directors to corporation or its shareholders for monetary damages for breach of directors' duties, provided that such provisions may not eliminate or limit any director's liability for self-dealing or corporate opportunity, for intentional misconduct or known violations of law, for unlawful distributions (KRS 271B.8-330, which adopts §8.33 of Act, may not be superceded by articles), or for acts or omissions occurring prior to date provision in articles limiting liability under section becomes effective (KRS 271B.2-020[2][d][4]). If shareholders wish to adopt supermajority shareholder voting provisions, they must include provisions in articles of incorporation. (KRS 271B.7-270).

Filing of Articles.—Original and two exact or conformed copies of articles must be filed with secretary of state. (KRS 271B.1-200[9]). One copy is then filed with and recorded by county clerk in which registered office of corporation is situated. (KRS 271B.1-200[10]). Scrivener information pursuant to KRS 382.335 is required on articles of incorporation and some other documents required by Act. Unless registered agent signs articles, corporation must deliver registered agent consent with articles. (KRS 271B.2-020[4]).

Incorporation Tax.—Domestic corporation having capital stock divided into shares must pay into State Treasury, at time of incorporation, organization tax based upon number of shares authorized by its articles of incorporation at following rates (KRS 136.060[1]): 1¢ for each share up to and including 20,000; 1/2¢ for each share in excess of 20,000 up to and including 200,000; 1/5¢ for each share in excess of 200,000. Minimum tax in any case, $10. (KRS 136.060[5]).

When domestic corporation amends its articles by changing authorized number of its shares, tax on shares authorized by amendment must be computed at rates set forth above. If tax so computed exceeds tax paid on basis of number of shares authorized prior to amendment, excess tax must be paid when amendment is filed. (KRS 136.060[2]).

See note at head of Digest as to 1998 legislation covered.

See Topical Index in front part of this volume.

CORPORATIONS . . . *continued*

Domestic corporation existing prior to July 1, 1946, which, by amendment after that date, changes its name, increases its powers, enlarges its scope, or prolongs its corporate life, must on filing such amendment, pay organization tax at rates above set forth, on so much of its entire capital stock as has not theretofore borne tax. (KRS 136.060[3]).

Consolidated or merged corporation formed under Kentucky law is not required to pay any organization tax on number of shares of its capital stock on which organization tax has been paid by its constituent corporations prior to consolidation or merger, but such organization tax must be paid at rates hereinbefore set forth on any increase in number of shares of capital stock of consolidated corporation over aggregate number of shares of constituent corporations prior to consolidation or merger. (KRS 136.060[4]).

When domestic corporation consolidates or merges with foreign corporation under Kentucky law, organization tax must be paid at rates hereinbefore set forth on number of shares of capital stock of foreign corporation. (KRS 136.060[4]).

No corporation, organized with shares of capital stock, may exercise any corporate powers in Kentucky until the organization tax (if any) due from it has been paid, and upon such payment it must file statement thereof with Secretary of State. (KRS 136.060[5]).

Filing Fees.—

Secretary of State.—Filing of: articles of incorporation or amendments or restatements of articles—$40; articles of merger or share exchange—$50; amended and restated articles—$80; articles of dissolution—$40; articles of revocation of dissolution—$15; annual report—$15; certificate of existence or authorization—$10. (KRS 271B.1-220).

County Clerk.—$8 for filing with county clerk all documents specified in KRS 271B.1-220 for first three pages and $2 for each additional page. (KRS 64.012). Clerk may also require prepayment of postage for returning recorded corporate documents. (KRS 382.240). These fees include County Clerk charge of up to $1 for each instrument recorded, regardless of whether instrument is returned by mail. Postage, if any, charged by clerks should be confirmed prior to recordation.

License to do Business.—Domestic corporation's existence begins with filing of articles with Secretary of State unless articles specify delayed effective date. (KRS 271B.2-030). Foreign corporation's authority to transact business in state begins with issuance of certificate of authority by Secretary of State. (KRS 271B.15-050). KRS 271B.1-280, based on §1.28 of Act, authorizes Secretary of State to issue certificate of existence for domestic corporation or certificate of authorization for foreign corporation to anyone. Certificate shall set forth name, duration if less than perpetual, that all fees, taxes and penalties which are collected by Secretary of State and which affect existence have been paid, that most recent annual report has been filed, and that articles of dissolution have not been filed. Subject to any reservation stated therein, certificate is conclusive evidence of corporation's existence or authorization to do business in state. (KRS 271B.1-280[3]).

Organization.—KRS 271B.2-050 adopts §2.05 of Act without material variation.

Paid In Capital Requirements.—None. (KRS 271B.6-210). See subhead Issuance of Stock, infra.

Amendment of Articles.—KRS 271B.10-010 to .090 adopt §§10.01 to 10.09 of Act without material variation.

Increase or Decrease of Authorized Capital Stock.—See subhead Amendment of Articles, supra.

Bylaws.—KRS 271B.2-060 and .2-070 adopt §§2.06 and 2.07 of Act. KRS 271B.10-200 and 220 adopt §§10.20 and 10.22 of Act, relating to bylaw amendments, without material variation. §10.21 of Act, permitting "supermajority" shareholder quorum and voting provisions in bylaws is omitted. "Supermajority" provisions are permitted, but must be set forth in articles of incorporation. (KRS 271B.7-270).

Stock.—§§6.01 and 6.02 of Act adopted. (KRS 271B.6-010 and 020).

Stock Certificates.—§6.25 of Act adopted. (KRS 271B.6-250). §6.26 of Act, permitting uncertificated shares, adopted. (KRS 271B.6-260).

Issuance of Stock.—§6.20 of Act, regarding subscriptions, adopted. (KRS 271B.6-200). §6.21 of Act, regarding issuance, adopted but subsection (b) rewritten and subsection (e) omitted insofar as they relate to issuance of stock for promissory notes or services to be performed; substitute provisions, based on Ky. Const. §193, provide that shares may be issued only for equivalent consideration consisting of money paid, labor done, or property actually received, and all fictitious increase of shares shall be void. (KRS 271B.6-210[2]). Shares issued in consideration of unsecured promissory note are void. (728 S.W.2d 529). New subsections [5 and 6] added to KRS 271B.6-210 to create presumption that consideration received in excess of par value upon issuance of par stock deemed to be consideration for issuance of share dividends and to direct directors to designate either consolidated net income of corporation or consideration presumably received for issuance of shares as consideration received upon declaration of share dividends. §6.23 of Act, relating to share dividends, adopted with similar qualification requiring calculation of deemed consideration. (KRS 271B.6-230). §6.28 of Act, relating to expense of issuance, adopted with non-substantive variation. (KRS 271B.6-280).

Transfer of Stock.—§6.27 of Act, relating to transfer restrictions, adopted with variation that restriction, even if improperly noted, may be enforceable against holder or transferee with actual knowledge. (KRS 271B.6-270). See category Business Regulation and Commerce, topic Commercial Code. §7.07 of Act, relating to fixing record date, adopted. (KRS 271B.7-070).

Uniform Simplification of Fiduciary Security Transfers Act has not been adopted.

Uniform Commercial Code.—1972, 1977 and 1994 amendments adopted with variations. (KRS c. 355). See category Business Regulation and Commerce, topic Commercial Code.

Stock Transfer Tax.—None.

Shareholders.—Cc. 6 and 7 of Act governing general rights of shareholders adopted without significant variation unless noted under separate subheads. §6.30 of Act, relating to preemptive rights, substantially adopted with special transition provisions recognizing preemptive rights to shareholders of corporations incorporated prior to effective date of Act in certain situations. (KRS 271B.6-300[4]).

Shareholders' Actions.—§7.40 of Act adopted with additional requirement that person commencing action must fairly and adequately represent shareholders' interests in enforcing corporation's right. (KRS 271B.7-400[1]). Dec. 1989 amendments to Revised Model Act by ABA Committee on Corporate Laws to §7.40 of Act and proposing new §§7.41 to 7.47 not adopted. Kentucky Rules of Civil Procedure do not have rule equivalent to Rule 23.1 of Federal Rules of Civil Procedure. No requirement exists that person commencing action post security for expenses of action.

Shareholders' Liabilities.—§6.22 of Act adopted. (KRS 271B.6-220). "Double liability" attaches only to ownership of shares of investment companies. (KRS 291.115).

Shareholders' Meetings.—§§7.01 to .27 of Act adopted without significant variations (KRS 271B.7-010 to -270), except: Shareholders' meetings must be called by holders of at least 33$\frac{1}{3}$% of shares, unless other percentage is called for in articles of incorporation (KRS 271B.7-020[2]); shareholder action by unanimous written consent without meeting authorized unless prohibited by articles of incorporation (KRS 271B.7-040[1]); unanimous consent of shareholders is effective as of delivery of last necessary writing to secretary, unless other date is specified (KRS 271B.7-040[4]); shareholder may revoke consent prior to delivery of votes required to take action (KRS 271B.7-040[5]); articles of incorporation may authorize any action, other than election of directors, by consent of at least 80% but less than all of shareholders, even action on certain fundamental changes requiring not less than ten days advance written notice if notice given, but prompt notice of any action taken by less than unanimous vote shall be given to non-consenting shareholders (KRS 271B.7-040[2], [7] and [8]); §7.20 of Act adopted with omission of subsection (d) (KRS 271B.7-200); proxy appointments and proxies by cablegram, telegram, photographic or equivalent reproduction are specifically authorized (KRS 271B.7-220[b], -240[1]); revocation of proxy appointment is effective upon receipt by secretary (KRS 271B.7-220[6]); shares held by corporation may be voted by president, proxy appointed by him, or other person designated by board of directors, and special provisions govern voting by administrator, executor, guardian, fiduciary, or receiver (KRS 271B.7-240[6] to [9]); pledged shares must be voted by pledgor until transferred into name of pledgee (KRS 271B.7-240[10]); quorum and voting requirements presently in effect shall govern vote to amend articles of incorporation provisions relating to quorum and voting requirements (KRS 271B.7-270[2]); and cumulative voting for directors mandatory (KRS 271B.7-280).

Voting Trusts.—§§7.30 and 7.31 of Act adopted. (KRS 271B.7-300, -310).

Directors.—Subchapter A of c. 8 of Uniform Act adopted. (KRS 271B.8-010 to -100) without significant variation, except: Cumulative voting is mandatory pursuant to Ky. Const. §207 (KRS 271B.7-280; 8-080[3]); §8.09 of Act, relating to court-ordered removal of directors, omitted; and, only two directors required in order to stagger terms of office (KRS 271B.8-060).

Directors Meetings.—Subchapter B of c. 8 of Act adopted. (KRS 271B.8-200 to -250).

Powers and Duties of Directors.—See subheads Directors, supra, and Liabilities of Directors, infra. §8.30 of Act, regarding general standards for discharging duties, adopted with variations described in subhead Liabilities of Directors, infra.

Liabilities of Directors.—§8.30 of Act adopted (KRS 271B.8-300) with following variations: Director shall discharge his duties in good faith, "on an informed basis," and in manner he "honestly" believes to be in best interests of corporation (KRS 271B.8-300[1]); director shall be considered to act on "informed basis" if he makes, with care ordinarily prudent person in like position would exercise under similar circumstances, inquiry into corporation's business and affairs or into particular action to be taken or decision to be made (KRS 271B.8-300[2]); standard of "honest" belief is substituted for "reasonable" belief (KRS 271B.8-300[3]); nonuniform additions to statute provide further that action of any director shall not be basis for monetary damages or injunctive relief unless (1) director breached duties under KRS 271B.8-300, (2) in case of monetary damages, breach constituted willful misconduct or wanton or reckless disregard for best interests of corporation and its shareholders (KRS 271B.8-300[5]); and plaintiffs have burden of proving breach, willfulness, wantonness or recklessness and legal causation by clear and convincing evidence (KRS 271B.8-300[6]); but nothing in KRS 271B.8-300, or its predecessor section KRS 271A.202, eliminates or limits liability of directors for acts prior to July 15, 1988 (KRS 271B.8-300[7]). §8.33 of Act adopted (KRS 271B.8-330) with 1986 technical changes allowing compliance with KRS 271B.8-300 as defense.

Officers.—Subchapter D of c. 8 of Act adopted. (KRS 271B.8-400 to .8-440). KRS 271B.8-420 contains nonuniform standards of officers' conduct comparable to those applicable to directors. See subhead Liabilities of Directors, supra.

Indemnification of Directors and Officers.—Subchapter E of c. 8 of Act adopted (KRS 271B.8-500 to -580) with following variation: §8.58(a) of Act replaced by provision that KRS 271B.8-500 to -580 do not prevent adoption in bylaws or by agreement by vote of shareholders or disinterested directors, or otherwise, of other indemnification rights. (KRS 271B.8-580[1]).

Principal Office.—Articles of incorporation must set forth mailing address of principal office. (KRS 271B.2-020[1][d]).

Resident Agent.—Chapter 5 of Act adopted, KRS 271B.5-010 through .5-040, with following variation. Agent must sign appointment or deliver written acceptance to Secretary of State before appointment is effective. (KRS 271B.5-010[2]).

See note at head of Digest as to 1998 legislation covered.

See Topical Index in front part of this volume.

CORPORATIONS ... *continued*

General Powers of Corporations.—Chapter 3 of Act adopted (KRS 271B.3-010 to -040), with addition that presence or absence of corporate seal on official documents shall not affect legality or validity thereof (KRS 271B.3-020[2]).

Dividends.—§6.40 of Act adopted (KRS 271B.6-400) with addition that indebtedness not considered liability for purposes of determinations under subsection (3) (§6.40[c]) of Act, if its terms provide that payment of principal and interest are made only if and to extent that payment of distribution to shareholders could be made. If indebtedness is issued as distribution, each payment of principal or interest is treated as distribution effect of which is measured on date payment is actually made. (KRS 271B.6-400[7]). §6.23 of Act, relating to share dividends, adopted, with variation that share dividends may not be made without consideration (KRS 271B.6-230); KRS 271B.6-210(5) and (6) set forth method for determining deemed consideration.

Unclaimed Dividends.—See category Property, topic Absentees, subhead Escheat.

Sale or Transfer of Corporate Assets.—C. 12 of Act adopted without material variation. (KRS 271B.12-010 and .12-020).

Books and Records.—Subchapter A of c. 16 of Act adopted (KRS 271B.16-010 to .16-040) with 1986 technical change to §16.020(f) (KRS 271B.16-020[6]).

Reports.—Subchapter B of c. 16 of Act adopted (KRS 271B.16-200 to .16-220) except: §16.20 of Act replaced with provision that corporation required to send its most recent financial statements showing in reasonable detail its assets and liabilities and results of its operations to any shareholder or holder of voting trust certificates upon written request (KRS 271B.16-200); §16.21(b) of Act omitted; subsections 5 through 7 of §16.22(a) of Act omitted; last sentence of §16.22(d) omitted; and June 30 substituted for Apr. 1 as last date in §16.22(c) for submission of annual reports (KRS 271B.16-220[3]).

Corporate Bonds or Mortgages.—See subheads General Powers of Corporations and Sale or Transfer of Corporate Assets, supra.

Merger and Consolidation.—C. 11 of Act adopted (KRS 271B.11-010 to -070), with addition to §11.07 of Act based on Ky. Const. §200 which requires that upon merger between Kentucky corporation and foreign corporation with foreign corporation surviving, Kentucky courts retain jurisdiction over corporate property within state as if transaction had not taken place (KRS 271B.11-070[2][c]). Consolidations no longer authorized by statute. Merger of one or more domestic or foreign limited liability companies or limited partnerships allowed with one or more domestic corporations. (KRS 271B.11-080).

Share Exchanges or Acquisitions.—See subhead Merger and Consolidation, supra.

Antitakeover Provisions.—Nonuniform antitakeover statute, referred to as Shareholder Protection Act and applicable to most corporations with 500 or more beneficial shareholders and principal office located in Kentucky, requires approval of majority of disinterested directors or affirmative vote of 80% of all shares and two thirds of disinterested shares for approval of merger or other business combination with any 10% shareholder or other corporation which after transaction would be 10% shareholder. (KRS 271B.12-200 to -230). Special voting requirements do not apply if fair price standards are met. (KRS 271B.12-220[2]). Business combinations with interested shareholders prohibited for period of five years after such party became shareholder in many circumstances. (KRS 271B.12-210[3]). Business combination of capital stock, franchises or property of two or more railroad, telegraph, bridge or other common carrier companies owning parallel or competing lines or structures is prohibited (Ky. Const. §201; 144 Ky. 324, 138 S.W. 291) but telephone companies are permitted to make such combination upon strict compliance with conditions imposed (KRS 278.510).

Tender Offers.—See subhead Merger and Consolidation, supra.

Dissolution.—C. 14 of Act adopted (KRS 271B.14-010 to -070) with following variations: Original and three copies of articles of dissolution must be filed with secretary of state (KRS 271B.14-030[1]); secretary of state shall forward one copy to commissioner of revenue (KRS 271B.14-030[2]); dissolution does not alter corporation's federal or state tax obligations (KRS 271B.14-050[2][h] and KRS 271B.14-060[4]); claims against dissolved corporations are barred unless proceedings are commenced within two years after publication of notice (KRS 271B.14-070[2][c] and .14-070[3]); §14.20(1) of Act omitted; notices concerning administrative dissolution are sent by first class mail to corporation's registered office, rather than by procedure described in §5.04 of Act (KRS 271B.14-210[1], [2], 14-220[2], 14-230[1]); reinstatement following administrative dissolution may occur at any time after effective date rather than only within first two years (KRS 271B.14-220[1]); appeals made to circuit court of county where corporation's principal office is located, or, if foreign corporation, to county where registered office is located (KRS 271B.14-070[2]); "oppressive" omitted from equivalent of §14.30(2)(ii) (KRS 271B.14-300[2][6]); §14.30(2)(iv) of Act omitted; actions by attorney general lie in Franklin County (Frankfort) (KRS 271B.14-310).

Insolvency and Receivers.—§§14.32 and 14.40 of Act adopted. (KRS 271B.14-320, -400).

Close Corporations.—No special provisions adopted.

Appraisal.—C. 13 of Act adopted (KRS 271B.13-010 to -310) with following variations: In any business combination subject to Shareholder Protection Act (KRS 271B.12-200 to -230), "fair value" shall be at least amount required to be paid pursuant to KRS 271B.12-220(2) (KRS 271B.13-010[3]); §13.02(a)(4)(iii) of Act, relating to preemptive rights, omitted; shareholder may also dissent from any transaction subject to Shareholder Protection Act (KRS 271B.12-200 to -230) or exempted from that act by KRS 271B.12-220(2) (KRS 271B.13-020[1][e]); under KRS 271B.13-200(1) corporation need only provide copy of statute to persons entitled to notice of dissenters' rights on shareholder's request; §13.22(b) of Act modified to require notice sent ten days after proposed corporate action was authorized by shareholders or, if shareholder approval was not required, by board of directors (KRS 271B.13-220[2]);

and §13.25(b)(5) of Act omitted. See also subheads Merger and Consolidation and Share Exchanges or Acquisitions, supra.

Foreign corporations may not be allowed to do business in Kentucky on conditions more favorable than those prescribed by law for domestic corporations. (Ky. Const. §202).

Authority to Transact Business.—§§15.01 through 15.05 of Act adopted, KRS 271B.15-010 to -050, with following variation. Agent must sign application or deliver written consent. (1998 Acts HB 666[10]). Monetary penalties for transacting business without certificate of authority: $2 per day, not to exceed $500 per year. (KRS 271B.15-020[4]).

Name.—§15.06 of Act adopted (KRS 271B.15-060) with addition that name must be distinguishable from name of domestic limited partnership and foreign limited partnership registered to do business in Kentucky, and assumed name filed with secretary of state pursuant to KRS 365.015 (KRS 271B.15-060[2][e]).

Registered Agent.—§§5.01 to 5.04 of Act adopted, KRS 271B.5-010 to -040, with following variation. Agent must sign appointment or deliver written consent. (KRS 271B.5-010[2]).

Service of Process.—§15.10 of Act adopted. (KRS 271B.15-100).

Withdrawal and Revocation of Authority.—§15.20 of Act, relating to withdrawal, adopted. (KRS 271B.15-200). §15.30 of Act, relating to revocation, adopted (KRS 271B.15-300) with following variations: "deliver" is changed to "file" (KRS 271B.15-300[1]); §15.30(2) of Act omitted; and remaining subsections renumbered. §§15.31 and 15.32 of Act adopted (KRS 271B.15-310, 320) except that service of notice is to be effected by first class mail to corporation's registered office (KRS 271B.15-320).

Taxation of Corporate Property.—The ordinary business corporation is assessed and taxed as natural person. (KRS 132.220, 250; 136.020). See category Taxation, topics Property (Ad Valorem) Taxes, subhead Real and Personal Property Taxable and Corporation License Taxes.

Returns for assessment must be made as of Jan. 1 in each year and filed with property valuation administrator of county where property located by Mar. 1 (KRS 132.220), except in case of: (1) Certain public service corporations assessed by Department of Revenue; and (2) certain kinds of taxpayers, such as banks, trust companies, building and loan associations, turnpike companies, railroads, owners or bailees of distilled spirits, etc., covered by special provisions which require reports to Department of Revenue or other tribunal or officer charged with duty of assessment.

The taxable situs of real estate and tangible personalty is its actual location (KRS 132.200, .220, .250), but mere temporary location of tangibles for transient purposes does not fix taxable situs (134 Ky. 99, 119 S.W. 749; 181 Ky. 675, 205 S.W. 789).

Intangibles of a domestic corporation are taxable where its registered office is located, and intangibles of a foreign corporation, which have acquired a business situs in Kentucky (KRS 132.190[1]), are taxable where its principal office for Kentucky is located. (Compare 236 Ky. 629, 33 S.W.2d 690). All such intangibles must be listed for taxation accordingly. (KRS 132.190[4]).

Taxation of Corporate Stock.—The holders of stock in a corporation, whether domestic or foreign, need not list their shares for ad valorem taxation so long as such corporation and its subsidiaries pay taxes to Kentucky on at least 75% of their total property, wherever located; except that bonds and obligations of U.S. and its possessions, and bonds and obligations of Commonwealth of Kentucky and its instrumentalities, and its political subdivisions and their instrumentalities are excluded from computation of total property for purposes of exemption. (KRS 136.030).

Other corporate stocks owned by a corporation are taxed in same manner and to same extent as its intangibles generally.

Franchise Tax.—License tax is imposed on right to exist as corporation and to do business in Kentucky. It is levied alike on domestic and foreign corporations that are not subject to a tax on franchise. Alternative method of computing license tax is provided where apportionment provisions do not fairly measure taxpayer's capital in state. Annual license tax rate is $2.10 on each $1,000 of capital stock represented by property owned or business done in Kentucky. Minimum tax $30. (KRS 136.070[5]). Corporations with gross income of $500,000 or less entitled to credit of $1.40 per $1,000 of initial $350,000 of capital employed in business. (KRS 136.070[6]).

Total capital of each corporation subject to tax is apportioned to Kentucky by property, payroll and sales factors in ratio of 1:1:2 before tax applied. (KRS 136.070[2], [3]). Exemption provided for book value of stock and other securities of subsidiary corporations held if corporation being taxed has its commercial domicile in Kentucky and owns stock in other corporations with value of at least 50% of its total assets. (KRS 136.071).

Reports.—Each corporation liable for corporation license tax must, on or before Apr. 15 or 15th day of fourth month following close of its fiscal year, report to Department of Revenue, on prescribed forms, information required as basis for computing and assessing corporation license tax. (KRS 136.080 to .100).

Payment.—After tax is assessed, Revenue Cabinet must notify corporation by mail of amount fixed, and tax must be paid in 30 days from date of notice, or protest may be filed and hearing before Cabinet, with proceedings for review by State Tax Commission and by courts after exhausting administrative remedies, which must be strictly followed. (KRS 136.110).

License tax must be paid to Revenue Cabinet by check or money order payable to State Treasurer. (KRS 136.110). Heavy penalties are imposed for default in making required reports and payments. (KRS 136.050).

Separate franchise tax is imposed alike on corporations, associations, partnerships and individuals engaged in any public or quasi-public service. For that reason, this tax is discussed elsewhere. (See category Taxation, topic Taxes, subhead Public Service Corporation Property Tax.)

Financial Institutions.—Franchise tax substantially similar to license tax on corporations is imposed on financial institutions which solicit business from 20 or more persons in Kentucky or have receipts attributable to sources in Kentucky equal to $100,000 or more. Rate of tax is 1.1% of net capital (as defined in KRS 136.515) with

CORPORATIONS . . . *continued*
minimum tax of $300. (KRS 136.510). Principal differences between financial institutions franchise tax and franchise tax on other corporations, supra, are: (1) apportionment ratio is 1:1:1 for financial institutions (KRS 136.525); and (2) report due on or before Mar. 15 (KRS 136.545).

Income tax on corporations, see category Taxation, topic Income Tax.

Professional corporations may be organized under KRS c. 274 by those rendering personal services to public of a type which requires a license or other legal authorization, and which prior to Act could not be performed by corporation. Includes, but is not limited to, public accountants, certified public accountants, chiropractors, osteopaths, physicians, surgeons, dentists, podiatrists, chiropodists, architects, veterinarians, optometrists, and attorneys-at-law. Incorporation does not alter professional responsibility or privilege nor does it insulate principal from malpractice liability.

Deeds.—See category Property, topic Deeds.

Nonstock, nonprofit corporations without capital stock may be formed by one or more persons for any lawful purpose, such as civic, athletic, recreational or social, not involving pecuniary gain. Act does not apply to cooperatives. KRS 273.161 to .390, "Nonprofit Act", contains special provisions applicable to articles of incorporation, powers, membership and agent for service, and incorporates portions of Act for profit with respect to holding of real estate, amendment of articles and dissolution. (KRS 273.161 to .390). Such corporations can be organized for charitable, educational, civic, religious, or like purposes, but not for labor unions or trade associations. (KRS 273.167).

Model Non-Profit Corporation Act not adopted.

Business trusts defined, and procedure for organizing, operation and terminating same in KRS 386.370.

Limited Liability Companies.—See topic Limited Liability Companies.

JOINT STOCK COMPANIES:

There are no provisions for the organization of joint stock companies, and the members thereof are individually liable for the obligations of such companies. See topic Associations. As to professional corporations, see topic Corporations, subhead Professional Corporations.

Business trusts defined, and procedure for organization, operation and terminating same, in KRS 386.370.

LIMITED LIABILITY COMPANIES:

Kentucky Limited Liability Company Act, effective July 15, 1994, permits formation of limited liability companies ("LLCs"). Act is codified in KRS 275.

Name.—Must contain words "limited liability company", "limited company" or abbreviations "LLC" or "LC". If professional LLC, name must contain words "professional limited liability company", "professional limited company" or abbreviations "PLLC" or "PLC". (KRS 275.100).

Purpose.—May be organized for any lawful purpose, including provision of professional services. (KRS 275.005).

Powers.—Except as limited by KRS c. 275, its articles of organization or operating agreement, LLC has power to do all things necessary or convenient to carry out its business and affairs. (KRS 275.010).

Formation.—By one or more persons by delivering executed articles of organization to Secretary of State for filing. (KRS 275.020).

Articles of Organization.—Must set forth: (1) name satisfying above-listed requirements; (2) street address of initial registered office and name of initial registered agent; (3) mailing address of initial principal office; and (4) statement that LLC will be managed by manager(s) or by its members. If PLLC, articles must designate professional services to be practiced. Articles must be accompanied by written consent of initial registered agent to serve in that capacity. Articles may include any other matter permitted in operating agreement and not inconsistent with law. (KRS 275.025).

Amendments to Articles of Organization.—Unless articles or operating agreement provide otherwise, amendment of articles to: (1) change management from members to managers or managers to members requires unanimous vote of members; (2) delete name of registered agent, or address of registered office or principal office requires action by any manager or (if no manager) member if statement of change is on file with Secretary of State; and (3) make any other changes requires vote of majority of managers, or if management vested in members, members. (KRS 275.030).

Filing Fees.—Articles of organization-$40; application for certificate of authority as foreign LLC-$90; amendment of articles of organization-$40; restatement of articles of organization-$40; amendment and restatement of articles of organization-$80; articles of dissolution-$40; change of registered agent, registered office or both-$10; registered agent's change of registered office-$10 per LLC, not to exceed total of $1,000; change of address of principal office-$10; reservation of name-$15; transfer of reserved name-$15; application for use of indistinguishable name-$20; application for registered name-$36; application for renewal of registered name-$36; articles of merger-$50; amended certificate for authority-$40; certificate of withdrawal-$40; articles of correction-$20; certificate of existence or authorization-$10; reinstatement following administrative dissolution-$100; annual report-$15; and any other document required or permitted to be filed by KRS c. 275-$15. (KRS 275.055).

Operating Agreement.—Members may agree among themselves how business and affairs of LLC shall be conducted. Many provisions of enabling law may be varied by operating agreement. (KRS 275.015).

Admission of Members.—Person(s) who deliver articles of organization to Secretary of State need not be members. (KRS 275.020). If acquiring LLC interest directly from LLC, person admitted as member upon compliance with operating agreement; if issue not addressed in operating agreement, admission is dependent upon written consent of all members. (KRS 275.275). Assignee of LLC interest is admitted upon compliance with operating agreement and, unless operating agreement provides otherwise, consent of majority-in-interest of members. (KRS 275.255, KRS 275.265).

Assignment of Membership Interest.—Unless otherwise provided in operating agreement, membership interest is assignable in whole or part. Such assignment does not dissolve LLC and does not entitle assignee to become member but conveys only right to receive distributions which assignor would have received. Unless assignee becomes member, assignor continues to be member until removed by other members. (KRS 275.255).

Voting of Members.—Unless otherwise provided in operating agreement, consent of majority-in-interest of members is required to amend written operating agreement, authorize manager or member to contravene written operating agreement, or amend articles to change management of company from members to managers or managers to members. Unless otherwise provided in KRS c. 275, articles or operating agreement, consent of majority-in-interest of members or, if managed by managers, managers is required to decide any matter connected with business affairs of LLC. (KRS 275.175).

Management.—Unless articles of organization vest management of LLC in manager(s), management of business and affairs of LLC vests in members. If articles vest management in manager(s), manager(s) shall have exclusive power to manage business and affairs of LLC, except to extent otherwise provided in KRS c. 275, articles or operating agreement. Unless otherwise provided by articles or operating agreement, managers: (1) shall be elected or removed upon consent of members entitled to cast majority of votes to be cast by members; (2) need not be members or natural persons; and (3) unless sooner removed or resign, hold office until appointment of successor. (KRS 275.165).

Liability to Third Parties.—Except as specifically set forth in KRS c. 275, members and managers, as such, are not liable for obligations of LLC. (KRS 275.150). Member, as such, is not proper party to proceeding by or against LLC, unless proceeding is to enforce member's right against or liability to LLC or as otherwise provided in operating agreement. (KRS 275.155).

Contributions.—Interest in LLC may be issued in exchange for cash, property, services rendered, or promissory note or other obligation to contribute cash or property or to perform services. (KRS 275.195). Member's promise to contribute to LLC enforceable only if written. If member fails to make required contribution, member shall be obligated, at LLC's option, to contribute cash equal to portion of value of stated contribution not made. Unless operating agreement provides otherwise, obligation of member to contribute may be compromised only upon unanimous consent of members. However, creditor of LLC who extends credit or otherwise relies upon member's signed contribution obligation before compromise thereof may enforce original obligation. (KRS 275.200).

Allocation of Profits and Losses.—Profits and losses of LLC are allocated among members and classes thereof in manner provided in operating agreement. If written operating agreement does not provide otherwise, profits and losses shall be allocated on basis of agreed value of member's contribution to extent received by LLC and not returned to member. (KRS 275.205).

Distributions.—All allocated among members and classes thereof as provided in writing in operating agreement. If operating agreement does not provide otherwise in writing, each member shares on basis of agreed value of member's contributions to extent received by LLC and not returned to member. (KRS 275.210). Unless written operating agreement provides otherwise, no member has right to receive any distribution in any form other than cash, and no member may be compelled to accept asset in kind from LLC to extent that percentage of asset distributed to member exceeds percentage that member would have shared in cash distribution equal to value of property. (KRS 275.220). No distribution may be made by LLC if after giving effect thereto (1) LLC would be unable to pay its debts as they come due or (2) LLC's assets would be less than sum of its liabilities plus, unless otherwise provided in operating agreement, amount that would be necessary (if LLC were to be dissolved at time of distribution) to satisfy preferential rights of other members which are superior to rights of member receiving distribution. (KRS 275.225).

Voluntary Withdrawals.—Unless otherwise provided in written operating agreement, member has no right to withdraw from LLC. If written operating agreement does not specify time to withdraw, member cannot withdraw without consent of all remaining members. (KRS 275.280).

Cessation of Membership.—Person ceases to be member of LLC upon: (1) voluntary withdrawal; (2) assignment of person's interest in LLC to one who becomes member; (3) removal by vote of other members in accordance with operating agreement or upon sale of person's interest; (4) unless otherwise provided in operating agreement or by consent of majority-in-interest of remaining members, upon person's involvement in certain bankruptcy-related or similar proceedings; (5) unless otherwise provided in operating agreement or by consent of majority-in-interest of remaining members, upon person's death or entry of order adjudicating person incompetent; (6) certain other instances relating to type of entity which person is (i.e., trust, corporation, other LLC). (KRS 275.280).

Dissolution occurs upon first of following: (1) expiration of term of LLC set forth in articles of organization, if any, or upon occurrence of events, specified in articles of organization or operating agreement; (2) written consent of majority-in-interest of members; (3) entry of judicial decree of dissolution; or (4) filing of certificate of dissolution by Secretary of State. (KRS 275.285). Procedure for winding up affairs of LLC set forth in KRS 275.300, 275.305 and 275.310.

Merger.—Unless otherwise provided in operating agreement, LLC may merge with one or more other LLCs or other business entities, with either LLC or other entity being survivor. (KRS 275.345). Plan of merger must be approved by majority-in-interest of members, and by any other business entity by vote required by laws applicable to it. (KRS 275.350). Requirements for plan of merger set forth in KRS 275.355. Entity surviving merger must deliver to Secretary of State articles of merger which satisfy requirements of KRS 275.360. Upon consummation of merger, surviving entity succeeds to all rights and obligations of merged entities. (KRS 275.365).

See note at head of Digest as to 1998 legislation covered.

See Topical Index in front part of this volume.

KY – 4

LIMITED LIABILITY COMPANIES ... *continued*

Conversion of Partnership.—Partnership or limited partnership may be converted to LLC. (KRS 275.370).

Foreign LLC Qualification.—Foreign LLC must obtain certificate of authority prior to transacting business within Kentucky. (KRS 275.386). Certificate obtained by applying to Secretary of State in accordance with KRS 275.395.

PARTNERSHIPS:

Uniform Partnership Act adopted in 1954 without substantial variation. (KRS 362.150 to .360). See Uniform and Model Acts section. KRS 362.200, which adopted §11 of uniform act and provided that admission by partner concerning partnership affairs is binding on partnership, was repealed effective July 1, 1992 when Kentucky Rules of Evidence became effective. Revised Uniform Partnership Act (1992-1994) not adopted.

Formation.—No formalities, filing or recording required.

Name.—Unless name of partnership includes real name of at least one of partners, partnership must file certificate of assumed name. (KRS 365.015). See also category Intellectual Property, topic Trademarks and Tradenames. Partnership may sue and be sued in its common name. (KRS 362.605).

Limited Partnership.—Uniform Limited Partnership Act (1976) with 1985 amendments adopted without substantial variation. (KRS 362.401 to 362.527). See Uniform and Model Acts section. KRS 362.437(2) defines several activities which do not constitute taking part in business in order to subject limited partner to liability.

Limited Liability Partnerships.—Effective July 15, 1994, Kentucky amended its Uniform Partnership Act to allow for creation of registered limited liability partnerships ("LLPs"). Partnership becomes LLP by filing with Secretary of State statement which satisfies requirements of 1994 Ky. Acts c. 389 §01. Except for liability arising from his or her own negligence, wrongful acts or misconduct, partner in LLP is not liable for obligations of LLP. (KRS 362.220). Name of LLP must include words "registered limited liability partnership" or end with abbreviation "LLP". (KRS 362.565). Prior to transacting business in Kentucky, foreign limited liability partnership must register with Secretary of State in accordance with KRS 362.585.

Out of State Partnerships.—No special registration requirements apply to general partnerships organized under laws of foreign state, but special requirements do apply to foreign limited partnerships. Foreign limited partnership authorized to do business in state only after registration with Secretary of State, designation of domestic process agent, and payment of recording fee of $60. (KRS 362.499). Foreign limited partnership must select fictitious name for transacting business in state or obtain written consent of holder of corporate or other holder of trade name to use own name if own name is indistinguishable from name of existing domestic or foreign corporation or name held under trade name statute, KRS 365.105. (KRS 365.015).

BUSINESS REGULATION AND COMMERCE

BANKS AND BANKING:

Uniform Commercial Code adopted. (KRS c. 355). See topic Commercial Code. General laws regulating organization and management of corporations apply to banks, trust companies and combined bank and trust corporations unless inconsistent with special provisions or otherwise made inapplicable. (KRS 287.050; 271B.17-010).

Regulated by Department of Financial Institutions which is headed by Commissioner of Financial Institutions. (KRS 287.011; 287.690; 287.854). Offices of Department of Financial Institutions located at 477 Versailles Road, Frankfort 40601. Department also regulates affairs of trust companies, savings and loan associations, consumer loan companies, investment and industrial loan companies, credit unions and mortgage loan companies and administers general laws relating to securities (blue sky laws). (KRS 287.011[2]; KRS c. 294).

Private Banking.—Only corporations may conduct private banking business in state. (KRS 287.030).

Shareholders' Liability.—Holders of shares of stock in banks have same type of liability to bank and creditors thereof as do shareholders of private business corporations. Such liability is limited to payment of authorized or subscribed consideration upon original issuance and liability for his own act or conduct. (KRS 271B.6-220).

Bank Holding Companies.—Multibank holding companies are allowed subject to restriction on acquisition of newly formed banks. (KRS 287.900[2]). No individual or bank holding company can control banks holding more than 15% of total deposits and member accounts in offices of federally insured depository institutions in Kentucky. (KRS 287.900[3]).

Deposits.—General provision authorizes banks to receive deposits and allow interest thereon. (KRS 287.180). Officers prohibited from receiving deposits or assenting to receipt of deposits with knowledge that bank is insolvent. (KRS 517.100). Violation of section is felony punishable by imprisonment from one to five years (KRS 532.060), and fine of not less than $1,000 nor greater than $10,000, or double gain from transaction, whichever is greater (KRS 534.030). Separate authorization is provided to allow banks to pay any amount deposited by minor to minor (KRS 287.380), and, subject to their charters, to pledge assets or provide surety bonds as collateral security for governmental deposits made with them (KRS 287.330). Deposits subject to reserve requirements on demand deposits as mandated by Board of Governors of Federal Reserve System. (KRS 387.300). Collections are governed by Uniform Commercial Code. See topic Commercial Code.

Unclaimed Deposits.—Demand and time deposits, sums payable on money orders escheat to state if abandoned for seven years; funds or other property held in safe deposit boxes or other safekeeping arrangements escheat to state if abandoned for seven years (KRS 393.060[1] and [3]); and sums payable on travelers checks escheat after 15 years from issuance. (KRS 393.060[2]). See also category Property, topic Absentees, subhead Escheat.

Collections are governed by Uniform Commercial Code. See topic Commercial Code.

Investments by banks and trust companies of their own funds are regulated by KRS 287.100, 287.110, 287.310; of trust funds by KRS 287.225, 287.230 and 287.240. Permissible investments include owning or operating discount brokerage service or travel agency. (KRS 287.100). Banks can hold and own personal property. (KRS 287.105). See also category Estates and Trusts, topic Trusts, subhead Uniform Common Trust Fund Act.

Banks and trust companies are authorized to: be appointed, and act, as fiduciaries (KRS 287.210[1], KRS 395.005); act as agent for transaction of any business or management of estates, collection of rents, accounts, interest, dividends, notes, bonds, securities for money and debts, and demands of every character (KRS 287.210[2]); receive on deposit and for safekeeping gold, silver, jewelry, money, and other personal property of every kind (KRS 287.210[3]); and effective June 1, 1997 participate in interstate merger transactions (KRS 287.920). Only banks may: accept for future payment drafts or bills of exchange drawn upon them by their customers; issue letters of credit authorizing holders thereof to draw drafts upon them or their correspondents at sight or on time, and accept or discount acceptances. (KRS 287.190).

Four or more banks, trust companies or national banks may form fiduciary investment company for investment management of funds held in fiduciary capacity. (KRS 386.510 to 386.600).

Uniform Common Trust Fund Act not adopted.

Credit unions organized under supervision of Commissioner of Financial Institutions. (KRS c. 290). Credit unions authorized to charge interest rates of 2% per month, rate which is often used for "most favorable lender" purposes. (KRS 290.435).

Savings and loan associations may be organized under supervision of Commissioner of Financial Institutions. (KRS c. 289).

Industrial loan companies may be formed which meet requirements and obtain approval of Commissioner of Financial Institutions may be formed. Loans may be made in amounts up to $7,500 at interest rates up to 7%, which may be discounted or charged in advance. Loan period may not exceed five years and 32 days. Industrial loan companies may offer revolving credit plans, if secured by first or second mortgage on residential property. (KRS 291.410 to .600).

Consumer loan companies may be established and make loans, subject to supervision of Commissioner of Financial Institutions. (KRS c. 288). Licensed consumer loan companies may make loans at special rates. See topic Interest, subhead Small Loans.

Foreign Banks.—Banks chartered in other states and national banks having their principal place of business in other states may lend money in state without qualification or approval but such banks may not receive deposits or transact any other kind of banking business in state unless they have merged with domestic bank pursuant to merger transaction approved by Department. (KRS 287.030). Detailed listing is provided of activities related to making loans in state which may be undertaken without rendering foreign banking or lending organizations subject to requirements relating to qualification to do business in state and to state and local taxation. (KRS 287.670 to 287.680).

See also categories Estates and Trusts, topics Executors and Administrators, Trusts; Family, topic Guardian and Ward.

Reports and Tax on Deposits.—State and national banks, trust companies, federally chartered foreign banks and domestic branches of foreign banks must report to Revenue Cabinet, on or before Jan. 21, amount of deposits of persons, firms and corporations subject to taxation in state as of Jan. 1, and pay on or before Mar. 1 tax thereon of 1/1000 of 1%, which may be deducted from such deposit in each case. (KRS 132.030, 132.040 and 136.500).

BILLS AND NOTES:

Uniform Commercial Code adopted. See topic Commercial Code for variations from Official Text and citation.

Special Requirements.—No special requirements as to form are set for notes because of their purpose or intended use. Nonnegotiable note payable to order of maker and indorsed by him constitutes promise to pay face amount to party to whom delivered or assigns. (KRS 371.070). Failure to list note or bond on intangible property tax return when required constitutes defense to payment thereof until taxes, penalties and accrued interest thereon have been paid. (KRS 132.300). See category Taxation, topic Property (Ad Valorem) Taxes, subhead Real and Personal Property Taxable.

Judgment Notes.—A provision in a note authorizing a confession of judgment thereon is void (KRS 372.140), but the insertion of such void provision does not render the note itself void or affect its negotiability (KRS 355.3-104[1][c]). Appearance under such power is criminal offense. (KRS 372.990).

Attorney Fees.—Provisions in any writing which create debt, or lien on real property, obligating debtor to pay reasonable attorney fees in event of default are enforceable to extent paid or agreed to be paid to other than salaried employee of creditor. (KRS 411.195).

Special defenses against holders in due course of consumer paper are recognized. See topic Consumer Protection.

BILLS OF LADING:

See topic Carriers.

BILLS OF SALE:

See topic Sales.

See note at head of Digest as to 1998 legislation covered.

See Topical Index in front part of this volume.

BLUE SKY LAW:

See topic Securities.

BROKERS:

Business of real estate brokers and sales associates employed by them is regulated by KRS c. 324. Business of mortgage loan brokers regulated by KRS c. 294.

Uniform Commercial Code adopted. (KRS c. 355). See topic Commercial Code.

Real Estate Brokers.—Act creates Real Estate Commission and requires that all brokers and sales associates shall be licensed by Commission and mandates six hour annual continuing education for all active agents licensed after June 19, 1976. (KRS 324.281; 324.020). License fees: Broker and sales associate, license fee set by Commission, not to exceed $30. (KRS 324.070). License may be suspended or revoked following hearing, by Commission, from whose findings appeal lies to Circuit Court. (KRS 324.160; KRS 324.170; KRS 324.210). Licenses must be renewed annually by written request with failure to renew resulting in expiration and fine not to exceed $200. (KRS 324.090). Commission may obtain injunction against unlicensed persons acting as brokers. (KRS 324.020[5]). Application for license as sales associate or broker must be made on form prescribed by Commission. Examination and successful completion of school instruction required for license. (KRS 324.040, 324.045; 324.046). Bond not required. Licensees must carry errors and omissions insurance. (KRS 324.395).

If Commission has reciprocity agreement with other state, broker or sales associate holding license from another state with licensing and educational standards deemed sufficient for minimal competence may be issued license without examination. (KRS 324.141).

Advertising governed by statute and commission regulations. (KRS 324.117). All contract deposits must be held in escrow account maintained in Kentucky, with interest, if any, used as agreed to in writing by parties. (KRS 324.111).

Written brokerage contract is required. See topic Frauds, Statute of.

Mortgage Loan Brokers.—Each person who for compensation or gain holds himself out as agent for prospective borrowers or prospective lenders with respect to loans to be secured by mortgage lien on single family residence, including condominium or apartment dwelling with four or fewer units required to obtain license from Commissioner of Department of Financial Institutions before transacting business in state. (KRS 294.030; 294.010). Applicants supply information required in verified application. (KRS 294.032). Investigation fees for initial application—$300 for principal office and $150 for each branch office; initial licensing fee $450 for principal office and $250 for each branch office in Kentucky (license fees prorated if submitted in second half of year). (KRS 294.034[1]). Annual renewal fees in same annual rates payable by June 20th each year. (KRS 294.034[3] and [4]). Surety bond in amounts not less than $100,000 for each mortgage loan company and $50,000 for each broker required. (KRS 294.060). Mortgage loan brokers' practices regulated, including rates (KRS 294.110 and 294.120), disclosures (KRS 294.115), and escrow accounts (KRS 294.130). Licenses subject to suspension by Commissioner upon proof that mortgage broker has or is about to violate law. (KRS 294.090, 294.190 and 294.200).

Criminal Penalties.—
Penalties for Violation of KRS C. 294.—(KRS 294.990).
Insolvent Brokers in Margin Transactions.—Broker in business of buying or selling, upon margin, stocks, bonds, grain, produce or cotton, and charging commissions therefor, who, being insolvent, with knowledge of that fact, accepts from customer ignorant of such insolvency, deposits of money, stocks, bonds, securities or other things of value, to be used as margin for purchase of stock, bonds, grain, produce or cotton, otherwise than in payment of or security for existing indebtedness, thereby causing customer to lose property or money so deposited, shall be guilty of Class D felony. (KRS 434.320, 434.340).

Pledge or Disposition of Securities Without Customer Consent.—Broker who has in his possession money or securities belonging to customer and pledges or disposes of them without customer's consent guilty of Class D felony. (KRS 434.330, 434.340).

Insurance Brokers.—See category Insurance, topic Insurance Companies.

Broker-Dealers in Securities.—See topic Securities.

Loan Brokers.—See topic Consumer Protection.

Payment of Taxes.—As to duty of stock and bond brokers to pay taxes due from customers, see category Taxation, topic Property (Ad Valorem) Taxes, subhead Assessment.

BULK SALES:

Art. 6 of Uniform Commercial Code repealed in 1992. No other statutory provision. See category Debtor and Creditor, topic Fraudulent Sales and Conveyances; also topic Commercial Code, this category.

CARRIERS:

This digest deals only with carriers in intrastate commerce.

Supervision.—The Railroad Commission, under Ky. Const. §209 (157 Ky. 357, 163 S.W. 239), and under KRS, cc. 276 and 277, has extensive powers of control over railroads, water carriers, and express companies. Transportation Cabinet has control over carriers by air. (KRS c. 183). As to carriers by motor vehicle, see category Transportation, topic Motor Vehicles, subhead Motor Vehicle Carriers. (KRS c. 281).

Other carriers, such as telephone and telegraph companies, natural gas transportation companies, and water districts/commissions are brought under jurisdiction and control of Public Service Commission as to services, rates, tolls and charges. (KRS c. 278).

Licenses.—Operators of air carriers must be licensed by Federal Aviation Administration. (KRS 183.050). Other carriers must obtain from Public Service Commission certificate of convenience and necessity before furnishing public utility other than

electric (KRS 278.020) and certificate of environmental compatibility for generation of electricity (KRS 278.025).

Rates.—As to carriers under Railroad Commission: written statement of rates must be furnished shipper within reasonable time after demand (KRS 276.140); deviation from rate schedules prohibited, but special contract rates permitted, if uniform (KRS 276.150); rate schedules must be filed with Commission and made available for inspection by public (KRS 276.130); rates subject to approval by Commission (KRS 276.170; KRS 276.180).

Rates of other carriers are subject to control of Public Service Commission and must be filed with Commission. (KRS 278.160; KRS 278.190; KRS 278.270).

Discrimination.—Unjust discrimination and unreasonable preferences prohibited; carriers under Railroad Commission (KRS 276.290; 276.300); other utilities (KRS 278.170).

Limiting Liability.—Exemption from common-law liability is prohibited. (Const. §196). By statute, initial carrier is made responsible for loss or damage to shipments over lines of connecting carriers, and it may not by contract exempt itself from such statutory liability. (KRS 276.470).

Bills of lading and other documents of title governed by Uniform Commercial Code. (KRS 355.7-).

Liens.—Carriers lien conferred by Uniform Commercial Code, effective July 1, 1960. (KRS 355.7-307, 355.7-308).

Employers' Liability.—As to employees in intrastate commerce, railroads are subject to an Employers' Liability Law, similar to Federal Employers' Liability Act, codified at 42 USC § 51, applying in interstate commerce. (KRS 277.310).

Motor Vehicle Carriers.—See category Transportation, topic Motor Vehicles.

COMMERCIAL CODE:

Uniform Commercial Code adopted effective July 1, 1960 and codified as c. 355 of KRS. Official Article and section numbers retained, following decimal point (e.g., §2-201 of Code as published in Uniform and Model Acts section codified as KRS 355.2-201).

1962 Official Text adopted.

1966 Official Amendments adopted.

1966 Official Optional Amendments to §§1-209, 7-209 and 9-105 adopted.

1972 Official Amendments adopted. See subhead Variances from 1962, 1972, 1977, 1987, 1989 and 1990 Official Text, infra for variations from official text.

1973 Official Amendments adopted.

1977 Official Amendments adopted. See subhead Variances from 1962, 1972, 1977, 1987, 1989 and 1990 Official Text, infra for variations from official text.

1987 Official Amendments adopted. See subhead Variances from 1962, 1972, 1977, 1987, 1989 and 1990 Official Text, infra for variation from official text.

1989 Official Amendments Article 4A adopted; Article 6 repealed.

1990 Amendments to Art 2A adopted. See subhead Variances from 1962, 1972, 1977, 1987, 1989 and 1990 Official Text, infra for variations from text.

1990 Amended Art. 3 and Conforming and Miscellaneous Amendments to Arts. 1 and 4 adopted.

1991 Amendment to Art. 3 adopted.

1994 Revision of Art. 8 adopted.

1994 and 1995 Amendments to Arts. 1, 4, 5 and 9 conforming to Art. 8 adopted.

1995 Amendments to Art. 5 not adopted.

Options in 1962, 1966, 1972, 1977, 1986 and 1989 Official Texts have been exercised as follows:
§2-318, 1966 alternative A adopted;
§2A-216, alternative A adopted;
§4-106, alternative A to subsection (2) adopted;
§4-202(1)(b), optional phrase adopted;
§5-112(1), optional phrase omitted;
§5-114, optional sections (4) and (5) omitted;
Article 6, Alternative A, repeal, adopted;
§7-204, optional subsection (4) for reference to local statutes, omitted;
§7-403(1)(b), optional phrase adopted;
§9-203, optional section (4) adopted, and reference made to KRS cc. 190, 226, 287, 288, 290, 291, 359, and 360.
§9-302(3)(b), alternative A adopted;
§9-401, third alternative 1972 subsection (1) adopted with revision of subsection (c) (see subhead Variances from 1962, 1972, 1977, 1987, 1989 and 1990 Official Text infra). Alternative subsection (3) not adopted;
§9-402, optional language in subsections (3) and (5);
Optional §9-407 adopted with variations (see subhead Variances from 1962, 1972, 1977, 1987, 1989 and 1990 Official Text infra).

Variances from 1962, 1972, 1977, 1987, 1989 and 1990 Official Text appear in:
§1-105(2), words "perfection provisions" substituted for "policy and scope" and reference to §9-102 deleted.
§1-110 official comments consulted in construction and application of KRS 355.
§1-201(3) omits "and 2A-207".
§1-201(9), sentence added which reads: "All persons who sell minerals or the like (including oil and gas) at wellhead or minehead shall be deemed to be persons in the business of selling goods of that kind."
§2-316(3), new subsection (d) added excluding implied warranties that farm animals are free from disease or sickness unless seller knows of diseased or sick condition.
§2A-103(1)(e), deletes "if the total payments to be made under the lease contract, excluding payments for options to renew or buy, do not exceed $25,000."

COMMERCIAL CODE ... *continued*

§2A-108(4)(b), deletes "and the lessee claiming unconscionability has brought or maintained an action he knew to be groundless."

§2A-201(1)(a), changes $1,000 to $500.

§2A-521(3), adds "writ of possession."

New section 2A-110 provides that official comments may by consulted in construction and application of Article 2A.

§2A-524(1), 1990 amendment not adopted.

Art. 8, 1994 revision adopted.

§9-105, subsection (1)(n) omitted; definitions for "identification number" (taxpayer identification number assigned by Internal Revenue Service or for individual, either Social Security Account numbers or code consisting of first three letters of last name and birth date in MM/DD/YY format) and (Kentucky Lien Information System) added;

§9-105(h) omits commodity controls;

§9-109(3), first sentence omits "or supplies";

§9-109 (3)(b) added to define equine interests as "farm products", whether or not debtor is engaged in farming operations.

§9-204(2), subsection (4)(a) of 1962 Official Text concerning effect of after-acquired property clause on future crops retained as subsection (2)(a) with balance of subsection (2) set forth as subsection (b);

§9-301(2), 20 days allowed instead of ten;

§9-302(1)(g), additional exception added for security interest in property, including after-acquired property, of railroad or public utility if described in mortgage or security agreement filed in accordance with provisions for recording mortgages; 1972 clause (1)(g) redesignated (1)(h); 1994 clause (1)(h) redesignated (1)(i);

§9-302(5), nonstandard subsection added exempting public utilities subject to regulation by Public Service Commission and rural electric and rural telephone cooperative corporations from filing provisions of Part IV and providing that perfection of security interest for such entities can be accomplished only through recordation of a mortgage in accordance with KRS 382.340;

§9-307, nonstandard provision added as subsection (2) relating to sales of pledged tobacco at tobacco warehouses; nonstandard provision added as subsection (3) relating to sales of grain or soybean crops to holders of grain storage licenses; nonstandard provision added as subsection (4) relating to sales of livestock at licensed stock yards; nonstandard provision added as subsection (6) relating to sales of race horses at public auction; official subsection (2) renumbered as subsection (5); official subsection (3) redesignated as subsection (7);

§9-312(4), 20 day period provided instead of ten;

§9-319, nonstandard section added requiring that party possessing security interest against livestock or grain which has been sold free of liens and encumbrances must pursue remedies against seller to judgment or dismissal with prejudice before pursuing remedies against purchaser or selling agent;

§9-401(1)(b), clauses added excepting collateral of coal or accounts arising from sale of coal; nonstandard provision added giving separate indexing of fixture filings and mortgage instruments.

§9-401(1)(c) requires filing in office of county clerk of county of debtor's residence if debtor is resident of state or, if debtor is nonresident of state, then in office of Secretary of State, Frankfort, Kentucky 40601.

§9-401(5) and (6), official subsection (5) not adopted and official subsection (6) replaced with nonstandard subsection (5) which specifies residency for different classifications of debtors. Individual debtors are deemed resident of county in which debtor's principal place of business is located and if debtor has no place of business in state, then debtor is deemed nonresident for purposes of filing. General partnerships are deemed resident in county of which principal place of business is located, but if no place of business in state, then debtor is nonresident for purposes of filing. Domestic limited partnerships deemed resident in county in which its "office" is located as set forth in certificate of limited partnership filed with Secretary of State or recent amendment. Domestic limited partnership whose office is not located in state is deemed nonresident. Foreign limited partnerships authorized to do business in state deemed resident of county in which office of its process agent is located as set forth in designation or most recent amendment thereto filed with Secretary of State. Domestic business, nonprofit and professional service corporations and limited liability companies deemed resident of county in which registered office is located as set forth in most recent filing with Secretary of State. Foreign corporations and foreign limited liability companies authorized to transact business in state deemed resident of county in which registered office is located as set forth in most recent filing with Secretary of State. Cooperative corporations organized under KRS c. 272 deemed resident of county in which principal business is transacted as set forth in articles of incorporation or most recent amendment thereto filed with Secretary of State. Rural electric and rural telephone cooperative corporations organized under KRS c. 279 deemed resident of county in which principal offices are located as set forth in articles of incorporation or most recent amendment thereto filed with Secretary of State. Domestic business trust organized under KRS c. 386 deemed resident of county in which principal place of business is located as evidenced by recordation of declaration of trust in that county pursuant to KRS 386.420. Domestic credit union deemed resident of county in which its principal place of business is located as set forth in articles of incorporation or most recent amendment filed with Secretary of State. Any other organization deemed resident of county in which its principal place of business in state is located, except that any limited partnership or corporation not organized under Kentucky law and not authorized to do business in state, or any organization without place of business in state, deemed nonresident for purposes of filing;

Kentucky Lien Information System. §9-401A creates dual filing requirement, for filings made after Jan. 4, 1999, by requiring informational filing with Secretary of State. Informational filings will create statewide, internet accessible database.

§9-402(1), financing statement must include debtor identification number (TIN for business). Financing statement covering crops growing or to be grown must describe production season, or financing statement deemed to describe crops produced in production season which ends 12 months after filing date of financing statement, and

financing statement may cover no more than one production season. Carbon, photographic or other reproduction of security agreement or financing statement filed in any other state may be filed in Kentucky. Clauses added excepting financing statements covering coal or accounts arising from sale of coal from requirement that financing statement covering minerals comply with subsection (5);

§9-402(3), subsections (1), (2) and (3) redesignated as subsections (a), (b) and (c) and in subsection (c), filings to be in "the same office as" real estate records;

§9-402(5), clause relating to transmitting utility deleted and words "in the same office as" inserted before "real estate records"; clauses added excepting financing statements covering coal or accounts arising from sale of coal;

§9-402(7), debtor required to notify secured party in writing of change of name, identity or corporate structure to begin four month continuation period;

§9-403(5), continuation statement must include debtor's identification number; standard subsection (5) deleted and replaced with cross-reference to KRS 64.012 where fees are set forth. See subhead Fees on Filing and Certification, Tax on Filing, infra;

§9-403(6), standard subsection (6) is deleted and nonstandard subsection inserted in its place which provides that real estate mortgages, which are effective as fixture filings under KRS 355.9-402(6), remain effective as fixture filing until mortgage is released or satisfied of record in mortgage records or its effectiveness otherwise terminates as to real estate;

§9-403(7), optional language omitted; clauses added excepting financing statements covering coal or accounts arising from sale of coal;

§9-404(1), first sentence relating to financing statements concerning consumer goods deleted; termination statement must identify original financing statement by file number, debtor's identification number and date; uniform fee for filing and indexing separate statement of assignment complying with KRS 355.9-404(1) is $3;

§9-404(2), official subsections (2) and (3) renumbered (3) and (4) and nonofficial subsection (2) inserted requiring secured party to file termination statement with appropriate office within 15 days after secured transaction has terminated even in absence of demand by debtor and upon failure to do so, secured party may be liable to debtor for greater of $25 or any loss caused to debtor by such failure;

§9-404(3), filing officer authorized to send statement to last known address of party entitled to receive it;

§9-404(4), official subsection (3) omitted and replaced with uniform fee for filing and indexing termination statement in amount of $1, $3 for financing statements filed prior to July 1, 1966;

§9-405, fees for filing and indexing set forth in separate section, KRS 64.012, see subhead Fees on Filing and Certification, Tax on Filing, infra;

§9-405(2), assignment must include debtor's identification number; clauses added excepting filings covering coal or accounts arising from sale of coal from assignment indexing requirements;

§9-406, statement of release must include debtor's identification number; fees for filing set forth in separate section KRS 64.012, see subhead Fees on Filing and Certification, Tax on Filing, infra;

§9-407, fees for information set forth in separate section KRS 64.012, see subhead Fees on Filing and Certification, Tax on Filing, infra. Filing officer and employees are absolved from personal liability as result of erroneous information furnished pursuant to section;

§9-501(3)(b), KRS 355.9-505 in its entirety may not be waived or varied;

§9-504(3), written statement by consumer renouncing or modifying right of notification ineffective.

§10-103 not adopted.

§10-104 not adopted.

Forms.—Usual UCC forms in use with following additions: add debtor identification number (TIN for business; for natural persons, first three letters of last name and birth date in MM/DD/YY format); to continuation or termination statement, add "Financing Statement was filed [date]." (KRS 355.9-403[3];-.9-404[1]). No officially prescribed forms in use. Some county clerks may require address within county to appear before filing financing statements.

Fees on Filing and Certification, Tax on Filing.—County clerk's fees: $17 ($8 filing, $6 release and postage, and $3 tax) for filing and indexing financing or continuation statement. (KRS 64.012 and 142.010). $5 for filing and indexing termination statement and sending or delivering termination statement. (KRS 64.012). $1 additional filing fee for each motor vehicle registered or required to be registered in state. (KRS 186.045; 64.012). $1 for Kentucky Lien Information System filing; $8 fee for filing assignment. (KRS 64.012). County clerk entitled to fee of $6 for giving certificate under KRS 335.9-407 listing effective financing statements and assignments and $5 for providing certified copy of each filed financing statement or statement of assignment. (KRS 64.012). Secretary of State's fees: $11 (includes $3 for later filing termination statement) for each filing of financing statement (KRS 355.9-401[1]); $8 for filing continuation statement; $8 for each amendment to financing statement); $8 for filing each assignment, $8 for each release or partial release, and $5 for certificate with seal and 50¢ per page for providing certified copy of any document or affixing seal to certificate (KRS 14.090[1]; KRS 64.012).

Tax of $3 applies to filing of every financing statement or security agreement with county clerk but not with Secretary of State. (KRS 142.010).

See also topics: Banks and Banking, Bills and Notes, Brokers, Carriers, Contracts, Factors, Frauds, Statute of, Sales, Securities, Warehousemen; categories Business Organizations, topic Corporations; Civil Actions and Procedure, topic Limitation of Actions; Debtor and Creditor, topics Assignments, Fraudulent Sales and Conveyances, Liens, Pledges; Documents and Records, topics Records, Seals; Mortgages, topic Chattel Mortgages.

CONDITIONAL SALES:

See topic Sales.

CONSIGNMENTS:

See topic Factors.

See note at head of Digest as to 1998 legislation covered.

See Topical Index in front part of this volume.

CONSUMER PROTECTION:

Broad Consumer Protection Act declares unlawful all unfair (defined for purposes of Act as "unconscionable"), false, misleading or deceptive acts or practices in conduct of any trade or commerce. (KRS 367.110 to 367.300 and 367.990). Enforcement and supervisory powers placed in Department of Law. (KRS 367.150). Attorney General granted broad investigation powers (KRS 367.240) and, on petition, is authorized to seek and obtain restraining order or temporary or permanent injunction of unfair, false, misleading or deceptive acts or practices (KRS 367.190). Courts granted additional authority to make additional orders or judgment including restoration of moneys, appointment of receiver for business, or revocation of license or certificate authorizing person to engage in business in state. (KRS 367.200-367.220). Civil penalty to Commonwealth of $2,000 per violation authorized for unlawful practices, or $10,000 per violation when victim is aged 60 or older (KRS 367.990[2]) and fine up to $500 or imprisonment up to 12 months or both for concealing, falsifying documentary material subject to investigation by Attorney General or intentionally falsifying, withholding, etc. documents, records or materials from investigation (KRS 367.900[3] and .990[4]; 532.090[1]; 534.040[2]).

Uniform Deceptive Trade Practices Act not adopted.

Unsolicited goods delivered to person deemed gift. (KRS 365.710).

Referral sales outlawed. (KRS 367.350).

Buying clubs and vacation clubs regulated and their contracts subject to being cancelled under KRS 367.395-367.405.

Home solicitation sales regulated with three business day revocation period. (KRS 367.410 to 367.450).

Sales of land for recreation and retirement use regulated under supervision of Attorney General. (KRS 367.470-367.486).

Solicitors of magazines, encyclopedias, bibles, periodicals, etc., required to file statement with county clerk; fee for filing statement $5. (KRS 367.510 to 367.530).

Solicitors for charitable and civic purposes must file IRS Form 990, if applicable, or notice of intent to solicit with Attorney General. (KRS 367.657).

Business Opportunity.—See topic Franchises.

Loan Brokers.—Persons who arrange or offer to arrange or advise concerning loan of money or credit card or line of credit for consideration may not collect advance fee. (KRS 367.380[4]; 381.381). Most regulated lenders and all business loans exempted. (KRS 367.380[4]).

Unlicensed health care practitioners shall use academic title or claim possession of academic degree only if accredited, and honorary degree only if disclosed. (KRS 367.825-367.826).

Pyramid distribution plans outlawed. (KRS 367.830-367.834).

Rental-Purchase Agreements.—Disclosure requirements imposed on agreements for use of personal property by consumers for initial period of four months or less, automatically renewable, and permitting ultimate purchase. (KRS 367.976-367.985). Definition of regulated instrument excludes Art. 9 security agreements, non-consumer leases, credit sales governed by federal truth-in-lending regulations, home solicitation sales, and retail installment sales under KRS 371.210.

Fresh meat produced outside U.S. and sold by retailer, wholesaler, distributor or processor generally must be so identified to purchaser. (KRS 367.855-367.857).

New car lemon bill mandates arbitration of warranty claims arising in first 12,000 miles or one year after sale or lease. (KRS 367.840-367.846). New motor vehicle manufacturers must offer informal dispute resolution procedures (arbitration) to purchasers who have disputes relating to unsatisfactory warranty repairs, malfunctions and other problems with performance of purchased vehicle during first two years or 25,000 miles of ownership. (KRS 367.860-367.870).

See also topic Sales; category Transportation, topic Motor Vehicles.

Health spa establishments must file registration statement with Attorney General's Consumer Protection Division and comply with regulation of their business dealings with consumers. (KRS 367.905-367.930).

Holder in due course defense abolished for consumer purchase money loan contracts not affected by FTC trade regulation rule. (KRS 367.600-367.610).

Plain Language Statutes.—Insurance policies for homeowners, automobile, accident and health, life and other forms of personal insurance must be in English and readable and understandable by persons of average intelligence and education. (KRS 304.14-440; 304.14-435). Insurance policy simplification provisions provided for in KRS 304.14-420 to 304.14-450.

CONTRACTS:

Common law rules apply generally, but see topic Frauds, Statute of. Uniform Commercial Code adopted (KRS c. 355); see topic Commercial Code. Also see topic Consumer Protection; categories Documents and Records, topic Seals; Family, topics Infants, Husband and Wife.

Guaranty contract must be written on, or expressly refer to, instrument guaranteed to be valid unless it is in writing signed by guarantor and sets out maximum aggregate liability and termination date. (KRS 371.065[1]). Guaranty may cover unspecified amounts of interest accruing on, and fees, charges and costs of collecting, guaranteed indebtedness. (KRS 371.065[2]).

Surrogate parenting contracts are void. (KRS 199.590[4]).

FACTORS:

Business of receiving and selling goods consigned or otherwise entrusted for sale is not regulated business in state.

Uniform Commercial Code adopted. (KRS 355.1-101 to 355.11-108). See topic Commercial Code.

License Requirements.—None.

Liens.—Governed by Uniform Commercial Code.

Consignment Agreements.—No provision for recording or filing but see Art. 9 of Uniform Commercial Code. (KRS 355.9-101 et seq.).

FRANCHISES:

Uniform Franchise and Business Opportunities Act.—Not adopted.

Business Opportunity.—Sale of Business Opportunity Act, KRS 367.801-367.819, regulates opportunities to offer, sell or distribute goods or services supplied in whole or in part by offeror when offeror obtains initial required consideration of not less than $500 from purchase or lease of opportunity, offeror has represented that investor can earn net profit from opportunity, and offeror has represented based on offeror's knowledge that market demand will enable investor to earn profit from opportunity, or offeror has provided locations or assistance in finding locations for operation of opportunity, or offeror has represented that there is guaranteed market or buy-back program for product offered to investor. (KRS 367.801[5]). Offerors who do not qualify for exemption under KRS 367.807 must register with Division of Consumer Protection of Office of Attorney General and post bond of not less than $75,000. (KRS 367.815; 367.807; 367.805).

Motor Vehicle Franchises.—Relationship between manufacturers or importers of new motor vehicles and motor vehicle dealers regulated. (KRS 190.010-190.990). Statutes administered by Motor Vehicle Commission. (KRS 190.058-190.059).

FRAUDS, STATUTE OF:

KRS 371.010 provides that unless some memorandum or note thereof is in writing, signed by party to be charged, or by his authorized agent, no action shall be brought to charge any person: (1) Upon representation concerning character, credit, etc., of another, made with intent that such other may thereby obtain credit, money or goods; (2) upon promise to pay debt contracted during infancy, or ratification of any such promise or contract made during infancy; (3) upon promise of personal representative as such to answer out of his own estate any liability of his decedent; (4) upon promise to answer for debt, default or misdoing of another; (5) upon any agreement in consideration of marriage, except mutual promises to marry; (6) upon any contract for sale of real estate or any lease thereof for term longer than one year; (7) upon any agreement which is not to be performed within one year from making thereof; (8) upon any agreement for commission or compensation for sale or lease of real estate or for assisting another in sale or lease of real estate; or (9) upon any promise, contract, agreement, undertaking or commitment to loan money, to grant, extend or renew credit, or make any financial accommodation to establish or assist new or existing business enterprise, but subsection does not include credit card credit or consumer transactions. It is not necessary to express consideration for agreement in writing. Consideration may be proved or disproved by parol or other evidence.

KRS 371.090 provides that no person shall be bound as surety of another by act of agent unless authority of agent is in writing signed by principal. For other limitation on guaranty contracts, see topic Contracts.

Sales of Personalty.—See topic Commercial Code. KRS 355.2-201 expresses requirements as to sales of goods of value of $500 or more.

Contracts for sale of standing trees or timber, to be enforceable, must be in writing, or some memorandum thereof must be in writing, signed by the person to be charged, or his authorized agent. (KRS 371.100).

Part performance may take agreement out of statute only if agreement is not to be performed within one year. (300 Ky. 69, 187 S.W.2d 1015).

INTEREST:

Legal rate in absence of agreement fixing rate is 8%. (KRS 360.010). Instrument does not bear interest unless provided in such instrument. (KRS 355.3-112).

Maximum Rates.—Any party or parties may agree in writing for higher rates, as follows: (a) Up to 4% in excess of discount rate on 90-day commercial paper in effect at Federal Reserve Bank in Federal Reserve District where transaction consummated or 19%, whichever is less, on money due or to become due where original principal amount is $15,000 or less; and (b) at any rate on money due or to become due where original principal amount exceeds $15,000 unless another law of state provides another maximum rate. (KRS 360.010[1]).

Banks.—State or national bank may, however, charge a minimum of $10 interest on any loan made by it in this state (KRS 360.010[2]) and state chartered banks may charge any rate on loans less than $15,000 allowed to national banks (KRS 287.214; see 12 U.S.C. §85). Bank or trust company may collect interest in advance to maturity of loan (KRS 287.215) and bank or trust company may charge up to 1¾% per month pursuant to revolving credit plan (KRS 287.740). See topic Banks and Banking.

Credit Unions.—State chartered credit unions may make loans to members, and charge interest at rate not to exceed 2% per month on unpaid balances. (KRS 290.435).

Installments of interest may be made payable at fixed times and if not then paid they bear interest just as principal if contract expressly so provides. (90 Ky. 340, 13 S.W. 249).

Time-price differential rule, holding that owner of real or personal property may set credit price for sale without regard to usury limit, recognized in line of cases. (309 Ky. 295, 217 S.W.2d 641; 58 Ky. 663).

Judgments.—Interest runs on judgment at rate of 12% compounded annually from its date, but judgment for accruing interest on written obligation bears interest according to instrument, whether higher or lower than 12%. Court may direct, after hearing with due notice, that judgment for unliquidated damages bear interest at lesser rate. (KRS 360.040).

Interest on open account runs from date when account is liquidated by demand, or by rendering account to debtor. (285 Ky. 727, 149 S.W.2d 22).

Small Loans.—Persons licensed to make small loans may contract in writing, for interest at rate of 3% per month on unpaid balance up to $1,000, 2% per month on unpaid balance exceeding $1,000 but not exceeding $3,000, but where original amount

INTEREST... *continued*

of loan exceeds $3,000 rate is limited to 2% per month on unpaid balance. Loan period may not exceed 60 months and 15 days if loan is $3,000 or less and may not exceed 120 months if loan is in excess of $3,000. (KRS 288.530; 288.580).

Securities broker-dealers exempt from usury statutes for credit granted on debit balance secured by securities. (KRS 292.545).

Pawnbrokers are limited to 2% per month on unpaid balances, plus reasonable service fee not to exceed ¹/₅ of value of loan per month. (KRS 226.080).

Usury.—Taking, receiving, reserving or charging more than authorized interest constitutes forfeiture of entire interest when knowingly done. Borrower may recover twice amount of interest paid under usurious agreement if action brought within two years of date of usurious transaction. (KRS 360.020). Corporations, except those whose principal asset is ownership of a one or two family dwelling, may not plead usury as a defense. (KRS 360.025). Limited partnerships, limited liability companies and business trusts also may not plead defense of usury, with similar exception. (KRS 360.027). Defense of usury is available against holder in due course of negotiable paper. (255 Ky. 339, 73 S.W.2d 1105).

Requirement by insurance company lending money that borrower insure his life or that of another or his property with such company, and pay premiums during continuance of loan, and assign policy as security, is not usurious, if premiums are not higher than charged to other persons. (KRS 360.030). Statute may be invalid, see 22 F.Supp. 233, because of improper legislation adoption.

Contracts made and to be performed in other states, if valid there, will be enforced in Kentucky, even though they would be usurious if made in Kentucky. (307 Ky. 612, 211 S.W.2d 831).

All unfair, false, misleading or deceptive acts or practices are declared unlawful by KRS 367.170. See topic Consumer Protection.

LICENSES, BUSINESS AND PROFESSIONAL:

Various occupations are subjected to a license tax (KRS c. 137)—some of them purely as a revenue measure—others, by way of regulation, e.g., real estate brokers (KRS c. 324); race tracks (KRS 137.170).

Likewise cities and towns, if so authorized by their charters, may collect city license taxes on motor vehicles as a revenue measure and as a police regulation. (229 Ky. 186, 16 S.W.2d 1034; 229 Ky. 722, 17 S.W.2d 1017; 225 Ky. 123, 7 S.W.2d 833).

Licenses for hunting and fishing must be obtained by all nonresidents of Kentucky, and by residents not hunting on their own lands. (KRS 150.170). Detailed information may be obtained from Department of Fish and Wildlife Resources, Frankfort.

Commercial Travelers.—State imposes no license requirements.

See also topic Securities; categories Insurance, topic Insurance Companies; Transportation, topic Motor Vehicles.

Collection Agencies.—No legislation, but debt adjusters and debt adjusting is unlawful. (KRS 380.010 to 380.990).

MONOPOLIES, RESTRAINT OF TRADE AND COMPETITION:

State antitrust statute ("Little Sherman Act") declares every contract, combination in form of trust or otherwise, or conspiracy, in restraint of trade or commerce in state to be unlawful and further declares that it is unlawful for any person or persons to monopolize or attempt to monopolize or combine or conspire with any other person or persons to monopolize any part of trade or commerce in state. (KRS 367.175). Activities of legitimate labor unions, agricultural or horticultural cooperative organizations (KRS 272.295) and consumer organizations, and individual members thereof, public utilities, and any activities authorized or approved under any federal or state statute or regulation are exempt from coverage of Act. (KRS 367.176). Attorney General authorized to bring action to recover civil penalty on behalf of Commonwealth up to $5,000 or $200 per day for violations of KRS 367.175 in addition to penalties contained in KRS 367.990. (KRS 367.990[8]). Prior to adoption of statute it had been held that contract in unreasonable restraint of trade was void (276 Ky. 666, 124 S.W.2d 1019), but reasonable restraint of competition was legal (277 Ky. 301, 126 S.W.2d 165).

Unfair Trade Practices.—KRS 365.020; 365.040 to .070 forbid anyone doing business in Kentucky to: (1) discriminate between different localities by selling or distributing goods at different rates (transportation costs considered) with intent to destroy or prevent competition; or (2) make secret payments or rebates or extend secretly any special services or privileges to the injury of competitor "where such payment or allowance tends to destroy competition." Contracts made in violation of act are illegal and no recovery thereon is allowed. KRS 365.030 prohibiting below cost sales has been ruled unconstitutional. (764 S.W.2d 80).

Any person or corporation, private or public, may maintain an action to enjoin a violation of the act and, if injured thereby, for the recovery of damages, and on proving actual damages, may recover three times the amount thereof. (KRS 365.070).

A corporation or firm violating the act is subject to severe penalties. Partners, officers, directors and agents of any firm or corporation aiding in the violation are guilty of misdemeanor and subject to like civil liability. The penalty for each violation is a fine of from $100 to $1,000, imprisonment not exceeding six months, or both. Remedies given in the act are cumulative. (KRS 365.070[3]).

Special Acts govern regulation of motor vehicle dealers (KRS 190.010 to.080) and transfer of motor vehicle installment sale contracts (KRS 190.090 to .140). Southern Dairy Compact governing sale and marketing of milk adopted. (KRS 260.670-260.672).

Resale Price Contracts.—Special acts govern resale price of cigarettes. (KRS 365.260-365.380). Special acts concerning milk (KRS 260.675-260.760) and alcoholic beverages (KRS 244.380-244.420) have been ruled unconstitutional (691 S.W.2d 893) and preempted by federal antitrust statutes (635 S.W.2d 319) respectively.

Franchises.—See topic Franchises.

RESTRAINT OF TRADE:

See topic Monopolies, Restraint of Trade and Competition.

SALES:

Uniform Commercial Code adopted: Art. 2 of Code replaces Uniform Sales Act. (KRS 355.2-).

Contracts of Sale of Personalty.—No unusual requirements exist with general application concerning formality, validating or size of type. For requirements that some sales contracts be in writing, see topic Frauds, Statute of. For requirements applicable to consumer sales contracts, see topic Consumer Protection; and subhead Retail Credit Sales, infra this topic.

Bills of Sale.—No set forms prescribed. Any instrument showing intention is sufficient.

Product Liability.—Three theories of liability recognized: ordinary negligence (294 S.W.2d 534); "strict liability" as set forth in §402A of Restatement 2d, Torts (402 S.W.2d 441); and contract liability for breach of warranty under Uniform Commercial Code. Lack of privity of contract is defense in breach of warranty action brought by one not in family or household and not guest of buyer. (KRS 355.2-318; 695 S.W.2d 411).

Product Liability Act states certain evidentiary presumptions and sets certain limitations upon introduction of evidence and amounts of liability in actions brought for or on account of personal injury, death or property damage caused by or resulting from manufacture, construction, design, formulations, development of standards, preparation processing, marketing, etc. of any product. (KRS 411.300 to 411.350). Rebuttable presumptions established that any product was not defective if injury, death or property damage occurred more than five years after date of first sale to first consumer or more than eight years after date of manufacture and that product was not defective if its design, methods of manufacture and testing conformed to generally recognized and prevailing standards in state of art at time design prepared and product manufactured. (KRS 411.310). Manufacturer's liability for damages limited to damages resulting from use of product in original, unaltered and unmodified condition. (KRS 411.320[1]). Manufacturers not liable for any damages if plaintiff's unauthorized alteration or modification was substantial cause of injury or if plaintiff failed to exercise ordinary care in use of product. (KRS 411.320[2 & 3]). Wholesalers', distributors' and retailers' liability for injuries caused by products not manufactured by them limited to circumstances when express warranty breached or when they knew or should have known product was defective. (KRS 411.340).

Retail Credit Sales.—Retail seller of tangible chattels other than motor vehicles, sold primarily for personal, family or household use, must furnish copy of contract to buyer. (KRS 371.210; 371.220). Contract required to contain notice to buyer, in at least ten point bold type, not to sign unless all blank spaces filled in and until he has read same, and that he is entitled to a copy of the contract. (KRS 371.220). If copy of contract not delivered or mailed to buyer before goods delivered buyer may rescind contract and is entitled to refund of down payment. (KRS 371.220). Contract must contain names and addresses of seller and buyer, description of goods, cash sale price, amounts of down payment, difference between down payment and cash sale price, insurance premium, if any (stating type of insurance and terms of coverage), official fees, principal balance and time price differential, number of installments, amount of each, and due date of payment. (KRS 371.220). Contract need not be contained in one document. (KRS 371.230). Buyer has right to prepay in full unpaid time balance and is entitled to refund credit specifically set out in statute. (KRS 371.260). Amendment of contract and refinancing charge provided for. (KRS 371.270). Subsequent purchases may be consolidated with earlier, but each subsequent purchase treated as an individual contract. (KRS 371.290).

Retail charge agreements for open-end credit sales are covered by act, with specific requirements as to form set forth. (KRS 371.300-371.330).

"Time price differential" may be contracted for and received under either retail installment contract or retail charge agreement. No maximum rate provided in statute. (KRS 371.260; 371.300[3]).

Installment sales of motor vehicles regulated in detail by KRS 190.090-190.140.

Consumer Protection.—Unsolicited goods delivered to person deemed gift to person with no obligation to return. (KRS 365.710). See subhead Retail Credit Sales, supra and topic Consumer Protection; category Transportation, topic Motor Vehicles. Revised Uniform Deceptive Trade Practices Act adopted with variations. See topic Consumer Protection.

Bulk Sales.—See topic Commercial Code.

Sales of Motor Vehicles.—See category Transportation, topic Motor Vehicles, subheads Titles and Sales.

SECURITIES:

Uniform Commercial Code.—Adopted. See topic Commercial Code.

Supervision.—Administrator is Commissioner of Department of Financial Institutions, 477 Versailles Road, Frankfort, 40601.

Uniform Securities Act (see Uniform and Model Acts section) adopted. (KRS 292.310 to 292.991). Kentucky Act contains numerous variations from Uniform Act and order of sections is different.

Deviations From Uniform Act:

Not Adopted.—Following provisions of Uniform Securities Act are not found in Kentucky Act: §§201(c); 202; 203(b); 204; 205(b); 206; 208; 211; 215; 302; 304(b)(6); 305; 401(b)(6); 402(2) and (3); 502; 607; 702-705; 707; 802-807; 909-911.

Significant additions to Uniform Act provisions include:

Brokers, Dealers, Agents and Advisers.—Written examination may be required before registration as broker-dealer, agent, investment adviser or investment adviser representative (KRS 292.330[4]), and director may consider ratio between net capital and aggregate indebtedness for registration applicants (KRS 292.330[5]). Amount of surety bond may be up to $25,000 but bond not required if net capital exceeds

See note at head of Digest as to 1998 legislation covered.

See Topical Index in front part of this volume.

SECURITIES . . . *continued*

$100,000 (KRS 292.330[6]). Fidelity bonds up to $250,000 in penal amount may also be required. (KRS 292.330[7]). Renewal applications may be made contingent upon updated information. (KRS 292.330[10]). Registration fees, either initial or for annual renewal, are $120 for each broker-dealer, $100 for each investment adviser, and $50 for each agent and investment adviser representative. Covered advisers must make notice filing with Commissioner. (KRS 292.330[2]). Fee is $50 for transfer of agent or investment adviser representative. (KRS 292.330[11]).

Registration by Notification (KRS 292.350) is available for non-issuer distribution securities if previously offered and sold outside of state. (KRS 292.350[1][b]). Statement for registration by notification must contain name and address of managing underwriters and description of plan of distribution (KRS 292.350[2][g]) and identify any adverse order, judgment or decree relating to security by court or by S.E.C. (KRS 292.350[2][i]).

Registration by Coordination.—Statement must contain amount of securities to be offered in state (KRS 292.360[2][b]), other states in which registration statement has been or is expected to be filed (KRS 292.360[2][c]), identification of any adverse order, judgment or decree previously entered by any court or by S.E.C. relating to offering, any other documents as Commissioner may require (KRS 292.360[2][d]) and registration fee required by KRS 292.330.

Registration by Qualification.—Statement must contain one copy of latest prospectus or offering circular (KRS 292.360[2][a]), actual amount received and to be received by directors and officers (see §304[b][2] of Uniform Act) if more than $15,000 (KRS 292.370[2][c]), cost basis of property to be acquired with proceeds (KRS 292.370[2][h]), other states in which registration statement has been or is expected to be filed (KRS 292.370[2][k]), identification of any adverse order, judgment or decree previously entered by any court or by S.E.C. relating to offering (KRS 292.370[2][l]), opinion of counsel must state whether or not offering will comply with 1933 Act requirements (KRS 292.370[2][o]), and certain financial information depending upon maximum amount of proceeds to be received in offering (KRS 292.370[2][p]). Commissioner may require undertaking for registrants by qualifications of keeping securities registered up to five years and that issuer forward audited annual financial statements to holders during period securities are registered. (KRS 292.380[4]).

Examination fee of $125 is required in addition to registration fee ($60-$1,200). (KRS 292.380[5]).

Bases for stop order also include commissions or fees exceeding 20% of offering or such other amount specified in guidelines adopted by North American Securities Administration Association. (KRS 292.390[1][j]).

Exempt securities include securities issued by rural electric and rural telephone cooperative corporations (regulated by KRS c. 279), any security issued or guaranteed by U.S. or any state, any security commissioner expressly by rule or order finds registration is not necessary or appropriate in public interest or for protection of investors, and certain stock and patronage refunds issued by cooperative corporations. (KRS 292.400). Insurance policies, annuity contracts and variable annuity contracts issued by any insurance company are exempted from definition of "security". (KRS 292.310[18]).

Exempt transactions include stock dividends, securities issued in connection with reorganizations, mergers, etc. and certain securities of subsidiary or affiliated corporations. (KRS 292.410). Before certain securities may be issued as exempt securities, claim of exemption must first be filed with Commissioner. (KRS 292.415[1]). Commissioner has authority to determine whether security or transaction is entitled to exemption. May request Commissioner to make ruling by submitting verified statement and $250 filing fee. (KRS 292.415[3]). Certain verified statements required to support claim for exemption of issues transaction. (KRS 292.420).

Limitations.—Three-year limitations period applies for civil actions instead of two-year period in §410(e) of Uniform Act. (KRS 292.480[3]).

Tender Offers.—No statutory regulation after July 15, 1986.

Franchising, Pyramid Sales, Etc.—Offers of business opportunities regulated by KRS 367.801-367.819. Pyramid sales schemes have been held violative of Consumer Protection Act, KRS 367.110 to 367.390. (511 S.W.2d 224). See topic Consumer Protection, subhead Broad Consumer Protection Act. See also topic Franchises.

Uniform Simplification of Fiduciary Security Transfers Act not adopted.

Uniform Securities Ownership by Minors Act not adopted.

Insurance Company Stock.—See category Insurance, topic Insurance Companies.

WAREHOUSEMEN:

Elaborate provisions define warehousemen and their powers, duties, rights and liabilities as such, and deal with (1) warehouses generally, (2) oil warehouses, (3) grain warehouses, (4) tobacco warehouses, (5) "Unbonded Farm Agricultural Warehouses" and (6) "Self-Service Storage Facilities". (KRS cc. 359, 251, 248).

Uniform Commercial Code adopted. See topic Commercial Code.

Warehouse Companies.—A warehouse company may be organized as a corporation with power to guarantee warehouse receipts issued by itself or by other warehouse companies. Such guaranty is governed by insurance laws of state and is subject to regulation by Department of Insurance. (KRS 359.170).

Bonds.—Person to whom grain warehouseman's license is issued must file (1) in office of county clerk bond with good surety, conditioned upon faithful performance of duty as public grain warehouseman (KRS 359.060), and (2) with Department of Agriculture bond issued by surety company authorized to do business in state, or in lieu of bond, certificate of deposit or irrevocable letter of credit. (KRS 251.430, 251.440, 251.451).

Licenses.—Grain warehouseman must obtain annual license from county clerk; fee, $1. (KRS 359.050). Separate license from Department of Agriculture required; fees range from $200 to $500. (KRS 251.430). Special warehouse storing distilled spirits and wine must secure license; fee, $125 per year. (KRS 243.030). Tobacco warehouse must secure license; for $500 per year; bonded warehouse $1,000 per year. (KRS 248.290).

Liens and warehouse receipts, and many rights, duties and liabilities of warehousemen are governed by Art. 7 of Uniform Commercial Code (KRS c. 355.7-101 et seq.). See topic Commercial Code.

CITIZENSHIP

ALIENS:

Property.—For summary of common and statutory law, see 201 Ky. 513; 256 S.W. 1106.

Alien may be a distributee of personal estate of an intestate as though he were a citizen, (KRS 391.030) and may take and hold any personal property, except chattels real, unless he is an enemy (KRS 381.320).

An alien, not being an enemy, shall, after he has declared his intention to become a citizen of U.S. according to forms required by law, be enabled to recover, inherit, hold and pass by descent, devise or otherwise, any interest in real or personal property in same manner as if he were a citizen of Kentucky. (KRS 381.290). Any alien who shall have purchased or contracted to purchase or who shall hold or have title to real property and who shall become a citizen of U.S. before same is escheated by a proper procedure (which may be at any time after expiration of eight years from time title is acquired by nonresident alien) and any purchaser, lessee, heir or devisee of him, if citizen of U.S., who shall before property is escheated become owner thereof by purchase or inheritance, shall take and hold same free and released from any right or claim of Commonwealth by reason of such person having been alien. (KRS 381.300). Any alien not enemy residing in Kentucky may take and hold any lands for purpose of residence or occupation by him or his servants, or for purpose of any business, trade or manufacture, as long as he remains resident of state. (381.320.)

Any person whose spouse is a citizen of U.S. and any person whose father or mother at his birth was citizen of U.S., although born elsewhere, may take and hold both real and personal property by devise, purchase, descent or distribution. (KRS 381.310).

Real estate in Kentucky passing to a nonresident alien by descent or devise may be held by such alien for a period of eight years after final settlement of estate of decedent from whom acquired, and during such period may be held and alienated by such nonresident alien, and, if he be a minor, may be sold by proper proceedings in conformity to laws regulating sales of infants' real estate, if commenced within such period of eight years. (KRS 381.330).

If a nonresident alien obtaining possession of real estate acquired by descent or devise dies before such eight year period expires, the alien's rights thus acquired pass by descent or devise; if to a citizen of the United States, then as fully as if such alien had himself been a citizen, but if to an alien, then to be held for him and disposed of by him within such eight year period. (KRS 381.300; 381.340).

Title by Descent from Alien.—It is no bar in itself to a claimant of title by descent that an intestate ancestor through whom claimant derives descent is or has been an alien. (KRS 391.060).

Escheat.—Except as otherwise provided in law, any real estate of nonresident alien may be escheated to state for office found or other act at any time after expiration of eight years after he acquired title. (KRS 381.300[1]; 201 Ky. 513, 256 S.W. 1106).

CIVIL ACTIONS AND PROCEDURE

ACCORD AND SATISFACTION:

No general statute on subject. Common-law principles apply. (226 Ky. 109, 9 S.W.2d 1091; 230 Ky. 509, 20 S.W.2d 276). When claim is in dispute and debtor delivers check stating in full payment of claims and creditor endorses check without objection, creditor accepts accord and satisfaction. (944 S.W.2d 314).

If a sum smaller than the debt is paid in full satisfaction of claim not yet due, payment satisfies claim; but if due, payment of smaller sum than acknowledged and uncontested debt will not satisfy it, unless based upon valuable consideration, such as composition with creditors wherein other creditors likewise compromise their claims.

Uniform Commercial Code adopted. See category Business Regulation and Commerce, topic Commercial Code.

Compromise.—If a claim is disputed, a less amount paid in compromise operates to discharge liability thereon.

Pleading.—Defense must be pleaded. (CR 8.03).

ACTIONS:

Term action includes proceedings in any court. Kentucky Rules of Civil Procedure (CR) similar to Federal Rules of Civil Procedure (FRCP) have been adopted. See topic Practice.

Equity.—No distinctions made between actions seeking legal or equitable remedies, except in District Court whose jurisdiction excludes matters in equity. (KRS 24A.120[1]).

Forms of Action.—CR 2 substantially identical to FRCP 2.

Condition precedent to maintaining action against city for injury resulting from defects in any bridge, street, sidewalk, alley or other public thoroughfare therein is that claimant must, within 90 days of such injury, give written notice of such claim to city in manner and with detail prescribed by KRS 411.110; 299 Ky. 87, 184 S.W.2d 890, 440 S.W.2d 265.

Commencement.—See topics Process, Pleading.

Parties.—CRs 17, 18, 19, 20 and 21 substantially identical to federal counterparts.

ACTIONS . . . *continued*

Class Actions.—CR 23 substantially identical to FRCP 23. Uniform Class Actions Act not adopted.

Intervention.—CR 24 substantially identical to FRCP 24.

Interpleader.—CR 22 is substantially identical to FRCP 22(1). Equivalent to FRCP 22(2) not adopted.

Third Party Practice.—CR 14 substantially identical to FRCP 14.

Joinder of Causes of Action.—CR 18 substantially identical to FRCP 18.

Splitting Causes of Action.—CRs 20.02 and 42.02 substantially identical to FRCPs 20(b) and 42(b) respectively.

Consolidation of Actions.—CR 42.01 identical to FRCP 42(a).

Severance of Actions.—CR 41 substantially identical to FRCP 41.

Stay of Proceedings.—CR 43.03 authorizes trial judge, in his discretion, to order postponement of trial on basis of absence of evidence or of witness.

Abatement and Revival.—CR 25 substantially identical to FRCP 25 except that time for revival is not fixed, but depends upon applicable statutes. All actions for personal injury or injury to property survive except actions for slander, libel, criminal conversation, and so much of action for malicious prosecution as is intended to recover for personal injury. (KRS 411.140). Excepted actions or claims die with person, either plaintiff or defendant.

Limitation of.—See topic Limitation of Actions.

Small Claims.—See category Courts and Legislature, topic Courts.

Termination of Actions.—May occur by dismissal or by judgment. CRs 41, 54, 55 and 56 similar to federal counterparts.

Prohibited Actions.—None. Every person shall have remedy by due course of law in court for injuries done him in his lands, goods, person or reputation. (Ky. Const. §14).

Administration.—See category Estates and Trusts, topic Executors and Administrators.

Direct Actions Against Insurer.—See category Transportation, topic Motor Vehicles, subhead Direct Actions.

Submission of Controversy.—See topic Submission of Controversy.

Action lies against Commonwealth in favor of those with lawfully authorized written contracts with Commonwealth for actions, including enforcement of or breach of contract, in Franklin Circuit without jury. (KRS 45A.245). Action lies against Commonwealth before statutory Board of Claims in favor of persons who have sustained damages to person or property as proximate result of negligence of Commonwealth, its departments or agencies, or its officers, agents or employees while acting in scope of their employment. Recovery is limited to $100,000 for single claim or $250,000 if single act results in multiple claims but damages not allowed for collateral or dependent claims, mental distress or pain and suffering. (KRS 44.070).

Privity no longer required in action by buyer against manufacturer for personal injuries and property loss suffered as result of defect in product. (402 S.W.2d 441). Privity remains requirement in claims for breach of warranty. (KRS 355.2-318).

APPEAL AND ERROR:

General.—

Courts.—Courts with appellate jurisdiction, in descending order, are Supreme Court, Court of Appeals, and Circuit Court. Supreme Court and Court of Appeals have, with certain very limited exceptions, appellate jurisdiction only. Circuit Courts, in addition to hearing appeals from District Courts, serve as trial courts of general jurisdiction. Rules for appellate procedure are found in Rules 72-76 of Kentucky Rules of Civil Procedure (CR). Kentucky Rules of Civil Procedure are patterned generally after Federal Rules of Civil Procedure. See topic Practice.

Appeals Allowed.—At least one appeal is allowed as matter of right in all cases, civil and criminal, except from judgments of acquittal in criminal cases (other than for purposes of securing certification of law) and from that portion of judgment dissolving marriage. (Const. §115; KRS 22A.020[3]). Appeals after first appeal are discretionary with next higher appellate court. (CR 76.20).

Appeal Bond.—No appeal bond is required. Filing fees are required which vary from court to court. No filing fee exceeds $150. There are no costs except filing fee. (CR 76.42[2][a]).

Stay of Proceedings.—Stay of proceedings on appeal is not automatic. Injunction judgments are stayed at discretion of appellate court. (CR 62.02; 65.08). Monetary judgments may be stayed as matter of right by giving adequate supersedeas bond for full amount of judgment plus costs, interest, and damages. (CR 62.03; 73.04). 10% penalty is imposed upon appellant who has superseded judgment and after first appeal seeks further appellate relief without success. (KRS 26A.300).

Extent of Review.—Appellate review is limited to issues of law, except issues of fact found by jury may be set aside where flagrantly or palpably against evidence or unsupported by evidence of probative value. Findings by court may be set aside where clearly erroneous. (CR 52.02; 500 S.W.2d 405; 336 S.W.2d 343).

Character of Hearing.—All appeals from one court to another (as opposed to appeals from rulings of administrative agencies, see subhead Administrative Agencies, Boards, Etc., infra) are upon record and not by trial de novo. (Const. §115).

Appeals from District Courts.—Review is by appeal to Circuit Court from final action of District Court. (KRS 23A.080).

How Taken.—Appeal from District Court to Circuit Court in civil cases is taken by filing notice of appeal and paying filing fee within 30 days after date of judgment or order was entered, or within 30 days from entry of order granting or denying certain timely post-judgment motions (CR 72.02; 73.02), or within ten days from date of judgment in Small Claims Division (KRS 24A.340). Cross appeals are permitted. (CR 74.01). Appeal must be perfected within 30 days after date of filing of first notice of appeal. (CR 72.08). Perfection includes filing of appellant's statement of appeal (concise statement of appellant's legal questions and propositions shall not exceed ten pages). (CR 72.06; 72.10). Appellee has 30 days after date on which appellant's brief is filed in which to file its counterstatement (not exceeding ten pages). (CR 72.12). Record on appeal from District Court includes entire original record of proceedings in District Court. Record need not be certified until Court of Appeals grants motion for review of Circuit Court's action. (CR 72.04).

Appeals from Circuit Court.—Appeal lies as matter of right to Court of Appeals from judgment or final order in all actions originating in Circuit Court, except from judgments imposing sentence of death or imprisonment for life or for 20 years or more, in which cases appeal lies directly to Supreme Court. (Const. §110). Within ten days from time notice of appeal to Court of Appeals has been filed, any party may file motion in Supreme Court for transfer of case directly to that court. (CR 74.02[1]). Filing motion for transfer to Supreme Court suspends running of time to perfect appeal in Court of Appeals. (CR 74.02[3]). Motion for transfer to Supreme Court will be granted only upon showing that case is of great and immediate public importance.

How Taken.—In civil cases where appeal lies as matter of right, filing fee must be paid to, and notice of appeal must be filed with clerk of Circuit Court within 30 days after date judgment or final order was entered or within 30 days from entry of order granting or denying certain timely post-judgment motions. (CR 73.02; 77.04[2]). Failure to file timely notice of appeal or cross-appeal shall result in dismissal (CR 73.02[2]) and frivolous appeal may result in award of damages and single or double costs to appellee (CR 73.02[4]). In criminal cases different form of notice must be filed within ten days from entry of judgment or final order. (R.Cr. 12.04). Cross-appeal may be taken and must be filed within ten days after last day allowed for notice of appeal. (CR 74.01). Appeal from Circuit Court judgment in case originally appealed from District Court is taken by filing motion for discretionary review within 30 days after Circuit Court judgment is entered. (CR 76.20[2][a]). Response to such motion may be filed within 20 days. (CR 76.20[5]). If granted, appeal shall proceed as if taken as matter of right. (CR 76.20[9]). Following notice of appeal appellant and appellee designate such untranscribed portions of proceedings before Circuit Court as they wish prepared in record on appeal. (CR 75.01). Circuit Court Clerk must, within ten days after filing of transcript of evidence by court reporter, or within 30 days from first notice of appeal if trial proceedings were taken solely by video recordation or if there were no proceedings to transcribe (which period may be extended by appellate court upon motion and showing of good cause) prepare original record and upon completion so certify to parties. (CR 73.08; CR 75.07[5]). Record remains with Circuit Court for use by parties until all briefs are completed. (CR 75.07[7]). Appellant has responsibility to insure that Circuit Court clerk prepares and certifies record in timely fashion. Within 20 days after filing notice of appeal, appellant shall file with Court of Appeals prehearing statement, and prehearing conference may be had. (CR 76.03). After prehearing conference Court of Appeals may designate appeal as Special Appeal (CR 76.05) in which short position papers are filed instead of briefs. Appeals are perfected by causing Circuit Court Clerk's certification of record to be filed with clerk of appropriate appellate court, and by filing appellant's brief (which may be either printed or typed) in appellate court within 30 days from Circuit Court Clerk's certification that record has been prepared. (76.02). Appellee's brief must be filed within 30 days after appellant's brief, and appellant may file reply brief within 15 days. (CR 76.12[2]). Circuit Court Clerk thereafter forwards record to appellate court. Certain special rules apply in appeals where videotape equipment is used to record lower court proceedings; principal difference is that appellant's brief must be filed within 60 days after certification of record on appeal by Circuit Court Clerk, and appellee's brief must be filed within 60 days after appellant's brief. (CR 98).

How Decided.—Unless waived by all parties or unless Court of Appeals enters order dispensing with oral argument, Court of Appeals hears all parties on oral argument. (CR 76.16). Court of Appeals sits in panels of three judges each. (SCR 1.030). All decisions are by written opinion, although only certain opinions are published. (KRS 21A.070[2]).

Post-Decision Motions.—Petitions for rehearing or modification or extension of opinion are permitted and must be filed within 20 days after date on which opinion is issued. (CR 76.32). Responses are permitted and must be filed within 20 days after date on which petition is filed. (CR 76.32).

Appeals from Court of Appeals.—Motion for discretionary review by Supreme Court of final order entered in appellate case decided by Court of Appeals must be filed within 20 days after date of order or opinion for which review is sought, or, if post-decision motion was filed in Court of Appeals, within 20 days after denial of post-decision motion or 20 days after final order or opinion disposing of case. (CR 76.20[2][b]). Each respondent may file response to motion within 20 days after motion is filed. Cross motions are permitted. (CR 76.21). If motion is denied, decision appealed from shall be affirmed; if granted appeal shall be perfected and prosecuted as appeals taken as matter of right. (CR 76.20[9]). Cross appeals are permitted. (CR 74.01). Appellant has 30 days from date of entry of order granting review to file brief, which may be printed or typewritten. (CR 76.12). Appellee has 30 days to file brief and appellant has 15 days to file reply brief. (CR 76.12).

How Decided.—Supreme Court hears oral argument in all cases unless oral argument is dispensed with by order of Supreme Court. (CR 76.16). Decision is by entire court. (SCR 1.020[1]).

Post-Decision Motions.—Petitions for rehearing or modification or extension of opinion are permitted. Motions must be filed within 20 days after date of opinion. (CR 76.32). Responses are permitted and must be filed within 20 days after date petition is filed. (CR 76.32).

Administrative Agencies, Boards, Etc.—Procedures generally applicable to administrative hearings, records of proceedings, and orders or decisions of state administrative agencies are provided in KRS c. 13B; appeals from orders or decisions of administrative commissions, agencies, or boards are generally taken to Circuit Court. Form of proceeding is considered original action and not appeal. (KRS 23A.010). For example, review of decision of Board of Claims is taken to Circuit Court of county where hearing conducted or, if claim less than $500, claimant may file in District

APPEAL AND ERROR... *continued*

Court where claim arose (KRS 44.140); Kentucky Board of Tax Appeals: Franklin Circuit Court or Circuit Court where taxpayer resides (KRS 131.370); Public Service Commission: Franklin Circuit Court (KRS 278.410); Commissioner of Department of Financial Institutions: Franklin Circuit Court (KRS 292.490).

BONDS:

Bonds required or permitted in civil actions or proceeding differ depending upon particular proceeding. Typical uses include to stay appeal, obtain restraining order or temporary injunction (CR 65.05), attach or replevy property, discharge writ of attachment or replevin or warrant of distress and sue as nonresident plaintiff. Governmental units exempt from requirement to give bond in such proceedings. (KRS 454.190; CR 81A). Clerk of appropriate court prepares bonds to be taken therein and is empowered to refuse any surety deemed insufficient. (KRS 30A.060[2]). Jailers may prepare bail bonds for incarcerated prisoners. (KRS 431.5305).

Sureties.—Surety, who may be individual or surety company (KRS 304.21-050), must be resident of Kentucky (KRS 454.185) or be certified as sole surety (KRS 304.21-060). Sureties must be worth double sum to be secured beyond amount of surety's liabilities, and must have property liable to execution in Kentucky equal to sum secured; two or more sureties on same bond must meet these qualifications in aggregate. (KRS 454.185). Officer taking surety upon bond may require surety to make affidavit of qualifications. (KRS 454.180).

Trust companies and banks, authorized to act in fiduciary capacities, need no surety in their own fiduciary bonds, other than their capital stock, which is pledged by law. However, court, in its discretion, may require additional surety. (KRS 287.220).

All public or fiduciary bonds must be limited as to surety in definite penal sum, to be fixed by court or officer approving bond but not less than estimated value of estate fiduciary is in charge of, with right in such court or officer to increase penal sum of bond or require its renewal with other or additional sureties. (KRS 62.060).

No person, which includes corporation, partnership, registered limited liability partnership and limited liability company (KRS 446.010[26]), can be bound as surety of another, by act of agent, unless authority of such agent is in writing signed by his principal (KRS 371.090).

If a bond in a judicial proceeding is adjudged defective, a new and sufficient one may be executed within such reasonable time as the court may fix, with same effect as if originally executed. (KRS 454.175).

Enforcement.—Any person beneficially interested may sue on bond, but others likewise interested must be made parties either as plaintiffs or as defendants. (CR 17.01, 19.01). Surety may sue principal or cosurety on bond after payment due (KRS 412.140), but creditor must also be made defendant (KRS 412.150). Statute of limitations for enforcement against surety of bonds given in judicial proceedings is seven years after accrual of action (KRS 413.220); generally, limitation is five years with respect to fiduciary bonds (KRS 413.230).

CERTIORARI:

This writ is not used in Kentucky. For discretionary review by Supreme Court of final order of Court of Appeals, see topic Appeal and Error, subhead Appeals from Court of Appeals. For discretionary review by Court of Appeals of final order of Circuit Court sitting as appellate court, see topic Appeal and Error, subhead Appeals from Circuit Court, catchline How Taken.

CHARITABLE IMMUNITY:

See topic Damages.

COMMISSIONS TO TAKE TESTIMONY:

See topic Depositions and Discovery.

COSTS:

Costs in court proceedings are fixed by statute and taxed by clerk of court, subject to revision by circuit judge with imposition of penalty for illegal charge. (KRS 64.410; 64.460). Generally, successful party, though liable to officials for his own costs, is entitled to recover his costs against losing party, to be awarded in judgment. (KRS 453.040[1]). Exceptions to general rule apply for defendants who are necessary nominal parties and may apply to actions between partners, tenants in common or joint tenants and actions for settling distribution and division of deceased persons' estates, to settle partnerships and settle or enforce trusts. (KRS 453.040 [1 and 2]).

Personal representative, curator, conservator, assignee, guardian or trustee, if unsuccessful, shall be liable for costs to extent of fiduciary's assets. (KRS 453.140).

In civil actions brought by Commonwealth, in actions brought to challenge assessment or collection of taxes, and in appeals initiated by Commonwealth from administrative review board decisions, prevailing party, subject to judicial approval and discretion, may recover court costs for necessary attorneys' fees (\$40 per hour maximum) and expenses of experts up to total of \$10,000. (KRS 453.010; KRS 453.255; KRS 453.260).

Reasonable attorneys' fees may be awarded as costs to extent actually incurred (but not for salaried employee) in action after default on writing which creates debt or creates lien on real property, if writing so provides. (KRS 411.195).

Security for Costs.—Former requirements for cost bonds from nonresidents of state or private corporations before commencing proceedings in courts have been repealed. To stay enforcement of judgment on appeal, appellant must give supersedeas bond with good and sufficient surety, amount of which includes coverage of costs in judgment and costs on appeal. (CR 62.03; 73.04).

Liability of Attorney.—No provision exists. Former provision which required attorney for plaintiff to give security for costs was repealed in 1996.

DAMAGES:

Common law generally prevails as to compensatory damages.

Punitive damages are specifically recoverable by statute in some actions, e.g., for wrongful death (KRS 411.130); by surviving spouse or child of person killed by use of deadly weapon (KRS 411.150); for striking by certain weapons (KRS 411.020); or where defendant acted toward plaintiff with oppression, fraud or malice (KRS 411.184); in private insurance actions (KRS 411.560[4]; or in action against newspaper (KRS 411.051). Punitive damages not recoverable for breach of contract. (KRS 411.184[4]). In all other actions, punitive damages recoverable only upon clear and convincing evidence defendant acted with oppression, fraud or malice. (KRS 411.184[2] and [5]). Where property is wrongfully distrained for rent, owner may recover treble damages. (KRS 383.020). In action for waste, treble damages may be recovered of tenant. (KRS 381.350, 381.400).

Comparative Negligence Rule.—Pure form adopted judicially. (673 S.W.2d 713). Uniform Comparative Fault Act not adopted. Jury must, under instructions, apportion damages by degree of contribution to causation by joint trespassers or tortfeasors, including third party defendants. (KRS 411.182).

Charitable Immunity.—Doctrine of charitable immunity abrogated, (348 S.W.2d 930). Officers, directors, trustees and volunteers of charitable organizations receive limited immunity if they are not compensated for their services. (KRS 411.200).

Sovereign Immunity.—Commonwealth has partially waived sovereign immunity allowing awards up to \$100,000 per individual claimant (and up to \$250,000 if single act results in multiple claims, total award to be equitably divided among claimants) granted by statutory Board of Claims for damages to person or property for negligence of Commonwealth, its departments or agencies or their officers, agents or employees while acting in scope of employment. (KRS 44.070). Damages not allowed for collateral or dependent claims, mental distress or pain and suffering. (KRS 44.070[1]). Sovereign immunity not extended to negligent performance of ministerial acts by state employees. (e.g., 793 S.W.2d 823). Claim barred if not presented to Board of Claims within one year from time it accrued or, in personal injury cases, two years from injury. (KRS 44.110). Claims made are tried before Board and appeals heard by Circuit Court on basis of record created before Board. (KRS 44.086, 44.140). Action lies against Commonwealth in favor of those with lawfully authorized written contracts with Commonwealth, such actions to be brought in Franklin Circuit Court. (KRS 45A.245).

Limited waiver of sovereign immunity implicit in Board of Claims Act does not apply to counties which are entitled to defense of sovereign immunity for damages from performance of governmental functions and for damages from performance of discretionary functions. (327 S.W.2d 98). Cities and municipal corporations (e.g. board of health, sewer districts) are not protected by doctrine of sovereign immunity (805 S.W.2d 133) except in exercise of regulatory functions (687 S.W.2d 144) and with respect to traffic control devices (KRS 44.071). State agencies and county governments may acquire motor vehicle and workers compensation insurance without waiving immunity (KRS 44.055; 67.180, 67.185) and claims can be made against such policies.

No-Fault Insurance.—See category Transportation, topic Motor Vehicles, subhead No-Fault Insurance.

Uniform Contribution Among Tortfeasors Act (Revised) not adopted. KRS 412.030 allows contribution among wrongdoers where wrong is mere act of negligence and involves no moral turpitude. Apportionment is permitted between all parties against whom claims have been made and all persons released by claimant. (KRS 411.182).

See category Estates and Trusts, topic Death, subhead Action for Death.

DECLARATORY JUDGMENTS:

See topic Judgments.

DEPOSITIONS AND DISCOVERY:

Rules substantially similar to Federal Rules have been adopted and amended periodically to conform generally to existing federal practice. See also topic Practice.

Deposition of any party or other person may be taken by plaintiff upon notice served 30 days or more after action commenced, or within that time by leave of court, and by defendant at any time after action commenced. (CR 30.01).

Uniform Foreign Depositions Act not adopted.

Kinds.—Deposition of witness or party may be taken upon oral examination on notice (CR 30); or upon written questions with notice (CR 31); provision is also made for: interrogatories to parties (CR 33), production for inspection or copying (CR 34), requests for admission (CR 36), physical and mental examination of persons (CR 35)—all substantially similar to Federal Rules except CR 30.02 contains more specific provisions than Federal Rule 30(b) for video depositions and no specific authorization for telephonic or remote depositions. Each party limited to serving 30 interrogatories and 30 requests for admission on each other party without order of court. (CR 33.01).

Within State for Use within State.—See subhead Before Whom Taken, infra.

Within State for Use Elsewhere.—See subhead Before Whom Taken, infra.

Outside of State for Use within State.—See subhead Before Whom Taken, infra.

Before Whom Taken.—By written stipulation of parties, deposition may be taken before any person. (CR 29).

Within State for Use Within State.—In absence of stipulation, depositions taken within state to be used in its courts must be taken before examiner; judge, clerk, commissioner, or official reporter of a court; notary public (CR 28.01) or before such persons as may be prescribed by special statute; e.g., commissioned officers of U.S. Armed Forces, under KRS 384.080.

Within State for Use Elsewhere.—Depositions taken within state for use elsewhere are governed, generally speaking, by the laws of the jurisdiction to which the court belongs. CR 28.03 provides for such taking by production of commission or proof of

DEPOSITIONS AND DISCOVERY . . . *continued*
notice duly served to judge of district court of district where witness resides and issuance of subpoena thereon.

Outside State for Use Within State.—Depositions may be taken outside state for use within state before a commissioner appointed by the Governor of state where taken or before any other person empowered by commission directed to him by consent of parties or order of court or before judge, justice of peace, mayor, or notary public, or by commissioned officers of Armed Forces under certain circumstances, or as authorized by state where deposition taken. (CR 28.02).

Commissions.—See subhead Before Whom Taken, supra.

Purpose.—Depositions may be taken upon oral examination or written questions for discovery or for use in evidence, or both (CR 26.01), and may be used as evidence at trial if court finds witness is more than 100 miles from place of trial, is absent from state, occupies one of certain enumerated positions, is dead, is of unsound mind, is prevented from attending for certain enumerated causes, or that justice requires use in exceptional circumstances (CR 32.01).

Perpetuating Testimony.—Depositions may be taken before action by resident, or by nonresident having interest in real property in state, to perpetuate testimony, by filing verified petition in circuit court of county of residence of expected adverse party or in which real estate is situated. (CR 27.01). Provision is also made for taking depositions in trial court pending appeal to perpetuate testimony for use in event of further proceedings in trial court. (CR 27.02).

Certain actions equitable in nature may be tried by deposition. (CR 43.04[1]).

Attendance of witness may be compelled by subpoena by clerk of court or other authorized officer; similar provision is made for subpoena duces tecum under rules substantially same as Federal Rule 45 (a) and (b). (CR 45.01, 45.02). Subpoena may be served by any person who may serve summons, or by any person over 18 years of age, by delivering or offering to deliver a copy to the person to whom it is directed. (CR 45.03). Resident may be required to attend only in county where he resides, is employed, or transacts his business in person, or at such other place as fixed by order of court. (CR 45.04). Witness subpoenaed outside county of residence to be paid mileage. (KRS 421.015).

Compelling Attendance of Witnesses.—See subhead Attendance of Witness May Be Compelled, supra.

Examination of Witnesses.—Deponent may be examined upon any matter not privileged relevant to subject matter of action including existence, custody, etc., of tangible items, location of persons having knowledge of relevant facts, and insurance agreements. Fact that testimony may be inadmissible is not ground for objection, if testimony is reasonably calculated to lead to discovery of admissible evidence. (CR 26.02). Protective orders may be made by court, upon motion and notice. (CR 26.03).

Return.—Officer taking deposition must certify thereon that witness was duly sworn by him and that deposition is a true record of the testimony given and must promptly deliver or send the deposition by registered mail to the clerk of the court where action pending, for filing. (CR 30.06). Where deposition taken on written questions, copies of notice and interrogatories received by officer must be attached to deposition. (CR 31.02). Submission to and signing by witness is required only upon written request of party. (CR 30.05).

Forms.—The following forms, in use prior to adoption of Civil Rules, may be substantially followed.

Form

Deposition on Questions.—After style of court and case, use following caption:

The depositions of John Doe and Richard Roe, taken on behalf of the plaintiff, in an action now pending in the Jefferson Circuit Court, wherein John Jones is plaintiff and Richard Smith is defendant. The said Richard Roe, having been first duly sworn, deposes as follows:

(Here follows the deposition, which after having been read to the witness must be subscribed by him, unless all parties expressly waive reading and signature).

When all the depositions are taken and signed, let the officer taking them add the following certificate, varying it to suit names and facts:

The State of Ohio }
County of Hamilton } ss.

I, John Smith, a notary public in and for the county and state aforesaid, do certify that the above and foregoing depositions of John Doe and Richard Roe were taken before me, at my office in the city of Cincinnati, County of Hamilton, and State of Ohio, on the tenth day of November, 19. . . ., upon the questions and cross-questions hereto annexed; that said witnesses were each sworn by me that the evidence they should give in the action should be the truth, the whole truth, and nothing but the truth, before giving their testimony; that the testimony of each of said witnesses was written by me in their presence (or if either of the witnesses wrote his own testimony, state the fact, and that it was so written in the presence of the officer), read to and subscribed by him in my presence. I further certify that at the taking of said deposition neither party was present in person, nor represented by agent or attorney (or if both parties, or either party, attended, state the fact). My commission expires on the . . . . . . day of . . . . . ., 19. . . . .

John Smith, Notary Public. (Seal.)

Deposition on Notice.—The form of caption and certificate should be the same as above, substituting the word "notice" for "questions" wherever it occurs, and particularly stating in certificate which of parties attended at examination. If taken by consent, without notice, certificate should state that fact.

If the notice specifies the hours between which the depositions are to be taken, the certificate should state them likewise.

EQUITY:

See topic Actions.

EVIDENCE:

See topic Depositions and Discovery.

Witnesses.—Kentucky Rules of Evidence (KRE), patterned after Federal Rules of Evidence state rules of competency of witnesses and testimony. (KRS 422A.0101 to 422A.1104).

Privileged Communications.—Communications between lawyers and clients. (KRE 503). Husbands and wives (KRE 504), clergymen and penitents (KRE 505), counselors and clients (KRE 506) and psychotherapists and patients (KRE 507) are protected by qualified privileges. State, sister states and U.S. may claim privilege to protect identity of informers. (KRE 508). Except as provided by constitution, statute, or rules of evidence or other rules promulgated by Supreme Court, no person has privilege to refuse to be witness, or to disclose any matter, or to produce any object or writing, or to prevent another from being witness. (KRE 501).

Privilege exists for confidential communications to certified public accountant or public accountant but does not excuse compliance with validly issued subpoena or summons or limit investigations by state board of accountancy or by quality review committees. (KRS 325.440).

Husband and Wife.—Spouse of party has privilege to refuse to testify against party and party has privilege to prevent spouse from testifying as to events occurring after date of marriage, but no privilege exists when sufficient evidence has been introduced to support finding that spouse conspired or acted jointly in commission of crime charged or when one spouse is charged with wrongful conduct against person or property of other spouse, minor child of either, resident in household of either, or bystander to conduct affecting persons named. Court may refuse to allow privilege in any proceeding if interests of minor child would be adversely affected. (KRE 504).

Communications or Transactions with Infants or Persons Since Deceased or Incompetent.—Evidence which is otherwise competent is not inadmissible solely because it consists of statements of infants, persons who have died, or who are incompetent. Statements which constitute hearsay, as defined in KRE 801(c), may be admissible under exceptions provided in KRE 801A to 806.

Self-incrimination.—A witness may not be compelled to incriminate himself. (Ky. Const., §11; KRS 421.225).

Bribery or intimidation or corruption or retaliation against witness is punishable felony. (KRS 524.020, 524.040, 524.055). Harassing or tampering with witness is misdemeanor. (KRS 524.045, 524.050). Official proceedings need not be pending at time of offense for conduct to be actionable.

Compelling Attendance.—Subpoenas for attendance at hearing or trial may be served at any place in state, but deposition of certain witness may be used in place of personal attendance, unless witness failed when subpoenaed to appear for deposition. (CR 45.05). Mileage fee allowed for witness subpoenaed outside county of residence. (KRS 421.015). See topic Depositions and Discovery.

Compelling Testimony.—If witness refuses to testify, or to be sworn or to give deposition, he may be imprisoned until he testifies, or until final disposition of case. (KRS 421.140; caveat, 712 S.W.2d 363, limitation on court's contempt power declared unconstitutional).

INJUNCTIONS:

Injunctions may be issued to prevent commission of illegal or unconscionable act, to compel that act be taken, or to protect status quo while rights of parties are decided.

Writ of injunction is abolished. In its stead, Circuit Court by interlocutory order or by final judgment, may enjoin or command doing of act in question. (CR 65.01). CR 65 in its separate parts is comparable to, but not identical with, FRCP 65. See topic Practice. CR 65 authorizes issuance of restraining orders, temporary injunctions and final injunctions and provides procedures for interlocutory review in Court of Appeals and Supreme Court. Unlike Federal Rule 65, CR 65 does not provide for automatic expiration of restraining orders after ten days nor require immediate hearing following issuance of restraining order. Restraining orders, unlike temporary injunctions, may be issued without notice; restraining orders, however, may not be mandatory. (CR 65.01).

Jurisdiction.—Circuit Court is only court of original jurisdiction authorized to issue injunction or restraining order. (CR 65.01). Any Circuit Court with jurisdiction over parties and subject matter sufficient to support action relating to subject matter may issue restraining order, temporary injunction or permanent injunction. Restraining order, temporary injunction or permanent injunction may be issued only at commencement of or during pendency of civil action in Circuit Court. (CR 65.03).

Prerequisites.—

Restraining Order.—Applicants must clearly show by verified complaint or affidavit that their rights are being or will be violated by adverse party, that they will suffer immediate and irreparable injury, loss or damage before notice can be served and hearing had, and that applicant's attorney has made effort to give notice to adverse party and has stated reasons why notice shall not be required. (CR 65.03). Injury is regarded as irreparable if there is no certain pecuniary standard for measurement of damages. (350 S.W.2d 454). Every restraining order granted without notice shall define injury, state why it is irreparable, and show why order was granted without notice. (CR 65.03).

Temporary Injunction.—Notice must be given and movants must clearly show by verified complaint, affidavit or other evidence that their rights are being or will be violated by adverse party and that they will suffer immediate and irreparable injury, loss or damage pending final judgment in action or that acts of adverse party will tend to render such final judgment ineffectual. (CR 65.04). In determining whether to issue temporary injunctive relief, court must determine whether plaintiff has shown irreparable injury, weigh equities involved, including possible detriment to public interest, harm to defendant, and whether injunction will merely preserve status quo, and evaluate complaint to see whether substantial question has been presented. (575 S.W.2d 695). Order is void which grants mandatory injunction that in effect gives plaintiff entire relief sought in action, unless notice be given and opportunity to be heard be afforded to defendant affected by such order, before it is made. (107 Ky. 419, 54 S.W. 732).

See note at head of Digest as to 1998 legislation covered.

See Topical Index in front part of this volume.

KY – 13

INJUNCTIONS . . . *continued*

Permanent injunction may be entered as part of final judgment in action on merits of cause. (CR 65.01).

Procedure.—Restraining order may be granted without notice at commencement of action or during pendency thereof by judge of court in which action is pending, or by district judge of that judicial district if circuit judge is absent, or in their absence from county, by district court trial commissioner of that county if he is attorney, or by any circuit judge if no judge of circuit court in which action is pending is present in his judicial circuit. (CR 65.03). Temporary injunction may be granted by Circuit Court in which action is pending on motion. (CR 65.04).

Bond must be secured prior to issuance of temporary injunction or restraining order. (CR 65.05).

Appellate Review.—If circuit court grants, denies, modifies, or dissolves temporary injunction, such action in any of these cases may be reviewed upon application to Court of Appeals to grant or to dissolve or to reinstate injunction pendente lite. (CR 65.07, 65.08).

If the circuit court, in its final judgment, dissolves a temporary injunction previously issued in case, upon request of party aggrieved, that court must provide in judgment that within 20 days thereafter party aggrieved may apply to Court of Appeals, to revise judgment and to determine extent to which and conditions upon which injunction shall continue in force pending appeal. (CR 65.07, 65.08).

Any party adversely affected by order of Court of Appeals may move Supreme Court to vacate or modify order. Motion must show extraordinary cause. (CR 65.09).

See also category Employment, topic Labor Relations.

JUDGMENTS:

Kentucky Rules of Civil Procedure (CR) are based on Federal Rules of Civil Procedure with conforming amendments from time to time, and variations to conform to state court system. Judgment is written order of court which determines all or some of claims in action. (CR 54.01). Any judgment which adjudicates less than all claims in action and which does not state that there is no just reason for delay and that it is final with respect to claim adjudicated is interlocutory and subject to revision before entry of final judgment. (CR 54.02). Some miscellaneous practice statutes affect rights to seek judgment and enforcement and revival of judgments (see subheads infra). Circuit or district judge required to enter written judgment or order within 90 days from date of submission. (KRS 454.350). Judge's failure to comply with time limits does not render judgment or order void, but authorizes mandate or writ from higher court to issue order or, as last resort, removal of offending jurist by judicial retirement and removal commission. (KRS 454.350; SCR Part IV; 653 S.W.2d 652).

Judgments by confession are permitted only upon personal appearance of defendant (KRS 454.090-454.100), or offer made in pending suit to confess judgment for part of amount claimed (CR 68).

Judgment by consent or agreement of parties is valid and enforceable. (283 Ky. 317, 141 S.W.2d 265).

Judgment on compromise is valid. (CR 68).

Judgment on pleadings is authorized. (CR 12.03). Provision also made for directed verdict and judgment notwithstanding verdict. (CR 50).

Summary Judgment.—Provision is made for summary judgment, substantially similar to that made in Federal Rule 56. (CR 56). Standard for grant is stricter than under Federal Rule. (807 S.W.2d 476). In addition, special provision is made for summary judgment in following instances: (1) surety against principal or co-surety for money paid; (2) client against attorney for money or property received; (3) party or officer against surety for costs; (4) party against officer for money or property received, and damages; and (5) in cases specially authorized by statute. (KRS 418.005).

Declaratory Judgments.—Act, but not Uniform Act, adopted. (CR 57; KRS 418.005-418.090).

Default judgments are authorized. Court, commissioner or jury may hear proof and assess damages. (CR 55.01). Default judgment shall not be entered against Commonwealth or U.S. unless claimant establishes right to relief by satisfactory evidence. (CR 55.04).

Offer of Judgment.—Defendant more than ten days before trial may serve upon adverse party an offer to allow judgment to be taken against him with costs then accrued. Offer may be conditioned upon defendant's failure in his defense. Offer cannot be withdrawn before acceptance and before elapse of ten-day period. (816 S.W.2d 1991). Offer not accepted within ten days is deemed withdrawn and evidence thereof is not admissible. If judgment obtained by offeree is not more favorable than offer, the offeree must pay costs incurred after offer made. (CR 68).

Vacation or Modification.—Judgment rendered in trial court may be altered, amended or vacated by it (CR 59.05, 60), or reversed or modified by Court of Appeals (KRS 22A.060), or by Supreme Court (KRS 21A.050). Trial court may relieve party from final judgment for following reasons: (1) Mistake, inadvertence, surprise, or excusable neglect; (2) newly discovered evidence; (3) perjury or falsified evidence; (4) fraud affecting proceedings; (5) judgment is void; (6) judgment has been satisfied, released, or discharged, or prior judgment upon which it has been based is properly reversed or vacated; or (7) any other reason of extraordinary nature. Motion must be made within reasonable time and in cases of 1, 2, and 3 above, not more than one year after judgment was entered. (CR 60.02).

Lien.—Final judgment for recovery of money in state or federal court shall act as lien upon all real estate in which judgment debtor has any ownership interest located in any county in which judgment creditor files notice of judgment lien with county clerk, county clerk enters notice in lis pendens record, judgment creditor sends notice of judgment by first class mail to judgment debtor with required wording and judgment debtor certifies on notice filed with clerk that statute has been complied with. (KRS 426.720). Personal judgments against sheriffs and other collectors of public monies or their sureties create lien on their property. (KRS 135.100; 283 Ky. 462, 141 S.W.2d 867). As to lien of execution, see category Debtor and Creditor, topic Executions. As to lis pendens notice, see KRS 382.440, 382.510.

Revival.—Not necessary upon death of defendant after sale of his property under execution. (KRS 426.550, 426.555[1]). Before sale, levy of execution is suspended until revived against personal representative or successor of defendant after lapse of six months from time of qualification of his first representative, though if property be of perishable nature, or cost of keeping it ought to be avoided, reviver may be had upon rule in action after ten days notice, served in same manner as summons. (KRS 426.555). After recovering judgment, death of plaintiff in judgment will not prevent issuance of execution, but execution must be in favor of his representative or successor, if there be one, or if judgment be recovered by several parties, execution must be issued in favor of those surviving, and where all of them be dead, execution must issue in favor of representative of last survivor. (KRS 426.551). Judgment, or levy of execution thereunder, may be revived against a real representative (i.e., an heir or devisee of lands) after 12 months from defendant's death. Reviver may be by order based upon show-cause rule after ten days notice thereof, served like a summons. (KRS 426.555). See category Debtor and Creditor, topic Executions.

Each successive issuance of execution within 15 years after judgment or from date of last execution issued acts as a revival of the judgment. (KRS 413.090[1]).

Assignment.—Certain assignments of judgments are recognized by statute, e.g., to sureties (KRS 412.090) and to officer holding execution (KRS 426.380).

Equitable assignments of judgments are recognized in practice by filing in the court that rendered the judgment an informal written assignment of judgment proved by oath of attesting witness in open court or by acknowledgment before an officer authorized to take acknowledgments of deeds. Thereafter the judgment or any execution thereon will run in name of judgment plaintiff for benefit of assignee.

Satisfaction.—Upon return of execution showing judgment satisfied, clerk must enter on judgment: Satisfied by execution. Party or his attorney receiving satisfaction of judgment otherwise than by execution, must make, date and sign this entry in judgment: Satisfied in full. Court may compel entry of satisfaction to be made. (CR 79.02).

Bar.—Actions on judgments are barred after lapse of 15 years from date of last execution issued thereon, although limitations period may differ in certain specified situations (KRS 413.090[1]), and judgment barred in state or country where rendered is barred here unless rendered in favor of resident of Kentucky who had cause of action from time it accrued (KRS 413.330).

Judgment Based on Constructive Service.—If defendant constructively served is deprived of property because of judgment, court shall retain control over and not dispose of property or proceeds for one year, unless plaintiff executes bond with surety approved by court, to effect that if defendant shall procure vacation or modification of judgment, plaintiff shall restore to defendant any property or money obtained under such judgment, restoration of which shall be adjudged (CR 4.11), and defendant may obtain any relief (such as new trial, relief from judgment or order) available to party personally served (CR 4.10). Provision for bond does not apply to judgments in favor of State. (CR 81A).

Judgment for Attorney's Fees.—See topic Costs; category Business Regulation and Commerce, topic Bills and Notes.

Judgment Notes.—See category Business Regulation and Commerce, topic Bills and Notes.

Actions on judgments where no property found must be brought in county in which judgment was rendered, or in which defendant resides or is summoned. (KRS 452.440).

Foreign Judgments.—Recognized and enforced per Revised Uniform Enforcement of Foreign Judgments Act. (KRS 426.950-426.990). See subhead Revised Uniform Enforcement of Foreign Judgments Act, infra.

Revised Uniform Enforcement of Foreign Judgments Act printed in Uniform and Model Acts section adopted in part. (KRS 426.950-426.990). §§1-6 of Act adopted without material variation. §§7-10 of Act not adopted. Must pay amount otherwise provided for filing suit to file foreign judgment. (KRS 426.970). No execution or other process shall issue until 20 days after date foreign judgment is filed. (KRS 426.960[3]).

LIMITATION OF ACTIONS:

Actions must be brought within following periods after respective causes of action accrue:

Eighteen years: Action to determine paternity under KRS 406.021(1). (KRS 406.031).

Fifteen years: Action to recover real estate (KRS 413.010), except that seven years adverse possession bars action (KRS 413.060); action on judgment or decree (KRS 413.090[1]) (limitation running from last issue of execution thereon for collection of judgment debt as distinguished from costs [See 299 Ky. 729, 187 S.W.2d 289]); actions on recognizance, bond or written contract, official bond of public officer or bond posted by individuals appointed by court or authority of law (such as receivers, conservators, trustees, etc.), or on bonds for payment of money or performance of undertakings (such as appeal, injunction, supersedeas, attachment, payment of costs, replevin, etc. bonds), except when shorter period provided for specific purposes (KRS 413.090. See 241 Ky. 541, 44 S.W.2d 518). (*Caveat*, absent fraud, action against personal representative or any distributee must be brought within two years from date of order of discharge of personal representative. [KRS 396.205].) As for actions on sales contracts, see infra, subhead Four Years.

Accrual of Cause of Action.—Valid contract to devise property is not broken until death of contracting party. (299 Ky. 719, 187 S.W.2d 264).

Ten years: Probate of will; action for which no other limitation is prescribed (KRS 413.160). Action for relief or damages on ground of fraud or mistake is barred after

LIMITATION OF ACTIONS . . . *continued*
ten years after making of contract or perpetration of fraud, regardless of time of discovery. (KRS 413.130[3]).

Eight years: In product liability action, rebuttable presumption lies that product was not defective if injury, death or property damage occurs more than eight years after date of manufacture. (KRS 411.310). Action for wrongful death or damage to person or property from deficiency in construction components, design, planning, supervision, inspection or construction of any improvement to real property, occurring within seventh year from substantial completion, must be brought within one year from date of injury or eight years after substantial completion, whichever is sooner. (KRS 413.135[2]). (*Caveat*, predecessor statute twice held unconstitutional. [808 S.W.2d 809; 704 S.W.2d 179]). Also, note apparent conflict with KRS 413.120[13] in subhead Five Years, infra.)

Seven years: Action against sureties on any contract or bond or action on judgment or decree against a surety on which no execution has issued in seven years. (KRS 413.220).

Action for damages to property or personal injury or death arising from deficiency in construction components, design, planning, supervision, inspection or construction of any improvement to real property must be brought within seven years following substantial completion of such improvement. (KRS 413.135[1]). (*Caveat*, apparent conflict created by KRS 413.135[2], which allows additional time to bring action for injury occurring during seventh year from substantial completion. See subhead Eight Years, supra.)

Five years: Action against surety for executor, administrator, guardian or curator, or for sheriff to whom decedent's estate has been transferred (KRS 413.230); action on contract not in writing, express or implied; on draft or bill of exchange; on sealed or unsealed negotiable promissory note actually negotiated (241 Ky. 541, 44 S.W.2d 518); on open or stated account (any item due more than five years barred, but due date is computed from Jan. 1 following date of purchase [KRS 413.130]); for fraud or mistake (time running from discovery, but time may not exceed ten years from transaction); for injury to real or personal property or injury by trustee to rights of beneficiary (KRS 413.120); proceeding by state for retrospective assessment of particular intangibles, namely, money in hand, notes, bonds, shares of stock, accounts or other credits, secured or unsecured (KRS 132.290); to enforce liability created by statute not fixing different limitation, including action to recover taxes (115 Ky. 239, 72 S.W. 1090); for penalty or forfeiture under statute not fixing different limitation; to enforce liability of steamboat or other vessel; to foreclose liens securing street improvement bonds authorized in cities of certain classes; action for personal injuries against builder of home or other improvements, cause to accrue at time of original occupancy (*Caveat*, note apparent conflict with KRS 413.135, in subheads Seven Years and Eight Years, supra.); to enforce liability of bail; for injury to rights not arising on contract and not otherwise enumerated (KRS 413.120); action to enforce lien for unpaid installments of unemployment compensation (KRS 341.300).

In product liability action, rebuttable presumption lies that product was not defective if injury, death or property damage occurs more than five years after sale to first consumer. (KRS 411.310).

Four years: Action for breach of contract for sale of goods, unless parties have, by sales agreement, reduced period; but period may not be reduced to less than one year. (KRS 355.2-725).

Three years: Action on county bonds which have been called for payment (KRS 413.110); action for recovery of real property, after removal of disability (KRS 413.020). Civil action under Uniform Securities Act. (KRS 292.480[3]).

Two years: Action for taking, detaining or injuring personal property, including action for specific recovery. (KRS 413.125). Action for no-fault insurance benefits for injury other than death (period runs from date injured person suffers loss and knows, or should know, loss was caused by accident but action must be commenced within four years of date of accident) (KRS 304.39-230[1]); action for tort liability arising out of use of motor vehicle not limited by no-fault insurance act (period runs from date of injury or death or date of last benefit payment made by no-fault carrier, whichever is later) (KRS 304.39-230[6]); action on state warrant which has been called for payment (KRS 413.110); actions which accrued against deceased person during life if no personal representative appointed (KRS 396.011) (*caveat*, see subhead Six Months, infra); actions by or against common carriers by rail or water, based on overcharges or undercharges, and actions for damages before Railroad Commission (KRS 276.500); actions for recovery of usurious interest paid (KRS 360.020); action by party aggrieved by decision of district court admitting will to probate or rejecting will, within two years of decision of district court (KRS 394.240); action against personal representative or any distributee (period runs from date of order of discharge of personal representative [KRS 396.205]).

One year: Action for personal injury or death not covered by longer limitation period (481 S.W.2d 668); for libel, slander, malicious prosecution, conspiracy, arrest, seduction, criminal conversation, breach of promise of marriage or negligence or malpractice of physician or surgeon; for escape of prisoner arrested on civil process; for recovery of stolen property or its value or damages against thief or any accessory; for killing or injuring of cattle by railroad or other corporation and for recovery of usury (KRS 413.140). Conflict exists with respect to recovery of interest paid; see subhead Two Years, supra. Action for survivor's no-fault insurance benefits (period runs from date of death resulting from accident or four years from date of accident, whichever occurs first). (KRS 304.39-230[2]). Action in tort or contract for professional service malpractice. (KRS 413.245). Action in Board of Claims for damages caused by negligence of Commonwealth, its departments or agencies or its officers, agents or employees while acting in scope of employment. (KRS 44.110). See topic Damages, subhead Sovereign Immunity. For claims against estate of decedent, see category Estates and Trusts, topic Executors and Administrators, subhead Presentation of Claims.

Accrual of Cause of Action.—Cause of action accrues for professional services malpractice when injury was discovered or should have been discovered. (KRS 413.245; 459 S.W.2d 166). Same rule applies to product liability actions for personal injury from latent disease caused by exposure to harmful substance. (580 S.W.2d 497).

Six months: Actions, other than claims in favor of U.S., State of Kentucky or any subsidiaries thereof or as to security proceedings to enforce any mortgage, pledge, lien or other security interest or proceedings to establish liability of decedent under policy of liability insurance, which accrued against deceased person during life (period runs from date personal representative appointed; two years from date of death if no representative is appointed) (KRS 396.011).

Uniform Commercial Code adopted, (KRS c. 355), but bulk sales article repealed. See category Business Regulation and Commerce, topic Commercial Code.

Actions Not Specifically Provided For: Action for liability created by statute when no other period provided, five years. (KRS 413.120). Action for injury to rights, not arising under contract and not otherwise enumerated, five years. (KRS 413.120). Action for relief not provided by statute and not otherwise provided for, ten years. (KRS 413.160).

Limitation statutes do not apply to express trust that is both continuing and subsisting or to action by vendee in possession to obtain conveyance of real property. (KRS 413.340; 849 S.W.2d 534).

Commencement of Action.—An action is commenced on date of first summons or process issued thereon in good faith from court having jurisdiction of cause of action. (KRS 413.250; CR 3). Good faith requirement is missing if service not attempted in due course.

New Actions.—If an action is commenced in due time and in good faith in any court or other tribunal, and upon defense being made the court adjudges that it has no jurisdiction of the action, plaintiff may, within 90 days from time of such judgment, commence a new action in the proper court or other appropriate tribunal. The time elapsed between commencing the two actions is not counted in applying any statute of limitation. (KRS 413.270).

Foreign Causes of Action.—When cause of action has arisen in another state or country and by its laws action thereon is barred by limitation shorter than that prescribed by Kentucky, action thereon in Kentucky is barred by such shorter period of limitation, regardless of residence of the parties. (KRS 413.320).

Extension of Time.—If an act required to perfect a cause of action is restrained by injunction or other lawful means, or through vacancy in office, absence of officer or his refusal to act, the time covered by such restraint is not counted as part of limitation period, and this applies also where collection of judgment or commencement of action is stayed by injunction. The period of such stay is not counted in computing limitation. (KRS 413.260). Written agreements entered into in good faith and at arms length to extend limitations period for filing of civil actions are enforceable. (KRS 413.265).

Disability of Plaintiff.—Actions for recovery of real property may be brought by former disabled person or person claiming through him within three years after disability removed (KRS 413.020), but no later than 30 years from time right of action first accrued (KRS 413.030). To extend statutory period to bring action, disability must have existed when cause of action first accrued. (KRS 413.020). In all other actions, if person entitled to bring action was disabled when cause of action accrued, applicable period of limitation does not begin to run until disability removed, or until death. (KRS 413.170). Intervening inception of disability does not toll running of statute. (246 Ky. 404, 55 S.W.2d 39).

Absence or Concealment of Defendant.—If resident defendant is absent from Kentucky when a cause of action accrues the statute runs from the date of his return, and if he obstructs prosecution of the action by departing from state, absconding or concealing himself or other indirect means, time of such obstruction is not included in the period within which action shall be commenced. (KRS 413.190). Cited statute does not apply to defendants not residing in Kentucky when cause of action accrued. (299 Ky. 751, 187 S.W.2d 281).

Death of Defendant.—All claims against decedent's estate which arose before death, if not barred by other limitation before death, barred against estate, personal representatives and heirs and devisees unless presented within one year if personal representative appointed or within two years after decedent's death if no personal representative appointed. (KRS 396.011). No claims barred by limitation which would expire during six month period from decedent's death (KRS 396.045) (*caveat*, except for limitations imposed by KRS c. 396). With consent of all successors with affected interests personal representative may waive any limitation available to estate. (KRS 396.065). Actions commenced before death must be revived against estate of deceased defendant within one year from death. (KRS 395.278).

Interruption of Statutory Period.—Statutory period commences anew upon new promise in substitution for old (294 Ky. 664, 172 S.W.2d 457), or part payment (299 Ky. 664, 186 S.W.2d 797).

Revival of Barred Claims.—A debt barred by limitations cannot be revived by mere partial payment. There must be actual acknowledgment of debt and promise, either oral or written, to pay, and any action must be based on new promise. (226 Ky. 301, 10 S.W.2d 1095; 285 Ky. 128, 147 S.W.2d 70).

Contractual limitations are enforced where period is not unreasonably short. (276 Ky. 132, 122 S.W.2d 990).

Record Memorandum of Extension.—The period of limitation upon actions (required to be brought within 15 years) on any bond or obligation for the payment of money secured by a lien, may not be prolonged or extended as against purchasers or creditors without notice (246 Ky. 225, 54 S.W.2d 906), unless the promisor and the holder of the lien before 15 years after maturity of the debt enter a memorandum on the margin of the record of the deed or mortgage, attested by the clerk, showing that the debt is extended, and for what time it is extended, and the amount still due thereon. Clerk's fee, 25¢. (KRS 413.100).

Pleading.—Ordinarily defense of limitation must be pleaded. This is always the safe course (293 Ky. 627, 169 S.W.2d 823), but a motion to dismiss complaint may be sustained in exceptional cases, e.g., fraud cases where plaintiff, suing after five years

See note at head of Digest as to 1998 legislation covered.

See Topical Index in front part of this volume.

LIMITATION OF ACTIONS . . . *continued*

from commission of fraud complained of, fails to state facts showing that he could not discover the fraud within the five year period (236 Ky. 217, 32 S.W.2d 971; 297 Ky. 257, 180 S.W.2d 93). Defense may be raised by motion to dismiss if fact that limitations period has run is clear on face of complaint. (429 S.W. 2d 860).

Notice to City.—See topic Actions.

PARTITION:

Jurisdiction and Venue.—Suit by person desiring partition of land held jointly with others, or by person desiring allotment of dower or curtesy, or by person with 20% or more ownership interest in closely held farm or partnership must be brought in circuit court of county in which land or greater part thereof lies. (KRS 381.135).

Proceedings.—Commissioners are appointed to determine division or allotment thereof according to rights of parties. Registered land surveyor must perform survey according to determination, signed and sealed, unless such survey exists. (KRS 381.135).

Partition in Kind or Sale.—Where equitable partition of land cannot be made, court may order sale and division of proceeds. (271 Ky. 84, 111 S.W.2d 579).

PLEADING:

Kentucky Rules of Civil Procedure (CR) govern pleading in all civil actions, except for special statutory proceedings, such as claims in Small Claims Division of District Court (see category Courts and Legislature, topic Courts, subhead Small Claims Courts), petitions for dissolution of marriage (see category Family, topic Dissolution of Marriage, subhead Pleading), sales of realty of persons under disability (see category Family, topic Guardian and Ward, subhead Real Estate), and cases placed on "Economical Litigation Docket" in certain circuit courts (see topic Practice, subhead Economical Litigation Docket) for which proceedings statutory provisions prevail over inconsistent procedures set forth in Rules. (CR 1[2]). Rules are patterned on Federal Rules of Civil Procedure with modifications for peculiarities of state practice. See topic Practice. No differences apply to pleadings seeking equitable relief from those seeking relief at law.

Form of Pleadings.—All pleadings and papers other than exhibits, computer printouts and printed briefs shall be typewritten, double spaced in black ink with 1½ inch margin on left side on unglazed paper not greater than 8½ inches by 11 inches in size. (CR 7.02[4]).

Pleadings permitted are: Complaint and answer; reply to counterclaim denominated as such; answer to cross-claim; third party complaint; third party answer; and where ordered by court, reply to answer or third party answer. (CR 7.01).

Complaint and other claims for relief must contain short statement of claim and demand for judgment. Claim for unliquidated damages shall not recite amount of alleged damages other than allege that damages exceed jurisdictional amount. Party may obtain information as to amount claimed by interrogatories; amount claimed shall not exceed last amount stated in answer to interrogatories. (CR 8.01).

Counterclaim or Set-off.—Pleading must state as a counterclaim any claim which at the time of serving the pleader has against any opposing party, if it arises out of the transaction or occurrence that is the subject matter of the opposing party's claim, and does not require for its adjudication the presence of third parties of whom the court cannot acquire jurisdiction, except claim need not be stated if such claim is subject of another pending action. (CR 13.01). Counterclaims may be permitted as to any claim against opposing party not arising out of transaction or occurrence that is subject matter of opposing party's claim. Reply may not contain such counterclaim. (CR 13.02).

Reply.—Permitted on order of court to an answer or a third party answer; without court order a reply is required to a counterclaim denominated as such. (CR 7.01).

Demurrer has been abolished; but matters formerly asserted by special and general demurrers may be raised by motion. (CR 7.02[3], 12.02).

Amended or Supplemental Pleadings.—Party may amend once as a matter of course at any time before responsive pleading is served, or if no responsive pleading is permitted and action has not been placed upon trial calendar, party may amend any time within 20 days after pleading is served; otherwise, amendment may only be made by leave of court or by consent of adverse party. (CR 15.01; 479 S.W.2d 6). Leave to amend shall be freely given when justice so requires. (CR 15.01). Amendments to conform to evidence may be made on motion even after judgment. (CR 15.02).

Supplemental pleadings setting forth transactions, occurrences or events which have happened since the pleading to be supplemented, may be permitted by the court on motion. (CR 15.04).

Service of pleadings and motions must be made upon a party. If he is represented by an attorney, the service must be made on the attorney. Service may be made by delivering or mailing a copy to his last known address, or if no address is known, by leaving a copy with the clerk of the court. (CR 5.02).

Time.—Answer must be served within 20 days after service of summons on defendant, or within 20 days after the service of a pleading stating a cross-claim against the party answering. Reply to a counterclaim must be served within 20 days after service of the answer or, if a reply is ordered by the court, within 20 days after service of the order, unless the order otherwise directs. (CR 12.01).

Response to amended pleading must be made within time remaining for response to original pleading or ten days after service, whichever is longer. (CR 15.01).

Proof of Claims.—In sending claims to Kentucky for suit, clear statement of claim and its origin, nature and amount in detail should be furnished, and original note, contract, etc., upon which claim is based should be forwarded.

Economical Litigation Docket.—Supreme Court has adopted supplemental rules, CR 88-97, to be applied in few circuits and divisions identified by Supreme Court order for all contract, personal injury, property damage, property rights and termination of parental rights cases filed in designated circuits and divisions.

Small Claims.—See category Courts and Legislature, topic Courts.

Frivolous Claims.—Attorney's or party's signature on pleading warrants that to best of his or her knowledge, information and belief, pleading is well-grounded in fact and warranted by existing law or good faith argument for extension, modification or reversal of existing law, and is not interposed for any improper purpose. (CR 11). Bad faith is not required before sanction imposed. (746 S.W.2d 85). Malicious prosecution action also lies for asserting frivolous claim in either civil or criminal action. (621 S.W.2d 895). Signing attorney must be attorney actually representing party. (621 S.W.2d 895). Standard for determining adequacy of attorney's inquiry is "reasonableness under the circumstances". (746 S.W.2d 85).

PRACTICE:

Practice is regulated by Rules of Civil Procedure, patterned on Federal Rules as amended periodically with modifications relevant to state practice.

Discovery, in addition to provisions of Civil Rules, is allowed: in actions for recovery of specific personal property (KRS 425.106); against garnishee (KRS 425.511); on return of no property found (KRS 426.381). See also category Debtor and Creditor, topic Executions.

Filing Discovery Documents with Court.—Interrogatories, requests for production or inspection, requests for admission and subpoenas shall not be filed with court. Party responsible for serving those documents shall retain originals and become custodian. (CR 5.06[1]).

Demand for Admission of Facts.—Written request for admission of facts or of genuineness of documents may be made after action commenced. Facts not denied are deemed admitted. (CR 36.01). Expense of proving documents or facts after denial of validity, including reasonable attorney's fees, may be charged to party denying. (CR 37.01). Court may order answer or amended answer. (CR 36.01). Each party limited to serving 30 interrogatories and 30 requests for admission on each other party without order of court. (CR 33.01).

Direct Actions Against Insurer.—See category Transportation, topic Motor Vehicles, subhead Direct Actions.

Economical Litigation Docket.—Supreme Court has adopted supplemental rules, CR 88-97, to be applied in few circuits and divisions identified by Supreme Court order for all contract, personal injury, property damage, property rights and termination of parental rights cases filed in designated circuits and divisions.

Videotape Records and Transcripts.—At option of individual circuit judges, videotape equipment may be used in place of reporter to record proceedings in civil and criminal cases. Procedures for use of equipment and use of resulting recording as transcript on appeal governed by CR 98.

Small Claims.—See category Courts and Legislature, topic Courts.

See also topics Actions, Appeal and Error, Depositions and Discovery, Injunctions, Judgments, Pleading, Process; category Debtor and Creditor, topics Attachment, Executions, Garnishment.

PROCESS:

Action is commenced by filing of complaint and issuance of warning order or summons thereon. (CR 3.01). Process is regulated by Kentucky Rules of Civil Procedure (CR) patterned after Federal Rules of Civil Procedure. See topic Practice.

General Requisites.—Process may not issue until plaintiff's complaint is filed. (CR 4.01[1]). Officer need not serve process in civil case unless party obtaining it deposits with clerk who issues it the cost of service, not exceeding $5, or secures right to sue in forma pauperis. (KRS 64.080). As a means of bringing a defendant into court, service of process may be actual or constructive. Summons and copy of complaint must be served together. (CR 4.04[1]).

By Whom Issued.—Clerk of court in which action properly brought, issues summons. (CR 4.01).

Who May Serve.—Summons may be served by registered or certified mail, return receipt requested (CR 4.01[1][a]; see subhead Service by Mail, infra) or may be served by any person authorized by law to serve (CR 4.01[1][b]). Persons so authorized include county sheriff (KRS 454.140), any person appointed by him (KRS 70.050) or at request of plaintiff, coroner, jailer or constable (KRS 454.140), or special bailiff appointed by court to serve particular process or order (KRS 454.145).

Personal Service on Individual.—Summons is served by delivering or, if acceptance refused, by offering to deliver copy to person to be summoned or by delivery to agent authorized by appointment or by law to receive service of process for such individual. (CR 4.04[2]).

Personal service on unmarried infant is on guardian; or if none, on father or mother within state; or if none, on person having control of unmarried infant. If there are no such individuals or if all foregoing are plaintiffs, clerk must appoint guardian ad litem for service. (CR 4.04[3]).

Personal Service on Incompetent.—Same as on infant.

Personal service on domestic or foreign corporation is made by serving officer or managing agent thereof or chief agent in county where action is brought, or any other agent authorized by appointment or law to receive service on its behalf. (CR 4.04[5]). Any process may be served on registered agent appointed by corporation, or if corporation fails to appoint or maintain registered agent or agent cannot be served by reasonable diligence, process may be served on secretary of corporation by registered or certified mail, return receipt requested. (KRS 271B.5-040[2]; 273.3644[2]). Process may be served on foreign corporation by serving Secretary of State under Long Arm Statute (KRS 454.210; see subhead Long Arm Statute, infra), or by serving corporation's registered agent in Kentucky or, if foreign corporation has no registered agent or agent cannot be served by reasonable diligence by serving secretary of foreign corporation by registered or certified mail, return receipt requested. (KRS 271B.15-100[2]). These are alternate methods of serving process on foreign corporation. (KRS 271B.5-040[3]; 271B.15-100[4]; 690 S.W.2d 393). Process for corporation formerly, but no

See note at head of Digest as to 1998 legislation covered.

See Topical Index in front part of this volume.

PROCESS . . . *continued*
longer, qualified to do business in state may be served on Secretary of State. (KRS 271B.15-200[3]; 273.363).

Personal service on partnership or association, subject to suit under common name, is made by serving member, managing agent, or agent authorized by appointment or law to receive service on its behalf. (CR 4.04[4]). Domestic limited partnership must maintain agent for service of process. (KRS 362.407[2]). Foreign limited partnership must maintain registered agent; if registered agent's authority has been revoked or agent cannot be found or served with reasonable diligence, can serve Secretary of State. (KRS 362.497[1]).

Service outside Kentucky upon certain defendants is authorized either by certified mail with return receipt requested or upon delivering copy of summons to defendant by person over 18 years of age. Such service without appearance does not authorize personal judgment. (CR 4.04[8]). See subhead Long Arm Statute, infra, for alternate method of service which does authorize personal judgment.

Service by Mail.—At direction of initiating party and payment of costs, clerk shall mail copy of summons and complaint by registered or certified mail, return receipt requested, to address set forth in caption on complaint or to alternate address set forth in written instructions. Service by registered or certified mail is complete only upon delivery of envelope to addressee. Return receipt is proof of time, place and manner of service. (CR 4.01[1][a]).

For service by mail in Small Claims cases in District Court, see category Courts and Legislature, topic Courts, subhead Small Claims Courts.

Constructive Service.—Following parties may be constructively served: (1) Nonresident individual absent from state, (2) corporation, partnership or association subject to suit under common name, having no agent in state known to plaintiff upon whom summons may be served, (3) individual absent from state four months or who has departed with intent to delay or defraud creditors, (4) individual who has left county of residence to avoid service of summons or has so concealed himself that summons cannot be served, (5) individual whose name and place of residence are unknown to plaintiff. (CR 4.05).

In such cases plaintiff or attorney must file affidavit with clerk stating one or more of grounds above mentioned and, except in case of (5), last known address of defendant, or, in case of (2), last known address of one upon whom service might be had, or his ignorance of such fact. If affidavit is made by other than plaintiff, it must state affiant's connection with plaintiff and affiant's belief that plaintiff is ignorant of such facts as are unknown to affiant. (CR 4.06). Thereupon clerk makes warning order upon complaint warning defendant to appear and defend within 50 days (CR 4.05), and must appoint attorney for defendant (CR 4.07).

Neither plaintiff nor attorney may be appointed or may suggest name of warning order attorney. It is duty of warning order attorney to make diligent efforts to inform defendant by mail concerning pendency and nature of action and to report result of efforts to court within 50 days after appointment. If attorney cannot inform defendant concerning action or if he learned that defendant is under disability, must so report and make affirmative defense if he can, or report to court that he cannot. No judgment can be rendered against defendant for whom warning order is made until defense or report has been filed. (CR 4.07).

Defendant constructively summoned deemed to have been summoned on 30th day after entry of warning order and action proceeds accordingly. (CR 4.08).

Substituted service is allowed in certain classes of cases, such as suits against foreign insurance companies (see category Insurance, topic Insurance Companies), suits under the "Blue Sky Law" (see category Business Regulation and Commerce, topic Securities), and suits against nonresident owners or operators of motor vehicles (see category Transportation, topic Motor Vehicles) or nonresident real estate brokers (see category Business Regulation and Commerce, topic Brokers). But in a suit against insurance company, held that right to have substituted service is confined to cases involving contracts entered into or transactions had in Kentucky and does not extend to contracts entered into or transactions had in another state. (277 Ky. 320, 126 S.W.2d 468).

Service by publication on creditors of decedent may be had in actions for settlement of decedents' estates. (KRS 395.520). As to effect of such service on creditor failing to appear, see KRS 395.535. As to time, mode and medium of publication, see KRS 424.110 to 424-210.

Proof of Service.—Postal return receipt showing time and place of delivery or official return of officer whose name appears on summons, endorsed thereon, is proof of service. (CR 4.01).

Long Arm Statute.—Personal jurisdiction granted courts over nonresidents who act directly or by agent as to claims arising from person's: (1) Transacting any business in state; (2) contracting to furnish goods or services in state; (3) causing tortious injury by act or omission in state; (4) causing tortious injury in state by act or omission outside state if person regularly does or solicits business or engages in other persistent course of conduct or derives substantial revenue from consumption of goods or services in state; (5) breach of express or implied warranty in state resulting from sale outside state when seller knew person injured would use, consume or be affected by goods in state and seller also regularly does or solicits business or engages in persistent course of conduct in state or derives substantial revenue from goods used or consumed in state; (6) owning or using real property in state if claim arises from voluntary ownership, use or possession of property; (7) contracting to insure person or property in state; (8) committing sexual intercourse in state which causes birth of child if certain conditions met. Nonresident defined by Act to include individuals, partnerships, corporations, personal representatives, and other legal entities. Process to be served on nonresident in any county or on Secretary of State as statutory agent for nonresident. Venue lies in county where plaintiff resides or where claim arose. (KRS 454.210; see 302 F. Supp. 174).

Nonresident Motorist.—See category Transportation, topic Motor Vehicles.

Service on Holiday or Sunday.—See category Introduction, topic Holidays.

REPLEVIN:

Common law action of replevin has been superceded by statutory writ of possession procedures under KRS c. 425 (194 Ky. 648, 240 S.W. 363), by secured party's self-help remedy under Uniform Commercial Code (see category Business Regulation and Commerce, topic Commercial Code), and by statutory attachment and garnishment procedures (see category Debtor and Creditor, topics Attachment and Garnishment). Discussion under this topic describes writ of possession practice.

Proceedings.—Plaintiff may upon filing complaint or at any time prior to judgment in action move court for writ of possession. Motion shall be verified or supported by affidavit and shall set forth following: (1) Showing of basis of claim and that plaintiff is entitled to possession and if based on written instrument, copy of same must be attached to; (2) showing that it is wrongfully detained by defendant, how possession was acquired by defendant and reason for detention to plaintiff's best knowledge and belief; (3) description of property and statement of its value; (4) statement of location of property and if property is located in private place, creditable showing of probable cause based upon credible and reliable information supporting belief property is located therein; (5) that it has not been taken for tax, fine or seized under execution or if so seized it is exempt from such seizure. (KRS 425.011).

Plaintiff must make demand in writing at or after time suit is filed by delivering such demand and copy of complaint, motion and summons to defendant or by sending them to defendant by registered or certified mail, return receipt requested, to last known place of residence at least seven and not more than 60 days before such order of possession is sought. Demand must inform defendant that he has seven days in which to petition court for hearing, or in which amount claimed in complaint must be paid in full, and that unless hearing is set or amount paid, writ of possession will issue. Demand must identify court in which suit has been filed, grounds therefor, date of demand, amount claimed, and name and address of plaintiff and his attorney. Affidavit must be filed evidencing compliance with this subsection prior to issuance of writ. Circuit court clerk will issue writ of possession upon compliance with this statute unless defendant has requested hearing. (KRS 425.012).

Writ of possession shall contain statutory requirements (KRS 425.046), and if there is request by defendant or intervening party for hearing, writ shall then issue if plaintiff establishes before judicial officer probable validity of claim and files bond for double value of property (KRS 425.031; 425.036; 425.111).

If immediate possession or order restraining defendant from transferring, encumbering, concealing, or impairing value of property is desired, ex parte writ of possession is available if affidavit shows great or irreparable injury as described in KRS 425.076, or plaintiff may at or after filing of motion apply for temporary restraining order which shall be issued if there is showing that there is immediate danger that property will be transferred, concealed or moved or substantially impaired in value. (KRS 425.066, 425.071).

Officer executing writ must retain property for ten days and if defendant does not retake possession, shall deliver same to plaintiff. (KRS 425.010).

Levy.—Officer executing writ of possession shall take possession of property and remove same to place of safe keeping, or upon order of court or officer appointed by court, install keeper for property. (KRS 425.091).

Repossession.—During ten days property is held by officer, defendant may regain possession by executing bond in amount equal to plaintiff's bond or if no judicial determination, then for value of property as stated in plaintiff's complaint. (KRS 425.116).

All bonds shall have sufficient surety and either party may take exception to other's sureties. Plaintiff must take exception within ten days after defendant files bond and defendant must take exception within ten days after writ of possession is executed. (KRS 425.121).

Claims of Third Persons.—Third person claiming property may prevent plaintiff from taking possession or regaining possession in same manner as defendant. (KRS 425.116).

Judgment or Order.—Judgment may include damages for taking and withholding of property. (89 Ky. 388, 12 S.W. 772). Ultimate right to possession must abide result of suit, but if either plaintiff or defendant wrongfully converts or disposes of property so that it cannot be reached, person so wrongfully converting is liable to wronged party for value of property thus wrongfully converted.

Sale.—Property taken under writ of possession may be sold by order of court during pendency of action if, by reason of its perishable nature or cost of keeping it, sale would be beneficial to parties. (KRS 425.101[2]).

SEQUESTRATION:

See categories Business Organizations, topic Corporations; Debtor and Creditor, topics Attachment, Executions, Fraudulent Sales and Conveyances, Garnishment, Receivers.

See category Business Regulation and Commerce, topic Frauds, Statute of.

STAY OF EXECUTION:

See topic Appeal and Error; category Debtor and Creditor, topic Executions.

SUBMISSION OF CONTROVERSY:

Parties to a question that might be the subject of a civil action, may, without action, state the question and the facts upon which it depends, and present a submission thereof to any court which would have jurisdiction if an action had been brought, but it must appear by affidavit that the controversy is real and the proceedings in good faith to determine the rights of the parties. The court must thereupon decide the matter as if an action were pending. (KRS 418.020-418.030).

VENUE:

Venue in civil actions is prescribed by KRS 452.400-452.505 and by KRS 452.700.

See note at head of Digest as to 1998 legislation covered.

See Topical Index in front part of this volume.

VENUE . . . *continued*

(A) Actions affecting real property must generally be brought in county in which land or some part thereof is located: (1) For recovery of land or some estate or interest therein; (2) for partition of land except in settlement of decedent's estate; (3) for sale of land under mortgage, lien or other encumbrance, except in satisfaction of debts of decedent; (4) for injury to land (KRS 452.400) (as distinguished from any injury to crops growing on land) (223 Ky. 751, 4 S.W.2d 717).

(B) Various other actions ordinarily transitory in nature, are localized and must be brought in certain designated counties. (KRS 452.400; 223 Ky. 751, 4 S.W.2d 717).

(C) Other transitory actions must be brought in the county in which defendant resides, or in which one of several defendants resides or is summoned. (KRS 452.480).

Venue for consumer protection action set forth in KRS 367.220.

Venue for determination of disability and guardianship for disabled set forth in KRS 387.520.

Venue for administration of trusts set forth in KRS 386.680-386.690.

Venue in paternity action set forth in KRS 406.151.

Certain exceptions to these general rules exist in case of suits against common carrier or corporation. (KRS 452.450, 452.455).

Change of Venue.—Parties to any suit may by consent have an order in or out of court for its removal to any other court. A party to any civil proceeding triable by a jury in a circuit court may have a change of venue to a circuit court of an adjacent county (KRS 452.050), upon showing that he cannot have fair and impartial trial by filing verified motion setting forth grounds relied on (KRS 452.010; KRS 452.030). Court may hear evidence and arguments at hearing. Granting motion in discretion of court and will be granted when justice so requires. (KRS 452.030). Change of venue may be taken from district court in one county to district court of another county under like limitations and restrictions. (KRS 452.700).

Contract Provisions.—No specific authority on enforceability of provisions in agreement fixing venue. Provisions in agreement fixing forum are given effect unless provisions attempt to oust state of judicial jurisdiction or are unfair or unreasonable. (583 S.W.2d 97; 556 F. Supp. 819).

COURTS AND LEGISLATURE

COURTS:

United States District Courts.—Kentucky is divided into two judicial districts, known as Eastern and Western Districts. (28 USC §97). It is authorized nine District Judges, commissioned respectively, four to serve in Eastern District, four to serve in Western District, and one to serve in either district or both of them. (28 USC §133).

Division of business in each district among judges is determined in accordance with 28 USC §137.

Eastern District.—Clerk's office: Lexington 40501.

Counties Composing Eastern District.—Anderson, Bath, Bell, Boone, Bourbon, Boyd, Boyle, Bracken, Breathitt, Campbell, Carroll, Carter, Clark, Clay, Elliott, Estill, Fayette, Fleming, Floyd, Franklin, Gallatin, Garrard, Grant, Greenup, Harlan, Harrison, Henry, Jackson, Jessamine, Johnson, Kenton, Knott, Knox, Laurel, Lawrence, Lee, Leslie, Letcher, Lewis, Lincoln, Madison, Magoffin, Martin, Mason, McCreary, Menifee, Mercer, Montgomery, Morgan, Nicholas, Owen, Owsley, Pendleton, Perry, Pike, Powell, Pulaski, Robertson, Rockcastle, Rowan, Scott, Shelby, Trimble, Wayne, Whitley, Wolfe and Woodford.

Court sits at Ashland, Covington, Frankfort, Lexington, London and Pikeville.

Western District.—Clerk's office: Louisville 40201.

Counties Composing Western District.—Adair, Allen, Ballard, Barren, Breckinridge, Bullitt, Butler, Caldwell, Calloway, Carlisle, Casey, Clinton, Christian, Crittenden, Cumberland, Daviess, Edmonson, Fulton, Graves, Grayson, Green, Hancock, Hardin, Hart, Henderson, Hickman, Hopkins, Jefferson, Larue, Livingston, Logan, Lyon, Marion, Marshall, McCracken, McLean, Meade, Metcalf, Monroe, Muhlenberg, Nelson, Ohio, Oldham, Russell, Spencer, Simpson, Taylor, Trigg, Todd, Union, Warren, Washington, and Webster.

Court sits at Louisville, Paducah, Owensboro and Bowling Green.

Judicial System of State.—Judicial power of Commonwealth (excepting as to impeachments alone which are brought by House of Representatives and tried by Senate) is vested in one unified Court of Justice which is divided into a Supreme Court, a Court of Appeals, trial courts of general jurisdiction known as Circuit Courts, and trial courts of limited jurisdiction known as District Courts. (Ky. Const. §§109, 66-68).

Supreme Court.—

Seat of Court and Clerk's Office.—In state capitol building, Frankfort, Kentucky 40601.

Jurisdiction.—Supreme Court has appellate jurisdiction only, except it shall have power to issue all writs necessary in aid of its appellate jurisdiction or complete determination of any cause or as may be required to exercise control of Court of Justice. (Ky. Const. §110). Direct appeals from judgments of Circuit Court imposing sentence of death or life imprisonment or imprisonment for 20 years or more mandated by Constitution. Otherwise, Supreme Court to have such appellate jurisdiction as provided by its Rules. (Ky. Const. §110). All causes and proceedings pending before old Court of Appeals as of Jan. 1, 1976 transferred to Supreme Court as of that date, (1974, c. 84) and all records of old Court of Appeals involving proceedings of that court from Oct. 1793 through Dec. 1975 entitled to same dignity as records of Supreme Court from and after Jan. 1, 1976 (KRS 21A.100).

Rule-Making Power.—Supreme Court's power includes prescribing rules governing its appellate jurisdiction, practice and procedure in all judicial courts, and admission to and discipline of members of Bar. (Ky. Const. §117).

Power to Certify Law.—Supreme Court may answer questions of law certified to it by U.S. Supreme Court, or U.S. Court of Appeals or U.S. District Court or by highest appellate court of any other state or District of Columbia on any issue of Kentucky law determinative of cause in requesting court. (CR 76.37).

Court of Appeals.—

Seat of Court and Clerk's Office.—Clerk, Court of Appeals, 360 Democrat Drive, Frankfort, Kentucky 40601-9229.

Jurisdiction.—Court of Appeals exercises appellate jurisdiction from final and interlocutory judgments, convictions, orders or decrees of circuit courts except for judgment dissolving marriage. (Const. §111; KRS 22A.020).

Circuit Courts.—

Seats of Court and Clerks' Offices.—State is divided into 56 judicial circuits (KRS 23A.020) with court held in each county (Ky. Const. §112). Court is held, and clerks' offices located, in county courthouse or in other county owned facilities approved by Supreme Court. (KRS 26A.100).

Circuit courts are courts of record and have original jurisdiction of all matters, both in law and equity, of which jurisdiction is not exclusively delegated to some other tribunal. They have jurisdiction in all cases where title to real estate is in question, in contested probate matters, and cases in equity. Except in cases involving title to or affecting real estate, contested probate matters and matters in equity, value in controversy exclusive of interest and costs must exceed $4,000. (23A.010; 24A.120[1][a]). They have appellate jurisdiction of judgments and final orders of District Courts. (23A.080). Circuit Courts are authorized to review actions and decisions of most administrative agencies, special districts and boards, such proceedings being original actions not appeals. Chief Justice of Supreme Court or Supreme Court may establish family court within any judicial circuit, which as part of circuit court may have either exclusive jurisdiction in all matters assigned to family court, or concurrent jurisdiction with district courts. (Const. §§110, 116; KRS 23A.010[5]; 23A.110[4]; 24A.010[6]; 24A.120[2]). Family court jurisdiction includes cases involving domestic or family issues or dissolution of marriage, child custody, visitation, support and equitable distribution, adoption and termination of parental rights, domestic violence (including emergency protective orders), noncriminal juvenile matters (including juvenile mental inquests and self-consent abortions), paternity and matters under Uniform Reciprocal Enforcement of Support Act (URESA), dependency, abuse, or neglect, and status offenses (including truancy, unmanageable children, and runaways). (KRS 23A.110[3]).

By KRS 26A.020 provisions are made for selection of special judge of Circuit Court, when regular judge is absent, deceased, or incapable of affording party fair or impartial trial or will not impartially decide application for change of venue.

Judicial Circuits.—

Adair County: Twenty-ninth Circuit; court sits at Columbia.

Allen County: Forty-ninth Circuit; court sits at Scottsville.

Anderson County: Fifty-third Circuit; court sits at Lawrenceburg.

Ballard County: First Circuit; court sits at Wickliffe.

Barren County: Forty-third Circuit; court sits at Glasgow.

Bath County: Twenty-first Circuit; court sits at Owingsville.

Bell County: Forty-fourth Circuit; court sits at Pineville and Middlesboro.

Boone County: Fifty-fourth Circuit; court sits at Burlington.

Bourbon County: Fourteenth Circuit; court sits at Paris.

Boyd County: Thirty-second Circuit; court sits at Ashland.

Boyle County: Fiftieth Circuit; court sits at Danville.

Bracken County: Nineteenth Circuit; court sits at Brooksville.

Breathitt County: Thirty-ninth Circuit; court sits at Jackson.

Breckinridge County: Forty-sixth Circuit; court sits at Hardinsburg.

Bullitt County: Fifty-fifth Circuit; court sits at Shepherdsville.

Butler County: Thirty-eighth Circuit; court sits at Morgantown.

Caldwell County: Fifty-sixth Circuit; court sits at Princeton.

Calloway County: Forty-second Circuit; court sits at Murray.

Campbell County: Seventeenth Circuit; court sits at Newport. Part of session held at Alexandria.

Carlisle County: First Circuit; court sits at Bardwell.

Carroll County: Fifteenth Circuit; court sits at Carrollton.

Carter County: Thirty-seventh Circuit; court sits at Grayson.

Casey County: Twenty-ninth Circuit; court sits at Liberty.

Christian County: Third Circuit; court sits at Hopkinsville.

Clark County: Twenty-fifth Circuit; court sits at Winchester.

Clay County: Forty-first Circuit; court sits at Manchester.

Clinton County: Fortieth Circuit; court sits at Albany.

Crittenden County: Fifth Circuit; court sits at Marion.

Cumberland County: Twenty-ninth Circuit; court sits at Burkesville.

Daviess County: Sixth Circuit; court sits at Owensboro.

Edmonson County: Thirty-eighth Circuit; court sits at Brownsville.

Elliott County: Thirty-seventh Circuit; court sits at Sandy Hook.

Estill County: Twenty-third Circuit; court sits at Irvine.

Fayette County: Twenty-second Circuit; court sits at Lexington.

Fleming County: Nineteenth Circuit; court sits at Flemingsburg.

Floyd County: Thirty-first Circuit; court sits at Prestonburg.

Franklin County: Forty-eighth Circuit; court sits at Frankfort.

Fulton County: First Circuit; court sits at Hickman.

Gallatin County: Fifty-fourth Circuit; court sits at Warsaw.

Garrard County: Thirteenth Circuit; court sits at Lancaster.

Grant County: Fifteenth Circuit; court sits at Williamstown.

Graves County: Fifty-second Circuit; court sits at Mayfield.

Grayson County: Forty-sixth Circuit; court sits at Leitchfield.

Green County: Eleventh Circuit; court sits at Greensburg.

Greenup County: Twentieth Circuit; court sits at Greenup.

Hancock County: Thirty-eighth Circuit; court sits at Hawesville.

Hardin County: Ninth Circuit; court sits at Elizabethtown.

Harlan County: Twenty-sixth Circuit; court sits at Harlan.

Harrison County: Eighteenth Circuit; court sits at Cynthiana.

Hart County: Tenth Circuit; court sits at Munfordville.

Henderson County: Fifty-first Circuit; court sits at Henderson.

Henry County: Twelfth Circuit; court sits at Newcastle.

See note at head of Digest as to 1998 legislation covered.

See Topical Index in front part of this volume.

COURTS . . . *continued*

Hickman County: First Circuit; court sits at Clinton.
Hopkins County: Fourth Circuit; court sits at Madisonville.
Jackson County: Forty-first Circuit; court sits at McKee.
Jefferson County: Thirtieth Circuit; court sits at Louisville.
Jessamine County: Thirteenth Circuit; court sits at Nicholasville.
Johnson County: Twenty-fourth Circuit; court sits at Paintsville.
Kenton County: Sixteenth Circuit; court sits at Covington. Part of session held at Independence.
Knott County: Thirty-sixth Circuit; court sits at Hindman.
Knox County: Twenty-seventh Circuit; court sits at Barbourville.
Larue County: Tenth Circuit; court sits at Hodgenville.
Laurel County: Twenty-seventh Circuit; court sits at London.
Lawrence County: Twenty-fourth Circuit; court sits at Louisa.
Lee County: Twenty-third Circuit; court sits at Beattyville.
Leslie County: Forty-first Circuit; court sits at Hyden.
Letcher County: Forty-seventh Circuit; court sits at Whitesburg.
Lewis County: Twentieth Circuit; court sits at Vanceburg.
Lincoln County: Twenty-eighth Circuit; court sits at Stanford.
Livingston County: Fifty-sixth Circuit; court sits at Smithland.
Logan County: Seventh Circuit; court sits at Russellville.
Lyon County: Third Circuit; court sits at Eddyville.
Madison County: Twenty-fifth Circuit; court sits at Richmond.
Magoffin County: Thirty-sixth Circuit; court sits at Salyersville.
Marion County: Eleventh Circuit; court sits at Lebanon.
Marshall County: Forty-second Circuit; court sits at Benton.
Martin County: Twenty-fourth Circuit; court sits at Inez.
Mason County: Nineteenth Circuit; court sits at Maysville.
McCracken County: Second Circuit; court sits at Paducah.
McCreary County: Thirty-fourth Circuit; court sits at Whitley City.
McLean County: Forty-fifth Circuit; court sits at Calhoun.
Meade County: Forty-sixth Circuit; court sits at Brandenburg.
Menifee County: Twenty-first Circuit; court sits at Frenchburg.
Mercer County: Fiftieth Circuit; court sits at Harrodsburg.
Metcalfe County: Forty-third Circuit; court sits at Edmonton.
Monroe County: Twenty-ninth Circuit; court sits at Tompkinsville.
Montgomery County: Twenty-first Circuit; court sits at Mt. Sterling.
Morgan County: Thirty-seventh Circuit; court sits at West Liberty.
Muhlenberg County: Forty-fifth Circuit; court sits at Greenville.
Nelson County: Tenth Circuit; court sits at Bardstown.
Nicholas County: Eighteenth Circuit; court sits at Carlisle.
Ohio County: Thirty-eighth Circuit; court sits at Hartford.
Oldham County: Twelfth Circuit; court sits at Lagrange.
Owen County: Fifteenth Circuit; court sits at Owenton.
Owsley County: Twenty-third Circuit; court sits at Booneville.
Pendleton County: Eighteenth Circuit; court sits at Falmouth.
Perry County: Thirty-third Circuit; court sits at Hazard.
Pike County: Thirty-fifth Circuit; court sits at Pikeville.
Powell County: Thirty-ninth Circuit; court sits at Stanton.
Pulaski County: Twenty-eighth Circuit; court sits at Somerset.
Robertson County: Eighteenth Circuit; court sits at Mount Olivet.
Rockcastle County: Twenty-eighth Circuit; court sits at Mount Vernon.
Rowan County: Twenty-first Circuit; court sits at Morehead.
Russell County: Fortieth Circuit; court sits at Jamestown.
Scott County: Fourteenth Circuit; court sits at Georgetown.
Shelby County: Fifty-third Circuit; court sits at Shelbyville.
Simpson County: Forty-ninth Circuit; court sits at Franklin.
Spencer County: Fifty-third Circuit; court sits at Taylorsville.
Taylor County: Eleventh Circuit; court sits at Campbellsville.
Todd County: Seventh Circuit; court sits at Elkton.
Trigg County: Fifty-sixth Circuit; court sits at Cadiz.
Trimble County: Twelfth Circuit; court sits at Bedford.
Union County: Fifth Circuit; court sits at Morganfield.
Warren County: Eighth Circuit; court sits at Bowling Green.
Washington County: Eleventh Circuit; court sits at Springfield.
Wayne County: Fortieth Circuit; court sits at Monticello.
Webster County: Fifth Circuit; court sits at Dixon.
Whitley County: Thirty-fourth Circuit; court sits at Williamsburg and Corbin (KRS 23.060).
Wolfe County: Thirty-ninth Circuit; court sits at Campton.
Woodford County: Fourteenth Circuit; court sits at Versailles.

District Courts.—

Seats of Court and Clerks' Offices.—State is divided into 59 judicial districts (KRS 24A.030) with same boundaries as judicial circuits except that: Nelson County, part of tenth judicial circuit, is fifty-seventh judicial district; Marshall County, part of forty-second judicial circuit, is fifty-eighth judicial district; and Ballard and Carlisle Counties, part of first judicial circuit, are fifty-ninth judicial district. See subhead Circuit Courts, catchline Judicial Circuits, supra. Court is held in each county. (Ky. Const. §113).

Clerks of circuit courts also serve as clerks for District Courts. (KRS 30A.010[1]). District Courts are courts of record having continuous session and exercising limited original jurisdiction. (KRS 24A.010).

Jurisdiction.—District Courts exercise exclusive original jurisdiction of all: (1) Offenses designated as misdemeanors, unless joined in indictment with felony, and all violations of city or county ordinances, except those denominated as felonies or capital offenses or offenses punishable by imprisonment in penitentiary by state statutes (KRS 24A.110; 26A.030[1]); (2) all civil cases in which amount in controversy does not exceed $4,000, exclusive of interest and costs, except matters affecting title to real estate and matters of equity (KRS 24A.120); (3) uncontested probate matters (KRS 24A.120); and (4) all matters relating to juveniles or minors (KRS 24A.130), except for matters for which jurisdiction is vested in other courts, such as child support matters incident to dissolution of marriage (divorce) proceedings (KRS 403.210). District Courts exercise jurisdiction to examine any charge alleging felony or capital offense (to determine if probable cause exists for trial in Circuit Court) and may upon motion and for good cause shown, reduce charge of felony to misdemeanor. (KRS 24A.110[3], [4]).

Fees.—Filing fees and miscellaneous costs for civil cases filed in Circuit Court and District Court are set by rules of Supreme Court. (KRS 23A.200; KRS 24A.170). Filing fee for civil complaint in Circuit Court is $95 in nonjury action and $120 in jury action; filing fee for civil complaint in District Court is $40. Where amount in controversy is $1,500 or less (Small Claims Division of District Court), filing fee is $15, and $20 filing fee applies to cases not filed in Small Claims Court in which amount in controversy is $500 or less. $25 filing fee applies to probate, guardianship, paternity and certain other matters. (KRS 23A.200; 24A.170). Jury fee for civil trial in Circuit Court is $25 (see supra) and jury fee for civil trial in District Court is $12.50. (KRS 29A.330). Additional fees will be charged for additional filings and other matters and court is authorized to require payment of additional costs in cases requiring extraordinary services. Filing fee is $55 for appeal from District Court to Circuit Court; $55 fee also applies where case is transferred from District Court to Circuit Court when counterclaim or cross-claim exceeding jurisdiction of District Court is filed. In civil cases, clerk may require additional deposit of $5 to cover plaintiff's fees. (KRS 64.080). Court costs for criminal cases in Circuit Court are $75. (KRS 23A.205). Parties and counsel should consult clerk of courts above for total of applicable fees and costs.

Small Claims Courts.—Small claims division is established in each district court (see subhead District Courts, supra) with civil jurisdiction concurrent with district court (except for libel, slander, alienation of affections, malicious prosecution and abuse of process claims) when damages or personal property claimed do not exceed $1,500 exclusive of interest and costs or when claim involves contract or agreement relating to purchase of goods or services of value of not in excess of $1,500 exclusive of interest and costs. (KRS 24A.230). Division may enter all orders or judgments authorized for district courts except for provisional remedies, such as attachments, garnishments, replevin, etc. (KRS 24A.230). Assigned claims and class action claims may not be filed in division (KRS 24A.240[2]); persons engaged in business of lending money at interest and collection agents may not file claims for collection in division (KRS 24A.240[3]), and no person may file more than 25 claims per business location in division in any one year (KRS 24A.250[1]). Attorneys are permitted to represent parties but their participation is not required. (KRS 24A.240[1]).

Action commenced by filing claim on form provided by clerk of division where defendant or his agent resides or is doing business (KRS 24A.260) (Quaere—service on nonresident defendants. See category Civil Actions and Procedure, topic Process, subhead Long Arm Statute.). Upon filing of claim, court sets time for hearing on date not less than 20 nor more than 40 days after service of process and clerk institutes process by sending notice as authorized by statute or procedural rule. (KRS 24A.280[2]). See category Civil Actions and Procedure, topic Process. Continuances granted only in interests of fairness and justice. (KRS 24A.280[3]). Counterclaims stating facts showing claim arising out of same subject matter as plaintiff's claim and within jurisdictional limits of division heard with plaintiff's claim. (KRS 24A.290). No other formal pleadings necessary and no pretrial discovery allowed. (KRS 24A.300). Action removed to regular docket of district court if counterclaim is filed which exceeds jurisdiction of small claims division, or if defendant entitled to jury trial claims right to jury, or if court deems action too complex for simplified procedures. (KRS 24A.310). All claims in division are tried to court without jury (KRS 24A.320) and hearing and disposition of matters is informal (KRS 24A.330). Appeal from judgment of division lies to circuit court in judicial circuit where division is located as in other appeals from district court. (KRS 24A.340).

LEGISLATURE:

Meets biennially in Jan. of even years (Const. §36) for no more than 60 legislative days per session (Const. §42).

Special or Extraordinary Sessions.—Governor may call special sessions limited to subjects identified by Governor in proclamation. (Const. §80).

Initiative.—No provision for.

Referendum allowed with respect to legislation classifying personal property for ad valorem taxation at a rate lower than applies to real estate. (Const. §171).

Lobbyists.—Lobbying defined in KRS 6.611(26). Legislative agents, i.e., lobbyists, and their employees required to register with Kentucky Legislative Ethics Commission by KRS 6.807. Legislative ethics regulated by KRS 6.601 to 6.829. Executive agency lobbying and registration regulated by KRS 11A.201 to 11A.246.

REPORTS:

Official Reports.—Volumes of reported decisions are named and cover periods, as follows:

Hughes, one volume, 1785-1801; Sneed, one volume, 1801-1805; Hardin, one volume, 1805-1808; Bibb, four volumes, 1808-1817; A. K. Marshall, three volumes, 1817-1821; Littell, five volumes, 1821-1824; Littell's Selected Cases, one volume, 1795-1821; T. B. Monroe, seven volumes, 1824-1828; J. J. Marshall, seven volumes, 1828-1832; Dana, nine volumes, 1832-1840; Ben Monroe, 18 volumes, 1840-1858; Metcalf, four volumes, 1858-1863; Duvall, two volumes, 1863-1865; Bush, 14 volumes, 1865-1879; Kentucky Reports, cited Ky., since 1879. Official Ky. Reports and advance sheets were discontinued in 1951, with volume 314.

Unofficial Reports. —Kentucky Law Reporter, in 32 volumes reported all decisions of Kentucky Court of Appeals and Superior Court (which no longer exists) from 1880 to 1908.

Kentucky Opinions, in 13 volumes, contains decisions of Court of Appeals not officially reported, from 1864 to 1886.

See note at head of Digest as to 1998 legislation covered.

See Topical Index in front part of this volume.

KY – 19

REPORTS . . . *continued*

Decisions of Kentucky Court of Appeals and Kentucky Supreme Court from June, 1886 to date are reported in Southwestern Reporter and in separately bound Kentucky Decisions (West Pub. Co.).

Digests.—Kentucky Digest (West Pub. Co.) covers all reported Kentucky cases.

STATUTES:

Official compilation of Kentucky Revised Statutes dated 1970 is supplemented with periodic replacement volumes and annual pocket supplements. Bobbs-Merrill Publishing Co. has been designated publisher of the official compilation under supervision of Legislative Research Commission.

An unofficial edition of Revised Statutes, with supplements, is published by Banks-Baldwin Law Pub. Co.

Session laws published by Legislative Research Commission as Kentucky Acts. Kentucky Rules of Civil Procedure and Rules of Criminal Procedure promulgated by Supreme Court, with amendments, are published with Kentucky Revised Statutes and in separate volumes by West Pub. Co. and by Banks-Baldwin.

Uniform acts which have been adopted are: Anatomical Gift (1970); Arbitration (1984); Business Corporation, revised (1988); Certification of Questions of Law (1978); Child Custody Jurisdiction (1980); Commercial Code (1960, 1990); Conservation Easement (1988); Controlled Substances (1972); Criminal Extradition (1960); Disclaimer of Transfers by Will, Intestacy or Appointment (1974); Disclaimer of Transfers Under Nontestamentary Instruments (1980); Disposition of Community Property Rights at Death (1974); †Division of Income for Tax Purposes (1953, 1985); †Durable Power of Attorney (1972); Revised Enforcement of Foreign Judgments Act (1990); †Fiduciaries (1930); Insurers Liquidation (1920); *Interstate Family Support (1996); Judicial Notice of Foreign Laws (1942); Limited Partnership (1988); Management of Institutional Funds Act (1976); †Marriage and Divorce (1972); †Motor Vehicle Accident Reparations (1974); Partnership (1954); Paternity (1964); Photographic Copies of Business and Public Records as Evidence (1952); Revised Principal and Income (1992); *Reciprocal Enforcement of Support (Revised) (1972); Recognition of Acknowledgments (1970); Rendition of Prisoners as Witnesses in Criminal Proceedings (1976); Residential Landlord and Tenant (1974; 1984, available for adoption by units of local government only); †Rules of Evidence (1992); †Securities (1961, 1972); Simultaneous Death (1942); Testamentary Additions to Trusts Act (1966); To Secure Attendance of Witnesses from Within or Without a State in Criminal Proceedings (1952); Trade Secrets (1990); Transfers to Minors Act (1986); Trustees' Powers (1976); †Veterans' Guardianship as Revised (1942).

†Adopted with significant variations or modifications. See appropriate topics as to Acts within scope of Digests volume.

*Revised Uniform Reciprocal Enforcement of Support Act repealed in favor of Uniform Interstate Family Support Act, KRS 407.5101 to 407.5902, but only effective upon date United States Congress requires adoption of latter uniform act. (KRS 407.480).

For text of Uniform Acts falling within the scope of the Martindale-Hubbell Law Digests see Uniform and Model Acts section.

UNIFORM LAWS:

See topic Statutes.

CRIMINAL LAW

BAIL:

See topic Criminal Law.

CRIMINAL LAW:

Principal criminal laws of Commonwealth found in penal code in KRS cs. 500 to 534, and in sections of Unified Juvenile Code, KRS cs. 600 to 645. These laws are supplemented by specific prohibitions in KRS cs. 431 to 441 and at ends of other KRS Chapters, such as KRS 189.990 to 189.933 which provide penalties for violation of regulatory provisions previously set forth in KRS c. 189, traffic regulations. Most matters of procedure governed by separate Rules of Criminal Procedure (R Cr.) and sections of Unified Juvenile Code.

All offenses may be prosecuted by indictment and felonies must be so prosecuted. (Ky. Const. §12). All offenses, except those required by law to be prosecuted by indictment, may be prosecuted by information, complaint or uniform citation. (R Cr. 6.02).

Indictment is found by grand jury, presented to court in presence of grand jury, and warrant or summons issued thereon. (R Cr. 5.20, 6.52).

Bail.—All prisoners shall be bailable upon sufficient security, except in cases of capital offenses when proof is evident or presumption of guilt great; habeas corpus shall not be suspended except during rebellion, invasion or when public safety requires. (Ky. Const. §16). Procedures for bail before and after conviction pending appeal provided in R Cr. 4.02 to 4.36. Commercial bail bond business is prohibited. (KRS 439.560).

Uniform Criminal Extradition Act in effect. (KRS 440.150 to 440.420).

Interstate Compact for Supervision of Parolees and Probationers in effect. (KRS 439.560).

DEBTOR AND CREDITOR

ASSIGNMENTS:

All bonds, bills or notes for money or property are assignable. (KRS 371.040).

Any assignment, pledge or other transaction (regardless of form) intended to create a security interest in personal property, including goods, documents, instruments, chattel paper, accounts receivable or contract rights, is governed by Uniform Commercial Code. (KRS 355.9-101 et seq.). The same is true as to any sale of accounts receivable, contract rights or chattel paper. See category Business Regulation and Commerce, topic Commercial Code.

All the foregoing claims are assignable at law. In addition, other claims have been held assignable in equity, such as claims to fund in court (231 Ky. 298, 21 S.W.2d 457), claims of insurance companies, by way of subrogation, to value of property destroyed by tort (218 Fed. 315) and claims for value of property wrongfully taken by defendant's tort (139 Ky. 402, 58 S.W. 987).

Unliquidated claims for personal injuries due to defendant's tort have been held not assignable either at law or in equity. (228 Ky. 679, 15 S.W.2d 461). Once claim is liquidated, it is assignable by subrogation. (517 S.W.2d 737).

Suit on assigned claims in cases not covered by KRS 371.040, must be brought in name of assignor for use and benefit of assignee, or assignor must be made party defendant. Suit by assignee against assignor, where claim has been assigned, must state amount paid by assignee to assignor and seek to recover that amount. (KRS 371.050). Both assignor and assignee must be joined in suit on claim assignable in equity. (231 Ky. 298, 21 S.W.2d 457). Due diligence in prosecution of original obligor is necessary in order to hold assignor. If note is nonnegotiable, maker must be prosecuted to insolvency at first term of court after maturity of note. (113 Ky. 147, 67 S.W. 260).

Instrument Transferring Title.—No particular form of written instrument is required, and no writing is necessary except in case of (1) assignments between husband and wife, (2) assignments of wages, (3) assignments covered by Uniform Commercial Code, and (4) assignments of notes secured by recorded instruments.

Assignment by endorsement of obligations to pay money or like obligations is sufficient to pass title between the parties. (KRS 371.040).

Recording is not required except: (1) In case of transfer of personal property between husband and wife (KRS 404.020), (2) where lien notes secured by recorded instrument are assigned (KRS 382.290), and (3) for transfer of property without transfer of possession (KRS 378.040). Assignment of recorded liens may be made by assignor personally noting said assignment on recorded instrument in clerk's office which is to be attested by clerk or by recordable instrument which sets forth date of note assigned, brief description of note, name and address of assignee, and deed book and page of instrument wherein lien or mortgage is recorded and complies with clerk's indexing system. (KRS 382.290; 382.335; 382.430). Filing required where assignment covered by Uniform Commercial Code.

Notice.—No notice to debtor or obligor is required for validity of assignment. Giving of notice of assignment of nonnegotiable bonds, bills or notes may affect ability of nonconsumer obligor to assert defenses he has against original obligee against assignee. See KRS 371.040; 355.9-206(1). Consumer obligor's defenses may not be so affected. See category Business Regulation and Commerce, topic Consumer Protection, subhead Holder in Due Course.

Assignment between husband and wife is not valid, as to third persons, unless in writing, acknowledged and recorded as in case of chattel mortgages. (KRS 404.020; 205 Ky. 450, 266 S.W. 43). This applies to intangibles as well as tangibles. (285 Ky. 125, 147 S.W.2d 67).

Assignment of Wages.—No assignment of wages to be earned or paid in the future where the consideration is less than $200 is valid unless contract is in writing stating terms, date of maturity of debt, and full name and address of assignee, or if assignee is nonresident, name and address of some person in Kentucky upon whom process may be served. The assignment is not valid except as to fixed or definite amount of wages earned or to be earned within 90 days from date of instrument, and must be assented to by employer to be valid against him. Penalty for violation by assignee is fine of $50 to $200. National and state banks, trust companies and credit unions are exempt from foregoing provisions. (KRS 371.110-371.150).

Person licensed to engage in small loan business and taking assignment of future wages as security may not collect from borrower's employer, at any one time, more than 10% of amount then owing to borrower by employer (KRS 288.570).

ATTACHMENT:

Actions in Which Allowed.—General attachment may be had, where grounds therefor exist, in any action for recovery of money. (KRS 425.301). Special provisions govern procedure for prejudgment attachment or garnishment of earnings. (See topic Garnishment, subhead Earnings.)

Courts Which May Issue Writ.—Writs may be issued from circuit courts or district court which has jurisdiction over subject matter of claim for money. (KRS 425.301).

In Whose Favor Writ May Issue.—Remedy by attachment is available to any plaintiff, including nonresident and foreign corporation.

Against Whom Writ May Issue.—Property of any defendant in civil action is subject to attachment, unless exempted by statute. (See topic Exemptions.) Writ may issue against any person holding property of defendant (KRS 425.316); as for example funds due governmental employees (KRS 427.130).

Claims on Which Writ May Issue.—Claim must be for recovery of money. It is not necessary that claim sued on should have accrued or become payable in Kentucky, if otherwise court has jurisdiction.

Before debt or liability on contract becomes due, equitable action may be brought for indemnity, and attachment against defendant's property may be obtained by order of court on grounds similar to those hereinafter stated and after bond given. (KRS 425.306).

Attachment may also be issued in action for recovery of money due on contract, judgment for award, if defendant therein has no property in this state subject to execution or not enough thereof to satisfy plaintiff's demand and collection of such demand will be endangered by delay in obtaining judgment and return of no property found. (KRS 425.301[2]).

ATTACHMENT . . . *continued*

Limitations Upon Right to Attach.—Attention is called to limitations imposed by following laws, upon right to attach goods covered by negotiable documents unless such documents are impounded by court: (a) Uniform Commercial Code (KRS 355.7-602); (b) U.S. Code, title 49, §103, affecting order bills of lading issued in interstate commerce; and (c) securities transferable in manner set forth in Uniform Commercial Code (KRS 355.8-320).

Grounds of attachment, other than as heretofore stated, are that defendant, or one or more of several defendants: (1) Is foreign corporation or nonresident of state; or (2) has been absent from state for four months; or (3) has departed from state with intent to defraud his creditors; or (4) has left county of his residence to avoid service of summons; or (5) so conceals himself that summons cannot be served upon him; or (6) is about to remove or has removed his property, or material part thereof out of this state, not leaving enough therein to satisfy plaintiff's claim, or claims of said defendant's creditors; or (7) has sold, conveyed, or otherwise disposed of his property, or suffered or permitted it to be sold, with fraudulent intent to cheat, hinder or delay his creditors; or (8) is about to sell, convey, or otherwise dispose of his property with such intent. But attachment may not be granted on sole ground that defendant is foreign corporation or nonresident of this state except in action on debt or demand arising on contract or judgment or award. (KRS 425.301; 154 Ky. 162, 156 S.W. 1079).

Proceedings to Obtain.—Person seeking prejudgment order of attachment must file written motion for order under oath and set forth nature of plaintiff's claim, that it is just, sum plaintiff believes he ought to recover and existence of any ground for issuance set forth in KRS 425.306. (KRS 425.307). Order may issue ex parte by judge, commissioner or other officer appointed by court for these purposes if plaintiff shows by affidavit that great and irreparable injury will result if issuance of order delayed until hearing held and posts bond with one or more sufficient sureties. (KRS 425.308; KRS 425.309). Otherwise plaintiff must deliver written demand, along with copy of complaint, motion and summons, to debtor or send them by registered or certified mail, return receipt requested, to debtor's last known residence not less than seven nor more than 60 days before order sought. Demand shall give debtor seven days to petition court for hearing or pay claim in full and shall state that unless hearing requested or claim paid, order will be sought to subject debtor's property to payment of claim. Affidavit of compliance with this procedure necessary. (KRS 425.301).

Attachment Bond.—Must be in amount not less than double amount of plaintiff's claim and be executed by one or more sufficient sureties. (KRS 425.309). Surety not required on bond posted by any domestic bank, savings and loan institution, or member of Farm Credit System as defined in 12 U.S.C. §2002. (KRS 425.001).

Levy.—Statutes provide no procedure for levy of order of attachment. General practice follows procedure for levy of writ of possession. See category Civil Actions and Procedure, topic Replevin, subhead Levy.

Indemnity.—Bond required of plaintiff to obtain writ of attachment covers damages sustained by defendant which are proximately caused by operation of levy of writ of attachment. (KRS 425.309).

Lien and Priorities.—Several orders of attachment against earnings have priority according to date of service on employer. (KRS 425.506[2]). Former statute setting priorities between different attachments on other property has been repealed and no corresponding new statute has been enacted. Rule appears to be that priorities determined by date of levy upon property (42 Ky. 199) unless several deliveries made to same officer and his deputies in which case priority governed by dates of delivery to officer and deputies. (45 Ky. 414).

Notice Required to Preserve Lien of Attachment.—In order to preserve lien of attachments upon real estate of defendants affected thereby, memorandum giving style and nature of case, amount of attachment, names of parties, and description of real estate attached, must be filed in clerk's office of county in which land is located. (KRS 382.440-382.470; 345 F. Supp. 342).

Release of Property.—Defendant may dissolve attachment by posting bond with sufficient surety equal to plaintiff's claim. (KRS 425.309).

Vacation or Modification.—Defendant may file motion for order quashing attachment and is entitled to immediate hearing. (KRS 425.302).

Sale.—Statutes provide no procedure for sale of attached property. General practice follows procedure for sale of property subject to writ of possession. See category Civil Actions and Procedure, topic Replevin, subhead Levy.

Third Party Claims.—Statutes do not provide procedures for third party claims. See category Civil Actions and Procedure, topic Replevin, subhead Claims of Third Persons for comparable procedures with respect to writs of possession.

CREDITORS' SUITS:

General principles of equity apply to creditors' suits, subject to extension of such principles: (1) By KRS 426.381, which authorizes proceeding in equity to enforce, by attachment without bond, judgment upon which there has been execution issued and returned and property, if any, found is sufficient to satisfy judgment and (2) by KRS 378.060 to 378.100 which constitute preferential transfer in contemplation of insolvency as assignment of all property of debtor for benefit of all creditors under jurisdiction of circuit court. See also topics Fraudulent Sales and Conveyances, Garnishment; category Estates and Trusts, topic Executors and Administrators.

EXECUTIONS:

Writs of execution may be issued upon any judgment rendered by court of record and not barred by limitation. (KRS 426.010; KRS 426.035).

Kinds of execution are: (1) Fieri facias or writ of execution upon personalty and realty (KRS 426.020 and CR 69.03); (2) judicial sale of mortgaged real property, see category Mortgages, topic Mortgages of Real Property, subhead Enforcement; (3) post judgment attachment (KRS 426.010 and CR 69.02); (4) post judgment garnishment (KRS 425.501 and CR 69.02); and (5) venditoni exponas on sale of property by sheriff or other person (KRS 426.440 and CR 70). Statute preserves all other appropriate writs of execution allowable by ancient practice of courts of chancery (KRS 426.430) but body execution probably not preserved. See subhead Body Execution, infra.

Exemptions.—See topic Exemptions.

Time for Issuance.—Execution may issue at any time within 15 years after judgment (KRS 413.090), except that unless otherwise ordered by the court, no execution may be issued on any judgment until after ten days from its rendition (KRS 426.030). Execution upon surety required within seven years. (KRS 413.220). As to execution upon decedent's estate, see category Estates and Trusts, topic Executors and Administrators, subhead Presentation of Claims.

Stay.—Except in certain cases, such as judgments enforcing a lien or judgments against a lawyer or agent or collecting officer for money collected and withheld and certain other cases specified by law, an execution may be replevied for three months, at any time before sale, by the defendant giving to the officer an obligation to the plaintiff, with good security for the amount thereof, including interest, costs, and half commissions. If replevin bond is not paid at maturity, execution may issue against the estate of defendant and surety, upon which no security can be taken, and sale must be for cash. No other stay of execution is provided for by law. Similar bond to stay execution of judgment may be executed in clerk's office, before execution issues, for debt, interest and costs. (KRS 426.450 to 426.480).

Lien.—The ordinary writ of execution (fieri facias) is not a lien upon either personalty or realty of the execution defendant except from the time it is placed in the hands of the proper officer for execution. (KRS 426.120). In order to preserve such lien as against subsequent purchasers or lessees or incumbrances of defendant's real estate without notice, a memorandum thereof, giving necessary details, must be filed in the county clerk's office of the county in which the land is located. This applies also to executions issued by United States courts. (KRS 382.440-382.470). For judgment lien, see category Civil Actions and Procedure, topic Judgments.

Levy.—Levying officer must make return to court which specifies: (1) execution satisfied; (2) no property found; (3) property sold; or (4) property not sold for lack of bidders. (KRS 426.040). Special provisions are made as to executions levied on livestock (KRS 426.310) or on property jointly owned by defendant and another (KRS 426.680).

Officer holding execution must levy on sufficient property to make amount of execution, and sell first personalty (not exempt) and next land to raise amount of execution. Sale must be on terms of three months time, and purchaser must execute bond with good surety, to be approved by the officer, bearing interest from date of sale.

Return.—All executions are returnable within 30 days after levy but in no event more than 60 days after issue. (KRS 426.040).

When execution issues from court of another county, the sheriff must report any levy thereof upon land for record in the circuit court clerk's office of his county. (KRS 426.110).

Priorities.—Executions issued against same person take precedence in order in which they come into hands of officer. (KRS 70.370; 426.120).

Claims of Third Persons.—A sale under execution of real or personal property on which a bona fide encumbrance created prior to the execution exists gives to the purchaser no title to the property but a mere lien thereon, subject to the encumbrance, for the purchase price under execution sale with 10% per annum interest from date of execution sale. Such lien is enforceable in equity, and execution defendant may redeem property by payment of original encumbrance and discharge of purchaser's lien. (KRS 426.290).

Joint owner may not be deprived of property levied on except for purpose of inventory and appraisal; execution creditor has lien on property enforceable in equity and, upon affidavit that creditor believes property is about to be removed from county, sold, or disposed of, court may order officer to possess property unless forthcoming bond executed. (KRS 426.680).

Satisfaction.—See subheads Levy, supra; Sale, infra.

Sale.—Any interest in land, legal or equitable, vested or contingent, in possession, reversion or remainder, absolute or defeasible, may be taken and sold under execution. (KRS 426.190). Personal property is to be levied on and sold prior to levy on and sale of real property. (KRS 426.130).

Officer making sale of land under execution must sell at the court house door of the county in which the land lies. He can sell only so much land as will satisfy the execution. Before making the sale, he must advertise the time and place thereof, by written notice, describing the land, posted at the court house door and in three other public places in the vicinity of the land to be sold, for fifteen days next preceding the sale. (KRS 426.200). Defendant who has interest in several tracts of land can designate tract to be sold. (KRS 426.210). Sheriff will convey title of land to purchaser if land not redeemed and redemption period had expired. (KRS 426.250). Purchaser may file motion to obtain possession of land. (KRS 426.260).

Personal estate may be sold at or near the place of levy, ten days after levy thereon, provided time and place of sale and description of property be first advertised by posting written or printed notices ten days preceding, at three of the most public places in vicinity of place of sale. (KRS 426.160).

All public sales of any kind of property, the appraised value of which is $100 or more, when sold under execution or judgment or decree, must, unless otherwise agreed by the parties thereto, be advertised in a newspaper of bona fide circulation (paid subscriptions) published in the county of such sale at least once a week for three consecutive weeks next preceding day of sale; provided that in counties where there is a daily newspaper, publication of such notice of sale for three consecutive days (excluding Sunday) next preceding day of sale is sufficient. Advertisement must state time, place and terms of sale and describe property to be sold. (KRS 426.560).

Redemption.—Land sold under execution must be appraised before the sale by disinterested intelligent householders of the county appointed by the officer making the sale and if it does not bring two-thirds of such appraised value, the execution defendant has a right to redeem it within one year from the sale by paying the

See note at head of Digest as to 1998 legislation covered.

See Topical Index in front part of this volume.

KY – 21

EXECUTIONS . . . *continued*

purchase price at the execution sale with 10% per annum interest thereon. Upon occurrence of sale for less than two-thirds appraised value, judgment debtor entitled to remain in possession until right of redemption expires and purchaser is entitled to deed and possession at that time. (KRS 426.200-426.250).

Such right of redemption may itself be sold under execution. (KRS 426.240).

Mortgage and Other Sales Distinguishable.—Real estate sold under judgment or decretal sale for debt other than on execution must in like manner be appraised before sale and is likewise subject to redemption upon substantially same terms with like right to sell right of redemption. (KRS 426.520-426.540).

There is no right of redemption of personal property sold under execution or decretal sale. Purchaser at sale of land for less than two-thirds appraised value shall receive immediate writ of possession and deed containing lien in favor of defendant reflecting his right to redeem during year. (KRS 426.530).

Supplementary Proceedings.—After return of "no property found": (1) Execution plaintiff may bring equitable action based on such return, in which attachment may be issued without affidavit or bond and made writ of garnishment. Full disclosure by garnishee and execution defendant may be compelled and court may compel surrender of any property discovered by appropriate writ or process of contempt. (KRS 426.381). (2) Execution plaintiff, by amended and supplemental petition in same action, may have judgment redocketed and join with judgment debtor any person believed to be indebted to him or to hold money or property for him. Thereupon case is transferred to equity and court may enforce full discovery and subject to judgment any property discovered. (KRS 426.381). (3) Execution, plaintiff may file petition in equity to subject to judgment any real estate to which judgment defendant has legal or equitable title, even though property is in adverse possession of another, who must be made defendant. (KRS 372.070). (4) Court may enforce surrender of property, money or securities therefor discovered during action or during enforcement of judgment proceedings and may use its contempt power to enforce surrender thereof from defendant. (KRS 426.384). Garnishees must appear and disclose sums owing to defendant and upon failure to do so may be proceeded against as in contempt. (KRS 425.511).

Judgment plaintiff may also file in office of clerk of court which rendered the judgment an affidavit showing date of judgment, amount due thereon and that a named garnishee is indebted to the judgment defendant or holds property belonging to him. Thereupon plaintiff may obtain a writ of garnishment without bond and proceed as in the case of a garnishment before judgment. (KRS 426.511). See topic Garnishment.

Revivor of Execution.—Death of defendant after sale of his property under execution does not call for revivor. It must be conveyed as if defendant were living. The levy of an execution, under which sale has not taken place, is not discharged by defendant's death. It is merely suspended thereby until revived as in case of proceedings taken to revive judgments. (KRS 426.555).

Death of one defendant does not prevent execution against a surviving defendant. (KRS 426.553).

Death of judgment plaintiff does not require same proceedings for revivor of execution as in case of death of judgment defendant. An affidavit will suffice as in case of judgment. (KRS 426.551, 426.552).

As to corresponding provisions in case of decretal sales, compare KRS 426.550.

Body execution (capias ad satisfaciendum) abolished (Acts 1976, c. 91, §46) but contempt powers of court may be sought against defendant refusing to surrender property (KRS 426.384).

EXEMPTIONS:

Personal Property.—Following personal property of individual debtor resident in Kentucky is exempt from execution, attachment, garnishment, distress or fee bill: Household furnishings, jewelry, personal clothing and ornaments not to exceed $3,000; tools, equipment and livestock, including poultry, of person engaged in farming not to exceed $3,000; one motor vehicle and its necessary accessories including one spare tire not exceeding $2,500; professionally prescribed health aids of debtor or dependent of debtor (KRS 427.010[1]); earnings, see subhead Earnings, infra (KRS 427.010[2]); tools necessary in trade for individual debtor not exceeding $300 in value and one motor vehicle not exceeding $2,500 in value and its accessories of mechanic or other service or repair artisan are similarly exempt, (KRS 427.030); professional library, office equipment, instruments, furnishings and one motor vehicle not exceeding $2,500 in value and accessories of minister, attorney, physician, surgeon, chiropractor, veterinarian, or dentist are similarly exempt (KRS 427.040); benefits payable by any assessment, cooperative life or casualty insurance company or by any fraternal benefit society (KRS 427.110); police and firefighters' pension fund in cities of first, second, third or fourth classes, with exception of child support obligations (KRS 427.120; 427.125); award made under crime victim's reparation law; payment on account of wrongful death under certain conditions, payment not to exceed $7,500 on account of personal bodily injury of debtor or individual of whom debtor is dependent but awards for pain and suffering or compensation for actual pecuniary loss not included within this exemption; retirement allowances in accumulated contributions accrued under Kentucky state employees' retirement system or Kentucky teachers' retirement system; right or interest in qualified individual retirement account, annuity, deferred compensation account, pension, profit-sharing, stock bonus or other retirement plan which qualifies for deferral of income tax until date benefits are distributed to extent of amounts thereon more than 120 days before bankruptcy and not subject to court order for maintenance or support (KRS 427.150[2]; 61.690; 161.700); public assistance grants for aid to families with dependent children, elderly, blind or disabled (KRS 205.220); unemployment compensation rights, with exception of child support obligations (KRS 341.470); workers' compensation claims and payments with exception of child support obligation pursuant to KRS 403.212 (KRS 342.180). Following additional property is exempt to extent reasonably necessary for support of debtor and debtor's dependents: Money or property constituting awards for alimony, support or maintenance; assets held, payments made and amounts payable under stock bonus, pension, profit-sharing, annuity plans or contract; payment on account of wrongful death of individual of whom debtor was dependent; payment in compensation of loss

of future earnings of debtor or individual of whom debtor is or was dependent. (KRS 427.150[1] and [2][b] and [d]). Debtor who has filed for bankruptcy under provisions of Federal Bankruptcy Code entitled to additional general exemption not to exceed $1,000 to be applied toward any property in bankruptcy estate. (KRS 427.160).

Real Property.—In addition to exempt personalty, there is exempt from sale under execution, attachment or judgment individual debtor's aggregate interest, not to exceed $5,000 in value, in real or personal property used by debtor as principal residence or in burial plot for debtor or dependent. Exemption does not apply if debt or liability existed prior to purchase of property or erection of improvements thereon. (KRS 427.060).

Federal Bankruptcy Code exemptions not authorized. (KRS 427.170).

Substitution.—There is no provision giving a debtor who does not possess articles specifically exempted right to hold money or other property exempt in lieu thereof.

Debts Against Which Exemption Not Allowed.—Husband not entitled to exemption as against decree awarding alimony (166 Ky. 91, 178 S.W. 1164) nor to executions, attachments or garnishments issued for collection of maintenance for minor children (KRS 427.045). No exemption against debts of public officers to state, arising through defalcation (187 Ky. 260, 218 S.W. 740); no exemption against landlord's lien on growing crop for money or supplies furnished toward raising crop (KRS 383.110); state has specific lien on property for taxes (KRS 134.420).

Waiver of Exemption.—Personal property exemption may not be waived in advance. (73 Ky. 156). Real property exemption cannot be waived except in formal writing. (KRS 427.100).

Necessity of Claiming.—Burden of proof on debtor to prove specific property is subject to exemption. (175 Ky. 513, 194 S.W. 545; KRS 425.501).

Earnings.—Maximum amount of any aggregate disposable earnings, as defined in KRS 427.005 to include wages, salary, commissions, bonus, etc. as reduced by any amounts required by law to be withheld, which may be subjected to garnishment may not exceed lesser of 25% of disposable earnings for week or amount by which disposable earnings for week exceed 30 times current minimum hourly wage under Fair Labor Standards Act of 1938. (KRS 427.010[2]).

Restriction does not apply to amounts due under any order of court for support of any person, under any order of any bankruptcy court pursuant to c. 13 of Bankruptcy Code, or under any debt due for any state or federal tax. (KRS 427.010[3]).

Effect of Exemptions Under Foreign Law.—Exemptions provided by law of state where wages earned and payable apply to all garnishments served in Kentucky and debtor may plead them except where personal service effected in Kentucky, where defendant was bona fide resident of Kentucky when subject debt arose, or where defendant was bona fide resident of Kentucky when cause of action arose. (KRS 427.050).

See topic Garnishment.

Special exemptions include: certain insurance benefits (KRS 427.110); police and firefighter's pension funds in cities of first, second, third and fourth classes, before or after payment to beneficiary, with exception of child support obligations (KRS 427.120); public assistance grants for aid to families with dependent children, elderly, blind or disabled (KRS 205.220); growing crops, in certain cases (KRS 426.170); teacher's retirement funds, with exception of child support obligations (KRS 161.700); unemployment compensation rights, with exception of child support obligations (KRS 341.470); workmen's compensation claims and payments, with exception of child support obligation pursuant to KRS 403.212 (KRS 342.180).

Homestead Exemption.—See topic Homesteads.

Uniform Exemptions Act not adopted.

FORECLOSURE:

See topic Liens; category Mortgages, topic Mortgages of Real Property.

FRAUDULENT SALES AND CONVEYANCES:

Uniform Fraudulent Conveyance Act not adopted.

Lack of Valuable Consideration.—Every gift, conveyance, assignment or transfer made by a debtor of or upon any of his estate without valuable consideration therefor is void as to all his then existing liabilities, but is not on that account alone void as to creditors whose debts or demands are thereafter contracted, nor as to purchasers with notice of the voluntary alienation or charge (KRS 378.020); and though it be adjudged to be void as to a prior creditor, it is not therefore deemed to be void as to such subsequent creditors or purchasers (KRS 378.020; 217 Ky. 164, 289 S.W. 213).

It makes no difference under the statute that the debtor making a gift of his property may have ample estate outside of Kentucky that could be subjected to the payment of his debt. (203 Ky. 127, 261 S.W. 868). Nor does the fact that the gift is to the debtor's wife and amounts only to a reasonable provision for her out of his estate affect the rights of existing creditors. (166 Ky. 61, 178 S.W. 1146).

Intent to Hinder, Delay or Defraud.—Every gift, conveyance, assignment or transfer of or charge upon a debtor's estate made by him with intent to delay, hinder or defraud creditors, purchasers or other persons, and every bond or other evidence of debt given or action commenced or judgment suffered with like intent, is void as against such creditors, purchasers and other persons. This provision does not affect the title of a purchaser for a valuable consideration unless it appears that he had notice of the fraudulent intent of his immediate grantor or of the fraud rendering void the title of such grantor. (KRS 378.010).

Transfers to hinder or evade collection of taxes also condemned. Payment of full consideration by transferee is defense against seizure. (KRS 131.550).

Transfers of Personalty Without Change of Possession.—As to personal property, every voluntary alienation of or charge upon personal property is void as to a purchaser without notice, or any creditor prior to the lodging for record of such transfer or charge in the office of county clerk of county where alienor or person creating charge

FRAUDULENT SALES AND CONVEYANCES ... *continued*
resides, unless actual possession in good faith accompanies such alienation or charge. (KRS 378.040).

Pretended Loans of Personality.—Where any loan of personal property is pretended to have been made to any person with whom (or those claiming under him) possession has remained for five years, or where any reservation or limitation by way of condition, reversion, remainder, or otherwise, is pretended to have been made in the alienation of such property so possessed, the absolute right is deemed to be with the possession in favor of a purchaser without notice, or any creditor of the person so remaining in possession, unless the written evidence of the loan, reservation or limitation be duly recorded in the county where the person resides, before the possession is taken, or unless it is contained in a properly recorded will. (KRS 378.050).

Transfers Operating as Assignments for Benefit of Creditors.—Any sale, mortgage, assignment, act or device resorted to by debtor, in contemplation of insolvency or with design to prefer one creditor over another, operates as assignment and transfer of all property of debtor and inures to benefit of all creditors. (KRS 378.060).

Transfers Between Husband and Wife.—See category Family, topic Husband and Wife.

Remedy of Aggrieved Person.—When any real property has been fraudulently conveyed, transferred or mortgaged by a debtor, any party aggrieved thereby may, without waiting to reduce his claim to judgment and return of "No property found," file a petition in equity against the parties to such fraudulent transfer or conveyance or mortgage, or their representatives or heirs, alleging facts which show their right of action, and alleging such fraud or the facts constituting it, and describing the property and seeking to subject it. When such a petition is filed, a lis pendens is thereby created upon the property so described, and the suit progresses and is determined as other suits in equity and as though it had been brought upon a return of "No property found," as required prior to the enactment of this statute. (KRS 378.030).

Lis Pendens.—In order to prevail as against subsequent purchasers, lessees or incumbrancers of such real estate for value and without notice, the plaintiff must file a lis pendens statement in the office of county clerk of county in which such real estate or greater part thereof lies, giving description of real estate and reference to action, and name of person whose right, title or interest, therein is involved or affected. Where real estate consists of tracts lying in different counties, separate notice must be filed in each county, as to tract lying in that county. (KRS 382.440).

Sequestration of Estate.—Detailed provisions are made by KRS 378.060-378.090 for sequestering the estate of the debtor, including fraudulent or preferential transfers thereof, and distributing same among creditors generally, subject to the preferences in distribution prescribed by KRS 378.090.

By KRS 378.080, writ of ne exeat may be granted in this case.

Bulk Sales.—Art. 6 of Uniform Commercial Code repealed in 1992. No other statutory provision.

GARNISHMENT:

Statutes govern remedy whereby creditor may reach property of debtor in possession of third party. Garnishment recognized as post judgment remedy (KRS 425.501; CR 69.02) but same type of relief available through attachment procedure (KRS 425.301). See topic Attachment.

Property Which May Be Reached.—Any property or claim which is subject to attachment or execution is subject to garnishment when held for debtor by another. (KRS 425.501). Special provisions govern procedure for prejudgment garnishment which is treated as form of attachment (see topic Attachment), garnishment of wages (see subhead Earnings, infra) and garnishment against security which is transferable matter in manner set forth in KRS 355.8-320. (See KRS 425.126.)

Jurisdiction.—Court having jurisdiction to issue execution in particular action has sole jurisdiction to issue garnishment. (58 Ky. 97). Personal jurisdiction over employer is sufficient since employee may claim wages wherever employer may be found. (476 S.W.2d 197).

Proceedings to Obtain.—After entry of final judgment in personam against debtor, judgment creditor may file affidavit signed by him or his agent or attorney in office of clerk of court in which judgment was entered showing date of judgment, amount due thereon, that one or more persons hold property belonging to or are indebted to judgment debtor and obtain order of garnishment to be served upon garnishee in accordance with Rules of Civil Procedure. (KRS 425.501).

Answer of Garnishee.—Each garnishee summoned shall appear in person or by affidavit served and filed as above set out disclosing any sums, whether due or not, owed defendant and any property of defendant in control or in possession of garnishee and in case of corporate garnishee, any shares of stock therein held by or for benefit of defendant. If garnishee defaults, court may compel appearance for examination by process of contempt or it may hear proof of debt owing or property held by garnishee and make order in relation thereto as if what is so proved had appeared on examination of garnishee. (KRS 425.511).

Practice.—Garnishee may pay any money owing to defendant by him, not exceeding plaintiff's claim and costs, to officer having in hand order of attachment, or may pay it into court or to such person as court may direct and to that extent garnishee is discharged from liability to defendant, and he is not subjected to costs beyond those caused by his resistance of claim against him, and if he make true disclosure and payment as required by law, he is allowed his costs. (KRS 425.516).

Court may compel payment or delivery of property by garnishee or garnishee may give bond for forthcoming of property and retain possession pending final order. (KRS 425.521).

Adverse Claims.—When answer of garnishee shows property claimed belongs to one not party, court must order such claimant brought before it. (56 Ky. 625; 70 Ky. 116). If garnishee fails to disclose adverse claim, he is liable to adverse claimant, notwithstanding judgment against him as garnishee. (62 Ky. 186).

Judgment.—If garnishee fails to make disclosure satisfactory to plaintiff, he may be made defendant in suit by petition or amended petition, and plaintiff may proceed against garnishee in same manner as defendant might proceed in action against garnishee to recover property held or debt owing by garnishee. (KRS 425.526).

Earnings in excess of amount exempt (see topic Exemptions) are subject to garnishment.

Salaries or sums due to state, county, school board and city officers and employees and all sums owing to any person by state or any agency or department thereof, or by any county school board, city or county, are subject to attachment or garnishment. (KRS 427.130).

Earnings are defined in KRS 427.005 to include wages, salary, commissions, or bonus. Plaintiff must file affidavit as hereinbefore set forth and must file order of garnishment containing information set forth in KRS 425.506. Each order of garnishment of earnings creates lien on all nonexempt earnings earned during pay period in which order served and such succeeding pay periods designated in order. Priority among garnishments is based according to date of service on employer and each inferior order shall take effect as if served at commencement of next succeeding pay period. (KRS 425.506). No employer may discharge any employee by raising of fact that his earnings have been subjected to garnishment for any one indebtedness (KRS 427.140), and fine up to $1,000 and imprisonment up to one year may be imposed for violation of this provision (KRS 427.990).

Exemptions.—See topic Exemptions.

HOMESTEADS:

Homestead exemption is allowed to debtor or dependent of debtor in real or personal property to extent of $5,000 if property used as permanent residence in state but exemption does not apply against debt which existed prior to purchase of property or erection of improvements thereon. (KRS 427.060).

Limitation of value of property which may be held exempt is $5,000, including improvements. (KRS 427.060).

Limitation of Area.—None.

Debts or Liabilities Against Which Exemption Not Available.—The exemption is not available in case of suit brought to enforce a lien for purchase money of the land claimed or to enforce a mortgage thereon given by the owner, in which his wife joins, nor in any case where debt or liability being enforced existed prior to purchase of land or erection of improvements thereon. (KRS 427.060; 163 Ky. 502, 173 S.W. 1108).

Designation of Homestead.—No particular form of words in a deed is necessary to create a homestead and there is no requirement of filing or recording a claim of homestead. But specific provisions are made for valuation and allotment of homestead. (KRS 427.080-427.100).

Claim of Exemption.—Where debtor inherits land, a reasonable time is allowed him to establish and claim homestead therein. (230 Ky. 696, 20 S.W.2d 734).

Homestead claim may be asserted even after sale under execution, where sheriff did not observe statutory requirements. (255 Ky. 221, 72 S.W.2d 1037).

Waiver, Alienation or Encumbrance of Exemption.—No express relinquishment of the homestead is necessary in deed or mortgage of the property, if words are used which purport to convey the entire estate; but no mortgage, release or waiver of homestead exemption is valid unless in writing subscribed by husband and wife, and acknowledged and recorded in the same manner as conveyances of real estate. (KRS 427.100).

It has been held, however, that a husband may convey his homestead without his wife joining in the deed, subject only to her dower right therein. (117 Ky. 695, 78 S.W. 915).

Loss of Exemption.—Common law applies. Whether unoccupied property has been abandoned as homestead depends on facts. (247 Ky. 105, 56 S.W.2d 710).

Proceeds of sale of homestead are exempt pending intended investment in a new homestead. (229 Ky. 728, 17 S.W.2d 1022).

Sale to pay debts of deceased husband may be made subject to rights of widow and children (KRS 427.070) or if property sought to be sold is in opinion of appraisers worth more than $5,000 and is not divisible without great diminution in value, it may be sold for not less than $5,000 and that amount paid to defendant (KRS 427.090).

Rights of Surviving Spouse and Family.—The homestead is for use of the debtor's widow so long as she occupies it as a home, and unmarried infant children have right of joint occupancy. In like manner, the wife's homestead is for benefit of surviving husband and her children, under like situation. (KRS 427.070; 230 Ky. 143, 18 S.W.2d 961).

JUDGMENT NOTES:

See category Business Regulation and Commerce, topic Bills and Notes.

LEVY:

See topics Attachment, Executions.

LIENS:

Uniform Commercial Code has been adopted. (KRS 355.1-101 et seq.). See category Business Regulation and Commerce, topic Commercial Code.

Agisters and livery stable keepers or persons feeding or grazing cattle for compensation have lien on cattle for one year for reasonable charges for keeping, caring for, feeding and grazing cattle. (KRS 376.400). "Cattle" includes horses, mules, asses, oxen, sheep, hogs or goats. (KRS 446.010[6]).

Aircraft.—Liens on aircraft are created exactly as for motor vehicles. (KRS 376.281). See subhead Repairmen, infra.

Architects and Landscape Architects.—Architect who builds, repairs or improves property of another under such circumstances that mechanic's or materialmen's lien

LIENS . . . *continued*

may be imposed on property, shall, from proceeds of any payment received from owner, pay in full all persons who have furnished material or performed labor on property. Payments will be made pro rata if payment by owner is not sufficient to pay all bills. (KRS 376.070). Professional architects and professional landscape architects given liens similar to mechanics liens. (KRS 376.075; 323.010[3]; 323A.010[3]). KRS 376.075 appears to overrule case stating that no mechanic's or materialmen's lien is created in favor of architect who does not build, repair or improve property but merely prepares plans or drawings. (75 Ky. 75).

Artisans.—Persons who repair radios, phonographs and other electrical appliances have lien on articles on completion of repair for agreed or reasonable charges for parts, supplies, accessories and labor. Liens may be enforced by action or articles may be sold after 30 day notice to owner. (KRS 376.430). Persons performing work on watches, clocks or jewelry have lien on article for amount due for work. Articles may be sold after 30 day notice to owner if account not paid within six months. (KRS 376.290).

Boats and Watercraft.—Any boat remaining in possession of one who has performed labor, repairs or furnished accessories or supplies may be sold to pay charges which have been due for more than 30 days. Procedures for sale are prescribed statutorily. (KRS 376.280). Officers or employees, except captain, aboard steamboat or other vessel have lien on vessel, tackle, furnishings and apparel for wages due and said lien has priority over all other debts of owner or other liens; mechanics, trades people have like liens for work and supplies furnished to vessel. (KRS 376.360).

Bondholders.—Statutory mortgage lien exists in favor of all bond and coupon holders for municipal hospitals and appurtenances (KRS 216.140), waterworks and appurtenances (KRS 96.400), and industrial buildings (KRS 103.250) until payment in full of principal of bonds.

Child Support.—Cabinet for Human Resources has lien or levy for unpaid child support, enforceable against all real and personal property of obligor, if he has failed to make child support payment in amount equal to support payable for one month and child support has been assigned to Cabinet of Human Resources. (KRS 205.745). Lien or levy is superior to any mortgage or encumbrance created after notice of lien or levy is recorded and lien or levy shall have first priority over any other lien assigned by any other agency, association or corporation. (KRS 205.745).

Cleaners, Launderers and Tailors.—Any person who cleans, presses, glazes, alters or repairs clothing or household goods has lien on articles remaining in possession to secure reasonable or agreed upon charges. If charge is not paid within 90 days article may be sold after notice to customer. (KRS 376.300). Notice must be by registered letter stating time and place of sale mailed 30 days in advance of sale. (KRS 376.300). Persons who store clothes or household goods have similar lien. If charges have not been paid for 12 months, articles may be sold with notice to owner. (KRS 376.310). Notice as required above is registered letter stating time and place of sale and must be mailed 15 days in advance of sale. (KRS 376.320).

Employees.—When property of any business, either by its own act or by operation of law, is assigned for benefit of its creditors or comes to be distributed among them, there is lien on all such property securing wages due employees (excluding chief officer, directors and stockholders), and in case of railroad, there is lien securing claims for materials and supplies furnished for its operation. (KRS 376.150). Such liens are superior to lien of any mortgage or other encumbrance thereafter created, and in case of employees, to extent of wages coming due within six months before event stated, are also superior to any mortgage or encumbrance theretofore created. (KRS 376.160, 376.170-376.190).

Frozen food locker plant owner has lien on contents of each locker, compartment or space for payment of locker rental, processing or other charges. Ten days after written notice by certified mail, return receipt requested, of foreclosure, owner may sell contents of locker for their reasonable value. (KRS 221.100).

Keepers of hotels, inns, boarding house or houses of private entertainment have lien on baggage and personal property owned and brought in by person receiving board, nursing, care or attention of landlord for contract price or reasonable price. (KRS 376.340). Person holding such lien may have district court in county where debt created issue warrant directed to sheriff, constable or town marshal authorizing him to seize property described in affidavit supplied by lienholder. If property has been removed with consent of landlord, lien shall continue no longer than ten days from removal. (KRS 376.350).

Garagemen or those in business of storing or towing motor vehicles have lien for reasonable charges for same as long as vehicle remains in lienholder's possession. Vehicle may be sold after 45 days to pay for charges after not less than ten days advance notification by certified mail of time and place of sale. This lien is subject to prior recorded liens. (KRS 376.275).

Levees.—Lien exists for cost of establishment, construction, reconstruction, repair, enlargement, extension and maintenance of any levee against land within territory protected by levee, superior to all other liens except liens for taxes. (KRS 266.180).

Mine Reclamation.—Lien is created by KRS 350.575 for those expending money for restoration, reclamation, abatement or control of adverse effects of past coal mining on land on which work was done. Special provisions for creation and enforcement of lien are set out by statute.

Motor vehicle taxes including liens for license taxes, excise taxes, motor fuel taxes or other motor vehicular taxes may be filed by bureau of vehicle regulation with county clerk. (KRS 281.602).

Motor Vehicles, Local Government Lien.—Local government shall possess lien on motor vehicle impounded pursuant to KRS 82.625 for all fines, penalties, towing, handling, storage charges and fees imposed thereon. Such lien is superior to all other liens on vehicle. (KRS 82.625).

Service Fee of Stallion, Jack or Bull.—Any licensed keeper of stallion, jack or bull has lien for payment of service fee upon get of stallion, jack or bull for one year after birth. (KRS 376.420).

Real Estate of Public Assistance Recipient.—KRS 98.013 provides for lien in favor of any first class city on real estate owned or thereafter acquired by any recipient of general assistance through city's department of public welfare. Lien includes all amounts paid recipient. Director of public welfare must record said lien in office of county clerk in county where property is located in order for it to be effectual against any mortgage, purchase or judgment creditor without actual notice. Lien is not enforceable while real estate is occupied by surviving spouse or until she remarries, or is occupied by dependent child, provided no action is brought to settle estate.

Repairmen.—Automobile, aircraft and boat repairmen have prior lien for repairs, accessories or supplies furnished. (384 S.W.2d 302). Lien is not lost by removal of automobile or aircraft from repairmen's possession if statement similar to that for mechanic's lien is filed within six months. (*Query,* as to loss of lien on boats where possession relinquished.) When charges have been due over 30 days, vehicle, aircraft or boat may be sold, after advertisement. (KRS 376.270, 376.280, 376.281). *Caveat:* Motor vehicle sale and registration transfer pursuant to these statutes has been held unconstitutional by one court (378 F.Supp. 491) but in light of more recent authority statute is considered constitutional. (See 436 U.S. 149; slip op. C 80-0548 [W.D. Ky. Feb. 11, 1981]; OAG 84-154.) Equipment, machine, machinery and motor repairmen have possessory lien for charges, which is lost upon relinquishing possession, unless lien statement is filed in office of county clerk in county of owner's residence within three months. (KRS 376.440).

Road Construction by Public Road Districts.—Assessment made by board of directors of public road district against each owner of property abutting upon road improvement shall become lien on property of such owner and shall be prior and superior to all other liens except those of taxes. (KRS 184.130).

Sanitation District—Bondholder's Lien.—Statutory mortgage lien exists upon all property of sanitation district in favor of holders of Sanitation District Bonds, to secure payment of bonds and coupons. (KRS 220.420). Bonds are issued under KRS 220.380.

Savings and loan association lien applies on every share of stock of savings and loan association which is not fully paid up to ultimate value fixed by articles of incorporation and for such other charges as may be lawfully incurred thereon. (KRS 289.301). By-laws of association may prescribe manner of enforcing lien.

Unemployment Compensation—Lien on Property of Employer.—Lien is created in favor of Cabinet for Human Resources upon all property, real and personal, then owned or subsequently acquired, of any employer from whom contributions, interest or penalties are or may be due under KRS 341.260 of Unemployment Compensation Act. (KRS 341.310). Lien on any property of employer also exists for any unpaid contributions which has same force and effect of mechanics' lien (see subhead Mechanics' Liens, infra), and lien on gas, oil or other mineral leasehold (KRS 376.140), by reason of labor performed (KRS 341.315).

Vendor's liens upon lands sold and not fully paid for are recognized as originating in equitable principles regardless of express reservation in deed. They are not created but are rather restricted by KRS 382.070, which requires that in order to preserve such lien as against bona fide creditors and purchasers deed must state what part of consideration remains unpaid. This statute has no effect as to parties or volunteers claiming under them. (103 Ky. 710, 46 S.W. 219; 233 Ky. 673, 26 S.W.2d 551).

Veterinarians.—Any licensed veterinarian who performs professional services for animal by contract with or written consent of owner or agent has lien for reasonable value of services provided. (KRS 376.470). Lien dissolved unless statement filed in county clerk's office as provided in KRS 376.475 and enforced as provided in KRS 376.110, 376.120 and 376.130. Veterinarians may also sell any unclaimed animal after ten days to pay for charges after notification to owner by certified mail of time and place of sale. (KRS 257.105).

Liens upon water craft for wages of all officers and employees thereon, except captain, and lien thereon for work done on such craft and materials furnished in connection therewith to mechanics and materialmen are provided. (KRS 376.360).

Workers' Compensation.—All rights of compensation by Workers' Compensation Act, KRS c. 342, shall have same preference or priority for whole thereof against assets of employer as is allowed by law for any unpaid wages for labor. (KRS 342.175).

Liens and other remedies for sellers of goods are provided by Sales Article of Uniform Commercial Code. (KRS 355.2-101 et seq.).

See also topics Attachment, Executions, Pledges; categories Business Regulation and Commerce, topics Commercial Code, Factors, Warehousemen; Civil Actions and Procedure, topic Judgments; Legal Profession, topic Attorneys and Counselors; Mortgages, topics Chattel Mortgages, Mortgages of Real Property; Property, topics Dower, Landlord and Tenant; Taxation, topic Property (Ad Valorem) Taxes, subhead Lien.

Federal Liens.—Act similar to original Uniform Federal Tax Lien Registration Act adopted with variations (KRS 382.480 to 382.500) to provide that proper place for filing notices of tax liens, and other liens such as in favor of Environmental Protection Agency, on real and personal property are to be filed in office of county clerk of each county within which property subject to lien located, that clerks shall record such notices in federal tax lien notice file or encumbrance book or federal lien notice file or encumbrance book, and that discharge of lien is filed in same office where original notice filed. Revised Uniform Federal Tax Lien Registration Act and Uniform Federal Lien Registration Act not adopted.

Defrauding secured creditors by destroying, removing, concealing, transferring, encumbering or otherwise dealing with property subject to security interest to hinder enforcement of interest is misdemeanor unless collateral value in excess of $100 in which case offense is felony. (KRS 517.060).

See note at head of Digest as to 1998 legislation covered.

See Topical Index in front part of this volume.

LIENS . . . *continued*

Waiver, Loss or Extinguishment.—Governed by common law principles, except where statute creating specific lien imposes conditions by which lien may be lost, waived or extinguished.

Enforcement.—Liens, including mortgages, are enforced generally by suits in equity. Procedure of strict foreclosure is not sanctioned, but mortgagee may take possession for account of mortgagor after default and abandonment. (KRS 426.525). In certain cases affecting personal property, such as security agreements or deeds of trust, vendor or trustee may sell under express power in written instrument. (160 Ky. 557, 169 S.W. 986; 293 Ky. 637, 169 S.W.2d 820). See Uniform Commercial Code. Aliter as to lands. (KRS 381.190).

Mechanics' Liens.—A general law (KRS 376.010-376.130) gives mechanics and materialmen, upon conditions therein stated, a lien, dating from the commencement of work, upon the improvements and the interest of the contracting owner in the land for work done and material furnished. Where the work is done by contract with a lessee for term of years, in making additions or improvements to the leased estate, the lien claimant may remove such additions or improvements if he can do so without material injury to previous improvements. (KRS 376.040; 19 K.L.R. 386, 40 S.W. 685). Subcontractors and laborers also have liens under this statute not to exceed, in aggregate, original contract price agreed on between owner and original contractor. Provision is made for protection of purchasers and mortgagees. By KRS 376.140, person furnishing work, supplies, machinery or other things of value to lessee of oil, gas or other mineral lease, for use in improving leasehold, is given lien on lessee's entire interest to secure payment.

Provision is made by KRS 376.010 for protection of owners and lienholders or other persons in interest in land by requiring materialman or mechanic who has not contracted directly with owner or his agent to give notice to owner or his authorized agent, within following time limits after last item of work or material is furnished: 75 days for claims less than $1,000; 120 days for claims over $1,000; 45 days for claims of any amount for improvements made to either single or double family dwelling or appurtenances unless owner-occupant has paid another for such improvements prior to receipt of such notice. Provision for single or double family dwelling applies only to construction pursuant to contract. (KRS 376.010[4]). Lien waived by mechanic or materialman who has not contracted directly with owner, or owner-occupant, if such written notice not given within such time periods.

Lien may be enforced by a suit in equity by any one holding such lien, and all others may file and prove their claims without pleading. Lien is lost unless a prescribed statement under oath of claim of lien is filed in county clerk's office within six months from time claimant ceases work or furnishes material, copy of statement is sent by regular mail to owner within seven days of filing with county clerk's office, and suit is brought thereon within 12 months after filing such claim, with extension of time for suit in case of debtor's death within 12-month period, for six months from such death. Lien statement shall include name, address of claimant, or if claimant is corporation, name and address of process agent. If no name or address is included, service in action involving real property shall be on person signing statement. (KRS 376.080; 376.090. See 184 Ky. 244, 211 S.W. 765; 201 Ky. 45, 255 S.W. 846; 211 Ky. 536, 277 S.W. 836; 211 Ky. 809, 278 S.W. 105; 213 Ky. 741, 281 S.W. 988, and later cases).

It is a penal offense for owner of property to misapply proceeds of sale or mortgage to discharge of mechanic's or materialman's lien thereon, where time allowed for filing and recording such lien claims has not expired at time of such sale or mortgage, and also for contractor or other person engaged in building, repairing or improving property to fail to apply payments made to him on account thereof, to discharge of such lien of mechanics or materialmen, unless in either case such lien shall have been waived or released in writing. (KRS 376.050-376.070; 376.990).

Prior real estate mortgage, recorded without knowledge of party's intent to file mechanic's lien statement, takes precedence over subsequent mechanic's lien. (394 S.W.2d 930).

Professional engineers and land surveyors given similar lien. (KRS 376.075).

Public Improvements.—Persons who perform or furnish labor, materials or supplies, including rental equipment, for construction or improvement of any canal, railroad, bridge, public highway or other public improvement in Kentucky, by contract with the owner or by subcontract thereunder, have a lien on all the property and franchises of the owner, except as to property owned by the state, subdivision or agency thereof or by any city, county, urban-county government, or charter county government in which event lien attaches to funds due to contractor from owner of property improved. Such lien is for full contract price of labor, materials and supplies furnished, and is superior to all other liens thereafter created, provided (1) that person intending to perform or furnish labor, materials or supplies must file in clerk's office of county written statement setting forth what he has contracted to furnish and price thereof, (2) within 30 days after last day of last month in which any labor was performed or materials or supplies furnished, claimant must file in county clerk's office statement, verified by affidavit, setting forth amount for which and project on which lien is claimed, and attested copy must be delivered to owner. (KRS 376.195-376.230).

Proper county clerk's office for filing statement in case of bridge, highway or other property of state, county or city is in county in which owner's seat of government is located. In other cases, required statements must be filed in each county where claim accrues. (KRS 376.230).

Mechanics' liens on public improvements are enforced by proper proceedings in equity, to which other lienholders shall be made parties. (KRS 376.260). If court action is filed to enforce lien on public improvements and owner of property is state, subdivision or agency thereof, or city, county, urban-county, or charter county government, that owner shall be given notice of court action to enforce lien, but that owner shall not be required to respond to or participate in court action. (KRS 376.260). All suits for enforcement of mechanics' liens on public improvements shall be instituted in Circuit Court of county in which is located property on which improvement is made, except where property is owned by public university in which event, suit shall be instituted in Circuit Court of county in which is located main campus of public university. (KRS 376.250).

Contractors on public works are almost invariably required to give surety bonds for compliance with their contracts. In specific instances (e.g., county road contracts and contracts of certain classes of cities), a surety bond is required by law, but there is no statute of general application on the subject.

Attachment Lien.—See topic Attachment.

Attorney's Lien.—See category Legal Profession, topic Attorneys and Counselors.

Collateral Security.—See topic Pledges.

Execution Lien.—See topic Executions.

Judgment Lien.—See category Civil Actions and Procedure, topic Judgments.

Landlord's Lien.—See category Property, topic Landlord and Tenant.

Liens on Exempt Property.—See topic Exemptions.

Liens on Homestead.—See topic Homesteads.

Real Estate Mortgage Lien.—See category Mortgages, topic Mortgages of Real Property.

Tax Lien.—See category Taxation, topic Property (Ad Valorem) Taxes, subhead Lien.

PLEDGES:

Pledges are among the security devices governed by Uniform Commercial Code. (KRS 355.9-). See category Business Regulation and Commerce, topic Commercial Code.

Attachment.—Any interest of pledgor or pledgee in things pledged is subject to attachment. Pledgee is responsible only for reasonable care in preservation of thing pledged. Pledgee of note must use ordinary diligence to collect it at maturity.

Trust Receipts.—Governed by Uniform Commercial Code. (KRS 355.9-).

RECEIVERS:

In general conduct of receivership, such as issuing receiver's certificates, etc., court is governed by general equitable principles.

Jurisdiction and Proceedings.—Circuit court, in exercise of its equitable jurisdiction, may sequester property of defendant by appointing receiver to take charge thereof, subject to regulations and conditions prescribed by statute as to receivership generally, by KRS 381.420 as to actions against tenant committing waste, and by KRS 378.080 as to preferential transfers by insolvent debtor.

Court may appoint receiver, on motion of any party to action who shows that he has, or probably has, right to, lien upon or interest in any property or fund involved in action, that is in danger of being lost, removed or materially injured. Court may order and coerce delivery of such property or fund to its receiver. (KRS 425.600).

Order appointing or refusing to appoint receiver is deemed final order for purposes of appeal to appellate court. (KRS 425.600).

Eligibility and Competency.—Excepting personal representatives, guardians, curators and committees of persons of unsound mind, neither party to action nor his attorney, nor any person interested therein, may be appointed receiver. (KRS 31A.080[2]).

Qualification.—Receiver, before acting, must take oath to perform duties faithfully, and must give bond therefor in such sum and to such person as the court shall direct. (KRS 31A.080; 31A.020; 31A.030).

Powers and Duties.—Receiver has, under control of court, power to bring and defend actions; to take and keep possession of property; to receive rents, collect debts, and generally to do such acts with respect to property as court may authorize. (KRS 425.600[2]).

Discharge.—Regularly appointed receivers under KRS c. 31A hold office for four years, unless sooner removed at pleasure of court. (KRS 31A.080[1] and 31A.010).

As to receivership to preserve assets of going corporation, see KRS 271B.14-310 through 271B.14-330. As to receivership of corporation that has become insolvent or has its capital impaired or has violated law under which it was organized, see category Business Organizations, topic Corporations.

Consumer Protection Matters.—See category Business Regulation and Commerce, topic Consumer Protection.

SUPPLEMENTARY PROCEEDINGS:

See topic Executions.

DISPUTE RESOLUTION

ALTERNATIVE DISPUTE RESOLUTION:

Constitution allows General Assembly to enact laws concerning arbitration. (Const. §250).

Uniform Arbitration Act adopted. See topic Arbitration and Award. Common law and voluntary mediation procedures also in use.

Mandatory Dispute Resolution.—

Labor Relations.—Labor commissioner has duty to investigate and mediate labor disputes. (KRS 336.151). Commissioner is authorized to create boards to which disputes between employers and employees may be submitted for mediation. (KRS 336.140). Information received by mediator relating to labor dispute is confidential. (KRS 336.153). Prior to representing or agreeing to represent party to any labor/management negotiation or arbitration, any individual, partnership, association or corporation who represents, advises or acts as consultant or spokesman for any party to dispute must notify Secretary of Labor of that intent and be certified. (KRS 336.156). Secretary maintains roster of qualified arbitrators and insures that persons listed on roster comply with rules and regulations pertaining to arbitration, ethical standards and procedures. (KRS 336.1662 and 336.1663).

See note at head of Digest as to 1998 legislation covered.

See Topical Index in front part of this volume.

KY – 25

ALTERNATIVE DISPUTE RESOLUTION . . . *continued*

Motor Vehicle Warranties.—Manufacturers of motor vehicles required to offer arbitration (informal dispute resolution procedures) to buyers to settle disputes relating to unsatisfactory warranty repairs, malfunctions and other problems arising during first two years or 25,000 miles of ownership. (KRS 367.860 to 367.870). Buyers of new motor vehicles required to pursue arbitration of warranty claims arising in first 12,000 miles or one year before seeking judicial relief. (KRS 367.842[4]). Any mechanisms established in compliance with 16 C.F.R. Part 703 satisfies Kentucky requirements so long as it provides each party right to oral hearing. (KRS 367.867).

Miscellaneous.—Provision in motor vehicle liability insurance policy agreeing to arbitrate all future disputes not binding. (KRS 304.20-050). In divorce proceedings, court, at request of either party shall, or sua sponte may, order conciliation conference. (KRS 403.170). Fire department fee for services disputes involving fee in excess of $500 shall be submitted to arbitration. (KRS 75.450[2][c]).

Voluntary Dispute Resolution.—Statutory provisions authorizing include:

Workers Compensation Act allows for binding mediations and arbitration which may provide that decision of arbiter is not subject to review by Administrative Law Judge as long as alternative dispute resolution is part of bargained agreement which does not diminish rights of any parties under Workers Compensation Law. (KRS 342.277).

Discrimination in Housing Conciliation Agreement may provide for binding arbitration of dispute. Arbitration may award any appropriate relief including monetary relief. (KRS 344.605).

Kentucky Insurance Arbitration Association establishes nonprofit organization to provide mechanism for reimbursement among reparations obligors of losses paid as basic or added reparations for motor vehicle torts. (KRS 304.39-290).

Attorney and Client.—Legal negligence claims of $10,000 or less may be resolved by submission to binding arbitration. (SCR 3.800). Fee disputes between attorney and client and fee disputes between attorneys may be resolved by submission to binding arbitration. (SCR 3.810). Mediation and arbitration procedures to resolve other disputes between attorneys by submission to mediation, binding arbitration or nonbinding arbitration established in SCR 3.815.

Solid waste management conflicts concerning host community collection and disposal fees and other issues related to municipal solid waste management facility sifting and operations, except issues related to permit conditions imposed by cabinet may be resolved by negotiation, mediation or arbitration. (KRS 147A.030).

Department of Mines and Minerals provides for mediation at option of well operator when well operator has been unable to reach agreement with surface owners concerning proposed use of land. (KRS 353.5901).

ARBITRATION AND AWARD:

Uniform Arbitration Act adopted and effective for agreements to arbitrate made subsequent to July 12, 1984. (KRS 417.045-417.240). Agreements to arbitrate disputes entered into prior to July 13, 1984 are governed by common law principles. (KRS 417.230).

Deviations from Uniform Act (see Uniform and Model Acts, Part III).—§1 of Act excludes coverage for collective bargaining agreements and other employer-employee agreements and insurance contracts but Act applies to arbitration provisions between two or more insurers, including reinsurers. (KRS 417.050).

§7(a), arbitrators may issue subpoenas. (KRS 417.110[1]).

§7(d), reference is to circuit court. (KRS 417.110[4]).

§8(a), certified mail substituted for registered mail. (KRS 417.120[1]).

§10, award of attorneys' fees to prevailing party allowed if provision therefor contained in agreement. (KRS 417.140).

§12(c), reference in first clause is to ground 12(a)(1) instead of ground 12(a)(5). (KRS 417.160[3]).

§15, omitted.

§18, references are to county. (KRS 417.210).

§22, omitted.

§24, omitted.

See also topic Alternative Dispute Resolution.

Mandatory Arbitration.—See topic Alternative Dispute Resolution, subhead Mandatory Dispute Resolution, catchline Motor Vehicle Warranties.

DOCUMENTS AND RECORDS

ACKNOWLEDGMENTS:

Uniform Recognition of Acknowledgments Act adopted to supplement other provisions. (KRS 423.110 to 423.190). See Part III, Uniform and Model Acts section.

Within state: County clerk, notary public or deputy of any county clerk may take. (KRS 382.130; 382.250; 423.010). Fees: clerk, $2; notary, not more than 50¢. (KRS 64.012, 64.300).

Outside state but within United States: Judge, clerk or deputy clerk of court; notary public; mayor; secretary of state; justice of peace; or commissioner authorized to take acknowledgment of deeds. Official seal required. (KRS 423.110; 382.140).

Outside the United States: Any foreign minister, secretary of legation, officer in U. S. consular service, secretary of foreign affairs, notary public or judge or clerk of a superior court of nation where taken. Official seal required. (KRS 382.150). Officer of foreign service of U.S., consular agent or other person authorized by regulation of U.S. Department of State to perform notarial acts in place. (KRS 423.110).

Officers in U.S. Armed Forces.—Any commissioned officer in active service of U.S. Armed Forces may take acknowledgments, affidavits, or depositions of (a) members of U.S. Armed Forces, wherever located, (b) merchant seaman serving outside U.S. limits, (c) persons outside U.S. limits by official U.S. permission, assignment or direction, or (d) any other person authorized by regulation of Armed Forces to perform notarial acts. Certificate showing date of acknowledgment and that person appearing before certifying officer acknowledged instrument is sufficient and officer's official

signature is prima facie evidence that person acknowledging is within purview of statute. Acknowledgments so taken previous to enactment of statute are validated. (KRS 384.080; KRS 423.110).

General Requirements as to Taking.—Officer is liable on bond for failure to use reasonable care to identify person acknowledging. Showing that imposter acknowledged instrument creates prima facie case of negligence. (123 Ky. 437, 96 S.W. 801).

General Requirements of Certificate.—Requirement that Kentucky notary's certificate state date of expiration of his commission (KRS 423.010) has been held merely directory (22 K.L.R. 1169, 60 S.W. 186). Official seal of officer taking acknowledgment in Kentucky not required.

Married women acknowledge like other persons; no separate examination required.

Attorneys in Fact.—No special requirements, but form provided. See subhead Forms, infra.

Corporations.—No special requirements, but form provided. See subhead Forms, infra.

Foreign Acknowledgments.—Uniform Recognition of Acknowledgments Act adopted as supplement to other provisions. See subheads Outside the United States and Officers in U.S. Armed Forces, supra.

Effect.—Proper acknowledgment or proof entitles an instrument to be admitted to record. (KRS 382.130 et seq.).

Proof by Subscribing Witness.—Recordable writings, not acknowledged by parties before authorized officials, may be admitted to record, if executed and acknowledged by parties before two subscribing witnesses, upon proof of such execution and acknowledgment before any officer authorized to take acknowledgments by oath or affidavit of the two subscribing witnesses that instrument was executed and acknowledged before them by parties thereto, or by like proof of one subscribing witness, who proves also attestation of other, or by like proof of two witnesses that both subscribing witnesses are dead and like proof of signature of one of them and of grantor or grantors, or by like proof of two witnesses that both subscribing witnesses are out of state, or that one of them is so absent and other is dead, and like proof of signature of one of witnesses and of grantor or grantors or on certificate of county court clerk in Kentucky or of any notary public that instrument had been acknowledged or proven before him in one of methods above set forth. (KRS 382.130). Affidavit required of witness may be made anywhere before any officer authorized to take acknowledgments (KRS 382.130-382.150; 423.080) or depositions (CR 28).

Where deed is proven for record by persons other than the subscribing witnesses, officer's certificate must state names and addresses of witnesses making proof. (KRS 382.160).

Authentication of official character and genuineness of signature of Kentucky notary is by certificate under seal of county clerk in county in which notary is qualified to act. (KRS 423.020). Fee, not more than 50¢. (KRS 64.300). No special requirements for authentication of official character or genuineness of signature of officer taking acknowledgment outside of Kentucky, but in practice resort is frequently had to authentication as provided by act of Congress or law of official's own state. General authentication requirements are set forth in KRE 901.

As to whether or not particular instruments need to be acknowledged, see categories Debtor and Creditor, topic Assignments; Mortgages, topic Mortgages of Real Property; Property, topic Deeds. As to jurat to affidavits, see topic Affidavits.

Forms.—Following short forms of certificates of acknowledgment are authorized by KRS 423.110 to 423.190 for use within or outside state. Words "acknowledged before me" mean (1) that person acknowledging appeared before person taking acknowledgment, (2) that he acknowledged that he executed instrument, (3) that person acknowledging instrument executed it for purposes stated and/or with authority to act in capacity stated, and (4) that person taking acknowledgment either knew or had satisfactory evidence that person acknowledging was person named in instrument or certificate. (KRS 423.150).

Forms

For an Individual Acting in his Own Right:

STATE OF . . . .

COUNTY OF . . . .

The foregoing instrument was acknowledged before me this (date) by (name of person acknowledged).

My Commission expires (for Notary Public).

(Signature of Person Taking Acknowledgment)

(Title or Rank)

(Serial Number, if any)

For a Corporation:

STATE OF . . . .

COUNTY OF . . . .

The foregoing instrument was acknowledged before me this (date) by (name of officer or agent, title of officer or agent) of (name of corporation acknowledging) a (state or place of incorporation) corporation, on behalf of the corporation.

My commission expires (for Notary Public).

(Signature of Person Taking Acknowledgment)

(Title or Rank)

(Serial Number, if any)

For Partnership:

STATE OF . . . .

COUNTY OF . . . .

The foregoing instrument was acknowledged before me this (date) by (name of acknowledging partner or agent), partner (or agent) on behalf of (name of partnership), a partnership.

My commission expires (for Notary Public).

(Signature of Person Taking Acknowledgment)

ACKNOWLEDGMENTS . . . *continued*
(Title or Rank)
(Serial Number, if any)

For an Individual Acting as Principal by an Attorney-in-Fact:
STATE OF . . . .
COUNTY OF . . . .
The foregoing instrument was acknowledged before me this (date) by (name of attorney in fact) as attorney in fact on behalf of (name of principal).
My commission expires (for Notary Public).
(Signature of Person Taking Acknowledgment)
(Title or Rank)
(Serial Number, if any)

By any Public Officer, Trustee, or Personal Representative:
STATE OF . . . .
COUNTY OF . . . .
The foregoing instrument was acknowledged before me this (date) by (name and title of position).
My commission expires (for Notary Public).
(Signature of Person Taking Acknowledgment)
(Title or Rank)
(Serial Number, if any)

Validating Acts.—See KRS 382.230; 207 Ky. 391, 269 S.W. 318; 209 Ky. 806, 273 S.W. 476.

Alternative to Acknowledgment or Proof.—No statutory provision.

AFFIDAVITS:

May be made before the following officers:

Within State.—Following officers authorized to administer oaths and affirm statements of affiant: any examiner, judge, clerk, commissioner, official court reporter and notary public; other persons may be authorized by law for special circumstances. (CR 43.13, 28). Agent or attorney for person may administer oath to such person but must state circumstances in affidavit. (CR 43.13[1]). County clerk's fee for same, $2. (KRS 64.012). Notary public's fee, 50¢. (KRS 64.300).

Outside State but Within United States.—Commissioner appointed by Governor of state where taken, person specially commissioned, judge of court, justice of peace, mayor of city, or notary public. (CR 28.02, 43.13[1]).

Persons in or with U. S. Armed Forces.—Before commissioned officers of U. S. Armed Forces as prescribed for acknowledgments. (KRS 384.080). See topic Acknowledgments.

General Requirements as to Administration.—See topic Acknowledgments.

General Requirements of Jurat.—Certificate of officer is proof of time and manner of affidavit being made. (CR 43.13(2)). No proof of officer's commission or qualification is required, except that certificate of Kentucky notary should state when his commission expires (KRS 423.010), but statute held merely directory (22 K.L.R. 1169, 60 S.W. 186).

Affidavit of Agent or Attorney.—Any affidavit which the code requires or authorizes a party to make may, unless otherwise expressed, be made by his agent or attorney, if he be absent from the county or mentally incapable of taking oath, or physically unable to attend before officer. (CR 43.13(1)).

Use.—Affidavit may be used to verify pleading; to prove service of summons, notice or other process in action; to obtain provisional remedy (such as arrest and bail, order for immediate delivery of personal property, attachment, injunction, receivership, etc.) or examination of witness, stay of proceedings or warning order; or upon motion; and in certain other exceptional cases allowed by law. It may also be used to prove for record execution and acknowledgment of recordable instruments. (KRS 382.130 and 423.080).

Form.—The declaration must be a written statement, subscribed and sworn to before a proper officer, whose certificate must be separate and must follow signature of affiant. (CR 43.13). Where affidavits are filed in suits, the style of the court and case is made the caption of the affidavit, otherwise the state and county in which executed is all that is shown.

A form in general use is as follows:

Form
Affidavit
[Style of proceeding]
or
Commonwealth of Kentucky
County of . . . .
The affiant, John Doe, first being duly sworn, deposes and says:
1. . . . .
2. . . . ., etc.
Further the affiant sayeth not.

. . . .
(signature)
COMMONWEALTH OF KENTUCKY
COUNTY OF . . . . } SS
The foregoing instrument was acknowledged before me this . . . . . day of . . . . . ., 19 . . . . by (name).
My Commission expires . . . . (for Notary Public)
. . . .
Name and Title of Officer

Alternative to Affidavit.—No statutory provision.

NOTARIES PUBLIC:

Qualification.—Must be 18 years or older, a resident of county from which application made, and of good moral character. (KRS 423.010).

Authentication.—See topic Acknowledgments.

Seal.—To be recorded, instruments acknowledged out of state must be under seal, but certificates on affidavits made in state for use within state need not be certified under seal. See topic Acknowledgments.

Powers and Duties.—Notary may administer oaths and take acknowledgments of deeds, mortgages, etc., and has important powers and responsibilities with respect to protest of commercial paper.

Territorial Extent of Powers.—Jurisdiction is limited to county for which appointed, but notary in any county may qualify and act as notary in any other county on compliance with KRS 423.020 and subject to its conditions.

Expiration of Commission.—Certificate must state date of expiration of his commission (KRS 423.010), and ought to show venue of act certified. Failure to state date of expiration of commission is not fatal to instrument or certificate (22 K.L.R. 1169, 60 S.W. 186), nor does failure in certificate to show venue invalidate it (113 F. 443), nor does omission of jurat invalidate affidavit actually signed and sworn to (202 Ky. 751, 261 S.W. 277; 655 S.W.2d 503).

Fees.—Not more than following amounts may be charged: attestation, protestation or taking acknowledgment and certifying under seal, 50¢; recording same in book kept for that purpose, 75¢; each notice of protest, 25¢; administering oath and certificate thereon, 20¢. (KRS 64.300).

Commissioners of deeds may take acknowledgment or proof of any instrument, except will, if instrument is required by law of this state to be recorded. May administer any oath or take any affirmation necessary to discharge of official duties; may take and certify depositions. (KRS 423.080).

Officers of U. S. Armed Forces.—See topic Acknowledgments.

RECORDS:

County clerk is officer having charge of records relating to conveyances and encumbrances upon property (various sections of KRS c. 382), wills (KRS 394.300), statutory liens (KRS 376.080, 376.100, 376.110, 376.230), corporations with registered office in county (duplicate of copy filed with Secretary of State, see e.g. KRS 271B.1-200[10]), assumed names of individuals, general partnerships, including registered limited liability partnerships, limited partnerships, business trusts, corporations and limited liabilities companies doing business in county (KRS 365.015), U.C.C. financing statements (KRS 355.9-401), records of title to roads, maps etc. (KRS 178.320), records of licenses of grain warehousemen (KRS 359.050), changes of name (KRS 401.040), marriage licenses (KRS 402.230), etc. Uniform Commercial Code (1962 Official Text) has been adopted (KRS c. 355), with 1972 and 1977 Official Amendments; see category Business Regulation and Commerce, topic Commercial Code.

Recordable Instruments.—No deed conveying any title to or interest in land, for a longer time than five years, nor any agreement in consideration of marriage, nor deed of trust or mortgage, is valid against a purchaser for a valuable consideration without notice, or any creditor, until such deed is acknowledged or proved according to law and lodged for record. The term "creditors," as used above, includes all creditors and not merely those who have acquired liens. (KRS 382.080, 382.270; 102 Ky. 434, 43 S.W. 205).

A contract for the sale of land or any interest therein, or an option to buy or offer to sell land or any interest therein, may be recorded when duly acknowledged or proved for record. (KRS 382.090, 382.100).

Place of Recording.—Instruments affecting real property must be recorded in county where land, or greater part thereof, is located. (KRS 382.110). *For list of Counties and County Seats see first page for this state in Volume containing Practice Profiles Section.*

Requisites for Recording.—The clerk may not record any deed conveying any interest in real estate equal to or greater than a life estate unless it plainly specifies and refers to the next immediate source from which the grantor derived title, and in referring to former conveyance, states office, book, and page, when recorded and date thereof, e. g. (following description) "being the same property conveyed to the grantors by A. B. by deed dated January 1, 1900, and recorded in the office of the Jefferson County Clerk in Deed Book 500, page 100." This requirement does not apply to deeds made by any court officer in his official capacity. (KRS 382.110).

Instruments executed in state to be recorded only when acknowledged or proved as provided in KRS 382.130. (See topic Acknowledgments.) Instruments executed out of state to be acknowledged in same manner. (KRS 382.140).

No county clerk may receive or record any instrument not executed or acknowledged prior to July 1, 1962 (other than financing statement filed under Uniform Commercial Code—Opinion Ky. Atty. Gen., 62-263) conveying or granting any interest in or lien upon real or personal property, or relating to organization or dissolution of private corporation, unless instrument bears name and address and signature or facsimile thereof of person who prepared it. (KRS 382.335[1]). No county clerk shall receive or permit recording of any instrument not executed or acknowledged prior to July 1, 1970 which conveys grants, assigns or otherwise disposes of real estate or any interest therein unless such instrument contains mailing address of grantee or assignee. (KRS 382.335[2]). Those provisions do not apply to wills or statutory liens in favor of state (KRS 382.335[3]) and receipt and recordation by clerk without compliance with these provisions shall not prevent such record of filing of instrument from becoming notice as otherwise provided by law, nor impair admissibility of record as evidence (KRS 382.335[5]).

Note: Regulations adopted in 1998 with proposed effective date of Mar. 1, 1999 establish additional standards for documents presented for recording in offices of County Clerks. (725 KAR 1:070, eff. 3/1/99). Standards include: (a) size—$8^{1}/_{2}$ by 11 inch pages, except maps, plats, drawings, wills and instruments whose size otherwise set by law; (b) margins—1 inch side, top and bottom margins but with 2 inches at top of first page and at bottom of last page; (c) clarity—dark ink on white paper without

See note at head of Digest as to 1998 legislation covered.

See Topical Index in front part of this volume.

RECORDS . . . *continued*

background color, images or writing; (d) type-printed eight point standard non-cursive font type; and (e) paper—at least 20 pound, bond paper, not bound or continuous form and without superfluous decorations such as wax, ribbons or seals. Instruments created, certified or accepted for filing or recording by U.S. government or government of any nation or state are exempt from regulation. (725 KAR 1:020[6]).

See also category Business Regulation and Commerce, topic Commercial Code.

Recording Fees.—Deeds, mortgages and leases $9 ($12 with tax) plus $2 for each page over three. Deed of release, real property options, lis pendens and mechanics $9, federal tax lien $8, state tax liens $5 (no tax) plus $2 for each page over three. Original financing statement $14 ($17 with tax) which includes $5 for filing termination statement (KRS 64.012); if collateral includes Kentucky licensed motor vehicles, clerk collects $17 for noting lien on certificate of title (KRS 186A.190[7]); continuation statements and assignments of financing statements $9 (KRS 64.012).

In addition to fees in KRS 64.012, clerk may require prepayment of postage for returning recorded instrument. (KRS 382.240). These fees include County Clerk charge of up to $1 for each instrument recorded, regardless of whether instrument is returned by mail. Postage, if any, charged by clerks should be confirmed prior to recordation.

Recording Tax.—See category Taxation, topic Taxes, subhead Real Estate Conveyance Tax.

Foreign Conveyances or Encumbrances.—Recordable when acknowledged before officer authorized to take acknowledgments outside of Kentucky, and official seal affixed. (See topic Acknowledgments.)

Effect of Record.—Certified copies of all instruments legally recorded are prima facie evidence in all courts and tribunals of this state.

Torrens Act has not been adopted.

Transfer of Decedent's Title.—Where decedent leaves will, its probate in the proper District Court affords only evidence of transfer of title to real estate required by Kentucky law.

Where decedent does not leave a will, persons claiming title to real estate by the laws of descent must, before recording any deed to such real estate, file with the clerk of the county court to whom such deed is presented for record, an affidavit of a grantor therein or of any one of the heirs at law or next of kin of the decedent, or an affidavit of two persons resident in Kentucky, each of whom has personal knowledge of the facts, setting forth: (1) The name of the decedent; (2) date of his death; (3) whether he was married or single, and if married the name of the surviving spouse; (4) the place of decedent's residence at the time of death, if known to affiant; (5) that decedent died intestate; (6) the names, ages and addresses, so far as known or ascertainable, of all of decedent's heirs at law and next of kin who inherited such real estate, the relationship of each to said decedent and the interest in the real estate inherited by each of them. Such affidavit must be recorded by the clerk in the record of deeds and indexed in the general index of deeds in his office in the name of the decedent as grantor, and in the name of each of such heirs at law or next of kin as grantees, as though such names had occurred in a deed of conveyance from the deceased to his said heirs at law or next of kin. The clerk is forbidden to receive for record any deed of an intestate's real estate by a person or persons claiming to have inherited the same until such an affidavit is presented to him, but the law provides that nothing therein shall be construed to invalidate the recording as legal notice of any such deed lodged for record prior to the filing of such affidavit. Any person wilfully or fraudulently making affidavit to any statements which he knows to be false is subject to fine or imprisonment or both, and is also liable to any person injured by the making, filing, recording or use of such affidavit. (KRS 382.120; 832.990[2]).

Filing Under Commercial Code.—Kentucky adopted 1962 official version of and 1966, 1972 and 1977 official amendments to U.C.C. Version of §9-401(1), subsection which governs proper place to file financing statement, is patterned after "third alternative subsection" proposed for §9-401(1) with words "county clerk" inserted in (1)(a). Subsection (1)(c) provides in pertinent part: "(c) In all other cases, if the debtor is a resident of this state in the office of the county clerk of the county of the debtor's residence or, if the debtor is a nonresident of this state then in the office of the secretary of state of the Commonwealth of Kentucky". (KRS 355.9-401[1]). Subsection 9-401(5) sets forth 11 specific clauses for determining residency of different kinds of debtors: Individual debtor deemed to be resident of county in which his principal place of business is located; domestic business corporation, domestic limited liability company, foreign business corporation and foreign limited liability company authorized to transact business in this state are each deemed resident of county in which its registered office is located as set forth in most recent corporate filing with Secretary of State; Kentucky limited partnership deemed resident of county where its office is located, as set forth in certificate of limited partnership; general partnership deemed resident of county in which its principal office is located but if office is not located in state, partnership deemed nonresident; comparable provisions set forth for business trusts, credit unions, cooperative and nonprofit corporations and other types of entities. (KRS 355.9-401[5]). In addition to filings required by §9-401, informational only filing does not convey notice or constitute perfection required with Secretary of State for indexing in centralized Lien Information System. Filing requirements do not apply to fixture filings where collateral is goods intended to be fixtures nor to timber, minerals, oil and gas, coal, or accounts, other than accounts arising from sale of coal. (KRS 355.9-401A[1]).

Fees on Filing; Tax.—County clerk's fees: $14 for filing and indexing financing statement (KRS 64.012), including $5 filing and indexing termination statement (see KRS 64.012), $8 for filing continuation statement or assignment (KRS 64.012). Secretary of State's fees: $13 (includes $5 for later filing of termination statement) for each financing statement (KRS 355.9-401[1]); $8 for each amendment to financing statement; $8 for each assignment and $8 for each release or partial release. $1 for informational filings in centralized Lien Information System. (KRS 355.9-401A[2]). County clerk's fee for providing certification under KRS 355.9-407 is $5 and $5 for each certified copy of financing statement or assignment. (KRS 64.012). Secretary of State's fee for providing certification under KRS 355.9-407 is $5 for certificate with seal and 50¢ per page

for providing certified copy of any document or affixing seal to certificate. (KRS 14.090[1]).

Tax of $3 applies to filing of every financing statement or security agreement in county clerk's office. (KRS 142.010). In addition, clerk may require prepayment of postage for returning recorded financing statement or security agreement. (KRS 382.240). These fees include County Clerk charge of up to $1 for each instrument recorded, regardless of whether instrument is returned by mail. Postage, if any, charged by clerks should be confirmed prior to recordation.

Vital Statistics.—Records of births, deaths, marriages, divorces, annulments and adoptions are prepared by local registrars and forwarded periodically for permanent record to Office of Vital Statistics, Cabinet for Human Resources in Frankfort. (KRS 213.031; 213.036). Certified copies of records on file with Office of Vital Statistics available upon request for births and deaths. (KRS 213.131). Other records available for research or administrative purposes under certain conditions. (KRS 213.131[4]). Requests for copies of records should be directed to State Registrar, Office of Vital Statistics, Vital Records, 275 East Main Street, Frankfort, Kentucky 40621. Fee for copy of any certificate on record may not exceed $9 (KRS 213.141[1]); no fee charged military service veterans for certificates of birth or death required for certain claims against government (KRS 213.141[4]). Telephone information concerning availability of records and procedures may be available from (502) 564-4212.

Records of marriages are kept in offices of county clerks which issued licenses. (KRS 402.230). Records of dissolutions of marriage, annulments, etc. contained in final court judgments maintained by clerks of circuit courts entering decrees. (KRS cc. 403, cc. 30A).

Establishing Birth Record.—Establishing record of birth not recorded at time of occurrence is governed by administrative regulations. (KRS 213.056). In case proof becomes necessary, rules of evidence established by Cabinet for Human Resources apply. (KRS 213.056[1]).

Lis Pendens.—Notice of pendency of action required to be filed in county clerk's office in county where real property located for any action involving interest in real property in order to provide constructive notice to third parties. Notice must include (i) number of action; (ii) style of action; (iii) name of person whose interest affected; and (iv) description of real property. (KRS 382.440 and 382.450). Certified copy of any matter in reference to bankruptcy should be filed in county clerk's office wherein lands of bankrupt are located and recorded in general deed index in name of bankrupt, as grantor, and trustee or receiver (if any), as grantee. (KRS 382.510).

SEALS:

A seal or scroll is not necessary to give effect to deed or other writing. Unsealed writings stand on same footing with sealed writings. (KRS 371.020). This statute does not apply to negate any other law requiring state or county seal or seal of court, corporation or notary to any writing.

A scroll may be used by a corporation or individual in the execution of a deed. (36 Ky. [6 Dana] 37).

Corporate Seal.—General powers authorize every corporation to have and use corporate seal, KRS 271B.3-020(1), but provide that neither absence nor presence of seal on any writing adds to or detracts from legality or validity of any writing. (KRS 271B.3-020[2]). Absence of corporate seal does not affect entitlement of writing to be filed by Secretary of State. (KRS 271B.1-200[7]).

Effect of Seal.—The fact that an instrument is sealed does not preclude impeachment thereof for lack of consideration. (KRS 371.030).

Uniform Commercial Code in effect. (KRS c. 355). See KRS 355.2-203 as to seals.

TORRENS ACT:

See topic Records.

VITAL STATISTICS:

See topic Records.

EMPLOYMENT

EMPLOYER AND EMPLOYEE:

See topic Labor Relations.

LABOR RELATIONS:

Department of Workplace Standards of Labor Cabinet regulates wages, hours, and safety of employees.

Hours of Labor.—Persons under 18 may not work more than five hours continuously without 30-minute lunch period. (KRS 339.270). No employee may be required to work more than four hours without ten minute rest period, in addition to lunch period. (KRS 337.365). Reasonable lunch break required not sooner than three hours after beginning of shift nor later than five hours after beginning of shift. (KRS 337.355).

Wages, which as defined includes commissions and earned bonuses, payable to employees, as defined to include all persons permitted to work with limited exceptions, must be paid in legal tender of U.S. or in checks on demand deposit accounts (KRS 337.010; Const., §244). Not less than local "prevailing wage", as determined by Commissioner of Department of Workplace Standards, must be paid on public works costing more than $250,000, adjusted annually. (KRS 337.010; 337.530).

Employers of ten or more persons, who pay by check and make deductions from salaries or wages due employees, must furnish, at time of payment, a statement showing amount and purpose of each deduction made. (KRS 337.070). No employer shall withhold any part of employee's wages except to extent authorized by law, by employee in writing or by employer-employee contracts. (KRS 337.060). Mandatory tip pools prohibited. (KRS 337.065).

LABOR RELATIONS . . . *continued*

Every employer must pay employees as often as semi-monthly all wages or salary earned by such employees to day not more than 18 days prior to date of payment. No employer may exempt itself from this provision by special contract. (KRS 337.020). Time for payment is 15 days for all employers engaged in mining. (KRS 352.540).

Employees who leave or are discharged must be paid all earned wages on next regular payday or within 14 days of dismissal or leaving, whichever is later. (KRS 337.055). Violation of section renders employer liable for civil penalties up to $1,000 and twice amount withheld. (KRS 337.385; 337.990).

Non-transferable scrip, tokens, drafts, orders or coupons, redeemable in merchandise, may be issued at the request of any employee, but such scrip, etc., is redeemable in lawful money on any legal settlement day or pay day. (KRS 337.040).

As to assignments of wages, see category Debtor and Creditor, topic Assignments.

Wage and hours laws adopt minimum wage rate set out in 29 U.S.C. §206(a)(1). (KRS 337.275). Time and one-half required for all hours over 40 in work week except for retail and hotel and motel employees and those exempted from federal overtime coverage by 29 U.S.C. §§213(b)(1), 213(b)(10) and 213(b)(17), and except for employees of private nonprofit childcare facilities under KRS c. 199. (KRS 337.285).

Exemptions from all coverage under statutes provided for: agricultural employees; executives, supervisory and outside sales personnel; U.S. gov't. employees; domestic servants if only one in household; certified learners, apprentices, workers with disabilities and students; employees of small retail stores, service industries, hotels, motels and restaurants and family employees in all such establishments; baby-sitters and home companions for sick or elderly; newspaper persons; employees of organized nonprofit camp, religious or nonprofit educational conference center if in operation less than seven months a year; and certain state employees. (KRS 337.010[2][a]).

Commissioner of Workplace Standards given enforcement duties and powers under wage and hour laws (KRS 337.275 to 337.405) and civil penalties provided for violation of various sections of wage and hours statutes (KRS 337.990). Order or decision of Commissioner may be appealed in accordance with KRS c. 13B. (KRS 337.310).

Child Labor.—Children under 14 years of age may not be employed in certain establishments, and during the school term may not be employed at all unless in program supervised and sponsored by child's school district and approved by Department of Education under regulations of Department of Workplace Standards. Children as young as 11 years old may be employed as caddies on public or private golf courses. (KRS 339.225). Certain rigid requirements are made for employment of children between 14 and 18. (KRS 339.230). There are other regulations for other children. (KRS 339.210-339.990).

Female Labor.—No provisions.

Discrimination in employment by employers, labor organizations and employment agencies and in apprenticeship programs and in advertisements for employment on basis of race, color, religion, national origin, sex, disability or age over 40 unlawful. (KRS 344.030-344.110). Enforcement by Human Rights Commission in coordination with federal agencies. (KRS 344.150-344.190). Civil action available, regardless of whether employee files complaint with Human Rights Commission. (KRS 344.450). Specific prohibition of discrimination in payment of wages on basis of sex. (KRS 337.423). Civil rights protection extended to smokers and others who use tobacco products, but individual must comply with any workplace policy concerning smoking. (KRS 344.040).

Discrimination against persons with physical disabilities prohibited; protection extended to any person with AIDS. (KRS 207.130 et seq.). Enforced through administrative proceedings or civil action. (Id.). (With regard to disability discrimination potential conflict exists between KRS 344.010 et seq. and KRS 207.130 et seq.)

Employer may not retaliate or discriminate against employee who files claim for workers' compensation benefits. (KRS 342.197). Enforced through civil action. (Id.).

Employer may not require applicant or employee to waive, arbitrate or otherwise diminish any existing or future claim, right or benefit under Kentucky or federal statutory law. (KRS 336.700).

Labor Unions.—Employees may organize, designate representatives for collective bargaining, strike, engage in peaceful picketing and assemble collectively for peaceful purposes. Neither employers nor employees may engage in unfair acts or resort to violence, intimidation, threats, or coercion. (KRS 336.130). Kentucky has no statewide "right to work" law. Cities cannot enact local "right to work" ordinances. (391 S.W.2d 360).

Labor Disputes.—Commissioner of Department of Workplace Standards has duty to inquire into and endeavor to settle labor disputes (KRS 336.151; 336.010); may create boards to which disputes may be submitted on request (KRS 336.140). Employers, employees, and their representatives have duty to meet and confer to resolve disputes. (KRS 336.152).

Injunctions will lie to restrain violence, personal injury or damage to property after hearing on petition accompanied by affidavit that such acts have occurred or to prohibit picketing in violation of no-strike clause in contract. (KRS 336.130[3]; 411 S.W.2d 935). Affidavit specifying acts of violence, etc. and prior hearing apparently not required to restrain picketing in violation of no-strike clause. (KRS 336.130[3]). Submission of false affidavit concerning acts of violence, etc. is punishable as form of perjury. (KRS 336.130[4]; 523.030).

Employer-Employee Relations Act.—A comprehensive statute dealing with employer-employee relations extends the functions and duties of the Commissioner of Department of Workplace Standards and of Department of Workplace Standards, creates Kentucky Occupational Safety and Health Standards Board and Kentucky Apprenticeship and Training Council. Another Act prescribes certain duties of employers and employees, provides for safety standards and devices, and deals with payment of wages and apprenticeship agreements. (KRS, Title XXVII, Labor, cc. 336, 337, 338, 343).

Occupational safety and health standards, including federal standards, have been adopted and enforced by board within Department of Workplace Standards. (KRS 338.011 to 338.195; 803 KAR c. 2). Standards apply to all employers, employees and places of employment in state except those subject to regulatory authority of Occupational Safety and Health Administration (OSHA) of U.S. Department of Labor and federal government employees. (KRS 338.021). Employees reporting violations are statutorily protected. (KRS 358.121). Administrative proceedings provided for enforcement (KRS 338.081) or Commissioner of Workplace Standards may request civil or criminal action including injunction in court to restrain substantially dangerous acts and practices (KRS 338.133).

Worker's Compensation Act provides for compensation for injury, occupational disease, or death, which arises out of and in course of employment, without regard to fault as cause of injury, occupational disease, or death. (KRS 342.610[1]; 342.620; 342.610[5]; 342.001[1]; 342.0011[2]; 342.0011[5]). Psychological, psychiatric or stress-related changes excluded unless direct result of physical injury. (KRS 342.001[1]). Employer's liability under Act is exclusive. (KRS 342.690).

Employers and Employees Applicable.—Term "employers" as used in Act means any person having one or more employees, except those engaged solely in agriculture. Included as an employer are states and local governments and school districts. (KRS 342.630).

"Employees" exempt from Act are: persons employed as domestic servants in private home by employer who has less than two regularly employed employees working 40 hours or more per week; persons employed for 20 consecutive days or less in maintenance, repair, remodeling or similar work in or about private home of an employer, if employer has no other employees subject to Act; any person performing services in return for aid and/or sustenance from religious or charitable organization; any person for whom rule of liability for injury or death is provided under laws of U.S., except those persons covered under Title IV, P. L. 91-173, 91st Congress, commonly referred to as Black Lung Benefits of the Federal Coal Mine Health and Safety Act of 1969, or as am'd; any person employed in agriculture; any person who would otherwise be covered but who elects not to be covered; any person participating in voluntary carpool or vanpool program; any member of religious sect that adheres to established tenets opposing benefits if members of sect have longstanding practice of providing for dependent members. (KRS 342.650). Employer may elect that coverage apply to exempt employees. (KRS 342.660).

Acceptance or Rejection of Act.—Act is mandatory for those employers not specifically excluded, and employee is considered covered under Act unless he specifically elects not to be covered or is exempt. (KRS 342.630; 342.650). Assets of employers who are not exempted and who have not purchased insurance or qualified as self-insurers (KRS 342.340) subject to lien in favor of Uninsured Employers Fund from time certificate is filed (KRS 342.770). Award on such claim is statutorily liquidated to be present value of all probable payments, discounted by 4% and may be pursued by Attorney General on behalf of state. (KRS 342.790).

Reports to Board.—Employers subject to Act required to keep records of all injuries, fatal or otherwise, received by employees in course of employment. Report of every injury to employee causing absence from work for more than one day must be sent to Board in Frankfort within one week of injury and knowledge. Follow-up reports also required. (KRS 342.038). Injury report must be sent to workers' compensation carrier or other party responsible for payment of benefit within three days from date employer receives notice of incident. (KRS 342.038[3]).

Notice of Claim, Time for and Contents.—Notice of an accident shall be given to employer as soon as practicable after happening thereof, and no proceeding shall be maintained unless application for resolution of claim shall have been made within two years after date of accident, or in case of death, within two years after such death or, in case voluntary payments have been made, within two years after suspension of such payments or two years after date of accident whichever is later. (KRS 342.185). Claim resulting from work-related exposure to human immunodeficiency virus barred unless notice of injurious exposure is given to employer as soon as practicable after happening thereof and application for adjustment of claim is filed within five years from date of exposure. (Id.).

In case of occupational disease, time for filing claim is three years after last injurious exposure to occupational hazard, or after employee first experiences distinct manifestation of disease, whichever last occurs. Three year limitation also applies to occupational disease claims resulting in death. Maximum time limit remains five years from last injurious exposure regardless of when disease manifests itself, except in radiation disease or asbestos related disease cases time limit is 20 years from last injurious exposure. (KRS 342.316). Printed copies of claim forms will be provided by Workers' Compensation Board, Frankfort, Kentucky 40601.

Hearings on Claims.—Act is administered by Workers' Compensation Commissioner. (KRS 342.260). Arbitrators are empowered to resolve disputes through benefit review conferences. (KRS 342.270). Case may be transferred or appealed to Administrative Law Judge (ALJ) for hearing. (KRS 342.270; 342.275). Disputes shall be determined in summary manner. (KRS 342.260). There is provision for appeal to Workers' Compensation Board and to Court of Appeals. (KRS 342.285; 342.290).

Benefits.—Injured employee entitled to prompt medical rehabilitation services to accomplish feasible, practical and justifiable physical rehabilitation and to vocational rehabilitation of up to 52 weeks, or longer on order of ALJ or arbitrator after hearing. (KRS 342.710). Employee suffering from occupational injury or disease, in addition to income compensation, is entitled to select medical treatment at employer's expense. (KRS 342.020). Income benefits for total disability are set at 66²/₃rds of employee's average weekly wage, maximum 100% and minimum 20% of state average weekly wage. Income benefits for permanent, partial disability, based on 66²/₃rds of employee's average weekly wage, maximum 75% of state average weekly wage multiplied by permanent impairment rating published by AMA times a factor set forth in statute. (KRS 342.730). If injury results in death within four years, lump sum of $25,000 payable to estate, from which burial expenses and costs of transportation are paid. (KRS 342.750). State average weekly wage determined annually by Commissioner. (KRS 342.740; 342.143). Income and other benefits for occupational "black lung" covered specifically. (KRS 342.732).

All fees of attorneys and physicians are subject to approval by ALJ or arbitrator, subject to statute and administrative regulations, and attorney's fee may not exceed 20% of award, but no more than $2,000 for services performed up to and including determination by arbitrator. Upon appeal of arbitrator's determination or Order of ALJ, fees fixed at no more than 20% of first $25,000 increase in benefits, 10% of next $10,000,

See note at head of Digest as to 1998 legislation covered.

See Topical Index in front part of this volume.

KY – 29

LABOR RELATIONS . . . *continued*
and 5% of additional increase with maximum of $10,000. (KRS 342.320). Employer's attorney's fees also capped. (Id.).

To Whom Compensation for Death Payable.—If injury causes death, income benefits shall be payable to (a) widow or widower during widowhood or widowerhood and to (b) surviving children until any such child dies, marries, or reaches age of 18. Child who originally qualified as dependent by virtue of being less than 18 may upon reaching age 18 continue to qualify if he satisfies tests of being physically or mentally incapable of self support and actual dependency. Enrollment in educational institution up to age of 22 will entitle child to benefits. Also entitled to benefits is (c) each parent, if actually dependent, and, (d) brothers, sisters, grandparents and grandchildren, if actually dependent. (KRS 342.750). In addition, lump sum payable to estate if injury results in death within four years.

Enforcement of awards is by action in Circuit Court of County in which injury occurred. (KRS 342.305).

Occupational diseases are covered by Workers' Compensation Act. See subhead Worker's Compensation Act, supra. To be covered, disease must arise out of and in course of employment, have causal connection with work conditions and be traced to employment as proximate cause. (KRS 342.620[2]; 342.0011[2]).

Employers' Liability Act.—Common carriers by railroad and their employees, while engaged in intrastate commerce in Kentucky, are subject to the terms of an Employers' Liability Law substantially similar to the Federal Employers' Liability Law. (KRS 277.310-277.320).

Public Works.—Contractors and subcontractors engaged in construction of public works are subject to strict regulation in respect to selection of employees, wages, hours of work and overtime. (KRS 337.505-337.550).

Unemployment Compensation.—See category Taxation, topic Unemployment Compensation Tax.

For eligibility, unemployed worker must: (a) Make claim; (b) register for work; (c) be able to work or be enrolled in approved training program; (d) serve one-week waiting period; (e) have earned sufficient base-period wages, determined by formula, and (f) not be disqualified by reason of enumerated acts. (KRS 341.350-341.370).

Benefits, based on wages earned in base period (quarter) are determined annually by Secretary of Human Resources on basis of average monthly employment for previous year, not exceeding lesser of 26 times weekly benefit or one third of base period wages. (KRS 341.380).

Liens of Employees.—See category Debtor and Creditor, topic Liens.

WORKERS' COMPENSATION LAW:

See topic Labor Relations.

ENVIRONMENT

ENVIRONMENTAL REGULATION:

Kentucky statutory and regulatory provisions relating to environment treat specifically problems of water, air and noise pollution control, solid and hazardous waste disposal, coal and surface mining reclamation, clay mining reclamation and use, storage and application of pesticides.

General supervision of environment is placed in Natural Resources and Environmental Protection Cabinet (Capital Plaza Tower, Frankfort, Kentucky 40601), with exception of storage, use and application of pesticides and storage of fertilizer which are supervised by Department of Agriculture, and on-site sewage disposal systems which are regulated by Cabinet for Human Resources.

Jurisdiction over air pollution control is held concurrently by Natural Resources and Environmental Protection Cabinet and local Boards of County Air Pollution Control Districts. In counties with concurrent jurisdiction, standards and facilities must equal or exceed state standards. (KRS 224.20-130). Local boards are granted broad powers including issuance, suspension and revocation of permits, collection of permit fees, enforcement of violations and assessment of fines. (KRS 77.005 et seq.). Concurrent jurisdiction exists for Jefferson County (Louisville).

Petroleum Storage Tank Environmental Assurance Fund Commission established by statute to administer funds intended to reimburse expense of corrective action required by release of motor fuels from underground storage tanks. (KRS 224.60-100 et seq.). Commission abolished and duties transferred to Office of Petroleum Storage Tank Environmental Assurance Fund, attached to Public Protection and Regulation Cabinet, by Executive Orders of Governor, Nos. 96-485, 96-591. Annual fee levied of $30 per tank for purpose of funding administration program. (KRS 224.60-150).

Cabinet and Governor are advised by Environmental Quality Commission, composed of seven members appointed by Governor. (KRS 224.01-100, 224.01-110). Commission serves as forum for exchange of information and ideas relating to natural environment. (KRS 224.01-110).

Environmental Board controls and manages Environmental Trust Fund. Board is composed of secretary of Natural Resources and Environmental Protection Cabinet, chairman of Environmental Quality Commission, and six members at large appointed by Governor. (KRS 224.01-210). Fund may be used to support research and development, education or training necessary to guide development of environmental policy. (KRS 224.01-205).

Kentucky Infrastructure Authority assists governmental agencies with construction and acquisition of infrastructure projects including those for pollution abatement. (KRS 224A.035, 224A.011[15]). Affairs of Authority are managed by eight member board which for administrative purposes is attached to Finance and Administration Cabinet. (KRS 224A.030). Authority is empowered to levy tax of not more than 2% on purchase of water service or sewer service in state, and may make loans or grants to assist construction of infrastructure projects. (KRS 224A.070). Agriculture Water Quality Authority is multidiscipline peer group that establishes state-wide and regional agriculture water quality plans. (KRS 224.71-100 through 224.71-145). Authority consists of eleven members and is administratively attached to Natural Resources and Environmental Protection Cabinet.

Cabinet is designated as state agency for purpose of following federal acts: Water Pollution Control Act, Clean Air Act, Solid Waste Disposal Act, Resource Conservation and Recovery Act, and Surface Mining Control and Reclamation Act. (KRS 224.16-060).

Prohibited Acts of Pollution.—Cabinet has adopted standards of air and water quality, air and noise emissions and generation, handling and disposal of solid and hazardous waste in form of administrative regulations to implement statutory prohibitions. Cabinet has adopted standards for reclamation of surface coal mining operations.

Air pollution, in contravention of emission standards, ambient air standards, or rules and regulations of Cabinet, is prohibited. (KRS 224.20-110). Vehicle emissions regulated. (KRS 224.20-710 to KRS 224.20-765). Air emission fees for administering air quality program mandated by Title V of Clean Air Act Amendments authorized by statute. (KRS 224.20-050).

Water pollution in contravention of standards, rules, regulations of Cabinet, or which alters physical, thermal, chemical, biological, or radioactive properties of waters of Commonwealth in a manner detrimental to public health or welfare, animal, aquatic or marine life, present or future uses of public water supply, or recreational, commercial, industrial, agricultural or other use of water is prohibited. (KRS 224.01-010[34], 224.70-110). Discharges from boats are specifically regulated. (KRS 235.420 to 235.470).

On-site sewage disposal systems regulated by Cabinet for Human Resources ("CHR"). (KRS 211.350-211.380). Service of septic tanks and transportation and disposal of septic tank waste is also regulated by CHR. (KRS 211.970-211.982; 211.995; 224.10-194).

General criminal statute (KRS 438.060) prohibits placing in any stream, dam, pool or pond any substance rendering waters unfit or producing a stench, and prohibits placing carcass of any beast in any water course, or within 25 yards of any water course, spring or pond.

Water resources of Commonwealth shall be put to their most beneficial use. (KRS c. 151). To ensure continued growth and economic well being of Commonwealth and to advance safety, happiness and welfare of people, Commonwealth is specifically empowered to protect rights to use and availability of water and to prevent harmful overflows from flooding. (KRS 151.110).

Wild Rivers System.—Development and use of land along designated portions of Cumberland River, Red River, Rockcastle River, Green River, Big South Fork of Cumberland River, Martins Fork of Cumberland River, Rock Creek, Little South Fork of Cumberland River and Bad Branch of Poor Fork of Cumberland River is restricted and regulated by Natural Resources and Environmental Protection Cabinet. Construction and change-of-use permits required. (KRS 146.200-146.990).

Solid and hazardous waste generation and disposal regulated. (KRS 224.01-010; KRS 224 subchapters 40 through 50). Special waste (e.g., mining and utility wastes, sludge, cement kiln dust, etc.) regulated. (KRS 224.50-760). Solid waste landfills for disposal of limited quantities of hazardous waste must meet requirements of Natural Resources and Environmental Protection Cabinet. (KRS 224.43-614). Hazardous waste generators required to compile and retain records regarding wastes and to report activities to local government officials (KRS 224.46-510) and subject to assessments to fund hazardous waste management fund (KRS 224.46-580). Local government solid waste management plans required by KRS c. 109. Permits required for waste disposal facilities. (KRS 224.40-305; 224.46-520). Manifest system adopted for transport of hazardous wastes. (KRS 224.46-560; 224.46-570). Underground storage tanks regulated. (KRS 224.60-100 through 224.60-160). Open dumps regulated. (KRS 224.40-100). Agricultural wastes and hazardous wastes in amounts determined not harmful to public are exempt from regulation. (KRS 224.46-540). Labeling required for rigid plastic containers and bottles sold in state. (KRS 224.50-585). Waste tires regulated. (KRS 224.50-820 to 224.50-846).

Release or threatened release of hazardous substance, pollutant or contaminant into environment required to be reported to Cabinet. (KRS 224.01-400[6], [7], [9],[10], and [11]). Cabinet to establish contingency plan for response to release or threatened release of hazardous substance, pollutant or contaminant. (KRS 224.01-400[14]). Cabinet authorized to bring action for recovery of response costs against persons liable for release and Cabinet has lien for response costs against real and personal property of person liable for release. (KRS 224.01-400[15]and [23]). Cabinet may designate hazardous substances, pollutants and contaminants and is required to prepare inventory of sites where releases of same have occurred. (KRS 224.01-400[2] and [17]). Criteria for cleanup of release enumerated in KRS 224.01-400(21). Defenses and limitations to liability determined in accordance with Comprehensive Environmental Response Compensation and Liability Act and Federal Clean Water Act. (KRS 224.01-400[25]).

Noise pollution regulated by multi-section acts involving licensing, regulation, standards, product labeling and abatement and insulation standards with state and local enforcement. (KRS 224.30-050 et seq.). Emission of noise from boundaries of property or moving vehicle which interferes with another's enjoyment of life is prohibited. (KRS 224.30-050).

Pesticide use may be restricted by Department of Agriculture by regulation when necessary to prevent injury. (KRS 217B.010-217B.990). No person may apply any pesticide professionally without license issued by Department. (KRS 217B.070). Right of way and aerial applicators must provide surety or liability insurance to protect persons damaged. (KRS 217B.130).

Enforcement of general environment statutes is vested in Cabinet. Agents of Cabinet are authorized to enter upon public and private property to inspect and investigate compliance or noncompliance with law. Persons engaged in regulated activity must file descriptive information as required by Cabinet and may be required to install self-monitoring equipment. Cabinet may require performance bond. (KRS 224.10-100; 224.40-650; 224.46-520). Scope of regulatory powers described. (KRS 224.46-530). Emergency power specified. (KRS 224.46-580[3] and [15]; 224.01-400).

See note at head of Digest as to 1998 legislation covered.

See Topical Index in front part of this volume.

KY – 30

ENVIRONMENTAL REGULATION... *continued*

Procedures for administrative hearings for consideration of orders and complaints, and provisions for appeal of final Cabinet orders and determinations are detailed. (KRS 224.10-420 to 224.10-470, KRS 151.182-151.186, and KRS 350.0301-350.032).

Penalties.—Civil penalties up to $25,000 per day and injunction lie for discharging any substance into any waters of Commonwealth which causes or contributes to violation of water quality standards (KRS 224.70-110; 224.99-010[1]; 224.99-020), for failure to monitor and report on introduction of incompatible pollutants into publicly owned sewage treatment works (KRS 224.73-120; 224.99-010[1]; 224.99-020), or for emitting or discharging into air any contaminant which causes or contributes to violation of air quality standards (KRS 224.20-110; 224.99-010[1]; 224.99-020) or for violating hazardous waste management provisions of Chapter (KRS 224.99-010[5]).

Civil penalties of up to $5,000 per day and injunction lie for violations of waste disposal or waste facility permit laws, water purification, or noise pollution provisions and for failures to perform other duties imposed by Chapter. (KRS 224.99-010[2]).

Knowing violations of water, air, sewage and waste disposal provisions constitute Class D felony, and carry fine of up to $25,000 and/or imprisonment for up to five years for each day in violation. (KRS 224.99-010[4] and [6]). Knowing violations of noise pollution act constitute Class A misdemeanor. (KRS 224.99-010[3]).

Civil and criminal enforcement actions for water or air pollution may be brought in Franklin Circuit Court (Frankfort) or in county where violation occurs by Cabinet's Office of Legal Services or, at request of secretary, by Attorney General. (KRS 224.99-020).

Additional civil liability provided in favor of Commonwealth for destruction, death or injury to fish or other wildlife, resulting from violation of any orders, rules, regulations, or determinations of Cabinet. (KRS 224.01-070).

Criminal littering as defined in KRS 512.070 is Class A misdemeanor carrying maximum imprisonment of 12 months (KRS 532.090) and/or $500 fine for individual (KRS 534.040 [2][a]) or $10,000 for corporation (KRS 534.050[1][b]). Civil penalties of up to $5,000 per day per violation may be assessed for violations of c. 350 (KRS 350.990). Civil penalties of not less than $5,000 nor more than $25,000 per day for mining without permit. (KRS 350.990[2]). Knowing and willful violations of c. 350 may constitute Class A misdemeanors or Class D felonies. (KRS 350.990[4]-[8]).

Permits.—Permit issued by Cabinet must be held before discharging any sewage into water or emitting any matter into ambient air, constructing or operating waste disposal site or facility, or installing air pollution control device. (KRS 224.10-100[19]).

Permits also required for withdrawal of public water from stream, lake, ground water source or other body of water with certain exceptions (KRS 151.140) and construction in, along or across floodway of any stream (KRS 151.250, 151.310).

Surface Mining Reclamation.—No person may engage in surface coal mining operations without first obtaining permit from Cabinet (KRS 350.060) and filing reclamation bond (KRS 350.064). Reclamation standards detailed at KRS 350.405 to KRS 350.455. Reclamation bond will be released upon reclamation to satisfaction of Cabinet in accordance with schedule set forth in statutes and regulations. (KRS 350.093). Cabinet may revoke permit or forfeit bond for violations of reclamation standards. (KRS 350.130). Cabinet may issue permit authorizing disposal of coal combustion by-products at surface coal mining operations. (KRS 350.270).

Exemptions.—Cabinet may grant exemptions from its regulations where serious hardship would otherwise occur and measurable impact on quality of ambient air or water of Commonwealth will not be produced. (KRS 224.10-270).

Interstate Compacts.—Kentucky has entered into Ohio River Valley Water Sanitation Compact with states of Illinois, Indiana, New York, Ohio, Pennsylvania, Tennessee, and West Virginia. (KRS 224.18-760). Additional agreements with Tennessee are authorized by KRS 224.18-785. Interstate Water Sanitation Board through its three members are authorized to serve as Commonwealth's representative on boards of interstate commissions and to enforce provisions of compacts. (KRS 224.18-710; 224.18-715). Kentucky has adopted provisions of Interstate Compact on Air Pollution. (KRS 224.18-200). Four commissioners appointed by Governor and Secretary of Natural Resources and Environmental Protection Cabinet members of Interstate Air Pollution Control Commission to carry out terms of Compact. (KRS 224.18-210). Kentucky has joined Interstate Environmental Compact to deal with ecological systems and environmental problems which cross state lines. (KRS 224.18-100-224.18-110). Kentucky has enacted and entered into Interstate Mining Compact. (KRS 350.300).

Tax exemptions provided for certified pollution control facilities. (KRS 224.01-300-224.01-310). See category Taxation, topic General Sales and Use Tax, subhead Exemptions from Sales and Use Taxes.

ESTATES AND TRUSTS

ADMINISTRATION:

See topic Executors and Administrators.

ADVANCEMENTS:

See topic Descent and Distribution.

ALLOWANCES:

See topic Executors and Administrators.

CLAIMS:

See topic Executors and Administrators.

DEATH:

If a resident of Kentucky goes from state and does not return to it for seven successive years, a presumption of his death arises. (KRS 422.130). This does not supersede common law presumption of death after seven years' absence unheard from, but is merely declaratory of common law as far as it goes. (240 Ky. 172, 41 S.W.2d

935; 300 Ky. 797, 190 S.W.2d 479; 2 F. Supp. 365). Substantially common law rule as to presumption is provided by an escheat statute. (KRS 393.050). Determination by federal agency or service of death is prima facie evidence in courts and before agencies of state. (KRS 422.135). Both statutory and common law presumptions are rebuttable. (252 Ky. 793, 68 S.W.2d 393).

Uniform Simultaneous Death Act has been adopted. (KRS, c. 397).

Uniform Survival and Death Act.—Not adopted.

Action for Death.—An action lies for death of a person caused by negligence or wrongful act of another. (Const. §241; KRS 411.130). Action must be brought by personal representative of decedent (KRS 411.130), within one year after death occurred (KRS 413.140), and recovery is distributed according to statutory directions (KRS 411.130; 127 Ky. 55, 104 S.W. 1011). Damages recoverable include funeral expense and loss of earning power (307 Ky. 135, 210 S.W.2d 340), and pain and suffering of deceased before death (KRS 411.133). In wrongful death for minor, surviving parent may recover for loss of affection and companionship in addition to other elements. (KRS 411.135).

Surviving spouse and child under 18 of one killed by careless, wanton or malicious use of firearms or certain other deadly weapons have a right of action for such death. (KRS 411.150).

Personal representative permitted to recover both for wrongful death and for personal injuries suffered prior to death. (KRS 411.133).

No statutory limitation may be placed on the amount recoverable for death. (Const., §54).

As to award under Workmen's Compensation Act, see category Employment, topic Labor Relations.

As to death from faulty design of building, see category Civil Actions and Procedure, topic Limitation of Actions.

Survival of Tort Actions.—Causes of action for personal injury or property damage survive, except actions for slander, libel, criminal conversation, and so much of action for malicious prosecution as is intended to recover for personal injury. (KRS 411.140).

Death Certificate.—See category Documents and Records, topic Records, subhead Vital Statistics.

Uniform Anatomical Gift Act (1970) adopted with modifications. (KRS 311.165 to 311.235). Addition to §1 defines "transplantable organ" as including kidney, liver, lung, heart, and bone marrow and excludes other body parts. (KRS 311.165[5]). Nonuniform additions to Uniform Act prohibit profiting from trade in transportable organs (KRS 311.171) and condemn prohibited acts as criminal offenses with fines up to $500,000 and imprisonment up to ten years (KRS 311.990[27-31]).

Uniform Anatomical Gift Act (1987) not adopted.

Living Wills.—See topic Wills, subhead Living Will.

DECEDENTS' ESTATES:

See topics Descent and Distribution, Executors and Administrators, Wills; category Debtor and Creditor, topic Homesteads.

DESCENT AND DISTRIBUTION:

See also topic Executors and Administrators; category Property, topic Dower.

Real and personal property are subject to slightly different treatment.

Real Estate.—Undevised real estate of decedent descends, subject to right of homestead, and subject also to right, if any, of dower or curtesy, to kindred in following order: (1) To children and/or descendants of deceased children; (2) to parents equally or all to surviving parent; (3) to brothers and sisters and/or descendants of deceased brothers and sisters; (4) to surviving spouse; (5) if none of aforementioned, one moiety of estate to paternal and other to maternal kindred, in following order: (a) first, to grandfather and grandmother equally if both are living; but if one is dead, entire moiety shall go to survivor; if no grandfather or grandmother, then (b) to uncles and aunts and/or their descendants, if none, then (c) to great-grandfathers and great-grandmothers, in same manner prescribed for grandfather and grandmother above, if none, then (d) to brothers and sisters of grandfathers and grandmothers and their descendants; and so on in other cases without end, passing to nearest lineal ancestors and their descendants; (6) if there is no such kindred of one of parents, whole goes to kindred of other. If there is neither paternal nor maternal kindred, whole goes to kindred of surviving spouse, as if he or she had survived and died entitled to estate. (KRS 391.010). Special sections govern disposition of real property acquired with proceeds of or income from community property. (KRS 391.210 to 391.260).

Descendants of person who if living would be entitled to inherit, take per stirpes share of such deceased ancestor. (KRS 391.040).

Ancestral Estates.—When person dies intestate without issue, owning real estate of inheritance which was gift of either of his parents, such parent, if living, inherits it. (KRS 391.020[1]). If decedent was under 18 and died without issue, having title to real estate derived by gift, devise, or descent from one of his parents, whole descends to that parent, and that parent's kindred, as hereinbefore directed; if none, then in like manner to other parent and his or her kindred; but kindred of one may not be so excluded by kindred of other parent if such kindred are more remote than grandfather, grandmother, uncles and aunts of intestate and their descendants. (KRS 391.020[2]).

Aliens.—See category Citizenship, topic Aliens.

Personal Estate.—Surplus personalty of intestate, left after payment of funeral expenses, charges of administration and debts, subject to right, if any, of dower or curtesy, to same persons to whom real estate of intestate would descend, with these exceptions: (a) Personal estate of infant distributed as though he died after attaining full age; (b) alien may be distributee of personal estate; (c) personal property or money on hand or in bank up to $7,500 exempt from distribution upon application of surviving spouse, or if none, of surviving children. (KRS 391.030). Exemption also applies to surviving spouse of person dying testate. (KRS 391.030[4]). See topic Executors and Administrators, subhead Allowances. Special sections govern disposition of property under community property laws of another state. (KRS 391.210; 391.260).

See note at head of Digest as to 1998 legislation covered.

See Topical Index in front part of this volume.

DESCENT AND DISTRIBUTION . . . *continued*

Surviving Spouse.—Rights of surviving spouse to inherit surplus real estate and surplus personalty set forth under category Property, topic Dower. If decedent left no children, parents, or brothers or sisters or descendants of deceased brothers or sisters surviving, surviving spouse takes all real estate. (KRS 391.010). See subhead Real Estate, supra. Conviction of felony in connection with taking life of decedent causes forfeiture of all interest in and to property of decedent, including right to take under decedent's will, as joint tenant with rights of survivorship or as beneficiary of any insurance policy. (KRS 381.280). If surviving spouse is alien, certain restrictions apply. See category Citizenship, topic Aliens.

Collaterals of the half-blood inherit half as much as those of whole blood, or as ascending kindred, when they take with either. (KRS 391.050).

Posthumous child of decedent takes as though born in decedent's lifetime, if born within ten months of decedent's death. (KRS 391.070).

Illegitimates.—For purpose of intestate succession, illegitimate child may inherit by, through and from natural mother. (KRS 391.105). Illegitimate child may also inherit by, from and through natural father if natural parents married before or after birth of child, even if marriage void, or adjudication of paternity before death of father or after upon clear and convincing proof. (KRS 391.105; 635 S.W.2d 316; 896 S.W.2d 15). Issue of illegitimate child may inherit through such child. (87 Ky. 216, 8 S.W. 337). Natural father may inherit from and through illegitimate child. (799 S.W.2d 5).

Adopted Child.—See category Family, topic Adoption.

Determination of Heirship.—When property passes by intestate succession, or under will to beneficiary not named, proceeding may be had in district court to determine persons entitled. Adversary action may be commenced in circuit court. (KRS 391.035).

Advancements.—Any real or personal property or money, given or devised by parent or grandparent, to descendant, must be charged to descendant, or those claiming through him in division and distribution of undevised estate of parent or grandparent; and such party receives nothing further therefrom until other descendants made proportionately equal with him, according to his descendable and distributable share of whole estate, real and personal, devised and undevised. Advancement estimated according to value of property when given. Maintaining or educating, or giving of money to child or grandchild, without view to portion or settlement in life, not deemed advancement. (KRS 391.140).

Advancement made to distributees not taken as part of decedent's personal estate in estimating distributable share of widow or widower. (KRS 391.140). Gift from one spouse to other, even though called "advancement," not within this statute. (286 Ky. 504, 151 S.W.2d 369).

Desertion; Divorce.—Spouse who voluntarily leaves other and lives in adultery forfeits all right and interest in property of other, unless he or she afterward reconciles and they live together as husband and wife. (KRS 392.090). Decree of dissolution of marriage bars all future distributive rights in estate of former spouse. (KRS 392.090).

Renunciation.—See topic Wills, subhead Renunciation.

Election between curtesy or dower and distributive shares, see topic Wills.

Escheat.—Property of person dying intestate without heirs or distributees, or whose heirs, distributees, devisees or legatees do not claim same within seven years after death, escheats to state subject to debts and liabilities of deceased. (KRS 393.040).

Uniform Probate Code.—Not adopted.

ESTATES:

See category Property, topic Real Property.

EXECUTORS AND ADMINISTRATORS:

Jurisdiction and Venue.—Probate proceedings held in and letters of administration issued by district court of county in which: (1) Decedent resided at death, if resident of Kentucky; or (2) if residence on military reservation or fort, in any adjacent county thereto; or (3) if not then resident of Kentucky, (a) in county in which land, if any devised or owned by decedent, or part thereof, is located, or (b) if no land in Kentucky devised, or owned, in county in which he died or in which estate or part thereof located or where there is debt or demand owing to him. (KRS 394.140, 395.030).

Preferences in Right to Administer.—When decedent leaves no will or no qualified person named in will who can execute its provisions, letters of administration must be issued to following named persons or their nominees respectively (if qualified) in following order: (1) Surviving husband or wife or suitable administrator nominated by such spouse; (2) or if surviving husband or wife does not nominate suitable administrator, one or more of those next entitled to distribution as court deems best suited to manage estate. (KRS 395.040). Preferential right of administration or of nominating administrator not absolute (185 Ky. 449, 215 S.W. 86; 239 Ky. 263, 39 S.W.2d 258); it may be waived, but without legal cause one entitled can not be deprived of right to administer (246 Ky. 338, 55 S.W.2d 20) or to nominate suitable person (178 Ky. 573, 199 S.W. 58; 240 S.W.2d 593). If decedent's surviving spouse and relations fail to apply for administration within 60 days of death, court may grant administration to creditor or any other person, except to master or other commissioner whose duty it is to settle accounts of personal representative. If will later produced and proved, administration theretofore granted ceases. (KRS 395.040).

Eligibility and Competency.—Any resident of Kentucky over 18 years of age, resident under 18 years of age (if will specifically directs appointment of minor [KRS 395.080]), any national bank located in Kentucky having fiduciary powers, and any Kentucky bank or trust company incorporated under and authorized by Kentucky law to act as fiduciary, may qualify as executor or administrator. (KRS 395.005).

Nonresident of legal age may be appointed executor or administrator if related to decedent by consanguinity, marriage, adoption, or spouse of such person so related. (KRS 395.005). Nonresident personal representative must designate resident of county of probate as process agent. (KRS 395.015).

Foreign corporation may not act as executor or administrator of one who died domiciled in Kentucky or as testamentary trustee under will of such decedent. (O.A.G. 62-1141).

Application for Appointment.—Applicant for appointment as executor or administrator must file written application in duplicate under oath, stating names of decedent's surviving spouse and all heirs at law, or such as are known, their post office addresses, if known, date of decedent's death, in general terms of what the estate consists and probable value of personal and real estate, and any indebtedness owed to decedent by applicant. Executor named in will may omit names and addresses of heirs at law unless requested by court. Application of nonresident must include designation of resident of county where administration pending as process agent for actions against estate or against him accrued in administration thereof. Clerk must mail duplicate copy of application to Commissioner of Revenue. (KRS 395.015[1]).

Notice and Hearing.—In case of intestacy, or where administrator with will annexed or de bonis non to be appointed, if no surviving spouse, or if such spouse waives right to appointment or not qualified to act and does not nominate suitable administrator and there are two or more resident heirs at law entitled to appointment, court must appoint time for hearing application for appointment. (KRS 395.015[2]). At least five days written notice by certified mail, of hearing must be given to surviving spouse and all known heirs residing in Kentucky, except where gross amount involved is less than $5,000, court may dispense with notice. (KRS 395.016).

Qualification.—Executor, administrator or other fiduciary must take oath and give bond sufficient to secure value of decedent's whole estate. (KRS 62.060).

Exemption from Surety on Bond.—Every fiduciary, must provide surety on his bond unless, on petition of interested party, court satisfied all interests are protected or if will or trust directs no surety required. (KRS 395.130). Capital stock sufficient security for corporate fiduciary unless court or party in interest demands additional security. (KRS 287.220[2]).

District court judge must annually inquire into solvency of sureties and require new bond or additional surety where necessary for protection of estate. (KRS 395.640; 395.160).

Issuance of Letters.—Before entering on execution of his trust, executor or administrator must receive letters of appointment from district court having jurisdiction. (KRS 395.105). At time of appointment he may (but is not required to) designate attorney who will represent him in matters relating to trust, and if done notices to such fiduciary must also be sent by court to such attorney. (KRS 395.145).

Removal.—Grounds: residence out of state without appointing agent for service of process; insanity or other incapability of discharging trust; bankruptcy, insolvency or failing circumstances; failure to give additional security when required (KRS 395.160); neglect or refusal to file inventory or account on date fixed by court (KRS 395.255).

Special Kinds of Administration.—Provision made for: Administrator with will annexed, if will names no executor or named executor cannot or does not qualify (KRS 395.050); administrator de bonis non, if personal representatives die and decedent was intestate (KRS 395.060); curators (q.v.); ancillary administrators (see subhead Foreign Executors or Administrators, infra).

Curators.—Curator may be appointed to take charge of decedent's estate during contest over probate of will or while court delayed in granting letters testamentary or of administration. (KRS 395.410-395.430).

Public Administrators.—District court of each county must appoint public administrator, to whom it may commit estates as to which no one will qualify as administrator or apply for administration, within 60 days after death. (KRS 395.380-395.400).

Inventory and Appraisal.—Personal representative must file in district court, within two months after qualification, inventory in duplicate of estate coming into his hands, original to be recorded by clerk and duplicate mailed by clerk to Commissioner of Revenue. (KRS 395.250).

Personal representatives accountable only for such estate as comes or may come into their hands for administration (KRS 395.290), but may be held responsible by action on their bonds for failure to use due diligence in collecting or managing estate (KRS 395.300).

Settlement Suit.—Provision made for settlement suit in circuit court when appears genuine issue concerning correct settlement of estate or right of beneficiary or creditor to receive payment. (KRS 395.510-395.515).

Assets for Payment of Debts.—Decedent's property, whether real or personal (except property exempted to widow and infant children, see subhead Allowances, infra), constitutes assets for payment of his debts. (KRS c. 396).

General Powers and Duties.—Representative has such duties as required by law or ordered by court. (KRS 395.105; 395.195-395.220). See also subhead Sales, infra.

Notice to Creditors.—At least once a month, each probate court clerk must publish in newspaper having general circulation in county, list of all fiduciary appointments made since preceding publication, with name and address of each decedent or ward, name and address of fiduciary, date of appointment, name and address of fiduciary's attorney, if any, and date by which claims of creditors must be presented. (KRS 424.340).

Presentation of Claims.—In action pending at decedent's death, which action survives at law, substitution of personal representative for decedent, or motion therefor, constitutes presentation of claim. (KRS 396.015[2]). No action may be brought on claim against estate until claim presented in manner set forth in KRS 396.015. (KRS 396.035). All claims against decedent's estate which arose before death of decedent, excluding claims of U.S., state or any subdivision thereof, whether due or to become due, absolute or contingent, liquidated or unliquidated, founded on contract, tort, or other legal basis, if not previously barred by other statutes of limitations, are barred against estate, personal representative, and heirs and devisees of decedent, unless brought within six months of appointment of personal representative or within two years after decedent's death if no personal representative appointed. (KRS 396.011; 396.205). This section

See note at head of Digest as to 1998 legislation covered.

See Topical Index in front part of this volume.

EXECUTORS AND ADMINISTRATORS . . . *continued*
does not affect any proceedings to enforce security interest securing decedent's obligation or on property of estate, to extent of security, or proceedings to establish liability of decedent or personal representative, to extent of liability insurance. (KRS 396.011[2]).

Proof of Claims.—To participate in distribution, claimant must deliver or mail to personal representative or file with court clerk written statement of claim. (KRS 396.015). Personal representative may require claimant's affidavit or other evidence that, to claimant's knowledge, claim justly due, no payments made thereon and no offsets against same; or if payments made or offsets exist, nature and amount of each must be shown by evidence or stated in affidavit. (KRS 396.026).

Approval or Rejection of Claims.—Personal representative may mail notice to claimant of allowance or disallowance of claim, and, if decision changes, must notify claimant. (KRS 396.055). Disallowance of claim irreversible if statute of limitations has run. (KRS 396.055). When claim rejected in whole or in part by mailed notice warning of impending bar, action to enforce must be commenced within 60 days. (KRS 396.055). Personal representative's failure to mail notice to claimant 60 days after time for original presentation of claims constitutes notice of allowance, except court may disallow claim for cause shown. (KRS 396.055[1]). Judgment against personal representative to enforce claim is allowance of claim. (KRS 396.055[2]).

Payment of Claims.—Six months after date of appointment, personal representative may pay allowed claims in order of priority. (KRS 396.075[1]). Personal representative may pay any claim not barred, with or without formal presentation, but personally liable to any other claimant whose claim is allowed and is injured by such payment if payment prior to six month limit and adequate security for refund not obtained, or payment made due to negligence or willful fault of personal representative and injured claimant deprived of priority. (KRS 396.075[2]).

If any allowed claim, unmature, contingent or unliquidated, matures prior to distribution, it must be paid as matured and absolute claims of same class. (KRS 396.115[1]).

Priorities.—Claims against insolvent estates paid in following order: (1) Costs and expenses of administration; (2) funeral expenses; (3) debts and taxes with preference under federal and state laws; (4) all other claims. No preference given to any claim over others within same class. (KRS 396.095). If estate insufficient, each claimant entitled to receive equal proportionate share of claim. If preference or security allowed in another jurisdiction but not this state, benefited creditor may receive only balance of claim from local assets. (KRS 396.175[2]).

Sales.—Power of sale of property, real or personal, conferred by will on executor or trustee, may be exercised according to its terms. (KRS 395.200-395.220; 250 Ky. 584, 63 S.W.2d 776). Power so conferred upon executors, if not restricted personally, may be exercised by surviving executor (KRS 395.060) or administrator d. b. n., c. t. a. (KRS 395.050). Unless authorized by express terms of will, personal representative has no power to sell real estate. (KRS 395.220). In order to enforce sale of property for payment of debts representative must bring suit in circuit court for settlement of decedent's estate or move district court for order of sale. (KRS 389A.010-389A.025; 395.510-395.550).

In all cases, personal representative, when satisfied sale in best interests of estate, may sell at public or private sale, and at fixed price or for best price obtainable, and for cash or on such terms as personal representative may determine, any part or all of personal property belonging to estate, except (a) tangible personalty set apart as exempt to surviving spouse; (b) property specifically bequeathed, when sale not necessary to pay debts, provided that sale may be made with consent of legatee; (c) property suitable for distribution in kind or where such distribution is demanded prior to sale; (d) property sought to be sold contrary to provisions of will, unless sale is necessary to pay debts and charges or its retention will probably cause great loss to estate. Prior court order authorizing or setting conditions for sale of personal property not necessary. (KRS 395.200).

Actions by Representative.—Representative may sue on claims of decedent. (CR 17.01). As to revival of actions commenced by decedent, see topic Actions. Action commenced by representative may be continued by successor. (KRS 395.280). If person dies prior to expiration of time for bringing action and action survives, personal representative may bring action after expiration date, if commenced within one year of representative's qualification. (KRS 413.180[1]). If person dies prior to accrual of action and personal representative qualifies more than one year after decedent's death, representative deemed qualified on last day of one year period. (KRS 413.180[2]).

See topic Death for wrongful death action by representative.

See subhead Settlement Suit, supra.

Actions Against Representatives.—No suit may be brought against executor or administrator until after two months from qualification of first personal representative of estate except against executor de son tort or upon denial by fiduciary in writing of claim by alleged creditor. (KRS 395.270). After two months creditor may bring suit on claim against personal representative, unless claim had previously been denied by personal representative, in which case creditor may bring suit earlier. (KRS 395.270). All claims pending against decedent at time of death, if not barred by other limitation period, must be brought within six months from date of appointment of personal representative or within two years from date of death if no representative appointed or be barred. (KRS 396.011). Application to revive action for or against deceased pending at date of death must be made within one year after death. (KRS 395.278). Notwithstanding any other statute to contrary, no cause of action, except fraud, on any unbarred claim may be brought against personal representative or distributee after two years from date of order of discharge of personal representative. (KRS 396.205). See category Civil Actions and Procedure, topic Limitation of Actions.

Allowances.—Personal property or money of decedent, on hand or in bank to amount of $7,500 exempt from distribution and sale and set apart by district court to surviving spouse, or if no surviving spouse to surviving children. Surviving spouse, or children if no surviving spouse, may select personal property up to $7,500 in value. (KRS 391.030).

On petition of surviving spouse, before appointment of administrator, district judge having jurisdiction may authorize by order surviving spouse to withdraw from any bank or other depository not exceeding $1,000 belonging to deceased spouse's estate. (KRS 391.030[2]).

Widow's Quarantine.—Surviving spouse entitled to share of rents and profits of deceased spouse's real estate equal to share in real estate itself and must hold dwelling house, yard, garden, stable and lot in which it stands and orchard adjoining any of aforesaid premises until dower or curtesy assigned. (KRS 392.050).

Intermediate and Final Accounting and Settlement.—Executor, administrator or curator must, within two years after appointment and annually thereafter or whenever required by court, render accounting to and make settlement with court appointing him. (KRS 395.610). Informal settlement allowed from fiduciary who is sole beneficiary of estate or upon verified waiver from all beneficiaries of estate if no beneficiary is under disability. (KRS 395.605). No verified waiver required from non-residuary legatee who received legacy; cancelled check or signed receipt attached to settlement sufficient. (KRS 395.605[2]). District court must make settlements with personal representatives in his county (KRS 395.600) and must make written report of settlement to circuit clerk (KRS 395.620).

Clerk must indorse on settlement report time of filing and hearing date. (KRS 395.620). At hearing or in interval exceptions thereto may be filed. (KRS 395.615). If no exceptions filed and report made according to law, report must be approved and recorded. If exceptions filed, must be hearing thereon. Settlement so made and recorded prima facie evidence between parties interested. (KRS 395.630).

Not less than ten days prior to date of hearing, clerk, at cost of estate, must cause notice of filing of settlement to be published in newspaper of general circulation in county, or with court's approval, fiduciary must give at least ten days written notice by mail to all unpaid creditors and distributees. (KRS 395.625).

At expiration of trust, every fiduciary must fully account and pay estate over to persons entitled thereto. Such account must list all unpaid creditors whose claims were allowed and all creditors whose claims were disallowed. (KRS 395.610).

Except in case of corporate fiduciaries supervised by state or federal banking authorities, no account of any fiduciary may be approved until after exhibition to court for its examination of securities shown in account as being in fiduciary's hands or certificate of bank having possession thereof or in which they have been deposited for safekeeping, and also certified bank statement showing funds to credit of trust. (KRS 395.610).

As to procedure when fiduciary neglects or refuses to file inventory or account when due by law or when ordered by court, see KRS 395.255, 395.990.

Notwithstanding provisions regulating settlement with district court, where suit in equity for settlement of decedent's estate or trust estate brought pursuant to KRS 395.510-395.550, circuit court thereafter has exclusive jurisdiction over such settlements. (Compare 221 Ky. 396, 298 S.W. 975; 227 Ky. 670, 13 S.W.2d 1025). In such cases clerk of circuit court must make and file certificate of each approved settlement. (KRS 395.650). Fiduciary may file proposed final settlement prior to actual delivery of estate assets. Any exceptions to settlement heard by court while fiduciary has assets in hand. (KRS 395.617).

In case of property subject to escheat, estate must be settled within one year or as soon thereafter as practicable. (KRS 393.030).

Distribution.—Law allows personal representatives two years to distribute residue of estate without accounting for interest except as collected by them (KRS 395.310), but they may distribute after six months from qualification (KRS 395.190). Specific pecuniary legacies must be paid within one year and carry interest thereafter. (KRS 394.520). If doubt as to sufficiency of assets for proposed distribution, personal representatives should require refunding bond from persons to whom distribution made, and if suit brought in circuit court for settlement, safe course is to await regular distribution under orders of court. (227 Ky. 670, 13 S.W.2d 1025).

Distribution Not Feasible.—Provision made for distribution of funds payable to curator appointed for distributee to whom not feasible or permissible to make payment because of absence from last known place of residence for period of one year and who is not known to have been living during that time. (KRS 395.410-395.440). Similar provision made for disposition of funds due convict. (KRS 387.290). In proper circumstances circuit court may appoint receiver to accept and manage funds due distributee. (141 Ky. 455, 132 S.W. 1039).

Distribution if Abroad.—No specific provision. However, KRS 395.410 may cover such instances. This section and those following provide for appointment of curator. If situation does not apply it is probable that application for appointment of receiver to protect property should be made in circuit court. Administrator or executor could then, pursuant to order of court, turn over funds to receiver who would hold, manage and protect them pending return of the distributee.

Liabilities of Representatives.—Unless otherwise provided in contract, personal representative not individually liable on contract if acting in fiduciary capacity in administration of estate, unless he fails to reveal representative capacity and identify estate in contract. (KRS 396.185[1]). Representative individually liable for obligations arising from ownership or control of estate or for torts committed in course of administration due to personal fault. (KRS 396.185[2]). All claims may be asserted against personal representative in fiduciary capacity, regardless of individual liability. (KRS 396.185[3]). Failure to plead or defend action cannot render representative liable for more than amount of his decedent's assets chargeable to him; and he is liable only for amount of such unadministered assets remaining in his hands. (KRS 395.290).

Successor representative may maintain action against former representative, his sureties and representatives, for damages or debts arising from maladministration or omissions of predecessor. (KRS 395.300).

Up to two years from qualification, representative charged with interest realized on assets; after two years, charged with interest on surplus assets in his hands. (KRS 395.310).

Compensation of representatives may not exceed 5% of value of personal estate plus 5% of income collected, except that court may allow additional compensation for unusual and extraordinary services in connection with real estate or with estate or inheritance taxes claimed against property not part of estate. (KRS 395.150, construed in 292 Ky. 701, 168 S.W.2d 24).

See note at head of Digest as to 1998 legislation covered.

See Topical Index in front part of this volume.

KY – 33

EXECUTORS AND ADMINISTRATORS ... *continued*

When Administration Unnecessary.—Provision made for dispensing with administration of estate of decedent (1) by agreement of all beneficiaries when no debts or claims owed by or made on estate, or (2) when spouse survives and probate estate less than $7,500 plus claims of preferred creditors. Person applying per alternative (1) must advertise for creditors in newspaper of general circulation each week for six weeks and must post bond for benefit of creditors in amount of personal estate. District court must be satisfied provision made for paying inheritance and estate taxes before granting petition to dispense by agreement. (KRS 391.030; 395.450-500).

Small Estates.—See subhead When Administration Unnecessary, supra.

Foreign Executors or Administrators.—Foreign executors or administrators have no right, merely by virtue of appointment in foreign jurisdiction, to act in Kentucky, or to resort to Kentucky courts to enforce claims asserted by them. (91 Ky. 88, 15 S.W. 4). Their rights are those recognized by comity or by express statute in Kentucky. In absence of Kentucky administration, they may sell and transfer personal property in Kentucky, and sell and transfer stocks in Kentucky corporations by proceeding in conformity with requirements prescribed for Kentucky fiduciaries. See supra, subhead Sales.

Foreign representative cannot sue in Kentucky except for collection of debt. (KRS 395.170[1]). Must be administration in Kentucky before suit can be brought for any other purpose. If no resident representative, foreign representative of nonresident decedent may prosecute actions in Kentucky for recovery of debts due decedent, but no judgment may be rendered in any such action until plaintiff gives bond as required to pay any debt due by decedent to any resident of Kentucky to extent of assets coming into plaintiff's hands. (KRS 395.170[2]). If resident representative of nonresident decedent appointed, resident representative alone has power to sue, but Kentucky debtor paying debt to foreign representative, without notice of appointment of Kentucky representative is discharged from debt to extent of such payment. (KRS 395.170[4]; 179 Ky. 695; 201 S.W. 20).

See also topic Wills, subhead Foreign Probated Wills.

Uniform Fiduciaries Act (1930) adopted in 1942 with substantial modifications. (KRS 386.100 to 386.150).

Revised Uniform Principal and Income Act adopted (1992). (KRS 386.191 to 386.349).

Uniform Simplification of Fiduciary Security Transfers Act not adopted.

Uniform Anatomical Gift Act adopted with insignificant modifications. (KRS 311.165 to 311.235). See topic Death.

Uniform Probate Code not adopted.

FIDUCIARIES:

Term "fiduciary" as used in KRS c. 395 includes executors, administrators, curators, guardians, conservators, trustees and testamentary trustees and associations and corporations where appointed by or accountable to district court and any other individual or corporation holding funds or otherwise acting in fiduciary capacity. (KRS 386.010; 395.001).

See topics Executors and Administrators, Trusts; category Family, topic Guardian and Ward.

INTESTACY:

See topic Descent and Distribution.

TRUSTS:

Neither Uniform Trusts Act nor Uniform Probate Code adopted.

Kinds.—General common law and equity principles recognize express trusts and constructive trusts. Resulting trusts abrogated by statute as fraud against existing creditors of person paying consideration (KRS 381.170) except where grantee takes deed in own name without consent of person paying consideration or unless grantee in violation of same trust purchases lands deeded with effects of another or grantee recognizes debt to those contributing purchase money (29 Ky. L. Rep. 885, 96 S.W. 794; 121 S.W. 1002); principle extended to personal property (269 S.W.2d 219). Charitable trusts recognized if gift, etc. made to organization devoted to charitable, religious or like purpose or if gift clearly made for charitable or humane purpose. (KRS 381.260).

Creation.—No particular form or language necessary for creation of express trust so long as intention to create trust clearly manifested and beneficiary and property both identified by either settlor or trustee. (279 Ky. 334, 130 S.W.2d 809; 277 Ky. 245, 126 S.W.2d 127). Parol trusts for both personalty and realty may be enforced. (293 Ky. 565, 169 S.W.2d 617). Trusts will not fail for want of trustee. (250 Ky. 1, 61 S.W.2d 904). Attempted trust may fail if settlor fails to divest himself of control of corpus or retains absolute power to revoke. (272 S.W.2d 666). Failure to place active duty or responsibility upon trustee may cause trust to fail. (299 S.W.2d 629).

Appointment of Trustee.—Any person or organization competent to enter into contract may serve as trustee of inter vivos trust. (KRS 395.001). No person may serve as testamentary trustee except upon appointment by district court exercising probate jurisdiction. (KRS 24A.120[b]).

Eligibility and Competency.—Any resident of Kentucky over 18 years of age, any national bank located in Kentucky having fiduciary powers, any state bank or trust company incorporated in Kentucky and authorized by Kentucky law to act as such, and any nonresident of legal age who is related to decedent by consanguinity, marriage, adoption, or spouse of such person so related may be testamentary trustee. (KRS 395.005).

Foreign corporation may serve as fiduciary, except as limited by KRS 395.001 and KRS 395.0005. (O.A.G. 62-1141).

Qualification.—Testamentary trustees must take oath (KRS 62.030) and furnish bond with surety (KRS 62.060).

Removal of Trustee.—Common law fiduciary duties prevail with power in district court to remove. (KRS 395.160). Trustee of trust less than $25,000 exclusive of income may petition district court for distribution to beneficiaries and discharge of trust. (KRS 386.185).

General powers and duties of trustees with respect to administration of trusts governed by KRS c. 386. Uniform Trusts Act not adopted. Uniform Trustees' Powers Act adopted at KRS 386.800-386.845.

Testamentary trustee of real estate, under conditions justifying it in opinion of court, may make long term lease of trust property covering period which may extend beyond duration of trust, where term of trust is indeterminate and term of lease is reasonable under circumstances of particular case. (255 Ky. 244, 73 S.W.2d 41).

As to release of power in trust, see KRS 386.095.

Sales.—Various provisions made for the sale of real estate held in trust. (KRS 389A.010-389A.045).

Trustee of express trust may sell and convey any interest in real estate held in such trust, in all cases where circuit court, under existing or future laws, would have jurisdiction to order judicial sale thereof. Sale must be made on terms and conditions for best interest of trust estate. (KRS 389A.020). Without previous judicial proceeding or judgment, interest in real estate held by fiduciary for ward, or by more than one person or by unknown heir may be sold by private sale subject to circuit court approval. (KRS 389A.032). Action for approval of sale must be brought pursuant to KRS 389A.030 and 389A.035. Act does not limit trustee's power to sell and convey real estate where authorized by instrument creating trust or otherwise authorized by law to do so. Real estate held by trustee as security for debt cannot be sold except under judgment of court, unless debtor joins in writing evidencing sale. (KRS 381.190).

Investments and changes of investments are regulated by KRS c. 386. When bank or trust company acts as "fiduciary" under instrument reserving in grantor or vesting in investment advisory committee, etc., any power to direct acquisition, disposition, or retention of investments or to authorize acts proposed by fiduciary, then fiduciary not liable for (1) loss resulting from compliance with grantor's or investment advisory committee's directions, or (2) loss resulting from failure to take action proposed by fiduciary requiring prior authorization of grantor or investment advisory committee, if fiduciary timely sought but failed to obtain prior authorization. (KRS 287.275[1]). Fiduciary not obligated to perform investment reviews or make investment recommendations to extent grantor or investment advisory committee has authority to make investment decisions. (KRS 287.275[2]). KRS 287.275 not applicable to fiduciary acting pursuant to instrument containing provisions inconsistent with section. (KRS 287.275[3]). See also category Business Regulation and Commerce, topic Banks and Banking. Revised Uniform Principal and Income Act adopted. (KRS 386.191 to 386.349).

Securities in Name of Nominee.—Any bank or trust company acting as fiduciary may have securities registered in own name, or name of nominee. (KRS 287.225).

Bequests and Devises to Inter Vivos Trusts.—See topic Wills.

Accounting.—No routine duty of testamentary trustees to render accounts to court or other official (KRS 395.610); trustees' actions may be reviewed in judicial proceedings (KRS 386.675).

Compensation.—Trustee of estate (where not covered by contract), may receive for services 6% of income collected, plus annual commission of 3/10 of 1% of fair value of real and personal estate in care of fiduciary; however, at option of fiduciary, in lieu of annual commission on principal, he may have commission not exceeding 6% of fair value of principal distributed, paid at time of distribution. Court may allow additional compensation for unusual or extraordinary services not normally incident to care and management of estate. (KRS 386.180, construed in 292 Ky. 701, 168 S.W.2d 24; KRS 387.760).

Final Settlement and Discharge.—Final settlements of testamentary trustees not required. See subhead Accounting, supra.

Uniform Common Trust Fund Act not adopted. Authorization for and regulation of common trust funds found in KRS 287.230-287.235.

Revised Uniform Principal and Income Act adopted in 1992. (KRS 386.191 to 386.349).

Uniform Fiduciaries Act (1930) adopted in 1942 with substantial modifications. (KRS 386.100 to 386.150).

Uniform Simplification of Fiduciary Security Transfers Act not adopted.

Uniform Testamentary Additions to Trusts Act repealed in 1998. (KRS 394.075).

Uniform Trustees' Powers Act adopted in 1976. (KRS 386.800 to 386.845).

Gifts to Minors.—See category Family, topic Infants.

Spendthrift trusts valid as to income and principal unless self-imposed. Exceptions in favor of creditors, in case of spendthrift's liability for taxes, necessities, child support or maintenance. (KRS 381.180).

Accumulations.—Provision for accumulation of income for period not contravening statute relating to restraint on alienation valid. (131 Ky. 609, 115 S.W. 739).

Perpetuities.—See category Property, topic Perpetuities.

Pour Over Trusts.—See topic Wills, subhead Bequests and Devises to Inter Vivos Trusts.

Renunciation.—Trust may be terminated by consent of all beneficiaries when continuance not necessary to carry out material purpose of settlor. (238 S.W.2d 142; 554 S.W.2d 397). Irrevocable trust revocable with consent of settlor and all beneficiaries. (727 S.W.2d 408).

Uniform Disclaimer of Transfers Under Nontestamentary Instruments Act adopted in 1980. (KRS 394.035).

Business trusts defined, and procedure for organization, operation and terminating same in KRS 386.370 to 386.440.

See note at head of Digest as to 1998 legislation covered.

See Topical Index in front part of this volume.

WILLS:

Uniform Probate Code not adopted.

Testamentary Capacity.—Every person of sound mind, 18 years of age or older, may by will dispose of his real or personal estate to which he may be entitled at his death. Will effectively disposes of property acquired after execution of will. (KRS 394.020). Person under 18 years of age can make will only (1) in pursuance of power specifically given to that effect and (2) if parent, he or she may appoint guardian for child by will. (KRS 394.030).

Testamentary Disposition.—Testator may dispose of any estate, right or interest in real or personal estate that he may be entitled to at his death, which would otherwise go to heirs or personal representatives. (KRS 394.020). No limitation imposed on bequests to charities or religious institutions.

Execution.—No will valid unless in writing, with name of testator subscribed thereto by himself or by some other person in his presence and by his direction. If will not written wholly by testator, subscription must be made or will acknowledged by testator in presence of at least two credible witnesses, who must subscribe their names to will in presence of testator and in presence of each other. (KRS 394.040). No absolute requirement that both witnesses sign at same time or in presence of each other if acknowledged by testator upon witness' signing. (233 Ky. 23, 24 S.W.2d 902).

Validity of will not affected by fact that attesting witness, competent at time of attestation, subsequently becomes incompetent to testify. (KRS 394.210).

Statutorily approved form for execution and attestation of self-proved will set forth infra, under Form for self-proved will.

Form of Attestation.—No set form required, but wording in form set out in subhead Self-Proved Will, infra, recommended.

Holographic wills recognized. (KRS 394.040; 166 Ky. 421, 179 S.W. 389).

Nuncupative Wills.—Statutory provisions recognizing validity of unwritten will for personal property for soldiers in actual service or mariners at sea repealed effective June 16, 1972.

Revocation.—Testator's marriage does not revoke previously made will or codicil. (KRS 394.090). Testator's divorce or annulment of testator's marriage after executing will revokes any disposition or appointment of property made by will to former spouse, and any nomination of former spouse as fiduciary, unless will expressly provides otherwise. (KRS 394.092). Property not passing to former spouse under KRS 394.092 passes as if former spouse predeceased testator; provisions conferring some power upon former spouse are interpreted as if former spouse predeceased testator. Will speaks at time of testator's death. (KRS 394.330). Divorce does not revoke will making no bequest or devise to former spouse. (KRS 394.092). Will may also be revoked by later will or codicil, by writing executed like will, declaring intention to revoke, or by testator or someone in his presence and by his direction tearing, burning, obliterating, canceling or destroying instrument or signature thereto with intent to revoke. (KRS 394.080).

Will once revoked revived by reexecution of revoked will or execution of codicil for that purpose with all formalities required for original execution, but only to extent intention to revive shown. (KRS 394.100). Will revoked by divorce revived by testator's remarriage to former spouse. (KRS 394.092).

Testamentary Gifts to Subscribing Witnesses or Their Spouses.—If will attested by person to whom or to whose spouse any beneficial interest in estate devised or bequeathed, and will cannot otherwise be proved (see 170 Ky. 316, 185 S.W. 1133), such person deemed competent witness; but such devise or bequest void, unless witness entitled to share of estate of testator if will not established, in which case he receives so much of his share as does not exceed value of that devised or bequeathed (KRS 394.210).

Bequests and Devises to Inter Vivos Trusts.—Trust instrument may be incorporated in will by reference if properly identified. If trust instrument amended subsequent to date of testator's will, operative effect of will not changed by amendment. (245 S.W.2d 914).

Uniform Testamentary Additions to Trusts Act adopted in 1996. (KRS 394.075).

Probate.—Wills proved before district court (KRS 394.140. See also KRS 24A.120[b]), and deposited and recorded in office of clerk of that court (CR 79.05[2]). As to venue of probate proceedings, see topic Executors and Administrators.

Person offering will for probate must file verified application for probate, stating testator's residence at death and facts necessary to establish court's jurisdiction and, as far as known, names, ages and post office addresses of testator's surviving spouse and, if required by court, heirs at law. Application for probate may be combined with application for appointment as executor or administrator with will annexed. (KRS 394.145).

Person offering will may cause summons to be issued requiring any person interested to appear and show cause why will should not be probated. (KRS 394.170). Court may fix date for hearing and summon persons interested to appear then (KRS 394.180) or it may proceed to probate or reject will without summoning anyone (KRS 394.220).

Two modes of procedure allowed—one, ex parte (common form), and second, inter partes (solemn form). Only difference in legal effect is in procedure to review or vacate judgment of district court. (274 Ky. 99, 118 S.W.2d 200).

No person is, on account of being executor of will, incompetent as witness for or against it. (KRS 394.200).

Creditor, or creditor's spouse, may be competent witness for or against will attested by him or her which charges testator's estate with payment of creditor's debt. (KRS 394.200).

Where witnesses unavailable, will may be probated on proof by at least two credible disinterested witnesses of handwriting of purported testator; or upon sufficient proof of such handwriting; but court may require additional proof of pertinent facts and circumstances. (KRS 394.235). See subhead Self-Proved Will, infra.

Ten year limitation (see category Civil Actions and Procedure, topic Limitation of Actions) applies to original probate of wills (KRS 413.160; 395.010; 96 Ky. 313, 28 S.W. 497), but not to ancillary probate in Kentucky of wills properly probated in other states (119 Ky. 488, 84 S.W. 548; see also 130 Ky. 445, 113 S.W. 490).

When paper probated as will and later will discovered, proceedings may be instituted in court probating earlier will to vacate its judgment and to probate later will, provided such proceedings instituted within ten years after testator's death. (KRS 394.295; 255 Ky. 695, 75 S.W.2d 353. Compare 272 Ky. 147, 113 S.W.2d 1133 as to procedure).

As to procedure and evidence required for probate of lost will, see 458 S.W.2d 759.

No will admissible in evidence until probated by court having jurisdiction. Such probate is conclusive, except as to jurisdiction of court, until superseded, reversed or annulled. (KRS 394.130; 286 Ky. 768, 151 S.W.2d 1017; 255 Ky. 27, 72 S.W.2d 712).

Self-Proved Will.—Attested will may at time of execution or thereafter be made self-proved by acknowledgment of testator and witnesses before officer authorized to administer oaths. Self-proved wills may be admitted to probate without testimony of any subscribing witness, but otherwise treated no differently than will not self-proved. (KRS 394.225). For form to self-prove attested will subsequent to execution, see KRS 394.225(2). Execution and attestation before notary public, or other officer authorized to take oaths, in format substantially similar to statutory form below will allow will to be admitted to probate without testimony of any subscribing witness:

Form

I, ____________, the testator, sign my name to this instrument this ______ day of ________, 19__, and being first duly sworn, do hereby declare to the undersigned authority that I sign and execute this instrument as my last will and that I sign it willingly (or willingly direct another to sign for me), that I execute it as my free and voluntary act for the purposes therein expressed, and that I am eighteen (18) years of age or older, of sound mind, and under no constraint or undue influence.

____________ (Testator)

We, __________, __________, the witnesses sign our names to this instrument, being first duly sworn, and do hereby declare to the undersigned authority that the testator signs and executes this instrument as his last will and that he signs it willingly (or willingly directs another to sign for him), and that each of us, in the presence and hearing of the testator and in the presence of the other subscribing witness, hereby signs this will as witness to the testator's signing, and that to the best of our knowledge the testator is eighteen (18) years of age or older, of sound mind, and under no constraint or undue influence.

____________ (Witness)

____________ (Witness)

THE STATE OF ____________
COUNTY OF ____________

Subscribed, sworn to and acknowledged before me by ________, the testator and subscribed and sworn to before me by ________, and ________, witnesses, this ____ day of ________.

(Signed) ____________

(OFFICIAL CAPACITY OF OFFICER)

Living Will.—Kentucky Living Will Directive Act adopted 1994. (KRS 311.621 to 311.643). Any person 18 years or older of sound mind and with decisional capacity may make written living will directing any or all of following: (a) direct withholding or withdrawal of life-prolonging treatment; or (b) direct withholding or withdrawal of artificially provided nutrition or hydration; or (c) designate one or more adults as surrogate or successor surrogate to make health care decisions on grantor's behalf. (KRS 311.623). Living will directive must be honored by grantor's family, regular family or attending physician and any health care facility in which grantor is patient. (KRS 311.623[2]). Notification to emergency medical responder or paramedic, of person's wish not to be resuscitated, only recognized if on standard form or identification approved by Kentucky Board of Medical Licensure, in consultation with Cabinet for Human Resources. (KRS 311.623[3]). Individuals also have common law right to refuse medical treatment, including nutrition and hydration. (858 S.W.2d 698). Surrogate may make any health care decisions which grantor could make individually if grantor had decisional capacity; decisions must be made in accordance with grantor's desires as indicated in advance directive. (KRS 311.629).

Living will directive must be in writing, dated, and signed by grantor or at his direction, either witnessed by two or more adults in grantor's presence and in presence of each other, or acknowledged before notary public or other person authorized to administer oaths. Witnesses must be 18 years old and following may not serve as witnesses: (a) grantor's blood relative; (b) beneficiary of grantor under Kentucky descent and distribution statute; (c) employee of health care facility where grantor is patient, unless employee serves as notary public; (d) grantor's attending physician; or (e) any person directly financially responsible for grantor's health care. (KRS 311.621[1]; KRS 311.625[2]). Surrogate may resign any time by giving written notice to grantor; to immediate successor surrogate, if any; to attending physician; or to any health care facility then waiting for surrogate to make health care decision. (KRS 311.625[3]).

Revocation of living will directive accomplished by (a) writing, signed and dated; (b) oral statement of intent by grantor with decisional capacity in presence of two adults, one of whom must be health care provider; or (c) destruction of document by grantor or some person in grantor's presence and at grantor's direction. Any revocation effective immediately. (KRS 311.627[3]). Oral statement by grantor with decisional capacity to revoke advance directive overrides any previous written advance directive. (KRS 311.627[2]). Notwithstanding advance directive, life sustaining treatment and artificially provided nutrition and hydration must be provided to pregnant woman unless medical certainty procedures (a) will not maintain woman in such way as to permit unborn child's continuing development and live birth; (b) would be physically harmful to woman; or (c) prolong severe pain which cannot be alleviated by medication. (KRS

See note at head of Digest as to 1998 legislation covered.

See Topical Index in front part of this volume.

WILLS . . . *continued*
311.629[4]). Grantor or responsible party of grantor responsible for notifying health care provider of advance directive. (KRS 311.633).

Following, in order of priority, may make health care decisions for adult without decisional capacity who has not executed advance directive: (a) patient's judicially appointed guardian if medical decisions within scope of guardianship; (b) patient's spouse; (c) patient's adult or majority of adult children; (d) patient's parents; (e) patient's nearest living relative or majority of relatives of same relation. (KRS 311.631). Persons acting in good faith under advance directive exonerated from criminal and civil liability. (KRS 311.635).

Living will directive must be substantially in following form (KRS 311.625), and may include other specific directions which are in accordance with accepted medical practice and not specifically prohibited by any other statute. Invalidity of any other specific direction shall not affect directive. (KRS 311.625).

FORM

LIVING WILL DIRECTIVE

My wishes regarding life-prolonging treatment and artificially provided nutrition and hydration to be provided to me if I no longer have decisional capacity, have a terminal condition, or become permanently unconscious have been indicated by checking and initialing the appropriate lines below. By checking and initialing the appropriate lines, I specifically:

____ Designate __________ as my health care surrogate(s) to make health care decisions for me in accordance with this directive when I no longer have decisional capacity. If __________ refuses or is not able to act for me, I designate __________ as my health care surrogate(s).

Any prior designation is revoked.

If I do not designate a surrogate, the following are my directions to my attending physician. If I have designated a surrogate, my surrogate shall comply with my wishes as indicated below:

____ Direct that treatment be withheld or withdrawn, and that I be permitted to die naturally with only the administration of medication or the performance of any medical treatment deemed necessary to alleviate pain.

____ DO NOT authorize that life-prolonging treatment be withheld or withdrawn.

____ Authorize the withholding or withdrawal of artificially provided food, water, or other artificially provided nourishment or fluids.

____ DO NOT authorize the withholding or withdrawal of artificially provided food, water, or other artificially provided nourishment or fluids.

____ Authorize my surrogate, designated above, to withhold or withdraw artificially provided nourishment or fluids, or other treatment if the surrogate determines that withholding or withdrawing is in my best interest; but I do not mandate that withholding or withdrawing.

In the absence of my ability to give directions regarding the use of life-prolonging treatment and artificially provided nutrition and hydration, it is my intention that this directive shall be honored by my attending physician, my family, and any surrogate designated pursuant to this directive as the final expression of my legal right to refuse medical or surgical treatment and I accept the consequences of the refusal.

If I have been diagnosed as pregnant and that diagnosis is known to my attending physician, this directive shall have no force or effect during the course of my pregnancy.

I understand the full import of this directive and I am emotionally and mentally competent to make this directive.

Signed this ____ day of __________, 19___.

____
LIVING WILL GRANTOR

____
ADDRESS

In our joint presence, the grantor, who is of sound mind and eighteen (18) years of age, or older, voluntarily dated and signed this writing or directed it to be dated and signed for the grantor.

WITNESS __________ ADDRESS __________

WITNESS __________ ADDRESS __________

OR:

STATE OF KENTUCKY)
__________ COUNTY)

Before me, the undersigned authority, came the grantor who is of sound mind and eighteen (18) years of age, or older, and acknowledged that he voluntarily dated and signed this writing or directed it to be signed and dated as above.

Done this _____ day of __________, 19___.

____
NOTARY PUBLIC

MY COMMISSION EXPIRES: __________

Execution of this document restricts withholding and withdrawing of some medical procedures. Consult Kentucky Revised Statutes or your attorney.

Durable Health Care Power.—See category Property, topic Powers of Attorney.

Contest.—Action may be brought in circuit court of same county from every action of district court admitting will to record or rejecting it, provided party appealing has interest in estate of decedent entitling him to do so. (KRS 394.240). Same procedure is used to obtain interpretation or reformation of will. (KRS 394.240). (As to right of testator's widow, see 186 Ky. 486, 217 S.W. 365.) Such action must be filed in circuit court within two years from rendition of district court judgment. (KRS 394.240). Proceeding in form of civil action and plaintiff is required to join all necessary parties. (KRS 394.260). Notice of action to be filed by plaintiff and indexed in county clerk's office. (KRS 394.240[2]).

Filing action in circuit court, unless taken within 12 months, does not prevent appointment of executor or administrator by district court, or settlement, distribution and division of decedent's estate. (KRS 394.250). Circuit court may enter order restraining further distribution and division of estate. (KRS 394.250).

In circuit court trial de novo. Final decision in circuit court, subject to appeal to Court of Appeals, bars any other proceeding to question probate or rejection of will, but this does not preclude court of justice from its jurisdiction to impeach final decision for any reason that would give jurisdiction over any other judgment at law, e.g., fraud or lack of jurisdiction. (KRS 394.260; 286 Ky. 768, 773, 151 S.W.2d 1017).

Legacies.—If will fixes no time for payment, pecuniary legacies become payable and interest bearing one year after probate of will. (KRS 394.520; 228 Ky. 73, 14 S.W.2d 397). Legatees may sue for settlement of estate six months after qualification of representative. (KRS 395.510). Conversion of money or property or proceeds of property, devised to testator's heirs, into other property not ademption unless intent of testator. Devisee receives value of property unless contrary intent of testator shown. (KRS 394.360). For other actions, see topic Executors and Administrators, subhead Actions Against Representatives.

Unclaimed legacies escheat to Commonwealth after seven years. (KRS 393.020).

Lapse.—If devisee or legatee predeceases testator, leaving issue who survive testator, such issue take parent's share, unless will indicates different intent. (KRS 394.400). When devise to several as class, or as tenants in common, or joint tenants, and one or more of devisees predecease testator and others survive, shares of those that die go to their descendants, if any; if none, to surviving devisees, unless will indicates different intent. (KRS 394.410[1]). Devise to children embraces grandchildren where no children and no other construction will give effect to devise. (KRS 394.410[2]). If devise to several as joint tenants with right of survivorship, share of deceased devisee divided amongst such as survive. If all such joint tenants predecease testator, property devolves as if devised to several as tenants in common. (KRS 394.410[3]).

Children living when will executed may be disinherited simply by testator disposing otherwise of all his property. (KRS 394.382[1]; see 226 Ky. 42, 10 S.W.2d 474.) But mere attempt to exclude heir from inheritance ineffectual without some other disposition of testator's estate. (KRS 394.382; 184 Ky. 466, 212 S.W. 423; 262 Ky. 798, 91 S.W.2d 513).

Child or children born or adopted after execution of will receives share of estate equal in value to what child would receive if testator died intestate (see topic Descent and Distribution) unless: (1) Omission appears intentional from will; (2) when will executed testator had one or more children and devised substantially whole estate to other parent of omitted child; or (3) evidence outside will relating to transfers to omitted child during life of testator show intent that those transfers be in lieu of testamentary provision. (KRS 394.382[1]). Pretermitted child or children's shares satisfied by taking ratably from interest of heirs, devisees and legatees. (KRS 394.382[2]). As to rights of posthumous child to estate in remainder, see KRS 381.140. As to his rights and liabilities to contribution, see KRS 394.460; 394.470.

Election.—Surviving spouse may, within six months after probate or within six months after deposition of any contest arising from probate, renounce will of deceased spouse and take dower or curtesy share of estate as if no will, except share in real estate held in fee simple directly or beneficially by decedent at time of death is only in one-third of such real estate. (KRS 392.080). Such renunciation must be acknowledged before and left for record with county clerk in county where probate made or acknowledged before subscribing witness and proved before and left with county clerk. Copy of renunciation must be filed with clerk of court in which probate made. Time for election may be extended for additional six month period by order of district court, but no such extension may be granted unless applied for before expiration of original six months period. (KRS 392.080).

On proper application in behalf of insane widow, chancellor may exercise right of election for her. (243 Ky. 202, 47 S.W.2d 1059). Presumably same procedure applies on behalf of insane husband surviving his wife.

Contribution.—When widow's dower or widower's curtesy taken from estate devised to devisee, such devisee receives contribution on principles of KRS 394.420 to 394.490, unless different intent appears in will. (KRS 394.480).

Contract to Make Will.—Agreement to will property though not effective as will, if based upon legal consideration is valid and enforceable in action for its breach. (299 Ky. 103, 184 S.W.2d 579). Cause of action accrues at death of promisor. (299 Ky. 721, 187 S.W.2d 259). If contract executed after June 16, 1972, contract established only by provisions in valid will stating material provisions of contract, by express reference in valid will to contract and evidence proving provisions of contract, or by writing signed by decedent evidencing contract. (KRS 394.540[1]; 856 S.W.2d 892). Execution of joint will or mutual wills not evidence of contract not to revoke will or wills. (KRS 394.540[2]; 856 S.W.2d 892).

Renunciation.—Surviving spouse may renounce will and receive share under KRS 392.020 (see subhead Election, supra), but such action limits interest in real estate to one-third. (KRS 392.080). Renunciation must be made within six months after probate of will, but such period may be extended on application to district court. (See Uniform Disclaimers of Transfers by Will, Intestacy or Appointment Act, KRS 392.080.) Surviving spouse who renounces will may claim $7,500 exemption provided by KRS 391.030.

Beneficiary of any testamentary instrument, joint tenant, heir, next of kin, devisee, legatee, person succeeding to disclaimed interest, or appointee under power of appointment exercised by testamentary instrument may disclaim interest to any property or interest therein by filing written disclaimer in district court prior to acceptance of property or interest or benefit thereunder and within nine months after date of death of decedent. (KRS 394.610-394.680). No disclaimer by living person's legal representative, except for person's attorney-in-fact, shall be made unless court with jurisdiction of estate has authorized disclaimer. (KRS 394.610). No disclaimer by person's attorney-in-fact shall be made unless instrument governing attorney-in-fact's authority expressly authorizes disclaimer. (KRS 394.610). Nontestamentary instruments or contracts may be disclaimed within nine months after event determining beneficiary or his interest. (KRS 394.035).

See note at head of Digest as to 1998 legislation covered.

See Topical Index in front part of this volume.

KY – 36

WILLS . . . continued

Foreign Executed Wills.—Real and personal estate in Kentucky of person domiciled outside of Kentucky may be disposed of by will executed according to law of testator's domicile. (KRS 394.120).

Statutes do not prohibit nonresident's will from original probate in Kentucky if property located in Kentucky.

Foreign Probated Wills.—When will of nonresident relative to any estate in Kentucky is probated outside Kentucky, authenticated copy and certificate of probate thereof may be offered to district court having jurisdiction to probate such will in Kentucky. (KRS 394.150). When so offered, court must presume, in absence of evidence to contrary, that will was duly executed and admitted to probate as will in state or county of testator's domicile, and must admit such copy to probate as will in Kentucky. (KRS 394.150).

Simultaneous Death.—See topic Death, subhead Uniform Simultaneous Death Act.

Testamentary guardian, or alternatively, limited guardian or conservator, or both may be nominated by will of surviving parent (KRS 387.040), and appointed by District Court (KRS 387.070). See category Family, topic Guardian and Ward, subhead Eligibility and Competency.

Testamentary Trusts.—See topic Trusts.

Uniform Anatomical Gift Act adopted with insignificant modifications. (KRS 311.165 to 311.235).

Uniform Disclaimer of Transfers by Will, Intestacy or Appointment Act adopted in 1974. (KRS 394.610 to 394.680).

FAMILY

ADOPTION:

Department for Social Services within Cabinet for Families and Children establishes criteria for and regulates adoption. (KRS 199.472; 905 KAR c.1).

Any person of any age may be adopted. Any person over 18 who is a resident of or who has resided in Kentucky for 12 months immediately preceding filing may file in circuit court of his county petition for leave to adopt child. (KRS 199.470[1]).

Consent Required.—Voluntary and informed consent of living parent or parents of child born in lawful wedlock or mother of child born out of wedlock, or father of child born out of wedlock if paternity legally established or if affidavit filed stating affiant is father of child; but such consent not required if (a) parent(s) adjudged mentally disabled not less than one year before filing of petition; (b) parental rights have been terminated; (c) living parents divorced and parental rights of one have been terminated and consent has been given by parent having custody; or (d) biological parent has not established parental rights as required by KRS 625.065. (KRS 199.500[1]). No consent of biological parents required if it is pleaded and proved that parent has (a) abandoned child for 90 days or more; (b) inflicted or allowed to be inflicted serious, non-accidental physical injury or emotional harm; (c) failed for six months or more to provide essential parental care and protection; (d) caused or allowed child to be sexually abused or exploited; or (e) for reasons other than poverty alone, failed continuously or repeatedly to provide essential food, clothing, shelter, medical care or education for child. (KRS 199.502[1]). Minor parent who is party defendant may consent to adoption but guardian ad litem for minor parent appointed. If adoptee is 12 or over, his or her consent must be given in court, unless waived by court. Consent may not be given within 72 hours after birth of child. Consent given at 72 hours after birth shall be final and irrevocable 20 days after placement approval by Secretary of Cabinet, or 20 days after consent if placement approval was given prior to signing of consent, if approval is required. (KRS 199.500). If adoptee over 18, only adoptee's consent necessary. (KRS 405.390). Statutory procedure for involuntary termination of parental rights of either or both parents in case of neglected, abandoned or abused child. (KRS 625.050 to 625.120).

Conditions Precedent.—No petition for adoption of child may be filed until child has lived continuously in home of petitioner for at least 90 days immediately prior to filing of petition, unless child is placed in home of petitioner by Cabinet, by child placement agency licensed by Cabinet, or with written approval of Secretary of Cabinet, in which case petition may be filed at time of placement. No petition shall be filed unless prior to filing, child has been placed for adoption by child-placement agency, by Cabinet or with written approval of Secretary of Cabinet but no approval is necessary if petitioner is stepparent, grandparent, sister, brother, aunt or uncle of child sought to be adopted or if child is placed by agency from another state with written consent of Secretary. (KRS 199.470).

Jurisdiction is vested in Circuit Court. (KRS 199.470[1]). Action is in personam. (395 S.W.2d 588).

Venue is in county of petitioner's residence. (KRS 199.470[1]).

Petition.—Husband or wife of petitioner must join, unless petitioner is married to biological parent of adoptee, but this requirement may be waived by court. (KRS 199.470[2]).

Following persons must be made defendants: (a) adoptee; (b) biological living parents of child under 18 if child is born in lawful wedlock or if child born out of wedlock, its mother and its father if (i) father is known and identified by mother by affidavit, (ii) prior to entry of final order in termination proceeding he has asserted paternity in action, to custodial agency, or to petitioner within 60 days after birth, (iii) his name is affixed to birth certificate, (iv) he has commenced judicial proceeding claiming parental rights, (v) he has contributed financially to support child, or (vi) he has married mother of child or lived openly with child or with mother of child; however, neither parent, if parental rights have been terminated; (c) child's guardian, if any; (d) if custody of child has been transferred to Cabinet or other person, agency or institution, then it must be named. If biological parents, mother, or if paternity is established, then father (see [b]) are defendants, no guardian ad litem need be appointed. (KRS 199.480). If proposed adoptee is 18 or over, he or she alone need be made defendant. (KRS 405.390). Service on all necessary defendants same as in other civil cases (CR 4; see category Civil

Actions and Procedure, topic Process), except child under14 in custody of Cabinet, agency, institution, or individual, shall be served by serving Cabinet. (KRS 199.480[2]).

Petition must contain allegations regarding, inter alia, name, birth date and place, age, and residence of petitioner and adoptee, date of marriage of petitioner, relationship of child to petitioner, name by which adoptee to be known after adoption, description of adoptee's property, name and address of legitimate adoptee's living parents, or of mother, if illegitimate, and father if paternity legally established or by affidavit, and of child's guardian. Certified copies of any orders terminating parental rights must be filed with petition. Any consents must be filed prior to entry of adoption judgment. Copy of any placement approval by Secretary of Cabinet or Secretary's designee must be filed with petition. (KRS 199.490).

Procedure.—Circuit clerk forwards two copies of petition to Cabinet for investigation and report, which must be rendered within 90 days from placement of child or 90 days after petition filed, whichever is longer, unless period is extended by court. If Cabinet is party defendant, its reports, if it files no other pleadings, are considered answer to petition. (KRS 199.510).

Hearing is private. (KRS 199.515).

Decree.—The court must not enter judgment of adoption of a minor child unless it finds that facts stated in petition are established; all legal requirements, including jurisdiction have been met; petitioners are of good moral character and good reputation in community, and are able properly to maintain and educate child; that child is suitable for adoption; and that its best interests would be promoted thereby. If judgment of adoption is entered, it must set forth all jurisdictional facts and adjudge that child shall thenceforth be deemed to have legal status of child of petitioners. (KRS 199.520).

If petition for adoption is denied, child may be returned to custody of Cabinet, individual, institution, or agency (if any) previously having charge of it; otherwise court must certify case to juvenile session of District Court for appropriate action, and District Court must advise Cabinet of pendency of such action. (KRS 199.550).

Appeal.—Party to adoption proceeding aggrieved by final order therein may appeal to Court of Appeals as in other equity actions. (KRS 199.560).

Record.—Files and records of court in adoption proceedings are not open to copy or inspection by persons other than parties to such proceedings, their attorneys, or representatives of Cabinet, except upon order of court expressly permitting inspection. (KRS 199.570). Upon entry of final order, record may be opened to adult adopted person only, but only with written consent of biological parents and written order of court, or if biological parents are deceased or cannot be located, by written order of court. (KRS 199.572). No person having charge of such records may furnish any copy thereof or disclose names of any parties appearing therein except on order of court. (KRS 199.570[1]). Replacement birth certificate shall show residence of adoptive parents as birthplace of child but, if requested by adoptive parents, replacement certificate shall contain location of birth, hospital and name of doctor or midwife. (KRS 199.570[3]). Health history of biological parents and blood relatives, if known, shall be given to court and adoptive parents not later than date of adoption, and to adult adopted person if requested in person or in writing. (KRS 199.520[4]). Cabinet is to make diligent effort to notify adoptive parent, if adopted person is minor, adult adopted person, or adult adoptable person of information received from biological parent, biological sibling, or provider of medical services which has affected or may affect physical or mental health of genetically related persons. (KRS 199.525[1]). Cabinet shall submit health history received under (KRS 199.525[1]) to Clerk for Circuit Court and Clerk shall place health history in adoption case file. (KRS 199.525[2]).

Name.—Judgment of adoption changes name of child to conform to prayer of petition, without reference to former name. (KRS 199.520[1]).

Effect of Adoption.—Adoptee is considered natural child of adoptive parents as if born of them for purposes of inheritance, succession and other considerations. Except where biological parent is spouse of adoptive parent, child has no legal relationship to its biological parents. (KRS 199.520[2]). Adoptee cannot inherit from or through blood relatives. (406 S.W.2d 151).

Setting Aside Adoption.—Adoption may be annulled on petition filed within five years after judgment and on proof that adoptee reveals traits of ethnological ancestry different from those of adoptive parents, of which latter had no information prior to adoption; no attack may be made based on procedure or substance of adoption suit after one year from entry of judgment of adoption. (KRS 199.540).

Surrogate Parenting Contracts.—No person, agency, institution, or intermediary may be party to contract compensating woman for her artificial insemination and subsequent termination of parental rights to child born as result of such insemination; contract is void. (KRS 199.590).

Interstate Compact on Placement of Children has been adopted. (KRS 615.030).

ALIMONY:

See topic Dissolution of Marriage, subheads Temporary Maintenance for Spouse, Permanent Maintenance for Spouse.

COMMUNITY PROPERTY:

System does not obtain in Kentucky.

DESERTION:

See topics Dissolution of Marriage, Husband and Wife; categories Estates and Trusts, topic Descent and Distribution; Property, topic Dower.

DISSOLUTION OF MARRIAGE:

This subject is covered in KRS c. 403. Absolute divorce is now called dissolution of marriage. Kentucky statute based in part on Uniform Marriage and Divorce Act.

Grounds for Dissolution of Marriage.—Sole basis for dissolution is irretrievable breakdown of marriage relationship. (KRS 403.110[5]; 403.170[3]). Determination whether marriage is or is not irretrievably broken is judicial function based on evidence

DISSOLUTION OF MARRIAGE ... *continued*

and not mere agreement of parties. (564 S.W.2d 220). For grounds for declaration of invalidity of marriage, or annulment, see topic Marriage, subhead Annulment.

Grounds for Legal Separation.—Judgment for separation or divorce from bed and board may be rendered for any cause that allows divorce or for any other cause that court in its discretion deems sufficient. (KRS 403.050).

Citizenship Requirements.—None.

Residence Requirements.—One of parties, at time action is commenced, must be resident of state and residence must have been maintained in state for 180 days next preceding filing of petition. (KRS 403.140[1]). Being stationed in state while a member of armed services may constitute residence (KRS 403.140[1]), but mere domicile or legal residence is insufficient (300 Ky. 237, 188 S.W.2d 439). Temporary absence from state does not defeat requirement otherwise met. (663 S.W.2d 219). Fact of sufficient residence must be proved by testimony of one or more credible witnesses, who may be petitioner or respondent. (KRS 403.025).

Jurisdiction.—Courts having general equity jurisdiction may grant decree of dissolution of marriage or legal separation and no jury may be impaneled. (KRS 403.010). Court of Appeals has no jurisdiction to reverse judgment of Circuit Court dissolving marriage. (KRS 22A.020[3]).

In connection with jurisdiction as affecting validity in other states of Kentucky divorce, see 181 U.S. 155; 325 U.S. 226. See also 211 Ky. 799, 278 S.W. 121, and 325 U.S. 279.

Venue.—Action for maintenance or dissolution must be brought in county where husband or wife usually resides. (KRS 452.470).

Process.—Petition for dissolution may be joint. (KRS 403.150[3]). If petition filed by one party, service must be in accordance with provisions of Civil Rules (KRS 403.150[4]), by personal service, constructive service or warning order (CR 4.01 to 4.16).

Pleading.—Action is commenced by filing verified petition for dissolution of marriage or legal separation. Petitioner, or petitioners, must allege that marriage is irretrievably broken and set forth: Age, occupation, social security number, and residence of each party and his length of residence in state; date of marriage and its place of registry; fact that parties are separated and date of separation; names, ages and addresses of any living infant children of marriage and whether wife is pregnant; any arrangements as to custody, visitation, and support of children and maintenance of spouse; and, relief sought. If either party alleges domestic violence and abuse (as defined in KRS 403.720), petitioner must certify existence and status of any domestic violence protective orders. (KRS 403.150[2]).

A recommended form for petition is as follows:

Form

.... Circuit Court
Mary Doe   Petitioner
vs.   Petition for Dissolution of Marriage
Henry Doe   Respondent
IN RE: The marriage of Mary Doe and Henry Doe (and custody and support of two infant children, if applicable)
Petitioner, Mary Doe, for her cause of action herein, states as follows:
1. (facts as to 180 day residency)
2. (facts as to age, occupation and address of petitioner)
3. (facts as to age, occupation and address of respondent, or joint petitioner who is denominated as respondent)
4. (facts as to date of marriage, etc.)
5. (facts as to separation, etc.)
6. (facts as to living infant children and pregnancy)
7. (facts as to arrangements for custody, etc. of children and for maintenance of a spouse, and if no arrangement made, statement to that effect)
8. The marriage of Mary Doe and Henry Doe is irretrievably broken.
9. (facts concerning property and ability of one spouse to provide for support and maintenance, if desired).
10. (facts concerning domestic violence and abuse, if applicable).
WHEREFORE, Petitioner, Mary Doe, demands (or Petitioner and Respondent demand):
A. Dissolution of marriage of Petitioner and Respondent.
B. (Prayer concerning custody of infant children)
C. That marital property be legally divided between Petitioner and Respondent in just proportions.
D. (Prayer for child support and maintenance both temporary and permanent if desired), as the Court may deem reasonable.
E. (Prayer for restoration of name if desired)
F. (Prayer for costs and reasonable attorney's fee) and for all other orders and relief to which Petitioner (or Petitioner and Respondent) may be entitled.

....
signature of attorney for Petitioner
....
signature of Petitioner

[Jurat for petitioner's signature, or signatures of petitioner and respondent if both parties join, see category Documents and Records, topic Acknowledgements.]

Response if filed may also be verified (KRS 403.150[4]) and only defense to action is denial that marriage is irretrievably broken (KRS 403.170[2]; 403.150[5]).

Petitioner or attorney must file with petition information on forms supplied by Office of Vital Statistics in Cabinet for Health Services. (KRS 213.116[4]).

Practice.—If minor children who are issue of marriage exist, no testimony (other than temporary motions) until 60 days have elapsed from first of date of service of summons or appointment of warning order attorney. (KRS 403.044).

Uncontested allegation that marriage is irretrievably broken may be considered by court upon hearing (KRS 403.170[1]) or by upon findings and recommendation of Commissioner of court (CR 53). In contested case court shall consider all relevant factors in hearing or hearings, may order conciliation conference, and shall determine whether marriage is irretrievably broken. (KRS 403.170[2]). No decree can be entered that marriage is irretrievably broken until parties have lived apart, or under same roof without sexual cohabitation, for 60 days. (KRS 403.170[1]). Finding of irretrievable breakdown is determination that there is no reasonable prospect of reconciliation. (KRS 403.170[3]).

Restraining orders and temporary injunctions are available. (KRS 403.160[3] and 403.160[5]).

When wife is pregnant at time petition is filed, court may continue case until pregnancy is terminated. (KRS 403.150[7]).

Judgment or Decree.—Decree of dissolution of marriage and decree of legal separation are final when entered in accordance with Civil Rules. (KRS 403.130[1]). No jurisdiction for appeal of decree of dissolution of marriage to Court of Appeals. (KRS 22A.020[3]).

Decree of legal separation operates as to property thereafter acquired, and as to personal rights and legal capacities of parties, as decree of dissolution of marriage, except that neither may marry again during lifetime of other, and legal separation does not bar curtesy, dower or distributive right, and it may be revised or set aside at any time by court rendering it. (KRS 403.050, 403.042).

Decree of legal separation may be converted to decree of dissolution of marriage after one year on motion of either party. (KRS 403.230[1]).

Temporary Maintenance for Spouse.—Temporary maintenance (alimony) is available on motion of either party with supporting affidavit when court has personal jurisdiction over both parties. (KRS 403.160[1]). Temporary injunctions or restraining order pursuant to civil rules may be sought. (KRS 403.160[3]). Temporary order or temporary injunction terminated by final decree. (KRS 403.160[6]). For grounds for temporary maintenance, see subhead Permanent Maintenance for Spouse, infra.

Allowance for Prosecution of Suit.—Court during action, upon decree of dissolution and after termination may, after considering financial resources of both parties, assess reasonable amount of costs and attorney's fees. Attorney's fees for services rendered before, during and after action may be granted directly in name of and collected directly by attorney. (KRS 403.220).

Permanent Maintenance for Spouse.—If dissolution action was based upon constructive service of absent spouse, permanent alimony may be sought upon motion with supporting affidavit after final decree. (KRS 403.200[1]). Maintenance or support once granted may be modified upon showing of changed circumstances so substantial and continuing as to make terms unconscionable. (KRS 403.250[1]). Unless otherwise expressly agreed or provided in decree, death of either party or remarriage of party receiving maintenance terminates obligations for future payments. (KRS 403.250[2]).

Grounds for maintenance are: insufficient property, including marital property, available to provide for reasonable needs; or inability of spouse to support himself through appropriate employment, or condition or circumstances of child for whom spouse is custodian make it inappropriate for spouse to be required to seek employment outside home. (KRS 403.200[1]). Court to grant maintenance for amounts and for periods of time as court deems just after considering: financial resources available to spouse seeking maintenance; time necessary to acquire sufficient education or training for appropriate employment; standard of living during marriage; duration of marriage; age, and physical and emotional condition of spouse seeking maintenance; and ability of spouse from whom maintenance is sought to meet his needs while meeting those of spouse seeking maintenance. (KRS 403.200[2]). Fault is not a ground for granting maintenance but may be considered in determining amount of maintenance granted. (498 S.W.2d 134).

Division of Property of Spouses.—Written separation agreement between parties is encouraged, is binding upon court, except provisions for custody, support, and visitation of children, and will be enforced unless court, after considering economic circumstances of parties and other relevant evidence produced by parties, finds its provisions unconscionable. Provisions set forth verbatim or by reference in decree of dissolution or legal separation. (KRS 403.180). KRS 403.190 sets forth factors for court-ordered declaration of separate property of parties and division of "marital property." Fault may still be factor in division, see 460 S.W. 2d 821, at 826, although section provides marital misconduct not to be regarded. (KRS 403.190[1]).

Change of Wife's Name.—If no children born of marriage, wife's maiden name shall be restored by court. If child or children born, name may be restored on her motion. (KRS 403.230[2]).

Custody of Children.—Matters relating to child custody may be subject of separate action in court of competent jurisdiction or may be considered during dissolution of marriage proceeding upon inclusion of demand in petition. (KRS 403.420[4]; 403.140[1][d]). Separate proceeding for custody is instituted upon verified petition and action is designated "In re the Custody of (name or names of infant children)." (KRS 403.130[2]). Factors for court to consider in assuming jurisdiction over initial or modification decree of child custody are set forth in Uniform Child Custody Jurisdiction Act, adopted as KRS 403.400 to 403.630. See Uniform and Model Acts section of this Digest. Custody matters to be determined in accordance with best interests of each child with equal consideration to each parent and to de facto custodian, but court to consider, among other relevant factors: Wishes of parent or parents and any de facto custodian; wishes of child as to his custodian; interaction and interrelationship of child with parent or parents, siblings and other persons; child adjustment to home, school and community; mental and physical health of all concerned; and information, records and evidence of domestic violence as defined in KRS 403.720. (KRS 403.270). Court may not consider conduct of proposed custodian which is not likely to affect child adversely. (647 S.W.2d 790). Custodian's abandonment of family residence shall not be considered when abandonment was due to threatened or actual physical harm to that party from spouse. (KRS 403.270[4]). Joint custody to parents authorized if in best interests of child. (KRS 403.270[5]). Temporary custody order may be sought (KRS 403.280[1])

DISSOLUTION OF MARRIAGE . . . *continued*
and court may order investigation by friend of court or child agency (KRS 403.300). Child custody proceedings given priority on court dockets. (KRS 403.310[1]). Parent not granted custody is entitled to reasonable visitation rights unless court finds such rights would seriously endanger child's physical, mental, moral or emotional health, and court empowered to modify visitation rights in accordance with child's best interests. (KRS 403.320). Custody decree, once entered, shall not be modified for two years except upon court's belief of serious danger to child's physical, mental, moral or emotional health or custodian appointed under prior decree has placed child with de facto custodian (KRS 403.340[1]), or pursuant to Uniform Child Custody Jurisdiction Act (KRS 403.340[2]). Criminal penalties relating to custody are set forth in KRS 509.070.

Allowance for Support of Children.—Separate proceeding for support may be instituted upon verified petition (KRS 403.130[2]), or motion for temporary child support may be filed in dissolution or separation proceeding (KRS 403.160[2]). State guidelines for child support awards mandated by Title I of Family Support Act of 1988, 42 USC §667, set forth in KRS 403.211-403.213. When parent who fails to support child is not obligated to provide support by court order, Cabinet for Families and Children may determine parents' child support obligations through administrative proceedings. (KRS 405.430). Court may enforce temporary support order with temporary injunction. (KRS 403.160[3]). Child support obligations, unless otherwise agreed in writing or otherwise provided in decree, terminate upon emancipation of child, but if child turns 18 and emancipated because of age, not because married while high school student, support required while high school student, but not beyond completion of year in high school when child turns 19 (see topic Infants) but not by death of parent obligated to support child. (KRS 403.213[3]). When parent obligated to provide support dies, amount of support may be modified, revoked, or commuted to lump sum payment, to extent just and appropriate in circumstances. (KRS 403.213[3]).

Service of process may be had under long-arm statute upon person whose marital domicile is in state if he removes himself from state to avoid support obligations. (KRS 454.275).

Remarriage.—Decree of dissolution of marriage authorizes either party to marry again. (KRS 403.010). Decree of legal separation bars remarriage of both parties during life of other. (KRS 403.050).

Foreign divorce is recognized and enforced but Kentucky can always examine foreign decree for necessary jurisdiction. (211 Ky. 799, 278 S.W. 121). Uniform Divorce Recognition Act not adopted.

Separation agreements are encouraged, enforced in accordance with terms if not found unconscionable, and may be either set out in full or incorporated by reference in decree of dissolution of marriage. (KRS 403.180). See subhead Division of Property of Spouses, supra.

Antenuptial Contracts.—See topic Husband and Wife.

DIVORCE:

See topic Dissolution of Marriage.

GUARDIAN AND WARD:

Minors.—District courts have jurisdiction over appointment and removal of guardians, limited guardians and conservators for minors and management and settlement of their accounts. (KRS 387.020[1]). Guardian may be appointed to care for person and financial resources of minor. (KRS 387.020[3]). Limited guardian may be appointed to care only for person of minor. (KRS 387.020[4]). Conservator may be appointed to care for financial resources of minor. (KRS 387.020[5]). If minor resides in Kentucky, jurisdiction exercised in county of minor's residence or, in case of testamentary guardianship, in county where will probated. (KRS 387.020[1]). If minor nonresident, jurisdiction in county where minor has real or personal property located. If property located in more than one county, district court which first takes proceedings for appointment of guardian, limited guardian or conservator retains jurisdiction. (KRS 387.020[3]).

Uniform Probate Code not adopted.

Selection of Guardian.—Last surviving parent of minor may by will nominate guardian, or alternatively limited guardian, or conservator, or both. (KRS 387.040). Testamentary guardian or conservator of estate must, however, be also appointed by proper order of district court. (KRS 387.070).

Minor 14 years of age or older may nominate own guardian, limited guardian or conservator provided compliance with certain prescribed formalities (KRS 387.050), and guardian appointed before ward attains age of 14 may be superseded by guardian appointed on nomination of ward after attaining that age (141 Ky. 278, 132 S.W. 541).

In appointing guardian, limited guardian, or conservator, district court must appoint any person or entity whose appointment in best interest of minor, taking into consideration (1) ability of person or entity to manage and preserve minor's estate, and (2) person or entity nominated by will of last surviving parent or person nominated by minor if 14 years of age or older. (KRS 387.032).

Eligibility and Competency.—Any interested person or entity may petition for appointment of guardian. (KRS 387.025). Any guardian will be removed if moves out of Kentucky, becomes incapable of or fails to discharge duties, or district court deems removal in best interest of ward. (KRS 387.090). As to powers of nonresident guardians or conservators, see subhead Foreign Guardian or Conservator, infra. Exactly the same provisions are made for appointment of public guardians as in case of public administrators (see category Estates and Trusts, topic Executors and Administrators), except that sheriff may not act as guardian. (KRS 395.380).

Appointment of Guardian.—Any interested person may petition court for appointment of guardian or limited guardian for unmarried minor or for appointment of conservator for minor owning real or personal property. (KRS 387.025[1]-[2]). Petition must set forth name, address and date of birth of minor; name and address of minor's spouse, if any; name and address of minor's parents, or if minor has no living parent, names and addresses of minor's adult next of kin; name and address of individual or facility having custody of minor; facts and reasons supporting need for guardianship, limited guardianship, or conservatorship for minor; description and approximation of value of minor's real and personal property and other financial resources; name and address of petitioner; name and address of petitioner's attorney, if any; and name and address of person or entity desiring appointment as guardian, limited guardian, or conservator. (KRS 387.025[3]). Petition must be accompanied by verified application of person or entity desiring appointment setting forth name, address, and age of applicant; applicant's relationship to minor, if any; whether applicant has ever been convicted of crime; and applicant's qualifications to serve as guardian, limited guardian, or conservator. (KRS 387.025[4]). Duplicate copy must be mailed by clerk to Secretary of Revenue Cabinet. Court must appoint time for hearing petition and application; notice of hearing must be given minor if more than 14 years of age and to each person or entity required to be named in petition not less than five days prior to hearing. (KRS 387.025[5]). District court, after hearing, issues letters of appointment. (KRS 387.070[1]).

Qualification.—Guardian or conservator may not act until he has given bond to state, with surety approved by court, for faithful performance of trust. (KRS 387.070—see same statute for exceptions).

Inventory.—Within 60 days after appointment, guardian or conservator must file inventory of ward's estate coming into his hands, supplementing it as to additional property within like period, if any comes to his knowledge. (KRS 387.100).

Powers and Duties.—Guardian or limited guardian has powers and responsibilities of parent regarding ward's support, care and education, but not personally liable for ward's expenses and not liable to third persons by reason of relationship for acts of ward. (KRS 387.065[1]). Guardian or limited guardian must take custody of person of ward and establish ward's place of abode within Kentucky and must take reasonable care of ward's personal effects. (KRS 387.065[2]). Guardian or limited guardian may receive money payable for support of ward, consent to medical care for ward, consent to ward's marriage, adoption or military enlistment and expend funds of ward's estate for support of persons legally dependent on ward. (KRS 387.065[3]). Guardian, limited guardian or conservator may expend without court authorization (unless limited by court) income or principal of estate for support, care and education of ward (unless parent legally obligated and able to supply). (KRS 387.065[5]-[6]). Guardian or conservator may also apply income and principal for payments of taxes, claims and expenses of guardianship and in accordance with 387.065 for support, care and education of ward or ward's dependent. (KRS 387.125[1]). Guardian or conservator may sell ward's personal property without court authorization but must comply with provisions regarding fiducial sales of property in KRS c. 389A. (KRS 387.125[3]). Guardian or conservator may institute or defend actions, claims, or proceedings for protection of ward's estate. (KRS 387.125[6]). Guardian or conservator may lease real property for term no longer than seven years unless otherwise approved by court. (KRS 387.125[7]). See KRS 387.135 and 387.137 for limited guardian and conservator powers and duties as reflected above.

At age of 18, guardian or conservator must distribute funds to ward unless ward then disabled or partially disabled. (KRS 387.065[8]; 387.137).

Guardian may act for ward in cases where application made to dispense with administration in certain cases of small estates. (KRS 395.480). See category Estates and Trusts, topic Executors and Administrators.

Kentucky guardians may not remove ward's property from state without obtaining permission from district court of county in which qualified. (KRS 387.200).

Investments.—See KRS c. 386; and category Estates and Trusts, topic Trusts.

Securities in Name of Nominee.—See category Estates and Trusts, topic Trusts, subhead Securities in Name of Nominee.

Real Estate.—Guardian or conservator holding funds for investment may invest in real estate upon approval of district court (KRS 386.020[1]); may lease real property for term no longer than seven years unless otherwise approved by district court (KRS 387.125[7]); may sell real property by proceeding under KRS 389A.010 to 389A.045 (KRS 387.125[3]). Without previous judicial proceeding or judgment, interest in real property held by fiduciary for ward may be sold by private sale subject to court approval. (KRS 389A.032).

Liabilities of Guardian.—Guardian, conservator and sureties liable for waste. (KRS 387.080[2]). Other liabilities same as those of executors and administrators (q. v.). Guardian liable up to $2,500 for unemancipated child's willful defacing of property if joined as defendant subject to cumulative limit of $10,000. (KRS 405.025). Neither limit applies for purposes of motor vehicle negligence liability. (KRS 405.025[2]; 186.590).

Accounts.—Guardian or conservator must file accounts of execution of guardian's or conservator's trust. Accountings subject to provisions governing fiduciary accountings (KRS 395.610 to KRS 395.657 and KRS 395.990) except (1) accounting of guardian or conservator must be filed one year after appointment of guardian or conservator, and annually thereafter unless ward's net estate is $5,000 or less, in which case accounting must be made on biennial basis, and (2) each accounting for estates with net value over $5,000 must include plan for preserving and maintaining ward's estate (KRS 387.175).

Termination of Guardianship.—Guardian, limited guardian, or conservator may be removed by district court if becomes insane, moves out of Kentucky, becomes incapable of discharging trust, fails to discharge duties or court deems removal in best interest of ward. (KRS 387.020; 387.090). Guardian may resign trust on application. (KRS 387.090; 395.325).

Disabled Persons.—District courts have exclusive jurisdiction over all proceedings involving determination of disability, modification of order, appointment and renewal of guardians and conservators, and management and settlement of their accounts. (KRS 387.520). Venue per KRS 387.520(2), (3).

District court can appoint bonded curator for any person deeming himself unfit to manage his property or business because of age or physical disability and weakness. (KRS 387.320).

Petition for appointment of limited guardian, guardian, limited conservator or conservator for individual allegedly disabled, called "respondent", may be filed by interested

See note at head of Digest as to 1998 legislation covered.

See Topical Index in front part of this volume.

GUARDIAN AND WARD . . . *continued*
party or entity or by individual needing guardianship or conservatorship. Petition must set forth: Petitioner's relationship; interest; name and address and name and address of petitioner's attorney, if any; name and address; date of birth, if known; interest; name, place of residence, date of birth, and nature or degree of disability of respondent; facts and reasons supporting need for guardianship and conservatorship; names and addresses of respondent's next of kin, if known; description and approximate value of respondent's financial resources including government benefits, insurance settlements, and anticipated yearly income, if known; name, address, qualifications, and relationship, if any, to respondent of individual proposed as guardian or conservator; and name and address of any person or entity appointed by respondent as respondent's attorney-in-fact under durable power of attorney as defined in subsection (1) of §2 of this Act, or as respondent's surrogate to make health care decisions under advanced directive. (KRS 387.530). Prior to hearing on petition, there must also be filed, by either employee of licensed facility where respondent resides or by court-appointed person or agency, "interdisciplinary evaluation report" containing specified information. (KRS 387.540[4]). Court must appoint time for hearing within 30 days of application; notice of hearing must be given petitioner, respondent, their attorneys, respondent's next of kin, person with whom or facility at which respondent resides, and proposed guardian or conservator at least 14 days prior to hearing. (KRS 387.550). At hearing convened to determine disability of respondent, respondent has right to court-appointed counsel (KRS 387.560) and trial by jury (KRS 387.570).

Court may appoint as limited guardian, guardian, limited conservator or conservator any suitable person or any entity, public or private, capable of conducting active guardianship or conservatorship program. Unless no other suitable person is available and willing, court shall not appoint any public or private entity directly providing services to respondent. (KRS 387.600[1]). Any person desiring appointment shall file written application under oath, stating name, address, qualifications and relationship to respondent. (KRS 387.530[2]). Prior to appointment, court must make reasonable effort to question respondent concerning his preference and any preference indicated shall be given due consideration. If respondent has attorney in fact, then that must be treated as indication of preference to have attorney in fact appointed and said preference shall be given due consideration. Court must appoint person or entity best qualified and willing to serve. (KRS 387.600[2]).

Foreign guardian or conservator of ward not Kentucky resident may, by application to district court having jurisdiction, be authorized to sue for, recover and remove to ward's domicile, ward's personal estate in Kentucky. (KRS 387.185).

Gifts to Minors.—See topic Infants; category Courts and Legislature, topic Statutes.

Uniform Fiduciaries Act adopted with substantial modifications. See KRS c. 386.

Uniform Simplification of Fiduciary Security Transfers Act not adopted.

Uniform Veterans' Guardianship Act adopted. (KRS 388.190-388.390).

Compensation.—Guardians, limited guardians, and conservators receive reasonable compensation for services rendered and reimbursements for reasonable expenses. Compensation shall not exceed fees provided to trustees of estates as provided in KRS 386.180. (KRS 387.111).

HUSBAND AND WIFE:

See also categories Estates and Trusts, topic Descent and Distribution; Property, topics Curtesy, Deeds, Dower, Real Property.

During marriage, neither spouse has any interest in property of other owned at time of marriage or acquired after marriage. (KRS 404.010[1]). As to marriage previously contracted, law in force at time material to inquiry should be consulted. (104 Ky. 48, 46 S.W. 524; 104 Ky. 77, 47 S.W. 195).

Disabilities of Married Women.—Last of specific disabilities (relating to ability to convey real property and making promissory notes) removed effective June 21, 1974.

Separate Property.—Wife's estate is liable for her debts and responsibilities contracted or incurred before marriage, and for such contracted after marriage, except as indicated in cc. 404 and 392. (KRS 404.010[2]; 267 Ky. 816, 103 S.W.2d 269).

A married woman may acquire and hold property, real and personal, by gift, devise or descent or purchase (KRS 404.020[1]), and may in her own name, as if she were unmarried, sell, encumber and dispose of her personal property (KRS 404.020[1]).

Husband is not liable for wife's debt or responsibility contracted before or after marriage, except to extent that he has received property from or by her by virtue of marriage, and except, further, that husband is liable for necessaries furnished wife after marriage. (KRS 404.040). However, husband entitled to credit for deceased wife's debt in determining distributive shares of estate. (KRS 140.090). Otherwise neither consort is liable, by virtue of marriage, for other's obligations. Husband is personally liable for expenses of wife's funeral. (241 Ky. 322, 43 S.W.2d 1017).

Beneficial interest of married woman in life insurance policy or proceeds thereof inures to her separate use and that of her children, independently of her husband or his creditors. (KRS 304.14-340[1]).

Contracts.—Husband and wife may contract with each other as with other persons. (KRS 404.010, 404.020).

Married woman may make contracts, sue and be sued, as single woman, and may convey her own property to her husband without circumlocution. (292 Ky. 723, 167 S.W.2d 847). She may have power and right to rent out her real estate, and collect, receive and recover in her own name rents thereof, and make contracts for improvement thereof. (KRS 404.020).

A gift, transfer or assignment of personal property between husband and wife is not valid as to third persons unless in writing and acknowledged and recorded as required in case of chattel mortgages. (KRS 404.020[2]; 205 Ky. 450, 266 S.W. 43). This applies to intangibles. (285 Ky. 125, 147 S.W.2d 67).

Wife may, without consent of husband, take out insurance on life of husband or children. Premiums deemed to have been part of her separate estate. (KRS 304.14-340[2]).

Antenuptial contracts are enforceable and favored (236 Ky. 809, 34 S.W.2d 442) if in writing (KRS 371.010[5]), full disclosure has been made of extent of property owned by each party (711 S.W.2d 860) and other principles of contract law satisfied.

Actions.—A married woman may sue or be sued as though unmarried (KRS 404.060[1]), and may bring or defend certain actions for her husband (KRS 404.060[2, 3]). She may sue her husband on contract (143 Ky. 94, 136 S.W. 127) and for injury to her separate property (215 Ky. 154, 284 S.W. 1042), and for personal injuries (262 S.W.2d 480, 481). Presumably same rights and inhibitions attach to husband. Spouse and child abuse actions recognized with equitable remedies available. (KRS 403.715-403.785). Married woman is liable for her own torts as if unmarried.

Agency.—No reason is perceived why either husband or wife may not act as agent or attorney in fact for the other. (See KRS 404.030.)

Conveyance or Encumbrance of Property.—Either spouse may sell, convey or encumber his or her lands and chattels real, but the right of the other spouse to curtesy or dower is not affected thereby unless he or she joins in the instrument or releases the right by separate instrument. (KRS 404.030). As to sale or mortgage of property with one spouse free of dower or curtesy right of the other, see category Property, topic Dower. Gift or assignment of personal property must be recorded to bind third parties. (KRS 404.020[2]).

Children.—See topic Infants, subhead Support of Minor.

Desertion and Nonsupport.—It is felony punishable by imprisonment from one to five years or by fine not to exceed $10,000 for parent intentionally to desert minor in circumstances endangering life or health of minor. (KRS 530.040; 532.060[2][d]; 534.030). Persistent failure to provide support which person can reasonably provide and which he has duty to provide by virtue of court or administrative order to minor or other child adjudged mentally disabled or indigent spouse may be punished either as misdemeanor, or in flagrant cases, as felony with imprisonment up to five years. (KRS 530.050; 532.060).

Revised Uniform Reciprocal Enforcement of Support Act adopted with modifications conforming to local procedure. (KRS 407.100-407.360). Civil enforcement by Circuit or District Court. (KRS 407.170). Revised Uniform Reciprocal Enforcement of Support Act repealed in favor of Uniform Interstate Family Support Act, KRS 407.5101 to 407.5902, but only effective upon date United States Congress requires adoption of latter uniform act. (KRS 407.480).

Civil remedy available to deserted wife is by action for support. See topic Dissolution of Marriage. As to effect of desertion on right of inheritance see category Estates and Trusts, topic Descent and Distribution.

Community property system does not apply in Kentucky. Uniform Disposition of Community Property Rights at Death Act adopted. (KRS 391.210 to 391.260).

INFANTS:

Minors of both sexes attain their majority at age of 18, except for purchase of alcoholic beverages and for care of disabled children. (KRS 2.015). Until then, their parents are entitled to their services or their earnings, unless they have been emancipated. (KRS 405.010; 198 Ky. 330, 248 S.W. 892).

When any deposit is made by minor in his name, bank may pay him amount deposited. (KRS 287.380).

An infant is liable for necessaries.

Voting age is 18. (Ky. Const. §145).

Emancipation.—Marriage does not remove disability of infancy (160 Ky. 432, 169 S.W. 891), but married infant may be plaintiff or defendant in action without appointment of guardian ad litem or necessity of bringing suit by guardian or next friend. Judgment may be rendered against married infant. (CR 17.02).

Disabilities.—Usual common-law disabilities apply. KRS 389A.010 establishes provisions for sale of realty of persons under disability.

Ratification of Contracts.—Common law rules govern infants as to their capacity to contract and their right to disaffirm contracts, provided, however, that war veterans, under 18 years of age, borrowing money from the Federal Government, under Federal law enacted for their benefit, are bound by their contracts making and securing such loans. In such cases the borrower and his spouse, though under 18 years old, are deemed of full age. (KRS 384.090). Minors may borrow money from banks for educational purposes; instrument must have approval of parent or guardian and of financial officer of institution of learning. (KRS 287.385).

Actions.—Unmarried minors may sue by guardian or next friend. If sued, defense must be made for them by guardian or guardian ad litem, and no judgment may be rendered against an infant until such defense is made or a report filed showing inability to make defense after a careful examination of case. (CR 17.03). Service under CR 5.01 shall be made on person bringing or defending action. (CR 17.03). Court has discretion to require parent or guardian of infant defendant to pay attorney's fees and costs. (KRS 405.027). Parents of child may jointly maintain action for loss of services or earnings of infant child as result of injury wrongfully or negligently inflicted upon child. (KRS 405.010).

Support of Minor.—Both parents of child have duty of nurture and education of infant and of dependent children over age 18 with permanent physical or mental disability, but father is primarily liable for nurture and education of his infant children and for any unmarried child over 18 so long as child is full-time high school student, but not beyond completion of school year during which child reaches age 19. (KRS 405.020). Legal obligation to support terminates when child reaches 18. (KRS 403.213[3]; 413 S.W.2d 887). Age limitation does not void contract for support of child over 18. (418 S.W.2d 740).

Parental Responsibility.—Parent liable up to $2,500 (cumulative total $10,000) for unemancipated child's willful defacing of property if joined as defendant. (KRS 405.025[1]). Payment will not bar criminal proceedings against minor for balance not paid by parent or guardian. (KRS 405.025[1]). Parent who signs application for motor

See note at head of Digest as to 1998 legislation covered.

See Topical Index in front part of this volume.

INFANTS ... *continued*

vehicle operator's license for infant liable jointly and severally with infant for negligence. (KRS 186.590). Parental immunity from infants' claims in tort is largely abandoned. (465 S.W.2d 921).

Adoption.—See topic Adoption.

Desertion.—Parental rights of either or both legitimate parents may be terminated for neglect, desertion or abuse. (KRS 625.090).

Guardianship.—See topic Guardian and Ward.

Uniform Transfers to Minors.—1983 Uniform Transfers to Minors Act adopted (KRS 385.012 to 385.252) in substantially form set out in Part III, except age 18 designated as age "minor" becomes "adult" in §1.

Uniform Securities Ownership by Minors Act not adopted.

Interstate Compact for Placement of Children has been adopted. (KRS 615.030).

MARRIAGE:

Males and females under age of 18 but over age of 16 cannot lawfully marry, except, with permission of parents, surviving parent or guardian, or in cases of pregnancy, with consent of district court judge. In no case, except that of pregnancy which requires permission of district court, may males and females under age of 16 marry. (KRS 402.020).

Consent Required.—When either contracting party is under 18 years of age but over 16 years of age, and not before married, no license may issue without written consent of such party's father, mother, or custodian, personally given or certified in writing and attested by two subscribing witnesses and proved by oath of one of such witnesses. No license shall issue if either party to marriage is under age of 16, unless in case of pregnancy district court orders issuance of license. (KRS 402.210). Pregnant female under 18 unable to obtain consent of parent or guardian may apply to District Court for permission to marry which may be granted in judge's discretion. (KRS 402.020).

Medical Examination.—None required.

License.—No marriage may be solemnized without a license therefor, issued by county clerk of county where female resides at time, except that it may be issued by any county clerk when she is 18 years or over or widow, and it is issued on her application in person or by writing signed by her. (KRS 402.080).

Notice or publication of banns is not required.

Ceremonial marriage may be solemnized only by ministers or priests of any denomination in regular communion with any religious society, judges and justices of Court of Justice, retired judges and justices of Court of Justice except those removed for cause or conviction of felony, county judges/executive and such justices of peace and fiscal court commissioners as Governor or county judge/executive may authorize. (KRS 402.050[1]). But where either party belongs to religious society having no officiating priest or minister whose usage is to solemnize marriage at usual place of worship, marriage may be solemnized by consent given in presence of such society. (KRS 402.050[1][c]). At least two persons, in addition to parties and person solemnizing marriage, must be present at every ceremony. (KRS 402.050[2]).

Reports of Marriages.—Person solemnizing marriage must, within one month, return license to county clerk of county where license issued, with certificate of marriage over his signature, giving date and place of marriage and names of at least two of persons present. (KRS 402.220). County clerk must keep record of marriages and index thereto. (KRS 402.230).

Record.—See category Documents and Records, topic Records, subhead Vital Statistics.

Common law marriages contracted in Kentucky are not generally recognized as valid, but they are so considered for the purposes of recovery and distribution under special provisions of Workmen's Compensation Act. (243 Ky. 694, 49 S.W.2d 571; 275 Ky. 559, 122 S.W.2d 137). Common law marriages contracted elsewhere are recognized if valid in State where contracted, unless marriage is between members of same sex. (KRS 402.040; 245 Ky. 399, 53 S.W.2d 725).

Marriage by proxy or by written contract is not authorized in Kentucky.

Prohibited Marriages.—Following marriages are prohibited and declared void: (1) Between persons who are nearer of kin to each other by consanguinity than second cousins, whether of whole or half blood (KRS 402.010); (2) with person who has been adjudged mentally disabled (KRS 402.020[1][a]); (3) where there is husband or wife living, from whom person marrying has not been divorced (KRS 402.020[1][b]); (4) when not solemnized or contracted in presence of authorized person or society unless either party believed such authority existed (KRS 402.020[1][c]); (5) between members of same sex (KRS 402.020[1][d]); (6) between more than two persons (KRS 402.020[1][e]); (7) of male or female under 18 years of age, but over 16 years of age, except with consent of parent or guardian, or in case of pregnancy, with consent of district court judge, pregnancy is only instance where marriage of persons under age of 16 is recognized, and then, only with district court order. (KRS 402.020[1][f]).

Heavy penalties are provided for violation of prohibitions above outlined. (KRS 402.990).

Issue of all illegal or void marriages are considered as if born in lawful wedlock. (KRS 391.100). Issue of bigamous marriage is legitimate. (266 Ky. 176, 98 S.W.2d 483).

Foreign Marriages.—Marriage valid in state where solemnized is valid in Kentucky unless marriage is between members of same sex. (KRS 402.040).

Annulment.—Circuit Courts exercising equity jurisdiction may decree a marriage invalid or void in following circumstances: (a) Party lacked capacity to consent to marriage at time marriage was solemnized because of mental incapacity or infirmity, or influence of alcohol, drugs or other incapacitating substances, or a party was induced to enter into marriage by force or duress or by fraud involving essentials of marriage; (b) party lacks physical capacity to consummate marriage by sexual intercourse, and other party did not at time marriage was solemnized know of incapacity; (c) marriage is

prohibited; or (d) at instance of next friend where person was under 18 but over 16 years of age at time of marriage, and consent of father, mother, guardian, or other person having charge of care not obtained, or if under 16 marriage not conducted with permission of district court. (KRS 403.120[1]; 402.030).

Actions for annulment must be brought within 90 days after petitioner obtains knowledge of conditions described in (a) or (b) above, within one year after petitioner obtains knowledge that marriage was prohibited when solemnized (KRS 403.120[2]), and before cohabitation following 18th birthday (KRS 402.030). Where doubt is felt concerning validity of marriage, court may on petition of either party affirm or avoid it except party over age cannot bring petition against party underage. (KRS 402.250).

Issue of illegal or void marriages are considered to be born in lawful wedlock. (KRS 391.100).

Antenuptial Contracts.—See topic Husband and Wife.

INSURANCE

INSURANCE COMPANIES:

Insurance Code comprised of 50 topical subtitles is codified as Chapter 304 of Revised Statutes. Assessment or cooperative insurance is generally dealt with separately in KRS Ch. 299.

Supervision by Commissioner of Insurance who is head of Department of Insurance. (KRS 304.2-020). Commissioner's address is 229 West Main Street, Frankfort, Kentucky 40602. Information may be obtained by writing Department of Insurance, P.O. Box 517, Frankfort, Kentucky 40602.

Financial institutions authorized to engage in insurance agency activities (KRS 304.9-135[1]) must comply with all applicable requirements in insurance code (KRS 304.9-135[2]). Officers and employees of financial institutions prohibited from delaying or impeding customer's transactions in order to influence selection or purchase of insurance. (KRS 304.9-135[3]).

Rates of all types of insurance, except life insurance, annuities, ocean marine insurance, accident and health insurance, reinsurance, assessment or cooperative insurance, and individual and group workers' compensation self-insurance (KRS 304.13-021) shall be determined in competitive market by insurer (KRS 304.13-051). Rates in noncompetitive market, as determined by order of Commissioner (KRS 304.13-041), shall be made by insurer in accordance with rate standards of KRS 304.13-031. In competitive market every insurer shall file rates and supplementary rate information with Commissioner not later than 15 days after first use of rates. (KRS 304.13-051). In noncompetitive market every insurer shall file rates, supplementary rate information, and supporting information (KRS 304.13-061) with Commissioner not later than 30 days before effective date of rates (KRS 304.13-051). Existing rates in noncompetitive market may be disapproved by Commissioner pursuant to rating standards of subtitle 13, KRS c. 304, subject to right of appeal under KRS 304.2-370. (KRS 304.13-071). If change in competitive market rates, manuals or underwriting rules results in 25% increase or decrease in rates of any insured risk in any territory, all such rates must be approved by Commissioner. (KRS 304.13-051[5]). Each health insurers' policy must be filed with Commissioner and adhered to, may be changed as insurers may deem proper, but Commissioner's order required for premium rate increase. (KRS 304.17-380; KRS 304.17-383; KRS 304.17A-095). Life insurers' rates regulated in accordance with specified tables under KRS 304.15-340, except that adjusted premiums shall be operative in accordance with KRS 304.15-342 at option of insurer from July 15, 1982, or in any case on Jan. 1, 1989. Title insurers' rates regulated by KRS 304.22-020.

KRS 304.17A-020 creates Kentucky Health Purchasing Alliance for purpose of negotiating best rates for health coverage for Alliance members. Certain state and government employees are required to join Alliance and membership for other persons and employers with 50 employees or less is optional. (KRS 304.17A-010[17], [23]). Health plans must be renewable and limitations placed on preexisting conditions exclusions. Department of Insurance defines five standard health care benefit plans. (KRS 304.17A-160).

Annual statements must be filed by each authorized insurer (as defined in KRS 304.1-100) before Mar. 1 of each year for affairs of year ending Dec. 31 preceding. Commissioner may suspend or revoke authority of any insurer failing to file annual statement when due. (KRS 304.3-240[4]).

Policies.—
Approval.—Policies, annuity contract forms, application forms (where required and which will be a part of issued policy or contract), printed rider or indorsement forms, and forms of renewal certificates must be filed with Commissioner and approved before delivery or issuance for delivery in state. (KRS 304.14-120[1]). Health insurance filings must be made under KRS 304.17A-200 to 304.17A-260. Exceptions made for surety bonds, specially rated inland marine risks or to certain unique policies, riders, indorsements or forms. Filing may be made by rating organizations for certain insurers. (KRS 304.14-120[1]).

Filing must be made not less than 60 days in advance of any delivery in state. If not disapproved or earlier affirmatively approved, or if Commissioner has not extended time, by notice, for approval or disapproval, form so filed shall be deemed approved. Expiration of 30 day extension period shall be deemed approval also. Commissioner may at any time, after notice and for cause shown, withdraw any approval. (KRS 304.14-120[2]). Specific grounds for disapproval enumerated in KRS 304.14-130 include exclusion of, or discrimination in, coverage for HIV or AIDS infection and whether premium charged is unreasonable in light of benefits provided.

Standard or uniform provisions are required for policies of all kinds in KRS 304.14-150 and for policies, contracts and certificates of different kinds of insurance in subtopic of Code devoted thereto. Commissioner may waive required use of particular provision in particular policy. (KRS 304.14-140[1]). He may approve any substitute provision which is not less favorable to insured or beneficiary (KRS 304.14-140[2]) or which contains substantially similar provisions and is required by law of domicile of foreign or alien insurer (KRS 304.14-140[3]).

See note at head of Digest as to 1998 legislation covered.

See Topical Index in front part of this volume.

INSURANCE COMPANIES . . . *continued*

Additional policy provisions and contents allowed. (KRS 304.14-160). Policies must be legible and intelligible, meeting requirements of KRS 304.14-430 to 304.14-450 and Commissioner-promulgated regulations. (KRS 304.14-420). Insurance policies and claim related information must be written in English. (KRS 304.14-435). Special surplus line legend required on policy. (KRS 304.10-090).

Claims.—All claims under any insurance contract must be paid within 30 days with failure to settle within such time resulting in statutory interest and attorney fee entitlement. (KRS 304.12-235). Unfair claims settlement practices described in KRS 304.12-230.

Discrimination.—Insurers other than life or health prohibited from unfair discrimination in favor of particular persons or between insureds or subjects having substantially like insuring risks, exposure factors or expense elements. (KRS 304.12-080[1]). Particular discrimination provisions apply to life insurers (KRS 304.12-080[2]) and health insurers (KRS 304.12-080[3]). Specific testing and underwriting procedures prescribed for HIV infection and related matters. (KRS 304.12-013).

KRS 304.17A-150 contains antidiscrimination provision which prohibits insurer from encouraging employer to exclude certain employees from health insurance coverage.

Rebates, discounts, abatements, credits or reduction of premium stated in policy, special favors and advantages are prohibited except as provided for in applicable filing with Commissioner. (KRS 304.12-090).

Additional unfair trade practices and frauds regulated and prohibited in subtitle 12. KRS 304.12-010 to 304.12-250. Commissioner given authority, after notice and hearing, to cause institution of action to restrain or enjoin continuance of any method, act or practice, defined in Code or not, which is determined to be unfair, deceptive or not in public interest. (KRS 304.12-120-304.12-130). Purchase of insurance policy is purchase of service covered by Consumer Protection Act. (KRS c. 367; 759 S.W. 2d 819).

KRS 304.47-020(2) condemns "fraudulent insurance act" where aggregate of claim, benefit or money is less than or equal to $300 as misdemeanor, punishable by not more than one year in prison, fine, or both. "Fraudulent insurance act" includes filing or pursuing false insurance claims or aiding another to file or pursue false insurance claim. (KRS 304.47-020[1][A], [C]).

Liens.—No separate provision in Code.

Agents and Brokers.—Agents, solicitors, consultants, administrators, managing general agents, and adjusters licensed and regulated by KRS 304.9-010 to 304.9-470. Reinsurance intermediaries licensed and regulated by KRS 304.9-700 to 304.9-759. Brokers licensed and regulated in subtitle relating to surplus lines, KRS 304.10-010 to 304.10-210.

Agent.—In order to obtain license, applicant must be 18 years of age or over, must be bona fide resident of state, submit evidence from appointing insurer or three unrelated persons of trustworthiness, reliability and good character, must have high school education or equivalent, must have completed 40 hour course of instruction prescribed by insurance commissioner and passed written examination, unless exempt from examination for reasons specified in KRS 304.9-107 or 304.9-170, must provide evidence of liability insurance or penal bond in minimum amount of $10,000 per erroneous act or failure to act or agreement to assume responsibility by insurer for whom he is exclusive agent and must show appointment by authorized insurer subject to issuance of license. (KRS 304.9-105). Once licensed, agent must remain bona fide resident of state and must not use license principally for purpose of writing controlled business, and must be appointed as agent by authorized insurer. (KRS 304.9-100; 304-9-120 to 304.9-140). Referral fees restricted. (KRS 304.9-136). Agents or solicitors for whom exam is required as condition of licensure and who are not otherwise exempted must complete 24 hours of commissioner-approved continuing education courses of which 12 must be classroom hours in each two-year period beginning July 1 and ending June 30 two years later. (KRS 304.9-295). Providers of continuing education courses must pay fee for approval of course content at rate of $5 per hour of content, minimum $10. (KRS 304.4-010; 806 KAR 4:010[12]). Nonresidents may be licensed as life insurance agents under conditions specified in KRS 304.9-140. Firm or corporation may be licensed as agent if it maintains place of business in state and principals named in application meet requirements for individual licenses. (KRS 304.9-130). Temporary licenses available under certain conditions. (KRS 304.9-300 to 304.9-310). Agent under KRS 304.9-120, except life and health agents, must maintain accessible place of business in state where his licenses and licenses of solicitors employed by him must be displayed and where he must maintain complete records of transactions available to Commissioner. (KRS 304.9-390). Biennial license fees of resident agent of $40 for each insurer represented; nonresident life agent fee $50 biennially. (KRS 304.4-010; 806 KAR 4:010[6]).

Managing General Agent.—In order to obtain license, resident applicant must hold general insurance agent's license and be appointed by each authorized insurer represented. Nonresident applicant must hold nonresident general lines insurance license and be appointed by each insurer represented. Nonresident managing general agents subject to same restrictions as nonresident agents. If any unauthorized insurers are represented, applicant must also hold surplus lines broker license. Initial licenses issued to expire on Mar. 31, 1988 and biennially thereafter. Biennial license fee of $100. (KRS 304.9-085; 304.4-010; 806 KAR 4:010[7]).

Solicitor.—In order to obtain license, applicant must meet same requirements as set for agent's license (see catchline Agent, supra), except must show employment by licensed resident agent subject to issuance of license instead of appointment by authorized insurer. (KRS 304.9-105). Once licensed, solicitor must remain bona fide resident of state and must not use license for principal purpose of writing controlled business. (KRS 304.9-100[2]; 304.9-120). Biennial license fee, $40. (KRS 304.4-010; 806 KAR 4:010[8]). Solicitor may not be concurrently licensed to more than one agent and shall not have authority to bind risks or countersign policies. (KRS 304.9-380).

Consultant must be 25 years of age or over, have had not less than five years of actual experience as a licensed agent with respect to kinds of insurance to be covered by license or other special training or experience, have thorough knowledge of kind of insurance to be covered, must pass written examination, must be competent, trustworthy under highest fiduciary standards, financially responsible and of good reputation and must have insurance policy coverage with aggregate liability of $50,000, and deposit $10,000 as bond with Commissioner. (KRS 304.9-320; KRS 304.9-330). Biennial license fee, $100. (KRS 304.4-010; 806 KAR 4:010[10]).

Administrator.—Persons who collect premiums for or who settle or adjust claims on life or health, or annuity, benefit plans required to hold current license. (KRS 304.9-051 and 304.9-052). Applicants must be 21 or over, competent, trustworthy, reliable and of good reputation, have attained educational level acceptable to Commissioner and be financially responsible. Initial licenses expire Mar. 31, 1987 and revised biennially thereafter. Firm or corporation may be licensed as administrator if persons authorized to act meet requirements for individual licenses. Nonresident administrators deemed to appoint Secretary of State as agent for service of process. (KRS 304.9-052). Administrators may only act under written agreement with insurer and hold funds of insurer in fiduciary capacity. Books, records and written agreement of administrator to be retained for five years after involved transaction. Advertising must be approved in advance by insurer. Notification of administrator's involvement to insureds required. Compensation on basis of claims experience prohibited. (KRS 304.9-371 to 304.9-377).

Adjuster, as defined in KRS 304.9-070, must be 21 years or over, resident of Kentucky or resident of another state with reciprocal provisions, be full-time salaried employee of licensed adjuster or insurer, law graduate or have special experience or training, must be trustworthy and of good reputation, have passed written examination and must maintain in state office accessible to public (KRS 304.9-430). Firm or corporation may be licensed as adjuster if each individual who will exercise powers is also qualified for license as adjuster. (KRS 304.9-430[3]). Special exception applies for nonresidents in state to investigate or adjust particular loss or for adjustment of series of losses resulting from common catastrophe. (KRS 304.9-430[4]). Biennial license fee, $50. (KRS 304.4-010; 806 KAR 4:010[9]). Salaried employees of domestic insurers exempt from fee. (KRS 304.9–430[1]).

Broker's license may be issued to any person who has held current general lines agent's license continuously for at least three years, who has been deemed competent and trustworthy in surplus lines by Commissioner, who maintains office and represents at least three casualty and property insurers in state, who gives evidence of financial responsibility for errors and omissions of $500,000 per occurrence and $1,500,000 in aggregate, and who posts bond in penal sum of $20,000. (KRS 304.10-120; 304.10-140). Brokers shall maintain and keep available to Commissioner in their offices full records of each surplus lines coverage procured for five years after issuance (KRS 304.10-160) and shall file with Commissioner on forms provided on or before Apr. 1 of each year, verified annual statement of all surplus lines transacted in previous calendar year (KRS 304.10-170). Biennial license fee, $100. (KRS 304.4-010; 806 KAR 4:010[7]).

Process Agent.—Secretary of State designated irrevocable attorney for receipt of process for each authorized foreign or alien insurer, each domestic reciprocal insurer, and each domestic Lloyd's insurer and each qualified self-insurer. (KRS 304.3-230). Service upon unauthorized insurers shall be upon Secretary of State. (KRS 304.3-230[3]; 304.11-040). Service upon authorized domestic insurers is same as upon domestic business corporation. (KRS 304.3-230[4]; 271B.5-040).

Investments regulated for domestic insurers by KRS 304.7-010 to 304.7-360. Investments of foreign insurers shall be as permitted by laws of domicile if of a quality substantially equal to quality required of domestic insurers. (KRS 304.7-330).

Foreign Insurance Companies.—Right to do business in state contingent upon issuance of certificate of authority (KRS 304.3-070) issued by Commissioner; qualifications for issuance of certificate generally same as for domestic insurers but foreign insurer must have been issuing own policies as authorized insurer in domicile for at least three years, or be wholly owned subsidiary of an insurer previously authorized in Kentucky, successor in interest to authorized insurer, or be organized solely for purpose of insuring against special hazards to property or liability for which adequate provision is not made by previously authorized insurers (KRS 304.3-090). Commissioner may suspend certificate of authority for specified acts or omissions of insurer. (KRS 304.3-200).

Foreign or alien applicant must include in application, in addition to information required of domestic insurers on forms supplied by Commissioner, name and address of person to whom lawful process to be forwarded, a certificate of public insurance supervising official of its state or country of domicile showing that it is authorized or qualified for authority to transact in such state or country kinds of insurance proposed in Kentucky, a certificate as to deposit for maintenance of action (alien only), and a certificate as to deposit in state, or an approval of Commissioner for deposit out of state, of eligible assets equal to minimum required capital stock or minimum required basic surplus. (KRS 304.3-150[7] to [10]; 304.3-060[4]; 304.3-140[3]).

Fee of $500 charged for issuance of original certificate of authority, $100 for each annual renewal (KRS 304.4-010; 806 KAR 4:010[3]); restrictions provided on amount and character of real estate and mortgage investments for domestic insurers applicable to foreign and alien insurers if allowable by laws of domiciliary jurisdiction (KRS 304.7-330).

Conduct of insurance business in state without required certificate of authority bars maintenance of actions in state courts, either directly or indirectly, to enforce any right, claim or demand arising therefrom but does not relieve insurer of liability to defend (KRS 304.3-060[4]) and renders insurer liable for premium tax equal to 2% of gross premiums charged and penalty of 25% if not paid before Mar. 1 of year after year of collection (KRS 304.11-050). Commissioner empowered to institute action through Attorney General to enjoin business without certificate of authority. (KRS 304.11-030[4]).

No separate reports required of foreign or alien insurers; no separate requirements set for withdrawal.

Taxation of Foreign Insurers.—Annual premium tax of 2% levied on foreign life, foreign stock other than life and foreign mutual other than life companies, except cooperative or assessment, based on report on or before Mar. 1. (KRS 136.330 to 136.350). Beginning Jan. 1, 2000, every life insurance company must make irrevocable selection to be taxed under KRS 136.320 or 136.330. (KRS 136.335). Fire insurers pay additional tax of 3/4 of 1% of premiums. (KRS 136.350; 136.360). Health insurance contract or contracts for state employees not subject to tax under KRS 136.340 and

See note at head of Digest as to 1998 legislation covered.

See Topical Index in front part of this volume.

KY – 42

INSURANCE COMPANIES . . . *continued*
136.350. Estimated payments due June 1 and Oct. 1 in addition to Mar. 1 if yearly amounts of tax, including tax on workman's compensation premiums, exceeds $5,000 and penalty provided if not paid when due. (KRS 136.377).

Retaliatory Laws.—Code includes requirement that Commissioner impose obligations, prohibitions, or restrictions of whatever kind upon foreign or alien insurer or upon its agents or representatives doing business or seeking to do business in state equivalent to discriminatory or onerous requirements imposed upon Kentucky domestic insurers in domiciliary jurisdiction of foreign or alien insurer. (KRS 304.3-270; KRS 91A.080[5]).

Premium Tax.—For taxation of foreign and alien insurers, see subhead Foreign Insurance Companies, supra. Taxable capital and taxable reserves of domestic life insurers are taxed at rates of 70¢ and 1 mill respectively plus 30¢ on each $100 of taxable capital for county and city taxes in lieu of other taxes. (KRS 136.320[3]-[5]). Annual 2% premium tax applies to other domestic insurance companies with 3/4 of 1% additional tax imposed upon fire insurers. (KRS 136.340-136.360). Health insurance contract or contracts for state employees not subject to tax under these sections. In addition to any such premium taxes, every domestic, foreign, or alien insurer (other than life or health insurers) must collect premium surcharge at $1.50 per $100 of premiums on coverage to policyholders, to be reported and remitted by insurer to Revenue Cabinet on 20th of each month; rate to be adjusted Jan. 1, 1992. (KRS 136.392). Cities, counties, and urban county governments may elect to impose license fees or taxes on privilege of engaging in business of insurance and Commissioner shall impose equal premium tax on foreign insurers if foreign state retaliates against Kentucky insurer because of this provision. (KRS 91A.080[5]).

Privilege Tax.—Fee of $100 charged each foreign and domestic insurer upon filing annual statement, or additional or supplemental statement, each year. (KRS 304.4-010; 806 KAR 4:010[1]). No other privilege taxes levied.

Uniform Insurers Liquidation Act substantially adopted with numerous variations, omissions and additional matters. Insurers rehabilitation and liquidation covered by KRS 304.33-010 to 304.33-600.

Direct Actions Against Insurer.—See category Transportation, topic Motor Vehicles, subhead Direct Actions.

No-Fault Insurance.—Plan adopted. (KRS 304.39-010 et seq.). See category Transportation, topic Motor Vehicles, subhead No-Fault Insurance.

Plain Language.—See subhead Policies, supra; category Business Regulation and Commerce, topic Consumer Protection.

SURETY AND GUARANTY COMPANIES:

Such companies are subject to general provisions of corporation statutes (KRS c. 271B) and to general provisions of insurance code relating to domestic and foreign insurers (KRS c. 304, subtitle 21).

Insurance commissioner is directed to send a certified list of all insurers who have been granted a certificate of authority to transact surety business in state to county clerk of each county, and such lists, updated annually, are to be maintained as public records in such clerks' offices. (KRS 304.21-020).

Bonds of corporate surety companies authorized to transact surety business in state are sufficient to meet requirements for all forms of undertakings, recognizances, guaranties and other obligations. (KRS 304.21-050). Any insurer which executes any surety contract estopped to deny its corporate power to execute contract or assume liability. (KRS 304.21-080).

See category Civil Actions and Procedure, topic Bonds.

See also category Business Organizations, topic Corporations, subhead Shareholders' Actions.

INTELLECTUAL PROPERTY

TRADEMARKS AND TRADENAMES:

KRS 365.561 through 365.613 ("1994 Act") (effective July 15, 1994) (provisions codified in succession with numbers ending in .##1, .##3, and .##7), repeals KRS 365.560 through 365.625 (provisions codified in succession with numbers ending in .##0 and .##5), except as to matters arising before or pending on effective date of 1994 Act. (Acts 1994, c. 468, §19). Federal Lanham Act is persuasive authority for interpreting and construing 1994 Act. (KRS 365.561).

Common Law Protection.—Nothing in 1994 Act adversely affects rights or enforcement of common-law rights in marks acquired in good faith. (KRS 365.611). Principles of unfair competition allow user of name or mark to enjoin use of deceptively similar name or mark if so similar as to infringe upon good will and reputation. (445 S.W. 2d 135).

Who May Acquire Trademark.—Juristic person (defined to include firm, partnership, corporation, union, association, or other organization capable of suing or being sued) or natural person, and legal representatives, successors, or assigns of such person, may apply for and obtain registration. (KRS 365.563[5]-[7]).

What May Be Used.—Any word, name, symbol, or device may be used as trademark or service mark to identify, distinguish, and indicate source of goods or services including, but not limited to, distinctive package or container of any kind, or any combination: (1) used in any manner on goods or on containers or displays associated with goods or on tags or labels affixed to goods or, if nature of goods makes placement on goods impracticable, then on documents associated with goods or their sale; or (2) used or displayed in sale or advertising of services. (KRS 365.563). Mark must not consist of (1) immoral, deceptive, or scandalous matter; (2) matter which may disparage or falsely suggest connection with person (living or dead), institutions, beliefs, or national symbols, or bring them into contempt or disrepute; (3) flag or coat of arms or other insignia (or any symbolization thereof) of U.S., any state or municipality, or any foreign nation; (4) name, signature, or portrait of living individual without consent; (5) merely descriptive or deceptively misdescriptive or primarily geographically descriptive

or primarily surname; (6) matter so resembling mark used previously as to be likely to cause confusion or mistake or to deceive. (KRS 365.567). "Use" prerequisite to registration is bona fide use in ordinary course of trade. (KRS 365.563[8]).

No false brand may be used on anything sold with intent to deceive purchaser. (KRS 325.100).

Registration.—File verified application at following address: Office of Secretary of State, Trademark Department, P.O. Box 718, Frankfort, Kentucky 40602-0718; telephone (502) 564-2848; facsimile (502) 564-4075. Application must be made on prescribed form with facsimile of mark as actually used in triplicate, setting forth: (1) name and business address, (2) state of incorporation (if any), or if partnership, state in which organized and names of general partners; (3) goods or services on or in connection with which mark is used, and mode or manner in which mark is used in connection with goods or services; (4) class of goods or services; (5) date of first use anywhere; (6) date of first use in Kentucky; and (7) statement that applicant is owner, that mark is in use, and that no other person has right to use mark in identical or similar form or has federal or Kentucky registration of mark in identical or similar form. Application fee is $10 per class of goods/services payable to Kentucky Secretary of State. Application must be signed by applicant or person authorized to sign on applicant's behalf. (KRS 365.571).

Upon filing, Secretary of State's office examines application and may request additional pertinent information or request amendments to application, or may require applicant to disclaim exclusive rights in un-registrable component of mark otherwise registrable; applicant may voluntarily disclaim component of mark sought to be registered. Disclaimer does not affect rights in disclaimed matter if disclaimer has acquired distinctiveness (secondary meaning). If applicant is not entitled to registration, Secretary will advise and state reasons therefor; applicant shall have reasonable period of time to reply or amend application. Examination procedure continues until Secretary finally refuses registration or applicant fails to timely reply or amend. Upon Secretary of State's final refusal of registration, applicant may appeal to Franklin Circuit Court, which may order Secretary to register mark. Franklin Circuit Court's final decision appealable. Concurrent applications pertaining to identical or confusingly similar marks for same or related goods or services are accorded priority by order of filing. Rejected applicants can bring action to cancel registration on grounds of prior or superior rights to mark. (KRS 365.573). Certificate issued by Secretary of State is admissible in any Kentucky court as evidence of registration. (KRS 365.577).

Timber dealer may adopt brand by filing writing and prescribed form with county clerk of county in which his principal place of business is located, and posting copies thereof in designated places. (KRS 364.070).

Assignment.—Mark and registration or application is assignable with goodwill of business in which mark is used, or with that part of goodwill of business connected with use of and symbolized by mark. Assignment must be duly executed in writing and, upon payment of $5 recording fee, may be recorded with Secretary of State who will issue new certificate of registration for remainder of term in name of assignee. Assignment is void as against subsequent purchaser for valuable consideration without notice unless recorded within three months after date of assignment or prior to subsequent purchase. Registrants and applicants may record certificate of change of name of registrant or applicant upon payment to Secretary of $5 recording fee. Written and duly executed instruments relating to registered mark or pending application (e.g. licenses, security interests, or mortgages) may be recorded by Secretary. Recordation of such instruments constitutes rebuttable presumption of execution of assignment or other instrument. Photocopies are acceptable for recording if certified by any party thereto or successor as true and correct copy of original. (KRS 365.583).

Protection Afforded.—Term of registration is five years, renewable for additional five-year terms upon application filed within six months prior to expiration of term and upon payment of $5 renewal fee to Secretary. Registration in effect prior to effective date of statute continues in effect for remainder of unexpired term. Secretary of State has responsibility to notify registrants (at last-known address) of necessity of renewing registrations at least six months prior to expiration date. (KRS 365.581).

Infringement.—Owner of registered mark can enjoin manufacture, use, display, or sale of counterfeits or imitations thereof. Court may award profits or damages, and order that counterfeits or imitations be delivered up for destruction. In cases where party commits wrongful acts with knowledge of prior registration or in bad faith, court may award to prevailing party treble profits or damages plus reasonable attorneys' fees. (KRS 365.603). Infringement of timber dealer's brand is forbidden (KRS 364.080); criminal penalties for use of false brand on items sold with intent to deceive (KRS 365.100) and for violation of KRS 365.110, which forbids dealer or merchant to apply to any package label bearing name of any manufacturer without written authority, fine of $10 to $50 for each offense. (KRS 365.990).

Cancellation.—Secretary of State will cancel any registration: (1) upon request of registrant or assignee of record; (2) if registration not renewed; (3) when court has found that mark has been abandoned, that registrant is not owner, that registration was improperly granted or fraudulently obtained, that mark is generic name of goods or services or portion thereof for which it has been registered, or that registered mark is so similar to federal registration prior to application date and not abandoned so as to be likely to cause confusion or mistake or to deceive; and (4) which court orders canceled on any other ground. (KRS 365.591).

Tradenames.—"Trade name" defined as any name used by person to identify his business or vocation. (KRS 365.563[4]). No person or general or limited partnership, business trust, corporation, limited liability partnership or limited liability company may do business in Kentucky under assumed name, or any name or style other than his or its real name as defined in KRS 365.015(1) unless and until certificate of assumed name is executed, acknowledged and recorded in county clerk's office in county where such business is conducted or, in case of general and limited partnerships, limited liability companies, business trusts, corporations and limited liability companies, with Secretary of State's office with copy filed in county where entity deemed resident under KRS 355.9-401, which copies are to be filed with county clerk after stamped "filed" by Secretary of State. (KRS 365.015[3]). For corporations, certificate can be executed by any authorized person. For business trust it must be signed by trustees. For limited

TRADEMARKS AND TRADENAMES . . . *continued*

partnership it must be executed by general partner. For general partnership, including registered limited liability partnership, it must be executed by at least one partner authorized to do so by partners. For limited liability company, by member or manager authorized to act. No certificate of assumed name filed with Secretary of State shall set forth assumed name which is not distinguishable upon records from any other name, previously filed and on record with Secretary of State. (KRS 365.015[2]). Assumed name is effective for five years and may be renewed for successive terms. (KRS 365.015[4]). General partnerships shall file amendment, signed by all partners, to assumed name certificate to reflect change in identity of partners. Secretary of State entitled to $20 fee for filing such statement and county clerk $8. (KRS 365.015[6]; 64.012). Contracts made without compliance with these provisions are not void. (218 Ky. 128, 290 S.W. 1028). Fine of $25 to $100 and imprisonment of ten to 30 days or both may be imposed for any violation of KRS 365.015, assumed name statute with each day of continuing violation constituting separate offense. (KRS 365.990[1]).

TRADE SECRETS:

Uniform Trade Secrets Act, with 1985 Amendments, adopted without material variation effective July 13, 1990. See Part III, Uniform and Model Acts Section. (KRS 365.880 to 365.900).

Common law protection available, at least against appropriation by persons in fiduciary relationship such as employee. See 507 S.W.2d 166.

LEGAL PROFESSION

ATTORNEYS AND COUNSELORS:

Kentucky lawyer may not practice unless he or she is member in good standing of integrated State Bar. (SCR 3.030).

Jurisdiction over Admission.—Supreme Court has power to prescribe rules for admission to practice. (Const. §116). Board of Bar Examiners is charged with responsibility of administering examination to qualified applicants. (SCR 2.000[3]).

Copies of rules and forms for making application to take bar examination may be obtained from clerk of Supreme Court, Frankfort, Kentucky 40601.

Eligibility.—Applicant for admission to practice must be of good moral character and general fitness requisite for attorney and take oath to support state and federal constitutions. (SCR 2.010). Application will be denied if submitted for primary purpose of using admission in state to obtain admission in, or circumvent admission requirements of, some sister state or District of Columbia. (SCR 2.015).

Provision is made by KRS 21A.130 and SCR 2.000 for appointment by Supreme Court of Board of Bar Examiners and by SCR 2.040 for appointment by Supreme Court of Committee on Character and Fitness, charged with duty of investigating each applicant and reporting thereon to Board.

Each person who intends to apply for admission to Bar by examination must file with Clerk of Supreme Court in Frankfort verified application form provided by Board of Bar Examiners no later than Oct. 1 for succeeding Feb. examination or Feb. 1 for succeeding July. Application shall contain personal information, information concerning general and legal education, involvement in civil or criminal proceedings, history of applications for admission to bars of sister states, and other information required by Board of Bar Examiners or Character and Fitness Committee. Fees for application, examination and character investigation must accompany application in amount of $375, $475 or $575 depending on when filed (see subhead Registration as Law Student, infra); $625 if filed by attorney admitted to bar in another state. (SCR 2.020). Any applicant whose application to bar of another state has been refused for any reason is ineligible to take bar examination in Kentucky unless refusal was based on failure to pass bar examination in that state. (SCR 2.020[7]). Character and Fitness Committee required to advise Board of Bar Examiners not less than three months prior to date of examination of names and addresses of applicants for examination and at least ten days prior to bar examination certify to Secretary of Board of Bar Examiners of names and addresses of applicants who are qualified, to take bar examination. (SCR 2.040). Decision of Character and Fitness Committee on eligibility of applicant is final unless on motion of applicant made within 60 days after notice of decision has been mailed to applicant's last known address. Supreme Court upon review of record over-rules decision. (SCR 2.040; 2.060). Character and Fitness Committee may recommend to Court Conditional Admission on terms set forth in written agreement. (SCR 2.042). Character and fitness determination valid for three years. Recertification after three years (from date of certification to date of examination) requires submission of form and $75 fee. (SCR 2.025).

Registration as Law Student.—No requirement. Law student who has completed second year of law school may register for character and fitness determination. Fee is $275 if filed no later than June 1 after completion of second year. (SCR 2.016). Application for character and fitness registration for bar examination; however, registration fee for bar examination when law student has previously filed character and fitness application is $200, but fee for applicant who has not filed application for character and fitness registration as law student is $575. (SCR 2.020).

Educational Requirements.—Applicant for bar examination must have been graduated, with J.D. or equivalent professional degree, from law school approved by A.B.A. or Association of American Law Schools. (SCR 2.070). Prior to or at time of examination, each applicant must certify completion of course in ethics but in exceptional cases Character and Fitness Committee may waive requirement. (SCR 2.090[1]). No person shall sit for bar examination unless person has passed Multi-State Professional Responsibility Exam with scaled score of 75 or higher. (SCR 2.080). Similar criteria not required from applicants for admission on motion after admission and practice in another state. See subhead Admission Without Examination, infra.

Petition for Admission.—See subhead Eligibility, supra.

Examination.—Except as hereinafter stated, every applicant for admission must pass Multi-State examination administered by National Conference of Bar Examiners with scaled score of 132 or higher and must pass essay examination given by Board of Bar Examiners on 14 enumerated topics specified by Supreme Court with general average of 75% or higher. (SCR 2.090[4]). Applicant who has taken Multi-State examination in another jurisdiction within three years of application may transfer score of 132 or higher and need only take essay portion of examination. (SCR 2.090[4]). Applicant who fails bar examination may reapply for next scheduled bar examination on provided form accompanied by fee of $50. $150 examination fee is required of applicants who failed bar examination. (SCR 2.022). Essay examination subjects may include administrative law and procedure; conflict of laws; contracts; constitutional law; corporations; criminal law and procedure; civil procedure; domestic relations; real and personal property; federal taxation; torts; Uniform Commercial Code; wills and trusts; evidence. (SCR 2.090[1]). Special accommodations available for disabled applicants. (SCR 2.091). Certification of passing grade to Supreme Court, approval of recommendation for admission by Supreme Court or any Justice hereof during vacation, payment of bar association dues, $25 Certificate of Admission fee and administration of oath precede issuance of certificate. (SCR 2.095, 2.100). Within 12 months after admission, each person admitted to Bar must complete 15 hour "New Lawyer Skills Program", (SCR 3.652[5]) unless person admitted for five years to bar of another state or person has attended mandatory new lawyer training program of at least 12.5 credits, including two ethics credits, offered by bar association of another state and approved by Director. (SCR 3.652[7]).

Clerkship in lawyer's office before admission is not required.

Admission Without Examination.—Any person who has been admitted to highest court of District of Columbia or some other state and who has been engaged in active practice of law for five of seven years preceding application may be admitted to bar of Kentucky without examination provided that applicant meets all requirements for admission to bar as provided for in rules, including proof that district or state in which applicant has performed major portion of professional activities has comparable provisions for admission without examination. Active engagement in teaching of law considered active engagement in practice of law. Application for admission to be filed with clerk of Supreme Court together with fee of $850. (SCR 2.110).

Examination by Committee on Character and Fitness is required pursuant to SCR 2.040.

Limited Certificate of Admission.—Attorney who is not member of bar of Kentucky but is member of bar in another state or District of Columbia and who performs legal services in state solely for employer, its parents, subsidiaries, or affiliates is required to file sworn statement with Clerk of Supreme Court providing scholastic and professional information. Application fee of $500 and current dues to Kentucky Bar Association and statement of employer must accompany application. Upon approval, Court issues certificate of limited admission to practice law in state subject to duties and obligations of licensed members of bar and bar association but subject to restrictions that such persons may practice solely for employer and affiliates and may not appear as attorney of record in any court of state without regularly licensed co-counsel. (SCR 2.111).

Admission Pro Hac Vice.—Person licensed to practice in another state but not Kentucky shall be permitted to practice case in state only if he subjects himself to jurisdiction and rules of court governing professional conduct and engages licensed Kentucky attorney as co-counsel. Co-counsel's presence shall be necessary at all trials and at other times when required by court. (SCR 3.030[2]).

Attorneys associated with organized public defender programs or organized legal services programs sponsored, approved or recognized by Kentucky Bar Association may upon motion for restricted admission and submission of $25 fee, be allowed to practice with program for 18 months, or duration of employment, whichever shorter, if graduate of accredited law school, admitted to practice in highest court of another state, and able to evidence necessary moral character and fitness. (SCR 2.112).

Regulation and Licenses.—In addition to prescribing rules for admission, Supreme Court has power to promulgate rules governing its appellate jurisdiction, rules for appointment of commissioners and other court personnel, rules of practice and procedure for all judicial courts in state, and rules governing discipline of members of bar. (Const. §116). Supreme Court has power to provide for organization, government and membership of state bar and to adopt rules and regulations to govern conduct and activity of state bar and its members. Pursuant to this authority, Court may authorize Kentucky Bar Association to conduct hearings, administer necessary oaths, take testimony under oath, compel attendance of witnesses, and compel production of records and other evidence incident to disciplining of members of bar. (KRS 21A.150, 21A.160). Rules adopted by Court pursuant to this authority are found in Rules of Supreme Court. (SCR 3.010-3.830).

Disabilities.—Certain public officers are prohibited from engaging in private practice of law while in office, to wit: Governor and Lieutenant Governor (KRS 11.120); attorney general (KRS 15.015); all judges of Supreme Court, Court of Appeals, Circuit Courts, and District Courts (Const. §123). Certain clerks and other local officers are prohibited from maintaining law partnerships with attorneys or sharing office space with attorneys. (KRS 61.098).

No statute prohibits attorney from becoming surety for client, other than restrictions contained in Code of Professional Responsibility, principles of which have been recognized and accepted as sound statement of standard of professional conduct required of all members of bar. (SCR 3.130).

Liabilities.—Attorney employed to attend to professional business who neglects to attend to business after being paid for services, or who attends to business negligently is liable to client for damages and costs sustained by reason thereof, and if fee was paid, is liable for refund of fee. (KRS 411.165). Client security fund established and administered by Bar Association to provide partial indemnification for victims of fraudulent or dishonest acts by members of bar. (SCR 3.820). Binding arbitration provided for claims of legal negligence involving claims of $10,000 or less. (SCR 3.800). Also see category Civil Actions and Procedure, topic Costs.

Compensation.—As to fees taxed as costs, see category Civil Actions and Procedure, topic Costs.

See note at head of Digest as to 1998 legislation covered.

See Topical Index in front part of this volume.

KY – 44

ATTORNEYS AND COUNSELORS . . . *continued*

Contracts between attorney and client for part of recovery are champertous and void (KRS 372.060), but contracts for fee measured by amount or value recovered are recognized as valid (112 Ky. 712, 66 S.W. 751).

Fee agreements between attorney and client are generally not regulated, except as set forth in Kentucky Rules of Professional Conduct, see subhead Disbarment or Suspension, infra, and except in Workmen's Compensation cases. (KRS 342.320). No fee allowed against insolvent estate. (KRS 453.210). Procedures for arbitration of fee disputes between attorney and client and between attorneys are found in SCR 3.810. See category Dispute Resolution, topic Arbitration and Award.

Court in which case is pending will on timely application protect attorney from being discharged without payment of his proper fee, before allowing substitution of other counsel. (186 Ky. 713, 218 S.W. 258).

Lien.—Attorneys have lien on all claims, except those of state, put into their hands for suit or collection, or upon which suit has been instituted for amount of any fee which may have been agreed upon by parties or in absence of such agreement, for reasonable fee. If action is prosecuted to recovery, attorney shall have lien upon judgment recovered, legal costs excepted, for such fee. If records show name of attorney, defendant in action shall have notice of lien, but if parties before judgment in good faith compromised or settled their differences without payment of money or other thing of value, attorney shall have no claim against defendant for any part of fee. (KRS 376.460).

Attorney Ethics.—Kentucky Rules of Professional Conduct (SCR 3.130) are based on Model Rules of Professional Conduct adopted by House of Delegates of American Bar Association. Significant variations from Model Rules include: Rule 1.6 adopted with non-uniform subparagraph (b)(3) authorizing disclosure of confidential information "to comply with other law or a court order"; Rule 3.3 adopted without subparagraph (a)(3); Rules 7.1 through 7.5 adopted with variations relating to lawyer advertising which is regulated and monitored by Attorneys Advertising Commission; Rule 8.3 (reporting professional misconduct) not adopted. Minor changes made to many other Model Rules to conform to local law and to eliminate potential ambiguity.

Disbarment or Suspension.—Disciplinary cases instituted by filing complaint with Director of Kentucky Bar Association or by independent investigation by inquiry tribunal established by SCR 3.140. (SCR 3.160). Temporary suspension or probation authorized on petition of Inquiry Tribunal supported by affidavit indicating misappropriation of funds, conviction of Class A misdemeanor or mental disability or addiction affecting physical or mental fitness. (SCR 3.165). Automatic suspension upon conviction of felony. (SCR 3.166). Proof in disciplinary matters is taken before trial committee which files report with Board of Governors which makes findings of unprofessional conduct or not. (SCR 3.170-3.380). Findings and recommendations of Board of Governors forwarded to Supreme Court, where Attorney General acts as counsel for Bar Association. (SCR 3.390-3.450). Attorney licensed in Kentucky may be disciplined as result of professional disciplinary action taken in another jurisdiction. (SCR 3.435). When attorney has been suspended, disbarred or has abandoned his practice without notifying his clients, special commissioner may be appointed by Supreme Court to protect clients' interests. (SCR 3.395). Commissioner's power includes taking possession of attorney's files and records for purposes of inventory, evaluation, delivery to clients or new attorneys representing clients. (SCR 3.395[2]).

Unauthorized Practice.—Except in case of nonresident attorney admitted pro hac vice, it is misdemeanor to practice law, as defined in SCR 3.030(2), without license. (KRS 524.130). Supreme Court may prevent unauthorized practice by contempt proceedings, after written notice from Director of Kentucky Bar Association. (SCR 3.460). Appearance in Small Claims Division of District Court by officer or manager of corporation or partnership which is party to case is not unauthorized practice. (SCR 3.020). See category Courts and Legislature, topic Courts, subhead Small Claims Courts. Representation before any administrative tribunal or court by paralegal assistant under direction and supervision of lawyer pursuant to court rule or decision is not unauthorized practice of law. (SCR 3.700[3]).

Trust companies regularly engaged in drafting wills, deeds, trust instruments, and other legal documents, as agents or fiduciaries for compensation, and giving legal advice to makers of such documents, are engaged in unlawful practice of law. (393 S.W.2d 778). Lay corporate employees may not prepare mortgage for employer even though no compensation paid. (476 S.W.2d 177).

Mandatory Continuing Legal Education.—Every attorney in practice more than one year other than incumbent judges shall attend annual minimum of 12.5 hours in approved continuing legal education courses. (SCR 3.661; 3.666). At least two of 12.5 hours must specifically address topics of legal ethics, professional responsibility or professionalism. (SCR 3.661). Members may carry forward any excess attendance over 12.5 hours from two preceding years to satisfy minimum requirement for any educational year. (SCR 3.661[4]; SCR 3.666). Failure to meet CLE requirements is grounds for suspension from practice of law in Kentucky. (SCR 3.668[2]). Suspension procedures upon hearing before Supreme Court are set forth in SCR 3.669.

Specialty Certification Requirements.—Lawyer may communicate fact of practice in fields of law or fact of concentration of practice but lawyer may not use any form of "certified specialist", "expert", or "authority" in advertisement or statement regarding his or her practice unless: if admitted to patent practice with U.S. Patent and Trademark Office, may use "patent attorney"; if certified by appropriate government agency for admiralty practice, may use "admiralty" or "proctor on admiralty"; or if achieved certification from organization qualifying under 496 U.S. 91, may communicate fact so long as lawyer retains certification and good standing with organization. (SCR 3.130[7.40]).

Professional Corporations.—See category Business Organizations, topic Corporations, subhead Professional Corporations.

Legal Interns.—Legal internship program authorizes students who have successfully completed ⅔ of academic hour requirements for first degree in law in, and any graduate of, approved law school to provide legal services to, and may appear in certain legal proceedings on behalf of, persons financially unable to employ counsel and Commonwealth. Student prohibited from engaging as intern unless participating in legal aid program or clinical program of approved law school and until written approval for his participation has been filed with clerk of Supreme Court, clerk of Circuit Court in county where law school is located, and with clerk of each court for which student or graduate is to appear. (SCR 2.540).

MINERAL, WATER AND FISHING RIGHTS

MINES AND MINERALS:

Supervision.—

Surface coal mining operations, including surface impacts of underground coal mines, oil shale mining, and clay mining are regulated by Natural Resources and Environmental Protection Cabinet (Capital Plaza Tower, Frankfort, Kentucky 40601). (KRS 350.050; 350.240; 350.600).

Mine safety and blasting are regulated by Department of Mines and Minerals in Public Protection & Regulation Cabinet (P.O. Box 14080, Lexington, Kentucky 40512). (KRS 351.020[2]).

Oil, gas and salt water wells regulated by Department of Mines and Minerals. (KRS 353.200).

Operation of Mines.—

Underground and Surface Mines.—Construction and operation of underground and surface coal and clay mines, education, certification and annual recertification of miners, underground miners, mine foremen, assistant mine foremen, mine inspectors, electrical inspectors, mine safety inspectors, shotfirers and coal mine electricians, and specifications for equipment used in such mines are specified in Chs. 351 and 352 of KRS. No person may be assigned work duties for purpose of mining coal unless he holds either certificate of competency and qualification issued by Board of Miner Training, Education and Certification or miner trainee permit issued by Commissioner of Department of Mines and Minerals. (KRS. 351.102).

Surface mining statute requires persons wishing to engage in surface coal mining operations to obtain permit from Cabinet (KRS 350.060) and to reclaim land (KRS 350.100; 350.405-350.470). See category Environment, topic Environmental Regulation.

Safeguarding of Employees.—Statutes provide for comprehensive safety regulations and various reports, which must be made to Department of Mines and Minerals. Surface and underground mine safety analysts must hold current mine foreman's certificates, pass examination and have five years' applicable mine experience. Mine safety analysts authorized to enter mine site, confer with foreman as to mine conditions and employee work practices, and advise mine management, employee representatives, and Commissioner of Department of Mines and Minerals concerning hazardous conditions, and make recommendations and to assist in improving safety of mines and work habits. (KRS 351.242). Mine analyst program to be coordinated with appropriate federal officials to avoid duplication of efforts. (KRS 351.242). Miners must be paid their wages in lawful money twice each month. (KRS 352.540).

Inspection of Mines.—Each mine must be inspected at least once every six months and more often if funds permit and whenever any danger to workmen may exist. (KRS 351.140). Duties of mine inspectors set out in KRS 351.140.

Oil, gas and salt water wells are regulated under KRS c. 353. Well operators must submit operations and reclamation plans and must have surface owner's consent prior to drilling. (KRS 353.5901). As to regulation of pipelines, see category Business Regulation and Commerce, topic Carriers.

Mineral Leases.—Lease of oil, gas, coal or mineral rights for longer than five years must be recorded. (KRS 382.080; see category Property, topic Landlord and Tenant).

Oil and Gas Leases.—Special provisions authorize the consolidation of oil and gas leases to be executed by guardians of minors (KRS 353.240-353.260), by guardians or conservators of wards (KRS 387.700[4]), and in cases where contingent future interests are involved, by trustees under court appointment, as provided in KRS 353.210-353.230, 353.300-353.380.

Taxes.—State tax equal to 4½% of market value of petroleum produced annually is imposed. (KRS 137.120). Tax is collected through transporter of petroleum. (KRS 137.140).

Severance tax is levied on coal at rate of 4½% of gross value of all coal severed and/or processed but not less than 50¢ per ton. (KRS 143.020). Certificate of registration must be obtained before severing coal in state (KRS 143.030[1]) and cash bond or corporate surety bond may be required (KRS 143.050). Late payments of tax draw interest at rate revised annually to equal bankers' prime interest rate. (KRS 143.080; 131.010[6]; 131.183). Corporate officers personally liable for tax. (KRS 143.085). Nonpayment of tax, or falsified or altered certificate declared to be misdemeanor. (KRS 143.990).

MORTGAGES

CHATTEL MORTGAGES:

Governed by Secured Transaction Article of Uniform Commercial Code. (KRS 355.9-101 to 355.9-507). As to special provisions governing retail credit sales contracts, see category Business Regulation and Commerce, topic Sales.

Special provisions are made with respect to chattel mortgages by Kentucky public utility corporations (KRS 382.340), and liens on motor vehicles (see category Transportation, topic Motor Vehicles, subhead Liens).

Forms.—See category Business Regulation and Commerce, topic Commercial Code.

COLLATERAL SECURITY:

See category Debtor and Creditor, topic Pledges.

See note at head of Digest as to 1998 legislation covered.

See Topical Index in front part of this volume.

MORTGAGES OF PERSONAL PROPERTY:

See category Business Regulation and Commerce, topic Commercial Code.

MORTGAGES OF REAL PROPERTY:

Lien theory obtains. Title remains in mortgagor. (250 Ky. 617, 63 S.W.2d 796).

Execution.—A mortgage is an ordinary deed, containing a clause of defeasance, and it should be executed and acknowledged as a deed.

As to matters which must be set forth in order to entitle mortgage to be recorded, see infra, subhead Recording.

Where mortgagor is married, his or her spouse must join in mortgage in order to bar dower or curtesy rights and should waive his or her right of homestead therein.

Recording is not essential to validity of mortgage as between parties, but in order to be effective as against bona fide purchaser for value from, or creditors of, mortgagor, it must be acknowledged or proved and recorded or lodged for record in office of county clerk of county where land is situated. (KRS 382.270). See also category Documents and Records, topic Records.

There are special provisions for recording mortgages executed by domestic public service corporations. (KRS 382.340).

Recording of a mortgage or deed of trust is forbidden unless (1) it sets forth name, county and state of residence and postoffice address, including county, of person owning debt secured thereby and liable for taxes thereon (KRS 382.430); (2) states date and maturity of obligations theretofore or forthwith issued and secured thereby (KRS 382.330); and (3) sets forth name and address of person who prepared instrument with signature or facsimile (KRS 382.335). By KRS 382.110 any "deed of conveyance of any interest in real property equal to or greater than a life estate is not entitled to be recorded unless the deed plainly specifies and refers to the next immediate source from which the grantor derived title to the property or the interest conveyed therein." Inasmuch as there may be difference of opinion (not resolved by court decision) as to whether or not mortgage or deed of trust falls within this section better practice is to include in instrument reference to immediate source of mortgagor's or grantor's title. See also category Documents and Records, topic Records, subhead Requisites for Recording.

Master forms may be recorded containing standard covenants, conditions, obligations, powers, etc., which may be incorporated by book, page and date reference in later mortgages recorded in same county. Master form must be entitled "Master form recorded by [name]" but need not be acknowledged before admitted to record. (KRS 382.295).

Recording Tax and Fees.—No mortgage can safely be treated as legally recorded until recording tax of $3 required by KRS 142.010 is paid. In addition, clerk's fee for recording mortgage is minimum of $9 ($12 including tax) for first three pages and $2 for each page over three. (KRS 64.012). Clerk's fees for recording deeds of assignment and deeds of release are $9 plus $3 for marginal notation on each assigned or released mortgage. (KRS 64.012). Clerk may also require prepayment of postage for returning recorded mortgage. These fees include County Clerk charge of up to $1 for each mortgage recorded, regardless of whether mortgage is returned by mail. Postage, if any, charged by clerks should be confirmed prior to recordation. (See also categories Documents and Records, topic Records; and Taxation, topic Real Estate Conveyance Tax.)

As to future issues of bonds under "open-end" mortgages, the required statement as to date and maturity of additional obligations must be placed of record before such additional obligations are issued. (KRS 382.380).

Trust deeds are sometimes used instead of direct mortgage from debtor to creditor. Substantially same principles apply as in mortgages.

Parol Evidence as to Character of Instrument.—An instrument, in form an absolute conveyance, if intended merely as security for debt, will be treated as a mortgage, and intention may be shown by parol without allegation of fraud or mistake. (148 Ky. 531, 146 S.W. 1094).

Future advances or indebtedness may be secured by mortgage. (279 Ky. 153, 130 S.W.2d 48). Any lender's future advances, including under line of credit or revolving credit plan, may be covered by mortgage if mortgage by its terms expressly so provides and states maximum additional indebtedness which may be secured. (KRS 382.520; 382.385). See subhead Priorities, infra.

Priorities.—Bona fide deeds of trust or mortgages take effect (in absence of notice, actual or implied) in order in which acknowledged or proved and recorded. (KRS 382.280). Lien for delinquent taxes can obtain priority over prior recorded mortgage. (KRS 134.420). Priority of lien under mortgage providing for future advances determined by whether advances were obligatory or discretionary. (560 S.W.2d 239).

Assignment.—Provision is made for noting of record the assignment of obligations secured by mortgage or deed of trust, except railroad mortgages securing bonds payable to bearer. But assignment must give the name, residence, and postoffice address of the assignee. (KRS 382.290; 382.430).

Release of lien can be made on the record only by the person appearing of record to be the holder of the obligation secured by the lien so released. All other releases declared void. (KRS 382.290).

Satisfaction.—See subhead Discharge of Lien, infra.

Discharge of Lien.—Liens of mortgages or trust deeds may be discharged by entry on margin of record, by deed of release, or by marginal entry record. (KRS 382.360). Action lies in district or circuit court against lienholder who does not release lien of record within 30 days from date of satisfaction. Lienholder who fails to release may be liable to owner for up to $500 plus actual expenses, including attorney fees, incurred by owner in securing lien release. Former lienholder shall send copy of lien release by mail to last known address of property owner within seven days of release. (KRS 382.365). Violation shall result in payment of $50 to fee owner plus actual expenses.

Failure to list for taxation any note or bond secured by mortgage, which is subject to taxation, may be pleaded in defense of any action thereon, but such defense is taken away upon payment of the required tax with penalties and interest. (KRS 132.300).

Foreclosure.—See subhead Enforcement, infra.

Enforcement.—Liens of mortgages and trust deeds upon realty can be enforced only by decree in equity. (KRS 381.190). Common law or strict foreclosure forbidden, but mortgagee after default may take possession of abandoned mortgaged property for purpose of preserving and maintaining same, harvesting crops or letting same, all for account of mortgagor. (KRS 426.525).

Property must be appraised before judicial sale thereof, and if it does not bring two-thirds of such appraised valuation, the owner may redeem within one year from sale by paying the purchaser the purchase money and 10% per annum interest thereon. If property sells for less than two-thirds appraised value, purchaser entitled to immediate writ of possession and deed continuing lien in favor of defendant reflecting defendant's right to redeem within year. Redemption right may itself be sold either at decretal sale or under execution issued for unpaid balance of judgment. (KRS 426.520-426.540).

Sales.—No sale of real estate by trustee under deed of trust or pledge to secure payment of debts shall be valid, nor pass title of property specified in such deed or pledge, unless sale thereof be made in pursuance of judgment of court of equity, or shall be made by assignee under voluntary deed of assignment, or grantor shall join in conveyance to purchaser. (KRS 381.190). Assignee for benefit of creditors, generally, has power to convey and pass all right and title to same which assignor had at date of deed of assignment. Sale must be made as court may direct. (KRS 379.090).

Deficiency Judgment.—In action to enforce mortgage, judgment may be rendered for sale of property and against defendant personally if before court on personal service or entry of appearance. (KRS 426.005).

Following is acceptable form of mortgage of land:

Form

This mortgage between . . . . . ., of the first part, and . . . . . ., of the second part whose address is . . . . . (post office address for mortgagee necessary, including county of residence): Witnesseth that, in order to secure the payment of the debt hereinafter mentioned said first party both hereby sell and convey unto said second party all his interest in a certain lot of land in . . . . . . county, Kentucky, described as follows, to wit: (Describe land) being the same (or, a part of the same) land conveyed by . . . . . . to . . . . . ., by deed dated . . . . . ., and recorded in deed book . . . . . ., page . . . . . ., in the office of the clerk of the . . . . . . county court: (give next immediate source of title, whether by deed, will or inheritance, showing how title was derived by grantor). To have and to hold said land, with its appurtenances, unto said second party, his heirs and assigns forever, with covenant of general warranty and against all encumbrances; but this conveyance is upon the following conditions, to wit: The said first party has this day executed his . . . . . promissory note of even date herewith to said second party, for the sum of . . . . . . dollars, with a final maturity date of . . . . with interest payable semi-annually at . . . .%. Said second party resides in . . . . county in the state of . . . . and his post office address is . . . . in such state. (Any or all the following additional agreements may be inserted here. The said parties further agree: (1) that if said first party shall for ten days fail to make any payment of interest at maturity thereof, or shall fail to pay any taxes or assessments on said land when due, or shall fail to keep said property insured as herein provided, said second party may, at his option, treat the whole debt secured by this mortgage as due and payable, and proceed to enforce the lien of this mortgage by suit; (2) said first party shall keep the improvements on said land insured for the benefit of said second party, in some solvent company for not less than $. . . . . ., and in case of failure so to do, said second party may so insure said improvements, and all premiums paid for such insurance shall become a part of the mortgage debt hereby secured, with interest from date of payment; (3) said first party shall punctually pay all taxes and assessments assessed against said property, and, in default of such payment, said second party may pay same, and all such payments shall become a part of the mortgage debt hereby secured, with interest from the date of such payments). Now, if said first party shall well and truly pay and discharge said indebtedness and interest at maturity, and shall well and truly keep and perform all the agreements herein set out, then this conveyance shall be void, otherwise, to remain in full force and virtue; In testimony whereof, witness the signature of said first party this . . . . . . day of . . . . . ., A. D., 19 . . . . .
(signature)
(acknowledgment)

This mortgage has been prepared by . . . . whose address is . . . .
. . . .
Signature of scrivner

PROPERTY

ABSENTEES:

Care of Property.—Provision is made for appointment of curator to protect and preserve estate of a person absent from his last known place of residence for one year and not known to have been living during that time. Such appointment is made by District Court having jurisdiction to appoint personal representative for such absentee, if deceased. (KRS 395.410[2]). Application must be made by some relative, creditor or debtor of absentee, or by some person in possession of or interested in his property or rights. (KRS 395.430). Definite procedure is prescribed after required notice by newspaper publication and by letter to absentee at last known address. Curator must collect and safely keep assets of absentee, and he may pay debts, invest funds and, under order of court, sell perishable or other goods. (KRS 395.420[2]). He must give bond (KRS 395.410[3]) and render accounts to court (KRS 395.610). Appeal from order appointing curator is allowed as in case of appointment of administrators, but appeal does not suspend powers of curator. (KRS 395.440).

Process Agent.—For service of process on foreign and domestic corporations and other entities, see category Civil Actions and Procedure, topic Process.

Person Serving in or with U. S. Armed Forces or as Merchant Seaman.—Where such a person has provided no adequate power of attorney for another to act for him,

---

See note at head of Digest as to 1998 legislation covered.

See Topical Index in front part of this volume.

ABSENTEES . . . *continued*
and has been reported or listed as missing, interned or beleaguered, besieged or captured by an enemy, a conservator of his estate may be appointed by District Court of county of his legal domicile or where such property is situated. (KRS 384.050, 384.070). As to adequacy and legal effect in such cases of existing power of attorney, see KRS 384.010-384.040. Conservator must give bond and has same powers as guardian of infant or conservator of mentally disabled person. (KRS 384.060).

Escheat.—Subject to specific exceptions, unclaimed real estate or tangible property of intestate decedent escheats to state after seven years. (KRS 393.020). Unclaimed intangible property held by life insurance company (KRS 393.062) or held by or issued by business association after seven years (KRS 393.064, 393.090). Unclaimed money paid into court (KRS 393.100) and funds held by Federal government (KRS 393.068), escheat after five years; unclaimed parimutuel tickets escheat after two years. (KRS 393.095). Presumption of death after seven years. (KRS 393.050, 422.130). Holder of abandoned property required to report to Department of the Treasury annually by Nov. 1 for 12 month period ending July 1 of that year. (KRS 393.110). Escheated property may be reclaimed from state. (KRS 393.140).

See categories Business Regulation and Commerce, topic Banks and Banking, subhead Unclaimed Deposits; Citizenship, topic Aliens, subhead Escheat; Estates and Trusts, topic Descent and Distribution, subhead Escheat, also topic Wills, subhead Unclaimed Legacies.

ADVERSE POSSESSION:

Adverse possession of lands exists where the person in actual possession claims the property for himself against the world.

Character and Duration of Possession.—Adverse possession, if actual, open, notorious, peaceable, and continuous for the period required under the Statutes of Limitation to defeat an action for its recovery (see category Civil Actions and Procedure, topic Limitation of Actions) ripens into a title in fee simple, but all these elements must concur. (412 S.W.2d 869; 158 Ky. 316, 164 S.W. 964).

When Notice Necessary.—Possession of street, alley or public easement in city or town or of public road in county does not become adverse until written notice of adverse claim is given. (KRS 413.050).

Easements.—Same principles apply as in case of the property itself in which easement is claimed.

Disabilities.—Adverse possession by joint tenant never presumed but may be established by proof of unequivocable nature. Other disabilities same as those which suspend running of limitations. See category Civil Actions and Procedure, topic Limitation of Actions.

CONVEYANCES:

See topic Deeds.

CURTESY:

As to marriages contracted before Mar. 15, 1894, the right of curtesy in lands acquired prior to that date (30 K.L.R. 1127, 100 S.W. 236; 299 Ky. 538, 186 S.W.2d 16) exists substantially as at common law (104 Ky. 48, 46 S.W. 524; 104 Ky. 77, 47 S.W. 195; 165 Ky. 306, 176 S.W. 1173). As to marriages contracted and as to lands acquired, since Mar. 15, 1894, husband has same right in deceased wife's real estate as widow has in estate of husband. (299 Ky. 538, 186 S.W.2d 16). See topic Dower.

Release and Bar.—Same as Dower (q.v.).

Election between curtesy and testamentary provisions, see category Estates and Trusts, topic Wills.

Distributive share of husband in estate of wife, real or personal, see category Estates and Trusts, topic Descent and Distribution.

DEEDS:

Any interest in lands (but not a mere expectancy, 198 Ky. 256, 248 S.W. 530) not in the adverse possession of another may be conveyed by deed, and no estate of inheritance or freehold or for a term of more than one year may be conveyed except by deed or will. (KRS 382.010).

See topic Real Property for types of estates.

Execution.—Deed must be in writing and signed by grantor (KRS 371.010) and contain mailing addresses of grantor and grantee, statement of full consideration and sworn notarized certificate signed by grantor and grantee (or respective agents thereof) that consideration reflected in deed is full consideration paid (KRS 382.135). In case of transfer by gift, or with nominal or no consideration, sworn notarized certificate shall recite that transfer is by gift and set forth estimated cash value of property. Deed filing requirements shall not apply to deeds (1) which convey utility easements only; (2) transfer property through court action pursuant to divorce proceedings; (3) convey right-of-ways that involve governmental agencies; (4) convey cemetery lots; and (5) correct errors in previous deeds conveying same property from same grantor to same grantee. In case of transfer by will or intestate succession, personal representative shall file affidavit with county clerk of each county in which any property is located containing names and addresses of persons receiving property interests and full or fair estimated market value of interests received. (KRS 382.135). Acknowledgment is not essential to validity as between parties, but deed must be acknowledged or proved in order to be recorded. (See infra, subhead Recording.) In order to bar dower or curtesy, spouse of grantor must execute and acknowledge deed. For circumstances in which spouse must join, see topics Dower, Curtesy; category Family, topic Husband and Wife.

Seal is not necessary in case of a deed by an individual (KRS 371.020), or of a corporation (KRS 271B.3-020).

Conveyance by Married Woman.—See category Family, topic Husband and Wife.

Conveyance by Attorney.—See topic Powers of Attorney.

Short Covenants.—A covenant by a grantor in a deed that he will "warrant the property hereby conveyed" or words of like import, or the words "with warranty" or "with general warranty" in any deed have the same effect as if the grantor had covenanted that he, his heirs and personal representatives would forever warrant and defend property unto grantee, his heirs, personal representatives and assigns against claims and demands of all persons whatever. Covenant by grantor that he will specially warrant property conveyed, or words of like import, or words "with special warranty" in any deed have same effect as if grantor had covenanted that he, his heirs and personal representatives, would forever warrant and defend property unto grantee, his personal representatives and assigns against claims and demands of grantor, and all persons claiming or to claim by, through or under him. (KRS 382.030; 382.040).

Quitclaim Deed.—A conveyance which contains no covenant of warranty, and particularly a conveyance made "without warranty," is a mere quitclaim deed, conveying only such title as the grantor actually has. (See 221 Ky. 593, 597, 299 S.W. 201, reviewing authorities.)

Recording is not essential to the validity of a deed as between the parties; but in order to be effective against bona fide purchasers for value without notice or creditors of the vendor the deed must be acknowledged or proved and recorded or lodged for record in the office of the clerk of the court of the county in which the land, or the greater part thereof, is situated. (KRS 382.270; 382.110). Statute applies in favor of all subsequent creditors and such antecedent creditors as have secured some equity in the property prior to recording of deed. (251 Ky. 377, 65 S.W.2d 83). As to requisites for recording, see category Documents and Records, topic Records.

Deed conveying life estate or greater interest must refer to next immediate source of title, with office, book and page of recordation, and date thereof. (See category Documents and Records, topics Records, Acknowledgments.)

As to recording release of lien see KRS 382.360.

Recording Tax and Fees.—No deed is legally lodged for record until recording tax of $3 (KRS 142.010) is paid thereon (KRS 382.260).

In addition, tax of 50¢ for each $500 of value is imposed for privilege of transferring title to real property. Computation is made on actual purchase price or in case of gift, on property's fair market value. (KRS 142.050). Tax not imposed on transfers (1) to or from U.S. or political subdivision if transfer is by gift or for nominal consideration; (2) to provide or release security of debt; (3) to correct previously recorded deed; (4) between husband and wife, or between former spouse as part of divorce proceeding; (5) on sale for delinquent taxes; (6) to partition property; (7) pursuant to merger or consolidation between and among corporations, partnerships, including registered limited liability partnerships, limited partnerships; or limited liability companies; (8) conversion of general partnership or registered limited liability partnership or limited partnership into limited liability company; (9) between subsidiary and parent corporation for no consideration, nominal consideration, or in sole consideration of cancellation of surrender of either corporation's stock; (10) under foreclosure proceeding; (11) between person and corporation, general partnership, limited partnership, registered limited liability partnership, or limited liability company in amount equal to portion of value of real property transferred that represents proportionate interest of transferor in entity to which property transferred, if transfer for nominal consideration; (12) between parent and child or grandparent and grandchild with nominal consideration; (13) by corporation, general partnership, limited partnership, registered limited liability partnership or limited liability company to person as owner or shareholder, upon dissolution of entity, in amount equal to portion of value of real property transferred that represents proportionate interest of person to whom property transferred, if transfer for nominal consideration; (14) between trustee and successor trustee; (15) between limited liability company and any of its members; (16) to trustee (as defined in KRS 386.800) to be held in trust or from trustee to beneficiary of trust if grantor is sole beneficiary of trust, grantor is beneficiary of trust and direct transfer from grantor of trust to all other individual beneficiaries of trust would have qualified for exemption pursuant to one of exemptions previously enumerated herein, or direct transfer from grantor of trust to all other individual beneficiaries of trust would have qualified for exemption pursuant to one of exemptions previously enumerated herein. (KRS 142.050[7-9]). Deed must recite full consideration or fair market value or facts which show why transfer tax not applicable. (KRS 382.135).

Clerk's fee for recording deed is minimum of $8 ($11 including tax) plus $2 per page for each page over three. (KRS 64.012). Clerk may also require prepayment of postage for returning recorded deed. (KRS 382.240). Jefferson County Clerk charges $1 for each deed recorded, regardless of whether deed is returned by mail. Postage, if any, charged by other clerks should be confirmed prior to recordation. See also category Documents and Records, topic Records.

Operation and Effect.—See subhead Recording.

Full consideration must be stated on deeds to Commonwealth. (KRS 45.450).

Adjustment of Taxes.—Holder of legal title, holder of equitable title, and bailee or claimant in possession of property on assessment date (Jan. 1) shall each be liable for taxes assessed thereon; as between themselves, holder of equitable title has primary obligation to list property and pay taxes thereon whether or not property is in his possession at time of payment.

The following is a sufficient form of deed; no special requirements apply for corporations or married persons:

Form

This Deed made this . . . . day of . . . . . ., 19 . . . . between A. B. of (address), of the first part and C. D. of (address), of the second part. Witnesseth, That for and in full consideration of (State consideration showing what, if any, part thereof is unpaid, and stating that "to secure the payment of which a lien is hereby retained" if vendor's lien intended) the receipt whereof is hereby acknowledged, said first party does hereby sell and convey unto said second party a certain lot or parcel of land located in . . . . County, Kentucky, described as follows, to wit: (Describe land) being the same (or a part of the same) property conveyed by . . . . . . to . . . . . . by deed dated . . . . . . and recorded in deed book . . . . . . page . . . . . . in the office of the clerk of . . . . . . County, Kentucky. (Give next immediate source of title, whether by deed, will or inheritance,

See note at head of Digest as to 1998 legislation covered.

See Topical Index in front part of this volume.

KY – 47

DEEDS . . . *continued*

showing how title was derived by grantor). To Have and to Hold, Said land, with its appurtenances, unto said second party, his heirs and assigns forever, with covenant of General Warranty; and said first party further covenants with said second party, his heirs and assigns, that said first party is lawfully seized of said land in fee simple, and has full right and power to convey the same, and that said land is free from all encumbrances: In Witness Whereof, said first party has hereunto set his hand on the day and date first above written (signature of grantor). (Acknowledgment of signature of grantor—see category Documents and Records, topic Acknowledgments).

Certificate of Consideration: Being first duly sworn, the undersigned state that the consideration set forth in the foregoing Deed is true and correct and is the full consideration paid for the above described property. (Signature of each of the grantor and grantee or agent of each). (Acknowledgment of each signature—see category Documents and Records, topic Acknowledgments). This instrument prepared by (signature or facsimile signature and typewritten, printed or stamped name and address of scrivener of deed).

DEEDS OF TRUST:

See category Mortgages, topic Mortgages of Real Property.

DOWER:

If spouse dies intestate, survivor has estate in fee of one-half of surplus real estate of which decedent, or anyone for use of decedent, was seized of estate in fee simple at death, and an estate for life in one-third of real estate of which decedent, or anyone for use of decedent, was seized of estate in fee simple during coverture but not at death, unless right to such interest has been barred, forfeited, or relinquished. Survivor also has estate in one-half of surplus personalty. (KRS 392.020). Lien theory of dower rejected. (480 S.W.2d 173). As to dower right on renunciation of will, see category Estates and Trusts, topic Wills, subhead Election.

Surviving husband has same rights in land of deceased wife if marriage was contracted or if land was acquired after Mar. 15, 1894. (KRS 392.010, 392.020). See topic Curtesy.

Release.—Surviving spouse is not endowed of lands sold or mortgaged before marriage (though not conveyed) or sold after marriage by deed in which he or she joined, or to satisfy lien for purchase money, or any lien created before marriage, but his or her right to dower or curtesy attaches to surplus of land or of proceeds if such proceeds have not been disposed of by deceased spouse in his or her lifetime. (KRS 392.040).

Bar.—An absolute divorce bars dower. (KRS 392.090). It is not barred by sale of husband's land under execution.

Sale Free of Dower.—By proceedings in equity, a married person may be empowered to sell or mortgage his or her land free of any dower or curtesy right of spouse who is confirmed mentally disabled person (KRS 392.140) or wife may be empowered to sell or mortgage her land free from any dower or curtesy right of husband who has been adjudged mentally disabled. (KRS 404.050. Compare prior law [K. S. 2131] in light of cases reported in 294 Ky. 122, 137, 171 S.W.2d 41, 49).

Election between dower and testamentary provision, see category Estates and Trusts, topic Wills.

ESCHEAT:

See topic Absentees, subhead Escheat; categories Business Regulation and Commerce, topic Banks and Banking, subhead Unclaimed Deposits; Citizenship, topic Aliens; Estates and Trusts, topics Descent and Distribution, subhead Escheat, Wills, subhead Unclaimed Legacies.

LANDLORD AND TENANT:

Kinds of Tenancy.—Statutes deal separately with tenancies at will, by sufferance, or for a term. (KRS c. 383).

Uniform Residential Landlord and Tenant Act not adopted statewide; KRS 383.500 authorizes cities, counties and urban-county governments to enact provisions of Uniform Residential Landlord and Tenant Act (as codified in KRS 383.505-383.715) in its entirety and without amendment.

Leases.—A lease of land for more than one year is within the Statute of Frauds (KRS 371.010) and may not be made except by deed (KRS 382.010). Delivery and acceptance by lessee necessary for validity. (477 S.W.2d 814).

However, recovery of reasonable rental allowed in absence of written contract. (KRS 383.090).

Security Deposits.—Except in cities, counties and urban-county governments which are under Uniform Residential Landlord and Tenant Act, no statutory provisions regulate security deposits.

Recording.—Lease of real property for a longer period than five years must be acknowledged or proved and recorded or lodged for record in office of county clerk in which land, or greater part thereof, is situated, in order to be effective against bona fide purchaser for value without notice from, or creditors of, lessor. (KRS 382.080). Recording fee is $9 ($12 including tax under KRS 142.010) for first three pages, $2 for each page over three and $3 for each marginal notation. (KRS 64.012). Clerk may also require prepayment of postage for returning recorded lease. (KRS 382.240). These fees include County Clerk charge of up to $1 for each lease recorded, regardless of whether lease is returned by mail. Postage, if any, charged by clerks should be confirmed prior to recordation. (KRS 64.012). See topic Deeds; also category Documents and Records, topic Records, subhead Requisites for Recording. However, tenant's possession of leased premises is itself notice to all world, putting purchasers upon inquiry to ascertain nature and extent of tenant's rights even including option to renew lease or to purchase leased property. (200 Ky. 387, 255 S.W. 79; 203 Ky. 90, 261 S.W. 883).

Rents.—Even in absence of written contract, landlord entitled to reasonable satisfaction for use and occupation of his land. (KRS 383.090).

An assignment of a lease or an interest thereunder, by a tenant at will or by sufferance, or a tenant who has a term less than two years, unless consented to in writing by the landlord, operates as a forfeiture to the landlord, entitling him to reenter and take possession. (KRS 383.180).

Liabilities of Tenant.—Unless expressly provided to the contrary by the writing, the tenant's agreement to repair or leave premises in repair does not bind him to erect buildings thereon, destroyed by fire or other casualty without his fault or neglect; nor is the tenant, unless he otherwise contracts, liable for rent, during the remainder of his term, of any leased building so destroyed. (KRS 383.170).

If a tenant for life or years commits voluntary waste, he is subject to action of waste, in which treble damages may be recovered, and he can lose thing wasted. (KRS 381.350).

Rent may be recovered by distress, attachment, or action, and bears interest at 6% per annum from time it is due. (KRS 383.010).

Liens.—Landlord has superior lien on fixtures, household furniture and other personal property of tenant or undertenant from time possession is taken under lease and where real estate is rented for farming or coal mining purposes. Lien extends also to produce thereof. Lien secures four months rent due or to become due, but not rent more than four months overdue; in case of lease for farming or coal mining purposes it secures rent due or to become due for one year but not rent more than eleven months overdue. If any such property is removed from leased premises, openly and without fraudulent intent, and not returned, landlord's lien continues for only 15 days from date of removal. Landlord may enforce lien against such property wherever found. Landlord's lien is subordinate to valid liens on property existing when it was brought on the premises. (KRS 383.070, 383.080).

Termination of Tenancy.—Usual common law principles apply, except where covered by Uniform Residential Landlord and Tenant Act. (KRS 383.695). Removal, transfer or abandonment of rented personal property to defraud landlord is misdemeanor. (KRS 434.225).

Tenant Holding Over.—Tenant for a term of one year or more, who holds over after his term expires, may, within 90 days from expiration of his term, abandon leased premises or be evicted therefrom, but after 90 days lease renews itself by operation of law so as to bind both landlord and tenant for one year from original date of expiration, and so on from year to year until tenant abandons premises or is turned out of possession or makes new contract. (KRS 383.160).

Tenancy for less than one year, under like holding over continued for 30 days, is renewed for 60 days from original expiration, and so on from time to time until the tenant abandons the premises or is turned out of possession or makes a new contract. (KRS 383.160).

Dispossession.—Summary remedies by writs of forcible entry and/or detainer are given for recovering possession of the leased premises. (KRS 383.200-383.285).

Distress.—Summary remedies in nature of attachment for rent are given landlord for recovery of rent due or for securing rent to become due or for agreed share of crops. (KRS 383.010-383.030).

LEASES:

See topic Landlord and Tenant.

PERPETUITIES:

KRS 381.215 provides: "No interest in real or personal property shall be good unless it must vest, if at all, not later than twenty-one years after some life in being at the creation of the interest. It is the purpose of this section to enact the common law rule against perpetuities, except as hereinafter modified by KRS 381.215 to 381.223." Exceptions: Trusts created as part of stock, bonus, pension, disability or death benefit, or profit sharing plan for benefit of employees. (KRS 381.217). Violation of rule is determined by actual rather than possible events. (KRS 381.216).

Estates in fee simple determinable and possibilities of reverter are abolished, with certain limitations and exceptions set out in the statutes. (KRS 381.218-381.222).

See category Estates and Trusts, topic Trusts.

A reasonable restraint upon the alienation of real property may be imposed for a reasonable time. (230 Ky. 141, 18 S.W.2d 957).

Accumulations are permitted, unless in violation of Rule against Perpetuities. (131 Ky 609, 115 S.W. 739).

PERSONAL PROPERTY:

Tenancy by entireties recognized. (See 389 S.W.2d 904.)

POWERS OF ATTORNEY:

Attorneys in Fact.—An agency to contract for sale of land may be created by parol (191 Ky. 75, 229 S.W. 132; 147 Ky. 159, 143 S.W. 1027), but power of attorney to convey land must be in writing and acknowledged and recorded or lodged for record as deed. As between principal and agent, contract for commission for sale or lease of real estate must be in writing. (KRS 371.010[8]).

No agency created by written power of attorney, given by one who at time of execution thereof, or thereafter became, member of U.S. Armed Forces, merchant seaman serving outside limits of U.S. or person outside said limits by permission, assignment or direction of any department or official of U.S. government in connection with any war activity, is revoked or terminated by death of principal as to agent or any other person who, without actual knowledge or actual notice of such death, acted in good faith in reliance on such power. No report or listing of principal as "missing" or "missing in action" constitutes or may be interpreted as constituting actual notice of death or of any facts indicating such death. (KRS 384.010 to .040).

Uniform Durable Power of Attorney Act not adopted.

Durable Powers.—General power of attorney may provide that it shall be exercisable notwithstanding subsequent disability or incapacity of principal, and, unless it

POWERS OF ATTORNEY . . . *continued*

states time of termination, notwithstanding lapse of time since execution of instrument, provided writing contains words, "this power of attorney shall not be effected by subsequent disability or incapacity of the principal, or lapse of time," or "this power of attorney shall become effective upon the disability or incapacity of the principal," or similar words expressing intent of principal. (KRS 386.093).

Health Care Powers.—Adult with decisional capacity may designate one or more adults as health care surrogate to make medical decisions. See KRS c. 311. See also category Estates and Trusts, topic Wills, subhead Living Will.

REAL PROPERTY:

All titles to land in Kentucky are allodial and, subject to the state's right of eminent domain and of escheat, owned entirely and absolutely by their respective owners. (KRS 381.020).

Any interest in or claim to land may be disposed of by deed or will, except that a sale or conveyance of land at the time in the adverse possession of another is champertous and void. (KRS 372.070, 382.010). Any estate in lands may be made to commence in future by deed as by will. (KRS 381.040). As to necessity and requirements of recording, see category Documents and Records, topic Records.

Presumption is in favor of conveyance in fee simple or such estate as grantor had. (KRS 381.060). Estates tail at common law are converted into estates in fee simple. (KRS 381.070).

Unless a different purpose is plainly expressed, a deed or will containing a limitation contingent upon a person dying "without heirs" or "without children" or "issue," or words of like import, must be construed as a limitation to take effect when such person shall die, unless the object on which the contingency depends is then living, or, if a child of his body, such child be born within ten months next thereafter. (KRS 381.080).

Court of equity may, in exercise of its equitable discretion, postpone decretal sale of a contingent estate, where present sale would involve its sacrifice (143 Ky. 730, 137 S.W. 201; 144 Ky. 172, 137 S.W. 859), but sale under execution is authorized (KRS 426.190).

No sale of real estate by trustee under deed of trust for payment of debts is valid, nor does trustee's conveyance thereof pass title unless: (1) Made pursuant to a judgment of court; or (2) made by an assignee under a voluntary deed of assignment (pursuant to KRS c. 379); or (3) the maker of such deed of trust or pledge join with the trustee in a writing evidencing such sale (KRS 381.190).

Contracts for sale of standing trees or timber, to be enforceable, must be in writing signed by person to be charged, or his authorized agent. Title to such trees or timber passes when marked with purchaser's brand. (KRS 371.100; 364.120).

Rule in Shelley's Case is not recognized in Kentucky, being clearly superseded by KRS 381.090. (215 Ky. 14, 284 S.W. 109).

Joint tenancy is recognized but common law right of survivorship between joint tenants abolished. (KRS 381.120). One or more joint tenants of real property may partition interest in real property during lifetime by deed or other instruments unless property is residential real property that is owned exclusively by husband and wife as joint tenants with right of survivorship and actually occupied by them as principal residence. (KRS 381.120).

Tenancy by Entireties.—Unless expressly provided for in conveyance or devise to husband and wife, there is no mutual right to the entirety by survivorship between them, but they take as tenants in common. (KRS 381.050).

Foreign Conveyances or Encumbrances.—Kentucky law controls mode of execution and acknowledgment or proof, as well as validity and effect of a devise, conveyance or encumbrance of real property situated in this State, and recordability of any conveyance or encumbrance thereon, or probate of any will affecting Kentucky real property. (311 Ky. 59, 223 S.W.2d 374).

Condominiums are recognized and regulated by Horizontal Property Law. (KRS 381.805 to 381.910). Uniform Condominium Act not adopted.

Aliens.—See category Citizenship, topic Aliens.

See also topics Curtesy, Deeds, Dower, Landlord and Tenant; categories Civil Actions and Procedure, topic Partition; Debtor and Creditor, topic Homesteads; Documents and Records, topic Records; Family, topic Husband and Wife; Mortgages, topic Mortgages of Real Property.

Uniform Simplification of Land Transfers Act not adopted.

TAXATION

Subject to exemptions provided, all property having situs in Kentucky is taxable for public purposes and all taxes upon property of same class shall be uniform. (Ky. Const. §171). General Assembly may authorize local governmental units to impose and collect various taxes and license fees. (Ky. Const. §181). Summaries of principal taxes administered by Revenue Cabinet arranged alphabetically by topic, following topic Administration.

ADMINISTRATION:

State Taxes.—Kentucky Revenue Cabinet exercises all administrative functions for revenue and tax laws levied for state purposes. Information, forms and waivers, etc., may be obtained by contacting Kentucky Revenue Cabinet, 200 Fair Oaks Lane, Frankfort, Kentucky 40602 (502-564-4580).

County, School and Municipal Taxes.—Local governmental agencies impose and collect various taxes, including property (ad valorem) taxes, occupational license taxes on net profits and utility gross receipts taxes. For information concerning taxes in Louisville and Jefferson County, contact Louisville and Jefferson County Revenue Commission, 734 West Main Street, Louisville, Kentucky 40202 (502-574-4900); for information concerning taxes in Lexington and Fayette County, contact Lexington Fayette Urban County Government Revenue Department, 200 East Main Street, Lexington, Kentucky 40507 (606-258-3340).

Assessment.—Income taxes may be assessed following audit by Revenue Cabinet. (KRS 141.420[2]). Revenue Cabinet may issue jeopardy assessments upon specific grounds for any taxes reasonably believed due (KRS 131.150[1]), and may proceed to collect same through garnishment, attachment or other legal proceedings (KRS 131.1510[2]). For inheritance taxes, see topic Inheritance Tax, subhead Administration and Enforcement. For property taxes, see topic Property (Ad Valorem) Taxes, subhead Assessment.

Protest of Taxes Assessed by Revenue Cabinet.—Any assessment by Cabinet of value of property or of additional taxes due set forth in written notice from Cabinet becomes due and payable unless protested in writing by taxpayer within 45 days of date of notice. (KRS 131.110).

Aggrieved taxpayer must within 45-day period file with Revenue Cabinet written protest with supporting statement, setting forth grounds for such protest and information upon which it is made. Upon written request Cabinet may extend time for filing supporting statement if it appears that delay is necessary and unavoidable, and its refusal to make such extension may be reviewed in same manner as in case of protested assessment. At time of filing both protest and supporting statement, taxpayer may request ruling on protest as filed, or request conference with Cabinet or its agent, which conference must be granted in writing stating time set therefor. Taxpayer may appear at conference in person or by representative. Additional conferences may be held by mutual consent. After considering protest, Cabinet or its agent must issue final ruling thereon, which must be mailed to taxpayer. Taxpayer may request final ruling anytime after filing timely protest and supporting statement. When requested, Cabinet must issue such ruling within 30 days from receipt of request.

Board of Tax Appeals, consisting of three members appointed by Governor, is vested with exclusive jurisdiction to hear and determine final rulings, orders and determinations of any agency of state or county government affecting revenue and taxation. Any party aggrieved by any ruling, order or determination of any state or county agency charged with administration of any taxing or licensing measure may appeal to Board by filing written complaint or petition of appeal with Board within 30 days from date agency's ruling is mailed. (KRS 131.340). Revenue Cabinet may appeal local property assessment as being too low. In such proceeding, Board forwards Cabinet's certification of value of property to interested parties and Cabinet's value becomes prima facie value for appeal. (KRS 131.340).

Appeals to Board of Tax Appeals are de novo and conducted in accordance with procedure for administrative hearings in KRS 13B.010 to 13B.130. (KRS 131.340). Current procedures published in 802 KAR 1:010. Proceedings before Board must be officially reported, except appeals of unmined mineral assessments. (KRS 131.355). Board must make written findings to support its decisions or orders. In case of any appeal, any taxes, interest, or penalty paid and found by Board to be in excess of that legally due must be refunded to taxpayer. (KRS 131.360).

Appeals from final orders of Board of Tax Appeals may be made to Franklin Circuit Court or to circuit court in county in which aggrieved party resides or conducts business, or in case appealed from county board of supervisors, to circuit court of county where appeal originated. If appeal is from order sustaining assessment, collection of tax may be stayed by filing of supersedeas bond.

Penalties.—

Uniform Civil Penalty Act set forth at KRS 131.180 provides following penalties unless otherwise provided for separate taxes: (1) failure to make timely return or report, unless such failure due to reasonable cause (as defined in KRS 131.010[9]), carries 2% penalty every 30 days or fraction thereof not to exceed 20% of entire tax; (2) failure to withhold or collect any tax as required, or failure to timely pay tax computed as due on return or report or timely pay at least 75% of tax determined due by Revenue Cabinet, without reasonable cause, carries 2% penalty every 30 days or fraction thereof not to exceed 20% of tax; (3) failure to timely pay installment of estimated tax or underpayment of declaration of estimated tax, without reasonable cause, carries 10% penalty; (4) failure or refusal to make and file report or return or furnish any information requested in writing by Revenue Cabinet may result in assessment of tax up to twice amount estimated to be due plus 5% penalty for each 30 day period or fraction thereof that return or report not filed not to exceed 50% of tax assessed; (5) failure or refusal to pay tax within 45 days of due date if not protested carries 2% penalty every 30 days or fraction thereof; (6) failure to obtain in timely manner any identification number, permit, license or other like document from Cabinet, unless such failure is due to reasonable cause, carries penalty of 10% of any cost or fee required to be paid for such document; (7) deficiency due to negligence carries 10% penalty; (8) deficiency due to fraud carries 50% penalty; (9) tendering of check to Cabinet which is not paid when presented results in penalty equal to 10% of check unless failure to honor payment result of error by person other than taxpayer; (10) failure to make timely return or report or make timely payment, within time or in manner required by law where not otherwise specially provided, carries penalty equal to 2% of total tax due each 30 days or fraction thereof plus interest at bank prime rate.

Corporate officer or other person who becomes liable for payment of any tax shall also be liable for all applicable penalties and interest (KRS 131.180[13]).

Real and Personal Property Tax.—Criminal: fraudulent evasion carries three times amount of tax. (KRS 132.570). Civil: $500 for failure to furnish complete list of property; 10% of tax with 1/2% interest per month on previously omitted property voluntarily listed; 20% of tax with interest at rate adjusted annually to equal banks' prime rate on previously omitted property involuntarily listed. (KRS 132.290; 132.183 and 132.990).

Inheritance and Estate Tax.—If tax is not paid within 18 months after death, interest is charged at rate equal to adjusted prime rate charged by banks, rounded to nearest full percent; 5% discount if tax paid in nine months from death. Criminal: $50 to $500 or up to 12 months in jail or both for defrauding court appointed appraiser. (KRS 140.210, 140.990[4]). Personal representatives or other persons subject to Uniform Civil Penalty Act for violations of inheritance and estate tax provisions. (See catchline Uniform Civil Penalty Act, supra.) (KRS 140.991; 131.180).

See note at head of Digest as to 1998 legislation covered.

See Topical Index in front part of this volume.

KY – 49

ADMINISTRATION . . . *continued*

Income Tax.—Civil: failure to make payment on or before date prescribed carries interest as part of tax at rate determined annually as equal to bankers' prime rate on each installment until paid (KRS 141.985); violation of any income tax provision contained in KRS c. 141 subjects taxpayer to Uniform Civil Penalty Act, catchline supra, within this subhead. Criminal: 50% of deficiency if due to fraud; fine of $500-$5,000 or one to five years in penitentiary or both. (KRS 141.990; 131.180).

Sales and Use Tax.—Failure or refusal to file carries twice estimated tax plus 10% of entire assessment; failure to make timely return without good cause carries 5% penalty every 30 days not to exceed 25% of entire tax; failure to make timely payment incurs interest at 6% per annum; failure to pay assessment incurs 10% interest per month. Criminal: $10-$100 or not more than 30 days in jail or both for doing business without permit or giving resale certificate to evade tax. (KRS 139.930).

Excise Taxes.—Covering motor carriers and dealers of gasoline and special fuels: subject to Uniform Civil Penalty Act, catchline supra, within this subhead. (KRS 138.290 and .990; 131.180).

Corporation and Utility Tax.—Corporation treated like individual unless otherwise specially provided. Corporation failing to pay assessment is delinquent and incurs 10% penalty with 10% interest per annum plus $50 per day for every day of delinquency. Utility failing to make timely payment incurs 20% penalty with 8% interest per annum; $1,000 for failure to make timely utility reports. (KRS 136.050 and .990).

Tax Amnesty Program has been discontinued.

Taxpayer Bill of Rights.—Following rules apply to administration of taxes subject to jurisdiction of Revenue Cabinet: (1) taxpayer has right to be represented by attorney or accountant in any Cabinet proceeding; (2) Cabinet must perform audits and conduct conferences only at reasonable times; (3) taxpayer has right to record Cabinet conferences; (4) penalty and interest are waived if taxpayer's failure to file timely return or make payment is due to written advice from Cabinet not subsequently invalidated; (5) taxpayers have right to receive copy of any audit; (6) taxpayer may enter into installment payment agreement upon written request or inability to pay; (7) taxpayer is entitled to receive extension of time for Kentucky provided IRS has given similar extensions; (8) taxpayers may seek damages in action filed before Kentucky Board of Claims for willful, reckless and intentional disregard of taxpayer's rights; and (9) taxpayers have right to privacy of Kentucky tax returns and reports. (KRS 131.041 to 131.081; 131.183; 131.500; 131.580 and 131.110).

Uniform Federal Lien Registration Act Amended not adopted. Non-uniform federal lien act adopted at KRS 382.480 and 387.490.

ALCOHOLIC BEVERAGE TAXES:

Alcoholic beverages taxes imposed pursuant to KRS c. 243.

CIGARETTE TAXES:

Cigarette taxes imposed pursuant to KRS 138.140.

COAL SEVERANCE TAX:

See category Mineral, Water and Fishing Rights, topic Mines and Minerals, subhead Taxes.

CORPORATE STOCK TAX:

See category Business Organizations, topic Corporations.

CORPORATION LICENSE TAXES:

See category Business Organizations, topic Corporations. Corporate organization tax imposed pursuant to KRS 136.060.

ESTATE TAX:

Estate tax imposed is equal to amount of state death tax credit claimed on federal estate tax return, less inheritance tax assessed net of discount. (KRS 140.130).

FINANCIAL INSTITUTIONS STATE FRANCHISE TAX:

See category Business Regulation and Commerce, topic Banks and Banking, subhead Reports and Tax on Deposits.

GASOLINE AND SPECIAL FUELS TAXES:

Gasoline Tax.—Gasoline "received" in Kentucky taxed pursuant to KRS 138.220 and 138.344. License provision adopted to prevent avoidance of tax by motor carriers purchasing gasoline outside state. (KRS 138.655-138.725).

Liquified petroleum gas tax imposed pursuant to KRS 234.320.

Motor carrier fuels tax is imposed by KRS 138.660 and 138.6601.

Special Fuels Tax.—Tax on fuels other than gasoline used to propel vehicles on public highways is imposed by KRS 138.660.

GENERATION SKIPPING TAX:

Kentucky has no generation skipping tax.

GIFT TAX:

None; but inheritance tax applies to gifts in contemplation of death or to take effect at or after death. (See supra, subhead Inheritance Tax.)

INCOME TAX:

Income tax is imposed by KRS c. 141 on individuals, business trusts, joint stock companies, fiduciaries and corporations (except certain specialized corporations, e.g., banks, insurance companies, building and loan associations. Limited liability companies treated as corporations for federal income tax purposes treated as corporations for Kentucky income tax purposes. (KRS 141.208[c]). Income of partnership or limited liability company treated as partnership for federal income tax purposes is not taxed to entity, but members are taxed on their respective shares of partnership or limited liability company net income. (KRS 141.208[b], 141.206).

Returns on calendar year basis must be made on or before Apr. 15 of following year; returns on fiscal year basis on or before 15th day of the fourth month following close of fiscal year. Forms of return may be obtained from Revenue Cabinet, Frankfort, to which payment of tax must be made (KRS 141.160, 141.220) by check or money order payable to State Treasury of Kentucky (Cabinet Regulation).

Persons reasonably expecting income in excess of $5,000 other than from wages subject to withholding, with estimated tax in excess of $500 from such sources, and gross income such as to require annual return, must file estimate, on or before Apr. 15, June 15, Sept. 15, or Jan. 15 (determined by period when minimum income first met), with part payment of estimated tax. Proportionate payment is based on time of making first estimate. (KRS 141.300, 141.305).

Returns are required from single individuals and married couples with adjusted gross income of $5,000 or more, from blind or over 65 individuals with adjusted gross income of $5,000 or more, from married couples, both of whom are over 65, with combined adjusted gross income of $5,400 or more, and from blind and over 65 individuals with adjusted gross income of $5,000 or more: except any individual with $5,000 or more of self-employment income must file return and any nonresidents of state with any gross income from Kentucky sources and total gross income of $5,000 or more must file return. (KRS 141.180).

Taxes are payable on filing of returns determined without regard to extensions. (KRS 141.220).

Individuals in military and public health service of U.S. may defer filing return or paying tax until 12 months after termination of service in area designated as combat zone by presidential proclamation without penalty or interest. (KRS 141.215).

Income Taxed—Individuals.—Tax is levied on "net income" determined pursuant to KRS 141.010 as follows: Beginning with "gross income" as defined in §61 of federal Internal Revenue Code as of Dec. 31, 1997 ("IRC") minus deductions allowed by IRC §62 (as modified for depreciation by KRS 141.0101); exclude income taxation of which is prohibited by state and U.S. constitution and federal and state statutes (KRS 141.010[10][a]); exclude federal and local retirement annuities accrued or accruing prior to Jan. 1, 1998 (KRS 141.021); exclude income from Railroad Retirement Act supplemental retirement annuities and include interest income on state and local obligations of other states (KRS 141.010[10][b], [c]); exclude picked up employee pension contributions made pursuant to IRC §414(h) (KRS 141.010[10][d]); exclude social security and railroad retirement benefits subject to federal income tax and money received as damages from "Agent Orange" exposure from persons serving in Vietnam (KRS 141.010[10][e]); exclude income received for services as precinct worker for training or working at polls; exclude amount paid for health insurance fee for taxpayer, taxpayer's spouse and dependents; exclude any amount paid during year for insurance for long-term care; exclude capital gains attributable to property taken by eminent domain; exclude any amount received by tobacco producer as result of national settlement agreement between tobacco industry and states' Attorney General or any federal legislation relating thereto; include for years ending before Jan. 1, 1991 federal tax refunds or credits during taxable year and deduct for years ending before Jan. 1, 1991 federal income tax paid for years ending before Jan. 1, 1990 to arrive at "adjusted gross income" (KRS 141.010[10][f], [g]); deduct to arrive at "net income" standard deduction allowed by KRS 141.081 or value of leasehold interest of property contributed to charitable organization used as temporary living quarters for homeless family and all deductions allowed in c. 1 of IRC applicable to Kentucky, plus deductions allowed by IRC §214 (working parents deduction) as it existed on Dec. 31, 1975, except: (1) deduction allowed for state income taxes paid, (2) deduction for value of distributive shares of estate of decedent unless deduction not claimed on inheritance tax return, (3) deduction for personal exemptions allowed under IRC §151, and (4) deduction not allowed for dues to organization(s) determined to have violated civil rights laws of Kentucky. Also deduct charitable contribution of property created by personal efforts of taxpayer if provisions of KRS 141.0201 are satisfied. (KRS 141.0201). Individuals domiciled in, or who maintain abode and spend more than total of 183 days of taxable year in state are taxed on their income from all sources but allowed credit for income taxes paid to another state on production of evidence of such payment. (KRS 141.070). Payments received by person displaced by state land acquisition programs are considered income for purposes of state's personal income tax law, corporation tax law or other state tax laws; such payments not considered as income or resources of any public assistance recipient and not deducted from amount of aid to which recipient otherwise entitled. (KRS 56.610, 56.740).

Rate.—Entire net income is subject to tax at following rates: 2% on first $3,000; 3% on next $1,000; 4% on next $1,000; 5% on next $3,000; 6% on all in excess of $8,000, less applicable credits. (KRS 141.020).

Exemptions.—In lieu of exemptions, tax credit is allowed in computing normal tax. Credits are: unmarried person, $20; married person filing separate return, $20, and additional $20 if return is separate, other spouse has no Kentucky gross income and is not dependent of another taxpayer; married persons filing joint return, $40; for each dependent, $20; additional $40 credit for taxpayer over 65 (or spouse over 65 without gross income and not dependent of another), additional $40 credit if taxpayer or spouse is blind; for fiduciary other than estate, $2; for estate, $20; for Kentucky National Guard member, additional $20. (KRS 141.020[3]). Credit of $100 allowed to any employer for each person hired if that person has been classified as unemployed by Human Resources Cabinet for at least 60 days prior to employment by taxpayer provided that person remains employed for at least 180 consecutive days during taxable year in which credit is claimed. (KRS 141.065).

Tax credits available for portion of investment in state-sponsored venture capital entity (KRS 154.20-340 to -370); also available for household dependent care services (20% of IRC amount) and low income (graduated scale $0-$25,000). (KRS 141.067 and 141.066).

See note at head of Digest as to 1998 legislation covered.

See Topical Index in front part of this volume.

INCOME TAX. . . *continued*

Tax credits available for amounts paid as job development assessment fees by employees of new business financed by depressed counties economic development authority in order to retire authority's bonds. (KRS 154.22-070).

Optional tax table may be developed by Cabinet specifying classes of taxpayers eligible.

Nonresidents carrying on a business, trade, profession, occupation or other activity in this state or owning therein tangible property or such intangible property as has acquired a business situs in Kentucky, are taxed at same rates on the net income derived therefrom, less credits reduced proportionately in the ratio which the nonresident's net income in Kentucky bears to his total net income from all sources. Formulas set for credits when spouse has no Kentucky income. However, exemption granted resident of foreign state which grants similar exemption to Kentucky resident on income earned in such state. (KRS 141.020).

Income Taxed—Corporations.—Tax is levied on "taxable net income" of domestic corporations and foreign corporations doing business in Kentucky (except financial institutions [other than banker's banks under KRS 287.135]), state and federal savings and loan associations making loans to members only, banks for cooperatives, production credit associations, insurance companies, including farmers' and other mutual casualty insurers, corporations exempted from federal income tax by IRC §501 and other religious, educational, charitable or like corporations not organized or conducted for pecuniary profit). For tax years after Dec. 31, 1989, rates are: 4% of first $25,000 of taxable net income; 5% of excess to $50,000; 6% of excess to $100,000; 7% of excess to $250,000; and 8.25% of amount of taxable net income in excess of $250,000. (KRS 141.040[3]). "S" corporations defined in IRC §1361(a) exempt from tax, except they must pay tax at foregoing rates (unless exempt from federal tax under IRC §1374) if net capital gain exceeds $25,000 and exceeds 50% of taxable income for taxable year and taxable income for year exceeds $25,000. (KRS 141.040).

"Taxable net income" for corporations is determined pursuant to KRS 141.010 as follows: Beginning with "gross income" as defined by IRC §61 as of Dec. 31, 1995, and modified by depreciation adjustments of KRS 141.0101, but excluding accelerated cost recovery provisions relating to safe harbor leases (IRC §168[f][8]), (1) exclude income exempt from taxation by Kentucky constitution and federal laws, (2) exclude dividend income received after Dec. 31, 1969, (3) include interest income derived from obligations of other states, (4) exclude 50% of gross income derived from disposal of coal covered by IRC §631(c), (5) include for lessors income tax payments made by lessees and exclude such payments from gross income of lessees, (6) include income determined due under consolidated or combined return provisions of KRS 141.205, and (7) ignore provisions of IRC §281, to obtain Kentucky gross income. Then to obtain "net income" deduct value of leasehold interest of property contributed to charitable organization used as temporary living quarters for homeless family and all deductions allowable to corporations under c. 1 of IRC as of Dec. 31, 1995, except for (a) State taxes paid to other states or District of Columbia, Puerto Rico or any territory or possession of U.S. or any foreign country, (b) deductions allowed by IRC §§243, 244, 245 and 247, (c) ignore provisions of IRC §281, (d) exclude deductions allocable to income either exempt or not taxed in state, (e) exclude expenses related to safe harbor leases, IRC §168(f)(8), and (f) exclude deduction for dues to organizations determined to have violated civil rights laws of Kentucky. With respect to taxable years beginning before Jan. 1, 1994, for property placed in service before Jan. 1, 1990, in lieu of full ACRS deductions provided in IRC §168 and §179, reasonable allowance for depreciation, exhaustion, wear and tear, and obsolescence of property used in trade or business is allowed as follows: (i) depreciation on property placed in service prior to Jan. 1, 1981 is computed as in IRC §167, using method elected when property was first placed in service or as changed and approved by IRS; (ii) depreciation on non-recovery property placed in service on or after Jan. 1, 1981 is computed as in IRC §167 as in effect on Dec. 31, 1980; (iii) depreciation on recovery property placed in service before Aug. 1, 1985 by corporations with taxable years beginning on or after July 1, 1984 and before Aug. 1, 1985 is calculated either (a) by dividing total IRC §168 deductions by 1.4 or (b) by using allowed or allowable deductions as calculated under IRC §167; (iv) depreciation on transition property placed in service on or after Jan. 1, 1981 and before Aug. 1, 1985 and first reported in taxable year beginning on or after Aug. 1, 1985 is computed by straight line method over remaining useful life of assets. Taxpayer can treat cost of property placed in service on or before July 1, 1985 as expense as provided in IRC §179 in effect on Dec. 31, 1981, with limit of $5,000 as to aggregate cost. Taxpayer can elect to treat cost of property placed in service on or after Aug. 1, 1985 as expense as provided in IRC §179 in effect on Dec. 31, 1980. For property placed in service after Dec. 31, 1989, depreciation and expense deductions allowed under IRC §168 and §179 in effect on Dec. 31, 1989 are allowed. (KRS 141.0101). For taxable years beginning after Dec. 31, 1993, amounts of depreciation and election to expense deductions, basis of assets, and gain or loss from sale or other disposition of assets is same for Kentucky purposes as determined under c. 1 of IRC. (KRS 141.010[3]). For property placed in service before first day of first taxable year beginning after Dec. 31, 1993, and owned by taxpayer on first day of first taxable year beginning after Dec. 31, 1993, special transition rules apply for including net difference between adjusted Kentucky basis and adjusted federal basis in gross income. (KRS 141.010[12]-[14]). For tax years ending on or after Dec. 31, 1995, corporation subject to tax in Kentucky may elect to file consolidated Kentucky corporation income tax return if corporation is member of affiliated group as defined in IRC §1504(a) and return includes all members of affiliated group. (KRS 141.200). Election is binding on both Cabinet and affiliated group for eight years. (KRS 141.200[3][d]). Net income apportioned between Kentucky and other states based substantially on Uniform Division of Income for Tax Purposes Act (KRS 141.120, see Part III of this volume) is "taxable net income"; apportionment factor weighs sales, property and payroll in ratio of 2:1:1 (KRS 141.120[8]). For ability of multiple corporations engaged in unitary business to file combined returns, see 889 S.W.2d 788 and KRS 141.120(11).

Credit of $100 is allowed to any employer for employment of each person who has been classified as unemployed by Human Resources Cabinet for at least 60 days prior to employment by employer, provided that person remains employed for at least 180 consecutive days during taxable year in which credit is claimed. (KRS 141.065).

Approved companies entering into financing agreements with Kentucky economic development authority are entitled to certain tax credits (or for some approved companies; amounts applied as estimated tax payments) against Kentucky income tax. (KRS 154.22-050, -060; 154.26-090; 154.28-090; 141.400; 141.403). Approved companies entering into service and technology agreements with Kentucky depressed counties economic development finance authority are entitled to tax credit (or estimated tax payment) against Kentucky income tax. (KRS 154.24-110, -120; 141.407).

Certain certificated air carriers which have made investment in state entitled to general tax credit. (KRS 144.125). Fifty percent credit available for investment in qualifying waste recycling and composting equipment. (KRS 141.390).

Qualified farming operations allowed accelerated depreciation deductions for new buildings and equipment purchased to enable participation in certain networking projects and to establish or expand secondary food-producing facilities in Kentucky. (KRS 141.0101[11]). Qualified farm operation also entitled to certain nonrefundable credits against Kentucky income tax on any income generated by qualified farming operation's participation in networking project. (KRS 141.412).

Withholding.—Employers subject to withholding provisions similar to those in Federal law. (KRS 141.310-141.340). Bond may be required in no greater amount than $50,000. (KRS 141.310). Cabinet may require taxpayers whose average withholding liability exceeds $25,000 to remit tax by electronic fund transfer. (KRS 131.155).

INHERITANCE TAX:

Inheritance tax is governed by KRS c. 140, the salient features of which are as follows:

Taxable Property.—Tax at progressive rates levied on transfer of property, having Kentucky situs, which passes by will or by intestacy laws of state, or by sale or gift in contemplation of death, including: (1) All property in state's jurisdiction belonging to its inhabitants; (2) all tangible personal property of such inhabitants, wherever located, that has not acquired situs for taxation outside Kentucky; (3) all intangible property of any nature, belonging to persons domiciled in Kentucky except partnership property located in another state and subject to inheritance or estate tax in that state; (4) all intangible property of any nature, belonging to nonresidents, which has acquired business situs in Kentucky; (5) all real property or interest therein within Kentucky; (6) all tangible personal property, having acquired situs in Kentucky and not taxable elsewhere, belonging to nonresidents (KRS 140.010); (7) proceeds of life insurance policies payable on death of assured, resident in Kentucky, whether payable to assured or his estate, or some other designated beneficiary, except that such proceeds payable to designated beneficiary or beneficiaries including testamentary or inter vivos trustee other than assured or his estate, or to trust for benefit of such beneficiaries (409 S.W.2d 518), and proceeds of any life insurance policy issued by or through Federal Government, or pension or annuity payments made to surviving spouse under Fed. R.R. Retirement Act, are tax-free (KRS 140.030[2]); (8) obligations of contractual nature due from one dying resident in Kentucky, "payable at or after death," unless affirmatively shown that decedent, during life, received substantially equivalent consideration therefor (KRS 140.030[1]); (9) property having Kentucky situs, transferred by decedent (whether resident or nonresident) in contemplation of death or to take effect in possession or enjoyment at or after death, including transfers under which transferor retains (a) possession or enjoyment of property so transferred or its increase, (b) power to designate persons to take property or its income, except in case of bona fide sale for adequate consideration, or (c) property conveyed in trust, over which settlor has power of revocation exercisable by will (KRS 140.020); (10) property passing by survivorship between joint tenants or tenants by entireties (KRS 140.050).

Tax imposed when any person or corporation subject to tax becomes beneficially entitled in possession of or expectancy to any property or income thereof by such transfer. (KRS 140.010).

Rates and exemptions vary according to following classification of beneficiaries (see KRS 140.070 for description of beneficiary classification and applicable tax rate, and KRS 140.080 for applicable exemption by classification):

Class A includes parent, surviving spouse, child by blood, stepchild, child adopted during infancy, child adopted during adulthood who was reared by decedent during infancy and grandchild who is issue of child by blood, issue of stepchild, issue of child adopted during adulthood who was reared by decedent during infancy, issue of child adopted during infancy, brothers, sisters, half-brothers, or half-sisters. Inheritance tax being phased-out for Class A beneficiaries. Exemptions, if decedent died prior to July 1, 1995 are: Surviving spouse total inheritable interest; infant child by blood or adoption, or child by blood or adoption, who has been declared mentally disabled, $20,000; any other member of class, $5,000, except brothers, sisters, half-brothers, half-sisters, $1,000. During phase-out, Class A beneficiaries entitled to exemption equal to greater of pre-July 1, 1995 exemption or phase-out percentage of inheritable interest. Phase-out percentage based on date of death. For decedents dying: from July 1, 1995 through June 30, 1996, 25%; from July 1, 1996 through June 30, 1997, 50%; from July 1, 1997 through June 30, 1998, 75%; on or after July 1, 1998, 100%.

Tax Rates: 2% on amount by which amount or value of transfer exceeds exemption, if any, applicable and does not exceed $20,000; 3% on next $10,000 or part thereof (excess over $20,000 up to $30,000); 4% on next $15,000 or part thereof (excess over $30,000 up to $45,000); 5% on next $15,000 (excess over $45,000 up to $60,000); 6% on next $40,000 (excess over $60,000 up to $100,000); 7% on next $100,000 (excess over $100,000 up to $200,000); 8% on next $300,000 (excess over $200,000 up to $500,000); 10% on all over $500,000.

Class B includes nephew, niece, nephew or niece of the half blood, son-in-law, daughter-in-law, aunt or uncle or great-grandchild who is grandchild of child by blood, of stepchild or of child adopted during infancy. Exemption, $1,000. Rates: 4% on first $10,000 or part thereof; 5% on next $10,000 or part thereof (excess over $10,000 up to $20,000); 6% on next $10,000 or part thereof (excess over $20,000 up to $30,000); 8% on next $15,000 or part thereof (excess over $30,000 up to $45,000); 10% on next $15,000 or part thereof (excess over $45,000 up to $60,000); 12% on next $40,000 or part thereof (excess over $60,000 up to $100,000); 14% on next $100,000 or part thereof (excess over $100,000 up to $200,000); 16% on excess over $200,000.

See note at head of Digest as to 1998 legislation covered.

See Topical Index in front part of this volume.

INHERITANCE TAX . . . *continued*

Class C includes any educational, religious or other institutions, societies or associations, or any cities, towns or public institutions not qualifying for complete exemption (see subhead Exempt Transfers, infra) and all persons not included in Class A or Class B. Exemption, $500. Rates: 6% on first $10,000 or part thereof; 8% on next $10,000 or part thereof (excess over $10,000 up to $20,000); 10% on next $10,000 or part thereof (excess over $20,000 up to $30,000); 12% on next $15,000 or part thereof (excess over $30,000 up to $45,000); 14% on next $15,000 or part thereof (excess over $45,000 up to $60,000); 16% on excess over $60,000.

Exempt Transfers.—Following transfers are entirely exempt: Transfers to educational, religious or other institutions, societies or associations whose sole object and purpose are to carry on charitable, educational or religious work; transfers in trust for any charitable purpose; transfers to cities, towns or public institutions in Kentucky for public purposes. (KRS 140.060).

Tax does not apply to any gratuity pay, death compensation or other award or benefit paid by federal government to surviving spouse or heirs of person by reason of his service in U.S. armed forces. (KRS 140.015).

Tax also does not apply to value attributable to employer's contributions receivable by beneficiary from employees' trusts meeting requirements of IRC §401(a), or from retirement annuity contracts purchased under plan described in IRC §403(a), or from retirement annuity contract purchased for employee by employer which is an IRC §170(b)(1)(A)(ii) or (vi) organization exempt from tax under IRC §501(a), or under Ch. 73 of tit. 10 of U.S. Code or to value of annuity receivable by beneficiary (other than executor) under individual retirement account (IRC §408[a]), individual retirement annuity (IRC §408[b]), or retirement bond (IRC §409[a]). (KRS 140.063).

Administration and Enforcement.—Revenue Cabinet supervises collection, has power to sue in Kentucky or elsewhere, requires necessary reports from representatives or beneficiaries. An executor or administrator must file duplicate of inventory with Revenue Cabinet. (KRS 140.160. See also category Estates and Trusts, topic Executors and Administrators).

On request of interested party, district court must appoint appraiser for succession tax purposes. Appraiser, after notice and hearing, must file report of appraisement in court and copy with Revenue Cabinet. His compensation may not exceed 1/10 of 1% of appraised value. (KRS 140.170).

After investigation, Revenue Cabinet may change value of the property subject to succession taxes and advise representatives of estate thereof. (KRS 140.170).

Succession taxes must be assessed at full and fair cash value of property transferred. Personal representatives, trustees and beneficiaries personally liable for inheritance taxes to extent of property so transferred coming into their hands (KRS 140.190) and representatives or trustees may not deliver any bequest or distributive share before collecting tax thereon (KRS 140.220). Such taxes are lien on property transferred and on all property in hands of personal representative or trustee until paid or bond therefor given as provided in KRS 140.190 and 140.210. Personal property acquired by bona fide purchaser for value not affected by lien, but owner of securities may not have them transferred to him by issuing corporation until permit granted by Revenue Cabinet and filed with such corporation. (KRS 140.190).

Deductions.—In computing estate value to determine amount or value particular beneficiaries entitled to receive, only following deductions allowed: (1) Decedent's debts other than those secured by property outside Kentucky's tax jurisdiction and those barred by limitation; (2) taxes accrued and unpaid on decedent's property other than taxes on property outside Kentucky's tax jurisdiction; (3) death duties paid to foreign countries; (4) federal estate taxes paid, in proportion assessed on property in Kentucky; (5) special assessments which are lien on property taxable in Kentucky; (6) funeral, monument and cemetery lot maintenance expenses actually paid, not exceeding $5,000; (7) commissions of executor or administrator in amount actually allowed and paid; (8) costs of administration, including reasonable attorney's fees. (KRS 140.090).

Valuation Date.—Value of assets determined for estate and inheritance tax purposes as of date of death. (KRS 140.010; 140.100[2]).

Valuation of Particular Transfers.—Present value of future, contingent or limited estates or interests is determined according to specified U.S. mortality tables, applying rate of 4% per annum. (KRS 140.100[2]).

When annuity or life estate terminated by death and tax thereon not fixed, its value for taxation is amount of annuity or income actually paid or payable to annuitant or life tenant while entitled thereto. Tax on such annuities and life interests must be paid out of corpus unless otherwise provided by "terms of the will." (KRS 140.100[3]). (*Query:* As to constitutionality of tax on remainderman measured by amount life tenant consumed while living.)

Contingent or defeasible estates in expectancy taxed at applicable rate based on "the happening of the most probable contingencies or conditions named in the will, deed, trust agreement." Provision made for refund if property ultimately should vest in persons taxable at lower rate or exempt from taxation. (KRS 140.110).

When Due; Interest.—Tax becomes due at death of decedent, payable within 18 months (KRS 140.210) and constitutes lien on property transferred and on all property acquired by executor, administrator or trustee. (KRS 140.190[3]). (*Query:* As to validity of that portion of law which attempts to fix lien on property given to A for tax due from B on gift to A.)

If tax paid within 18 months no interest charged; if paid within nine months discount of 5% allowed. If tax not paid within 18 months, interest charged at rate equal to adjusted prime rate charged by banks, rounded to nearest full percent. Bond required of fiduciary not paying tax in 18 months. (KRS 140.210; 131.010[6]; 131.183).

Returns and Reports.—Return must be filed with Revenue Cabinet within 18 months after death of decedent, or at time of payment of tax, whichever is earlier. (KRS 140.160). Where real estate of decedent transferred to another person so as to become subject to tax, executor, administrator or trustee must inform Revenue Cabinet within six months after his appointment, or, if fact not then known to him, within one month after it becomes known. (KRS 140.180).

Foreign Representative.—If no administration in Kentucky, foreign executor or administrator, or foreign grantee of property which is subject of taxable transfer by decedent, may apply directly to Revenue Cabinet for ascertainment of tax without necessity of local administration. If tax not adjusted within six months after decedent's death, proper district court, on application of Revenue Cabinet, must appoint administrator in Kentucky. (KRS 140.270).

Taxable Transfers.—Every transfer by grantor or donor of material part of estate, without adequate valuable consideration within three years prior to death, or made in nature of final disposition of estate, is prima facie deemed made in contemplation of death and therefore taxable. (KRS 140.020).

Property passing by exercise of power of appointment, or by failure to exercise such power, taxable as though person taking had inherited from donee of power. Transfer of property by power of appointment may be taxed either upon creation of power or upon exercise of power. (525 S.W.2d 68). Provision made for regulating exemptions allowed as deductions. (KRS 140.040).

Joint deposits, including certificates of deposit, in bank and real or personal property held in joint names of two or more persons or held as tenants by entirety, with remainder to survivor, taxable at death of one of them, to extent of such decedent's interest therein, computed as if absolute owner of equal fractional interest therein. (KRS 140.020[3]; KRS 140.050).

Credit allowed where property transferred to decedent within five years of death and tax paid thereon. (KRS 140.095).

Life insurance company may pay proceeds of taxable insurance on decedent's life, or balance due at death of decedent on annuity contract, to person entitled thereto, on mailing notice to Revenue Cabinet in such form as it prescribes, setting forth fact of such payment. Cabinet may dispense with notice requirement where policy for less than $1,000. (KRS 140.260).

Under reciprocal arrangements, Revenue Cabinet, on finding that intangible personal property of nonresident decedent physically located in Kentucky, must communicate such information to proper taxing officials of state of decedent's domicile (KRS 140.270), and another state, in which nonresident was domiciled at death, may by suit in Kentucky enforce its claim for death taxes due it from such nonresident's estate (KRS 140.280).

Reciprocal agreements with other states having same legislative policy may be made to accomplish following results: (1) immunity from taxation in Kentucky of intangible property of nonresident decedent (domiciled in United States) held by Kentucky trustee if jurisdiction of decedent's domicile grants similar immunity to estates of deceased residents of Kentucky; (2) immunity from taxation in Kentucky of intangible personal property of deceased resident of Kentucky held in trust in another jurisdiction if such jurisdiction levies succession tax but grants immunity in respect of intangible property of its resident decedents held by Kentucky trustee. In either event immunity from taxation in Kentucky conditioned on evidence presented that tax has been or will be paid to such other jurisdiction. (KRS 140.275).

Interstate Co-operation.—When domicile is in dispute, a compromise may be made by Revenue Cabinet. (KRS 140.285).

Waivers required for transfer of stock of resident decedent, regardless of place of transfer, or domicile of corporation. Waivers must be obtained for transfer of stock of nonresident decedent in most Kentucky corporations. Where waiver not required for transfer of stock of nonresident decedent, Kentucky corporation may make transfer upon receipt of affidavit (Revenue Form 803) from personal representative. Forms for requests for waivers vary, and they, with other information, may be obtained from Revenue Cabinet, Inheritance and Estate Tax Section, Frankfort, KY 40620. (Rulings issued pursuant to authority contained in KRS 140.240, 140.250.)

Access to safety deposit boxes to which decedent in his lifetime had access either for himself or as agent for renter of box is regulated by stringent rules. (KRS 140.250).

MARIJUANA AND CONTROLLED SUBSTANCES TAX:

Tax imposed on each dealer engaging in manufacture, importation, transportation, distribution, acquisition, purchase, storage, use or possession of certain quantities of marijuana and controlled substances pursuant to KRS 138.870 to 138.889. Tax stamps, labels or other tax indicia must be purchased from Cabinet and affixed to marijuana and controlled substance to evidence payment of tax. (KRS 138.874).

MOTOR CARRIER FUELS TAX:

See topic Gasoline and Special Fuels Taxes, subhead Motor Carrier Fuels Tax.

MOTOR VEHICLE USAGE TAXES:

Tax at rate of 6% of "retail price" (see next paragraph), minimum $6, levied on use in state of every motor vehicle unless exempted. Tax collected by county clerk upon original registration in state or transfer of ownership of vehicles previously registered. Credit given for similar taxes paid in other states which give similar credit for substantially identical taxes paid in this state. Refund available if new vehicle replaced or purchase price refunded within 60 days by selling dealer or within 90 days by manufacturer or as result of formal arbitration or litigation or in case of manufacturer when ordered to do so by dispute resolution system established under KRS 367.865 or 16 C.F.R. 703 because of malfunction or defect. (KRS 138.460). Exemptions from tax provided for: (a) Vehicles sold to U.S., state or any political subdivision thereof; (b) vehicles sold to educational or charitable institutions; (c) motor vehicles previously registered or titled when being sold or transferred to licensed dealers for resale; (d) vehicles sold by licensed and registered dealers to nonresident members of Armed Forces stationed in state; (e) commercial vehicles with capacity of more than nine passengers owned by nonresident and used primarily in interstate commerce and registered under KRS 186.145; (f) vehicles previously registered in state transferred between husband and wife or parent and child, stepparent and stepchild or grandparent and grandchild; (g) transfers when only business name has changed; (h) transfers between proprietorship and corporation or limited liability company or between corporation and limited liability company, within six months of time corporation dissolves; (i) transfers

See note at head of Digest as to 1998 legislation covered.

See Topical Index in front part of this volume.

KY – 52

MOTOR VEHICLE USAGE TAXES . . . *continued*
under will, court order or by descent and distribution; if vehicles were previously registered in Kentucky; (j) transfers without consideration by subsidiary corporation to parent or between limited liability company and any of its members; (k) interest of partner when other interests transferred to him; (l) vehicles repossessed by secured party if held for resale only; and (m) vehicles transferred to insurance company in settlement of claim if junked or held for resale only. (KRS 138.470).

"Retail price" of motor vehicles subject to tax determined as follows: for new vehicles, dealer demonstrator vehicles, previous model year vehicles and certain U-Drive-It vehicles, retail price is total consideration given at time of purchase or thereafter, including any trade-in allowance as attested to by affidavit. If affidavit not available to establish total consideration given, retail price is 90% of manufacturer's suggested retail price with all equipment and accessories and including transportation charges, not including that portion of vehicle attributable to equipment or adaptive devices necessary to facilitate or accommodate operator or passenger with physical disabilities, but with no allowance for value of trade-in vehicle; for used vehicles being registered for first time in Kentucky by new resident, retail price is average trade-in value appearing in automotive reference manual prescribed by Revenue Cabinet if model appears, or $100 for vehicles no longer listed; for used vehicles registered outside Kentucky purchased outside Kentucky by Kentucky resident for Kentucky registration, retail price is total consideration given at time of purchase or thereafter, including average trade-in value given in automotive reference manual prescribed by Revenue Cabinet; for used vehicles previously registered in Kentucky sold in Kentucky and certain U-Drive-It vehicles sold in Kentucky, retail price is total consideration given, excluding any trade-in allowance (KRS 138.450, KRS 138.450[10], KRS 186A.115); and trucks with gross weight in excess of 10,000 pounds retail price is 81% of manufacturers' suggested retail price with all equipment and accessories and including transportation charges (KRS 138.460). Motor vehicle dealer who operates service department may register vehicle to be used exclusively as loaner vehicle for use of its customer and pay 6% tax upon fair lease value in accordance with KRS 138.460.

POLLUTION ABATEMENT AUTHORITY TAX:

Tax of not more than 2% of gross bill may be levied on every purchase of water service and sewer service in state. (KRS 224A.070[5]). Funds received earmarked for grants to local governmental units to assist in construction or acquisition of water, sewer or utility projects. (KRS 224A.040).

PROPERTY (AD VALOREM) TAXES:

Real and Personal Property Taxable.—Subject to exemptions hereinafter noted, all property having a situs in Kentucky is taxable. (Ky. Const. §171).

Taxable situs of property generally is thus fixed: (1) Real property in county, city and taxing district where located. (KRS 132.220;132.200). (2) Tangible personal property, in county, city and taxing district where it has acquired a taxable situs. (KRS 132.220, 132.200). Temporary location for transient purposes does not fix taxable situs. (134 Ky. 99, 119 S.W. 749; 181 Ky. 675, 205 S.W. 789). (3) Intangibles at residence of real or beneficial owner (not at residence of fiduciary or agent in possession) or, if they have acquired a business situs in Kentucky, in county of such situs. (KRS 132.190). Intangibles of Kentucky resident integrated into separate business activity outside Kentucky may, under certain circumstances, not have situs in Kentucky. See 479 S.W.2d 15. (4) A fiduciary holding intangibles for a real or beneficial owner residing out of Kentucky need not list them or pay taxes thereon, except in case of a personal representative pending settlement of his decedent's estate, before such nonresident legatee or beneficiary is entitled to receive his share. (KRS 132.190; 142 Ky. 365, 134 S.W. 914; 134 Ky. 121, 119 S.W. 774).

Resident is defined as any person who has taken up place of abode within state with intention of continuing to abide in state. Any person who had his actual place of abode in state for most of 12 month period preceding date assessment is to be made is deemed resident. (KRS 132.010).

Exemptions.—Following classes of property are exempt from all taxation: public property used for public purposes; real property owned and occupied by, and personal property owned by, religious institutions; nonprofit burial grounds; charitable and nonprofit educational institutions; public libraries, their endowments and maintenance income; household goods used in home; crops grown in year in which assessment is made; and first $6,500 of value of real property maintained as permanent residence by owner who is 65 years of age or older or totally disabled. Procedures provided whereby persons 65 years of age and older must apply for homestead exemption provided by Ky. Const. §170 (KRS 132.810; Ky. Const. §170); bonds of state, counties, municipalities, taxing and school districts (Ky. Const. §171); value or amount of unmanufactured agricultural products to extent of value, or amount, of any unpaid nonrecourse loans thereon granted by U.S. or any agency thereof (KRS 132.200[6]). Revenue bonds issued under Appropriation Act and interest thereon exempt from all taxation by Commonwealth and subdivision (KRS 36.370); shares of stock (942 S.W.2d 893); intangible property of financial institutions paying tax under KRS 136.300 (KRS 136.300).

Following classes of property are subject to taxation for state purposes only and are not taxable by counties, cities, school or other taxing districts (KRS 132.200 unless otherwise noted): (1) Farm implements and farm machinery owned and used by person actually engaged in farming and used in his farm operation; (2) livestock, ratite birds and domestic fowls; (3) capital stock of savings and loan associations; (4) machinery, whether owned or leased, actually engaged in manufacturing and products in course of manufacture (which includes printing, publishing and distributing newspaper or operating job printing plant), and raw material actually on hand at plant for purpose of manufacture; (5) commercial radio, television and telephonic equipment directly used or associated with electronic equipment which broadcast electronic signals to antenna; (6) unmanufactured agricultural products on hand at plants of manufacturing concerns or in possession of producer or any agent of producer to which such products have been conveyed or assigned for purpose of sale (cities and counties but not other taxing districts may tax other unmanufactured agricultural products); (7) money in hand, notes, bonds, accounts and other credits, whether secured or unsecured; (8) all privately-owned leasehold interests in industrial buildings owned and financed by tax-exempt governmental unit or by other tax-exempt statutory authority through revenue bonds except that local tax exemption does not apply to value of leasehold interest created through private financing; (9) certified pollution control facilities; (10) certified alcohol production facilities; (11) tangible personal property located in foreign trade zone as designated under 19 U.S.C. §81; (12) historic motor vehicles as defined in KRS 186.043; (13) certified fluidized bed energy production facilities; (14) unregistered motor vehicles held in licensed dealer inventory on assignment under KRS 186A.230; (15) machinery and equipment used to recycle waste materials; (16) new farm machinery and other equipment held in retailer's inventory for sale under floor plan financing arrangement by "retailer"; (17) new boats and new marine equipment held in registered dealer's inventory under floor plan financing arrangement; (18) financial institution deposits (KRS 132.030); (19) annuities or present right to receive income, excluding future lump sum payments, for life or lives or other indeterminate period (KRS 132.2151); (20) accounts receivable, notes, bonds, credits and other intangible property rights arising out of business transactions substantially performed outside state, patents, trademarks, copyrights, and licensing or royalty agreements, intercompany intangible property receivables due from "affiliates companies", tobacco base allotments (KRS 132.020[4]); (21) brokers' accounts receivable (KRS 132.050); (22) vested and contingent interests in retirement plans qualified for exemptions under federal income tax laws (KRS 132.043); (23) deposits in savings accounts at credit unions (KRS 132.047); (24) aircraft not used to transport persons or property for hire if approved by local taxing authority; (25) "taxable capital" and "taxable reserves" of domestic life insurance companies except that county and city where principal office is located may impose tax of 15¢ per $100 of taxable capital (KRS 136.320).

Property of Kentucky Educational Savings Plan Trust and income therefrom exempt from all taxation by Commonwealth and subdivisions; interest earned on any money paid by any participant is exempt from Kentucky income tax. (KRS 164A.370).

Funds of fraternal benefit societies organized or licensed under KRS c. 304-.29, exempt from all state, county, district, municipal and school taxes; real estate and office equipment not so exempt. (KRS 304.29-241).

Unmanufactured agricultural products, other than those specified in (6) above, are subject to local taxation by cities and counties each at rate not exceeding 1½¢ on each $100 of all unmanufactured tobacco and not exceeding 4½¢ on each $100 of all other unmanufactured agricultural products not at plant for manufacturing purposes. (KRS 132.200).

There are no special provisions for members of Armed Forces. See, however, subhead Income Tax, infra.

State Tax Rates.—Except as otherwise provided, rates are 31½¢ per $100 of value of all real property directed to be assessed for taxation and 45¢ per $100 of value of all other property directed to be assessed for taxation. (KRS 132.020). Real property rate must be reduced to compensate for any increase over 4% in aggregate assessed value of real property over preceding year's assessment; rate must be increased to compensate for any decreased assessment so that revenue produced will remain steady. (KRS 132.020[6]). Special tax rates (all set forth in KRS 132.020, except as otherwise noted) as exceptions to above are provided as follows: 1½¢ per $100 of all tobacco; 1½¢ per $100 of value of privately-owned leasehold interests in industrial revenue bond developments owned and financed by tax-exempt governmental units except that rate does not apply to value of leasehold interest created through private financing; 25¢ per $100 of money in hand, notes, bonds, accounts, other credits, secured or unsecured; 1½¢ per $100 of unmanufactured agricultural products; 1½¢ per $100 of aircraft not used to transport persons or property for hire; 1/10 of 1¢ per $100 of farm implements and farm machinery used in farm operations; 1/10 of 1¢ per $100 of livestock and domestic fowls; 1/10 of 1¢ per $100 upon tangible personal property located in foreign trade zone as designated in 19 U.S.C. §81; 15¢ per $100 of machinery actually engaged in manufacturing, and commercial radio, television and telephonic equipment used directly in broadcasting to antenna, and certified pollution control facilities; 1/10th of 1¢ per $100 of certified alcohol production facilities and fluidized coal energy production facilities; 25¢ per $100 of value of historic motor vehicles as defined in KRS 186.043; 1½¢ per $100 of accounts receivable, notes, bonds, credits, and other intangible property rights arising out of or created in course of business transactions performed outside of state, patents, trademarks, copyrights and licensing and royalty agreements, shares of capital stock of and accounts receivable, notes, bonds, credits, nondomestic bank deposits and other intangible personal property due from "affiliated companies"; 1/10th of 1¢ per $100 of value of intangible assets of financial institutions, 5¢ per $100 of finished goods, raw material and work in process inventory; 5¢ per $100 of retailer's inventory; 1/10 of 1¢ per $100 on deposits in financial institutions (KRS 132.030); see category Business Regulation and Commerce, topic Banks and Banking, subhead Reports and Tax on Deposits; 10¢ per $100 of brokers' accounts receivable from margin transaction customers (KRS 132.050); 1/10 of 1¢ of goods in original packages or fungible goods in bulk, in public warehouses awaiting transshipment to in- or out-of-state location (KRS 132.095); 70¢ per $100 of "taxable capital" for calendar year beginning before 2000, 56¢ per $100 of taxable capital for calender year 2000, 42¢ per $100 of taxable capital for calendar year 2001, 28¢ per $100 of taxable capital for calendar year 2002, 14¢ per $100 of taxable capital for calendar year 2003, and 1/10 of 1¢ per $100 of taxable capital for calendar year 2004, and 1/10 of 1¢ per $100 of "taxable reserves" of domestic life insurance in lieu of all other state taxes (KRS 136.320); 1/10 of 1¢ per $100 of any right or interest, vested or contingent, in retirement plan exempt under federal income tax laws (KRS 132.043); 1/10 of 1¢ per $100 of savings accounts in credit unions in lieu of all other state taxes (KRS 132.047); 10¢ per $100 of assessed value on railroads operating solely within Kentucky (KRS 132.020[11]). Motor vehicles are subject to centralized ad valorem tax system using rates equalized on Jan. 1, 1983 assessments in various counties. (KRS 132.487). County clerks are to collect motor vehicle ad valorem tax at time of annual registration renewal or transfer on all vehicles registered by them. (KRS 134.800; 186.021).

Local Tax Rates.—For cities, counties and special taxing districts and other municipalities for other than school purposes, maximum rates for property taxes vary by population as follows: for cities with populations of 15,000 or more, rate not to exceed

See note at head of Digest as to 1998 legislation covered.

See Topical Index in front part of this volume.

KY – 53

PROPERTY (AD VALOREM) TAXES... continued

$1.50 per $100, for populations of 10,000 to 14,999, rate not to exceed $1 per $100, for populations under 10,000, rate not to exceed 75¢ per $100, and for counties and taxing districts, rates not to exceed 50¢ per $100. (Const. 157). Most cities, counties and districts do not charge taxes equal to these maximum rates and by statute are prohibited from doing so. (KRS 132.023; 132.027). Any levy of tax rate which increases revenue for agency other than state, other than through net assessment growth, is subject to recall vote on petition. (KRS 132.017). Special rates applied by state law of: 1¹/₂¢ per $100 of nonexempted (see item [6] in subhead Exemptions, supra) unmanufactured tobacco and 4¹/₂¢ per $100 of other nonexempted unmanufactured agricultural products (KRS 132.200); 15¢ per $100 of "taxable capital" of domestic life insurance companies for county and city purposes but not school or other district purposes (KRS 136.320). Cities and counties may enact additional tax to fund specific projects upon public vote in favor of each project and tax. (KRS 65.125).

Assessment.—All property not exempt by Constitution must be assessed at 100% fair market value (Const. §172; 391 S.W.2d 694), except General Assembly may provide for assessment of land used for agricultural and horticultural purposes according to land's value for such use (Const. §172A). Owners of agricultural and horticultural lands, as defined in KRS 132.010[9-11], which have been devoted exclusively to agricultural or horticultural use for at least five successive years may petition for valuation for taxing purposes at agricultural or horticultural value and defer taxation on higher value. (Ky. Const. §174; KRS 132.450[2]). Owners who have petitioned for and have been granted zoning classification other than agricultural or horticultural may not petition. Corporate owners, except those organized primarily for agricultural or horticultural purposes are excluded from provisions. When land which is valued and taxed as agricultural or horticultural land is converted to any other use, that portion of land upon which use is changed is subject to tax for succeeding year at its fair cash value. (KRS 132.454).

Unmined coal, oil and gas reserves and any other mineral or energy resources which are owned, leased or otherwise controlled separately from surface real property are assessed by Cabinet at no more than fair market value in place as separate and distinct interest. (KRS 132.820).

Provisions made for local governments to grant, on application, assessment moratorium for up to five years to encourage repair, rehabilitation, restoration or stabilization of existing improvements on property. (KRS 99.600-99.605; 132.452).

Real property generally is assessed by property valuation administrators in each county. Provision is made for public review of real property tax rolls during period in early May each year following public notice (KRS 133.045) and for review or correction at instance of taxpayer or of taxing authorities (KRS cc. 132, 133). Revenue Cabinet generally assesses personal property and has large powers of supervision and correction as to real property, and also as to countywide assessments. (KRS c. 133). It also has exclusive right to assess properties of certain kinds of corporations and public utilities as hereinafter pointed out. See infra, subhead Public Service Corporation Property Tax.

Jan. 1 is assessment date for state, county and school district taxes on all forms of property. (KRS 132.220). Cities have their own procedures for assessment and collection of taxes, with different taxing dates for cities of different classes, but any city may use assessments made by county property valuation administrator or Revenue Cabinet of property located within its limits except for levy and collection of ad valorem taxes on motor vehicles for which cities shall use assessment required by KRS 132.487(5). (KRS 132.285).

Taxpayer must list his real property with county property valuation administrator for assessment between Jan. 1 and Mar. 1; persons having interest in intangible and tangible personal property must list such property with county property valuation administrator or with Revenue Cabinet between Jan. 1 and May 15 in each year (KRS 132.220), except in cases of returns to and assessments by Revenue Cabinet. See infra, subhead Public Service Corporation Property Tax. Property valuation administrator maintains and certifies lists of real property additions and real property deletions to property tax rolls for each taxing district. (KRS 132.015). Stock, bond and other security brokers in State required to report securities and market values held as of Jan. 1 of each year and pay intangible tax of customer thereon. (KRS 132.060; 132.070).

Provision is made for compulsory retrospective assessment of omitted property by proceedings instituted by Revenue Cabinet in county where omitted property is liable to assessment. (KRS 132.330-132.350). Appeals from assessment on omitted property may be taken by either party to circuit court of county and thence to Court of Appeals. (KRS 132.340).

Omitted property is subject to interest on tax at rate adjusted annually to equal banks' prime rate from date tax would have been delinquent had property been listed, plus penalty of 10% if voluntarily listed, or 20% if not voluntarily listed. Omitted property is subject to retroactive assessment for five years from date when it became omitted. When property is assessed retroactively by action, an additional penalty of 20% of original tax, interest and penalty, may be imposed. (KRS 132.290; 131.010).

Review of Assessment.—

Real Property.—When it appears to Revenue Cabinet that assessment in any district is not in compliance with law, it may order re-assessment of all or part of property in such district. (KRS 132.660). Revenue Cabinet may reopen assessments of personal property within five years of assessment to determine if assessment was at fair cash value. (KRS 132.360).

Taxpayer aggrieved by administrator's assessment on real property may appeal by requesting conference with administrator or deputy. If taxpayer is still aggrieved, appeal may be made to board of assessment appeals by letter or written petition filed with county clerk no later than one workday following end of inspection period. Appeal from action of Board may be taken to Kentucky Board of Tax Appeals unless taxpayer failed to either appeal to county board of assessment appeals or appear before board either in person or by designated representative. (KRS 133.120). See topic Administration, subhead Board of Tax Appeals.

Appeals from Cabinet assessments of unmined coal, oil and gas reserves, and any other mineral or energy resources owned, leased or otherwise controlled separately from surface real property, are made pursuant to KRS c. 131 in manner similar to public

service franchises. (KRS 132.820[5]). See subhead Public Service Corporation Property Tax, catchline Review of Assessment by Revenue Cabinet, infra.

Personal Property.—Taxpayer approved by Revenue Cabinet's reassessment of personal property may protest to Revenue Cabinet and utilize administrator remedy procedures available under KRS 131.110 and 131.340. (KRS 132.360).

Payment.—Taxes are due annually on Sept. 15 after date fixed for assessment, except in case of assessments made by Revenue Cabinet, as to which see infra, subhead Public Service Corporation Property Tax and except as to taxes on money in hand, deposits in out of state banks, and unmanufactured tobacco, which are due on second succeeding Sept. 15 after assessment. If paid before Nov. 1 after due date, discount of 2% is allowed. If not paid by Jan. 1 following due date 2% on unpaid tax is added. After Feb. 1 in same years penalty is 10% of the tax. If tax collection schedule is delayed through no fault of taxpayer, Revenue Cabinet may revise collection schedule. Penalties and costs are provided for further delays (KRS 134.020), but in certain extreme conditions Governor may by proclamation, applicable to one or more counties or to entire state, extend time for payment of any taxes or interest or both (KRS 134.030).

The owner of any property on which a tax has become delinquent, or the person liable for such tax, may request the officer authorized to collect to receive payment from any other person or corporation, and on receiving payment the officer must, on request of the payer, issue a certificate of transfer of the tax claim. Such certificate confers on the transferee the priority of lien and all rights and powers as to enforcement or collection that the taxing authority would have had, and the transferee may also enforce the lien by action in any court of competent jurisdiction. (KRS 134.090-134.130).

Appropriate agency can authorize refunds or credits within two years from payment date for ad valorem taxes provided taxpayer follows appropriate administration remedy provision. (KRS 134.580).

Collection.—Sheriff is collector of state, county, and district property taxes, unless otherwise provided, and commences collection after receipt of tax bills from county clerk. (KRS 134.140). In addition to methods of enforcing collection of tax claims hereinafter described, KRS c. 135 provides other procedures for collection of public claims by action.

Lien.—Property taxes of state and of each county, city or other taxing district constitute lien on property assessed for five years following date when they became delinquent, and also on any real property owned by delinquent taxpayer when such claim for delinquent taxes thereon is offered for sale. Lien is for amount of delinquent taxes, with interest, penalties, costs, etc., and has priority over any other obligation or liability to which property may be subjected. (KRS 134.420). Except as otherwise provided for specific taxes, all state, county and district taxes which are collected locally become delinquent on Jan. 1 following their due date. (KRS 134.020[3]). Lien for other taxes administered by Cabinet created when taxpayer neglects or refuses to pay after demand and lien attaches to all property but lien does not have priority over subsequent perfected purchase money security interest. (925 S.W.2d 185; KRS 134.420[2]). Lien remains in force for ten years from date notice of tax lien is filed by Revenue Cabinet with appropriate county clerk. Holder of legal or equitable title and claimant or bailee in possession of property on assessment date are all responsible for taxes though sale may be made before year expires. Between parties, holder of equitable title required to list and pay tax on property. (KRS 134.060).

An inchoate lien on real estate to secure state, county and district taxes exists from date when assessment thereof should have been made, which lien is perfected by subsequent proceedings for assessment and ascertainment of taxes due, but in case of retrospective assessments rights of bona fide purchasers except of real property acquired in meantime are not prejudiced. (KRS 134.420). Same principle applies generally in case of city taxes. (Compare KRS 91.560; 91A.070).

Sale.—When a tax becomes delinquent the collector is authorized to first distrain personal property of delinquent taxpayer and sell it for cash. (KRS 134.430[2]). If personal property sufficient to satisfy tax bill is not found in county, tax claim must be advertised and offered for sale if there is any real estate subject to lien of tax claim. (KRS 134.430[3]).

The collecting officer must purchase tax claim on behalf of taxing authority if no other person will pay in cash full amount of tax claim. (KRS 134.450).

On consummating the sale of the tax claim, the collecting officer must issue to the purchaser a certificate of delinquency which, to the full amount of interest, penalties and costs continues to be a personal debt of the delinquent taxpayer, and the lien of the tax continues. (KRS 134.450[1], 134.460; 134.470).

No action to enforce the certificate of delinquency may be brought until one year after issuance thereof and any such action must be brought within five years after expiration of one year period. After one year period has expired owner of certificate may bring personal action thereon against delinquent taxpayer, bring proceedings to enforce lien of tax claim or sue in personam for personal judgment and in rem for enforcement of statutory lien. (KRS 134.470).

Prior to sale of property in lien under certificate of delinquency, tax claims collected thereby bear interest from date of issuance until collected, at rate of 12% per annum. (KRS 134.460).

Redemption.—Where property is sold pursuant to a judgment of foreclosure of lien, no appraisement is required and there is no right to redemption, except that where the taxing authority acquires real estate property may be redeemed at any time before Revenue Cabinet gives deed to purchaser, by paying to county court clerk amount due at time property was acquired, plus subsequent costs and 12% per annum interest. (KRS 134.510).

Public Service Corporation Property Tax.—Every corporation, association, partnership or person performing any public service, in addition to other taxes imposed, must annually pay a tax on its operating property to state and (except as hereinafter stated) a local tax thereon to county, city, town and taxing district wherein it exercises a franchise to conduct any public service business. (KRS 136.120).

Valuation and Assessment.—Revenue Cabinet has sole power to value and assess all the property, including the franchise, of every corporation, association or person performing any public service. (KRS 136.120).

See note at head of Digest as to 1998 legislation covered.

See Topical Index in front part of this volume.

PROPERTY (AD VALOREM) TAXES . . . *continued*

The property of all such taxpayers must be classified by Cabinet as operating tangible (including franchise), non-operating tangible and non-operating intangible. Non-operating intangible property within taxing jurisdiction of Kentucky is taxable for state purposes only at same rate as intangible property of non-franchise taxpayers. Tangible property, whether operating or non-operating, is subject to state and local taxes at same rate as tangible property of other taxpayers not performing public services. (KRS 136.120). For rates, see subheads State Tax Rates and Local Tax Rates, supra.

Cabinet determines fair cash value of operating property of public service corporation as unit. In case of public service corporation with property or routes only in Kentucky, operating property is allocated within Kentucky as provided below. In case of public service corporation with property or routes in and outside of Kentucky, fair cash value of operating property is apportioned to Kentucky based on average of property factor (which must reflect amount of operating property in Kentucky compared to operating property everywhere) and business factor (which must reflect use of operating property in Kentucky compared to use of operating property everywhere). (KRS 136.160). Operating property so apportioned to Kentucky is allocated within Kentucky as provided below.

Cabinet must allocate assessment of operating property in Kentucky among local taxing authorities in proportion to location of operating property and length of lines or routes. (KRS 136.170).

Non-operating tangible and non-operating intangible property of such taxpayers is valued by Revenue Cabinet as if such property were being valued by property valuation administrator in county where property has taxable situs. (KRS 136.160[3]). Assessed value of non-operating tangible property is allocated to local taxing authority where property is situated. (KRS 136.170).

Special provision is made for taxation of watercraft owned by water transportation companies. (KRS 136.181-136.186).

Review of Assessment by Revenue Cabinet.—Revenue Cabinet, immediately after fixing value of operating property and other property of public service corporation for taxation, must notify corporation of valuation and amount of its assessment for state and local purposes. (KRS 136.180). Pending outcome of any appeal, taxpayer must pay tax based on taxpayer's estimate of true value; upon final determination of valuation, taxpayer must pay any additional tax plus interest from date tax would have been due if no appeal taken. (KRS 136.180).

When the valuation of operating property and other property of public service corporation has been finally determined, Cabinet must immediately certify unless otherwise specified to county clerk of each county in which any portion of operating property or non-operating tangible property assessment of corporation is liable to local taxation amount of property liable for local tax. County clerk must file certificate of valuation in his office and certify to proper collecting officer of county, city or taxing district amount for collection. For local taxes on property of railroad or railway companies operating solely in Kentucky, Cabinet also to compute annually multiplier to be applied against local tangible property tax rates. Multiplier equals statewide locally taxed business tangible property divided by total statewide business personal property. For determining local taxes to be collected for railroad carlines, Cabinet to calculate annually aggregate local rate for each local taxing district. Rate is statewide tangible tax rate multiplied by fraction with numerator being commercial and industrial tangible property assessment subject to full local rates and denominator being total commercial and industrial tangible personal property assessment. (KRS 136.180).

Reports.—Every public service corporation must annually, between Dec. 31 and Apr. 30, make and deliver to Revenue Cabinet at Frankfort report in form prescribed by Cabinet, showing such facts as listed in KRS 136.130 or as Cabinet may request. Report must cover 12 months ending Dec. 31, but Cabinet may change date of report to conform to any change in date established by Federal regulations. If corporation is in hands of receiver or other person by order of court, report must be made by receiver or other person. Revenue Cabinet may grant public service company 30 day extension to file if good cause exists, taxpayer's request is before due date, and taxpayer reports any change in property of $50,000 or more. (KRS 136.130).

Railroad corporation owning or operating a railroad out of Kentucky need report for tangible property assessment only such proportion of its rolling stock as its railroad mileage in Kentucky bears to its total railroad mileage. (KRS 136.140).

In case of failure to report, Cabinet may ascertain required facts and values in such manner and by such means as it deems proper, at cost of corporation in default. (KRS 136.150).

Substantial penalties are prescribed for willful failure or refusal to make required reports or for delinquency in payment of taxes. (KRS 136.990).

Local Taxes.—Operating property of public service corporation, whether domestic or foreign, is taxable in each county, city or district where operating property is located or through or into which its lines or routes pass or are operated, in proportion which operating property or length of its lines or routes in such county, city or district bears to total operating property or length of its lines in Kentucky. (KRS 136.170). Railroad bridges spanning any river constituting state boundary are localized for taxation in county or city where located. (KRS 136.200).

PROVIDER TAX:

Tax of 2% of gross revenues received by all providers of hospital services, nursing facility services, intermediate care facility services for mentally retarded, licensed home health care services and health maintenance organization services. (KRS 142.303, 142.307). Tax of 1.5% until June 30, 1997, 1% from July 1, 1997 until June 30, 1998, and 0.5% from July 1, 1998 until June 30, 1999 on gross revenues received by all providers of physician services. After June 30, 1990, no tax imposed on physician services. (KRS 142.309). Provider is any person receiving gross revenues for provision of health care items or services in Kentucky, excluding any facility operated by federal government. (KRS 142.301). Tax also imposed on pharmacies and other persons who dispense or deliver certain outpatient prescription drugs. (KRS 142.311).

RACE TRACKS:

Race tracks subject to license taxes imposed pursuant to KRS 137.170, 138.570 and 138.480 in lieu of all other taxes to state or any subdivision thereof. (KRS 137.190). Excise tax on certain types of racing imposed by KRS 138.510.

REAL ESTATE CONVEYANCE TAX:

Tax of $3 is collected by county clerk in addition to other taxes and fees described herein upon recording of filing of each power of attorney to convey real or personal property, on each mortgage, financing statement or security agreement, on each conveyance of real property and on each lien or conveyance of coal, oil, gas or other mineral right or privilege. (KRS 142.010). In addition, tax of 50¢ for each $500 of value is imposed for privilege of transferring title to real property. Computation is made on actual purchase price or in case of gift on property's fair market value. (KRS 142.050). Tax not imposed on transfers: (1) to U.S., state or political subdivision for no consideration or nominal consideration; (2) to provide or release security of debt; (3) to confirm or correct previously recorded deed; (4) between husband and wife or between former spouses as part of divorce proceeding; (5) on sale for delinquent taxes or assessments; (6) to partition property; (7) pursuant to merger of corporations, partnerships or limited liability companies; (8) between subsidiary and parent corporation for no consideration, nominal consideration or in sole consideration of cancellation or surrender of either corporation's stock; (9) under foreclosure proceeding; (10) between person and corporation, general partnership, limited partnership, registered limited liability partnership, or limited liability company in amount equal to portion of value of real property transferred that represents proportionate interest of transferor of property in entity to which property transferred, if transfer for nominal consideration; (11) between parent and child or grandparent and grandchild for nominal consideration; (12) by corporation, general partnership, limited partnership, registered limited liability partnership, or limited liability company to person as owner or shareholder upon dissolution of entity in amount equal to portion of value of real property transferred that represents proportionate interest of individual transferee, if transfer for nominal consideration; (13) to trustee (as defined in KRS 386.800) to be held in trust or from trustee to beneficiary of trust if grantor is sole beneficiary of trust, grantor is beneficiary of trust and direct transfer from grantor of trust to all other individual beneficiaries of trust and direct transfer from grantor of trust to all other individual beneficiaries of trust would have qualified for exemption pursuant to one of exemptions previously enumerated herein, or direct transfer from grantor of trust to all other individual beneficiaries of trust would have qualified for exemption pursuant to one of exemptions previously enumerated herein; (14) between trustee and successor trustee; (15) between limited liability company and any of its members. (KRS 142.050[7]). No deed may be considered legally lodged for record until tax has been paid thereon. (KRS 382.260).

SALES AND USE TAXES:

Sales Tax.—Tax of 6% of gross receipts is imposed upon all retailers for privilege of making retail sales and leases of tangible personal property. (KRS 139.200; KRS 139.340). Tax must be collected by retailer from consumer and constitutes debt of retailer to state. (KRS 139.210). Gross receipts from rentals or leases entered into or renewed after July 31, 1985 are subject to tax. (KRS 139.532).

Use Tax.—Complementary use tax of 6% is imposed on tangible personal property purchased outside Kentucky for storage, use or consumption in state (KRS 139.310) unless sales tax at least equal to that in Kentucky has been paid and taxing state grants similar credit for sales tax paid Kentucky (KRS 139.510). Use tax payable by rental vehicle certificate holder (KRS 281.615) regularly engaged in renting or leasing motor vehicles to retail customers may be paid at rate of 6% of fair market rental of vehicle, but not less than actual charges, and tax may be passed on to customers (KRS 138.463).

Exemptions from Sales and Use Taxes.—Excluded from computation of amount of taxes are receipts from sale, storage, use or consumption of: (1) Gasoline and special fuels taxed under KRS c. 138, motor vehicles taxed under KRS 138.460 and distilled spirits, wine and malt beverages taxed under KRS c. 243 (KRS 139.050[3]); (2) sales for resale or of permanent lodgings (KRS 139.100); (3) blood or human tissues such as corneas, bones or organ transplants (KRS 139.125); (4) property purchased for resale or for shipment or use solely outside state (KRS 139.150); (5) tangible personal property which Constitution or laws of U.S. or Constitution of state prohibit being taxed, such as sales or use by federal government, sales in or use in interstate or foreign commerce (KRS 139.470[1]); (6) returnable and nonreturnable containers when sold without contents to persons who fill and re-sell containers with contents (KRS 139.470[2][a]); (7) returnable containers when sold with contents in retail sale of contents or when resold for refilling (KRS 139.470[2][b]); (8) tangible personal property for performance of fixed sum, fixed fee contract for public works executed prior to Feb. 5, 1960 (KRS 139.470[3]); (9) occasional sale (KRS 139.470[4]); (10) tangible personal property sold to common carriers for use outside state (KRS 139.470[5]); (11) tangible personal property sold through coin-operated bulk vending machines for 50¢ or less by retailer primarily engaged in making such sales (KRS 139.470[6]); (12) property or services sold to or used solely in governmental functions by any agency of state government or any county, city or local government district (KRS 139.470[7]); (13) natural gas, electricity, fuel oil, bottled gas, coal, coke, wood, or sewer services or water sold to Kentucky residents for use in heating, water heating, cooking, lighting or other residential uses (KRS 139.470[8]); (14) any rate increase for school taxes or other charges or surcharges added to total amount of residential telephone bill (KRS 139.470[9]); (15) prescription medicines, medical oxygen purchased for private use, or prosthetic devices and physical aids (KRS 139.472); (16) tangible personal property sold to out-of-state agency, organization, or institution exempt from sales and use tax in its state of residence when that agency, organization or institution gives proof of its tax exempt status to seller and seller maintains file of such proof (KRS 139.470[10]); (17) newspaper inserts or catalogs purchased for use outside Kentucky and delivered outside Kentucky by seller's vehicle, common carrier or U.S. Postal Service; (18) rolling stock and locomotives, including materials necessary for operation (KRS 139.480[1]); (19) coal for manufacture of electricity (KRS 139.480[2]); (20) all energy or energy-producing fuels used in course of manufacturing, processing, mining or refining to extent cost of

See note at head of Digest as to 1998 legislation covered.

See Topical Index in front part of this volume.

SALES AND USE TAXES . . . *continued*
energy or fuels exceeds 3% of cost of production (KRS 139.480[3]); (21) livestock of kind products of which ordinarily constitute food for human consumption if sale made for breeding or dairy purposes and either by or to person regularly engaged in business of farming (KRS 139.480[4]); (22) poultry for breeding or egg business (KRS 139.480[5]); (23) farm workstock for use in farming operations (KRS 139.480[6]); (24) seed for farming, feed for livestock and poultry (KRS 139.480[7]); (25) commercial fertilizer sold to or used by farmers regularly engaged in producing food for human consumption (KRS 139.480[8]); (26) machinery used directly in manufacturing or processing production process for new and expanded industry (processing production includes: processing and packaging of raw materials, in-process materials, and finished products; processing and packaging of farm and dairy products for sale; and extraction of minerals, ores, coal, stone and natural gas) and replacement machinery which will increase consumption of recycled materials at facility by 10% or more (KRS 139.480[10]); (27) farm machinery and repair and replacement parts thereof used exclusively in farming operations but not including motor vehicles (KRS 139.480[11]); (28) certified pollution control facilities defined in KRS 224.01-300 and, through June 30, 1994, all materials, supplies, repair and replacement parts for such facilities used in steel making process (KRS 139.480[12]); (29) tombstones and other grave markers (KRS 139.480[13]); (30) on-farm facilities and components for grain or soybean storing, drying, processing or handling (KRS 139.480[14]); (31) gasoline and other fuels used to operate farm machinery, on-farm grain or soybean drying facilities, on-farm poultry or livestock facilities, on-farm ratite facilities or on-farm facilities (KRS 139.480[16]); (32) textbooks and course materials used in course of study in nonprofit educational institution (KRS 139.480[17]); (33) property comprising coal fired plants to make ethanol for gasohol; (34) aircraft, repair and replacement parts and supplies used in interstate commerce for conveyance of property or passengers for hire (KRS 139.480[19]); (35) property used in constructing or modifying blast furnaces (through June 30, 1994) (KRS 139.480[21]); (36) food or food products purchased for human consumption with federally issued food stamps (KRS 139.480[22]); (37) property certified as fluidized bed energy production facility (KRS 139.480[20]); (38) charges for admission to historical sites designated in National Register by U.S. Department of Interior operated by nonprofit organization and of sales of materials, supplies and services to nonprofit organization used to restore, maintain or operate such historical site (KRS 139.482); (39) ships and vessels, including property used in repair or construction of, supplies and fuel consumed in operation of and supplies consumed by crew members aboard ships and vessels used primarily in transportation of property and conveyance of persons for hire (KRS 139.483); (40) most grocery store sales of food for human consumption, but candy, confectionery and chewing gum, alcoholic beverages, cocktail mixes, soft drinks and sodas, medicines, tonics, vitamins, and dietary supplements, bottled water, pet foods, and take out or carry out prepared foods and foods sold through nonmechanical self-service vending systems not included within this exemption (KRS 139.485); (41) sales of property or services to educational, charitable or religious bodies if used solely for such purposes and sales of food to students in school cafeterias and lunchrooms or sales other than athletic tickets by nonprofit, school sponsored organizations (KRS 139.495); (42) first $1,000 in any year of sales by individuals and nonprofit organizations incident to garage or yard sales or fund raising events so long as sales are made by individuals or nonprofit organizations not engaged in business of selling (KRS 139.496); (43) sale or use of horses, or interest or shares in horses, provided purchase or use is made for breeding purposes only, or of stallion services, or of horses less than two years of age at time of sale, provided sale is made to nonresidents of Kentucky and horse is transported out of state following sale or training period in state (KRS 139.531); (44) lease or rental of films to commercial theaters charging sales tax on admission charges (KRS 139.484); (45) on-farm facilities used exclusively for raising poultry or livestock (KRS 139.480[15]); (46) industrial supplies (KRS 139.470[11]); (47) property in this state upon which similar sales tax has been levied by another state in amount equal to or greater than amount of tax imposed in Kentucky (KRS 139.510); (48) machinery and equipment used to recycle waste materials (KRS 139.480[23]); (49) farm chemicals used in production of crops as business, or in raising and feeding of livestock or poultry, products of which ordinarily constitute food for human consumption (KRS 139.480[8]); (50) ratite birds, eggs to be used in agricultural pursuit for breeding and production of ratite birds, feathers, hides, breeding stock, eggs, meat, and ratite by-products and certain items used in ratite breeding (KRS 139.480[24]); (51) embryos and semen used in reproduction of livestock, that ordinarily constitutes food for human consumption, if sale is made to person engaged in farming (KRS 139.480[25]); (52) llamas and alpacas to be used as beasts of burden or in agricultural pursuits, and feed, feed additives, insecticides, fungicides, herbicides, etc. and on-farm facilities, used therein (KRS 139.480[26]); and (53) buffaloes to be used as beasts of burden or in agricultural pursuit (KRS 139.480[27]); aquatic organisms sold directly to or raised by person regularly engaged in business of producing agriculture products (KRS 139.480[28]); and water sold to person regularly engaged in business of farming and used to produce crops, produce milk for sale, or raise and feed livestock or poultry or ratites, llamas, alpacas, buffalo or aquatic organisms (KRS 139.480[29]).

Motion picture company filming in Kentucky during any 12 month period is entitled to refundable tax credit equal to sales and use tax paid for purchases made in connection with filming or production, provided reporting procedures complied with. (KRS 139.538 to 139.5386).

Morticians, undertakers and funeral directors are consumers of caskets and vaults used in their service, tax to be paid when purchased by morticians, undertakers or funeral directors. (KRS 139.5313).

Retailer selling tangible personal property for storage, use or other consumption in this state must register with department, and make application for permit. (KRS 139.390, 139.240).

Credit for sales taxes available for certain certificated air carriers which have made substantial investment in state. (KRS 144.120).

Returns are required to be filed with Revenue Cabinet on or before 20th day of month following each calendar month. Seller, retailer, or other person purchasing tangible personal property which is subject to tax which has not been paid, must file return. Taxes are payable monthly and must be remitted with return. (KRS 139.540, 139.550, 139.580). Cabinet may require taxpayers whose average monthly liability for tax exceeds $25,000 to remit tax by electronic fund transfer. (KRS 131.155). Cabinet may audit returns and must assess any tax deficiency within four years from date return was filed. (KRS 139.620).

For Regulations governing Sales and Use Tax write Revenue Cabinet, Frankfort Kentucky 40602.

Utilities gross receipts are taxable under sections of general sales and use tax, supra; limited exemption applies to sales of energy or energy producing fuels used in manufacturing, processing, mining, or refining. (KRS 139.480).

SPECIAL FUELS TAX:

See topic Gasoline and Special Fuels Taxes, subhead Special Fuels Tax.

STAMP TAX:

No stamps required by state law on any written instruments, but stamps required on containers or packages of beer, wines, spirituous liquors, cigarettes, etc. See topic Sales and Use Tax.

UNEMPLOYMENT COMPENSATION TAX:

Unemployment compensation tax, in form of "contributions" is imposed by KRS c. 341. Act applies to any employing unit (as defined in KRS 341.060 and 300 Ky. 1, 187 S.W.2d 821) which has in any calendar quarter in either current or previous calendar year paid for service in covered employment (as defined in KRS 341.050 with exemptions in KRS 341.055) wages of $1,500 or more. (KRS 341.070).

Definition "covered employment" includes service in Kentucky and in interstate commerce performed by common law employees, corporation officers, other personal services provided by persons who do not have a substantial investment in non-transportation facilities and some individuals employed by state agencies and some nonprofit organizations. Particular coverage provisions are coordinated with coverage of Federal Unemployment Tax Act. (KRS 341.050). Exemptions from "covered employment" include agricultural labor as defined in federal act, domestic service, most state agency employees, intrafamily service, most services performed for foreign governments, and international organizations, student nurses, interns, insurance agents, minor newspaper carriers, minor unrelated services and student aid services in college or vocational schools. Particular exemption provisions are coordinated with federal act. (KRS 341.055).

Basic rate for employers is 3% (2.7% for employers who become subject to KRS c. 314 on or after Jan. 1, 1999) of wages paid until employer has been subject to tax for 12 consecutive calendar quarters as of computation date (not exceeding $8,000 per annum paid any employee; but if "wages" as defined in Federal Unemployment Tax Act is amended to include remuneration in excess of $4,200 KRS c. 341 adopts same), then subject to reduction as and when justified by employer's benefit experience. There is no tax on employees. (KRS 341.030, 341.270).

Contributions must be remitted quarterly by the employer, to the Division of Unemployment Insurance. (KRS 341.260 and administrative regulations).

Nature and history of tax and status of lien securing it are discussed in 299 Ky. 224, 184 S.W.2d 963.

UNIFORM FEDERAL LIEN REGISTRATION ACT AMENDED:

See topic Administration, subhead Uniform Federal Lien Registration Act Amended.

USE TAX:

See topic Sales and Use Taxes.

TRANSPORTATION

MOTOR VEHICLES:

Commercial vehicles regulated by Department of Vehicle Regulation within Transportation Cabinet, State Office Building, Frankfort, Kentucky 40601. (KRS 186.005[1]). Motor vehicles other than commercial vehicles regulated by Transportation Cabinet, State Office Building, Frankfort, Kentucky 40601 and by Justice Cabinet, Credit Union Building, 417 High Street, Frankfort, Kentucky 40601. (KRS 186.005[1]). Commercial and noncommercial motor vehicles alike are registered by County Clerks under regulations promulgated by Department or one or other of Cabinets. (KRS 186.020).

Vehicle license required, renewable annually during driver's birth month for all motor vehicles under 6,000 lbs., including motorcycles, and on or before Apr. 1 for commercial vehicles in excess of 6,000 lbs., provided that apportioned vehicles will be registered on staggered basis to be established by regulation. (KRS 186.020; 186.170; 186.050; 186.151; 186.170; 186A.035). License required for trailers, semi-trailers, manufactured homes and recreational vehicles, other than those regulated by Motor Carrier Act (for which license may be required under KRS c. 281), or privately owned trailers used for transporting boats, luggage, personal effects, or farm products, supplies or equipment (KRS 186.650-186.700). Number plate must be displayed at rear except for semitrailer-tractor for which display upon front required. (KRS 186.170). County clerks prohibited from renewing or transferring registration for motor vehicle if ad valorem tax thereon is due and not paid. (KRS 185.021). See category Taxation, topic Taxes, subhead Rates. County clerks prohibited from renewing or issuing registration if motor vehicle is not insured in accordance with KRS 304.39-080. (KRS 186.021). If insurance for vehicle is canceled or not renewed, and owner does not provide proof of insurance after notice from department, vehicle registration is revoked. (KRS 186A.040). In such case, owner must pay fee and show proof of insurance to have registration reinstated. (KRS 186.180).

Separate registration requirements if vehicle owned or leased by U.S. or local governmental unit. (KRS 186.060; 186A.080).

No special statutory provision for members of Armed Forces.

See note at head of Digest as to 1998 legislation covered.

See Topical Index in front part of this volume.

MOTOR VEHICLES . . . *continued*

Mobile homes, manufactured homes and recreational vehicles dealers and manufacturers must be licensed or certified by licensure and certification boards. (KRS 227.620; 227.565).

Operator's Licenses.—Minimum age for operator's license is 16. (KRS 186.440). Licenses issued initially for time until operator reaches age 21 (KRS 186.531[1]) and then licenses are renewable every four years during month of birth. (KRS 186.4101). Fee, $8 or $18 for combination motor vehicle—motorcycle license, $12 for four-year motorcycle renewals. (KRS 186.410, 186.531). Instruction permit may be obtained for one year period from clerk. Licensed operator at least 21 years of age must occupy seat aside holder of instruction permit, when vehicle is in operation. (KRS 186.450).

Examination of initial applicants by State Police required, but persons holding valid license from another state which grants reciprocity to Kentucky licensees exempt from new examination. (KRS 186.480).

Except in cases of hardship, any person under age of 18 not high school graduate or not successfully participating in school or not being schooled at home not eligible for license (KRS 186.440[2]); 16 and 17 year old students who drop out of school or are academically deficient may have their licenses revoked or denied (KRS 159.051; 186.560[10]). Students under 18 who apply for instruction permit must prove they are high school graduates or are still in school. (KRS 186.440[2]).

Any person who fails to attend certain drivers' training courses within one year of being issued initial license will have driving privilege suspended until driver attends traffic school. (KRS 186.410).

Manufacturer or dealers license required.

Drivers of commercial motor vehicles, as defined in 49 U.S.C. App. §2716 and as supplemented by regulations of State Transportation Cabinet, to include vehicles designed to transport 16 or more persons, certain hazardous materials and others having vehicles defined in federal law, required to have one but not more than one license. (KRS 281A.020).

Members of Armed Forces exempt when operating official vehicle in course of service if furnished with operator's permit by U.S. (KRS 186.420).

Commercial Drivers' Licenses.—No person who drives commercial motor vehicles may have more than one driver's license. (KRS 281A.060). Holder of commercial driver's license considered to hold valid Kentucky license issued per KRS 186.412. (KRS 281A.170[6]). Transportation Cabinet issues commercial drivers licenses. (KRS 186.412[2]). Commercial vehicle is motor vehicle which is designed to carry property and meets weight standards set by 49 U.S.C. App. §2716 and Transportation Cabinet; designed to carry 16 or more passengers including driver; transporting of hazardous materials; or any other vehicle Transportation Cabinet requires to be operated by licensed commercial driver. (KRS 281A.010[7]). School bus operators must have commercial driver's license. (KRS 189.540[3]). KRS 281A does not apply to emergency equipment operators, military vehicles if operator is licensed by military and is in uniform in pursuit of military purpose, drivers of agricultural transporters operated by private carrier within 150 highway miles of point of origin or drivers of self-powered recreational vehicle. (KRS 281A.050). Qualification for license: resident of Kentucky, holds valid operator's license issued per KRS 186.412 and has passed state police administered maximum federal knowledge and skill tests for driving commercial vehicles. (KRS 281A.130 and .160). Person who has been resident of Kentucky for 30 days shall not drive commercial vehicle under another jurisdiction's commercial driver's license. (KRS 281A.140). Commercial license issued with clarification, endorsements and restriction. (KRS 281A.170). Commercial license normally expires after four years. (KRS 281A.170[4]). License issued to those 21 or over; if issued to person 18-21 certain restrictions apply, such as license marked with "I" restriction limiting driver to Kentucky intrastate commerce and depending on class of vehicle. (KRS 281A.120; 281A.170[4]). Current commercial vehicle operators holding valid Kentucky operator license eligible for grandfathering under KRS 281A.200. Grandfather permit runs from Jan. 1, 1991 to Apr. 1, 1992. Licenses issued per 281A.200 expire in birth month and year of regular operator's license. (KRS 281A.200). Purpose of KRS c. 281A is to implement Federal Commercial Motor Vehicle Safety Act of 1986.

Motorcycle License.—Operation of motorcycle on public highways prohibited except when operator is in possession of valid operator's license. (KRS 189.285). Protective headgear required for persons under age 21, persons operating motorcycle under instruction permit, persons operating motorcycle under motorcycle or motor vehicle-motorcycle license held for less than one year, and persons who do not show proof of health insurance at time of application for license to operate motorcycle without protective headgear. (KRS 189.285; 189.865). Instruction permit available for one year period for motorcycle operation. (KRS 186.450[2]).

Moped License.—Operation of mopeds on public highway prohibited without operator's license. (KRS 186.410).

Titles.—Registration of vehicle ownership must be made with county clerk in county of residence (or in county of principal operation if owned by nonresident or by other than individual) before operation of vehicle on public highways permitted. (KRS 186.020). Owner must apply to bureau of vehicle regulation, through county clerk in appropriate county for certificate of title in his name. (KRS 186A.065; 186A.120-186A.170). Reciprocity for registration and fee exemptions provided nonresidents operating vehicles properly registered in another state (KRS 186.140) and for motor carriers (KRS 281.835). Persons moving to state must register vehicle in state within 15 days. (KRS 186.020; 186.150; 186A.095). Registration and titling of new motor vehicles requires delivery to clerk of bill of sale and/or manufacturer's certificate of origin. (KRS 186.020; 186A.115[3] [a]). Registration and titling of motor vehicles previously registered in another state requires delivery to clerk of proof of insurance, certificate of title or bill of sale and registration receipt. (KRS 186.020; 186A.115[3] [a]). For sale of vehicles titled and registered in state, see subhead Sales, infra.

Last registered owner of vehicle deemed to be owner for purpose of enforcing regulatory statutes (KRS 189.228; 189.752) but Sales Article of Uniform Commercial Code (KRS 355.2-101 et seq.) determines ownership for purposes of tort liability (455 S.W.2d 52). KRS c. 186A rather than general law of sales, govern issue of who owns motor vehicle for insurance purposes. (762 S.W.2d 414). Copy of registration receipt shall be kept in owner's possession and, except for motorcycles, copy must be kept in vehicle for inspection. (KRS 186.170).

Sales.—Delivery of title and, in some cases, notarized affidavit setting forth total and actual consideration paid for motor vehicle to county clerk necessary to evidence sale of vehicle previously registered in state to new owner. (KRS 186.190; 138.450; 186.200). Upon presentation and payment of $3 fee, clerk issues registration transfer. (KRS 186.190; 186.200). Registration receipt and bills of sale must be accompanied by completed assignment and warranty of title and application for new title. (KRS 186A.215). Retail installment sales regulated in detail. Finance charges limited and buyer permitted to anticipate payments. (KRS 190.090-190.140).

As to tax on sales of motor vehicles, see category Taxation, topics Sales and Use Taxes and Motor Vehicle Usage Taxes.

Previous owner-user's name must be supplied to prospective purchaser by dealers or salesmen. (KRS 190.080[2]).

Odometer tampering prohibited. (KRS 190.260-190.320).

Liens.—Security interest in motor vehicles governed by motor vehicle registration statutes (KRS cc. 186 and 186A) and Uniform Commercial Code (KRS c. 355). Except when vehicle is in dealer's inventory (344 S.W.2d 383), perfection, assignment and discharge of security interest and other liens on motor vehicles are effected solely by notation on certificate of title by county clerk in county of debtor's residence or, if debtor is nonresident, in county in which vehicle is principally situated or operated; if debtor is other than natural person, KRS 355.9-401(5) governs determination of debtor's county of residence; if debtor does not reside in Kentucky, notation done with county clerk in county where property is principally situated or operated. (KRS 186A.190). Secured party perfects security interest by submitting standard title lien statement to county clerk along with required fees and either application for first title for vehicle or dealer's existing certificate of title. (KRS 186A.195). Clerk enters secured party's name, mailing address and zip code along with date lien noted into automated title system so that title when issued by Department of Vehicle Regulation carries information on up to two liens. (KRS 186A.190 and 186A.195). County clerk entitled to charge $10.50 per motor vehicle for noting and perfecting security interest, $3 of which is transmitted to state treasurer. (KRS 186A.190[7]). Clerk retains original of lien statement and sends copy to secured party. (KRS 186A.190[6]). Perfected security interests in motor vehicles may be assigned by filing statement of assignment with county clerk in county where lien statement filed (KRS 186.045) and paying fee of $8 (KRS 64.012). On termination of lien or security interest, secured party has obligation to file termination statement within ten days with clerk, with copy to debtor, and clerk discharges security interest by notation on title. (KRS 186.045). Secured party subject to penalty up to $250 if individual or $500 if corporation for each offense for failure to file termination statement within ten days. (KRS 186.045[2]; 186.990[1]); 534.040[2]; 534.050[1].

Identification Marks.—Felony to alter or remove serial numbers or other identification marks of maker; unlawful to deal with or possess car so altered.

Operation Prohibited.—Motor vehicles may not be operated anywhere in state by persons under influence of alcohol or other substance which impairs driving ability. (KRS 189A.101[1]). Motor vehicle may not be operated anywhere in state while blood alcohol concentration is 1/10 of 1% or greater, or for persons under 21, 2/100 of 1% or greater, as determined by blood or breath analysis. (KRS 189A.010[1]; KRS 189A.005[1]). Presence of alcohol concentration less than 5/100 of 1% raises presumption that operator is not under influence of alcohol. Presence of 5/100 of 1% or greater, but less than 1/10 of 1%, raises no presumption that operator is, or is not, under influence. (KRS 189A.010[2]). Presence of 5/100ths of 1% or more by weight of alcohol in blood requires minimum four hour detention following arrest. (KRS 189A.110). Penalties for first offense within five year period can include fines to $500 or imprisonment to 30 days, or both (KRS 189A.010[4]), pretrial suspension of operator's license (KRS 189A.060) and revocation of license for 90 days (KRS 189A.070). Motor vehicles may not be operated on public highways by person not holding valid operator's license. (KRS 186.410; 186.990[3]). Additional $20 fine shall be collected for deposit into brain injury trust fund established pursuant to KRS 211.476. (KRS 189A.010[10]). Operator's license shall be revoked or denied for not less than five years upon conviction for murder or manslaughter resulting from operation of motor vehicle, and for six months for first offense and for one or two years for second and subsequent offenses, for perjury or making false affidavit on forms relating to operation of motor vehicles or vehicle regulation, hit and run driving, motor vehicle theft, second and subsequent failures to obtain and maintain liability and no-fault insurance coverage, or conviction of fraudulent use of driver's license, or conviction of operating motor vehicle, motorcycle, or moped without operator's license, or if person is under 18 years old and has dropped out of school or is academically deficient. (KRS 186.560). Various prohibitions in addition to size and weight limits (see subhead Size and Weight Limits, infra), apply to operation of vehicles with chains, lugs, solid tires and regrooved or recut tires. (KRS 189.190 to 189.205).

Implied consent law adopted whereby operator, or person in physical control of vehicle, deemed to have agreed to one or more tests of alcohol or drug content. First instance of refusing to take test results in revocation of license for six months. (KRS 189A.103; KRS 189A.107).

Equipment Required.—Regulated by KRS 189.080-189.140. Use of seat belts is required (KRS 189.125[6]) for failure of which driver is subject to $75 fine (KRS 189.990[25]). Use of child restraint systems, or infant seats, is required (KRS 189.125[3]); violation punishable by $50 fine (KRS 189.990[24]).

Size and Weight Limits.—Regulated by KRS c. 189.

Lights Required.—Regulated by KRS 189.040, 189.050.

Inspection.—Inspection required by certified inspector (designated by county sheriff) of every vehicle, except new motor vehicles sold by licensed dealer, brought into state before application for new registration and certificate of title may be submitted to county clerk. (KRS 186A.115).

See note at head of Digest as to 1998 legislation covered.

See Topical Index in front part of this volume.

KY – 57

MOTOR VEHICLES ... *continued*

Trucks and semi-trailers are subject to special regulations as to speed, size and load limits. See KRS c. 189.

Accidents.—Operator of any vehicle involved in accident resulting in injury to or death of any person or resulting in damage to another vehicle or other property has duty to stop, notify law enforcement officer, ascertain extent of injury or damage, render reasonable assistance to injured person or persons, and provide, if requested, registration information on vehicle and names of owner, occupants and operator, and render written report of accident to Justice Cabinet, Department of State Police within ten days if accident involved personal injury or death or property damage exceeding $500. (KRS 189.580; 189.635). If operator of vehicle incapacitated, another occupant in vehicle at time of accident capable of making report shall do so. State police may require operator to render supplemental reports and may require witnesses of accidents to render reports. (KRS 189.635). Failure to comply with statutory requirements is violation punishable by fine. (KRS 189.990[1]). Law enforcement officers investigating scene of accident are required to file written report of accident within ten days after investigation. (KRS 189.635).

Parking lot operators are liable as bailees for hire for safekeeping of automobiles, and may not contract to avoid liability. (KRS 189.700-189.720).

Owner's Liability.—The owner of a car is not liable for the negligence of others unless he was present in the car or the car was operated by his servant or agent within the scope of authority and duty, except that joint and several liability with a minor under 18 for the negligence of such minor is imposed on: (1) An owner who causes or knowingly permits such minor to drive his motor vehicle on a highway; (2) any person giving or furnishing a motor vehicle to such minor; and (3) a parent, guardian or employer of such minor who signed on behalf of such minor an application on which he was licensed. (KRS 186.590). The "family purpose doctrine" is applied in Kentucky. (235 Ky. 749, 32 S.W.2d 324).

Guests.—Owner or operator is liable for injury to or death of guest resulting from negligence in operation. (243 Ky 533, 534, 49 S.W.2d 347).

Proof of Financial Responsibility.—See subhead No-Fault Insurance, infra, for description regarding mandatory insurance coverage. Motor vehicle operators license may be suspended for nonpayment within 60 days of final judgment rendered by court in Kentucky or other state upon cause of action arising out of ownership, maintenance or use of motor vehicle unless judgment creditor consents in writing that operator be allowed to maintain license. (KRS 187.400-410).

Insurance.—See subhead No-fault Insurance, infra, for description regarding mandatory liability insurance coverage. All liability policies issued in state must have uninsured motorist coverage unless insured affirmatively rejects such coverage in writing. (KRS 304.20-020). County clerks may not register or renew registration for vehicles which are not covered by mandatory insurance or other security. (KRS 186.021). Insurance companies required to notify Department of Vehicle Regulation monthly of cancellations or nonrenewals of insurance coverages during previous month except those whose nonrenewal was at end of policy with term of six months or longer and who failed to make payment for renewal of policy. (KRS 304.39-085). On notification of cancellation or nonrenewal of mandatory coverage, insured must provide proof of new insurance to Department of Vehicle Regulation or county clerk within 30 days or face fine up to $1,000, revocation of vehicle registration and 90 days in jail, and for second or subsequent offense, revocation of operator's license, fine of at least $1,000 and not more than $2,500 and 180 days in jail. (KRS 186A.040; 304.99-060).

No-Fault Insurance.—Comprehensive no-fault insurance plan, based on Uniform Motor Vehicle Accident Reparations Act, adopted effective July 1, 1975 to provide "basic reparation benefits" to insured for net losses suffered by him and his additional insureds for personal injuries and limiting right to sue for general damages. Claims for property damage are excluded from no-fault insurance plan. (KRS 304.39-010 to 304.39-340).

Specific sections of chapter in insurance code provide as follows: All operators and users of motor vehicles, other than motorcycle operators and passengers who are exempted from mandatory coverage of law, are deemed to have consented to certain limitations upon their tort rights unless they have affirmatively rejected benefits of Act in writing. (KRS 304.39-060; 304.39-040).

Motor vehicle registrants are required to procure insurance coverage of not less than $25,000 for all damages arising out of bodily injury sustained by one person and not less than $50,000 for all damages arising out of bodily injury sustained by all persons in one accident and $10,000 for all damages arising out of destruction of property or $60,000 coverage for all damages of any kind arising out of one accident. (KRS 304.39-080; 304.39-110). Self insurance may be provided in lieu of policy in certain circumstances. (KRS 304.39-080; 187.600).

General damages not recoverable by suit unless accident results in medical expenses which exceed $1,000, or injury or disease consists in whole or in part of permanent disfigurement, fracture to bone, compound, comminuted, displaced or compressed fracture, loss of body member, permanent injury within reasonable probability, permanent loss of bodily function, or death. (KRS 304.39-060). Two year statute of limitation applies to bring suit for general damages when suit allowed. (KRS 304.39-230). See category Civil Actions and Procedure, topic Limitation of Actions, subheads Two Years and One Year. Insurers required to offer up to $40,000 in added reparations benefits coverage, deductibles to basic reparations benefits in amounts of $250, $500, and $1,000, and under insured motorist coverage in amount equal to bodily injury liability purchased.

Procedures.—Act establishes assigned claims plan to provide basic reparation benefits to specified persons and procedure for operation of such plan; establishes procedure for payment of basic reparation benefits; provides penalties for late payments; prohibits assignment of benefits except under specified conditions; provides procedure for exchange of medical and other evidence with respect to claims; establishes Kentucky Insurance Arbitration Association for purpose of loss shifting; grants Commissioner of Insurance certain regulatory powers; provides penalties for failure to procure insurance required by Act; and requires 10% premium rate reduction for one year.

Foreign vehicle registered in home state or country, displaying license plates and operated by one holding certificates of registration required by home state exempt from registration for not exceeding reciprocal period. (KRS 186.140).

Vehicle properly registered in another state operating into or through Kentucky in interstate commerce under certificate or permit issued by Interstate Commerce Commission is exempt from registration fees and weight and excise taxes, provided state of owner's principal place of business grants Kentucky operators a like exemption and reciprocity agreement has been entered into between foreign state and Kentucky. (KRS 281.835).

Nonresident operator, duly licensed in his home state and having license in his immediate possession may operate a vehicle, including motorcycle or moped, in this state without having Kentucky instructor's permit or operator's license if home state extends reciprocal privilege. Similar privilege, with some restrictions, extended to nonresident over 16 whose home state does not require license. (KRS 186.430).

Direct Actions.—Action against insurer by injured person not allowed, until after judgment obtained against insured (330 S.W.2d 412; KRS 426.381), but judgment against uninsured motorist is not required before recovery on uninsured motorist coverage (477 S.W.2d 811).

Actions Against Nonresidents.—The Secretary of State is made agent for service of process in suits brought in Kentucky courts against nonresident operator or owner of motor vehicle arising out of accident or collision or damage caused in Kentucky thereby. (KRS 188.020-188.060; 434 S.W.2d 316).

Motor Vehicle Carriers.—Commercial vehicles and common carrier must have certificate of convenience and necessity, and contract carriers of persons and property in intrastate commerce, and in interstate commerce, insofar as permitted by U.S. Constitution, are subject to regulation and control of Bureau of Vehicle Regulation within Department of Transportation. (KRS 281.610, 281.695; 186.005).

Contract carrier must have permit, and common necessity. Each certificate and permit must be renewed annually before Jan. 1, with $25 fee. (KRS 281.011; 281.615; 281.650). Carrier must furnish bond, insurance policy or certificate of insurance insuring each vehicle owned or leased by carrier, in a liability amount based on capacity of vehicle and type of commodity carried. (KRS 281.655). (Carrier may be exempted from this requirement on showing of financial responsibility.)

Rates, fares and charges of carriers must be reasonable, and service must be adequate. (KRS 281.675). Common carrier must maintain on file with Bureau, schedule of rates, fares, charges, and classifications, and time schedule, if any, of vehicles operated under certificate. Copies must be available for inspection at designated public places. Similar provision exists with respect to contracts of contract carriers. (KRS 281.680). Common carriers must adhere to schedule on file; contract carriers must not discriminate in charges. (KRS 281.685).

Nonresident carriers must appoint agent for service of process in Kentucky before operating in state and keep information as to agent current with Bureau. (KRS 281.710). Bureau furnishes license plates appropriate to operation. (KRS 281.720). Act prescribes maximum working hours for drivers which may, but need not be, identical with federal regulations adopted by U.S. Department of Transportation. (KRS 281.730).

In order to prevent avoidance of state gasoline tax, provision is made for licensing of motor carriers, amount being based on mileage in state. (KRS 138.655 to 138.7291). Certificate holders and permit holders prohibited from advertising under any names other than names in which certificates or permits issued. (KRS 281.802). Persons advertising services for intrastate transportation of household goods must include certificate or permit number issued by bureau of vehicle regulation in advertisement. (KRS 281.802).

Transportation Department may issue motor carrier safety ratings and may require maintenance of satisfactory safety rating. (KRS c. 281).

Commercial Drivers' Licenses regulated in detail, see subhead Operator's Licenses, catchline Commercial Drivers' Licenses, supra.

Motor Vehicle Fees and Taxes.—Annual registration fees for motor vehicles are as follows: (county clerk's fee, $1 additional) (KRS 186.050): motorcycles $9, plus $7 for each sidecar attachment thereto; passenger vehicles (not more than nine passengers), farmers' trucks, gross weight 38,000 lbs. or less, school and church buses, and certain other vehicles, $11.50; commercial vehicles (excluding those engaged in hauling passengers for hire and operating under certificates of convenience and necessity) registration fees ranging from $11.50 to $1,260, according to gross weight. All registration fees 50% greater if vehicle not equipped wholly with pneumatic tires. Reduced fee for certain vehicles having gross weight over 18,000 lbs. In addition to county clerk's fees, registration fees for trailers drawn by vehicles licensed under KRS 186.050(1) (generally passenger vehicles) and camping trailers, travel trailers, etc., $4.50; all other trailers, $19.50; no fee for privately-owned trailers used to carry boats, luggage, farm products, etc.

For motor vehicles required to be titled, application for certificate of title must be accompanied by $6 fee (KRS 186A.130) unless title is needed in less than five working days in which case fee is $25 (KRS 186A.170[1]; 186A.130[3]).

Fee for manufacturer or dealers plate is $25 and $14.50 for additional plates. (KRS 186.070).

Proportional registration of commercial vehicles authorized under interstate agreements for vehicles operated in Kentucky and in other states. (KRS 186.050[13]).

Tax on Sale or Use of Motor Vehicles.—See category Taxation, topics Sales and Use Taxes and Motor Vehicle Usage Taxes.

Gasoline Tax.—See category Taxation, topic Gasoline and Special Fuels Taxes, subhead Gasoline Tax.

Lemon Law.—See category Business Regulation and Commerce, topic Consumer Protection.

See note at head of Digest as to 1998 legislation covered.

See Topical Index in front part of this volume.

LOUISIANA LAW DIGEST REVISER

Phelps Dunbar, L.L.P.
Texaco Center
400 Poydras Street
New Orleans, Louisiana 70130-3245
Telephone: 504-566-1311
Fax: 504-568-9130, 504-568-9007
Email: info@phelps.com
Baton Rouge Office: 445 North Boulevard, Suite 701, 70802-5707. Mailing address: P.O. Box 4412, 70821-4412. Telephone: 225-346-0285. Fax: 225-381-9197. Email: info@phelps.com

Reviser Profile

History: The firm of Phelps Dunbar was founded in New Orleans in 1853 by Joseph M. Dirrhammer who, with John Hansen Kennard, admitted to practice in 1858, formed the firm of Dirrhammer & Kennard. After several successor firms and changes in firm name, the firm became Phelps, Dunbar, Marks & Claverie in 1943 and became Phelps, Dunbar, Marks, Claverie & Sims in 1955. In 1990, the firm name was changed to simply Phelps Dunbar.

Although one of the oldest and largest firms in Louisiana, Phelps Dunbar is a successful combination of old traditions with young and progressive ideas of a modern law practice. While based in New Orleans, the firm's practice is national and international in scope.

Since 1972, it has grown from 32 lawyers to 215 lawyers. The firm has also opened new offices since 1984 in Baton Rouge, Louisiana; Jackson, Mississippi; Tupelo, Mississippi; Houston, Texas; and London, England.

Areas of Emphasis: Phelps Dunbar is a full service law firm which has developed departmental specialization in most phases of the law, including Corporations, Taxation, Banking, Securities, Bankruptcy, Real Estate, Admiralty, Aviation, Insurance, Antitrust, Construction, Railroads, Oil & Gas, Probate, Estate Planning, News Media, Patents, Copyrights, Legislative Counseling Gaming, Environmental Counseling and General Litigation.

Since the early 1920's the firm has followed a policy of selecting as associates only graduates who possess high academic accomplishments and of selecting its partners from among its outstanding associates thus assuring the firm of excellent legal talent and high morale.

Client Base: The clients of Phelps Dunbar are as diverse as its departments of specialization can service. Most of the clients are corporate leaders in their various fields although there are many individual clients concerned with Estate Planning, Taxation and Probate. Many of the corporate clients have had long association with the firm, one since 1875, some since the 1890's and many for eighty years or more.

Firm Activities: The firm's partners and associates are encouraged to and do participate in worthwhile civic, charitable and educational fields and to participate in legal education programs and bar activities at the local, state and national levels. Ten of the firm's partners have served as Adjunct Professors, some for as long as 25 years, in the law schools of Louisiana and Mississippi.

Management: The firm is managed by a Policy and Planning Committee composed of seven partners elected annually by the partners. This committee exercises broad supervision over the affairs of the partnership. The support staff for the firm's 215 lawyers comprises 325, including 60 paralegals. The day-to-day management of the firm, however, is carried out by the Chairman of the Policy and Planning Committee, one partner designated as Chairman of the Operations Committee, and the Administrator and Assistant Administrator.

Significant Distinctions: Louisiana Supreme Court Justices: William W. Howe, 1869-72; John H. Kennard, 1871-72 and Charles E. Fenner, 1880-93. President, American Bar Association: William W. Howe, 1897-98; President, Maritime Law Association of the United States: John W. Sims, 1980-82; George W. Healy III, 1992-1994. United States District Judges: Blake West and Jack M. Gordon who assumed the bench in 1971. Presidents, Board of Administrators, Tulane University: Charles E. Fenner, 1893-06; Esmond Phelps, 1926-50. President, Board of Trustees, University of Louisiana: John H. Kennard, 1880-84. Members, Board of Administrators, Tulane University: Walker B. Spencer, 1895-1941; Ashton Phelps, 1955-72; and John G. Weinmann, 1981-   . Dean, Tulane Law School: Charles P. Fenner 1914-21.

The firm of Phelps Dunbar and its predecessor firms have been Revisers of the Louisiana Law Digest since 1931.

LOUISIANA LAW DIGEST

(The following is a list of all Categories and Topics, including cross-references, covered in this Digest.)

LOUISIANA LAW DIGEST

Revised for 1999 edition by

PHELPS DUNBAR, L.L.P., of the New Orleans and Baton Rouge Bars.

(References are to title and section or title and chapter of the Louisiana Revised Statutes of 1950 unless otherwise indicated; C.C. indicates Revised Civil Code, 1870; C.C.P. indicates Code of Civil Procedure; C.Cr.P. indicates Code of Criminal Procedure; C.E. indicates Code of Evidence; Ch. C. indicates Children's Code; citations are to articles of the Codes. Subsequent statutes are cited by year and number of Act. Const. indicates the Constitution of the State of Louisiana of 1974, effective January 1, 1975 unless otherwise noted. Certain provisions of the Constitution of 1921 are continued as statutes. Parallel citations to the Southern Reporter begin with 104 La. and 9 La. App. See also category Courts and Legislature, topic Statutes.)

Note: Revision includes Acts 1—76 of the 1998 Regular Session effective August 15, 1998 unless otherwise indicated. Legislature meets annually but sessions in even-numbered years are reserved for fiscal matters. This revision contains all acts passed in 1998 Regular Session and in the First Extraordinary Session of 1998 (Acts No. 1–170), with effective date of June 16, 1998 for enactments of that extraordinary session unless otherwise noted.

INTRODUCTION

GOVERNMENT AND LEGAL SYSTEM:

The State of Louisiana is a constituent state of the United States of America. For further discussion of the U.S. federal system, see Introduction to the Federal Government of the United States at the beginning of this volume. A great many laws are promulgated by the federal government of the United States and are not reflected in the topics below. See the Introduction to this volume for references to the federal law topics covered.

Unlike the other 49 constituent states of the United States, Louisiana has a civil law system with roots in Roman, Spanish and French law. For information on the courts and legislature of Louisiana, see category Courts and Legislature.

HOLIDAYS:

Legal holidays, in addition to Sundays, are: Jan. 1, Jan. 8, 3d Mon. in Jan., Jan. 19, 3d Mon. in Feb., Good Friday, last Mon. in May, June 3, July 4, Aug. 30, first Mon. in Sept., 2d Mon. in October; Nov. 1, Nov. 11, 4th Thurs. and Fri. in Nov., Dec. 25; day of national or state observance of Martin Luther King, Jr.'s birthday; inauguration day in Baton Rouge; Mardi Gras in parishes of East Baton Rouge, Orleans, Plaquemines, St. Bernard, Jefferson, St. Charles, Lafayette, St. Tammany, Iberia, St. Martin, Ascension, St. James, Washington and St. John the Baptist, Calcasieu, Jefferson Davis, St. Landry, Evangeline, Cameron, Assumption, Acadia, Vermilion, St. Mary, Iberville, Pointe Coupee, Lafourche, West Baton Rouge and East and West Feliciana (T. 1, §55, as am'd Act 346 of 1988), and in all municipalities where so declared. Sat. is holiday in parish of Orleans, city of Baton Rouge, and all parishes of 2nd and 6th congressional districts except Ascension and in Calcasieu and Jefferson Davis parishes. For banking holidays, see category Business Regulation and Commerce, topic Banks and Banking. Offices of clerks of district, parish and city courts are closed on Jan. 1, 3rd Mon. of Feb., Good Friday, Memorial Day, last Mon. of May, July 4, Labor Day, Nov. 1, Nov. 11, 4th Thurs. and Fri. of Nov., Christmas Eve Day, Christmas Day, and New Year's Eve Day. (T. 1, §55[E], as am'd Act 607 of 1986). Offices of district court clerks are to be closed on Martin Luther King's Birthday observance day, and offices of clerks of city courts and parish courts may be closed on that day with approval of chief judge. (T. 1, §55[E][1][c], added Acts 495, 534 and 698 of 1993). Mardi Gras Day and Martin Luther King's Birthday are holidays for clerk of city court of Hammond and clerk of city court for Sulphur, Ward Four. (T. 1, §55[E], as am'd Act 153 of 1986 and Act 333 of 1992). Mardi Gras is legal holiday for clerks of court in parishes of East and West Feliciana, East Baton Rouge, Iberville, Pointe Coupee, West Baton Rouge, St. John the Baptist, St. Charles, Lafourche, St. Mary, Assumption, Terrebonne, St. Martin, Ascension, St. James, St. Tammany, St. Bernard, Jefferson Davis, Livingston, Acadia, Vermilion, Calcasieu, Orleans and Tangipahoa. (T. 1, §55[E][1][a][iii], am'd Act 22 of 1996 First Ex. Sess.). Clerks may close in emergency situations with prior judicial approval and subsequent official notice. (T. 1, §55[E][2], added Act 464 of 1984). Specified business operations and sale of certain consumer goods on Suns. are prohibited, with certain exemptions. (T. 51, §§191-194, as am'd Act 586 of 1985). Birthday of Martin Luther King, Jr. may be state employee holiday every other year. (T. 1, §55[B][2], as am'd Act 838 of 1985).

No election may be held on Christmas Day, Holy Saturday, Easter, Yom Kippur, Rosh Hashanah, or Passover. (T. 18, §1951, am'd Act 168 of 1972).

Holidays Falling on Sunday.—If Dec. 25, Jan. 1 or July 4 is Sunday, next day is a holiday.

Holidays Falling on Saturday.—If Dec. 25, Jan. 1 or July 4 falls on Sat., preceding Fri. is holiday.

OFFICE HOURS AND TIME ZONE:

Louisiana is in the Central (GMT −06:00) time zone. Office hours are generally from 8:30 a.m. to 5 p.m.

BUSINESS ORGANIZATIONS

AGENCY:

The rights and liabilities of principal and agent are, in general, similar to those at common law, although in Civil Code, agents are called mandatories and contract of agency is called mandate, type of legal representation of another. Civil Code provisions on mandate comprehensively restated in Act 261 of 1997 (eff. Jan. 1, 1998), amending and reenacting C.C. arts. 2985 through 3032.

Who May Act as Agents.—Emancipated minors may be appointed agents. (C. C. 3001). Married women may act as mandatories. (C. C. 1787).

ASSOCIATIONS:

A corporation unauthorized by law or by an act of Legislature may acquire and possess estates and have common interests. (C. C. 446, as am'd Acts 446 and 459 of 1978).

Co-operative associations, with or without capital stock, may be incorporated for marketing of sea food products and by-products. (T. 12, §451 et seq.).

Associations of producers of agricultural products, for the purpose of promoting the intelligent and orderly marketing of agricultural products through cooperation and to make distribution as direct as can be efficiently done between producer and consumer, are permitted. (T. 3, §§121 et seq., as am'd Acts 87-91 of 1966).

Transfers.—Where property is acquired by one or more persons acting for and in the name of an unincorporated association for religious, charitable or educational purposes, upon due incorporation of association, a transfer made by said persons, or survivors in case of death of one or more, to incorporated association vests title as fully as if made by all, free of claims of heirs of decedent or decedents. In case of death of said persons before formal transfer, title vests in said association provided it had possession as owner during life time of said trustees or subsequently for ten years. (T. 12, §207). Unless part of incorporation of association which is governed by T. 12, §207, or otherwise provided by its organizational documents, unincorporated nonprofit associations may donate, sell and encumber immovable property upon authorization by majority of members voting at special meeting. (C. C. Art. 446, as am'd Act 352 of 1980).

Actions.—An unincorporated association has the right to sue in its own name, and appears through its president or other authorized officer. (C.C.P. 689). It may be sued in its own name alone, but its members may be sued jointly with it. (C.C.P. 738).

Professional Associations.—See topic Corporations, subhead Professional Corporations.

CORPORATIONS:

By Act 105 of 1968, Ch. 1 ("Business Corporations Law," §§1-72), Ch. 2 ("Non-Profit Corporation Law," §§101-155) and Ch. 3 ("Foreign Corporations Law," §§201-245), of Title 12, were repealed, and Ch. 1 ("Business Corporation Law," §§1-178), Ch. 2 ("Non-Profit Corporation Law," §§201-269) and Ch. 3 ("Foreign Corporation Law," §§301-321) were adopted with an effective date of Jan. 1, 1969. §7 of Act provides that provisions shall be effective as to all corporations incorporated or authorized to transact business in this state whether prior or subsequent to Act. §8 provides that every corporation incorporated prior to Jan. 1, 1969, and every other person shall conclusively be deemed to have accepted all of provisions of Act unless written notice to contrary is filed with Secretary of State before Apr. 1, 1969; however, validity or effectiveness of such notice is not recognized by Act.

Limited Liability Companies.—See topic Limited Liability Companies.

General Supervision.—There is no corporation commission or commissioner having general supervision over business corporations in Louisiana, except that office of Secretary of State serves in this capacity to a limited extent.

Purposes.—Any lawful business purposes, except banking and insurance in all of their several forms, operating homesteads or building and loan associations, practicing law (except as provided in T. 12, c. 8), and business governed by special laws or prohibited by law. (T. 12, §22).

Name.—Name shall contain word "Corporation," "Incorporated," "Limited" (or abbreviations thereof), "Company" or "Co." (not preceded by "and" or "&"), unless railroad, telegraph or telephone company, and must be distinguishable from reserved or actual name of any other corporation, domestic nonprofit corporation or foreign corporation, or tradename registered with Secretary of State, except in specified cases including that charter of otherwise similar corporation has been revoked, or consisting of words deceptively or falsely suggesting charitable or nonprofit nature. (T. 12, §23, as am'd Act 296 of 1997). Name cannot include "bank," "banking," "banker," "savings," "safe deposit," "trust," "trustee," "building &/and loan," "homestead," "assurance," "casualty," "redevelopment corporation," "electric cooperative," "insurance" (except independent insurance agency), or "credit union." Name also may not include "doing business as" or "d/b/a". Secretary of State must obtain evidence that ten day written notice of application for certificate of incorporation has been given to State Board of Registration for Professional Engineers and Land Surveyors, if name includes "engineer," "Engineering," "surveyor" or "surveying." Name of intended corporation may be reserved upon request with Secretary of State for fee of $5. (T. 12, §23, as am'd Act 983 of 1993). Although no statutory provision so provides, telephone or written request for availability of name is usually honored by office of Secretary of State.

Term.—Duration of corporation is perpetual unless otherwise specified in articles. (T. 12, §24).

See note at head of Digest as to 1998 legislation covered.

See Topical Index in front part of this volume.

CORPORATIONS... *continued*

Incorporators.—One or more natural or artificial persons capable of contracting may form corporation. There are no requirements as to citizenship or residence of incorporators. (T. 12, §21).

Articles of incorporation, either acknowledged or by authentic act (see category Documents and Records, topic Acknowledgments), must be in English language and signed by each incorporator or by agent duly authorized by document attached to articles.

Articles must contain (a) Name of corporation; (b) purpose(s) or statement that purpose is to engage in any lawful activity for which corporations may be formed under T. 12, c. 1; (c) duration, if other than perpetual (but see subhead Term, supra); (d) aggregate number of shares; (e) if only one class of shares, par value or a statement that all shares are without par value; (f) if shares are divided into classes, number and par value (or a statement that shares are without par value) of shares of each class; designation of each class and each series of each preferred or special class; preferences, limitations and relative rights of each class and variations between series; authority of board to amend articles to fix preferences, limitations and relative rights of each class and to establish and fix variations of rights between series of any preferred and special class and any of these powers may be made dependent upon facts ascertainable outside articles, so long as process of determination is made clear in articles; and (g) full name and post office address of each incorporator. (T. 12, §24, as am'd Act 914 of 1997).

Articles may contain (a) Preemptive rights of shareholders or any class of shareholders (T. 12, §72 shall be deemed included in articles if articles provide: "Shareholders shall have preemptive rights."); (b) powers or rights of corporation, directors, shareholders or any class of shareholders; (c) provisions, under certain limitations, for reversion of unclaimed dividends (cash, property or share) and reclassification shares; (d) limitations on personal liability of officers or directors, except as to breach of duty of loyalty, bad faith, intentional wrongdoing, personal benefit and the like; and (e) any other provision not prohibited by law. (T. 12, §24, as am'd Act 261 of 1987). Actions alleging violation of preemptive rights must be brought within five years of issuance of shares to which those rights apply. (T. 12, §72[B], added by Act 44 of 1991, eff. June 23, 1991).

Filing of Articles of Incorporation.—Articles or multiple original thereof must be filed with Secretary of State with initial report (required by T. 12, §101) and may be delivered in advance for filing as of a specified date and time within 30 days after delivery (T. 12, §25). Initial report (T. 12, §101) must be signed by each incorporator or his agent (authorization to be annexed to report) and must set forth (a) Location and post office address of registered office; (b) full name and post office address of each registered agent; and (c) names and post office address of each director, if selected, otherwise a supplemental report, in similar form, must be filed when directors are selected. If they are in compliance with corporation code, Secretary of State shall record articles and initial report, and issue certificate of incorporation. Corporate existence commences with issuance of certificate; however, if articles are filed within five days (exclusive of legal holidays) of execution of articles (by acknowledgment or authentic act), corporate existence commences as of time of execution. Multiple original of articles and initial report, or copies certified by Secretary of State, with copy of certificate of incorporation, must be filed with recorder of mortgages of parish of registered office within 30 days of filing of articles with Secretary of State. (T. 12, §25, as am'd Act 88 of 1983). If articles of incorporation or initial report should be inaccurate, or defectively executed or acknowledged, corrected articles or report may be filed. (T. 12, §35, added Act 442 of 1982).

Addresses in initial report must be location and municipal address, if any, not post office box only. (T. 12, §101, as am'd Act 459 of 1976).

Corporation incorporated in one jurisdiction including Louisiana and foreign jurisdictions may change jurisdiction of its incorporation while maintaining its corporate existence. (T. 12, §164, as am'd Act 466 of 1983).

Fees must be paid in advance to Secretary of State as follows: $50 for filing and recording articles of incorporation, or amendments thereto; or dissolutions, reinstatement or merger proceedings; fee includes all certificates and certified copies required for filing with appropriate clerk of court. Additional certified copies and certificates furnished upon request at cost of $10, or certificate only for $5. (T. 12, §171, as am'd Act 235 of 1983). Any other certificate is $5, except resignation or appointment of registered agent, change of registered office or appointment of officers and directors ($10); or annual report ($12). (T. 12, §171).

Paid in Capital.—If provided for in articles, corporation cannot incur debts or transact business except incidental to organization, obtaining of subscriptions or payment for shares, until paid-in capital is paid in full. (T. 12, §26).

Amendment of Articles.—Two-thirds vote of voting power present, or such larger or smaller vote, not less than a majority of voting power present or total voting power, as articles may require, is necessary for amendment of charter, including reclassification of stock. If amendment would adversely affect rights of stockholders of any class or series, such stockholders are entitled to vote as a class on amendment, whether or not they are entitled to vote under articles of incorporation, and same proportionate vote of such stockholders as of stockholders having right to vote is required to pass amendment, in addition to required vote of stockholders having right to vote. Unless otherwise provided in articles, shareholders' rights are not adversely affected unless amendment (otherwise as permitted by articles): (a) Alters or abolishes preferential rights; (b) creates, alters or abolishes any redemption rights; (c) alters or abolishes preemptive rights; (d) creates or alters (other than abolish) restrictions on stock transfer; (e) excludes or limits voting rights, except for limitation by voting rights of new shares being authorized on an existing or new class; and (f) alters or abolishes dividend rights, except by rights of new shares being authorized of an existing or new class. (T. 12, §31, as am'd Act 849 of 1990).

After adoption of amendment, articles of amendment shall be executed by president or vice-president or other person authorized by shareholders (a copy of which resolution or consent shall be annexed to articles) and by secretary or treasurer or any assistant secretary or assistant treasurer, and must be acknowledged by president, vice-president or other authorized person, or be in form of an authentic act. Articles must contain amendment, date and manner of adoption, number of shares of each class or series represented at meeting and voting for and against (T. 12, §32); in case of reclassification of stocks, (a) number of shares of par value and par value thereof and number having no par value, and (b) if shares are divided into classes, number of shares of each class, par or no par value of shares of each class, designation of each class and series of each preferred or special class, preferences, etc. of each class and series, and authority of board of directors to amend articles to fix rights, preferences and limitations of shares and variations of rights between series of preferred or special classes. Directors may also act with respect to numbers of shares issued and related matters. (T.12, §33, am'd Act 612 of 1989). Following reclassification, aggregate allotted value of issued shares cannot exceed stated capital. (T. 12, §54).

Articles of amendment or multiple original thereof, must be filed with Secretary of State and multiple original or copy certified by Secretary of State must be filed in mortgage office of parish of registered office. (T. 12, §32). See subhead Filing of Articles of Incorporation, supra, for similar provisions for predelivery of Articles of Amendment and effective date thereof.

Powers.—Corporation may perform any act necessary or proper to accomplish its purposes as expressed or implied in articles, or incidental thereto, which are not repugnant to law. (T. 12, §41). Corporations are specifically authorized to have a seal, to have perpetual existence (unless otherwise provided in articles, but see subhead Term, supra), to sue and to be sued, to acquire, hold, use and alienate or encumber property of any kind including own shares (unless otherwise provided in articles or by law), and shares, memberships or other interests of other businesses; to make contracts and guarantees; borrow and lend money, conduct business in this state or elsewhere, make by-laws, elect officers and establish pension plans, stock bonus and like plans, provide indemnity and insurance (T. 12, §83), make donations, and do any lawful business in time of war or national emergency. (T. 12, §41, as am'd Act 914 of 1997).

Corporations, domestic or foreign organized to develop and transmit electric power, have right to expropriate for rights of way, power plant sites and necessary buildings (T. 19, §2) and to mortgage transmission lines and extensions though not completed (T. 45, §§124, 125).

By-laws.—Unless specified in articles, board of directors may make and alter by-laws, not inconsistent with articles or law, subject to shareholders' power to change or repeal such by-laws. Emergency by-laws may be adopted by board of directors under specified conditions. (T. 12, §28).

Stock.—Corporations have power to create two or more kinds of stock of such classes and series with such designations, limitations, conversion rights, preferences, and voting powers or restrictions or qualifications as shall be stated in articles of incorporation. Stock may be with or without par value. Unless otherwise provided in articles, corporation may issue fractional shares, and board of directors may issue script for fractional shares. (T. 12, §51). Unless articles provide otherwise, corporation may issue convertible securities and stock purchase rights. (T. 12, §56). Corporation may purchase or redeem its shares out of surplus or out of stated capital. (T.12, §55, as am'd Act 175 of 1988).

Stock certificates must be signed by president and secretary or by such officers as articles or by-laws provide. Certificate must state: (a) State or incorporation; (b) name of registered holder; (c) number and class of shares; (d) par value or statement that shares have no par value; (e) name of corporation; (f), if shares of more than one class authorized, rights, voting powers, preferences and restrictions granted to or imposed upon shares of each class, and authority of board of directors to establish other series and fix relative rights, preferences and limitations of shares of any class or series; (g) if for fractional shares, limitations and restrictions thereon (other than voting rights), or that corporation will furnish upon request a summary thereof. If articles or by-laws restrict transfer of shares, reference to such restriction must be stated on certificate, or summarized, or referred to with information as to where such may be inspected. Where certificate is countersigned by transfer agent and a registrar, signature of corporation's officers may be facsimile. (T. 12, §57).

Issuance of Shares.—Par value shares may be issued initially for consideration expressed in dollars, not less than par value, as fixed by board. No-par shares may be issued for consideration expressed in dollars as fixed by board, or by majority vote of voting power present if provided in articles, or by incorporators as to initial shares. Consideration must be paid in cash, property or services actually rendered and shares shall not be issued for check (unless certified) or note of purchaser until actually paid. (T. 12, §52, am'd Act 436 of 1974).

Control Share Acquisitions.—Limitations on voting power of persons acquiring control shares as defined imposed. Unless articles of incorporation provide otherwise, person acquiring control shares has only voting rights guaranteed by statute, which are in turn determined by resolution voted upon by all disinterested shareholders. Special shareholders meeting may be called to consider such resolution. If acquiring person is accorded full voting rights, other shareholders may have dissenters' rights to fair cash value of their shares, defined as highest price paid per share by acquiring person in control share acquisition. (T. 12, §§135-140.2, as am'd Act 613 of 1990). "Safeguard period" defined and regulated. (T. 12, §§130-130.2, added Act 914, eff. July 23, 1991). Foreign corporations are subject to similar, but not identical, procedures.

Transfer of Stock.—See category Business Regulation and Commerce, topic Commercial Code.

Uniform Securities Ownership by Minors Act not adopted.

Uniform Simplification of Fiduciary Security Transfers Act adopted. (T. 9, §§3831-3840).

Stock Transfer Tax.—No State tax.

Stockholders.—Shareholders have only such preemptive rights as fixed in articles. (T. 12, §72). Unless as otherwise provided in articles and referred to in certificates, each share shall be in all respects equal to every other share. (T. 12, §51).

Stockholders' Liabilities.—Subscriber to or holder of shares not liable to corporation or its creditors other than to comply with terms of subscription. Shareholders who

See note at head of Digest as to 1998 legislation covered.

See Topical Index in front part of this volume.

LA–2

CORPORATIONS . . . *continued*
knowingly or without reasonable care consented to or voted for issuance of shares for property or services which were grossly overvalued, are liable to corporation for benefit of creditors or shareholders. Shareholder may be liable up to amount of an unlawful dividend or distribution of assets received by him. (T. 12, §93).

Stockholders' Meetings.—Unless otherwise provided in articles or by-laws, annual and special meetings of shareholders may be held anywhere within or without state, and notice of time, place and purpose of meeting must be given at least ten days but not more than 60 days prior to meeting date. Notice may be waived in writing. If more than 18 months elapse without annual meeting, any shareholder may call meeting at registered office. Special meetings may be called at any time by president or board of directors. On written request of one-fifth of total voting power (or such greater or lesser proportion as fixed in articles or by-laws), secretary must call a special meeting at registered office not less than 15 nor more than 60 days after receipt of such request. Secretary or transfer agent must certify list of shareholders entitled to vote as of record date. (T. 12, §73). Cumulative voting is allowed where articles so provide. (T. 12, §75). Shareholder may vote by written proxy filed with secretary before meeting, which proxy is not revoked by shareholder's death unless written notice thereof is received by officer maintaining list of shareholders before exercise of proxy. Unless otherwise provided, proxy may be revoked at will and validity ceases 11 months after date of execution. No proxy shall be valid in excess of three years from date of execution. (T. 12, §75). Statute provides for non-exclusive methods by which proxies may be granted. (T. 12, §75[C][6], added Act 983 of 1993).

Voting trusts are authorized for period not exceeding 15 years extendable for ten years. (T. 12, §78).

Directors.—There must not be less than one natural person who is director. If not fixed in articles or by-laws, number of directors shall be number named in initial report. Number, classification, qualifications, compensation, terms of office (not to exceed five years), manner of election, time and place of meetings, and powers and duties of directors may be fixed in by-laws. Upon vacancy, remaining directors, even if not constituting quorum, may fill vacancy for unexpired term; however shareholders may fill vacancy at special meeting called prior to action by directors. There are no requirements as to share ownership by directors or as to citizenship or residence of directors. If not provided in articles or by-laws, directors serve term of one year and until their successors are chosen and qualified. (T. 12, §81, as am'd Act 914 of 1997).

Directors' Meetings.—Meetings of directors may be held within or without state, as decided by majority vote. Notice of meeting must be given as provided in by-laws. Majority of board is necessary for a quorum.

Director may vote by proxy if, but not unless, it is so provided in articles, but proxy may be given only to a shareholder or another director. (T. 12, §81).

Powers and Duties of Directors.—All corporate power is vested in and business and affairs of corporation are managed by board of directors. Board of directors may designate committees, consisting of one or more directors, who may exercise powers to extent provided in resolution, articles or by-laws. Directors may take any action by unanimous consent signed by all directors or all members of committee. (T. 12, §81, as am'd Act 914 of 1997).

Liabilities of Directors and Officers.—Directors and officers stand in a fiduciary relationship to corporation and shareholders. Officers and directors may be liable (a) if corporation transacts business before paid in capital is received; or (b) if, knowingly and without reasonable care, they consent to issuance of shares in violation of law, or for property or services grossly overvalued. If directors knowingly, or without reasonable care, consent to unlawful dividend or distribution of assets, or to unlawful redemption of shares, they may be liable to corporation and its shareholders. (T. 12, §92[D]). Directors may rely in good faith on records of corporation, upon reports presented by corporation's officers or directors, by any committee of board of directors, or by certain experts selected with reasonable care by board or any committee or any officer having authority to make such selection. (T.12, §92[E], am'd Act 612 of 1989, eff. July 6, 1989). Directors may be indemnified by corporation, and indemnity may be through wholly-owned subsidiary, not regulated by Commissioner of Insurance. (T. 12, §83, as am'd Act 561 of 1986, eff. July 2, 1986). Any action against directors and officers for breach of their duties short of intentional conduct must be brought within one year of alleged act of one year of date alleged act is discovered or should have been discovered; if intentional conduct, respective periods are two years. (T. 12. §96, added Act 1101 of 1997, eff. July 14, 1997).

Officers.—Board of directors must elect a president, secretary, and treasurer and may elect one or more vice-presidents. Unless otherwise provided in articles, no officer need be a director and any two offices may be combined in one person. If officers are listed in articles or amendment thereto, municipal address, not post office box only, must be included for each officer.

Officers and agents shall have such authority and perform such duties as may be prescribed in by-laws, or determined from time to time by board of directors.

Any officer or agent may be removed by board of directors without prejudice to his contract rights.

Articles may provide for election of certain or all of officers by certain class of shareholders or directors.

President, vice-president or manager of any domestic or foreign corporation doing business in this state has power, in name of corporation, to authorize institution of any suit, to direct issuance of conservatory writs and to bond property in custodia legis and may, on behalf of corporation, execute any bond in connection with any legal proceedings and make any affidavit required by law or rules of court; but this authority may be modified, limited or denied by articles or by-laws or by resolution of board of directors. (T.12, §82, as am'd Act 102 of 1989).

Liabilities of Officers.—See subhead Liabilities of Directors and Officers, supra.

Reports.—An initial report is required. (See subhead Filing of Articles of Incorporation, supra.)

Annual report must be filed with Secretary of State on or before anniversary date of incorporating in Louisiana. Report must be signed by president, treasurer or other proper officer, or by two directors, and state: (a) Post office address and municipal address or location of registered office; (b) name and post office address and municipal address or location of registered agents; (c) name and post office address of each director and officer; and (d) number of issued shares of each class. (T. 12, §102, am'd Act 103 of 1992, eff. June 5, 1992).

Upon request of any stockholder of record, corporation must, once in every calendar year, send to such stockholder a verified report containing above information contained in last annual report preceding said request, together with a condensed balance sheet (showing inter alia and separately amount of stated capital, capital surplus and earned surplus). (T. 12, §102). Penalty of $50, recoverable by stockholder, is imposed on officers neglecting to send such report within 15 days after receiving said request, for every day that they neglect to do so. (T. 12, §172).

For failure to make and file an initial report, annual report, or articles, with Secretary of State within 15 days after written request by Secretary of State a penalty of $50, recoverable by Attorney General or District Attorney, is imposed on corporation for every day that it neglects to file such report. (T. 12, §172).

Registered Office.—Every corporation must continually maintain an office in state, to be known as registered office, location and post-office address or which must be stated in initial report. Registered office may be changed by vote of directors, in which case notice of change must be filed with Secretary of State and mortgage office of parish of new registered office within 30 days; and if notice is not filed within 30 days after registered office is vacated, office of Secretary of State is considered as registered office of corporation. If office is changed to another parish, notice must be filed in mortgage office of both parishes. Registered office is considered as domicile of corporation. (T. 12, §104).

Books and Records.—Corporation must keep at its registered office or at its principal place of business in or outside of state (a) books and accounts showing amounts of its assets and liabilities, receipts and disbursements, and gains and losses, and (b) records of proceedings of shareholders, directors, and committees of board; and must keep, at above stated offices or office of its transfer agent, a share register or stock certificate record showing names of shareholders, their addresses, number and classes of shares held by each, and certificate date.

Upon at least five days written demand, any one or more shareholders, except business competitor, who are holders in aggregate of at least 5% of all outstanding shares for at least six months, are entitled to examine for any proper or reasonable purpose, any and all of records and accounts of corporation. If shareholder is interposed for business competitor, or owns stock or is otherwise interested in business competitor, he or it must own not less than 25% of all outstanding shares for period of six months before exercise of privilege.

Right of inspection may be conferred upon holders of bonds, debentures and other obligations, subject to restriction by articles, by-laws, or majority of voting power of shareholders. (T. 12, §103, as am'd Act 841 of 1984, eff. July 13, 1984).

Registered Agent.—Corporation must maintain at least one registered agent which may be individual resident of this state, partnership authorized to practice law in this state, professional law corporation, or business corporation or foreign corporation authorized to do business in this state. Name and post office address of agent must be stated in initial report along with notarized affidavit of agent accepting designation as agent. Notice of change of registered agent, or name of corporate or partnership registration agent (within 30 days), must be filed with Secretary of State and mortgage office of parish of corporation's domicile, by either corporation or agent. Upon resignation of agent, within 30 days corporation must file with Secretary of State and mortgage office, certificate executed by president, secretary, or vice-president, stating name and post office address of successor agent. (T. 12, §104, as am'd Act 99 of 1988).

Revocation of Articles and Franchise.—If corporation fails to designate and maintain registered office or registered agent for 90 days, or fails to file annual report for three consecutive years, Secretary of State must revoke articles of incorporation and franchise, with 30 days prior notice to corporation. Corporation status may not be revoked if corporation brings itself into good standing. (T. 12, §163[C], as am'd Act 298 of 1997). Attorney General may seek similar relief if franchise was procured through fraud, or corporation has abused authority, or was not authorized to be formed under appropriate statute. Reinstatement of corporate status is possible under certain conditions. (T. 12, §163, as am'd Act 88 of 1983 and Act 714 of 1984).

Sale or Transfer of Corporate Assets.—Voluntary sale, lease, exchange, or other disposition of all or substantially all of a corporation's assets may be authorized only by a two-thirds (or such lesser proportion, not less than a majority of voting power present or total voting power, as articles may provide), if corporation is not insolvent, or by vote of two-thirds of entire board of directors, if corporation is insolvent. Notice to shareholders of meeting must state: "Dissenting shareholders who comply with the procedural requirements of the Business Corporation Law of Louisiana will be entitled to receive payment of the fair cash value of their shares if the transaction to be considered is effected upon approval by less than 80% of the corporation's total voting power." Suit to enjoin such sale must be brought within 90 days after corporate action authorizing such disposition. (T. 12, §121, as am'd Act 849 of 1990).

Dividends.—Board of directors may declare dividends in cash, property or shares out of surplus (except earned surplus reserved by board, T. 12, §62B), except (1) when insolvent or would thereby become insolvent, or (2) when such would be contrary to restrictions in articles. If no surplus is available, dividends may be paid out of net profits for current or preceding fiscal year, under certain restrictions. No dividend may be paid in shares other than with treasury shares, without transfer to stated capital from surplus of (1) an amount not less than aggregate par value of shares issued, and (2) an amount determined by directors in respect to no-par shares issued. Dividends in shares of a class may not be paid to shareholders of another class unless permitted by articles or authorized by a majority of voting power present of holders of shares of class in which payment is to be made. (T. 12, §63).

Unclaimed Dividends.—See subhead Articles of Incorporation, supra; also category Property, topic Absentees.

See note at head of Digest as to 1998 legislation covered.

See Topical Index in front part of this volume.

LA – 3

CORPORATIONS... *continued*

Merger or Consolidation.—Merger, consolidation or share exchange with surviving corporations may be achieved as follows: (1) Board of directors of each business, nonprofit or foreign corporation which desires to merge or consolidate shall either enter into agreement of merger or consolidation signed by majority of directors of each corporation, or adopt resolution approving agreement of merger or consolidation, and if agreement prescribes changes in articles of surviving corporation, agreement must comply with T. 12, §54A (see subhead Amendment of Articles, supra) to extent applicable; (2) agreement must be approved by shareholders of foreign corporation in accordance with law under which such was formed; (3) agreement must be approved by two-thirds (or by such larger or smaller proportion, not less than majority of voting power present or total voting power, as articles may provide) of voting power of shareholders present at any annual or special meeting, for which notice has been given, which notice must, if applicable, state: "Dissenting shareholders who comply with the procedural requirements of the Business Corporation Law of Louisiana will be entitled to receive payment of the fair cash value of their shares if the merger or consolidation is effected upon approval by less than 80% of the corporation's total voting power", and to which notice must be annexed copy or summary of agreement; and if such prescribes change in articles of surviving corporation, which change, if in form of amendment, would entitle class or series of shares to vote as class, agreement must also be approved by such vote by shareholders of such class or series as would be required for amendment; (4) secretary or assistant secretary of each corporation must certify on agreement fact of approval by shareholders, and approved and certified agreement must be signed and acknowledged by president or vice-president of each corporation; (5) approval of shareholders of surviving corporation is not required if articles of surviving corporation are not amended, if shares of such corporation to be issued or delivered do not exceed 15% of shares of same class outstanding prior to agreement, and in certain other instances, and secretary or assistant secretary must certify on agreement that approval is not required and reasons therefor; (6) adopted, certified and acknowledged agreement or, in lieu thereof, certificate of merger or consolidation must be filed with Secretary of State who, after payment of all taxes, fees and charges, shall record same, endorsing thereon date and, if requested, hour, of filing, and issue certificate of merger or consolidation. Agreement certificate may be delivered in advance to Secretary of State for filing as of specified date within 30 days of delivery. Duplicate original of certificate of merger or consolidation must be filed with mortgage office in each parish in which corporate party has its registered office, and in conveyance records of each parish in which corporate party has immovable property, title to which is transferred as result of agreement. (T. 12, §§111-112, added Act 849 of 1990). Share exchange with surviving corporation governed by statute. (T. 12, §116, added Act 849 of 1990).

Parent corporation owning at least 90% of outstanding shares of each class of a subsidiary corporation may (a) merge itself into such subsidiary by filing with Secretary of State a certificate signed and acknowledged by its president or vice-president and secretary or assistant secretary, setting forth a copy of resolution of board of directors and date thereof, and stating that resolution has been approved by parent's shareholders in manner and by vote prescribed in T. 12, §112C or that no approval is required by virtue of T. 12, §112(E); or, (b) merge subsidiary into itself by filing with Secretary of State certificate signed by such officers setting forth copy of resolutions of board of directors effecting such merger and date of adoption thereof. Duplicate original certificate issued by Secretary of State must be filed in mortgage office of each parish in which corporate party has its registered office and in conveyance office of each parish where corporations own immovable property. Copy of certificate must, within 20 days of filing with Secretary of State, be mailed to each minority shareholder of each subsidiary. Surviving corporation's name may be changed by merger resolution.

In case of consolidation into new corporation, articles and initial report are in usual form except corporations consolidating shall be named as incorporators, articles and report must be signed and acknowledged by president or vice-president and secretary or assistant secretary of each corporation, and articles must state shares, obligations, cash or other consideration to be delivered to shareholders or manner of converting shares into securities of new corporation.

"Business combinations" as defined are subject to special vote of 80% of voting stock and two-thirds of votes of those other than "interested shareholder" as defined. (T. 12, §§132-134, added Act 841 of 1984, eff. July 13, 1984).

Merger or consolidation are effective when agreement, certificate, or articles and initial report are filed with Secretary of State and upon compliance with laws under which any foreign corporation is formed, or upon later effective date, not exceeding 30 days, stated in agreement or certificate. (T. 12, §§111-115).

Commissioner of Insurance must approve merger, consolidation or acquisition of control of domestic insurer. (T. 22, §731, as am'd Act 767 of 1975).

Dissolution.—Voluntary dissolution, conducted with or without court supervision, must be authorized by majority vote of voting power of shareholders present, or by such larger vote as articles require. If without supervision of court, shareholders may appoint liquidators but appointment is not effective until notice is published at least once in local newspaper (copy thereof with affidavit of publisher must be filed with Secretary of State), and certificate, signed and acknowledged by president or vice-president and secretary or assistant treasurer must be filed with Secretary of State, which certificate must also be filed with mortgage office of parish of corporation's registered office. If shareholders do not approve liquidation out of court, corporation must file petition with court which shall name liquidator. (T. 12, §§141-142, as am'd Act 849 of 1990). If corporation is not doing business and owes no debts, it may be dissolved by filing of affidavit with Secretary of State executed by shareholders, or by incorporator if no shares have been issued. Filing shareholders or incorporator become personally liable for claims against corporation. Secretary of State must reinstate corporation so dissolved only upon court order so directing him. (T.12, §142.1, as am'd Act 142 of 1989).

On petition of Attorney General, district court may order dissolution of corporation which has violated anti-trust law. (T. 51, §139, as am'd Act 366 of 1975).

Shareholder(s) owning not less than 20% of outstanding shares for six months, a majority of directors, a judgment creditor when execution has been returned "nulla bona," or a receiver, may institute involuntary proceedings on specified grounds including: (a) Corporate assets are insufficient to pay liabilities; (b) objects of corporation have failed; (c) liquidation would be beneficial to shareholders; (d) management is deadlocked; (e) shareholders are deadlocked, but only if irreparable injury to corporation or shareholders is being suffered or is threatened and court determines dissolution is warranted after due regard for rights of other shareholders, employees and public; (f) corporation has failed to commence business for one year following incorporation or suspended business for one year; (g) corporation has committed gross and persistent ultra vires acts; (h) corporation articles and franchise have been annulled, vacated or forfeited by judgment under T. 12, §163; or (i) receiver has been appointed. Provision is also made for dissolution of corporation having only two shareholders, each owning one half the shares and those shareholders are engaged in joint venture between themselves and corporation. (T. 12, §143, as am'd Act 269 of 1985).

Proceedings for dissolution take effect when appointment of liquidator by shareholders becomes operative or when court has appointed liquidator. (T. 12, §141).

When proceeding for dissolution takes effect, all rights, powers and duties of officers and board of directors are vested in liquidator or liquidators appointed by shareholders or court, and authority and duties of officers and directors of corporation cease except as, in opinion of liquidator or liquidators, it is necessary that they be continued. (T. 12, §141). At any time before corporate existence ceases, voluntary dissolution may be terminated by such vote of shareholders as was required to commence proceedings, and certificate must be filed with Secretary of State and Recorder of Mortgages, and with court, if under supervision thereof, and notice must be published as aforesaid. (T. 12, §149).

Liquidator for out of court dissolution must prepare annual report of assets and liabilities, disposition of assets and anticipated tax year of final accounting and distribution, which must be made available to any shareholder on request. (T. 12, §145, am'd Act 312 of 1976).

Tender Offers.—Board of directors, when evaluating tender offer or offer to make tender or exchange offer or to effect merger or consolidation, may consider factors other than consideration being offered. (T. 12, §92[G]). See also subheads Control Share Acquisitions and Merger or Consolidation, supra.

Insolvency and Receivers.—See category Debtor and Creditor, topic Receivers.

Close Corporations.—No special statutory provisions.

Appraisal.—Prior to or at meeting of shareholders, dissenting shareholder must file written objection (and must vote against such action) to authorization by shareholders for sale, lease or exchange of all of corporation's assets, or for merger or consolidation, unless authorization was by vote of at least 80% of total voting power, except right of dissent does not exist in case of (1) Sale under court order; (2) sale for cash with distribution to shareholders within one year; or (3) with respect to action on merger or consolidation, by shareholders holding shares of any class which were either listed on a national exchange or held by less than 2,000 stockholders unless articles provide otherwise or shares of such shareholders were not converted by merger or consolidation solely into shares of surviving or new corporation. If merger is pursuant to T. 12, §112H (short form merger by parent corporation) subsidiary's shareholders may dissent without regard to proportion of voting power approving merger.

Procedures are established for deposit in escrow of certificates and to enforce shareholder's right to receive payment for shares; however, court may not enter order staying proposed corporate action (but see subhead Sale or Transfer of Corporate Assets, supra). (T. 12, §131, as am'd Act 433 of 1975).

Business development corporations to promote prosperity of State of Louisiana are authorized and are formed generally in same manner as business corporations. (T. 51, §1101 et seq.).

Act 49 of 1969 authorizes formation of industrial development corporations as defined in federal Small Business Investment Act of 1958.

Nonprofit corporations are regulated by T. 12, c. 2. Model Non-Profit Corporation Act not adopted. Same fees as listed for ordinary corporations. (T. 12, §263, as am'd Act 235 of 1983). Nonprofit corporation may reincorporate as business corporation by following requisite procedures. (T. 12, §165, added Act 642 of 1986). Annual reports are required for nonprofit corporations. ($5 filing fee must accompany annual report, except for churches. (T. 12, §205.1, as am'd Act 22 of 1990). Charter may be revoked for failure to file required reports. (T. 12, §262.1, added Act 309 0f 1995). Change of name, office or agent may be accomplished by inclusion in annual report, but notice of change of office must be recorded in both new and old parish. (T. 12, §236, added Act 333 of 1991). Articles of incorporation must include location and address of registered office, not simply post office box; names and addresses of registered agents, not simply post office box; and names, addresses and terms of office of initial directors, not simply post office box. (T. 12, §203[B], as am'd Act 291 of 1997).

Nonprofit public corporations for development of trade and business in municipalities and parishes are authorized. (T. 51, §1151 et seq.).

Quasi-public nonprofit corporations may be created. (T. 12, §202, as am'd Act 122 of 1979).

Real estate investment trusts are authorized. (T. 12, §§491-493, as am'd Act 526 of 1977).

Professional Corporations.—Professional law corporations may be organized pursuant to General Business Corporation Law, subject to statutory limitation, and authority of Supreme Court to regulate practice of law. (T. 12, §§801-815, am'd Act 535 of 1985). Professional medical corporations may be organized pursuant to Business Corporation Law, subject to specified modifications and limitations, and subject to regulation by Louisiana State Board of Medical Examiners. (T. 12, §§901-915, as am'd Act 172 of 1979). Professional dental corporations may be organized pursuant to Business Corporation Law, subject to special modifications and limitations and subject to regulation by Louisiana State Board of Dentistry. (T. 12, §§981-995, am'd Act 400 of 1979). Professional accounting corporations may be organized pursuant to Business

CORPORATIONS . . . *continued*

Corporation Law, subject to special modifications and limitations and subject to regulation by Louisiana State Board of Certified Public Accountants. (T. 12, §§1001-1015, am'd Acts 82 and 83 of 1972). Professional Nursing Corporations may be organized pursuant to Business Corporation Law, subject to special modifications and limitations and regulation by State Board of Nurse Examiners. (T. 12, §§1071-1085, added Act 730 of 1977). Professional Architectural Corporations are permitted subject to regulation by Board of Architectural Examiners. (T. 12 §§1086-1101, added Act 225 of 1979). Professional optometry corporations are permitted subject to regulation by Board of Optometry. (T. 12, §§1110 to 1124, added Act 404 of 1980). Professional psychology corporations are permitted subject to regulation by State Board of Examiners of Psychologists. (T. 12, §§1111-1125, added Act 523 of 1980). Professional architectural-engineering corporations are permitted subject to regulation by State Board of Architectural Examiners and State Board of Registration for Professional Engineers and Land Surveyors. (T. 12, §§1171-1181, added Act 465 of 1983). Business corporation may convert to professional corporation upon compliance with statutory requirements governing particular professional corporation. (T. 12, §173, as am'd Act 182 of 1989).

Homesteads and Savings and Loan Corporations.—Laws relating to incorporation, powers, capitalization, membership, records, reports, liabilities, regulation, operation, merger and dissolution of homestead and savings and loan associations has been recodified. (T. 6, c. 9). See category Business Regulation and Commerce, topic Banks and Banking.

Foreign corporations may not transact business in state without obtaining certificate of authority from Secretary of State. (T. 12, §301). Foreign corporation is not considered to be transacting business in state by maintaining or defending suits; holding directors' or shareholders' meeting; maintaining bank accounts; maintaining offices or agencies for transfer of its securities; soliciting or procuring orders if such must be accepted outside state; creating evidence of debt, mortgages or liens; collecting debts; transacting interstate or foreign commerce; conducting isolated transactions; acquiring or disposing of property not as part of regular business activity; or, if a foreign bank (state or national bank), mutual savings bank or fund society, insurance company, or other such entity, when acquiring loans, secured or unsecured, maintaining depository or pledgeholder agreements, servicing loans, or acquiring property by foreclosure or in lieu of foreclosure and disposing thereof. Above listing not exclusive. (T. 12, §302, as am'd Act 751 of 1972).

Foreign corporation must file application in duplicate (triplicate if banking corporation) with, and on form prescribed by, Secretary of State stating: (1) Name of corporation and state or country of incorporation as well as federal tax identification number (its absence does not invalidate application), along with certificate of good standing from incorporating state (not certified copy of articles or certificate of incorporation), with original signature and dated within 90 days of submission for certificate of authority (T. 12, §304[A] and [C], as am'd Act 335 of 1991); (2) if name of corporation does not conform to requirements (T. 12, §303, as am'd Act 88 of 1983), name of corporation with word, abbreviation or distinguishing term which it elects to add thereto for use in this state; (3) address of principal office in state or country of incorporation and of principal business office outside this state; (4) address of principal business establishment and registered office in this state and name of its registered agent in this state at such address; (5) nature of business to be transacted in this state if it does not propose or is not permitted to transact in this state business of every nature authorized by its articles; (6) names and addresses of its directors and officers; (7) other information required by Secretary of State (T. 12, §304, as am'd Act 266 of 1985). Secretary of State must obtain evidence that ten day written notice of application for certificate of incorporation has been given to State Board of Registration for Professional Engineers and Land Surveyors, if name includes "engineer," "engineering," "surveyor" or "surveying." Copy of articles or certificate of incorporation, authenticated by proper officer of state or country of incorporation, must be filed with application. (T. 12, §304, as am'd Acts 477 and 685 of 1974). Foreign corporation authorized to do business in state with no business establishment in state is deemed to have principal business establishment at address of its registered agent in state. (T. 12, §304[A][4], as am'd Act 983 of 1993).

Fee to be paid Secretary of State is same as that for domestic corporations. (See subhead Fees, supra.) Corporation must pay authorization tax based upon proportion of authorized capital stock which its gross assets employed in this state bear to total gross assets, (1) of $50 if either (a) aggregate par value of such proportion of authorized shares with par value exceeds $25,000, or (b) number of such proportion of authorized shares without par value exceeds 10,000; or (2) $10 otherwise. (T. 12, §316).

Unless certificate of authority obtained, foreign corporation transacting business in this state may not present judicial demand before any court of this state, but is not prevented from defending any action, suit or proceeding in this state. Attorney General may file suit against corporation transacting business without certificate of authority, for all fees and taxes which would have been imposed by law if it had qualified, plus all penalties. (T. 12, §314).

Corporation must file annual report stating: (1) Name; (2) address of registered office in this state, if changed since last report, (3) address of its principal office in state or country of incorporation, and its principal office outside this state, if changed since last report; (4) name of registered agent, if changed since last report; (5) names and addresses of officers and directors; and (6) municipal address of present business establishment. Report must be filed with Secretary of State on or before anniversary date of qualifying to transact business, except first annual report shall be filed on or before anniversary date of qualifying to transact business in Louisiana in year next succeeding calendar year in which certificate of authority was issued. (T. 12, §309, as am'd Act 103 of 1992, eff. June 5, 1992).

Corporation must maintain resident agent to receive service of process and registered office which may be same as its business office. Corporation must keep at its business office in or outside this state, or if no such business office exists, at its principal place of business, wherever located, records showing properties and business

transactions in this state (including accounts of assets and liabilities, receipts and disbursements, and gains and losses, and, if subject to severance taxes, a complete account of its severances in this state). (T. 12, §308, as am'd Act 526 of 1982).

Control share acquisitions are governed by legislation similar to that in place for domestic corporations. (T. 12, §§140.11 through 140.17, added Act 173 of 1988, eff. June 29, 1988).

Corporation may withdraw by procuring certificate of withdrawal upon filing with Secretary of State an application in duplicate originals executed by designated officers on form prescribed by Secretary of State, stating: (1) Name and state or country of incorporation; (2) that corporation is not transacting business in state; (3) that corporation surrenders its authority to transact business in state; (4) that corporation revokes authority of resident agent in this state, and consents to service of process upon Secretary of State in any action arising out of any business transacted in state; (5) address for mailing by Secretary of State of any process served on corporation; (6) such other information as required by Secretary of State. Upon approval of application, and payment of all fees, charges, taxes, etc., as evidenced by certificates of Collector of Revenue and of Administrator of Division of Employment Security, Department of Labor, Secretary of State issues certificate of withdrawal. (T. 12, §312). Termination of withdrawal proceedings may be effected by requisite notice to Secretary of State. (T. 12, §312.1, added Act 647 of 1986). Advance fee of $50 for recordation is required. (T. 12, §316, added Act 649 of 1986).

Secretary of State may revoke certificate of authority for enumerated causes. (T. 12, §313, as am'd Act 717 of 1984, eff. July 12, 1984). Errors in certificate of authority may be corrected by certificate of correction. (T. 12, §307.1, added Act 268 of 1985). Amended certificates may be obtained, but must contain evidence of any name change issued by incorporating jurisdiction. (T. 12, §307[B], as am'd Act 335 of 1991).

On petition of Attorney General, district court may order ouster of corporation from state and liquidation of property and affairs if in violation of anti-trust laws. (T. 51, §139, as am'd Act 366 of 1975).

Franchise Tax.—Tax accrues on first day of calendar or fiscal year used by corporation. Every domestic and every foreign corporation, exercising its charter, or qualified to do business or actually doing business in this state, or owning or using any part or all of its capital, plant, or any other property in this state, as further defined in T. 47, §601, must by 15th day of third month, following month in which tax accrues, make verified report and pay to Collector of Revenue tax of $3 for each $1,000 of capital stock, surplus, undivided profits and borrowed capital, if any, on excess over $300,000; $1.50 for each $1,000 below $300,000. (T. 47, §601, and §609, as am'd Act 59 of 1986, eff. Jan. 1, 1987). Collector may grant extensions by virtue of federal extensions. (T. 47, §612, as am'd Act 104 of 1985). Minimum tax, $10. Basis for computation in case of domestic or foreign corporation is determined by taking arithmetical average of: (1) Ratio that net sales in Louisiana and other revenue attributable to Louisiana bears to total net sales in regular course of business and other revenue, and (2) ratio of value of property in Louisiana to value of all property. Minimum tax is $10, and in no case may tax be based on amount less than assessed value of property in state. Penalty for willfully false or fraudulent return is 50% of tax. Delinquency penalty is 5% of tax for each 30 days, not to exceed 25% of tax. Attorney's fee of 10% of tax, interest and other penalties is allowed, and interest at 6% per annum runs from date tax is due until paid. Recordation in mortgage records by Collector of Revenue of statement of delinquent tax operates as first lien, privilege and mortgage on all property of corporation. Corporations exempt are: Labor, agricultural and horticultural corporations; mutual savings banks, national banking corporations and certain state banks; building and loan associations; fraternal beneficiary societies, orders or associations; nonprofit cemetery companies; religious, charitable, scientific, literary and educational corporations; business leagues, chambers of commerce, real estate boards or boards of trade; civic leagues; nonprofit clubs; local benevolent life insurance associations; ditch or irrigation companies; mutual or cooperative telephone companies; insurance corporations paying premium tax under T. 22; farm associations and their related financing organizations; voluntary employees' beneficiary associations; local teachers' retirement fund associations. (T. 47, §608, as am'd Act 103 of 1985). Bank holding companies and public utility holding companies may deduct certain investments in subsidiaries. (T. 47, §§601-616, am'd Act 119 of 1973). Exemption may be provided for new industrial establishments or new corporate headquarters located in state. (T. 47, §§3202-3205, as am'd Act 3 of 1985).

Natural gas pipe line companies pay additional annual franchise tax of 1% of gross receipts. (T. 47, §§1031-1040).

Forms for franchise tax reports may be obtained from Secretary of State on request.

Business License Tax.—See category Business Regulation and Commerce, topic Licenses, Business and Professional.

Income Tax.—See category Taxation, topic Income Tax.

Deeds.—See category Property, topic Deeds.

Forms for Domestic Corporation.—There are no prescribed forms.

Forms for Foreign Corporation.—Printed forms of applications for certificates of authority and withdrawal are furnished, without charge, by Secretary of State, Baton Rouge, on application therefor.

Model Non-Profit Corporation Act.—Not adopted. See subhead Nonprofit Corporations, supra.

Unincorporated Associations.—Dissolution of unincorporated associations, confirmation of their purpose and disposition of their assets is regulated. (T. 12, §§501-505, as am'd Act 907 of 1985).

JOINT STOCK COMPANIES:

No special provisions of law.

Professional Corporations.—See topic Corporations, subhead Professional Corporations.

See note at head of Digest as to 1998 legislation covered.

See Topical Index in front part of this volume.

LIMITED LIABILITY COMPANIES:

Recognized and governed by T. 12, §§1301-1369, added Act of 1992, eff. July 7, 1992, as supplemented by Act 475 of 1993, eff. June 9, 1993, which also amended C.C. 2352 and 2636 and T. 9, §§3431, 3434, 3435 and 3445; and as am'd by Act 847 of 1995. Such companies may be dissolved by affidavit filed with Secretary of State, if company is no longer doing business and owes no debts. (T. 12, §1335.1, as am'd Act 102 of First Ex. Sess. of 1998, eff. May 5, 1998).

PARTNERSHIPS:

General.—Partnership is juridical person created by contract and distinct from its partners which may include all persons, trustees, succession representatives and unincorporated associations. (C. C. Art. 2801). Unless otherwise stipulated, partners participate equally in profits, commercial benefits and losses, but if agreement stipulates as to participation in only one of profits, benefits, losses or distribution of assets other than capital contribution, partners participate equally in all categories. (C. C. Arts. 2803 and 2804). Name does not have to include name of any partner. (C. C. Art. 2805). With written agreement, immovable property may be acquired by partnership, and such is effective as to third persons if partnership contract is filed with Secretary of State. (C. C. Art. 2806). Unanimous consent is required to amend agreement, to admit partners, or to terminate or permit withdrawal, if partnership is constituted for term. (C. C. Art. 2807). Majority, or as stipulated, may manage partnership. (C. C. Art. 2808). Partner is liable for his virile share of debts but may plead discussion of partnership assets. (C. C. Art. 2817).

Withdrawal.—Partner ceases to be member upon death, interdiction, relief under C. 7 of Bankruptcy Code, seizure without release of his interest under Art. 2819, expulsion or withdrawal, or as provided in agreement. (C. C. Art. 2818). Unless otherwise provided in agreement, majority of partners must agree to expulsion for just cause. (C. C. Art. 2820).

For just cause, partner may withdraw from partnership constituted for term (C. C. Art. 2821) and must give reasonable notice if there is no term (C. C. Art. 2822).

Termination.—Unless provided by law, partnership terminates by unanimous consent, judgment of termination, relief to partnership under C. 7 of Bankruptcy Code, reduction to one member, expiration of term, attainment or impossibility of object, or in accordance with partnership agreement. (C. C. 2826, as am'd Act 797 of 1981 and Act 273 of 1982).

Unless otherwise provided in agreement, partnerships are liquidated in same manner and according to same rules as corporations. (C. C. Art. 2834).

Limited Partnership.—Partnerships in commendam consist of one or more general partners and one or more limited partners. (C. C. Art. 2837). Name of partnership must include "limited partnership", "partnership in commendam" or other identification, and must not imply that limited partner is general partner. (C. C. Art. 2838). Limited partner becomes liable as general partner if he permits his name to be used in manner implying he is general partner, or if he knew or should have known of such use and did not take reasonable steps to prevent use, but not if name had been included in name of predecessor business entity. (C. C. 2839, as am'd Act 429 of 1984). Agreement must describe contribution of limited partner, its agreed value or method of determination, and time or circumstance when contribution is to be made. (C. C. Art. 2840). Written agreement must be filed with Secretary of State. (C. C. Art. 2841). Limited partner must restore any distribution that renders partnership insolvent. (C. C. Art. 2842). Limited partner becomes liable as general partner if he participates in management or administration or conducts any business with third persons on behalf of partnership. (C. C. Art. 2844). Limited partner does not incur such liability for one or more of following kinds of activity: Consulting with and advising partner on business matters, or acting as surety for partnership, or approving or disapproving amendment of agreement, or acting as employee, officer, director, shareholder of corporate general partner (C. C. 2845 and 2846, as am'd Act 429 of 1984), or voting for continuation, dissolution or liquidation of partnership, alienation, lease or encumbrance of all or substantially all of partnership assets, or incurrence of indebtedness, other than in ordinary course of business, change in nature of business, or admission, expulsion, withdrawal of partners or selection or removal of managing partners. (C. C. Art. 2847). Limited partnership terminates by retirement from partnership, or death, interdiction or dissolution of sole or any general partner, unless partnership is continued with consent of remaining general partners under right in contract of partnership or if, within 90 days after such event, all remaining partners agree in writing to continue partnership and to appointment of one or more general partners if necessary or desired. (C.C. 2826, as am'd Act 273 of 1982).

Registered Limited Liability Partnerships.—Defined and regulated by T. 9, §§3431-3433 and 3441-3447, added Act of 1992, eff. July 7, 1992 and by C.C. 2352 and 2636; T. 9, §§3431, 3434, 3435 and 3445, all as am'd, Act 475 of 1993, eff. June 9, 1993 and Act 847 of 1995).

Joint Venture.—Joint venture for exploration, development or operation of mineral rights does not create partnership absent express agreement.

Registering.—Secretary of State maintains Central Registry for Contracts of Partnership, in which original or certified copy of agreement must be filed to affect third persons. (T. 9, §3402). To be filed, agreement must contain name of partnership, municipal address of its principal place of business, and name and address of each general and limited partner. (T. 9, §3403, as am'd Act 100 of 1988). Amendments must also be filed in same manner. (T. 9, §3404). Secretary of State issues certificate of registry. (T. 9, §3405). Original or certified copy of agreement and copy of certificate of registry must be filed with recorder of mortgages of principal place of business. (T. 9, §3406). Documents may be delivered for registry prior to effective date with specified date and hour for registry. (T. 9, §3407). Filing within five days after execution, exclusive of holidays, is deemed filed for registry as of date of execution. (T. 9, §3408).

Annual Reports.—Partnerships that have written agreement of partnership are required to file annual report with secretary of state and pay annual fee of $25. (T. 9, §§3409, 3410, 3428, added Act 989 of 1997).

Foreign Partnerships.—Any partnership formed under any law other than Louisiana may only enjoy rights, privileges and juridical status of Louisiana partnership by registering with Secretary of State statement showing its name, jurisdiction of formation, designated agent for service of process with municipal address, name and address of at least one general partner who gives consent as to service of process, principal place of business outside this State, principal place of business within this state (if any), whether partnership intends to own immovable property in state, and whether any partner seeks to have limited liability recognized in Louisiana. Statement must be accompanied by certificate of partnership or articles of partnership and amendments, and affidavit of general partner certifying correctness of information, genuineness of documents and his authority. (T. 9, §3422, as am'd Act 338 of 1986). To own immovables, or have limited partners, copy of partnership agreement need not be filed but must be provided within 30 days of request by secretary of state. (T. 9, §3423, as am'd Act 479 of 1987). Failure to maintain agent for service of process constitutes designation of Secretary of State. (T. 9, §3424). Amendments to articles should be filed and termination of registration may be made by authorized partner. (T. 9, §§3426 and 3427, as am'd Act 340 of 1986).

BUSINESS REGULATION AND COMMERCE

BANKS AND BANKING:

See also topic Commercial Code.

General supervision over banks is exercised by Commissioner of Financial Institutions. (La. Banking Law, T. 6, §1 et seq., Act 719 of 1984, effective Jan. 1, 1985).

Stock.—The shares of any state bank may be divided into classes, with voting powers, preferences, rights or restrictions as provided in articles as approved by commissioner. (T. 6, §251).

Fees.—Semiannual assessment is levied against each institution by Commissioner. (T. 6, §331).

Capital Requirement.—Subscribed capital requirements as follows: $500,000; commissioner may require greater amount of capital if he reasonably deems it necessary for safe, sound and proper operation of bank; requirement inapplicable to bank organized solely to effect merger with existing bank. (T. 6, §215).

Cash Reserves.—Must maintain cash reserves as specified by Commissioner following requirements of Federal Reserve System. (T. 6, §301).

Deposits.—State banks may offer any type of deposit account, interest bearing or not, consistent with provisions of La. Banking Law, rules and regulations of commissioner, and federal rules and regulations, including individual and joint deposits, minor's deposits, and deposits in trust. (T. 6, §242 and §§311-317). See also subhead Decedents' Property, infra.

Control and disposition of safety deposit boxes in name of two or more persons, and of associations, corporations, trusts or agents, are specified. (T. 6, §§320-326, am'd Act 357 of 1989).

Unclaimed Deposits.—Deposits uncalled for and unnoticed by depositor for ten years must be reported to Collector of Revenue, and must be delivered to him after time specified. Revised Uniform Disposition of Unclaimed Property Act adopted. (T. 9, §§151-188).

Decedents' Property.—No bank, banker, trust company, warehouseman or other depositary and no person, corporation or partnership having on deposit any monies, credits, or other things of value for a person deceased and no corporation, the stock or registered bonds of which were owned by person deceased may deliver or transfer such monies, credits, stocks, bonds or other things to any heir or legatee of such deceased person, unless the tax thereon has been paid or unless it has been judicially determined that no taxes are due. Otherwise person or corporation so making delivery or transfer is liable for tax unless made prior to written notice of death, or made to succession representative submitting certified copies of letters issued by a court of competent jurisdiction, or to surviving spouse, heirs or legatees pursuant to certified copy of judgment, or of contents of safety deposit box, whether listed or not, to aforesaid persons under same conditions. (T. 47, §2413, am'd Act 704 of 1975). Every executor must cause an inventory to be taken and no monies, securities, property and effects of deceased may be delivered to said executor until inventory has been made and filed in court in proceedings in which he is acting as executor. (T. 47, §2413). However, bank, credit union, homestead association, or other depository may pay to surviving spouse up to $10,000 out of deposits of deceased spouse without court order or judgment and without determining whether or not inheritance tax is due. Surviving spouse must give affidavit that total funds withdrawn from all depositories does not exceed $10,000. Receipt of surviving widow is full release and discharge of bank or depository from liability for amount paid. (T. 9, §§1513, 1514, am'd Act 54 of 1984). Bank or other depository may pay funds to surviving spouse solely in name of surviving spouse but must notify collector of revenue within seven days of payment. (T. 9, §1513C, added Act 316 of 1976).

Bank may transfer deposit of deceased person to heirs or succession representative on written receipt and production of certified copy of letters or of judgment of court of competent jurisdiction putting heirs in possession. (T. 6, §325).

Alternative Deposits.—In case of joint deposits under names of two or more persons, funds of which are payable to either or any of depositors, a bank is not liable for paying balance to any of surviving depositors, but if bank has received notice in writing of death of any such account owner it shall thereafter report payments made out of account within one week after payment is made. (T. 6, §312, am'd Act 118 of 1988).

Deposits in Trust.—When a depositor in trust for another dies, and bank is without notice of existence and terms of the trust, bank may pay the funds therein to person for whom deposit was made. (T. 6, §314).

See note at head of Digest as to 1998 legislation covered.

See Topical Index in front part of this volume.

LA – 6

BANKS AND BANKING . . . *continued*

Adverse claimant to deposit without court order or bond need not be recognized by bank, except where depositor is fiduciary for claimant, who shows by affidavit reasonable cause to apprehend misappropriation by fiduciary. (T. 6, §315).

Uniform Common Trust Fund Act has not been adopted.

Withdrawals.—State banks may pay deposits of customers in accordance with terms of deposit contract. (T. 6, §325). Deposits of minors may be withdrawn by minor or other person in accordance with terms of written instructions given at time of opening account. (T. 6, §313).

Checks.—See topic Commercial Code.

Any person who, with intent to defraud, obtains money, credit, goods or anything of value by drawing or uttering a check or draft on a bank or depositary, knowing there are not sufficient funds therein to pay same, is guilty of a misdemeanor. (T. 14, §71).

Parties in consumer credit transaction may agree to additional charge to consumer's account if consumer tenders NSF check in payment of such account, not to exceed 5% of check amount of $15, whichever is smaller. (T. 9, §3529, added Act 473 of 1981).

Forgeries.—See topic Commercial Code.

Holidays for financial institutions are: Sundays; New Year's Day; Independence Day; Labor Day; Thanksgiving Day; and Christmas Day. Whenever Dec. 25, Jan. 1, July 4, or Nov. 11 falls on Sun., next day is holiday; whenever they fall on Sat., preceding day is holiday; but in either event banks may choose to remain open. Financial institution at its option may be open or closed on Sat. Optional holidays due to severe weather conditions are allowed. (T. 6, §128, am'd Act 281 of 1991). See also category Introduction, topic Holidays, but specific banking provisions are "entire and exclusive" with reference to any other statutory authorities.

Set-Off.—La. Banking Law establishes statutory right of set-off in favor of banks supplementing any rights bank may have pursuant to contract with customer or under UCC 9. (T. 6, §316, am'd Act 137, effective Sept. 1, 1989). Statutory set-off does not apply to funds in IRA or other tax-deferred account. (T. 6, §316[A]).

Collections.—See topic Commercial Code.

Investments are regulated by T. 6, §§241, 242 (am'd Act 134 of 1989), and 243 (am'd Act 55 of 1986).

"Savings Bank"—La. Banking Law suppressed classification of banks as "savings banks". (T. 6, §1 et seq., Act 719 of 1984 effective Jan. 1, 1985). State savings and loan associations may use terminology "savings bank" as part of corporate name. (T. 6, §712, am'd Act 163 of 1986).

Holding Companies.—Eff. Jan. 1, 1985, holding companies may own or control more than one banking institution. Bank holding company is defined as any company directly or indirectly owning or controlling 25% or more of any class of voting shares of any bank, or which controls election of majority of bank directors, or for whose shareholders 25% or more of bank's voting stock is held in trust. Bank holding companies also limited in acquisition of "nonbank banks" (T. 6, §521, added Act 108 of 1985) and with regard to minority shareholders' rights in acquisitions of more than 10% of stock must make same offer to all shareholders (T. 6, §517, as am'd Act 127 of 1985).

Mergers.—Authorization and procedures for mergers and consolidations are provided by law, subject to shareholder approval. Effective date of merger, recognition of surviving bank, rights of dissenting shareholders and other matters are provided for in T. 6, §§351-355, 376 (am'd Act 93 of 1988). Commissioner may authorize acquisition, merger or consolidation of impaired financial institution. (T. 6, §§970-974, am'd Act 975 of 1986).

Branches.—State banks may establish branches anywhere in state with approval of Commissioner. (T. 6, §501 et seq., am'd Act 39 of 1988).

Interstate Banking.—Beginning Jan. 1, 1989, national reciprocal interstate banking is permitted. (T. 6, §533, am'd Act 686 effective July 7, 1989).

Financial Service Center Banks may be organized in state and are authorized to extend credit outside state without limitation regarding amount of interest charged. (T. 6, §§541-548, added by Act 808 of 1987).

Savings and Loan Associations.—Organization, powers, investments, loans and other actions of savings and loan associations are specified in La. Savings and Loan Association Law and regulated by Commissioner of Financial Institutions. (T. 6, §§701 et seq.).

Credit Unions.—Organization, powers, investments, loans and other actions of credit unions are specified and regulated by Commissioner of Financial Institutions. (T. 6, §641 et seq).

Foreign building and loan associations are permitted to conduct business only in accordance with laws governing local associations, but no foreign association can do business until it procures from Commissioner of Financial Institutions a certificate of authority and public necessity to do so. To procure such authority, foreign association must first deposit with State Treasurer $100,000 in cash or in bonds of the U.S., or Louisiana and file with Commissioner of Financial Institutions a certified copy of its charter, constitution and by-laws and other rules and regulations showing its manner of doing business, together with statement such as is required annually from local building and loan associations and a written instrument agreeing that citations or other legal process may issue against it from any parish in this state and be served on Commissioner either personally or by leaving a copy thereof at an office of Commissioner. Commissioner must mail copy of any paper served on him to home office of such association. Issuing of certificates of authority and public necessity is discretionary with Commissioner and depends upon needs of community and service to public interest. Foreign building and loan associations need not so qualify to participate in mortgages with local banking institutions or to purchase mortgages pursuant to commitments made with local banking institutions or to purchase mortgages if original loan was made by local banking institution. (T. 6, §§891-898).

See also topic Sales.

BILLS AND NOTES:

See topic Commercial Code.

Holidays.—Promissory notes, bills of exchange and commercial paper, maturing on Sunday, holiday or half holiday, required by law or commercial usage to be protested, are due on first day (not a Sunday or legal holiday or half holiday) succeeding day of maturity. In computing delay allowed for giving notice of non-acceptance or nonpayment holidays and half holidays do not count, and if day following protest is holiday or half holiday, next day is computed as first day after protest. For purposes of protecting or otherwise holding liable any party to bill, check or note which is not paid before 12 o'clock noon on any half holiday, a demand or acceptance or payment may be made and notice of protest given on next succeeding secular or business day. Person receiving and collecting check, bill or note, due on half holiday, is not guilty of neglect and does not incur liability in not presenting same on that day. Payment certification or other transaction by bank in this state, otherwise valid, is not rendered invalid because done on holiday or half holiday. (T. 30, §3-806).

Special Requirements.—A note secured by real estate or chattel mortgage must be paraphed by the notary before whom the act of mortgage was executed, but the notarial paraph for identification does not destroy negotiability.

Where a lost instrument is made foundation of a suit or defense, loss must have been publicly advertised within a reasonable time thereafter unless a commercial bond has been furnished in amount equal to face value of note plus 25% thereof. (C. C. 1832, as am'd Act 331 of 1984, eff. Jan. 1, 1985). When note secured by mortgage on immovable property has been lost or destroyed, holder in action to cancel mortgage may prove demand by affidavit without hearing in open court, unless court directs otherwise. (T. 9, §2782.2, added Act 963 of 1986).

Judgment notes are not recognized.

Attorney's fees clauses are enforceable. (30 La. Ann. 398). Consumer Credit Law limits attorney's fees to 25% of unpaid debt. (T. 9, §3530).

Special Defenses.—See topic Consumer Protection.

BILLS OF LADING:

See topic Carriers.

BILLS OF SALE:

Not required.

BLUE SKY LAW:

See topic Securities.

BROKERS:

Real estate brokerage and operation is regulated by statute requiring license, bond and supervision by state board. (T. 37, c. 17). Licenses required for those engaged in other brokerage business, graduated according to volume of business done in preceding year. See topic Factors, subhead Business License Tax.

See also topic Commercial Code.

BULK SALES:

See category Debtor and Creditor, topic Fraudulent Sales and Conveyances.

CARRIERS:

Carriers are supervised, controlled and regulated by Public Service Commission, which has charge of rates also.

Duties and Liabilities.—Carriers are bound to provide for the safekeeping and preservation of the things entrusted to them (C. C. 2751), and are liable for things shipped or received for shipment (C. C. 2752) and for loss or damage of things entrusted to their care unless they can prove loss or damage caused by accident or uncontrollable events (C. C. 2754).

Carrier may be sued at point of delivery or shipment or at domicile of carrier for all freight which it may fail, refuse or neglect to deliver or for damages done thereto. (T. 13, §3231).

Every claim for loss or damage to property or freight must be adjusted and paid within 30 days in case of shipments wholly within state and within 60 days in case of shipments from without state, after filing claim with agent at point of destination of shipment. (T. 45, §§1097-1098). But see Act 70 of 1972, which requires settlement of all claims for damage to goods resulting from transporting property within 60 days after filing claim. (T. 45, §1097).

Limitation of liability and discrimination are governed by the usual rules.

Privilege is given carrier for freight money, taxes, storage, etc., and if articles carried are destroyed or lost without fault of carrier he has privilege on insurance money, provided he gives notice to owner within 30 days after loss or before insurance is paid. (C. C. 3217).

Improper disclosures concerning shipments prohibited. (T. 45, §§1091, 1092).

Unclaimed freight can be sold. (T. 45, §§1101-1103).

Bills of Lading.—See topic Commercial Code.

COMMERCIAL CODE:

Uniform Commercial Code has not been adopted. Legislature has enacted commercial laws incorporating Arts. 1, 3, 4, 5, 7 and 8 (T. 10, as am'd Acts 164 and 165 of 1978 and Act 1133 of 1992, eff. July 1, 1993), and Art. 9 (T. 10, c. 9 enacted Act 528 of 1988, am'd Act 135 of 1989 effective Jan. 1, 1990) of U.C.C. with following material variances (Articles of U.C.C. are referred to in Commercial Law as Chapters):

Chapter I. General Provisions:

Section 1-101: Title changed to read "Commercial Laws."

See note at head of Digest as to 1998 legislation covered.

See Topical Index in front part of this volume.

COMMERCIAL CODE . . . *continued*

Section 1-103: Amended to provide that other laws of Louisiana shall apply unless displaced by particular provisions of Commercial Laws;

Section 1-105: Amended to delete references to Sections in Articles 2 and 6 which are not incorporated (T. 10, §1-105 am'd Act 135 of 1989);

Section 1-106: Amended to delete clause beginning, ". . . . . but neither consequential . . . . ." in Subsection (1) considered contrary to Louisiana law (C.C. 1934), and deletes Subsection (2) as unnecessary in view of Article 423 of Code of Civil Procedure;

Section 1-109: Deleted as contrary to Louisiana policy;

Section 1-201: "Bill of lading" amended to refer to "marine or land transportation"; "Conspicuous", last sentence deleted; "Delivery" incorporates phrase "actual or constructive, from one person to another"; "Notice", last two sentences deleted; also deletes definitions of "Action". "Aggrieved Party", "Agreement," "Bank," "Contract," "Defendant," "Fault," and "Genuine,"

Section 1-206: Deleted as covered by Articles 2277, 2278 and 2441 of Civil Code; (Article 2 of U.C.C. omitted).

Chapter 3—Commercial Paper:

Section 3-105: Subsection (2) amended to read "A promise or order is conditional if the instrument . . . . .";

Section 3-112: Subsection (c) amended to add ". . . . ., or to furnish financial information, or to do or refrain from doing any other act for the protection of the obligation expressed in the instrument not involved in the payment of money on account of the indebtedness evidenced by the instrument; or . . . . ." ;

Section 3-116: Subsection (b) amended to read "(b) if not in the alternative, is payable to all of them and may be negotiated or discharged only by all of them, but may be enforced by any one of them, the others being considered necessary parties only in accordance with Article 643 of the Louisiana Code of Civil Procedure."

Section 3-118: Subsection (c) replaced by the text of N.I.L. §17(7);

Section 3-122: Subsection (4) separated and made a new Section 3-123;

Section 3-201: Word "security" is deleted from Subsection (2). Donative transfers inter vivos of negotiable instruments, otherwise governed by special form requirements of Civil Code, are governed by standard provisions of Art. 3 of Uniform Commercial Code. (T. 10, §3-201 [4], added Act 452 of 1982);

Section 3-207: "Minor" used instead of "infant" in Subsection (1), and phrase "the declaration of a constructive trust" is deleted from Subsection (2);

Section 3-305: "Minority" used instead of phrase "infancy and emancipated minority" in Subsection (1) and Subsection (2) (b) amended to read ". . . . . as renders the obligation an absolute nullity";

Section 3-416: Subsection (6) deleted for possible conflict with Louisiana law (Cf. 13 Tul. L. Rev.);

Section 3-419: Subsections (1) and (2) amended to read: "(1) When a drawee to whom an instrument is delivered for acceptance refuses to return it on demand; or when a person to whom an instrument is delivered for payment refuses on demand either to pay or to return it; or when a person pays an instrument on a forged indorsement, he is liable to the true owner. (2) In an action against a drawee under subsection (1) the measure of the drawee's liability is the face amount of the instrument. In any other action under subsection (1) the measure of liability is presumed to be the face amount of the instrument." Subsection (3) amended to delete phrase "in conversion" and omit reference to Sections 3-205 and 3-206;

Section 3-501: Incorporates 1966 Amendment of U.C.C.

Section 3-602: Amended to read "A discharge of any party provided by this Chapter is not effective . . . . .";

Sections 3-802, 3-803 and 3-804: Deleted;

Section 3-806: Added to retain provisions as to holidays, see topic Bills and Notes, subhead Holidays;

Section 3-807: Added to read "A non-negotiable bill of exchange, promissory note, or other non-negotiable obligation for the payment of money, made within Louisiana, shall not be received as evidence of a debt when the whole sum is expressed in figures unless it is accompanied by proof that it was given for the sum therein expressed. The cents or fractional parts of a dollar may be in figures.";

Chapter 4—Bank Deposits:

Section 4-105 of Commercial Laws amended to include within definition of "bank" savings and loan association and credit union when performing banking functions in check collection process only. (T. 10, §4-105[g], added Act 137 of 1981).

Section 4-402: Last three sentences of U.C.C. deleted to conform with Louisiana jurisprudence, 123 So. 126;

Section 4-405: "Interdiction" used instead of "incompetence";

Chapter 5—Letters of Credit:

Section 5-103: Second sentence of Subsection 1(a) amended to read: "A credit shall clearly state whether it is revocable or irrevocable and in the absence of such statement shall be presumed to be irrevocable." Subsection (3) omits definitions of "Contract for Sale";

Section 5-107: Subsection (4) amended to read "Unless otherwise specified and subject to the provisions of R.S. 10:5-109 . . . . .";

Section 5-109: Subsection 1(a) amended to delete "for sale or other transaction";

Section 5-112: "Except" clause deleted from second sentence of Subsection (1);

Section 5-114: Phrase "for sale or other contract" deleted in Subsection (1), (2), and Subsections (4) and (5) were deleted:

Chapter 7—Documents of Title:

Section 7-101: Title changed to read: "Commercial Laws—Documents of Title". Word "depositary" instead of "bailee" is used in this section and other sections of Chapter 7.

Section 7-102: Definition of "receipt of goods" added as subsection (1)(h).

Section 7-102: Subsection (3) left blank as §7-102(3) of U.C.C. is deleted.

Section 7-204: Subsections (3) and (4) left blank as corresponding subsections of U.C.C. deleted.

Section 7-205: "in good faith" substituted for "in the ordinary course of business".

Section 7-209: Changed to read: "(1) A warehouseman has a lien on the goods covered by a warehouse receipt or on the proceeds thereof in his possession for charges for storage or transportation, demurrage and terminal charges, insurance, labor, or charges present or future in relation to the goods, and for expenses necessary for preservation of the goods or reasonably incurred in their sale pursuant to law. If the person on whose account the goods are held is liable to the warehouseman for like charges or expenses in relation to other goods and it is stated in the receipt that a lien is claimed for such charges and expenses, the warehouseman also has a lien against the goods covered by the receipt for such other charges and expenses whether or not the other goods have been delivered by the warehouseman. But as to a person to whom a negotiable warehouse receipt is duly negotiated a warehouseman's lien is limited to charges in an amount or at a rate specified on the receipt or if no charges are so specified then to a reasonable charge for storage of the goods covered by the receipt subsequent to the date of the receipt.

(2) The warehouseman may also reserve a security interest against the depositor for a maximum amount specified on the receipt for charges other than those specified in Subsection (1), such as for money advanced and interest. Such a security interest is governed by the chapter on Secured Transactions (Chapter 9). (T. 10, §7-209, am'd Act 135 of 1989 effective Jan. 1, 1990).

(3)(a) A warehouseman's lien for charges and expenses under Subsections (1) or (2) is also effective against any person who so entrusted the depositor with possession of the goods that a pledge of them by him to a good faith purchaser for value would have been valid but is not effective against a person as to whom the document confers no right in the goods covered by it under Section 7-503.

(b) A warehouseman's lien on household goods for charges and expenses in relation to the goods under Subsection (1) is also effective against all persons if the depositor was the legal possessor of the goods at the time of deposit. 'Household goods' means furniture, furnishings and personal effects used by the depositor in a dwelling.

(4) A warehouseman loses his lien on any goods which he voluntarily delivers or which he unjustifiably refuses to deliver."

Section 7-403: In subsection (1)(b), following words are deleted: "but the burden of establishing negligence in such cases is on the person entitled under the document".

Section 7-502: In subsection (1)(c), words "agency or estoppel" are deleted.

Section 7-504: Subsections (2), (3) and (4) of U.C.C. section are deleted.

Section 7-509: Words "contract to sell" substituted for "contract of sale".

Section 7-601(2): Word "concursus" substituted for "interpleader".

Chapter 8—Investment Securities. (T. 10, §8-101 am'd Act 135 of 1989 to include 1977 official Amendments, effective Jan. 1, 1990):

Section 8-101: Title changed to read "Commercial Laws—Investment Securities".

Section 8-204: Art. 8-204 of U.C.C. is modified slightly to require that restrictions comply with Corporate Code. (T. 12, §§57 and 210).

Section 8-501: Added to provide that law does not enlarge powers of infants or other persons lacking full legal capacity.

(Arts. 6 and 10 of U.C.C. omitted.)

Chapter 9—Secured Transactions

Section 9-101—Title changed to read: "Commercial Law—Secured Transactions".

Section 9-102—Consignments added to subsection (1); definitions added in subsection (4) to reflect La. terminology.

Section 9-103—Adds rules applicable to deposit accounts in subsection (7).

Section 9-104—Defines exception applicable to transfers by government agencies with cross-reference to T. 39, §1421(a) and (2). Subsections (h), (k) and (l) deleted. Subsection (m) added to except application as to public utility corporations.

Section 9-105—Subsection (N) deleted. References to Article 2 deleted in Subsection (3).

Section 9-111—Reference to Article 6 deleted.

Section 9-113—Deleted.

Section 9-114—Substantially rewritten to conform to La. law on consignment.

Section 9-206—Reference to Article 2 in subsection (2) deleted.

Section 9-207—Subsection (2)(c) deleted.

Section 9-305—Adds specific rules for perfection of security interest in life insurance, beneficiary interest under trust, and in deposit account established with third party.

Section 9-312—Subsection 2 deleted.

Section 9-313—Differences in subsection (2) relate to La. property law. See topic Real Property. Subsection (4)(c) deleted.

Section 9-315—Definition of "product" added.

Section 9-401—If filing is necessary to perfect security interest under T. 10, §9-103, filing with Clerk of Court of any parish, or Recorder of Mortgages in Orleans Parish, will suffice.

Section 9-402—Form of financing statement reads as follows:

Name of debtor (or assignor) _____

Address _____

Social Security number/taxpayer identification number _____

Name of secured party (or assignee) _____

Address _____

(1) This financing statement covers the following types (or items) of property: (Describe) _____

(2) (Check if applicable) The above goods are fixtures on (or where appropriate substitute either "The above minerals or the like (including oil and gas) or accounts will be financed at the wellhead or minehead of the well or mine located on _____)" real estate described on an attachment hereto.

(If the debtor does not have an interest of record) The name and social security number or taxpayer identification number, as applicable, of a record owner of the real estate concerned is _____

See note at head of Digest as to 1998 legislation covered.

See Topical Index in front part of this volume.

COMMERCIAL CODE . . . *continued*

(3) (If products of collateral are claimed) Products of the collateral are also covered.

Signature of Debtor

(Use Whichever
is Applicable) (or use "Assignor" if applicable)

Signature of Secured Party

(or use "Assignee" if applicable)

Subsection (6) deleted. In subsection, note that La. requires social security number or taxpayer identification number.

Section 9-403—La. filing rules contemplate filing with clerks and transmission to Secretary of State, who shall maintain master index of all financing statements, continuation statements, assignment, releases, termination statements, and other statements. (T. 10, §9-403[6], Act 528 of 1988, am'd Act 135 of 1989).

Section 9-409—Added authorizing Secretary of State to prescribe forms to be used for filing.

Section 9-508—Self-help repossession generally prohibited in La.

Section 9-505—Subsection (1) deleted.

Section 9-408—Adds special provisions applicable to use of executory process to enforce security interest.

Sections 9-601 through 9-605 contain La. transition rules (T. 10, §§9-601—9-605, added Act 135 of 1989, am'd Act 598 of 1989).

1973 Official Amendment adopted.

1977 Official Amendments not adopted, except as noted above.

Uniform Commercial Code Art. 9 has been enacted effective July 1, 1989. (T. 10, c. 9, enacted Act 528 of 1988). Comments and explanatory notes to be prepared during interim period by Louisiana State Law Institute, and additional technical corrections bill is expected to be enacted before effective date.

CONDITIONAL SALES:

See topic Sales.

CONSIGNMENTS:

See topic Factors.

CONSUMER PROTECTION:

Unsolicited merchandise deemed gift to recipient, who may enjoin sender from billing or requesting payment. (T. 51, §461, added Act 10 of 1970). Member of organization making retail sales to its members may notify organization of termination of his membership, and merchandise delivered after 30 days following receipt of notice by certified letter is deemed a gift; however, provision does not relieve member from liability to organization for breach of contract. (T. 51, §462, added Act 10 of 1970). Advertising, promotion and sale of time share plans are regulated. (T. 9, §§1131.1-1131.27, added Act 552 of 1983).

Any person who signs purchase agreement in excess of $150 with itinerant door-to-door salesman (no fixed place of business and peddles from house to house) can withdraw within three days of signing agreement counting from day after agreement was signed. (T. 9, §2711).

Louisiana Consumer Credit Law (Act 454 of 1972), effective Jan. 1, 1973, regulates all types of consumer credit transactions. (T. 9, §§3510-3568, as am'd Act 365 of 1983). Law establishes maximum charges on consumer loans, consumer credit sales, negotiable instruments after negotiation or if instrument is not negotiated within 35 days of date of making, negotiable instruments after maturity, revolving charge accounts, revolving loan accounts with lender credit cards, delinquency charges, and deferral charges. (T. 9, §§3519-3526, as am'd Acts 501 and 502 of 1980). Parties in consumer credit transaction may agree to additional charge to customer's account if consumer tenders NSF check in payment of such account, not to exceed 5% of check amount or $15, whichever is smaller. Such charge is in addition to other authorized delinquency charges under Consumer Credit Act. (T. 9, §3526.1, added Act 473 of 1981). Law provides for consumer prepayment of unpaid balance at any time without penalty and with rebate of unearned finance or credit service charges. (T. 9, §§3528-3529, as am'd Act 365 of 1983). Law provides for limitation of attorney's fees to 25% of unpaid debt on default, prohibits use of multiple agreements to obtain higher credit service charges, requires negotiable instruments to bear legend "negotiable paper" on face thereof, makes promissory notes in connection with home solicitation sales non-negotiable, requires 30 days notice in specified form to consumer of assignment of negotiable instrument before original assignee may become holder in due course, provides for refinancing scheduled payment which is twice as large as average of earlier payments without penalty which must be designated as "balloon payment", and prohibits referral sales agreements with consumer. (T. 9, §§3530-3537, as am'd Acts 333, 554 and 808 of 1985; §3535 repealed, Act 66 of 1985). Law regulates home solicitation sales with provisions for cancellation by consumer, for form of sales agreements, and requirements on part of consumer. (T. 9, §§3538-3541). Law regulates credit life insurance, credit health and accident insurance, and property insurance required by extender of credit in consumer credit transaction, and effective Jan. 1, 1975, regulates premiums that may be charged for insurance. (T. 9, §§3542-3549). Law provides remedies and penalties, including nonenforcement or modification of agreements containing "unconscionable" clauses, refund of service or finance charges and three times such charges plus attorney's fees if violation of law was intentional or not in good faith, correction of violation if violation was in good faith, correction of self-discovered violations, and criminal penalties. (T. 9, §§3551-3553). Law is administered by Commissioner of Financial Institutions, who licenses all persons, except supervised financial organizations, making supervised loans defined as loans in which finance charge exceeds 10% simple interest per annum. (T. 9, §§3557-3561). Collection practices are regulated including contact between lender and persons other than consumer, and number of contacts between lender and consumer. (T. 9, §3562). Law requires persons making consumer credit sales, consumer leases or consumer loans, etc., to file notification in specified form prior to Jan. 31 of each year and pay fee of at least $10. (T. 9, §§3563-3565, as am'd Act 808 of 1985). Extenders of credit prohibited from discriminating against persons because of race, color, religion, national origin, sex or marital status, or from requiring any major or emancipated minor to meet credit qualification standards not required of other persons similarly situated. (T. 9, §3583 as am'd Act 161 of 1978).

Unfair Trade Practices and Consumer Protection Law (Act 759 of 1972. T. 51, §§1401-1418) makes unlawful unfair methods of competition and unfair or deceptive acts or practices in conduct of any trade or commerce (T. 51, §1405), establishes Governor's Consumer Protection Division (T. 51, §1403) which may make rules and regulations interpreting provisions of act subject to approval of Permanent Advisory Board on Consumer Protection and Attorney General (T. 51, §1405), and authorizes Attorney General to enforce Act (T. 51, §1404). Exemptions are provided to transactions regulated by certain other regulatory agencies, publishers, owners, etc. of advertising media under certain circumstances, a seller of a product and service using advertising or promotional material supplied by manufacturer or other person from whom seller purchases product or service unless seller refuses to provide to Attorney General name and address of such manufacturer or other person and seller must agree to cease disseminating advertisement or promotional material, and conduct which complies with T. 15 U.S.C., §45(a)(1). (T. 51, §1406). Provision is made for action by any person for violation of act to recover actual damages, and if violation was with knowledge after notice by Director of Division or Attorney General, court must award treble damages plus attorney's fees and costs. If such action is groundless and brought in bad faith, court may award attorney's fees and costs to defendant. Action must be brought within one year of date of transaction or act giving rise to right of action. (T. 51, §1409). Director of Division and Attorney General are authorized to accept voluntary compliance which must be filed in district court in parish of violator's domicile, to make investigative demands and depositions enforceable by court action and use other procedures provided by Constitution and laws of State. (T. 51, §§1410-1415). Provision is made for a $5,000 civil penalty for violation of an injunction issued under law. (T. 51, §1416). District attorneys may enforce act under supervision of Attorney General. (T. 51, §1417). Law is made applicable to all consumer transactions which are evidenced by a writing signed by consumer in state or when a merchant negotiates in state or by mail, telephone or otherwise for a transaction with a consumer. (T. 51, §1418).

Design and construction of mobile homes, and licensing of dealers provided for. (T. 51, §911, as am'd Act 589 of 1979).

Residential Truth in Construction Act requires contractor to deliver specified Notice of Lien Rights to owner or agent for execution before construction. (T. 9, §§4851-4855, added Act 237 of 1976).

Banks and other credit companies are prohibited from disseminating specific information as to credit transactions except pursuant to subpoena duces tecum or other order but only after giving immediate notice by certified or registered mail to person, and except provision of general information to credit reporting company or another business entity having legitimate business need for information. (T. 9, §3571, added Act 252 of 1976).

Fraudulent sale of kosher food is prohibited. (T. 40, §608.2, added Act 722 of 1977)

Promotional contests involving sales presentations are regulated. (T. 51, §§1721-1722, added Act 527 of 1983).

Rental referral agencies are regulated by T. 51, §§1700-1704.

Dance studios are regulated by T. 51, §§1551-1566. (Act 533 of 1979).

Sale of bedding and upholstered furniture is regulated. (T. 40, §§1191-1208).

Work-at-home solicitation is regulated. (T. 51, §1711, added Act 830 of 1980).

Plain Language Law.—No "Plain Language Law" adopted.

CONTRACTS:

See also topic Commercial Code.

Louisiana law of contracts is not derived from Common Law, rather it is derived from French Civil Code. Title IV of Louisiana Civil Code, dealing with "Conventional Obligations" contains provisions relating to: General principles (C.C. 1756-1759); natural obligations (C.C. 1760-1762); kinds of obligations (C.C. 1763-1820); transfer of obligations (C.C. 1821-1830); proof of obligations (C.C. 1831-1853); extinction of obligations (C.C. 1854-1905); contracts generally (C.C. 1906-1917); contractual capacity (C.C. 1918-1926); consent (C.C. 1927-1947); vices of consent (C.C. 1948-1965); cause (C.C. 1966-1970); object and matter (C.C. 1971-1977); third party beneficiaries (C.C.. 1978-1982); effects of contracts (C.C. 1983-2012); dissolution (C.C. 2013-2024); simulations (C.C. 2025-2028); nullity (C.C. 2029-2035); revocatory and oblique actions (C.C. 2036-2044); and interpretive rules (C.C. 2045-2057). For specific types of contracts, see appropriate topics.

Venue for actions on contract in parish of execution of contract or where work was performed or was to be performed. (C.C.P 76.1, added Act 217 of 1991). In public contracts as defined, provisions as to choice of law and choice of forum other than Louisiana are null; contracting party may waive prohibition, but laws of same session (1992) are in conflict on issue of waiver. (T. 38, §2196, added Act 75 of 1992, eff. June 5, 1992; T. 9, §2778, added Act 582 of 1992, eff. June 30, 1992).

FACTORS:

Any factor, broker, commission merchant, middleman or other person or corporation acting as commission merchant, or undertaking to sell for another any goods, wares, merchandise, sugar, cotton, rice, or any other agricultural produce, must render a true and correct account of the sales thereof within fifteen days of the date of said sales, which statement must give the name and address of the person or corporation to whom sold and dates of said sales. (T. 51, §5). Cotton merchants purchasing from farmers must register with Commissioner of Agriculture and provide bond of $50,000. (T. 3, §700 et seq., as am'd Act 888 of 1985).

Bond.—Commission merchants who sell in this state on commission or buy as agent or broker any farm products, fish, oysters, shrimp, crabs, game or fur skins must furnish bond to Commissioner of Agriculture, etc., in the sum of $1000. (T. 51, §§1-4).

False Statements, Etc.—It is misdemeanor to render a false statement or account of a sale of cotton or other agricultural product, or falsely to represent that such products are held for future sale when sold, or when they are held on consignment, to sell,

See note at head of Digest as to 1998 legislation covered.

See Topical Index in front part of this volume.

LA – 9

FACTORS ... *continued*
without rendering a complete account, showing price, grade, and name and address of purchaser, or with intent to defraud consignor, to make a false charge, report of condition, or statement. (T. 3, §500).

Lien.—Factor has lien on movables entrusted to him for sale and on proceeds and unpaid purchase money, which is prior to lien of attachment. If factor becomes insolvent, consignor may reclaim goods consigned or if sold has lien on unpaid price thereof. (C. C. 3247-8).

Recordation of Contracts.—There are no provisions as to filing or recording consignment agreements or notices of factors' liens.

Business license tax levied on all factorage, brokerage or commission businesses ranges from a minimum of $30 when the gross annual commissions are less than $5,000 to a maximum of $4,000 when such commissions are $500,000 or more, twenty-two classes being provided for. (T. 47, c. 3).

FRANCHISES:

No special legislation. Uniform Franchise and Business Opportunities Act not adopted.

FRAUDS, STATUTE OF:

See also topic Commercial Code.
No statute as such. Analogous provisions are:

Transfer of immovable property must be in writing; but if a verbal sale or other disposition of such property be made, it is good against the vendor and vendee who confesses it when interrogated on oath, provided actual delivery has been made of the immovable. (C. C. 2275).

Sale of movables verbally is valid, but all verbal agreements relative to movable property, and all verbal contracts for payment of money where value is in excess of $500 may be proved by two or more witnesses, or one witness and other corroborative circumstances. (C. C. 2277, 2441). Verbal sale of movables without delivery cannot affect rights of third persons. (C. C. 2247).

Parol evidence is not received to prove any promise to pay: (1) A judgment of any court, in or out of this state, for the purpose of taking same out of prescription, or reviving it after prescription has run; (2) any debt or liability of one deceased in order to take it out of prescription, or to revive it after prescription has run; (3) the debt of a third person; (4) any debt or liability evidenced by writing, when prescription has already run. But in all these cases the acknowledgment or promises must be in writing, signed by the party to be bound, or by his agent or attorney in fact specially authorized in writing so to do. (C. C. 2278).

INTEREST:

Legal rate on or before Sept. 12, 1980, is 7% until Sept. 12, 1980, then 10% until Sept. 11, 1981, and 12% until Jan. 1, 1988 and thereafter two points over coupon issue yield equivalent as calculated by commissioner of financial institutions. (C.C. 2924, as am'd Act 275 of 1997).

Maximum rate which may be contracted for is 12% (C. C. 2924 as am'd Act 142 of 1982), except that domestic and foreign corporations, limited partnerships, foreign limited partnerships and partnerships in commendam, may agree to pay any rate of interest (T. 12, §603, as am'd Act 210 of 1977). Any person borrowing funds for commercial or business purposes may agree to pay interest in excess of maximum conventional rate otherwise applicable and to pay interest on interest (T. 9, §3509, added Act 665 of 1981 and C.C. 2924, as am'd Act 458 of 1984), and may agree that interest rate may vary from time to time without making condition potestative or destroying negotiability (T. 9, §3509.1, added Act 361 of 1982).

Simple conventional interest on loans secured in whole or part, directly or indirectly, by immovable property, may not exceed 12% per annum. (T. 9, §3503, as am'd Act 205 of 1979). Interest on obligations secured directly or indirectly, in whole or part, by mortgage on immovable property insured by Federal Housing Administration, may be enforced pursuant to §245 of National Housing Act. (T. 9, §3508, added Act 582 of 1979). Similar exemption provided for Veterans' Administration loans and FHA loans. (T. 9, §3504, as am'd Act 764 of 1979). Wrap-around mortgages are also exempt if nominal interest in wrap-around does not exceed lawful rate for conventional loans. (T. 9, §3508, as am'd Act 764 of 1979). Graduated payment mortgages are also exempt if interest rate is not greater than lawful rate and if unpaid principal does not increase as result of deferred interest, exclusive of taxes, insurance and other non-finance charges, to amount greater than 150% of original face amount of note and mortgage. (T. 9, §3504, as am'd Acts 424 and 767 of 1982). Obligation secured by mortgage on immovable (real) property, when mortgagee is former owner of property, may bear rate of interest agreed upon by parties within maximum limitations permitted for federally insured financial institutions, but subject to ceiling of 17%; no defense of usury if so authorized. (T. 9, §3504, added Act 261 of 1982). Adjustable rate mortgages as defined are also exempt from laws on usury and interest on interest. (T. 9, §3504 [D], added Act 424 of 1982). Retail installment contract may include finance charge not in excess of specified rates between 1.5% and 2.25% based on model year of motor vehicle. (T. 6, §957, as am'd Act 110 of 1980).

Discount.—Any rate of interest can be collected by way of discount provided that interest from maturity may not exceed 8%. This does not apply, however, to banks of state or to consumer credit transactions as defined by Consumer Credit Law. (C. C. 2924, am'd Act 454 of 1972).

Judgments.—Legal interest attaches from date of judicial demand on all judgments sounding in damages "ex delicto" (T. 13, §4203), except as to state, its agencies and political subdivisions, as to which it is 6% (T. 13, §5112, as am'd Act 509 of 1985). Interest may run from date sum of money or damages for delay of performance is due. (C.C. 2000, as am'd Act 137 of 1985).

Compound interest is not permitted, unless amount is added to principal and a new contract made except as provided by Consumer Credit Law, for agricultural purposes, in matters preempted by federal law or regulation, or as provided in regulations of state commissioner of financial institutions. Original stipulation for compound interest invalid. (C. C. 1939, as am'd Act 822 of 1981 and Act 673 of 1982).

Small Loans.—See subhead Consumer Credit Law, infra.

Consumer Credit Law (Act 454 of 1972) specifies maximum loan finance charges for consumer loans, revolving charge accounts, and credit card accounts (T. 9, §§3519-3524), maximum delinquency and deferral charges (T. 9, §§3525-3526), privilege to consumer to prepay without penalty and with rebate of unearned loan or credit service charges (T. 9, §§3527-3529), and provides that insurance costs must be included in computation of maximum finance charges (T. 9, §3542). See topic Consumer Protection.

Consumer Credit Opportunity Law.—Extenders of credit prohibited from discriminating against natural persons solely because of race, color, national origin, sex or marital status, and from requiring natural persons to meet credit qualifications not required of other persons similarly situated. (T. 9, §3581 et seq., added Act 705 of 1975.)

Credit Cards.—Any seller or issuer of credit cards honored by seller engaged in extension of consumer credit on open account may impose, after 25 days following receipt of statement by consumer, a finance charge not exceeding $1^1/_2$% per month on all amounts unpaid from month to month. (Act 313 of 1970).

Credit union may charge rate as provided in by-laws and approved by commissioner of financial institutions, on loans to members. (T. 6, §654, as am'd Act 436 of 1982).

Usury.—Person paying usurious interest may recover same by suit within two years after payment. (C. C. 2924). Entire interest forfeited if over lawful rate. (T. 9, §3501: 274 So.2d 150).

Consumer Credit Law (Act 454 of 1972) permits recovery of finance charges and three times such finance charges plus attorney's fees if extender of credit violated law intentionally or was not in good faith. Action must be brought within 60 days of final payment of consumer credit contract or within one year of date of violation in case of a revolving loan or revolving charge account. (T. 9, §3552). Violation of law is a misdemeanor. (T. 9, §3553).

Defense of usury may not be invoked by domestic or foreign corporation organized for profit, limited partnership and partnership in commendam or in certain instances by those receiving loans for commercial or business purposes. (T. 12, §703, as am'd Act 458 of 1984).

LICENSES, BUSINESS AND PROFESSIONAL:

Large number of occupations and businesses are licensed, and occupational license tax collected, by local governments. Local governmental occupational taxes may include attorneys. (T. 47, §§341-363, as am'd Act 1017 of 1986). State occupational license taxes repealed by Act 567 of 1981, effective Jan. 1, 1982. Detailed information as to local licenses available from various parishes, cities and towns. Persons engaged in rendering financial planning and management service for individuals must be licensed by Director of Division of Occupational Standards. (Added Act 423 of 1970). Contractors are licensed by State Licensing Board for Contractors. (T. 37, §§2151 et seq., am'd Act 82 of 1976).

Commercial Travelers.—No license is imposed on traveling salesmen representing jobbers or wholesalers, who do not carry with them goods for sale, but only take orders therefor, and deliver said orders to their employer, at store or permanent place of business to be filled in the manner usual to the jobbing or wholesale trade. (T. 47, §368). Salesmen displaying samples at a display room, however, must be licensed. (T. 47, §372, am'd Act 218 of 1972).

The following special licenses are levied:

A tax of 2% of gross receipts from intrastate business is imposed on "public utilities," excluding, however, persons engaged in any business or operations on navigable waters. (T. 47, §§1001-1010).

Traffic in liquor is subject to tax on liquor sold, and manufacturers and dealers require licenses or permits for which various fees are charged. (T. 26, §71; T. 26, §§791-797, added Act 128 of 1972). For regulations, write Collector of Revenue, Baton Rouge. There is an additional graduated tax for Parish of Orleans. (T. 26, §492).

Traffic in beer and wine is subject to tax on beverages sold and dealers must obtain licenses or permits. (T. 26, §§271, 341). In Parish of Orleans there is an additional state license of varying proportions. (T. 26, §492).

Traffic in bottled soft drinks is subject to a tax on selling price and a requirement that dealers obtain licenses. (T. 47, §§881-908).

Automobile service clubs must be licensed by Insurance Commissioner. (T. 22, §1751 et seq., as am'd Act 260 of 1975).

Poll takers required to register with Secretary of State. (T. 14, §325, am'd Act 602 of 1972).

Persons engaged in business of selling checks must be licensed. (T. 6, §1031 et seq., am'd Act 324 of 1972).

Cotton brokers must obtain certificate of authority from Commissioner of Agriculture and post $50,000 bond. (T. 3, §§700-705, am'd Act 888 of 1985).

Aircraft must be registered with Aircraft Registrar of Department of Transportation and dealers must be licensed with Registrar. (T. 2, §1 et seq., added Act 889 of 1985).

Collection Agencies.—No legislation.

See also categories Insurance, topic Insurance Companies; Taxation, topic Chain Store Tax.

MONOPOLIES, RESTRAINT OF TRADE AND COMPETITION:

Contracts, combinations, trusts, or conspiracies to restrain trade, fix or limit amount or quantity of any article, commodity, or merchandise to be manufactured, mined, produced or sold in state, or to influence trade in any manner so as to affect prices, are illegal. Penalty for violation is fine and imprisonment and in case of corporation revocation of charter or forfeiture of right to do business in state (T. 51, §121 et seq., as am'd Act 366 of 1975).

See note at head of Digest as to 1998 legislation covered.

See Topical Index in front part of this volume.

MONOPOLIES, RESTRAINT OF TRADE AND COMPETITION . . . *continued*

Agreement or conspiracy to fix price of products of soil, such as fruit, nuts or vegetables is felony, punishable by fine or imprisonment or both. (T. 51, §§140-141).

Manufacturer or wholesale distributor of motor vehicles may not require that purchases be financed through designated finance company (T. 51, §§661-668). When commerce will be lessened or a monopoly created, no person shall sell or lease goods with agreement or understanding that purchaser or lessee shall not use goods of a competitor of vendor or lessor and no person shall sell commercial machines or equipment without providing a manual containing diagrams, instructions and parts lists sufficient to permit user to repair items where such refusal compels user to obtain repairs from seller. (T. 51, §124 as am'd Act 669 of 1970).

Unfair sales of certain merchandise below cost are misdemeanors. (T. 51, §§421-427).

Cancellation or failure of renewal of franchise between refiner and retailer of motor gasoline requires 90 day notice except under specified circumstances; and retailer is not permitted to cancel franchise during its term unless retailer has failed to comply substantially with any essential and reasonable requirements of franchise or with any other condition, stipulation or provision of franchise, unless grounds for cancellation are such which do not require notice of cancellation or otherwise provided by law. Either party may obtain injunction, specific performance, damages and attorney's fees. Retailer may require refiner to re-purchase tires, batteries and other accessories, and may recover for loss of good-will if refiner has used 90 day cancellation. Action for cancellation or non-renewal must be brought within two years thereof. (T. 51, §§1451-1454, added Act 628 of 1974).

Marketing of agricultural, horticultural, floricultural, aquicultural, or vegetable products produced in this state, except milk and other specified products, is regulated through Commissioner of Agriculture. (T. 3, §552.1 et seq., added Act 500 of 1978).

Certain noncompetition agreements are permitted in limited circumstances. (T. 23, §921, am'd Act 639 of 1989).

Resale Price Agreements.—See category Intellectual Property, topic Trademarks and Tradenames.

Motion Picture Fair Competition Act adopted by Act 663 of 1977. (T. 37, §§2901-2905, as am'd Act 366 of 1980).

NEGOTIABLE INSTRUMENTS:

See topic Bills and Notes.

RESTRAINT OF TRADE:

See topic Monopolies, Restraint of Trade and Competition.

SALES:

(N.B.: Wholesale revision of Civil Code articles on sales effected by Act 841 of 1993, but not effective until Jan. 1, 1995 and not included in 1994 edition of Digest.)

Three circumstances must concur to the perfection of the contract of sale, to-wit: the thing sold, the price and the consent. (C. C. 2439).

The sale of a thing belonging to another person is null; it may give rise to damages when the buyer knew not that the thing belonged to another person. (C. C. 2452). If, at moment of sale, thing sold is totally destroyed, sale is null; if there is only part of thing destroyed, purchaser has choice either to abandon sale or to retain preserved part, by having price thereof determined by appraisement. (C. C. 2455).

Mortgage in favor of homestead or savings and loan or other associations subject to T. 6, §§701 et seq., may not be cancelled or removed from public records, or be in any manner affected by sale in succession, liquidation, insolvency, receivership, bankruptcy or partition proceedings, unless prior to application or petition for sale at least ten days written notice of sale is given to association by registered or certified mail. (T. 6, §833, am'd Act 689 of 1977).

Lease purchase of specified mobile equipment having dealer cost of not less than $3,000 per unit, may be designated as lease without necessity of filing chattel mortgage. (T. 9, §3509.2 added Act 208 of 1983).

Consideration.—The price of the sale must be certain, that is to say, fixed and determined by the parties. It ought to consist of a sum of money, otherwise it would be considered as an exchange. It ought to be serious, that is to say, there should have been a serious and true agreement that it should be paid. It ought not to be out of all proportion with the value of the thing; for instance the sale of a plantation for a dollar could not be considered as a fair sale; it would be considered as a donation disguised. (C. C. 2464).

Transfer of Title.—Sale is complete between the parties and the property is of right acquired by the purchaser as soon as there exists an agreement for the object and for the price thereof, although the object has not yet been delivered or the price paid. (C. C. 2456).

Promise to sell is, in general, specifically enforceable (C. C. 2462), but if earnest money is given either party may recede from the agreement by paying a proportional penalty (C. C. 2463).

As soon as the agreement is complete, the article is at the risk of the buyer (C. C. 2467), except that the seller is responsible for due and reasonable care (C. C. 2468). Where the seller delays delivery, he is absolutely responsible. (C. C. 2470).

Obligations of Seller.—The seller is bound to two principal obligations, that of delivering and that of warranting the thing he sells. The warranty has two objects: the first is the buyer's peaceable possession of the thing sold, and the second is the hidden defects of the thing sold, or its redhibitory vices. (C. C. 2475-6).

If the seller, knowingly and dishonestly, has sold the property of another person, he shall be obliged to reimburse to the buyer all expenses, even of embellishments of luxury, that the buyer has been at improving the premises. (C. C. 2510).

Whether seller is bound in warranty, or not, by agreement, buyer becomes subrogated to seller's rights and actions in warranty. (C. C. 2503).

Product Liability.—Louisiana courts have applied the articles on redhibition (C. C. 2520-2540) in products liability cases. A seller who does not know of defect is only bound to repair, or to restore purchase price if repair is impossible, less value of use by purchaser. If seller is held liable, he has right of action against manufacturer for losses despite any provisions of franchise or other agreement. (C. C. 2531, as am'd Act 673 of 1974). Courts have allowed damages where seller is also manufacturer on ground that manufacturer is presumed to know of defect. (129 La. 838, 56 So. 906). Recent jurisprudence indicates that functional equivalent of strict liability in tort will be available in product liability cases in Louisiana. (259 La. 599, 250 So.2d 754; 262 La. 80, 262 So.2d 377). Neither negligence nor privity of contract need be established.

Neither warranty of fitness, strict liability nor liability of any kind without negligence applies to physicians, hospitals and blood banks in supplying human blood and blood components or transplantation of human or animal tissue containing viral diseases undetectable by appropriate laboratory tests. (T. 9, §2797, as am'd Act 204 of 1982; C. C. 2322.1, added Act 611 of 1981; C. C. 1764, as am'd Act 301 of 1968).

Provision in contract for sale of equipment or machinery to be incorporated in construction project, as defined, which excludes consequential damages is null. Construction project definition excludes industrial or agricultural projects such as shipbuilding, energy conversion or generation, forestry, paper, sugar or chemical production, fixed platform fabrication, or various mineral activities. (T. 9, §2775, as am'd Act 564 of 1984).

Warranties.—If new motor vehicle does not conform to express warranty and consumer so reports and makes vehicle available for repair, manufacturer must repair. After four or more unsuccessful attempts at repair, manufacturer must at its option either replace with comparable vehicle or refund entire purchase price less reasonable use allowance. (T. 51, §§1941-1946, added Act 228 of 1984).

Right of dissolution of contract of sale is an accessory of credit representing the price, and if held by several persons all must join in suit for dissolution, but any one can become subrogated to rights of person refusing by paying amount due him. (C. C. 2561).

Formalities Required.—Movables may be sold by oral contract, bill of sale not necessary to pass title. All sales of immovables must be in writing, and, in order to have effect against third persons, must be recorded. (C. C. 2440-2).

Printed Contracts.—No statutory requirement as to type size in printed contracts.

Lesion.—If corporeal immovable has been sold for less than half of its true value, vendor may, at any time within four years, rescind sale for this reason alone. (C. C. 2589, et seq., as am'd Act 222 of 1985).

The vendor may reserve the right of redemption within a period not longer than ten years by return of the purchase price. (C. C. 2567 et seq.).

The succession of a living person cannot be sold. (C. C. 2454).

Consumer Protection.—See topic Consumer Protection.

Conditional sales of railroad or street railroad equipment, or rolling stock, are valid as against third persons, if evidenced by instruments duly acknowledged and recorded, provided each locomotive, engine or car so sold has the name of the vendor, lessor, or bailor plainly marked on each side thereof, followed by the word owner, lessor or bailor, as the case may be. Conditional sales of tank cars valid without above requirements. (T. 45, §§611-612, 1241-1244).

As to other property, reservation of title in vendor is ineffective and full title passes to vendee. (121 La. 152, 46 So. 193). However, conditional sale contracts, made out of the state and valid where made, will be recognized and given effect. (See 152 La. 622, 94 So. 138.)

"Endless Chain".—Sales of merchandise by "endless chain" plan constitute misdemeanor unless permit of Louisiana Securities Commission first obtained. (T. 51, §§361-371).

"Bankrupt," etc., Sales.—So-called insurance bankruptcy, removal, etc., sales must be licensed by mayor. False statement in application punishable by fine and/or imprisonment. No goods may be ordered in contemplation of selling same at, or during such sale. (T. 51, §§31-41)

"Bond for deed" sales of encumbered property are unlawful without first providing written guarantee, recorded in mortgage office, by lienholder to release property on payment by purchaser of stipulated mortgage release price. Payments by purchaser must be made to bank designated as escrow agent. Vendor cannot require promissory note to represent purchase price. (T. 9, §§2941-2947). Buyer under "bond for deed" contract is deemed owner for purposes of homestead exemption from property taxes. (C.C. 447[B], added Act 640 of 1995).

Bulk Sales.—See category Debtor and Creditor, topic Fraudulent Sales and Conveyances.

Retail Credit Sales.—No act adopted regulating such sales except with reference to motor vehicles.

Sales of Motor Vehicles.—See category Transportation, topic Motor Vehicles.

SECURITIES:

Art. VIII of Uniform Commercial Code has been adopted as "Commercial Laws—Investment Securities." (T. 10, §8-101 et seq., added Act 165 of 1978). See topic Commercial Code.

Sales of securities are governed by Louisiana Securities Law. (T. 51, §701 et seq., as am'd Act 722 of 1985). Issuance of securities by public entities is regulated by special statute. (T. 39, §§1431-1437, added Act 34, 1st Ex.Sess., 1983).

Supervision is by Commissioner of Financial Institutions, who is also Commissioner of Securities.

Regulatory Powers of Supervising Authority.—Commissioner regulates security dealers and salesmen, and investment advisors, including suspension or revocation of their registration, regulates registration of securities by qualification or notification, unless security or transaction is exempt, including issuance of stop orders denying effectiveness or suspending or revoking effectiveness of any registration, may disqualify

SECURITIES . . . *continued*
exemption from regulation of specified securities, may adopt rules or regulations exempting transactions, and has other authority with respect to administration of Law including investigations, issuance of subpoenas, and conduct of hearings. (T. 51, §§703-711, as am'd Act 722 of 1985).

Prerequisites to Sales or Offerings.—See subhead Regulatory Powers of Supervising Authority, supra.

Securities to Which Act Applicable.—"Security" means any note, stock, treasury stock, bond, debenture, evidence of indebtedness, certificate of interest or participation in any profit-sharing agreement, collateral-trust certificate, preorganization certificate or subscription, transferable share, investment contract, voting-trust certificate, certificate of deposit for security, fractional undivided interest in oil, gas, or other mineral rights, any put, call, straddle, option, or privilege on any security, certificate of deposit, or group or index of securities (including any interest therein or based on value thereof); or, in general, any interest or instrument commonly known as "security", or any certificate of interest or participation in, temporary or interim certificate for, receipt for, guarantee of, or warrant or right to subscribe to or purchase, any of foregoing.

"Security" does not mean: Any insurance or endowment policy or annuity contract nor any variable annuity contract as provided for and regulated under T. 22 and issued by life insurance company licensed to do business in state of Louisiana; currency, or any note, draft, bill of exchange, loan participation or bankers acceptance, or any other evidence of indebtedness issued by bank other than shares of such institution; or any right, interest, or instrument or class or type of right, interest, or instrument which Commissioner, by rule or regulation, excludes from definition of security.

Exempt Securities.—Registration requirements do not apply to any of following securities: (1) Any security, issued or guaranteed by U.S., any state, any political subdivision of a state, or any agency, authority, public corporation, or other instrumentality of one or more of foregoing, including any underlying or separate security which secures any of foregoing securities. Pursuant to Secondary Mortgage Market Enhancement Act of 1984, T. 51, §708(1) does not apply to securities issued by any person, trust, corporation, partnership, association, business trust, or business entity created pursuant to or existing under laws of U.S. or any state which is offering securities pursuant to §106(a)(1) or (2) of that Act; (2) any security issued or guaranteed by Canada, any Canadian province, any political subdivision of any such province, any agency or corporate or other instrumentality of one or more of foregoing, or any other foreign government with which U.S. currently maintains diplomatic relations, if security is recognized as valid obligation by issuer or guarantor; (3) any security issued by or guaranteed by any bank organized under laws of U.S., or any bank, savings institution, or trust company organized and supervised under laws of Louisiana, including any interest or participation in any common trust fund or similar fund maintained by any such bank exclusively for collective investment and reinvestment of assets contributed thereto by such bank in its capacity as trustee, executor, administrator, or guardian; (4) any security issued by and representing interest in or debt of, or guaranteed by, any federal savings and loan association or any building and loan or similar association organized under laws of Louisiana and authorized to do business in this state; (5) any security issued by bona fide agricultural cooperative; (6) any security issued or guaranteed by any federal credit union or any credit union, industrial loan association, or similar association organized and supervised under laws of Louisiana; (7) any security issued or guaranteed by any railroad, other common carrier, public utility, or holding company which is subject to jurisdiction of Interstate Commerce Commission and other conditions; (8) securities listed or approved for listing upon notice of issuance on New York Stock Exchange or American Stock Exchange or security designated or approved for designation as national market system security by National Association of Securities Dealers, Inc. or any other stock exchange or market system approved by Commissioner, and all securities senior or equal in rank to such securities, any security represented by subscription rights which have been so listed, or any warrant or right to purchase or subscribe to any of foregoing, but Commissioner, in public interest, may disqualify some or all securities listed on such stock exchange or market system from the exemption; (9) promissory notes maturing in not more than nine months from date of issuance, provided that said securities are not offered for sale by means of advertisements publicly disseminated in news media or through mails; (10) notes issued in connection with acquisition of real or personal property or renewals thereof, if such notes are issued to sellers of and are secured by all or part of real or personal property so acquired; (11) any security of issuer if it has class of securities registered under §12 of Securities Exchange Act of 1934 which has been so registered for three years immediately preceding offering date, under specified conditions. (T. 51, §708, as am'd Act 722 of 1985).

Exempt Transactions.—T. 51, §109 exempts transactions involving judicial sales, transactions involving certain pledgees, transactions not involving issuer, underwriter or affiliate of issuer, transactions by certain affiliates, transactions pursuant to or exempted from Securities Act of 1933 subject to approval by Commissioner, transactions involving stock dividends or other distributions not involving any consideration other than sales of fractional interests, transactions involving sale of securities to banks, savings institutions, trust companies and other institutions and dealers, transactions involving exchanges with existing security holders of issuer or subsidiary under specified conditions, stock option bonus or other plans involving no consideration other than services, qualified employee stock purchase plans, offers but not sales of securities for which registration statement has been filed under Securities Act of 1933, transactions incident to judicially approved reorganization, transactions involving certain mergers and other reorganizations, and between certain parent and subsidiary corporations, transactions in connection with certain pooled income funds, and other transactions exempted by Commissioner, including Private Offering Exemptions in Rule 1 of Art. D, Reg. 1 of Commissioner. (T. 51, §709, as am'd Act 722 of 1985).

Registration of Securities by Notification.—Specified types of securities may be registered by notification with Commissioner by filing registration statement prescribed by Commissioner which may include Form A, Uniform Application, and other documents and information or copy of prospectus filed with Securities and Exchange Commission. (T. 51, §705[D], as am'd Act 722 of 1985).

Registration of Securities by Qualification.—Securities not entitled to registration by notification must be registered by qualification with Commissioner by filing registration statement prescribed by Commissioner which may include Form A, Uniform Application, and other specified information and documents or, under specified conditions, copy of registration statement and other information filed with Securities and Exchange Commission together with Form A, Uniform Application. (T. 51, §705[B], as am'd Act 722 of 1985).

Small Issues and Nonprofit Issuer Registration.—Limited registration statements are provided for small issues (up to $1,000,000 as permitted by Commissioner) and nonprofit issues. (T. 51, §705, as am'd Act 722 of 1985).

Registration Fees.—Generally 1/10 of 1% of aggregate price of securities, but not less than $100 and not more than $1,000, plus $250 for expenses of Commissioner.

Take-Over Offers.—See category Business Organizations, topic Corporations, subhead Tender Offers.

Registration of Broker-Dealers, Agent-Salesmen and Investment-Advisors.—Broker-dealers, agent-salesmen, investment-advisors and loan brokers must be registered with Commissioner by filing verified application. Dealers and salesmen must pass written examination. (T. 51, §703, as am'd Act 722 of 1985).

Bonds.—Broker-dealers must post surety bonds up to $10,000 unless waived by Commissioner. (T. 51, §703, as am'd Act 722 of 1985).

Records.—Dealers, salesmen and investment advisors must keep records of all security transactions as required by Commissioner. (T. 51, §703, as am'd Act 722 of 1985).

Liabilities.—Any person who (a) offers or sells a security in violation of section requiring registration of broker-dealer or agent-salesmen, section requiring registration of security or sections requiring registration by qualification or notification, except sales of exempt securities or exempt transactions; (b) offers or sells a security in violation of Act or a security the registration of which was revoked or suspended; or (c) offers or sells a security by means of an untrue statement of a material fact or by omitting to state a material fact, is liable to purchaser for consideration paid, interest, costs and attorney fees, less income received from security. Liability may extend to persons controlling seller, partners, officers or directors of seller, employees and broker-dealers or agents materially aiding in sale. Suit must be brought within two years after contract of sale. (T. 51, §§712-714, as am'd Act 722 of 1985).

Uniform Simplification of Fiduciary Security Transfers Act adopted. (T. 9, §§3831-3840).

Uniform Securities Ownership by Minors Act not adopted.

STATUTE OF FRAUDS:

See topic Frauds, Statute of.

WAREHOUSEMEN:

Art. VII of Uniform Commercial Code has been adopted as "Commercial Laws—Documents of Title". (T. 10, §7-101 et seq., added Act 164 of 1978). See topic Commercial Code.

Licensing.—Before transacting business, a proprietor lessee, or manager of a warehouse must procure from district court of parish where warehouse is situated a certificate that he is transacting business as public warehouseman under laws of state, which shall be issued upon written petition stating locality, name of warehouse or warehouses, name of each person individually or member of firm interested as owner or principal in its management, or names of president, secretary and treasurer if a corporation. Said certificate revocable by court upon summary proceedings upon written complaint to court setting forth particular violation. Bond must be given with good and sufficient security approved by court for $5,000, or $25,000 in municipality of 50,000 or more population, which must be renewed every two years from date of approval. When one bond of $25,000 has been furnished no further bond need be furnished to qualify in another parish or municipality. There is penalty for every day business is carried on without certificate. In addition, warehouseman who violates any provisions of law is guilty of criminal offense. (T. 54, §§111-117).

Reports.—Operator of warehouse must file with Supervisor of Public Accounts detailed monthly reports on or before fifteenth day of month and may not engage in business of selling or distributing any goods subject to excise, license or privilege taxes. (T. 54, §182).

CITIZENSHIP

ALIENS:

Aliens, except enemy aliens (T. 42, §32 as am'd Act 472 of 1974), are not subject to restrictions.

See, however, category Employment, topic Labor Relations.

CIVIL ACTIONS AND PROCEDURE

ACCORD AND SATISFACTION:

Compromise must be in writing or recited in open court and capable of being transcribed from record. Agreement recited in open court confers upon parties right of judicial enforcement, although substance may thereafter be written in more convenient form. (C. C. 3071, as am'd Act 782 of 1981). It has force of adjudication and cannot be attacked for error of law or lesion, but error of calculation may be corrected. May be annulled for error in person or on matter in dispute, for fraud or violence, or when made in execution of title which is null unless parties expressly compromised on nullity. Compromise entered into on false documents is null. (C. C. 3078-81).

Content of compromise may be unenforceable if it conceals public hazard or information related to it, unless information is trade secret. (C.C.P. 1426, as am'd Act 49 of 1995, eff. in prospective manner only Aug. 15, 1995).

See note at head of Digest as to 1998 legislation covered.

See Topical Index in front part of this volume.

LA – 12

ACCORD AND SATISFACTION . . . *continued*

A power to receive includes that of giving a receipt in acquittance. (C. C. 2999).

Dation en paiement (giving in payment) is an act by which debtor gives a thing to creditor in payment of a sum due (C. C. 2655); delivery is essential (C. C. 2656); made by insolvent husband to wife to replace her dotal and paraphernal effects is valid as against other creditors and is favored by law (22 La. Ann. 327).

Pleading.—Defense should be specially pleaded. (C.C.P. 1005).

ACTIONS:

Actions are divided into personal, real and mixed. (C.C.P. 422).

Personal action is one brought to enforce obligation against obligor personally and independently of property which he possesses. This action is grounded on one of four causes which give rise to personal obligations, which are contracts, quasi contracts, offenses and quasi offenses. (C.C.P. 422).

Real actions are those brought to enforce rights in, to, or upon immovable property. Three principal real actions are petitory, possessory and hypothecary. Petitory action is brought by person not in possession claiming title to real estate against person who is in possession of property or claims ownership adversely. (C.C.P. 3651, 3652). Possessory action is brought by person who claims to be restored to or maintained in possession of real estate against party who has evicted him or disturbed his possession. (C.C.P. 3655, 3656). Hypothecary action is brought by creditor against property which has been hypothecated to him by his debtor, in order to have it seized and sold for payment of his debt. (C.C.P. 3721-3743). Mortgagee may sue any person who, without mortgagee's consent, buys, sells or otherwise converts mortgaged immovables. (T. 9, §5382, am'd Act 107 of 1980).

Equity.—All actions are brought in the same courts and no distinction is made between law and equity. Louisiana has never adopted a separate court of equity.

Conditions precedent to bringing an action differ according to the nature of the action. For instance, in an action for a passive breach of contract, the plaintiff must, as a condition precedent to bringing the action put the defendant in default; not so, in an action for an active breach. (C. C. 1933). The plaintiff is not required to make an amicable demand upon the debtor unless required by particular statute. (C.C.P. 421). His failure to do so can only affect his right to claim costs of court.

An action is commenced by filing a petition to a court of competent jurisdiction. (C.C.P. 421). See topic Pleading; also topic Process.

Parties.—An action can only be brought by one having a real and actual interest which he asserts. (C.C.P. 681). Necessary and indispensable parties are defined and factors for their characterization are provided. (C.C.P. 641-646, as am'd Act 662 of 1995). Persons other than those made parties to original action may be made parties to reconventional (counterclaim) demand, whether this be permissive or compulsory joinder. (C.C.P. 1064, as am'd Act 858 of 1995).

Class Actions.—Effective July 1, 1997 and applicable only to actions filed on or after effective date, class action provisions amended to track closely Rule 23 of Federal Rules as it stood in 1997. Prerequisites to any class action are (1) numerosity such that joinder is impracticable; (2) common questions of law or fact; (3) claims or defenses of representatives are typical; (4) representatives will fairly and adequately represent class; and (5) class definition may be made objectively in terms of ascertainable criteria, such that court may determine constituency of class for purposes of conclusiveness of any rendered judgment. (C.C.P. 591, as am'd Act 839 of 1997, eff. July 1, 1997). Three forms of federal class actions are recognized, viz., limited fund or inconsistent adjudication class under FRCP 23(b)(1); class appropriate for final injunctive or declaratory relief under FRCP 23(b)(2); and class concerning common questions of law or fact that predominate over individual, making class action superior vehicle to resolve controversy, as under FRCP 23(b)(3). (C.C.P. 591, as am'd Act 839 of 1997, eff. July 1, 1997). Fourth type of class action is also recognized, when parties to settlement request certification under third category above, even though requirements are not otherwise met. (C.C.P. 591[B][4], as am'd Act 839 of 1997, eff. July 1, 1997). Provisions consistent with Federal Rules of Civil Procedure for certification procedure, case management, judgment settlement and the like. Specific provisions on suspension of statute of limitation while class action request is pending or while action after certification is pending; specific provisions for derivative actions. (C.C.P. 592 through 596, 611 through 617, as am'd Act 839 of 1997, eff. July 1, 1997).

Intervention.—Any third party may intervene in a suit when he has an interest in the success of either party to the suit or an interest opposed to both. (C.C.P. 1091).

Interpleader.—Concursus proceeding may be invoked to require persons having competing or conflicting claims to money, property, or mortgages or privileges on property to assert their respective claims against all other parties to proceeding. (C.C.P. 4651).

Third Party Practice.—Defendant in principal action or in reconvention may implead any person, including a co-defendant who may be liable to him for all or part of principal demand. As to demands connected to principal demand, third party defendant may reconvene against plaintiff or third party plaintiff and plaintiff may assert demand against third party defendant. Co-party may bring cross-claim against any other co-party. (C.C.P. 1071 et seq., added Act 63 of 1983).

Joinder.—Separate actions may be cumulated or joined in same demand, provided one of them does not preclude, or is not inconsistent with, another and each action is brought in proper venue. (C.C.P. 461-463).

Severance.—Where defendants are sued on the same cause of action, severance is within the discretion of the trial judge. (C.C.P. 465).

Splitting cause of action is not permitted; that which is not demanded in the first action will be held to be waived. (C.C.P. 425).

Consolidation of suits before same court and involving common issues may, in discretion of court, be ordered. (C.C.P. 1561).

Abatement and Revival.—Death of party does not abate action unless it is strictly personal to him. (C.C.P. 428). Legal successor is substituted for deceased party by motion. (C.C.P. 801-804). Succession representative may bring "survival action" for damages of deceased tort victim if statutory representatives do not survive him. (C.C. 2315.1, as am'd Act 675 of 1987).

Abandonment.—Where plaintiff, at any time before final judgment, allows three years to elapse without taking any steps to prosecute his demand, he is considered as having abandoned same. Rule does not apply to succession proceeding: (1) Which has been opened, (2) in which representative has been appointed, or (3) in which testament has been probated. Provision operative without formal order, but court may authorize contradictory hearing before dismissal. Supporting affidavit of inactivity must be filed, and motion must be served on plaintiff, who has 30 days from service to move to set aside dismissal. Discovery is deemed to be step that defeats showing of inactivity. (C.C.P. 561, as am'd Act 1221 of 1997, eff. July 1, 1998 and applicable to all pending actions).

Trials.—Separate trials of liability and damages are permitted. (C.C.P. 1562, added Act 534 of 1983). Preference in scheduling may be given to party over 70 or terminally ill. (C. C. P. 1573, added Act 106 of 1990).

Jury Trials.—Jury trial may be had in civil matters when either party timely prays therefor not later than ten days after service of last pleading directed to such issue. Jury trial not available in: (1) Suit where no individual petitioner's cause of action exceeds $50,000; (2) suit on unconditional obligation to pay specific sum of money unless defense is forgery, fraud, error or failure of consideration; (3) summary, executory, probate, partition, mandamus, habeas corpus, quo warranto, injunction, concursus, worker's compensation, emancipation, tutorship, interdiction, curatorship, legitimacy, filiation, annulment or divorce proceeding; (4) proceeding to determine custody, visitation, alimony or child support; (5) proceeding to review action by administrative or municipal body; (6) suit on admiralty or general maritime claim under federal law brought in state court under federal "savings to suitors" clause, if plaintiff has designated suit as maritime claim; (7) other cases where jury trial is specifically denied by law, such as those against political subdivisions (which, however, may choose to waive prohibition). (C.C.P. 1732 as am'd Act 661 of 1993; T. 13, §5101 et seq; T. 13, §5105[c], as am'd Act 598 of 1995; T. 13, §5105[D], as am'd Act 63 of 1996 First Ex. Sess.). Parties may stipulate that fewer than all issues are to be tried by jury (C.C.P. 1736, as am'd Act 534 of 1983), and separate trials of liability and quantum may be ordered (C.C.P. 1562, as am'd Act 534 of 1983). Court may order, with consent of all parties, that separate trial on damages precede trial on liability. (C.C.P. 1562, as am'd Act 289 of 1985). Similarly, separate trial on insurance coverage may be held unless material factual dispute as to insurance coverage duplicates issue relative to liability or quantum; separate trial of insurance coverage is to court alone. (C.C.P. 1562[D], added Act 72 of 1992). Peremptory challenges to jurors must be made in side bar conference. (C.C.P. 1766 [D], added Act 703 of 1990). Ordinary jury is 12 unless parties stipulate six. (C.C.P. 1761, as am'd Act 534 of 1983). If jury is 12, nine must concur unless parties stipulate otherwise; if jury is six, five must concur unless parties stipulate otherwise. (C.C.P. 1797, as am'd Act 534 of 1983). Directed verdicts and judgments n.o.v. are permitted, and jury verdict may take form of general verdict, special verdict or general verdict accompanied by answers to interrogatories. (C.C.P. 1810-1813, as am'd Act 534 of 1983). Additur and remittitur are also permitted. (C.C.P. 1814, added Act 173 of 1989). Court may on its own motion or motion of any party grant mistrial after hearing on issue. (C.C.P. 1631[C], added Act 411 of 1995). Jury's findings are not binding on appellate court (see topic Appeal and Error), and thus jury trial use is more limited than in other states. Compulsory reconventional demand (counterclaim), triable by jury may be so tried even if main demand is not triable by jury. (C.C.P. 1731, as am'd Act 661 of 1995).

Jurors may have copies of instructions in deliberation room, and may take notes and have those in deliberation room as well. (C.C.P. 1792 and 1794, as am'd Act 668 of 1997).

Limitation of.—See topic Limitation of Actions.

Small Claims.—See category Courts and Legislature, topic Courts.

Administration.—See category Estates and Trusts, topic Executors and Administrators.

Direct Actions.—See category Transportation, topic Motor Vehicles, subhead Direct Actions.

APPEAL AND ERROR:

Appellate jurisdiction of Supreme Court extends only to: (1) Cases in which law or ordinance has been declared unconstitutional and (2) cases in which defendant has been convicted of capital offense and death penalty has actually been imposed. (Const., art. 5, §5, as am'd Act 844 of 1980, voter approved Nov. 11, 1980). When constitutionality of statute is at issue, attorney general must be given notice. (T. 13, §4448, added Act 1004 of 1985).

Courts of Appeal.—Except as otherwise provided, appeal lies to courts of appeal in all cases of which Supreme Court is not given exclusive appellate jurisdiction. Appeal from family, juvenile, parish and city courts as well as district courts lies to courts of appeal. Appeal from justice of peace courts lies to parish court or if none, district court of parish where justice of peace court is situated. All appeals are heard on record made up in trial court, with exception of appeals from justice of peace courts, which are tried de novo without further appeal allowed. (C.C.P. 5001-5002, as am'd Act 46 of 1979; Const., art. 5, §10).

How Taken.—Appeal may be taken either by motion in open court, by written motion or by petition. (C.C.P. 2121).

Time for Taking.—Limitation for taking suspensive appeal from judgment of district court is 30 days from either: (1) Expiration of delay for applying for new trial (seven days from signing of judgment or, when notice of judgment is required by C.C.P. Art. 1913, from mailing of notice of judgment exclusive of legal holidays); (2) refusal to grant new trial where notice thereof not required; or from (3) date of mailing of notice

See note at head of Digest as to 1998 legislation covered.

See Topical Index in front part of this volume.

LA – 13

APPEAL AND ERROR . . . *continued*

of refusal to grant new trial or judgment NOV, when notice required. (C.C.P. 1914[C], as am'd Act 657 of 1995; C.C.P. 2123). Usual limitation for taking devolutive appeal is 60 days from applicable date as above; appellees seeking to have judgment modified, revised or reversed as to any other party may take appeal within usual delays or within ten days of mailing by clerk of first devolutive appeal in case, whichever is later. (C.C.P. 2087, as am'd Act 174 of 1977). When one party has filed motion for new trial or motion for judgment NOV, delays for appeal do not begin for any party until they run for party requesting such post-judgment relief. (C.C.P. 2087, as am'd Act 658 of 1995). Appeal periods are suspended if case is removed to federal court and resume upon remand. (C.C.P. 2087[D] and 2123[C], as am'd Act 609 of 1997).

Appeals from parish, city or justice of peace courts, whether suspensive or devolutive, must be taken within ten days from judgment or from service of notice of judgment where necessary. (C.C.P. 5003, added Act 46 of 1979).

Person who could have intervened in trial court may appeal, whether or not any other appeal has been taken. (C.C.P. 2086).

Perfecting appeal divests trial court of jurisdiction except for certain ministerial matters. (C.C.P. 2088[10], as am'd Act 126 of 1983).

Appeals taken before disposition of all posttrial motions are premature, but become effective upon denial of such motions. (C.C.P. 2087[D], 2123[C], added Act 1056 of 1997).

Stay of Proceedings.—Suspensive appeal stays execution; devolutive appeal does not. (C.C.P. 2123, 2124).

No suspensive appeal allowed from judgment appointing or removing tutor or curator of minor, interdict or absentee or of a vacant succession or other administrator of succession nor from judgment relating to custody or alimony. (C.C.P. 2122, 4068, 2974, 3943, 4548).

Only suspensive appeal may be taken from judgment granting or refusing annulment of marriage, separation or divorce. (C.C.P. 3942).

If Supreme Court denies application for writ of certiorari, or denies application for re-hearing of its own decision, it may stay execution of appellate court judgment pending timely application for certiorari or appeal to U. S. Supreme Court. (C.C.P. 2166 and 2167, as am'd Act 163 of 1982).

Bond.—Security to be furnished for suspensive appeal from: (1) Money judgment shall be equal to amount of judgment, including interest allowed by judgment to date security is furnished; (2) judgment distributing fund in custodia legis shall be sufficient to cover costs; (3) all other judgments shall be amount sufficient to satisfy judgment and damages resulting from suspension of execution. No security is required for devolutive appeal. (C.C.P. 2124, am'd Act 307 of 1989; see also T. 23, §1351, as am'd Act 707 of 1979). Security may be by bond or by encumbrance of immovable property. (C.C.P. 5121.1, added Act 200 of 1984).

Scope of Review.—All appeals to Supreme Court are on both law and facts except in criminal cases or otherwise provided by Constitution. (Const., art. 5, §5). Appeals to Court of Appeals are on both law and fact except as limited to law by Constitution or as provided by law with regard to administrative agency decisions. (Const., art. 5, §10).

Judgment on Appeal.—Appellate court may render any judgment which is just, legal, and proper on record. (C.C.P. 2164). In civil matters only, when judgment of district court is reversed or modified, and one of three judges dissents, case may be reargued before panel of at least five judges and majority must concur to render judgment. (Const., art. 5, §8, as am'd Act 844 of 1980, voter approved Nov. 11, 1980).

Rehearing.—Within 14 days of rendition of judgment by appellate court or Supreme Court in criminal matter, or within 14 days of mailing of notice of judgment of Court of Appeal in civil matter, rehearing may be requested. (C.Cr.P. 922, C.C.P. 2166, as am'd Act 451 of 1983).

Abandonment of appeal takes place when parties fail to take step in prosecution or disposition for period of one year. (C.C.P. 561, 2165; Unif. Rules, Cts. of App., VII).

Fees.—Filing fee in civil cases before Supreme Court is $150. (T. 13, §126, as am'd Act 104 of 1986). Filing fee in courts of appeal for filing record of appeal is $100; for writ application, $50; for rehearing application, $70. (T. 13, §352, as am'd Act 104 of 1986).

BONDS:

All bonds required either by law or by order of court to be furnished in any judicial proceeding may be made payable to the clerk of court. Personal surety may furnish immovable property in parish where proceeding was brought, as security for bond for civil court costs including jury costs; surety must present to clerk assessment certificate, homestead exemption waiver, and mortgage executed in clerk's favor. (T. 13, §843.2, added Act 413 of 1983).

When litigant has furnished a bond that is insufficient in amount or incorrect by reasons of errors or omissions, he may correct such insufficiency, error or omission and furnish new or additional bond; any new bond so furnished and any supplementary or additional bond has the same effect as to principal and surety as the original bond. (C.C.P. 5124). Adverse party may rule party furnishing bond into court to show cause why bond should not be deemed insufficient or invalid. (C.C.P. 5123).

If original bond is found insufficient or invalid, party furnishing same has right within four judicial days thereafter to furnish new or supplemental bond. Should new bond be found insufficient or invalid, party furnishing it is entitled to furnish second new or supplemental bond within four days. If that bond is insufficient or invalid, party furnishing it may not correct defects. (C.C.P. 5124-5126).

Sureties.—Bond may not be accepted unless each surety thereon makes oath that he is worth over and above his debts and obligations in assets that can be subjected to levy under execution the amount for which he has bound himself, and unless principal makes oath that he is informed and believes that this is the case; this does not apply to surety companies authorized to do business in the state. When party furnishing bond is plaintiff, a cash bond may be furnished in lieu of other security. (C.C.P. 5121-5122).

Sureties on all bonds must pay where principal fails to pay promptly or within 30 days from amicable demand in writing, or be penalized with 10% attorneys' fees, if suitor recovers full amount claimed. (T. 9, §3902).

No bond is required for notary who is attorney. (T. 35, §72, as am'd Act 943 of 1988, eff. Aug 1, 1988).

Enforcement.—Any person in interest may sue upon a bond furnished in a judicial proceeding. (C.C.P. 5121). Debtor and surety may be joined in the same suit. (C. C. 3051).

CERTIORARI:

The Supreme Court, courts of appeal, and each of the judges thereof, subject to review by the court of which he is a member, and each district judge throughout the state may in aid of their respective jurisdictions, original, appellate, or supervisory, issue writs of certiorari. (Const., art. 5, §2).

Supreme Court may issue writ of certiorari to any state court in aid of its supervisory jurisdiction. (Const., art. 5, §5).

Each Court of Appeal has power to certify to Supreme Court any question of law arising in any case pending before it, and thereupon Supreme Court may either give binding instructions or decide case upon whole record. (Const., art. 5, §11).

Proceedings.—Party wishing to obtain the writ addresses his sworn petition to the higher tribunal stating the reasons for which he seeks the writ annexing thereto certified copy of inferior judge's order or ruling, judge's reasons therefor, and pleadings, and copy of petition must be mailed to inferior judge and adverse parties. (La. Sup. Ct. Rule X).

Stay.—If Supreme Court denies application for writ of certiorari, it may stay execution of appellate court judgment pending timely application for certiorari or appeal to U. S. Supreme Court. Similar authority if it denies application for re-hearing of own decision. (C.C.P. 2166 and 2167, as am'd Act 163 of 1982).

CHARITABLE IMMUNITY:

See topic Damages.

COMMISSIONS TO TAKE TESTIMONY:

See topic Depositions and Discovery.

COSTS:

In New Orleans all costs must be paid in advance before the services required are performed. Elsewhere a deposit in an amount established by local rules is required at time of filing suit.

Unless the judgment provides otherwise costs are paid by the party cast. (C.C.P. 1920).

Appellate court may tax costs of both courts or any part thereof against any part. (C.C.P. 2164).

Security for Costs.—The defendant can require security for costs, the amount to be fixed by the court, and should the plaintiff fail to furnish security as ordered by the court his suit will be dismissed as in case of nonsuit. In parishes outside of Orleans, the demand must be made before pleading. (T. 13, §1215).

Forma Pauperis.—Bond for costs or current payment of costs may be dispensed with in case of poverty of litigant. (C.C.P. 5181-5188).

DAMAGES:

Generally, Louisiana courts award damages recognized by common law. However, punitive or exemplary damages are not awarded except under specific statutory provisions therefor. Such damages are awardable: (1) Upon proof that injuries upon which action is based were caused by wanton or reckless disregard for rights and safety of others by defendant whose intoxication while operating vehicle was cause in fact of resulting injuries (C.C. 2315.4); or (2) upon proof that injuries were caused by wanton and reckless disregard for rights and safety of claimant through criminal sexual activity which occurred when victim was 17 or younger, regardless of whether dependent was prosecuted for act (C.C. 2315.7, added Act 831 of 1993, eff. June 22, 1993). Damages may include loss of consortium, service and society, recoverable by same persons who would have had cause of action for wrongful death of injured person (mutually exclusive preferred classes in order of: [1] Surviving spouse or children; [2] parents; [3] siblings; [4] grandparents). Father or mother who have abandoned child, as defined, has no such action. (C.C. 2315, 2315.1, 2315.2, latter two provisions as am'd Act 1317 of 1997, eff. July 15, 1997 and applicable only to causes of action arising on or after that date). They may also include, as to specific relatives and under specific conditions, damages for experiencing harm to others. (C.C. 2315.6, added Act 782 of 1991). Contractual provisions for liquidated damages are enforceable, except that they may be held to increase interest charges on contracts to pay money to extent of violating law of usury. Except in proceedings on contracts, promissory notes, open accounts, other negotiable instruments, for alimony or child support, on tax claim or in garnishments, specific amount of damage may not be pleaded. (C.C.P. 893, 1032 and 1703, as am'd Act 443 of 1988, eff. Jan. 1, 1989).

Sovereign Immunity.—No immunity for state, state agency, nor political subdivision from suit and liability in contract or injury to person or property. (Const., Art. 12, §10). However, by series of special legislative provisions, public defendants enjoy special treatment in personal injury matters, viz., structured payment plans (T. 13, §5114, added Act 450 of 1985); limited vicarious liability based on employment relationships (T. 42, §§1441.1-1441.4, added Act 451 of 1985); limitation on amount awardable to $500,000 except medical care and loss of earnings (T. 13, §§5106 and 5109, as am'd Act 63 of 1996 First Ex. Sess.); and limitations on strict liability rules (T. 9, §2800, added Act 454 of 1985).

Charitable Immunity.—Immunity denied. (289 So.2d 88). No person rendering care gratuitously and in good faith at scene of emergency, or who moves injured person to

DAMAGES . . . *continued*
place of medical care, is liable for damages, but immunity does not apply when damages result from business relationship, intentional or gross negligence, and immunity is personal to assisting person. (T. 9, §2793, added Act 600 of 1975). No nurse, physician, dentist or surgeon who renders gratuitous service at scene of emergency is liable for any act or omission in rendering such service.

Dram Shop Liability.—Liability denied. Holder of liquor permit or his employees is not liable to person of legal age for injury or death to him or others caused by intoxication. Social host is similarly treated. (T. 9, §2800.1, added Act 18 of 1986, eff. June 6, 1986).

Medical malpractice damages may be limited upon qualification with Residual Malpractice Insurance Authority, and there are special provisions with respect to future medical care expenses and settlements in that regard. (T. 40, §§1299.39-1299.48, as am'd Act 239 of 1985). Blood and tissue bank services are subject to special regulation, and are not considered as selling product or subject to strict liability rules. (C.C. 2322.1 and T-9, §2797, as am'd Act 1091 of 1990).

No-Fault Insurance.—See category Transportation, topic Motor Vehicles, subhead No-Fault Insurance.

Uniform Contribution Among Tortfeasors Act.—Not adopted.

Comparative Negligence Rule.—C.C. Arts. 2103, 2323 and 2324, and C.C.P. Art. 1811 provide for "pure" comparative negligence. As amended in 1996, C.C. Arts. 2323 and 2324 provide in most cases for several rather than solidary liability with each wrongdoer liable only for his percentage of fault, regardless of immunity or insolvency of others. Same percentage of fault is applicable to subrogee, when it has been applied to subrogor. (C.C. 2324.2, added Act 771 of 1989, eff. July 9, 1989).

See categories Business Regulation and Commerce, topic Interest, subheads Maximum Rate, and Discount; Estates and Trusts, topic Death, subhead Action for Death.

DECLARATORY JUDGMENTS:

See topic Judgments.

DEPOSITIONS AND DISCOVERY:

Rules governing depositions and discovery have been adopted from pertinent provisions of Federal Rules of Civil Procedure. By Act 574 of 1976 articles have been renumbered and comprise C.C.P. 1429-1456.

Discovery through depositions may be obtained regarding any matter not privileged which is relevant to subject matter involved in pending action, whether it relates to claim or defense of party seeking discovery or to claim or defense of any party, including existence, description, nature, custody, condition, and location of any books, documents, or other tangible things and identity and location of persons having knowledge of any discoverable matter. It is not ground for objection that information sought will be inadmissible at trial if information sought appears reasonably calculated to lead to discovery of admissible evidence. (C.C.P. 1422).

Attorney of record representing party may not be deposed except under extraordinary circumstances, and then only by court order after contradictory hearing. (C.C.P. 1452, as am'd Act 767 of 1981).

Outside of State for Use within State.—All provisions relative to taking of depositions upon oral examination or depositions upon written interrogatories apply equally whether deposition is to be taken in state or in another state, except that compulsory process for appearance of deponent is governed by law of place where deposition taken. (C.C.P. 1435).

Depositions de bene esse may be taken upon giving reasonable notice in writing to every other party to the action. Notice should state time and place for taking deposition, and name and address of each person to be examined. After notice is served, upon motion seasonably made by any party or by person to be examined and upon notice and for good cause shown, court in which action is pending may make an order that deposition shall not be taken or that it may be taken only at some designated time or place other than that stated in notice, or that it may be taken on written interrogatories, or that certain matters shall not be inquired into, or that scope of examination shall be limited to certain matters, or that examination shall be held with no one present except parties to action and their officers or counsel, or that after being sealed, deposition shall be opened only by order of court, or that secret processes, developments, or research need not be disclosed, or that parties shall simultaneously file specified documents of information enclosed in sealed envelopes to be opened as directed by court; or court may make any other order which justice requires to protect party or witness from annoyance, embarrassment, oppression or undue expense.

The officer before whom the deposition is to be taken must put the witness on oath and must personally, or by someone acting under his direction and in his presence, record the testimony of the witness. Such officer may be shorthand or court reporter, or notary. Testimony must be taken stenographically and transcribed unless parties agree otherwise. All objections made at time of examination to qualifications of officer taking deposition, or to manner of taking it, or to evidence presented, or to conduct of any party, and any other objection to proceedings must be noted by officer upon deposition. Evidence objected to must be taken subject to objections. In lieu of participating in oral examination, parties served with notice of taking deposition may transmit written interrogatories to officer who must propound them to witness and record answers verbatim.

When the testimony is fully transcribed, the deposition must be submitted to the witness for examination and must be read to or by him unless such examination and reading are waived by the parties. Any changes in form or substance which the witness desires to make must be entered upon the deposition by the officer with the statement of the reasons given by the witness for making them. The deposition must then be signed by the witness unless the parties by stipulation waive the signing, or the witness is ill or absent from the parish or county where the deposition was taken and cannot be found, or refuses to sign. If the deposition is not signed by the witness, the officer must sign it and state on the record the fact of the waiver, or of the illness or absence of the witness, or the fact of the refusal to sign, together with the reason, if any, given therefor. Video deposition is exempt from reading and signing requirements. (C.C.P. 1445, as am'd Act 295 of 1990).

The officer must certify on the deposition that the witness was duly sworn by him and that the deposition is a true record of the testimony given by the witness. He must then securely seal the deposition in an envelope, endorsed with the title of the action and marked "Deposition of (here insert name of witness)" and promptly send it by registered or certified mail to party at whose request deposition was taken, who shall become custodian of deposition. Original deposition shall not be filed in record, but made available to all other parties for inspection or copying. (C.C.P. 1426, 1433, 1434, 1436, 1445, and 1446, as am'd Act 388 of 1989, eff. June 30, 1989).

Depositions upon written interrogatories may be taken after commencement of action by any party of any person including party. Party desiring to take deposition upon written questions shall serve them upon every other party with notice stating name and address of person who is to answer them, if known, and if name is not known, general description sufficient to identify him or particular class or group to which he belongs, and name or descriptive title and address of officer before whom deposition is to be taken. Deposition upon written questions may be taken of public or private corporation or partnership, or association, or government agency in accordance with provisions of C.C.P. 1442. Within 30 days after notice and written questions are served, party may serve cross-questions upon all other parties. Within ten days after being served with cross-questions, party may serve redirect questions upon all other parties. Within ten days after being served with redirect questions, party may serve recross-questions upon all other parties. Court may, for cause shown, enlarge or shorten time periods stated above. (C.C.P. 1448).

Copy of notice and copies of all questions served shall be delivered by party taking deposition to officer designated in notice, who shall proceed promptly to take testimony in response to questions and to prepare, certify, and file or mail deposition, attaching thereto copy of notice and questions received by him. When deposition is filed party taking it shall promptly give notice thereof to all other parties. (C.C.P. 1449).

When answer to interrogatory may be derived from business records as easily by serving party as by party served, it is sufficient answer to specify and make available those records, with sufficient particularity to permit serving party to locate information. (C.C.P. 1460, as am'd Act 450 of 1982).

Depositions may be taken by telephone if agreed upon by every party to suit. (C.C.P. 1436.1, added Act 205 of 1986).

Interrogatories and their answers, document requests and responses, and requests for admissions and responses need not be filed in record except in limited circumstances. (C.C.P. 1474, as am'd Act 388 of 1989, eff. June 30, 1989).

Perpetuating Testimony.—Person who desires to perpetuate his own testimony or that of another person, regarding any matter that may be cognizable in any court of this state may file verified petition in court in which anticipated action might be brought stating that petitioner expects to be party to action, cognizable in court of this state but is presently unable to bring it or cause it to be brought, subject matter of expected action and his interests therein, facts that he desires to establish by proposed testimony and his reasons for desiring to perpetuate it, names or description of persons he expects will be adverse parties and their addresses so far as known, names and addresses of persons to be examined and substance of testimony which he expects to elicit from each, and shall ask for order authorizing petitioner to take depositions of persons to be examined named in petition, for purpose of perpetuating their testimony. (C.C.P. 1429).

Petitioner shall thereafter serve notice upon each person named in petition as expected adverse party, together with copy of petition, stating that petitioner will apply to court, at time and place named therein, for order described in petition. Notice must be served at least 20 days before hearing, but if such service cannot be made with due diligence, court may make such order as is just for service by publication or otherwise, and shall appoint for persons not served attorney who shall represent them, and in case they are not otherwise represented, shall cross-examine deponent. If any expected adverse party is minor or incompetent, court shall appoint attorney to represent him. (C.C.P. 1430).

If court is satisfied that perpetuation of testimony may prevent failure or delay of justice, it shall make order designating or describing person whose deposition may be taken and specifying subject matter of examination and whether deposition shall be taken upon oral examination or written interrogatories. (C.C.P. 1431). If court is satisfied there is substantial possibility that person whose testimony is sought will die or be too incapacitated to testify before contradictory hearing can be held, it may grant perpetuation of testimony ex parte. (C.C.P. 1430.1, added Act 53 of 1989).

In Aid of Execution of Judgment.—Deposition of third party who may have financial records of judgment debtor may be allowed by court to aid in execution of judgment. (C.C.P. 1433, 1469.2, 2451.1, as am'd and added Act 1000 of 1990).

Production of Documents.—Party may request production of documents for inspection, and party who produces them must do so as they are kept in usual course of business, organized to correspond with categories of request. (C.C.P. 1462, as am'd Act 451 of 1982). Specific provisions govern requests for production of medical records. (C.C.P. 1465.1, added Act 823 of 1993; T. 13, §§3715.1, 3715.3, 3734[E] and [F]; C.F. 510[E], all as am'd Act 988 of 1993). No order compelling production of medical records may be granted without certification that copy of proposed order or subpoena has been delivered to custodian of records or his attorney. (C.C.P. 1469.1, added Act 1046 of 1986). Subpoenas to permit inspection of tangible things permitted. (C.C.P. 1463[B], added Act 410 of 1995).

Before Whom Taken.—Depositions must be taken before an officer authorized to administer oaths, who is not an employee or attorney of any of the parties or otherwise interested in the outcome of the case. (C.C.P. 1434).

Compelling Attendance of Witnesses.—A witness who is a resident of this state may be required to attend an examination to take his deposition only in the parish in which he resides or is employed or transacts his business in person, or at such other convenient place as may be fixed by order of court. A nonresident witness, temporarily in this state, may be required to attend an examination to take his deposition only in the parish that he is served with a subpoena, or at such other convenient place which may

See note at head of Digest as to 1998 legislation covered.

See Topical Index in front part of this volume.

LA – 15

DEPOSITIONS AND DISCOVERY . . . *continued*

be fixed by order of court. (C.C.P. 1436). If witness resides out of this state, the law of the place where the deposition is to be taken will govern the compulsory process to require the testimony and appearance of such witness. (C.C.P. 1435).

Uniform Foreign Depositions Act has been adopted. (T. 13, §§3821, 3822). Additional sections have been added to provide for taking of depositions in another state, territory, district or foreign jurisdiction in a pending action in this state or in a matter cognizable by court of this state, by notice, letter rogatory, or manner stipulated by parties; and, with respect to actions pending in foreign jurisdictions, for compelling of attendance of witnesses or production of documents. (T. 13, §§3823, 3824, added Act 37 of 1966).

Form of notary's return (not statutory) usually used where deposition is upon written interrogatories is as follows:

Form

United States of America.

State of . . . . . .

County of . . . . . .

No. . . . . . .

John Doe ......District Court for the

vs. Parish of . . . . .

Richard Roe. State of Louisiana.

Answers of . . . . . . of . . . . . ., State of . . . . . ., a witness on behalf of . . . . . ., to Interrogatories and Cross-Interrogatories propounded to him.

I.

In answer to Interrogatory No. 1, the witness says: (Here insert his answers). (Same with each Interrogatory and Cross-Interrogatory).

. . . .

(Witness signs here).

(If there are more than one witness, the answers to the interrogatories and cross-interrogatories are given for each in the form above indicated).

(At the conclusion of the depositions the following return is made by the Notary):

To the Honorable, the . . . . . . District Court for the Parish of . . . . . ., State of Louisiana.

I, ..., a Notary Public duly commissioned and qualified in and for the Parish of . . . . ., State of . . . . ., authorized by the laws of said State to administer oaths and to take the depositions of witnesses, hereby certify that I caused to appear before me on the . . . . . . day of . . . . . ., 19. . . ,. . . . . ., the witness for the . . . . . . in the above cause; that said witness was by me first duly sworn to testify the truth, the whole truth and nothing but the truth in answer to the interrogatories propounded to him; that the attached interrogatories and cross-interrogatories were thereupon propounded to said witness by me, said authority, his answers thereto being reported in my presence in shorthand and thereafter transcribed in typewriting; that the transcript thereof was then read over by the said witness and sworn to and subscribed by him in my presence; that the foregoing pages contain a true and correct transcript of the deposition of said witness as thus given.

I further certify that I am not of counsel or related to any of the parties to this cause, or in the employ of any of them, and that I am in nowise interested in the result of said cause.

In Witness Whereof, I have hereunto affixed my hand and set my seal of office at . . . . . ., Parish of . . . . . ., State of . . . . . ., on this . . . . . . day of . . . . . ., 19. . . .

. . . .

Notary Public

Use of Deposition.—At trial or upon hearing of motion or interlocutory proceeding, any part or all of deposition, so far as admissible under rules of evidence applied as though witnesses were then present and testifying, may be used against any party who was present or represented at taking of deposition or who had reasonable notice thereof for purpose of contradicting or impeaching testimony of deponent as witness. Deposition of officer, director or managing agent or person designated to testify on behalf of public or private corporation, partnership, or association or government agency which is party, may be used by adverse party for any purpose. Deposition of witness whether or not party may be used by any party for any purpose if court finds that witness is dead, or that witness is at greater distance than 100 miles from place of trial or hearing, or is out of state, unless it appears that absence of witness was procured by party offering deposition, or that witness is unable to attend or testify because of age, illness, infirmity or imprisonment, or that party offering deposition has been unable to procure attendance of witness by subpoena; or upon application and notice that such exceptional circumstances exist as to make it desirable, in interest of justice and with due regard to importance of presenting testimony of witnesses orally in open court, to allow deposition to be used. If only part of deposition is offered in evidence by party, adverse party may require him to introduce any other part which in fairness should be considered with part introduced and any party may introduce any other parts. Substitution of parties does not affect right to use depositions previously taken. When action in any court of state or of U.S. or of any state has been dismissed and another action involving same subject matter is afterward brought between same parties or their representatives or successors in interest, all depositions lawfully taken and duly filed in former action may be used in latter as if originally taken therefor. (C.C.P. 1450).

Non-stenographic Recordation of Testimony.—Testimony at deposition may be recorded by other than stenographic means, in which event notice shall designate manner of recording, preserving and filing deposition, and may include other provisions to insure that recorded testimony will be accurate and trustworthy. If order is made, party may nevertheless arrange to have stenographic transcription made at his own expense. Videotaped deposition may be taken and used just as any other deposition, without court order, but certified shorthand reporter must also be present unless waived by all parties. (C.C.P. 1440, as am'd Act 295 of 1990).

Deposition of an Organization.—Party may in his notice name as deponents public or private corporation or partnership or association, or government agency and designate with reasonable particularity matters on which examination is requested. Organization so named shall designate one or more officers, directors, or managing agents, or other persons who consent to testify on its behalf, and may set forth, for each person designated, matters on which he will testify. Person so designated shall testify as to matters known or reasonably available to organization. This does not preclude taking of deposition by other procedures as authorized by rules. (C.C.P. 1442).

Special Notice.—Leave of court is not required for taking of deposition by plaintiff if notice states that person to be examined is about to go out of state and will be unavailable for examination unless his deposition is taken before expiration of 15-day period ordinarily required, and sets forth facts to support statement. Plaintiff's attorney shall sign notice, and his signature constitutes certification by him that to best of his knowledge, information, and belief, statement and supporting facts are true. If party shows that once he was served with notice under this article he was unable, through exercise of diligence to obtain counsel to represent him at taking of deposition, deposition may not be used against him. (C.C.P. 1439).

Protective Orders.—Under authority of C.C.P. 1426, protective orders are available for specific listed circumstances. However, such orders may not be issued to limit discovery or seal records relating to public hazard or information permitting public to protect against such hazard, unless information is trade secret. (C.C.P. 1426, as am'd Act 49 of 1995, eff. in prospective manner only Aug. 15, 1995).

EQUITY:

See topic Actions.

EVIDENCE:

Witnesses.—Subject to testimonial privileges generally, and specifically as to husband-wife privilege, attorney-client privilege, physician-patient privilege, priest-penitent privilege, informant-prosecuting attorney privilege, trade secrets and political vote privilege, contained in c. 5 of La. Code of Evidence, eff. Jan, 1, 1993 (old law applicable to communications made prior to that date).

A witness either residing or employed in this state may be subpoenaed to attend a hearing or trial held anywhere in the state, but no subpoena issues if witness resides and is employed outside parish and more than 25 miles from court where hearing or trial conducted, unless by order of court accompanied by deposit with court of statutory witness fees and expenses. (C.C.P. 1352, as am'd Act 23 of 1961; T. 13, §3661, as am'd Act 145 of 1991).

Legislators and legislative personnel cannot be compelled to be witnesses, except in felony cases, during legislative session and at other specified times. (T. 13, §3667.1, am'd Act 177 of 1974). Governor cannot be compelled to be witness except under narrow circumstances. (T. 13, §3667.2, added Act 591 of 1977).

Communications to recognized religious authorities relating to matrimonial rights or status may be privileged. (T. 13, §3734.2, added Act 127 of 1983).

Communications to crime-stoppers organizations relative to alleged criminal activities are privileged. (T. 15, §477.1, added Act 790 of 1985).

Witnesses to authentic acts as relates to contracts executed before a notary public must be at least 14 years of age. (C. C. 2234).

Witnesses to wills must be at least 16 years of age and cannot be insane, blind or persons declared incompetent by criminal laws. Deaf persons also cannot be witnesses to wills, except as to statutory wills under T. 9, §§2442 and 2444. (C. C. 1591-93, as am'd Act 711 of 1979 and Act 198 of 1983).

See also topic Depositions and Discovery.

Presumptions.—Portions of Code of Evidence provide with respect to treatment of presumptions in civil proceedings. (C.E. 301 to 308, added Act 577 of 1997).

INJUNCTIONS:

Injunctions are granted generally for all causes for which injunctions are allowed in other jurisdictions. (C.C.P. 2298, 3601, 3663, 3944). Temporary restraining order may not be used in place of preliminary injunction to arrest seizure and sale of property. (C.C.P. 2752, as am'd Act 812 of 1988).

The sheriff may be enjoined from paying plaintiff the proceeds of property seized if a third person opposes said payment, alleging he is entitled to be paid in preference to plaintiff. (C.C.P. 2299, as am'd Act 23 of 1961).

If property be seized and a third person claims ownership, such third person may obtain an injunction preventing judicial sale before adjudication of claim of ownership. (C.C.P. 1092, as am'd Act 92 of 1962).

If sale of property by executory process or following seizure under writ of fieri facias, is enjoined, court may award damages, including attorney's fees. (C.C.P. 2751, as am'd Act 302 of 1981; C.C.P. 2298, as am'd Act 301 of 1981).

Courts shall generally issue injunctions in all cases where irreparable injury, loss or damage may otherwise result, or in cases specially provided by law. (C.C.P. 3601, as am'd Act 34 of 1969).

Procedure.—No injunction may issue without notice to the opposite party or parties and an opportunity given for hearing. (C.C.P. 3602).

Upon an application being made to the court for a preliminary writ of injunction, court may order the defendant to show cause on a date and hour fixed not less than two nor more than ten days after service of the order, why a preliminary writ should not issue; but if it appear by verified petition or affidavit to the court that immediate and irreparable injury, loss or damage will result to applicant before notice can be served and hearing had, and upon certification by applicant's attorney of efforts to give notice to adverse party, court may in its discretion issue temporary restraining order upon applicant furnishing bond in such amount as court may fix. Such temporary restraining order must be filed in clerk's office and entered of record. It is effective only from time of service or of actual knowledge of issuance thereof; and must by its terms expire within time prescribed by court, not to exceed ten days, unless extended for like periods, or extended for longer period with consent of restrained party. (C.C.P. 3602-

INJUNCTIONS . . . *continued*
3605, as am'd Act 204 of 1985). However, temporary restraining order issued in conjunction with rule nisi for preliminary injunction prohibiting spouse from disposing or encumbering community property, or harming other spouse or child, or removing child from jurisdiction of court, in suit for separation or divorce remains in force until hearing is held on rule for preliminary injunction. (C.C.P. 3604, as am'd Act 770 of 1982). Matter of issuance of preliminary injunction must then be fixed for hearing and party obtaining temporary restraining order must then proceed with application for preliminary injunction, or if he fails to do so court will dissolve restraining order. Upon two days' notice to party obtaining temporary restraining order or preliminary injunction or upon such shorter period as court may prescribe, opposite party may appear and move for dissolution or modification of such order. (C.C.P. 3606 and 3607). Upon hearing for preliminary injunction or dissolution or modification of temporary restraining order or preliminary writ of injunction court may hear such application upon verified pleadings and supporting affidavits or may take proof as in ordinary cases. If proof is by affidavit applicant must deliver true copies of supporting affidavits to defendant at least twenty-four hours before time fixed for hearing or such shorter time as court may order. Defendants must also deliver true copies of affidavits to be used by them before time fixed for hearing. Additional affidavits may be allowed by court. (C.C.P. 3609).

Bond.—A preliminary injunction or temporary restraining order will not issue except on applicant furnishing bond (unless bond is dispensed with by law) in such amount as court fixes. (C.C.P. 3610).

Disobedience of or resistance to any lawful restraining order or writ of injunction may be punished as a contempt of court. (C.C.P. 3611).

Appeal.—There is no appeal from order relating to temporary restraining order. Appeal may be taken as matter of right from order or judgment relating to preliminary or final injunction, but such order or judgment shall not be suspended during pendency of appeal unless court in its discretion so orders. Any appeal from order or judgment related to preliminary injunction must be taken and bond furnished within 15 days. (C.C.P. 3612).

Suspensive appeal is allowed from any restraining order or injunction restraining enforcement of any Constitutional provision or act of Legislature. (T. 13, §4431).

Labor Disputes.—Issuance of temporary restraining orders and preliminary injunctions in labor disputes is drastically limited. (T. 23, §§841-849).

JUDGMENTS:

Interlocutory judgments do not determine the merits; they are pronounced on preliminary matters in the course of the proceedings. Definitive or final judgments are such as determine merits in whole or in part, and have force of res adjudicata. (C.C.P. 1841).

If, after case has been set for trial, plaintiff does not appear, defendant may obtain judgment of dismissal, and the court determines whether the dismissal is with or without prejudice. (C.C.P. 1672). Court may also, on own motion, dismiss action without prejudice when all parties thereto fail to appear on trial day; in event of such dismissal and claim of pending settlement, either party may reinstate action within 60 days if settlement does not occur. (C.C.P. 1672[A][2], added Act 1058 of 1997).

In case of jury trial court must give judgment within three legal days if general verdict returned, but if special verdict returned, court is allowed same time for deliberation as in trial without jury. (C.C.P. 1916).

In cases taken under advisement, notice of rendition of interlocutory order or judgment must be mailed by clerk, regardless of written request therefor. (C.C.P. 1914, as am'd Act 61 of 1983). Notice of signing of default judgment against defendant on whom there was no personal service or on whom there was service through secretary of state and who filed no exceptions or answer, shall be served on defendant or secretary of state by sheriff. (C.C.P. 1913[A], as am'd Act 700 of 1992).

Directed verdicts are available in jury trials, or by equivalent motion to dismiss in judge trials, in general accord with Federal Rules of Civil Procedure interpretations. (C.C.P. 1810). Judgments notwithstanding verdict also available as alternative to request for new trial. (C.C.P. 1810.1, added Act 41 of 1982). Remittitur or additur is permitted, but only if issue of quantum is clearly separable from other issues in case. (C.C.P. 1814, added Act 178 of 1989).

Judgment must be signed by judge except as otherwise provided by law. (C.C.P. 1911, am'd Acts 87 of 1974).

Judgment signed by judge on separate trial of issue of liability is final, appealable judgment. (C.C.P. Art. 466, added Act 598 of 1980).

Delay for applying for new trial shall be seven days, exclusive of legal holidays. Delay commences to run on day after judgment was signed, except when notice of judgment is required, delay commences to run on day after clerk has mailed or sheriff served notice of judgment. (C.C.P. 1974, as am'd Act 520 of 1974).

All judgments affecting real estate must specifically describe such real estate. (C.C.P. 1919). If owner of immovable property has name similar to that of judgment debtor, he may file affidavit of distinction. (T. 9, §5501, added Act 839 of 1985).

Judgments may be amended at any time by trial court to alter phrasology or to correct errors of calculation. (C.C.P. 1951).

Default Judgments.—If defendant has not appeared and filed pleadings within time allowed therefor (see topic Pleading), a judgment by default may be entered by oral motion in open court or written motion mailed to court. Judgments by default in district court may be confirmed after two days, exclusive of holidays, after being entered, and final judgment obtained upon production of proper proof. Judgments by default, on promissory note, other negotiable instrument, or open accounts, can be confirmed by affidavit of correctness thereof. (C.C.P. 1701, 1702, 4896). Preliminary default before confirmation is not required in city court or parish court when amount in dispute is $3,000 or less. In those proceedings and in district court proceedings, when sum is due on open account, negotiable instrument or other conventional obligation, deficiency judgment derived therefrom, or when amount sought is that authorized under R.S. 9:2782 for NSF check, hearing in open court not required. Plaintiff submits proof required and proposed judgment; within 72 hours, judge must sign judgment or set down for hearing. (C.C.P. 4902, as am'd Act 456 of 1982; C.C.P. 4903, added Act 456 of 1982; C.C.P. 1702, as am'd Act 285 of 1986). In such cases, certification of compliance with procedure is required. (C.C.P. 1702.1, added Act 507 of 1984). When demand is based on claim of personal injury, sworn narrative report of physician or dentist may be offered in lieu of testimony. (C.C.P. 1702, as am'd Act 266 of 1983). When defendant in action for divorce, by sworn affidavit before any notary public, acknowledges receipt of petition and waives citation, service, all delays, trial notice and appearance, judgment by default may be entered on day affidavit is filed and confirmation may take place without hearing in open court. (C.C.P. 1701 and 1702, as am'd Act 219 of 1986). In certain actions for divorce (passage of certain time after separation), judgment is without hearing unless ordered by judge. (C.C.P. 1702[E], added Act 271 of 1987). When default is to be confirmed against state or its political subdivisions, notice of entry of default judgment must be given before confirmation. (C.C.P. 1704[C] and [D], added Act 155 of 1986, eff. June 28, 1986).

Declaratory Judgments.—Uniform Declaratory Judgments Act has been enacted. (C.C.P. 1871-1883).

Confession of Judgment.—Judgment may not be confessed prior to maturity of obligation, except for purpose of executory process. (T. 9, §3590, added Act 518 of 1978).

Rule for Judgment.—At any time after answer filed, plaintiff may by motion, submit to court question of right to summary judgment or judgment on the pleadings. No appeal lies from dismissal of motion. These proceedings do not lie in actions for divorce, separation or annulment of marriage, or in any case where community, paraphernal or dotal rights are involved in action between husband and wife, except in special case of divorce after judgment of separation when all parties are represented by counsel. (C.C.P. 969, as am'd Act 219 of 1986). Summary judgment may be rendered on liability alone even when there is genuine issue as to damages. (C.C.P. 966, as am'd Act 89 of 1984).

Summary proceedings may be used for trial or disposition of following matters only: (1) Incidental question arising in course of litigation: (2) application for new trial; (3) issue which may be raised properly by exception, contradictory motion, or rule to show cause: (4) action against surety on judicial bond after judgment has been obtained against principal, or against both principal and surety when summary proceeding against principal is permitted; (5) homologation of judicial partition, of tableau of distribution or account filed by legal representative, or of report submitted by auditor, accountant, or other expert appointed by court; and opposition to any of foregoing, to appointment of legal representative, or to petition for authority filed by legal representative; (6) habeas corpus, mandamus, or quo warranto proceeding; (7) determination of rank of mortgages and privileges on property sold judicially, and of order of distribution of proceeds thereof; (8) child support, custody, and visitation for minor child; support for spouse; injunctive relief; use and occupancy of family home; use of community or personal property; and support between ascendants and descendants; (9) annulment of probated testament; and (10) other matters permitted by law. (C.C.P. 2592, as am'd Act 1009 of 1990, eff. Jan. 1, 1991). Also, intervention in executory proceedings when third person claims mortgage or privilege on property seized and seeks to assert his right to share in distribution of proceeds of sale (C.C.P. 2643, as am'd Act 92 of 1962); in proceeding for failure to pay tax and judgment prohibiting further pursuit of business (T. 47, §401); ejectment proceedings against tenants (C.C.P. 4732).

Recordation.—The effect of the recordation of a judgment expires in ten years from the date upon which it is recorded. They must be reinscribed within this period. If not, they will become junior to all such judgments, mortgages or liens as may have been inscribed between the time of the original inscription and the date of the reinscription of the judgment in question.

Lien.—A judgment is not a lien on real estate until it is recorded as a mortgage, but when so recorded it becomes a lien on all real property of the judgment debtor in the parish in which it is recorded. (C.C. 3322). It is not a lien on personal property until a levy thereon under execution.

Revival.—Money judgment is prescribed ten years after signing by trial court, or from rendition by appellate court, unless revived. Any party interested in judgment may, at any time before it is prescribed, have it revived by citation to defendant or his representative from court which rendered judgment. Revival continues judgment in force for ten years, and judgment may be revived as often as desired. (C.C. 3547, C.C.P. 2031).

Satisfaction of Judgment.—No particular form is used. As a general rule, counsel for plaintiff makes the notation "docket satisfied." giving the date and signing his name on the page of the entry of the particular case in the clerk's docket, whereupon the clerk issues a certificate of satisfaction of docket, which upon production to the recorder of mortgages is sufficient authority for the cancellation of the inscription of the judgment on the mortgage records.

Foreign Judgments.—Judgments rendered in different courts of the United States import full proof in courts of this state if copy of them which is offered be certified by judge of court of record of district or political subdivision in which judgment is kept, authenticated by seal of court, or certified by public officer having seal of office in such place, authenticated by his seal. (C.C.P. 1395, 28 U.S.C.A. §1738).

When judgments derive from foreign state or country, they may be authenticated by certificate of secretary of embassy, legation, consul or consular agent, or other officer of U.S. Foreign Service stationed there, authenticated by his seal. (C.C.P. 1395).

Judgments Against State.—Any single money judgment against state up to $100,000 may be satisfied from Final Judgments Fund with attorney general's approval, following procedure in statute. Interest on judgment ceases to accrue upon tender by state or 30 days after judgment if final, whichever is earlier, if judgment creditor pursues this remedy. (T. 13, §§5131-5, as am'd Act 575 of 1982). Confirmation of default judgment against state or political subdivisions cannot be made until 15 days after notice of entry of default judgment. (C.C.P. 1704[C] and [D], added Act 155 of 1986, eff. June 28, 1986).

See note at head of Digest as to 1998 legislation covered.

See Topical Index in front part of this volume.

JUDGMENTS . . . *continued*

Uniform Enforcement of Foreign Judgments Act has been adopted as supplementary method to enforce foreign judgments. (T. 13, §§4241-4247, added Act 464 of 1985).

Offer of Judgment.—Procedure somewhat similar to FRCP 68 available, permitting either party as settlement device to offer to permit judgment to be entered prior to trial. If claimant rejects and receives more than 25% below offered amount, or if defendant rejects, and more than 25% above offered amount is awarded at trial, rejecting party is liable for costs (not including attorney fees) after rejection of offer. (C.C.P. 970, as am'd Act 354 of 1997).

LIMITATION OF ACTIONS:

See also category Business Regulation and Commerce, topic Commercial Code.

As to prescription by which ownership of property is acquired, see topic Adverse Possession.

Periods of prescription which operate to release debts are as follows:

One Year Period.—Following actions are prescribed after one year: All delictual (tort) actions, prescription to commence from day injury or damage is sustained; and when damage is to real property, prescription to commence from day owner of property acquired, or should have acquired, knowledge of damage. Prescription runs against absentees and incompetents, including minors and interdicts, unless there is legislatively-established exception. (C.C. 3492-3, 3468, as am'd Act 173 of 1983, eff. Jan. 1, 1984). There is such exemption as to minors and interdicts in product liability cases. (C.C. 3492, as am'd Act 621 of 1992). Actions for injury or death against any physician, chiropractor, dentist, psychologist, optometrist, nurse, licensed midwife practitioner, community blood or tissue center or hospital duly licensed by state, must be brought within one year of occurrence or of discovery of injury but not later than three years after occurrence. (T. 9, §5628, as am'd Acts 818 and 983 of 1995). Similar provision and time periods for accountants and attorneys (T. 9, §§5604 and 5605, added Act 683 of 1990), and for insurance agents, brokers, solicitors or similar licensees (T. 9, §5606, added Act 764 of 1991). Moreover, special prescriptive period of three years from Sept. 7, 1990 established for all claims against attorneys and accountants arising from conduct prior to that date. (T. 9, §§5604, 5605, as am'd Act 611 of 1992). Action by beneficiary against trustee is prescribed in one year after rendition of final account, or one year after attainment of age 18. (T. 9, §2234, as am'd Act 309 of 1980). Action in redhibition (rescission of sale) against "good faith" seller of residential immovable property is prescribed in one year from delivery. (C.C. 2534, as am'd Act 172 of 1995).

Two Years Period.—Actions by or against common carriers for collection or recovery of freight charges or for loss of or damage to freight are prescribed by two years from date of shipment. (T. 45, §1100).

Action for violation of building restrictions must be brought in two years. (C. C. Art. 781, added Act 170 of 1977).

Informalities of legal procedure connected with sale at public auction of real or personal property made by sheriff, auctioneer or other person authorized by court so to sell are prescribed against after lapse of two years, or five years where minors or interdicts were part owners. (C. C. 3543).

Two years limitation may be applicable to action to remove building encroaching on public way. (T. 9, §5627, added Act 350 of 1979).

Actions under uninsured motorist provisions must be brought in two years from date of accident. (T. 9, §5629).

Action by heir or legatee not recognized in judgment of possession must be brought in two years from finality of judgment of possession against any third person acquiring interest in immovable by onerous title from person recognized as heir or legatee. (T. 9, §§5630-5631, added Act 721 of 1981).

Actions against succession representatives, tutors and curators for defective sale or mortgage of property must be brought within two years of sale or mortgage if sale or mortgage was court approved. (T. 9, §5632, added Act 374 of 1990, eff. July 10, 1990).

See also categories Business Regulation and Commerce, topics Securities, subhead Liabilities; Monopolies, Restraint of Trade and Competition; and Transportation, topic Motor Vehicles, subhead Financial Responsibility.

Three Years Period.—The following actions are prescribed by three years: (1) Action for recovery of compensation for services rendered, including payment of salaries, wages, commissions, tuition fees, professional fees, fees and emoluments of public officials, freight, passage, money, lodging and board; (2) action for arrearages of rents and annuities; (3) action on money lent; (4) action on open account ([1], [2], [3], and [4], C.C. 3494, as am'd Act 147 of 1984, eff. June 25, 1984); (5) action by succession creditors against other creditors or legatees (C.C. 1188, 1431); (6) tax inscriptions (T. 33, §3746); (7) action for refund of overpaid taxes (T. 47, §§263, 1623); (8) action by client against attorney for return of papers delivered to him for purposes of law suit (C.C. 3496, as am'd Act 173 of 1983); (9) action to recover underpayments or overpayments of royalties from mineral production, except for state-owned properties (C.C. 3494[5], added Act 1031 of 1986); (10) action for contributions made to education or training of spouse, reckoned from date of signing of divorce judgment or declaration of nullity. (C.C. 120, added Act 1008 of 1990, eff. Jan 1, 1991). This prescription runs from day payment is exigible and accrues to past due payments even if there is continuation of labor, supplies or other services, as applicable. (C.C. 3495, as am'd Act 173 of 1983). Prescription runs against absentees and incompetents, including minors and interdicts, unless there is legislatively-established exception. (C.C. 3468, as am'd Act 173 of 1983). All changes effected by Act 173 of 1983 eff. Jan. 1, 1984.

Four Years Period.—Four years' prescription applies to special actions—as action of minor against tutor respecting acts of tutorship; action of lesion (C. C. 340, 1876) as well as to redhibition (rescission of sale) actions as to residential or commercial immovable property if not subject to shorter time (C.C. 2534, as am'd Act 266 of 1997, with one-year grace period from Aug. 15, 1997).

Five Years Period.—The following actions are prescribed by five years: (1) Action for annulment of testament; (2) action for reduction of excessive donation; (3) action for rescission of partition and warranty of portions; (4) actions on negotiable instruments and on promissory notes whether negotiable or not, which prescription commences from day payment is exigible (C.C. 3498, as am'd Act 901 of 1993, eff. July 1, 1993); (5) action for arrearages of alimony and child support (C.C. 3497.1, added Act 147 of 1984, eff. June 25, 1984). Prescription suspended in favor of minors during minority, but otherwise runs against absentees and interdicts. (C.C. 3497, 3468, as am'd Act 173 of 1983, eff. Jan. 1, 1984).

Public sale by sheriff of lands of record as owned by foreign corporation, made under attachment carried on in parish where lands are situated and maintained by judgment of court, and sale recorded in conveyance records of said parish, is valid by prescription after five years from date of recordation. Running of prescription may be interrupted by filing of suit for property. (T. 9, §§5641, 5642).

Actions against contractor and/or surety on public works prescribe in five years from date of substantial or acceptance, whichever is first, or default. (T. 38, §2189, as am'd Act 250 of 1975).

Will must be probated within ten years of death of testator or testatrix or within five years of judicial opening of succession, whichever first occurs. (T. 9, §5643 and C.C.P. 2893, both as am'd Act 316 of 1981).

Action to recover for asbestos abatement prescribes five years after completion of work or discovery of manufacturer, whichever is later. (T. 9, §5644, added Act 728 of 1985).

Action to make executory arrearages in spousal support or installment payments awarded for contributions made to education or training of spouse is prescribed by passage of five years. (C.C. 3497.1, as am'd Act 605 of 1997, eff. July 3, 1997).

Ten Years Period.—All personal actions, except those above enumerated, are prescribed by ten years. (C. C. 3499, as am'd Act 173 of 1983, eff. Jan. 1, 1984). Money judgment is prescribed by ten years unless prescribed earlier by law of state where rendered. May be revived for ten additional years by action commenced before lapse of prescriptive period. (C. C. 3501, as am'd Act 173 of 1983, eff. Jan. 1, 1984). Judgments in favor of state prescribe in ten years. (T. 9, §5685, as am'd Act 407 of 1984). Action to set aside sale of immovable on ground of lack of authorization of agent signing deed, is prescribed by ten years. (T. 9, §5681, as am'd Act 595 of 1979). Except as otherwise provided by law, action for rescission or nullity of agreement or contract is prescribed in ten years. (C. C. Art. 2221, as am'd Act 308 of 1980). Actions against any person performing land surveying, architectural or construction services are prescribed by ten years unless fraud is shown. (T. 9, §2772, as am'd Act 712 of 1990). Action against contractor or architect for construction, renovation or repair of defects in buildings and other works is prescribed in ten years. (C.C. 3500, as am'd Act 173 of 1983, eff. Jan. 1, 1984).

Title in religious groups receiving and using conditional donation in keeping with condition is quieted after ten years uninterrupted possession and such use. (T. 9, §2321, am'd Act 205 of 1984).

Will must be probated within ten years of death of testator or testatrix or within five years of judicial opening or succession, whichever first occurs. (T. 9, §5643 and C.C.P. 2893, both as am'd Act 316 of 1981).

Actions against persons for sexual abuse or physical abuse resulting in permanent impairment or permanent physical injury or scarring of minor subject to ten-year limitation which does not begin to run until minor reaches majority. (C.C. 3498.1 as am'd Act 503 of 1995).

Actions to make executory arrearages of child support are subject to liberative prescription period of ten years. (C.C. 3501.1, added Act 605 of 1997, eff. July 3, 1997).

Thirty Years Period.—Action for recognition of right of inheritance and recovery of whole or part of succession is subject to prescription of 30 years, running from day of opening of succession. (C.C. 3502, as am'd Act 173 of 1983, eff. Jan. 1, 1984).

What Law Governs.—Prescription provided by Louisiana law applies to obligation arising under laws of another jurisdiction which is sought to be enforced in Louisiana; but when contract or obligation has been entered into, or judgment rendered, between persons who reside out of this state, which is barred by statute of limitations of place where obligation is to be performed or judgment executed, same is barred by prescription in Louisiana, upon debtor who is thus discharged subsequently coming into this state. (C. C. 10, as am'd Act 173 of 1983, eff. Jan. 1, 1984).

Waiver of Prescription.—The right to plead prescription cannot be renounced until it is acquired. (C. C. 3449).

Interruption of Period of Prescription.—Citation upon, or acknowledgment by, one debtor in solido interrupts prescription as to all. Citation upon heir of debtor in solido does not interrupt prescription as to other heirs or co-debtors. (C. C. 3503, as am'd Act 173 of 1983, eff. Jan. 1, 1984). Citation of principal interrupts prescription as to surety. (C. C. 3504, as am'd Act 173 of 1983, eff. Jan. 1, 1984). Filing of suit in court of competent jurisdiction and proper venue interrupts prescription, but when suit filed in incompetent court, or in improper venue, prescription is interrupted only as to defendants served with process within prescriptive period. (C. C. 3462, added Act 187 of 1982). Payment by debtor of interest or principal of obligation constitutes acknowledgment of all other obligations including notes of co-debtors in solido pledged to secure that obligation. (T. 9, §5807, am'd Act 119 of 1975).

Revival of Barred Debts.—A debt barred by limitations may be revived only by written acknowledgment. (C. C. 2278).

Contractual limitations shortening the time within which action must be brought are permitted. (C. C. 3471, added Act 187 of 1982).

Pleading.—Prescription must be pleaded, which may be done at any stage of proceedings before final judgment. (C. C. 3452). If plea is made in appellate court, plaintiff may demand remand to trial court for trial of exception. (C.C.P. 2163). Creditor or other interested person may plead prescription although debtor has renounced it. (C. C. 3453).

Peremption is period of time fixed by law for existence of right which, if not timely exercised, is extinguished upon expiration of peremptive period. Peremption need not be pleaded, as it may be supplied by court on own motion any time prior to final judgment. Peremption may not be renounced, interrupted or suspended. (C. C. 3458-3461, added Act 187 of 1982).

See note at head of Digest as to 1998 legislation covered.

See Topical Index in front part of this volume.

LIMITATION OF ACTIONS... *continued*

See also category Debtor and Creditor, topic Fraudulent Sales and Conveyances.

PARTITION:

See also category Property, topic Real Property.

No one can be compelled to hold property with another, unless the contrary has been agreed upon; any one has a right to demand the division of a thing held in common, by the action of partition. (C. C. 1289 and 807, latter added Act 990 of 1990, eff. Jan. 1, 1991). Stipulation never to partition is invalid. (C. C. 1297). Can agree not to partition for limited time, not over 15 years. (C.C. 1300; T. 9, §1702, added Act 477 of 1987; C.C. 807, added Act 990 of 1990, eff. Jan. 1, 1991). No prescription to action of partition. (C. C. 817, added Act 990 of 1990, eff. Jan. 1, 1991). Mineral servitudes and royalties are subject to partition. (T. 31, art. 172, et seq.). Property held in indivision may be partitioned at demand of person having share in full ownership, though there may be other shares in naked ownership and usufruct. Person having only share in naked ownership or only in usufruct does not have this partition right, though naked owner and usufructuary of same share may combine in demand and be treated as full owner of that share. (C.C. 543, as am'd Act 535 of 1983).

Partition is voluntary or judicial; voluntary when made by consent; judicial when made by authority of court. (C. C. 809).

Whenever a party to a partition is an unrepresented absentee, minor or mental incompetent, or the interested parties cannot agree, the partition must be judicial. (C.C.P. 4602).

It is also definitive or provisional; definitive means permanent and irrevocable; provisional when made provisionally of certain things before the rest can be divided, or of everything when parties are not in situation to make an irrevocable partition. (C. C. 1295).

Each coheir may demand in kind his share of the movables and immovables belonging to the succession, unless creditors have made seizure or opposition, or a majority of the coheirs are of opinion that a sale of the property is necessary. (C. C. 811).

Judicial partition may be made in kind or by sale, latter after notice to counsel of record, curators and persons appearing in proper person. (C.C.P. 4607, as am'd Act 832 of 1990). Suit must be brought where property is situated. (C.C. 1290; C.C.P. 80). Petition for partition of property in succession must be filed in succession proceeding. (C.C.P. 3461). Appraisement may be ordered by judge. (C.C.P. 4604). If it is found that property is not conveniently divisible, sale may be ordered. (C. C. 811). If it is possible to divide in kind, notary is appointed by judge to proceed with partition. (C. C. 1345). Notary must give written notice to all interested parties within 15 days of his appointment. (C. C. 1347). Property is then made up in equal lots (C. C. 1364) and drawn for by parties (C. C. 1367). Record of these proceedings is homologated by court after ten days from service of rule to show cause on all other parties and no opposition filed. (C.C.P. 4609-4610).

Rescission.—Partitions may be rescinded for lesion (or inequality) of more than one-fourth of the true value. (C. C. 814).

PLEADING:

Petition.—Actions in district courts are commenced by petition with caption setting forth name of court, title and number of action, designation of pleadings and names of first party on both sides with indication of other parties (C.C.P. 853), stating articulately in numbered paragraphs facts which constitute cause of action (C.C.P. 854), and concluding with prayer for relief desired or alternative relief (C.C.P. 891) and signed by attorney filing same, showing his address (C.C.P. 863). Petition must include names, surnames and domiciles of parties and concise statement of all causes of action arising out of material facts that are subject matter of litigation, along with street address for receipt of service of all items involving litigation. (C.C.P. 891, as am'd Act 48 of 1991). Petition may not include specific amount of damages, except in claims on contracts, notes, tax claims, garnishments, open accounts or alimony and child support. (C.C.P. 893, am'd Act 724 of 1989, eff. July 8, 1989). If specific amount of damages is necessary to establish jurisdiction of court, right to jury trial, lack of possible federal diversity jurisdiction or for other purposes, general allegation to that effect is permissible and sufficient. (C.C.P. 893, as am'd Act 332 of 1992).

Pleading requirements generally are relaxed in justice of peace courts, city and parish courts, with exception that pleadings must be in writing in parish court where amount in dispute is more than $1,000 and in city court where amount in dispute is more than $500. (C.C.P. 4901-4902, 4911).

Petitions for damages resulting from medical malpractice must first have been submitted to medical review panel, and may not contain prayer for specific amount of damages. (T. 40, §1299.41 et seq.).

Citation issued by the clerk of court, under seal, is served by sheriff. (C.C.P. 1291). Citation must be accompanied by certified copy of petition.

Answer.—Fifteen days (ten days, or 15 days if served through Secretary of State, in justice of peace courts, in parish court where amount in dispute is more than $1,000 but less than $3,000, and in city court where amount in dispute is more than $500 but less than $3,000; C.C.P. 4915, added Act 46 of 1979), after service of citation are allowed for filing pleadings by defendant. If service is made upon nonresident under T. 13, §3201, default judgment may not be entered until 30 days after filing of affidavit of service by mail or delivery to defendant. (T. 13, §3205). Defendant must admit or specifically deny each material allegation of fact and must specially plead any affirmative defenses. (C.C.P. 1001-1006).

In suits on open accounts, promissory notes or other negotiable instruments, if no answer be filed, ex-parte affidavit to correctness of account is sufficient to obtain judgment. (C.C.P. 1702).

Defendant may make a demand in reconvention as to any cause of action he may have against plaintiff, regardless of connexity; and must make such demand or face his judicator bar if demand arises out of subject matter of principal demand. (C.C.P. 1061, as am'd Act 521 of 1990, eff. Jan. 1, 1991). He may include plea of compensation or setoff (C.C.P. 1062), and may bring in third persons, such as warrantors, who may be

liable to him on principal demand. (C.C.P. 1111, 1112). He may also intervene, to join with plaintiff, or defendant, or to oppose both (C.C.P. 1091 et seq.); or party may cross-claim against co-party (C.C.P. 1071 et seq., added Act 63 of 1983).

Declinatory exceptions (C.C.P. 925), and dilatory exceptions (C.C.P. 926) must be filed at same time either prior to or in answer, or prior to confirmation of default judgment. (C.C.P. 928, as am'd 1055 of 1997). Peremptory exceptions (C.C.P. 927) may be pleaded at any stage of proceeding prior to submission of case for decision, and may be filed with declinatory exception or with dilatory exception, or both (C.C.P. 928, as am'd Act 60 of 1983). When exception is filed prior to trial, it will be tried prior to or at trial. (C.C.P. 929, as am'd Act 1055 of 1997).

Reply.—When defendant alleges new facts in his answer these are considered as denied by plaintiff; neither replication nor rejoinder is permitted. (C.C.P. 852).

Amendment.—Without leave of court, by plaintiff before service of answer, and by defendant within ten days of service of answer. Otherwise, leave of court or consent of adverse party must be obtained. (C.C.P. 1151).

Demand for Judgment on Pleadings.—Judgment may be asked for on face of pleadings by rule, except in matters of divorce, separation from bed and board, annulment of marriage, or in any case where the community, paraphernal or dotal rights of a married woman may be involved. (C.C.P. 965-969).

Demand for Summary Judgment.—Any party may move for summary judgment, on ground there is no genuine issue of fact, based upon pleadings, depositions, admissions and affidavits, if any. Summary judgment not allowed in those same matters in which judgment on the pleadings not allowed. (C.C.P. 966, 967, 969). By 1996 amendments to C.C.P. 966, summary judgments are said to be favored and motions for them are to be construed to secure just, speedy and inexpensive determination of every action. (C.C.P. 966, as am'd Act 9 of 1996 First Ex. Sess.). Pending motion must be ruled upon at least ten days before trial. (C.C.P. 966, as am'd Act 9 of 1996 First Ex. Sess.). Summary judgment, having effect of partial final judgment, may be granted on liability alone although there is genuine issue as to quantum. (C.C.P. 966, as am'd Act 89 of 1984). Summary judgment may also be rendered dispositive of particular issue, theory of recovery, cause of action, or defense, in favor of one or more parties, even though granting does not dispose of whole case. (C.C.P. 966[E], as am'd Act 483 of 1997, eff. July 1, 1997).

Documents.—It is not necessary that a document on which a demand is founded be filed, and when annexed it is not necessary to serve copy. (C.C.P. 1311).

Claims.—If suit is to be brought, information should be furnished as to names and residences of plaintiff and defendant and facts that make up cause of action, e.g., in case of goods sold and delivered, itemized statement of account, giving dates, details of goods and amounts. In case of open account, affidavit of correctness thereof, before any competent officer, should be furnished, as such affidavit constitutes prima facie proof and is sufficient for judgment by default. (C.C.P. 1702). Provisions for proof of contents of lost or damaged instruments are made. (T. 13, §§3740 and 3741, added Act 172 of 1986).

Small Claims.—See category Courts and Legislature, topic Courts.

Frivolous Claims.—Pleadings and discovery requests deemed to be improper as defined are subject to potential sanctions after hearing, as to counsel or party or both. (C.C.P. 863 and 1420, as added Act 442 of 1988, eff. Jan. 1, 1989). Provision is similar to F.R.C.P. Rule 11, but contains "grace period" for withdrawal of pleadings filed within 60 days of expiration of statute of limitations and also requires hearing before imposition of sanctions.

Filing by Facsimile Transmission.—Filing any paper in civil action by facsimile transmission is permitted, so long as filing by hard copy within five days and $5 transmission fee over and above filing fee. (T. 13, §850, added Act 463 of 1991).

Motion to strike may be filed at any time; former ten-day requirement repealed. (C.C.P. 964, as am'd Act 1055 of 1997).

PRACTICE:

In civil matters, practice is governed by the Code of Civil Procedure and the various statutes.

Procedure to be followed by state administrative agencies in adoption of rules and in making administrative decisions and rules governing review thereof are set forth in T. 49, §§951-968.

Discovery.—Parties are granted right to various discovery devices, pursuant to Code of Civil Procedure. (C. C. P. 1421-1474). Discovery devices include depositions upon oral examination and upon written interrogatories, interrogatories to parties, motions for production or inspection, and physical and mental examination of parties. Interrogatories propounded to another party are limited to 35 and then additional 35 by ex parte motion during entire proceeding, including subparts. Lesser number may be imposed by local rule; greater number requires leave of court. (C.C.P. 1457, as am'd Act 1315 of 1997).

Depositions.—See topic Depositions and Discovery.

Demand for Admission of Facts.—Parties have right to demand sworn written admissions of facts and genuineness of documents. Failure to deny facts or genuineness of documents, within 15 days usually, constitutes admission thereof, and subsequent proof of facts denied or genuineness denied subjects party denying same to payment of reasonable expenses for making proof, including attorney's fees, unless good reasons existed for denial or admission sought was not of substantial importance. (C. C. P. 1466-1468, 1472).

Direct Actions Against Insurer.—See category Transportation, topic Motor Vehicles, subhead Direct Actions.

Small Claims.—See category Courts and Legislature, topic Courts.

See also topics Actions, Appeal and Error, Depositions and Discovery, Injunctions, Judgments, Pleading, Process; category Debtor and Creditor, topics Attachment, Executions, Garnishment.

See note at head of Digest as to 1998 legislation covered.

See Topical Index in front part of this volume.

PROCESS:

Governed by rules in Louisiana Code of Civil Procedure and T. 13, §3471 et seq. It is ordinary, executory and summary.

Ordinary when citation takes place and all delays and forms of law observed. Executory when seizure is obtained against property of debtor, without previous citation, by virtue of act or title importing confession of judgment. Summary when carried on with rapidity, and without observance of formalities required in ordinary cases, as when courts provide for administration of vacant successions; child custody, support, alimony and visitation matters; determination and award of attorney fees; and property of minors and absent heirs. (C.C.P. 851, 2591, 2592, 2631).

Generally no process can be had on legal holidays, except for the issuance of conservatory writs, such as attachment, sequestration, provisional seizures, injunction. (C.C.P. 288, 323). See category Introduction, topic Holidays.

Service of process must be requested within 90 days of filing, unless waived by defendant, or suit is subject to involuntary dismissal. (C.C.P. 1201[C], added Act 518 of 1997, eff. Jan. 1, 1998).

Who May Serve.—Citations and all other legal process, whether issued by clerk, sheriff or constable, must be served by sheriffs and constables throughout state, except if sheriff is interested party, if office of sheriff is vacant or if sheriff is disqualified by law in which case process is served by constable or by officer appointed by court. (T. 13; §§3471, 3476, as am'd Act 159 of 1979). When sheriff has not served within five days of receipt or is unable to serve, court may appoint any person over age of majority residing within state to serve. (C.C.P. 1293, as am'd Act 210 of 1984).

Service on individual is made when proper officer tenders citation or other process to individual or leaves same at individual's dwelling house or usual place of abode with person of suitable age and discretion residing in domiciliary establishment. (C.C.P. 1232, 1234, as am'd Act 355 of 1985). Service on representative, such as attorney, may be made on secretary, as defined, in attorney's office. (C.C.P. 1235, as am'd Act 45 of 1991). Personal service on individual who is named in several capacities is sufficient for all such capacities, if clearly alleged. (C.C.P. 1237, added Acts 851 and 1237 of 1995).

Curator ad hoc may be appointed upon whom service may be made for an absentee. But an absentee may by notarial act deposited with sheriff provide for additional legal mode of service on himself.

Process against domestic or foreign corporation may be served on either of its agents for service of process. (See category Business Organizations, topic Corporations.) In case of failure to designate such agents, or in case of vacancy or inability to serve, process may be served on any officer, director or resident agent named in articles or in last report to Secretary of State, or on any employee of suitable age and discretion found in corporation's registered office or in any place where it is doing business. If officer whose duty it is to make service is unable, after diligent search, to locate any of such persons, service may be made by registered mail or on Secretary of State or some other person designated by him, who must forward papers to corporation at its last known address. (C.C.P. 1261, as am'd Acts 859 and 1237 of 1995, 1262; T. 12, §104). Fee of $10 for service on Secretary of State. (T. 49, §225, as am'd Act 314 of 1985).

Service on State and Political Subdivisions.—In suits against State or State agency, process may be served on attorney general or person in his office over 16 and on agency head. In suits against political subdivisions, service may be obtained on person designated and registered with Secretary of State as agent for service of process and in absence of such designation, on district, parish or city attorney or other proper person depending upon identity of named defendant. (T. 13, §5107, as am'd Act 586 of 1983).

Service on Nonresidents.—Process on nonresidents (individuals, partnerships, associations and other legal or commercial entities not domiciled in state, and foreign corporations), who transact any business in state, contract to supply services or things in state, cause injury or damage by act or omission in state, cause injury or damage through act or omission outside of state if he regularly does business or engages in other persistent course of conduct or derives revenue in this state, has interest in real right or immovable in this state, who is charged with nonsupport of child, parent, spouse or former spouse domiciled in this state with whom nonresident formerly resided in this state, against whom parentage and support of child is alleged, when child was conceived by nonresident while in this state, or manufactured product or component which caused injury in this state, if product's finding its way into this state could have been foreseen, may be served with process by counsel for plaintiff by mailing certified copy of citation and petition to defendant by certified or registered mail, or by actual delivery to defendant by individual authorized by court or authorized by law of place where service is made with respect to service of process of any of its courts of general, limited, or small claims jurisdiction. (T. 13, §3201 et seq., as am'd Acts 331 and 943 of 1995). Catchall provision permits exercise of personal jurisdiction over nonresident on any basis consistent with state or federal constitution. (T. 13, §3201[B], added Act 418 of 1987). Service on nonresident motorist may be made through secretary of state. (T. 13, §§3474 and 3475, as am'd Act 151 of 1990).

Same method of service may be used with respect to nonresident who resided in state and who owes support to child or spouse or former spouse domiciled in state. (T. 13, §3201[f], added Act 734 of 1977).

Service on minor, if emancipated, is made through personal or domiciliary service on minor; if unemancipated, through personal or domiciliary service on his legal representative. If unemancipated minor is legitimate issue of living parents not divorced nor judicially separated, father or, in event of his absence or mental incompetency, mother, is party through whom service is made. If one or both parents are dead, parents are divorced or judicially separated, or minor is illegitimate, service is made through court-appointed tutor. When minor has no tutor and action is brought against him, court will appoint attorney to represent him. (C.C.P. 731, 732, 1235, 5091). See category Family, topics Guardian and Ward and Infants.

Service on incompetent person, who has been interdicted, is made through personal or domiciliary service on his curator. If incompetent person has no curator, but is interdicted or committed to or confined in mental institution and action is brought against him, court will appoint an attorney as his legal representative. (C.C.P. 733, 1235, 5091). See category Family, topic Guardian and Ward.

Service on partnership is made by personal service on partner. Personal service on any employee of suitable age and discretion will constitute service on partnership, if officer attempting to make service certifies that he was unable to serve partner after diligent efforts to do so. (C.C.P. 1263).

Service on foreign corporation may be made as follows: (a) On any agent whom the corporation may have designated as agent for the service of process—wherever found; (b) if such agent cannot be found, upon any regularly employed agent or employee of the corporation, of suitable age and discretion in any office which corporation may have established and maintains in this state; (c) if corporation has failed to appoint and maintain agent for service of process, or such agent cannot be found, and said corporation has not established and maintained an office in state, service may be ordered to be made on Secretary of State; (d) by personal service on its "counsel of record"; (e) by certified mail under T. 13, §3204 if subject to long-arm statute. (C.C.P. 1261, as am'd Act 37 of 1988; 1262; T. 12, §104; T. 13, §3471).

Service of process upon foreign insurer transacting business in state without authority, may be made upon Secretary of State. (T. 22, §1253).

Service on unincorporated association is made by personal service on appointed agent, if any, or in his absence, on managing official at any place where business of association is regularly conducted. In absence of all managing officials, service may be made by personal service on any member of association. (C.C.P. 1264).

Service by Publication.—There is no provision for service by publication, except in case of monition to clear title. (T. 13, §§4941-4951).

Service on physician may be made when physician is not party to action by service on any clerical employee. (C.C.P. 1236, added Act 778 of 1975).

Service on Attorney.—After civil action is begun, service may be made on attorney of record. (C.C.P. 1313). Subsequent to service of original petition, any pleadings, documents or notices which may be served by mail or delivery to attorney of record may also be made by delivering copy by means of telephonic facsimile communication device, which shall then be shown by certificate filed in record. (C.C.P. 1313, as am'd Act 249 of 1997; T. 13, §3471[8], added Act 524 of 1989). Service may also be made on attorney under C.C.P. 5091 if service cannot be made on nonresident by registered or certified mail or actual delivery. (T. 13, §3204[B], as am'd Act 205 of 1995). But service can no longer be made on counsel of record after final judgment disposing of all litigated issues. (C.C.P. 1314, as am'd Act 268 of 1997).

Long Arm Statute.—See subhead Service on Nonresidents, supra.

Proof of Service.—Sheriff endorses on copy of citation date, place and method of service, and signs and returns copy to clerk of court. If service is made on nonresident under T. 13, §3204, individual serving process must file affidavit showing method of mailing and annexing return receipt, or showing date, place and manner of delivery if process actually delivered to defendant.

Nonresident Motorist.—See category Transportation, topic Motor Vehicles.

REPLEVIN:

No such writ.

SEQUESTRATION:

The conservatory writ, sequestration, is a mandate of court, ordering the sheriff to take into his possession and keep a thing of which another person has the possession, until after the decision of a suit, in order that it be delivered to him who shall be adjudged entitled to have property or possession of that thing.

Grounds for Issuance of Writ.—Sequestration may be issued when one claims the ownership or right to possession of property, or a mortgage lien or a privilege thereon, if it is within the power of the defendant to conceal, dispose of or waste the property or the revenues therefrom, or remove the property from the parish, during the pendency of the action. (C.C.P. 3571, 3663).

Sequestration also provided with regard to leased movables upon default of lessee. (T. 9, §3261-3271).

Proceedings.—Except when ordered by court by its own motion, writ of sequestration is secured by filing petition, accompanied by affidavit, and bond. Affidavit must show facts necessary to establish one or more of grounds for issuance of writ. (C.C.P. 3501).

Property Subject to Sequestration.—All species of property, real or personal, as well as revenue proceeding from same, may be sequestered. (C.C.P. 3571; T. 9, §§3261-3271).

Release of Property.—Defendant may secure release of property by furnishing security for the satisfaction of any judgment that may be rendered against him. (C.C.P. 3507, T. 9, §§3261-3271). Written agreement to hold seizing authority harmless for wrongful seizure may be substituted for security at discretion of sheriff, if property is not seized to enforce mortgage, lien or privilege. (C.C.P. 3507.1, added Act 593 of 1985).

Delivery of Property to Plaintiff.—If defendant does not file bond within ten days, plaintiff may, by filing similar bond, secure delivery of the property to himself. (C.C.P. 3576, T. 9, §§3261-3271).

Sale of Property.—Perishable property may be sold without advertisement or appraisement. (C.C.P. 2333).

SERVICE:

See topic Process.

STAY OF EXECUTION:

See topics Appeal and Error, Injunctions; category Debtor and Creditor, topic Executions.

See note at head of Digest as to 1998 legislation covered.

See Topical Index in front part of this volume.

SUBMISSION OF CONTROVERSY:

No statutes authorize submission of controversy to court on agreed statement of facts but courts generally allow such submission.

VENUE:

Ordinarily, suits must be brought in the court having jurisdiction over defendant's domicile. (C.C.P. 42). Action for revendication of real estate, or for seizure and sale of real estate under an act of hypothecation importing confession of judgment, or for enforcing legal or judicial mortgage against third possessors, or actions for sequestration may be brought either where any portion of the property is situated or at defendant's domicile. (C.C.P. 72, as am'd Act 1055 of 1997, 42). Actions for labor performed or supplies or materials furnished, or for improvements made upon any real estate, may be brought in court having territorial jurisdiction of the property or at defendant's domicile. (T. 13, §3233).

Venue of actions against a qualified foreign corporation is parish where its designated principal business establishment is located or in parish designated as principal business establishment in application to do business in state (C.C.P. 42, as am'd Act 487 of 1990) and against unqualified foreign corporation, in parish where process may be served upon it. Venue of actions against foreign or alien insurer is East Baton Rouge Parish. (C.C.P. 42, as am'd Act 23 of 1961).

In matters relating to succession, where succession opened. In matters relative to partition of real property, where property situated. In matters relative to partnership, while continuing, where it is established, or if there are several establishments, where obligation was entered into. In matters relative to failure, in court where failure declared. In matters relative to warranty, in court of principal action. Where defendants are foreigners, or have no known place of residence in the state, where they are found. Where defendants are joint or solidary obligors, at domicile of any one of them. (C.C.P. 73, am'd Act 117 of 1989). Against sureties on official bonds, in parish in which bond was filed. Actions involving real estate (immovable property), where property is situated or at defendant's domicile. (C.C.P. 42, 71-79, 80, as am'd Act 195 of 1989). Actions involving matters over which business office had supervision, where business office located or at defendant's domicile. (C.C.P. 77, as am'd Act 117 of 1989). Actions to revoke donation of immovable property or relative to lease of immovable property, where property is situated. (C.C.P. 80, am'd Act 893 of 1989 and Act 541 of 1989). To obtain child custody, in parish where either party is domiciled or parish of last matrimonial domicile. To change or modify custody, or to modify support award, in parish where person awarded custody or support is domiciled or parish where original decree was rendered. (C.C.P. 74.2, as am'd Act 417 of 1987). For political subdivisions to enforce collection of open account, parish of its location, parish where services were rendered or any other parish permitted by law. (T. 13, §3241, added Act 333 of 1986). Actions on contract may be brought in parish where executed or parish where any work was performed or was to be performed. (C.C.P. 76.1, added Act 217 of 1991). Actions to partition community property, resolve claims arising from either former matrimonial regime or from co-ownership of former community property may be brought as incident to action which would result in termination of regime or in parish where immovable property is situated or, as to movable property, in parish of domicile of either spouse. (C.C.P. 82, as am'd Act 1055 of 1997).

Venue for divorce or annulment is non-waivable and must be either in parish where either party is domiciled or in parish of last matrimonial domicile. (C.C.P. 3941, as am'd Act 1009 of 1990, eff. Jan. 1, 1991).

Suits on fire, life, marine, medical protective, accident, sick benefit insurance or vehicle collision insurance policies may be brought at domicile of insured or where loss occurred; or in case of life insurance, at domicile of deceased or his beneficiary; or in case of accident insurance, at domicile of insured or in parish where accident occurred, or in parish where accident policy was written; and in case of sick benefits, at place where claimant resides at time of his sickness. These rules apply to suits on policies of fraternal orders and mutual benefit societies. (C.C.P. 45, 76).

Nonresident owners of plantations may be sued for wages due laborers and others, in the parish in which the work was performed. (T. 23, §637).

Steamboats, railroads, and other public carriers doing business in Louisiana may be sued for non-delivery of freight at point of delivery or at point of shipment or domicile of carrier. (T. 13, §3231).

If cause of action arose from a trespass or an offense or quasi-offense action may be brought in parish where wrongful conduct occurred or damages sustained. (C.C.P. 74).

District courts in all parishes bordering on Gulf of Mexico have concurrent jurisdiction to enforce statutes for protection of aquatic life. In case of illegal operation of vessel registered in any such parish, venue is proper in such parish against vessel and all persons subject to prosecution for such operation. (T. 13, §3240, added Act 82 of 1975).

Choice of venue outside Louisiana not permitted in construction contracts, subcontracts, and purchase orders for public and private works projects. (T. 9, §2779, added Act 217 of 1991).

Change of venue may be sought where action is brought in an improper venue (C.C.P. 121), when a party cannot obtain a fair trial (C.C.P. 122) or for forum non conveniens (C.C.P. 123). Limited forum non conveniens transfers available between city and district courts. (C.C.P. 124 and 4854, added Act 600 of 1985). Except in maritime actions, change of venue may be granted upon showing that action is predicated solely on federal statute and based on acts or omissions outside state. (C.C.P. 123, as am'd Act 818 of 1988, eff. July 18, 1988).

COURTS AND LEGISLATURE

COURTS:

United States District Courts.—(28 U.S.C. §98).

Middle District.—Clerk's office: Baton Rouge 70801. Composed of parishes of Ascension, East Baton Rouge, East Feliciana, Iberville, Livingston, Pointe Coupee, St. Helena, West Baton Rouge and West Feliciana.

Court sits at Baton Rouge.

Eastern District.—Clerk's office: New Orleans 70130. Composed of parishes of Assumption, Jefferson, Lafourche, Orleans, Plaquemines, St. Bernard, St. Charles, St. James, St. John the Baptist, St. Tammany, Tangipahoa, Terrebonne and Washington.

Court sits at New Orleans.

Western District.—Clerk's Office: Shreveport 71102.

Alexandria Division is composed of parishes of Avoyelles, Catahoula, Grant, La Salle, Rapides, and Winn.

Lafayette Division is composed of parishes of Acadia, Iberia, Lafayette, St. Martin, St. Mary, and Vermilion.

Lake Charles Division is composed of parishes of Allen, Beauregard, Calcasieu, Cameron, Jefferson Davis and Vernon.

Monroe Division is composed of parishes of Caldwell, Concordia, East Carroll, Franklin, Jackson, Lincoln, Madison, Morehouse, Ouachita, Richland, Tensas, Union and West Carroll.

Opelousas Division is composed of parishes of Evangeline and St. Landry.

Shreveport Division is composed of parishes of Bienville, Bossier, Caddo, Claiborne, De Soto, Natchitoches, Red River, Sabine and Webster.

Deposit of $120 is required in each district on commencing action in civil causes; deposit of $90 for each estate administered on filing Chapter 13 proceeding and $500 if Chapter 11 proceeding.

Supreme Court of Louisiana.—Supreme Court has general supervisory jurisdiction over all inferior courts. It has exclusive original jurisdiction in all disciplinary proceedings. See also category Civil Actions and Procedure, topics Appeal and Error, Certiorari.

Court sits at New Orleans.

Parish, City and Justice of Peace Courts.—With certain exceptions, jurisdiction of parish, city and justice of peace courts is limited to actions in which amount of dispute does not exceed $10,000 for city and parish courts and $2,000 for justice of peace courts. (C.C.P. 4842-4844, am'd Act 186 of 1990 and C.C.P. 4911, as am'd Act 299 of 1989). $5,000 limit is applicable to city court in Ville Platte. (C.C.P. 4842[A] and 4843[C], as am'd Act 193 of 1997, eff. Jan. 1, 1998). City courts in New Orleans and in any municipality with population between 20,050 and 24,000 have concurrent jurisdiction with district court in cases where amount in dispute or value of property involved does not exceed $20,000. (C.C.P. 4843[D], as am'd Act 466 of 1995). City courts in territorial jurisdiction of greater than 50,000 population have concurrent jurisdiction with district courts as to actions by political subdivisions for abatement of violations of law or ordinance, regardless of amount. (C.C.P. 4843[C], added Act 186 of 1990). City courts in which population of territorial jurisdiction is less than 50,000 have concurrent jurisdiction with district courts when amount in dispute does not exceed $15,000; same jurisdiction applies to city courts of Bossier City, Lake Charles, Monroe, Hammond, Houma, Shreveport and Lafayette. (C.C.P. 4843[E] and [F], added Acts 193 and 323 of 1997 provided as to Lafayette eff. on Jan. 1, 1998). Concurrent jurisdiction of Baton Rouge City Court is $20,000. (C.C.P. 4843[F], added Act 323 of 1997). Concurrent jurisdiction of Plaquemine City Court is $25,000. (C.C.P. 4843[F], added Act 407 of 1997). City courts have jurisdiction in eviction actions limited to rentals up to $150 per day, $500 per week, $1,500 per month, $18,000 per year. (C.C.P. 4845, as am'd Act 301 of 1983). Justice of peace courts have concurrent jurisdiction with district court in cases in which amount in dispute does not exceed $2,000; if greater demand in amended or supplemental pleading, court must transfer action. (C.C.P. 4911, as am'd Act 692 of 1992). Justice of peace courts also have jurisdiction over eviction suits concerning leased residential premises regardless of amount involved and eviction suits concerning leased commercial premises and leased farmlands where monthly rental does not exceed $2,000 per month, regardless of amount of rent due or rent for unexpired term of lease. (C.C.P. 4912, as am'd Act 544 of 1991). Parish and city courts have jurisdiction over incidental actions of any amount. (C. C. P. Arts. 4831-4847, as am'd Act 823 of 1982 and Act 448 of 1987). In parish and city courts, procedure is essentially same as that for district courts. (C.C.P. 4901-4903, as am'd Act 156 of 1986). However, parish and city courts may permit oral pleading by rule when amount in dispute is $2,000 or less. (C.C.P. 4901, as am'd Act 249 of 1987).

In addition to amount limitations, these courts do not have jurisdiction in actions: (1) Involving title to immovables, (2) right to public office or position, (3) in which plaintiff asserts civil or political rights under federal or state constitutions, (4) claims for annulment, divorce, separation of property or alimony, (5) succession, interdiction, receivership, liquidation, habeas corpus, or quo warranto proceedings, (6) in which state or political subdivision is defendant, (7) involving tutorship, curatorship, emancipation and partition, and (8) other actions as provided by law. (C. C. P. Art. 4847, as am'd Act 361 of 1990, eff. Jan. 1, 1991).

In addition, justice of peace courts do not have jurisdiction over executory proceedings, adoption, tutorship, emancipation or partition proceedings, nor may issue injunctive orders except to arrest execution of its own writ or to enforce execution of judgment of justice of peace court or made executory by it. (C. C. P. Art. 4913, as am'd Act 545 of 1991). Parish courts have concurrent jurisdiction with district courts in proceedings for injunctive relief brought by political subdivision to enjoin law violations. (C.C.P. 4845.1, added Act 152 of 1986, eff. June 28, 1986).

Justice of peace courts do not have jurisdiction in rem or quasi in rem. (C. C. P. Art. 4913, as am'd Act 156 of 1986).

Principal actions in which defendants have right to jury trial may be transferred to district court, but jury trial is waived with respect to incidental actions filed in these courts. (C. C. P. Art. 4872, as am'd Act 46 of 1979).

In all justice of peace cases, and in district courts with concurrent jurisdiction, claim may be stated orally to clerk and no written pleadings are required except in executory proceedings or for attachment or sequestration for which affidavit is required. Court may require completion of forms or execution of affidavits. All exceptions must be included in answer to be filed within ten days of service of citation, or 15 days if served through Secretary of State. Failing answer, judgment of default may be entered without prior default. In actions on open accounts, promissory notes, negotiable instruments or other conventional obligations, prima facie proof may be by affidavit. Notice of judgment necessary when defendant was not served personally and made no appearance, in

See note at head of Digest as to 1998 legislation covered.

See Topical Index in front part of this volume.

LA – 21

COURTS . . . *continued*

cases taken under advisement, or court does not sign judgment immediately and party requests notice. Delay for applying for new trial is three days exclusive of holidays, but this procedure is not allowed in justice of peace courts.

Appeals from parish and city courts are to court of appeal. Appeals from justice of peace courts are to parish court, and, if none, to district court, in which case is tried de novo and from which there is no further appeal except for supervisory jurisdiction by court of appeals. Delay for appeal is ten days from date of judgment or service of required notice, or from denial of motion for new trial for city and parish courts and 15 days for justice of peace courts. (C.C.P. 4924 and 5002, as am'd Act 156 of 1986).

Courts for the Parish of Orleans—City of New Orleans.—

Court of Appeal.—Fourth Circuit Jurisdiction: Appellate only extending to: (1) All civil matters, (2) all matters appealed from family and juvenile courts, and (3) all criminal cases triable by jury, except those in which defendant has been convicted of capital offense and death penalty has actually been imposed for which appellate jurisdiction is in Supreme Court. Criminal appellate jurisdiction limited to questions of law. Civil appellate jurisdiction extends to law and facts, except as limited to questions of law by Constitution or as provided by law in review of administrative agency determinations. Covers Parishes of Orleans, Plaquemines and St. Bernard; domiciled in New Orleans. (Const. art. 5, §§5 and 10, as am'd Act 843 of 1980, voter approved Nov. 11, 1980; T. 13, §312, as am'd Act 3 of 1981, eff. May 1, 1982). See category Civil Actions and Procedure, topic Appeal and Error, subhead Courts of Appeal.

Civil District Court.—Jurisdiction: Exclusive general and original probate jurisdiction, and original civil jurisdiction in all cases where amount in dispute or fund to be distributed shall exceed $100, exclusive of interest, and exclusive jurisdiction in suits involving immovable property, right to office or other public position, civil or political rights, probate and succession matters, when state or political corporation or subdivision or a succession is a defendant, and of appointment of receivers and liquidators. (Const., art. 5, §16). See subhead Parish, City and Justice of Peace Courts, supra.

Criminal District Court.—Exclusive jurisdiction for trial and punishment of all crimes, misdemeanors, offenses committed within Parish of Orleans; and appellate jurisdiction in all cases tried before Juvenile Courts, or Recorders Courts of New Orleans.

City Courts.—First and Second City Courts sit in New Orleans. See subhead Parish, City and Justice of Peace Courts, supra.

Municipal Court.—Four municipal judges sit as committing magistrates and to try violations of city ordinances other than traffic ordinances.

Traffic Court.—Four judges sit as committing magistrates and to try violations of ordinances regulating traffic upon city streets.

Juvenile court has jurisdiction of trial of all children under 17 years of age alleged to be in need of supervision or of care, or when charged with crime, except certain serious crimes enumerated in Const. art. 5, §19 and triable under adult procedure or transferrable to adult court. (C.J.P. art. 15).

Appeal lies to appropriate court of appeal, but no appeal shall lie from judgment refusing to adjudicate child to be delinquent. (C.J.P. arts. 97-8). Appeals must be taken within 15 days of judgment. (C.J.P. art. 99). Appeal does not stay judgment unless trial or appellate court directs otherwise. (C.J.P. art. 103).

Courts Outside of New Orleans.—

Courts of Appeal.—State is divided into five circuits, each subdivided into election districts, as follows:

First Circuit.—1st Dist.: Parishes of Ascension, Assumption, Iberville, Lafourche, Pointe Coupee, St. Mary, Terrebonne and West Baton Rouge. 2d Dist.: Parish of East Baton Rouge; 3d Dist.: Parishes of East Feliciana, Livingston, St. Helena, St. Tammany, Tangipahoa, Washington and West Feliciana.

Second Circuit.—1st Dist.: Parishes of East Carroll, Franklin, Madison, Morehouse, Quachita, Richland, Tensas and West Carroll, divided in two subdistricts for election purposes; 2d Dist.: Bienville, Bossier, Caldwell, Claiborne, Jackson, Lincoln, Union, Webster and Winn. 3d Dist.: Parishes of Caddo, DeSoto and Red River, divided in two subdistricts for election purposes. (T. 13, §312, as am'd Act 1069 of 1992, eff. July 14, 1992).

Third Circuit.—1st Dist.: Parishes of Avoyelles, Catahoula, Concordia, Grant, LaSalle, Natchitoches, Rapides, and Sabine. 2d Dist.: Parishes of Allen, Beauregard, Calcasieu, Cameron, Jefferson Davis and Vernon. 3d Dist.: Parishes of Acadia, Evangeline, Iberia, Lafayette, St. Martin, St. Landry and Vermilion.

Fourth Circuit.—1st Dist.: Parish of Orleans; 2nd Dist.: Parish of Plaquemines; 3rd Dist.: Parish of St. Bernard.

Fifth Circuit.—1st Dist.: Parish of Jefferson; 2nd Dist.: Parish of St. James and that portion of Parish of St. John the Baptist east of Mississippi River; 3rd Dist.: Parish of St. Charles and that portion of Parish of St. John the Baptist west of Mississippi River. (T. 13, §312, as am'd Act 3 of 1981, eff. May 1, 1982).

Court of Appeal, First Circuit, is domiciled in City of Baton Rouge.

Court of Appeal, Second Circuit, is domiciled in City of Shreveport.

Court of Appeal, Third Circuit, is domiciled in City of Lake Charles.

Court of Appeal, Fourth Circuit, is domiciled in City of New Orleans.

Court of Appeal, Fifth Circuit, is domiciled in City of Gretna.

Jurisdiction: Appellate only extending to: (1) All civil matters, (2) all matters appealed from family and juvenile courts, and (3) all criminal cases triable by jury, except those in which defendant has been convicted of capital offense and death penalty has actually been imposed for which appellate jurisdiction in Supreme Court in that instance. Criminal appellate jurisdiction limited to questions of law. Civil appellate jurisdiction extends to law and facts, except as limited to questions of law by Constitution or as provided by law in review of administrative agency determinations. (Const. art. 5, §§5 and 10, as am'd Act 843 of 1980, voter approved on Nov. 11, 1980).

Sessions of the Courts of Appeal are held at their respective domicilies only.

District Courts.—Original jurisdiction in all civil and criminal matters except as otherwise provided. They have unlimited and exclusive original jurisdiction in all felony cases, and in cases involving immovable property, and in all probate and succession matters, and in all cases where state, parish, municipality or other political corporation, or a succession, is a party defendant, in all cases involving right to office or other political position, civil or political rights, and of all proceedings for appointment of receivers or liquidators to corporations or partnerships. (Const., art. 5, §16).

District courts have concurrent original jurisdiction with courts of limited jurisdiction as follows: (1) With parish courts, in cases where amount in dispute or value of property involved does not exceed $5,000 (C.C.P. 4842) and in proceedings instituted by political subdivisions for injunctive relief with respect to acts which may violate applicable law (C.C.P. 4845.1, added Act 152 of 1986, eff. June 28, 1986); (2) with city courts other than First and Second in New Orleans, Ville Platte, Plaquemine, Bossier City, Shreveport, Lafayette, Monroe and Eunice, where amount in dispute or value of property involved does not exceed $10,000 (C.C.P. 4843, as am'd Act 770 of 1985); and (3) with justice of peace courts, where such amount or value does not exceed $1,200 (C.C.P. 4844, as am'd Act 823 of 1982).

Outside of Parish of Orleans, there are 40 judicial districts, parishes included are as follows:

First District: Caddo.
Second District: Claiborne, Bienville and Jackson.
Third District: Lincoln and Union.
Fourth District: Quachita and Morehouse.
Fifth District: West Carroll, Richland and Franklin.
Sixth District: East Carroll, Madison and Tensas.
Seventh District: Catahoula and Concordia.
Eighth District: Winn.
Ninth District: Rapides.
Tenth District: Natchitoches.
Eleventh District: DeSoto and Sabine.
Twelfth District: Avoyelles.
Thirteenth District: Evangeline.
Fourteenth District: Calcasieu.
Fifteenth District: Acadia, Lafayette and Vermilion.
Sixteenth District: St. Mary, Iberia and St. Martin.
Seventeenth District: Lafourche.
Eighteenth District: Iberville, West Baton Rouge and Pointe Coupee.
Nineteenth District: East Baton Rouge.
Twentieth District: East Feliciana and West Feliciana.
Twenty-first District: Tangipahoa, Livingston and St. Helena.
Twenty-second District: Washington and St. Tammany.
Twenty-third District: Ascension, Assumption and St. James.
Twenty-fourth District: Jefferson.
Twenty-fifth District: Plaquemines.
Twenty-sixth District: Bossier and Webster.
Twenty-seventh District: St. Landry.
Twenty-eighth District: La Salle.
Twenty-ninth District: St. Charles.
Thirtieth District: Vernon.
Thirty-first District: Jefferson Davis.
Thirty-second District: Terrebonne.
Thirty-third District: Allen.
Thirty-fourth District: St. Bernard.
Thirty-fifth District: Grant.
Thirty-sixth District: Beauregard.
Thirty-seventh District: Caldwell.
Thirty-eighth District: Cameron.
Thirty-ninth District: Red River.
Fortieth District: St. John the Baptist. (All contained in T. 13, §477, as am'd Act 21 of 1982).

Parishes

Acadia Parish: Fifteenth District; court sits at Crowley.
Allen Parish: Thirty-third District; court sits at Oberlin.
Ascension Parish: Twenty-third District; court sits at Donaldsonville.
Assumption Parish: Twenty-third District; court sits at Napoleonville.
Avoyelles Parish: Twelfth District; court sits at Marksville.
Beauregard Parish: Thirty-sixth District; court sits at DeRidder.
Bienville Parish: Second District; court sits at Arcadia.
Bossier Parish: Twenty-sixth District; court sits at Benton.
Caddo Parish: First District; court sits at Shreveport.
Calcasieu Parish: Fourteenth District; court sits at Lake Charles.
Caldwell Parish: Thirty-seventh District; court sits at Columbia.
Cameron Parish: Thirty-eighth District; court sits at Cameron.
Catahoula Parish: Seventh District; court sits at Harrisonburg.
Claiborne Parish: Second District; court sits at Homer.
Concordia Parish: Seventh District; court sits at Vidalia.
DeSoto Parish: Eleventh District; court sits at Mansfield.
East Baton Rouge Parish: Nineteenth District; court sits at Baton Rouge.
East Carroll Parish: Sixth District; court sits at Lake Providence.
East Feliciana Parish: Twentieth District; court sits at Clinton.
Evangeline Parish: Thirteenth District; court sits at Ville Platte.
Franklin Parish: Fifth District; court sits at Winnsboro.
Grant Parish: Thirty-fifth District; court sits at Colfax.
Iberia Parish: Sixteenth District; court sits at New Iberia.
Iberville Parish: Eighteenth District; court sits at Plaquemine.
Jackson Parish: Second District; court sits at Jonesboro.
Jefferson Parish: Twenty-fourth District; court sits at Gretna.
Jefferson Davis Parish: Thirty-first District; court sits at Jennings.
Lafayette Parish: Fifteenth District; court sits at Lafayette.
Lafourche Parish: Seventeenth District; court sits at Thibodaux.
LaSalle Parish: Twenty-eighth District; court sits at Jena.
Lincoln Parish: Third District; court sits at Ruston.
Livingston Parish: Twenty-first District; court sits at Livingston.

See note at head of Digest as to 1998 legislation covered.

See Topical Index in front part of this volume.

COURTS . . . *continued*

Madison Parish: Sixth District; court sits at Tallulah.

Morehouse Parish: Fourth District; court sits at Bastrop.

Natchitoches Parish: Tenth District; court sits at Natchitoches.

Orleans Parish: Court sits at New Orleans.

Ouachita Parish: Fourth District; court sits at Monroe.

Plaquemines Parish: Twenty-fifth District; court sits at Pointe-a-la-Hache.

Pointe Coupee Parish: Eighteenth District; court sits at New Roads.

Rapides Parish: Ninth District; court sits at Alexandria.

Red River Parish: Thirty-ninth District; court sits at Coushatta.

Richland Parish: Fifth District; court sits at Rayville.

Sabine Parish: Eleventh district; court sits at Many.

St. Bernard Parish: Thirty-fourth District; court sits at Chalmette.

St. Charles Parish: Twenty-ninth District; court sits at Hahnville.

St. Helena Parish: Twenty-first District; court sits at Greensburg.

St. James Parish: Twenty-third District; court sits at Convent.

St. John the Baptist Parish: Twenty-ninth District; court sits at Edgard.

St. Landry Parish: Twenty-seventh District; court sits at Opelousas.

St. Martin Parish: Sixteenth District; court sits at St. Martinville.

St. Mary Parish: Sixteenth District; court sits at Franklin.

St. Tammany Parish: Twenty-second District; court sits at Covington.

Tangipahoa Parish: Twenty-first District; court sits at Amite.

Tensas Parish: Sixth District; court sits at St. Joseph.

Terrebonne Parish: Thirty-second District; court sits at Houma.

Union Parish: Third District; court sits at Farmerville.

Vermillion Parish: Fifteenth District; court sits at Abbeville.

Vernon Parish: Thirtieth District; court sits at Leesville.

Washington Parish: Twenty-second District; court sits at Franklinton.

Webster Parish: Twenty-sixth District; court sits at Minden.

West Baton Rouge Parish: Eighteenth District; court sits at Port Allen.

West Carroll Parish: Fifth District; court sits at Oak Grove.

West Feliciana Parish: Twentieth District; court sits at St. Francisville.

Winn Parish: Eighth District; court sits at Winnfield.

City Courts have been conferred by Legislature with civil jurisdiction in cities where combined population of city and ward or wards of parish were situated is more than 5,000.

City Courts have been established in following cities: Abbeville, Alexandria, Bastrop, Baton Rouge, Bogalusa, Bossier City, Bunkie, Crowley, Eunice, Hammond, Jennings, Lafayette, Lake Charles, Minden, Monroe, Morgan City, Natchitoches, New Iberia, Rayne, Ruston, Shreveport, Springhill, Sulphur, Ville Platte and West Monroe. (T. 13, §1952).

City courts may establish small claims divisions which are not courts of record. Civil subject matter jurisdiction over cases up to $2,000. (T. 13, §5202 [A], as am'd Act 298 of 1985). Neither depositions nor interrogatories are permitted in such divisions.

See subhead Parish, City and Justice of Peace Courts, *supra.*

Parish Courts.—In Jefferson Parish, First Parish Court has jurisdiction east of Mississippi River and Second Parish Court has jurisdiction west of Mississippi River. Parish Court for Parish of Ascension may sit in Donaldsonville, Gonzales and Sorrento.

See subhead Parish, City and Justice of Peace Courts, *supra.*

Justice of Peace Courts.—Any parish, other than Orleans, may be divided into not more than six nor less than three justice of peace wards.

See subhead Parish, City and Justice of Peace Courts, *supra.*

Mayor's Courts.—Mayors or other municipal officers have been vested with jurisdiction over violation of municipal ordinances.

Juvenile Courts.—Juvenile jurisdiction is vested in special juvenile or family courts, created by law for Caddo, Orleans, Jefferson and East Baton Rouge parishes; or in district courts in other parishes. (Ch. C. art. 302). Court exercising juvenile jurisdiction has jurisdiction of trial of all children under 17 years of age alleged to be in need of supervision or of care, or when charged with crime except certain serious crimes enumerated in Const. art. 5, §19 and triable under adult procedure or transferable to adult court. (Ch. C. art. 303).

Appeal lies to appropriate court of appeal, but no appeal shall lie from judgment refusing to adjudicate child to be delinquent. (Ch. C. arts. 330-331). Appeals must be taken within 15 days of judgment. (Ch. C. art. 332). Appeal does not stay judgment unless trial or appellate court directs otherwise. (Ch. C. art. 336).

Small Claims Courts.—See subheads Courts for the Parish of Orleans—City of New Orleans, catchline City Courts: Courts Outside of New Orleans, catchlines Justice of Peace Courts, and City Courts.

LEGISLATURE:

Regular sessions convening in odd-numbered years are general in nature and convene at noon on last Mon. in Mar. for 60 legislative days during 85 calendar days. Regular sessions convening in even-numbered years are fiscal only in nature and convene at noon on last Mon. in Apr. for 30 legislative days during 45 calendar days. No measure levying new tax or increasing existing tax may be enacted during regular session in odd-numbered year. There are provisions for extraordinary or emergency sessions. (Const. art. 3, §2).

Lobbyists.—Regulated by T. 24, §§51-55.

REPORTS:

The decisions of the Supreme Court of Louisiana are to be found in the following reports: Martin, twenty volumes. Old and New Series Louisiana, nineteen volumes. Robinson, twelve volumes. "Louisiana Annual Reports." 1-52 "Louisiana Reports" beginning vol. 104 and running consecutively through Volume 263 in 1972, when official volumes were discontinued. These decisions are now printed in Southern Reporters.

Decisions of Courts of Appeal are to be found in Orleans Court of Appeal Reports (Vols. 1 to 14) and Louisiana Courts of Appeal Reports (Vols. 1 to 19). Current appellate decisions (1928 to present) are printed in Southern Reporters.

The decisions of the Courts of Appeal are to be found in the Orleans Court of Appeal Reports (Vols. 1 to 14) and Louisiana Courts of Appeal Reports (Vols. 1 to 19). Southern Reporter contains decisions from 1928 on.

Louisiana decisions are also reported in Southern Reporter.

Digests.—Louisiana Digest (West Pub. Co.), with pocket parts, covers reported Louisiana decisions.

STATUTES:

The Revised Statutes of 1950, Revised Civil Code, Code of Civil Procedure and Code of Criminal Procedure, are official. West Publishing Company publishes an unofficial edition of the foregoing, entitled West's Louisiana Statutes Annotated.

Uniform Acts which have been adopted are: Anatomical Gift (1968); Blood Tests to Determine Paternity (1972); Child Custody Jurisdiction Act (1978); Controlled Substances (1972); Declaratory Judgments (1948); Disposition of Unclaimed Property, Revised (1972); Enforcement of Foreign Judgments (1985); Federal Tax Lien Registration (1966); Fiduciaries (1924); Foreign Acknowledgments (1916); Foreign Depositions (1922); Foreign Executed Wills (1912); Foreign Probated Wills (1916); Insurers Liquidation (1948); Judicial Notice of Foreign Laws (1960); Management of Institutional Funds (1976); † Principal and Income (Revised) (1964); Proof of Statutes (1922); Reciprocal Enforcement of Support Act (1952; 1966); Simplification of Fiduciary Security Transfers (1960); To Secure the Attendance of Witnesses From Without a State in Criminal Proceedings (1936); † Trade Secrets Act (T. 31, §§1431-1439, added Act 462 of 1981, deleting §3[b] of Uniform Act); Transfers to Minors (1988); Unauthorized Insurers (1940); Veterans' Guardianship (1932); Vital Statistics (1942).

See also category Business Regulation and Commerce, topic Commercial Code.

† Adopted with significant variations. See appropriate topics.

For text of Uniform Acts falling within the scope of the Martindale-Hubbell Law Digests see Uniform and Model Acts section.

UNIFORM LAWS:

For list of Uniform Acts in force in this state see topic Statutes. For text of Uniform Acts within the scope of the Martindale-Hubbell Law Digests see Uniform and Model Acts section.

CRIMINAL LAW

BAIL:

See topic Criminal Law.

CRIMINAL LAW:

A Criminal Code (Tit. 14) and a separate Code of Criminal Procedure, as supplemented by Ancillaries (Tit. 15) are in effect.

Indictment or Information.—Prosecution for capital crime must be on presentment or indictment by grand jury. Prosecution for other offenses may be by indictment or by information filed in open court or office of clerk. (Code Criminal Procedure, arts. 382-384). Under certain circumstances, attorney for witness before grand jury may be present. (C.Cr.P. 433(A), as am'd Act 725 of 1986). In capital case, jury need not be sequestered if there is joint motion that it should not be. (C.Cr.P. 791[B], as am'd Act 1172 of 1995).

Bail.—A person accused of crime is entitled to bail in all cases except where he is charged with a capital offense and proof of his guilt is evident or presumption thereof great. Bail is permitted after conviction where a maximum sentence of five years or less is imposed and court may grant bail if more than five years. (Const., art. 1, §18; Code Criminal Procedure, arts. 312-314).

If mental capacity is put at issue, lack of sufficient capacity must be proven by clear and convincing evidence. (C.Cr.P. 648[A], as am'd Act 755 of 1990).

Change of Venue.—Criminal court may first select jury in another parish to which it might transfer venue in capital cases, and then transfer after selection. (C.Cr.P. 623.1, added Act 82 of 1991).

Capital Sentencing.—Sentencing in capital case is through separate hearing, in which jury must be instructed that governor has constitutional authority to alter sentence of death or life imprisonment. (C.Cr.P. 905.2, as am'd Act 551 of 1995, contingent upon voter approval of constitutional amendment in late 1995). Following plea or conviction in capital case, court may order upon joint motion entry of sentence of life imprisonment and not hold sentencing hearing. (C.Cr.P. 557 and 905, as am'd Act 434 of 1995).

Interstate Compact for Supervision of Parolees is in effect. (T. 15, §574.14).

DEBTOR AND CREDITOR

ASSIGNMENTS:

See category Business Regulation and Commerce, topic Commercial Code. Uniform Commercial Code Art. 9 enacted effective Jan. 1, 1990. (Act 528 of 1988; am'd Act 135 of 1989).

Both corporeal objects and incorporeal things (e.g., a debt, inheritance, etc.) may be sold or assigned, as may also a thing yet to come but not in existence (e.g., unborn issue of an animal) or an uncertain hope. (C. C. 2449-51).

Form and Requisites.—There are no formal requisites for an assignment. Title to movables may be transferred by oral or written contract, although sales of immovables must be in writing and must be recorded in order to have effect against third persons. (C. C. 2440-2).

See note at head of Digest as to 1998 legislation covered.

See Topical Index in front part of this volume.

ASSIGNMENTS . . . *continued*

Accounts receivable may be assigned without notice to debtor where assignor has filed in conveyance office of parish in which assignor has place or places of business specified notice of assignment setting forth intention to assign accounts receivable to certain assignee. (T. 9, §§3101-3111, am'd Acts 37 of 1985, 242 of 1988 and 77 of 1989, latter eff. June 6, 1989). Future accounts receivable may also be assigned. (T. 9, §3102[D], added Act 319 of 1983).

Transfer of title to credits, rights, or other choses in action has the effect of delivery as between the transferrer and transferee. (C. C. 2642). By "title is meant the material evidence, written or other, of the incorporeal right, such as can serve as evidence of the right in a court of justice. (129 La. 382, 386, 56 So. 324). But the transferee is only possessed as regards third persons after notice has been given to the debtor of the transfer having taken place or after the acceptance of the transfer by the debtor in an authentic act. Partial transfer and assignment is effective as to debtor without notice. (C.C. 2643, as am'd Act 97 of 1985).

The sale or transfer of a credit includes everything which is an accessory to the same; as suretyship, privileges and mortgages. (C. C. 2645).

Assignment of Wages.—Voluntary assignment, sale or transfer of earnings is permitted, but not enforceable against employer without his consent except in certain instances. (T. 23, §731, as am'd Act 204 of 1983).

ATTACHMENT:

Actions in Which Allowed.—Attachment is a conservatory writ and may be obtained in any action for a money judgment. (C.C.P. 3542).

In Whose Favor Writ May Issue.—Attachment may be obtained by any plaintiff, including a nonresident or foreign corporation.

Against Whom Writ May Issue.—Attachment may issue against resident or nonresident.

Claims on Which Writ May Issue.—Attachment may issue on an unmatured claim or a claim which is not payable in the state.

Grounds.—Attachment may be granted on ground that debtor: (1) Has departed from state permanently, or is about to do so before judgment can be obtained and executed against him; (2) is nonresident who has no agent for service of process within state; (3) conceals himself with intention to avoid citation; (4) with intent to defraud creditors, or to give unfair preference to some of them, has mortgaged, assigned or otherwise disposed of his property, or part thereof, or is about to do so; (5) has converted his property into money or other evidences of debt, with intent to place it out of reach of creditors, or is about to do so. (C.C.P. 3541).

In case of an unmatured claim, attachment may issue on any of the aforementioned grounds or on the ground that the debtor is about to remove his property out of the state before the debt becomes due. (C.C.P. 3543).

In case of a money demand against a nonresident, attachment lies regardless of nature or origin of claim, liquidated or unliquidated character or certainty or uncertainty of amount demanded. (C.C.P. 3542).

Attachment on ground of nonresidence lies against a foreign corporation which has not qualified in the state, but not against one which has qualified. (152 La. 1075, 95 So. 227).

Property Subject to Seizure.—A creditor may obtain a seizure against all property belonging to the debtor, whether same be in debtor's possession or in that of third person. (C.C.P. 3503, 2411).

Proceedings.—Attachment issues upon filing of petition showing grounds for writ, with verification or affidavit by creditor, his counsel or agent. (C.C.P. 3501). *Caveat:* Fuentes v. Shevin, 407 U.S. 67, 92 S. Ct. 1983, 32 L. Ed. 2d 556 (1972), held notice and an opportunity to a hearing prior to seizure of property constitutionally essential under due process clause.

Attachment may be obtained by leave of court on affidavit and giving bond, provided the usual petition is filed on the next day. (C.C.P. 3502).

Bond.—Creditor must file bond equal to debt, exclusive of interest and costs; except that bond need not exceed $250, unless court orders otherwise, where nonresidence is sole ground of attachment. (C.C.P. 3544).

Issuance of Writ.—Writ may issue on legal holiday (C.C.P. 288), and whether or not debt is liquidated or has matured. (C.C.P. 3542, 3543).

Levy on personal property is made by sheriff taking physical possession of same; on real property by placing keeper on property or, by service of notice of seizure upon owner, filing of notice with recorder of mortgages for parish and entry of data regarding the filing with recorder of mortgages and description of property in sheriff's seizure book. (T. 13, §§3851-3861, as am'd Act 32 of 1960).

Release.—Defendant may secure release of attachment by filing bond in amount exceeding by one-fourth the value of property attached or the amount of the claim, whichever is less. (C.C.P. 3507, 3508).

Sale.—Property attached, except perishables, may be sold only under execution after judgment. (C.C.P. 3510).

Preferences between attachments are in order of dates of service of writs.

Dissolution.—Attachment may be dissolved on rule to show cause. (C.C.P. 3506).

Third Party Claims.—Third person may intervene to protect interest in property attached. If such person claims ownership of property, sale may be enjoined; if he claims a prior lien, sale is not enjoined but rights of parties are referred to proceeds of sale. (C.C.P. 1092, 1094, 1098, 2592, 2643).

Vacation or Modification.—If value of property seized under attachment exceeds what is reasonably necessary to satisfy plaintiff's claim, defendant may secure release of excess.

CREDITORS' SUITS:

Not known in Louisiana.

EXECUTIONS:

Execution of judgments belongs to the courts by which the causes have been tried in the first instance. (C.C.P. 2251). It is the duty of the party wishing to avail himself of the judgment to procure its execution.

Exemptions.—See topic Exemptions.

Time for Issuance.—Execution may issue only properly when delay for suspensive appeal has elapsed; recordation of judgment prior to that time does not begin execution proceedings. (C.C.P. 2252, as am'd Act 523 of 1985).

Holidays.—Sheriff may not execute writ, mandate or order on legal holiday, except attachment, sequestration, fieri facias, executory process or injunction.

Definitive judgments rendered on appeal may be executed as soon as a certified copy is filed in the trial court. (C.C.P. 2251). No execution can issue on a judgment after a suspensive appeal has been taken and an appeal bond furnished. (C.C.P. 2123, 2126). Execution issued before the expiration of delays within which a suspensive appeal may be taken is irregular, and if a suspensive appeal is subsequently taken, the writ and seizure made thereunder may be vacated and avoided. In such a case the party causing the writ to issue bears the cost of issuing said writ and also subjects himself to a possible action in damages. If no suspensive appeal is taken within the prescribed delays, irregularity in the writ is cured. (C.C.P. 2252).

Application for execution is made to the clerk of court. (C.C.P. 2253). Deposition of third party holding financial records may be allowed by court in aid of execution of judgment. (C.C.P. 1433, 1469.2 and 2451.1, as am'd and added Act 1000 of 1990).

Writs of execution differ according to the nature of the judgment to be executed. (C.C.P. 2253). Where judgment directs delivery of an estate, clerk issues a writ of possession by which the sheriff is charged with placing successful party in possession. If party condemned to quit real property refuses to go, sheriff must proceed to carry out the order using force if necessary. (C.C.P. 2501). If judgment orders delivery of a thing and if the thing is concealed or carried out of the jurisdiction, or if judgment orders the doing or refraining from something specified other than delivery of a thing, and party condemned refuses or neglects to comply, party in whose favor judgment was rendered may obtain on contradictory motion an order to distrain property of the debtor, an order adjudging debtor in contempt, or a judgment for damages. (C.C.P. 2502). Where judgment orders payment of a sum of money, judgment creditor may obtain from the clerk a writ of fieri facias. (C.C.P. 2253, 2291). This writ directs sheriff to seize property of debtor and to sell same to satisfy judgment. (C.C.P. 2291). It may be accompanied by garnishment against third person. (C.C.P. 2411). If sale is enjoined as wrongful, court may award damages, including attorney's fees. (C.C.P. 2298, as am'd Act 301 of 1981).

The sheriff is charged with the duty of executing. (C.C.P. 321).

Levy on personal property is made by sheriff taking physical possession of same. Notice of seizure must be served on judgment debtor, attorney of record, or attorney appointed by court. (C.C.P. 2293). Levy on real property is made constructively by service of notice of seizure on defendant, recordation of notice in mortgage office and entry on sheriff's records. (T. 13, §§3851-3880).

Return.—Execution from a court of record must be returned within one year from its issuance, unless property has been seized within such period. (C.C.P. 2294).

Priorities.—Seizing creditors obtain privilege according to order of their seizures. (C.C.P. 2292).

Intervention may be asserted by a third person claiming ownership of property seized or liens superior or inferior to lien of the seizing creditor. (C. C. P. 1092, as am'd Act 92 of 1962).

Advertisement and Sale.—Three days exclusive of holidays after giving notice of seizure, sheriff must proceed to advertise. (C.C.P. 2331). Perishable property may be sold without advertisement or appraisement. (C.C.P. 2333).

Sales of real estate must be advertised at least twice; sales of personal property must be advertised at least once. (C.C.P. 2331). Description by lot and subdivision, or by municipal number, or by section, township and range, and reference to conveyance recordation, is legally sufficient. (T. 43, §211, added Act 46 of 1986, eff. Jan. 1, 1987). Property must be appraised and sold at public auction. (C.C.P. 2332). If sale does not bring two-thirds of appraised value, there must be second offering and sheriff must readvertise sale in same manner as new sale, and with same delays, and property must be sold for whatever it brings in cash. (C.C.P. 2336). Whether new sale or second sale, highest bid must be sufficient to discharge costs, and all mortgages, liens and privileges superior to that of seizing creditor. (C.C.P. 2337).

Redemption.—There is no right of redemption of property sold under execution.

Seizure of Rights of Action.—Creditor may seize rights and interest of a litigant in pending law suit by serving notice on parties to the action, by which seizing creditor acquires a lien or preference on whatever is realized by the debtor out of the suit. (T. 13, §§3864-3868).

Supplementary Proceedings.—On proper petition, the court may order an examination of a judgment debtor concerning his property. Failure to submit to examination or answer proper questions may be punished as contempt. (C.C.P. 2451-2456).

See also category Civil Actions and Procedure, topic Injunctions.

EXEMPTIONS:

The following are exempt from seizure: The tools, instruments, and books necessary to trade, calling or profession of debtor, whereby he makes all or part of livelihood; rights of personal servitude, of use or habitation of usufruct of the estate of minor child, and income from dotal property; wedding or engagement rings up to value of $5,000; clothing, bedding, linen, china, non-sterling silverware, glasses, living, bedroom, dining room suites, heating and cooling equipment, one noncommercial sewing machine, equipment for required therapy, washers, dryers, cooking stove, kitchen utensils, pressing irons, refrigerator, freezer, and one cow used by debtor or family; family portraits, arms and military accoutrements; musical instruments played or practiced on by debtor

EXEMPTIONS . . . *continued*
or family; and poultry and fowl for family use. (T. 13, §3881, as am'd Act 532 of 1985). Exemptions with respect to tangibles do not apply as to chattel mortgages and certain repairmen's liens, so long as property is properly described. (T. 13, §3885, as am'd Act 56 of 1983, and T. 9, §§4501 and 4502, as am'd Acts 93 and 94 of 1979). Exemption for tools and instruments of trade does not extend to motor vehicles and trailers, except for one pickup truck or utility vehicle weighing less than three tons, one trailer, used in debtor's trade, and one motor vehicle not possessing any luxury characteristics and not used solely for transportation to and from work. (T. 13, §3881, as am'd Act 108 of 1983).

The foregoing exemptions do not apply in favor of a lessee as against his lessor. (30 La. Ann. 157). As to exemptions from lessor's lien see topic Landlord and Tenant.

In c. 11 bankruptcy cases, exempt property is only that property and income exempt under law of this state and §522 of Bankruptcy Code. Property upon which debtor has voluntarily granted lien is not exempt from seizure or forced sale under process of law, to extent of balance due on debt secured thereby. (T. 13, §3881 [B], as am'd Act 670 of 1982).

Creditor may seize beneficiary's interest in trust only (1) when it is subject to voluntary alienation by beneficiary or (2) to extent beneficiary has donated property to trust, directly or indirectly. (T. 9, §2004, as am'd Act 253 of 1997).

See topic Homesteads.

Debts Against Which Exemptions Not Allowed.—Personal property exemptions are not available against claims for taxes or assessments levied pursuant to law, debts contracted for purchase price of exempt property, moneys due for rent or claims secured by chattel mortgage or pledge of the exempt property.

Waiver of Exemption.—Personal property exemption may be waived in writing.

Earnings.—75% of disposable earnings for any week are exempt, as defined to classify disposable earnings as that portion remaining after deductions in usual course of business for retirement and insurance coverages and debts to employer; minimum exemption of 30 times federal minimum hourly wage in effect at time earnings are payable or multiple or fraction thereof if pay period is greater or less than one week. (T. 13, §3881, as am'd Act 155 of 1991).

Insurance.—The proceeds or avails or dividends (up to certain monetary limit) of all life, including fraternal and co-operatives, health and accident insurance, annuity insurance and endowment insurance are exempt from all liability for any debt, except for debt secured by a pledge of policy, or any rights under such policy that may have been assigned; or any advance payments made on or against such policy. (T. 22, §§646, 647 as am'd Act 910 of 1990). Widow or heirs who have renounced succession may, nevertheless, claim proceeds of policies. If no heirs, expenses of funeral, last illness and administration must be paid from proceeds.

Pensions, Annuities, etc.—All pensions and all proceeds of and payments under annuity policies, individual retirement accounts, Keogh plans, simplified employee pension plans and others qualified under Internal Rev. Code (IRAs, Keoghs and like to extent that contributions thereto were tax exempt, plus interest or dividends) are exempt from all liability from debt except for alimony and child support. But no contribution to such fund is exempt if made within one year of filing for bankruptcy or within one year of filing of writ of seizure against such plan. (T. 20, §33[1], as am'd Act 362 of 1983). All gratuitous payments made by employers to employees or former employees, or their widows, heirs or beneficiaries, are also exempt from all but alimony and child support obligations. (T. 20, §33[2]).

Homestead Exemption.—See topic Homesteads.

FORECLOSURE:

See topic Liens; category Mortgages, topic Mortgages of Real Property.

FRAUDULENT SALES AND CONVEYANCES:

Annulment.—Obligee has right to annual act of obligor, or result of failure to act of obligor, made or effected after right of obligee arose, that causes or increases obligor's insolvency. (C.C. 2036, eff. Jan. 1, 1985). Obligor deemed insolvent when total of liabilities exceeds total of fairly appraised assets. (C.C. 2037, eff. Jan. 1, 1985). Obligee may annul onerous contracts under certain conditions. (C.C. 2038, eff. Jan. 1, 1985). Obligee may attack gratuitous contract made by obligor whether or not other party to contract knew that contract would cause or increase obligor's insolvency. (C.C. 2039, eff. Jan. 1, 1985). Action of obligee must be brought within one year from time he learned or should have learned of act or failure to act, but not more than three years from act. (C.C. 2041, eff. Jan. 1, 1985). Obligee may not annul contract of obligor in regular course of business. (C.C. 2040, eff. Jan. 1, 1985). Obligee must join obligor and third persons, who can plead discussion of obligor's assets. (C.C. 2042, eff. Jan. 1, 1985). If obligor establishes right to annul, such right is exercised only to extent that it affects obligee's rights. (C.C. 2043, eff. Jan. 1, 1985). Obligee may exercise obligor's right when he refuses to do so, unless it is strictly personal, if obligor causes or increases insolvency by his refusal. (C.C. 2044, eff. Jan. 1, 1985).

Bulk Sales.—Only limited bulk sales provisions in force, applicable to sale of motor vehicle dealership. (T. 9, §2961, added Act 961 of 1992). Prior, more expansive provisions were repealed by Act 377 of 1991 (formerly T. 9, §§2961-2968).

See also category Taxation, topic Property (Ad Valorem) Taxes, subhead Payment.

GARNISHMENT:

Caveat: Fuentes v. Shevin, 407 U.S. 67, 92 S. Ct. 1983, 32 L. Ed. 2d 556 (1972), held notice and an opportunity to a hearing prior to seizure of property constitutionally essential under due process clause.

Garnishment process may be issued in aid of attachment, if the attaching creditor has reason to believe that a third person has possession of money or other property belonging to the defendant. The process, with appropriate interrogatories must be served on the third person. (C.C.P. 2412).

Garnishment process may also be used in aid of execution of a judgment under a writ of fieri facias. (C.C.P. 2411).

Reply of Garnishee.—Within 15 days (five days in City Court) after service of citation and interrogatories, the garnishee must file sworn answers thereto, otherwise there is prima facie case made against him that he is indebted to defendant for amount of claim plus costs, and interest. (C.C.P. 2412, 2413). Interrogatories served on garnishee must include questions which when answered will inform court as to whether defendant debtor is employed by garnishee, his wage rate, manner paid, and other judgments or garnishments; if no longer employed, where and by whom debtor is presently employed and residing, if known to garnishee. (T. 13, §3924, as am'd Act 532 of 1982).

Traverse of Reply.—The reply of the garnishee may be traversed by the attaching creditor and the issue raised is tried by the court. (C.C.P. 2414). Traverse of reply of garnishee must be made within 15 days after service of notice of reply on party issuing garnishment. (C.C.P. 2414).

Seizure.—If garnishee declare in his reply that he has property, etc., of debtor in his possession, the court can order that it be turned over to sheriff or constable, as the case may be.

Wages, salary, etc., may be garnished, in which case the court, after a hearing, fixes the portion which is exempt (see topic Exemptions) and provides for payment to the garnishing creditor out of the balance. Indebtedness to employer may be given priority over garnishment. (T. 13, §§3921-3927). No person lending money at more than 10% per annum may garnish any legally exempt salary or wages of debtor in attempt to force payment of debt, under penalty of imprisonment. (T. 20, §32). Worker may not be discharged because of single garnishment, and has remedy for reinstatement and back pay. Worker may be discharged if earnings are subjected to three or more garnishments for unrelated debts in two-year periods, other than garnishment resulting from accident or illness causing loss of ten or more consecutive days at work. (T. 23, §731, as am'd Act 204 of 1983).

See topic Exemptions, subhead Earnings.

HOMESTEADS:

Constitution of 1974.—Legislature required to provide for exemption from seizure and sale, as well as waivers and exclusions, to at least $15,000 in value of a homestead, as provided by law. (Const., art. 12, §9).

There is exempt from seizure and sale by any process whatever, except as hereinafter mentioned, homestead bona fide owned by debtor and occupied by him, consisting of land, not exceeding 160 acres, buildings and appurtenances, whether rural or urban, to total value of not more than $15,000. If homestead exceeds $15,000 in value, beneficiary is entitled to that amount in case sale of homestead under legal process realizes more than that sum; if sale does not realize more than that sum, above costs and expenses, it is void. Benefit of exemption may be claimed by surviving spouse or minor child or children. (T. 20, §1, as am'd Act 446 of 1977).

See also category Family, topic Husband and Wife.

Registration.—Sworn declaration must be recorded in order to be valid. (T. 20, §1, as am'd Act 446 of 1977).

Debts Excluded from Exemption.—Property exempted as homestead cannot be sold to enforce any judgment, execution, or decree except for: (1) Purchase price of property or any part of such purchase price; (2) labor, money and material furnished for building, repairing or improving homesteads; (3) liabilities incurred by any public officer of fiduciary, or any attorney at law, for money collected or received on deposit; (4) taxes or assessments; (5) rent which bears a privilege on said property; (6) amount due homestead or building and loan association for loan made on security of the property; (7) amount due for money advanced on security of mortgage on the property. If at time of loan mentioned in (6) or granting of mortgage mentioned in (7) borrower or mortgagor was married and not separated from bed and board of spouse, homestead is bound only if latter consented to loan or mortgage. (T. 20, §1, as am'd Act 446 of 1977).

Waiver.—Any person entitled to a homestead may waive the same by signing a written waiver thereof; provided that if such person be married and not separated from bed and board from the other spouse, the waiver is not effective unless signed by the latter. Right to sell homestead property shall be preserved, but no sale shall impair rights of creditors thereon. All such waivers must be recorded in mortgage records of parish where homestead is situated. Such waiver may be either general or special and has effect from time of recording. (T. 20, §1, as am'd Act 446 of 1977).

JUDGMENT NOTES:

Not recognized.

LEVY:

See topics Attachment, Executions.

LIENS:

Equitable liens are unknown in Louisiana. Liens and privileges exist only when specially granted by law.

Liens or privileges are given by law on both movables and immovables, to certain classes of creditors, those in the same class being paid pro rata in case of deficiency of assets.

Except as result of judicial sales in executory proceedings or execution of judgments, lien or privilege is not cancelled, removed from public record, or affected by private or public sale in any succession, liquidation, insolvency, bankruptcy, receivership or partition proceeding. (T. 9, §5031, as am'd Act 894 of 1981).

Attorney's Lien.—See category Legal Profession, topic Attorneys and Counselors.

Banker's Lien.—See category Business Regulation and Commerce, topic Banks and Banking.

Carrier's Lien.—See category Business Regulation and Commerce, topic Carriers.

Chattel Mortgage Lien.—See category Mortgages, topic Chattel Mortgages.

See note at head of Digest as to 1998 legislation covered.

See Topical Index in front part of this volume.

LIENS . . . *continued*

City of New Orleans has a lien on immovable property for charges incurred by it in cutting weeds and noxious growths upon any lot or sidewalk. Notice must be served upon owner for ten days before city can cut said weeds, or if owner is unknown notice may be given by advertisement for two days. (1918, act 136). Said city also has a lien on immovable property abutting on a street for the paving of said street or the sidewalks thereof.

Collateral Security.—See topic Pledges.

Liens on Homestead.—See topic Homesteads.

Judgment Lien.—See category Civil Actions and Procedure, topic Judgments.

Landlord's Lien.—See category Property, topic Landlord and Tenant.

Liens on Exempt Property.—See topic Exemptions.

Liens on movables are given as follows: To the overseer of a plantation, for salary for the current year, on the crop and its proceeds; to those furnishing necessary supplies to a plantation for the current year, for the cost thereof, on the crop and its proceeds; to workmen, for repairs made to movables, for the charges for such repairs, but only so long as possession of such movables is retained; to lessors of immovables and to laborers, for wages, on crops of the current year, and on furniture and implements of farming; to pledgees, for the amount for which pledged, on pledges in their possession; a depositor or bailor, for the amount thereof, on the sales price of the movable deposited, if the same be sold; to one expending money for preservation of a movable, on the thing preserved, for the money so expended; to the seller, for unpaid purchase price, on the movable sold while it is in possession of the purchaser; to an innkeeper, for his charges, on the movables of the guest, while they are on the premises; to a carrier for his charges, on the movable carried, while in possession of the carrier, and also on proceeds of insurance of the movable carried. (C. C. 3217).

In general, liens on movables exist until the debt is satisfied or extinguished by prescription, except as otherwise stated.

Other liens are granted to: (a) cleaners or storers of carpets (T. 9, §§4681-4686); (b) drayman or hauling company (T. 9, §4601, as am'd Act 296 of 1985); (c) furnisher of feed for livestock used by contractor or subcontractor in construction or repair of public roads, under contract of over $500 (T. 9, §§4921-4923); (d) furnisher of feed or medicine for race horses (T. 9, §4661) or veterinarian who provides medical services (T. 9, §4661, as am'd Act 843 of 1985); (e) lumber workers (T. 9, §§4621-4622); (f) moss gatherers (T. 9, §4641); (g) saw mill and planing mill employees (T. 9, §§4621-4622); (h) sugar mill employees (T. 9, §4721); (i) threshermen (T. 9, §§4521-4523, am'd Act 202 of 1972); (j) vendors of cotton seed (T. 9, §4542); and (k) vendors and producers of agricultural and dairy products (C. C. 3227; T. 9, §4541 and §5021), makers or repairers of movable goods (T. 9, §4502, am'd Act 359 of 1983); (l) operators of self-service storage facilities for payment of rent and other charges for storage of movables on premises (T. 9, §§4756-4760, added Act 506 of 1981). No lien applicable to fresh or frozen food products. (T. 9, §4544 as am'd Act 609 of 1978).

Ship or vessel liens are given for damage caused by neglect or fault of operator thereof where injury occurs within territorial jurisdiction of State of Louisiana. (T. 34, §§801-817).

Vendor of property destroyed by fire has lien on funds due or to become due under insurance policies. To protect lien, written notice of claim and statement of amount due under oath must be given insurer before payment. (T. 9, §§4581-4582)

Garages.—Any person operating garage or place where automobiles or other machinery are repaired, or parts made therefor, regardless of whether automobile, etc., be physically in such establishment during making of such repairs or of parts therefor, or regardless of by whom same be attached, has lien upon automobile, truck or machinery for repairs made or parts furnished and for labor performed upon same, for period of 120 days, and is entitled to enforce this lien and privilege by writ of sequestration without furnishing security. If estimate was given, written authorization must be obtained to exceed estimate. This lien and privilege is superior to all other privileges except vendor's lien and privilege, chattel mortgage previously recorded, or bona fide purchasers to whom possession has been given and by whom price has been paid without notice of privilege. (T. 9, §4501, as am'd Act 949 of 1988). If vehicle subject to superior privilege is seized and sold, proceeds over amount necessary to satisfy debt secured by superior privilege are payable to repairman. (T. 9, §4501[C], added Act 949 of 1988).

Hospital Lien.—Hospitals providing services to an injured person have a lien on total amount of any recovery by person from another person on account of such injury, or on net amount payable to an insurance company under a contract providing for indemnity or compensation to injured person. Lien is subject to privilege of attorney. Lien becomes effective by giving written notice by certified mail, return receipt requested, to injured party, to his attorney, to person liable, to insurance company insuring person liable, and to insurance company obligated to pay indemnity or compensation to injured person. Any person who receives a notice before payment of any sums, subject to lien, to injured person, his attorney, heirs, or legal representative, is liable to hospital for amount of its lien but not in excess of amount paid. (T. 9, §§4751-4755). Physicians and chiropractors have similar right for expenses of care under workers' compensation. (T. 23, §1142, as am'd Act 107 of 1986).

Mechanics' Liens.—See subhead Liens on Immovables—Private Works Act, infra.

Liens on Immovables—Private Works Act.—Effective Jan. 1, 1982, following persons have privilege on immovable to secure obligations of owner arising out of work on immovable: (1) Contractors, for price of their work; (2) laborers or employees of owner, for price of work performed at site; (3) sellers, for price of movables sold to owner which become component parts of immovable, or are consumed at site, or consumed in machinery or equipment used at site; (4) lessors, for rent of movables used at site and leased by written contract; and (5) registered or certified surveyors, engineers or licensed architects employed by owner, for price of professional services rendered in connection with work. (T. 9, §4801, as am'd Act 724 of 1981). Following persons have claims against owner and contractor to secure payment of obligations arising out of performance of work under contract (and these claims against owner are also secured by privilege on immovable on which work is performed): (1) Subcontractors, for price of their work; (2) laborers or employees of contractors or subcontractor, for price of work performed at site; (3) sellers, for price of movables sold to subcontractor or contractor that become component parts of immovable, or are consumed at site or in machinery or equipment used at site; (4) lessors, for rent of movables used at site and leased to subcontractor or contractor by written contract (T. 9, §4802, as am'd Act 724 of 1981); and (5) prime consultant registered or certified surveyors or engineers, or licensed architects, or their professional subconsultants (T. 9, §4802[A][5], added Act 41 of 1989, eff. June 15, 1989). Owner is relieved of these claims and securing privileges when bond has been given and maintained by contractor as required by law (T. 9, §4812) and proper notice of contract and bond has been given (T. 9, §4811). To be entitled to assert claim, lessor of movable must deliver copy of lease to owner and contractor within ten days of time movables are first placed on site. (T. 9, §4802[G], as am'd Act 724 of 1981).

Work Performed by General Contractor.—Written notice of contract between general contractor and owner should be filed before work begins, identifying parties, immovable, price of work and when payment is to be made. Sufficient description by lot, square, subdivision, township and range required; street or mailing address alone is insufficient. (T. 9, §4831[C], as am'd Act 589 of 1983). Privilege is not available without such notice when price exceeds $25,000. (T. 9, §4811, as am'd Act 724 of 1981). Bond is also required, in following amounts: (1) If price is $10,000 or less, 100% of price; (2) if price is between $10,000 and $100,000, 50% of price but not less than $10,000; (3) if price is between $100,000 and $1,000,000, 1/3 of price but not less than $50,000; and (4) if price is more than $1,000,000, 25% of price but not less than $333,333. Bond includes both payment and performance, unless latter is expressly excluded. (T. 9, §4812, as am'd Act 724 of 1981). Up to total amount of bond, liability of surety is unconditional, without benefit of discussion or division. Priorities of payment established in statute if amounts due exceed bond. Action must be brought against surety within one year after expiration of time specified in T. 9, §4822 for claimants to file statement of claim or privilege. (T. 9, §4813, as am'd Act 724 of 1981).

Claims and Privileges.—Privileges are effective as to third persons when notice of contract is filed or when work is begun, as statutorily defined. Third persons may conclusively rely upon affidavit made by engineer, surveyor, architect or building inspector employed by government or lending institution, of inspection of immovable at specified time showing no work had begun, provided affidavit is filed before or within four business days after execution of affidavit. (T. 9, §4820, as am'd Acts 904 and 999 of 1988).

Privileges granted by Private Works Act rank among themselves and as to other mortgages and privileges as follows: (1) Privileges for ad valorem taxes or local assessments for public improvements against property are first; (2) privileges of laborers or employees of owner, contractor and subcontractor rank next and equally with each other; (3) bona fide mortgages or vendor's privileges effective as to third persons before privileges granted by Private Works Act rank next in accordance with their respective rank as to each other; (4) privileges of sellers, lessors and subcontractors rank next and equally with each other; (5) privileges of contractors, surveyors, engineers and architects rank next and equally with each other; (6) other privileges and mortgages rank next in accordance with their respective rank as to each other. (T. 9, §4821, as am'd Act 724 of 1981).

Preservation of Claims and Privileges.—If notice of contract is filed, persons claiming privilege have 30 days after filing of notice of termination of work or its substantial completion to file statement of claim and deliver to owner copy of statement of claim, except contractor, who has 60 days. (T. 9, §4822[A], as am'd Act 685 of 1988, eff. Jan. 1, 1989). If notice of contract is not filed, claimants must file statement of claims within 60 days of filing notice of termination of work or of substantial completion or abandonment of work, if notice of termination is not filed. (T. 9, §4822[C], as am'd Act 724 of 1981). Contents of statement of claims and definition of termination of work and substantial completion are provided in Act.

Extinguishment of Claims and Privileges.—Privileges granted by Private Works Act, and claims against owner or contractor, are extinguished if not timely and properly preserved as provided in statute, or if claimant fails to institute action against owner for enforcement within one year after expiration of time given in statute for filing statement of claim or privilege to preserve it. (T. 9, §4823, as am'd Act 724 of 1981). Effect of filing claim ceases as to third persons unless notice of lis pendens is filed within one year of claim. (T. 9, §4833, as am'd Act 711 of 1985). Extinguishment of claim against owner does not extinguish statutory claims against contractor. If surety on bond is surety for owner, filing of bond extinguishes privilege but does not affect owner's personal liability. If contractor files bond, both privilege and personal liability of owner to particular claimant are extinguished. (T. 9, §4823 [D] and [E], as am'd Act 724 of 1981).

Enforcement.—Owner or other interested party may convoke concursus proceeding and cite all persons who have preserved claims, and must cite owner, contractor and surety if not otherwise parties, to establish validity and rank of claims and privileges. (T. 9. §4841, as am'd Act 724 of 1981). In such proceeding, proof of delivery at site by claimant asserting sale of movables is prima facie evidence that movables became component parts of immovable, or were used on immovable, or in machinery or equipment used at site in performing work. (T. 9, §4842, as am'd Act 724 of 1981).

A contractor or subcontractor who defaults on any contract for the construction, erection or repair of any building, structure or other improvement, and who has applied any money received on account on said contract other than to the settlement of bills for material and labor furnished thereunder, is guilty of a misdemeanor. (T. 14, §202).

Wells.—Person performing labor or services in drilling well in search for oil, gas or water, or in operation of oil, gas or water well, or in construction, operation or repair of any flow lines or gathering lines connected to well or pipeline owned by well operator, or doing any trucking, towing, dredging or making any repairs, or furnishing fuel, material or supplies used on or in connection with drilling of well, has lien and privilege for amount which is due him, cost of preparing and recording lien and 10% attorney's fees, on well and lease, on all oil produced therefrom and stored on lease and on all machinery, appurtenances, appliances, structures, etc., thereto attached for drilling, equipment and operation of such lease. Laborer's lien primes that of furnisher of

See note at head of Digest as to 1998 legislation covered.

See Topical Index in front part of this volume.

LA – 26

LIENS . . . *continued*
materials or supplies. (T. 9, §4861, as am'd Act 949 of 1984). Notice setting forth nature and amount must be filed in mortgage records of parish where property is located within 180 days after last day of performance of labor or service or from date of delivery of materials and supplies. Such lien is superior to all other liens and mortgages, except taxes or bona fide vendor's privilege or other mortgages or liens existing and recorded when work has begun. (T. 9, §4862, as am'd Act 191 of 1986). Lien prescribes one year from date of recordation. (T. 9, §4865). Sequestration without bond granted on oath to amount due. (T. 9, §4866). Owner has right to bond lien by depositing with clerk of court in parish in which lien is recorded bond with surety, or federally insured certificate of deposit, for amount equal to claim, 10% attorney's fees, plus one-fourth. (T. 9, §4867, as am'd Act 519 of 1985).

Railroad Supplies.—Any person who has furnished supplies, materials or labor that entered into the construction, maintenance or repair of the permanent roadbed and structure of a railroad, has a lien and privilege upon the roadbeds, tracks, rights of way and franchises of such railroad. (T. 9, §4901). This lien exists without necessity of recordation and exists for period of 12 months from date of delivery of such materials or supplies, or performance of such labor, and has preference over all liens, mortgages or encumbrances of any character whatsoever. (T. 9, §§4902, 4903).

Contracts for public works, where over $1,000 require bond for 50% of contract price with surety approved by official representative, and must be recorded in office of recorder of mortgages not later than 30 days after work begins. (T. 38, §2241). Carriers of materials and supplies may also be entitled to lien. (T. 38, §2241, as am'd Act 344 of 1975 and Act 244 of 1985). Acceptance shall be executed by architect or engineer upon completion and may be executed upon substantial completion. (T. 38, §2244.1). Materialmen, suppliers or workmen having direct contractual relationship with subcontractor and not with contractor must give written notice of claim to contractor, or file sworn statement of amount due with said authority and record same in office of recorder of mortgages within 45 days after recordation of acceptance or notice of default. (T. 38, §2247, as am'd Act 16 of 1962). Architects, engineers and lessors of movable property engaged by contractor or subcontractor may also assert lien. (T. 38, §2242, as am'd Act 158 of 1986). Where notice of concursus proceedings is served on debtor recording statement he must object to solvency of surety within ten days or said public authority is relieved of personal liability. (T. 38, §2244). Hold harmless or indemnity agreements in public contracts in favor of public bodies are restricted. (T.38, §2216, am'd Act 333 of 1989, eff. June 27, 1989). See also category Civil Actions and Procedure, topic Limitation of Actions, subheads One Year Period, Five Years Period.

Form for Claim or Recordation.—The statutes do not describe any particular form to be used in making claim for and recording a mechanic's lien. The following may be used, although the wording thereof must necessarily be altered to suit the case:

Form

State of . . . . . .

County (or Parish) of . . . . . .

Personally before me, the undersigned authority, a Notary Public, in and for the County (or Parish) of . . . . . ., State of . . . . . ., duly commissioned and qualified, there came and appeared . . . . . ., of . . . . . ., State of . . . . . ., who being first duly sworn did depose and say:

That under a contract entered into by affiant with . . . . . ., who is a contractor and is engaged in the construction of a building located on a certain parcel of land owned by . . . . . ., consisting of Lot No. . . . . . ., in Square No. . . . . . ., bounded by . . . . . ., ..., ..., and . . . . . . Streets, in the City of . . . . . ., County (or Parish) of . . . . . ., State of . . . . . ., affiant sold and delivered to said contractor on the above described premises certain materials of the value of . . . . . . dollars, all as shown in detail on the statement of account annexed hereto and made a part hereof, which said statement describes in detail the materials furnished and the dates of delivery and the prices thereof; that said materials were actually used in the construction of the aforesaid building which is the property of the owner of said parcel of land; that the full amount shown on said statement is justly due and owing to affiant and that nothing has been paid on account thereof.

Sworn to and subscribed this . . . . . . day of . . . . . ., 19. . . . . .

. . . .
Notary Public.

To be sufficient, description of property may not consist of street or mailing address alone, but should include lot, square, subdivision, and in some instances, township and range.

Real Estate Mortgage Lien.—See category Mortgages, topic Mortgages of Real Property.

Owners Association Lien.—Residential and commercial owners association with respect to lots in subdivision may record sworn detailed statement of charges, expenses and dues imposed upon lot in accordance with recorded restrictions, servitudes and obligations affecting subdivision. Such preserves lien for period of five years after date of recordation. (T. 9, §§1145-1148, added Act 583 of 1979).

Tax Lien.—See category Taxation, topic Property (Ad Valorem) Taxes, subhead Tax Liens.

Vendors of immovables have a lien thereon for unpaid purchase money, which must be recorded in order to affect third persons. (C. C. 3271). Lien is not extinguished nor subordinated to other mortgages or liens when obligation is assumed by new obligor, notwithstanding release of original obligor. (T. 9, §5384, as am'd Act 585 of 1980).

Creditors of successions and particular legatees have for three months after decedent's death a privilege as to property of successions of such decedents when heirs or residuary legatees accept the successions without administration. Creditors of the heirs or residuary legatees who so accept the successions have a like privilege over property of the heirs of residuary legatees, other than property received from the succession. (T. 9. §§5011, 5012).

To affect real property, affidavits supporting these privileges must be recorded in mortgage records of parish where realty is situated within three months of decedent's death, and they are pre-empted unless suit thereon be filed within three months of rendition of judgment of possession, or if no succession opened, within three months of recordation of privilege. Both privileges are subordinate to pre-existing mortgages or other privileges. (T. 9, §§5013-5016).

Registration.—Privileges on movables are valid without registration unless otherwise specifically provided. Privilege on immovable must be recorded in parish where immovable is located in order to affect third persons. (C. C. 3273-4).

Redemption.—There is no right of redemption of property sold under foreclosure of a lien.

MECHANICS' LIENS:

See topic Liens.

PLEDGES:

See also category Business Regulation and Commerce, topic Commercial Code.

Every lawful obligation may be enforced by the auxiliary obligation of pledge.

If the principal obligation be conditional, that of the pledge is confirmed or extinguished with it; and if the obligation is null, so also is the pledge. (C. C. 3136-38).

Except as hereinafter stated, it is essential to a contract of pledge that the creditor be put in possession of the thing given to him in pledge and consequently, that actual delivery of it be made to him. (C. C. 3152).

Debtor may pledge claim against another person by transferring it in act of pledge and delivering to creditor note or instrument proving its existence, without endorsement. (C. C. 3156, as am'd Act 315 of 1981).

The pledge invests the creditor with the right of causing his debt to be satisfied by privilege and in preference to other creditors out of the product of the pledged property. (C. C. 3157).

Except in the case of a pledge of notes, bills of exchange, bills of lading, stocks, bonds, or other written obligations, it is required that the pledge, to be valid against third persons, should be proved by a written instrument, in which shall be stated the amount of the debt intended to be secured and the situation and nature of the thing given in pledge. (C. C. 3158).

Claims, credits, obligations and incorporeal rights in general, evidenced by written instrument or muniments of title, may be pledged in same manner as other property, and pledge is valid as to all persons without delivery of claim, credit, obligation or incorporeal right to pledgee. To obligate obligor to pay amount due thereunder to pledgee, notice of pledge must be given in writing to obligor or be acknowledged in writing by him. (T. 9, §§4321-4323).

In the case of promissory notes, bills of exchange, bills of lading, stocks, bonds or written obligations of any kind, it is sufficient that the debtor should deliver to the creditor the notes, bills of exchange, bills of lading, etc., without any further formalities. (C.C. 3158, am'd Act 137 of 1989, effective Sept. 1, 1989). Additional alternative methods of pledging promissory notes, and of pledging nonnegotiable instruments, are also available. (T. 9, §§4330-4334, added Act 243 of 1988, am'd Act 348 of 1989).

See also category Business Regulation and Commerce, topic Commercial Code.

Rents, royalties, overriding royalties, bonuses and other payments and rights accrued, accruing or to accrue under mineral leases and other contracts relating to minerals may be pledged by written instrument identifying right pledged, lands affected, and debt and/or future obligations secured, and pledge is valid as to all persons without delivery. To have effect other than between immediate parties, pledge must be recorded in mortgage records where land is situated. To obligate lessee or obligor to pay to pledgee, certified copy of instrument of pledge, if by authentic act, or multiple original, if by private act, must first be delivered to lessee or obligor, or lessee or obligor must first acknowledge notice of pledge in writing. No transfer assignment or termination of right of pledgee under a pledge is binding upon any person dealing with pledgee until 30 days after delivery to him of certified or duplicate copy of such act. (T. 31, arts. 197-205, as am'd Act 269 of 1979).

Pledge or assignment of rents or lease or both may be made by lessor in act of mortgage or separate written instrument which becomes operative as to debtor upon written notification by assignee, and, if such relates to immovable property, it has effect upon registry of original or certified copy in conveyance office where property is located. (T. 9, §4401, as added Act 321 of 1980).

Warehouse Receipts.—See category Business Regulation and Commerce, topic Commercial Code.

Fruits of the pledge are deemed part of the pledge and remain in the hands of the pledgee. He cannot, however, appropriate them to his own use. He is bound to give an account of them to the debtor, or to deduct them from what may be due him. (C. C. 3168).

Remedies of Pledgee.—Independently of a contract, the pledgee cannot in case of failure of payment, dispose of the pledge until he has obtained a judgment against the pledgor in the ordinary course of law. But the pledgor may authorize the sale or other disposition of the property pledged, in such manner as may be agreed upon, without the intervention of the courts. (C. C. 3165). It cannot, however, be agreed that in case of failure to pay the debt the pledge shall belong to the pledgee. (150 La. 482, 90 So. 769).

Purchase of Pledge.—While it is not entirely clear how far the pledgee may go with respect to purchasing the pledge (see 107 La. 236, 31 So. 733; 130 La. 843, 58 So. 636), it would seem that he may purchase at sale by his agent at public place after due notice to pledgor.

RECEIVERS:

Are appointed by district courts of state, after trial, to take charge of property and business of corporations, domiciled in this state, and of property of foreign corporations located in this state, in cases and under following conditions: When requested by stockholders owning 20% of entire outstanding shares for more than six months when management or shareholders are deadlocked; by any shareholder or creditor when officers or directors grossly mismanaging affairs of corporation or committing gross and

See note at head of Digest as to 1998 legislation covered.

See Topical Index in front part of this volume.

LA – 27

RECEIVERS . . . *continued*

persistent ultra vires acts; at instance of stockholder or creditor, when property abandoned and no one authorized to take charge of and conduct corporation's affairs; at instance of any creditor having judgment, when corporation is insolvent or when execution has issued on judgment and has been returned nulla bona; at instance of creditor when property seized under judicial process by fraud or collusion between officers, directors, stockholders and any creditor; at instance of stockholder when majority of stockholders are violating rights of minority shareholders and endangering their interests; or, if a foreign corporation, upon above grounds, or on application of a duly appointed liquidator or receiver of state or country of incorporation. (T. 12, §§151 and 317).

Jurisdiction.—State district court in parish where domestic corporation has its registered office or where foreign corporation has designated registered office in state or where property of foreign corporation is situated if it has no designated registered office, has jurisdiction to appoint receiver for such corporation. (C.C.P. Art. 42).

Proceedings.—Application for appointment of a receiver is made by petition to proper court as above. Court may enjoin corporation, its directors, officers, stockholders and agents from disposing of corporate property or changing status of its affairs pending trial of matter. Court may appoint temporary receiver and stay other proceedings against corporation's property. Matter is determined by court in a summary manner without intervention of a jury. (T. 12, §753).

Eligibility and Competency.—Receiver may be shareholder, director or officer, but cannot be a person of specified relationships with court and judge. (T. 12, §§144, 151).

Qualification.—Receiver must give such bond for faithful performance of his duties as is fixed by court. (T. 12, §151).

Powers and Duties.—Receiver has powers of judicial liquidator (T. 12, §146 C) and court may authorize any receivers of any corporation, in order to carry on business of corporation, to borrow or obtain money on certificates of indebtedness to be taxed as costs of court. Sum so obtained shall bear a privilege on all of property real or personal and income of corporation to be paid by preference and priority over all other creditors of corporation—save a mortgage on immovable property and vendor's privileges antedating certificates. (T. 12, §152).

Compensation.—Not specified.

Discharge.—Procedure not specified.

REDEMPTION:

See topics Executions, Liens; categories Mortgages, topic Mortgages of Real Property; Taxation, topic Property (Ad Valorem) Taxes, subhead Redemption.

SUPPLEMENTARY PROCEEDINGS:

See topic Executions.

TRUSTEE PROCESS:

See topic Garnishment.

USURY:

See category Business Regulation and Commerce, topic Interest.

DISPUTE RESOLUTION

ALTERNATIVE DISPUTE RESOLUTION:

Mandatory Dispute Resolution.—Not generally required, except in few instances (e.g., workers' compensation).

Voluntary Dispute Resolution.—Encouraged and available, particularly in family matters. See topic Arbitration and Award. Specific provisions governing voluntary alternative dispute resolution may be found in T. 9, §§4101 through 4112, added Act 1451 of 1997.

ARBITRATION AND AWARD:

With the exception of matrimonial cases (C. C. 140, 2427), any controversy, whether suit has begun or not, may be submitted to arbitration. (C.C. 3099-3132, as am'd Act 571 of 1985). Statute of limitations tolled as to any matter so submitted until termination of authority of arbitrators. (C.C. 3105, as am'd Act 782 of 1984).

Uniform Arbitration Act not adopted.

Contracts to Arbitrate Future Disputes.—Any provision in any written contract to settle by arbitration a controversy arising out of contract or refusal to perform whole or part thereof is valid, irrevocable and enforceable except upon such grounds as exist at law and equity for the revocation of any contract. Any proceeding brought in violation of arbitration agreement may be stayed by court in which proceeding is pending upon application of one of the parties. Party aggrieved by alleged failure to perform may petition any court having jurisdiction over the parties and upon a finding that the making of arbitration agreement or failure to perform same is not an issue shall order parties to proceed in accordance with terms of contract. (T. 9, §§4201-4203).

Powers of Arbitrators.—Arbitrators may summon in writing any person to attend before them or as a witness and in a proper case to bring any book, record or paper deemed material as evidence. If persons refuse or neglect to attend, court may compel attendance. Arbitrators may also petition court for taking of depositions. (T. 9, §§4206-4207).

Award and Enforcement Thereof.—Award must be in writing and signed by arbitrators or majority of them. Within one year after award made any party may apply to court for order confirming award. Notice of application in writing must be served upon adverse party or his attorney five days before hearing thereof. The award may be vacated or modified by court and court may direct a rehearing by arbitrators where award vacated. (T. 9, §§4209-4211).

Judgment on award is docketed as if it were rendered in an action and has the same force and effect and is subject to all provisions of law relating to a judgment in an action. It may be enforced as ordinary judgment. Appeals may be taken as in ordinary action. (T. 9, §§4212, 4214-4215).

Foregoing provisions do not apply to contract of employment of labor or contract for arbitration controlled by valid legislation of the U. S. not subject to above provisions. (T. 9, §4216).

MANDATORY DISPUTE RESOLUTION:

See topic Alternative Dispute Resolution.

DOCUMENTS AND RECORDS

ACKNOWLEDGMENTS:

Uniform Acknowledgments Act has been adopted with slight variations and sections 4, 5 and 6 omitted. (T. 35, §§511-513). Uniform Foreign Acknowledgments Act has been adopted with slight variations. (T. 35, §§551-555).

May be taken by following officers:

Within state: Notary public or recording officer. Fee varies from $1 to $5.

Without state but within United States, its Territories and District of Columbia: Judge; justice of the peace; notary public; any officer authorized to take acknowledgments where he acts. (T. 35, §5, as am'd Act 320 of 1980, §513).

Without United States: Ambassador, minister, envoy or chargé d'affaires, secretary, of legation, consul general, consul, vice consul or commercial agent of U.S., in country to which he is accredited; any officer of U.S., notary public or commissioner or other agent of Louisiana authorized to take acknowledgments, if such officer has official seal, and is commissioned or accredited to act where acknowledgment is taken. (T. 35, §9 as am'd Act 240 of 1980). Commissioned officer of U.S. Army, Navy, Marine Corps or Coast Guard may take acknowledgments in foreign country.

The authentic act, which is full proof of the agreement contained in it against the contracting parties and their heirs or assigns, is, as relates to contracts, that which has been executed before a notary public or other officer authorized to execute such functions in the presence of two witnesses, aged at least 14 years, or of three witnesses if a party be blind. If a party does not know how to sign, the notary must cause him to affix his mark to the instrument. (C. C. 2234, 2236). Forms of authentic acts will be found under categories Mortgages, topics Chattel Mortgages, Mortgages of Real Property; Property, topic Deeds.

All acts passed before any notary public or commissioner for State of Louisiana and two witnesses in District of Columbia, or any state of U.S., other than Louisiana, and any commissioned officer of U.S. Army, Navy, Marine Corps or Coast Guard have same force and effect as authentic acts executed in this state. (T. 35, §§6, 7, 453).

Every instrument executed before any ambassador, minister, chargé d'affaires, secretary of legation, consul general, consul, vice-consul, or commercial agent has the full force and effect of an authentic act executed in Louisiana; it is not necessary that officer be assisted by two witnesses, attestation, seal and signature of the officer of themselves being sufficient. (T. 35, §9).

Affidavit of subscribing witness or of grantor of instrument makes prima facie proof and serves in lieu of acknowledgment. (C. C. 2253; T. 13, §3720).

Married women acknowledge as though single; separate examination not necessary. (T. 35, §512).

Requisites of Certificate.—Officers are not required to state the date of expiration of commissions in certificates of acknowledgment.

No requirement that seal be affixed by Louisiana officer nor, except as hereinbefore indicated, by officer outside of state.

Authentication.—No authentication is required for certificates of acknowledgments taken in this state, in foreign country by officers above mentioned, or in United States by notaries public for Louisiana. Where acknowledgment is taken in Louisiana for use elsewhere and authentication is required, clerk of district court in parish of notary's qualification authenticates his certificate. Fee, $1. Secretary of State will also authenticate notary's qualification (fee $2). If for use in foreign country, certification of clerk of court may, however, be required.

Effect.—An instrument acknowledged or proved according to law may be admitted to record or read in evidence without further proof. (C. C. 2242, 2253).

Forms of Acknowledgment.—The following is the usual form used within the State of Louisiana:

Forms

State of Louisiana:
Parish of . . . . . . :

Be it known, That on this . . . . . . day of the month of . . . . . ., 19. . . . . ., before me, the undersigned authority, personally came and appeared . . . . . ., to me personally known and known by me to be the person whose genuine signature is affixed to the foregoing document, who signed said document before me and in the presence of the two witnesses whose names are thereto subscribed as such, being competent witnesses, and who acknowledged, in my presence and in the presence of said witnesses, that he signed the above and foregoing document as his own free act and deed and for the uses and purposes therein set forth and apparent.

In witness whereof, the said appearer has signed these presents and I have hereunto affixed my hand and seal, together with the said witnesses on the day and date first above written.

(This acknowledgment must be signed by the party making the same, by the two witnesses to the execution of the document and by the officer.)

The forms provided by the Uniform Acknowledgments Act and the Uniform Foreign Acknowledgments Act may be used.

ACKNOWLEDGMENTS . . . *continued*

Form of Proof by Witness

State of . . . ., County (or Parish) of . . . . . .

Personally before me, the undersigned authority, a Notary Public in and for the County (or Parish) of . . . . . ., State of . . . . . ., there came and appeared . . . . . ., a subscribing witness to the foregoing document, well known to me, Notary, who being first duly sworn, did depose and say:

That he knows . . . . . ., the individual described in and who executed the foregoing document; that he was present and saw said . . . . . . execute the same, and that he thereupon, at the same time, subscribed his name as witness thereto.

. . . .

Affiant.

Sworn to and subscribed before me, this . . . . . . day of . . . . . ., 19. . . .

. . . .

Notary Public.

———————

Alternative to Acknowledgment or Proof.—No statutory provision.

AFFIDAVITS:

Affidavits may be executed before any officer authorized under the law of the place where taken to administer oaths.

Persons serving in or with armed forces or Coast Guard may execute affidavits before any commissioned officer in active service of armed forces or Coast Guard. (T. 35, §7).

Jurat.—No requirement as to necessity of seal of officer or of statement of date of expiration of officer's commission.

Authentication.—No requirement for authentication where affidavit is to be used in jurisdiction other than that in which taken.

Use of Affidavit.—An ex parte sworn statement cannot, generally speaking, be used in evidence.

Form

State of . . . . . ., Parish (or County) of . . . . . .

Personally before me, the undersigned authority, a Notary Public in and for the Parish (or County) of . . . . . ., State of . . . . . ., duly commissioned and qualified, there came and appeared . . . . ., who, being first duly sworn, did depose and say:

(Insert statement of Affiant).

. . . .

(Signature of Affiant).

Sworn to and subscribed before me this . . . . . . day of . . . . . ., 19. . . .

. . . .

Notary Public.

———————

Alternative to Affidavit.—No statutory provision.

NOTARIES PUBLIC:

Qualification.—Any citizen of state or resident alien 18 years of age or over may be appointed notary public in and for parish of his residence or of principal office. (T. 35, §191, as am'd Act 517 of 1985). Notary Public having principal office in parish other than residence may qualify in both parishes if he meets requirements of each parish. (T. 35, §671, added Act 654 of 1975). After appointment by Governor and before receiving commission, notary must take oath and must furnish bond in favor of Governor for $5,000, said bond to be conditioned for faithful performance of all duties required by law of notary. (T. 35, §191, as am'd Act 451 of 1977).

Person licensed to practice law in Louisiana who is notary in any parish may exercise functions of notary in every parish. (T. 35, §191[P], added Act 125 of 1984). Non-lawyer notaries generally limited to parish of their appointment, but number of special provisions authorize such persons to exercise functions in adjacent parishes. (T. 35, §191[A] through [T], added Acts 333 and 1028 of 1995).

Ex officio notaries with powers limited to administering oaths and receiving sworn statements may be appointed in certain departments such as Public Safety and Justice. (T. 35, §§391-401, as am'd Act 36 of 1991).

Disbarred or suspended attorney is not qualified or eligible nor is he allowed to exercise function of notary public. (T. 35, §14, added Act 301 of 1976).

Authentication.—See topic Acknowledgments.

Seal.—No requirement that notary have seal except that applicant for commission as notary public for Parish of Orleans must produce to Governor for deposit in office of Secretary of State "the impress of his official seal." (T. 35, §255). Acts of foreign notaries also need not be certified under hand and official seal of notary; such acts have same effect without further proof of signatures as if made before Louisiana notary. (T. 35, §5, as am'd Act 313 of 1981).

Powers and Duties.—Notaries public have power, within their several parishes, to make inventories, appraisements, partitions, to receive wills, make protests, matrimonial contracts, conveyances, and generally all contracts and instruments of writing; to hold family meetings and meetings of creditors; to receive acknowledgments of instruments under private signature; to affix the seals upon the effects of deceased persons, and to raise the same; and all acts executed by them, in conformity with the provisions of art. 2234 of the civil code, shall be authentic acts. Oaths and acknowledgments, in all cases, may be taken or made by or before any notary public duly appointed and qualified in this state. Notaries have power to receive wills in which they are named as administrator, executor, trustee, attorney for administrator, executor or trustee, attorney for heir legatee, or for estate. (T. 35, §2, as am'd Act 427 of 1982).

Notarial acts must be made and executed in any place within jurisdictional limits of notary. (T. 35, §10, as am'd Act 460 of 1974).

Notaries must include social security number or employer identification number in act conveying, leasing or encumbering immovable property, but absence of number does not affect validity. (T. 35, §17, as am'd Act 322 of 1991, eff. Jan. 1, 1992).

They must not pass or execute any act for the sale, transfer or exchange of any real estate unless the taxes due on the same be first paid, to be shown by tax collector's receipt or certificate for that purpose. (T. 9, §§2901, 2921, 2922).

Notary must file with assessor a copy of act of sale of Orleans property within 15 days. (T. 35, §281 as am'd Act 43 of 1964).

Recordation.—Notaries must record every deed of sale, donation or any sort of conveyance of immovable property within 48 hours in the parish of Orleans and within 15 days in other parishes. Before passing any act or deed of sale, they must demand a certificate from the register of conveyance, if in the parish of Orleans, showing that the vendor has not alienated in any other way the property to be sold. (T. 9, §2928; C. C. 2255). Authentic acts by an Orleans notary relating to real property outside Orleans Parish, and all acts, contracts and instruments, except chattel mortgages, filed with recorder of mortgages or register of conveyances in Orleans Parish must be filed first with custodian of notarial records in Orleans Parish who is entitled to a fee of $5 per instrument. (T. 35, §323 as am'd Act 663 of 1984).

Keeping of Records.—In city of New Orleans, notaries must keep their records in a brick building and when notary officially ceases to be such, either by death, removal or otherwise, his records must be deposited and preserved in central office of notarial records of city of New Orleans. At end of each calendar year, Orleans notaries must index, bind, and deposit with Custodian of Notarial Records original of authentic acts affecting Orleans real estate and passed before them during that year and registered or recorded in Conveyance and Mortgage Offices: such deposit to be made not later than July 1 of following year, commencing July 1, 1967. Custodian shall charge $5 for each act deposited. (T. 35, §323, as am'd Act 663 of 1984). In all other parishes, notaries must deposit at once their records in office of clerk of district court in parish. (C. C. 2251, 2252, 3370).

Territorial Extent of Powers.—Limited to particular parish or parishes for which appointed. (T. 35, §2). Notaries admitted to practice of law have statewide jurisdiction. (T. 35, §191[P], added Act 125 of 1984).

Certificate of Authority.—See topic Acknowledgments, subhead Authentication.

Officers of the U. S. Armed Forces.—Every mortgage, sale, lease, transfer, assignment, power of attorney, oath, affirmation, or affidavit executed by a member of armed forces or Coast Guard of U.S. before a commissioned officer in active service of armed forces or Coast Guard shall have same force and effect as if made or executed before a notary in Louisiana. Instrument must bear signature of such officer, proper designation of his rank and branch of service or subdivision thereof. Such instruments and testaments and trusts executed before any judge advocate under 10 U.S.C. §801 or Defense Department or Coast Guard civilian attorney have same force as if executed before notary in Louisiana. (T. 35, §7, as am'd Act 50 of 1991, eff. June 25, 1991).

RECORDS:

All matters relating to real estate, including liens, and chattel mortgages must be recorded in office of Recorder of Mortgages or Register of Conveyances in the parish where the property is situated to affect third persons. Authentic acts by an Orleans notary relating to real property outside Orleans Parish, and all acts, contracts and instruments, except chattel mortgages, filed with recorder of mortgages or register of conveyances in Orleans Parish must be filed first with custodian of notarial records in Orleans Parish who is entitled to a fee of $5 per instrument. (T. 35, §323). *For list of Parishes and Parish Seats see first page for this state in Volume containing Practice Profiles Section.*

Fees of clerk of court, who is ex officio registrar and recorder, are as follows (except in parish of Orleans): For filing any document of record, $2; for recording act under private signature acknowledged by official other than parish recorder, 75¢ per 100 words or minimum of $3 per page; for recording any instrument when required by law, 75¢ per 100 words or minimum of $3 per page; for making copies, 75¢ per 100 words; for attesting, $2; for certificate of mortgage in one name and one property with seal, $10 for first name, $5 for each additional name and 75¢ for each additional 100 words in excess of 150; for chattel mortgage or crop lien certificate for one property, $5 for first name and $3 for each additional name, and 75¢ for each 100 words in excess of 150; for cancelling real estate or chattel mortgages, $3; for cancelling crop lien, $4 (T. 13, §844, as am'd Act 86 of 1982); for recording chattel mortgage, $5; for document of one or two pages, $2 per page for third, fourth or fifth page, and then $1 per page for all additional pages (T. 9, §5353, as am'd Act 181 of 1986).

Fees for filings in conveyance office are generally $5 for each page of act in full, plus $2 for each additional lot in sale, except $6 for each page of leases and application for redemption from state Land Office, $7 for process verbal of sheriff's sale, $10 per page for Department of Highways sale and expropriation, and $15 for resubdivision or rezoning order. Fees for filing in mortgage office are $6 for mortgages, vendor's liens, assumptions and assignments, plus $2 for each additional description; $6 for materialman's lien plus $1 for each statement; $6 for recording one page judgment plus $1 for each additional page; $5 per page for charters, partnership filings, marriage contracts, powers of attorney, UCC financial statement, bond mortgages and indentures, donations or revocations, and other documents; $4 for chattel mortgages plus $2 for each 100 words over 100 words; $4 for acceptance or default of contracts plus $1 per additional page; $6 for federal tax lien or discharge.

All above fees may be increased up to 10% by clerk at his discretion. (T. 13, 841[D] and 844[F], added Act 317 of 1986).

Inter vivos donations of immovables must be registered within time prescribed for registry of mortgages in conveyance records of parish where immovable is situated. (T. 9, §2371; C. C. 1554, as am'd Act 798 of 1981).

Servitudes.—Servitude or right of way agreement obtained after Aug. 1, 1970, for installation of facilities, is effective only with regard to grantor, grantee and their heirs, successors and assigns, unless a plat, sketch or aerial photograph showing approximate location of facility is recorded with agreement in conveyance records of parish in which property is located. (T. 9, §2726).

See also category Mineral, Water and Fishing Rights, topic Mines and Minerals.

———————

See note at head of Digest as to 1998 legislation covered.

See Topical Index in front part of this volume.

RECORDS . . . *continued*

Torrens Act.—Not adopted.

Transfer of title of decedent, whether resident or nonresident, is accomplished by judgment of district court in probate proceedings sending heir or devisee into possession, a copy of which judgment, certified by clerk of court, is registered in conveyance records of parish where real estate is situated.

Vital Statistics.—Births, deaths, marriages and other records are prepared locally and filed with State Registrar, Division of Vital Statistics, Department of Health and Human Resources, 325 Loyola Avenue, New Orleans, Louisiana 70112. Copies of records are available from that office for following fees: $6 for certified copy of original birth certificate or "long form" copy; $5 for issuance of regular death certificate; $10 for filing of delayed death or birth certificate; $5 for certified copy of marriage, delayed birth or death certificate, and $5 for marriage license. Instructions and forms will be provided by that office for filing delayed certificate of birth. (T. 40, §§32-79, as am'd Act 347 of 1985).

See also category Estates and Trusts, topic Wills, subhead Central Registry for Wills.

SEALS:

Seals are not required for the validity of contracts or any other written instruments in this state. They have no effect as importing consideration.

TORRENS ACT:

Not adopted.

VITAL STATISTICS:

See topic Records.

EMPLOYMENT

EMPLOYER AND EMPLOYEE:

See topic Labor Relations.

LABOR RELATIONS:

Age discrimination in employment is prohibited as to persons from 50 through 69 years of age. (T. 23, §893 et seq., am'd Act 846 of 1985; §976 repealed). Discrimination in compensation, terms, conditions or privileges of employment is prohibited, whether on basis of race, color, religion, sex or national origin, unless pursuant to affirmative action plan; claimant may seek general or special compensatory damage on that basis, as well as back pay, restoration of employment, related benefits, reasonable attorney's fees and court costs, but must pay attorney's fees, damages and costs if claim frivolous. (T. 23, §1006, added Act 709 of 1983).

Employer: must pay in cash 4% interest on cash deposit required of employee (T. 23, §891); must not coerce employee to refrain from joining labor organization (T. 23, §824) and contract having such effect is void (T. 23, §823); must not require employee to agree not to engage in competing business upon termination of employment except in limited situations (T. 23, §921); on public buildings must employ bona fide citizens and qualified voters (T. 38, §§2185, 2186); must not, if employing twenty-five or more, adopt rule for discharge of employees or rejection of applications on any age limit under fifty years, except where system of old age pensions has been adopted by employer (T. 23, §§892, 893).

Servant attached to person or family may leave or be discharged without assigning cause. (C.C. 2747). Laborer on plantation or in manufacture cannot leave or be discharged before end of term of hiring without assigning good cause (C.C. 2748) and employer discharging without good cause must pay wages for full term (C.C. 2749).

Employer may not discharge employee for jury service. (T. 23, §965, added Act 469 of 1974).

Persons denied employment solely because of assignment or garnishment of wages may recover reasonable damages. (T. 23, §731, as am'd Act 204 of 1983).

Employers may not discriminate against persons who have asserted claims under state or federal workmen's compensation laws. (T. 23, §1361, added Act 704 of 1980). Claims of such discrimination which are determined to be frivolous lead to reasonable damage awards, including attorney's fees and costs. (T. 23, §1361[E], added Act 638 of 1993, eff. June 15, 1993).

Civil Rights Act for Handicapped prohibits discrimination against and denial of employment and other benefits to handicapped persons who have cause of action against any person engaging in discriminatory actions for all relief including compensatory damages, attorneys' fees and costs. Action must be brought within 180 days from date of discovery but not in excess of one year from date of discriminatory act. (T. 46, §§2251-2256, added Act 665 of 1980).

Employment of aliens is regulated. (T. 23, §§991, 992.1, 992.2 and 995, as am'd Act 894 of 1985).

Absent proof of bad faith as defined, employer is immune from civil liability for providing accurate information about current or former employee's job performance to prospective employer who inquires; similar immunity given to prospective employer if he hires person based on that information, against later claim for negligent hiring or retention. (T. 23, §291, added Act 632 of 1995).

State has "whistle-blower" statute to protect employees against reprisals for revealing certain violations of law. (T. 23, §967, added Act 1104 of 1997, eff. July 14, 1997).

Children.—Employment of minors is regulated. (T. 23, §§151-290). Minors not apprentices may not work in specified places or any place, or in any occupation, dangerous to life or limb or injurious to health or morals. Commissioner of Labor determines, after public hearing, which occupations are hazardous. (T. 23, §161).

Minors over 16 years old may enter into apprenticeship agreements approved by Department of Labor. (T. 23, §§381-391).

With written consent of parent, any minor may participate in theatrical or musical performance sponsored by nonprofit organization or public body, and, with consent of Louisiana Film Commission, may participate in commercial movies produced or filmed in state. (T 23, §253).

Labor Unions.—Employees have right of self organization and are free to designate a representative of their own choosing to negotiate terms and conditions of their employment. (T. 23, §822). Right to work as agricultural laborer cannot be denied on account of membership or nonmembership in any labor union, (T. 23, §§881-889).

No person is required, as condition of employment, to become or remain member of any union or to pay any dues, fees, assessments or other charges to union. (T. 23, §§981-987, added Act 97 of 1976).

Wages.—Public service corporations and employers of ten or more persons in manufacturing, boring for oil or mining must pay employees, except clerical force and salesmen, at least twice a month, pay days being two weeks apart as near as practicable. Term employee does not include individual employed in bona fide executive, administrative, supervisory or professional capacity. (T. 23, §633).

Employer: must pay in current money on pay day full face value of checks, tickets, etc., redeemable wholly or partly in merchandise (T. 51, §§301-303); must pay employee on discharging him if employee so demands (T. 23, §§631-632); must not require employee to forfeit wages when discharged or quitting or assess fines against employee (T. 23, §§634-636).

Upon demand of employee after discharge or resignation, employer must pay wages (including fringe benefits) within three days, or be liable either for 90 days wages or wages to date of payment, whichever is lesser, and in event suit is filed after such period, all costs including reasonable attorney's fees. (T. 23, §§631 and 632, and §640, as am'd Act 317 of 1977).

Employer may pay up to $6,000 to surviving spouse of employee, or to children if employee leaves no surviving spouse upon receipt of specified affidavit, provided no divorce proceeding is pending. (T. 9, §1515, am'd Act 604 of 1992). Employer must give notice to Department of Revenue and Taxation and forward copy of release.

Act 65 of 1968 prescribes payment of prevailing wages in particular area (as determined by Commissioner of Labor) on all projects of state or its agencies, and local political subdivisions are authorized to adopt ordinances and resolutions governing contracts let by them (T. 38, §2301).

Assignment of Wages.—See category Debtor and Creditor, topic Assignments.

Non-competition Clauses.—Clauses restricting competition of employees after termination are limited by statute. (T. 23, §921, as am'd Act 937 of 1995, eff. June 28, 1995).

Workmen's Compensation.—Subject of compensation for injured employees is governed by T. 23, c. 10. Coverage is for all persons performing services arising out of and incidental to employment in course of employer's trade, business or occupation, but bona fide president, vice-president, secretary and treasurer owning not less than 10% of stock of corporation, sole proprietor, or partner, may waive provisions of Act. (T. 23, §1035, as am'd Act 465 of 1979). Act also covers employees suffering disability or death resulting from occupational disease but such claims must be filed within six months of specific dates. (T. 23, §1031.1, as am'd Act 666 of 1980). Degenerative disc disease, spinal stenosis, arthritis, mental illness and heart-related or perivascular disease are specifically excluded from definition of occupational disease. (T. 23, §1031.1[B], as am'd Act 454 of 1989, eff. Jan. 1, 1990).

Employees performing work on private residential premises of householder and employees of private unincorporated farm when employee's net earnings are $1,000 or less and total net earnings of all employees on farm do not exceed $2,500 are not covered by compensation, when such work is not incidental to nor arises out of any trade, business or occupation of such householder or farmer. (T. 23, §1035[B], as am'd Act 246 of 1995, eff. June 14, 1995). Householder not liable as employer or principal under Act, but any person engaged in business of supplying persons to do work on private residential premises is liable under Act. (T. 23, §1035, as am'd Act 827 of 1981). Real estate brokers are also exempt from coverage. (T. 23, §1047, added Act 829 of 1982). Part-time employees are defined, and average weekly wages calculated, according to number of hours actually worked; and benefits are based on that calculation. (T. 23, §1021, am'd Act 1, 1st Ex.Sess., 1983 and Act 926 of 1985).

Act may also apply as to employees working outside Louisiana. (T. 23, §1035.1, added Act 583 of 1975).

In cases where Act applies, compensation is paid regardless of whether or not injury was caused by the negligence of employer. Compensation denied if employer proves injury caused by employee's willful attempt to injure himself or another, by intoxication, by deliberate failure to use guard or protection provided to him, or if employee is initial physical aggressor in unprovoked physical altercation, unless excessive force is used in retaliation against initial aggressor. (T. 23, §1081, am'd Act 1, 1st Ex.Sess., 1983). Upon proof of intoxication, causal relationship to injury is presumed unless employee disproves it. (T. 23, §1081, as am'd Act 454 of 1989, eff. Jan. 1, 1990).

A principal contractor is liable to the employees of a subcontractor for compensation but is subrogated to any rights they may have against others. Such an employee may elect to secure compensation from his employer. (T. 23, §§1061-1063).

Employee may claim compensation without affecting his claim for damages against a third person causing the injury, and employer may sue such person for amount which he has paid or become obligated to pay as compensation. Any fault allocated to party immune due to employment status serves to reduce claim for reimbursement by employer or compensation insurer. (T. 23, §1101[A], as am'd Act 15 of 1996 First Ex. Sess.). In any such action damages recovered must be apportioned between employer and employee, claim of employer having precedence. No compromise by employer or employee is binding upon and does not affect the rights of the others unless assented by him. (T. 23, §§1101, 1103).

If employee or dependent compromises with third person with written approval of employer or insurer, latter remains liable for compensation in excess of amount of compromise. Without such approval, employee or dependent forfeits right to any compensation from employer or insurer over amount of compromise; employee can regain right to excess compensation by paying over to employer out of compromise amount

LABOR RELATIONS . . . *continued*

enough to reimburse compensation benefits paid to that time, up to limit of 50% of compromise amount. (T. 23, §1102, am'd Act 1, 1st Ex.Sess., 1983). If, after intervention by employer or insurer, third-party defendant does not obtain approval of employer or insurer of settlement with employee, third-party defendant must reimburse employer or insurer for benefits paid. (T. 23, §1102[C], as am'd Act 852 of 1984).

Compensation right is exclusive of all other rights against employer, or any principal or any officer, director, stockholder, partner or employee of employer or principal, unless not acting in course or scope of employment or partnership was formed to evade provisions of Act. (T. 23, §§1032 and 1101, as am'd Act 147 of 1976 and Act 454 of 1989, latter eff. Jan. 1, 1990). Overruling contrary court decision, punitive damages also declared excluded by Compensation Act, with prospective effect from June 17, 1995. (T. 23, §1032, as am'd Act 432 of 1995). Act does not apply to uncompensated officers and directors of nonprofit associations. (T. 23, §1046, added Act 295 of 1976).

An employer must furnish all necessary medical and hospital services and medicines and replacement or repair of any prosthetic device damaged in accident and reasonable expense of burial not to exceed $5,000. (T. 23, §1203 and §1210, as am'd Act 55 of 1995). Physicians' and chiropractors' fees must be reasonable and agreed to by parties or approved by Director or court. Lien for their payment exists. (T. 23, §1142, as am'd Act 107 of 1986). Reimbursement level for medical or hospital services, and for drugs and supplies, is controlled by schedule. (T. 23, §1034.2, as am'd Act 938 of 1988, eff. Jan. 1, 1989).

Compensation for either temporary or permanent total disability is 66⅔% of wages during period of disability; such disability may be found only when employee cannot engage in any self-employment or gainful occupation for wages, regardless of its nature and specifically including any odd lot employment, sheltered employment or employment while working in any pain. (T. 23, §1221[1] and [2], am'd Act 1, 1st Ex.Sess., 1983). Compensation termed "supplemental earnings benefits" is available to disabled workers who cannot earn 90% or more of wages at time of injury; these benefits amount to 66⅔% of difference between average monthly wages at time of injury and such wages earned thereafter or which employee is able to earn. Such benefits are payable for up to 520 weeks, due in any week in which employee cannot earn 90% of prior wage amount. They terminate at end of any two-year period commencing after termination of temporary total disability, unless during that two-year period such benefits have been payable during at least 13 consecutive weeks. Such benefits also terminate when employee retires or begins to receive social security old age benefits, subject to minimum award of 104 weeks regardless of retirement or social security benefits. (T. 23, §1221[3], as am'd Act 926 of 1985, eff. Jan. 1, 1986). Compensation for loss of parts of body vary both as to percentage of wages and period of weeks, and are termed "partial disability benefits". Other losses not specified may be compensated by court up to 66⅔% of wages during 100 weeks. Inguinal hernia is treated separately with requirement of notification to employer promptly and treatment by physician within 30 days after accident. (T. 23, §1221[4], as am'd Act 945 of 1985).

No compensation is paid for the first week after the injury is received; except that in cases where disability from injury continues for six weeks or longer, after date of the accident, compensation for the first week must be paid after six weeks have elapsed. (T. 23, §1224).

Benefits for permanent total disability may be reduced by benefits from federal Social Security or employer-fund disability plans. Supplemental earnings benefits or benefits for temporary or total permanent disability are not payable for any week in which employee receives unemployment compensation, and no benefits of any nature are payable if federal worker's compensation benefits are received. (T. 23, §1225, as am'd Act 1, 1st Ex.Sess., 1983).

Compensation for death within two years after last treatment resulting from accident is by weekly payments varying according to number and relationship of beneficiaries and extent of dependency. Payments continue to spouse until death or remarriage but lump sum of two years payments due on remarriage. Payment to incapacitated child continues during incapacity. Payment to other dependent children continues until age 18, death, or marriage, but may continue to age 23 while a student in accredited educational institution. Payments to other dependents continue during dependency or until death. If there are no legal dependents entitled to benefits under any state or federal compensation system, each surviving parent is entitled to lump sum of $20,000. (T. 23, §§1231, 1232 and 1233, as am'd Act 431 of 1992).

Payments must be made at time and place of payment of wages, except the parties may agree to longer interval not exceeding one month, and court may approve interval of payment over one month. At option of employee, payments may be mailed to designated address. (T. 23, §1201). Any voluntary payments during disability or to dependents, not due, may, subject to court's approval, be deducted. (T. 23, §1206).

Maximum compensation to be paid for injuries between Sept. 1, 1996 and Aug. 31, 1997 is $349 and minimum is $93, based on average weekly wage of all employment subject to Employment Security Law, computed to nearest dollar. If wage of employee is less than minimum, he is entitled to average weekly wage. (T. 23, §1202, as am'd Act 926 of 1985). For injuries occurring on or after July 1, 1983, maximum weekly compensation is fixed at 75% of average weekly wage in all state employment (as opposed to maximum of 66⅔% of average weekly wage for injuries prior to that date). Minimum remains at 20% of average weekly wage figure, but minimum is not applicable to supplemental earnings benefits or partial disability benefits. (T. 23, §§1202, 1221, as am'd Act 1, 1st Ex.Sess., 1983).

Employer and employee may compromise and settle bona fide disputes by agreement under supervision of administrative hearing officer. (T. 23, §§1271-1273). Such agreement must have employer's consent as well as insurer and employee; lump sum payment, if any, must be in best interest of parties; and six months must have elapsed after termination of temporary total disability.

Compensation may be commuted in a lump sum by agreement of parties, if approved by court as reasonably complying with statutory provisions, but payments due may not be discounted at a greater rate than 8% per annum nor paid without approval of court, under penalty of liability for one and one-half times the statutory rate of compensation. (T. 23, §1274). Commutation does not preclude employee from making further claim if disability extend beyond contemplated period. (198 La. 921, 5 So.2d 288).

Record keeping and voluntary arbitration functions, as well as general supervision of Act and safety and rehabilitation matters, are established in state Office of Worker's Compensation Administration and its director. When parties have dispute over claim, they may file proceedings with administrative hearing officer. Any dissatisfied party may seek relief from court of appeal. (T. 23, §1310.2 et seq., added Act 938 of 1988, eff. Jan. 1, 1990). Initial mediation of claim is provided. (T. 23, §1310.3, as am'd Act 348 of 1995, eff. June 16, 1995). See category Dispute Resolution, topic Alternative Dispute Resolution.

Claims for payments are barred unless parties agree to payments to be made or formal claim has been filed with state administrative office within one year after accident, death, development of injury or last payment. Such time period is three years in case of supplemental earnings benefits, to run from last benefit payment of any type. In all cases, claim must be filed two years after accident resulting in delayed development of injury. (T. 23, §1209, as am'd Act 1, 1st Ex.Sess., 1983). Claims filed with state administrative office presumed timely if received on first legal day following expiration of due date. (T. 23, §1209[B], added Act 884 of 1985). Medical benefit claims are subject to similar time limitations (one year from accident or three years from last payment). (T. 23, §1209[B], added Act 926 of 1985). Failure to pay claims within designated periods of 14, 30 and 60 days after appropriate notice or finality of judgment subjects employer or insurer to varying penalties up to 24% and to reasonable attorney's fees, if such failure is arbitrary, capricious or without probable cause. (T. 23, §1201.2, as am'd Act 1, 1st Ex.Sess., 1983).

Hearing officer proceedings under Act are summary, and procedure for appeal is governed by C.C.P. (T. 23, §§1311-1320, as am'd Act 1, 1st Ex.Sess., 1983). For injuries after Jan. 1, 1990, administrative hearing officer system in place, with appeals to appellate court bypassing district court. Default judgments may be entered and confirmed. Fees payable by claimant to attorney must be approved by director or court and then constitute lien. They must not exceed 20% of first $20,000 of any award and 10% of part of award over $10,000. (T. 23, §1141, as am'd Act 609 of 1995). Final judgment may be modified by hearing officer with approval of all parties, and hearing officer shall review case at any time after six months of rendition of judgment and issue recommendation. (T. 23, §1331, as am'd Act 1, 1st Ex.Sess., 1983). Rehabilitation of injured employee may be ordered by hearing officer at expense of employer or insurer for up to 26 weeks, and may be extended for another 26 weeks; possibility of rehabilitation must be assessed prior to adjudication of permanent disability. (T. 23, §1226, added Act 1, 1st Ex.Sess., 1983). Examination by vocational rehabilitation expert may be ordered on good cause shown. (C.C.P. 1464, as am'd Act 324 of 1991).

Nonresident employer, who comes within the Act and who does not carry compensation insurance or own real property in this state worth at least $100,000 must furnish evidence of current insurance or must deposit with State Treasurer securities in an amount approved by Louisiana Insurance Rating Commission or give bond to secure payment of compensation. (T. 23, §§1181-1182, as am'd Act 266 of 1987).

Workmen's Compensation Second Injury Fund provided for reimbursement to employers hiring employees who have a specified permanent, partial disability when employee sustains a second injury. Workmen's compensation insurers and self-insured employers required to contribute specific percentage of gross premiums received or which would have been paid if insured at level fixed by governing board. (T. 23, §1371, et seq., as am'd Act 188 of 1995, eff. June 12, 1995).

Groups of five or more employers may institute group self-insurance funds pursuant to requirements of Compensation Act. (T. 23, §1192 et seq., as am'd Act 13 of 1991, eff. June 14, 1991).

Self-insured program is subject to initial certification by commissioner of insurance, for fee of $1,500; and to annual review, for fee of $300. (T. 22, §1078[B], added Act 18, 1st Ex.Sess., 1983). Insurance coverage is mandatory absent self-insurance arrangements or special statutory exemptions, such as for municipalities. (T. 23, §1168). State-operated fund is available. (T. 23, §§1391-1415, added Act 814 of 1991).

Unemployment Compensation.—An unemployed individual is eligible to claim benefits provided he registers for work at and continues to report to a state employment office; is able to and is available for work; has been unemployed for a waiting period of one week; and, has previously been paid during his base period (as defined in Act) wages for insured work equal to at least one and one-half time wages paid to him in that calendar quarter in which his wages were highest. (T. 23, §1600, am'd Act 2 of 1st Ex.Sess., 1983). Unemployed individual who is otherwise eligible may not receive benefits for specified period for certain reasons, such as: Leaving former employment without good cause; being discharged for misconduct; failing to apply for or accept suitable work; becoming unemployed due to labor dispute; receiving or seeking unemployment benefits under laws of another state or U.S.; receiving payments under private retirement or pension plan; and making misrepresentations in order to obtain benefits. (T. 23, §1601, as am'd Acts 566 and 596 of 1985).

WORKERS' COMPENSATION LAW:

See topic Labor Relations.

ENVIRONMENT

ENVIRONMENTAL REGULATION:

General Supervision.—Department of Environmental Quality has jurisdiction of environmental protection pursuant to Louisiana Environmental Quality Act, including regulation of air quality, water pollution control, regulation of solid waste disposal, and regulation of hazardous wastes. (T. 30, §§1051-1150.79, as am'd Acts 306, 329, 347, 479, 781, 942 of 1986, T. 32, §§1501-1520, T. 33, §7556, T. 36, §§231-239, 351-359, T. 40, §5, as am'd Act 449 of 1979). Coastal Zone Management Program, Department of Natural Resources, designates various agencies, depending upon intended usage, to issue permits with respect to land use in coastal zone of state. (T. 49, §§213.1-213.22). Department of Wildlife and Fisheries regulates recreational and commercial hunting, fishing, trapping, and recreational boating. (T. 56, §§3-700.5, T. 36, §§601-610).

See note at head of Digest as to 1998 legislation covered.

See Topical Index in front part of this volume.

LA – 31

ENVIRONMENTAL REGULATION . . . *continued*

Prohibited Acts of Pollution.—Generally, all persons are prohibited from discharging contaminants into air and water, to transport, store, etc., radioactive materials, to cause pollution by solid wastes, or to transport, store or otherwise handle hazardous wastes, contrary to rules and regulations of Department of Environmental Quality. Underground injection of hazardous wastes is regulated by Department of Natural Resources. (T. 30, §4.1 et seq., added Act 389 of 1981, am'd by Act 609 of 1985).

Enforcement.—Enforcement of regulations and laws concerning environmental affairs is generally by Department of Environmental Quality through civil suits for damages, cease and desist orders, compliance orders, or by attorney general with respect to criminal actions. Officials may conduct on-site investigations under some circumstances without advance notice or warrant. (T. 30, §1061.1, added Act 655 of 1982, am'd by Act 97 of 1983). When order is final but not complied with, attorney general may institute ex parte petition in 19th Judicial District Court (East Baton Rouge Parish) to make order judgment of court and to make it executory. (T. 30, §1073, as am'd Act 254 of 1988, eff. July 6, 1988). Appeals by aggrieved persons are only to 19th Judicial District Court (East Baton Rouge Parish) within 30 days of ruling or action. (T. 30, §2050.21, as am'd Act 1143 of 1997).

Penalties may be assessed as follows: (1) When person willfully or knowingly discharges, emits, or disposes in contravention of statute, regulations or permit, substance which does or could endanger human life or health, conviction of felony and fine of up to $1,000,000 or cost of cleanup and $100,000 per day of violation plus costs or up to ten years at hard labor or both except for discharge of certain air contaminants; or discharges substance which does not endanger human life or health, conviction of misdemeanor and fine of up to $25,000 per day or imprisonment for not more than one year or both. Misdemeanor verdict is responsive to charge of felony. (T. 30, §1073[F], as am'd 942 of 1986; §1073[F][1]added by Act 942 of 1986). General penalty provisions for violation of Act or orders of commission include civil penalty up to $25,000 a day for each day of violation and each act of violation and conviction of misdemeanor, and up to $50,000 a day for failure to comply with cease and desist orders. (T. 30, §18 and §1073 [E] as am'd Act 320 of 1983). Any amounts paid as fines are credits toward any eventual judgment or settlement in civil suit for damages. (T. 30, §1073, as am'd Act 318 of 1987, eff. July 6, 1987). Persons who violate hazardous waste control permits may also be punished by fines up to $100,000 per day or imprisonment at hard labor up to ten years, or both. (T. 30, §1137 [G], as am'd Act 146 of 1982). Civil suits for damages resulting from violations may be brought by Department in name of state, but any amount paid as penalty for violation is credit toward judgment or settlement in that suit. (T. 30, §1073 [B], as am'd Act 97 of 1983).

Careless transportation of hazardous materials is punishable both criminally and civilly. (T. 32, §1519, added Act 327 of 1984). Upon showing of reckless disregard, punitive damages are awardable. (C.C. 2315.1, added Act 335 of 1984). "Hazardous waste site" includes entire contaminated area and may extend beyond facility's boundary. (T. 30, §1148[C], added by Act 329 of 1986). Fuel containing hazardous waste regulated by Department of Environmental Quality (T. 30, §1136[A][8], added by Act 781 of 1986).

Permits.—Permits with respect to environmental affairs are issued by Department. Persons may not import hazardous wastes and permits to dispose of hazardous wastes generated in foreign country may not be granted. (T. 30, §1137.1, added Acts 260 and 694 of 1983).

Coastal Zone Management Program designates various agencies, depending upon intended usage, to issue permits with respect to lands in coastal zone of state, with coordination through Department of Natural Resources. (T. 49, §§213.1-213.12, as am'd Acts 512 and 705 of 1983).

Permits for surface mining of coal and transport, treatment, storage or disposal of hazardous wastes, necessary from Department of Natural Resources. (T. 30, §§901 et seq., am'd Acts 121 and 748 of 1980). Permits for transport, treatment, storage or disposal of hazardous waste necessary from Department of Natural Resources. (T. 30, §§1131-1149.50, as am'd by Acts 306, 781, and 942 of 1986).

Hazardous Waste Tax.—Tax by weight is imposed on disposal and storage of hazardous waste, as defined. One-time tax of $2 per dry weight ton of hazardous waste content of Louisiana land was imposed as of July 1, 1984. For future waste disposal or storage more than 90 days for incineration at sea, tax of $10 per dry weight ton is imposed for waste disposed at sites on which generator's act or process produced waste and $20 per dry weight ton for waste disposed at other sites. Tax on "extremely hazardous waste" is $25 per dry weight ton, as defined. Tax on hazardous and extremely hazardous substances increases $1 per year until 1998. Reciprocal tax calculation imposed: Same tax as in generating state as minimum. (T. 30, §§1149.21, 1149.32 and T. 47, §§821-832, as am'd Act 655 of 1988, eff. July 1, 1988).

ESTATES AND TRUSTS

ADMINISTRATION:

See topic Executors and Administrators.

ADVANCEMENTS:

See topic Descent and Distribution, subhead Collation.

ALLOWANCES:

See topic Executors and Administrators.

CLAIMS:

See topic Executors and Administrators; category Civil Actions and Procedure, topic Pleading.

DEATH:

There is a presumption of a person's death after absence lasting five years or more. (C.C. 54, as am'd Act 989 of 1990, eff. Jan. 1, 1991).

Survivorship.—When several persons perish in a common disaster and there is no evidence of survivorship, presumption of survivorship is determined by age alone. (C.C. 936-938, as am'd Act 526 of 1985). Presumption may be altered or negated by testator in will by providing that property shall devolve as if testator had survived as to heir, legatee or trust beneficiary of trust. (C.C. 1521, as am'd Act 583 of 1985). Ninety-day survivorship clause in testament is permitted. (C.C. 1521, as am'd Act 680 of 1987).

Action for death lies in favor of surviving spouse and child or children of decedent or either such spouse or such child or children; if none, in favor of surviving parents or parent; if none, in favor of surviving brothers and sisters; if none of above, surviving grandparents, or any of them. Father or mother who has abandoned child, as defined, has no such cause of action. Action must be brought within one year. Damages are recoverable for death of decedent, and damages sustained by survivors bringing action, but are not limited by law. (C.C. 2315.1 and 2315.2, as am'd Act 1317 of 1997, eff. July 15, 1997 and applicable only to causes of action arising on or after that date). Succession representative may bring "survival action" for damages of deceased tort victim if statutory representatives do not survive him. (C.C. 2315.1, as am'd Act 675 of 1987). Surviving spouse, parent or child involved in killing of deceased may not bring action and does not exclude successive classes of beneficiaries. (C.C. 2315.5, as am'd Act 180 of 1991).

Death Certificate.—See category Documents and Records, topic Records, subhead Vital Statistics.

Uniform Anatomical Gift Act adopted. (T. 17; §2351, et seq., am'd Act 311 of 1985).

See topic Wills, subhead Living Will.

DECEDENTS' ESTATES:

See topics Descent and Distribution, Executors and Administrators, Wills; category Debtor and Creditor, topic Homesteads.

DESCENT AND DISTRIBUTION:

Note: Significant revisions to certain portions of Civil Code relative to seizin, opening of successions, acceptance and renunciation, payment of debts, types of testamentary dispositions and probate procedure are made by Act 1421 of 1997, but only eff. as of July 1, 1999.

When person dies and leaves no will, property descends to various persons by law depending upon classification of property as community or separate property of deceased. Community property of deceased is inherited by his descendants (C. C. 888, added Act 919 of 1981); or if he leaves no descendants, by his surviving spouse in full ownership (C. C. 889, added Act 919 of 1981). Descendants include persons born of marriage, those adopted and those whose filiation to parent has been established in manner provided by law, and their own descendants who may represent them if they died before deceased. (C. C. 3556[8], as am'd Act 919 of 1981). Separate property of deceased is inherited, in successive order if they survive him, by his descendants; his brothers or sisters or their descendants; his parents; his surviving spouse; his ascendants; and other collateral heirs. (C. C. 891-6, added Act 919 of 1981).

Share of community property inherited by descendants is subject to usufruct of surviving spouse. (C. C. 890, added Act 919 of 1981). See subhead Surviving Spouse, infra.

Rights of each of these various classes of heirs are as follows:

Descendants succeed to property of their ascendants in equal portions and by heads if they are in same degree, and by roots if all or some of them succeed by representation. (C. C. 888, added Act 919 of 1981). They inherit both separate and community property to exclusion of other heirs, subject to usufruct rights of surviving spouse. In vitro human embryos have inheritance rights of children if subsequently they develop into unborn children later born in live birth. (T. 9, §§121-133, added Act 964 of 1986; C.C. 26, as am'd Act 125 of 1987, eff. Jan. 1, 1988).

Parents; Brothers and Sisters.—If deceased leaves no descendants but is survived by father, mother or both, and by brother or sister, or both, or descendants of last, brothers and sisters or their descendants succeed to separate property of deceased, subject to usufruct in favor of surviving parent or parents. If both parents survive deceased, usufruct is joint and successive. Parent includes one legitimately filiated to deceased or filiated by legitimation or by acknowledgment under C. C. 203 or by judgment under C. C. 209, or who has openly and notoriously treated child as his own and has not refused to support him. (C. C. 891, added Act 919 of 1981). If deceased leaves neither descendants nor parents, his brothers or sisters or their descendants succeed to his separate property in full ownership to exclusion of other ascendants and other collaterals. (C. C. 892, added Act 919 of 1981). If deceased leaves neither descendants, nor brothers or sisters or their descendants, his parent or parents succeed to separate property to exclusion of other ascendants and other collaterals. (C. C. 892, added Act 919 of 1981).

Property that devolves to brothers or sisters is divided among them equally if they are all born of same parents. If they are born of different unions, it is equally divided between paternal and maternal lines of deceased: Brothers or sisters fully related by blood take in both lines and those related by half-blood take each in his own line. If there are brothers or sisters on one side only, they take entirety to exclusion of all relations in other line. (C. C. 893, added Act 919 of 1981).

Brothers and sisters of deceased, or their descendants, inherit in their own right or by representation, as regulated by laws referring to latter. (C. C. 881-7, added Act 919 of 1981).

Surviving Spouse.—Share of community, undisposed of by deceased, is inherited by surviving spouse if there are no descendants. (C. C. 889, added Act 919 of 1981). If deceased leaves descendants, his or her undisposed of share of community is inherited by such descendants. Community share inherited by descendants is subject to usufruct of surviving spouse, unless deceased has disposed of that share adversely to interest of

DESCENT AND DISTRIBUTION . . . *continued*
surviving spouse. Usufruct terminates when surviving spouse contracts another marriage, unless confirmed by will for life or for shorter period. (C. C. 890, added Act 919 of 1981). Such usufruct is legal usufruct, and does not impinge on forced share of descendants. Deceased may by testament grant usufruct for life or for shorter period to surviving spouse over all or part of his separate property, regardless of inheriting heir. (C. C. 890, as am'd Act 445 of 1982). This usufruct is also legal usufruct, not impingement on legitime of forced heirs, but they may seek security. (C. C. 890, as am'd Act 445 of 1982; C.C.P. 3154.1, added Acts 911 and 919 of 1981). Property subject to such usufruct includes pension or retirement plan payments, if community property. (C.C. 890, as am'd Act 1075 of 1990, eff. July 27, 1990).

If deceased died rich leaving spouse in necessitous circumstances, marital portion in varying amounts may be available, subject to maximum of $1,000,000. (C.C. 2434, as am'd Act 289 of 1987).

Adopted Children.—See category Family, topic Adoption.

Illegitimate Descendants.—Illegitimate children may be legitimated by subsequent marriage of parents if acknowledged by them as their children. They may be legitimated by father or mother by act before notary and two witnesses. (C.C. 200, as am'd Act 480 of 1983). Illegitimates may be acknowledged by declaration executed before notary and two witnesses or by registration of birth or baptism. Prior to declaration, party is entitled to notification by notary of certain rights and obligations. (T. 9, §392, as am'd Act 6 of First Ex. Sess. of 1998, eff. July 1, 1998). And illegitimate children may prove their filiation in action brought within one year of death of parent or within 19 years after child's birth, whichever first occurs. (C. C. 208 and 209, as am'd Act 527 of 1982). Judgments in such actions must be recorded by clerk in conveyance records and are effective against third persons from date of recordation. (T. 13, §914.1, added Act 425 of 1982). Once filiation of such children is established in one of foregoing manners, they have same rights as legitimate children. (C. C. 888, added Act 919 of 1981). Such establishment of filiation would have same effect as to other relations, such as ascendants and siblings and other collaterals.

Ascendants.—If deceased leaves neither descendants, nor brothers, sisters, or descendants from them, nor parents, nor spouse not judicially separated, his other ascendants succeed to his separate property. If ascendants in paternal and maternal lines are in same degree, property is divided into two equal shares, one of which goes to ascendants on paternal side, and other to ascendants on maternal side, whether number of ascendants on each side is equal or not. In this case, ascendants in each line inherit by heads. If there is in nearest degree but one ascendant in two lines, such ascendant excludes ascendants of more remote degree. (C. C. 895, added Act 919 of 1981). No representation is permitted in ascending line. (C. C. 883, added Act 919 of 1981).

Ascendants, to exclusion of all others, inherit immovables given by them to their children or their descendants of more remote degree who die without posterity. If immovable has been alienated, but price is still due in whole or part, ascendants have right to receive price. They also succeed to right of reversion on happening of any event which child or descendant may have inserted as condition in his favor in disposing of immovable. (C. C. 897, added Act 919 of 1981). Ascendants inheriting immovables take them subject to all mortgages which donee may have imposed on them, and ascendants exercising right of reversion are bound to contribute to payment of succession debts, in proportion to value of objects given. (C. C. 898, added Act 919 of 1981).

Collaterals.—If deceased leaves neither descendants, nor brothers, sisters, or descendants from them, nor parents, nor spouse not judicially separated, nor other ascendants, his other collaterals succeed to his separate property. Among collateral relations, nearest in degree excludes all others. If there are several in same degree, they take equally and by heads. (C. C. 896, added Act 919 of 1981).

Representation is fiction of law, effect of which is to put representative in place, degree and rights of person represented. (C. C. 881, added Act 919 of 1981). Representation takes place ad infinitum in direct line of descendants. It is permitted in all cases, whether children of deceased concur with descendants of predeceased child, or whether, all children having died before him, descendants of children are in equal or unequal degrees of relationship to deceased, but is limited with respect to claims of predeceased forced heirs to representation of those forced heirs who would not have been 23 at time of decedent's death. (C.C. 882, as am'd Act 147 of 1990, eff. July 1, 1990). There is no representation in ascending line. (C. C. 883, added Act 919 of 1981). In collateral line, representation is permitted in favor of children and descendants of brothers and sisters of deceased, whether they succeed in concurrence with uncles and aunts, or whether, brothers and sisters of deceased having died, their descendants succeed in equal or unequal degrees. (C. C. 884, added Act 919 of 1981).

In all cases in which representation is permitted, partition is made by roots; if one root has produced several branches, subdivision is also made by roots in each branch, and members of same branch take by heads. (C. C. 885, added Act 919 of 1981). Only deceased person may be represented. (C. C. 886, added Act 919 of 1981). One who has renounced his right to succeed to another may nonetheless enjoy representation with respect to that other. (C. C. 887, added Act 919 of 1981).

Afterborn Children.—Child in mother's womb is considered born for all purposes of its own interest: it takes all successions opened in its favor since its conception, provided it be capable of succeeding at moment of birth. Child legitimated by a marriage posterior to its conception takes only those successions which are opened since the marriage of the father and mother. (C. C. 954). Child must be born alive in order to inherit. (C. C. 955).

Unworthy Heirs.—Unworthiness of heirs for designated reasons may be established according to C.C. 964-975.

Death in Common Disaster.—See topic Death, subhead Survivorship.

Collation of goods is the supposed or real return to the mass of the succession made by an heir of that which he has received in advance of his share. (C. C. 1227). Children or grandchildren coming to the succession of ascendants must collate what they have received by donation inter vivos and cannot claim legacies unless the donations and legacies have been made expressly as an advantage over other coheirs. (C. C. 1228). Collation is always presumed where it has not been expressly forbidden. (C. C. 1230). Dispensation from obligation of collating may be made in instrument in which gift is made, in later authentic act or in valid last will. (C.C. 1232 and 1501, as am'd Act 246 of 1986). One obliged to collate may renounce succession and retain gift. If, however, remaining amount of inheritance should not be sufficient for legitimate portion of other children, including in succession of deceased property which person renouncing would have collated, had he become heir, he shall then be obliged to collate up to sum necessary to complete such legitimate portion. (C. C. 1237). To make legitimate descendants liable to collation, they must appear in quality of heirs to succession of ascendants from whom they have received gift or legacy. (C. C. 1238). Collation is made in kind when gift itself is returned and by taking less when donee diminishes portion he inherits by value of gift. (C. C. 1252, 1253). If immovable has been given and is still in donee's possession, donee has choice of making collation in kind or by taking less, unless donor has prescribed otherwise. (C. C. 1255). But in case of movables, donee is bound to collate for them by taking less according to their value at time of donation. (C. C. 1283). Collation of money may be made in money or by taking less. (C. C. 1285). Gifts not exceeding disposable portion of decedent's estate (see topic Wills, subhead Forced Heirs) are not taken into consideration in determining distribution of estate where it was expressly provided by donor that they should be over and above forced portion of donee.

Forced Heirs.—See topic Wills, subheads Forced Heirs, and Disinherison.

Escheat.—In default of blood or adopted relations, or spouse not judicially separated, estate of deceased belongs to state. (C. C. 902, added Act 919 of 1981).

See also topic Executors and Administrators.

ESTATES:

See category Property, topic Real Property.

EXECUTORS AND ADMINISTRATORS:

Administration of the estate of a decedent is necessary if the heir does not accept simply and unconditionally. (C. C. 1058).

Acceptance of Succession.—Though succession be acquired by heir from moment of death of deceased, his right is in suspense until he decides whether he accepts or rejects it. If heir accepts he is considered as having succeeded to deceased from moment of his death; if he rejects it he is considered as never having received it. Heir who accepts is considered as having succeeded to deceased from moment of his death not only for part of succession belonging to him in his own right, but for parts accruing to him by renunciation of his coheirs in succession of deceased. (C. C. 946, 947, 976, T. 9, §§5011-5016).

Unconditional acceptance by heir binds him personally for payment of all debts of succession, as if he had contracted them himself. (C. C. 1013). Heir may accept only part of succession, but such acceptance has same effect as to debts of succession as if he had accepted entire succession. (C. C. 986, as am'd Act 249 of 1981). All acceptances presumed to be with benefit of inventory (see subhead Benefit of Inventory, infra) unless there is personal obligation in petition for possession or separate instrument. (T. 9, §1421, added Act 602 of 1986).

Placing Heirs or Legatees in Possession.—Heirs of intestate may be recognized and sent into possession of his property without administration of his succession when none of creditors of succession has demanded its administration, on ex parte petition of (1) Those of heirs who are competent, if all of these accept succession unconditionally; (2) legal representative of incompetent heirs if all of heirs are incompetent and legal representative has been appointed therefor; or (3) surviving spouse in community of deceased, if all of heirs are incompetent and no legal representative has been appointed for some or all of them. In such cases, surviving spouse in community of deceased may be recognized by court as entitled to possession of community property. (C.C.P. 3001 and 3004, am'd act 23 of 1961). When testament has been probated, court may send legatees into possession of their respective legacies without administration of succession, on their ex parte petition, when all of legatees are either competent or are acting through their qualified legal representatives, all competent residuary legatees accept succession unconditionally, and none of creditors of succession has demanded its administration. In such cases, surviving spouse in community of testator may be recognized by court as entitled to possession of community property. (C.C.P. 3031 and 3033). In either intestate or testate succession, creditors thereof may demand security from heirs, residuary legatees or surviving spouse for payment of claims (C.C.P. 3007, 3034) as may particular legatees for payment of their legacies (C.C.P. 3035).

Benefit of Inventory.—The heir may, in all cases, claim the benefit of inventory, by which is meant the privilege of being liable for the charges and debts of the succession only to value of effects thereof. (C. C. 1032, 1054, 1058). All acceptances are presumed to be under benefit of inventory absent contrary written indication. (T. 9, §1421, added Act 602 of 1986). It shall not be necessary for minor heirs to make any formal acceptance of succession that may fall to them, but such acceptance shall be considered as made for them with benefit of inventory by operation of law and in all respects have force and effect of formal acceptance. (C. C. 977).

When the succession is accepted under benefit of inventory it is administered by an administrator appointed by the court.

Jurisdiction.—District courts have jurisdiction of opening of successions. (Const., art. 5, §16).

Venue is in the parish: (1) of the domicile of the decedent; (2) if he had no domicile or residence in this state, where he owns real property, or if none, where he owns movable property. (C.C.P. 2811).

Preferences in Right to Administer.—When an administratorship or dative testamentary executorship is claimed, preference in appointment is given in order as follows: (1) best qualified among surviving spouse, competent heirs or legatees, or legal representatives of any incompetent heirs or legatees; (2) best qualified among nominees of those in (1) above; (3) best qualified among creditors of deceased or co-owner of immovable property with deceased. (C.C.P. 3098, as am'd Act 29 of 1993).

See note at head of Digest as to 1998 legislation covered.

See Topical Index in front part of this volume.

LA – 33

EXECUTORS AND ADMINISTRATORS . . . *continued*

Attorney for Executor.—Designation of attorney for executor is binding on executor and heirs. (T. 9, §2448, added Act 250 of 1986).

Eligibility and Competency.—A woman, whether married or single, may act as executrix or administratrix (T. 9, §51) but a minor may not act in either capacity (C.C.P. 3097). An interdict, convicted felon or one who is unfit because of bad moral character is disqualified. Strangers are disqualified except when named testamentary executor. (C.C.P. 3097).

A nonresident who has appointed resident agent for service of all process related to succession may serve as executor or administrator, provided appointment is filed in succession proceedings. (C.C.P. 3097, as am'd Act 4 of 1964). Statute implies a foreign corporation may also serve, if permitted by charter, and appointment of resident agent be made.

Qualification of Representative.—After inventory has been taken, or sworn descriptive list of decedent's property filed, person who has been named administrator or dative testamentary executor gives bond, which must exceed by one-fourth value shown on inventory or on descriptive list. (C.C.P. 3151, 3153). If bond is secured by personal sureties, they must be residents of state though not of parish where security is given and must have unencumbered property in state amply sufficient to secure bond. (C.C.P. 3155.1, added Act 236 of 1986). Administrator or executor must then take oath for faithful performance of his duties. (C.C.P. 3158). Testamentary executor need not give bond unless required by provisions of will or petition of creditor, or heir or surviving spouse in community. (C.C.P. 3153).

Administrators of Vacant Successions.—A succession is defined as vacant when no one has claimed it or all heirs are unknown or have renounced succession. (C.C. 1095). When no qualified person has applied for appointment as administrator of a vacant succession within three months, court may appoint attorney-at-law as administrator. (C.C.P. 3121, as am'd Act 530 of 1974). Role of public administrator in parishes with over 100,000 population is fulfilled by state Department of Revenue and Taxation. (T. 9, §1581; T. 36, §458).

General Powers and Duties.—Succession representative is fiduciary with respect to succession, and shall have duty of collecting, preserving, and managing property of succession in accordance with law. He shall act at all times as prudent administrator and shall be personally responsible for all damages resulting from his failure so to act. (C.C.P. 3191, as am'd Act 4 of 1964). Upon order of court, they may sell succession property at public or private sale to pay debts or legacies (C.C.P. 3261-3264) without priority between real and personal property and may borrow funds and mortgage or encumber succession property with court approval. (C.C.P. 3228, as am'd Act 203 of 1995). Household goods as defined may be sold at appraised value without advertisement. (C.C.P. 3287, added Act 724 of 1985). Nonresident succession representative may execute power of attorney appointing resident to represent him in all acts of his administration provided power of attorney is filed in succession proceeding. (C.C.P. 3191 as am'd Act 4 of 1964). Succession representative may by power of attorney designate person to manage in his stead, and that person in turn may appoint substitute if power of attorney permits. (T. 9, §1517, added Act 284 of 1985). Representative may bring "survival action" on behalf of deceased tort victim, when statutory representatives do not survive victim. (C.C. 2315.1, as am'd Act 675 of 1987).

Majority of heirs may be sent into possession of property prior to homologation (approval) of final tableau of distribution after contradictory hearing with administrator. (C.C.P. 3362, as am'd Act 209 of 1986).

Uniform Fiduciaries Act adopted with slight variations. (T. 9, §§3801-3814; §3803 repealed, Act 444 of 1960).

Uniform Principal and Income Act.—Revised Uniform Principal and Income Act forms basis of La. R.S. 9:2141 et seq.; however, certain departures are made where provisions of Uniform Act are not in conformity with general laws of Louisiana.

Uniform Simplification of Fiduciary Security Transfers Act adopted. (T. 9, §§3831-3840).

Uniform Anatomical Gift Act.—Adopted. (T. 17, §2351, et seq.).

Claims against estates under administration should be presented for approval in writing to the executor or administrator. (C.C.P. 3241). No particular form of claim is necessary.

Succession representative to whom claim against succession has been submitted must within 30 days acknowledge or reject claim in whole or part. Failure of succession representative either to acknowledge or reject claim within 30 days of date it was submitted to him shall be considered rejection thereof. Acknowledgment of claim by succession representative shall (1) Entitle creditor to have his claim in succession representative's petition for authority to pay debts or in his tableau of distribution for payment in due course of administration; (2) create prima facie presumption of validity of claim even if it is not included in succession representative's petition for authority to pay debts or in his tableau of distribution; and (3) suspend running of prescription against claim as long as succession is under administration. (C.C.P. 3241-3245).

Should he decline to recognize the claim, the creditor may file suit against the succession representative and obtain a judgment, to be paid in the ordinary course of administration. (C.C.P. 3246). If there is no danger of the claim becoming prescribed, the creditor may, instead of filing suit, await the filing of an account by the executor or administrator and then assert his claim by way of opposition. (C.C.P. 3336).

Form.—No particular form required (C.C.P. 3241) except to suspend running of prescription as follows:

Form

To: . . . . . . duly qualified (administrator or executor) of the estate of . . . . . ., at . . . . . ., Louisiana:

This is to notify you that I, ..., domiciled at (give full address), am a creditor of the Succession of . . . . . ., in the amount of . . . . . . Dollars ($. . . . . .), representing (short statement of facts on which claim is based, and if based on written instrument, annex copy thereof, or if written instrument is lost or destroyed, a statement of such loss or destruction). (If claim secured, describe security and property affected thereby).

This formal proof of claim is (delivered to you personally) (mailed to you by certified or registered mail) on this . . . . . . day of . . . . . ., 19. . . . ., in compliance with Article 3245 of the Louisiana Code of Civil Procedure.

. . . .

State of . . . . . .
Parish (or County) of . . . . . .

BEFORE ME, the undersigned authority, personally came and appeared . . . . . ., who, being duly sworn deposed and said that he has read the above and foregoing formal proof of claim against the Succession of . . . . . ., and that all the statements therein contained are true and correct.

Sworn to and subscribed before me this . . . . . . day of . . . . . ., 19. . . .

. . . .
Notary Public

Payment of Claims.—No debts of the decedent can be paid without the authorization of the court. The administrator or executor presents to the court an account or tableau of distribution setting forth the payments and disbursements which he proposes to make. Court order is not required for publication of notice of filing of tableau of distribution. (C.C.P. 3303, as am'd Act 204 of 1986). All parties interested are notified by publication to show cause within seven days why account so filed should not be approved. (C.C.P. 3304, as am'd Act 280 of 1980). Opposition may be filed at any time before homologation and shall be tried as summary proceeding. (C.C.P. 3307, as am'd Act 23 of 1961). Judgment thereon is subject only to suspensive appeal. (C.C.P. 3308). If no oppositions are filed within seven days account is, upon production of satisfactory evidence by administrator or executor, approved and homologated, and funds ordered distributed in accordance therewith. (C.C.P. 3307, as am'd Act 280 of 1980). Dation en paiement (deed in lieu) is permissible for secured or unsecured debts. (T. 9, §§1471-1473, as am'd Act 564 of 1988).

Debts are preferred in following order: expenses of funeral; charges imposed by law; expenses of last sickness; wages of servants for one year past and the current year; amounts due to retail dealers, for provisions and supplies for the decedent and his family during the six months preceding death, or due to keepers of inns or boarding houses for the year preceding death; and salaries of clerks. (C. C. 3191).

Sales.—On petition of administrator or executor, the court may order private or public sale of movable or immovable property without priority, to pay debts or legacies. (C.C.P. 3271 and 3281). Private sales of movable property may be made ten days after only one advertisement; immovable property, seven days after latter of two advertisements. (C.C.P. 3282-3284, am'd Act 626 of 1972; T. 43, §203, as am'd Act 627 of 1972). Sales of motor vehicles at appraised value in inventory list may be made without advertisement. (C.C.P. 3288, added Act 237 of 1986). Public sales are made in manner provided for judicial sales in execution of judgments. See category Debtor and Creditor, topic Executions.

Stocks and bonds may be sold at private sales under order of court. (C.C.P. 3285).

Leases.—Court may authorize lease of property limited to one year absent consent of heirs or legatees. Mineral leases may be authorized for more than one year but court must state minimum bonus and minimum royalty which must be not less than one-eighth. Notice must be published once in parish of succession proceedings and also in parish where property is located for mineral lease. Publication must be at least seven days prior to court authorization. (C.C.P. 3226 and 3229, am'd Act 131 of 1974).

Actions.—There is no suspension of the right to sue on claims against a decedent's estate. Action must be brought within three years after distribution of assets in order that claim may participate in assets distributed.

Suit against succession representative or his surety because of fault in course of administration must be brought within two years of date of judgment homologating final account: except in case of embezzlement or payment not in accordance with final account. Period not suspended by minority of claimant. (T. 9. §5621).

Allowances.—Whenever surviving spouse or minor children of deceased person are left in necessitous circumstances, and do not possess in their own rights property to amount of $1,000, surviving spouse or legal representatives of children are entitled to demand and receive from succession of deceased, sum, which added to amount of property owned by them, or either of them, in their own right, will make up sum of $1,000, which amount must be paid in preference to all other debts, except those secured by vendor's privilege, conventional mortgages, and expenses incurred in selling property. Surviving spouse shall have and enjoy usufruct of amount so received from deceased's succession, until remarriage or death, which amount afterwards vests in and belongs to children or other descendants of deceased. (C. C. 3252, as am'd Act 711 of 1979).

If either husband or wife die rich, leaving survivor in necessitous circumstances, latter has a right to take out of succession of deceased what is called marital portion; that is, one-fourth of succession in full ownership if there be no children, and same portion in usufruct only, when there are not more than three children; and if there be more than three children, survivor, whether husband or wife, shall receive only child's share in usufruct, and is bound to deduct from this portion legacy left by deceased to spouse and payments due spouse as result of death. During administration, court may provide for fixed allowance of marital portion. (C. C. Arts. 2432-2437, as am'd Act 710 of 1979). Marital portion is limited to $1,000,000. (C.C. 2434, as am'd Act 289 of 1987).

Marital portion may be placed in trust. (T. 9, §§1851-1854, added Act 67 of 1977).

Decedents' Property.—See same subhead under category Business Regulation and Commerce, topic Banks and Banking.

Accounts of administration must be rendered annually and at other times ordered by court. (C.C.P. 3331). Ten days notice of hearing on final account must be given by service of copy of account and notice of prospective homologation upon each heir or residuary legatee, which notice, except for final account, may be served by ordinary

See note at head of Digest as to 1998 legislation covered.

See Topical Index in front part of this volume.

LA – 34

EXECUTORS AND ADMINISTRATORS . . . *continued*
mail and final account may be served by certified or registered mail. (C.C.P. 3335, as am'd Act 36 of 1966).

Compensation.—Executor allowed reasonable amount as is provided in testament in which he is appointed; administrator allowed such reasonable amount as is provided by agreement between administrator and surviving spouse, and all competent heirs or legatees of deceased. In absence of specified testamentary amount or agreement with survivors, executor or administrator is entitled to fee of 2½% on value of estate, as appraised in inventory. (C.C.P. 3351, as am'd Act 281 of 1982).

If there are two or more executors or administrators, commission is apportioned among them as court directs. (C.C.P. 3352).

A testamentary executor who is legatee receives commission unless will provides to contrary. If legacy and compensation of executor together exceed disposable portion, executor shall receive only disposable portion. (C.C.P. 3353).

When Administration Unnecessary.—See subhead Small Estates, infra.

Small Estates.—When Louisiana domiciliary dies intestate leaving property in Louisiana having gross value of $50,000 or less; it is not necessary to open judicially succession if there is no immovable property and sole heirs are descendants, ascendants, brothers, sisters or descendants thereof, or surviving spouse. (C.C.P. 3421, as am'd Act 582 of 1980; C.C.P. 3431, as am'd Act 111 of 1995). Competent major heirs and surviving spouse, if any, may submit to inheritance tax collector their affidavit setting forth date of death; domicile at death; fact of intestacy; fact of no immovable property; deceased's marital status; names and addresses of surviving spouse and heirs and relationship of latter; and, brief description of movable property left by deceased showing value of each item thereof at date of death. (C.C.P. 3432). When inheritance tax collector certifies that inheritance tax is paid or that no inheritance taxes are due, affidavit is full and sufficient authority for transfer of stocks and bonds and payment or delivery of any money or property, described therein, by any corporation, person, bank or depositary, free of claim by collector. (T. 47, §2410, as am'd Act 582 of 1980; C.C.P. Arts. 3433 and 3434). Public administrators may administrate small successions under defined procedure. (C.C.P. 3431, as am'd Act 701 of 1990). See also category Business Regulation and Commerce, topic Banks and Banking, subhead Decedents' Property.

Distribution If Abroad.—No express statutory provision.

Foreign and Ancillary Administration.—See topic Wills, subhead Foreign Wills.

INTESTACY:

See topic Descent and Distribution.

PROOF OF CLAIMS:

See topic Executors and Administrators; category Civil Actions and Procedure, topic Pleading.

TRUSTS:

Kinds Recognized.—Donations inter vivos or mortis causa in trust for educational, charitable, literary, or religious purposes may be made. Trustees, on acceptance, may incorporate and have, in addition to power especially given in trust instrument, general authority of administration. In event of failure of trustee, Governor appoints substitute, who is subject to all duties and limitations as provided in instrument creating trust. (T. 9, §§2271-2279).

Louisiana Trust Code (T. 9, §§1721-2252) authorizes express private trusts, whether inter vivos or testamentary, which (unless trust instrument which stipulates a term provides an earlier termination) terminate: (1) At death of last surviving income beneficiary or 20 years from death of settlor, whichever is last to occur, if at least one settlor and one income beneficiary are natural persons; (2) at death of last surviving income beneficiary or 20 years from creation of trust, whichever is last to occur, if none of settlors is a natural person but at least one income beneficiary is a natural person; (3) at expiration of 20 years from death of last settlor, if at least one settlor but none of income beneficiaries is a natural person; or (4) at expiration of 50 years from creation of trust if neither settlors nor income beneficiaries are natural persons. (T. 9, §1831, as am'd Act 164 of 1987). Heirs, legatees or assignees of designated beneficiary are not considered beneficiaries for purpose of fixing maximum allowable term. (T.9, §1801, as am'd Act 110 of 1989). If trust instrument stipulates longer term than permitted, trust enforced to maximum allowable term. (T. 9, §1832). If no term stipulated, trust terminates upon death of last natural income beneficiary, but if income beneficiary is not natural person, then 20 years from death of last natural settlor, or 20 years from creation of trust if none of settlors is natural person. (T. 9, §1833).

Legitime, or forced portion (see topic Wills, subhead Forced Heirs), may be placed in trust under certain restrictions. (T. 9, §§1841-1845, and 1847, as am'd Act 160 of 1979). Trust may be created upon proceeds of life insurance. (T. 9, §1881). Class trusts in favor of some or all of direct descendants or collateral descendants of whatever degree may be created, and if trust instrument so provides, interest to each beneficiary shall be held in separate trust after class has closed. (T. 9, §1891 as am'd Act 682 of 1997, §§1892-1906). Membership in class trusts may be by representation. (T. 9, §§1892-1895, as am'd Act 582 of 1985 and Act 284 of 1988). Employers may create trusts for benefit of employees for any term or for indefinite terms. (T. 9, §§1921-1922). Mixed private and educational, charitable or religious trusts are permitted. (T. 9, §1951). Public trusts, with state, parish, municipality or subdivision thereof as beneficiary, are authorized. (Act 135 of 1970). Marital portion under C. C. 238, whether in full property, usufruct or any portion thereof, may be placed in trust. (T. 9, §§1851-1854, as added Act 67 of 1977).

Creation.—Testamentary trust must be created in one of forms prescribed for donations mortis causa. (T. 9, §1751). Inter vivos trust may be created only by authentic act or by act under private signature executed in presence of two witnesses and duly acknowledged by settlor or attesting witness. (T. 9, §1752). No particular language is required and instrument may incorporate by reference terms of an existing trust. (T. 9, §§1753 and 1754). If trust affects immovable property, it or extract of it must be filed in public records. (T. 9, §2092, as am'd Act 257 0f 1995). See also category Family, topic Guardian and Ward, subhead Management of Property.

Complete or Partial Refusal.—Beneficiary may refuse all or any part of interest in trust. Settlor may stipulate effect of refusal, and if he does not, Trust Code provides for its effect. (T. 9, §§1988, 1990, as am'd Act 79 of 1983).

Substitute Beneficiary.—Must be in being and ascertainable on date of creation of trust, though class may be substitute beneficiary. Trust instrument may provide that interest of principal beneficiary who is descendant of settlor and dies intestate without issue during trust or at termination will vest in one or more of settlor's descendants in being and ascertainable at death of such principal beneficiary (T. 9, §1975, as am'd Act 455 of 1982). Except as to legitime, same provision may be made even as to such person who provides otherwise in his testament. (T. 9, §1973, as am'd Act 254 of 1997). Trust instruments may provide for successive substitutions. (T.9, §1973, as am'd Act 111 of 1989). Interest of beneficiary may be conditioned upon surviving settlor for short period of time specified by C.C. 1521. (T. 9, §2011, as am'd Act 413 of 1995).

Appointment of Trustee.—One or more trustees, alternates or successors may be designated in instrument, or, in absence of designation, may be appointed by court. (T. 9, §1785). Provisional trustee may be appointed by court upon application of interested person or upon court's own motion. (T. 9, §1786). Trustee, in his capacity as such, can be beneficiary of another trust. (T.9, §1801, as am'd Act 110 of 1989).

Eligibility and Competency.—Trustee may be natural persons having full capacity to contract and citizens of U.S., or federally insured depositories organized under state or federal law, subject only to restrictions for national banks or trust company organized under Louisiana law. Resident aliens may also be trustees. (T. 9, §1783, as am'd Act 1400 of 1997, eff. July 15, 1997). With respect to trust for mixed private and charitable purposes, trustee may also be nonprofit corporation or trust for educational, charitable, or religious purposes that is designated as income or principal beneficiary. (T. 9, §1783, as am'd Act 215 of 1995).

Qualifications.—Unless dispensed with by instrument, individual trustee must furnish security. (T. 9, §2171). Upon application of interested person, court may compel trustee to furnish security (T. 9, §2172) or may increase, diminish or dispense with security (T. 9, §2173).

Removal of Trustee.—Trustee may be removed in accordance with trust instrument or by court for sufficient cause shown. (T. 9, §1789, as am'd Act 627 of 1968). After removal, trustee must deliver property but retains right to preserve property until delivery. (T. 9, §2069, added Act 358 of 1995).

General Powers and Duties.—Trustee must administer solely in interest of beneficiary (T. 9, §2082) and exercise care and skill of man of ordinary prudence (T. 9, §2090). He cannot be principal officer of corporation in which trust funds are invested, or of other legal entity in which those funds are invested, unless settlor authorizes it. (T. 9, §2097, as am'd Act 251 of 1997). Unless otherwise provided by trust instrument, trustee may divide trust into two or more separate trusts. (T. 9, §2030, added Act 344 of 1995).

Investments.—Unless instrument provides otherwise, trustee is not limited in investments except by prudent man rule. If authorized or directed to invest in U.S. government securities, trustee may invest in money market mutual fund of such securities, unless instrument specifies otherwise. (T. 9, §2127, as am'd Act 178 of 1986).

Sales.—Unless provided otherwise by instrument, trustee may sell trust property (and settlor cannot forbid sale of realty for period beyond 15 years from his death); may enter into leases of trust property, either as lessor or lessee, for term in excess of term of trust; may mortgage or pledge trust property; and may compromise, arbitrate and abandon claims. (T. 9, §§2118-2121). Corporate or individual trustee may not buy or sell property in which trustee has interest, or to himself as trustee of another trust, unless with court approval after contradictory hearing. (T. 9, §2085, as am'd Act 359 of 1990, eff. July 10, 1990).

Modification.—If, subsequent to creation of a trust, circumstances change so that literal compliance with terms of trust is impractical, impossible or illegal, court may direct trust to be administered in manner to accomplish most effectively general purpose of trust. (T. 9, §§2331-2337). Proper court may also order termination of trust under certain circumstances, including when trust estate is less than $25,000. (T. 9, §2026, as am'd Act 665 of 1991). Proper court may permit termination or modification of trust, or deviation from provisions concerning its administration if its continuance or compliance with its provisions would defeat or substantially impair its purposes. (T. 9, §§2026, 2064, as am'd Act 252 of 1997).

Uniform Management of Institutional Funds Act adopted. (T. 9, §2337.1 et seq.).

Securities in Name of Nominee.—Trustee may hold stock in name of nominee but is liable for loss resulting from nominee's acts. (T. 9, §2124). Unless otherwise provided in trust instrument, corporate trustee may deposit securities in clearing corporation. (T. 9, §2124.1, added Act 346 of 1983).

Legacies to Inter Vivos Trust.—Unless restricted or denied by instrument, settlor or other person may add to trust estate by donation inter vivos or mortis causa, with approval of trustee. (T. 9, §§1931-1936). When trust anticipates future annual additions and refers to annual exclusion from federal gift tax, dollar limitation is amount of exclusion in effect in year in which donation is made to trust. (T. 9, §1937, added Act 423 of 1982).

Accounting.—Trustee must render to beneficiary annual accounts and a final account showing receipts, disbursements and itemization of property at end of year. (T. 9, §2088). Trustee required to furnish information requested by beneficiary and permit beneficiary or authorized person to examine accounts. (T. 9, §2089).

Compensation.—Unless otherwise provided in instrument or waived, trustee entitled to reasonable compensation. (T. 9, §2181).

Common Trust Funds.—Unless otherwise provided in instrument, and with consent of co-trustees, trustee may establish common trust funds. (T. 9, §2128, as am'd Act 159 of 1974).

See note at head of Digest as to 1998 legislation covered.

See Topical Index in front part of this volume.

TRUSTS . . . *continued*

Designation of Attorney.—Designation of attorney for trust in instrument is binding. In absence of designation or if named attorney is incapable of acting, beneficiaries may select attorney unless trustee is natural person qualified under T. 9, §1783, and then trustee may select attorney. (T. 9, §241, as am'd Act 622 of 1983).

Revised Uniform Principal and Income Act forms basis of La. R.S. 2141 et seq.; however, certain departures are made where provisions of Uniform Act are not in conformity with general laws of Louisiana. Trust instrument can grant trustee equitable discretion in apportionment of receipts and expenditures. (T.9, §2142, as am'd Act 114 of 1989).

Gifts to Minors.—See category Family, topic Infants.

Uniform Fiduciaries Act adopted with slight variations. (T. 9, §§3801-3814, §3803 repealed, Act 444 of 1960).

Uniform Simplification of Fiduciary Security Transfers Act adopted. (T. 9 §§3831-3840).

Accumulations.—In absence of contrary stipulations in instrument, trustee required to distribute income at least every six months. (T. 9, §1962). Settlor may stipulate distribution of income or place discretion in trustee (T. 9, §§1961, 1963, 1964, as am'd Act 767 of 1997), except with respect to legitime in trust where income must be paid to forced heir at least once each year (T. 9, §1841).

Perpetuities.—See category Property, topic Perpetuities.

WILLS:

Note: Comprehensive changes in types of testamentary dispositions are made by Act 1421 of 1997, but only effective as of July 1, 1999.

Note: In Louisiana the expression "donation mortis causa" is used solely with respect to testamentary gifts, the "donation mortis causa" of the common law not being recognized. See 105 La. 705, 30 So. 233.

Testamentary Capacity.—To make a donation mortis causa one must be able to comprehend generally nature and consequences of disposition he is making. (C.C. 1477, as am'd Act 363 of 1991). Married woman may make donation mortis causa of real or personal property.

A minor over sixteen years can make a will as though a person of full age. (C. C. 1476). Other provisions relative to capacity to give and receive inter vivos and mortis causa, as well as procedure for proof of undue influence, are contained in C.C. 1470-1483, as am'd Act 363 of 1991.

Forced Heirs.—Law reserves to certain descendants of owner of property, who are termed "forced heirs", certain portion of estate, termed "legitime", of which they cannot be deprived by donations, inter vivos or mortis causa, unless there is just cause to disinherit them. In case there are forced heirs, only following portions of estate may be disposed of by will or donation: Three-fourths if there is one child under age of 23 or one child of any age, who, because of mental incapacity or physical infirmity, is permanently incapable of taking care of his person or property; one half if there are two or more such children. (C.C. 1493, am'd Act 77 of 1996 First Ex. Sess.). Limited representation of such heirs permitted, if predeceased and would have satisfied these criteria at time of decedent's death. Legitime is diminished by renunciation of forced heir; part of those who renounce becomes part of disposable portion; legitime of other heirs not affected. (C.C. 1500, am'd Act 77 of 1996 First Ex. Sess.). If heir is disinherited or declared unworthy of succeeding, legitime is determined by number of other forced heirs of deceased living or represented. (C.C. 1500, as am'd Act 77 of 1996 First Ex. Sess.). Dispositions in excess of portions above stated are reduced accordingly. (C.C. 1493-5, 1502).

Decedent may delegate authority to executor to allocate specific assets to satisfy legacy expressed in terms of quantum or value, in order to satisfy forced portion. (C.C. 1302, 1573, 1725 as am'd Act 448 of 1982).

To determine the reduction to which donations inter vivos or mortis causa are liable, an aggregate is formed of all the property belonging to the donor or testator at the time of his decease; to that is fictitiously added all property disposed of by donation inter vivos, according to its value at the time of the donor's decease in the condition in which it was at the period of the donation. The debts due by the estate are deducted from this aggregate amount and the disposable quantum is calculated on the balance, taking into consideration the number of forced heirs. Life insurance proceeds on life of donor and premiums paid therefor are not included in calculation, but if payable to forced heir, are to be credited in satisfaction of his forced share. (C.C. 1505, as am'd Act 77 of 1996 First Ex. Sess.). Donations inter vivos made more than three years prior to death of donor are not included in calculation. (T. 9, §2372, as am'd Act 402 of 1995, eff. Jan. 1, 1996). Donations inter vivos to spouse of previous marriage during existence of that marriage are not included in calculation. (T. 9, §2373). Benefits payable by reason of death, disability, retirement or termination of employment under plans of deferred compensation adopted by public employer, or under plans qualified under §§401 or 408 of Internal Revenue Code, and employer and employee contributions under such plans, are not included in calculation, but any such amounts payable to forced heir are to be credited in satisfaction of his forced share. (C.C. 1505, as am'd Act 77 of 1996 First Ex. Sess.). Payments under IRA to beneficiary similarly excluded, but if payable to forced heir are credited against his forced share. (T. 9, §2448, added Act 600 of 1986).

Testamentary bequests are all reduced pro rata in the absence of any provision to the contrary in the will after which donations inter vivos are reduced until legitime is made up, last donation in point of time being taken first (C.C. 1507, 1508, as am'd Act 77 of 1996 First Ex. Sess.). Donated property returned in kind by donee remains subject to real rights created by operation of law or onerous title. Action for return of property extends only to donees and their successors by gratuitous title. Heirs do not have right to claim immovable which has been donated and then alienated by onerous title by donee and if donee retains possession, can only regain property subject to real rights conventionally or legally created. (C.C. 1264, 1270, 1281, 1516, 1517, 1518, as am'd Act 869 of 1984, and C.C. 1568, as am'd Act 527 of 1985). Donation of movable is completely null if donor divests himself of all his property, not leaving enough for own subsistence; similar donation of immovable is null, unless donee alienates immovable by onerous title. In latter case, donor retains right to seek value of donation against donee. (C.C. 1498, as am'd Act 77 of 1996 First Ex. Sess.).

Louisiana forced heirship rules apply to immovable property in state unless deceased was domiciled outside state at time of death and left no forced heirs domiciled in this state at time of death. (C.C. 3533, as am'd Act 257 of 1997).

Disinherison.—Although all other heirs may be excluded by mere omission or disinherison without cause, a forced heir may be deprived of the legitime only by specific disinherison for legal cause.

A child may be disinherited and deprived of his or her legitime if he or she has: (1) Struck or raised his hand to strike the parent, but a mere threat is not sufficient; (2) been guilty, towards a parent, of cruelty, of a crime or grievous injury; (3) attempted to take the life of either parent; (4) accused a parent of any capital crime, except high treason; (5) refused sustenance to a parent, having means to afford it; (6) neglected to take care of a parent become insane; (7) refused to ransom a parent when detained in captivity; (8) used any act of violence or coercion to hinder a parent from making a will; (9) has refused to become security for a parent, having the means, in order to take him out of prison; (10) being a minor, married without the consent of his or her parents; (11) been convicted of felony for which law provides that punishment could be life imprisonment or death; (12) known how to contact parent but failed to do so without just cause for two years after majority, unless child is in armed services. (C.C. 1621, as am'd Act 465 of 1985).

Ascendants other than parents may disinherit their descendants for first nine causes and 11th and 12th causes hereinabove enumerated. (C.C. 1622, as am'd Act 334 of 1987).

A disinherison to be valid must be made in one of the forms prescribed for testaments, and the testator must express for what reasons he disinherits the heir in question. Disinherited heir must prove cause for disinherison did not exist, or prove reconciliation after it occurred, to avoid its effects. Proof of reconciliation must be clear and unequivocal, evidenced in writing, and signed by testator. (C.C. 1624, as am'd Acts 82 and 367 of 1989, latter eff. June 29, 1989).

See topic Descent and Distribution for provisions relative to proof of unworthiness of intestate heirs.

Formalities of Execution.—There are four classes of donations mortis causa or testament, to wit: (1) Nuncupative or open testaments; (2) mystic or sealed testaments; (3) olographic testaments; (4) statutory testaments. (C.C. 1574 and T. 9, §2442).

Nuncupative testament may be made by public act or by act under private signature.

The nuncupative testament by public act must be received by a notary public in the presence of three witnesses residing in the place where the will is executed, or five witnesses not residing in the place. The testament must be written by the notary as it is dictated. It must then be read to the testator in the presence of the witnesses. Express mention must be made of the whole, observing that all the formalities must be fulfilled at one time, without interruption and without turning aside to other acts. (C. C. 1578). The testament must be signed by the testator, or if he does not know how or is not able to sign, express mention of his declaration and of the cause which hinders him to sign must be made in the act. The testament must also be signed by the witnesses or by one for all, if others can not write. (C. C. 1579-80).

The nuncupative testament under private signature must be written by the testator himself, or by any other person from his dictation, even by one of the witnesses, in the presence of five witnesses residing in the place where the will is received or in the presence of seven witnesses residing out of that place; or it will suffice if in the presence of the same number of witnesses the testator presents the paper on which he has written his testament or caused it to be written out of their presence, and declare to them that that paper contains his last will and testament. (C. C. 1581). In either case the testament must be read by the testator to the witnesses, or by one of the witnesses to the rest in the presence of the testator. It must be signed by the testator, if he knows how or is able to sign, and by the witnesses, or at least by two of them in case the others know not how to sign, and those of the witnesses who do not know how to sign must affix their mark. (C. C. 1582). In the country it suffices for the validity of the nuncupative testament under private signature that the testament be passed in the presence of three witnesses residing in the place where the testament is received, or of five witnesses residing out of that place, provided that in this case a greater number of witnesses cannot be had. (C. C. 1583).

Sealed or mystic testament is made in the following manner: The testator must sign his dispositions, whether he has written them himself or has caused them to be written by another person. The paper containing those dispositions, or the paper serving as their envelope, must be closed and sealed. The testator must present it, thus closed and sealed, to the notary and to three witnesses or he must cause it to be closed and sealed in their presence. Then he must declare to the notary in the presence of the witnesses, that the paper contains his testament, written by himself, or by another by his direction, and signed by him, the testator. The notary must then draw up the act of superscription which must be written on that paper or the sheet which serves as its envelope, and that act must be signed by the testator, and by the notary and the witnesses. (C. C. 1584). All that is prescribed as aforesaid must be done without interruption or turning aside to other acts. In case the testator, by reason of any hindrance which has happened since the signing of the testament, cannot sign the act of superscription, mention of the declaration made by him must be made, but it is not necessary to increase the number of witnesses. (C. C. 1585). Those who are not able to write or sign their names cannot make dispositions in the form of a mystic testament. (C. C. 1586).

Olographic testament is that which is written by the testator himself. In order to be valid it must be entirely written, dated and signed by the testator without its being subject to any other formality. (C. C. 1588).

Statutory testaments may be executed as follows:

1. By person who knows how to sign his name and knows how to and is physically able to read, by written instrument, dated and executed in presence of notary and two competent witnesses. Testator must declare or signify to them that instrument is his last will and sign his name at end of will and each other separate page, and execute with notary and witnesses following, or substantially similar, declaration:

See note at head of Digest as to 1998 legislation covered.

See Topical Index in front part of this volume.

LA – 36

WILLS . . . *continued*

"The testator has signed this will at the end and on each other separate page, and has declared or signified in our presence that it is his last will and testament, and in the presence of the testator and each other we have hereunto subscribed our names this . . . . . day of . . . . . ., 19. . . . . ."

2. By person unable to sign because of physical infirmity, by written instrument dated and executed in presence of notary and two witnesses. Testator must declare or signify that instrument is his last will, that he is unable to sign because of physical infirmity, and must affix his mark at end of will and on each other separate page. In presence of testator and each other, notary and witnesses must execute following, or substantially similar, declaration:

"The testator has declared that he knows how to sign his name but is unable to sign his name because of a physical infirmity and he has affixed his mark at the end and on each other separate page of this will and declared or signified in our presence that this is his last will and testament and in the presence of the testator and each other we have hereunto subscribed our names this . . . . . day of . . . . . ., 19. . . . . ."

Will may be in braille or other similar mode.

3. By person whose sight is impaired so that he cannot read or who does not know how to read and whether or not he is able to sign his name, in form similar to above but will must be read aloud by notary in presence of testator and two competent witnesses, and witnesses must follow reading on copies of will. Testator must then declare or signify that he heard reading and that will is his last will, and must sign his name at end of will and on each other separate page. If he is unable to sign, he must declare or signify such to notary and witnesses and declare cause thereof, and must affix his mark at end of will and on each separate page. In presence of testator and each other, notary and witnesses must sign following, or substantially similar, declaration:

"Read aloud by the notary in the presence of testator and each other, such reading having been heard by the testator and followed on copies of the will by witnesses, signed at the end and on each other separate page, (or if not signed by the testator, the statement of his declaration or signification that he cannot sign his name and the cause that hinders him from signing) and declared or signified by testator, in our presence, to be his last will and testament, and in the presence of testator and each other we have hereunto subscribed our names on this . . . . . day of . . . . . ., 19. . . . . ."

4. By person who knows how to and is physically able to read braille, by instrument in braille dated and signed by testator in presence of notary and two witnesses. Testator must declare or signify to them that instrument is his last will and sign will at end and on each other separate page. In presence of testator, and each other, notary and witnesses must sign following, or substantially similar, declaration, in writing and not in braille:

"The testator has signed this will at the end and on each other separate page, and has declared or signified in our presence that it is his last will and testament, and in the presence of the testator and each other we have hereunto subscribed our names this . . . . . day of . . . . . ., 19. . . . . ."

If testator is unable to sign his name, testator must also declare or signify to notary and witnesses that he is unable to sign because of physical infirmity, and shall affix his mark at end of will and each other separate page. In presence of testator, and each other, notary and witnesses must sign following, or substantially similar, declaration, in writing and not in braille:

"The testator has declared that he knows how to sign his name but is unable to sign his name because of a physical infirmity and he has affixed his mark at the end of each other separate page of this will, and declared or signified in our presence that this is his last will and testament and in the presence of the testator and each other we have hereunto subscribed our names this . . . . . day of . . . . . ., 19. . . . . ."

(T. 9, §§2442 and 2443, as am'd Acts 744 of 1980, 246 of 1984, and 58 of 1989, latter eff. Jan. 1, 1990).

Witnesses.—The following persons are incapable of being witnesses to testaments: (1) Persons under age of 16; (2) insane or blind persons; (3) persons whom criminal laws declare incapable of exercising civil functions; (4) deaf persons, except as to statutory wills under T. 9, §§2442 and 2444. Neither can testaments be witnessed by those who are constituted heirs or named legatees, under whatsoever title it may be, provided that this qualification does not apply to the mystic testament. (C. C. 1591-1593, as am'd Act 198 of 1983). If testament is witnessed by heir or legatee, it is not null except as to any legacy to that heir or legatee, and this exception applies to all testaments, regardless of when made. (C.C. 1592, as am'd Act 6 of 1989, eff. June 6, 1989).

Witness to statutory will must meet above qualifications, must know how to sign his name and to read required attestation clause, and physically able to do both. If testator's sight is impaired, witnesses must also know and be able to read will as written, if not in braille. (T. 9, §§2442 and 2443, as am'd Act 744 of 1980).

Revocation and Annulment.—Testaments are revocable at the will of the testator. (C. C. 1690). Revocation must be in one of the forms prescribed for a testament (C. C. 1692) or may be by intentional destruction of the will by the testator (168 La. 303, 121 So. 874).

Testament is revoked by subsequent birth, legitimation or subsequent adoption of child unless testament provides to contrary. (C. C. 1705, as am'd Act 209 of 1974). If will is made after conception of child and provides for such child and child is born after testator's death, will remains valid. (154 La. 1060, 98 So. 874).

After a testament has been probated it may be annulled, at the suit of any party interested, on the ground that it is defective in form, or that the testator was incapable, or that the dispositions are contrary to law. This right of attack prescribes after the legatees have been in possession for five years. (C. C. 3542; 162 La. 22, 110 So. 75).

Testament may be annulled upon proof it is product of influence by legatee or another person that so impaired volition of testator as to substitute volition of legatee or other person for volition of testator. (C.C. 1479, added Act 363 of 1991).

Probate.—No testament can have effect unless presented to the judge of the parish in which succession is opened. (C. C. 1644). Proceeding to open succession shall be brought in district court of parish where deceased was domiciled at time of his death. If deceased was not domiciled in this state at time of his death, his succession may be opened in district court of any parish where immovable property of deceased is situated, or movable property of deceased is situated if he owned no immovable in state at time of his death. (C.C.P. 2811). Nuncupative testaments by public act do not require proof in order that their execution may be ordered; they are full proofs of themselves. (C. C. 1647). Nuncupative testaments under private signature cannot be executed until they have been proven by declaration on oath of at least three witnesses who were present when they were made. (C.C.P. 2884). Execution of mystic testaments cannot be ordered until they have been in like manner proved by declaration on oath of at least three of witnesses who were present at act of superscription. (C.C.P. 2885). If any of witnesses to nuncupative testament under private signature or to mystic testament be dead, incapacitated, or absent or cannot be located, so that it is impossible to procure number prescribed by law for proving testament, it will be sufficient to prove it by declaration of living witnesses who are in state. If notary and all witnesses are dead, absent, incapacitated or cannot be located, probate is by two witnesses who recognize signature of testator or notary or the two witnesses. (C.C.P. Art. 2886, as am'd Act 106 of 1980). As to private nuncupative and mystic testaments, written affidavit may be used in lieu of oral testimony for probate. (C.C.P. 2884 and 2886, as am'd Act 270 of 1987). Olographic testament must be acknowledged and proved by declaration of two credible persons, who must attest that they recognize testament as being entirely written, dated and signed in testator's handwriting. Testimony of such persons may be given in form of affidavit executed after death of testator before notary and two witnesses, unless court orders person to appear and testify; such affidavits to be filed in probate proceedings; affidavit procedure not permitted when genuineness of will is judicially contested. (C.C.P. 2883, as am'd Act 594 of 1983). Statutory testaments cannot be executed until they have been proved by declaration on oath of notary and one witness to will or both witnesses to will. If notary or any witnesses be dead or absent or cannot be located, will may be proved by declaration on oath of notary, witness or witnesses living and in state. If notary or none of witnesses living in state or are incapacitated, will may be proved by declaration on oath of two credible persons that they recognize testator's signature or signature of notary or of the two witnesses. Such declarations may be made in form of affidavits and filed in proceedings unless court requires attendance in person. (C.C.P. 2887, as am'd Act 106 of 1980). With leave of court, petitioner may take deposition of witnesses. (C.C.P. 2889, as am'd Act 26 of 1985). When probate is by affidavit, process verbal ordinarily required may be dispensed with. (C.C.P. 2890, as am'd Act 393 of 1984).

Probate proceedings are usually instituted by the executor or the universal legatee and may be ex parte. There is no requirement that heirs or legatees be cited.

Time for Probate.—Will must be probated within five years of judicial opening of succession. (T. 9, §5643 and C.C.P. 2893, both as am'd Act 247 of 1986).

Self-proved Wills.—Nuncupative wills by public act do not require proof of execution unless there is allegation of forgery. (C. C. Art. 1647, C.C.P. Art. 2891).

Legacies.—*Note:* As of July 1, 1999, under changes wrought by Act 1421 of 1997, three types of legacies will be (1) general, (2) universal and (3) particular; other changes under same act with same effective date. Until July 1, 1999, there are three types of legacy: (1) Universal, (2) under universal title and (3) particular. (C. C. 1571). A universal legacy is one by which the testator gives the whole of his estate. (C. C. 1606). If the universal legatee accepts, he is bound for all debts of the estate and must discharge all particular legacies. (C. C. 1611). The legatee under universal title takes under the will a certain portion of the estate or a certain portion of the realty or personalty. (C. C. 1612). He is liable for a pro rata part of the debts and particular legacies. (C. C. 1614). All other legacies are particular. (C. C. 1625). They are discharged in preference to all other gifts mortis causa. (C. C. 1634). The particular legatee is not personally liable for debts, but legacy is subject to reduction. (C. C. 1642). In all types of legacies, legatees may demand delivery immediately after testator's death. (C. C. 1608, 1609, 1613, 1627). Decedent may delegate authority to executor to allocate specific assets to satisfy legacy expressed in terms of quantum or value. (C. C. 1302, 1573, 1725, as am'd Act 448 of 1982). Legacies may be revoked by language or conduct of testator, or deemed revoked when legatee bills or attempts to bill testator. (C.C. 1691, as am'd Act 354 of 1987).

Proof of Suggestion or Captation.—With repeal of C.C. 1492 eff. July 1, 1990, prohibition against evidence of hatred, anger, suggestion or captation causing legacies is removed. Standard and quality of proof in such cases is governed by C.C. 1478-1483, as am'd Act 363 of 1991.

Unclaimed Legacies.—See category Property, topic Absentees, subhead Monies Due Absentee.

Lapse of Legacies.—If a legacy lapses through death or incapacity of the legatee, it goes to the lawful heirs (C. C. 1709) or the universal legatee (C. C. 1704), except when the legacy is made jointly to two or more persons, in which case the survivor takes all (C. C. 1707-8).

Legacies to Inter Vivos Trusts.—See topic Trusts, subhead Legacies to Inter Vivos Trust, supra.

Foreign Wills.—Uniform Foreign Executed Wills (T. 9, §2401) and Foreign Probated Wills (T. 9, §§2421-2425) Acts have been adopted. Changes of verbiage in the latter act do not appear to change the requirements in any material respects.

Simultaneous Death.—See topic Death, subhead Survivorship.

Testamentary Trusts.—See topic Trusts.

Central Registry for Wills.—Secretary of State has central registry for name, address and social security number of testator and location of testament. Registry is optional and to be in strict confidence. Fee for registration $10. Fee for information $10, available to any person presenting satisfactory evidence of death of testator. (T. 9, §§2446-2447, added Act 222 of 1981).

See note at head of Digest as to 1998 legislation covered.

See Topical Index in front part of this volume.

LA – 37

WILLS . . . *continued*

Living Will.—Declaration to authorize withdrawal or withholding of life-sustaining procedures in terminal and irreversible condition is recognized in form prescribed. (T. 40, §1299.58, am'd Act 187 of 1985).

FAMILY

ADOPTION:

Any adult or child may be adopted. Age of adopter, procedure and other essentials differ according to age of adoptee.

Adoptees Over Seventeen.—Any person 18 years of age or over may adopt any person over age of 17. Adoption is by notarial act before recorder or notary public, signed by adopter and adoptee, and if adoptee is unemancipated minor by his or her parents or legal custodian. If person to be adopted is interdicted major, act must be signed by adoptive parent or parents and appointed curator. (T. 9, §461, as am'd Act 68 of 1983). Court approval, after confidential proceedings, is required when adoptive parent or parents are younger than person to be adopted. (T. 9, §461, as am'd Act 124 of 1988, eff. Jan. 1, 1989). Special provisions are made where parental authority has ceased. (T. 9, §§425 and 427, as am'd Act 303 of 1988, eff. July 7, 1988). Act is then recorded by clerk of court (in Parish of Orleans by register of conveyance) in special book kept for that purpose. Name of adoptee may be changed in act of adoption. Adoptions prior to effective date of act are validated. (T. 9, §461, as am'd Act 714 of 1978, and §462).

Adoptees Under Seventeen.—Any single person 18 years of age or older, or married couple jointly, may petition to adopt child. (T. 9, §422, as am'd Act 714 of 1978).

Consent or legal surrender by legitimate parents is required, except when court has adjudged abandonment by one parent and the other legitimate parent consents in writing to his or her spouse's petition for adoption (T. 9, §422), or when spouse of legitimate parent having legal custody of adoptee, or grandparent with legal custody, petitions for adoption and the other legitimate parent has refused or failed to pay decreed support of adoptee for one year, or is a nonresident and has failed to support adoptee for one year after adverse judgment of custody or has failed to visit or communicate with child for two years (T. 9, §422.1, as am'd Act 887 of 1985). Detailed provisions for voluntary surrender for private adoption are contained in T. 9, §§422.3-422.14 (as am'd Act 702 of 1987, eff. July 9, 1987). Surrendering parents must provide adoptive parents with certain non-identifying medical genetic information. (T. 9, §422.13, added Act 717 of 1981). Father of illegitimate child may establish right to oppose adoption of child by acknowledging child as his by signing birth certificate or executing authentic act of acknowledgment and recording it prior to act of surrender, decree of abandonment or judgment terminating mother's rights. (T. 9, §422.14, am'd Act 725 of 1985). Voluntary surrender can only be made by domiciliary of state, or to domiciliary of state if surrendering party is non-domiciliary. (T. 9, §422.5, as am'd Act 473 of 1987, eff. Jan. 1, 1988).

Jurisdiction and venue is in either court of domicile of petitioner or that of parent or legal custodian or in parish of surrender of adoptee or of declaration of abandonment or termination of parental rights. (T. 9, §423, as am'd Act 426 of 1983).

Petition with all exhibits must be served by registered mail on Department of Health and Human Resources and on agency having legal custody of child. Petition must also be served on each of living parents unless child legally surrendered or declared abandoned by court of competent jurisdiction. Petition must state: (1) Name, address, age, occupation and marital status of each petitioner; (2) name of child; (3) place and date of child's birth; (4) name and address of parent or legal custodian; (5) how child entered petitioners' home; (6) relationship between petitioner and child and other information. (T. 9, §§424-425).

Proceedings.—Department of Health and Human Resources submits confidential report of its findings concerning health, character and suitability of child and health, character and financial fitness of petitioner. When petitioner is spouse of legitimate parent of child and child has lived in home of petitioner for period of at least six months, department need only report on availability of child for adoption; but where child in that situation is 13 or over, department shall also investigate physical and mental condition of child and suitability of petitioner's home for adoption. (T. 9, §427, as am'd Act 387 of 1983). Court appoints time and place for hearing, and judge upon examining report and interrogating parties may grant or refuse interlocutory decree. (T. 9, §§427-428).

Final decree of adoption may be petitioned for after child has lived with adopter for at least one year but not less than six months after interlocutory decree granted. Procedure to obtain final decree same as for interlocutory decree and a second confidential report must be submitted by Health and Human Resources Department. Petition for final decree must be filed within two years of interlocutory decree or latter becomes null and void. In certain limited situations, final decree may be rendered at first hearing. (T. 9, §§431-432, 434, as am'd Act 410 of 1983).

Name of adoptee under 17 may be changed in decree, surname to be same as adopter. (T. 9, §435). See also subhead Adoptees Over Seventeen, supra.

Effect of Adoption.—Children lawfully adopted and their issue become forced heirs of their adoptive parents but retain their rights as heirs of their blood relatives to same extent as other children. See category Estates and Trusts, topic Wills, subhead Forced Heirs. They inherit from relatives of adoptive parents as if legitimate child of latter. Blood relatives, subject to certain exceptions, are divested of all rights of inheritance and relieved of legal duties with regard to adopted and legal issue. (C. C. 214).

Voluntary Registry Act.—State has voluntary registry act permitting adopted person, biological mother and biological father (if he has legitimated or formally acknowledged child or signed voluntary abandonment and release for child's adoption) to file information affidavit with state agency seeking to be matched with persons filing similar affidavit, i.e., adoptee with biological parent or biological parent with adoptee. No such registration permitted until 25 years from birth of adoptee. If both adoptee and younger

sibling adopted by same parents, then no such registration until adoptee is over 25 and sibling is over 18. If requesting affidavits match, state agency puts parties into contact with each other. Mandatory counselling session upon filing of affidavit. (T. 40, §§91-99, added Act 40 of 1982).

Interstate Compact on Adoption and Medical Assistance adopted. (T. 46, §1795, added Act 810 of 1985).

ALIMONY:

See topic Divorce.

COMMUNITY PROPERTY:

See topic Husband and Wife.

DESERTION:

See topics Divorce, Husband and Wife.

DISSOLUTION OF MARRIAGE:

See topic Divorce.

DIVORCE:

Termination of Marriage.—Marriage terminates only upon death of either spouse, divorce, judicial declaration of nullity or issuance of court order authorizing spouse of person presumed dead to remarry, as provided by law. (C.C. 101, as am'd Act 1009 of 1990, eff. Jan. 1, 1991).

Grounds for Divorce.—Except in case of covenant marriage, divorce shall be granted upon rule to show cause filed by spouse when either spouse has filed petition for divorce and upon proof that at least 180 days have elapsed from service of petition or from written execution of written waiver of service, and that spouses have lived separate and apart continuously for at least 180 days prior to filing of rule. (C.C. 102, as am'd Act 1380 of 1997). Divorce shall also be granted upon petition of spouse and proof that (1) spouses have been living separate and apart continuously for period of six months or more on date petition is filed; or (2) other spouse has committed adultery; or (3) other spouse has committed felony and has been sentenced to death or imprisonment at hard labor. (C.C. 103, as am'd Act 918 of 1991). Cause of action for divorce is extinguished by reconciliation of parties. (C.C. 104, added Act 1009 of 1990, eff. Jan. 1, 1991). Matters incidental to divorce proceedings may also be determined therein, such as custody, visitation, support for child or spouse, injunctive relief, use and occupancy of family home or other property. (C.C. 105, added Act 1009 of 1990, eff. Jan. 1, 1991).

In case of covenant marriage, which parties may agree to enter after required counselling, grounds for divorce are more restrictive and separation from bed and board is available prior to divorce. (T. 9, §§224, 225, 234, 245, as am'd Act 1380 of 1997, eff. July 15, 1997; and T. 9, §§272 through 275, added Act 1380 of 1997, eff. July 15, 1997).

Effect of Divorce.—Judgment of divorce terminates community property regime retroactively to date of filing of petition in action in which judgment of divorce is rendered, but without prejudice to rights of third parties validly acquired in interim. (C.C. 159, as am'd Act 1009 of 1990, eff. Jan. 1, 1991).

No Judicial Separation from Bed and Board.—With revisions effected by Act 1009 of 1990, eff. Jan. 1, 1991, judicial separation is no longer available. Divorce proceedings as outlined above take place of former judicial separation proceedings.

Residence Requirements.—For purposes of divorce action, if spouse has established and maintained residence in state for period of six months, there is rebuttable presumption of domicile in state in parish of such residence. (C.C.P. 10 [A][7], as am'd Act 1009 of 1990, eff. Jan. 1, 1991).

Jurisdiction over divorce proceedings is vested in district courts. (Const., art. 5, §16). No devolutive appeal is allowed; suspensive appeal must be taken within 30 days after judgment. (C.C.P. 3942).

Hearings in divorce proceedings, and with respect to incidental matters, may be in chambers upon showing of good cause and with mutual consent. (T. 9, §314, am'd Act 1009 of 1990, eff. Jan. 1, 1991). Judgment dismissing divorce petition under C.C. 102 shall be rendered upon joint application of parties and payment of costs, or upon contradictory motion of plaintiff. (C.C.P. 3958, added Act 628 of 1993).

Absent Defendant.—In any action for divorce where defendant is absent from the state or his or her whereabouts are unknown or in case of reconvention when plaintiff is absent and in actions for divorce based on a judgment for separation when the adverse party was absent from the state or his or her whereabouts were unknown, the court having jurisdiction over the cause must, upon application by plaintiff, appoint an attorney at law to represent such absent party and all proceedings must be had contradictorily with said attorney at law and any judgment may be rendered against the attorney which might be rendered against his principal if he were present in person in open court. (C.C.P. 5091, 5098).

Order to Obtain Property.—After filing of petition for divorce, court may grant to either spouse order or injunction without bond requiring sheriff or police to accompany petitioning spouse to marital domicile or elsewhere to obtain personal property such as wearing apparel of spouse or children, food and eating utensils, and other items deemed necessary by court for safety and well-being of petitioner and children. (T. 9, §§373-374, added Act 1009 of 1990, eff. Jan. 1, 1991).

Spousal Support.—In proceeding for divorce or thereafter, court may award interim periodic support to party or final, periodic support to party free from fault prior to filing of proceeding to terminate marriage, based on needs of that party and ability of other party to pay. (C.C. 111, as am'd Act 1078 of 1997, eff. Jan. 1, 1998). This spousal support, as of Jan. 1, 1998, replaces concept of alimony. Court must consider all relevant factors in determination of level of support, including needs of parties; income and means of parties, including liquidity; financial obligations of parties; earning capacity; effect of child custody on earning capacity; time necessary for claimant to acquire appropriate education, training or employment; health and age of parties; duration of

DIVORCE . . . *continued*

marriage; and tax consequences. (C.C. 112[A], as am'd Act 1078 of 1997, eff. Jan. 1, 1998). Support is limited to one third of obligor's net income. (C.C. 112[B], as am'd Act 1078 of 1997, eff. Jan. 1, 1998). Interim periodic allowance may be awarded, but shall not extend beyond 180 days from rendition of divorce judgment, except for good cause shown. (C.C. 113, as am'd Act 1078 of 1997, eff. Jan. 1, 1998). Award of periodic support may be modified upon change of circumstances and terminated if no longer necessary, but subsequent marriage of obligor spouse is not change of circumstances. (C.C. 114, as am'd Act 1078 of 1997, eff. Jan. 1, 1998). Obligation of spousal support is extinguished upon remarriage of obligee, death of either party or judicial determination that obligee has cohabited with another person of either sex in manner of married persons. (C.C. 115, as am'd Act 1078 of 1997, eff. Jan. 1, 1998). Obligation of final spousal support may be modified, waived or extinguished by judgment, by authentic act or by act under private signature acknowledged by obligee. (C.C. 116, as am'd Act 1078 of 1997, eff. Jan. 1, 1998). Right to claim after divorce obligation of spousal support is subject to preemptive period of three years, running from latest of (1) day judgment of divorce is signed or (2) day judgment terminating prior judgment of spousal support is signed, if that judgment was in action commenced either before signing of judgment of divorce or within three years of it or (3) day last payment was made, when obligation is initially performed by voluntary payment within periods described in (1) or (2) above and no more than three years has elapsed between payments. (C.C. 117, as am'd Act 1078 of 1997, eff. Jan. 1, 1998). Except for good cause shown, judgment awarding, modifying or revoking interim spousal support allowance is retroactive to date of judicial demand. (T. 9, §321, as am'd Act 1078 of 1997, eff. Jan. 1, 1998). Judgment or order for spousal or child support shall not be recorded; if record, shall be cancelled and does not have effect of judicial mortgage. (T. 9, §322, as am'd Act 1078 of 1997, eff. Jan. 1, 1998). Judgment decreeing support due and executory may be recorded and shall be judicial mortgage. (T. 9, §323, as am'd Act 1078 of 1997, eff. Jan. 1, 1998). When judgment is rendered to make past due alimony executory, court must award attorney fees and costs to prevailing party, except for good cause shown. (T. 9, §375). Order for past due alimony is retroactive to filing date of petition unless good cause shown. (T. 9, §310, added Act 166 of 1984). Award for support not to be changed unless party shows change of circumstances of one party, which is not established by judgment for past due support. (T. 9, §311, as added Act 41 of 1985).

Division of Property of Spouses.—See subhead Property, infra.

Property.—Divorce carries with it separation of goods and effects. (See topic Husband and Wife.) After filing of petition for divorce, and contradictory hearing, either spouse may be awarded occupancy of family home, if community property, and use of community movables or immovables pending partition of community property, based upon relative economic status of parties and best interest of family. Court may also award spouse given custody of children of marriage use and occupancy of family residence, even if it is separate property of other spouse, based on economic status of parties and best interest of family. (T.9, §374, added Act 1009 of 1990, eff. Jan. 1, 1991). Such award is made pending partition of community property or for 180 days after termination of marriage, whichever first occurs. (T. 9, §374[A], as am'd Act 965 of 1995). Such award or actual use does not require payment of rent to other spouse. Party against whom divorce has been pronounced loses all advantages or donations other party may have conferred by marriage contract or since, and party at whose instance judgment has been obtained preserves all those to which such party would have been entitled; and this takes place even if such donations were reciprocally made, but rule does not apply in cases of mutual fault. (C.C. 141, as am'd Act 99 of 1990).

Custody of Children.—In divorce proceeding or thereafter, court shall award custody of child in accordance with best interest of child. (C.C. 131). If parents agree, court shall award custody in accordance with their agreement unless best interest of child dictates otherwise. (C.C. 132). In absence of agreement, or if agreement is not in child's best interest, award shall be joint unless sole custody in one parent is shown by clear and convincing evidence to serve best interest of child. (C.C. 132). If award of joint custody or sole custody to either parent would result in substantial harm to child, court shall award custody to another person with whom child has been living in wholesome and stable environment, or to any other person able to provide such environment. (C.C. 133). Court must consider all relevant factors in determining best interest of child; representative list is given in statute. (C.C. 134). Custody hearing may be closed to public. (C.C. 135). Child custody mediation procedures authorized and qualifications for mediators fixed by statute. (T. 9, §§331 et seq., as am'd Act 287 of 1995).

Reasonable visitation rights are awardable to non-custody parent, unless after hearing court finds visitation would not be in child's best interest. (C.C. 136[A]). Other relatives and stepparents and stepgrandparents may seek visitation rights under extraordinary circumstances, to be determined by statutory list of factors to determine best interest of child with respect to such request. (C.C. 136[B], as am'd Act 57 of 1995).

Non-suspensive appeals are permitted from custody and visitation orders. (C.C.P. 3943, as am'd Act 261 of 1993).

In child custody matters, evaluation of party or of child by mental health professional may be ordered. (T. 9, §331, as am'd Act 261 of 1993). Mediation of differences between parties may be ordered. (T. 9, §332, as am'd Act 261 of 1993). Award of joint custody is outlined by statute; joint custodians are obligated to confer with respect to best interest of child. (T. 9, §§335 and 336, as am'd Act 261 of 1993). Violations of custody or visitation orders may be found and punished, including with restrictions on visitation. (T. 9, §§341-343, as am'd Act 261 of 1993).

Access to records and information pertaining to minor child not denied to parent solely because he or she is not child's custodial or domiciliary parent. (T. 9, §351, as am'd Act 261 of 1993).

Interim support allowance for child may be allowed when demand for final support is pending. (C.C. 141). Child support allowances can be modified upon proof of change of circumstances. (C.C. 142). If child support is in specific amount per child, award terminates when child reaches majority or is emancipated unless child is full-time student in good standing at secondary school, is not 19 and is dependent upon either parent; if award is in aggregate for several children, termination occurs when youngest child reaches age of majority and is not in conditions described above. (T. 9, §315.22, added Act 261 of 1993). Statutes specify certain obligations, such as health care insurance. (T. 9, §315.4).

Provisional custody by mandate may be given by parents acting jointly or by single custodial parent, limited to one year's duration at a time. (T. 9, §§951-954, as am'd Act 235 of 1995).

Maintenance of Children.—Parents, by the very act of marrying, contract together the obligation of supporting, maintaining and educating their children, and the children's right to such support, maintenance and education is not affected by separation or divorce. (C. C. 135, 227).

When judgment is rendered to make past child support executory, or to enforce visitation order, court must award attorney fees and costs to prevailing party, except for good cause shown. (T. 9, §375, added Act 1009 of 1990, eff. Jan. 1, 1991).

Failure to pay child support may result in revocation of hunting and fishing licenses. (T. 9, §§315.30-315.38, added Act 751 of 1995).

Duration of Temporary Restraining Order.—In suit for divorce, temporary restraining order issued in conjunction with rule nisi for preliminary injunction prohibiting spouse from disposing of or encumbering community property or harming other spouse or child, or removing child from jurisdiction of court, remains in force until hearing on rule nisi. (C.C.P. 3604, as am'd Act 770 of 1982).

Protective Orders in Domestic Abuse Situations.—Protective orders and other relief are available in cases of domestic abuse as defined, not including negligent injury and defamation, whether proceeding for separation or divorce has been filed or not. (T. 46, §§2121-2125 and §§2131-2139, as am'd Acts 406 and 407 of 1983).

Remarriage.—Where divorce is granted on ground of adultery, guilty party is now permitted to marry his or her accomplice. (Act 625 of 1972, repealing C. C. 161).

Foreign Divorces.—Uniform Divorce Recognition Act repealed 1954, act 616.

Annulment of Marriage.—See topic Marriage.

GUARDIAN AND WARD:

Persons Entitled to Tutorship.—During marriage father is administrator of minor's estate and mother when father is mentally incompetent, committed, interdicted, imprisoned or an absentee. (C.C. 221; C.C.P. 4501; C.C.P. 4502, as am'd Act 566 of 1975). Parents enjoy usufruct of minor's estate but right does not extend to donations to child unless specifically so provided in donation. (C.C. 226, as am'd Act 714 of 1985). Mother is tutrix of illegitimate child not acknowledged by father or acknowledged by him without her concurrence. If both have acknowledged, court selects one as tutor. (C.C. 256, as am'd Act 215 of 1983). Parents of mother are considered first on death of mother of illegitimate who has not been acknowledged by father. (C. C. Art. 536, as am'd Act 536 of 1979).

Upon death of either parent, tutorship of minor children belongs of right to surviving parent, but survivor must qualify as provided by law. (C.C. 248, as am'd, Act 30 of 1960). Father or mother dying last, or parent who is curator of spouse, can appoint a tutor by will or by having made a declaration before death, executed before a notary public and two witnesses. (C.C. 257). Judge may for good reasons refuse to confirm tutorship given by surviving father or mother and appoint someone else in his or her stead. (C.C.P. 4062). When tutor has not been appointed by father or mother dying last, or if tutor is not confirmed or is excused, tutor appointed from among qualified ascendants in direct line, collaterals by blood within third degree and surviving spouse of minor's father or mother dying last. (C.C. Act 263, as am'd Act 429 of 1976). If there is no ascendant, nearest of kin in collateral line is entitled to tutorship. (C.C. 267).

A minor not emancipated is placed under a tutor after dissolution of marriage of his parents or their separation from bed and board. (C. C. 157 and 246). During marriage, fathers and mothers have enjoyment of estate of their children; but in such case property belonging to children cannot be sold or mortgaged or any other step taken in regard to it, except with same formalities as are prescribed in case of minors represented by tutors, father during marriage occupying place and being clothed with powers of tutor. (C.C.P. 4501).

The party who is entrusted with care of children, in case of divorce or separation, is of right their natural tutor, as though the other party had died. When parents have been awarded joint custody, they are natural co-tutors of child with equal authority and solidary responsibility, unless modified by their own agreement with court approval. (C. C. 250, as am'd Act 695 of 1983). Either parent in joint custody situation may appoint tutor of children's property; if both appoint, tutor appointed by parent administers portion of children's estate attributable to appointing parent; court decides which shall administer other portions. (C.C. 258, as am'd Act 680 of 1992).

Eligibility.—The following persons cannot be tutors: Minors, except father and mother; persons interdicted, or shown on contradictory hearing to be mentally incompetent, a convicted felon, indebted to minor (not applicable to father and mother); an adverse party to a suit with minor (other than father and mother); or a person contradictorily proved to be incapable because of physical or mental condition, or bad moral character. (C.C.P. 4231).

Appointment, recognition or confirmation of tutors must be made by the judge of the parish where the surviving parent or parent awarded custody of the minor is domiciled, and in other cases where the minor has his domicile, if he has a domicile in the state, or if he has no domicile in the state, by the judge of the parish where any real estate of is situated, or if none, where movable property is situated. If parents are awarded joint custody of minor, they must petition jointly for appointment as co-tutors in district court of parish in which divorce or separation proceedings were instituted or in parish of domicile of minor if specified in joint custody agreement. (C.C.P. 4031, as am'd Act 764 of 1990). When minor is without tutor, any person who has claim against him may apply to competent judge to request that attorney at law be appointed to represent minor. (C.C.P. 4232).

Tutorship of mentally retarded person may be continued beyond age of majority until revoked by court of domicile. Title of such a proceeding is "Continuing Tutorship of (Name of Person), A Mentally Retarded Person." (C.C. art. 356, as am'd Act 714 of 1974).

GUARDIAN AND WARD . . . continued

Bonds.—All tutors may give bond in lieu of special or general mortgage. If not natural tutor, bond must be of duly authorized surety company, or covered by Louisiana state, political subdivision or municipal, or U.S. bonds or domestic loan or homestead association shares properly insured deposited as directed by court, certificates of deposit of approved banks, or by at least two personal sureties signing in solido each of whom is state resident and owns unencumbered property in state sufficient to secure bond. (C.C.P. 4132, am'd Act 136 of 1985). Judge fixes amount and may allow substitution of securities. (C.C.P. 4136).

A parent, qualified as tutor or not, may secure his obligations to his minor child be general or special mortgage or by bond of the type authorized for other sureties, or by bond in addition to legal mortgage if so ordered. (C.C.P. 4134, 4135). Bond may be increased or diminished; but when only asset of minor is contested damage claim, court may postpone furnishing of security until claim is recovered. (C.C.P. 4131, as am'd Act 146 of 1985). With court authorization, legal mortgage may be subordinated to conventional mortgage. (C.C.P. Art. 4137, added Act 389 of 1980).

Where no person will accept tutorship and give bond, court may dispense with bond. (C.C.P. 4463). Court may also dispurse with bond requirement in small tutorship proceedings (property with gross value of $20,000 or less). (C.C.P. 4463, as am'd Act 45 of 1990).

Inventory.—Applicant for tutorship must have an inventory of minor's property made within ten days after signing of court order. Itemized description of property, sworn to, may take place of formal inventory.(C.C.P. 4101, as am'd Act 344 of 1983).

Management of Property.—Matters affecting minor's interest submitted for determination to court by tutor contradictorily with undertutor, or with undertutor's concurrence, by ex parte order. (C.C.P. 4271). Ability to invest, reinvest or withdraw funds limited and subject to court approval in most instances. (C.C.P. 4270, 4272, as am'd Act 122 of 1995). Tutor may place some or all of minor's property in trust if authorized by court. (C.C.P. Art. 4269.1, added Act 276 of 1980). Whenever court renders monetary judgment or judgment of possession of property in favor of minor, it may include orders to insure that funds or property are used for minor's benefit. (C.C.P. 4521, added Act 296 of 1984).

Sales.—Tutor may sell minor's property at public or private sale by petitioning court, and, in absence of concurrence by under-tutor, by taking rule on under-tutor. (C.C.P. 4271, 4301-4342).

Leases.—Court may authorize lease of minor's property, limited to term of tutorship. (C.C.P. 4268, am'd Act 133 of 1974).

Accounts.—Tutor must render an annual account of his administration and at other times ordered by the Court, and a final account after expiration of or upon revocation of his tutorship. (C.C.P. 4391, 4392).

Agreements Between Tutor and Minor.—Every agreement which may take place between tutor and minor arrived at age of majority, is null and void unless same was entered into after rendering of a full account and delivery of vouchers, whole being made to appear by receipt of person to whom account was rendered ten days previous to agreement. (C. C. 339).

Absence of Tutor.—A tutor who is a nonresident or who is about to leave the state permanently must execute a power of attorney appointing a resident to represent him and this power of attorney must be filed in the tutorship proceeding. Agent may be authorized by the absent tutor to represent him in all matters relating to tutorship. A resident tutor who will be temporarily absent may similarly appoint such an agent. (C.C.P. 4273 as am'd Act 4 of 1964).

Investments.—See category Estates and Trusts, topic Trusts.

Fees allowed tutors are fixed by court not to exceed 10% of annual revenues from minor's property, unless increased by court on proper showing. (C.C.P. 4274, as am'd Act 36 of 1966)

Uniform Veterans' Guardianship Act has been adopted. (T. 29, §§351-373, as am'd).

Insane person or one incapable of handling his estate through infirmity may have curators appointed in interdiction proceedings to administer the interdict's estate. (C. C. 389 et seq.). Spouse or relative is entitled to curatorship. (C.C. 390, C.C.P. 4550). Interdict is treated like a minor who is under a tutor, and rules respecting the tutorship of a minor generally apply to curatorship. (C.C.P. 4554). Curator may obtain court approval to place interdict's property in trust. Interdict must be sole beneficiary, trustee must be named, maximum spendthrift restraints must be imposed, and trust is subject to termination at option of interdict upon judicial termination of interdiction or in event of interdict's death. Upon creation of trust, curator is entitled to no further commissions with respect to trust property. (C.C.P. 4554.1, added Act 272 of 1983).

Curator with limited powers may be appointed after court inquiry into specific disabilities of incapacitated person. Limited curator's powers are restricted to those necessary to provide for needs of incapacitated person; rights of person may be infringed only in least restrictive manner. Judgment of limited interdiction must set forth specific powers of limited curator. (C. C. 389.1, added Act 167 of 1981).

By power of attorney, competent person may nominate curator of his person, property or both, should he be later interdicted. Court must appoint person so nominated, unless otherwise disqualified or deemed not in best interest of interdict. (C.C.P. 4550, as am'd Act 304 of 1981).

Under specified conditions, including consent of interdict's spouse and heirs of first degree, curator may continue to make donations in limited amounts to descendants to continue interdict's policy of making gifts prior to interdiction, up to limit of $10,000 annually to each (T. 9, §1022, as am'd Act 143 of 1991), and may make donations to charitable and nonprofit organizations (T. 9, §1023, added Act 68 of 1979, and §1031) or to collaterals or their descendants when interdict has no spouse or direct descendants (T. 9, §1024, added Act 299 of 1991, eff. July 3, 1991).

Foreign Tutors.—Upon producing proof of appointment, tutors or guardians of minors residing out of Louisiana are entitled to sue for and recover any property, rights or credits belonging to minors in this state, upon producing satisfactory evidence of appointment as aforesaid, without being under necessity of qualifying as tutors according to laws of Louisiana, when no tutor has been appointed in Louisiana. (C.C.P. 4431, 4433). They cannot, however, remove from state property of any minor unless foreign tutor petitions and obtains judgment of court of parish where property is situated upon certain stated conditions. (C.C.P. 4432, as am'd Act 36 of 1966).

Uniform Fiduciaries Act adopted with slight variations. (T. 9, §§3801-3814, §3803 repealed by Act 444 of 1960).

Uniform Simplification of Fiduciary Security Transfers Act adopted. (T. 9, §§3831-3840).

Uniform Child Custody Jurisdiction Act adopted. (T. 13, §§1700-1724, added Act 513 of 1978).

HUSBAND AND WIFE:

Matrimonial regime governing ownership and management of property of spouses may be legal, contractual or partly legal and partly contractual. Legal matrimonial regime is that specified by law in C. C. Arts. 2325 et seq., as am'd Act 565 of 1980. (See subhead Community Property, infra.)

Antenuptial Contracts.—Matrimonial agreement establishing separate regime or modifying or terminating legal regime may be executed by spouses as to all matters not prohibited by public policy, either before marriage, or during marriage, to subject themselves to legal regime, and during marriage may terminate or modify regime upon approval of court upon joint petition, or within first year of moving into and acquiring domicile in state. (See also subhead Separate Property, infra.) Such agreements may not renounce or alter marital portion or established order of succession; nor may spouses limit as to third persons right that one spouse alone has under legal regime to obligate community or to alienate, encumber or lease community property. Agreement must be by authentic act or act under private signature and duly acknowledged, and is effective as to third persons when filed in parishes in which immovable property is situated and parishes of domicile as to movable property. Unless fully emancipated minor cannot enter matrimonial agreement without concurrence of father and mother, or parent having legal custody, or tutor. (C. C. Arts. 2325-2333).

Divorce.—Judgment of divorce terminates community property regime retroactive to date of filing of action. (C.C. 159, as am'd Act 1009 of 1990, eff. Jan. 1, 1991).

Disability of Married Women.—All disabilities are removed in so far as separate property of the wife is concerned. (T. 9, §§101-105; T. 6, §28).

Separate property of spouse consists of property acquired prior to establishment of community property regime, acquired by spouse with separate things or with separate and community things when value of community things is inconsequential, acquired individually by inheritance or donation, acquired as damages from other spouse for breach of contract or fraud or bad faith in management of community, acquired as damages of indemnity in connection with management by spouse of separate property, and acquired as result of voluntary partition of community during existence of community property regime. (C. C. 2341, as am'd Act 921 of 1981). Declaration of separate property may be contested by other spouse unless he concurs in act, and by creditors, but where there has been declaration, transfer by onerous title may not be set aside. (C. C. Art. 2342). Donation of interest in community to other spouse transforms interest into separate property of donee, and, unless otherwise provided in act of donation, equal interest of donee becomes separate property and natural and civil fruits and minerals produced from or attributed to property given as well as bonuses, delay rentals, royalties and shut-in payments arising from mineral leases, become donee's separate property. (C. C. 2343, as am'd Act 921 of 1981). Personal injury damages are also separate property of spouse, but portion of damages attributed to expenses incurred by community as result of injury, or in compensation of loss of community earnings except that accrued after termination of community, is community. (C. C. Art. 2343).

Separate property regime is established by agreement excluding legal regime or by judgment of separation. (C. C. Art. 2370). Each spouse enjoys and disposes of separate property without concurrence of other spouse. (C. C. Art. 2371). Spouse is solidarily liable with other spouse for family necessities. (C. C. Art. 2372). Except as provided by agreement, each spouse contributes to expenses in proportion to his means. (C. C. Art. 2373).

Spouse may obtain judgment of separation of property if community is threatened by fraud, fault, neglect or incompetence of other spouse or disorder of affairs of other spouse, which judgment is retroactive to day of filing of petition without prejudice to rights acquired in interim. (C. C. Arts. 2374 and 2375). Creditors may intervene to object to separation or modification of regime on grounds of fraud and may file action in one year to annul judgment. (C. C. Art. 2376). Partition of community property may be sought by incidental demand in separation proceeding. (C.C. 150, added Act 225 of 1986).

Community Property.—Unless modified or terminated by agreement, legal regime of community of acquets and gains applies to spouses domiciled in this state. (C. C. Art. 2334). Each spouse owns present undivided one-half interest in community. (C. C. Art. 2336). Spouses may without court approval voluntarily partition community property in whole or in part during existence of community regime; things acquired by such partition are separate property. (Partition effective against third persons when filed for registry as provided in C. C. 2332. (C. C. 2336, as am'd Act 282 of 1982), Spouse may not alienate, encumber or lease to third person undivided interest in community or particular thing thereof prior to termination of community. (C. C. Art. 2337). Community property is that acquired during community through effort, skill or industry of spouse, or acquired with community things or with community and separate things unless classified as separate property by C. C. Art. 2341, or donated to spouse jointly, or natural and civil fruits of community, or for damages to community property, or all other property not classified as separate. (C. C. Art. 2338). Natural and civil fruits of separate property, minerals produced from or attributable to separate property, and bonuses, delay rentals, royalties and shut-in payments from mineral leases are community unless reserved by spouse by declaration by notarial act or private acts duly acknowledged which is effective as to fruits of immovables when registered in conveyance records of parishes where property is located, and in parish of domicile as to

HUSBAND AND WIFE . . . *continued*
movables. (C. C. Art 2339, as am'd Act 565 of 1980). There is rebuttable presumption that things are community. (C. C. Art. 2340). One spouse may transfer separate property to other, with stipulation that it shall become community. Transfer by onerous title must be in writing, and by gratuitous title must be by authentic act. By such transfer, property is transformed into community property. (C. C. 2343.1, added Act 921 of 1981). Separate or community obligation may be satisfied from community property and from separate property of spouse incurring obligation. (C. C. Art. 2345). Each spouse may manage, control or dispose of community things unless otherwise provided by law. (C. C. Art. 2346). Concurrence of spouses is required with respect to alienation, encumbrance or lease of family home and furniture and furnishings therein, all of assets of community enterprise, and movables issued or registered by law in names of spouses jointly. (C. C. Art. 2347). Spouse may expressly renounce right of concurrence and management of community enterprise, which may be irrevocable for stated term not to exceed three years. (C.C. 2348, as am'd Act 554 of 1984, eff. Jan. 1, 1985). Renunciation of right to concur may include future-acquired property within applicable time limit. (C.C. 2348, as am'd Act 622 of 1984, eff. Jan. 1, 1985). Spouse may nonetheless reserve right of concurrence as to specifically described community immovable property. (C. C. 2348, as am'd Act 132 of 1981). Donation of community requires concurrence of spouses except for usual or customary gifts of value commensurate with economic position of spouses. (C. C. Art. 2349). Spouse who is sole manager of enterprise may alienate, encumber, or lease movables unless issued in name of other spouse or as required by law. (C. C. Art. 2350). Spouse has exclusive right to manage, alienate, encumber, or lease movables issued or registered in his name as provided by law. (C. C. Art. 2351). Spouse who is partner has exclusive right as to management, etc., of partnership interest. (C. C. Art. 2352). Alienation, encumbrance or lease of community without required concurrence is relatively null. (C. C. Art. 2353). Spouse is liable for loss or damage caused by fraud or bad faith in management of community. (C. C. Art. 2354). By summary proceedings, court may authorize one spouse to act alone if in best interests for family and other spouse is unable or arbitrarily refuses to concur. (C. C. Art. 2355). Community terminates on death of spouse, or by judgment of divorce, or separation from bed and board, or separation of property. (C. C. Art. 2356). Obligations of spouse may be satisfied from property of former community after termination, and spouse is liable for obligations of other spouse up to value of community disposed of for purposes other than satisfaction of community obligations. (C. C. Art. 2357). By written act spouse may assume responsibility for one-half of each community obligation incurred by other spouse, and may dispose of community without incurring further responsibility for obligations incurred by other spouse. (C. C. Art. 2357.1). Reimbursement by one spouse to other may be had on termination of community. (C. C. Art. 2358). Reimbursement shall be made from patrimony of spouse who owes reimbursement. (C.C. 2358.1, added Act 1991 of 1990). Obligations for common interest of spouses or for other spouse is community obligation. (C. C. Art. 2360). There is presumption that obligations incurred during regime are community. (C. C. Art. 2361). Alimentary obligations under law are deemed community. (C. C. Art. 2362). Separate obligations are those incurred before or after regime, or during but not for common interests or for other spouse, those resulting from intentional wrongs not for benefit of community, and those incurred for separate property of spouse to extent such does not benefit community, family or other spouse. (C. C. Art. 2363). On termination of community, spouse is entitled to one-half of value of community property used to satisfy separate obligation of other spouse or to acquire, use, improve or benefit separate property of other spouse (C. C. Arts. 2364 and 2366), and one-half of value of separate property used to satisfy community obligations to extent of community assets unless for ordinary and customary marriage expenses and support, maintenance and education of children in which case reimbursement is not limited to community assets (C. C. Art. 2365). If community property is seized as result of criminal act by one spouse not perpetrated for community benefit, other spouse is entitled to reimbursement upon termination of regime for one half of value at time of seizure. (C.C. 2364.1, added Act 499 of 1997). Spouse is entitled to one-half of value of separate property used for acquisition, use, improvement or benefit of community (C. C. Art. 2367), and one-half of enhanced value of separate property of other spouse as result of uncompensated labor or industry of spouses (C. C. Art. 2368). Special rules of accession and reimbursement apply when community assets are used to make improvements on separate property and vice versa. (C.C. 2367.1 and 2367.2, added Act 933 of 1984). Spouses owe each other accounting, which right prescribes in three years from termination of community. (C. C. Art. 2369). After termination of community property regime, provisions governing co-ownership apply unless there is contrary provision of law or juridicial act. (C.C. 2369.1, added Act 991 of 1990). Principles governing management of former community property are provided. (C.C. 2369.2 through 2369.8, eff. Jan. 1, 1996). If spouses are unable to agree on partition of community property or settlement of claims between them, either spouse on termination of matrimonial regime may institute proceeding to make that determination. In proceeding, each party files descriptive list of all assets and liabilities; other party must traverse or concur in other's list; court may appoint experts to assist in assessing value; court then partitions property and liabilities according to value at time of trial. If party fails to file list, other party may file rule to show cause why its list should not be deemed to constitute judicial determination of assets and liabilities; court may grant request or extend time for filing by other party. (T. 9, §2801[1][a], as am'd Act 35 of 1997). In those few parishes that have family courts, those courts have exclusive jurisdiction of such actions. (T. 13, §1415, added Act 35 of 1997). Allocation of liability to one spouse requires that spouse to discharge that obligation. If allocation is inequitable, difference may be made up by present or deferred payment of money. In certain circumstances, allocation by lot is permitted or court may order private sale. Partition by licitation is permitted only as last resort. (T. 9, §2801, added Act 439 of 1982).

When petition for divorce has been filed, either spouse may obtain judgment decreeing separation of property by rule and upon proof of living separate and apart without reconciliation for 30 days from date of or prior to filing of divorce petition. (C.C. 2374, as am'd Act 627 of 1993). Even absent filing of divorce petition, judgment decreeing separation of property may be had on petition of either spouse when spouses have lived separate and apart continuously for six months. (C.C. 2374[D], added Act 25 of 1993).

Contracts.—A married woman, whether a resident of this state or not, is competent to contract debts, purchase, sell and mortgage and to bind and obligate herself personally, and with reference to her separate property; to sell, alienate or otherwise dispose, and to mortgage and pledge, or otherwise encumber, her separate property for the benefit of herself, her husband, or any other person, and to bind herself, personally, as surety for her husband or any other person. (T. 9, §§101-103). She may also open bank accounts, deposit funds therein and withdraw the same by check as though unmarried. (T. 6, §28).

See also category Business Regulation and Commerce, topic Interest, subhead Consumer Credit Opportunity Law.

Actions.—A married woman has the right to appear in court and to sue and to be sued and joinder of her husband is not necessary. (T. 9, §102). Spouses may not use each other except for causes of action pertaining to contracts, matrimonial regimes, restitution of separate property, divorce, declaration of nullity, spousal or child support and child custody. (T. 9, §291, as am'd Act 1009 of 1990, eff. Jan. 1, 1991).

Desertion and Non-support.—Desertion or intentional non-support by husband of destitute wife or by either parent of destitute minor children constitutes criminal neglect, punishable by fine of not more than $500, or imprisonment for not more than six months. Court may direct fine to be paid to wife or tutor or custodian of minor, or may order defendant to pay weekly alimony and enter into recognizance with surety conditioned for payment thereof. Failure to pay such alimony may be punished as contempt and amount of fine ordered paid to wife, tutor or custodian of minor. (T. 14, §§74, 75, as am'd Act 116 of 1975).

Uniform Reciprocal Enforcement of Support Act adopted with immaterial variations. (Civil enforcement by juvenile courts of state. (T. 13, §§1641-1699, as am'd Act 288 of 1966 to conform with recommendation of National Conference).

See also category Estates and Trusts, topic Descent and Distribution.

INFANTS:

Age of majority, 18 for both sexes. (C. C. 29, am'd Act 125 of 1987). Tutorship of mentally retarded person may be continued beyond age of majority until revoked by court of domicile. (C. C. 355 and 358, as am'd Act 216 of 1979). In such cases, retarded person is permanent minor, except that after age 18, unless formally interdicted, person has legal capacity of minor granted emancipation conferring power of administration. (C.C. 359, as am'd Act 714 of 1974). Name changes governed by law. (T. 13, §4751, as am'd by Act 201 0f 1995).

Parental rights of abused or neglected child may be terminated in proceedings brought by district attorney. (T. 13, §§1600-1605, as am'd Act 400 of 1985).

Contract for surrogate motherhood (agreement of person not married to contributor of sperm to carry child to term and then surrender it) prohibited. (T. 9, §2713, added Act 583 of 1987).

Adoption.—See topic Adoption.

Emancipation is of two kinds: (1) Emancipation conferring power of administration, which may be granted to minor fifteen years of age by father, or by mother if no father, by notarial act. Minor thus emancipated has full administration of his estate and may pass all acts necessary to such administration, grant leases, receive revenues and monies due him and give receipts for same, but he cannot bind himself legally for any sum exceeding amount of one year of his revenue, nor can he alienate, affect or mortgage his immovables without authorization of court on recommendation of his tutor or administrator of his estate. (C. C. 370, 371, 373, as am'd Act 346 of 1972). He cannot donate inter vivos except by marriage contract in favor of person to be married. When engaged in trade he is considered as being of full age for all acts relative to such trade. This emancipation may be revoked whenever minor contracts engagements which exceed limits prescribed by law. (C. C. 365-378). (2) Emancipation by marriage, which subjects minor to same rules as hereinbefore enumerated, but, if below 16 years, he cannot alienate, affect or mortgage immovable property without consent of court. This emancipation cannot be revoked. (C. C.379-384). Minor 16 years or older may be judicially emancipated. (C. C. 385, added Act 155 of 1976).

Parental Responsibility.—Father and mother, and after death of either, survivor, are responsible for damage occasioned by minor. (C.C. 2318, as am'd Act 578 of 1984; also 308 So.2d 270).

Contracts of minors not emancipated are valid if made with the intervention of their tutors and the assent of a family meeting where such is required. When the minor has no tutor or one who neglects to supply him with necessaries for his support a contract or quasi contract for providing him with what is necessary for those purposes, is valid. (C. C. 1922, 1923, eff. Jan. 1, 1985).

Minors may consent to medical treatment without parental authorization. (T. 40, §§1095-6, added Acts 182 and 183 of 1972).

Minors may deposit money in bank and draw the same out (T. 6, §278) and may subscribe for, transfer stock or shares in any building, loan, or homestead association or society, as if he or she had attained age of 18 years, provided that, in case of minor less than ten years, parents or survivor may act without tutorship proceedings (T. 6, §765).

Uniform Transfers to Minor Act adopted (eff. Jan. 1, 1988).

Uniform Securities Ownership by Minors Act not adopted.

Actions.—Tutor appointed by court of this state is proper plaintiff to sue to enforce right of unemancipated minor, when (1) One or both parents are dead; (2) parents are divorced or judicially separated; or (3) minor is illegitimate child. Father, as administrator of estate of his minor child, is proper plaintiff to sue to enforce right of unemancipated minor who is legitimate issue of living parents who are not divorced or judicially separated. Mother, as administratrix of estate of her minor child, is proper plaintiff in such action, when father is mentally incompetent, committed, interdicted, imprisoned or absentee; with judicial permission, mother may represent minor when father fails or refuses to do so. (C.C.P. 683, as am'd Act 106 of 1992, eff. June 5, 1992). Suit against minor is brought against same parties under same conditions, or if none, against appointed attorney. (C.C.P. 732, as am'd Act 106 of 1992, eff. June 5, 1992).

Sale of minor's property, see topic Guardian and Ward.

See note at head of Digest as to 1998 legislation covered.

See Topical Index in front part of this volume.

LA – 41

INFANTS . . . *continued*

Uniform Child Custody Jurisdiction Act adopted. (T. 13, §§1700-1724, added Act 513 of 1978).

Comprehensive Children's Code adopted by Act 235 of 1991 and am'd by Act 251 of 1995, eff. Jan. 1, 1996).

MARRIAGE:

Marriage is legal relationship between man and woman created by civil contract. (C.C. 86, as am'd Act 886 of 1987, eff. Jan. 1, 1988).

Requirements for contract of marriage are: (1) Absence of legal impediment; (2) marriage ceremony; and (3) free consent of parties, expressed at ceremony. (C.C. 87, as am'd Act 886 of 1987, eff. Jan. 1, 1988). Legal impediments are existence of valid marriage (C.C. 88), and certain degrees of relationship, such as ascendants and descendants and collaterals within fourth degree, whether of whole or half blood (C.C. 90). Persons of same sex may not contract marriage with each other. (C.C. 89).

Covenant marriage may be entered after required counselling, and grounds for divorce in such marriage are more restrictive than in non-covenant marriages; separation from bed and board is available prior to actual divorce. (T. 9, §§272 through 275, added Act 1380 of 1997, eff. July 15, 1997, and also applicable by election of parties to preexisting marriages).

Minimum Age for Marriage.—Ordained ministers of gospel and judges or magistrates entrusted with power of celebrating marriages are prohibited to marry minor without written consent of both parents or judicial authorization. (T. 9, §211, added Act 886 of 1987, eff. Jan. 1, 1988).

Consent Required.—Minors of either sex must have received consent of both parents or survivor of them, and if both dead, consent of tutor. (T. 9, §211, added Act 886 of 1987, eff. Jan 1, 1988). But marriage between minors is not void or voidable because contracted without such consent. (C.C. 87, as am'd Act 886 of 1987, eff. Jan. 1, 1988).

Licenses to celebrate marriages in the Parish of Orleans are issued by state registrar of vital records and judges of city courts, and in other parishes, by clerks of court. License application must contain social security number or statement that no such number has been issued. (T. 9, §224[A][6], added Act 8 of First Ex. Sess. of 1998, eff. Apr. 24, 1998). Licenses for marriage may be issued in any parish, regardless of place of ceremony or domicile of parties. (T. 9, §222, as am'd Act 81 of 1990). However, marriage celebrated without issuance of license is valid and not subject to annulment, only penalty being assessed against the officiant. (C.C. 87). Within his respective jurisdiction, any judge may celebrate any marriage for which lawful license has been issued, regardless of parish of issuance. (T. 9, §203).

Medical examination of male and female within ten days of application for license, with physician's certificate that examinee is free of venereal diseases, and presentation of birth certificate or equivalent, are conditions precedent to issuance of license. (T. 9, §226, 230).

Ceremonial Marriage.—Ceremony is necessary to constitute valid marriage. (C.C. 87).

Marriages may be celebrated by registered minister of gospel or priest of any religious sect, by justices of Supreme Court at any place within state, by judges of court of appeal at any place within their circuit, by district judges at any place within their district, and by judges of city, family and juvenile courts at any place within parish where court is situated, even if judge is retired. (T. 9, §203).

Marriage must be celebrated in presence of two witnesses of full age and act of celebration must be made and signed by person who celebrates same, parties and witnesses. (C.C. 87, 91; T. 9, §244). These requirements are directory only. (C.C. 91).

Delay of 72 hours between issuance of license and marriage ceremony is required; may be waived upon certificate issued by certain authorized judges. (T. 9, §241).

Name.—Marriage does not change name of either spouse; married person may use surname of either or both spouses. (C.C.P. 3947, added Act 836 of 1987). In voter registration, woman may use hyphenated surname. (T. 18, §111[B], as am'd Act 317 of 1988).

Record.—See category Documents and Records, topic Records, subhead Vital Statistics.

Common Law Marriages.—Marriage by private agreement, express or implied, not recognized in this state. (C.C. 87).

Marriages by procuration are not allowed. (C.C. 92).

Nullity and Annulment.—Marriage is absolutely null if contracted without ceremony, by procuration or in violation of impediment. Judicial declaration not required, but action to recognize nullity may be brought by any interested person. (C.C. 94, as am'd Act 886 of 1987, eff. Jan. 1, 1988). Marriage is relatively null when consent of one of parties is not freely given, and such marriage may be declared null upon application of party whose consent was not freely given. Marriage may not be declared null if that party confirmed marriage after recovering his liberty or regaining his discernment. (C.C. 95, as am'd Act 886 of 1987, eff. Jan. 1, 1988).

Absolutely null marriage produces civil effects in favor of party who contracted it in good faith, for as long as party remains in good faith. When cause of nullity is one party's prior undissolved marriage, civil effects continue in favor of other party, regardless of whether latter remains in good faith, until marriage is pronounced null or latter party contracts valid marriage. Marriage contracted by party in good faith produces civil effects in favor of child of parties. (C.C. 96, as am'd Act 886 of 1987, eff. Jan. 1, 1988). Relatively null marriage produces civil effects until it is declared null. (C.C. 97, as am'd Act 886 of 1987, eff. Jan. 1, 1988). In proceeding seeking declaration of nullity, court may award party incidental relief afforded in divorce proceeding, such as custody, support and visitation. (C.C. 151 and 152, added Act 108 of 1993, eff. Jan. 1, 1994).

Foreign Marriages.—Marriage valid by law of state where contracted is valid in Louisiana, unless parties were domiciled in Louisiana at time of marriage and marriage was prohibited by Louisiana law.

Marital Portion.—If spouse dies leaving survivor in necessitous circumstances, marital portion in varying amounts may be due, but subject to maximum of $1,000,000. (C.C. 2434, as am'd Act 289 of 1987).

MARRIED WOMEN:

See topics Husband and Wife, Marriage; categories Civil Actions and Procedure, topic Evidence, subhead Witnesses; Debtor and Creditor, topic Homesteads; Documents and Records, topic Acknowledgments; Estates and Trusts, topics Executors and Administrators, Wills; Property, topic Dower.

INSURANCE

INSURANCE COMPANIES:

Title 22 is the Louisiana Insurance Code. When Insurance Code is silent, Business Corporation Code applies. (T. 22, §40, added Act 715 of 1981).

General supervision of the insurance business is vested in the Commissioner of Insurance. (T. 22, §2). He must make examinations at specified intervals of all insurers doing business in the state. (T. 22, §1301 as am'd Act 702 of 1979). Expenses of these inspections are borne by companies. (T. 22, §1304). Self-insured health and accident plans are subject to special regulation. (T. 22, §§3001-3017, as am'd and added Act 902 of 1990). Attorney general is charged with providing legal representation to Commissioner, and may also seek writ of mandamus to force Commissioner to take certain actions. (T. 22, §743, as am'd Act 382 of 1991; T. 22, §1468, added by Act 383 of 1991, both eff. July 6, 1991).

Domestic insurer must obtain approval of Commissioner before applying for admission to another state. (T. 22, §1461, added Act 454 of 1976).

Insurance Holding Company System Regulatory Law adopted by Act 794 of 1991.

Name.—Names deceptively similar to those of other companies are specifically forbidden. (T. 22, §32).

Reports.—Every insurer authorized to do business in the state must, before Mar. 1, file a true statement of its condition, transactions and affairs as of the preceding Dec. 31. Such statements must be made on forms furnished by Commissioner of Insurance. (T. 22, §1451). All insurers must also file a report for license tax purposes prior to each March 1 certifying to amount of annual gross premiums received during preceding year. (T. 22, §1070).

Owner of more than 10% of shares of domestic insurer or officer of domestic insurer must file reports with Commissioner of Insurance. Unfair profits derived from purchase and sale or sale and purchase within six months may be recovered by company. (T. 22, §§1525-1533, added Act 8 of 1966).

Policies.—Insurance Code sets forth a number of matters that must be included in life insurance policies, (T. 22, §170, as am'd Act 547 of 1981); in annuities and endowment contracts (T. 22, §173); group life insurance policies (T. 22, §179); health and accident policies (T. 22, §§212-215, as am'd Act 513 of 1983); industrial insurance policies (T. 22, §§251-259); and fraternal benefit contracts (T. 22, §§549-550). Life insurance policies must state that insured has ten days to examine policy, during which he may return policy and receive refund of any premium advanced by him. Provisions inapplicable to non-renewable trip-travel insurance policies. (T. 22, §170[A][10], added Act 661 of 1981). Fire insurance companies must use Louisiana standard form of fire insurance policy which is set forth in Code. (T. 22, §691). Policies equalling or exceeding standard fire policy may be used in lieu of it, or standard fire policy may be attached in its entirety to another policy. (T. 22, §691.2, added Act 133 of 1986, eff. June 26, 1986). Clauses in fire policies requiring additional insurance or coinsurance are prohibited in certain cases. (T. 22, §694, as am'd Act 115 of 1963). All basic policy forms, other than surety bond forms, must be filed with and approved by Commissioner of Insurance. (T. 22, §620). Louisiana Insurance Underwriting Association, composed of all insurers writing Louisiana property insurance, empowered to issue fire and extended coverage insurance for property in coastal areas. (T. 22, §§1431-1446, as am'd Act 584 of 1974).

Insurers are prohibited from paying benefits to person criminally responsible for death, disablement or injury of individual insured or person judicially determined to have participated in intentional, unjustified killing of insured. (T. 22, §613, as am'd Act 743 of 1987).

Liability insurers are subject to direct action by party injured by insured's conduct and must be joined with insured as defendant except in exceptional cases (insolvency or bankruptcy of insured, inability to serve process on insured, immunity of insured or when insured is deceased). (T. 22, §655, as am'd Act 584 of 1992).

See also category Business Regulation and Commerce, topic Consumer Protection.

Proof of Loss and Penalties.—All insurers must furnish upon written request forms of proof of loss. (T. 22, §650). If death claims under life policies are not paid within 60 days after receipt of proof of death and insurer has no just cause for not paying, amount due shall bear 8% per annum interest until paid. (T. 22, §656 as am'd Act 477 of 1980). Health and accident benefit claims must be paid within 30 days of receipt of proof of claim under penalty of insurer paying double the benefits due, plus reasonable attorney's fees unless reasonable grounds exist for not doing so. (T. 22, §657). Any court of competent jurisdiction in parish of insured's domicile (except justice of peace courts) may hear claims for penalties. (T. 22, §657, as am'd Act 872 of 1990, eff. July 25, 1990). All other types of claims must be settled within 30 days after proof of loss, and are subject to penalty of 10% on amount found to be due from insurer to insured or $1,000, whichever is greater, plus reasonable attorney's fees, when failure to pay claim is found to be arbitrary, capricious or without probable cause. (T. 22, §658, am'd Act 879 of 1992). On fire claims, payment period is suspended during official arson investigation. Louisiana Insurance Guaranty Association, composed of specified types of insurers, empowered to assess members specified amounts in order to pay unpaid claims of insolvent insurers. (T. 22, §§1375-1394, added Act 81 of 1970).

See note at head of Digest as to 1998 legislation covered.

See Topical Index in front part of this volume.

LA – 42

INSURANCE COMPANIES . . . *continued*

Payment of Cash Surrender Values.—Delay of six months may be invoked in payment of cash surrender values, but interest must be paid after first 30 days. (T. 22, §168[A][2], as am'd Act 951 of 1991).

Rates.—Louisiana Insurance Rating Commission, consisting of Commissioner of Insurance and six citizens of Louisiana appointed by the Governor. (T. 22, §§1401-1422, as am'd Act 228 of 1985). Under supervision of Louisiana Insurance Rating Commission, Louisiana Rating and Fire Prevention Bureau, which is composed of all stock fire insurance companies doing business in state, fixes equitable and nondiscriminating mandatory rates of premium to be charged on fire and extended coverage insurance and on other coverages usually written by fire insurers on property other than motor vehicles. These rates must be approved by Louisiana Insurance Rating Commission. Bureau also inspects every risk, files written survey thereon, defines safest method of constructing buildings and supervises installation of electric and heating apparatus. (T. 22, §1405, as am'd Act 429 of 1974). Commission determines and fixes mandatory rates to be charged on all casualty insurance risks, including vehicle insurance. (T. 22, §1406, as am'd Acts 241 and 242 of 1983). Every insurer, except as to inland marine risks not written according to manual rates or rating plans, must file all manuals, rate plans, etc., with appropriate divisions. (T. 22, §1407 as am'd Act 136 of 1966). Any action taken by Commission is subject to review in District Court for Parish of East Baton Rouge after hearing before Commissioner of Insurance. (T. 22, §1361).

Discrimination.—Unfair discrimination in favor of particular individuals or persons, or between insureds or subjects of insurance having substantially like insuring risk and exposure factors, or expense elements, in the terms and conditions of any contract, or in the rate of premium charged therefor, or in the benefits payable is specifically forbidden. (T. 22, §§652, 1214, am'd 1954, act 87). Certain types of preferences in issuance of group insurance are prohibited. (Act 320 of 1970).

Rebates of premiums on life insurance, annuity or health and accident insurance, other than as provided for in such policy, which are made as an inducement to such insurance, and the giving, selling or purchasing or so offering anything of value whatsoever not specified in the contract as an inducement to such insurance are specifically prohibited. (T. 22, §1214, am'd 1954, act 87).

Agents and Brokers.—Insurance agents, brokers and solicitors must be authorized and licensed by Commissioner of Insurance. (T. 22, §§1113, 1166, 1170, 1260). In addition to licensing requirements, a new applicant for license as a general life, health or accident insurance agent must submit to written examination by Commissioner of Insurance (T. 22, §1114), but temporary license may be issued to agent of combination life insurer. (T. 22, §1214, as am'd Act 362 of 1980). Nonresident may be licensed provided that state in which such person lives accords same privilege to Louisiana citizen. (T. 22, §1116).

No person may act as agent or representative for companies not authorized to do business in Louisiana. (T. 22, §§1112, 1252, am'd Act 238 of 1972).

All insurance contracts including those issued as result of agent accepting application or producing policy either as casualty insurance assigned risk under T. 22, §1417 et seq., for Louisiana Joint Reinsurance Association under T. 22, §1406.1 et seq., or for Louisiana Insurance Underwriters Association under T. 22, §1431 et seq. (other than life, health and accident or annuity insurance), covering any property or insurable interests or business activities within state, must be counter-signed by resident agent, who must receive commission, but agent may give power of attorney to licensed solicitor to sign when it is impossible or impracticable for agent to sign, or may authorize insurer to countersign by applying or imprinting agent's name or agent may apply or imprint his name in lieu of manually signing policy. Commissioner may approve waiver of countersigning for replacement policies. (T. 22, §1171, Act 132 of 1979). Agents cannot countersign policy in blank. (T. 22, §1177). Agents may not divide profits with unlicensed persons. (T. 22, §1174).

Companies may not pay adjuster any fee in excess of regularly fixed salary. (T. 22, §1451).

Process Agent.—Domestic Insurers must appoint registered agents for service of process. (T. 22, §32). Foreign Insurers must appoint Secretary of State agent for service of process (T. 22, §985). Transacting of business in state by foreign or alien insurer without certificate of authority or delivery of policy of such insurer to Louisiana resident is equivalent to appointment by such insurer of Secretary of State to be its agent for service of process. (T. 22, §1253).

Investments are governed by §§841-853 of Title 22, as am'd Act 251 of 1983.

Foreign Insurance Companies.—Any foreign or alien insurer, including reciprocals, Lloyds and fraternals, but excluding nonprofit funeral insurance and life, health and accident insurers on the cooperative or assessment plan, may be admitted to transact business in this state. (T. 22, §§941, 981). To qualify, company must file with Commissioner of Insurance: (1) application setting forth its name, location of home office, type of insurer, organization date, kinds of insurance it proposes to transact in state and such other information as Commissioner of Insurance deems necessary; (2) copy of its charter or articles of incorporation certified by proper official of its domicile; (3) copy of its by-laws or constitution certified by its proper officers; (4) copy of the applications and insurance contracts it proposes to write in this state; (5) copy of its last annual statement; (6) copy of the last report of examination certified by a proper supervisory official; (7) certificate from proper official of its domicile that it is duly incorporated or organized and is presently authorized to write kinds of insurance which it proposes to write in this state; (8) instrument appointing Secretary of State agent for service of process; (9) such other documents as Commissioner of Insurance may require. (T. 22, §982). To receive certificate of authority, insurer must also meet minimum capital and surplus requirements for similar domestic insurers (as to which see T. 22, §§71, 72, 121, 122, 254, 294, 495, 1021-1025, 1028), have its funds invested in accordance with laws of its domicile, make required deposit with State Treasurer and file a certificate from proper official of its domiciliary state showing that a deposit has been made there of not less than $100,000 as authorized by law of domiciliary state (T. 22, §983, as am'd Act 74 of 1969). See also subhead Reports, supra.

Commissioner of Insurance has power to refuse, suspend or revoke certificate of authority after 30 days notice of a foreign or alien insurer on finding that violations of Code exist. (T. 22, §987).

Unauthorized insurer cannot file actions or proceedings in state courts to enforce right, claim or demand arising out of business transacted in state. (T. 22, §1254).

See also category Civil Actions and Procedure, topic Process.

Unauthorized Insurers False Advertising Process Act adopted to subject foreign insurers to jurisdiction of Commissioner and courts of this state in connection with false advertisements and for service of process upon such insurers through Secretary of State. (T. 22, §§1231-1235).

Reciprocity.—Domestic companies are forbidden to insure lives in other states without qualifying in such states where such states require their companies to qualify in Louisiana to insure lives there. (T. 22, §1251).

Retaliatory Law.—Where laws of any other state impose on insurers of this state doing business in such state taxes, fines, penalties or other obligations additional to or in excess of those imposed by Louisiana upon insurers organized under the laws of other states, the same taxes, fines, penalties and other obligations are imposed upon all insurers of such state doing business in Louisiana. (T. 22, §1079).

Taxes.—Insurance business is subject to license tax based on annual gross premiums, as follows: on companies issuing life, accident, health, service, endowment or annuity policies, $140 per gross annual premiums of $7,000 or less and $225 for each additional $10,000 or fraction thereof (T. 22, §1062, as am'd Act 3, 1st Ex. Sess. of 1984); on companies issuing fire, marine and transportation policies, $180 per gross annual premiums of $6,000 or less and $300 for each additional $10,000 or fraction thereof (T. 22, §1063, as am'd Act 3, 1st Ex. Sess. of 1984); on companies issuing plate glass and boiler insurance, $60 per gross annual premiums of $6,000 or less and $66.67 for each additional $10,000 or fraction thereof (T. 22, §1064); on companies issuing casualty, surety, fidelity or other insurance, $180 per gross annual premiums of $6,000 or less and $185 for each additional $10,000 or fraction thereof (T. 22, §1065, am'd Act 42 of 1974). License taxes are to be remitted on quarterly basis to Commissioner of Insurance. (T. 22, §1071, as am'd Act 16, 1st Ex.Sess., 1983).

If insurer invests one-sixth or more of its total assets in bonds of state or its subdivisions, or in mortgages on property in state, or on loans to Louisiana residents or corporations, or in stock of domestic homestead, building and loan associations, tax is only one-third of above amounts. (T. 22, §1068).

Surcharge of not more than 20% of premiums is levied through malpractice liability insurers for Patient's Compensation Fund. (T. 40, §§1299.44, as am'd Act 183 of 1976).

Workmen's compensation insurers must contribute 1% of gross premiums to Second Injury Fund. (T. 23, §1377, added Act 165 of 1974). Such insurers are also subject to assessment of percentage of compensation benefits actually paid to fund operation of state Office of Worker's Compensation Administration, precise amount to be determined by regulations issued by director of office. (T. 23, §1291.1, added Act 29, 1st Ex.Sess., 1983).

Municipal and parochial corporations in state are authorized to impose a license tax based on gross annual premiums. (T. 22, §1066). There is an additional tax of 1 1/4% per annum on gross annual premiums of fire insurers, proceeds of which are used to pay salary and expenses of state fire marshal. (T. 22, §1077, as am'd Act 446 of 1968). There is an additional tax of 1/4% on annual premiums received for fire insurance covering property in this state. (T. 22, §1080). Assessment of up to 1% of gross direct premiums received from this state may be levied for expenses of Commission, and other public funds. (T. 22, §1419, am'd Act 323 of 1974).

Legal reserve of life insurance companies organized under laws of Louisiana is exempt from taxation. (Const., art. 7, §21).

Direct Actions Against Insurer.—See category Transportation, topic Motor Vehicles, subhead Direct Actions.

See also category Business Organizations, topic Corporations.

Uniform Insurers Liquidation Act.—Adopted. (T. 22, §§757-763).

SURETY AND GUARANTY COMPANIES:

See topic Insurance Companies.

INTELLECTUAL PROPERTY

TRADEMARKS AND TRADENAMES:

Whenever any individual, firm, partnership, corporation, association, union or other organization has adopted or used any trademark, service mark, trade name to identify goods made or sold by him, to identify services of one person, or to identify his business, vocation, or occupation, it is unlawful to counterfeit or imitate label, etc. Trademark may be registered by filing with Secretary of State application in form prescribed by Secretary of State containing specified information and payment of fee of $25, together with fee of $2 per page and $10 for certification of documents. Registration is effective for ten years and may be renewed for ten years by filing application with payment of fee of $25. (T. 9, §§211-224). Reservation may be made for 60 days by payment of $5 fee.

A manufacturer or seller of beverages or food in containers identified by any mark or device, may file a description of such device with the clerk of the civil district court in the parish of his principal place of business, and print the same once a week for five consecutive weeks in a newspaper published in the same parish, to protect the mark or device. When these requirements have been complied with, it is a misdemeanor or refill such containers, or to mutilate such marks or devices, or to use the same in any manner. (T. 51, §§241-243).

Assignment.—Trademark may be assigned with good will of business by written instrument recorded with Secretary of State for fee of $25. (T. 51, §217, as am'd Act 235 of 1983).

Tradenames.—Partnership or person doing business under fictitious name must file with register of conveyances in New Orleans or with clerk of court in other parishes a

See note at head of Digest as to 1998 legislation covered.

See Topical Index in front part of this volume.

TRADEMARKS AND TRADENAMES . . . *continued*
certificate giving full names and addresses of partners or person so doing business, and pay fee of 25¢. Failure to do so is a misdemeanor. (T. 51, §§281-284).

TRADE SECRETS:

Uniform Trade Secrets Act adopted in 1981, Act 462, but with deletion of §3(b) from Uniform Act.

Actual or threatened misappropriation of trade secrets as defined may be enjoined. (T. 51, §1432). In addition to or in lieu of injunctive relief, complainant may recover damages for actual loss, or for unjust enrichment. (T. 51, §1433). Attorney's fees may be awarded to prevailing party. (T. 51, §1434). Court must preserve secrecy of alleged trade secret by reasonable means. (T. 51, §1435). Action for misappropriation must be brought within three years after misappropriation is discovered or by exercise of reasonable diligence should have been discovered; continuing misappropriation is considered single claim. (T. 51, §1436). Statutory provisions replace conflicting tort, restitutionary and other state laws pertaining to civil liability for misappropriation of trade secret. (T. 51, §1437). Chapter of statutes is to be applied and construed to effectuate its general purpose to make uniform law with respect to trade secrets among states enacting it. (T. 51, §1438).

LEGAL PROFESSION

ATTORNEYS AND COUNSELORS:

The Supreme Court has, by rule, integrated the bar of Louisiana. All practicing attorneys must be members of the Louisiana State Bar Association. Mandatory CLE requirements have been in place since 1988.

Admission.—A committee of the Supreme Court has charge of admissions to the bar.

Attorney Ethics.—ABA Model Rules of Professional Conduct not officially adopted, but Louisiana rules are very similar. (T. 37, c. 4 App., following §218).

Eligibility.—Applicant must, in addition to passing state bar examination, be citizen or resident alien of U.S., 18 years of age, and of good moral character and must have graduated from law school that is approved by American Bar Association. Applicant must file his application, on prescribed form, with Committee on Bar Admissions, along with $50 fee, at least 45 days prior to examination. Application must be prepared in applicant's own handwriting and must be executed under oath.

Examination.—Committee on Bar Admissions conducts Bar examinations semi-annually and designates dates and places of examinations. Multi-State Bar Examination is not used except commencing Aug. 1, 1984, all applicants must pass Multi-State Professional Responsibility Examination.

Registration as Law Students.—No statutory requirement.

Foreign Attorneys.—An applicant who is a member of bar of another state must meet same conditions as are imposed on other applicants.

Admission Pro Hac Vice.—Subject to certain limitations, members of bars of other states may appear temporarily in courts of Louisiana.

Licenses.—Supreme Court issues licenses to successful applicants to Bar. License fee is $25. Practitioners of less than three years must pay $40 per year to Louisiana State Bar Association. Practitioners of more than three years must pay $100 per year.

Suretyship.—Attorney may act as surety except on bail bonds. (T. 15, §88).

Lien.—Attorneys have privilege, and are ranked second among privileged creditors, for law charges in succession proceedings. (C. C. 3254, 3276). By written contract, attorney may acquire fee or interest in subject matter in claim or suit, in which contract attorney and client may stipulate that neither may settle or otherwise dispose of suit without written consent of other, and any settlement or other disposition without such consent is null and void if contract is filed with clerk of court in parish where suit is pending, or is to be brought, or where client is domiciled. (T. 37, §218, as am'd Act 670 of 1975).

Fees.—Where parties agree in writing that debtor shall be liable for creditor's attorney's fees in fixed or determinable amount, creditor is entitled to that amount as part of damages. (C.C. 1935, as am'd Act 483 of 1983).

Unauthorized Practice.—No person shall practice law unless an active member in good standing of Louisiana State Bar Association.

It is not "practice of law" for partnership, corporation or other legal entity to assert claim, not exceeding $5,000 or defense pertaining to open account or promissory note, or suit for eviction of tenants, on its own behalf in courts of limited jurisdiction through duly authorized partner, officer or representative. (T. 37, §212 [C], as am'd Act 673 of 1992).

Trustee in discussing creation of trust with any settlor may not influence selection of attorney. (T. 9, §2241, as am'd Act 622 of 1983).

Discipline.—Supreme Court has exclusive original jurisdiction over disciplinary proceedings against a member of bar. (Const., art. 5, §5).

Attorneys are prohibited from paying money or giving any other thing of value to any person for purpose of obtaining representation of any client. (T. 37, §219, added Act 759 of 1977).

Professional Corporation.—See category Business Organizations, topic Corporations, subhead Professional Corporations.

MINERAL, WATER AND FISHING RIGHTS

MINES AND MINERALS:

Louisiana Mineral Code (T. 31, art. 1, et seq., as am'd Act 660 of 1983), consolidates laws applicable and related to mineral law. Code covers landowner's rights in minerals (arts. 4-16), nature of mineral rights and capacity, authority and formalities necessary for their creation (arts. 18-20), nature, prescription and use of mineral servitude (arts. 21-79, as am'd Act 589 of 1975), nature, creation, extinction, prescription and alternation of mineral royalty (arts. 80-104), executive rights to grant mineral leases (arts. 105-113), nature and creation of mineral leases, and obligations of lessor, obligations of lessee, transactions involving lessee's interest, termination and remedies for violation of lease, leases involving outstanding mineral rights, and privilege of lessor (arts. 114-148), effect of expropriation upon mineral rights (arts. 149-152, as am'd Act 348 of 1980; T. 41, §1338, added Act 371 of 1980), effect of possession and acquisitive possession (arts. 153-163), creation, ownership and partition of mineral rights and consequences of co-ownership, and effect of partition of land upon mineral rights (arts. 164-187, as am'd Act 1047 of 1986 and Act 647 of 1988), rights of usufructuaries in minerals (arts. 188-196, as am'd Act 589 of 1975 and Act 245 of 1986), pledge or mortgage of mineral rights (arts. 197-205), cancellation of extinguished mineral rights from public records (arts. 206-209), and protection of purchasers of production and method of compelling payment for production (arts. 210-212.31, as am'd Act 660 of 1983). Owners of mineral production payments and royalty owners who claim refusal of mineral lessees to make timely payments must give written notice to obligor of such failure as prerequisite to judicial demand. Obligor has 30 days after receipt in which to pay. Failure without reasonable cause given may double amount otherwise due. (T. 31, §§212.21 through 212.23, added Act 249 of 1982). When mineral lease is extinguished prior to expiration of primary term, former lessee must, within 90 days after extinguishment, record act evidencing expiration in official records of all parishes where lease is recorded. Failure to do so causes lessee to be liable to person in whose favor right or lease expired for all damages incurred therefrom and reasonable attorney's fee. (T. 31, §§206-207, as am'd Act 358 of 1982).

Lessee is required to provide complete address in lease. If he does not keep address information current, lessor may constitute Secretary of State as lessee's agent. (T. 30, §112, added Act 303 of 1984). Lessee must notify lessor within 90 days after cessation of production that lease has terminated. (T. 30, §102, added Act 559 of 1984).

Mineral Code also provides regulation of lignite and coal development and mining plans. (T. 30, §§11, 61, 115, 178, 191, 195 and 213, as am'd Act 203 of 1983).

An agreement by owners of mineral rights for joint exploration and production of minerals must be filed in conveyance records of parishes where land is located, to bind third parties. Declaration signed by parties or by general operator or agent of parties may be filed in lieu of agreement, but declaration must state where agreement can be found; by paying fee, any person may require agreement to be recorded in full. (T. 9, §§2731-2733, as am'd Act 325 of 1985).

Effective Jan. 1, 1984, payors of royalties must provide specified statutory information when royalty checks are issued, including lease identification number, date of sales, total sales, owner's final realizable price per barrel or MCF, total amount of taxes and like. (T. 31, §212.31, added Act 660 of 1983).

Mortgage of mineral rights may designate keeper or method of selection of keeper in event of seizure of property. Mortgage may specify compensation of keeper, reducable for court, and keeper has full power of administration, including operations, of property. (T. 9, §§5106-5110, added Act 546 of 1974).

State Mineral Board is agency to receive, sell and otherwise contract with regard to royalties in kind. (T. 30, §§142 and 143, as am'd Act 592 of 1979). Commissioner authorized to establish production incentive fund and to make production incentive or bonus payments to producers of 7½% of gross value received by applicant up to 750 barrels per day. (T. 31, §701, et seq., added Act 501 of 1974).

Upon request of owner, an electric log filed with Commissioner of Conservation remains confidential for a period of one year for wells shallower than 15,000 feet, or two years for wells 15,000 feet deep or deeper, which periods may be extended for a like period. No release by Commissioner to third persons is required of logs of offshore wells. (T. 44, §1, am'd Act 4 of 1973, Ex. Sess.).

Certain indemnity or "hold harmless" clauses in contracts pertaining to drilling are declared null, to extent such clause requires defense or indemnification when there is negligence or fault (strict liability) on part of indemnitee, its agent or employee, or independent contractor directly responsible to indemnitee. Such clauses in operating or farmout agreements as defined are not prohibited. (T. 9, §2870[D], as am'd Act 237 of 1982). Public utilities, forestry industry and companies who drill with Frasch Process are exempt from provisions, as are instances of liability for radioactive exposure and arising out of containment of well blowouts. Master or general service agreements, or blanket contracts, providing for future indemnity are specifically prohibited. Act does not apply to contracts providing indemnity executed prior to Sept. 11, 1981. (T. 9, §2780, as am'd Act 33 of 1981 First Extraordinary Session).

Conservation of oil and gas resources and regulation in case of overproduction are provided for and regulated by State Dept. of Conservation.

It is a misdemeanor to prospect for oil and state lands without consent of State Mineral Board (T. 30, §212) or on private property without consent of owner (T. 30, §217).

The Natural Resources and Energy Act of 1973 authorizes Commissioner of Conservation to develop programs and regulations for equitable distribution of energy supplies in state, for conservation of energy and prevention of waste thereof, and for mandatory allocation of use of fuels. Commissioner is authorized to supervise, regulate and control production, transportation, distribution, sale and use of intrastate natural gas, except ethane and heavier hydrocarbons and synthetic gas from coal, lignite or petroleum coke. Priorities are established for use of fuels. Intrastate natural gas transporters may be required to use uniform system of accounting, and to transport natural gas of others. Commissioner may regulate rates, charges and services of intrastate natural gas transporters, who may expropriate private property if issued a certificate of transportation by Commissioner. Intrastate gas transporters may be ordered by Commissioner to improve their facilities, may not abandon facilities without approval of Commissioner, and may be required to obtain approval of Commissioner before construction or extension of facilities. Approval of Commissioner is required for connection of an intrastate natural gas system with another pipeline system. Commissioner is authorized to plan, construct, finance, lease, and sublease pipeline systems, expropriate mineral leases, gas supplies and reserves, oil refineries, minerals, mineral rights and pipelines; and allocate or ration all natural gas and other hydrocarbons received as "in kind" royalties by private land and mineral owners and by state. Upon declaration by Governor of a state of emergency

See note at head of Digest as to 1998 legislation covered.

See Topical Index in front part of this volume.

LA – 44

MINES AND MINERALS . . . *continued*
as result of extreme shortages of natural gas under specified circumstances, Commissioner must establish a plan for statewide emergency conservation, allocation, rationing, and storage of intrastate natural gas, with specified priorities. Commissioner may supervise, regulate and control minimum sales prices of intrastate natural gas direct to industrial users and public utilities except sales by utilities to other users, if contract involves more than one billion cubic feet within a 12 month period or a lesser volume determined by Commissioner. Natural gas companies are required to file schedules showing prices for sales of intrastate natural gas and 30 days notice of changes must be given to Commissioner and public. Reports must be filed with Commissioner in prescribed form. Commissioner may investigate violations and failure to comply with a subpoena of Commissioner is subject to a fine of $1,000 and/or one year imprisonment. A rehearing may be applied for within 30 days after issuance of an order by Commissioner and if such is applied for and denied, party may file for a review by district court having jurisdiction by filing a petition within 60 days after denial of rehearing or date when application for rehearing may be deemed to have been denied by failure of Commissioner to act upon application within 30 days of its filing. Review by court may cover only objections contained in application for rehearing filed with Commissioner. Act also provides for a Louisiana Energy Commission, and provides for application of act to intrastate liquefied petroleum gas. (T. 30, §§501-692, am'd Act 250 of 1985).

Development of geothermal resources is regulated by Department of Natural Resources. (T. 30, §§800-809, added Act 134 of 1976).

Natural Gas Pricing Act is administered through assistant secretary of office of Conservation, Department of Natural Resources. (T. 30, §§1002-1007, as am'd Act 594 of 1978). Right of action is provided in favor of former purchaser/recipient deprived of natural gas by compulsory reallocation (except by emergency declared by governor) against ultimate industrial users and/or ultimate local distributor knowingly availing themselves of reallocated natural gas. (T. 30, §§411-414, added Act 674 of 1977).

Taxes.—General severance tax is imposed on oil at rate of 12.5% of value, as defined in section, at time and place of severance, subject to reduction as to wells of limited production (T. 47, §633[7] as am'd Act 2 of 1994); oil severance tax from certified stripper wells suspended in any month in which average monthly price is less than $20 per barrel (T. 47, §633[7][c][i][bb], added Act 2 of 1994, eff. June 1, 1994); on distillate, condensate or similar resources at rate of 12.5% of gross value at time and place of severance; on natural gasoline, casinghead gasoline, other natural gas liquids, ethane, and methane recovered after separation of oil, distillate, or condensate at 10¢ per barrel of 42 gallons: on butane and propane recovered through processing gas at rate of 5¢ per barrel of 42 gallons (T. 47, §633[8], am'd Act 6 of 1973. Ex. Sess.): on gas at rate of 10¢per 1,000 cubic feet, at rate of 3¢ per 1,000 cubic feet if produced from a well determined by Department of Conservation and Collector of Revenue to have a specific limited production generally determined by a casinghead pressure of 50 pounds per square inch or less, at rate of 1³/₁₀¢ per 1,000 cubic feet if well is incapable of producing 250,000 cubic feet of gas per day (T. 47, §633[9], as am'd Act 387 of 1990); on sulphur at rate of $1.03 per 2,240 lbs.: on salt at rate of 6¢ per 2,000 lbs.; on coal at rate of 10¢ per 2,000 lbs.: on lignite at rate of 10¢ per 2,000 lbs.; on ores at rate of 10¢ per 2,000 lbs.; on marble at rate of 20¢ per 2,000 lbs.; on stone at rate of 3¢ per 2,000 lbs.; on gravel at rate of 6¢ per 2,000 lbs.; on sand at rate of 6¢ per 2,000 lbs.; on shells at rate of 4¢ per 2,000 lbs.; and on salt content in brine or solution when used in manufacture of other products and not marketed as salt at rate of ¹/₂¢ per 2,000 lbs. (T. 47, §631 et seq., as am'd Act 10 of 1st Ex. Sess. of 1984).

Credit may be allowed for severance taxes by amount of first use taxes paid by taxpayer. (T. 47, §647, as am'd Act 394 of 1979).

Exemption from all severance tax is provided as to oil or gas new discovery wells as defined, spudded after Sept. 30, 1994 and completed between that date and Sept. 30, 1996; suspension of tax lasts 24 months or until recovery of payout of well cost, whichever first occurs. (T. 47, §648.1-648.4, added Act 2 of 1994, eff. June 1, 1994).

Royalties and severance tax under present or future state leases may be suspended as to production by tertiary recovery projects. (T. 30, §127.1, added Act 644 of 1983; T. 47, §633.4, added Act 643 of 1983).

Owners of oil, gas or mineral property as defined are immune from liability to any person who unlawfully enters that property, in absence of showing of gross negligence or intent to injure. (T. 9, §§2800.4[A][1] and [A][4], and 2800.4[E], as am'd and added Act 889 of 1993).

See also category Environment, topic Environmental Regulation.

MORTGAGES

CHATTEL MORTGAGES:

For general provisions as to both chattel mortgages and mortgages on real property, see topic Mortgages of Real Property.

For chattel mortgages on vehicles, see also category Transportation, topic Motor Vehicles. Uniform Commercial Code Art. 9 enacted (Act 528 of 1988, am'd Act 135 of 1989) effective Jan. 1, 1990. See category Business Regulation and Commerce, topic Commercial Code. For mortgage of movables used in commercial and industrial activity, see topic Mortgages of Real Property, subhead Conventional Mortgages.

Requisites of Instrument.—Chattel mortgage must be in writing setting out full description of property mortgaged so that it can be identified, and stating when obligation shall mature. Property mortgaged must be accurately described and its location must be stated, but failure to state location does not affect validity of mortgage if model or serial number given. (T. 9, §5352, as am'd Act 701 of 1987 and Act 920 of 1988). Mortgage may limit recourse against mortgagor. (C. C. Art. 3291, as am'd Act 238 of 1980).

Sufficiency of Description of Property.—Mortgage on lumber, logs, staves, crossties, tiles, bricks, loose cotton, cotton seed and its by-products, livestock, poultry, stocks of merchandise, furniture, fixtures, equipment, inventory, or other things in bulk but changing in specifics, with location set out, is valid, and proper description in bulk is sufficient for all purposes. (T. 9, §5351, am'd Act 312 of 1972 and Act 920 of 1988, §5352; T. 32, §710, as am'd Act 419 of 1983).

Recording.—Chattel mortgage is valid as between parties as of date of their signing written act of mortgage. Instrument must be notarized, but need not be witnessed or be signed in presence of notary public. Executory process foreclosure requires instrument be passed by authentic act executed before notary public and two witnesses or by private act duly acknowledged by party or subscribing witness before notary public. In order to affect third persons either multiple original of mortgage or notice of security interest must be recorded in office of recorder of mortgages in parish in which mortgagor has place of business. (T. 9, §5353, as am'd Act 920 of 1988). Lien is effective from filing for recordation, which filing is notice to all persons in state. However, holders of chattel mortgages cannot enforce their rights against bona fide purchasers from dealers, wholesalers or retailers duly licensed to sell type of merchandise covered by mortgage. Lien primes all mortgages, liens, privileges or preferences arising subsequent to recordation. (T. 9. §§5353-5355, as am'd Act of 189 of 1986 and Act 920 of 1988). Certified copy of mortgage may be recorded in lieu of original. (T. 9, §5353, as am'd Act 703 of 1975). See also category Documents and Records, topic Records, subhead Fees.

Recorded collateral chattel mortgage on changing inventory primes vendor's privilege arising from sale to dealer after recordation of such mortgage except as to bona fide retail purchaser. (T. 9, §5354.1, as am'd Act 283 of 1985 and Act 920 of 1988). Special rules of recordation and effectiveness govern chattel mortgages on mobile homes. (T. 9, §§1149.1 et seq., as am'd Act 574 of 1984).

Holders of Foreign Security Interests.—Ordinarily holders of security interests created out-of-state must file such interest of record in East Baton Rouge Parish within 60 days of notice that property transferred into state. If such interest is created on movable property subject to titling under foreign motor vehicle statute, recordation requirement does not apply, provided certificate of title has been issued and clearly shows creation of such security interest in state where title was issued. (T. 9, §§5353 [G], as am'd Act 920 of 1988, 5353 [J], 5354).

Reinscription.—Chattel mortgage or notice of security interest must be reinscribed before expiration of one year after date of last installment provided for in mortgage, or five years after date of execution, whichever is later, or ten years as to collateral chattel mortgages; and thereafter every two years. Fee $2. (T. 9, §5356, am'd Act 920 of 1988).

Floating Stock.—Stocks of merchandise in retail, wholesale and manufacturing establishments, furniture, fixtures, equipment, inventory, or other things in bulk, but changing in specifics, may be subject of chattel mortgage; however, effect of mortgage ceases as to articles disposed of by mortgagor up to time of foreclosure, but attaches to purchases made to supply their place. (T. 9, §§5351, 5352, am'd Act 920 of 1988).

Incorporeal Rights.—Chattel mortgage may provide lien on incorporeal rights incidental or accessory to mortgaged property or its use, such as proceeds from sale, lease, insurance loss or condemnation. (T. 9, §5386, added Act 985 of 1988).

Attachment of Mortgaged Property to Immovable.—When movable property previously mortgaged is located on immovable property in such manner as to make it immovable, it nevertheless remains movable in so far as such mortgage is concerned and shall not pass by sale of immovable, and no sale or mortgage of immovable property affects or impairs lien of chattel mortgage or remedies for its enforcement. (T. 9, §5357, as am'd Act 728 of 1978; see also T. 6, §1862 as am'd Act 728 of 1978).

Removal of Property.—It is a misdemeanor for the owner of mortgaged movable property to remove it from the parish where it was located at the time the mortgage was executed without the consent of the mortgagee. (T. 9, §5359).

Purchaser from nonresident of his parish takes subject to the mortgage, and unless he obtains from the seller an affidavit that the property is not mortgaged he is liable to mortgagee for debt secured by property. (T. 9, §5362 as am'd Act 731 of 1988).

Satisfaction may be entered of record by mortgagee or holder of mortgage note, or release may be granted in form used for release of mortgage on immovable. (See topic Mortgages of Real Property.) Fee of recorder, $1. (T. 9, §5356).

Cancellation.—Except as to judicial sale, no chattel mortgage may be cancelled, removed from public records or affected by public or private sale in any succession, liquidation, insolvency, receivership, bankruptcy or partition proceeding. (T. 9, §5251, added Act 356 of 1980).

Foreclosure.—A chattel mortgage is ordinarily foreclosed in same manner as conventional mortgage on real estate and same rules apply with respect to deficiency (T. 9, §5363); however, special streamlined procedures are available to certain creditors as to certain chattels other than household goods (T. 6, §§965-967, added Act 235 of 1992, eff. Jan. 1, 1993 but not effective in Orleans Parish). See topic Mortgages of Real Property. Foreclosure by executory process is permitted whether mortgage is by authentic act or by act under private signature duly acknowledged (T. 9, §5363), and whether transfer or negotiation of bearer paper is by authentic act or by act under private signature duly acknowledged (T. 13, §4102, added Act 178 of 1982). Party enforcing right to seizure and sale of motor vehicle located out of state may use procedural laws of that state or of Louisiana. If he does so, he may at his option return vehicle to Louisiana and sell it at private sale without appraisal if permitted by mortgage instrument. Such sale satisfies debt and does not permit deficiency judgment. (C.C.P. 2725, as am'd Act 106 of 1986). Ex parte repossession of mobile homes permitted if home has been abandoned, mortgagor has not paid minimum of two consecutive monthly payments, and petition in court of competent jurisdiction has been filed seeking ex parte order authorizing secured party to proceed. Bond must be posted, affidavit of abandonment completed, and satisfactory proof of mortgage must be shown. Ten-day notice on front door of mobile home prior to repossession as well as newspaper advertisement. Mortgagor may waive some of these requirements. (T. 9, §5363.1, added Act 367 of 1983).

Redemption.—There is no right of redemption.

Form.—There is no statutory form of mortgage. Following is sufficient:

Form

(Caption: "Collateral Chattel Mortgage" in ten bold type, if appropriate)

CHATTEL MORTGAGES ... *continued*

United States of America: State of Louisiana: Parish of . . . . .: Before me, ..., a notary public duly commissioned and qualified within and for the parish of . . . . . ., State of Louisiana, and in the presence of the witnesses hereinafter named and undersigned, personally came and appeared . . . . ., resident of . . . . ., who declared and acknowledged to me notary, that . . . . . justly, truly and legally indebted unto . . . . . in the just and full sum of . . . . . . dollars, lawful money of the United States of America; and for the reimbursement of which sum, and as evidence of said indebtedness . . . . . . made and subscribed . . . . . certain . . . . . . promissory note . . . . . . for the sum of . . . . . .dollars, made payable to the order of . . . . . . as follows: . . . . . . and bearing interest at the rate of . . . . . .% per annum from . . . . . . until paid, interest payable annually, interest and principal payable at . . . . . .; which said promissory note . . . . . . after having been paraphed "Ne Varietur" by me, notary, of even date herewith, to identify . . . . . herewith . . . . . been delivered to . . . . ., who . . . . . . present, accept . . . . . . this act of mortgage and acknowledge . . . . . . due receipt of said note . . . . . . And now, in order to secure the full, punctual, and final payment of said note . . . . . . at maturity together with all interest accrued thereon, and furthermore, to secure the payment and reimbursement of any and all attorney's fees, costs, charges and expenses that may be incurred or paid, in the event that it becomes necessary to place said note . . . . . . at maturity in the hands of an attorney at law for collection, by suit or otherwise, which attorney's fees are hereby fixed at the sum of . . . . . .% of the aggregate amount due on said note, the said . . . . . . do . . . . . . by these presents specially mortgage, affect and hypothecate unto and in favor of the said . . . . . ., and to inure to the benefit of any future holder or holders of said note . . . . . . the said . . . . . . being here present and accepting the following described property to-wit: (insert description sufficient to identify property, giving statement of location). Being the same property which the present mortgagor acquired . . . . . . The said property to remain mortgaged, affected and hypothecated until the full and final payment of the said note . . . . . . in principal, interest, attorney's fees, costs, charges and expenses aforesaid. And the said mortgagor . . . . . . do . . . . . by these presents hereby bind and obligate . . . . . . heirs and assigns not to sell, alienate, deteriorate, encumber the said property herein mortgaged to the prejudice of this mortgage; nor to remove said property out of this parish without the written consent of the mortgagee. And the said mortgagor . . . . . . further declare . . . . . . that . . . . . . consent . . . . . . agree . . . . . . and stipulate that in the event such promissory note . . . . . . not paid at maturity, it shall be lawful for the said mortgagee . . . . . ., and . . . . . . do . . . . . . hereby authorize the said mortgagee . . . . . ., or any future holder or holders of said note . . . . . ., to cause all and singular the property hereinbefore described and mortgaged to be seized and sold under executory or other legal process, issued by any court of competent jurisdiction, without appraisement to the highest bidder paying cash, in the manner and form provided by and pursuant to the provisions of the laws of the state; the said mortgagor . . . . . . hereby confessing judgment in favor of the said mortgagee . . . . . . of any future holder or holders of said note . . . . . . for the full sum thereof in principal, interest, attorney's fees, costs, charges and expenses of whatsoever nature; and hereby expressly waiving (1) the benefit of appraisement of said property in the event of its seizure and sale under judicial process, as required by Arts. 2332, 2336, 2723 and 2724, Louisiana Code of Civil Procedure; (2) the three days delay and notice to the debtor required by Arts. 2639 and 2721, Louisiana Code of Civil Procedure; (3) the notice of seizure required by Arts. 2293 and 2721, Louisiana Code of Civil Procedure; (4) the three days delay required by Arts. 2331 and 2722, Louisiana Code of Civil Procedure; and (5) the benefits of the other provisions of Arts. 2331, 2722 and 2723, Louisiana Code of Civil Procedure, not specifically mentioned above. Mortgagee or his agent may act as consent keeper and the sheriff, constable or justice of the peace making the seizure shall be released from liability on account thereof. And the said mortgagor . . . . . . hereby specially declared that . . . . . . the true and lawful owner . . . . . . of the movable property hereinabove described and mortgaged, and that same has not been heretofore alienated by the present mortgagor. According to certificate of the clerk of court and ex-officio recorder in and for the parish of . . . . . . (in parish or Orleans, "recorder of mortgages for the parish of Orleans") annexed hereto it appears that said property is clear of all encumbrances (or certificate may be waived as follows: "The parties hereto waive the mortgage certificate in the name of the mortgagor and exonerate me, notary, from all responsibility for the non-production of same and its nonannexation to this act"). Thus done and passed at . . . . . ., in the parish of . . . . . ., State of Louisiana, on this . . . . . day of . . . . . ., A. D. 19. . . . ., in the presence of . . . . . . and . . . . . ., two competent witnesses, who sign these presents with appearers and me, notary, after due reading of the whole.

Witnesses:

. . . .
. . . .
                                    . . . . .Notary Public.

The following is the form of paraph to be written across the face of the note by the notary public:

Ne Varietur—For identification with an Act of Chattel Mortgage passed before me this . . . . . . day of . . . . . ., 19. . . . . ., at . . . . . ., State of . . . . . .
                                    . . . .
                                    Notary Public.

Above form should be modified if used as collateral mortgage to state maximum amount of future advances.

The usual security clauses contained in real estate mortgages (see topic Mortgages of Real Property) may be included.

For form where mortgagor is a corporation and form of sale and mortgage, see category Property, topic Deeds.

Statutory form of notice of security interest is as follows (T. 9, §5353[C], as am'd Act 920 of 1988):

FORM

"Notice of Security Interest

Date _____

(Mortgagor) has granted a Louisiana chattel mortgage/Louisiana collateral chattel mortgage. The obligation secured by the mortgage is in favor of . . . . and payable at . . . . . . and matures on . . . . or is otherwise described as follows:

_____

The chattel mortgagor's domicile, registered office, or principal place of business, as applicable, is

_____
(Street Address)
_____
(City)
_____
(Parish)

The chattels mortgaged are generally described as follows:
_____
(Specific Items)
_____
(Inventory)
_____
(Masses or Assemblages)
_____
(Other)

The holder of the obligation at the time of the filing of this notice is _____ whose business address is
_____
(Street Address)
_____
(City)
_____
(Parish and/or County)
_____
(State)
_____
(Chattel Mortgagor)
_____
Holder of Obligation
Secured by Chattel Mortgage
or Collateral Chattel Mortgage"

Notice is not required to be notarized or witnessed.

COLLATERAL SECURITY:

See category Debtor and Creditor, topic Pledges.

MORTGAGES OF PERSONAL PROPERTY:

See topic Chattel Mortgages.

MORTGAGES OF REAL PROPERTY:

Mortgage Defined.—Generally, mortgage is nonpossessory right created over property to secure performance of obligation. (C.C. 3278). Mortgage gives mortgagee, upon failure of obligor to perform obligation that mortgage secures, right to cause seizure of property and sale in manner provided by law and to have proceeds applied to satisfaction of obligation in preference to claims of others. (C.C. 3279). Mortgage is indivisible real right that burdens entirety of mortgaged property and follows property into whatever hands it may pass. (C.C. 3280).

Limited Nature.—Mortgage may be established only as authorized by legislation. (C.C. 3281).

Accessory Nature.—Mortgage is accessory to obligation it secures. Mortgagee may thus enforce mortgage only to extent that he may enforce obligation it secures. (C.C. 3282).

Kinds of Mortgages.—Mortgage is conventional, legal or judicial, and with respect to manner in which it burdens property, is general or special. (C.C. 3283). Conventional mortgage is established by contract; legal, by operation of law; and judicial, by law to secure judgment. (C.C. 3284). General mortgage burdens all present and future property of mortgagor; special mortgage burdens only certain specified property of mortgagor. (C.C. 3285).

Mortgageable Property.—Only things susceptible of mortgage are: (1) corporeal immovable with its component parts; (2) usufruct of corporeal immovable; (3) servitude of right of use; (4) lessee's rights in lease of immovable; and (5) property made susceptible of conventional mortgage by special law, such as chattel mortgages, railroad property and ships under construction. (C.C. 3286, as am'd Act 649 of 1992, eff. July 1, 1993; T. 9, §§5521-5537).

Conventional Mortgages.—Conventional mortgage may be established only by written contract, but no special words are required. (C.C. 3287). Contract must state precisely nature and situation of each of immovables or other property; amount of obligation; and must be signed by mortgagor. (C.C. 3288). Contract need not be signed by mortgagee, whose consent is presumed and whose acceptance may be tacit. (C.C. 3289). Conventional mortgage may be established only by person having power to alienate property so mortgaged. (C.C. 3290). Special mortgage given by contract over property mortgagor does not own is established when property is acquired by mortgagor; general conventional mortgage is permitted only when expressly provided by law. (C.C. 3291). Conventional mortgage may be established to secure performance of any lawful obligation, even one for performance of act, and conventional mortgage may have term and be subject to condition. (C.C. 3293).

Future Property.—Mortgage may secure obligations that may arise in future. Mortgage has effect between parties from time it is established and as to third persons from

---

See note at head of Digest as to 1998 legislation covered.

See Topical Index in front part of this volume.

MORTGAGES OF REAL PROPERTY . . . *continued*
time contract of mortgage is filed for registry. Promissory note or other evidence of indebtedness secured by mortgage of future property need not be paraphed for identification with mortgage, nor need it recite that it is secured by mortgage. Mortgage continues until terminated by mortgagor if obligation no longer exists, or upon extinguishment in some other lawful manner. (C.C. 3298, as am'd Act 779 of 1992).

Extinction.—Mortgage is extinguished: (1) by extinction or destruction of thing mortgaged; (2) by confusion as result of obligee's acquiring ownership of thing mortgaged; (3) by prescription of obligations mortgage secures; (4) by discharge through execution or other judicial proceeding in accordance with law; (5) by consent of mortgagee; (6) by termination of mortgage as provided by law; and (7) when all obligations, present and future, for which mortgage is established have been incurred and are extinguished. (C.C. 3319).

Legal mortgages exist in favor of minors, persons interdicted and absentees, against property of their tutors and curators to secure fidelity of their administration. This mortgage results from recordation of bond given by tutor or curator, as case may be, or when no bond is given from recordation of abstract of inventory of property and effects of minor, interdict or absentee. (C.C.P. 4061, 4101, 4134). Forfeitures of property bonds to secure appearance of criminal defendants have effect of mortgage. (T. 15, §85.1, added Act 342 of 1983).

Judicial mortgage, resulting from the recordation of a judgment, operates against all property mortgagable under C.C. 3286 of judgment debtor which he may own at time of recordation, or may subsequently acquire. (C.C. 3300, 3302, 3303).

The recordation of a foreign judgment will not operate as a mortgage unless or until that judgment has been made executory by a tribunal of this state. (C.C. 3305). Judgments of federal district courts in Louisiana, or those of other districts registered in accordance with 28 USC §1963, do operate as judicial mortgages without being made executory. (T. 13, §4204, as am'd Act 986 of 1988).

Recordation.—Mortgage must be recorded in the office of the recorder of mortgages for the parish wherein the property lies, in order to be effective against third persons, unless parties agree in writing that recordation shall not occur. (C.C. 3370, as am'd Act 666 of 1987). If debtor has immovable property lying in more than one parish, inscription must be made in office of recorder of mortgages for each parish. (C. C. 3346-7). For recording fees, see category Documents and Records, topic Records. Disposition of original instrument after record is same as in case of deed. (See category Property, topic Deeds.) Mortgages must include social security number or employer identification number of mortgagor, but absence of number does not affect validity. (T. 9, §5141, as am'd Act 322 of 1991, eff. Jan. 1, 1992). Clerk may not refuse to accept for recordation instrument which lacks social security number or taxpayer identification number, however. (T. 9, §5141[D], added Act 39 of 1993).

Mortgage of movables used in commercial or industrial activity must be recorded in same manner as chattel mortgage. (T. 9, §5369, added Act 235 of 1980 repealed effective July 1, 1989 by Act 528 of 1988, see category Business Regulation and Commerce, topic Commercial Code).

Mortgage inscription may be cancelled by presentation to mortgage office of original note or notes marked paid if notes are paraphed for identification with mortgage as required by Art. 3384 of Civil Code. (T. 9, §5167, added Act 579 of 1974). If note is lost or destroyed, procedure for cancellation by use of affidavit exists. (T. 9, §5168, as am'd Act 362 of 1991).

Except as to judicial sales in executory proceedings or execution of judgments, no conventional or judicial mortgage may be cancelled, removed from public records or affected by public or private sale in any succession, liquidation, insolvency, receivership, bankruptcy or partition proceeding. (T. 9, §5251, as am'd Act 894 of 1981).

Priorities.—Among creditors the rank of mortgages is determined by the time of their recordation. (C. C. 3329). Regarding collateral mortgages, see T.9, §5550 et seq., added by Act 137 of 1989, effective Sept. 1, 1989.

Reinscription.—Except in the case of legal mortgages, and in certain other cases expressly provided by statute, mortgages maturing less than nine years from date, to preserve their effect as against third persons, must be reinscribed every ten years. Where obligations secured mature after nine years, reinscription is not necessary until six years after maturity of last obligation. (C. C. 3369).

Foreclosure.—Extra-judicial sale is not permitted. Mortgage must be foreclosed through courts in order to provoke sale. There are two modes of foreclosure: (1) Ordinary process and (2) executory process.

Ordinary process involves the filing of a suit with citation to the debtor and the usual delay for answering, followed by a judgment as in ordinary cases, the judgment recognizing the lien of the mortgage. Thereafter, a writ of fieri facias is issued and the property sold, the mortgage creditor being paid with preference out of the proceeds.

Executory process may be invoked when the mortgage has been granted in an authentic act, executed before a notary and two witnesses, in which the obligor declares and acknowledges the obligation, whether then existing or thereafter to arise, to which the mortgage relates. (C.C.P. 2631). Executory proceeding to enforce mortgage may be brought in parish where property located or of defendant's domicile. (C.C.P. 2633 as am'd Act 117 of 1989). Holder of mortgage note files in court a petition to which he attaches original note and certified copy of mortgage, whereupon court enters an order for issuance of executory process. (C.C.P. 2634). Notice of demand is served upon debtor (C.C.P. 2639), and if payment is not made within three days, writ of seizure and sale addressed to sheriff is issued, whereupon mortgaged property is seized. Notice of seizure is served on debtor, and three days thereafter property is advertised for sale. Advertisement is run once a week for 30 days, and property is then sold at public auction by sheriff, plaintiff being paid with preference out of proceeds. (C.C.P. 2721 et seq). *Caveat:* Fuentes v. Shevin, 407 U.S. 67, 92 S. Ct. 1983, 32 L. Ed. 2d 556 (1972), held notice and an opportunity to a hearing prior to seizure of property constitutionally essential under due process clause. But see Buckner v. Carmack, 272 So.2d 326, in which Louisiana Supreme Court distinguished Louisiana executory process from Fuentes condemnation.

Person desiring notification of seizure of specific immovable property must file request for such notice in mortgage records, stating legal description of property, name of owner and name of person desiring notice. $10 fee for such recordation. Desire for such notice will appear on mortgage certificate, and sheriff should then notify. But failure to notify does not invalidate sale or affect rights of seizing creditor. (T. 13, §3886, added Act 615 of 1982).

Action to annul sale of immovable property by reason of any objection to form of proceedings or lack of authentic evidence must be filed before sheriff files proces verbal or filed sale in conveyance office. (T. 13, §4112, added Act 681 of 1975).

If mortgage is legal, judicial, or conventional, foreclosing creditor may ignore any sale of property made by mortgagor and proceed as though mortgagor still had title and was in possession. (C.C.P. 3741).

Evidence in authentic form is required to support order for executory process in cases provided by law. By this is meant properly certified copy or duplicate original of act of mortgage, mortgage note properly paraphed by notary, certified copy of authorizing or ratifying resolution of corporate board of directors for mortgage on corporate property, certified copy of contract of partnership authorizing execution of mortgage, etc. (C.C.P. 2635 and 2626, as am'd Acts 177, 185 and 259 of 1982). Certain kinds of evidence need not be submitted in authentic form: Evidence as to proper party defendant, or necessity for appointing attorney to represent unrepresented defendant, or agreement to extend or modify obligation to pay, or written notification of default, or name change, merger, purchase and assumption of financial institution, or name change or death of any party, or breach of condition in mortgage, or of advances made by holder of collateral mortgage note or note for future advances. (C.C.P. 2637, as am'd Act 161 of 1989, eff. June 22, 1989). If mortgage is collateral mortgage, existence of actual indebtedness may be shown by petition with evidence of handnotes attached. (C.C.P. 2637, as am'd Act 185 of 1983). Authentic evidence requirements also not applicable to holders of bearer paper with reference to transfer, assignment, pledge or negotiation of such paper. (T. 13, §4102, added Act 178 of 1982). Proper form for certifying copies when required may be found in T. 13, §4102. (Added Act 178 of 1982). Signatures of endorsers, guarantors and others on instruments secured by mortgage are presumed genuine, and written evidence of assignment, pledge, or transfer of instrument shall be deemed authentic for purposes of executory process. (T.9, §4422, added Act 292 of 1989).

If defendant in executory proceeding arrests seizure and sale of property by injunction and court determines seizure to be wrongful, damages may be awarded, including attorney's fees. (C.C.P. 2751, as am'd Act 302 of 1981). Security must accompany request to enjoin seizure and sale except in specified instances. (C.C.P. 2753, as am'd Act 341 of 1983).

Except as provided in articles of partnership, person authorized to execute mortgage on behalf of partnership may, for purposes of executory process, execute confession of judgment in act of mortgage without execution of articles of partnership by authentic act. (C. C. 2814, as am'd Act 888 of 1981).

In an application for executory process against property mortgaged by a corporation, a copy of resolution of board of directors authorizing execution of mortgage signed and certified by secretary or such copy attached to original act of mortgage and certified by notary before whom act was passed, or by custodian of notarial records in Orleans Parish or Clerk of Court in parishes other than Orleans, is sufficient evidence of authority of officer or agent to execute same and no authentic or further proof of such authority or of existence of corporation or board of directors or of personnel or authority of board to grant such authority is necessary. (T. 13, §4103, as am'd Act 489 of 1986; C.C.P. 2636).

When debtor's succession is not under administration or has not been accepted by heirs, mortgage creditor may proceed in rem contradictorily with heirs or against an attorney at law appointed by court to represent the succession. (C.C.P. 2672-2674).

Person designated by parties in mortgage instrument or in another acknowledged instrument, or by mortgagee or agent if so provided in such instrument, shall be designated keeper of property, but owner of home and of property containing not more than four dwelling units must be designated keeper during his occupancy. (T. 9, §§5136-5140.1, as am'd Act 226 of 1977).

Deficiency Judgment.—Creditor may obtain deficiency judgment either by converting executory proceeding into ordinary proceeding or by separate suit. (C.C.P. 2772).

When seizing creditor takes advantage of waiver of appraisement contained in act of mortgage and proceeds of sale are insufficient, debt nevertheless stands discharged. (T. 13, §4106).

Redemption.—There is no right of redemption after foreclosure sale.

Deeds of trust are not permitted in Louisiana, except that a mortgage may be given to secure the payment of two or more bonds, notes, or other obligations and in such mortgage a trustee for the holders of the obligations may be named as mortgagee and vested with full power to enforce the mortgage for the benefit of the holders of the obligations. (T. 9, §§5301-5302). Such mortgage may also pledge incorporeal movables such as credits and other claims. The provisions of law relative to substitutions, fidei commissa and trust dispositions shall not affect such mortgages. Such mortgage may provide that the trustee shall not be obliged to foreclose unless the holders of a designated portion of the obligations specified in the mortgage shall request the trustee to act. Such mortgage may be enforced by seizure and sale or otherwise as trustee deems expedient. The interest of the holders of the obligations is in common and indivisible, and in the event of foreclosure and sale of the mortgaged property, they are entitled to participate pro rata in the proceeds. (T. 9, §§4303-4307).

Form of Mortgage.—It is advisable that a Louisiana notary or commissioner should prepare a mortgage, or that preparation should be in charge of local counsel. The following form is in use:

Form

United States of America: State of Louisiana: parish of Orleans: city of New Orleans. Be it known, That on this . . . . . . day of the month of . . . . . . in the year of our Lord 19. . . . . ., before me, ..., a notary public, duly commissioned and qualified, in and for this city and the parish of Orleans, therein residing, and in the presence of the

See note at head of Digest as to 1998 legislation covered.

See Topical Index in front part of this volume.

MORTGAGES OF REAL PROPERTY . . . *continued*

witnesses hereinafter named and undersigned, personally came and appeared: (state name of party) hereinafter referred to as "Mortgagor," of full age of majority and a resident of the Parish (or County) of . . ., State of . . . . . ., who, being first duly sworn, did depose and say:

(Here give the marital status required by T. 35, §11 following forms suggested in title Deeds, q.v.).

Which said appearer declared and acknowledged that he is justly and truly indebted unto . . . . . ., of full age of majority and a resident of the parish (or county) of . . . . ., State of . . . . . ., hereinafter referred to as "Mortgagee," in the full and true sum of . . . . . dollars, for the reimbursement whereof he has made and subscribed his one certain promissory note for the sum of . . . . . . dollars, to the order of and endorsed in blank by himself, dated . . . . . and made payable at the . . . . ., ... after date, with interest thereon at the rate of . . . . . per cent, per annum from . . . . . . until paid, interest payable annually, which said note, after having been paraphed "Ne Varietur" by me, notary, to be herewith identified, has been delivered unto . . . . . ., mortgagee, who hereby acknowledges receipt of said note.

If on default it shall become necessary to place said note in the hands of an attorney at law for collection, or to recover the amount due on said note, or any part thereof, or any other amount due by the mortgagor under the terms thereof, through legal proceedings of any character, the said mortgagor binds himself to pay the fees of the attorney at law who may be employed for that purpose, which fees are hereby fixed at the sum of . . . . . . per cent, of the amount due on said note.

Now, in order to secure the full and punctual payment of said note and interest when same shall be due, together with said attorney's fees, and to secure the faithful performance of all of the obligations hereinafter mentioned and the reimbursement and payment of premiums of insurance, taxes and assessments and interest due thereon, and all costs and charges hereinafter specified, the said mortgagor declared that he does, by these presents, mortgage, affect and specially hypothecate, in favor of the said mortgagee and to inure to the use and benefit of any and all holder or holders of said promissory note, the said mortgagee being here present and accepting, the following described property, to-wit: (Here insert description of property with reference to acquisition, that is, "being the same property that was acquired by purchase by . . . . . ., Mortgagor, from . . . . . ., as per act passed before . . . . . ., Notary Public, dated . . . . . ., registered in the Conveyance Records of . . . . . Parish, Louisiana, in Book . . . . . ., Folio . . . . . .").

The said property so to remain mortgaged and hypothecated until the full and final payment of the aforesaid promissory note in capital and interest and of all amounts secured by this mortgage, the said mortgagor binding himself and his heirs not to sell, alienate or encumber the same to the prejudice of these presents.

The mortgagor hereby confesses judgment in favor of said mortgagee for the full amount thereof, principal and interest, together with all fees, costs, charges, expenses, insurance premiums, taxes and assessments that may become due, in accordance with the terms hereof, and consents, agrees and stipulates that in the event the said promissory note is not punctually paid at its maturity, either fixed or determined as hereinafter provided, or in the event any sum due hereunder is not punctually paid when due, it shall be lawful for and he does hereby authorize the said mortgagee to cause all and singular the said hereinabove described and herein mortgaged property to be seized and sold under executory or other legal process, issued by any competent court, without appraisement, mortgagor hereby expressly waiving (1) the benefit of appraisement of said property in the event of its seizure and sale under judicial process, as required by Arts. 2332, 2336, 2723 and 2724, Louisiana Code of Civil Procedure; (2) the three days delay and notice to the debtor required by Arts. 2639 and 2721, Louisiana Code of Civil Procedure; (3) the notice of seizure required by Arts. 2293 and 2721, Louisiana Code of Civil Procedure; (4) the three days delay required by Arts. 2331 and 2722, Louisiana Code of Civil Procedure; and (5) the benefits of the other provisions of Arts. 2331, 2722 and 2723. Louisiana Code of Civil Procedure, not specifically mentioned above; and does further agree that in the event of any such sale the property may be sold at the option of the mortgagee either as a whole or in such lots and parcels as the said mortgagee may elect.

The said mortgagor declared that he does agree and stipulate as follows:

First: To keep the buildings and improvements on the above described and herein mortgage property constantly insured against loss by fire in an amount not less than . . . . . . dollars, until the full and final payment of said note, and all amounts due hereunder, in companies acceptable to the mortgagee, and to transfer such insurance and deliver the policies to the mortgagee, hereby authorizing said mortgagee to cause said insurance to be effected upon his default.

Second: To pay, punctually when due, all taxes and assessments which may be levied on said mortgaged property, hereby authorizing said mortgagee to pay same on mortgagor's default.

Third: In the event the mortgagor fails to effect the insurance above provided, or to transfer and deliver same as above stipulated, or fails to pay taxes or assessments as above provided, and the mortgagee effects such insurance and pays the premiums due therefor, or pays the taxes or assessments above referred to, the amounts so paid by mortgagee shall immediately become due and payable by the mortgagor to the mortgagee, with interest at the rate of eight (8%) per cent, per annum until paid, and such amounts with interest as aforesaid shall, up to the sum of . . . . . . dollars, be deemed a part of the debt secured by this Act of Mortgage; Provided, however, that none of the above provisions shall be construed as obliging the mortgagee to effect such insurance or pay the premiums therefor, or pay the taxes or assessments above referred to, or as making the mortgagee liable for loss, damage or injury, in the event the mortgagee fails so to do.

Fourth: In the event of the happening of any one or more of the following events, termed events of default, to wit: (a) Default in the payment of the principal or interest of said note when due; (b) Default in the performance by mortgagor of any one of the above covenants and agreements relating to procuring and transferring of insurance, delivery of policies, and payment of taxes or assessments; (c) Application by the mortgagor for a respite; (d) Voluntary application by the mortgagor to be adjudicated a

bankrupt; (e) Institution of proceedings against mortgagor to have him declared an involuntary bankrupt; (f) Institution of proceedings against mortgagor looking to the appointment of a receiver or syndic; (g) Seizure of the property herein mortgaged, or any portion thereof, under a writ of attachment, or fieri facias, or other legal process; then, the whole indebtedness hereby secured shall, at the option of the mortgagee, at once become due and exigible.

The failure of the mortgagee to exercise any option to declare the maturity of the principal debt, or any other sums hereby secured, shall not be taken or deemed a waiver of right to exercise such option or declare such maturity as to such past or any subsequent violation of any of said covenants or stipulations.

All covenants by mortgagor in favor of mortgagee and all rights hereby conferred on mortgagee shall enure to the benefit of any present or future holder or holders of said note.

The mortgagor does hereby waive, in favor of the mortgagee, as regards the property hereinabove described and hereby mortgaged, any and all homestead exemptions to which he is or may be entitled under the Constitution and Laws of the State of Louisiana.

And now, to these presents, came and intervened Mrs. . . . . . ., wife of said mortgagor, being duly authorized by her said husband, who declared that she hereby joins her said husband in the waiver of homestead exemptions hereinabove stipulated.

According to the certificates of the Register of Conveyances and Recorder of Mortgages (outside the Parish of Orleans, the Clerk of Court and Ex-Officio Register of Conveyances and Recorder of Mortgages, it being noted, however, that Clerks of Court are not required by law to issue Conveyance Certificates and that some Clerks make a practice of not so doing and that it is not essential to the Act outside the Parish of Orleans that a Conveyance Certificate be annexed), in and for the Parish of . . . . . ., State of Louisiana, annexed hereto, it appears that said property has not been heretofore alienated by the present mortgagor, and is free of all encumbrances (except such alienations or encumbrances as may be listed on the Conveyance and Mortgage Certificates which should be enumerated here). [Or certificates may be waived. See topic Chattel Mortgages].

All State and City (or Parish) taxes up to and including the taxes due and exigible in the year of . . . . . . are paid, as per tax researches annexed hereto.

Thus done and passed at . . . . . ., in the Parish (or County) of . . . . . ., State of . . . . . . on the day and in the month and year first hereinabove written, in the presence of . . . . . . and . . . . . ., competent witnesses, who have hereunto signed their names with the said appearers and me, Notary, after due reading of the whole.
Witnesses:

. . . .

. . . .
                                                                    Mortgagor.
                                                                . . . .
                                                             Wife of Mortgagor.
                                                                . . . .
                                                                    Mortgagee.
                                                                . . . .
                                                                 Notary Public.

_____

Names of parties, witnesses and notary must be printed or typed under their respective signatures. See also category Property, topic Deeds, subhead Community Property.

Municipal address of property, if any, must be recited in description of property, along with social security number of employer tax identification number of mortgagor. (T. 35, §17).

Mortgages of specified rural property must contain prepayment clause pursuant to T. 9, §§5321-5326, as am'd Act 308 of 1983.

Any of the security clauses and the homestead waiver contained in the above form may, of course, be omitted, as the parties may desire.

The following is the form of paraph to be written across face of mortgage note by Notary Public:

Ne Varietur—For identification with an Act of Mortgage passed before me this . . . . . . day of . . . . . ., 19. . . ., at . . . . . ., State of . . . . . .

                                                                . . . .
                                                                 Notary Public.

_____

Where mortgagor is a corporation, describe officer executing instrument as indicated in category Property, topic Deeds, and make other variations required by the situation.

Act of Sale and Mortgage.—For form see category Property, topic Deeds.

Assignment of Mortgage.—Transfer of note secured by mortgage carries the mortgage with it, but endorsement of note must be evidenced by authentic act to preserve right to invoke executory process. No transfer, assignment or termination of right of mineral right is effective upon person dealing with mortgagee until 30 days after delivery to third person of certified or duplicate original copy of said act. (T. 31, art. 205).

Satisfaction of Mortgage.—Following form of full and complete release of mortgage is in general use:

Form

State of . . . . . .
Parish (or County) of . . . . . .
Personally before me, the undersigned authority, a Notary Public in and for the Parish (or County) of . . . . . ., State of . . . . . ., there came and appeared . . . . . ., of full age of majority and a resident of . . . . . ., State of . . . . . ., who exhibited to me, Notary, as fully paid, cancelled and acquitted, a promissory note drawn and subscribed by . . . . . ., to the order of and endorsed by . . . . . ., for the sum of . . . . . . dollars, dated the . . . . . . day of . . . . . ., 19. . . ., identified by . . . . . ., Notary, on the . . . . . . day of . . . . . ., 19. . . ., with an Act of . . . . . ., passed before him on said date and secured by mortgage granted in said Act upon the property more fully described in said Act.

And the said appearer declared that the said described note having been fully paid, he does hereby, as the last holder thereof, grant a full release of the above recited mortgage

_____

See note at head of Digest as to 1998 legislation covered.

See Topical Index in front part of this volume.

MORTGAGES OF REAL PROPERTY . . . *continued*

which secured its payment, hereby authorizing and requesting the Recorder of Mortgages (or outside New Orleans, the Clerk of Court and Ex-Officio Recorder of Mortgages) for the Parish of Orleans, State of Louisiana, to cancel and erase entirely on his records the inscription of said mortgage as the same appears recorded in his office in Book . . . . . ., Folio . . . . . .

Whereupon, I, the said Notary, have canceled the signatures and notarial paraph on the said note and have annexed said note to the margin hereof for future reference.

Thus done and passed at . . . . . ., State of . . . . . ., on the . . . . . . day of . . . . . ., in the presence of . . . . . . and . . . . . ., the undersigned competent witnesses, who have signed hereto with the said appearer and with me, Notary, after due reading of the whole.

Witnesses:

. . . .

. . . .
                                                                        Appearer.

                                                                        . . . .
                                                                        Notary Public.

If a portion, represented by a note, of the mortgage indebtedness has been paid, and a partial release is to be granted as to all of the mortgaged property, substitute in the foregoing form, at the appropriate place, the following:

"And the said appearer declared, that the said described note having been paid, he does hereby, as last holder thereof, release the above recited mortgage so far as securing the payment of said note only, but no further, hereby authorizing and requesting the Recorder of Mortgages (or outside of New Orleans, Clerk of Court and Ex-Officio Recorder of Mortgages) for the Parish of . . . . . ., State of Louisiana, to make mention of the partial release of mortgage herein granted as aforesaid, on the margin of the record of said mortgage in his office, in Book . . . . . ., Folio . . . . . ."

If a portion of the note evidencing the mortgage indebtedness has been paid, omit the words "as fully paid, cancelled and acquitted" and substitute at the appropriate place the following:

"And the said appearer declared, that the sum of . . . . . . dollars having been paid on the principal of the above described note, he does hereby, as last holder thereof, release the above recited mortgage so far as securing the payment of said amount thus paid only, but no further, hereby authorizing and requesting the Recorder of Mortgages (or Clerk of Court and Ex-Officio Recorder of Mortgages) for the Parish of . . . . . ., State of Louisiana, to make mention of the partial release of mortgage herein granted as aforesaid, on the margin of the record of said mortgage, in his office, in Book . . . . . ., Folio . . . . . ."

"Whereupon, I, the said Notary, have paraphed said note for identification with this Act of Partial Release, and have delivered same to said appearer, who hereby acknowledges receipt thereof."

If only a portion of the mortgaged property is to be released, omit the words "as fully paid, cancelled and acquitted," if there has been only a payment on account of the mortgage note, and substitute, at the appropriate place, the following:

"And the said appearer declared that the sum of . . . . . . dollars having been paid on account of said note (or, if an entire note has been paid, say 'the said described note having been paid'), he does hereby, as last holder thereof, release the above recited mortgage so far as same bears upon the following described property, to-wit: (Insert description of property to be released from mortgage)

but no further, hereby authorizing and requesting the Recorder of Mortgages (or Clerk of Court and Ex-Officio Recorder of Mortgages) for the Parish of . . . . . ., State of Louisiana, to make mention of the partial release of mortgage herein granted as aforesaid, on the margin of the record of the said mortgage in his office, in Book . . . . . ., Folio . . . . . ."

If the note has been only partly paid, the following clause should be added and the note paraphed as above indicated:

"Whereupon, I, the said Notary, have paraphed said note for identification with this Act of Partial Release and have delivered same to said appearer, who hereby acknowledges receipt thereof."

In this case the form of paraph to be written across the face of the note by the notary is as follows:

Ne Varietur—For identification with an Act of Partial Release of Mortgage passed before me this . . . . . . day of . . . . . ., 19. . . ., at . . . . . ., State of . . . . . .

                                                                        . . . .
                                                                        Notary Public.

See also subhead Assignment of Mortgage, supra.

Chattel Mortgages.—See topic Chattel Mortgages.

See also categories Business Regulation and Commerce, topic Sales; Property, topic Powers of Attorney, subhead Conveyance or Mortgage by Attorney.

PROPERTY

ABSENTEES:

Curator of Absentee's Property.—Absent person is one who has no representative in state and whose whereabouts are unknown and cannot be ascertained by diligent effort. If such person owns property, court may upon petition of interested party and showing of necessity, appoint curator to manage property. (C.C. 47, as am'd Act 989 of 1990, eff. Jan. 1, 1991; T. 9, §§3421-3445, added Act 989 of 1990, eff. Jan. 1, 1991). Such curator has power of both administration and disposition over property, as provided by law (T. 9, §§3437 through 3440, added Act 989 of 1990, eff. Jan. 1, 1991); but when absentee is spouse in community, curatorship is limited to separate property (C.C. 48, as am'd Act 989 of 1990, eff. Jan. 1, 1991).

Legal Capacity of Absentee.—Creation of curatorship does not deprive absentee of juridical capacity, but his own acts of disposition of immovable property are not effective toward curator or third persons unless filed in public records of parish of location of immovable property. (C.C. 49, as am'd Act 989 of 1990, eff. Jan. 1, 1991).

Termination.—Such curatorship terminates when absentee appoints person to represent him in state, when his whereabouts are known, or when he dies. (C.C. 50, as am'd Act 989 of 1990, eff. Jan. 1, 1991). Curatorship also terminates when judgment of declaration of death is rendered, due to presumption of death due to long absence. (C.C. 51, as am'd Act 989 of 1990, eff. Jan. 1, 1991).

Accounting.—Upon termination of curatorship, curator must account for management and restore property to formerly absent person or his successors. (C.C. 52, as am'd Act 989 of 1990, eff. Jan. 1, 1991). When curator acquires knowledge of termination of curatorship, he must file notice to that effect in curatorship proceeding; acts of administration or disposition after termination are valid until filing of that notice. (C.C. 53, as am'd Act 989 of 1990, eff. Jan. 1, 1991).

Declaration of Death.—Person satisfying definition of absentee for five years is presumed dead, and upon petition by interested party, court shall render declaration of such death and determine effective date of death. (C.C. 54, as am'd Act 989 of 1990, eff. Jan. 1, 1991). Such declaration opens succession as of date of death so determined, and property devolves under applicable law of succession. (C.C. 55, as am'd Act 989 of 1990, eff. Jan. 1, 1991). If person reappears, he is entitled to recover his property that still exists in condition in which it is found, from those who took it as his successors, or from their transferees by gratuitous title; and he may also recover net proceeds of things alienated and for diminution of value of things resulting from their encumbrance. (C.C. 57, as am'd Act 989 of 1990, eff. Jan. 1, 1991).

Management of Community.—When spouse is absentee, other spouse may be authorized by court to manage, alienate or lease community property that otherwise absentee would have exclusive right to administer. (C.C. 2355.1, added Act 989 of 1990, eff. Jan. 1, 1991).

Presumption of Death.—When person has disappeared under circumstances such that death seems certain, his death is considered to have been established even though his body has not been found. (C.C. 30, added Act 989 of 1990, eff. Jan. 1, 1991).

Attorney for Absentee.—If absent defendant has not been served with process or has not made general appearance, court will appoint attorney to represent such absent person. (C.C.P. 5091).

Monies Due Absentee.—Holder of money or other abandoned property must report such property to Secretary of Department of Revenue and Taxation and deliver it to him after time specified. Revised Uniform Disposition of Unclaimed Property Act adopted. (T. 9, §§151-182, as am'd Act 829 of 1986).

Estates of Military Personnel.—Property of military personnel missing under circumstances strongly indicating death and whose "death" has been accepted by military authorities may be turned over to heirs forthwith. (T. 9, §1441).

Partition by Co-Owner.—Owner of undivided interest in immovable property may sue for partition against absentee or unknown co-owner, with court appointing attorney to represent such co-owner. (C.C.P. 4623).

ADVERSE POSSESSION:

Adverse possession is termed "acquisitive prescription" in Louisiana.

Immovables.—Continuous and uninterrupted possession of an immovable for ten years under just title acquired in good faith will establish ownership, even as against absentees and incompetents, including minors and interdicts. (C.C. 3474, added Act 187 of 1982). Such possession for 30 years establishes ownership without need of title and regardless of good faith. No prescription as between husband and wife, parents and children during minority, tutors and minors during tutorship, and curators and interdicts during interdiction. (C.C. 3469, added Act 187 of 1982).

Movables.—Uninterrupted possession of a movable for three years in good faith and under just title establishes ownership. Such possession for ten years establishes ownership without need of title or good faith. (C. C. 3490, 3491).

Easements.—Apparent servitudes may be acquired by ten years peaceful and uninterrupted possession in good faith and just title, and by 30 years uninterrupted possession without title or good faith. (C. C. 742, as am'd Act 514 of 1977).

CONVEYANCES:

See topic Deeds.

CURTESY:

Unknown to the law of Louisiana. See category Estates and Trusts, topic Descent and Distribution, subhead Surviving Spouse.

DEEDS:

There is no statutory form of deed in Louisiana. See topic Real Property for types of estates.

Execution.—A deed, or act of sale of real estate, must be signed by the vendor, and, as a matter of practice, is usually signed by the vendee. The vendee's signature, however, is not essential, as an act of ownership is sufficient evidence of acceptance. The act should contain, first, the date and place where passed; the names, surnames and qualities of the contracting parties; their marital status; description of property; price of transfer, and terms and conditions, if sale be on credit. To prove itself it should be in authentic form, that is, passed before notary public and two witnesses. Names of parties, witnesses and notary must be printed or typed under their respective signatures. (T. 35, §12, am'd 1954, act 430).

Deed must contain total sales price, amount of mortgage, correct names and addresses of vendor and vendee, and municipal or street address of property. (T. 47, §2328; T. 35, §17).

See categories Debtor and Creditor, topic Homesteads; Family, topic Husband and Wife, subhead Community Property.

Conveyance by Attorney in Fact.—See topic Powers of Attorney, subhead Conveyance or Mortgage by Attorney.

DEEDS . . . *continued*

Tax Certificates.—Any party to act of conveying real property outside limits of municipal corporation having population of over 300,000, may obtain certificate showing whether state, parish, municipal and levee district taxes have been paid, and certificate is conclusive evidence of payment when annexed to act. (T. 9, §§2901-2904, as am'd Act 651 of 1978). In cities of over 300,000 population similar certificates evidencing full payment of paving or local improvement assessments must also be attached, but future installments may be assumed by purchaser. (T. 9, §§2921-2927). In such cities, state, parish, municipal and levee district taxes for the year in which transfer takes place, may be assumed by purchaser when same could not be paid on date of transfer. (T. 9, §2925).

Recording.—In order to operate as notice to third persons, instrument must be recorded in office of register of conveyances in parish where property is situated. (C. C. 2442; T. 9, §2721). For recording fees see category Documents and Records, topic Records.

The record of an act under private signature purporting to be a sale or exchange of real property has no effect against creditors or bona fide purchasers unless previous to being recorded it is acknowledged by the party or proved by the oath of one of the subscribing witnesses and the certificate of such acknowledgment is signed by the parish recorder, a notary, or a justice of the peace and recorded with the instrument. (C. C. 2253, 3367).

Forms.—For warranty deed the following may be used:

Form

UNITED STATES OF AMERICA

State of . . . . . .

Parish (or County) of . . . . . .

Be It Known, That on this . . . . . . day of the month of . . . . . ., in the year . . . . . .,

Before me, ..., a Notary Public duly commissioned and qualified in and for the Parish (or County) of . . . . . ., State of . . . . . ., therein residing, and in the presence of the witnesses hereinafter named and undersigned,

Personally came and appeared:

. . . . . . (State name of vendor), of full age of majority and a resident of . . . . . ., State of . . . . . ., who, being first duly sworn, did depose and say:

(Here give marital status and permanent mailing address as required by T. 35, §11 and T. 35, §12 in somewhat following form: "that he has never been married"; or "that he has been married but once and then to . . . . . ., who is now living and residing with him in the City of . . . . . ., State of . . . . . . at . . . . . .," or "from whom he was divorced by judgment of the . . . . . . Court in the proceedings entitled . . . . . . and bearing the docket number . . . . . . of said court on the . . . . . . day of . . . . . ., 19. . . ."; or "that he has been married twice, by first marriage to . . . . . ., who died on the . . . . . . day of . . . . . ., 19. . . ., and by second marriage to . . . . . ., from whom he is living separate and apart"; or whatever marital status may be, giving in all cases Christian and family name of other spouse).

and who declared that he does, by these presents, grant, bargain, sell, transfer, assign, setover, abandon and deliver, with all legal warranties and with full substitution and subrogation in and to all the rights and actions of warranty which he has or may have against all preceding owners and vendors, unto . . . . . . (State name of vendee and give marital status and address as in case of vendor), here present, accepting and purchasing for himself, his heirs and assigns, and acknowledging due delivery and possession thereof, all and singular the following described property, to-wit: (Here insert description of property with reference to acquisition).

To Have and to Hold the above described property unto the said purchaser, his heirs and assigns forever.

This sale is made and accepted for and in consideration of the price and sum of . . . . . . Dollars, which the said purchaser has well and truly paid in ready and current money to the said vendor, who hereby acknowledges the receipt thereof and grants full acquittance and discharge therefor.

According to the certificates of the Register of Conveyances and Recorder of Mortgages (outside the Parish of Orleans, the Clerk of Court and Ex-Officio Register of Conveyances and Recorder of Mortgages, it being noted, however, Clerks of Court are not required by law to issue Conveyance Certificates and that some Clerks make a practice of not so doing, and that it is not essential to the Act outside the Parish of Orleans that a Conveyance Certificate be annexed), in and for the Parish of . . . . . ., State of Louisiana, annexed hereto, it appears that said property has not been heretofore alienated by the present Vendor, and is free of all encumbrances (except such alienations or encumbrances as may be listed on the Conveyance and Mortgage Certificates which should be enumerated in the Act itself).

All State and City (or Parish) taxes up to and including the taxes due and exigible in the year of . . . . . . are paid, as per tax researches annexed hereto.

Thus Done and Passed at . . . . . ., State of . . . . . ., on the day and in the month and year first hereinabove written, the presence of . . . . . . and . . . . . ., the undersigned competent witnesses who have signed these presents together with said appearers and me, Notary, after due reading of the whole.

Witnesses:

. . . . Vendor.

. . . . Vendee.

. . . .
Notary Public.

Description of property must include municipal number, if any. (T. 35, §16, added Act 444 of 1979).

When grantor is a corporation, after name and residence of officer executing deed, insert: "who declared that he is . . . . . . of . . . . . ., a corporation organized under the laws of the state of . . . . . ., domiciled in . . . . . ., and that he appears and acts herein for and on behalf of said . . . . . ., hereinafter sometimes called 'vendor,' being duly authorized hereunto under and by virtue of a resolution of the board of directors of vendor, passed at a meeting held on . . . . . ., 19. . . ., a duly certified copy whereof is annexed hereto and made a part hereof; which said appearer, acting in his capacity aforesaid, declared that vendor does, by these presents, grant, etc." (continuing as in preceding form).

If certificates and tax researches are waived, the following clause may be used in the appropriate place: "The parties hereto waive the production of mortgage, conveyance and other certificates and relieve me, Notary, from any and all responsibility in connection therewith."

Quitclaim deed may be in same form as warranty deed, except that for words of alienation in such deed substitute "remise, release, sell, convey and quitclaim, without any warranty whatsoever, not even for the return of the purchase price."

Act of Sale and Mortgage.—The following form is frequently used:

(Preamble same as in warranty deed above) who declared to me, notary, that he does by these presents, grant, bargain, sell, convey, transfer, assign, set over, abandon and deliver, with all legal warranties and with full substitution and subrogation in and to all the rights and actions of warranty which he has or may have against all preceding owners and vendors, unto (name, address, domicile and marital status of vendee), here present, accepting and purchasing for himself, his heirs and assigns, and acknowledging due delivery and possession thereof, all and singular the following described property, to-wit: (description of property).

To have and to hold the above described property unto the said purchaser, his heirs and assigns forever.

This sale is made and accepted for and in consideration of the price and sum of . . . . . . dollars, in part payment whereof said vendee has paid in ready and current money the sum of . . . . . . dollars to the said vendor, who hereby acknowledges the receipt thereof and grants full acquittance and discharge therefor, and for the balance of said purchase price, to-wit: the sum of . . . . . . dollars, the said purchaser has furnished . . . . . . promissory note . . . . . ., each for the sum of . . . . . ., dated . . . . . . and payable . . . . . ., bearing interest at the rate of . . . . . . per cent per annum from . . . . . . until paid, which said note . . . . . . after having been paraphed "Ne Varietur" by me Notary, to be identified herewith . . . . . . delivered to the said vendor, who hereby acknowledges the receipt thereof. (The remaining portion of the act may be drafted following the form under Mortgages, except, of course, it is not necessary to repeat the description of the property. Retention of vendor's lien may be expressed by inserting immediately before the words, "the said mortgagor declared that he does by these presents, mortgage, affect and specially hypothecate," the words, "vendor's lien and privilege are retained, and").

Community Property.—See category Family, topic Husband and Wife. Wife must sign mortgage in all parishes in order to waive homestead exemption from seizure of $15,000. (Const. of 1921, art. 11, §§1-4; Const., art. 11, §9, and art. 14, §34). See also category Debtor and Creditor, topic Homesteads.

DEEDS OF TRUST:

See category Mortgages, topic Mortgages of Real Property.

DOWER:

As it exists at common law is unknown in Louisiana. See category Estates and Trusts, topic Descent and Distribution, subhead Surviving Spouse.

ESCHEAT:

See topic Absentees; categories Business Regulation and Commerce, topic Banks and Banking, subhead Unclaimed Deposits; and Estates and Trusts, topic Descent and Distribution, subhead Escheat.

LANDLORD AND TENANT:

All corporeal things are susceptible of being let out, movable as well as immovable, excepting those which cannot be used without being destroyed by that very use. (C. C. 2678). Leases of movables governed by Lease of Movables Act, providing comprehensively for definition and regulation of financed leases as defined; permissible charges; remedies after default; including limited self-help repossession; insurance; and miscellaneous requirements. (T. 9, §§3301-3342, as am'd Act 592 of 1985, eff. July 13, 1985).

Leases may be by written or verbal contract. (C. C. 2683). If no term is specified, a lease of a house is presumed to be by the month. (C. C. 2685); of a country estate by the year (C. C. 2687). If tenant continues on a farm for a month after lease expires lease is renewed for a year (C. C. 2688); if in a house for a week, lease is renewed for a month (C. C. 2689).

Lease must be recorded to affect bona fide purchaser of real property. (C. C. 2264). Extract of lease may be recorded rather than entire lease. Extract must include names and signatures of lessor and lessee; date of execution; brief description of leased premises; term; reference to renewal or purchase options, if any. (T. 9, §2721.1, added Act 1053 of 1986). Acquirer of property takes subject to prior recorded leases and provisions therein for payment of commissions. (T. 9, §2721, as am'd Act 974 of 1992). Mere possession is not equivalent to recordation. (30 La Ann. 436). Property description must include municipal number, if any. (T. 35, §17, added Act 578 of 1985).

Obligations of Lessor.—Landlord or lessor must deliver thing leased in good condition to tenant or lessee; maintain the thing in condition to serve for use for which leased; cause tenant to be in peaceable possession; make during the lease all repairs which may accidentally become necessary. (C. C. 2692-3). Lessor is liable for any damages to lessee from defects in leased premises, whether or not he knew of them. (C. C. 2695). But lessee may, by stipulation in lease, exempt lessor from liability for unknown defects. (T. 9, §3221). Landlord or his successor must return any security deposit to lessee within one month of termination, unless all or part retained to remedy lessee's default. (T. 9, §§3251-3254 as am'd Act 578 of 1985). When lessee has been constructively evicted or when premises are rendered uninhabitable through no fault of lessee, lessor must mitigate his damages. (T. 9, §3260, added Act 906 of 1993).

See note at head of Digest as to 1998 legislation covered.

See Topical Index in front part of this volume.

LA – 50

LANDLORD AND TENANT . . . *continued*

Obligations of Lessee.—Lessee or tenant is bound to enjoy thing leased as good administrator, according to use for which it was intended by lease; to pay rent at terms agreed on: to make following repairs at his expense, if it becomes necessary, during lease: to hearth, back of chimney and chimney casing; to plastering of lower part of interior walls; to pavement of rooms, when partially broken, but not when in state of decay; replace window glass, when broken accidentally, but not when broken either in whole or in their greatest part by a hail storm or by any other inevitable accident; to windows, shutters, partitions, shop windows, locks and hinges, and everything of that kind, according to the custom of the place. (C. C. 2710, 2716). Lessee of dwelling liable for reasonable attorney fees for failure to pay rent within 20 days following delivery of written demand. (T. 9, §3259, added Act 478 of 1978).

Rights of Lessee.—Tenant or lessee has right to sub-lease, unless contrary agreement. (C. C. 2725). Has right to remove improvements and additions made by him, with consent of owner. (C. C. Art. 493, added Act 180 of 1979).

Lessee may mortgage lease, but without affecting lessor's rights. Mortgage not good against third persons until recorded. (T. 9, §5102).

Violation of Lease.—A party violating a lease of land is liable for damages equal to the market value of average crop, which could be grown on such land located in immediate vicinity. Third person enticing, aiding or abetting violation by tenant is subject to solidary liability. (T. 9, §§3201-3203). Cancellation of lease of movable, and sequestration thereof provided for. (T. 9, §§3261-3271, added Act 114 of 1974).

Lien.—Landlord or lessor has, for the payment of his rent and other obligations of lease, a right of pledge on movable effects of lessee or tenant or on those of third persons, unless transiently upon the leased premises, except clothes and linen of lessee and those of his wife and family, his bed, bedding and bedstead and those of his wife and family; his arms, military accoutrements, and the tools and instruments necessary for the exercise of the trade or profession by which he gains his living and that of his family: cooking stoves and utensils of stove, plates, dishes, knives, forks, spoons, pots, pans, and other cooking utensils, and dining table and chairs necessary for lessee and family. (C. C. 2705-2708). This right of pledge extends to property of sublessee on leased premises, up to amount subtenant owes to lessee. (C. C. 2706). If property seized is that of third person, he may recover property by intervention in sale proceeding under C.C.P. 1092. (C.C. 2707, am'd Act 66 of 1984). On failure or death of lessee using property for mercantile purpose, right limited to rent for six months after death or failure against original lessee. (T. 9, §3241).

Landlord's lien has priority over a chattel mortgage, when the chattel mortgage is recorded after the property has been put upon the leased premises. (157 La. 39, 101 So. 864). Lessor of land for mobile home or manufactured housing may collect fees from mortgagees. (T. 9, §3259.1, added Act 531 of 1985).

Seizure of Property for Rent.—When lessor sues for rent whether same is due or not, he may obtain sequestration of such property without security, and it is sufficient for him to swear that it is within lessee's power to conceal, dispose of, or waste the property or revenues therefrom, or remove same from the parish, and thereby destroy the privilege. (C.C.P. 3571, 3572, 3575). The lessee is permitted to obtain release of sequestered property by furnishing security equal to $1^1/_4$ value of property, or $1^1/_4$ amount of claim whichever is the lesser. (C.C.P. 3507). Perishable property may be sold without advertisement or appraisement. (C.C.P. 2333, 3513). If rent paid when due, lessor must pay costs of sequestration proceeding. (C.C.P. 3572).

The lessor may seize, even in hands of a third person, property of lessee which lessee removed from the premises, without lessor's consent, within 15 days of removal, or so long as property remains in custodia legis, if property was removed by sheriff or other court officer. (C. C. 2709, am'd Act 30 of 1960).

Dispossession.—Lessor, desiring to obtain possession of leased premises on termination of lease by limitation, nonpayment of rent or other breach, must demand in writing that tenant remove within five days from delivery of notice. If lease has no definite term, notice must be given five days before termination. If lease is for definite term, notice must be given 30 days before end of term. (C.C.P. 4701). Lessee may waive notice requirements in writing in lease, and if so, lessor may institute eviction proceedings without notice. (C.C.P. 4701, as am'd Act 713 of 1981). If tenant refused to comply with notice, or has waived requirement of notice, lessor may cause him to be cited summarily to show cause, within two days after service of rule, why he should not be condemned to deliver up possession. (C.C.P. 4731, 4732). Upon reasonable belief that premises are abandoned as defined, lessor may take possession after notice and before court order. (C.C. 4731, as am'd Act 684 of 1991). If on trial of rule, tenant is adjudged to deliver up possession but does not comply within 24 hours thereafter, justice or judge who rendered judgment must forthwith issue his warrant directed to constable, marshal or sheriff, commanding him forthwith to deliver to lessor full possession by clearing premises of any property therein, in presence of two witnesses. On obtaining warrant, officer may, if necessary, break open doors, windows or gates of leased premises in order to put lessor in possession. (C.C.P. 4733, 4734; T. 9, §3322, as am'd Act 344 of 1990).

Uniform Residential Landlord and Tenant Act.—Not adopted.

LEASES:

See topic Landlord and Tenant.

PERPETUITIES:

The Louisiana law does not countenance the suspension of absolute ownership of or of the power to alienate real or personal property. The creation of future estates is not permitted, but all estates must vest immediately. (C. C. 1520). Private educational, charitable or religious trusts and mixed educational, charitable and religious and private trusts are authorized. (T. 9, §1721 et seq.). A trust instrument may provide for substitute principal beneficiaries, including a class, if principal beneficiary should die intestate and without descendants. (T. 9, §§1972-1977, am'd Act 160 of 1974).

PERSONAL PROPERTY:

Tenancy by the entirety in personalty not permitted by laws of Louisiana. (C. C. 494). Leases of movable (personal) property are governed by special provisions. (T. 9, §3302 et seq., as am'd Act 213 of 1986).

POWERS OF ATTORNEY:

A mandate, procuration or power of attorney is an act by which one person gives power to another to transact for him and in his name, one or several affairs. (C. C. 2985).

The object of the mandate must be lawful, and the power conferred must be one which the principal himself has a right to exercise. (C. C. 2987).

The procuration is gratuitous unless there has been a contrary agreement. (C. C. 2991).

A power of attorney may be given, either by a public act or by a writing under private signature, even by letter. It may also be given verbally, but of this testimonial proof is admitted only conformably to the rules applicable to ordinary contracts. (C. C. 2992).

It may be either general for all affairs or special for one affair only. (C. C. 2994). Person may by power of attorney nominate curator of his person, his property or both, should he later be interdicted. Court must appoint person so nominated unless otherwise disqualified or deemed not in best interest of interdict. (C.C.P. 4550, as am'd Act 304 of 1981).

The power must be express and special for the following purposes: to sell or to buy; to incumber or hypothecate; to accept or reject a succession; to contract a loan or acknowledge a debt; to draw or indorse bills of exchange or promissory notes; to compromise or refer a matter to arbitration; to make health care decisions; to make transaction in matters of litigation; and in general where things to be done are not merely acts of administration, or such as facilitate such acts. Neither property nor its location need be specifically described. (C. C. 2997, as am'd Act 184 of 1990).

Action to set aside document containing statement that power of attorney is attached thereto, on ground that executing party was without authority or that power of attorney is otherwise invalid, is prescribed by ten years from date on which document was recorded, even though power of attorney is not actually attached to recorded document. (T. 9, §5682, added Act 481 of 1982).

Expiration of Agency.—Power of attorney terminates: When revoked by principal, when agent resigns or renounces power, upon death of principal or agent, upon issuance of order of relief in bankruptcy in favor of principal or agent, upon interdiction of agent, upon qualification of curator after interdiction of principal, upon occurrence of resolutory condition stipulated in power, or when purpose for which power given is destroyed or disposed of by principal. Unless otherwise provided by its terms, power is not terminated by principal's incapacity, disability or other condition making express revocation impossible or impractical. Persons entitled to protection of public records may rely upon recorded power until terminated of record. (C. C. 3027, as am'd Act 303 of 1981).

If principal die or lose civil rights, acts done by agent before knowledge of such fact are valid and bind principal. (C. C. 3032).

Express mandate from one spouse to another authorizing transactions with specified creditor may be revoked only by delivery of written revocation. (T. 9, §3850, added Act 511 of 1978).

Conveyance or Mortgage by Attorney.—An act of sale or mortgage of real estate may be executed by an attorney in fact. The power of attorney in such a case must be express (C. C. 2997), but need not be either by authentic act or by act under private signature duly acknowledged, and may be given any sort of writing, even by letter (C. C. 2992). Nevertheless it is customary to grant such a power of attorney by authentic act or act under private signature duly acknowledged. A suggested form of such authentic act is as follows:

Form

UNITED STATES OF AMERICA
STATE OF . . . .
COUNTY OF . . . .

BE IT KNOWN, That on this . . . . . day in the month of . . . . ., in the year . . . . . ,

BEFORE ME, ..., a Notary Public duly commissioned and qualified in and for the State and County aforesaid, therein residing and in the presence of the witnesses hereinafter undersigned,

PERSONALLY CAME AND APPEARED:

. . . . . ., of full age of majority and a resident of the City of . . . . ., County of . . . . . ., State of . . . . . ., who declared that he has made and appointed and does by these presents make, nominate, ordain, authorize, constitute and appoint, and in his place and stead depute and put . . . . . . to be appearer's true and lawful attorney in fact, giving and by these presents granting unto the said attorney full power and authority for appearer, and in appearer's name and behalf, and to appearer's use

(Here are included powers granted. Power to sell or mortgage real estate must be specifically granted and description of real estate must be set forth in Power of Attorney)

and generally to do and perform all and every other act, matter and thing whatsoever as shall or may be requisite or necessary in the premises, as in the sole discretion of said attorney may seem requisite or proper, all as fully, amply and effectually, and to all intents and purposes with the same validity as if all and every such act, matter, or thing, were or had been particularly stated, expressed and especially provided for, or as appearer could or might do if personally present; also with full power of substitution and revocation; and the said appearer hereby agrees to ratify and confirm all and whatsoever the said attorney shall lawfully do or cause to be done by virtue of this Act of Procuration.

Thus done and passed in my notarial office in the City of . . . . ., County of . . . . ., State of . . . . . ., on the day and date aforesaid, in the presence of the undersigned competent witnesses, who hereunto sign their names as such, together with the said appearer and me Notary, after due reading of the whole.

See note at head of Digest as to 1998 legislation covered.

See Topical Index in front part of this volume.

LA – 51

POWERS OF ATTORNEY . . . *continued*
WITNESSES:

. . . .
                                                              APPEARER
. . . .

. . . .
NOTARY PUBLIC
—————————

REAL PROPERTY:

This state does not recognize any of the common law estates, such as tenancy in common, joint tenancy, tenancy by the entirety, etc., the law being in this respect based on the French civil law and not the English common law.

There is, however, in this state a species of ownership which is similar to the common law life estate. That is the usufruct that a person has on property, of which the naked ownership is vested in another. Where two or more persons own in common, such ownership is termed as ownership in indivision or in joint ownership.

Ownership in Indivision.—Ownership of same thing by two or more persons is ownership in indivision. In absence of other provisions of law or juridical act, shares of all co-owners are presumed to be equal. (C.C. 797, added Act 990 of 1990, eff. Jan. 1, 1991). Co-owners share fruits and products of things held in co-ownership in proportion to their ownership; when such fruits or products are produced by co-owner, others are entitled to shares after deduction of costs of production. (C.C. 798, added Act 990 of 1990, eff. Jan. 1, 1991). Co-owner is liable to other co-owners for any damage to thing held in indivision through his fault. (C.C. 799, added Act 990 of 1990, eff. Jan. 1, 1991). Co-owner may take necessary steps for preservation of thing without concurrence of any other co-owner. (C.C. 800, added Act 900 of 1990, eff. Jan. 1, 1991). Use and management of thing is determined by agreement of all co-owners. (C.C. 801, added Act 990 of 1990, eff. Jan. 1, 1991). Co-owner may freely lease, alienate or encumber his share, but consent of all co-owners is required for similar actions as to entire thing. (C.C. 805, added act 990 of 1990, eff. Jan. 1, 1991). Reimbursement of expenses of one co-owner in proportion to shares of other owners is required. (C.C. 806, added Act 990 of 1990, eff. Jan. 1, 1991).

Partition.—No one may be compelled to hold thing in indivision with another unless contrary has been provided by law or juridical act, and any co-owner has right to demand partition of thing held in indivision; partition may be excluded by agreement for up to 15 years. (C.C. 807, added Act 990 of 1990, eff. Jan. 1, 1991). Partition may not be obtained when use of thing is indispensable for enjoyment of another thing owned by one or more of co-owners. (C.C. 808, added Act 990 of 1990, eff. Jan. 1, 1991). Mode of partition may be determined by agreement of all co-owners, but in absence of such agreement, co-owner may demand judicial partition. (C.C. 809, added Act 990 of 1990, eff. Jan. 1, 1991). Partition may be in kind, by licitation or by private sale. (C.C. 810-811, added Act 990 of 1990, eff. Jan. 1, 1991). Real rights are not affected by partition in kind or by licitation; when thing is partitioned in kind, real right burdening share of co-owner attaches to part of thing allotted to him. (C.C. 812-813, added Act 990 of 1990, eff. Jan. 1, 1991). Extrajudicial partition may be rescinded on account of lesion if value of part received by co-owner is less by more than one fourth of fair market value of portion he should have received. (C.C. 814, added Act 99 0 of 1990, eff. Jan. 1, 1991). Action for partition is not subject to any prescriptive period. (C.C. 817, added Act 990 of 1990, eff. Jan. 1, 1991).

Building restrictions are governed by C. C. 775-783, added Act 310 of 1980). Building restrictions terminate as provided in act which establishes them. In absence of such provision, restrictions may be wholly or partially amended or terminated by agreement of owners representing more than one-half of land area affected if restrictions have been in effect for 15 years or more, or by agreement of owners representing two-thirds of affected land area and two-thirds of number of owners of affected land if restrictions have been in effect for more than ten years. (C.C. 780, as am'd Act 129 of 1983).

Civil Rights Act for Handicapped prohibits discrimination against handicapped persons with respect to all forms of real estate transactions. Handicapped persons may bring action for all relief including compensatory damages, attorneys' fees and costs. Action must be brought within 180 days from date of discovery but not in excess of one year from date of discriminatory act. (T. 46, §§2251-2256, added Act 665 of 1980).

Condominiums are permitted under Louisiana Condominium Act. (T. 9, §§1121-1142, as am'd Act 552 of 1983).

Real estate investment trusts are authorized. (T. 12, §§491-493).

See also topics Curtesy, Deeds, Dower, Landlord and Tenant; categories Business Organizations, topic Associations; Business Regulation and Commerce, topic Consumer Protection; Civil Actions and Procedure, topic Partition; Debtor and Creditor, topic Homesteads; Family, topic Husband and Wife; Mortgages, topic Mortgages of Real Property; Documents and Records, topic Records.

TRUST DEEDS:

See category Mortgages, topic Mortgages of Real Property.

TAXATION

General supervision is in Collector of Revenue (T. 47, §651) and in Louisiana Tax Commission as to property taxes (T. 47, §1837, as am'd Act 385 of 1977). Taxpayer's Bill of Rights exists. (T. 47, §15, added Act 136 of First Ex. Sess. of 1998, eff. May 5, 1998.

ADMINISTRATION:

New Industry Exemption.—Upon recommendation of State Board of Commerce and Industry, Louisiana Tax Commission may enter into contracts with new manufacturing establishments under certain conditions, granting exemption from corporation franchise tax, corporation income tax, sales and use tax, and other taxes imposed on like business. (T. 47, §§3201-3206, as am'd Act 381 of 1976).

Penalties.—With reference to taxes imposed in T. 47, Subtitle II, §§21-1700 (income, sales, occupational license, vehicle registration license, corporation franchise, general severance, reforestation severance, royalty gas excise tax, petroleum products, tobacco, soft drinks, alcoholic beverages, utilities, chain store, power use and gift taxes), interest is added to delinquent taxes at rate of $1\frac{1}{4}$% per month from due date until paid. (T. 47, §1601, as am'd Act 853 of 1982). For failure to timely file returns for such taxes, penalty of 5% per month not to exceed 25% is added. (T. 47, §1602). If return is filed with less than full remittance, penalty is assessed only on amount not paid. (T. 47, §1602, as am'd Act 43 of 1986, eff. Oct. 1, 1986). Delinquencies bearing penalties under $5,000 not due to negligence of taxpayer may be waived by secretary of Revenue Department; over that amount, approval of tax appeal board required. (T. 47, §1603, as am'd Act 43 of 1986, eff. Oct. 1, 1986). Additionally, fine of not more than $500 or imprisonment for not more than six months may be imposed if income tax return is not filed within 90 days after final date for filing. (T. 47, §107). For failing to file return or for making incorrect return under circumstances indicating willful negligence or intentional disregard of rules and regulations, but with no intent to defraud, there is additional charge of 5% of tax due or $10, whichever is greater. (T. 47, §1604.1). If return is false, fraudulent or grossly incorrect under circumstances indicating intent to defraud, penalty of 50% of tax found due is charged. (T. 47, §1604). Wilful failure to report or wilful false return can result in criminal penalties of $1,000 or imprisonment for not more than one year or both. (T. 47, §1642). If tax is collected by distraint procedure, there is additional $10 penalty. (T. 47, §§1601-1605.1).

Ad valorem taxes bear interest at rate of 10% per annum from date such taxes are due until paid. (T. 47, §2101, as am'd Act 615 of 1974).

Inheritance taxes bear interest at rate of $\frac{1}{2}$% per month commencing nine months after death of decedent and 1% per month beginning 12 months after death of decedent. Running of interest on tax due from individual heir, legatee or donee may be stopped by payment of tax with interest. Interest may be remitted if beneficiary is ignorant of inheritance or if there is bona fide contest of succession. Extension of time within which inheritance taxes may be fixed and paid, without interest or penalty, may be granted by court upon showing of reasonable cause. If succession is required to file federal estate tax return, court must grant extension of time not to exceed 15 months after date of decedent's death. (T. 47, §2420 as am'd Act 202 of 1973).

Unemployment compensation taxes bear interest at rate of 1% per month from due date and penalty on both contributions and interest of 5% for each month, not to exceed aggregate penalty of 25%. (T. 23, §1543).

Parishes, municipalities and other taxing authorities impose various other penalties with respect to specific taxes levied by them.

Suits for Refund of Tax Paid Under Protest.—Suits for refund of taxes paid under protest, after appropriate notice to collector, may be brought only in state court. (T. 47, §1576[B] and [C], as am'd Act 245 of 1983).

ALCOHOLIC BEVERAGES TAX:

Alcoholic beverages tax is imposed by T. 26, §§341-741. Surcharge imposed by Act 7 of 1st Ex. Sess. of 1984 repealed by Act 855 of 1985.

AUTOMOBILE RENTAL TAX:

Tax of $2\frac{1}{2}$% of total amount of short-term (less than 29 days) automobile rental contract is imposed from Aug. 1, 1990 through June 30, 2000. (T. 47, §550).

BUSINESS LICENSE TAXES OR FEES:

See categories Business Regulation and Commerce, topics Factors, Licenses, Business and Professional; Insurance, topic Insurance Companies.

CHAIN STORE TAX:

Chain stores operating in Louisiana are subject to an annual graduated license tax by parishes and/or municipalities at a rate fixed by total number of units in chain, whether or not located in parish, municipalities or Louisiana, at following rates: not more than 10 stores, $10 per store; 11 to 35 stores, $15 per store; 36 to 50 stores, $20 per store; 51 to 75 stores, $25 per store; 76 to 100 stores, $30 per store; 101 to 125 stores, $50 per store; 126 to 150 stores, $100 per store, 151 to 175 stores, $150 per store; 176 to 200 stores, $200 per store; 201 to 225 stores, $250 per store; 226 to 250 stores, $300 per store; 251 to 275 stores, $350 per store; 276 to 300 stores, $400 per store; 301 to 400 stores, $450 per store; 401 to 500 stores, $500 per store; more than 500 stores, $550 per store. (T. 47, §10, added Act 487 of 1975).

CORPORATE FRANCHISE TAX:

Corporation Franchise Tax.—See category Business Organizations, topic Corporations. Statute of limitations on actions by state concerning returns suspended if there is failure to file return. (T. 47, §1580[C], added Act 1348 of 1997, eff. July 15, 1997 and applicable to tax periods beginning after Dec. 31, 1997).

DRAINAGE TAX:

Drainage Taxes.—An acreage tax of 25¢ may be imposed on land in a drainage district to defray organization expenses of district. (T. 38, §1619). When plan for reclamation has been approved by district court, board of commissioners of district may levy a tax on all lands in district to which benefits have been assessed to pay cost of carrying out of improvements shown on plan. (T. 38, §§1602-1675).

Gravity drainage or subdrainage district may levy an acreage tax not exceeding 50¢ per acre per year. (T. 38, §1770).

Such districts may levy acreage tax not exceeding 35¢ per acre per year for maintaining, improving and repairing gravity drainage systems. (T. 38, §1901).

ESTATE TRANSFER TAX:

Estate Tax.—Estate transfer tax fixes an additional tax to maximum amount of credit allowed by U.S. Internal Revenue Code for state death taxes in determination of federal estate taxes, so that difference between such credit and amount of state inheritance tax (if less) must be paid to state. (T. 47, §2431, et seq., as am'd Act 315 of 1972 and Act 202 of 1973). Estate transfer tax return must be filed where estate tax transfer tax is due or where value of net estate amounts to $60,000 or more, within nine months after date of death or prior to filing federal return, whichever comes first. (T. 47, §2436, am'd Act 202 of 1973).

Apportionment Against Inter Vivos Dispositions.—Estate tax apportionment law enacted. (T. 9, §§2431-2438).

Interstate Co-operation.—No statutory authorization.

GARBAGE TAX:

Garbage tax of 5 mills on dollar per year may be levied on all taxable property in a garbage district to provide and maintain garbage collection and disposal service. (T. 33, §§8001-4).

GAS CONSUMPTION TAX—MANUFACTURERS' TAX CREDIT:

Manufacturers tax credit for gas consumption allowed at rate of 2¢ per 1,000 cubic feet in excess of 25,000 cubic feet, to certain manufacturers and municipalities using gas in operation of a manufacturing establishment. (T. 47, §7, am'd by Act 117 of 1976).

GASOLINE AND SPECIAL FUELS TAXES:

Gasoline tax is imposed by T. 47, §§711-727, 714.1, am'd Act 11 of 1st Ex. Sess. of 1984, 771-788 and 1681 et seq.

Special fuels tax is imposed by T. 47, §§801-815, as am'd Act 475 of 1985. Gasohol as defined is exempt. (T. 47, §802.1, added Act 793 of 1979).

GIFT TAX:

Gift tax is levied on all gifts inter vivos and on transfers for inadequate consideration to extent of value in excess of consideration. Annual exclusion: $10,000 per donee (T. 47, §1205[A], as am'd Act 773 of 1985, eff. after Dec. 31, 1985); lifetime exemption: $30,000. Rate of tax: 2% on taxable gifts up to $15,000; 3% on taxable gifts exceeding $15,000. In years after Dec. 31, 1991, all gifts to spouse are exempt from gift tax. (Act 236 of 1987). Tax is computed on total of gifts, in excess of exemptions, during tax year and all preceding tax years, and tax for particular year is excess of tax so computed over gift taxes paid for previous years. Each donor and donee must make return to Collector of Revenue and tax thereon paid for gifts made during preceding calendar year on or before Apr. 15 of each year. Collector may accept federal extensions to extend time to file state return. (T. 47, §1208, as am'd Act 104 of 1985). If donor fails to pay tax it is collectible from donee within 30 days after notice of assessment is served on him. (T. 47, §1201-1212, am'd Act 569 of 1972). Gifts by either spouse to third parties is considered made half by each for purposes of gift tax. (T. 47, §1205[C], added Act 201 of 1983). Valuation may be made by Collector according to IRS table for valuation of usufruct. (T. 47, §1203[A][2], added Act 10 of 1994, eff. July 1, 1994).

HAZARDOUS WASTE TAX:

Tax by weight is imposed on disposal and storage of hazardous waste as defined. One-time tax of $2 per dry weight ton of hazardous waste content of Louisiana land was imposed as of July 1, 1984. For future waste disposal or storage more than 90 days for incineration at sea, tax of $30 per dry weight ton is imposed for waste disposed at sites on which generator's act or process produced waste and $60 per dry weight ton for waste disposed at other sites. Tax on "extremely hazardous waste" as defined is $100 per dry weight ton. Reciprocal tax imposed: Same tax as in generating state as minimum tax on transportation of such materials also imposed. (T. 30, §1149.21 and T. 47, §§821-823, am'd Act 391 of 1990, eff. Aug. 1, 1990).

INCOME TAX:

Income tax on individuals is imposed at following rates: 2% on amount by which net income exceeds credits and exemptions applicable but does not exceed $10,000; 4% on next $40,000 or part thereof (excess over $10,000 up to $50,000); 6% on excess over $50,000. State individual and joint income tax schedule cannot exceed rates set forth in T. 47, §32 on Jan. 1, 1974; and federal income taxes paid must be allowed as a deduction. (Const., art. 7, §4). Nonresidents are taxed on income earned within or derived from Louisiana sources. (T. 47, §32). Combined personal exemptions and standard deductions are: Single person $6,000 ($4,500 after Dec. 31, 1982); married joint return and qualified surviving spouse, $12,000 ($9,000 after Dec. 31, 1982); married separate return, $6,000 ($4,500 after Dec. 31, 1982), and head of household, $12,000 ($9,000 after Dec. 31, 1982); each allowable exemption for dependents, $1,000; taxpayer who is blind, sustained loss of one or more limbs, is mentally retarded or is deaf, additional $1,000; but beginning with taxable years after Dec. 31, 1982, combined personal exemption and standard deduction is deducted from lowest (2%) tax bracket and any excess is deducted from middle (4%) bracket. (T. 47, §§79, and 294 and 296, as am'd Act 1, 2d Extraordinary Session, 1983). $6,000 of annual retirement income received by persons 65 or over is exempt from state income tax. (T. 47, §44.1, added Act 880 of 1981). All social security and railroad retirement income is exempt from state income tax. (T. 47, §44.2, added Act 298 of 1984). Credit of $25 may be allowed per child for educational expenses. (T. 47, §297, added Act 209 of 1979). Exemptions of nonresidents apportioned in ratio of Louisiana income to all income. Net income of corporations is taxed at rate of 4% on first $25,000, 5% on next $25,000, 6% on next $50,000, 7% on next $100,000, 8% on excess of $200,000. (T. 47, §32, as am'd Act 2 of 1977, First Extraordinary Session). Pending voter approval of constitutional amendment in Nov., 1984, corporate deduction for federal income tax paid limited to $1,000 for state income tax purposes. (T. 47, §§55 and 241, as am'd Acts 4 and 15 of

1st Ex. Sess. of 1984). Corporations are permitted credits for creation of new jobs for certain persons, with carryover provisions from Jan. 1, 1980. (T. 47, §287.749 added Act 16 of 1st Ex. Sess. of 1986). Corporations are required to pay estimated tax for taxable year in specified installments if estimated tax for taxable year can reasonably be expected to be $1,000 or more. (T. 47, §287.654, added Act 16 of 1st Ex. Sess. of 1986). Income received by individuals or corporations actively and primarily engaged in business of operating steamships as carriers of goods or passengers in interstate or foreign commerce or on high seas excluded from gross income and exempt. Withholding is required by every employer making payment of wages taxable by Louisiana, at rate of 1.5% of amount by which employee's wages exceed exemptions and credits unless employee provides employer with withholding exemption certificate in such form and pursuant to such regulations as prescribed by commissioner. (T. 47, §112, as am'd Act 454 of 1974). Declaration of estimated tax is due from individuals whose income tax liability can reasonably be expected to exceed $200 after credit for withholding taxes. (T. 47, §116, as am'd Act 502 of 1975). Partnerships must file information return. (T. 47, §201, as am'd Act 459 of 1975).

Statute of limitations on actions by state concerning returns suspended if there is failure to file return. (T. 47, §1580[C], added Act 1348 of 1997, eff. July 15, 1997 and applicable to tax periods beginning after Dec. 31, 1997).

For tax years beginning after Dec. 31, 1976, and prior to Jan. 1, 1983, there is provided alternative method of taxation of individuals, resident or nonresident, based upon federal income tax liability for same period with respect to adjusted gross income attributable to state. Computation of tax is determined by tables but may not exceed rates stated above. (T. 47, §§290-299, as am'd Act 288 of 1983; T. 47, §§298 [B]and [C] repealed Act 1, 2d Extraordinary Session 1983, effective for taxable years after Dec. 31, 1982).

Individual income tax returns are due May 15 if on calendar year basis and on 15th day of fifth month after close of fiscal year. Corporate income tax returns are due Apr. 15 if on calendar year basis and on 15th day of fourth month after close of fiscal year. (T. 47, §103, as am'd Act 60 of 1986, eff. for tax years beg. after Jan. 1, 1986). Forms furnished by Collector of Revenue, to whom returns are made and taxes paid. Collector may accept extensions on federal returns as extension on state return. (T. 47, §103[O], as am'd Act 104 of 1985).

Those required to file state income tax return are: (1) Individual having gross income for taxable year of $12,000 or more, regardless of tax table income; (2) individual having tax table income of $4,500 or more, if single, or married filing separate return; or (3) individual having tax table income of $9,000 or more, if married filing joint return or filing as head of household or qualifying widow or widower with dependent child. (T. 47, §101[A], as am'd Act 630 of 1985). Beginning with taxable years after Dec. 31, 1982, individuals required to file tax returns are: Single or married filing separate return with tax table income of $4,500 or more; married filing joint return, head of household or qualified widow or widower with dependent child having income of $9,000 or more. (T. 47, §292.1, as am'd Act 1, 2d Extraordinary Session, 1983).

Effective May 29, 1997, creation of no-return concept is authorized, permitting certain taxpayers subject to withholding to be exempt from filing personal income tax return. (T. 47, §296.1).

INHERITANCE TAX:

Inheritance tax is levied on all inheritances, legacies and donations in contemplation of death (T. 47, §2401) but tax is to be phased out in stages and will be completely repealed for deaths occurring after June 30, 2004 (T. 47, §§2401, 2403, as am'd Act 818 of 1997).

Valuation is as of date of death or, alternative date up to six months from date of death. (T. 47, §2403, as am'd Act 457 of 1975).

Rates and exemptions vary according to classification of beneficiaries and amount of gift, as follows:

Class 1. Surviving spouse, descendant by blood or affinity, direct ascendant or adopted child: For persons dying prior to 1984, first $5,000 exempt, 2% on next $20,000 or part thereof; 3% on excess over $25,000. Effective Jan. 1, 1984, first $10,000 exempt if death occurs during calendar 1984; first $15,000 exempt if death occurs during 1985; first $20,000 if death occurs during 1986; first $25,000 if death occurs during or after 1987; rate of tax 2% on first $20,000 over applicable exemption; 3% on excess over applicable exemption plus $20,000. (T. 47, §§2402[a] and 2403, as am'd Act 874 of 1982). In years after Dec. 31, 1991, all gifts and inheritances to and by surviving spouse are exempt from gift and inheritance tax. (Act 236 of 1987).

Class 2. Collateral relations, including brothers or sisters by affinity: First $1,000 exempt; 5% on next $20,000 or part thereof; 7% on any excess thereof.

Class 3. State of Louisiana or political subdivision; all donations for public purposes exempt. (T. 47, §2402).

Class 4. All others: First $500 exempt; 5% on next $5,000 or part thereof; 10% on any excess thereof. (T. 47, §§2402, am'd Act 543 of 1972 and 2403).

Inheritance tax covers property of residents or nonresidents in Louisiana, and personal property of Louisiana residents wherever located. (T. 47, §2404, am'd Act 512 of 1972).

Donations and legacies to charitable, religious or educational institutions located in Louisiana, and to those located in any state or territory whose laws grant reciprocal exemptions to donations and legacies to any such institutions located in this state are exempt. Proceeds of life insurance, retirement or pension plan, or trust receivable by any beneficiary other than decedent's estate are excluded from property subject to inheritance tax. (T. 47, §2402, as am'd Act 159 of 1975, §2404).

Inheritance tax return on forms provided by Collector of Revenue must be filed if inheritance tax is due or gross estate amounts to $15,000 or more. Original return must be filed in succession record, and duplicate original with required documents must be filed with collector of revenue within nine months after date of death or at time for filing of a Federal Estate Tax Return when it is required. (T. 47, §2425, am'd Act 511 of 1988). Extensions of time to file federal returns may be treated as state extensions. (T. 47, §2420, as am'd Act 104 of 1985).

See note at head of Digest as to 1998 legislation covered.

See Topical Index in front part of this volume.

INHERITANCE TAX . . . *continued*

Where no administration ordered a full statement of properties and values must be presented to the court and the tax collector within nine months from death or discovery of will. (T. 47, §2408, am'd Act 202 of 1973).

Tax must be paid within nine months after decedent's death, and if not so paid there is a penalty of one-half of 1% per month for three months and 1% a month thereafter, unless beneficiary was ignorant of inheritance or extension of time has been granted by judge having jurisdiction of succession. (T. 47, §2420, am'd Act 202 of 1973).

Collector of revenue is tax collector. (T. 47, §2417, am'd Act 202 of 1973).

Where estate does not exceed $50,000, collector of revenue may fix tax on affidavit only. (T. 47, §2410, as am'd Act 582 of 1980).

No tax is levied on intangibles belonging to a decedent not domiciled in Louisiana, no matter how such intangibles are held or used in Louisiana. (T. 47, §2404).

IRRIGATION TAX:

Irrigation tax not in excess of 10¢ per acre per year, may be imposed on land in irrigation district. (T. 38, §2116).

LEVEE TAXES:

Tax of ¼ mill may be levied on property to cover costs of land and improvements used or destroyed for levee purposes. (Const., of 1921, art. 16, §6 con't. as statute). Tax of 5 mills may be levied on all taxable property in alluvial portions of levee districts for constructing and maintaining levees. Board of Levee Commissioners of Orleans Levee District may levy tax not in excess of 2½ mills. These taxes may be increased by vote of taxpayers. (Const., art. 6, §39).

PROPERTY (AD VALOREM) TAXES:

Taxable Property.—All real property situated in this state and all personal property having situs in this state is taxable unless specially exempted by law.

Notes, judgments, accounts and credits of nonresidents originating from business done in this state have taxable situs here. (T. 47, §1702).

Effective Jan. 1, 1973, all ad valorem property taxes levied by State of Louisiana were repealed. Constitution of 1974 (art. 7, §19) limits state taxation on property for all purposes to 5¾ mills per dollar of assessed valuation.

Rates of taxation, per dollar of assessed valuation, are limited or permitted by the Constitution as follows:

Municipal tax for all purposes, seven mills, but municipality which is exempt from payment of parish taxes or which under legislative authority, maintains its own schools, may levy up to ten mills; and rate may be increased upon majority vote for that purpose. (Const., art. 6, §27). Additional special tax not exceeding one mill by municipalities of 75,000 or over to be used for three platoon police system authorized. Additional special tax not exceeding 1½ mills by municipalities of between 15,000 and 30,000 for municipal employees' benefits authorized except for policemen, firemen, and elective officers. This does not apply to City of New Orleans. (Const. of 1921, art. 14, §12, con't. as statute by Const., art. 14, §16). Municipalities operating under home rule or special charters may levy tax on real property for constructing specified public works. (Const. Art. 6, §36; Act 179 of 1975).

Parish Tax.—For general purposes Parishes may levy up to four mills per dollar, except that Orleans Parish may levy up to seven mills and Jackson Parish may levy up to five mills. Rates may be increased upon majority vote in election for that purpose. Except in Orleans, rate of parish tax is reduced by one-half on property in municipality having a population over 1,000 and which providing and maintaining a system of street paving. (Const., art. 6, §26).

Special Adjustment.—Millages are adjusted upon re-assessment of properties in accordance with Art. 7, §23 of Constitution.

Additional Taxes.—Political subdivisions may levy special taxes for public improvements if approved by majority vote. (Const., art. 6, §32).

Delinquency and Lien.—Taxes on immovable property become delinquent after Dec. 31 of year for which levied, bearing interest thereafter at 10% per annum. (T. 47, §2101). Lien expires three years after tax becomes delinquent. (T. 47, §2111).

Exemptions.—(A) All public property; (B) property owned by non-profit corporation or association exclusively for religious, burial, charitable, health, welfare, fraternal or educational purposes and declared exempt from federal and state income tax, property of bona fide labor organizations, and property of lodge or club organized for charitable or fraternal purposes, of non-profit corporations promoting trade, travel and commerce, and of trade, business, industry or professional society or association, if such is owned by non-profit corporation or association organized under laws of Louisiana for that purpose, but property under (B) is not exempt if owned for commercial purpose unrelated to exempt purpose of corporation or association; (C) cash on hand or on deposit, stocks and bonds (except bank stocks, tax on which is paid by bank), obligations secured exclusively by Louisiana property and notes or other evidence thereof, loans by life insurance companies secured solely by their policies, legal reserve of domestic insurance companies, loans secured by homestead or building and loan association to its members secured only by stock of association, debts for merchandise or articles of commerce or for services, obligations of Louisiana or its political subdivisions, personal property used in homes or on loan in a public place, irrevocably dedicated burial places of individuals for themselves or their families, agricultural products owned by producer, agricultural machinery and other agricultural implements, animals on farm, property of agricultural fair associations, property of cultural, Mardi Gras carnival or civic activities without profit to owners, rights-of-way for state highways, boats using gasoline for fuel, commercial fishing vessels for human consumption, ships and oceangoing tugs, towboats and barges in international trade and domiciled in state ports (except for port dues and except as to vessels in coastal trade); (D) raw materials, goods, and other commodities imported into state from outside U.S. while on public property of port authority or docks of common carrier where such first entered state, or while imports (other than minerals and ores of same kind as mined or produced in state and manufactured articles) are held in original form in bales or other original packages, and raw materials held in bulk for new material inventory of manufacturers

and processors solely for those purposes, or while held by an importer in original form and agricultural products in bulk (except those held by retailer as stock in trade); raw materials, goods and other commodities held for export to point outside of U.S.; property moving in inter-state commerce and stored while in transit through or over state for a final destination outside state; but property described in (D) must be reported to tax authorities, whether or not exempt; (E) motor vehicles used on Louisiana highways except for general or special taxes levied by municipalities or districts created by same unless exemption is allowed by municipalities; and (F) new manufacturing establishments or additions to manufacturing establishments by contract with State Board of Commerce and Industry with approval of governor, for an initial term of up to five years and a renewal term of up to five additional years. (Const., art. 7, §21). Crop dusting aircraft are included in definition of agricultural equipment. (T. 47, §1707, am'd Act 215 of 1980).

Homestead exemption is $7,500 of assessed valuation. (Const. art. 7, §20, as am'd Act 844 of 1980 with voter approval, and Act 432 of 1981).

There is no exemption for members of armed forces.

Residential solar energy equipment may be exempted. (T. 47, §1706, added Act 591 of 1978).

Assessment.—Property is assessed by percentage of fair market value specified at 10% for land, 10% for improvements for residential purposes, 25% for public service properties other than land, and 15% for other property. Agricultural, horticultural, marsh and timber land is assessed 10% of use value, and legislature may provide similarly for buildings of historic architectural importance. (Const. Art. 7, §18, as am'd Oct., 1979). Tax Commission determines capitalization rate, not less than 12%, for determining use value of agricultural lands. (T. 47, §2307A[3], as am'd Act 29 of 1981 First Extraordinary Session). Special assessment for five years may be allowed for structures in downtown, historic or economic development district. (T. 47, §§4311-4319, added Act 445 of 1983).

Corporations, with the exception of banks, are assessed directly on property, real and personal, owned by them.

Stock of state and national bank assessed to shareholders at domicile or location of bank at 15% of their value as determined by assessing authorities. Federal joint stock land banks assessed similarly at 15% of their value. All taxes so assessed must be paid by bank but it may collect same from shareholders or transferees. (T. 47, §§1967-1972).

Every taxpayer must file sworn list of his properties with tax assessor within 45 days after receipt of forms from assessor, or by Apr. 1, whichever is later, except for Jefferson Parish in which forms must be filed within 45 days after receipt from assessor. (T. 47, §2324, as am'd Act 695 of 1981). Failure estops him from contesting assessment. (T. 47, §1956).

Assessment rolls in parishes other than Orleans must be completed before July 1. Notice of completion is given by publication in newspaper, after which rolls are exposed in office of tax assessor for inspection and correction for 15 days. (T. 47, §1987). Assessment rolls in Orleans Parish must be completed by Aug. 1 of tax year and exposed for inspection and correction for 15 days thereafter. (T. 47, §§1987, 1992).

Manufacturers, retailers and wholesalers whose gross merchandise sales exceed $15,000 must keep inventories of assets in state showing quantity, description and value as of Jan. 1, and record of purchases and sales, such records to be open for inspection by tax assessor or any other taxing authority. (T. 47, §1961).

Assessors must place on assessment list all property subject to taxation, including merchandise or stock in trade on hand during preceding year. Inventory value of such merchandise is arrived at by computing cost or purchase price at point of origin, plus carrying charges to point of destination, and average value arrived at is basis for fixing assessable value. Crops, whether growing or gathered, are considered attached to the realty while in first hands. In assessing mercantile firms such value must be placed on stock in trade, cash and money at interest, as will represent fair average of capital employed. Nonresidents must keep in the state all books and papers pertaining to business transacted therein. (T. 47, §§1951-1961).

Holder of mortgage may demand separate assessment of mortgaged property. (T. 47, §1963).

Louisiana Tax Commission may correct or change any assessment at any time before taxes are actually paid. (T. 47, §1990).

Review of Assessment.—Objections to excessive valuation made by taxpayer during time rolls are open for inspection or correction are presented to board of reviewers for parish. (T. 47, §1992, as am'd Act 75 of 1983). Appeals of determinations of board must be made to Louisiana Tax Commission. (T. 47, §§1992 and 1989, as am'd Acts 383 and 384 of 1977). Appeal lies from decision of tax commission to district court of parish of location of property or domicile of commission, but said suit must be instituted in 30 days. (T. 47, §1989, as am'd Act 384 of 1977 and Act 609 of 1982). In Parish of Orleans public hearings during ten day period are had before Orleans Parish Board of Reviewers and revision by Louisiana Tax Commission must be completed by Oct. 15. (T. 47, §1997).

Payment.—Dates of payments of ad valorem taxes vary throughout parishes. However, payment in all cases must be paid on or before Dec. 31 of year in which assessment made. If holder of mortgage requests, notice of delinquent taxes must be given an opportunity to pay taxes within 20 days after notice. (T. 47, §2180.1, added Act 585 of 1984). Ad valorem taxes on movables involved in bulk sales are due ten days prior to transfer. (T. 47, §2101, as am'd Act 853 of 1985).

Collection of tax imposed by state or political subdivision may not be restrained; tax declared illegal may be recovered by taxpayer. (T. 47, §1989). Procedure provided for recovery of taxes paid under protest. (T. 47, §1998, as am'd Act 272 of 1995, eff. July 1, 1995).

Following year in which taxes are due, collector must give notice to delinquent, advertise for sale of property in manner provided for judicial sales, and sell property on day of sale without appraisement, all as provided by law. (Const., art. 7, §25).

Any delinquent ad valorem tax due to the state or to any political subdivision may be paid to said taxing authority in installments, and interest at the rate now or hereafter fixed by law must be collected on each installment separately at the time of the payment of such installment. (T. 47, §2106).

See note at head of Digest as to 1998 legislation covered.

See Topical Index in front part of this volume.

PROPERTY (AD VALOREM) TAXES . . . *continued*

Amount assessed by ordinance to cover improvements is due upon passage and if not paid within 30 days, parish may proceed against assessed property and owner for assessment plus 20% attorney's fees and interest to be fixed by police jury. (T. 33, §3687, as am'd Act 484 of 1970).

Tax Liens.—Copy of assessment roll must be filed with Recorder of Mortgages for the Parish of Orleans by Oct. 15 of each year. In the other parishes copy of assessment roll must be filed in the office in which mortgage records of each parish are kept on or before Nov. 15 in each calendar year. (T. 47, §1993). From the day the assessment roll is filed in the mortgage office it acts as a lien on each specific piece of real estate therein assessed. (T. 47, §1993).

State, its subdivisions and municipalities have first lien and privilege on all personal property for payment of all taxes on personal property in all judicial or insolvency proceedings, receiverships or liquidation. (T. 47, §2175).

Tax Sales.—No sale of property for taxes can be set aside for any cause except on proof of payment of taxes for which the property was sold, unless the proceeding to annul is instituted within six months from the service of notice of sale, which notice shall not be served until the time for redemption has expired, or within five years from the date of the recordation of the tax deed if no notice is given. (Const., art. 7, §25).

Redemption.—Real estate or immovable property sold for taxes can be redeemed within three years from date deed registered upon payment of tax, costs and 5% thereon, with interest at 1% per month. (Const., art. 7, §25 and T. 47, §§2171 et seq., as am'd Act 270 of 1995, eff. Dec. 31, 1995).

Municipal corporations may lease property acquired for taxes and, upon payment of all taxes, paving or local improvement assessments shall issue certificate of redemption. (T. 33, §2864, am'd Act 74 of 1966).

Subrogation to Tax Lien.—After taxes become delinquent, any person may pay same and take subrogation therefor; but when payment is made by person not holding a bond or note secured by mortgage or privilege on the property, written consent of taxpayer must be filed with tax collector. Interest so acquired may be assigned, but written evidence of assignment must be filed with tax collector. Person subrogated can request sheriff in writing to sell the property for his account, and such sale is conducted same as a tax sale. (T. 47, §2105).

REAL ESTATE CONVEYANCE TAX:

None.

SALES AND USE TAXES:

Louisiana levies 4% tax on sales at retail, use, consumption, distribution, lease or rental and storage for use and consumption, in state of tangible personal property and sale of services in state. (T. 47, §§302, 321). Telecommunications services as defined are subject to tax, but not to advance collection requirement. (T. 47, §§301, 306, 332 and 1003, as am'd Act 388, eff. Aug. 1, 1990). State tax is collected in advance by supplier of retail dealer. (T. 47, §306, as am'd Act 867 of 1985). Electricity generation tax repealed by Act 9 of 1973. Ex. Sess., eff. Jan. 1, 1974. Additional sales and use taxes are locally imposed by several parishes.

Exemptions include gasoline, steam, water (not including water in bottles, etc.), electric power or energy and any materials and energy sources used to generate electric power for resale or used by industrial manufacturing plant for self-consumption or cogeneration, newspapers, fertilizer and containers for farm products sold to farmers, natural gas; all energy sources when used for boiler fuel except refinery gas; new trucks, automobiles and aircraft withdrawn from stock by new vehicle and aircraft dealers for use as demonstrators; drugs prescribed by physician or dentist; orthotic and prosthetic devices and wheelchairs prescribed by physicians or licensed chiropractors for personal consumption or use; ostomy, ileostomy, or colostomy device or similar devices; patient aids and medical devices prescribed by physician or licensed chiropractor for home use; food sold for preparation and consumption in home; sales of tangible personal property, admission fees and parking fees associated with charitable events, and newspapers published by religious organizations (T. 47, 305.14[A][1], as am'd Act 39 of 1994); package food requiring further preparation by purchaser; sales of meals to staff and students of educational institutions, hospitals, mental institutions, to boarders in rooming houses and occasional meals consumed on premises of educational, religious or medical organizations, though not sales to outsiders or general public; materials, fuel and equipment used for crawfish production (T. 47, §305, as am'd Act 364 of 1987). Services, installation and repair of cable television paid by subscriber are exempt. (T. 47, §305.16, added Act 593 of 1974). Sales to "Boys State" and "Girls State" are exempt. (T. 47, §301, as am'd Act 20 of 1996). Sales to churches and synagogues are exempt. (T. 47, §301[8][d], added Act 28 of 1996). Qualified exemptions are granted to certain farm products, farm equipment up to $50,000, livestock at certain public sales, claimed racehorses, pesticides, fertilizers and containers used for farm products, new automobiles, insulin, new aircraft and component parts for ships, vessels, barges, drilling ships, drilling barges, commercial fishing vessels of 50 tons load displacement and over built in Louisiana and for proceeds of their sale. (T. 47, §305, as am'd Acts 145, 787, and 179 of 1979; T. 47, §305.1, as am'd Act 56 of 1982). Credit may be allowed for tax paid on sale and use of article in another state. (T. 47, §303). State and local sales and use tax is not applicable to sale at retail, purchase, lease or importation of motor vehicles to be stored, used or consumed for lease or rental, so long as lease is at reasonable market rates (T. 47, §305.36, added Act 415 of 1982), nor is state sales and use tax applicable to diesel fuel and butane used or consumed for farm purposes (T. 47, §305.36, added Act 820 of 1982). Demonstrator trucks, automobiles and airplanes are exempt. (T. 47, §305[8], added Act 516 of 1977). Taxes are not imposed on sales of monetized bullion having total value of $1,000 or more, or with respect to aircraft, equipment and parts purchased by commuter airlines domiciled in state. (T. 47, §305.21, as am'd Act 637 of 1979). New vehicles furnished by dealers to schools and colleges on free loan basis for use in driver education programs are exempt. (T. 47, §305.25, added Act 507 of 1978). Antique airplanes privately owned and not used commercially are exempt from all taxes. (T. 47, §6001, added Act 567 of 1980).

Sales and use taxes do not apply to vessels leased for mineral production beyond territorial limits of state, or for providing of services for such production (T. 9, §305.17, added Act 818 of 1975), or to property purchased for use in offshore areas, exact location of which is unknown at time of purchase (T. 47, §305.10, as am'd Act 631 of 1985).

Refund of sales tax permitted on tangible personal property destroyed in a natural disaster. (T. 47, §315.1, am'd Act 60 of 1973).

Certain sales and purchases by blind persons are exempt. (T. 47, §305.15, added Act 61 of 1973).

Sales and use taxes do not apply to capital mass transit equipment and to gasohol containing mixture of at least 10% alcohol if distilled in state from agricultural commodities and dyed color designated by Department of Revenue and Taxation. (T. 47, §§305.27-28, as am'd Act 443 of 1985).

State and local sales and use taxes do not apply to purchases by state or any of its political subdivisions. (T. 47, §301[8][a]and [e], as am'd Act 1029 of 1991, eff. Sept. 1, 1991). State sales and use taxes also do not apply to sale, use, storage or lease of energy conservation property as defined. (T. 47, §305.31, added Act 516 of 1981), nor to purchase of construction materials for operation of nonprofit retirement centers as defined (T. 47, §305.33, added Act 876 of 1981), nor to purchases made by waterworks districts (T. 47, §305.34, added Act 883 of 1981). State sales and use taxes do not apply to purchases over $100 by public housing authorities. (T. 47, §305.35, added Act 891 of 1981). Neither state nor local sales and use taxes apply to retail sale, use, consumption, distribution or storage for consumption of items of intangible personal property by sheltered workshop for mentally retarded. (T. 47, §305.38, added Act 242 of 1982). State sales and use taxes do not apply to direct consumer purchases of butane, propane or other liquefied petroleum gases for private residential purposes of cooking and heating (T. 47, §305.39, as am'd Act 622 of 1985, eff. July 1, 1986), nor to diesel fuel and butane, propane or other liquefied petroleum gases used for farm purposes (T. 47, §305.37, as am'd Act 621 of 1985, eff. July 1, 1986 and Act 511 of 1985). Such taxes do not apply to commercial fishing boat operators and owners. (T. 47, §305.20[A], added Act 687 of 1984). Such taxes also do not apply to purchases of specialty items of carnival and other nonprofit organizations (T. 47, §305.40, added Act 439 of 1985); or to admission ticket sales by dance, drama or performing arts groups (T. 47, §305.40, added Act 513 of 1985). Ducks Unlimited chapters, and other organizations dedicated to conservation of migratory waterfowl on North American continent, are exempt from state and local tax. (T. 47, §305.40, added Acts 512 and 835 of 1985). Chemical supplies used in printing are similarly exempt. (T. 47, §305.40, added Act 847 of 1985). Supplies and equipment reasonably necessary for operation of "free hospital" as defined are also exempt. (T. 47, §301[7], [10], [18], [21], added Act 5 of 1994, eff. July 1, 1994). Many exemptions are periodically suspended by Legislature. (T. 47, §§302, 331, as am'd Act 20 of 1994, eff. July 1, 1994).

Activities in domed stadiums and other publicly-owned facilities also enjoy limited exemptions from sales tax for admission tickets, parking and facility tours. (T. 39, §§467-468, added Act 2 of 1985).

Board of Appeals for Local Sales and Use Taxes has jurisdiction of all appeals for tax assessments or refunds. Request for review must be filed within 30 days of assessment. (T. 33, §2890.1 et seq., added Act 737 of 1985).

Refunds are authorized within three years of sale, lease or rental of corporeal movable property paid for or under Medicare. (T. 47, §315.2, added Act 25 of 1994).

SEVERANCE TAX:

Severance tax is levied on timber at rate of 2¹/₄% of value and on pulp wood at 5% of value as determined by Forestry and Tax Commissions. (T. 47, §633, as am'd Act 460 of 1975). Tax of 6% in lieu of other taxes levied on forest products grown on lands reforested under contracts with Department of Conservation or Forestry Commission. (T. 56, §§1541-1543). Severance tax on salt water shrimp, 15¢ per barrel of 210 pounds of shrimp, providing out of state shipments, other than by common carrier, shall pay 50¢ per barrel of 210 pounds. (T. 56, §505). Severance tax imposed on skins or hides taken from wild furbearing animals or alligators. (T. 56, §§251-276). See also category Mineral, Water and Fishing Rights, topic Mines and Minerals.

SOFT DRINK AND SYRUP TAX:

Tax of 2³/₄% of wholesale price of bottled soft drinks, and soft drink syrups, reduced to 2¹/₂% on July 1, 1981. Tax is collected by means of stamps or crowns affixed to taxable articles. (T. 47, §881, as am'd Act 788 of 1980). Unadulterated fruit juices exempt from tax. (T. 47, §§882 and 883, am'd Act 116 of 1973).

STAMP TAX:

None except on tobacco and soft drinks.

TOBACCO TAX:

Tobacco tax is imposed by T. 47, §§841-869, as am'd Act 390 of 1990, eff. Aug. 1, 1990.

UNEMPLOYMENT COMPENSATION TAX:

Unemployment Compensation Tax is imposed on employers who in any calendar quarter paid wages of $1,500 or more or who employed at least one individual for some portion of a day in any 20 different calendar weeks and others who elect to come within act. (T. 23, §1472). Tax rate varies based upon employer's reserve ratio and fund factor. (T. 23, §1536). Employees are not required to contribute. All Louisiana employers, regardless of number of employees, must make initial report of status and number of employees and must also give notice of termination or change of business. Employers subject to tax must make quarterly returns and pay tax to Administrator of Employment Security, Department of Labor, Baton Rouge. Checks in payment should be made payable to "Office of Employment Security."

See note at head of Digest as to 1998 legislation covered.

See Topical Index in front part of this volume.

LA – 55

TRANSPORTATION

MOTOR VEHICLES:

General supervision by Department of Public Safety, Motor Vehicle Division, Baton Rouge, Louisiana 70806. Department of Highways has power to supervise, regulate and control traffic. (T. 32, §§2, 702, am'd Act 96 of 1972).

Vehicle License.—Private passenger vehicles are subject to an annual registration license tax which is collected by Department of Revenue, Motor Vehicle Division each two years in advance in even numbered years. Commissioner may provide for staggered registration. (T. 47, §532, am'd Act 23 of 1974). Applicant for registration must declare insurance coverage and produce evidence if required. (T. 32, §862, as am'd Act 510 of 1980). On private passenger vehicles purchased in odd numbered years, a proportionately reduced license tax is collected for operation of such vehicle during such odd numbered year. Amputees and blind veterans of Second World War and post-1950 military service, who are La. citizens and who receive veterans financial assistance in purchasing automobiles, are exempt from this tax. No other exemptions for Armed Forces. (T. 47, §463, as am'd Act 318 of 1962). Street rods may be registered under special provisions. (T. 32, §§451-454, added Act 587 of 1980). Most other vehicles are subject to license tax which is collected annually. Certain farm equipment, municipal passenger coaches, and self-propelled off-road construction vehicles are exempt. (T. 47, §479, as am'd Act 188 of 1972; T. 41, §502, am'd Act 533 of 1972). Certificate, or photocopy, must be on display in vehicle or presented for inspection within five days. (T. 47, §506, am'd Act 8 of 1975). License plates must be displayed at height not less than 12 inches from ground in clearly visible position. (T. 47, §507). Every motor vehicle registered in state must be inspected for required safety equipment at least annually. (T. 32, §1304, am'd Act 227 of 1983).

Operator's license required. Licenses are issued by Dept. of Public Safety, Drivers License Division. (T. 32, §402). License valid until operator's birthday in fourth year from year of issuance unless revoked for cause. Licenses to operate vehicles other than passenger vehicles and two axle trucks must be renewed annually. (T. 32, §412, am'd Act 311 of 1978). Person under 18 not licensed as chauffeur. Minors 15 years of age or over may obtain driver's license or power cycle license and minors 17 years of age or over may obtain Class B chauffeur's license only with consent of either parent or by tutor or other person having custody, and license may be denied on request of person having custody of minor. (T. 32, §407, as am'd Act 48 of 1976). Parent must sign declaration of insurance coverage with respect to minor. (T. 32, §871, as am'd Act 510 of 1980). Members of Armed Forces not required to have license if operating vehicle of such agency, have operator's license issued by such agency and are on official duty. (T. 32, §420). Licensed driver charged with traffic violation may deposit license in lieu of bail bond. (T. 32, §411, am'd Act 185 of 1976). Suspension of driving privileges may occur upon proof of certain level of intoxication; level is lower for those under 18. (T. 32, §661.1 [C][1][c], added Act 20 of 1994, Third Ex. Sess.).

Titles.—Certificates of title are issued by Commissioner. Application for certificate of title must be on form prescribed by Commissioner, sworn to before Notary Public or Commissioner's assistants, and must be accompanied by previous owner's certificate of title duly endorsed with sale and assignment or other satisfactory evidence of title. (T. 32, §707).

Sales are effected by vendor endorsing sale and assignment on his certificate of title and delivering same to purchaser who must file application for new certificate of title within five days after delivery of vehicle. (T. 32, §705, as am'd Act 186 of 1983, §707). Any person transferring motor vehicle, whether by sale, lease or otherwise, must give written notice to Collector of Revenue on form provided by him within 15 days of transfer (T. 47, §510, as am'd Act 362 of 1975) and must provide signed statement that odometer mileage is correct. (T. 32, §726.1, added Act 564 of 1972). Retail installment contracts involving sale of motor vehicles subject to certain requirements (T. 6, §951 et seq., as am'd Act 244 of 1983) and effective Jan. 1, 1973, additional requirements with regard to form and assignment of promissory notes similar to Consumer Credit Law. Motor vehicle manufacturers, distributors, dealers and lessors are regulated and licensed through Motor Vehicle Commissioner. (T. 32, §§1251-1259, as am'd Act 911 of 1985).

Warranties.—If new motor vehicle does not conform to express warranty and consumer so reports and makes vehicle available for repair, manufacturer must repair. After four or more unsuccessful attempts at repair, manufacturer must at its option either replace with comparable vehicle or refund entire purchase price less reasonable use allowance. (T. 51, §§1941-1946, added Act 228 of 1984). If motor vehicle does not conform to express warranty and consumer complies with foregoing provisions, reasonable attorney's fees must be awarded with judgment in his favor. (T. 51, §1947, added Act 169 of 1985).

Liens and Encumbrances.—See category Debtor and Creditor, topic Liens, subhead Garages. Chattel mortgages on vehicles must be in writing either by authentic act or by private act duly authenticated and must set out obligations secured, exact sum and maturity, and full description of vehicle mortgaged, including following data insofar as it may exist with respect to particular vehicle; make, year, model, type of body, motor number, manufacturer's serial number, license number and year of Louisiana plates currently in effect on vehicle at date of mortgage and location of vehicle. Duplicate original must be recorded with Commissioner who must also receive at same time mortgager's certificate of title on which he enters notation of chattel mortgage. Effective date and priority of mortgage as against third persons is date of its execution by parties if mortgage is noted on certificate of title within 15 days by Commissioner and if not noted within 15 days, date of delivery to Commissioner. (T. 32, §710, am'd Act 964 of 1985). Floor plan mortgages are allowed in specified manner.

Motor vehicles remain subject to chattel mortgages when located on immovable property but mobile homes may become immovable upon recordation of specified documents. (T. 32, §710 [N] as am'd Act 728 of 1978).

Upon satisfaction of mortgage, mortgagee or any holder may present Certificate of Title to Commissioner, and request that he note on said certificate and his records a cancellation of notation of chattel mortgage. Commissioner shall comply if satisfaction appears genuine. (T. 32, §708, as am'd Act 162 of 1976).

Chattel mortgages on vehicles are also governed in all other respects by laws applying to chattel mortgages generally. See categories Business Regulation and Commerce, topic Commercial Code; Mortgages, topic Chattel Mortgages.

Operation Prohibited.—By person under 15 years of age (T. 32, §416); by person under 17 between hours of 11 p.m. and 5 a.m. on Mon. through Thurs., and between 12 o'clock midnight and 5 a.m. on Fri. through Sun. (T. 32, §416.1, as am'd Act 775 of 1981); of vehicle not registered, equipped, licensed or operated in accordance with law (T. 32, §§51-53); of vehicle or combination of vehicles exceeding size, weight and load limitations (T. 32, §54). Vehicles operated in violation of law may be impounded. (T. 32, §392). Transportation of hazardous materials is regulated. (T. 32, §§1501-1517, as am'd Acts 113, 497, and 549 of 1985; T. 40, §1471, as added Act 721 of 1979).

Size and Weight Limits.—Regulated by T. 32, §§379-388, 462, as am'd Act 936 of 1985.

Equipment Required.—Regulated by T. 32, §§190, 190.1, 301-377, am'd by Act 113 of 1977.

Lights Required.—Regulated by T. 32, §§301-332.

Seat Belts.—State requires seat belts and their use for front-seat passengers; $25 fine; limited comparative negligence effect. (T. 32, §295.1, added Act 377 of 1985, eff. July 1, 1986).

Accidents.—Driver involved in accident causing injuries or death or property damage apparently exceeding $100 must, within 24 hours, forward report to Division of State Police, or, if accident occurred in incorporated city or town, to police department thereof. (T. 32, §398). Driver must stop after all accidents and must render aid in any accident resulting in the death or personal injury of another. (T. 32, §414).

Punitive damages are awardable if injuries are caused by wanton or reckless disregard of safety of others by defendant whose intoxication while driving motor vehicle is cause of those injuries. (C.C. 2315.1, added Act 511 of 1984).

Owner's Liability.—Family purpose doctrine not applied, but under C. C. 2318 father is liable for damages occasioned by negligent driving of automobile by his unemancipated minor child residing with him. (11 La. App. 485, 124 So. 160). C. C. 2318 imposes liability on mother after death of father and also on tutor. Liability of one spouse for conduct of other in operating automobile is covered by law relative to matrimonial regimes. Generally, if spouses have community regime, all obligations incurred by spouse are presumed to be community and can be discharged from community property or separate property of tortfeasor spouse. (C. C. 2357, 2360). Even if spouses have separate property regime, spouse is solidarily liable with other spouse who incurs obligation for necessaries for spouse or family. (C. C. 2372). There is no general owner-consent statute in this state imposing liability upon owner for negligent operation of vehicle with his consent.

Guests.—There is no statute restricting liability for injury to a guest.

Financial Responsibility.—Operator of every motor vehicle involved in accident in which any person is killed or injured or in which property of any person including himself is damaged in excess of $500 must, within ten days of accident, give evidence to Department of Public Safety of financial responsibility consisting of automobile liability policy having $5,000-$10,000 bodily injury coverage and $5,000 property coverage, or bond having $5,000-$10,000 bodily injury coverage and $5,000 property coverage. (T. 32, §§861, 871, as am'd Act 229 of 1985). On failure to do so, Department must suspend license of operator, impound license plate and all registrations of owner of vehicle involved unless security in sum determined by Department is furnished to it. (T. 9, §863 as am'd Act 282 of 1983). Suspension lasts until security deposited, or until release from liability or final adjudication of nonliability filed with Department, or until one year has elapsed with no action for damages having been instituted. Knowing operation without such security in force, or allowing such operation by owner, is punishable by $500 fine upon conviction. (T. 32, §865, added Act 926 of 1981, eff. Jan. 1, 1982). In addition, fee of $15 must be paid before any license may be reinstated. Nonresident involved in accident must meet above requirements or have operating privilege revoked and notice thereof sent to state in which nonresident resides if law of said state provides, as law of Louisiana does, for reciprocal suspension of licenses and registrations of residents failing to meet financial responsibility laws of other states. Nonresident and resident must also give proof of financial responsibility upon first conviction of driving while intoxicated, under influence of drugs, etc. (T. 32, §§871-878 and 896, as am'd Acts 273 and 510 of 1980).

Automobile liability policies must pay to their insured who is legally entitled to recover from owner or operator of an uninsured vehicle or vehicle insured by insolvent insurer amount of damages, bodily or otherwise, in not less than limits of bodily injury liability provided by policy, and subrogation of liability insurer is provided for such amounts paid. Insured may reject such coverage or may demand increase of coverage up to limits of policy liability coverage. (T. 22, §1406, am'd Act 623 of 1977). Action must be brought within two years of accident. (T. 9, §5604, added Act 444 of 1977).

Insurance in limits of $10,000/$20,000/$10,000, or binder for same, or cash or security deposit with state treasurer is required for all self-propelled motor vehicles registered for operation upon highways and roads of state. (T. 32, §§861-864, as am'd Act 237 of 1984). Information on existence of such coverage available from Department of Public Safety for $15 fee. (T. 32, §871, as am'd Act 496 of 1985).

No-Fault Insurance.—Not adopted.

Automobile Service Clubs.—Regulated by Insurance Commissioner. (T. 22, §§1751-1770, as am'd Act 260 of 1975).

Nonresident owner of vehicle duly licensed in home state and displaying proper license plates may operate vehicle in Louisiana if home state accords like privilege to Louisiana vehicles. Where no such reciprocal arrangement exists Commissioner may grant permission to nonresidents for occasional or casual trips in Louisiana. Nonresident regularly employed in or carrying on business in state and owning and operating motor vehicle in such business must register same like a resident. (T. 47, §§511, 512 and 513, as am'd Act 300 of 1974). If no reciprocal agreement exists, nonresident owner of truck must obtain 48 hour permit from commissioner and pay $25 fee. (T. 47, §511.1, added

MOTOR VEHICLES . . . *continued*

Act 267 of 1975). Nonresident operator of vehicle cited for traffic violation need not post bond if state of his residence is party to Interstate Traffic Violations Compact. (T. 32, §§1426-1431).

Action against nonresident, arising out of accident while he or his authorized agent or employee is operating motor vehicle on highway, may be commenced by service of citation and copy of petition on Secretary of State, and sending notice of service together with copy of petition and citation to defendant by registered mail or certified with receipt requested. (T. 13, §§3474, 3475, as am'd Act 353 of 1977).

Direct Actions.—Injured person or his heirs or survivors have right of direct action against liability insurer, or against both insurer and its insured jointly and in solido, if policy issued or delivered in Louisiana or if accident or injury occurred in Louisiana and whether or not liability policy excludes such direct action. Venue of direct action suit lies either in parish where accident or injury occurred or under ordinary rules of venue. Insured must be joined with insurer in direct action, except in certain circumstances (insolvency or bankruptcy of insured, inability to serve insured or immunity of insured). (T. 22, §655, as am'd Act 934 of 1988, eff. Jan. 1, 1989).

Unclaimed Vehicles: Storage and Disposition.—T. 32, §521, am'd Act 461 of 1974.

Motor vehicle carriers regulated by Public Service Commission. (T. 45, c. 4). Must have special license, and when operated over fixed route must have certificate of public convenience and necessity. (T. 45, §164). Fee of $10 per vehicle or combination must be paid between Jan. 1 and Feb. 1 of each year. (T. 45, §169, as am'd Act 184 of 1977). Commission may enact rules, procedures, penalties, charge fees. (T. 45, §169A, added Act 304 of 1972). Must file bond to indemnify passengers and others injured by operation. (T. 45, §§173-176). Liable for negligent damage to highways. Foreign vehicle operating on regular route must have state license and permit. (T. 47, §513). Vehicle used as motor carrier may be operated only by licensed chauffeur. Person in charge of vehicle used in business of transporting passengers must be licensed as operator or chauffeur and vehicle must have "for hire" license plates. (T. 45, §181).

License plates and registration certificate may not be issued to common carrier, contract carrier or charter carrier without certificate by Public Service Commission that carrier is entitled thereto. (T. 45, §§178-180).

Gasoline Tax.—See category Taxation, topic Gasoline and Special Fuels Taxes.

RAILROADS:

See category Business Regulation and Commerce, topic Carriers.

MAINE LAW DIGEST REVISER

Pierce Atwood
One Monument Square
Portland, Maine 04101-1110
Telephone: 207-791-1100
Fax: 207-791-1350
Email: info@PierceAtwood.com

Reviser Profile

History and Areas of Practice: Northern New England's largest law firm, Pierce Atwood is a full service firm experienced in handling complex legal matters in the areas of Corporate, Commercial and Securities Law, Environmental and Natural Resources Law, Health Care, Insurance Law and Regulation, Intellectual Property, International Law, Labor and Employment Law, Public Utilities and Energy Regulation, Real Estate Law, Taxation, Estate Planning, Legislation and Litigation. With offices in Portland and Augusta, Maine, and Newburyport, Massachusetts, the firm provides a full range of legal services. In a number of areas, including Environmental and Natural Resources Law, Bankruptcy and Creditors' Rights, Intellectual Property Law, Federal Court Litigation, Energy Regulation and Labor Law, the firm's practice extends throughout the country and abroad.

Client Base: Pierce Atwood's client base includes numerous Fortune 500 companies, public utilities, venture capital concerns, medium and small business entities, municipal corporations, and real estate developers, as well as individuals. The firm's litigation practice involves the representation of both individuals and businesses. Pierce Atwood is also actively involved in pro bono legal matters.

Firm Philosophy: Pierce Atwood prides itself on providing the highest quality of legal advice in an efficient manner consistent with the needs of its clients and the economic pressures they face. The firm's size allows its lawyers to develop extensive and concentrated experience and specialization in a broad range of areas likely to be relevant to clients' needs. The firm then works with its clients to ensure that particular matters are staffed and handled by attorneys knowledgeable in the pertinent area.

Significant Distinctions: Pierce Atwood enjoys an internationally recognized reputation in the region. Firm members have served with distinction in various governmental, civic, and charitable functions. For example, one partner is a member of the EPA's National Environmental Justice Advisory Council and an arbitrator for the Inter-American Commercial Arbitration Commission and was a member of Vice President Gore's Environmental Advisory Team to Assist with Bolivian Presidential Transition. Another partner was special counsel for the United States of America before the International Court of Justice at The Hague, is the past chairman of the ABA Committee on Judiciary, and has served as a Regent and Treasurer and is the past President of the American College of Trial Lawyers. One lawyer served with distinction as Chief Justice of Maine's Supreme Judicial Court. Other partners have served as counsel for the Governor, counsel in the Office of Tax Legislative Counsel, in the United States Treasury Department, as Mayor of Portland, as Deputy Attorney General and Chief of the Natural Resources Division for the State of Maine, as members of the Portland City Council and in other civic and community activities. Many members of the firm have published books and articles and lectured on a wide variety of legal topics. The firm has contributed significantly to the development of the law in a variety of legal areas.

MAINE LAW DIGEST REVISER

Pierce Atwood
One Monument Square
Portland, Maine 04101-1110
Telephone: 207-791-1100
Fax: 207-791-1350
Email: janice@PierceAtwood.com

Reviser Profile

MAINE LAW DIGEST

(The following is a list of all Categories and Topics, including cross-references, covered in this Digest.)

MAINE LAW DIGEST

Revised for 1999 edition by

PIERCE ATWOOD, of the Portland Bar.

(References, unless otherwise indicated, are to titles and sections of Maine Revised Statutes Annotated of 1964. M.R.C.P. indicates the Maine Rules of Civil Procedure. M.R.E. indicates Maine Rules of Evidence. M.R. Probate P. indicates Maine Rules of Probate Procedure. Parallel citations to the Atlantic Reporter begin with 77 Me.)

Note: Includes legislation passed through the first special session of the 118th Maine Legislature.

INTRODUCTION

GOVERNMENT AND LEGAL SYSTEM:

The State of Maine is a constituent state of the United States of America. For further discussion of the U.S. federal system, see Introduction to the Federal Government of the United States at the beginning of this volume. A great many laws are promulgated by the federal government of the United States and are not reflected in the topics below. See the Introduction to this volume for references to the federal law topics covered.

Like all but one of the United States, Maine has a common law legal system, with roots in English common law. For information on the courts and legislature of Maine, see category Courts and Legislature.

HOLIDAYS:

Legal and bank holidays are: Jan. 1; 3d Mon. in Jan.; 3d Mon. in Feb.; 3d Mon. in Apr.; last Mon. in May, but if U.S. Government designates May 30th as date for observance of Memorial Day, 30th of May; July 4; 1st Mon. in Sept.; 2d Mon. in Oct.; Nov. 11; 4th Thurs. in Nov.; Dec. 25; any day of thanksgiving, mourning or disaster, proclaimed or appointed by Governor or President of U.S. If Jan. 1, July 4, Nov. 11 or Dec. 25 falls on Sun., following Mon. is bank holiday. (T. 4, §1051; T. 9-B, §141).

Legality of Transactions on Sunday.—Sales of motor vehicles (T. 17, §3203) and motor homes (T. 17, §3203-A) prohibited (T. 17, §3203). Operation of business, travel and recreation on Sun. governed by T. 17, §3204.

OFFICE HOURS AND TIME ZONE:

Maine is in the Eastern Standard (GMT −05:00) time zone. Office hours are generally from 9 a.m. to 5 p.m.

BUSINESS ORGANIZATIONS

AGENCY:

Rules of common law apply.

ASSOCIATIONS:

Actions.—Organized unincorporated society or association may sue in name of its trustees for time being, and may maintain action at law, though defendant or some of defendants are members of same society or association. (T. 14, §2).

Liabilities.—Members of unincorporated associations may be liable on contracts made by associated persons. (514 A.2d 807).

Partnerships.—See topic Partnerships.

Professional Associations.—See topic Corporations, subhead Professional Corporations.

CORPORATIONS:

Maine Business Corporation Act, T. 13-A, became effective Jan. 1, 1972. Act is based in large part upon ABA Model Business Corporation Act (1960). Due to number of substantial variances from Model Act, it is not feasible to specifically enumerate such variances here.

General Supervision.—Maine Business Corporation Act ("MBCA") is administered by Secretary of State. (T. 13-A, §1303). Address: Secretary of State, State House Station 101, Augusta, ME 04333-0101.

Purposes.—Generally, corporation may be organized for purpose of carrying on any lawful business. (T. 13-A, §401). Purpose need not be stated in Articles of Incorporation. (T. 13-A, §404).

Name.—May not imply that corporation is organized for any purpose for which corporation may not be organized under MBCA. Name may not be same as, or deceptively similar to, name of any domestic or foreign corporation, limited partnership, limited liability company, or limited liability partnership, or any reserved, registered or any of foregoing, or any trademark or service mark registered in Maine. (T. 13-A, §301). Name may not consist of obscene, contemptuous, profane or prejudicial language, promote abusive or unlawful activity or falsely suggest association with public institutions. (T. 13-A, §301). Name may be reserved by filing application with Secretary of State. If Secretary of State finds name available, name will be reserved for 120 days. (T. 13-A, §302). Interim reservation available for ten days. (T. 13-A, §302). Reserved name may not be renewed, but after expiration of reservation period, name may be reserved by same or different applicant. (T. 13-A, §302). Right to use of name may be transferred by filing notice of transfer with fee of $20. (T. 13-A, §§302, 1401). For other filing fees, see subhead Filing Fees, infra.

Term of Corporate Existence.—Perpetual. (T. 13-A, §202).

Incorporators.—One or more incorporators may file Articles of Incorporation. Incorporators need not be residents of Maine. (T. 13-A, §402).

Articles of Incorporation.—Only one copy need be filed. Must set forth name; location in Maine; address of initial registered office; name of initial clerk; either number of initial directors (and if selected and if powers of incorporator are to terminate upon filing of articles, names and addresses of person or persons to serve as directors until first annual meeting or until successors elected and qualify) or following statement in haec verbae: "There shall be no directors initially; the shares of corporation will not be sold to more than 20 persons; the business of the corporation will be managed by the shareholders;" relevant information regarding shares (if one class only, state total number of authorized shares, par value of each share, or statement that shares are to be without par value; if two or more classes, must designate each class of shares, as to each class must specify total number of authorized shares and par value of shares or statement that shares are to be without par value; if shares of preferred or special class to be issued in series, must state whether shares have par value or no par value, and must either designate each series and specify relative rights, preferences and limitations [to extent that such is to be specified in articles] or set forth any authority of board of directors to establish and designate series within any class and determine relative rights, preferences and limitations among such series). Articles must also summarize aggregate par value of authorized shares having par value and total number of authorized shares without par value. Articles may also include other provisions authorized or required by MBCA to be included in articles, bylaws, agreements, instruments or other provisions not inconsistent with law or contrary to public policy. Articles must be signed by each incorporator with incorporators' addresses typed beneath or opposite signature, and by clerk as required by T. 13-A, §304(2-A). (T. 13-A, §403).

Filing of Articles.—Articles should be filed with Secretary of State, State House Station 101, Augusta, ME 04333-0101.

Incorporation Tax.—Payable to Secretary of State upon filing Articles of Incorporation, based upon capitalization as follows: Par value stock: $30 for each $100,000 up to $2,000,000; between $2,000,000 and $20,000,000, $600 plus $150 per million dollars in excess of $2,000,000; in excess of $20,000,000, $3,300 plus $70 per million dollars in excess of $20,000,000. No par value stock: 1¢ per share up to 20,000 shares, but not less than $30; between 20,000 and 2,000,000 shares, $200 plus ½ ¢ per share in excess of 20,000; in excess of 2,000,000 shares, $10,200 plus ¼ ¢ per share in excess of 2,000,000 shares. (T. 13-A, §1403).

Filing Fees.—Articles of Incorporation, $75 plus fee based on amount of capital stock (see subhead Incorporation Tax, supra); application to reserve corporate name, $20; application to register corporate name, $20 per month; application to renew registration of registered name, $155; assumed name statement, $105 (or, if true corporate name is not available, pursuant to T. 13-A, §301, $20); application of foreign corporation for authority to do business in state, $180; statement changing clerk or registered office, $20; notice of resignation of clerk, $20; fee for filing annual report for domestic or foreign corporation, $60. (T. 13-A, §1401).

License to Do Business.—Foreign corporations must be authorized to do business in State. (T. 13-A, §1201). Foreign corporation may apply for such authority by filing application and certificate of good standing and $180 fee. (T. 13-A, §§1202, 1401). Upon filing of application, foreign corporation is authorized to do business in State. (T. 13-A, §1203).

Organization.—Filing of Articles constitutes corporation's charter and authority to do business. (T. 13-A, §406). Incorporators manage corporation and may adopt bylaws and elect directors, unless initial directors have been named in Articles. Before or after filing of Articles, organizational meeting must be held to elect initial directors who will serve until first annual meeting (if meeting of incorporators), to elect officers (if meeting of directors), to adopt bylaws, etc. Meeting may be held without call if unanimously agreed, or upon call. (T. 13-A, §407).

Paid in Capital Requirements.—No requirements upon incorporation.

Amendment of Articles.—Corporation may amend Articles from time to time by filing articles of amendment. (T. 13-A, §§802, 807). Articles may also be amended by incorporator (or by ⅔ of incorporators if more than one) prior to election of initial directors (if directors not named in Articles) or prior to organizational meeting of board of directors (if directors named in Articles). (T. 13-A, §803). Directors may amend with respect to registered office or clerk and to reduce authorized shares as result of share cancellations. Clerk authorized to change registered office. (T. 13-A, §804). All amendments except those permitted by §§803 and 804 require action of directors and shareholders in accordance with procedures set forth in T. 13-A, §805. Articles may also be amended by unanimous written consent of shareholders without necessity of directors' resolution. (T. 13-A, §805). Certain amendments affecting class of shares require class voting. (T. 13-A, §806).

Increase or Decrease of Authorized Capital Stock.—Stated capital can be reduced in following ways: (i) direct reduction by shareholder vote (T. 13-A, §522); (ii) retirement or cancellation of reacquired shares (other than redeemable shares redeemed or purchased) (T. 13-A, §521); (iii) redemption or repurchase of redeemable shares (T. 13-A, §520); and (iv) cancellation of redeemable shares purchased or redeemed. (T. 13-A, §520).

With respect to direct reduction of stated capital by shareholder vote, corporation may only reduce stated capital if such reduction is not accompanied by any action requiring amendment to Articles and is not accompanied by retirement or cancellation of shares. Board of directors adopts resolution specifying amount of proposed reduction and manner in which reduction to be effected and directing that reduction be

CORPORATIONS . . . *continued*
submitted to shareholder vote. Written notice of meeting, specifying that purpose of meeting is to consider reduction of stated capital, must be given to each shareholder. Majority vote of outstanding shares of each class required regardless of whether such shares are entitled to vote under Articles. Reduction not permitted if stated capital after reduction would be equal to or less than aggregate preferential amounts payable in event of involuntary liquidation, or less than aggregate par value of all issued shares having par value. (T. 13-A, §522).

Stated capital is increased in following ways (i) issuance of par value stock, to extent of par (T. 13-A, §513); (ii) consideration received on issuance of no par stock (unless portion allocated to capital surplus in accordance with MBCA) (T. 13-A, §513); (iii) discretionary board action transferring surplus, capital or earned, to stated capital (T. 13-A, §513); and (iv) by required transfer from surplus, capital or earned, to stated capital caused by issuance of share dividends from authorized but unissued shares or amendment to Articles increasing par value or liquidation preferences of outstanding shares.

Bylaws may contain any provisions for regulation and management of corporation not inconsistent with law or Articles. Any provision which could appear in bylaws may be included in Articles. (T. 13-A, §601).

Stock.—Corporation has power to create and issue number of shares stated in Articles. Shares may be divided into one or more classes. Classes may consist of shares with or without par value, with such designations, preferences, limitations and relative rights as stated in Articles. Articles may limit or deny voting rights of, or provide special voting rights for, shares of any class to extent not inconsistent with MBCA. Articles may provide for redemption, cumulative, noncumulative or partially cumulative dividends, dividend preferences or preferences upon liquidation, or convertible shares. If more than one class, shares of each class must be designated so as to distinguish them from shares of other classes. Shares not preferred as to dividends or other distributions may not be designated as preferred shares. (T. 13-A, §501). If Articles provide, shares of any preferred or special class may be divided into and issued in series. (T. 13-A, §502).

Stock Certificates.—Certificates must be signed by any two of: president, vice president, clerk, secretary or assistant secretary of corporation, or by such other two officers as are designated in bylaws; and may be sealed with corporate seal. If certificate countersigned by clerk, transfer agent or assistant transfer agent or registered by registrar, other than corporation itself or employee, any other signature on certificate may be facsimile. If corporation is authorized to issue shares of more than one class, certificate must contain full statement of designations, preferences, limitations and relative rights of shares of each class authorized to be issued or must state that corporation will furnish such statement upon request and without charge. If corporation authorized to issue preferred or special class in series, variations in relative rights and preferences between shares of each series so far as they have been fixed and determined, and authority of board to fix and determine relative rights and preferences of other series must also be contained on such statements. Certificates must also state that corporation organized under laws of Maine, name of person or persons to whom issued, number and class of shares, designation of series, if any, and par value or statement that shares are without par value. (T. 13-A, §511). Shareholder agreements must be conspicuously referred to on face or back of certificates. (T. 13-A, §618).

Record Date.—Board may set record date not more than 60 days in advance of shareholder meeting or in advance of dividend distribution. For shareholder meetings, said date may not be less than ten full days, or if close corporation, not less than three full days, prior to date on which action requiring such determination is to be taken. If no date set, day next preceding date on which notice of meeting is mailed, or day next preceding date on which resolution declaring dividend is adopted, as case may be, is deemed record date. If provided by bylaws, directors may, in lieu of fixing record date, close stock transfer books for stated period; said period may not exceed 60 days, and, with respect to shareholder meeting, books must be closed at least ten days, or if close corporation, not less than three days, immediately preceding meeting. (T. 13-A, §606).

Stock Transfer Tax.—None.

Shareholders.—Unless otherwise provided in Articles, holders of shares of any class having voting rights have certain statutory preemptive rights in event of proposed sale or exchange by corporation of additional shares of same class, grant by corporation of any options or rights to purchase shares of same class, or proposed sale or exchange by corporation of any securities convertible into or carrying option to purchase shares of same class. (T. 13-A, §623). If, after Sept. 1, 1985, corporation shall adopt provision in its Articles or bylaws requiring greater than 10% of shares entitled to vote to call special meeting, then upon application of not less than 10% of shares entitled to vote, Superior Court may order special meeting held. (T. 13-A, §603). Articles may provide for cumulative voting. If so, statutory procedure applies. (T. 13-A, §622). Certain shareholders have right to inspect and copy corporate books and records during normal business hours. (T. 13-A, §626).

Shareholders' Actions.—Shareholder may not commence or maintain derivative proceeding unless shareholder (i) was shareholder of corporation at time of act or omission complained of or became shareholder through transfer by operation of law from one who was shareholder at that time, and (ii) fairly and adequately represents interests of corporation in enforcing right of corporation. (T. 13-A, §629). Moreover, shareholder may not commence derivative proceeding until (i) written demand has been made upon corporation to take suitable action, and (ii) 90 days have expired from date that demand was made unless shareholder has earlier been notified that demand has been rejected by corporation or unless irreparable injury to corporation would result by waiting for expiration of 90-day period. (T. 13-A, §630). If corporation commences inquiry into allegations made in demand or complaint, court may stay any derivative proceeding for period court determines appropriate. (T. 13-A, §631). Derivative proceeding may not be discontinued or settled without court's approval. (T. 13-A, §633).

Shareholders' Liabilities.—Shareholder liable for distribution or payment received from corporation if corporation was insolvent or thereby rendered insolvent, or if shareholder had reason to know that such distribution or payment was contrary to MBCA or to Articles. (T. 13-A, §624).

Shareholders' Meetings.—Written notice stating place, day and hour of meeting and, in case of special meeting or when otherwise required by MBCA, purposes for which meeting is called, shall be delivered not less than ten nor more than 60 days (or in case of close corporation, not less than three nor more than 60 days) before date of meeting. Notice of adjourned meeting need not be given if meeting adjourned for less than 30 days, time and place of adjourned meeting is announced when adjournment is taken, and no new record date is fixed for meeting. (T. 13-A, §604). Record date for determining shareholders shall not be more than 60 days in advance. (T. 13-A, §606). Shareholders' list need not be arranged by classes and series of stock held. (T. 13-A, §607). Shareholders' list must be available at least ten days, or in case of close corporation, three days, prior to date of meeting. (T. 13-A, §607). Shareholder whose shares are pledged entitled to vote until shares transferred on corporate records to pledgee or nominee of pledgee. (T. 13-A, §613).

Voting Trusts.—Shareholders may create revocable or irrevocable voting trusts for purpose of conferring upon trustee right to vote or represent shares for period not exceeding 21 years. Voting trust must be created by written agreement and by transferring shares to trustee. Corporation must enter fact that shares are subject to voting trust on corporate records. Trust certificates are issued by trustees to shareholders who transfer shares in trust. (T. 13-A, §619).

Directors.—Close corporation of 20 or less shareholders need not have board of directors if expressly provided for in Articles. (T. 13-A, §701). Otherwise, must have at least three directors, unless two or fewer shareholders, in which case number of directors may not be less than number of shareholders. (T. 13-A, §703). No maximum number of directors provided by statute. Directors need not be residents of Maine, nor shareholders of corporation. (T. 13-A, §702). Directors hold office until succeeding annual meeting, except when directors are elected to staggered terms as permitted under T. 13-A, §705. Directors elected by shareholders. (T. 13-A, §704). Power to fill vacancies created by increase in authorized number of directors is reserved to shareholders acting at annual meeting or special meeting called for that purpose, unless expressly delegated to directors by shareholder resolution or bylaws. (T. 13-A, §706). All other vacancies filled by majority vote of remaining directors, unless Articles or bylaws reserve such power to shareholders. (T. 13-A, §706).

Classes.—Articles may provide that directors be divided into either two or three classes. Special provisions apply if cumulative voting for directors authorized by Articles. If corporation authorized to issue more than one class of shares, Articles may confer upon holders of one or more specified classes of shares right to elect all directors, or any specified number of them, or directors of any class or classes established by Articles, other than classification by term of office. (T. 13-A, §705).

Directors' Meetings.—Meetings may be held at any place within or without state, unless bylaws provide otherwise. Time and place for meetings may be fixed by bylaws, or, if not fixed by bylaws, by directors. Telephonic meetings authorized. Regular meetings may be held without notice if time and place of meetings are fixed by bylaws or board; special meetings require at least three days notice unless bylaws otherwise provide. (T. 13-A, §§708, 709). Majority of directors then in office constitutes quorum unless greater proportion required by Articles or bylaws. However, if fewer directors in office than one-half number of directors fixed by bylaws or Articles, directors then in office may transact no other business than filling of vacancies on board. (T. 13-A, §710). Unless otherwise provided by Articles or bylaws, action by unanimous written consent authorized for any action required to be taken at directors' meeting. (T. 13-A, §711).

Powers and Duties of Directors.—In general, business and affairs of corporation is managed by board of directors. Close corporations may be managed by shareholders if Articles of Incorporation so provide. Directors must exercise powers and discharge duties in good faith with view to interests of corporation and of shareholders and with that degree of diligence, care and skill which ordinarily prudent men would exercise under similar circumstances in like positions. Directors may in considering best interests of corporation and shareholders, consider effects of any action upon employees, suppliers and customers, and upon communities in which offices or establishments of corporation are located, and all other pertinent factors. (T. 13-A, §716). "Good faith" on part of officer or director requires exercise of reasonable business judgment after reasonable inquiry into facts. (T. 13-A, §102[14]).

Liabilities of Directors.—Directors are not personally liable for monetary damages for failure to discharge any duty as director unless director found not to have acted honestly or in reasonable belief that action was in or not opposed to best interests of corporation or shareholders. (T. 13-A, §716). Directors who vote for or assent to improper or illegal declaration of dividends, distributions of assets, or purchase or redemption of shares, may be held jointly and severally liable for amount or value of such dividends, distributions or payments. (T. 13-A, §720).

Officers.—Required officers consist of president and treasurer. Board of directors or bylaws may provide for other officers. Officers elected by board of directors or, if Articles expressly provide, by shareholders. (T. 13-A, §714).

Indemnification of Directors and Officers.—Statute provides for indemnification, either optional or mandatory, of directors, officers, employees or agents of corporation or any person serving at request of corporation as director, officer, trustee, partner, fiduciary, employee or agent of another corporation, partnership, joint venture, trust, pension or other employee benefit plan or other enterprise against all expenses, including attorneys' fees, judgments, fines and amounts paid in settlement in connection with any threatened, pending or completed action, suit or proceeding, whether civil, criminal, administrative or investigative, brought by reason of such person's status. Indemnification prohibited if person finally adjudicated (i) not to have acted honestly or in reasonable belief that actions were not against best interest of corporation or shareholders (or in case of person serving as fiduciary of employee benefit plan or trust, not to have acted in best interests of that plan or trust, or its participants or beneficiaries);

CORPORATIONS . . . *continued*

(ii) with respect to any criminal action or proceeding, to have had reasonable cause to believe conduct was unlawful; or (iii) with respect to matters asserted by or in right of corporation, liable to corporation, unless court determines person fairly and reasonably entitled to indemnity notwithstanding such liability. Indemnification required in all cases where director, officer, employee or agent successfully defends any actions, suit or proceeding or any claim, issue or matter therein. Corporation has power to purchase and maintain insurance on behalf of any person who is or was director, officer, employee or agent of corporation, or is or was serving at request of corporation as director, officer, trustee, partner, fiduciary, employee or agent of another corporation, partnership, joint venture, trust, pension or other employee benefit plan or other enterprise against any liability asserted against that person and incurred by that person in any such capacity, or arising out of that person's status as such, whether or not corporation would have power to indemnify that person. (T. 13-A, §719).

Principal Office.—Clerk must maintain registered office at some fixed place within Maine. Registered office need not be corporation's place of business. (T. 13-A, §304). Foreign corporation must also maintain registered office within Maine. (T. 13-A, §1212).

Resident Agent.—Each domestic corporation must maintain clerk who is natural person resident in Maine. Clerk need not be director or officer. (T. 13-A, §304). Each foreign corporation must maintain registered agent who may be either individual resident in Maine whose business or residential address is same as corporation's registered office, or domestic or foreign corporation authorized to do business in state whose registered office is same as registered office of corporation. (T. 13-A, §1212).

General Powers of Corporations.—Subject to MBCA and any other applicable law, in addition to specific powers enumerated by statute, corporations have all powers necessary or convenient to effect purposes of corporation or further business in which corporation may lawfully be engaged. Articles of Incorporation need not list any of such powers. (T. 13-A, §202). Ultra vires abolished with three exceptions: (i) proceedings by shareholders to enjoin action; (ii) proceedings by corporation, directly or in representative action, against directors or officers; and (iii) proceedings by attorney general to dissolve corporation or to enjoin corporation from transaction of unauthorized business. (T. 13-A, §203).

Dividends.—Board may declare and pay dividends on outstanding shares in cash or in property, including shares of other corporations. Dividends may not be declared or paid (i) when corporation is insolvent or payment would render corporation insolvent; or (ii) when there are contrary restrictions in Articles of Incorporation. Following general limitations also apply: (i) dividends may be paid in cash or property only "out of" unreserved and unrestricted earned surplus or "out of" unreserved and unrestricted net earnings of current fiscal year and next preceding fiscal year taken as single period, except as otherwise provided by statute; and (ii) except as otherwise provided in Articles corporation engaged in exploitation of natural resources or other wasting assets may declare and pay dividends out of depletion reserves. (T. 13-A, §514). Statute provides authority for payment of accrued, cumulative dividends out of capital surplus even if corporation has no earned surplus or if earned surplus would be insufficient to permit payment of those dividends. Applies only to shareholders having cumulative preferential right to receive dividends in discharge of their cumulative dividend rights. (T. 13-A, §516).

Unclaimed Dividends.—See category Property, topic Absentees.

Sale or Transfer of Corporate Assets.—Sale of all or substantially all of corporation's assets other than in usual and regular course of business requires prior approval of shareholders. Sale must be authorized in following manner: (i) board adopts resolution recommending sale, and directing submission thereof to shareholder vote at either annual or special meeting; (ii) written notice of meeting given to each shareholder of record stating the purpose of meeting is to consider proposed sale, accompanied by accurate summary of material terms of proposed sale, containing conspicuous statement of dissenter's rights, and mailed to each shareholder whether or not entitled to vote; and (iii) at meeting, shareholders may authorize sale by majority vote of outstanding shares entitled to vote (unless class voting applies, in which case authorization requires majority vote of each class entitled to vote as class and of total outstanding shares entitled to vote). Articles may prescribe greater vote. Sale may also be authorized by unanimous written consent of shareholders. (T. 13-A, §1003).

Books and Records.—Corporation must keep accurate books and records of account and written minutes of shareholder, directors and committee proceedings. Corporation must also keep record of shareholders, containing name, address and number and class of shares held by each shareholder of record. Shareholder records must be kept at corporation's principal place of business or at office of clerk, transfer agent or registrar. Corporations other than close corporations must prepare balance sheet and profit and loss sheet as of close of most recent fiscal year within five months after close of fiscal year. (T. 13-A, §625).

Reports.—Every Maine corporation and every foreign corporation authorized to do business in state must file Annual Report with Secretary of State with three exceptions: (1) corporations that have been "excused" under statute; (2) religious, charitable, educational or benevolent corporations; and (3) corporations organized under specific non-stock corporation statutes. Annual reports must be filed by June 1 of each year and must contain: (1) name and jurisdiction of incorporation; (2) address of registered office in Maine, name of clerk or registered agent and, in case of foreign corporation, address of registered or principal office in jurisdiction of incorporation; (3) brief statement of character of business in which corporation is engaged in Maine, if any; and (4) name and address of president, treasurer, clerk or registered agent, and directors (or if there are no directors, shareholders). (T. 13-A, §1301).

Corporate Bonds or Mortgages.—Corporation may issue convertible bonds or debentures. (T. 13-A, §524). Corporations have power to mortgage property. (T. 13-A, §202).

Merger and Consolidation.—Corporations may merge or consolidate with other domestic, as well as foreign, corporations. (T. 13-A, §§901, 906). Requirements for approval include: (1) approval by board of directors of plan of merger or consolidation; (2) submission of plan of merger or consolidation to shareholders' meeting (special or annual); (3) special notice requirements for shareholders' meeting; and (4) affirmative vote of absolute majority of outstanding shares entitled to vote thereon, unless class voting provisions apply. Articles may prescribe greater vote. (T. 13-A, §902). Merger permitted without shareholder vote if plan of merger does not amend Articles of Incorporation of surviving corporation and shares of any class of stock of surviving corporation to be issued under plan of merger do not exceed 15% of shares of surviving corporation of same class outstanding immediately prior to date of merger. (T. 13-A, §902). Articles of Merger or Consolidation must be filed with Secretary of State with fee of $80. If merger or consolidation increases total authorized capital stock, additional amount required (see subhead Incorporation Tax, supra) which may not be less than $35. If change in corporation's purposes, additional $20 due. If new or surviving corporation is foreign corporation, fee for authority to do business in Maine also required. All fees paid to Secretary of State. (T. 13-A, §1401).

Dissolution.—Three methods of nonjudicial dissolution available: (1) by incorporators; (2) by unanimous written consent of shareholders; and (3) by shareholder vote. (T. 13-A, §§1101-1103). Judicial dissolution may be initiated by shareholders, creditors, corporation itself or Attorney General. (T. 13-A, §1115).

Procedure.—Voluntary dissolution by incorporators accomplished by filing articles of dissolution. (T. 13-A, §1101). Voluntary dissolution by unanimous written consent of shareholders accomplished by filing intent to dissolve. (T. 13-A, §1102). Voluntary dissolution by shareholder vote accomplished in following manner: (1) either (a) board of directors adopts resolution recommending that corporation be dissolved, and directing that question of dissolution be submitted to shareholder vote at annual or special meeting, or (b) shareholders owing at least 20% of all outstanding shares entitled to vote on dissolution may, in writing, propose dissolution of corporation and call upon board to submit their proposal to vote of shareholders; if directors fail or refuse for more than 30 days, shareholders proposing dissolution may call shareholder meeting; (2) written notice must be given to each shareholder of record entitled to vote at dissolution meeting stating that one purpose of such meeting is to consider dissolution; (3) affirmative vote of two-thirds shares entitled to vote required unless articles require greater percentage or class voting provisions apply; (4) upon adoption of resolution at shareholder meeting, statement of intent to dissolve must be filed with Secretary of State. (T. 13-A, §1103).

Upon filing of statement of intent to dissolve, corporation must cease business, except as may be necessary for winding up; corporate existence continues until filing date of articles of dissolution, or until decree of dissolution has been entered by court. (T. 13-A, §1105).

Articles of Dissolution.—After all debts, liabilities and obligations of corporation have been paid and discharged, or adequate provision has been made therefore, and all remaining property and assets of corporation have been distributed to shareholders, articles of dissolution are filed. Upon filing of articles of dissolution, corporate existence ceases with certain exceptions. (T. 13-A, §1110).

Insolvency and Receivers.—In dissolution proceedings, court may appoint liquidating receiver. (T. 13-A, §1117).

Close Corporations.—Defined as corporation with shares formed under laws of Maine which, at any given time, has 20 or less shareholders. (T. 13-A, §102). Articles of incorporation of close corporation may provide that corporation to be managed by its shareholders rather than by directors. (T. 13-A, §701). Articles of close corporation may provide that any shareholder or holder of any specified number, proportion or class of outstanding shares may dissolve corporation at will or upon occurrence of any specified event or contingency. (T. 13-A, §1114).

Appraisal rights available in following situations: (1) in connection with dissenters' rights resulting from merger, consolidation, sale of all or substantially all of corporation's assets not in usual and regular course of its business, or any other action as to which right to dissent is expressly given by MBCA (T. 13-A, §909); or (2) in connection with control transactions. See subhead Control Share Acquisitions, infra.

Foreign Corporations.—Foreign corporation may not do business in Maine until authorized to do so under statute. (T. 13-A, §1201). Foreign corporation may apply for authority to do business by executing and delivering for filing with Secretary of State application with fee of $180. Application must be accompanied by certificate of good standing from proper officer of jurisdiction of incorporation. Certificate of good standing must have been made not more than 90 days prior to delivery of application for filing. (T. 13-A, §§1202, 1401). Foreign corporation may own real estate without necessity of qualifying to do business within state. (T. 13-A, §1201). Foreign corporation which does business in Maine without required authority liable for all fees and penalties which would have been imposed under MBCA. In addition, such corporation liable to state for $25 per day for each day it fails to pay such fees and penalties. (T. 13-A, §1214). Foreign corporation which is authorized to do business in state must file annual report. (T. 13-A, §1301, see subhead Reports, supra). Foreign corporation authorized to do business in state must maintain registered agent and registered office. (T. 13-A, §1212).

Taxation of Corporate Property.—Same rules as apply to taxation of individuals except that personal property of manufacturing, mining, smelting, agricultural and stock raising corporations, and corporations organized for purpose of buying, selling and leasing real estate shall be taxed to corporation in place where situated except for personal property employed in trade (taxed in place where employed) and for property owned, leased or controlled by mining company (taxed at mine site). (T. 36, §§602 & 603). Reimbursement from state available for property tax paid on certain business property. See category Taxation, topic Property Taxes, subhead Real and Personal Property Taxable.

Taxation of Corporate Stock.—None.

Franchise Tax.—Repealed.

Income Tax.—See category Taxation, topic Income Tax.

Corporate Unitary Income Tax.—To extent corporation has income derived from unitary business carried on by two or more members of affiliated group, Maine net

CORPORATIONS . . . *continued*

income of such corporation is determined by apportioning that part of federal taxable income of entire group which derives from unitary business. (T. 36, §5102[8]).

In case of affiliated group of corporations engaged in unitary business, preferential corporate tax rates apply only to first $250,000 of Maine net income of entire group. (T. 36, §5200).

Corporate members of affiliated group engaged in unitary business must file combined report. (T. 36, §5220[5]).

Jurisdiction.—Foreign corporation not registered with Secretary of State but doing business in Maine subject to jurisdiction by Maine courts over act committed outside state. (404 A.2d 564).

Professional Corporations.—Corporation may be organized for purpose of performing any professional service which requires obtaining of license or other legal authorization prior to performing such services. Included would be accountants, chiropractors, dentists, doctors, architects, veterinarians, life insurance agents, attorneys, and others. (T. 13, §§701-716).

Maine Nonprofit Corporation Act.—T. 13-B, effective Jan. 1, 1978. Act is patterned after Maine Business Corporation Act, with variations.

Control Share Acquisitions.—Statute provides that when person or group acting in concert becomes "controlling person" (e.g., person or group acting in concert that has voting power over at least 25% of shares in any class entitled to elect director) such person or group must notify shareholders that control transaction has occurred. Shareholders may then demand payment for fair value of their shares under statutory procedures. Corporations may opt out of statute if articles of incorporation provide that statute not applicable. Statute does not apply to corporations not registered or traded on national exchange or not registered with Securities and Exchange Commission. (T. 13-A, §910).

Limited Liability Companies.—See topic Limited Liability Companies.

JOINT STOCK COMPANIES:

Not specifically authorized by statute.

LIMITED LIABILITY COMPANIES:

Limited liability companies authorized effective Jan. 1, 1995. (T. 31, §§601-762).

PARTNERSHIPS:

Uniform Partnership Act adopted. (T. 31, §§281-323).

Name.—Mercantile partnership must file certificate with city clerk setting forth names and residences of partners, and nature of business and name under which business is transacted. (T. 31, §1).

Limited Partnerships.—Maine Revised Uniform Limited Partnership Act adopted effective Jan. 1, 1992. Maine Revised Uniform Limited Partnership Act, T. 31, §§401-530. Follows substance, purpose and scope of Revised Uniform Limited Partnership Act (1976, with 1985 Amendments). Numerous material deviations from text of Revised Uniform Act have been made.

Limited Liability Partnerships.—Authorized. (T. 31, §§801-876).

BUSINESS REGULATION AND COMMERCE

BANKS AND BANKING:

Uniform Commercial Code and Consumer Credit Code adopted. Revised Art. 3 (designated Art. 3-A in Maine) has been adopted with minor variation from Uniform Act. Art. 4A of Uniform Commercial Code has been substantially adopted with technical modifications to conform to Maine statutory conventions. (T. 11, §§4-1101 to 4-1507). Conforming amendments also adopted with technical modification. (T. 11, §1-105[2]). Art. 4 also adopted. See topics: Commercial Code, Consumer Credit.

Regulated by T. 9-B. All state financial institutions, are supervised by Bureau of Banking. (T. 9-B, §§111, 121, 131). Superintendent has authority to prohibit officer or director of financial institution from participating in banking industry. (T. 9-B, §232).

Title 9-B organized as follows: (1) General Provisions, (2) Bureau of Banking, (3) Organization and Structure of Financial Institutions, (4) Powers and Duties of Financial Institutions, (5) Savings Banks (repealed), (6) Trust Companies (repealed), (7) Savings and Loans (repealed), (8) Credit Unions, (9) Industrial Banks, (10) Other Financial Entities, (11) Specialty or Limited Purpose Financial Institutions, (12) Foreign Banks.

Note: In 1997 Legislative Session, Maine Legislature enacted Universal Bank Charter with goal of creating single, universal bank charter. Because Universal Bank Charter was emergency legislation, it became effective upon signing by Governor.

With respect to newly-formed state-chartered institutions, differentiation between trust companies, savings banks or savings and loan associations will no longer exist. Rather, all institutions will be referred to as "universal banks". However, there will be no reduction in powers for existing trust companies, savings banks or savings and loan associations.

Notwithstanding generic powers of newly formed financial institutions under Maine law, Universal Bank Charter does provide for several "specialty" or "limited purpose" financial institutions set forth in §11 of Banking Code. Pursuant to 9-B M.R.S.A. §1211, non-depository trust company may be chartered to perform activities that are generally limited to trust or fiduciary matters. Pursuant to 9-B M.R.S.A. §1221, merchant bank may be chartered to perform lending and investing activities, as well as trust or fiduciary matters. Merchant banks are not permitted to engage in deposit activities. (9-B M.R.S.A. §1221). Uninsured bank may be chartered pursuant to 9-B M.R.S.A. §1231. Uninsured bank does not accept retail deposits and is not insured by FDIC. (9-B M.R.S.A. §1231).

Franchise Tax.—Financial institutions that have Maine net income or Maine assets and sufficient state presence are subject to franchise tax even if institution is treated for federal income tax purposes as partnership, S corporation, or entity disregarded as separate from its owner.

Deposits.—

Form.—May be made in trust for another, made jointly in names of two or more persons with or without rights of survivorship, made in name of minor. (T. 9-B, §427).

Death.—Deposits of decedent under $1,000 may be paid to survivors or creditors without liability to executor or administrator if payment made more than six months after decedent's death and no personal representative has been appointed. (T. 9-B, §427 [8]). Financial institution may pay orders drawn by decedent prior to death from funds on deposit if presentation is made within 30 days of order and for subsequent periods, provided actual notice of death of drawer has not been received. (T. 9-B, §427[11]).

Demand Deposits.—Financial institutions may accept demand deposits from individuals and others. (T. 9-B, §421-A).

Deposits by Minor.—Deposits in name of minor are property of minor and financial institution has discretion to pay such deposits to minor or his guardian. (T. 9-B, §427).

Fiduciary Deposits.—In absence of notice of terms of trust, upon death or disability of fiduciary, bank may pay either to fiduciary's executor, administrator, conservator or guardian, or to substituted fiduciary, or to beneficiary (or to parent, guardian or person standing in *loco parentis* to beneficiary who is under age 15). Foregoing is subject to §6-111 of Uniform Probate Code. (T. 9-B, §427; T. 18-A, §6-111).

Insurance.—All state financial institutions shall take any action necessary to have deposits or accounts insured by FDIC. (T. 9-B, §422).

Joint Deposits.—Subject to §6-112 of Uniform Probate Code, financial institution is released from further liability if it makes payment to either depositor, whether other is living or not, or to legal representative of survivor of such depositors if proofs of death are presented showing that decedent was last surviving party or if there is clear and convincing evidence that no rights of survivorship were intended when account was created. (T. 9-B, §427). Joint deposits become property of surviving party or parties, unless clear and convincing evidence of different intention at time account was created. (T. 9-B, §427; T. 18-A, §6-104). Joint deposits may be pledged in whole or in part by those authorized to make withdrawals therefrom, unless contrary to specific terms of deposit or account. (T. 9-B, §427).

Transfer.—Deposit or accounts are transferable by written assignment accompanied by delivery of evidence of deposit or account. (T. 9-B, §427).

Unclaimed Deposits.—Definition and disposition of abandoned funds controlled by Unclaimed Property Act. (T. 33, §§1951-1980).

Branch Banking.—Subject to certain conditions, branch offices may be established anywhere in state. Prohibited branches and satellite facilities governed by T. 9-B, §339-A.

Mobile branches are permitted in certain rural areas. (T. 9-B, §339).

Satellite facilities are governed by T. 9-B, §§334-339-A. Notice requirements are also included in those sections. Satellite facilities operated by financial institutions not authorized to do business in this State are expressly prohibited. (T. 9-B, §339-A[2]).

Collections.—Uniform Commercial Code adopted. (T. 11, Art. 4).

Set-Off.—Bank cannot set off past due indebtedness against deposit intended to be held in trust, if intention communicated to bank or circumstances such as to charge bank with knowledge of intention. (98 Me. 448, 57 A. 799).

Industrial banks authorized. Individual loan must not exceed 4% of total capital and reserves for direct loans and 15% of total capital and reserves for indirect loans. Limitation inapplicable to obligations of U.S. and of Maine. (T. 9-B, §918[1]).

Banking emergency may be proclaimed by Governor and thereupon Superintendent of Bureau of Banking may regulate and restrict payments by banks. (T. 9-B, §§151-152).

Uniform Common Trust Fund Act enacted with substantial variation. (T. 18-A, §§7-501 to 7-503). Applies to fiduciary relationships in existence on Sept. 1, 1951 or thereafter established. (T. 18-A, §7-503). Nonuniform variations to §1 of Uniform Act include authorization of common trust funds for purpose of furnishing investments to affiliated banks; definition of "common trust fund" to include any trust or fund maintained by bank or trust company exclusively for collective investment or reinvestment of money contributed thereto by bank or trust company, or affiliate thereof, as fiduciary, including trustee of any employee benefits trust or fund; definition of "fiduciary" to include trustees, executors, administrators, guardians and custodians under Uniform Transfers to Minors Act. (T. 18-A, §7-501). Nonuniform variations to §2 of Uniform Act include: adoption of Maine-specific notice and service provisions and placement of jurisdiction in Superior Court or probate court, in county where accountant has its principal place of business, as proper forum for accountant petitioning for court approval of its accounting. (T. 18-A, §7-502). §§3 through 6 of Uniform Act not enacted in Maine.

Foreign Banks.—Foreign financial institution holding company, foreign bank or foreign bank holding company may establish or acquire more than 5% interest in Maine financial institution or financial institution holding company or any financial institution holding company controlling, directly or indirectly, Maine financial institution only with prior approval of Superintendent of Banking. (T. 9-B, §§1013, 1015). Exceptions to prior approval requirement may exist when Maine financial institution, Maine financial institution holding company or financial institution holding company controlling Maine financial institution engages in closely related activity or establishes subsidiary or when Maine financial institution holding company or financial institution holding company controls Maine financial institution holding company or acquires or establishes subsidiary, if certain conditions are met. (T. 9-B, §1015). Foreign bank or trust company may serve in fiduciary capacity to extent that Maine banks are permitted to serve as fiduciaries in state in which such foreign bank is organized. Such foreign bank must designate Secretary of State as attorney for service of process and otherwise qualify in manner of other foreign corporations, and must file certificate within 90 days of application from official supervising banks where foreign bank was organized

---

See note at head of Digest as to 1998 legislation covered.

See Topical Index in front part of this volume.

BANKS AND BANKING . . . *continued*

indicating that it is duly authorized, that it has authority to act in fiduciary capacity and that foreign state grants similar authority to banks of this State. (T. 18, §§4161-4163-A).

Mutual Financial Institution Conversions.—Conversion of mutual financial institution into mutual holding company governed by T. 9-B, §§1051-1055.

Community Development Credit Union.—Community development credit unions were developed in 1997 to promote economic revitalization for low income wage earners. (T. 9-B, §§131, 817, 827).

BILLS AND NOTES:

Uniform Commercial Code adopted. See topic Commercial Code.
Uniform Consumer Credit Code adopted. See topic Consumer Credit.

Judgment Notes.—Confessions of judgment authorized in consumer credit transaction agreement are void. (T. 9-A, §3-306). See topic Consumer Credit.

Attorney Fees.—Provision requiring maker to pay all expenses attendant to enforcing payment of note is not against public policy. (154 A.2d 161). No statutory provisions.

BILLS OF LADING:

See topic Carriers.

BILLS OF SALE:

No specific statutory provisions. See generally topic Sales.

BLUE SKY LAW:

See topic Securities.

BROKERS:

Brokers and producers are generally regulated under various statutes and administrative regulations. See topic Licenses, Business and Professional.

Insurance Producers.—The Maine Insurance Code defines insurance producer as one who solicits, takes application for, negotiates, effects, procures, delivers, renews, binds or receives commissions for policies of insurance. (24-A M.R.S.A. §1402[6]). Insurance producers are licensed by Superintendent of Insurance.

Real Estate Brokers.—Licensed by Real Estate Commission. (T. 32, §§13003, 13061).

Salvage Brokers.—Person, firm or corporation engaged in buying, selling, distributing or warehousing distressed merchandise, whether or not in combination with other merchandise, which does not operate food salvage establishment must obtain license from Commissioner of Agriculture, Food and Rural Resources. (T. 22, §§2152, 2167).

Misc. Brokers.—Securities broker-dealers, sales representatives and investment advisers are licensed by Securities Administrator. (T. 32, §§10301-10314). See topic Securities.

Brokers of agricultural commodities are licensed by the Commissioner of Agriculture, Food and Rural Resources. (T. 7, §§451-460).

Uniform Commercial Code adopted. See topic Commercial Code.

CARRIERS:

Minimally regulated at state level. Some municipal regulations. Ferries are subject to regulation and control of Public Utilities Commission. (T. 35-A, §§102, 103).

See also category Transportation, topic Motor Vehicles, subhead Motor Vehicle Carriers.

Uniform Commercial Code adopted. See topic Commercial Code.

Bills of Lading.—Uniform Commercial Code governs. (U.C.C. §§7-101-7-603). Optional phrase in §7-403 omitted. For other options and deviations from U.C.C., see topic Commercial Code.

Liens.—Uniform Commercial Code governs. (U.C.C. §§7-307, 7-308).

Unclaimed Baggage and Merchandise.—Freight and baggage transported by carrier which remains unclaimed for six months after arrival may be sold at auction. Public notice is required. (T. 33, §§1701-1702). Common carriers may sell unclaimed perishable goods or livestock after complying with statutory notice requirements. (T. 33, §§1703-1704).

Hazardous Substances and Materials.—Transportation of hazardous substances is subject to certain provisions of Uniform Hazardous Substances Labeling Act. (T. 7, §§501-513). That act does not apply to carriers who, while lawfully transporting hazardous substance, permit Commissioner of Agriculture, upon request, to copy any records showing transactions in and movement of articles. (T. 7, §509). Transportation of hazardous materials is also subject to hazardous material control law pursuant to which 49 C.F.R. parts 107, 171-174, 177-180, 387 and 397 have been adopted by reference. (T. 25, §§2101-2106-A; Dept. of Pub. Safety, Bureau of State Police Reg. c. 6). See also subhead Railroads, infra.

Disputed Title.—Common carrier is authorized to delay transportation of property for up to five days if title to such property is claimed by person other than consignor or consignee. (T. 33, §1751).

Taxation.—Certain common carriers may claim refund of fuel tax. (T. 36, §§2909, 3215).

Railroad Crossings.—Vehicles transporting certain hazardous materials and passenger buses are required to stop at railroad crossings. (T. 29-A, §2076[3]).

Railroads.—State may after hearing acquire railroad line for sale, lease or contract to operator by obtaining federal regulatory approvals or by eminent domain, to ensure safe, efficient, reliable service. (T. 23, §§7101-7156).

Applications for financial assistance from state or for permission to acquire or construct additional rail lines governed by T. 23, §7320.

Transport of Hazardous Materials.—Any person transporting by rail more than 25 tons of certain hazardous materials at one time required to register annually and pay fee of 15¢ per ton of hazardous materials transported, payable quarterly, or $25,000 payable at time of registration. (T. 38, §1319-I).

Major Modifications of Rail Service.—Any railroad which files I.C.C. petition or proposal concerning sale, merger, abandonment or embargo of any rail line in Maine shall concurrently file copy of same with Department of Transportation. Any person or entity which proposes to acquire or construct additional railroad line in Maine or provide rail service over extended or additional railroad line, and which files petition or proposal with I.C.C. to do so shall file copy of same with Department of Transportation. (T. 23, §7104).

COMMERCIAL CODE:

Uniform Commercial Code adopted effective Dec. 31, 1964. (T. 11, §§1-101-10-108). Arts. 1, 2, 4, 6 and -7 based on 1962 Official Text which is printed in Uniform and Model Acts section. Art. 6, Bulk Transfers, repealed effective June 30, 1992. Art. 2A, Leases, based on 1987 and 1990 Official Text, effective June 30, 1992. (T. 11, §§2-1101—2-1531). Art. 3, Commercial Paper (1962 Official Text), repealed and replaced by Revised Art. 3, Negotiable Instruments (designated Art. 3-A in Maine) (T. 11, §§3-1101—3-1605), effective Oct. 13, 1993. Maine's Art. 3-A is substantial enactment of Uniform Art. 3 with minor variations. Art. 4-A, Funds Transfers, based on 1989 Official Text, effective June 30, 1992. (T. 11, §§4-1101—4-1507). Art. 5 (designated Art. 5-A in Maine) is based on 1994 Official Text, effective Sept. 19, 1997. Art. 8 (designated Art. 8-A in Maine) is based on 1994 Official Text, effective Sept. 19, 1997. Art. 9, Secured Transactions, is based on 1972 Official Text, effective Jan. 1, 1978. Art. 10, Transition Provisions, similar to Art. 11 of Official Text. See Part III for Official Text.

Address of Secretary of State.—Secretary of State, State House Station 101, Augusta, ME 04333-0101.

Options in Official Text have been exercised as follows: §2A-216, alternative C adopted; §3-121, alternative A adopted; §4-106, optional phrase adopted; §4-202(1)(b), optional phrase adopted; §4-212, optional paragraph adopted; §7-204, optional subsection (4) for reference to local statutes omitted; §7-403(1)(b), optional phrase omitted; §9-401(1), first alternative subsection (1) adopted; §9-401(6), deleted; optional §9-407 adopted; 2A-216, alternate C adopted.

Variances from 1962 Official Text.—In addition to purely formal changes made to conform to standard Maine legislative drafting practices, following variances and additions to 1962 Official Text are found in the Maine statute: §1-102, subsection (5) deleted; §1-109 omitted; §1-201(30), cross reference to §1-102 deleted; §1-201(33), "or his nominee" inserted; §1-201(46) omitted; §1-207(2), adds accord and satisfaction does not apply to renumbered subsection (1); §1-209, 1966 Official Optional Amendment not adopted; §2-107(1), "timber" deleted; §2-107(2), "or of timber to be cut" inserted before "is a contract"; §2-108 added which reads: "The procurement, processing, distribution or use of whole blood, plasma, blood products, blood derivatives and other human tissues such as corneas, bones or organs for the purpose of injecting, transfusing or transplanting any of them into the human body is declared to be, for all purposes, the rendition of a service by every person participating therein and, whether or not any remuneration is paid therefor, is declared not to be a sale of such whole blood, plasma, blood products, blood derivatives or other tissues, for any purpose, subsequent to October 1, 1969."; §2-313(1)(b), second sentence has been inserted which reads: "In the case of consumer goods sold by a merchant with respect to such goods, the description affirms that the goods are fit for the ordinary purposes for which such goods are used"; §2-313(1)(c), "whole of the" deleted; §§2-314(1) and 2-314(3), "by section 2-316" in lieu of "(Section 2-316)"; §2-316(5) provides that disclaimer of warranties of merchantability or fitness for a particular purpose unenforceable as to consumer goods, including mobile homes; §2-316(5)(a) provides that violation of §§2-314, 2-315 or 2-316 arising from retail sale of consumer goods and services constitutes violation of Unfair Trade Practices Act; §2-318, lack of privity no defense in any action against manufacturer, seller or supplier of goods for breach of warranty, if plaintiff was person whom defendant might reasonably have expected to use, consume or be affected by goods; §2-607, subsection (7) added stating that subparagraph (3), paragraph (a) shall not apply where remedy is for personal injury resulting from any breach; §2-702, 1966 Official Amendment adopted; §2-725, following paragraph added to subsection (2): "A cause of action for personal injuries arising under this Article for breach of warranty occurs when the injury takes place and is governed by the limitation of action period under Title 14 section 752"; Revised Art. 3 and conforming amendments thereto adopted; §4-106, optional language adopted; §4-202, optional language adopted; §4-204, 1962 Official Text Amendment adopted; §4-212, optional subsection (2) adopted; §7-209, 1966 Official Amendment not adopted. Conforming amendments to repeal of Art. 6 have been made.

Variations from 1972 Official Text.—In addition to purely formal changes made to conform to standard Maine legislative drafting practices and changes resulting from adoption of Art. 8 (as revised by 1994 revision project), following variances and additions to 1972 Official Text are found in Maine statute: §9-102(1), after "provided in" add "section 9-103 on multiple state transactions in"; §9-103(1)(d)(iii) substitute "section 9-307, subsection (3)" for "(subsection (2) of Section 9-307)."; §9-103(3)(a) after "trailers" insert "mobile homes" before "rolling stock"; §9-103(3)(b) after "located," add "when the last event occurs on which is based the assertion that the security interest is perfected or unperfected"; §9-103(6) omitted; §9-104(a), after "United States" add "such as the Ship Mortgage Act, 1920"; §9-104(e), insert following after "agency": "other than an Indian tribal government"; §9-104(k), after "part of" add "any of the following:"; §9-109(4), add following sentence before last sentence: " 'Inventory' includes timber to be cut."; §9-111, repealed in conformity with repeal of Art. 6; §9-203(4) reads: "A transaction, although subject to this Article, is also subject to the applicable provisions of Title 9-A, or to Title 30, sections 3961 and 3965, and in the case of conflict between the provisions of this Article and any

COMMERCIAL CODE . . . *continued*
such statute the provisions of such statute control. Failure to comply with any applicable statute has only the effect which is specified therein." §9-301(2), time for filing with respect to purchase money security interest is 20 days after debtor receives possession of collateral; §9-302, 1977 conforming amendment adopted; §9-302(1)(d), reads: "A purchase money security interest in consumer goods where the amount financed, as defined in Title 9-A, section 1-301, subsection 5, is less than $2,000, but fixture filing is required for priority over conflicting interests in fixtures to the extent provided in section 9-313.": §9-302(3)(b), omits "of this state" and lists "Title to motor vehicles, Title 29, Chapter 7" in lieu of bracketed material; §9-304, 1977 conforming amendment adopted; §9-305, 1977 conforming amendment adopted; §9-306(2), after "Article" insert "or Article 8" before "otherwise provides"; §9-306(3), after "section" in last sentence, insert "and in Article 8" before "a security interest"; §9-307(1), insert after "business," "other than a person buying timber, logs or pulpwood from a person engaged in timbering operations or from a person dealing in timber, logs or pulpwood and"; §9-307(2), repealed; §9-309, 1977 conforming amendments adopted; §9-312, 1977 conforming amendment adopted; §9-312(4), substitute "20 days" for "ten days"; §9-401(1), in subsection (1)(a), insert "or is crops growing or to be grown," after "Section 9-103," and "concerned" after "real estate," after subsection (1)(a), insert subsection (1)(a-1) reading as follows: "(a-1) When the collateral is farm products, a filing may be made with the Secretary of State in accordance with procedures adopted under Title 5, section 90-A." §9-401(1)(b), bracketed material reads: "Secretary of State"; §9-401(6), omitted; §9-402(1), at end of first sentence insert"; provided that, for purposes of this section, if the collateral is a mobile home as defined in Title 10, section 1402, subsection 2, the description of collateral shall include the location designated by the debtor in the security agreement as the place at which the mobile home is, or is to be, located."; third sentence, after "subject to" add section 9-103, subsection (5), "or covers crops growing or to be grown"; 9-402(1) last sentence, insert "legible" before "carbon"; 9-402(2), delete "(subsection 7)", add second sentence which reads: "The secured party is not required to file a new financing statement to perfect or continue to perfect a security interest after such change of name, identity or corporate structure of the debtor"; §9-402(3), insert "Mailing" before "address," in item 3, delete "and this financing statement is to be filed [for record] in the real estate records"; §9-402(5), after "Section 9-103" add "or covering crops growing or to be grown"; and delete "must recite that it is to be filed [for record] in the real estate records" and "[sufficient if it were contained in a mortgage of real estate to give constructive notice of the mortgage under the law of this state]"; §9-402(6)(c), delete "other than a recital that it is to be filed in the real estate records"; §9-402(7), delete sentence beginning "Where the debtor so changes his name . . ."; §9-403(3), insert "and if the continuation statement covers timber to be cut, minerals or the like, including oil and gas, or accounts subject to section 9-103 subsection (5), or crops growing or to be grown or fixtures, it shall contain the name of the record owner." after "the original statement is still effective,"; insert "Unless an assignment is a matter of record," before "a continuation statement signed by a person"; §9-403(4), insert at end of last sentence, "In addition, if the financing statement is filed in the office of a register of deeds and contains the name of a record owner of real estate, the filing officer shall also index the statement according to the name of the record owner of the real estate. The index may be made up of the statements themselves, copies thereof, separate cards or otherwise.", delete "In addition" from beginning of second sentence; §9-403(5), fee for filing, indexing and furnishing filing data for original financing statement filed on or after July 1, 1993 is $20, except that filing fee at registry of deeds is $8 for first page and $2 for each page thereafter (T. 33, §751), with $3 surcharge for each document recorded (T. 33, §752). Fee for filing, indexing and furnishing filing data for continuation statement or any amendment to continuation statement shall be $10, except that filing fee at registry of deeds is same as if original were filed on or after July 1, 1993; §9-403(7) in its entirety is as follows: "When a financing statement, continuation statement, termination statement, statement of assignment or a statement of release covers timber to be cut or covers minerals or the like, including oil and gas, or accounts subject to sections 9-103, subsection (5), or covering crops growing or to be grown, or is filed as a fixture filing, the filing officer shall index it under the names of the debtor and any owner of record shown on the financing statement in the same fashion as if they were the mortgagors in a mortgage of the real estate described, and under the name of the secured party as if he were the mortgagee thereunder."; §9-404(1) in its entirety is as follows: "(1) The following provisions apply to the sending or filing of termination statements: (a) With respect to financing statements filed prior to April 1, 1970: Whenever there is no outstanding secured obligation and no commitment to make advances, incur obligations or otherwise give value, the secured party must within 30 days from the date on which the foregoing first occurs send the debtor a statement that he no longer claims a security interest under the financing statement, which shall be identified by file number. A termination statement signed by a person other than the secured party of record must include or be accompanied by the assignment or a statement by the secured party of record that he has assigned the security interest to the signer of the termination statement. The fee for filing and indexing such an assignment or statement thereof shall be $3. If the affected secured party fails to send such a termination statement he shall be liable to the debtor for $10, and in addition for any loss caused to the debtor by such failure. (b) With respect to financing statements filed on or after April 1, 1970: Whenever there is no outstanding secured obligation and no commitment to make advances, incur obligations or otherwise give value, the secured party must within 30 days from the date on which the foregoing first occurs, file a termination statement stating that the secured party no longer claims a security interest under the financing statement, which must be identified by file number. A termination statement signed by a person other than the secured party of record must include or be accompanied by the assignment or a statement by the secured party of record that the secured party has assigned the security interest to the signer of the termination statement. The fee for filing and indexing such an assignment or statement thereof is $3. If the affected secured party fails to file such a termination statement, the secured party is liable to the debtor for $25, and in addition for any loss caused to the debtor by such failure."; §9-404(3), fee for filing and indexing termination relating to financing statement filed after Apr. 1, 1970 and prior to July 1, 1993, is $10 if acknowledgment copy of UCC-1 form is used and $15 if terminated by filing UCC-3 amendment form; no fee for filing and indexing termination statement with respect to financing statement filed on or after July 1, 1993. Fee for termination of financing statement that was filed prior to Apr. 1, 1970 is $2. Register of deeds receives fee of $8 for first record page and $2 for each additional record page with respect to filing and indexing termination statement (T. 33, §751), plus $3 per document surcharge (T. 33, §752); §9-405(1), uniform fee for filing, indexing and furnishing filing data for financing statement indicating assignment is $5, except that filing fee at registry of deeds is $8 for first page plus $3 per document surcharge and $2 for each page thereafter; §9-405(2), reads as follows: "A secured party may assign of record all or a part of his rights under a financing statement by filing in the place where the original financing statement was filed of a separate written statement of assignment signed by the secured party of record and setting forth the name of the secured party of record and the debtor, the file number and the date of filing of the financing statement and the name and address of the assignee and containing a description of the collateral assigned. A copy of the assignment is sufficient as a separate statement if it complies with the preceding sentence. On presentation to the filing officer of such a separate statement, the filing officer shall mark such separate statement with the date and hour of the filing. He shall note the assignment on the index of the financing statement, or in the case of a fixture filing, or a filing covering timber to be cut, or covering minerals or the like, including oil and gas, or accounts subject to section 9-103, subsection (5), or covering crops growing or to be grown, he shall index the assignment under the name of the assignor as grantor and, he shall index the assignment of the financing statement under the name of the assignee. The uniform fee for filing, indexing and furnishing filing data about such a separate statement of assignment shall be $3. Notwithstanding the provisions of this subsection, an assignment of record of a security interest in a fixture contained in a mortgage effective as a fixture filing, section 9-402, subsection (6), may be made only by an assignment of the mortgage in the manner provided by the laws of this State other than this Title." §9-406, insert "Unless an assignment is a matter of record, a statement of release signed by a person other than the secured party of record must be accompanied by a separate written statement of assignment signed by the secured party of record and complying with section 9-405, subsection (2), including payment of the required fee," in place of third sentence; uniform fee for filing and noting statement of release is $3 in all cases; §9-407(1), substitutes "statement of release" for "statement or release"; §9-407(2) reads as follows: "Upon the written request of any person, the filing officer shall issue an information request report, in such form as the Secretary of State may approve, showing whether there is on file on the date and hour stated therein any presently effective financing statement naming a particular debtor and any statement of assignment thereof and if there is, giving the date and hour of filing of each such statement and the names and addresses of each secured party therein. The uniform fee for an information request report is $5, plus $.50 for each page of the report after the first page. Upon request the filing office shall furnish a copy of any filed financing statement, continuation statement, termination statement, statement of assignment or statement of release for a fee of $2 plus $.50 for each page of the copy after the first page."

"Notwithstanding this subsection, if the filing officer is a municipal clerk or a register of deeds, issuance of the certificate of information is discretionary.

"Upon reasonable request and within the existing ability of the office of the Secretary of State to respond, the filing officer shall furnish to any municipal clerk, without charge and for municipal purposes only, a copy of any filed financing statement, continuation statement, termination statement, statement of assignment or statement of release. The uniform fee for certification is $5 for a short-form certificate and $10 for a specially worded certificate."; §9-409, insert following section; "The Secretary of State may provide an expedited service for the processing of documents in accordance with this Part. If the service is provided, the Secretary of State shall establish by rule a fee schedule and governing procedures in accordance with the Maine Administrative Procedure Act. All fees collected as provided by this section must be deposited into a fund for use by the Secretary of State in providing an improved filing service."; §9-410, insert following section: "The Secretary of State may provide public access to the database of the Department of the Secretary of State through a dial-in modem, public terminals and electronic duplicates of the database. If access to the database is provided to the public, the Secretary of State may promulgate rules in accordance with the Maine Administrative Procedure Act to establish a fee schedule and governing procedures."; §9-411, insert following section: "*1. Informational publications.* The Secretary of State may establish by rule in accordance with the Maine Administrative Procedure Act (Section 8001 et seq. of title 5) a fee schedule to cover the cost of printing and distribution of publications and to set forth the procedures for the sale of these publications.

"*2. Fund; fees deposited.* All fees collected pursuant to this section must be deposited in a fund for use by the Secretary of State for the purpose of replacing and updating publications offered in accordance with this Part and for funding new publications."; §9-412, insert following section: "The Secretary of State may accept electronic filings of federal tax liens. The Secretary of State may establish by rule in accordance with the Maine Administrative Procedure Act (Section 8001 et seq. of title 5) the procedures and standards for electronic filings of federal tax liens." §9-413, insert following section: "The Secretary of State has the power and authority necessary to administer this Part and perform the duties imposed. These powers include, without limitation, the power to:

(1) Make rules consistent with this Part;

(2) Prescribe forms for all documents required or permitted to be filed with the Secretary of State and to refuse to file documents not utilizing the prescribed forms to the extent possible; and

(3) Refuse to file any document that is not clearly legible or may not be clearly reproducible photographically."; §9-504(1), insert "or lease" after "for sale" and "selling,"; §9-504(2), delete "contract rights" preceding "chattel paper"; §9-504(3), insert ", except in the case of consumer goods," after "shall be sent by the secured party to the debtor, if"; §9-505(2) reads: "In any other case involving consumer goods or any other collateral, a secured party in possession may, after default, propose to

COMMERCIAL CODE... *continued*
retain the collateral in satisfaction of the obligation. Written notice of such proposal shall be sent to the debtor if he has not signed after default a statement renouncing or modifying his rights under this subsection. In the case of consumer goods, no other notice need be given. In other cases, notice shall be sent to any other secured party from whom the secured party has received, before sending his notice to the debtor or before the debtor's renunciation of his rights, written notice of a claim of an interest in the collateral. If the secured party receives objection in writing from a person entitled to receive notification within 21 days after the notice was sent, the secured party must dispose of the collateral under §9-504. In the absence of such written objection, the secured party may retain the collateral in satisfaction of the debtor's obligation."

Variations from 1989 Official Text: §4A-205(a)(2) and (3) (designated §4-1205[1][b] and [c] in Maine code) reads as follows: "(b) If the funds transfer is completed on the basis of a payment order that erroneously instructed payment to a beneficiary not intended by the sender or that was an erroneously transmitted duplicate of a payment order previously sent by the sender, the sender is not obliged to pay the order and the receiving bank is entitled to recover from the beneficiary any amount paid to the beneficiary to the extent allowed by the law governing mistake and restitution.

(c) If the funds transfer is completed on the basis of a payment order erroneously instructing payment in an amount greater than the amount intended by the sender, the sender is not obliged to pay the order to the extent the amount received by the beneficiary is greater than the amount intended by the sender. In that case, the receiving bank is entitled to recover from the beneficiary the excess amount received to the extent allowed by the law governing mistake and restitution." §4A-302(3) (designated §4-1302 in Maine code) reads as follows: "(3) Unless subsection (1), paragraph (b) applies or the receiving bank is otherwise instructed, the bank may execute a payment order by transmitting its payment order by first class mail or by any reasonable means. If the receiving bank is instructed to execute the sender's order by transmitting its payment order by a particular means, the receiving bank may issue its payment order by the means stated or by any equivalent means." Conforming technical amendment to Art. 1 adopted.

Variations from 1987 and 1990 Official Text: In addition to formal changes made to conform to standard Maine legislative drafting practices, following variances and additions to 1987 and 1990 Official Text are found in Maine statute: §2A-103(e), end with "$25,000"; §2A-103(h), after "lease contract" add "including mobile homes"; §2A-104, subsection (1)(a) reads: "Certificate of title statute of this State;"; §2A-109, in subsection (1), substitute "when the party represents that that party is insecure" for "when he [or she] deems himself [or herself]insecure"; §2A-201, in subsection (4)(a), substitute "specifically' for "specially"; §2A-209(1), after "claims arising therefrom." add "In a finance lease that is a consumer lease, supplier's ability to disclaim, exclude or modify any implied warranties of merchantability and fitness of a particular purpose or to exclude and modify the consumer's remedies for breech of those remedies is subject to §2A-316, subsection (5)"; §2A-214(5), add "In a consumer lease that is not a finance lease, the lessor's ability to disclaim, exclude or modify any implied warranties of merchantability and fitness for a particular purpose or to exclude or modify the consumer's remedies for breach of those warranties is subject to and governed by the terms and provisions of §2A-316, subsection (5)"; §2A-216, Alternative C adopted; §2A-221, delete text after "the lease contract is avoided;" add "and (2) After delivery in a consumer lease, if the goods are lost or destroyed: (a) If the lessee is not in default under the lease, the lessee may provide substitute goods of at least equal kind and quality satisfactory to the lessor and continue the lease. Permission to substitute goods may not be unreasonably withheld by the lessor. Any insurance proceeds paid with respect to the goods must be applied to the purchase of the substitute goods; or (b) At the consumer's option, any insurance proceeds must be paid to the lessor and, in such an instance, the lessee remains liable only for the insurance deductible plus any amounts otherwise due to the lessor because of any prior default by the lessee under the terms of the lease."; §2A-303(8), at end add "The lessor's remedies with regard to a prohibited transfer or a transfer that results in default are subject to the duty of the lessor to mitigate damages."; §2A-510(2), delete "But" at beginning of second sentence and add the word "shall" after "the aggrieved party" and substitute word "reinstate" for "reinstates"; §2A-511(1), in first sentence, word "to" is used instead of word "or" after "reasonable instructions received from the lessor", probably an error; §2A-516(3)(a), insert "Except in the case of a consumer lease," before "within a reasonable time", delete word "over" after word "remedy"; §2A-516(3)(b), delete word "except" before "in the case of a consumer lease," delete all text after "within a reasonable time after the lessee receives" and insert "discovers or should have discovered any default, the lessee shall notify either the lessor or any assignee of the lessor. By notifying one of these parties the lessee preserves any remedy against any of the parties; and"; §2A-524(1), delete "After default by the lessee under the lease contract of the type described in §2A-523(1) or §2A-523(3)(a) or, if agreed, after other default by the lessee, the lessor may" at beginning of section and add "A lessor aggrieved under section 2-1523, subsection (1) [§2A-523(1)] may"; §2A-525(3), substitute "if possible" for "if it can be done"; §2A-528, in title of section delete words "failure to pay" and "other default"; §2A-529(5), delete all text before "a lessor who is held not entitled" and insert "After a lessee has wrongfully rejected or revoked acceptance of goods, has failed to pay rent then due or has repudiated (section 2-1402) [§2A-402]". Revised Art. 3 (designated Art. 3-A in Maine) and conforming amendments to other Arts. adopted.

Variations from 1994 Official Text.—Only purely formal changes have been made to conform to standard Maine legislative drafting practices.

Filing Fees.—See category Documents and Records, topic Records, subhead Filing Under Commercial Code.

Forms.—See end of this Digest.

See also topics: Banks and Banking, Bills and Notes, Brokers, Carriers, Contracts, Factors, Frauds, Statute of, Sales, Securities, Warehousemen; categories Business Organizations, topic Corporations; Civil Actions and Procedure, topic Limitation of Actions; Debtor and Creditor, topics Assignments, Fraudulent Sales and Conveyances, Liens, Pledges; Documents and Records, topics Records, Seals; Mortgages, topic Chattel Mortgages.

CONSUMER CREDIT:

Uniform Consumer Credit Code (1974 Act) adopted effective Jan. 1, 1975.

Maine Consumer Credit Code, T. 9-A, §§1-101-11-121, follows the substance, purpose and scope of Uniform Consumer Credit Code. Code is administered by Bureau of Consumer Credit Protection. Major changes in organization and numerous material deviations from text of Uniform Code have been made. Because of number of deviations from Official Text, it is not feasible to specifically list such deviations here.

Maine Act organized as follows:
Art. I.—General Provisions and Definitions.
Art. II.—Finance Charges and Related Provisions.
Art. III.—Regulation of Agreements and Practices.
Art. IV.—Insurance.
Art. V.—Remedies and Penalties.
Art. VI.—Administration.
Art. VII.—Repealed.
Art. VIII.—Truth-in-Lending.
Art. IX.—Consumer Credit Transactions Secured by First-Lien Mortgages.
Art. X.—Credit Services Organizations.
Art. XI.—Rental-Purchase Practices.

Disclosure of consumer credit terms covered by T. 9-A, §§8-201—8-209.

Portions of Maine Insurance Code, T. 24-A, are incorporated in Article IV of Consumer Credit Code, replacing provisions of Uniform Code.

CONSUMER PROTECTION:

In addition to Maine Consumer Credit Code discussed under topic Consumer Credit, following consumer protection legislation exists in Maine:

Fair Credit Reporting Act.—T. 10, §§1311-1329, regulates consumer reporting and investigative consumer reporting, disclosure of information to consumers by consumer reporting agencies, and provides procedures for correcting inaccurate or misleading information.

Financial Planner's Disclosure.—Financial planner required to disclose to consumer any direct or indirect interest he has, or any potential financial gain he stands to make, if consumer makes recommended investment. (T. 32, §§9751-9754).

Home Solicitation Sales.—T. 32, §§4661-4671 allows consumer to avoid contract entered into as result of salesman's direct contact with consumer by means of personal visit or telephone call or otherwise without consumer soliciting contract or call. Contract must be written, signed by both parties, and contain date of transaction, terms of sale, mailing address of seller's permanent place of business, statement of limitation and consumer's right to avoid transaction. Contract must be provided to consumer immediately following signature. Contract may be avoided by written notice and consumer may demand within 20 days of such notice that seller take possession of any goods, at consumer's residence, and if seller fails to do so within 20 days, goods become property of consumer. In making sale, seller may not misrepresent material fact, create false impression or make false promises. Violations punishable by fine of not more than $2,000 (or $10,000 if defendant is organization) or imprisonment for not more than one year or both. (T. 32, §4667; T. 17-A, §§1252, 1301). Violation also constitutes violation of Unfair Trade Practices Act. (T. 32, §4670). See subhead Unfair Trade Practices Act, infra.

New Housing.—Judicially recognized implied warranty of habitability from builder-vendor to initial purchaser. (407 A.2d 294).

Home Construction Contracts.—Any home construction contract for more than $1,400 in materials or labor must be in writing and signed by contractor and homeowner or lessee. Homeowner or lessee must receive copy of executed contract, which must contain certain specified information and provisions, prior to any work performance. (T. 10, §1487).

Change orders must be in writing, signed by both parties, detail changes in original contract that result in revised contract price, and state previous and revised contract price. (T. 10, §1488).

Exemptions from requirements of T. 10, §§1487, 1488 permitted only if contractor specifically informs homeowner or lessee of rights and parties mutually agree to nonconforming contract or change order. (T. 10, §1489).

Penalties.—Any violation is prima facie evidence of violation of Unfair Trade Practices Act, and is civil violation subject to forfeiture of not less than $100 or more than $1,000. Two years limitation period applies, running from date of occurrence of violation. (T. 10, §1490).

Debt Collection.—Debt collection businesses regulated by T. 32, §§11001-11054.

Credit Cards.—T. 9-A, §§8-301 and 8-302 prohibit issuance of credit cards except in response to request or application therefor and limit liability of card holder for unauthorized use of credit card to maximum of $50. Such limitations applicable only if card is accepted credit card, issuer gave adequate notice of potential liability, issuer has provided cardholder with description of means by which issuer may be notified of loss or theft of card, unauthorized use occurs before card holder has notified issuer, and issuer has provided method whereby user of card can be identified as person authorized to use it. If above conditions are not met, holder not liable for any unauthorized use. Maximum monthly finance charge is finance charge set forth in agreement between consumer and creditor. (T. 9-A, §2-402). Maine Consumer Credit Code—Truth in Lending Act regulates various aspects of credit cards, including determination of finance charges and annual percentage rate, disclosure requirements, and billing. (T. 9-A, §§8-101—8-404). When travel agent furnishes travel services to consumer, provider of travel services may not impose surcharge on travel agent or reduce travel agent's commission as result of consumer's use of credit card. (T. 10, §1142).

See note at head of Digest as to 1998 legislation covered.

See Topical Index in front part of this volume.

CONSUMER PROTECTION . . . continued

Manufacturer's Rebate.—Any person advertising availability of manufacturer rebate form must make forms available to consumer at time of sale. (T. 10, §§1231-1233).

Solar Energy Equipment Warranty Act.—T. 10, §§1491-1494, establishes warranty for sale and installation of solar energy equipment. Violations punishable by fine. In addition, violation of Act constitutes violation of Unfair Trade Practices Act. (T. 5, §§206-214).

Unfair Trade Practices Act.—T. 5, §§206-214 prohibits unfair and deceptive trade practices, and provides for enforcement by Attorney General's department and private enforcement by injured consumers.

"Unsolicited goods" statute adopted whereby person who receives unsolicited merchandise may refuse delivery or deem it gift and use it or dispose of it in any manner without obligation to sender. (T. 33, §1101).

Uniform Deceptive Trade Practices Act.—Adopted. See T. 10, §§1211-1216. See topics Interest, Sales, Consumer Credit.

Warranties on New Motor Vehicles.—Business practices between consumers and automobile manufacturers governed by motor vehicle "lemon law". (T. 10, §§1161-1165). Under Maine Lemon Law, manufacturer, its agent or authorized dealer must make repairs necessary to conform vehicle to express warranties if consumer reports nonconformity during term of express warranties, within two years of delivery date, or during first 18,000 miles, whichever is earlier. If, after reasonable number of attempted repairs, vehicle is still nonconforming, manufacturer must replace vehicle or make refund to consumer. Consumer may reject replacement and receive instead refund. (T. 10, §1163). See category Transportation, topic Motor Vehicles, subhead Sales.

Warranties and Disclosures on Used Motor Vehicles.—Sales of used motor vehicles governed by Used Car Information Act. Dealer must provide written statement warranting that used vehicle successfully passed inspection and disclosing numerous other matters specified by statute. (T. 10, §§1471-1478). See category Transportation, topic Motor Vehicles, subhead Sales.

Audiotext Service Charges.—Regulation of charges, and disconnections from failure to pay such charges, from use of telephone informational services, including 900 numbers. (T. 35-A, §§801-808).

Rent-to-Own Arrangements.—Governed by T. 9-A, §§11-101 to 121.

Plain Language.—Consumer loan and lease agreements between resident consumers and supervised lenders and lessors in Maine must be "written in a clear and coherent manner using words with common and everyday meanings" and "appropriately divided and captioned by its various sections." Not applicable to loans exceeding $100,000, or to leases in which capitalized cost of leased property exceeds $100,000, or to language or arrangements otherwise required by law. Certification of compliance available from Office of Consumer Credit Regulation, or, in case of agreements from supervised financial organizations, Bureau of Banking. Application fee $25. Certification bars legal proceeding against lender. Consumer lease is lease of goods to consumer for personal, family or household purposes, which is for term exceeding four months and which is not made pursuant to lender credit card. (T. 10, §§1121-1126).

Deceptive Trade Practices.—Uniform Deceptive Trade Practices Act adopted. (T. 10, §§1211-1216). In addition, engaging in "deceptive business practices" is crime punishable by fine of up to $2,000 or imprisonment for up to one year or both. (T. 17-A, §901).

Automated Telephone Solicitations.—Prohibited except for one call per day between hours of 9 a.m. and 5 p.m. Regulated by T. 10, §§1498-1499.

Cable Television.—Various consumer protections and rights are provided under T. 30-A, §3010 including right to credit or refund for service interruption of six or more consecutive hours.

Commodities.—T. 10, §§2621-2629 regulates sale of commodities including misrepresentation of quantity, method of sale, pricing, delivery tickets required for sales from bulk, information required on packages, advertising and conformity to national method of sale, packaging and labeling regulations.

Weighing and Measuring Devices.—Weighing and measuring equipment used by dealers or repairmen must be tested and calibrated annually by state sealer. (T. 10, §2654). Retail vehicle tank metering devices may be tested by certain registered repairmen. (T. 10, §2654-A).

Motor Vehicle Dealers, etc..—Conduct of motor vehicle dealers, manufacturers, brokers, factory branches, factory representatives, distributors, wholesalers, etc. is regulated by T. 10, §§1171-1176.

Telefacsimile Transmission.—Unsolicited transmission of telefacsimile message seeking charitable contributions or promoting purchase or rental of real property, goods or services is prohibited. Violation constitutes unfair trade practice. (T. 10, §1496).

Transient Sales.—Transient sellers of consumer merchandise regulated by T. 32, §§4681-4690. All transient sellers must register with Department of Business, Occupational and Professional Regulation and make security deposit (unless waived in accordance with statute).

Business Opportunities.—Mandatory disclosure and registration requirements for seller of business opportunity. (T. 32, §§4691-4700-B).

CONTRACTS:

Uniform Commercial Code adopted with variations. (T. 11, §§1-101—10-108). See topics Commercial Code, Consumer Credit, Consumer Protection, Frauds, Statute of, Sales; categories Documents and Records, topic Seals; Family, topic Infants.

FACTORS:

Governed by Uniform Commercial Code. See topic Commercial Code.

License Requirements.—None.

FRANCHISES:

Uniform Franchise and Business Opportunities Act.—Not adopted.

Alcoholic Beverages.—Franchises for wholesale sales of malt liquor, wine and low-alcohol spirits governed by T. 28-A, §§1401-1408 and 1451-1465.

Business Opportunities.—Sales of business opportunities governed by T. 32, §§4691-4700-B.

Cable Television.—Municipalities responsible for franchising and regulating cable television systems pursuant to guidelines set forth in T. 30-A, §§3008, 3010.

Motor Fuel.—Franchises for motor fuel dealerships governed by T. 10, §§1451-1457.

Motor Vehicles.—Franchises for motor vehicle dealerships governed by T. 10, §§1171-1186.

Farm Machinery.—Franchises for farm equipment and machinery dealerships governed by T. 10, §§1285-1298.

Power Equipment, Machinery and Appliances.—Franchises for power equipment, machinery and appliances governed by T. 10, §§1361-1370.

FRAUDS, STATUTE OF:

No action is maintainable to charge an executor or administrator on a special promise to answer damages out of his own estate; to charge any person upon any special promise to answer for the debt, default or misdoings of another, or upon an agreement made in consideration of marriage, or that is not to be performed within one year from the making thereof, or upon any contract to pay debt after discharge therefrom under bankruptcy law of U.S., or assignment or insolvent laws of this state, or by reason of any misrepresentation or assurance concerning character, conduct, credit, ability, trade or dealings of another unless made in writing and signed by party to be charged thereby, or by some person thereunto lawfully authorized. (T. 33, §51). No action shall be maintained on any contract made by minor unless he, or some person lawfully authorized, ratified it in writing after he arrived at age of 18 years, except for necessaries or real estate of which he has received title and retains benefit. (T. 33, §§51-53).

Any minor 16 or over who takes loan from New England Higher Education Assistance Foundation is of full legal capacity for such purpose. (T. 33, §52).

Agreements as to Wills.—Uniform Probate Code adopted, effective Jan. 1, 1981. (T. 18-A, §§1-101-8-401). Rule requiring certain contracts to be in writing in order to support action thereon has been extended to any agreement to give, bequeath or devise by will any property, whether real, personal or mixed. (T. 33, §51[7]).

Agreements as to Business.—Any agreement to refrain from carrying on or engaging in any trade, business, occupation or profession for any term of years, or within any designated territory, or both, is unenforceable unless the agreement or some memorandum thereof is in writing and signed by the person to be charged. (T. 33, §51[8]).

Contracts of Sale.—Any contract for sale of lands, tenements or hereditaments, or of any interest in or concerning them is unenforceable unless contract thereof is in writing and signed by party to be charged. (T. 33, §51[4]).

Part performance by person seeking to enforce unwritten contract may take it out of statute of frauds on ground of equitable estoppel based on equitable fraud. (351 A.2d 845).

Uniform Commercial Code adopted and governs contracts for sale of personal property. (T. 11, §§1-206 and 2-201).

Commercial Code.—See topic Commercial Code.

INTEREST:

Maximum legal rate on loan made by financial institution, in absence of agreement in writing establishing different rate is 6% per year. (T. 9-B, §432). Maximum rate in consumer credit transactions established under Consumer Credit Code, T. 9-A. Finance charge in consumer loans other than open end credit, calculated according to actuarial method, may not exceed equivalent of following: Total of (i) 30% per year on that part of unpaid balance of amount financed that is $2,000 or less, (ii) 24% per year on that part of unpaid balance of amount financed that is more than $2,000 but does not exceed $4,000, and (iii) 18% per year on that part of unpaid balance of amount financed that is more than $4,000. (T. 9-A, §2-401). Finance charge in consumer credit sales other than open end credit, calculated according to actuarial method, may not exceed equivalent of greater of either of following: (a) Total of (i) 30% per year on part of unpaid balance of amount financed that is $1,000 or less, (ii) 21% per year on part of unpaid balance of amount financed that is more than $1,000 but does not exceed $2,800, and (iii) 15% per year on part of unpaid balance of amount financed that is more than $2,800; or (b) 18% per year on unpaid balance of amount financed. Nor may finance charge on certain home improvement credit transactions exceed 18%. Certain minimum charges may be made. (T. 9-A, §2-201; Rule 220). Note payable at future date with interest greater or less than 6% draws such interest until maturity but after maturity draws 6% unless rate after maturity provided for therein. (67 Me. 540). Interest is allowable on account only by agreement or after demand (22 Me. 116) but is recoverable on balance of account stated from date of settlement (32 Me. 256). Interest not allowed on money collected until demand. (24 Me. 343). Compound interest not allowed unless expressly stipulated for. (90 Me. 206, 38 A. 138; 91 Me. 340, 40 A. 132). Finance charge on transaction to finance or refinance acquisition of, or secured by, manufactured housing, not involving security interest in real estate may not exceed greater of: (a) Rate 2% greater than maximum rate established by federal regulations under VHA, 38 USC §1819(f) or (b) 18% per year. However, in event no specific maximum rate is established by federal regulation, this provision will not apply. (T. 9-A, §2-201[10], §2-401[8]). Finance charge on consumer credit sale of motor vehicle sold on or after Jan. 1, 1994 may not exceed 18% per year on unpaid

INTEREST . . . *continued*
balance of amount financed. (T. 9-A, §2-201[9-A]). Balloon payments in consumer credit transaction other than open end credit governed by T. 9-A, §3-308. See topic Consumer Credit.

Judgments.—Interest after judgment equals 15% for cases in which damages claimed or awarded do not exceed $30,000 District Court jurisdictional limit. For other actions, interest equals coupon issue yield equivalent of average accepted auction price for last auction of 52-week Treasury bills settled immediately prior to date from which interest is calculated, plus 7%. (T. 14, §1602-A). Interest before judgment equals 8% for cases in which damages claimed or awarded do not exceed $30,000 District Court jurisdictional limit, except cases involving contract or note containing provision relating to interest. For other actions, interest equals coupon issue yield equivalent of average accepted auction price for last auction of 52-week treasury bills settled immediately prior to date from which interest is calculated, plus 1%. (T. 14, §1602).

Small Loans.—See topic Consumer Credit and supra, this topic.

Usury.—See topic Consumer Credit and Introductory Paragraph, supra, this topic.

LICENSES, BUSINESS AND PROFESSIONAL:

Licenses are required for numerous businesses and occupations. (T. 32). Following is partial list of business and professional activities that are licensed.

Transient Sales of Consumer Merchandise.—Every person, including self-employed, or those who employ one or more transient sellers of consumer merchandise must acquire registration from Department of Professional and Financial Regulation. (T. 32, §4682). Transient seller must disclose by prescribed form registration number and permanent business address in advertisements and on receipts. (T. 32, §4682-B). Registration must be renewed annually. (T. 32, §4684-A). Application fee is $25. Original and renewal registration fee $75. Security deposit of $10,000 or anticipated yearly gross revenues in state, if less, must be made with Department; deposit may be by bond and may be waived by Department, with advice of Attorney General of state, on application. (T. 32, §§4685-4685-A). Towns and municipalities may also regulate transient sales of consumer merchandise. (T. 32, §4683).

Traveling circus, amusement show and amusement device must have state license. Fee for circus outdoors or under tent, $500; for circus indoors, $300; for amusement show, carnival, thrill show, ice show, rodeo or similar performance indoor or outdoor, $300; for each amusement device, $50; for circus produced by nonprofit charitable organization, license required but no fee. (T. 8, §502).

Food establishments, except for eating establishments and certain storage facilities, must be licensed by Commissioner of Agriculture, Food and Rural Resources. (T. 22, §2167).

Eating establishments must be licensed by Department of Human Services. (T. 22, §2492).

Debt collection businesses must pay $400 biennially and be licensed by Superintendent of Consumer Credit Protection. (T. 32, §11031).

Social workers must be licensed by State Board of Social Worker Licensure. (T. 32, §7051).

Chiropractors must be licensed by Board of Chiropractic Examination and Registration. (T. 32, §551).

Collection Agencies.—Governed by T. 32, §§11001-11054. License and bond required.

Massage therapists must be licensed by Department of Professional and Financial Regulation. (T. 32, §§14301-14311).

Money transmitters must be licensed by Director of Office of Consumer Credit Regulation. (T. 32, §§6101-6129).

MONOPOLIES, RESTRAINT OF TRADE AND COMPETITION:

Contract, combination in form of trust or otherwise, or conspiracy in restraint of trade or commerce is class C crime. (T. 10, §1101). Monopolization, attempt to monopolize and combination or conspiracy to monopolize is class C crime. (T. 10, §1102). No person engaged in commerce may acquire, directly or indirectly, whole or any part of stock, other share capital, or assets of another person also engaged in commerce in Maine where effect of such acquisition may substantially lessen competition or create monopoly. (T. 10, §1102-A). Up to $100,000 civil penalty may be assessed against violator of §1101 or §1102. (T. 10, §1104). Action to recover civil penalty from alleged violator bars criminal prosecution based on same conduct and vice versa. (T. 10, §1104).

Persons, corporations, etc., manufacturing, producing, refining or mining article or product which enters into general use and consumption may not form trust or enter into combination contrary to public policy. (T. 13, §171).

Unfair Sales.—Retailer may not, with intent to injure competitors or destroy competition, advertise, offer to sell or sell at retail any article of merchandise at less than cost. Similar restriction is imposed on wholesalers with respect to sales, etc., at wholesale. (T. 10, §§1204-A, 1207).

Unfair Trade Practices Act.—Unfair methods of competition and unfair or deceptive acts or practices in conduct of trade or commerce are unlawful. Act construed in accordance with interpretations given by Federal Trade Commission and federal courts to §5(a)(1) of Federal Trade Commission Act. (T. 5, §207). Actions permitted under laws as administered by regulatory boards or officers acting under statutory authority are exempt. (T. 5, §208). Attorney General may promulgate rules and regulations and enforces Act. Actions by injured consumers authorized. Right to trial by jury. (T.5, §§206-214).

Uniform Franchise and Business Opportunities Act.—Not adopted. See topic Franchises.

Business Opportunities.—See topic Franchises.

Franchises.—See topic Franchises.

Cooperative marketing associations or corporations organized for sole purpose of marketing fish, fish products or agricultural products of state are not to be deemed illegal. (T. 13, §171).

Cooperative agreements among hospitals for sharing, allocation or referral of patients, personnel, instructional programs, support services and facilities or medical, diagnostic or laboratory facilities or procedures or other services traditionally offered by hospitals, and are not to be deemed illegal when properly certified. (T. 22, §§1881-1888).

SALES:

Uniform Commercial Code adopted. (T. 11, §§2-101 to 2-725). See topic Commercial Code.

Contracts of Sales.—See topics Commercial Code, Frauds, Statute of.

Bills of Sale.—See topic Commercial Code.

Product Liability.—Sale of goods in defective condition unreasonably dangerous to user or consumer may be liable for physical harm caused by such defect. (T. 14, §221). Lack of privity is no defense. (462 A.2d 1144).

Retail Credit Sales.—See category Transportation, topic Motor Vehicles, subhead Sales.

Consumer Protection.—See topic Consumer Protection.

Bulk Sales.—See topic Commercial Code; category Debtor and Creditor, topic Fraudulent Sales and Conveyances.

Sale of Business Opportunities.—Mandatory disclosure and registration requirements for seller of business opportunity. (T. 32, §§4691-4700-B).

Sales of Motor Vehicles.—See category Transportation, topic Motor Vehicles.

SECURITIES:

Revised Maine Securities Act governs securities, broker-dealers, sales representatives and investment advisors. (T. 32, §§10101-10713). Uniform Commercial Code adopted. See topic Commercial Code.

Supervision.—Securities Administrator: Christine A. Bruenn, State House Station 121, Augusta, Maine 04330.

Regulatory Powers of Supervising Authority.—Authority to make rules (T. 32, §10703), enforce act (T. 32, §10602), investigate (T. 32, §10601), in addition to other grants of specific and general powers.

Securities to Which Act Applies.—Security under Act means any note; stock; treasury stock; bond; debenture; evidence of indebtedness; certificate of interest or participation in any profit-sharing agreement; any limited partnership interest; collateral-trust certificate; preorganization certificate or subscription; transferable share, investment contract; voting-trust certificate; certificate of deposit for security; documents of title to and certificates of interest in oil, gas or other mineral lease or in payments out of production under such lease, right or royalty; any put, call, straddle or option entered into national securities exchange relating to foreign currency; any put, call, straddle or option on any security, certificate of deposit or group or index of security, including any interest therein or based on value thereof; or, in general, any interest or instrument commonly known as "security" or any certificate of interest or participation in, temporary or interim certificate for, receipt for, guarantee of, or warrant or right to subscribe to or to purchase, any of foregoing. "Security" does not include any insurance or endowment policy or annuity contract under which insurance company promises to pay money either in lump sum or periodically for life or some other specified period or any interest in contributory or noncontributory pension or welfare plan subject to United States Employee Retirement Income Security Act of 1974. (T. 32, §10501).

Registration Requirement.—Person may not offer or sell any security in Maine unless security is registered under Revised Maine Securities Act, security or transaction is exempt under Revised Maine Securities Act, or security is federal covered security. (T. 32, §10401).

Exempt Securities.—(a) Any security issued, insured or guaranteed by U.S., or any agency thereof but not including any security payable solely from revenues to be received from nongovernmental industrial or commercial enterprise unless guaranteed by person whose securities are exempt under certain provisions; (b) any security issued, insured or guaranteed by Canada or any subdivision, or instrumentality thereof if recognized by issuer, insurer or guarantor as valid obligation; (c) any security issued by and representing interest in or direct obligation of, or guaranteed by any depository institution or holding company, deposit accounts of which are insured by Federal Deposit Insurance Corporation or Federal Savings and Loan Insurance Corporation or deposit insurance fund expressly authorized by state; (d) any security issued by and representing interest in or direct obligation of, or guaranteed by, any federal credit union or any credit union organized under laws of Maine, shares of which are insured by National Credit Union Share Insurance Fund or deposit insurance fund expressly authorized by state; (e) any security issued by and representing interest in or direct obligation of, or guaranteed by, any insurance company authorized to do business in state but this exemption does not apply to annuity contract, investment contract, etc., under which promised payments are not fixed in dollars, but are substantially dependent upon investment results of segregated fund or account invested in securities; (f) any security issued or guaranteed by any railroad, other common carrier, public utility or other holding company which is subject to jurisdiction of United States Interstate Commerce Commission, registered holding company under United States Public Utility Holding Company Act of 1935 or it subsidiary, or regulated in respect of its rates and charges by U.S. or any state, or regulated with respect to issuance or guarantee of security by governmental authority of U. S., any State, Canada or any Canadian province or territory; (g) equipment trust certificates in respect of equipment leased or conditionally sold to person, if securities issued by that person would be exempt; (h) any security listed or approved for listing upon notice of issuance on designated national market system, any other security of same issuer of senior or equal rank,

See note at head of Digest as to 1998 legislation covered.

See Topical Index in front part of this volume.

ME – 9

SECURITIES . . . *continued*
called for by subscription rights, or any warrant or right to purchase or subscribe to any of foregoing; (i) any option issued by clearing agency registered as such under United States Securities Exchange Act of 1934 if security, etc., underlying option is registered under this Act, is exempt from this subsection or is otherwise not required to be registered under this Act; (j) any security issued by any person organized and operating not for private profit, but exclusively for religious, educational, benevolent, charitable, and certain other nonprofit purposes or by person exempt from tax under §§501(c) (2)—(10), (19), 501(e), 501(f) or 528, of United States Internal Revenue Code of 1954 provided no net earnings of issuer inure to benefit of any person; (k) any commercial paper which arises out of current transaction proceeds of which have been or are to be used for current transactions and which evidences obligation to pay cash within nine months of date of issuance, exclusive of days of grace, or any renewal of that paper which is likewise limited or any guarantee of that paper of any such renewal; (l) any security issued in connection with employee stock purchase, pension, savings, option, profit sharing or similar employees benefit plan; and (m) membership or equity interest in, or retention certificate or like security given in lieu of cash patronage dividend issued by cooperative organized and operated as nonprofit membership cooperative under laws of any state when not traded to public. (T. 32, §10502).

Exempt Transactions.—(a) Any isolated nonissuer transaction; (b) any nonissuer transaction in outstanding security if issuer of security has class of securities registered pursuant to United States Securities Exchange Act of 1934, §12(b) or 12(g) and has been subject thereto for period of no less than 90 days or has filed and maintained with administrator for period of not less than 90 days information comparable to that information required under United States Securities Exchange Act; (c) any nonissuer transaction, in outstanding security if Moody's, Standard and Poor's, Fitch's or any other nationally recognized securities manual designated by administrator, has contained for not less than 90 days balance sheet of issuer not more than 18 months old and profit and loss statement for fiscal year preceding or most recent year of operation; (d) any nonissuer transaction, affected by or through licensed broker-dealer pursuant to unsolicited order or offer to buy but broker-dealer may be required to provide proof that was unsolicited; (e) any transaction between issuer or other person on whose behalf offering of security is made and underwriter or among underwriters; (f) any transaction in bond or other evidence of indebtedness secured by real estate mortgage, deed of trust, personal property security agreement or by agreement for sale of real or personal property, if entire mortgage, deed of trust or agreement, together with all bonds or other evidences of indebtedness secured thereby as offered and sold as unit; (g) any transaction by personal representative, executive, administrator, sheriff, marshal, receiver, trustee in bankruptcy, guardian or conservator acting in their official capacities; (h) any transaction executed by bona fide secured party without purpose of evading this act; (i) any offer or sale of security to financial and institutional investor or to broker-dealer; (j) any offer or sale of preorganization certificate or subscription if no commission is paid for soliciting any prospective customer, no public advertising or general solicitation is used, and number of subscribers does not exceed ten and no payment is made by any subscriber; (k) any offer or sale of preorganization certificate or subscription agreement issued in connection with organization of depository institution if under supervision of governmental official or agency; supervision includes ability to require disclosures of prospective investors, impound proceeds from sale of preorganization certificates, or, until organization of depository institution completed, require refund to investors if depository institution does not obtain grant of authority from government; (l) any transaction pursuant to offer to existing security holders of issuer including persons who at time of transaction are holders of convertible securities, nontransferable warrants or transferable warrants exercisable within not more than 90 days of issuance, if (1) no commission or other remuneration, other than standby commission, is paid or given, directly or indirectly, for soliciting any security holder in this State, or (2) prior to any offer in this State, notice, specifying terms of offer, is filed with administrator together with consent to service of process required by §10704 and filing fee of $300 for each security being offered in this State and administrator does not by order disallow exemption within next five full business days; (m) transaction involving offer, but not sale, of security where United States Securities Act of 1933 or rule of United States Securities and Exchange Commission allows preeffective offers to be made if registration statements required under federal and state law have been filed but are not effective and no stop refusal or suspension order has been entered by administrator or United States Securities and Exchange Commission and no public proceeding or examination is pending; transaction involving offer but not sale if registration statement has been filed under revised Maine Securities Act but is not effective, neither United States Securities and Exchange Commission nor administrator had entered stock refusal or delay order nor is such order pending, and security is entitled to exemption from registration requirement of United States Securities and Exchange Act of 1933; (n) any transaction involving distribution of securities of issuer to security holders of another person in connection with merger, consolidation, exchange of securities, sale of assets or other reorganization to which issuer or other person, or their parent or subsidiary are parties; (o) any transaction involving offers or sales of one or more promissory notes directly secured by first lien on single parcel of real estate which is used for residential or commercial purposes and participation interest in notes and where notes and participation interest originated by depository institution are offered and sold provided that minimum aggregate sales price paid by each purchaser shall not be less than $250,000, each purchaser shall pay cash within 60 days of sale, and each purchaser shall buy for that person's own account only; allowed where notes and participation interests are originated by mortgagee approved by HUD; allowed where involving non-assignable contracts to buy or sell securities which contracts are to be completed within two years; (p) any offer or sale of securities of corporation organized under laws of Maine if number of holders of securities does not and will not in consequence of sale exceed ten, exclusive of financial and institutional investors, and if securities have not been offered to public by general advertisement and general solicitation; (q) any offer or sale of securities of corporation organized under laws of this state if number of holders of securities of entity, exclusive of financial and institutional investors, will in consequence of sale exceed ten, but will not, in consequence of sale, exceed 25 in number and if securities sold in reliance on subsection have not been offered to public by general advertisement or general solicitation. Person relying on this exemption shall file with administrator notification for exemption which will require name, address and telephone number of issuer, state and date of incorporation of issuer, name, address and telephone of persons who may respond to inquiries about issuer, location at which books and records of issuer will be kept and whether they will be available for inspection by shareholders; description of all classes of securities of issuer, including newly authorized classes of securities, providing number of authorized units of each class, par value per unit and number of units of each class as are issued and outstanding; description of class of securities as shall be offered for sale, including number of units authorized, par value per unit, number of units currently outstanding, number of units being offered for sale; number of units outstanding and price at which each unit is offered for sale, description of rights of holders of securities offered pursuant to this exemption, including voting rights and if cumulative or noncumulative liquidation rights, preemptive rights and any other rights or limitations applicable to securities; date of annual meeting of shareholders will be held, location and time of meeting, description of how shareholders will be notified and if annual financial statement and report of activity will be available to shareholders; brief description of how proceeds of offering will be used and if proceeds shall be returned to investors if minimum amounts are not raised by specific date; brief description of issuer's plan of business and whether business is currently operational; and list of significant risks assumed by investor, including management experience, competitive and economic factors, net worth position of issuer and improbable or limited opportunity for release of securities. Copy of notification shall be made available to each offeree of securities sold in reliance on this exemption and shall contain such legends as administrator prescribes; (r) any transaction by issuer not involving any public offering within meaning of United States Securities Act of 1933 and rules promulgated under that Act, including, but not limited to, any transaction exempt from regulation with United States Securities and Exchange Commission and any transaction constituting nonpublic offering under rules adopted by administrator if no later than 15 days after first sale in this State of security in reliance on exemption from registration provided in this subsection, issuer shall file with administrator notice on United States Securities and Exchange Commission Form D, as amended, and consent to service of process required by §10704, and pay filing fee of $300. (T. 32, §10502).

Federal Covered Securities.—"Federal covered security" means any security described as covered security in Securities Act of 1933. (T. 32, §10501[2-A]).

Federal Covered Securities under §18(b)(2) of Securities Act of 1933.—Federal covered security may not be offered or sold in Maine in reliance on §18(b)(2) of Securities Act of 1933 unless there is on file with administrator currently effective notice filing and consent to service of process required by §10704. Notice filing requirements are as follows: (1) Person authorized to register security under Securities Act of 1933 shall file with administrator notice, upon form prescribed by administrator, and consent to service of process required by §10704, signed by issuer of security, and pay filing fee of $500; and (2) to maintain currently effective notice filing, person authorized to register security under Securities Act of 1933 shall file with administrator, no later than expiration date of currently effective notice filing, notice, on form prescribed by administrator, and pay filing fee of $500. (T. 32, §10505[1]).

Federal Covered Securities under §18(b)(4)(D) of Securities Act of 1933.—Notice filing requirements for federal covered securities offered or sold in Maine in reliance on §18(b)(4)(D) of Securities Act of 1933 are set forth in §10502(2)(R). (T. 32, §10505[2]).

Other Federal Covered Securities.—Unless administrator provides otherwise by rule, any other federal covered security may be offered and sold in Maine in reliance on its being federal covered security without filing notice or payment of fee. (T. 32, §10505[3]).

Registration of Securities.—There are three types of registration: by notification, coordination and qualification. (T. 32, §§10401-10404). $500 filing fee for each security offered is charged, except, in case of registration by qualification, for offering for which total amount raised is less than $1,000,000, filing fee is $300 for each security offered. (T. 32, §10405). Registration must be filed with securities administrator.

Registration by Notification.—Any security whose issuer and predecessors have been in continuous operation for at least five years if (1) there has been no defaults during current fiscal year or within three preceding fiscal years in payment of principal, interest or dividends on any security of issuer with fixed maturity or fixed interest or dividend provision; and (2) issuer or any predecessors in past three years had average net earnings, determined in accordance with generally accepted accounting practices, (i) which are applicable to all securities without fixed maturity or fixed interest or dividend provision outstanding at date registration statement is filed and which equal at least 5% of amount of such outstanding securities, as measured by maximum offering price or market price on date, selected by registrant, within 30 days before date of filing registration statement, whichever is higher, or book value on day, selected by registrant, within 90 days of date of filing registration statement to extent that there is neither readily determinable market price nor cash offering price; (ii) which, if issuer and any predecessors have not had any security, as described previously, outstanding for three full fiscal years, which equal at least 5% of amount, as described previously, of all securities which will be outstanding if all securities being offered or proposed to be offered, whether or not they are proposed to be registered or offered in this state, are issued; and any security other than document of title to certificate of interest or participation in oil, gas or mining title or lease or in payments out of production under such title or lease, registered for nonissuer distribution if any security of same class has been registered under Revised Maine Securities Act or security being registered was originally issued under exemption under Revised Maine Securities Act. (T. 32, §10402).

Registration by Coordination.—Any security for which registration statement has been filed under United States Securities Act of 1933 may be registered by coordination in connection with same offering. Registration statement shall contain two copies of latest former prospectus filed under United States Securities Act, and, if required by administrator, copy of articles of incorporation and bylaws or their equivalent, copy of

See note at head of Digest as to 1998 legislation covered.

See Topical Index in front part of this volume.

ME – 10

SECURITIES . . . *continued*

any agreement with or among underwriters, copy of any indenture and specimen or copy of security and other documentation as required under statute. (T. 32, §10403).

Registration by Qualification.—Any security may be registered by qualification. Registration statement shall contain information concerning issuer, directors and officers and other information as required under statutes. (T. 32, §10404).

Registration of Broker-Dealers/Sales Representatives.—Any person engaged in effecting securities transaction for account of others or own account must be licensed unless exempted (T. 32, §§10301, 10501); initial fee and renewal fees required ($200 for broker-dealer, $40 for sales representative, and $200 for investment advisor) (T. 32, §10306); licensee subject to examination (T. 32, §10307); sales representative cannot act for more than one broker-dealer or issuer unless affiliated or authorized by administrator (T. 32, §10308[4]).

Liabilities.—Person offering for sale securities in violation of statute is liable to purchaser for purchase price, interest and cost. Purchaser in violation of statutes may be liable for damages to seller. Other statutory and equitable remedies may be imposed. (T. 32, §§10602-10605).

Uniform Commercial Code adopted. See topic Commercial Code.

Uniform Securities Ownership by Minors Act not adopted.

Commodities.—Sale of commodities, commodity contracts or commodity options regulated by T. 32, §§11201-11313.

WAREHOUSEMEN:

Uniform Commercial Code adopted. See topic Commercial Code.

CITIZENSHIP

ALIENS:

Property.—Aliens may take, hold, convey and devise real estate or any real estate interest. (T. 33, §451).

Knowingly employing illegal alien is state Class E crime. (T. 26, §871). Illegal aliens may not receive unemployment benefits. (T. 26, §1192[11]). Superior Court has sole jurisdiction over applications for naturalization. (T. 14, §6451).

CIVIL ACTIONS AND PROCEDURE

ACCORD AND SATISFACTION:

Common law rules apply. Defense available only when actual performance accepted.

Acceptance of money or other valuable consideration, however small, in full satisfaction of demand, bars subsequent action thereon. (T. 14, §155).

Compromise.—No settlement, general release or statement by injured person in hospital or sanitarium made within 30 days of injury admissible in evidence at trial of action to recover damages except as obtained by police officers or motor vehicle inspectors in performance of duties, by family members or by or for injured person's attorney. Such settlements and general releases null and void. (T. 17, §3964). This does not apply to agreements entered into under Workmen's Compensation Law and approved by Workers' Compensation Board.

Pleading.—In pleading to a preceding pleading, party must affirmatively set forth accord and satisfaction. (M.R.C.P. Rule 8[c]).

Uniform Commercial Code adopted. See category Business Regulation and Commerce, topic Commercial Code.

ACTIONS:

Supreme Judicial Court has promulgated Maine Rules of Civil Procedure (cited M.R.C.P.) governing commencement and prosecution of civil actions in District Courts and Superior Courts and appeals to Supreme Judicial Court sitting as Law Court. These rules in general conform to Federal Rules of Civil Procedure with significant alterations that are needed for adaptation to state practice and some changes believed advisable for Maine courts.

Equity.—See subhead Forms of Action, infra.

Forms of Action.—One form of civil action; formal distinction between law and equity abolished. (M.R.C.P. 2).

Conditions Precedent.—

Maine Tort Claims Act.—Notice of claim must be filed within 180 days after cause of action accrues except for good cause shown. (T. 14, §8107). Suit must be filed within two years of accrual. (T. 14, §8110).

Maine Health Security Act.—Claimant must serve notice of claim upon defendant and court. (T. 24, §§2853, 2903[1][A]). Claimant must submit claim to prelitigation screening panel. (T. 24, §§2851, 2903[1][B]).

Insurance Subrogation.—Insurer must serve notice on insured of intent to commence suit in name of insured at least ten days prior to asserting claim. (M.R.C.P. 17[c]).

Commencement.—Action may be commenced by (1) service of summons and complaint, or (2) filing complaint with court. Method 1 requires filing of complaint within court 20 days after service. Method 2 requires filing of return of service within 90 days after filing of complaint. (M.R.C.P. 3).

Parties.—Action must be brought in name of real party in interest. (M.R.C.P. 17[a]). Executor, administrator, guardian, bailee, trustee of express trust, one who has contracted for benefit of third party, or one authorized by statute may sue in own name. (M.R.C.P. 17[a]). Insurer who has paid part or all of claim may sue in insured's name after serving notice of action on insured ten days before bringing action and attaching notice and return to complaint. (M.R.C.P. 17[a],[c]). Person subject to

process must be joined as party if (1) complete relief cannot be accorded in person's absence or (2) person claims interest in subject matter and disposition in person's absence may (i) impair or impede person's ability to protect that interest, or (ii) leave any other party at risk of multiple or inconsistent obligations. (M.R.C.P. 19[a]). If person has not been joined, court shall order joinder. (M.R.C.P. 19[a]). If person refuses to join as plaintiff, person may be made defendant. (M.R.C.P. 19[a]). If person cannot be joined, court may dismiss action if equity and good conscience require. (M.R.C.P. 19[b]). Pleading asserting claim for relief must identify known persons described above who are not joined and explain. (M.R.C.P. 19[c]). Misjoinder not ground for dismissal; parties may be dropped or added by order of court on own or any parties' motion. (M.R.C.P. 21).

Class Actions.—Prerequisites to class action are: class so numerous that joinder of all members is impractical; questions of law or fact common to class; claims or defenses of representative parties typical of claims or defenses of class; representative parties will fairly and adequately protect interests of class. (M.R.C.P. 23[a]).

If above are satisfied, class action is maintainable if: prosecution of separate actions would create risk of inconsistent adjudication which would establish incompatible standards of conduct for party opposing class or adjudications as to individual members would dispose of others' interests or impair their ability to protect their interests; party opposing class has acted or refused to act on grounds generally applicable to class; or common questions of law or fact predominate so that class action is superior to other actions. (M.R.C.P. 23[b]).

Court must determine whether class is maintainable as soon as practicable after commencement of action. (M.R.C.P. 23[c][1]). Court shall direct best notice practicable under circumstances, including individual notice to all members identifiable through reasonable effort. (M.R.C.P. 23[c][2]). Notice must advise members that: court will exclude individual from class if individual requests by specific date; judgment whether favorable or not will apply to all members who do not request exclusion; and any member may appear through own counsel. (M.R.C.P. 23[c][2]).

Class action shall not be dismissed or compromised without approval of court and notice to all members as court directs. (M.R.C.P. 23[e]).

Intervention.—Shall be of right upon timely application when statute confers unconditional right to intervene or when applicant claims interest in subject of action and applicant is situated so that disposition of action may impair or impede applicant's ability to protect that interest, unless interest is adequately represented by other parties. (M.R.C.P. 24[a]). Permissive upon timely application when applicant's claim or defense and main action have question of law or fact in common. (M.R.C.P. 24[b]). Must be made by motion served upon parties. (M.R.C.P. 24[c]).

Interpleader.—Stakeholder may bring action of interpleader against two or more claimants, and defendant stakeholder may bring in claimant not party to action. (M.R.C.P. 22). Stakeholder may deposit fund with court or commit to escrow upon agreement of parties and be dismissed from action. (609 A.2d 711; 297 A.2d 87).

Third Party Practice.—Any time after commencement of action defendant may cause complaint and summons to be served on person not party who is or may be liable to defendant for all or part of plaintiff's claim against defendant. (M.R.C.P. 14[a]). Plaintiff may do same for counterclaim. (M.R.C.P. 14[b]). Third party defendant may assert against plaintiff any defenses which third-party plaintiff has to plaintiff's claim. (M.R.C.P. 14[a]). Plaintiff must assert any claim against third-party defendant arising out of transaction or occurrence that is subject matter of plaintiff's claim against defendant. (M.R.C.P. 14[a], 13[a]). Any party may move for severance, separate trial, or dismissal of third-party claim. (M.R.C.P. 14[a]).

Joinder of Causes of Action.—Joinder of any claims against opposing party permissible whether legal or equitable. (M.R.C.P. 18[a]). Party must make all claims arising out of same aggregate of operative facts. (570 A.2d 1205). Defendant must bring all claims as counterclaims against opposing party if claim arises out of transaction or occurrence that is subject matter of opposing party's claim and does not require presence of third parties of whom court cannot acquire jurisdiction. (M.R.C.P. 13[a], 586 A.2d 1263).

Splitting Causes of Action.—Court may order separate trials for convenience, to avoid prejudice, or to prevent embarrassment or delay. (M.R.C.P. 20[b], 42[b]).

Consolidation of Actions.—Pending actions involving common question of law or fact may be consolidated. (M.R.C.P. 42[a]).

Severance of Actions.—See subhead Splitting Causes of Action, supra.

Stay of Proceedings.—Grant of stay rests in sound discretion of court. (395 A.2d 453).

Abatement and Revival.—No personal action shall be lost by death of either party, but shall survive for personal representative. (T. 18-A, §3-817). Upon death of party, motion for substitution must be made within 90 days after suggestion of death is made on record by service of statement of fact of death. (M.R.C.P. 25[b], [c]). Court may allow action to continue upon motion for substitution in cases of incompetency or transfer of interest. (M.R.C.P. 25). Real action does not abate upon death or marriage of party. (M.R.C.P. 80A[e]).

Limitation of.—See topic Limitation of Actions.

Small Claims.—See category Courts and Legislature, topic Courts.

Termination of Actions.—Plaintiff may voluntarily dismiss by filing notice of dismissal before service by adverse party of answer or motion for summary judgment, whichever first occurs. (M.R.C.P. 41[a][1]). Action may be dismissed by filing stipulation of dismissal signed by all parties, unless receiver appointed. (M.R.C.P. 41[a][1]). Otherwise, action may only be dismissed upon order of court upon terms and conditions deemed proper. (M.R.C.P. 41[a][2]). No settlement of action on behalf of infant by next friend or defended on infant's behalf by guardian or guardian ad litem shall be valid unless approved by court. (T. 14, §1605, M.R.C.P. 17A).

Prohibited Actions.—Breach of promise to marry. (T. 14, §854). Alienation of affections. (T. 19, §167). Wrongful birth of healthy child. (T. 24, §2931).

See note at head of Digest as to 1998 legislation covered.

See Topical Index in front part of this volume.

ACTIONS . . . *continued*

Administration.—See category Estates and Trusts, topic Executors and Administrators.

Direct Actions Against Insurer.—See category Transportation, topic Motor Vehicles, subhead Direct Actions.

APPEAL AND ERROR:

See also topic Practice.

Appeals to Supreme Judicial Court.—All appellate review of civil actions from Superior Court by Supreme Judicial Court sitting as Law Court is by appeal. Cases also may be reported to that court. (M.R.C.P. 72). In addition, questions of law may be certified by federal court to Supreme Judicial Court. (M.R.C.P. 76B). Procedure on appellate review by Law Court is governed in general by M.R.C.P. 72-76A. Appeals from District Court foreclosure judgments are directly to Supreme Judicial Court. (T. 14, §1901). Appeals from final decision of Public Utilities Commission on questions of law or nonfinal decisions as to reasonableness of charge or constitutionality of commission ruling are also directly to Supreme Judicial Court. (T. 35-A, §1320[1], [5]). Parties in interest may seek review by Law Court of decisions of Appellate Division of Workers' Compensation Commission, Workers' Compensation Board or one of its hearing officers, but Law Court's review of such petitions is discretionary. (M.R.C.P. 73[i], [j], T. 39-A, §322).

Extent of Review.—Supreme Judicial Court, sitting as Law Court may review facts and set aside findings only if clearly erroneous.

Time for Taking Appeal.—An appeal is taken by filing a notice of appeal within 30 days after the entry of the judgment appealed from. (M.R.C.P. 73[a]). Appeal from Worker's Compensation Board or hearing officer must be made within 20 days after receipt of notice of filing of decision. (T. 39-A, §322).

Appeals to Superior Court.—Appeals from decisions of district courts must be taken within 30 days. (M.R.C.P. 76D, T. 14, §1901).

Extent of Review.—Superior Court reviews facts and sets aside findings only if clearly erroneous. (M.R.C.P. 76D). De novo jury trials can be held on forcible entry and detainer action appeals from District Court. (M.R.C.P. 80D[f][2]). De novo hearings are also held in Superior Court on appeals from assessments of State Tax Assessor. (T. 36, §151).

Appeals from Juvenile Court.—Appeals from order in juvenile court to Superior Court must be taken within five days or such time as Supreme Judicial Court provides by rule. (T. 15, §3402[5]).

Appeals (trial de novo) from Probate Court.—Appeals from probate court must be taken to Supreme Judicial Court (T. 18-A, §1-308) within 30 days after decree (M.R. Probate P. 73).

Appeals from State Agency Decisions.—Review of final agency action or failure of agency to act proceeds by filing petition for review in Superior Court within 30 days after receipt of notice if taken by party to agency proceeding; within 40 days by other aggrieved parties; and within six months of expiration of time within which agency should have acted for failure to act. (T. 5, §11002).

Appeals from Other Governmental Action.—Review of other governmental action or failure to act proceeds by filing of complaint in Superior Court within 30 days after action or refusal to act, unless otherwise specified by statute. (M.R.C.P. 80B). Complaints on failure to act must be brought within six months after time in which action should reasonably have occurred.

Appeal Bond.—Neither bond for costs nor supersedeas bond required.

Stay of Proceedings to Enforce Judgment.—No execution upon judgment until 30 days after entry or until time for appeal has expired. (M.R.C.P. 62[a]). Taking of appeal operates as automatic stay of execution. (M.R.C.P. 62[e]).

BONDS:

In action on bond in a penal sum, when jury finds condition broken, they estimate plaintiff's damages, and judgment is entered for penal sum, but execution is issued for such damages and costs. (T. 14, §6601).

Sureties.—Surety bonds are authorized in civil and criminal cases if duly executed by surety company authorized to do business in Maine. (T. 4, §1054).

Limitation of Actions.—Actions against sureties on bonds in criminal cases must be brought within one year after default of principal. (T. 14, §754).

Sureties on official bonds may appear and defend in suits against their principals, whenever such sureties may ultimately be liable upon such bonds. (T. 14, §6602).

Suits on probate bonds of any kind payable to the judge may be originally commenced by any person interested in estate or other matter for which bond was given, either in probate court in which bond was filed or in superior court of that county. (T. 18-A, §8-309).

CERTIORARI:

Writ of certiorari not available. Proceedings in nature of certiorari may be brought to review action of government agency. (M.R.C.P. 80B, 81[c]).

CHARITABLE IMMUNITY:

See topic Damages.

COSTS:

Filing fees, fees for service of process, witness fees, and travel expenses allowed to prevailing party in action unless court otherwise directs. (T. 14, §1502-B; M.R.C.P. 54). Court may also allow reasonable costs for expert witness fees and expenses, cost of medical reports, visual aids and costs of depositions. (T. 14, §1502-C). Clerk shall tax costs under T. 14, §1502-B; other costs determined at hearing. (T. 14, §1502-D).

Court may waive all or part of costs if they cause significant financial hardship on any party. (T. 14, §1502-D).

Attorney General recovers litigation costs, including court costs, reasonable attorney fees, and reasonable expert witness fees, when prevailing in certain proceedings. (T. 14, §1522).

DAMAGES:

Common law generally prevails as to compensatory damages. Punitive damages allowed at jury's discretion only if defendant acts with actual malice (i.e., ill will) or where conduct is so outrageous that malice can be implied. Reckless disregard for circumstances is insufficient to establish implied malice. Proof of malice must be by clear and convincing evidence. (494 A.2d 1353). Statutes allow double, treble or other exemplary damages in number of cases for waste by part owners, life tenants, etc., and for willful injury to ornamental grounds, trees, agricultural products, etc. (T. 14, §§7551, 7552, 7552-A, 7556, 7560). Except for demand for liquidated damages, demand in Superior Court civil case cannot include dollar amount or figure; prayer shall be for damages reasonable in premises. (T. 14, §52).

Charitable Immunity.—Doctrine prevails unless charity insured in which case liability limited to amount of policy. (T. 14, §158). Directors, officers, volunteers of charitable organizations are immune from civil liability in negligence actions arising from acts or omissions occurring within course and scope of charitable organization's activities. (T. 14, §158-A).

Comparative Negligence Rule.—Adopted 1965. (T. 14, §156). Uniform Comparative Fault Act not adopted.

Sovereign Immunity.—Maine Tort Claims Act removes defense of sovereign immunity for certain tort claims, provides procedures for making claims and limits recovery to $300,000 for all claims arising out of single occurrence. (T. 14, §§8101-8118).

Uniform Contribution Among Tortfeasors Act (Revised) not adopted.

See category Estates and Trusts, topic Death, subhead Actions for Death.

DEPOSITIONS AND DISCOVERY:

Governed by Maine Rules of Civil Procedure. These rules in general conform to Federal Rules of Civil Procedure. See topic Practice.

Within State for Use Within State.—Generally conforms to Federal Rules of Civil Procedure. Absent leave of court, ten days written notice must be given to all parties prior to deposition. Court on ex parte application and for good cause shown may prescribe shorter notice. (M.R.C.P. 30[b][1]).

Within State for Use Elsewhere.—Upon application, certified by member of Maine bar, to clerk of courts in county where deponent resides or is employed or transacts business in person, party may take deposition in Maine upon oral examination pursuant to laws of foreign jurisdictions for use therein. (M.R.C.P. 30[h]). Contents of application prescribed. (M.R.C.P. 30[h][3]). Parallel rule for depositions upon written questions. (M.R.C.P. 31[d]).

Outside of State for Use Within State.—Depositions may be taken within another state, or within a territory, or in a foreign country (1) on notice before a person authorized to administer oaths therein, (2) before a person appointed or commissioned by court, or (3) pursuant to a letter rogatory. (M.R.C.P. 28[b]).

Before Whom Taken.—Within state, notary public or person appointed by court. (M.R.C.P. 28[a]). Outside state, see subhead Outside of State for Use Within State, supra.

Compelling Attendance of Witness.—A resident of Maine who is not party or officer of party may not be required to travel to attend examination outside county where he resides or is employed or transacts his business in person, or distance of more than 100 miles one way, whichever is greater unless court otherwise orders. Nonresident may be required to attend in county where he is served or within 100 miles therefrom or at other convenient place fixed by court. (M.R.C.P. 45[c][3]).

Examination of Witnesses.—Governed by M.R.C.P. 30(c). Substantially similar to Federal Rules.

Discovery.—Substantially identical to Federal Rules.

Demand for Admission of Facts.—Substantially identical to Federal Rules. Request must be set forth above response. (M.R.C.P. 36).

Interrogatories.—Substantially identical to Federal Rules. Only one set of interrogatories may be served upon another party absent leave of court. (M.R.C.P. 33[a]).

Uniform Foreign Depositions Act not adopted.

EVIDENCE:

Rules of Evidence.—Pursuant to rule-making authority given it in 1974 under T. 4, §39-A, Supreme Judicial Court has adopted, prescribed and promulgated Maine Rules of Evidence (cited M.R.E.) effective Feb. 2, 1976. Rules, subject to legislative abrogation, supersede all laws in conflict with them. These rules in general conform to federal rules of evidence with significant variations reflecting legal principles in accord with public policy of State of Maine. (M.R.E. 601). See also subhead Witnesses, infra; topic Depositions and Discovery.

Witnesses.—Every person is competent to be witness except as otherwise provided. (M.R.E. 601[a]). Person disqualified to be witness if incapable of expression concerning matter so as to be understood by judge and jury either directly or through interpretation by one who can understand witness, or is incapable of understanding duty to tell truth. (M.R.E. 601[b]). Personal knowledge required for nonexpert witnesses. (M.R.E. 602). Oath or affirmation required. (M.R.E. 603).

Parties are competent to testify in their own behalf, and husband or wife of either party may be witness.. (T. 16, §53). Judge presiding at trial may not testify as witness. (M.R.E. 605). Member of jury may not testify as witness in case in which he is sitting as juror. (M.R.E. 606).

See note at head of Digest as to 1998 legislation covered.

See Topical Index in front part of this volume.

EVIDENCE . . . *continued*

Husband or wife of accused is competent witness in criminal cases except in regard to marital communications (T. 15, §1315) construed to mean confidential communications (284 A.2d 91).

Privileged Communications.—Lawyer-client privilege. (M.R.E. 502). Physician and psychotherapist-patient privilege. (M.R.E. 503). Husband-wife privilege. (M.R.E. 504). Religious privilege. (M.R.E. 505). Political vote privilege. (M.R.E. 506). Trade secret privilege. (M.R.E. 507). Governmental privileges. (M.R.E. 508). Privilege to refuse to disclose identity of informer. (M.R.E. 509). Confidentiality of communications between licensed social workers and clients. (T. 32, §7005). Statutory privilege for school social workers and counselors. (T. 20-A, §4008). Privileged communications to sexual assault counselors. (T. 16, §53-A). Privileged communications to victim advocate. (T. 16, §53-B).

Communications or Transactions with Persons Since Deceased or Incompetent.—Statements constituting hearsay, as defined in M.R.E. 801, may be admissible under exceptions provided in M.R.E. 804. Hearsay statement by person under 16 describing any incident involving sexual act or sexual contact performed with or on minor by another shall not be excluded as evidence in criminal proceeding if court finds person's mental or physical well-being will more likely than not be harmed if person were to testify in open court and statement is made under oath subject to all rights of confrontation, has been recorded by court-approved means and is made in presence of judge. (T. 15, §1205). Husband-wife privilege (M.R.E. 504), physician and psychotherapist-patient privilege (M.R.E. 503), school social worker and counselor-client privilege (T. 20-A, §4008), licensed social worker-client privilege (T. 32, §7005) and statutory confidentiality of certain other information are abrogated in relation to required reporting, cooperation with government agency or guardian ad litem in investigation or other child protective activity or giving evidence in child protection proceeding (T. 22, §4015).

In all criminal trials accused shall, at his own request but not otherwise, be competent witness. Accused shall not be compelled to testify on cross-examination to facts that would convict or furnish evidence to convict him of any other crime than that for which on trial. Fact accused does not testify in own behalf shall not be taken as evidence of guilt. (T. 15, §1315).

Self-incrimination.—No defendant can be compelled to testify in any action when pleadings imply or charge criminal offense, traffic infraction or civil violation for possession of marijuana. If he offers himself as witness, he waives his privilege of not incriminating or testifying against himself, but his testimony cannot be used in evidence against him in any criminal prosecution, traffic infraction proceeding or civil proceeding for possession of marijuana involving same subject matter. (T. 16, §201).

Compelling Attendance.—See topic Depositions and Discovery.

Uniform Rendition of Prisoners as Witnesses in Criminal Proceedings Act enacted. (T. 15, §1461-1471).

INJUNCTIONS:

Availability of injunction as remedy governed generally by common law.

Jurisdiction.—Superior court, law court, and U.S. district court can issue injunctions.

Prerequisites.—Temporary restraining orders may be granted without notice to adverse party if it is made to appear clearly from specific facts shown by affidavit or verified complaint that immediate and irreparable injury will result unless it is granted before notice can be served and hearing held. Applicant's attorney must also certify to court efforts, if any, made to give notice and reasons supporting claim that no notice should be required. Preliminary injunction can be granted only upon notice to adverse party and hearing. Application for preliminary injunction may be included in complaint or may be made by motion. Every restraining or injunctive order must set forth reasons for its issuance, be specific in terms, and describe in reasonable detail and without reference to any other document act or acts to be restrained. (M.R.C.P. 65).

Procedure relating to temporary restraining orders and preliminary injunctions governed by Rule 65 of Maine Rules of Civil Procedure. This rule in general conforms to Rule 65 of Federal Rule of Civil Procedure. See topic Practice.

Bond.—No restraining order or preliminary injunction will issue except upon giving of security by applicant, in such sum as court deems proper, provided, however, that for good cause shown and recited in order, court may waive giving of security. Surety upon land or undertaking under this rule submits to court's jurisdiction and irrevocably appoints clerk of court as surety's agent. Surety's liability may be enforced on motion without necessity of independent action. Motion and its notice may be served on clerk of court who mails copies forthwith to persons giving security. (M.R.C.P. 65[c]).

Temporary Injunction.—See subheads Prerequisites and Procedure, supra.

There are several statutory grants of right to seek injunction including state enforcement of laws (1) regulating professions such as, among others, occupational therapists (T. 32, §2276[3]) and physical therapists (T. 32, §3118[2]); accountants (T. 32, §12276), foresters (T. 32, §5019); (2) protecting consumers (T. 5, §209); (3) protecting defined environmental areas such as, among others, Allagash Wilderness Waterway (T. 12, §674), Saco River Corridor (T. 38, §967) and (4) protecting health, safety or general welfare of persons or property arising from discharge, emissions or deposit of any materials into any waters, air or land of state constituting substantial and immediate danger (T. 38, §348). Actions for injunctions relating to land use violations governed by Rule 80K of Maine Rules of Civil Procedure.

Statutory grants of right of private party to seek injunctions are provided in areas of: commercial relations involving, among others, trademark and tradenames (T. 10, §1530) and sale of business opportunities (T. 32, §4700); domestic relations involving abuse (T. 19, §765); and labor relations (T. 26, §5). Some statutory grants of right to seek injunction contain provisions relating to procedure such as availability of ex parte orders and dissolution of injunctions.

JUDGMENTS:

See also topic Practice.

Judgments are entered forthwith by the clerk upon a general verdict of a jury or otherwise upon order of the court. In general, judgments issue in the same manner as in the Federal Courts. (M.R.C.P. 58). Docketing of orders or judgments is governed by M.R.C.P. 79(a).

See also topic Actions.

Actions.—Venue for civil actions on judgment rendered by any court of record in State may be brought in county where it was rendered or in county in which either party resides. (T. 14, §503).

Liens.—Filing of execution in registry of deeds creates lien in favor of judgment creditor. Notice by certified or registered mail to judgment debtor on or before 20th day after filing or recording required. (T. 14, §4651-A).

Declaratory Judgments.—Uniform Act adopted. (T. 14, §§5951-5963).

Vacation or Modification.—M.R.C.P. 60 entitled "Relief from Judgment or Order" governs method for relief from judgment and is very similar to Federal Rules.

Default Judgments.—M.R.C.P. 55 entitled "Default" governs entries of default and default judgments and is similar to Federal Rule of Civil Procedure 55.

A defendant living out of state, defaulted in an action without an appearance or other service than a newspaper publication, may within six months after the levy of an execution on his real estate or the sale of a right of redemption, bring an action for relief from the judgment in such action, and he may redeem from such levy or sale within three months after the relief is denied, or after final judgment in the action if the relief is granted. If such judgment is in his favor the amount thereof must be allowed toward such redemption notwithstanding a conveyance of such estate by the creditor. (T. 14, §2351).

Judgments by Confession.—Bill in equity is never taken pro confesso against infant defendant. (65 Me. 352).

Judgments by Consent.—Consent judgments cannot be modified or vacated absent claim of fraud or mistake by consenting party. (444 A. 2d 361 [Me.], cert. denied, 459 U.S. 831).

Revival.—Writ of scire facias was abolished in M.R.C.P. 81(c).

Summary Judgments.—M.R.C.P. 56 governing summary judgments is similar to Federal Rule of Civil Procedure 56.

Judgments on Pleadings.—M.R.C.P. 12(c) governing motions for judgment on pleadings is similar to Federal Rule of Civil Procedure 12(c).

Offer of Judgment.—M.R.C.P. 68 is similar to Federal Rule of Civil Procedure 68.

Assignments.—When judgment has been assigned for valuable consideration, and bona fide, in writing, and levy of execution issued on such judgment has been made, and creditor dies after levy, assignee may bring action in court issuing execution, requiring debtor to show cause why another executor should not issue on same judgment, in name and/or benefit of said assignee. (T. 14, §2020). If such judgment is not discharged, assignee may bring civil action in his or her own name. (T. 14, §2021).

Confession of Judgment.—Negotiability of instrument is not affected by term authorizing confession of judgment on instrument if it is not paid when due. (T. 11, §3-1104[1][c][ii]).

Satisfaction.—No form of satisfaction is prescribed. The following may be used: "Judgment and costs fully paid and satisfied. No further action by either party for the same cause."

Judgment Notes.—No statutory provisions.

Uniform Enforcement of Foreign Judgments Act adopted. (T. 14, §§8001-8008).

LIMITATION OF ACTIONS:

Civil actions must be brought within following periods:

Six years: The general statute of limitations is for six years. Exceptions to six year statute are listed in following paragraphs. (T. 14, §752).

No limit: Actions for sexual abuse of minor under age of 16 may be commenced at any time after cause of action accrues.

Twenty years: Any real action (T. 14, §801); or action on witnessed promissory note or on contract or liability under seal or on bills, notes, or other evidences of debt issued by bank (T. 14, §751). Rebuttable presumption that judgment of U.S. court or state court of record, or of district court in this state paid and satisfied after 20 years. (T. 14, §864). See also category Estates and Trusts, topic Descent and Distribution.

Fifteen years: Actions against validity of governmental taking of real estate for nonpayment of property taxes recorded after Oct. 13, 1993 must be commenced within 15 years following expiration of period of redemption. For tax liens recorded on or before Oct. 13, 1993, action must be commenced within 15 years following expiration of period of redemption or no later than July 1, 1997. (T. 36, §946-A).

Twelve years: Actions for sexual abuse of minor between ages of 16 and 18 must be brought within 12 years after cause of action accrues or within six years of time person discovers or should have discovered harm, whichever occurs later. (T. 14, §752-C).

Four years: Actions for malpractice or professional negligence against duly licensed architects or engineers must be commenced within four years of discovery but in no event more than ten years after substantial completion of construction contract or of services unless valid contract provides for other limitation period. (T. 14, §752-A).

Actions for professional negligence against duly licensed land surveyors must be commenced within four years of discovery, but in no event more than 20 years after completion of plan or professional services. (T. 14, §752-D).

Three years: Actions for injury or death against health care providers and health care practitioners. Actions for injury or death against health care providers and practitioners by minors must be brought within six years after cause of action accrues or within three years after minor reaches age of majority, whichever first occurs. Cause of action accrues on date of act or omission giving rise to injury, unless cause of action involves leaving foreign object in body or failure of sterilization procedure, in which

LIMITATION OF ACTIONS . . . *continued*
case cause of action accrues when plaintiff discovers or reasonably should have discovered harm. (T. 24, §2902).

No action for injury or death against health care providers and health care practitioners may be brought until written notice of claim served upon person accused of professional negligence. (T. 24, §2903). Statute of limitations tolled from date upon which notice of claim served or filed with Superior Court until 30 days following day upon which claimant receives notice of findings of panel. (T. 24, §2859).

Two years: For assault and battery, false imprisonment, libel, slander. (T. 14, §753). Actions for wrongful death. (T. 18-A, §§2-804[b]). Actions for claims against governmental entity or its employees under Maine Tort Claims Act. (T. 14, §8110). However, notice of claim must be filed within 180 days. (T. 14, §8107). Actions for claims against ski area or tramway owners or operators, as defined under T. 26, c. 5, subchapter V-A, arising out of participation in skiing, or hang gliding or use of tramway therewith. (T. 14, §752-B). Action for damages caused by intoxicated individual brought against person who served alcohol. However, notice of claim must be given within 180 days. (T. 28-A, §§2514, 2513). Action by debtor against creditor for unlicensed consumer lending of open-end credit. (T. 9-A, §5-201[2]). See also category Employment, topic Labor Relations, subhead Workers' Compensation Act.

One year: For escape; action against bail, bondsmen of poor debtor or person adjudged trustee. (T. 14, §§851, 754). Action by debtor against creditor for unlicensed consumer lending of loans other than open-end credit line. One year commences on date of last scheduled payment under loan agreement. (T. 9-A, §5-201[2]).

Nine months: All claims against decedent's estate which arose before death of decedent are barred unless presented within earlier of nine months of decedent's death or four months following notice by publication. (T. 18-A, §3-803[b]). All claims against decedent's estate which arise at or after decedent's death are barred unless presented within later of nine months after decedent's death or four months after claim arose. (T. 18-A, §803[b]).

New Action.—When a summons fails of service or return by unavoidable accident, or officer's negligence, or the action is defeated for any matter of form, or by death of either party, plaintiff or his executor or administrator may commence a new action on same demand within six months. If either party dies before or within 30 days after time expires, action may be commenced within 20 months after representative is appointed. (T. 14, §§855, 856).

In actions upon mutual accounts, time runs from last item proved. (T. 14, §852).

Actions are deemed commenced when summons and complaint are served or when complaint is filed with court, whichever occurs first. (T. 14, §553).

Uniform Commercial Code.—Adopted. §2-725 provides four year statute of limitations for breach of any contract for sale. Action accrues when breach occurs, regardless of aggrieved party's lack of knowledge.

Disabilities.—If a person entitled to bring an action is a minor, insane, imprisoned or outside the limits of the United States when the cause of action accrues, the action may be brought within the time limited by statute after the disability is removed. (T. 14, §853). In case of real action, extension is for ten years after disability removed. (T. 14, §807).

Concealment by Defendant.—If person, liable to any action, fraudulently conceals cause thereto, or if fraud is committed which entitles any person to action, action may be commenced at any time within six years after person entitled thereto discovers he has just cause of action, except in cases of fraudulent transfer. (T. 14, §859).

Absence or Insolvency.—If a party is out of state when action accrues against him, time runs from when he comes into the state; if the action accrues before he leaves the state, the time he is absent if therefrom is not reckoned; if a person is adjudged insolvent after an action, provable in insolvency, accrues against him, time of insolvency proceedings is not to be reckoned. (T. 14, §866). See also category Property, topic Absentees.

Causes Arising Outside the State.—No action may be brought by any person whose cause of action has been barred by the laws of any state, territory or country while all the parties have resided therein. (T. 14, §866).

Revival of Barred Debts.—Claims barred by the statute of limitations can be revived by written acknowledgment, signed by the party to be charged, or by part payments on account. (T. 14, §§860, 863).

Contractual limitations are permitted; but life insurance company may not limit time from bringing action against it to less than three years. (T. 24-A, §2525).

Pleading.—The statute of limitations is an affirmative defense, which must be pleaded in order to be available. (M.R.C.P. 8[c]).

PARTITION:

Persons seized of, or having a right of entry into, real estate in fee simple or for life, as tenants in common or joint tenants may be compelled to divide same by writ of partition to superior court. (T. 14, §6501). Person interested and not named in petition, and not so notified as to enable him to appear earlier, may, in discretion of court, be permitted to appear and defend at any time before final judgment. (T. 14, §6504). If judgment is for partition, court appoints three or five commissioners to make same. (T. 14, §6511).

Maine has statutory partition (T. 14, §6501 et seq.) and equitable partition (T. 14, §6051 [7]). Persons seized of or having right of entry into real estate in fee simple or for life, as tenants in common or joint tenants and those in possession or having right of entry for term of years, as tenants in common, may bring civil action for partition. (T. 14, §§6501-02).

Jurisdiction and Venue.—Action for partition may be brought in Superior or District Court in county where real estate is situated. (T. 14, §6502).

Proceedings.—Complaint must clearly describe estate, state proportion claimed and give names and residences of tenants in common (T. 14, §6502), and must state "TITLE TO REAL ESTATE IS INVOLVED" directly beneath designation of pleading. (M.R.C.P. 10[a]). Service of process shall be made as in other civil actions and notice by publication shall be given to tenants whose identity or whereabouts are unknown. (T. 14, §6503). Person interested and not named in complaint may, in discretion of court, be permitted to appear and defend. (T. 14, §6504).

Partition in Kind or Sale.—Statutory partition provides for division of real estate. (T. 14, §6501). If parcel of greater value than party's share or cannot be divided, may be assigned to one party by his payment to other party. (T. 14, §6515). Equity partition allows sale. (430 A.2d 37, 39).

PLEADING:

Pleading is governed by Maine Rules of Civil Procedure which are patterned after Federal Rules. See topic Practice.

Proof of Claims.—For purpose of bringing suit copy of original documents sufficient; if claim on open account, should be itemized and include dates, full and exact names of parties and residences, together with statement of nature of claim; location of real estate and personal property helpful for attachment.

Small Claims.—See category Courts and Legislature, topic Courts.

PRACTICE:

Practice is governed by Maine Rules of Civil Procedure. These rules in general conform to Federal Rules of Civil Procedure.

Maine Administrative Procedure Act, T. 5, §§8001-11008, governs rule making, advisory rulings, adjudicatory proceedings, and judicial review with respect to agencies as defined by T. 5, §8002(2).

Direct Actions Against Insurer.—See category Transportation, topic Motor Vehicles, subhead Direct Actions.

Small Claims.—See category Courts and Legislature, topic Courts.

See also topics Actions, Appeal and Error, Depositions and Discovery, Injunctions, Judgments, Pleading, Process; category Debtor and Creditor, topics Attachment, Executions, Garnishment.

PROCESS:

M.R.C.P. 4, 4A and 4B, based on Federal Rules of Civil Procedure form basis for procedural rules and method of service of process in commencement of a civil action. Civil actions are commenced by service of a summons and complaint or by filing a complaint with court. See topic Practice.

General Requisites.—Summons must bear signature or facsimile signature of clerk, be under seal of court, contain name of court and names of parties, be directed to defendant, state name and address of plaintiff's attorney, and time within which defendant must answer, and must notify him that in case of his failure to answer, judgment by default will be rendered against him for relief demanded in complaint. (M.R.C.P. 4[a]). Complaint must contain caption setting forth name of court and county, title of action, docket number and word "complaint." Title of action shall include names of all parties. Complaint must be dated. If claim involves title to real estate, words "TITLE TO REAL ESTATE IS INVOLVED" must be included beneath designation. (M.R.C.P. 10[a]). All claims must be made in separate numbered paragraphs. (M.R.C.P. 10[b]).

By Whom Issued.—Summons may be procured in blank form from Clerk of Courts and filled out by plaintiff's attorney. (M.R.C.P. 4[b]).

Service by Mail.—Service may be made by mailing copy of summons and complaint to person to be served together with two copies of notice and acknowledgment form and return envelope, postage prepaid, addressed to sender. If no acknowledgment of service under this paragraph received by sender within 20 days after date of mailing, service of summons and complaint must be made in person as permitted by Rule 4 or by statute. (M.R.C.P. 4[c][1]).

Who May Serve.—Service is made by Sheriff or Deputy Sheriff within county or by some person specially appointed by court for that purpose. (M.R.C.P. 4[c][2]).

Personal Service on Individual.—Service can be made either by delivering copy of summons and complaint to defendant personally or, upon motion and order, by leaving them at usual place of abode with some person of suitable age residing there or by delivering copy of summons and complaint to agent authorized by appointment or by law to receive service of process. (M.R.C.P. 4[d][1]).

Personal Service on Infant.—Service made on infant and also on guardian, if within state, and if not, to father or mother or other person with whom infant resides or as provided by court order. (M.R.C.P. 4[d][2]).

Personal Service on Incompetent Person.—Service made on guardian or competent member of family with whom incompetent resides or if living in institution, to director of institution, or as provided by court order and also on incompetent unless otherwise ordered. (M.R.C.P. 4[d][3]).

Personal service upon county, town, city, U.S. or other public corporation other than State of Maine—upon officers designated in Rule. (M.R.C.P. 4[d][4-7]).

Personal Service on Partnership.—Service must be made on all partners by delivering copy of summons and complaint to any general partner or managing or general agent of partnership, or by leaving copies at office or place of business of partnership within state, or to any agent, attorney in fact or other person authorized by Rule or Statute. (M.R.C.P. 4[d][10]).

Personal Service on Domestic Corporation.—Service is made: (a) On any officer, director or general agent; or, if none found, on any person in actual employment of corporation; or, if none found, on Secretary of State, provided plaintiff's attorney also sends copy of summons and complaint to corporation by registered or certified mail, addressed to corporation's principal office as reported on latest annual return; or (b) on any agent or attorney in fact authorized by appointment or statute to accept service. (M.R.C.P. 4[d][8]).

See note at head of Digest as to 1998 legislation covered.

See Topical Index in front part of this volume.

PROCESS . . . *continued*

Personal Service on Association.—Service must be made on all members.

Personal Service on Foreign Corporation.—Service on any officer, director or agent within state or at any office or place of business of corporation within state or by service on any agent or attorney authorized by appointment or statute to accept service. (M.R.C.P. 4[d][9]).

Personal Service in Action for Guardianship or Conservatorship.—Ward served in person. (T. 18-A, §5-309). Spouse, adult children and parents served by certified mail. (T. 18-A, §§5-309, 5-405).

Service on State of Maine.—Service made by delivering copy of summons and complaint to Attorney General or deputies either personally or by registered or certified mail, return receipt requested, and in actions attacking validity of order of staff officer or agency not made party by also sending copy of summons and complaint by ordinary mail to such officer or agency. (M.R.C.P. 4[d][11]).

Service on State Officer or Agency.—Service made, as appropriate, either by method prescribed for personal service on individual (M.R.C.P. 4[d][1]) or by delivering copy of summons and complaint to officer, director or manager of public corporation or to any member of public body, agency, or authority (M.R.C.P. 4[d][7]) and by sending copy of summons and complaint by ordinary mail to Attorney General (M.R.C.P. 4[d][12]).

Service on Trustees of Express Trust.—Service made in any action for claim of relief against trust, except action by beneficiary, by delivering copy of summons and complaint to any trustee or by leaving same at office or place of business of trust within state, or by delivering copy of summons and complaint to any agent or attorney in fact authorized by appointment or statute to receive service on behalf of trust, provided any further notice required by statute shall be given. (M.R.C.P. 4[d][13]).

Personal Service Outside the State.—Service in same manner as if such service were made within state, by any person authorized to serve civil process by laws of place of service, or by person specially appointed to serve. Affidavit of person making service filed with court stating time, manner and place of service. (M.R.C.P. 4[e]).

Service outside state by mail allowed where service cannot, with due diligence, be made personally within state. Service may be made by registered or certified mail, return receipt requested, with instructions to deliver to addressee only, in following cases where pleading demands: (1) Judgment affecting interest or title in real or personal property within state; or (2) judgment for divorce or annulment. (M.R.C.P. 4[f]).

Service by Publication.—Court, on motion and showing that service cannot, with due diligence, be made by another prescribed method may order service by publication in following instances: (1) actions affecting title to property within state; or (2) divorce or annulment actions.

Notice must be published once a week for three successive weeks in designated newspaper of general circulation in county where action is pending. In addition, service is made by mail to defendant's last known address of copy of order as published. First publication of summons is made within 20 days after order allowing it is granted. Service is complete on 21st day after first publication. Plaintiff files with court affidavit that publication has been made (M.R.C.P. 4[g]).

Long Arm Statute.—Jurisdiction of state courts may be founded upon: (1) Transaction of any business in state; (2) doing or causing tortious act to be done or causing consequences of tortious act to occur within state; (3) ownership, use or possession of any real estate situated in state; (4) contracting to insure any person, property or risk located within state at time of contracting; (5) conception resulting in paternity; (6) contracting to supply services or things within state; (7) maintaining domicile in state subject to marital or family relationship out of which arises claim for divorce, alimony, separate maintenance, property settlement, child support or child custody, or commission in state of any act giving rise to such claim; (8) acting as director, manager, trustee or other officer of corporation incorporated in or having its principal place of business in state; (9) maintaining any other relation to state or to persons or property which affords basis for jurisdiction by courts of state consistent with Constitution of U.S. Service of process upon person subject to jurisdiction of courts of state by operation of long arm statute may be made by personal service of summons on defendant outside state. (T. 14, §704-A). Extended personal jurisdiction for interstate child support actions. (T. 19, §2851).

Proof of Service.—Officer making service writes on process date on which and person on whom service was made. Plaintiff's attorney files proof of service with court within time during which person served must respond to process. (M.R.C.P. 4[h]).

Uniform Child Custody Jurisdiction Act (service requirements). (T. 19-A, §§1701-1725).

Uniform Interstate Family Support Act adopted. (T. 19, §§2801 et seq.).

Expedited Process for Commencement of Paternity Actions (service requirements). (T. 19-A, §§1601-1614).

Refer to c. XI of Maine Rules of Civil Procedure for special rules for form of process in following actions: divorce and annulment (M.R.C.P. 80); real actions (M.R.C.P. 80A); review of governmental action (M.R.C.P. 80B); review of final agency action (M.R.C.P. 80C); forcible entry and detainer (M.R.C.P. 80D); administrative inspection warrants (M.R.C.P. 80E); traffic infractions (M.R.C.P. 80F); civil violations (M.R.C.P. 80H); search warrants for Schedule Z drugs (M.R.C.P. 80I); warrants for surveys and tests (M.R.C.P. 80J); land use violations (M.R.C.P. 80K); jury trial de novo in small claims appeals to Superior Court (M.R.C.P. 80L).

Nonresident Motorists.—See category Transportation, topic Motor Vehicles.

REPLEVIN:

Goods unlawfully taken or detained from the owner or person entitled to the possession thereof, and goods attached on mesne process or taken on execution claimed by a person other than the defendant in the suit in which they are attached or taken, may be replevied by such owner or person. (T. 14, §7301).

Proceedings.—Action for replevin must be commenced by filing complaint, together with motion for approval of replevin and replevin bond. Motion shall be supported by affidavit setting forth facts which demonstrate that there is reasonable likelihood that plaintiff will prevail in replevin action. Replevin bond must have sufficient sureties, in double actual value of goods to be replevied. (T. 14, §7303). Order of replevin (unless ex parte) will be entered only after notice to defendant and hearing. (M.R.C.P. 64). If value of goods exceeds $30,000, action must be brought in superior court for county where they are detained; if it does not exceed $30,000, before any district court of said county. (T. 14, §7302).

Repossession.—For ex parte replevin orders, defendant on two day's notice to plaintiff may move for return of replevied property. Court then holds hearing on replevin where plaintiff bears burden of proof.

If defendant is entitled to return of replevied goods, court shall order plaintiff to return goods plus pay costs and damages from taking. (T. 14, §7304). Beasts distrained to obtain satisfaction for damages claimed to be done by them, may also be replevied. (T. 14, §7401).

SEQUESTRATION:

There is no statutory authority or case law on subject of sequestration.

SUBMISSION OF CONTROVERSY:

When questions presented by appeal to law court can be determined without examination of all pleadings, evidence and lower court proceedings, parties may prepare and sign statement of case. (M.R.C.P. 74[d]). In cases where all parties appearing request, superior court may report any action to law court for determination where there is agreement as to all material facts and question of law is of sufficient importance. Any such action will be heard and determined in manner provided in case of appeals. (M.R.C.P. 72).

VENUE:

Personal and transitory actions, except foreign attachment, shall be brought, when parties live in state, in county where any plaintiff or defendant lives, except that in trustee actions it must be brought in county where some trustee lives; and when no plaintiff lives in state, in defendant's county, or in either case, in county where cause of action took place. Corporations may sue and be sued in county in which they have an established place of business, or in which plaintiff or defendant, if a natural person, lives. There are special provisions relative to actions on sheriff's and coroner's bonds, judgment debts and actions by or against counties, towns, parishes or school districts. Action may be dismissed for improper venue with double costs to defendant. (T. 14, §501-507).

Change of Venue.—Presiding Justice of Superior Court or Chief Justice of Superior Court may transfer any civil action or proceeding from Superior Court in one county to another county. Transfer may also be by consent of all parties to civil proceeding with prior consent of Chief Justice of Superior Court. (T. 14, §508). In District Court, transfer may be made by court on motion or its own initiative for convenience or in interest of justice. (T. 4, §155).

Contract Provisions.—No statute or case law.

Mandatory Venues.—Certain actions may be brought in designated venues:

Administrative Appeals.—In Superior Court for county where petitioners reside or have principal place of business, agency has principal place of business, or subject activity or property is located. (T. 5, §11002).

Forcible Entry and Detainer.—In division of District Court where property is located. (T. 4, §155).

Attachment.—If brought in District Court, must be in division in which plaintiff, defendant or subject property resides. (T. 4, §155).

Divorce, Separation, Annulment or Support.—Court where either plaintiff or defendant resides. (T. 4, §155).

Domestic Abuse.—Division of District Court in which either plaintiff or defendant resides. (T. 19, §763).

Enforcement of Money Judgment.—Against resident in division of District Court where debtor resides or keeps place of business; against nonresident individual in division where debtor is commorant; against nonresident corporation in any division in which civil summons could be served on debtor or in which action resulting in judgment could have been brought; except that enforcement of consumer debt judgment must, at creditor's option, be in division where debtor resides or transaction took place. (T. 14, §3121-A[1]). If civil order of arrest issues or motion for contempt is filed, action must be transferred to division in which debtor resides. (T. 14, §3121-A[2]).

Guardianship for Incapacitated Person.—In place where incapacitated person resides; if court has ordered institutionalization, then also may be brought in court issuing such order. (T. 18-A, §§5-302, 5-313).

Protective Proceeding for Disabled Person.—In place where disabled person resides or, if nonresident, where he has property. (T. 18-A, §5-403).

Guardianship for Minor.—Where minor resides. (T. 18-A, §§5-205, 5-211).

Protective Proceeding for Minor.—Where minor resides or, if nonresident, where he has property. (T. 18-A, §5-403).

Protective Petition for Infant.—In District Court where infant legally resides or child is present. (T. 22, §4031).

Limited Partnership Agreement (Petition for Execution, Amendment or Certificate).—In Superior Court for county in which limited partnership has registered office or, if no registered office in Maine, then in Kennebec County Superior Court. (T. 31, §425).

Motor Vehicle Dealer Complaint about Location of New Dealership by Manufacturer.—In Superior Court for county in which plaintiff dealership is located. (T. 10, §1174-A).

Partition or Quiet Title of Real Estate.—In District or Superior Court for county in which real estate is located. (T. 14, §§6502, 6651).

See note at head of Digest as to 1998 legislation covered.

See Topical Index in front part of this volume.

VENUE . . . continued

Replevin.—If goods are worth less than District Court jurisdictional maximum, then in division for county where goods are detained; if value exceeds jurisdictional maximum, then in Superior Court for county where goods are detained. (T. 14, §7302).

Arbitration Award Order Application.—In Superior Court specified in arbitration agreement or in court where prior hearing was held; otherwise in Superior Court for county where adverse party resides or has place of business or, if nonresident, in court of any county; subsequent applications to court hearing initial application. (T. 14, §5944).

COURTS AND LEGISLATURE

COURTS:

United States District Court.—Clerk's offices: Portland 04101, Bangor, 04402-1007. Maine constitutes one judicial district. Court held at Portland and Bangor. Cases arising in counties of Androscoggin, Cumberland, Knox, Lincoln, Oxford, Sagadahoc and York to be filed and ordinarily tried at Portland. Cases arising in counties of Aroostook, Franklin, Hancock, Kennebec, Penobscot, Piscataquis, Somerset, Waldo and Washington to be filed and ordinarily tried in Bangor.

Supreme Judicial Court.—Clerk's office: Portland, 04112-0368. As Law Court, it is highest court. Seven members. Jurisdiction of Law Court is of cases on appeal from inferior courts including certain interlocutory rulings, questions of law arising on reports of cases or on agreed statement of facts, cases presenting question of law, cases requesting equitable relief, motions to dissolve injunctions, and questions arising in nature of habeas corpus, mandamus and certiorari. (T. 4, §57). Questions of law may be certified by federal court to Law Court. (T. 4, §57, M.R.C.P. 76B). Single justices of Supreme Judicial Court have concurrent jurisdiction with Superior Court over requests for equitable relief. (T. 4, §105).

Superior Court.—Established by Laws 1929, c. 141, has original jurisdiction in all matters either original or appellate formerly exercised by Supreme Judicial Court except those powers exercised by Supreme Judicial Court sitting as Law Court and except matters within jurisdiction of District Court. (T. 4, §105).

Place of sitting.—

Androscoggin County: court sits at Auburn.
Aroostook County: court sits at Caribou and Houlton.
Cumberland County: court sits at Portland.
Franklin County: court sits at Farmington.
Hancock County: court sits at Ellsworth.
Kennebec County: court sits at Augusta.
Knox County: court sits at Rockland.
Lincoln County: court sits at Wiscasset.
Oxford County: court sits at South Paris.
Penobscot County: court sits at Bangor.
Piscataquis County: court sits at Dover-Foxcroft.
Sagadahoc County: court sits at Bath.
Somerset County: court sits at Skowhegan.
Waldo County: court sits at Belfast.
Washington County: court sits at Machias.
York County: court sits at Alfred.

Probate Courts.—In each county there is a court of probate with judge and register. Probate court has jurisdiction of administration of estates of deceased persons, wills, guardianships, adoptions, change of name, and such other matters as may be conferred by law. It has concurrent jurisdiction in equity with Supreme Judicial Court of all matters relating to administration of deceased persons, to wills and to trusts which are created by will or other written instrument. (T. 4, §252).

State District Courts.—State is divided into 30 Divisions over which 13 District Courts have same civil and criminal jurisdiction as that exercised by municipal courts and trial justices which were in existence on effective date of creating act. Jurisdiction of District Courts is governed by T. 4, §152. District Courts have exclusive jurisdiction over: (1) Mental health commitment hearings and mental retardation certification hearings under T. 34-B, §§5462-5478; (2) habitual truancy actions under T. 20-A, §§3272-3273 and 5051-5053, and (3) small claims actions under T. 14, §§7481-7486. In addition, they have original jurisdiction concurrent with Superior Court over: (1) All civil actions when no equitable relief is demanded and damages claimed do not exceed $30,000; (2) all civil actions to enforce liens under T. 10, §3251 et seq. and T. 35-A, §706; (3) actions for divorce, annulment or separation and proceedings under T. 19-A, §101 et seq.; (4) actions to quiet title to real estate under T. 14, §§6651-6658; (5) actions to quiet title to real estate under T. 36, §946; (6) actions for breach of implied warranty and covenant of habitability under T. 14, §6021; (7) actions to foreclose mortgages under T. 14, §6321, et seq.; (8) actions for restitution under T. 5, §213 (unfair trade practices); (9) actions for illegal evictions under T. 14, §6014; (10) actions for foreclosures of mortgages and for redemption; (11) actions to compel specific performance, to cancel and to compel discharge of written contracts upon full performance or payment; (12) actions for relief from fraud, duress, unjust enrichment, trust, accident or mistake; (13) actions for nuisance or waste; (14) actions concerning partnerships or between partners or part owners of real or personal property; (15) actions regarding property matters between spouses under T. 19, §166 until Oct. 1, 1997, thereafter T. 19-A, §806; (16) civil actions for redelivery of goods not able to be replevied or for reaching property not able to be attached, not able to be taken on execution, or conveyed in fraud of creditors; (17) actions concerning vested or contingent interests in or liens on specific property or otherwise affecting title to real property; (18) actions to compel compliance with court orders; (19) actions seeking equitable relief through equitable defense, counterclaim, cross-claim or responsive pleading or reply under M.R.C.P.; (20) actions to enforce access to health care under T. 22, §1715; (21) proceedings for equitable relief and impose penalties involving violations of environmental ordinances, regulations or laws; and (22) receipt of guilty pleas in criminal cases with maximum imprisonment terms of one year or more.

District Courts also have original jurisdiction concurrent with Superior Court to grant equitable relief in proceedings involving consent to minor's abortion under T. 22, §1597-A. Chief Judge sets trial terms, although court in continuous session. Appeal is to Superior Court except from judgment in foreclosure action where appeal is directly to Supreme Judicial Court. (T. 14, §1901).

Districts.—13 districts are as follows with place for holding court shown in parentheses after name of each division:

First District: divisions of Eastern Aroostook (Caribou); and Western Aroostook (Madawaska, Fort Kent).
Second District: divisions of Central Aroostook (Presque Isle) and Southern Aroostook (Houlton).
Third District: divisions of Southern Penobscot (Bangor); Western Penobscot (Newport).
Fourth District: divisions of Northern Washington (Calais); Southern Washington (Machias).
Fifth District: divisions of Central Hancock (Ellsworth); Southern Hancock (Bar Harbor) and Waldo (Belfast).
Sixth District: divisions of Bath-Brunswick (Bath, West Bath, or Brunswick); Lincoln (Wiscasset) and Knox (Rockland).
Seventh District: divisions of Northern Kennebec (Waterville); Southern Kennebec (Augusta).
Eighth District: division of Southern Androscoggin (Lewiston/Auburn).
Ninth District: divisions of Southern Cumberland (Portland); Northern Cumberland (Bridgton).
Tenth District: divisions of Eastern York (Biddeford or Saco); Western York (W. York) and Southern York (York).
Eleventh District: divisions of Northern Androscoggin (Livermore Falls); Northern Oxford (Rumford) and Southern Oxford (South Paris).
Twelfth District: divisions of Somerset (Skowhegan); Franklin (Farmington).
Thirteenth District: divisions of Piscataquis (Dover-Foxcroft); Northern Penobscot (Millinocket); Central Penobscot (Lincoln). (T. 4, §154).

Court Alternative Dispute Resolution Service established to provide mediation in Superior and District Courts. (T. 4, §18-B).

Justices of the Peace.—Chief Judge may authorize any attorney at law licensed to practice in state to receive complaints, issue process for arrest, issue search warrants, endorse commitment certificates, who shall be called justice of peace. Authorized to act only in district of residence. (T. 4, §161).

Small Claims Courts.—Governed by T. 14, §§7481-7486, small claims are any right of action cognizable by court, not involving title to real estate, in which debt or damage claimed does not exceed $4,500 exclusive of interest and costs. Procedure governed by rules of procedure adopted by law court. Alternative, not exclusive, proceeding. District court has jurisdiction. District court has power to grant monetary and equitable relief. Equitable relief limited to orders to return, reform, refund, repair or rescind. Small claim must be brought in district court division where transaction occurred, where defendant resides, where defendant has place of business or, if defendant is corporation or partnership, where registered agent resides. Judgment obtained is res judicata as to amount in controversy. Appeal of adverse decision only recourse. If defendant not indigent, minimum $15 monthly installment payment for money judgment enforcement may be assessed.

JUSTICES OF THE PEACE:

Appointments of justice of peace are no longer authorized. (T. 5, §82). See also topic Courts and category Documents and Records, topic Notaries Public.

LEGISLATURE:

Meets annually: First Regular Session convenes on first Wed. of Dec. in odd-numbered years and usually lasts until third Wed. in June; Second Regular Session convenes on first Wed. after first Tues. in Jan. in even-numbered years and usually lasts until third Wed. in Apr. Times for adjournment may be extended. Proposed legislation is considered during First Regular Session. Consideration of legislation is limited for legislators to emergency and financial matters during Second Regular Session. (Const. Art. IV, Pt. 3, §1; T. 3, §2).

Special Sessions.—May be convened by Governor or by President of Senate and Speaker of House with consent of majority of members of each political party. Special sessions typically last three to four days. (Const. Art. V, Pt. 1, §13; Art. IV, Pt. 3, §1).

Referendum and Initiative.—Constitution provides for both. (Const., Art. IV, Pt. 3, §§17-22).

Lobbyists.—Regulated by T. 3, §§311-326.

REPORTS:

Cases decided by Supreme Judicial Court, sitting en banc as a law court are reported in Maine Reports, beginning with vol. 1. First nine generally cited as Greenleaf's Reports. Maine decisions are also reported in the Atlantic Reporter. Maine Reports discontinued as of 1966; replaced by Maine Reporter which collects cases decided by Supreme Judicial Court as reported in Atlantic Reporter.

Digest.—Maine decisions are digested in the Atlantic Digest and in Lawrence's Maine Digest, which has been brought down through Vol. 146 (1950-51) of the Maine Reports by a Vol. III published in Dec., 1953. Also in West's Maine Digest. See also topic Statutes.

STATUTES:

Latest revision is 1964 Maine Revised Statutes Annotated. Subsequent acts are in session laws.

Uniform Acts adopted are: Anatomical Gift Act (1969); (T. 22, §§2901-2910); Arbitration (1967) (T. 14, §§5927-5949); Attendance of Witnesses from Without a

---

STATUTES . . . *continued*

State in Criminal Proceedings (1939) (T. 15, §§1411-1415); Child Custody Jurisdiction Act (1979) (T. 19-A, §§1701-1725); Civil Liability for Support (1955) (T. 19-A, §§3501-3506); Commercial Code (1964) (T. 11, §§1-101-9-507); Commercial Code for Investment Securities (1998) (T. 11, §§8-1101—8-1511); Commercial Code for Letters of Credit (1998) (T. 11, §§5-1101—5-1117); Common Trust Fund (1979) (T. 18-A, §§7-501-7-503); Condominium Act (1983) (T. 33, §§1601-201 to 1604-118); Conservation Easement Act (1985) (T. 33, §§476-479-B); Consumer Credit Code (1975) (T. 9-A, §§1-101-11-121); Criminal Extradition Act (1929) (T. 15, §§201-229); Deceptive Trade Practices (1969) (T. 10, §§1211-1216); Declaratory Judgments Act (1941) (T. 14, §§5951-5963); Determination of Death Act (1983) (T. 22, §§2811-2813); Disclaimer of Property Interests (1979) (T. 18-A, §2-801); Disclaimer of Transfers by Will, Intestacy or Appointment (1975) (T. 18-A, §2-801); Disclaimer of Transfers Under Nontestamentary Instruments (1975); Division of Income for Tax Purposes (1989) (T. 36, §§5210-5211); Durable Power of Attorney (1991) (T. 18-A, §§5-501-5-506); Enforcement of Foreign Judgments (1975) (T. 14, §§8001-8008); Federal Lien Registration (1988) (T. 33, §§1901-1907); Fraudulent Transfer (1986) (T. 14, §§3571-3582); Guardianship and Protective Proceedings (1979) (T. 18-A, §§5-101 et seq.); Health-Care Decisions (1995) (T. 18-A, §§801-817); Interstate Arbitration of Death Taxes (1949) (T. 36, §§3911-3924); Interstate Compromise of Death Taxes (1949) (T. 36, §3981); Interstate Family Support (1993) (T. 19-A, §§2801-3401); Joint Obligations (Model) (1966) (T. 14, §§11-17); Judicial Notice of Foreign Law (1939) (T. 16, §§401-406); Jury Selection and Service (1970) (T. 14, §§1211-1219); Limited Partnership Act (1973) (T. 31, §§401-414); Management of Institutional Funds (1993) (T. 13, §§4100-4109); Motor Vehicle Certificate of Title and Anti-theft (1969) (T. 29, §§2350-2461); Partnership (1973) (T. 31, §§281-323); Paternity (1967) (T. 19-A, §§1551-1651); Photographic Copies of Business and Public Records as Evidence (1963) (T. 16, §456); Premarital Agreement (1987) (T. 19-A, §§601-611); Probate Code (1979) (T. 18-A, §§1-101-8-401); Recognition of Acknowledgments Act (1969) (T. 4, §§1011-1019); Rendition of Prisoners as Witnesses in Criminal Proceedings (1967) (T. 15, §§1461-1471); Rights of the Terminally Ill (1989) (T. 18-A, §5-701); Rules of Evidence (1979); Simultaneous Death (1979) (T. 18-A, §2-805); State Administrative Procedure Act (Model) (1977) (T. 5, §§8001-11008); Testamentary Additions to Trusts (1963) (T. 18-A, §2-511); Trade Secrets (1987) (T. 10, §§1541-1545); Transfer on Death Security Registration (1998) (T. 18, §§6-301—6-312); Transfers to Minors (1988) (T. 33, §§1651-1674); Trustees' Powers (1981) (§§7-401-7-405); Unclaimed Property (1998) (T. 33, §§1951-1980) (see category Property, topic Absentees).

Uniform Commercial Code adopted. See category Business Regulation and Commerce, topic Commercial Code.

For text of Uniform Acts falling within the scope of the Martindale-Hubbell Law Digest see Uniform and Model Acts section.

CRIMINAL LAW

BAIL:

See topic Criminal Law.

CRIMINAL LAW:

Maine Criminal Code effective May 1, 1976. (T. 17-A, §§1-1357).

The state laws relating to crimes and criminal procedure conform to the principles of common law. Statutes deal with particular crimes.

Most crimes classified as A, B, C, D or E and maximum sentence of fine or imprisonment is based on class.

Indictments.—All criminal prosecutions must be on indictment by grand jury, except for contempt of court, or when prosecution utilizing charging instrument other than indictment is expressly authorized by rule of court, or in proceedings before district court, district court acting as juvenile court and courts therefrom. (T. 15, §701).

Bail.—No person before conviction shall be bailable for any capital offense when proof is evident or presumption great. (Me. Const., Art. I, §10). Eligibility for bail and procedures relevant thereto governed by Maine Bail Code. (T. 15, §§1001-1102).

Uniform Criminal Extradition Act adopted with numerous variations. (T. 15, §§201-229).

Uniform Act for Out-of-State Parolee Supervision.—Enacted. (T. 34-A, §§9801-9864).

Uniform Rendition of Prisoners as Witnesses in Criminal Proceedings Act enacted. (T. 15, §1461-1471).

DEBTOR AND CREDITOR

ASSIGNMENTS:

Common law requirements govern assignment of rights, debts or choses in action except where governed by statute.

Uniform Commercial Code adopted, contains statutory provisions on this topic. See category Business Regulation and Commerce, topic Commercial Code. Any assignment, pledge or other transaction (regardless of form) intended to create a security interest in personal property, including goods, documents, instruments, chattel paper, accounts receivable or contract rights is governed by Uniform Commercial Code. Art. 9 also governs sale of accounts receivable, contract rights or chattel paper. See category Business Regulation and Commerce, topic Commercial Code.

Instrument Transferring Title.—No special requirements. Witnesses and acknowledgments are not required but acknowledgment required if instrument recorded although financing statements under Uniform Commercial Code need not be acknowledged. (T. 33, §203).

Filing and Recording.—No requirements other than for wages, except as imposed by Commercial Code (T. 11), and trademarks law (T. 10, §1525).

Notice.—Consumer is authorized to pay original creditor until she receives notification of assignment of rights to payment pursuant to consumer credit transaction which clearly identifies rights assigned. (T. 9-A, §§3-203, 9-306). See category Business Regulation and Commerce, topics Consumer Credit and Commercial Code. Insurer assuming or transferring obligations or risks on contracts of insurance in some circumstances must give statutory notice to or obtain prior approval of policyholders. (T. 24-A, §§761-766).

Form.—There is no statutory form of assignment. Assignments of estates in land must be in writing. (T. 33, §162).

Licenses.—Many state issued licenses are not assignable. Reference should be made to statutes governing particular licenses.

Assignment of Prizes.—Right to Tri-State Lotto prize over $5,000 not assignable, except payment of prize drawn may be paid to another person as provided in §416-A. (T. 8, §416).

Assignment of Wages.—No assignment of wages is valid against any person other than parties thereto, unless such assignment is recorded by clerk in office of Secretary of State; and no such assignment shall be valid against employer unless he has actual notice thereof. If employment is in unorganized place, record should be in registry of deeds. (T. 26, §627).

Assignment of wages for child support obligation has absolute priority over previously recorded court ordered assignments in satisfaction of money judgment. (T. 26, §627). Creditor may not take assignment of earnings of consumer for payment or as security for payment of debt arising out of consumer credit transaction. (T. 9-A, 3-305). Assignment in violation of this section unenforceable by assignee of earnings and revocable by consumer. Assignments of unemployment compensation benefits are void, except as to amounts deducted or collected under T. 26, c. 13. (T. 26, §1044). Claims for workers' compensation are not assignable except for payment of support or reimbursement of general assistance. (T. 39-A, §106).

ATTACHMENT:

See generally M.R.C.P. 4A., T. 14, §§4101-4613.

Actions in Which Allowed.—All civil actions. (M.R.C.P. 4A, T. 14, §4151).

Courts Which May Issue Writ.—Real and/or personal property may be attached on writ issued by Superior Court or District Court. (T. 14, §§4151, 4452).

In Whose Favor Writ May Issue.—May issue in favor of resident, nonresident or foreign corporation.

Against Whom Writ May Issue.—Against any resident of the state or against any nonresident having property in the state. Quasi in rem jurisdiction affecting only property attached can be based upon attachment of property within state. Attachment not available before judgment in action against consumer for debt arising from consumer credit transaction as defined by T. 9-A, §1-301(12). (M.R.C.P. 4A[a]).

Proceedings to Obtain.—No property, including real estate, may be attached unless such attachment is for specified amount approved by court. (M.R.C.P. 4A[c]). Except as provided in M.R.C.P. 4A(g), order may be entered only after notice to defendant, hearing and finding by court that it is more likely than not that plaintiff will recover judgment, including interest and costs, equal to or greater than aggregate sum of attachment and any insurance, bond or other security and any property or credits attached by other writ of attachment or by trustee process. Attachment of property must be within 30 days of order approving attachment. (M.R.C.P. 4A[c]). Motion for approval of attachment to be supported by affidavits. (M.R.C.P. 4A[c], [i]). Defendant opposing motion for approval of attachment shall file opposition within 21 days after filing of motion, unless another time is set by court. (M.R.C.P. 4A[c], M.R.C.P. 7[c]).

M.R.C.P. 4a(g) provides that order approving attachment may be entered ex parte only if court finds: (1) it is more likely than not plaintiff will recover judgment equal to or greater than aggregate sum of attachment and any insurance, bond or other security, and any property or credits attached by other writ of attachment or by trustee process, and either (2) clear danger that if notified in advance defendant will remove property from state or will conceal it or will otherwise make it unavailable to satisfy judgment or (3) immediate danger that defendant will damage or destroy property. Motion for ex parte attachment must be supported by affidavit. Such affidavit shall be upon affiant's own knowledge, information or belief. (M.R.C.P. 4A[i]). Attachment must be recorded.

Approval of Limited Attachment or Substituted Security.—Upon appropriate showing by party whose property is to be attached, court shall specify that attachment to issue solely against particular property or credits. If, at hearing on motion to approve attachment, party whose property is to be attached tenders cash or bond equal to amount of attachment to be approved, and deposits or files same with court, court may order any prior attachment dissolved and no further attachment shall issue absent showing that cash or bond has become inadequate or unavailable as security. (M.R.C.P. 4A[d]).

Civil Judgment.—Nonexempt real or personal property may be attached following entry of civil action judgment and prior to issuance of writ of execution upon judgment by filing attested copy of court order in registry of deeds for county in which property is located or proper place pursuant to T. 11, §9-401. Such filing constitutes perfection of attachment. Party whose property is so attached must be immediately notified by certified letter mailed by attaching party to last known address. (T. 14, §4151).

Levy.—If on real estate then within five days after attachment officer must file in registry of deeds in county where some part of estate lies an attested copy of his return relative to such attachment with value of property he is commanded to attach. (T. 14, §4454).

If attachment is of personal property, officer must take possession of it either by removing the property or putting in a keeper. (T. 14, §4152).

See note at head of Digest as to 1998 legislation covered.

See Topical Index in front part of this volume.

ATTACHMENT . . . *continued*

Optional Method.—Any interest in real or personal property, not exempt from attachment, may be attached by filing in registry of deeds for county in which property is located or proper place pursuant to T. 11, §9-401(1) attested copy of court order approving real or personal property attachment provided filing is made within 30 days of court order approving attachment (T. 14, §4154).

Indemnity.—Officer may require indemnity before levying.

Attachment Bond.—Any attachment made on an original writ, issued upon judgment by default against absent defendant, continues for one year and 60 days after judgment is rendered, when no bond is given; and when bond is given it continues for 60 days after such bond is filed with clerk of court. Bond must be deposited with clerk of court, who decides upon sufficiency of its sureties, subject to appeal. (T. 14, §§4701, 4702).

Priorities.—Creditor first attaching may exhaust the amount covered by his attachment; but subsequent creditors may petition court for permission to defend prior suits. (T. 14, §201).

Sale.—Personal property may be sold by consent of debtor and creditor, proceeding as if it were a sale on execution. (T. 14, §4351).

Perishable goods may be sold without consent of debtor before or after entry of actions. Procedure for sale set forth in the statutes. (T. 14, §4352). Upon motion of either party, court may order personal property to be sold and proceeds held as security for claim involved. (T. 14, §4353).

Duration of Attachment.—Attachment of real or personal property continues during time within which appeal may be taken from judgment and during pendency of appeal. When judgment becomes final by expiration of time for appeal, by dismissal of appeal, or on certificate of decision from Superior Court or Law Court, attachment continues for 60 days, with some exceptions. (T. 14 §§1601, 4601; M.R.C.P. 62[f]). In addition to other provisions of law, attachments of real or personal property may be enforced and duration extended as provided by T. 14, §§3131, 3132 and 4651.

Release of Property.—Attachments are dissolved: (1) when judgment for defendant has become final by expiration of time for appeal; (2) by dismissal of appeal or on certification of decision from law court; (3) by decree of insolvency on debtor's estate before levy or sale on execution; (4) by insolvency proceedings commenced within four months as provided in insolvency law; (5) by reference of action and all demands between parties thereto by rule of court and judgment on report of referees; (6) by amendment of complaint, by consent of parties, so as to embrace larger demand than it originally did, and judgment for plaintiff thereon, unless record shows that no claims were allowed plaintiff not originally stated in complaint; (7) by delivery to officer of bond to plaintiff in penal sum not exceeding amount of attachment, with approved sureties, conditioned that within 30 days after judgment, or after adjournment, defendant will pay plaintiff or his attorney amount of judgment, with costs, such bond to be approved as to penal sum and sureties by plaintiff or court; and (8) by lapse of 60 days after final judgment without enforcement. (T. 14, §§4601, 4602, 4613). Ex parte attachment may be dissolved or modified without submitting to personal jurisdiction upon motion by defendant on two days notice; plaintiff has burden of justifying any finding which defendant has challenged by affidavit. (M.R.C.P. 4A[h]).

Third Party Claims.—Attachment may be made by party bringing counterclaim, crossclaim, or third-party complaint in same manner as upon original claim. (M.R.C.P. 4A[e]).

CREDITORS' SUITS:

A remedy in equity is given to reach and apply to debts, any property or interest of a debtor which cannot be attached on writ or taken in execution in a suit at law or any property or interest conveyed in fraud of creditors. (T. 14, §6051[11]).

See topic Fraudulent Sales and Conveyances.

EXECUTIONS:

May be issued on judgments of Superior Court or District Court after 24 hours from time judgment has become final by expiration of time for appeal, dismissal of appeal, or on certificate of decision from law court, unless court has, pursuant to rule, ordered earlier execution, and is returnable within three years. No first execution may be issued after one year, from time judgment has become final as above except where judgment is rendered on default against defendant absent from state, in which case first execution may be issued within not less than one nor more than two years from time of judgment. (T. 14, §§4651-4652). Where judgment is rendered against absent defendant in personal action who has no actual notice, execution may not issue until one year after entry of judgment unless plaintiff gives defendant bond in double amount of damages and costs, conditioned to repay to defendant any part of judgment from which he may ultimately be relieved. (T. 14, §4701). Alias or pluries executions may be issued within ten years after day of return of preceding execution and not afterwards. (T. 14, §4653).

Where execution is not issued within time prescribed, an order on motion may be issued against defendant to show cause why execution should not issue. (T. 14, §4654).

Exemptions.—See topic Exemptions.

Stay.—Except as hereinbefore indicated, there is no stay of execution in the absence of appeal. Execution may be ordered immediately for cause shown pending appeal or post trial motion as long as no representation is made that party intends to appeal or make such motion. (M.R.C.P. 62[c]). See category Civil Actions and Procedure, topic Appeal and Error.

Lien.—Filing of execution with registry of deeds (real estate) or proper places for perfecting security interest in personal property pursuant to T. 11, §9-401, within one year after issuance of execution creates lien in favor of judgment creditor, and is in amount sufficient to satisfy judgment together with interests and costs. Lien becomes void and loses its status as perfected security interest unless judgment creditor notifies judgment debtor by certified or registered mail sent to last known address on or before 20th day after filing or recording of existence of lien. (T. 14, §4651-A).

Levy by Appraisal.—Real estate which is attachable may be taken on execution, by causing it to be appraised by three disinterested persons, one chosen by creditor, one by debtor (or by creditor if debtor after reasonable time neglects to do so), and one by officer having execution for service. Such appraisers must state value of estate appraised and describe it in return made and signed by them on back of execution or annexed thereto. (T. 14, §§2001-2003).

Levy by Sale.—Real estate may be taken on execution and sold at public auction to highest bidder. (T. 14, §§2201-2209). Equity of redemption may be levied on and sold. (T. 14, §2252).

Return.—On levy by execution officer, in return, shall state substantially time when land was taken on execution and give information about appraisers and appraisal. (T. 14, §2005). Officer who sells executed property must file return which describes each article sold and price at which it sold. (T. 14, §4758).

Priorities.—Proceeds of sale of executed property are applied to discharge multiple judgments in order which writs of execution or attachment were served. (T. 14, §5001).

Claims of Third Persons.—Personal property, subject to claim of third person, may be attached, held and sold as if unencumbered. (T. 14, §§4251-4256). Procedure is same as in case of attachment. See topic Attachment.

Satisfaction.—Proceeds of sale of executed property applied to pay changes and satisfy execution. Residue, if any, to other creditors who have attached property, and then to debtor. (T. 14, §§4759, 5001).

Sale.—All attachable real or personal property, not exempted by statute, may be sold on execution. (T. 14, §4751). All personal property taken on execution must be held by officer at expense of debtor for four days and sold within 14 days of seizure. (T. 14, §4752). Officer shall post notice of time and place of sale at least 48 hours prior to sale. (T. 14, §4753).

Redemption.—Real estate levied or sold upon execution may be redeemed at any time within one year from the date of the levy of sale. (T. 14, §2251). Personal property sold on execution can not be redeemed, except in cases of (1) sales of mill or building sold as chattels personal, in which case such property may be redeemed at any time within one year after sale (T. 14, §4760); and (2) franchise sold on execution, which may be redeemed at any time within three months (T. 14, §4854).

Supplementary Proceedings.—Judgment creditor may subpoena judgment debtor to appear before judge of District Court to determine judgment debtor's ability to satisfy judgment. Subpoena must set forth time and place for disclosure hearing; order to produce any documents requested by judgment creditor; warning that failure to obey subpoena may result in arrest; and notification of debtor's right to be heard on ability to pay. (T. 14, §3122). Debtor may be subpoenaed to disclose not more than once every six months, or by court order. (T. 14, §3124). Failure of debtor to appear can result in issuance of civil order of arrest. Under civil order of arrest, debtor arrested and brought to disclosure hearing. (T. 14, §§3134-3135). Failure to comply with any court order can result in citation for contempt. (T. 14, §3136). At hearing, debtor must disclose assets and sources of income. Court has broad power to order installment payment plan from assets, subject to certain maximum amounts, and to modify same. (T. 14, §§3127-3131). Court may order third party to withhold funds of debtor, subject to notice and hearing requirements. (T. 14, §3127-A). Court can order provisional installment payment pending sale of property. (T. 14, §3130). Court can order nonexempt property turned over to creditor in satisfaction; court may order sale of property not divisible if value exceeds debt or if debtor and creditor cannot agree. (T. 14, §3131). Court may order lien on debtor's interest in nonexempt personal property (T. 14, §3132); and upon two or more successive defaults in installment payment plan or failure to appear in response to hearing subpoena may order debtor's employer to pay creditor directly (T. 14, §3127-B). Employer must respond by form answer served upon employer and withhold previously ordered installment amounts. (T. 14, §3127-B). If debtor fails to comply with any order, creditor may complain in writing and court may punish by contempt. (T. 14, §3136). Employer may not discharge employee because of such order. (T. 14, §3127-B). All property sold under court order must be accounted for by affidavit by judgment creditor to court. (T. 14, §§3130-3131). Fees and costs of service to be added to judgment. (T. 14, §3126).

EXEMPTIONS:

In addition to homestead exemption (see topic Homesteads), there are a large number of personal property exemptions from attachment and execution, specified with particularity and in many cases limited in amount. (T. 14, §§4421-4426). Exemptions apply except to extent property fraudulently conveyed by debtor. (T. 14, §4422). Corporation may not claim any personal property exemption.

Substitution.—There is no provision authorizing debtor who does not own articles specifically exempted to hold other articles or money exempt in place thereof.

Debts Against Which Exemptions Not Allowed.—Debtors interest in property other than residence, generally not exempt from claims secured by purchase money security interests in such property. (T. 14, §4425[2]).

Pensions.—Interest of employee in any group annuity or pension trust effected by employer is exempt from attachment, execution levy, trustee process or other legal or equitable process. (T. 24-A, §2432).

Homestead Exemption.—See topic Homesteads.

See also topic Garnishment.

FRAUDULENT SALES AND CONVEYANCES:

Equitable action applies to property fraudulently conveyed. (T. 14, §6051[11]). Attachments and levies may be made on land fraudulently conveyed by debtor. (T. 14, §2014). Deceptive business practices punishable by fine or imprisonment. (T. 17-A, §901).

See note at head of Digest as to 1998 legislation covered.

See Topical Index in front part of this volume.

ME – 18

FRAUDULENT SALES AND CONVEYANCES . . . *continued*

Uniform Fraudulent Transfer Act.—Adopted. (T. 14, §§3571-3582). Material variances from Uniform Act: Action must be brought within six years after transfer made or obligation incurred. (T. 14, §3580). Creditor's damages limited to double value of property concealed or transferred. (T. 14, §3578).

Uniform Commercial Code.—Adopted. (T. 11, §§1-101—10-108). Maine has repealed §§6-101—6-110 (Bulk Transfers). See category Business Regulation and Commerce, topic Commercial Code.

GARNISHMENT:

Garnishment, by that name, does not exist; but trustee process has same effect. Garnishment allowed for spouses and ex-spouses of retired military personnel by order of court to satisfy child support order and spousal support order. (T. 19, §2604).

Trustee Process.—In connection with commencement of any personal action except actions only for specific recovery of goods and chattels, for malicious prosecution, for slander by writing or speaking, or for assault and battery, trustee process may be used in superior court, or district court except that no person shall be adjudged trustee for any amount due from him as defendant's earnings. (T. 14, §2601; M.R.C.P. 4B). Trustee process not available before judgment in action against consumer for debt arising from consumer credit transaction as defined in T. 9-A, §1-301(12). (M.R.C.P. 4B[a]).

Venue.—The action is brought in the county in which any trustee resides. In divorce action action must be brought in county in which court has jurisdiction over parties. (T. 14, §2604).

Service.—Service of summons to trustee is in like manner and with same effect as other process (see category Civil Actions and Procedure, topic Process). Among other things, trustee summons shall contain specified amount for which goods or credits of defendant are attached on trustee process and state name of justice or judge who entered order approving trustee process and date thereof. (M.R.C.P. 4B[b], [c]).

Who May Be Made Trustees.—Corporations may be made trustees. (T. 14, §2608). Executors and administrators may be made trustees (T. 14, §2619) and also persons receiving fraudulent conveyances of personal property (T. 14, §2629).

No person may be adjudged trustee by reason of: (1) Any negotiable paper accepted, made or endorsed by him unless held under fraudulent conveyance void as to defendant's creditors; (2) anything received or collected by him as officer, by force of legal process; (3) money in his hands as public officer; (4) money or other thing due on contingency; (5) any debt due from him on judgment while he is liable to execution thereon; (6) any amount due from him to principal defendant, as wages for his personal labor, or that of his wife or minor children. Moreover, wages of minor children and of women are not, in any case, subject to trustee process on account of any debt of parent or husband; (7) when service was made by leaving copy and payment made on negotiable security given before actual notice of (or reasonable ground of belief) of such service; (8) any amount due for board furnished a member of legislature while in attendance thereon; (9) renting by bank or trust company of safe deposit box or on account of contents thereof; (10) any money deposited with him in a broker's trust account, except to extent provided in T. 32, §13178. (T. 14, §2602).

Duties of Trustee.—The trustee must appear and file a written disclosure within 20 days after service and submit to an examination under oath upon which and such other evidence as is introduced he is either charged for a specified amount, or discharged. (M.R.C.P. 4B[e]). He may be defaulted and adjudged trustee for nonappearance. (T. 14, §2614).

Unmatured Claims.—Money or other thing due absolutely may be attached before it has become payable but the trustee is not required to pay before the time fixed by contract. (T. 14, §2628).

Setting Off Taxes.—Any municipal corporation summoned as trustee may set off taxes due it from the principal defendant. (T. 14, §2609).

Proceedings To Obtain.—No trustee summons may be served unless attachment on trustee process for specified amount has been approved by order of court. No order of approval unless notice to defendant, hearing and finding that is more likely than not that plaintiff will recover judgment, including interest and costs, in aggregate sum equal to or greater than amount of trustee process and any insurance, bond or other security, and any property or credits attached by writ of attachment or other trustee process available to satisfy judgment. Action may be commenced only by filing complaint with motion for approval of attachment on trustee process. Motion for ex parte order shall be accompanied by certificate of plaintiff's attorney of amount of insurance, bond, or other security, and other attachment or trustee process available to satisfy judgment. Motion and affidavits with notice of hearing thereon shall be served upon defendant at same time and in same manner that summons and complaint are served. Trustee process shall be served within 30 days after date of order approving such process. Defendant opposing motion for approval of attachment on trustee process shall file opposition within 21 days after filing of motion, unless another time is set by court. (M.R.C.P. 4B[c], M.R.C.P. 7[c]).

Order approving trustee process may be entered ex parte when court finds: (1) that it is more likely than not that plaintiff will recover judgment in amount equal to or greater than aggregate sum of trustee process and any insurance, bond or other security, and property or credits attached by writ of attachment or other trustee process, available to satisfy judgment and, either (2) clear danger that if notified in advance defendant will withdraw goods and credits from state or will conceal or will otherwise make them unavailable to satisfy judgment or (3) there is immediate danger that defendant will dissipate credit or damage goods. (M.R.C.P. 4B[i]). Motion for ex parte order shall be supported by affidavit and attorney's certificate as to insurance, bond, or other security and any other attachment or trustee process. (M.R.C.P. 4B[i]). Affidavit shall be on affiant's own knowledge, information and belief. (M.R.C.P. 4B[i]).

Approval of Limited Attachment on Trustee Process or Substituted Security.—Upon appropriate showing by party whose property to be attached by trustee process, court shall specify that attachment to issue solely against particular goods or credits. If, at hearing on motion, party whose property to be attached tenders cash or bond equal to amount of attachment to be approved, and deposits or files same with court, court may order any prior attachment dissolved and no further attachment shall issue absent showing that cash or bond has become inadequate or unavailable as security. When two or more defendants alleged to be jointly and severally liable, one or more of defendants may tender cash or bond to satisfy total amount plaintiff entitled to recover against all defendants. (M.R.C.P. 4B[d]).

Practice.—On two days notice to plaintiff, defendant whose goods or credits have been attached on trustee process pursuant to an ex parte order may appear, without submitting to personal jurisdiction, and move dissolution or modification of trustee process. Plaintiff has burden of justifying any finding in ex parte order which defendant has challenged by affidavit. (M.R.C.P. 4B[j]).

Bank Accounts.—Maximum of $100 of demand bank accounts of defendant held by any one trustee are exempt from ex parte trustee process. (M.R.C.P. 4B[i]).

Duration of Attachment on Trustee Process.—Attachment on trustee process continues during time within which appeal may be taken from judgment and during pendency of appeal. When judgment for plaintiff becomes final by expiration of time for appeal, by dismissal of appeal, or on certificate of decision from Superior Court or Law Court, attachment continues for 60 days. (T. 14, §§1601, 4601; M.R.C.P. 62[f]). But compare T. 14, §2956 which states that when person adjudged trustee, if goods, effects and credits in his hands not demanded by virtue of execution within 30 days after final judgment, attachment is dissolved and they are liable to another attachment.

HOMESTEADS:

Limitation of Value.—Not to exceed $12,500 in real or personal property that debtor or dependent of debtor uses as residence or in cooperative that owns property that debtor or dependent of debtor uses as residence; provided that if minor dependents of debtor have their principal place of residence with debtor, debtor's interest may not exceed $25,000, and if debtor's interest is held jointly with any other person debtor's interest may not exceed lesser of $12,500 and product of debtor's fractional share multiplied by $25,000. If debtor or dependent of debtor is 60 years old or older or physically or mentally disabled and unable to engage in substantial gainful employment debtor's interest may not exceed $60,000 or lesser of $60,000 and product of debtor's fractional interest multiplied by $120,000. (T. 14, §4422).

Limitation of Area.—No provision.

Debts or Liabilities Against Which Exemption Not Available.—Claims secured by real estate mortgages on or security interests in residence or claims of certain lien creditors who perform labor or furnish labor or materials. (T. 14, §4425).

Designation of Homestead.—No provision.

Claim of Exemption.—No provision.

Waiver of Exemption.—No statute provision for form of release. Ordinary form of deed with joinder of spouse containing clause: "relinquishing and conveying all rights by descent and all other rights in the premises conveyed" releases homestead rights.

Loss of Exemption.—No provision.

Alienation or Encumbrance.—No provision.

Proceeds of Sale.—Proceeds from sale of exempt property exempt for six months from date of receipt for purpose of reinvesting in residence. (T. 14, §4421).

Rights of Surviving Spouse and Family.—Surviving spouse domiciled in Maine or minor and dependent children entitled to homestead allowance of $5,000. (T. 18-A, §2-401).

LIENS:

Enforcement.—Statutory liens are enforced by attachment. Liens on houses, buildings, appurtenances, wharves, piers and lots may also be enforced in action in Superior or District Court where liened property is situated provided action is commenced within 120 days after last of labor or services are performed or labor, materials or services are so furnished (T. 10, §3255), absent 90-day extension where owner dies, is adjudicated bankrupt or warrant of insolvency issues against estate within 120 days and before commencement of action. (T. 10, §3255). Land rent is lien on buildings. (T. 10, §3452).

Liens on Vessels.—Labor and materialmen have a lien upon materials until they become part of a new vessel, and upon vessel for four days after it is launched, or for four days after completion of contract under which such labor or materials are furnished. Domestic vessels are subject to a lien to any part owner or other person to secure payment for labor and materials necessary for their repair, provisions, stores and other supplies necessary for their employment, use of a wharf, dry dock or marine railway, or for advances made for same. Last named lien continues two years and is enforced by proceedings in U. S., but not in state, courts. (T. 10, §§3851-3852).

Miscellaneous Liens.—Persons engaged in following occupations have lien for their services upon product of their labor or materials: (1) Digging, hauling, or furnishing lime rock; (2) cutting or dressing granite in any quarry; (3) mining, quarrying, or manufacturing slate in any quarry (T. 10, §3651); (4) furnishing labor or wood for manufacturing or burning bricks (T. 10, §3201); (5) cutting, peeling, yarding or hauling hemlock bark, cord wood or pulp wood or cooking for persons so engaged (T. 10, §3606); (6) cutting, hauling, rafting or driving logs or lumber, shoeing horses or oxen, or repairing property employed in such cutting, etc., or cooking for persons so engaged (T. 10, §3601); (7) cutting cord wood or any wood used in the manufacture of pulp (T. 10, §3606); (8) manufacturing, cutting wood for, and hauling last blocks, railroad ties or ship knees, spool timber, and cooking for persons so engaged (T. 10, §3607); (9) furnishing corn or other grain or fruit for canning or other preservation (T. 10, §3301); (10) laborer in any tannery on any hides and skins or in any capacity about establishment (T. 10, §3551); (11) owners of stallions have lien on colts foaled in State to secure payment of service fee for use of stallion in begetting same, continuing until colt is six months old (T. 10, §3351); (12) persons furnishing pasturage, food and shelter to animals (T. 10, §3352); (13) marina and boatyard storage facility owner on

See note at head of Digest as to 1998 legislation covered.

See Topical Index in front part of this volume.

ME – 19

LIENS . . . *continued*
property stored at facility for rent, labor and other charges (T. 10, §1383); (14) there is lien for taxes on all real estate and upon personal property of nonresidents (T. 36, §§552, 602); (15) persons harvesting or pressing hay have lien for their labor (T. 10, §§3401-3402); (16) persons furnishing monumental work under contract have lien continuing two years, to be enforced by attachment (T. 10, §3701); (17) persons who perform labor or furnish materials, constructing, altering or repairing wharves or perform services as architects, surveyors or engineers (T. 10, §3251); (18) also on mortgages and mortgaged estates for costs of foreclosure; (19) on stray animals for damages done (T. 33, §1060); (20) on wagons, carts, sleighs and other vehicles, and aircraft and parachutes, for labor in manufacturing or repairing, which takes precedence of all other claims (T. 10, §3801); (21) on land on which services have been rendered by landscape gardeners (T. 10, §3501); (22) on watches, clocks, jewelry, cleaned, repaired or pressed clothes, electric motors, small motors 20 horsepower or less, radios, other electronic equipment, appliances, and musical instruments for labor and materials expended thereon (T. 10, §§3951-3953); (23) for providing hospital care (T. 10, §3411); (24) producer of potatoes upon processed forms thereof for his labor, care and expense of growing and harvesting (T. 10, §§3321-3331); (25) employee may have lien on employer's real estate or personal property for wages or medical benefits lost due to employer's failure to implement agreed health plan (T. 26, §629-B); (26) State, upon commercial real estate for costs incurred in abatement, cleanup or mitigation of hazardous substance (T. 38, §1371); (27) sanitary district for unpaid sewer and drainage service assessments (T. 38, §§1205, 1208); (28) water utility against landlord of multi-unit residential rental property on property for cost of water utility services (T. 35-A, §6111); (29) real estate licensees (T. 10, §3251); (30) upon shares and dividends of credit union member to extent of any loan made to and any dues or charges payable by that member (T. 9-B, §827); (31) operator of self-service storage facility on all personal property stored within leased space, for rent, labor or other changes (T. 19, §1374); (32) on contents of safe deposit box for use of any safe or box in vaults of any bank or safe deposit company (T. 10, §3751).

Mechanics' Liens.—Person who performs labor or furnishes labor or materials including repair parts of machines used, or performs services as surveyor, architect, real estate licensee, engineer, owner-lessor, or owner-supplier of equipment used in erecting, altering, moving or repairing house, building or appurtenances, public building, wharf or pier, or in selling any interest in land, improvements or structures, by virtue of contract with or by consent of owner, has lien thereon, and on land on which it stands, and on any interest such owner has in same, to secure payment thereof, with costs. If owner of building has no legal interest in land on which building is erected, lien attaches to building. (T. 10, §3251). To preserve such lien claimant must within 90 days from time he ceases to labor, furnish materials or perform services file with registry of deeds of county or registry district in which premises are located true statement under oath in form prescribed by statute of amount due, except where labor, materials, or services are furnished by contract with owner of property affected (T. 10, §3253), and bring suit within 120 days after last of labor is performed or materials furnished. If claimant is real estate licensee, claimant must also notify by certified mail bona fide purchaser before she takes title to premises. (T. 10, §3255). If labor or materials were not furnished by contract with owner of property, he may prevent such lien for labor, services or materials not then furnished by giving written notice to person performing or furnishing same that he will not be responsible. Lien may be enforced only to extent of balance due person with whom owner directly contracted, but defense is available only with respect to sums paid by owner to person with whom he directly contracted where payment was made prior to commencement of action to enforce lien or written notice in statutory form to owner from person performing or furnishing labor, materials or services. Defense does not apply where labor, materials or services are performed or furnished for business, commercial or industrial purposes unless owner resides on premises affected. Any person who is bona fide purchaser for value of house, building or appurtenances, public building, or wharf or pier or building thereon, takes title free of mechanics lien unless before purchaser takes title person performing or furnishing labor, materials or services has filed statement under oath (T. 10, §3253) or notice (T. 10, §3255) in office of registry of deeds of county or registry district in which premises are located (T. 10, §§3251-3265). Lien may be enforced by labor organization on behalf of its members; such action may not be dismissed or compromised without court approval. (T. 10, §§3266-3269).

Public Works.—The State Highway Commission has authority to require a bond for protection of persons who furnish labor and materials for construction of state and state-aid highways. (133 Me. 389, 179 A. 297).

Uniform Commercial Code adopted. (T. 11, §§1-101—10-108). See category Business Regulation and Commerce, topic Commercial Code.

Uniform Federal Lien Registration Act adopted. (T. 33, §§1901-1907).

Attorney's Lien.—No provision.

Collateral Security.—See topic Pledges.

Execution Lien.—See topic Executions.

Judgment Lien.—See category Civil Actions and Procedure, topic Judgments.

Liens of Exempt Property.—See topic Exemptions.

Landlord's Lien.—See category Property, topic Landlord and Tenant.

Real Estate Mortgage Lien.—See category Mortgages, topic Mortgages of Real Property.

Liens on Homestead.—See topic Homesteads.

Tax Lien.—See category Taxation, topic Property Taxes, subhead Lien.

PLEDGES:

Whoever has a lien on or a pledge of any personal property in his possession not covered by Uniform Commercial Code may enforce it by sale in manner provided in contract creating such lien or pledge or in manner provided by statute. (T. 10, §4001).

Remedies of Pledgee.—After trial and final adjudication, court may order sale of property with proceeds to amount owed paid to pledgee and balance, if any, to pledgor. (T. 10, §4008).

Uniform Commercial Code adopted. See category Business Regulation and Commerce, topic Commercial Code.

RECEIVERS:

Jurisdiction.—Superior Court holds general equitable power to appoint receiver. (T. 14, §6051). May also be appointed as matter of right under contract. (575 A.2d 731). Other specific statutory authority to appoint receiver includes: appointment of long-term care receiver (T. 22, §§7931-7938); appointment of receiver of facilities and providers of services funded in whole or in part by Department of Human Services (T. 34-B, §§13001-13008); and appointment of receiver to administer estate of missing and absent persons. See category Property, topic Absentees.

Proceeding.—Accompanied by motion in connection with civil action. Available pendente lite.

Statutory procedure repealed with enactment of corporate law. Equitable receivership available. Corporate law has procedure for judicial dissolution. (T. 13-A, §§1115-1123).

DISPUTE RESOLUTION

ALTERNATIVE DISPUTE RESOLUTION:

Court Alternative Dispute Resolution Service.—Maine Supreme Judicial Court issued following Rules for Referral of Cases to the Court Alternative Dispute Resolution Service (CADRES):

Mandatory Mediation Referrals.—Following cases are referred to CADRES for mediation unless court grants waiver: (1) all contested domestic relations matters except for protection from abuse cases, paternity cases filed by DHS, and child protective cases; (2) all small claims matters; (3) all requests for environmental enforcement mediation pursuant to T. 38, §347-A; (4) all requests for land use mediation pursuant to T. 5, §314.

Discretionary Mediation Referrals.—Court may refer any contested civil action for mediation by mediator agreed to by parties or, in absence of agreement, to CADRES.

Additional Disputes Requiring Mandatory Dispute Resolution.—

Agricultural Cooperatives.—Agricultural marketing and bargaining matters remaining in dispute between handlers of agricultural commodities and qualified associations 30 days prior to contract date submitted by parties to required mediation. Any time prior to commencement of required mediation, handler and qualified association may mutually agree to obtain or may unilaterally obtain mediator's services. At end of mediation, mediator shall promptly prepare report, recommending either resumption of bargaining for period of time not to exceed two days or submission of all matters still in dispute to arbitration. (T. 13, §1958-B).

Public Works Construction.—Dispute between State and public works contractor that cannot be settled must be submitted to alternative dispute resolution (ADR) or binding arbitration. If unsatisfied with ADR, State or contractor may submit dispute to binding arbitration. Mandatory ADR does not apply to public improvements under supervision of Department of Transportation. (T. 5, §1749).

Motor Vehicle Disputes.—All motor vehicle manufacturers shall submit to arbitration if requested by consumer within two years from date of original delivery to consumer of new motor vehicle or during first 18,000 miles of operation, whichever occurs first. (T. 10, §1169).

Alternative Dispute Resolution Project Administrative Order.—Maine Supreme Judicial Court issued Administrative Order establishing pilot project for civil actions in Androscoggin, Aroostook, Kennebec, Oxford, Penobscot and Sagadahoc Counties for period actions filed on or before June 30, 1997. Experimental Rule 16B, which applies to Kennebec and Sagadahoc Counties, establishes procedure for "early" (prediscovery) ADR intervention. *Note:* Project was terminated by Administrative Order dated Aug. 12, 1997. Cases filed on or after July 1, 1997 shall proceed under M.R.Civ.P. 16A. Experimental Rule 16C applies to Androscoggin and Aroostook Counties and establishes procedure for "later" (at discovery midpoint) ADR intervention. Penobscot and Oxford Counties are control group; civil actions in those counties conducted under existing M.R.C.P. Experimental Rules 16B and 16C replace Rule 16 in counties in which they apply.

Voluntary Dispute Resolution.—Effective June 21, 1993, Interim Advisory Committee on Dispute Resolution in Public Sector assists state, municipal and other governmental entities in developing plans and policies for negotiated rulemaking and dispute resolution as recommended in final report of Commission to Study the Future of Maine's Courts. (T. 4, §1).

Referee in Personal Actions.—All controversies which may be subject of personal action, may be submitted to one or more referees, by articles of agreement acknowledged before notary public, report of referee to be rendered to court agreed upon in articles of submission. Such submission may not be revoked except by mutual consent. Award may be by majority of referees. Court may accept, reject or recommit report. Either party may appeal such judgment. (T. 14, §§1151-1155).

Environmental Enforcement Actions.—If Department of Environmental Protection brings enforcement action in District Court, either party may request arbitration any time before alleged violator appears to answer department's complaint. (T. 38, §347-A[4][E]).

Radiation Protective Act.—All parties to dispute under Act may agree to submit to arbitration or other ADR; governor of each party state shall appoint arbitrator. (T. 22, §679-A). Act incorporates Texas Low-Level Radioactive Waste Disposal Compact, Art. IV, §4.05(7).

State Employee Labor Relations.—Act provides for mediation procedures if either party to controversy requests such services prior to arbitration or on motion of Maine Labor Relations Board (MLRB). If parties unable to effect settlement through mediation, they may jointly agree to call upon MLRB for fact-finding services. If parties

See note at head of Digest as to 1998 legislation covered.

See Topical Index in front part of this volume.

ME – 20

ALTERNATIVE DISPUTE RESOLUTION . . . *continued*

have not resolved controversy after fact-finding, either party may petition MLRB to initiate compulsory final and binding arbitration. (T. 26, §979-D).

Workers' Compensation.—Workers' Compensation Board recognizes as valid and binding any provisions in collective bargaining agreements calling for ADR, including mediation and binding arbitration. (T. 39-A, §110).

See topic Arbitration and Award.

ARBITRATION AND AWARD:

Uniform Arbitration Act adopted. (T. 14, §§5927-5949). Restricted to contracts entered after Oct. 6, 1967. Act does not apply to automobile liability insurance policy provision for arbitration of claim under uninsured motorist coverage.

Mandatory Arbitration.—Disputes between: (1) alcoholic beverage manufacturers and wholesalers over value of franchise upon cancellation, nonrenewal, amendment or transfer (T. 28-A, §1457[2]); (2) contractors and State of Maine on public works projects except DOT projects. (T. 5, §1749).

DOCUMENTS AND RECORDS

ACKNOWLEDGMENTS:

Uniform Recognition of Acknowledgments Act adopted. (T. 4, §§1011-1019). In addition, certificate of acknowledgment taken in state other than Maine is presumed to be in form prescribed by laws of such state if it contains words "notary public", name of notary public, and name of state in which acknowledgment was taken. (T. 4, §1014-A).

Acknowledgments may be taken by following officers (T. 33, §203):

Within state: Notary public, attorney admitted to practice in Maine.

Outside state but within U.S.: Clerk of court of record having seal, notary public, or commissioner appointed by Maine Governor for purpose or commissioner authorized in state where acknowledgment taken.

Outside U.S.—Minister, consul or vice-consul of U.S. or notary public in any foreign country.

Persons in U.S. Armed Forces may acknowledge before any officer of rank of Lieutenant or higher in Army, U.S. Marine Corps or Air Force or Ensign or higher in Navy or Coast Guard. (T. 33, §203).

General Requirements as to Taking.—Notary public may not perform notarial act for notary public's spouse, parent, sibling, child, spouse's parent or child's spouse with certain exceptions provided by statute. (T. 4, §954-A). Notary public may not take acknowledgment of instrument by or to bank or corporation of which notary is stockholder, director, officer or employee if notary is party to such instrument. (T. 4, §954, T. 33, §203).

General Requirements of Certificate.—Notaries public required to maintain and affix seal of office; not required to state date of expiration of commission. (T. 4, §951).

Married women acknowledge like other persons; no special requirements.

Attorneys-in-Fact.—No special requirements.

Corporations.—Unless notary is party to instrument to be notarized, notary who is stockholder, officer, employee or agent of corporation may acknowledge instrument. Such notary may administer oath to any other stockholder, officer, employee or agent of such corporation. (T. 4, §954, T. 33, §203).

Authentication.—No statutory provisions.

Acknowledgments may also be accomplished in manner provided by Uniform Recognition of Acknowledgments Act. (T. 33, §203; T. 4, §§1011-1019).

Effect of Acknowledgment.—Instruments to be recorded in registry of deeds must be acknowledged, except those issued by court, plans, notices of foreclosure, financing statements as provided in T. 11, §9-401 and notices of liens for internal revenue taxes and certificates discharging such liens. (T. 33, §203).

Proof by Subscribing Witness.—When grantor or lessor dies or leaves state without acknowledging her deed, its execution may be proved by subscribing witness before any court of record in state. (T. 33, §301).

Forms.—Short Forms of Acknowledgment set forth in Uniform Recognition of Acknowledgments Act are authorized by statute. (T. 4, §1016). Following form is also in common use:

Corporation acknowledgment:

State of . . . . . ., County of . . . . . ., ss.:   (Date.)

Then personally appeared the above-named (name of officer who signed the document, with his title and name of corporation) and acknowledged the foregoing instrument to be his free act and deed in his said capacity and the free act and deed of said corporation.

Before me, ...
(Notary Public).

Validating Acts.—Records of deeds and other instruments made prior to Jan. 1, 1990, containing defective acknowledgments are validated under T. 33, §352. See also T. 33, §203.

Alternative to Acknowledgment or Proof.—Alternatives to acknowledgment under certain circumstances are provided under T. 33, §§301-306.

AFFIDAVITS:

Affidavits may be taken by a notary public or any other officer authorized to administer oaths, including officers of Armed Forces in special cases. (T. 4, §§1011, 1056). Attorneys at law duly admitted and eligible to practice in courts of State have all powers of notaries public. (T. 4, §1056).

Affidavits supporting motion for attachment must be on personal knowledge, information or belief, and affiant must state that he believes every statement made on information or belief to be true. (M.R.C.P. 4A[i]).

Form.—The certificate or caption of an affidavit may be in the following form:

Form

State of Maine,

County of . . . . . ., ss.

Be it known, that on this . . . . . . day of . . . . . ., before me, A. B., a notary public for the State of Maine, residing in the . . . . . . of . . . . . ., in said county, duly commissioned and sworn, and by law authorized to administer oaths and affirmations, personally appeared . . . . . ., of . . . . . ., to me well known, and known to be the person he represents himself to be, who being by me duly sworn, did make the following (or foregoing) affidavit by him subscribed.

In testimony whereof I have hereunto set my hand and affixed my seal of office the day and year first above written.

(Seal).   (Official Signature).

(If the officer has a seal he must affix it to the certificate).

Alternative to Affidavit.—No statutory provisions.

NOTARIES PUBLIC:

Qualification.—Maine resident 18 years of age. Oath must be taken before Dedimus Justice. All attorneys admitted to practice in Maine have powers of notaries public and are authorized to do all acts which may be done by notaries public. (T. 4, §1056).

Authentication.—See topic Acknowledgments, subhead Authentication.

Seal.—Notary public may keep official seal bearing name exactly as it appears on notary's commission, words "Notary Public" and "Maine" (or abbreviation, "Me."). (T. 4, §951).

Powers and Duties.—When authorized by the laws of Maine or of any other state or country to do any official act, notary may administer any oath necessary to completion or validity thereof. (T. 4, §951).

He may on behalf of any person interested, present any bill of exchange or other negotiable paper for acceptance or payment to any party liable therefor; notify indorsers or other parties thereto; record and certify all contracts usually recorded or certified by notaries; and in general, do all acts which may be done by notaries public according to the usages of merchants, and authorized by law; he shall note all mercantile and marine protests when requested and shall record all such protests by him noted and done in his official capacity. (T. 4, §§952, 953). Resident notaries public may solemnize marriages in Maine. (T. 19-A, §655).

Notary public shall not perform notarial act if any interest may affect impartiality except specified instances. (T. 4, §§954, 954-A).

Notary shall maintain records of all notarial acts performed. (T. 4, §955-B).

Territorial Extent of Powers.—Notaries may act officially anywhere in Maine.

Expiration of Commission.—Notary not required to give date commission expires.

Fees.—No fixed schedule of fees, except charge of $1.50 in course of lawsuit for notification of parties, making of certificate and recording proceedings.

Officers of U.S. Armed Forces.—Have notarial powers provided in Uniform Recognition of Acknowledgments Act. (T. 4, §§1011 et seq.).

RECORDS:

Deeds of real estate, life estates, entailed estates, and leases for more than two years or for indefinite term, must be recorded in registry for county in which land lies to be valid against any person but lessor or grantor, heirs and devisees, and persons having actual notice thereof. Memorandum of lease may be recorded in lieu of lease. (T. 33, §201). No time for recording fixed. Uniform Commercial Code adopted, T. 11, §§1-101—10-108, see category Business Regulation and Commerce, topic Commercial Code. Recorded deed, lease or other written instrument relating to real estate takes precedence over unrecorded attachment and seizures on executions. (T. 14, §4454, T. 33, §201).

Recordable Instruments.—See introductory paragraph, supra.

Place of Recording.—See introductory paragraph supra, and subhead Filing Under Commercial Code, infra. *For list of Counties and County Seats, see first page for this State in Volume containing Practice Profiles section.* Oxford County and Aroostook County have two registry districts; territorial definition of Oxford County registry districts in T. 33, §702, Aroostook County districts in T. 33, §703.

Requisites for Recording.—Deeds and other written instruments, excepting plans, notices of foreclosure of mortgages, instruments issued by court of competent jurisdiction and duly attested by proper officer thereof and financing statements as provided in T. 11, §9-401, before being recorded must be acknowledged by persons executing same or one of them or by attorney executing same. (T. 33, §203). Instrument acknowledged in accordance with Uniform Recognition of Acknowledgments Act accepted. (T. 33, §203).

Recording Fees.—At registry of deeds, $8 first page; $2 each subsequent page. Additional fees may be charged if recording requires indexing of more than four names. (T. 33, §751).

Recording Taxes.—See category Taxation.

Foreign Conveyances and Encumbrances.—See category Property, topic Real Property, subhead Foreign Conveyances or Encumbrances.

Effect of Record.—Maine has race-notice system. Duly recorded conveyances of right, title and interest are effectual against prior unrecorded conveyances as if they purported to convey actual title. (T. 33, §201).

Torrens system has not been adopted.

See note at head of Digest as to 1998 legislation covered.

See Topical Index in front part of this volume.

RECORDS . . . *continued*

Transfer of Decedent's Title.—Prior to Jan. 1, 1981, if deceased died testate, register of probate will record abstract of portions of will covering real estate in registry of deeds of all counties in which deceased owned real estate, provided will or petition for probate indicates location of real estate. If deceased died intestate, no documents filed in registry of deeds. Probate records must be examined. Executors and administrators not required to file any documents with register of deeds. Since Dec. 31, 1980, register of probate will file certificate and abstract in registry of deeds. (T. 18-A, §1-504). Personal representatives convey by deed of distribution or deed of sale, both statutorily prescribed. (T. 18-A, §715, T. 33, §§775[3-A]—[3-D]). Foregoing applies to real estate of nonresident decedent, but in such case ancillary administration is necessary and if decedent died testate copy of will must be recorded in this state. (See category Estates and Trusts, topic Wills.)

Filing Under Commercial Code.—Proper place to file to perfect security interest is as follows: (a) When collateral is timber to be cut or minerals or like, including oil and gas, or accounts resulting from sale of minerals or like, including oil and gas, at wellhead or minehead, or unharvested crops, or when financing statement is fixture filing and collateral is goods which are or are to become fixtures, then in appropriate registry of deeds; (b) when collateral is farm products, in Secretary of State's office pursuant to T. 5, §90-A; or (c) in all other cases, in Secretary of State's office. To perfect security interest in any collateral, including fixtures, of transmitting utility file in Secretary of State's office. (T. 11. §9-401).

Fee for filing with Secretary of State original financing statement (UCC-1) $20; continuation, partial release, assignment or amendment (UCC-3) $10; termination if UCC-1 filed prior to July 1, 1993 and UCC-1 acknowledgment copy used $10; if UCC-1 filed prior to July 1, 1993 and UCC-3 used $15; if UCC-1 filed on or after July 1, 1993 no fee. Fee for filing with registry of deeds $8 first page, $2 each additional page.

Vital Statistics.—Reports of births, deaths and marriages must be made to town or city clerk. (T. 22, §§2701-2844). Copies of birth, death and marriage certificates may be obtained from town or city clerk or from State of Maine Office of Vital Records, Augusta, Maine 04333. Fee $10, each additional copy $4 if custodian satisfied that applicant has direct, legitimate interest. (T. 22, §§2701, 2706). State of Maine Office of Vital Records also maintains voluntary acknowledgments of paternity. (T. 22, §2701).

Establishing Birth Record.—Record relating to birth may be corrected by filing with town or city clerk affidavit of person required by law to furnish information for original record or of one or more credible persons having knowledge of case. (T. 22, §2705). Individual having no recorded birth certificate may establish birth record by submitting to town or city clerk record made at time of birth or testimony of individuals familiar with facts. (T. 22, §2764).

Lis Pendens.—No statutory provision or court rule.

SEALS:

Seals required as by common law. Recital that instrument is sealed by or bears seal of person signing, or is given under hand and seal of person signing, or is intended to take effect as sealed instrument is sufficient to give effect of sealed instrument, except on stock certificates or if otherwise required by law on public documents. (T. 1, §72). Statute of limitations for personal action on contracts or liabilities under seal is 20 years after cause of action accrues, except as governed by Commercial Code. (T. 14, §751).

Corporate Seals.—Seal of corporation may, but need not, be affixed to document executed in accordance with §104 and its absence will not impair its validity. (T. 13-A, §107).

Effect of Seal.—Presence of corporate seal is prima facia evidence document was so executed. (T. 13-A, §107).

Uniform Commercial Code adopted. See category Business Regulation and Commerce, topic Commercial Code.

EMPLOYMENT

LABOR RELATIONS:

Unlawful for employer to charge fee for application for employment. Penalty of not more than $500 for each violation. (T. 26, §594). Persons, corporations, or partnerships engaged in practically all lines of general business including public utilities, are required to pay weekly to employees wages earned by them to within eight days of date of payment. Municipalities must pay wages bi-weekly unless otherwise agreed to by employee. If any payday is missed, all employers must pay hourly wages due employee on or before employee's next regular payday. (T. 26, §621). Employer cannot exempt itself from this by contract. (T. 26, §623). Violation is punishable by fine of not less than $100 nor more than $500 per violation. Judgment for unpaid wages includes reasonable interest, liquidated damages in amount double recovered wages, and costs of suit, including reasonable attorney's fee. (T. 26, §626-A). Does not apply to cooperative corporations or associations if employee is stockholder and does not request corporation to pay him weekly. (T. 26, §623). Unlawful for employer to allow any agreement that permits employee compensation (unless earned in agriculture or in private home) to be returned to employer for any reason other than payment of loan, debt or advance, payment of merchandise purchased from employer, employee-paid benefits, or rent or utility-related expense of company-owned building. (T. 26, §629). Employee leaving employment shall be paid in full within defined reasonable time after demand. Any loan or future earnings advance may be deducted if employee signs statement. (T. 26, §626). Employer, upon written demand, must state reasons for termination within 15 days or suffer $50-$500 penalty. Employee may bring action to enforce this law, and employer may also be required to reimburse employee for costs of suit and attorney fees, if employee is successful. (T. 26, §630). Employer setoffs and counterclaims in collective bargaining context regulated. (T. 26, §626-B). Employee has right to review personnel file and can collect costs of suit (including reasonable attorney's fee) for enforcing such right. (T. 26, §631). Employer recovery of overcompensation limited to 10% of subsequent net pay without employee's written permission except that overcompensation can be fully deducted from any wages due voluntarily terminated employee. (T. 26, §635).

Severance Pay.—Industrial or commercial employers of 100 or more, in certain circumstances, liable for severance pay on relocation or termination of business at rate of one week's pay for each year of employment. "Employer" defined to include parent corporation of corporate subsidiary. (T. 26, §625-B).

Former employees of certain terminated employers within state entitled to wages for maximum of two weeks for work performed out of Maine Wage Assurance Fund. (T. 26, §632).

Wage rates for women must be the same as those paid to men for comparable work in same establishments. (T. 26, §628).

Minimum wage is set at $4.25 per hour, unless federal minimum wage exceeds $4.25, in which case it matches federal minimum wage, up to maximum of $5.15. Tip credits may not exceed 50% of minimum wage. (T. 26, §664).

Overtime rate for all hours actually worked in excess of 40 hours is $1^1/_2$ times regular hourly rate except in certain enumerated employments. (T. 26, §664).

Minors under 18 years of age, enrolled in school, cannot work more than 50 hours per week, ten hours per day or six consecutive days when school is not in session; when school is in session, minor cannot work more than 20 hours per week or four hours per day (with exception for authorized school closure or last school day of week). Minors under 16 years of age can work maximum of 40 hours per week, eight hours per day or six consecutive days when school is not in session; 18 hours per week, three hours per day or six consecutive days when school is in session. Hours of employment are limited. Restrictions not applicable to persons holding high school diploma, equivalency certificate or emancipated minor. Seasonal theatrical and film acting employment and some agricultural and fishing employment are excepted on approval by Superintendent of Schools. (T. 26, §774).

Employment of minors prohibited in certain hazardous occupations when under 18 years of age and in certain other occupations when under 16 and 14 years of age. Employment of minors under 16 and 15 years of age is permissible in certain establishments such as amusement parks and establishments selling frozen dairy products. (T. 26, §§771-773).

Employer must post in accessible place printed notice of labor laws and must keep time record for every minor under 18 years of age in most occupations or suffer $50-$2,500 penalty. (T. 26, §§701-704).

Work permits required in some cases. (T. 26, §§775-785).

Violation of sections pertaining to restricted employment of minors and work permits is punishable by fines of not less than $250 nor more than $50,000 per violation. (T. 26, §781).

Assignment of Wages.—See category Debtor and Creditor, topic Assignments.

Medical or eye examinations required of employee or applicant by employer must be paid for by employer. Violation is punishable by fine of not more than $50 per violation. (T. 26, §592).

Drug Testing.—Substance abuse testing of applicants and employees by employers governed by T. 26, §§681-690. Applies to hiring of employees to work outside of State if contract governed by Maine law. (T. 26, §681).

Labor Disputes.—Blocking delivery of certain necessary supplies or equipment to any enterprise prohibited. Violation punishable by fine of up to $250 or imprisonment up to 30 days or both. (T. 17, §3606). Hiring professional strikebreakers illegal. Violation is punishable by fine of not more than $300 per violation or imprisonment up to 180 days or both. (T. 26, §§851-856). Employment interviews and medical examinations of job applicants prohibited at employer work site during labor dispute. Violation is punishable by fine of not more than $10,000 for each day violation continues. Possession of firearms at off-site interview locations, except by certain authorized security guards, is Class D crime. (T. 26, §595). During strike, employer must notify insured employees before canceling group health insurance policy. (T. 26, §634).

Employee rest breaks of 30 consecutive minutes must be given by employer of more than two people on duty simultaneously after six consecutive hours of work, except if otherwise agreed upon or if nature of work allows frequent breaks. (T. 26, §601). Violation is punishable by fine of $100-$500 per violation. (T. 26, §602).

Labor Unions.—Collective bargaining fully recognized; no "right to work" law. As to state employees, regulated by T. 26, §§979-979-Q. As to municipal employees, regulated by T. 26, §§961-974.

Fair Employment Practice Act.—Unlawful for any employer, employment agency or labor organization to refuse to hire or to discriminate against any individual on account of race, color, sex, sexual orientation, physical or mental disability, religion, ancestry, age or national origin or because of previous assertion of claim or right under workers' compensation laws with respect to compensation, hire, promotion, tenure, terms, conditions or privileges of employment or related matters, except where based on bona fide occupational qualifications. (T. 5, §§4571-4576). Word "sex" includes pregnancy and medical conditions which result from pregnancy. (T. 5, §4572-A). Unlawful for any employer to require or permit, as condition of employment, any employee to retire at or before specified age or after completion of specified number of years of service. (T. 5, §§4574-4575).

Sexual Harassment Program.—Employers to implement sexual harassment program including training for employees in workplaces with 15 or more workers. (T. 26, §§806-807). All employers must post and distribute annually information on illegality of sexual harassment and on complaint process. (T. 26, §807).

Family Medical Leave.—Unless employed at permanent work site with fewer than 25 employees, any employee employed by same employer for 12 consecutive months is entitled to up to ten consecutive work weeks of family medical leave, paid or

See note at head of Digest as to 1998 legislation covered.

See Topical Index in front part of this volume.

LABOR RELATIONS . . . *continued*

unpaid, in any two years. Thirty days notice required unless precluded by medical emergency. (T. 26, §§843-848).

Work-Related Manslaughter.—Person is guilty of manslaughter if, while in direct and personal management or control of employment, place of employment or employee, such person intentionally or knowingly violates state or federal occupational safety or health standard, and violation causes death of employee, if death was reasonably foreseeable consequence of violation. (T. 17-A, §203).

Discrimination for tobacco use outside employment prohibited. (T. 26, §597).

Workers' Compensation Act.—(T. 39-A, §101 et seq.).

Administration of Act.—Workers' Compensation Board responsible for general supervision of administration of Act, management of Board employees and rule making. (T. 39-A, §151). Eight member board comprised of four management and four labor members; appointed by governor, reviewed by joint standing committee of legislature, confirmed by legislature. (T. 39-A, §151). Executive director, responsible for day-to-day operations, serves at Board's pleasure. (T. 39-A, §152).

Trouble Shooter Program.—Trouble shooters attempt to prevent or resolve disputes through facilitating communication between and providing information for all parties who have impact on workers' compensation system. (T. 39-A, §153[2]).

Mediation.—Mandatory upon filing notice of controversy or other indication of controversy. (T. 39-A, §313).

Arbitration.—Available if parties mutually agree in writing. (T. 39-A, §314).

Independent Medical Examinations.—Board establishes list of approved medical examiners. (T. 39-A, §312). To be eligible, during previous year medical examiner may not have examined employee at request of insurance company, employer or employee. If parties agree on selection of medical examiner, findings are binding. If parties fail to agree on selection, Board assigns medical examiner and findings are adopted unless clear and convincing contrary evidence in record. Medical examiner may not be employee's health care provider and may not have treated employee for injury in question.

Hearings.—Hearing officers appointed by and serve at pleasure of Board. (T. 39-A, §152). Hearing officer's decisions reviewable by Board upon motion of hearing officer if issue of significance to workers' compensation system. (T. 39-A, §320). Any party may appeal hearing officer or Board decision to Law Court. Law Court has discretion to decline to hear appeal. (T. 39-A, §322).

Obligation of Employer.—Every employer must secure payment of compensation through insurance contract, self-insurance, or group self-insurance. (T. 39-A, §§401-407). Certain employers engaged in domestic services or agricultural industry excepted. (T. 39-A, §401[1]). Failure to secure coverage may subject employer to class D criminal charges, $10,000 civil penalty and suspension of authority to do business. (T. 39-A, §§401[3], 324[3]).

Effect on Employees of Employer's Compliance.—Employee of complying employer, except illegally employed minor, waives right to common law action against employer, and employer is exempt from, all actions involving personal injuries arising out of and in course of employment, or for death resulting from those injuries. (T. 39-A, §104, 408).

Notice of injury must be given to employer stating time, place, cause, and nature of injury, together with address of person injured, within 90 days of injury, or there can be no proceedings under act. (T. 39-A, §301). But want of notice does not bar proceedings under act, if employer or his agent had knowledge of injury. Any time during which employee is unable by reason of physical or mental incapacity to give said notice or fails to do so on account of mistake of fact, is not included in 90-day period. In case of death of employee within 90-day period, there is allowed for giving said notice three months after such death. (T. 39-A, §302).

Reports by Employers.—Employer who has received notice of, or has knowledge of, injury causing loss of time or requiring services of physician must, within seven days thereafter, report to Board such injury, average weekly wage of injured employee and such other particulars as Board requires, and must also report employee's resumption of employment and wages or earnings at time. (T. 39-A, §303).

Reports by Employees.—In addition to notice of injury requirements employees receiving compensation under Act who return to employment or engage in new employment after injury must make written report of such employment to Board and to previous employer within seven days of return to work, including name of employee, his employer and amount of weekly wage received or to be received. (T. 39-A, §308).

Statute of Limitations.—Employee's claim for compensation is barred unless agreement or petition is filed within two years of injury or if employee is paid by employer or insurer without employer or insurer filing notice of controversy, within two years of such payment. Time during which employee is physically or mentally incapacitated to make such claims is not included in said period. In case of death of employee, there must be allowed for filing said petition one year after such death. No petition of any kind may be filed more than six years following date of latest payment under Act. (T. 39-A, §306).

Status of Claims.—Employee may not waive rights to compensation under Act. Claims for compensation are not assignable or subject to attachment or liable in any way for debts of the claimant except certain support or general assistance obligations. (T. 39-A, §106). Such claims have preference over unsecured debts of the employer. (T. 39-A, §108).

Benefits.—

Total or Partial Incapacity.—While incapacity for work is partial, employer must pay employee 80% of difference between before injury and after injury after-tax weekly wage. (T. 39-A, §213). While incapacity for work is total, employer must pay employee 80% of after-tax weekly wage. (T. 39-A, §212). For either partial or total incapacity, maximum benefit is greater of $441 or 90% of state average weekly wage. (T. 39-A, §211). Compensation paid for duration of disability if injury is in excess of 15% to body. In all other cases, maximum duration of benefits 260 weeks. (T. 39-A, §213). Benefits may be terminated if employee refuses bona fide job offer. (T. 39-A, §214). 15% threshold and 260 week limit may be adjusted annually. (T. 39-A, §213).

Death.—If death results from injury, employer must pay dependents who were wholly dependent on employee's wages for support, 80% of employee's after-tax weekly wage for 500 weeks. Maximum weekly benefit is greater of $441 or 90% of State average weekly wage. If dependent's spouse becomes dependent of another, benefits cease upon payment to spouse of balance of benefits up to $500. Remaining weeks of payment are payable to other dependents of employee. If dependent was only partially dependent on employee's wages for support, payment will be reduced proportionately. If, at expiration of 500 week period, any dependent person is less than 18 years old, benefits must continue until that person reaches age of 18. (T. 39-A, §215).

Medical, Surgical and Other Aids.—Reasonable and proper medical, surgical and hospital services, nursing, medicines and mechanical, surgical aids, as needed, must be paid for by employer. Board to establish reimbursement schedules. (T. 39-A, §§206 and 209).

Benefit Payment.—First payment due within 14 days of when employer has notice of injury or death. Subsequent payments due weekly. If no ongoing dispute and payment 30 days late, $50 per day added to amount owed to employee. Memorandum of payment must be sent to Board upon making first payment. Payments may be reduced or discontinued if employee returns to work or receives pay increase. If employee has not returned to work, and no order or award of compensation or compensation scheme has been entered, payments may be reduced or discontinued by providing employee with 21 days written notice. If payment scheme already entered, benefits may only be reduced or discontinued upon Board order; payments must continue during appeal process until all appellate proceedings completed and order entered by Board. (T. 39-A, §205).

Settlement of Claims.—By permission of Board, lump sum settlement may be approved six months after date of injury. Such settlement releases employer and insurance carrier from all further claims. (T. 39-A, §352).

Injuries Outside of State.—Remedies under Act are exclusive as regards injuries occurring outside of State to worker hired within State unless contract specifically provides otherwise. (T. 39-A, §102[11][A][2]).

Occupational Diseases.—Certain occupational diseases come within provisions of Act. (T. 39-A, §601-615). Special provisions apply to asbestosis. (T. 39-A, §614). Information regarding identity and risks of chemicals in work place must be provided to employees. (T. 26, §§1709-1725).

Workers' Compensation Rating System.—See category Insurance, topic Insurance Companies, subhead Workers' Compensation Rating System.

Unemployment Compensation.—Available to employees of certain employers as defined in T. 26, §1043.

If eligible, employee may receive compensation for total unemployment ranging from minimum of $12 per week to maximum of 52% of employee's annual average weekly pay, plus $10 weekly supplement for each unemancipated dependent child up to 50% of employee's individual weekly benefit. (T. 26, §1191). Partial unemployment benefits also available for amount of weekly benefit minus weekly earnings in excess of $25. (T. 26, §1191). Conditions of eligibility prescribed by statute, generally requiring filing claim, registering for work, being able, and available for full-time work, serving waiting period of one week of total or partial unemployment, and having earned wages. (T. 26, §1192). Disqualification for benefits results if employee voluntarily left work without good cause attributable to that employment, refuses to accept work, falsifies his application, is absent from work due to incarceration for conviction of criminal offense, or was discharged for misconduct or crime, or if unemployment due to work stoppage because of certain labor disputes or is receiving pension or wages, terminal pay, vacation pay or holiday pay. Employee not disqualified if decision to leave voluntarily caused by illness, spousal transfer, acceptance of another job which fails to materialize or domestic abuse if employee makes reasonable efforts to preserve employment. (T. 26, §1193).

Retraining of Dislocated Workers.—Provision providing financial support for certain dislocated workers repealed but grandfathered for those enrolled in training programs prior to Mar. 31, 1995. (T. 26, §§1043, 1196).

Occupational Safety and Health Act.—All state, county, municipal, school district and other political corporation employers are subject to rules and regulations for working conditions formulated by Board of Occupational Safety and Health. Violations punishable by fine. (T. 26, §§561-571). All agricultural workers in state entitled to be reasonably free of hazards to their safety and health. (T. 26, §§580-581).

ENVIRONMENT

ENVIRONMENTAL REGULATION:

Legislation.—Governed by T. 38, §§341-A-2312; T. 7, §§601-625; T. 12, §§681-689, 900-908, 4807-4807-G; T. 30-A, §§4301-4359, 4401-4407, 4451-4452, 4454-4457, 4461-4469; T. 37-B, §§791-806.

General Supervision.—Department of Environmental Protection, comprised of Commissioner of Environmental Protection and ten-member Board of Environmental Protection, is vested with general supervisory powers over air, water, solid and hazardous waste, land development site selection and control, and mining and rehabilitation of land. (T. 38, §§341-A, 361-A, 541, 581, 1301, 1317, 1361, 1401, 1601, 1651, 1841, 2301). State House Station 17, Augusta, ME 04333.

Prohibited Acts of Pollution.—No person, or entity may discharge pollutants, including oil and hazardous matter, into any stream, river, pond, lake, ground, surface or tidal waters or into ambient air nor install or operate surface or subsurface waste water disposal system without first obtaining license. (T. 38, §§413, 543, 568, 590, 1317-A). Discharges of certain dioxens and furans in detectable quantities as defined. (T. 38, §420). Discharges of oil and petroleum products are prohibited, although Department may license discharges of waste contaminated with oil under certain circumstances, if treated. (T. 38, §543). No person may discharge air contaminants which contribute to violation of established air quality standards. (T. 38, §591). Air and water discharges of mercury in excess of state standards are prohibited. (T. 38,

See note at head of Digest as to 1998 legislation covered.

See Topical Index in front part of this volume.

ENVIRONMENTAL REGULATION...*continued*

§§420, 585-B). Maine is signatory to New England Interstate Water Pollution Control Compact, and member of Interstate Commission. (T. 38, §491-A).

Enforcement.—Department of Environmental Protection (DEP) and Attorney General may enforce violations of laws and regulations administered by DEP. (T. 38, §§347-A, 348). Enforcement actions may be resolved by administrative consent with Attorney General's and Board's approval, civil or criminal prosecution by Attorney General, administrative enforcement or civil prosecution by DEP with Attorney General's approval. (T. 38, §347-A). Municipalities may enforce state sludge spreading and storage permits under some circumstances. (T. 30-A, §4452, T. 38, §1305).

Penalties.—Civil penalties for violations of Maine environmental laws other than hazardous waste violations range from $100 to $10,000 per violation per day. Hazardous waste civil penalties are capped at $25,000 per violation per day. If economic benefit resulting from violation exceeds these penalties, penalty may be increased to amount up to twice economic benefit per day of violation. Supplemental environmental projects may be performed in lieu of other civil fines under some circumstances. Criminal penalties must be more than $100, less than $25,000 and may include up to one year in jail. Criminal penalties for tampering and falsification can be as high as $10,000 and six months in jail. (T. 38, §349). Criminal penalties for some hazardous waste violations can include fines of $50,000 per day. (T. 38, §1319-T).

Permits.—Required for discharges of waste (T. 38, §§413, 414, 414-A); for installation of plumbing or subsurface waste water disposal system (T. 30-A, §4215); for air emissions (T. 38, §590); for certain activities in or adjacent to coastal sand dunes, coastal wetlands, mountain areas, freshwater wetlands, great ponds, rivers, streams, brooks, wildlife habitats (T. 38, §480-C); for construction of projects of state or regional significance that may substantially affect environment (T. 38, §483-A); for medium borrow pits (T. 38, §490-C [notice of intent]); for certain rock quarries (T. 38, §490-Y [notice of intent]); for construction of projects including over 20,000 square feet of impervious surface on five or more acres of disturbed area in certain watersheds (T. 38, §38, §420-D); log storage or transport of logs or pulpwood from islands to mainland (T. 38, §418); for lead-based paint activities including assessments and deleading (T. 38, §§1291-1297); solid waste facility construction, alteration and operation (T. 38, §1306); handling hazardous waste or operating hazardous waste facility site (T. 38, §1319-R); operation, installation or replacement of oil storage and terminal facilities (T. 38, §§545, 563). License fee is imposed upon all oil terminal facilities (with certain exceptions) for each barrel of oil or petroleum product transferred (T. 38, §551). Coastal and Inland Surface Oil Clean-up Fund and Ground Water Oil Clean-up Fund established from license fees to assist in oil spill cleanup. (T. 38, §551, 569-A). License required for mooring in Maine waters of oil tankers not waiting for scheduled loading or unloading of cargo. (T. 38, §560).

Hazardous Substance Sites.—Governed by T. 38, §§1361-1371.

Forfeiture of Property.—All real estate used or intended to be used, and all money, negotiable instruments and securities intended to be used in violation of hazardous substance provisions subject to forfeiture to State. (T. 38, §1370).

Lien on Real Estate.—All costs incurred by State for abatement, cleanup or mitigation of hazards due to uncontrolled substance site, including interest and penalties, shall be lien against real estate of responsible party. Lien on real estate encompassing site shall have priority over all encumbrances filed after July 7, 1987. Lien on other real estate shall have priority over all encumbrances filed after creation of lien under this section. (T. 38, §1371).

State Acquisition of Property.—State may acquire property necessary to conduct remedial actions in response to threat at uncontrolled substance site. (T. 38, §1364).

Water Classification Program.—All Maine waters classified in accordance with standards established by legislature. Quality classification of body of water determines allowable levels of pollutant discharges, and extent to which other activities tending to degrade of water quality may be undertaken. (T. 38, §§464-470).

ESTATES AND TRUSTS

ADMINISTRATION:

See topic Executors and Administrators.

DEATH:

Presumption of Death.—Person is presumed to be dead when he is absent and unheard of for five years. (T. 18-A, §1-107[3]). See also category Property, topic Absentees.

Survivorship.—Uniform Simultaneous Death Act adopted. Differs from Uniform Act in that 2d section is limited to testamentary dispositions and does not apply to all dispositions as does 2d section of Uniform Act. (T. 18-A, §§2-805).

Actions for Death.—If injuries cause immediate death, or death without conscious suffering, an action may be maintained within two years by and in name of personal representative of deceased person for benefit of widow or widower and children, or if neither, of heirs. Damages awarded may include all pecuniary injuries resulting from such death to persons for whose benefit action is brought, reasonable expenses of medical, surgical and hospital care and treatment, reasonable funeral expenses and amount not exceeding $150,000 for loss of consortium, including damages for emotional distress. (T. 18-A, §2-804[b]; 104 Me. 109, 71 A. 476). Where death follows period of conscious suffering as result of personal injury, tortfeasor is liable for both: (1) Damages for death, recoverable for benefit of widow or widower and children plus reasonable expenses, and also (2) damages recoverable at common law (which cause of action survives—see category Civil Actions and Procedure, topic Actions). But there can be only one recovery for same injury. (T. 18-A, §2-804[c]).

Death Certificate.—See category Documents and Records, topic Records, subhead Vital Statistics.

Uniform Anatomical Gift Act.—See topic Wills.

Uniform Determination of Death Act.—Adopted 1983. (T. 22, §§2811-2813).

Living Wills.—See topic Wills.

DESCENT AND DISTRIBUTION:

Uniform Probate Code, including 1975 Official Amendments, adopted. (T. 18-A, §§1-101-8-401). 1977 and 1979 Official Amendments not adopted.

See also topic Executors and Administrators.

Part of intestate estate not passing to surviving spouse or entire estate if there is no surviving spouse, passes as follows: (1) To issue of decedent, to be distributed per capita at each generation; (2) if no surviving issue, to decedent's parent or parents equally; (3) if no surviving issue or parent, to issue of parents or either of them to be distributed per capita at each generation; (4) if no surviving issue, parent or issue of parent, but decedent is survived by one or more grandparents or issue of grandparents, half of estate passes to paternal grandparents if both survive, or surviving paternal grandparent, or to issue of paternal grandparents if both are deceased to be distributed per capita at each generation; other half passes to maternal relatives in same manner; but if there be no surviving grandparent or issue of grandparents on either paternal or maternal side, entire estate passes to relatives on other side in same manner as half; (5) if no surviving issue, parent or issue of parent, grandparent or issue of grandparent, but decedent is survived by one or more great-grandparents or issue of great-grandparents, half of estate passes to paternal great-grandparents who survive, or to issue of paternal great-grandparents if all are deceased, to be distributed per capita at each generation; other half passes to maternal relatives in same manner; but if no surviving great-grandparent or issue of great-grandparent on either paternal or maternal side, entire estate passes to relatives on other side in same manner as half. (T. 18-A, §2-103).

Community Property Options in Official Text have not been adopted.

Variations from Official Text.—§2-801(b) substitute "nine months" for "six months", §2-803 optional provision adopted. §3-108 amended to provide that for decedents dying before Jan. 1, 1981, no informal probate or appointment proceeding, other than proceeding to probate will previously probated at testator's domicile and appointment proceedings relating to estate in which there has been prior appointment, may be commenced more than 20 years after decedent's death, with certain exceptions. §3-306(b) optional provision of 1979 Official Amendments not adopted. §3-914 unclaimed assets disposed of according to Unclaimed Property Act. (T. 33, §§1801-1820, 1851-1875).

Surviving spouse takes as follows: (1) If no surviving issue or parent of decedent, entire intestate estate; (2) if no surviving issue but decedent is survived by parent or parents, first $50,000, plus 1/2 of balance of intestate estate; (3) if there are surviving issue all of whom are issue of surviving spouse also, first $50,000, plus 1/2 of balance of intestate estate; (4) if there are surviving issue one or more of whom are not issue of surviving spouse, 1/2 of intestate estate. (T. 18-A, §2-102).

Half blood inherits as whole blood. (T. 18-A §2-107).

Posthumous Children or Other Issue.—No provision.

Illegitimates.—Person born out of wedlock is child of mother; that person is also child of father if: (i) Natural parents participated in marriage ceremony before or after birth of child, even though attempted marriage is void; or (ii) father adopts child into his family; or (iii) father acknowledges in writing before notary public that he is father of child, or paternity is established by adjudication before death of father or is established thereafter by clear and convincing proof, but paternity so established is ineffective to qualify father or his kindred to inherit from or through child unless father has openly treated child as his and has not refused to support child. (T. 18-A, §2-109). Persons born out of wedlock are included in class gift terminology in wills and trusts as child of father if person is openly and notoriously so treated by father or is so recognized by testator or settlor. (T. 18-A, §2-611).

Adopted Children.—See category Family, topic Adoption.

Determination of Heirship.—No provision.

Advancements.—If person dies intestate as to all his estate, property which he gave in lifetime to heir treated as advancement against latter's share of estate only if declared in contemporaneous writing by decedent or acknowledged in writing by heir to be advancement. For this purpose property advanced is valued as of time heir came into possession or enjoyment of property or as of time of death of decedent, whichever first occurs. If contemporaneous writing by decedent established value of property advanced, that value shall apply. If recipient of property fails to survive decedent, property is not taken into account in computing intestate share received by recipient's issue, unless declaration or acknowledgment provides otherwise. (T. 18-A, §2-110).

Renunciation.—Uniform Disclaimer of Transfers by Will, Intestacy or Appointment Act adopted, as part of Uniform Probate Code. (T. 18-A, §2-801).

Election.—Surviving spouse of person who dies domiciled in Maine has right of election to take 1/3 of "augmented estate". (T. 18-A, §§2-201-2-207).

Escheat.—If decedent left neither surviving spouse nor kindred, real and personal property escheats to state. (T. 18-A, §2-105). Uniform Transfer on Death Security Registration Act 1997, c. 627, §1, effective June 30, 1998. (T. 18-A, §§6-301—6-312).

EXECUTORS AND ADMINISTRATORS:

Uniform Probate Code, including 1975 Official Amendments, adopted. (T. 18-A, §§1-101-8-401). 1977 and 1979 Official Amendments not adopted.

Uniform Fiduciaries Act not adopted.

Uniform Principal and Income Act not adopted.

Uniform Simplification of Fiduciary Security Transfers Act repealed.

Uniform Anatomical Gift Act adopted. (T. 22, §§2901-2909).

TRUSTS:

There can be no trust concerning lands, except trusts arising or resulting by implication of law, unless created or declared by some writing signed by party or his attorney.

See note at head of Digest as to 1998 legislation covered.

See Topical Index in front part of this volume.

TRUSTS . . . *continued*

(T. 33, §851). Title of a purchaser for a valuable consideration or a title derived from levy of an execution cannot be defeated by trust unless purchaser had notice thereof. Record of instrument creating trust in registry where land lies is regarded as such notice. (T. 33, §852). Where real estate is conveyed in mortgage or in trust to two or more persons with power to appoint a successor to one deceased, it is held in joint tenancy unless otherwise expressed. See also category Property, topic Perpetuities.

Uniform Probate Code, including 1975 Official Amendments, adopted. (T. 18-A, §§1-101-8-401). 1977 and 1979 Official Amendments not adopted.

Variations from Official Text.—§7-101 registration of trusts permissive not mandatory. UPC §7-104 omitted; new §7-104 providing for jurisdiction over unregistered trusts. §7-407 prohibitions and requirements applicable to trusts which are private foundations.

Common trust funds provided for. (T. 18-A, §§7-501-7-503).

Transfers to Minors.—Uniform Transfers to Minors Act adopted. (T. 33, §§1651-1674).

Uniform Simplification of Fiduciary Security Transfers Act repealed.

Uniform Disclaimer of Transfers by Will, Intestary or Appointment Act adopted, as part of Uniform Probate Code. (T. 18-A, §2-801).

Uniform Disclaimer of Transfers under Nontestamentary Instruments Act adopted, as part of Uniform Probate Code. (T. 18-A, §2-801). Uniform Prudent Investors Act adopted. (T. 18-A, §§7-301—7-302).

Uniform Principal and Income Act not adopted.

Uniform Fiduciaries Act not adopted.

Uniform Trustees Powers Act adopted. (T. 18-A, §§7-401-7-406).

Perpetuities.—See category Property, topic Perpetuities.

WILLS:

Uniform Probate Code, including 1975 Official Amendments, adopted. (T. 18-A, §§1-101-8-401). 1977 and 1979 Official Amendments not adopted.

Community Property Options in Official Text have not been adopted.

Variations from Official Text.—§2-801(b) substitute "nine months" for "six months", §2-803 optional provision adopted. §3-108 amended to provide that for decedents dying before Jan. 1, 1981, no informal probate or appointment proceeding, other than proceeding to probate will previously probated at testator's domicile and appointment proceedings relating to estate in which there has been prior appointment, may be commenced more than 20 years after decedent's death, with certain exceptions. §3-306(b) optional provision of 1979 Official Amendments not adopted, §3-914 unclaimed assets disposed of according to Unclaimed Property Act. (T. 33, §§1801-1820, 1851-1875).

Uniform Disclaimer of Transfers by Will, Intestacy or Appointment Act adopted. (T. 18-A, §2-801).

Uniform Rights of the Terminally Ill Act adopted, but with substantial changes from Model Act. Competent individual at least 18 years old may execute, in presence of two witnesses, declaration directing that life-sustaining procedures and artificially administered nutrition and hydration be withheld or withdrawn. (T. 18-A, §§5-701-5-714).

Living Wills.—See subhead Uniform Rights of the Terminally Ill Act, supra. Uniform Transfer on Death Security Registration Act 1997, c. 627, §1, effective June 30, 1998. (T. 18-A, §§6-301—6-312).

FAMILY

ADOPTION:

(T. 18-A, §§9-101-9-401).

Any person may be adopted, regardless of age. (T. 18-A, §9-301).

Consent Required.—Written consent by: Adoptee if 14 years or older; legal custodian or guardian, except that Judge of Probate may overrule unreasonable lack of consent; each living parent; and if no living parent, guardian or legal custodian. (T. 18-A, §9-302). Consent, not required from putative father or legal father who is not biological father, who received notice and failed to respond, parents whose parental rights have been terminated, parents who have executed surrender and release, or parents of adoptee aged 18 years or older. Petition for adoption must be pending before consent is executed. (T. 18-A, §9-302).

Conditions Precedent.—Court may require that child shall have lived for one year in home of proposed adopter under supervision of Dept. of Human Services or licensed adoption agency before adoption is granted. (T. 18-A, §9-304).

Jurisdiction.—Judges of probate court have jurisdiction of adoption proceedings.

Venue.—If adoptee is placed by licensed child-placing agency or Department, petition must be filed in county in which petitioner resides; adoptee resides or was born; or in which placing agency is located. For non-agency/nondepartmental adoptions, county in which adoptee resides; county in which petitioner resides; or where consent has been filed. (T. 18-A, §9-104).

Petition.—Forms are supplied by probate court of county having jurisdiction.

Proceedings.—Upon filing of petition for adoption of minor, court shall direct State Dept. of Human Services to conduct study of whether child is proper subject for adoption and whether proposed home is suitable and report to court regarding same within 60 days. (T. 18-A, §9-304[a]). Court may waive requirement of study and report if (1) court has report with sufficient current information or (2) petitioner is blood relative of child to be adopted. (T. 18-A, §9-304[a]). Certified copy of birth certificate must accompany petition. (T. 18-A, §9-304). Adoption papers on or after Aug. 8, 1953 are confidential, subject to release by Probate Judge. (T. 18-A, §9-310).

State Registrar maintains voluntary contact file for adoptees and natural parents. (T. 22, §2706-A). Adoption Assistance Compact protects interests of some children whose adoptive parents move out of state or who are adopted by residents of another state. (T. 22, §4171).

Decree.—If judge determines that adoption is in best interests of adoptee, court enters decree that includes new name of adoptee. Decree must order that from that date adoptee is child of petitioner and must be accorded status set forth in §9-105. If court determines that it is in best interests of adoptee, court may require that names of adoptee and petitioner remain confidential. (T. 18-A, §9-308).

Name.—Request for amended birth certificate is filed with petition. (T. 18-A, §9-303).

Effect of Adoption.—Adopted person is child of adopting parent and not of natural parents except that adopted child will also inherit from natural parents and their respective kin if adoption decree so provides, and except that adoption of child by spouse of natural parent has no effect on relationship between child and either natural parent. (T. 18-A, §2-109[1]).

Setting Aside Adoption.—Judge of Probate may annul adoption on petition of two or more persons showing that adoption was obtained by fraud, duress, error or illegal procedures or court finds other good cause consistent with best interests of adoptee. (T. 18-A, §9-315).

Foreign Adoption.—Adoption of a child in any other state according to laws of that state has same force and effect in Maine as to inheritance and all other rights and duties as if in this state. Decree of finalized adoption from foreign country may serve as basis for Maine decree of adoption. (T. 18-A, §9-312).

Private Adoptions Involving Interstate Placements.—Any person or agency bringing child into state for purposes of adoption or taking child out of state for purposes of adoption must obtain from Dept. of Human Services certification of compliance with T. 22, c. 1153. (T. 18-A, §9-311).

DISSOLUTION OF MARRIAGE:

See topic Divorce.

DIVORCE:

(T. 19, §§661-752).

Grounds for Divorce.—Divorces may be granted by superior court and district court on following grounds: adultery; impotence; extreme cruelty; utter desertion continued for three consecutive years next prior to commencement of action; gross and confirmed habits of intoxication from use of intoxicating liquors or drugs; nonsupport, where one spouse being of sufficient ability to provide for other, grossly, wantonly, or cruelly refuses or neglects to provide suitable maintenance for complaining spouse; cruel and abusive treatment; irreconcilable differences; or mental illness requiring confinement in mental institution for at least seven consecutive years prior to commencement of action. (T. 19-A, §§102, 902). If divorce is sought on grounds of cruel and abusive treatment, plaintiff must not only show cruel and abusive conduct on part of spouse, but must also prove that such conduct caused plaintiff physical or mental injury or that continuation of marriage relationship would jeopardize physical or mental health. (161 Me. 289, 211 A.2d 583) Where irreconcilable differences are alleged, and other party denies it, court may order both to see professional counselor. Court may not grant divorce when parties seek to procure divorce for fraudulent purposes. (T. 19-A, §901).

The running of the period necessary for divorce on the ground of desertion is not necessarily stopped by a mere visit of one of the parties to the other if no cohabitation took place.

Grounds for Legal Separation.—District Court and Superior Court have jurisdiction to enter separation decree: (1) Upon petition of married person who lives apart or who desires to live apart from spouse for period in excess of 60 continuous days; or (2) upon joint petition of married couple who live apart or who desire to live apart for period in excess of 60 continuous days.

No judicial separation decree shall be granted where parties seek to procure decree for fraudulent purposes. (T. 19-A, §851). Courts will refer parties to mediation prior to contested hearing where parties have minor children. (T. 19-A, §§851, 251).

Residence Requirements.—Plaintiff is resident of this State and parties were married in this State; plaintiff is resident of this State and parties resided in this State when cause of divorce accrued (T. 19-A, §901); plaintiff has resided in this State in good faith for six months before action is commenced; or defendant is resident of state (T. 19-A, §901). Wife is competent to obtain separate domicile for purpose but it must be a bona fide residence. Any member of Armed Forces on active duty stationed in Maine or spouse may file complaint for separation, support or annulment without otherwise meeting residency requirements. (T. 19, §102).

Jurisdiction.—District court has concurrent original jurisdiction with superior court for action of divorce and annulment. District court has concurrent original jurisdiction with superior court for petitions for judicial separation. (T. 19A, §103).

Venue of matrimonial actions is in county or judicial division where either party resides, except that if petitioner has left county or judicial division in which parties lived together and respondent still lives in that county or judicial division, then petitioner must file in that county. (T. 19-A, §851).

Process.—Subject to the special provisions of M.R.C.P. 80, divorce actions are commenced like other civil actions. Attachment and trustee process may be used in connection with the commencement of the action. Service must be made upon a resident defendant by delivery to him in hand, unless the court otherwise orders. Service may be made upon nonresidential defendant by registered or certified mail. (M.R.C.P. 4[f]). For nonresident defendants or ones whose residence is unknown service is by publication as provided in other actions.

Pleading.—Defendant may counterclaim for divorce, annulment, separate support, or determination of parental rights and responsibilities. (M.R.C.P. 80[b]).

See note at head of Digest as to 1998 legislation covered.

See Topical Index in front part of this volume.

DIVORCE . . . *continued*

Practice.—Court may at any time refer parties to mediation on any issues. Mediation is mandatory in contested divorces involving minor children, unless no issues of fact exist and all unresolved issues are questions of law. (T. 19-A, §251).

Judgment or Decree.—Trial court may, upon motion, grant final judgment of annulment or divorce during pendency of appeal period provided no cause for delay exists and rights of parties will not be prejudiced. (T. 19-A, §§752, 906).

Divorce is denied where parties seek to procure divorce for fraudulent purposes. (T. 19-A, §901).

Condonation not absolute defense, but discretionary with court. Recrimination is comparative not absolute defense. (T. 19-A, §902).

Decree is absolute; there is no interlocutory judgment or decree.

Temporary Alimony.—Court may, while action is pending, make provision for either spouse's separate support. (T. 19-A, §904).

Allowance for Prosecution of Suit.—Court may, while action is pending, order either spouse to pay other spouse, or attorney for other spouse, sufficient money for defense or prosecution thereof. (T. 19-A, §904).

Permanent Alimony.—Court may decree to either spouse alimony payable out of estate of other, and may order spouse to pay for defense or prosecution of hearings on alimony. Court may order one spouse's real estate, or rents and profits therefrom, to be assigned to other spouse for life. In lieu of alimony, court may decree specific sum to be paid. Court may, at any time, alter, amend, or suspend decree for alimony or for specific sum, but court may not increase alimony if divorce decree prohibited increase. Pending petition to enforce decree of alimony, or decree for payment of money instead thereof, for support of minor children, for support pending action or for payment of counsel fees, or for alteration of decree as to support or custody of children, court may order either spouse to pay to other spouse, or to counsel for other spouse, sufficient money for prosecution or defense thereof. (T. 19-A, §952). On motion to enforce alimony decree or other order of support, court may issue summary process and find defaulting party guilty of contempt and may order execution and judgment, garnishment, attachment or any other method of enforcement permissible in civil action. (T. 19-A, §§952, 2601-2668).

Division of Property of Spouses.—Court has broad powers over disposition of marital property. All property acquired subsequent to marriage and prior to judicial separation or divorce is presumptively marital property unless otherwise shown. If divorce decree fails to dispose of marital property, omitted property deemed held by both parties as tenants in common. Either party may move court at any time to set aside or divide property. All rights in real estate acquired by divorce decree effectual against any person when decree or abstract thereof is filed in registry of deeds for county or registry district where real estate situated. Claim of nonowner spouse to real estate as "marital property" does not affect owner spouse's title until nonowner spouse records in appropriate registry of deeds either: (1) Copy of divorce complaint, (2) clerk's certificate of divorce complaint, or (3) divorce decree or abstract thereof. Parties must submit abstracts necessary to implement decree with any final decree submitted to court or decree shall name party responsible for preparing abstract and parties shall pay required filing fee. Recording of said decree or abstract has effect of quitclaim deed. When divorce granted out of state, plaintiff or plaintiff's attorney must record duly authenticated copy of decree in registry of deeds in each of counties where real estate is situated. (T. 19-A, §953).

Change of Name.—Court may allow either spouse to change that person's own name. (T. 19-A, §1051).

Custody of Children.—When parents are living apart court may award allocated parental rights and responsibilities, shared parental rights and responsibilities or sole parental rights and responsibilities, according to best interest of child. (T. 19-A, §§1653-1654). Maine has adopted Uniform Child Custody Jurisdiction Act. (T. 19-A, §§1701-1725).

Allowance for Support of Children.—Court may order either parent of minor child to contribute reasonable and just sums as child support payable weekly, monthly or quarterly. Court shall also order either parent to provide child support beyond child's 18th birthday if child is attending secondary school. (T. 19-A, §1653). Support guidelines based on child support table adopted by Department of Human Services creates rebuttable presumption of amount to be paid. (T. 19-A, §2005).

Remarriage.—No restrictions on marriage of persons who have been divorced.

Foreign Divorces.—Divorce decree out of state according to law of state where rendered by court having jurisdiction of cause and of both parties, is valid in Maine except where residents of this state go out of it for purpose of obtaining divorce for causes which occurred here while parties resided here and which do not authorize divorce in this state. (T. 19-A, §907).

Separation Agreements.—Marital settlement agreement that is not incorporated by reference in final judgment of divorce may nevertheless be valid if fair and not contrary to public policy. (71 A.2d 514).

Antenuptial Contracts.—See topic Husband and Wife.

GUARDIAN AND WARD:

Uniform Probate Code, including 1975 Official Amendments, adopted. (T. 18-A, §§1-101-8-401). 1977 and 1979 Official Amendments not adopted.

Additions to Official Text.—Under §5-105 limited guardians may be appointed by court with fewer than all powers and duties of guardians.

T. 18-A, §5-303(b) requiring appointment of visitor, guardian ad litem or attorney if incapacitated person not already represented, and requiring appointment of attorney if incapacitated person contests any aspect of guardianship proceeding. T. 18-A, §5-310 repealed (Apr. 8, 1994) and new §5-310-A enacted governing appointment of temporary guardian, requiring post-appointment expedited hearing. T. 18-A, §5-407 requires appointment of attorney for incapacitated person, if not already represented who

wishes to contest any aspect of conservatorship proceedings. T. 18-A, §5-408-A enacted governing appointment of temporary conservator, requiring post-appointment expedited hearing if incapacitated person contests any aspect of temporary conservatorship.

Person with substantial interest in nursing care or boarding facility (T. 22, §§1817 and 7801) may act as guardian for resident of such facility only if person is also: a spouse, adult child, parent or relative with whom incapacitated person resided for more than six months prior to filing of petition for appointment of incapacitated person (T. 18-A, §5-311[c]).

Delegation of Guardian's Authority.—Parent or guardian of minor or incapacitated person, by properly executed power of attorney, may delegate to another person, for period not exceeding six months, his or her powers regarding care, custody or property of minor or incapacitated person, except power to consent to marriage or adoption. (T. 18-A, §5-104). Power delegated that would otherwise expire will automatically be extended for parent or guardian who is member of U.S. Armed Forces Reserve and under order to active duty for more than 30 days until 30 days after active duty order ends or court so provides. (T. 18-A, §5-104[b]).

Uniform Fiduciaries Act not adopted.

Uniform Simplification of Fiduciary Security Transfers Act repealed.

HUSBAND AND WIFE:

Disabilities of Married Women.—Married woman has, in general, same rights and liabilities as man. All disabilities of coverture have been removed.

Separate Property.—A married person may hold any property, real or personal, as that person's separate property. (36 Me. 64; T. 19-A, §§801-802).

Contracts.—A married woman may contract with her husband or any other person as though unmarried and may become bound as surety.

Antenuptial Contracts.—Maine Uniform Premarital Agreement Act (T. 19-A, §§601-611), differs from Uniform Act in that Maine Act does not include severability provisions of Uniform Act, §17, and provides that premarital agreement is void 18 months after parties to agreement become biological or adoptive parents, unless written amendment is executed stating agreement remains in effect or altering agreement. Latter provision does not apply to premarital agreements executed on or after Oct. 1, 1993. (T. 19-A, §606).

Actions.—A married woman may sue or be sued without joinder of her husband. She cannot, however, be arrested on mesne process or execution. (T. 19-A, §805). Either spouse may sue other in tort. (412 A.2d 71). Wife may bring bill in equity against her husband for recovery, conveyance, transfer, payment or delivery to her of any property exceeding $100 in value, standing in his name, of which he has legal title, or which is in his possession or under his control but which belongs to wife; and husband has same rights against his wife. (T. 19-A, §806; 118 Me. 337, 108 A. 105).

Agency.—Either spouse may act as attorney in fact for the other.

Conveyance or Encumbrance of Property.—Married person, widow or widower may convey separate property, real or personal, without joinder or consent of spouse, except that real estate conveyed to person by his or her spouse cannot be conveyed without joinder of spouse, unless such real estate was conveyed to him or her as security for or in payment of bona fide debt due to him or her from spouse. (T. 19-A, §801, 92 A. 489).

Conveyance by one spouse in which other does not join releases any rights and interests by descent which latter may have in property conveyed unless latter files required notice of claim in registry of deeds where land is located within statutorily prescribed time. (T. 33, §§470-475). Signature of nonowner spouse is not required on conveyance for value dated after Dec. 31, 1980, unless nonowner spouse has filed claim in registry of deeds during divorce proceeding. (T. 33, §480). See also topic Divorce.

Desertion.—T. 19-A, §851(1) repealed; §851(3) repealed. No statutory provision regarding desertion. See provision regarding judicial separation. (T. 19-A, §851; LD. 407).

T. 19-A, §§2801-3401 enacted Uniform Interstate Family Support Act without repealing 1968 Uniform Reciprocal Enforcement of Support Act. Uniform Civil Liability for Support Act (T. 19-A, §§3501-3506) adopted. Civil enforcement by action in district or superior court. (T. 19-A, §§2601-2608).

INFANTS:

Age of majority is 18 for both sexes. (T. 1, §§72, 73).

Emancipation.—Infant is not emancipated by marriage. However, married person, widow or widower of any age may dispose of real and personal estate by will and may own, manage, mortgage and convey real or personal property. (T. 19-A, §§801-802).

Disabilities.—Disability of nonage lifted at age 18. (T. 1, §72). Drinking age 21. (T. 28-A, §§2, 2051).

Ratification of Contracts.—No action can be maintained against any minor on any contract made by him, unless he, or some person lawfully authorized, ratified it in writing after he arrived at the age of 18 years, except for necessaries or real estate of which he has received the title and retains the benefit and except with respect to contracts furthering his higher education. (T. 33, §52).

Actions.—Infants must sue by prochein ami, or guardian ad litem, except in bastardy process. (41 Me. 460). Infants defend by guardian, and not by prochein ami. (T. 18-A, §5-209). Abrogation of parental immunity in tort. (409 A.2d 634).

Support of Minor.—Parents obligated to support children in need. (T. 19-A, §1504).

Parental Responsibility.—Parents jointly liable with minor (7 through 17) who lives with parents for willful or malicious damage up to $800 if child would have been liable as adult. (T. 14, §304). Parent or guardian of minor or incapacitated person, by properly executed power of attorney, may delegate to another person, for period not

See note at head of Digest as to 1998 legislation covered.

See Topical Index in front part of this volume.

INFANTS . . . *continued*

exceeding six months, his or her powers regarding care, custody or property of minor or incapacitated person, except power to consent to marriage or adoption. (T. 18-A, §5-104). Power delegated that would otherwise expire will automatically be extended for parent or guardian who is member of U.S. Armed Forces Reserve and under order to active duty for more than 30 days until 30 days after active duty order ends or court so provides. (T. 18-A, §5-104[b]).

Adoption.—See topic Adoption.

Uniform Transfers to Minors Act adopted (T. 33, §§1651-1674), repealing Maine Uniform Gifts to Minors Act. In addition to purely formal changes made to conform to standard Maine legislative drafting practices, Maine statute contains following variances and additions to 1983 Official Text: §1(11), "minor" means individual who has not attained 18 years of age; §7(b), delete "must be made" and add "shall be paid"; §18(c), after "written notice" add "of resignation"; §20(1), delete "21" and add "18", and after "Section 4 or 5" add "unless the transferor has specified in writing in the transferring instrument that the transfer shall not occur until the minor attains a later age, not to exceed 21 years of age. The following words or their substantial equivalent must appear in the transferring instrument: 'The custodian shall transfer __ _____ (description of property) to _____ (name of minor) when _____ (he or she) reaches the age of __ (age at which transfer will occur)' " (T. 33, §1660); §22(a), after "as" delete "now"; §24 not adopted; §25 not adopted; §26 not adopted; §27 not adopted.

MARRIAGE:

Consent Required.—If either party is under 18, certificate cannot issue without notifying judge of probate in county in which minor resides of filing of this intention; and written consent from that judge to issue license. Judge of probate shall issue decision within 30 days of receiving notification of intention to marry. (T. 19-A, §652).

Notice of intention to marry must be filed with town clerk, as follows: if both parties are residents of state, at residence of each; if only one is a resident, at such party's residence; if both are nonresidents, where marriage is to be solemnized. Clerk issues certificate not less than three days thereafter. Parties must submit application for recording notice of intention to marry, including signed certification that information recorded is correct and applicants are free to marry under Maine law. Applicants' signatures must be acknowledged before official authorized to take oaths. Application open for public inspection in clerk's office. Certificate of genetic counseling from physician must be filed with notice of marriage intentions between man and daughter of his father's brother or sister, or corresponding marriage by woman. Notice may be filed by either party to proposed marriage. While statute does not require personal appearance many clerks require one of applicants to appear either at time of filing or at time of issuance of certificate. (T. 19-A, §651).

Divorced person who files notice of intention to marry must file therewith a certificate or certified copy from clerk of court which granted divorce, showing title and location of court, names of parties, which party obtained divorce, cause therefor and when decree became absolute. (T. 22, §2801).

Medical Examination.—None required.

License.—Certificate is delivered to person performing ceremony before same is begun. Certificate must be signed by person performing ceremony, both parties to intended marriage and two witnesses. Certificate is void if not used within 90 days after filing notice of intention to marry. (T. 19-A, §§652, 654).

Waiting Period.—Three days. May be waived by judge of probate court, supreme judicial court, superior court, or district court upon hearing and finding it expedient that marriage be solemnized without delay and payment of $10 fee to probate, supreme judicial, superior, or district court. (T. 19-A, §652).

Ceremonial Marriages.—Ceremony may be performed by resident Justices, resident judges, resident lawyers admitted to Maine bar, justice of peace or notary public residing in this state, ordained minister of gospel, cleric or person licensed to preach by association of ministers, religious seminary or ecclesiastical body, whether resident or nonresident of State and whether or not citizen of U.S. (T. 19-A, §658). Quaker marriages are valid. (T. 19-A, §655).

Ceremony must be performed in presence of at least two witnesses besides person officiating. (T. 19-A, §656).

Marriage solemnized before known resident of state professing to be duly authorized is not invalid because of lack of authority, nor is marriage invalidated by omission or informality in entering intention of marriage; provided marriage is in other respects lawful and is consummated with full belief of either party that they are lawfully married. (T. 19-A, §657).

Reports of Marriages.—Person performing ceremony must make record of marriage and forward original certificate to clerk who issued same within seven days following date such marriage was solemnized, and if marriage was solemnized elsewhere than at residence of parties, return a copy of certificate to clerk of town where marriage was solemnized. (T. 22, §2802).

Record.—See category Documents and Records, topic Records, subhead Vital Statistics.

Common Law Marriages.—Not recognized. (254 A.2d 46).

Proxy Marriages.—No provision.

Marriages by Written Contract.—No provision.

Prohibited Marriages.—No man shall marry his mother, grandmother, daughter, granddaughter, sister, brother's daughter, sister's daughter, father's sister, mother's sister, daughter of his father's brother or sister or daughter of his mother's brother or sister; corresponding prohibitions as to marriage by woman. Man may marry daughter of his father's brother or sister only after filing certificate of genetic counseling signed by physician. Corresponding restriction for woman. (T. 19-A, §701). Persons of same sex may not contract marriage. (T. 19-A, §701).

No person impaired by reason of mental illness or mental retardation to extent that he lacks sufficient capacity to make responsible decisions concerning his person or property is capable of contracting marriage. Polygamous marriages are void. (T. 19-A, §701).

Foreign Marriages.—Any marriage performed in another state that would violate provisions of T. 19-A, §701 if performed in this State is not recognized in this State and is considered void if parties take up residence in this State. (T. 19-A, §701).

Annulment.—When the validity of a marriage is doubted either party may file a libel as for divorce and the court may decree it annulled or affirmed. (T. 19-A, §752). Annulment may be decreed on account of parties being within prohibited degrees of consanguinity (in which case issue is illegitimate) or on account of insanity or idiocy. (T. 19-A, §752). Marriages prohibited in §701 if solemnized in this State, are absolutely void without legal process. (T. 19-A, §751). Marriage may also be annulled when either party has husband or wife of prior marriage still living, but if second marriage was contracted in good faith believing prior husband or wife dead, or that former marriage was void or divorce decreed, that fact is stated in decree and issue of such marriage begotten before commencement of suit are legitimate issue of parent capable of contracting. (T. 19-A, §752). No time specified by statute within which annulment for nonage must be brought.

Antenuptial Contracts.—See topic Husband and Wife.

INSURANCE

INSURANCE COMPANIES:

Regulated by T. 24, §§2301–2332-6 and T. 24-A, §§1-6816.

Supervision by Superintendent of Insurance.

Rates governed by T. 24-A, §§2301-2387-B.

Annual statement filed with Superintendent of Insurance.

Annual audit of insurers required and annual audited financial report must be filed with Superintendent of Insurance. (T. 24-A, §221-A).

Policies.—General requirements of T. 24-A, §§2401-2452 apply to all policies. Simplification of policy language and approval by Superintendent of Insurance. (T. 24-A, §§2439-2445). T. 24-A, §§2501-2555 govern life insurance and annuity contracts. T. 24-A, §§2601-2629 govern group life insurance. T. 24-A, §§2670-2680 set forth Preferred Provider Arrangement Act of 1986. T. 24-A, §§2701-2754 govern health insurance contracts. T. 24-A, §§2771-2774 govern licensure of medical utilization review entities. T. 24-A, §§2801-2847-F govern group and blanket health insurance. T.24-A, §§2848-2850-D govern continuity of health coverage. T. 24-A, §§2851-2864 govern credit life and credit health. T. 24-A, §§2881-2888 govern group legal services insurance. T. 24-A, §§2901-2910-A govern casualty insurance. T. 24-A, §§2911-2924 govern cancellation of auto insurance. T. 24-A, §2927 governs personal automobile insurance and rental vehicle coverage. T. 24-A, §§2931-2940 govern mass marketing of casualty and property insurance. T. 24-A, §§3001-3007 govern standard fire insurance policies. T. 24-A, §§3020-3022 govern deposit notes. T. 24-A, §§3030-3034 govern lien of mortgages on policies. T. 24-A, §§3048-3056 govern cancellation of property insurance. T. 24-A, §§3101-3105 govern surety insurance contracts. T. 24-A, §3201 governs title insurance. T. 24-A, §§5001-5015 govern Medicare supplement insurance. T. 24-A, §§5051-5056 govern nursing home care and long-term care insurance.

Insurance Information and Privacy Protection Act.—Guidelines for insurers collection, use and disclosure of information gathered in connection with insurance transactions. (T. 24-A, §§2201-2220).

Unfair Claims Practices.—Claim settlement practices of insurers, except health, life and workers compensation, regulated by statute, enforceable by Superintendent of Insurance and private civil action. (T. 24-A, §§2164-D, 2436-A).

Late Payment.—Claims must be paid or disputed or additional information requested within 30 days (60 days for fire claims) after proof of loss is received by insurer and ascertainment of loss is made by agreement or arbitration. Claim for attorneys fees and interest accrues for insurer's failure to pay timely undisputed claim. (T. 24-A, §2436).

Discrimination.—Rate discrimination is prohibited. (T. 24-A, §§2159, 2162). Discrimination prohibited against blind persons (T. 24-A, §2159-A), or mentally or physically disabled (T. 24-A, §2159-A), or persons infected with HIV (T. 24-A, §§2159, 2452, 2526-A, 2629, 2750, 2846, 4120, 4121-A, 4229) or on basis of genetic information or testing for health insurance or unfair discrimination for life, disability or long-term care (T. 24-A, §2154-C).

Maternity Benefits.—Health insurance plans must provide same maternity benefits for unmarried women as for married policyholders with maternity coverage (T. 24-A, §2741), coverage on expense incurred basis must begin at moment of birth (T. 24-A, §2743).

Tie-In Sales.—Prohibition against tying purchase of desired type of insurance or contract for credit to additional insurance purchases. (T. 24-A, §§2168-A–2168-B).

Rebates.—Prohibition against rebate as inducement to purchase insurance. (T. 24-A, §§2160, 2162). Exceptions from this prohibition. (T. 24-A, §§2161–2162).

Dividends.—Prohibition against making payment of policy dividend conditioned upon renewal of policy. (T. 24-A, §2162-A).

Liens.—Priority liens on policies regulated by T. 24-A, §§2729-A, 2836, 2910-A, 4243.

Producers, Agents and Brokers.—Regulated by T. 24-A, §§1401-1447 and 1901-1912. Producers, agents, managing general agents, brokers, consultants, adjusters and insurance administrators must be licensed by Superintendent of Insurance.

See note at head of Digest as to 1998 legislation covered.

See Topical Index in front part of this volume.

INSURANCE COMPANIES . . . *continued*

Market Assistance Plan.—Insurance Superintendent can request insurer voluntarily to participate in market assistance plan, providing insurance at agreed-upon rate to persons or groups unable to obtain coverage. (T. 24-A, §2325-A).

Process Agent.—As a condition to transacting business within state, resident agent must be irrevocably appointed to receive process. (T. 24-A, §421).

Investments.—Regulated by T. 24-A, §§1101-1162-A.

Foreign insurance companies must meet same reserve requirements as domestic insurers and can sell only types of insurance authorized for domestic insurers. (T. 24-A, §406). Must maintain deposit in state in amount not less than $100,000 actual market value, or in lieu thereof provide Superintendent of Insurance certificate from official of some other state to effect that such deposit is maintained in that state. (T. 24-A, §412). Application for certificate of authority is filed with Superintendent of Insurance, and must be accompanied by certificate of insurance department of its state of domicile, showing that it is authorized to transact kinds of business in that state or country of domicile, that it proposes to transact in Maine. (T. 24-A, §413). Fee for filing this application is $1,000. (T. 24-A, §601).

Retaliatory Laws.—If any state imposes any taxes, licenses, or fees (except agent, producers or brokers licensing fees and other administrative fees) on Maine insurers which are greater than those imposed on domestic insurers, same are imposed upon insurers from such state. (T. 24-A, §428).

Premium tax at the rate of 2% is imposed on all gross direct premiums on contracts written on risks located or resident in state deducting therefrom return premiums and dividends paid to policyholders. Fire insurance companies subject to additional tax of 1.4% of gross direct premiums for fire risk insurance written in state less return premium thereon and policyholder dividends. Tax collected quarterly. (T. 36, §§2513, 2513-A, 2519; 2521-A; T. 25, §2399). Captive insurers subject to different tax scheme. (T. 36, §2513-B). Large domestic disability insurers subject to different tax structure. (T. 36, §2513). Premium tax rate of 2% upon all gross direct premiums written on risks located or resident in State for workers' compensation insurance, less return premiums and dividends paid. (T. 36, §2523). Surplus lines insurers tax rate is 3% per year on all gross direct premiums. (T. 36, §2513).

Direct Actions Against Insurer.—See category Transportation, topic Motor Vehicles, subhead Direct Actions.

Insurance Inspections.—Furnishing or failure to furnish insurance inspection will not subject insurer to liability for damages for injury, death or loss occurring as result of act or omission in course of inspection. (T. 14, §167).

Insurance and Banking.—Authorized financial institutions and credit unions or affiliates thereof may act as insurance agent, broker or consultant and may employ, affiliate with or hire as third party agent licensed insurance producer or agency, broker or consultant. (T. 9-B, §448, T. 24-A, §1443-A). Supervised lenders may become licensed and may act as insurance agency, broker or consultant for sale of insurance products. (T. 9-A, §§4-401, 4-407). Financial institutions and credit unions have power to engage in any activity that federally chartered financial institutions and credit unions have under federal law. (T. 9-B, §§416, 828, T. 24-A, §212-A).

Risk Retention Groups.—Regulated by T. 24-A, §§6091-6104.

Workers' Compensation Rating System.—Regulated by T. 24-A, §§2381-2387-B.

SURETY AND GUARANTY COMPANIES:

Any insurer duly authorized to transact surety insurance in Maine may be accepted as surety upon bond of any person or corporation required by laws of state to execute a bond. If such insurer furnishes satisfactory evidence of its ability to provide all security required by law, no additional security may be exacted, but other surety or sureties may in discretion of official authorized to approve such bond be required, and such surety company may be released from its liability upon same terms and conditions as are by law prescribed for release of individuals. (T. 24-A, §3102). Insurer must attach power of attorney to every bond it executes through attorney-in-fact in this state, unless bond is executed by officer of insurer. (T. 24-A, §3105).

Foreign surety companies are entitled to do business in the state only on compliance with statutory provisions. Among other things such a company must appoint agent in this state for service of process. (T. 24-A, §421).

INTELLECTUAL PROPERTY

TRADEMARKS AND TRADENAMES:

Any person who adopts and uses mark in this state, subject to limitations set forth, may register trademark. (T. 10, §1522).

What May Be Used.—Mark distinguishing goods or services of applicant may not be registered if deceptive, or if it falsely suggests connection to persons or institutions, consists of U.S. or state insignia, comprises name of living individual without consent, confusingly similar to another mark, or consists of or comprises corporate or limited partnership name, unless with consent to use mark similar to name. Marks, in addition, may not be registered absent proof of acquired distinctiveness if merely descriptive or deceptively misdescriptive of goods or services, primarily geographically descriptive or deceptively misdescriptive (except in certain cases) or primarily merely surname. (T. 10, §1522).

Registration.—Application must be made to Secretary of State, accompanied by specimen of mark in triplicate and $50 fee for first class, $10 for each additional class payable to Treasurer of State. Application must be signed and verified by applicant. (T. 10, §1522). Application must set forth manner in which mark is used in connection with goods and services and class of goods and services, date first used and statement that to best of applicant's knowledge and belief applicant is owner of mark.

Assignment.—Assignable by written instrument, which may be recorded with Secretary of State upon payment of $40 to Treasurer of State. (T. 10, §1525).

Protection.—Registered mark, or any copy thereof, may not be used, or reproduced, etc., in connection with sale of goods and services, without consent of registrant. (T. 10, §1529).

Infringement.—Infringer liable to owner of registered mark for statutory damages not to exceed $2,000, and, in exceptional cases, attorneys fees; common law, and criminal remedies also available. (T. 10, §§1531, 1532).

Tradenames.—Before transacting business in state under assumed name corporation must file statement setting forth corporate name, assumed name and address of registered office. Corporation failing to comply may be enjoined from continued use of assumed name. (T. 13-A, §307).

TRADE SECRETS:

Uniform Trade Secrets Act adopted. (T. 10, §§1541-1548).

Commercial Feeds.—Commercial Feed Law (T. 7, §§711-724) makes it Class E crime to use for one's own advantage or to reveal trade secrets concerning commercial feeds obtained pursuant to law (T. 7, §722).

Community Right-to-Know Act.—Exceptions to Right-to-Know Act (T. 22, §§1696-A–1696-H) prohibiting disclosure of trade secrets (T. 22, §§1696-D, 1696-F).

Environmental Laws.—Limited exceptions from certain reporting requirements for trade secrets and prohibitions against using or revealing trade secrets obtained pursuant to various environmental laws. (T. 7, §§508[2], 606[2][C]; T. 26, §1716; T. 38, §1310-B).

LEGAL PROFESSION

ATTORNEYS AND COUNSELORS:

State bar is not integrated.

There are no distinctions between attorneys and counselors.

Bar Associations.—Each county has a bar association. There is also a state bar association.

Bar Rules.—Maine Bar Rules, including Code of Professional Responsibility, promulgated by Supreme Judicial Court.

Board of Overseers of Bar appointed by Supreme Judicial Court to oversee conduct and discipline of attorneys admitted to practice.

Jurisdiction over admission is in the Supreme Judicial Court.

Registration As Law Student.—No Requirement.

Eligibility.—Applicant for admission to Maine Bar must have graduated with bachelor's degree from accredited college or university or successfully completed at least two years' work as candidate for that degree at accredited college or university and (i) graduated from American Bar Association accredited law school; (ii) graduated from law school accredited by U.S. jurisdiction in which it is located, then admitted to practice by examination in one or more jurisdictions within U.S. and actively practiced there for at least three years; (iii) graduated from foreign law school with legal education equivalent to that provided by ABA accredited law schools; or (iv) successfully completed two thirds of requirements for graduation from ABA accredited law school and then pursued study of law in office of attorney within state for at least one year. (T. 4, §803).

Petition for Admission.—Applicant may register with board of examiners by filing application obtained from board, together with fee during following time periods: for Feb. examination, between preceding Oct. 15 and preceding Dec. 20; for July examination, between preceding Mar. 15 and preceding May 20. Applicant must also submit proof of good moral character. (Me. Bar Admission Rules 5, 6, 9).

Examination.—Conducted by Board of Bar Examiners each Feb. and July at locations announced by Board. (Me. Bar Admission Rule 10). $20 fee for requesting application forms. $500 application fee for applicant admitted for more than one year in any other jurisdiction. $250 application fee for all other applicants. (Me. Bar Admission Rule 6). Multi-state Bar Examination comprises ^{4}/₁₁ths of examination score; general examination, which may include questions from Multi-state Essay Examination, comprises 7/₁₁ths of score. General examination topics include: Maine Rules of Civil and Criminal Procedure, Maine Rules of Evidence, Maine Code of Professional Responsibility. Examination may also include numerous other topics. (Me. Bar Admission Rule 10). Each person admitted after July 1, 1987, required to have obtained scale score of 75 on Multistate Professional Responsibility Examination. (Me. Bar Admission Rule 11).

Applicant who has (i) been admitted by examination to practice in one or more other U.S. jurisdictions and who has been in active practice of law for at least three of preceding five years or (ii) taken Multi-state Bar Examination within the 61 months prior to current administration of examination, may elect to take only first day of examination. Applicant who has achieved "useable" Multi-state Bar Examination score may be admitted on basis of further modified written examination under certain conditions. (Me. Bar Admission Rule 10).

Clerkship.—Not Required.

Admission Without Examination.—No longer allowed in any case. (T. 4, §807).

Admission Pro Hac Vice.—Attorney of another state may be admitted temporarily on motion. (T. 4, §802).

Licenses.—Annual registration fee depending on length of time admitted and active status, payable to Board of Overseers of Bar.

Privileges.—Lawyer-client privilege recognized. (M.R.E. 502).

Disabilities.—None.

Liabilities.—See category Civil Actions and Procedure, topic Costs.

Compensation.—Fees governed by Me. Bar Rules 3.3, 8 & 9. Fees may not be "excessive". (Me. Bar Rule 3.3[a]). Contingent fee agreement must be in writing in

---

See note at head of Digest as to 1998 legislation covered.

See Topical Index in front part of this volume.

ATTORNEYS AND COUNSELORS . . . *continued*

duplicate, and signed by attorney and by each client. Contingent fees not permitted in criminal cases, divorce, annulment or separation proceedings or where method of determination of attorney's fees is expressly provided by statute or regulation. (Me. Bar Rule 8).

Disbarment or Suspension.—Any person may submit written complaint alleging attorney misconduct to Board of Overseers of the Bar. Complaint is investigated by Bar Counsel who makes initial determination of whether sanctionable misconduct exists. If complaint is not dismissed by Bar Counsel due to lack of sanctionable misconduct, Bar Counsel will present complaint to Grievance Commission appointed by Board. If disciplinary panel of Grievance Commission finds serious misconduct, panel will either issue public reprimand or direct Bar Counsel to commence disciplinary proceedings before single justice of Supreme Judicial Court. Public reprimands are reviewable by such single justice. Board has burden of proof in disciplinary proceedings before single justice who hears such proceedings de novo. Bar counsel may also seek determination by Board whether attorney is incapacitated from continuing practice by reason of mental infirmity or addiction to drugs or intoxicants. (Me. Bar Rule 7-7.3).

Champerty.—Person is guilty of champerty if, with intent to collect by civil action a claim, account, note or other demand due, or to become due to another person, he gives or promises anything of value to such person. This provision does not apply to agreements between attorney and client to prosecute civil action on contingent fee basis. (T. 17-A, §516).

Unauthorized Practice.—Persons not admitted to bar forbidden to practice. Prohibition does not apply to person representing self in court or to range of other narrow exceptions. Unauthorized practice of law is Class E crime. Under rules of Supreme Judicial Court, senior law student attending ABA approved law school may appear in state courts on behalf of state agencies or under supervision of organizations providing legal services to indigent. (T. 4, §807).

Mandatory Continuing Legal Education.—None. Registered attorneys should endeavor to complete 12 hours annually with at least one hour primarily concerned with issues of professional responsibility. (Me. Bar Rule 3.11).

Specialty Certification Requirements.—Lawyer not permitted to publicly represent or imply that she is recognized, designated, or certified specialist, except (1) lawyer admitted to practice before U.S. Patent and Trademark Office may use designation "Patents", "Patent Attorney", or "Patent Lawyer"; (2) lawyer engaged in trademark practice may use designation "Trademarks", "Trademark Attorney", or "Trademark Lawyer"; and (3) lawyer engaged in admiralty practice may use designation "Admiralty", "Procter in Admiralty", or "Admiralty Lawyer". However, lawyer may communicate that his practice is limited to particular fields. (Me. Bar Rule 3.8).

Professional Association (or Corporation).—See category Business Organizations, topic Corporations, subhead Professional Corporations.

Attorney Ethics.—Derived from ABA Model Rules of Professional Conduct, California Rules of Professional Conduct. (Me. Bar Rule 3). Lawyers who have direct supervisory authority over another lawyer shall make reasonable efforts to ensure that other lawyer conforms to Code of Professional Responsibility. (Me. Bar Rule 3.13).

MINERAL, WATER AND FISHING RIGHTS

MINES AND MINERALS:

Operation of Mines.—No person may engage in mining activity without obtaining approval from Maine Board of Environmental Protection or Maine Department of Environmental Protection. (T. 38, §§482, 483-A, 485-A). All mining activity must include safety and reclamation provisions for affected land or otherwise comply with approval. Board may require bond to assure compliance with T. 38, c. 3. Persons engaged in mining activity must reclaim affected land in accordance with approved plan. (T. 38, §490). Persons expending more than $25,000 in one calendar year for mineral exploration must register with state geologist. (T. 12, §550). Separate provisions for borrow pits over five acres and rock quarries over one acre. (T. 38, §§490-A-490-M, 490-W-490-EE).

Prohibitions.—Engaging in mining or advance exploration activity without approval. (T. 38, §§482, 483-A). Mining of uranium or thorium. (T. 38, §489-B).

State Owned Lands.—Natural Resources Information and Mapping Center and agencies having jurisdiction over state-owned lands have jurisdiction over mineral exploration and development activities on state-owned lands including permits, fees and leases. (T. 12, §§549-549-C).

Safeguarding Employees.—No provisions.

Inspection of Mines.—Provision contained at T. 38, §§347-C, 490-G (borrow pits), and 490-AA (rock quarries).

Oil and Gas.—Provision contained at T. 12, §549-B.

Taxes.—See category Taxation.

MORTGAGES

CHATTEL MORTGAGES:

Uniform Commercial Code and Consumer Credit Code adopted. See category Business Regulation and Commerce, topics: Commercial Code, Consumer Credit.

Filing.—See category Business Regulation and Commerce, topic Commercial Code, subhead Variations from 1972 Official Text, §9-401(1).

Forms.—Forms of Chattel Mortgages or Security Agreement vary widely according to circumstances of transaction. Therefore, it is not feasible to provide standard form here. Commercial Code forms at end of this digest are in use.

Consumer Credit Code.—Maine has adopted Uniform Consumer Credit Code, several provisions of which affect Chattel Mortgages. See category Business Regulation and Commerce, topic Consumer Credit.

COLLATERAL SECURITY:

See category Debtor and Creditor, topic Pledges.

MORTGAGES OF PERSONAL PROPERTY:

See topic Chattel Mortgages.

MORTGAGES OF REAL PROPERTY:

Supreme Judicial Court, Superior Court and District Courts have concurrent original full equity jurisdiction as to mortgages and redemption thereof. Title theory applies.

Execution and Recording.—Mortgages are executed and recorded like other deeds and for same fees.

Conditions usually set forth in mortgage deed itself, but may be made by absolute conveyance with bond or other separate instrument of defeasance to mortgagor executed as part of transaction. (T. 33, §501).

Recording Fees.—See category Documents and Records, topic Records.

Taxes.—See category Taxation.

Trust deeds not in ordinary use.

Future Advances.—Mortgage may cover future advances if it states it secures future advances and specifies total amount of obligations it may secure. Subsequent lienor may limit priority of future advances by notice to mortgagee; mortgagor may limit amount of advances by notice to mortgagee. (T. 33, §505 applies to mortgages recorded on or after Jan. 1, 1994.)

Priorities.—If mortgagee institutes foreclosure proceedings, owner of subsequent mortgage can get assignment of prior mortgage and debt by paying amount owed and foreclosure costs. (T. 14, §6205). Interest of prior mortgagee with superior priority not affected by foreclosure by junior mortgagee. (T. 14, §6321). Subject to certain conditions (see subhead Future Advances, supra), with respect to any mortgage recorded on or after Jan. 1, 1994 which secures future advances, future advances have priority of original mortgage. (T. 33, §505).

Subordination Agreements.—May use subordination agreements to control order of priority.

Assignment.—Word "assign" is sufficient to transfer mortgage of real estate without words "sell, transfer and convey". (T. 33, §770).

Possession of Mortgagee.—Mortgagees may enter or recover possession before or after breach of condition, unless agreement to contrary, but in such case, if mortgage is afterwards redeemed, must account for rents and profits from time of taking possession. (T. 33, §502).

Release.—Can discharge mortgage by deed of release. Ordinary quitclaim deed of premises specifying that object is to release premises from incumbrance of mortgage sufficient. (104 Me. 527, 72 A. 491).

Satisfaction and Discharge.—Must discharge mortgage by written discharge acknowledging satisfaction thereof and signed and acknowledged by mortgagee, executor, administrator, assignee or, in some cases, attorney. (T. 33, §§551, 553-A). When recorded, discharge has same effect as release deed. If mortgagee, after full performance of condition of mortgage, fails to discharge mortgage within seven days after requested, fined $10 to $50, to be recovered in civil action. (T. 33, §551). All discharges must be recorded by written instrument and acknowledged as required of other instruments to be recorded. No discharges permitted by entry in margin of instrument to be discharged. (T. 33, §551). If mortgagee fails to discharge mortgage on residential, owner-occupied, one to four family dwelling, 30 days after receiving payment, attorney licensed to practice in Maine may discharge mortgage by executing and recording affidavit in registry of deeds containing specific information. (T. 33, §553-A).

Foreclosure.—Mortgagee or his assignee, after breach of condition, may bring foreclosure by following methods: (1) action at law for possession; (2) obtaining possession and holding premises by written consent of mortgagor or person holding under him; (3) entering, peaceably and openly, unopposed in presence of two witnesses and taking possession of premises; (4) giving public notice in newspaper of general circulation in county where premises situated, if any, or if not, in newspaper of general circulation in adjoining county, three weeks successively, of claim by mortgagee on such real estate, describing premises intelligibly, naming date of mortgage and stating condition breached by reason whereof he claims foreclosure, and causing copy of said printed notice, and name and date of newspaper in which it was last published, to be recorded in registry of deeds in which mortgage should be recorded within 30 days after last publication; or causing attested copy of such notice to be served on mortgagor or his assignee by sheriff, and causing notice and return to be recorded within 30 days after service (used if possession not desired); (5) bill in equity (in special cases). In all cases notice of fact and method of foreclosure in form prescribed by law must be recorded within 30 days in registry of deeds. (T. 14, §§6201-6203). Foreclosure proceedings by civil action in Superior Court or District Court also available. (T. 14, §§6321-6325).

Acceptance by mortgagee of anything of value on account of mortgage debt from mortgagor or one claiming under him, except income from mortgaged premises while in possession, after foreclosure is begun and before expiration of time for redemption constitutes a waiver of foreclosure proceeding unless written agreement to contrary. (T. 14, §6204). With respect to mortgages on mortgagor's primary residence, mortgagee may not accelerate maturity of obligation or otherwise enforce mortgage without first providing notice and 30 day period to cure. (T. 14, §6111).

Sale.—Express provision for "Statutory Power of Sale" may be included or incorporated by reference in mortgages granted by corporations, partnerships, limited liability companies and trusts. (T. 14, §6203-A; T. 33, §501-A). For mortgage executed on

See note at head of Digest as to 1998 legislation covered.

See Topical Index in front part of this volume.

MORTGAGES OF REAL PROPERTY . . . *continued*

or after Oct. 1, 1993, mortgage must state it is given primarily for business, commercial or agricultural purpose for power of sale to be used. (T. 14, §6203-A). Special restrictions if mortgage given by trust. (T. 14, §6203-A).

Deficiency Judgments.—To bring action for deficiency after exercise of power of sale, holder of mortgage must notify mortgagor in writing of intention to foreclose and of liability for deficiency 21 days before date of sale and sign affidavit of mailing of such notice within 30 days after foreclosure sale. (T. 14, §6203-E.). After public sale pursuant to T. 14, §§6321-23, any deficiency shall be assessed against mortgagor and court will issue execution therefore. (T. 14, §6324).

Redemption.—Mortgagor has one year after first publication or service of notice or acquiring of possession by mortgagee, or, except in case of sales made under Statutory Power of Sale, from date of sale, in which to redeem, and if property not redeemed within such time, right of redemption foreclosed. (T. 14, §§6202, 6204). Redemption period for foreclosure by civil action of mortgages executed on or after Oct. 1, 1975 is 90 days from date of judgment of foreclosure and sale. For mortgages executed prior to Oct. 1, 1975, period of redemption is one year from date of judgment. (T. 14, §6322).

Escrow Accounts.—If funds held in escrow by lender for payment of taxes or insurance premiums, lender must pay interest. (T. 9-A, §3-312; T. 9-B, §429). Mortgage deed must contain provisions for payment of interest on escrow accounts if mortgage on one-four unit owner-occupied residential property and loan requires payment into escrow account. (T. 33, §504).

Form.—Statutory short form adopted. (T. 33, §§761-775).

Forms

Mortgage Deed:
A. B. of . . . ., ... County, ..., (being unmarried) for consideration paid, grant to C. D. of . . . ., ... County, ..., with mortgage covenants, to secure the payment of . . . . dollars in . . . . years . . . . with . . . . per cent interest per annum, payable in . . . . installments, as provided in . . . . note of even date, the land in . . . ., ... County . . . .

(description and encumbrances, if any)

This mortgage is upon the statutory condition, for any breach of which the mortgagee shall have the remedies provided by law.

E. F., spouse of the Grantor, releases all rights in the premises being conveyed.

Witness . . . . hand and seal this . . . . day of . . . .
(here add acknowledgment)

Assignment of Mortgage:
C.D., holder of a mortgage from A.B. to C.D., dated . . . . . ., recorded . . . . in the . . . . County Registry of Deeds, Book . . . . . ., Page . . . . . ., assign said mortgage and the note and claim secured thereby to E.F.

Witness . . . . hand and seal this . . . . day of . . . . (here add acknowledgment)

Partial Release of Mortgage:
C.D., the holder of a mortgage by A.B. to C.D., dated . . . . . ., recorded . . . . in the . . . . County Registry of Deeds, Book . . . . . ., Page . . . . . ., for consideration paid, release to A.B., all interest acquired under said mortgage in the following described portion of the mortgaged premises:
(description)

Witness . . . . hand and seal this . . . . . day of . . . . . (here add acknowledgement)

Discharge of Mortgage:
C.D., holder of a mortgage from A.B. to C.D., dated . . . . ., recorded . . . . in the . . . . . County Registry of Deeds, Book . . . . ., Page . . . . ., acknowledge satisfaction of the same.

Witness . . . . hand and seal this . . . . . . day of . . . . . (here add acknowledgment)

Chattel Mortgages.—See topic Chattel Mortgages.

PROPERTY

ABSENTEES:

Care of Property of Absentee.—If a person entitled to or having interest in property in Maine, or to whom debts or obligations are owing from persons within state, has disappeared or absconded from place where he was last known to be, his whereabouts are unknown, and he has no agent in Maine, or if such person has disappeared without providing for his wife and minor children dependent on him for support and it is not known where he is or he is known to be outside of state, receiver may be appointed by court to take charge of his property, collect debts due to him, sell, lease or invest his property, pay charges for support of wife and minor children and pay debts of such absentee. (T. 18-A, §§8-101-8-110). Eight years after absentee's disappearance, his interest in property ceases and it must be distributed as though he had then died intestate. (T. 18-A, §§8-112-8-113). If, however, receiver is not appointed within seven years after absentee's disappearance, time limited to accounting for, or for distribution of absentee's property, or for barring actions related thereto, is one year after date of receiver's appointment. (T. 18-A, §8-114).

See also category Estates and Trusts, topic Death.

Process Agent.—Following persons and entities are required to appoint agent for service of process, or are subject to service of process made on state official, as condition to being licensed to do business or appointed in fiduciary capacity: Foreign consumer creditors (T. 9-A, §1-203), out-of-state credit unions with branch in Maine

(T. 9-B, §816), foreign corporations (see category Business Organizations, topic Corporations) (T. 13-A, §1212), domestic limited partnerships and nonresident general partners thereof (T. 31, §§407, 409, 410), foreign limited partnerships (T. 31, §§500, 501), domestic limited liability companies and nonresident members or managers thereof (T. 31, §§607, 722, 723), domestic limited liability partnerships (T. 31, §807), foreign limited liability partnerships (T. 31, §§861, 862), domestic nonprofit corporations and nonresident directors thereof (T. 13-B, §§304, 306, 307), foreign nonprofit corporations (T. 13-B, §§1209, 1212) foreign fiduciaries (T. 18, §4162), foreign insurance companies, agents, brokers, adjusters and consultants (T. 24-A, §§421, 2104), foreign public accountants (T. 32, §12263), foreign surety companies (T. 24-A, §421), sellers or promoters of business opportunities (T. 32, §4700-A), investment advisers, broker-dealers and sales representatives of securities (T. 32, §10305), employers of transient sellers of consumer merchandise (T. 32, §4689), unit owners subject to Unit Ownership Act (T. 33, §569), nonresident polygraph examiners (T. 32, §7165), foreign electric utilities (T. 35-A, §3140).

Escheat.—Unclaimed estate passes to state. (T. 18-A, §2-105).

Unclaimed Property.—Uniform Unclaimed Property Act (1995 Act) has been adopted, effective July 1, 1998. (T. 33, §§1951-1980). Where Maine law deviates from Uniform Act, comments are provided to explain deviation. Effective July 1, 1998, Maine's prior Unclaimed Property Act, T. 33, §§1801-1875, has been repealed. See category Estates and Trusts, topic Descent and Distribution, subhead Escheat.

In case of partition of real estate, if any owner resides without the state, having no agent therein, court may appoint agent to act for him. (T. 14, §6505).

Review of Default Judgment Against Absentee.—See category Civil Actions and Procedure, topic Judgments.

Executions.—Execution shall not be issued upon default judgment in personal action against absent defendant until one year after entry of judgment unless bond is given. (T. 14, §4701, M.R.C.P. 62).

ADVERSE POSSESSION:

Acquisition of title through possession of real estate inconsistent with title of another.

Character of Possession.—Possession must be actual, open, notorious, hostile, under claim of right, continuous and exclusive. (T. 14, §§810, 816; 652 A.2d 90). If possession of land by mistake as to boundary line is open and notorious, hostile nature of claim is established if all other elements of adverse possession present. (T. 14, §810-A).

Duration of Possession.—20 years. (T. 14, §801). No action may be commenced after 40 years. (T. 14, §815).

Easements.—May acquire by adverse use, but owner can prevent by giving public notice. (T. 14, §812).

Disabilities.—Person who is minor, mentally ill, imprisoned or absent from U.S., or one claiming under him, may bring action within ten years after disability removed. (T. 14, §807).

CONVEYANCES:

See topic Deeds.

CURTESY:

Curtesy is abolished. (T. 18-A, §2-113).

As to distributive share of surviving spouse in estate of deceased spouse, see category Estates and Trusts, topic Descent and Distribution.

DEEDS:

Execution.—Must be signed and delivered in order to pass title to real estate. Grantee's full mailing address must be included, but error in or omission thereof will not affect validity or recordability of deed. (T. 33, §§456, 457). Instrument to be recorded must include printed or typed name of each party signing, including person taking acknowledgment. (T. 33, §651-A). Witnesses desirable and usual, but not required by statute. Trusts created under Maine State law are not recognized as entities capable of holding or conveying title to real property in their own names. There is recent legislation that validates certain conveyances to and from trusts by deeming such conveyances to have been made to or from trustees of such trusts and preserving claims for limited time for those adversely affected. (T. 33, §851-A). See topic Real Property for types of estates, see category Family, topics Husband and Wife, and Divorce for circumstances in which spouse must join. Seal not required.

Recording.—To be valid as against any person other than parties thereto, persons claiming under them or those having actual notice thereof, deed for conveyances of estate in fee simple, fee tail or for life, or leases for more than two years or for an indefinite term must be recorded in registry of deeds for county where land lies. (T. 33, §201).

Deed must be duly acknowledged by at least one grantor or by his attorney executing same to be recorded (T. 33, §203); if grantor dies or leaves state without acknowledging or refuses to acknowledge, execution may be proved by subscribing witness to have deed recorded (T. 33, §301). Instrument acknowledged according to Uniform Recognition of Acknowledgments Act accepted. (T. 33, §203).

In all cases, certificate of acknowledgment must be indorsed on deed. (T. 33, §306).

Recording Fees.—See category Documents and Records, topic Records.

Operation and Effect.—Deeds offered for recording must be accompanied by declaration in duplicate signed by parties or authorized representatives under penalties for perjury and indicating taxpayer identification numbers of grantor and grantee, declaring consideration for property transferred. (T. 36, §4641, et seq.). If transfer declared not subject to tax, must state reason therefor. (See T. 36, §4641-C for specific exemptions.) Declaration must include tax map and parcel number, or indicate no map

---

DEEDS . . . *continued*

exists, and evidence of compliance with withholding tax. Certain deeds exempt. (T. 36, §4641-D).

Taxes.—See category Taxation, topic Real Estate Transfer Tax. Exceptions to real estate transfer tax requirement: (1) Conveyances by or to U.S., State of Maine, or any of their instrumentalities, agencies or subdivisions, but only governmental entity exempt (except in case of certain deeds to Department of Transportation from nonprofit land conservation organizations in which case both parties exempt); (2) mortgage or mortgage discharge; (3) partial release of mortgage deed; (4) deed in lieu of foreclosure; (5) deed which, without additional consideration, confirms, corrects, modifies or supplements previously recorded deed; (6) deed dated or acknowledged prior to Oct. 1, 1975 and offered for recording after that date; (7) deed of distribution made pursuant to T. 18-A; (8) deed without actual consideration between husband and wife, or parent and child, and deeds between spouses in divorce proceedings; (9) tax deeds; (10) certain deeds of partition; (11) certain deeds pursuant to mergers; (12) certain deeds between parent corporation and its subsidiary; family corporation and its stockholders; partnership and its partners; or limited liability company and its stockholders; (13) deed pursuant to U.S. Bankruptcy Code; (14) certain deeds to and from trustee of trust; (15) certain deeds to charitable conservation organizations; (16) deed to limited liability company, when grantor or grantee owns interest in limited liability company in same proportion as grantor's or grantee's interest in or ownership of real estate being conveyed. (T. 36, §§4641-C, 4641-D).

Forms.—Statutory short forms adopted. (T. 33, §§761-775).

Forms

Warranty Deed:

A. B. of . . . . . . County, ..., (being unmarried), for consideration paid, grant to C. D. of . . . ., . . . County, ..., with Warranty Covenants, ... the land in . . . ., ... County, Maine.
(description and encumbrances, if any)
E. F., spouse of said grantor, releases all rights in the premises being conveyed.
Witness . . . . hand and seal this . . . . day of . . . . (here add acknowledgment)

Quitclaim Deed With Covenant:

A. B. of . . . ., ... County, ..., (being unmarried) for consideration paid, grant to C. D. of . . . ., ... County, ..., with quitclaim covenant the land in . . . ., ... County, ...
(description and encumbrances, if any)
E. F., spouse of said grantor, releases all rights in the premises being conveyed.
Witness . . . . hand and seal this . . . . day of . . . . (here add acknowledgment)

Quitclaim Deed Without Covenant or Release Deed:

A. B. of . . . ., ... County, ..., (being unmarried) for consideration paid, release to C. D. of . . . ., ... County, ..., the land in . . . ., ... County, ...
(description)
E. F., spouse of said grantor, releases all rights in the premises being conveyed.
Witness . . . . hand and seal this . . . . day of . . . . (here add acknowledgment)

DOWER:

Dower is abolished. (T. 18-A, §2-113).

Election.—See category Estates and Trusts, topic Descent and Distribution.

ESCHEAT:

See topic Absentees, subhead Escheat; categories Business Regulation and Commerce, topic Banks and Banking, subhead Unclaimed Deposits; Estates and Trusts, topic Descent and Distribution, subhead Escheat.

LANDLORD AND TENANT:

Tenant is entitled to exclusive possession in absence of agreement to contrary. (83 Me. 550, 22 A. 469). In written and oral leases of dwelling unit, landlord deemed to warrant dwelling fit for human habitation. If warranty broken, tenant may file complaint against landlord, containing allegations specified by statute, in District or Superior Court. (T. 14, §6021). If court finds allegations true, it may, in addition to other remedies which exist: (1) order landlord to repair unsafe or unhealthful conditions, (2) order rebate by landlord or deduction from amounts tenant owes of rent paid in excess of fair value of use and occupancy for period condition existed, (3) authorize tenant to vacate temporarily without payment of rent to allow repairs, and (4) enter further orders as court deems necessary; court may not award consequential damages. (T. 14, §6021). Written agreement in which tenant accepts specified conditions for reduction in rent or other fair consideration is binding, but any other agreement by tenant to waive foregoing rights is void. (T. 14, §6021).

Landlord cannot force tenant of dwelling unit to waive certain rights granted by statute through rules or provisions in lease agreement. Provisions which absolve landlord from liability for negligence, require tenant to pay landlord's legal fees to enforce rental agreement, require tenant to give lien on property or require tenant to acknowledge fairness of agreement or rules, are unenforceable. Applies to rental agreements entered into or renewed on or after Nov. 1, 1991. (T. 10, §9097-A; T. 14, §6030).

Subletting without authority voids lease at option of landlord. (85 A. 404). Landlord may file petition for protection of rental property or tenants from harm posed by tenant. (T. 14, §6030-A).

Uniform Commercial Code Art. 2A adopted. (T. 11, §2-1101 et seq.).

Kinds of Tenancy.—Maine recognizes tenancies for term of years, periodic tenancies for month to month or year to year and tenancies at will.

Leases.—No estate in lands greater than a tenancy at will can be created unless in writing. (T. 33, §162). Leases for more than two years or for indefinite period must be acknowledged and recorded in district where land lies to be valid against third persons without actual notice. (T. 33, §201).

Security Deposits.—For residential rental unit may not exceed two months rent. (T. 14, §6032). Landlord may not commingle security deposits with assets and must hold deposits in account beyond claims of creditors. (T. 14, §6038). Landlord must return portion of security deposit due with statement of reasons for any portion retained within time, not to exceed 30 days, specified in written lease or within 21 days after termination of tenancy at will or surrender and acceptance of premises (T. 14, §6033); willful retention of security deposit entitles tenant to double amount of withheld deposit plus attorneys' fees and court costs (T. 14, §6034). Landlord may retain security deposit to cover costs of storing and disposing of unclaimed property, nonpayment of rent or nonpayment of utility charges. (T. 14, §6033). Landlord may sell property abandoned by tenant to cover same costs, subject to procedures of T. 14, §6013, and remit balance to State. When landlord's interest in rental unit terminates, must transfer security deposits to successor in interest and notify tenant or return funds to tenant. (T. 14, §§6035, 6038). Landlord has obligation to mitigate damages caused by defaulting tenant. (T. 14, §6010-A). Exemptions for conflicting provisions in federally guaranteed mortgages and owner-occupied buildings of five or less units. (T. 14, §6037).

Landlord must provide tenant with written receipt for each rental payment and each security deposit payment received partially or fully in cash, unless tenancy for dwelling unit in owner-occupied building of five dwelling units or less. (T. 14, §§6022, 6023).

Recording.—Fee of $8 for first page, $2 for each additional page, plus surcharge of $3 per document. (T. 33, §§751, 752). Lease considered recorded for all purposes if memorandum of lease recorded which is executed and acknowledged by one lessor, names all parties to lease, describes property, states date and term and gives any provisions concerning renewals, extensions or options to purchase; need not describe rent. (T. 33, §201).

Rent.—Actions for arrears of rent subject to six-year statute of limitations. (T. 14, §752). Court must deduct from amount of rent due difference between rent and fair value of use and occupancy for period during which landlord fails to remedy condition which renders premises unfit for human habitation if tenant gives written notice of such condition, did not cause condition and rental payments were current when notice given. Rebuttable presumption that rental price is fair value of premises free from condition rendering it unfit for human habitation. (T. 14, §6010). Landlord must mitigate damages upon tenant's default by making reasonable efforts to re-rent. (T. 14, §6010-A). Penalty for late payment of rent for residential unit (more than 15 days past due) limited to 4% of one month's rent and cannot be assessed unless tenant had written notice at lease term commencement. (T. 14, §6028). Can increase rent for residential units only after 30 days' written notice to tenant; cannot waive this requirement. (T. 14, §6015).

Utility may not demand payment from tenant for service to tenant because of landlord's failure to pay for that service and may disconnect service only after affording tenant notice and opportunity to assume payment responsibility. If tenant assumes responsibility and pays for utility services, can deduct amount paid from any rent due landlord. (T. 14, §6024-A; T. 35-A, §706).

Lien.—When lease of land made to erect buildings thereon, such buildings and all interests of lessee are subject to lien and liable to be attached for rent due. If attachment made within six months after rent becomes due, effective against any transfer by lessee. (T. 10, §3451).

Termination of Tenancy.—Tenancies at will must be terminated by 30 days written notice by either party, except seven days written notice may be given by landlord where he can show tenant or invitee has caused intentional and substantial damage to premises, permitted nuisance within premises or violated law regarding tenancy, or where payment of rent is seven or more days in arrears. Seven day notice must indicate specific ground claimed for issuing notice and, where rent arrearage is claimed, must state that payment of full amount due before expiration of notice negates notice. (T. 14, §6002). After three good faith attempts to serve tenant, service of seven day notice can be accomplished by leaving notice at tenant's last and usual place of abode and mailing to tenant's last known address. (T. 14, §6002). Parties may consent to termination on other terms. 30 days notice must be made to expire on rent day unless tenant in arrears. When tenancy terminated, tenant liable to forcible entry and detainer unless has paid, after service of notice, rent that accrued after termination of tenancy. (T. 14, §6002). Tenants holding under lease or contract subject to process of forcible entry and detainer at expiration or forfeiture of term, without notice, if begun within seven days from expiration or forfeiture of term. (T. 14, §6001). Evictions other than by forcible entry and detainer illegal; tenant can recover costs, attorneys fees and greater of actual damages or $250. (T. 14, §6014).

Distress.—No statutory provisions for distress for rent; it has been practically superseded by attachment.

Uniform Residential Landlord and Tenant Act not adopted.

LEASES:

See topic Landlord and Tenant.

PERPETUITIES:

Common law rule against perpetuities applies, except as modified in certain major respects by T. 33, §101.

Employee trusts removed from the operation of the rules against perpetuities and restraints on alienation. (T. 26, §841). See also category Estates and Trusts, topic Trusts.

PERSONAL PROPERTY:

No statutory provision for tenancy by entirety in personalty. Corporate securities held in name of two or more people as joint tenants or with right of survivorship shall be deemed to be held in estate in joint tenancy as at common law. (T. 33, §901).

POWERS OF ATTORNEY:

Attorneys in Fact.—No special formalities of execution required.

Deeds or mortgage of real estate may be executed by attorney in fact acting under power of attorney under seal which should be recorded in county in which land is situated.

Uniform Durable Power of Attorney Act.—Adopted with variations. (T. 18-A, §§5-501 to 5-506).

REAL PROPERTY:

No estate in lands greater than tenancy at will and no trust in lands can be created unless by written instrument except trusts resulting by implication of law. (T. 33, §§162, 851).

Conveyances not in mortgage and devises of land to two or more persons create estates in common, unless otherwise expressly stipulated. Joint tenancy may be created, but intention must be clearly shown. Deeds naming two or more grantees as joint tenants construed as vesting fee simple estate in them with survivorship. Owner may create joint tenancy between himself and one or more other persons by a conveyance to himself and such persons with appropriate language expressing intent. (T. 33, §159). Person seized of land as tenant in tail may bar entail by conveyance in fee. (T. 33, §156). Deed of release or quitclaim conveys grantor's estate. (T. 33, §161).

Tenancies by entirety not recognized. (88 Me. 17, 33 A. 652).

Rule in Shelley's Case abolished. (T. 33, §158).

Foreign Conveyances or Encumbrances.—Conveyance or encumbrance executed and acknowledged in conformity with law of state where executed is valid in Maine; see Uniform Recognition of Acknowledgments Act. (T. 4, §§1011-1019).

Condominiums.—Permitted under Unit Ownership Act. (T. 33, §§560-587).

Uniform Condominium Act adopted, but numerous variations. (T. 33, §§1601-101—1604-118).

Trespass.—New scheme of marking property enacted in 1996. Property may be posted with signs or marked with paint, at intervals no greater than 100 feet and at all vehicular access points. Persons entering posted property without permission are guilty of criminal trespass. (T. 17-A, §§402, 404).

See also topics Curtesy, Deeds, Dower, Landlord and Tenant; categories Civil Actions and Procedure, topic Partition; Debtor and Creditor, topic Homesteads; Family, topic Husband and Wife; Mortgages, topic Mortgages of Real Property.

TAXATION

ADMINISTRATION:

Property taxation is dealt with in T. 36, §§201-1610.

State Tax Assessor has general supervision of administration of assessment and taxation laws. (T. 36, §§201, 301). Taxes on real estate and personal property are assessed and collected by cities and towns independently and property within unorganized territories assessed and collected by State Bureau of Revenue Services and State Tax Assessor respectively. (T. 36, §§302, 703, 709, 709-A, 801, 1602). Taxes on telecommunications personal property owned or leased by telecommunication business assessed and collected by State Tax Assessor and by municipal assessor for persons not a telecommunications business. (T. 36, §457). Municipalities meeting assessment standards promulgated by State Tax Assessor have option of joining other municipalities in primary assessing area. (T. 36, §303). Assessment is by local boards of assessors, or municipal officers or assessors. (T. 36, §§703, 709, 709-A, 1602). State and county taxes are apportioned among cities and towns and share of state and county tax of each city and town is included in assessment of city or town taxes. (T. 36, §§208, 251-52, 383, 507, 709, 714).

Penalties.—Following penalties imposed under Title 36:

Failure to File Return When Due.—If return filed before or within 30 days after taxpayer receives formal demand that return be filed, penalty of $25 or 10% of tax due (whichever greater). If return filed later than 30 days after demand, penalty of 100% of tax due. If return not filed and jeopardy assessment issued, penalty of 100% of tax due. (T. 36, §187-B).

False Return.—If return is materially incorrect due to negligence or intentional disregard of law (without intent to defraud), penalty of $25 or 25% of deficiency (whichever greater). If due to fraud with intent to evade tax, penalty of $75 or 75% of deficiency (whichever greater). (T. 36, §187-B).

Failure to Pay.—Penalty of 1% of unpaid tax (whichever greater) for each month during which failure continues up to maximum of 25% of unpaid tax (whichever greater). For failure to pay assessment for which no further review available, penalty of 25% of tax due (whichever greater), if payment not within ten days of demand for payment. (T. 36, §187-B).

Substantial Understatement.—If return results in underpayment of tax, any portion of which is due to "substantial understatement", (without negligence, intentional disregard of tax laws or fraud), penalty imposed of $5 or 1% of that portion of underpayment (whichever is greater) for each month or fraction of month during which failure to pay that portion of underpayment continues, up to maximum of $25 or 25% (whichever is greater). "Substantial understatement" is defined by statute. (T. 36, §187-B).

Insufficient Funds.—Penalty of $10 or 1% of payment amount (whichever greater).

Electronic Funds Transfers.—Penalty of lesser of 5% of tax due or $5,000 imposed for failure to remit taxes by electronic funds transfer when required to do so by assessor. In addition to particular penalties, State imposes additional interest charge for

each month and standard penalties for all tax delinquencies. Penalties waived or abated under some circumstances. (T. 36, §§186, 187-B).

ALCOHOLIC BEVERAGE TAXES:

Excise Tax on Malt Liquor, Wine and Low-Alcohol Spirits.—Imposed by T. 28-A, §1652.

State Liquor Tax.—Imposed by T. 28-A, §1651.

CIGARETTE AND TOBACCO PRODUCTS TAX:

Cigarette Tax.—Imposed by T. 36, §§4361-4382.

Tobacco Products Tax.—Imposed on tobacco products other than cigarettes by T. 36, §§4401-4407.

ESTATE TAX:

Note.—New estate tax applicable for estate of person whose death occurs after June 30, 1986. (T. 36, §§4061-4079). Old inheritance and estate taxes applied to earlier deaths. (T. 36, §3402).

Generally new estate tax equal to amount of federal estate tax credit for state death taxes. (T. 36, §§4063-4064).

Apportionment Against Inter Vivos Dispositions.—No apportionment statute.

Interstate Co-operation.—Uniform Act on Interstate Arbitration of Death Taxes adopted. (T. 36, §§3911-3924). Uniform Act on Interstate Compromise of Death Taxes adopted. (T. 36, §§3981-3985). Uniform Division of Income for Tax Purposes Act adopted. (T. 36, §§5210-5211).

EXCISE TAXES:

Following are three excise taxes:

Commercial Forestry Excise Tax.—Imposed by T. 36, §§2721-2727.

Mining Excise Tax.—Imposed by T. 36, §§2851-2865. Such tax is in lieu of property tax.

Watercraft Excise Tax.—Imposed by T. 36, §§1501-1506.

FRANCHISE TAX:

Imposed on certain financial institutions (including certain pass-through entities) by T. 36, §5206.

GASOLINE AND SPECIAL FUELS TAXES:

Gasoline Tax.—Imposed by T. 36, §2903.

Inventory tax on internal combustion fuel held by retailers imposed by T. 36, §2916-A, effective Apr. 1, 1989.

Special Fuel Tax.—Imposed by T. 36, §§3201-3219.

GIFT TAX:

None.

INCOME TAX:

T. 36, §§5101-5403 imposes an income tax on individuals, trusts and estates and corporations, and franchise tax on financial institutions.

Tax applies to entire taxable income of resident individuals, taxable income of nonresident individuals derived from sources within state and Maine net income of corporations and financial institutions attributable to their operations within state. Compensation paid by U.S. for service in armed forces of U.S. performed by nonresident does not constitute income derived from sources within state. Taxable income of estates and trusts taxed at rates set for resident individuals. (T. 36, §§5111, 5160).

Taxable income of residents is federal adjusted gross income less deductions and exemptions provided and subject to statutory modifications. (T. 36, §§5121, 5122, 5125, 5126). All resident individuals are entitled to standard deduction tax credit, amount depending on filing status. (T. 36, §5124-A). Resident individuals are allowed personal exemption tax credits for each exemption to which entitled for taxable year for federal tax purposes. Amount subject to annual adjustment. (T. 36, §5126).

Taxes are returned and paid at same time as federal income taxes. Payments are made to State Tax Assessor.

Minimum tax imposed. (T. 36, §5203-A).

Every person with income tax liability of more than $500 for prior or current tax year must pay estimated tax. (T. 36, §§5228-5234).

Corporate rate assessed against Maine net income is 3.5% for income not over $25,000; $875 plus 7.93% of excess over $25,000 for income $25,000 to $75,000; $4,840 plus 8.33% of excess over $75,000 for income $75,000 to $250,000; and $19,417 plus 8.93% of excess over $250,000 for income $250,000 or more. (T. 36, §5200). Individual tax rate dependent upon filing status. (T. 36, §5111).

Corporate Unitary Income Tax.—See category Business Organizations, topic Corporations, subhead Income Tax.

Maine Seed Capital Tax Credit Program.—See category Business Organizations, topic Corporations, subhead Maine Seed Capital Tax Credit Program.

INHERITANCE TAX:

No longer applicable.

MAHOGANY QUAHOG TAX:

Imposed by T. 36, §§4711-4718.

PRODUCE TAXES:

Blueberry Tax.—Imposed by T. 36, §§4301-4318.

Potato Tax.—Imposed by T. 36, §§4601-4606.

See note at head of Digest as to 1998 legislation covered.

See note at head of Digest as to 1998 legislation covered.

See Topical Index in front part of this volume.

PROPERTY TAXES:

Real and Personal Property Taxable.—All real estate and personal property is taxable except as is specifically exempted by law. (T. 36, §§502, 551). Personal estate, for purposes of taxation, includes all tangible goods and chattels wheresoever they are and telecommunications personal property is subject to state, but not local tax. (T. 36, §§457, 601). All property not exempt is subject to tax as of each Apr. 1. (T. 36, §502).

Exemptions from taxation with respect to certain classes of property include public property, property affected with public use, certain pollution control facilities, public obligations, property used for religious, literary, scientific or benevolent and charitable purposes, property of posts of veteran organizations, American National Red Cross, certain fraternal organizations, chambers of commerce or boards of trade, all items of individually owned personal property (with certain exceptions), household furniture, wearing apparel, tools, musical instruments, etc., domestic animals and fowls, agricultural products, certain property of members of the armed forces in active service, war veterans and their widows or blind persons, mines property in interstate transportation held by common carrier, vessels and pleasure boats, vehicles exempt from excise tax, certain farm machinery, pollution control facilities and stock in trade obtained as trade-in. Excise tax on mining of metallic minerals in lieu of property tax. Various statutory restrictions apply. (T. 36, §§652-53, 655-56, 2851-63, 2865-66).

Industrial inventories, stock in trade, agricultural produce and forest products and livestock exempt from municipal property taxation. Stock in trade includes certain unoccupied manufactured homes. (T. 36, §655). Further provision for reimbursement to municipalities of revenue loss resulting from said exemptions. (T. 30, §5056).

Reimbursement.—Taxpayers may claim reimbursement from state for up to 12 years for property taxes paid to local taxing jurisdictions with respect to certain qualified business property first placed in service, or constituting construction in progress, in Maine after Apr. 1, 1995. Reimbursement is not available, or is limited, with respect to certain taxpayers and certain property. Taxpayers seeking reimbursement must obtain assessment information from municipality and file claim form with state tax assessor within 60 days after tax is paid. (T. 36, §§6651-6659).

Assessment.—Real estate is assessed to owner or person in possession thereof on Apr. 1 in place where it is situated. (T. 36, §§502, 553). Real property of unknown owner is assessed as other property, except owner is indicated as "unknown". (T. 36, §557-A). Abuttors receive copy of notice required to run for three consecutive weeks in newspaper of general circulation in county where property is located, describing property and fact of assessment to unknown owner. (T. 36, §557-A). Forest land may be taxed on basis of potential for annual wood production. (T. 36, §§571-584-A). Where value of recreational use lease of land exceeding 100 acres exceeds value of tree growth extractable on sustained basis, land is not considered used for growth of forest products and is removed from taxation applicable thereto. (T. 36, §574-A). Farms and open spaces may be taxed in accordance with current use. (T. 36, §§1101-1118). Personal property within state or owned by residents of state and located without state, except in certain specified cases set forth in statute, is assessed to owner in town where owner resides on Apr. 1 (T. 36, §§602, 603). Machinery and other personal property brought into state after Apr. 1 and prior to Dec. 31 by any person upon whom no personal property tax was assessed on Apr. 1 must be taxed as other personal property in town in which used for first time. (T. 36, §611).

Buildings and mobile homes on leased land or on land not owned by owner of buildings are considered real estate for purposes of taxation and taxed in place where said land is located. (T. 36, §551).

Before making assessment, assessors may give notice, in writing, by mail or other reasonable means directed to last known address to all persons liable to taxation to furnish lists of all estates, real and personal, of which they were possessed on Apr. 1. If notice is given by mail, failure to make such return precludes right to seek abatement and any appeal unless taxpayer shows that taxpayer was unable to make return at time appointed. (T. 36, §706). Failure to answer proper inquiries as to nature, situation and value of taxable property precludes right to appeal. (T. 36, §706).

Property in unorganized territory of State assessed by Bureau of Revenue Services. (T. 36, §§302-303).

Payment.—Time for payment is set by municipality by meeting. (T. 36, §505). Property taxes generally are payable to particular municipality care of tax collector. (T. 36, §§505, 709, 709-A). Municipalities by meeting may provide discount for early payment. (T. 36, §505).

Professional Assessment Firms.—Guidelines to be established by State Tax Assessor. Each firm must employ at least one certified Maine assessor. (T. 36, §330).

Omitted Assessments and Reassessments.—Whenever within three years from last assessment any estates liable to taxation have been omitted from assessment, or any tax is invalid or void for error in assessment, assessors for time being may, by supplement to invoice and valuation and list of assessments, assess such estates their proportion of tax. Such supplemental assessments must be committed to collector for time being with certificate under hands of assessors stating that they were omitted and that powers in previous warrant are extended thereto, and collector has same power, and is under same obligation to collect them, as if they had been contained in original list; and all assessments are valid, even though by such supplemental assessment whole amount exceeds sum to be assessed by more than 5%. (T. 36, §713). Supplemental assessments also permitted for unorganized territories. (T. 36, §1331).

Review of Assessment.—Abatements may be made by assessors within one year from commitment if on assessor's own initiative or within 185 days upon written application stating grounds, or by municipal officers on written application stating grounds after one year but within three years or on their own initiative, but municipal officers cannot grant abatement for error in valuation. (T. 36, §841). Municipal officers, or State Tax Assessor for unorganized territory may, within three years, abate real and personal taxes for persons who cannot pay due to infirmity or poverty or if death, absence or insolvency make tax uncollectable. Municipal officer and State Tax Assessor may extend three year period for abatement. (T. 36, §841). Written application for abatement is deemed denied within 60 days after filing if no notice of decision issues and taxpayer does not consent in writing to extension of time within that period. (T. 36, §842). Appeal of decision of assessor or deemed denial is to local board of assessment review where municipality has adopted that board or to primary assessing area board of review if primary assessing area has adopted that board. (T. 36, §843). Appeal of decision of local board of assessment review is to Superior Court within 30 days, and in case of deemed denial taxpayer may appeal to Superior Court within 30 days. (T. 36, §843). With respect to nonresidential property or properties with equalized value of $1,000,000 or greater (either separately or in aggregate) either party may appeal decision of local board of assessment review or primary assessing area board of assessment review to State Board within 60 days or after application is deemed denied. (T. 36, §843).

Unless municipality or primary assessing area has adopted board of assessment review appeal is to county commissioners within 60 days, except owner of nonresidential property with equalized valuation of $1,000,000 or more (either separately or in aggregate) has option to appeal to State Board. (T. 36, §844). Taxpayer may appeal deemed denial to either Superior Court within 30 days and either party may appeal decision of county commissioners to Superior Court within 30 days. (T. 36, §844). County commissioners may establish County Board of Assessment Review to hear all appeals to county commissioners. (T. 36, §844). Appeals are deemed denied when decision is not made within 60 days of date application is filed and applicant has not agreed to delay. (T. 36, §§843, 844).

Appeals with regard to tree growth or farm and open space tax determinations may be made to State Board of Property Tax Review. (T. 36, §§583, 1118). State Board of Property Tax Review must hold hearing de novo for all appeals of assessments involving nonresidential property with value of $1,000,000 or greater (either separately or in aggregate). (T. 36, §273). State Board of Property Tax Review has its own procedural rules. To appeal assessment, taxpayer must first pay amount of taxes equal to taxes paid in preceding tax year (provided that amount does not exceed current amount due) or amount of taxes in current year not in dispute, whichever is greater. Payment requirements do not apply to property valued at less than $500,000. (T. 36, §§843-844).

Lien.—Real estate is subject to a lien to secure payment of all taxes legally assessed on real estate, and such lien takes precedence over all other claims on said real estate and interest therein and continues until said taxes are paid. (T. 36, §552). Personal property is subject to lien to secure payment of all taxes legally assessed on personal property and, when perfected, such lien takes precedence over all other claims on personal property, except in certain circumstances, and continues until taxes paid or lien otherwise terminated by law. (T. 36, §612).

Sale.—In case the tax on real estate remains unpaid on the first Monday in February next following the assessment, the collector must, at 9 a.m. on that day, sell at public auction, to the highest bidder, so much of such real estate or interest therein as is necessary to pay the tax with interest and all charges. Sale must be at office of collector or at place where last preceding annual municipal meeting was held. (T. 36, §1071).

In case of resident owners, notice of sale may be given by posting notices thereof at least six weeks, and not more than seven weeks, before date of sale. In case of nonresident owners, collector must publish notices in some newspaper published in county where such real estate lies three weeks successively, beginning at least six weeks before date of sale. If no newspaper is published in said county, notices must be published in like manner in the state paper. In all cases, collector must file with municipal clerk a copy of each notice with certificate thereon that he has given notice of intended sale as required by law. Such copy and certificate must be recorded by clerk. (T. 36, §1071).

After land is advertised, and at least ten days before day of sale, collector must notify owner, if resident, or occupant thereof, if any, of time and place of sale by delivering to him in person, or by registered mail with receipt demanded, or leaving at his last and usual place of abode, a written notice signed by him stating time and place of sale and amount of taxes due. In case of nonresident owner, such notice must be sent by mail to the last and usual address, if known to collector, at least ten days before day of sale. (T. 36, §1073). Tax collector must sell at public auction, to highest bidder, so much of real estate as is necessary to pay tax due, together with certain enumerated costs. (T. 36, §1074).

When real estate is so sold for taxes, collector must, within 30 days after sale, lodge with municipal treasurer: (1) A certificate under oath, designating quantity of land sold, names of owners of each parcel, names of purchasers, and what part of amount due on each parcel was tax and what cost and charges; and (2) a deed to the purchasers of each parcel sold. The treasurer must put such deeds on file in his office and after (but not before) the expiration of two years from day of sale deliver each deed to grantee therein or his heirs, provided owner, mortgagee, or any person in possession or other person legally taxable therefor does not within such time redeem estate. (T. 36, §1076).

As to personal property tax liens, T. 11, §§9-501 to 9-507 generally apply, except municipality has no right to propose to retain property in satisfaction of lien, as provided under T. 11, §9-505, and collection procedure is optional and does not affect alternate collection procedures authorized by law. (T. 36, §612).

Redemption.—Any person to whom the right belongs may, at any time within two years from date of sale, redeem any real estate or interest therein sold for taxes by paying into the town treasury, for the purchaser, the full amount certified to be due, with interest on the whole at rate of 8% a year from date of sale. (T. 36, §1078).

Alternative Method of Enforcing Lien.—Officer to whom a tax has been committed for collection, may, after expiration of eight months and within one year of commitment, give to person against whom tax is assessed, or leave at his last and usual place of abode, or send by certified mail, return receipt requested, to his last known address, notice in writing signed by said officer stating amount of tax, describing real estate on which assessed, alleging that lien is claimed and demanding payment of tax within 30 days after service of notice. After expiration of said 30 days and within ten days thereafter said officer must record in registry of deeds of county or registry district where said real estate is situated, certificate signed by him setting forth amount of such tax, description of real estate on which assessed and allegation that

See note at head of Digest as to 1998 legislation covered.

See Topical Index in front part of this volume.

ME – 33

PROPERTY TAXES . . . *continued*

lien is claimed on said real estate, that demand for payment of said tax has been made in accordance with statutes, and that said tax remains unpaid. At time of recording certificate, tax collector must file with municipal treasurer true copy of certificate and mail such copy by certified mail, return receipt requested, to each record holder of mortgage on said real estate, addressed to him at his last known address. (T. 36, §942). Special alternative procedures apply to time-share units. (T. 36, §942-A).

Filing of said certificate in registry of deeds creates tax lien mortgage on real estate described therein to town in which real estate is situated, having priority over all other mortgages, liens, attachments and encumbrances of any nature, and giving town all rights usually incident to mortgagee, except right of possession. If taxes, with interest and costs, are not paid within 18 months after filing of certificate, mortgage is deemed to have been foreclosed and right of redemption to have expired. Municipal treasurer shall notify party named in tax lien mortgage not less than 30 nor more than 45 days prior to foreclosing date by certified mail, return receipt requested, of impending automatic foreclosure. (T. 36, §943). If tax, interest and costs are paid within redemption period, mortgage may be discharged in manner provided for discharge of real estate mortgages. (T. 36, §943).

Special provision is made for redemption by the record owner, or the record holder of a mortgage or his assigns, in cases where the aforementioned notice was not given and also for waiver of automatic foreclosure, as provided above, and instituting an action of foreclosure before right of redemption has expired. (T. 36, §§943-945).

Discharge of tax lien given after redemption right expires terminates title derived by municipality one year after recording of such discharge. (T. 36, §943).

Special statutory provisions apply to the assessment and collection of taxes in plantations, unorganized territories and unincorporated places and on wild lands, and with respect to forest land, farm and open space land, aircraft and mobile homes, watercraft and commercial forestry excise tax. (T. 36, §§571-584-A, 1084-1121, 1181-1331, 1481-1491, 1501-1506, 1601-1610, 2721-2727).

Penalties, set forth in T. 36, §§891-1084, include provision for action and attachment by municipality, interest, and arrest and commitment to jail until payment.

REAL ESTATE TRANSFER TAX:

Grantor and grantee must each pay tax upon privilege of transferring and receiving title to real property at rate of $1.10 for each $500 or fractional part thereof, of value of property transferred. Certain deeds exempt. (T. 36, §4641-A).

RECYCLING ASSISTANCE FEE:

Imposed by T. 36, §4832.

SALES AND USE TAXES:

Sales taxes are imposed by T. 36, §§1751-2113. Rate is 7% of value of liquor and food sold in licensed establishment, 7% of value of rental of living quarters, 10% of value of rental, for period of less than one year, of automobile, 7% of value of prepared food sold in certain establishments licensed for on-premises consumption of liquor and 5.5% of value of all other tangible personal property and taxable services. Value is measured by sale price. Rental of automobile for one year or more taxed at 5.5% of sum of (a) total monthly lease payment multiplied by number of payments, (b) amount of equity involved in any trade-in, and (c) value of any cash down payment. (T. 36, §1811). Tax is added to sales price.

Sales Subject to Tax.—All retail sales of tangible personal property, including electricity and certain non-custom computer programs and taxable services. Taxable services are defined as rental of living quarters, sleeping or housekeeping accommodations in hotels, rooming houses, tourist or trailer camps; telephone or telegraph service; extended cable television service; fabrication services; rental of video tapes and video equipment; and rental or lease of automobile. (T. 36, §§1811, 1752 [17-A]). Also, casual sales of certain motor vehicles, watercraft and aircraft. (T. 36, §1764). Sales tax is imposed on only net sales price of farm tractor, motor vehicle, aircraft, boat, chain saw, self-propelled vehicles used to harvest lumber, livestock trailer, camper trailer or special mobile equipment where sale involves trade-in. (T. 36, §1765). Exemptions include: Tax on "use" of telecommunications equipment (including lease or rentals). (T. 36, §1752[18-B]).

Exemptions.—Sales that Maine is prohibited from taxing by Maine or U.S. Constitution; sales to municipal, state or federal governments or their agencies, if wholly owned by them; food products considered grocery staples (including milk, meat, fruit and others but not including, for example, malt or vinous liquors, soft drinks, dietary supplements or snack food); ships' stores; medicines for humans sold on prescription; prosthetic devices, including certain hearing aids and eyeglasses, among others; certain school, hospital congregate care facility and nursing home meals; seed, feed, hormones, fertilizer, pesticides, insecticides, fungicides, weed killers, defoliants, litter, and medicines used in agricultural production; bait of commercial fisherman; fuel when used for domestic purposes including coal, oil, gas and first 750 kilowatts per month of electricity; certain motor fuels; sales of water for domestic purposes; sales of all fuel used in burning blueberry fields; sales of fuel and electricity used at manufacturing facility; sale of returnable containers when sold with contents; containers, labels, etc., when sold for use in packing property to be sold; publications issued at average intervals not exceeding three months; sales of automobiles used in driver education programs; sales of automobiles to amputee veterans; certain sales of motor vehicles and watercraft to nonresidents; sales to certain research centers, schools and churches; rental charges by certain camps, schools, hospitals and nursing homes; certain rentals for continuous period of more than 28 days; sales to community mental health facilities; sales to incorporated private nonprofit residential child care institutions; sales of funeral services; sales to nonprofit youth organizations whose primary purpose is to provide athletic instruction in nonresidential setting, or to councils and local units of incorporated nonprofit national scouting organizations; certain sales of tangible personal property, to construction contractors, which are to be physically

incorporated in and become permanent part of real property for sale to any organization or government agency provided exemption under T. 36, §1760; sales to incorporated hospitals, incorporated nonprofit nursing homes and boarding care facilities licensed by Maine Department of Human Services, and nonprofit certified home health care agencies; sales to local branches of incorporated international nonprofit charitable organizations that provide medical supplies and equipment to persons on free loan basis; sales to community action agencies; sales to incorporated nonprofit organizations where sole purpose is to fulfill wishes of children with life-threatening diseases when family or guardian is financially unable to do so; sales to emergency shelter and feeding organizations; sales of any water or air pollution control facility; resale of motor vehicles, special mobile equipment, livestock trailers or aircraft or isolated transaction involving sale of same except farm tractors and lumber harvesting vehicles or loaders by owner to corporation, partnership, LLC or LLP in which seller is majority owner; sale of replacement or repair parts of aircraft, used by scheduled airline, based in state, that is regularly used in service regulated by C.A.B. or by 49 U.S.C. §1371; machinery and equipment for use by purchaser directly and primarily in production of tangible personal property intended to be sold or leased for final use or consumption; machinery and equipment used by purchaser directly and exclusively in research and development in experimental or laboratory sense; sales of machinery, equipment, instruments and supplies for use by purchaser directly and primarily in biotechnology applications; medical equipment and supplies used by diabetics; certain sales through coin operated vending machines; sales of tangible personal property for care of seeing eye dogs; sales of used mobile and modular homes; sales of new mobile and modular homes, exemption limited to 50% of value; sales of property, including automobiles and watercraft, purchased and used by present owner outside state, provided certain conditions are satisfied; residential facilities for medical patients and their families; sales to incorporated, nonprofit volunteer search and rescue organizations; sales of tangible personal property and taxable services by schools and by school-sponsored organizations where profits benefit those schools or organizations or are used for charitable purpose; sales of tangible personal property to incorporated nonprofit monasteries and convents for use in their operation and maintenance; sales to incorporated nonprofit organizations whose primary purpose is to provide support systems for single-parent families; sales to local branches of incorporated nonprofit organizations whose purpose is to construct low-cost housing for low-income people; sales to incorporated nonprofit institutions conducting research solely for Maine Science and Technology Commission and receiving funding under T. 5, c. 385; sales to incorporated nonprofit organizations whose sole purpose is to create and maintain registry of Vietnam veterans; sales to incorporated nonprofit organizations whose primary purposes are to promote public understanding of hearing impairment and to assist hearing-impaired persons by dissemination of information, and referral and coordination of community resources for hearing-impaired; sales to credit unions organized under Maine law; sales to nonprofit ambulance corps and fire departments; sales to regional planning commissions and councils of government; sales of certain instrumentalities of interstate or foreign commerce; sales to incorporated nonprofit historical societies and museums; sales to licensed, incorporated nonprofit nursing schools and day-care centers; sales to certain church affiliated nonprofit residential homes for adults; sales to any nonprofit free public lending library; sales to incorporated nonprofit veterans' memorial cemetery associations; certain sales of railroad track materials; sales of items purchased with federal food stamps; sales to incorporated nonprofit hospice organizations which provide program for physical and emotional needs of terminally ill patients; sales of self-help literature related to alcoholism or alcoholics anonymous groups; sales of tangible personal property to be physically incorporated in and become part of portable classroom for lease to certain schools; sales to certain educational organizations which provide educational programs designed to teach young people how to make decisions about drugs, alcohol and interpersonal relationships; sales to incorporated nonprofit animal shelters of tangible personal property used in maintenance or operation of those shelters; sales to nonprofit organizations for development of housing for low income people; sales of tree seedlings for use in commercial forestry; sales of tangible personal property, other than fuel or electricity, that becomes ingredient or component part of, or that is consumed or destroyed or loses its identity directly and primarily in either production of tangible personal property for later sale or lease, other than lease for use in this state, or production of tangible personal property pursuant to contract with U.S. Government or agency thereof; sales of meals or lodging to employees at their place of employment as credit towards wages; sales to certain nonprofit eye banks; sales of organic bedding materials for farm animals and hay. (T. 36, §1760). Sales of certain depreciable machinery and equipment used directly and primarily in commercial agricultural, commercial aquaculture or commercial fishing. (T. 36, §2013).

When and by Whom Payable.—Tax is levied on consumer. When added to sale price, tax is debt of purchaser to retailer, recoverable in same manner as purchase price. (T. 36, §1753). Tax collected by retailer is held in trust by retailer for State of Maine and is personal debt of retailer to State. (T. 36, §1953). Retailer files report of previous month's sales with State Tax Assessor on or before 15th of each month or with Assessor's permission at other intervals. Retailer filing report and having tax liability in excess of $250,000 for prior calendar year required to pay assessor amount equaling 80% of tax liability for corresponding month in prior year or 80% of retailer's liability for actual month. Payments credited against tax due with monthly reports. (T. 36, §1951-A). Tax is due and payable at time of sale. (T. 36, §1952). Tax on sale or use of any vehicle is paid at time and place of registration, except where dealer has collected tax in full. (T. 36, §1952-A).

Use Tax.—Tax at same rate as sales tax on storage, use or other consumption in this state of tangible personal property or taxable services purchased at retail sale. Person so storing, etc., is liable for tax until paid or until he has taken receipt from seller duly authorized by Assessor showing seller has collected sales or use tax, in which case seller is liable therefor. (T. 36, §§1861-1862).

SARDINE TAX:

Imposed by T. 36, §§4692-A-4699-A.

See note at head of Digest as to 1998 legislation covered.

See Topical Index in front part of this volume.

STAMP TAX:

None.

UNEMPLOYMENT COMPENSATION TAX:

Unemployment compensation tax, termed "contributions," is imposed on every employer who or which, during current or preceding calendar year, has paid wages of $1,500 or more or has had in employment one or more individuals for some portion of day in each of 20 different weeks. Standard rate of tax is 5.4% of wages paid by him, but rate may be varied in accordance with experience record of employer. There is no tax on employees and employers may not deduct any part of their own "contributions" from wages of employees. Returns must be made and tax shown thereby paid quarterly to State Bureau of Employment Security. Employers must also pay additional amount of 4/10 of 1% of wages paid by employer with respect to employment. (T. 26, §§1043, 1221).

UNIFORM FEDERAL LIEN REGISTRATION ACT:

Adopted. (T. 33, §§1901-1907).

TRANSPORTATION

MOTOR VEHICLES:

See T. 29-A.

Secretary of State, State House Station 29, Augusta, ME 04333, has general supervision of motor vehicle laws and regulations.

Vehicle license required annually. Number plates must be displayed front and rear. (T. 29-A, §452). Manufacturer or dealer selling motor vehicle may attach to rear plate holder temporary plates good for 14 days or if purchaser is nonresident member of armed services, for 20 days. (T. 29-A, §462). Fuel use identification decals required on vehicles of specified size and use. (T. 29-A, §525).

Sales.—Maximum finance charge on consumer credit sale of motor vehicle sold after Jan. 1, 1994 is 18% per annum. (T. 9-A, §2-201[9-A]). Disclosure rules relative to manufacturer's suggested retail price, transportation charges and any charge for extra services or equipment not included in manufacturer's retail price. (T. 29-A, §953; T. 10, §§1191-1193). Business practices of motor vehicle manufacturers, distributors and dealers regulated. (T. 10, §§1171-1186). Business practices between manufacturer and consumer are governed, in part, by "lemon law". (T. 10, §§1161-1169). Warranty and disclosure of information (e.g., "substantial collision damage") required in used car sales. (T. 10, §§1471-1478). Warranty contents and disclosure of information specified for sale or transfer of used all-terrain vehicles. (T. 12, §7855).

Titles.—Certificate of title required at first registration and every change of registration, except for vehicles with model year prior to 1984. (T. 29-A, §§651-652). Certificate to show: Date issued, owner's name and address, lien holders, title number and description of vehicle. (T. 29-A, §658).

Operator's License.—Effective July 1, 1993, operator's license issued to persons under 65 years of age expires on sixth birthday following date of issuance; $27 ($38 commercial license) fee required. Operator's license issued to person 65 years of age or older expires on fourth birthday following date of issuance; $18 fee required ($25 commercial license). (T. 29-A, §1406). Persons 15 years of age or older may apply for instruction permit except that persons under 18 must complete driver education course. Instruction permit entitles driver to drive motor vehicle for 18 months when accompanied by licensed driver at least 20 years of age who has held valid drivers license for two consecutive years. Persons under 21 cannot apply for license until three months have passed since issuance of instruction permit and person has completed minimum of 35 hours of driving, including five hours of night driving. (T. 29-A, §1304). Persons under 16 years of age not eligible for operator's license, but may apply for special restricted license. (T. 29-A, §1251). See catchline Special Restricted License, infra. Persons under age of 18 may acquire operator's license only upon successful completion of driver education course and examination. (T. 29-A, §1351). Persons of age 17 or over may acquire license on completion of written examination and physical examination demonstrating ability to operate vehicle. (T. 29-A, §1301). At time operator first renews license after attaining age of 40 years, must take vision test. Operator must thereafter take vision test every second renewal until reaching 62. After reaching 62, operator must take vision test upon each renewal. (T. 29-A, §1303). Within 30 days of establishing Maine residency, new resident must apply for Maine license. (T. 29-A, §110). Operators license must be specifically endorsed to permit operation of motorcycles. (T. 29-A, §1254). Reexamination of accident-prone, incompetent or unqualified drivers may be required. (T. 29-A, §§1308-1309). Members of U.S. armed forces on active duty, if otherwise qualified, may without payment of fee acquire license which remains valid until 30 days after discharge or release. (T. 29-A, §1255).

Special Restricted License.—Persons 15 years of age who complete driver education course may apply for special restrictive license for educational or employment need. (T. 29-A, §1256).

Provisional License.—Original driver's license issued to new applicant 21 years of age or older is provisional license for one year period. If person convicted of motor vehicle violation during provisional license period, mandatory suspension ranging from 60 to 120 days (depending upon whether it is first, second or third offense) shall be imposed. (T. 29-A, §2471). License issued to applicant under age of 21 is provisional license for period of two years following date of issue or until licensee attains age of 21 whichever is later. If person convicted of motor vehicle violation during first year of juvenile provisional license issued before Aug. 1, 1998, or within two years of license issued after July 31, 1998, mandatory suspension ranging from 60 to 120 days as above. Juvenile provisional licensee who operates vehicle with any amount of alcohol in blood is subject to mandatory one year suspension for first offense and two year suspension for second offense. Additional 180-day mandatory suspension if passenger was under 21. Licensee must submit to chemical test if probable cause to believe person has operated motor vehicle with any amount of alcohol in blood.

Failure to submit to such test carries mandatory 18 month suspension for first refusal and 30 month suspension for second and each subsequent refusal. (T. 29-A, §2472). Additional 180-day mandatory suspension applies if passenger was under 21. (T. 29-A, §§2472, 2521).

Liens.—Security interests in motor vehicles are listed on certificate of title as well as on separate certificate of lien. (T. 29-A, §701).

Identification Marks.—Unlawful knowingly to deal with, conceal or possess motor vehicle from which serial number of other identification has been removed or altered to conceal or misrepresent identity of vehicle. (T. 29-A, §2105). Name of owner or lessee of truck tractors must be displayed thereon in letters not less than 2½" in height. (T. 29-A, §1951).

Operation Prohibited.—By person under age of 21 with any amount of alcohol in blood or whose license has been suspended or revoked. (T. 29-A, §2472).

Size and Weight Limits.—Regulated by T. 29-A passim.

Equipment Required.—Regulated by T. 29-A passim. Child safety seat required for children under four. Seatbelts required for persons under 18. (T. 29-A, §2081).

Lights Required.—Regulated by T. 29-A, §§1904-1909, 2067). Motorcycles and motor driven cycles (moped) required to have lighted headlamp when in motion. (T. 29-A, §2062).

Inspection at official inspection stations required annually and vehicle must carry official inspection sticker. Not applicable to vehicles owned and registered in another state, certain vehicles in transit, farm tractors, certain farm trucks, certain antique motor vehicles and certain commercial trailers and semitrailers. (T. 29-A, §§1751-1770).

Signals for turning, stopping, or decrease of speed given by signal light, mechanical device or hand: (1) Left turn, hand and arm extended horizontally; (2) right turn, hand and arm extended upward; (3) stop or decrease speed, hand and arm extended downward. (T. 29-A, §2071).

Parking.—Motor vehicle must not be parked on travelled portion of any public way when it is practicable to park or leave such vehicle off such way. Vehicle must not be parked on public way, unless at least ten feet on the main traveled portion opposite such vehicle is left for free passage, and operator of any approaching vehicle has clear view of way for 300 feet beyond parked vehicle before approaching within 200 feet of such vehicle. Vehicle must not be parked on specific portions of public way that are included in limited access highway. (T. 29-A, §2068). Vehicle parked so as to interfere with snow removal or normal movement of traffic may be towed away at owner's expense. (T. 29-A, §2069).

Abandoned vehicles are regulated by T. 29-A, §§1851-1860. Vehicles considered abandoned if owner or lien holder fails to retrieve vehicle and pay all reasonable charges for towing, storage and authorized repair within 14 days of notification by mail or publication. Ownership of vehicle may pass to person on whose property abandoned vehicle is located. (T. 29-A, §1856). Vehicle abandonment on public way is traffic infraction. (T. 29-A, §1858). Vehicle abandonment on island is Class E crime. (T. 29-A, §1860).

Accidents.—Driver of vehicle involved in accident resulting in personal injury or property damage in apparent amount of $500 or more must immediately give notice to state police officer, nearest state police office, sheriff's office, deputy sheriff, office of municipal police department, or municipal police officer. Failure to comply with reporting requirements is grounds for suspension of license and is Class E crime. (T. 29-A, §2251).

Owner's Liability.—No statutory provision, but general rule is that liability of owner must be based on agency or some retention of right of control of automobile. (See definition of owner in T. 29-A, §101.)

Guests.—There is no statute restricting liability for injury to gratuitous guest.

Proof of Financial Responsibility.—Every operator or owner of vehicle except governmental vehicles, dealer vehicles and registered vehicles for hire (T. 29-A, §1601) must maintain insurance or proof of financial responsibility in amount of $50,000 for bodily injury or death to any one person, $100,000 for bodily injury or death to two or more persons in one accident, $25,000 for injury to or destruction of property in one accident and $1,000 per person for medical payments, and must produce evidence of same upon demand to law enforcement officer (T. 29-A, §§1601-1605-A). Law enforcement officers required to demand proof of insurance or financial responsibility from persons stopped for moving violations or involved in accidents. Violation for failure to provide proof of financial responsibility to law enforcement officer dismissed if violator provides proof of insurance or financial responsibility in effect at time of violation prior to date for filing answer to complaint. Violation punishable by fine not less than $100 nor more than $500 and suspension of operator license and motor vehicle registration. (T. 29-A, §1601). Proof of financial responsibility must be required by Secretary of State of any person convicted of violating financial responsibility maintenance requirements. (T. 29-A, §1601[7-A]). Proof may be furnished by: (a) Filing with Secretary of State certificate of insurance company or surety company qualified to do business in this state that it has issued motor vehicle policy or bond carrying coverages as above stated; (b) deposit of money or securities in like amount; (c) in case of corporation, satisfying Secretary of State as to financial responsibility. (T. 29-A, §1605). Secretary of State may waive requirement of filing such proof at any time after three years from date of request for compliance. (T. 29-A, §1602). These provisions apply to nonresidents as well as residents and to accidents in other states by Maine residents. (T. 29-A, §1609). Operating license or registration of persons with certain previous convictions will be suspended until financial responsibility requirements are met. (T. 29-A, §1603).

Insurance.—Compulsory for registration. (T. 29-A, §402). See subhead Proof of Financial Responsibility, supra.

Foreign vehicles, duly licensed in home state, are exempt from Maine license requirements, provided that no vehicle operated commercially at site in Maine or used in intrastate transport of persons, merchandise or materials may be exempt without

MOTOR VEHICLES . . . *continued*

written reciprocity agreement. (T. 29-A, §109). Nonresident-owned semitrailers, drawn by Maine registered power units, are allowed in intrastate commerce without Maine registration or reciprocity agreement. (T. 29-A, §109). Reciprocal and apportioned registrations authorized. (T. 29-A, §157). (Repealed.) Within 30 days of establishing Maine residency, new resident must apply for Maine registration. (T. 29-A, §351).

Motor trucks or trailers traveling only in interstate commerce and owned in a state wherein an excise tax shall have been paid on said vehicle, which state grants to Maine-owned trucks or trailers an exemption, are exempt from excise taxes levied by this state. (T. 36, §1483).

International Registration Plan.—Maine is member of International Registration Plan. (T. 29-A, §§531-532).

Driver License Compact.—Maine is party state to Driver License Compact. (T. 29-A, §§1451-1471).

Nonresident Operator.—Same reciprocal provision as apply to foreign vehicles.

Action against nonresident arising out of operation of vehicle or aircraft in state may be commenced by service of process on Secretary of State. Notice of such service and copy of process must be sent to defendant by registered mail. (T. 29-A, §108).

Direct Actions.—No provision for direct actions against insurer.

Motor Vehicle Carriers.—Motor vehicles carrying passengers for hire or transporting freight, merchandise or household goods for hire within State must obtain operating authority license from Secretary of State. Vehicles used primarily for transportation of passengers for hire need not obtain separate license as freight or merchandise carrier. $25 fee must accompany permit application. (T. 29-A, §552). Motor vehicles used for conveyance of passengers and interchangeably for conveyance of passengers and property shall pay $23 fee. Certain combination vehicles must obtain general commodity permits from Secretary of State. (T. 29-A, §2354). Motor vehicles transporting freight, merchandise or household goods must also display identification device prescribed by Secretary of State. Annual fee for such device, $8. (T. 29-A, §553). Motor vehicles required to be registered for rent, lease or livery must obtain insurance or indemnity bond, or provide evidence of self-insurance. Persons violating these provisions guilty of Class E crime. (T. 29-A, §1612). Certain motor vehicles transporting freight or merchandise for hire are exempt from permit and vehicle identification requirements. (T. 29-A, §556). Transportation of hazardous materials is regulated. (T. 25, §§2102-A—2106-A; T. 29-A, §2076). Operating vehicle in excess of its registered weight is Class E crime, penalty imposed. (T. 29-A, §2356).

Motor Vehicle Taxes.—Sales and use tax, if applicable, and local excise tax must be paid prior to registration of vehicle. (T. 29-A, §409; T. 36, §1486).

Registration Fees.—Regulated by T. 29-A, §501.

Gasoline Tax.—See category Taxation, topic Gasoline and Special Fuels Taxes.

Lemon Law.—See category Business Regulation and Commerce, topic Consumer Protection, subhead Warranties on New Motor Vehicles.

COMMERCIAL CODE FORMS

See also categories Business Regulation and Commerce, topic Commercial Code; Mortgages, topic Chattel Mortgages.

Financing Statement.—Form UCC-1:

This FINANCING STATEMENT is presented to a filing officer for filing pursuant to the Uniform Commercial Code:	3 Maturity date (if any):
1 Debtor(s) (Last Name First) and address(es) 2 Secured Party(ies) and address(es)	For Filing Officer (Date, Time, Number, and Filing Office)

4 This financing statement covers the following types (or items) of property:

ASSIGNEE OF SECURED PARTY

Name

Address

Check ☐ if covered: ☐ Proceeds of Collateral are also covered ☐ Products of Collateral are also covered No. of additional Sheets presented:

Filed with: . . . .

Date . . . .

By . . . .
                                        Signature(s) of Debtor(s)

Filing Officer Copy—Alphabetical

Statement of Continuation, Partial Release or Assignment.—Form UCC—3:

This STATEMENT is presented to a filing officer for filing pursuant to the Uniform Commercial Code.	3 Maturity date (if any):
1 Debtor(s) (Last Name First) and address(es) 2 Secured Party(ies) and address(es)	For Filing Officer (Date, Time, Number, and Filing Office)

This statement refers to original Financing Statement No. . . . .
Date Filed . . . . , 19. . . .

A. Continuation . . . . .☐	B. Partial Release . . . .☐	C. Assignment . . . .☐	D. Other: . . . .☐
The original financing statement between the foregoing Debtor and Secured Party, bearing the file number shown above, is still effective.	From the collateral described in the financing statement bearing the file number shown above, the Secured Party releases the following:	The Secured Party certifies that the Secured Party has assigned to the Assignee whose name and address is shown below, Secured Party's rights under the financing statement bearing the file number shown above in the following property:	

Dated: . . . . , 19. . . .   By: . . . .
                                                 (Signature(s) of Secured Party(ies)

Filing Officer Copy—Alphabetical

See note at head of Digest as to 1998 legislation covered.

See Topical Index in front part of this volume.

MARYLAND LAW DIGEST REVISER

Venable, Baetjer and Howard, LLP
(A Limited Liability Partnership Including Professional Corporations)
1800 Mercantile Bank & Trust Building
Two Hopkins Plaza
Baltimore, Maryland 21201-2978

Telephone: 410-244-7400

Fax: 410-244-7742

Email: info@venable.com.

Internet: www.venable.com.

Reviser Profile

History: The firm was founded in 1900 by Richard M. Venable, a law school professor, civic leader and distinguished lawyer, and by two of his former pupils, Edwin G. Baetjer and Charles McHenry Howard. After a half century of gradual internal growth, the firm made its first acquisition in 1951 with the addition to its partnership ranks of H. Vernon Eney, one of Maryland's most outstanding lawyers. A firm of tax practitioners headed by Jacques T. Schlenger was acquired in 1963, and a firm of labor law specialists headed by A. Samuel Cook was added in 1970.

In 1981 an office was opened in Washington, D.C. by the current chairman and senior partner, Benjamin R. Civiletti, former Attorney General of the United States, and the firm now operates offices in McLean, Virginia; and Rockville and Towson, Maryland. The Washington office is known as Venable, Baetjer, Howard & Civiletti. As of September 30, 1997, the firm had 264 lawyers representing over 110 colleges and 45 different law schools.

Areas of Practice: Venable, Baetjer and Howard, LLP offers a full range of legal services in the fields of Corporate, Banking and Business Law; Securities Regulation; Municipal Financing; Bankruptcy and Creditors' Rights; Intellectual Property; Copyright and Computer Law; Labor and Employee Relations; Litigation; Environmental and Energy Law; Health Care and Hospital Law; Real Estate; Estates and Trusts; Franchise Law; Electronic Marketing and Distribution; Communications; Federal Administrative Law; Taxation; Antitrust, Products Liability and Trade Regulation; Publishing Law; Immigration; Patents; Copyrights; and Government Contracts. The firm is organized into three separate divisions designated as Business, Government and Labor-Litigation, with subdivisions of specialty within each division.

Client Base: Venable's clients rely on the experience and good judgment of our lawyers for assistance in achieving solid and practical business solutions. We represent large financial, manufacturing, transportation, mass media, and high technology companies throughout the Washington-Baltimore area and nationwide. We also counsel small businesses, nonprofit organizations, charitable groups, and individuals.

Firm Activities: The firm encourages its partners and associates to become involved in bar association activities and other pursuits devoted to the improvement of the administration of justice as well as civic and *pro bono publico* work. Five partners have served as presidents of the Maryland State Bar Association and one as president of the Virginia Bar Association. Many of the partners and associates serve on the boards of educational, religious and eleemosynary institutions.

The firm is a member of the "5% club", a group of businesses and professional enterprises in the Baltimore and Washington areas pledged annually to contribute to charities at least 5% of their previous year's net income. Over the years, the firm has lent significant support to the two local law schools; it has endowed two lecture series at the University of Maryland School of Law, one in memory of Harry N. Baetjer and the other in memory of Stuart H. Rome, both deceased partners, and the moot courtroom at the University of Baltimore School of Law has been given in memory of the late H. Vernon Eney.

Significant Distinctions: In addition to Mr. Civiletti's service as Attorney General of the United States, other partners and associates over the years have devoted themselves to important public service: John Marshall Butler and Paul S. Sarbanes were elected to the United States Senate, the latter having previously served in the House of Representatives; Francis D. Murnaghan, Jr., was appointed to the United States Court of Appeals for the Fourth Circuit; J. Frederick Motz and Benson Everett Legg were named to the U.S. District Court for the District of Maryland; William D. Quarles to the Circuit Court for Baltimore City and Joseph H.H. Kaplan to the Circuit Court for Baltimore City; Susan H. Gauvey was named U.S. Magistrate Judge to the District for the District of Maryland; Richard W. Emory and Paul F. Strain have served as Deputy Attorney General of Maryland, and numerous attorneys in the firm have served as Assistant Attorneys General and on the staff of the United States Attorney for the District of Maryland.

Venable, Baetjer and Howard LLP

(A Limited Liability Partnership Including Professional Corporations)

1800 Mercantile Bank & Trust Building

Two Hopkins Plaza

Baltimore, Maryland 21201-2978

Telephone : 410-244-7400

Fax : 410-244-7742

Email : info@venable.com

Internet : www.venable.com

Reviser Profile

MARYLAND LAW DIGEST

(The following is a list of all Categories and Topics, including cross-references, covered in this Digest.)

MARYLAND LAW DIGEST

Revised for 1999 edition by

VENABLE, BAETJER and HOWARD, LLP, of the Baltimore Bar.

(References to numbered articles, unless otherwise indicated, are to Michie's Code, 1957 Edition. Beginning at First Extraordinary Session in 1973, Maryland General Assembly has proceeded to recodify state law into separate subject matter codes. As of close of 1994 legislative session, there had been enacted following separate codes: Agriculture, Business Occupations and Professions, Business Regulations, Commercial Law, Constitutions, Corporations and Associations, Courts and Judicial Proceedings, Education, Environment, Estates and Trusts, Family Law, Financial Institutions, Health-General, Health Occupations, Insurance (eff. Oct. 1, 1997), Labor and Employment, Natural Resources, Public Utility Companies, Real Property, State Finance and Procurement, State Government, State Personnel and Pensions, Tax-General, Tax-Property and Transportation. These codes are cited herein as "agric. art.," "bus. occ. art.," "bus. reg. art.," "comm. law art.," "const. art.," "corps. art.," "courts art.," "ed. art.," "env. art.," "est. & tr. art.," "fam. law art.," "fin. inst. art.," "health-gen. art.," "health occ. art.," "ins. art.," "lab. emp. art.," "nat. res. art.," "pub. util. comp. art.," "real prop. art.," "state fin. and proc. art.", "st. gov't art.," "st. pers. and pens. art.," "tax-gen. art.", "tax-prop. art." and "trans. art." They are being published by Michie Co. as separate volumes, superseding 1957 Edition of Annotated Code of Maryland. "R. P." indicates Maryland Rules of Procedure (officially cited "Md. Rules"). [See category Civil Actions and Procedure, topic Practice herein.] "Comar" indicates Code of Maryland Regulations. R. Prof. Con. indicates Rules of Professional Conduct as adopted by Court of Appeals. Session laws are cited by year and chapter number. Parallel citations to Atlantic Reporter begin with 64 Md.)

Note: This revision covers all legislation signed by the Governor through July 1, 1998.

INTRODUCTION

GOVERNMENT AND LEGAL SYSTEM:

The State of Maryland is a constituent state of the United States of America. For further discussion of the U.S. federal system, see Introduction to the Federal Government of the United States at the beginning of this volume. A great many laws are promulgated by the federal government of the United States and are not reflected in the topics below. See the Introduction to this volume for references to the federal law topics covered.

Like all but one of the United States, Maryland has a common law legal system, with roots in English common law. For information on the courts and legislature of Maryland, see category Courts and Legislature.

HOLIDAYS:

Legal holidays are Jan. 1, Jan. 15 (unless U.S. Congress designates another day for observance of Martin Luther King, Jr.'s Birthday), Feb. 12, 3d Mon. in Feb., Mar. 25, Good Friday, May 30, July 4, 1st Mon. in Sept., Sept. 12, Oct. 12, statewide general election days, Nov. 11, 4th Thurs. in Nov., Dec. 25, special days appointed by Governor or President. (art. 1, §27). Banking institutions may elect to remain open for business on Feb. 12, Mar. 25, Sept. 12, election days or specially proclaimed holidays. If state and federal governments observe legal holidays on different dates, bank may observe either or both. (fin. inst. art. §5-705).

Banks may elect to remain closed on some or all Sats. (fin. inst. art. §5-706).

Holiday Falling on Saturday.—For state employees, if holiday falls on Sat., preceding Fri. is holiday. (art. 89, §28).

Holiday Falling on Sunday.—If holiday falls on Sun., following Mon. is holiday. (art. 1, §27).

Legality of Transactions on Saturdays, Sundays and Holidays.—Uniform Commercial Code governs effect of holiday on commercial paper. (comm. law art. tits. 3 and 4). Acts done on holidays are not void. (85 Md. 547, 37 A. 222). Post-1967 contracts made on Sun. in Wicomico County are enforceable. (art. 27, §499). As to pre-1967 Sun. contracts, see 253 Md. 451, 253 A.2d 353.

For effect of holiday on computation of time, see category Civil Actions and Procedure, topic Pleading, subhead Time.

OFFICE HOURS AND TIME ZONE:

Maryland is in the Eastern (GMT −05:00) time zone. Office hours are generally from 9 a.m. to 5 p.m.

BUSINESS ORGANIZATIONS

AGENCY:

Common law rules apply to relation of principal and agent in absence of legislation.

For requirement that certificate be filed by agent or other person doing business under name other than his own, see category Intellectual Property, topic Trademarks and Tradenames.

ASSOCIATIONS:

Formation.—Association is formed by articles of association, which is private compact between parties.

Rights and Powers.—Substantially same as those of corporation.

Liabilities.—Substantially same as those of corporation. (177 Md. 333, 9 A.2d 755). Money judgment is enforceable only against assets of association, not against assets of individual members. (courts art. §§11-105).

Professional Associations.—See topic Corporations, subhead Professional Corporations.

Actions.—Unincorporated association or joint stock company having recognized group name may sue or be sued in such name in action affecting common property, rights and liabilities. No such action abates because of change in membership or dissolution. (courts art. §6-406). Creditor of person engaged in mercantile, trading, or manufacturing business as agent or doing business or trading under any designation, title, or name other than person's own name who fails to file certificate required under §1-406 of corp. & assoc. article, may bring action against person or name, title, or designation under which business is conducted and service on person shall be valid. (courts art. §6-406.1). Associations and joint stock companies are sued and, and process is

served on them, under statutes relating to corporations. Judgment is enforceable only against assets of association, not against assets of individual member or shareholder. (courts art. §11-105). See topic Corporations; category Civil Actions and Procedure, topics Process, Venue.

Dissolution.—No special provision.

Real Estate Investment Trusts.—See topic Joint Stock Companies.

Limited Liability Companies.—See topic Corporations.

CORPORATIONS:

Revision Commissions which undertook revision of Md. Corporation Law, subsequently enacted in 1951 and 1967, considered Model Business Corporation Act as proposed by Committee on Corporate Laws of Section of Corporation, Banking and Business Law of American Bar Association in 1950 and adopted (albeit in every instance with changes) a few details suggested by that Model Act; Md. General Corporation Law is, however, generally and substantially divergent from Model Act. Concept of corporate "distribution" as defined in §1.40(6) of Revised Model Act has been substantially adopted in Md.

Law was substantially reorganized in 1975 recodification, effective July 1, 1975. References are to Corporations and Associations Article of Code unless otherwise indicated.

General Supervision.—State Department of Assessments and Taxation, 301 W. Preston St., Baltimore 21201, has general charge of corporations. For charter information, call (410) 225-1340.

Purposes.—Generally, corporation may be formed for any one or more lawful purposes. If purpose makes corporation subject to special provision of law, it must comply therewith. (§2-101).

Name must indicate corporate status, as by containing word "company," "corporation," "incorporated" or "limited," or abbreviation of one of such words; it must not contain word which indicates organization for purpose not contained in charter; it must not be same as or misleadingly similar to name of another domestic corporation, limited partnership, limited liability partnership, or limited liability company or registered or qualified foreign corporation, limited partnership, limited liability partnership, or limited liability company, or as name then reserved or registered with Dep't of Assessments and Taxation. (§1-502–505). Foreign corporation with name that is same or misleadingly similar to name of Md. corporation or one registered or qualified to do business in Md. may register or qualify and transact business under disclosed assumed name. (§2-106). Availability of name may be ascertained by inquiry to Dep't of Assessments and Taxation. If several names are to be checked, inquiry should be in writing.

Exclusive right to use of specified name may be reserved by person intending to organize Md. corporation, by Md. corporation proposing to change name, by foreign corporation intending to register or qualify to do business in Md., or by registered or qualified foreign corporation proposing to change name. Reservation is made by filing signed application and paying $7 fee to Dep't of Assessments and Taxation. Reservation lasts for 30 days and may be renewed or transferred (by filing notice of transfer executed by applicant (§§1-505, 1-203). Corporation of another state may register its name, so long as it is not same or misleadingly similar to name of Md. corporation, limited partnership, limited liability partnership, or limited liability company or registered or qualified foreign corporation, limited partnership, limited liability partnership, or limited liability company with name already reserved or registered, by filing application and certificate of good standing in home state and paying $50 fee to Dep't of Assessments and Taxation. Registration is effective until close of calendar year and may be renewed annually by application filed with $50 fee between Oct. 1 and Dec. 31. (§§7-101, 1-506, 1-203). Tradenames "other than the person's own name" must be registered with Dep't. of Assessments and Taxation prior to commencement of operation of business. (§1, subtitle 5).

Term of Corporate Existence.—Perpetual unless otherwise provided by law or by charter. (§2-103). If existence is limited, corporation must comply with §3-519 before existence expires.

Incorporators.—Any one or more adult individuals who need not be residents of state. (§2-102[a]).

Articles of Incorporation.—Articles must be signed by incorporators, either acknowledged before notary public or contain statement that incorporators acknowledge articles to be their act, and must include: (1) Name and address of each incorporator and statement that he is 18 or older and is forming corporation under general laws of state of Md.; (2) name of proposed corporation; (3) purposes for which corporation is

---

See note at head of Digest as to 1998 legislation covered.

See Topical Index in front part of this volume.

CORPORATIONS . . . *continued*

formed; (4) address of principal office of corporation; (5) name and address of resident agent; (6) total number authorized shares, number and par value of shares each class or statement as to no par, aggregate par value of all shares of all classes having par value; (7) if shares divided into classes, description of each class with preferences, conversion and other rights, voting powers, restrictions, limitations as to dividends, qualifications and terms and conditions of redemption of each class; (8) number of directors and names of those who will act until successors are elected and qualify. Articles may include: (1) Any lawful provision defining, limiting and regulating powers of corporation, directors and stockholders or holders of any class of securities; (2) lawful restrictions upon transferability of shares of any class; (3) any provision authorized to be included in bylaws; (4) any provision which requires for any purpose greater proportion of votes than otherwise required by law; (5) any provision which requires for any purpose lesser proportion of votes than otherwise required by law, but not less than majority of votes entitled to be cast on matter; (6) provision which divides directors into classes and specifies terms; (7) provision for cumulative voting; (8) provision which varies in accordance with §2-405.2(a) standards for liability of directors and officers of corporation for money damages. (§§2-102[a], 2-104, 1-302[a]). Pursuant to §§1-208 and 2-405.3, any entity required to maintain resident agent must first obtain such person's written consent and file such consent with Department of Assessments and Taxation.

Filing of Articles.—Articles must be filed for record with Dep't of Assessments and Taxation. (§2-102). When Dep't accepts charter document it endorses date and time of acceptance, records document in its own records, transmits document to clerk of court in county where principal office is located (who must record it in corporate records), and issues certificate acknowledging acceptance and date and time thereof. (§1-202). Filings may be made by "facsimile device" except where sum of recordation and transfer taxes and filing fees exceeds $500. (§1-201). Fees and taxes must be paid by VISA or MASTERCARD when filing by fax. Dep't of Assessments and Taxation fax number is (410) 333-7097. Standard form of fax cover sheet available on request. Fax filings considered expedited service and require additional fees.

Errors in documents (including errors in execution) filed with Dep't of Assessments and Taxation may be corrected by filing certificate of correction identifying document by title, parties' names, date filed, and identifying error. Certificate of correction may not: (1) Alter board or stockholders resolution; (2) effect change that fails to comply with requirements of Md. General Corporation Law at time document to be corrected was filed; (3) change effective date of document; (4) alter any right or liability accrued before filing of certificate of correction, except those existing because of error when there has been no rightful and detrimental reliance on original document. Certificate of correction must be executed in same manner as document to be corrected was required to be executed. (§1-207).

Incorporation Tax or Fee.—Organization and capitalization fee payable by every domestic corporation (except those specifically mentioned below), at or before time of incorporation, at rates based on authorized capital stock, as follows: Not over $100,000, $20; between $100,000 and $1,000,000, $20 plus $1 for each $5,000 or fraction thereof over $100,000; between $1,000,000 and $2,000,000, $200 plus $10 for each $100,000 or fraction thereof over $1,000,000; between $2,000,000 and $5,000,000, $300 plus $15 for each $500,000 or fraction thereof over $2,000,000; over $5,000,000, $390 plus $20 for each $1,000,000 or fraction thereof over $5,000,000. Stock without par valued at $20 per share for purpose of organization and capitalization fee. Same rates apply in case of increase of capital stock, including increase through merger or consolidation. Minimum tax in case of merger or consolidation is $20. Organization and capitalization fee on corporations without capital stock, savings and loan associations and credit unions is $20. (§1-204). Fee payable to Dep't of Assessments and Taxation.

Filing Fees.—Recording fee of $20 must be paid to Dep't of Assessments and Taxation at time of filing articles of incorporation. Filing fees for other documents governed by §1-203. Processing articles, filed in person on expedited basis requires additional filing fee of $30. If certified copy of articles desired, fee is $6 for certification and $1 per page for each duplicate certified copy made at same time, fee is $1 for certification and $1 per page. Certified copies requested on expedited basis require additional filing fee of $20 per copy. (§1-203). Filings by fax machine (see subhead Filing of Articles, supra) subject to regular fees plus charge for expedited basis.

License to Do Business.—Corporations as such do not require license to do business other than certificate of acceptance of charter or qualification as foreign corporation. License for type of business may be required. See subhead Filing of Articles, supra.

Organization.—Directors named in charter to act until first annual meeting hold organization meeting to adopt bylaws, elect officers and transact other business. (§2-109).

Paid-In Capital Requirements.—No requirement that any part of capital be paid in before organization or commencing business.

Amendment of Articles.—Procedure for amendment of articles of incorporation where stock is outstanding or subscribed for is for directors to pass resolution declaring amendment advisable and to call meeting of stockholders, who must approve same by affirmative vote of two-thirds of votes entitled to be cast, unless lesser percentage, but not less than majority, is provided for in charter. (§§2-604, 2-104[b][5]). Articles of amendment must then be executed on behalf of corporation (see §1-301) and filed with Dep't of Assessments and Taxation, and recording fee of $20 (and capitalization fee if authorized capital is increased) must be paid. (§§2-610, 1-203). Effectiveness of articles of amendment can be postponed for up to 30 days after filing and acceptance. (§§2-610.1, 2-611). For contents of articles of amendment, see §2-607.

In case of non-stock corporation, charter or bylaws may provide for approval of amendment by any number of members. (§5-202[b][6]).

In case of stock corporation, if there are no shares outstanding or subscribed for entitled to vote, prior to first meeting incorporators may file amended charter; at or after first meeting, directors may amend. (§2-603). Directors, without shareholder approval, may amend articles to delete word "The" or geographical location, to abbreviate or substitute for abbreviation words "corporation", "incorporated", "company", or "limited", or if corporation is registered as open-end investment company under Investment Company Act of 1940, may change corporate name or name or other designation of any class or series of its stock. (§2-605). Proposed amendment may be abandoned before effective date by majority of board and by notice to Dep't of Assessments and Taxation (if articles of amendment have been filed). (§2-612).

Increase or Decrease of Authorized Capital.—Authorized capital stock may be increased or decreased by articles of amendment adopted as outlined in preceding paragraphs with certain additional information. (§2-602[b]). Shares acquired by corporation, that are shares subject to redemption or convertible shares, are retired automatically and assume status of authorized but unissued stock. (§2-310). Open-end investment company, if authorized by charter, may increase authorized capital by action of directors and by filing articles supplementary with Dep't of Assessments and Taxation. (§§2-105[c]; 2-208.1).

Bylaws.—Every corporation must have bylaws for regulating government of corporation and for administration of its affairs. Bylaws may contain anything not inconsistent with law or charter. (§2-110). After organization meeting of board of directors, power to make, alter or repeal bylaws is vested in stockholders except to extent such power is vested in directors by charter or bylaws. (§2-109[b]).

Corporate Seal.—See category Documents and Records, topic Seals, subhead Corporate Seal.

Stock.—Corporation may create one or more classes of stock, with or without par value, and with such preferences, dividends, rights of redemption, voting powers, restrictions and qualifications as are deemed desirable. (§2-105).

Stock Certificates.—Each stockholder is entitled to certificate signed by chairman of board, president or vice-president and by secretary, assistant secretary, treasurer or assistant treasurer. It may but need not be sealed with corporate seal. Signatures may be manual or facsimile, and seal may be facsimile or other form. Certificate must state name of corporation, name of stockholder and class and number of shares represented. If more than one class of stock authorized, certificate must contain full statement or summary of designations and any preferences, conversion and other rights, voting powers, restrictions, limitations as to dividends, qualifications, and terms and conditions of redemption of each class (and differences between rights and preferences of series, if any, of preferred or special class) or state that corporation will furnish such information to any stockholder on request and without charge. (§2-210). For uncertificated shares, see subhead Stockholders, infra. Future services or obligation to pay may constitute payment for stock, convertible securities, warrants, or option. (§2-206). Stock certificate may not be issued until stock is fully paid. (§2-210). Shares issued for future services, labor, or payment may be escrowed or transfer may be restricted in other ways until performance. If there is no performance, shares may be cancelled in whole or in part. (§2-206). For uncertificated shares, see subhead Stockholders, infra.

Issuance of Stock.—Corporation may generally issue stock or securities convertible into stock that are authorized by charter, if issuance does not violate charter or bylaws. (§§2-201, 2-204[a]). When stock is outstanding, directors may not issue additional stock or convertible securities unless: (1) Charter permits directors to authorize issuance; (2) charter does not require stockholder approval and actual value of consideration received is at least equal to par or (in case of nonpar stock) stated capital for outstanding shares of same class or (in case of convertible securities) par or stated capital of stock which will result from conversion (if greater than par, stated capital or principal amount of convertible securities); or (3) issuance is submitted to and approved at meeting of stockholders; but issuance of stock as stock dividend and issuance as part of reclassification of stock or of consolidation or merger are excepted. (§2-204[b]-[e]). Before issuance, directors must, with certain exceptions, adopt resolution authorizing issuance, setting minimum consideration or formula for ascertainment thereof, describing any non-money consideration and stating its actual value or value below which it will not fall (which value is conclusive absent actual fraud). Stock so authorized may be issued as fully paid and nonassessable, even if value of consideration is less than par. (§2-203).

Transfer of Stock.—Uniform Commercial Code adopted. (comm. law art. tit. 8). See category Business Regulation and Commerce, topic Commercial Code.

Record date for ownership of stock for fixing dividend, voting or other rights may be fixed by directors unless bylaws provide otherwise. Date shall be within 90 days of date of action, payment or allotment and, in case of stockholders' meeting, not less than ten days prior to meeting. Books may be closed against transfers for period not longer than 20 days preceding meeting of stockholders, dividend payment date or other action; and, in case of stockholders' meeting, closing must be at least ten days before date of meeting. If record date not set and transfer books not closed, record date for notice of or voting at stockholders' meeting is later of close of business on day notice mailed or 30th day before meeting; and record date for dividend or allotment is closing on day of declaratory resolution, provided payment may not be made more than 60 days thereafter. For adjourned meetings, see subhead Stockholders' Meetings, infra. (§2-511).

As to special provisions relating to transfer of stock of close corporations, see subhead Close Corporations, infra.

Uniform Securities Ownership by Minors Act not adopted.

Uniform Simplification of Fiduciary Security Transfers Act adopted. (est. & tr. art. §§15-301 to 15-311).

Stock Transfer Tax.—None.

Stockholders.—Absent charter or bylaw provision to contrary, corporation may authorize issuance of shares without certificates, provided stockholders are sent written statement containing information that must be placed on certificate pursuant to §2-211. (§2-210[c]). Otherwise, every stockholder has right to stock certificate (§2-210), right to inspect bylaws, minutes of stockholders' meeting, any voting trust agreement on file and annual statement of corporation, right also (unless corporation is open-end investment company) to obtain statement of all securities issued during 12 months preceding

CORPORATIONS . . . *continued*
request (§2-512), and right to elect directors, adopt bylaws and all such other rights reserved to stockholders by charter or by statute or generally accorded to stockholders. Stockholders holding 5% of any class of stock for period of six months have right to inspect and copy stock ledger and books of account and to demand statement of affairs. (§2-513).

If authorized by charter or bylaws, board may, by resolution, adopt procedure permitting beneficial owner of stock to elect, by certification, treatment as record owner. Resolution must specify certain information, including class of shares affected, form and effect of certification, time limit for certification, if any, plus any other desirable provision. (§2-514).

Unless charter provides otherwise, stockholder does not have preemptive rights with respect to: (1) Stock issued at initiation of enterprise; (2) stock issued for fair value in exchange for non-money consideration; (3) stock offered to stockholders and unsubscribed for; (4) treasury stock sold for fair value; (5) stock issued under articles of merger; (6) non-voting stock issued for fair value; (7) stock issued to officer or employee after two-thirds vote of stockholders; and (8) other issuance where preemptive rights impracticable. (§2-205[a]). Unless charter expressly grants such rights, stockholder does not have any preemptive right to subscribe to any additional issue of stock or security convertible into additional issue of stock. (§2-205[a]). If stockholder is granted preemptive right, he or she may waive such right and, if in writing, such waiver is irrevocable even though not supported by consideration. (§2-205[b]).

Md. corporation operating under federal or state license may limit or restrict transferability of capital stock to, and ownership by, aliens and may restrict alien's right to vote stock when statute granting license limits ownership or control by aliens. (§5-703[b]).

Stockholders' Liabilities.—Stockholder who knowingly receives illegal distribution is liable for contribution to directors who are liable to corporation for that distribution. (§2-312[b]).

Stockholders' Meetings.—Meetings held at time and place specified in bylaws or fixed by directors pursuant to bylaws. If bylaws permit, annual meeting may be set by directors on any day within 31 day period specified in bylaws. At least ten days' notice to stockholders necessary. Must have annual meeting and such special meetings as president or majority of directors or other specified persons may call. Meetings may be held anywhere in U.S. (§§2-501 to 2-504). If charter or bylaws so provide, annual meeting not required of corporation registered under Investment Company Act of 1940 unless election of directors by stockholders is required by that Act. (§2-501). If registered investment company is required to have meeting it must be held within 120 days of event requiring meeting under Investment Company Act of 1940, and special meeting called for that purpose is deemed annual meeting. (§2-501). Informal action by unanimous written consent of stockholders is permitted. (§2-505). Meeting convened on date announced may be adjourned from time to time without further notice to date not more than 120 days after original record date. (§2-511[d]). Failure to hold annual meeting does not invalidate corporate existence or affect any otherwise valid corporate act. (§2-501).

Voting.—Each share entitled to one vote unless charter otherwise provides. (§2-507[a]). Fractional shares and scrip permitted. (§2-214). Cumulative voting in election of directors may be authorized in charter. (§2-104[b][7]). In absence of specific provision of law or charter, quorum requires presence in person or by proxy of majority of shares outstanding and entitled to be cast and majority of votes cast is sufficient to approve matter. (§2-506[a]). Special provisions in case of non-stock corporation are contained in §5-206. Voting by proxy is authorized, but proxy not valid more than 11 months after date unless containing specific provision contra. (§2-507[b]). Specific procedures established for authorizing proxies. (§2-507[c] and [d]). Proxy without interest is revocable. (110 Md. 468, 73 A. 281). Voting rights may be conferred by charter on any securities of corporation. (§2-105[a][7]).

Unless secretary is given written notice to contrary, where shares are registered in names of two or more persons, vote of one binds all, and if more than one vote, majority binds all; even-split vote causes shares to be voted proportionately unless additional vote is cast by court-appointed person. (§2-508[c]).

Directors.—Except in case of close corporation (see applicable subhead), business and affairs of corporation are managed under direction of board. (§2-401[a]). Powers of corporation, save those reserved by charter, bylaws or law, are exercised by or under direction of board. (§2-401[b]). Each corporation must have at least three directors at all times unless there is no stock outstanding (in which case one director is permissible) or unless there are less than three stockholders (in which case there must be at least as many directors as there are stockholders). (§2-402[a]). Number of directors may be increased or diminished by stockholders through amendment of bylaws, or by directors if bylaws so provide. (§2-402[b], [c]). No statutory requirements as to stock ownership, citizenship or residence of directors. (§2-403). Directors are elected by stockholders at annual meeting. (§2-404[b][1]). Unless charter or bylaws provide otherwise plurality of all votes cast at meeting where quorum present is sufficient to elect director. (§2-404[d]). Directors may be divided into classes, but no director may be elected for longer period than five years and terms of at least one class must expire each year. (§2-404[b][2]). Unless contrary to charter, majority of shares entitled to vote may remove director with or without cause and elect successor except stockholders of any class or series entitled to elect separately one or more directors may elect successor to fill board vacancy resulting from removal of director elected by that class or series. Director elected by class or series, however, can be removed without cause only by vote of majority of shares of class or series. If there is cumulative voting and less than entire board is to be removed, director cannot be removed without cause over opposed votes sufficient to elect him. (§§2-406, 2-407[a][1]). Unless charter or bylaws provide otherwise, majority of remaining directors may fill vacancy on board not caused by increase in number of directors; majority of entire board may fill vacancy so created, except that if stockholders of any class or series are entitled to separately elect one or more directors, majority of remaining directors, or sole remaining director, elected by that class or series may fill any vacancy among directors elected by that class or series. (§2-407[b]).

Directors' Meetings.—Bylaws determine place and time of directors' meetings and notice required. Directors' meetings need not be held in state. Board or committee thereof may meet via conference telephone. (§2-409). Informal action by unanimous written consent is permitted. (§2-408[c]).

Unless bylaws provide otherwise, majority of entire board is quorum. Notwithstanding bylaws, quorum may not be less than one-third of board or less than two directors, or if there is only one director, that will constitute quorum. Unless statute, charter or bylaws provide for greater proportion, action may be taken by majority of quorum. (§2-408). Director present at meeting presumed to have assented to action taken unless he (1) announces dissent at meeting, and (2) it is entered in minutes or written dissent is filed with secretary before adjournment or forwarded to secretary by certified mail, return receipt requested, bearing U.S. Postal Service postmark, within 24 hours. Director who votes in favor of action or fails to make dissent known at meeting cannot later dissent. (§2-410).

Powers and Duties of Directors.—Directors may exercise all powers of corporation except such as by law, charter or bylaws are reserved to stockholders. (§2-401[b]). If bylaws so provide, directors may elect executive or other committee of one or more directors and delegate to it any or all powers of directors except: (1) Power to authorize dividends or distributions on stock; (2) recommend action to stockholders; (3) amend bylaws; (4) approve merger or exchange; (5) classify or issue stock unless classification or issuance is pursuant to formula or plan adopted by board. (§2-411).

Directors must perform duties in good faith, in manner reasonably believed in corporation's best interest and with care of ordinary prudent man in like circumstances. In performance of duties, director may rely on others (including officers, employees, lawyers and other professionals, experts and board committees), if director has reasonable belief in their competence and reliability. Director meeting these standards avoids liability save for unfair transaction in which director is interested and which is not ratified by disinterested majority of board or holders of majority of disinterested shares. (§2-405.1; courts art. §5-348). See subhead Interested Director Transactions, infra.

Interested Director Transactions.—Contracts between corporation and (1) director; (2) other corporation sharing common director; or (3) other corporation controlled by director are not void or voidable because of interest, common directorship or presence and vote of interested director if majority of disinterested directors or majority of disinterested shareholders ratify contract or if transaction is fair. Interested directors and/or stock they or interested corporation own may be counted towards quorum at meeting ratifying transaction. Burden of proving fairness placed on person asserting fairness. Burden of proof inapplicable to fixing of compensation. (§2-419).

Liabilities of Directors.—Director who performs his duties in accordance with standard of care specified in §2-405.1 has no liability by reason of being or having been director. (§2-405.1[c]; courts art. §5-348). Charter may expand or limit liability of director to corporation for money damages but may not limit liability to extent that (i) he received improper benefit or profit, (ii) he is adjudicated to have been guilty of active and deliberate dishonesty which was material to cause of action or (iii) he was director of certain banking and/or financial institutions. (§2-405.2; courts art. §5-349).

Directors who vote for or assent to illegal "distribution" as defined in §§1.40(6) and 6.40 of Revised Model Act are jointly and severally liable to extent of illegality, unless charter of corporation limits liabilities of directors as provided in §2-405.1, supra. Director held liable to corporation for improper distribution is entitled to contribution from similarly liable directors and from stockholders who knowingly receive illegal distribution. (§§2-301, 2-309, 2-311, 2-312). See subhead Powers and Duties of Directors, supra.

Director or officer of corporation may not knowingly and willfully authorize or consent to issuance of unauthorized stock or convertible securities of corporation, or issuance of stock or convertible securities of corporation not in compliance with laws relating to issuance, nor may he authorize or consent to false entry concerning issuance into corporate books. (§2-216[a]). Violation is misdemeanor subject to criminal penalties. (§2-216[c]).

Indemnification.—Substance of Model Business Corporation Act, §5 (1980 version) adopted with Md. amendments. Major variation: Termination of proceeding by conviction, nolo contendere plea or probation prior to judgment creates rebuttable presumption that director did not meet standard of care. (§2-418).

Officers.—Except in case of close corporation (see applicable subhead), corporation must have president, secretary and treasurer and may have one or more vice-presidents, assistant secretaries and assistant treasurers. (§2-412). If permitted by bylaws, person may hold more than one office but may not serve concurrently as president and vice-president. (§2-415[a]). Except in case of close corporation (§4-102), person holding more than one office may not act in more than one capacity to execute, acknowledge or verify instrument requiring execution, etc. of more than one officer (§2-415[b]). Directors choose and remove officers and fill vacancies, unless bylaws provide otherwise. (§2-413[a]).

Loans to Officers.—Corporation may lend to or guarantee obligation of officer or employee without interest and without security if, in board's judgment, corporation is benefitted thereby or if loan is advanced against indemnification. (§2-416[a]).

Principal Office.—Corporation must have principal office in state, which must be named in charter, and in case of change of location, certified copy of resolution authorizing same must be filed for record with Dep't of Assessments and Taxation. (§2-108).

Resident Agent.—Corporation must have at least one resident agent who is either citizen actually residing in state or Md. corporation. Resolution authorizing change of resident agent or statement as to his change of address must be filed for record with Dep't of Assessments and Taxation. (§2-108). Entity may not designate resident agent without first obtaining that person's written consent and filing consent with Department of Assessments and Taxation. (§2-405.3).

General Powers of Corporations.—Unless otherwise provided by law or charter, corporation has following powers: (1) To have perpetual existence; (2) to sue and be sued; (3) to have, use and alter and abandon common seal; (4) to transact business

See note at head of Digest as to 1998 legislation covered.

See Topical Index in front part of this volume.

CORPORATIONS . . . *continued*

within and without state; (5) to make contracts and guarantees, incur liabilities and borrow money; (6) to transfer and dispose of assets; (7) to issue bonds, notes, etc. and secure them by mortgage of assets; (8) to acquire, hold and deal with real and personal property; (9) to acquire, hold, use and dispose of stock or obligation of or interest in other corporation, association, partnership or individual; (10) to acquire (subject to statutory limitations) own stock and securities; (11) to invest surplus, lend and take and hold real and personal property as security; (12) to be promoter, partner, member, associate or manager of partnership, joint venture, trust or other enterprise; (13) to make gifts or contributions as authorized by directors out of profits and for use of governmental or charitable institution; (14) to elect officers and appoint agents, define duties and prescribe benefits thereof; (15) to adopt, alter and repeal bylaws; (16) to exercise powers set forth in charter or granted by law; and (17) otherwise to act consistent with law to promote its purposes. (§2-103).

Dividends may not be paid when corporation is insolvent or when payment will render it insolvent on application of standards of insolvency in §6.40 of Revised Model Act. (§2-311).

Stock dividends may be issued on capitalization from surplus of par value of new shares, or, if stock is without par value, then upon capitalization from surplus of amount of stated capital to be fixed by directors, in either case plus such additional sums from surplus as directors may prescribe. Split-up or division of issued shares without change in aggregate stated capital is not to be treated as "stock dividend" for this purpose. (§2-309).

Open-end mutual fund may redeem less than $500 in shares from stockholder if notice given. (§2-310.1).

Unclaimed Dividends and Stock Interests.—Governed by Md. version of Uniform Disposition of Abandoned Property Act. (comm. law art. tit. 17). See category Property, topic Absentees.

Sale or Transfer of Corporate Assets.—Corporation may transfer assets (§3-102[a][8]), but if transfer is of all or substantially all property and assets, transfer must be recommended by directors of transferor and approved by affirmative vote of two-thirds of its shares outstanding and entitled to vote (unless lesser percentage, but not less than majority, is prescribed by charter) and articles of transfer filed. (§§3-104, 3-105, 3-107, 3-109). But see subhead Corporate Take-Over, infra. If articles provide, proposed consolidation, merger, share exchange or transfer of assets may be abandoned before effective date by majority vote of board of one corporate party to articles, or, unless articles provide otherwise, by majority vote of board of each corporate party to articles. Abandonment does not affect contracts by any corporate party to transaction. (§3-108). When articles filed, corporation must submit property certificate for each county where corporation owns interest in land, giving deed reference or other description and stating consideration paid for transfer. (§3-112; tax-prop. art §§12-104[a], 13-204). See category Documents and Records, topic Records, subheads Recording Fees and Tax on Recordation. Procedure is provided whereby stockholder may demand and receive payment of fair value of stock if corporation transfers all or substantially all assets as above. (§§3-201 to 3-213).

Books and Records.—Corporation must keep complete books and records of accounts and of transactions and minutes of proceedings of stockholders, directors and executive or other committees, if any. Books and records may be in written or other readily retrievable form; minutes must be recorded in writing, but may be kept in reproduced form. (§2-111). Stock ledger must be maintained. (§2-209). President or other officer named in bylaws must prepare annually full and true statement of affairs of corporation including balance sheet statement of operation, submit same at annual stockholders' meeting and file same within 20 days thereafter at principal office in state. (§2-313). Owner or owners of 5% of any class of stock who have held such stock for six months may inspect books and stock ledger and demand statement of corporation's affairs. (§2-513[a]). Stockholders in close corporation have broader rights of inspection. (§§4-403, 4-404).

Reports.—Every domestic corporation, limited liability company, limited liability partnership, or limited partnership, and every foreign corporation, limited liability company, limited liability partnership, or limited partnership, subject to jurisdiction of state must file with Dep't of Assessments and Taxation, on or before Apr. 15 each year, report in such form and containing such information as may be required by regulations of Dep't. (tax-prop. art. §11-101).

With annual report domestic or foreign corporation must pay report fee of $100, except that no report fee is required of charitable institutions and nonstock corporations. For savings and loan associations, banking institutions and credit unions, annual report fee is $100. (§1-203).

Businesses entering into contracts with state which exceed, in aggregate, $100,000 during any calendar year, are required to file certain information, including listing of beneficial owners of 5% or more of business. (state fin. & proc. art. §13-221).

Corporate Bonds or Mortgages.—Corporation may issue bonds, notes and other obligations and secure same by mortgage or deed of trust of all or any part of assets. (§2-103[7]). Corporation's charter may confer voting or other rights on holders of bonds, notes or other securities. (§§2-104[b][1], 2-105[a][7]). Mortgage, pledge or creation of security interest in any or all assets may be made without stockholder approval or filing of articles of transfer, unless charter or bylaws provide otherwise. (§3-104[a][2]).

Merger, Consolidation and Share Exchange.—Md. corporations may merge or consolidate with or participate in share exchange (as successor or corporation whose stock is acquired) with other Md. corporation, with corporations of any other state, laws of which permit such transactions, or with Md. or foreign business trust. In addition, Md. corporations may merge into Md. or foreign limited partnerships with Md. or foreign limited liability companies. (§§1-101, 3-102). Procedure is for board to adopt resolution setting forth terms and conditions of transaction and declaring it advisable, to call meeting of stockholders, to secure approval of two-thirds (unless lesser percentage, not less than majority, is prescribed by charter) of shares of each corporation at duly called stockholder's meeting (§3-105) and to execute and file articles of consolidation, merger or share exchange with Dep't of Assessments and Taxation (§§1-301[a], 3-107, 3-109). But see subhead Corporate Take-Over, infra. Merging or consolidating corporation must submit property certificate for each county where it owns interest in land, and it may be required to pay recordation tax. See subhead Sale or Transfer of Corporate Assets, supra. (For rights of dissenting stockholders, see §§3-201 to 3-213.) Merger if no stock outstanding or not involving reclassification, change of rights of outstanding stock or amendment to charter of surviving corporation and not involving issuance of more than 20% of theretofore outstanding shares of same class does not require approval of stockholders of surviving corporation. (§3-105[a][5]). Merger of 90% owned subsidiary into parent where charter of parent not amended does not require approval of stockholders of either corporation and may be accomplished on vote of majority of all directors provided that minority shareholders of subsidiary have rights of dissenting stockholders. (§§3-105[a][1], 3-106). Unless waived by all minority stockholders, parent corporation must, at least 30 days before filing articles of merger, give notice of transaction to shareholders of record on that day or record date fixed not more than ten days prior thereto. (§3-106[d]). Certified copy of document effecting merger or consolidation must be filed with Dep't of Assessments and Taxation, and survivor must file property certificate under §3-112 and informational certificate as to any merger or consolidation of foreign corporations owning property in Md. (§3-117). At time of filing articles of merger, consolidation or share exchange, parties must pay recording fee of $20 and filing fee of $4 for each certificate, for each county in which any of consolidating or merged corporations or transferor corporation or corporation whose shares are acquired in share-exchange has principal office or owns interest in land. (§§1-203, 3-111, 3-112). If successor in consolidation, merger, or transferor in transfer of assets, or corporation whose stock is acquired in share exchange is Md. corporation, transaction is effective when Dep't of Assessments and Taxation accepts articles, unless articles specify later time (up to 30 days after articles accepted). (§3-113[a]). If consolidation or merger provides for increase in authorized capital stock, capitalization fee on increased capital must be paid. (§1-204[f][2]). See subhead Incorporation Tax or Fee, supra.

Corporate Take-Over.—Former take-over statute, §§11-703, 11-901 to 11-908, declared unconstitutional. (547 F.Supp. 522 [D.Md. 1982]). Tit. 11, subtit. 9 repealed as of July 1, 1986. 1983 special legislative session produced special voting requirements act as new subtit. 6, which provides that "business combination" may not be entered into without approval of: (1) 80% of outstanding shares; and (2) two-thirds of outstanding shares that are disinterested in business combination. This voting requirement is in addition to any other requirements contained in other statutes or corporation's charter. (§3-602).

Statute's focus is "business combination" with one who is "interested stockholder". "Interested stockholder" is defined to include any person, other than corporation itself or any subsidiary, that is: (1) Beneficial owner, directly or indirectly, of 10% or more of voting power of corporation after date that corporation had 100 or more beneficial owners of its stock; or (2) affiliate or associate of corporation that, at any time within prior two years and after date that corporation had 100 or more beneficial owners of its stock, was beneficial owner, directly or indirectly, of 10% or more of voting power of corporation. (§3-601[j]). "Business combination" includes: (1) Merger, consolidation or share exchange, except one that does not alter shareholders' contract rights or convert shares, with (a) any interested stockholder or (b) any other corporation that is, or would be after transaction, affiliate of one who was interested stockholder prior to transaction; (2) sale, lease, transfer or disposition in any 12 month period, other than in ordinary course of business or pursuant to dividend or other method affording substantially proportionate treatment to voting stockholders, to any interested stockholder or affiliate thereof, of assets of corporation or any subsidiary that have aggregate value of 10% or more of market value of corporation's outstanding stock or its net worth; (3) issuance or transfer by corporation or any subsidiary to any interested shareholder or affiliate thereof, of equity securities of corporation or any subsidiary having value of more than 5% of corporation's market value, except pursuant to exercise of warrants or purchase rights offered pro rata or on some similar basis to all stockholders; (4) adoption of any plan or proposal for liquidation or dissolution of corporation in which anything but cash will be received by interested stockholder or affiliate thereof; (5) any reclassification of securities or recapitalization or any merger, consolidation or share exchange with any subsidiary that has effect of increasing by 5% or more of total number of outstanding shares proportionate amount of outstanding shares of corporation or any subsidiary that is directly or indirectly owned by interested stockholder or affiliate thereof; (6) receipt by any interested shareholder or affiliate other than corporation or its subsidiaries of benefits, directly or indirectly, of any loan, advance, guarantee, pledge or other financial assistance or any tax credit or other tax advantage provided by corporation or its subsidiaries. (§3-601[e]). Other significant definitions contained in statute.

Super-majority vote required by §3-602 does not apply if: (1) Price and/or consideration received on both aggregate and per-share basis meet certain very detailed requirements that establish minimum price and form of payment; (2) certain standards are met with respect to past performance in payment of dividends; and (3) interested stockholder has not received certain types of benefits. (§3-603[b]). Further, under certain enumerated conditions, corporation's board of directors may elect to exempt corporation from super-majority requirements, or to qualify circumstances under which corporation would be subject to requirements. Depending on circumstances of such election, stockholder approval may be required, and articles supplementary, setting forth terms and method of adoption, must be filed with Dep't of Assessments and Taxation. (§3-603[c], [d]). In addition, unless corporate charter provides otherwise, super-majority requirements do not apply to close corporation, corporation having fewer than 100 shareholders, investment company registered under federal Investment Co. Act of 1940, corporation with interested stockholder that became interested stockholder inadvertently if such stockholder, as soon as possible, divests of shares to become disinterested stockholder and if it was not interested stockholder within preceding five years except by inadvertence, or corporation whose original articles of incorporation or charter amendment, as adopted after June 30, 1983, provide for exemption from scope of requirements. Any post June 30, 1983 vote to amend charter

See note at head of Digest as to 1998 legislation covered.

See Topical Index in front part of this volume.

MD – 4

CORPORATIONS . . . *continued*
must meet 80% and two-thirds "disinterested stockholder" requirements of statute and is not effective until 18 months after stockholder vote. Such charter amendment may not apply to any business combination with stockholder who became interested on or before day of vote. (§3-603[e]). Unless exemption under §3-603(c)(d) or (e) applies, corporation may not engage in business combination with interested stockholder for five years after most recent date on which interested stockholder became such. (§3-602[a]).

Shareholders' appraisal rights for transactions governed by super-majority requirements or exempted from requirements in accordance with §3-603(b) are to be determined in accordance with minimum price requirements of §3-603(b) (§3-202[b]).

Control Share Acquisition Statute.—"Control shares" of corporation acquired in "Control Share Acquisition" have no voting rights except to extent approved by holders of two-thirds of outstanding shares disinterested in transaction, even if charter would otherwise permit smaller proportion of votes to prevail. (§3-702[a][1][2]). Statute does not apply if corporation so provides by charter or bylaw provision adopted before acquisition. (§3-702[b]). "Control shares" are shares owned or controlled by acquiring person which would enable him to vote for election of directors in any one of following ranges of voting power: (i) One-fifth or more but less than one-third of all voting power, (ii) one-third or more but less than majority, or (iii) majority. Control shares do not include shares which person is entitled to vote solely by virtue of revocable proxy. (§3-701[d]). "Control Share Acquisition" means acquisition, directly or indirectly, of control shares either through ownership or through acquisition of power to direct exercise of voting power but does not include acquisition of shares: (i) Made before Nov. 4, 1988 or under contract made prior to that date, (ii) under laws of descent and distribution, (iii) under satisfaction of pledge or other security interest created in good faith and not for purpose of circumventing statute or (iv) under merger, consolidation or share exchange complying with law if target corporation is party thereto. (§3-701[e]). Control Share Acquisition also does not include any acquisition by acquiring person of ownership of or right to vote shares which would fall within any of ranges defined as control shares, if person's possession in that range has been previously authorized by stockholders or is entitled to one of exemptions mentioned above. (§3-701[e][3]). Shares acquired within 90 days or shares acquired under plan to make Control Share Acquisition are considered to have been acquired in same acquisition. (§3-702[e]). Statute does not apply to acquisition of control shares of: (i) Close corporations, (ii) corporations with less than 100 stockholders or (iii) investment company registered under Investment Company Act of 1940. (§3-702[c]).

Any person proposing to make or who has made Control Share Acquisition may deliver "acquiring person statement" to corporation setting forth certain information specified by statute. (§3-703). Acquiring person may also request special meeting of stockholders to determine voting rights to be accorded control shares at time of delivery of acquiring person statement. Unless it determines that there is not adequate financing to make acquisition, board of directors is required to call special meeting of stockholders if acquiring person provides copy of any agreement for outside financing needed to make acquisition and agrees to pay expenses of holding meeting. (§§3-704 and 705). If special stockholders' meeting is required, board must provide acquiring person statement to stockholders with notice of meeting and statement setting forth position or recommendation of board or that it has no position or recommendation. (§3-706).

Unless charter or bylaws provide otherwise, if voting rights for control shares are not approved, corporation may redeem any or all control shares for 60-day period beginning on date of meeting at which voting rights are denied, except control shares for which voting rights have been approved in prior transaction. (§3-707). If acquiring person statement is not delivered to board of directors, 60-day period is extended to period beginning on 11th day after Control Share Acquisition is made and ending 60 days after statement is delivered. Redemption must be made at fair value, i.e., is price determined as of date of last acquisition of control shares by acquiring person or price in effect on date of meeting approving voting rights. (§3-707).

Unless charter or bylaws provide otherwise, before Control Share Acquisition has occurred, if voting rights for control shares are approved at stockholders' meeting and acquiring person is entitled to exercise or direct exercise of majority of all voting power, all stockholders of corporation other than acquiring person have right to require corporation to repurchase their stock for fair value, which may not be less than highest price per share paid by acquiring person in Control Share Acquisition. (§3-708).

Dissolution.—Corporation having stock outstanding may obtain voluntary dissolution after action by directors and affirmative vote of two-thirds (unless lesser percentage, not less than majority, is prescribed in charter) of stock outstanding and entitled to vote. (§3-403). Notice of dissolution must be mailed to all known creditors and employees no less than 20 days prior to filing articles of dissolution. (§3-404). Articles of dissolution must be filed with Dep't of Assessments and Taxation (§3-406, 3-407) and recording fee of $20 plus additional fee of $30 paid (§1-203). Involuntary dissolution may be had upon petition in equity court: (1) By stockholders controlling 25% of votes for director election, when directors or stockholders are deadlocked; (2) by any stockholder who may vote in director election, when stockholder deadlock prevents director election at two consecutive annual meetings, or when acts of directors or controlling persons are illegal, oppressive, or fraudulent; or (3) for insolvency (see subhead Insolvency and Receivers, infra). (§3-413). Special provision applies to close corporation. (§4-602). Certain transfers of real property to stockholders made upon dissolution are exempt from transfer and recording taxes. Transfer exempt from taxes if it is to stockholder who is: (1) Original shareholder; (2) certain relative of original shareholder; or (3) person acquiring shares by gift or devise from original shareholder. (tax-prop. art. §§12-108[q], 13-207[a][10]).

Insolvency and Receivers.—In event of insolvency, stockholder or creditor may have equity court declare corporation dissolved and may procure appointment of receiver to liquidate corporation. (§§3-413[c], 3-415). In strong case, court of equity will appoint receiver to prevent fraudulent or gross mismanagement and wasting of corporate assets by officers and directors. (155 Md. 549, 142 A. 885).

Close Corporations.—Md. corporation is granted election to be treated as "close corporation." Election must be made in original charter or in charter amendment approved by unanimous vote of stockholders. (§4-201). Subsequent election by charter amendment no longer to be treated as close corporation requires unanimous consent of stockholders. (§4-203). Close corporation must initially have one director, but may elect after organization to have no board of directors, in which case stockholders manage business and affairs by direct action and exercise all powers of directors. (§§4-301 to 4-303). Under unanimous stockholders' agreement contained in charter, bylaws or separate written instrument, stockholders may regulate any aspect of corporate affairs or of stockholder relations. Stockholder subsequently acquiring stock by gift or bequest from assenting party or with actual knowledge of agreement is bound by unanimous stockholders' agreement, and agreement may be enforced by equity court. (§§4-101[c], 4-401). Close corporation need have but one officer, who can execute documents in more than one capacity (§4-102); unless stockholder requests one, it may dispense with annual stockholders' meeting. (§4-402). Charter documents and stock certificates must disclose close corporation status. (§4-202). Unless stockholders have agreement regulating transfer of stock, statute invalidates transfer without unanimous stockholder consent. (§4-503[b]). Broader rights of stockholder inspection are provided than in general corporation law. (§§4-403, 4-404). In event of disagreement among stockholders, petition may be filed for judicial dissolution. (§4-602). Consolidation, merger, transfer of assets, acquisition of corporation's stock in share exchange, require approval of all stockholders. (§4-601).

Appraisal.—Stockholder who objects to consolidation, merger or sale of all or substantially all corporate assets, or to amendment of corporate charter altering contract rights of any outstanding stock and substantially adversely affecting his rights where right to do so not reserved in charter, or where his stock is to be acquired in share exchange, or where transaction is "business combination" governed by §3-602 or §3-603(b) (see subhead Corporate Take-Over, supra), is entitled to demand and receive fair value of his stock. (§§3-201 to 3-213). Statutory procedures must be strictly followed. Most important conditions precedent require that (1) written objection to proposed action be submitted at or prior to stockholders' meeting, or within 30 days after notice or waiver of notice of merger of subsidiary into corporation owning 90% of stock, and (2) written demand for payment be made on survivor or transferee corporation within 20 days of consolidation, merger, sale or charter amendment. See subhead Merger, Consolidation and Share Exchange, supra. (§3-203). Statutory provisions constitute exclusive remedy and preclude injunctive relief. (155 Md. 66, 141 A. 425). Objecting stockholder ceases to have rights of stockholder with respect to stock (except right to payment) and he receives no dividend as of date for determining fair value. (§§3-202, 3-204). Special provisions apply to appraisal rights in conjunction with "business combinations" governed by special voting requirements. (§§3-202, 3-602, 3-603[b]).

Foreign Corporations.—Foreign corporation seeking to do intrastate business in Md. must qualify with Dep't of Assessments and Taxation by certifying to Dep't its address and name and address of resident agent, and paying qualification fee of $50. (§§1-203, 7-203). Unless qualified to do intrastate business, foreign corporation shall register with Dep't before doing interstate business, by certifying to Dep't its address and name of resident agent; no charge. (§7-202). Foreign corporation not required to qualify, which owns income producing real or tangible personal property in Md. acquired other than by foreclosure, must register to do interstate business. (§7-202.1). Insurance companies subject to regulation under Md. insurance laws, railroads, federal credit unions and national banks (if main office is located in Md.) are exempt from registration and qualification requirements. (§7-201). Foreign corporation registered or qualified and subject to suit in Md. must maintain resident agent and mailing address, both of which have been certified to Dep't of Assessments and Taxation. Such certificate may certify address of principal office in state, and if so, corporation must certify subsequent change of address or discontinuation of office. Certificate must be signed by president or vice-president. (§7-205). Within 60 days after amendment to charter changing its name, merging, consolidating or dissolving, qualified or registered foreign corporation must file, with Dep't of Assessments and Taxation, officially certified statement showing action and date taken, and executed by official who has custody of record. (§7-206). Representative of successor corporation must also file affidavit indicating whether corporation merging out of existence or consolidating owns interest in land in Maryland.

Failure to Comply.—Penalties are provided for failure to register or qualify, including prohibition on maintenance of suit in state court and fines on corporation and on officers and agents. (§§7-301, 7-302). Failure to file certificate as to charter amendment subjects corporation to penalty of $5 plus $1 for each ten days or fractional part of ten days during failure to comply continues. (§7-303). Failure to qualify, register or file certificate or report does not affect validity of contract. (§7-305). Foreign corporation required to qualify or register may not benefit from any statute of limitations in action either arising out of contract made or liability incurred while doing business without having complied or instituted while doing business without having complied. (courts art. §5-204).

Effect of Compliance.—Compliance with registration or qualification requirements does not of itself render foreign corporation subject to suit in state, nor may it be construed as consent to be sued where corporation would otherwise not be subject to suit (§7-210); however, by doing intrastate, interstate or foreign business in state, corporation assents to state laws (§7-105).

Reports.—Foreign corporation, limited liability company, limited liability partnership, or limited partnership doing business in state or owning property therein must file annual report. (tax-prop. art. §11-101). Failure to file may lead to forfeiture of right to do intrastate business. (§7-304). See subhead Reports, supra.

Foreign corporation, savings and loan association, national banking association, or credit union subject to jurisdiction of state must pay to Dep't of Assessments and Taxation at time of filing annual report filing fee of $100. Nonstock corporation or charitable institution pays no fee. Insurance company pays annual filing fee of $25 to Insurance Commissioner. (§1-203).

See note at head of Digest as to 1998 legislation covered.

See Topical Index in front part of this volume.

MD – 5

CORPORATIONS . . . *continued*

Real Property.—No restrictions on right of foreign corporation to acquire or hold real property.

Foreign corporation may be sued in state, on any cause of action if it maintains principal place of business in state; otherwise on cause of action arising from acts enumerated in long-arm statute. (courts art. §§6-102, 6-103). See category Civil Actions and Procedure, topic Process, subhead Personal Service Outside the State.

Taxation.—Foreign corporations doing business in state are subject to income tax on income earned in state and are also subject to property tax, sales and use taxes and miscellaneous license taxes for certain types of business or occupations. Foreign corporations are not required to pay qualification tax or annual franchise tax, except public utilities such as railroad, telephone, telegraph, oil pipeline, gas and electric companies are subject to gross receipts tax. See category Taxation, topic Franchise Taxes, subhead Public Service Company Franchise Tax.

Surrender of Authority.—Registration or qualification of foreign corporation may be terminated by filing with Dep't of Assessments and Taxation application for termination, executed by president or vice-president and stating: (1) Name of corporation and address of any principal office in state; (2) name and address of resident agent; (3) that corporation is no longer transacting intrastate or interstate business in state, as case may be; (4) that corporation wishes to terminate qualification or registration to do such business, as case may be; and (5) that all required reports have been filed and all taxes have been paid. Certificates as to payment of taxes must accompany application. (§7-208).

Taxation of Corporate Property.—Same as taxation of property of individual, except that Dep't of Assessments and Taxation assesses tangible personal property and operating property (except land) of public utilities. (tax-prop. art. §8-201). Appeal from assessment by Dep't, must be taken to Md. Tax Court within 30 days of mailing of final assessment; appeal bond required. (tax-gen art. §13-510, tax-prop. art. §14-514). Appeal from Tax Court to circuit court. (tax-gen art. §13-532). Intangible property of corporations not taxed.

Taxation of Corporate Stock.—Corporate stock of domestic corporation (other than airline or air freight company) under jurisdiction of Public Service Commission subject to property tax assessed by Dep't of Assessments and Taxation. (tax-prop art. §8-109[d]). See subhead Stock Transfer Tax, supra.

Franchise Tax.—See subhead Reports, supra. No annual franchise tax on capital of domestic or foreign corporations.

Domestic and foreign savings banks and savings and loan associations, trust companies, commercial banks and other financial institutions pay franchise tax on net earnings in lieu of income tax, but special exceptions exist for international financial transactions. See category Taxation, topic Franchise Taxes, subheads Public Service Company Franchise Tax, Franchise Tax on Financial Institutions, Franchise Tax on Savings and Loan Associations. (tax-gen art. tit. 8). Utilities such as oil pipeline, gas and electric companies pay special franchise tax measured by gross receipts. (tax-gen art. tit. 8, subtit. 4). Gross receipts tax due and payable quarterly. (tax-gen. art. §8-405).

See category Taxation, topic Administration, subhead Penalties.

See also subhead Incorporation Tax or Fee, supra.

Model Non-Profit Corporation Act not adopted, but see tit. 5 of corps. art., parts of which are modeled on Act.

Income tax applicable to corporations except those which pay franchise tax and small business corporations which have elected subchapter S treatment. See category Taxation, topic Income Tax.

Real Estate Investment Trusts.—Covered by tit. 8 of corps. art. See topic Joint Stock Companies.

Professional Corporations.—Professional Service Corporation Act authorizes individual or group of individuals, duly licensed or otherwise legally authorized to render professional service, to incorporate and become shareholders of professional corporation. (§§5-101 to 5-134). Name in charter must contain Professional Corporation, Chartered, Professional Association, P.A., P.C., or CHTD. (§5-106[a]). If professional corporation ceases to render professional services, it must amend articles of incorporation to convert into general corporation. (§5-123). By charter amendment, stockholders of professional corporation may change status to general corporation. (§5-117.1). When amendment becomes effective, corporation may not conduct business allowed only by title 5 of corps. art.

Consumer Cooperative Corporation.—Md. Consumer Cooperative Act authorizes cooperative organized as stock or non-stock corporation, for purpose of acquiring, producing, manufacturing, furnishing, or distributing goods or services for mutual benefit of members. (§§5-5A-01 to 5-5A-30).

Deeds.—See category Property, topic Deeds.

Organized Crime.—Attorney General may bring civil proceeding to forfeit charter of Md. corporation or to revoke permit of foreign corporation where certain persons related to corporation are, with knowledge of president and majority of board of directors, involved in organized crime. (§1-405[b]).

Cooperative Housing Corporations.—Regulated by tit. 5, subtit. 6B.

Limited Liability Companies.—See topic Limited Liability Companies.

JOINT STOCK COMPANIES:

No general legislation. See topic Associations, subhead Actions. References are to Corporations Art. of Code unless otherwise indicated.

Limited Liability Companies.—See topic Corporations.

Real Estate Investment Trusts.—Unincorporated trust or association in which real property is acquired, held, managed, administered, controlled, invested, or disposed of for benefit and profit of holders of transferable shares of beneficial interest is permitted. (tit. 8). Declaration of trust must be filed with Dep't of Assessments and Taxation; it must clearly indicate that trust is real estate investment trust and must include number of trustees, names of those persons who will serve as trustees until first meeting of shareholders, name and address of resident agent, number of shares authorized, and provisions for annual meeting and election (at least every three years). (§8-202). Unless waived by Comptroller, trust must file bond, cash or approved securities, to secure payment of taxes. (§8-204). Amendment of declaration of trust requires board to adopt resolution setting forth amendment, notice to shareholders, and affirmative vote or written consent of two-thirds of shares, unless declaration requires lesser vote or gives trustees power to amend to qualify under Internal Revenue Code. (§8-501).

Powers.—Real estate investment trust has perpetual existence and broad general statutory powers similar to those of corporation, not including, however, power to use and apply land for farming, agricultural, horticultural or similar uses. (§§8-301, 8-302[b]).

Requirements.—At least 75% of assets must be represented by real estate, mortgages or mortgage related securities, government securities, cash and cash equivalent items, including high-grade short term securities and receivables. (§8-302[a]). Declaration of trust may permit more than one class of beneficial shares. Trustees may classify or reclassify unissued beneficial shares after filing articles supplementary with Dep't of Assessments and Taxation. Certain information must be included on stock certificate if more than one class of stock is authorized. (§8-203). Trust must submit annual report, including financial statements certified by independent accountant, to shareholders at or before annual meeting and place report on file at principal office, and it must permit inspection of records at any reasonable time by Dep't. (§§8-401, 8-402).

Limited liability is provided for. (§8-601). Declaration of trust may include provision limiting liability to trust or shareholders for money damages. (courts art. §5-350[c]). Corporate charter may include similar provisions. (§2-405.2).

Taxation.—Taxed as corporation, except that income tax imposed on corporation is imposed only on undistributed income, provided that trust complies with §§856 to 858 of Internal Revenue Code and at least 90% of taxable income, without regard to capital gains, is distributed within taxable year or before time prescribed for filing return; otherwise all net income taxable. Taxes are lien on property of trust. Distributions to beneficial owners are treated as investment income. (tax-gen art. §§10-304 to 10-308).

Merger.—Md. real estate investment trust may merge into Md. or foreign business trust or Md. or foreign corporation or such entities may merge into it. (§8-501.1). Procedure is for board of trustees to adopt resolution declaring transaction advisable and setting forth its terms and conditions, to submit proposal at duly called annual or special meeting of shareholders (§§2-501 to 2-504, 8-501.1), to secure approval of two-thirds of entitled votes except if declaration of trust provides that lesser proportion, not less than majority, will suffice (§8-202[c]), and to execute and file articles of merger with Dep't of Assessments and Taxation (§§8-501.1, 3-109, 1-301). Dep't shall then prepare certificates of merger specifying name of each party to articles, name and principal place of business of successor, and time articles accepted by Dep't; certificates shall be forwarded to and recorded by clerk of court for each county where merging trust or corporation, other than successor, owns interest in land. (§8-501.1[j]). Objecting trust shareholders have same rights as objecting shareholder of Md. corporation. (§§3-201 to 3-213). Merging trust or corporation must submit property certificate for each county where it owns interest in land. Merger not involving reclassification, change of rights of outstanding shares or amendment of declaration of trust of successor trust, nor issuance or delivery of more than 15% of outstanding shares of same class does not require approval of shareholders of successor trust. (§§8-501.1, 1-101). Upon filing articles of merger, parties must pay recording fee of $20 and filing fee of $4 for each certificate submitted. (§§8-501.1, 1-203). If successor is Md. real estate investment trust, merger effective when Dep't accepts articles unless articles specify later date (up to 30 days permissible); if successor foreign corporation or business trust, or Md. business trust, merger effective when Dep't accepts articles or time specified by law of state where successor organized. (§8-501.1). See topic Corporations, subhead Merger, Consolidation and Share Exchange.

Professional Associations.—See topic Corporations, subhead Professional Corporations.

See also topics Associations, Corporations.

LIMITED LIABILITY COMPANIES:

Maryland Limited Liability Company Act adopted. (tit. 4A).

Name must contain either words "limited liability company" or abbreviation: "L.L.C.", "LLC", "L.C.", or "LC". Right to use name forfeited unless limited liability company files certificate every five years with State Department of Assessments and Taxation. (§§4A-208; 1, subtitle 5). Name may be reserved. (§§4A-209; 1, subtitle 5).

Purpose.—Any lawful purpose except acting as insurer. (§4A-201).

Formation.—Any person may execute and file Articles of Organization with State Department of Assessments and Taxation. (§4A-202). Articles of Organization must contain name, purpose, address of principal office in Md., and name and address of resident agent, and may contain any other lawful provision. (§4A-204). Certificate of Correction, see §4A-205. Execution of Articles and Certificates, see §§2-405.3, 4A-206. Principal office and resident agent, see §4A-210.

Limited Liability.—No person with interest in limited liability company is personally liable for obligations of limited liability company, solely by reason of interest. (§4A-301). Individual who renders professional service as employee is liable as if sole practitioner. (§4A-301.1).

Acts of Members.—Articles of Organization may provide for limited authority of members to act for company. Otherwise, each member is agent of company for purpose of its business. (§4A-401).

Operating Agreement.—May establish management, share of assets and earnings, assignment and new members, certificates of interest in company, and amendment of Operating Agreement. Operating Agreement need not be in writing. Unless otherwise provided, all members must agree to amendment of Operating Agreement. (§4A-402).

See note at head of Digest as to 1998 legislation covered.

See Topical Index in front part of this volume.

LIMITED LIABILITY COMPANIES . . . *continued*

Voting.—Members vote in proportion to interests in profits; majority governs. (§4A-403).

Transactions by Member.—Unless otherwise provided, member may lend money and transact other business with company just as nonmember. (§4A-405).

Finance.—Contribution may be cash, property, services rendered, or promissory note or other binding obligation to contribute cash or property or to perform services. (§4A-501). Unless otherwise provided, profits and losses allocated in proportion to capital interest, and distributions made in proportion to right to share in profits. (§4A-503).

Membership and Interests.—Membership interest is personal property. (§4A-602). Assignment governed by §§4A-601 through 4A-607.

Merger governed by §§4A-701 through 4A-710. Unless otherwise provided in Operating Agreement, limited liability company may merge into other limited liability company, limited partnership, stock corporation, or business trust having transferable unit of beneficial interest, or vice versa. (§4A-701). Member who objects to merger has same rights as stockholder under tit. 3, subtit. 2. (§4A-705).

Derivative Actions.—Member may bring derivative action to same extent that stockholder may bring derivative action under corporation law. Members with authority to bring action must have refused to bring action or be unlikely to bring action. (§4A-801). If action is successful or plaintiff receives anything, court may award reasonable expenses, including attorneys' fees. (§4A-804).

Dissolution and Winding Up.—Dissolution occurs upon events specified in Articles of Organization or Operating Agreement, at time specified by unanimous consent of members, or at time of entry of decree of judicial dissolution, except as otherwise provided in operating agreement, or at time limited liability company has no members for 90 days. (§4A-902). Dissolution causes winding up unless remaining member consents, or, if there is more than one remaining member, remaining members unanimously consent to continuation of limited liability company except after judicial decree of dissolution. (§4A-902). Limited liability company continues until terminated in accordance with §4A-908. (§4A-901). Termination occurs on later of date Articles of Cancellation are filed or effective date of Articles of Cancellation. Limited liability company continues to exist for purpose of paying debts, collecting and distributing assets, and doing other acts required to wind up. (§4A-908). Upon winding up and termination, assets are distributed to creditors of limited liability company, and then to members in proportion to adjusted capital interests. (§4A-906).

Foreign limited liability companies generally governed by law of state of organization. (§4A-1001). Registration is required and must set forth name, state of organization, date of formation, general character of business in Md., name and address of resident agent in Md., statement appointing State Department of Assessments and Taxation as resident agent if needed, and address of office required to be maintained in state of organization or principal office. (§4A-1002). Foreign limited liability company doing business in Md. without registering subject to penalty of $200, and each member and agent guilty of misdemeanor and subject to fine of $1,000. Unregistered foreign limited liability company doing business in Md. may not maintain suit unless above penalty paid and company or successor either complies with registration requirements, or is no longer doing business in Md. (§4A-1007). Following activities do not constitute doing business: being involved in suit or similar proceeding, holding meetings that concern internal affairs, maintaining bank accounts, conducting isolated transactions, foreclosing mortgages, acquiring title through default, holding such property, or selling such property. Owning other income-producing real or tangible personal property is considered doing business. (§4A-1009).

PARTNERSHIPS:

References are to Corporations Article of Code unless otherwise indicated.

Revised Uniform Partnership Act, 1997 version, adopted. (tit. 9A).

Limited Partnership.—Revised Uniform Limited Partnership Act, 1976 version, adopted with Md. amendments. (tit. 10).

Registration requirements for foreign limited partnerships became effective July 1, 1985. (§10-1104).

Intentional major variations from 1976 Uniform Act include following (all references are to Corporations Article):

"Consent" is defined as writing consenting to specified act or event. (§10-101[c]).

Certificate of cancellation is included within definition of "certificate." (§10-101[b]).

"Foreign Limited Partnerships" include those formed under laws of foreign country. (§10-101[f]).

Name may only be reserved for 30 days. (§10-103).

Partnership books of Md. limited partnership must be kept at its principal office in Md. (§§10-104, 10-108, 9-402).

Limited partnerships may not act as insurers. (§10-106).

Limited partnership certificates are filed with Dep't of Assessments and Taxation, and must set forth limited partnership's name, address of principal office, name and address of resident agent, name and address of each general partner, latest date limited partnership to dissolve and any other matters partners determine to include. (§2-405.3).

Amendments must be promptly made in event of material inaccuracies. List of specific events requiring amendment deleted from Md. version. (§10-202). Typographical errors, errors in transcription and technical errors in limited partnership certificates may be corrected by filing certificates of correction. (§10-202.1). If amendment made within 30 days after general partner knew or should have known of inaccuracy, general partner not liable for inaccuracy. (§10-207[b]).

Unless partnership agreement provides otherwise, limited partnerships may merge with Md. or foreign limited partnerships, or limited liability companies, corporations having capital stock or business trusts having transferable units of beneficial interest. (§10-208).

Certificate of cancellation must contain list of dates of each amendment. (§10-203).

Person erroneously believing himself to be limited partner is only liable to another who reasonably relies on that person's general partner status if person knew or should have known that certificate was never filed or that he was inaccurately referred to therein as general partner. (§10-304).

Unless otherwise provided, profits and losses, as well as distributions, are made on basis of value of contribution of each partner. (§§10-503, 10-504).

Withdrawing partner gets fair share of partnership interest without regard to right to share in distributions. (§10-604).

§607 rewritten to refer to limitations on return of contributions (rather than on distributions). (§10-607).

Assignment by partner of all interests in partnership interest does not create substitution of partner. (§10-702).

Upon death or disability of general partner, guardian, personal representative, or successor automatically becomes limited partner. General partner automatically becomes limited partner upon doing of certain acts. (§10-704).

"Cause" must be shown before court can wind up affairs of limited partnership. (§10-803).

Foreign limited partnership may not conduct any business in Md. which domestic limited partnership is prohibited from doing by Md. law. (§10-901).

Foreign limited partnership doing business but not registered in Md. may not sue in Md. unless it pays penalty for failure to register ($200) and either registers or proves it is no longer doing business in Md. (§10-907).

General partner or agent of unregistered foreign limited partnership doing business in Md. is guilty of misdemeanor and subject to fine up to $1,000. (§10-907).

Activities permissible without "doing business" in Md. are listed. Ownership of nonexempt income-producing real or tangible personal property in state is "doing business". (§10-909). By doing business in Md. foreign limited partnership assents to Md. laws (§10-910), but registration by itself does not subject foreign limited partnership to suit in Md. nor operate as consent to be sued (§10-911).

Derivative actions are possible to same extent as for stockholders under Md. corporations law. (§10-1001). One is entitled to bring derivative action if partnership status devolved on him by operation of law. (§10-1002).

§§208, 209 and 605 (second sentence) of Uniform Act were not adopted.

Limited Liability Partnerships.—Md. Uniform Partnership Act amended to include limited liability partnerships. (1994, c. 494).

Formation.—Partnership formed under tit. 9 may register as limited liability partnership by filing with Dep't of Assessments and Taxation certificate setting forth name, purpose, address of principal office in Md., and name and address of resident agent. (§9A-1001[a]). Partnership qualifies as limited liability partnership when certificate filed or at such later time as specified in certificate. (§9A-1001[b]). Amendment to certificate must be in writing, filed with Dep't of Assessments and Taxation, and executed by authorized person. (§9A-1001[c], [d]). Registration may be withdrawn at any time by filing withdrawal notice executed by one or more authorized partners. (§9-1001[e]). Status of partnership not affected by admission or withdrawal of partners, provided business continues in same name without liquidation of partnership affairs. (§9-1001[f]). Principal office and resident agent, see §9-1005.

Name must contain either words "limited liability partnership" or abbreviation: "L.L.P." or "LLP" as last words or letters of name. (§9A-1003[1]). Name may be reserved. (§9-1004).

Limited Liability.—Partner in limited liability partnership not liable for debts and obligations of partnership arising from negligent or wrongful act or omission of another partner, employee, or agent of partnership occurring while partnership is limited liability partnership. (§9A-306[c]). Partner liable if negligent in appointing, supervising, or cooperating with other partner, employee, or agent. (§9A-306[c], [d][1]). Partner liable, in contract or tort, for debts and obligations of partnership relating to contracts made by partnership prior to registration as limited liability partnership, unless registration consented to in writing by other party to contract. (§9A-306[d][3]). Partnership and its assets remain liable for all partnership debts and obligations. (§9A-306[d][2]). Statute not intended to limit authority of regulatory body that licenses professionals.

Powers.—Partnership, including limited liability partnership, may conduct its business and have and exercise powers granted by tit. 9 in any state, territory, district or possession of U.S. or in any foreign country. (§9A-106[c]).

Choice of Law.—Legislature intends that legal existence of limited liability partnerships formed under tit. 9A be recognized outside state of Md. and that Md. laws governing limited liability partnerships transacting business outside Md. be granted protection of full faith and credit under U.S. Const. (§9A-106[c]). Internal affairs of partnerships, including limited liability partnerships, governed by Md. law. (§9-106[d]).

Foreign limited liability partnerships generally governed by law of state of organization. (§9A-106[b]). Registration is required and must set forth name, state of organization, general character of business in Md., name and address of resident agent in Md., statement appointing Dep't of Assessments and Taxation as resident agent if needed, and address of office required to be maintained in state of organization or principal office. (§9A-1101[b]). Certificate of Correction, see §9A-1104. Certificate of Cancellation, see §9A-1105. Foreign limited liability partnership doing business in Md. without registering subject to penalty of $200 and each member and agent guilty of misdemeanor and subject to fine of $1,000. (§9A-1106[d]). Unregistered foreign limited liability partnership doing business in Md. may not maintain suit unless above penalty paid, and partnership or successor either complies with registration requirements, or is no longer doing business in Md. (§9A-1106[a]). Following activities do not constitute doing business: being involved in suit or similar proceeding, holding meetings that concern internal affairs, maintaining bank accounts, conducting isolated transactions, foreclosing mortgages, acquiring title through default, holding such property, or selling such property. Owning other income-producing real or tangible personal property is considered doing business. (§9A-1108).

See note at head of Digest as to 1998 legislation covered.

See Topical Index in front part of this volume.

MD – 7

BUSINESS REGULATION AND COMMERCE

BANKS AND BANKING:

Financial Institutions Article effective as of July 1, 1980. References are to article unless otherwise indicated.

Uniform Commercial Code adopted. (comm. law art. tit. 4). See topic Commercial Code.

General Supervision.—Commissioner of Financial Regulation, 501 St. Paul Place, 13th Floor, Baltimore, Maryland 21202, has supervision over state banking institutions, which are regulated under tits. 1 to 5. For powers and duties, see tit. 2, subtit. 1. Savings and loan associations are regulated. See category Business Organizations, topic Corporations.

Preferred Stock.—Commercial bank may, with approval of Bank Commissioner, issue preferred stock, which may be convertible into common stock except in certain instances. Preferred stockholders may be entitled to cumulative dividends not exceeding 6% per annum on par value of stock, and no dividends may be paid on common stock until cumulative dividends on preferred stock have been paid in full. (§3-302).

Deposits.—State banking institutions may receive deposits and pay interest thereon. (§§3-206, 3-207, 4-206). Savings banks may pay interest only out of profits. (§4-303[a]). Savings and loan associations may pay dividends or interest only from current earnings, earned surplus, expense fund or as otherwise provided by law. (§9-404). Provisions in multiple-party account agreements for certain transfers on death are nontestamentary. Funds in such accounts pass under agreement or, in absence of provision, to survivors. (§1-204, est. & tr. art. §1-401). Common law altered. (§1-204).

Unclaimed Deposits and Property.—Except for demand, savings, or matured time deposits subject to court order, such deposits with banking and financial organizations and business associations, and share accounts or deposits with savings and loan associations inactive for five years, and sums payable on certified checks, drafts, certificates of deposit and money orders, and funds and personal property removed from safe deposit boxes after expiration of lease period, when unclaimed for five years and sums payable on traveler's checks unclaimed for 15 years, are governed by Uniform Disposition of Abandoned Property Act. For purposes of imposing service charge holder may consider money order dormant after one year. But deposits in banking organizations not considered abandoned if depositor has engaged in any credit, trust or other deposit transaction with organization within five years. Depositor must be issued notice by first class mail to last known address and has 30 days to respond. (comm. law art. tit. 17, subtit. 3).

Confidential Financial Records.—Banks, trust companies, savings and loan associations, credit unions, and other organizations that are chartered under Md. banking laws and subject to supervision of Bank Commissioner, may not disclose customer's financial records (checks, drafts, statements, credit items, debit items, and any information regarding loans) unless customer approves, or customer is deceased or disabled and representative or guardian is court-appointed, in response to certain requests by Dep't of Human Resources to confirm customer's eligibility for public assistance or institution received request or subpoena for information from child support enforcement administration of the Dep't of Human Resources (§1-302) or in response to subpoena (§1-304). Willful violation is misdemeanor punishable by fine up to $1,000. (§1-305). Financial records may be examined by CPA during audit, by State's Attorneys in certain instances, by agent of supervisory agency, by other enterprises or consumer reporting agency during ordinary exchange of credit information, in published data (when customer cannot be identified), and in connection with mortgagee estoppel certificates and in connection with request by customer for extension of credit with affiliated financial institution. (§1-303).

Statements to Depositors.—Banking institutions, credit unions and savings and loan associations are required to furnish written information to customers concerning terms of interest-bearing accounts upon demand and when account is opened. (§§5-302, 6-401, 9-403).

Banks, savings banks, savings and loan associations must provide borrower with annual statement of escrow account balance. (comm. law art. §12-109[b][3]).

Collections.—Uniform Commercial Code adopted. (comm. law art. tit. 4).

Trust companies are given additional powers. (§3-207).

Common trust funds may be formed by trust company to provide for collective investment of money held by it as fiduciary. (tit. 3, subtit. 5).

Uniform Common Trust Fund Act not adopted.

Savings institution may not have capital stock, but must be mutual association, unless organized as subsidiary savings bank pursuant to tit. 4, subtit. 9. (§4-401). Under limited circumstances, mutual association may be converted to capital stock association. (§§9-611, 9-612). Conversion of mutual association to credit union governed by tit. 9, subtit. 11. May own and let for hire vaults or safe deposit boxes and, in accordance with rental agreement, may permit deposits of property, and may, with prior approval of Bank Commissioner, exercise same corporate and fiduciary powers as trust company. (§4-206). May have checking accounts as well as savings accounts. (248 Md. 461, 237 A.2d 45).

Industrial Banks.—Special statutory provisions, administered by Commissioner of Consumer Credit, govern finder's fees, consumer loans under tit. 12, subtit. 8 of comm. law art., installment loans under §12-103(c) of comm. law art., persons engaged in business of sales finance company, and mortgage loan lenders (tit. 11). Alternative lending authority provided by comm. law art. tit. 12, subtits. 9 and 10. See topic Interest.

State Banks.—Except for such institutions not in business of accepting deposits or retaining funds in deposit accounts, state chartered banking institutions must be members of Federal Deposit Insurance Corporation. (§5-509). By authorization of Bank Commissioner and specified board, state banks may engage in additional banking

activities and bank-related services under same conditions and restrictions as national banks. (§5-504). State bank may merge with, consolidate with, or transfer assets of Maryland savings and loan association under limited circumstances. (§3-702).

Foreign Banks.—Except as permitted by Tit. 5, Subtits. 9, 10 and 11, foreign bank or savings and loan association may not maintain office in state to solicit deposits or to conduct banking, savings or trust business and must obtain permit to operate office or electronic terminal in state unless office or electronic terminal is authorized under federal law or Title 5. (§§12-201, 12-207). Foreign bank or affiliated corporation may not become bank holding company. (§12-204). But foreign bank may carry on some functions of banking institution. (38 Op. Att'y Gen. 104). As to right of foreign trust company to act as fiduciary in Md., see categories Estates and Trusts, topics Executors and Administrators, Trusts; Family, topic Guardian and Ward.

Out-of-State Bank Holding Companies.—Under Tit. 5, Subtit. 9, out-of-state bank holding company or subsidiary may acquire and hold all voting shares of single new bank in Md. if approved by Bank Commissioner, who must evaluate holding company's application under certain specific criteria. (§5-905). Under Subtit. 10, out-of-state bank holding company may establish branches in Md. if certain conditions are met. (§5-1003). Under Subtit. 11, out-of-state bank holding company may acquire one or more Md. savings and loan associations and convert them into commercial bank. Newly-created bank will operate with same rights and restrictions as Md. bank. (§5-1105[a]).

Credit Unions.—Regulated by Bank Commissioner under §6-102. For powers, see tit. 6. All state chartered credit union accounts must be insured by Md. Credit Union Insurance Corporation or by National Credit Union Administration Share Insurance Program. (§6-601). Credit unions may receive deposits from and make loans to members (§6-207, tit. 6, subtit. 5), may set own dividend rate (§6-402).

Interest.—See topic Interest.

Equal Credit Opportunity.—Illegal to discriminate on basis of sex, marital status, race, color, religion, national origin, age, handicap, geographic area, or neighborhood in extension of credit. (comm. law art. §§12-113, 12-701 to 12-708).

Mortgage brokers and bankers regulated, business restricted. (tit. 12, subtit. 5). Fees subject to restrictions. (comm. law art. §§12-801 to 12-809).

Taxation.—See category Taxation, topic Franchise Taxes, subheads Franchise Tax on Financial Institutions, and Franchise Tax on Savings and Loan Associations. Credit unions exempt from taxation by State or local subdivision. (§6-103).

Prohibited Acts.—Include deceptive representations and advertisements, restrictions on financial dealings with competitors, and various other acts. (§5-807).

Automated Teller Machines.—Operator of automated teller machine installed after Jan. 1, 1995 must evaluate safety of proposed automated teller machine location and meet certain lighting requirements; must also provide written notice of basic safety precautions to customers. For automated teller machines installed prior to Jan. 1, 1995, compliance is optional until July 1, 1995, with certain exceptions. (§1-207).

BILLS AND NOTES:

Uniform Commercial Code adopted. (comm. law art. tit. 3). See topic Commercial Code.

Special Requirements.—No special requirements as to recitals in notes of particular classes or based on particular considerations.

Judgment Notes.—Term authorizing confession of judgment if note not paid when due does not affect negotiability. (comm. law art. §3-112[1][d]). But negotiability is lost if note authorizes confession of judgment before maturity. (158 Md. 587, 149 A. 270). If authorization permits confession of judgment before maturity, note not negotiable. (34 Md. App. 350, 367 A.2d 102). Confessed judgment clause invalid or prohibited in many consumer transactions, e.g., in door-to-door sale (comm. law art. §14-302[4]), consumer loan (comm. law art. §12-311[a][1]), or note given as part of retail credit account (comm. law art. §12-507[b]). Confessed judgment clauses that waive consumer's right to assert legal defense not permitted in any contract related to consumer transaction. (comm. law art. §13-301[12]). See topic Interest, subhead Maximum Rate; category Civil Actions and Procedure, topic Judgments, subhead Judgment by Confession.

Attorney's fee clause enforceable (160 Md. 57, 152 A. 815) and note remains one for sum certain (comm. law art. §3-106[1][e]).

Special Defenses.—See topics Consumer Protection, subhead Assignments, Sales, subhead Retail Installment Sales.

BILLS OF LADING:

See topic Carriers.

BILLS OF SALE:

See topic Sales.

BLUE SKY LAW:

See topic Securities.

BROKERS:

Uniform Commercial Code adopted. (comm. law art. tits. 1 to 10). See topic Commercial Code.

In absence of special agreement to contrary, broker employed to buy, sell, lease, or mortgage real estate, etc. or to procure loan entitled to commission when person procured enters into binding written contract acceptable to and signed by employer. (real prop. art. §14-105). Broker also entitled to customary commission when he procures person ready, willing and able to purchase upon terms authorized and advises owner of fact and gives opportunity to complete sale. (127 Md. 512, 96 A. 642).

See note at head of Digest as to 1998 legislation covered.

See Topical Index in front part of this volume.

BROKERS . . . *continued*

Licenses.—See appropriate categories, e.g., Insurance, topic Insurance Companies. For general requirements, see art. 56.

Bond.—None required.

Real Estate Brokers.—Real Estate Commission has supervision over licensing and activities of real estate brokers. Applicant for license must have three years experience as real estate salesman or be qualified to practice law and must pass written examination. (bus. occ. art. §16-305). Licensee must prove completion of 12 hours of approved continuing education every two years to have license renewed unless Commission waives requirement; beginning in 1996, requirement increases to 15 hours. (bus. occ. art. §16-315). Licensee participating in residential real estate transaction as seller's agent, buyer's agent, or cooperating agent must make written disclosure of representation of seller or lessor to prospective buyer or lessee not later than first scheduled face-to-face contact. (bus. occ. art. §16-528).

Employment agency must obtain annual license from Commissioner of Division of Labor and Industry. (bus. reg. art. tit. 9). Entities directly providing part-time employment or which do not charge any fee to or do not require contract with applicants are excluded from definition of employment agencies. (bus. reg. art. §9-101).

Insurance Agents and Brokers.—See category Insurance, topic Insurance Companies.

BULK SALES:

Uniform Commercial Code adopted. (comm. law art. tit. 6). See topic Commercial Code.

See also category Business Organizations, topic Corporations, subhead Sale or Transfer of Corporate Assets.

CARRIERS:

Uniform Commercial Code adopted. (comm. law art. tits. 1 to 10). See topic Commercial Code.

Carriers Regulated by Public Service Commission.—For details and extent of regulation, see art. 78.

Rates.—Intrastate rates must be just and reasonable and must be approved by Public Service Commission. Commission may also fix rates. (pub. util. comp. art. §4-102). Mass Transit Administration may fix rates for carriers under its jurisdiction. (trans. art. §§7-505; 7-506).

Discrimination in rates or service prohibited. (pub. util. comp. art. §4-503).

Limiting Liability.—Carrier may limit liability by contract with shipper. (106 Md. 472, 67 A. 1099).

Bills of Lading.—Uniform Commercial Code adopted. (comm. law art. tit. 7). Criminal provisions for certain acts set out in comm. law art. §§18-201 to 18-207.

Motor Vehicle Carriers.—See category Transportation, topic Motor Vehicles.

COMMERCIAL CODE:

Uniform Commercial Code (see Uniform and Model Acts section) enacted in 1963 in its entirety with provision that it take effect on Feb. 1, 1964. It appeared as art. 95B prior to recodification effective July 1, 1975 as comm. law art. tits. 1 to 10. Section numbers of art. 95B and comm. law art. correspond to those of 1962 official text.

1966 Official Amendments.—Not adopted except §§2-702(3), 3-501(3), 7-209(3).

1972 Official Amendments.—Adopted to take effect on Jan. 1, 1981.

1977 Official Amendments.—Adopted effective July 1, 1986.

1987 Official Text of Article 2A.—Adopted to take effect Jan. 1, 1995 (with conforming amendments to §§1-105, 1-201[37]and 9-113). (1994, c. 535).

1989 Official Amendments.—Adopted to take effect on July 1, 1991.

1990 Official Amendments to Article 2A.—Adopted to take effect Jan. 1, 1995. (1994, c. 535).

Intentional variations from official text of Uniform Commercial Code are as follows:

§1-102(5)(b) provides words of neuter gender refer to any gender.

§1-103 provides that age of majority as to capacity to contract is 18. See revisors note following comm. law art. §10-104.

§2-314 defines seller to include manufacturer, dealer and/or retailer and abolishes privity in any action brought by buyer against said parties. Implied warranty also applies to leased goods.

§2-315 provides that implied warranty of fitness for particular purpose also applies in certain bailments and leases.

§2-316 is made inapplicable by §2-316.1 to sales of consumer goods and services. Language used by seller of consumer goods or services to attempt to modify or exclude implied warranties is unenforceable, although seller may recover damages resulting from breach from manufacturer. Implied warranties may be modified or excluded for sale of certain used automobiles. Language used by manufacturer of consumer goods to limit or modify consumer's remedy for breach of manufacturer's express warranties is unenforceable unless he provides reasonable and expeditious means of performing warranty obligations. (§2-316.1).

§2-318 adds to buyer's household and house guests: "any other ultimate consumer or user of the goods or person affected thereby."

§2-702(3) provides seller's right to reclaim is not subject to rights of lien creditor, see note to 1966 Official Amendments, supra.

§3-305 provides holder in due course also takes instrument free from claims and defenses of maker of purchase money instrument obtained by certain time-share developers.

§§3-512 to 3-514 added to give holder of dishonored check right to send notice of dishonored check to drawer following ten days of nonpayment. Drawer of check is liable for collection fee of up to $25. (§3-512). These provisions provide alternative to any other right of recourse. (§3-514).

§4-406 as adopted deleted "or holds . . . to the customer" and changed "fourteen calendar days" to "14 business days". (§4-406[2][b]).

§4A-206(a) as adopted omits "or other third-party communication system" from first sentence and inserts "funds-transfer" preceding "system" in every instance.

§6-106(4) provides for appointment of receiver to take custody of and distribute agreed purchase price paid into circuit court.

§6-107(3) amended to require delivery of notice to Comptroller of State in addition to other persons in text.

§6-108(3)(b) amended so that auctioneer must give notice to Comptroller of State in addition to creditors and those who assert claims against transferor.

§7-204(4) is omitted in its entirety.

§8-401(3) is additional subsection which provides options to issuer of uncertificated securities upon receipt of instruction requesting registration of pledge.

§9-301(2) provides 20 day grace period to perfect purchase-money security interest.

§9-301(2A) provides ten day grace period to perfect nonpurchase money security interest.

§9-301(4) not enacted.

§9-302(1)(d) provides exemption from filing financial statement for purchase money security interest in consumer goods having purchase price not in excess of $1,500 per item.

§9-302(1)(h) provides that no financing statement need be filed for grant of security interest in certain mortgages.

§9-307(1) designates official text (A) and added paragraph (B) to remove liability from person performing auction services for seller of farm products even though that person knows of perfected security interest in farm products.

§9-307(2) provides that consumer goods must have original purchase price not in excess of $1,500 per item in order for buyer to take free of security interest.

§9-307(3) not enacted.

§9-312(4) provides 20 day grace period to perfect purchase-money security interest.

§9-313 did not adopt 1972 amendment to this section but conforms to 1962 official text.

§9-401(1) enacted using third alternative with following modifications: (a) eliminated reference to all collateral except crops; filing for crops is to be made in office of clerk of circuit court; (b) eliminated reference to financing statement filed as fixture filing; filing is to be made in land records in office of clerk of circuit court in county where mortgage would be filed; (c) filing is to be made in office of Dep't of Assessments and Taxation; (d) this subsection was added to provide that §9-401(1) could not be construed to invalidate any financing statement properly filed in good faith prior to July 1, 1995.

§9-401(5) provides filing is to be made with office of Dep't of Assessments and Taxation and also provides that priorities supplied by §9-313 apply to such filings.

§9-401(7) added to provide that "county" as used in this section includes Baltimore City. Fee for filing with court clerk, or with Dep't of Assessments and Taxation currently (1) $10 for release nine pages or less; (2) $20 for any other instrument nine pages or less; (3) $20 for instrument, regardless of length, involving solely principal residence; and (4) $75 for any other instrument ten pages or more. (real prop. art. §3-601). Circuit courts for some counties and Baltimore City also require 50¢ fee for postage and handling.

§9-401(8) allows filing with Dept. of Assessments and Taxation to be made by facsimile transmission as provided in corps. art. §1-201 "or by electronic data interchange."

§9-401.1 provides for transitional refiling procedures as to any later modification statement which relates to financing statement filed prior to July 1, 1971.

§9-401.2 provides for transitional refiling procedures as to any later modification statement which relates to financing statement filed prior to July 1, 1995.

§9-402(1) provides that when financing statement is filed only with Dep't of Assessments and Taxation under §9-401(1)(c), statement shall identify (1) county in which each debtor's principal place of business is located; (2) each debtor's county of residence, or (3) shall indicate that neither (1) nor (2) applies.

§9-402(5) refers to "a financing statement filed as to collateral which is or is to become fixtures" instead of "fixture filings (§9-313)." Financing statement under this subparagraph must recite that it is "to be recorded in the land records."

§9-402(6) changes financing statement filed as a "fixture filing" to "financing statement covering goods that are or are to become fixtures." Subdivisions (c) and (d) refer to recording in land records instead of filing in real estate records.

§9-402(9) adds various requirements concerning size, form and contents and printing or typing of financing or continuation statement, or assignment, termination or release statement (e.g., 8 point or elite type, black letters on white paper, sheet not larger than 8½ x 14", with two-inch margin top and bottom and one-inch margin on sides); also concerning additional fee for statement not otherwise readily subject to photostating or microfilming and applicability of recordation tax. For form of financing statement, see category Mortgages, topic Chattel Mortgages.

§9-403(2) provides that financing statement filed after June 30, 1978 is effective for 12 years. §9-403(2) provides that security interest perfected by filing and existing at time insolvency proceedings are commenced remains perfected until latter of termination of insolvency proceedings plus 60 days or date when it otherwise would have lapsed. §9-403.1 provides that 12 year effectiveness applies only to financing and continuation statements filed after June 30, 1978.

§9-403(3) provides that filing of continuation statement within six months prior to expiration of original extends effectiveness for 12 years. Filing officer may ordinarily remove record of lapsed statement from files after six years or immediately if photographic record is retained. §9-403(3) as adopted omitted last sentence of official text relating to filing officer's retention of certain continuation statements.

§9-403(4) adds to duties of filing officer concerning recording, indexing and redelivery of financing or continuation statement.

§9-403(5) refers to real prop. art. §3-601 for fees. See subhead Filing Fee, infra.

§9-403(7) adopted optional language and reference to owner of record omitted.

See note at head of Digest as to 1998 legislation covered.

See Topical Index in front part of this volume.

COMMERCIAL CODE . . . *continued*

§9-404(1) covers financing statements filed after Jan. 1, 1981 and omits word "signed" following "statement of assignment" in third sentence.

§9-404(2) adds to duties of filing officer concerning recording, indexing and redelivery of termination statement.

§9-404(3) refers to real prop. art. §3-601 for filing fees for termination. See subhead Filing Fee, infra.

§9-405(1) adds to duties of filing officer and refers to real prop. art. §3-601 for filing fee (see subhead Filing Fee, infra).

§9-405(2) adds "the record reference" to data to be supplied for assignment and adds to duties of filing officer concerning recording, indexing and delivery of statement of assignment. Last sentence refers to real prop. art. §3-601 for filing fee. See subhead Filing Fee, infra.

§9-406 adds "the record reference and the date of filing" to data to be supplied in statement of release and adds "with its record reference" to what is to be marked upon margin of index of filing of financing statement. Last sentence refers to real prop. art. §3-601 for filing fees. See subhead Filing Fee, infra.

§9-407 subjects creditor to $100 fine if creditor charges fee to record and then fails to record document in 30 days or fails to return fee. See commentary following tit. 10 in 1975, c. 49.

§9-503 designates official text (1) and added subsection (2) which provides that if secured party elects to proceed by judicial process it may be done by writ of replevin or otherwise.

§9-504(3) conforms to 1962 official text.

§10-109 provides that unlapsed financing or continuation statements filed prior to Jan. 1, 1981 remain effective for period provided in comm. law art. in effect at date of filing. Continuation statements on previously filed financing statements to be filed in accordance with new provisions. (§10-109[2]). For filings after Jan. 1, 1981, names and addresses of debtor and secured party govern dates and places of filing. (§10-109[4]).

Options and alternatives in 1962 official text and Permanent Editorial Board's 1966 and 1972 recommendations for optional amendments have been exercised as follows:

§1-209: 1966 official optional amendment not enacted.

§2-318: 1966 official optional amendment alternative A adopted with addition to buyer's household and house guests of "any other ultimate consumer or user of the goods or person affected thereby."

§3-121: alternative B adopted.

§3-501(3): 1966 amendment adopted.

§4-106: optional phrase omitted.

§4-202(1)(b): optional clause adopted.

§4-212: optional subsection (2) adopted.

§6-102(3): includes restaurants and sellers of alcoholic beverages.

§6-106: optional section adopted with variations in subsection (4) indicated under subhead Intentional Variations.

§6-107(2): optional paragraph (e) adopted.

§6-108(3): optional paragraph (c) adopted.

§6-109: optional subsection (2) omitted.

§7-204: optional subsection (4) omitted.

§7-209(3): 1966 amendment adopted.

§7-403(1)(b): optional clause adopted.

§9-203(4): refers to other statutes which also regulate loans and retail installment sales such as Consumer Loan Law, and Retail Installment Sales comm. law art. title 12, subtitles 3 and 6 and provides that, in event of conflict, those statutes prevail.

§9-302(3)(b): refers to other statutes, which provide for central filing of, or require notation on certificate of title of, security interest.

§9-401(1): third alternative subsection (1) adopted with variations indicated under subhead Intentional Variations.

§9-401(3): alternative subsection (3) not adopted.

§9-401(6) adopted.

§9-402(5): optional language relating to description of real estate not adopted.

§9-407: official text not adopted, see subhead Intentional Variations, supra.

§10-104(2): optional subsection (2) adopted with reference made to est. & tr. art. §§15-301 to 15-311.

§11-101 adopted as §10-105(2) with 1972 amendments effective Jan. 1, 1981.

§11-102 adopted as §10-106.

§11-103 adopted as §10-107.

§11-104 adopted as §10-108.

§11-105 official text not adopted but similar provision adopted as §10-109, see subhead Intentional Variations, supra.

§11-106 adopted as §10-110.

§11-107 adopted as §10-111.

§11-108 adopted as §10-112.

Place of Filing.—See subhead Intentional Variations, supra, §9-401(1).

Filing Fee.—§§9-403(5), 9-404(3), 9-405(1), (2) and 9-406 refer to real prop. art. §3-601, which fixes uniform fees as provided under subhead Intentional Variations supra. (§9-401[7]).

Recordation Tax.—Exempt from tax are liens or encumbrances upon vehicles and vessels which are filed with Motor Vehicle Administration or Department of Natural Resources, mechanics' liens, crop liens, certain purchase money deeds of trust or purchase money mortgages, assignments of mortgages or deeds of trust, judgments, releases, orders of satisfaction, certain Uniform Commercial Code security agreements, certain refinancing agreements where refinanced property is mortgagor's principal residence, certain supplemental and previously recorded instruments, and instruments transferring property between certain relatives, most transfers to state, state agencies or other political subdivisions are also exempt from recordation tax, participation agreement showing interest in note, mortgage or deed of trust based on prior recorded loan to mortgagor or grantor under deed of trust. Also exempt is any instrument transferring real property from cooperative housing corporation on its termination to owner of cooperative interest in corporation, under certain conditions. (tax-prop. art. §12-108). Other filed financing statements subject to tax. (tax-prop. art. §12-108). See category Documents and Records, topic Records, subhead Tax on Recordation.

See also topics: Banks and Banking, Bills and Notes, Brokers, Carriers, Contracts, Factors, Frauds, Statute of, Sales, Securities, Warehousemen; categories Business Organizations, topic Corporations; Civil Actions and Procedure, topic Limitation of Actions; Debtor and Creditor, topics Assignments, Fraudulent Sales and Conveyances, Liens, Pledges; Documents and Records, topics Records, Seals; Mortgages, topic Chattel Mortgages; Transportation, topic Motor Vehicles.

CONDITIONAL SALES:

See topic Sales.

CONSIGNMENTS:

See topic Factors.

CONSUMER PROTECTION:

References are to Commercial Law Article of Code unless otherwise indicated.

Consumer protection legislation generally administered by Division of Consumer Protection in Office of Attorney General, 7 N. Calvert St., Baltimore 21202, which may adopt rules, regulations and standards. (§§13-201 to 13-205).

Unfair or Deceptive Trade Practices.—Uniform Deceptive Trade Practices Act not adopted.

Unfair or deceptive trade practices, prohibited in sale, lease or bailment (or offer therefor) of consumer goods, realty or services, in extension of consumer credit, or in collection of consumer debts, whether or not any consumer is actually deceived or damaged, include: (1) False or misleading oral, written or visual representations; (2) untrue representations of sponsorship, character, quality or quantity; (3) deceptive failure to state material facts; (4) false disparagement; (5) offers without intent to sell or to fulfill demand (unless expressly limited); (6) false representations concerning price reduction or comparative price; (7) false statement of need for services or goods; (8) false statement of discount prices; (9) misrepresentation or concealment of material fact in connection with promotion or sale, merchant's subsequent performance, or violation of consumer protection act or order thereunder; (10) solicitation over telephone without first stating name and trade name, purpose of conversation, goods and services offered; (11) use of scheme in telephone sales that misrepresents solicitor's true status or purpose; (12) use of confessed judgment clause waiving consumer's right to assert legal defense in contract related to consumer transaction; (13) violations of various other provisions of tits. 10, 13 or 14 of comm. law art. or of Energy Conservation Building Standards Act, art. 78, §54-I. (§§13-301 to 13-303). Insurance and body shops are regulated by Automotive Crash Parts Act. (§§14-2301 to 14-2304).

Vacation Club Membership.—It is deceptive trade practice for sales agent to violate requirements of §§14-2401 to 14-2403. Contract to purchase vacation club membership, which includes plans that provide accomodations in certain time-share units, campgrounds, and condominiums, must contain following statement in at least 14-point bold-faced type which appears immediately before and on same page as signature of purchaser: "You may cancel this contract without penalty or obligation within 10 days from the date of this contract. If you decide to cancel this contract, you must provide notice of the cancellation in writing to (the sales agent) at (address of sales agent). Any attempt to obtain a waiver of your cancellation rights is unlawful. Cancellation entitles you to a refund of all moneys within 15 business days after receipt of notice of cancellation." (§14-2402[d][1]).

Door-to-Door Sales.—It is unfair and deceptive trade practice to violate provisions of Maryland Door-to-Door Solicitations Act. (§§14-2601 to 14-2603). Act prohibits receipt of more than $200 through door-to-door solicitation of consumers. Solicitor must give consumer pledge form, inform consumer of his right to rescind pledge at any time and that pledge is not enforceable, notify consumer that solicitor may not accept at time of solicitation any money including amount of pledge that equals or exceeds $200, inform consumer of right to refund if requested within 30 days after contribution, provide disclosure statement prior to acceptance of solicitation, and, if requested, within 30 days of request mail to consumer at no charge financial statement of person for whom solicitation is made. (§14-2603). Pledge form must contain following information: (1) name of solicitor; (2) name and address of party on behalf of whom solicitation was made; (3) statement of purpose for which contribution will be used; (4) disclosure statement as provided in §14-2601(f); (5) date and amount of door-to-door solicitation; (6) name and address of consumer; and (7) statement of consumer's right to rescind and method of rescission. Pledge is not enforceable contract. Request for refund must be by certified mail, return receipt requested. Refund must be made within ten days after receipt of request. (§14-2603[f]).

Other General Prohibitions and Requirements.—Certain referral sales plans are prohibited. (§13-304). Person may not notify another of prize, award or selection for receipt of thing of value, other than trading stamps, certain retail sales and certain games of skill competitions, or Md. State Lottery tickets, conditioned on purchase or submission to sales promotion unless retail price of prize offered does not exceed greater of $40 or lesser of 20% of purchase price of goods and services that must be purchased or $400. However, this limited exception does not apply to offer of prize requiring person either to pay any money to participate in or to submit to sales promotion effort, or to prize promotion involving award of prizes by chance. (§13-305). If gift offered in exchange for business is unavailable when properly claimed, offeror must give certificate and subsequently redeem with same or similar gift. (§13-306). Unless repair to home appliance is done under service contract or after quotation of flat price or firm estimate, bill itemizing hourly labor rate, time used and cost of parts is required. (§13-307). Electrical consumer product must bear mark of certified testing lab; and electrical extension cord must be labeled for maximum amperes safely conducted. Violations may be misdemeanors subject to fine. (§§13-308, 13-309). Sellers of reserved seat tickets, other than nonprofit organizations, must display seating

CONSUMER PROTECTION . . . *continued*
plan showing obstructions. (§13-310). Seller may not condition sale upon buyer's entry into service contract. (§13-311). "Earn at home" ads for mass mailing campaigns illegal if money advances solicited or no compensation paid. (§13-314).

Unit Pricing.—With certain exceptions (including described small businesses), one who sells, offers or displays consumer commodity at retail must disclose unit price, as defined, if consumer commodity is sold only by units or is prepackaged or retail-packaged and in one of following categories: (1) Foods, condiments, cooking oils, etc.; (2) paper products; (3) wrapping products; (4) soaps, detergents, cleansing aids, etc. Disclosure not required if seller is then disclosing as to 90% of commodities subject to disclosure. (§§14-101 to 14-104). Provision is made for public institution of compliance proceedings. (§14-106).

Consumer Debt Collection.—Certain acts prohibited in collection or attempted collection of alleged debt: (1) Use or threat of force or violence; (2) threat of criminal prosecution, unless transaction involved criminal violation; (3) disclosure of or threat to disclose information known to be false affecting debtor's reputation for credit worthiness; (4) contacting debtor's employer before final judgment on delinquent debt, except as permitted by statute; (5) disclosure of or threat to disclose to person known to have no legitimate business need, other than debtor, debtor's spouse or minor debtor's parent, of information affecting debtor's reputation, whether or not for credit worthiness, except as permitted by statute; (6) communication with debtor or relative in abusive or harrassing manner; (7) use of obscene or grossly abusive language in communication with debtor or relative; (8) attempt or threat to enforce right known to be nonexistent; or (9) use of communication falsely simulating legal or judicial process or falsely appearing to be issued by government or lawyer. Violator is liable for damages, including damages for emotional distress. (§§14-201 to 14-204). See topics Licenses, Business and Professional, subhead Collection Agencies; Interest, subhead Maximum Rate.

Bank or other financial institution may not offset property or money in savings or checking account for settlement of delinquent consumer debt, unless authorized by customer in writing or by order of court. (§§15-701, 15-702).

Door-to-Door Sales.—It is unfair or deceptive trade practice for person engaged in door-to-door sale of consumer goods or services with purchase price of $25 or more, inclusive of interest and service charges, to: (1) Fail to furnish buyer with (a) fully completed receipt or copy of contract at time of execution, in same language used in oral sales presentation and giving date and name and address of seller, and (b) readily visible statement (as described) advising of right to cancel before midnight of third business day following transaction; (2) fail to furnish buyer at time of sale with completed notice of cancellation, in duplicate and in form specified; (3) fail to complete notice of cancellation with specified information; (4) include confession of judgment or waiver of certain rights; (5) fail to inform buyer orally at time of sale of right to cancel; (6) misrepresent buyer's right to cancel; (7) fail to honor valid notice of cancellation by buyer and, within ten business days, to refund payments, return goods traded in, and cancel any negotiable instrument or security interest; (8) negotiate or transfer evidence of indebtedness given by buyer before midnight of fifth business day following transaction; (9) fail, within ten business days of receiving buyer's notice of cancellation, to notify buyer of intent to repossess or abandon goods; (10) solicit sale or order without initially expressly revealing identity of solicitor, trade name, nature of goods or services offered (written information stating above information must be displayed); or (11) use scheme misrepresenting solicitor's true status or mission. (§14-302). Violation permits buyer to cancel sale by notifying seller in any manner. (§14-303). Violator is liable to affected person for damages and reasonable attorneys' fees; wilful violator is guilty of misdemeanor and subject to fine and imprisonment. (§§14-304, 14-305). See also subhead Unfair or Deceptive Trade Practices, supra.

Telephone Solicitations.—Regulated by Maryland Telephone Solicitations Act. (§§14-2201 to 14-2205).

Consumer Products Guaranty Act.—Act requires certain disclosures to be made by person making available consumer goods or services with actual cash price of more than $10 and making guaranty. (§§14-403, 14-401). Act sets forth duties and defenses of guarantor. (§14-404, 14-405). Attorney General is authorized to enforce Act (§14-406), but policy of encouraging voluntary and informal settlement procedures is stated, and use of such procedures is promoted. (§14-407). Service contracts voluntary on buyer's part and designation of service representatives by guarantors specifically permitted. (§14-408).

Prescription Drugs.—On request by consumer in person or by telephone, licensed pharmacist must disclose current price of prescription drug sold by pharmacy. (health occ. art. §12-502).

Pharmacist may substitute generically equivalent drug for prescribed brand name product, unless prescriber expressly directs otherwise or price to purchaser is not less. Dep't of Health and Mental Hygiene must establish, revise and distribute formulary of equivalent drug products. (health occ. art. §12-508).

Health Maintenance Organizations.—Advertising by HMOs must meet requirements of health-gen. art. §19-714.

Assignments.—Any holder of consumer credit contract is subject to all claims and defenses which debtor has against seller; notice of this fact must be given in sales contract. (§14-1302).

False Advertising.—Person may not advertise falsely in conduct of business, trade or commerce or in provision of any service. To determine if advertisement is misleading, both representations and failure to reveal material facts are to be considered. Violator is subject to penalty of up to $500, recoverable by Attorney General for state in civil action brought after opportunity to defendant to show cause why action should not be commenced. Compliance with rules and regulations of and statutes administered by Federal Trade Commission or any unit of state government is defense. Statute does not apply to television or radio station broadcasting advertisement or to publisher of printed advertisement and does not modify private litigation rights. (tit. 11, subtit. 7).

Layaway Sales Act.—Seller must: (1) Give buyer written contract, signed by all parties, containing certain required terms, and stating all agreements between parties; (2) hold for buyer, or agree to deliver on agreed date, conforming goods; (3) permit buyer to cancel within seven days after contract was entered, without penalty or obligation, and thereupon refund all payments and return goods traded in; (4) give written receipt for certain payments; (5) comply with request by buyer for statement of account within ten days; (6) deliver goods identical to those selected when buyer has made all payments in accordance with agreement. Buyer may cancel without obligation or penalty, and receive full refund of payment and return of goods traded in; (1) Within seven days after date of contracting, or (2) if seller violates any of above-listed requirements, at any time before buyer accepts goods. Otherwise, buyer may cancel at any time before delivery, but seller may then retain as liquidated damages lesser of 10% of price or amount paid before cancellation. Seller may cancel and retain those same liquidated damages if buyer defaults, which is defined as 15 days delinquency on scheduled payment; however, liquidated damages limitation does not apply if goods were specially ordered to buyer's specification. Seller may not increase layaway price, and must credit to buyer any reduction in price charged for goods made within ten days after execution of contract. Seller who makes sale in willful violation of subtitle is liable to buyer for penalty of three times amount paid by buyer, plus reasonable attorneys fees, in addition to refund provision above. (§§14-1101 to 14-1110). See topic Sales, subhead Retail Installment Sales.

Credit Cards.—Revolving credit agreements regulated by §12-903.

Vendors may not record address or telephone number. Also vendors are not permitted to record credit card number as condition of acceptance of personal check. However, vendor may request display of credit card for identification purposes. (§13-317).

Consumer credit reporting extensively regulated. (§§14-1201 to 14-1218).

Miscellaneous Special Provisions.—Special protection is afforded to consumers transacting for fine prints (§§14-501 to 14-505), gold and silver items (§§14-601 to 14-608), secondhand watches (§§14-701 to 14-706), used radios and televisions (§§14-801 to 14-803), kosher products (§14-901 to 14-909), automotive repair (§§14-1001 to 14-1009) and health club services (§§14-12B-01 to 14-12B-08). Contracts for sale of new vehicles must contain price, manufacturer's code or stock number and description of extra items or any charge not included in base price. (trans. art. §15-311). Dealers offering mechanical repair contracts on vehicles must maintain adequate insurance reserves. (trans. art. §15-311.1). Unfair and deceptive trade practice to change mileage on odometers. (comm. law art. §13-301; trans. art. §22-415). Unfair and deceptive trade practice to fail to correct nonconformity, defect or condition within 30 days of receipt by manufacturer of customer notification, or to replace vehicle or refund purchase price, under Automotive Warranty Enforcement Act: bad faith violations may result in award of up to $10,000 in damages to consumer. (§§14-1501 to 14-1504). Prior waiver of certain rights to hearing or opportunity to be heard before replevin of property subject to security interest is invalid. (§14-1303). Unsolicited merchandise sent is considered unconditional gift to recipient, as is merchandise sent by membership sales organization after 30 days following execution of return receipt attached to member's notice of membership termination. Sender's continued billing may be enjoined at expense of losing party. (§14-1304). Unsolicited credit card not accepted until person in whose name card is issued signifies acceptance in writing or uses card; until acceptance, issuer bears risk of loss, theft or unauthorized use. (§14-1305). Duration of service contract is extended for certain days appliance is in custody of service contractor for upkeep or repair. (§14-1306). Credit card issuer must notify cardholder of subpoena for information. Notice sent to last address is sufficient. (§13-312). Certain insulating material offered for sale must meet minimum fire retardancy standards and report must be filed with state fire marshal. (§13-313). Certain attic fans must contain protective devices. (§13-315). Seller of ladder capable of conducting electrical current must affix to ladder warning to that effect. (§14-1307). Seller of color photographic film must enclose sufficient processing instructions to enable commercial processor to identify proper chemical and developing procedures. (§14-1308).

Consumer Loans.—Under Md. Consumer Loan Law, upon full repayment of consumer loan lenders must furnish borrowers with written statement identifying loan transaction and stating that loan has been paid in full, mark all loan documents indelibly with words "paid" or "cancelled", release any mortgage or security, and restore any pledge or certificate of title. (§12-308). Similar requirements apply to credit grantors. (§12-1024).

Enforcement and Penalties.—Except where other express provision governs, following procedures for enforcement are available: (1) Consumer subjected to violation may file written complaint with Consumer Protection Division; (2) Division must investigate and may refer complaint to Federal Trade Commission; (3) Division may seek cooperation of licensing authorities and contracting departments of state in connection with investigation of licensee or contractor; (4) Division may dismiss complaint if it determines there are no reasonable grounds for finding violation; (5) other rights and remedies of consumer not foreclosed. (§13-401). If Division finds reasonable grounds to believe violation has occurred, it may attempt conciliation; terms of conciliation agreement may be embodied in written assurance of discontinuance or settlement agreement, signed by Division and each party, which does not constitute admission of violation. If Division determines that violations are causing immediate, substantial and irreparable harm, Attorney General may seek ex parte or interlocutory injunction without conciliation. Failure to adhere to any such assurance or agreement is violation of Consumer Protection Act. (§13-402). After service of statement of charges upon alleged violator and public hearing, if Division determines there has been violation, it may issue cease and desist order and order for affirmative action by violator. Division may issue cease and desist order without first conducting hearing. (§13-403[d][1]). However, order must grant respondent opportunity to request hearing, which must be held within seven days from the date on which request is made. (§13-403[d][3] &[4]). It may also institute civil action to preserve status quo or to obtain compliance with order. (§13-403). Division may submit dispute to arbitration under Uniform Arbitration Act and may institute program for voluntary arbitration of consumer disputes. (§13-404). Attorney General has subpoena powers, and information

See note at head of Digest as to 1998 legislation covered.

See Topical Index in front part of this volume.

MD – 11

CONSUMER PROTECTION . . . *continued*
obtained is inadmissible in later criminal proceedings against person providing evidence. (§13-405). Apart from procedure for public hearing and subsequent order, Attorney General may, on seven days notice to violator, institute action for injunction, in which court may enter any order necessary to prevent violation or to restore property acquired by violation or appoint receiver where there has been wilful violation. (§13-406). Attorney General may recover costs of any action brought for use of state. (§13-409). Actions by state for recovery of civil penalty or for criminal fine or imprisonment are also possible. (§§13-410, 13-411). Above procedures are not exclusive. (§§13-407, 13-408).

Plain Language Law.—No plain language statute.

See also topics Interest, Sales.

CONTRACTS:

Uniform Commercial Code adopted. (comm. law art. tit. 1-10). See topic Commercial Code.

Unless Md. law provides otherwise, no unit of municipal (art. 23A, §1A) or county government (art. 25, §1A; art. 25B, §13A) may raise defense of sovereign immunity on written contract executed by authorized official or employee. Punitive damages disallowed on county or municipal contracts. (art. 23A, §1A; courts art. §5-507[a]; art. 25, §1A; courts art. §5-508[a]; art. 25B, §13A; courts art. §5-510; art. 25A, §1A; courts art. §5-323). Claim on state, county or municipal contracts must be brought within one year from date claim arose or within one year of completion of contract giving rise to claim, whichever is later. (art. 23A, §1A; art. 25, §1A; art. 25A, §1A; art. 25B, §13A).

FACTORS:

Uniform Commercial Code adopted. (comm. law art. tits. 1 to 10). See topic Commercial Code.

License Requirements.—Factor must procure traders' license in each county or Baltimore City where he opens or carries on fixed place of business. (bus. reg. art. tit. 17, subtit. 18).

Consignment Agreements.—No statutory requirements with respect to filing or recording consignment agreements. Even so, in view of Uniform Commercial Code, comm. law art. §2-326(3), prudent consignor should record "agency record" certificate or file financing statement. (comm. law art. §2-326[3][c]).

Purchaser without notice that consignee is not authorized to sell and receive payment takes as against owner, though purchaser has notice that seller is only consignee. (comm. law art. §11-804).

If goods or possessory document taken as security for preexisting debt, then he who takes them, even with knowledge that he takes from consignee, has interest held by pledgor, unless he takes with notice that consignee has no authority to pledge, in which case no interest whatever passes, and claim for setoff of debt due by consignee is not allowed against owner in favor of pledgee. (comm. law art. §§11-805, 11-806).

Consignee's Lien.—Consignee has lien on goods for money or negotiable instrument given to or for use of shipper or consignor, unless he has notice that such person is not true owner. (comm. law art. §11-802). Consignee of agricultural products has lien for bona fide advance in money or goods to consignor on security of consignment. (comm. law art. §11-808[c]).

Consignee holding possessory document considered true owner for purpose of contract with third person for sale or for deposit of goods as security for money or negotiable instrument, unless third person knows consignee not true owner. (comm. law art. §11-803).

Conversion of consigned goods or proceeds by consignee or his agent or employee is misdemeanor punishable by fine up to $1,000 or imprisonment up to six months or both. Failure to pay over proceeds of sale, less commissions, within five days after receipt and after demand is prima facie evidence of conversion. (comm. law art. §11-809).

Consignments of agricultural products give only special right to sell and deliver to bona fide purchaser for valuable consideration, and no mortgage, pledge or deposit passes title. (comm. law art. §11-808).

Works of fine art become bailment property when delivered to art dealer on consignment and are not subject to claims, liens or security interests of creditors of art dealer. (comm. law art. §§11-8A-01 to 11-8A-04).

FRANCHISES:

References are to bus. reg. art. tit. 14 unless otherwise indicated.

Registration.—Any person offering to sell franchise in Md., or to Md. resident must be registered with Securities Commissioner. (§14-214[a]).

Application.—Registration application consists of offering prospectus which must contain following information about franchisor: (1) Names under which franchisor doing or intends to do business and of parent or affiliated company; (2) principal business address and that of State agent authorized to receive process; (3) business form; (4) identity and business experience of persons affiliated with franchisor; (5) statement noting whether any party identified in prospectus was convicted of felony or held liable for fraud, embezzlement, fraudulent conversion or misappropriation of property or is subject to order of SEC or securities administrator of any state denying registration to or revoking registration under securities decree or is subject to order of FTC or is subject to injunctive or restrictive order relating to business activity; (6) length of time franchisor has conducted business of type offered, granted franchises and granted franchises of different type; (7) recent financial statement and statement of any material changes; (8) copy of proposed franchise agreement; (9) franchise fee charged, proposed application of proceeds of fee and formula for fee if fees are not consistent; (10) list of all fees paid by franchisee; (11) termination, renewal, and option purchase clauses; (12) obligations of franchisee to purchase or lease from designated sources; (13) obligations of franchisee to purchase or lease in accordance with specifications or from approved suppliers; (14) terms of financing arrangements; (15) assignment of franchise agreement; (16) earning claims with supporting data; (17) arrangements with public figures; (18) information regarding presently operating franchises; (19) territory; (20) authorization for Commissioner to examine franchisor's financial records; (21) irrevocable consent to suit in Md. and appointment of Commissioner as attorney to receive service of process; and (22) such other information as Commissioner may require. (§14-216).

Books and Records.—Maintenance of complete set of books, records and accounts of sales required to sell. (§14-224).

Escrow or Bond.—Upon failure of franchisor to demonstrate to Commissioner that adequate financial arrangements have been made to fulfill franchisor's obligations to provide items included in offering, Commissioner may require escrow or impound fees paid by franchisee until obligations satisfied. (§14-217).

Exemptions.—Following may be exempted from registration: (1) Offer or sale by franchisee or by subfranchisor of entire area franchise for own account; (2) any transaction by executor, administrator, sheriff, receiver, bankruptcy trustee, guardian or conservator; (3) offer or sale of franchise substantially similar to franchise owned by offeree; and (4) other exemptions determined by Commissioner. (§14-214).

Filing Fee.—Application for registration filing fee is $500, for renewal is $250 and for amendment $100. All must be signed and verified by franchisor. (§§14-215, 14-219, 14-220). Registration becomes effective at noon of 30th business day after filing application (§14-218) and remains effective for one year. (§14-219).

Liability.—Person is liable to purchaser if franchise sold in violation of §14-214 or by means of untrue statement of material fact or material omission. (§14-227[a]). Franchisee may sue in law or equity to recover damages (§14-227[b]) and franchisor subject to imprisonment up to five years or $10,000 fine or both (§14-228). No waiver of liability of franchisor allowed. (§14-226).

Material Change.—Franchisor must give Commissioner written notification by application to amend, of any material change in information contained in application. Effective date of amendment to be determined by Commissioner. (§14-220).

Offering Prospectus.—Proposed offering prospectus must state in 10-point type that registration does not constitute approval and must accompany application. (§14-216). Commissioner may accept application and prospectus required by federal government agency, government agency of another state, or approved by association of administrators of state franchise laws. (§14-215).

Powers of Commissioner.—Commissioner may: (1) Upon violation of tit.14, order franchisor to stop further sales and may bring suit in circuit court to enjoin violative acts and enforce compliance within three years after violative act; (2) make public or private investigations; and (3) publish information concerning violation. (§§14-207 to 14-210).

Prospective Franchisee.—Unlawful to sell any franchise subject to registration without first providing prospective franchisee, at earlier of (1) prospective franchisee's first personal meeting with franchisor to discuss sale of franchise, or (2) ten business days prior to execution of contract or payment of fee relating to sale of franchise, copy of prospectus with all related agreements. (§14-223).

Renewal.—Upon submitting to Commissioner registration renewal statement accompanied by prospectus at least 15 business days before expiration, registration may be renewed for additional one year periods. Effective date of renewal is noon of day on which registration was due to expire. (§14-219).

Stop Order.—Revocation of registration may occur if Commissioner finds any of following: (1) Noncompliance with regulations; (2) offer of franchise would constitute deceit or fraud on purchaser; (3) any person identified in application is convicted felon or subject to order or has civil judgment entered against him, as described in §14-216, whose involvement in sale of franchise creates unreasonable risk to potential purchasers; (4) prospectus has material inaccuracy, is incomplete or contains false or misleading statement of material fact or material omission; (5) any person found to be engaging in false, fraudulent or deceptive practices in connection with offer of franchise; (6) financial condition of franchisor would affect ability to fulfill obligations to franchisee; and (7) noncompliance with escrow or bond requirements. (§14-221). Commissioner must notify applicant of entry of stop order, its basis, and that upon receipt of written request matter will be set for hearing within 15 days. Stop order may be vacated or modified. (§14-222).

FRAUDS, STATUTE OF:

All estates or interests in land, leasehold or freehold, except leasehold estates not exceeding one year, created by parol are at will only. Assignment of estate or interest in land must be in writing. (real prop. art. §§5-101 to 5-103).

Sales of land made by sheriff under fieri facias are within statute of frauds (10 G. & J. 294), but judicial sales are not (214 Md. 230, 133 A.2d 450; 39 Md. 299).

No action may be brought in following cases unless agreement, or note or memorandum thereof, in writing is signed by party to be charged or someone duly authorized by him: (1) Upon promise of personal representative to answer for damages out of his own estate (est. & tr. art. §8-109[i]); (2) upon promise to answer for debt, default or miscarriage of another; (3) upon agreement made upon consideration of marriage; (4) upon agreement not to be performed within one year (art. 39c, §1); or (5) upon contract for sale or disposition of land or interest therein (real prop. art. §5-104). Writing must also show consideration for agreement, except in case (2) above, where consideration may be shown by parol. (courts art. §10-907).

All declarations of trust and all assignments of beneficial interests in trusts respecting land must be in writing. (real prop. art. §§5-105, 5-106).

Contracts of Sale.—Uniform Commercial Code adopted. See topic Commercial Code. Contract for sale of goods for price of $500 or more not enforceable unless there is sufficient writing, except when: (1) Contract is for specially manufactured goods with reasonable indication that goods are for buyer; (2) party against whom enforcement is sought admits contract formation; or (3) payment has been made and accepted, or goods have been received and accepted. Between merchants, written confirmation, sufficient to bind sender and received within reasonable time, satisfies requirement as

See note at head of Digest as to 1998 legislation covered.

See Topical Index in front part of this volume.

MD – 12

FRAUDS, STATUTE OF . . . *continued*

against receiving party who has reason to know of its contents, unless receiving party sends written objection within ten days after receipt. (comm. law art. §2-201).

Part Performance.—Part performance of substantial nature will take case out of Statute of Frauds and render contract enforceable. (183 Md. 334, 37 A.2d 843; 164 Md. 594, 165 Atl. 812). Contract must be clear and definite, and act done must likewise be clear and definite and directly referable to particular agreement. (291 Md. 224, 434 A.2d 1015).

INTEREST:

Constitution fixes legal rate at 6% unless otherwise provided by legislature. (Const. art. III, §57). References are to sections of Commercial Law Art. of Code unless otherwise indicated.

Interest defined in various subtitles regulating loan and credit extension, see infra.

Maximum rate is 6% on unpaid balance unless otherwise provided (§12-102), but lender may charge 8% under written agreement (§12-103[a][1]). Loan secured by certificate of deposit may bear interest at rate not to exceed 2% above certificate's rate. (§12-103[a][2]). As practical matter, however, credit deregulation measures enacted by 1982 and 1983 sessions of General Assembly will be statutory provisions under which most lenders will extend credit.

1982 credit legislation, effective for loans made, renewed or refinanced after July 1, 1982, permits maximum 24% per annum simple interest on following transactions unless otherwise indicated: (1) Unsecured loans and loans secured by pledge of collateral other than savings account (§12-103[a][3]); (2) installment loans not secured by real property (§12-103[c]); (3) secondary mortgage loans (but origination fee may be charged in some instances) (§12-404[d]); (4) closed end credit accounts (24% on accounts made on or after July 1, 1982) (§12-505[a][3]); (5) open end retail accounts (may not exceed 2% per month) (§12-506[a][3]); (6) installment sales contracts for new and used motor vehicles under two years old (§12-609[f]); (7) installment sales contracts for other consumer goods (§12-610[3]); (8) loan renewals or extensions made by sales finance companies (§12-634[c] & [d]); loans by state-chartered credit unions made before Oct. 1, 1994 (fin. inst. art. §6-507[b]). For consumer loans not exceeding $6,000 made, renewed or refinanced after July 1, 1982, maximum monthly rate varies with original principal amount and unpaid principal balance per schedule in §12-306(a)(6). No maximum rate on loan to corporation or commercial loan in excess of $15,000, if not secured by residential real property, or in excess of $75,000, if secured by residential real property. (§12-103[e]). Lender who requires borrower to make false or misleading statement that loan is commercial loan is subject to treble damages. (§12-106.1). Qualified securities dealers who extend credit to customers may charge interest at any rate on debit balance if debit balance is payable on demand and if secured by securities. (§12-103[f]).

Interest is defined to include loan fees, service and carrying charges, discounts, time-price differentials, investigator's fees, points and origination fees. (§12-101[e]). Not considered as interest are certain types of late charges, certain prepayment penalties, governmental fees and charges, investigation and supervision fees on loans secured by inventory or accounts receivable, securities broker's service charge, and expenses charged by lender and not retained by lender for attorney's fees, governmental taxes and charges, loan insurance premiums and premiums paid for insuring life or health of borrower. Fees and charges otherwise includable as interest paid by developer to lender for purpose of making loans available to home buyers are not interest except such fees may be charged as interest if §12-108 is applicable. (§12-105). Lender may not charge borrower or other person any point or fraction of point, except where loan is made under federal law and is secured by mortgage or deed of trust insured or guaranteed by federal agency, or where loan is to corporation or is commercial loan in excess of $15,000 not secured by residential real property, or in excess of $75,000 secured by residential real property (§12-108[a]), or except where permitted or required pursuant to federal or Md. law providing for program of mortgage purchases or by federal agency, including GNMA, FNMA, FHLMC, etc., or state or local agency under certain conditions. State and local loan programs subject to one point limit. (§12-108[b], [c]).

Extensive consumer protection measures apply regarding repossession and redemption of goods (§12-115); refinancings and consolidations of loans (§12-116); elimination of holder in due course status of assignee of consumer debt (§§12-117, 14-1302); charging of variable interest on loans not secured by real property (§§12-118,12-505.2, 12-610.2); prohibition of or restriction on balloon payments in certain transactions (§§12-103[a][3] & [c], 12-306[a][7], 12-505.3, 12-634; fin. inst. art. §6-507[b][5]). Computation of interest and fees allowed are regulated. (§§12-306, 12-307). Disclosure statement quoting statutes and providing certain information required. (§12-308). Criminal penalties apply to overcharges not due to accidental or bona fide error of computation, and to knowing and willful participation in violation by member, officer, director, employee, or agent of licensed lender. (§12-316). Lender may not retain any interest or compensation if excess interest, discount or other charge is willful. Treble overcharge in damages allowed for non-willful overcharges not corrected before next payment. (§12-313).

1983 credit legislation adds two new subtitles to comm. law art. without changing existing subtitles. (See discussion supra.) "Credit grantors" have option of extending credit either under one of new subtitles or under prior law, but each transaction must comply with all provisions of subtitle elected. (§§12-914, 12-1014). New provisions, which cover revolving credit transactions (Subtit. 9) and closed end credit transactions (Subtit. 10), employ term "credit-grantor" to make clear application not only to banks and traditional lenders, but also to retailers and others who extend credit and make loans in course of business (§12-901). New subtitles cover all types of loans and borrowers, but certain consumer protections apply only to credit or loans extended to consumers for personal, household or family purposes.

Subtit. 9 governs extensions of credit such as bank and retail credit cards, credit card cash advances, overdraft or credit checking and lines of credit, including telephonic, electronic and automated teller transactions. (§12-902). Revolving credit plan may be secured by any collateral acceptable to credit grantor including real property,

except that revolving line of credit accessible by use of credit card may not be secured by lien on residential real property. (§12-902). Interest rate is capped at 24% per year simple interest but may vary with index. (§§12-903, 12-904). Interest rate, as varied, may apply to purchases or loans made prior to date that rate changed. (§12-904). §12-904(a) provides that charges contained in revolving credit plan agreement may vary according to index or formula that (1) is made readily available to and verifiable by borrower, (2) is beyond control of credit grantor, and (3) may be within control of borrower. Subsection (d) provides that if formula under (a)(3) is used to measure credit risk, periodic percentage rate of interest or finance charges (1) shall be lower for consumer borrower measured as more credit worthy and (2) if formula considers delinquency or arrearages, may not be raised unless consumer borrower is at least two months in arrears in payment. Balloon payments prohibited. (§12-903). Finance charge or interest may not be imposed if balance is paid in full within 25 days after end of billing period or, if there is no balance at beginning of billing period, on purchases added to account during billing period. (§12-903).

If credit agreement does not impose certain special fees, e.g., annual membership charge, transaction charge or minimum charge level, and if agreement provides, credit grantor may impose interest or finance charge from date of purchase. (§§12-903, 12-905). Sellers of goods or services are limited to imposing only one special fee, which must be foregone if interest is charged from date of purchase. (§§12-903, 12-905). Certain actual, verifiable fees incurred but not retained by credit grantor may also be charged to consumer borrower, and if credit grantor is depository institution that extends credit by demand deposit or overdraft loan arrangement, it may impose customary service charges. (§§12-905, 12-907). All credit grantors may allow deferral of scheduled payment and assess deferral charge. (§12-908).

Credit grantor may require consumer borrower to purchase certain property, title or credit loss insurance if loan is secured, but purchase of certain other types of insurance is consumer's option. Premiums are not considered interest or finance charges. (§12-909).

Non-consumer borrowers may be subject to higher interest rates on payments or portions thereof in default, and all borrowers may, under certain circumstances, be subject to late or delinquency charges which are not considered interest or finance charges. Assessment of such charges is regulated. (§12-910).

Credit grantor may impose different terms on debt arising out of purchases and that arising out of loans unpaid and, provided proper notice is given, may amend terms to alter amount of interest, fees or repayment due or method of computation. Upon proper notice, new terms may apply to any indebtedness that arose prior to date of change. (§§12-906, 12-912).

Licensing, investigatory, enforcement and penalty provisions of fin. inst. art. tit. 11, subtit. 3, and tit. 11, subtit. 5, continue to apply to subject institutions under 1983 enactment, unless credit grantor or extension of credit is exempt. (§12-915). Commissioner of Consumer Credit administers subtitle, but authority does not extend to depository institutions. (§12-916). Penalties for knowing or wilful violations are set forth (§§12-917, 12-918), but credit grantors are not liable for noncompliance if error is corrected within certain time and under certain conditions. (§12-920). Statute of limitations for actions for violation of subtitle is six months after credit extension has been repaid in full. (§12-919).

If consumer borrower is in default, certain specific procedures must be followed for repossession, sale, redemption or application of proceeds, but requirements may not apply in certain cases of fraudulent or wrongful conduct by borrower or in event of prior repossession and redemption. (§12-921).

Subtit. 10, which governs closed end credit transactions, permits credit grantor to charge up to 24% simple interest per year, which rate may vary with same type of objective index described above. (§§12-1003, 12-1004). (But see §12-306[a][6], enacted in 1982 session, which permits effective interest rate of up to 33% on certain closed end consumer loans.)

Credit grantor may charge certain other loan fees, finder's fees or other charges, provided that sum thereof does not exceed 10% of underlying loan, and may charge reasonable fees for services rendered or expenses incurred; provided, however, that such fees may be charged to consumer borrower only in certain instances. (But see §12-1005[a].) Such fees and charges are not considered interest. (§12-1005). Certain other fees and costs may be assessed in event of default. (§12-1011).

If loan to consumer under Subtit. 10 is secured by collateral other than lien on residential real property, balloon payments at maturity are prohibited. If loan is secured by secondary lien on residential real property, balloon payment at maturity is permitted in certain circumstances. (§12-1003[c]).

Deferral of scheduled payments is permitted, as is fee therefor. (§12-1006). Credit grantor may require consumer borrower to purchase certain types of insurance in certain circumstances, but other types are optional with consumer. Premiums for such insurance are not considered interest. (§12-1007). Non-consumer borrowers may be required to pay certain higher interest rates on payments in default, and all borrowers may, under certain circumstances, be subject to late or delinquency charges (provided, however, that consumer loan agreement must so state). Such charges are not considered interest. (§12-1008).

Consumer borrower may prepay Subtit. 10 loan without penalty. (§12-1009). If consumer refinances, charge may be imposed. (§12-1010). For non-consumer loans, credit grantor may charge fees for extension, deferral, prepayment or refinancing. (§12-1012).

Subtit. 10, like Subtit. 9, supra, sets forth various provisions for licensing, regulation, enforcement, penalties and repossession. (§§12-1015—12-1021).

Lenders are subject to licensing, regulation enforcement and penalty assessment by Commissioner of Consumer Credit and Bank Commissioner as applicable. See specific comm. law art. provisions discussed supra, and fin. inst. art. tits. 11 and 12.

Disclosure statements setting forth principal, total finance charge as defined in federal Truth-in-Lending Act in dollars (if loan payable on demand, on per diem basis), rate in percent and payments in addition to interest must be furnished to borrower prior to execution of loan contract, unless loan under Md. Higher Education Loan Program, loan made to corporation or commercial loan in excess of $15,000, if

INTEREST . . . *continued*

not secured by residential real property, or in excess of $75,000, if secured by residential real property. (§12-106). Compliance with disclosure provisions of Federal Truth-in-Lending Act and regulations sufficient. (§12-106[b][3], [b][4]). Lenders receiving monthly payments on more than five loans secured by real property must notify each borrower at least annually of prior payments of principal, amount considered as interest, and amount of principal remaining unpaid. (§12-106[c]).

Bonds, notes and other written obligations to pay specified sum of money bear interest from date, if "with interest" or "with interest from date" be written therein or thereon; otherwise, from either date of demand or date of accrual of cause of action, in accordance with Uniform Commercial Code. (§§3-118[d], 3-122[4]).

Judgments and decrees generally bear interest at 10% from rendition. Money judgments for loan debt not secured by realty may carry contract rate until originally-scheduled maturity date. (courts art. §§11-106, 11-107, 11-301).

Open Accounts.—Interest does not run as matter of right, but may be allowed in such amount as is fair in discretion of jury, or court, if case is tried without jury. (213 Md. 509, 132 A.2d 582; 245 Md. 524, 226 A.2d 565).

Mortgage Secured Loans.—From Feb. 23, 1979 any loan secured by first mortgage or first deed of trust on residential real property or interest therein may carry interest at any rate if there is written agreement between lender and borrower setting forth rate, if there is no prepayment penalty, if not refinancing of loan secured by first mortgage or first deed of trust on any interest in residential real property (unless lender is banking institution, national bank association, federal savings bank, or federal or state savings and loan association or credit union, or other exceptions apply), and if lender does not require payment of any interest in advance except any points otherwise permitted. (§12-103[b]). Lender may charge interest at rate permitted by federal law if loan made in compliance with federal law, secured by mortgage or deed of trust, and insured or guaranteed in full or part by FHA, VA or other federal agency or instrumentality. (§12-103[d]). From June 1, 1974 lending institution lending on security of first mortgage or deed of trust or residential real property and maintaining escrow account must pay interest on such account at greater of regular passbook rate or 3%, unless lender uses direct reduction method; does not apply if loan purchased by out-of-state lender under certain federally insured mortgage programs if purchaser services loan itself. Lender or lender's assignee may not impose collection fee or service charge on maintenance of escrow account on first mortgage or first deed of trust. (§12-109.2). Lender imposing fees on borrower for settlement services or document review services performed by lender-designated attorney for loan on borrower's primary residence must make certain written disclosures. (§§12-119, 12-120).

Secondary Mortgage Loans.—Person making loans, not to corporate borrowers or for business purposes or commercial investment, where loan or deferred purchase price is secured in whole or part by mortgage, deed of trust, security agreement or other lien on Md. residential real property subject to lien of one or more prior encumbrances other than ground rent or leasehold interest, must be licensed under or exempt from licensing requirements of tit. 12, subtit. 3 of fin. inst. art. (§§12-401, 12-402). Interest ceiling is 24% per annum simple interest providing certain conditions are met. Lender may take interest in advance on full amount of loan for entire period; balloon payments permitted only on residential real property with mandatory postponement options given to borrower. (§§12-404, 12-404.1). In certain circumstances, consumer protection measures apply. (§§12-116, 12-117, 12-118). Loans regulated in extensive detail. Criminal penalties apply to wilful violation by lender, officer, employee or other person. (§12-414). See subhead Maximum Rate, supra. Subordinate mortgage loans made under credit grantor subtitles are not subject to these restrictions. (§§12-913.1, 12-1013.1).

Insurance premium loan carrying charges may not exceed 1.15% per 30 days, and initial service charge may not exceed $20. (ins. arts. 23-504, 23-304, 23-305).

Usury.—Defined as charging by lender of interest in amount greater than allowed by comm. law art. tit. 12, subtit. 1. (§12-101[k]). Person guilty of usury must forfeit three times excess of interest and charges collected above legal interest and charges or $500, whichever is greater. Usury cannot be claimed or pleaded if lender, within 30 days of execution of loan, gives notice and modifies contract rate to legal rate. (§12-114). Usury cannot be claimed or pleaded against assignee or holder for bona fide and legal consideration without notice of usury in creation or assignment of instrument (§12-112) or against anyone where loan has been satisfied for six months (§12-111). Usury law applies to loan document executed outside Md. if loan is to Md. resident and secured by property located in Md. (§12-114[c]).

Discrimination prohibited, with certain exceptions. (§§12-113, 12-305 [consumer loans]). Equal Credit Opportunity Act, administered by Commissioner of Consumer Credit except for actions relating to certain banks which are administered by State Bank Commissioner, prohibits discrimination on basis of sex, marital status, race, color, religion, national origin or age (assuming ability to contract). Violation of Federal Equal Credit Opportunity Act is violation under Maryland statute. (§§12-701 to 12-707).

See also topic Sales, subheads Retail Installment Sales, Retail Credit Accounts, Sales Finance Companies.

LICENSES, BUSINESS AND PROFESSIONAL:

General license laws of state are contained in bus. reg. art. License laws relating to alcoholic beverages are contained in art. 2B. Clerks of circuit courts issue all traders' licenses (bus. reg. art. tit. 17, subtit. 18) and marriage licenses (fam. law art. §2-405). License laws relating to grain dealers contained in agric. art. tit. 13. Most businesses and some occupations are required to obtain licenses. State licensing authorities may require individual applying for license to disclose whether individual has ever been convicted of controlled dangerous substance offense (i.e., drug offense) on or after Jan. 1, 1991, and if applicant has been so convicted, licensing authorities may (i) refuse to issue license to individual, or (ii) issue license subject to certain terms and conditions. (art. 41, §§1-403—1-409, art. 27, §§298A, 639[d], 641[a], 641A[d]). Before any

license may be issued or renewed, applicant must certify that he has paid all undisputed taxes and unemployment insurance contributions or has provided for payment in manner satisfactory to unit responsible for collection. (bus. occ. art. §1-203).

Applicant for issuance or renewal of license or permit must certify that all taxes, including unemployment insurance contributions, have been paid. (bus. occ. art. §1-203).

Accountants.—Licensing requirements contained in Business Occupations Article (bus. occ. art.), tit. 2.

Architects.—Licensing requirements contained in bus. occ. art., tit. 3.

Barbers.—Licensing requirements contained in bus. occ. art., tit. 4.

Cigarette Manufacturing.—Licensing requirements contained in bus. reg. art. §§16-201 to 16-207, 16-210, 16-212, 16-214 and tax. gen. art. 12-104, 12-201, and 13-825(h)(1).

Cosmetologists.—Licensing requirements contained in bus. occ. art., tit. 5.

Electricians.—Licensing requirements contained in bus. occ. art., tit. 6.

Foresters.—Licensing requirements contained in bus. occ. art., tit. 7.

Hearing Aid Dealers.—Licensing requirements contained in bus. occ. art., tit. 8.

Heating, Ventilation, Air Conditioning and Refrigeration Contractors.—Licensing requirements contained in bus. reg. art. §§9A-101, 9A-302, 9A-306, and 9A-309.

Interior Designers.—Licensing requirements contained in bus. occ. art., tit. 8.5.

Landscape Architects.—Licensing requirements contained in bus. occ. art., tit. 9.

Lawyers.—Licensing requirements contained in bus. occ. art., tit. 10.

Mortician.—Licensing requirements contained in health occ. art. §§7-301 to 7-321.

Pilots.—Licensing requirements contained in bus. occ. art., tit. 11.

Plumbers.—Licensing requirements contained in bus. occ. art., tit. 12.

Private Detectives.—Licensing requirements contained in bus. occ. art., tit. 13.

Professional Engineers.—Licensing requirements contained in bus. occ. art., tit. 14.

Professional Land Surveyors.—Licensing requirements contained in bus. occ. art., tit. 15.

Home Improvement Contractors.—Licensing requirements contained in bus. reg. art. tit. 8.

Real Estate Appraisers.—Licensing requirements contained in bus. occ. art. tit. 15.5.

Real Estate Brokers.—Licensing requirements contained in bus. occ. art., tit. 16.

Security Systems Technicians.—Licensing requirements contained in bus. occ. art. §§17-101 to 17-601; bus. reg. art. §8-301(d)(4) and (5).

Commercial Travelers.—Nonresident traveling salesmen, sample merchants and representatives of foreign mercantile or manufacturing concerns need no license to make sales to or solicit orders from licensed merchants. (bus. reg. art. §17-804). With certain exceptions hawker's and peddler's license is required for sales to public. (bus. reg. art. tit. 17, subtit. 9).

Nonresident Businesses.—Nonresident home improvement contractors, heating, ventilation, air conditioning, and refrigeration contractors, construction contractors, and plumbers and gas fitters are required to pay license fees. (bus. reg. art. §§8-301, 8-303, 9A-301, 9A-305, 17-602, 17-603, 17-1503, 17-1504).

Gasoline dealers must be licensed (bus. reg. art. tit. 17, subtit. 18) and are subject to special regulation (bus. reg. art. tit. 10, subtit. 3 [Motor Fuel Inspection Law]). See also topic Monopolies, Restraint of Trade and Competition, subhead Gasohol and Gasoline Products Marketing Act.

Mortgage bankers and brokers must be licensed and must file $50,000 surety bond with Bank Commissioner. (fin. inst. art. §§12-501 to 12-507).

Franchises.—Offer of franchise in Md. or to Md. resident must be registered with Securities Commissioner. (bus. reg. art. tit. 14). See topic Franchises.

Fur Dealers.—Exempt from license if furs or pelts were taken legally from wild by that person. (nat. res. art., §10-506[f]).

Residential service agency required to obtain license. (health gen. art. 19-4A-01 to 19-4A-10). Residential service agency is any nongovernmental business employing or contracting with individuals to provide home health care for compensation to unrelated sick or disabled individual in residence of that individual.

Collection Agencies.—Collection agencies licensed by Collection Agency Licensing Board, division of Office of Commissioner of Consumer Credit. (bus. reg. art. §7-301). In addition to annual license fee of $400, surety bond of $5,000 must be posted. (bus. reg. art. §§7-302 to 7-304). Certain debt collection practices forbidden. See topic Consumer Protection, subhead Consumer Debt Collection.

MONOPOLIES, RESTRAINT OF TRADE AND COMPETITION:

Art. 41 of Md. Declaration of Rights prohibits monopolies. Common law prohibits restraint of trade. (258 Md. 419, 266 A.2d 1). Md. Antitrust Act (comm. law art. tit. ll, subtit. 2) complements federal law governing restraints of trade, unfair competition and unfair, deceptive and fraudulent acts or practices (§11-202; 36 Md. L. Rev. 323), but permits suit by indirect purchasers (§11-209[b]). Enumerated activities are exempt. (§11-203). Attorney General may institute criminal and civil enforcement proceedings, and final judgment or decree in such proceedings (but not consent judgment or decree entered before testimony is taken) is prima facie evidence against defendant in private action for treble damages. (§§11-207, 11-209, 11-210). If Maryland brings criminal action under subtitle 2 of title 11, or U.S. brings criminal action under federal antitrust law, any civil action under §11-209 related to subject matter of criminal action must be brought within one year after conclusion of criminal action or within four years

MONOPOLIES, RESTRAINT OF TRADE AND COMPETITION . . . *continued*
after cause of action accrued, whichever is later. Certain conduct is specifically permitted. (§11-204[b]).

See also topic Consumer Protection; category Intellectual Property, topic Trademarks and Tradenames.

Sales Below Cost.—No retailer or wholesaler may, with intent to injure competitor or destroy competition, advertise, offer to sell or sell at retail or wholesale any item of merchandise at less than cost as defined in Act. Circuit courts have jurisdiction to enjoin any act so prohibited. Act does not apply: (1) To bona fide clearance sales, if so advertised and goods so marked and sold; (2) to prompt sales necessary to forestall loss; (3) where merchandise is imperfect or damaged or is being discontinued, if so advertised, marked and sold; (4) to sales in final liquidation of business; (5) to sales for charitable purposes or to relief agencies; (6) to contract sales to departments of government or governmental institutions; (7) to sales by officer acting under order or direction of court; (8) where price is set in good faith to meet competition. (comm. law art. tit. 11, subtit. 4). Statutory formula for determining costs held unconstitutional as applied to merchant whose costs were less than formula. (197 Md. 586, 80 A.2d 267).

Cigarette Sales Below Cost Act contains special provisions governing retail and wholesale sales of cigarettes, which are not covered by general Md. Sales Below Cost Act. (comm. law art. tit. 11, subtit. 5).

Resale Price Agreements.—See category Intellectual Property, topic Trademarks and Tradenames.

Gasohol and Gasoline Products Marketing Act governs oral or written agreements between distributors of gasohol and gasoline products and retail dealers under which dealers obtain right to use trademark, tradename, service mark, etc. or to occupy premises. (comm. law art. tit. 11, subtit. 3). See also topic Licenses, Business and Professional, subhead Gasoline Dealers.

NEGOTIABLE INSTRUMENTS:

See topic Bills and Notes.

SALES:

References are to Commercial Law Article of Code unless otherwise noted.

Uniform Commercial Code adopted. (comm. law art. tit. 2). See topic Commercial Code.

Sales Below Cost Act.—See topic Monopolies, Restraint of Trade and Competition.

Contracts of Sale.—No statutory regulation as to type size in printed contracts generally; however, in retail installment sale agreements, certain matters must be printed in 12-point bold type or larger. See subhead Retail Installment Sales, infra.

Bills of Sale.—Uniform Commercial Code adopted.

Conditions or Warranties.—Uniform Commercial Code adopted. See topic Commercial Code, subhead Intentional Variations, for limitations on attempts to exclude warranties. (§§2-316, 2-316.1).

Improvements to Real Property.—Unless properly excluded, there are implied warranties to original purchaser of newly constructed private dwelling unit for one year that improvements are free from faulty materials, constructed in workmanlike manner according to sound engineering standards and fit for habitation. In case of structural defects, warranty expires two years from date of completion, delivery, or taking of possession. (real prop. art. §§10-203 and 10-204).

Product Liability.—Manufacturer or supplier of dangerous or harmful product may be liable for negligence if it knows of danger and fails to warn user (198 Md. 414, 84 A.2d 81; 221 Md. 476, 158 A.2d 110), or if it represented unsafe product to be safe (221 Md. 105, 156 A.2d 442); but, except as modified by Uniform Commercial Code, it will not be liable for breach of warranty unless there is privity (181 Md. 614, 31 A.2d 316). Under Uniform Commercial Code, express or implied warranty extends from manufacturer, dealer and retailer to family, household and guests of purchaser and to any other ultimate consumer or user of goods or person affected thereby, if it is reasonable to expect person to use, consume or be affected and if person is personally injured by breach. (§§2-314, 2-318). Attempt by seller or manufacturer of consumer goods or services to modify or exclude express or implied warranties is unenforceable. (§2-316.1). Defenses available in tort action, such as contributory negligence and assumption of risk, may be asserted in breach of warranty actions. (See 260 Md. 190, 271 A.2d 744; 279 Md. 371, 368 A.2d 993.)

§402A of Restatement (Second) of Torts providing for strict liability in tort for seller of defective and unreasonable dangerous consumer goods has been adopted by case law, 278 Md. 337, 363 A.2d 955.

Transfer of Title.—Uniform Commercial Code adopted.

Delivery.—Uniform Commercial Code adopted.

Stoppage in Transitu.—Uniform Commercial Code adopted.

Remedies of Seller and Buyer.—Uniform Commercial Code adopted.

Defenses Against Lender.—Licensed lender who knowingly participates in financing sale of goods or services used primarily for personal, family or household purposes is subject to all claims and defenses of borrower against seller arising from such sale. (§12-309).

Conditional Sales.—Uniform Commercial Code adopted. No recordation tax. No statutory requirement as to type size in printed contract. Absent specific agreement to contrary, person in lawful possession of property has right of possession superior to person with legal title by virtue of security interest pursuant to conditional sales contract or other security agreement. Such legal title no defense to charge of theft. (art. 27, §343).

Lease of chattels, designed to accomplish purposes of conditional sale, must be recorded as conditional sale contract. (190 Md. 182, 57 A.2d 796).

Land Installment Contracts.—References are to Real Property Article of Code unless otherwise indicated. Executory agreement under which purchaser agrees to pay purchase price of improved or unimproved and subdivided real property to be used or improved and used as dwelling in five or more payments subsequent to any down payment and under which vendor retains title as security is governed by real prop. art., tit. 10, subtit. 1. There must be complete written contract signed by all parties. Purchaser must be given and give receipt in form specified for copy of instrument at or before signing. Purchaser must also be given and give receipt for copy signed by seller. Purchaser has unconditional right to cancel until he signs and receives copy signed by seller. Before purchaser signs and receives copy, seller must deliver receipt in form specified for any payment or deposit made by purchaser. (§§10-102[a] to [e]). Within 15 days after contract signed by both parties, vendor must record it among land records of county where property lies; otherwise purchaser may cancel. (§10-102[f]). Contract must contain information specified, and must recite certain information in tabular form. (§10-103[b]). Application of installment payments is prescribed (§10-103[c]), and vendor may not place or hold mortgage on property in amount greater than balance due under contract, nor may mortgage require payments in excess of contract installments (§10-103[d]). When contract recorded, property is deemed to be held by record owner of title, subject to rights of purchaser. (§10-104). When 40% of purchase price paid, or sooner if contract so provides, purchaser may demand grant of premises, on condition that he execute purchase money mortgage. Periodic principal and interest payments required by mortgage may not exceed land contract installments unless mortgagor consents. Deed and mortgage executed pursuant to purchaser's demand supersede land installment contract. (§10-105). Purchaser may cure default under contract before date designated in vendor's notice to terminate contract. (§10-106). Vendor must deliver statement of account to purchaser at least annually (in Jan.) or on demand no more than twice a year and when 40% of purchase price paid. (§10-107). Purchaser may enforce law by suit in equity, and may be awarded reasonable attorneys' fees. (§10-108). Special notice required for contract involving some subdivisions in Prince George's County. (§10-701).

Retail Credit Accounts.—References are to Commercial Law Art. of Code unless otherwise indicated. Retail credit accounts made in Md. must comply with comm. law art. See topic Interest, subhead Maximum Rate, for summary of 1983 legislation dealing with open-end credit transactions. Account considered made in Md. regardless of situs if: (1) Seller offers or agrees in Md. to sell to resident buyer, (2) resident buyer accepts or offers to buy in Md., (3) oral or written solicitation to sell originates outside Md. but is forwarded to and received by resident buyer, or (4) verbal or written solicitation to buy originates in Md. from resident buyer and is forwarded to and received by outside retail seller. (§12-502[b]). Retail credit account may be established by seller or financial institution only on request of or with consent of buyer. (§12-503[a]). Discrimination on basis of sex, marital status, age (over 18) or geographic area or neighborhood is prohibited. Questionnaire may not refer to race, creed, color or national origin of applicant. (§12-503[b]). Alimony or child support received by buyer must be considered as income. (§12-503[c]). Seller or financial institution establishing account must confirm fact in writing in form specified. (§12-503[d]). Retail credit account agreement must be in writing and either be signed by buyer or reasonable attempt have been made to obtain buyer's signature; certain information must be contained in application form for account and supplied upon establishment of account. (§12-503[e]). Before first payment and within 40 days after each purchase, holder of account must inform buyer in writing of certain information (§12-503[f]), and certain other information must be supplied in writing within 40 days after each payment (§12-503[g]). Buyer under open-end account may request annually amount of finance charges collected by holder during preceding calendar year; holder must respond within 30 days. (§12-503[h]). Buyer whose credit balance on open-end account exceeds $1 must receive monthly statement; and if balance remains same after four consecutive monthly statements, holder must send buyer check or money order in full amount. (§12-506.1). Holder of account must disclose address and telephone number on each billing statement. (§12-503[i]). Maximum finance charges on open-end and closed-end accounts are prescribed. No membership or other fee except that specified in subtitle may be charged on open-end accounts. (§§12-504 to 12-506). Unintentional and good faith failure to comply with §§12-504 to 12-507 may be corrected within ten days after holder becomes aware of such failure. (§12-513[b]). Promissory note taken as part of retail credit account must refer to account and is subject, if assigned, to defenses of buyer against establisher of account; note may not contain confession of judgment. (§12-507). Account agreement may contain provision for payment of reasonable attorneys' fees only, fees to be set by court. (§12-508). Notwithstanding agreement to contrary between seller and issuer of credit card, seller may offer cash discount to cash customers. (§12-509). Buyer may inquire in writing about status of account, and holder of account must answer within 60 days or forfeit finance charges. (§12-510). Buyer may assert billing error in writing within 60 days of receipt of statement, and holder must acknowledge in writing within 30 days of buyer's inquiry and, within 60 days and before action to collect, make corrections and notify buyer thereof or send buyer statement of reasons why account is correct. Until holder complies, he may not communicate unfavorable credit information concerning buyer based on buyer's failure to pay disputed account. Failure to comply subjects holder to civil penalties as follows: if there is no billing error, holder forfeits finance charge in connection with disputed amount from date of buyer's inquiry; if there is billing error, holder is liable for damages resulting from failure to comply. (§12-511). Buyer cannot be charged fee for reply to account status inquiry or billing inquiry. (§12-511.1). Buyer cannot waive benefits of retail credit accounts law. (§12-512). General penalty for violation of law is forfeiture of finance charges (§12-513[a]), and knowing violation is misdemeanor punishable by fine up to $100 (first offense) or up to $500 (subsequent offense) (§12-515). Complaint of violation is filed with Commissioner of Financial Regulation, who may investigate and may hold hearing after ten days written notice to defendant. If Commissioner finds violation, he must issue cease and desist order, which is appealable under Md. Administrative Procedure Act. Commissioner may not issue cease and desist order against incorporated bank, savings institution or trust company, against savings and loan association or against federal or state-chartered credit union. (§12-514). See topic Interest, subhead Maximum Rate, for discussion of additional regulation.

See note at head of Digest as to 1998 legislation covered.

See Topical Index in front part of this volume.

MD – 15

SALES . . . *continued*

Retail installment sales of goods whose price is $25,000 or less are governed by comm. law art. tit. 12, subtit. 6, and tit. 12, subtit. 10. See topic Interest, subhead Maximum Rate, for discussion of additional regulation. Bona fide C.O.D. transactions, and those regulated by Md. Layaway Sales Act (see topic Consumer Protection) not governed by subtit. 6. (§12-601[1][3]). Seller or sales finance company may not make false, misleading or deceptive statement in advertisement relating to finance, delinquency or extension charges or to security interest, collateral, terms or conditions on which it will make or finance installment agreement. (§12-602). Discrimination on basis of sex, marital status, age (over 18), geographic area of residence or neighborhood of residence prohibited. (§12-603). Installment sale agreement must be evidenced by complete written instrument, signed by all parties before seller delivers goods. (§12-604). Seller must deliver exact copy of agreement to buyer at or before time buyer signs: he must also deliver copy signed by seller within 15 days after buyer signs, or agreement and instruments signed by buyer are void, and seller must refund all payments and deposits. Until buyer signs agreement and receives copy signed by seller, he has unconditional right to cancel and receive refund of payments and deposits made; during cancellation period, seller must deliver receipt for any payment or deposit, which receipt must be in form specified. (§§12-605[a]-[c]). Acknowledgment of delivery of copy of agreement must be printed in 12-point type or larger, and, if contained in agreement, must be printed immediately below signature and independently signed. (§12-605[d]). Agreement must contain specified information. (§12-606). If agreement does not contain information required by §§12-604 to 12-606, or if seller fails to deliver copy to buyer, holder may not collect finance, delinquency or collection charges from buyer. (§12-630[a]). Certain provisions, including confession of judgment and assignment of wages, are prohibited. (§12-607). If instrument contains prohibited provision, provision is void, and holder may not collect any finance, delinquency or collection charge. (§12-630[d]). Special provisions apply to catalog sales. (§12-608). Detailed provisions prescribe maximum finance charges, additional charges allowable, charges which may be made for insurance, refunds of charges which must be made in certain instances, etc. (§§12-609 to 12-616, 12-619, 12-620, 12-623). If excessive finance charge is imposed by agreement, holder cannot collect any finance, delinquency or collection charge (§12-630[a]); however, unintentional and good faith failure to comply with §§12-609 to 12-612 may be corrected within ten days (§12-630[c]). If buyer is charged for insurance, holder or assignee must deliver copy of policy or certificate within 25 days after delivery of goods or within five days after assignment. (§12-613[c]). If buyer must make payment in addition to down payment before he has right to delivery, he may cancel before delivery or tender of goods by seller, and seller must refund at least 90% of all payments made within ten days. If buyer is entitled to delivery because of down payment and before any further payment but refuses to accept goods, all or part of down payment may be forfeited as provided in agreement. (§12-615). Person receiving payment on account of agreement must give receipt on request, or without request if payment is in cash. (§12-617[a]). Unless buyer receives written notice of assignment of agreement, he may pay or notify last known holder, and such payment or notice is binding on assignee. (§12-617[b]). Add-on contract is permitted. (§12-618). Notwithstanding provision in agreement to contrary, buyer may prepay without penalty, and holder must refund specified portion of finance charge. (§§12-612 [consumer goods], 12-620). Holder is required to deliver copy of agreement and statement of account within ten days after receipt of request from buyer; statement must be supplied free, except that fee of 50¢ may be charged for statement supplied within 60 days after prior statement. (§12-621). After buyer has paid all sums due and upon request, holder must deliver within 15 days to buyer, surety and each owner of collateral signed statement of discharge and instruments of release. (§12-622). Detailed provisions govern repossession. (§§12-624 to 12-627). Promissory note taken as part of installment sale must refer to agreement, and if assigned, is subject to defenses which buyer might assert against seller or sales finance company (except buyer's acknowledgment or receipt of copy of agreement is conclusive in favor of assignee without actual knowledge to contrary). (§§12-628, 12-630[b]). Buyer may not waive benefits of retail installment sales law. (§12-629). Complaint of violation is filed with and handled by Commissioner of Consumer Credit same as for violation of retail credit account law. Knowing violation of comm. law art. §§12-602 to 12-631 is misdemeanor punishable by fine up to $100 (first offense) or up to $500 (subsequent offense). (§12-636[a]). See topic Interest, subhead Maximum Rate, for discussion of additional regulation.

Sales Finance Companies.—Person, other than banking institution, engaged in business of acquiring, investing in or lending money or credit on security of interests in: (1) Installment sale agreements made between others; (2) retail credit account transactions made between others; or (3) certain home improvement transactions made between others, must be licensed by Commissioner of Consumer Credit. (fin. inst. art. tit. 11, subtit. 4). Such licensee may renew or extend time for payment of any installment of or whole of installment sale agreement or may refund previously paid installment, if written agreement is signed and delivered as specified. (comm. law art. §§12-632, 12-633). Licensee may charge for renewal, extension, or refund up to specified maximum interest rates. (§12-634). Licensee must permit buyer to prepay without penalty and must refund unearned finance charges. (§12-635). Violation of comm. law art. §§12-632 to 12-635 is misdemeanor punishable by fine up to $500 or imprisonment up to six months or both. (§12-636[b]). See topic Interest, subhead Maximum Rate, for discussion of additional regulation.

See also topic Interest; categories Mortgages, topic Chattel Mortgages; Transportation, topic Motor Vehicles, subhead Liens and Security Interests.

Consumer Protection.—See topic Consumer Protection.

Bulk Sales.—Uniform Commercial Code adopted. (comm. law art. tit. 6). See also category Debtor and Creditor, topic Fraudulent Sales and Conveyances.

Sales of Motor Vehicles.—See category Transportation, topic Motor Vehicles.

Distress or Going Out of Business Sale.—Going out of business sales and other such sales governed by tit. 11, subtit. 11. (§11-1101[c]). Inventory describing each item for sale, quantity of each, and regular and sale prices of each must be filed with Division of Consumer Protection of Attorney General's Office before conducting sale. (§11-1104). Anyone advertising such sale may not conduct sale for more than 60 days, order and receive any goods for purpose of selling them at sale, or sell goods not listed on inventory. (§11-1103).

SECURITIES:

Uniform Securities Act (see Uniform and Model Acts section) has been adopted in substance under title "Maryland Securities Act". (corps. art. tit. 11). In 1997, Maryland revised Maryland Securities Act to conform to National Securities Market Improvements Act of 1996. Following additional material insertions, changes and omissions have been made to Uniform Act.

§201(c):	Registration of investment advisers and investment adviser representatives required. (corps. art. §11-401[b]). Investment adviser defined in §11-101(h). Act covers financial planning activities that do not involve securities (i.e., art, bullion, collectibles). (corps. art. §11-101[g][1]).
§202(a):	Provisions dealing with registrations of investment advisers. (corps. art. §11-405[a]). Registration of broker-dealer does not automatically constitute registration of any agent. (corps. art. §§11-405, 11-406).
§202(b):	Applicant for initial or renewal registration as broker-dealer shall pay filing fee of $250. Applicant for initial or renewal registration or transfer of registration as agent shall pay filing fee of $35. Applicant for initial or renewal registration as investment adviser shall pay filing fee of $300. Applicant for initial or renewal registration or transfer of registration as investment adviser representative shall pay filing fee of $50. (corps. art. §11-407). Central Registration Depository exclusive method of agent registration, transfer and termination for Md. When application denied or withdrawn, Commissioner retains filing fee (corps. art. §11-407).
§202(d):	Commissioner may require by rule or order minimum capital for registered broker-dealer and minimum financial requirements for investment advisor. (corps. art. §11-409).
§302:	Prospectus required in connection with offers and sales of securities registered by notification. (corps. art. §11-502[c]).
§303:	Privilege of coordination extended to securities qualified for exemption under federal regulations adopted under §3[b] or 3[c] of the Securities Act of 1933. (corps. art. §11-503[d]).
§304(d):	Use of prospectus in connection with sale of securities registered by qualification made mandatory. (corps. art. §11-504[d]).
§305(b):	Filing fee is 0.1% of maximum aggregate offering price, with $500 minimum and $1,500 maximum, except that any filing made pursuant to exemption under Md. Securities Act requires $100 fee. Fee retained if application is withdrawn before effective date or stop-ordered. (corps. art. §11-506).
§305(g):	Omitted.
§305(h):	Omitted.
§402(b)11:	Offer directed to not more than 35 persons in state during any 12 consecutive months (other than certain institutional investors) is exempt if seller reasonably believes all buyers are purchasing for investment and if no advertisement or general solicitation is used, but Commissioner may, by rule or order, increase or decrease number of offerees permitted or waive conditions as to their investment intent. (corps. art. §11-602[9]). Exemption from registration by coordination with 17 C.F.R., Parts 230.505 and 506, permitted by rule. Manually-signed Form D must be filed within 15 days of first sale. (COMAR 02.02.04.15). Separate transactional exemption by COMAR 02.02.04.12 requires filing of and compliance with Md. forms. Local issuer exemption with certain restrictions permitted by COMAR 02.02.04.11.

Securities not originally registered in Md. may be offered or sold by or through registered broker-dealer if: (1) Offer or sale is not for benefit of issuer or 10% owner; (2) security is not part of unsold allotment taken for benefit of issuer or 10% owner; and (3) stop order or similar order or injunction is not in effect. (corps. art. §11-602[13]). Securities traded under NASDAQ may be exempted from registration requirement. (corps. art. §11-601[12]). Commission may exempt transactions exempted by SEC under §§3[b] or 4[2] of Securities Act of 1933. (corps. art. §11-602[15]).

Supervision.—Securities Commissioner, Securities Division, State Law Department, 200 St. Paul Place, 20th Floor, Baltimore, Maryland 21202.

Subdivision offerings not specifically dealt with by Md. Securities Law.

Franchising.—Franchisors offering franchises in state must register with State Division of Securities and provide copy of registration to potential franchisees at earlier of first personal meeting or ten business days prior to execution of contract or payment

See note at head of Digest as to 1998 legislation covered.

See Topical Index in front part of this volume.

MD – 16

SECURITIES . . . *continued*

of consideration. Civil and criminal penalties are provided for violations of Act. (bus. reg. art. tit. 14, subtit. 2).

Business Opportunity Act.—Sellers of products or services (other than one-time sale of business) intended to enable purchaser to start business (such as pyramiding arrangements, or transactions in which seller agrees to provide or assist purchaser in obtaining accounts or retail outlets, seller agrees to purchase buyer's products made using seller's supplies or services, or seller represents that buyer will derive income in excess of price paid to seller) must register with Division of Securities and provide copy of registration to potential buyer at earlier of first personal meeting or ten days prior to signing contract or accepting consideration. Civil and criminal penalties apply for violations. (bus. reg. art. tit. 14, subtit. 1).

Uniform Commercial Code adopted. (comm. law art. tits. 1 to 10). See topic Commercial Code.

Uniform Simplification of Fiduciary Security Transfers Act adopted. (est. & tr. art. tit. 15, subtit. 3). Uniform Commercial Codes does not repeal act. (comm. law art. §10-104).

Uniform Securities Ownership by Minors Act not adopted.

Maryland Uniform Transfer-on-Death Security Registration Act adopted. (1994, c. 644).

Tender Offers.—See category Business Organizations, topic Corporations.

STATUTE OF FRAUDS:

See topic Frauds, Statute of.

TRUST RECEIPT SECURITY:

Uniform Commercial Code adopted. (comm. law art. tits. 1 to 10). See topic Commercial Code.

WAREHOUSEMEN:

Uniform Commercial Code adopted. (comm. law art. tit. 7). See topic Commercial Code.

Bonds.—None required.

Licenses.—Must procure annual license from clerk of court where located. Fee is $30 to $150 per year depending upon size of town or city in which warehouse is located. (bus. reg. art. §§17-1202, 17-2203).

Warehouse Receipts.—Uniform Commercial Code adopted. (comm. law art. tit. 7). Criminal provisions for certain acts set out in comm. law art. §§18-101 to 18-401.

Lien.—Uniform Commercial Code adopted.

Notice to Customer Storage Household Goods.—Every moving and storage firm and every warehouse used for storage of household goods, prior to rendering service and in application for service or in separate written statement (12-pt. type or larger), must notify customer that he should obtain insurance. Violation is misdemeanor punishable by fine up to $5,000 or 30 days in jail or both. (bus. reg. art. §17-1204).

CITIZENSHIP

ALIENS:

Alien may not qualify as executor or administrator unless he is spouse of decedent and permanent resident of U.S. (est. & tr. art. §5-105[b]).

Property.—Aliens, not enemies, may own, sell, devise, dispose of, or otherwise deal with property in same manner as if they were citizens by birth. (real prop. art. §14-101).

Distribution to heir or legatee who is nonresident of U.S. will not be made if it appears that nonresident will not have full benefit, use or control of property to which he is entitled. Instead, property will be ordered paid to board of education of county or Baltimore City for use of public schools. Provision is made for subsequent repayment without interest to claimant or legal representative. (est. & tr. art. §9-108).

See also category Business Organizations, topic Corporations, subheads Stock, Stockholders.

CIVIL ACTIONS AND PROCEDURE

ACCORD AND SATISFACTION:

Uniform Commercial Code adopted. (comm. law art. tits. 1 to 10). See category Business Regulation and Commerce, topic Commercial Code.

Compromise.—Compromise of disputed claim is binding. (See 113 Md. 111, 77 A. 130.) Compromise of undisputed claim by which less than full performance is accepted in full satisfaction is not binding even though evidenced by receipt in full, unless supported by collateral or new consideration or unless under seal. (58 Md. 67). This result may differ for certain contracts. (comm. law art. §2-209).

Pleading.—Must be specially pled as affirmative defense. (R.P. 2-323[g][1]).

ACTIONS:

Equity.—Effective July 1, 1984, law and equity distinction abolished for purposes of pleadings, parties, court sittings and dockets but does not affect right to jury trial. (R. P. 2-301).

Forms of Action.—Md. Rules, effective July 1, 1984, provide for one form of action known as "civil action". (R. P. 2-301). Special rules apply for ejectment (12-101); eminent domain (12-201 to 12-213); foreclosure (14-201 to 14-210); habeas corpus (15-301 to 15-312); injunction (15-501 to 15-505); mandamus (15-701); mechanics' lien (12-301 to 12-308); and detinue and replevin (12-601 to 12-602).

Conditions Precedent.—Notice of claim must be given to certain municipal corporations and counties. See topic Limitation of Actions, subhead Municipal Corporations. Arbitration is prerequisite to medical malpractice suit. See category Dispute Resolution, topic Arbitration and Award, subhead Medical Malpractice. Prior notice of intention to file mechanics' lien is required before certain mechanics' lien actions. See category Debtor and Creditor, topic Liens, subhead Mechanics' Liens.

Commencement.—See topics Process, Pleading.

Parties.—Court rules permit great liberality in joining, adding or dropping parties. (R. P. 2-211 to 2-214).

Class Actions.—When there is common question of law or fact and joinder of numerous members of class is impracticable, one or more representatives with claims or defenses typical of those of class and who will fairly and adequately protect interests of all may sue or be sued on behalf of all. (R. P. 2-231[a]).

Intervention may be had upon timely motion as of right if applicant's interest is not adequately represented and applicant may be bound by judgment or if he would be adversely affected by disposition of property subject to control of court; otherwise where there is common question of law or fact. (R. P. 2-214[a]). Federal or state government, or political subdivision, or officer or agent of any of them, may be permitted to intervene as permitted when constitutional provision, charter provision, statute, ordinance, regulation, executive order, requirement or agreement challenged or relied upon as defense. (R. P. 2-214[b][2]). Special rules apply to intervention in juvenile causes. (R. P. 11-122).

Interpleader is available by complaint for interpleader, counterclaim or cross claim. Complaint must specify nature and value of property and may be accompanied by payment or tender of property into court. (R. P. 2-221).

Third Party Practice.—Defendant may bring in third party who is or may be liable to him for all or part of plaintiff's claim by serving summons, third party claim and copies of previous pleadings. If defendant files third party claim more than 30 days after time for filing answer, any other party may move to strike it or to sever it for separate trial, and court must grant motion unless there is showing late filing does not prejudice other parties. (R. P. 2-332).

Joinder of Causes of Action.—Joinder of causes of action liberally permitted. Plaintiff may join in one action, as either independent or alternate claims, as many claims as he may have against defendant. (270 Md. 397, 311 A.2d 776). Claims involving different plaintiffs or defendants may be joined whenever any question of law or fact is common to all and asserted right to relief arises out of same transaction or occurrence. (R. P. 2-212).

Splitting Causes of Action.—Cause of action may not be split. (212 Md. 526, 129 A.2d 827).

Consolidation of Actions.—Court may consolidate actions involving common question of law or fact or common subject matter. (R. P. 2-503). By order of transferor court, action or any claim or issue in action may be transferred from one judicial circuit to another judicial circuit where action may have been brought and similar actions are pending. (R.P. 2-327[d]).

Severance of Actions.—Court has discretion to order severance at request of party or on its own initiative. (R. P. 2-503[b]).

Stay of Proceedings.—Court has discretion to order stay of proceedings pending determination of another proceeding that may affect issues raised. (254 Md. 541, 255 A.2d 73). Court may, upon motion of party or its own initiative, stay proceedings pending resolution of question of law. (R. P. 2-502).

Abatement and Revival.—Actions at law survive death of either party; actions in equity survive death of either party if court can grant effective relief in spite of death. (courts art. §6-401). Slander actions abate upon death of either party unless appeal has been taken from judgment for plaintiff. (courts art. §6-401).

Limitation of.—See topic Limitation of Actions.

Small Claims.—See category Courts and Legislature, topic Courts, subhead District Courts.

Release of tort claim for personal injury signed within five days after injury is voidable within 60 days. (courts art. §5-305.1). During first 15 days confinement in hospital, no attempt can be made to obtain settlement or general release from injured person, and any settlement or release so obtained cannot be used in evidence. (courts art. §5-305.1). Personal injury release does not discharge subsequent tortfeasor who is not party to release, and whose responsibility for injuries is unknown at time of execution of release or who is not specifically identified in release. (courts art. §5-305.1).

Termination of Actions.—Voluntary dismissal of action must be upon order of court unless notice is filed before adverse party files answer or motion for summary judgment or stipulation of dismissal signed by all parties who have appeared is filed. (R. P. 2-506). If party has filed counterclaim before service of motion for voluntary dismissal, dismissal is not permitted over party's objection unless counterclaim can remain independently. Costs must be paid by dismissing party. (R. P. 2-506). Action may also be terminated by order of court for lack of jurisdiction or failure to prosecute. (R. P. 2-507).

Prohibited Actions.—Actions for breach of promise to marry, except in cases of pregnancy, are barred. (fam. law art. §3-102). Actions for alienation of affections are barred. (fam. law art. §3-103).

Administration.—See category Estates and Trusts, topic Executors and Administrators.

Direct Actions Against Insurer.—See category Transportation, topic Motor Vehicles, subhead Direct Actions.

APPEAL AND ERROR:

Court of Appeals and Court of Special Appeals are highest appellate courts. See category Courts and Legislature, topic Courts.

See note at head of Digest as to 1998 legislation covered.

See Topical Index in front part of this volume.

APPEAL AND ERROR . . . *continued*

Rules of Court Govern Appeals.—Appeals for both Court of Appeals and Court of Special Appeals are governed by tit. 12 of courts art. and R. P. tit. 8. Certain interlocutory orders are appealable. (courts art. §12-303).

Time Allowed for Taking.—Sole method of securing review by Court of Appeals is by direct appeal, or application for leave to appeal where allowed by law, pursuant to Maryland's Uniform Certification of Questions of Law Act, or by writ of certiorari. (R. P. 8-301). Petition for writ of certiorari may be filed: (1) If appeal to Court of Special Appeals taken, either before or after Court of Special Appeals has rendered decision, but not later than 15 days after mandate, or (2) not later than 30 days after entry of final judgment of circuit court acting in appellate capacity. (R. P. 8-302; courts art. §12-305). Notice of appeal to Court of Special Appeals must be filed within 30 days from date of judgment or order appealed from. (R. P. 8-202). Court of Special Appeals may certify question of law or entire case to Court of Appeals. (R. P. 8-304). Appeal from final action of administrative agency shall be filed within 30 days from date of action appealed from or 30 days from sending or receipt of notice where such are required. (R.P. 7-203).

Method of Taking.—Appeal to Court of Special Appeals taken by filing notice of appeal in lower court. (R. P. 8-201). In civil cases other than juvenile causes and prisoner applications seeking relief relating to confinement or conditions of confinement, and except where expedited appeal is elected under 8-207, information report must be filed by appellant within ten days of filing notice of appeal. Each appellee may file supplemental information report within seven days of service of appellant's report. (R.P. 8-205). Within 20 days after filing appellant's information report, court must enter order that appeal proceed without pre-hearing conference or that pre-hearing conference be held. (R. P. 8-206). Pre-hearing conference held to discuss settlement, dismissal, limitation of issues, contents of record and record extract, continuance of appeal, times for filing briefs, and other matters. Judge shall enter order reciting actions taken and agreements reached. Judge who conducts pre-hearing conference shall not sit on panel assigned to hear case. Both information report and pre-hearing conference are regarded as disclosed for settlement purposes only. (R. P. 8-206). Unless directed otherwise, lower court must transmit record to Court of Special Appeals within 60 days of date of order directing that appeal proceed without pre-hearing conference, or within 60 days from date of order following pre-hearing conference, or, in cases involving juvenile causes and prisoner applications seeking relief relating to confinement or conditions of confinement, within 60 days of filing notice of appeal. (R. P. 8-412). For appeal to Court of Special Appeals or Court of Appeals, all original papers (or certified copy if lower court retains originals) filed in lower court, docket entries and transcripts, constitute record, except papers parties stipulate shall be omitted. Upon determination and order of lower court that originals should be kept in lower court, clerk shall transmit certified copy of original papers. Parties may file agreed statement of case in lieu of pleadings and evidence with approval of lower court, where questions on appeal can be decided by Court without reviewing evidence. Parties are strongly encouraged to agree to such statement. (R. P. 8-413). In civil cases, appellant must prepare and file record extract unless otherwise ordered by court. Unless parties stipulate as to contents within 15 days after record is filed, appellant must serve appellee with designation of portions of record to be included in extract, and appellee has ten days to designate additional portions to be included. Appellant then has five days to designate and serve on appellee further additional portions. Extract must include judgment appealed from, any opinion or charge of lower court, and other parts of record as are designated by parties. (R. P. 8-501).

Court of Special Appeals has expedited appeals procedure that may be chosen by agreement of both parties within 20 days of filing notice of appeal. Procedure involves limitations on length of brief and oral argument. (R. P. 8-207).

Where appeal is to Court of Appeals, record consists of record filed in Court of Special Appeals and record of, any proceedings in Court of Special Appeals. (R.P. 8-413[a]).

Within 40 days after filing of record in Court of Appeals or Court of Special Appeals, appellant must file brief; appellee must file brief within 30 days after filing of appellant's brief. Appellant may file reply brief any time within 20 days after filing of appellee's brief, but not later than ten days before argument. In Court of Appeals, 20 copies of each brief must be filed; in Court of Special Appeals, 15 copies of each brief must be filed. Two copies of each brief and record extract must be served on each party. (R. P. 8-502).

Appeal Bond.—No requirement that bond be filed to cover costs. As to supersedeas bond, see subhead Stay of Proceedings, infra.

Stay of Proceedings.—With certain exceptions, appellant may stay execution of civil judgment by filing supersedeas bond or other security with clerk of lower court any time before satisfaction of judgment. (R. P. 8-422). If such bond has been filed, no further bond required during pendency of review by Court of Appeals. (R. P. 8-422[e]).

Extent of Review.—Ordinarily, appellate court will not decide question which was not decided by lower court, but appellate court may decide question not presented in lower court if decision is desirable for guidance of lower court or to avoid further appeals. (R. P. 8-131[a]). In cases tried without jury, appellate court may review both law and evidence, but judgment of trial court will not be set aside on evidence unless clearly erroneous, and due regard will be given to opportunity of trial court to judge credibility of witnesses. (R. P. 8-131[c]). In law actions tried with jury, verdict of jury is conclusive (245 Md. 540, 226 A.2d 556), and only factual question is whether there was sufficient evidence to warrant submitting case to jury (183 Md. 233, 37 A.2d 312).

Character of Hearing.—Review is on record of proceedings below. (180 Md. 651, 26 A.2d 812).

Judgment or Order on Appeal.—Clerk of Court issues mandate to lower court 30 days after filing of opinion or entering of order or judgment by Court. (R. P. 8-606).

BONDS:

Bonds required to be filed in any action are governed by Md. Rules. (R. P. 1-401 to 1-406). All bonds may be approved by clerk or, upon refusal, by court. (R. P. 1-402[b]). In lieu of sureties on bonds, court may accept other security for performance of bond. (R. P. 1-402[e]).

Sureties.—Surety companies authorized to do business in Md. accepted as sufficient surety. If any surety on bond of personal representative, guardian, trustee, clerk or register conceives himself in danger of suffering from suretyship, he may demand counter security. Granting order for additional security is in discretion of court. (est. & tr. art. 6-102, 15-115; R. P. 1-402, 1-403, 10-702, 13-107).

Surety on bond of fiduciary or public official may be relieved by application to court. (R. P. 1-403, 13-107).

Enforcement.—Where bond is to state, action may be in name of state for benefit of party in interest. (R. P. 1-402[c]).

CERTIORARI:

Where final judgment has been rendered by circuit court after appeal from district court and party shows by petition that review is necessary to secure uniformity of decisions or that special circumstances render it desirable and in public interest, Court of Appeals may grant review by issuing writ of certiorari. (courts art. §12-305). Petition for writ of certiorari may be filed no later than 30 days after entry of judgment or disposition of post-trial motion. (R. P. 8-302[b]).

Except in certain instances (courts art. §12-202), where case or proceeding is pending in or decided by Court of Special Appeals after appeal from circuit court, orphans' court, or Md. Tax Court, party may petition Court of Appeals for certiorari. Petition may be filed before or after decision but not later than time prescribed by Maryland rules. (courts art. §12-201; R. P 8-302[a]). Court of Appeals may issue writ of certiorari on own motion in same cases. (courts art. §12-201). Court of Appeals must grant certiorari if it finds, on vote of number of judges required by rule (not more than three), that review is desirable and in public interest. Writ may issue before or after decision of Court of Special Appeals. Reasons for denial of writ must be stated in writing. (courts art. §12-203).

Court of Special Appeals may certify question of law or entire case to Court of Appeals which may accept by issuing writ of certiorari. (R. P. 8-304).

Writ of certiorari available to challenge actions of lower tribunal alleged to be unconstitutional or taken without jurisdiction. (R. P. 8-301 to 8-303; 273 Md. 486, 331 A.2d 55).

CHARITABLE IMMUNITY:

See topic Damages.

COMMISSIONS TO TAKE TESTIMONY:

See topic Depositions and Discovery.

COSTS:

Costs usually assessed against nonprevailing party. (R. P. 2-603; R. P. 3-603). Costs of appeal awarded to prevailing party unless court orders costs allocated among parties. (R. P. 8-607).

Specific provisions as to costs and fees are contained in courts art., tit. 7. §§7-101 to 7-104 govern proceedings in Court of Appeals and Court of Special Appeals; §§7-201 to 7-208 govern proceedings in circuit courts, including criminal proceedings; §§7-301, 7-302 govern proceedings in district courts. State Court Administrator fixes uniform costs and fees for Court of Appeals, Court of Special Appeals, and circuit courts, subject to approval of Bd. of Public Works. (§§7-102, 7-202). §7-201(b) provides for waiver of costs in Circuit Court in cases of indigency. R. P. also contain provisions for waiver of costs. (R. P. 8-201[b]).

Security for Costs.—Not required.

Special Situations.—If court grants motion for order compelling discovery or for protective order and determines that opposition to motion was without substantial justification, court shall require person whose conduct necessitated motion or party or attorney who advised action (or both) to pay reasonable expenses incurred in obtaining order, including attorney's fees, unless justice requires otherwise. (R. P. 2-433[c]). If court denies such motion and determines motion was made without substantial justification, court shall require moving party or attorney to pay such expenses, unless justice requires otherwise. (R. P. 2-433[c]). As sanction for failure to obey orders for discovery, or failure to make discovery pursuant to rules, court on motion after opportunity for hearing shall require responsible party or attorney (or both) to pay reasonable expenses caused by such failure, including attorney's fees, unless failure was substantially justified or justice requires otherwise. (R. P. 2-433[a]). In civil action, if court finds conduct of any party in maintaining or defending any proceeding was in bad faith or without substantial justification, court may require offending party or its attorney (or both) to pay costs and reasonable expenses to offended party, including reasonable attorney's fees. (R. P. 1-341).

DAMAGES:

Common law generally prevails as to compensatory damages. In personal injury actions in which cause of action arose on or after July 1, 1986, $350,000 limit for noneconomic damages, including pain and suffering, impairment, disfigurement, loss of consortium. In personal injury and wrongful death actions in which cause of action arose on or after Oct. 1, 1994, $500,000 limit for noneconomic damages. Limitation on noneconomic damages will increase by $15,000 on Oct. 1 of each year beginning Oct. 1, 1995. "Noneconomic damages" in wrongful death actions includes mental anguish, emotional pain and suffering, loss of society, companionship, comfort, protection, care, marital care, filial care, parental care, attention, advice, counsel, training, guidance or education. (courts art. §11-108). Statutory limit does not apply to wrongful death actions which arose before Oct. 1, 1994. (329 Md. 533, 620 A.2d 905).

DAMAGES . . . *continued*

Punitive damages allowed in non-intentional tort actions only upon clear and convincing proof of actual malice. Degree of malice needed to recover punitive damages in other actions vary. (325 Md. 420, 601 A.2d 633).

Sovereign Immunity.—Limited waiver of state's sovereign immunity in tort claims to extent of insurance coverage. (st. gov't art. §§12-101 to 12-110). Limited waiver of immunity of both state and local governments for negligent use of motor vehicles. (trans. art. §17-107[c]). Limited waiver of liability for local governments and their employees for tortious conduct. Local governments not liable for punitive damages, but may indemnify government employee subject to punitive damages award with certain exceptions. (courts art. §5-303). For contract actions, see category Business Regulation and Commerce, topic Contracts.

Charitable Immunity.—Doctrine of charitable immunity presently prevails (249 Md. 233, 238 A.2d 863) but legislative and judicial exceptions exist. Immunity of hospitals and nursing homes exists only if insured for not less than $100,000 and only as to excess over insurance limits. (health-gen. art. §19-354, courts art. §5-632[c]). Agents of charitable organizations (and athletic clubs, civic leagues or organizations, cooperative housing corporation and homeowners' associations) immune from personal liability under some circumstances. (courts art. §5-312). Insurer of charitable institution may not assert defense of charitable immunity for claim covered by insurance policy. (ins. art. §19-103; 17 Md. L. Rev. 159). Defense of charitable immunity must be asserted as affirmative defense. (R.P. 2-323[g]).

Comparative Negligence Rule.—Not adopted.

Good Samaritan Law.—Enumerated persons are not liable for civil damages resulting from any professional act or omission not amounting to gross negligence committed in rendering free assistance: (1) At scene of emergency; (2) in transit to medical facility; (3) through communication with persons rendering emergency assistance. Person not enumerated in rendering free emergency assistance at scene of emergency not liable if he acts in reasonably prudent manner and relinquishes care when licensed or certified person is able to assume responsibility. (courts art. §5-603). Limited immunity for health care provider and physician volunteers who work at charitable organizations that provide health care services. (courts art. §5-606).

See category Estates and Trusts, topic Death, subhead Action for Wrongful Death.

No Fault Insurance.—See category Transportation, topic Motor Vehicles, subhead Insurance.

DECLARATORY JUDGMENTS:

See topic Judgments.

DEPOSITIONS AND DISCOVERY:

Court of Appeals has adopted broad rules for taking of depositions, including rules for videotape or audiotape depositions. (R. P. 2-401 to 2-419). These rules may be availed of before (R. P. 2-404) or after (R. P. 2-411) filing suit. Depositions may be taken for purpose of discovery, for use as evidence or to perpetuate testimony.

Within State for Use Within State.—Depositions may be taken under Md. Rules, as detailed below.

Within State for Use Elsewhere.—Where mandate, writ or commission is issued out of court of record of foreign jurisdiction, or where upon notice or agreement, witness in Md. must be deposed, witnesses may be compelled to appear and testify in same manner and by same process and proceeding as for depositions taken for proceeding in Md. (courts art. §9-401).

Outside of State for Use Within State.—Md. Rules make provision for depositions outside state, as detailed below. See subheads Before Whom Taken; Compelling Attendance of Witnesses, infra.

De Bene Esse.—Depositions may be taken de bene esse. (R. P. 2-404).

Perpetuating Testimony.—Depositions may be taken to perpetuate testimony before or after filing suit. (R. P. 2-404, 2-411).

Pending Proceedings.—At any time after jurisdiction has been obtained over defendant or over property which is subject of proceeding, but not earlier than day for defendant's initial pleading, party may, upon proper notice without leave of court, take deposition of person, whether party or not, on oral examination, written questions or by telephone, for purpose of discovery or for use as evidence in proceeding or for both purposes. (R. P. 2-411, 2-417, 2-418). Leave of court is also required to depose person previously deposed in same action and person in prison. (R. P. 2-411).

Before Proceedings.—Person who desires to perpetuate testimony may have deposition taken in Md. upon notice to persons against whom deposition is expected to be used. If deposition of minor or incompetent is to be taken, notice must be given to individual and parent, guardian or other person having care or custody of person or estate of individual. (R. P. 2-124[b], 2-404). Court within whose jurisdiction deposition is to be filed may, on motion of person taking deposition, authorize notice by publication, registered mail or otherwise on nonresident and may appoint attorney to represent nonresident at examination. Notice must be filed in circuit court of any county in which expected adverse party resides. (R. P. 2-404).

Before Whom Taken.—Within state, depositions taken before any person authorized to administer oath. Within any other state, territory, district or possession of U.S., depositions taken before officer authorized to administer oaths by laws of U.S. or place where deposition taken or before person appointed by court where action is pending. In foreign state or country, depositions taken: (1) On notice before any person authorized to administer oath in place where deposition is taken, either by laws of that place or by laws of U.S., or (2) before person commissioned by court, or (3) pursuant to letter rogatory issued by court. (R. P. 2-414).

No deposition may be taken before relative, employee, attorney or counsel of party, or relative or employee of attorney or counsel, or before person financially interested in proceeding, unless objection waived. (R. P. 2-414[d], [e]).

Parties may stipulate in writing to take depositions before any person at any time or place, on any notice and in any manner. (R. P. 2-401[g]).

Notices.—Ten days notice in writing to every other party to proceeding required for deposition on oral examination; but court may enlarge or shorten time. Notice must state time and place of deposition, and name and address of each person to be examined, or if name not known, general description sufficient to identify him or his class or group. If deposition to be video or audiotaped, notice must specify method of recording, and if video or audio deposition of expert is taken for use at trial, notice must so state. (R. P. 2-412).

Compelling Attendance of Witnesses.—Upon request of party entitled to issuance of subpoena, clerk must issue completed subpoena or provide blank form to be completed and returned for signing. (R. P. 2-510). Subpoena must be served at least ten days before date of deposition. (R. P. 2-412[a]). Subpoena commanding production of documentary evidence may be issued without order of court, but, on motion of person from whom discovery is sought and for good cause shown, court may pass order to limit scope of examination or protect person or party. (R. P. 2-403, 2-510). Subpoena commanding production of documentary evidence must be served at least 30 days before date of deposition. (R. P. 2-412[c]). Nonparty resident of Md. required to attend only in county where he resides or is employed or is engaged in business in person, or at other convenient place fixed by court. Nonparty, nonresident deponent may be required to attend only in county where personally served or within 40 miles from place of service or at other convenient place fixed by court. Where examination held out of state, witness compelled to attend and testify in accordance with law of place of examination. Party deponent, in addition to places provided above, may be required to attend in county where action pending. (R. P. 2-413).

Examination of Witnesses.—For deposition on oral examination, examination and cross-examination proceed as at trial. Scope of cross-examination need not be limited to scope of direct. Objections as to manner of taking deposition, form of questions or answers, oath of affirmation, conduct of parties, or other error that might be obviated or removed if objected to at occurrence waived unless timely made during deposition. Officer must put witness on oath and personally, or by one acting under his direction and in his presence, record testimony. Testimony must be transcribed unless parties agree or court orders otherwise. (R. P. 2-415). In lieu of participating in oral examination, parties may transmit written interrogatories to officer, who must take responsive testimony and prepare, certify and file or mail deposition, attaching copy of notice and interrogatories. (R. P. 2-417).

Refusal to Answer.—Examination completed to extent practicable. Thereafter, on reasonable notice to affected parties, proponent may apply to court within whose jurisdiction deposition taken or to court where action pending for order compelling answer. (Similar procedure exists for refusal to answer written interrogatory.) Evasive or incomplete answer treated as failure to answer. (R. P. 2-432). Court may refuse to hear discovery dispute unless party certifies effort made to resolve dispute. (R. P. 2-431). When motion granted, court requires refusing deponent or party, or party or attorney advising refusal, or both of them to pay expenses of obtaining order, including attorney's fees if court finds that opposition to motion was without substantial justification, unless justice requires otherwise. When motion denied, court requires moving party or attorney or both to pay expenses of opposing motion, including attorney's fees, if court finds that motion was without substantial justification, unless justice requires otherwise. (R. P. 2-433[c]).

Signing and Certification of Deposition.—Deposition must be submitted to witness for correction and signing, absent waiver by witness and by parties. If witness desires to make corrections to transcript to conform it to testimony, changes must be made on separate sheet and attached by officer to transcript. If not signed by witness within 30 days, officer must sign and state on record why deponent has not signed. Any objections to corrections made by witness to transcript are waived unless motion to suppress corrections is made with reasonable promptness after corrections are filed. (R. P. 2-415).

Return.—Officer must certify on transcript that witness was duly sworn and that transcript is true record of testimony, and must seal deposition in envelope bearing title of proceeding and marked "Deposition of (name of witness)". Documents or things produced for inspection or offered as exhibits during examination shall, upon request of party, be marked for identification and returned with deposition; rule provides for substitution of copies for originals. On payment of reasonable charges, officer must furnish copy of deposition to party or deponent. (R. P. 2-415).

Use of Depositions.—Part or all of deposition may be used at trial or on hearing of motion or in interlocutory proceeding, if admissible under rules of evidence, applied as if witness present and testifying, as follows: (1) Any party may use deposition to impeach deponent as witness; (2) deposition of party or officer, director, or person designated to testify for party may be used by adverse party for any purpose; (3) deposition of witness may be used by any party for any purpose against other party present or represented at taking of deposition or having notice thereof, if court finds (a) that witness is dead, (b) that witness is out of jurisdiction (and absence not procured by party offering deposition), (c) that witness is unable to attend or testify because of age, physical or mental illness, infirmity or imprisonment, (d) that party offering deposition has been unable to procure attendance of witness by subpoena, or (e) upon motion and notice, that exceptional circumstances exist. Videotape depositions of treating or consulting physician, or expert witness, may be used for any purpose even if witness is available to testify, if deposition notice stated that deposition was for use at trial. If only part is offered, adverse party may require introduction of all other parts, which in fairness should be considered, and any party may introduce any other parts in accordance with Rule. (R. P. 2-419).

Form.—No statutory form. Following is sufficient:

Form
[Caption]

Pursuant to notice (or agreement or commission annexed), the deposition (upon oral examination) (upon written questions) of . . . . . . was taken at . . . . . ., City of . . . . . .,

---

DEPOSITIONS AND DISCOVERY . . . *continued*

State of . . . . . ., on the . . . . . . day of . . . . . ., 19. . . . . ., at . . . . . . o'clock A.M., before . . . .

Appearances: (insert names of counsel present)

Stipulations [optional]: It is stipulated and agreed by and between counsel for the respective parties that the reading and signing of this deposition by the witness is waived.

It is further stipulated and agreed that the filing of this deposition with the Clerk of the Court is waived.

* * * * *

. . . . . ., being duly sworn to tell the truth, the whole truth and nothing but the truth, was examined and testified as follows:

* * * * *

(Signature of witness, unless waived)

State of . . . . . ., City of . . . . . .:

I, ..., a . . . . . . in and for the State and City aforesaid, do hereby certify that the within named . . . . . ., personally appeared before me at the time and place herein set out, and, after having been duly sworn by me according to law, was interrogated by counsel.

I further certify that the examination was recorded by me and then transcribed to the within typewritten matter in a true and accurate manner, and that the same is a true record of the testimony given by the witness.

[optional] I further certify that the stipulations contained herein were entered into by counsel in my presence.

I further certify that I am not of counsel to any of the parties, nor an employee of counsel, nor related to any of the parties, nor in any way interested in the outcome of this action.

(Signature and title of examining officer)

EQUITY:

See topic Actions.

EVIDENCE:

See topic Depositions and Discovery.

Witnesses.—Competency is governed by common law rules, except that incapacity to testify does not result from interest in action or from conviction of crime, except that conviction of perjury absolutely and forever disqualifies convicted person as witness. (courts art. §§9-101, 9-104). In criminal trial age of child may not be reason for precluding child from testifying. (courts art. §9-103).

See also topic Depositions and Discovery.

Privileged Communications.—Person may not be compelled to testify in violation of attorney-client privilege. (courts art. §9-108). Privilege does not extend to facts learned by attorney but not communicated or confided by client. (227 Md. 8, 174 A.2d 768). Client may waive privilege. (132 Md. 397, 104 A. 40; 24 Md. App. 588, 335 A.2d 171). Confession or communication to minister, clergyman or priest of established church made in confidence by one seeking spiritual advice or consolation is privileged. (courts art. §9-111). Client may waive privilege.

Communications to physician other than psychiatrist are not privileged. (249 Md. 200, 238 A.2d 875, cert. denied, 393 U.S. 928, 59 Md. App. 392, 475 A.2d 1235). Communications to psychiatrist, psychiatric-mental health nursing specialist or licensed psychologist relating to diagnosis or treatment of mental or emotional disorder are privileged, except in certain cases such as commitment proceedings, malpractice, or defective delinquent proceedings, and proceedings where mental condition is put in issue by way of claim or defense. Patient may waive privilege. (courts art. §§9-109, 9-109.1).

Subject to numerous exceptions similar to psychiatrist or psychologist privilege, communications between individual and licensed certified social worker are privileged. (courts art. §9-121).

State secrets and information acquired by public officers are generally privileged. (177 Md. 168, 9 A. 2d 235; 30 Op. Att'y Gen. 125).

Communications and materials made available to licensed certified public accountant by client are subject to privilege with limited exceptions. (courts art. §9-110).

Persons employed by newspaper, journal, or radio or television station, press association, news agency, or wire service in news gathering or disseminating capacity do not have to reveal sources of news or information. (courts art. §9-112). Court may compel disclosure from one otherwise protected by privilege if (i) information is relevant to significant legal issue, (ii) information could not be otherwise obtained from alternative source, and (iii) there is overriding public interest in disclosure. (courts art. 9-112[d]).

Husband and Wife.—Wives and husbands of parties litigant are competent and may be compelled to testify in civil and criminal cases (courts art. §9-101[2]), but husband and wife are in no case competent to disclose any confidential communication made by one to other during marriage, nor can husband or wife be compelled to testify as adverse witness in criminal proceeding involving spouse, except in proceedings involving abuse of child under 18 or, in limited circumstances, if charge involves assault and battery in which spouse is victim. (courts art. §§9-105, 9-106). Spouse incompetency rule inapplicable when confidential communication constitutes threat or crime against other spouse. (37 Md. App. 180, 376 A.2d 1144).

There is rebuttable presumption that child is legitimate child of man to whom mother was married to at time of conception. Presumption may be rebutted by testimony of person other than mother or her husband. (fam. law art. §5-1028).

Communications or Transactions with Persons Since Deceased or Incompetent.—Party to proceeding by or against personal representative, heir, devisee, distributee or legatee as such, or by or against incompetent person, may not testify concerning any transaction with or statement made by dead or incompetent person, personally or through agent since dead, unless called by opposite party, or unless testimony of dead or incompetent person has been given already in same proceeding concerning same transaction or statement. (courts art. §9-116).

Children as Victims.—Abused child may testify outside courtroom via closed circuit television if judge determines that defendant's presence will cause child serious emotional distress such that child cannot communicate. (courts art. §9-102). In juvenile or criminal proceeding, courts may admit into evidence out of court statements of child-victim in cases of child abuse, rape, or assault with intent to commit rape if those statements are made to licensed physician, psychologist, or social worker. (courts art. §9-103.1).

Self-incrimination.—Witness may refuse to answer question on ground of self-incrimination and failure to testify in criminal proceeding on this basis does not create presumption against him. (courts art. §9-107; Md. Decl. of Rts., art. 22). Chemical test may be administered, and results are admissible in prosecution for drunken driving under prescribed conditions. (courts arts. 10-302, 10-306). All persons driving on Md. roads deemed to have consented to take chemical test, but person may not be compelled to submit to such test, and no presumption arises because of refusal to submit. (courts arts. 10-305[c], 10-309). Persons involved in motor vehicle accidents resulting in death or life threatening injuries may be compelled to submit to alcohol testing by police officers at accident scene. (trans. art. §16-205.1). Fact of refusal to submit to chemical test is admissible at trial only where material and relevant to matter other than defendant's guilt or innocence. (322 Md. 376, 587 A.2d 1102; courts art. §§10-302 to 10-309). Motor vehicle laws provide for suspension of operator's license if, inter alia, refusal made. (trans. art. §16-205.1). See category Transportation, topic Motor Vehicles, subhead Operator's License.

Character witness having adequate basis can give personal opinion as to character. (courts art. §9-115).

INJUNCTIONS:

Injunctions governed by Md. Rules. (R. P. 15-501 to 15-505). Injunction may be issued by court in any type of case if specially prayed, and at any stage of proceeding upon application or court's own motion. (R. P. 15-502). Statute prohibits issuing injunction against certain acts in labor dispute (lab. emp. art. §§4-307 to 4-318), and rules cited do not apply to labor disputes or domestic relations cases (R. P. 15-502).

Prerequisites.—Ex parte injunction will be granted if it appears from facts shown by affidavit or verified pleading that immediate, substantial and irreparable injury will result before adversary hearing can be had; otherwise injunction will not issue unless adverse party has had prior notice and opportunity to be heard. (R. P. 15-504, 15-505). Injunction will not be refused on ground applicant has adequate remedy at law for damages unless adverse party gives bond or satisfies court that he has property to answer for damages. (R. P. 15-502[c]).

Procedure.—In civil action, pleadings and other proceedings are same as in any other action. Complaint must set forth sufficient grounds upon which claim for injunction is founded. (R. P. 2-301, 2-302, 2-305).

Bond frequently but not always required. Bond required for ex parte or interlocutory injunction except in cases of hardship or application by state agency. (R. P. 15-503). Bonds governed by R. P. 1-401 to 1-406.

Temporary Injunction.—Interlocutory injunction may be issued after adversary hearing but before determination on merits. (R. P. 15-501).

Ex parte injunction expires in ten days as to resident or 35 days as to nonresident, but upon application made before expiration, court may extend for like period. Party so enjoined may request hearing on two days notice. (R. P. 15-504).

JUDGMENTS:

Judgment by confession may be entered by clerk on filing by plaintiff of complaint, accompanied by written instrument authorizing confession of judgment for liquidated amount and supported by affidavit of plaintiff or someone on his behalf stating amount due and address of defendant. (R. P. 2-611).

Immediately on entering such judgment, clerk must issue notice informing defendant of entry and of latest time for filing motion to open, modify or vacate judgment. (R. P. 2-611). For requirements as to service, see topic Process. Motion to vacate, open or modify judgment must be made within 30 days after service or summons (60 days if service made upon SDAT or out of state, 90 days if service made outside U.S.). (R. P. 2-611[c]; R. P. 2-321[a], [b]). Any motion must be heard promptly, and if court finds there is substantial and sufficient basis for actual controversy as to merits, court must order judgment opened, modified or vacated. (R. P. 2-611[d]).

If notice not served despite reasonable efforts to effect service, court must, after considering plaintiff's affidavit setting forth efforts to effect service, provide for notice to defendant in manner provided for by R. P. 2-122. (R. P. 2-611[b]).

Unless court orders otherwise, property cannot be sold in execution of confessed judgment and wages or debt are not to be remitted by garnishee to judgment creditor until expiration of time for debtor to move to open judgment and disposition of motion. (R. P. 2-611[e]).

Judgment by Consent.—Party may submit to judgment by consent. (R. P. 2-612).

Judgments on Pleadings.—No special provision for judgment on pleadings, except provisions for motion to dismiss. (R. P. 2-322).

Summary Judgment.—Plaintiff or defendant may at any time move for summary judgment on all or part of action on ground that there is no genuine dispute as to any material fact and he is entitled to judgment as matter of law. If motion filed before date of adverse party's initial pleading, it must be supported by affidavit; if filed later in proceeding, supporting affidavit is not required, but is good practice. Affidavit must show that affiant is competent to testify, must be made on personal knowledge and must set forth facts admissible in evidence. Response must state with particularity facts that are disputed. When motion for summary judgment is supported by affidavit or other statement under oath, party opposing motion must support response with affidavit or other written statement under oath to controvert any fact in motion. Upon hearing motion, court may grant or deny summary judgment or may enter order

See note at head of Digest as to 1998 legislation covered.

See Topical Index in front part of this volume.

MD – 20

JUDGMENTS . . . *continued*
limiting issues at trial to matters genuinely in dispute. (R. P. 2-501). No summary judgment is available in actions for divorce, annulment or alimony. (R. P. 9-208).

Judgment non obstante veredicto is provided for by R. P. 2-532.

Declaratory Judgments.—Uniform Act adopted. (courts art. §§3-401 to 3-415).

Default Judgment.—If defendant fails to plead on time, order of default may be entered against him by court on written request of plaintiff. (R. P. 2-613). Defendant may move to vacate order within 30 days of entry by stating reasons for failure to plead and basis for defense to claim. Court must vacate if it finds substantial and sufficient basis for actual controversy as to merits and that it is equitable to excuse failure. (R. P. 2-613).

Docketing.—After jury verdict or court decision allowing only recovery of costs or specified amount of money or denying relief, clerk must enter judgment by record on file jacket, docket book or docket within file. After entry of judgment, clerk must record and index judgment except judgment denying relief without costs. (R. P. 2-601).

Vacation or Modification.—Any party may move for new trial within ten days after entry of judgment. (R. P. 2-533). Upon motion within ten days after entry of judgment, court may receive additional evidence or may amend judgment or its findings or statement of reasons. (R. P. 2-534). Court may exercise revisory power and control over judgment if motion filed within 30 days, and if action tried without jury, may take any action that could be taken under R. P. 2-534. Otherwise, court may exercise revisory power upon motion at any time in case of fraud, mistake or irregularity. (R. P. 2-535).

Lien.—(For special rules applicable to district court judgments, see category Courts and Legislature, topic Courts, subhead District Courts.) If money judgment is indexed and recorded, judgment of circuit court is lien on real and certain leasehold property in county (or Baltimore City) where rendered, from date of judgment. (courts art. §11-402; R. P. 2-621). Circuit court judgment can be made lien in other county by sending certified copy of docket entries to clerk in that county; lien commences from date of filing such docket entries in that county. (courts art. §11-402; R. P. 2-622). Judgment of Court of Appeals, Court of Special Appeals, another circuit court of state, court of U.S. or any court entitled to full faith and credit constitutes lien in any county from date of receipt of certified copy of judgment by clerk in that county, to same extent as judgment entered by court in which property located. (R. P. 2-621, 2-623). Leases from year to year and leases for terms of not more than five years and not renewable do not constitute liens on real property. (courts art. §11-402). Execution or attachment may issue within 12 years from date of judgment or date of renewal. (R. P. 2-625). Renewal may be had at any time before expiration of judgment by filing notice of renewal. (R. P. 2-625). Execution upon judgment is not lien upon chattels until levy, and then only upon chattels included in levy. (courts art. §11-403).

Revival.—Judgment for sum certain expires 12 years from date of entry or most recent renewal. At any time before expiration of judgment, judgment holder may file notice of renewal and clerk shall enter judgment renewed. (R. P. 2-625).

Assignment.—Assignee of judgment may file assignment in court where judgment entered or recorded, and following filing, assignment may be enforced in name of assignee. (R. P. 2-624).

Satisfaction.—Upon receiving all amounts due on judgment, judgment creditor must furnish debtor and clerk with written statement of satisfaction which must be filed by clerk. (R. P. 2-626[a]). If judgment creditor fails to comply with R. P. 2-626(a), debtor may file motion for order declaring judgment satisfied. (R. P. 2-626[b]).

Actions on Judgments.—Action may be brought on judgments including foreign judgment. (182 Md. 577, 35 A.2d 449).

Foreign Judgments.—Debt of record entered in court in U.S. or foreign country may be proved by official transcript of entire record under seal of custodian and court or office where record made. (courts art. §10-601). Copy of authenticated foreign judgment filed with clerk of district court where judgment is $2,500 or less. (courts art. §11-802).

Uniform Foreign Money-Judgments Recognition Act adopted. (courts art. §§10-701 to 10-709).

Uniform Enforcement of Foreign Judgments Act adopted. (courts art. §§11-801 to 11-807).

Judgment Notes.—See category Business Regulation and Commerce, topic Bills and Notes.

Judgments Arising from Use of Motor Vehicle.—See category Transportation, topic Motor Vehicles.

LIMITATION OF ACTIONS:

Uniform Commercial Code adopted. (comm. law art. tits. 1 to 10). See category Business Regulation and Commerce, topic Commercial Code.

Actions must be brought within following periods after respective causes of action accrue:

Twenty Years.—To recover possession of corporeal freehold or leasehold estate in land, time running from beginning of adverse possession. (courts art. §5-103[a]). Landlord's claim to rent under lease or to reversion in property. (real prop. art. §8-107). Claim for damages incurred from error in land survey must be brought within earlier of 20 years of survey or three years after error discovered. (courts art. §5-112). See also subhead Improvements to Real Property, infra.

Twelve Years.—Action on any of following specialties must be filed within 12 years after cause of action accrues, or within 12 years from date of death of last to die of principal debtor or creditor, whichever sooner: (1) Promissory note or other instrument under seal; (2) bond, except public officer's bond; (3) judgment; (4) recognizance; (5) contract under seal; (6) any other specialty. Payment of principal or interest on specialty suspends operation of limitations for three years thereafter. Limitations do not apply to specialty taken for use of state. (courts art. §5-102). Promissory note or other instrument must meet certain standards to be considered under seal. (275 Md. 151, 338 A.2d 275).

Ten Years.—See subhead Improvements to Real Property, infra.

Seven Years.—To recover lands for breach of condition subsequent or termination of fee simple determinable estate. If breach or termination occurred before July 1, 1969, action must be commenced or entry made by July 1, 1976. (real prop. art. §6-103). On claim for state, county or city taxes where other period not prescribed. (tax-gen. art. §13-1103).

Five Years.—On public officer's bond (except state may sue on such bond at any time). (courts art. §5-104).

Four Years.—On contract of sale of personal property under Uniform Commercial Code—Sales. (comm. law art. §2-725). For collection of sales, amusement, fuel and use taxes, except that proof of fraud or gross negligence will remove bar of statute. (tax-gen. art. §13-1102).

Three Years.—Any civil action at law for which another period not provided by Code. (courts art. §5-101). Prosecution for welfare and Medicaid fraud. (courts art. §5-106[h] and [i]). Prosecution for certain vehicular homicide crimes. (courts art. §5-106[n]). In action for wrongful death, three years from death, except if death caused by occupational disease, whereupon shorter of ten years from death or three years from time cause of death discovered. (courts art. §3-904[g]; see also lab. emp. art. §9-902[d], in case where Workmen's Compensation claim involved). Contempt-of-court action for default on court ordered spousal or child support. (courts art. §5-111). Action to invalidate transfer of property between spouses by prejudiced creditors of transferor's spouse. (fam. law art. §4-301[d]). Action for practicing, attempting to practice or offering to practice medicine without license. (courts art. §5-106[q]). Actions under Maryland Tort Claims Act. (st. gov't art. §12-106). See also subhead Improvements to Real Property, infra.

Two Years.—Action for breach of express or implied warranties in sale of improvements to real estate. (real prop. art. §10-204). Prosecutions for unlawful use of driver's license or fraudulent use of false name when applying for driver's license. (courts art. §5-106[c]). Prosecution for violation of state election laws, conflict of interest laws, or criminal malfeasance, misfeasance, or nonfeasance by state or local official. (courts art. §5-106[f]).

One Year.—Actions for libel, slander, or assault (courts art. §5-105); prosecution for misdemeanor not punishable by confinement in penitentiary by statute (courts art. §5-106[a]); prosecution for fine, penalty or forfeiture (courts art. §5-107). Claims on municipal, county or state contracts must be brought within one year from date claim arose or within one year of completion of contract giving rise to claim, whichever is later. (st. gov't art. §12-202). See category Business Regulation and Commerce, topic Contracts.

Nine Months.—Claims against estate of decedent must be presented within earlier of nine months after death or two months after notice sent to creditors in form required under §7-103 notifying creditor that claim will be barred unless presented within two months after notice is sent. For deaths occurring on or after Oct. 1, 1992, claims must be presented by earlier of six months after decedent's death or two months after notice given. (est. & tr. art. §8-103[a]).

Six Months.—Claim against estate based on conduct of or contract with personal representative barred unless action commenced within six months of date claim arose. (est. & tr. art. §8-103[a], [c]). All other claims against estate of decedent dying after Oct. 1, 1992 must be presented within earlier of six months after death or two months after notice is sent. Where personal representative disallows claim in whole or part, claimant must file petition for allowance or commence action against personal representative or distributees within 60 days after mailing of notice of disallowance. (est. & tr. art. §8-107).

Action or levy under Uniform Commercial Code—Bulk Transfers. (comm. law art. §6-111).

Action for usury must be brought no later than six months after loan paid. (comm. law art. §12-111; see category Business Regulation and Commerce, topic Interest, subhead Maximum Rate, for other limitations under various credit statutes).

Malpractice.—Generally, action for injury arising from professional services of health care provider must be brought within shorter of five year period from commission of injury or three year period from discovery thereof. If claimant under 11 at time injury committed, time period commences when claimant reaches age 11, unless action is for injury to reproductive system or injury caused by foreign object negligently left in claimant's body; in either of these cases, and claimant under 16 years old at time of injury, limitations period begins to run at age 16. Filing of claim with Health Care Arbitration Office constitutes filing of action. See category Dispute Resolution, topic Arbitration and Award, subhead Medical Malpractice. (courts art. §5-109).

Securities Act.—Civil liability must be enforced by action commenced within three years after contract of sale, except that specified actions by buyer against seller must be brought within one year after violation or discovery thereof, but no later than three years after contract of sale. (corps. art. §11-703[f]).

Improvements to Real Property.—Except for cause of action against manufacturer or supplier for personal injury or death caused by asbestos or for property damage to property owned by government or educational institutions, no cause of action for damages accrues, and person may not seek contribution or indemnity for damages, when death, personal injury or injury to property resulting from defective or unsafe condition of improvement to real property occurs more than 20 years after date entire improvement becomes available for intended use. When defendant is architect, professional engineer or contractor limit is ten years. Cause of action for such injury accrues when injury or damage occurs, and action must be filed within three years thereafter. Provisions do not apply if defendant is in actual possession and control of property when injury occurs. (courts art. §5-108).

See note at head of Digest as to 1998 legislation covered.

See Topical Index in front part of this volume.

MD – 21

LIMITATION OF ACTIONS . . . *continued*

Death from Occupational Disease.—Action for damages for death arising from occupational disease must be filed within three years of discovery of facts from which it was or should have been known that occupational disease was proximate cause of death, but in any event not later than ten years from date of death. (courts art. §5-113).

Actions Not Specifically Provided For.—Any civil action at law for which no specific period provided by Code is governed by general three-year statute. (courts art. §5-101).

New Actions.—No provision for extending time to permit new action after previous action disposed of otherwise than on merits.

Foreign Causes of Action.—Normally limitations is matter to be determined by law of forum, and Md. statute applies to suit brought in state. (108 Md. 693, 71 A. 312). If product liability cause of action arose in foreign jurisdiction and cause of action barred there by reason of lapse of time, action cannot be brought in Maryland unless plaintiff is resident of Maryland. (courts art. §5-115).

Disability or Absence of Plaintiff.—When cause of action subject to limitation under courts art. §§5-101 to 113 accrues in favor of minor or mental incompetent, he must file action within lesser of three years or applicable period of limitations after disability removed, except where statute of limitations has more than three years to run at time of removal. Imprisonment, absence from state or marriage do not extend statute. (courts art. §5-201). Landlord under disability when 20 year period for rent or reversion expires has two years after removal of disability to assert rights. (real prop. art. §8-107).

Absence or Concealment of Defendant.—Person absenting himself from state or removing from county to county after contracting debt to avoid creditors (but not if for reasons of convenience, and not if he leaves assets with trustee to pay creditors) does not have benefit of limitations contained in courts art. tit. 5. If debtor is out of state when cause of action accrues, time runs only from his return. (courts art. §5-205).

Death.—For limitations on suits against personal representative, heirs or legatees, see subhead Nine Months, supra, and appropriate subheads under category Estates and Trusts, topic Executors and Administrators.

Fraud.—If knowledge of cause of action is kept from party by fraud of adverse party, cause of action accrues at time when party discovered, or by exercise of ordinary diligence should have discovered, fraud. (courts art. §5-203).

Interruption of Statutory Period.—Time between filing and dismissal of petition of insolvent debtor not counted so as to defeat claim against him. (courts art. §5-202).

Part payment or acknowledgment, oral or written, has following effect: (1) If statute has not run, time extended for three years from date of payment or acknowledgment; (2) if claim barred, it is revived for three years, except that express promise to pay is necessary to revive specialty debt. (177 Md. 43, 7 A.2d 186).

Contractual Limitations.—In sales contracts governed by U.C.C., parties may by original agreement reduce limitations to not less than one year, but may not extend limitations. (comm. law art. §2-725 [1]).

Pleading.—Limitations must be pleaded as affirmative defense. (R. P. 2-323[g][16]).

Municipal Corporations.—No action against local government can be brought for unliquidated damages unless written notice of time, place and cause of alleged injury is presented in person or by registered mail within 180 days (after injury) to city solicitor of Baltimore City or county executive, county council, county commissioners or corporate authorities of municipal corporation (notice to be given to county solicitor or county attorney in Anne Arundel County, Baltimore County, Harford County, and Prince George's County). Court may, upon motion and for good cause, entertain suit in absence of required notice, unless defendant shows its defense was prejudiced thereby. (courts art. §5-304).

PARTITION:

Any joint tenant, tenant in common or concurrent owner may require partition, and if property cannot be divided without loss or injury to parties in interest, sale will be ordered. (real prop. art. §14-107; R. P. 12-401). Right of petitioner does not depend on extent of his interest. (140 Md. 121, 117 A. 108). Tenancy by entireties cannot be severed by act of one spouse. (253 Md. 525, 253 A.2d 367).

Grounds.—It is sufficient that plaintiff desires division of property. (See real prop. art. §14-107; 228 Md. 624, 180 A.2d 878.) Bill of Partition cannot be made to settle title disputes or serve as action for ejectment. (188 Md. 581, 53 A.2d 555; 60 Md. 139).

Jurisdiction and Venue.—Equity courts have inherent power to partition either personal or real property (212 Md. 565, 130 A.2d 737; 3 Bland 184), and circuit courts have statutory power to partition any real property interest, either legal or equitable. (real prop. art. §14-107). However, jurisdiction to partition property is confined to cases where property interests are concurrent. (138 Md. 211, 114 A. 55). Suit should be brought in court in county where land lies. (courts art. §6-203). Orphans' court has power to partition distributions. (est. & tr. art. §9-107).

Proceedings.—Suit is instituted by bill in equity. Any person holding mortgage or other encumbrance or undivided interest in property may be made party. Unless all parties waive appointment of commissioners, court determining partition to be proper will commission not more than five nor less than three persons to value and divide property. (real prop. art. §14-107; R. P. 12-401[c]). Commissioners' report must be served on all parties who have appeared, and exceptions thereto must be taken within ten days. (R. P. 12-401[c]). Upon confirmation of commissioners' report, court enters final decree of partition or orders sale and division of proceeds. In former case, decree operates as conveyance and no deed is necessary. In latter, deed is executed by person appointed by court. (real prop. art. §14-107[c]). Personal representative or one or more heirs or legatees may petition orphans' court prior to closing of estate for partition of distribution. (est. & tr. art. §9-107).

Partition in Kind or Sale.—Partition is in kind unless it appears that property cannot be divided without loss or injury to parties interested, when partition may be by sale. (est. & tr. art. §9-107[b]; real prop. art §14-107[a]). Co-tenant entitled to compensation for improvements made on land to extent enhanced value of property at time of sale. (29 Md. App. 521, 349 A.2d 655).

PLEADING:

Maryland adopted new rules of procedure effective July 1, 1984. See also topic Practice.

Pleadings Permitted.—Pleadings allowed are complaint, answer, counter-claim, cross-claim, third-party complaint, and answer to counter-claim, cross-claim, or third-party complaint. Court may order reply to answer. Demurrers abolished. (R. P. 2-302).

Complaint.—Clear statement of facts and demand for judgment for relief necessary to constitute cause of action. (R. P. 2-305). Must be divided into separately numbered paragraphs, each containing single set of circumstances to extent possible. Each cause of action must be set forth in separately numbered count. Relief in alternative may be demanded and request for such other or further relief as case may require is good practice. (R. P. 2-303).

Answer.—For each averment, defendant must specifically admit, deny, or state that defendant is without knowledge or information sufficient to form belief as to truth of averment. (R. P. 2-323[c]). When action in any count is breach of contract, debt or tort, and claim is for money only, party may answer that count by general denial of liability. (R. P. 2-323[d]).

Counterclaim.—Party against whom claim is asserted may plead as counterclaim any claim he has against any opposing party. Counterclaim may claim relief exceeding amount of, or different in kind from, initial claim. If counterclaim requires presence of additional parties, court will order them to be brought in if jurisdiction can be obtained. (R. P. 2-331).

Reply.—Replications are abolished. (R. P. 2-302).

Demurrer.—Demurrers are abolished. (R. P. 2-302).

Amended or Supplemental Pleadings.—Amendment freely permitted unless court directs otherwise. Party may file amendment up to 15 days before scheduled trial date. Thereafter, amendment may be filed only by written consent of adverse party or by leave of court. Within 15 days after service of amendment, any other party may file motion to strike. (R. P. 2-341).

Affidavits of Merits.—Affidavit used in summary judgment cases. (See topic Judgments.) Supporting affidavit required in certain special cases, such as attachment. (R. P. 2-115[a]). When application made for ex parte injunction, either affidavit or verified pleading required. (R. P. 15-504). In divorce action involving alimony, maintenance, or support (including child support), current financial statements under affidavit must be filed by both parties. (R. P. 9-203).

Affidavits of Defense.—Not used except in summary judgment cases. See topic Judgments.

Bill of Particulars.—Replaced by motion for more definite statement, which may be made when pleading to which answer is permitted is so vague or ambiguous that party cannot reasonably frame answer. Motion must point out defects complained of and details desired. (R. P. 2-322[d]).

Verification not required except where specifically required by statute or rule. (R. P. 1-301[f]). Verification required, for example, in mandamus cases. (R. P. BE40, BE41). Where application made for ex parte injunction, either verification or affidavit required. (R. P. 15-504). Divorce pleading must be signed by party (R. P. 9-203), but verification not required.

Service of initial pleading is generally by sheriff. (R. P. 2-123). See topic Process. Service of subsequent pleadings is generally upon party's lawyer, by delivery or Mail. (R. P. 1-321).

Filing.—Pleadings must be filed with clerk of court. (R. P. 1-322). Pleading after original pleading will not be accepted for filing unless accompanied by admission, waiver or certificate of service on opposite party or his attorney. (R. P. 1-323).

Time.—Defendant must answer within 30 days after service, with certain exceptions. Where service is made outside state, initial pleading due 60 days from completion of service if made within U.S. or 90 days if beyond. (R. P. 2-321). Motion or other pleading requiring ruling of court or compliance by party enlarges time to 15 days after disposition by court or compliance by party. (R. P. 2-321[c]). Responses to motions must be filed within 15 days of service, or within time allowed for party's original pleading, whichever is later. (R. P. 2-311). Counterclaim, cross-claim, or third party claim must be filed within 30 days after time for filing answer. Otherwise, any party may file motion to strike within 15 days of service of counterclaim, cross-claim or third party claim. Court must grant motion to strike unless there is showing that delay does not prejudice other parties. (R. P. 2-331; 2-332).

Computation.—To compute period of time after event, day of event not included; Sats., Suns. and legal holidays counted only when period of time allowed is more than seven days. When last day would fall on Sat., Sun. or legal holiday, period extends to first day thereafter not such a day. (R. P. 1-203[a]). To compute latest day for performance of act required by statute, rule of procedure or court order to be performed prescribed number of days prior to event, all prior days counted (including Sats., Suns. and legal holidays). Latest day included unless Sat., Sun. or legal holiday, in which case latest day is first preceding day not Sat., Sun. or legal holiday. (R. P. 1-203[b]).

Service by Mail.—Whenever party must do some act within prescribed period after service upon party of notice or other paper, and service is made by mail, three days will be added to prescribed period. (R. P. 1-203[d]).

Frivolous Claims.—Attorneys are prohibited from bringing or defending proceeding unless there is basis that is not frivolous. (r. prof. con. 3.1, R. P. Appendix). All courts have power to impose sanctions against party, attorney or both that maintain or defend proceeding in bad faith or without substantial justification. (R. P. 1-341).

PLEADING . . . *continued*

Small Claims.—See category Courts and Legislature, topic Courts, subhead District Courts.

PRACTICE:

Civil and criminal practice in Court of Appeals, Court of Special Appeals, circuit and district courts is governed by Md. Rules. (R. P.).

Discovery.—

Depositions may be taken by oral examination (R. P. 2-415[b]), by telephone (R.P. 2-418) or by written interrogatories (R. P. 2-417). Deposition may be recorded by videotape and audiotape. (R. P. 2-416). See topic Depositions and Discovery. District court may order deposition, upon good cause shown, for party desiring to perpetuate own testimony or that of another party or witness (R. P. 3-431); otherwise, in district court actions, deposition may be taken only by written stipulation of parties (R. P. 3-401). Discovery and production of documents for inspection and reproduction is provided for in rules. (R. P. 2-422, 3-421[a][3]). In district court, documents discoverable limited to written instruments upon which claim or defense founded, signed or recorded statement given to adverse party, and reports of experts. (R. P. 3-421[a][3]).

Interrogatories may be served at any time by any party upon any other party in circuit court cases. Except to demand supplementary answers to interrogatories previously filed, party may not, without leave of court, serve more than one set of interrogatories or more than 30 interrogatories (including subsidiary or incidental interrogatories). (R. P. 2-421[a]). Interrogatories must be answered in writing, under oath and signed within later of 30 days after service or 15 days after date on which answering party's initial pleading or motion is required. (R. P. 2-421[b]). Motion for order compelling discovery must be filed with reasonable promptness. (R. P. 2-432). Answers may be used as permitted by rules of evidence. Option to produce business records in certain circumstances is provided. (R. P. 2-421). Limited written interrogatories are permitted in most cases before district court. (R. P. 3-421).

Demand for Admission of Facts.—Any party (except in district court) may serve upon any other party written request to admit genuineness of any relevant document or truth of any relevant matters of fact. Copies of documents must be supplied. Facts or genuineness are deemed admitted unless denied or other response or objection made within later of 30 days of service of request or 15 days after date on which party's initial pleading or motion is required. After refusal to admit genuineness or truth, demanding party who proves genuineness or truth may apply for reasonable expenses and attorneys' fees incurred in making proof. Demanding party may move for determination by court of sufficiency of answers or objections, and appropriate orders and awards of expenses may be made by court. (R. P. 2-424).

Direct Actions Against Insurer.—See category Transportation, topic Motor Vehicles, subhead Direct Actions.

Small Claims.—See category Courts and Legislature, topic Courts, subhead District Courts.

See also topics Actions, Appeal and Error, Injunctions, Judgments, Pleading, Process; categories Debtor and Creditor, topics Attachment, Executions, Garnishment; Dispute Resolution, topic Arbitration and Award.

PROCESS:

Civil action commenced by filing complaint. (R. P. 2-101). Clerk issues summons for each defendant in state forthwith upon commencement of action and delivers it to sheriff or other person designated by plaintiff. (R. P. 2-112). Upon request of plaintiff, additional summons issues against any defendant. (R. P. 2-112).

General Requisites.—Summons should be authenticated with seal of court, it should be signed by clerk, and should contain name of court and assigned docket reference, name and address of party requesting summons, name and address of person to be served, date of issue, time within which summons must be served, time within which defendant must respond, notification that failure to respond within time allowed may result in judgment by default or granting relief sought, and time within which return of service must be made. (R. P. 2-114).

By Whom Summons Issued.—Clerk of court. (R. P. 2-112).

Who May Serve.—Sheriff. (R. P. 2-123). Competent person over 18 years of age, including attorney of record, but not party, may execute process. Person other than sheriff executing process must make appropriate return by affidavit. Employee of party may serve process. (R. P. 2-123, 2-126; 249 Md. 94, 238 A.2d 251).

Personal Service on Individual.—Service may be made by delivery of process to party to be served or to agent authorized by appointment or by law to receive process. (R. P. 2-124[a]).

Personal Service on Infant.—Same as on adult, except copy must be left with parent, guardian, or other person having care or custody of infant if there be such parent, guardian or other person within jurisdiction of court. (R. P. 2-124[b]).

Personal Service on Incompetent Person.—Same as on competent person, except copy should be left with person having care of person or estate of incompetent if there be such person within jurisdiction of court. (R. P. 2-124[b]).

Personal Service on Partnership.—Partners must be sued as individuals to reach individual assets, and each must be served as individual.

Personal Service on Corporation.—In case of either domestic or foreign corporation, process may be served on resident agent or president, secretary or treasurer. If corporation has no resident agent or good faith attempt to serve resident agent, president, secretary or treasurer is unsuccessful, process may be served upon manager, any director, vice president, assistant secretary or assistant treasurer, or if none of above, upon anyone with express or implied authorization to accept service. (R. P. 2-124[c]).

If corporation required to have resident agent has no resident agent, or if two attempts on different business days to serve process on resident agent are unsuccessful, process may be served upon Dep't of Assessments and Taxation. (R. P. 2-124[c]).

Director of Dep't must forward copy to defendant at known mailing address or principal place of business. (courts art. §6-307).

Foreign or domestic insurance companies, reciprocal exchanges and interinsurers, surplus-line insurers and fraternal beneficial associations may be sued by service on Insurance Commissioner. (art. 48A, §§57, 197, 205[a], 347; R. P. 2-121[d]). Nonresident individuals, partnerships or corporations must file irrevocable consent to service of process on secretary of Real Estate Commission with their applications for real estate brokers license; and division of fees or holding of deposits in any real estate transaction in state is deemed consent without filing. (bus. occ. art. §§16-514, 16-515).

Every applicant for registration of securities under Md. Securities Act and every issuer proposing to offer security in state through agent must file irrevocable consent appointing Securities Commissioner as attorney to receive process in any noncriminal suit, action or proceeding arising under state securities law. (corps. art. §11-802).

Wherever insurance, surety or bonding company has accredited agent in state, it may sue or be sued on its policies, and service on agent is sufficient. (courts art. §6-306).

Personal Service on Association.—Same as service on corporation. (R. P. 2-124[c]).

Personal Service on Joint Stock Company.—Same as service on corporation. (R. P. 2-124[c]).

Personal Service on Foreign Corporation.—Same as service on domestic corporation. (R. P. 2-124[c]).

Personal Service Outside the State.—Where personal jurisdiction is authorized by courts art. tit. 6 (see subhead Long Arm Statute, infra), defendant may be served where found, within or without state. (courts art. §6-304). Service outside state is generally same as inside state and is governed by R. P. 2-121. Service may also be made in manner prescribed by court, or prescribed by foreign jurisdiction if reasonably calculated to give actual notice. (R. P. 2-121[a]).

Service by Mail.—In lieu of personal service, service within or without state may be by certified mail, endorsed "Restricted Delivery -Show to whom, date, address of delivery." (R. P. 2-121[a]).

Substituted Service.—Service upon Dep't of Assessments and Taxation, Insurance Commissioner, Securities Commissioner, Secretary of Real Estate Commission, with notice to defendant, is permitted depending upon circumstances. See subhead Personal Service on Corporation, supra.

Service on Defendant Who Seeks to Evade or Resists Service.—Evading domiciliary, resident or one who maintains principal place of business in state may be served upon court order by mailing summons, original pleading, and all papers filed with it to defendant at last known residence and delivering each to person of suitable age and discretion at place of business, dwelling house or usual place of abode of defendant. Affidavit that person has acted to evade service required. (R. P. 2-121[b]).

Where person resists service of civil process by threat or force, officer serving process must leave copy with responsible person at premises if possible, or post copy as near premises as practicable; such service effective as actual personal service. (courts art. §6-303).

Service on Defendant Whose Whereabouts Are Known, In Rem or Quasi In Rem Proceeding.—Same as service for obtaining personal jurisdiction over defendant. (R. P. 2-122).

Service on United States or Its Officer, Employee or Agent is as prescribed in R. P. 2-124(k) and (l).

Service by Publication.—In in rem or quasi in rem proceedings where whereabouts of defendant unknown, service may be by mailing notice to defendant's last known address and: (1) Publication of notice, (2) posting of notice by sheriff at or near courthouse door, or (3) by posting of notice by sheriff on conspicuous place on land. (R. P. 2-122[a]). Mailing and publication or posting to be completed at least 30 days before defendant's initial pleading due. (R. P. 2-122). Plaintiff must file affidavit to satisfy court of good faith efforts to locate defendant. (R. P. 2-122[a]). Proof of publication is by certificate of publisher filed in proceeding. (R. P. 2-126[b]).

In cases for divorce, annulment, or alimony, same service shall be had as in other cases. (R. P. 9-202).

Long Arm Statute.—Court may exercise personal jurisdiction as to any cause of action over person domiciled in, served with process in, organized under laws of, or maintaining place of business in state. (courts art. §6-102). Court may exercise personal jurisdiction over person who directly or by agent: (1) Transacts any business or performs any character of work or service in state; (2) contracts to supply goods, food, services or manufactured products in state; (3) causes tortious injury in state by act or omission in state; (4) causes tortious injury in or outside state by act or omission outside state, if person regularly does or solicits business, engages in any other persistent course of conduct in state or derives substantial revenue from goods, food, services or manufactured products used or consumed in state; (5) has interest in, uses or possesses real property in state; or (6) contracts to insure or act as surety for or on any person, property, risk, contract, obligation or agreement located, executed or to be performed within state at time contract is made, unless parties otherwise provide in writing. Where jurisdiction is based solely upon enumerated acts, person may be sued only on cause of action arising from enumerated acts. (courts art. §6-103). Breadth of long arm statute is to permit personal jurisdiction to extent permitted by federal Constitution. (311 Md. 496, 536 A.2d 633; 277 Md. 220, 352 A.2d 818).

Domestic Relations Cases.—In cases arising out of marital relationship or involving child support, alimony, or counsel fees, where plaintiff resides in Md. at time suit filed, court may exercise personal jurisdiction over nonresident defendant who has been personally served according to rules of procedure, if: (1) Md. was matrimonial domicile of parties immediately before separation, or (2) obligation to pay child or spousal support or counsel fees arose under Md. law or under agreement executed by one of parties in Md. (courts art. §6-103.1). Court may exercise personal jurisdiction over nonresident defendant alleged to be father in paternity proceeding if: (1) Mother

PROCESS . . . *continued*
resides in Md. when suit filed; (2) father is personally served with process; and (3) act of conception is alleged to have occurred in Md. (courts art. §6-103.2).

Proof of Service.—Proof of personal service is by notation on sheriff's return or by affidavit filed with clerk. Proof of service by mail is by affidavit with original return receipt attached. Proof of service by publication is by certificate of publisher filed with clerk. (R. P. 2-126).

Nonresident Motorist.—No specific legislation.

REPLEVIN:

Replevin procedure is governed by Md. Rules (R. P. 12-601 and 12-602).

Replevin is possessory action ex delicto founded on tortious detention or taking of personal property for which damages are allowed. (253 Md. 669, 253 A.2d 736; 201 Md. 433, 94 A.2d 639). It is appropriate remedy for person from whom goods have been obtained by fraud, including purchase by insolvent with no reasonable expectation of paying for goods. (69 Md. 276, 14 A. 666). It may be brought not only by owner, but also by one who has special property and right of possession, such as factor or bailee. (183 Md. 105, 36 A.2d 677). It is usual remedy for tenant to recover goods distrained upon by landlord where, for any reason, distraint is illegal.

Goods in custodia legis cannot be replevied. (9 G. & J. 220).

Proceedings.—District court has exclusive original jurisdiction, subject to right to demand jury trial. (courts art. §§4-401, 4-402). Action may be brought in county where defendant resides, is regularly employed or has place of business, or in county where goods sought to be replevied are located. (courts art. 6-201). Action is instituted by filing statement of claim, alleging that defendant unjustly detains property and claiming return of property. Statement may claim damages for detention. (12-601). Statement may be accompanied by petition for injunctive relief. (courts art. §4-401[6]). Clerk issues show cause order to defendant. Hearing on show cause order may be held no earlier than seven days after date of service upon defendant. If defendant fails to appear, property may be seized by sheriff. (12-601). If court determines at hearing that plaintiff, with reasonable probability, is entitled to return of property claimed, writ of replevin issues upon filing by plaintiff of approved replevin bond. (12-601). Replevin bond is in amount fixed by court, is payable to state for use of any person having interest in property sought, is conditioned for successful prosecution of action and return of property if adjudged and fulfillment of any judgment. (12-601). Writ of replevin must specifically describe property to be replevied. (12-601). Defenses to action of replevin are: (1) Defendant did not take property; (2) right to possession of property is in defendant; or (3) right of possession of property is in third party. (12-601). If writ issues, defendant may plead, and case proceeds to trial. If writ is denied, action proceeds in detinue. (12-602).

If demand for jury trial is filed, district court retains jurisdiction to conduct hearing on show cause order, enforce injunctions, and issue, renew and receive returns upon writ of replevin. Action is transmitted to circuit court only after writ is returned that property sought is seized or eloigned and time for filing of defendant's notice of intention to defend (15 days after service of summons and statement of claim, R. P. 3-307[b]) has expired. (courts art. §4-402[e][2]).

If property owner subject to statutory lien institutes replevin action and establishes right to writ issuance but for lien, court shall issue writ. At trial, court shall determine amount of lien claim, if any. If lienholder prevails at trial, award may include reasonable attorney's fees and property or lien amount. (comm. law art. §16-208).

Repossession.—No provision for return of property to defendant prior to final judgment in his favor.

Claims of Third Persons.—Defendant may plead right to property in third person. At trial, burden is on plaintiff to show title and right of possession superior to that of defendant or third person. (226 Md. 136, 172 A.2d 494). Action on replevin bond shall be brought in name of state to use of equitable plaintiff. (12-602).

Judgment or Order.—Verdict awards possession of property and must state separately value of property and amount of damages, if any, for detention. (12-601).

SEQUESTRATION:

See category Debtor and Creditor, topics Attachment, Executions.

SERVICE:

See topic Process.

STAY OF EXECUTION:

See topic Appeal and Error; category Debtor and Creditor, topic Executions.

SUBMISSION OF CONTROVERSY:

No special provision for submission of controversy on agreed-upon issues. Parties must file action and move for summary judgment. (R. P. 2-501).

VENUE:

References are to Courts Art. of Code unless otherwise indicated.

Individual.—Civil action must generally be brought in county or Baltimore City where defendant resides, carries on regular business, is employed or habitually engages in vocation. (§6-201[a]).

Special Cases, Additional Venue.—(1) Divorce—where plaintiff resides; (2) annulment—where plaintiff resides or marriage was performed; (3) replevin or detinue—where property is located; (4) action relating to custody, guardianship, maintenance or support of child—where father, alleged father, mother or child resides; (5) action for possession of real property—where land is located; (6) negligence action—where cause of action arose; (7) attachment on original process—where property is located or garnishee resides; (8) action for nondelivery or injury to goods against captain of vessel—where goods are received on board or are to be delivered. (§6-202). See also R. P.T41 (ejectment), R. P. 9-201 (divorce, alimony, annulment), provisions of which are additional to places in §6-202 where venue is proper.

Exceptions.—General rule does not apply to following actions, which must be brought as indicated: (1) Certain actions relating to interest in land (partition, enforcement of charge or lien, eminent domain, trespass, waste)—in county or Baltimore City that all or any portion of subject matter is located (if property lies in more than one county, court where proceedings first brought); (2) adoption proceeding—in county that petitioner is domiciled or has resided for at least 90 days, where licensed child placement agency having legal or physical custody of adoptee is located, where adoptee is domiciled (if he is related to petitioner by blood or marriage or is adult), or where equity court has continuing jurisdiction over custody of adoptee; (3) action to recover damages against railroad for injury to livestock—in county where injury occurred (§6-203); (4) administrative or judicial probate-in county where decedent was domiciled at time of death or, where decedent-not domiciled in Maryland, in county where petitioner believes is situs of largest part in value of decedent's property in Maryland at time of death (R. P. 6-111).

Multiple Defendants.—If no single venue is applicable to all defendants, all may be sued where any one could be sued or where cause of action arose. (§6-201[b]).

Nonresident or Absent Persons.—Nonresident individual may be sued in any county or Baltimore City. (§6-202[11]). Person absconding from county or leaving state before statute of limitations has run may be sued where found. (§6-202[12]). In local action where defendant cannot be found where subject matter is located, he may be sued in any county where general rule of venue permits. (§6-202[13]).

Domestic or foreign corporation is subject to same venue as is individual and may also be sued where it maintains its principal offices in state. (§6-201[a]). If corporation has no principal place of business in state, it may additionally be sued where plaintiff resides. (§6-202[3]). Suit on bond against corporate surety may additionally be brought where bond is filed or contract is to be performed. (§6-202[6]). Suit for damages against railroad company for injury to livestock must be brought where injury occurred. (§6-203[d]). Action by Attorney General to forfeit charter of Md. corporation or to revoke permit of foreign corporation for involvement in organized crime may be brought anywhere corporation is doing business. (corps. art. §1-405[d]).

Actions in Rem or Local Actions.—See subhead Exceptions, supra.

Change of Venue.—In action at law in circuit court, including issues from orphans' court, appeal from Workmen's Compensation Commission, and action transferred from district court for jury trial, upon suggestion by affidavit of any party (and not of counsel) that he cannot have fair and impartial trial in county in which action is pending, or upon motion of any party where all judges in county are disqualified to sit under Maryland Constitution court must transmit record to court in some other county if court finds there is reasonable ground for suggestion. (R. P. 2-505). In criminal proceedings, upon suggestion in writing under oath of any party that he cannot have fair and impartial trial in court in which case is pending, court shall transmit case to another court having jurisdiction for trial, except that in non-capital cases, court shall transmit case only if it is satisfied that suggestion is true or that there is reasonable ground for it. Second removal may be obtained by same procedure. (R. P. 4-254).

When action is filed laying venue in wrong county, court shall, upon proper objection to venue, dismiss action, or transfer action to court in proper county if justice so requires. (R. P. 2-327[b]).

Waiver.—Failure to assert improper venue by way of motion to dismiss prior to filing of answer operates as waiver. (R. P. 2-322[a][2]).

COURTS AND LEGISLATURE

COURTS:

References are to Courts and Judicial Proceedings Article of Code unless otherwise indicated.

United States District Court.—Clerk's office: U.S. Court House, 101 W. Lombard St., Baltimore 21201.

Deposit for costs required: $120 in civil or admiralty cases; $160 minimum in bankruptcy cases ($800 for filing under c. 11).

State Courts.—Judicial power vested in Court of Appeals, Court of Special Appeals, circuit courts, orphans' courts, and district courts. (Const. art. IV, §§1, 14A; courts art. §§1-301, 1-401, 1-501, 1-601). In criminal cases juries are judge of law and facts except that courts may pass upon sufficiency of evidence necessary to sustain conviction. (Md. Decl. of Rts., art. 23). All courts authenticate, under their respective seals, by their clerks; except orphans' courts authenticate by registers of wills. (Const. art. IV, §1; courts art. §2-201, est. & tr. art. §2-208).

Court of Appeals of Maryland.—Court of Appeals sits at Annapolis. There are seven judges, one from each of the seven appellate judicial circuits. (1994, c. 103, subject to ratification). (Const. art. IV, §14).

Jurisdiction.—Jurisdiction includes: (1) To review by way of certiorari proceeding pending in or decided by Court of Special Appeals on appeal from circuit court, orphans' court or Md. Tax Court (see subhead Maryland Tax Court, infra) either (a) on its own motion, or (b) where party has filed petition for certiorari before or after decision of Court of Special Appeals but not later than 15 days after its mandate, with exception of cases in which Court of Special Appeals has denied or granted leave to appeal in post conviction, bail-related habeas corpus, or inmate grievance commission proceeding; where final judgment entered following guilty plea in circuit court; where circuit court issued order revoking probation; (2) to review by way of certiorari final judgment of circuit court on appeal from district court if review is necessary to secure uniformity or other special circumstances make review desirable and in public interest; (3) exclusive appellate jurisdiction with respect to question certified under Uniform Certification of Questions of Law Act; and (4) exclusive appellate jurisdiction over cases where death penalty imposed. (§§12-201 to 12-203, 12-305, 12-307; R. P. 8-306[c][1]). Court may answer questions of law certified by federal courts or appellate

COURTS . . . *continued*

courts of any other state or by Court of Special Appeals and may certify questions of law to appellate courts of any state. (§§12-602, 12-603). Reasons for denial of writ of certiorari must be in writing. (§12-203).

Court of Special Appeals.—Court of Special Appeals sits at Annapolis in panels of three, but may order hearings en banc. There are 13 judges, six from state at large, and one each from seven special appellate judicial circuits. (§§1-402 to 1-403).

Jurisdiction.—Except for certified questions of law, criminal cases where death penalty imposed, and review by certiorari, Court of Special Appeals has exclusive initial appellate jurisdiction over any reviewable judgment, decree, order or other action of circuit court or orphans' court. (§12-308). Appeals subject to further review in Court of Appeals by certiorari, either before or after decision of Court of Special Appeals, if deemed desirable and in public interest by Court of Appeals. (§§12-201, 12-203). (See category Civil Actions and Procedure, topic Certiorari.) Court of Appeals may certify questions of law to highest court of any state. (§12-602). See subhead Maryland Tax Court, infra.

Circuit courts of counties have original and exclusive jurisdiction of cases in equity and at law of cases civil and criminal above jurisdiction of district court, jurisdiction of appeals from district court and certain administrative agencies, and concurrent jurisdiction at law with district court in cases involving $2,500 to $25,000 except where district court has exclusive jurisdiction regardless of amount. (§§1-501, 4-401, 4-402, 4-405). See subhead District Courts, infra. Original and exclusive jurisdiction is also given in most juvenile cases except in Montgomery County where District Court has jurisdiction in juvenile causes. (§§3-801[c], 3-804, 4-403). Circuit courts have jurisdiction over certain criminal offenses otherwise in jurisdiction of district courts if circuit court has jurisdiction over other offenses arising from same circumstances. (§4-302).

Circuits and Counties.—

First Judicial Circuit: Worcester, Somerset, Dorchester and Wicomico Counties.
Second Judicial Circuit: Caroline, Talbot, Queen Anne's, Kent and Cecil Counties.
Third Judicial Circuit: Baltimore and Harford Counties.
Fourth Judicial Circuit: Allegany, Garrett and Washington Counties.
Fifth Judicial Circuit: Carroll, Howard and Anne Arundel Counties.
Sixth Judicial Circuit: Montgomery and Frederick Counties.
Seventh Judicial Circuit: Prince George's, Charles, Calvert and St. Mary's Counties.
Eighth Judicial Circuit: Baltimore City. (Const. art. IV, §19).

Counties.—

Allegany County: Fourth Circuit; court sits at Cumberland.
Anne Arundel County: Fifth Circuit; court sits at Annapolis.
Baltimore County: Third Circuit; court sits at Towson.
Calvert County: Seventh Circuit; court sits at Prince Frederick.
Caroline County: Second Circuit; court sits at Denton.
Carroll County: Fifth Circuit; court sits at Westminster.
Cecil County: Second Circuit; court sits at Elkton.
Charles County: Seventh Circuit; court sits at LaPlata.
Dorchester County: First Circuit; court sits at Cambridge.
Frederick County: Sixth Circuit; court sits at Frederick City.
Garrett County: Fourth Circuit; court sits at Oakland.
Harford County: Third Circuit; court sits at Bel Air.
Howard County: Fifth Circuit; court sits at Ellicott City.
Kent County: Second Circuit; court sits at Chestertown.
Montgomery County: Sixth Circuit; court sits at Rockville.
Prince George's County: Seventh Circuit; court sits at Upper Marlboro.
Queen Anne's County: Second Circuit; court sits at Centreville.
St. Mary's County: Seventh Circuit; court sits at Leonardtown.
Somerset County: First Circuit; court sits at Princess Anne.
Talbot County: Second Circuit; court sits at Easton.
Washington County: Fourth Circuit; court sits at Hagerstown.
Wicomico County: First Circuit; court sits at Salisbury.
Worcester County: First Circuit; court sits at Snow Hill.

Orphans' court in Baltimore City and each county except Montgomery and Harford have jurisdiction over matters related to administration of estates of deceased persons. (Const. art. IV, §40; est. & tr. art. §§2-102, 2-103). Judges of circuit courts of Montgomery and Harford counties sit as orphans' courts for those counties. (Const. art. IV, §20). Judgment of orphans' court may be appealed to Court of Special Appeals. (§12-501). Except in Montgomery and Harford Counties, appeal from orphan's court may also be taken to circuit court as trial de novo. (§12-502).

Probate court has jurisdiction to determine title to personal property valued at not more than $20,000 includable in estate that is subject of proceeding before court. (est. & tr. §1-301).

District Courts.—State is divided into 12 districts; each district contains one or more counties; there is at least one district judge resident in each county. (Const. art. IV, §41B; §§1-602, 1-603). Administrative judge of district, with approval of chief judge, may appoint commissioners to issue warrants of arrest, to set bail and to release suspects on their own recognizance. (§2-607).

District court has exclusive original criminal jurisdiction where person at least 16 or corporation is charged with violating vehicle law or State Boat Act, or person at least 18 or corporation is charged with misdemeanor, or specified theft crime, violation of ordinance or rule or other act punishable by fine, imprisonment, or other penalty (if not felony), violation of bad check laws (whether felony or misdemeanor), violation of laws governing credit card offenses (whether felony or misdemeanor), violation of laws governing forgery and counterfeiting (whether felony or misdemeanor), violation of laws governing fraudulent insurance acts, or violation of laws governing false workers' compensation claims (§4-301), concurrent original criminal jurisdiction with circuit court where penalty may be confinement for three years or more or fine of $2,500 or more and in certain felonies (§4-302[d]), and criminal jurisdiction to try juvenile case if juvenile court waives jurisdiction or offender elects and offense is otherwise within its jurisdiction (§4-303). Criminal defendant may demand jury trial if

penalty may be imprisonment for more than 90 days; case then goes to circuit court. However, defendant may be denied jury trial if prosecutor recommends and judge agrees to maximum penalty of 90 days imprisonment and judge agrees not to increase bond if appeal taken. State may not demand jury trial. (§4-302[e]). District court has jurisdiction to conduct preliminary hearing in felony case. (§4-304).

With certain exceptions, it has exclusive original jurisdiction in following civil cases: (1) Action in tort or contract where claim does not exceed $25,000; (2) replevin action; (3) attachment before judgment where claim does not exceed $25,000; (4) action involving landlord and tenant, distraint or forcible entry and detainer; (5) grantee suit under real prop. art. §14-109; (6) petition for injunction relating to property claimed in replevin action or action of distress prior to seizure; (7) petition for injunction filed by tenant in action under real prop. art. §8-211 or local rent escrow law or by person in action under real prop. art. §14-120; (8) petition for injunction filed by county or municipality including Baltimore City, for enforcement of local health, housing, fire, building, electric, licenses and permits, plumbing, animal control, and zoning codes; (9) proceedings for forfeiture or return of moneys involved in gambling or controlled dangerous substances seizure where amount involved, excluding interest and attorneys' fees, where recoverable, does not exceed $20,000; (10) proceedings for various municipal infractions and zoning violations, violations of certain ordinances of charter counties and Baltimore City, violations of certain Washington Suburban Sanitary Commission rules and regulations, violations of ordinance or regulation enacted by county without home rule for which civil penalty is provided, civil infraction authorized to be prosecuted by sanitary commission, certain subdivision violations, and violations of certain liquor laws; (11) proceeding for civil penalty for violation of §8-1401 of nat. res. art., or regulations thereunder, involving prohibited disposal of used oil; (12) proceeding for civil penalty for violation of art. 41, §2-101(c-1) relating to conservation of resources; and (13) proceeding to enforce civil penalties for violations of lab. emp. art. §§5-101 to 5-901, where amount involved not more than $20,000 (Maryland Occupational Safety and Health Law). (§§4-401, 4-402). Court has concurrent jurisdiction with circuit court over cases seeking protection from domestic violence and in such proceeding has power of court of equity. (§4-404). It has no other equity jurisdiction, no jurisdiction to render declaratory judgment and no jurisdiction to try title to realty. (§4-402). Its civil jurisdiction is concurrent with jurisdiction of circuit courts where amount in controversy exceeds $2,500 but does not exceed $25,000 exclusive of prejudgment or postjudgment interest, costs, and attorney's fees if attorney's fees are recoverable by law or contract. (§§4-401, 4-402). In class actions, separate claims of class members may be aggregated to meet $2,500 minimum controversy amount. (§§4-402[d], 4-405). District court of Montgomery County also has jurisdiction in juvenile cases. (§4-403).

In civil cases, if amount in controversy exceeds $10,000, there is right to transfer to circuit court for jury trial. (§4-402). Civil juries consist of six jurors. (§8-306).

District court has exclusive jurisdiction over small claims, defined as civil actions involving under $2,500, and certain landlord tenant actions where amount of rent claimed is under $2,500. (§4-405). Small claims actions governed by R. P. 3-701.

All sums referred to above in this subhead are exclusive of attorneys' fees recoverable by law or contract.

Appeal is taken to circuit court for county (or Baltimore City) in which judgment was rendered. Party in civil case or defendant in criminal case may appeal from final judgment by filing order for appeal with clerk of district court within 30 days. State may appeal from final judgment in criminal case upon allegation that trial judge failed to impose sentence specifically required by code. In civil case involving more than $2,500 or when parties agree, appeal is on record; otherwise appeal is de novo. (§§12-401, 12-403).

District court is court of record. (§1-601). Promptly after entry, clerk must record and index judgment, except judgment denying all relief without costs, in judgment records of court. (R. P. 3-601[d]). Judgment entered in Baltimore City recorded and constitutes lien upon judgment debtor's real estate in Baltimore City from date of entry of judgment if entered in Baltimore City, or from date of recording if received from another county. Outside Baltimore City, judgment constitutes lien upon real estate of judgment debtor in county only when certified Notice of Lien of Judgment has been recorded in circuit court in that county. (R. P. 3-621).

Jurisdiction uniform throughout state (Const. art. IV, §41A), except that Montgomery County District Court also has jurisdiction over juvenile causes (§4-403).

Maryland Tax Court.—Md. Tax Court, administrative rather than judicial body, consists of five judges, one from Eastern Shore, one from Western Shore, one from Baltimore City and two at large. (tax-gen. art. §§3-102, 3-106). Provided that all remedies before assessing or taxing authorities and other administrative bodies are exhausted, court has jurisdiction to hear de novo appeals in all tax cases and has power to modify or change any valuation, assessment, classification, tax or final order appealed from. (tax-gen. art. §§3-103, 13-523). Final order of tax court may be appealed to circuit court. (tax-gen. art. §13-532).

LEGISLATURE:

Meets each year for no longer than 90 days, beginning second Wed. in Jan., and by three-fifths vote may extend session not more than 30 days. (Const. art. III, §§14-15). Governor may call extraordinary sessions up to 30 days. (Const. art. II, §16; art. III, §15). Referendum is provided for. (Const. art. XVI).

Lobbyists.—Lobbyist or person acting on behalf of lobbyist may not establish political committee for purpose of soliciting or transferring contributions from any person to Governor, Lieutenant Governor, Attorney General, Comptroller, or member of General Assembly, or candidate for election to office of Governor, Lieutenant Governor, Attorney General, Comptroller, or member of General Assembly. (art. 33, §13-201).

REPORTS:

Judicial Reports of Md. are contained in Harris and McHenry's Reports, Vols. 1 to 4, from 1658 to 1799; Harris and Johnson, 7 Vols., from 1800 to 1826; Harris and Gill, 2 Vols., from 1826 to 1829; Gill and Johnson, 12 Vols., from 1829 to 1842; Gill's

REPORTS . . . *continued*
Reports, 9 Vols., from 1843 to 1851; and Md. Reports, from 1851 to date and Md. Appellate Reports from 1967 to date. There are also 3 Vols. of Bland's, and 4 Vols. of Md. Chancery Reports.

Unofficial Reports.—Md. decisions are reported in Atlantic Reporter, from 1885 to date.

Digests are: Norris, Brown & Brune, one vol., 1 H. and McH. to 12 G. and J., and 1 to 3 Bland; Stockett, Merrick & Miller, one vol., 1 Gill to 8 Md., and 1 to 4 Md. Chancery; Brantly, 2 Vols. covering 1 H. & McH. to 76 Md., supplement I covering 77 to 88 Md., and supplement II covering 89 to 105 Md.; Carter, 2 vols., 106 to 147 Md. (comprising supp. III to Brantly's); Tiffany, one vol. covering 148 to 157 Md. (comprising supp. IV to Brantly's), and one vol. covering 158 to 167 Md. (comprising supp. V to Brantly's); West Publishing Co. Key Number Digest from year 1658 to date.

STATUTES:

General laws of Md. are contained in Michie's Code, 1957, supplemented to include laws as enacted; however, since 1973 certain subject matter codes have been separately enacted and published by Michie Co. in volumes superseding 1957 edition of Code. See Key at beginning of Md. Law Digest. Session laws are also published each year after passage by legislature.

Code of Public Local Laws (1930) was final consolidated version of laws of all political subdivisions of state. Includes all such laws up to and including those passed at 1929 session of legislature. Following counties have adopted more recent official Codes incorporating both public local laws and, for home rule counties, local ordinances: Allegany (1983 & Supp. 1995); Anne Arundel (1986 & Supp. 1995); Annapolis (1986 & Supp. 1994); Baltimore County (1991 & Supp. 1995); Baltimore City (1983 & Supp. 1994); Calvert (1986 & Supp. 1991); Caroline (1965 & Supp. 1980); Carroll (1976 & Supp. 1991, 1992, and 1993); Cecil (1989 & Supp. 1995); Charles (1988 & Supp. 1992); City of Cumberland (1990); Dorchester (1987 & Supp. 1994); City of Cambridge (1976); Frederick (1979 & Supp. 1995); Garrett (1985 & Supp. 1994); Harford (1986 & Supp. 1995); Howard (1995 & Supp. 1995); Kent (1994 & Supp. 1995); Montgomery (1994 & Supp. 1995); Prince George's (1991 & Supp. 1993); Queen Anne's (1983 & Supp. 1986-1995); St. Mary's (1978 & Supp. 1994); Somerset (1994); Talbot (1977 & Supp. 1990); Washington (1991); Wicomico (1978 & Supp. 1995); Worcester (1994).

Code of Public Local Laws of Baltimore City (1979 & Supp. 1991 & 1993 Interim Cum. Supp. 1994); Baltimore City Code (1976 with 1983 Replacement Volume & Supp. 1993, 1994 Cum. Supp.).

Baltimore City Charter was last published in bound volume with Public Local Laws in 1949, but charter as revised in 1964 has been published in pamphlet form with amendments, most recently in 1993. Charters of certain counties are published with their respective Codes of Public Local Laws.

Baltimore City Code (1976 with 1983 Replacement Volume & Supp. 1993, 1994 Cum. Supp.) contains all general ordinances enacted by Mayor and City Council of Baltimore and in effect on June 1, 1983.

Administrative rules and regulations are published in Code of Maryland Regulations, supplemented by Maryland Register. (Md. Code Ann., State Government Art., Title 10, Subtitle 1, Title 7, Subtitle 2).

Uniform Acts promulgated by the National Conference of Commissioners on Uniform State Laws which have been adopted are: Acknowledgment (1941); Acknowledgment Act Amendment (1961); Anatomical Gift (1968); †Arbitration Act (1965); Attendance of Witnesses from Without the State in Criminal Proceedings (1955); Certification of Questions of Law (1972); Child Custody Jurisdiction (1975); †Commercial Code (1963; 1980); Contribution Among Tortfeasors (1939 version) (1941); †Controlled Substances (1970); Criminal Extradition (1937); Declaratory Judgments (1945); †Determination of Death Act (1982); †Disclaimer of Property Interests (1978); Disposition of Unclaimed Property (1966) (MD title: Maryland Uniform Disposition of Abandoned Property); Enforcement of Foreign Judgments (1987); Estate Tax Apportionment (1964 Revised Act) (1965); Facsimile Signatures of Public Officials (1960); Federal Lien Registration Act (Revised Act, 1967); Fiduciaries (1929); Foreign Depositions (1922); Foreign Money-Judgments Recognition (1963); Fraudulent Conveyance (1920); Fresh Pursuit (1937); Insurers' Liquidation (1941); Inter-Party Agreement [Model] (1931); Interstate Arbitration of Death Taxes (1945); Interstate Compromise of Death Taxes (1945); Interstate Family Support (1996); (MD Title: Maryland Uniform Interstate Family Support Act); Limited Partnership (1918), †1976 version (1981); Machine Gun (1933); Management of Institutional Funds (1973); Out-of-State Parolee Supervision (1937); Partnership (1916); Photographic Copies of Business and Public Records as Evidence (1951); †Post Conviction Procedure (1958); Preservation of Private Business Records (1957); †Principal and Income (1939; Revised Act, 1965); †Public Defender [Model] (1971; effective Jan. 1, 1972); Reciprocal Transfer Tax (1929); Remedies for the Unauthorized Practice of Law [Model] (1961); †Securities (1962); Act for the Simplification of Fiduciary Security Transfers (1960); Simultaneous Death (1941); State Administrative Procedure [Model; 1961] (1957); Testamentary Additions to Trusts (1959); Trade Secrets Act (1989); Transfers to Minors (1989); Unclaimed Property Act (1981).

Other Uniform Acts adopted are: Transfer-on-Death Security Registration Act (1994).

†Adopted with significant variations or modifications. See appropriate topics.

For text of Uniform Acts falling within scope of Martindale-Hubbell Law Digests, see Uniform and Model Acts section.

UNIFORM LAWS:

For list of Uniform Acts in force, see topic Statutes. For text of Uniform Acts within scope of Martindale-Hubbell Law Digests, see Uniform and Model Acts section.

CRIMINAL LAW

BAIL:

See topic Criminal Law.

CRIMINAL LAW:

Art. 27 of Code contains general criminal statutes. Common law applicable to local circumstances still in effect except as changed by statute. (Decl. of Rights art. 5). Local acts may relate to particular counties or cities only.

Indictment or Information.—Misdemeanor may be prosecuted on information. Felony may be prosecuted on indictment, or on information after finding of probable cause at preliminary hearing or waiver of hearing by defendant. Defendant must be notified of right to request hearing but waives by failing to request hearing within ten days after initial appearance. When felony prosecuted on indictment, hearing required only if court so orders. (art. 27, §592). District court has jurisdiction to conduct preliminary hearings. (courts art. §4-304). Offenses within jurisdiction of district court, including certain felonies (see category Courts and Legislature, topic Courts, subhead District Courts) may be prosecuted on information. (R. P. 4-201).

Bail.—Sheriff or deputy may take bail bond in case of criminal offense not punishable by confinement in penitentiary, in penalty not exceeding $300 (unless specific fine or penalty is prescribed for offense, when bond must be for highest penalty or fine), with condition that person must appear in court when writ is returnable and not depart without leave of court. (art. 87, §6). District court judges (art. 27, §616½[b]) and commissioners (courts art. §2-607) authorized to make pretrial release determination, and determination may be made at district court level regardless of seriousness of offense. Chief judge of district court may provide for interim bail pending initial appearance. Denial of release by commissioner subject to review by district court judge. (R. P. 4-216[b],[g]). Circuit court may revoke or amend pretrial release order of district court. (R. P. 4-216[i]).

If crime charged is punishable by death or life imprisonment, pretrial release is discretionary; otherwise, accused entitled to release, and release on own recognizance permitted where court is of opinion that accused will appear in court as required. (art. 27, §638A; R. P. 4-216). District court judges may not grant pretrial release to defendant charged with certain crimes of violence if defendant is on parole, probation, or mandatory supervision for another crime of violence. (art. 27, §616½[l]). If court determines release on recognizance is unwarranted, conditions of release may be imposed, stated in writing or on record and based on enumerated factors. Condition may include release into custody of designated person, release under supervision of probation officer, restriction on travel or association or residence, or execution of bail bond, either unsecured, secured by greater of $25 or 10% of full penalty amount, or secured in full penalty amount. (art. 27, §616½[b]; R. P. 4-216[d]). Court may also require as condition of pretrial release that defendant be monitored by private home monitoring device. (art. 27, §616½[m]). Accused is ineligible for release on personal recognizance and bail may be refused where accused is charged with certain enumerated serious crimes while already on bail arising from previous accusation of enumerated crime. (art. 27, §616½[c]). Accused may remain on bail pending appeal in discretion of trial court. (R. P. 4-348). Affidavit required of bail bondsman (R. P. 4-217[d][2]), and circuit court may license bondsmen (R. P. 16-817).

Capital Punishment.—Applies to offenses committed on or after July 1, 1978. (1978, c. 3, §3). Separate sentencing proceeding determines punishment upon conviction of first degree murder, if state has given required written notice of intention to seek death sentence and of aggravating circumstances it relies on. Proceeding held before same jury which convicted defendant unless: (1) Defendant waives sentencing jury, or (2) defendant convicted upon plea of guilty, defendant convicted without jury, original jury has been discharged, or, review of original sentence of death by court of competent jurisdiction has resulted in demand for resentencing, in which case special sentencing jury must be impaneled. Fact finder considers enumerated aggravating and enumerated and other mitigating factors; death penalty is imposed if fact finder: (1) Determines beyond reasonable doubt that one of aggravating factors exists, (2) determines by preponderance of evidence that mitigating circumstances do not outweigh aggravating circumstances, and, if jury, is able to agree within reasonable time. Findings must be written and jury findings signed by foreman. (art. 27, §§412, 413; R. P. 4-343). Automatic review of death sentence by Court of Appeals provided; trial judge must submit prescribed report including recommendation as to appropriateness of death sentence. (art. 27, §414; R. P. 4-343). Court of Appeals is no longer required in appeal of sentence of death to determine whether sentence is excessive or disproportionate to penalty imposed in similar cases. (art. 27, §414). State is prohibited from imposing death penalty against incompetent inmates (art. 27, §75A), mentally retarded persons (art. 27, §412), and individuals under 18 when murder was committed (art. 27, §412). Statute imposing death penalty has been held constitutional. (287 Md. 695, 415 A.2d 830). Defendant has choice of execution by intravenous administration of lethal substances or gas. (art. 27, §627).

Criminal Injuries Compensation Act provides for awards to compensate victims of crime. (art. 26A). In addition, courts have authority to order convicted persons in certain cases to respond in restitution for victims' financial losses and medical expenses. Court may also order restitution for pecuniary or property losses paid or compensated for by third-party payor or medical expenses paid by governmental entity and reimbursement for funeral expenses for deceased criminal victims. Restitution to victim takes priority over third-party payor, unless third party payor has fully compensated victim, and governmental restitution. (art. 27, §640).

Criminal Offenders.—HIV testing—victim notification. (art. 27, §855).

Criminal Justice Information System established along with Criminal Justice Information Advisory Board to regulate collection and dissemination of criminal records. (art. 27, §§742 to 755).

Declaration of Victim's Rights Act provides that victims of crime have constitutional right to be treated with dignity throughout all phases of criminal justice process

See note at head of Digest as to 1998 legislation covered.

See Topical Index in front part of this volume.

MD – 26

CRIMINAL LAW ... *continued*
and have right to be informed of, and attend, and be heard at criminal justice proceedings. (art. 47).

Domestic Violence Act of 1994 adopted through various provisions of art. 27, courts & jud. proc. art., and fam. law art. (1994, c. 728).

Uniform Criminal Extradition Act adopted. (art. 41, §§2-201 to 2-228).

Uniform Act to Secure Attendance of Witnesses from Without a State in Criminal Proceedings adopted. (courts art. §§9-301 to 9-306).

Uniform Controlled Substances Act adopted with numerous variations, omissions and additional material as Md. Controlled Dangerous Substances Act. (art. 27, §§276 to 303).

Uniform Post Conviction Procedure Act adopted with numerous variations. (art. 27, §§645A to 645J). Complementary rules of procedure adopted. (R. P. 4-401 to 4-408).

Model Public Defender Act adopted with significant modifications. (art. 27A).

Organized Crime.—See category Business Organizations, topic Corporations. Attorney General may also bring civil proceeding to enjoin operation of business under enumerated circumstances, including where controlling person is involved in organized crime. (corps. art. §1-405[c]).

Sentencing procedures for multiple jurisdiction cases contained in art. 27, §690(c).

Sentencing procedures for second-time offenders in crimes of violence contained in art. 27, §§643 and 643B; art. 41, §§4-507, 4-511(d) and 4-516.

Victim and Witness Relocation Program established in art. 10, §§41B and 41D; st. gov't. art. §9-1705; 1993, c. 204, §20; and art. 27, §770.

DEBTOR AND CREDITOR

ASSIGNMENTS:

Uniform Commercial Code adopted. (comm. law art. tit. 1-10). See category Business Regulation and Commerce, topic Commercial Code.

Generally speaking, rights, debts and choses in action are assignable. (R. P. 2-241[a][3]; 274 Md. 404, 335 A.2d 89).

Instrument Transferring Title.—No particular form of assignment is necessary. (206 Md. 168, 110 A.2d 661). In order for assignee of chose in action to sue in his own name, assignment must be in writing by person authorized to make assignment. If obligation is under seal, assignment should be under seal in order for assignee to sue in his own name (comm. law art. §15-402[a]); and action against obligor requires assignor's certification before notary, in writing on obligation, that at time of assignment amount sued for was still owing. Assignee generally retains rights against assignor if he cannot recover from obligor, unless failure to recover is due to his own negligence or default. (comm. law art. §15-402).

Filing.—Not required except in case of judgment, which may be filed in court where entered or recorded. (R. P. 2-624; R. P. 3-624).

Recording.—Not required.

Notice.—Not required except where required by any policy of insurance, or in cases of partial assignment (195 F. Supp. 222); until notified to pay assignee, debtor is authorized to pay assignor (comm. law art. §9-318[3]).

Effect.—Assignee takes title and interest of assignor and is subject to same legal or equitable defenses as could have been made against assignor. (256 Md. 520, 261 A.2d 753). If assignment is in writing by person authorized to make same, assignee may in his own name sue or execute against obligor; otherwise assignee must proceed in name of assignor.

Assignment of Wages.—Assignment of wages not valid unless: (1) In writing, signed by assignor, acknowledged by him before notary public for county in which he resides and entered on same day by clerk of district court; (2) executed and acknowledged as aforesaid by assignor's spouse, if any; (3) including affidavit that assignor has not paid and will not pay, directly or indirectly, more than 6% per annum on any sum borrowed; (4) within three days from execution and acknowledgment, copy is served in same manner as summons on assignor's employer. Assignment of wages to be earned in whole or in part more than six months after making of assignment is void. Action for enforcement of invalid assignment may be enjoined on petition of assignor or employer. (comm. law art. §§15-301 to 15-305). Assignment of wages is void if as security for usurious contract or loan. (comm. law art. §12-110).

Assignment of accounts receivable and sales of accounts receivable are governed by Uniform Commercial Code. (comm. law art. tit. 9).

Assignments of claims under workmen's compensation law are not valid until issuance and delivery of warrant or voucher. (lab. emp. art. §9-732).

Assignment to Nonresident.—It is unlawful for creditor who is citizen of Md. to assign claim against Md. resident for purpose of having claim collected by attachment in foreign court or with intent to deprive debtor of exemptions from execution, unless creditor, debtor or person owing money to be attached is beyond jurisdiction of Md. courts. Violation is misdemeanor, and creditor is subject to fine not exceeding $50. Creditor is liable to debtor for debt collected by assignee outside Md. and for costs. Creditor also forfeits right to exempt his own wages or property from execution if writ of execution is issued against him for collection of these amounts. (comm. law art. §§15-501 to 15-503).

ATTACHMENT:

Actions in Which Allowed.—Attachment before judgment may issue in contract or tort action (courts art. §§3-303, 3-304), whether claim mature or unmatured (courts art. §3-302), in court of law or equity (courts art. §3-301).

Courts Which May Issue Writ.—Writ may be issued by court with jurisdiction, including district court. (courts art. §§3-301, 3-302, R.P. 2-115, 3-115).

In Whose Favor Writ May Issue.—Any plaintiff may obtain attachment. (courts art. §§3-301, 3-302).

Against Whom Writ May Issue.—Attachment may issue against any defendant as to whom sufficient grounds exist. (courts art. §§3-301, 3-303). Salary of state or local government employees or officers subject to attachment. (comm. law art. §15-607).

Claims on Which Writ May Issue.—It is not necessary that claim sued on be mature. (courts art. §3-305).

Grounds.—Attachment may issue on: (1) judgment or decree (courts art. §3-301; R. P. 2-641; R. P. 3-641); or (2) before judgment if (a) debtor is nonresident (or corporation having no resident agent in state) and either court could exercise personal jurisdiction over debtor, or action involves claims to property in state which property is to be attached, or action is any other in which attachment is constitutionally permitted; (b) debtor has acted to evade service; (c) debtor has absconded or is about to abscond from state, or has removed or is about to remove from his place of abode within state with intent to defraud creditors; (d) debtor has or is about to assign, dispose of, conceal, or remove any or all of his property from state with intent to defraud creditors, or has fraudulently contracted or incurred debt or obligation that is subject of action; (e) debtor is deceased and adult nonresident heir is entitled to land or interest in land against which attachment is sought; or (f) debtor is not licensed under Maryland Home Improvement Law but is required to be, and action arises out of home improvement transaction.

Proceedings to Obtain.—(1) On judgment or decree, writ of execution will be issued by clerk of court upon written request by judgment creditor accompanied by instructions to sheriff specifying debtor's address, amount and date of judgment, property to be levied, its location and whether property is to be left where found or removed (R. P. 2-641; R. P. 3-641); (2) on attachment before judgment, plaintiff must file following: (a) request for order directing issuance of writ, (b) complaint, (c) affidavit verifying facts set forth in complaint and stating grounds for entitlement to writ. Upon entry of order and filing of bond, clerk issues writ of attachment. (R. P. 2-115, 3-115). When writ directs levy of property, procedure follows R. P. 2-641 and 2-642, or R. P. 3-641 and 3-642. (R. P. 2-115[d], 3-115[d]). Plaintiff must have made reasonable efforts to notify defendant where request for attachment accompanies complaint and defendant cannot be served. (R. P. 2-115 [e]; R. P. 3-115[f]).

Attachment Bond.—Bond is required in amount of all costs, claims and damages that may be awarded defendant or claimant of property by reason of attachment. (R. P. 2-115[c]; R.P. 3-115[c]).

Levy and Property Subject.—All property of defendant wherever situated may be attached, including credits not yet due, property or credits of defendant in hands of another, and debt due defendant upon judgment or decree. (courts art. §§3-301, 3-305). Exceptions: proceeds of certain life insurance and annuity contracts (art. 48A, §385), fraternal order benefits (art. 48A, §328), and benefits under Workmen's Compensation Law prior to delivery of voucher (lab. emp. art. §9-732).

Greater of $145 per week or 75% of disposable wages due are exempt. In Caroline, Kent, Queen Anne's, and Worcester counties, greater of 75% of disposable wages due or 30 times federal minimum hourly wage then in effect is exempt. Medical insurance payments deducted from wages by employer are exempt. (comm. law art. §15-601.1). Preceding exemptions do not apply to attachment for income tax due state. (comm. law art. §15-602[b]). Exemption of wages from income tax claim is $50 plus $15 for each exemption (per week). (tax-gen. art. 13-811[d][2]). Attachment on wages constitutes continuing lien on present and future wages until judgment, interest, and costs are satisfied. (comm. law art. §15-602). Procedure instituted for employer to withhold wages subject to attachment. (comm. law art. §15-603; R.P. 2-646, 3-646).

Wages of nonresidents are attachable to same extent as residents. (comm. law art. §15-601[b]).

No levy can be made against property of estate, although security interests may be enforced in appropriate proceedings. (est. & tr. art. §8-114).

With few exceptions, certificated securities may be attached only if actually seized or surrendered to issuer. Uncertificated securities registered in name of debtor or certificated securities surrendered to issuer may not be attached except by legal process at issuer's chief executive office. (comm. law art. §8-317).

Debtor's rights in collateral may be attached. (comm. law art. §9-311).

Creditors of husband may attach money or restrain by injunction payment of money deposited to wife's credit if prejudicial to their rights. (fam. law art. §4-301).

Indemnity.—Sheriff directed to remove property from premises or to exclude others may require judgment creditor to file bond for expenses. (R. P. 2-641[c]; R. P. 3-641[c]).

Lien and Priorities.—Levy or laying of attachment creates inchoate lien on property, effects and credits of debtor in hands of garnishee or coming into hands of garnishee thereafter until trial. Lien is perfected by final judgment, and then relates back to time of levy or laying of attachment. (283 Md. 701, 393 A.2d 1356.) Several attachments take priority in order of levy; sheriff should levy on attachments in order in which they are placed in his or her hands, and courts will protect against levy in improper order. (91 Md. 613, 46 A. 960; 70 Md. 448, 17 A. 274).

Release of Property.—Attachment may be dissolved upon judgment for garnishee or dissolved by defendant's appearance and filing of bond in value of goods attached or plaintiff's claim, whichever is less, conditioned upon satisfaction of judgment for plaintiff. (R. P. 2-115; R. P. 3-115). Upon timely motion by defendant, property may be released from attachment if (1) complaint dismissed, (2) plaintiff fails to comply with attachment rules, (3) plaintiff fails to demonstrate probability of success on merits, (4) property of sufficient value to satisfy claim remains, (5) undue hardship to defendant who delivers alternate property of sufficient value, or (6) property is exempt. (R. P. 2-115[g]; R. P. 3-115[h]).

Sale.—Attached property before judgment must be retained while action pending unless otherwise ordered by court. At request of either party, court may direct sale of

---

See note at head of Digest as to 1998 legislation covered.

See Topical Index in front part of this volume.

ATTACHMENT . . . *continued*

perishable property. (R. P. 2-115[i]; R. P. 3-115[j]). For procedure in sale, see topic Executions.

Condemnation.—When judgment is entered in favor of plaintiff, court must order sale of attached property to extent necessary to satisfy judgment. If personal jurisdiction not obtained over defendant, judgment is in rem only against attached property and its entry and satisfaction will not bar another action for any unpaid balance of claim. (R. P. 2-115[k]; R. P. 3-115[1]).

Third Party Claims.—Claimant should file motion requesting attached property to be released. Notice must be given to judgment creditor and judgment debtor (if possible), who may file response to motion. Hearing on motion must be specifically requested. (R. P. 2-115[h], 2-643[e], [f]; R. P. 3-115[i], 3-643[e], [f]).

Vacation or Modification.—See supra subhead Release of Property.

CREDITORS' SUITS:

In practice, only creditors suits are for dissolution of corporation (corps. art. §3-413[c]), appointment of receiver (comm. law art. §§15-101, 15-103), or to vacate fraudulent conveyances (comm. law art. §§15-210 to 15-214).

EXECUTIONS:

Court where judgment entered or properly recorded with clerk may issue writ of execution upon written request of judgment creditor. (R. P. 2-641, 3-641). Court may issue attachment on judgment or decree instead of any other form of execution. (courts art. §3-301). Sheriff to whom any writ of execution is directed may seize and sell legal or equitable interest of defendant in real or personal property and distribute proceeds. (courts art. §11-501).

Kinds of Execution.—Writ of fieri facias directs sheriff to seize chattels and lands of judgment debtor to satisfy judgment or decree. (See 243 Md. 224, 220 A.2d 922; 185 F.Supp. 867; 2 Poe, Pleading and Practice [Tiffany Ed.] §§626 to 627). Writ of possession used to compel persons in possession of lands to deliver possession to persons who purchased at execution or foreclosure sale. (See 270 Md. 715, 313 A.2d 453.) Attachment on judgment also considered form of execution. (231 Md. 105, 189 A.2d 103). See topic Attachment.

Exemptions.—See topic Exemptions.

Time for Issuance.—Execution may issue any time within 12 years from date of entry of money judgment or most recent renewal thereof. (R. P. 2-625, 3-625).

Stay.—Appellant may stay execution pending appeal by filing supersedeas bond; if bond filed on appeal to Court of Special Appeals, no further bond required pending appeal to Court of Appeals but either court may increase, decrease or fix amount of bond, enter order as to surety or security on bond, or enter order as to other security. (R. P. 8-422). See category Civil Actions and Procedure, topic Appeal and Error.

In proper case, court may enter injunction against execution (180 Md. 545, 26 A.2d 18); court has power to issue order staying execution upon its own judgment (110 Md. 47, 72 A. 461). Court may grant stay for discharged bankrupt. (171 Md. 280, 189 A. 281). In practice, stay may be entered by agreement. (2 Poe, Pleading and Practice [Tiffany Ed.] §648).

Lien.—No lien on chattels until levy and then only on chattels included in levy. (courts art. §11-403). Recordation of money judgment itself constitutes lien on real estate within jurisdiction. (R. P. 2-621, 3-621). See category Civil Actions and Procedure, topic Judgments.

Levy on chattels is by actual seizure by sheriff or constable. (208 Md. 115, 117 A.2d 864; 74 Md. 602, 22 A. 1104). Levy on other property is by such seizure as character of property permits. Thus, levy on interest in real estate is by sheriff or constable going upon land, notifying defendant or tenant in possession of purpose of visit and making reasonably descriptive written schedule of property seized. (194 Md. 51, 69 A.2d 797). Levy upon growing crops is by proper notification to defendant and endorsement on levy. (88 Md. 601, 42 A. 201).

Return.—Following levy, sheriff must promptly file return with schedule. (R. P. 2-642[e], 3-642[e]).

Priorities.—Sheriff must serve writs in order in which they come into his hands, and must pay proceeds of sale to judgment creditors in same order. (224 Md. 138, 166 A.2d 916). But in case of land, priority of liens is in order in which judgments entered, and time of issuance and service of writs immaterial. (21 Md. 439; 8 G. & J. 35).

Claims of Third Persons.—In case of attachment on judgment, third person claiming property levied upon should file motion in court for release. If requested, court must promptly hold hearing on motion with notice to judgment creditor and debtor. (R. P. 2-643[e], [f]; 3-643[e], [f]).

Satisfaction.—Judgment creditor whose judgment has been satisfied shall furnish to judgment debtor and file with clerk written statement of satisfaction; if creditor fails to do so, debtor may file motion for order declaring judgment satisfied. In both cases, clerk shall enter judgment satisfied. (R. P. 2-626, 3-626).

Sale.—Sheriff can sell any legal or equitable interest or estate of defendant in any lands, tenements or hereditaments (courts art. §11-501), and purchaser takes as good title as defendant had (real prop. art. §14-103).

Sheriff must give prior notice of time, place and terms of sale. In case of sale of interest in property, notice must be posted on courthouse door or bulletin board in immediate vicinity of courthouse door and printed in newspaper in county where property located at least (1) ten days before sale of personal property, or (2) 20 days before sale of real property. Sheriff may recover costs of publication from defendant, or, if he is unable to pay, from plaintiff. (courts art. §11-502). Sale may be set aside, upon petition of debtor, if selling price so grossly inadequate as to shock conscience. (282 Md. 631, 386 A.2d 784).

Redemption.—No right of redemption of property sold under execution.

Supplementary Proceedings.—On request of judgment creditor, filed no earlier than 30 days after entry of judgment, court where judgment was entered or recorded may order debtor to appear for examination before judge or examiner. Any other person may also be ordered to appear if court satisfied by affidavit or other proof that person has property of debtor, is indebted to debtor for sum certain or has knowledge of concealment, fraudulent transfer or withholding of assets belonging to debtor. (R. P. 2-633, 3-633).

EXEMPTIONS:

State constitution authorizes legislature to exempt reasonable amount of debtor's property from execution. (Const. art. III, §44).

Selective Exemptions.—$3,000 cash or property of any kind if, within 30 days from date of attachment or levy by sheriff, debtor so elects. (courts art. §11-504[b][5]).

Specific Exemptions.—In addition to property selected, also exempt are all wearing apparel, books, tools, instruments or appliances not to exceed $2,500 in value necessary for practice of any trade or profession except those kept for sale, lease or barter; all money payable in event of sickness, accident, injury, or death of any person (including compensation for loss of future earnings but excluding disability income benefits if judgment is for necessities contracted for after disability incurred); professionally prescribed health aids and debtor's interest, not to exceed $500 in value, in personal property; certain rights and interests in retirement plans. (courts art. §11-504).

Bankruptcy Exemptions.—Md. debtor not entitled to claim federal bankruptcy exemption but may claim $2,500 in value of debtor's aggregate interest in any real or personal property. (courts art. §11-504).

Debts Against Which Exemptions Not Allowed.—None of above exemptions applies to levy for nonpayment of taxes or impairs vendors lien for purchase money, tax lien of mortgage, deed of trust or other security interest or mechanic's lien. (courts art. §11-507).

Exemptions do not apply to wage attachments, certain domestic relations orders, and certain creditors and assets of bankruptcy cases filed before Jan. 1, 1988. (courts art. §§11-504[e], 11-504[h][iii]).

Waiver of Exemption.—Wage exemptions, selective exemptions and specific exemptions above may not be waived. (comm. law art. §§15-601.1, 15-602[c]; courts art. §11-504[d]).

Life or annuity policy proceeds, including cash surrender and loan values, where policy is made for benefit of or assigned to spouse, children or dependent relative, exempt from claims of creditors based on obligations created after June 1, 1945 except where debtor pledged policy as security for such debt. (art. 48A, §385; est. & tr. art. §8-115). Money payable by fraternal benefit society exempt. (art. 48A, §328; est. & tr. art. §8-115).

Wages.—Greater of $145 per week or 75% of net wages due are exempt (non-waiveable) except against claim of state for income taxes. In Caroline, Kent, Queen Annes, and Worchester counties, greater of 75% of net wages due or 30 times federal minimum hourly wage then in effect. Medical insurance payments deducted from employee's wages by employer are exempt. (comm. law art. §15-601.1). Exemption from income tax claim is $50 plus $15 per exemption per week. (tax-gen. art. 13-811[d]). Wages are subject to lien and levy under nonsupport order. (fam. law art. §§10-120 to 10-126). See category Family, topic Husband and Wife, subhead Desertion or Nonsupport.

See also topic Attachment, subhead Levy and Property Subject.

FORECLOSURE:

See topic Liens; category Mortgages, topics Chattel Mortgages, Mortgages of Real Property.

FRAUDULENT SALES AND CONVEYANCES:

Uniform Fraudulent Conveyance Act adopted. (comm. law art. §§15-201 to 15-214). Acts which constitute fraudulent sale or conveyance are set forth therein.

Preferences, payments and transfers which would be void or fraudulent under state insolvency laws or bankruptcy laws if made by natural person are to like extent void and fraudulent if made by corporation and may be set aside by its receiver. (corps. art. §3-418[b]).

Remedies.—Statute makes provision for remedies for defrauded creditors. (comm. law art. §§15-209 to 15-211). Creditors may have sale or conveyance set aside by suit in equity. (156 Md. 65, 143 Atl. 644).

Bulk Sales.—Uniform Commercial Code adopted. (comm. law art. tit. 6). See category Business Regulation and Commerce, topic Commercial Code.

GARNISHMENT:

Property of debtor in hands of third person may be attached. Practice is to levy attachment upon property in hands of third person. (R. P. 2-645, 3-645). See topic Attachment.

Rights and Duties of Garnishee.—Garnishee must file answer within 30 days after service of writ of garnishment, admitting or denying that garnishee is indebted to judgment debtor or has possession of property of judgment debtor, and specifying amount and nature of any debt and describing any property. Certain exceptions exist to 30 day time limit for filing answer in circuit court. (R. P. 2-321, 2-645[e], 3-645[e]). Garnishee may assert any defenses that garnishee may have to garnishment and any defenses judgment debtor could assert. After answering, garnishee may pay any garnished indebtedness into court and may deliver to sheriff any garnished property, which is then treated as if levied upon by sheriff. (R. P. 2-645[e]; R. P. 3-645[e]). If garnishee fails to file answer within specified time, judgment creditor may obtain default judgment against garnishee. (R. P. 2-645[f], 2-613; R. P. 3-645[f], 3-509). If garnishee files timely answer, judgment creditor has 30 days to file reply contesting answer. If timely reply not filed, all matters set forth in garnishee's answer are treated

GARNISHMENT . . . *continued*

as established, and court may enter judgment upon request of judgment creditor, judgment debtor or garnishee. If timely reply is filed, matter proceeds as if original action between judgment creditor as plaintiff and garnishee as defendant, and is governed by rules applicable to civil actions. (R. P. 2-645[g]; R. P. 3-645[g]).

Judgment creditor may serve garnishee with interrogatories pursuant to R. P. 2-421 and 3-421; they must contain notice that unless answered within 30 days after service or within time for filing answer to writ, whichever is later, garnishee may be held in contempt of court and may require garnishee to pay reasonable attorney's fees and costs. (R. P. 2-645[h], 3-645[h]).

Judgment debtor may seek release of garnished property in accordance with R. P. 2-643, 3-643 before entry of judgment, provided that motion to exempt property from execution pursuant to R. P. 2-643(d), 3-643(d) must be filed within 30 days after service of writ of garnishment. (R. P. 2-645[i], 3-645[i]).

Judgment against garnishee is limited to value of property of judgment debtor established by judgment creditor to be in hands of garnishee, not exceeding amount owed under creditor's judgment against debtor and enforcement costs. (R. P. 2-645[j], 3-645[j]). Test of garnishee's liability is that he has property, funds or credits in his hands belonging to debtor for which debtor might maintain suit. (144 Md. 660, 125 A. 529).

Garnishment against property held in bank, trust company, savings bank or savings and loan by husband and wife jointly not valid unless both are judgment debtors, and garnishment against such property held by one party in trust for another not valid unless both are judgment debtors. (courts art. §11-603).

Earnings.—See topic Exemptions, subhead Wages.

HOMESTEADS:

Limited homestead exemption for executions by Maryland court officials and for bankruptcy proceedings under U.S. Bankruptcy Code. (11 U.S.C.A. §522[d]; courts art. §11-504[f]; 18 B.R. 132). See topic Exemptions.

JUDGMENT NOTES:

See category Business Regulation and Commerce, topic Bills and Notes.

LEVY:

See topics Attachment, Executions.

LIENS:

Uniform Commercial Code adopted. (comm. law art. tits. 1 to 10). See category Business Regulation and Commerce, topic Commercial Code. References are to Commercial Law Art. of Code unless otherwise indicated.

Aircraft, Boats, Mobile Homes and Motor Vehicles.—Any person who, with consent of owner, has custody of aircraft, boat or motor vehicle and who, at request of owner, provides service to or materials for vehicle, has lien on vehicle for charges incurred for repair, rebuilding, storage, parts, accessories, etc. (§16-202). Surrender or delivery of property discharges lien against third person without notice of lien, but not against owner or third person with notice. (§16-204). Aircraft lien subordinate only to rights of holder of bill of sale, contract of conditional sale, conveyance or mortgage or assignment of mortgage. (§16-205[a]). Boat lien subordinate to preferred ship mortgages filed with Secretary of Transportation before boat is sold pursuant to §16-207; boat lien subordinate only to security interest lawfully perfected, except for boat sold pursuant to §16-207. (§16-205[c]). Motor vehicle lien subordinate only to security interest lawfully perfected, except for motor vehicle lien when vehicle is sold pursuant to §16-207. (§16-205[b]). If owner disputes charge, he may institute judicial proceedings, which stay execution under lien; he may also repossess property on filing of corporate bond for double amount of charge claimed. (§16-206). If charges remain due and unpaid for 30 days and lienor is in possession, he may sell property at public sale after giving prescribed notice at convenient location between hours of 10 a.m. and 6 p.m. If lienor delivers vehicle or mobile home to third party for storage, and storage charges remain due and unpaid for 30 days, third party is deemed to hold perfected security interest and may sell vehicle or mobile home in same manner as lienor. (§16-207). For manner of perfecting security interest in motor vehicle or vessel, see categories Mortgages, topic Chattel Mortgages, subhead Boats; Transportation, topic Motor Vehicles, subhead Liens and Security Interests.

Commercial Real Estate Brokers.—Liens established by real prop. art. §§14-301 to 14-313.

Hotel.—Keeper of hotel, motel, inn, or boarding house has lien on baggage and other property belonging to or under control of guest or boarder on premises, for charges due or to become due for price or value of food or accommodation, amount of any loan or advance, or amount provided by cashing check, draft, etc. If charges giving rise to lien are unpaid 15 days after they become due, he may sell property. (§16-502).

Person taking in boarders or lodgers has similar lien on furniture or other property on premises for contract price of room or board. (§16-503).

Hospital which furnishes medical or other services to patient injured in accident not covered by Workmen's Compensation Act has lien on 50% of recovery or sum which patient or heirs or personal representative collect in judgment, settlement or compromise of claim against another. Charges secured may not exceed those allowed by Workmen's Compensation Commission for services to persons under Act. Lien is subordinate to attorney's lien for professional services for collecting or obtaining damages. (§16-601). Clerk of circuit court maintains hospital lien docket, indexed in name of injured patient. (§16-605). Person making payment to patient without paying lien may be liable to hospital for one year from date of payment. (§16-603).

Artisans and Tradesmen.—Artisan, including laborer, mechanic, repairman, tradesman, or drycleaner and launderer who, with consent of owner, has possession of goods for repair or other work, has lien on goods for costs of work done. Goods may be sold at public or private sale if costs of work done remain due and unpaid 90 days

after completion of work or retrieval date for drycleaner and launderer; alternatively, goods may be disposed of in any manner if costs giving rise to lien are due and unpaid nine months after laundered or drycleaned goods are due to be retrieved from storage. Artisan, drycleaner or launderer must post notice that unretrieved goods in above circumstances are subject to sale or disposal. (§§16-301, 16-302).

Condominium.—Assessments for common expenses may be enforced by imposition of lien pursuant to Md. Contract Lien Act. (real prop. art. §11-110 [d]).

Livestock.—Owner or operator of livery stable or other establishment giving care or custody to livestock has lien for board and other expenses. (§16-401).

Veterinarian giving care or custody to animal or performing medical or other services to animal may notify owner that animal is ready for delivery and, if animal not claimed within 10 days after prescribed notice is given, may sell animal or turn it over to animal welfare agency or to responsible private person. If notice given pursuant to §16-701(a), veterinarian or commercial boarding kennel operator, and custodian receiving animal, incur no liability upon sale or disposal of animal. (§16-701).

Waiver, Loss or Extinguishment.—Lienholder should retain possession of article or goods or may be held to have surrendered lien. (§16-204).

Enforcement of Liens.—Most liens on personal property enforced by public sale after certain time has elapsed and after sale has been appropriately advertised, as indicated under applicable subheads.

Mechanics' Liens.—Every building erected, and every building repaired, rebuilt or improved to extent of 15% of its value is subject to lien for payment of all debts contracted for work done and for materials furnished for or about same, including: digging wells, installing swimming pools, sodding, seeding or planting of shrubs, trees, plants, flowers, etc., and grading, filling, landscaping and paving. (real prop. art. §9-102).

Machines, wharfs, bridges subject to lien in same manner as buildings. (real prop. art. §9-102[c]). Term "building" is defined to include any unit of nonresidential building leased or sold separately as unit, e.g., one store within shopping center. (real prop. art. §9-101; see 293 Md. 575, 446 A.2d 55).

Lien for installation of water lines, sewers or streets in subdivided developments applies pro rata to developed lots and improvements. (real prop. art. §9-102[b]).

Lien extends to ground covered and so much adjacent ground held by same owner as is necessary for ordinary purposes of such building. Boundaries of land appurtenant may be set by written contract between owner of land and fabricators filed with clerk of circuit court. (real prop. art. §9-103[a], [b]).

If repairs or improvements are to single condominium unit in horizontal property regime, lien extends only to such unit. (real prop. art. §11-118[a]).

If building is erected or repaired, rebuilt or improved to extent of 25% of its value, by tenant for life or for years, or by person employed by such tenant, lien applies to his interest. (real prop. art. §9-103[c][2]).

If building not finished, lien attaches to extent of work done or material furnished. (real prop. art. §9-103[c][1]).

If contract made with anyone except owners of lot or agent, written notice substantially similar to following must be given personally or by registered or certified mail to owner or his agent within 90 days after work done or materials furnished:

"NOTICE TO OWNER OR OWNER'S AGENT
OF INTENTION TO CLAIM A LIEN"

. . . .
(SUBCONTRACTOR)
DID WORK OR FURNISHED MATERIAL FOR OR ABOUT THE BUILDING GENERALLY DESIGNATED OR BRIEFLY DESCRIBED AS . . . .
. . . . THE TOTAL AMOUNT EARNED UNDER THE SUBCONTRACTOR'S UNDERTAKING TO THE DATE HEREOF IS $. . . . .
OF WHICH $. . . . . IS DUE AND UNPAID AS OF THE DATE HEREOF. THE WORK DONE OR MATERIALS PROVIDED UNDER THE SUBCONTRACT WERE AS FOLLOWS: (INSERT BRIEF DESCRIPTION OF THE WORK DONE AND MATERIALS FURNISHED, THE TIME WHEN THE WORK WAS DONE OR THE MATERIALS FURNISHED, AND THE NAME OF THE PERSON FOR WHOM THE WORK WAS DONE OR TO WHOM THE MATERIALS WERE FURNISHED.)
I DO SOLEMNLY DECLARE AND AFFIRM UNDER THE PENALTIES OF PERJURY THAT THE CONTENTS OF THE FOREGOING NOTICE ARE TRUE TO THE BEST OF THE AFFIANT'S KNOWLEDGE, INFORMATION AND BELIEF.

. . . .
(INDIVIDUAL ON BEHALF OF
SUBCONTRACTOR)

ON BEHALF OF   . . . .
(SUBCONTRACTOR, IF NOT AN
INDIVIDUAL)
(INSERT IF
SUBCONTRACTOR IS NOT AN
INDIVIDUAL)
(real prop. art. §9-104).

If owner unavailable or dead (and successors not appearing in public records), notice may be effected by posting front of building in presence of competent witness. Notice effective when mailed, even if received after expiration of 90 day period. (See 287 Md. 348, 412 A.2d 996.)

Notice.—Filing of petition with clerk of court where land or any part thereof is located constitutes notice to purchaser that lien may be perfected. (real prop. art. §9-102[e]).

Giving credit or receiving notes or other securities is not waiver of lien. (real prop. art. §9-110).

Duration.—To establish lien, petition must be filed with clerk of circuit court where land is situated within 180 days after work or materials furnished. Petition must include: (1) Name and address of petitioner and owner; (2) nature of, amount of and time when work or materials furnished; (3) name of person for whom work or materials furnished; (4) sum claimed; (5) description of land and, if applicable, (6) statement of notification

LIENS . . . *continued*

to owner pursuant to real prop. art. §9-104. If petition filed against two buildings of same owner, petitioner must designate sum claimed on each building. (real prop art. §9-105). Petitioner must also file affidavit.

Waiver.—Executory contract between contractor and subcontractor may not waive or require subcontractor to waive right to claim mechanic's lien. (real prop. art. §9-113).

Upon filing of petition, court issues order directing owner to show cause within 15 days. Owner must appear at stated time or file answer and counteraffidavit before that time; otherwise, facts in petitioner's affidavit are deemed admitted. Court may make final order establishing or denying lien or it may enter interlocutory order upon finding of probable cause of petitioner's entitlement to lien. Order must: (1) Establish lien; (2) describe property; (3) state amount of lien; (4) state amount of bond owner may file to remove lien; (5) assign trial date within six months; (6) order may require petitioner to post bond. (real prop. art. §9-106). If part of land is located in another county, petitioner may create lien there by filing certified copy of docket entries of court order. (real prop. art. §9-107).

Upon foreclosure, if proceeds of sale are insufficient, each lien is satisfied in amount proportioned to amount it bears to total liens. (real prop. art. §9-108).

Right to enforce lien expires at end of one year from filing of petition. During this time, claimant may file petition to enforce lien or execute on bond. (real prop. art. §9-109).

Redemption.—No right of redemption of property sold under mechanic's lien.

Public Works.—Unless bond or other security is required by federal law or regulation or as condition of federal assistance, contractor constructing public work for state or subdivision not required by state to obtain bid bond or other security with bid or offer if contract price is expected to be $100,000 or less; performance bond not required if contract price is $100,000 or less. (state fin. and proc. art. §13-216).

Revised Uniform Federal Tax Lien Registration Act adopted. (real prop. art. §§3-401 to 3-405).

Attachment Lien.—See topic Attachment.

Attorney's Lien.—See category Legal Profession, topic Attorneys and Counselors.

Collateral Security.—See topic Pledges.

Execution Lien.—See topic Executions.

Judgment Lien.—See category Civil Actions and Procedures, topic Judgments.

Landlord's Lien.—See category Property, topic Landlord and Tenant.

Liens on Exempt Property.—See topic Exemptions.

Liens on Homestead.—See topic Homesteads.

Real Estate Mortgage Lien.—See category Mortgages, topic Mortgages of Real Property.

Tax Lien.—See category Taxation, topic Income Tax, subhead Lien.

Lien on Wages for Nonsupport.—See category Family, topic Husband and Wife, subhead Desertion or Nonsupport.

MECHANICS' LIENS:

See topic Liens.

PLEDGES:

Uniform Commercial Code adopted. (comm. law art. tit. 1-10). See category Business Regulation and Commerce, topic Commercial Code. Generally, pledge of consigned goods conveys only rights of consignee. (comm. law art. §§11-805, 11-806).

Agricultural Products.—Every pledge of agricultural products by commission merchant to whom products were delivered for sale for use and benefit of grower or producer is null and void without consent of grower or producer. (comm. law art. §11-808[b]).

Corporate Stock.—Stockholder of record of pledged shares may vote such shares absent agreement between pledgor and pledgee to contrary. (corps. art. §2-508[b]).

Repledge.—It is misdemeanor to repledge or rehypothecate any stocks, bonds or other securities held as security for money lent or advanced to owner of securities, without consent of pledgor. (art. 27, §215).

Remedies of Pledgee.—Pledgee should retain possession of goods in order to maintain lien. (47 Md. 88). Pledgee may sell goods without judicial process after reasonable notice to debtor to redeem. (27 Md. 354).

Pawnbrokers.—Pawnbrokers must get license if acting as secondhand precious metal object dealers. (bus. reg. art. tit. 12, subtit. 2).

In Baltimore City, license, bond and other regulations affecting pawnbrokers are set out in Baltimore City Code, art. 15, §§76 to 87, as amended.

RECEIVERS:

Receivers are fiduciaries governed generally by provisions of est. & tr. art. tit. 15. Fiduciary does not include receiver for purposes of est. & tr. art. §15-102, powers of fiduciary. Procedure may be governed by one of several subtitles of Md. Rules. R. P. subtit. 10 applies to receivers of property of minor or disabled person. R. P. subtit. 13 applies to trustees appointed by court and to receivers of property of minor or disabled person, and to receivers appointed under general authority of equity court to liquidate business or affairs of debtor or to receivers in certain statutory proceedings to dissolve corporations, but not to receivers in other specified statutory proceedings unless court orders compliance.

Banking institution may be taken into custody by Bank Commissioner, who may act as receiver. (fin. inst. art. tit. 5, subtit. 6). Receiver may be appointed for fraternal benefit society in certain instances. (art. 48A, §351). Federal Savings and Loan Insurance Corporation or Maryland Deposit Insurance Fund Corporation has absolute right to be appointed conservator or receiver of savings and loan association insured by it. (fin. inst. art. §9-709). Trust company may act as receiver. (fin. inst. art. §3-207[8]).

Where corporation is voluntarily dissolved, director, shareholder or creditor may petition equity court to take jurisdiction of liquidation, and court may continue directors as trustees or appoint one or more receivers. (corps. art. §3-411). Where action is brought by shareholders for involuntary dissolution of corporation, court may appoint one or more receivers pending final determination upon whether to dissolve; if it appears that corporation should be dissolved, court must appoint one or more receivers to supervise liquidation. (corps. art. §3-414). Where action is brought by shareholder or creditor to dissolve corporation on grounds it is unable to meet debts as they mature, and court determines that corporation is unable, court must appoint one or more receivers to supervise liquidation. (corps. art. §3-415).

Jurisdiction.—Equity courts.

Proceedings.—Appointment is procured by petition to court. (R. P. 13-106).

Eligibility and Competency.—Receiver must be disinterested person as between parties. (67 Md. 222, 9 A. 632). Receiver and each attorney, accountant or appraiser he desires to employ must inform court whether he has had certain relationships with or interests in debtor or secured creditor. (R. P. 13-302).

Qualification.—Receiver governed by R. P. subtit. 13 must give bond in amount not exceeding probable value of estate less value of certain securities or money deposited in financial institution and land which fiduciary lacks power to sell or convey. (R. P. 13-107).

Powers and Duties.—Receiver does not have general powers of fiduciary set forth in est. & tr. art. §15-102. R. P. subtitles 10 and 13 both prescribe duties for receivers. Statutory receiverships may carry particular powers or duties, e.g., corps. art. §3-418, prescribing powers of receiver in voluntary or involuntary corporate dissolution proceedings.

Compensation.—No general statute as to compensation of receivers. Amount of compensation is within discretion of court. (169 Md. 501, 182 A. 273). Rate depends upon difficulty of work and value of estate involved.

Discharge.—Receiver will be discharged by court after purposes for which he was appointed have been realized and his accounts approved.

REDEMPTION:

See topics Executions, Liens; categories Mortgages, topic Mortgages of Real Property; Taxation, topic Property Taxes.

SUPPLEMENTARY PROCEEDINGS:

See topic Executions.

TRUSTEE PROCESS:

See topics Attachment, Garnishment.

USURY:

See category Business Regulation and Commerce, topic Interest.

DISPUTE RESOLUTION

ALTERNATIVE DISPUTE RESOLUTION:

Mandatory Dispute Resolution.—Claims for medical injury against licensed or authorized health care providers exceeding concurrent jurisdiction of district court (currently $20,000) must be submitted to arbitration administered by Health Claims Arbitration Office. Limited judicial review is available to modify, correct or vacate award or assessment of costs thereunder. (courts art. §§3-2A-01 to 3-2A-09).

Uniform Arbitration Act governs enforcement of arbitration agreements, except those between employers and employees. (courts art. §§3-201 to 3-234). This Act provides for stays of proceedings, orders to arbitrate, and limited judicial review of arbitration decisions.

See also topic Arbitration and Award.

ARBITRATION AND AWARD:

Uniform Arbitration Act adopted. (courts art. §§3-201 to 3-234). Unless expressly provided by parties, Uniform Act does not apply to arbitration agreement between employers and employees. (courts art. §3-206). Arbitration of labor disputes may be sought by Commissioner of Labor and Industry. (lab. emp. art. §§4-101 to 4-220). Arbitration of pending actions is governed by Uniform Act. (R. P. 15-101).

Form and Requisites of Submission.—Submission should be in writing. (courts art. §3-206; R. P. 15-101).

Contracts to Arbitrate Future Disputes.—Prior to adoption of Uniform Arbitration Act in 1965, agreement to arbitrate was valid, but enforcement was difficult because of rule that unless agreement had been consummated by award, it would not bar suit at law or in equity. (147 Md. 161, 127 A. 746). Special statute provides for arbitration of disputes between employers and employees. (lab. emp. art. §§4-101 to 4-220).

Rescission.—Since adoption of Uniform Arbitration Act in 1965, party must observe agreement to arbitrate to same extent as any other contract. (courts art. §3-206).

Powers of Arbitrators.—Arbitrators have only such powers as are specified in submission, and if they exceed those powers, award is void. (186 Md. 669, 48 A.2d 447).

Award and Enforcement Thereof.—Award is binding and conclusive upon parties, and suit may be instituted upon award. (courts art. §3-202; 217 Md. 539, 144 A.2d 69). Application to arbitrator to correct or modify award must be made within 20 days after delivery of award to applicant. (courts art. §3-222). Petition in court to correct or modify award must be filed within 90 days after delivery of award to applicant. (courts art. §3-223). Petition to vacate award must be filed within 30 days after delivery of copy of award to petitioner. (courts art. §3-224).

See note at head of Digest as to 1998 legislation covered.

See Topical Index in front part of this volume.

ARBITRATION AND AWARD . . . *continued*

Judgment on Award.—In cases of arbitration of pending actions, judgment is entered by clerk after award is confirmed, modified or corrected by court. (R. P. 15-101, courts art. §3-228). In cases of arbitration out of court, upon application of party, court must confirm award, unless within 90 days after award grounds are urged for vacating, modifying or correcting award. (courts art. §§3-223, 3-227). Judgment is entered upon order confirming, modifying or correcting award and may be enforced as any other judgment. (courts art. §3-228).

International Commercial Arbitration Act adopted. (courts art. §§3-2B-01 to 3-2B-09). Circuit courts have jurisdiction to enforce agreements or orders calling for arbitration, to enter judgments on arbitration and to recognize and enforce awards rendered in foreign country. (courts art. §§3-203, 3-204).

Medical Malpractice.—All claims and actions against anyone licensed or authorized to provide health care services in Md., including licensed certified social worker-clinical, which exceed concurrent jurisdiction of district court (currently $20,000) must be submitted to arbitration administered by Health Claims Arbitration Office. Arbitration award may be rejected and judicial review sought. However, arbitration may be waived under certain circumstances. (courts art. §§3-2A-01 to 3-2A-09).

DOCUMENTS AND RECORDS

ACKNOWLEDGMENTS:

Uniform Acknowledgment Act adopted. (st. gov't art., Title 19, subtitle 1). Notarial Acts Before Commissioned Officers. (st. gov't art., Title 19, subtitle 2). Uniform Recognition of Acknowledgments Act not adopted. Acknowledgments may be made as follows:

Within State.—Before: (1) Judge of court of record; (2) clerk or deputy clerk of court having seal; (3) notary public; (4) master in chancery. (st. gov't art., §19-102).

Outside State but Within United States.—Before: (1) Clerk or deputy clerk of any federal court; (2) clerk or deputy clerk of any court of record; (3) notary public. (st. gov't art., §19-103).

Outside United States.—Before: (1) Ambassador, minister, chargé d'affaires, counselor to or secretary of legation, consul general, consul, vice-consul, commercial attaché or consular agent of United States accredited to country where acknowledgment is made; (2) notary public of country where made; (3) judge or clerk of court of record of country where made. (st. gov't art., §19-104).

Persons in or with U. S. Armed Forces.—Before any commissioned officer of any branch of U. S. Armed Forces by any person who is: (1) Member or spouse or dependent of member of such armed forces; (2) merchant seaman outside U.S.; (3) outside U.S. at direction of government in connection with activity pertaining to war in which U.S. is then engaged. Place of execution need not be stated. Signature, serial number, rank and branch of service should appear. Retroactive so as to validate such acknowledgments previously made. (st. gov't art., §19-111).

General Requirements as to Taking.—Officer taking acknowledgment should know or have satisfactory evidence that person making acknowledgment is person described in and who executed instrument. (st. gov't art., §19-105).

General Requirements of Certificate.—Certificate of officer taking acknowledgment must contain officer's: (1) Signature; (2) official seal, if such exists; (3) title; and (4) if officer is notary public, date commission expires. (st. gov't art., §19-108).

Married Women.—No special requirements. (st. gov't art., §19-106).

Attorneys in Fact.—No special requirements as to acknowledgments by attorneys in fact, except that Uniform Acknowledgment Act prescribes form. (st. gov't art., §19-107).

Corporation may acknowledge by president or vice-president or by its appointed attorney. (corps. art. §1-303).

Foreign Acknowledgments. — Uniform Acknowledgment Act adopted. (st. gov't art., Title 19, subtitle 1).

Effect of Acknowledgment.—Instruments, except residential leases (real prop. art. §4-101[a][2]), relating to real estate, mortgages and bills of sale will not be accepted for record unless acknowledged (real prop. art. §4-101[a]). Acknowledgment does not entitle paper to be received in evidence without further proof, although certified copy of recorded paper may be offered in evidence without further proof (courts art. §10-204).

Proof by Subscribing Witness.—No provision by which proof by subscribing witness may be substituted for acknowledgment.

Authentication.—No authentication necessary whether acknowledgment is made within or without state but in U.S. If acknowledgment is made outside U.S. before notary public or judge or clerk of court of record, certificate must be authenticated as provided in Uniform Acknowledgment Act. (st. gov't art., §19-109). If required by law of place where acknowledgment is to be used, authentication of signature and seal of notary public or other official may be obtained from clerk of circuit court of county. Fee, $1. (courts art. §2-212).

Forms.—In addition to forms set forth in Uniform Acknowledgment Act (st. gov't art., Title 19, subtitle 1), the following may be used:

Forms

Acknowledgment of Deed by Individual:
State of Maryland, ... County, to wit: I hereby certify, that on this . . . . . ., in the year . . . . ., before the subscriber, (here insert style of officer taking the acknowledgment), personally appeared (here insert name of the person making the acknowledgment), and acknowledged the foregoing deed to be his act. (Officer before whom acknowledgments are made must sign in his official capacity). (real prop. art. §4-204[a]).

Acknowledgment of Deed by Corporation:
State of Maryland, ... County, to wit: I hereby certify, that on this . . . . . ., in the year . . . . . ., before the subscriber (here insert style of officer taking acknowledgment), personally appeared (here insert name of the person making the acknowledgment) who acknowledged himself to be the (here insert the word "Vice-" if appropriate) President of (here insert name of the corporation) (the "Corporation") and that he, as such officer, being authorized so to do, executed the foregoing deed for the purposes therein contained by signing the name of the Corporation by himself as such officer [and certified that this conveyance is not part of a transaction in which there is a sale, lease, exchange or other transfer of all or substantially all of the property and assets of the Corporation]. (Bracketed material should be included unless instrument being acknowledged is a confirmatory deed filed in connection with articles of transfer or articles of merger.) (corps. art. §3-114; real prop. art. §14-113).

Acknowledgment of Deed by Husband and Wife:
State of . . . . . . County, to wit: I hereby certify, that on this . . . . . . day of . . . . ., in the year . . . . . ., before the subscriber, (here insert official style of person taking acknowledgment), personally appeared (here insert name of husband), and (here insert name of married woman making acknowledgment), his wife, and did each acknowledge the foregoing deed to be their respective act. (real prop. art. §4-204[b]).

Acknowledgment of Deed Taken Outside Maryland:
State of . . . . . . County, to wit: I hereby certify, that on this . . . . . . day of . . . . ., in the year . . . . . ., before the subscriber, (here insert official style of officer taking acknowledgment), personally appeared (here insert name of person making acknowledgment), and acknowledged the foregoing deed to be his act. In testimony whereof I have caused the seal of the court to be affixed, (or have affixed my official seal), this . . . . . . day of . . . . . ., A. D. . . . . . . (Seal of court). (real prop. art.§4-204 [c]).

Alternative to Acknowledgment or Proof.—See topic Affidavits, subhead Verification.

Validating Acts.—There have been numerous acts validating defective acknowledgments previously made in connection with transfer of real or personal property. In addition, acknowledgments of persons taken before commissioned officers of U.S. Armed Forces are validated. (st. gov't art., §§19-201 to 19-205).

Unless certain formal requisites of instrument recorded before Jan. 1, 1973 were challenged in judicial proceeding commenced by July 1, 1973, failure to comply with such formal requisites, including proper acknowledgment, has no effect. Unless same formal requisites of instrument recorded on or after Jan. 1, 1973 are challenged in judicial proceeding commenced within six months after it is recorded, failure to comply with formal requisites has no effect. (real prop. art. §4-109).

AFFIDAVITS:

Within State.—Affidavit may be made before anyone authorized to administer oath (R. P. 1-304), such as notary public (st. gov't art., §18-105) or judge. Fee may be up to $2 for original notarized act, and lesser amount for copies. (st. gov't art., §18-112).

Outside State but Within United States.—Affidavits may be made before anyone authorized by law of place where made. Notary public of another state presumed authorized to take affidavit in absence of showing to contrary. (25 Md. 402).

Outside the United States.—Affidavits may be made before anyone authorized by law of place where made. (1 Bland 352).

Persons in or with U. S. Armed Forces.—See topic Acknowledgments, which law is equally applicable to affidavits.

General Requirements as to Administration.—No particular requirements as to making affidavit. Oath is sufficient if made by affirmation (art. 1, §9), or by requiring person to hold up hand in recognition of solemnity of act (art. 1, §11). It is better practice, but not required, for affiant to sign affidavit. In proceedings governed by Md. Rules of Procedure, signing paper containing statement is sufficient if one of the following representations is included therein: Generally: "I solemnly affirm under the penalties of perjury that the contents of the foregoing paper are true to the best of my knowledge, information and belief." Personal knowledge: "I solemnly affirm under the penalties of perjury and upon personal knowledge that the contents of the foregoing paper are true." (R. P. 1-304).

General Requirements of Jurat.—Notaries required to have seal or stamp with which to authenticate. (st. gov't art., §18-108). In practice, office of person before whom made should appear in certificate, and officer taking affidavit should affix seal if he or she has one. (See 52 Md. 483; 25 Md. 402.) Person administering oath must certify as to date of expiration of commission. (st. gov't art., §18-108[c]).

Use of Affidavit.—Generally there is no right to use affidavit in evidence. (207 Md. 401, 114 A.2d 639).

Form

State of . . . . . ., County of . . . . . ., to wit: I hereby certify that on this . . . . . . day of . . . . . . in the year . . . . . . before me, the subscriber, (here insert style of officer taking affidavit) personally appeared (here insert name of person making affidavit) and made oath in due form of law that to the best of his knowledge, information and belief (here insert matters to be contained in affidavit). (Signature of affiant).

Subscribed and sworn to before me on the day and year first above written. (Signature of officer taking affidavit and seal).

Alternative to Affidavit.—See subhead Verification, infra.

Verification in lieu of affidavit or acknowledgment is allowed for corporate papers (corps. art. §1-302) or documents perfecting security interest (comm. law art. §9-402) filed with Dep't of Assessments and Taxation or papers filed with register of wills or orphan's court (est. & tr. art. §1-102).

NOTARIES PUBLIC:

Qualification.—Must be at least 18 years old, of good moral character and integrity, approved by local state senator, live or work in that state, and, if living in Md., be resident of district of approving Senator. Appointment is by Governor and commission is obtained from clerk of circuit court. (st. gov't art., §§18-101 to 18-103). Out-of-state individuals may be appointed notaries by Governor on approval of application by Secretary of State; Secretary of State is irrevocably deemed to be out-of-state notary's agent for service of process. (st. gov't art., §18-101[B]).

Authentication.—See topic Acknowledgments, subhead Authentication.

Bond.—None required.

Seal.—Must have seal. (st. gov't art., §18-108).

Powers and Duties.—Generally, notaries have power to authenticate official acts, deeds, conveyances, affidavits, etc., under notarial seal and to take acknowledgments in any county of Md. They have power to administer oaths, and certificate of notary under seal is sufficient evidence of notary having administered oath in character as notary public. Notary may take testimony and must keep record of official acts. (st. gov't art., §§18-101 to 18-112).

Territorial Extent of Powers.—State-wide; notary may act in county other than that for which appointed. (st. gov't art., §18-109).

Expiration of Commission.—Certificate of acknowledgment should state date when commission expires. (st. gov't art., §18-108[c]). Four year term. (st. gov't art., §18-103[c]).

Certificate of Authority.—See topic Acknowledgments, subhead Authentication.

Fees.—For original notarial act, not to exceed $2; and lesser amount for all other services. (st. gov't art., §18-112.)

Officers of U. S. Armed Forces.—May take acknowledgments, administer oaths and perform other notarial acts for: (1) Person in Armed Forces within or without U.S.; (2) merchant seaman without U.S.; or (3) civilian employee of federal government on duty outside U.S. in connection with war. (st. gov't art., §§19-201 to 19-202).

RECORDS:

Note: In 1985 session, Maryland Legislature added new article to Maryland Code to be entitled "Tax-Property Article". This Article is intended to revise, restate and recodify laws of State relating to property tax, recordation tax and transfer tax matters generally. Effective date of this Article is Feb. 1, 1986.

In Baltimore City, Clerk of Circuit Court has charge of land records; in counties, respective clerks of circuit courts for jurisdictions have charge of land records. (real prop. art. §3-301). Microfilm copies are recorded with State Archivist, Annapolis. (real prop. art. §3-303).

Uniform Commercial Code adopted. (comm. law art. tit. 1-10). See category Business Regulation and Commerce, topic Commercial Code, subheads Intentional Variations, Filing Fee.

Recordable Instruments.—Deeds, mortgages and other instruments creating estate in land above seven years, mechanics' liens and similar documents affecting title to real or personal property must be recorded. (real prop. art. §§3-101, 9-105). Any instrument affecting property may be recorded. Recording of such instrument constitutes constructive notice from date of recording. (real prop. art. §3-102).

Place of Recording.—Deeds and mortgages of land are recorded by county circuit court clerks, and in Baltimore City by Clerk of Circuit Court. They must be recorded in county or city where land affected lies; and if land lies in more than one jurisdiction, they must be recorded in each such jurisdiction. (real prop. art. §3-103). *For list of counties and county seats, see first page for this state in Volume containing Practice Profiles Section.*

Requisites for Recording.—Except in Baltimore, Cecil, Charles, Dorchester, Harford, Howard, Montgomery, St. Mary's, Washington, and Worcester Counties, deed or other instrument effecting change in ownership may not be received for record until property transferred on assessment books of county where located; and transfer on assessment books in certain counties requires prior payment of all public taxes, assessments and charges on property transferred and of all taxes on personal property in county due by transferor, if all county land owned by transferor is being transferred. (real prop. art. §3-104[a], [b]). In Baltimore City, no document effecting transfer except leases for less than seven year term may be recorded until lien certificate procured from city and all liens shown as due on certificate are paid and affidavit of transfer provided. Not applicable if transfer only adds parties to title. (Balto. City Code art. 28, §10). Exception to requirement of prepayment of personal property taxes is provided for grant by or on behalf of mortgagee, lien creditor, trustee of deed of trust, judgment creditor, trustee in bankruptcy, receiver or other court-appointed officer in insolvency or liquidation proceeding, for straw deed or supplementary instrument in certain counties, and for certain deeds transferring property to Anne Arundel County, to Frederick County, to Carroll County and, as of July 1, 1981, to Baltimore County. (real prop. art. §3-104[c]). Property may be transferred on record in July, Aug. or Sept. without required payment of taxes by permitting attorney to file statement regarding maintenance of real estate tax escrow account. (real prop. art. §3-104[c]). Other miscellaneous and special local requirements are set out in real prop. art. §3-104, including provision which prohibits recordation of any deed, mortgage, or deed of trust in any county or Baltimore City after Jan. 1, 1991, unless it bears certification of attorney at law that instrument has been prepared by attorney or under attorney's supervision, or certification that instrument was prepared by one of parties named in instrument. (real prop. art. §3-104[f][1]). Except for security agreements filed in accordance with §9-402 of Maryland Uniform Commercial Code, consideration payable, including amount of any mortgage or deed of trust assumed by grantee, or principal amount of secured debt incurred, must be described in recitals or acknowledgment of any instrument of writing or in affidavit under oath accompanying such instrument signed by party to such instrument. (tax-prop. art. §12-104).

Payment of Taxes as Condition Precedent.—See subhead Requisites for Recording, supra.

Recording Fees.—For recording deeds, mortgages, financing statements, and other instruments required to be filed among land records and financing statement records, in Baltimore City and in any county having block index system and grantor-grantee index system, fee is $4 per page or portion thereof, with minimum charge of $10 per instrument, plus $1 for each name to be indexed and $1 for each additional block. In other counties, fee is $4 per page or portion thereof with minimum charge of $10 per instrument, and $1 per name indexed. For recording short releases of all kinds, $3 plus $1 for each name to be indexed. (real prop. art. §3-601[b]). Any printed recordable instrument must be printed in not less than eight-point type and in black letters on white paper of sufficient weight and thickness to be clearly readable; and any typewriting must be in black letters not less than elite type; and document must be readily subject to photostating, otherwise clerk may charge three times regular charge. (real prop. art. §3-104[e]). Unless name of every signer of instrument is typed or printed directly above or below signature there is additional fee of $1. (real prop. art. §3-104[d]).

Tax on Recordation.—

Recordation Tax.—Recordation tax rates are applied to each $500 or fraction thereof of consideration payable or of principal amount of debt secured for instrument of writing. Consideration includes amount of any mortgage or deed of trust assumed by grantee or to which property conveyed is subject. Mayor and City Council of Baltimore City or governing body of county may set recordation tax rate. (tax-prop. art. §12-103[a],[b]). Maryland state law no longer establishes county rates to be used in absence of action by such local bodies. (tax-prop. art. §12-103). Exempt from tax are liens or encumbrances upon vehicles and vessels which are filed with Motor Vehicle Administration or Dep't of Natural Resources, mechanics' liens, crop liens, certain purchase money deeds of trust or purchase money mortgages, assignments of mortgages or deeds of trust, judgments, releases, orders of satisfaction, participation agreements showing interest in note, mortgages or deeds of trust based on prior recorded loan to mortgagor or grantor under deed of trust, certain Uniform Commercial Code security agreements, certain refinancing agreements where refinanced property is mortgagor's principal residence, certain supplemental and previously recorded instruments, and instruments transferring property between certain relatives. Also exempt from the tax are certain transfers of corporate property between related corporations, certain corporate or partnership conveyances of property upon dissolution, merger, consolidation, liquidation or termination, land installment contracts, options to purchase real property, deeds conveying title to real property where recordation was previously paid on contract of sale between same parties, transfers to certain public agencies, leases of seven years or less, and articles of merger or consolidation of foreign corporations and transfers from partnership to limited liability company. (tax-prop. art. §12-108). Counties and Baltimore City authorized to enact certain exemptions from recordation or transfer taxes on conveyance of owner-occupied residential property. (tax-prop. art. §§12-103[b], 13-408). Where instrument is filed with Dep't of Assessments and Taxation pursuant to corps. art. §3-107, tax is, in case of single debtor that has place of business in state and in case of multiple debtors all of whom have principal place of business in same county in state, rate set by county in which debtors' principal place of business is located, in case of single debtor that has no place of business in state but resides in state and in case of multiple debtors none of whom has principal place of business in state but all of whom reside in same county in state, rate set by county in which debtors reside and in case of single debtor that has no place of business in state and does not reside in state and in case of multiple debtors not covered above, rate of $1.65 per $500 or fraction thereof. (tax-prop. art. §12-103[d]).

Transfer Tax.—There is state transfer tax of 0.5% on consideration on instruments conveying title to real property or leasehold interests for more than seven years which are recorded. (tax-prop. art. §13-203). Exemption is available for transfers to organizations with principal purpose of preservation of agricultural land. (tax-prop. art. §13-207[b]). Also exempt are certain transfers of corporate property between related corporations, certain corporate or partnership conveyances of property upon dissolution, merger, consolidation, liquidation or termination, and deeds conveying title to real property where recordation was previously paid on contract of sale between same parties. (tax-prop. art. §13-404). For sale of improved residential real property to individual who has never owned in state residential real property that has been individual's principal residence who will occupy property as principal residence, rate of transfer tax is 0.25% of consideration payable for instrument of writing and transfer tax shall be paid entirely by seller. (tax-prop. art. §13-203). Land assessed for agricultural use and transferred for nonagricultural purposes subject to 5% agricultural transfer tax on consideration where land transferred is 20 acres or more; for transfer of less than 20 acres of agricultural land assessed for agricultural use or as unimproved agricultural land, rate of tax is 4%; and for transfer of less than 20 acres of agricultural land assessed as improved agricultural land or agricultural land with site improvements, rate of tax is 3%. Tax declines 25% each consecutive year property tax paid on basis of nonagricultural use assessment. (tax-prop. art. §13-303). Agricultural land transfer tax plus interest and lien in such amount imposed on transfers involving nonagricultural improvements if required notice of intent not filed. (tax-prop. art. §13-305[c]). See category Taxation, topic Property Taxes, subhead Taxable Property, catchline Assessment. In addition to above, some counties impose transfer tax as follows: In Howard County, 1% of actual consideration (How. Co. Code, §20.401); in Montgomery County, 1% of consideration on unimproved property, 0.25% of consideration on transfer of improved residential property if consideration is less than $40,000, 0.5% if consideration is $40,000 or more but less than $70,000 and 1% if consideration is $70,000 or more; 1% of consideration on transfer of improved commercial property; transfers of land assessed for farm use is at variable rates (Mont. Co. Code, §§52-21 to 52-27); in Prince George's County, 1.4% (P.G. Co. Code, §10-188); in Baltimore County, 1.5% with exemption of $22,000 for owner-occupied residential real estate (Balto. Co. Code §§33-127); in Anne Arundel County, 1% (A.A. Co. Code, art 6, §7-101); in Kent County, 0.5% (Code of Pub. Local Laws of Kent Co. §152-13); in Talbot County, 1.5% for consideration over $50,000 authorized (Code of Pub. Local Laws of Talbot Co. §6-6.1[a]).

See note at head of Digest as to 1998 legislation covered.

See Topical Index in front part of this volume.

RECORDS . . . *continued*

Division of Taxes.—In agreement for sale of property, it is presumed, in absence of agreement or law to contrary, that parties intended that federal and state stamp taxes and state and local transfer taxes be shared equally between grantor and grantee. This does not apply to mortgages or deeds of trust. (real prop. art. §14-104).

Foreign Conveyances or Encumbrances.—Instrument conveying Md. property may not be recorded unless executed and acknowledged as required by laws of this state. See topic Acknowledgments; category Property, topic Deeds.

Effect of Record.—Where two or more deeds or mortgages convey same lands or chattels real, one first recorded is preferred, if grantee accepted deed in good faith and without constructive notice by possession under unrecorded deed and for good and valuable consideration. (real prop. art. §3-203). See category Property, topic Deeds.

Torrens Act not adopted.

Transfer of decedent's title to real estate is shown by orphans' court records and by deed executed by personal representative, indexed under decedent's name in grantor index. (est. & tr. art. §9-105).

Filing under Commercial Code.—See category Business Regulation and Commerce, topic Commercial Code, subheads Intentional Variations (comm. law art. §9-401[1][b]), Filing Fee.

Vital Statistics.—Reports of births and deaths must be filed with Secretary of Health and Mental Hygiene on forms supplied. Administrative head of institution where child is born must file birth certificate within 72 hours after birth and must satisfy special requirements in case of unwed mothers. (health-gen. art. §4-208). Copies are maintained by health officers of counties or by Baltimore City Commissioner of Health. Secretary and courts maintain duplicate permanent records of marriages. Secretary receives and indexes reports of divorces and annulments from clerks of courts. Secretary furnishes certified or abridged copy of records of birth, death or of marriage performed after June 1, 1951; records of marriages may be, and records of early marriages or of divorces and annulments must be, certified by clerks of court. (health gen. art. tit. 4, subtit. 2).

Fees.—Certified or abridged copies or search report of birth, death or marriage certificates, $6 for each copy. (health gen. art. §4-217[c]).

Establishing Birth Records.—Secretary of Health and Mental Hygiene has power to make rules governing registration and delayed registration of births. (health-gen. art. §§4-203, 4-210). Forms and instructions may be secured from Division of Vital Records, 201 W. Preston St., Baltimore 21201.

Ordering Copies of Birth and Death Certificates.—Send request, together with $6 check or money order payable to Division of Vital Records, 4201 Patterson Avenue, Baltimore 21215. Request for birth certificate must include full name of person, birthdate, birthplace, father's full name and mother's maiden name. Request for death certificate must include deceased's full name and date and place of death. Applicant should state name, relationship and purpose for which record is intended. Fee is for search and one copy, if found, or statement that none is on record. Additional copies are $6 per copy.

Immunization Registry.—Dep't of Health and Mental Hygiene is required to develop and implement registry of child immunizations for all children in state between birth and age of six years. (health-gen. art. §18-109).

SEALS:

Conveyance of real property before Jan. 1, 1973 required seal. On or after Jan. 1, 1973, seal not required. (real prop. art. §4-109). Seal not required on will. (est. & tr. art. §4-102).

Uniform Commercial Code adopted. (comm. law art. tit. 1-10). See category Business Regulation and Commerce, topic Commercial Code.

Corporate Seal.—Whenever corporate seal required on any document by Md. law, or whenever Md. corporation required by any law to affix corporate seal to document, requirement may be satisfied by placing word "seal" adjacent to signature. (corps. art. §1-304). Corporate seal not required on deed or other instrument notwithstanding any provision to contrary in corporation's charter, bylaws, etc. (real prop. art. §4-101). Mere presence of corporate seal on document does not make it sealed instrument, but extrinsic evidence is admissible to show whether use of seal was intended to make instrument a specialty. (23 F. Supp. 137). Each certificate which represents any corporate security may be sealed with actual corporate seal or facsimile of it or in any other form. (corps. art. §2-212).

Effect of Seal.—Affirmation of seal on document is itself consideration (3 Md. 67), but in practice no one relies on seal alone to establish consideration. Contract specifically stated to be under seal is specialty, as to which period of limitations is 12 years instead of three years. (courts art. §5-102). Inclusion of "seal" in preprinted form is sufficient to make instrument one under seal. (307 Md. 142, 512 A.2d 1044). Person entitled to sue or liable to be sued on instrument but for seal may sue or be sued notwithstanding such seal, on instruments executed on or after June 1, 1914. (art. 75, §3).

TORRENS ACT:

Not adopted.

VITAL STATISTICS:

See topic Records.

EMPLOYMENT

EMPLOYER AND EMPLOYEE:

See topic Labor Relations.

LABOR RELATIONS:

References are to Labor and Employment Article of Code unless otherwise indicated. Division of Labor and Industry within Dep't of Licensing, Labor and Regulation has jurisdiction over labor matters, except that Dep't of Employment and Training has jurisdiction over unemployment and certain training and manpower matters. (§2-102).

Hours of Labor.—Employer of child under 18 must have work permit. (§3-205). Child under 14 may not be employed, with some exceptions. (§3-209).

Child under 16 may not be permitted to work more than four hours on school day or 23 hours in school week; nor more than eight hours on nonschool day or 40 hours in nonschool week; nor between 9 P.M. and 7 A.M. between Memorial Day and Labor Day nor between 8 P.M. and 7 A.M. after Labor Day through day before Memorial Day. Bona fide work-study hours not counted toward permitted maximum hours of work. Commissioner of Labor and Industry may grant exception to hour restriction if: (1) Parents or guardian give written permission and (2) Commissioner determines there is no hazard to health or welfare of child or problem fulfilling school graduation requirements. (§3-211).

Child under 18 may not spend more than 12 hours in combination of school hours and work hours per day; child under 18 must have at least eight consecutive hours of nonwork, nonschool time each day; but Commissioner of Labor and Industry may grant exception to hourly restriction in certain circumstances. Child under 18 may not be permitted to work more than five hours without 30 minute nonwork interval. (§3-210).

Employer must post notices of maximum hours and scheduled hours for child labor. (§3-214).

Violation of Child Labor subtitle punishable by fine or imprisonment. (§3-216).

Wages.—Every employer of one or more employees must pay minimum wages unless employees are excluded. Beginning July 1, 1975, minimum wage for employee subject to Md. Wage and Hour Law, whether or not also subject to federal Fair Labor Standards Act, is highest minimum wage set forth in Fair Labor Standards Act. If employees are not subject to Federal Fair Labor Standards Act but are subject to Maryland Wage and Hour Law, employer may pay training wage, if applicable, authorized under Fair Labor Standards Act. (§3-413). Employees covered are entitled to one and one-half times hourly rate for hours worked in excess of 40 (§§3-415[a], 3-420). Excluded from minimum wage law are persons employed in: (1) Agriculture, under certain conditions; (2) managerial or professional capacities; (3) charitable or nonprofit organizations on gratuitous basis; (4) any business, if employee under 16 and working 20 hours or less a week; (5) outside or commission sales; (6) any business, if age 62 or over and working 25 or less hours a week; (7) canning, packing or processing food, poultry or seafood; (8) business of immediate family member; (9) motion picture and legitimate theatres; (10) restaurants, taverns, drive-ins, drug stores grossing $250,000 or less; (11) any business, if employed as part of public school special education training program for mentally, emotionally or physically handicapped; (12) organized camp in nonadministrative capacity. (§3-403). Certain classes of employees are exempt from overtime provisions; agricultural employees exempted by overtime provisions of federal Fair Labor Standards Act must receive one and one-half times hourly rate for hours worked in excess of 60. (§3-420). With some exceptions, state employees are allowed compensation for hours worked in excess of 40. (§3-420).

In construction of public works where state funds constitute 50% or more of funds used or where local public body so resolves, wages paid must be not less than prevailing wages paid for similar work in locality. (state fin. and proc. art. §§17-201 to 17-205).

Every employer must establish regular pay periods and pay employees (except executive, administrative and professional employees) at least once every two weeks or twice a month in cash or by check. Employer must: (1) Notify employee when hired of pay rate and regular payday; (2) give notice of changes of payday or of decreases in pay rate at least one pay period in advance; (3) furnish each employee with statement of gross earnings and deductions (which deductions may be made only in specified instances); (4) upon termination of employment, pay employee all wages due for work prior to termination on or before regular payday. (§§3-503 to 3-505). Violations by employer subject to criminal or civil monetary penalties. False statements by employee subject to criminal fine. (§3-508). Commissioner of Labor and Industry may attempt to resolve violations by informal means of mediation and conciliation; may institute proceedings to collect moneys unlawfully withheld; such moneys are paid to employee without cost to employee. Commissioner authorized to enter into reciprocal agreements with labor departments of other states to collect moneys unlawfully withheld by out-of-state employers. (§§3-506 to 3-507).

Railroad company may not withhold any part of wages of employees for benefit of any relief association or members thereof. (art. 23, §238).

Wages of employee, and health, welfare and pension contributions contracted for in place of wages, earned not more than three months prior to assignment for benefit of creditors by or institution of insolvency proceeding against employer are to be paid in full out of estate after payment of costs and expenses of administration of trust or insolvency proceeding which court approves. (comm. law art. §15-102[b]).

See category Debtor and Creditor, topic Assignments, subhead Assignment of Wages.

Child Labor.—Child under 14 may not be employed or permitted to work. (§3-209). Child 14 or 15 may not be employed during school hours, and is prohibited from being employed in many occupations including manufacturing, mechanical, construction, industrial, airports, railroads or maritime, or any occupation found to be dangerous or injurious to health, morals, safety, or welfare unless child found to be incapable of profiting from further education, or unless enrolled in work-study or similar program where employment is integral part of such program, or where minor employed in purely office work or duties performed outside of rooms where goods are manufactured or produced, or if, after investigation, minor is issued exception by Commissioner if determined that work performed and area in which performed not hazardous. (§3-213).

Child under 18 may not be employed in many occupations including blast furnaces, commercial docks and wharves, certain occupations on commercial vessels, railroads, electrical work, manufacture or processing of alcoholic beverages, various manufacturing processes, except where enrolled in work-study or similar program where employment is integral part of such program, or where minor employed in purely office work performed outside of rooms where goods are manufactured or produced. (§3-213).

See note at head of Digest as to 1998 legislation covered.

See Topical Index in front part of this volume.

MD – 33

LABOR RELATIONS ... *continued*

Special permit may be issued for minor of any age to be employed as model, performer, or entertainer. (§3-207).

Commissioner of Labor and Industry may temporarily suspend any or all child labor laws in event of emergency or major disaster proclaimed by governor. (§3-102[b]).

Hours of labor regulated for children under 18. See subhead Hours of Labor, supra.

Commissioner of Labor and Industry authorized to conduct reasonable inspections of any place of employment to ensure compliance. (§3-204).

Violation of Child Labor subtitle punishable by fine or imprisonment. (§3-216).

Person under 21 working in business where alcoholic beverages are sold subject to special provisions in Anne Arundel, Baltimore, Carroll, Dorchester, Kent, Queen Anne's and Prince George's Counties. (art. 2B, §12-302).

Work permit must be issued to child under 18 and must be kept on file by employer. (§3-206).

Female Labor.—Labor laws apply equally to both sexes; wage and salary discrimination for work of comparable character on basis of sex prohibited. (§3-304). See subhead Discrimination, infra. Employers required to treat disabilities caused or contributed to by pregnancy or childbirth in same way as other temporary disabilities are treated. (art. 49B, §17).

Discrimination.—Unlawful for employer, employment agency or labor organization to discriminate against any individual on basis of race, color, religion, sex, age, national origin, marital status, or physical or mental handicap unrelated in nature and extent so as to preclude performance of employment. Localities may have established other protected statuses. Unlawful to discriminate against one who opposed practices made unlawful by statute or participated in proceeding under law. Not unlawful: to discriminate based on bona fide occupational qualification, to establish dress and grooming standards directly related to job, for certain sectarian educational institutions to discriminate on basis of religion, or to observe terms of bona fide seniority system or employment benefit plan except as to hiring. (art. 49B, §16).

Enforcement action initiated when person files complaint with federal, local, or state Commission on Human Relations within six months of alleged violation of law, or on Commission's initiative. (art. 49B, §9A). If probable cause to believe discrimination has occurred is found, Commission investigates and attempts to eliminate discrimination by agreement. If no agreement, public hearing held. Respondent may answer complaint, appear at hearing with counsel, submit testimony, examine and cross-examine witnesses. Hearing examiner may dismiss complaint, issue cease and desist order, order action to conform to law, order reinstatement or hiring with or without back pay, or grant nonmonetary relief. Monetary relief reduced by interim amounts earned or earnable, and limited to two years plus time between Commission's final determination and appellate decision. No cause finding generally appealable to circuit court. (art. 49B, §§9 to 11). Commission may institute litigation in equity court to enforce order. (art. 49B, §12). Misdemeanor to make malicious unfounded complaint. (art. 49B, §12).

Labor Unions.—Union's right to organize and to bargain collectively recognized. Yellow dog contracts against public policy and unenforceable. (§§4-302 to 4-304). No "right to work" law. Union must report to Commissioner of Labor and Industry by Jan. 10 all collective bargaining agreements which terminate during year. (§4-111).

Labor Disputes.—Anti-injunction law. (§§4-301 to 4-316). Division of Labor and Industry has limited power to mediate and arbitrate labor disputes and to hold consent elections and decertification elections. (§§4-201 to 4-220). Labor disputes arising within jurisdiction of Metropolitan Transit Authority may be submitted to arbitration board for final and binding arbitration. (trans. art. §7-602). Employment, recruiting, or furnishing of professional strikebreakers unlawful. (§4-403).

Military Service.—State and local governments must afford employees who return from military service reemployment rights as per art. 64A, §19B and art. 24, §10-101.

Workers' Compensation Act (tit. 9 lab. & emp. art.) provides for creation of Workers' Compensation Commission and requires every employer having one or more employees subject to Act to be certified as self-insurer or to carry insurance in order to compensate employees for injuries or death incurred. (§9-402). Prior to issuance of license or permit by state or any county or municipality to employer for activity in which he may employ one or more employees, employer must file with issuing authority certificate of compliance with Title 9, issued by Workers' Compensation Commission, or must provide workers' compensation insurance policy or binder number. (§9-105).

To Whom Applicable.—Act applies to every person and every state or local public agency that has one or more employees subject to Act. Unless exempt, employees covered are: (1) Every person, including minor, under any contract of hire or apprenticeship, and all helpers of employees actually or constructively known to employer, whether paid by employer or employee; (2) every paid officer of corporation except officers of close corporation or certain officers of farm corporation and certain officers of professional service corporations who elect not to be covered and whose employer serves notice upon insurance carrier and Commission; (3) any full-time employer, partner or sole proprietor who elects to be covered and who serves notice upon insurance carrier and commission; (4) every employee of political subdivision, public agency or public official, whether elected or appointed, and every member of volunteer fire department, police department or civil defense corps, except as exempted; (5) every person performing services for remuneration in course of business of employer at time of injury, if such person does not maintain separate business in relation to this service, if service is not to public and if person is not himself employer subject to Act; (6) every person who regularly sells or distributes newspapers; (7) any regularly employed apprentice or trainee while receiving training or instruction related to employment outside regular working hours; (8) any person receiving remuneration from farmer or dairy farmer for services performed; (9) any person employed as domestic servant in private home and earning $750 or more in cash in any calendar quarter from any single household; (10) volunteer aids, student teachers and student interns; (11) any person on jury duty in nonfederal court. (§§9-201 to 9-236). Exempt employees are: (1) Any person employed for not more than 30 consecutive work days to do maintenance, repair and remodeling work at private home or at employer's place of business, if employer has no other employees subject to Act; (2) any person performing services in return for

subsistence only, received from religious or charitable organization; (3) any person for whom rule of liability for injury or death is provided by laws of U.S.; (4) casual employees or persons employed wholly outside Md., with several exceptions; (5) in Allegany, Carroll, Charles, Frederick, Garrett, Queen Anne's, St. Mary's, Somerset, Washington and Worcester counties, any members of volunteer fire departments, police departments, civil defense corps, rescue squads, advanced life support units or other volunteers for public agencies (except that coverage may be provided by County Council or Commission to members of volunteer fire departments, rescue squads and advanced life support units in Allegany, Garrett, Charles, St. Mary's, Somerset, Washington, and Worcester counties pursuant to §34[e]); (6) any person riding in vanpool provided by employer if vanpool is insured, excluding driver of vehicle; (7) licensed real estate salespersons and associate real estate brokers, affiliated with licensed real estate broker under written agreement paid on commission basis only and qualifying as independent contractor for federal tax purposes; (8) certain owner operators of motor vehicles entering certain written agreements with motor carriers. Nonresident employee and employer temporarily within state exempt if covered under similar law of other state, if other state law provides reciprocal exemption. (§§9-201-9-236). After July 1, 1979, Act applies to officers and enlisted men of state militia while in "state active duty". (§9-215). Act also applies to any employer and his employees who jointly accept provisions of Act. (§9-215).

Notice of Injury and Claim.—Written notice of injury should be given to employer within ten days of accident or, in case of hernia or death, within 30 days. Employer should report accident and injury to Workers' Compensation Commission within ten days of receipt of notice. (§9-707). Claim should be filed by employee with Workmen's Compensation Commission within 60 days after date of accidental injury. Claim is barred if not so filed unless excused by Commission. (§9-709). Failure to file claim within two years constitutes complete bar, with some exceptions. In event of death, claim must be filed within 18 months from date of death. (§9-710). In cases of occupational disease, notice should be given within one year of date employee knows or has reason to believe that he is suffering from such disease, unless excused by Commission. Claim must be filed within two years unless waived by employer, except claim in case of pulmonary dust disease must be filed within three years. (§9-705). Claim for injury caused by ionizing radiation must be filed within two years of actual knowledge of injury. Claim must be on form prescribed by Commission. (§9-709). Employee may not be discharged solely because he files claim for compensation. (§9-1105).

Investigation.—Commission should investigate claim and, upon application of either party, hold hearing. Hearing is before member of Commission. Commission must make or deny award within 30 days after submission of claim or conclusion of hearing. (§§9-714, 9-736).

Rates of Compensation for Injuries.—(1) Permanent total disability: 66.6% of average weekly wage, but not more than 100% of "average weekly wage of the State of Maryland" nor less than $25 per week (unless established weekly wages are less, in which event compensation is equal to weekly wages), subject to annual cost of living adjustment, during continuance of disability (§9-637); (2) temporary total disability: 66.6% of average weekly wage, but not more than 100% of "average weekly wage of the State of Maryland" nor less than $50 per week (unless established weekly wages are less, in which event compensation is equal to weekly wages), during continuance of disability (§9-621); (3) permanent partial disability: for awards of less than 75 weeks, 33.3% of average weekly wages, but no more than $80 per week for claims arising out of events occurring on or after Jan. 1, 1988 and no more than $82.50 per week for claims occurring on or after Jan. 1, 1989 (§9-628); for awards equal to or greater than 75 weeks but less than 250 weeks, 66.6% of average weekly wages, but no more than 33.3% of average weekly wage of Md. (§9-629); for awards of 250 weeks or more, 66.6% of average weekly wages, but no more than 75% of average weekly wage of Md.; but in no case less than $50 per week (unless established weekly wages are less, in which case compensation is equal to weekly wages), period of compensation fixed by schedule based on character of injury (§9-627); (4) hernia: special provisions apply (§§9-633 and 9-634); (5) temporary partial disability: 50% of difference between average weekly wage and lower post-accident earning capacity, but not more than 50% of "average weekly wage of the State of Maryland" (§9-615). Compensation under (3) and (4) paid in addition to and consecutively with compensation under (2). Unpaid compensation under (1) (up to $45,000), and (4) survives death from cause not compensable under tit. 9 and is paid to surviving dependents, spouse or minor children. If compensable injury causes death within seven years from date of accident, benefits are payable in amounts and to persons specified, right to unpaid compensation surviving death of recipient. (§§9-678 to 9-682). Employee unable to perform previous work entitled to vocational rehabilitation for not more than 24 months, during which period he is compensated as if temporarily totally disabled. (§§9-670 and 9-674). In addition, employer must provide hospital, medical, surgical and similar services as required by Commission. (§9-660).

Subsequent Injury Fund established for payment of certain benefits to employees having permanent impairment and incurring subsequent disability by reason of compensable personal injury. Employers or their insurance carriers pay 5% on all awards against them for permanent disability or death approved on or after June 1, 1963 and before July 1, 1987, and 6¹/₂% on all awards approved on or after July 1, 1987. Fund held, managed and disbursed by State Treasurer. (§§9-802 and 10-214).

Loss or loss of use of both hands, or both arms, or both feet, or both legs, or both eyes or of any two thereof constitutes permanent total disability in absence of conclusive proof to contrary. (§9-636). Person having previously lost or lost use of hand, arm, foot, leg or eye may waive in writing right to compensation for preexisting partial disability upon subsequent accidental injury. (§9-657).

Rates of Compensation for Death.—(1) Without dependent persons: medical and hospital payments as required by Commission, and funeral expenses to maximum of $2,500 (plus assessment not to exceed $4,500, levied by Commission to supplement Uninsured Employers' Fund); (2) with wholly dependent persons: hospital, medical and funeral payments and, in addition, 66.6% average weekly wage, but not less than $25 (unless established weekly wages are less) nor more than 100% of "average weekly wage of the State of Maryland", for period of total dependency with aggregate amount to be not less than $45,000; (3) with partly dependent persons: hospital, medical and

---

See note at head of Digest as to 1998 legislation covered.

See Topical Index in front part of this volume.

LABOR RELATIONS . . . *continued*
funeral payments and, in addition, 66.6% of average weekly wage, but not more than 66.6% of "average weekly wage of the State of Maryland", for period of partial dependency with aggregate amount not to exceed $17,500. (§§9-681 to 9-682).

Where employer fails to secure payment of compensation for injured employees and dependents as provided in Act, employee may sue at common law, and in such suit, defenses of assumption of risk and contributory negligence and fellow servant doctrine are abolished. (§9-509[c]). Criminal penalties also provided for noncomplying individual employers and for officer responsible for general management of noncomplying corporate employer. (§9-1107[c]). Prosecution against employer for failing to maintain workers' compensation insurance must be brought within one year after (1) Commission finds, by order, that employer was uninsured, or (2) uninsured employer's fund makes payment. (courts art. §5-106[k]).

Uninsured Employers' Fund created to provide for payment of awards against uninsured defaulting employers. Fund established and maintained by assessments levied by Director of Fund Board against applicable employers who have failed to secure required insurance or insured employers whose payment of compensation abated by death of claimant. (§§9-1001 to 9-1010).

Occupational Diseases.—Any disease contracted as result of and in course of employment expressly included within Workers' Compensation Act and compensable thereunder. (§§9-101 and 9-502).

Employer's Liability Act.—Part of Workers' Compensation Act. See above.

Unemployment Compensation.—Unemployed individual eligible to receive benefits for 26 weeks if able to, available for, and actively seeking work, if he has registered and reports for work at employment office (with certain exceptions), if he has made claim, if he has been paid for two calendar quarters wages for insured work that total one and one-half times upper limit of division of high quarter wages as to which he qualifies and if he has been paid at least $576.01 for insured work during his high quarter. Employee of educational institution, governmental entity on behalf of such educational institution, or nonprofit organization temporarily unemployed because of established and customary unpaid sabbatical or vacation period disqualified. (§§8-901 through 8-903). Coverage includes domestic service, service not in course of employer's trade or business, agricultural labor, employment by governmental entities of state or its political subdivisions, except when performed by inmate of custodial or penal institution, certain services performed outside U.S., Canada, or Virgin Islands, and employment by certain educational institutions. (§§8-202 through 8-221). Weekly benefits range from $25 to $250, depending on amount of wages paid in high quarter of base period; additional allowances paid for up to five dependent children under 16 years of age verified by social security number or birth certificate. (§8-803). Individual disqualified for certain number of weeks or eligible only for partial benefits if unemployment due to voluntary quitting, gross misconduct, aggravated misconduct, disciplinary measures, stoppage because of labor dispute, if employee fails to apply for or accept suitable work, if he is receiving benefits under another unemployment insurance law or from pension, annuity or retirement payments or if he is receiving severance pay, except if claimant's job was abolished. In event employer pays retirement benefit in form of lump sum payment due to layoff or shutdown of operations, or if within 30 days of receiving lump sum payment claimant provides secretary with proof that payment has been placed in qualified retirement plan, benefit amount not deductible from unemployment insurance benefits. (§§8-1001 through 8-1008). Extended benefits are available to eligible individuals who have exhausted regular benefits during certain periods of high national or state unemployment. Extended benefits limited in certain circumstances if claimant files interstate claims, is disqualified for regular benefits, or does not seek or accept suitable work. (§§8-1101 to 8-1108).

Occupational Safety and Health.—State act similar to federal. (§§5-102 through 5-205). Standards must be at least as stringent as federal. (§5-309). Enforcement by Commissioner of Labor and Industry. (§§5-201—5-217). Federal employers excluded. (§8-212).

Lie Detector Tests.—Employer may not require applicant or employee to submit to lie detector test as condition of employment or continued employment. All applications for employment must contain notice in §3-702. Prohibition inapplicable to federal government or agency thereof, law enforcement agencies of state, counties, or municipal corporations and correctional officers of Baltimore City Jail and Baltimore County, Cecil County, Charles County, Harford County, St. Mary's County, and Washington County Detention Centers, employees of Washington County Detention Center and Calvert County Jail who have direct personal contact with inmates, and employees of Division of Correction assigned to Special Internal Investigative Unit expressly authorized by Commissioner of Correction.

Medical Information.—Applicant may not be required to answer any questions, written or oral, pertaining to any physical, psychological, or psychiatric illness, disability, handicap or treatment unless it bears direct, material and timely relationship to applicant's ability to perform job. (§3-701). Employer may not discharge or discriminate based upon information gained through employee's participation in group medical coverage but may use medical information which: (1) bears direct, material and timely relationship to employee's fitness for job or (2) substantially differs from that falsely provided by employee in job application. (§5-604). Employer who requires any employee, contractor, or other person to be tested for job-related reasons for use or abuse of any controlled dangerous substance or alcohol must have specimen tested at approved laboratory and must permit employee to request independent test of urine or blood sample. Laboratories must comply with federal cutoff standard for positive testing. Employer must provide to employee who tests positive copy of laboratory results, copy of employer's policy on substance or alcohol use or abuse, written notice of any intent to take disciplinary action or terminate employee, and copy of section permitting employees to request independent test of same sample, within 30 days from date test performed. (health-gen. art. §17-214.1).

See also category Business Regulation and Commerce, topic Brokers, subhead Employment Agency.

WORKERS' COMPENSATION LAW:

See topic Labor Relations.

ENVIRONMENT

ENVIRONMENTAL REGULATION:

General Supervision.—Responsibility for execution of Md.'s environmental laws is primarily shared by two state departments, Dep't of the Environment (2500 Broening Highway, Baltimore, 21224) and Dep't of Natural Resources (Tawes State Office Building, 580 Taylor Ave., Annapolis 21401). Former has authority in areas of air quality (env. art. tit. 2), noise (env. art. tit. 3), toxic, carcinogenic and flammable substances (env. art. tit. 6), water management (env. art. tit. 4), geothermal resources (env. art. tit. 5), controlled hazardous substances (env. art. tit. 7), radiation (env. art. tit. 8), water pollution (env. art. tit. 9), wetlands and riparian rights (env. art. tit. 16), deep and strip mining (env. art. tit. 15), and sanitary facilities (bodies politic and corporate created by municipalities to acquire, maintain and operate water, sewer, and/or solid waste systems) (env. art. tit. 9). Latter has general authority in areas of fish and fisheries (nat. res. art. tit. 4), forests and parks (nat. res. art. tit. 5), aquaculture (nat. res. art. tit. 4, subtit. 11A), and wildlife (nat. res. art. tit. 10). Responsibility for regulation of hazardous materials (health gen. art. §§22-501 to 22-508) and nuisance control rests with Dep't of Health and Mental Hygiene (201 W. Preston St., Baltimore 21201).

Maryland Environmental Service, body politic and corporate, provides water supply and waste purification and disposal services to public and private instrumentalities; it is unit within Dep't of Natural Resources and serves as staff for Hazardous Waste Facilities Siting Board. (nat. res. art. §§3-101 to 3-130).

Maryland Environmental Trust, charitable in nature, is established to encourage and promote conservation and environmental study and improvement and to motivate public to support environmental efforts. (nat. res. art. §§3-201 to 3-211).

Maryland Lead Paint Poisoning Commission is established to research lead poisoning prevention and remediation, to promulgate regulations to prevent lead poisoning, and to consult with Dept. of Environment on lead testing standards. (env. art. §§6-801 to 6-852).

Department of the Environment is responsible for development of program for response to emergency oil spillage in waters of State. (env. art. §4-406).

Environmental Trust Fund is created, assets of which consist primarily of proceeds of environmental surcharge levied on each kilowatt hour of electric energy generated in state. Fund is administered by Secretary of Natural Resources to carry out provisions of Power Plant Siting and Research Program, basically designed to provide for required electric power production with minimum adverse environmental impact. (nat. res. art. §§3-301 to 3-307).

Maryland Clean Water Fund is created to identify, monitor and regulate discharge of effluents into waters of State, particularly into Chesapeake Bay. Fund will be administered by Dep't. of the Environment, and will be funded by application fees, permit fees and civil or administrative penalties. (env. art. §9-320).

Drinking Water Loan Fund is created to provide financial assistance to local governments for water supply systems and related costs. (env. art. §9-1605.1).

Maryland Clean Air Fund is created to fund activities related to identifying, monitoring, and regulating air pollution. (env. art. §2-107).

Oil Contaminated Site Environmental Cleanup Fund is created to fund cleanup of sites and groundwater contaminated with oil and to help upgrade and replace underground storage tanks. (env. art. §§4-701 to 4-708).

Northeast Maryland Waste Disposal Authority is created to develop and implement plan for disposal of solid waste. (nat. res. art. §3-903).

Federal-State Mine Reclamation Fund is created to promote reclamation of abandoned mines. Fund is administered by Dep't of Natural Resources and will be funded by federal grants. (nat. res. art. §7-903).

Controlled Hazardous Substance Task Force is created to develop and implement strategy for future reduction, treatment and disposal of controlled hazardous substances. (env. art. §7-205.1). Task Force will remain in effect until Sept. 30, 1995.

Maryland Environmental Policy Act requires that all state agencies prepare environmental effects reports (impact statements) in conjunction with requests for legislative actions significantly affecting quality of environment. (nat. res. art. §§1-301 to 1-305).

Prohibited Acts of Pollution.—

Air.—"Air pollution" is defined as presence in outdoor atmosphere of substances in such quantities and of such duration that they are or will with reasonable certainty be injurious to human, plant, or animal life or to property, or will unreasonably interfere with proper enjoyment of property of others. (env. art. §2-101[b]). Dep't of the Environment required to promulgate primary and secondary ambient air quality standards identical to federal standards, except where none exist or upon request of local government bodies for more restrictive standards. Dep't may establish ambient standards for pollutants for which no national standards have been promulgated and shall promulgate emission standards limiting emissions from particular sources including requirements to assure continuous emission reduction. In areas where attainment of federal ambient air quality standards is achieved, emission standards shall be no more restrictive than necessary to attain and maintain such federal ambient standards, except such restriction does not apply for: (1) New source performance standards; (2) federal standards for prevention of significant deterioration; (3) national emission standards for hazardous pollutants; (4) emissions of substances for which no federal ambient standards promulgated; or (5) political subdivision that requests more restrictive standard. (env. art. §§2-301 to 2-304). Governor may issue executive order upon advice of Secretary of the Environment, proclaiming air pollution emergency and may, subject thereto, require immediate elimination of specifically identifiable sources of pollution. (env. art. §2-105).

Federally required motor vehicle emission control devices may not be altered or removed, nor may vehicle be operated without such devices if originally so equipped except in certain circumstances. (trans. art. §22-402.1). Dep't of the Environment is empowered to establish Low Emissions Vehicle Program, functionally equivalent to

See note at head of Digest as to 1998 legislation covered.

See Topical Index in front part of this volume.

MD – 35

ENVIRONMENTAL REGULATION . . . *continued*

California program under certain conditions, but may not require sale or use of specific vehicle fuels other than those certified by EPA. (env. art. tit. 2, subtit. 7).

Noise.—Dep't of the Environment is responsible for developing environmental noise standards, developing plan to attain and maintain those standards, coordinating state programs, and keeping records on sound limits adopted. (env. art. §§3-103, 3-401). Noise control regulations that apply to Dep't of Transportation facilities are jointly adopted by Dep'ts of Transportation and the Environment. (env. art. §3-401[d][2]). With certain minor exceptions, any county or municipality may adopt noise control regulations equal to or more stringent than state standards. (env. art. §3-105). Specific laws require establishment of noise zones and plans to reduce or eliminate "impacted land use areas" by administrators of all licensed airports. (trans. art. tit. 5, subtit. 8).

Administrator of Motor Vehicle Administration adopted regulations establishing maximum sound level limits for operation of existing and new motor vehicles; emergency vehicles exempt. (trans. art. §§22-601, 22-604, 22-605). No person may operate, and no owner may permit operation of, vehicle in manner to exceed limits so established. (trans. art. §§22-602, 21-1117). No person may sell or lease any vehicle manufactured after July 1, 1974 with maximum sound level potential exceeding limits established for new vehicles; no vehicle manufactured after July 1, 1974 may be titled or registered in state unless, when first sold for purposes other than resale, it complies with limits set for new vehicles. (trans. art. §22-606). Manufacturer, distributor, importer or agent must file, for each make and model sold in state, certificate with Motor Vehicle Administration that vehicle complies with noise control law. (trans. art. §22-608). Every motor vehicle having internal combustion engine must be equipped with exhaust muffler system in good working order, and no muffler bypass device may be used. (trans. art. §22-402). No person may modify exhaust system or other noise abatement device of vehicle to be operated in state so that noise exceeds that emitted by vehicle as originally manufactured; nor may person operate vehicle so modified in state. (trans. art. §22-609). No person may sell or offer muffler or other device which, when installed, will permit operation with greater sound level emission than that emitted from vehicle as originally manufactured. Manufacturer of such device must file certificate that his products sold in state comply with noise control law. (trans. art. §22-610).

Dep't of Natural Resources has published maximum sound level limits and enforcement regulations for operation of motor-driven off-highway vehicles in state parks, forests and other lands subject to Dep't jurisdiction and for operation generally of new motor-driven off-highway vehicles wherever operated. (nat. res. art. §5-209). No person may sell or lease such vehicle if it is new and has maximum sound level potential exceeding limits. Manufacturers, distributor, importer or agent must file certificate under oath with Dep't of Natural Resources that each make and model sold in state complies with noise control law. (nat. res. art. §5-209[d]). Dep't has published sound level limit regulations for operation of pleasure craft on state waters. (nat. res. art. §8-704[f]).

Solid Waste.—It is unlawful to manage industrial waste in manner which pollutes waters of state. (env. art. §9-224). Sewage sludge disposal is regulated by Dep't of the Environment (env. art. §9-230 et seq.), which also administers sewage sludge utilization fund (env. art. §9-244). Handling of hazardous waste, termed "controlled hazardous substances," are closely regulated by env. art. tit. 7, subtit. 2, and rules and regulations thereunder. No one may store or dispose of, or transport for storage or disposal, controlled hazardous substances except in permitted facility and no one may falsify required information. (env. art. §7-265). Transfer of hazardous material is regulated by env. art. tit. 7, subtit. 2, and rules and regulations thereunder.

Water.—It is unlawful to discharge any pollutant into waters of state unless in compliance with env. art. tit. 9 and rules and regulations thereunder. (env. art. §9-322). Person discharging or permitting discharge of oil must report incident immediately to Dep't of the Environment regardless of whether appropriate federal authority is also notified. (env. art. §§4-405, 4-410 to 411). It is unlawful to distribute, possess, sell, apply, or offer to sell or apply any antifouling paints containing tributyltin with certain exceptions. (agric. art. §§5-901 to 5-906). Special provisions govern pollution control of Chesapeake, its tributaries and surrounding wetlands (env. art. tit. 5, subtit. 11 and nat. res. art. tit. 8, subtit. 18; agric. art. tit. 8, subtits. 6, 7), sediment and waste control in Severn and Patuxent River watersheds (env. art. tit. 4, subtit. 3), flood prevention, conservation, sediment and erosion protection and urban development in Patuxent River Watershed (nat. res. art. tit. 8, subtit. 13) and land clearing and construction in designated Atlantic coast beach erosion control district (nat. res. art. §8-1102).

Enforcement.—

Air Quality.—Upon violation of Air Quality Control Act, or any standard or regulation, Dep't of the Environment may serve upon alleged violator written notice by certified mail of violation specifying facts and law involved and either requiring violator to appear and show cause at hearing or ordering compliance within specified time. Appeal from order is directly to circuit court in accordance with art. 10 and Md. Rules. (env. art. §§2-602 to 2-604, 2-607). Dep't may seek injunctive relief, civil penalty, or criminal penalty. (env. art. §§2-609 to 2-610.1). Criminal penalties available for knowing violations. (§2-609.1). Dep't may grant temporary fuel variance from rule, regulation or order. (env. art. §§2-501 to 2-505). Air Quality Control Act gives rise to no actionable rights, findings of fact or presumptions of law for benefit of any person other than state. (env. art. §2-106).

Noise.—Sound level limits for various categories of land use set by Dep't of the Environment, and regulations promulgated by Dep't in connection therewith, are to be enforced by said Dep't, using facilities and services of appropriate local agencies to maximum extent possible. (env. art. §3-403). All units of state government having jurisdiction over facility or engaging in activity which may result in emission of noise must comply with federal, state and interstate noise control requirements. (env. art., §3-503). Regulations concerning noise control in areas near state and non-state owned airports are to be enforced by State Aviation Administrator or political subdivision in which airport is located. (trans. art. tit. 5, subtitle 8).

Solid Waste.—Upon finding that waters of state are polluted by discharge of sewage sludge or handling of industrial waste so as to create likelihood of menace to public health or comfort, Secretary of the Environment may issue order to cease polluting. (env. art. §§9-220 to 9-224). Upon issuance of such order, industrial facility that does not have disposal permit is required to obtain one. (env. art. §9-224[c]). Failure to obey order results in civil penalty. (env. art. §9-268). After notice and hearing, Dep't of the Environment may revoke or suspend permit for violation of controlled hazardous substance law. (env. art. §7-257). Dep't of the Environment may also sue to enjoin violation. (env. art. §7-263). Violations are punishable by civil and criminal penalties. (env. art. §§7-265 to 267).

Water Quality.—Upon violation of env. art. tit. 9 or any rule or regulation promulgated thereunder, Dep't of the Environment must serve upon alleged violator written complaint. Notice by publication permitted. Alleged violators have all rights of parties in contested case hearings under Administrative Procedure Act. Appeal from final decision is directly to circuit court in accordance with art. 10, and Md. Rules. (env. art. §§9-334 to 9-343). Civil and criminal penalties and injunctive relief available. (env. art. §§9-339, 9-342, 9-343). Upon violation of env. art. tit. 4 attorney general may prosecute violator. (env. art. §4-502). All common law, equitable, and statutory rights in any person survive to allow suppression of nuisances or abatement of pollution. (env. art. §4-403).

Private Action.—State, state agencies, political subdivisions and their agents, and private persons have standing to bring action for mandamus or equitable relief, including declaratory relief, against officer or agency of state or political subdivision for failure to perform nondiscretionary duty arising from environmental laws, or for failure to enforce such laws, including whether permit or order has been unlawfully issued or is being violated. Procedural and standing requirements imposed. Subtitle does not create new cause of action or authorize suit for money damages, but does not abrogate any previously existing actions. Court must approve compromise or discontinuance of suit, and may award costs including attorney and witness fees against plaintiff acting in bad faith. (nat. res. art. §§1-501 to 1-508).

Penalties.—

Violation of Air Quality Control Act, or any standard or regulation thereunder, or any order of Dep't of the Environment, is civil offense carrying penalty of not more than $25,000 per day except that Secretary of Dep't of the Environment authorized to adopt rules and regulations specifying situation in which violator is subject to noncompliance penalty similar to §120 of Clean Air Act. (env. art. §§2-610, 2-612). Also, Dep't may seek injunctive relief. (env. art. §2-609). Dep't may settle any claim for penalty and remit 75% of any penalty paid where within three years violation has been removed or order met. (env. art. §2-610[c]). Also, Dep't may impose administrative penalties of up to $2,500 per violation, not to exceed $50,000 total, but only upon providing alleged violator with written notice of proposed action and opportunity for informal meeting. (env. art. §2-610.1). Criminal penalties available for knowing violations. (env. art. §2.609.1). Any violator may submit plan for compliance and, if approved, will not be considered in violation so long as plan is followed. (env. art. §2-611).

Violations of Solid Waste Law.—Violations of solid waste laws generally subject to same penalties as violations of Water Pollution Control laws, except for violations of sewage sludge requirements or laws concerning infectious waste in landfills. (env. art. §9-268). Violations of sewage sludge laws subject to civil penalties of $10,000 per day, not to exceed $50,000, and/or administrative penalties of $1,000 per violation, not to exceed $50,000 total. (env. art. §§9-269 to 9-270). For violations of hazardous waste laws, following are felonies punishable by fine not to exceed $100,000, five years imprisonment, or both: (1) Storing or disposing of any controlled hazardous substance, except in permitted facility; (2) transporting for treatment, storage or disposal of any controlled hazardous substance, except to permitted facility; (3) falsifying information required under law, regulations, or permit; and (4) authorizing, directing or permitting any of above offenses. (env. art. §7-265). Knowing violations subject to $250,000 fine and/or 15 years imprisonment. Violations are punishable by administrative penalty of not more than $25,000 per day of violation, not to exceed $100,000 total. (env. art. §7-266[b]). In addition, violations are punishable by civil penalty not to exceed $25,000. (env. art. §7-266[a]). Except for knowing violations, violations are misdemeanors punishable by not more than $25,000 per day of violation and imprisonment not to exceed one year or both for first offense, and $50,000 per day of violation, imprisonment of not to exceed two years, or both after first conviction. (env. art. §7-267).

Violation of Noise Control Law.—Wilful violation of Environmental Noise Control Act or of regulation or order issued thereunder, is civil offense carrying penalty of not more than $10,000 per day. Dep't of the Environment may also seek injunctive relief. Secretary of the Environment may settle any claim and may remit 75% of penalty paid, where violator eliminates violation or satisfies order within one year. Any violator may submit plan for compliance and, if approved, will not be considered in violation so long as plan is followed. (env. art. §§3-405 to 3-407).

Violation of Water Pollution Control Law.—Violation of env. art. tit. 9, or of rule, regulation, order or permit issued pursuant thereto, makes violator liable to penalty of not more than $10,000 per day, recoverable in civil action. Violation is also misdemeanor punishable by fine of not more than $25,000 or by imprisonment for not more than one year or both; in addition, violator may be enjoined. Conviction for second or later offense is subject to fine of not more than $50,000 per day of violation or imprisonment not exceeding two years or both, and to injunction. Each day of violation is separate offense. Person knowingly making false statement in document or report filed or required to be maintained, or knowingly rendering monitoring device inaccurate, is subject, upon conviction, to fine not exceeding $10,000 or to imprisonment for not more than six months or both. In addition, Dep't of the Environment may assess civil penalty of $1,000 per day, not exceeding total of $50,000, after hearing and finding that violation exists. Refusal or failure to pay latter penalty subjects violator's real and personal property to lien in favor of state. (env. art. §§9-342, 9-343).

Dep't of the Environment must charge and collect compensatory fee from person responsible for any oil spillage; and person is liable to third party for damage to real or personal property. (env. art. §§4-408, 4-409). Violation of licensing requirements for oil transfer facility is misdemeanor, punishable by fine up to $10,000 plus any accrued but unpaid license fees. (env. art. §4-411[e]). Violation of prohibition against discharge of oil from ship or of duty to report oil discharge is misdemeanor, punishable by criminal penalties of $50,000 and/or one year imprisonment, and/or civil penalties of $25,000 per violation. (env. art. §§4-410, 4-417 to 4-418). Vessel discharging oil may be held in port until penalty is paid, and penalty is lien on vessel. (env. art. §4-418). In addition, unless

---

See note at head of Digest as to 1998 legislation covered.

See Topical Index in front part of this volume.

ENVIRONMENTAL REGULATION . . . *continued*

otherwise provided by statute, violation of env. art. tit. 4 is misdemeanor subject to fine of not more than $500 or imprisonment of not more than three months, or both. (env. art. §4-501). Violators may also be subject to civil penalties of $10,000 per day of violation, up to total of $100,000. (env. art. §4-417[d]).

Special penalties for sewage treatment plants of up to $5,000 (administrative) or $25,000 (civil) per month. (env. art. §9-342.1).

Violation of law regulating antifouling paints is misdemeanor punishable by fine not exceeding $2,500. (agric. art. §5-906).

Violation of Geothermal Resources Law.—Violator of requirements of subtitle 8A of nat. res. art. subject to civil penalty not exceeding $10,000. Also, Department may seek injunction through Attorney General. (env. art. §5-608).

Permits.—

Air Quality Control.—Persons responsible for installations (source capable of generating, causing or reducing emissions) must register with Dep't of the Environment, except where installation is one for which permit to operate is obtained or where installation is of type specified as not required to obtain permit to construct. Where proposed changes will result in inaccuracy of registered information, re-registration is prerequisite. Change in ownership requires new registration. (Comar 26.11.02.02). Unless exempted by Dep't of the Environment, owner or operator must report by telephone to Dep't onset and termination of occurrence of excess emissions lasting or expected to last for one hour or more from installation requiring permit to operate. Dep't may require written report. (Comar 26.11.01.07). No person may construct, modify or alter installation without first obtaining permit to construct from Dep't, unless it is on list of excepted installations. No person may cause or allow certain listed installations to be used or operated without first having obtained permit to operate from Dep't. Permit requirements do not apply to: Changes, repairs or maintenance which cannot change quality, nature or quantity of emissions; machinery and equipment normally used in mobile manner; boilers used exclusively for operation of steam engines related to farm and domestic use; generating stations constructed by electric companies; actual construction of buildings (apart from emission producing machinery they house); nor parking garages or parking lots. (env. art. §§2-401 to 2-403; Comar 26.11.02).

Solid Waste.—Permit required to install, materially alter or materially extend water supply system, sewerage system, or refuse disposal system installed, altered, or extended after July 1, 1988. (env. art. §9-204). Sewage sludge utilization permit required (env. art. §9-231). Facility permit and reports required for those who own, establish, operate or maintain controlled hazardous substance facilities. (env. art. §7-232). Transporters, drivers and vehicles must be certified to transport controlled hazardous substances. (env. art. §7-249). Permit required for hazardous material transfer facility. (env. art. §§7-102 to 7-103). Hazardous Waste Facilities Siting Program transferred to Dep't of the Environment from Dep't of Natural Resources. (env. art. §§1-406, 7-401 to 7-413).

Water Quality Control.—Oil transfer facility must be licensed by Dep't of Environment. (env. art. §4-411). Vessel carrying or receiving more than 25 barrels of oil and discharging or receiving cargo of bulk oil in state must post bond of $500 per gross ton of vessel with Dep't of Environment. Failure to post bond is misdemeanor; vessels presenting evidence of financial responsibility to Dep't of Environment are exempt. (env. art. §4-407). Person may not engage in specific commercial or industrial operation involving transfer, storage, separating, removing, treating or disposing of oil or other unctuous substance without permit from Dep't of Environment. (env. art. §4-405).

Person may not construct defined facility (oil terminal and related facilities) in coastal area without permit from Dep't of Environment. (Coastal Facilities Review Act, env. art. tit. 14, subtit. 5).

Permit must be obtained from Dep't of the Environment in situations which will result in discharge of pollutants, or increase in such discharge, into state waters, including underground waters. Administration may apply effluent and pretreatment standards for introduction of certain pollutants by industrial users into publicly owned treatment works. (env. art. §§9-322 to 9-332).

Well may not be drilled until Dep't of the Environment issues permit. (env. art. §9-1306). Well drillers must be licensed. (env. art. tit. 13). Permit from Dep't of Environment required for appropriation or use of state waters, whether surface or underground, or for commencement of construction of structure which may appropriate or use such waters, other than use for domestic and farming purposes. (env. art. §5-502). Permit from Dep't of Environment required for construction, reconstruction or repair of reservoir, dam or waterway obstruction, or for making change in waterway obstruction, or for changing course, current or cross section of construction and operation of certain agricultural drainage systems, stream or other nontidal waters. Exception for certain small ponds, certain streams, and removal or demolition of residential structures. (env. art. §5-503). Permit from Dep't required for construction, reconstruction, change or addition to conduit, pipeline, cable, trestle, etc. in bed or waters of Potomac River. (env. art. §5-504).

Permit from Dep't of the Environment required to install or alter any water supply system, sewerage system, refuse disposal system for public use, refuse disposal system that is solid waste acceptance facility, and sewerage sludge utilization system. (env. art. §§9-204, 9-231). Dep't must approve plans for water and sewerage service before subdivided land is marketed or any permanent building is erected thereon. (env. art. §9-206).

Waterworks, wastewater works and industrial wastewater works are classified, and qualifications of superintendents who are authorized to manage each class are set. Dep't of the Environment regulates superintendents for waterworks, wastewater works, and industrial wastewater works. (env. art. tit. 12).

Wetlands.—With limited exceptions, person may not dredge or fill on state wetlands without license from Board of Public Works. (env. art. §16-202). Secretary of Environment may promulgate rules and regulations for dredging, filling, removing or otherwise altering or polluting private wetlands. (env. art. §16-302). Person proposing to conduct activity on any wetlands not authorized by such rules and regulations must apply for permit from Secretary; Secretary must advise applicant of extent of state wetlands involved in proposed activity and must indicate method of compliance with license requirements above, hold hearing, and render decision. In granting permit, Secretary

may impose conditions or limitations and may require bond. (env. art. tit. 16, subtit. 3). Permit is required to undertake any regulated activity in nontidal wetlands. Certain mitigation and best management practice requirements must be met. (env. art. tit. 5, subtit. 9).

Pesticides.—Distribution, sale, delivery or transportation of pesticides is subject to regulation by Secretary of Agriculture. (agric. art. tit. 5, subtitles 1, 2). Person desiring to distribute, sell, deliver or transport may be required to register pesticide annually. (agric. art. §5-105). Certain applicators, including public agencies, and consultants must obtain permits and certificates, and places of business engaged in application and consulting must obtain licenses. (agric. art. §§5-206 to 5-210.5).

Geothermal resources defined as natural heat of earth higher than 120° fahrenheit, energy resulting from such heat, medium containing heat and minerals or other products obtained from naturally heated material but excluding hydrocarbon substances. Permit from Dep't of Environment required to conduct exploration for geothermal resources, and to appropriate, use, or construct facility for appropriation or use of resources. (env. art. tit. 5, subtit. 6).

Seismic Operations.—Permit from Dep't. of Environment required to conduct seismic operations in state and prohibiting use of explosives in seismic operations conducted on waters and tributaries of Chesapeake Bay. (env. art. §14-107).

Appalachian States Low-Level Radioactive Waste Compact entered into. (env. art. §§7-301 to 7-306).

Asbestos removal may be performed only by businesses licensed by Dep't of Environment. (env. art. tit. 6, subtit. 4).

Lead paint abatement contracting, training, and inspecting may be performed only by businesses/persons accredited by Dep't of the Environment. (env. art. §§6-1001 to 6-1005).

Lead Poisoning Prevention Program established in 1993. Set up Commission to promulgate abatement regulations for residential rental properties constructed before 1950. (env. art. §§6-807 to 6-809). Such properties must be registered with Dept. of Environment by Dec. 31, 1995. (env. art. §§6-811 to 6-813). Owners must test and abate lead hazards by first change in occupancy after Feb. 24, 1996 according to specified standards. (env. art. §§6-815 to 6-822). Owners must provide lead hazard information to new renters on execution of any lease after Feb. 24, 1996 and to old renters no later than May 23, 1996. (env. art. §6-823). Bases of owner liability statutorily defined. (env. art. §§6-826 to 6-841). Established Lead Poisoning Prevention Fund, funded by annual fees paid by affected properties and by penalties paid by violators to Dept. of Environment. (env. art. §§6-843 to 6-845). $10 per day administrative penalty for properties not registered. (env. art. §6-849). $250 per day civil penalty for violation not cured within 20 days of notice. $15,000 civil penalty for knowing violation. (env. art. §6-850).

Interstate Environment Compact adopted. (nat. res. art. §3-501).

Ocean Beach Replenishment Fund established. (nat. res. art. §§8-1103 to 1104).

Susquehanna River Basin Compact entered into. (env. art. §5-301). Potomac River Basin Compact repealed. (1987, c. 234).

Radon Testing.—Regulated by env. art. §8-305.

ESTATES AND TRUSTS

ADMINISTRATION:

See topic Executors and Administrators.

ADVANCEMENTS:

See topic Descent and Distribution.

ALLOWANCES:

See topic Executors and Administrators.

CLAIMS:

See topic Executors and Administrators; category Civil Actions and Procedure, topic Pleading.

DEATH:

Uniform Absence as Evidence of Death and Absentees' Property Act repealed. See category Property, topic Absentees.

Definition.—Death occurs when, based on ordinary standards of medical practice, individual has sustained irreversible cessation of circulatory and respiratory functions or of all functions of entire brain (including brain stem). Definition is applicable for all purposes, including civil and criminal proceedings. Death must be pronounced before vital organs are removed for transplantation. (health gen. art. §§5-201 to 5-202). This statute represents Uniform Determination of Death Act with minor variations.

Survivorship.—Uniform Simultaneous Death Act adopted. (courts art. §§10-801 to 10-807). If descendant, ancestor or descendant of ancestor fails to survive decedent by 30 days he is deemed to have predeceased decedent for purposes of intestate succession. If time of death of decedent or of descendant, ancestor or descendant of ancestor, or of both, cannot be determined, person deemed not to have survived decedent by 30 days for purposes of intestate succession. (est. & tr. art. §3-110). Legatee, other than spouse, who fails to survive testator for 30 days is deemed to predecease testator absent will provision creating contrary presumption. (est. & tr. art. §4-401).

Action for Wrongful Death.—Only one action may be maintained against person whose wrongful act causes death of another. (courts art. §3-904[f]). Where cause of action arose in Md., suit must be brought in names of all persons who are or may be entitled to damages (viz., wife, husband, parent and child of decedent or, if no such persons, then any person related to decedent by blood or marriage who was wholly dependent upon him), whether or not they join in action, names of those not joining

---

DEATH . . . *continued*
being preceded by words: "to the use of . . . ." (R. P. 15-1001). Such action must be commenced within three years after death unless death caused by occupational disease, in which case action must be commenced within ten years of death or three years after cause of death was discovered, whichever is shorter. (courts art. §3-904[g]; see also art. 101, §58 regarding liability of third party other than employer). Action against estate of decedent must be commenced within six months after date of decedent's death, or within two months after representative delivers written notice to creditor, whichever is shorter (unless claim is covered by insurance) (est. & tr. art. §§8-104[d][e], 8-103[a]). For estates of decedents dying before Oct. 1, 1992, period is nine months after date of death, or within two months after representative delivers written notice to creditor, whichever is shorter. Where wrongful act causing death occurred outside state, substantive law of state of occurrence is applied. (courts art. §3-903[a]). For death of spouse or minor child, damages are not limited to pecuniary loss but may include damages for mental anguish, emotional pain and suffering, and loss of society, companionship, care, guidance, etc. (courts art. §3-904[d]). For death of unmarried child not minor (21 yrs. or younger or parent contributed 50% or more of support) damages not limited to pecuniary loss but may include damages for mental anguish, emotional pain and suffering, loss of society, companionship, guidance etc. (courts art. §3-904[e]). Action for expenses and pain and suffering of person whose death was not instantaneous must be brought by his executor or administrator. (See 104 Md. 332, 65 A. 49.) Funeral expenses of decedent not exceeding $5,000 (amount allowed under est. & tr. art. §8-106[b]) may be recovered. (est. & tr. art. §7-401[x][2]). There is no other statutory limitation on amount of recovery for death.

Living Wills.—See topic Wills, subhead Living Will.

Death Certificate.—See category Documents and Records, topic Records, subhead Vital Statistics.

Uniform Anatomical Gift Act adopted. (est. & tr. art. §§4-501 to 4-512).

DECEDENTS' ESTATES:

See topics Descent and Distribution, Executors and Administrators, Wills; category Debtor and Creditor, topic Homesteads.

DESCENT AND DISTRIBUTION:

References are to Estates and Trusts Article of Code unless otherwise indicated.

Real property and personal property both pass directly to personal representative for administration and distribution (§1-301) as follows:

Entire estate, or if there be surviving spouse, excess over share of spouse (see subhead Surviving Spouse, infra), descends and is distributed as follows, each class of which member is living taking to exclusion of subsequent classes: (1) To surviving issue by representation; (2) to surviving parents equally or, if only one, to that one; otherwise, to issue of parents by representation; (3) one-half to surviving paternal grandparents equally or, if only one, to that one; otherwise, to issue of paternal grandparents by representation; and one-half to surviving maternal grandparents equally or, if only one, to that one; otherwise, to issue of maternal grandparents by representation; if pair of grandparents or their issue fail to survive, their one-half is distributable as provided for other one-half; (4) one-quarter to each pair of great-grandparents equally or to survivor of each pair or, if neither survives, to issue of pair by representation; if any pair of great-grandparents and issue fails to survive, its one-quarter is distributable as provided for other three-quarters; (5) to living stepchildren equally (and issue of deceased stepchildren by representation), if born to non-divorced legal spouse. (§§3-103, 3-104). "Issue" is defined as every living lineal descendant except lineal descendant of living lineal descendant. (§1-209). If descendant, ancestor or descendant of ancestor fails to survive decedent by 30 days, he is deemed to have predeceased decedent and is not entitled to rights of heir. (§3-110). See topic Death, subhead Survivorship.

Degrees of kindred computed by civil law method by counting from decedent up to common ancestor and then down to claimant. (§1-203).

Surviving spouse takes: One-half if there is minor surviving child; $15,000 and one-half of residue if there is surviving issue, but no surviving minor child, or if there is no surviving issue, but surviving parent; whole estate if there is no surviving issue or parent. (§3-102). Person cannot be surviving spouse if person: (1) Is validly and absolutely divorced from decedent, or if marriage validly annulled; (2) voluntarily appears in foreign proceeding where decedent obtained absolute divorce or annulment, even if not recognized in Md.; (3) was remarried after decedent obtained decree of divorce or annulment; or (4) was convicted of bigamy while married to decedent. (§1-202).

Half blood and whole blood relatives of same degree share alike. (§1-204).

Posthumous child of intestate takes as though born in his lifetime, but posthumous child of another cannot take in his own right. (§3-107).

Illegitimate children and their issue inherit from mother and from each other as though born in lawful wedlock. They inherit from father only if father has been adjudicated such, acknowledges in writing or openly and notoriously recognizes that he is such, or marries mother and orally acknowledges that he is such, or adopts child. (§§1-207, 1-208).

Artificial Insemination.—Child conceived by artificial insemination of married woman with her husband's consent is considered legitimate. Consent of husband presumed. (§1-206[b]).

Adopted children treated as natural children of adopting parents and not as children of either natural parent, unless adopted by spouse of natural parent. (§1-207). See category Family, topic Adoption.

Determination of Heirship.—No special proceedings.

Advancements.—Property given to heir during lifetime is treated as advancement only if declared or acknowledged by heir or donor in writing as such. Advancement to heir other than surviving spouse does not increase share of surviving spouse. (§3-106).

Family Allowance.—See topic Executors and Administrators, subhead Allowances.

Election.—Dower and curtesy have been abolished. (§3-202).

Renunciation.—Md. Uniform Disclaimer of Property Interests Act adopted. (§§9-201 to 9-209). See topic Wills.

Nonresidents.—As to distribution to nonresidents of U.S., see category Citizenship, topic Aliens.

Escheat.—If intestate leaves no surviving spouse or relations entitled to take, entire estate is paid to board of education of county or Baltimore City for use of public schools, or, if intestate was recipient of long-term care benefits under Maryland Medical Assistance Program at time of death, to Department of Health and Mental Hygiene. Provision is made for subsequent repayment without interest to relative or personal representative of relative within fifth degree. (§3-105).

Uniform Disposition of Unclaimed Property Act adopted. (comm. law art. tit. 17). See category Property, topic Absentees.

See also topic Executors and Administrators.

ESTATES:

See category Property, topic Real Property.

EXECUTORS AND ADMINISTRATORS:

References are to Estates and Trusts Article of Code unless otherwise indicated.

Upon death, legal title to all real and personal property passes directly to personal representative for administration and distribution. (§1-301). "Personal representative" means executor or administrator. (§1-101[p]). Title 6 of Maryland Rules contains rules governing opening and administration of estates and various forms to be used.

Letters of administration may be granted administratively by register of wills or judicially by orphans' court of county or city in which decedent was domiciled, or, if not domiciled in Md., where largest part of decedent's property in Md. is located. (§§5-101, 5-103; R. P. 6-111[a]).

Preferences in Right to Administer.—Preference given in granting administrations as follows: (1) Personal representatives named in will admitted to probate; (2) surviving spouse and children of intestate decedent; or surviving spouse of testate decedent; (3) residuary legatees; (4) relations entitled to share in estate in following order: children of testate decedent; grandchildren; parents; brothers and sisters; (5) other relations who apply; (6) largest creditor who applies; (7) any person having pecuniary interest who applies; (8) any other person. (§5-104).

Right to administer may be renounced but may not be delegated. (§5-105; 107 Md. 357, 68 Atl. 573). Subject to priorities, persons entitled to serve may consent to another's serving. (R. P. 6-313, 6-314).

Personal representative of personal representative not entitled to administer estate of first decedent but must take action to protect it and to have new personal representative appointed. (§6-304).

Eligibility and Competency.—Qualifications same for executor or administrator. Trust company or corporation authorized by law to be personal representative can act. (§5-105[a]). No person under 18 years of age, mentally incompetent, convicted of serious crime or not citizen of U.S., unless spouse of decedent and permanent resident, can act. No full-time judge of state, federal or probate court, and no register of wills or clerk of court may serve unless surviving spouse or related to decedent within third degree. (§5-105[b]). Nonresident may act, but must file with register of wills instrument designating agent on whom process may be served. (§5-105[b]). See also category Business Regulation and Commerce, topic Banks and Banking.

Bond.—Penalty sum fixed by court or register of wills in amount not exceeding probable maximum value of personal estate less value of any posted collateral and any cash made subject to order of court. (§6-102[e]). Penalty sum may be increased or decreased at court's discretion for good cause at any time during administration. Surety may be corporation authorized to act as surety in Md. or individual approved by register. No bond save for taxes and debts of testator will be required if testator by will excuses bond or if all interested persons waive bond. For cause shown, additional bond may be required. National banking association and trust company not required to give bond. (§6-102). For form of bond see R. P. 6-312.

Oath.—No oath or affirmation required, only verification under penalties of perjury, which is required on petition for probate, inventories, accounts and other documents reciting facts. (§§1-102, 5-206).

Issuance of Letters.—After petition for probate acted upon and bond filed, certificate of letters of administration is issued by register of wills. (§§6-103, 6-104).

Removal.—Personal representative is subject to removal by Orphan's Court after hearing establishing misrepresentation of facts leading to appointment; wilful disregard of court order; incapacity or inability to effectively discharge duties and powers; mismanagement of property; failure to maintain designated agent for service of process; inexcusable failure to perform material duty. (§6-306). After notice and hearing, personal representative may exercise only powers of special administrator. (§§6-306[c], 6-403). Upon written application, any of personal representative's powers and duties may be suspended. (§6-301).

Special kinds of administration, such as c.t.a., d.b.n., ad colligendum, durante minoritate, pendente lite and ancillary, abolished effective Jan. 1, 1970. (§12-102). Upon petition, suitable person giving bond may be appointed special administrator to protect property pending appointment of personal representative or of successor personal representative. (§§1-101[t], 6-401).

Public Administrators.—No such office.

Inventory and Appraisal.—Inventory of all real and personal property, tangible and intangible, including debts owed decedent, listing fair market value and any encumbrance, must be filed by personal representative within three months after his appointment. (§7-201). Listed corporate stocks, over the counter securities, debts owed decedent, including bonds and notes, and bank and savings and loan accounts may be appraised by personal representative. Other property must be appraised either by one or more official appraisers appointed by register or by one or more special appraisers

See note at head of Digest as to 1998 legislation covered.

See Topical Index in front part of this volume.

EXECUTORS AND ADMINISTRATORS . . . *continued*
employed by personal representative. (§7-202). Value assigned to any inventory item may be revised upon petition. (§7-204).

General Powers and Duties.—Personal representative is made fiduciary by statute and must take possession or control of decedent's real and personal estate and, after paying debts and taxes, must settle and distribute estate and file accounts within time provided. (§§7-101, 7-102). If conferred by will or statute, personal representative may exercise power without application to, approval or ratification by orphans' court. (§7-401). Unless limited by will or by court order, in addition to powers conferred by will, common law or statute, personal representative has broad general powers, including: to retain assets in form received from decedent; to perform contracts; to deposit funds in checking accounts, insured interest-bearing accounts or short term loan arrangements; to vote stocks; to hold securities in name of nominee; to insure estate property; to compromise obligations; to pay taxes and expenses; to sell or exercise stock subscriptions or options; to consent to or oppose reorganizations, dissolutions or liquidations; to pay funeral expenses as provided in §8-106; to employ auditors and investment advisors; to prosecute and defend legal actions; to continue unincorporated businesses for four months (which period can be extended by court order in proceeding in which all interested persons are parties); to incorporate any business of decedent; to exercise options in insurance contracts; to pay valid claims and discharge mortgages and security interests; to convey redeemable reversions to owners of leasehold estates; to grant releases of mortgages and security interests; to make partial and final distributions in cash or in kind during administration; to invest in, sell, mortgage, pledge, exchange or lease property; to borrow money; to extend or renew obligations owed to estate; and to designate self on any document as executor or administrator as case may be. (§7-401). Where power is not conferred by will or by §7-401, order of court must be obtained. (§7-402). Good faith purchaser or mortgagee is protected and is not required to see to proper application of assets paid to personal representative. (§7-404).

Notice of appointment must be given to heirs and legatees, notifying persons who object to appointment or to probate of will to file objections within six months of appointment, unless extended by law; certificate of publication of such notice must be filed with register. (§7-103; R. P. 6-311). Within 20 days after appointment, personal representative must deliver to register text of published notice and list of names and addresses of heirs and legatees, to whom register will send copy of notice. (§7-104). Notice of appointment must be published once a week for three weeks in newspaper of general circulation in county of appointment. (R. P. 6-331).

Notice to creditors is contained in notice of appointment and must be published in local newspaper once a week for three successive weeks, notifying creditors to present claims within earlier of six months after decedent's death or two months after personal representative gives required notice by mail. For deaths before Oct. 1, 1992, notice must state that claims must be presented within earlier of nine months after death or two months after notice. (§7-103; R. P. 6-311). Personal representative is required to make reasonably diligent effort to identify and locate creditors and give notice by mail. (R. P. 6-401).

Presentation of Claims.—Claims may be made by filing with register or personal representative or by filing suit. (§8-104[c]; R. P. 6-413). Currently, creditors must file claim or commence suit within earlier of nine months after decedent's death or two months after personal representative gives required notice, or be barred from suing either personal representative or distributees, but period of limitation does not apply to actions covered by insurance to extent of insurance, nor to claims against Md. Automobile Insurance Fund. nor to foreclosure of lien claims. (§§8-103, 8-104). For estates of decedents dying before Oct. 1, 1992, period is nine months from decedent's death.

Proof of Claims.—Claimant should file with personal representative verified written statement of claim, including basis, name and address of claimant, amount claimed, date due if unmatured, nature of contingency, if any, and description of security, if any; or claimant may file verified written statement with register of wills, with copy to personal representative, in substantially following form (R. P. 6-413):

Form

[R. P. 6-413]
In the Estate of: ____________________ Estate No: ________
Date: ________

CLAIM AGAINST DECEDENT'S ESTATE

The claimant certifies that there is due and owing by the decedent in accordance with the attached statement of account or other basis for the claim the sum of $________.

I solemnly affirm under the penalties of perjury that the contents of the foregoing claim are true to the best of my knowledge, information, and belief.

____________________ Name of Claimant	____________________ Signature of claimant or person authorized to make verifications on behalf of claimant
____________________ Name and Title of Person Signing Claim	____________________ Address
	____________________
	____________________ Telephone Number

FILED: ____________________
RECORDED:
Claims Docket Liber ____________________ Folio ____________________

Approval or Rejection of Claims.—If personal representative intends to disallow claim, personal representative must notify each claimant who has filed verified statement of claim that it has been disallowed, in whole or in part, or that he will petition court for determination. Notice of disallowance must warn claimant to petition court for allowance or to commence suit against personal representative or distributees within 60 days or be barred. If personal representative takes no action on claim duly presented, claimant can petition orphans' court which can allow or disallow, in whole or in part, claim presented. (§8-107).

Payment of Claims.—Currently, six months after decedent's death, personal representative pays claims as allowed in order of priority. For estates of decedents dying before Oct. 1, 1992, period is nine months from decedent's death. Personal representative may pay barred claim only if permitted by will and may pay unbarred claim whether or not formal verified proof of claim filed. (§§8-102, 8-108). Personal representative is personally liable to unpaid claimant whose claim is allowed where personal representative made payments to others within six month period without requiring payees to give security or where he wilfully or negligently made payments depriving injured claimant of priority. (§8-108). Personal representative may give notice of meeting of all creditors to be held in not less than ten days for purpose of having claims approved in whole or in part under direction and control of court; personal representative's payment of such claims in accordance with court order is protected. (§8-109). Upon proof of unmatured claim, unless compromised, court will direct reservation and investment of sufficient amount. (§8-110). Secured claimant may receive payment in full if he surrenders security, or file claim and receive full amount less value of security, or foreclose security and file claim for deficiency, so long as he files within requisite nine or six-month period. (§8-111). Contingent claim must be filed within requisite nine or six-month period or be forever barred; if filed, it can be provided for by court order which reserves assets or which makes distributees liable to pay same. (§8-112). In allowing claim, personal representative may deduct counterclaim. (§8-113).

Priorities.—If assets insufficient to pay all claims, payment is in following order: (1) Fees due register of wills; (2) costs and expenses of administration; (3) funeral expenses not to exceed $3,500 except by special order of court; (4) commissions of personal representatives and licensed real estate salesmen and reasonable attorneys fees; (5) family allowance; (6) taxes due by decedent; (7) reasonable medical, hospital and nursing expenses of last illness; (8) rent owed by decedent for not more than three months in arrears; (9) wages, salaries or commissions for services performed within three months prior to decedent's death; (10) old age assistance claims under art. 88A, §77; (11) all other claims. (§8-105). No preference as to claims of same class, nor as to matured claims over unmatured claims.

Sales may be made without application to, approval of, or ratification by court. (§7-401[n]). Sale need not be reported or confirmed, but details must be included in initial or subsequent administration account. (§§7-302, 7-303). Personal representative may sell redeemable ground rent after written notice from tenant of intention to redeem, without approval of court. (§7-401[r]).

Actions by Representative.—Representative may commence and prosecute any personal action at law or in equity which decedent might have commenced and prosecuted, except actions for slander. (§7-401[x]). If suit is for wrong resulting in death of decedent, personal representative may recover, in addition to other damages, amount not to exceed $2,000 for funeral expenses. (§7-401[x]). Similarly, representative may continue action by decedent pending at time of death. (R. P. 2-241).

Actions Against Representative.—Personal representative may be sued in any action which could have been brought against decedent, except for slander. (§7-401[x]). Without filing claim, action may be commenced against estate within earlier of six months from decedent's death or two months after personal representative gives notice by mail. (§§8-103; 8-104[d]). For estates of decedents dying before Oct. 1, 1992, period is nine months from decedent's death. Other than action for personal injuries or wrongful death caused by decedent for which process had been served, actions must be brought within above time limits (unless claim is covered by insurance or by Md. Automobile Insurance Fund). (courts art. §3-902[c]; est. & tr. art. §§8-103[e], 8-104[d], [e]). Action pending when decedent died may be continued against representative by motion of successor, opposing, or affected third party, without presentation as claim. (R. P. 2-241).

Allowances.—$5,000 to surviving spouse and $2,500 for each unmarried dependent child under 18 available in both testate and intestate estates, and exempt from inheritance tax. (§3-201). Upon receipt of allowance for unmarried child of decedent under 18 who is not also child of surviving spouse, surviving spouse shall distribute allowance as provided in §13-501.

Election of surviving spouse to take statutory share in lieu of share left by will must be exercised within seven months after date of first appointment of personal representative under will unless extended by court order. (§3-206). In lieu of property left by will, surviving spouse may elect to take one-third share of net estate if there are surviving issue, or one-half if not. (§3-203). Net estate calculated without deduction for federal and Md. estate tax and penalties and interest thereon. (§§3-203, tax-gen. art. §7-308).

Widow's Quarantine.—No provision.

Intermediate Accountings.—Unless time extended, personal representative must render account within nine months from date of appointment and every six months thereafter until estate closed by filing of final account, and at other times as ordered by court. (§7-305). For estates of decedents dying before Oct. 1, 1992 and on or after May 19, 1989, initial period is later of ten months after date of death or nine months of notice of appointment. Upon filing account, personal representative must file certificate that he has mailed or delivered notice of such filing to all interested persons. (§7-301).

Exceptions to account must be filed within 20 days of court's approval. (§7-501).

Final Accounting and Settlement.—Final account must be filed upon termination of appointment. (§7-305). Unless time extended for good cause, all assets must be distributed within time for rendering first account (within nine months of appointment). (§7-101[b]).

Consent Settlement.—No special provisions. After charges known, proposed distribution mailed or delivered by personal representative to interested distributees must be objected to within 30 days, or right to object is lost. (§9-104[e]). In event of objection, personal representative may apply to court to make distribution. (§9-112).

Distribution.—With some exceptions, shares of legatees abate in following order: (1) Property not disposed of by will; (2) residuary legacies; (3) general legacies other than (4), (5) or (6) hereof; (4) general legacy to dependents; (5) general legacy to creditor in

See note at head of Digest as to 1998 legislation covered.

See Topical Index in front part of this volume.

EXECUTORS AND ADMINISTRATORS . . . *continued*

satisfaction of just debt; (6) general legacy to surviving spouse; (7) specific and demonstrative legacies. (§9-103). Personal representative must give deed or assignment to evidence distribution in kind. (§9-105). No priority in abatement between real and personal property, and abatement in each class is apportioned. Upon petition, court may partition undivided interests of heirs or legatees in property of estate. (§9-107). Upon distribution, personal representative may, but need not, obtain release from distributee. (§9-111). Fiduciary must distribute assets having values at dates of distribution amounting to no less than amount of legacy as determined for federal tax purposes, except where will directs otherwise. (§11-107). For statutory form of personal representative's deed, see real prop. art. §4-202(g). For distribution of legacies, see topic Wills. For distributions to minors, see category Family, topic Infants, subhead Distributions.

Distribution if Abroad.—Where distributee is nonresident of U.S. and, because of local conditions, would not have benefit or use or control at its full value of funds distributable to him, court may order distribution to board of education of county or Baltimore City for use of public schools. Provision is made for subsequent repayment without interest to claimant or legal representative. (§9-108).

Closing of estate occurs automatically with approval of final account; termination of appointment may be accomplished by request in final account or by court order entered upon petition filed more than six months after appointment, with notice to all interested persons and, if requested within 20 days of notice, hearing. (§10-101). If no action involving personal representative is pending one year after close of estate, he is automatically discharged from ordinary liability to all interested persons. (§10-103).

Liabilities.—Personal representative is made fiduciary by statute and must settle and distribute estate in accordance with will and estates and trusts article as expeditiously and with as little sacrifice in value as is reasonable. (§7-101). Representative's liability to third parties arising from administration is that of agent for disclosed principal. (§8-109[a]). Representative is not individually liable on contracts (unless agreed to) or for torts (absent personal fault) connected with administration. (§8-109[b] and [c]).

Heir or legatee liable to creditor up to value of distribution if estate closed and claim not barred. (§10-102). See subhead Presentation of Claims, supra. Claim against heir or legatee for property improperly distributed barred after three years from death of decedent or one year from date of distribution, whichever is later. (§§9-106[b], 10-103[b]). Liability may exist for share of estate taxes under Md. Uniform Estate Tax Apportionment Act. (tax gen. art. §7-308).

Compensation of Representatives.—Unless larger measure is provided by will, court may allow such commissions as it deems appropriate, but not to exceed 9% on property valued at $20,000 or less and $1,800 plus 3.6% of excess over $20,000 for property valued at greater than $20,000. (§7-601[b]). For estates of decedents dying before Jan. 1, 1992, fee simple real estate, (but not income thereon for estates of decedents dying on or after July 1, 1974 only), is excluded from estate in computation of commissions, but court may allow commissions not to exceed 9% on real estate sold by personal representative. (§7-601[d]). For estates of decedents dying on or after Jan. 1, 1992, fee simple real property is treated as property subject to administration upon which personal representative's compensation may be computed. (§7-601). Fees paid to broker are expense of administration and not deducted from commissions. (§7-601[d]). If will provides stated compensation additional compensation shall be allowed if provision is deemed insufficient by court. (§7-601[a]). Personal representative must give notice to all unpaid creditors and interested persons of commissions and counsel fees, including expenses of litigation, requested and basis for same and of right to hearing; any request for hearing must be filed within 20 days, otherwise court approval is final in absence of fraud, material mistake or substantial irregularity in proceeding. (§§7-502, 7-602, 7-603). For estates of decedents dying before July 1, 1989, 9% and 3.6% commission ceilings were 10% and 4%, respectively, but commissions were reduced by tax on commissions which has been repealed in estates of decedents dying after 7/1/89.

Tax on Commissions.—Prior to repeal, all ordinary commissions allowed were subject to tax of 1% on first $20,000 of estate and one-fifth of 1% on balance or 10% of total commissions allowed, whichever was greater. Tax due and payable despite fact representative may waive commission or receive legacy in lieu thereof. Tax payable only once on same property. Repealed effective for estates of decedents dying after July 1, 1989. Commissions attributable to personal representative were accordingly higher than currently, i.e., 10% on first $20,000 of probate estate and 4% on balance.

Administration of Small Estates.—Provision is made for expeditious and inexpensive settlement of estates of decedents who die either testate or intestate, where probate assets do not exceed $20,000 in gross value. No bond generally required unless estate exceeds priority expenses. If death occurs before Oct. 1, 1992, claims must be presented by earlier of nine months from date of decedent's death or 30 days after personal representative gives notice by mail. For estates of decedents dying before Oct. 1, 1992, period is six months or 30 days. If administrative expenses, allowable funeral expenses of decedent and family allowances equal known assets of estate, it can be settled immediately without notice to creditors. (§§5-601 to 5-606). Rules of procedure and forms for administration of small estates are set forth in R. P. 6-201 to 6-222.

When Administration Unnecessary.—Life insurance company may pay proceeds of policy without administration where total estate including insurance does not exceed $1,000. (art. 48A, §382).

Small Estates.—See subheads Administration of Small Estates, When Administration Unnecessary, supra. Also see R. P. 6-201 et seq.

Foreign Executors or Administrators.—Foreign personal representative of nonresident decedent need not take out letters in Md. for any purpose, but may exercise all powers and sue and be sued, subject to any statute or rule as to nonresidents. (§§5-501, 5-502). Where real or leasehold property is in Md., foreign personal representative must publish notice to creditors and show name of agent for service of process as to each county or Baltimore City where property located, whereupon creditor has six months from date of first publication to file claim or, if death occurs on or after May 19, 1989, earlier of six months from date of decedent's death or two months after foreign representative gives notice by mail. (§5-503[b]). For estates of decedents dying before Oct. 1, 1992, period is nine months from date of decedent's death or two months after

notice by mail. To fix inheritance tax, foreign representative files with register of wills, in county where it is believed largest part (in value) of property is located, authenticated copy of appointment and will, if any, and verified application which schedules property and its appraised value. (§5-504; R. P. 6-501).

Uniform Anatomical Gift Act adopted. (§§4-501 to 4-512).

Uniform Fiduciaries Act adopted. (§§15-201 to 15-211).

Uniform Principal and Income Act.—See topic Trusts, subhead Revised Uniform Principal and Income Act. Generally, expenses during administration are charged against principal, and income is determined under rules applicable to trustee. (§§7-304, 14-201 to 14-214).

Uniform Act for the Simplification of Fiduciary Security Transfers adopted. (§§15-301 to 15-311). Uniform Commercial Code does not repeal this Act. (comm. law art. §10-104).

Successor Corporate Fiduciaries Act. See §§15-1A-01 to 15-1A-05.

FIDUCIARIES:

See topics Executors and Administrators, Trusts; categories Family, topic Guardian and Ward; Property, topic Real Property.

INTESTACY:

See topic Descent and Distribution.

PROOF OF CLAIMS:

See topic Executors and Administrators.

TRUSTS:

References are to Estates and Trusts Article of Code unless otherwise indicated. Pensions and retirement funds are extensively regulated in Art. 73B.

Kinds.—Common law prevails. Express trusts, resulting trusts and constructive trusts are all recognized and enforced. (144 Md. 465, 125 Atl. 162).

Creation.—No special requirements except that express trust of real estate must be evidenced by writing signed by grantor. (7 Gill & J. 157).

Spendthrift trusts which secure income and principal against creditors are valid, but one may not create such a trust in his own favor. (116 Md. 655, 82 Atl. 831; 87 Md. 161, 39 Atl. 613). Maryland Discretionary Trust Act authorizes creation of trust for benefit of one who may someday become disabled or otherwise need state or federal assistance. (14-401 to 14-408).

Charitable trusts are recognized by statute and may be enforced by Attorney General or any interested person. (§14-301). Certain acts are prohibited in administration of charitable trusts. (§14-303). Procedure provided for modification of charitable remainder trusts to conform with Internal Revenue Code. (§14-304). For article on charitable trusts in Md., see 1 Md. L. Rev. 105.

Disclaimer of property interests, including future interests, governed by Uniform Disclaimer of Property Interests Act. (§§9-201 to 9-209). See topic Wills.

Appointment of Trustee.—No special requirements. Practice is to appoint by deed or will without court involvement. Equity court will make appointment rather than allow trust to fail for want of trustee. (171 Md. 547, 190 Atl. 215). Court may also authorize transfer of estate from one trustee to another. (R. P. 10-711).

Eligibility and Competency.—No special requirements. Trustee may be individual or corporation authorized to act as fiduciary. Foreign trust company may act as trustee. (16 Op. Att'y Gen. 70). No judge of any state court or federal court and no register of wills or clerk of court may start to serve as trustee after Jan. 1, 1970 unless he is surviving spouse or related to grantor within third degree. (§14-104).

Qualification.—If appointed by court, trustee may be required to give bond; otherwise no such requirement. Court-appointed noncorporate trustee may be required to give bond even though excused by trust instrument. (R. P. 10-702).

Removal of Trustee.—Court of equity must remove trustee who: (1) Willfully misrepresents material facts resulting in appointment or other action by court; (2) willfully disregards order of court; (3) shows incapability to properly perform duties of office; or (4) breaches his duty of good faith or loyalty. Court may remove trustee who: (1) Negligently fails to file bond; (2) negligently fails to obey court order; or (3) fails to perform duties or to competently administer trust. (R. P. 13-702). Trustee may resign with court approval after filing account and providing notice to interested persons, or without court involvement if so provided in instrument and trustee is not otherwise under court order. (R. P. 10-711).

General Powers and Duties of Trustees.—Except as limited by trust instrument or court order, trustee has, in addition to powers existing at common law, power, without court approval, to invest in, sell, mortgage, exchange or lease any property, and other broad powers similar to those granted by statute to personal representative. (§15-102). See topic Executors and Administrators, subhead General Powers and Duties. Separately recorded statement of fiduciary powers, as well as terms of any writing in existence, may be incorporated by reference into will or trust instrument. (§4-107).

Sales.—In absence of provision in instrument or court order to contrary, trustee has power to sell any property. (§15-102[c]). If power of trustee is questioned, court of equity may take jurisdiction of trust and order sale. (R. P. 14-301 to 14-306).

Investments.—Regulated by court rule and by statute. Prudent Investor Rule adopted. (1994, c. 602). If estate consists entirely of cash not in excess of $75,000, trustee subject to jurisdiction of court may apply for court order authorizing deposit in insured financial institution. (R. P. 10-705). In addition to powers conferred by statute or by trust instrument, trustee has broad powers without court approval to invest in any property and to deposit funds in checking accounts and in insured interest-bearing accounts. (§15-102). Code sets forth nonexclusive list of lawful investments. (§15-106). Otherwise, there is no authorized list of investments. Corporate trustee may invest fiduciary funds in no-load open-end mutual fund even if trustee receives compensation

TRUSTS . . . *continued*

from fund provided compensation is disclosed. (§15-106). See also category Family, topic Guardian and Ward, subhead Investments.

Uniform Management of Institutional Funds Act adopted. (§§15-401 to 15-409).

Securities in Name of Nominee.—Trustee subject to court jurisdiction must register securities in his name as fiduciary subject to order of court, except that he may register them in name of nominee if so authorized by trust instrument or by order of court. (R. P. 10-704). Trustee not subject to court jurisdiction may hold security in name of nominee. (§15-102[x]).

Uniform Fiduciaries Act adopted. (§§15-201 to 15-211).

Uniform Act for the Simplification of Fiduciary Security Transfers adopted. (§§15-301 to 15-311). Uniform Commercial Code does not repeal act. (comm. law art. §10-104).

Common trust funds provided for. (fin. inst. art. tit. 3, subtit. 5).

Revised Uniform Principal and Income Act (1962 Act) adopted. (§§14-201 to 14-214). Md. Act differs by excluding §§10 and 12, by being applicable to legal life tenant and remainderman in absence of contrary agreement or direction, and by excluding from application of §6(a) stock splits and stock dividends with respect to any interest or estate in existence prior to June 1, 1965. Except for §6(a), Act applies to trusts or estates no matter when they came into existence.

Gifts to Minors.—See category Family, topic Infants.

Accounting.—Trustee liable at all times for account of his stewardship. (27 Md. 368, 92 Am. Dec. 637). Trustee administering estate under supervision of equity court must file inventory of assets within 60 days after appointment or assumption of jurisdiction and must file accounts once each year. (R. P. 10-707).

Compensation.—Whether appointed by court or by will or deed, trustee is entitled to 6% of income from real estate and 6.5% upon first $10,000 of other income, 5% upon next $10,000, 4% upon next $10,000, 3% upon any excess, plus annual commissions of four-tenths of 1% of first $250,000 of corpus, one-fourth of 1% of next $250,000, three-twentieths of 1% of next $500,000, and one-tenth of 1% of excess of corpus. Usual commissions are allowed for selling real property. In absence of special circumstances, one-half of 1% is allowed upon final distribution. Amount specified is subject to provisions to any valid agreement, and court having jurisdiction may increase or diminish for cause and may allow special compensation for services of unusual nature. For trust accounts, trustee which is bank, loan association or member of Md. bar may charge increased commissions if specified requirements are satisfied. (§14-103).

Discharge.—Trustee may be discharged upon completion of purposes for which trust created, but should secure release from beneficiaries. If appointed by court, trustee must be discharged by court order. (§15-111).

Accumulations.—Valid up to time limit fixed by rule against perpetuities. (See, e.g., 199 Md. 264, 86 A.2d 504.)

Statute of Uses repealed. Notwithstanding, executory interests and powers of appointment are valid, subject to rule against perpetuities. (real prop. art. §2-116).

Perpetuities.—See category Property, topic Perpetuities.

Pour Over Trusts.—Life insurance, legacies and death benefits of any kind may be made payable to inter vivos or testamentary trusts. (§§4-411, 4-412, 11-105). See also topic Wills, subheads Bequests and Devises to Inter Vivos Trusts, Bequests and Devises to Testamentary Trusts.

Termination of Small Trusts.—If trust has fair market value of less than $50,000, corporate trustee may terminate trust upon giving notice and receiving no objection to termination. (§14-107).

WILLS:

References are to Estates and Trusts Article of Code unless otherwise indicated. Maryland Rules, Title 6 refers to recently adopted Title 6 of Maryland Rules of Procedures affecting decedent's estates and are referred to as R.P. 6-101 et seq.

No will is valid unless, at time of acknowledgement or execution, testator was 18 years of age or older and was legally competent to make will. (§4-101).

Testamentary Disposition.—Generally, no limitations upon testator's disposition of his property. Testator may not create perpetuity, with certain exceptions. (§§11-102, 11-103). See category Property, topic Perpetuities.

Surviving spouse may elect statutory share. (§3-203). Pretermitted child, or issue thereof, entitled to statutory share in certain circumstances. (§3-301).

Married woman cannot by will deprive husband of rights given him by law in her property; and husband cannot by will take away wife's rights in his property. (95 Md. 56, 51 Atl. 823). See also subhead Election, infra.

Joint bank account is non-testamentary and is effective under fin. inst. art. §1-204. (§1-401).

Execution.—Will must be in writing and signed by testator, or by some other person for him, in his presence and by his express direction, and must be attested and subscribed in presence of testator by two or more credible witnesses. (§4-102; 38 Md. 417). Will need not show addresses of witnesses, but petition for probate must state addresses of witnesses to will. (§5-201[f]).

Attestation Clause.—No attestation clause necessary, but existence eliminates necessity to prove execution by verified statement of person having personal knowledge. (§5-303). In practice, following is used:

Form

Signed, sealed, published and declared by the above-named testator as and for his last will and testament in the presence of the undersigned, who, at his request, in his presence and in the presence of each other, have hereunto subscribed our names as witnesses.

Holographic will valid if made outside U.S. by person serving in U.S. Armed Forces, but such is void after one year after testator's discharge unless testator has died or does not then possess testamentary capacity. (§4-103).

Nuncupative Wills.—Except for holographic wills, no nuncupative will is valid. (Official Comment to §4-103).

Revocation.—Will can be revoked: (1) By provision in subsequent validly executed will (a) revoking prior will, either expressly or by necessary implication, or (b) expressly republishing existing earlier will revoked by intermediate will; or (2) by burning, cancelling, tearing or obliterating of same by testator or in his presence and by his direction and consent; or (3) by testator's subsequent marriage followed by birth, adoption or legitimation of child who survives testator; or (4) as to provisions in wills for spouse only, by final decree of absolute divorce or annulment. (§4-105). Revocation provisions of §4-105 apply only to acts occurring on or after Jan. 1, 1970. (§12-102[d]). There is no revocation merely by subsequent birth, adoption or legitimation of child. (§3-301). Woman's will not revoked simply by subsequent marriage. (76 Md. 369, 25 Atl. 307).

Revival.—Will expressly revoked by subsequent will is not revived by revocation of subsequent will, unless prior will is still in existence and is republished with requisite formalities. (§4-106). If occurring prior to Jan. 1, 1970, revocation of subsequent will is evidence of intention to revive previous will and raises presumption that previous will is revived, which presumption may be strengthened or rebutted by evidence of attending circumstances and probable motive of testator. (20 Md. 357; 177 Md. 97, 8 A.2d 922).

Testamentary Gifts to Subscribing Witnesses.—Legacy to attesting witness is valid, and witness is competent to prove will. (114 Md. 336, 79 Atl. 600; Official Comment to §4-102).

Bequests and Devises to Testamentary Trusts.—Pour over trusts valid. Legacy not invalidated because testamentary trust not in existence at time instrument creating legacy was executed if will creating testamentary trust was executed before death of testator creating legacy to trust and will is offered for probate prior to, or within nine months of testator's death and admitted to probate. Termination of trust does not invalidate legacy. (§4-412). See also topic Trusts, subhead Pour Over Trusts.

Bequests and Devises to Inter Vivos Trusts.—Pour over trusts valid. Trust instrument may be amended or modified subsequent to date of testator's will without invalidating legacy. (§4-411). See also topic Trusts, subhead Pour Over Trusts.

Testamentary Guardians.—See category Family, topic Guardian and Ward.

Deposit of will during testator's lifetime is permitted. (§4-201).

Probate.—Will must be probated administratively by register of wills or judicially by orphans' court of county or Baltimore City where decedent was domiciled, or, if not domiciled in Md. and if no probate elsewhere, then where petitioner believes largest part of decedent's property in Md. is located. (§§5-101, 5-103). Petition for probate is filed requesting either administrative probate or judicial probate. (§§2-206, 5-201, 5-203, 5-206). Probate information booklet can be obtained from Register of Wills. Most estates can be opened administratively, but judicial probate, with notice and hearing before appointment, may be required if requested or circumstances prevent administrative probate. (§5-402; R. P. 6-302). Small estates up to $20,000 of probate assets are governed by similar but more simplified procedures. (§5-601; R. P. 6-201).

Following Notice of Appointment, Notice to Creditors and Notice to Unknown Heirs published by three successive weekly insertions, interested persons (primarily heirs and legatees) have six months from date of death or two months from date of notice, whichever is earlier, to file objections to appointment or to probate of will. Creditors currently may present claims by earlier of six months after date of decedent's death or two months after personal representative gives notice by mail. (§§7-103 to 7-103.1; R. P. 6-209, 6-311). For estates of decedents dying before Oct. 1, 1992, period is earlier of nine months after date of death or two months after notice by mail. Within 20 days of appointment, personal representative must deliver to register text of published notice and list of interested persons; thereupon, within five days, register must deliver or forward copy of notice by certified mail to each heir and legatee. (§§7-103, 7-104, 2-210; R. P. 6-316, 6-317).

Self-proved Wills.—In proceeding for administrative probate, witnesses to will need not appear before register if will has proper attestation clause or if verified statement is filed by person having personal knowledge of circumstances of execution, stating that named witnesses were in fact attesting witnesses. (§5-303; R. P. 6-152).

Contest.—Whether or not petition for probate has been filed, verified petition to caveat will may be filed at any time within six months following first appointment of personal representative under will, in which event judicial probate proceeding becomes mandatory. (§5-207; R. P. 6-431). Different will subsequently offered for probate may be challenged before later to occur of: (a) Three months after probate of subsequent will, or (b) six months after first appointment of personal representative under will. Action taken after administrative probate is binding as to all interested persons, unless request for mandatory judicial probate under §5-402 is filed within six months of administrative probate or unless, upon request filed within 18 months of decedent's death, court finds that petitioner was previously unaware of later discovered will, or that he was not given notice, or that there was fraud, mistake or substantial irregularity in prior probate proceeding. (§5-304). Judicial probate proceeding may be reopened for reasons contained in §5-304. (§5-407).

In terrorem clause penalizing interested person for contesting will is void if probable cause exists for instituting proceedings. (§4-413).

Legacies are payable within nine months of grant of letters unless time is extended for good cause. (§§7-101[b], 7-305). Unpaid legatees may petition orphans' court to require personal representative to account and pay legacies. (60 Md. 229). "Legatee" is defined as person entitled to any real or personal property under will and includes trustee but not beneficiary of trust. (§1-101[l]). Unless will otherwise provides, legatee other than spouse who fails to survive testator by 30 days is deemed to have predeceased testator absent will provision creating contrary presumption. (§4-401). Specific legatee is entitled to net income and is chargeable with repairs and expenses relating to management of specific property. (§7-304).

See note at head of Digest as to 1998 legislation covered.

See Topical Index in front part of this volume.

WILLS . . . *continued*

Renunciation.—Md. Uniform Disclaimer of Property Interests Act (est. & tr. art. tit. 9, subtit. 2), enacted to take effect July 1, 1978, is modeled after Uniform Disclaimer of Property Interests Act, with §1(a) derived from Uniform Disclaimer Transfers by Will, Intestacy or Appointment Act and §1(b) derived from Uniform Disclaimer of Transfers under Nontestamentary Instruments Act, with following material variations:

§1: Gives right to disclaim, in whole or in part, right of succession or transfer of any property and interest, including future interests, joint tenancies, and appointed property, arising under testamentary and nontestamentary instruments, or by intestacy. Right to disclaim survives death of person having it. Tenant by entireties may disclaim as separate interest, interest which would otherwise devolve by right of survivorship only if spouse affixes written consent. Personal representative of deceased person, attorney in fact of person, or guardian of property of minor or disabled person, may disclaim on behalf of that person 30 days after delivering or mailing written notice to all interested persons. (§9-201).

§2: Disclaimer shall be filed within nine months after right of succession or transfer arises or, if future interest, after right to possession is vested, and shall be filed with Register of appropriate county (if applicable) and trustee or other holder of legal title. Disclaimer of interest in real property shall also be recorded among land records of county where property is located. (§9-202).

§4(a): Unless devolution to disclaimant is expressly conditioned on disclaimant's survival of deceased owner or donee of power of appointment, property interest arising under testamentary instrument, by testamentary exercise of power of appointment, or by intestacy, devolves directly to persons who would have taken if disclaimant had died, intestate, domiciled in State of Maryland, owning property or interest, immediately before deceased owner or donee. (§9-204[a]).

§4(b): Unless devolution to disclaimant is expressly conditioned on disclaimant's survival to effective date of nontestamentary instrument or contract, property interest arising under such instrument or contract, by nontestamentary exercise of power of appointment, devolves directly to persons who would have taken if disclaimant had died, intestate, domiciled in State of Maryland, owning property or interest, immediately before effective date of instrument or contract. (§9-204[b]).

§4(c): §9-204(f) of Md. Act excludes reference to "written waiver of right to disclaim" and provides that creditors of disclaimant have no interest in disclaimed property. Other subsections added by Md. Act (§9-204[c], [d], [e] and [g]) provide that disclaimer is irrevocable, that disclaimer of power extinguishes power, that disclaimer relates back to death of deceased owner or donee, or effective date of nontestamentary instrument or contract, and that property interest subject to joint tenancy or tenancy by entireties which is disclaimed devolves as if disclaimant predeceased other joint tenant or tenant by entireties.

§5: Right to disclaim exists notwithstanding spendthrift provision. (§9-205[b]).

§7: Interest existing on July 1, 1978 as to which time for filing disclaimer has not expired may be disclaimed within time provided in §9-202 or before Apr. 1, 1979, whichever period is greater. (§9-207).

Unclaimed Legacies.—Personal representative may petition orphans' court to distribute unclaimed legacy to county board of education for use of public schools. (§§9-108, 9-112). Uniform Disposition of Unclaimed Property Act adopted. (comm. law art. tit. 17). See category Property, topic Absentees. See also topic Executors and Administrators, subheads Distribution, Distribution if Abroad.

Lapse.—If legatee predeceases testator, legacy does not lapse, but goes directly to those persons who would have taken had legatee died, testate or intestate, owning property; it is not subject to deceased legatee's debts or to second administration. (§4-403). If will was executed prior to Jan. 1, 1970, legacy to person who predeceases testator will pass to legatee's intestate heirs. (§12-102[d]).

Children may be disinherited, but law does not favor such disposition; intention to disinherit pretermitted child, or issue thereof, must be expressly stated in will. (§3-301[b][4]; 8 Gill 46).

If will provides for existing child, but makes no provision for child subsequently born, adopted or legitimated by testator, any such child, or issue of any such deceased child, subsequently born, adopted or legitimated who survives testator and is not expressly excluded by terms of will is entitled to lesser of (1) same share of estate which he would have taken if testator had died intestate, or (2) aggregate value of all legacies to children and issue of any deceased child divided by number of children who survive testator and deceased children leaving issue entitled to share. Issue of pretermitted child who did not survive testator may take by representation. (§§3-301, 3-302).

Election.—Dower and curtesy are abolished. (§3-202). In lieu of share left by will, surviving spouse may elect to take statutory share by renunciation and election in writing filed in court within seven months after date of first appointment of personal representative under will unless time extended by court order. (§§3-203 to 3-208; 8-103). Right of election is personal, but court having jurisdiction may by order exercise such election for minor or person under disability. (§3-204).

Contribution.—In event of diminution of estate by widow's election and renunciation, legatees must contribute ratably to elective share. (§3-208). Where afterborn children share in estate, legacies of children and issue of deceased children must contribute proportionately. (§3-303).

Foreign Executed Wills.—Will executed outside Md. is valid if executed in conformity with law of Md., or of place of execution, or of testator's domicile. (§4-104). Will or copy should accompany petition for probate. (§5-201).

Foreign Probated Wills.—Copy of will recorded pursuant to laws of another state or country, duly authenticated by register or record keeper and under seal of court or office where recorded, is sufficient evidence of will. Foreign personal representative, without taking out ancillary letters, may exercise in Md. all powers of his office. (§§5-501, 5-502). Where estate has property in Md. subject to Md. inheritance tax, foreign personal representative must file with register of wills in county where largest part in value of property is believed to be located copy of his appointment and of any will (authenticated pursuant to 28 USCA §1738), together with verified application describing all Md. property of estate, valuing it and giving basis for determined value. Register must fix

inheritance tax. (§5-504). Until he pays or secures payment of inheritance tax and files receipt or evidence of security among permanent records of court, unpaid tax obligation is lien on property of estate; lien lasts four years from date of decedent's death. (§5-505). See topic Executors and Administrators, subhead Foreign Executors or Administrators.

Living Will.—Living wills regulated by health-gen. art. tit. 5, subtit. 6. Any competent person at least 18 years old can execute written declaration to provide or withhold future health care or to appoint agent to make future health care conditions under specific circumstances. Written declaration must be dated, signed by or at direction of declarant, and witnessed by two people acting in good faith. At least one witness must not be entitled to any financial benefit from declarant's death. Oral declaration may be valid if made in presence of attending physician and documented as part of declarant's medical record. Written or oral advance directive becomes effective once attending physician and one other physician certify in writing that declarant is incapable of making informed decision. Unless specified, advance directive allows withholding of life-sustaining procedures, including artificial nutrition and hydration and cardiopulmonary resuscitation. (health-gen. art. §5-602). Advance directive can contain statement giving consent to gift of all or any part of declarant's body for purpose specified by statute. (health-gen. art. §5-604.1). Declaration may be revoked. (health-gen. art. §5-604). Persons following declaration's procedures are exempt from liability. (health-gen. art. §5-609). Declarations made in other states are effective to degree allowed under Maryland law if executed in compliance with laws of either Maryland or state where executed. (health-gen. art. §5-617). Optional forms provided. (health-gen. art. §5-603).

Simultaneous Death.—See topic Death, subhead Survivorship.

Testamentary Trusts.—See topic Trusts.

Uniform Anatomical Gift Act adopted. (est. & tr. art. §§4-501 to 4-512).

FAMILY

ADOPTION:

Family Law Article effective as of July 1, 1984. References are to article unless otherwise indicated.

Adoption procedure governed by Md. Rules. (R. P. 9-101 to 9-112).

Who May Adopt.—Any adult, even though single or unmarried. (§5-309). Married persons must act jointly unless separated under circumstances giving rise to divorce or annulment or petitioner's spouse is consenting natural parent of individual to be adopted or petitioner's spouse is incompetent. (§5-315).

Who May Be Adopted.—Any person, whether minor or adult although only minor can be placed under guardianship. (§5-307).

Consent Required.—Except when natural parents' rights terminated by valid judicial proceeding, consent must be obtained from: (1) Natural mother; (2) natural father; and (3) person to be adopted if ten years of age or older. Where natural parents' rights terminated by valid judicial proceeding, consent must be obtained from: (1)Executive head of child placement agency which has been awarded guardianship of individual and (2) person to be adopted if ten years of age or older. (§5-311). Consent may be revoked within 30 days after consent signed, except individual to be adopted may revoke consent before final decree is entered. (§5-311). Natural parent consent valid only if it contains notice of right to revoke consent. Consent of minor parent valid only if accompanied by affidavit of court-appointed attorney certifying that consent is knowingly and willingly given. (§5-314). Where there is clear and convincing evidence of (i) abandonment of child (i.e., identity of child's natural parents unknown and no one has claimed to be child's natural parent within two months of alleged abandonment), (ii) adjudication in prior juvenile hearings that child is in need of assistance or neglected, abused or dependent child, or (iii) certain circumstances exist, parental consent not required when in best interests of child. (§5-313).

Conditions Precedent.—Person to be adopted must be physically within Md. or subjected to jurisdiction of equity court. (courts art. §6-203[e]).

Counseling.—In independent adoption, natural parents must be advised of right to independent legal counsel and adoption counseling. Court may order adoptive parents to pay reasonable fees. (§5-320).

Jurisdiction.—Circuit court sitting in equity, except for child who is under jurisdiction of any juvenile court other than juvenile court for Montgomery County and who previously has been adjudicated to be child in need of assistance. Family Division to be established in each circuit court, where feasible. (§1-201).

Venue.—Any court having continuous jurisdiction over person to be adopted, or court of county, or Baltimore City, in which: (1) Petitioner is domiciled; or (2) petitioner has resided for at least 90 days; or (3) licensed child placement agency having custody or control of person to be adopted is located; or (4) person to be adopted is domiciled, if he is related to petitioner by blood or marriage or is adult; or (5) equity court has continuing jurisdiction over custody of person to be adopted. (courts art. §6-203[e]).

Petition.—Petition must be signed and verified by petitioner and spouse, if any, and must contain following: (1) Name, address, age, business or employment, and employer of petitioner and spouse, if any; (2) name, sex, date and place of birth of person to be adopted, and names, residences and ages of parents; (3) name, age and address of any children of both petitioner and spouse, and relationship to petitioner of person to be adopted; (4) statement of how person to be adopted was located; (5) if person to be adopted is minor, names and addresses of persons having legal or physical care, custody or control since birth, and period of time of such care; (6) explanation if spouse of petitioner does not join in petition; (7) explanation if consent required by law not filed with petition; (8) name of, address of and reference to proceeding appointing guardian, if any, with right to consent to adoption; (9) facts known to petitioner that may entitle person to be adopted or parent of such person to appointment of attorney by court; (10) any change of name desired. Petitions for guardianship, terminating natural parental rights, are provided for. (R. P. 9-103; §5-317).

See note at head of Digest as to 1998 legislation covered.

See Topical Index in front part of this volume.

ADOPTION . . . *continued*

Notice.—Petitioner must give notice of filing of petition to each person whose consent is required, unless their consent is filed with petition. (§5-322).

Proceedings.—Upon filing petition, court enters show cause order thereon unless all parties entitled to service have joined in petition. If parent of child to be adopted is under disability, attorney must be appointed and must make investigation of facts and report to court. Court may in any case conduct investigation or cause one to be made. (R. P. 9-105, 9-106; §5-323). Court must hold hearing before entering final decree. (§5-324.1). Proceedings may be preceded by petition for guardianship, effect of which is to terminate natural parental rights, duties and obligations. (§5-317). Guardianship may be granted only after necessary investigations and hearings and with consent of each living natural parent of child, except as in cases of abandonment, neglect, or if it is in individual's best interests. (§5-313; 5-317). Court must hold such hearing on petition for adoption as justice requires, with such privacy as it directs. (R. P. 9-109).

Decree may be interlocutory or final, in discretion of court. Interlocutory decree has all effects of final decree unless and until revocation, which may be any time before final decree, except that custody shall not be granted under interlocutory decree for longer than one year. Interlocutory decree must be reviewed within one year of entry or amendment or extension thereof. (R. P. 9-108-9-111; §5-308). Final decree may not be entered before the later of 30 days after birth of adopted person or 30 days after consent signed. (§5-324; R. P. 9-111). Attorney or firm may not represent both adoptive parent or child placement agency and natural parent. (§5-323).

Name.—Court may order change of name in decree. (R. P. 9-111).

Effect of Adoption.—Adopted person, whether minor or adult, becomes to all intents and purposes natural child of petitioner and is entitled to all privileges and subject to all obligations of child born in lawful wedlock to petitioner. Adopted person inherits through and as representative of adopting parent and lineal or collateral kindred of adopting parent in same manner as child by birth of adopting parent. In event of death of adopted child intestate, property passes in same manner as if adopted child had been born in wedlock to adopting parent. Natural parent is freed of all legal duties and obligations to adopted person and is divested of all rights with respect to such person. Adopted child loses all rights of inheritance from natural parents and their natural lineal or collateral relatives and vice versa, unless natural parent is married to adopting parent. Term "child," "heir," "issue," "descendant" or equivalent in deed, grant, will or other instrument is held to include adopted child, unless contrary intent plainly appears by express terms, whether such instrument executed before or after interlocutory or final decree of adoption. If instrument executed before June 1, 1947, this provision applies to those adopted after that date. (§5-308; est. & tr. art. §§1-205, 1-207). Siblings separated by adoptive placement or foster care may be granted sibling visitation rights upon decree by court, after petition and hearing, if necessary, if visitation is in best interests of children. (§5-525.2).

Setting Aside Adoption.—Any party may appeal to Court of Special Appeals from either interlocutory or final decree. Final decree may be set aside for fatal jurisdictional or procedural defects, only if petition is filed within one year following entry of final decree. (§§5-325, 5-330).

Public Assistance.—Dep't of Human Resources may, in its discretion, continue support to parents who adopt child formerly under foster care. (§5-530). Regardless of income, individual approved by private or public adoption agency may apply for subsidy to local Dep't of Social Services if he seeks to adopt child legally free for adoption who has been determined by local Dep't of Social Services to require medical assistance, medical care or subsidy due to physical or mental disability, age, emotional disturbance, race, ethnicity or sibling relationships. (§§5-401 to 5-415). Subsidy may not be denied to eligible child with previously unknown condition and may not be discontinued because child is moved to another state. (§5-408[a], [d]). If adoptive parent dies or is incapacitated, subsidy may be continued to another adult who is qualified to assume responsibility for child and does so. (§5-408[e]). Adoptive parent is entitled to reimbursement by state for certain expenses for independent or interlocutory adoption of child if department determines that child should not be returned to biological parents, child cannot be placed with adoptive parents without providing assistance and except where it would be against best interest of child, previous adoption attempts were made without assistance and were unsuccessful. (§5-410.1).

Interstate Compact on the Placement of Children enacted. (§§5-601 to 5-611).

Mutual Consent Voluntary Adoption Registry established. Natural parents, adult adoptees and adult natural siblings may register willingness to have identifying information released to each other. (§§5-4A-01 to 5-4A-07).

ALIMONY:

See topic Divorce.

COMMUNITY PROPERTY:

System does not obtain.

DESERTION:

See topics Divorce, Husband and Wife.

DISSOLUTION OF MARRIAGE:

See topic Divorce.

DIVORCE:

Subject governed by Courts Article, Family Law Article and Maryland Rules 9-209, 9-210.

References are to Family Law Article unless otherwise indicated.

Grounds for absolute divorce are: (1) Adultery (neither plea of recrimination nor condonation is bar, but either is factor for court to consider); (2) desertion for at least 12 consecutive months prior to filing suit without reasonable expectation of reconciliation; (3) voluntary separation, without cohabitation, for 12 consecutive months prior to filing suit and with no reasonable expectation of reconciliation; (4) conviction of felony or misdemeanor and sentence of at least three years or indeterminate sentence in penal institution, 12 months of which have been served; (5) uninterrupted separation, without cohabitation, for two years prior to filing suit; (6) permanent and incurable insanity, proved by testimony of two or more physicians competent in psychiatry, provided that insane spouse has been confined in institution for at least three years prior to suit; (7) cruelty of treatment, without reasonable expectation of reconciliation; (8) excessively vicious conduct, without reasonable expectation of reconciliation. (§7-103).

Grounds for limited divorce, are: Cruelty or excessively vicious conduct to complainant or minor child; desertion; voluntary separation beyond any reasonable expectation of reconciliation. (§7-102). Court may require, as condition precedent, that parties participate in reconciliation efforts. (§7-102).

Domestic Violence Act of 1994 adopted. (1994, c. 728). See category Criminal Law, topic Criminal Law.

Evidence.—Order or decision (or compliance with order or decision) under domestic violence subtitle to fam. law art. (§4-501 et seq.) is not admissible in divorce proceeding (§7-103.1).

Residence Requirements.—When grounds arose outside Md., plaintiff or defendant must have resided in state for one year preceding suit (§7-101[a]); where ground is insanity, one party must have been actual resident of state for two years preceding suit (§7-103[A][6]).

Jurisdiction.—Equity courts have jurisdiction, but juvenile or criminal court may have concurrent jurisdiction. Family Division to be established in each circuit court, where feasible. (§1-201). Residence of either party gives court jurisdiction. (193 Md. 164, 66 A.2d 381). Court may exercise long arm jurisdiction over nonresident defendant in civil proceeding arising from marital relationship where defendant is personally served, and where: (1) Md. was matrimonial domicile of parties immediately before separation or (2) obligation to pay child or spousal support or counsel fees arose under Md. law or agreement executed by one of parties in Md. (courts art. §6-103.1).

Venue.—Bill must be filed where plaintiff resides, or where defendant resides, is regularly employed or has place of business, or, in addition, in case of annulment, where marriage sought to be annulled was performed. (courts art. §§6-201[a] and 202[1], [2]; R. P. 9-201).

Process.—Same process as is had in other actions is had in divorce action (R. P. 9-202); service on nonresident whose whereabouts unknown may be by publication pursuant to R. P. 2-122. See category Civil Actions and Procedure, topic Process, subhead Service by Publication.

Pleading.—Bill must be signed by plaintiff in person and answer by defendant in person. Supplemental bill alleging grounds arising subsequent to original bill may be filed. In all actions in which alimony, maintenance, or support, including child support, is claimed, litigants must file current financial statements unless agreement on amount of alimony, maintenance or support is alleged to exist. (R. P. 9-203).

Practice.—No final decree entered except upon oral testimony by plaintiff before examiner, master, or in open court. (§1-203[c]). In uncontested cases testimony taken before examiner or master unless court directs otherwise. (R. P. 2-541[b], 9-208). Divorce cannot be granted on testimony of plaintiff alone; corroboration by at least one other witness is necessary. (§7-101). In action in which testimony has been concluded for more than 90 days without entry of final decree, additional testimony must be offered which is sufficient to justify conclusion that no change has occurred since prior testimony. (R. P. 9-208). Neither offer to reconcile, nor refusal by other spouse, is defense or bar to divorce. (§7-104).

Court may grant absolute divorce forever, legal separation forever or for limited time, and may grant legal separation when absolute divorce is prayed. (§§7-102, 7-103). Separation or settlement agreement may be incorporated into decree. (R. P. 9-210).

Temporary alimony may be awarded pending suit. (§11-102).

Allowance for Prosecution of Suit.—Court at any time may allow either spouse sum for expenses of litigation, including counsel fees, after considering financial need and justification for suit or defense. Reimbursement may be ordered for expenses already paid. (§11-110). See subhead Allowance for Support of Children, infra.

Permanent Alimony.—Court may award alimony to either spouse for limited period in decree granting limited or absolute divorce or annulment. (§11-101). Amount and duration in discretion of court after considering financial needs, ability to be self-supporting, time necessary to find suitable employment, standard of living during marriage, duration of marriage, monetary and nonmonetary contributions of each party to family, circumstances leading to separation, age and physical and mental condition, etc. (§11-106). Alimony may be awarded for indefinite period if spouse cannot reasonably be expected to become self-supporting or differences in standard of living will be unconscionably disparate. (§11-106). Decree may be modified from time to time. (§11-107). Right to alimony ceases on remarriage of recipient or death of either party. (§11-108). Separate agreement providing for final disposition of alimony is binding on court. (§11-101[c]).

Division of Property of Spouses.—Court granted power to make certain disposition of property (§§8-201 to 8-213); Md. court may exercise this authority after foreign divorce if one spouse domiciled in Md. when foreign proceeding commenced, and foreign court exercised no jurisdiction over that spouse or property at issue (§8-212). When granting annulment, divorce or separation as to personal property, court may order partition or sale of jointly owned property, but may not transfer ownership from one party to other when granting annulment or absolute divorce; court has same powers as to real property. (§8-202). When granting absolute divorce, court shall determine value of "marital property" acquired during marriage other than by inheritance or gift (§§8-201[e], 8-203); court may grant monetary award as adjustment of equities of parties concerning marital property, based on enumerated factors, including monetary and nonmonetary contributions of each spouse; military pensions must be considered as any retirement benefit. (§§8-203[b], 8-205). Court may allocate costs of maintaining health insurance coverage and require continuation of reinstatement of health insurance

See note at head of Digest as to 1998 legislation covered.

See Topical Index in front part of this volume.

MD – 43

DIVORCE . . . *continued*
coverage. (§12-102). When granting separation or divorce, court may determine which property is "family home" (§8-201[c]) and "family use personal property" (§8-201[d]) as defined, and may make orders as to use or possession of such property regardless of how it is titled or owned. (§§8-206 to 8-208). This authority is to be exercised to continue familiar environment for children, to permit continued use of such property by parent with custody of children, and in consideration of best interests of children and parties. (§8-206). Authority may be exercised pendente lite. (§§8-207, 8-208). Decree subject to modification (§8-209), and may not be for more than three years without extension by court (§8-210). Rights under decree cease if spouse granted such rights remarries. (§8-210). See category Estates and Trusts, topic Descent and Distribution, subhead Surviving Spouse.

Change of Wife's Name.—Request for change of name should be included in bill and in testimony. If requested, final decree must include restoration of spouse's former name, absent some illegal, fraudulent, or immoral intent. (§7-105).

Custody of Children.—Whether divorce is decreed or denied, court may determine who shall have custody and guardianship of children and support them, and may at any time annul, vary or modify order as to children. (§1-201). Court may award custody of minor child to either parent or joint custody to both parents. (306 Md. 290, 508 A.2d 964). Neither parent is presumed to have superior right to custody. (§5-203). Child 16 or over subject to custody decree may petition court to amend decree to change custody. (§9-103). Court may appoint attorney to represent children. (§1-202). Grandparent may petition court for reasonable visitation rights. (§9-102). If party to custody or visitation order unjustifiably denies or interferes with visitation rights, court may reschedule visitation, modify custody or visitation order to ensure compliance, and assess costs or counsel fees against interfering party. (§9-105). Court may require parties in action for divorce to participate in educational seminar designed to assist parents in minimizing disruption divorce causes in lives of their children. (§7-103.2).

Uniform Child Custody Jurisdiction Act enacted. (§§9-201 to 9-224).

Allowance for Support of Children.—Court may make allowance for support of children pending suit or thereafter and may change decree with respect thereto from time to time. (§§1-201, 12-101, 12-104). Each party is required to notify court and any support agency ordered to receive payments within ten days of change in address or employment. (§12-101[c][1]). Court shall use statutory child support guidelines in proceedings to establish or modify child support, pendente lite or permanent. (§§12-201 to 12-204). Except in certain circumstances, court shall immediately authorize service of earnings withholding order for all child support orders. (§10-122.1). Child Support Enforcement Administration may request, and court may order, employer or labor union to provide information and assistance to locate absent parent or to enforce parent's support liability. (§12-105). Court may issue withholding order on earnings of party defaulting in payment of court ordered child or spousal support. (§§10-120 to 10-135).

Remarriage.—No prohibition.

Foreign Divorces.—No statutory provision.

Absolute Divorce after Legal Separation.—Party who has obtained legal separation on ground of abandonment not estopped from subsequently obtaining absolute divorce although grounds insufficient to justify absolute divorce at time separation granted. (§7-103[e]; R. P. 9-203).

Separation Agreements.—Any deed, agreement or settlement between husband and wife respecting alimony, support, property rights or personal rights is binding and enforceable (§§8-101, 8-201[e]) and does not bar action for divorce, whether cause for divorce existed at time of or arose subsequent to time of execution, or whether at time of execution parties were living together or apart (§8-102). Where agreement makes provision for care, custody, education or maintenance of children, court may modify agreement in this respect. (§8-103). Court may also modify provisions as to support, or alimony between spouses unless there is express waiver by either spouse or agreement specifically provides otherwise. (§8-103).

Annulment of Marriage.—See topic Marriage.

GUARDIAN AND WARD:

References are to Estates and Trusts Article of Code unless otherwise indicated.

Father and mother are joint natural guardians of their minor child. (fam. law art. §5-203). Orphans' courts and circuit courts (in equity) have concurrent jurisdiction over minors. (§13-105). Family Division to be established in each circuit court, where feasible. (fam. law art. §1-201). Circuit courts have exclusive jurisdiction over disabled persons. (§13-105). Court may appoint guardian of property of minor or disabled person. (§§13-201 to 13-222). If court determines that property or benefits require protection or management, or funds are necessary for support and welfare of minor, it appoints guardian of property of minor or disabled person. (§13-201). Court may appoint guardian of person of minor or disabled person. (§§13-702 to 13-710). If neither parent is serving and no testamentary appointment has been made, court may appoint guardian of person of unmarried minor. (§13-702). Consent to guardianship may be revoked within 30 days after consent signed. (fam. law art. §5-317). For disabled person, see §§13-704 to 13-710. Special provisions apply to guardian of Veterans Administration beneficiary. (§§13-801 to 13-806). See also Md. Rules as to fiduciaries. (R. P. 10-101 to 10-712).

Selection of Guardian.—Court appoints guardian of property in following order of priority: (1) Foreign-appointed guardian or committee or other fiduciary; (2) person or corporation nominated by minor or disabled person who was over 16 and of mental capacity; (3) spouse; (4) parent(s); (5) person or corporation nominated by will of deceased parent; (6) children; (7) would-be heir; (8) nominee of institution providing care; (9) nominee of governmental agency paying benefits; (10) any other person deemed appropriate by court. (§13-207[a]). Guardian of person of unmarried minor may be appointed by will of surviving parent. (§13-701). Guardian of person of disabled person determined according to priorities listed in §13-707.

Eligibility and Competency.—Nonresident person or trust company may act as guardian upon designation of person or trust company to receive service of process. (§§13-207[d], 13-707[d]). No employee or official of local social services, State Department of Human Resources or Office on Aging may be appointed guardian. (§13-207[e]).

Appointment of guardian is procured in equity by petition. (§13-201[a]). Appointment by orphans' court is procured in same manner or may be made by court upon its own initiative. (§§13-201, 13-702, 13-705; R. P. 10-105 to 10-712). Petition for adoption in circuit court may be preceded by petition for guardianship. (fam. law art. §5-317).

Standby guardian of person or property of minor may be appointed by court upon petition by parent of minor when there is significant risk that petitioner will die or become incapacitated within two years of filing of petition. (§§13-901 to 13-908).

Inventory.—See subhead Accounts, infra.

Qualification.—No formalities. Bond not mandatory but may be required of natural person unless excused by appointing instrument or unless estate is less than $10,000. (§13-208).

Powers and Duties.—Guardian of property has broad general duties and powers with respect to administration and distribution of minor's or disabled person's property without application to court or court authorization or confirmation. (§§13-213, 13-214). Powers include power to sell, mortgage, lease, borrow money and other general fiduciary powers. (§§13-213, 13-214, 15-102; R. P. 10-703, 10-108[b]). Court may grant to guardian of person only those powers necessary to provide for demonstrated need of disabled person. (§13-708).

Investments.—If estate consists entirely of cash not in excess of $75,000, guardian may apply for court order authorizing deposit in insured financial institution. (R. P. 10-705). Unless limited by court order, guardian of property appointed by court has broad powers without court approval to invest in any property and to deposit funds in checking accounts and in insured interest-bearing accounts. (§§15-102, 15-106; R. P. 10-108[6], 10-703, 13-403). See also category Estates and Trusts, topic Trusts, subhead Investments.

Securities in Name of Nominee.—For fiduciary estates subject to court jurisdiction, order granting authority must be obtained from court. (R. P. 10-704[a][2]). Fiduciaries not subject to court jurisdiction may hold securities in name of nominee but fiduciary may be liable for wrongful act of nominee. (§15-102[x]). See category Estates and Trusts, topic Trusts, subhead Securities in Name of Nominee.

Real estate may be sold, invested, exchanged, leased or mortgaged without court order or confirmation. (§15-102[c]).

Liabilities of Guardian.—Liabilities and responsibilities are same as those of trustee or other fiduciary. (§§13-212, 13-216). Subject to provisions of Md. Rules, termination does not relieve guardian from liability. (§13-220[b][2]). Person involved in filing petition for appointment of guardian of person or participating in good-faith report, investigation or judicial proceeding relating thereto is immune from civil liability or criminal penalty. (§13-710[a]).

Accounts.—Equity court will require guardian it appoints to file inventory of assets within 60 days after appointment or assumption of jurisdiction and to file accounts once each year. (R. P. 10-705[d], 10-706, 10-707). Guardian appointed by orphans' court must file inventory with court 60 days after appointment and must file annual account with court. (R. P. 10-206, 10-208, 10-712). Upon death of guardian, guardian's personal representative must render account of ward's estate and apply for appointment of successor. (§13-220[c]). Unless time is extended by court order guardian must submit final account and proposal for final distribution within 90 days of termination of guardianship. (R. P. 10-209, 10-710, 10-207[e], 10-711[f]). Guardian of person must file annual report with court stating address and health status of disabled, non-minor person, guardian's plan to maintain well-being of person, and need for continuance, cessation or alteration of guardianship. (§13-708[b][7]; 293 Md. 685, 447 A.2d 1244, cert. denied, 459 U.S. 1147).

Removal of Guardian.—Court must remove guardian and appoint successor, after notice and hearing, for reasons of misrepresentation leading to appointment, willful disregard of court order, incapacity or breach of duty of good faith; court may do so for reasons of negligence or failure to completely perform any fiduciary duty. (R. P. 13-701, 10-208, 10-712).

Termination of Guardianship.—Court, upon petition, notice and hearing, may terminate guardianship if it finds that minority or disability has ceased or that minor or disabled person is dead or for other good cause. (§§13-220, 13-221; R. P. 10-209).

Insane Persons.—Circuit courts have exclusive jurisdiction. (§13-105). Upon petition, notice and hearing, court appoints guardian for disabled person. (§§13-105, 13-201, 13-704). For provisions concerning admission of mentally disabled persons into institutions, and release therefrom, see health-gen. art. §§10-601 to 10-813.

Foreign Guardians.—Foreign guardian may represent ward in Md. and exercise all powers of office without being appointed by Md. court but must file designation of Maryland resident to receive process for him. (§§13-222, 13-707[d]).

Gifts to Minors.—See topic Infants.

Uniform Fiduciaries Act adopted. (§§15-201 to 15-211).

Uniform Act for the Simplification of Fiduciary Security Transfers adopted. (§§15-301 to 15-311). Uniform Commercial Code does not repeal this Act. (comm. law art. §10-104).

HUSBAND AND WIFE:

Husband and wife are both sui juris as between themselves and with respect to other persons.

Disabilities of Married Women.—All disabilities removed. (See fam. law art. §4-201 et seq.; Md. Const., Declar. of Rights art. 46.)

Separate Property.—Property belonging to woman at time of marriage and all property she may acquire or receive after marriage is protected from debts of husband. (fam. law art. §4-301[d]). Similarly, property of husband is his own and free from claims of wife or her creditors. (fam. law art. §4-301[c]).

See note at head of Digest as to 1998 legislation covered.

See Topical Index in front part of this volume.

HUSBAND AND WIFE . . . continued

Contracts.—No restrictions on contracts made by married woman or husband, and they may contract with each other as freely as with third persons. (fam. law art. §§4-204, 4-205). Husband is no longer liable for debt or contract incurred or entered into by his wife on his credit. (fam. law art. §4-302 repealed by c. 360, H.B. 38).

Antenuptual agreements.—Settling or barring rights in real or personal property valid if full disclosure is made of worth or property to be waived or if waiving party has adequate knowledge of such worth. Absent disclosure or knowledge, if property rights waived are unfairly disproportionate to worth of property at time agreement is made, burden is on party relying on agreement to prove it was entered into voluntarily, freely and with full knowledge of effect and meaning. Substantial proof of valid waiver is receipt of independent legal advice by waiving party. (fam. law art. §§8-201 to 213; 298 Md. 552, 471 A.2d 705; 248 Md. 47, 234 A.2d 865).

Actions.—Married woman may sue or be sued in own name without restriction. (fam. law art. §§4-204, 4-205). In suit against married woman, no judgment or decree may be entered against her husband. (fam. law art. §§4-204 to 4-205). Husband not liable upon contract made by wife in own name and on own responsibility, or for tort committed by wife out of his presence and without his participation or sanction. (fam. law art. §4-301). Common law action for criminal conversation abolished. (287 Md. 585, 414 A.2d 929).

Husband and wife may sue each other in contract (fam. law art. §§4-204[5], 4-205[a]), but not for personal tort (152 Md. 247, 136 A. 534), but spousal immunity does not apply to action for outrageous, intentional tort (283 Md. 334, 390 A.2d 77).

Agency.—One spouse may appoint other to act as agent or attorney. (fam. law art. §4-204).

Conveyance or Encumbrance of Property.—Husband or wife may convey, transfer or encumber separate personal or real property without consent or joinder of other. (fam. law art. §4-203; est. & tr. art. §3-202). See category Property, topic Deeds, subhead Straw Deeds.

Desertion or Nonsupport.—Any person who without just cause willfully neglects to provide for support of his or her spouse or minor child, or deserts such child, is guilty of misdemeanor and may be prosecuted on information of State's Attorney. Before trial, with consent of traverser, or after conviction, court may, instead of imposing punishment or in addition thereto, make order for weekly payments to spouse or for child, which order constitutes lien on wages; and upon notice, employer must remit such amount to probation department, Child Support Enforcement Administration of Dep't of Human Resources or designated local agency. (fam. law art. §10-201 et seq.). Except in certain circumstances, court shall immediately authorize service of earnings withholding order for all child support orders. (fam. law art. §10-122).

Maryland Uniform Interstate Family Support Act (fam. law art. §§10-301-10-348).

Community property law inapplicable.

INFANTS:

Age of majority is 18 for both sexes. "Adult" is person 18 or over. "Minor," as pertains to legal age and capacity, is person under 18. (art. 1, §24). Alcoholic beverages may be sold only to persons 21 or older. (art. 2B, §12-108).

Emancipation.—Upon marriage, minor obtains certain rights, such as right to join with spouse who has reached age of majority in deed, deed of trust, mortgage, lease, note or financing statement. (est. & tr. art. §13-503[a]). Upon reaching age 15, minor may contract for annuity or life or health insurance, or for property, casualty and surety insurance on own property or interests, and minor not entitled to rescind, avoid, or repudiate contract, or any exercise of right or privilege because of his minority; however, neither minor nor minor's estate being administered by guardian is bound by unperformed agreement to pay insurance premium. (est. & tr. art. §13-503[c]). Receipt from minor who is sole owner of or has right to withdraw funds from account in financial institution is valid release of institution from payment to minor on account. (est. & tr. art. §13-504).

Disabilities existing at common law, such as those relating to capacity to contract and right to vote, still prevail. (comm. law art. §1-103; art. 33, §3-4[b][2]).

Ratification of Contracts.—Contract not beneficial to infant is not merely voidable but void ab initio and may not be ratified. Contract beneficial to infant or uncertain as to benefit or prejudice is voidable at election of infant and may be ratified upon infant's coming of age. Ratification may be either by express confirmation upon coming of age or by some act, such as acceptance of benefits, which would make it inequitable not to bind infant. Voidable contract may be disaffirmed by minor (1) during minority, or (2) if not ratified, within reasonable time after majority, or by minor's privies in blood. (comm. law art. §1-103; 49 F. Supp. 611 [D. Md. 1943]).

Medical treatment may be consented to as if adult by minor who is married or parent or is seeking advice concerning drug abuse, alcoholism, venereal disease, pregnancy or contraception not amounting to sterilization, is examined for treatment, or to obtain evidence of sexual assault, or initial medical screening and physical examination on and after admission of minor into detention center, or if, in judgment of physician, obtaining of consent of other person would adversely affect person's life or health. (health-gen. art. §20-102). Minor may not refuse treatment for drug abuse or alcoholism in inpatient alcohol or drug abuse treatment program certified under Title 8 of health-gen. art. for which parent or guardian has given consent. (health-gen. art. §20-102[c-1]). Minor age 16 or older has capacity to consent to consultation, diagnosis, and treatment concerning mental or emotional disorder. (health-gen. art. §20-104). Physician treating consenting minor not liable civilly or otherwise solely by reason of lack of capacity of minor to consent as above, nor is parent, guardian, or custodian liable for costs of treatment. (health-gen. art. §§20-102, 20-104). Under some circumstances, physician has option to inform spouse, parent, custodian or guardian of treatment given to minor. (health-gen. art. §§20-102, 20-103, 20-104). Physician may not perform abortion on unmarried minor unless first giving notice to parent or guardian except if minor does not live with, and reasonable efforts have been unsuccessful to give notice to, parent or

guardian, or such notice, in professional judgment of physician, may lead to physical or emotional abuse of minor. (health gen. art. §20-103). Attorney General for Maryland, however, has opined that health gen. art. §20-103 is unconstitutional and unenforceable. (75 Op AG No. 90-041). Amendment allowing physician to perform abortion upon mature minor or if in best interests of minor adopted. (health gen. art. §20-103).

License to sell alcoholic beverages may not be issued except by special order of judge. If license is issued, minor is liable for trade debts as though of full age. Parent responsibility unaffected. (art. 2B, subtitle 12A).

Actions.—Infants may sue by guardian or next friend and defend by guardian, or if no guardian, by attorney appointed by court in each case. (R. P. 2-202[b], [c]). Parent who is sole custodian of minor has exclusive right to sue for period of one year following accrual of cause of action. (R.P. 2-202[b]). Generally, any action brought by next friend may be settled by same, but, if next friend is not parent or person in loco parentis, settlement must be approved by parent or other person responsible for child or, if there is no such parent or person, by court in which suit is brought. (courts art. §6-405). If minor or other person on behalf of minor recovers on tort claim $2,000 or more, person responsible for payment of money must make payment by check payable to order of designated person, "trustee under Title 13 of the Estates and Trusts Article . . . for [minor]." Trustee must deposit check in financial institution. Withdrawal is allowed only by minor upon attaining majority, by personal representative of deceased minor, or upon order of circuit court. (est. & tr. art. §§13-401 to 13-407).

Parental Responsibility.—In any juvenile cause, judge may award judgment of restitution in favor of wronged person and against parent for damage, destruction or theft of property or for medical or funeral expenses caused by child under 18 if damage or expense was caused during commission of delinquent act. Judgment may not exceed: (1) Lesser of $5,000 or fair market value of property stolen or destroyed; (2) lesser of $5,000 or amount of damage or decrease in value of property, not to exceed fair market value of property or $5,000; or (3) lesser of $5,000 or reasonable medical or funeral expenses incurred. Absolute limit is $5,000 against any one child or his parents for acts arising out of single incident. Parent must be given opportunity to be heard and present evidence. Judgment enforced as other money judgment. (Crimes and Punishment art. §851).

Adoption.—See topic Adoption.

Custody.—See topic Divorce, subhead Custody of Children.

Absent Parents.—See category Property, topic Absentees, subhead Absent Parents.

Distributions.—Any person, including personal representative or trustee, who is under duty to pay money or deliver tangible personal property to minor may pay or deliver to guardian. If none or none known (payor not under duty to inquire), he may pay or deliver not exceeding $5,000 (amount or value) per annum to parent or grandparent with whom minor resides. If none, he may pay or deliver not exceeding $5,000 to parent or other person in loco parentis or deposit it in financial institution in sole name of minor (withdrawable only on court order or upon attainment of majority). Person receiving for minor must apply money to support and education of minor and preserve any excess money or tangible chattels until majority. Payor need not see to proper application of money or property. (est. & tr. art. §13-501). Personal representative, with approval of court, may distribute to minor who has no guardian by: (1) Depositing money in bank or insured savings and loan association subject to order of court; (2) transferring "custodial property" to custodian under Uniform Gifts to Minors Act; or (3) transferring tangible property to appropriate responsible person under conditions set forth in court order. If guardian has been appointed, personal representative may make payment to guardian upon filing of authenticated copy of authority. (est. & tr. art. §9-109).

Revised Uniform Gifts to Minors Act repealed.

Uniform Transfers to Minors Act adopted. (est. & tr. art. §§13-301 to 13-324). Applies to transfers of custodial property made July 1, 1989 if purported to have been made under Uniform Gifts to Minors Act or instrument designates custodian under Uniform Gifts to Minors Act or Uniform Transfer of Property Act of other state. (est. & tr. art. §13-321). Transfers of custodial property made before July 1, 1989 validated notwithstanding that transfer may not have been made under Uniform Gifts to Minors Act. (est. & tr. art. §13-322). Act is not exclusive method for making transfers to minors. (est. & tr. art. §13-323).

Uniform Securities Ownership by Minors Act not adopted.

Maryland Discretionary Trust Act adopted. (1994, c. 418).

Interstate Compact on Placement of Children enacted. (fam. law art. §§5-601 to 5-611).

Veterans.—War veteran or member of armed services who is minor may mortgage, buy or sell real estate, execute notes or perform other acts necessary to obtain benefits of Servicemen's Readjustment Act, and release claims. (est. & tr. art. §13-503[b]).

MARRIAGE:

Consent Required.—Male or female under 16 may not marry except (i) with consent of parent or guardian, accompanied by certificate of licensed physician that female is pregnant or has given birth to child. (fam. law art. §2-301[b]). Male or female 16 or 17 may marry (i) with consent of parent or guardian, who must swear that person to be married is at least 16 years old, or (ii) without consent of parent or guardian, but with certificate of licensed physician that female is pregnant or has given birth to child. (fam. law art. §2-301[a]).

License.—Marriage license obtained from clerk of circuit court for jurisdiction in which marriage is to be performed. (fam. law art. §2-402). License fee is $10, but county may set additional fee. (fam. law art. §2-404).

Before clerk may issue license, one of contracting parties must appear personally, apply for license and be examined under oath, and license may not be delivered by clerk until after 48 hours from time of application therefor, unless otherwise ordered by judge of circuit court in jurisdiction in case where at least one party is bona fide resident of state. Notarized statement may be substituted for personal appearance before clerk

MARRIAGE . . . *continued*

where neither party is resident of county where marriage to be performed. Court may waive 48-hour provision on request of party who is member of U.S. Armed Forces or who is Maryland resident. (fam. law art. §§2-402, 2-405).

Application information to be provided by applicant(s) to clerk includes: (i) full name, place of residence, and age of each party; (ii) whether parties are related by blood or marriage and, if so, in which degree of relationship; (iii) marital status of each party; and (iv) whether either party married previously, and date and place of each death or judicial determination that ended any former marriage. (fam. law art. §2-402[b]). If one party has been divorced, it is not necessary to submit copy of decree, but in practice divorced person must appear before clerk and answer questions before license will be issued.

If legal impediment to marriage exists, clerk must refuse to issue license until ordered by court to do so. (fam. law art. §2-405[f]).

Ceremonial Marriage.—Any minister or official of religious order or body authorized by rule or custom of such order or body to perform marriages may solemnize marriage in Md., and so may clerk or designated deputy clerk of circuit court. (fam. law art. §§2-406[a], 2-410). Person performing marriage must sign certificate and return one to married couple and one to clerk issuing marriage license. No provisions as to witnesses. Special rules for signing and disposition of marriage certificates for Society of Friends or Quaker marriages. (fam. law art. §2-409).

Marriage must be performed within six months after issuance of license. (fam. law art. §2-406[b]).

Reports of Marriages.—Person performing marriage must file certificate with clerk issuing license within five days after ceremony. (fam. law art. §2-409[b]). Clerk must make report at set intervals to Secretary of Health and Mental Hygiene of all licenses, divorces, and annulments granted by court. (fam. law art. §2-503).

Record.—See category Documents and Records, topic Records, subhead Vital Statistics.

Common law marriage not permitted, but if valid where contracted will be recognized. (20 Md. App. 369, 315 A.2d 816).

Proxy Marriages.—Not authorized.

Marriages by Written Contract.—Not authorized. (See 35 Md. 361.)

Prohibited Marriages.—Only marriage between man and woman is valid. (fam. law art. §2-201). Marriage void within enumerated degrees of consanguinity or affinity. (fam. law art. §2-202; 22 Md. 468). Prohibition on interracial marriage repealed.

Foreign Marriage.—Marriage valid where performed is valid in Md. (129 Md. 131, 98 A. 358).

Annulment.—Annulment procedure governed by Md. Rules. (R. P. 9-201—9-210). When court convicts one or both spouses of bigamy or of marrying within prohibited degree, judgment of conviction annuls marriage, provided that transcript of docket entries of criminal proceedings is recorded in records of circuit court of same county at instance of any interested person. (R. P. 9-209).

Venue.—County where plaintiff resides, or where defendant resides, is regularly employed or has place of business, or county where marriage was performed. (R. P. 9-201).

Children.—Child born or conceived during marriage is presumed legitimate. (est. & tr. art. §1-206[a]).

MARRIED WOMEN:

See topics Husband and Wife, Marriage; categories Civil Actions and Procedure, topic Evidence, subhead Witnesses; Debtor and Creditor, topic Homesteads; Documents and Records, topic Acknowledgments; Estates and Trusts, topics Executors and Administrators, Wills; Property, topic Dower.

INSURANCE

INSURANCE COMPANIES:

Insurance companies are under control of Maryland Insurance Administration, headed by Insurance Commissioner, 501 St. Paul Pl., Baltimore 21202. (§2-101). Effective 10/1/97, provisions relating to insurance have been recodified and transferred to new article, Insurance Article. References are to Insurance Article ("ins. art.") unless otherwise indicated.

Approval of Insurance Commissioner required for certain purchases, mergers, or other acquisitions of domestic insurers or certain other persons. (§§7-301-7-600). Extraordinary dividends or distributions of certain insurers regulated. (§7-706).

Annual statements must be filed with Insurance Commissioner on or before Mar. 1, accompanied by fee of $25. (§§2-112, 4-116). Late fee of $100 per day applies up to and including Mar. 10 ($150 per day thereafter). Audited financial report for year ending Dec. 31 due on or before June 1. Late fee of $100 per day applies up to and including June 1-June 10 (both inclusive) ($150 per day thereafter). Extension for good cause shown granted for ten days for either annual statement or audited financial report. (§4-116[a]).

Policies.—Extensive statutory provisions govern policy forms for all types of insurance. Forms must be filed with and approved by Insurance Commissioner. See ins. art., Title 11 and subdivisions thereof for various types of insurance. Variable life insurance and annuity contracts are authorized.

Rates.—All rates for surety, fidelity, casualty, liability, compensation, property, marine, inland marine, title, fire and allied lines must be approved by Insurance Commissioner. Rating organizations must obtain license from Commissioner. Provision made for review by courts of any order or decision of Commissioner. (§§2-202, 2-209, 11-205).

Certificate of Authority.—Domestic and foreign insurers must meet certain requirements as to capital, surplus, deposit of securities; they must file articles of incorporation and bylaws with all amendments; they must annually obtain certificate of authority from Commissioner. (§§4-101—4-116). Fee for original certificate of authority is $1,000; annual renewal fee for foreign insurers and domestic insurers with executive office in state is $500. Fee for annual renewal for domestic insurers with executive office outside state $2,500 to $11,000, except for those with out-of-state executive office prior to 1/1/29. Fee for reinstatement of certificate of authority is $500. Fee for filing articles of incorporation is $25. Fee for filing bylaws or amendments is $10. (§2-112[a]).

Accounting records and most assets of domestic companies must be kept within state. (§4-115).

Discrimination unlawful, with certain exceptions. (§27-208).

Rebates unlawful, with certain exceptions. (§§27-209, 27-212).

Insurance fraud involving value of $300 or more is felony subject to fine of $500 to $10,000 (or three times value of claim, whichever is larger), and subject to imprisonment up to 15 years, or both. (§§2-401—2-408).

Liens.—No provision for lien on policies.

Agents, Solicitors and Brokers.—Insurance agents and solicitors must have annual certificates of qualification, brokers must give bond, and continuing education required for renewal of certificate. (§10-101, see Title 10, subtitle 1 generally). Out-of-state broker may negotiate insurance on subjects of insurance in Md. on same terms and on payment of same fees as law of such other state imposes on citizens of Md. engaged in like business in such state. (§10-119).

Persons authorized by certificate of qualification issued by Insurance Commissioner and designated Managing General Agents may under certain conditions manage all or part of insurance business of insurer. (§8-201, see Title 8, subtitle 2, generally). Those activities expressly prohibited by managing agents are detailed in §8-209.

Surplus line broker or insured who obtains insurance from unauthorized insurer must file report with Insurance Commissioner. (§§3-301—3-327).

Applicant for certificate of qualification as agent or broker must pass written examination, with certain exceptions, and be otherwise qualified in terms of character, study programs and experience. (§§10-112, 10-103). Upon denial of application, applicant may have hearing before Commissioner and appeal to courts. (§§2-210—2-215).

Certificate of agent or broker may be suspended or revoked and penalty may be imposed for cause after notice and hearing, with right of appeal to courts. (§§10-126, 2-210—2-215).

Certificate fee for agent is $25 to $50 and $50 for biennial renewal; for broker it is $40 to $80 and $80 for biennial renewal; for surplus line broker it is $100 and $200 for biennial renewal. (§2-112[a][4]).).

Lloyds Underwriters may not organize or do business in Md., but insurers may, if otherwise permitted, place surplus line coverages in and cede reinsurance to foreign or alien Lloyds organizations. (§4-102[d][2]).

Process Agent.—Each insurer, each surplus line broker, and each fraternal benefit society, before being authorized to do business in Md., must irrevocably appoint Insurance Commissioner as agent to receive service of process. (§§4-107, 3-318[b], 3-319[d], 8-407). Process may also be served on domestic insurer as on other domestic corporation. (corps. art. §1-401; R. P. 2-124[c]). See category Civil Actions and Procedure, topic Process, subhead Personal Service on Corporation.

Insurance, surety or bonding company having accredited resident agent in Md. may be sued on its policies through service on such resident agent. (courts art. §6-306).

Unauthorized or alien insurer who solicits or issues contracts to Md. residents, or who otherwise transacts insurance business in Md. is deemed to appoint Insurance Commissioner as agent to receive service of process. (§4-206; see also courts art. §6-103 [b][6]).

Investments.—Life insurance companies must invest amount not less than required minimum paid-in capital stock in cash, or in bonds of or guaranteed by U.S., or in bonds of Md. or of any other state, or in Md. municipal bonds, and they must invest amount not less than entire reserves as defined in §5-511(b) in various other restricted classes of reserve investments. (§§5-501—5-511). Insurers other than life insurers must invest amount not less than required minimum paid-in capital stock and surplus, not less than 60% in bonds of or guaranteed by U.S. or in Md. state or Md. municipal bonds and balance in bonds of any other state, or in certain Md. mortgages or deeds of trust or in certain ground rents; and they must invest amount not less than 50% of unearned premium and loss reserves in certain other classes of reserve investments. (§5-607, see generally §§5-601—5-609). Investments of foreign or alien insurers may be as permitted by law of domicile but must be of quality substantially as high as is required of domestic insurers. (§§5-502, 5-602).

Reinsurance.—Domestic insurer may reinsure all or any part of particular risk and, with approval of Commissioner, may reinsure all or bulk of insurance in force. (§§5-903, 3-124, 3-125). Licenses and activities of reinsurance companies regulated. (§§8-501—8-520).

Liability Insurance.—All liability insurance policies issued in Md. must provide that bankruptcy or insolvency of insured shall not release insurer from liability. (§19-102). All liability policies issued to charitable institutions must provide that insurer shall be estopped from asserting defense of charitable immunity as to any claim covered by policy. (§19-103).

Compulsory motor vehicle liability insurance and certain no-fault coverage is in effect. (trans. art. §17-101; art. 48A, §§19-501—19-514). See category Transportation, topic Motor Vehicles, subhead Insurance.

Mutual insurance companies regulated by §§3-101 to 3-128.

Fraternal benefit societies regulated by §§8-401—8-468. See also subhead Foreign Insurance Companies, infra.

Health maintenance organizations, regulated by health-gen. art. tit. 19, subtit. 7, are authorized by Insurance Commissioner and subject to supervision of Commissioner and Dep't of Health and Mental Hygiene. They are not generally subject to insurance law and do not pay taxes on premiums. (health-gen. art., 19-706).

Health Insurance.—Extensive health insurance reforms set forth in courts & jud. proc. art. §3-2A-02; health-gen. art. §§19-706, 19-1501 through 19-1516, 19-1601

INSURANCE COMPANIES . . . *continued*
through 19-606, 19-714, 19-716, 19-729; health-occ. art. §1-209. Maryland Health Care Access and Cost Commission established to: (1) develop health care cost containment strategies; (2) facilitate public disclosure of medical claims data; (3) develop medical care database, resource management systems, and uniform set of benefits to be included in comprehensive standard health benefit plan; (4) develop payment system for health care services; and (5) establish standards for operation and licensing of electronic claims clearinghouses. (health-gen. art. §19-1502). Commission shall assess fee on all insurers and certain health care practitioners and self-insured groups. (health-gen. art. §19-1515).

Nonprofit health service plans regulated. (§§1-202, 5-101, 5-102). Certain educational and religious organizations and community foundations may make annuity agreements with donors. Authority of Insurance Commissioner to issue permits for such annuity agreements expires 9/30/99. (§16-114).

Except as otherwise provided, health insurance plan issued by nonprofit health center, health insurer or group or blanket health insurer may not contain non-duplicative provisions or coordinating coverage provisions with individually issued specified disease or intensive care policy. (§15-104).

Group Health Insurance contracts must offer option to continue coverage to surviving or divorced spouse and dependent children, and to employees who are involuntarily terminated. (§§15-404, 15-407—15-409). Employers must offer dependent coverage to eligible employees and to all eligible dependents of all eligible employees but need not contribute to premiums. (§17-209). Carriers must establish annual open enrollment period for self-employed individuals for at least 30 consecutive days in each six-month period. (§§15-411, 15-210).

When insurer intends to withdraw product from state market, must give Commission 90 days' notice; 180 days' notice required before insurer withdraws completely. (§27-603).

Coverage of preexisting conditions and long-term care benefits regulated by §§16-214, 15-208, 642 to 649.1, 701. Maryland Partnership for Long-Term Care Program provides long-term care benefits for enrollees. (health-gen. art. §§15-401 to 15-407, 647).

Health insurance for women with breast implants regulated by §15-105.

AIDS Insurance Assistance Program established to help HIV-positive individuals retain insurance coverage. (health-gen. art. §§15-201 to 15-205).

Coverage for mental illness regulated by health-gen. art. §19-703.

Medical Mutual Liability Insurance Society, non-stock corporation to issue policies of insurance against medical malpractice, funded initially by one-time tax on all physicians for privilege of practicing in state, established by 1975 legislative session, c. 544. (§§24-201—24-210).

Policies insuring health care providers (courts art. §3-2A-01) must be consistent with title 3, subtitle 2A of courts art., and must authorize insurer to settle claims within policy limits if paid solely by insurer. Insurer may make payments to claimants, within policy limits, before disposition of claim without admission of liability, damages or other prejudice. (§19-104).

Purchase of voting security or entering into agreement to merge or consolidate with or otherwise acquire control of foreign nonprofit health service plan or HMO authorized to do business in Maryland requires approval of Insurance Commissioner under certain circumstances and is regulated under Title 7, subtitles 3 and 4, §§7-109, 7-502, 7-306, and health-gen. art. §§19-711.2 to 19-711.3.

Legal Mutual Liability Insurance Society of Md. authorized. Effective upon finding by Insurance Commissioner, after consultation with state bar association, that substantial number of attorneys are or within six months will be unable to obtain malpractice insurance, lack of which affects Md. residents' ability to obtain adequate legal representation, creates mutual liability insurance company to indemnify person suffering injury resulting from rendering or failure to render legal services. Participation voluntary. (§§24-101—24-105).

Maryland Credit Union Insurance Corporation, under supervision of Bank Commissioner, insures all state-chartered credit union accounts after July 1, 1976. Foreign credit unions which are authorized to do business in Md. and have principal place of business in Md. may also be members. (fin. inst. art. §§7-101 to 7-117).

Insurance premium finance companies are regulated by §§23-101—23-506.

Risk Retention Groups.—Formed pursuant to Federal Liability Risk Retention Act and regulated by §§25-101-25-111.

Foreign Insurance Companies.—Foreign insurers may not engage in insurance business in Md. or maintain office or representative to solicit or service any kind of insurance in Md. unless expressly authorized by certificate of authority issued by Insurance Commissioner. Foreign insurer must meet capital and surplus requirements and must file with application for initial certificate of authority: (1) Copy of articles of incorporation with all amendments; (2) copy of bylaws with all amendments; (3) latest annual statement; (4) report of last examination certified by insurance supervisory official of domicile; (5) certificate of supervisory official of domicile that company is authorized to transact kinds of insurance proposed to be transacted in Md.; (6) certificate of supervisory official of domicile that company has deposited $100,000 in trust for protection of policyholders; (7) power of attorney authorizing Insurance Commissioner to receive service of process; (8) for alien insurer, copy of appointment of authority of U.S. manager. (§§4-108[3], 4-101—4-118). Similar provisions apply to foreign fraternal benefit societies. (§8-424). No insurer may be authorized to do business in Md. if it has or uses name confusingly similar to name of insurer already authorized. (§4-102). Foreign insurer authorized to do business in Md. may become domestic insurer by complying with laws relating to formation and organization of domestic insurer and designating place in Md. as principal place of business. (§3-126).

Retaliatory Law.—If by laws of any other state, taxes, licenses and other fees, in aggregate, and fines, penalties, deposit requirements or other material obligations, prohibitions or restrictions, additional to or in excess of those imposed by Md. laws on insurance companies of such other state, are imposed on insurance companies of Md. doing business or seeking to do business in such state, like obligations or prohibitions are imposed by Md. upon insurance companies of other state doing business in Md. Excepted from retaliation are personal income taxes, ad valorem taxes and special purpose assessments as to anything other than property insurance. (§6-301, see generally Title 6, subtitle 3).

Premium Tax.—Every insurance company must pay tax on new and renewal gross direct premiums allocable to state and written during preceding calendar year at rate of 0% of consideration for annuities and 2% of all other premiums (except property insurance written by domestic mutual insurance companies and wet marine and transportation contracts). Tax rate on premiums for property insurance written by domestic mutual insurance companies is 1%. Unauthorized insurers other than certain wet marine and transportation insurers must pay tax of 3% on gross premiums. (§§4-209, 6-102—6-104). Following deductions from gross direct premiums allocable to state are allowed, to extent allocable to taxable premiums: (1) Returned premiums (not including surrender values); (2) dividends paid or credited to policy-holders, or applied to purchase additional insurance or to shorten premium paying period; (3) returns or refunds made or credited to policy-holders because of retrospective ratings or safe driver rewards. (§§6-102—6-104). For all taxable years beginning after June 30, 1976 declaration of estimated tax must be filed with Insurance Commissioner on or before Apr. 15 of current taxable year, and 25% must be paid with each quarterly declaration. (§6-106).

"Insurance company" means: (1) Person engaged as principal in writing insurance, surety, guaranty or annuity contracts (except nonprofit hospital service plan corporations and fraternal beneficiary associations), including mutual insurance companies (except domestic mutual fire insurance companies), title insurance and credit indemnity companies, and (2) attorneys-in-fact for reciprocal exchanges or interinsurers. "Premiums" includes consideration for surety, guaranty and annuity contracts, dividends on life insurance policies which have been applied to purchase additional insurance or to shorten premium paying period, and so much of gross receipts of title insurance companies as is derived from business of insurance or guaranty, but does not include premiums payable weekly on policies covering weekly disability benefits. (§§1-101, 6-101, 6-102).

Domestic insurance companies are entitled to tax credit for annual franchise tax, and in addition, life insurance companies having home offices in state are entitled to credit for fees paid to Insurance Commissioner for valuing life insurance policies, not to exceed 15% of total amount of taxes. (§6-105).

Every insurance company subject to tax must file with Insurance Commissioner, on or before Mar. 15 in each year, report of new and renewal gross direct premiums written during preceding calendar year. (§§6-107, 6-113). Tax remaining, after crediting amount paid with declaration under §6-106, must be paid to Insurance Commissioner at time for filing report and, if not paid, company is subject to penalty of 5% and interest at monthly rate of 1/12 of adjusted annual federal rate (in effect on Jan. 1 of tax year) established by Secretary of Treasury pursuant to §6621 of IRC, from date when report was due. (§§6-107, 6-108).

Additional assessments after reports are filed are provided for. (§6-109). Companies may appeal from additional assessments to tax court. (§6-110).

As to premium tax payable by brokers, see subhead Agents, Solicitors and Brokers, supra.

Privilege Tax.—See subhead Certificate of Authority, supra.

Direct Actions Against Insurer.—See category Transportation, topic Motor Vehicles, subhead Direct Actions.

Rehabilitation and Liquidation.—Special delinquency proceedings constitute sole method of liquidating, rehabilitating, reorganizing or conserving insurer. (§§9-201—9-225).

Maryland Insurance Guaranty Association, to which all licensed insurers in lines other than life and health insurance, mortgage guaranty insurance, and annuities must belong, obligated to pay certain claims against insolvent insurers. (§§9-303—9-316).

Unclaimed funds held and owing by insurance company are governed by Uniform Disposition of Unclaimed Property Act. (comm. law art. tit. 17).

Uniform Insurer's Liquidation Act adopted. (§§9-201, 9-203, 9-207, 9-218 to 9-220, 9-226, 9-227).

No-Fault Insurance.—See category Transportation, topic Motor Vehicles, subhead Insurance, catchline No-Fault Insurance.

SURETY AND GUARANTY COMPANIES:

See also topic Insurance Companies.

Organization.—Surety and guaranty companies may be incorporated under general corporation laws, upon complying with applicable provisions of insurance law (21-101, 21-102, 9-407). Minimum capital stock is $250,000.

Assets; Reserves; License.—Stock company must have surplus assets, in excess of capital stock, of $375,000 to obtain original certificate and must thereafter maintain surplus assets of at least $250,000. Mutual company writing assessable policies must have assets totalling at least $250,000 and exceeding by $125,000 required reserves and other liabilities. (3-101—3-128). Company must obtain license or certificate from Insurance Commissioner before doing business in Md. (art. 4-101). It must also maintain certain designated reserves. (§5-205).

Rights and Powers.—Surety or guaranty company can execute any bond, undertaking or recognizance and guarantee performance of any act, duty or obligation or refraining from any act as required by any law, rule or regulation of any municipality, board, body, department, court, judge or public officer. (21-101[a] to [c]).

Foreign companies may do business in Md., unless state of incorporation prohibits Md. company from doing business in that state. (4-101—4-118).

Taxation.—Subject to same taxation as other businesses, except income tax, and also to annual tax of 2% on all new and renewal gross direct premiums. (§§6-102—6-104).

See note at head of Digest as to 1998 legislation covered.

See Topical Index in front part of this volume.

MD – 47

INTELLECTUAL PROPERTY

TRADEMARKS AND TRADENAMES:

Trademark or service mark may be adopted and used by any person, including any individual, firm, partnership, corporation, association, union or other organization. (bus. reg. art. §1-401).

What May Be Registered.—Any word, name, symbol or device to identify goods made or sold by person and to distinguish them from goods made or sold by others, except that which: (1) Is immoral, deceptive or scandalous; (2) disparages, falsely connects or brings into contempt or disrepute persons, living or dead, institutions, beliefs or national symbols; (3) comprises or simulates flag, coat of arms or other insignia of U.S., or of any state, municipality or foreign nation; (4) consists of or comprises name, signature or portrait of living individual, without his written consent; (5) is merely descriptive or geographically descriptive or deceptively misdescriptive or merely surname, unless mark has become distinctive as evidenced by five years continuous use prior to application (although still subject to attack in litigation [214 Md. 325, 135 A.2d 289]); or (6) so resembles mark registered in Md. or mark or tradename previously used in Md. and not abandoned as to be likely to confuse, deceive or cause mistake. (bus. reg. art. §1-404).

Registration.—Application filed in office of Secretary of State, on form furnished, to be accompanied by filing fee of $50 and three specimens or reproductions of trademark or service mark. Application should include following information: (i) name and business address of applicant, and if corporation, state of incorporation; (ii) goods or services in connection with which mark used; (iii) way applicant uses mark with goods or services; (iv) class under bus. reg. art. §1-405 to which goods or services belong; (v) date when mark first used anywhere and in Maryland; and (vi) statement that applicant is owner of mark and no other person has right to use either identical, or substantially similar, mark in Maryland. (bus. reg. art. §1-406). Certificate of registration, when issued, includes information required by application and is effective for ten years; it may be renewed within six months prior to expiration, upon filing form and paying $50 renewal fee. Successive ten year renewal permitted. (bus. reg. art. §§1-409, 1-410).

Assignment recorded upon payment of $10 fee to Secretary of State. Assignment void against subsequent purchaser for value without notice unless recorded within three months after date thereof or prior to subsequent purchase. (bus. reg. art. §1-411).

Cancellation occurs upon failure to renew, or voluntary request, or court order, or upon finding by court of abandonment, nonownership, improper grant, fraud or confusing similarity with prior mark registered in U.S. Patent Office. (bus. reg. art. §1-412).

Protection Afforded.—Certificate of registration admissible in evidence as proof of registration in court action or proceeding in state. (courts art. §§10-101 to 10-103, 10-204).

Infringement.—Any person who: (1) Uses without consent any reproduction, counterfeit or colorable imitation of registered mark, where such use is likely to cause confusion, mistake or deception as to origin of goods, or (2) knowingly reproduces, counterfeits or colorably imitates registered mark and applies same to labels, signs, packages, wrappers or advertisements in connection with sale or distribution of goods or services in state may be enjoined and is potentially liable in civil action by owner for all profits derived and damages suffered. Courts may order any such counterfeits or imitations to be delivered to officer of court or to plaintiff or to be destroyed. (bus. reg. art. §1-414).

Tradenames.—For definition, see bus. reg. art. §1-401. Tradenames not registered with Secretary of State. (bus. reg. art. §1-404[d]). Anyone doing mercantile trading or manufacturing business as agent or doing business under name not his own, must, prior thereto, file with Department of Assessments and Taxation certificate in form prescribed in statute. Fee for filing tradename is $10 plus $1 for each name to be indexed and $12 for each amendment, cancellation, or renewal certificate. (corps. art. §1-406). Failure to file such certificate renders owner liable to suit by any creditor in name under which business is conducted, and all property possessed, used or acquired in business is liable to seizure and sale under execution. Willful execution and filing of false certificate punishable by fine of up to $1,000, imprisonment of up to one year or both. (corps. art. §1-406[H]).

It is unlawful and punishable by fine for any person, corporation, association, etc., with intent to defraud, to trade or transact business in state under name, tradename or title same as or similar to that used first by other person, corporation, etc. This does not apply to individuals possessing similar names. (bus. reg. art. §1-415).

Gasoline Products Marketing Act.—See category Business Regulation and Commerce, topic Monopolies, Restraint of Trade and Competition.

TRADE SECRETS:

Uniform Trade Secrets Act has been adopted in substance under title "Maryland Uniform Trade Secrets Act" (comm. law art. §11-1201-1209) with following change.

§7: Act does not waive or limit any common law or statutory defense or immunity possessed by state personnel as defined under st. gov't art. §12-101. (comm. law art. §11-1207[b] [2]).

LEGAL PROFESSION

ATTORNEYS AND COUNSELORS:

Business Occupations Article effective as of Oct. 1, 1989. References are to this article unless otherwise indicated.

Jurisdiction over admissions exercised by Court of Appeals and State Board of Law Examiners, consisting of seven lawyers appointed by Court of Appeals. (§§10-201 to 10-202). Court has promulgated Rules Governing Admission to Bar of Md. (hereafter "Rule"). Board of Law Examiners has adopted Board Rules (hereafter "Board Rule").

Eligibility.—Applicant must be 18 years of age and citizen of U.S. before admission but need not be 18 years old or citizen in order to take examination. (§§10-207 and 10-209). Candidate must furnish proof of good character and reputation, which is investigated by character committee of practicing lawyers appointed by Court of Appeals. (Rule 5).

Registration As Law Student.—At any time after pre-legal studies, person may file application for admission to bar for purpose of determining if there are any current impediments to applicant's admission. (Rule 2[c][1]).

Educational Requirements.—Candidate must have successfully completed academic work necessary to meet minimum requirements for admission to ABA-approved law school, and must have degree of juris doctor or equivalent from law school. (§10-207; Rules 3, 4). Rule 4(b) permits waiver in special cases. Candidate must also complete course on legal professionalism. (Rule 11. *Note:* This rule expired on Dec. 31, 1995. Court of Appeals extended requirement, effective Jan. 1, 1996.)

Petition for Admission.—Admission is by petition to Court of Appeals; but petition is on printed form and is purely formal matter once candidate has passed examination and been approved by character committee, unless exceptions are made by any citizen during 30-day period set forth in conditional order of admission. (§10-208, Rules 10, 12).

Examination.—State Board of Law Examiners conducts and marks examinations, which are held twice a year. Time and place are fixed by Board. (Rule 7). At present, examinations held in Feb. and July during last Tues. and Wed. of each month. Exam consists of Multistate Bar Examination (MBE) and essay test on: Agency, business associations, commercial transactions, constitutional law, contracts, criminal law and procedure, evidence, family law, Md. civil procedure, professional responsibility, property and torts. Candidate must achieve either (1) score of 70% on Board test and scaled score of 120 on MBE, or (2) combined score of 70%. Board will carry over score of 140 or greater of any candidate on MBE taken in another jurisdiction at same or immediately preceding administration. (Board Rules 3, 4).

Clerkship.—None required.

Special Admission.—Members of bar of any state, district or territory of U.S., who for five out of past seven years, or for total of ten years at any time, have been regularly engaged as practitioners in jurisdiction or jurisdictions in which applicants were admitted to practice, judges of courts of record, or full time teachers of law at law school approved by ABA, may be admitted after examination and proof that they are of good character and reputation and that they intend to practice and to have office for practice of law or to teach law full time in Md. at law school approved by ABA and after examination as to state law. (§10-210; Rule 13; Board Rule 5). Petitioner must complete course on legal professionalism, as required by Rule 11. *Note:* This rule expired on Dec. 31, 1995. Court of Appeals extended requirement, effective Jan. 1, 1996. (Rule 13[o]).

Mandatory Continuing Legal Education.—No requirements at present.

Admission Pro Hac Vice.—Upon granting of written motion filed by attorney of record admitted to practice in Md., nonresident attorney may be specially admitted for limited purpose of appearing and participating as co-counsel with movant in any case pending in any state court, agency or commission. Attorney whose special admission is moved must certify number of times he had been specially admitted during preceding 12 months. Specially admitted attorney may participate in court, agency or commission proceedings only if accompanied by Md. counsel, unless latter's presence waived by presiding judge or officer. (§10-215; Rule 14). No papers will be accepted by federal district court unless signed by resident counsel except in pro se proceeding. (U.S. Dist. Ct. Local R. 102).

Licenses.—No license requirement other than admission to practice by Court of Appeals. No annual license fee, but annual payments into Clients' Security Trust Fund and Disciplinary Fund required. Amounts set each year by Court of Appeals. (§10-311; R. P. 16-811; 16-702).

Privileges.—No special privileges other than right to practice law in all courts of state. Attorney not exempt from jury service. (courts art. §8-209).

Disabilities.—Attorney or solicitor may not be surety on appeal or injunction bond or security for costs, but may be surety on attachment bond. (52 Md. 614).

Liability.—Attorney is liable for damage which results from his failure to execute business entrusted to him with ordinary care and diligence and with fair average degree of professional skill and knowledge. (181 Md. 606, 31 A.2d 312). See category Civil Actions and Procedure, topic Costs.

Clients' Security Trust Fund has been authorized by statute and established by rule of Court of Appeals to reimburse losses caused by defalcations of attorney. (§10-310 to 313; R. P. 16-811).

Attorney Trust Accounts.—Each lawyer or law firm must maintain account for deposit of trust money. (§§10-301 and 302). Attorney trust account must be maintained at approved financial institution in interest or non-interest bearing account. (§10-302). Trust monies too small or being held for too short time period to generate at least $50 interest or such larger amount attorney judges is necessary to equal cost of administering account, must be pooled by attorney and interest earned must be paid quarterly to Maryland Legal Services Corporation. (§10-303). Any lawyer willfully violating is guilty of misdemeanor and on conviction is subject to disciplinary proceedings under Rules and fine not over $5,000 or imprisonment not over five years or both. (§10-307; 280 Md. 21, 371 A.2d 129).

Malpractice Insurance.—Legal Mutual Liability Insurance Society of Md. authorized to provide legal malpractice insurance whenever Insurance Commissioner, after consulting with state bar association, determines that substantial number of attorneys unable to procure such insurance. (§§24-101—24-109). See category Insurance, topic Insurance Companies.

Compensation.—Right to compensation and amount depend upon contract, express or implied, and may be recovered in quantum meruit. Contingent fees are allowed except in domestic relations and criminal matters. (R. Prof. Conduct 1.5).

Lien.—Attorney has lien on actions, suits and proceedings of attorney's client from time they are commenced and on judgments and awards entered in favor of attorney's

See note at head of Digest as to 1998 legislation covered.

See Topical Index in front part of this volume.

ATTORNEYS AND COUNSELORS . . . *continued*
client. Lien extends to attorney's fees and compensation specially agreed on with client, if services for such fees and compensation produced funds to which lien is applicable. Attorney's lien is not subordinate to any other lien or claim except prior lien based on salaries or wages due to employees for work which is related to or part of award, order, decree or judgment, or lien against client for state taxes due. (§10-501).

Resignation.—Application to resign may be submitted only to Court of Appeals and must be in writing, giving reasons. No resignation allowed when attorney subject of investigation or when disciplinary proceedings pending. Resignation effective upon entry of order accepting it by Court of Appeals. (R. P. 16-712). Reinstatement possible. (R. P. 16-714).

Disbarment.—Attorney Grievance Commission administers discipline and inactive status of attorneys under R. P. 16-702. Disciplinary Fund finances operation of grievance system. Appointed Bar Counsel is chief executive of system and receives and records every complaint. (R. P. 16-704, 16-706). Inquiry Panel and Review Board may consider complaint not summarily dismissed. (R. P. 16-705—16-707). Reprimand or formal charges may result. (R. P. 16-606). Charges are filed on behalf of Grievance Commission in Court of Appeals, which may transmit to any court and designates judges to hear charges and clerk responsible for maintaining record of proceeding. Hearing court makes findings of fact and conclusions of law and files same with Court of Appeals. Court of Appeals hears exceptions, answers and recommendations respecting sanctions, and orders disbarment, suspension, reprimand, placing attorney on inactive status, dismissal of charges, or remands case. (R. P. 16-709—16-711). Attorney being investigated or proceeded against may consent to disbarment upon affidavit stating his recognition that he could not successfully defend disciplinary proceedings. Reinstatement is possible. (R. P. 16-712, 16-714).

Unauthorized Practice.—No person may practice law without having been admitted to bar, except officer of corporation, employee designated by officer of corporation, partner in business partnership, or employee designated by partner, or employee designated by owner of sole proprietorship may appear on behalf of corporation in civil suit in district court involving claim not exceeding $2,500 and not based on assignment to corporation of interest of another. (§10-206). Attorney admitted to highest court of another state permitted to act as corporate house counsel in Md., but is limited to giving advice to corporation, and may not appear in court or before state agency or commission unless attorney is specially admitted. (§10-206). Practice of law is deemed to include giving of advice in administration or probate of estates in orphans' courts. (§10-101). Model Act Providing Remedies for Unauthorized Practice of Law has been adopted with amendment providing role for Bar Counsel. See subhead Disbarment, supra. (§§10-401 to 10-407).

It is unlawful for corporation or voluntary association to hold itself out as engaged in practice of law or to solicit employment in connection with rendition of legal services. Violation is punishable by fine of not more than $500, and each officer or employee may be similarly fined. Prohibition does not apply to business of examining and insuring titles to real property, to collection or adjustment of mercantile claims, or to insurance corporations defending insured under policy of insurance (art. 27, §14) or to officer of corporation representing corporation in certain civil actions (art. 27, §14A).

Judge of state court (other than orphans' court of Harford and Montgomery Counties, and with certain limitations, Baltimore City and Prince George's and Calvert Counties), clerk of court, register of wills, employee of clerk or register, bailiff of any court, officer or employee of juvenile court, sheriff or deputy sheriff, or warden or deputy warden of any jail or penitentiary may not practice as attorney except such officials in Montgomery County and Harford County may assist in preparing certain legal documents and in Prince George's County, registrar of wills may prepare or assist in preparation of certain documents. (art. 10, §§27, 28, 30; courts art. §1-203; est. & tr. art. §§2-109, 2-202).

Professional Association (or Corporation).—Professional Service Corporation Act authorizes lawyer or group of lawyers to incorporate. (corps. art. §§5-101 to 5-134).

Attorney Ethics.—Maryland has adopted modified version of American Bar Association Model Rules of Professional Conduct. (R. P. 16-812, R. P. Appendix).

MINERAL, WATER AND FISHING RIGHTS

MINES AND MINERALS:

Laws administered by Bureau of Mines, part of Dep't of Natural Resources. (env. art. §15-201). Main office of Bureau must be in Garrett or Allegany County. (env. art. §15-201). Land Reclamation Committee advises with respect to open-pit mining. (env. art. §15-204).

Operation of Mines.—Rules and regulations governing mining activity set out in env. art. §§15-401 to 15-406.

Strip mining governed by regulations set out in env. art. §§15-501 to 15-513.

Surface mining of minerals other than coal governed by regulations set out in env. art. §§15-801 to 15-834.

Deep mining regulated by env. art. §§15-601 to 15-618.

Safeguarding of Employees.—Many provisions throughout nat. res. art. tit. 7 for safeguarding employees. Person may not work in mine without supervision until he has satisfied operator that he can work without endangering lives of fellow workers. Each miner must examine his working place and keep it in safe condition; he must immediately cease work and leave his place if he finds it has become dangerous, installing plain danger signal to warn others. Miners must notify foreman of dangerous or unsafe condition known to them. Acts endangering lives or health of employees or security of mine property are forbidden. Bureau of Mines may define special duties relating to security of life or property, and each employee must observe such duties. Operator must direct attention of each worker to general and special rules and regulations and to any exit and escapeway of mine in which he works. (env. art. §15-404).

Inspection of Mines.—Bureau of Mines may inspect mines and issue orders to require correction of danger or removal of persons or closing of mine. (env. art. §15-311).

Oil and Gas.—Dep't of Natural Resources enforces provisions relating to drilling, production and underground storage of oil and gas in state. (env. art. §§14-101 to 14-103). Person may not drill any well or dispose of any product of well without permit from Dep't. (env. art. §14-104). Drilling for oil or gas in waters of Chesapeake Bay or any of its tributaries is prohibited except under certain circumstances, and explosives may not be used in seismic operations on Bay or its tributaries. (nat. res. art. §8-817, env. art. §§14-106 to 14-109). Wells can be no closer than 1,000 feet to property boundary line except (1) under special circumstances after hearing, (2) by agreement with owners of oil and gas on adjacent land. Dep't prescribes distances between wells. (env. art. §14-112). Owner or operator of gas well may not willfully take gas unless it is metered by standard metering system. (env. art. §14-119). Special statutory provisions govern underground storage of natural and artificial gas and petroleum products in Prince George's County. (env. art. §§14-201 to 14-209). Md. has joined Interstate Oil and Gas Compact. (env. art. §§14-401 to 14-404). Special provisions govern leasing of state oil and gas resources. (nat. res. art. §§5-1701 to 5-1703).

Mine Railroads.—Such corporations can condemn rights of way and construct necessary railroads not more than ten miles in length. Legislature may at any time regulate, modify or change control, use, and estate of any railroad constructed by such corporation in manner deemed equitable to corporation and necessary to accommodation of public travel or use of railroad. (Formerly art. 23, §§168 to 178, deemed apparently obsolete by Legislature and transferred to Session Laws to avoid inadvertent substantive effect its repeal might have.)

Abandoned Mine Drainage Control Act is set out in env. art. §§15-701 to 15-706.

Abandoned Mine Reclamation Act is set out in env. art. §§15-1101 to 15-1109.

Interstate Mining Compact enacted and entered into. (env. art. §§15-901 to 15-902).

MORTGAGES

CHATTEL MORTGAGES:

Chattel mortgages generally obsolete, replaced by use of security agreements and financing statements governed by UCC. UCC governs chattel mortgage used as security device. (comm. law art. tit. 9). See category Business Regulation and Commerce, topics Commercial Code, Sales, subhead Retail Installment Sales.

Chattel mortgage is transfer of legal title in designated personal property as security for debt or obligation. Until discharged, it is lien upon property, and, if properly recorded, is good against subsequent lienors. (comm. law art. §9-301).

What May Be Mortgaged.—Any chattels. (98 Md. 645, 57A. 20).

Motor Vehicles.—See category Transportation, topic Motor Vehicles, subhead Liens and Security Interests.

Boats.—Security interest in vessel perfected by notation on certificate of title. Owner creating interest must deliver existing certificate together with application for new certificate to Dep't of Natural Resources; secured party must pay $15 fee. Dep't then issues new certificate to secured party. Interest perfected as of time of creation if delivery and payment made to Dep't within 30 days; otherwise interest perfected upon delivery and payment. Upon satisfaction of debt, secured party must send certificate of title and release to owner and copy of release to Dep't within 15 days; upon request of owner, and receipt of certificate of title and release, new certificate is issued to owner. Assignee of secured party's interest should procure new certificate. Special rules apply to vessel subject to security interest brought into state. (nat. res. art. §§8-728 to 8-736).

Fixtures.—Uniform Commercial Code adopted. For priorities in relation to fixtures, see comm. law art. §9-313.

Filing.—See category Business Regulation and Commerce, topic Commercial Code.

Recording.—Uniform Commercial Code adopted. To perfect assignment of security interest in mortgage, transfer must be recorded in land records. (real prop. art. §7-101[b]). As to recording fee, see categories Business Regulation and Commerce, topic Commercial Code; Documents and Records, topic Records. As to recording tax, see subhead Taxation, infra.

Satisfaction or Discharge.—Uniform Commercial Code adopted. Mortgage discharged by release signed by mortgagee describing collateral to be released, name and address of debtor and secured party, and recording reference of financing statement. (comm. law art. §9-406).

Foreclosure by Court Proceedings.—Uniform Commercial Code adopted. Court foreclosure rarely used. (R. P. 14-201—14-209). For description of foreclosure by court proceeding, see topic Mortgages of Real Property.

Sale by Mortgagee.—Uniform Commercial Code adopted. In all mortgages of personal property situated in state, foreclosure may be under: (1) Power of sale, i.e., clause in mortgage authorizing mortgagee or other person named to sell mortgaged property; (2) assent to decree, i.e., provision in mortgage whereby mortgagor assents to passing of decree for sale of property; or (3) court order where mortgage contains neither power of sale nor assent. In case (1) or (2), record holders of at least 25% of mortgage debt must consent or apply for sale. (R. P. 14-202, 14-205).

Where foreclosure is under power of sale or assent to decree, person named in mortgage to make sale must do so under supervision of court of equity for county or Baltimore City where property lies and must: (1) Docket suit if under power of sale, or file petition to foreclosure if under assent to decree and file mortgage or certified copy as exhibit; (2) give bond approved by court or clerk; (3) publish notice of time, place and terms of sale; (4) send notice by certified mail to mortgagor, present record owner and, under some circumstances, subordinate mortgagee, not less than ten nor more than 30 days before sale. Sale must be ratified and confirmed by court. (R. P. 14-203, 14-206, 14-207).

Where mortgage contains neither power of sale nor assent, procedure similar to assent except process, answer, and hearing required as in equity. Court may decree sale if payment not made in reasonable time provided. (R. P. 14-205).

See note at head of Digest as to 1998 legislation covered.

See Topical Index in front part of this volume.

MD – 49

CHATTEL MORTGAGES . . . *continued*

Where sale does not fully satisfy mortgage debt and interest, plaintiff may, within three years after final ratification of sale, apply for and obtain decree in personam for balance due. (R. P. 14-205; comm. law art. §9-501-502).

Redemption.—Uniform Commercial Code adopted. No right of redemption after bona fide sale. (224 Md. 408, 423-24, 168 A.2d 358 cert. denied 368 US 830).

Foreign Mortgages.—Uniform Commercial Code adopted.

Taxation.—See category Documents and Records, topic Records, subhead Tax on Recordation. Purchase money mortgages, assignments of mortgages, and security agreements on vehicles or vessels which are filed with Motor Vehicle Administration or Dep't of Natural Resources are exempt from recordation tax. (tax-prop. art. §12-108[b]).

Form of Security Agreement.—Following form is illustrative only and must be modified to meet situation.

Form

THIS SECURITY AGREEMENT, Made this . . . . day of . . . . . ., 19 . . . . by . . . . . ., Debtor, and . . . ., Secured Party.

NOW, THEREFORE, THIS SECURITY AGREEMENT WITNESSETH, That in consideration of the mutual covenants herein contained, Debtor hereby grants to Secured Party a security interest under the Maryland Uniform Commercial Code in all of the Debtor's present and future accounts, chattel paper, contract rights, documents of title, equipment, inventory and general intangibles (hereinafter called "Collateral"), to secure the sum of $. . . . . ., which the Secured Party hereby agrees to advance, and all additional sums hereafter advanced by Secured Party to Debtor from time to time as agreed upon. Debtor shall be entitled to retain possession and to process, use, sell or otherwise dispose of any of the Collateral hereunder, but the security interest hereby created shall continue in the proceeds and products of any such Collateral, and in any other personal property hereafter acquired, whether as additions to or replacements or substitutes for such Collateral or otherwise.

Debtor Warrants: (insert warranties desired; include a warranty as to Debtor's residence or chief place of business in Maryland).

Debtor Covenants and Agrees: (insert covenants desired).

Upon default by Debtor in the payment of the principal or interest of any liability or obligation secured hereby or in the performance of any covenant or agreement herein contained, or if any warranty or statement of the Debtor is not true, Secured Party may declare all liabilities and obligations secured hereby immediately due and payable and, in addition to any other rights and remedies available, may take possession of Collateral or proceeds and exercise any and all rights and remedies granted under the Maryland Uniform Commercial Code to a Secured Party upon a default.

WITNESS our hands and seals.

. . . .
Debtor Secured Party

Form of Financing Statement.—Only original need be filed. It should consist of black letters, at least eight point print or elite type, on white paper, not larger than 8½" x 14" in size, with two-inch margin top and bottom and one-inch margin on sides. (comm. law art. §9-402[9]). Effective July 1, 1995, financing statement filed only at State Department of Assessments and Taxation must identify county of debtor's principal place of business or residence in state or, if debtor has no principal place of business or residence in state, financing statement should so state. (comm. law art. §9-402). No official form. Following is acceptable:

Form

FINANCING STATEMENT

For Filing Officer—(Date, Time, No. and Office)

. . . .

☐ To Be ☐ Not to Be Recorded in Land Records

This financing statement is presented to a filing officer for filing pursuant to the Maryland Uniform Commercial Code.

1. Debtor and address: . . . .
2. Secured Party and address: . . . .
3. This Financing Statement covers the following types of personal property: (describe)
4. The proceeds of collateral ☐ are ☐ are not covered.
5. The products of collateral ☐ are ☐ are not covered.
6. (If collateral is crops) The above described crops are growing or are to be grown on: (describe real estate)
7. (If collateral is goods which are or which are to become fixtures) The above described goods are affixed or to be affixed to: (describe real estate)
8. (If collateral is timber to be cut) The above timber is standing on: (describe real estate)
9. (If collateral is minerals or the like or certain accounts) The above minerals or accounts will be financed at the wellhead or minehead or well or mine located on: (describe real estate)
10. (If debtor has no interest of record in real estate) A record owner is: (name)
11. This transaction ☐ is subject ☐ is not subject to recordation tax on the principal amount of $. . . . .

DEBTOR SECURED PARTY

. . . .

(type or print names beneath signatures)

PLEASE RETURN TO: (name and address)

. . . .

(comm. law art. §9-402).

Form of Statement of Continuation, Partial Release, Assignment, or Termination.—Same requirements as to type, spacing, etc. as for financing statement. No official form. Continuation statement must identify original statement by file number, state that original statement still effective, and be signed by secured party. (comm. law art. §9-403[3]). Release must be signed by secured party (if not secured party of record, release must be accompanied by written assignment signed by secured party of record) and contain name and address of debtor and secured party, description of collateral released, and file number, record reference and date of filing of financing statement. (comm. law art. §9-406). Assignment must be signed by secured party, contain name of secured party of record and debtor, name and address of assignee, description of collateral, and must identify financing statement by file number, record reference and date of filing. (comm. law art. §9-405). Termination statement must be signed by secured party or assignee and identify financing statement by file number and (except for consumer goods) record reference. (comm. law art. §9-404).

COLLATERAL SECURITY:

See category Debtor and Creditor, topic Pledges.

MORTGAGES OF PERSONAL PROPERTY:

See topic Chattel Mortgages; category Business Regulation and Commerce, topic Commercial Code.

MORTGAGES OF REAL PROPERTY:

References are to Real Property Article of Code unless otherwise indicated.

Mortgage is transfer of legal title to mortgagee as security for indebtedness. Mortgagor retains only equitable interest in property or equity of redemption. Equity of redemption passes to personal representatives of intestate. (est. & tr. art. §1-301). Heirs, devisees, personal representatives or assigns take all rights of mortgagor. (§1-103). Equity of redemption is subject to dower and curtesy as to estates of persons dying before Jan. 1, 1970. It is liable for debts and may be seized and sold in execution. (courts art. §11-501).

Deed of real estate absolute on its face is considered mortgage if there is defeasance in writing, but such defeasance must be recorded with deed. (§7-101[a]).

Execution.—Mortgage or deed of trust executed prior to July 1, 1974 must be signed, sealed and acknowledged; on or after July 1, 1974, seal or attestation not required if mortgage or deed of trust is in accordance with codified Statute of Frauds. (§4-101). Mortgage or deed of trust is invalid (except as between parties thereto) unless there is endorsed or attached oath or affirmation of mortgagee or secured party that consideration recited is true and bona fide. No purchase money mortgage or deed of trust (except where mortgage or deed of trust is given to seller in transaction to secure payment of all or part of purchase price) is valid, either as between parties thereto or as to any third parties, unless there is endorsed thereon or attached thereto oath or affirmation of secured party stating that actual sum of money advanced at closing transaction by secured party was paid over and disbursed by secured party to either borrower or person responsible for disbursement of funds at closing at time no later than complete execution and delivery of mortgage or deed of trust by borrower; lender may, however, deliver net proceeds if certain conditions met. Affidavit is required for only that part of loan that is purchase money, and if affidavit not given, mortgage or deed of trust is invalid only to extent of part of loan that was purchase money. Such affidavits are not applicable on or after July 1, 1974 to mortgages or deeds of trust where loan is business loan and usury laws (comm. law art. §12-103[e]) permit any rate of interest (§4-106).

Effective date of mortgage or deed of trust is date of delivery, which is presumed to be date of last acknowledgment, if any, or date stated in mortgage, whichever is later. (§3-201).

Recording.—Mortgage or deed of trust, when recorded, takes effect from its effective date as against mortgagor, his personal representatives, all purchasers with notice and all creditors of mortgagor with or without notice. (§3-201). Deed includes any deed, grant, mortgage, deed of trust, lease, assignment and release, pertaining to land or property, including interest in rents and profits from rents. (§1-101[c]). Interest created by deed granting, assigning, or otherwise transferring interest in rents or profits arising from property is perfected upon recordation regardless of terms of assignment and without assignee being required to take any further affirmative action. (§3-204).

Every mortgage, deed of trust or other instrument which also affects personal property shall be recorded among land records only. If interested party requests, index of financing records provided for in Uniform Commercial Code shall include notation that instrument has been recorded among land records, and instrument shall be indexed in general alphabetical index for land records. Such notation and indexing shall have same effect as if instrument were recorded in full among financing records. (§3-301).

Recording Fees.—In Baltimore City and in all counties, fee (i) $10 for release nine pages or less; (ii) $20 for any other instrument nine pages or less; (iii) $20 for instrument, other than as provided in (i), regardless of length, involving solely principal residence; (iv) $75 for any other instrument ten pages or more. (§3-601). Deed includes any deed, grant, mortgage, deed of trust, lease, assignment and release, pertaining to land or property, including interest in rents and profits from rents. (§1-101[c]). Interest created by deed granting, assigning, or otherwise transferring interest in rents or profits arising from property is perfected upon recordation regardless of terms of assignment and without assignee being required to take any further affirmative action. (§3-204).

Taxes.—See category Documents and Records, topic Records, subhead Tax on Recordation. Exempt from recordation tax are security agreements on vehicles and vessels which are filed with Motor Vehicle Administration or Department of Natural Resources, mechanics' liens, crop liens, certain purchase money deeds of trust or purchase money mortgages, assignments of mortgages or deeds of trust, judgments, releases, orders of satisfaction, participation agreements showing interest in note, certain Uniform Commercial Code security agreements, certain refinancing agreements where refinanced property is mortgagor's principal residence, certain instruments transferring property between spouses or former spouses in accordance with property settlement or divorce

See note at head of Digest as to 1998 legislation covered.

See Topical Index in front part of this volume.

MD – 50

MORTGAGES OF REAL PROPERTY ... *continued*

decree, certain supplemental and previously recorded instruments, and instruments transferring property between certain relatives. Also exempt from tax are certain transfers of corporate property between related corporations, certain corporate or partnership conveyances of property upon dissolution, liquidation or termination, land installment contracts, options to purchase real property, deeds conveying title to real property where recordation was previously paid on contract of sale between same parties, transfers to certain public agencies, leases of seven years or less, certain articles of merger, and articles of consolidation and transfer of property from partnership to limited liability company if members of limited liability company and their allocation of profits and losses are identical to partners of converting partnership. (tax-prop. art. §12-108).

Trust Deeds.—Deed of trust may be used as substitute for mortgage. See subheads Execution, supra, Future Advances, infra.

Future Advances.—

Mortgage executed prior to July 1, 1974 is lien for principal sum which appears on face of mortgage and is particularly mentioned and expressed to be secured thereby at time of executing same. Mortgage executed on or after July 1, 1974 is lien for principal sum which appears on face of mortgage and is particularly mentioned and expressed to be secured thereby, without regard to when advanced or readvanced. If after date of mortgage any sum is advanced or readvanced, priority for sum dates from date of mortgage regardless of whether advance or readvance was obligatory or voluntary under terms of mortgage. (§7-102).

Mortgage or deed of trust executed on or after July 1, 1974 is lien on property for principal sum of money up to aggregate principal sum appearing on face and expressed to be secured thereby, without regard to whether or when advanced or readvanced except that there is no necessity for recitation of principal sum for mortgages or deeds of trust to guarantee party secured against loss from being obligee of third party, or to indemnify party secured against loss from being endorser, guarantor, or surety, or secure guarantee or indemnity agreement. Where any sum of money is advanced or readvanced subsequent to date of mortgage or deed of trust, priority for such sum of money shall date from date of mortgage or deed of trust as against rights of intervening purchasers, mortgagees, trustees under deeds of trust or lien creditors, regardless of whether advance or readvance was obligatory or voluntary under terms of mortgage or deed of trust. (§7-102; see §15-102[11]).

After-Acquired Property.—Only under certain circumstances will mortgage of after-acquired property be valid in Md. After-acquired property clause will be strictly construed and property must clearly fall within provision. (144 Md. 654, 125 A. 40; 55 F.2d 211; 217 Md. 337, 143 A.2d 62; 19 Md. L. R. 294).

Priorities.—Recorded mortgage or deed of trust takes effect from its effective date as against mortgagee or trustee of any mortgage or deed of trust executed and delivered subsequent to such effective date unless subsequent mortgagee or trustee: (1) Has accepted delivery of such mortgage or deed of trust in good faith, without constructive notice through possession, and for good and valuable consideration, and (2) has recorded such mortgage or deed of trust first. (§3-203).

Mortgage or deed of trust to secure purchase money is preferred to any previous judgment against purchaser, provided such mortgage or deed of trust recites that sum so secured is in whole or in part purchase money for property purchased or otherwise recites that it is purchase money mortgage or deed of trust. (§7-104).

Subordinate mortgagee may record in separate docket request to receive notice of proposed foreclosure sale. (§7-105[c]). Failure of subordinate mortgagee to record request for notices does not affect duty of holder of superior mortgage to provide necessary notice except that holder of superior interest does not have duty to provide notice to condominium council of unit owners or homeowners association that has not filed request for notice. (§7-105).

Payment of Notes.—Title to all promissory notes and other instruments secured by mortgage is conclusively presumed to be vested in person holding record title to mortgage. As to payments made after July 1, 1974, after assignment of mortgage has been recorded, payment made by original mortgagor to assignor will be effective to reduce or discharge note or debt, unless such mortgagor has received actual notice of assignment prior to payment. (Also applies to payment by transferee of mortgaged property except where assignment of mortgage is of record at effective date of transfer of mortgaged property). (§7-103).

Subordination agreements honored if adequately evidenced. (243 Md. 480, 221 A.2d 361).

Assignment.—Mortgage may be assigned by lengthy assignment or by brief indorsement on instrument (to be recorded). (§§3-106, 4-203). Clerk records assignment with attachment containing names of parties to original mortgage and reference to where mortgage recorded. (§3-106). Short form is as follows:

Form

I hereby assign the within mortgage to the assignee, ... Witness my hand this . . . . . . day of . . . . . . 19. . . . . (§4-203[a]).

As to mortgages or assignments executed on or after July 1, 1974, grant of security interest in mortgage as security for payment of indebtedness or performance of obligation is governed by Uniform Commercial Code, but to perfect security interest, assignment of mortgage must be recorded in county where mortgage is recorded, and no financing statement need be filed. (§7-101). See subhead Payment of Notes, supra.

Release.—Mortgage or deed of trust may be released at option of clerk by short form of indorsement written upon record; or release may be endorsed on mortgage or deed of trust which is recorded; or party may present evidence of indebtedness marked "paid," which clerk may index and record; or release may be by long form in separate instrument, setting forth names of parties and date and record reference to instrument being released, which is recorded; or party may present original mortgage marked "paid" or "cancelled" by mortgagee or agent, which clerk may index and record; or party may present canceled check evidencing final payment, which clerk may index and record, if: (1) 60 days have passed since final payment, party sent secured party copy of §3-105

and notice that if no release is received in 30 days party will obtain release by presenting canceled check, and 30 days have passed since notice was mailed, (2) canceled check contains name of secured party, account number of debt (if any), and words indicating check represents payment in full, and (3) party presents affidavit by member of Md. Bar that mortgage or deed of trust has been satisfied, that notice described above was sent, and setting forth recording reference for original mortgage or deed of trust, is attached to check; or party executes and acknowledges certification of satisfaction if form prescribed by statute. (§3-105). Short form of release is as follows:

Form

I hereby release the within (or above) mortgage (or deed of trust). Witness my hand, etc. (§4-203[b]). See §§4-203(e) and 3-105(d)(5) for partial release.

Release of part of property allowed by execution and acknowledgment of partial release on separate instrument. (§3-105[f]).

Person responsible for disbursing funds at settlement must furnish buyer and seller at settlement with copy of recorded release of mortgage or deed of trust; but where such person properly disburses all funds entrusted to him within five days from delivery of deed, he need furnish such copy only upon specific request of buyer or seller. (§7-106[b]). Holder of lien or agent, on payment in satisfaction of lien, must furnish original copy of executed release upon written request from person responsible for disbursement of funds in connection with grant of title to property; release must be mailed or delivered within seven days of receipt of currency, certified or cashier's check or money order in payment of debt, or within seven days after clearance of other commercial paper given in payment. (§7-106[d]).

Satisfaction.—Payment of mortgage debt constitutes satisfaction, and mortgagor by equity proceeding can thereafter compel mortgagee to execute release. (56 Md. 421). See §7-106(e).

Foreclosure.—Mortgages of real or personal property situated in Md. may be foreclosed under (1) power of sale, i.e., clause in mortgage authorizing mortgagee or any other person named therein to sell mortgaged property, or (2) assent to decree, i.e., provision in mortgage whereby mortgagor assents to passing of decree for sale of property. (§7-105[a]). In each case record holders of at least 25% of mortgage debt must consent or make application for sale, and process, answer or hearing is not required. Mortgages may also be foreclosed where there is neither power of sale nor assent to decree, in same manner as mortgage containing assent to decree, except that (1) process, answer and hearing are required, (2) 25% requirement is inapplicable, and (3) court, under certain circumstances, may order sale before final decree. Action to foreclose mortgage under power of sale may only be instituted by natural person authorized to exercise power. (R. P. 14-201—14-205).

Where foreclosure is under power of sale, person named in mortgage to make sale must do so under supervision of court of equity for county or Baltimore City where property lies. Such person must: (1) Docket suit in appropriate equity court and file verified statement of mortgage debt together with mortgage or certified copy as exhibit; (2) give bond approved by clerk or court and publish notice of time, place and terms of sale (15 days notice required for real property, once a week for three successive weeks; five days notice for personal property); and (3) not less than ten nor more than 30 days before sale, send notice by certified mail, return receipt requested, bearing U.S. Postal Service postmark to mortgagor, present record owner and holder of subordinate mortgage, deed of trust, judgment or other subordinate recorded or filed interest who has filed appropriate request to receive notice. Sale must be ratified and confirmed by court. Failure to give notice to record owner or subordinate mortgagee does not invalidate title of purchaser; failure to give notice to mortgagor does not invalidate sale if person conducting sale gives affidavit or return receipt that such notice to mortgagor has been given prior to ratification by court. (§7-105; R. P. 14-203, 14-206).

Where foreclosure is under assent to decree, procedure is substantially same. Mortgagee files petition to foreclose in equity and files verified statement of mortgage debt together with mortgage or certified copy as exhibit. If default has occurred, court will enter decree ordering that property be sold forthwith and appointing trustee or trustees to make sale. Trustee must give bond and sell property pursuant to terms, including notice, fixed by court. Sale must be ratified by court. (R. P. 14-203, 14-206).

Strict foreclosure is seldom if ever used.

Deed of trust may be foreclosed in same manner as mortgage, except that foreclosure to be made by trustee appointed by deed or successor and 25% rule inapplicable. (R. P. 14-202[c], 14-210).

All purchasers at foreclosure sale have same rights and remedies against tenants of mortgagor as mortgagor had, and said tenants have same rights and remedies against purchaser as against mortgagor on date mortgage was recorded. If mortgage so authorizes and required advertisement of sale so discloses, foreclosure sale is subject to tenancies entered into after recording of mortgage. Any lease so continuing shall be unaffected by sale, except that purchaser shall become landlord, as of date of sale, on ratification of sale. (§7-105[f]).

Sales.—See subhead Foreclosure, supra.

Deficiency Judgment.—Decree in personam for deficiency shown by auditor's account may be obtained against mortgagor, provided motion therefor is made within three years from date of ratification of auditor's account. (R. P. 14-208).

Moratorium.—None.

Redemption.—Equitable right of redemption inherent in every mortgage transaction, regardless of form. (93 Md. 164, 48 A. 461). It must be exercised within reasonable time after forfeiture or be lost. (32 Md. 421). Right is divested by valid mortgage foreclosure sale. (153 Md. 50, 137 A. 509). Application to reopen judgment rendered in tax sale foreclosure proceeding granted only for lack of jurisdiction or fraud in conduct of proceedings to foreclosure. (tax-prop. §14-845).

Stale Mortgages.—Presumption that mortgage or deed of trust which remains unreleased of record has been paid off if 12 years after date of last payment called for in said instrument or any amendment or modification thereto have elapsed, or 40 years after date of record of such instrument have elapsed when date of last payment called for in such instrument cannot be ascertained and if no action has been brought to enforce lien

MORTGAGES OF REAL PROPERTY . . . *continued*
of said instrument within time periods set out above and no continuation statement has been filed within one year before expiration of applicable time period, lien created by such instrument shall terminate, shall no longer be enforceable against property, and shall be extinguished. (§7-106[c]).

Form for mortgage of fee simple property is as follows:

Form

This Mortgage, Made this . . . . . . day of . . . . . . in the year 19. . . . by and between . . . . . . of . . . . . . in the State of Maryland, of the first part, Mortgagor, and . . . . . . of the second part, Mortgagee: Whereas, Mortgagor is indebted to Mortgagee in the full and just sum of $. . . . . ., etc.

Now this Mortgage Witnesseth, that in consideration of the premises and of the sum of $1, the said . . . . . . do . . . . grant and convey unto . . . . . . heirs and assigns in fee-simple, all . . . . . . lot . . . . or parcel . . . . of ground situate and lying in the . . . . . . aforesaid, and described as follows, to wit:—Beginning for . . . . . . block . . . .

To have and to Hold the aforesaid parcel . . . . of ground, and premises unto and to the proper use and benefit of . . . . . . heirs and assigns forever. Together with the buildings and improvements thereupon, and the rights, alleys, ways, waters, privileges, appurtenances and advantages thereto belonging or in anywise appertaining.

Provided, that if the said . . . . . . executors, administrators or assigns, shall well and truly pay, or cause to be paid, the aforesaid principal sum of . . . . . . dollars and all the installments of interest thereon, when and as each of them shall respectively be due and payable as aforesaid, and shall perform each and all of the covenants herein on . . . . . . part to be performed, then this mortgage shall be void.

And the said Mortgagor . . . . . hereby assent . . . . . . to the passage of a decree for the sale of the property hereby mortgaged, such sale to take place only after a default in any of the covenants or conditions of this mortgage as herein provided; and the said Mortgagor . . . . . . hereby also authorize the said Mortgagee . . . . . ., ... personal representatives, or assigns, or . . . . . . duly authorized Attorney or Agent of the said Mortgagee . . . . . ., ... personal representatives, or assigns, after any default in the covenants or conditions of this mortgage, to sell the hereby mortgaged property. Any such sale, whether under the above assent to a decree or under the above power of sale, shall be under the provisions of The Real Property Article of the Public General Laws of Maryland and under Subtitle W of the Maryland Rules of Procedure or under any other General or Local Law and of the State of Maryland relating to mortgages, or any supplement, amendment, or addition thereto. And upon any such sale of said property, the proceeds shall be applied as follows: (1) to repayment of all expenses incident to said sale, including, but not limited to, reasonable counsel fees and a commission to the party making the sale of said property equal to the commission allowed Trustees for making sale of property by virtue of a decree of a Court having equity jurisdiction in the State of Maryland; (2) to the payment of all claims of the said Mortgagee . . . . . ., ... executors, administrators or assigns hereunder whether the same shall have matured or not; (3) and the surplus (if any there be), to the said Mortgagor . . . . . ., ... heirs, personal representatives or assigns, or to whoever may be entitled to the same.

And it is agreed, that until default be made in the premises, the said part . . . . of the first part . . . . . . executors, administrators or assigns, shall possess the aforesaid property upon paying, in the meantime, all taxes and assessments, public dues and charges levied or assessed, or to be levied or assessed, on said hereby mortgaged property, which taxes, mortgage debt and interest, public charges and assessments, ... the said part . . . . of the first part covenant . . . . to pay when legally payable.

And the said part . . . . of the first part further covenant to insure, and pending the existence of this mortgage to keep insured, the improvements on the hereby mortgaged property to the amount of at least . . . . . . dollars, and to cause the policy to be effected thereon to be so framed or endorsed as in case of fire, to inure to the benefit of the said . . . . . . executors, administrators or assigns, to the extent of . . . . . . lien or claim hereunder.

Witness . . . . . . hand and seal . . . .
Test: . . . . (Seal).
. . . . (Seal).

State of Maryland, City or County of . . . . . ., ss.:
I hereby certify, that on this . . . . . . day of . . . . . . in the year 19. . . . before me, ... of the State of Maryland, in and for the . . . . . . aforesaid, personally appeared . . . . . ., the mortgagor . . . . named in the foregoing mortgage and . . . . . . acknowledged the aforegoing mortgage to be . . . . . . act. At the same time also appeared . . . . . ., mortgagee, and made oath in due form of law, that the consideration set forth in said mortgage is true and bona fide as therein set forth and that the loan sum secured hereby has been paid over and disbursed by the mortgagee unto the mortgagor or the person responsible for disbursing of funds in the closing transaction or their respective agent at a time no later than the final and complete execution of this mortgage.

For variation of form of affidavit of consideration, see subhead Execution, supra.
For statutory form of mortgage, see §4-202(h).

Terms of any unexecuted declaration of provisions, covenants and conditions which has been recorded among county land records may be incorporated into mortgage or deed of trust recorded in same land records by specific reference to said declaration and by giving its record reference. Intention to incorporate must be clear, and mortgagor must be given copy of declaration when mortgage executed. (§7-108). Any change or modification to mortgage or deed of trust does not extinguish existing lien. (§7-111[a]). If change or modification increases principal secured above amount appearing on face of mortgage or deed of trust (1) existing lien priority of original document shall continue as to principal sum secured immediately before modification, and (2) lien priority for increase in principal sum shall date from date of modification. (§7-111[b]).

Interest chargeable in connection with loans secured by first mortgage or first deed of trust on residential real property is any amount as long as loan agreement and terms meet certain criteria. (comm. law art. §12-103[b]). See category Business Regulation and Commerce, topic Interest, subhead Mortgage Secured Loans. As to charging of points, see category Business Regulation and Commerce, topic Interest, subhead Maximum Rate.

Secondary Mortgage Loans.—Lender, other than regulated bank or savings and loan association, or insurance company, must be licensed by Commissioner of Consumer Credit unless lender falls within one of specified exemptions. (fin. inst. art. §11-502). See category Business Regulation and Commerce, topic Interest.

Chattel Mortgages.—See topic Chattel Mortgages.

PROPERTY

ABSENTEES:

Common law presumption of death after seven years absence abolished. (courts art. §3-102),

Care of Property.—Circuit courts have jurisdiction over protection and administration of property of absentees, as in case of disabled persons. (courts art. §§3-101 to 3-110; est. & tr. art. §§13-105[b], 13-201 to 13-222). Uniform Absence as Evidence of Death and Absentees' Property Act repealed for actions commenced Jan. 1, 1974 and thereafter.

Process Agent.—Md. corporation must have resident agent. (corps. art. §2-108[a][2]). Otherwise, no duty to appoint agent for service of process, except in special situations such as foreign corporation doing business in state or nonresident executor, administrator or guardian acting in state. See categories Business Organizations, topic Corporations; Estates and Trusts, topic Executors and Administrators; Family, topic Guardian and Ward.

Escheat.—Uniform Disposition of Unclaimed Property Act adopted, with amendments fixing presumptions of abandonment after five years for bank deposits (other than those subject to court order), share accounts, checks, drafts, safe deposit box contents, and most other types of unclaimed funds and property and after 15 years for travelers checks. (comm. law. art. tit. 17). But see category Business Regulation and Commerce, topic Banks and Banking, subhead Unclaimed Deposits and Property.

See also categories Business Regulation and Commerce, topic Banks and Banking, subhead Unclaimed Deposits and Property; Estates and Trusts, topics Descent and Distribution, subhead Escheat, Wills, subhead Unclaimed Legacies.

Absent Parents.—Child Support Enforcement Administration of Department of Human Resources maintains records on parents who have or appear to have deserted children, whether or not recipients of public assistance. (fam. law art. §12-105).

ADVERSE POSSESSION:

Title to real estate may be acquired through possession inconsistent with title of another.

Character of Possession.—Actual enclosure no longer necessary to prove possession. Acts of exclusive use and ownership, other than enclosure, may be given in evidence to prove possession. (courts art. §10-909[c]). Possession must be proved with clarity and precision. It must be adverse, actual, open, notorious, exclusive, hostile, under claim of title or ownership, unbroken, continuous and uninterrupted. Acts of use and ownership relied on must be consistent with claim of ownership against entire world. Possession or occupancy of part of tract of land under color of title to whole tract usually is claim to possession of whole tract. (152 Md. 174, 136 A. 537; 206 Md. 485, 112 A.2d 675).

Duration of Possession.—Full period of 20 years. (courts art. §5-103).

Easements.—Easement may be acquired by prescription through adverse, exclusive and uninterrupted use for 20 years. (60 Md. 74).

Rents reserved out of particular property are extinguished where no demand or payment of rent has been made for more than 20 years. (real prop. art. §8-107).

Disabilities.—Person who is minor or mental incompetent at time action accrues has lesser of three years or applicable remaining period after coming of age or sound mind to file action. Imprisonment, absence from state and marriage are no longer such disabilities as will toll running of limitations. (courts art. §5-201). Where tenant acquires title for failure of demand or payment of specific rent reserved for period of 20 years, landlord under any legal disability at end of 20-year period has two years after removal of disability to assert rights. (real prop. art. §8-107).

Quieting Title.—Any person in actual or constructive (if vacant) peaceable possession, regardless of whether hostile outstanding claim is being actively asserted, may bring suit in equity in county where property lies to quiet title. Proceedings may seek decree that plaintiff has absolute ownership and right of disposition of property, and defendant may be enjoined from asserting otherwise. (real prop. art. §14-108).

CONVEYANCES:

See topic Deeds.

CURTESY:

Estate of curtesy abolished. (est. & tr. art. §3-202; 259 Md. 1, 267 A.2d 209).

DEEDS:

References are to Real Property Article of Code unless otherwise indicated.
See topic Real Property for types of estates.

Execution.—Every deed conveying real estate, executed prior to Jan. 1, 1973, must be signed and sealed by grantor or bargainer and should be attested by at least one witness. All deeds conveying property, executed on or after Jan. 1, 1973, which contain names of grantor and grantee, description of property sufficient to identify same with reasonable certainty, and interest or estate intended thereby to be conveyed, are sufficient if executed, acknowledged and, where required, recorded; lease sufficient without acknowledgment. (§4-101[a]). Where deed has been signed by grantor, absence of seal or attestation does not affect validity. Corporate seal not required for execution of deed

See note at head of Digest as to 1998 legislation covered.

See Topical Index in front part of this volume.

MD – 52

DEEDS . . . *continued*
or other instrument. (§4-101[b]). See category Documents and Records, topic Acknowledgments, subhead Validating Acts. See also categories Estates and Trusts, topic Executors and Administrators, subhead Distribution; Family, topic Husband and Wife, subhead Conveyance or Encumbrance of Property.

Recording.—No estate of inheritance or freehold, or any declaration or limitation of use, or any estate above seven years, shall pass or take effect unless deed conveying same is executed and recorded. Rule does not apply to certain leases and when other methods of transfer permitted by law, e.g., articles of transfer by corporation. (§3-101). See topic Landlord and Tenant, subhead Leases.

Instrument affecting both real and personal property recorded among land records only. (§3-301[a]). If interested party requests, index of financing records provided for in Uniform Commercial Code includes notation that instrument has been recorded among land records, and instrument is indexed in general alphabetical index for land records. Such notation and indexing have same effect as if instrument recorded in full among financing records. (§3-301[b]). Mortgage can be effective as financing statement. See comm. law art. §9-402(6).

Deed must be recorded among land records of circuit court of Baltimore City or each county in which land lies. (§3-103). With certain exceptions, no deed recorded or transferred on assessment books until taxes due on real property and, if all realty owned in Baltimore City or county is being transferred, personal property taxes due by transferor paid. (§3-104[b]). Deeds, deeds of trust and mortgages to be recorded must contain certificate as to preparer. (§3-104[f]). See category Documents and Records, topic Records.

Recording Fees.—For any deed or other instrument required to be recorded among land records and financing statement records, for instruments required to be recorded with Dep't of Assessments and Taxation: (i) $10 for release nine pages or less; (ii) $20 for any other instrument nine pages or less; (iii) $20 for instrument, other than as provided in (i), regardless of length involving solely principal residence; (iv) $75 for any other instrument ten pages or more. (§3-601).

Operation and Effect.—Recorded deed takes effect from effective date as against grantee of deed executed and delivered subsequently, unless such grantee accepted delivery: (1) In good faith and without constructive notice through possession of prior grantee; (2) for good and valuable consideration; and (3) records deed first. (§3-203).

Effective date of deed is date of delivery, presumed to be later of date of last acknowledgment, if any, or date stated on deed. Recorded deed takes effect from effective date as against grantor, his personal representatives, purchasers with notice, and creditors of grantor with or without notice. (§3-201).

No words of inheritance necessary to create fee simple estate. Every conveyance passes fee unless contrary intention is expressed or necessarily implied. (§4-105).

Deed not construed to create joint tenancy unless expressly so providing. (§2-117).

Possession under unrecorded deed constitutes constructive notice of what inquiry of possessor would disclose as to existence of unrecorded deed, provided possession inconsistent with record title. (§3-202).

Deeds by Attorney.—If attorney appointed by power of attorney, power must be executed and acknowledged as deed and recorded with or prior to deed. Agent or attorney must describe himself in deed and sign and acknowledge as such. Power of attorney deemed revoked when revocation recorded in office where deed should be recorded. (§4-107).

Conveyances by Corporation.—Sale or transfer of real property of Md. corporation as part of transaction involving sale of all or substantially all of corporate assets is accomplished by articles of transfer or articles of consolidation or merger, pursuant to general corporation law. (corps. art. tit. 3, subtit. 1). Deed by Md. corporation which contains certification by person executing deed on behalf of corporation that conveyance not part of sale, lease, exchange or other transfer of all or substantially all property and assets of corporation is valid and effective whether or not there has been compliance with corps. art. tit. 3, subtit. 1. Deed by Md. corporation executed and recorded before Jan. 1, 1979 not invalid solely because of noncompliance with corps. art. tit. 3, subtit. 1, unless proceedings to set deed aside were commenced on or before July 1, 1979. (§14-113).

Straw Deeds.—Abolished in most cases. Interest in property may be conveyed by one or more persons, as grantors, to themselves alone, or to himself or themselves and another person or persons, as grantees, in life tenancy, with or without powers, in joint tenancy, tenancy in common or tenancy by entireties, without use of straw man. Interest in property held by husband and wife in tenancy by entireties may be conveyed: (1) By both acting jointly, to themselves, to either of them individually, or to themselves and another person or persons, in joint tenancy or tenancy in common; (2) by both acting jointly, to either husband or wife and another person or persons in joint tenancy or tenancy in common; and (3) by either acting individually to other in tenancy in severalty, without use of straw man. (§4-108).

Taxes.—See category Documents and Records, topic Records, subhead Tax on Recordation.

Form.—Following form of special warranty deed may be used:

Form

This Deed, Made this . . . . . . day of . . . . . . in the year 19. . . . by . . . . . . of the first part and . . . . of the second part; witnesseth, that in consideration of (actual consideration including value of mortgage assumed, must be stated here, in acknowledgment or in separate affidavit under oath) . . . . . . the said part . . . . of the first part . . . . . . do . . . . grant and convey unto said part . . . . of the second part . . . . . . heirs and assigns, in fee simple, all that lot or parcel of ground . . . . . . situate, lying and being in . . . . and described as follows, that is to say: (Here insert description).

Together with the buildings and improvements thereupon, erected, made or being: and all and every, the rights, alleys, ways, waters, privileges, appurtenances and advantages, to the same belonging, or anywise appertaining.

To have and to hold the said lot of ground and premises, above described and mentioned, and hereby intended to be conveyed: together with the rights, privileges, appurtenances and advantages thereto belonging or appertaining unto and to the proper use and benefit of the said part . . . . of the second part . . . . . . heirs and assigns in fee simple. And the said part . . . . of the first part hereby covenant . . . . that . . . . he . . . . will warrant specially the property hereby granted: and conveyed: and that . . . . he . . . . will execute such further assurance of said land as may be requisite.

Witness the hand . . . . and seal . . . . of said grantor . . . . .

Test:

Witness signs here. . . . . (Seal).

(Acknowledgment). . . . . (Seal).

To be recorded, deed must bear certification of attorney that deed was prepared by attorney or under attorney's supervision, or certification that deed was prepared by one of parties named in deed. (§3-104[f]).

Deed, or separate affidavit accompanying deed, must state actual amount of consideration paid, including value of mortgage assumed. (tax-prop. art. §12-104).

DEEDS OF TRUST:

See category Mortgages, topic Mortgages of Real Property.

DOWER:

Estate of dower abolished. (est. & tr. art. §3-202; 259 Md. 1, 267 A.2d 209).

ESCHEAT:

See topic Absentees, subhead Escheat; categories Business Organizations, topic Corporations, subhead Unclaimed Dividends and Stock Interests; Business Regulation and Commerce, topic Banks and Banking, subhead Unclaimed Deposits and Property; Estates and Trusts, topics Descent and Distribution, subhead Escheat, Executors and Administrators, subhead Distribution, Wills, subhead Unclaimed Legacies; Insurance, topic Insurance Companies, subhead Unclaimed Funds;.

LANDLORD AND TENANT:

References are to Real Property Article of Code unless otherwise indicated.

Kinds of Tenancy.—Lease may be for fixed term, for periodic term, at will, at sufferance or per autre vie.

Application for Residential Lease.—Fees charged certain residential tenants limited to sums actually expended for credit check and other expenses arising out of application. Application must contain statement explaining any liabilities incurred upon signing. (§8-213).

Leases.—Leases for terms of more than one year must be in writing and signed by party creating lease (§§5-101, 5-102); for more than seven years must be executed, acknowledged and recorded like deed, but, if not recorded, are still valid and binding: (1) Between original parties to lease and their personal representatives; (2) against creditors of original parties; and (3) against other person who claims by, through or under original party and who acquires interest claimed with actual notice of lease or at time when tenant (or anyone claiming by, through or under tenant) is in such actual occupancy as to give reasonable notice. (§3-101). For statutory form of lease, see §4-202(i). Tenant's possession under lease for not more than seven years gives notice of his rights. (100 Md. 387, 59 A. 648). Lease carries with it implied covenant of quiet enjoyment. (§8-204). As to lease of single or multi-family dwelling unit, landlord must assure that tenant may peaceably and quietly enter upon leased premises at beginning of term; if landlord fails to provide possession of dwelling unit at beginning of term, rent is abated until possession is delivered, and tenant may, upon written notice to landlord, terminate lease, in which event landlord must return all deposits; whether or not lease is terminated, landlord is liable for consequential damages suffered after tenant gives notice of inability to enter premises. (§8-204[a]-[e]). In Baltimore City, lease of dwelling, whether oral or in writing, carries with it implied warranty of fitness for human habitation. Such warranty continues throughout tenancy, and tenant's action for breach may be maintained affirmatively or as defense in landlord's action of summary ejectment or distress for rent. (Code Pub. Local Laws, 1983 Replacement Volume, 1995 Cum. Supp.).

Residential leases, except for leases which arise after sale of owner-occupied residential property where seller and purchaser agree that seller may remain in possession of property for period of not more than 60 days after settlement (§8-201[b]), may not contain: (1) Confessed judgment clauses; (2) provisions whereby tenant agrees to waive right or remedy provided by law; (3) late payment penalties exceeding 5% (different provisions for weekly rental payments); (4) provisions whereby tenant waives right to jury trial; (5) provisions for notice to quit less than legal period; (6) provisions authorizing landlord to take possession of leased premises or tenant's personal property therein without benefit of formal legal process; or (7) any provision indemnifying or exonerating landlord from liability arising from his fault or negligence on common areas. Provisions for automatic renewal for more than one month must be set apart distinctly and provide space for written acknowledgment by tenant; if unacknowledged, provision is unenforceable by landlord. Forbidden provisions are unenforceable and, if included in lease after July 1, 1975 or attempted to be enforced thereafter, allow tenant to recover actual damages, including reasonable attorney's fees. (§8-208).

After Jan. 1, 1975, landlord offering more than four dwelling units for rent at one location by means of written leases must provide copy of proposed form of lease to any prospective applicant who requests it in writing. Lease offered by such landlord must state agreement of parties as to condition of premises and specific obligations of parties as to heat, gas, electricity, water and repair. Lease may not contain provision authorizing landlord to take possession of premises or tenant's personal property except pursuant to law or provision allowing landlord to bring eviction or give notice to quit as retaliation against tenant for participation in tenant organization. (§8-203.1).

Name of owner of residential property or management entity, along with address and telephone number, must be posted by owner in conspicuous place on property, or information must be included in written lease or in rent receipt. (§8-210).

See note at head of Digest as to 1998 legislation covered.

See Topical Index in front part of this volume.

MD – 53

LANDLORD AND TENANT . . . *continued*

Recording.—Lease for longer period than seven years must be recorded as deed, but memorandum of lease may be recorded in lieu of entire lease, and lease is valid and binding as to certain parties even though not recorded. See subhead Leases, supra. (§3-101). Recording requirement not applicable to lease for initial term of not more than seven years, where each renewal term is for seven years or less and where renewal may be effected or prevented by party to lease or his assigns. (§3-101[c]). See topic Deeds.

Rent is generally matter for agreement between parties.

After July 1, 1974, every landlord of residential property must maintain records system showing dates and amounts of rent paid and that receipt was given for each cash payment. (§8-208.2).

When lessee applies for renewal under covenant and cannot produce satisfactory evidence showing payment of rent, landlord may recover three years rent and no more before renewal is had. (§8-111).

When there has been no demand for or payment of rent growing out of any kind of lease for more than 20 consecutive years, such rent will be presumed conclusively to be extinguished and landlord may not set up claim to rent or to reversion in property. Landlord under disability has two years from removal of disability to assert rights. (§8-107).

Where residential dwelling unit, whether publicly or privately owned or single or multiple unit, is leased for human habitation (not farm tenancy), and where condition or defect constitutes, or if not corrected will constitute, fire hazard or serious and substantial threat to life, health or safety of occupants, rent escrow remedy is provided to tenant. Tenant must notify landlord of defect in writing by certified mail, landlord must have actual notice of defect, or landlord must be given written notice of violation, condemnation, etc., by government agency. Landlord has reasonable time (as determined by court, but period longer than 30 days presumed unreasonable) to repair or correct. Tenant may raise issue of rent escrow either affirmatively or defensively. Relief is conditioned on tenant's payment of rent into court and on tenant's not having been subject of more than specified number of complaints for rent due and unpaid in prior year. In addition to any other remedy, if landlord has not repaired defects within 90 days after court finds that defects exist, tenant can seek injunctive relief. (§8-211). Local subdivision ordinance comparable in subject matter supersedes state law. For Baltimore City, see Code Pub. Local Laws, 1976 with 1983 Replacement Volume, 1995 Cum. Supp.

Security Deposits.—Effective July 1, 1972, security deposits for residential leases may not exceed two months rent or $50, whichever is greater, and must be deposited by landlord in banking or savings institution within 30 days of receipt. Within 45 days after end of tenancy, except where tenant evicted, ejected for breach or abandons premises, landlord must return deposit to tenant together with (if deposit is $50 or more) interest less any damages rightfully withheld. (Applies to all security deposits held by landlord with simple interest accruing from July 1, 1972 to July 1, 1980 at 3% and accruing after July 1, 1980 at 4%, interest accruing from later of July 1, 1972 or date of receipt.) Security deposit may be withheld for unpaid rent, damage due for breach of lease or damage to leased premises in excess of ordinary wear and tear (tenant having right to be present when premises are inspected to determine if such damage was done); if any portion withheld, landlord must present to tenant, within 30 days after termination of tenancy, written list of damages with statement of costs actually incurred. Where tenant evicted, ejected for breach or abandons, tenant must demand, within 45 days, return of deposit. Landlord must then send tenant list of damages and costs within 30 days of notice, and return deposit with interest but less costs within 45 days of notice, or forfeit right to withhold any part. In certain instances landlord may be liable for treble damages plus reasonable attorney's fees. (§8-203). See §15-102(18).

Smoke Detectors.—Required in sleeping areas. Landlord generally responsible for installation, repair or replacement, but refundable deposit may be required of tenant. Upon request, special detectors must be made available to hearing impaired tenants; hotels shall have at least one special detector for every 50 units. Insurers may not raise section as policy defense. (art. 38A, §12A).

Lien.—Except as indicated below, there is no lien without distraint. Where tenant makes assignment for benefit of creditors, or has his property taken by receiver under court decree in insolvency proceeding, landlord has perfected lien on all distrainable property of tenant for rent due not more than three months prior thereto, although no actual distraint levied. (comm. law art. §15-102[c]).

Where growing crops are reserved as rent, said rent is lien on crops. (§8-115[a]). In St. Mary's, Prince George's, Charles, Calvert and Worcester counties, where growing crops are reserved as rent or landlord makes advances on crops to be grown, such rent and advances are lien on crops, provided contract making advances is written and executed by landlord and tenant. Lien is not divested by sale by tenant, personal representative of deceased tenant, assignment of tenant in bankruptcy or insolvency, or by process of law. (§8-115[b]-[c]).

Termination of Tenancy.—In counties, except Montgomery County, landlord must give tenant written notice to quit of at least one month where tenancy is by month, or one week where tenancy is by week, three months where tenancy (including tobacco farm tenancies) is from year to year, and six months in case of all other farm tenancies. (§8-402[b][1], [4]). These notice provisions do not apply to Baltimore City. In Montgomery County, landlord must give two months written notice where residential tenancy is at least month to month but less than from year to year, except in case of single family dwellings. (§8-402[b][4][iii]). No written agreement between parties may provide for longer period for notice by tenant than for notice by landlord in order to terminate tenancy. (§8-501).

In Baltimore City, with certain exceptions, local law requires that landlord give tenant written notice of 60 days in case of tenancy for period less than year or in case of tenancy at will, at sufferance or pur autre vie, and of 90 days in case of tenancy from year to year; in all said cases and in cases where exceptions apply, tenant must give landlord at least 30 days notice. Parties must give notice or lease continues from term to term. (Code Pub. Local Laws, 1976 with 1983 Replacement Volume, 1995 Cum. Supp.).

In action of distress, after sale of all goods levied, landlord, at his election, may obtain order terminating residential lease where term is 15 years or less, provided tenant is served or twice returned non est. (§8-324).

Where term is seven years or less, fire or other unavoidable accident rendering improvements untenantable terminates tenancy. (§8-112). See subhead Destruction of Premises, infra.

Extensive requirements concerning termination of tenancy of renter for inauguration of condominium regime. (tit. 11). 180 days written notice required concurrent with first offer to purchase to tenant. (§§11-102.1, 11-136). Form of notice in statute. (§11-102.1). Tenant need not vacate until later of expiration of lease or 180 days, except for breach of lease, but exceptions provide for extension of tenancy for up to three years for certain types of tenants. (§§11-102.1, 11-137). See topic Real Property, subhead Condominiums.

Retaliatory evictions or increases in rent are prohibited where residential premises are leased, but local ordinances can supersede state statute. (§8-208.1).

Holding Over.—Unless stated otherwise in written lease and initialed by tenant, tenant permitted to hold over takes week to week tenancy if week to week before holding over; otherwise takes tenancy from month to month. Unless lease otherwise provides, tenant unlawfully holding over is liable for actual damages, such damages to be not less than apportioned rent for holdover period at lease rate. (§8-402).

Dispossession.—Procedures are provided for landlord's dispossession of tenant upon failure to pay rent (§8-401) or for wrongful holding over (§8-402) or where lease gives landlord right to repossession for breach of lease (§8-402.1). (In Baltimore City, see Code Pub. Local Laws, 1976 with 1983 Replacement Volume & Supp. 1993, 1994 Cum. Supp.) Where dispossession is sought because of nonpayment of rent, and except where tenant has received repeated summons with complaints for unpaid rent (in Balto. City, multiple judgments required), at any time before execution of eviction order, tenant has right to redemption of leased premises upon payment of all due rent and costs. (§§8-401[c] [5], 8-401[e]; Code Pub. Local Laws of Balto. City, 1976 with 1983 Replacement Volume, 1995 Cum. Supp.). Tenant or landlord may appeal to circuit court within ten days of judgment and if tenant, by giving bond (cases of holding over) (§8-402[b][2]; Code Pub. Local Laws of Balto. City, 1976 with 1983 Replacement Volume & Supp. 1993, 1994 Cum. Supp.) or two days of judgment and if tenant, by giving bond (cases of nonpayment of rent) (§8-401[f]; Code Pub. Local Laws of Balto. City, 1976 with 1983 Replacement Volume, 1995 Cum. Supp.).

Where jurisdiction is forbidden district court, as in actions to try title to real property (courts art. §4-402), or in ground rent ejectment (§8-402.2), common law action of ejectment must be pursued in circuit court of county where disputed land lies (courts art. §6-203).

Distress.—Landlord may distrain for unpaid rent in action at law by filing verified petition in district court. No distress available unless under written lease for more than three months or tenancy at will or periodic tenancy that has continued more than three months. (§8-302; Code Pub. Local Laws of Balto. City, 1976 with 1983 Replacement Volume, 1995 Cum. Supp.). Levy extends to all goods on leased premises, whether property of tenant or another (§8-306[a]), except: (a) Goods of subtenant or third party, where lease is more than 15 years (§8-306[b]); (b) certain tools, instruments, books and files of tenant used in trade or profession (§8-307[a]); (c) goods of tenant subject to prior recorded security interest under Uniform Commercial Code, unless landlord pays balance due holder of security interest (§8-307[b]). Where lease names either husband or wife as tenant, goods belonging to either or both are subject to levy as if both named tenants. (§8-326). If lease for more than three months is assigned, assignee liable to distress as if named tenant; goods of assignee on premises are subject to levy. (§8-329). Third person whose goods have been levied must petition to have goods excluded from levy within seven days thereof; otherwise goods are conclusively presumed to be goods of tenant. (§8-311). Within six months of distress action, landlord can obtain order to follow goods of tenant which tenant has removed. (§8-315). Appeal from any final order or deficiency judgment must be taken within 14 days, but such appeal does not stay subsequent distress for rent falling due after original distress petition unless tenant files appeal bond approved by court. (§8-332).

Action for waste is provided for by statute. (§14-102).

Fixtures.—Right of tenant to remove fixtures erected by him under one demise or term not lost or impaired by acceptance of new lease of same premises without intermediate surrender of possession. (§8-114). Lien may be given on furnishings or equipment affixed to real estate. (comm. law art. §9-313). See category Mortgages, topic Chattel Mortgages. Uniform Commercial Code adopted.

Destruction of Premises.—Unless otherwise provided in lease, when improvements on property rented for term of not more than seven years become untenantable through fire or unavoidable accident, tenancy terminates and all rent ceases on payment of proportionate rent to date of fire or accident. (§8-112).

Unless otherwise provided expressly in lease, covenant by lessee to leave premises in good repair does not compel erection of similar buildings or payment therefor if destruction by fire or otherwise was without lessee's negligence or fault. (§8-113).

Exculpatory clause in lease, whereby tenant covenants to indemnify or hold harmless landlord, or to preclude or exonerate landlord from any or all liability to tenant or another for injury, loss, damage or liability arising from omission, fault, negligence or other misconduct of landlord on or about leased premises or common areas used in connection therewith and not within exclusive control of tenant, deemed against public policy and void. No insurer may claim right of subrogation by reason of invalidity of such provision. (§8-105).

Redemption.—Provision is made for redemption of lease for longer than 15 years, created on or after Apr. 8, 1884 at option of tenant, after notice to landlord, for sum equal to capitalization of rent at rate set forth below; provision does not apply to lease for business purposes for term not exceeding 99 years; lease of property improved or to be improved by apartments, condominiums or cooperatives is lease for business use. (§8-110).

Ground Rents.—Law set out in real prop. art. at §§8-101, 8-102. Irredeemable rents can no longer be created. See subhead Redemption, supra. If lease was executed on or

LANDLORD AND TENANT . . . *continued*
after July 1, 1971, it is redeemable at any time after expiration of three years from its date; if executed on or after July 1, 1982 or between July 1, 1969 and July 1, 1971, at any time after five years from its date; if executed before July 1, 1969, at any time. As to leases executed between Apr. 8, 1884 and Apr. 5, 1888, redemption price may be some sum specified in lease not to exceed 4% capitalization of rent; if after Apr. 6, 1888 and before July 1, 1982, capitalization rate not to exceed 6%; if after July 1, 1982, capitalization rate not to exceed 12%. (§8-110). If tenant has power to redeem from trustee or other person who does not have power of sale, redemption may nevertheless be had in accordance with R. P. Y70-Y79. (§8-110[d]; 110 Md. 619, 73 A. 887).

If six months rent in arrears and landlord has right to reenter for nonpayment, he may, 30 days after sending tenant bill for unpaid rent, bring action for possession under §14-108.1; but before entry of judgment landlord must give written notice of pending entry of judgment to all mortgagees of lease who have recorded request for notice of judgment among land records before entry of judgment. Property is discharged from lease unless tenant or person claiming under lease pays ground rent and costs and commences action for relief from judgment within six months after execution of judgment. (§8-402.2).

Renewal.—Court of equity may enter judgment for renewal of lease with covenant for renewal, including 99 year lease. (§8-108).

Condominiums.—Extensively regulated by Maryland Condominium Act. (tit. 11). Uniform Condominium Act not adopted. See topic Real Property, subhead Condominiums.

Uniform Residential Landlord-Tenant Act not adopted.

LEASES:

See topic Landlord and Tenant.

PERPETUITIES:

Common law rules in force (est. & tr. art. §11-102), except that limited "wait and see" doctrine and saving provision reducing age contingency to 21 adopted by statute (est. & tr. art. §11-103), and except that there is no violation of Rule in case of trust created by employer as part of pension, stock bonus, disability, death benefit, profit-sharing, retirement, welfare or other plan for employees or their beneficiaries, or in case of legacy or conveyance for cemetery perpetual care of $5,000 or less, or in case of transfer of assets from one charitable corporation to another, contingent on future event, or in case of trusts for charitable purposes, or in case of trust in which governing instrument states that Rule Against Perpetuities does not apply and under which trustee has certain specified powers (est. & tr. art. §11-102), or in case of uncertain donees of gift for charitable uses, provided will directs formation of corporation to take gift and corporation is formed within 12 months (est. & tr. art. §4-409).

Accumulations of income permitted up to period of perpetuities. (See 199 Md. 264, 86 A.2d 504.)

PERSONAL PROPERTY:

Husband and wife may acquire personal property as tenants by entireties. Conveyance to husband and wife is presumed held as tenants by entirety unless contrary is designated, and property purchased with entirety money is also entirety property. (225 Md. 241, 170 A.2d 303).

Instrument shall not be construed to create joint tenancy unless instrument in writing expressly provides that property is to be held in joint tenancy. (real prop. art. §2-117).

POWERS OF ATTORNEY:

Attorneys in Fact.—Attorney in fact may be appointed by power of attorney as at common law. Power may be general or special, authority of attorney in fact depending in each case on language of power. (53 Md. 28). Power of attorney to attorney at law with reference to recovery of tort damages, signed within five days of injury, is voidable within 60 days. (court art. §5-305.1[A]).

Power of attorney should be executed by principal with same dignity required of any act which attorney may be called upon to perform, i.e., if attorney is to sign paper under seal, power should be under seal, and if attorney is to execute paper under oath, power should be verified.

Power of attorney to execute deed must be executed in same manner as deed and recorded with or prior to deed or it may be recorded on day after deed is recorded provided it is acknowledged and dated on or before date on which deed is executed. (real prop. art. §4-107). Unless otherwise provided by power, attorney in fact may exercise power during any period of disability or incompetence or uncertainty as to whether principal is dead or alive. (est. & tr. art. §13-601).

Where principal has died or become incompetent, attorney in fact may nonetheless bind representatives of principal, provided he acts in good faith under power, without actual knowledge of death or disability. (est. & tr. art. §13-602).

For appointment of health care agent, see category Estates and Trusts, topic Wills, subhead Living Will.

REAL PROPERTY:

References are to Real Property Article of Code unless otherwise indicated.

British Statutes are no longer in force except to extent enacted by General Assembly and contained in Code. (§14-115).

All common law estates in real property are still recognized, except that rule in Shelley's Case has been abolished (est. & tr. art. §11-104), contingent remainders are indestructible (est. & tr. art. §11-101), and person seized of estate tail may grant and sell it as if seized of estate in fee simple (§2-102). Possibilities of reverter and rights of entry are alienable but, if created after July 1, 1969, are limited to 30 years duration. Possibilities of reverter and rights of entry existing on July 1, 1969 are invalidated unless notice of intention to preserve is recorded as prescribed; however, these limitations do not apply to state or its subdivisions. (§§6-101 to 6-105). No deed, devise or other writing may be construed to create estate in joint tenancy unless it is expressly provided in instrument that property is to be held in joint tenancy. (§2-117). Deed or devise to husband and wife creates tenancy by entireties unless otherwise provided. (193 Md. 391, 67 A.2d 258). Property interests may be granted by one or more persons to themselves alone, or to himself or themselves and any other person, as grantees, in life tenancy, with or without powers, joint tenancy, tenancy in common, or tenancy by entirety without using intermediate strawman. Husband and wife may grant property held in tenancy by entirety by acting jointly (i) to themselves, to either individually, to either and another, or to themselves and another, in joint tenancy or tenancy in common, and (ii) by either acting individually to other in tenancy in severalty, without using intermediate strawman. (§4-108). See topic Deeds. Co-tenant who receives rent from third party must account to other co-tenants for rent over and above his proportionate share. (§14-106).

Rule in Shelley's Case.—Abolished. (est. & tr. art. §11-104).

Statute of Uses repealed. Notwithstanding, executory interests and powers of appointment are valid, subject to rule against perpetuities. (§2-116).

Action for waste provided by statute where waste is committed or permitted by mortgagor, life tenant, tenant for years or at will, periodic tenant, tenant in common, joint tenant or other person in possession of land. Person committing waste may be sued even after transfer of his estate. Waste committed after injunction is subject to penalty of double damages, payable in part to injured party, applied in part as fine. Court may also imprison violator. (§14-102).

Foreign Conveyances or Encumbrances.—Instruments affecting real estate located in Md. must be executed in accordance with laws of Md. in order to be valid.

Land Installment Contracts.—See category Business Regulation and Commerce, topic Sales.

Condominiums.—Uniform Condominium Act not adopted. Sections of horizontal property act effective July 1, 1981, amended substantially effective July 1, 1982, phase in at different times (see §11-142). Properties to become subject to condominium regime must be registered with Secretary of State by filing and updating promptly public offering statement, which must be refiled annually, including specified information, which must be delivered to initial purchaser, who has absolute right of rescission exercisable within specified time periods. Contract for initial sale of unit to member of public (including occupying tenant) may not be entered into until public offering statement is registered and ten days after all amendments then applicable to public offering statement are filed. (§§11-126, 11-127). Tenants have right of first refusal and right to receive lesser of actual moving expenses or $750. (§11-136). Special rights afforded to "designated household". (§11-137). Local governments may, in certain instances, add additional rights or exercise right of first refusal. (§§11-139, 11-140). On resale, seller must furnish purchaser, not later than 15 days prior to closing, with copy of declaration, bylaws, rules, regulations, various disclosures and descriptions, and certificate containing designated information. (§§11-135). Declaration (§11-103) and bylaws (§11-104) must contain designated information, and, together with condominium plat, must be recorded (§11-105). Each unit has all incidents of real property (§11-106) and undivided interest in common elements (§11-107). Council of unit owners, which governs affairs of condominium (§11-109), must, with limited exceptions, maintain insurance thereon (§11-114), and must register with Dep't of Assessments and Taxation (§11-119). Unless declaration or bylaws state otherwise, rules and regulations adopted after Jan. 1, 1984 are subject to procedural requirements; unit holders are granted hearing and disapproval rights (§11-111). Condominium unit owners are authorized to meet in specified area, subject to reasonable rules, to consider and discuss matters relating to operation of condominium. Governing bodies and committees of condominiums are required to allow unit and lot owners to comment on specified matters during specified meetings, subject to certain rules enacted by governing bodies. (§§11-108 and 11-109). Disputes are governed by statutory procedures set forth in §11-113. Assessment of each condominium unit is based on value of such unit rather than on proportionate value of whole property. (tax-prop. art. §§8-104, 8-207). Developer must appoint resident agent, who can be changed by unit of council owners, for service in suits against unit of council owners or arising in relation to common elements. (§11-119). Unless greater percentage (or lesser, if condominium is restricted to nonresidential uses) is provided in declaration, condominium may only be terminated by 80% vote. (§11-123). See topic Landlord and Tenant, subhead Termination of Tenancy.

Time Sharing.—Time shares of real estate regulated by §§14-2401 to 14-2403 of comm. law art.

Mobile Home Parks.—Mobile homes and mobile home parks governed by tit. 8A.

Farmland.—Land actively used for farm or agricultural purposes assessed at 50% of its use value. (tax-prop. art. §8-209). Land assessed as farmland which is converted to other use may be subject to agricultural transfer tax. Buyer of land liable or potentially liable for tax must be so notified in contract of sale or seller liable to buyer for tax amount. (tax-prop. art. §§8-209, 13-301 to 13-308). See also categories Documents and Records, topic Records, subhead Tax on Recordation, catchline Transfer Tax; Taxation, topic Property Taxes, subhead Taxable Property, catchline Assessment.

Stale Contracts of Purchase and Options.—No recorded contract of sale for real property is enforceable or is encumbrance on title of such property, when buyer is not in possession, as against persons other than original parties thereto, unless within five years after date set out in recorded contract for delivery of deed, action or proceedings are commenced to enforce contract. (§10-401).

When recorded instrument creates option to purchase real property, which according to its terms has expired, and one year has elapsed since time of expiration and no conveyance or other instrument has been recorded showing that option has been exercised, then recorded instrument creating option ceases to be notice, either actual or constructive, to any person or to put any person on inquiry as to existence or exercise of option. (§10-402).

Cooperative Housing.—Regulated by corps. art. tit. 5, subtit. 6B.

Homeowners Associations.—Regulated by Maryland Homeowners Association Act. (tit. 11B).

See note at head of Digest as to 1998 legislation covered.

See Topical Index in front part of this volume.

REAL PROPERTY . . . *continued*

New Home Builders.—Effective Jan. 1, 1991, regulated by New Home Warranty Act which requires, among other things, that new home builders disclose to purchasers and owners of new homes whether or not they participate in new home warranty security plans. (§§10-601—10-610).

Custom Home Sales.—Regulated by Maryland Custom Home Protection Act. (tit. 10, subtit. 5).

Building Codes.—As of 8/1/95, BOCA National Building Code (with some modifications) will serve as Maryland Building Performance Standards; local jurisdictions have authority to modify standards. (art. 83B, §§6-401 to 6-406).

See also topics Curtesy, Deeds, Dower, Landlord and Tenant; categories Business Regulation and Commerce, topic Sales; Civil Actions and Procedure, topic Partition; Family, topic Husband and Wife; Mortgages, topic Mortgages of Real Property.

TRUST DEEDS:

See category Mortgages, topic Mortgages of Real Property.

TAXATION

ADMINISTRATION:

Note: In 1988 session, Maryland Legislature added new article to Maryland Code to be entitled "Tax-General Article" (tax-gen. art.). This Art. is intended to revise, restate and recodify laws of State relating to certain taxes generally. Effective date of this Art. is Jan. 1, 1989.

Tax-prop. art. and tax-gen. art. are general governing statutes of this topic Taxation. Property is subject to state, county and municipal taxes.

Supervision.—Comptroller of Treasury, State Treasury Building, Annapolis 21404, has general supervision of administration of income tax, estate tax, sales and use tax, motor fuel tax, among others.

State Dep't of Assessments and Taxation, 301 W. Preston St., Baltimore 21201, has general supervision of administration of following taxes: Property taxes (review of assessments), corporation tax and franchise taxes.

Local Taxes.—Certain local taxes are imposed by individual counties. County income ("piggyback") taxes of between 20% and 60% are imposed. (tax-gen. art. §10-106). For local taxes on real property transfers, see category Documents and Records, topic Records.

Applicable State Interest Rate.—Applicable interest rate is determined annually by Comptroller in accord with statutory guidelines and may differ for refunds and amounts owed state, equal to greater of 13% or three percentage points above prime interest rate for money owed state. (tax-gen. art. §13-604).

Refund of Taxes.—Claim for refund of property, state or local taxes erroneously or mistakenly paid must be filed within three years of payment. (tax-prop. art. §14-915). Claim for refund of general taxes must be filed with agency to which paid within three years of payment. (tax-gen. art. §§13-901, 13-1104; art. 24, §9-711). State income tax and financial institution franchise tax refund claim or claim for credit of overpayment may not be filed after periods of limitations for filing claims as provided in §6511 of IRC. If such claim is allowed it may not exceed amount of State tax resulting from application of limits in §6511 of IRC. (tax-gen. art. §13-1104[c]). Taxpayer has one year from date of finality of assessment for tax year to claim refund of personal property taxes as to which taxpayer was entitled to exemption. (tax-prop. art. §14-915). Interest at applicable state interest rate allowed if overpayment not attributable to mistake or error by taxpayer. (tax-gen. art. §13-603). Interest on refund claims must be computed beginning 45 days after filing of claim. (tax-gen. art. §13-603). Appeal from denial of refund claim may be taken to Md. Tax Court within 30 days from receipt of notice of disallowance (tax-gen. art. §13-510); as to further appeal, see category Courts and Legislature, topic Courts, subhead Maryland Tax Court. Claim for refund of "special" taxes not acted upon within six months is deemed to be disallowed and may be appealed. (tax-gen. art. §13-510). No allowed refund claim is paid until all other state taxes due by taxpayer have been paid in full. (tax-gen. art. §13-905). For refund of sales or use tax, see topic Sales and Use Tax.

Penalties.—All references are to tax-gen. art. unless otherwise indicated.

Real and personal property taxes in arrears on Oct. 1 generally bear interest of ⅔ of 1% per month or fraction thereof until paid. However, some jurisdictions impose different rates. (tax-prop. art. §§14-602, 14-603). See also subhead Sales and Use Tax. Failure to report cost or market value of personal property results in penalty of 20% of escaped property. (tax-prop. art. §14-705).

Failure to pay tax when due subjects taxpayer to assessment of additional penalty not exceeding 10% of unpaid tax, or 25% for nonpayment of financial institution franchise tax and tobacco tax. (§13-701). Failure to provide income and expense information on certain income-producing real property may result in penalty of $100 per day, up to maximum of 0.1% of value of property. (tax-prop. art. §8-105).

Tax on insurance premiums and deposits for perpetual fire insurance, due on or before Mar. 15, bears monthly interest thereafter at applicable state interest rate and delinquent payer is subject to 5% penalty. (art. 48A, §§636, 637).

Inheritance tax bears interest at applicable state interest rate. Where there is no formal administration of estate and tax has not been paid 30 days after due date, interest begins on original due date. (§13-601). Interest on estate tax begins nine months after date of death.

Corporation which is subject to Md. jurisdiction, and firm or individual against whom assessment has been made for property taxes, that fails to file annual report on or before Apr. 15 is subject to initial penalty of ¹⁄₁₀ of 1% of assessments plus 2% of initial penalty for each 30 days or fraction thereof that default continues; initial penalty must not be less than $30 nor greater than $500. (tax-prop. art. §14-704). Dep't of Assessments and Taxation may grant extension up to 60 days. Request for extension must be filed on or before day return is due. (tax-prop. art. §14-704). Foreign corporation which

fails to file any report required by law, after demand and notice by Dep't of Assessments and Taxation, forfeits right to do intrastate business. (corps. art. §7-304).

Charter of corporation that fails to pay tax due by Oct. 1 is subject to annulment and forfeiture through notice and publication procedure initiated by Comptroller after Sept. 30 of following year. Forfeiture and revival procedures set forth in corps. art. §§3-503 to 3-520.

Recordation Tax.—Any person recording instrument without paying tax, or incurring additional debt secured by previously recorded instrument without paying additional tax, or willfully misrepresenting actual consideration by affixing evidence of greater or lesser tax paid, is subject to fine up to $500 or sentence up to six months in jail. (tax-prop. art. §§14-1010 to 14-1012).

Income tax and estimated tax payments paid after extension granted or additional amounts found due carry interest at applicable state interest rate. (§§13-601, 13-602). Taxes not paid when due bear penalty up to 25% as fixed by Comptroller plus interest at applicable state interest rate, on unpaid tax and penalty until paid. (§13-701). Willful failure to file income tax return subjects taxpayer to $5,000 fine or five years imprisonment or both. (§13-1001). Failure of corporation or individual to file declaration of estimated tax on prescribed date, failure to pay installments when due or failure to estimate tax equal to 90% of tax due subjects taxpayer to penalty up to 25% as fixed by Comptroller plus interest at applicable state interest rate. No interest assessed on penalty tax. (§§13-701, 13-702, 13-605). Willful preparation of false or fraudulent return subjects person assisting or acting in representative capacity for taxpayer to fine up to $5,000 or sentence up to five years imprisonment or both. (§13-1004). Willful preparation of fraudulent return subjects taxpayer or officer submitting return on behalf of corporation to prosecution for perjury and 50% penalty not to exceed 100% of underpayment of tax. (§§13-703, 13-1002). Failure by employer to file required withholding tax returns subjects employer to fine up to $5,000 or sentence up to five years imprisonment or both. (§13-1007). Failure to furnish employee with correct withholding statement subjects employer to $50 penalty for each failure in addition to criminal penalties. (§§13-706, 13-1007). Willful failure to provide information or providing false information on withholding certificate subjects person to fine up to $500 and/or six months imprisonment. (§13-1007).

Sales tax and use tax not paid when due bear penalty of 10% of unpaid tax plus interest per month at applicable state interest rate, until paid. (§§13-601, 13-701). Fraudulent failure to file return subjects taxpayer to 100% penalty. (§13-704). Failure to file return and pay tax assessment within ten days of receipt of final notice and demand subjects taxpayer to 25% penalty. (§13-709). Retailer who sells without sales and use tax license is subject to fine up to $100. (§13-1016). Any taxpayer or officer of corporate taxpayer who willfully fails to collect or pay over tax, file returns, or who files false return, is subject to fine up to $5,000 or up to five years imprisonment or both. (§§13-1001, 13-1003, and 13-1006). Any taxpayer or officer of corporate taxpayer who willfully fails to keep required records or uses false sales tax number is subject to fine up to $1,000 or up to one year imprisonment or both. (§13-1008).

Admissions and amusement tax not paid bears penalty of 10% plus interest at applicable state interest rate until paid or penalty of 100% plus interest at applicable state interest rate, if failure to file is with intent to defraud. (§§13-701, 13-704). If payment not made within 30 days after notice of delinquency, additional penalty of 25% due. (§13-708). Willful failure to file return or to pay taxes or keep records or willful false statement or misleading omission subjects taxpayer to fine up to $500 or up to six months imprisonment or both. (§§13-1001, 13-1003, 13-1005, 13-1008).

Motor fuel and motor carrier taxes not paid when due bear penalty of not greater than $25. (§13-701). Fraudulent failure to file return bears penalty of 100% of unpaid tax. (§13-703).

Tobacco tax not paid bears penalty of 25% plus interest per month at applicable state interest rate. (§13-701). Willful possession, sale or offer to sell unstamped cigarettes subjects taxpayer to fine up to $1,000 or up to one year imprisonment or both for each day possession continues. (§13-1014).

Alcoholic beverages tax not paid subjects manufacturer, wholesaler or retailer to fine up to $10,000 or up to five years imprisonment or both. (§13-1009).

General penalties include fine up to $500 for negligent failure to furnish required information (§13-1023); fine up to $5,000 and up to 18 months imprisonment, or both, for willful or intentional evasion of any tax or failure to file required reports or giving of incorrect or misleading information. (§13-1024).

Limitations.—Unless otherwise specifically prescribed, action for collection of all state, county or city taxes must be commenced within seven years of due date or assessment date. (tax-gen. art. §13-1103). Action to collect sales and use taxes must be brought within four years, except that proof of fraud or gross negligence (25% or more of tax due not paid) will remove bar of statutory period. (tax-gen. art. §13-1102).

ADMISSIONS AND AMUSEMENT TAX:

Note: References are to tax-gen. art.

Any county or municipal corporation may impose tax on gross receipts derived from any admissions and amusement charges in that county or municipal corporation. In addition Maryland Stadium Authority may impose tax on gross receipts derived from any admissions or amusements for admission to facility owned or leased by Stadium Authority. (§4-102). Admissions and amusement tax is applicable to receipts derived from admission to place, use of game for entertainment, use of recreational or sports facility, use or rental of recreational or sports equipment and merchandise, refreshments, or service sold or served in connection with entertainment at nightclub or room in hotel, restaurant, hall or other place where dancing privileges, music or other entertainment are provided. (§4-101). County may not impose tax on gross receipts from any source within municipal corporation located within that county if municipal corporation imposes admissions and amusement tax on gross receipts or specifically exempts any gross receipts from admissions and amusement tax. (§4-103). Rate of tax for counties and municipal corporations shall not exceed 10% of gross receipts; Stadium Authority's rate shall not exceed 8% of gross receipts. If gross receipts are also subject to sales and use tax, counties and municipal corporations may not set rate that exceeds 10% when combined with sales and use tax. If gross receipts are also subject to admissions and amusement tax by Stadium Authority, rate cannot exceed 10% when combined with tax

ADMISSIONS AND AMUSEMENT TAX... *continued*

imposed by Stadium Authority. (§4-105). Following are exempt: (1) Gross receipts derived from place where dancing is prohibited and only entertainment provided is from mechanical music, radio or television; (2) gross receipts from live boxing or wrestling match; (3) concerts or theatrical events presented or offered by nonprofit groups; (4) gross receipts derived from admission charges to or for use of facility or equipment in connection with bingo game operated in accordance with art. 27, §260; (5) bowling alley; (6) charter fishing boat; (7) gross receipts used exclusively for charitable, educational or religious purpose, or for volunteer fire company or nonprofit rescue squad, or fraternal, service, or veterans organization, or agricultural fair; and (8) gross receipts used for cost of prizes or winnings distributed as part of commercial bingo game operations in Anne Arundel County. Any county may exempt community associations, nonprofit organizations and performing arts organizations. (§§4-103, 4-104).

Tax return is due on or before tenth day of month that follows month in which person received gross receipts. (§4-201). Person must keep complete and accurate records for four years. (§4-202).

ALCOHOLIC BEVERAGE TAX:

Alcoholic beverage tax is imposed by tax-gen. art. §§5-101 et seq.

BOXING AND WRESTLING TAX:

Boxing and wrestling tax is imposed by tax-gen. art. §§6-101 et seq.

CHAIN STORE TAX:

Chain store tax is imposed by bus. reg. art. tit. 17, subtit. 18.

ESTATE TAX:

Note: All references are to tax-gen. art. unless otherwise indicated.

Tax is also imposed upon transfer of "Maryland estate" of each "decedent" (defined as resident of Md. or one who left real or tangible personal property in Md.). (§7-302). Tax is equal to amount, if any, by which credit under federal estate tax law exceeds aggregate of state death taxes payable out of Md. estate of decedent. (§7-304). Tax is imposed on amount of credit not satisfied by payment of Maryland inheritance tax. Tax not reduced by failure of personal representative to preserve maximum state death tax credit allowable under federal law. (§7-304). Tax limited to amount by which its timely payment under federal law would reduce federal estate tax payable. (§7-304). Tax is payable nine months after date of death. (§7-305). Interest at applicable state interest rate, from due date to date of payment. (§13-601). Comptroller may grant alternative payment schedule for tax in form of payment plan on case-by-case basis. (§7-307). Tax is paid to Comptroller of Treasury when estate tax return is filed with register of wills. (§7-306).

Apportionment Against Inter Vivos Dispositions.—Uniform Estate Tax Apportionment Act adopted. (§7-308).

Interstate Co-operation.—Uniform Acts on Interstate Arbitration of Death Taxes (§§7-104 et seq.) and Interstate Compromise of Death Taxes (§§7-118 et seq.) adopted.

FRANCHISE TAXES:

Note: All references are to tax-gen. art. unless otherwise indicated.

Public Service Company Franchise Tax.—Annual state tax of 2% of gross receipts is levied on public service companies engaged in telegraph, telephone, oil pipeline, electric, or gas business in Md.; gross receipts does not include gross charges from sale by public service company of Internet access service by which connection is provided between computer and Internet. Allocation formula is provided for such companies operating in several states. Report due Mar. 15; payment due with each return. (§§8-401 to 8-405). Declaration of estimated tax must be filed on or before June 1 of current taxable year if tax for year is estimated to exceed $1,000. Fifty percent of estimated tax is then due and payable. Underpayment (estimated payment by less than 45% of tax due for full taxable year) subject to interest calculated from due date of estimated tax payment until date of final tax payment for taxable year at applicable state interest rate. (§§8-401, 8-404, 8-405, 13-602).

Franchise Tax on Financial Institutions.—All domestic and certain other financial institutions are subject to franchise tax at rate of 7% of net earnings allocable to Md. Tax is imposed on commercial banks, credit companies, finance companies, international banking facilities, loan companies, mortgage companies, safe deposit companies, savings banks, savings and loan associations, trust companies and any company competing with national banks in Md. (§§8-101, 8-203, 8-204). Each covered institution must file quarterly estimated tax return with Dep't of Assessments and Taxation. (§8-209). Finance companies making loans to farmers, SBIA corporations, subchapter S corporations, and REMIC's are exempt. (§8-101). Special deduction authorized for international financial transactions. (§8-205). Principal amount of tax increment financing bonds, interest payable thereon, their transfers and any income or profit derived therefrom must be included in net earnings of financial institutions to extent required by §§128 and 128A of IRC for purposes of measuring state franchise tax. (art. 41, §14-211). Every financial institution must file declaration of estimated tax within five months of beginning of tax year if its tax is expected to exceed $1,000. Fifty percent of estimated tax is then due and payable. Tax return due by 15th day of third month after end of institution's fiscal year. (§§8-209, 8-210).

Franchise Tax on Savings and Loan Associations.—Such institutions are subject to tax rate of .013% of total withdrawal value of deposits of such institutions. (§8-301 et seq.).

GENERATION SKIPPING TRANSFER TAX:

Note: References are to tax-gen. art.

Generation skipping transfer tax (§7-401 et seq.) imposes tax on certain generation skipping transfers occurring at time of and as result of death of individual. (§7-402). It picks up any allowable federal credit on taxable termination attributable to Maryland

property passing with respect to decedents for whom federal return is required to be filed on or after 1/1/89. (§7-403).

GIFT TAX:

None, but inheritance tax applies to gifts in contemplation of death or intended to take effect at or after death. (tax-gen. art. §7-201).

INCOME TAX:

Note: All references are to tax-gen. art. unless otherwise indicated.

Imposed on individuals and corporations by §10-102. Forms and information may be procured from Comptroller of Treasury, State Treasury Building, Annapolis 21404.

Taxable net income of resident is taxpayer's federal adjusted gross income ("AGI"), modified as herein set forth, less deductions and personal exemptions hereinafter set forth. Taxpayer's federal AGI is increased by: (i) interest or dividends on obligations of any state or political subdivision (other than Md.) less related expenses; (ii) wages from and interest or dividends on obligations of any authority or instrumentality of U.S. or any foreign government which by law or treaty are exempt from federal income tax but not from state income tax; (iii) ordinary income portion of lump sum distribution allowable as deduction from federal AGI under §402(e)(3) of IRC, and, to extent treated as ordinary income, 40% of capital gain portion of distribution as provided in §402(a)(2) of IRC and giving effect to §401(e)(1)(D) of IRC; (iv) oil depletion allowance as claimed and allowed under §613 or 613A of IRC; (v) pickup contributions of retirement or pension system member; (vi) enterprise zone wage credit; (vii) reforestation and timber stand modification; (viii) amount of credit allowed under §10-703 if credit is based upon taxes paid by S corporation to state which does not recognize federal S corporation tax treatment; (ix) certain net operating losses; (x) 50% of sum of items of federal tax preference as determined and defined in §10-222; and (xi) expenses attributable to operating certain child care and day care facilities. Taxpayer's federal AGI is reduced by: (i) distribution to beneficiary of accumulated income on which fiduciary has paid income tax; (ii) dividends and interest from U.S. obligations, including such amounts received from mutual funds; (iii) any amount included in federal AGI under §62 of IRC for employer-provided official vehicle used in accordance with law by member of state, county or local police or fire department; (iv) payments from pension plan for injuries or disabilities received by policemen and firemen; (v) income derived from Development Credit Corporation of Md.; (vi) income due to withdrawal from Keogh Plan if state taxes previously paid; (vii) payments received under fire, rescue or ambulance personnel length-of-service award programs; (viii) for any eligible low-income taxpayer, earned income as defined in §32(C)(2) of IRC; (ix) included profit from sale or exchange of bonds issued by state or subdivisions; (x) to extent included, amounts received by individuals under Tit. II of Social Security Act or Tier I benefits under Railroad Retirement Act; (xi) relocation and assistance payments under real prop. art. §12-201 et seq.; (xii) pickup contributions for members of retirement or pension system; (xiii) included refunds of any state or local income taxes paid; (xiv) income exempted from state income tax by federal law or treaty; (xv) any income derived from intangible personal property held in Md. in trust for benefit of nonresident or corporation not doing business in state; (xvi) overseas military pay; (xvii) certain military retirement pay; and (xviii) up to $1,200 of salary of lesser-earning spouse of two-earner married couple filing jointly. (§10-207). Taxpayer's federal AGI also reduced by, if over 65 or if individual or spouse is totally disabled, lesser of pension payments or annual benefit received by Md. retirees from Social Security for prior calendar year. (§10-209). Subject to abrogation, taxpayer's federal AGI is reduced by: (a) not more than $3,000 for all expenses actually incurred and not itemized in computing federal taxable income by adoptive parents who adopt child with special needs as defined in §222 of IRC through public child welfare agency or licensed, not-for-profit private adoption agency; (b) not more than $2,000 for adoption of child without special need as defined in §473(c)(1) and (2) of Social Security Act; (c) up to $1,000 in expenses incurred each taxable year by employers in providing readers for blind employees and up to $5,000 in expenses incurred each taxable year by blind individuals in obtaining reader for personal use or use in their employment; (d) expenses incurred for purchase and installation of conservation tillage equipment; (e) expenses for household and dependent care; (f) fair market value of donated art works not deductible from federal AGI with several limitations including requirement that taxpayer derive at least 50% of income from sales of art works produced by taxpayer; (g) donated farm products to gleaning cooperatives; (h) upon election of taxpayer, historic structure preservation expenses; (i) expenses for reforestation or timber stand improvement activity; (i-1) $3,500 if individual is qualifying volunteer fire, rescue, or emergency medical services member for taxable year; (j) gross income of child included in parent's gross income under §1(a)(7) of IRC unless child is required to file income tax return or would have been required to if not for §1(i)(7) of IRC; (k) unreimbursed automobile travel expenses incurred while serving as volunteer for organizations providing medical, health or nutritional care described in §170 of IRC, while providing assistance (other than transportation) to handicapped individuals (as described in §190 of IRC) attending state community college, or while serving nonprofit volunteer fire company; (l) amount by which employer business deduction for employee wages and salaries under §280C(a) of IRC (relating to targeted jobs credit) is disallowed (§10-208); (m) cost of poultry or livestock manure spreading equipment used in accordance with approved nutrient management plan; and (n) $3,500 if individual is qualifying volunteer police officer.

Deductions.—Individual who has itemized his deductions for federal income tax purposes may deduct sum of such itemized deductions reduced as required by IRC and for state and local taxes deducted. (§10-218). Federal deductions which are eliminated, reduced, or changed to credit during taxable year does not affect deduction for state income tax during that year. (§10-221). Resident for less than full year can deduct only items expended during his residence in Md. Nonresident can claim deductions only to extent they are allocable to taxable income. Standard deduction of 15% of Md. adjusted gross income, not to be less than $1,500 ($3,000 on joint return or for head of household or surviving spouse) or not to exceed $2,000 ($4,000 on joint return or for head of household or surviving spouse), may be taken by certain individuals in lieu of itemized deductions. (§10-217, 10-220, 10-221).

See note at head of Digest as to 1998 legislation covered.

See Topical Index in front part of this volume.

INCOME TAX . . . *continued*

Personal Exemptions.—Individual taxpayer allowed exemption of $1,200 for each personal and dependent exemption for which he is entitled to deduction for federal tax purposes in corresponding tax year. Additional (i) $1,750 exemption for taxable year beginning after Dec. 31, 1997 but before Jan. 1, 1999; (ii) $1,850 exemption for taxable year beginning after Dec. 31, 1998 but before Jan. 1, 2000; (iii) $1,850 exemption for taxable year beginning after Dec. 31, 1999 but before Jan. 1, 2001; (iv) $2,100 exemption for taxable year beginning after Dec. 31, 2000 but before Jan. 1, 2002; and (v) $2,400 exemption for taxable year beginning after Dec. 31, 2001; exemption is allowed for dependent who is at least 65 years old on last day of taxable year. Additional $1,000 exemption allowed for each individual who is at least 65 years old on last day of taxable year or blind. Fiduciary allowed $200 exemption. For tax returns for periods less than one year, exemptions apportioned based on number of months included in taxable period. Nonresident receiving credit for taxes paid to other state receives proportion of exemption equal to adjusted gross income in Md. divided by federal adjusted gross income. (§§10-211 to 10-214).

Rates of tax on taxable net income of resident and on net income of nonresident taxable in Md. are 2% on first $1,000, 3% on second $1,000, 4% on third $1,000, and 4.875% for taxable year beginning after Dec. 1, 1997 but before Jan. 1, 1999; 4.85% for taxable year beginning after Dec. 31, 1998 but before Jan. 1, 2001, 4.8% for taxable year beginning after Dec. 31, 2000 but before Jan. 1, 2002; and 4.75% for taxable year beginning after Dec. 31, 2001 on excess over $3,000. (§10-105). For amounts in excess of $150,000 (for spouses filing jointly, surviving spouse, or head of household) or $100,000 (for other individuals) will be taxed at 6%. (tax-gen. art. §10-105). Counties and Baltimore City are required to impose upon their respective residents local income tax in form of surtax of not less than 20% nor more than 60% of state income tax liability. (§10-106). Local income tax surcharge is 50% as to Baltimore City and all counties, except as follows: Worcester County, 20%; Baltimore, Alleghany, and Montgomery Counties, 55%; Talbot and Prince George's Counties, 60%.

Credit against income tax allowed equal to 50% of earned income tax credit under §32 of IRC not to exceed income tax imposed without taking into account state personal property tax credit. (§10-704).

Residents are persons domiciled in state on last day of taxable year or who for more than six months of taxable year maintain place of abode in state, whether domiciled in state or not. (§10-101). Provision is made for allocation where person is resident for part of year. (§10-220).

Nonresidents are taxed on federal adjusted gross income reduced by nonresident's income other than income derived from tangible property, real or personal, located in state and from business, trade, profession or occupation wholly carried on in state, and from business, occupation, profession, or trade carried on within and without Md. to extent allocable to Md. under method required by Comptroller and of certain portions of military pay received by certain military personnel for active service outside U.S. and from lottery prizes or winnings from any other wagering derived in Md. (§10-210). Nonresident's federal itemized deductions and state exemptions are multiplied by fraction with Md. adjusted gross income as numerator and federal adjusted gross income as denominator. Comptroller may require different method to compute Md. itemized deductions. (§10-219). In computing adjustment under §§10-206-10-210, nonresident shall allocate state income derived in connection with business, occupation, profession, or trade by separate accounting or other method that Comptroller requires. (§10-401). Wages earned by nonresident in Md. exempt from tax if two states agree in writing to allow reciprocal exemptions from tax and from withholding. (§§10-806, 10-907).

Abatement of Tax.—Income tax will be abated in case of individual who dies while in active service in military if such death occurs while in combat or from wound or disease incurred while so serving or in case of individual who dies while employed in military or as civilian employee of U.S. if death occurred outside U.S. as result of terrorism or military action. (§13-908).

Tax may be withheld from wages of nonresident. (§10-907).

Corporations are taxed 7% of portion of Maryland modified income allocable to this State, according to business carried on in state and elsewhere. Corporations may allocate income to Md. by separate accounting if practical or by three-factor apportionment fraction weighing property and payroll equally and assigning double weight to sales. (§§10-105, 10-402). Maryland modified income of corporation is taxable income as defined in laws of U.S., increased by (1) net capital loss carry-back; (2) state or local income taxes; (3) interest or dividends (less related expenses) on obligations or securities of other states or their subdivisions; (4) federal tax exempt income; (5) oil percentage depletion allowance; (6) enterprise zone wage credit; (7) reforestation and timber stand modification; (8) net operating loss modification; and (9) unlicensed child care facility expenses. (§§10-304 to 10-306). Income is reduced by (i) refund of state income tax; (ii) included profit from sale or exchange of bonds of State of Md. or its political subdivisions; (iii) dividends from foreign subsidiary if taxpayer owns 50% or more of stock; (iv) amounts included by operation of §78 of IRC; (v) includible percentage of dividend income received from certain affiliated DISC's (as defined in §992[a] of IRC) equivalent to percentage excludable if DISC were not qualified under §992(a) (this exclusion applicable only if 50% of DISC net taxable income is subject to Md. taxation); (vi) expenses incurred for purchase and installation of conversation tillage equipment; and (vii) other miscellaneous subtractions. (§10-307).

Partnerships, S corporations and limited liability companies that have one or more nonresident shareholders, partners or members ("nonresidents") and have nonresident taxable income are subject to 5% tax on each nonresident's distributive or pro rata share of nonresident taxable income of partnership, S corporation or limited liability company. Tax is treated as imposed on nonresident and paid by partnership, S corporation or limited liability company. Tax paid may not exceed nonresident's share of cash flow. (§§10-102.1, 10-104).

Estates and Trusts.—Personal representatives of estate of decedent who died domiciled in Md. subject to state and county income tax and allowed $600 exemption. (§§10-102, 10-103, 10-212). Fiduciary of trust subject to state and county income tax, and allowed $200 exemption, if trust created by, or consists of property transferred by, will of decedent who died domiciled in Md., if creator of trust is resident of Md., or if trust principally administered in Md. (§§10-101[h], 10-103, 10-212).

Returns and Payment.—Returns must be filed with Comptroller on or before Apr. 15, or 15th day of fourth month following close of fiscal year, and full amount of tax must be paid at time of filing return. Husband and wife who file joint federal return must file joint return. (§§10-820, 10-807). Corporate income tax returns must be filed on or before Mar. 15, or 15th day of third month following close of fiscal year. (§10-821). Partnerships must file income tax returns on Form 501. (§10-814). Limited liability companies must file income tax returns as partnership if taxable under IRC §761 or as corporation if taxable under IRC Subchapter C. (§10-819). Last return of decedent must be filed by Apr. 15 of year following date of death. (§10-808). Extensions for filing of up to six months (one year for persons abroad) may be granted but taxpayer must pay interest, at applicable state interest rate, per month for period during extension when taxes remain unpaid. (§§10-823, 13-601). Returns are audited by Comptroller, and additional taxes may be assessed within three years after return was filed or within three years after due date of return, whichever is later; except assessment can be made at any time in case of false or fraudulent return or failure to file return or to report subsequent increases in federal taxable income. (§§13-1101, 13-401). Appeal may be made to Md. Tax Court within 30 days after notice of assessment is mailed. (§13-510).

Withholding and Payment of Estimated Tax.—Withholding of tax at source and remitting quarterly (or monthly if amount is $400 or more) is required. (§10-822). Fiduciary distributing taxable income to nonresident alien must withhold. (§10-905). Employer is required to supply withholding statement to individuals by Jan. 31 and to Comptroller by Feb. 28. (§10-911). Every individual receiving taxable income not subject to withholding is required to file quarterly declarations of estimated tax beginning Apr. 15 of year for which tax is due, unless tax liability on gross income not subject to withholding does not exceed $100 for individual taxpayer as well as every individual who receives income of $500 or more in cash or property as result of wagering, contest, lottery, raffle, or use of gambling machine, unless tax to be withheld under §10-906. (§10-815). Farmers and fishermen file declaration on succeeding Jan. 15, and may file return and pay tax by succeeding Mar. 1 in lieu thereof. (§10-820[c]). To avoid penalty, estimated tax must be at least 100% of prior year's tax or 90% of tax ultimately due. (§13-602). Quarterly payments of estimated tax must consist of at least 25% of estimated income tax shown on declaration for taxable year. (§10-902). In order to implement provisions, out-of-state employers may be required to post security. (§13-811).

Lien.—Unpaid tax, interest, and penalties constitute lien, in favor of state, extending to all property and rights to property. (§13-805). Notice of lien must be filed to prevail against subsequent mortgagee, pledgee, buyer or judgment creditor. (§13-809). Notice of lien on salary or wages must be given to employer. (§13-811).

Specially Exempt Organizations.—Following are specifically exempt from income tax: (1) Common trust funds, as defined by §3-501 of fin. inst. art.; (2) organization that is exempt from taxation under §408(e)(1) or §501 of Internal Revenue Code; (3) financial institution that is subject to financial institution franchise tax; (4) person subject to taxation under Title 6 of insurance article; (5) partnership, as defined in §761 of Internal Revenue Code; (6) S corporation; (7) investment conduit or special entity; or (8) limited liability company as defined under Title 4A of Corporations and Associations Article to extent that company is taxable as partnership, as defined in §761 of Internal Revenue Code. (§10-104). Tax exempt organization must make its Federal returns available for inspection. (§10-818).

INHERITANCE TAX:

Note: All references are to tax-gen. art. unless otherwise indicated.

With exceptions hereinafter stated, tax is imposed on privilege of receiving property that passes from decedent and has taxable situs in Md. (§7-202). Property subject to inheritance tax includes: (1) Property that passes by will or under intestate laws of state, at or after death of decedent, in trust or otherwise, to or for use of another person; (2) property in which, at death, decedent had interest as joint tenant; and (3) except for bona fide sale for adequate and full consideration in money or money's worth, property that passes by inter vivos transfer by decedent, in trust or otherwise if: (a) transfer is made in contemplation of death, (b) transfer is made by decedent within two years before death, (c) transfer is intended to take effect in possession or enjoyment at or after death of decedent, or (d) under transfer, decedent retained any dominion over transferred property during life of decedent including retention of beneficial interest, power of revocation or power of appointment by will or otherwise. (§7-201).

Exemptions.—Property having value of $1,000 or less passing to any one person; real property passing from decedent to surviving spouse or first $100,000 of property other than real property passing between such persons; interest in property that passes by right of survivorship; insurance payable to named beneficiary; death benefit excludable from estate under §11-105 of est. & tr. art.; annuity or other payment under public or private employee's pension plan if payment is not taxable for Federal estate tax purposes; receipt of family allowance that surviving spouse and minor children are allowed under §3-201 of est. & tr. art.; receipt of property for grave maintenance (up to $500); receipt of property to or for use of organization exempt from taxation under §501(c)(3) of IRC or that is deductible under §2055 of IRC provided corporation is incorporated under laws of this State or conducts substantial part of all its activities in Maryland or in District of Columbia or has its principal place of business in state which does not impose death taxes on property passing to charitable organization of this State; property passing from decedent's estate which qualifies under §5-601 of est. & tr. art. as small estate; property that is income, including gains and losses, accrued on probate assets after date of death of decedent; and property passing to state, county or municipal corporation of state. (§7-203).

Valuation.—Value of property subject to tax is appraised value stated in inventory required to be filed under §7-225. (§7-207). Personal property may be reappraised prior to distribution. (est. & tr. art. §§7-203, 7-204). Provision is made for valuing life estates and other interests less than absolute. (§§7-208, 7-209).

See note at head of Digest as to 1998 legislation covered.

See Topical Index in front part of this volume.

INHERITANCE TAX . . . *continued*

In case of joint tenancy, where interests are not otherwise specified or fixed by law, interest passing is determined by dividing value of property by number of joint tenants. (§7-209).

Valuation date is date of death or date of reappraisal. (est. & tr. art. §7-201). Valuation of contingent or remainder interest may be either as of date of death or date when preceding estate terminates. (§7-210).

Rates of tax are: 1% of clear value of property passing to or for use of grandparent, parent, spouse, child or other lineal descendant of decedent or any stepchild or stepparent; 1% of value to corporations if all stockholders of corporation consist of surviving spouse, parents, lineal descendants, stepparents, stepchildren, and spouses of lineal descendants; and also 1% on joint savings account passing by survivorship to spouse of lineal descendant, up to aggregate of $2,000 for all accounts held jointly with spouse, excess taxed at 10% (if interest vested on or after June 1, 1975). Tax rate for property passing to or for use of any other person is 10%. (§7-204).

Lien.—Tax is lien on real estate for four years from date of distribution. (§13-806[b]).

Payment.—Tax on distributive shares and legacies is due and must be paid to register of wills at time of filing of administration account showing distribution. (est. & tr. art. §7-307). Comptroller may grant alternative payment schedule in form of payment deferral or installment payment plan, not to exceed five year period, for inheritance tax, if payment of tax on normal due date would require party liable for tax to sell small business, or any interest in small business owned in whole or part by decedent. (§7-218). For date account is due, see category Estates and Trusts, topic Executors and Administrators, subhead Intermediate Accountings.

Executors, administrators, trustees, agents, fiduciaries and other persons making distribution of any property subject to tax are charged with payment thereof. (§7-215).

Interest.—Unpaid taxes bear interest beginning 30 days after date tax is determined. (§13-601).

Nonresidents.—Property passing on death of nonresident decedent is liable for tax if property has taxable situs in Md. (§7-202).

No tax is imposed on intangible property passing from nonresident if, at time of transfer, distribution or other disposition of such property, state, territory or country of such person's residence: (1) Did not impose transfer tax or death tax on intangible property of residents of Md. or (2) allowed reciprocal exemption. (§7-203).

Waivers for transfer of intangible personalty not required by Md. law.

MORTGAGE TAX:

See category Documents and Records, topic Records.

MOTOR CARRIER TAX:

Motor carrier tax is imposed by tax-gen. art. §§9-201 et seq.

MOTOR FUEL TAX:

Motor fuel tax is imposed by tax-gen. art. §§9-301 et seq.

NATURAL GAS TAX:

See category Mineral, Water and Fishing Rights, topic Mines and Minerals.

PROPERTY TAXES:

Note: All references are to tax-prop. art. unless otherwise indicated.

Taxable Property.—All property, other than intangible personal property, located in Maryland is subject to assessment and property tax upon owner of property. (§6-101[a]). Other than certain intangible personal property owned by corporation which is subject to assessment and property tax, intangible personal property is not subject to such tax. (§6-101[b]).

Property Owner's Bill of Rights enacted in 1990. (§§1-401-1-403).

Exemptions.—(1) Property owned by U.S., Md. or any political subdivision devoted to governmental use (§7-210); (2) property owned by religious organization used exclusively for public religious worship, as convent or for educational purposes (§7-204); (3) nonprofit cemeteries and mausoleums (§7-201); (4) property owned by nonprofit hospital (§7-202); (5) personal property initially leased by nonprofit hospital for more than one year (§7-202); (6) property (but not exceeding 100 acres of pertinent land) owned by any nonprofit organization and used exclusively for charitable or educational purpose (§7-202); (7) property of veterans' organizations (§7-234); (8) property owned by Chesapeake Bay Foundation (§7-203); (9) property operated as nonprofit continuing care facility for aged (§7-206); (10) dwellings of certain blind individuals and surviving spouses (§7-207); (11) dwellings of certain disabled veterans and their surviving spouses (§7-208); (12) property owned by nonprofit fire companies (§7-209); (13) property of historic societies (§7-214); (14) property owned by housing authority (§7-215); (15) property owned by Boy and Girl Scouts (§7-233); (16) property owned by community water systems (§7-205). Interest in property in international trade center if state or agency or instrumentality of state owns property and makes negotiated payments in lieu of tax payments. (§7-211).

Tangible personal property of certain credit unions and certain savings and loans (§7-228), and of certain banks (§7-221).

Certain manufacturing property; certain vessels, aircraft and motor vehicles, agricultural products and commodities under certain conditions; farming implements and livestock, except in certain counties; tangible personal property located at owner's residence, other than property used in connection with any business, occupation or profession; hand tools of mechanics and artisans; and business personal property in certain counties. (§§7-219 et seq.).

Procedures are established to apply for exemption of real property. (§7-103).

Assessment.—Property, real and personal, subject to ordinary taxation is valued and assessed for purposes of state and county or city taxation by supervisors of assessments appointed by Dep't of Assessments and Taxation. (§§2-105, 8-201, 8-202).

Property Tax Credit.—Baltimore City, certain counties and cities located within those counties are required or, in certain cases, have option to grant single mandatory credit against full amount of tax on certain types of property. (§§9-301 et seq.). Credit against real property taxes levied by state or local government is given to certain homeowners by reason of low income. Credit is not available to individuals whose net worth exceeds $200,000. Taxpayer must apply to Dep't of Assessments and Taxation for credit. (§§9-101, 9-104). Credit against rent paid subject to similar income and net worth limits of renters 60 or older, or disabled, or meeting income guidelines and living with one or more dependent children. (§9-102). Homeowner's property tax credit for occupants of independent living units subject to real property taxation at continuing care facilities for aged. (§9-104). Credit for businesses located in enterprise zones. (§9-103). Counties are empowered to grant property tax credits for land dedicated to "open space", for structures using solar energy, geothermal energy, or certain energy conservation components, for nonprofit community associations, civil leagues or organizations, or recreational or athletic organizations, and for agricultural land. (§§9-203, 9-206, 9-208, 9-305). Baltimore City and each county authorized to grant property tax credit for improvement of real property used exclusively for specified day care services by licensed provider. (§§9-213, 9-214). There is property tax credit for surviving spouses of certain veterans (§9-218), and credit is also provided statewide to landlords who rent to elderly or disabled at reduced rent. Mandatory property tax credit for conservation property (as defined in §9-107) against all property tax that would otherwise be due. Credit allowed for 15 years. Taxpayer must apply to Dep't of Assessments and Taxation for credit. (§9-107). Local tax credits are also allowed in some counties and municipalities for certain unsold, unrented or unoccupied new or rehabilitated dwellings. (§9-207). Credit allowed all homeowners limits to 15% per year increase in tax due to increased assessment unless property increased in value due to rezoning, transfer of title, substantial change in use, extensive improvements or prior year assessment clearly erroneous. (§§9-104, 9-105).

Governing body of municipal corporation or county may grant, by law, property tax credit for certain personal property used in research or testing facility. (§9-223).

Dep't of Assessments and Taxation values, assesses and taxes for purposes of state, county and city taxation: (1) Operating property, except land, of railroads or public utilities; (2) tangible personal property of corporation; (3) intangible personal property subject to taxation under §6-101; and (4) distilled spirits. (§8-201).

All real and personal property is required to be assessed at full cash value on date of finality. (§§8-107, 8-102). In case of real property only, full cash value adjusted by state growth factor of approximately 50% so that tax rate applies to approximately 50% of full cash value. (§8-103). Full cash value redetermined in event of transfer, zoning change, substantially completed improvement, change in use or character, subdivision or prior error. All real property reviewed, inspected and revalued triennially; resulting increases phased in over three year period. (§8-104). However, where residential property is rezoned, valuation and assessment may be based on residential use. (§§8-226, 8-228).

Special provision is made for assessment of operating property of railroads, public utilities, and other transportation property. (§§6-103, 7-230, 8-108). Guidelines for assessment of real property include provisions covering farm lands, marshlands, mobile homes, open space easements, woodlands, country clubs, and planned developments. Certain specified improvements may be excluded in determining value. (§§8-209 et seq.). In addition, Dep't of Assessments and Taxation may reduce assessments on certain damaged or threatened residential real property, and assessment of damaged property may not be increased unless property is restored, if replacement is comparable to lost property. (§§8-230, 8-231). With certain exemptions, where land assessed for agricultural use is transferred for nonagricultural purposes, agricultural transfer tax is imposed. See category Documents and Records, topic Records, subhead Tax on Recordation, catchline Transfer Tax. Income producing property may be valued by income capitalization method or any other appropriate method and submission of income and expense statement for property may be required. (§8-105). For method of assessment of value of personal property see §8-107. For assessment and valuation of public utility property and railroad property see §§8-108 and 8-109. For valuation of inventory of domestic business see §8-110.

Provision is made for reduction of taxes as of semiannual dates of finality of real or personal property either partially or totally damaged. (§10-304). Notice must be given to owner or other appropriate person of real property assessment, who then has right to appeal: (1) Before existing valuation is increased or decreased; (2) before any classification is changed; (3) establishment of initial real property value; (4) decision on assessment appeal or petition to change existing real property value or classification; and (5) revaluation or reclassification, if valuation or classification has been appealed but not finally determined. (§8-401).

Review of Assessment.—Any taxpayer, city, county, municipal corporation or Attorney General may, with respect to any property assessed by supervisor, demand hearing before supervisor of assessments as to value or classification if written appeal made within 45 days after date of notice. Transferee of property transferred after date of finality and before beginning of next tax year has 60 days after transfer to protest assessment for ensuing year. (§14-502). Within 30 days of final notice of assessment, further appeal can be filed with Property Tax Assessment Appeal Board. Thirty day limitation may be waived by Appeal Board by reason of physical inability of taxpayer. (§14-509). Rules of Property Tax Assessment Appeal Board to be issued by its administrator, in compliance with provisions of Administrative Procedure Act. (§3-108). After exhausting administrative remedies, any taxpayer, city, county, municipal corporation, Attorney General, or Dep't of Assessments and Taxation may appeal value or classification determination made by Property Tax Assessment Appeal Board to Md. Tax Court. Appeals to Md. Tax Court may also be made from final actions taken by Dep't of Assessments and Taxation with respect to taxes assessable by it. All appeals to Md. Tax Court must be taken by petition filed within 30 days of final decision or mailing of notice, as case may be. (§14-512). As to appeal from Md. Tax Court, see §14-513. As to appeal from Circuit Courts for county in which property located, see §14-515.

See note at head of Digest as to 1998 legislation covered.

See Topical Index in front part of this volume.

MD – 59

PROPERTY TAXES . . . *continued*

Unless taxpayer files bond with collecting agency, appeal will not stay or affect collection or enforcement of assessment or classification. (§14-514). Upon final determination of appeal, excess over amount properly chargeable is refunded with interest. (§14-611).

Provision is made for decrease or abatement of assessment after date of finality to correct erroneous and improper assessments and prevent injustice. (§8-419).

Rates of Tax.—Real and personal property owners pay full state, county and/or city rate prevailing at time. (§§6-301, 6-302). County's tax rate in certain municipalities may be less than general county rate to adjust for municipal property taxes paid by municipal residents. (§§6-305, 6-306). State property tax rate for personal property provided in State Finance & Procurement Article §8-134.

Levy, Payment, etc.—County or city authorities must annually levy county and city taxes at respective rates fixed for each taxable year (July 1-June 30). (§§1-101[ii], 6-204, 6-305, 6-306). Taxes on real property are imposed as of date of finality (Jan. 1) or semiannual or quarterly dates of finality (Apr. 1; July 1; Oct. 1); and taxes on personal property are imposed as of date of finality. (§8-416).

All state, county or city property taxes for taxable year are due on or after July 1 and are overdue and bear interest if not paid on or before Sept. 30. (§10-102). As general rule (although there are exceptions) interest on county or municipal corporation property tax is at rate of 2/3of 1% per month or fractional part thereof. (§14-603). Certain political subdivisions allow specified discounts for payment prior to Oct. 1. (§10-301).

As general rule, all property tax must be collected on or before seven years from date tax is due. Any judgment entered may be enforced or renewed as any other judgment. (§14-1101).

Lien.—Unpaid real property taxes are first lien on property from date they become payable. (§14-804[a]). All unpaid taxes on personal property are liens on personal property and on real property of owner of personal property; except that lien will attach to real property only after notice has been recorded and indexed among judgment records in county where land lies, or is recorded and indexed on tax rolls. (§14-804[b]).

Sale of property for nonpayment of state, county or city taxes must be made under §§14-801 et seq. Local collector of taxes mails notice to last owner on tax roll at least 30 days prior to commencement of advertisement of sale. (§14-812). Type and duration of publication notice differs by county. (§14-813). Sale by public auction at time and place stated in ad. (§14-817). Payment of accrued taxes, interest, penalty and sale costs required by day after sale; other terms set by collector. (§14-818). Collector gives purchaser certificate of sale, which is assignable. (§§14-820, 14-821).

Redemption.—Party having interest in property sold by collector may redeem property during redemption period, by paying to collector amount required with interest thereon. Certain expenses of purchaser may also be payable. (§14-827). Generally, holder of certificate of sale may institute proceeding in circuit court after six months from date of sale to foreclose all rights of redemption, but right to redeem continues until finally barred by decree in such proceeding. (§§14-829, 14-833, 14-844).

Taxation of Property of Corporations.—Stock of most domestic corporations is not subject to assessment and taxation. (§6-101[b]). Their real property is subject to assessment in county and, if applicable, municipal corporation or special tax district where it is situated. (§5-102[a]). Tangible personal property is generally subject to assessment in county and, if applicable, municipal corporation in which it is permanently located. (§5-102[b]). However, stock in business of manufacturing or commercial business is subject to assessment in county and/or municipal corporation in which business is carried on. (§5-102[c]).

Where "corporation" is defined as corporation entitled to property tax exemption pursuant to contract with State, all intangible personal property owned by corporation (so defined) is subject to assessment and property tax, except as exempt by said contract. (§6-101[b]).

For bonus and franchise taxes on corporations, see category Business Organizations, topic Corporations. For franchise tax on savings banks and building and loan associations, see topic Franchise Taxes, subhead Franchise Tax on Financial Institutions, infra. See also category Business Organizations, topic Joint Stock Companies, subhead Real Estate Investment Trusts.

REAL ESTATE CONVEYANCE TAX:

See category Documents and Records, topic Records.

REVISED UNIFORM FEDERAL TAX LIEN REGISTRATION ACT:

Revised Uniform Federal Tax Lien Registration Act adopted. (real prop. art. §§3-401 to 3-405).

SALES AND USE TAX:

Note: All references are to tax-gen. art. unless otherwise indicated.

Sales and use tax is imposed on retail sale in state or use in state, of tangible personal property or taxable service. (§11-102). Retail sale is defined as sale of title or possession of tangible personal property or sale of taxable service. Taxable sales of tangible personal property also include sales for use or resale in form of real estate by builder, contractor, or landowner. (§11-101[e]). Tangible personal property subject to sales and use tax includes right to occupy room or lodgings as transient guest, farm equipment, wall-to-wall carpeting that is installed into real estate, and coal, electricity, oil, nuclear fuel assemblies, steam and artificial or natural gas. (§11-101[h]). Taxable service includes fabrication, printing or production of tangible personal property by special order, commercial cleaning or laundering of textiles, cleaning of commercial or industrial building, certain telephone services pay-per-view television, credit reporting, or security service. (§11-101[j]). Term "use" is defined as exercise of right or power to use, consume, possess or store that which is acquired by sale. (§11-101[k]).

Counties may impose sales or use tax on sale of fuels, any utilities, any space rentals or any controlled dangerous substance (unless sale is made by person who registers and complies with art. 27, §281). (§11-102).

Exempt sales include: (1) Certain items used for agricultural purpose; (2) certain items bought for farmers; (3) certain agricultural products; (4) cylinder demurrage charge; (5) sales to cemetery company as described in §501(c)(13) of IRC; (6) sales to credit union; (7) sales to nonprofit charitable, educational or religious organization located in state which is not unit of U.S., except for American National Red Cross or in adjacent jurisdictions which operates within State on regular basis which contains reciprocal exemption for Maryland nonprofit organizations; (8) sales under $500 to nonprofit incorporated senior citizens' organization located in state which receives state or local funding; (9) sales to volunteer fire, ambulance or rescue squads located in state; (10) sales by church or religious organization; (11) sales by gift shops in state mental hospitals; (12) sales by hospital thrift shops staffed by volunteers which sell only donated goods; (13) sales of Md. and U.S. flags; (14) sales of food for human consumption by vendor who has no facilities for consumption on premises (but not including alcoholic beverages, soft drinks, or candy); (15) sales of food stamp items; (16) certain sales of food by vendor who has facilities for consumption on premises but also operates grocery store at that location; (17) sales of food at hospital when food charge included in regular room rate; (18) sales of food by church or religious organization; (19) meal plan food sales by school or college; (20) sales of food to support veterans' organizations; (21) food sales used to support volunteer fire or ambulance company or rescue squad; (22) sale of food or beverage in vehicle being operated in Md. in course of interstate commerce; (23) sale of seafood or crab prepared for non-immediate consumption; (24) certain fuels for residential use; (25) marine equipment and machinery used in loading, unloading and handling of cargo in interstate or foreign commerce; (26) television broadcast film or tape; (27) sales of aircraft, motor vehicle, railroad rolling stock, or vessel which is used primarily to cross state lines in interstate or foreign commerce; (28) sales of replacement part for any item listed in No. 27 above; (29) sale of motor vehicle other than house or office trailers that will be titled or registered in another state; (29.1) lease of motor vehicle that is leased for period of at least one year; (30) casual and isolated sales of less than $1,000 by person not regularly selling tangible personal property or taxable service; (31) certain capital transactions including: (a) transfers of tangible personal property to corporation upon its organization in exchange for stock, (b) transfers of tangible personal property in reorganization under §§368(a), 371 or 374 of IRC, (c) liquidating distribution, (d) contribution to capital of partnership or limited liability company, and (e) distribution of property by partnership to partners or by limited liability company to members; (32) sales of machinery or equipment used to produce bituminous concrete or electricity or fuel used to operate that machinery; (33) sales of certain machinery and equipment used in manufacturing or research and development; (34) sales of certain medical supplies and medicines to or by physician or hospital; (35) sales of hemodialysis drugs or devices by licensed pharmacist; (36) items for compensating for blindness; (37) decoders for captioned television programs; (38) telecommunication devices adopted specifically for hearing impaired; (39) artificial eyes, hearing devices or limbs; (40) wigs or hairpieces needed as a result of documented medical or surgical treatment; (41) colostomy or ileostomy devices; (42) corrective eyeglasses; (43) orthopedic or surgical appliances prescribed by physician; (44) batteries for artificial hearing device, larynx, transcutaneous nerve stimulator, or electrically powered wheelchair; (45) replacement cord for artificial hearing devices; (46) crutches; (47) wheelchair; (48) hospital bed; (49) oxygen tent; (50) other sickroom equipment; (51) equipment installed into motor vehicle for handicapped persons; (52) baby oil or baby powder; (53) sanitary napkins or tampons; (54) any service by sawmill of wood products for mine use in which miner retains title; (55) diesel fuel for use in reclamation of land that has been mined for coal by strip or open pit mining; (56) resales of mobile homes, and tax on first sale of mobile home is based on 60% of price (§11-104[d]); (57) tangible personal property or taxable service that nonresident acquires before property or service enters state and uses for 30 days or less for personal enjoyment or in presentation of exhibit, sporting event or other public performance or display; (58) precious metal bullion and coins; (59) photographic material and certain other art works for production of items used in composition or printing; (60) printing and sale of newspapers that are distributed free of charge; (61) direct mail advertising literature and mail order catalogues that will be used outside state; (62) documents of federal, state or local governments; (63) certain property for use in another state, including property merely stored in Md., certain tangible personal property to be incorporated in real property in another state, and images, videotape or other optical or digital forms or electronic signals generated from these images to cable or other nonbroadcast television network, if images are intended for viewing outside state; (64) property used for research and development; (65) items used for harvesting seafood; (66) personal, professional or insurance service that is not taxable service and involves sale of property as inconsequential element for which no separate charge is made; (67) custom computer software services; (67.1) sale of optional computer software maintenance contract if buyer does not have right, as part of contract, to receive at no additional cost software products that are separately priced and marketed by vendor; (68) sales to state or political subdivision of state (but not including sale of construction materials to contractors); (69) sales of admission when gross receipts are subject to admission and amusement tax; (70) sale of communication service that is not taxable service and which is subject to federal excise tax under §4251 of IRC; (71) sale of motor fuel subject to motor fuel tax or motor carrier tax; (72) sale of motor vehicle subject to motor vehicle excise tax under §13-809 or §13-811 to transp. art.; (73) rental of motion picture, motion picture trailer, or advertising poster for display at theater when gross receipts from activity are subject to admissions and amusement tax; (74) sale of vessel that is subject to excise tax under §8-716 of nat. res. art.; (75) sales in which buyer already paid sale and use tax when purchased; (76) tangible personal property or taxable service to extent buyer pays another state tax on sale or gross receipts; (77) deliverable end item testing equipment under U.S. Department of Defense contract awarded by bid after June 1, 1986; (78) transportation service; (79) water that is delivered to buyer through pipes or conduits; (80) sale to nonprofit organization made to carry on its work if organization is qualified as tax exempt under §501(c)(4) of I.R.C., and is engaged primarily in providing program to render its best efforts to contain, clean up, and otherwise mitigate spills of oil or other substances occurring in U.S. coastal and tidal waters; and (81) sale to elementary or secondary school in state or nonprofit parent-teacher organization or other nonprofit organization within elementary or secondary school in state for sale of magazine subscriptions in fund-raising campaign, if net proceeds are used solely of educational benefit of school or its students, including sale

See note at head of Digest as to 1998 legislation covered.

See Topical Index in front part of this volume.

MD – 60

SALES AND USE TAX . . . continued

resulting from agreement or contract with organization to participate in fund-raising campaign for percentage of gross receipts under which students act as agents or salespersons for organization by selling or taking orders for sale. Property used in other states prior to use in Md. is given 10% credit against purchase price for each full year of foreign usage. No use tax is payable on item on which Md. sales tax has been paid. (§§11-201 to 11-224).

Rates of tax are: (1) 1¢ on sales of 20¢; (2) 2¢ on sales of 21¢ to 40¢; (3) 3¢ on sales of 41¢ to 60¢; (4) 4¢ on sales of 61¢ to 80¢; (5) 5¢ on sales of 81¢ to $1; and (6) 5¢ on each $1 plus 1¢ on each 20¢ or fraction thereof in excess of $1. (§11-104).

Tax of 5% is imposed on gross receipts from vending machine sales. (§11-104). Vendor may not collect tax as separately stated item. (§11-405).

Tax of 8% imposed on rental or lease of rental truck. (§11-104).

Reports and Payment.—License is required of any person engaging in business of vendor in state or out of state. (§11-702). Application for license shall be submitted to Comptroller of Treasury. (§11-703). Vendor is trustee for state and is liable for collection of sales and use tax for and on account of state. (§11-401). For each sale sales and use tax shall be stated and charged separately from sales price and shown separately in record of sale. (§11-302). There is rebuttable presumption that any sale in state is subject to sales tax. (§11-103). Special provision is made for sales through vending machines. (§11-405).

Returns must be made and tax paid for each calendar month by 21st day of succeeding calendar month, to Comptroller of Treasury. (§11-502). Vendors receive credit for collection expense of 1.2% of first $4,200 of gross tax remitted and 0.6% thereafter. (§11-105). Comptroller may require vendor to post security. (§13-825[g]). Unpaid tax is lien on all property of person liable for payment with force of judgment lien upon recordation of lien notice in judgment docket. (§§13-805—13-810).

Whenever sale on which tax was paid is rescinded, vendor must refund tax to purchaser, and vendor is entitled to refund from Comptroller (if application made within four years of payment of tax). (§§11-403, 13-901[g], 13-1104[g]). Whenever taxpayer has erroneously or illegally paid tax, he may also apply for refund. Beginning 45 days after Comptroller receives claim for refund, claimant is paid applicable state interest rate unless refund claim is attributable to error or mistake of claimant that is not attributable to state or unit of state government (§13-603).

Records of taxable sales must be kept for four years. (§11-504). President, vice-president, treasurer, and any officer of corporation owning more than 20% of stock are personally liable for corporation's sales and use tax. (§11-601).

Any taxpayer may apply to Comptroller for revision of tax assessed against him within 30 days of mailing of assessment to his last known address. If tax is paid, application for refund must also be filed within same 30-day period. Comptroller must act promptly on application and notify taxpayer of action. Within 30 days of mailing of notice of such action, taxpayer may request formal hearing. Comptroller must grant hearing and notify taxpayer of decision. Taxpayer may then appeal within 30 days of mailing of notice to Md. Tax Court. (§§13-508 to 13-510).

Notice by certified mail, return receipt requested, bearing U.S. Postal Service postmark, must be given by purchaser from or assignee of any vendor to Comptroller at least ten days prior to taking possession of or paying thereafter for whole stock of merchandise or fixtures of business of vendor (purchased other than in ordinary course of trade and business) stating price, terms and conditions of sale, whether or not sales tax is due. (§11-505).

STAMP TAX:

None, except in case of instruments to be recorded. See category Documents and Records, topic Records.

TAX ON EXECUTORS' AND ADMINISTRATORS' COMMISSIONS:

See category Estates and Trusts, topic Executors and Administrators, subhead Tax on Commissions.

TAX ON COMMERCIAL APPLES:

Tax on commercial apples is imposed by agric. art., §10-406.

TITLING TAXES:

Boat titling tax is imposed by nat. res. art. §8-716.

Motor Vehicle Titling Tax.—See category Transportation, topic Motor Vehicles.

TOBACCO TAX:

Tobacco tax is imposed by tax-gen. art. §§12-101 et seq.

UNEMPLOYMENT COMPENSATION TAX:

Unemployment compensation tax or "contribution" is imposed on each employing unit which for some portion of day has or had in employment one or more individuals. (lab. emp. art. §8-101[n], 8-607).

Tax applies only to first $8,500 of wages paid. (lab. emp. art. §8-607[b]). Employer contributions regulated by lab. emp. art. §§8-606 to 8-613. Standard rate is 7.4%. (lab. emp. art. §8-608). No tax on employees. Returns must be made and tax paid quarterly to Employment Security Administration, 1100 N. Eutaw St., Baltimore 21201. (lab. emp. art. §8-607[e]).

USE TAX:

See topic Sales and Use Tax.

See also categories Business Organizations, topic Corporations; Business Regulation and Commerce, topic Banks and Banking; Documents and Records, topic Records; Estates and Trusts, topic Executors and Administrators; Insurance, topic Insurance Companies; Transportation, topic Motor Vehicles.

TRANSPORTATION

MOTOR VEHICLES:

References are to Transportation Article of Code unless otherwise indicated.

Supervision.—State Motor Vehicle Administration, 6601 Ritchie Highway, N.E., Glen Burnie 21062.

Vehicle license plate or validation tab required annually. (§13-412). Renewal time may be staggered. (§§13-912 and 15-108). Registration and plates expire on midnight of date indicated on registration card. (§13-412). Registration number plates are obtained from Motor Vehicle Administration or, in certain circumstances, dealer licensed under transp. art., title 15 (§13-410), and must be displayed front and rear on motor vehicle but only rear on motorcycle or trailer (§§13-410, 13-411). Members of U.S. Congress, except for members elected from Maryland, and nonresident members of Armed Forces serving on active duty in state, adjoining state, or D.C. are exempt. (§§13-402[e]; 13-402.1[c]).

Operator's license required (§16-101); must be renewed every five years upon passing vision test (§16-115). Renewal time may be staggered. (§§13-912 and 15-108). For licenses issued and renewed before Dec. 31, 1989, there are six major classes of licenses based on type vehicle being operated, as follows: Class A, tractor trailers; Class B, trucks over 25,000 pounds, excluding tractor-trailers; Class C, buses; Class D, automobiles, stationwagons and trucks up to 25,000 pounds, excluding tractor-trailers, buses up to 25,000 pounds and vanpool vehicles; Class E, motorcycles (§16-104); and mopeds (§§16-104; 16-104.2). For noncommercial licenses issued or renewed after Jan. 1, 1990, there are four major classes of licenses as follows: Class A, tractor trailers; Class B, trucks over 26,000 pounds, excluding tractor trailers; Class C, any vehicle 26,000 pounds or under excluding motorcycles; Class M, motorcycles. (§16-104.1). Operator's license obtained from Motor Vehicle Administration after written and driving tests. (§16-110). Conviction for controlled dangerous substance offense may affect right to obtain or retain license. (art. 41, §1-404). Person under 18 may not be licensed, except person 16-17 may be issued noncommercial Class B, C, or M license after completing approved driver education course, and Class E license must also complete motorcycle safety course. (§16-103). Person at least 15 years, nine months may be issued learner's permit, which authorizes driving when accompanied and supervised by driver at least 21 years old and licensed three years. Person may take tests for license 14 days after receiving learner's permit. (§§16-103[c], 16-105). Person 16-17 may be issued provisional license if person has learner's permit 14 days and has passed licensing tests and paid fees. Generally, provisional license holder may drive between 12:00 a.m. and 5:00 a.m. only under supervision of licensed driver at least 21 years old, and may drive unrestricted at other times. Holder of provisional license entitled to receive regular license: (1) Upon becoming 18, or (2) upon application after holding provisional license 18 months without being convicted of traffic violations enumerated in §16-402. Provisional license shall expire 60 days after licensee's 21st birthday. (§§16-111.2, 16-113, 16-113.1, 16-115).

Application of person under age of 18 must be signed and verified by parent, or guardian, or if applicant has no parent or guardian or is married, by employer or another adult. (§16-107).

Any driver gives implied consent to chemical test of alcohol concentration of person's blood or breath. License suspended 120 days (1st offense) to one year (2nd or subsequent offense) upon refusal to submit to such test. Driver involved in motor vehicle accident resulting in fatality, where driver reasonably believed to be driving intoxicated or while under influence of alcohol, will be required to submit to chemical test. (§16-205.1). License suspended or revoked on conviction of certain offenses involving driving while intoxicated, while intoxicated per se or under influence of drugs or alcohol. (§16-205). Motor Vehicle Administration may impose restrictions prohibiting driver from driving while any alcohol in blood. (§16-113[g]).

License may be refused, suspended, or revoked under point system for motor vehicle law violations. Revoked license may not be reinstated without reexamination, except for licenses revoked under §16-404 or 16-405. (§§16-401 to 16-407). Motor Vehicle Administration may require drivers convicted of moving violation to attend driver improvement or alcohol education program. (§16-212). New drivers aged 18 or older must complete three-hour alcohol and drug education course. (§§16-103.1, 16-212.1).

Members of Armed Forces.—See subhead Operation Prohibited, infra.

Driver Education Program has been established for persons 15 to 17. Program in schools implemented by regulations of State Board of Education, endorsed by Secretary of Transportation. Program in licensed drivers' schools implemented by regulations of Motor Vehicle Administration, endorsed by State Superintendent of Schools. (§§16-501 to 507, 509).

Titles.—Owner must procure certificate of title from Motor Vehicle Administration (§13-101.1), but may obtain vehicle license without such certificate (§13-109). To obtain certificate of title, or vehicle license in absence thereof, owner must pay excise tax of 5% of fair market value of automobile. (§13-809). State, municipal and certain other vehicles are exempt from 5% tax. (§13-810). See subhead Motor Vehicle Taxes, infra. Certificate of title optional for farm or special mobile equipment. (§13-103).

Sales.—It is unlawful to sell used motor vehicle for which certificate of title not issued. (§13-112[e]). If transferee of vehicle is licensed dealer who holds vehicle for sale, transferee dealer must obtain new certificate of title through former owner. (§13-113[a]). Transferee of other new or used vehicle must obtain old certificate from transferor, surrender it, and obtain new certificate from Motor Vehicle Administration. (§13-112). See also category Business Regulation and Commerce, topic Consumer Protection, subhead Miscellaneous Special Provisions.

Distributors.—Manufacturers of passenger vehicles manufactured in U.S. and distributors of foreign-made passenger vehicles engaged in business in Md. are licensed and regulated. Certain activities including coercion of dealers, false advertising and price discrimination are criminal offenses. (§§15-201 to 15-213).

Liens and security interests should be entered on certificate of title immediately and certificate delivered to Motor Vehicle Administration with proper filing fee. (§§13-107[a][3], 13-107[b], 13-203). Motor Vehicle Administration may prevent fraud on

---

See note at head of Digest as to 1998 legislation covered.

See Topical Index in front part of this volume.

MOTOR VEHICLES . . . *continued*

lienholder by refusing to issue new certificate of title or refusing to transfer vehicle registration and license to transferee. (§§13-110, 13-406). Security interest is perfected as of creation if delivery and payment of fee are completed within ten days, otherwise as of time of delivery and payment. (§§13-202 to 13-204). No recordation tax is payable in connection with lien or encumbrance filed with Motor Vehicle Administration. (§13-202). Secured party may obtain new certificate of title upon repossession. (§§13-114[b], 13-114[c]). See categories Business Regulation and Commerce, topics Commercial Code, Sales, subhead Conditional Sales; Debtor and Creditor, topic Liens, subhead Aircraft, Boats, Mobile Homes and Motor Vehicles.

Identification Marks.—Prohibited wilfully to remove or falsify identification number of vehicle or engine or knowingly to deal with or possess item so altered. Prohibited to remove vehicle license plate or registration card from vehicle or to affix unauthorized plate, with intent to conceal or misrepresent identity of vehicle or owner. (§14-107). Fraudulently altering or forging certificate of title, registration card, permanent vehicle license plate, or permit, or knowingly using such altered or forged item is prohibited. (§14-110).

Every truck, truck tractor and bus must be distinctively identified (visible from 50 feet) with name, trade name or company logo and city and state of owner or operator. (§22-404.3). Dealer prohibited from placing insignia, logo or other plates advertising name of dealer on vehicle unless certain conditions met. (§15-313[d]). In lieu of city and state names, company unit number, ICC number, or state agency number are permitted. Excepted are gas, electric, telegraph, telephone or water company trucks; trucks of five tons capacity or less; farm trucks; farm tractors; farm area motor vehicles; school buses; and vehicles used to transport money or commercial paper. (§22-404.3). Propane fueled vehicles must display certain decals. (§22-404.4). Motor vehicles equipped with power booster system must display decal. (§22-404.5).

Operation Prohibited.—Person who does not have valid license not permitted to drive vehicle upon Md. highways except: (1) U.S. government officer or employee operating government vehicle on government business, or member of U.S. Congress from state other than Md. who resides in state; (2) nonresident in possession of license issued to him by his state of residence to drive type of vehicle he is driving, if he is at least same age as that required of Md. resident to drive vehicle he is driving; (3) person driving road machine, farm tractor or farm equipment temporarily operated on highway or certain dock equipment in specified locations; (4) person on active duty with Armed Forces or U.S. Public Health Service, or his dependent, if such person possesses valid license for type of vehicle driven issued by state of domicile; (5) for 30 days, person returning from active duty outside U.S. with Armed Forces, or his spouse, child, or dependent returning from residence with him, if such person possesses valid license issued by Armed Forces for type of vehicle driven; (6) new resident of state during first 30 days of residency if new resident is in possession of license issued to him by former state to drive type of vehicle he is driving, and if he is at least same age as that required by Md. to drive type of vehicle he is driving; (7) nonresident student enrolled in school in Md. or bordering state, or serving medical internship in Md., who is in possession of license issued to him by his state or residence to drive type of vehicle he is driving, provided state of his residence extends same privileges to Md. residents; (8) member of Md. National Guard driving military vehicle in line of duty if issued Md. National Guard operator's identification card for type of military vehicle driven; and (9) nonresident of U.S. if he has valid license issued to him by his country or residence to drive type of vehicle he is driving, and if he is at least same age as that required by Md. to drive type of vehicle he is driving. (§16-102).

Unlawful for person who is intoxicated, intoxicated per se or under influence of alcohol, narcotic or other drug to drive or attempt to drive. (§21-902).

Unlawful for person to operate or permit operation of uninsured motor vehicle without having form and minimum benefits of security required by §17-103. (§17-107).

Unlawful to drive if driver and each occupant under 16 years old not restrained by seat belt. (§22-412.3). Unlawful to drive or ride on motorcycle unless wearing protective headgear. (§21-1306[b]).

Unlawful to transport children of certain ages or below certain weight in certain vehicles without child safety seat or other designated safety belt or harness. (§22-412.2). Violation is moving violation (primary offense).

Unlawful to drive while wearing, in one or both ears, earplugs, headset, or earphones attached to radio, tape player, or other audio device, except for certain emergency vehicles. (§21-1120).

Size and Weight Limits.—Regulated by §§24-101 to 24-114. Semitrailers up to 53 feet permitted on certain roads. (§24-104.2).

Equipment Required.—Regulated by §§22-101 to 22-418. Administrator of Motor Vehicles must approve certain equipment before it may be displayed, sold or delivered in state.

Lights Required.—Regulated by §§22-201 to 22-232.

Inspections.—Seller of used motor vehicle, except one selling to dealer, spouse, parent, child or co-owner must obtain certificate of inspection by authorized dealer or facility, certifying that minimum standards for equipment and mechanisms satisfied. Transferee cannot obtain permanent vehicle license or certificate of title without presenting inspection certificate to Motor Vehicle Administration. (§§23-101, 23-106, 23-107). Inspection facilities licensed by Automotive Safety Enforcement Division of State Police. (§23-103).

Preventive Maintenance Program.—Preventive maintenance required for certain trucks, tractors, buses and multi-purpose vehicles. (§§23-301 to 23-305).

Traffic Regulations.—Regulated by §§21-101 to 21-1412.

Accidents.—Driver must stop, give name, address, and registration number of vehicle he is driving and, on request, exhibit operator's license. Driver must render aid to any injured person, including seeing to transportation to doctor or hospital when necessary or requested. If driver collides with unattended vehicle, must stop and either locate operator or owner of damaged vehicle and give name and address of driver and owner of striking vehicle or leave in conspicuous place in struck vehicle written notice of name and address of driver and owner of striking vehicle. Failure to comply with above

requirements is misdemeanor. Where there is injury to or death of person, driver and/or owner must within 15 days forward written report of accident and evidence of liability insurance to Motor Vehicle Administration. If operator is physically incapable of making report, or is unavailable or refuses to do so, owner of vehicle must make report. False report or failure to report is misdemeanor and, in event of injury to person, is ground for suspension or revocation of all licenses and motor vehicle registrations of person in default. (§§20-101 to 20-109, 27-101). Driver of each vehicle involved in accident resulting in bodily injury or death of person shall immediately return to and remain at scene of accident until he has complied with §20-104. (§20-102). Report need not be filed if police have investigated accident and filed report with State Police. (§20-107[f] [1]).

Liability of Owner.—Owner is liable for negligence of others only when present in car operated by person under his control or car operated by his servant or agent within scope of authority and duty. Family car doctrine is not recognized. (139 Md. 557, 116 A. 68). Person who owns vehicle or who employs or otherwise directs driver may not knowingly permit operation in any manner contrary to law. (§26-102).

Vehicle registration may be suspended if owner permits vehicle to be driven by individual whom owner knows to have had license suspended or revoked for certain alcohol or drug-related violations. Numerous exceptions apply. (§13-705.1).

Guests.—No statute restricting liability for injury to gratuitous guest, and guest has been allowed to recover. (177 Md. 657, 11 A.2d 640).

Liability of Physician.—Physician who renders gratuitous emergency medical aid at scene of accident not liable in absence of gross negligence. (courts art. §5-603). See category Civil Actions and Procedure, topic Damages, subhead Good Samaritan Law.

Proof of financial responsibility is required in following cases:

Rental and Leasing of Vehicles.—Rent v. lease distinguished. (§18-101). Rent is for 180 days or less. Lease is for 180 days or more. Owner of vehicle must maintain proof of financial responsibility of owner and operator in order to keep vehicle registration. (§18-102).

Required Security in All Other Cases.—See subhead Insurance, infra.

Insurance.—

Compulsory Insurance.—Owner of Md. registered vehicle must maintain liability insurance policy providing coverage of at least $20,000 for bodily injury to or death of one person, $40,000 for any two or more persons, and $10,000 for property damage, and containing at least minimum no-fault insurance coverages required by insurance code. (§§17-103, 17-104). Other form of security may be accepted in lieu of policy. (§17-103[a][2] & [3]). Person notified of suspension of registration must voluntarily surrender all evidence of registration within 48 hours until required coverage is obtained. (§17-106). As to foreign vehicle, see subhead Foreign Vehicle, infra.

No-Fault Insurance.—Unless waived by affirmative written waiver of first named insured, all motor vehicle liability insurance policies must provide medical, hospital and disability benefits of at least $2,500 covering insured, members of insured's family residing in household, passengers injured in insured's vehicle, persons injured while using insured's vehicle with expressed or implied permission of insured, pedestrians injured by insured's vehicle and individuals injured in or on any other vehicle operated by muscular power in accident involving insured's vehicle. These provisions do not apply to taxicabs or commercial buses. (art. 48A, §539). Benefits are payable without regard to fault and without regard to collateral sources of benefits, and insurer has no right of subrogation. (art. 48A, §540). Right of any person to claim and sue for damages and losses sustained by such person as result of motor vehicle accident is not affected by no-fault insurance statute (art. 48A, §542), but benefits cannot be duplicated under third party's liability policy (art. 48A, §543). Excluded from no-fault coverage include: intentionally-caused accidents, injuries occurring while voluntarily in vehicle known to be stolen, while in commission of felony, or while fleeing pursuing police vehicle; certain economic loss benefits with respect to motorcycles; injuries to person occupying, or struck as pedestrian by, uninsured motorist vehicle owned by member of person's immediate family; and injuries to nonresident pedestrian in accident outside of state. (art. 48A, §545). All Maryland residents' insurance policies with collision coverage automatically extend that coverage to passenger cars rented by insureds named in policy for period of 30 days or less. Notice must be in bold type. (art. 48A, §541[d][4]). Insurers must provide certain information regarding rates and other matters to insureds. (art. 48A, §244D).

Md. Automobile Insurance Fund.—Effective Jan. 1, 1973, Fund supersedes Unsatisfied Claim and Judgment Fund. (art. 48A, §§243, 243A).

Persons denied insurance by private carriers for reasons other than nonpayment of premiums may acquire from Md. Automobile Insurance Fund statutory minimum compulsory liability insurance coverage. (art. 48A, §243B). Md. Automobile Insurance Fund does not cover vehicles leased to nonresidents or principally garaged out of state. (art. 48A, §243B[k]). Insurance by Fund may be denied or cancelled for nonpayment of premiums or suspension or revocation of insured's driver's license; but if policy covers spouse or other household member, cancellation cannot affect coverage of such innocent person. (art. 48A, §243D). Policy must be renewed if holder completes three years without chargeable traffic accident and with only one point for moving violations under point system. (art. 48A, §243C[d]).

Certain claims against unidentified persons and persons not covered by motor vehicle liability insurance may be made against Md. Automobile Insurance Fund (art. 48A, §243H) to extent of statutory minimum compulsory liability insurance coverage less certain deductions. (art. 48A, §243H,I).

Rate Classification and Cancellation.—Insurance companies must give 45 days notice to insured of cancellation, nonrenewal increase in premiums, or reduction in coverage, stating certain information including reason for action. Insured has right of appeal to Insurance Commissioner and further right of judicial review. (art. 48A, §240AA). At time of issuance or renewal, insurer must provide policyholder with clear statement of rate classification. (art. 48A, §242[c][4]). Insurer may not refuse to underwrite passenger motor vehicle solely because insured was previously insured by Maryland Automobile Insurance Fund. No insured may be retained in higher premium classification as result of claims record or points record for more than three years from date of last claim or last point; however, insurer may remove discount. (art. 48A,

See note at head of Digest as to 1998 legislation covered.

See Topical Index in front part of this volume.

MOTOR VEHICLES . . . *continued*

§242[c][7]). Insurer may reduce rates for motor vehicle personal injury and property coverage based on actuarial justification to person age 55 or older who has completed successfully within last two years certified course in accident prevention. (art. 48A, §242[c][8]). Insurance may not be cancelled, refused or terminated due to traffic violation or accident more than three years old on date policy or renewal is effective. (art. 48A, §234A[d]).

Nationwide Intercompany Arbitration Agreement.—Every automobile liability or physical damage insurer doing business in Md. must be member. Insurers must arbitrate and settle claims between themselves in accordance with terms of Agreement and rules promulgated thereunder. (art. 48A, §547).

Industry Automobile Insurance Association consisting of all licensed motor vehicle liability or physical damage insurers; membership required. (art. 48A, §243M).

Foreign vehicle registered in owner's place of residence and displaying license plates issued therefor may be operated without registration in Md., provided that vehicle not used for transportation of persons for hire, not regularly operated in carrying on business within Md., not designed or used primarily for transportation of property, and not in custody of resident for more than 30 days in any registration year. (§13-402.1[a]). Member of Armed Forces need not register passenger vehicle in Md. if registered in state of residence (§13-402.1[c]). Nonresident student attending Md. school need not register, provided home state extends same privileges to residents of Md. and student meets financial responsibility requirements. (§13-402.1[d]). Nonresident temporarily maintaining or occupying dwelling in Md. for more than 30 days may obtain nonresident permit upon application within ten days after 30 days. (§13-402.1[e]). Nonresident member of U.S. Congress residing in Md. need not register or obtain vehicle license during term. (§13-402[e]). Nonresident working on seasonal crop operations on farm need not register or obtain license plates for motor vehicle or trailer validly registered and bearing valid license plates issued by another state, provided nonresident obtains exemption permit from Motor Vehicle Administration. (§13-402[d]).

Nonresident Operator.—Nonresident student enrolled in accredited school in Md. and possessing valid driver's license of state or county of domicile may operate motor vehicle in Md. if state or country of domicile extends same privilege to Md. residents. Nonresident may drive only vehicle of class which he is licensed to drive in place of domicile. (§16-102[a][5]).

Direct Actions.—Action by injured person against insurer not allowed. In case where insured is charitable institution, insurer may be joined, but action may be tried only after judgment is obtained against insured. (219 Md. 422, 149 A.2d 768).

Motor vehicle carriers regulated by Public Service Commission. Must operate over fixed route, have special license and secure certificate of public convenience and necessity. (trans. art. §13-423; pub. util. comp. art. §§9-201-9-206). For heavy-duty vehicles that do not operate over fixed routes, special safety requirements apply. (trans. art. §25-111). Taxicabs also regulated by Public Service Commission. (pub. util. comp. art. §10-201).

Company van pools are regulated by §13-934 and require no permit from Public Service Commission. (pub. util. comp. art. §9-201).

Tax for Use and Maintenance of Roads.—There is motor carrier's road tax equivalent to rate per gallon of motor vehicle fuel tax calculated on amount of fuel consumed in state. (tax-gen. art. §§9-202, 9-204, 9-213).

Motor Vehicle Taxes.—Property taxes need not be paid on motor vehicles. (tax-prop. art. §7-301).

In addition to other taxes, there is excise tax for issuance of each original certificate of title and each subsequent certificate of title and for each motor vehicle, trailer, or semitrailer in interstate operation and registered without certificate of title (excluding certain house and office trailers, vehicles transferred for no consideration to members of immediate family or to heir, legatee or distributee, or from individual to partnership or corporation in which he has interest, fire engines, ambulances, vehicles owned by federal government and vehicles owned by state or any political subdivision, or certain organizations or for certain purposes, vehicles transferred involuntarily by certain transactions, or vehicles transferred in certain corporate transactions and certain special purpose vehicles owned by coal company), at rate of 5% of fair market value of vehicle except that excise tax of $50 is imposed on trailers exempt from titling. (§§13-808 to 13-810).

Gasoline Tax.—See category Taxation, topic Motor Fuel Tax.

Off-Road Vehicles.—Secretary of Natural Resources promulgated rules and regulations, effective Dec. 25, 1974, concerning operation of off-road vehicles on property owned or controlled by Dep't of Natural Resources. (Comar 08.01.03.06). Every off-road vehicle to be used on such property must be registered and provided with identification by Dep't. (nat. res. art. §5-209).

Judgments Arising from Use of Motor Vehicle.—If resident or nonresident fails within 30 days to satisfy final judgment upon cause of action arising out of ownership, maintenance or use of vehicle, person obtaining judgment or his representative may forward to Motor Vehicle Administration certified copy of judgment and certificate of facts relating thereto (on form provided by Administration), and Administration will suspend license and registration and any nonresident's operating privilege of judgment debtor. Suspension continues until judgment is stayed or satisfied in full. Exceptions are provided, including case where insurer is obligated to but does not pay judgment and case of insurer which has gone into liquidation. (§§17-201 to 17-209).

See also category Business Regulation and Commerce, topic Consumer Protection.

RAILROADS:

See category Business Regulation and Commerce, topic Carriers.

MASSACHUSETTS LAW DIGEST REVISER

Professor Richard M. Perlmutter
Suffolk University Law School
41 Temple Street
Boston, Massachusetts 02114
Telephone: 617-573-8153
Fax: 617-573-8143
Email: rperlmut@acad.suffolk.edu

Associate Revisers:
David S. Romantz and Herbert N. Ramy
Instructors, Suffolk University Law School

Research Assistants:
Vincent J. Froio, Jr. and Richard Reilly
Suffolk University Law School

Reviser Profile

Richard M. Perlmutter has been a Professor of Law at Suffolk University Law School, Boston, Massachusetts since 1976, teaching courses in Contracts, Equity, Remedies, Advanced Contracts, Sports Law, and Negotiation for Lawyers. He is a *cum laude* graduate of Harvard University Law School and a *magna cum laude* graduate of Tufts University. Prior to joining the Suffolk Law School Faculty, Professor Perlmutter served as law clerk to the Justices of the Massachusetts Superior Court and engaged in the private practice of law in Boston for more than ten years, specializing in real estate, business, regulated industries and health facilities law. Professor Perlmutter is coauthor of a casebook on Contract law and has lectured on that subject as well as commercial law, negotiation for lawyers and legal professional ethics. He was admitted to the Massachusetts Bar in 1967 and is a member of the Boston, Massachusetts and American Bar Associations and the Sports Lawyers Association. Professor Perlmutter has served as an arbitrator under the auspices of the American Arbitration Association and consults regularly with several Massachusetts law firms within his areas of expertise on appellate and other matters.

David S. Romantz and Herbert N. Ramy: David S. Romantz became the Director of Legal Methods at the Cecil C. Humphreys School of Law at the University of Memphis in July 1998. Previously he taught Legal Practice Skills at Suffolk University Law School. He is a *cum laude* graduate of University of Michigan and of Suffolk University Law School, where he served as Notes Editor of the Law Review. Mr. Romantz is a member of the Massachusetts, New York and Federal Bars. Herbert N. Ramy is *cum laude* graduate of the University of Massachusetts and of Suffolk University Law School, where he served as Comment Editor of the Transnational Law Review. Following graduation Mr. Ramy clerked for the Massachusetts Superior and Appeals Courts before returning to Suffolk Law School to teach in the Legal Practice Skills Program. He is a member of the Bars of Massachusetts, Maine and the Federal First Circuit.

Research Assistants: Vincent J. Froio, Jr. is a graduate of University of New Hampshire and is enrolled in the Suffolk Law School High Technology concentration. Richard Reilly holds a B.A. from California State University in Northridge and serves as Production Editor of the Suffolk University Law Review.

Suffolk University Law School was founded in 1906 as an evening law school providing access to the legal profession to ethnically diverse and less privileged persons in the Boston area community. In 1999 Suffolk will move from its Beacon Hill location to a new, state-of-the-art building in downtown Boston, within steps of the Massachusetts State Capitol, Boston City Hall and State and Federal Courts. Its urban location provides unique educational opportunities to its more than 1,500 day and evening division students. The Law School and its library, with more than 300,000 volumes and full computer research resources, is an integral and important part of the Boston and Massachusetts legal communities. Long recognized throughout New England as a trainer of highly qualified legal practitioners and jurists, Suffolk now numbers students from more than 40 states and 7 foreign countries, including graduates of more than 340 colleges and universities. Its alumni network of more than 13,000 attorneys, more than 70 resident full time faculty members and a 60 person adjunct faculty of distinguished practicing lawyers and judges have earned the Law School national recognition. Suffolk University Law School is fully accredited by the American Bar Association and the Association of American Law Schools.

MASSACHUSETTS LAW DIGEST

(The following is a list of all Categories and Topics, including cross-references, covered in this Digest.)

MASSACHUSETTS LAW DIGEST

Revised for 1999 edition by

PROFESSOR RICHARD M. PERLMUTTER, assisted by David S. Romantz and Herbert N. Ramy, Instructors, Vincent J. Froio, Jr. and Richard Reilly, Suffolk University Law School, Boston.

(Citations, unless otherwise indicated, refer to 1988 Official Edition Massachusetts General Laws, as am'd. Session laws are cited by year and chapter number. Parallel citations to the North Eastern Reporter begin with 139 Mass. "SJC" is used as abbreviation for Supreme Judicial Court; "BMC" is used as abbreviation for Boston Municipal Court. "Mass. R. Civ. P." refers to Massachusetts Rules of Civil Procedure; "MRAP" refers to Massachusetts Rules of Appellate Procedure; "Mass. R. Dom. Rel. P." refers to Massachusetts Rules of Domestic Relations Procedure; "CMR" refers to Code of Massachusetts Regulations "Unif. Prob. Ct. Prac." refers to Uniform Probate Court Practice.)

Note: This revision covers Acts of 1998 adopted and approved by Governor through August 10, 1998, up to Chapter 221.

Note: Readers are advised that the full text of every opinion of the Massachusetts Supreme Judicial Court and the Appeals Court is available at the Massachusetts Lawyers Weekly Internet site: "http://www.masslaw.com".

INTRODUCTION

GOVERNMENT AND LEGAL SYSTEM:

The Commonwealth of Massachusetts is a constituent state of the United States of America. For further discussion of the U.S. federal system, see Introduction to the Federal Government of the United States at the beginning of this volume. A great many laws are promulgated by the federal government of the United States and are not reflected in the topics below. See the Introduction to this volume for references to the federal law topics covered.

Like all but one of the United States, Massachusetts has a common law legal system, with roots in English common law. For information on the courts and legislature of Massachusetts, see category Courts and Legislature.

Preliminary Note.—During periods of crisis, governor may proclaim state of emergency (c. 33 App. §13-5) and exercise extensive legislative powers (c. 33 App. §§13-5—13-7). Executive orders are cited herein E.O. followed by number. Middlesex county form of government abolished by St. 1997, c. 48. Hampden and Worcester counties abolished, effective July 1, 1998, or at earlier date of 30 days after commissioner of revenue certifies, in writing, that county failed to make required payment on outstanding bond or note. (St. 1997, c. 48).

HOLIDAYS:

Legal holidays are Jan. 1, 3d Mon. in Jan., 3d Mon. in Feb., Mar. 17 (in Suffolk County only), 3d Mon. in Apr., last Mon. in May, June 17 (in Suffolk County only), July 4, first Mon. in Sept., 2d Mon. in Oct., Nov. 11, Thanksgiving Day and Christmas Day. (c. 4, §7[18]).

Holiday Falling on Sunday.—When a holiday falls on Sunday, the following day is a holiday. (c. 4, §7[18]; c. 136, §13[2]).

Legality of Transactions on Holiday.—Sun. laws apply for entire day, or on day following if day falls on Sun., on all legal holidays except Jan. 1, 3d. Mon. in Jan., 3d Mon. in Feb., Mar. 17, 3d Mon. in Apr., May 20, June 17, 2d Mon. in Oct., and Nov. 11 after 1 P.M., and transactions thereon are subject to Sun. laws and are therefore void unless they constitute works of charity or necessity or works falling within exception to Sun. laws. Retail stores may open at any time on Memorial Day, July Fourth, and Labor Day. Performance of work directly connected to retail sales on these days allowed. All types of lawful goods except alcoholic beverages may be sold. (c. 136, §16). If day set for town meeting falls on holiday, meeting postponed until following day. (c. 4, §7[18]; c. 136, §§13-15).

When last day for doing act falls on Sunday or holiday, the act may be done on next succeeding secular or business day. (c. 4, §9).

Saturdays.—State offices are closed all day on Saturdays unless kept open under special approval. When day or last day for performance of any act authorized or required to be performed at a state office falls on a Saturday when such office is closed, the act may be performed on next succeeding business day. (c. 30, §24).

Banks may close on Saturdays, and any act in connection with such banks which is required to be performed on a Saturday may be done on the next succeeding business day.(c. 167, §21).

A city or town may close any municipal office, and any act which is required to be performed on a Saturday may be performed on the next succeeding business day. (c. 41, §110A). SJC, Superior Court, Land Court, Probate Court, registries of deeds and offices of county commissioners may be closed on Saturdays. (c. 213, §4).

Sundays.—See c. 136. Sun. is common day of rest. Work done is ordinarily prohibited. (c. 136, see especially §5). Many exceptions exist to this general rule. Certain businesses may remain open on Sun. as provided by statute and various specified activities are not prohibited. (§6). Banks may conduct banking operations on Suns. (c. 136, §6[55]). Retail stores may open at any time on Suns. Performance of work directly connected to retail sales on Suns. allowed. All types of lawful goods except alcoholic beverages may be sold. (c. 136, §16). Kosher wine, however, may be sold by licensee who observes Sat. as Sabbath and who sells or delivers kosher meat or fish. (c. 138, §33). No employee who works in shop or store dealing in retail sales of goods (except alcoholic beverages) which employs more than seven persons, including proprietor, or who works in store which qualifies for exemption under c. 136, §§6 (25, 27), 16 may be required to work on such Suns. and work done must be compensated at not less than 1½ times regular rate; violations are punishable by fine under c. 149 (§§180A, 180). Sun. exemptions do not apply to Christmas if Christmas falls on Sun. (c. 136, §6[50]). Sabbatarian exemption allows secular place of business to remain open on Sun. if natural person in control of business conscientiously believes that Sat., should be observed as Sabbath, and causes all businesses which he may control in commonwealth to remain closed for secular business during 24 hour period he believes should be observed as Sabbath. (§6[8]).

OFFICE HOURS AND TIME ZONE:

Massachusetts is in the Eastern (GMT −05:00) time zone. Office hours are generally from 9 a.m. to 5 p.m.

BUSINESS ORGANIZATIONS

AGENCY:

Common law rules generally prevail.

ASSOCIATIONS:

Formation.—Associations not included in topic Joint Stock Companies are formed by agreement among members. There are no statutes especially governing their formation or dissolution, generally. There are statutory provisions governing formation of some specific types of associations. See General Index to Mass. Gen. Laws under Associations regarding specific types. Condominium Associations are governed by c. 183A, §§1-21. Specific provisions that must appear in Condominium Associations bylaws are set out in c. 183A, §11. Fraternal benefit societies are under control of commissioner of insurance and are governed in part by statutes applying to insurance corporations. (c. 176).

Rights and Powers.—Members of an association have property rights in the assets of such association. (318 Mass. 649, 63 N.E.2d 571).

In becoming a member of an unincorporated association, order or society, one submits himself to the jurisdiction of that body, and consents to be bound by its bylaws and to accept liability to expulsion in accordance with its laws, rules and usages as one of incidents of membership. (157 Mass. 128, 31 N.E. 776). After member has exhausted all remedies within organization, equity will require unincorporated association to obey its own rules. (311 Mass. 473, 42 N.E.2d 280).

Unincorporated associations as such are incapable of holding real estate, but a deed to such an association, all the members of which can be ascertained, may be construed as a grant to the persons associated, as tenants in common. (140 Mass. 31, 2 N.E. 687). It is better, however, that legal title be taken and held by trustees for that purpose. Associations may not practice law. (c. 221, §46).

Liabilities.—Members are liable for acts and contracts of association which they participated in, authorized, or ratified, where association is nonprofit making. (287 Mass. 376, 191 N.E. 661, overruled on other grounds, 354 Mass. 242, 237 N.E.2d 10). Where association is one for profit liability of members is regulated by ordinary principles of partnership.

Liability of Members of Professional Societies.—Members of professional societies or nonprofit corporations whose sole voting member is professional society composed of licensed medical practitioners, and hospital staffs are not liable for damages as result of acts or omissions performed within scope of duty as member provided action was undertaken in good faith and with reasonable belief that action or inaction was warranted. (c. 231, §85N).

Actions.—Unincorporated association, other than labor union (386 Mass. 314, 435 N.E.2d 1027), cannot be party to litigation. All members must be joined as parties. If members too numerous to be joined, number of members properly representative of all may sue or be sued as representatives of class (358 Mass. 682, 266 N.E.2d 651). Labor union may sue and be sued as legal entity. (386 Mass. 314, 435 N.E.2d 1027).

Dissolution.—Dissolution is accomplished in accordance with bylaws or rules of association. In the absence of provisions relative to dissolution, the property of the association is divided pro rata among the members. See generally c. 182 for dissolution of certain trusts. See Uniform Partnership Act §§29-43 (c. 108A) for dissolution of partnerships.

Supervision.—Commissioner of insurance has power to examine affairs of fraternal benefit societies from time to time, and in the event of mismanagement may request attorney general to commence court action to enjoin society from transacting business and for appointment of receiver and dissolution of society. (c. 176, §§33, 36-37). See topic Joint Stock Companies, subhead Statement.

Professional Associations.—See topic Corporations, subhead Professional Corporations.

Massachusetts Business Trust.—See topic Joint Stock Companies.

CORPORATIONS:

Domestic business corporations, in general, are governed by Business Corporation Law, c. 156B (BCL) and all citations, unless otherwise indicated, refer to that chapter.

See note at head of Digest as to 1998 legislation covered.

See Topical Index in front part of this volume.

CORPORATIONS . . . *continued*

Special Corporations.—Other chapters of General Laws govern formation and business of corporations formed to carry on following businesses and activities: Banking, including savings and cooperative banks and credit unions, cc. 167-172A; insurance, including surety companies, fraternal benefit societies and hospital and medical service corporations, cc. 174A-178 (note, c. 175, §174E is hereby repealed); professional practice, c. 156A; limited liability companies, c. 156C; cooperative ventures, c. 157; railroads and other utilities, cc. 159-166; charitable and other nonprofit activities, c. 180. Foreign corporations are governed by c. 181. C. 182 governs so-called "Massachusetts business trusts" i.e., trusts with transferrable shares, commonly used for business activities. See topic Joint Stock Companies.

General supervision of corporations is vested in state secretary. Address is: Secretary of the Commonwealth, Corporations Division, One Ashburton Place, 17th floor, Boston, Massachusetts 02108. Telephone number for general information is (617) 727-9640 or (617) 727-2850. Best hours for calling are between 8:45 a.m. and 12:00 p.m. Division has promulgated rules and regulations covering practice with respect to business, foreign, professional and nonprofit corporations, business trusts and limited partnerships. Nonprofit medical service corporations are regulated by commissioner of insurance. (c. 176B, §1).

Purposes.—Corporation organized under c. 156B may, with certain exceptions, conduct any lawful business except businesses noted above as being governed by other chapters of General Laws. (§3).

Powers.—Except as otherwise provided in its articles of organization, every business corporation shall have power in furtherance of its corporate purposes to: (a) Have perpetual succession unless its duration is limited by special law or its articles of organization; (b) sue and be sued; (c) have corporate seal; (d) elect or appoint directors, officers, employees and agents, fix their compensation, define their duties and obligations and indemnify them; (e) purchase, lease or otherwise acquire, hold, use and otherwise deal in and with, real or personal property, wherever situated; (f) sell or otherwise dispose of, or mortgage, encumber or create security interest in, its property, wherever situated; (g) purchase or otherwise acquire, hold, vote, employ, sell, lend, lease or otherwise dispose of, mortgage, pledge and otherwise deal in and with, bonds and other obligations, shares, or other securities or interests issued by others (but unless authorized by special act, not acquire or hold more than 10% of total capital stock of any domestic railway or gas company located in same city or town as place of business of corporation, except that corporation having its principal place of business in commonwealth may acquire and hold more than 10% of stock of domestic corporation carrying on business of gas company within commonwealth [c. 156, §5; c. 164, §31]); (h) make contracts, give guarantees, incur liabilities, borrow money, and issue its notes, bonds and other obligations, and secure them by mortgage or security interest in its property; (i) lend money, invest its funds, and hold real and personal property as security therefor; (j) do business in any jurisdiction within or without U.S.; (k) make donations, irrespective of corporate benefit; (l) pay pensions, establish and carry out pension, profit-sharing, share bonus, share purchase, share option, savings, thrift and other benefit plans for its directors, officers and employees and those of any other corporation, 50% of voting stock of which is owned by it; (m) purchase or otherwise acquire, hold, sell, lend or otherwise dispose of, pledge, use and otherwise deal in and with its own shares; (n) participate as subscriber in exchanging of certain insurance contracts; (o) be incorporator of other corporations; (p) exercise all powers necessary or convenient to effect any or all of purposes for which corporation is formed; provided that no such power shall be exercised in manner inconsistent with BCL or General Laws of commonwealth (§9). Corporation may be partner in any business which it could conduct itself. (§9A). Corporation may make contract of guarantee and suretyship, whether or not in furtherance of contracting corporation's purposes; provided (1) that contract necessary or convenient to conduct, promotion or attainment of business of (a) corporation all of outstanding stock of which is owned by contracting corporation, (b) corporation which owns all of outstanding stock of contracting corporation, or (c) corporation all of outstanding stock of which is owned by corporation which owns all of outstanding stock of contracting corporation, and (2) that board of directors of contracting corporation has determined that contract necessary or convenient to conduct, promotion or attainment of contracting corporation's purposes (§9B). SJC or Superior Court may, on information by attorney general at relation of state secretary, enjoin assumption or exercise of any franchise or privilege or transaction of any kind or business not authorized by articles of organization and law. (§10).

Name.—Corporate name must indicate incorporation and must not be same as, or so similar as to be likely to be mistaken for, name or tradename of (or reserved for) another domestic corporation or any corporation, firm, association or person which or who is, at time either of formation of corporation or of change of name of existing corporation, or was within three years prior thereto, carrying on business in commonwealth, unless, in case of similar name, written consent thereto of such other corporation, etc., is filed with state secretary. (§11). Availability of name may be checked by telephone but not reserved thereby. (Phone: [617] 727-9640). Corporate name may be reserved for 30 days upon written request and payment of fee determined annually by secretary of administration, currently $15. (§11[c], [d]). Upon written request and payment of additional fee determined annually by secretary, currently $15, state secretary may extend reservation for 30 days. See also category Intellectual Property, topic Trademarks and Tradenames.

Terms of corporate existence may be perpetual or limited.

Incorporators.—It is not required that any of incorporators be citizens or residents of Massachusetts. One incorporator is sufficient; if natural person, incorporator must be least 18 years of age. (§12). After corporation is formed but prior to initial issue of stock, incorporator(s) may exercise all rights of stockholders and take any action required or permitted by law, articles of organization or by-laws to be taken by stockholders. (§44). Any action required or permitted to be taken at any meeting of incorporators may be taken without meeting if written consents are filed with corporate records. (§12). Corporation can be incorporator. (§9[o]).

Organization.—One or more persons or corporations, as incorporators, may hold meeting at which (or execute written consent by which) bylaws are adopted and initial directors and officers are elected. (§12). Resident agent may also be elected and any other action taken which might be taken by stockholders after articles become effective. (Id.). Incorporators sign articles of organization (on form supplied by state secretary) in which must be set forth following: (1) That incorporators (stating their names and addresses) associate themselves to form corporation; (2) name of corporation; (3) purposes; (4) number of shares and par value, if any, of each class of stock authorized for issuance; and (5) if more than one class of stock is authorized, distinguishing designation for each class and, prior to issuance of any shares of class, if shares of any other class are outstanding, description of preferences, voting powers, qualifications, and special or relative rights or privileges of that class and of each series then established within any class. Articles may state: (1) Any restrictions imposed upon transfer of shares of stock; (2) provision eliminating or limiting personal liability of directors to corporation or its stockholders for certain acts; and (3) any other lawful provision for conduct and regulation of business and affairs of corporation, for its voluntary dissolution, or for limiting, defining or regulating its powers or powers of its directors, stockholders or any class of its stockholders. Following information must also be contained in articles but does not constitute permanent part thereof: (1) Street address of initial principal office in Massachusetts; (2) names and addresses of initial directors and officers; (3) fiscal year; and (4) name and business address of resident agent, if any. (§§12 and 13).

Filing Articles of Organization.—Articles are submitted to state secretary and upon endorsement of his approval, and payment of fee, articles are deemed filed. State secretary shall cause photographic or other copy to be made of articles showing his approval endorsed thereon and shall deliver same to corporation. (§6). Articles become effective when filed unless they specify later date not more than 30 days after filing date. (§12). Corporate existence begins when articles become effective. (Id.). Certified statement of fact of incorporation by state secretary is conclusive evidence of incorporation. (Id.).

Incorporation tax or fee is determined by commissioner of administration, currently $200 minimum. (§114[a]).

Filing Fees.—None initially in addition to incorporation fee set forth above.

Paid-in Capital Requirements.—None.

Amendment of Articles.—Pursuant to §70, corporation may, by vote of majority of each class of stock outstanding and entitled to vote thereon, authorize amendment of its articles of organization effecting any one or more of following: (1) Increase or reduction of authorized capital stock; (2) change of par value of authorized shares; (3) change of authorized shares with par value into any number of shares without par value, or exchange thereof pro rata for any number of shares without par value; (4) change in number of authorized shares without par value or exchange thereof pro rata for greater or lesser number of shares without par value; (5) change in number of authorized shares with par value, or exchange thereof pro rata for greater or lesser number of shares with par value; (6) change of authorized shares without par value into any number of shares with par value, or exchange thereof pro rata for any number of shares with par value; (7) change of its corporate name. However, any amendment which impairs or diminishes preferences, voting powers, restrictions, qualifications, special or relative rights or privileges of any outstanding shares must be authorized by at least two-thirds vote of shares affected. (§§70 and 71). All references to authorized shares include both unissued and outstanding shares. (§70).

Pursuant to §71 corporation may, by vote of two-thirds, or lesser proportion (but not less than majority) if articles of organization so provide, of each class of stock outstanding and entitled to vote thereon, authorize any amendment of its articles of organization; provided, only, that any provision added to or changes made in its articles of organization by such amendment could have been included in, and any provision deleted thereby could have been omitted from, original articles of organization filed at time of such meeting. If amendment adversely affects rights of any class of stock, vote of same proportion of such class, voting separately, is necessary. Series of any class affected differently than any other series of same class are treated, together with similarly affected series of same class, as separate class.

Holder of adversely affected shares who objects in prescribed manner and does not vote for amendment has statutory remedy of appraisal. (§76). Shares are deemed adversely affected only if amendment (otherwise than as permitted by articles of organization): (a) Alters or abolishes his preferential rights; (b) creates, alters or abolishes right of redemption of his stock; (c) alters or abolishes his preemptive rights; (d) creates or alters (other than to abolish) restrictions on transfer of his stock; or (e) excludes or limits right of such holder to vote on any matter except as such right may be limited by voting rights given to new shares then being authorized. (§§76 and 77). Whenever by virtue of any change or exchange, shares with par value become outstanding, aggregate par value of such shares may not exceed capital shown on balance sheet with respect to outstanding shares changed or exchanged plus any surplus that may be appropriated to capital in connection with change or exchange. (§70).

After any meeting at which any amendment is adopted, articles of amendment (on forms supplied by state secretary) signed by president or vice president and by clerk or assistant clerk, setting forth such amendment must be submitted to state secretary (§72), and, unless said articles specify later effective date not more than 30 days after filing, amendment is deemed effective upon his approval and payment of appropriate filing fee. (§§6 and 72). Fees for filing articles of amendment are determined annually by commissioner of administration, currently $100 minimum. (§114[b]).

Directors or stockholders by vote of majority of each class entitled to vote may authorize restatement of articles of organization. (§74). Amendments to articles may be effected by restatement provided that such amendments may be and such restatement is, as case may be, lawfully adopted in accordance with §70 or §71. Restated articles (on form supplied by state secretary), signed by president or vice president and clerk or assistant clerk, must be submitted to state secretary after meeting at which adopted. Restated articles (which are deemed to supersede original articles and any amendments thereto) are effective upon filing or at later effective date (not more than 30 days after such filing) specified in articles. (§74). Fee for filing restated articles of

See note at head of Digest as to 1998 legislation covered.

See Topical Index in front part of this volume.

MA – 2

CORPORATIONS . . . *continued*
organization determined annually by commissioner of administration, currently $200 minimum. (§114[c]).

Amendments to articles of organization pursuant to plan of reorganization confirmed under federal statutes relating to reorganization of corporations may be authorized by decrees or orders of reorganization court; articles of amendment in such cases are signed by court-authorized persons and manner of filing with state secretary, payment of fees and effectiveness are same as in case of amendments authorized by stockholder action. (§§73, 114[b]).

Certificates (on forms supplied by state secretary) of change in date of annual meeting, fiscal year, principal office of corporation in commonwealth, officers or directors, or resident agent must be filed with state secretary. (§53). Failure or refusal to file such certificate within 30 days of such change shall forfeit not more than $500. (§§53 and 113). Such changes are not deemed amendments of articles of organization. There is no filing fee. See subhead Reports, infra.

Bylaws.—Corporation may make bylaws which may contain any provisions not inconsistent with law or articles of organization for regulation and management of affairs of corporation. (§16). Power to make, amend or repeal bylaws is in stockholders, provided that if authorized by articles of organization, bylaws may provide that directors may also make, amend or repeal bylaws in whole or in part, except with respect to any provision thereof which by law, articles of organization or bylaws, requires action by stockholders. (§17). Not later than time of giving notice of meeting of stockholders next following making, amending or repealing by directors of any bylaw, notice thereof stating substance of such change shall be given to all stockholders entitled to vote on amending bylaws. Any bylaw adopted by directors may be amended or repealed by stockholders. (§17).

Stock may be issued with par value or without par value in one or more classes or series with such lawful preferences, voting rights, restrictions and qualifications as are set forth in articles of organization. Stock of any class may be divided into series if so provided in articles of organization. Variations in preferences, voting powers, qualifications, and special or relative rights or privileges of: (1) Any class of stock before issuance of any shares of that class or (2) one or more series within class before issuance of any shares of that series are permitted and must be fixed by articles of organization or, to extent authorized by articles, by directors. Each series of class shall have distinguishing designation. If directors establish series and fix its rights, certificate of vote must be filed with state secretary signed under penalties of perjury by president or vice president and clerk or assistant clerk. (§26). If shares of any series established by directors are restored to status of authorized but unissued shares pursuant to §21A, shares may be reissued by vote of directors, either as shares of same class and series or as shares of one or more other series within same class, terms of which are determined by directors in accordance with §26. In case of restored shares reissued by directors as shares of same series, corporation need not submit certificate of vote to state secretary. (§26).

Fractional shares or scrip in lieu thereof may be issued. (§28).

Stock certificates must be signed by chairman, president or vice president and treasurer or assistant-treasurer and bear statement of number of shares and class and designation of series thereof represented. (§27). Facsimile signatures are permissible if certificate is signed by either independent transfer agent or independent registrar. Every stock certificate issued after Sept. 30, 1965 by corporation while it is authorized to issue more than one class of stock must set forth upon face or back of certificate either: (1) Full text of special and relative rights of each class and series authorized, or (2) statement of existence of such special and relative rights and statement that corporation will furnish copy thereof upon written request and without charge. (§27[b]). Shares which are subject to any restriction on transfer pursuant to articles of organization, by-laws or any agreement to which corporation is party must, if issued after Sept. 30, 1965, have restriction noted conspicuously on certificate and also must have set forth upon face or back of certificate either: (1) Full text of restriction, or (2) statement of existence of restriction and statement that corporation will furnish copy thereof upon written request and without charge. (§27[c]). Unless prohibited by articles of organization or by-laws, board of directors may authorize any or all series and classes of shares to be uncertificated. However, if any holders of series or class of shares are entitled to hold certificated shares, all other holders of such series or class may hold certificated shares. (§27[d], am'd 1987, c. 247). New certificates in place of those alleged to have been lost, mutilated or destroyed may be issued, subject to c. 106, §8-405, on conditions (including sufficient bond with or without surety) determined by directors subject to by-laws. (§29).

Issuance of Stock.—Capital stock may be issued for cash, property (tangible or intangible), services or for debt, note or expenses. (c. 282, §18). Stock issued for cash may be paid for in full before issue or by installments; in latter case, certificate must be stamped to show percentage of amount paid and balance payable stating manner and time of payment and statement that shares are subject to forfeiture if unpaid. As each installment is paid, certificate should be stamped accordingly. (§19). Amount to be paid in for stock having par value must not be less than par value of shares at date of issue. (§18). Time, place and proportions of cash payments, whether in full or by installments, may be determined by directors. (§22). Detailed statutory provisions apply in case of refusal or neglect to pay subscriptions and installments. (§§24 and 25). No stock may be issued unless cash, so far as due, or property, services or expenses for which it was authorized to be issued, has been actually received or incurred by, or conveyed or rendered to corporation, or is in its possession as surplus (§21); nor is a note or other evidence of indebtedness (secured or unsecured) of person to whom stock is issued deemed payment for stock issued (§18); and president, treasurer and directors voting therefor are jointly and severally liable to any stockholder for actual damages caused him by such issue (§60). Any unissued capital stock from time to time authorized under articles of organization may be issued by vote of stockholders, or by vote of directors under authority of by-laws or a vote of the stockholders, which vote may be adopted before or after stock is authorized. (§21).

Reacquisition of Stock.—Shares of stock previously issued which have been reacquired by corporation, may, unless articles or by-laws otherwise require, be restored to status of authorized but unissued shares by vote of stockholders or of directors, without amendment of articles. (§21A).

Transfer of Stock.—Covered by Uniform Commercial Code. (c. 106, §§8-101 through 8-407).

Closing of Transfer Books.—Directors may fix record date, not more than 60 days before date of meeting, payment of dividend or other distribution, or last day on which consent or dissent of stockholders may be expressed, for determining stockholders entitled to participate; or directors may close for such purposes transfer books for all or any part of such period. If no record date is fixed and transfer books are not closed: (a) Record date for determining stockholders having right to notice of or vote at meeting of stockholders is at close of business on day next preceding day on which notice is given, (b) record date for determining stockholders for any other purpose is at close of business on day on which board acts with respect thereto. (§42).

Stock transfer tax repealed as of May 1, 1954.

Preemptive Rights.—Stockholders have no preemptive rights unless specifically set forth in articles of organization or bylaw adopted and amendable by stockholders only. (§20).

Derivative Suits.—No stockholder may maintain any derivative suit against stockholders, directors or officers, as such, unless he owned stock in corporation at time of act or default complained of or his stock devolved upon him thereafter by operation of law from one who was stockholder at such time. (§46).

Close Corporations.—Stockholders in corporation deemed to be "close corporation" owe one another substantially same fiduciary duty in operation of enterprise that partners owe to one another. (367 Mass. 578, 328 N.E.2d 505; 370 Mass. 842, 353 N.E.2d 657; 402 Mass. 650, 524 N.E.2d 849). Fiduciary duty owed to minority shareholders in close corporation does not prevent controlling group of shareholders from exercising substantial discretion regarding business policy. (423 Mass. 461, 464, 668 N.E.2d 351, 354).

Stockholders' Liabilities.—Stockholders to whom corporation makes any distribution (other than stock of corporation) if corporation is, or is thereby rendered, insolvent are liable to corporation for amount of such distribution or amount exceeding what could be distributed without rendering corporation insolvent, but only to extent of amount paid or distributed to them respectively. Stockholder who pays on judgment or otherwise more than his proportionate share of such liability has claim for contribution. (§45).

Stockholders' meetings may be held in commonwealth or elsewhere in U.S. to extent permitted by articles of organization. (§35). Annual meeting date fixed or determined in manner provided by bylaws shall be within six months after end of fiscal year. (§33). No change shall be made within 60 days before such date.

Seven days written notice of stockholder's meeting must be given by clerk or assistant clerk, or other person authorized by bylaws, or empowered by §34 to call special meetings, to stockholders entitled to vote and other stockholders entitled to notice under articles of organization or bylaws; notice must state time, place and purposes of meeting. (§36). Any stockholder may waive notice of meeting before or after meeting by writing filed with records of meeting. (§§36 and 37). Special meetings may be called by president or directors, and shall be called by clerk, or in case of death, absence, incapacity or refusal of clerk by any other officer, on written application of one or more stockholders holding at least 10%, 40% if class of voting stock is registered under Securities Exchange Act of 1934, of stock entitled to vote. (§34). In case no officer is able and willing to call special meeting, Supreme Judicial or Superior Court, upon application of one or more stockholders who hold at least 10%, 40% or other percentage specified in articles of organization or bylaws if class of voting stock is registered as above, of voting stock, may authorize one or more of them to call meeting. (§34).

Action by stockholders may be taken without meeting if all stockholders entitled to vote on matter consent in writing filed with records of meetings of stockholders. (§43).

Voting.—Unless articles of organization or bylaws otherwise provide, majority in interest of all stock outstanding and entitled to vote constitutes quorum. (§39). Articles of organization or bylaws may provide for greater proportion of vote for certain action than is required by BCL, in which case articles or bylaws control. (§8[a]). With respect to action on which BCL requires vote of each class of stock, articles of organization or bylaws may provide that two or more classes shall vote as single class, in which case, articles or bylaws control, except that no class or series adversely affected by amendment to articles of organization (§§71, 74) shall be deprived of right to separate vote (§8[b]). Corporation may not directly or indirectly vote its own stock but this does not limit right of corporation to vote its stock held by it in fiduciary capacity. (§40). Stockholders entitled to vote have one vote for each share and proportionate vote for fraction of share. (§41). In corporations having two or more classes or series of stock, variations in voting powers of different classes or series may be fixed. (Id.). Voting by proxy, dated not more than six months before meeting, is permitted. (Id.). Notwithstanding this provision, proxy coupled with interest sufficient in law to support irrevocable power need not specify meeting to which it relates. (§41). Ballot for elections by stockholders is required if requested by stockholder entitled to vote. (§§47 and 48). Stock on which overdue demanded installments are unpaid cannot be voted. (§41).

Voting Trusts.—There is no statutory provision, but voting trusts have been held valid. (355 Mass. 671, 247 N.E.2d 567). Written agreement between two or more stockholders or between one or more stockholders and one or more other persons may provide that shares held by such stockholders will be voted under procedures set forth in agreement. (§41A).

Directors and Officers.—Every corporation shall have president, treasurer, clerk, directors, and may have such other officers as bylaws authorize. (§48). Number of directors shall not be less than three, except that whenever there shall be only two stockholders, number of directors shall be not less than two and whenever there shall be only one stockholder or prior to issuance of any stock, number of directors shall be not less than one. (§47). Unless bylaws provide otherwise, treasurer and clerk are elected at annual meeting of stockholders and president is elected at next following

See note at head of Digest as to 1998 legislation covered.

See Topical Index in front part of this volume.

MA–3

CORPORATIONS . . . *continued*

meeting of directors. (§48). President must be director unless provided otherwise in bylaws. (§48). All other officers are chosen or appointed in accordance with provisions of bylaws or, in absence of such provisions, as may be determined by directors. (§48). Unless bylaws require, directors and officers need not be stockholders. (§48). Board of directors may be enlarged by stockholders at any meeting or, if authorized by bylaws, by vote of majority of directors then in office. (§§47, 48). All vacancies are filled by directors unless articles of organization or bylaws otherwise provide. (§52). Any officer may be required to give bond as bylaws prescribe or directors determine. (§48). Clerk or assistant clerk must record all proceedings of stockholders and, unless otherwise provided in bylaws, all proceedings of directors. (§48). Term of directors and president, treasurer and clerk is one year and until their successors are chosen and qualified, except that directors, by provision in articles, may be divided into classes, holding office from one to five years, term of at least one class expiring each year, and elected, if desired, by different classes of stock. (§50). Articles of organization may provide for termination of directors and officers elected by stockholders, upon specified events. (§50). Directors of corporation which has, or within 12 months has had, class of stock registered under Securities Exchange Act of 1934 as amended shall be classified into three classes of as equal number as possible, classes to hold office for one, two and three years, one class to be elected each year. (§50A[a]). Directors or 2/3ds of stockholders may elect exemption from classification requirement. (§50A[b][ii]). Unless articles of organization or bylaws provide otherwise, any director or officer may be removed with or without cause by body that elected him and director or officer elected by stockholders may be removed for cause by directors. Removal for cause requires notice and hearing. (§51).

There is no requirement that directors or officers be U.S. citizens, or residents of Massachusetts, except that clerk must be resident of commonwealth unless corporation has resident agent. (§48).

Directors' meetings may be held within or without commonwealth. (§56). Regular meetings may be held without notice at time and place fixed by bylaws or by board. (§56). Special meetings are held upon notice. (§56). Notice may be waived before or after meeting by writing filed with records of meeting. (§§56 and 58). Majority of directors in office constitutes quorum. (§57). Any action may be taken without meeting, if all directors consent thereto in writing filed with records of meetings of directors. (§59). Members of board of directors or any committee thereof may participate in meetings by means of conference telephone or similar communications equipment. (§59).

Powers and Duties of Directors.—Directors shall manage business and may exercise all powers of corporation, except such as by law, articles of organization or bylaws are conferred upon or reserved to stockholders. (§§47, 54). Corporation may provide in its articles of organization or bylaws for committees to be elected from and by its board of directors, and board of directors may, with certain statutory exceptions, delegate to any such committee some or all of its powers. (§55).

Liability of Directors and Officers.—Directors and officers of corporation who sign any statement or report required by BCL which is false in any material representation are jointly and severally liable to creditor of corporation who has relied upon false representation to extent of actual damage sustained by him by reason of reliance but not for debts contracted or contracts entered into after filing of statement or report in which such false statement is corrected. (§63).

President, treasurer, and directors who vote for issuance of stock in violation of law are jointly and severally liable to each stockholder for actual damages caused by such issuance. (§60).

Corporation may adopt provisions in its articles of organization to exempt or limit director's personal liability to corporation or its stockholders for monetary damages for breach of fiduciary duty notwithstanding any provision of law imposing such liability. (§13[b][1½]). Such provision, however, shall not eliminate or limit director's liability for: (i) Breach of director's duty of loyalty to corporation or its stockholders; (ii) director's acts or omissions not in good faith or involving intentional misconduct or knowing violation of law; (iii) director's vote for unauthorized distributions under §61 and §62 (described infra); or (iv) any transaction from which director derived improper personal benefit. (§13[b][1½]). No provision adopted pursuant to this clause shall eliminate or limit director liability for any act or omission occurring prior to date upon which such provision becomes effective. (§13[b]).

Incorporators and officers of corporation who sign any articles of organization, amendment, consolidation or merger false in any material respect are jointly and severally liable to any stockholder of corporation or resulting or surviving corporation for actual damage sustained by reason of reliance upon such statement, but not by reason of such reliance occurring after filing of corrected or amended articles of organization, etc. in which such false statement is corrected. (§64).

Anyone who knowingly makes, executes, files or publishes any report or statement required by corporation in this commonwealth (§68), or makes, executes or publishes in commonwealth any report or statement required by law of another state or country (§69) which is false in any material representation or whoever causes same to be done shall be punished by fine of not more than $5,000, imprisonment of not more than three years or both. (§§68 and 69).

Directors who vote for any distribution (other than distribution of shares of corporation) to one or more stockholders, whether by way of dividend, repurchase of corporation's stock or otherwise, in violation of articles of organization, are jointly and severally liable to corporation for excess of distribution over amount which could have been distributed without such violation, to extent such excess is not repaid. (§61). If corporation is or is thereby rendered insolvent, directors voting for such distribution, whether or not in violation of articles, are jointly and severally liable to corporation for amount of such distribution made while insolvent, or for amount by which distribution exceeds what could have been made without rendering corporation insolvent, to extent such distribution, or such excess, is not repaid. (§61). Directors who authorized distribution are not liable for distribution to stockholders if it could have been made without violating articles, or rendering corporation insolvent, at time authorized, even though subsequent payment causes such violation or insolvency. (§61).

Directors who vote for, and officers who knowingly participate in, loan of corporate assets to any director or officer are jointly and severally liable to corporation for any portion not repaid unless majority of directors who are not loan recipients or holders of majority of voting shares who are not loan recipients approve or ratify loan as in their judgment reasonably expected to benefit corporation. (§62).

There is right of contribution among officers and directors adjudged or ascertained to be liable upon same claim under any of above paragraphs regarding liability. (§66). However, it is complete defense to any claim under §§61-64, 66 or otherwise (except as expressly provided by statute) that director, officer or incorporator has performed duties as such, or as board committee member, "in good faith and in a manner he reasonably believes to be in the best interests of corporation, and with such care as ordinarily prudent person in a like position would use under similar circumstances" and he may rely on opinions and reports, including financial records, of officers or employees reasonably believed to be reliable and competent, counsel, accounts or other professionals or experts or, in case of director, board committees on which he does not serve, provided he does not have knowledge that would cause such reliance to be unwarranted. (§65). Determination of best interests of corporation includes consideration of interests of employees, suppliers, creditors and customers, economy of state, region and nation, community and societal considerations and long-term and short-term interests of corporation and stockholders, including possibility that these may be best served by continuing independence. (§65).

Directors, officers, employees and other agents of corporation, and persons who serve at corporation's request as directors, officers, employees, or other agents of another organization, or who serve at corporation's request in any capacity with respect to any employee benefit plan may be indemnified to extent authorized by articles of organization, or bylaw or vote adopted by stockholders. (§67). Except as otherwise provided in articles or bylaw, directors may authorize indemnification of employees, agents of corporation, officers, employees, or other agents of another organization, or who serve at corporation's request in any capacity with respect to any employee benefit plan. (§67). Indemnification includes payment by corporation of expenses incurred in defending civil or criminal action or proceeding in advance of final disposition of such action or proceeding, if person indemnified gives undertaking to repay such payment if later adjudicated to be not entitled to indemnification. (§67). Indemnification may be provided although person no longer officer, director, employee or agent of corporation or of such other organization or no longer serves with respect to corporation's employee benefit plan. (§67). No indemnification may be provided for any person with respect to any matter as to which he shall have been adjudicated not to have acted in good faith in reasonable belief that his action was in best interests of corporation or, to extent that such matter relates to service with respect to employee benefit plan, in best interests of participants or beneficiaries of such plan. Corporation may maintain insurance on behalf of any person who is or was director, officer, employee or other agent of corporation or is or was serving at request of corporation as director, officer, employee, or other agent of another organization or with respect to any employee benefit plan, against liability incurred in such capacity or arising out of his status as such, whether or not corporation would have power to indemnify him against such liability. (§67).

Limited Liability.—See topic Limited Liability Companies.

Officers.—See subhead Directors and Officers, supra.

Principal Office.—Articles of organization must specify initial principal office within commonwealth. (§13). Directors may from time to time change principal office. (§14).

Resident Agent.—Incorporators or directors may appoint resident agent as attorney upon whom process against corporation may be served. (§49).

Individuals with residence and place of business in commonwealth, domestic corporation or foreign qualified corporation which has office in commonwealth may be appointed resident agent. Appointment is effective upon filing with state secretary of articles of organization (in case of appointment by incorporators) or certificate of appointment (on form supplied by state secretary) signed by clerk with copy of directors' vote. Appointment may be revoked and new agent appointed by directors, in which event new certificate and vote must be filed. Resident agent must file certificate with state secretary of any change of agent's business address and may resign by giving corporation and secretary prescribed notice. (§49). Penalties are imposed for failure to have either clerk who is resident of commonwealth or resident agent. (§53).

Dividends.—See subheads Stockholders' Liabilities and Liability of Directors and Officers, supra.

Lists of dividends unclaimed for two years or more and names and last known addresses of persons to whose credit such dividends stand must, at least once in five years, be published in newspaper. (§31). See category Property, topic Absentees, subhead Escheat.

Sale or Transfer of Corporate Assets.—Every corporation may by vote of two-thirds, or lesser proportion (but not less than majority) if articles of organization so provide, of each class of stock outstanding and entitled to vote, authorize sale, lease or exchange of all or substantially all its assets. (§75[a]). Notice of meeting shall be given to each stockholder, whether or not entitled to vote. Stockholder consent to mortgage, pledge or granting of security interest in assets is not necessary unless required by articles of organization. (§75[b]). In case of consummated sale, lease or exchange, stockholder who objects in prescribed manner and does not vote in favor is entitled to appraisal and payment for his stock in accordance with §§86-98, inclusive. (§76).

Sale or transfer other than in ordinary course of business of all or substantially all of assets of corporation situated in Massachusetts gives rise to lien upon all such assets in favor of commonwealth to extent necessary to satisfy excise taxes, unless five days prior notice and tax returns are filed with commissioner of revenue ("commissioner") and at or prior to sale or transfer excise taxes are paid; lien may be waived by commissioner before or after transfer. (c. 62C, §51).

Any recordable instrument purporting to affect interest in real estate, executed in name of corporation by president or vice-president and treasurer or assistant treasurer

---

See note at head of Digest as to 1998 legislation covered.

See Topical Index in front part of this volume.

CORPORATIONS . . . continued

(who may be one and same person) shall be binding on corporation in favor of purchaser or other person relying in good faith on such instrument, notwithstanding inconsistent provisions of articles of organization, bylaws, certificate of incorporation, charter, special act of incorporation, constitution, or votes of corporation. (§115).

Books and Records.—Original, or attested copies of articles of organization, by-laws, and records of all meetings of incorporators and stockholders, and stock and transfer records (said attested copies and records being competent evidence in any court of commonwealth), containing list of all stockholders, their addresses and amounts of stock held by each, must be kept in commonwealth by every corporation at its principal office or office of its transfer agent, clerk or resident agent for inspection by stockholders. Copies and records need not all be kept in same office. Refusal or neglect of any officer or agent having charge of any of foregoing to exhibit them in legible form or submit list of stockholders to examination makes him and/or corporation liable to any stockholder for actual damages and SJC or Superior Court may order exhibition, but it is defense to action for damages or suit to order exhibition that actual purpose and reason for inspection sought were to secure, for purpose of sale, list of stockholders or to use list for purpose other than in interest of applicant, as stockholder, relative to affairs of corporation. (§32).

Reports.—Every corporation must submit to state secretary annually, within 30 days after its annual meeting, report of condition signed under penalties of perjury by officer. (§109). Penalties including dissolution may be decreed for failure to file. (§§101 and 112). Filing fee for this report is determined annually by secretary of administration, currently $85. (§114).

Certificate of any change in directors, president, treasurer or clerk must, within 30 days of change, be filed by clerk or assistant clerk with state secretary; penalties are imposed for failure to file. If corporation fails or refuses to file certificate of change within said 30-day period, any director or officer involved in change may evidence change by filing his own certificate stating therein that copy thereof has been mailed to corporation. (§53). Forms may be obtained from state secretary. No filing fee. (§114[g]).

Clerk or assistant clerk must file (on forms furnished by state secretary) certificate of change in fiscal year. (§38A). No filing fee. (§114[g]).

SJC may enjoin further prosecution of business until penalties have been paid and aforementioned reports and certificates have been filed. (§113). Criminal penalties are imposed for making, executing or publishing report which is knowingly false in any material representation. (§68). Criminal penalties are also imposed for publication of prospectus, book, notice, etc. which wilfully misstates corporate assets or financial affairs in order to influence apparent value of stock. (c. 266, §92). Creditor who relies on false report or statement may recover actual damages caused by such reliance from directors and officers who have signed report. (§63).

Clerk or assistant clerk must file with state secretary certificate of change of principal office in commonwealth. Such change is not effective until certificate filed. (§14). No filing fee. (§114[g]).

Domestic or foreign corporation doing business in Massachusetts must file information returns with commissioner on or before June 1 in each year with respect to Massachusetts residents or persons employed in Massachusetts to whom it has during preceding calendar year paid compensation, interest or annuities. Domestic corporation and foreign corporation doing business in Massachusetts must also file with commissioner annually on or before June 1 list of all Massachusetts residents and other persons deriving income in Massachusetts to whom it paid any income subject to taxation under c. 62 during preceding calendar year, stating amounts of such income paid by it. (c. 62C).

For returns which must be filed in connection with taxes payable by corporations, see infra, subhead Taxation, catchlines Domestic Corporations, and Foreign Corporations.

Errors in Filed Documents.—Error in any filed documents may be corrected by filing certificate of correction. (§6A). Corrected document takes effect day of filing original document. To those persons adversely or substantially affected by correction, document is effective from date of filing correction. (§6A).

Corporate Bonds or Mortgages.—For authorization required for mortgage of all assets see supra subhead Sale or Transfer of Corporate Assets.

Merger and Consolidation.—Two or more domestic corporations may consolidate to form new domestic corporation or merge into one of constituent corporations. (§78[a]). Such corporations enter into agreement of consolidation or merger which must set forth required information specified in §78. Agreement may contain any provisions that are permitted by BCL to be included in articles of organization. (§78[b][7]). Aggregate par value of shares with par value plus aggregate principal amount of any securities representing indebtedness of surviving or resulting corporations substituted for outstanding shares of constituent corporations must not exceed value of net assets of constituent corporations. (§78[b][6]). Agreement must be approved by vote of two-thirds, or lesser proportion (but not less than majority) if articles of organization so provide, of each class of stock of each constituent corporation entitled to vote at meeting called for purpose, provided that unless required by articles, merger agreement may be approved without stockholder action of surviving constituent corporation, by vote of its directors, if certain provisions of articles of organization of such corporation are not changed, shares to be issued pursuant to agreement do not exceed 15% of shares of such corporation of same class outstanding immediately before merger and issue by directors is properly authorized under §21. (§78[c]). At least 20 days notice of meeting must be given to each stockholder (whether or not entitled to vote). (§78[c][i][ii]). Resulting or surviving corporation must furnish copy of agreement to any stockholder of it or any constituent corporation upon written request and must keep original or attested copy at office in Massachusetts for inspection by such persons. (§78[d]). Articles of consolidation or merger must be filed with state secretary stating due adoption of agreement, names of constituent and resulting or surviving corporation, effective date and any charter amendments effected by agreement (or, in respect of resulting corporation, corporate purposes, authorized

capital, description of classes of stock if more than one, and any other lawful provisions which may be contained in articles of organization) and that copy of agreement will be furnished as aforesaid without charge. (§78[d]). Articles are signed by president or vice president and clerk or assistant clerk of each constituent, who must state under oath that agreement has been duly executed and approved. (§78[d][3][iii][d]).

One or more domestic corporations may consolidate or merge with one or more foreign corporations if laws of foreign state or states permit. (§79[a]). Resulting or surviving corporation may be organized under laws of state of any of constituent corporations. (§79[a]). Such corporations enter into agreement of consolidation or merger which must specify state under laws of which resulting or surviving corporation is to be organized. (§79[b]). Agreement must comply with laws of that state. (If Massachusetts, §78). If resulting or surviving corporation is to be organized under laws of foreign state, such corporation must: (1) Agree that it may be sued in commonwealth for any prior obligation of any constituent domestic corporation and of any constituent foreign corporation qualified to do business in commonwealth and for any obligation thereafter incurred by resulting or surviving corporation (including obligation to dissenting stockholders); and (2) appoint state secretary as its agent to accept service of process in action for enforcement of any such obligation. (§79[c]). Each of constituent corporations must adopt agreement of consolidation or merger in accordance with laws of state in which it is organized. (§79[c]). Resulting or surviving corporation must furnish copy of agreement to any stockholder of it or any constituent corporation upon written request and must keep original or attested copy at office in Massachusetts if it is Massachusetts corporation or otherwise wherever records of its stockholders' meetings are permitted to be kept. (§79[c][2]). Articles of consolidation or merger must be filed with state secretary stating substantially same information required in case of consolidation or merger of domestic corporation. Articles are signed by president or vice president and clerk or assistant clerk of Massachusetts constituents and corresponding officers of foreign constituents, who must state under oath that agreement has been duly executed and approved, or adopted, as required by laws of their respective states. (§79[c][3]).

Stockholders in domestic corporation which has voted to consolidate or merge under above provisions who objects in prescribed manner to consolidation or merger may demand from resulting or surviving corporation payment for his stock and appraisal thereof. (§85). However this does not apply to shareholders in surviving constituent corporation if merger did not require vote of stockholders of surviving corporation. (§85). Stockholder must before vote is taken file written objection to proposed action stating that he intends to demand payment for his shares if proposed action is taken, not vote in favor of action, and within 20 days after notice is mailed that merger or consolidation is effective, make written demand for payment for stock. (§§86-98, inclusive). Corporation upon which such demand is made shall pay him fair value of his stock within 30 days after expiration of period during which such demand may be made. (§89).

Domestic corporation owning at least 90% of each class of outstanding stock of domestic and/or foreign corporation and foreign corporation having such ownership of stock of domestic corporation may merge subsidiary into itself by vote of directors of parent if laws of any foreign state involved permit. (§82[a]). Vote must specify effective date of merger and, if parent does not own all of subsidiary's outstanding stock, terms and conditions of merger. Articles of merger must be filed with state secretary. (§82[b]). Articles must set forth vote and state effective date of merger, and in case of foreign parent, articles must contain: (1) Agreement of parent that it may be sued in commonwealth for any prior obligation of subsidiary and any obligation thereafter incurred by parent (including obligation to any dissenting stockholder of subsidiary); and (2) appointment of state secretary as its agent to accept service of process in action for enforcement of any such obligation. (§82[b]). Articles are signed by president (or vice-president) and clerk (or assistant clerk) of parent (or if parent is foreign corporation, by corresponding officers) who make affidavit that directors' vote was duly adopted and that parent owned at least 90% of stock of subsidiary. (§82[b]). Merger is effective upon filing of articles or upon later effective date (not more than 30 days after such filing) specified in articles. (§82[b]). If parent does not own all of stock of subsidiary, notice of merger must be given to each stockholder by registered or certified mail within ten days after effective date of merger. (§82[c]). Within 20 days after mailing of notice, each other stockholder may demand from parent payment for his stock and appraisal thereof. (§82[c]).

Voluntary association or trust, if at least 90% of certificates of participation or shares of each class are owned by domestic corporation, may be merged into such corporation. (§83[b]). Likewise voluntary association or trust owning at least 90% of each class of outstanding stock of domestic corporation may be merged into corporation. In both cases, written instrument or declaration of trust under which association or trust is formed or regulated must permit merger. (§83[b]). Corporation and association or trust enter into agreement which must state terms and conditions of merger, effective date and, if corporation does not own all of certificates or shares of association or trust, consideration to be paid by corporation with respect to each certificate or share not owned by it. (§83[b]). Agreement is approved by directors and executed by president (or vice-president) and treasurer (or assistant treasurer) of corporation and approved and executed by association or trust. (§83[c]). Copy of agreement must be furnished to any stockholder of corporation or holder of shares or participant in trust or association upon written request, and original or attested copy must be kept at office in Massachusetts for inspection by such persons. (§83[d]). Articles of merger must be filed with state secretary stating names of constituents, effective date and that corporation will furnish copy of agreement as aforesaid without charge. (§83[d][3]). Articles are signed by president (or vice-president) and clerk (or assistant clerk) of corporation and by authorized persons for association or trust, stating under penalties of perjury that requisite percentage of ownership exists and that agreement was duly approved. (§83[d][3]). Merger is effective when articles are filed or on later effective date as specified but not more than 30 days after such filing. (§83[d][3]). If corporation or association or trust does not own all of certificates, or shares or stock (as case may be) of other, corporation must send notice by registered or certified mail to holders of certificates or shares of association or trust (if corporation is parent) or to stockholders of corporation (if association or trust is parent) within ten days after effective date of

CORPORATIONS . . . *continued*

merger. (§83[f]). Within 20 days from mailing of notice, such holders may demand from corporation payment for their certificates or shares or their stock, as case may be, and appraisal thereof. (§83[f][3]).

Any corporation and foreign corporation as defined in c. 181, §1, may merge into one or more domestic limited liability companies or foreign limited liability companies. (§83A). If domestic entity is not surviving entity, that domestic corporation must file copy of certificate of consolidation or merger with state secretary within 30 days of transaction. (§83A).

With respect to all consolidations and mergers under BCL certified copy of articles of consolidation or merger or state secretary's certificate of filing of same must be filed within 20 days after effective date of consolidation or merger in registry of deeds in each district within commonwealth in which real property of constituent corporation, or association or trust is situated, except that no filing need be made with respect to real property of constituent corporation which is surviving corporation. (§§78[e]; 79[d]; 82[c]; 83[e]). In addition, when association or trust has merged into corporation, copy of articles of merger must be filed in office of clerk of city or town in which association or trust has its principal place of business. (§83[e]).

Acquisitions of stock of banking institutions are regulated specially by statute. (c. 167A, §4a).

Fee for consolidation or merger is determined annually by secretary of administration, currently $250 minimum. (§114[d]).

Tender Offers.—See category Business Regulation and Commerce, topic Securities, subhead Tender Offers.

Dissolution.—Corporation may, unless otherwise provided in its articles of organization, by vote of majority of each class outstanding entitled to vote, authorize petition (setting forth in substance grounds) for dissolution to be filed in SJC, or such petition may be filed by holders of not less than 40% of capital stock outstanding entitled to vote if directors are deadlocked in management of corporate affairs and stockholders are unable to break deadlock or if stockholders are deadlocked in voting power and no directors are elected; and after notice and hearing decree of dissolution may be entered. (§99). Corporation may be voluntarily dissolved by filing of articles of dissolution. (§100). Dissolution may be authorized by vote of two-thirds of each outstanding class of stock entitled to vote or by compliance with provisions of articles of organization. (§100[a]). Within 30 days after authorization notice must be given to commissioner of revenue. (§100[b]). Articles of Dissolution signed by president (or vice president) and clerk (or assistant clerk) must thereafter be filed with state secretary. (§100[c]). Dissolution is effective upon filing of articles or at later effective date (not more than 30 days after such filing) specified in articles provided state secretary has received certificate of commissioner of revenue that all taxes due under c. 62C have been paid or provided for. (§100[d]).

Corporation may also be dissolved by state secretary if corporation fails for two consecutive years to file reports with state secretary or tax returns with commissioner of revenue or pay taxes due under c. 62C, or provide for otherwise, or if state secretary is satisfied that corporation has become inactive and that its dissolution would be in public interest. (§101). State secretary shall give corporation at least 90 days' notice of proposed dissolution with copy to commissioner of revenue stating that corporation will be dissolved 90 days after notice or such later date as state secretary shall order. (§101). Notice shall state reasons for dissolution and corporation may request hearing within 60 days. (§101). If after hearing secretary finds cause, corporation shall be dissolved 30 days after notice of such finding is given to corporation. Corporation shall not be dissolved for failure to file reports or tax returns or tax payments if same are filed at least ten days before effective date of dissolution and state secretary has received certificate of commissioner of revenue that corporation is in good standing regarding returns due and taxes payable. (§101). Upon application by interested party state secretary may revive corporation for any purpose with or without limitation in time. (§108). Every corporation continues as body corporate for three years after its existence is terminated for other purposes by dissolution, expiration of its charter by limitation, or in any other manner, for purpose of prosecuting and defending suits and enabling it gradually to settle its affairs, dispose of and convey its property and distribute its net assets to its stockholders, but not to continue business for which established, and for purposes of any suit brought by or against it within or prior to said three years it continues beyond said period for further period of 90 days after final judgment in suit. (§102). At any time within three years (or within extension of said three year period by pendency of any suit) corporation may petition SJC or Superior Court for leave to distribute assets; and after notice by certified or registered mail to state secretary, commissioner of corporations and taxation and all known creditors and by publication for three successive weeks in newspaper of general circulation and hearing, court may authorize distribution and directors will not be liable therefor. (§103).

Insolvency and Receivers.—On application to SJC or Superior Court by creditor or stockholder, receivers may be appointed to wind up corporation, existence of which has been terminated for other purposes by dissolution, expiration of term of existence or other reason, and powers of such receivers and existence of corporation may be continued as long as court finds necessary for said purposes. (§104). Receivers may also be appointed if judgment has been recovered against corporation and it has neglected for 30 days after demand made on execution to pay or exhibit property sufficient to satisfy execution and it has been returned unsatisfied. (§105). Such receivers shall pay debts of corporation (ratably, if funds in their hands are insufficient, in manner directed by court) and distribute any balance remaining to former stockholders or legal representatives. (§106).

Reorganization.—Any plan of reorganization pursuant to any statute of U.S. confirmed by decree of court of competent jurisdiction may be carried out pursuant to such decree without further action by directors and stockholders. (§73). See subhead Amendment of Articles, supra.

Foreign Corporations.—Governed by c. 181 and § numbers herein refer to sections of that chapter. Foreign corporation is corporation organized other than under laws of Massachusetts. (§1). It may not undertake any type of business in Massachusetts

prohibited to domestic corporation. (§2). Every foreign corporation which does business in Massachusetts or which has usual place of business therein, or which owns or leases real estate therein without having such usual place of business, or which is engaged therein, permanently or temporarily, and with or without usual place of business therein, in construction, erection, alteration or repair of building, bridge, railroad, railway or structure of any kind, or in construction or repair of roads, highways or waterways, or in any other activity requiring performance of labor, shall be considered to be doing business in Massachusetts unless its activities within Massachusetts consist of no more than one or more of following: (a) Maintaining bank accounts; (b) maintaining or appointing trustees, depositaries, or agencies for holding, transfer, exchange or registration of its securities; (c) holding meetings of its directors or shareholders; (d) participating or appearing in any action or suit or any administrative or arbitration proceeding, or in settlement of claims or disputes; or (e) performing activities subject to regulations under c. 167 or c. 175, if foreign corporation has complied with provisions of applicable chapter or chapters. (§3).

Within ten days after commencement of doing business in Massachusetts, foreign corporation shall file with state secretary certificate (on form supplied by state secretary) signed under penalty of perjury by its president or vice-president and its clerk or assistant clerk or secretary or assistant secretary, accompanied by certificate of legal existence from state of domicile, setting forth: (1) Its exact name; (2) location of principal office; (3) brief description of activities within Massachusetts; (4) location of any local office and name and address of any resident agent; (5) names and residences of its president, treasurer, clerk or secretary and directors; (6) fiscal year; (7) date of organization and jurisdiction under which organized; (8) duration of existence; and (9) statement of fees imposed by jurisdiction under whose laws it is organized on corporations organized under Massachusetts law or their agents doing business in that jurisdiction. (§4). Any change in name, principal office location or description of corporate activities shall be reported to state secretary in amended certificate in required form, signed as aforesaid, within 60 days of effective date of such change. (§4). Filing fee for initial certificate is determined annually by secretary of administration, (§7), currently $300 minimum. Corporations from Texas, Oregon, Oklahoma, Alaska, and Mississippi are subject to higher fees. Every foreign corporation shall annually, on or before 15th day of third month after close of its fiscal year, submit report of condition with state secretary, on required form, signed by officer setting forth: (1) Its exact name; (2) location of principal office; (3) location of any local office and name and address of any resident agent; (4) names and residences of its president, treasurer, clerk or secretary and all directors and date upon which term of office of each expires; and (5) amount of authorized and issued capital stock, including number and any par value. (§4). Filing fee is determined annually by secretary of administration, (§7), currently $85.

No foreign corporation doing business in Massachusetts shall assume name or trade name of another corporation established under Massachusetts law, or of corporation wherever established, firm association or person carrying on business in Massachusetts at time of incorporation or change of name of subject corporation or within three years prior thereto, or assume name which is under reservation under laws of Massachusetts for another or proposed corporation wherever established, or assume name so similar to any of foregoing as to be likely to be mistaken for it, except with written consent of said corporation, etc. (§5). SJC or Superior Court shall have jurisdiction to enjoin such foreign corporation from doing business under name assumed in violation of any provision of this section, although initial or amended certificates may have been approved and filed. (§5). Availability of name may be checked by telephone ([617] 727-9640), and may be reserved only by writing. Name may be reserved for 30 days upon written request and payment of fee determined annually by secretary of administration, currently $15. Upon written request and payment of fee determined annually by secretary of administration, currently $15, state secretary will extend reservations for 30 days. (§5). See also category Intellectual Property, topic Trademarks and Tradenames.

If laws of any other jurisdiction impose on corporations organized under Massachusetts law or their agents doing business in Massachusetts any fees as condition of doing business in that jurisdiction in addition to or in excess of those imposed by this chapter upon foreign corporations and their agents, like fees shall be imposed by state secretary upon all foreign corporations organized under laws of such jurisdiction and their agents doing business in Massachusetts as long as such laws remain in force. (§8).

Every foreign corporation which fails to file initial certificate or amended certificate as required by §4 shall, for each such failure and for each year that each such failure shall continue, be fined not more than $500. (§9). Annual report of condition filed late subject to additional fee, currently $25. (§9). No such failure shall affect validity of any contract involving foreign corporation, but no action shall be maintained or recovery had in any of courts of commonwealth by foreign corporation as long as such failure continues. (§9). If foreign corporation fails to file report of condition within six months of date prescribed, state secretary shall give notice by certified mail to corporation of its default. If foreign corporation fails to comply within 30 days after such notice of default has been so mailed, it shall be fined not more than $10 for each day for 15 days after expiration of said 30 days, and not more than $200 for each day thereafter during which such default continues, or any lesser sum that court may deem just and equitable. (§9). Court may issue injunction restraining further prosecution of business of foreign corporation, and further exercise of any corporate rights, privileges or franchises in Massachusetts, until such penalties with interest and costs have been paid and until foreign corporation has filed all certificates and reports required by §4. (§9).

Any officer of foreign corporation who signs any statement or report required by this chapter which is false in any material representation and that he knows or has reason to know to be false shall be liable to creditor of foreign corporation who has relied upon such false representation to extent of actual damage sustained by him by reason of such reliance; provided that officer signing false report of condition shall not be liable to creditors for debts contracted or contracts entered into after filing of report of condition or corrected report of condition that is not false in any material representation. (§10). No liability shall be imposed under §10 upon any officer who shall have

CORPORATIONS . . . *continued*
discharged duties of his position in good faith and with degree of diligence, care and skill that prudent men would ordinarily exercise under similar circumstances in like position. (§11). In discharging his duties such person, when acting in good faith, shall be entitled to rely upon books of account of foreign corporation or upon written reports made to foreign corporation by any of its officers, other than such person, or by independent public accountant. (§11). Any officer who pays on judgment rendered on claim asserted under §10 shall be entitled to contribution from other officers against whom judgment has been entered on same claim or who shall be ascertained to be liable to plaintiff upon same claim. (§12). Whoever knowingly makes, executes, files or publishes any report or statement required by law to be made, executed, filed or published by foreign corporation in Massachusetts, or whoever causes same to be done, which report or statement is false in any material representation, shall be punished by fine of not more than $5,000 or by imprisonment for not more than three years, or both. (§13). Whoever knowingly makes, executes, files or publishes any report or statement required by law of another state or country to be made, executed, or published by foreign corporation, or whoever causes same to be done, within Massachusetts, which report or statement is false in any material representation, shall be punished by fine of not more than $5,000 or by imprisonment for not more than three years, or both. (§14).

Foreign corporations shall be liable to be sued and to have their property attached in same manner and to same extent as individuals who are residents of other states. (§15). Every foreign corporation doing business in Massachusetts which has not complied with provisions of §4 and every foreign corporation which has complied with such provisions but whose resident agent cannot, after diligent search by authorized legal agent, be found shall be deemed to have appointed state secretary as its attorney for service of process. (§15). Service of process in all judicial and administrative proceedings against foreign corporation doing business in Massachusetts may be made upon state secretary. Service of process in all judicial and administrative proceedings against foreign corporation formerly doing business in Massachusetts including one that has withdrawn from Massachusetts, may be made upon state secretary if proceeding involves liability alleged to have been incurred by foreign corporation while it was doing business in Massachusetts. (§15).

Withdrawal of Foreign Corporation.—Foreign corporation formerly doing business in Massachusetts may withdraw upon filing with state secretary certificate of withdrawal signed under penalties of perjury by its president or vice-president, and its clerk or assistant clerk or its secretary or assistant secretary or, if foreign corporation is in hands of receiver or trustee, by such receiver or trustee, in required form, setting forth: (1) Its exact name; (2) location of its principal office; (3) names and residences of its president, treasurer, clerk or secretary and directors; (4) date of fiscal year; and (5) that foreign corporation is not doing business in commonwealth. State secretary shall not receive for filing certificate of withdrawal unless it is accompanied by certificate of commissioner that all taxes due and payable by foreign corporation to commonwealth have been paid or provided for. Filing fee determined annually by secretary of administration, currently $100. (§16).

Taxation.—

All Corporations.—Generally, every business or manufacturing corporation, domestic or foreign, is taxable locally on its real estate, poles, underground conduits, wires and pipes. (c. 59, §§2, 5[16]). Real estate tax based on value as of Jan. 1. Buildings and other things erected on or affixed to land between Jan. 2 and June 30 of fiscal year preceding that to which tax relates deemed part of such real estate as of Jan. 1. (c. 59, §2A). In addition, machinery used in conduct of business and owned by or in possession of corporation which has not been classified as manufacturing corporation is subject to local taxation. Such machinery does not include stock-in-trade or refrigeration, air conditioning or accounting or administrative equipment. (c. 59, §5[16]). Machinery regularly used locally in course of business considered situated there for local tax purposes regardless of its physical location Jan. 1. Taxes on machinery used in transporting persons or goods must be apportioned to reflect amount of time machinery physically located in city or town. (c. 59, §18). Classification of corporations is made annually by commissioner of revenue ("commissioner"). (c. 58, §2). Commissioner may revoke classification and assess excise due retroactively. (396 Mass. 137, 484 N.E.2d 1005). Commissioner of Revenue may prescribe regulations necessary to carry out intent and purpose of cc. 62C, 60A, 62-65C, §10 of c. 121A and §21 of c. 138 and has done so with respect to taxation of corporations. (830 CMR §63 et seq.). All corporations not exempt under c. 59, §5, 3rd and 10th are also subject to annual excise tax on motor vehicles at any time during year registered in Commonwealth. (c. 60A, §1). All corporations also subject to excise (income) tax. See following paragraphs.

Domestic Corporations.—Defined as corporations subject to cc. 156, 156A, 156B or 180 which have privileges, powers, rights or immunities not possessed by individuals or partnerships, but excluding corporations organized under c. 157, §10 (agricultural cooperatives), domestic manufacturing corporations (defined in c. 63, §§38C, 38[K]& [l]), corporate regulated investment companies under IRC §851 (c. 63, §30, 1st), and corporations exempt from federal tax under IRC §501 (c. 63, §30, 1st). All domestic corporations doing business in Commonwealth must pay, as excise tax for each taxable year, $7 per $1,000 of value of its tangible property as determined under c. 63, §30 or its net worth as determined under c. 63, §8; 8.33% of its net worth or $400, whichever is greater. (c. 63, §32). Net income to be allocated to Massachusetts is corporation's "net income" as defined in c. 63, §§30-33, 38-38M, with modifications described in c. 63, §§38, 38A.

Actual rate determined each year by commissioner based on amount collected in previous year. (c. 63, §31B). "Tangible property corporation" is corporation whose tangible property situated in Massachusetts on last day of taxable year and not subject to local taxation is 10% or more of that portion of its total assets allocated to Massachusetts. (c. 63, §30, 10th). Book values are used for this computation. Assets are allocated to Massachusetts by subtracting from book value of all assets book value of tangible property subject to local taxation, and multiplying remainder by income allocation percentage determined under c. 63, §38. (c. 63, §30, 10th). Corporation which is not tangible property corporation is intangible property corporation. (c. 63, §30, 11th).

For a tangible property corporation, taxable tangible property is original cost less depreciation or amortization taken for shareholder reporting purposes of tangible property situated in Massachusetts on last day of taxable year and not subject to local taxation. (c. 63, §30, 7th). If corporation has transferred its tangible property to reduce its excise, commissioner may determine amount of its taxable tangible property on basis of average of such tangible property held during taxable year. (c. 63, §30, 7th).

For an intangible property corporation, taxable net worth is aggregate book value of its assets on last day of taxable year, less sum of (a) liabilities; (b) book value of tangible property situated in Massachusetts and subject to local taxation (less interest of any mortgagee therein); and (c) book value of investments in domestic subsidiaries representing 80% or more of their voting stock, multiplied by income allocation percentage determined under c. 63, §38. (c. 63, §30, 8th). In determining book value, commissioner may disallow any reserve which he deems not reasonable and proper. (c. 63, §30, 8th)

Special provisions apply to domestic corporations which are subsidiaries of or corporations otherwise closely affiliated with other corporations to ensure tax is imposed on true earnings of such domestic corporations. (c. 63, §33).

Net income is gross income less deductions, not credits, allowed under IRC, except for deductions allocable to one or more classes of income not included in corporations taxable net income pursuant to c. 63, §38(a). (c. 63, §40, 4th). Five percent of dividends not included in taxable net income shall be included pursuant to c. 63, §38(a). Net operating loss (nol) is amount by which deductions allowed under §30, 4th, exceed gross income for taxable year. (c. 63, §30, 5th). Nol's sustained after Dec. 31, 1989 are allowed as deduction in determining net income with following limitations: (1) 25% of net income for period between Dec. 31, 1990 and Dec. 31, 1991; (2) 50% of net income for period between Dec. 31, 1991 and Dec. 31, 1992; 75% of net income for period between Dec. 31, 1992 and Dec. 31, 1993; (4) 100% of net income for period after Dec. 31, 1993. (c. 63, §30, 5th[b]). Nol may not be carried forward more than five years and cannot be carried back. (c. 63, §30, 5th[b]). Carry over losses, determined under IRC §172 available during corporations first five years of existence provided that 50% of voting stock is not owned by another corporation. (c. 63, §30, 5th[c]). Corporations may deduct as adjustment to net income 95% of dividends received from corporations owned at least 15% by recipient corporation. (c. 63, §38[a][i]). Corporations may deduct amount equal to credit allowed under IRC §51 for wages deemed compensation paid in Massachusetts under c. 63, §38(e). (c. 63, §38I). In lieu of above deduction, business corporations may deduct, in addition to any other deduction allowable under c. 63, 25% of compensation paid to individuals employed in certified business facilities and living in area that either is currently classified as poverty area or had been previously classified as poverty area at time of original certification. (c. 63, §38F; 408 Mass. 18, 556 N.E.2d 371). Limited deduction is allowed for use of alternative energy sources. (c. 63, §38H). Business corporations may also deduct 25% of allowed deductions under IRC §170(e)(4) for research contribution to educational organizations in Massachusetts. (c. 63, §38J). For tax years beginning on or after Jan. 1, 1993, corporations may deduct 10% of cost of renovating abandoned building in economic opportunity area. (c. 63, §38O).

See §38(K) and (L), for tax requirements for defense and manufacturing corporations.

Gross income is federal gross income plus interest received on bonds or notes of any state, including Massachusetts, less deduction for capital losses to extent allowable by IRC. (c. 63, §30, 3rd).

Credits.—For expenditures incurred on or after Jan. 1, 1991, domestic or foreign corporation is allowed credit against its excise tax equal to sum of 10% of excess of qualified research expenses for taxable year over base amount; and 15% of basic research payments determined under §41(e)(1)(a) of Internal Revenue Code. (c. 63, §38M[a]). At election of taxpayer, credit allowed under §38M may be applied separately with respect to qualified research expenses and gross receipts attributable to defense and other activities. (c. 63, §38M[i]). Manufacturing corporations, or business corporations engaged primarily in research and development, or corporations primarily engaged in agriculture or commercial fishing allowed credit of 1% of federal income tax basis, after deduction of any federal tax credit taken, of certain tangible property acquired, constructed, reconstructed or erected during taxable year. (c. 63, §31A[a]). Manufacturing corporations, or business corporations engaged primarily in research and development, and agricultural or commercial fishing corporations are allowed 3% credit for tangible personal property. (c. 63, §31A[i]). One percent credit is not available for taxable years between Dec. 31, 1993 and Jan. 1, 1998. (c. 63, §31A[k]). Three percent credit is available only between taxable years Dec. 31, 1993 and Jan. 1, 1998. (c. 63, §31A[k]). (c. 63, §31A[l]). No corporation may claim 3% credit for more than five years. (c. 63, §31A). Manufacturing corporation, or business corporation engaged primarily in research and development, allowed credit of $500 multiplied by increase in number of certain full-time employees during taxable year. (c. 63, §31C). For "eligible business facility" (defined in c. 23B, §11) located in poverty area, business corporations allowed credit in amount determined by multiplying assessed value of facility's real property owned or leased by corporation, divided by $1,000, by excess of equalized property tax rate in locale over average equalized rate in Massachusetts. (c. 63, §38E). For tax years beginning on or after Jan. 1, 1993, corporation participating in "certified project" in economic opportunity area (defined in c. 23A, §3A) allowed credit of 5% of cost of property qualifying for §31A credit, in lieu of §31A credit. (c. 63, §38N). Effective with respect to tax years beginning on or after Jan. 1, 1983, maximum amount of credits otherwise allowable to corporation in any one taxable year may not exceed 50% of its excise tax liability. (c. 63, §32C). However, any unused credits may be carried over to subsequent tax years. (c. 63, §32C).

Investment Credit Requirements.—Credit of 1% of federal income tax basis of qualifying tangible property, after deduction for any federal tax credit taken, is allowed to manufacturing corporation, business corporation engaged primarily in research and development or corporation engaged primarily in agriculture or fishing. (c. 63, §31A[a]). For tax years ending on or after Dec. 31, 1993 through Dec. 31, 1995,

See note at head of Digest as to 1998 legislation covered.

See Topical Index in front part of this volume.

MA-7

CORPORATIONS . . . *continued*

investment tax credit is 3%. (c. 63, §31A[i]). No corporation may claim 3% credit for more than five years. (c. 63, §31A[1]). For tax years beginning on or after Jan. 1, 1996, credit is 1%. (c. 63, §31A[a]). Qualifying tangible property is tangible personal property and other tangible property including buildings and structural components thereof used and situated in Massachusetts which is either depreciable under IRC §167 and with useful life of four years or more, or considered recovery property under IRC §168. (c. 63, §31A[a], [i]). Property leased by corporation as lessor does not qualify. (c. 63, §31A[b]). Credit may not reduce tax below minimum but may be carried forward three years. (c. 63, §§31A[c], [g]). Pro rata recapture if property disposed of before end of useful life. (c. 63, §31A[e]).

Foreign Corporations.—Defined as corporations organized under laws of jurisdictions other than Massachusetts for purposes for which domestic corporation could be chartered under cc. 156, 156A, 156B or 180, and which have privileges, powers, rights or immunities not possessed by individuals or partnerships, but excluding corporations subject to tax under c. 157, §18 (agricultural cooperatives), foreign manufacturing corporations (c. 63, §42B), corporate regulated investment companies under IRC §851 (c. 63, §30, 2d), and corporations exempt from federal tax under IRC §501 (c. 63, §30, 2d). Except as follows, tax is same as for domestic corporations. Foreign corporation qualified to do business in Massachusetts or doing business in Massachusetts is subject to Massachusetts corporate excise tax. (See c. 63, §39.) Net income is apportioned to Massachusetts as provided in c. 63, §38. In determining whether foreign corporation is tangible or intangible property corporation, investments in foreign corporations not doing business in Massachusetts are subtracted from total assets. (c. 63, §30, 10th and 11th). Net worth of foreign intangible property corporation is such portion of its total net assets as book value of tangible assets situated in Massachusetts and not subject to local taxation, plus its intangible assets allocable to Massachusetts, bears to book value of its total assets. (c. 63, §30, 9th). Intangible assets allocable to Massachusetts are such portion of book value of all intangibles, less book value of investments in and advances to subsidiaries not doing business in Massachusetts, as is found by multiplying such amount by corporate income allocation percentage, determined under c. 63, §38. (c. 63, §30, 11th). In computing net-worth measure of foreign intangible property corporations, term "subsidiary corporations" means corporations in which taxpayer corporation owns 80% or more of voting stock. (c. 63, §30, 9th). Special provisions apply to foreign corporations which are subsidiaries of or otherwise closely affiliated with other corporations to ensure tax imposed on true earnings of such foreign corporations. (c. 63, §39A).

Liability for corporation excise tax extends to foreign corporations which were lessors of real estate or tangible personal property in Massachusetts at any time during taxable year. Lessee is jointly liable for tax. (c. 63, §39; c. 62C, §48).

S Corporations.—Domestic and foreign corporations qualified as S corporations under Federal Internal Revenue Code determine income and loss for Massachusetts for tax purposes as follows:

For taxable years ending on or after Dec. 31, 1988 but before Dec. 31, 1989 S corporations having total receipts less than $6 million for taxable year, or less than $9 million if average of total receipts for three consecutive taxable years immediately preceding current taxable year is less than $6 million, determine net income measure of excise by taking into account provisions of Code Subchapter S and include income in net income measure of Massachusetts tax only to extent such income taxed to S corporation under Code while S corporations having larger total annual receipts determine income or loss and include income in net income measure in same manner as other business corporations. (c. 63, §32D).

For taxable years ending on or after Dec. 31, 1989 (a) S corporations having total receipts for taxable year of less than $6 million determine net income measure and include income as described above for like S corporations, (b) S corporations having total receipts of $6 million or more for taxable year determine taxable net income under c. 62, not taking into account provisions of Code Subchapter S. Their net income is taxed at corporate level at rate of 3% if their total receipts equal or exceed $6 million but are less than $9 million or 4.5% if their total receipts equal or exceed $9 million. (c. 63, §32D).

Total receipts mean gross receipts or sales, less returns and allowances but not less cost of goods sold or of operations, plus dividends, interest, net capital gains, rental and all other income. (c. 63, §32D).

Consolidated Returns.—If two or more domestic business corporations or foreign corporations file a consolidated return of income federally, net income measure of their excises imposed under c. 63, §32 or §39 may, at their option, be assessed upon their combined net income, in which case excise will be assessed to all said corporations and collected from any one or more of them. (c. 63, §32B). Statutes do not authorize application of "unitary business" method in determining corporation's net income taxable by Massachusetts. (c. 63, §32B; c. 63, §§33, 39A, 42; 393 Mass. 490, 472 N.E.2d 259).

Banks, including banking associations, trust companies, federal or state savings and loan associations, savings and cooperative banks, and corporations authorized to do business of banking company under c. 172A are subject to tax of 12.54% of net income or, as to foreign country banks, apportioned net income as defined. (c. 63, §§1, 2).

Security Corporations.—In lieu of regular corporation excise levied under c. 63, §32 (domestic) and §39 (foreign), every corporation engaged exclusively in buying, selling, dealing in, or holding securities (except securities of DISC) on its own behalf and not as broker is eligible for special reduced annual excise as security corporation if it obtains proper classification by application filed with commissioner prior to end of its taxable year. (c. 63, §38B[a]). If such corporation is bank holding company under Internal Revenue Code, annual excise is .33% of its gross income or $456, whichever is greater. (c. 63, §38B[b]). Any corporation taxable under §38B shall not be subject to excise tax imposed by §§2, 32 or 39. (c. 63, §38B[c]).

Filing; Penalties; Abatement.—Corporate excise (income) tax returns must be filed with commissioner by 15th day of third month following close of taxable year. (c. 62C, §11[a]). Generally, extension of six months is available; longer extension, however, may be granted. (c. 62C, §19). Changes in taxable income as determined by

federal government must be reported to commissioner. (c. 62C, §30). Abatement of excess excise tax on basis of reduction in federal taxable income may be sought within one year of date of notice of final determination of reduction. (c. 62C, §§30, 37). Entire tax, less amounts previously paid with estimated returns, due on due date of return, and interest on unpaid amounts accruing before Jan. 1, 1993 is at 18% per annum, plus penalty of ¹/₂% per month of amount shown on return up to 25%. Additional penalty for failure to file return equal to 1% per month of tax required to be shown on return up to 25% of tax amount, with additional penalty tax for failure to show amount of tax required to be shown on return equal to ¹/₂% per month up to 25% of tax not shown if such tax not paid within 30 days following notice of tax due. (c. 62C, §§32, 33). Beginning Jan. 1, 1993, interest on unpaid amounts accrues at federal short-term rate under IRC §6621(b) plus 4%, compounded daily; interest on late payment penalties accrues from 31st day following notice of tax due; interest on late filing penalties accrues on due date of return. (c. 62C, §§32, 33). Applications for abatement of assessment of tax may be filed within three years from last day for filing corporate excise tax return, within two years from date tax was assessed or deemed to be assessed or within one year from any date on which tax was paid, whichever is later. (c. 62C, §37). If commissioner and taxpayer agree to extend period for assessment of tax, period for abatement will not expire prior to expiration of assessment period. (c. 62C, §37). Corporation may appeal to appellate tax board within 60 days after date of notice of decision of commissioner or six months after application for abatement is deemed denied under c. 58A, §6. (c. 62C, §39). Commissioner will waive or abate any portion of penalty or addition to tax attributable to taxpayer's reasonable reliance on erroneous written advice furnished by department of revenue officer or employee in response to specific written request. (c. 62C, §36B). In general, interest accruing before Jan. 1, 1993 on refund of taxes abated is at 18%, thereafter, interest accrues at federal short-term rate under IRC §6621(b) plus 4%, compounded daily. (c. 62C, §40). Commissioner may, after notice, make additional assessments within three years after date return was due or date return was filed, whichever is later, or six years if taxpayer omits gross income exceeding 25% of gross income and at any time in case of false or fraudulent returns or failure to file. (c. 62C, §26[b], [d]and [h]). Commissioner may allow taxpayers to satisfy liabilities in installment payments. (c. 62C, §37B). C. 62C, §31A imposes personal and individual liability after notification by commissioner on person liable for tax of corporation or partnership under c. 62B, §5; c. 64G, §7B; c. 64H, §16; or c. 64I, §17.

Note: Certain rates of income tax and minimum amounts of tax stated above for corporations include 14% surtax on statutory rates and amounts provided by 1969, c. 546.

Disclosure of Corporate Tax Information.—Generally, all corporations which file reports with Securities and Exchange Commission and are required to file tax returns in Massachusetts must file statements with Secretary of State by Mar. 1 each year, disclosing certain tax information including total tax paid and credits taken on most recent return. (c. 62C, §83). Information on such statements is public, although corporate identity not revealed.

Taxation—Declaration of Estimated Tax.—Corporations which can reasonably expect to have estimated tax exceeding $1,000 for taxable year must pay estimated tax in four installments, except as otherwise provided. (c. 63B, §2). In general, interest accruing before Jan. 1, 1993 on underpayment of any installment is at 18%; thereafter, interest accrues at federal short-term rate under IRC §6621(b) plus 4%, compounded daily. (c. 63B, §3). Officers, directors or employees wilfully responsible for failure of corporation to pay estimated tax installments are liable for taxes lost by Commonwealth plus $500 to $5,000 penalty. (c. 63B, §9). Procedures and requirements for making payments of estimated tax, in accordance with §§2-10 of c. 63B, for taxable years ending on or after Dec. 31, 1989, are contained in 830 C.M.R. 63B.2.2.

Corporate Trusts.—See c. 62, §8.

Professional Corporations.—Professional corporations may be formed by physicians, surgeons, psychologists, chiropractors, podiatrists, acupuncturists, registered nurses, engineers, electrologists, physical therapists, certified public accountants, public accountants, dentists, veterinarians, optometrists and attorneys. (c. 156A).

Model Non-Profit Corporation Act not adopted.

JOINT STOCK COMPANIES:

There are few statutory provisions governing joint stock companies; but voluntary associations under written instrument or declaration of trust and having transferable shares are regulated by c. 182, as amended.

Purposes.—No statutory provisions.

Formation.—On penalty of fine or imprisonment, trustees of such association must file instrument or declaration, and any amendments thereof, with state secretary (filing fee, currently $200) and with clerk of each town or city where it has usual place of business. If association owns or controls majority of shares of public utility or common carrier, it must also file with Department of Public Utilities. (c. 182, §§2 and 3). Annual reports must be filed thereafter with secretary (and Department, if applicable). (c. 182, §§4, 12).

Rights, Powers and Liabilities.—No statutory provisions.

Actions.—Such an association may be sued in its own name in an action at law for obligations incurred by duly authorized officer or trustee or agent thereof and for damages resulting from negligence of such officer or trustee or agent acting in performance of his duty, and its property is subject to attachment and execution as if it were corporation and service of process on one trustee is sufficient. (c. 182, §6). Otherwise suit must be brought as at common law. See topic Associations.

Dissolution.—No statutory provisions.

Massachusetts Business Trust.—These trusts are recognized as a form of voluntary association. See c. 182.

Statement.—Association with transferable shares must file annual report with state secretary. State secretary may seek to enjoin association which does not file from transacting business. (c. 182, §§12-14). Where association is one which controls public

See note at head of Digest as to 1998 legislation covered.

See Topical Index in front part of this volume.

JOINT STOCK COMPANIES . . . *continued*
utility companies or common carriers, it must file annual statement showing number of shares owned or controlled, and its records, etc., may be examined by department of public utilities. (c. 182, §§4, 7).

Tax Reports.—Every partnership, association, trust, estate, organization, society, club, governmental agency or any other entity doing business in Massachusetts must file information returns for Massachusetts income tax purposes as in case of domestic corporation (see topic Corporations, subhead Reports). (c. 62C, §8).

Professional Associations.—See topic Corporations, subhead Professional Corporations.

LIMITED LIABILITY COMPANIES:

Massachusetts Limited Liability Company Act became effective Jan. 1, 1996. Act is similar to §§101 to 1206 of Uniform Limited Liability Company Act. Unless otherwise noted, all references in this section are to General Laws c. 156C.

Name.—Limited liability company name shall contain words "limited liability company", "limited company", or abbreviation "L.L.C.", "L.C.", "LLC", or "LC". (§3). Reservation of specified name shall be made by filing with state secretary, any application specifying name to be reserved and name and address of applicant. (§4).

Purposes.—Limited liability companies may carry on any lawful business, trade, profession, purpose or activity. (§4).

Filing.—Organizers must file certificate of organization in office of state secretary containing name of limited liability company, Massachusetts address of office and resident agent for service of process, date of dissolution (if fixed), managers' names and addresses, name of any other person authorized to execute any documents to be filed with state secretary, general character of limited liability's business, and any other matters organizers determine necessary. (§12).

Cancellation of Certificates of Organization.—Cancelled upon dissolution and winding up of company or when there are fewer than two members, or upon filing of certificate of consolidation or merger if limited liability company does not "survive". (§14).

Filing Fees.—Fees for filing certification of organization and mandatory annual report is $500. (§12).

Liability to Third Parties.—Members or manager shall not be obligated personally for debts, obligations or liability of company solely as result of their status as member or manager. (§22). Regulating boards shall adopt regulations requiring designated amount of liability insurance to be maintained. (§65).

Liability to Company.—Member is obligated to perform any promise to contribute cash or property or to perform services, even if unable because of death or disability. May be required to contribute cash in lieu of other contribution. (§28).

Voting.—May be on per capita, number, financial interest, class group or any other basis. If operating agreement does not provide for voting rights of members, decision of members who own more than 50% of unreturned contributions to company shall be controlling. (§21).

Form of Contribution.—Contribution of member may be in cash, property, services rendered, or promissory note or other obligation to contribute cash, property, or to perform services. (§27).

Property.—Limited liability company interest is personal property. Member has no interest in specific limited liability property. (§37). Upon acceptance of c. 59, §5(16A) by any city or town, generally, all property owned by limited liability company, except real estate, poles, and underground conduits, wires and pipes, is exempt from local taxes, if limited liability company meets certain preconditions. (c. 59, §5[16A]).

Resignation of Members.—Regardless of whether operating agreement provides that member does not have right to resign, member may resign upon not less than six months' prior written notice to company and to each member and manager. If resignation violates operating agreement, limited liability company may recover from resigning member damages and offset damages against any amounts otherwise distributable to resigning members. (§36).

Dissolution.—Company is dissolved upon first to occur of following: time or event specified in operating agreement, written consent of all members, judicial dissolution, or death, insanity, retirement, resignation, expulsion, bankruptcy, or dissolution of member unless business of company is continued either by consent of all remaining members within 90 days following such event or pursuant to written right to continue or entry of decree of judicial dissolution. (§43). Procedures for winding up business of dissolved companies set forth in §45.

Foreign Limited Liability Companies.—Provisions relating to foreign limited liability companies contained in §§47 to 54.

Merger or Consolidation.—Provisions relating to merger or consolidation of two or more limited liability companies contained in §§59 to 63.

PARTNERSHIPS:

Uniform Partnership Act is in effect. (c. 108A).

Revised Uniform Limited Partnership Act is in effect. (c. 109). Fees for filing original certificates and amendments, withdrawals or cancellations are determined annually by secretary of administration, currently $200 and $100, respectively. Place of filing is in office of state secretary. (c. 109, §§8, 9, 61; 950 C.M.R. 108.17).

As to necessity of appointing agent where partnership composed of nonresidents, see category Property, topic Absentees, subhead Process Agent.

As to information returns which must be filed for Massachusetts income tax purposes, see topic Joint Stock Companies, subhead Tax Reports.

Limited Liability Partnerships.—Uniform Partnership Act, c. 108A, amended to include limited liability partnerships by c. 108A, §6. Unless otherwise indicated all references are to sections of c. 108A.

Formation.—Partnerships formed under c. 108A may register as limited liability partnership by filing registration statement with state secretary which includes name of partnership, principal office, federal i.d. number, statement of business or profession and list of names and addresses of partners. (§45). Name of limited liability partnership must end with words "registered limited liability partnership", "limited liability partnership" or abbreviation "L.L.P." or "LLP". (§46). Registration fee is $500. (§45).

Limited Liability.—Partner in limited liability partnership shall not be personally liable for debts and obligations of partnership, whether tort, contract or otherwise, arising while partnership is registered. (§15). Limitation of liability does not operate to limit personal liability of partner arising in whole or part by such partners own negligent acts. (§15).

Foreign Limited Liability Partnerships.—Laws of state in which foreign limited liability partnership registered entitled to full faith and credit and partnership governed by laws of state of incorporation. (§47). Foreign partnerships must register in same manner as domestic limited liability partnerships. (§47).

BUSINESS REGULATION AND COMMERCE

BANKS AND BANKING:

Uniform Commercial Code adopted. (c. 106). See topic Commercial Code.

Regulated as follows: Basic statutes are cc. 167, 167C, 167D, 167E, 167F, 167G which apply to all banking institutions including, as to certain matters, national banking associations, federal savings and loan associations and federal credit unions. In addition, bank holding companies are governed by c. 167A, mutual holding companies by c. 167H, electronic fund transfers by c. 167B, trust companies by c. 172, savings banks by c. 168, cooperative banks by c. 170, credit unions by c. 171, "Morris Plan" banks by c. 172A and deposits with others than banks for transmission to foreign countries by c. 169. Banks and banking are under supervision of commissioner of banks. (c. 167). The Mutual Savings Central Fund, Inc. established by c. 168 App., §1-1 also has certain supervisory powers over savings banks (c. 168 App., §2-1A), as has Co-Operative Central Bank over co-operative banks (c. 170, §26A; c. 170 App., §1-1). Board of bank incorporation also has supervisory powers over organization of savings banks (c. 168, §5), co-operative banks (c. 170, §4) and trust companies (c. 172, §6).

Stockholders.—Not liable to assessment.

Deposits.—

Limitation of Amount.—Generally, trust companies and savings and co-operative banks may receive demand, time and other deposits, without limitation (c. 167D, §3), and may sell serial or paid-up shares in denominations of $100 to $200 without limitation (Id. §4). See c. 167D, §3 for fees for accounts established for personal, family, or household purposes. Credit union members are limited to $100,000 in shares or deposits or both for individual members and $125,000 for joint accounts, exclusive of club deposits. These limits are increased in case of credit unions having assets of $4,000,000 or more to $150,000 and $200,000 and, in case of credit unions having assets of $30,000,000 or more, to $250,000 and $500,000. (c. 171, §30). Fraternal organizations, etc., eligible for credit union membership may have deposit accounts up to limits applicable to joint accounts for individual members, provided total deposits by organization do not exceed 25% of credit union's assets. (c. 171, §30). See c. 171, §41A for fees for accounts established for personal, family, or household purposes. Morris Plan banks may receive fully insured deposits of money upon certificates up to limit of $60,000 per depositor. (c. 172A, §§5, 5A).

Types.—Joint accounts are permitted in all banks in names of two or more persons, payable to depositors or survivor(s) of them. (c. 167D, §5). Funds on deposit in name of minor may, unless in violation of written agreement to which bank is party, be paid to minor or to another on his written order or to his legal representative or to either parent. (Id. §7). Deposits in trust may be made by one or two persons for another. Payments may be made to trustee or, if there are two trustees, to both or either or survivor of them. If no other notice of existence or terms of trust has been received in writing upon death of trustee or both trustees, account may be paid to beneficiary or his legal representative. (Id. §6). Time deposits may be received by all banks, which must send notice of maturity to depositor if maturity in excess of 30 days. (Id. §§2[1], 8). Bank that accepts demand deposits or NOW accounts must, upon request of depositor and without charge, return cancelled instruments of such accounts. (Id. §27).

Instrument establishing deferred compensation or retirement plan, trust or custodial account and designating beneficiary will be effective according to its terms notwithstanding statutory or common law testamentary disposition. (Id. §30).

Except as required by legal process, banks need not recognize adverse claims to deposits or securities held for any person unless adverse claimant gives bond of indemnity or files affidavit setting forth facts for reasonably believing that such person is his fiduciary and about to misappropriate deposit or securities. (Id. §31).

Written notice by certified mail must be given upon transfer of funds of depositor to reduce or extinguish debt owed by depositor to bank. (Id. §19). Debtor of bank may, with some exceptions, set off amount of deposit with bank if bank proceeds against debtor on such debt. (Id. §20).

Funds in deposit account of deceased depositor shall be paid to depositor's legal representative unless account less than $3,000 and no demand therefor made by representative, in which case may be paid to surviving spouse or next of kin upon presentation of death certificate and surrender of deposit book or other instrument evidencing deposit. (Id. §33).

No bank may impose any fee, other than reasonable returned check fee, against savings or checking account of person 65 or older or 18 or younger. (c. 167D, §2[1]). See c. 167D, §3 for fees for accounts established for personal, family, or household purposes.

Funds Availability.—Each banking institution as defined in c. 167D, §35 must disclose to account holders its policy regarding availability for withdrawal or use of

See note at head of Digest as to 1998 legislation covered.

See Topical Index in front part of this volume.

MA – 9

BANKS AND BANKING . . . *continued*
funds deposited by means of items other than cash. Obligation of foreign branch of bank to repay deposit in foreign currency governed by c. 167D, §36. Accounts include all asset accounts. Disclosures on availability requirements must be in accordance with provisions of Expedited Funds Availability Act, 12 U.S.C. 4001 et seq. and Regulation S promulgated thereunder. (c. 167D, §35).

Regulation of Consumer Transactions.—No bank shall engage in Massachusetts in unfair methods of competition or unfair or deceptive acts or practices involving consumer transactions (transactions between banks and natural persons involving primarily personal, family or household purposes). Commissioner has power to promulgate and enforce rules and regulations defining what constitutes unfair methods of competition or unfair or deceptive acts. (c. 167, §§2A-2G).

Truth-in-Savings Law.—All banking institutions must make certain disclosures to consumers opening accounts at such institutions. Commissioner authorized to issue implementing regulations. (c. 140E, §2).

Unclaimed Deposits.—Deposits as to which no communication from depositor has been received for three years are deemed to have been abandoned and escheat to commonwealth. (c. 200A, §3). See category Property, topic Absentees, subhead Escheat.

Collections.—See Uniform Commercial Code c. 106, Art. 4.

Trust Companies, Savings Banks, Co-operative Banks.—Trust companies and savings and co-operative banks are generally regulated and supervised by commissioner (see generally c. 167) and generally have equal banking powers. (c. 167, §1). Chapters governing location of main and branch offices (c. 167C), deposits and accounts (c. 167D), mortgages and loans (c. 167E), investments and other powers (c. 167F), and trust departments (c. 167G), generally apply to all three types of banking institutions. Establishment and operation of trust companies is governed by c. 172, of savings banks by c. 168, and of co-operative banks by c. 170. C. 167H authorizes mutual savings banks and mutual co-operative banks to establish mutual holding companies. Deposits in all savings banks certified by commissioner to be in sound and safe condition to continue business are fully insured by Mutual Savings Central Fund, Inc. (c. 168 App., §2-1) in excess of deposits insured by Federal Deposit Insurance Corp. (Id. §2-17). Shares in co-operative banks are fully insured by Co-Operative Central Bank (c. 170 App., §2-1) in excess of account balances insured by Federal Deposit Insurance Corp. (Id. §2-16). See subhead Deposits, supra. Savings banks and co-operative banks may merge with credit unions subject to approval of commissioner (see c. 168, §34F; c. 170, §26F). Articles of consolidation or merger must be filed with secretary of state. (c. 168, §34F).

Credit Unions.—See c. 171. Loan powers and limits of credit unions are governed by §§57-66. Preference is given to small personal loans but real estate mortgages and other types of secured loans may also be made. (§§57, 60-62, 65, 66). See subhead Deposits, supra. Credit unions may require 90 days' notice of withdrawal of shares or 60 days' notice of withdrawal of deposits. (§43). Deposits in trust may be made by one or two persons for another. Payments may be made to trustee or, if there are two trustees, to both or either or to survivor. If no other notice of existence or terms of trust has been received in writing upon death of trustee or both trustees, account may be paid to beneficiary or his legal representative. (§40). Joint accounts are permitted in names of two or more persons, payable to depositors or to survivors. (§39). Credit unions may offer special notice accounts (§34), receive term shares or deposits (§32), act as trustee or custodian under profit-sharing or retirement plan or IRA (§35) and, may authorize accounts that would allow withdrawals by negotiable or transferable instruments for purpose of making transfers to third parties. Such accounts shall be subject to regulations of commissioner. (§31). Deposits or shares of deceased shall be paid to legal representative unless total amount not greater than $3,000 and no demand therefor made by representative, in which case may be paid to surviving spouse or next of kin upon presentation of death certificate and passbook, if any. (§42). Deposits and shares of minor may be paid to minor, his parents or guardian. (§41). Insurance of deposits and shares provided by Massachusetts Credit Union Share Insurance Corp. (§6) or by National Credit Union Administration Share Insurance Fund (§§6, 77).

Foreign Banks.—See generally c. 167, §§38-43A. No foreign bank shall conduct banking business in commonwealth, except as provided in c. 167B, unless board of bank incorporation grants certificate to bank authorizing such activity. (c. 167, §38). Any foreign bank, which receives certificate pursuant to c. 167, §38, may, if authorized by laws of its jurisdiction of organization, merge or consolidate with Massachusetts bank or federal bank, subject to commissioner's approval. (c. 167, §39). Foreign banks, which establish branch through merger, consolidation, or purchase of assets or stock of Massachusetts bank, shall operate under supervision of commissioner and under same laws that govern operation of Massachusetts banks. (c. 167, §39).

Any out-of-state bank or out-of-state federal bank may establish and maintain branches through merger or consolidation with or purchase of assets or stock of any Massachusetts bank, subject to conditions set forth in c. 167, §39B. Out-of-state bank, which satisfies such conditions, shall operate same as Massachusetts branch under supervision of commissioner and subject to same laws governing activity of Massachusetts banks. (c. 167, §39B). Commissioner shall inspect and examine activities of foreign and out-of-state banks inside commonwealth, to determine financial status and compliance with applicable laws. For purpose of examinations, commissioner shall have access to vaults, books, and papers of out-of-state or foreign bank. (c. 167, §41). Commissioner shall maintain reports of such examinations and shall provide parent bank with copies of reports. (c. 167, §40). Additionally, each foreign bank, out-of-state bank, and out-of-state federal bank, which maintains Massachusetts branch, must register with commissioner. (c. 167, §40A).

Subject to approval of commissioner, foreign bank, out-of-state bank, or out-of-state federal bank, which does not have branch in commonwealth, may establish new bank without purchasing bank, in accordance with provisions of c. 167, §39B. However, jurisdiction in which foreign bank, out-of-state bank, or out-of-state federal bank has its principal place of business must allow Massachusetts bank to do same. (c. 167, §39C).

Banking association or corporation having principal office in another state may be authorized by board of bank incorporation to act as fiduciary in Massachusetts provided it is authorized to so act by laws of state where its principal office is located and such state has laws permitting Massachusetts banks to act in same capacity. Association or corporation holding such license and appointed fiduciary is subject to provisions of general law with respect to appointment of agents by foreign fiduciaries and to same taxes, obligations and penalties with respect to its activities as such fiduciary and property held by it in its fiduciary capacity as like corporations or associations having their principal office in Massachusetts, and such association or corporation must file agreement with board of bank incorporation to perform such obligations and pay such taxes and penalties. Any such association or corporation acting only in such fiduciary capacity as herein provided is not deemed to be transacting banking business in Massachusetts. (c. 167, §43).

Banking Emergencies.—As to power of Commissioner of Banks to proclaim and regulation of banks thereupon, see c. 167, §21.

Uniform Common Trust Fund Act adopted. (c. 203A). Corporate trustees use simplified procedures in collectively invested inter vivos trusts. (c. 167G, §3).

BILLS AND NOTES:

Uniform Commercial Code applies. (c. 106, §§3-101 to 3-605). No retroactive effect for c. 106, §3-118.

Days of Grace.—Uniform Commercial Code applies. (c. 106). C. 106, §3-506 repealed.

Special Requirements.—In action on contract, other than bill of exchange, for payment of money where contract is payable beyond limits of U.S., amount to be recovered is determined by current rate of exchange on due date with interest from that date. (c. 107, §10).

Protest of bill of exchange, note or order certified under hand and seal of notary public is prima facie evidence of facts stated in protest. (c. 107, §13).

C. 106, §3-122 repealed. See c. 106, §§3-401 to 3-420 for "Liability of Parties".

Consumer Notes.—If contract for sale of consumer goods on credit requires or involves execution of note, such note must have "consumer note" printed on face and holder of note cannot be holder in due course thereof within meaning of Art. 3 of c. 106. (c. 255, §§12C, 13I).

Judgment Notes.—Stipulation in note, contract or other instrument or in any writing relating thereto agreeing, or authorizing another person, to confess judgment in any action which may be brought thereon is void and any such judgment shall be set aside on motion of defendant. (c. 231, §13A). Any judgment entered in action upon note, contract or other instrument in which defendant waived or agreed to waive issue or service of process shall be set aside on motion of defendant unless service is actually made or seven days' notice of intention to enter action is given by registered mail. (c. 231, §13A).

Attorneys fees.—See topics Consumer Protection, Commercial Code.

BILLS OF LADING:

See topics Carriers, Commercial Code.

BILLS OF SALE:

See topics Sales, Commercial Code.

BLUE SKY LAW:

See topics Securities, Commercial Code.

BROKERS:

Common law rules of Agency generally prevail unless contract provisions specify otherwise.

Uniform Commercial Code adopted. (c. 106). See topic Commercial Code.

Insurance brokers. (See category Insurance, topic Insurance Companies.) Stock brokers. (See topic Securities.) Brokers of transportation by motor vehicles, see category Transportation, topic Motor Vehicles, subhead Motor Vehicle Carriers. Miscellaneous. (See topic Licenses, Business and Professional.)

Real Estate Brokers.—Unless contract specifies to contrary, broker engaged by owner ordinarily is entitled to commission when: (a) Broker produces purchaser ready, willing and able to buy on owner's terms, (b) purchaser enters binding contract with owner, and (c) purchaser completes transaction by closing title in accordance with contract terms unless failure of completion of contract results from wrongful act or interference of seller. (367 Mass. 622, 327 N.E.2d 727). Seller's scheme to obtain payment for property without paying commission constitutes bad faith dealing. (38 Mass. App. Ct. 221, 646 N.E.2d 1081 review granted by 420 Mass. 1105, 651 N.E.2d 410). Broker is entitled to commission only if his efforts are found to have been predominating efficient cause of sale or lease. (283 Mass. 420, 186 N.E. 547). If no closing occurs pursuant to contract, through no fault of landowner, broker not entitled to commission. (421 Mass. 537, 658 N.E.2d 687). Real estate brokers must be licensed and are subject to Board of Registration regulations. (c. 112, §§87PP-87DDD½). Brokers holding licenses subject to renewal on or after Jan. 1, 1999 must complete courses approved by Board of Registration. (c. 112, §87XX½). Brokers holding licenses renewed before Dec. 31, 2000 must attend 12 class hours and brokers holding licenses renewed on or after Jan. 1, 2001 must attend no less than six and no more than 12 class hours of approved curriculum. (c. 112, §87XX½, inserted by St. 1996, c. 369, §2). Continuing education requirement does not apply to foreign brokers provided that those brokers demonstrate continuing education in home state. (c. 112, §87XX½). Board of registration regulations do not apply to person acting for himself as owner, lessor, lessee, tenant or mortgagee. (c. 112, §87QQ).

Acceptance of "Net Listings" and other specified conduct have been prohibited. (c. 112, §87AAA).

See note at head of Digest as to 1998 legislation covered.

See Topical Index in front part of this volume.

MA – 10

BROKERS . . . *continued*

Only licensed brokers or salesmen may engage in business of finding dwelling accommodations for prospective tenants for fee. (c. 112, §87DDD¹/₂).

Broker not licensed to sell real estate entitled to commission on sale of personal property. (403 Mass. 291, 528 N.E.2d 1176).

Mortgage Brokers.—Persons engaged in business of mortgage broker or mortgage lender are required to obtain license from commissioner of banks and are subject to regulation. (c. 255E, §§1-10).

C. 255E does not apply to (a) certain banks and federal lending institutions, (b) persons engaged as employees of mortgage brokers or lenders, (c) persons who act as mortgage brokers for, or mortgage lenders who make, fewer than five loans within any 12 consecutive months, (d) certain nonprofit, public or independent educational institutions and nonprofit agencies assisting low to moderate income households in purchase or rehabilitation of residences of four units or less, (e) charitable organizations created by last will and testament before Jan. 1, 1950, which make no more than 12 mortgage loans during 12 month period. (c. 255E, §2).

BULK SALES:

See topic Commercial Code; category Debtor and Creditor, topic Fraudulent Sales and Conveyances.

CARRIERS:

Common carriers are largely regulated by department of public utilities. (cc. 159-161).

Rates.—Generally regulated by department of public utilities. (c. 159, §10).

Discrimination.—Unjustly discriminatory and unduly preferential rates and charges and, in general, giving of free service are prohibited. (c. 159, §§14, 14A and 15).

Limiting Liability.—As to goods, liability for loss or damage may be limited against risks, other than negligence or misconduct of carrier, by reasonable conditions in contract for carriage. (98 Mass. 239, 93 Am.Dec. 162; see also Uniform Commercial Code, c. 106, §7-309). As to passengers, rule, in general, is that carrier may not exonerate itself by contract from liability for all negligence. (227 Mass. 493, 116 N.E. 899; see also c. 159, §3).

Bills of Lading.—Uniform Commercial Code applies. (c. 106, §§7-101 to 7-105 and 7-301 to 7-603 but optional language of 7-403[1][b] omitted).

Motor Vehicle Carriers.—See category Transportation, topic Motor Vehicles.

Liens.—Carrier has lien on goods for transportation charges and for charges for storage reasonable time after their arrival. (199 Mass. 586, 85 N.E. 846). Goods not called for within one year after receipt at place of consignment may be sold at public auction for payment of transportation and storage charges and cost of sale. (c. 135, §6).

COMMERCIAL CODE:

Uniform Commercial Code was adopted (Sept. 21, 1957, c. 106), effective Oct. 1, 1958. 1966 Official Amendments not adopted. 1972 Official Amendments adopted effective Jan. 1, 1980. 1977 Official Amendments adopted effective Mar. 1, 1984. Art. 4A (Funds Transfers) adopted Oct. 25, 1991, effective Jan. 1, 1992. Art. 6 (Bulk Transfers), repealed by St. 1996, c. 160, §3. Adopted new Art. 2A (Leases) on Aug. 29, 1996.

1972 Official Amendments.—Adopted.

1977 Official Amendments.—Adopted.

1987 Official Text of Article 2A (Leases) and Conforming Amendments. —Adopted.

1989 Official Text of Article 4A (Funds Transfers).—Adopted.

1990 Official Amendments.—Adopted.

1991 Official Text of Revised Article 3 and Conforming Amendments.—Not adopted.

1994 Official Text of Revised Article 8 (Investment Securities) and Conforming Amendments.—Adopted, except for 8-601-8-603.

1995 Official Text of Revised Articles 3 and 4 and Conforming Amendments.—New Arts. 3 and 4, inserted by St. 1998, c. 24, §8, conform with Uniform Commercial Code, 1995 Official Text.

1995 Official Text of Revised Article 5 and Conforming Amendments.—Conforms with Uniform Commercial Code, 1995 Official Text, with no retroactive effect.

Material Variations from 1972 Official Text as amended.—

1-102: Omits (5).

1-105: Adopts 1987 amendment conforming to new Art. 2A, and 1989 amendment conforming to new Art. 4A on fund transfers.

1-109: Omitted.

1-201: 1987 amendment to (37) adopted. Omits (46). (30) omits reference to omitted subsection 1-102(5). (33) adds "or his nominee" after "person." Does not adopt 1990 amendments to (20), (24), or (43) to conform to Revised Art. 3. Current version of (20), (24), and (43) and line 226 consistent with 1995 Official Text.

1-209: Optional Section adopted in 1979.

2-207: Inserts "or different" after "additional." Replaces "Act" with "chapter."

2-312: Adds subsection: "(4) Unless otherwise agreed a seller makes no warranty under subsection (3) with respect to any claim for which the exclusive remedy of the claimant is by action against the United States in the Court of Claims or in the district courts of the United States."

2-316: Adds subsection: "(5) The implied warranties of merchantability and fitness shall not be applicable to a contract for the sale of human blood, blood plasma or other human tissue or organs from a blood bank or reservoir of such other tissues or organs. Such blood, blood plasma or tissue or organs shall not for the purposes of this Article be considered commodities subject to sale or barter, but shall be considered as medical services."

2-316A: New section: "The provisions of section 2-316 shall not apply to extent provided in this section. Any language, oral or written, used by a seller or manufacturer of consumer goods and services, which attempts to exclude or modify any implied warranties of merchantability and fitness for a particular purpose or to exclude or modify the consumer's remedies for breach of those warranties, shall be unenforceable.

Any language, oral or written, used by a manufacturer of consumer goods, which attempts to limit or modify a consumer's remedies for breach of such manufacturer's express warranties, shall be unenforceable, unless such manufacturer maintains facilities within the commonwealth sufficient to provide reasonable and expeditious performance of the warranty obligations.

Any language, oral or written, used by a seller or manufacturer of goods, which attempts to exclude or modify any implied warranties of merchantability and fitness for a particular purpose or to exclude or modify remedies for breach of those warranties, shall be unenforceable with respect to injury to the person. This subsection does not affect the validity under other law of an agreement between a seller or manufacturer of goods and services and a buyer that is an organization, allocating, as between them, the risk of damages from or providing indemnity for breaches of those warranties with respect to injury to the person.

The provisions of this section may not be disclaimed or waived by agreement." Amended in 1990 without apparent change.

2-318: Reworded: "Lack of privity between plaintiff and defendant shall be no defense in any action brought against the manufacturer, seller, lessor or supplier of goods to recover damages for breach of warranty, express or implied, or for negligence, although the plaintiff did not purchase the goods from the defendant if the plaintiff was a person whom the manufacturer, seller, lessor or supplier might reasonably have expected to use, consume or be affected by the goods. The manufacturer, seller, lessor or supplier may not exclude or limit the operation of this section. Failure to give notice shall not bar recovery under this section unless the defendant proves that he was prejudiced thereby. All actions under this section shall be commenced within three years next after the date the injury and damage occurs."

2A-104: 1(a) inserts reference to c. 90B and c. 90D.

2A-108: 4(b) after word "unconscionability", adds words "the court shall award reasonable attorney's fees to the party against whom the claim is made if the criteria of six E through six G, inclusive, of chapter two hundred and thirty-one are met."

2A-214A: New section: (1) provides that §2A-214 (exclusion or modification of warranties) does not apply to extent provided in this section. (2) Oral or written language in consumer lease, which attempts to exclude or modify lessee's remedies for implied warranties of merchantability and fitness for particular purpose, or attempts to exclude or modify remedies for breach of such warranties, is unenforceable. (3) Oral or written language in consumer lease, which attempts to limit or modify lessee's remedies for breach of manufacturer's express warranties, is unenforceable, "unless the manufacturer maintains facilities within the commonwealth sufficient to provide reasonable and expeditious performance of the warranty obligations." (4) Oral or written language in lease, attempting to exclude or modify implied warranties of merchantability and fitness for particular purpose, or to exclude or modify remedies for breach of said warranties, is unenforceable as to injury to person. (5) Prohibits agreements disclaiming or waiving provisions of this section.

2A-216: New section: In actions to recover damages for breach of express or implied warranties, or for negligence, lack of privity between defendant and plaintiff is not valid defense if manufacturer, supplier or lessor of goods might reasonably have expected plaintiff to use, consume or be affected by goods. Actions must be commenced within three years after date of injury and damage occurs.

2A-503: (3) inserts words "Subject to sections 2A-214A and 2A-216" before "consequential".

3-120: Did not adopt 1990 Official Amendment which replaced UCC 3-120 and 3-121 with 4-106. Repealed by St. 1998, c. 24, §8.

3-121: Retains alternative A of pre-1990 Official Text. Repealed by St. 1998, c. 24, §8.

3-501: Does not adopt 1966 Official Amendment.

3-803: Did not adopt 1990 Official Amendment which renumbered and restated UCC 3-803 with 3-119. Substitutes "receives notice that he is being sued" for "is sued," and "notice of the obligation" for "notice of the litigation." Repealed by St. 1998, c. 24, §8.

4-106: Did not adopt 1990 Official Amendment which renumbered UCC 4-106 as 4-107. Omits optional language "maintaining its own deposit ledgers" from pre-1990 Official Text. Adds second sentence: "The proper branch to which a stop-order should be directed is the branch where the customer's account is maintained and the effectiveness of a stop-order as to time (Section 4-303) is determined by the time when such branch receives the stop-order and has a reasonable time to act on it." Repealed by St. 1998, c. 24, §8.

4-202: (1)(b) adopts optional language "or directly to the depository bank under subsection (2) of section 4-212". Adopts optional 1(d). (2) omits "exercises ordinary care under subsection (a) by taking proper action"; (2) also substitutes "be seasonable" for "constitute the exercise of ordinary care." Repealed by St. 1998, c. 24, §8.

4-212: Adopts optional subsection (2) from pre-1990 Official Text. Omits "If the return or notice is delayed beyond the bank's midnight deadline or a longer reasonable time after it learns of the facts, the bank may revoke the settlement, charge back the credit, or obtain a refund from its customer, but it is liable for any loss resulting from the delay." Did not adopt 1990 Official Amendment which renumbered UCC 4-212 as 4-214. Repealed by St. 1998, c. 24, §8.

5-107: (2) omits "and acquires the rights of an issuer." Current version conforms with Uniform Commercial Code, 1995 Official Text, with no retroactive effect.

5-112: (1) omits optional language: "except as otherwise provided in subsection (4) of Section 5-114 on conditional payment." Current version conforms with Uniform Commercial Code, 1995 Official Text, with no retroactive effect.

See note at head of Digest as to 1998 legislation covered.

See Topical Index in front part of this volume.

COMMERCIAL CODE . . . *continued*

5-113: Omits (2)(b) in its entirety. Text of (a) subsumed under (2). Current version conforms with Uniform Commercial Code, 1995 Official Text, with no retroactive effect.

5-114: Omits optional (4) and (5). Adopted 1977 Official Amendment inserting "certificated" before "security" in (2) and (2)(a). Adopts 1994 conforming amendments. Current version conforms with Uniform Commercial Code, 1995 Official Text, with no retroactive effect.

5-116: Adopts 1972 conforming amendments. Current version conforms with Uniform Commercial Code, 1995 Official Text, with no retroactive effect.

6-100 et seq.: repealed by St. 1996, c. 160, §3.

7-204: Omits (4).

7-209: Does not adopt 1966 Official Amendment adding (3)(b).

7-210: (1) adds "in good faith for the purposes of avoiding or reducing loss and of effective realization" after "warehouseman" in fourth sentence.

7-308: (1) adds "in good faith for the purposes of avoiding or reducing loss and of effective realization" after "If the carrier" in fourth sentence.

7-403: (1)(b) omits optional language: ", but the burden of establishing negligence in such cases is on the person entitled under the document."

8-302: (2) adds "unauthorized or" before "wrongful."

8-308 to 8-321: Repealed by St. 1996, c. 170, §4.

8-408: Repealed by St. 1996, c. 170, §4.

9-104: (e) reworded: "to a security interest created or granted by a government or governmental subdivision or agency to the extent that the creation, validity, enforceability, perfection or priority of such security interest is expressly governed by any other general or special law; or".

9-109: (3) of current version reads: " 'farm products', if they are crops or livestock or supplies used or produced in farming operations or if they are products of crops or livestock in their unmanufactured states, such as ginned cotton, wool-clip, maple syrup, milk and eggs, and if they are in the possession of a debtor engaged in raising, fattening, grazing or other farming operations. If goods are farm products they are neither equipment nor inventory."

9-111: Repealed by St. 1996, c. 160, §4.

9-203: (4) specifies state laws to which transaction also subject. Current version amended by striking out, in line 1, word "section 4-208" and inserting in place thereof "section 4-210."

9-301: (2) reworded: "If the secured party files with respect to a purchase money security interest before or within twenty days after the debtor receives possession of the collateral, he takes priority over the rights of a transferee in bulk or of a lien creditor which arise between the time the security interest attaches and the time of filing."

9-302: (3)(b) substitutes "chapter ninety D;" for "the following statutes of this state;". Current version amended by striking out, in line 17, word "section 4-208" and inserting in place thereof "section 4-210."

9-307: (1) moves remainder of sentence beginning "takes free of a security interest created by his seller" to added (1)(a). Adds subsection: "(1)(b) takes free of a security interest created by a predecessor in interest of his seller if the buyer buys without knowledge of the security interest and for his own personal, family or household purposes."

9-312: (4) Substitutes "twenty days" for "ten days."

9-401: Adopts third alternative subsection (1). (1)(a) reworded following "or, consumer goods,": "then in the office of the clerk of the town where the debtor resides or if the debtor is not a resident of the commonwealth then in the office of the clerk of the town in which the goods are kept;". (1)(c) reworded: "in all other cases, in the office of the state secretary and in addition, if the debtor has a place of business in only one town of the commonwealth, also in the office of the clerk of such town, or, if the debtor has no place of business in the commonwealth, but resides in the commonwealth, also in the office of the clerk of the town in which he resides."

9-402: (5) adopts optional language "for record" and does not adopt remaining optical language.

9-403: Omits (7). (5) reworded: "The fee for filing, indexing and furnishing filing data for an original or a continuation statement or any amendment of either shall be set by the filing officer, but if an original financing statement any amendment thereof which is filed in a registry of deeds consists of more than one page the fee for filing and indexing the same and furnishing filing data with respect thereto shall be as set forth in sections thirty-eight and thirty-nine of chapter two hundred and sixty-two, but in no event shall any such fee be greater than ten dollars."

9-404: (1) specifies date of filing as July 1, 1979; (1) also substitutes "twenty-five dollars" for "one hundred dollars" in last sentence. (3) reworded: "The fee for filing and indexing a termination statement including sending or delivering the financial statement shall be set by the filing officer, except in registries of deeds, where it shall be four dollars, but in no event shall any such fee be greater than ten dollars."

9-405: (1) reworded: "A financial statement may disclose an assignment of a security interest in the collateral described in the financial statement by indication in the financing statement of the name and address of the assignee or by an assignment itself or a copy thereof on the face or back of the statement. On presentation to the filing officer of such a financing statement the filing officer shall mark the same as provided in subsection (4) of section 9-403. The uniform fee for filing and indexing and furnishing filing data for a financial statement so indicating an assignment shall be set by the filing officer, except in the registries of deeds where it shall be four dollars, but in no event shall any such fee be greater than ten dollars." (2) reworded penultimate sentence: "The uniform fee for filing, indexing and furnishing filing data about such a separate statement of assignment shall be five dollars, except in registries of deeds where it shall be four dollars."

9-406: Reworded last sentence: "The uniform fee for filing and noting such a statement of release shall be set by the filing officer, except in registries of deeds where it shall be four dollars, but in no event shall any such fee be greater than ten dollars."

9-407: Adopts optional (1) and (2). (2) reworded: "Upon request of any person, the filing officer, except the registers of deeds and assistant recorders of the land court, shall issue his certificate showing whether there is on file on the date and hour stated therein, any presently effective financing statement naming a particular debtor and any statement of assignment thereof and, if there is, giving the date and hour of filing of each such statement and the names and addresses of each secured party named therein. The fee for such a certificate shall be five dollars. Upon request, the filing officer shall furnish a copy of any filed financing statement, continuation statement, termination statement, statement of assignment or statement of release for a fee of two dollars and, if such statement consists of more than three pages, an additional fee of one dollar for the fourth and each succeeding page."

9-409: New section: "Unless a filing officer has notice of an action pending relative thereto, he may remove from the files and destroy:

(a) a lapsed financing statement, a lapsed continuation statement, a statement of assignment or release relating to either, and any index of any of them, one year or more after lapse; and

(b) a termination statement and the index on which it is noted, one year or more after the filing of the termination statement."

9-410: New section "(1) Financing statements, security agreements, continuation statements, amendments, termination statements, statements of assignment and statements of release which are filed in registries of deeds and which comply with the requirements of this Part shall be recorded and indexed in the manner provided in chapter thirty-six if they relate to unregistered land, and shall be registered in the manner provided in chapter one hundred and eighty-five if they relate to registered land. Each statement and amendment shall be indexed according to the name of the debtor and, if the statement shows the name of a record owner of the real estate which is other than that of the debtor, the statement shall also be indexed according to the name of such record owner. Except as provided in subsection (3), the fees for recording, indexing and registering shall be as provided in this Part.

(2) In addition to other requirements of this Part, a continuation statement, amendment, termination statement, statement of assignment or statement of release which is filed in a registry of deeds must refer to the record of the original financing statement by book and page if it related to unregistered land and by document number if it relates to registered land. The register of deeds shall enter upon the margin of the record of the original financing statement a notation of the record of the subsequent statement or amendment.

(3) If a person filing any financing statement, continuation statement, amendment, termination statement, statement of assignment or statement of release, furnishes the register of deeds a copy thereof, the register of deeds shall upon request note upon the copy the file number and date and hour of the filing of the original and deliver or send the copy to such person."

Forms.—See end of this Digest.

See also topics: Banks and Banking, Bills and Notes, Brokers, Bulk Sales, Carriers, Consumer Protection, Contracts, Factors, Frauds, Statute of, Sales, Securities, Warehousemen; categories Business Organizations, topic Corporations; Civil Actions and Procedure, topic Limitation of Actions; Debtor and Creditor, topics Assignments, Fraudulent Sales and Conveyances, Liens, Pledges; Documents and Records, topics Records, Seals; Mortgages, topic Chattel Mortgages; Transportation, topic Motor Vehicles.

CONDITIONAL SALES:

Art. 9 of Commercial Code applies, c. 106, §9-101 et seq. (superceding prior legislation dealing with conditional sales). See topic Commercial Code.

CONSIGNMENTS:

Covered by Commercial Code, c. 106, §§1-201(37), 2-326, 2-403(2) and (3), 9-114, and 9-408. See topic Commercial Code. As regarding fine art, any clause in consignment agreement waiving any provision of c. 104A is void. (c. 104A, §5).

CONSUMER PROTECTION:

See generally c. 6, §115A (unit pricing of packaged commodities); c. 12, §§11E, 11F (intervention by attorney general in legal proceedings on behalf of consumers in matters involving public utilities and insurance companies); c. 40, §8F (municipal consumer advisory commission); c. 90, §7N1/2 (sale, lease and repair of new motor vehicles); c. 93, §43 (unsolicited merchandise); c. 93, §48 (cancellation of consumer agreements); c. 93, §48B (travel services); c. 93, §§68A-68E (cancellation of credit service organization contracts); c. 93, §§50-68 (consumer credit reporting); c. 93A (consumer protection act; so-called "Baby FTC Act"); c. 93, §§78-88 (health club service contracts); c. 93, §§90-93 (consumer leasing); c. 93, §107 (customized wheelchair sales and warranties); c. 94, §§184B-184E (consumer products pricing practices); c. 106, §2-316A (prohibiting limitation or modification of UCC implied warranties and certain c. 106, §2-316 express warranties); c. 106, §2-318 (privity not required for warranty action); c. 106, §2A-214A (prohibiting exclusion or modification of implied warranties in consumer lease agreements); c. 112, §84B (requiring itemized list of funeral costs); c. 140, §§86-114C (loans); c. 140D (consumer credit cost disclosure); c. 140E (consumer account disclosure); c. 151B, §§1-10 (unlawful discrimination); c. 151C, §§1-5 (fair educational practices); c. 167B (electronic fund transfers); c. 231, §85J (treble damages for fraud in sale of personal property); c. 255, §12C (consumer note); c. 255, §12F (survival of consumers' defenses in consumer loan transactions); c. 255, §13I-J (default under consumer credit transactions); c. 255, §13K (contracts between certain schools and students); c. 255B (retail installment sales of motor vehicles); c. 255C (insurance premium finance agencies); c. 255D (retail installment sales and services); c. 265, §13C (assault in order to collect loan). See also topics Commercial Code, Interest, subhead "Truth-in-Lending" Law, Monopolies, Restraint of Trade and Competition, subhead Unfair Trade Practices, Sales, subhead Retail Installment Sales; categories Civil Actions and Procedure, topics Injunctions, subhead Consumer Protection, Limitation of Actions, subhead Within Four Years; Insurance, topic Insurance Companies, subhead Unfair Methods of Competition and Deceptive

See note at head of Digest as to 1998 legislation covered.

See Topical Index in front part of this volume.

MA – 12

CONSUMER PROTECTION . . . *continued*
Acts and Practices; Mortgages, topic Mortgages of Real Property; Transportation, topic Motor Vehicles, subhead Sales.

Unfair methods of competition and unfair or deceptive acts or practices in conduct of any trade or commerce are declared unlawful by c. 93A, §2(a). C. 93A has extensive application in consumer protection area and may be enforced by attorney general as well as by private parties. See topic Monopolies, Restraint of Trade and Competition, subhead Unfair Trade Practices, for detailed description.

Submission of baseless claim by attorney, on behalf of former officer, against corporation does not fall within scope of c. 93A. (425 Mass. 344, 680 N.E.2d 1163).

Consumer sales contracts are regulated by c. 255B, c. 255D, c. 93, §48; c. 140D, c. 255, §12C. Consumer retail installment sales contracts are subject to very detailed disclosure and cancellation provisions and limitations on interest rates. See topics Interest, subhead Small Loans, Sales, subhead Retail Installment Sales, for description.

UCC sales, leases, secured transactions, and commercial paper articles have been modified in several ways affecting consumers. Under c. 106, §2-316A "[a]ny language, oral or written, used by a seller or manufacturer of consumer goods and services, which attempts to exclude or modify any implied warranties of merchantability and fitness for a particular purpose or to exclude or modify the consumer's remedies for breach of those warranties, shall be unenforceable." Similar provisions, respecting limitations on modification and exclusion of implied warranties, govern in consumer lease agreements. (c. 106, §2A-214A). C. 255, §12C requires that promissory note executed in connection with contract for sale of consumer goods on credit have printed on face "consumer note" and holder of note cannot be holder in due course thereof within meaning of Art. 3 of c. 106. C. 255, §§13I-J, c. 255B, §20A and c. 255D, §§21-22 specify that secured creditor may not repossess collateral from consumer/debtor until he has given consumer/debtor notice of his intention to repossess and 21 day period to cure default. If creditor repossesses said collateral after 21 day period, debtor may still redeem collateral from creditor within 20 days of creditor's taking possession. Creditor may not repossess collateral without hearing unless default "is material and consists of the debtor's failure to make one or more payments as required by the agreement, or the occurrence of an event which substantially impairs the value of the collateral," and only if possession can be obtained without use of force or entrance upon debtor's property, unless debtor gives permission for such entrance. Consumer/debtor is not liable for any deficiency after repossession or acceptance of consumer goods by creditor if unpaid balance of debt under retail installment sale contract is $1,000 or less ($2,000 or less in case of motor vehicle retail installment sale contract or secured consumer loan not under retail installment sale contract). If unpaid balance is greater than $1,000 ($2,000 in case of motor vehicle retail installment sale contract or secured consumer loan not under retail installment sale contract), deficiency must be calculated using fair market value of collateral. (c. 255, §13J; c. 255B, §20B; c. 255D, §22). See also topic Commercial Code.

Consumer Reporting Agencies.—See generally c. 93, §§50-68. Conforms substantially to federal law. Principal differences under state law are: (1) Narrower definition of business transaction in section delineating permissible purposes (§51); (2) consumer may elect to have name excluded from list provided by consumer reporting agency by notifying agency (§51A); (3) consumer report may include bankruptcies that antedate report by less than 14 years (§52); (4) consumer reporting agency must disclose contents of information in its file and upon written request provide copy thereof and must disclose names of users (§56); (5) permits disclosures to consumers by certified mail (§57); (6) length of consumer statement disputing completeness or accuracy of item in file not limited to specific number of words (§58).

Fraud in Sale of Personal Property.—Seller of personal property by deceit or fraud is liable in tort to purchaser for treble damages. (c. 231, §85J).

Unfair Debt Collection Practices.—No creditor may collect personal debt by harassing or embarrassing debtor, by using instruments that simulate judicial process or by communicating with certain third parties without permission of debtor. Use of language on envelope that shows debt is being collected is considered communication to third party. (c. 93, §49). Regulations governing debt collection have been promulgated by attorney general. See 940 C.M.R. §7.01 et seq. See also c. 265, §13C (assault in order to collect loan).

Cancellation of Certain Contracts.—Agreement for sale or lease of goods, or rendering of services, or both, primarily for personal, family or household purposes in excess of $25 in value and which is consummated by party thereto at place other than address of seller or lessor, may be cancelled by buyer if he so notifies seller within three business days. Notice requirements, penalties and remedies for failure to comply are found in c. 93, §48. Each such agreement must contain following language in bold face type of minimum size of ten points: "You may cancel this agreement if it has been signed by a party thereto at a place other than the address of the seller, which may be his main office or branch thereof, provided you notify the seller in writing at his main office or branch by ordinary mail posted, by telegram sent or by delivery, not later than midnight of the third business day following the signing of this agreement." (c. 93, §48[B]). Attached to each such agreement must be Notice of Cancellation form conforming to statutory language. (c. 93, §48[B]). Forms and notices of right to cancel prescribed by Federal Trade Commission may be substituted for those required by c. 93, §48(B). Seller's right of reclamation of goods furnished buyer under cancelled contract is limited by statute. (c. 93, §48D). Seller of services must not commence services during three day cancellation period. (c. 93, §48[J]). Retail installment sales contracts may also be cancelled within three days pursuant to c. 255D, §14. Motor vehicle retail installment sales contracts may also be cancelled by purchaser in certain situations. (c. 255B, §13). Contracts between buyers and credit service organizations are governed by c. 93, §§68A-68E. Contracts between buyer and credit service organization must be in writing, dated, signed by parties and include following language near space for buyer's signature and in minimum of ten point bold face type: "You, the buyer, have the right to cancel this contract or agreement at any time prior to midnight of the third business day following the date thereon." (c. 93, §68D[a]). Notice of Cancellation form in minimum of ten point bold face type containing specific statutory language must be attached to contract or agreement. (c. 93, §68D[b]).

Technical, vocational, trade school contracts and similar contracts may be cancelled at any time and student receives refund under conditions described in c. 255, §13K.

Unit Pricing.—Pursuant to authority given to Massachusetts consumer council by c. 6, §115A, council has promulgated Unit Pricing Regulations (203 CMR 3.00 et seq.), which apply to all retail stores except those operated by person as his sole place of business, provided that such establishment has sales volume of less than $1,000,000 per year.

Unsolicited Goods.—Any person who receives unsolicited goods offered for sale, but not ordered by him, may treat them as an unconditional gift, and use or dispose of them without obligation. (c. 93, §43).

Credit Cards.—Liability for unauthorized use limited by statute. (c. 140D, §26). Credit card issuer holding funds of cardholder in deposit account may not apply them on debt arising from use of credit card without written agreement by cardholder. (c. 140D, §21). Upon receipt of proper written notification of billing error from cardholder issuer must comply with regulations promulgated under c. 140D, §29.

Credit card issuers are expressly authorized to charge annual fees, subject to disclosure, cancellation and related requirements. Applications, pre-approved written solicitations and certain printed advertisements intended to "aid, promote or assist . . . . in the issuance of a credit card" are required to contain various disclosures including, in part, finance charges expressed as annual percentage rate, whether rate can vary, and whether annual fee is imposed. All charges and fees must be disclosed. (c. 140D, §§4-5).

Flammable Sleepwear.—Massachusetts regulates hazardous and flammable substances pursuant to c. 94B, §1.

Fair Information Practices.—Governmental executive branch agencies and those contracting with them who maintain personal data systems are subject to extensive regulation designed to safeguard access to or dissemination of personal data. Executive office of health and human services and state agencies within executive office may submit personal data to DOR to establish and maintain Mass. Longitudinal Database for Research in Child Support Enforcement and Social Services Programs. (c. 66A).

Freedom of Information.—Custodians of public records must comply, within ten days of receipt, with request for inspection or copy of public record. Attorney general or appropriate district attorney may take measures deemed necessary to insure compliance with this requirement. Massachusetts Superior Court and SJC given jurisdiction to order compliance. (c. 66, §10[b]).

Plain Language.—Insurance policies issued to more than 50 policyholders in commonwealth must meet following standards: 50 minimum Flesch scale readability; print size at least ten point type, one point leaded; style, arrangement and overall appearance do not give undue prominence to any portion of text, endorsement or rider; table of contents or alphabetical subject index included; margins and ink to paper contrast do not unreasonably interfere with readability; organization of content and summary help understanding. (c. 175, §2B). Disclosures required by Truth-in-Lending law, see topic Interest, subhead "Truth-in-Lending" Law, must be clear and conspicuous (c. 140D, §8), and those required by chapter governing electronic fund transfers must be in readily understandable language (c. 167B, §8).

Sunshine Law.—All meetings of governmental bodies must be open to public, except for discussion of disciplinary matters, security matters and similar specified purposes, and private meeting may be held only after governmental body has voted in public to hold private meeting. (c. 39, §23B). Records must be kept of all meetings and must be made public in most circumstances. (c. 39, §23B). Supervision and maintenance of public service records is also governed by c. 66, §§1-18. On proof of failure to comply with statute, court order requiring compliance therewith shall issue. Such order may be sought by three or more registered voters, attorney general, or appropriate district attorney. Such complaint must be speedily determined and burden of proof is on respondent to establish compliance with statute. If complaint is filed within 21 days of date when action made public, such order may invalidate any action at any meeting held in violation of statute. Any order may also require records of any meeting to be made public unless determined that maintenance of secrecy is authorized. (c. 30A, §11A½; c. 34, §9G; c. 39, §23B, c. 66, §17C).

CONTRACTS:

Common law rules apply, modified by adoption of Uniform Commercial Code. (c. 106). See topic Commercial Code. For other modifications, see topics Consumer Protection, Sales; categories Documents and Records, topic Seals; Family, topic Infants, subhead Disabilities.

Agreement for offer to purchase real estate is binding in certain circumstances. (44 Mass. App. Ct. 274, 690 N.E.2d 460).

Court may apply second look doctrine at time of breach when determining enforceability of liquidated damages clause of real estate purchase and sale agreement. (44 Mass. App. Ct. 825, 694 N.E.2d 869).

FACTORS:

Uniform Commercial Code adopted. (c. 106). See also topic Commercial Code. U.C.C. governs, generally, rights of creditors of consignee of goods as against rights of consignor. (c. 106, §2-326), risk of loss of consigned goods (c. 106, §2-327), power of merchant to sell entrusted goods in ordinary course (c. 106, §2-403), and liens on or security interests in consigned goods (c. 106, §9-101 et seq.). In addition c. 104, §1, provides that consignee or factor having authority to sell consigned goods is deemed owner so as to give validity to bona fide contract of sale made by factor (but see c. 106, §2-403, dispensing with requirement of authority to sell). C. 104, §§2-6 govern liens on consigned goods. C. 106, §9-114 governs priority disputes between consignor and secured party who is or becomes creditor of consignee. Special statute on consignment of fine art takes precedence over any inconsistent provisions of U.C.C. or c. 104.

See note at head of Digest as to 1998 legislation covered.

See Topical Index in front part of this volume.

MA – 13

FACTORS . . . *continued*
(c. 104A, §§1-6). Criminal penalty provided for fraudulent sales and conversions by factors. (c. 266, §88).

License Requirements.—None.

Liens.—Covered by Uniform Commercial Code. (c. 106, §§2-326, 2-327, 2A-306, 2A-307 and 9-101 et seq.). Also, c. 104 (not repealed by U.C.C.) allows consignee to assert lien on consigned goods in possession of shipper for money advanced to shipper without notice that shipper is not owner (§2); permits consignee to assert lien on goods consigned by person entrusted with goods and having authority to sell or consign, if consignee had cause to believe such person was owner or had legal interest in goods to amount of lien (§3); allows creditor of consignee or factor to assert lien on pledged goods, or document representing goods, for money advanced to consignee or factor, subject to provisions of U.C.C. (§4); limits rights of creditor accepting pledge of consigned goods for antecedent debt of consignee or factor (§5); and provides that §§3-5 of c. 104 do not affect lien of consignee or factor for expenses in shipping and caring for goods, nor prevent owner from recovering goods under stated conditions (§6). Statute on consignment of fine art provides that consigned art is held in trust for consignor and is not subject to claim by creditor of consignee, provisions of U.C.C. to contrary notwithstanding. (c. 104A, §§3-6).

Consignment Agreements.—Covered by U.C.C. (c. 106, §2-326, §9-101 et seq.). As to agreements on consignment of fine art, any clause in such agreements waiving any provision of c. 104A is void. (c. 104A, §5).

FRANCHISES:

Uniform Franchise and Business Opportunities Act has not been enacted.

Amendments to and Revocation of Franchises.—Every charter, franchise or act of incorporation shall forever remain subject to revocation and amendment. (Const. Amend. Art. LIX).

Termination.—Legislature has not adopted limitations on right to terminate franchise agreements in general (381 Mass. 284, 408 N.E.2d 1370) but in some specific areas there are limits on right of certain franchisors to terminate franchise agreements without cause: motor vehicle dealerships (c. 93B, §4[3][e][4]) and gasoline marketing agreements by suppliers (c. 93E, §5A). Unconscionability of provision allowing termination without cause must be determined on case by case basis, focusing in large part on whether, at time of agreement's execution, contract provision could result in unfair surprise and was oppressive to allegedly disadvantaged party. (381 Mass. 284, 408 N.E.2d 1370). Clause is not automatically oppressive because it does not require cause for termination. (381 Mass. 284, 408 N.E.2d 1370). Clause which is clearly worded and not hidden in agreement may satisfy condition that it not be surprise. (381 Mass. 284, 408 N.E.2d 1370).

FRAUDS, STATUTE OF:

Unless contract or note or memorandum thereof is in writing and signed by party to be charged, or by some person duly authorized by him, no action shall be brought: (1) To charge executor, administrator, or assignee in insolvency on special promise to pay damages from his own estate; (2) to charge person on special promise to answer for debt, default, or misdoings of another; (3) on agreement upon consideration of marriage; (4) on contract for sale of real estate or interest therein; (5) on agreement not to be performed within one year from making of contract. (c. 259, §1). Consideration need not be expressed in writing but may be proved by any legal evidence. (c. 259, §2). New promise to pay debt barred by discharge in bankruptcy or insolvency must be in writing and signed by debtor or person duly authorized by him. (c. 259, §3). No action lies on representation concerning character, conduct, credit, ability, trade or dealings of another person unless made in writing and signed by party to be charged thereby or by one duly authorized by him. (c. 259, §4).

Contracts of Sale.—Uniform Commercial Code applies. See c. 106, §§1-206 (personal property), 2-201 (goods) and 8-319 (securities). Contract, oral or written, for sale or transfer of evidence of debt due from U.S. or individual State, or of stock, or interest in stock, of bank, company, city or village incorporated under U.S. or State law, is void unless vendor at time of contracting is owner or assignee thereof, or is authorized by owner or assignee to sell or transfer same. (c. 259, §6).

Part Performance.—Uniform Commercial Code applies to sale of goods. (c. 106, §2-201). Under some circumstances, part performance will validate contract for sale of land. (289 Mass. 1, 193 N.E. 737).

Guaranty Written on Commercial Paper.—Uniform Commercial Code applies. (c. 106, §§3-416 and 3-419).

Security Interest.—Enforceability governed by c. 106, §9-203.

Wills.—Agreements relative to making or revocation of will or codicil or to giving legacy or making devise must be in writing and signed by person whose executor or administrator is sought to be charged or by person duly authorized by him in writing. (c. 259, §§5, 5A).

INTEREST:

In absence of agreement or provision of law rate of interest is 6%. (c. 107, §3).

Maximum Rate.—See subhead Usury, infra.

Judgments.—Upon finding or verdict for plaintiff for pecuniary damages for personal injuries, consequential damages or damage to property, clerk of court is required to add to damages interest thereon at 12% per year from commencement of action. (c. 231, §6B, but see 406 Mass. 62, 545 N.E.2d 1168 as to prejudgment interest in action for conscious suffering and wrongful death of stabbing victim). In contract actions, clerk is required to add to judgment for pecuniary damages interest at contract rate, if established, and otherwise at 12% per year, from date of breach or demand, if established, and otherwise from commencement of action. (c. 231, §6C). Interest at 18% may be awarded by court upon finding that defenses, setoffs or counterclaims of other party were wholly insubstantial, frivolous and not in good faith. (c. 231, §6F). Judgment bears interest from day of entry thereof until payment. (c. 235, §8). Post-judgment interest is at rate provided for prejudgment interest. (c. 235, §8).

Open Accounts.—Unless money is by express agreement, usage or understanding payable at a fixed time, interest runs only from a demand for payment, and does not run on open or unliquidated accounts. (2 Cush. [56 Mass.], 475).

Small Loans.—Any rate of interest or discount may be reserved by special agreement, which, if for more than 6%, must be in writing (c. 107, §3) except that: (1) On loans of less than $1,000 made at a rate of more than 6% per annum, other than those hereinafter referred to, discharge may be secured on payment of principal and agreed interest if less than 18% a year or on payment of 18% interest if agreed rate higher than 18% for period expiring one year after maturity, and in either case interest at 6% after one year, plus not more than $5 for actual expenses of making and securing loan may be recovered (c. 140, §90); (2) whoever engages in business of making consumer loans of $6,000 or less must be licensed, and interest rates and provisions of loan must comply with regulations of commissioner of banks (c. 140, §96); (3) maximum rate of interest chargeable by pawnbrokers must be fixed by licensing authorities (c. 140, §78); (4) maximum rate of interest on motor vehicle retail installment sales, insurance premium financing and retail installment sale of other goods and services regulated by c. 255B, §14, c. 255C, §14 and c. 255D, §11, respectively.

Discharge of security interests, pledges, assignments of wages securing repayment of small loans conforms to Commercial Code requirements. (c. 140, §107).

Open-End Credit Transaction.—No creditor may collect finance charge equivalent to annual percentage rate greater than 18%, except that when commissioner establishes index rate greater than 18%, creditor may collect finance charge at any rate established by it. Commissioner establishes index rate quarterly. (c. 140, §114B). Creditor may collect finance charge of 50¢ for billing cycle if finance charge otherwise assessable less than 50¢. (c. 140, §114B). Disclosure requirements for open-end credit transactions are found in 209 C.M.R. 32.05. For authority to charge fees and related disclosure requirements see topic Consumer Protection, subhead Credit Cards.

Unfair Debt Collection Procedures.—See topic Consumer Protection, subhead Unfair Debt Collection Practices.

Mortgages.—See category Mortgages, topic Mortgages of Real Property, subhead Restrictions.

Usury.—Whoever charges interest over 20% per annum shall be guilty of criminal usury, unless rate is regulated under other provision of law or regulations thereunder, or loan is by any lender subject to control, regulation or examination by any state or federal regulatory agency. "Interest" is broadly defined to include all charges, brokerage fees and the like. Usurious loan may be voided by Supreme Judicial or Superior Court upon petition by borrower. Person may avoid effects of this law by notifying attorney general of his intention to engage in such transactions and keeping records with respect thereto. (c. 271, §49).

Life Insurance Policy Loans.—The interest on policy loans made by life insurance companies is limited to 8% or adjustable rate not exceeding higher of: (a) Monthly average of Moody's published corporate bond composite yield as of two months prior to when rate is being determined or (b) current rate being used to compute cash surrender values plus 1%. (c. 175, §142).

Premium finance agencies are regulated by statute (c. 255C) and are required to comply with Truth in Lending Law (c. 255C, §23).

Motor Vehicles Sales Finance Companies.—See topic Licenses, Business and Professional. Financing by installment contract, see category Transportation, topic Motor Vehicles, subhead Sales.

Retail Installment Sales.—See topic Sales, subhead Retail Installment Sales for licensing requirements and form and content of agreements.

"Truth-in-Lending" Law.—See c. 140D; 209 C.M.R. 32, which contains regulations promulgated pursuant to c. 140D by commissioner of banks. Conforms substantially to federal law and regulation. Principal differences under state law are: (1) Statute of limitations is four years (c. 260, §5A); (2) written acknowledgment of receipt signed by debtor only raises rebuttable presumption of disclosure in credit transactions in which security interest on real estate is created (c. 140D, §10[c]); (3) right of rescission expires four years after transaction consummated or upon transfer or sale of consumer's interest in real property (§10[f]); (4) disclosures must be made to customer upon creation of credit balance (§22); (5) automatic debiting must be authorized in separate agreement with specified disclosure (§21); (6) mandatory free ride period for retail goods or services purchased with credit card (§20); (7) finance charge cannot be collected unless periodic statements are mailed 15 days before earlier of end of next succeeding billing cycle or payment due date (§19); (8) all finance charges, without exceptions for small amounts, must be expressed as annual percentage rates (§12[a][4]); the accrual of finance or other charges during three-day rescission period is prohibited (§10[a]).

Violations of this law are also violations of c. 93A. (c. 140D, §34).

Credit Bureau Reports.—See topic Consumer Protection.

See also category Civil Actions and Procedure, topic Injunctions.

LICENSES, BUSINESS AND PROFESSIONAL:

Licensing of certain professions and occupations is governed by c. 112. Following professions and occupations, among others, require state registration and/or licensing: physicians and surgeons (§2), physicians assistants (§§9C-9K), podiatrists (§§13-22), athletic trainers and occupational/physical therapists (§§23A-23Q), respiratory therapists (§§23R-23BB), pharmacists (§§24-36), sellers of drugs (retail or wholesale) (§§36A-42A), dentists (§§43-53), veterinarians (§§54-60), architects (§§60A-60O), optometrists (§§66-73B), dispensing opticians (§§73C-73M), nurses (§§74-81C), professional engineers and land surveyors (§§81D-81T), embalmers and funeral directors (§§82-87), certified public accountants (§§87A-87E), barbers (§§87F-87S), cosmetologists (§§87T-87KK), sanitarians (§§87LL-87OO), real estate brokers and salesmen

See note at head of Digest as to 1998 legislation covered.

See Topical Index in front part of this volume.

MA – 14

LICENSES, BUSINESS AND PROFESSIONAL... *continued*
(§§87PP-87DDD ½), electrologists (§§87EEE-87OOO), radio and television technicians (§§87PPP-87VVV), certified health officers (§§87WWW-87ZZZ), waste water treatment facility operators (§§87AAAA-87BBBB), drinking water supply facility operators (§§87CCCC-87DDDD), chiropractors (§§89-97), landscape architects (§§98-107), nursing home administrators (§§108-117), psychologists (§§118-129A), social workers (§§130-137), speech-language audiologists (§§138-147), acupuncturists (§§148-162), allied mental health and human services professionals (§§163-172), real estate appraisers (§§173-195). Licensed mental health counselor who also holds license as social worker must designate which license governs their practice. (§165). Licensing of certain mortgage brokers and lenders governed by c. 255E.

C. 221, §§37-52 governs licensing of attorneys. See category Legal Profession, topic Attorneys and Counselors, subhead Annual Registration.

Under c. 140, cities and towns may require licenses or permits for many businesses and activities, including, among others: pool tables for hire and bowling alleys (§177), overnight camps and cabins (§§32A-32B), innholding (§§2-9), lodging houses (§§22-32), dogs (§§136A-147), firearm sales (§§121-128), dispensing food or beverages (§§21A-21F), public amusements (§181), and boating (§§194-196).

Mammography facilities are regulated and licensed under c. 111, §52.

Auctioneers are licensed under c. 100. Labeling, distribution, sale, storage, transportation, use and disposal of pesticides are regulated by c. 132B.

Physician's license may be cancelled by Massachusetts licensing authorities on ground that license was revoked by another state "for reasons substantially the same" as those for which such licenses are suspended in Massachusetts. (398 Mass. 571, 500 N.E.2d 268).

Motor Vehicles Sales Finance Companies.—(c. 255B, §§1-3). Any person, other than bank, national banking association, federal savings and loan association or federal credit union, engaged in financing motor vehicles must secure license from bank commissioner. Fees determined annually by secretary of administration. Each licensee is required to file annual report with commissioner. Copies of printed forms of retail installment contracts used must be filed with bank commissioner.

For financing by installment contract see category Transportation, topic Motor Vehicles, subhead Sales.

Commercial travelers need not be licensed.

Collection Agencies.—Person, partnership, association or corporation conducting collection agency, and not being Mass. attorney, must be licensed by commissioner of banks and must file with state treasurer $10,000 surety company bond (or deposit $10,000 cash in lieu thereof) conditioned on paying, on written demand, the proceeds of collection to the one for whom the collection was made. Upon renewal of license, bond must be $10,000 or two times average monthly net collections rounded to next highest thousand, whichever is greater, but in no event more than $25,000. (c. 93, §§24, 25). Failure to account on written demand, to pay within 30 days of written demand or to comply with terms of the statute is punishable by fine, imprisonment, or both. (c. 93, §28).

Documents resembling legal process cannot be used for collection purposes by attorneys or collection agencies. (c. 93, §49[d]).

Creditor, attorney or assignee shall not collect or attempt to collect debt incurred primarily for personal, family or household purposes in unfair, deceptive or unreasonable manner. (c. 93, §49)

Commissioner of banks may from time to time establish regulations for conduct of collection agencies. (c. 93, §24).

MONOPOLIES, RESTRAINT OF TRADE AND COMPETITION:

Illegal under c. 93, §§1-14A, known as Mass. Antitrust Act, when occurring and having competitive impact primarily and predominantly within Mass., and, where knowing violation with specific intent to injure, punishable by fine of not more than $100,000 if corporation or if any other person, by fine of not more than $25,000 or imprisonment of not more than one year, or both. (§10). For purposes of Act, jurisdictional burden rests upon party asserting jurisdiction where 10% of person's gross revenue is derived from transactions involving interstate commerce outside of New England. As to all other persons, party asserting lack of jurisdiction shall have burden of establishing same. (§3). Any person injured may recover damages sustained, together with costs of suit, including reasonable attorney's fees, and may be awarded up to three times damages sustained if court finds there was malicious intent to injure. (§12). Civil action by attorney general on behalf of natural persons in Mass. stays any civil action under c. 93 or c. 93A based in whole or in part on same complaint. (Id.). Actions under Act must be brought within four years after cause of action accrued. (§13).

Agreements to Discriminate on Basis of Race, Etc.—It is unlawful for any person doing business in Massachusetts to agree with any foreign government, foreign person or international organization to refuse, fail or cease to do business in Massachusetts with, or to refuse, fail or cease to do business with, any person or business in Massachusetts because of race, color, creed, religion, sex, national origin or foreign trade relationships. (c. 151E, §2). Proceedings may be brought by attorney general to restrain violations of this prohibition. Suit seeking damages or injunction may be instituted by persons injured by such violation; up to treble damages, costs and reasonable attorney's fees may be awarded if willful violation is found. Action must be brought within four years after cause of action has accrued. For purposes of act, action for continuing violation accrues at time of latest violation. (c. 151E, §3).

Unfair Trade Practices.—It is criminal offense for retailer or wholesaler, with intent to injure competitors or destroy competition, to advertise, offer to sell or sell merchandise at less than "cost" plus any sales tax. (c. 93, §14F). Exceptions are: Isolated transactions not in usual course of business; bona fide clearance sales (if advertised or offered or marked and sold as such); mark down sales after bona fide efforts to sell prior to mark down; sales of perishable merchandise to forestall loss; sales of damaged goods or goods sale of which is being discontinued (if advertised or offered or marked and sold as such); sales on final liquidation of business; sales for charitable purposes or to relief agencies; sales on contract to certain state and local agencies; sales in which price of merchandise is made in good faith to meet competition; and sales by fiduciary or other officer acting under court order. (c. 93, §14G). Special provisions apply to advertising, offering to sell or selling cigarettes at less than "cost." (c. 64C, §§12-21). Massachusetts also has undertaken to regulate private trade, business and correspondence schools. (c. 75C, §1 et seq.; c. 75D, §1 et seq.).

It is an unfair trade practice for any manufacturer, winegrower, farmer-brewer, importer or wholesaler of any alcoholic beverage to refuse to sell, except for good cause shown, any item having brand name, to any licensed wholesaler to whom such manufacturer, winegrower, farmer-brewer, importer, or wholesaler has made regular sales of such brand items during period of six months preceding any refusal to sell. (c. 138, §25E). When consumer uses credit card to purchase travel services, provider of travel services, not including air carriers, may not impose surcharge or reduce commission of travel agent. Imposing surcharge or reducing commission constitutes unfair or deceptive practice. (c. 93, §48B).

It is unfair trade practice for car dealer to force customer to purchase optional accessories installed by dealer. (c. 93B, §4[4][a]; 18 Mass. App. 733; 470 N.E.2d 142).

Regulation of Business Practice and Consumer Protection Act.—C. 93A imposes extensive requirements in connection with fair trade practices. Unfair methods of competition and unfair or deceptive acts or practices in conduct of trade or commerce are unlawful, by statute. Negligent misrepresentation of fact, truth of which is reasonably capable of ascertainment is unfair and deceptive act. (21 Mass. App. 229, 486 N.E.2d 737; rev. den. 396 Mass. 1106, 488 N.E.2d 1179). Mass. courts guided by Federal Trade Commission and federal courts interpretations of §5(a)(1) of Federal Trade Commission Act as from time to time amended. Mass. attorney general given authority to make rules and regulations interpreting and defining unfair methods of competition and unfair or deceptive acts or practices (such rules not to be inconsistent with rules, regulations and decisions of Federal Trade Commission and federal courts interpreting 15 U.S.C. §45[a][1]; c. 93A, §§2[b], [c]). Attorney general has promulgated regulations affecting business practices, landlord-tenant relations, and retail advertising.

Mass. attorney general is given power to seek court injunctions against unfair practices covered by Act and extensive investigatory powers including right to subpoena witnesses and documents. (c. 93A, §§4-7). On petition of attorney general, court may order dissolution, suspension or forfeiture of franchise of corporation which is habitual violator of such injunctions. (c. 93A, §8). Court may also order violator to pay civil penalty up to $5,000 for each violation, and reasonable costs of litigation including reasonable attorney fees. (c. 93A, §4). Willful violators of c. 93A, §2 regarding securities and futures contracts, may also be forced to pay between two and three times ascertainable loss (c. 93A, §4) but recovery for nonwillful violation is actual damages (c. 93A, §4). Statute does not apply to transactions or action otherwise permitted under laws administered by any regulatory board or officer acting under statutory authority of commonwealth or U.S. (c. 93A, §3).

Private remedies by way of complaint, counterclaim, cross-claim, or third party action are available to any person, other than person entitled to bring action under §11, who has been injured as a result of use or employment by another person of unfair or deceptive act or practice (c. 93A, §9) and to any person engaged in conduct of any trade or commerce who suffers loss of money or property as result of use or employment by another person so engaged of either unfair or deceptive act or practice or of unfair method of competition (c. 93A, §11). Unfair practice must have occurred primarily and substantially within state. (c. 93A, §11). Relief not available, however, in context of employer-employee relationship. (388 Mass. 8; 444 N.E.2d 1262). Also, statute not applicable in disputes between parties in same business venture. (421 Mass. 448, 657 N.E.2d 1267). Further, there appears to be no right of contribution among joint and several tortfeasors with regard to multiple damage assessments. (387 Mass. 841; 443 N.E.2d 1308). Injunctive relief is available only in Superior Court or, in some circumstances, Housing Court. (c. 185C, §3). See 366 Mass. 688, 322 N.E.2d 768, for pleading requisites of c. 93A action. Private enforcement by consumers (not businessmen) is subject to 30 day demand procedure in which consumer must reasonably describe offense and injury caused thereby and afford defendant opportunity to tender restitution. Demand requirements do not apply if claim asserted by way of counterclaim or cross-claim, or respondent does not maintain place of business or keep assets within commonwealth. (c. 93A, §9[3]). If court finds willful or knowing violation of c. 93A, §2 double or treble damages must be awarded. If loss of money or property not suffered, may obtain injunction if unfair practice may cause loss of money or property. (c. 93A, §§9[3] and 11). Reasonable attorneys' fees are also awarded to petitioners in all cases where violation of c. 93A, §2 is found. (c. 93A, §§9[4] and 11; see 26 Mass. App. 99, 524 N.E.2d 110). There is no right of jury trial under c. 93A (388 Mass. 307, 446 N.E.2d 674) however Superior Court judge may in his discretion submit c. 93A claim to jury (397 Mass. 230, 490 N.E.2d 1169).

In civil action under c. 93A, doctrine of exhaustion of remedies will not be strictly applied. (c. 93A, §9[6]).

NEGOTIABLE INSTRUMENTS:

See topic Bills and Notes.

RESTAURANT SMOKING RESTRICTIONS:

See category Health, topic Smoking Regulations.

RESTRAINT OF TRADE:

See topic Monopolies, Restraint of Trade and Competition.

SALES:

Uniform Commercial Code applies. (c. 106, §§2-101 through 2-725). See topic Commercial Code.

Conditional Sales.—Uniform Commercial Code applies. (c. 106, §§9-101 through 9-507). See topic Commercial Code.

Consumer Protection.—See topic Consumer Protection.

See note at head of Digest as to 1998 legislation covered.

See Topical Index in front part of this volume.

MA – 15

SALES . . . *continued*

Motor Vehicles.—See category Transportation, topic Motor Vehicles, subhead Sales.

Retail Installment Sales.—Any person (other than bank or savings and loan association) engaged in business of purchasing retail installment sales agreements must obtain license from commissioner of banks. (c. 255D, §2). Licensee must keep such books and records as will enable commissioner to determine whether licensee is complying with rules and regulations made by commissioner. Every licensee must preserve such books, accounts and records, for at least two years after making final entry with respect to any retail installment sale agreement, revolving credit agreement, or any sale made pursuant thereto. Any licensee neglecting to make annual report as required by regulation may be subject to fine of $50 for each day during which such neglect or failure continues. (c. 255D, §3).

Retailer cannot require buyer to use credit. (c. 255D, §10A).

Form and content of sales contracts are governed by c. 255D and "Truth-in-Lending" requirements of c. 140D. As to latter, see topic Interest, subhead "Truth-in-Lending" Law. Buyer may cancel contract until seller has signed and delivered or mailed to buyer copy of contract or within three business days if consummated at place other than seller's address, by sending proper notice. (c. 255D, §14). Notice of debtor's right to such cancellation must be set forth in contract and detachable Notice of Cancellation form conforming to statutory language must be attached to each contract signed by buyer at place other than address of seller. Federal Trade Commission forms and notices may be submitted. (c. 255D, §9). Holder of retail installment sale agreement, or other person acting in his behalf, is subject to real and personal defenses which buyer has against seller. (c. 255D, §25A). Retail installment sales contracts may not contain certain proscribed terms. (c. 255D, §§10 and 15). No installment seller may permit any person to become obligated to said seller under more than one retail installment sales agreement executed at same time. (c. 255D, §11[D]). Holder of retail installment agreement may, by agreement with buyer, refinance unpaid balance. Also retail installment sales agreements may be altered. Refinancing of unpaid balance and alteration of contract permitted subject to conditions of c. 255D, §§16-18A.

Repossession and Deficiency Judgments.—Governed by c. 255D, §§21-22.

Discrimination in Granting Credit.—Refusal to extend credit because of individual's age, sex, sexual orientation or marital status is unlawful except as permitted. Violations give rise to liability for actual damages, or, if none, special damages not to exceed $1,000 plus legal fees. (c. 151B, §4[14]). Retail store providing credit privileges may not refuse access solely because of person's being 62 or older. (c. 151B, §4[12]).

Massachusetts commission against discrimination issued regulations substantially similar to Federal Reserve Board's Regulation B barring discrimination on basis of race, color, religion, national origin, sex, sexual orientation, children, handicap, marital status, age (provided applicant has capacity to enter into binding contract) or fact that all or part of applicant's income derives from any assistance program in granting of credit. These guidelines implement c. 151B, §§4(3B), 4(10), 4(14), 5; c. 272, §98.

Concealment of Leased Property.—Selling, concealing or refusing to turn over personal property held under written lease or rental agreement, with intent to defraud, is criminal offense. (c. 266, §87).

"Fire, Closing Out" Sales, etc.—Persons conducting fire, closing out, removal and like sales must comply with special requirements designed to promote fair dealing with public, for violation of which fines are imposed. (c. 93, §§28A-28F). See also c. 266, §91.

Product Liability.—Lack of privity of contract is not a defense in action for breach of warranty or negligence brought against manufacturer or seller or lessor if plaintiff might reasonably have been expected to use, consume or be affected by goods. Manufacturer, seller, lessor or supplier may not exclude or limit operation of this section. Such actions must be commenced within three years after date injury or damage occurs. (c. 106, §§2-318, 2A-216).

Unit Pricing.—See topic Consumer Protection.

Bulk Sales.—Art. 6 (Bulk Transfers), repealed by St. 1996, c. 160, §3.

Sales Below Cost.—See topic Monopolies, Restraint of Trade and Competition.

SECURITIES:

Uniform Securities Act, 1956 version, (see Uniform and Model Acts section) adopted. (c. 110A). Short title is Uniform Securities Act. Rules and Regulations have been issued and are found in 950 C.M.R. Following are material insertions, changes and omissions.

§102(b): Investment advisory contracts and compensation omitted.

§102(c): Custody of client's securities or funds omitted.

§§201, 202, 203 and 204: Registration provisions include investment adviser representatives.

§201(d): Registrations expire on last day of calendar year.

§202(b): Filing fees for applicant for initial or renewal registration of broker-dealer, and for agent, including agent automatically registered pursuant to §202(a), determined annually pursuant to authority deriving from §412 by commissioner of administration, currently $300 and $40. Initial or renewal fees for investment advisor or representative, including representative automatically registered pursuant to §202(a), currently $300 and $50, respectively. Fee determined annually pursuant to authority deriving from §412 by commissioner of administration, currently $40, when agent transfers from one broker-dealer or issuer to another.

§202(d): Minimum capital for broker-dealers is set forth in §202(d).

§202(e): Surety bond omitted. Broker-dealer must be registered with Securities & Exchange Commission and comply with its net capital, customer protection and custody of securities, and reporting requirements.

§204(a): Secretary may order fines or censure, as well as denial, suspension or revocation of registration.

§204(a) (2) (E)-(G): Bases upon which secretary may order fine, censure or denial, suspension or revocation of registration include order by secretary denying, suspending or revoking registration as broker-dealer, agent, investment advisor or investment adviser representative, as well as, (i) order by securities administrator or agency of another state or Canadian province or territory, or of Securities and Exchange Commission, after notice and opportunity for hearing, denying, revoking or suspending license as broker-dealer, agent or investment advisor, (ii) order suspending or expelling applicant or registrant from membership in self-regulatory organization registered under either Securities Exchange Act of 1934 or Commodities Exchange Act; (iii) U.S. Postal Service fraud order; (iv) cease and desist order, issued after notice and opportunity for hearing by secretary, Canadian province or territory, Securities and Exchange Commission or Commodity Futures Trading Commission; (v) revocation, denial or suspension of registration by Commodity Futures Trading Commission; or (vi) finding that broker-dealer or any of its principals has engaged in any unethical or dishonest conduct in securities, commodities or insurance business.

§302: Registration by notification omitted.

§303: Registration by coordination adopted. (c. 110A, §302).

§304: Registration by qualification adopted. (c. 110A, §303).

§305: (c. 110A, §304); Uniform Act §305(b) (c. 110A, §304[b]): Filing fee for registration statement determined annually pursuant to authority deriving from §412 by commissioner of administration, currently 1/20th of 1% of Massachusetts portion of offering but not less than $300 nor more than $1,500.

§305(d): (c. 110A, §304[d]). No five year limitation.

§305(g): Escrow omitted.

§305(h): Form of subscription or sales contract omitted.

§305(k) (c. 110A, §304[i]): Filing fee for open-end investment company, determined annually, pursuant to authority deriving from §412, by commissioner of administration, currently $2,000 registration fee and $1,000 annual reporting fee.

§402(a)(1): Securities of Massachusetts or any subdivision thereof not exempt from §403 (filing of sales and advertising literature).

§402(a)(2): Does not include revenue obligations.

§402(a)(4): Also includes securities of corporations licensed to make small loans and subject to regulation by commissioner of banks under c. 140.

§402(a)(5): Omits annuity, investment or similar contracts dependent on investment results.

§402(a)(8): Includes securities also listed on Boston, Midwest, Pacific Coast, and Philadelphia Stock Exchanges or Chicago Board of Options.

§402(a)(12): Includes certain cooperatives organized under c. 157 or c. 157A.

§402(b)(2): Non-issuer distribution of securities registered under the Securities Exchange Act of 1934 is exempted from sections 301 and 403. (c. 110A, §402[b] [2]).

§402(b)(8): Institutional buyer includes but is not limited to (i) Small Business Investment Company under Small Business Investment Act of 1958; (ii) private business development company under §202(a)(22) of Investment Advisers Act of 1940; (iii) Business Development Company under §2(a)(48) of Investment Company Act of 1940; (iv) Qualified Institutional Buyer per 17 C.F.R. 230.144A(a); and (v) entity with total assets over $5 million and which is either (a) company not formed for specific purpose of acquiring offered securities or (b) organization under §501(c)(3) of Internal Revenue Code.

§402(b)(9): Transaction pursuant to offer directed to not more than 25 persons other than those designated in paragraph (8) in commonwealth during any period of 12 consecutive months is exempt if seller reasonably believes that all buyers are purchasing for investment. If any commission or other remuneration is paid to any person for soliciting any prospective buyer in commonwealth other than those designated in paragraph (8) notice must be filed with secretary at least ten days before receipt of consideration from or delivery of subscription agreement by any purchaser, and secretary has five full business days to disallow exemption.

Under c. 110A, §402(b)(13), secretary is empowered by rule or order to exempt other transactions.

§403: In exercising rule-making authority under this section as to any security, including state and local issues, state secretary may require filing of sales literature used, but may not require advance approval or advance filing, or any filing by issuers outside Massachusetts, and criminal penalties of c. 110A, §409 do not apply.

§407A: When secretary determines after notice and opportunity for hearing that someone has or is about to violate c. 110A, secretary may issue cease and desist order and order fine up to $10,000 per violation, accounting, disgorgement or other relief. Secretary may issue temporary cease and desist order before hearing when delay would irreparably harm public interest.

§408: Secretary may bring court action to enforce compliance with c. 110A, and court may grant injunction or restraining order and may order accounting, disgorgement, rescission or other relief, including appointment of receiver or conservator. Secretary may be required to post bond.

§410(a)(2): Damages in civil suit defined as amount that would be recoverable upon tender less value of security when buyer disposed of it and interest at 6% a year from date of disposition.

§410(e): No person may bring action for civil liability more than four years after discovery of violation of c. 110A.

§411: Judicial review may be obtained pursuant to c. 30A, §14.

Consumer Protection.—Consumer Protection Act (c. 93A; see topic Monopolies, Restraint of Trade and Competition, subhead Unfair Trade Practices, catchline Regulation of Business Practice and Consumer Protection Act) includes securities and contracts of sale of commodity for future delivery and provides for double or treble damages for willful violations in addition to civil penalty not in excess of $10,000 and payment of costs including reasonable attorneys fees. (c. 93A, §§1, 4, 9[3]).

Tender Offers.—Regulated by c. 110C. Statute applies to tender offers, open market purchases, solicitation of particular shareholders, or any other acquisition which would make offeror and his associates beneficial owners of more than 10% of any class of equity securities of corporation incorporated or having its principal place of business in Massachusetts ("take-over bids"). (§1). Take-over bid does not include,

See note at head of Digest as to 1998 legislation covered.

See Topical Index in front part of this volume.

SECURITIES . . . *continued*

among other things, offer made with consent of directors of target company and their recommendation of terms to all stockholders or offer for consideration consisting primarily of securities covered by current prospectus of effective registration statement under Securities Act of 1933, or offer by corporation to acquire its own securities or those of subsidiary in which it holds at least two-thirds of voting stock, or offer to acquire corporation having less than 25 stockholders. (§1). If offeror or target company is public utility, public utility holding company, bank or bank holding company or savings & loan holding company, and offer is subject to regulatory approval, Act does not apply. (§12). Term "offeror" does not include bank or broker-dealer lending funds in ordinary course of business or any person or firm providing advice or ministerial services to offeror and not otherwise participating in take-over bid. (§1).

Offeror shall not make take-over bid unless offeror publicly announces its terms, files with state secretary and target company, on date of commencement of take-over bid, requisite information (set forth in §§4, 5) and pays filing fee determined annually by secretary of administration, currently $1,000. (§2). Target company or any offeree, within five days of such filing and upon payment of fee, currently $250, and deposit not to exceed $750 for costs, may request state secretary to hold hearing, or, within ten days of such filing, state secretary may order hearing if he feels it to be appropriate for protection of offerees. (§§2, 6). If state secretary does not order hearing within ten days, or if hearing is ordered or requested and state secretary finds that intended offer does not, or after appropriate amendment would not, violate statute, offer may proceed. (§2). Hearing shall commence within 20 days of such filing and adjudication shall be made within 45 days of filing. (§6).

If take-over bid is made for less than all outstanding equity securities of any class and if number of securities depositing in response to bid is greater than number offeror has agreed to accept, offeror must take up and pay for securities pro rata, according to number of securities deposited by each offeree. If consideration offered is increased during take-over bid, increased consideration must be paid to all offerees. (§7).

Prohibited offers and provisions include offers not made to all shareholders of target company who are Massachusetts residents, offers not made on same terms as offers to other shareholders who reside outside of Massachusetts, offers which do not remain open for at least 15 days with right to extend such period; purchase of shares within 15-day period; and offer to offeree of payment of fee or commission not available to all offerees. (§7).

In addition, offer may not be made if offeror and his associates and affiliates hold 5% or more of target company's stock any shares of which were purchased within one year before proposed offer and before making any such purchase offeror either failed to announce publicly his intention to gain control of target company or otherwise failed to make fair and full disclosure of such intention to persons from whom he acquired shares. (§3).

Shares tendered may be withdrawn at any time up to five days prior to date for termination of offer. (§7).

Solicitation materials must be filed with secretary and delivered to target company on date of commencement of takeover bid. (§§2, 4).

Civil, criminal and injunctive penalties are provided. (§9). Offeror, target company and offerees have private rights of action for injunctive relief. (§9). Action must be commenced within three years after violation or within one year after discovery of facts constituting violation, whichever first expires. (§9[c]). Secretary has rulemaking powers. (§10).

Control Share Acquisitions.—Takeovers of Massachusetts corporations and foreign corporations with specified Massachusetts contacts are also regulated by Control Share Acquisitions Act, cc. 110D and 110E. Law applies to certain Massachusetts business corporations, certain gas and electric companies, and certain Massachusetts business trusts and voluntary associations with: (1) At least 200 shareholders, (2) principal office, place of business or substantial assets in Massachusetts and (3) either more than 10% of shareholders, or more than 10% of shares held by, residents of Massachusetts. Prior to Jan. 1, 1988, such entities may become subject to law by charter or by-law amendment or by Board vote. After that date, law will apply unless charter or by-laws provide otherwise. Foreign corporations meeting tests (1) and (3) above and having principal executive office and more employees or assets employed or located in Massachusetts than in any other state as of certain specified times may become subject to law by appropriate charter or by-law amendment.

Law applies whenever acquiror (as defined) makes or proposes to make control share acquisition (acquisition causing acquiror's ownership to exceed thresholds of 20%, 33⅓% or 50% of voting power of target, subject to certain exceptions). Shares acquired in control share acquisition will have voting rights only to extent granted by majority vote of shares which are not interested shares (as defined, generally shares owned by persons not allied with acquiror or with target company management). Law provides mechanism for acquiror to force shareholder vote by delivery of written statement containing specified information and undertaking to pay certain target company expenses of holding special shareholder meeting. Otherwise, vote occurs at next annual or special meeting. Other provisions of law provide for restoration of voting rights in transfer which is not control share acquisition, authorize articles or by-laws of Massachusetts corporations to force redemption of control shares if voting rights not granted or written statement not delivered and provide appraisal rights for dissenters in Massachusetts corporations if shareholders vote to grant majority voting power to acquiror.

Business Combinations.—C. 110F. Corporation shall not engage in any business combination with any interested stockholder for three years unless: (1) Directors approve such action prior to stockholder becoming interested, (2) interested stockholder owned at least 90% of voting stock at time transaction commenced, or (3) directors approve and two-thirds of voting stock of non-interested stockholders affirm such business combination. Interested stockholder includes any person other than corporation and certain affiliates and associates of corporation that own 5% or more of corporation's voting stock. (§3). Restriction does not apply if, among other things: (1) Corporation's charter provides it will not be governed by such provision; (2) stockholders elect not to be governed by such provision, provided such election is not

effective for 12 months and such election does not apply to any business combination between corporation and any person who became interested stockholder on or prior to date of election; (3) corporation does not have at least 200 stockholders; (4) corporation does not have principal office, place of business or substantial assets in Massachusetts and either more than 10% of its stockholders residing within Massachusetts or more than 10% of its shares held by Massachusetts residents; or (5) business combination is proposed prior to consummation or abandonment of transaction which is with or by person who was not interested stockholder during previous three years. (§2). Law also provides that no business combinations shall terminate or impair labor negotiated employment contracts. (c. 149, §20E).

Supervision.—Uniform Securities Act and take-over bids under c. 110C are supervised by Director, Securities Division, Office of the Secretary of the Commonwealth, John W. McCormack Building, 17th Floor, One Ashburton Place, Boston, Massachusetts 02108. Telephone: (617) 727-7190.

Uniform Commercial Code adopted. (c. 106). See topic Commercial Code.

Uniform Simplification of Fiduciary Security Transfers Act not adopted.

Uniform Securities Ownership by Minors Act not adopted.

STATUTE OF FRAUDS:

See Frauds, Statute of.

TRUST RECEIPT SECURITY:

See category Debtor and Creditor, topic Pledges.

WAREHOUSEMEN:

Bonds.—Licensees must give bond to state treasurer for faithful performance of their duties in amount and with sureties approved by commissioner of public safety or designee. (c. 105, §1). Provision is made for release of sureties on such bonds on notice. (c. 105, §2A).

Licenses.—§§1-6 of c. 105 provide for issuance, on application and public notice thereof, of licenses for maintenance of public warehouses by commissioner of public safety, or designee, to suitable persons or corporations established under laws of, and having their places of business within, commonwealth. License fee is determined annually by secretary of administration, currently $250. (c. 105, §1).

Persons or Massachusetts corporations having their place of business in Massachusetts may, without license, keep public warehouse on premises of any other person or corporation for storage under contract of goods, wares or merchandise of such other person or corporation. (c. 105, §2C).

Whoever maintains public warehouse without procuring license and giving bond shall be punished by fine of not more than $1,000 and subject to injunction. (c. 105, §2).

Books and Accounts.—Warehouseperson must keep account of all transactions concerning goods in his care. Books are open to inspection by any person interested in property to which entries relate. (c. 105, §5).

Insurance and Warehouse Receipts.—Licensed warehouseperson must, upon written request by party storing property, insure such property. Any warehouse receipt delivered to depositor of family, personal or household goods shall contain following notice conspicuously printed in at least eight point type: "The property which you are putting in storage is not covered by insurance against fire or theft. You may contact the warehouseman for instructions on placing insurance coverage for fire and theft on the deposited property." (c. 105, §4).

Penalties for false or misleading receipts or fraudulent use of receipts appear in c. 105, §§55-64.

Uniform Commercial Code applies. (c. 106, §§7-101 to 7-210; 7-401 to 7-603).

Lien.—Warehouseperson has lien against bailor on goods covered by warehouse receipt or on proceeds thereof in his possession for charges for storage or transportation (including demurrage and terminal charges), insurance, labor or charges present or future in relation to goods, and for expenses necessary for preservation of goods or reasonably incurred in their sale pursuant to law. (c. 106, §7-209[1]). Warehouseperson loses lien on any goods which are voluntarily delivered or of which delivery is unjustifiably refused. (c. 106, §7-209[4]). For provisions on enforcement of warehouseperson's lien, see c. 106, §7-210.

CITIZENSHIP

ALIENS:

Aliens may sue and be sued as citizens. Employment of certain aliens: students, visitors and persons not admitted for permanent residence, is punishable by fine of up to $500 unless admitted under work permit or employment authorized by U.S. attorney general. (c. 149, §19C).

Property.—Resident or nonresident aliens may hold and convey real property. (c. 184, §1).

CIVIL ACTIONS AND PROCEDURE

ACCORD AND SATISFACTION:

In general, common law principles apply.

Compromise.—Acceptance of a lesser amount for a disputed or unliquidated claim is a valid compromise. (6 Cush. 148, 60 Mass. 148).

Pleading.—An accord and satisfaction must be specially pleaded. (Mass. R.Civ.P., Rule 8[c]).

Uniform Commercial Code adopted. See category Business Regulation and Commerce, topic Commercial Code.

See note at head of Digest as to 1998 legislation covered.

See Topical Index in front part of this volume.

ACTIONS:

In 1996, District/Municipal Court Rules of Civil Procedure, which governed actions in District Court Department and Boston Municipal Court Department, were merged with Massachusetts Rules of Civil Procedure (Mass. R. Civ. P.). Procedure in Massachusetts trial courts is governed by: (1) Massachusetts Rules of Civil Procedure which apply to actions before single justice of Supreme Judicial Court or Appeals Court, and in following departments of Trial Court: Superior Court, Housing Court, Land Court, and Probate and Family Court in proceedings seeking equitable relief (In this Digest these departments are referred to as Superior Court, Housing Court, Land Court and Probate Court, respectively, to District Court and Municipal Court Proceedings, and in all civil suits whether in law or in equity, except as provided in Rule 81 (Mass. R. Civ. P. 1); (2) Massachusetts Rules of Domestic Relations Procedure (Mass. R. Dom. Rel. P.), which apply to proceedings for divorce, separate support, custody, annulment, spousal and child support, paternity and support for child born out of wedlock, and abuse prevention. All sets of rules are based on Federal Rules of Civil Procedure, with changes appropriate to Massachusetts needs or established Massachusetts practice. Both sets of rules follow same numbering system. Significant variations between District/Municipal Court and Superior Court practice due to statutory or other limitations on jurisdiction are noted below. Mass. Uniform Small Claims Rules have been adopted. Juvenile Court Rules adopted.

Forms of Action.—One form of action known as "civil action." (Rule 2). Substantive equitable remedies remain unaffected, including right to reach and apply assets of debtor. (c. 214, §3). See category Courts and Legislature, topic Courts.

District Courts are virtually without equity jurisdiction, but by statute equitable defenses going to entire case may be raised in District Courts. (c. 231, §31).

Commencement.—Civil action is commenced by: (1) Mailing complaint and entry fee to clerk by certified or registered mail; or (2) filing complaint and entry fee with clerk. (Rule 3). Actions brought for registration or confirmation (c. 185) are commenced by filing surveyor's plan and complaint on Land Court form (Rule 3).

Parties.—Rules 17-21, equivalent to Federal Rules except Rule 17(a) does not apply to right of insurer to sue in behalf of employee in workmen's compensation case (c. 152, §15) and insurer may sue in name of assured to whose rights it is subrogated (Rule 17); Rule 20 aggregates entry fees in certain cases.

With respect to actions against owners of residential premises for Sanitary Code violations, a tenant may join certain persons as parties pursuant to c. 111, §127N.

Class Actions.—Prerequisites for class action are equivalent to Federal Rule 23(a). Class action maintainable if prerequisites met, if common questions of law or fact predominate, and if class action is superior to other available methods. (Rule 23[b]). There is no Mass. equivalent to Federal Rules 23(b)(1), 23(b)(2) or 23(c); notice to class members is within court's discretion. (Rule 23[d]). Court approval required for dismissal or compromise. (Rule 23[c]). Rules 23.1 and 23.2 are equivalent to Federal Rules.

Class actions also maintainable under c. 93A, §11 on behalf of persons injured by unfair methods of competition or unfair or deceptive trade practices.

Uniform Class Actions Act not adopted.

Intervention.—Rule 24, equivalent to Federal Rule, but requires parties challenging constitutionality of legislative act or municipal ordinance to notify attorney general.

Interpleader.—Rule 22, equivalent to Federal Rule.

Impleader.—See infra, subhead Third Party Practice.

Third Party Practice.—Rule 14, equivalent to Federal Rule except third party complaint may be filed as of right within 20 days after service of answer. Rule excludes cases of registration and confirmation of title in Land Court.

Joinder of Claims and Parties.—Rules 18-21, equivalent to Federal Rules. District Courts have no jurisdiction over fraudulent conveyances.

Consolidation and Separate Trial.—Rule 42, substantially equivalent to Federal Rule, except that Mass. R. Civ. P. Rule 42(c) provides procedure for consolidation of cross actions pending in more than one District Court. Whenever related actions are pending in more than one division of same department of trial court, administrative justice of such department may order consolidation of such actions for purpose of trial, upon motion of any party. (c. 223, §2A). Pursuant to Rule 42(d), District Court may order separate trial of any claim, cross-claim, counter-claim, or third party claim.

Severance of Actions.—Rule 42(b) and Rule 19(b), substantially equivalent to Federal Rules, provide respectively for separate trial and for severance of parties as required for just adjudication.

Stay of Proceedings.—Execution upon judgment or proceedings taken for its enforcement shall be stayed until time for appeal has expired. Execution is also stayed pending appeal. (Mass. R. Civ. P. Rule 62; MRAP 6). See Nolan, 9A Mass. Practice, §986. See also topic Appeal and Error, subhead Stay of Proceedings; Appeal Bond. There are numerous statutes dealing with specific instances in which stay of proceedings is authorized. See Stay, General Index, Mass. Gen. Laws. See also category Property, topic Landlord and Tenant, subhead Dispossession.

Abatement and Revival.—In addition to actions which survive by common law, including most actions of contract (1 Pick. 71, 18 Mass. 71) there survive by statute actions of replevin, actions of tort for assault, battery, imprisonment or other damage to person, for medical expenses incurred by spouse, parent or guardian of injured person, for conversion, or for real or personal property damage, and actions against sheriffs for misconduct or negligence of themselves or their deputies. Actions which survive may be brought or prosecuted by or against personal representative of decedent. (c. 228, §1).

Substitution of representative of decedent is pursuant to Rule 25. Failure by surviving party to move for substitution within one year after date of approval of bond of decedent's representative will result in dismissal of action unless such failure was result of excusable neglect. Death of one of multiple parties is governed by Rule 25(a)(2).

If one of several parties dies before final judgment, action may be prosecuted by or against surviving plaintiff or defendant as case may be. (c. 228, §7); see also Mass. R. Civ. P. 25(a)(2)..

Termination of Actions.—Actions may be terminated by judgment (Rule 54); stipulation, voluntary and involuntary dismissal (with or without prejudice) (Rule 41); or by court or defendant's motion for lack of prosecution of any action which has remained upon docket for three years (Rule 41[b]).

Prohibited Actions.—No action for breach of contract to marry.

Amendments.—Rule 15, equivalent to Federal Rule, except amendment of right must be made prior to grant of order of dismissal, and provisions of Federal Rule 15(c) as to amendments changing parties are omitted.

Small Claims.—Uniform Small Claims Rules in effect. See category Courts and Legislature, topic Courts, subhead District Court and BMC, catchline Small Claims.

Removal From District Court.—When claim, counterclaim, or cross claim exceeds $25,000, not including interest, party against whom such claim, counterclaim or cross claim is brought may remove case to Superior Court by filing claim of trial in Superior Court with District Court, together with $100 filing fee (c. 231, §104) and $50 surcharge (c. 262, §2), and such surety as approved by other party or by clerk of District Court, payable to such other party to satisfy judgment for costs which may be entered in Superior Court within 30 days (c. 231, §104). Claim of trial by Superior Court must be filed within 25 days of service of pleading asserting claim, counterclaim, or cross claim (except that for compulsory counterclaims, claimant must request removal within five days of expiration of time allowed to assert counterclaim). (c. 231, §104). If claim, counterclaim, or cross claim is less than $25,000, case must be tried in District Court but party who would have been entitled to remove but for fact that $25,000 standard was not met may obtain de novo trial in Superior Court under retransfer provision of c. 231, §102C. See infra, subhead Removal from Superior Court.

Removal from Superior Court.—Superior Court may on its own motion or on motion of any party determine that if plaintiff prevails there is no reasonable likelihood that recovery will exceed $25,000 and court may thereupon transfer any civil action to District Court or BMC. (c. 231, §102C). Any party to transferred action aggrieved by finding or decision of District Court or BMC may as of right have case retransferred for determination by Superior Court. Request for retransfer or transfer to Superior Court must be filed with District Court within ten days after notice of finding or decision. (Id.). District court's disposition of case on summary judgment is "decision" for purposes of retransfer. (407 Mass. 31, 551 N.E.2d 903).

Actions for Medical Malpractice.—Must be heard initially by tribunal consisting of superior court justice, physician and lawyer for determination of whether or not plaintiff's evidence raises legitimate question of liability. If tribunal finds for defendant, plaintiff is barred from usual judicial process unless he files $6,000 bond for costs within 30 days of tribunal's finding. (c. 231, §60B). Awards for pain and suffering, loss of companionship, embarrassment and other items of general damage limited to $500,000 unless fact finder finds substantial or permanent loss or impairment of bodily function, substantial disfigurement or other special circumstances. (c. 231, §60H). Such awards must be itemized. (c. 231, §60F). Limits imposed on contingency fees. (c. 231, §60I).

Actions Against Public Bodies Based on Torts.—Must be brought in Superior Court. (c. 258, §3). Prerequisites include prior written claim to appropriate "executive officer" (c. 258, §1) within two years of injury; claim must be denied in writing or compromise or settlement not reached within six months before filing action (c. 258, §4). Certain claims, such as one based on intentional tort and one based on discretionary conduct, excepted. (c. 258, §10[c][b]). Public bodies, however, are not immune under §10(c) for wanton or reckless acts. (419 Mass. 278, 643 N.E.2d 1043). Public bodies include commonwealth, counties, cities, towns, districts and departments, offices, commissions, councils, boards, divisions, bureaus, institutions or agencies thereof but not authorities and other independent bodies politic and corporate. General release of employee of municipality or public body from liability also operates to release municipality against which derivative liability would also lie. (38 Mass. App. Ct. 70, 645 N.E.2d 44, further app. rev. denied, 419 Mass. 1107, 646 N.E.2d 1071).

Actions for Contribution.—Uniform Contribution Among Joint Tortfeasors Act in effect with minor variations. (c. 231B, §§1-4).

Actions Based on Defects.—No recovery can be had for personal injury or property damage due to defect or disrepair of public or private way unless proper notice is given to county, city, town or person obligated to repair way within 30 days after injury or removal of incapacity. (c. 84, §15, c. 81, §18). Commonwealth not liable for injury from insufficient railing on state highway, injury sustained on sidewalk, or construction or repair of highway. (c. 81, §18). No recovery can be had in actions founded on defective condition of private premises and adjoining ways caused by or consisting in part of ice or snow unless proper notice to owner is given within 30 days after injury or removal of incapacity. When defect is caused by ice or snow, failure to give notice is not defense unless defendant proves that he was prejudiced by such lack of notice. (c. 84, §§18-21).

Actions to Enforce Foreign Judgments.—New action required. Uniform Enforcement of Foreign Judgments Acts not in effect.

Limitation of.—See topic Limitation of Actions.

Right to Privacy.—See topic Injunctions, subhead Right to Privacy.

Actions by Developers Against Public Interest Groups.—Any action against party that is brought in response to that party's exercise of its right to petition under U.S. or state constitution is subject to special motion to dismiss. (c. 231, §59H). Special motion should be granted unless party against whom motion is brought shows: (1) moving party's exercise of its right to petition lacks factual support or arguable legal basis; and (2) moving party's actions caused injury. (c. 231, §59H). Motion may be filed within 60 days of service and costs are available to moving party if successful. (c. 231, §59H).

See note at head of Digest as to 1998 legislation covered.

See Topical Index in front part of this volume.

APPEAL AND ERROR:

Note: Massachusetts trial courts were organized and consolidated by 1978, c. 478. For description of present organization, see category Courts and Legislature, topic Courts, subhead Trial Court. Civil procedure is governed by Massachusetts Rules of Civil Procedure (Mass. R. Civ. P.), based largely on Federal Rules of Civil Procedure (see topic Practice).

Civil Appeals.—Civil appeals from decisions of Appellate Division of District Court, and of Housing, Land, Probate and Superior Courts, are governed by Massachusetts Rules of Appellate Procedure (MRAP), modelled substantially on Federal Rules of Appellate Procedure. Appellate review may be instituted by notice of appeal filed in lower court (MRAP Rule 3), in most cases within 30 days of entry of judgment (MRAP Rule 4), within 60 days if Commonwealth or officer or agency thereof is party, or by report, except from Appellate Division or Probate Court (see subhead Report; Interlocutory Review, infra), to following courts:

To Supreme Judicial Court.—Supreme Judicial Court (SJC), highest court in Commonwealth, has concurrent civil jurisdiction with Appeals Court (c. 211A, §10), but no civil appeal may be taken of right to SJC except from decision of single justice of SJC (see MRAP Rule 1[b]; but cf. c. 231, §112) and of any tribunal from which appeal must by law be brought in SJC (MRAP Rule 1[b]). SJC regulates appeal procedure to full court of single justice's relief denial from trial court interlocutory ruling. (MRAP Rule 1[b]; SJC Rule 2.21). Direct review, or further review following Appeals Court decision, will be permitted by SJC when majority of Appeals Court justices considering or deciding particular case determine such review to be in public interest, or when two SJC justices (for direct review) or three SJC justices (for further review) so determine. (c. 211A, §§10-11; MRAP, Rules 11 and 27.1). Party with right to remove its case to Superior Court after adverse decision by Appellate Division may not appeal to SJC prior to trial in Superior Court. (396 Mass. 303, 486 N.E. 2d 26). Filing Motions Requirement; call Jean M. Kennett, Clerk of Supreme Judicial Court for Commonwealth, 1412 New Court House, Boston 02108, Tel: (617) 557-1020; Fax: (617) 557-1145.

To Appeals Court.—Appeal may be taken to Appeals Court from decision of appellate tax board (c. 58A, §13; c. 211A, §10), Land Court, Housing Court or Superior Court (c. 211A, §10; c. 231, §113), Probate Court (c. 211A, §10), Appellate Divisions of District Court and Boston Municipal Court (c. 211A, §10; c. 231, §109) and criminal sessions of District Court and Boston Municipal Court (c. 211A, §10 as amended by 1992, c. 379, §66), except that Appeals Court may not review first degree murder convictions (c. 211A, §10). Appeals Court Clerk: Nancy Turck Foley, tel: (617) 725-8106.

To Superior Court.—Trial de novo may be had in Superior Court upon appeal from District Court within six days of entry of judgment. (c. 231, §97).

To Appellate Division.—Civil appeals from decisions of District and Municipal Courts to Appellate Division of those Courts are governed by District/Municipal Courts Rules for Appellate Division Appeal (DMRA). These rules govern appeals in all civil actions commenced and any court action occurring on or after July 1, 1994. (DMRA 1A).

Notice of appeal along with filing fee must be filed with clerk of trial court and served on all parties by appellant. (DMRA 3[a]). Notice of appeal must contain items set forth in DMRA 3. Notice of appeal must be filed within ten days after date of entry of judgment in case being appealed. (DMRA 4). Ten-day extension may be granted upon showing of excusable neglect or other good reason. (DMRA 4[c]).

Appeals may be made in three different forms: Expedited Appeal—appropriate when issues limited and clearly defined. (DMRA 8A Comments). Must be filed within 20 days of filing notice of appeal and must contain items set forth in DMRA 8A(a). Filing deadlines and parties to be served expedited appeal and briefs are set forth in DMRA 8A(b)(c). Objections timely made will automatically terminate expedited appeal. (DMRA 8A[b]). Agreed Statement of Case—may be used if expedited appeal fails; allows parties to frame issues for appeal in brief form. (DMRA 8B Comment). Parties must file with trial court agreed statement of case ("Asoc") within 30 days of filing notice of appeal or termination of expedited appeal. (DMRA 8B[b]). "Asoc" must contain items set forth in DMRA 8B(b). Statement deemed approved by trial judge unless within 15 days of filing trial judge enters disapproval order, to be served on all parties by clerk. (DMRA 8B[c]). Filing deadlines and parties to be served "Asoc" and briefs are set forth in DMRA 8B(d). Appeal on Record of Proceedings—appropriate if complex issues or dispute as to nature of issues. (DMRA 8C Comments). Parties must file and serve Appeal on Record of Proceedings ("Arop") within 30 days of filing notice of appeal or termination of procedures under Expedited Appeal or Agreed Statement of Case. (DMRA 8C[b]). "Arop" must contain items set forth in DMRA 8C(b). Filing deadlines and parties to be served "Arop" and Record are set forth in DMRA 8C(c-g).

General provisions for filing and service (DMRA 13); computation and extension of time (DMRA 14); briefs and other papers (DMRA 16-20); oral arguments (DMRA 22). See also c. 231, §108.

Notice of Appeal.—Massachusetts courts have no jurisdiction over party not named in notice of appeal. Time for filing notice of appeal runs from date of entry on docket even if notice is never mailed to counsel. (Mass. R. Civ. P. 77). Notice of appeal filed before timely post-trial motion under Rules 50(b), 52(b) or 59 is nullity and new notice required.

Procedure for appeals from adjudications and orders of commitment in proceedings brought pursuant to c. 119, §27 governed by Interim Supplemental Rules of Appellate Procedure in Care and Protection Cases. Claim of appeal must be filed with clerk of trial court within ten days of entry of adjudication or order of commitment. (Interim Supp. MRAP Rule 3[c], compare c. 119, §27).

Report; Interlocutory Review.—Review of trial court verdict or finding by reporting case to Appeals Court may be granted by trial court sua sponte or upon motion. (c. 231, §111; Mass.R.Civ.P., Rule 64). Trial court may also report case before trial or decision where parties agree in writing as to all material facts. (c. 231, §111; Mass.R.Civ.P., Rule 64). Report of case is treated for purposes of MRAP as notice of appeal, and plaintiff in civil action, defendant in criminal action, treated as appellant. (c. 231, §112A; MRAP, Rule 5).

Interlocutory review of finding or order of trial court available if court reports that its finding or order so affects merits of controversy that interlocutory determination by appellate court is desirable. (c. 231, §111; Mass.R.Civ.P., Rule 64). Interlocutory review of finding or order by single justice of SJC similarly available if justice reports that his findings or order so affects merits of controversy that matter ought to be determined by full SJC or Appeals Court. (c. 231, §112; Mass.R.Civ.P., Rule 64[a], [b]). Absent interlocutory report by trial court, any party aggrieved by interlocutory order of justice of Housing Court, Land Court, Superior Court or Probate Court (but not of SJC single justice) may file petition within 30 days of order in Appeals Court seeking relief from order. (c. 231, §118).

Stay of Proceedings; Appeal Bond.—Execution generally stayed until time for appeal expires; after appeal taken execution of judgment ordinarily stayed pending decision on appeal. Unless otherwise ordered, judgment not stayed in injunction, receivership action. (Mass.R.Civ. P., Rule 62). Application for stay of judgment or order of lower court pending appeal may be made to appellate court or to single justice thereof upon showing that application to lower court for relief is impracticable or has been denied. Stay of judgment or order may be conditioned upon filing of bond or other appropriate security in trial court. (See MRAP, Rule 6.)

Extent of Review.—Except in extraordinary case, only legal issues raised by parties below are subject to review. (388 Mass. 491, 446 N.E.2d 1385). In actions tried without jury, trial court's findings of fact will not be set aside unless clearly erroneous. (Mass.R.Civ.P., Rule 52). In actions to be tried, without jury, trial court must accept master's subsidiary findings of fact unless they are clearly erroneous, mutually inconsistent, unwarranted by evidence as matter of law, or are otherwise tainted by error of law. (Mass.R.Civ.P., Rule 53). To extent that court adopts them, findings of master are considered findings of court. (Mass.R. Civ.P., Rule 52).

Review of Administrative Decisions.—Judicial review of any administrative regulation, or of sufficiency of reasons for adoption as emergency regulation, is by action for declaratory relief under c. 231A, unless otherwise provided in particular instances. (c. 30A, §7). Ordinarily review of final decision of administrative agency in adjudicatory proceeding is instituted in Superior Court. (c. 30A, §14).

BONDS:

Requirements for giving of security by applicant for temporary restraining order or preliminary injunction (Mass. R. Civ. P. 65[c]), and for stay or injunction pending appeal (Mass. R. App. P. 6[b]) are same as in federal courts, except Mass. R. Civ. P. 65(c) also provides exemption from requirement of giving security to commonwealth, any political subdivision of commonwealth and any officer or agency of commonwealth or any political subdivision thereof. Defendant whose property has been attached in civil action may at any time dissolve attachment by giving bond with sufficient sureties. (c. 223, §120). Plaintiff, plaintiff's attorney, master in chancery, or court must approve bond. Sureties must satisfy plaintiff, or magistrate must find bond suffices to cover attachment allowing for defendant's debt. (c. 221, §§120, 125). Approval of bond requires written application to magistrate. (c. 223, §§121, 125). Bond may be required when appeal is taken from interlocutory or final judgment affecting injunction. (Mass. R. Civ. P. 62[c]). Mass. R. Civ. P. Rule 65.1 governs procedural requirements for security).

Sureties.—Requirements vary in accordance with type of bond, court rules and local practice.

Enforcement.—Massachusetts rule governing proceedings against sureties (Mass. R. Civ. P. 65.1) is same as federal rule. Judgment may be entered against surety for full penal sum of bond, but execution will issue only for amount provided by statute. (c. 235, §§9, 10).

CERTIORARI:

Jurisdiction.—SJC or Superior Court. (c. 249, §4).

Grounds.—Petitioner for certiorari must show: (1) Errors of law were committed (353 Mass. 540, 233 N.E.2d 316); (2) in judicial or quasi-judicial proceeding (administrative actions excluded [354 Mass. 759, 236 N.E.2d 87]) which is not according to course of common law and not otherwise reviewable by motion or appeal (see also c. 249, §4); (3) such errors appear on face of record and are so substantial and material that, if allowed to stand, will result in manifest injustice or substantial injury to petitioner; (4) lack of any other available remedy (318 Mass. 681, 63 N.E.2d 561; 355 Mass. 79, 242 N.E.2d 868). (See also c. 249, §4.)

Proceedings.—Civil action in nature of certiorari may be commenced in SJC or Superior Court within 60 days after close of proceedings complained of. (c. 249, §4). Writs of certiorari have been abolished and petitioner must file motion to obtain relief pursuant to Mass. R. Civ. P. (Mass. R. Civ. P. 60[b], 81[b]). Petition is addressed to sound discretion of court (349 Mass. 553, 210 N.E.2d 699), but party aggrieved by final judgment may appeal to full court of SJC or, from judgment in Superior Court, to Appeals Court (c. 211A, §10) unless direct review by SJC is required under c. 211A, §10A or §10B. See category Courts and Legislature, topic Courts.

Review.—Appropriate standard of review determined according to nature of action sought to be reviewed. (379 Mass. 794, 401 N.E.2d 113).

CHARITABLE IMMUNITY:

See topic Damages.

COMMISSIONS TO TAKE TESTIMONY:

See topic Depositions and Discovery.

COSTS:

Costs are awarded to prevailing party by statute and taxed by clerk of court. (c. 261, §§1, 19). Costs do not include attorney's fees unless granted by statute (e.g. c. 93A

See note at head of Digest as to 1998 legislation covered.

See Topical Index in front part of this volume.

COSTS . . . *continued*

and c. 231, §59H), but may include witness fees, entry fees, traveling expenses, premiums on bonds to dissolve attachment, expenses of taking depositions if reasonably necessary (Mass. R. Civ. P. 54[e]) and up to $500 for costs of plans, drawings, photographs and certified copies of records actually used at trial (c. 261, §25A). Court may award costs only after conducting hearing and making findings of reasonable necessity. (413 Mass. 320, 597 N.E.2d 404). With certain exceptions, plaintiffs in Superior Court recovering less than $100 receive no costs. (c. 261, §4). Costs may be doubled or trebled, excluding witness fees, copying costs and deposition costs. (c. 261, §11). Costs incurred in appeal may be allowed by court before which appeal is heard. (c. 261, §22). Costs may include expenses and attorney's fees when court finds that party has brought insubstantial, frivolous or bad faith claims or defenses. (c. 231, §§6E-6G and c. 231, §59H). Award of costs bears interest from date of order. (404 Mass. 112, 533 N.E.2d 1341). Costs recoverable against commonwealth allowed only by authority of statute. (409 Mass. 89, 564 N.E.2d 998). Costs may be imposed against commonwealth in civil actions initiated by commonwealth. (c. 261, §14).

Security for Costs.—Where no plaintiff is an inhabitant of Massachusetts, an endorser for costs, who is a responsible inhabitant, must be furnished. (c. 231, §42).

Liability of Attorney.—Attorney in case is not, as such, liable for costs, but where no plaintiff is inhabitant of Massachusetts, signature of attorney on complaint constitutes endorsement for costs. (183 Mass. 102, 66 N.E. 422).

Indigent Persons.—Upon filing an affidavit of indigency, court may grant a waiver, substitution or payment by commonwealth of normal fees and costs. (c. 35, §12; c. 261, §§27A-27G). Payment of court costs for indigent parties should be delivered to state treasurer. (c. 35, §12). Indigent party who recovers in excess of three times total amount of fees or costs waived or paid must repay total amount thereof to clerk or register of court. (c. 261, §27E).

DAMAGES:

Common law generally prevails as to compensatory damages except as noted.

Punitive damages are allowed only by statute. Instances of such statutes are: (1) At least double, and up to treble, damages plus reasonable attorney's fees for willful unfair trade practices (c. 93A, §§9 and 11); (2) certain frauds in selling goods at auction (c. 100, §12); (3) actions by third persons to recover gambling losses (c. 137, §1); (4) damages caused by dog after it is ordered to be restrained (c. 140, §159); (5) attorney who fails to pay over money collected (c. 221, §51); (6) minimum of $5,000 for willful or grossly negligent conduct resulting in death (liability of employer to employee excluded) (c. 229, §2; see category Estates and Trusts, topic Death, subhead Actions for Death); (7) willful damage to trees (c. 242, §7); (8) willful damage to farm property (c. 242, §7A); and (9) employer who retaliates against any person required to report child abuse or neglect who does so liable for treble damages, costs and attorneys' fees. (c. 119, §51A).

Comparative negligence rule has been adopted. (c. 231, §85). Contributory negligence does not bar recovery if plaintiff's negligence is not greater than total amount of negligence attributable to defendants, but any damages allowed shall be diminished in proportion to amount of negligence attributable to injured party. Defense of assumption of risk abolished. (c. 231, §85).

Wrongful Death.—See category Estates and Trusts, topic Death, subhead Actions for Death.

Charitable Immunity.—If tort is committed in course of any activity carried on to accomplish directly charitable purposes of body, liability in any cause of action shall not exceed $20,000 (exclusive of interest and costs). There is no such limitation if tort is committed in course of activities "primarily commercial in character" even though carried on to obtain revenue to be used for charitable purposes. (c. 231, §85K). No director, officer or trustee of charitable educational institution who is unpaid for such services shall be liable solely by reason of such services for harm to another resulting from good faith activities performed within scope of official duty unless damage or injury caused by wilful or wanton misconduct or said person's operation of motor vehicle. (c. 231, §85K).

Sovereign Immunity.—Scope defined by c. 258. Public departments and agencies, other than certain authorities and other independent public agencies (§1), are liable as if they were private individuals if negligent act or omission of public employee responsible was within scope of his office or employment (§2). But remedy does not extend to punitive damages or any damages in excess of $100,000 per plaintiff or to prejudgment interest (§2); to any claim based upon public employee's performance of, or failure to perform, discretionary act (§10); to any claim arising out of intentional tort (§10), to any claim arising out of collection of taxes or lawful detention of goods by law enforcement officer, or to several other claims (§10). Remedy is exclusive (§2) and requires that written claim be presented within two years, be denied in writing by executive office of public employer and civil action brought within three years, after cause of action arose (§4), except for claims asserted by third-party complaint, cross-claim, counterclaim or small claims against housing authorities (§4). Remedy precludes action against public employee or estate for injury caused by negligent or wrongful act committed within scope of office or employment, provided, however, that public employee provides reasonable cooperation to public employer in his defense. (§2). Superior Court has jurisdiction of all civil actions brought against public employer (§3), except that district court and housing court have jurisdiction over civil actions brought against housing authorities (§3). Small claims against housing authorities must be brought within three years. (§4).

No-Fault Insurance.—See category Transportation, topic Motor Vehicles, subhead No-fault Insurance.

Uniform Contribution Among Tortfeasors Act adopted with revisions. (c. 231B). Right of contribution exists in favor of joint tortfeasor who has paid more than his share of common liability. (c. 231B, §1). In determining pro rata shares, relative degrees of fault shall not be considered. (c. 231B, §2). Enactment of comparative negligence statute (c. 231, §85) did not repeal by implication this statute (395 Mass.

76, 478 N.E.2d 930). Contribution is available with respect to settlement entered into by tortfeasor to pro rata extent that amount paid was reasonable. (c. 231B, §1).

DECLARATORY JUDGMENTS:

See topic Judgments.

DEPOSITIONS AND DISCOVERY:

Uniform Foreign Depositions Act not adopted. Rules 26-37, Mass. R. Civ. P., Mass. and R. Dom. Rel. P. substantially similar to Federal Rules. Significant differences are noted as follows: Rule 29, broadens procedures which may be modified by stipulation; Rule 30, leave of court must be obtained if: (i) deposition is to be taken prior to expiration of 30 days after service of summons and complaint, (ii) there is no reasonable likelihood that recovery will exceed $5,000 if plaintiff prevails, (iii) action is pending in Superior Court and there has been trial in district court before transfer, (iv) there has been hearing before master, or (v) relief sought is custody of minor children, divorce, affirmance or annulment of marriage, separate support, or any like relief; Rule 30(b) seven days written notice of deposition is required and if production of documents and tangible items are required at taking of deposition, deposing party shall give at least 30 days written notice; and Rule 37, as applied by Probate and Dist./Mun. courts, in which contempt order may issue only if refusal to obey discovery order is willful and only willful failure to produce person for physical examination justifies imposition of sanctions; otherwise, Mass. R. Civ. P. 37 does not require willfulness. Rule 30A authorizes taking of audio-visual depositions and provides procedure to be followed. Depositions in actions not governed by Mass. R. Civ. P. is governed by c. 233, §§24-45.

Discovery Methods.—Discovery may be obtained by: depositions upon oral examination or written interrogatories; written interrogatories; production of documents or things; permission to enter upon land or property for inspection or other purposes; physical and mental examinations; requests for admission. (Rule 26[a]).

Scope of Discovery.—Parties may obtain discovery of any matter which is not privileged and which is relevant to subject matter of pending action. Information inadmissable at trial may be discovered if it appears reasonably calculated to lead to discovery of admissable evidence. (Rule 26[b]).

Materials Prepared for Trial.—May be discovered if party seeking discovery shows (a) substantial need of materials in preparing party's case and (b) party unable to obtain without undue hardship their substantial equivalent by other means. If discovery ordered, court shall protect against disclosure of mental impressions, legal theories, of representatives of party to litigation. (Rule 26[b][3]).

Supplementation of Responses.—Generally, party who has responded to discovery request has no duty to supplement response to include after-acquired information, except (1) as to question directly addressed to: identity or location of person with knowledge of discoverable matters, identity of expert witness, subject matter or substance of expert testimony, (2) response given was incorrect, when given, or is no longer correct and circumstances are such that failure to supplement is in substance known concealment, or (3) court order, agreement of parties, or new request to supplement. (Rule 26[e]).

Depositions of Persons Outside of State.—Deposition to obtain testimony or documents or other things may be taken outside commonwealth on reasonable written notice. Court may commission person to administer oath or may issue letter rogatory. (c. 223A, §10). As to persons before whom depositions may be taken, see Rule 28 (identical to Federal Rule 28).

Use of Depositions.—Rule 32 of Mass. Rules is substantially similar to Federal Rule 32 except that under Rule 32(a)(3)(b) deposition of witness found to be "out of The Commonwealth" may be used and that Mass. R.Civ.P.32(c) has not been abrogated as in Federal Rules.

Before Whom Taken.—Depositions shall be taken before an officer authorized to administer oaths under laws of commonwealth, of U.S., or before a person appointed by court in which proceeding is pending. Outside commonwealth depositions may be taken on notice before a person authorized to administer oaths in place in which examination is held by law thereof or by laws of U.S.; or before a person commissioned by court. (Rule 28).

Recording.—In actions governed by Mass. R. Civ. P. and Dist./Mun. R. Civ. P. recording by other than stenographic means permitted pursuant to Rule 30(b) (4) by order of court upon motion with notice and opportunity to be heard in opposition or by written stipulation of all parties. Where testimony is to be recorded by audio-visual methods, provisions of Rule 30A apply. In other actions electronic recording is permissible pursuant to c. 233, §30.

Production of Documents.—May be obtained upon request by party to any other party pursuant to Rule 34 (same as Fed. R. Civ. P. 34) in actions to which they apply. If request is made in conjunction with taking of deposition, 30 days written notice for compliance must be given to party (Rule 30[b][5]), but subpoena duces tecum to nonparty witness is governed by Rule 45.

Depositions may be taken by telephone, by leave of court upon motion with notice and opportunity to be heard in opposition or by written stipulation of all parties. (Rule 30[b][7]).

Audiovisual Depositions.—Oral deposition may be recorded by audio-visual methods by leave of court upon motion with notice and opportunity to be heard in opposition or by written stipulation of all parties. Except by leave of court, notice of taking audio-visual deposition shall not be served sooner than six months after commencement of action. Simultaneous stenographic record must also be prepared unless parties otherwise stipulate or upon court order. Upon motion with notice and opportunity to be heard court may in interest of justice allow introduction of audio-visual deposition as evidence. (Rule 30A).

Audiovisual Depositions of Experts.—Party may take oral deposition of own expert by audiovisual means and use as evidence at trial in place of oral testimony,

DEPOSITIONS AND DISCOVERY . . . *continued*

unless court orders otherwise. (Rule 30A[m]). Notice pursuant to Rule 30A must also state deposition will be recorded by audiovisual means for use at trial. (Rule 30A[m][3]).

Within Commonwealth for Use Elsewhere.—On application by any interested person, or in response to letter rogatory, Mass. court may order person domiciled or found within commonwealth to testify or to produce documents for use in proceeding pending outside commonwealth. (c. 223A, §11).

Perpetuating Testimony.—Rule 27 regulates taking of depositions for purposes other than discovery. It is identical in substance to Federal Rule 27.

Commissions.—Commissions are issued by the court. (Rule 28).

Compelling Attendance of Witnesses.—Witness may be compelled to attend deposition by subpoena issued pursuant to Rule 45. Service may be made by anyone over 18 who is not party. Subpoena may not be served before service of deposition notice (which is complete upon mailing). Unless by court order, no Massachusetts resident may be compelled by subpoena to attend deposition more than 50 airline miles from his home or place of work, whichever is nearest to place designated for taking of deposition.

Letters Rogatory.—Deposition may be taken outside U.S. before person appointed in response to letter rogatory. Letter should be addressed "To the Appropriate Authority in [insert name of country]". (Rule 28).

Interrogatories.—Any party may serve interrogatories on any other party; party can serve as of right no more than 30 interrogatories on any one party. (Rule 33[a]). Interrogatories may be served on plaintiff after action commenced, and on any other party with (or after) service of summons and complaint on that party. Party served must, within 45 days, answer each interrogatory, or state, in lieu of answer, objection and reasons for objection. Court may order further interrogatories which must be answered within 30 days of order's filing. (Rule 33[a]). If answer to interrogatory may be derived from business records, and burden of deriving answer is substantially same for both party served and party serving, it is sufficient answer to specify records concerned and afford party serving opportunity to examine them. (Rule 33[c]).

Production of Documents, Things, Entry Upon Land.—Any party may serve on any other party request to provide documents and tangible things, or to enter upon land for purpose within scope of discovery. (Rule 34[a]).

Examination of Persons.—If physical/mental condition of party, or person in party's custody, is in controversy, court may order, for good cause shown, that person submit to physical/mental examination. (Rule 35[a]). If party against whom order issued requests, party causing examination must deliver detailed written report of examination and is entitled to receive reports of any other examination of same condition. If party requests examination report, or deposes examiner, party waives any privilege regarding testimony of any person who has, or may, examine him or her in respect of same mental/physical condition; but does not otherwise waive right to object at trial to introduction of report of any part thereof. (Rule 35[b]).

Requests for Admissions.—Party may serve on any other party written request for admission of truth of any discoverable matter, including application of law to fact and genuineness of documents. (Rule 36[a]). Matter is admitted unless, within 30 days of service, party served denies matter, or serves written, signed objection. Defendant not required to serve answers or objections before expiration of 45 days after summons and complaint served unless court shortens time. (Rule 36[a]). Any matter admitted is conclusively established unless court, on motion, permits withdrawal or amendment of admission. (Rule 36[b]).

EQUITY:

See topics Actions, Practice.

EVIDENCE:

See topic Depositions and Discovery.

Witnesses.—

Caveat: SJC has not adopted proposed Rules of Evidence modeled after Federal Rules but has invited parties to cite such proposed Rules whenever appropriate.

Privileged Communications.—Confidential communications by client to attorney cannot be disclosed by attorney without client's consent, but client who voluntarily testifies may be asked whether he or she will waive privilege. (374 Mass. 320, 372 N.E.2d 764). All memoranda, communication and other work product made during certain mediation of disputes shall be confidential and shall not be subject to disclosure provided that they do not pertain to mediation of labor disputes in presence of mediator. (c. 233, §23C). Certain communications to priests, rabbis, ministers, and Christian Science practitioners are privileged. (c. 233, §20A).

Limited patient-psychotherapist privilege is recognized, except in proceedings for commitment of dangerous patient, in certain child custody, adoption and malpractice cases and in cases where party's mental or emotional condition is at issue. (20 Mass. App. 919; 478 N.E.2d 744, §20B [Judge, in certain child custody cases, has discretion to force disclosure of patient-psychotherapist communications.]). Psychotherapist privilege has been expanded to include communications with psychiatric nurse mental health specialist. (c. 233, §20B). Limited privilege is recognized for communications between licensed social worker and patient. (c. 112, §§135-135B). Social worker privilege applies only to disclosures "from a person", not to social worker's personal observations. (c. 112, §§135-135B, 398 Mass. 372, 496 N.E.2d 1368). Confidential communication between abused individual and domestic violence victim's counselor is privileged and in limited circumstances, is inadmissible and not subject to discovery. (c. 233, §20K).

Communications or Transactions with Persons Since Deceased or Incompetent.—In civil action, declaration of deceased person is not inadmissible as hearsay or as private conversation between husband and wife if court finds that it was made in good faith and on personal knowledge of declarant. (c. 233, §65). If party to action who has filed answers to interrogatories dies, so much of such answers as court finds have been made upon personal knowledge of deceased shall not be inadmissible as hearsay or self-serving if offered in evidence in said action by representative of deceased party. (c. 233, §65A). If suit against executor or administrator is supported by oral testimony of decedent's promise or statement, evidence of decedent's statements, memoranda, acts and habits tending to show improbability of alleged statement or promise are admissible. (c. 233, §66).

Self-Incrimination.—Privilege against self-incrimination exists. (Massachusetts Constitution, Declaration of Rights, Art. XII, G. L. c. 233, §20C; c. 3, §28).

Competency.—All persons of sufficient understanding may testify except that neither husband nor wife is allowed to testify to private conversation with other (except in desertion and nonsupport proceedings, paternity proceedings and child abuse [including incest] proceedings and as noted below) and (except as aforesaid) neither can be compelled to testify against other in criminal proceeding. Nor can unemancipated minor child living with parent testify against parent in criminal proceeding where victim not family member residing in household. (c. 233, §20). Person accused of crime is deemed competent witness at his own request only and his failure to testify creates no presumption against him. (id.). Religious belief is not necessary to render person competent as witness. (c. 233, §19). Nor does fact that person has been convicted of crime incapacitate him from acting as witness, but conviction may be shown as affecting witness' credibility, provided conviction is offered within statutory period of time. (c. 233, §21; 19 Mass. App. 257, 473 N.E.2d 708). Evidence of witness' record of conviction for traffic violation resulting in fine only may not be shown, unless he has been convicted of another crime within five years. (c. 233, §21). Party who calls witness is prohibited from impeaching witness' credit by evidence of bad character. (c. 233, §23; 367 Mass. 117, 324 N.E.2d 624).

Evidence may not be shown before any grand jury or court of rape victim's reputation with regard to sexual conduct. (c. 233, §21B).

Child, age three years, eight months, is competent to testify when child understands obligation to tell truth, although child is unable to explain meaning of "punishment". (c. 233, §20, 398 Mass. 325, 496 N.E.2d 652). Child, age five years, competent to testify where child understands importance of telling truth and punishment for not doing so although no oath taken. (36 Mass. App. 593, 633 N.E.2d 1062).

Testimony of mentally retarded person may be taken by alternative procedures if court determines person will suffer trauma or loss of functioning or communicative abilities. (c. 233, §23E[b][1]). In such case, familiar person may sit near witness and testimony may be taken outside of courtroom or videotaped outside presence of jury. (c. 233, §23E).

Oath or Affirmation.—Witness may be sworn according to ceremonies of his peculiar religion. Person not believer in any religion shall be required to testify truly under penalties of perjury, and evidence of his disbelief in existence of God may not be received to affect his credibility as witness. (c. 233, §19).

Foreign Criminal Cases.—Residents of this state may be compelled to attend as witnesses at criminal trials in state of Maine or in any adjacent state under penalty of not more than $300 fine by subpoena issued by any justice of peace, upon receipt of certificate from clerk of court of record in such other state that prosecution is there pending and that such resident is supposed to be material witness therein. (c. 233, §§12, 13).

Admissibility of Certain Out-of-Court Statements.—Under certain circumstances certain out-of-court statements by sexually abused children under age of ten admissible in abuse and custody cases. (c. 233, §§81, 82, 83).

INJUNCTIONS:

Jurisdiction.—SJC, Superior Court, Probate Court and Housing Court may in their discretion issue under their general equity powers restraining orders, preliminary or permanent injunctions, except that Superior Court has exclusive original jurisdiction of all actions in which injunctive relief is sought in any matter involving or growing out of labor dispute. (See Rule 65, Mass. R. Civ. P., based on Rule 65, Fed. R. Civ. P.; c. 214, §1; c. 215, §6; c. 220, §2; c. 185C, §3; and topic Practice).

Prerequisites.—Injunction never is issued except to prevent irreparable injury. (224 Mass. 152, 112 N.E. 853). Temporary restraining order may be granted without notice to adverse party if it clearly appears from specific facts shown by affidavit or by verified complaint that immediate and irreparable injury, loss or damage will result to applicant before adverse party can be heard. (See Rule 65[a], Mass. R. Civ. P., based on Rule 65, Fed. R. Civ. P.) Preliminary injunction requires notice. (Mass. R. Civ. P. §65[b]). Granting of preliminary injunction requires showing of irreparable injury, likelihood of success on merits, and balancing of risks to parties. (380 Mass. 609, 405 N.E.2d 106; 417 Mass. 329, 629 N.E.2d 1321). See subhead Misappropriation of Trade Secrets, infra.

Procedure.—Governed generally by Rule 65, Mass. R. Civ. P., based on Rule 65, Fed. R. Civ. P. Fee of $50 plus surcharge (see category Courts and Legislature, topic Courts, subhead Superior Court, catchline Filing Fees) is imposed for issuance of injunction. (c. 262, §§4, 4C). Appeals from interlocutory orders concerning injunctive relief governed by c. 231, §118.

Temporary Injunctions.—See supra, subheads Jurisdiction; Prerequisites.

Bond.—Governed by Mass. R. Civ. P., §65(c), equivalent to Federal Rule.

Labor Disputes.—Requirements generally governed by statute. (c. 214, §6; c. 149, §20C). See category Employment, topic Labor Relations.

Misappropriation of Trade Secrets.—Injunctive relief available to prevent taking, receiving, concealing, assigning, transferring, leasing, pledging, copying, or otherwise using or disposing of trade secret regardless of value. Preliminary injunction "shall" be granted against former employee using employer's trade secret in directly competitive capacity, where competition, conversion and use of trade secret are in violation of written employment agreement. (c. 93, §42A).

Unauthorized Use of Name, Portrait or Picture.—Injunctive relief available if such is used for advertising or trade purposes; damages and treble damages may also be awarded. (c. 214, §3A).

INJUNCTIONS . . . *continued*

Consumer Protection.—Injunctive relief available to any person who suffers loss as result of unfair or deceptive acts or practices. (c. 93A, §§9, 11). Injunction may be obtained by attorney general or aggrieved party against deceptive advertising. (c. 266, §91B).

Right to Privacy.—Superior Court has equitable jurisdiction to protect privacy rights against unreasonable, substantial, or serious interference therewith. (c. 214, §1B).

Unlicensed Mental Health or Health Professional, Sexual Contact.—c.12, §11L generally. Injunctive relief available to Attorney General against unlicensed mental health professional or unlicensed health professional for sexual contact with patient or client, or former patient or client. (c. 12, §11L[b]). Violation of injunction subject to criminal penalties or civil contempt. (c. 12, §11L[f]and [g]).

JUDGMENTS:

Mass. R. Civ. P. govern procedure in Superior Courts, District Courts, and Municipal Courts, and Mass. R. Dom. Rel. P. govern procedure in certain cases in Probate Court. Rules are substantially similar and, unless otherwise indicated, version appropriate for court in question should be consulted.

Judgments by Consent.—Consent judgments in certain motor vehicle cases are regulated by c. 231, §140A.

Judgments on Pleadings.—Rule 12(c), equivalent to Federal Rule; deleted in Mass. R. Dom. Rel. P.

Summary Judgments.—Rule 56, equivalent to Federal Rule; deleted in Mass. R. Dom. Rel. P.

Declaratory Judgments.—When an actual controversy has arisen, Supreme Judicial, Superior, Land and Probate Courts may make binding declarations of right, duty, status and other legal relations, before or after breach or violation. (c. 231A, §1). Superior Court has jurisdiction to enjoin, and to determine legality of, administrative practices and procedures of any municipal, county or state agency or official alleged to be in violation of Constitution of U.S. or Constitution or laws of commonwealth, or which are in consistent violation of rules or regulations promulgated under authority of such laws. (c. 231A, §2). See also Rule 57.

Default Judgments.—Rule 55, equivalent to Federal Rule; deleted in Mass. R. Dom. Rel. P.

Offer of Judgment.—Rule 68, substantially similar to Federal Rule; deleted in Mass. R. Dom. Rel. P.

Docketing.—See infra, subhead Entry.

Vacation or Modification.—Rules 59-60, substantially similar to Federal Rules, except that Mass. Rule 59 allows additur in court's discretion.

Lien.—Judgment is not lien, and no judgment or decree affecting the title to real estate has effect against third persons not having actual notice unless recorded in registry of deeds (or in case of registered land, registered [c. 185, §§86, 88]) with description of land, but such record may be made within 60 days if notice of pendency of action was so recorded and in case of unregistered land entry of ordinary attachment of real property in registry of deeds is considered notice of pendency of action (c. 184, §17; c. 185, §86). Judgment may be sued on in civil action.

Revival.—No statutory provisions.

Assignment.—A judgment may be assigned like any other chose in action.

Satisfaction.—Upon satisfaction of judgment entry thereof should be made in court. Judgment of court of record of U.S. or any state is presumed paid 20 years after rendition. (c. 260, §20).

Actions.—An action may be brought on a judgment.

Foreign Judgments.—A foreign judgment is proved by an authenticated copy of record. (c. 233, §69).

Interest.—Judgment bears interest from day entered at prejudgment rate. (c. 235, §8). Legal interest rate is 6%. (c. 107, §3). Prejudgment interest rate 12% per annum from date action commenced. (c. 231, §6B). In actions based on contractual obligations, court clerk must add interest to damages at contract rate or rate of 12% per annum from date of breach or demand or from date action commenced. (c. 231, §6C).

Judgments Nunc Pro Tunc.—Judgment of Supreme Judicial, Superior or Land Courts bears date as of date of entry, unless court orders it to be entered as of an earlier day than that of entry. (c. 235, §4).

Judgment on Frivolous Demurrer.—Rule 12, substantially similar to Federal Rule.

Entry.—Rule 58, substantially equivalent to Federal Rule.

Stay.—Rule 62, substantially similar to Federal Rule except that no execution shall issue upon judgment until time for appeal from judgment has expired; filing of appeal automatically stays execution. Automatic stay of Rule 62 is inapplicable to interlocutory or final judgment in action for injunction or in receivership action. For stay of such judgments, application to court must be made. (c. 231, §116). See also Mass. R. Dom. Rel. P. 62.

Uniform Enforcement of Foreign Judgments Act not adopted.

Uniform Foreign Money-Judgments Recognition Act adopted. (c. 235, §23A).

Judgment Notes and Contracts.—See category Business Regulation and Commerce, topic Bills and Notes.

LIMITATION OF ACTIONS:

Decedents' Estates.—For estates of decedents dying before Jan. 1, 1990, action against executor or administrator by creditor of deceased is barred unless creditor either: (a) Presents claim within four months of executor's or administrator's giving bond and, if disallowed, commences action within 60 days of notice of disallowance, or (b) commences action within nine months of executor's or administrator's giving bond, whichever is later; and unless, in either case, process is served by delivery in hand upon executor or administrator or service thereof accepted by him or notice stating name of estate, name and address of creditor, amount of claim, and court in which action has been brought is filed in proper registry of probate. (c. 197, §9).

Foregoing claim procedure is abolished for estates of decedents dying on or after Jan. 1, 1990. (c. 197, §9). See category Estates and Trusts, topic Executors and Administrators, subhead Presentation of Claims.

Notwithstanding foregoing, action for personal injuries or death, if commenced more than one year after date of death of deceased, may be brought against executor or administrator within three years next after cause of action accrues, provided any judgment recovered in action so brought may be satisfied only from policy of insurance or bond, if any, and not from general assets of estate (c. 197, §9A).

Uniform Commercial Code imposes four year limitation on actions for breach of contract under Code. (c. 106, §2-725). Actions for breach of warranty (at least with respect to personal injuries) may be commenced within three years after date injury and damage occurs. (c. 106, §2-318).

Uniform Fraudulent Transfers Act imposes four year statute of limitations for transfers made with actual intent to hinder, delay or defraud creditor, transfers made without receiving consideration of reasonable equivalent value under §6(a). One year limitation is imposed upon transfers arising under §6(b). (c. 254, §§5, 6, 10).

Personal Actions.—Actions are commenced by mailing complaint and fee to, or filing complaint and fee with, clerk. (Mass. R. Civ. P., Rule 3). Civil action is timely commenced under Mass. R. Civ. P., Rule 3 if postmark is within applicable statute of limitations. (878 F.2d 556). But see 412 Mass. 464 (civil action untimely when postmarked within statutory period prescribed by c. 30A, §14, but received and filed by clerk after expiration of statutory period). See also 71 F.3d 29 (action in Federal Court not commenced for limitations purposes either by mailing copy of complaint to district court or by facsimile transmission of incomplete copy of complaint). Actions must be begun within following times next after cause of action accrues:

Within 20 years: Actions on contracts under seal, on bills, notes, or other evidences of indebtedness issued by a bank, on promissory notes signed in the presence of an attesting witness, if brought by the original payee or his executor or administrator; actions on contracts not limited by any other statutory provision; and actions to recover for support of inmates in state institutions (c. 260, §1); also, judgments of courts of record within U.S. are presumed to be paid and satisfied at the expiration of 20 years (c. 260, §20).

Within six years: Actions on contracts, other than those to recover for personal injuries founded upon contracts or liabilities express or implied not included in §1, except judgments of courts of record of this or any other state or of U.S. (c. 260, §2).

Within four years: Actions against sheriffs for misconduct or negligence of their deputies (c. 260, §3); breach of contract of sale subject to reduction by agreement of the parties to not less than one year (c. 106, §2-725); actions arising under Mass. Antitrust Act (c. 93, §13) or any consumer statute, including c. 93A (c. 260, §5A). See also subhead Uniform Commercial Code, supra.

Within three years: Actions against commonwealth, certain political subdivisions, certain public employees under c. 258 (see topic Damages, subhead Sovereign Immunity); except as otherwise provided, actions for tort, actions of contract to recover for personal injuries and actions of replevin (c. 260, §2A); actions for assault and battery, false imprisonment, slander, libel, actions against sheriffs, deputy sheriffs, constables, or assignees in insolvency, for taking or conversion of personal property; actions of contract or tort for malpractice, error or mistake against hairdressers, operators and shops registered under c. 112, §§87T-87JJ; actions against cities, towns or counties for personal injuries or property damage arising out of operations of vehicle owned by, or under control of, city, town, or county; actions of tort for bodily injury or death from accidents where liability is by law required to be secured by motor vehicle liability bond or policy of insurance or by deposit with division of highways (c. 260, §4); actions of contract or tort for malpractice, error or mistake against attorneys, certified public accountants, public accountants (c. 260, §4); actions of contract or tort for malpractice, error or mistake against physicians, surgeons, dentists, optometrists, hospitals and sanitoria (in no event later than seven years after occurrence of event alleged to be cause of injury on which action based except where action based on leaving foreign object in body) (c. 260, §4); suits by judgment creditors to reach and apply obligation of insurer to judgment debtor, where judgment is in tort action for injury, death or property damage against officers or employees of, or arising out of operation of motor or other vehicles owned by, commonwealth, metropolitan district commission, or counties, cities or towns (c. 260, §4); and suits on motor vehicle liability bonds (c. 260, §4); actions of tort arising out of hit and run accidents may, notwithstanding any other provision of law, be commenced within six months after plaintiff learns of identity of defendant providing written notice of time, place and facts of accident is given to police and registrar of motor vehicles within 30 days after such accident and providing action is brought within three years after accident (c. 260, §4B); actions for negligence or breach of warranty (at least with respect to personal injuries) where Massachusetts Uniform Commercial Code applies (c. 106, §2-318); actions for personal injury or death against administrator or executor, or against decedent if no executor or administrator appointed (c. 197, §9A); actions against persons, cities, towns or counties for personal injury or property damage due to defect or disrepair of public way if notice given within 30 days (c. 84, §18); actions arising from violations of any law intended for protection of civil rights (c. 260, §5B). For actions of wrongful death generally, see category Estates and Trusts, topic Death, subhead Actions for Death. For actions under "Take-Over Bid" statute, c. 110C, see category Business Regulation and Commerce, topic Securities, subhead Tender Offers.

Within two years: Actions against guardians, trustees or conservators on any contract made or act done by them as such, except actions on probate bonds or in favor of estate or of any beneficiary or ward, or of commonwealth (c. 260, §11); or against fire insurance companies (c. 175, §99); actions to recover premiums paid to an insurance company when policy was procured through fraud, cause of action accruing

---

See note at head of Digest as to 1998 legislation covered.

See Topical Index in front part of this volume.

LIMITATION OF ACTIONS . . . *continued*
at date of issue of policy (c. 175, §181); claims for personal injury, death and property damage against Massachusetts Bay Transportation Authority (c. 161A, §21); claims under minimum fair wage law (c. 151, §20A); actions to recover damages for destruction of fine art (c. 260, §2C). See category Estates and Trusts, topic Death, subhead Actions for Death.

Within one year: Actions against executors or administrators on any contract made or act done by them as such, excepting actions on probate bonds or in favor of estate or of any beneficiary or ward, or of commonwealth (c. 260, §11); certain actions to recover back wages (c. 260, §4A). Actions, except consumer protection actions referred to in c. 260, §5A, for which limit is four years, for penalties or forfeitures under penal statute if brought by person to whom penalty or forfeiture is given in whole or in part, must be brought within one year after offence is committed; if penalty of forfeiture is given in whole or in part to commonwealth, action by commonwealth may be brought within two years. (c. 260, §5). For actions under "Take-Over Bid" statute, c. 110C, see category Business Regulation and Commerce, topic Securities, subhead Tender Offers. Actions for personal injury or death caused by Dalkon Shield intrauterine device must be brought against Dalkon Shield Claimants Trust no later than one year from date of certification by U.S. Dist. Ct. for E.D. Virg. or by six months from 7/1/95, whichever is later. (c. 260, §2E; 1995, c. 5, §§200, 358).

Within six months: See subhead Uniform Commercial Code, supra.

Within sixty days: Civil actions in nature of certiorari. (c. 249, §4).

Accounts.—In action on mutual and open account current, the action is deemed to accrue from the date of the last item proved. (c. 260, §6).

Counterclaims.—Limitation period applied to permissive counterclaim as if sued on at time complaint filed; no limitation applies to mandatory counterclaim not exceeding plaintiff's claim. (c. 260, §36).

Design, Planning and Construction.—Actions of tort for damages arising out of any deficiency or neglect in design, planning, construction or general administration of improvement to real property shall be commenced only within three years next after cause of action accrues; provided, however, that in no event shall such actions be commenced more than six years after earlier of opening of improvement to use, or substantial completion and taking of possession by owner. Same provisions apply to improvements to real property of public agency, except that no such action may be commenced more than six years after earlier of: (1) Official acceptance of project, (2) opening to public use, (3) acceptance by contractor of final estimate by public agency, or (4) substantial completion and taking of possession by public agency. (c. 260, §2B). Any action brought by or on behalf of any county, city, town, regional school district, housing authority, or commonwealth to recover cost of asbestos related corrective actions shall be commenced within six years of discovery. (c. 260, §2D).

New Actions.—If an action is seasonably begun and fails for defect in process, or for certain other reasons not affecting merits, or if judgment for plaintiff is vacated or reversed, a new action, if one lies, may be brought within a year, though period of limitation has elapsed. (c. 260, §32).

Foreign Causes of Action.—The plaintiff cannot maintain his suit if it has become barred by laws of any state or country while he resided there. (c. 260, §9). This rule does not apply, however, to action brought in commonwealth against defendant who has been subject at all relevant times to service of process in commonwealth, in which case out-of-state statute of limitations is not borrowed. (399 Mass. 533, 505 N.E.2d 526). Whether to apply statute of limitations of forum state or foreign state is decided by applying significant relationship test, and is no longer procedural question resulting in automatic application of forum state's statute. (419 Mass. 658, 647 N.E.2d 42). Forum selection clauses in contracts are enforceable if enforcement is fair and reasonable. (419 Mass. 572, 646 N.E.2d 741).

Disabilities of Plaintiff.—If plaintiff was minor or incapacitated by reason of mental illness when action accrued, time runs only from removal of disability. (c. 260, §7). "Discovery" rule, whereby action does not accrue until plaintiff has knowledge or sufficient notice that he was harmed and knowledge or sufficient notice of what cause of harm was, applies to psychotherapeutic malpractice (409 Mass. 239, 565 N.E.2d 780) and child sexual abuse (c. 260, §4C; 79 F.3d 1). In medical malpractice suits only, infant must commence action within three years or before ninth birthday, whichever is later, but in no event later than seven years after occurrence of event alleged to be cause of injury on which action based except where action based on having foreign object in body. (c. 231, §60D).

Absence or Concealment of Defendant.—Absence of defendant from commonwealth while in military service does not toll limitations statute if defendant retains domicile in commonwealth. (109 Mass. 40). Fact defendant nonresident does not toll statute if service available under long-arm statute or as nonresident motorist. (c. 223A, §6; c. 90, §3A; 372 Mass. 271, 361 N.E.2d 1247). Statute tolled if defendant is or becomes nonresident during period of nonresidency but no action may be brought on cause of action barred by laws of foreign jurisdiction while defendant resided there. (c. 260, §9). If person entitled to bring action dies before same is barred, or within 30 days thereafter, action may be brought by executor or administrator at any time within period within which deceased might have brought action or within two years of his giving bond, or within three years when executor or administrator knew or should have known of factual basis for claim. (c. 260, §10). If person liable to action dies before action is barred, action may be brought against executor or administrator within one year after death of deceased if within same year process has been served by delivery in hand upon executor or administrator or service thereof accepted by him or notice filed in proper registry of probate. (c. 197, §9).

Interruption of Statutory Period.—See subhead Absence or Concealment of Defendant, supra.

Revival of Barred Claims.—An acknowledgment or new promise, to be evidence of a new or continuing contract, must be in writing, signed by the party chargeable. (c. 260, §13). A part payment of principal or interest, though not evidenced by writing, may renew the contract as to the party making it, but is not sufficiently proved by an endorsement by the party to whom it is made. (c. 260, §14). An acknowledgment, new promise or payment by one does not affect his joint contractor or the latter's executor or administrator. (c. 260, §15).

Contractual Limitations.—Time within which action against common carrier on bill of lading may be brought may be limited by contract, provided limitation is reasonable. (285 Mass. 232, 189 N.E. 98).

Pleading.—Defense of statute of limitations may be raised by motion to dismiss or judgment on pleadings but ordinarily it must be specifically pleaded. (Mass. R. Civ. P. 8[c]; 396 Mass. 278, 485 N.E.2d 947).

Concealment of Action.—If the person liable fraudulently conceals the cause of action, the period prior to discovery of his cause of action by the plaintiff is excluded. (c. 260, §12).

Conditions Precedent.—As to limitation of time for giving notice as condition precedent to certain actions, see topic Actions.

Residence Outside State When Action Accrues.—If the defendant resides out of commonwealth when action accrues, statute runs only from his return; if after action accrues he leaves commonwealth, period of his absence, if such absence amounts to change of residence, is deducted. (c. 260, §9). Not so, however, if defendant can be served, under long arm statute or otherwise. See also subhead Absence or Concealment of Defendant, supra.

Real Actions.—Actions to recover lands or make entry thereon must be brought within 20 years after the right accrued, or within 20 years after the demandant or those under whom he claims were seized. (c. 260, §21).

Entry to constitute possession must be followed by at least one year's open and peaceable possession, or by an action begun upon such entry and seisin within one year after ouster. (c. 260, §28). 20 years bar applies to actions by the state with certain exceptions. (c. 260, §31).

No mortgage shall be foreclosed after expiration of 50 years from recording of same unless extension of same or affidavit that mortgage is not satisfied is recorded within last ten years of such period. (c. 260, §§33-35).

Workmen's Compensation.—Claim for workmen's compensation must be filed within four years of date of injury. (c. 152, §41).

Negligence.—See topic Damages.

PARTITION:

Jurisdiction and Venue.—Any person, except a tenant by entirety, owning a present undivided legal estate in land, not subject to redemption, may file a petition for partition in the Probate Court for any county where any part of land lies. Life tenant or tenant for years of whose term at least 20 years remains unexpired may, in discretion of court, have partition of fee. (c. 241, §§1, 2).

Proceedings.—Petition for partition shall be in alternative, praying for division of land or for either public or private sale of all or any part which court finds cannot be advantageously divided. (c. 241, §6). If court determines that petitioner is entitled to partition, commissioners will be appointed to make partition. (c. 241, §12). Notice of petition must be given either by personal service or by registered mail at least 14 days before return day to all respondents whose addresses are known and to each respondent whose address is not known by mailing notice to last known address at least 14 days before return day and by publishing notice once in each of three successive weeks in such newspaper as court shall order, last publication to be at least one day before return day. (c. 241, §8). Notice of petition must be recorded in registry of deeds for every registry district in which any of land lies. (c. 241, §7).

If any persons are not served personally and do not appear, or are minors or under any disability and have no guardian or other legal representative in this state, or if anyone whose name is unknown or who is unascertained or not in being appears to have an estate as co-tenant, the court will appoint a suitable person to act for him in proceedings. (c. 241, §9).

Partition in Kind or Sale.—Partition is made in kind if possible and, if not, by sale and a division of the proceeds (c. 241, §31) or by setoff upon payment of a just amount. (c. 241, §14).

Costs determined by court and paid by commissioners from proceeds in case of sale and by petitioner in case of division with right of contribution from other parties with vested interests. (c. 241, §22). Contribution from other parties shall be in proportion to interests of parties, unless court finds different proportion more equitable. (Id.).

Probate Court in which petition is brought has equity jurisdiction over all matters relating to partition and over distribution of proceeds of sale. (c. 241, §25).

PLEADING:

Mass. R. Civ. P. and variants thereof applicable to Departments of Trial Court are substantially similar to Federal Rules. See Rule 1, Mass. R. Civ. P. for scope of coverage. Mass. R. Civ. P. Rules govern all District and Municipal Court civil actions. (Rule 1A). Special and/or Supplemental Rules of Superior, Land, Housing, Probate & Family Departments and rules version applicable to respective courts should be consulted. Superior Court Department (617) 725-8130; Land Court Department (617) 227-7470; Administrative Office, Housing Court Department (617) 725-8483; Administrator Office, Probate and Family Court (617) 742-9743.

Pleadings Permitted.—Rules 7-15, substantially similar to Federal Rules, except in following principal particulars: Rule 7(a) permits trustee's answer under oath as response to trustee process; Rule 8(a), no jurisdictional statement required; Rule 8(b), signature to instrument and allegation that place is public way taken as admitted unless specifically denied; Rule 10(d) requires statement of each party's residence or usual place of business or statement that they are not known; Rule 11 requires all papers be signed by member of Mass. Bar who shall include telephone number; Rule 12(b)(8) allows defense of misnomer of party; Rule 12(b)(9) allows defense of pendency of prior action; Rule 12(b)(6) requires short, concise statement of grounds on which such defense is based; Rule 12(h) provides that defenses under 12(b), (2), (3), (4), (5), (8) and (9) are waived if not raised in defendant's initial response or amendment thereof

See note at head of Digest as to 1998 legislation covered.

See Topical Index in front part of this volume.

MA – 23

PLEADING . . . *continued*

as permitted by Rule 15(a); Rule 13, see subhead Counterclaim, Set-off, and Recoupment, infra.

Complaint and Answer.—Claim for relief, whether original claim, counterclaim, cross-claim or third-party claim must contain short and plain statement of claim and demand for judgment. (Rule 8[a]). Every pleading must contain caption with name of court, county, title of action, docket number, and designation as in Rule 7(a). (Rule 10[a]). Complaint only must include names of all parties. (Rule 10[a]). Each averment of claim or defense must be made in numbered paragraphs. Each claim founded in separate transactions and each defense other than denials must be stated separately. (Rule 10[b]).

Frivolous Claims.—Reasonable counsel fees and other defense costs and expenses may be awarded after hearing in civil action if court separately and distinctly finds "that all or substantially all" of claims, defenses, setoffs or counterclaims made by party represented by counsel "were wholly insubstantial, frivolous and not advanced in good faith." (c. 231, §6F). Frivolous claims advanced by parties not represented by counsel can give rise to award "representing . . . . reasonable costs, expenses and effort in defending against such claims." Awards can include prejudgment interest at 150% of 12% statutory rate set forth in c. 231, §6C. Court must specify in reasonable detail method of computing elements of any award. Assertion of novel or unusual argument or principle of law is not by itself sufficient ground for finding claim frivolous. Awards may not be entered in cases involving default judgment without appearance by defendant, nor in actions settled by parties thereto. Section does not focus on conduct of party prior to trial but on conduct of litigation. (391 Mass. 517, 462 N.E.2d 295). Good faith implies absence of malice and absence of design to defraud or seek unconscionable advantage. (403 Mass. 332, 529 N.E.2d 1334). Poor judgment does not constitute bad faith. (Id.). Party aggrieved by decision on motion made pursuant to c. 231, §6F may file appeal. (c. 231, §6G). See topic Appeal and Error.

Time.—Governed by Rules 6 and 12, equivalent to Federal Rules, except: Rule 6(a) omits bad weather exception, excludes weekends and holidays from computation only when period of time prescribed or allowed less than seven days, limits holidays to those in c. 4, §7, or designated by U.S. President, U.S. Congress or commonwealth; Rule 6(b) allows court to extend time by permitting in limited cases, required action by stipulation; Rule 6(c) provides that notice of hearing must be served on opponent not later than seven days before hearing (three days in Probate & Family Court).

Counterclaim, Set-off, and Recoupment.—Governed by Rule 13, substantially similar to Federal Rule except: compulsory counterclaim is not required if pleader's claim is based upon property damage arising out of collision or personal injury, including actions for consequential damages, or death, and Rule 13(j) governs counterclaims in actions transferred, appealed and removed to Superior Court; actions in Land Court for registration and confirmation and tax title foreclosures will not allow counterclaims, except by leave of court. (Rule 13[a]).

Amendments.—See topic Actions.

Verification.—Rule 11(a), substantially equivalent to Federal Rule. Rule 65 "Injunctions", substantially similar to Federal Rule, does not require attorney certification.

Service.—All orders, pleadings and motions must be served on each party. (Rule 5[a]). Service is generally on party's attorney, by delivery or mail. (Rule 5[b]).

Filing.—All papers must be filed with clerk of court within reasonable time after service, except for notices of deposition, deposition transcripts, requests for production under Rule 34 and responses to requests for production under Rule 34. (Rule 5[d]).

Interpleader is available under Rule 22 of Mass. R. Civ. P.

Claims for Collection.—In sending claims to Massachusetts for collection, the original instrument should be forwarded, if there be one and if the same is not in the possession of the party, a copy accompanied with reasons for the nonpossession of the original.

If it is upon an open account, the account must be fully itemized and not merely stated, as majority of complaints in such causes are upon account annexed. There should be full statement of facts. If haste is required in making attachment, send letter giving full names of all plaintiffs and defendants (in case of partnership, full names and residences of individual members of partnership, in case of corporation, exact corporate name and state of incorporation) and amount and nature of claim. Motion for ex parte attachment (or trustee process) requires affidavit of specific facts on affiant's knowledge, information and belief as to clear and immediate danger that property of defendant will be conveyed, removed, conceded or destroyed if prior notice given. (Rule 4.1). Court may require bond. (c. 246, §1). If claim is contested it must be proved either by deposition or witnesses. Where trustee fails to satisfy claim within 30 days of judgment plaintiff may commence action to have such satisfied from goods and estate of trustee. (c. 246, §45).

Small Claims.—See category Courts and Legislature, topic Courts, subhead District Court and BMC, catchline Small Claims.

PRACTICE:

Mass. R. Civ. P. govern vast majority of lower court civil cases, and are substantially similar to Federal Rules, with numerous minor variations necessitated by Massachusetts needs and by salutary or ingrained features of existing Massachusetts practice.

Probate Court Rules govern proceedings in Probate Court. Also see Mass. R. Dom. Rel. P. 101-103, 201-204, 401-408 (Prob. Ct. Supp.) and Uniform Practices (Prob. Cts.). Also, Mass. R. Civ. P. govern proceedings in Probate and Family Court seeking equitable relief. (Mass. R. Civ. P. 1). See category Family, topic Divorce, subheads Process, Pleading, Practice.

In addition, practice is regulated by various statutes contained in cc. 211-250, but Rules supersede great many of statutory procedural provisions set forth in those chapters.

Of these statutes, most important are c. 231 dealing with pleading and practice, c. 231A dealing with declaratory judgments, and c. 214 dealing with equity jurisdiction. Latest amendments should be consulted. See also c. 185 concerning Land Court.

Massachusetts Rules of Appellate Procedure govern both civil and criminal appeals. Civil appeals from District and Municipal Court decisions to those courts' Appellate Division governed by District/Municipal Courts Rules for Appellate Division Appeal (DMRA).

Supreme Judicial Court Rules conform to changes in practice and procedure introduced by Rules of Civil and Appellate Procedure. Principal effect of amendments is to tailor coverage of certain rules to criminal proceedings not covered by Rules of Civil and Appellate Procedure. In addition Rule 3:03 allows certain qualified law school students to appear in court on behalf of indigent parties under general supervision of member of bar.

Discovery.—Governed by Rules 26-37, substantially similar to Federal Rules. Party is limited to total of 30 interrogatories unless leave of court granted to file additional interrogatories. Parties may file more than one set of interrogatories provided aggregate does not exceed 30. Answers and objections due 45 days after service. (Rule 33). For other significant differences, see topic Depositions and Discovery. See also infra, subhead Demand For Admission of Facts.

Demand for Admission of Facts.—Under procedure equivalent to that under Federal Rules, party may request admission of matters within appropriate scope of discovery (Rule 36[a]); matter deemed admitted unless answered or objected to within 30 days of service. If other party fails to admit truth requested but requesting party proves such truth, he may apply to court for order requiring other party to pay his reasonable expenses, including reasonable attorney's fees, in making that proof. (Rule 37[c]).

Jury Trial.—Except for Worcester central District Court and any District Court in Essex county, there is no right of trial by jury, in civil cases, except in Superior Court. (c. 218, §§19A, 19B). Any party may demand jury trial of any issue triable of right by jury not later than ten days after service of last pleading directed to such issue. (Rule 38, Mass. R. Civ. P.; c. 231, §102C). Rule 38 applies to District Court proceedings only where jury trial in civil cases provided by statute. (Rule 38[e], Mass. R. Civ. P.; c. 218, §§19A, 19B).

Speedy Trials.—Superior Court may, on motion for cause shown, advance action for speedy trial. (c. 231, §59A). In any civil action in any court of Commonwealth in which one or more parties at time of commencement of proceedings is 65 years of age or older or during pendency of proceeding attains age of 65, court shall, upon motion of such person, advance proceeding for speedy trial. (c. 231, §59F). See also, malpractice cases (c. 231, §59C), election results (c. 231, §59D), housing and redevelopment authorities (c. 231, §59E).

Direct actions against insurer not permitted. (458 F.2d 1299).

Small Claims.—Governed under Uniform Small Claims Rules. See category Courts and Legislature, topic Courts, subhead District Court and BMC, catchline Small Claims.

PROCESS:

See also topics Actions, Appeal and Error; category Debtor and Creditor, topics Attachment, Garnishment.

Caveat.—Attachments of real and personal property available pursuant to c. 223, §42 et seq. Summary attachment declared unconstitutional (see category Debtor and Creditor, topic Attachment, catchline Caveat) and previous practice which allowed commencement of actions by serving writ of attachment or trustee process has been abolished. Rule 4.1, provides for notice and hearing in seeking attachment of real and personal property. Rule 4.2, provides similar procedure for attachments sought to be made of goods or credits by trustee process. For summary of attachment procedure in Superior Court and District Court, see category Debtor and Creditor, topic Attachment, subheads Grounds, and Proceedings To Obtain.

Generally.—Civil actions are commenced by: (1) Mailing to clerk of proper court by certified or registered mail complaint and entry fee prescribed by law, or (2) by filing such complaint and entry fee with such clerk. (Mass. R. Civ. P. 3). After action is commenced, plaintiff or his attorney delivers copy of complaint and summons for service to sheriff, deputy sheriff, or special sheriff or any other person duly authorized by law. Summons may be obtained in blank from clerk and filled in with appropriate information by plaintiff or plaintiff's attorney. (Mass. R. Civ. P. 4[a]).

Limits of Process.—Process runs throughout state. (c. 223, §20).

Who May Serve.—See infra, subhead Methods of Service.

Defaults.—Rule 55, substantially similar to Federal Rule except Rule 55(b)(1) requires that party seeking default judgment file affidavit that defendant is not infant, incompetent, or in military service.

Time for Service.—Written proof of service must be made promptly and within time during which person served must respond to process, ordinarily 20 days. (Rule 4[f]; see Mass. R. Civ. P. 12). Under Rule 5(f), any paper served by a party and required to be filed with court must be so filed within five days after service.

Methods of Service.—Service of process must be made by a sheriff, deputy sheriff, special sheriff, or any other person duly authorized by law. (Mass. R. Civ. P. 4; c. 220, §7; c. 221, §§70, 78). As to agreement to waive service or issue of process, see category Business Regulation and Commerce, topic Bills and Notes. *Caveat,* Rule 4 incorporates existing statutory requirements of service. In domestic relations cases, service may additionally be made by any other disinterested person, and service for contempt for failure to appear may be made by sheriff or police or other duly designated person at fee fixed by Probate Court. (Mass. R. Dom. Rel. P. 4[c]; c. 215, §34A).

1. Individuals.—An individual defendant is served by delivering summons and copy of complaint in hand, or by leaving same at his last and usual place of abode, or if he has none, with his agent, within commonwealth. (Mass. R. Civ. P. 4; 393 Mass. 789, 473 N.E.2d 1097). For district court actions, if service is made at last, and usual place of abode, officer making service shall mail by first class mail copy of summons to such

See note at head of Digest as to 1998 legislation covered.

See Topical Index in front part of this volume.

PROCESS . . . *continued*

last and usual place of abode. (c. 223, §31). In domestic relations case, service on individual within commonwealth must be by delivering summons and complaint in hand to defendant unless defendant is not amenable to personal service, when service may be by order of notice as prescribed by law. Service at last and usual place of abode and on agent are no longer authorized in domestic relations cases. (Mass. R. Dom. Rel. P. 4[d]). Personal service upon defendant while exercising his right to vote is invalid. (c. 223, §31A). Citations for contempt in proceedings for support of wife or children or under Uniform Interstate Family Support Act may be served by delivering copy of summons and complaint personally, or, by leaving copy of summons and complaint at defendant's last and usual place of abode and by mailing copies to defendant. (Mass. R. Dom. Rel. P. 4[d][2]).

2. Absent Defendants.—No personal action can be maintained against a person who is not an inhabitant of the state, unless he or his agent duly appointed under c. 227, §§5, 5A has been served with process within state or unless service has been made outside state (see Mass. R. Civ. P. 4[e] and c. 223A, §4), or unless effectual attachment of his property (including attachment by trustee process) is made on writ of attachment; and in case of attachment without personal service judgment is valid only to secure application of property attached to satisfaction of judgment. (c. 227, §1). Where no personal service is made on absent defendant or his agent, order of notice, by publication or otherwise, must be obtained. (c. 227, §7). In actions of contract against several defendants, if due service is made on one or more, but, owing to absence from state or other sufficient cause, not on others, action may proceed to judgment against those served. (c. 227, §15). Such judgment if unsatisfied is not bar to future action on same contract against those not served. (Id.). Counterclaim may be brought by defendant against nonresident plaintiff. (c. 227, §2).

Court may also exercise personal jurisdiction over a person domiciled in, organized under laws of, or maintaining his or its principal place of business in, state as to any cause of action. (c. 223A, §2). Court may exercise personal jurisdiction over a person, who acts directly or by an agent, as to cause of action in law or equity arising from person's: (a) transacting any business in state, including acts which relate to marriages (19 Mass. App. 228, 473 N.E.2d 209; 757 F.2d 448); (b) contracting to supply services or things in state; (c) causing tortious injury by act or omission in state; (d) causing tortious injury in state by act or omission outside state if he regularly does or solicits business, or engages in any other persistent course of conduct, or derives substantial revenue from goods used or consumed or services rendered, in state; (e) having interest in, using or possessing real property in state; (f) contracting to insure any person, property or risk located within state at time of contracting; (g) having lived as party to marriage contract within state for at least one year within two years immediately preceding commencement of action, where plaintiff continues to reside in state and action concerns certain obligations relating to marriage; or (h) having been subject to exercise of personal jurisdiction of Massachusetts court which resulted in child support order where plaintiff and child continue to reside in commonwealth and where plaintiff is pursuing modifications of such order or enforcement thereof (c. 223A, §3). Advertising product in publication distributed in state does not constitute transacting business therein. (375 Mass. 149, 376 N.E.2d 548). When service is authorized outside state it may be made, when reasonably calculated to give actual notice, (1) In any appropriate manner prescribed for service within state; (2) in manner prescribed by law of place in which service is made for service in that place in action in any of its courts of general jurisdiction; (3) by any form of mail addressed to person to be served and requiring signed receipt; (4) as directed by foreign authority in response to letter rogatory; or (5) as directed by court. (Mass. R. Civ. P. 4[e]; c. 223A, §6).

3. Infants and Insane Persons.—The practice is to require the same service upon infants and persons under guardianship or of unsound mind as upon other defendants and then to give notice to guardian, if any. (171 Mass. 303, 50 N.E. 612).

4. Corporations.—Service of process in action against municipal corporation may be made on treasurer or clerk. (Mass. R. Civ. P. 4[d][4]).

Services of process in an action against a domestic corporation may be made on officer, managing or general agent, or person in charge of business or other duly authorized agent, and if no such person is found, court, upon plaintiff's application, may issue order of notice in manner and form prescribed by law. (Mass. R. Civ. P. 4[d][2]). If, after diligent search, no person is found upon whom service of process may be made, service may be made upon state secretary. (c. 223, §37).

There are special provisions for service on parishes and religious societies and proprietors of wharves, general fields and certain real estate who are incorporated. (Id.)

In addition to service upon state secretary (c. 181, §15), any foreign corporation having its principal or usual place of business in commonwealth, or which is engaged in or soliciting business in commonwealth, may be served with process in same manner as domestic corporation (Mass. R. Civ. P. 4[d][2]; c. 223, §38). Constitutionality of this provision with regard to soliciting business has not been decided by SJC, but see 149 U.S. 194, and 205 U.S. 530. (See catchline Absent Defendants, supra.).

5. Voluntary Associations.—In actions against a voluntary association under a written instrument or declaration of trust with transferable shares service may be made on any trustee or like officer thereof. (c. 223, §40). Any other voluntary association can be sued at law only by serving all members thereof. (327 Mass. 409, 99 N.E.2d 155). If membership is too numerous, action can be brought against class representatives as long as class adequately represents membership. (Mass. R. Civ. P. 23.2). Unincorporated association subject to suit within state under common name may be served with process in same manner as domestic corporation. (Mass. R. Civ. P. 4[d][2]). (See category Business Organizations, topic Associations.)

6. Partnerships.—Service is made on partners individually in manner described above. (275 Mass. 120, 175 N.E. 159).

7. Service on Commonwealth or agency thereof is made by delivery of summons and complaint to Boston office of attorney general, and, in case of agency, to its office, its chairman, member, its secretary or clerk. Service may be effected by certified or registered mail. (Mass. R. Civ. P. 4[d][3]).

Agents for Service of Process.—Foreign corporation doing business or having usual place of business or owning or leasing real estate or engaged in construction or building projects in commonwealth must file with state secretary name and address of resident agent (c. 181, §4); and any such corporation which does business here without in fact appointing resident agent or whose resident agent cannot be found after diligent search or who refuses to act as such, is deemed to have appointed state secretary its attorney for service of process (c. 181, §15). Foreign insurance companies (c. 175, §151), and fraternal benefit societies (c. 176, §36), before being admitted to do business here must appoint commissioner of insurance such attorney.

Nonresidents and foreign partnerships doing business here must appoint an agent for service of process and, under certain circumstances in default of such appointment, service may be made on city or town clerk. (See category Property, topic Absentees; c. 227, §§5, 5A).

Nonresident Plaintiffs.—Complaints, summons, writs and other processes in which plaintiff is a nonresident must before entry be endorsed by some responsible person who is an inhabitant of state, such endorser is liable for all costs awarded against plaintiff. (c. 231, §§42-45, 47-48).

Nonresident Motorist.—For service of process growing out of a motor vehicle accident, see category Transportation, topic Motor Vehicles.

Long Arm Statute.—See subhead Methods of Service, catchline 2. Absent Defendants, supra.

REPLEVIN:

Although Massachusetts statutes providing for summary writs of replevin have not been repealed (c. 247) or amended, similar statutes in other states were held unconstitutional by U.S. Supreme Court in 407 U.S. 67. But see 416 U.S. 600; cf. 419 U.S. 601 (summary garnishment unconstitutional because bond only means of dissolution, no provision for early hearing and defendant deprived of use of property during proceeding). Furthermore, Mass. R. Civ. P. do not provide special procedure for replevin, and Reporter's Notes to Mass. R. Civ. P. 2, state that relief in nature of replevin is available under Rules, but that right to obtain immediate possession by summary process is abolished. However, c. 214, §3 does give SJC and Superior Court original and concurrent jurisdiction over actions to compel redelivery of goods and chattels taken or detained from owner. Mass. R. Civ. P., Rule 65.2 provides that in action brought pursuant to c. 214, §3 order that party redeliver goods may be made ex parte pursuant to Rule 65(a) and existing law governing temporary restraining orders or with notice and hearing pursuant to Rule 65(b) and existing law governing preliminary injunctions. Security required of applicant in amount determined by court to cover costs and damages to person wrongfully enjoined or restrained. (Mass. R. Civ. P. 65.2 and accompanying Reporter's Notes).

SEQUESTRATION:

Rarely used in this state. Still lies for enforcement of decrees. (c. 214, §4; 21 Mass. [4 Pick.] 507; 53 Mass. [12 Met.] 363). Preservation of property, title to which is in litigation, pending determination, may be accomplished by receivership. (215 Mass. 194, 102 N.E. 438). Chattels and choses in action may be sequestered. (147 Mass. 81, 17 N.E. 75).

See category Debtor and Creditor, topic Attachment.

SERVICE:

See topic Process.

STAY OF EXECUTION:

See category Debtor and Creditor, topic Executions, subhead Stay.

SUBMISSION OF CONTROVERSY:

Agreement as to facts is generally called "statement of the case" or "agreed statement". (Mass. R. App. P. 8[d]).

VENUE:

Local Actions.—Actions concerning land are local and must be brought where the land lies, except that actions for rent, use and occupation or breach of covenant are considered transitory. (c. 223, §3). If land lies in more than one county, action in most cases may be brought in either county. (c. 223, §12).

Replevin actions are local and must be brought where goods are detained. (c. 223, §4).

Transitory actions in SJC and Superior Court, if at least one party lives in Massachusetts, must (subject to certain exceptions) be brought in county where one of parties lives or has usual place of business. (c. 223, §1). Action on assigned claim other than negotiable instrument must be brought in any county in which it could have been brought by assignor. If neither party lives in commonwealth, action may be brought in any county. (c. 223, §1). In action in which trustee process is used, action may be brought in county where any trustee lives or has usual place of business, except that if all trustees live or have usual places of business in one county action must be brought in that county. (c. 246, §2). Subject to certain exceptions, actions in Superior Court for injuries received by reason of negligence which may not be brought in District Court must be brought in county where injury was received or where plaintiff lives or has usual place of business. (c. 223, §7).

Transitory actions in District Court (other than small claims proceedings, as to which see category Courts and Legislature, topic Courts, subhead District Court and BMC, catchline Small Claims) must be brought in any county where one of parties lives or has usual place of business or in judicial district adjoining judicial district in which one of parties lives or has usual place of business or, in action commenced by trustee process, in county where trustee lives or has usual place of business, and in either case, in judicial district (or adjoining judicial district thereto) therein where party or one of trustees lives or has usual place of business; except that action may be brought in BMC if venue otherwise exists under c. 218, §54 (c. 223, §2) and except that motor vehicle tort actions may be brought either in judicial district where one party lives, in judicial district adjoining and in same county as judicial district in which defendant lives or has his usual place of business, or, if one party lives in

See note at head of Digest as to 1998 legislation covered.

See Topical Index in front part of this volume.

MA – 25

VENUE . . . *continued*

Suffolk County, in BMC (c. 218, §21). Action against nonresident may be brought in District Court in county in which personal service on nonresident or attachment of his property is made. (c. 223, §2). Small claims proceedings may be brought in judicial district where either party lives or has his usual place of business or employment provided that action brought against landlords or lessors of land or tenements rented for residential purposes and arising out of such property or rental, may be also brought in judicial district in which property is located. (c. 218, §21).

Actions by or against an executor or administrator may be brought wherever testator or intestate might have sued or been sued at date of his decease. (c. 223, §11).

Change of Venue.—Provision is made for change of venue in case of error, possible prejudice, or improper venue for trustee process. (c. 223, §§13, 15; c. 246, §§3, 4A).

Witness.—See topic Evidence, subhead Witnesses.

COURTS AND LEGISLATURE

COURTS:

United States District Court.—Clerk's Offices: U.S. Post Office & Court House, 90 Devonshire St., Boston, MA 02109, tel: (617) 223-9152; Federal Building & Courthouse, 1150 Main St., Springfield, MA 01103, tel: (413) 785-0214; Harold D. Donohue Federal Building & Courthouse, 595 Main St., Worcester, MA 01608, tel: (508) 793-0552.

Massachusetts comprises one Federal District.

Sittings.—Court sits regularly at Boston, Worcester and Springfield.

Special sessions anywhere in district at discretion of any judge on request of party or otherwise.

Filing Fee.—On commencement of a civil action a filing fee of $150 is required.

Supreme Judicial Court.—Massachusetts Supreme Judicial Court, New Court House, Pemberton Square, Boston, MA 02108, tel: (617) 557-1000. Clerk of Supreme Judicial Court for the Commonwealth, Jean M. Kennett, tel: (617) 557-1020.

Generally.—Supreme Judicial Court is governed by c. 211.

Jurisdiction.—See also subhead Appeals Court, infra. SJC sitting en banc has appellate jurisdiction of questions of law arising before single justice of court, or in Appeals, Superior, Probate, Land and Housing Courts, or in appellate division of any District Court or of BMC, or from trial by jury in any of several district courts which are permitted by statute to conduct such trials, and authority to review orders or rulings of certain administrative bodies. Concurrent jurisdiction with Appeals Court. Where appellate review is not within jurisdiction of Appeals Court, then appellate review shall be directly to SJC. Supreme Judicial Court holds concurrent appellate jurisdiction with Appeals Court for determinations made with certain other court departments. (c. 211, §10). Additionally, further appellate review by Supreme Judicial Court may be decided where majority of Appeals Court justices certifies that case is of public interest or it furthers interest of justice, and three justices of Supreme Judicial Court authorize review. (c. 211, §11). See subhead Appeals Court, catchline Appellate Review. With exceptions noted under subhead Superior Court, catchline Civil Jurisdiction, SJC has original jurisdiction of all matters cognizable under general principles of equity, and may exercise equity powers in various special cases provided for by statute. Equity cases are tried before single justice of court, but court may direct issues to be framed for trial by jury, or may transfer for partial or final disposition in superior or probate court, respectively, any cause within concurrent jurisdiction of such court. It may also direct any cause within such concurrent jurisdiction brought in Superior or Probate Court, to be transferred in whole or in part to SJC. Court has jurisdiction to issue all writs and processes to such courts and to corporations and individuals which may be necessary to furtherance of justice and to regular execution of laws. (c. 211, §3). It has original jurisdiction, concurrent with Probate, Superior and Land Courts, of declaratory judgment proceedings. First Mon. of every month is a return day for writs and other processes. In addition to foregoing jurisdiction, court has original and exclusive jurisdiction of some special proceedings.

Court is always open in every county, and business may be transacted at any time; and in any county court may make orders, render judgments or decrees, and transact business in cases pending in any other county. Full court sits in Boston, see catchline Sittings of Full Bench, infra, and has jurisdiction of all matters that arise in, or that might be heard by it in, any county, and it may upon application and in its discretion, direct a case to be heard by full court sitting in any county and for commonwealth.

Sittings of Single Justice.—Justice of court sits in Boston to hear all matters within jurisdiction of a single justice, including cases in equity and motions arising therein in any county. Party must apply to justice to appoint time and place for hearing. (SJC Rule 2:07). Weekly list for hearing in Boston will be made up on which cases from any county may be set down, either by order of court, or by agreement of counsel and notice to clerk; or by written notice to all parties interested seven days at least before day of hearing and by filing with clerk, not later than day preceding hearing, affidavit of such notice. (SJC Rule 2.18). Matters will normally be heard in Boston, but single justice, in his discretion, may set any matter for hearing in any place within commonwealth. For rules governing practice before single justice see SJC Rules 2:01-2:20.

Sittings of Full Bench.—A law sitting of court for commonwealth is held in Boston on first Mon. of each month from Oct. through May. (SJC Rule 1:02).

Filing Fees.—$200 for application for further appellate review; $160 for entry of complaint, petition, or other action (single justice); $150 for entry of appeal to full bench per appellant; $50 for issuance of injunction or restraining order. Fees also apply to Appeals Court. (c. 262, §4). For surcharge see subhead Superior Court, catchline Filing Fees, infra.

Appeals Court.—Massachusetts Appeals Court, New Courthouse, Pemberton Square, Boston, MA 02108, tel: (617) 725-8106. Clerk: Nancy Turck Foley, tel: (617) 725-8106.

Generally.—Massachusetts Appeals Court is governed by c. 211A.

Jurisdiction.—Original jurisdiction over final orders of labor relations commission (§5); concurrent appellate jurisdiction with SJC with respect to determinations made in Appellate Tax Board, Superior Court, Housing Court, Land Court, Probate Court, BMC in jury session, BMC appellate division, Juvenile Court, District Court in jury session and District Court appellate division, except in review of convictions for first degree murder. (§10).

Appellate review if matter is within jurisdiction of Appeals Court shall be in first instance by Appeals Court except (a) whenever two justices of SJC issue an order for direct review either at request of party or at court's own initiative, upon finding that questions to be decided are: (1) Questions of first impression or novel questions of law which should be submitted for final determination by SJC, (2) questions concerning constitution of commonwealth or U.S. which have been raised in court of commonwealth, and (3) questions of such public interest that justice requires final determination by SJC; and (b) whenever Appeals Court as body or majority of justices thereof considering particular case certifies that direct review by SJC is in public interest. Appellate review is direct to SJC if matter not within jurisdiction of Appeals Court. (§10; MRAP 11).

Appeals Court may prior to or after final determination report any case or any question of law arising therein to SJC for determination if, in opinion of Appeals Court, unusual public or legal significance of matter or efficient administration of justice so requires. SJC may remand such case or questions to Appeals Court if no determination has been made by Appeals Court. SJC may transfer to Appeals Court any case or issue pending before it which has not been determined by Appeals Court, including those within SJC's original jurisdiction and its direct appellate jurisdiction. (§12).

There shall be no review by SJC of any matter within jurisdiction of Appeals Court which has been decided by Appeals Court, except: (a) where majority of justices of Appeals Court deciding case or Appeals Court as a whole certifies that public interest or interests of justice make further appellate review desirable, or (b) where leave to obtain further appellate review is specifically authorized by three justices of SJC for substantial reasons affecting public interest or interests of justice. Decision of panel of Appeals Court may be reviewed and revised by majority of justices of full court. Such review shall not be condition precedent to obtaining further appellate review by SJC. (§11).

Party aggrieved by interlocutory order of Superior Court, Housing Court, Land Court or Probate Court may, within 30 days of entry of order, petition single justice of Appeals Court seeking relief from such order. Relief, and whether hearing is granted, is at discretion of justice. (c. 231, §118). Party aggrieved by interlocutory order of Superior Court, Housing Court or Probate Court affecting preliminary injunction or party aggrieved by interlocutory order of single justice granting relief may, within 30 days of entry of order, appeal (as matter of right) to Appeals Court or SJC. (c. 231, §118).

Law governing presentation of cases to SJC for appellate review, except as to printing records and briefs, applies to presentation of cases to Appeals Court. (c. 211A, §13). See category Civil Actions and Procedure, topic Appeal and Error.

Sittings.—Court sits regularly in Boston second and third Mons., Oct. through May. (Appeals Ct. Rule 1.26).

Documents Submitted.—Rules regarding briefs submitted to Appeals Court have changed. (MRAP Rules 16 and 18). Consult Court Clerk to determine current rules. (MRAP Rule 16).

Trial Court.—See c. 211B. Trial Court consists of seven departments: Superior Court Department; Housing Court Department; Land Court Department; Probate and Family Court Department; Boston Municipal Court Department; Juvenile Court Department; District Court Department. (Each department is referred to by its court, e.g. Superior Court for Superior Court Department, and Probate and Family Court is referred to as Probate Court.) Generally, departments are further subdivided into divisions. See category Civil Actions and Procedure, topic Actions, subhead Consolidation and Separate Trial. See category Pleading for administrative offices telephone numbers.

Superior Court.—See c. 212.

Civil Jurisdiction.—In general, Superior Court has original jurisdiction of all civil actions, except those of which other courts are expressly given exclusive original jurisdiction. (c. 212, §4). It has exclusive original jurisdiction over claims against commonwealth, complaints for flowing lands, civil actions for foreclosure of mortgages and of other real and mixed actions not within jurisdiction of Land or District Courts (c. 212, §3) as well as over actions in which injunctive relief is sought in any matter involving or growing out of labor dispute (c. 214, §1). Superior Court has original and concurrent jurisdiction, with SJC, over all cases and matters of equity (c. 214, §1); Superior Court has original and concurrent jurisdiction, with SJC, Probate Court and Land Court, over actions for declaratory judgment (c. 231A, §1). Superior Court also has appellate jurisdiction of decisions of commission against discrimination (c. 151B, §6), of orders approved by associate commissioners of department of labor and industries (c. 149, §9), of decisions of certain municipal planning authorities including decisions of zoning boards of appeal (c. 40A, §17), of orders making betterment assessments (c. 80, §7), and of decisions and orders of governmental bodies not specifically mentioned above. In addition, Superior Court has jurisdiction to review orders of certain other governmental bodies not hereinabove specifically mentioned. Any civil action may be transferred by motion of party or on court's motion to District Court or in the Boston Municipal Court where action was filed for trial in Superior Court and there is no reasonable likelihood damages will exceed $25,000. (c. 231, §102C). Party aggrieved by decision of BMC or District Court after such transfer from Superior Court may have case retransferred for determination by Superior Court. (c. 231, §102C). Party aggrieved by decision of BMC or District Court in case which could not have been transferred to Superior Court in first instance may have case redetermined by Superior Court. (c. 231, §97).

Criminal Jurisdiction.—Superior Court has original jurisdiction of all crimes. (c. 212, §6).

See note at head of Digest as to 1998 legislation covered.

See Topical Index in front part of this volume.

MA – 26

COURTS . . . *continued*

Jury Trials.—Civil cases at law are tried before jury if either party so demands. Otherwise before justice of court alone. (Mass. R. Civ. P. 38). All criminal trials are before jury with qualification that defendants in other than capital cases may waive trial by jury. (c. 263, §6; Mass. R. Crim. P. 19).

Sittings (c. 212, §14).—

Barnstable County: at Barnstable. (508) 362-2511.
Berkshire County: at Pittsfield. (413) 499-7487.
Bristol County: at Taunton, at New Bedford, at Fall River. (508) 823-6588.
Dukes County: at Edgartown. (508) 627-4668.
Essex County: at Salem, at Lawrence, at Newburyport. (978) 744-5500.
Franklin County: at Greenfield. (413) 774-5535.
Hamden County: at Springfield. (413) 748-7649.
Hampshire County: at Northampton. (413) 584-5810.
Middlesex County: at Cambridge, at Lowell. (617) 494-4003.
Nantucket County: at Nantucket. (508) 228-2559.
Norfolk County: at Dedham. (781) 326-1600.
Plymouth County: at Plymouth, at Brockton. (508) 583-8250.
Suffolk County: at Boston. (617) 725-8175.
Worcester County: at Worcester, (508) 770-1899, at Fitchburg, (978) 345-2111.

Filing Fees.—$175 for filing complaint; $50 for issuance of injunction or restraining order; $20 for filing petition to county commissioners. (c. 262, §4A). There is also surcharge of $10 on any initial filing fee in any court except for entry of small claims action, for which surcharge is $4. (c. 262, §4C).

Probate Court.—See c. 215. For each county there is division of Probate Court.

Jurisdiction.—Probate Courts are courts of superior and general jurisdiction over matters within their jurisdiction. (c. 215, §2). Probate Court has jurisdiction of probate of wills and of granting administration of estates; of appointment of guardians and conservators; of changes of names by individuals; of petitions by married women concerning their separate estate and for matters relating to care, custody and maintenance of minor children; of paternity matters; of health care proxies; of petitions for adoption of children; and of partition of real estate held in common. (c. 215, §§3-4; c. 241, §2). Probate Court has original and concurrent jurisdiction in equity with SJC and Superior Court of all cases and matters of equity cognizable under general principles of equity jurisprudence. (c. 215, §6). Court also has concurrent jurisdiction in equity with SJC and Superior Court of all matters relating to administration of estates of deceased persons, to wills, to trusts and to guardianship and conservatorship and of any other matters of which Probate Court has jurisdiction. (c. 215, §6). Court also has concurrent jurisdiction with SJC and Superior Court and Land Court of declaratory judgment proceedings. (c. 231A, §1).

If more than one division of court has jurisdiction, court in which proceedings are first begun retains exclusive jurisdiction. (c. 215, §7). Petition for relief from interlocutory order may be made to single justice of Appeals Court. (c. 231, §118). Appeal of interlocutory order granting, continuing, modifying, refusing or dissolving preliminary injunction may as matter of right be made to Appeals Court. (c. 231, §118). Petition or appeal must be within 30 days of entry of interlocutory order. (c. 231, §118). Appeal of final decree or order must be made within 30 days of court entry and is to Appeals Court or, under certain circumstances, to full court of SJC. (c. 215, §9). See topic Practice. Appeal of allowance or disallowance of claims by commissioners in insolvency appointed by division of court is to Superior Court. (c. 198, §§2, 11).

Sittings (c. 215, §62).—By single judge at place and time appointed by Chief Justice.

Filing Fees.—Various filing fees apply. Amounts range from $30 to $100 except for filing petitions for allowance of account where fee based on number of years involved and size of account. (c. 262, §4B). For surcharge see subhead Superior Court, catchline Filing Fees, supra.

District Court and BMC.—See c. 218. Each county is divided into judicial districts. District Court consists of divisions, one for each judicial district. Each division of District Court may be referred to by name of principal place for holding of said court.

There are Municipal Courts established for different parts of City of Boston. Within their territorial limits these courts have same jurisdiction as District Courts, except that territorial district of BMC in civil matters is (with minor exceptions) entire County of Suffolk.

District and Municipal Courts have original jurisdiction, concurrent with Superior Court, in all civil actions seeking money damages. (c. 218, §19). Equity jurisdiction is limited to actions to enforce provisions of Sanitary Code (c. 218, §19C) and appeals from zoning boards of appeal (c. 40A, §17). These courts also have jurisdiction, concurrent with Superior Court, of actions in summary process (c. 218, §19; c. 239, §2). District and Municipal Courts have original jurisdiction, concurrent with Probate and Family Court Department over actions under c. 209D, found in St. 1995, c. 5, §87, Uniform Interstate Family Support Act. (c. 218, §19). They also have exclusive jurisdiction over proceedings transferred under c. 211, §4A. (c. 218, §19).

All of these courts have limited criminal jurisdiction. (c. 218, §26). District and Municipal Courts have original jurisdiction, concurrent with Superior Court, of following offenses: all violations of by-laws, orders, ordinances, rules and regulations, made by cities, towns and public officers, all misdemeanors (except libels), all felonies punishable by imprisonment in state prison for not more than five years, crimes referred to in c. 90, §§24G(a), 24(L)(1); c. 94C, §§32(a), 32A(a); c. 94C, §32J; c. 265, §15A; c. 266, §§16-19, 28, 49, 127; malicious destruction of private property under c. 266, §127; crimes of escape or attempt to escape from any penal institution, indecent assault and battery on child under 14, forgery of promissory note, or of order for money or other property, and of knowingly uttering as true such forged note or order. (c. 218, §26). Their territorial jurisdiction, both civil and criminal, is restricted, but executions issued by them can be served and must be obeyed in every county to which they are directed. They as a rule sit at least once a week for civil business, and usually sit daily for criminal business. All cases are heard by single justice without jury except where jury of six members is provided by c. 218, §27A.

Party against whom action is brought in District or Municipal Court which might have been brought in Superior Court or plaintiff against whom such counterclaim or cross-claim is asserted or defendant who asserts compulsory counterclaim may, if such party desires jury trial, remove case to Superior Court if claim exceeds $25,000, by filing within 25 days of service of process claim of trial in Superior Court and affidavit, together with appropriate entry fee and $100 surety bond, except that defendant asserting compulsory counterclaim must file within five days after time to file claim expires; otherwise such party waives jury trial. (c. 231, §§103-104). No bond is necessary for removal of auto tort case if payment of any judgment for costs is secured in whole or in part by motor-vehicle liability bond or policy or by deposit as provided in c. 90, §34D. If ad damnum in writ is less than $25,000, case must be tried in District Court and party who otherwise would have been entitled to remove case to Superior Court who desires trial in Superior Court must file said entry fee and bond within 30 days after notice of decision or finding. Proceedings in all District and Municipal Courts are governed by uniform rules. See category Civil Actions and Procedure, topic Actions. In any District or Municipal Court appeal may be taken on questions of law to appellate division of such court consisting of three judges, and thence to Appeals Court. (c. 231, §§108, 109). Appellate division of such court shall also hear claims for compensation of victims of violent crimes and civil motor vehicle infractions. (§108). In summary process actions, judgments rendered in District or Municipal Court may be appealed directly to Superior Court within ten days after entry of judgment. (c. 239, §5, see c. 231, §97).

Every division of District Court may hold criminal sessions with juries of six people for purpose of conducting jury trials in cases commenced in several divisions of criminal or juvenile offenses over which district courts have original jurisdiction. BMC may also hold such sessions for purpose of conducting jury trials in cases commenced in BMC or in divisions of District Court in Suffolk County. (c. 218, §27A). There is concurrent jurisdiction in superior and district courts for crime of intimidating witness. (c. 218, §26).

Filing Fees.—$100 civil complaint entry fee; $30 for filing petition to approve sureties; $30 for filing supplementary process. (c. 262, §2). For surcharge see subhead Superior Court, catchline Filing Fees, supra.

Restraining Orders and Protective Orders.—Legislature enacted domestic violence record system to track issued protective and restraining orders. (c. 209A, et al.). C. 218, §35A governs consideration of criminal records and domestic violence records under proceedings for misdemeanors made in district court.

Small Claims (c. 218, §§21-25).—Claims of $2,000 or less, in nature of contract or tort (other than libel or slander), even if recovery may be greater than such sum because double or treble damages may be awarded, or claims for property damage caused by motor vehicle regardless of amount, may be brought before District Court of district in which either plaintiff or defendant lives or has his usual place of business without summons and complaint or formal pleading on payment of entry fee of $14 (on claim of $500 or less) or $19 (on claims over $500), in each case plus surcharge and registry postage (§§21-22). Statement of claim is made to clerk and entered in concise form in docket. Service is made by registered mail. Costs may be entirely omitted in discretion of court (§22). Intended as alternative, not exclusive remedy; case may be removed to regular civil docket at request of either party or on motion of judge to avoid loss of appellate rights or jury trial. (396 Mass. 1013, 487 N.E. 2d 853). Rules of pleading and practice may be modified. (§§21, 22). Every cause begun under small claims procedure must be determined initially in District Court. Plaintiff beginning cause under this procedure waives trial by jury and right to appeal to jury of six in District Court. No such cause may be removed for trial in Superior Court, but defendant may, within ten days after receipt of court's finding, file in court where cause was determined claim of trial by jury of six in District Court and affidavit that there are questions of law and fact in cause requiring trial by jury, with specifications thereof, and that such trial is intended in good faith. (c. 218, §23). Claim of trial by jury must be accompanied by entry fee and $100 surety bond (or cash) to satisfy costs. Actions for property damage arising out of motor vehicle accidents commenced in district court shall not have res judicata or collateral estoppel effect. (c. 218, §23). (§23). Court shall waive bond requirement if satisfied that defendant has insufficient funds and appeal is not frivolous. (§23). Plaintiff's costs in any action begun by summons and complaint which might have been begun under foregoing procedure may be eliminated in whole or in part. (§25). Court may order payment to prevailing party of amount found due on or before day stated or by installments; may modify, extend or vacate such order; and may enforce such order by contempt proceedings. Procedure governed by Uniform Small Claims Rules.

Land Court.—See c. 185. Land Court, for registering title to real estate substantially according to so-called Torrens Systems, has exclusive original jurisdiction of all applications for registration of title to land within commonwealth, and power to hear and determine all questions arising upon such applications; of writs of entry and various petitions for clearing title to real estate; and of petitions for determining validity and extent of municipal zoning ordinances, by-laws and regulations; it has original concurrent general equity jurisdiction in matters relating to land, including appeals from planning board decisions (c. 185, §1[k]), except in cases of specific performance of contracts relating to same; it has exclusive original jurisdiction of proceedings for foreclosure of and redemption from tax titles; and it has original jurisdiction, concurrent with SJC and Superior and Probate Courts, of declaratory judgment proceedings. (c. 231A, §1). All causes are tried and questions of fact finally determined by court unless interested party within time limit claims trial by jury. (c. 185, §15). In case of such claim issues of fact are framed and tried before jury in Superior Court. Land Court may enforce its orders or decrees in same manner as decrees are enforced in equity. (c. 185, §§25, 25A). Questions of law arising in Land Court or on such trial in Superior Court may be taken on appeal to Appeals Court and in some instances to SJC. (c. 185, §15). Court sits at Boston, but may adjourn to other places. (c. 185, §1).

Filing Fees.—$100 for entry of original petition or writ. (c. 262, §39). For surcharge see subhead Superior Court, catchline Filing Fees, supra.

See note at head of Digest as to 1998 legislation covered.

See Topical Index in front part of this volume.

MA – 27

COURTS . . . *continued*

Housing Court.—See c. 185C. Housing Court consists of divisions for Hampden County, Worcester County, City of Boston, northeastern division including Essex County and certain Middlesex County municipalities and southeastern division including Bristol and Plymouth Counties. (c. 185C, §1).

Jurisdiction.—Divisions of Housing Court have common law and statutory jurisdiction concurrent with divisions of District Court and Superior Court of all crimes and civil actions, including all contract and tort actions, arising in their respective geographical boundaries, relating generally to health, safety or welfare of housing occupants or to enforce sanitary, building and fire codes and appeals from decisions of Boston Rent Board. (c. 185C, §3). Housing court also has jurisdiction over criminal prosecutions involving violations of fire code. (39 Mass. App. Ct. 285, 655 N.E.2d 386). All cases shall be tried before justice of Housing Court, except that jury is available where required by federal or state constitutions and defendant has not waived his right to trial by jury. (c. 185C, §21). Divisions of Housing Court are courts of superior and general jurisdictions, including concurrent equity jurisdiction, with reference to all cases and matters relating to housing within their jurisdiction. (c. 185C, §§2, 3). In Hampden County, division may hear appeal from zoning board of appeals or other special permit granting authority where decision concerns land in county. (c. 40A, §17).

Transfer of Cases.—Civil action within jurisdiction of Housing Court pending in another court may be transferred to Housing Court by any party.

Sittings (c. 185C, §4).—Hampden County division: at court house facilities of Superior Court within Hampden County. Boston City division: at Suffolk County court house. Worcester division in Worcester County courthouse and in certain district courthouses in county. Northeastern division: Lawrence with regular sittings in Lowell, Salem and Lynn, Peabody or Haverhill. Southeastern division: Taunton with regular sittings in Brockton, Fall River and New Bedford with at least two weekly sittings in each of Bristol and Plymouth County sites.

Filing Fees.—$60 for entry of action, filing third party complaint, other initial filings. (c. 185C, §19). For surcharge see subhead Superior Court, catchline Filing Fees, supra.

Juvenile Court.—Juvenile Court comprised of divisions in following counties: Suffolk, Barnstable and Town of Plymouth, Plymouth, Norfolk, Middlesex, Essex, Worcester, Franklin and Hampden, and Bristol. Within territorial limits of each division, each division exercises jurisdiction, exclusive of Municipal and District Courts located within territorial limits of division, over cases of juvenile offenders under 17, cases of neglected, wayward or delinquent children and equity jurisdiction in all cases and matters arising under c. 119 having to do with protection and care of children. (c. 218, §60). Within its jurisdiction Juvenile Court has same powers, duties and procedures as District Court and laws relating to District or Municipal Court apply to Juvenile Courts. (c. 218, §59). Procedures for prosecuting juveniles in juvenile and district courts have been amended. (See generally, c. 119, et al., and c. 120, et al.) Additionally, legislature enacted juvenile court rules regarding care and protection, guardianship and adoption of minor. (Juv. Ct. Rules 1-12).

Small Claims Courts.—See subhead District Court and BMC, catchline Small Claims.

LEGISLATURE:

Bicameral legislature composed of senate and house of representatives is known as general court. (Const., Part II, c. I, §I, Art. I). Convenes annually in Jan. (Const., Amendments, Arts. X, LXIV).

Special or Extraordinary Sessions.—The legislature may also meet at such times as it judges necessary and at call of governor with advice of council if welfare of Commonwealth requires it. (Const., Part II, c. II, §I, Art. V; Amendments, Arts. X, LXXV).

Initiative and Referendum.—There is constitutional provision for initiative and referendum. (Const., Amendments, Art. XLVIII, as am'd in part by Art. LXXIV). Attorney general may refuse to certify initiative petition which proposes to change internal procedures of general court insofar as such petition does not propose "law" within meaning of Art. XLVIII. (390 Mass. 593, 458 N.E.2d 734).

Lobbyists.—Any person deemed legislative agent must register as such with state secretary. (c. 3, §§39-41). Legislative agent is defined as person who for compensation or reward does any act to promote, oppose or influence legislation or governor's approval or veto thereof. Legislative agent includes person who, as part of his regular and usual business or professional activities and not simply incidental thereto, attempts to promote, oppose or influence legislation, or governor's approval or veto thereof, whether or not any compensation in addition to salary for such activities is received for such services; provided, however, that for purposes of this definition person shall be presumed to engage in activity covered by this definition in manner that is simply incidental to his regular and usual business or professional activities if he engages in any activity or activities covered by this definition for not more than 50 hours during any reporting period or receives less than $5,000 during any reporting period, for any activity or activities covered by this definition. (c. 3, §39).

Persons who influence legislation or decision of state executive branch officials concerning legislation, rates, rules, regulations and general standards, their employers and groups of organizations expending over $250 each calendar year to influence legislation or decision, must register with state secretary and make timely public filings of various expenditures. Penalties may be assessed for late filings. (c. 3, §§40, 44). See c. 3, §44 for group organization exempt from registration.

Registration as Lobbyist.—Any person deemed to be legislative agent for purposes of c. 3, §§39-41 must register as such with state secretary. (c. 3, §§39-41). Person employing or agreeing to employ legislative agent must, within one week after such employment or agreement, register such status with secretary of state. Agent must register within ten days. (c. 3, §40).

Further Filing.—Semi-annually, legislative agents and their respective employers and/or clients, must give itemized report on nature and extent of all expenses incurred in course of legislative agent's duration of employment, except any one day's expenditures under $35 for legislative agents need not be itemized. (c. 3, §47). Penalties for late filings. (c. 3, §§43, 47). No legislative agents may give any gift or pay for any meal, beverage or other item for public official or public official's family except if public official is member of legislative agent's family as defined by c. 3, §43. (c. 3, §43).

Organizational Activities.—Any group or organization that spends in excess of $250 during any calendar year to promote, oppose, or influence legislation, or governor's veto or approval thereof, must register itself, purposes of such organization, legislation which effects those purposes, and total amount of expenditures incurred in furtherance of such activities. This registration must be completed on or before Jan. 15 and July 15 of each year. (c. 3, §44). Appropriate forms shall be open to public inspection. (c. 3, §43). Penalties may be assessed for late filings. (c. 3, §44). See c. 3, §44 for group or organization exempt from registration.

REPORTS:

Quincy's Rep., 1 vol., 1761-1772; Tyng, 17 vols., 1804-1822; Pickering, 24 vols. 1822-1840; Metcalf, 13 vols., 1840-1847; Cushing, 12 vols., 1848-1853; Gray, 16 vols., 1854-1860; Allen, 14 vols., 1861-1867, Mass. Reps., beginning with vol. 97 published. Mass. Appeals Court Reps. beginning with Vol. 1 covering Dec., 1992 published. (Advance sheets published in Mass. Adv. Sh. and Mass. App. Ct. Adv. Sh. published currently.)

Massachusetts decisions are also reported in Northeastern Reporter.

Digests.—A digest prepared by Messrs. Bennett, Gray and Swift, with supplement, includes the Reports through 177 Mass.; a digest by M. H. Throop, with supplements, includes the Reports through 180 Mass.; an index digest by W. V. Kellen, with supplement, includes the Reports through 212 Mass., a digest by W. Ladd, published by Hildreth, includes, with supplements, Reports 212-310; a digest under the American digest system includes, with supplements, the Reports through 281 Mass.; a digest by West Publishing Co. now published includes, with supplements, current Reports.

STATUTES:

Latest official compilation of statutes is 1994 Official Edition of General Laws of the Commonwealth. General Laws, enacted effective Dec. 31, 1920 are latest revision of statutes of general application. Tercentenary Edition included all changes to Jan. 1, 1932. Official Edition of General Laws republished each even-numbered year, annual supplement published each odd-numbered year, and monthly cumulative pamphlet published each month of every year. Massachusetts General Laws are unofficially compiled and arranged in accordance with corresponding chapters and sections of General Laws, and annotated in "Annotated Laws of Massachusetts", now prepared and published by Lawyers Cooperative Publishing Company, and in "Massachusetts General Laws Annotated", now prepared and published by West Publishing Co.

Administrative rules and regulations are published in Code of Massachusetts Regulations, supplemented by Massachusetts Register. (c. 30A, §§6, 6A).

Code of Massachusetts Regulations and Massachusetts Register.—Prior to adoption, amendment or repeal of any agency regulation, public hearing is required if: (a) Violation of regulation is punishable by fine or imprisonment; (b) enabling legislation of agency or other law so requires; or (c) public hearing is required as matter of constitutional right. Public hearing need not be subject to provisions governing adjudicatory proceedings. Agencies are empowered to enact emergency regulations to remain in effect not more than three months which do not comply with notice and public hearing requirements. Even if public hearing is not required prior to adoption, amendment or repeal of any regulation, agencies must meet detailed notice requirements and afford interested persons opportunity to be heard. (c. 30A, §§2, 3, 3A).

State secretary required to print executive orders of general application, regulations, notices and other items of sufficient public interest in bi-weekly serial publication entitled "Massachusetts Register", which is available upon request of any person or group at price to be established independently of statutory charges of c. 262. Contents of Massachusetts Register shall be judicially noted and cited by volume and page number. At least one copy of Register must be maintained in prominent place at each agency office. (c. 30A, §§2-6B).

Uniform Acts.—Following Uniform Acts were adopted: *Acknowledgments (1894) (c. 183); Aircraft Financial Responsibility (1956) (c. 90); Anatomical Gift (1971) (c. 251); Arbitration (1960) (c. 251); Certification of Questions of Law (1971) (Sup. Jud. Ct. Rule 1:03); *Child Custody Jurisdiction (1983) (c. 209B); *Commercial Code (1957) (c. 106); Common Trust Fund (am'd 1969) (c. 203A); *Contribution Among Tortfeasors, Revised (1937) (c. 231B); *Controlled Substances (1971) (c. 94C); Custodial Trust (1993) (c. 203B); Declaratory Judgments (1945) (c. 231A); Durable Power of Attorney (1981) (c. 201B); Foreign-Money Judgments Recognition (1966) (c. 235); Fraudulent Transfer (1996) (c. 254); Insurers Liquidation (1939) (c. 175, §§180A to 180L); Interstate and International Procedure (1968) (c. 223A); Interstate Arbitration of Death Taxes (1943) (c. 65B); Interstate Compromise of Death Taxes (1943); *Interstate Family Support (1995) (c. 209D, §§1-101 to 9-902); Limited Partnership (1976, am'd 1985) (c. 108A); Management of Institutional Funds (1976) (c. 180A); *Model Real Estate Time-Share (1988) (c. 183B); *Motor Vehicle Certificate of Title and Anti-Theft (1972) (c. 90D); Partnership (1922) (c. 108A); Photographic Copies of Business and Public Records as Evidence (1952) (c. 233); Securities (1972) (c. 110A); Simultaneous Death (1941, am'd 1961) (c. 190A); Statutory Rule Against Perpetuities (1990) (c. 184A); Statutory Will (1987) (c. 191B); Testamentary Additions to Trusts (1963) (c. 203, §3B); Transfers to Minors (1986) (c. 201A).

*Adopted with significant variations or modifications.

For text of Uniform Acts falling within the scope of the Martindale-Hubbell Law Digests see Uniform and Model Acts section.

UNIFORM LAWS:

For list of Uniform Acts in force in this state see topic Statutes. For text of Uniform Acts within the scope of the Martindale-Hubbell Law Digests see Uniform and Model Acts section.

CRIMINAL LAW

BAIL:

See topic Criminal Law.

CRIMINAL LAW:

Crimes are defined by statute (see particularly cc. 264 to 274) and common law. Criminal procedure is governed by statute (see particularly cc. 263, 275-280) and Rules of Criminal Procedure effective July 1, 1979. (Mass. R. Crim. P.).

Access to Records.—Access to certain criminal records is restricted. (c. 6, §§172-175). Provision denying access to indices of criminal records (§172) unconstitutional (819 F. Supp. 89). Legislature enacted sex offender registry to track recidivism rates of sex offenders. (c. 6, §§178 et al.).

Indictment or Information.—Prosecution is by grand jury indictment in Superior Court (absent waiver of indictment) and by complaint in District Court. (Mass. R. Crim. P. 3-5).

Bail.—All crimes, except capital offenses and treason, are bailable on personal recognizance unless person authorized to admit to bail determines in exercise of his discretion that release will endanger safety of other persons or community or that release on personal recognizance will not assure defendant's appearance in court. (c. 276, §58; c. 264, §1).

Gun Control.—Carrying firearm without license or firearm identification card is punishable by imprisonment for not more than two years, and fine of not more than $500. (c. 269, §10[h]). Carrying firearms with or without license onto secondary school, college or university property without written authorization from institution administrators punishable by fine of no more than $1,000, prison term of no more than one year or both. (c. 269, §10[j]). Statutes governing licensing of firearms and firearm identification cards is controlled by c. 140, §§121-131C. Ban on sale of assault weapons made after 1994. (S.B. No. 1985).

Right to Counsel.—Right to counsel exists at every step of any criminal proceeding, including examination before grand jury. (c. 277, §14A).

Victims of Violent Crimes.—Victims of violent crimes or their dependents may be eligible for compensation by commonwealth for lost earnings, medical, funeral and other expenses up to $25,000. (c. 258C, §3[a]). Funeral expenses may not exceed $4,000. (c. 258C, §3[b][1]).

DEBTOR AND CREDITOR

ASSIGNMENTS:

Statutory provisions of this topic are covered by Uniform Commercial Code. (c. 106, §§2-210; 9-102; 9-104[d]; 9-206[1]; 9-302[1][e]; 9-302[2]; 9-311; 9-318; 9-405). See category Business Regulation and Commerce, topic Commercial Code.

Rights, debts and choses in action are in general assignable in accordance with common law rules. Home solicitation contracts and evidences of indebtedness arising from same and retail installment sales agreements (other than for motor vehicles) signed by buyer at place other than seller's address may not be assigned by seller or lessor until midnight of fifth business day following execution of such contracts. (c. 93, §48I; c. 255D, §9 [D 12]).

Where a claim has been assigned by an executor or administrator that fact should be set forth in the assignee's declaration or pleading. (c. 231, §6).

Instruments Transferring Title.—No special requirements. Witnesses and acknowledgment are not necessary, except that acknowledgment is required if the instrument is to be recorded.

Recording.—No requirement except for those specified in subhead Assignment of Wages and those required for assignment of security interests or sale of accounts or chattel paper security interests by Uniform Commercial Code.

Notice.—Prior assignee, in order to prevail against actual payment to a subsequent assignee, must prove that subsequent assignee had notice of prior assignment. (344 Mass. 160, 181 N.E.2d 673).

Where notice of the assignment has been given the debtor, the assignee of a part only of a chose in action may maintain a suit in equity on the assignment, joining the assignor and the debtor as defendants. (233 Mass. 20, 123 N.E. 103).

Effect.—Common law rules apply.

Assignment of Wages.—The statutory provisions on this topic are found in c. 154. No assignment of or order for future wages to secure a loan of less than $3,000 is valid for a period exceeding one year; nor, if the assignor is a married man, unless wife's written consent is attached thereto; nor against the employer until accepted in writing by him and with such recorded with the clerk of the town where the assignor lives, if a resident, and if not a resident where he is employed, nor is it valid unless it is substantially in the standard form set forth in §5. No such assignment will be recorded unless it states on its face that the sum of $10 per week as earned of the wages assigned is exempt from such assignment. (c. 154, §2).

No assignment of or order for future wages, other than one subject to the preceding paragraph, is valid for more than two years from making thereof, nor unless made to secure debt contracted prior to or simultaneously with execution of the assignment, nor unless executed in writing in form set forth in §5 and signed by assignor in person, stating date of execution, value of consideration furnished, and rate of interest. No such assignment is valid which does not state on face that three-quarters of assignor's wages are exempt from same. No such assignment is valid unless written acceptance of employer, and if assignor is married man, of his wife, is endorsed thereon or attached thereto (c. 154, §3), and copy delivered by assignee to assignor at date of execution; nor is it binding on employer until he has received copy of assignment and written account stating balance due and sums received by assignee giving date of every payment and whether it is interest, principal, or, in case of loan, payment on charge for making and securing (c. 154, §4). No assignment of future wages is valid against trustee process, unless before service of writ, assignment has been recorded in office of clerk of town where assignor resides at time of record (c. 154, §6). Union or craft dues or obligations, or subscriptions to nonprofit hospital service corporations, or to medical service corporation, or to charitable corporation, or payments or contributions toward cost of any insurance policy or annuity contract, or purchase of government bonds, or purchase of stock pursuant to employee stock purchase plan, federal or state chartered credit unions, or payroll deductions for bank accounts may be deducted from employee's wages in accordance with written requests from individual employees regardless of foregoing requirements provided that no such written request, except in case of labor or trade union or craft dues, shall be regarded as assignment valid against trustee process. (c. 154, §8).

Fee for Recording Assignments of Future Wages or Salary.—$1, subject to change by individual community. (c. 262, §34[2]). See topic Garnishment, subhead Earnings.

ATTACHMENT:

See also topic Garnishment.

Caveat.—Attachment available pursuant to c. 223, §42 et seq. Prejudgment attachment of real estate, under then existing statutes and rules, held unconstitutional insofar as not providing for notice, opportunity for hearing, and court approval prior to attachment. See 365 F. Supp. 1299; 349 F. Supp. 741. SJC Rule 1:04A, Mass. R. Civ. P. 4.1, and Mass. R. Dom. Rel. P. 4.1 provide revised attachment procedure, requiring notice and hearing, except on showing of limited exigent circumstances. (See 584 F.2d 559, 561; 462 F. Supp. 172, 183 n. 12.) SJC Rule 1:03A, Mass. R. Civ. P. 4.2, and Mass. R. Dom. Rel. P. 4.2 govern trustee process.

Actions in Which Allowed.—In all personal civil actions in which debt or damages are recoverable, property may be attached upon original writ and held as security to satisfy such judgment or decree as plaintiff may recover, but no attachment of real estate may be made on writ returnable before District Court unless damages demanded (determined by ad damnum of writ) exceed $20 (c. 223, §42) and, in action or suit for amount which is liquidated or ascertainable by calculation, no attachment by trustee process or otherwise may be made for larger sum than amount of claim and amount reasonably necessary to include interest and costs (c. 223, §42A).

Courts Which May Issue Writ.—All courts may issue writ of attachment. (c. 223, §§1-15).

In Whose Favor Writ May Issue.—Attachments may be made in suits by or against nonresidents as well as in suits by or against residents. (c. 227, §1).

Against Whom Writ May Issue.—See subhead In Whose Favor Writ May Issue, supra.

Claims on Which Writ May Issue.—There is no statutory requirement that claim sued on should be payable within state. No direct attachment will lie to secure claim not yet due.

In actions or claims against the estate of a deceased person there can be no attachment other than a "chip" (nominal) attachment (282 Mass. 45, 184 N.E. 677), except by permission of the Probate Court where the executor or administrator was appointed (c. 230, §7). (This section does not apply to creditor whose claim accrues after settlement of estate. [c. 197, §29].)

Attachment may issue in action for divorce (c. 208, §33) or separate support (c. 208, §12).

Grounds.—Plaintiff must show reasonable likelihood that he will recover judgment, including interest and costs, in amount equal to or greater than amount of attachment over and above any liability insurance shown by defendant to be available to satisfy judgment. If plaintiff seeks writ of attachment, ex parte, plaintiff must show in addition to above, either: (1) That person of defendant is not subject to jurisdiction of court in action; (2) there is clear danger that defendant if notified in advance of attachment of property will convey it, remove it from state or will conceal it; or (3) there is immediate danger that defendant will damage or destroy property to be attached. (Mass. R. Civ. P. 4.1).

Proceedings To Obtain.—Action in which attachment is sought may be commenced only by filing motion for approval of attachment along with complaint and affidavit in support of motion. Copies of motion, complaint, affidavit and notice of hearing must be served on defendant in manner provided by Mass. R. Civ. P. 4, at same time summons and complaint are served. Notice of hearing must inform defendant that by appearing to be heard on motion for approval of attachment he will not thereby submit himself to jurisdiction of court nor waive service of complaint and summons upon him in manner provided by law. Court approval, after hearing, is required. (Rule 4.1[c]). For ex parte attachment, plaintiff must also file certificate as to liability insurance available to satisfy judgment. (Rule 4.1[f]).

Attachment Bond.—No bond is required to obtain attachment, but attaching officer may require sufficient security if there is reasonable doubt as to ownership of personal property either before or after attachment. (c. 223, §45A).

There are certain restrictions on right to attach railroad cars and engines and steamboats in use making regular passages (c. 223, §43), ships and vessels (c. 223, §44), personal property used in printing and publishing a newspaper (c. 223, §45) and motor vehicles (c. 223, §44A).

Levy of Attachment on Real Estate.—Every original writ for attachment of real estate or any right or interest therein shall contain name and last known residence of each defendant. (c. 223, §62). Writ of attachment is not valid against subsequent good faith purchasers unless name in writ matches name under which owner of property acquired record title. (38 Mass. App. Ct. 627, 650 N.E.2d 1279 [misplaced hyphen destroyed priority]; c. 223, §66). Officer's return on writ that attachment has been made constitutes valid attachment as between parties of defendant's right, title and interest in unregistered real estate not exempt by law. No special description of land attached is required. To be effective against subsequent creditors or bona fide purchasers, attachment must be recorded at registry of deeds of district where land lies (c. 223,

ATTACHMENT . . . *continued*
§63). Attachment of registered land must be filed and registered in office of assistant recorder for registry district where land lies. (c. 185, §§78, 81).

Attachment of leasehold estate is allowed. (See 57 Mass. 318.) There is no prohibition against attachment of realty held in common (369 Mass. 665, 342 N.E.2d 712) or jointly held realty (345 Mass. 423, 187 N.E.2d 859) even though attaching party has claim against only one of owners. Real estate held by husband and wife as tenants by entirety cannot be attached and sold on execution by creditor of debtor spouse so long as property is principal residence of non-debtor spouse; provided that both spouses are liable for debts incurred on account of necessities furnished to either spouse or member of family. (c. 209, §1).

Attachment expires six years from recording date unless renewed for subsequent periods of six years. (c. 223, §114A).

If an encumbrance is removed after the attachment is made, it inures to the benefit of the attaching creditor. (c. 223, §70).

Real estate fraudulently conveyed, or which is held in trust for debtor, whereby he is entitled to a present conveyance, or which was acquired by debtor by a deed describing him as trustee, regardless of validity of trust or legal effect of designation as trustee, may be attached specially as property of debtor, but must be described by locality and name of person holding legal title. (c. 223, §67).

Levy of Attachment on Personal Property.—A perfected security interest in personal property, which from its bulk or other cause cannot be immediately removed, may be obtained by filing within three days after attachment a certified copy of writ and return of attachment in office of clerk of city or town, state secretary, or registry of deeds. (c. 223, §50; c. 106 §9-401). Wages and pensions may in certain actions be attached by trustee process (c. 246, §28), but $125 per week of wages and amounts held by trustee for defendant in pension exempt. See generally topic Garnishment.

Other personal property must be kept in possession of officer, who may put keeper over it on authorization of court therefor. To have keeper appointed, plaintiff must file affidavit with court stating facts which require such appointment and court must endorse its assent to appointment upon writ (c. 223, §48). Attached personal property may be kept on premises where found. (c. 223, §49). However, such property or keeper must be removed upon written request of defendant without unreasonable delay. (c. 223, §§48-49). If defendant in writing requests property to be left on premises, it cannot be removed until he has had reasonable opportunity to dissolve attachment by giving bond. Live animals and personal property liable to perish, or that cannot be kept without disproportionate expense, may be sold, and proceeds held subject to attachment (c. 223, §88), unless defendant deposits appraised value in money with attaching officer or gives bond with two sufficient sureties conditioned to pay appraised value of property (c. 223, §93).

Motor vehicle registered in the commonwealth may not be attached on mesne process in an action of contract except on consent in writing of a justice of the court where suit is commenced. (c. 223, §44A).

There can be no attachment of goods for which a negotiable document of title is outstanding, unless document be first surrendered to bailee or its negotiation enjoined. (c. 223, §72).

Personal property subject to mortgage, pledge, or lien or sold under conditional sale contract may be attached as if unencumbered, if creditor pays or tenders to mortgagee, pledgee, lienor, conditional vendor, or his assigns, amount for which property is so liable within ten days after demand. (c. 223, §74). If attaching creditor denies validity of any such encumbrance, encumbrancer or his assigns may be summoned as trustee and validity of encumbrance and amount due determined. If validity is upheld, attachment becomes void unless amount due is paid as ordered by court. (c. 223, §81).

Personal property owned by several jointly may, it seems, be attached on writ against one of them, but on appraisal and giving of bond by others must be surrendered to them. (c. 223, §§102-105). See 369 Mass. 665, 342 N.E.2d 712.

See also topics Garnishment, Exemptions.

Indemnity.—See subhead Attachment Bond, supra.

Lien.—A lien exists so long as a valid attachment remains in effect. (238 F.2d 683).

Priorities.—Successive attachments may be made in same or different suits upon same property, and take priority according to time. (Rule 4.1[e]). In case of real property, priority is in order of recording at Registry. Person claiming interest in property attached, by reason of subsequent attachment or otherwise, may by proper proceeding be admitted to contest validity of prior attachment on ground that amount demanded in first action was not justly due or was not payable when it was commenced. (c. 223, §§106-113).

Judgment creditors who have not attached have no rights in the debtor's property as against attaching creditors. (See generally Uniform Commercial Code, c. 106, §9-201.)

Release of Property.—Attachment may be dissolved by depositing with attaching officer sum equal to ad damnum in complaint or writ, or by giving bond with sureties or authorized surety company approved in writing by plaintiff, or approved by magistrate upon examination, with condition to pay amount plaintiff may recover within 30 days after final judgment and/or to pay amount of any special judgment within 30 days after entry thereof. (c. 223, §§120-129). Costs of obtaining bond may be recovered by prevailing defendant. (377 Mass. 522, 386 N.E.2d 1273). Attachment may be dissolved as to particular property by giving bond as above to pay value of such property, which is fixed by appraisal. (c. 223, §125). Attachment may be dissolved by appointment of receiver on complaint filed within four months (c. 223, §130), and by final judgment in favor of defendant after time for appeal has expired. If appeal has been duly claimed any attachment or other security as by bond shall stand until appellate review has been exhausted. (c. 223, §115). Attachment is also dissolved, except as to property alienated by him before death, by death of defendant, if administration is granted on his estate upon application made within one year after death. (c. 223, §116). Also if real property is attached and no service is made upon defendant, attachment is dissolved unless record shows that notice has been given to defendant within 60 days or such further time as court may allow after entry of case. (c. 223, §115A). Property remains subject to attachment for 30 days after execution may first issue unless attachment is sooner dissolved. (For property attached or judgment rendered in Nantucket County above period extended to 60 days.) (c. 223, §59).

Any bond may be executed by another person on behalf of party to suit, if it appears to magistrate approving it that there is good cause why it is not executed by such party. (c. 223, §133). Sureties on bond to dissolve attachment are released by principal's discharge in insolvency in proceedings instituted within four months after attachment, if original claim if proved in insolvency would have been barred by discharge of defendant. (c. 223, §124).

Attachments in all cases shall be dissolved, discharged, or reduced in whole or in part without order of court by any method provided in c. 223. (c. 223, §113A).

Sale.—Animals and perishable goods which have been attached may be sold after appraisal proceedings. (c. 223, §§87-101). Proceeds of such sale are held pending final judgment and are then distributed by court. (c. 223, §87).

Third Party Claims.—Attachment may be made by party bringing counterclaim, cross claim or third party complaint in same manner as upon original claim. (Mass. R. Civ. P. 4.1[d]).

Vacation or Modification.—

Ex Parte Attachments.—On two days notice to plaintiff, or on such notice as court prescribes, a defendant may move, without submitting his person to jurisdiction of court, for dissolution or modification of an ex parte attachment. At such hearing plaintiff has burden of justifying any finding in ex parte order which defendant has challenged by affidavit. (Mass. R. Civ. P. 4.1[g]).

Other Attachments.—On application to a justice of court to which process is returnable, an attachment found upon summary hearing of parties to be excessive or unreasonable may be ordered to be reduced or discharged, or part of property may be ordered to be released. (c. 223, §§113A, 114).

Liability of Attaching Officer.—The attaching officer becomes liable to the creditor for the goods attached. If attaching officer has sold on execution property attached, he shall be liable only for proceeds of sale after deducting legal fees and charges for attaching, keeping and selling such property. (c. 223, §117).

Property Liable to Attachment.—With limited exceptions (see subhead Equitable Attachment, infra and topic Exemptions), all real and personal estate liable to be taken on execution, except such personal estate as is considered from its nature or situation exempt according to principles of common law or which is by statute exempt, is liable to attachment. (c. 223, §42). C. 223, §42 specifically exempts from attachment such property as is exempt from execution under c. 235, §34.

Time of Making Attachment.—Attachment may be made within 30 days after order allowing attachment or, upon order of court, subsequent to expiration of 30-day period. (Mass. R. Civ. P. 4.1[a], [c], and [e]).

Equitable Attachment.—SJC and Superior Court, and Boston, Hampden and Worcester Housing Courts after entry of judgment, have jurisdiction to reach and apply debtor's property which cannot be attached or taken on execution or fraudulently conveyed. (c. 214, §3[6]-[9]; c. 223, §86A). Shares in domestic and foreign corporations cannot be attached in civil action in which only money damages are sought (c. 223, §71), but may be reached and applied to satisfaction of claims (c. 214, §3[7]). Choses in action and any property, right, title or interest, legal or equitable, within or without state, which cannot be taken on execution, may, without other ground of equitable jurisdiction, be reached and applied for satisfaction of debt. (c. 214, §3[6]). Civil action to reach and apply should not be confused with judgment creditors' bills to reach property that cannot be taken on execution. (215 Mass. 415, 102 N.E. 646).

Lis Pendens.—When litigation concerns title to or use or occupation of real property, party may create cloud on title to real property, thereby achieving some of practical effect of real estate attachment, by filing memorandum of lis pendens with local registry of deeds. (c. 184, §§15-17). No notice or hearing required. Constitutionality upheld under State Const. (383 Mass. 883, 420 N.E.2d 349); upheld under 14th Amend., Federal Const. (383 Mass. 559, 420 N.E.2d 343).

CREDITORS' SUITS:

By statute actions may be brought in Superior Court and SJC (initially in Superior Court, 373 Mass. 854; 364 N.E.2d 815): (a) To reach and apply in payment of debt any attachable property fraudulently conveyed (c. 214, §3 [8]); or any property or interest not reachable by attachment (whether in debtor's possession or not) if value ascertainable by means in court's ordinary procedure (c. 214, §3 [6]); (b) to reach and apply, to satisfy judgment for bodily or property damage or death, insurance company's obligation to judgment debtor if judgment unsatisfied for 30 days after rendered (c. 214, §3 [9]; cf. Mass. R. Civ. P. 69); and (c) to reach and apply shares in domestic and national corporations located or having general office in Massachusetts (whether plaintiff creditor or not). (c. 214, §3[7]).

Creditors' actions in accordance with usual equity practice may also be brought.

EXECUTIONS:

All money judgments are enforceable by writ (sometimes referred to as complaint) for execution. Mass. R. Civ. P. 69, Domestic Relations R. 69, c. 235, and c. 236 prescribe law applicable to executions. See Local Dist. Ct. R. 58.2 for procedure on satisfying judgment.

Execution based on judgment of sister state will issue after judgment in Massachusetts court and if plaintiff files with Massachusetts court transcript of record of judgment in earlier case under seal of court rendering it, attested by clerk of such court. (c. 235, §14).

Judgment from foreign country is enforceable in Massachusetts in same manner as judgment from sister state (see subhead Execution Based on Judgment of Sister State, supra) pursuant to c. 235, §23A (Uniform Foreign Money-Judgments Recognition Act).

Kinds of Executions.—Execution to enforce money judgment (c. 235) or judgment for costs. Execution for possession in summary process action. (c. 239, §3). Alias and

See note at head of Digest as to 1998 legislation covered.

See Topical Index in front part of this volume.

MA – 30

EXECUTIONS . . . *continued*
other successive executions are recognized. (c. 235, §17). For enforcement of judgment of small claims actions, see Mass. Uniform Small Claims Rules 7 and 9. See also subhead Body Execution, infra.

See category Property, topic Landlord and Tenant, subheads Holding Over, and Dispossession.

Exemptions.—See topics Exemptions, Garnishment.

Time for Issuance.—Execution shall not issue on judgment until all possible appellate review is exhausted. (c. 235, §16; Mass. R. Civ. P. 62).

Original execution in Superior Court and in District Courts may not issue after more than one year after party is first entitled to take it out. (c. 235, §17). No alias or other successive execution can be issued, unless within five years of return day of that which preceded it. (id).

If judgment remains unsatisfied after expiration of time for taking out execution, creditor may obtain new execution by motion to court or bring civil action thereon. (c. 235, §19).

Stay.—Rule 62 and c. 235, §16 provide automatic stay until appellate review exhausted or time for appeal has expired.

Lien.—Prior to levy there is no lien of an execution. The only lien possible before judgment is the lien of an attachment.

Property Subject to Levy.—With limited exceptions (see topic Exemptions) all property of the debtor may be levied upon. Gold and silver coin, currency and bank notes may be taken on execution. (c. 235, §§32, 33). Terms for 100 years or more, if 50 years or more remain unexpired, are regarded as real estate for levy of execution thereon. (c. 235, §46). Other terms for years are seized on execution in like manner as personal property, except that officer must give 14 days notice of time and place of sale by leaving written notice with debtor personally or at his last abode and by posting notice on listed premises. (id). All lands of debtor except homestead estate (c. 188, §§1 as am'd 1995, c. 297 §1, 1A; but see c. 236, §18) in possession may be taken on execution against him, including remainder or reversion, all his rights of entry in lands and of redeeming mortgaged lands, and all such lands and rights fraudulently conveyed with intent to defeat, delay, or defraud his creditors, and lands directly or indirectly paid for by him, record title to which has been retained by vendor or conveyed to third person with like intent, or on trust expressed or implied whereby debtor is entitled to present conveyance. (c. 236, §1). Property qualifying under homestead exemption is beyond reach of creditors to extent of $100,000. (c. 188, §1). Real property or manufactured home of persons 62 years old or older or of disabled person protected against execution of judgment to extent of $200,000. (c. 188, §1A). Real estate of deceased person may be taken on execution against executor or administrator in suit upon debt of deceased. (c. 236, §53).

If an execution is returned satisfied in whole or in part by sale of property not liable to execution and damages are recovered on account of the sale, a new execution shall issue in the amount remaining due. (c. 235, §20).

Levy of Execution on Real Estate.—An execution may be levied on real estate either by setting off the real estate at a value fixed by appraisal (c. 236, §§6-25), or by public sale and conveyance by the officer. (c. 236, §§26-30). If real estate levied on was not attached on mesne process, the officer must file in the registry of deeds at the time of making the levy a copy of the execution with memorandum thereon that the execution is in his hands for the purpose of taking the land, and no such taking is valid against a purchaser in good faith and for value until a copy is so deposited. (c. 236, §4). If the levy is not completed by set-off or sale within six years from the date on which notice of the execution was deposited in the registry of deeds, the levy is void as to any land within the registry district unless within the six-year period it is renewed at the registry of deeds. (c. 236, §49A). If land was attached on mesne process such a copy and memorandum must be so deposited within 40 days after judgment (c. 236, §49A) and attachment becomes void 40 days after said judgment unless the copy is so deposited. Seventy days are allowed if land attached is in Nantucket County and judgment was rendered in another county, or vice versa. (c. 236, §4). To be valid against third parties acting in good faith, execution and return in case of set-off and officer's deed in case of sale must be recorded in registry of deeds within three months after levy or sale has been completed. (c. 236, §§21, 27).

Return.—An original execution is returnable 20 years after judgment except that those against executors, administrators, trustees or fiduciary officers in their respective capacities are returnable within 60 days after date of execution; alias execution five years after date thereof. (c. 235, §§17, 23; c. 260, §20). Execution for possession of rented or leased residence shall not issue later than three months following judgment and is returnable within three months after date of issuance. (c. 235, §23).

Priorities.—If property is not already subject to an attachment or other lien, priority is in the order of the time of making levy. See c. 235, §44.

Conduct of Sale.—Officer authorized to serve execution shall make sale to highest bidder at public auction and convey all debtor's title to land or rights sold. (c. 236, §27).

Satisfaction.—Defendant may pay amount of execution or property may be sold through levy on the execution. See c. 236, §§26, 32.

Sale.—Sale of property, both real (c. 236, §§26-32) and personal (c. 235, §§36-45), with certain exemptions (see topic Exemptions) is provided for by statute. In case of personal property officer must give notice of time and place of sale by posting notices 48 hours at least before time of sale in public place in town where sale is to be made or by causing advertisement thereof to be published in newspaper published in town where debtor resides. (c. 235, §37). In case of real estate, written notice of time and place of sale must be delivered at least 30 days before sale to debtor, if he may be found in precinct, and must be posted in public place in town where land lies and in two adjoining towns; such notice must also be published in paper of town where land lies once in each of three successive weeks, first publication to be not less than 21 days before sale. (c. 236, §28).

Redemption.—Real estate set off or sold on execution may be redeemed within one year after the levy or sale. (c. 236, §33). Personal property may be redeemed prior to sale. (c. 235, §36).

Supplementary Proceedings.—(See c. 224, §§14-22.) Natural persons, corporations, trusts, societies, partnerships, associations and any other legal entities are subject to supplementary process and proceedings. Unpaid judgment creditor may file application for supplementary proceedings on which summons issues for debtor. Failure to appear in answer to summons constitutes contempt and if debtor is corporation or trust with transferable shares, court shall treat officer, trustee or agent served as contemnor. At hearing, debtor is examined as to his property and ability to pay. If court finds that debtor has property not exempt he may be ordered to produce it to satisfy judgment, interest and costs or to transfer or assign it to creditor. If court finds debtor able to pay, it may, after allowing debtor, if natural person, out of income not less than $125 per week or amount exempt under 15 U.S.C. 1671-1677 order debtor to pay judgment in full or by partial payments from time to time. Order may be made combining any of above orders. Unexcused failure to comply with order constitutes contempt, punishable by fine or imprisonment for not more than 30 days, but such punishment does not discharge debtor, and court retains jurisdiction until proceedings finally dismissed and may punish later violations. If court finds debtor is unable to pay or if creditor fails to appear, proceedings may be dismissed. If proceedings are dismissed, creditor may not within one year file new application on same judgment. Debtor may apply by petition for benefit of examination.

Creditor has burden of proof in showing existence of nonexempt property of debtor. (c. 224, §16).

Debtor may be imprisoned or fined on showing that he has conveyed or concealed property in fraud of creditors or has, since debt was incurred, gambled to extent of $100, or that he contracted debt with intent not to pay it. (c. 224, §19).

Imprisonment and supplementary proceedings are discharged by full payment of debt or by bankruptcy proceedings on proper application. (c. 224, §21).

Body Execution.—No person may be arrested on execution unless creditor makes application for certificate authorizing arrest supported by affidavit and proves to satisfaction of court that he believes and has reason to believe that judgment debtor intends to leave state. Debtor arrested on execution may give recognizance to appear within 30 days for examination relative to his property and ability to pay. He may also give notice that he desires to take oath that he does not intend to leave state, and must be examined in relation thereto. If court is satisfied that he does not intend to leave state, he will be discharged but he may be forthwith required to submit to examination. If he is not so discharged, he will be committed to jail until examination had, unless he recognizes or posts bail. (c. 224, §6). See also c. 224, §§24-25.

EXEMPTIONS:

Uniform Exemptions Act not adopted.

Personal Property Exempt from Execution.—Debtor is entitled to exemption of various items of personal property from seizure on execution, subject to specified dollar limits, including clothing, household furniture, livestock, tools, stock in trade, automobile, money for necessaries, homestead interests, cash savings deposits, and back wages for personal services or labor. (c. 235, §34).

Social Benefit Payments.—Numerous social benefits are exempt from attachment, in some instances subject to certain conditions, including funds of some relief societies and fraternal benefit societies (c. 176, §22); group life insurance proceeds, paid and unpaid (except debts arising from support obligations) (c. 175, §135); group annuity proceeds and benefits (except debts arising from support obligations under cc. 208, 209, 273), if contract so provides (c. 175, §§132C, 119A); disability insurance benefits to level of $35 per week except for necessities contracted for after insurance benefits have begun (c. 175, §110A); insurance and pension interests of insurance company employees and agents (c. 175, §§36-36B; see c. 175, §§132C and 110A); retirement funds of cooperative bank employees (except debts arising from support obligations) (c. 170, §32) and of credit union employees (except debts arising from support obligations) (c. 171, §33); workmen's compensation payments (except debts to veteran's agent or commissioner of veterans' services and/or debts arising from support obligation) (c. 152, §47); employment security benefits (except debts arising from support obligations) (c. 151A, §36); aid to families with dependent children (trustee process only) (c. 118, §10); and relocation assistance to persons displaced by eminent domain (c. 79, §6A).

Property Held by Government.—Commonwealth cannot be summoned as trustee under trustee process without statutory authorization. (362 Mass. 151, 285 N.E.2d 103. See also c. 41, §43A.) Various categories of property held by government are exempt, including wage deductions from public employees for payment to credit unions (c. 149, §178B); and property owned by governmental agencies performing proprietary duties, including housing authorities (c. 121B, §13) and Massachusetts Bay Transportation Authority (c. 161A, §2).

Earnings and Pensions.—Unpaid wages or salary for personal labor or services are exempt to extent of $125 per week except debts arising from support obligations. Wages held by trustee for defendant in pension exempt. (c. 246, §28). See topic Garnishment.

Real Property.—Exempt to extent of $50,000 in most cases except support obligations. See topics Executions, subhead Property Subject to Levy, Homesteads; and c. 236, §18.

Other Exemptions.—First $500 of bank account of natural person is exempt. (c. 246, §28A). Partner's interest in partnership property may not be attached except on claim against partnership. (c. 108A, §25[2][c]). Decedent's property may not be attached without permission of probate court. (c. 230, §7). Amounts deposited with state treasurer in lieu of compulsory automobile liability coverage cannot be attached except for payment of judgment. (c. 90, §34D).

Substitution.—Debtor is not entitled to hold other things exempt in place of those named.

See note at head of Digest as to 1998 legislation covered.

See Topical Index in front part of this volume.

MA – 31

EXEMPTIONS . . . continued

Debts Against Which Exemptions Not Allowed.—None.

Waiver of Exemption.—With certain exceptions, exemptions may be waived. (135 Mass. 401. But see, e.g., c. 151A, §36.)

Necessity for Claiming Exemption.—No special provisions. Exemptions should be claimed. (135 Mass. 401). Exemptions may be claimed by debtor and in certain circumstances by his wife, children, or representatives after death.

Trustee Process.—See topic Garnishment.

FORECLOSURE:

See topics Factors, Liens, Pledges; category Mortgages, topic Mortgages of Real Property.

FRAUDULENT SALES AND CONVEYANCES:

Legislature, in 1996, repealed Uniform Fraudulent Conveyance Act and enacted Uniform Fraudulent Transfer Act. (c. 109A). New law differs in some respects from Uniform Conveyance Act. Under UFTA, person who claims that transfer was invalid must show actual fraud, which is defined as actual intent to hinder, delay, or defraud any creditor of debtor, or constructive fraud, which may be found if transfer is made without supplying consideration of reasonable equivalent value. (c. 109A, §5). UFTA now imposes special statute of limitations for fraudulent transfers. (c. 109A, §10).

GARNISHMENT:

Trustee process used in Massachusetts for objects accomplished elsewhere by garnishment. See c. 246, to which statutory citations under this topic refer; Mass. R. Civ. P., Rule 4.2; and topic Attachment.

Caveat.—Prejudgment attachment by trustee process under then existing statutes and rules held unconstitutional, insofar as not providing for notice, opportunity for hearing, and court approval prior to attachment. See 349 F. Supp. 741; 365 F. Supp. 1299. Mass. R. Civ. P. Rules 4.1 and 4.2 provide revised attachment procedure applicable to goods, chattels and other property, designed to overcome constitutional deficiencies cited by federal courts. Under revised Rules providing for notice and hearing except in certain exigent circumstances, trustee process may now be used pursuant to c. 246, but only by court order upon motion in compliance with those Rules. See 584 F.2d 559, 561.

Property Which May Be Reached.—Goods, effects and credits of defendant entrusted to or deposited with a third person may be reached by trustee process except money held in any bank to meet payroll of defendant's employees (§20) and $500 of a natural person held in a bank in commonwealth. (§28A). Joint account shall be treated as if each depositor owned one half. (§28A). Debts due to defendant, if due absolutely and without contingency even though not yet payable (§24; §32[4]), or held by any person by conveyance void as to creditors of defendant (§25) as well as wages and pensions subject to certain exemptions (§28), may be attached by trustee process and held to satisfy final judgment. But person may not be adjudged trustee: (1) By reason of having drawn, made, accepted, or endorsed any negotiable instrument or other security which at date of summons was negotiable to holder in due course; (2) by reason of money received as sheriff or other officer, under execution or other process in favor of defendant; (3) by reason of money in his hands as public officer; (4) by reason of money or any other thing due from him to defendant, unless it is, at time of service of summons upon him, due absolutely and without any contingency; (5) by reason of judgment debt so long as he is liable to execution; (6) by reason of money or credits due for wages of defendant's wife or minor children; (7) by reason of money or credits due as wages or lay of seaman except those accruing to fisherman (§32); (8) by reason of money or credits due for wages of personal labor or services of defendant, except on claim reduced to judgment, and after court approval on ten days notice to defendant. (§32[8], Rule 4.2[a]). Various social benefit payments, and property held by government, are exempt from attachment. See topic Exemptions.

Jurisdiction and Venue.—Action must be brought in county in which one of trustees resides or has usual place of business (§2), but in inferior courts except BMC person may not be held to answer as trustee except in county in which he lives or has usual place of business (§4), provided, however, that if action could not be brought in that inferior court except because of residence or place of business of trustee, court may on motion of any party transfer case to any other inferior court in which action might have been commenced had there been no trustee named in writ (§4A).

Grounds.—Court must find reasonable likelihood that plaintiff will recover judgment, including interest and costs, in amount equal to or greater than amount of trustee process over and above any liability insurance shown by defendant to be available to satisfy judgment. If plaintiff seeks ex parte order approving trustee process, court must find also that either: (i) Defendant is not subject to jurisdiction of court, or (ii) clear danger that defendant if notified in advance of trustee attachment will remove goods or credits from state or conceal them, or (iii) immediate danger that defendant will dissipate, damage or destroy goods to be attached on trustee process. (Rule 4.2[g]).

Proceedings to Obtain.—Mass. R. Civ. P. and Rules of Domestic Relations, Rule 4.2, govern. Plaintiff must file motion for approval of attachment on trustee process, together with complaint and affidavit(s). Copies of all documents to be served on defendant. Notice of hearing must inform defendant that by appearing to be heard, he will not thereby submit himself to jurisdiction of court nor waive service of complaint and summons upon him. (Rule 4.2[c]). For ex parte attachment by trustee process, plaintiff must also file certificate as to liability insurance available to satisfy judgment. (Rule 4.2 [g]). Trustee process must be served within 30 days after order approving attachment. (Rule 4.2[c]).

Trustee process is not available in actions for specific recovery of goods and chattels, for malicious prosecution, for libel or slander, or for assault and battery. (Rule 4.2[a]). Trustee process may be used and any person may be summoned as trustee of defendant therein, except nonresident individuals having no usual place of business in this state and foreign corporations and associations having no such place of

business. Except in case of summons stating that action is on judgment, or in contract for personal services, or for goods sold and delivered, or for money due under contract in writing or in tort for damages on account of operation of motor vehicle not registered in this state, no summons ad damnum of which exceeds $1,000 may be served on any alleged trustee unless plaintiff, if other than Massachusetts governmental unit, has filed in court bond with surety company authorized to do business in this state as surety, or with sureties approved by justice, associate justice or special justice of court. Bond must be of such amount not less than $250 as court shall require and must be conditioned upon payment to defendant of amount not greater than penal sum. No bond required for actions to enforce child support, maintenance or alimony if proper procedure used. Summons must bear endorsement in specified manner of fact that required bond has been so filed. Cost of bond is taxed in plaintiff's costs if he prevails in action. (c. 246, §1).

If co-partners are summoned as trustees, service on one partner is sufficient. (§7).

Answer of Trustee (Garnishee).—Trustee must answer within 20 days under oath or statutory penalties of perjury disclosing fully what goods, effects and credits of defendant were in his hands when trustee was served (§§10, 11), and may be interrogated from time to time in writing upon oath. (§12).

Practice.—Trustee's answers are taken as true, but additional facts not inconsistent therewith may be proved (§16) and trustee may be interrogated through written interrogatories. He is liable for willfully false answer for full amount of judgment recovered in suit and interest thereon. (§19). Liquidated cross demands in favor of trustee may be set off. (§26). Trustee who does not answer may be defaulted for full amount of unsatisfied judgment against defendant. (§46). Trustee who answers may be allowed costs including counsel fees. (§68).

Adverse Claims.—A person claiming by force of assignment or otherwise goods, effects or credits in hands of alleged trustee, may be admitted to suit in order to determine his title. (§33). Person having interest by assignment or otherwise in money or credits attached may dissolve attachment by giving bond with sufficient sureties, and after filing of bond trustee is not liable to plaintiff for effects in his hands. (§§66 and 67).

Release of Property.—Attachment may be dissolved by filing surety company bond. (c. 223, §120). Defendant may move to dissolve or modify ex parte attachment on two days notice. (Rule 4.2[h]). See topic Attachment.

Judgment against trustee discharges him from all demands by defendant for all goods, effects and credits paid, delivered, or accounted for by trustee by force of such judgment. (c. 246, §43).

Earnings.—Attachment of wages or salary may be made only on action brought upon judgment and court permission, after notice, required. Court may shorten or waive notice requirement if it finds that justice would be unreasonably delayed or hindered. (§32[8]). Unpaid wages or salary for personal labor or services are exempt to extent of $125 per week, except debts arising from support obligations. Wages held by trustee for defendant in pension are exempt. (§28). Except for writ to satisfy support order, every writ of attachment of wages for personal labor or services or of such pension must contain statement of amount exempted under statute and direction to trustee to pay over exempted amount to defendant in same manner and at same time as such amount would have been paid if no attachment had been made. (§28; Rule 4.2[b]).

Monies in defendant's payroll account exempt from trustee process. Fine for depositing other funds therein to avoid process. (§20). Fine for suing resident debtor outside Massachusetts with intent of depriving him of protections afforded by commonwealth to wage earners. (§20A). $500 in any bank account of natural persons only is exempt from attachment by trustee process. Summons served on bank must describe this exemption. (§28A).

See topics Attachment, Exemptions.

HOMESTEADS:

See generally c. 188. Prior to 1977 homestead was little used because it was thought not applicable to joint property and because surviving spouse of deceased homesteader, with minor child, could not mortgage without guardianship and court approval. 1977, c. 791 made law applicable to joint property. However, in attempting to avoid need for surviving spouse to obtain court approval to mortgage, statute actually made it necessary to have court approval even while homesteader and spouse were both living (unless appropriate power was reserved in creating homestead). This was corrected by 1978, c. 539 and 1979, c. 248 but mortgages between Dec. 5, 1977 and Oct. 18, 1978 may still require court approval. Those made by surviving spouse with minor children still require court approval. In general, application and effect of statute as amended are unclear.

Estate of homestead to extent of $100,000 in land and buildings may be acquired by owner or owners of home or one or all who rightfully possesses premises by lease or otherwise, and occupies or intends to occupy said home as principal residence. Such estate shall be exempt from laws of conveyance, descent, devise, attachment, levy on execution and sale for payment of debts and legacies with specified exceptions. Owner of home for homestead purposes shall include sole owner, joint tenant, tenant by entirety or tenant in common; provided, that only one owner may acquire estate of homestead in any such home for benefit of his family; and provided further, that estate of homestead may be acquired on only one principal residence for benefit of family. Word "family" includes, for purposes of homestead statute, either parent and child or children, or husband and wife and their children, if any, or sole owner. (c. 188, §1 as am'd 1995, c. 297, §1).

Estate of homestead to extent of $200,000 per individual, whether declaration is filed individually or jointly, in real property or manufactured home may be acquired by person 62 years old or older or disabled if person occupies or intends to occupy property as principal residence. "Disabled" means having impairment meeting disability requirements for supplemental security income under 42 U.S.C. 1382c(a)(3)(A) and (C) in effect at time of filing. (c. 188, §1A). Extent of homestead limit applies to equity of homesteader and excludes amount of value mortgaged. (128 B.R. 321).

HOMESTEADS . . . *continued*

Limitation of Value.—$50,000. If premises claimed by judgment debtor as estate of homestead are in opinion of levying officer of greater value than $50,000 appraisers are appointed who must set aside so much of premises, including dwelling house, in whole or in part, as appears to be of value of $50,000 and residue of property may be levied upon. (c. 236, §18).

Limitation of Area.—None.

Debts or Liabilities Against Which Exemption Not Available.—Sale for taxes or attachment, levy or sale for debt contracted previous to acquisition or for purchase of homestead, decree for support of spouse or minor child or ground rent where buildings are on land not owned by owner of homestead. (§1). With respect to elderly or disabled homestead: Taxes, assessments and liens; first and second mortgages; debts or contracts incurred prior to filing of declaration of homestead protection; decree for support of spouse or minor child; or ground rent where buildings are on land not owned by owner of homestead. (§1A).

Designation of Homestead.—Homestead estate may be created by declaration in deed by which property is acquired or, after acquisition, by writing duly signed, sealed and acknowledged and recorded in registry of deeds in county where land is situated or in office of city or town clerk in city or town where manufactured home is located. (§2). Elderly or disabled homestead estate may be created by filing elderly or disabled person declaration of homestead protection together with original or certified copy of U.S. Social Security Administration disability award letter or licensed physician's letter certifying that person meets statutory disability requirements then in effect, at registry of deeds wherein such person resides. (§1A).

Probate court may issue judgment allowing spouse and minor children, if any, living apart from owner of homestead use and enjoyment of homestead. (§3).

Claim of Exemption.—No special provisions. See supra, subhead Designation of Homestead.

Release.—Estate of homestead may be terminated during lifetime of homesteader by: (1) Deed signed by homesteader and spouse not specifically reserving homestead or (2) release of homestead duly signed, sealed, acknowledged by homesteader and spouse, if any, and recorded in registry for county in which property located, except that as to homesteads created between Dec. 5, 1977 and Oct. 18, 1978 guardian's license is necessary to release rights of minor children unless homesteader reserved such power in creating estate; but conveyance which does not release homestead rights shall be valid to pass any title or interest beyond or subject to estate of homestead. (§7).

After death of homesteader, release by guardian under license of court is necessary to release interests of minor unmarried children. (§8).

Loss of Exemption.—No special statutory provisions.

Proceeds of Sale.—Proceeds of sale of homestead are not exempt prior to investment in another homestead. Proceeds of sale licensed by court may be apportioned by court among parties entitled thereto.

Rights of Surviving Spouse and Family.—At death of person holding homestead, homestead continues for benefit of surviving spouse and minor children until youngest child reaches 18 years and surviving spouse dies or remarries. (§4).

JUDGMENT NOTES:

See category Business Regulation and Commerce, topic Bills and Notes.

LEVY:

See topics Attachment, Executions.

LIENS:

The provisions of the common law as to liens are in force.

Waiver, Loss or Extinguishment.—Common law principles, and statutes as noted below, apply.

Personal Property.—Liens upon personal property are governed by c. 255.

Mechanics' and Materialmen's Liens.—*Note*: Legislature, in 1997, revised statutes governing mechanics liens. (c. 254).

Generally.—Law requires persons, who perform personal labor in erection, alteration, repair or removal of building, structure or improvement to real property, to file notice of written contract with registry of deeds in order to enforce lien against debtor. (c. 254, §§1, 2, 2A, 2B, 4, 5, 8). Moreover, law allows persons to enforce lien upon debtor for construction management and contractor services, as well as, rental equipment, appliances and tools. (c. 254, §2). Requirement for written contract caused confusion under prior law, and now legislature defines "written contract" as any written contract enforceable under laws of commonwealth. (c. 254, §2A).

Lien will automatically dissolve unless person entitled to enforce lien complies with statutory requirements. (c. 254, §§2, 4, 8). These requirements state that person must file just and true account of amount due creditor. (c. 254, §8). Time of filing "statement of the amount due" is at earliest date of: (a) 90 days after recording of notice of substantial completion under §2A, (b) 120 days after recording of notice of termination under §2B, or (c) 120 days after person entitled to enforce lien under §2 or anyone who performed or furnished labor, material, rental equipment, appliances or tools records in registry of deeds. (c. 254, §§2, 2A, 2B).

Any person who enters written contract to erect, alter, repair or remove building, structure or other improvement to real property or for furnishing material, rental equipment, appliances or tools must file under §2. Once work is sufficiently complete so that it can be occupied or utilized for its intended use, creditor seeking to enforce lien must file notice of substantial completion in registry of deeds. (c. 254, §2A). If, however, contract is terminated prior to filing of notice of substantial completion under §2A, creditor seeking to enforce lien, must file notice that contract was terminated. (c. 254, §2B).

Procedure to enforce lien is governed by §5. Statute requires that creditor seeking to enforce lien must bring action in superior or district court where land lies within 30 days after filing of required statements under §8. Otherwise, lien will be dissolved. (c. 254, §§5, 8). Additionally, lien will be dissolved, unless, creditor records in registry of deeds attested copy of complaint, which contains brief description of property, and statement of amount due. These documents must be filed within 30 days after commencement of action. (c. 254, §5). Court may enter order to sell property to satisfy lien under §5A. Priority of previous and subsequent creditors is governed under §7.

Subcontractors.—Provisions governing notice and filing of liens of subcontractors is outlined in §4.

Bond.—Any person entitled under c. 254 may record surety bond in statutory form, and thereafter no lien for labor and/or materials (except for liens of principals on bond) can attach under contract as to which bond is given. (c. 254, §12).

Prior Mortgages.—Mortgage existing and recorded prior to recording of notice of lien has priority to extent of amount advanced or unconditionally committed over lien under §§2, 3 and 4 for labor and/or materials used in erection, alteration, repair or removal of building or structure, which erection, etc., was actually begun before recording of mortgage. (c. 254, §7).

Attaching Creditor.—Rights of attaching creditor cannot prevail against lien for personal labor, nor against claim of lienor when notice of contract has been filed or recorded in registry of deeds prior to recording of attachment. (c. 254, §13).

Public Buildings and Railways.—No lien shall attach to any land, building or structure thereon owned by commonwealth (c. 254, §6) or (probably) on essential property of railroad or railway (226 Mass. 148, 115 N.E. 299), but officers or agents of state or any county, city or town contracting for public buildings are required to obtain sufficient security by bond or otherwise for payment by contractors and subcontractors for labor and materials, and rental of equipment, furnished or employed. Such security must be enforced by filing petition in equity within one year after day on which claimant last performed labor or furnished materials, etc., included in claim. In addition, claimant who is subcontractor must give written notice of claim to contractor within 65 days after day on which he last performed labor, etc. (c. 149, §29).

Other Real Property Liens.—There is statutory lien on real estate for taxes (see category Taxation, topic Property Taxes); for assessments for construction of sewers and sidewalks (c. 83, §§15, 16B, 27), removal of snow (c. 85, §6), sprinkling of streets (c. 40, §§16-18) and other local improvements (c. 80, §§12, 15, 16) for two years after last installment is committed to collector; for charges due to municipal utility (c. 164, §§58B, 58C); for drainage of swamps and lowlands (c. 252, §11); for cost of removal of obstructions in gaming houses (c. 271, §25); for certain improvements made by life tenant during his tenancy (c. 237, §38); for municipal water rates (c. 40, §§42A, 42B); on mills for damages by flowage, but such lien does not extend to any amount due more than three years before commencement of action therefor (c. 253, §14); in favor of railroads on real estate adjoining lines for erection and maintenance of fences (c. 160, §94); and in favor of city or town on real estate for cost of removing dangerous or illegal structure therefrom after refusal of owner, lessee or mortgagee in possession to do so (c. 143, §9). Equitable lien may be created upon real estate in certain circumstances. (373 Mass. 445, 368 N.E.2d 276). In absence of express agreement there is no lien in favor of vendor of real estate.

Hazardous Material Removal Lien.—Commonwealth has lien to secure removal costs and other liability from release of oil and hazardous materials. Except as to residential real property, lien has priority over any prior or subsequent encumbrances or levying creditor of owner of affected site and over any subsequent purchasers. (c. 21E, §13).

Condominiums.—Condominium unit owner's share of common expenses, which shall include costs of collection, including reasonable attorneys' fees, plus interest, late fees, and fines lawfully assessed by organization of unit holders, constitutes lien upon his unit. Organization of unit holders may assess to each unit owner cost of any energy conservation device installed in unit, not already separately metered for water and utilities, and his proportionate share of costs of water and other utilities, with certain provisions. (See c. 183A, §6.) Such lien shall have priority over all other liens, except municipal liens (in event of tax taking or foreclosure) or, with limited exceptions, first mortgage of record (in event of foreclosure). Organization of unit owners may assess cost of maintaining, repairing or replacing limited common area solely to owner of unit to which limited common area is designated, and assessment is enforceable as common expense. (c. 183A, §6). Condominium liens are also enforced pursuant to c. 254, §§5 and 5A.

Personal Property.—There are statutory liens on personal property as follows: Upon ships, their tackle, apparel and furniture in favor of pilots for services (c. 103, §17), and others for labor and materials furnished for construction, repairing, launching, and for provisions, stores and other articles furnished on account of vessel (c. 255, §§14-22) (if contract is maritime, enforcement only in federal courts; otherwise, enforcement by civil action in Superior Court [c. 255, §17]); in favor of persons pasturing, boarding or keeping horses and other domestic animals, placed with them by owner's consent, upon such animals (c. 255, §24); in favor of public garage owners upon automobiles placed with them by owner's consent (c. 255, §25); in favor of warehousemen (c. 106, §§7-209, 7-210), jewelers and watchmakers (c. 255, §31C); for storage of goods removed under summary process proceedings (c. 239, §4); in favor of aircraft mechanics and airport operators for landing and other charges (c. 255, §31E); upon paintings, photographs and like properties in favor of persons performing work on them (c. 255, §31F); in favor of railroads for feeding livestock (c. 272, §81); in favor of carriers for storage and transportation charges (c. 106, §§7-307, 7-308); in favor of factor or consignee for expenses of shipment and care of goods (c. 104, §§2, 3 and 6); in favor of manufactured housing communities operators for rental facilities, storage, and care of manufactured home sites (c. 255, §25A). Provisions made for enforcing these liens. (c. 255, §§26, 29, 31B).

Merchandise Liens.—Uniform Commercial Code applies. (c. 106, §§9-101 through 9-507).

See note at head of Digest as to 1998 legislation covered.

See Topical Index in front part of this volume.

MA – 33

LIENS . . . *continued*

Motor Vehicles.—Legislature amended rules regarding creation of security interest with motor vehicles. (c. 36, §21A).

Investment Securities.—Legislature revised laws governing investment securities and perfection of security interest. (c. 106, §§8-101, et al.). Security interest can be imposed upon investment property, which is generally defined as any security, whether certified or uncertified, security entitlement, securities account or commodities contract or account. (c. 106, §§9-115 and 9-203). To perfect security interest, perfecting party must have control over investment property. (c. 106, §§8-106 and 9-115). Control may be held where perfecting party gains possession, becomes entitlement holder, becomes registered owner, or in instances where commodity customer has granted security interest in commodity. (c. 106, §§8-106 and 9-115). See category Business Regulation and Commerce, topic Commercial Code.

Attorney's Lien.—See category Legal Profession, topic Attorneys and Counselors.

Processor's Lien on Materials.—There is a statutory lien for work, labor, and materials furnished in processing cotton, wool, silk, synthetic fibers or leather goods and hides, or of goods of which above form component part and processing of wood, metals, paper, paperboard, plastic and plastic compounds, covering addition of materials and labor furnished in printing, cutting, milling, extruding, combining and serving, as against goods in lienor's possession which extends to unpaid balance of account for work, labor and materials furnished in course of such process in respect of any other goods of same owner whereof lienor's possession has terminated. This lien has priority over any owner's title, lien, interest or encumbrance and may be surrendered or waived only by express written agreement of parties. (c. 255, §31A).

Hospital Charges.—Hospital may secure lien for its charges payable out of recoveries in tort liability cases by mailing by certified mail, return receipt requested, statutory notice of claim to injured person, his attorney, person alleged to be liable for accident, and any insurance carrier covering liability of such person. (c. 111, §§70A, 70B).

Death of Owner.—Foregoing liens are not dissolved by owner's death or conveyance of property, and subsist in favor of creditor's personal representatives.

MECHANICS' LIENS:

See topic Liens.

PLEDGES:

Covered by Uniform Commercial Code. (c. 106, §§1-201[32]; 8-306[4], 8-401 and 9-101 through 9-507). See category Business Regulation and Commerce, topic Commercial Code.

Trust Receipts.—Covered by Uniform Commercial Code. (c. 106 §§9-101 through 9-507). See category Business Regulation and Commerce, topic Commercial Code.

Unauthorized Sale.—It is a criminal offense to sell or dispose of collateral security before maturity of the debt without the authority of the pledgee. (c. 266, §85).

Public Pensions.—A pledge of a pension, annuity or retirement allowance from the state, or county, city or town, is void and pledgee is liable to fine. (c. 32, §92).

Attachments.—The pledgor's interest in the property pledged may by proper proceedings be attached. See topic Attachment. (c. 106, §§9-203 and 9-204).

RECEIVERS:

Jurisdiction.—Supreme Judicial and Superior Courts have general powers to appoint receivers. (c. 214, §1). (See also c. 156B, §104; c. 155, §52.)

Proceedings.—By statute receivers may be appointed inter alia: (1) For domestic corporation if execution against it is not satisfied within 30 days after demand (c. 156B, §105) or if its charter has expired or otherwise terminated, or if corporation has been dissolved under §§99, 100 or 101 (c. 156B, §104); (2) of property of absentee in certain cases (c. 200, §1 et seq.) (see category Property, topic Absentees, generally); (3) of property of out-of-state bank if insolvent, if its capital is impaired, if continuance of business would be hazardous to public or if it has exceeded its powers or failed to comply with any provision of law (c. 167, §42); and (4) for long term care facility subject to licensing under c. 11, §71 in case of emergency or when it does not have license or license application on file, or when license has been denied, revoked, or not renewed, or procedures to do so have been initiated and residents' security cannot be assured while matter is pending (c. 111, §72M-72U). (Mass. R. Civ. P. 66; Super. Ct. Rule 51).

Eligibility and Competency.—No special statutory requirements.

Qualification.—A receiver may be required to give bond. (c. 214, §17).

Powers and Duties.—Receivers appointed under general equity powers have no powers except such as are conferred upon them by the orders of the court. (c. 155, §52; 107 Mass. 1). Receivers appointed under statute have powers conferred by particular statute.

Compensation.—Discretionary with court.

Discharge.—The receiver is discharged by court decree issued under general equity power, after certain conditions met. (c. 223, §131). No order discharging receiver will be entered until he has settled his final account. (Mass. R. Civ. P. 66[e], Super. Ct. Rule 51).

Dissolution of Attachments.—The appointment of a receiver to take possession of property dissolves any attachment of property if complaint seeking appointment of receiver is filed within four months after attachment was made, unless court continues attachment. (c. 223, §130).

REDEMPTION:

See topics Executions, Liens; categories Mortgages, topic Mortgages of Real Property; Taxation, topic Property Taxes.

SUPPLEMENTARY PROCEEDINGS:

See topic Executions, subhead Supplementary Proceedings.

TRUSTEE PROCESS:

See topic Garnishment.

USURY:

See category Business Regulation and Commerce, topic Interest.

DISPUTE RESOLUTION

ALTERNATIVE DISPUTE RESOLUTION:

Mandatory Dispute Resolution.—Chief justice for administration and management of state trial court is given authority under c. 211B, §19 to create rules for mandatory alternative dispute resolution (ADR) program for civil actions in trial court. Parties to dispute are not bound by results of any mandatory ADR. (c. 211B, §19). As part of pilot program established in Bristol, Worcester and Suffolk counties, civil action will be screened for possible referral to qualified ADR program within 12 months of filing complaint. (c. 211B, §19). Similar programs may exist in several other Massachusetts counties. Options available for those screened for ADR are self-directed settlement negotiations, case evaluation, mediation, nonbinding arbitration, expert fact-finding and binding arbitration. (c. 211B, §19). Uniform Rules on Dispute Resolution set standards for court-connected alternative dispute resolution programs and include ethical standards for all neutrals providing dispute resolution services. (SJC Rule 1:18).

Mediation: Collective Bargaining Agreements.—When negotiations over collective bargaining agreements between public employees and their employers are at impasse before Board of Conciliation and Arbitration (board), board is required to appoint mediator within five days of determining impasse exists, or parties may agree on mediator. (c. 150E, §9). If impasse continues after 20 days of mediation, board is mandated to appoint fact finder. (c. 150E, §9). See also 457 CMR §2 et seq. for rules governing alternative dispute resolution before board.

Arbitration.—Uniform Arbitration Act adopted. See topic Arbitration and Award for reference to mandatory arbitration.

Voluntary Dispute Resolution.—Under Superior Court Rules, when agreement has been made to refer to arbitrator and filed in clerks office, clerk should issue rule relative to agreement. (Sup. Ct. Rule 52). Objections to acceptance of award under this rule must be made in writing setting forth specific grounds. (Sup. Ct. Rule 52).

With respect only to Charlestown Division of District Courts, informal resolution of cases is encouraged and clerk of that court is mandated to assist parties by providing mediation services whenever possible. (Standing Order I-92[II][F][1]).

Voluntary programs may exist in other Massachusetts court by administrative order.

Local Rule 16.4 of U.S. District Court for District of Massachusetts contains provisions governing ADR. At each judicial conference, judge or magistrate is required to inquire about settlement and potential for ADR. (Local Rule 16.4[B]). Judge or magistrate may, in their discretion refer case to ADR program available in district court. (Local Rule 16.4[C][1]). Available ADR forums listed under rule, although not exhaustive, include mini-trials, summary jury trials, and mediation. (Local Rule 16.4[C][2]-[4]). Judge or magistrate is not limited to these options. (Local Rule 16.4[C]).

Dispute Resolution Services.—There are variety of court annexed dispute resolution programs available. For more information, call clerk of courts for county in which case is pending.

There are also number of private companies in Massachusetts which offer ADR services. For more complete list of ADR providers see 1994 Directory of Massachusetts Alternative Dispute Resolution Providers, published by Boston Bar Association and Directory of Alternative Dispute Resolution Providers found on pages 261-262 of 1995 Massachusetts Lawyers Diary and Manual. See also listings in Martindale-Hubbell Dispute Resolution Directory.

ARBITRATION AND AWARD:

Uniform Arbitration Act adopted (c. 251) but does not apply to collective bargaining agreements to arbitrate. Judicial enforcement of arbitration provisions in labor contracts is available under similar statute. (c. 150C). Consolidation or severance of arbitration proceedings may be ordered by Superior Court under certain circumstances. (c. 251, §2A).

Form and Requisites of Submission.—Submission in writing to Superior Court. (§2). Applications to modify, correct, vacate or enforce award to be made by motion. (§15).

Contracts to Arbitrate Future Disputes.—Written contracts are enforceable. (§1).

Rescission.—Written contract to arbitrate subject to rescission or revocation only to extent applicable to any other contract. (§1).

Powers of Arbitrators.—Arbitrators have only powers specifically granted in agreement. (§3). If there are multiple arbitrators, such powers may be exercised by majority thereof unless otherwise provided by agreement or by c. 251. (§4). Arbitrators have powers to authorize discovery, and discovery under Rule 34, Mass. R. Civ. P. is permitted. (§7).

Award and Enforcement Thereof.—Award binding on parties, and court may be petitioned to confirm award. (§11). Application to arbitrator to modify, correct or clarify award must be made within 20 days after delivery of award. (§9). Petition to court to modify or correct award must be filed within 30 days after delivery of award. (§13). Petition to court to vacate award must be filed within 30 days after delivery of award except in cases of award procured by corruption, fraud or other undue means, in which case petition must be filed within 30 days after such grounds are or should have been known. (§12).

See note at head of Digest as to 1998 legislation covered.

See Topical Index in front part of this volume.

ARBITRATION AND AWARD . . . *continued*

Judgment on Award.—Judgment is entered upon granting of order confirming, modifying or correcting award and may be enforced as any other judgment. (§14).

Multiple Damages.—Arbitration awards not subject to c. 93A multiple damages. (411 Mass. 31, 576 N.E.2d 680).

Mandatory Arbitration.—Required in following cases, subject to relevant restrictions: (1) Claims by consumers against manufacturers of defective automobiles (c. 90, §7N¹/₂); (2) claims for compensation by abutting communities against developers of hazardous waste facility sites (c. 21D, §§14, 15); (3) claims by health care providers excluded from participation in medical malpractice self insurance fund (c. 175F, §11).

See also topic Alternative Dispute Resolution.

DOCUMENTS AND RECORDS

ACKNOWLEDGMENTS:

Uniform Acknowledgments Act was, with minor differences, incorporated into c. 183, §§29-42, with results discussed in following subheadings.

Within State.—Acknowledgments within the state must be before a justice of the peace or notary public. (c. 183, §30). Fee: Justice of peace 25¢. (c. 262, §1).

Outside State but Within United States.—Out of Mass. and in U.S., acknowledgments must be before justice of peace, notary public, magistrate (which includes, probably, mayor of a city), or commissioner appointed by governor of Massachusetts for purpose (as to commissioners outside state, see c. 222, §§4-7); or before any officer authorized by law of such other state to take proofs and acknowledgments of deeds if there is annexed certificate from secretary of state where officer resides under seal of such state, or from clerk of court of record in county where officer resides or took acknowledgment, authenticating authority of officer taking acknowledgment and genuineness of his signature. (c. 183, §§30, 33, 41). Acknowledgment taken in another state before notary public whose notarial stamp or seal is impressed to instrument is sufficient without certificate of authority. (c. 183, §30; 328 Mass. 242, 103 N.E. 2d 251).

Outside the United States.—If in a foreign country, acknowledgments must be before a justice of the peace, notary, magistrate, commissioner (as described in preceding paragraph), ambassador, minister, consul, vice-consul, chargé d'affaires, or consular officer or agent of U.S. accredited to such country. If made before U.S. official, there must be certification by him under his seal of office. (c. 183, §30).

Persons in U.S. Armed Forces.—Person serving in or with U.S. Armed Forces or dependent may acknowledge instruments before any active commissioned officer of such forces having rank of second lieutenant or ensign or any higher rank providing instrument contains statement that person executing instrument is serving in or with U.S. Armed Forces or is dependent of such person and includes serial number of person so serving. No authenticating certificate is necessary. Instruments so acknowledged outside Mass. have same effect as though taken before commissioner of Mass. appointed to take depositions in other states. (c. 222, §11).

General Requirements as to Taking.—No special statutory requirements. Arbitrator may not take acknowledgment on submission to arbitration. (20 Pick. 480). Attorney of interested party may take acknowledgment on deed. (303 Mass. 105, 20 N.E.2d 939). Grantor must actually state that instrument is executed as his free act and deed. (320 Mass. 410, 69 N.E.2d 806).

General Requirements of Certificate.—The validity of an acknowledgment for purposes of recording is not affected by the absence of an official seal (4 Cush. 260, 58 Mass. 260) or of statement indicating when commission of officer expires (c. 222, §8).

Husband and Wife.—Either spouse alone can provide acknowledgment in conveyance of property held as tenants by entirety. (8 Mass. App. 860, 398 N.E.2d 497). The acknowledgment of a married woman is taken as if she were single. (c. 183, §31).

Attorneys in Fact.—The law relative to the acknowledgment and recording of deeds applies equally to letters of attorney for the conveyance of real estate. (c. 183, §32).

Corporations.—No special requirements.

Foreign Acknowledgments.—Uniform Acknowledgments Act adopted, with exceptions noted above.

Effect of Acknowledgment.—Entitles deed to be recorded. (c. 183, §29).

Proof by Subscribing Witness.—When a grantor dies or departs from the state without acknowledging his deed, or refuses to acknowledge it, its due execution may be proved by proper proceedings be proved by the testimony of subscribing witness, or, if they are all dead or out of state, by proof of handwriting of grantor and subscribing witness, and certificate of such proof must be endorsed upon deed, which may then be recorded. (c. 183, §§34-37, 40). Before or pending such proceedings copy compared with original by register may be filed in registry of deeds, and such filing has for 30 days, or until seven days after termination of such proceedings, same effect as recording deed. (c. 183, §38). In order to prove execution of deed as above provided, there must be at least one attesting witness. (c. 183, §39).

Authentication.—Official character of officer taking acknowledgment in this state will in all cases be certified by state secretary (fee determined annually by secretary of administration) and also (if officer elects to file his signature with court clerk) by clerk (for civil business, in Suffolk County) of superior court (court of record) in any county where officer's signature is on file (customary fee, $3). As to acknowledgments taken outside of state, see subhead Outside State but within United States, supra. (c. 183, §33).

Forms

Begin in all cases with a caption showing the state and county where the acknowledgment is taken.

In case of natural persons acting in their own right: On this . . . . day of . . . . 19. . . ., before me personally appeared A. B. (or A. B. and C. D.), to me known to be the person (or persons) described in and who executed the foregoing instrument, and acknowledged that he (or they) executed the same as his (or their) free act and deed. (c. 183 App. Form 13).

In case of natural persons acting by attorney: On this . . . . day of . . . . . 19. . . ., before me personally appeared A. B., to me known to be the person who executed the foregoing instrument in behalf of C. D., and acknowledged that he executed the same as the free act and deed of said C. D. (c. 183 App. Form 14).

In case of corporations or joint-stock associations: On this . . . . day of . . . . 19. . . ., before me appeared A. B., to me personally known, who, being by me duly sworn (or affirmed), did say that he is the president (or other officer or agent of the corporation or association) of (describing the corporation or association) and that the seal affixed to said instrument is the corporate seal of said corporation (or association), and that said instrument was signed and sealed in behalf of said corporation (or association) by authority of its board of directors (or trustees), and said A. B. acknowledged said instrument to be the free act and deed of said corporation (or association). (c. 183 App. Form 15).

In case the corporation or association has no corporate seal, omit the words "the seal affixed to said instrument is the corporate seal of said corporation (or association), and that" and add, at the end of the affidavit clause, the words "and that said corporation (or association) has no corporate seal." (c. 183 App. Form 15).

In all cases add signature and title of the officer taking the acknowledgment.

Other forms are permitted. (c. 183, §42).

The certificate of acknowledgment may be on a separate paper annexed to the instrument. (c. 183, §30).

Alternative to Acknowledgment or Proof.—No statutory provision.

Curative Act.—Recorded instrument unacknowledged or defective as to acknowledgment is deemed fully effective absent suit on defect within ten years of recording. (c. 184, §24).

AFFIDAVITS:

Affidavits may be sworn:

Within State.—Before justice of peace or notary public. (c. 222, §1). If for use in proceeding in Massachusetts court, before clerk or assistant clerk of such court. (c. 221, §18).

Without State.—Before notary public duly commissioned and qualified by any other state or government, within jurisdiction for which commissioned, certified under official seal. (c. 233, §73). Also before commissioners, appointed by Massachusetts governor, in foreign countries and in states, territories, districts and dependencies of U.S., certified under official seal, when affidavit is to be used or recorded in Massachusetts (c. 222, §§4-6). Some case authority for recognizing oaths administered by clerk of foreign court if within his statutory authority and if his office and signature are certified. (338 Mass. 263, 155 N.E.2d 165).

General Requirements as to Administration.—Affidavit must be either sworn before qualified officer or verified by written declaration that it is made under penalties of perjury. (c. 268, §1A; see also Superior Court Rule 15 as to affidavits to be used in Superior Court). No statutory requirements as to administration of oath.

General Requirements of Jurat.—Official seal required only when affidavit sworn outside Massachusetts (c. 233, §73; c. 222, §6); preferred practice when sworn before Massachusetts officer. No requirement that date of expiration of commission be stated, but preferred practice. Jurat required by common law when affidavit is sworn, but when jurat not required by statute, notary's (unsigned) certificate qualifies statement as sworn statement. (143 Mass. 380, 9 N.E. 740; cf. 353 Mass. 551, 233 N.E.2d 723). Title of subscribing officer should be stated. (143 Mass. 380, 9 N.E. 740). Name of subscribing officer must be printed or typed below signature on sworn affidavit to be filed in Probate Court (c. 222, §8A) and preferably should be printed or typed on other affidavits.

Use of Affidavit.—Governed by rules of procedure and evidence.

Form.—No statutory form is prescribed. Customary form of sworn affidavit as follows:

Commonwealth of Massachusetts
[County], SS.
[Case caption]
I, ..., hereby state as follows:
[Statement of facts]

        [Signature of Affiant]

Subscribed and sworn to before me this   day of   , 19 .

    [Signature of Officer]

    [Typed name of Officer]
    [Title and Seal, if any]
    My commission expires . . . .

Customary form of affidavit signed without oath is:
Commonwealth of Massachusetts
[County], SS.
[Case caption]
I, ..., hereby state as follows:
[Statement of facts]
Signed under the penalties of perjury this . . . . day of . . . ., 19 . . . .

    [Signature of Affiant]

    . . . .

See note at head of Digest as to 1998 legislation covered.

See Topical Index in front part of this volume.

AFFIDAVITS . . . *continued*

Alternative to Affidavit.—Statement containing written declaration that it is made under penalty of perjury satisfies requirement of affidavit. (c. 268, §1A; 369 Mass. 175, 338 N.E.2d 834; 370 Mass. 243, 346 N.E.2d 861).

NOTARIES PUBLIC:

Seal.—A notary public is not required to use a seal (159 Mass. 193, 34 N.E. 173), except on lists of taxable property (c. 59, §31).

Powers and Duties.—Notaries public are authorized to take acknowledgments of deeds and other instruments and administer oaths or affirmations. (c. 222, §1).

A person over 14 may nominate his guardian before a notary public. (c. 201, §2). Notaries public have duties with respect to opening certain safe deposit boxes (c. 158, §17); and with respect to summoning witnesses (c. 233, §1).

Territorial Extent of Powers.—Every notary public is authorized to act throughout the commonwealth. (c. 222, §1).

Expiration of Commission.—Must state date of expiration of commission, but failure to do so does not invalidate action. (c. 222, §8).

Fees.—Statute permits the charging of fees in accordance with a specified schedule. (c. 262, §§1, 41, 43).

Commissioners of Deeds.—May be appointed by governor with extraterritorial powers. (c. 222, §§4-7).

Printing of Name.—Notary must print name below signature, but failure to do so does not invalidate action. (c. 222, §8).

Authentication.—See topic Acknowledgments, subhead Authentication.

RECORDS:

Recordable Instruments.—To affect persons other than parties, privies, or persons having actual notice, conveyances of estates in fee simple, fee tail or for life (see category Property, topic Deeds), certain leases or proper notices thereof (see category Property, topic Landlord and Tenant), mortgages, assignments of rents or profits, and assignments of mortgages of real estate (see category Mortgages, topic Mortgages of Real Property) are among those instruments which must be recorded (c. 183, §4) or, instrument, in case of registered land, registered (see subhead Registered Land, infra) in registry of deeds for county or district in which land is located.

Under c. 155, §8, and with respect to certain domestic and foreign corporations, any recordable instrument purporting to affect an interest in real estate, executed in name of corporation by president or vice-president and by treasurer or assistant treasurer, who may be one and same person, shall be binding on corporation in favor of purchaser or other person relying in good faith on such instrument, notwithstanding inconsistent provisions of articles of organization, certificate of incorporation, charter, special act of incorporation, constitution, by-laws, resolutions or votes of corporation. Comparable provision for domestic business corporations is c. 156B, §115 and for charitable corporations is c. 180, §10C. Comparable provision for trusts is c. 184, §34.

Place of Recording.—Instruments affecting real property must be recorded with registry of deeds for county where land is located, or district within county in cases of Berkshire, Bristol, Essex, Middlesex and Worcester. (c. 183, §4). *For list of Counties and County Seats see first page for this state in Volume containing Practice Profiles Section.* Financing statements are filed in accordance with the Uniform Commercial Code. (c. 106, §9-403).

Requisites for Recording.—Before a deed may be admitted to record there must be annexed to it or endorsed upon it a certificate of its acknowledgment by one or more of grantors or by attorney executing it or of proof of its due execution (c. 183, §§29, 30; see topic Acknowledgments), which certificate is recorded therewith, except that a copy of a deed not acknowledged may be filed in registry of deeds, where it will have same effect for 30 days as if recorded if deed is within that time duly proved and recorded or if after expiration of such 30 days proceedings to compel acknowledgment are still pending. Effect of such filing continues for seven days after termination of such proceedings (see topic Acknowledgments). (c. 183, §38).

No instrument conveying unregistered land shall be accepted for recording unless it (a) indicates that land is same as described in or conveyed by sufficiently identified prior recorded instruments or, (b) states that instrument does not create new boundaries, or (c) identifies land by reference either to a previously recorded plan recorded in same registry and sufficiently identified to locate plan, or by reference to a plan recorded with conveyance. Failure to comply does not invalidate instrument. (c. 183, §6A).

The law dealing with the acknowledgment and recording of deeds applies to letters of attorney for the conveyance of real estate. (c. 183, §32).

Every deed, mortgage or assignment of mortgage presented for record must contain or have endorsed on it the full name, residence and post office address of grantee, mortgagee, or assignee and, if deed and recital of amount of full consideration in dollars or nature of other consideration therefor. Address of land must be endorsed in margin of deed. Omission of these matters does not affect validity of deed, mortgage or assignment but may prevent recording thereof. (c. 183, §§6, 6B, 6C).

If instrument cannot be properly duplicated or a proper record thereof made, it may not be accepted for recording. (c. 36, §12A).

Recording fees are, with certain exceptions, as follows: Deed, $25 ($40 for registered land); mortgage, $20 plus, if deed or mortgage contains more than four pages, $1 for each page over four ($30 for registered land); mortgage foreclosure deed and affidavit, $35 ($70 for registered land); U.C.C. financing statement, continuation statement or amendment of either, $10; termination statement or assignment of financing statement, $4; municipal lien, $4; federal tax lien, registered land, $5; all other instruments, $10 ($30 for registered land); additional pages beyond four and additional marginal references, $1; plans (9¹/₂ x 14 inches or less), $10, with each additional sq. ft. or part, $3 ($20 for registered land). See c. 262, §§38, 39; c. 106, §§9-403-9-406. For fees paid to Registry of Deeds, add 40¢ for first ounce, 70¢ up to two ounces, and 25¢ each additional ounce up to 12 ounces for return postage. For fees paid to Land Court,

add one-time 52¢ postage charge. For fees paid to Land Court, number of pages does not affect charge imposed.

Copies of Instruments in Registry of Deeds.—Photostat copies, 75¢ per page, $1 per plan. (c. 262, §38).

Excise Taxes on Deeds.—Deeds or other written instruments that purport to convey ownership interests in real property with value, exclusive of liens, in excess of $100 are subject to excise tax of $2.28 for first $500 in value or fractional part thereof and $2.28 for each additional $500 in value or fraction or part thereof. Some county-specific differences in rates provided for by statute. This tax does not apply to any instrument or writing given to secure debt or to any deed, instrument or writing to which commonwealth or U.S. or any of their agencies are party. (c. 64[D], §1). There is also additional tax equal to 14% of tax imposed under provisions of said chapter. (Acts, 1969, c. 546, §23).

Foreign Conveyances or Encumbrances.—Conveyances executed outside the commonwealth must comply with the laws of the commonwealth. (c. 155, §§1, 8).

Effect of Record.—An unrecorded instrument of defeasance has no effect, except as against the maker of the instrument, his heirs and devisees, and persons having actual notice of it. (c. 183, §53).

The record of a deed or other instrument affecting title to land, duly acknowledged or proved, is conclusive evidence of delivery of such instrument, in favor of purchasers for value without notice. (c. 183, §5).

Certain formal defects cannot be raised after a deed has been recorded for ten years. (c. 184, §24).

Taxes.—See category Taxation, topic Stamp Tax.

Agreement for purchase and sale of real estate, or any extension thereof, must be acknowledged by a seller in order to be received for record, and such recorded agreement or extension must be extended by instrument recorded, or suit for its enforcement begun and memorandum thereof (like that described in c. 184, §15, or see category Property, topic Real Property, subhead Lis Pendens) recorded, within 90 days from date provided in agreement or extension for delivery of deed in order to be effective after such 90-day period against persons other than parties. (c. 184, §17A).

Other instruments which must be recorded include: Writ of entry or other proceeding or a judgment or decree therein affecting title to real estate or the use of buildings thereon (see category Property, topic Real Property); execution on judgment for possession (c. 237, §42); execution by virtue of which land is taken (see category Debtor and Creditor, topic Executions); decrees of Land Court (c. 185, §48); certificate of entry to foreclose mortgage (c. 244, §2) (see category Mortgages, topic Mortgages of Real Property); certificate of foreclosure sale under power of sale in mortgage (c. 244, §15); certificate of entry for breach of condition (c. 184, §19); notice of partition proceedings and final decree therein (c. 241, §7) (see category Civil Actions and Procedure, topic Partition); warrant for possession of property of absentee (see category Property, topic Absentees); notice of designation of property as homestead estate (c. 188, §2) (see category Debtor and Creditor, topic Homesteads); attachment on mesne process of land or leasehold in order that it be valid against subsequent attaching creditors or purchasers (c. 223, §63) (see category Debtor and Creditor, topic Attachment); conditional sale of heating apparatus, elevator apparatus or machinery, plumbing and fixtures which are attached to real estate (see category Business Regulation and Commerce, topic Sales); trusts concerning land, in order to give notice of trust to all the world (c. 203, §2) (see category Estates and Trusts, topic Trusts); building contracts, in order to secure lien upon land and building (c. 254, §30) (see category Debtor and Creditor, topic Liens); decrees of court discharging such liens (c. 254, §15); notice to prevent acquisition of easement (c. 187, §3) (see category Property, topic Adverse Possession); antenuptial contracts (c. 209, §26) (see category Family, topic Husband and Wife); tax collector's deed or instrument of taking (c. 60, §54) (see category Taxation, topic Taxes); statement of unpaid municipal water bills, in order to effect lien on real estate to which water is supplied (c. 40, §42A); chattel mortgages (c. 106, §9-302) (see category Mortgages, topic Chattel Mortgages, subhead Filing). Notices of federal tax lien or certificate of discharge of such lien (c. 36, §24); receipts for federal succession taxes (c. 36, §16) and petition, decree of adjudication and order approving trustee's bond under federal Bankruptcy Act (c. 36, §24A) may be recorded.

Affidavits of a person's married or unmarried status, kinship, or date of birth or death, purporting to relate to title of real estate, may be recorded in registry of deeds for county where land or any part thereof lies. (c. 183, §5A). Any such affidavit, in so far as its facts bear on the title to the land, is admissible in evidence in support of such title in any court in proceedings relating to such title. (ibid.).

A final decree in equity ordering conveyance or release to be made has, if recorded, same effect as though such conveyance, etc., were made and delivered. (c. 183, §§43 and 44, c. 209, §32D).

Fees.—See subhead Recording Fees, supra.

Registered Land.—Instruments affecting registered land, in lieu of recording, are presented to the recorder or assistant recorder of the Land Court. (c. 185, §§57-59). Fees for recordings relating to registered land are prescribed by c. 262, §39.

Torrens Act.—Land Court has exclusive original jurisdiction of, among other things, complaints for registration of titles to and easements in land held in fee simple and has power to hear and determine all questions arising upon complaints (c. 185, §1[a]), actions commenced pursuant to c. 208 and c. 209 excepted (c. 185, §1[a¹/₂]). It is court of record. Where title is contested contestants may claim jury trial at time of filing answer, and petitioner may claim jury trial within ten days after time allowed for such filing. (c. 185, §15). Issues of fact are then tried in Superior Court before jury. Questions of law arising in Superior Court or in connection with decree or otherwise in Land Court are appealable to Appeals Court or, subject to certain conditions, to SJC. (c. 185, §15).

The object of the court is to confirm and register land titles, and a decree to such effect, with few exceptions, binds the land and quiets the title thereto. (c. 185, §45).

Every applicant who receives certificate of title in pursuance of judgment of registration, and every subsequent purchaser of registered land who takes certificate of title for

RECORDS . . . *continued*

value and in good faith, holds same free from all encumbrances except those noted on certificate, and any of following encumbrances which may be existing:

(1) Liens, claims or rights arising or existing under laws or constitution of U.S. or of commonwealth which are not required by law to appear of record in registry in order to be valid against subsequent purchasers or encumbrances of record.

(2) Taxes, within three years after they have been committed to collector.

(3) Any highway, town way, or any private way laid out under the provisions of §21 of c. 82 if the certificate of title does not state that the boundary of such way has been determined.

(4) Any lease for a term not exceeding seven years.

(5) Any liability to assessment for betterments or other statutory liability which attaches to land in commonwealth as lien; but if there are easements or other rights appurtenant to parcel of registered land which for any reason have failed to be registered, such easements or rights remain so appurtenant notwithstanding such failure, and are held to pass with land until cut off or extinguished by registration of servient estate, or in any other manner.

(6) Liens in favor of U.S. for unpaid taxes arising or existing under I.R.C. of 1954, as am'd from time to time, and any other federal lien which may be filed in commonwealth. (c. 185, §§45 and 46).

(7) Liens in favor of commonwealth for unpaid taxes arising or existing under laws of commonwealth (c. 185, §46) (effective as to liens recorded on and after Jan. 1, 1985).

The law provides for an insurance fund based on an assessment of one-tenth of 1% of the assessed or court-determined value of land at time of original registration to indemnify persons who have without negligence sustained loss or damage, or been deprived of their estate by operation of land registration law. (c. 185, §§99-109).

Transfers of land are made by deed and surrender of registration certificates and issue of new certificates. (c. 185, §§57 and 62).

Registration of land is optional originally, but after such registration all instruments affecting the land, except wills or leases for a term not exceeding seven years, must be registered to have effect as conveyances or otherwise to affect the land. (c. 185, §57).

Transfer of Decedent's Title.—With respect to registered land, devisees or heirs at law may, after 30 days from granting of letters testamentary or of administration or at any time after entry of final decree on appeal therefrom, file a certified copy of the final decree of the Probate Court and of will, if any, in Land Court, which, after notice to all persons in interest and hearing, may grant new certificate of title to devisees or heirs at law. (c. 185, §97). With respect to unregistered land, there is no provision for recording to show title in devisees or heirs at law, except as this is shown by records of Probate Court. In case of intestacy, sworn petition for administration is customarily relied on for identity of heirs at law. As to when title of decedent passes, see category Estates and Trusts, topics Descent and Distribution, Wills, subhead Devises.

Vital Statistics.—City and town clerks must keep records of all births, deaths and marriages (c. 46, §1) and transmit certified copies of such records to state registrar (c. 46, §17), from whom certified copies of such copies may be obtained for fee determined annually by secretary of administration, currently $6, $11 for mail requests. Address requests to: Registry of Vital Records, 470 Atlantic Ave., Boston, MA 02210, (617) 753-8600. Reproduction of certified birth, marriage or death records of town clerk is prohibited except by certain officials in course of their official duties. (c. 46, §19A). Fee for city or town clerk's certificate of birth, marriage or death is $6, subject to change by individual community (c. 262, §34), but there may also be charge for actual expense of examining records and copying record required. Abstract copies of such records may be obtained free with letter of indigency. (c. 46, §26). In Boston certified birth, marriage, or death certificate available for $6 and abstracts not available.

Establishing Vital Records.—Town or city clerk has discretion to record birth, marriage or death not recorded when it occurred as required by law on the basis of (1) an affidavit containing the required facts made by person required by law to furnish information for an original record (in case of birth, includes parents and physician in charge) or credible person having knowledge thereof, (2) a certified copy of the record of any other town or city or (3) a written statement made at the time by any person since deceased required by law to furnish evidence thereof. (c. 46, §13). Usually clerk requires supporting written evidence made at or near the time, such as a church record.

Persons unable to furnish an affidavit for the establishment of a birth record may petition the city or town clerk for the recording of such birth. If clerk is not satisfied with evidence submitted by petitioner, petition and evidence may be submitted to a judge of probate court who may allow petition and order birth recorded. (c. 46, §13A).

Filing under Commercial Code.—When the collateral is equipment used in farming operation or farm products or accounts arising from the sale of farm products or consumer goods the financing statement is filed in the office of city or town clerk where debtor resides, or if debtor is not resident of state then in office of city or town clerk where goods are kept; if collateral is timber to be cut or minerals, including oil and gas, or the like, or if filing is fixture filing under c. 106, §9-313, financing statement is filed in office where real estate mortgage would be filed; and in all other cases financing statement is filed in office of secretary of state and also if debtor has only one place of business in state in office of clerk of such city or town, or if debtor has no place of business in state but resides in state also in office of city or town where he resides. Good faith filings made improperly may, with limitations, still be effective. (c. 106, §9-401). As to fees, see category Mortgages, topic Chattel Mortgages.

Evidence.—An official record kept within commonwealth, or entry therein, when admissible for any purpose, may be evidenced by official publication thereof or by copy attested by officer having legal custody of record or by his deputy. If record is kept in any other state, district, commonwealth, territory, or insular possession of U.S. or within Panama Canal Zone, Trust territory of Pacific Islands, or Ryukyu Islands, record or entry therein, when admissible for any purpose, may be evidenced by official publication thereof or by copy attested by officer having legal custody of record, or by his deputy and accompanied by certificate that officer has custody. Certificate may be made by judge of court of record having jurisdiction in governmental unit in which record is kept, authenticated by seal of court, or by any public officer having seal of office and having official duties in governmental unit in which record is kept, authenticated by seal of his office. (Mass. R. Civ. P., Rule 44[a][1]).

Foreign official record, or an entry therein, when admissible for any purpose, may be evidenced by official publication or copy thereof, attested by person authorized to make attestation, and accompanied by final certification as to genuineness of signature and official position (1) of attesting person, or (2) of any foreign official whose certificate of genuineness of signature and official position either (a) relates to attestation or (b) is in a chain of certificates of genuineness of signature and official position relating to attestation. Final certification may be made by secretary of embassy or legation, consul general, consul, vice consul, or consular agent of U.S. or a diplomatic or consular official of foreign country assigned or accredited to U.S. If reasonable opportunity has been given to all parties to investigate authenticity and accuracy of documents, court may, for good cause shown, admit an attested copy without final certification or permit foreign official record to be evidenced by an attested summary with or without a final certification. (Mass. R. Civ. P., Rule 44[a][2]).

Written statement that after diligent search no record of entry of a specified tenor is found to exist in records designated by statement, authenticated as provided in this chapter in case of a domestic record, or complying with requirements of this chapter for a summary in case of a record in a foreign country, shall be admissible as evidence that records contain no such record or entry. (Mass. R. Civ. P., Rule 44[b]).

Public records are defined by statute (c. 4, §7, cls. 26) and must be provided by custodian thereof to any person requesting such records.

SEALS:

An impression or stamping of a seal of a court, public office, public officer or corporation upon paper is as valid as if made on wax or wafer attached to such paper. (c. 4, §9B).

Corporate Seal.—No special provisions.

Uniform Commercial Code adopted. See category Business Regulation and Commerce, topic Commercial Code.

Effect of Seal.—Some common law distinctions between sealed and unsealed instruments still exist, i.e. sealed instruments import valuable consideration. With respect to sales of goods, however, see Uniform Commercial Code. Common law rule absolving undisclosed principal of liability on unsealed instrument is abrogated. (369 Mass. 150, 338 N.E.2d 335). Effective June 4, 1977 no instrument purporting to effect interest in land shall be void for lack of seals. (c. 183, §1A).

By statute (c. 4, §9A) a recital that the instrument is sealed by or bears the seal of the person signing the same or is intended to take effect as a sealed instrument is sufficient to give the instrument the legal effect of a sealed instrument without the addition of any seal of wax, paper or other substance or any semblance of a seal by scroll, impression or otherwise, except that the foregoing does not apply where the seal of a court or public officer is expressly required by constitution or statute to be affixed to a paper, nor does it apply to corporate stock certificates.

TORRENS ACT:

See topic Records.

VITAL STATISTICS:

See topic Records.

EMPLOYMENT

EMPLOYER AND EMPLOYEE:

See topic Labor Relations.

LABOR RELATIONS:

Principal statutes are cc. 149-152. Enforcement under direction of department of labor and industries (as to cc. 149, 150, 150B, and 151), labor relations commission (as to cc. 150A and 150E), dept. of employment and training (as to c. 151A), commission against discrimination (as to cc. 151B and 151C) and dept. of industrial accidents (as to c. 152).

Hours of Labor.—(See c. 136, §6[50] and c. 149, §§30-58, 39, 41, 45-51A, 52, 56-74, 60, 65-69, 73, 78, and 100-102.)

Most county and municipal employees and employees of persons engaged in public contract work restricted to eight hours work in any day, 48 hours in any week and six days in any one week, except in emergency. (c. 149, §§48-50A). State employees generally limited to eight-hour days and 40-hour weeks, with certain occupations exempted. (c. 149, §30A).

Private employers must generally allow 24 consecutive hours rest in every seven consecutive days to employees in manufacturing, mechanical or mercantile establishments, and to watchmen and guards in banks, except for persons employed in hotels, railroads, certain utility companies and certain other businesses. (§§48-50).

Restrictions are also imposed upon requiring private employees to work on Suns. or holidays, but exceptions are made as to certain businesses and occupations. (c. 136, §6[50] and c. 149, §§45-52). Employees likewise cannot be required to work on their sabbath or other holy days. (c. 151B, §4 [1A]).

Except for certain types of facilities, or as exempted by commissioner upon application, employers must allow 30 minutes for meal for each six hours of work in calendar day. (c. 149, §§100, 101).

Wages.—Wage of less than $4.75 per hour is illegal, unless commissioner of labor and industries expressly approves payment of lesser minimum wages in particular occupations. Effective Jan. 1, 1997, minimum wage is $5.25. (c. 151, §1 am'd 1995, c. 196 §1). Commissioner may not set minimum rates below $1.85 per hour except for learners, apprentices, ushers, ticket sellers and takers, janitors, golf caddies, and service people receiving more than $20 per month in tips. (§7 am'd 1995, c. 5, §74). Criminal

See note at head of Digest as to 1998 legislation covered.

See Topical Index in front part of this volume.

MA – 37

LABOR RELATIONS . . . *continued*
penalties for violations of between $50-$1,000, or ten-90 days imprisonment, or both (c. 150, §19), and civil remedies (§20) provided.

Premium Rates for Overtime Work.—Private employees entitled to time-and-one-half for work in excess of 40 hours weekly, but commissions, drawing accounts and incentive pay are excluded in computing regular rate, and certain specified occupations are exempted. (c. 151, §1A). Employees (other than executive, professional and administrative employees earning more than $200 per week) of retail store employing more than seven persons (including proprietor) entitled to time-and-one half for work performed on Sun. (c. 136, §6[50]). Most state employees entitled to time-and-one-half for work in excess of eight hours per day or 40 hours per week. (c. 149, §30B).

Weekly Payment of Wages.—It is crime for employer to fail to pay employees at least biweekly or to make interval between date of payment and last date on which wages were earned greater than six days. (c. 149, §148). Bona fide executive, administrative or professional employees may be paid biweekly, or semi-monthly, or monthly if they elect. Biweekly wage payment requirement not applicable in certain instances, including agricultural, but is applicable to payment of commissions when amount thereof has been determined and become due. Wages of involuntarily discharged employee must be paid on date of discharge; or, in Boston, as soon as payroll laws are complied with; except commissions may be paid when normally calculated. Wages earned but unpaid at time of voluntary termination of employment must be paid on next regular payday or, if none, by following Sat., unless employee is absent, in which case balance payable upon demand. Violation punishable by $500-$3,000 fine or up to two months imprisonment, or both. President, treasurer or other officer or agent involved in managing corporation is deemed to be employer, and so punishable. (§148). Injunctive relief, treble damages, costs and attorney's fees provided for violations of §148. (c. 149, §150). Employees may not be penalized for exercise of wage and hour rights. (§148A). When paying wages, employer must furnish payslip to employee showing: employer and employee names, date, hours worked, hourly wage, and deductions or increases made in pay period. (c. 149, §148). Employer in manufacturing, mercantile and certain other businesses may not deduct wages of employee coming late to work more than proportionately to time lost. (§152).

Tips.—Employees in certain service industries may not be required to pay over to their employer all or any part of their tips unless employer publicly displays sign stating percentage of tips, if any, which employees may retain. (c. 149, §159A).

Priority of Wage Claims.—Massachusetts insolvency statute repealed effective July 1, 1978. Priority given to wage claims not exceeding $100 against insolvent estates of deceased persons (c. 198, §1) and in settlement of estates by receivers (c. 206, §31).

Assignment of Wages.—See category Debtor and Creditor, topic Assignments.

Presumption of Employment.—For purposes of c. 149, individual performing any service, except services authorized under c. 149, is deemed employee unless showing made that individual is free from control and direction, services are performed either outside usual course of business of enterprise or outside of all places of business of enterprise, and individual is customarily engaged in independent occupation, profession, or business of same nature as services performed. Failure to withhold state or federal taxes, unemployment compensation, or worker's compensation, cannot be used to make required showing. Violation punishable by $100-$1,000 fine, or by two months imprisonment, or both. In case of violation by corporation, president, treasurer, and managing officer deemed employer. (c. 149, §148B). Civil remedies available. (c. 149, §150).

Child Labor.—(See c. 149, §§56-105.) Persons under 18 generally not permitted to work more than nine hours per day, more than 48 hours per week or more than six days per week; and child's hours of work each day must fall within period not exceeding ten consecutive hours in most cases (§§56, 67); but these strictures inapplicable to persons employed in professional, executive, administrative or supervisory capacities, and to personal secretaries. (§56). Upon written petition of not less than 60% of employees in place of employment where principal source of income is tips, Attorney General may allow periods of work to fall within period not exceeding 12 consecutive hours. (§56). Child's hours of labor may extend to 52 hours per week in certain types of seasonal employment during June to Oct., provided total hours in any year not exceed average of 48 hours a week for whole year, excluding Sun. and holidays. (§56). Children 14 or younger may be employed in agricultural labor for no more than four hours per day, nor more than 24 hours per week except if related by blood or marriage to owner or operator of farm on which employed. (§56). Children under 16 are not permitted to work on certain equipment (§61) and in certain occupations deemed overly hazardous, arduous or corruptive (§§62-64) or which might interfere unduly with their schooling (§§69-73). Substantial criminal and civil penalties against employers, parents and children are provided for violation of child labor laws (e.g., §§57, 78-83, 86, 90-92, 95, 97-98, 104).

Female Labor.—C. 149, §54 authorizes department of employment and training to regulate employment of women in core rooms of iron/steel foundries. However, Title VII of Civil Rights Act of 1964 preempts all state laws requiring employers to distinguish on basis of gender (except for bona fide occupational qualifications). (1971-72 Op.Atty.Gen. 134). No other restrictions.

Discrimination.—

Forbidden Practices.—C. 151B makes it unlawful to discriminate against persons on account of race, color, religious creed, national origin, sex, sexual orientation (unless such orientation involves minors as sex objects), age (over 40), ancestry or handicap, in connection with employment, tenure, terms and conditions of employment, membership rights in labor unions, or furnishing of bonds. (§4). Sexual harassment by employer or agent specifically defined (§1[18]) and prohibited (§4[16A]). Same-sex harassment is prohibited, regardless of sexual orientation of parties. (424 Mass. 285, 676 N.E.2d 45). Employer must make reasonable accommodation for qualified handicapped persons unless accommodation would impose undue hardship to employer's business. (§4[16]). Employment advertisements or job application inquiries which directly or indirectly express limitation based on protected class status are prohibited. (§4[3]).

Employer may not request information or discriminate against person refusing to provide information regarding (1) arrest not resulting in conviction, (2) first conviction for drunkenness, simple assault, speeding, minor traffic violation, affray or disturbing peace, (3) conviction of misdemeanor where conviction and incarceration, if any, ended five years or more prior, unless person has been convicted of another offense within prior five years. (§4[9]). Employer may not request information, nor refuse to employ, nor fire person for failing to inform regarding commitment to mental institution, provided person has been discharged and has psychiatric certification of mental competence. (§4[9A]).

No person may coerce, intimidate, or discriminate in any way against any person for opposing practices forbidden by c. 151B. (§4[4]-[4A]).

No person may coerce, intimidate, threaten or interfere with other person for having aided or encouraged any other person in exercise of right protected by c. 151B. (§4[4A]).

Employers may request conviction data and custody status from Criminal History Systems Board under limited circumstances. (c. 6, §167 et seq.).

Available Relief.—Complaint must be filed with commission against discrimination within six months of allegedly discriminatory act. (c. 151B, §5). Commission empowered to investigate and pass upon complaints of unlawful practices, to hold hearings, to issue subpoenas, and to promulgate rules and regulations. (§3). Voluntary mediation possible before investigation under Commission's regulations. If, after investigation, commission finds probable cause to credit allegations of complaint, and attempts at conciliation fail, single commissioner holds hearing on complaint. (§5). If unlawful practice found, commissioner issues cease and desist order, and such affirmative orders as may be necessary, as well as actual damages, attorney's fees and costs (but no punitive or multiple damages). (§5). Commissioner's decision reviewable before full commission (§3[6]), and then by expeditious judicial review in superior court (§6). Standards of review in c. 30A, §14.

Ninety days after filing complaint with commission, or sooner if commissioner assents in writing, but no later than "three years after unlawful practice occurred", complainant may bring civil action in Superior Court, Probate Court or Housing Court, which ends review by commission. (§9). In civil action, court may grant injunctive relief and actual and punitive damages and must, if it finds for complainant, award attorney's fees and costs. (§9). In actions for age discrimination, petitioner entitled to jury trial and, if practice committed knowingly, to at least double and up to treble damages. (§9). Actions for employment discrimination based on sex (418 Mass. 220, 636 N.E.2d 212) or handicap (419 Mass. 792, 647 N.E.2d 716) fall within state constitutional right to jury trial although arbitration provisions in employment contract will be binding at least in context of sexual discrimination. (42 Mass. App. Ct. 347, 677 N.E.2d 242). First Circuit has held jury trial required by Seventh Amendment in other c. 151B actions. (962 F.2d 120).

In addition there are following special antidiscrimination provisions:

On Account of Age.—Dismissing from employment, refusing to employ, discriminating against in compensation or other terms of employment or giving effect to agreement entered into on or after Sept. 1, 1984 requiring any such action with regard to person over age of 40 is forbidden. (c. 149, §§24A-24J, c. 151B, §4[1B]). Exceptions provided for bona fide seniority systems or employee benefit plans and mandatory retirement at age 65 of certain executives and faculty members. (c. 151B, §4[17]). Age discrimination is punishable under c. 151B and, in private sector, by fine up to $500. (c. 149, §24A). Contrary to Federal law, plaintiff may prevail by showing that employer's reason for termination decision was pretext. (419 Mass. 437, 646 N.E.2d 111).

Wage Disparities.—Payment to employee of salary or wages less than rates paid to employees of opposite gender for like or comparable work makes employer liable to underpaid employee for amount of underpaid wages, additional equal amount of liquidated damages, and reasonable attorney's fees; court action must be instituted within one year of alleged violation. (c. 149, §105A).

Maternity Leave.—Employer must give up to eight weeks of maternity leave (paid or unpaid) for purpose of giving birth or adopting child under 18 years of age, or under 23 years of age if mentally or physically disabled, to any eligible female employee on at least two weeks' notice of anticipated departure date and of intention to return. (c. 149, §105D). Commission Against Discrimination has promulgated regulations concerning pregnancy-related disabilities pursuant to c. 151B, §3, para. 5. Such disabilities must be treated like any other. (375 Mass. 160, 375 N.E.2d 1192).

Alternative Remedy for Race/Gender Discrimination.—Under c. 93, §102, any person denied same legal protections enjoyed by white male citizens, including right to make or enforce contracts, may sue in superior court for injunctive relief, compensatory and punitive damages, and, if successful, will be awarded attorney's fees and costs.

Alternative Remedy for Age/Handicap Discrimination.—Under c. 93, §103, any person, regardless of handicap or age, must, with reasonable accommodation, have same rights as other persons to make and enforce contracts.

Wrongful Discharge—Implied Covenant of Good Faith.—Employment relationship terminable "at-will" by employer or employee, absent express or implied term as to duration. (384 Mass. 659, 429 N.E.2d 21). Limited exception to "at-will" doctrine based on breach of implied covenant of good faith and fair dealing applies when employer discharges employee without cause with effect of depriving employee of compensation related to past services. (373 Mass. 96, 364 N.E.2d 1251). Goal of covenant is to deny employer financial windfall resulting from denial to employee of compensation for past services. (393 Mass. 231, 471 N.E.2d 47; 391 Mass. 333, 461 N.E.2d 796). Employee cannot recover unvested portions of employment compensation package based on implied covenant. (108 F.3d 5).

Violation of Public Policy.—Exception to "at-will" doctrine when employee discharged for asserting legally guaranteed right, doing what law requires, refusing to do what law forbids, or performing important public deeds, even though law does not absolutely require performance of deeds. (412 Mass. 469, 589 N.E.2d 1241; 410 Mass. 805, 575 N.E.2d 1107). Public policy must be derived from clearly articulated law (e.g. constitutions, statutes, regulations) and not from private professional codes. (412 Mass. 469, 589 N.E.2d 1241).

Where comprehensive statutory remedy for alleged wrong exists (e.g., Fair Employment Laws), employee may not assert wrongful discharge claim. (783 F. Supp. 713).

All Massachusetts employers, employment agencies, and labor organizations must have specific sexual harassment policies. (c. 151B, §3A).

See note at head of Digest as to 1998 legislation covered.

See Topical Index in front part of this volume.

LABOR RELATIONS . . . *continued*

Labor Unions and Disputes.—

Labor Relations Act.—C. 150A, modeled on National Labor Relations Act, gives employees (not including domestic workers) right to self-organization and collective bargaining. (§§2, 3, 3A). Domestic workers over age 17 and employed at least 16 hours per week have limited right to self-organization and collective bargaining. (§§3, 3A). See also category Business Regulation and Commerce, topic Securities, subhead Business Combinations.

Unfair labor practices by employers include: (1) Interference with or coercion of employees in their rights to self-organization, to bargain collectively and to engage in concerted activities for purpose of mutual aid or protection; (2) interference with or domination of either formation or administration of any labor organization; (3) discrimination in regard to hiring, tenure or any term or condition of employment on account of membership in labor organization (but union security clauses requiring union membership as condition of employment are valid and enforceable except in cases of employees unfairly denied union membership), and (4) refusal to bargain collectively with employees' chosen representatives. (§4).

Unfair labor practices by unions include: (1) Seizure or unlawful occupancy of private property as means of forcing settlement of labor dispute; (2) engagement in or authorization of any strike, slowdown, boycott or other concerted action for purpose of bringing about commission of unfair labor practice; (3) injuring trade or business of any person because such person has refused to commit unfair labor practice; (4) interfering with or coercing employees in selection of representatives for purpose of collective bargaining after labor relations commission has determined that employees involved do not desire to be represented by union; and (5) refusing to bargain collectively with any employer who has recognized union as exclusive bargaining agent. (§§4A-4B).

Commission authorized to hold hearings, conduct investigations, issue subpoenas and promulgate rules and regulations, all in aid of its primary functions to make appropriate unit determinations, certify labor unions as duly selected bargaining representatives of employees, adjudicate unfair labor practice petitions and determine any charge that employee has been unfairly denied admission to, or expelled from, membership in union. (§§5, 6 and 6A). Superior Court has jurisdiction to review final orders of commission. (§6).

Advertising and Hiring during Labor Disputes.—Advertising for or hiring of help during labor disputes is regulated, and knowing employment of professional strikebreakers during lockout or lawful strike is prohibited. (c. 149, §§22-23). Employment of civil defense personnel or armed guards during labor disputes regulated. (c. 149, §§23A-23B; c. 147, §30).

Dispute Settlement.—C. 150 provides for conciliation and arbitration of industrial disputes; c. 150B deals with peaceful settlement of industrial disputes posing threat to public health and safety, and c. 150C (based on Uniform Arbitration Act) governs enforcement of collective bargaining agreements to arbitrate.

Collective Bargaining for Public Employees.—C. 150E gives certain state, county and municipal employees, including certain personnel employed by judicial branch, right to form or join employee organizations for purposes of bargaining collectively on questions of wages, hours and other terms and conditions of employment.

"Right to Work" Law.—Massachusetts has no such law.

Injunctions.—In cases involving labor disputes, chief justice of superior court must designate three judge panel to hear any petition for injunctive relief. (c. 212, §30). C. 214, §6 forbids issuance of any restraining order or injunction, preliminary or permanent, in labor dispute, except after testimony in open court, with opportunity for cross-examination, and after findings of fact by court that: (a) Unlawful acts have been threatened and will be committed unless restrained, or have been committed and will be continued unless restrained; (b) substantial and irreparable injury to plaintiff's property will result; (c) greater injury will result to plaintiff from denial of relief than will be inflicted upon defendants by granting same; (d) plaintiff has no adequate remedy at law; and (e) public officers charged with duty to protect plaintiff's property are unable or unwilling to furnish adequate protection. Hearing must be preceded by personal notice to all known defendants and to chief of officers charged with protection of plaintiff's property, except that injunctive relief may be granted ex parte if principal representative or attorney of employees or labor organization participating in dispute was informed of time and place at which application for temporary restraining order would be presented (sufficiently in advance to appear in opposition thereto), or if plaintiff made every reasonable effort to give such notice but was unable to do so. (§6[2]). Despite procedural compliance, injunctive relief will be denied if plaintiff fails to make all reasonable efforts to settle by alternate means, or does not abide by legal obligations. (§6[4]). Notwithstanding foregoing, injunctive relief may be granted without reference to procedures outlined above whenever parties to jurisdictional dispute have voluntarily submitted to arbitration, and defendant has failed to abide by arbitration procedure, or to comply with terms of arbitration award, and engages in strike, picketing, boycott or other concerted interference against plaintiff. (c. 214, §6A).

Labor Unions.—May not operate unless statement filed with commissioner of labor and industries setting forth names and addresses of union's officers, its aims, scale of dues, fees, fines, assessments and officers' salaries. Labor unions having membership of more than 50 members also required to file annual statement with commissioner of receipts and expenditures of union. These reports open to public inspection. Fines provided for failing to file or making false statement, but filing with commissioner of duplicate of financial statement filed with U.S. Department of Labor is sufficient. (1946, c. 618, §§1-5, am'd 1949, c. 394). Labor unions may sue and be sued as legal entities. (386 Mass. 314, 435 N.E.2d 1027).

Workers' Compensation Act.—Contained in c. 152 and administered by dept. of industrial accidents. (c. 23E). Provides schedule of payments and other benefits to be made or provided by insurer of employer, including self-insurance group of which employer is member, (or by employer if self-insurer) to eligible employees in case of injuries (including certain diseases) sustained in course of employment and resulting deaths. (c. 152, §§26-51).

Employees not subject to act include officers and crew on vessels in interstate or foreign commerce, certain professional athletes, certain salespersons affiliated with real estate brokers, certain independent direct salespersons of consumer products working on commission, certain taxicab operators, persons covered by federal compensation law, and certain persons whose employment not in usual course of trade or business of employer. Provisions elective to employers of seasonal, casual or part-time domestic servants. (§1[4]).

Employee subject to act is eligible for compensation unless employee claimed common law right of action by written notice to employer at time of hiring or, if employer was not then insured, within 30 days after notice that employer had become insured. (§24). Employee may waive claim to common law right of action upon five days' written notice. (§24). Agreement by employee to waive statutory right to compensation invalid (§46), although employee can agree to binding arbitration of specific compensation claim as alternative to administrative proceeding (§10B). No proceedings for compensation may be maintained unless injured employee or, if employee deceased, legal representative or beneficiary, serves written notice upon employer or insurer as soon as practicable, and files claim within four years after employee became aware of causal relationship between disability and employment, or after employee died. (§41). Notice must be signed and must give time, place and cause of injury. (§42). Inaccuracy or want of proper notice will not bar employee if insurer not prejudiced thereby. (§44).

Compensation for incapacity not payable for injury which does not incapacitate employee five or more full days or for mental or emotional disability arising principally out of bona fide personnel action, except action for intentional infliction of emotional harm. (§29). Suits for negligence, assault and battery, intentional infliction of emotional distress are barred by exclusivity provisions of Workers Compensation Act. (422 Mass. 563, 664 N.E.2d 815). Exclusivity of act also precludes action against employer for common law claims of intentional or negligent infliction of emotional distress arising out of workplace sexual harassment. (422 Mass. 551, 664 N.E.2d 808).

Within seven days, excluding Suns. and legal holidays, after receipt of notice or knowledge of injury resulting in five or more days loss of work, employer must notify employee, insurer and division of administration of department of industrial accidents, on forms prescribed by division. (§6). Division of administration then informs employee of rights, benefits and obligations, monitors distribution of benefits, attempts to resolve disputes, and provides claim form to employee if dispute not resolved. (§6A). Within 14 days of receipt of employer's notice, or of employee's claim form, whichever is first, insurer must either commence weekly payments or notify division, employer and employee by certified mail that it will not pay and will contest claim for payment, specifying grounds and basis for such position and stating that to secure benefits employee must file claim with department. (§7[1]). Claim is filed with insurer, and with division of administration which attempts to resolve dispute by informal means and, if no resolution, refers claim to industrial accident board within 15 business days after receipt. (§10).

Claim then referred to administrative judge who must require conference within 28 days after claim received by board, and within seven days thereafter enter order requiring or denying payment or modification of benefits. (§10A). Fourteen days to appeal order for hearing before board member, to be held within 28 days of filing of appeal (§§10A, 11); 30 days to file for appeal before reviewing board (§11C). Appeal requires fee paid into special fund per §65. Fee waived for indigents. (§11C). Alternatively, at any time more than five days before conference, parties may agree to binding arbitration by independent arbitrator. (§10B). Orders, decisions and arbitration awards enforceable by Superior Court (§10[B][4]); appeals from reviewing board decisions go to Appeals Court. (§12). Filing of claim, acceptance of payment or submission to proceeding under c. 152 releases all claims of employee under common law against employer. (§23).

Employer may agree through collective bargaining to binding obligations and procedures respecting (a) benefits supplemental to those of §§34-36, (b) alternative dispute resolution system, (c) use of limited list of medical treatment providers, (d) use of limited list of impartial physicians, (e) light duty, modified job, or return to work program, (f) 24 hour health care program, (g) committees and procedures for worker safety, or (h) vocational rehabilitation or retraining program. (§10C).

Penalties for employer violation include fine and shutdown, public bidding prohibitions, exposure to lawsuits by competing bidders (§25C), criminal penalties (including imprisonment) (§§14[3], 25C), and recovery of amounts paid by Workers' Compensation Trust Fund to injured employees (§65). If insurer contests claim for benefits and loses or settles, it must pay employee's reasonable attorney's fees (c.152, §§10A-13A).

Occupational Diseases.—See subhead Workers' Compensation Act, supra.

Employers' Liability Act (c. 153) applies with certain limitations to recovery by injured employee against employer not covered by Workers' Compensation Act.

Unemployment Compensation.—Employment security benefits are governed by c. 151A and administered by department of employment and training. (c. 23, §91-N). Unemployed individual eligible for weekly benefits related to percentage of earnings during base period (c. 151A, §29) if (a) had wages of $2,000 during base period with certain provisions (see c. 151A, §24[a]); (b) capable of, available for and actively seeking employment; (c) has notified state employment office. (c. 151A, §24). Base period is last four completed calendar quarters before benefit year, but there are options to use other methods of determining base period. (See c. 151A, §1[a].) Duration of benefits generally limited to 30 weeks or 36% of individual's total wages during preceding year, whichever is less (c. 151A, §30), and benefits are paid out of fund contributed to by employers based on percentage of each employer's total payroll and on employment experience rate of each (c. 151A, §§13-18). Employer applying to state instrumentality for license to conduct profession, trade, business, or for license renewal, must certify his compliance with state contribution laws. (c. 151A, §19A). Benefits are extended if individual is attending vocational training course approved by director (§§24, 30) or during periods of heavy unemployment as determined by U.S. Secretary of Labor. (§30A). See category Insurance, topic Insurance Companies, subhead Universal Health Insurance.

Penalties.—Any employer, or officer or agent thereof, who (a) attempts to evade contribution, or payment in lieu of contribution, or (b) knowingly misrepresents in connection with contribution, or (c) refuses to make contribution required by commissioner of department of employment and training, or (d) makes deduction from wages to pay required contributions, or (e) attempts by threat or coercion to induce waiver of individuals' c. 151A rights, or to prevent testimony at c. 151A hearing, or (f) willfully

See note at head of Digest as to 1998 legislation covered.

See Topical Index in front part of this volume.

MA – 39

LABOR RELATIONS . . . *continued*
corrupts, or endeavors to intimidate, state officer acting pursuant to c. 151A, or willfully endeavors to impede due administration of c. 151A, is subject to substantial fines, imprisonment, or both. (c. 151A, §47). Any person who makes or assists in making false or misleading statement to obtain benefits for self or another subject to fine up to $10,000, imprisonment up to five years or both. (c. 151A, §47).

Miscellaneous.—

Change of Location.—Owner of every establishment employing 12 or more persons must give notice of change of location of operations in prescribed form to commissioner of labor and industries. (c. 149, §179B).

Corporate Takeovers.—Any employee of corporation having, or within 12 months having had, class of stock registered under Securities Exchange Act of 1934 as amended who is terminated within shorter of (a) 12 months from date of contested election of directors to facilitate voting control transfer, or (b) period from contested election to control transfer shall receive lump-sum termination payment of twice employee's weekly compensation multiplied by number of years of completed service in addition to any other payment due. (c. 149, §184).

Employee Training Grants.—Grants available to employers, employer groups, labor organizations, and training providers to provide education and training to existing employees and new workers. (c. 29, §2RR).

Employment Applications.—Applications for employment must contain statutorily prescribed notice informing applicant that lie detector testing is illegal. (c. 149, §19B[2(b)]). If employer seeks information concerning prior convictions, application must contain statutorily prescribed notice informing applicant that sealed arrest and conviction records need not be revealed. (c. 276, §100A).

Health, Welfare Benefits and Retirement Funds.—Such funds are regulated by law and must register and report annually. (c. 151D). Non-state and municipal employees entitled to 90 days extended health insurance coverage when they leave group plan due to total or partial closing of facility with 50 or more employees. (c. 175, §§110D, 110G; c. 176B, §6A; c. 176G, §4A). For commercial health plans, 90 day period begins at expiration of automatic 31-day continuation period required by c. 175, §110D. Employees covered by commercial or nonprofit, Blue Cross/Blue Shield (c. 176A) plan entitled to additional 39 weeks of coverage at own expense when involuntarily laid off (c. 175, §110G; c. 176B, §6A). Employers failing to comply become responsible as insurers.

Group life insurance coverage must continue for 31 days following termination of employment. (c. 175, §134[4]). Employees must be notified of conversion rights, if any. (c. 175, §134A). Divorced spouses of participants in certain group insurance plans are entitled to continued coverage until remarriage of participant or spouse unless divorce judgment provides otherwise. Notice of cancellation of coverage of divorced or separated spouse must be given. (c. 175, §110I; c. 176A, §8F; c. 176B, §6B; c. 176G, §5A). It is unlawful for employers to fail to make contributions to health or welfare funds or pension funds or other employee benefit funds in violation of terms of collective bargaining agreement. (c. 149, §181).

Industrial Homework.—C. 149, §§143-147H, prohibits manufacturing or processing of materials in home for employer unless commissioner of labor and industries has issued permit therefor to employer. Permits for certain specified homework not issued. (§144). Restrictions on homework inapplicable to domestic service (§143) and to organizations incorporated in Massachusetts for educational or philanthropic purposes (§147H). Penalties are provided for violation of law or regulations issued by commissioner. (§§147A, 147C, and 147G).

Leave from Work.—Upon request, employee of manufacturing, mechanical or mercantile establishment entitled to vote in election must be permitted to leave work for this purpose during the two hours after polls in voting precinct open. (c. 149, §178). Nontemporary employee must be granted leave of absence of up to 17 days per year without loss of position or benefits for training in ready reserves of U.S. armed forces. (c. 149, §52A). Veteran whose services not essential to public health and safety must be given leave of absence to participate in Veterans Day or Memorial Day exercises. (c. 149, §52A1/2). Employees must be given leave for jury duty (c. 234A, §60), with up to three days' pay for regularly employed person (c. 234A, §48). Eligible employee allowed 24 hours leave to participate in child's school activities, accompany child to medical or dental appointment, or accompany elderly relative to medical, dental, or professional service appointment. (c. 149, §52D; 29 U.S.C. §§2611-2612). Eligible employee must have worked 1,250 hours in preceding 12 months for employer, and employer must have minimum of 50 workers. (c. 149, §52D; 29 U.S.C. §§2611-2612).

Lie Detector Tests.—Use of lie detector tests (including polygraph and written tests) by any employer with respect to any employee or applicant for employment (even if administered outside Massachusetts) is punishable by fine of up to $1,500 or imprisonment of responsible officials for up to 90 days and is subject to civil action by aggrieved persons for injunctive relief, treble damages of at least $500 and attorneys' fees and costs. (c. 149, §19B).

Medical Examinations.—Employer may condition offer of employment on results of medical examination conducted solely for purpose of determining whether employee, with reasonable accomodation, is capable of performing essential functions of job. (c. 151B, §4[16(3)]). Employer must pay for examination (c. 149, §159B), and furnish copy of medical report to employee upon request (c. 149, §19A). If employee has reasonable expectation of doctor-patient confidentiality, disclosure of results to employer may trigger invasion of privacy action against both doctor and employer. (395 Mass. 59, 479 N.E.2d 113; 785 F.2d 352). Employer may not require HLTV-III antibody or antigen test as condition for employment—violation punishable as unfair practice under c. 93A, §2. (c. 111, §70F). For rules determining whether subjecting private employees to random drug testing violates c. 12, §11I or c. 214, §1B, see 418 Mass. 425, 637 N.E.2d 203.

See subhead Discrimination, catchline Forbidden Practices, supra, for restrictions on inquiring about criminal history, handicap, or other protected class status. Employers may be liable for negligent hiring or retaining dangerous persons. (401 Mass. 860, 520 N.E.2d 139; 26 Mass. App. Ct. 289, 526 N.E.2d 1309). Application forms seeking work history must state that applicant may include "any verified work performed on a voluntary basis". (c. 149, §52B). Use of consumer reports and investigative consumer reports (background and credit checks) regulated. (c. 93, §50 et seq.).

Personnel Records.—Employers are required to permit present and former employees upon written request to inspect and copy their personnel records and to submit written statements of explanation for inclusion in such records. Violation punishable by $500-$2,500 fine. (c. 149, §52C).

Plant Closings.—Employers utilizing financing issued, insured or subsidized by certain quasi-public agencies must agree to make good faith effort to provide longest practicable advance notice, and maintenance of income and health insurance benefits. At least 90 days' notice or equivalent benefits expected whenever possible. (c. 149, §182). See catchline Health, Welfare Benefits and Retirement Funds, supra, for insurance continuation provisions. Reemployment assistance fund to provide benefits as determined by regulations to be promulgated. (c. 151A, §§71A-H). Employers may be billed by state for cost of benefits. (§71H).

Toxic Substances.—Under c. 111F, employers (except certain research labs which obtain an exemption) in whose workplaces certain toxic substances are used must: (i) Label certain containers containing such substances, (ii) maintain and make available upon request to employees, unions and physicians material safety data sheets (minus trade secret information if exemption is obtained) for each substance, (iii) post notice in workplace regarding employees' rights under this law, (iv) instruct employees about proper handling of such substances, and (v) file copies of data sheets with Mass. department of environmental and quality engineering for possible public inspection. Violations are subject to fine of up to $250 per day. Willful violations are treated as misdemeanors subject to fine of up to $1,000 per day and/or imprisonment of up to 90 days. (c. 111F, §3).

Working Conditions.—Employer must provide proper lighting, ventilation, and sanitation in work rooms and proper heat from Oct. 15 to May 15. (c. 149, §§113, 117). Industrial and construction employers must provide drinking water. (c. 149, §106). Fire exits may not be locked or obstructed during working hours. (c. 149, §126). Employers cannot require employees to work more than six hours during calendar day without interval of at least 30 minutes for meal except in certain industries or with exemption. (c. 149, §§100, 101).

WORKERS' COMPENSATION LAW:

See topic Labor Relations.

ENVIRONMENT

ENVIRONMENTAL REGULATION:

General Supervision.—Most Massachusetts environmental agencies are organized under executive office of environmental affairs. (c. 21A). Department of environmental protection includes divisions of wetlands (overseeing inland and coastal wetlands), water supply, water pollution, air quality (overseeing air and noise pollution), hazardous waste, environmental analysis, solid waste disposal and hazardous waste facility siting. Department of environmental management includes divisions of waterways (overseeing dredging and filling in tidal areas and certain rivers and streams), forests and parks and water resources (overseeing water planning). There are also departments of food and agriculture; fisheries, wildlife and recreational vehicles; and Metropolitan District Commission. Executive office of environmental affairs includes divisions of conservation services, environmental policy act and review (overseeing Environmental Impact Report Review) and coastal zone management. Department of environmental protection also plans, establishes and manages programs to assess uses of water and to plan for future water needs in commonwealth with broad permitting and regulatory powers (c. 21G) and is charged with controlling air pollution by enforcing emissions standards for stationary sources and motor vehicle sources of air contamination (c. 111, §§142A-K as am'd by 1995, c. 39 §§7-9). Commissioner of department of environmental protection shall adopt regulations known as state environmental code. (c. 21A, §13).

Prohibited Acts of Pollution.—Operation of sources of direct or indirect pollution of water and air is broadly prohibited, except as licensed by permit. (c. 21, §42; c. 111, §§142A-H; also see regulations promulgated pursuant to these chapters). No filling or dredging of wetlands except after compliance with extensive regulatory process; see subhead Permits, infra. (c. 131, §40). No permit or financial assistance from state to certain projects, including those likely to cause significant damage to environment, granted until 60 days after public notice of final environmental impact report. (c. 30, §§61-62H and regulations promulgated thereunder). Also, dumping of rubbish on public land, in or near coastal or inland waters or on property of another is prohibited. (c. 270, §16). Willful depositing of solid waste into commercial container of another without permission is prohibited. (c. 266, §146). Abandoned underground residential tanks utilized exclusively for heating or heating water shall be drained and cleaned properly or removed as directed by fire department. (c. 148, §38A).

Enforcement.—Division of environmental protection of department of attorney general is empowered at request of appropriate agency or on own initiative to commence or intervene in all departmental proceedings, as well as to bring suits and actions, civil and criminal, to enforce all antipollution laws and regulations and to secure any common law right or remedy. (c. 12, §11D, c. 21G, §14). As alternative to any other civil penalty that may be prescribed by law, department of environmental protection may assess civil administrative penalty of not less than $100 for failure to comply with any provision of any regulation, order, license, or approval issued or adopted by that department or of any law that department has authority or responsibility to enforce. (c. 21A, §16). Department of environmental protection has similar powers to adopt regulations at any time and to impose penalties as to water management. (c. 21G, §§3, 14). Moreover, any ten citizens of commonwealth may petition superior courts for injunctive or declaratory relief in cases involving imminent damage to environment. (c. 214, §7A). Commonwealth may seek injunctive relief in Superior Court for violation of air pollution regulations adopted by department of environmental protection. (c. 111, §142A).

Penalties.—Discharge of pollutants into Massachusetts waters in contravention of permit requirements is punishable by fine of $2,500-$25,000 per day and/or jail sentence of up to one year; alternatively, commonwealth may bring civil action, seeking up to $25,000 per day. (c. 21, §42). Continuing violation of state environmental code is

See note at head of Digest as to 1998 legislation covered.

See Topical Index in front part of this volume.

MA – 40

ENVIRONMENTAL REGULATION . . . *continued*
punishable by fine of up to $25,000 per day and/or imprisonment for up to one year, or civil penalty of up to $25,000 per day. (c. 21A, §13). Violation of air pollution regulations, or permit, approval or order issued thereunder from department of environmental protection is punishable by fine of up to $25,000 and/or imprisonment for up to one year, or civil penalty of up to $25,000 for each violation. Superior Court may also enjoin violation. (c. 111, §§142A-142B). Violations of Massachusetts Water Management Act (c. 21G) may be punished by fine of not less than $1,000 and not more than $10,000 per day and/or imprisonment up to 180 days, or civil penalty of up to $25,000 per day. (c. 21G, §14). Violations of order issued under Massachusetts Water Management Act punishable by civil penalties under c. 21A, §16. (c. 21G, §14). Filling or dredging any wetland without permit is punishable by fine of not more than $25,000 per day and/or jail sentence of not more than two years, or civil penalty of up to $25,000 for each violation. (c. 131, §40). Disposal of dredged materials within marine boundaries of commonwealth without permit is punishable by fine of up to $25,000 per day and/or imprisonment, or civil penalty, of not more than $25,000 per day. (c. 21A, §14). Violation of c. 91, §§52-54, pertaining to transportation and dumping of dredged material in tide waters, or violation of any permit or license granted under these sections, is punishable by fine of up to $25,000 per day and/or imprisonment for up to one year, or civil penalty of up to $25,000 per day. (c. 91, §55). Violation of Hazardous Waste Management Act (c. 21C) may be punished by fine of $25,000 and/or two year jail sentence or civil penalty up to $25,000 for each day of violation. Knowing violation of §5 of c. 21C, relating to collection, storage, transportation, etc. of hazardous waste, may be punished by fine of not more than $100,000 and/or state prison imprisonment for not more than 20 years or in jail for not more than 2½ years for each such violation. (c. 21C, §10). Persons who violate any provision of Oil and Hazardous Material Release Prevention and Response Act (c. 21E) or any order or regulation thereunder, subject to civil penalty of $25,000 for each violation or may be punished by fine of not more than $25,000 and/or jail for not more than two years for each violation. (c. 21E, §11). Owner or operator of site or vessel who fails to give notice of release of hazardous material therefrom, may be punished by fine of not more than $100,000 and/or imprisonment in state prison for not more than 20 years or in jail for not more than 2½ years for each day violation continues. (c. 21E, §11). Fine of not more than $3,000 for first offense and not more than $10,000 for each subsequent offense shall be imposed for dumping of rubbish on public or private land and in or near coastal or inland waters. (c. 270, §16). Failure to drain and clean or remove abandoned underground residential tanks utilized exclusively for heating or heating water as required by c. 148, §38A punishable by fine up to $25,000 and/or imprisonment up to two years, or civil penalty up to $25,000 for each violation. (c. 148, §38H).

Civil Liability, Liens.—Owner or operator of site or vessel from or at which there is or has been release or threat of release of hazardous material, person who at time of disposal owned or operated site at or from which there is release or threat of release, transporter or person who arranged for transportation of hazardous material to or in site or vessel from which there is or has been release or threat of release, any person causing or legally responsible for release or threat of release of oil or hazardous material, is liable, without regard to fault, to commonwealth for all costs of assessment, containment and removal by commonwealth and for all damages for injury to and destruction or loss of natural resources and to any person for damage to real or personal property incurred or suffered as result of such release or threat. Liability to commonwealth for costs may be trebled. Liability may be apportioned among owners or responsible persons and may be avoided by showing that release or threat of release was caused by act of God, act of war or act or omission of third party other than employee, agent or person contractually related to otherwise liable party, provided that person seeking to avoid liability exercised due care, took reasonable precautions against third party acts or omissions and foreseeable consequences and gave notice of release or threat of release. (c. 21E, §5). Certain property owners, secured lenders, and fiduciaries including trustees, that have not caused or contributed to releases or threats of releases may partially be exempt from liability under recent revisions to c. 21E, but may be liable to commonwealth up to value of property following commonwealth assessment, containment, and response actions. (c. 21E, §5[b], [d]). Liability to commonwealth for its costs constitutes debt which becomes lien on all property owned by liable party when statement of claim filed or recorded, as to real estate in manner required for recording or registering encumbrances, and as to personal property in manner required by c. 106, §9-401. Lien has priority over all encumbrances on contaminated site. (c. 21E, §13).

Permits.—Permit is required for discharge of sewage, industrial waste or any other effluent or pollutant into Massachusetts waters, including groundwater. (c. 21, §43). Air emissions permits are required for large-scale heating plants, incinerators, nuclear energy utilization facilities, and large variety of manufacturing and commercial operations, pursuant to 310 CMR 7.00 et seq. Permits are required before any inland or coastal wetland may be filled or dredged. Latter permits may be obtained only by complying with procedure, which entails public hearings and approval by local conservation commission, mayor, or board of selectmen with possible appeal to department of environmental protection. (c. 131, §40). Permit from department of environmental protection is required before removal of dredged materials from marine boundaries and may be issued only after determination that such disposal will not unreasonably degrade or endanger marine environment or public health. (c. 21A, §14). Permit (and registration statement) is also required from department of environmental protection for water withdrawals and uses in excess of threshold volume. (c. 21G, §§5, 7). Permit is required for individual septic system from board of health and often from department of environmental protection as well. (c. 21A, §13; State Environmental Code Tit. 5, 310 CMR 15.00 et seq.). Permit is required from department of environmental protection—division of water pollution control for new connections to public sewer system which will add more than 15,000 gallons of sewage per day, and for increases of over 2,000 gallons of sewage per day from existing connections. (c. 21, §43 and regulations promulgated pursuant thereto). Permit is required from department of environmental protection—division of waterways to construct structure in stream on which federal, state or municipal funds have been spent for channel improvements or flood control (c. 91, §12A) or in great ponds (c. 91, §13), tidewater, tidelands or filled tidelands (c. 91, §14). Permit is required from department of environmental protection for collection, storage, transportation, treatment or disposal of hazardous waste. Persons licensed to transport hazardous wastes will be required to pay fee intended to cover cost of projects undertaken to assess, contain and remove releases of oil and hazardous materials. (c. 21C, §7). No hazardous waste treatment, storage, or disposal facility may be constructed without site assignment under c. 111, §150A. (c. 21C, §7). Authority to issue permits for sewage discharge within Metropolitan Sewage System has been transferred from Metropolitan District Commission to Massachusetts Water Resources Authority. (1984, c. 372). Registration required for commercial digging or drilling wells. (c. 21, §16). Certification required for operation of wastewater treatment facilities. (c. 21, §34C). See also c. 164, §69K, providing for certificates of environmental impact and public need with respect to electric, oil and natural gas facilities. Environmental impact report process under Massachusetts Environmental Policy Act (c. 30, §§61-62H) is supervised by secretary of executive office of environmental affairs. Permit from fire marshall is required for removal or relocation of underground tank which has been used for keeping or storage of flammable or combustible fluids. (c. 148, §38A).

Pesticides.—Labeling, distribution, sale, storage, transportation, use, and disposal of pesticides are regulated by c. 132B. See category Business Regulation and Commerce, topic Licenses, Business and Professional.

Septic Systems.—Requirements for septic systems in general and requirements for septic system inspection for conveyancing of property effective 3/31/95 are regulated by State Environmental Code Tit. 5, 310 CMR 15.00 et seq. and 1995, c. 38, §289. (c. 21A, §13). See also 1995, c. 38, §§300, 351. Since their enactment in 1995, State Environmental Code Tit. 5 regulations have been modified in attempt to ameliorate financial burden on certain property owners. Applicable volumes of Massachusetts Register should be consulted.

Use of Toxic Substances.—Certain users of specified toxic substances must submit reports to commonwealth disclosing levels of toxics use. (c. 21I).

UST Fund.—Owners or operators of leaking underground storage tanks may be eligible for reimbursement of eligible cleanup costs under commonwealth's UST fund. (c. 21J).

Wetlands.—Certain uses of wetlands subject to prohibition or regulation by local conservation commissions and department of environmental protection. (c. 131, §40).

ESTATES AND TRUSTS

ADMINISTRATION:

See topic Executors and Administrators.

ADVANCEMENTS:

See topic Descent and Distribution.

ALLOWANCES:

See topic Executors and Administrators.

CLAIMS:

See topic Executors and Administrators; category Civil Actions and Procedure, topic Pleading.

DEATH:

Common law presumption of death of person absent and not heard from for seven years is recognized. (42 Mass. [1 Met.] 204). See also category Property, topic Absentees.

Survivorship.—Uniform Simultaneous Death Act has been adopted, but does not apply to distribution of property passing under instrument, other than will, executed before Oct. 27, 1941. (c. 190A, §1).

Death Certificates.—See category Documents and Records, topic Records, subhead Vital Statistics.

Actions for Death.—(c. 229). Basis for recovery, which formerly was solely for tortfeasor's degree of culpability, now includes survivors' need for compensation. On all causes of action for wrongful death executor or administrator, on behalf of survivors and not estate, may recover fair monetary value (no floor or ceiling on amount) of decedent to persons entitled to receive damages recovered including compensation for loss of reasonably expected net income, services, protection, care, assistance, society, companionship, comfort, guidance, counsel and advice of decedent to persons entitled to damages recovered. (c. 229, §2). Grief of survivors not included. (400 Mass. 1003, 508 N.E.2d 842).

Person who: (1) By negligence causes death, or (2) by willful, wanton or reckless act causes death under circumstances that deceased could have recovered damages for personal injuries if death had not resulted, or (3) operates common carrier of passengers and by negligence causes death of passenger, or (4) operates common carrier of passengers, and by willful, wanton or reckless act causes death of passenger under such circumstances that deceased could have recovered damages for personal injuries if death had not resulted, or (5) is responsible for breach of warranty arising under Art. 2 of c. 106 which results in injury to person that causes death, shall be liable in damages in amount of: (1) fair monetary value of decedent to persons entitled to receive damages recovered (as set forth in §1) including, but not limited to, compensation for loss of reasonably expected net income, services, protection, care, assistance, society, companionship, comfort, guidance, counsel and advice, (2) reasonable funeral and burial expenses, and (3) punitive damages not less than $5,000 if death caused by willful, wanton or reckless conduct or gross negligence; except that: (1) liability of employer to person in his employment shall not be governed by this section, (2) person operating railroad shall not be liable for negligence in causing death of person while walking or being upon such railroad contrary to law or reasonable rules and regulations of carrier, and (3) person operating street railway or electric railroad shall not be liable for negligence for

See note at head of Digest as to 1998 legislation covered.

See Topical Index in front part of this volume.

MA – 41

DEATH . . . *continued*
causing death of person while walking or being upon that part of street railway or electric railroad not within limits of highway. Person shall be liable for negligence or willful, wanton or reckless act of agents or servants while engaged in his business to same extent and subject to same limits as he would be liable under this provision for his own act. Damages shall be recovered in action of tort by executor or administrator of deceased. For causes of action arising prior to Jan. 1, 1982, no recovery shall be had for death which does not occur within two years after injury which caused death; this limitation abolished as to causes of action arising subsequent to Jan. 1, 1982. (1981, c. 493). Action to recover damages shall be commenced within three years after from date of death or date that executor or administrator knew or should have known that basis for action exists, or within such time thereafter as provided by c. 260, §§4, 4B, 9 or 10. (c. 229, §2).

If person dies through injuries suffered because of defect on way or bridge, recovery of not more than $4,000 may be had from person or governmental unit responsible for repairing same if there was reasonable notice of want of repair and if tort action is commenced within two years after injury causing death. (c. 229, §1). See category Criminal Law, topic Criminal Law, subhead Victims of Violent Crimes.

Survival of Tort Actions.—In all cases recovery may be had against executor or administrator of person causing death even if such person dies before occurrence of death giving rise to right of recovery. (c. 229, §5A). In all cases amount recovered is distributed to next of kin if no spouse survives; to surviving spouse if no issue survive; if deceased is survived by spouse and by one child or by issue of one deceased child, one-half to surviving spouse and one-half to surviving child or his issue by right of representation; if deceased is survived by spouse and by more than one child, surviving either in person or by issue, one-third to surviving spouse and two-thirds to children or issue by right of representation. (c. 229, §1). In certain cases recovery may also be had on separate count for conscious suffering resulting from same injury causing death, but such damages, punitive damages and funeral expenses are assets of decedent's estate. (c. 229, §6). Damages for conscious suffering received in death action more than one year from date of deceased's death are new assets of estate within meaning of c. 197, §11. (c. 229, §6B). In hit and run cases action may be brought within six months of learning identity of defendant, but in no event more than three years after accident. (c. 260, §4B).

See also categories Civil Actions and Procedure, topic Damages; Employment, topic Labor Relations.

Living Wills.—See topic Wills, subhead Living Wills.

Uniform Anatomical Gift Act.—See topic Wills.

DECEDENTS' ESTATES:

See topics Descent and Distribution, Executors and Administrators, Wills; category Debtor and Creditor, topic Homesteads.

DESCENT AND DISTRIBUTION:

Real estate and personal property not disposed of by will, subject to rights of spouse of deceased (see infra, subhead Surviving Spouse) and to rights of homestead (see category Debtor and Creditor, topic Homesteads), go to children and to issue of any deceased child by right of representation; if no surviving child of intestate, then to all his other lineal descendents, in equal shares if of same degree, otherwise by right of representation; if no issue, then equally to father and mother or survivor of them; if no issue, father or mother, then to brothers and sisters and to issue of any deceased brother or sister by right of representation; if no surviving brother or sister of intestate, then to all issue of his deceased brothers and sisters, in equal shares if of same degree, otherwise by right of representation; if no issue, father or mother, or issue of father or mother, then to next of kin in equal degree, through nearest ancestor. (c. 190, §§2, 3). See infra, subhead Escheat. Degrees of kindred are computed according to rules of civil law; kindred of half blood inherit equally with whole blood in same degree. (c. 190, §4). Child born out of wedlock is heir of mother and of any maternal ancestor. (c. 190, §5). If parents intermarry and father acknowledges child as his, child deemed legitimate and is heir of father and any paternal ancestors. (c. 190, §7). (See infra, subhead Illegitimates.) As to inheritance by and from adopted persons, see category Family, topic Adoption. See also topic Executors and Administrators.

In case of intestacy, title to Massachusetts real estate vests in heirs at law on death of decedent, whether resident or nonresident, subject to right of administrator to sell or mortgage for payment of debts, taxes, administration expenses, etc., if applicable personal property of estate is insufficient. (c. 202, §§1, 28).

Doctrine of Worthier Title.—Abolished as applies to wills (c. 184, §33A) and inter vivos trusts (c. 184, §33B).

Surviving Spouse.—Election of dower must be filed in probate registry within six months after approval of bond of executor or administrator. (c. 189, §1). If surviving spouse fails to elect, he or she takes following shares of property not disposed of by will: if deceased leaves kindred but no issue and estate does not exceed $200,000, surviving spouse takes all; otherwise survivor takes $200,000 and one-half of remaining personal and real property (if personal property is insufficient to pay $200,000, interested party may petition to have survivor paid from sale or mortgage); if deceased leaves issue, survivor receives one-half of personal and of real property; if deceased leaves neither kindred nor issue, survivor takes all. (c. 190, §1).

Half Blood.—Kindred of half blood inherit equally with whole blood in same degree. (c. 190, §4).

Posthumous Children or Other Issue.—After born child takes as if alive at date of parent's death. (c. 190, §8).

Illegitimates.—Child born out of wedlock is heir of mother and of any maternal ancestor. (c. 190, §5). *Caveat:* Similar statute held unconstitutional in 430 U.S. 762; 97 S.Ct. 1459 (1977). Statutory requirement that parents intermarry to enable child born out of wedlock to inherit from father is unconstitutional, however, separate statutory requirements of acknowledgment or adjudication of paternity are constitutional. (380 Mass. 663, 405 N.E.2d 135). When paternity is conceded, right to inherit from natural father cannot be denied. (Id.). See also c. 190, §7. Child born out of wedlock declared legitimate in foreign state is legitimate child under law of commonwealth. (394 Mass. 306, 475 N.E.2d 395).

Adopted Children.—See category Family, topic Adoption.

Determination of Heirship.—Ordinarily, preferable method is petition for, and order of, distribution.

Advancements.—Real or personal property given by intestate in his lifetime to issue as advancement is considered part of intestate's estate. (c. 196, §§3, 4). Gifts and grants are held advancements if so expressed or charged in writing by intestate or acknowledged in writing by recipient. (c. 196, §5). Securities owned by deceased, value not more than $750 with any one issuer, cumulative value not more than $2,100, may after 30 days after death, if no executor or administrator has demanded payment and issuer has no notice of proceedings, be transferred to surviving spouse or adult child of deceased or to surviving mother or father. (c. 196, §9).

Election.—Surviving spouse must file election of dower in probate registry within six months after approval of administrator's bond. (c. 189, §1). If dower is claimed, intestate rights in real estate are waived. (Id.).

Election between distributive share and testamentary provision, see topic Wills, subhead Election.

Disclaimer.—See topic Wills, subhead Disclaimer.

Escheat.—If intestate leaves no kindred and no spouse, estate escheats to commonwealth, unless intestate veteran living in Soldiers' Home, in which case estate goes to Home. (c. 190, §3).

Dower.—See category Property, topic Dower.

Curtesy.—Merged with dower. See category Property, topic Dower.

ELECTION:

See topic Wills.

ESTATES (in property):

See category Property, topic Real Property.

EXECUTORS AND ADMINISTRATORS:

Uniform Probate Code not adopted.

Probate Court of each county has jurisdiction (with both general and equity powers) over administration of estate of person who, at his decease, was inhabitant of county and of nonresident leaving estate to be administered in county. (c. 215, §§3, 6).

Temporary Administration.—Probate Court may appoint as temporary executor or temporary administrator c.t.a. person named executor in will (c. 192, §13) or petitioner for administration c.t.a. (c. 193, §7A) for decedents dying on or after Jan. 1, 1978, if: (1) testator requests such appointment or (2) upon written assent of widow or husband and all heirs and next of kin of full age and capacity. Seven days notice of intent to seek appointment must be given to all heirs and next of kin unless appointment assented to as aforesaid. Counsel's certificate that notice given is prima facie evidence thereof. (c. 192, §13, c. 193, §7A). Temporary executor or administrator c.t.a. (hereinafter "temporary representative") may be exempted from giving surety on official bond if: (1) Widow or husband and all heirs and next of kin of full age and capacity assent thereto and testator so requests, or (2) upon assent of all devisees and legatees with present vested interests; and provided that temporary representative submit affidavit that estate exceeds amount of certain preferred claims and allowances. (c. 205, §4A).

Temporary representative must collect and preserve personal property and for that purpose may commence and defend suit; unless will directs otherwise, court may without notice authorize temporary representative to take charge of real property, to sell personal property, to invest, to pay certain preferred claims and to continue decedent's business; temporary representative may not make distributions except amounts allowed to widow or minors for necessaries. (c. 192, §14).

Powers of temporary representative cease upon approval of bond of executor or administrator c.t.a. but not later than 90 days after appointment unless extended by court pursuant to c. 192, §15 and thereupon he shall deliver all property to such executor or administrator c.t.a. (c. 205, §1). If all persons appointed executors or administrators c.t.a. are same persons as temporary representatives, no new inventory need be filed and they may account for temporary administration in their account as such executors or administrators c.t.a. (c. 192, §16). Temporary representative not so appointed must render inventory and account within 30 days of discharge or cessation of powers. (Id.). Special administrators with powers similar to temporary fiduciaries may be appointed without notice if emergency requires. (c. 193, §10).

For estates of decedents dying on or after Jan. 1, 1990, action may be brought against temporary representative within one year of date of death, but will be stayed until permanent representative is appointed. (c. 193, §15).

Preferences in Right to Administer.—If competent and willing to act, and found suitable by court, executor named in will is appointed by court. (c. 192, §4).

Unless court deems it proper to appoint another person, administration is granted to one or more of following persons, if competent and willing to undertake it, who are preferred in order named: widow or widower; next of kin or their guardians or conservators as court selects; principal creditors, if none of above are competent or seek appointment; if no known widow, widower, or next of kin is in commonwealth, public administrator. (c. 193, §1). Administration may be granted to one or more of next of kin or any suitable person if widow or widower and all next of kin resident in commonwealth of full age and capacity consent in writing. (c. 193, §2). In practice, any person named by one who is himself entitled to administration is appointed, provided proper notice is given and no objection is made. Probate Court may, on request of widow, widower or heir of deceased, grant letters of administration to applicant therefor after granting such letters to public administrator; letters testamentary or of administration with will annexed must be granted when will of deceased is allowed after grant of letters of administration to public administrator. When person to whom such letters are

EXECUTORS AND ADMINISTRATORS . . . *continued*
granted gives bond as required by law, powers of public administrator over estate cease. (c. 194, §7).

Eligibility and Competency.—Any individual (either sex, whether married or not [c. 209, §5]) of proper capacity or any duly authorized national bank or Massachusetts trust company may be appointed executor or administrator. Where minor is named as executor, administrator c.t.a. is appointed to hold office during minority unless another executor accepts trust. (c. 193, §8; c. 192, §6). Nonresident may be appointed executor, administrator, or trustee, but may not receive letter of appointment until he has, by writing filed in registry of probate, appointed resident agent upon whom service of legal process may be made. (c. 195, §8). As to competency of foreign bank, see category Business Regulation and Commerce, topic Banks and Banking, subhead Foreign Banks.

Petition for probate of will or letters of administration must be signed by petitioners personally, sworn to by one of them and accompanied by certified copy of death certificate. (c. 192, §1). Filing fee $50, plus $10 surcharge. (c. 262, §§40, 4C).

If it appears in petition for probate of will or letters testamentary that no widow, widower or heir at law is known, attorney general must be made party to proceedings. (c. 192, §1A).

Proceedings for Appointment.—Notice of petition for letters testamentary or of administration must be given in manner and form prescribed by probate court and usually may be made: either by personal service of notice on all persons interested or by mailing notice to all persons interested at least 14 days before return day (court sometimes requires earlier notice where person to be notified resides at distance) and by publishing citation at least seven days before return day in newspaper. Except where executor requests exemption from sureties on his bond, no notice of petition is necessary if all parties entitled thereto assent in writing or appear voluntarily or waive notice, nor if administration is granted to one or more of next of kin or any suitable person if widow or widower and all next of kin resident in commonwealth of full age and capacity consent in writing. (c. 193, §2).

For estates of decedents dying on or after Sept. 1, 1992, petition must include sworn statement that copy of petition and death certificate have been sent by mail to department of public welfare.

Appeal Period.—Person aggrieved may appeal to appeals court or, in certain circumstances, to SJC within 30 days after entry of decree by Probate Court. (c. 215, §9). Acts performed by fiduciary after entry of decree of appointment or authorizing him to sell, mortgage or lease real or personal property and prior to expiration of appeal period are valid as though appeal period had expired without any appeal in all instances where no appearance entered against such appointment, sale, mortgage or lease prior to entry of decree or where such appearance entered and withdrawn prior to entry of decree, notwithstanding fact that appeal may have been taken in said period. (c. 215, §9A).

Oath.—No requirement.

Bond.—Every executor or administrator is required to give bond before entering on his duties. (c. 205, §1). Failure to give bond within 30 days of appointment may be deemed resignation or declination. (c. 205, §8). Testator may not exempt executor or administrator c.t.a. from giving bond, but he may and usually does exempt fiduciary from sureties thereon. (c. 205, §§4, 4A, 5). Bond with personal sureties is usually 50% or 100% greater than value of personal estate. Sureties must be satisfactory to court and reside within commonwealth except that surety company authorized to do business within commonwealth may be surety. (c. 205, §9). Executor and administrator c.t.a. (whether or not resident here), may be exempted from giving sureties if testator so directs, or may be exempted if all interested persons of full age, except creditors, consent, provided in either case all creditors and guardians or conservators of interested persons under disability are notified as ordered by court (usually by publication). (c. 205, §4). Court may order additional bond or new bond with new sureties or increased penal sum in proper circumstances. (c. 205, §§13, 14). Court may, in any case, order sureties. (Id.). No surety is required upon bonds filed by domestic trust companies (c. 167G, §6) or by national banks located in commonwealth and permitted to act in fiduciary capacity (c. 205, §6A) nor, in actual practice, by foreign banks appointed here. (c. 167, §43). Filing fee for each bond, $30. (c. 262, §40).

Issuance of Letters.—Letters are issued after approval of bond. (c. 192, §4).

Removal.—Executor or administrator may be removed by Probate Court if he becomes insane or otherwise incapable of acting, or is otherwise unsuitable therefor, or if he resides outside commonwealth and neglects to render accounts or settle estate after being duly cited by Probate Court. (c. 195, §11). If new bond required by court not given executor or administrator may be removed. (c. 205, §16).

Special Kinds of Administration.—If no executor is named in will or if all executors are dead, incompetent or refuse to accept trust, or if executor named in will is minor at time of probate of will (see supra, subhead Eligibility and Competency), or neglects for 30 days after probate of will to give bond according to law, administrator with will annexed may be appointed. (c. 193, §7). If sole or surviving executor or administrator dies, resigns or is removed before having fully administered estate, administrator de bonis non may be appointed. (c. 193, §9). Court is not free to substitute its own selection for that of petitioner without affirmative reasons therefor. (352 Mass. 660, 227 N.E.2d 497).

Public Administrators.—Office of public administrator is created and governed by c. 194.

Inventory and appraisal must be filed by executor or administrator. (c. 205, §1). Temporary executor or administrator c.t.a. (see supra, subhead Temporary Administration) must file inventory when required by c. 192 or Probate Court. (c. 205, §1[8]). Every inventory required to be filed must include appraisal of property by executor or other fiduciary setting forth actual market values. On motion by executor or other fiduciary, before filing of inventory, or by any interested person after filing, court may appoint special appraisers if court finds it to be in best interest of estate. (c. 195, §6).

General Powers and Duties.—Executor or administrator has all powers and duties generally accompanying such office, except as restricted or otherwise provided by will or order of Probate Court, including right to sell personal property, compromise claims, make prudent investments, distribute in cash or in kind (c. 195, §5A) and, with consent of court, to sell or collect rents from realty, give or renew mortgages, etc. (c. 202, §§1-20A, 28,30) or compromise controversies with respect to will or administration of estate (c. 204, §§13, 14). He may be licensed to continue business for not more than one year from date of appointment; for cause court may extend authority beyond one year. (c. 195, §7). For deaths occurring after Jan. 1, 1997, executor may sign and file affidavit with registry of deeds stating no federal tax filing required. (c. 65C, §114).

Notice to Legatees.—Within three months after allowance of will and appointment and qualification of executor, he must by mail notify devisees and legatees named in will whose addresses are known to him and he must file affidavit in Probate Court showing names of those notified and addresses to which notices were mailed. (c. 192, §12).

Notice to Creditors.—No notice need be given to creditors except in case of estate which is declared insolvent. (c. 198, §5). For estates of decedents dying on or after Jan. 1, 1990 see subhead Proceedings for Appointment, supra.

Presentation of Claims.—For estates of decedents dying before Jan. 1, 1990, statement of claim containing prescribed information may be presented to executor or administrator within four months from date of giving bond. Claim is deemed presented upon its receipt by executor or administrator within this time period or upon its filing with register of probate. (c. 197, §9). If, at end of such four month period after giving bond, representative has no notice of demands sufficient to warrant his representing estate insolvent, he may pay debts of estate and is not personally liable for demands of creditors of which he had no notice. (c. 197, §2).

Actions against estate of decedent dying on or after Jan. 1, 1978 and before Jan. 1, 1990 are barred unless: either (1) claim is presented within four months from date of giving bond and action commenced within 60 days of its disallowance or (2) action is commenced within nine months from date of giving bond, whichever is later, and in either case before expiration of applicable period writ has been served in hand, service accepted or notice of action filed in registry of probate. Executor or administrator not held to answer action by creditor of deceased brought within any other or additional period of limitation for bringing such action hereinafter set forth unless, prior to expiration thereof, writ has been served or filed as aforesaid. (c. 197, §9).

For estates of decedents dying on or after Jan. 1, 1990, action by creditor must be commenced, and process served upon or accepted by executor or administrator, or notice of action filed in registry of probate, within one year of date of death. (c. 197, §9). If executor or administrator of such estate, at end of six month period after date of death, has no notice of demands sufficient to warrant his representing estate insolvent, he may pay debts of estate and is not personally liable for demands of creditors of which he had no notice. (c. 197, §2).

For estates of decedents dying on or after Sept. 1, 1992, if decedent received medical assistance under c. 118E while inpatient in nursing facility or other medical institution while 65 years or older, department of public welfare may present claims against estate within four months after approval of bond of executor or administrator by filing claim with registry of probate and delivering or mailing copy thereof to executor or administrator. (c. 197, §9).

Presentation of claim does not prevent running of short statute of limitations relating to suits against executor or administrator. Only remedy for disputed or disallowed claim is action against representative. (c. 197, §9).

Unliquidated Claims.—Creditor of deceased whose right of action does not accrue within one year after date of death may present claim to Probate Court at any time before estate is fully administered, and if Court determines claim is or may become justly due from estate, Court shall order executor or administrator to retain sufficient assets to satisfy claim. (c. 197, §13). Failure to petition for retention of assets in timely manner may constitute culpable neglect and bar late-filed claim. (c. 197, §10).

Proof of Claims.—No forms yet prescribed by courts, but claim must be in writing, including name and address of claimant, amount claimed, basis of claim, and description of security, if any. For estates of decedants dying on or after Jan. 1, 1990, notice must contain description of action filed and identify court in which filed. (c. 197, §9).

Approval or Rejection of Claims.—See supra, subhead Presentation of Claims. Interpreting pre-1990 version of statute, common law provides that failure of executor or administrator to mail notice of disallowance of claim within 60 days after expiration of four month period has effect of allowance. (18 Mass. App. 230, 464 N.E.2d 404, but see 395 Mass. 868, 482 N.E.2d 818, regarding authority of executor or administrator to change allowance of claim to disallowance). Allowed claims bear interest at legal rate from expiration of such period unless claim is based on contract specifying otherwise, in which case contract rate is applied. (c. 197, §9). Repealed for estates of decedents dying on or after Jan. 1, 1990. (1989, c. 329).

Payment of Claims.—Upon complaint filed, Probate Court may order payment of claims allowed as provided above to extent funds are available for payment. (c. 197, §9). See also infra, subhead Actions Against Representative. Repealed for estates of decedents dying on or after Jan. 1, 1990. (1989, c. 329).

Priorities and Insolvent Estates.—If Probate Court on representation of executor or administrator finds estate to be probably insolvent, it may appoint commissioners to receive and examine claims. (c. 198, §§2, 4). Notice to all known creditors is required (c. 198, §§5, 3) and, unless court extends time, all claims must be presented within six months after court's order appointing commissioners or requiring notice. (c. 198, §9).

In general, no action may be maintained against executor or administrator after estate has been represented insolvent, unless for claim entitled to preference which would not be affected by insolvency of estate or unless assets prove more than sufficient to pay all debts allowed. (c. 198, §31).

In insolvent estates, assets are applied to payment of debts in following order (no payments to be made to creditors of any class until all debts of preceding class of which executor or administrator had notice have been paid): (1) necessary expenses of last illness and funeral and expenses of administration; (2) debts entitled to preference under laws of U.S.; (3) public rates, taxes, child support arrears and excise duties; (4) debts due to division of medical assistance for estates of persons dying on or after 7/1/92, regardless of when assistance provided; (5) wages or compensation not exceeding $100

See note at head of Digest as to 1998 legislation covered.

See Topical Index in front part of this volume.

MA – 43

EXECUTORS AND ADMINISTRATORS . . . *continued*
for labor done within one year before death or judgment on such wages; (6) debts not exceeding $100 for necessaries furnished decedent or family within six months of death or judgment on such debts; (7) other debts. (c. 198, §1). Excess of claim over security prorates as independent claim. (312 Mass. 200, 43 N.E.2d 795). Payment of administrative expenses entitled to priority. (357 Mass. 225, 257 N.E.2d 447).

Preferential transfer by insolvent person within four months of death may be avoided by his executor or administrator, who may recover property or its value. (c. 198, §§10A, 10B).

Sales.—(c. 202). Neither executor, unless power is given him in will, nor administrator has power to sell real estate without license from Probate Court. (c. 202, §6). Court may set terms of sale. (69 Mass. [3 Gray] 205). Fee for petition for license to sell real estate, $50 plus $10 surcharge. (c. 262, §§40, 4C). If notice includes publication for three successive weeks, and no appearances entered against sale, price at which sale is licensed is conclusively presumed to be highest possible. (c. 202, §38). Both executors and administrators have full power to sell personal property without license. (295 Mass. 250, 3 N.E.2d 817). Release of Massachusetts estate tax lien on real estate required before license will be granted by Probate Court.

Actions by Representative.—Representative has right to sue on claims of decedent. In addition to actions which survive by common law, following actions survive: under c. 247; tort for assault, battery, imprisonment or other damage to person; for consequential damages arising out of injury to person and consisting of expenses incurred by husband, wife, parent or guardian for medical, nursing, hospital or surgical services in connection with such injury, for goods taken away or converted, or for property damage; and actions against sheriffs for misconduct or negligence. (c. 228, §1). Action to contest will is common law property right and survives death of contestant. (398 Mass. 817, 501 N.E.2d 504). In personal actions which survive, if sole plaintiff or defendant dies after commencement and before final judgment, action may proceed by or against executor or administrator, and appeal not entered before death may be entered thereafter. (c. 228, §4). Substitution of executor or administrator as party governed by Mass. R. Civ. P. (c. 228, §4A). Administrator de bonis non may be substituted for deceased or removed executor or administrator. (c. 230, §11).

Actions Against Representative.—See c. 197, §§1, 9. See supra, subhead Presentation of Claims; see category Civil Actions and Procedure, topic Limitation of Actions. If new assets are received after time for filing claim under §9 is barred, suit may be brought within four months after creditor has notice of receipt of such new assets and within six months after their actual receipt. (c. 197, §11). If action brought within time limit of §9 fails or is defeated for certain defects of form, plaintiff may bring new action for same cause within 60 days after determination. (c. 197, §12). Bill in equity will lie after year has expired if justice and equity require, but will not affect previous payments or distributions. (c. 197, §10). Notwithstanding §9, action for injuries or death may be commenced more than one year from date of death of deceased if commenced within three years from accrual of cause of action; any judgment recovered can be satisfied only out of proceeds of insurance policy or bond, if any, and not from general assets of estate. (c. 197, §9A). Executor or administrator not compelled to pay claim unless proved in action begun within one year after claim becomes payable. (c. 197, §14). In limited circumstances, transferee liability is available to creditors whose claims accrue after expiration of period of limitations. (c. 197, §§28-30).

Administrator de bonis non is liable to action by creditor for same period as provided in §9 for original executor or administrator (see supra, this subhead) less any time which has run against preceding officer but in any event for not less than two months from date of appointment, provided that this section is not applicable to claims already barred at date of appointment. (c. 197 §17). Repealed for estates of decedents dying on or after Jan. 1, 1990. (1989, c. 329).

In no case may action be brought against executor, administrator or administrator de bonis non before three months after giving bond, unless action is brought for recovery of demand which would not be affected by insolvency of estate or, after estate has been represented insolvent, for purpose of ascertaining contested claim, but in no case may action against administrator de bonis non be brought before six months after executor or administrator first appointed gave bond. (c. 197, §§1, 2A). Repealed for estates of decedents dying on or after Jan. 1, 1990. (1989, c. 329).

Estate of deceased person cannot be attached in suit against executor or administrator on debt due from deceased without consent of probate court. (c. 230, §7). Action against estate is valid if representative had legal existence when action commenced and had notice and filed answer for estate. (402 Mass. 92, 521 N.E.2d 721).

For actions which survive and substitution of parties, see supra, subhead Actions by Representative.

Except as hereinafter set forth, action against estate of decedent dying on or after Jan. 1, 1990 will be barred unless such action is commenced within one year after date of death and unless, before expiration of such period, process has been served upon or accepted by executor or administrator, or notice of action filed in registry of probate. Executor or administrator is not held to answer action by creditor of deceased commenced within any other or additional period of limitation for bringing such action provided by or under c. 197 unless before expiration of such period process has been served upon or accepted by executor or administrator, or notice of action filed in registry of probate. Foregoing rules also apply to trustee of trust, assets of which are subject as matter of substantive law to being reached by creditors of estate. See subheads Proceedings for Appointment and Presentation of Claims, supra for notice to be given to department of public welfare and presentation of claim by said department if decedent received medical assistance under c. 118E while age 65 or older. (c. 197, §9). Notwithstanding foregoing, action for injuries or death may be commenced more than one year after date of death of decedent if commenced within three years from accrual of cause of action; any judgment can be satisfied only out of proceeds of insurance policy or bond, if any, and not from general assets of estate. (c. 197, §9A).

Allowances may be made by Probate Court for immediate need of surviving spouse or minor children of deceased. (c. 196, §2). During pendency of petition relative to probate of will or appointment of administrator, court may, upon petition and after notice, make allowance for surviving spouse and children of deceased from property held by special administrator, not exceeding portion to which they would be finally entitled. (c. 193, §13).

Widow's Quarantine.—Widow or widower may remain in deceased spouse's house for six months after deceased spouse's death, rent free. (c. 196, §1).

Intermediate Accountings.—Every executor and administrator must render account at least once a year and at such other times as court requires, but may be excused in any year if court is satisfied that it is not necessary or expedient. (c. 206, §1). In practice, accounts are not filed annually.

Final Accounting and Settlement.—No fixed time within which final settlement must be made. (c. 206, §22). Before any account will be allowed, notice must be given to attorney general of Massachusetts if public charitable interests; to department of mental health in case of mentally ill persons or to department of mental retardation in case of mentally retarded persons and Veterans Administration if interested; to all legatees and devisees; to heirs; to all other persons entitled to share in estate. (c. 206, §24).

Distribution.—Unless otherwise provided in will, interest at 8% payable from one year after date of death. (c. 197, §§9, 20, SJC Rule 1:14). Executor or administrator may obtain decree for distribution to protect self. See also topic Wills, subhead Legacies. Probate Court may, upon application of executor or administrator, authorize him to deliver to parents of minor any funds to which minor is entitled and being held by administrator or executor, when sum is less than $1,000. (c. 215, §41A).

Distribution if Abroad.—If claimant is outside of U.S. and its territories, court may require personal appearance of claimant to assist in establishing identity, right and opportunity to receive fund. (c. 206, §27A). Special provisions may be made for payment of funds to distributee where it is not possible to assure his receipt of funds.

Disclaimer.—See topic Wills, subhead Disclaimer.

Liabilities.—Unless otherwise provided, executor or administrator is not personally liable on contract entered into in his fiduciary capacity unless he fails to disclose his representative capacity and identify estate; executor or administrator is individually liable in tort only if personally at fault. (c. 195, §17).

Compensation of Representatives.—Administrators and executors are entitled to compensation for services as court may allow. (c. 206, §16). No statutory rate, subject to changing local custom.

When Administration Unnecessary.—Insurance company which upon death of individual residing within commonwealth owes his estate aggregate sum not exceeding $10,000 under certain policies may, at any time not less than 60 days after death, pay such sum to his surviving spouse or, if none, to one or more of his heirs; provided that at time of such payment, no written claim for such sum has been received at company's home office from any executor or administrator of estate of such individual. Any payment made under such policies to person at least 18 years old constitutes full discharge of company from all liability thereunder. (c. 175, §187E).

Wages of deceased employee not in excess of $100 may be paid after 30 days to certain relatives if administration is not taken out. (c. 149, §178A).

Deposits in savings bank, co-operative bank, federally-chartered bank or credit union, or shares in credit union, with value of $3,000 or less and co-operative bank shares and savings accounts in savings banks with value of $3,000 or less may, under certain circumstances, be paid after 30 or 60 days to surviving spouse or next of kin. (c. 167D, §33; c. 171, §42).

Informal Administration of Small Estates.—If Massachusetts resident dies leaving estate consisting entirely of personal property, which may include motor vehicle, valued at not more than $15,000, surviving spouse, child, grandchild, parent, brother, sister, niece, nephew, aunt or uncle, if of full age and legal capacity and Massachusetts resident, or, if deceased resident in department of mental health or department of mental retardation or receiving certain public assistance, designee of department of mental health, department of mental retardation or department of public welfare, may, 30 days after decedent's death and no formal administration commenced, file statement with Probate Court on form furnished by court and act thereunder as voluntary administrator of estate. (c. 195, §16).

If decedent with small estate qualifying for informal administration under c. 195, §16 leaves will naming person as executor that person may, upon filing information required under §16, distribute estate according to terms of will. If such executor not Massachusetts resident, he must appoint resident agent. (c. 195, §16A).

Small Estates.—See supra, subheads When Administration Unnecessary and Informal Administration of Small Estates.

Foreign Executors or Administrators.—See generally c. 199A.

Foreign representative may, after expiration of 60 days from death of nonresident decedent, collect personal property owed to or owned by such decedent upon presenting affidavit prescribed by statute (c. 199A, §2); if such decedent owned tangible personal property located in commonwealth at time of death or had at any time within 12 months prior thereto place of abode located therein, foreign representative may not accept payment or delivery earlier than one month after filing proof of his authority with Probate Court and commissioner of revenue (c. 199A, §§2, 5). Payment or delivery made in good faith to foreign representative releases resident debtor to same extent as if made to local representative (c. 199A, §3) but cannot be made once resident creditors notify resident debtor of claim (c. 199A, §4). Upon filing of proof of authority as aforesaid, foreign representative has all powers of local representative acting in same capacity (c. 199A, §6) but such power is suspended with certain exceptions upon application for local administration (c. 199A, §7). Foreign representative who files proof of authority as aforesaid, receives property from resident, etc., is subject to jurisdiction of commonwealth under specified circumstances. (c. 199A, §§8, 9, 11). Foreign representative may, after six months and such notice as court may order, be licensed to sell real estate of nonresident decedent if no local administration is pending and no creditor or other person is prejudiced thereby; after satisfaction of all claims against estate in commonwealth, proceeds may be taken by him out of commonwealth to be accounted for in court of his appointment. (c. 202, §32). Foreign representative may, after three months and such notice as court may order, be licensed to receive or

See note at head of Digest as to 1998 legislation covered.

See Topical Index in front part of this volume.

MA – 44

EXECUTORS AND ADMINISTRATORS ... *continued*

sell personal property if no local representative has been appointed and foreign representative will be liable to account in jurisdiction where appointed. (c. 204, §3). Probate Court empowered to protect beneficial owners of bank and brokerage accounts held in commonwealth which allegedly have been converted by estate administrator of foreign domiciliary, even though property rights in accounts must ultimately be decided by courts in foreign country. (22 Mass. App. 689, 497 N.E.2d 26). See also topic Wills, subhead Foreign Probated Wills.

As to sale of real estate by foreign testamentary trustee, see topic Trusts.

Ancillary Administration.—Where administration is taken out on estate of deceased nonresident, his estate within commonwealth is, after payment of local debts, disposed of according to his last will; otherwise his real estate descends according to laws of commonwealth. (c. 199, §1). Residue of personal property is distributed according to laws of state or country of which he was inhabitant by Probate Court or, in its discretion, such residue may be transmitted to executor or administrator, if any, where deceased lived. (c. 199, §2). If nonresident dies insolvent, his estate within commonwealth must be so disposed of that all his creditors, within and without commonwealth, may receive equal proportions of their respective debts. (c. 199, §3). See also topic Wills, subheads Foreign Probated Wills, Health Care Proxy.

Uniform Fiduciaries Act not adopted.

Uniform Principal and Income Act not adopted.

Uniform Simplification of Fiduciary Security Transfers Act not adopted.

Uniform Anatomical Gift Act adopted, with minor variations. (c. 113, §§7-14).

FIDUCIARIES:

See topics Executors and Administrators, and Trusts; also category Family, topic Guardian and Ward.

INTESTACY:

See topic Descent and Distribution.

LIVING WILLS:

See topic Wills.

PROOF OF CLAIMS:

See topic Executors and Administrators; category Civil Actions and Procedure, topic Pleading.

TRUSTS:

Creation.—Trust concerning land can be created only by written instrument signed by person creating it or by his attorney (c. 203, §1) whereas trust of personal property may be oral (186 Mass 108, 71 N.E. 109). In wills and other written instruments, certain powers and discretions may be conferred on trustee by reference to statutory forms. (c. 184B).

Revocable Trusts.—Revocable inter vivos trust with income payable to settlor and with power of appointment and other interests reserved, is valid although not executed as will. (315 Mass. 457, 53 N.E.2d 113). Assets may form part of donor's estate for purposes of surviving spouse's election against will (390 Mass. 864, 460 N.E.2d 572) and are subject to creditors if donor's estate is insufficient to discharge debts (7 Mass. App. 633, 389 N.E.2d 768). In case of donor dying on or after Jan. 1, 1990, except as otherwise provided in c. 197, action by creditors against trustee will be barred unless commenced against trustee, executor or administrator within one year after date of death in manner provided in c. 197, §9. (c. 197, §9). See also topic Executors and Administrators, subhead Actions Against Representative. Inter vivos pour-over trust executed contemporaneously with execution of will is valid even though not funded until settlor's death. (393 Mass. 754, 473 N.E.2d 1084). Divorced spouse does not take under revocable pour-over trust funded entirely at time of decedent's death. (Id.).

Spendthrift Trusts.—Property may be placed in trust for beneficiary (other than settlor) with provision that neither income nor principal may be alienated or subjected to claims of creditors or dependents in advance of payment. (402 Mass. 707, 529 N.E.2d 394). Prohibition against involuntary alienation does not bar voluntary alienation absent express provisions to that effect. (Id.).

Employee Trusts.—Trust created by employer as part of stock bonus, pension, disability, death benefit or profit sharing plan for benefit of some or all of his employees is exempt from rule against perpetuities or rule against suspension of alienation for such time as may be necessary to accomplish purpose. (c. 203, §3A).

Charitable Trusts.—Trusts which are "private foundations" and "split interest trusts" are prohibited from acts of "self dealing," retaining "excess business holdings," making investments which jeopardize trust's exempt purposes and making "taxable expenditures" as terms are defined in IRC §§509, 4941, 4943, 4944, 4945, 4947. (c. 68A, §1). "Private foundations" and charitable trusts must distribute income sufficient to avoid tax liability under IRC §4942(a), (c. 68A, §2), unless otherwise ordered by court (c. 68A, §7).

Condominium Trusts.—See generally c. 183A.

Pour-over Trusts.—See topic Wills, subhead Bequests and Devises to Inter Vivos Trusts.

Trustees.—Any competent person of age may be trustee, subject to probate court's approval of suitability in case of testamentary trustee or other court appointee. Merger of otherwise qualified corporate trustee does not in all cases require new appointment. (342 Mass. 360, 173 N.E.2d 294). As to out of state corporate fiduciaries, see category Business Regulation and Commerce, topic Banks and Banking.

Dealing with Trustees.—If any money, securities or other personal property is paid, transferred or delivered to trustee, receipt of trustee is sufficient discharge and no person is bound to see to application of money, etc., by trustee. (c. 203, §20). Corporations and unincorporated associations are not bound to see to execution of any trust to which their shares are subject or to ascertain whether trust authorized transfer by holder, but they cannot knowingly participate in breach of trust. (c. 203, §21).

Compensation.—Reasonable compensation for trustee determined by court and may be apportioned between income and principal. (c. 206, §16). Customary charges by Boston banks are usually followed. Investment counsel charges are not normally allowed in addition to trustee's compensation.

Principal and Income.—Although distributions in cash or property are usually income, capital gains distributions by mutual funds are principal even if made in cash (346 Mass. 521, 194 N.E.2d 707) and distribution in stock of another corporation is income unless deemed by trustee to be essentially principal (c. 203, §21A).

Investments.—"Prudent man" rule is standard. No statutory provision regulates kinds of investments which trustees or other fiduciaries may make. Trust funds may be invested in participations in common trust fund created and administered by corporate fiduciary unless trust instrument or decree otherwise provides. (c. 203A, §§1, 2). Investments in mutual funds are not forbidden on ground of delegation. Fiduciaries may, if governing instrument permits, invest in certain investment funds holding U.S. government obligations. See c. 167G, §3(8). Any association or corporation authorized to do banking business and to exercise trust powers in commonwealth may invest funds which it holds in fiduciary capacity in any collective investment fund or common trust fund established by any affiliate of such association or corporation as defined in c. 167A, §1(e); and any such association or corporation may invest in any collective investment fund or common trust fund established by it pursuant to provisions of c. 167G or c. 203A funds held by any such affiliate in fiduciary capacity; provided that any such investment is not prohibited by any instrument, judgment, decree or order creating such fiduciary relationship. (c. 167G, §3[10A]).

Securities in Name of Nominee.—Any fiduciary, acting directly or through agent or custodian, may, under certain circumstances, register trust securities in name of partnership or corporate nominee even though trust instrument does not contain such authority. (c. 203, §14B).

Accumulations.—No statutory prohibition. Trustee may accumulate trust income for period equal to rule against perpetuities; in charitable trust, accumulation may be for any period which is not deemed unreasonable. (296 Mass. 298, 5 N.E.2d 550).

Accounting.—Testamentary trustee is obligated to render periodic accounts. Procedure for allowance is governed by c. 206, §24, Mass. R. Civ. P. 72, Unif. Prob. Ct. Prac. XV and XVI. Court may waive appointment of guardian ad litem if nonaccounting co-fiduciary adequately represents interests of persons whose interests would otherwise require such appointment. (Unif. Prob. Ct. Prac. XVIA). Inter vivos trustee may be required to account by any beneficiary. (352 Mass. 194, 224 N.E.2d 417).

Disclaimer.—See topic Wills, subhead Disclaimer.

Perpetuities.—See category Property, topic Perpetuities.

Judicial Termination.—Upon petition by trustee, any interested person or personal representative of decedent's estate, court may consolidate or terminate trust where costs of administration are such that continuation or establishment of trust would defeat or substantially impair its purposes. Distribution order shall specify shares in which both income and remainder beneficiaries may take except that marital trust shall be distributed only to surviving spouse. (c. 203, §25). Trust may be terminated if purpose fulfilled. (38 Mass. App. Ct. 308, 647 N.E.2d 722).

Uniform Common Trust Fund Act adopted. (c. 203A).

Uniform Testamentary Additions to Trusts Act adopted. (c. 203, §3B).

Uniform Principal and Income Act not adopted.

Uniform Prudent Investor Act.—Massachusetts is considering adopting some variation thereof.

Uniform Fiduciaries Act not adopted.

Uniform Simplification of Fiduciary Security Transfers Act not adopted.

WILLS:

Only person 18 years or more and of sound mind may make will. (c. 191, §1).

Testamentary disposition is not restricted as to amount which may be given to religious, charitable, etc., institutions except for spouse's right to elect statutory share (see infra, subhead Election).

Person over 18 may make gift of all or part of his body to take effect upon or prior to his death. Uniform Anatomical Gift Act (1968 Act) adopted. (c. 113, §§7-13).

Execution.—Will must be in writing, signed by testator (signature by cross alone suffices) or some person in his presence and by his express direction, and attested and subscribed in his presence by two or more competent witnesses. (c. 191, §1).

Any person of sufficient understanding is competent witness. (c. 191, §2). See infra, subhead Testamentary Gifts to Subscribing Witnesses.

Will executed in conformity with law at time of execution or (provided it is in writing and subscribed by testator) according to law of place of execution or of testator's domicile is valid. (c.191, §§4, 5).

Attestation Clause.—(c. 192, §2). I, the undersigned testator, do hereby declare that I sign (or direct another to sign for me) and execute this instrument as my last will, that I sign it willingly (or willingly direct another to sign for me) in the presence of each of said witnesses, and that I execute it as my free and voluntary act for the purposes herein expressed.

_____
Testator

We, the undersigned witnesses, each do hereby declare in the presence of the aforesaid testator that the testator signed (or directed another to sign for him and said person signed for him) and executed this instrument as his last will in the presence of each of us, that he signed it willingly (or willingly directed another to sign it for him), that each of us hereby signs this will as witness in the presence of the testator, and that to the best

See note at head of Digest as to 1998 legislation covered.

See Topical Index in front part of this volume.

WILLS ... *continued*
of our knowledge the testator is eighteen (18) years of age or over, of sound mind, and under no constraint or undue influence.

_____
Witness
_____
Witness

STATE OF _____
COUNTY OF _____
Subscribed, sworn to and acknowledged before me by the said testator and witnesses this ___ day of _____ A.D.

(Signed) _____
(Seal) _____
Official Capacity

See *infra*, subhead Probate.

Holographic wills are not recognized.

Nuncupative Wills.—Soldier in actual service or mariner at sea may make nuncupative will of personal property. (c. 191, §6).

Revocation.—Will can be revoked only by burning, tearing, canceling or obliterating with intent to revoke by testator or some person in his presence and at his direction; by some other writing executed as required for will; or by subsequent changes in testator's condition or circumstances from which revocation is implied by law. (c. 191, §8). Marriage operates as revocation unless will, itself, shows it was made in contemplation thereof, except so far as it exercises power of appointment which, in absence of such exercise, would not pass to heirs at law in case of intestacy. Unless will provides otherwise, purported disposition or appointment of property made by will of testator dying on or after Jan. 1, 1978 to former spouse is revoked by testator's divorce or annulment of marriage and property passes as if former spouse predeceased testator; provisions conferring powers of appointment or nominating spouse as fiduciary are likewise revoked. Provisions not applicable to will made under c. 191B Uniform Statutory Will Act—unless will otherwise provides. (c. 191, §9).

Revival.—Remarriage to former spouse revives provisions revoked solely by divorce or annulment. (c. 191, §9).

Testamentary Gifts to Subscribing Witnesses.—Beneficial devise or legacy in will of testator to subscribing witness or to husband or wife of such witness is void unless two other subscribing witnesses not similarly benefited thereunder. (c. 191, §2). See *supra*, subhead Execution.

Bequests and Devises to Inter Vivos Trusts.—Uniform Testamentary Additions to Trusts Act adopted. (c. 203, §3B). Trust may be amended after the execution of the will or the death of testator. (Id.; 341 Mass. 366, 170 N.E. 2d 350). See also topic Trusts, subhead Revocable Trusts.

Probate.—During testator's life, will may be deposited with register of probate. (c. 191, §10). Any person, other than register, having custody of will must deliver it within 30 days after notice of testator's death to court or executors named therein who must so deliver it. One neglecting without reasonable cause to deliver will after citation to do so may be committed to jail. (c. 191, §13). Person suspected of concealing will may be examined by court upon complaint of interested party. (c. 191, §14).

Probate Court for each county has jurisdiction over estates of persons who, at time of their death, resided in that county; as to nonresidents, Probate Court of any county where assets are located has jurisdiction. (c. 215, §3). See category Civil Actions and Procedure, topic Practice.

Allowance of will is secured by filing will in Probate Court, together with petition on required form, to which is annexed affidavit by at least one petitioner that statements therein made are true to best of his knowledge and belief and must be accompanied by certified copy of decedent's death certificate issued by public officer. (c. 192, §1). Notice must be given to surviving husband or wife and all heirs or next of kin (if none, to attorney general [c. 192, §1A]) and, in practice, to legatees and devisees, either by personal service or by publication and mailing. Petition for probate must state whether or not surviving husband or wife of deceased is under disability. If it appears by written consent of heirs or by satisfactory evidence that no person intends to object to probate, court may grant probate: (1) On testimony of one subscribing witness; affidavit of such witness taken before register may be received as evidence; (2) with respect to will executed or republished on or after Jan. 1, 1978, without testimony if self proved by affidavits of testator and witnesses in form prescribed by statute and made under seal and before officer authorized to administer oaths under laws of state where executed; (3) without testimony if executed, attested and made self-proved by affidavits of testator and witnesses (see subhead Attestation Clause, *supra*), each made under seal and before officer authorized to administer oaths under laws of state where executed; or (4) without testimony if assented to in writing by widow or husband of deceased and by all heirs at law and next of kin. (c. 192, §2). If on return day of citation issued upon petition anyone has entered appearance in opposition, question of allowance of will is set down for hearing at future date. Appeal must be claimed and filed within 30 days after entry of decree appealed from. (c. 215, §9).

Decree allowing will or compromise of will or adjudicating intestacy is, after one year from its rendition or final establishment, conclusive in favor of purchasers for value in good faith, without notice, from executors, administrators, guardians, conservators, legatees, heirs and devisees; in favor of executors, administrators, trustees, guardians and conservators who have settled their accounts in due form and in good faith disposed of assets according to law; and in favor of persons who have in good faith made payments to executors, administrators, trustees, guardians and conservators. But if subsequent decree reverses or qualifies original decree, heirs, distributees, devisees and legatees are held liable for any proceeds or assets of estate received by them. (c. 192, §3). Adjudication of fact of death is not conclusive. (c. 192, §3).

Register of probate may issue certificate of appointment to voluntary administrator or voluntary executor after payment of proper fee. (c. 195, §§16-16A). (See also topic Executors and Administrators.)

New form for simultaneous execution and attestation of will adopted. (c. 192, §2). See *supra*, subhead Attestation Clause.

Self-proved Wills.—See *supra*, subheads Probate, Attestation Clause.

Contest ordinarily must be in probate proceedings rather than by attack on will after probate.

Legacies may be recovered by bill in equity. (c. 197, §19). Interest is payable, unless otherwise provided in will, from date of expiration of period within which creditors may bring actions against executor or administrator or six months from date upon which distribution is required by trust instrument; rate of interest shall be set by SJC rules, but in absence of such rules, rate is 4%. (c. 197, §20).

Real estate of testator shall not be liable to be sold for payment of legacy by executor either under power in will or under license or order of court in such proceeding unless proceeding is filed in Probate Court within six years from testator's death. (c. 197, §19). There is different time period for legatee to bring action to recover legacy for which testator's real estate may be used for payment if testator died prior to 1972. (1972, c. 750, §1).

Unclaimed Legacies.—See category Property, topic Absentees, subhead Escheat.

Disclaimer.—See generally c. 191A. All citations in this subhead refer to said chapter.

Interests Disclaimable.—Beneficiary may disclaim any legal or equitable interest or estate, present, future or contingent, in real or personal property, any fractional share thereof, any power to appoint, consume, apply or expend property or any right, power or privilege thereto which would otherwise pass to disclaiming party by intestate succession, devise, legacy, bequest, by exercise or non-exercise of power of appointment, as beneficiary of trust or annuity or insurance contract, as surviving joint tenant or tenant by entirety (except as to portion allocable to his contributions), under any deed, assignment, or other inter-vivos conveyance or transfer, or in any other manner. (§§1, 2).

Procedure.—After creation of interest disclaimed, but not more than nine months after event determining final ascertainment of beneficiary and that interest is indefeasibly vested, clear and unequivocal signed written disclaimer should be filed with probate court or courts wherein fiduciary having control of property is required to account. Copy of disclaimer shall be delivered to person or entity having possession of disclaimed property. (§§3-5).

Disclaimers of interests in real property must be acknowledged as provided for deeds of realty and should be filed with appropriate registry of deeds or registry district. (§5).

Effect.—Disclaimed interests never vest in beneficiary. Disclaimers are effective according to their terms, irrespective of spendthrift restrictions or similar restraints imposed by any instrument, statute or rule of law, and are irrevocable. (§§7, 9).

Bars to Right to Disclaim.—Assignment, conveyance, encumbrance, pledge or other transfer or disposition of interest by beneficiary, or any contract therefor, or judicial disposition or sale before disclaimer; insolvency of beneficiary; signed written waiver of right to disclaim; and acceptance of interest will bar right to disclaim. (§8).

Devises.—On probate in Massachusetts of will devising Massachusetts real estate, whether resident or nonresident testator, title vests in devisees as of date of testator's death, subject to right of executor or administrator c. t. a. to sell or mortgage for payment of debts, taxes, administration expenses, etc., if applicable personal property of estate is insufficient. (c. 202, §§1, 28).

Lapses.—If issue of child or relation dying before testator survives testator, such issue takes same devise or legacy as such child or relation unless contrary intention is shown by will. "Child" and "issue" and "relation" include adopted children. Foregoing applies to class gifts whether death occurred before or after execution of will. (c. 191, §22).

Children.—Child or issue of deceased child not provided for by will or in testator's lifetime, whether born during testator's lifetime or after his death, is entitled to same share as in case of intestacy unless omission appears to have been intentional or testator provided for child during life time. Omitted child or issue may not share in testator's real property unless claim is filed in registry of probate within one year after date of approval of executor's bond. (c. 191, §20).

Guardian ad litem must be appointed to represent certain omitted heirs under disability.

Election.—Surviving spouse (except if deceased spouse had been deserted or was living apart for justifiable cause as established by decree of court) may, within six months after probate (or if validity of will is litigated, may, with consent of court on timely petition, within six months after termination of litigation) file in registry of probate written waiver of will's provisions and then (a) if testator leaves issue, surviving spouse is entitled to one third personal and real property; (b) if testator leaves kindred but no issue, surviving spouse is entitled to $25,000 and one half of remaining personal and real property, but in either case, (a) or (b), if elective share exceeds $25,000, surviving spouse takes $25,000 and income only for life from excess over that amount, personal property to be held in trust and real property to be vested in him or her for life; or (c) if testator leaves no issue or kindred, surviving spouse is entitled to $25,000 and one half remaining personal property and one half remaining real property, absolutely. (c. 191, §15). For these purposes, property may include assets of testator's revocable inter vivos trust. (390 Mass. 864, 460 N.E.2d 572).

Dower.—Surviving spouse not entitled to dower in addition to taking under provisions of will unless will shows contrary intention. (c. 191, §17).

Foreign Executed Wills.—See *supra*, subhead Execution.

Foreign Probated Wills.—Will allowed elsewhere may be allowed by probate court in any county where any property on which such will may operate exists upon production of copy of will and of probate thereof duly authenticated; will which by laws of place where made is valid without probate may be allowed upon production of copy of will or official record thereof duly authenticated. Affidavit stating names and residences of known heirs and next of kin of testator living at his death and their relationship to

WILLS . . . *continued*
testator must be presented. Notice of presentation for probate must be given by publication. (c. 192, §9). See also topic Executors and Administrators, subheads Foreign Executors or Administrators and Ancillary Administration.

Effect of Will.—Every devise carries all testator's interest in land unless contrary intention appears. (c. 191, §18). Will operates on all property possessed by testator at his death unless contrary intention appears (c. 191, §19) and may pass right of entry in case of disseisin (c. 191, §24).

Powers of Appointment.—c. 204, §§27-33 provide that, unless instrument creating power provides otherwise, power may be released in manner set forth in statute. Disclaimers of powers of appointment are treated in c. 191A. See supra, subhead Disclaimer. General residuary clause will not exercise power of appointment unless reference is made to powers of appointment or there is some other indication of intention to exercise power. (c. 191, §1A). Unless instrument creating power manifests contrary intent, power may be exercised to create less than absolute legal and equitable interests, including new powers of appointment. (c. 191, §1B).

Guardian ad Litem.—Appointment by court to represent interests of unborn or unascertained persons may be avoided by testamentary provision nominating person to represent such interests or requesting that such representation be dispensed with. (c. 206, §24).

See also category Family, topic Guardian and Ward.

Doctrine of Worthier Title.—Abolished. (c. 184, §33A).

Simultaneous Death.—See topic Death, subhead Survivorship.

Testamentary Guardian.—See category Family, topic Guardian and Ward, subhead Eligibility and Competency.

Uniform Anatomical Gift Act adopted. (c. 113, §§7-13). Lifetime gift of organs or tissue permitted if properly authorized.

Uniform Statutory Will Act adopted. (c. 191B).

Living Wills.—No legislation.

Health Care Proxy.—Every competent adult over age of 18 and of sound mind may appoint health care agent by executing health care proxy. Proxy must be in writing and signed by maker, or at his direction, in presence of two adult witnesses who must sign document. Appointed health care agent cannot act as witness. Health care proxy is presumed to be valid unless court determines otherwise. (c. 201D, §2). Probate Court has exclusion jurisdiction of all actions concerning health care proxies. (c. 215, §3). Valid foreign proxies are enforceable in Massachusetts. (c. 201D, §11).

Health care proxy shall identify principal and health care agent, indicate that principal intends agent to have authority to make health care decisions for principal, describe any limitations on agent's authority, and indicate that agent's authority shall become effective when it is determined that principal lacks capacity to make health care decisions. (c. 201D, §4). Determination of principal's capacity is to be made by attending physician according to accepted medical standards and must be in writing. (c. 201D, §6).

Agent has authority to make all health care decisions for principal including decisions about life-sustaining treatment, subject to any limitations in proxy. In making health care decisions, agent must consider medical alternatives and prognosis, principal's wishes if known, including his moral and religious beliefs, and if unknown, agent must act in principal's best interest. Health care providers must act according to agent's decision subject to any limitations in proxy, court order (c. 201D, §5), any objections by principal (c. 201D, §6), or physician's or health care facility's objections pursuant to c. 201D, §§14 and 15. However, health care proxy cannot permit suicide or mercy killing. (c. 201D, §12).

Health care proxy may be revoked by notifying agent or health care provider orally or in writing or by any other act evidencing specific intent to revoke. Proxy is automatically revoked upon execution of new proxy or divorce of principal if spouse is agent. Revocation must be recorded in principal's medical records. (c. 201D, §7).

Neither health care provider nor agent can be subject to criminal or civil liability if he acted in good faith while fulfilling his duty according to proxy. (c. 201D, §8).

If health care proxy has not been executed, health care provider may rely on informed consent of responsible parties acting on behalf of incompetent patient to extent permitted by law. Powers of attorney executed before this chapter was enacted Dec. 19, 1990 are valid to allow agent to make health care decisions for principal. (c. 201D, §16).

FAMILY

ADOPTION:

See generally c. 210; all citations, unless otherwise indicated, refer to said chapter. See also c. 119, §26(4), as amended effective Jan. 29, 1993, for authority of District and Juvenile Courts to terminate parental right to consent to adoption if in best interest of child based upon certain factors.

A person of full age (his spouse, joining) may (subject to certain exceptions) petition probate court in county where he (or if nonresident, where child) resides for leave to adopt as his child another person younger than himself (other than petitioner's spouse, brother, sister, aunt or uncle of whole or half blood). Minors may petition (or join spouse petition) for adoption of natural child of one of parties. (§1). Spouse must join petition for adoption. (§5A).

In any petition for adoption department of social services shall submit to court for verification that child is not registered with federal register for missing children and Massachusetts central register. (§5A).

Adoptive parents may sue for "wrongful adoption" based on misrepresentations made by adoption agency about child's pre-adoptive history. (421 Mass. 147, 653 N.E.2d 1104).

Consent Required.—Decree for adoption requires, inter alia, written consent of child if over 12; of child's spouse, if any; of lawful parents, may be previous adoptive parents, or surviving parent; or of mother alone if child born out of wedlock and not previously adopted. Such written consent may be executed no sooner than fourth day after birth of child to be adopted. It must be attested and subscribed before notary public in presence of two competent witnesses, one of whom must be selected by consenting person. Form of consent is set forth. Any consent or surrender outside commonwealth is valid if in accord with laws of state or country where executed. (§2).

Consent Not Required.—When petition for adoption filed by person having care and custody of child, Court may dispense with necessity of consent of persons named in §2 (other than child) if: (i) person to be adopted is at least 18 years old; or (ii) Court finds that allowance of petition for adoption is in best interest of child. Department of social services or any licensed child care agency may commence proceeding to dispense with need for consent to adoption of child in care or custody of such department or agency. (§3[a] and [b]). (On "care or custody" see c. 210, §3[b]; 25 Mass. App. Ct. 579, 521 N.E.2d 399.) If Department has only temporary custody of child, foster parents have standing to file adoption petition without consent of natural parents. (416 Mass. 791, 625 N.E.2d 1362). Such petition may be heard notwithstanding pendency of petition brought under c. 119 or c. 201 regarding same child. Justice may be assigned to hear simultaneous petitions regarding same child. If petition contested, court shall appoint counsel to represent child. (391 Mass. 572, 463 N.E.2d 324; §3[a] and [b]). To dispense with parental consent, court must find clear and convincing evidence parent currently unfit to further best interests of child. (414 Mass. 705, 610 N.E.2d 898). Some hearsay admissible to establish parental fitness provided parent has opportunity for rebuttal. (416 Mass. 510, 623 N.E.2d 1118). Hearsay statements of children under ten concerning sexual abuse may be admitted with certain conditions. (c. 233, §83; 419 Mass. 67, 643 N.E.2d 26). In care and protection proceedings in District and Juvenile Courts, termination of parental right to consent to adoption may be adjudicated if in child's best interest and certain conditions met. (c. 119, §26[4]). Court consideration of termination of parental rights required under certain circumstances with 13 factors to be considered by Court. (c. 210, §3[c]). Court can consider whether parent will correct condition that currently disables parent from furthering best interests of child. (36 Mass. App. Ct. 355, 631 N.E.2d 564). Court shall enter final order of adjudication and permanent disposition no later than 15 months after date case first filed with provisions for up to three month extension. (c. 119, §26[4]). Mass. Uniform Probate Practice X requires agency to submit written report consisting of information on biological parents, summary of agency's history with child, and agency's plan for child. Section Xa provides for tracking system for all termination proceedings brought under §3, including notice requirement and discretion to appoint counsel in contested cases. Notwithstanding mother's surrender of child born out of wedlock (§2) or termination of her right to withhold consent (§3), one adjudicated or timely claiming to be father of child is entitled to notice and right to petition for adoption under specified circumstances (§4A).

Conditions Precedent.—Child under 14 must (subject to waiver by court for cause) have resided with petitioner for at least six months. (§5A). At least one of following conditions must be met in case of child under 14: (1) Child placed with petitioner for adoption by department of social services or by agency authorized by department for such purpose; (2) petitioner blood relative of child being adopted; (3) petitioner stepparent of child being adopted; (4) petitioner nominated in will of deceased natural parent of child as guardian or adoptive parent; or (5) petition approved in writing by department of social services or authorized agency with rights of appeal to probate court in case of refusal to approve petition. (§2A).

Jurisdiction.—Probate Court. (§1). Residence within commonwealth by either child or petitioner. (§1).

Venue.—County where petitioner resides or, if petitioner is nonresident, county where child resides. (§1).

Petition.—Printed form supplied by register of probate.

Proceedings.—On petition for adoption of child under 14, unless sponsored by institution for care of children, notice must be given to department of social services. (§5A). Department shall file report within 30 days of notice unless court, on showing of departmental inability to report caused by circumstances beyond its control, grants up to 30 additional days to complete report. Court may appoint certain charitable corporations to file report after unexplained failure by department to report. (§5A). No decree may be entered until department or appointed corporation files report and until child has resided with petitioner for at least six months. Court may waive these conditions if one of petitioners is parent of child; residence requirement may be waived by court for cause. (§5A). If written consent is not submitted, order of notice is issued to persons who should have consented. (§4). Sworn statement must be filed by petitioners setting forth certain facts pertaining to each of them. (§6). Hearings shall be held in chambers on request, with only necessary parties and witnesses present; if hearing is contested, consent of other parties is required. (§6). In evaluating suitable support, court shall consider assurances by department of social services of adoption subsidy. (§6). See also New Uniform Practices of Probate Courts X, Xa and Xb for requirements as to administrative agency report and plan and as to tracking of adoption petitions and proceedings thereon.

Decree.—Gives child all rights of natural child except as stated under subhead Effect of Adoption. If petitioning adopting parent dies before entry of decree, probate court may enter decree nunc pro tunc to date of filing petition within three months of date of death. Decree has effect of decree of adoption. (§6B).

Name.—Court may decree such change of name as petitioner may request. (§6). Adopting parent may request change in child's birth records. (§6A). If such request has been made, town clerk receiving certificate of adoption must correct record of birth and notify adopting parent of change. Town clerk must, on judicial order or when requested by person seeking his own birth record or by person in proper official capacity, release information contained in original record; if record has been amended following adoption, information in original record may be issued only upon order of Probate Court for county where adoption granted or, if adoption granted outside commonwealth, upon order of court for county in which birth occurred. (c. 46, §13).

Records of Adoption.—All documents and all record books are unavailable for inspection unless court, for cause, otherwise orders. (§5c). Under certain conditions, placement agency shall release non-identifying information about biological parents. (§5D).

See note at head of Digest as to 1998 legislation covered.

See Topical Index in front part of this volume.

MA – 47

ADOPTION . . . *continued*

Out of State Decrees.—Resident parent of child born or adopted outside Massachusetts may present specified documentary evidence of birth or adoption to town clerk where parent was then domiciled for filing as evidence of such birth or adoption. (c. 46, §1B).

Effect of Adoption.—Adopted child inherits from his adopting parent and stands in same position with respect to kindred of such parent (including other adopted children, 291 Mass. 153, 197 N.E. 162) as natural legitimate child thereof. Adoption destroys right of inheritance from natural kindred except, after 1975, when adoption is by new spouse of surviving natural parent who remarries after death of other natural parent. All property of adoptive child passes to adoptive heirs. Court may decree that right of inheritance vests as of date petition filed. (§7). Words "child", "grandchild", "issue", "heir", "heir-at-law" or their respective equivalents in grant, devise or bequest in instrument executed after, but not before, Aug. 26, 1958, shall include adopted person to same extent as if born to adopting parent except where contrary intention appears. (§8). Trust's definition of grandchildren as "children of the body of" settlor's children excluded adopted grandchildren and their issue from trust. (37 Mass. App. Ct. 450, 640 N.E.2d 495).

Person adopted in another state or country in accordance with its laws is, upon proof of such fact, entitled in commonwealth to same rights of succession to property as if he had been adopted in commonwealth. (§9).

Setting Aside Adoption.—Parent who had no personal notice before decree of adoption and who had neither waived notice (§2) nor been subject of decree dispensing with notice (§3) may appeal from decree within one year after actual notice (§11). Adoption may be set aside for fraud or undue influence. (154 Mass. 574, 28 N.E. 1051).

Criteria.—In making orders for adoption, judge must consider need of child for loving and responsible parental care and all factors relevant to physical, mental and moral health of child. If parent of child requests religious designation for child, court may grant petition for adoption only to person of faith designated, unless not in best interest of child. (§5B).

Bringing Children into State for Purpose of Adoption.—Permit through written application accompanied by bond must be obtained before bringing into commonwealth any child for purpose of placing or boarding such child in family or home in commonwealth with view to adoption, guardianship, custody or care by any person other than relative. (c. 119, §36).

ALIMONY:

See topic Divorce.

COMMUNITY PROPERTY:

System does not obtain in Massachusetts.

DESERTION:

See topics Divorce, Husband and Wife.

DISSOLUTION OF MARRIAGE:

See topic Divorce.

DIVORCE:

See generally c. 208. All citations, unless otherwise indicated, refer to said chapter. Uniform Marriage and Divorce Act not adopted; but alimony and division of property are determined under §34, which is similar to Uniform Act, §307, Alternative A.

Grounds for Absolute Divorce.—Divorce may be adjudged for adultery; impotency; utter desertion continued for one year prior to filing of complaint; gross and confirmed habits of intoxication caused by voluntary, excessive use of liquor or drugs; cruel and abusive treatment; gross and cruel failure to support and maintain other spouse; irretrievable breakdown of marriage; sentence to confinement for life or for five years or more in federal penal institution or in penal or reformatory institution in any state; provided, however, that divorce shall be adjudged although both parties have cause, and defense of recrimination is abolished. (§§1, 2). If ground for divorce is irretrievable breakdown in marriage and parties file joint petition, affidavit that is jointly or separately executed and notarized executed separation agreement, divorce nisi shall enter 30 days after court approval of agreement. (§1A as am'd). One party may obtain divorce nisi on ground of irretrievable breakdown after hearing held no sooner than six months after filing of complaint. (§1B as am'd). Six-month waiting period may be waived, at election of court, to permit consolidation of this type of irretrievable breakdown action with opposing party's action under §1. (id.). Corroborating witnesses are not required except where necessary, e.g., in adultery cases where plaintiff does not have personal knowledge; in imprisonment cases where plaintiff was not present in court when defendant was sentenced. (Uniform Practices of Probate Courts, II).

Grounds for Legal Separation.—If spouse fails without justifiable cause to provide suitable support to other spouse or deserts other spouse, or if married person has justifiable cause for living apart, Probate Court may prohibit spouse from imposing any restraint on personal liberty of other and make orders for support of spouse and care and custody of children. (c. 209, §32).

Citizenship Requirements.—None.

Residence Requirements.—See infra, subhead Jurisdiction.

Jurisdiction.—Except as hereafter stated, basis of jurisdiction is marital domicile, and divorce may not be adjudged if parties have never lived together as husband and wife in this commonwealth nor for cause which occurred in another jurisdiction unless prior thereto parties had lived together as husband and wife in commonwealth and one of them lived in commonwealth at time when cause occurred. (c. 208, §4). However, if plaintiff has lived in commonwealth for one year last preceding filing of complaint, if cause occurred without commonwealth, or if plaintiff resides in commonwealth at time of filing and cause occurred within commonwealth, divorce may be adjudged for any cause allowed by law, unless plaintiff moved into commonwealth for purpose of obtaining divorce. (§5).

Venue.—Actions for divorce must be brought in Probate Court for county in which one party lives, except that if either party still resides in county where parties last lived together, action must be brought in that county; but, in event of hardship, court may transfer action to county where affected party resides. (§6).

Process.—Governed by Mass. R. Dom. Rel. P., Rule 4. Process shall be served by sheriff, deputy sheriff or by any other disinterested person; or, if outside commonwealth, by any individual permitted to make service under Massachusetts law or under law of place where service is to be made. Summons and complaint must be served together, and defendant may accept service by written endorsement of notarized acceptance of service on summons. If service is not so accepted service shall be made upon individual by delivering copy of summons and complaint to him personally, except for paternity contempt or modification complaints where service can be made by personal delivery or by leaving copy at defendant's last and usual place of abode and by mailing copies to defendant. If personal service cannot be made, then service may be made by publication once each week for three successive weeks in newspaper designated by register of court and by mailing. Proof of service shall be made to court promptly (within time during which defendant must respond, 20 days). (Rule 4[d]).

Pleading.—Rules 7-11, Mass. R. Dom. Rel. P. govern pleadings and appearances in actions for divorce. In addition, Probate Court Rules, Supplemental Rules and Uniform Practices of Probate Courts must be consulted with regard to special areas of pleading, especially where adultery or any other allegation derogatory to character or reputation of third person is alleged in pleading. In that event rules require certain preliminary procedures before name of third party may be disclosed on public record (see Supplemental Rule 404); and notice must be given to third party, who is then entitled to appear in action (Supplemental Rule 405). If plaintiff is seeking conveyance of real estate as part of divorce judgment, complaint should include specific demand therefor; otherwise affidavit of notice and proof of receipt by defendant must be filed at least seven days before hearing of case. (Uniform Practice XIV). If either party wishes to have stenographer appointed to take testimony, written request must be filed at least 48 hours before trial. (Probate Court Rule 18).

Practice.—Matrimonial actions are subject to Mass. R. Dom. Rel. P. and to Supplemental Rules, Uniform Practices of Probate Courts and Probate Court Rules. Temporary orders, e.g. support, vacate marital home, are generally subject to seven days' notice requirement. (Mass. R. Dom. Rel. P. 6). Within 45 days of receipt of summons where financial relief requested, parties must file with court and deliver to each other financial statements using prescribed forms. (Supplemental Rule 401). Interrogatories may be filed, but Probate Rule 27 requires motion that they be ordered answered. Spouse may be ordered to vacate marital home for up to 90 days (which may be extended) on finding that health, safety or welfare of moving party (or of any minor children) would be endangered or substantially impaired by failure to enter such order. (§34B). During pendency of divorce, court may appoint attorney to investigate and report to court and may direct that attorney or any other attorney to defend action. (§16).

Discovery.—Interrogatories and requests for production of documents may be served. (Mass. R. Dom. Rel. P. 33, 34). Parties have 30 days to respond, or 45 days if served with summons and complaint. Interrogatories in all sets combined may not exceed 30, including subsidiary interrogatories. (Mass. R. Dom. Rel. P. 33). Depositions may be taken upon seven days notice to parties. (Mass. R. Dom. Rel. P. 30). Attendance of witnesses may be compelled by subpoena. (Mass. R. Dom. Rel. P. 45). Financial statement may be requested upon ten days notice. (Supplemental Rule 401). No further request for financial statement may be made within 90 days of previous request without court order. (Supplemental Rule 401).

Judgment or Decree.—Judgment nisi is granted in first instance, to become absolute without further action by parties in 90 days, unless court otherwise orders for sufficient cause upon application of any interested party. (c. 208, §21, Mass. R. Dom. Rel. P. 58[c]). Nisi period is stayed by filing of appeal, only if claim of appeal is from that portion of judgment nisi that would dissolve marriage. Filing of appeal generally does not stay other aspect of appealed judgment or other order or judgment relative to custody or visitation, alimony, support or maintenance. (Mass. R. Dom. Rel. P. 62[g]). After judgment nisi, action may not be dismissed or discontinued on motion of either party except on such terms as court orders after notice to other party and hearing, unless written agreement to dismissal or discontinuance, signed by both parties, is filed. (§21). Under certain circumstances, judgment for separate support may require one party to make conveyance of land to other, and judgment itself may act to vest title if person fails to comply with order. (c. 209, §32D).

Temporary Alimony.—Under certain circumstances, court may order alimony pendente lite including health benefits. (c. 208, §17).

Allowance for Prosecution of Suit.—Court may require either party to pay into court amount to enable other party to maintain or defend action. (§17; Supplemental Rule 406).

Contempt.—Probate and Family Courts have power to enforce orders and punish contempt under general equity jurisdiction. (c. 215, §34). Rules of Domestic Relations Procedure apply to contempt actions. (c. 215, §34A). Probate Court is empowered to enforce its orders, including jail sentence for failure to comply with support order. (c. 215, §34). Criminal contempt requires finding of ability to pay when due and intentional failure to obey. (380 Mass. 137, 402 N.E.2d 1024). Presumption of entitlement to attorney's fees to plaintiff if contempt found. (c. 215, §34A). Where finding of contempt has been made, involving support or custody order, review of order must take place before jail confinement may be ordered. (c. 215, §34B).

Alimony.—Alimony may be awarded to either party upon or after divorce (c. 208, §34), and court's order remains subject to revision (§37). Temporary alimony may be awarded pending divorce. (§17). In determining amount of alimony court is required to consider specified factors and may consider certain additional factors. Required factors are: length of marriage, conduct of parties during marriage, age, health, station, occupation, amount and sources of income, vocational skills, employability, estate, liabilities

See note at head of Digest as to 1998 legislation covered.

See Topical Index in front part of this volume.

MA – 48

DIVORCE . . . *continued*
and needs of each of parties and opportunity of each for future acquisition of capital assets and income. Discretionary factors are: contribution of each of parties in acquisition, preservation or appreciation in value of their respective estates and contribution of each of parties as homemaker to family unit. If obligor has health insurance, in addition to any alimony, court shall order obligor either to exercise option of additional coverage in favor of spouse, obtain coverage for spouse, or reimburse former spouse for cost of health insurance. (§34).

Alimony improper in absence of finding of financial need. (422 Mass. 477, 664 N.E.2d 10).

Orders for alimony and support may be modified in discretion of probate court when party seeking modification shows change in circumstances. (c. 208, §37; 13 Mass. App. Ct. 189, 431 N.E.2d 591). Although remarriage of spouse receiving alimony does not per se terminate alimony, it makes prima facie case requiring judge to terminate payment in absence of extraordinary circumstances. (420 Mass. 820, 652 N.E.2d 589).

Division of Property of Spouses.—May be ordered in addition to or in lieu of alimony, following application of same factors (see subhead Alimony, supra). (§34). Court shall also consider present and future needs of dependent children. (§34). Court may not assign dependent children interest in marital property. (425 Mass. 693, 682 N.E.2d 865). Property in which one spouse holds title subject to division irrespective of when or how acquired. (372 Mass. 398, 361 N.E.2d 1305). In determining alimony, Court may consider earning potential, but neither professional degree nor increased earning capacity marital asset subject to equitable assignment. (399 Mass. 240, 503 N.E.2d 946). In divorce proceeding court cannot assign separate property of either husband or wife to third party such as minor child. (394 Mass. 749, 477 N.E.2d 402). Court may, however, assign, as property asset, percentage of party's future pension benefits, or allocate percentage of pension benefits attributable to period of marriage if and when they are received. (399 Mass. 754, 506 N.E.2d 879). Court may not delegate to parties equitable distribution of marital estate. (420 Mass. 854, 652 N.E.2d 610).

Change of Wife's Name.—Court granting divorce may allow woman to resume her maiden name or name of former husband. (§23).

Custody of Children.—Provision for care and custody of minor children may be made in proceedings for divorce or for legal separation (§19; c. 209, §37) or after judgment (§28). Absent emergency conditions, abuse or neglect, presumption is that parents share legal custody but not physical custody of minor children. (c. 208, §31). However, statutes do not limit power of court to make any order relative to custody of child if such order is in best interest of child. No presumption in favor of or against shared legal or physical custody at time of trial. (c. 208, §31). Significant consideration must be given to domestic violence in making custody orders. (39 Mass. App. Ct. 29, 653 N.E.2d 195). No court may give visitation rights to parent convicted of first-degree murder of child's other parent unless child consents. (c.c. 208, §28; 209, §37). Court must consider abuse of parent or child as factor contrary to child's best interest. (c. 208, §31A). Court's finding of abuse creates rebuttable presumption that placement with abuser not in child's best interest. (c. 208, §31A). Interstate child custody proceedings governed by c. 209B. Notwithstanding any provision of c. 209B to contrary, no child may be ordered or compelled to appear or attend child custody proceeding in another state when judge, after hearing, finds probable cause to believe that such child may be in jeopardy or exposed to risk of mental or physical harm by return to other state. (c. 209B, §11). Parties filing petition or complaint involving care or custody of child must file affidavit containing list of all other known proceedings involving child including certified copies of pleadings and determination of each proceeding held outside of commonwealth. (Trial Ct. Rules IV, Unif. Rule Req. Disclosure of Pending and Concluded Care or Custody Matters). If obligor has health insurance, court shall order obligor to provide any children with health insurance. (c. 208, §§20, 34).

Allowance for Support of Children.—Allowance for support and education of minor children and for support and education of children between 18 and 21 years of age who live with parent and are principally dependent on parent for support may be made in proceedings for divorce or for legal separation (c. 208, §19; c. 209, §37) or after judgment (c. 208, §28). Court must apply child support guidelines promulgated by Chief Justice when determining child support amount, and use of guidelines creates rebuttable presumption that amount is correct. (c. 208, §28). For children between ages 21 and 23, court may order maintenance, support and education if child is domiciled in home of parent and is principally dependent upon that parent for maintenance due to child's enrollment in educational program up to and including undergraduate college degree. (c. 208, §28; c. 209C, §9; c. 209, §37). Order for child support may be modified even after death of supporting parent. (37 Mass. App. Ct. 322, 640 N.E.2d 476). C. 119A governs enforcement of child support. Division of child support enforcement in department of revenue has enforcement power. (c. 14, §§1, 1A). Illegitimate child is constitutionally entitled to support from biological father between 18 and 21 years of age to same extent as child of divorced parents. (23 Mass. App. Ct. 590, 504 N.E.2d 659). Court has authority to order retroactive support from birth date and provision of health insurance in cases of illegitimacy. (29 Mass. App. Ct. 967, 560 N.E.2d 1288). Department of revenue has broad duties with respect to enforcing child support obligations including locating obligors, establishing paternity, collecting support payments, and enforcing support orders. (c. 119A, §§1-6). Department of revenue empowered to collect information from all commonwealth employers in enforcing child support obligations. (c. 119A, §14). In enforcing child support obligations, Department of revenue may require withholding of pension payments (c. 32, §§11, 19C), notify Registry of Motor Vehicles to prohibit issuance or renewal of license to operate (c. 90, §22), and notify employers to withhold income from obligor paychecks (c. 119A, §12).

Remarriage.—After judgment becomes absolute, parties may remarry. (c. 208, §24). If during lifetime of spouse with whom marriage is in force person enters into subsequent marriage, and such subsequent marriage contract was entered into by one of parties in good faith believing that former spouse was dead or that former marriage had been annulled by divorce or without knowledge of such former marriage, remarried persons shall, after impediment to their marriage has been removed, if they continue to live together as husband and wife in good faith on part of one of them, be held to have legally married from and after removal of such impediment. (c. 207, §§4, 6).

Foreign Divorces.—Divorce adjudged in another state by court having jurisdiction of cause and both parties is valid in Massachusetts, but divorce adjudged in another state is of no effect in Massachusetts if obtained by inhabitant of Massachusetts who goes into another state to obtain divorce for cause occurring in Massachusetts while parties were domiciled there or for cause which would not authorize divorce in Massachusetts. (§39). But see, as to constitutional limits, 334 U.S. 378; 334 U.S. 343.

Enforcement of Foreign Decrees.—Foreign decrees for allowance or alimony may be enforced in Massachusetts. (c. 208, §35).

Uniform Interstate Family Support Act adopted at c. 209D, provides for registration, modification and enforcement of foreign orders for spousal and child support. Statute is similar in most respects to Uniform Act with following noted modifications:

§207(c): Any action brought under former Uniform Reciprocal Enforcement of Support Act and is pending or was decided in Municipal Court Departments may be transferred to probate and family court by following procedures in this subsection;

§§3-307(b)(5) & 3-307(b)(6): substitutes two day notice requirement with five day notice requirement;

§3-310(a): requires commonwealth to establish state information agency under Act.

Separation Agreements.—Private agreements are valid as actions to dispose of property interests and as to provisions for support and maintenance if fair and entered into freely. (c. 208, §1A; 371 Mass. 433, 358 N.E.2d 432).

Separate Support.—Probate Court may after consideration of factors set forth in statute issue order for separate support although petitioner is not living apart from spouse. (c. 209, §32). In case of failure to obey separate support judgment, or to participate in community service program, probate judge may order jail sentence to be served during such hours as will permit person to continue employment. (c. 215, §34). When party unable to make support payment, court may order party to seek employment or to participate in community service or job training program. (c. 215, §34).

Antenuptial Contracts.—See topic Husband and Wife.

Domestic Violence.—Person abused by family or household member or by person in substantive dating relationship may file complaint requesting protection from abuse such as physical harm, fear of serious physical harm, forced sexual relations. (c. 209A, §1). Protection from abuse may include orders to refrain from abuse, to refrain from contacting plaintiff, to vacate household, to remain away from household and workplace, to pay temporary support, to pay monetary compensation and to attend batteror's treatment program. (c. 209A, §3).

Temporary Orders.—If plaintiff demonstrates substantial likelihood of immediate danger of abuse, court may enter temporary relief orders as it deems necessary, without prior notice to defendant. Defendant shall have opportunity for hearing on continuation of temporary orders no later than ten court business days after temporary orders entered. (c. 209A, §4). Upon issuance of temporary order, court must order immediate suspension and surrender of defendant firearms license and surrender of all firearms and ammunition within control, ownership or possession of defendant to law enforcement officers. (c. 209A, §3B).

Powers of Police.—Whenever law officer has reason to believe that family or household member has been abused or is in danger of being abused, such officer shall use all reasonable means to prevent further abuse. (c. 209A, §6). Law officer must notify abused person of rights to file complaint requesting protection from further abuse. (c. 209A, §6).

Stalking is crime. (c. 265, §43). Stalking defined as one who willfully and maliciously engages in knowing pattern of conduct or series of acts over period of time directed at specific person which seriously harms or annoys and makes threat with intent to place person in imminent fear of death or injury. (c. 265, §43[a]). Conduct includes threats made by telephone, mail, e-mail and facsimile. (c. 265, §43[a]).

GUARDIAN AND WARD:

Guardian may be appointed for minor, mentally ill or mentally retarded person; person unable to make or communicate informed decisions due to physical incapacity or illness or spendthrift; conservator may be appointed for person unable to care for property by reason of advanced age, mental weakness, mental retardation or physical incapacity. See generally c. 201. All citations, unless otherwise indicated, refer to said chapter.

Probate Court of county where ward resides or, if ward is nonresident, has property has jurisdiction over guardianship matters. (§1). Mentally retarded person is someone who is substantially limited in ability to learn or adapt, which limitations have resulted from inadequately developed or impaired intelligence. (§1).

Selection of Guardian.—Court may nominate and appoint guardian for minor under 14; minor over 14 may nominate guardian for appointment on approval of court. (§2). Father or mother by will may appoint guardian for minor child and such appointment shall be effective when guardian accepts appointment by filing bond in acceptable form. (§3). Special provisions apply to appointment of charitable organizations as guardians of minors.

Eligibility and Competency.—No special requirements. Court has power to determine whether guardian is fit person for guardianship. Nonresident is entitled to act as guardian and may be nominated as guardian in will. (§§30-31). Court is not free to substitute its own selection for that of petitioner without affirmative reasons, stated with particularity. (14 Mass. App. 685, 442 N.E.2d 421). Notice requirements of hearings in Probate Ct. R. 29b.

Appointment of Guardian.—Guardian is appointed by decree of Probate Court. Temporary guardian may be appointed without notice if court satisfied of emergency. (§14). Procedures for appointment differ depending on whether ward is minor, mentally retarded, mentally ill, or physically incapacitated. (§§2, 6-6B). Criminal offender record check required on persons 18 years or older residing in foster home before child may be placed in such home, except that in emergency placement check must be made within ten days of placement. (c. 28A, §10A). Physician's certificate must be filed to obtain appointment of guardian, except for minors. Examination must be within 30 days prior to entry of each decree, temporary or permanent. (Unif. Prob. Ct. Prac. XXII). Clinical

See note at head of Digest as to 1998 legislation covered.

See Topical Index in front part of this volume.

MA – 49

GUARDIAN AND WARD . . . *continued*
team report required in guardianships and conservatorships of mentally retarded; report must be dated and examinations must be within 180 days prior to filing of each petition, temporary or permanent. Requirement may be waived. (Unif. Prob. Ct. Prac. XXII[a]).

Any judge of Probate Court may appoint guardian ad litem to institute contempt proceedings against persons who fail to obey decrees of probate court involving care, custody or maintenance of minor children, and such guardian may personally serve any citation or capias throughout commonwealth. (c. 215, §56B).

Entry fee for petition of appointment, $50 plus $10 surcharge (except where petitioner certifies that ward's estate does not exceed $100, in which case there is no entry fee). (c. 262, §40).

Qualification.—Guardian must give bond in sum ordered by court; such bond must be with sureties except where testamentary guardian exempted by will. (c. 205, §§1, 5). Bond may be increased or decreased by court as value of assets increases or decreases. No oath is required.

Inventory.—Guardian must file inventory. (c. 205, §1).

Powers and Duties.—Guardian cares for and manages estate: collecting assets, paying debts, applying so much of estate as needed for maintenance and support of ward and family and representing him in actions where no guardian ad litem or next friend appointed. (§§37-43A; see also c. 202, §§21-26). Conservator has similar powers over ward's property.

Guardians of minors have custody of person of ward and care of ward's education, except that surviving parents shall have such care and custody unless court otherwise orders. Marriage of minor ends guardian's custody of person but not property of ward. (§5). Guardian of mentally ill, mentally retarded person or spendthrift has care and custody of person of ward. (§12). See infra under subhead Mentally Ill. Conservators have no custody over person.

Estate Planning.—Guardian shall have custody of all wills, codicils and other testamentary instruments executed by his ward. Probate Court may, after notice, authorize conservator or guardian (other than of minor) to take action or apply funds to minimize taxes and to provide for gifts to charities, relatives and friends. Such action may include (but is not limited to) release of certain interests, execution of revocable or irrevocable trusts extending beyond ward's lifetime, exercise of option to change beneficiaries of insurance policies, execution of disclaimers or renunciations, etc. Gifts may be made to prospective legatees, devisees or heirs apparent of ward or may be made to individuals or charities in which ward is believed to have interest. If ward's intentions cannot be ascertained, he will be presumed to favor reduction in taxes and partial distribution of his estate as provided. Guardian not required to include as beneficiary any person whom he has reason to believe would be excluded by ward. Order is effective for 12-month period. Similar applications may be made in subsequent years. (§38).

Investments.—Court may authorize guardian to purchase life insurance or annuities for ward with funds from estate. (§47A). See category Estates and Trusts, topic Trusts.

Real Estate.—License from Probate Court is required for sale of real estate. (§§37, 38; see also c. 202, §§21-26, 36-38). If notice includes publication at such times and in such newspapers as court orders, and no appearance entered against sale, price at which sale is licensed is conclusively presumed to be highest possible. (c. 202, §38).

Liabilities of Guardian.—Conservator or guardian subject to individual liability if fails to reveal representative capacity and identify estate, or if tort arises from administration of estate and conservator or guardian personally at fault. (c. 202, §37).

Accounts.—Annual accounts provided for unless excused by court. (c. 206, §1).

Termination of Guardianship.—Guardianship terminates on death of ward or death, resignation or removal of guardian. Guardianship of minor terminates when ward reaches 18. (§4). Guardianship of mentally ill or mentally retarded person or spendthrift may be terminated through petition to Probate Court that guardianship is no longer necessary. (§§13, 13A).

Mentally Ill.—Parent, two relatives or friends of mentally ill or mentally retarded person, any agency within executive offices of human services or educational affairs, or certain nonprofit organizations may petition Probate Court to appoint guardian. (§§6, 6A). Notice to allegedly mentally ill or mentally retarded person, his presumptive heirs, department of mental retardation, and, if interested, U.S. Veterans Bureau is required. (§7). Guardian of mentally ill person can be appointed, after hearing, on finding that he is incapable of caring for himself by reason of mental illness. (§6; 375 Mass. 394; 378 N.E.2d 951). Guardian may be appointed for mentally retarded person who can handle some but not all of his own affairs (7 Mass. App. 56; 385 N.E.2d 1024) but who is incapable of making informed decisions concerning his personal and financial affairs (§6A). Guardian or temporary guardian of mentally ill or mentally retarded person has no authority to commit ward to mental health or mental retardation facility unless, after hearing, court finds that same to be in best interests of ward and specifically authorizes such commitment (§§6, 6A, 14), after finding, beyond reasonable doubt that there is likelihood of serious harm to ward (377 Mass. 272; 385 N.E.2d 995). Special provisions apply to appointment of temporary guardian of mentally ill or mentally retarded person and authority of such temporary guardian to commit ward to mental health facility. (§14). Guardian has custody of person of ward, except married person (§24) and management of his estate and must give bond (§12).

Prior judicial approval is required before guardian may consent to administering or withholding of proposed extraordinary medical treatment. (385 Mass. 555, 432 N.E.2d 712). Absent emergency situation, committed mental patient must have been adjudicated incompetent, guardian appointed, and substituted judgment treatment decision made by judge before patient/ward can be forcibly medicated with antipsychotic drugs. (390 Mass. 489, 458 N.E.2d 308). Order approving treatment plan (after notice and hearing) should provide for periodic review and guardian should monitor treatment for substantial changes in ward's condition and circumstances warranting modification. (Id.). Special provisions apply to authority of guardian to consent to treatment with antipsychotic medication. (§§6, 6A, 14).

Foreign Guardians.—Foreign-appointed guardian producing transcript showing appointment and showing giving of bond and security double value of nonresident ward's property is entitled to receive from probate court of county in which ward's Massachusetts estate is situated letters of guardianship. (§30). Foreign appointed guardian or conservator may represent interests of foreign ward in any Massachusetts proceedings to determine rights in real or personal property in Massachusetts if no local guardian or conservator has been appointed. (c. 199A, §10). Person indebted to or in possession of property belonging to foreign ward may pay debt or deliver property to foreign guardian or conservator upon receipt of proof of appointment and affidavit and payment or delivery made in good faith upon such proof of authority and appointment releases debtor or person in possession as if payment made to local guardian or conservator. (c. 199A, §§2, 3). Nonresident individual is elegible for appointment as guardian, but nonresident guardian must appoint resident agent. (c. 195, §§8-10). As to foreign banks acting as guardians, see category Business Regulation and Commerce, topic Banks and Banking.

Armed Services Personnel Missing in Action or Prisoner of War.—Probate Court may, upon petition of relative or friend, appoint conservator of property of member of armed services who is missing in action or prisoner of war. (§16A). Conservator must give bond. (§19).

Persons Unable to Care for Property.—If person by reason of mental weakness or physical incapacity is unable properly to care for his property, Probate Court may, on his petition or, in first instance, that of friend, after notice to him, his heirs presumptive and, if interested, U.S. veterans' bureau and hearing, appoint conservator to have charge and management of his property subject to direction of court. (§§16, 17). Parent, two relatives or friends of mentally retarded person, certain nonprofit organizations or any agency within office of human services may petition Probate Court to appoint conservator. (§16B). Special provisions apply, in certain instances, to power of conservator of mentally retarded person. (§16B). Conservator has management of estate of ward and all laws relative to jurisdiction of probate court over estate of mentally ill persons under guardianship are applicable to estate of person under conservatorship. (§20). Temporary conservator may be appointed for person who by reason of mental weakness or physical incapacity is unable to care properly for his property if court finds that welfare of such person requires immediate appointment of temporary conservator. No separate petition is necessary for appointment of temporary conservator and all procedures incident to equitable proceedings and relief prior to final decree are applicable. (§21). Conservatorship may, upon petition, be discharged by court when it is no longer necessary. (§18).

Spendthrifts.—On petition of relative or department of public welfare, Probate Court may, after notice to alleged spendthrift and hearing, adjudge as spendthrift person who by drinking, gaming, idleness or debauchery so spends his estate as to expose himself or family to want and may appoint guardian. (§§8, 9).

Health Care Proxy.—See category Estates and Trusts, topic Wills.

Gifts to Minors.—See topic Infants.

Uniform Durable Power of Attorney Act adopted 1981 as c. 201B.

Uniform Fiduciaries Act not adopted.

Uniform Simplification of Fiduciary Security Transfers Act not adopted.

HUSBAND AND WIFE:

Married person coming from another state or country into this commonwealth has all rights, powers and obligations given to married persons by laws of this commonwealth. (c. 209, §28). Such person retains all property theretofore acquired under laws of another state or country, but future rights and liabilities are governed by laws of commonwealth. (c. 209, §29).

Disabilities of Married Women.—All disabilities of married women other than those hereinafter expressly mentioned have been removed.

Separate Property.—Real and personal property of any person upon marriage remain that person's separate property, and married person may receive, receipt for, hold, manage and dispose of property, real or personal, as if such person were sole. (c. 209, §1). Transfers of real and personal property between husband and wife are valid as if they were sole. (c. 209, §3). Work and labor performed by wife for persons other than husband and children is presumed to be for her separate account. (c. 209, §4).

Surname of Married Woman.—Wife may not be required to use husband's surname for purposes of voting records or any other records involving personal identification, including application for credit, provided that wife is generally known by surname other than husband's. (c. 151B, §4, cl. 15). Either party to marriage may adopt any surname. (c. 46, §1D).

Contracts.—Wife may contract in same manner as if she were sole and may contract with husband. (c. 209, §2). Wife may act as fiduciary and bind herself and estate which she represents without any act or assent of husband. (c. 209, §5). Either spouse may become liable as endorser on bill or note made by other as surety for other. (124 Mass. 108). Bill or note made by either, valid at its inception, is not extinguished by passing into hands of other. (209 Mass. 193, 95 N.E. 297).

Actions.—Married woman may sue or be sued without joinder of husband; one spouse can sue other in connection with contracts. (c. 209, §6). Common law doctrine of spousal immunity scaled back. Interspousal cases allowed for motor vehicle accidents (370 Mass. 619, 351 N.E.2d 526) and negligence in maintenance of real estate (381 Mass. 231, 409 N.E.2d 717).

Agency.—Either spouse may act as agent or attorney for other. (315 Mass. 199; 51 N.E.2d 965).

Conveyance or Encumbrance of Property.—Either spouse may convey individually. (c. 209, §1).

Desertion and Nonsupport.—Criminal proceedings may be brought against husband or wife who without just cause deserts or unreasonably fails to support spouse or minor child (c. 273, §1 et seq. as am'd 1995, c. 5, §§97, 98) and orders for support frequently have been given in such proceedings. See also infra, subhead Legal Separation, and topic Divorce; category Property, topic Absentees.

Uniform Reciprocal Enforcement of Support Act repealed. (1995, c. 5, §105).

See note at head of Digest as to 1998 legislation covered.

See Topical Index in front part of this volume.

MA – 50

HUSBAND AND WIFE . . . *continued*

Uniform Interstate Family Support Act adopted. (c. 209D; 1995, c. 5, §87).

Community property system is not observed in Massachusetts.

Antenuptial contracts designating certain property to remain or become that of husband or wife are void except as between parties, heirs and personal representatives unless recorded before, or within 90 days after, marriage. (c. 209, §§25, 26).

Conveyances.—Transfers of real and personal property between husband and wife are valid as if they were sole. (c. 209, §3). Conveyances of property to wife need not state that it is to her sole and separate use.

Conveyance to husband and wife creates tenancy in common and not joint tenancy unless instrument manifests clear intent to create joint tenancy. Tenancies by entirety recognized in Massachusetts. (c. 184, §7).

Torts.—Married woman is liable for her torts as though unmarried. (110 Mass. 238). Common law doctrine of interspousal immunity and c. 209, §6 do not bar suits by spouse for tort committed by one against other. (370 Mass. 619, 351 N.E.2d 526). Post divorce tort action may not be barred unless doctrine of issue preclusion may be invoked under certain specific circumstances. (402 Mass. 21, 520 N.E.2d 151).

Legal Separation.—If judgment has been entered that spouse has been deserted or is living apart from other for justifiable cause, and if he or she dies testate, other spouse is not entitled to waive provisions of will. (c. 209, §36).

Wife or husband who has been abandoned by spouse without sufficient maintenance may be authorized, upon motion to Probate Court and with notice, to dispose of spouse's property during period of abandonment as if moving party were sole. (c. 209, §30).

Liability for Debts.—Wife and her separate property are not liable for husband's debts, but if she has property to amount of $2,000 or more, she is jointly liable with him for debts due to amount of $100 in each case for necessaries furnished with her knowledge or consent to herself or family. (c. 209, §7). If wife vests husband with title to and possession of her property and permits him to hold himself out as owner, she is estopped to deny his ownership as against creditors to extent of debts incurred relying on his ownership. (235 Mass. 330, 127 N.E. 420). Husband is not liable upon cause of action which originated against wife prior to marriage (c. 209, §8) nor upon her separate contracts thereafter made (c. 209, §9), but she has same authority as at common law to pledge his credit for her support. (242 Mass. 245, 136 N.E. 350).

Interest of debtor spouse in principal residence of nondebtor spouse, held by entireties, not subject to seizure or execution by creditor; except that both spouses are liable jointly or severally for debts incurred for necessaries furnished either spouse or member of family. (c. 209, §1).

Husband an wife holding as tenants by entirety under deed dated prior to Feb. 11, 1980 may elect provisions of c. 209, §1, by recording election at registry of deeds. (c. 209, §1A).

Wife may do business on separate account without subjecting husband to liability for debts of her business. (c. 209, §9). Requirement for filing certificate to effectuate above has been abolished. (c. 209, §10). Except in cases involving incest, failure to pay child support, or violation of restraining order, spouses disqualified from testifying against one another. (c. 233, §20 as am'd 1995, c. 5, §94).

See also category Civil Actions and Procedure, topic Evidence, subhead Witnesses.

INFANTS:

Age of majority, 18. (c. 4, §7, cl. 51; c. 231, §85P).

Adoption.—Consent required from child above age 12. See also topic Adoption. (c. 210, §§2, 3).

Emancipation takes place when infant becomes 18 unless legally incapacited for some reason other than age. (c. 231, §85P). See c. 208, §28 for special support entitlement for children of divorced parents between 18-23.

Disabilities.—In general, infant has no power to contract except for maintenance and education. (6 Mass. 78). Minor age 16 or over may contract for motor vehicle liability insurance. (c. 175, §113K). Minor age 15 or over may contract for life or endowment insurance. (c. 175, §128). Minor, 12 years or older, who is certified by two or more physicians to be dependent on drugs, may consent to furnishing of hospital and medical care, other than methadone maintenance therapy, without disaffirmance because of minority. (c. 112, §12E). Physician, dentist or hospital not liable for care rendered without parental consent in emergency cases when delay in treatment will endanger life, limb, or mental well-being of patient. Minor may also effectively consent without disaffirmance to certain medical or dental care (except sterilization or abortion) when either care is of emergency nature or minor: (i) Is married, widowed or divorced; (ii) is parent of child; (iii) is member of armed forces; (iv) is pregnant or believes herself pregnant; (v) is living separate and apart from parents and manages own financial affairs; or (vi) reasonably believes he suffers from or has come into contact with disease dangerous to public health. Liability will not result for good faith reliance on minor's representations of legal ability to consent. Records and information concerning such care are confidential between minor and physician or dentist. (c. 112, §12F). See c. 112, §12S for requirements applicable to unmarried minors seeking abortion. Unemancipated minor living with natural or adopted parent shall not testify in any criminal proceeding against said parent where victim is not member of said parent's family and does not reside in said parent's household. (c. 233, §20).

Persons 18 or over may vote (Art. III, Mass. Const. Art. of Amend.); may not sell alcoholic beverages except in licensed establishment or knowingly possess, transport, or carry alcohol until age 21 except in course of employment (c. 138, §§34, 34C); may not consume alcohol until age 21 (c. 138, §34A); may execute valid will (c. 191, §1); may marry without parental consent (c. 207, §7); may donate blood without parental consent (c. 111, §184C); may make anatomical gifts to take effect at death or may make gift for transplant while living (c. 113, §8[a]); and may buy lottery ticket (c. 10, §29). Police officer may immediately seize driver's license of driver under 21 with blood alcohol percentage of .02 or greater. (c. 90, §24[1][f][2] as am'd 1995, c. 38, §115).

Ratification of Contracts.—Infant may ratify all contracts after majority (no writing needed). (14 Mass. 457).

Actions.—Infant may sue by guardian, if any, or next friend (no court appointment needed). (c. 201, §36). Guardian ad litem or next friend may upon request be appointed by court to protect interest of any minor, as well as others under disability. (c. 201, §1 et seq.).

See also topic Guardian and Ward.

Torts.—Infant is liable for torts (except for fraud in representing that he is of age [175 Mass. 513, 56 N.E. 574]) but not held to same standard of care as adult (346 Mass. 174, 190 N.E.2d 676).

Parents of infant or of adult child dependent on parents have cause of action for loss of consortium against any person legally responsible for causing infant or such child serious injury. (c. 231, §85X).

Imputed Negligence.—Negligence of parent or custodian is not imputed to infant. (c. 231, §85D).

Parental Liability.—Parents with custody of unemancipated child over age seven and under age 18 are liable up to $5,000 for damage caused by child's wilful acts resulting in property damage or injury or death. (c. 231, §85G). Parents with custody of unemancipated minor are responsible for legal fees incurred by minor in connection with criminal proceedings against him as court determines, not exceeding $300. (c. 119, §29A).

Support of Minors.—Unjustified failure or refusal to support minor child by person having legal obligation is subject to criminal sanction. (c. 273, §1). Human services department shall give due consideration to child's request to be placed outside home of any parent or guardian when there is history of abuse and neglect in such home by such parent or guardian. (c. 119, §39G as am'd 1995, c. 38, §138). It is felony for either parent of illegitimate minor child to neglect or refuse to contribute reasonably to such child's support and maintenance. (c. 273, §15 as am'd 1995, c. 5, §99). Court may order support for certain minors up to age 23. (c. 209C, §9; c. 208, §28). See topic Divorce for support of children of divorced parents.

Uniform Child Custody Jurisdiction Act adopted as c. 209B.

Uniform Transfers to Minors Act adopted as c. 201A. Age of majority under Act is 21. (c. 201A, §1).

Uniform Reciprocal Enforcement of Support Act repealed. (1995, c. 5, §105).

Uniform Interstate Family Support Act adopted as c. 209D; 1995, c. 5, §87.

Protection.—Through various courts, orders are available to protect physical or emotional welfare, or support needs, of minors in cases of: divorce (c. 208, §19); separation (c. 209, §37); family abuse (c. 209A); delinquency or other circumstances requiring special protections, such as child born to prison inmate (c. 119); desertion, nonsupport and illegitimacy (c. 273). Orders of foreign courts enforced in commonwealth. (c. 298, §5). Office for children has responsibility for those under 18, or under 22 if child has special needs. (c. 28A, §§2, 4). Social services must notify district attorney of instances of child abuse. (c. 119, §51B). See category Employment, topic Labor Relations, subhead Child Labor.

Uniform Securities Ownership by Minors Act not adopted.

Inheritance.—See category Estates and Trusts, topic Descent and Distribution.

Termination of Parental Rights.—See generally c. 119 (see also c. 210, Adoption). Upon petition of person alleging abuse or neglect of minor, court, upon finding of reasonable cause, may assign custody of minor to department of social services, licensed child care agency, or other qualified person. (c. 119, §24). Within 18 months of transfer of custody of minor, and periodically thereafter, committing court must reconvene to determine future status of minor, but court may later approve permanent placement. (c. 119, §29B). In assigning permanent custody away from natural parents, court must consider best interests of child and parental unfitness. (367 Mass. 631, 328 N.E.2d 854). Natural parents may not be deprived custody in absence of showing of "grievous shortcomings" that put child's welfare at risk. (383 Mass. 573, 421 N.E.2d 28).

MARRIAGE:

See generally c. 207. All citations, unless otherwise indicated, refer to said chapter.

Nonage.—Common law age of consent (12 females, 14 males) in effect (1 Gray [67 Mass.], 119), but marriage of person under age 18 may not be licensed or performed without court authority (§§7, 24, 25).

Consent.—Probate or District Court may authorize marriage of person under age 18 upon consent of parents or guardian, or without such consent in certain circumstances. (§25). Marriage of person of age of consent but under 18 is not subject to annulment even though licensing official and minister are subject to fine. (1 Gray [67 Mass.], 119).

License.—Persons intending to be married must personally (substitute is permitted in case of illness), or by either party if other is in armed forces or jail, file notice of intention to marry with clerk or registrar of any city or town at least three days before marriage. (§§19, 20). Each party must also file certificate of doctor as to medical examination made within 30 days prior to notice of intention. (§28A). License is to be issued three or more (but not more than 60) days after filing notice of intention of marriage and must be given to minister or official before marriage may be solemnized. (§28).

Marriage Ceremony.—Marriage may be solemnized by resident clergyman or nonresident in specified cases, or in ceremonies conducted by Quaker meetings or other assemblies specified, or according to usage of any other religious organization which may have filed certain information with secretary of state; also by justice of peace if also town, city or court clerk or registrar (including assistant clerk or registrar), or if designated by governor as authorized to perform same. (§§38, 39). Marriage believed to be valid by either party is not invalidated by celebrant who mistakenly or wrongfully professes his authority to perform it. (§42).

See note at head of Digest as to 1998 legislation covered.

See Topical Index in front part of this volume.

MA – 51

MARRIAGE . . . *continued*

Reports of Marriages.—Person solemnizing marriage must keep records and make certain returns to clerk or registrar of municipality issuing license. (§§39, 40). Content of record prescribed by statute. (c. 46, §1).

Common law marriages are not recognized. (127 Mass. 459).

Proxy Marriages.—Status of proxy marriages has not been determined by S.J.C. Not addressed by statute.

Marriages by Written Contract.—Marriage by virtue of written contract is not recognized. No action for breach of contract to marry. (§47A).

Prohibited Marriages.—No man may marry his mother, grandmother, daughter, granddaughter, sister, stepmother, grandfather's wife, grandson's wife, wife's mother, wife's grandmother, wife's daughter or wife's granddaughter, brother's or sister's daughter, father's or mother's sister. (§1). Corresponding prohibitions as to marriage of woman except that woman may not marry daughter's husband but may marry husband's father. (§2). Prohibitions apply even if marriage by which affinity was created was dissolved. (§3). Marriage prohibited as polygamous or because of affinity or consanguinity is void ab initio. (§§4, 8).

Marriage, contracted in commonwealth by party residing and intending to continue to reside in another state where such marriage would be void, is void in commonwealth. (§11).

If person residing and intending to continue to reside in commonwealth goes into another jurisdiction and there contracts marriage prohibited and declared void by laws of commonwealth, such marriage is void for all purposes in commonwealth. (§10).

Annulment.—Proceedings for annulling or affirming marriage may be brought by complaint in Probate Court in like manner as divorce proceedings. (§14; c. 215, §3). Plaintiff must have domicile or five years residence in commonwealth for annulment of foreign marriage. (§14). See category Civil Actions and Procedure, topic Practice.

Issue of Invalid Marriage.—Issue of marriage void by reason of consanguinity or affinity considered born out of wedlock. (§15). Issue of marriage which is void for nonage or mental illness, or void by reason of prior marriage which second spouse was unaware of or in good faith considered no bar, are legitimate issue of parent capable of marrying. (§§16, 17).

Divorce.—See topic Divorce.

Residence.—Residence within commonwealth not required, but before issuing license (certificate) to nonresident, officer must satisfy himself by requiring affidavits or otherwise that person is not prohibited from marrying by law of jurisdiction where he or she resides. (§12).

MARRIED WOMEN:

See topics Husband and Wife, Marriage; categories Debtor and Creditor, topic Homesteads; Documents and Records, topic Acknowledgments; Estates and Trusts, topic Executors and Administrators; Property, topics Absentees, Dower.

HEALTH

FOOD, DRUG AND COSMETICS:

Regulated by c. 94, §1 et seq.

HEALTH INSURANCE:

See also category Insurance, topic Insurance Companies.

Universal Health Insurance.—Division of health care finance and policy established to regulate certain rates of payment for health care services and formulate health care policy. (c. 118G, §2[a][b]). Uncompensated Care Trust Fund established to pay for uncompensated services provided by health care service providers. (c. 118G, §18). Small businesses may pool together when purchasing health insurance for employees. (c. 188G, §21).

Non-group Insurance.—See generally c. 176M.
Health Maintenance Organization.—See generally c. 176G.
Small Group Health Insurance.—See generally c. 176J.

PUBLIC HEALTH:

See generally cc. 17, 111, 112.

Physicians must comply with all registration requirements of c. 112, §2. Profiles, including all disciplinary actions, on licensed physicians made available to public, (c. 112, §5). Registered nurses must comply with all registration requirements of c. 112, §80B.

Public assistance for pregnant women and infants with inadequate health insurance available through "Healthy Start Program". (c. 111, §24D).

SMOKING REGULATIONS:

Smoking prohibited in public conveyances and transportation terminals. (c. 272, §43A). Possession and commercial use of cigarette vending machines regulated by c. 64C, §10. Municipalities may ban smoking in all public places, including restaurants, bars, workplaces and public forums under Home Rule Amendment to the Massachusetts Constitution. (Mass. Const. Amend. art. 2; 383 Mass. 152, 418 N.E.2d 335). Boston has banned smoking in restaurants but not in bars. (Public Health Commission, tel: [617] 534-4718).

INSURANCE

INSURANCE COMPANIES:

The business of insurance in general is governed by cc. 175, 176, as amended and is under supervision of Division of Insurance, 470 Atlantic Ave., Boston 02210-2223. Many provisions of c. 156B (Business Corporation Law) are incorporated into c. 175.

(c. 175, §30). Insurance company holding companies are regulated by special provisions. (c. 175, §§47A, 193L-N,S). C. 118F provides for universal health insurance.

Ten or more residents of state may form mutual or stock company. (c. 175, §§48, 48A). Capital and other financial requirements vary with type of company and types of insurance to be issued. (c. 175, §§48, 48A). License fee for organization determined annually by secretary of administration currently $1,025 ($150 renewal fee; $116 renewal of company license fee, $750 examination fee).

Except fraternal benefit societies and savings banks (where special provisions of cc. 176 and 178 apply) only domestic companies which have obtained certificate (c. 175, §32) and foreign companies which have obtained a license (c. 175, §151, Fifth) may engage in insurance business.

All companies must file elaborate annual statements (c. 175, §§25-27) and must underwrite specified types of insurance only (c. 175, §§47, 47A, 48, 48A). Any form of insurance policy issued to more than 50 policyholders in state, other than casualty or property insurance for business, professional or governmental operations, or certain life, accident or health insurance or annuities, must be filed for approval by insurance commissioner and must meet certain specifications as to readability, organization and appearance. (c. 175, §§2B, 193F). Standard form of fire insurance policy is required, but may be modified or added to by riders or by writing on margin or across face of policy. (c. 175, §99). Insertion of certain conditions or provisions in policies is prohibited. (c. 175, §§22-22C, 22E, 24A). Right of insurance companies to cancel or refuse to issue automobile insurance policies is limited. (c. 175, §§22C, 22E). See also c. 175, §113A. There is similar provision limiting cancellation of fire insurance policies. (c. 175, §§99, 193P).

Person paying consideration for life insurance contract need not have insurable interest in life of insured individual if organization qualified under §501(c)(3) of IRC is named irrevocably as owner and beneficiary.

Domestic companies may under certain conditions merge or consolidate with each other or with foreign companies. (c. 175, §§19A, 19B, 193S). Minority interests in subsidiary domestic insurance company may, under certain conditions, be acquired by parent company. (c. 175, §193Q).

Interlocking directorates are regulated. (c. 175, §193C). A domestic insurance company is regulated in its right to acquire stock in another insurance company. (c. 175, 193D).

Rebates, with stated exceptions, are prohibited. (c.175, §§182-184).

A beneficiary named in a policy of life or endowment insurance may sue thereon in his own name. (c. 175, §125).

If policyholder substantially complies with change of beneficiary policy requirements on lifetime annuity contract, exact compliance will be excused. (37 Mass. App. Ct. 357, 639 N.E.2d 1106).

An infant may not avoid or repudiate because of infancy any contract of life or endowment insurance in which he or certain near relations are beneficiaries, if he was 15 years of age when the contract was made. (c. 175, §128).

Joint Underwriting Association, which provides medical malpractice insurance, has been converted to Medical Professional Mutual Insurance Company. (1994, c. 330, am'd 1995, c. 63).

When family member is injured in auto accident, spouse and children are entitled to recover loss of consortium damages as separate "persons" who suffered "distinct" injuries. (392 Mass. 537, 467 N.E.2d 137). However, Commissioner of Insurance has authority to modify language of standard automobile insurance policy to remove separate per person limit for loss of consortium plaintiffs. (395 Mass. 765, 481 N.E.2d 1373). Negligent infliction of emotional distress claim of family member of passenger killed in auto accident is not claim for "bodily injury" for insurance coverage and therefore is subject to same per person limit as passenger's estate's wrongful death claim. (420 Mass. 587, 650 N.E.2d 793).

Commissioner of Insurance may approve standard automobile insurance policy where underinsured motorist provision not applicable to protect named insured when underlying bodily injury or death sustained by person not insured by policy. (420 Mass. 799, 652 N.E.2d 128).

Motorist who had Massachusetts auto policy with underinsured motorist coverage may not recover under higher underinsured motorist coverage in another household member's policy. (419 Mass. 144, 643 N.E.2d 435).

Blue Shield's prohibition of "balance billing" by doctors does not violate antitrust laws. (749 F.2d 922).

Homeowner's insurance policy excluding coverage of damages arising out of use of motor vehicle does not exclude claim against insured for negligent supervision of party resulting in negligent operating of motor vehichle by another insured, when considered together with clause providing that coverage applies separately to each insured. (398 Mass. 240, 496 N.E.2d 158).

Special rules apply to crime insurance. (c. 175, §102E).

Before making payments over $500, insurer must determine whether claimant subject to child support lien by examining information provided by Department of revenue or by sending department information regarding claimant ten days before payment. (c. 175, §24D).

Universal Health Insurance.—Commonwealth adopted version of Health Insurance Portability Act (P.L. 104-191) which limits power of employer/insurer to deny coverage because of preexisting condition (c. 176M, N). Where c. 175 is inconsistent with c. 176M, 176M governs.

C.118G establishes division of health care finance and policy. (§2). Division administers uncompensated care pool which provides health care coverage for uninsured. (§2[c]). C. 118G also provides for administration of uncompensated care trust fund and medical security trust fund for benefit of uninsured. (§§18, 20). Chapter also provides for small business health insurance pool to equalize employee health insurance costs for small business. (c. 118G, §21).

Both unincorporated business and corporate employers may receive tax credit for initiating employer paid health insurance programs. (c. 62, §6[f]).

Cc. 117A and 118E both contain provisions for medical care and assistance for those who qualify. (c. 117A, §§1-3, c. 118E, §§6A-6B).

See note at head of Digest as to 1998 legislation covered.

See Topical Index in front part of this volume.

INSURANCE COMPANIES . . . *continued*

Unfair Methods of Competition and Deceptive Acts and Practices.—Regulated by c. 176D. §3 of said act enumerates unfair methods of competition and unfair or deceptive practices. §3(9) proscribes certain unfair claims settlement practices. §3A prohibits specific unfair methods of competition and unfair or deceptive acts or practices by insurance companies. §4 contains further prohibitions pertaining to lending of money or extension of credit. C. 93A is also applicable to unfair or deceptive insurance practices. (373 Mass. 72, 365 N.E. 2d 802). See category Business Regulation and Commerce, topic Monopolies, Restraint of Trade and Competition, subhead Unfair Trade Practices.

Accident, dental and health insurance policyholders must be provided with copies of medical information used to deny liability. (c. 175, §108). All payments or denial of liability must be furnished promptly. (c. 175, §108[4]).

Insurance company may not deny coverage due to insured's failure to give seasonable notice of claim unless company is prejudiced thereby. (c. 175, §112). Insurer doing business in Massachusetts shall reveal limits of insured's policy to injured party making claim against insured. (c. 175, §112C).

Sale of Life Insurance or Annuity Policies.—Sale of life insurance or annuity policies to replace existing policy issued by another insurer governed by regulations promulgated by insurance commissioner based on model regulation developed by National Association of Insurance Commissioners. (c. 175, §204).

Medicare and Supplemental Coverage.—Policies providing supplemental coverage to Medicare must be approved by commissioner and meet certain standards promulgated by commissioner. Exception for employers and trade unions. (c. 175, §205).

Premium Finance Agreements.—Subject to regulation and full disclosure provisions similar to those applied to retail installment sales contracts. (c. 255C; c. 140D). Persons holding or acquiring such finance agreements, except banks including federal savings banks, sales finance companies and licensed small loans companies, must obtain licenses from commissioner of banks. (c. 255C, §2). In case of conflict between statute and c. 140D, Truth-in-Lending Law, latter controls. (c. 255C, §23). Violations of c. 255C are also violations of c. 93A, consumer protection law. (c. 255C, §6).

Excise Taxes.—Every domestic insurance company, except as otherwise provided, is subject to annual excise of 2% of gross premiums for all policies written or renewed, all additional premiums charged, and all assessments made during preceding calendar year, exclusive of reinsurance. Such excise is not imposed on life insurance companies with respect to amounts received as consideration for annuity contracts and business taxable under c. 63, §20, or on marine, or fire and marine, insurance companies with respect to business taxable under c. 63, §29A. In addition, such excise does not apply to premiums for policies written or renewed for insurance of property or interests in other states or countries where a tax is actually paid by company or its agents. (c. 63, §22). Marine and fire and marine companies are subject to special provisions. (c. 63, §29A). Foreign companies, except life insurance companies, with respect to business taxable under c. 63, §§20, 21, marine insurance or fire and marine insurance companies with respect to business taxable under c. 63, §29A, must annually pay excise upon gross premiums for all policies written or renewed, or additional premiums charged, and all assessments made during preceding calendar year for insurance of property or interests in commonwealth or which are subjects of insurance by contracts issued herein. Excise rate is 2%, but tax is to be not less in amount than would be imposed by laws of state or country under which such company is organized upon like insurance company incorporated in this commonwealth if doing business to same extent in such state or country. (c. 63, §23).

Life insurance companies authorized to transact business in Massachusetts must annually pay an excise of 2% upon premiums received during preceding calendar year. Life companies authorized to do business in commonwealth before Dec. 31, 1943, are subject to special provisions under which they transfer to basis of tax on premiums, in year tax computed on net value of policies that equals or exceeds tax so computed. (c. 63, §20 and notes following). Foreign life insurance companies in addition to foregoing tax must pay sum equal to excess over such excise of amount of tax which would be imposed in same year by laws of state or country under which such company is organized upon life insurance company incorporated in Massachusetts or upon its agents if doing business to same extent in such state or country. (c. 63, §21).

Domestic non-life companies must also pay tax equal to 1% of total gross investment income earned in preceding calendar year (c. 63, §22A), while domestic life companies not subject to tax under c. 63, §22A must pay investment privilege excise equal to 14% of net investment income computed in accordance with apportionment formula (c. 63, §§22B-22D).

Domestic life insurance companies are subject to assessments to pay expenses involved in the valuation of securities by the National Association of Insurance Commissioners. (c. 175, §14A).

Agents or Brokers.—Only persons who are licensed may act as agents or brokers. (c. 175, §§163, 166). Savings bank employees selling life insurance must also be licensed as agents. (c. 178A, §4). No license to issue to employee of bank or mortgage company which was not itself licensed prior to Oct. 11, 1972. (c. 175, §174E). Agent's license issued only on written notice by company authorized to transact business in commonwealth of appointment of person who meets requirements of statute to act as its agent in commonwealth. Resident of other state may qualify for license as such agent of domestic company. Resident of state granting similar license to Massachusetts residents may qualify for license as agent of authorized foreign company, but must do business through licensed resident agents of such company. (c. 175, §163). Only residents of commonwealth or of states granting like privileges to residents of commonwealth may be licensed as brokers. (c. 175, §166). Licenses expire every three years, but may be renewed on payment of fee. (c. 175, §§163, 166).

Special brokers may be licensed to negotiate insurance contracts against specified hazards on property or interests here in foreign companies not authorized to transact business here. (c. 175, §168). Otherwise, licenses apply only to insurance underwritten by companies authorized to do business here. (c. 175, §§163, 166).

There are special license provisions relative to partnerships. (c. 175, §173).

Insurance agent may offset funds due an insured for return premiums against amounts due him from insured. (c. 175, §187B).

Insurance advisers are subject to license and other requirements. (c. 175, §177B).

Coercion.—No person engaged in the business of financing the purchase of real or personal property, or of lending money on the security of real or personal property shall require that insurance on such property be placed with a particular agent, broker or insurance company, provided that such person may nevertheless approve or disapprove of insurance company and terms and conditions of policy selected. (c. 175, §193E). Nor may owner of residential property be compelled to continue or renew fire insurance policy in excess of amount of outstanding mortgage (c. 175, §95A), although mortgagee may require insurance in amount not in excess of replacement cost (c. 183, §66). Charges for credit life and credit health and accident insurance are limited by statute. (c. 255B, §10; c. 255C, §14A; c. 255D, §26; c. 255, §§12F, 12G).

Discrimination.—When insurance policy, certificate or service contract provides for reimbursement or payment for any professional services performed by any person, licensed under c. 112, such reimbursements or payments shall not be denied because of race, color or creed nor shall any insurer permit any unfair discrimination to said persons. (c. 175, §193K). Life insurance companies may not discriminate in amount of premium or in any other term of policies on account of race (c. 175, §122), nor may any such company permit discrimination in favor of individuals between insurants of same class and equal expectation of life (c. 175, §120). Life insurance policies may not be refused for sole reason of mental retardation, if insured is at least three years old and policy amount is exactly $1,500, or blindness or primarily because of exposure to DES. (c. 175, §§120A-120C). Certain medical and hospital insurance policies may not be refused by reason of blindness, deafness or exposure to DES. (c. 175, §108A; c. 176A, §8E; c. 176B, §§4D, 4E). No discrimination on basis of blindness, physical impairment or mental retardation is permitted except where based on sound actuarial principles or related to actual experience (c. 175, §193T) and no discrimination on basis of exposure to DES (c. 175, §108C; c. 176A, §8E; c. 176B, §4E). No discrimination on basis of being victim of abuse as defined by c. 209A, §1 in policies for residential property insurance, accident or sickness insurance, and life or endowment insurance, (c. 175, §§95B, 108G, 120D), or in terms or conditions of hospital service plans (c. 176A, §3A), or medical service plans (c. 176B, §5A). No medical malpractice insurer shall discriminate against any eligible health care provider based upon specialty practiced, however premium charges may be based upon reasonable classifications of risks associated with specialty. (c. 175, §193U).

Foreign Companies.—Before license is issued to foreign company to engage in insurance business here it must inter alia file copy of charter and statement of condition, satisfy the commissioner that its condition is equal to required standard, appoint him attorney for service of process, and appoint a resident of state its agent. (c. 175, §151).

Commissioner may for cause revoke license. (c. 175, §5). Every foreign corporation must notify commissioner forthwith of all changes in name, location, capital, organization and certain other matters. (c. 175, §23A). Company organized under laws of foreign country must make a deposit with state treasurer or officer of another state equal to capital required for domestic companies. (c. 175, §155). Commissioner may publish fact that unlicensed foreign company is without license and is not amenable to suits in Massachusetts for collection of policies, etc. (c. 175, §160B).

Foreign company may make contracts of insurance on lives, property or interests therein, and annuity or pure endowment contracts and suretyship contracts with residents, only by lawfully constituted and licensed resident agents, and all insurance instruments delivered in Massachusetts, except life endowment policies, annuity or pure endowment contracts and accident or health policies, must be countersigned by such a resident agent. (c. 175, §157).

Plain Language.—See category Business Regulation and Commerce, topic Consumer Protection, subhead Plain Language.

Retaliatory Laws.—If laws of any other state impose on Massachusetts insurance companies doing business there burdens and restrictions in excess of those imposed on foreign corporations by Massachusetts law, like burdens, etc., are imposed on companies of said state doing business here. (c. 175, §159). Such reciprocity likewise determines imposition of retaliatory taxes. (c. 63, §24A).

Variable Annuity Insurance.—Policies may be issued by life companies, subject to commissioner's approval. (c. 175, §§132G, 132H).

No-fault Insurance.—See category Transportation, topic Motor Vehicles, subheads Insurance, No-fault Insurance.

Uniform Insurers Liquidation Act, adopted. (c. 175, §§180A to 180L).

SURETY AND GUARANTY COMPANIES:

Surety companies, agents and brokers are subject to all applicable provisions of c. 175 governing insurance. (c. 175, §107).

Rights and Powers.—A corporation organized in Massachusetts to guarantee the fidelity of persons in positions of trust and to act as surety on official bonds may insure the fidelity of persons holding public or private positions of trust and may, if approved by the court, obligee or person competent to approve such bond, act as joint or sole surety upon the official bond or other undertaking in civil or criminal procedure of any person or corporation to the United States, the commonwealth, any county, city, town, judge of probate, or public officer, or to any corporation or association; and may act as joint or sole surety upon any undertaking conditioned upon performance of any duty, or performance or nonperformance of any act specified in bond, and upon bonds to indemnify against loss any person who is responsible as surety for performance by others of any office or trust. (c. 175, §105). If by law two or more sureties are required upon any obligation upon which company is authorized to act as surety, it may act as joint or sole surety. (Id.). Provisions applicable to insurance companies in general apply to these corporations. See topic Insurance Companies.

Foreign Companies.—Foreign corporation of this class may do business, through lawfully constituted and licensed resident agents, only after deposit of not less than

See note at head of Digest as to 1998 legislation covered.

See Topical Index in front part of this volume.

MA – 53

SURETY AND GUARANTY COMPANIES... *continued*
$100,000 with state treasurer, or officer of another state for protection of its policyholders in U.S. (c. 175, §106), filing of power of attorney constituting commissioner of insurance its agent for service of process and compliance with other conditions set forth in c. 175, §151. (See topic Insurance Companies.) Elaborate annual statements must be filed.

INTELLECTUAL PROPERTY

TRADEMARKS AND TRADENAMES:

Note:—Massachusetts has adopted Model Trademark Act, effective April 1, 1974.

What May Be Used.—It is unlawful for any person, firm, corporation or association, except agencies or instrumentalities of the U. S. Government, in selling goods, to use words or abbreviations "Army," "Navy," "Marine Corps," "Marines," "Coast Guard," "Government," "Post Exchange," "P. X.," "G. I." or any words or phrases which may lead public to believe business owned, operated or managed by U. S. Government, except that such words may be used in corporate name of corporation as name of charitable corporation if approved by state secretary. (c. 110, §4B). No person, society, association, or corporation shall knowingly assume, adopt or use name of benevolent, humane, fraternal, charitable or labor organization, or name which is colorable imitation thereof. (c. 266, §71A). No individual, association or partnership may use word "corporation" or "incorporated" or any other word or phrase which may lead public to believe that such party is corporation. (c. 110, § 4A). No person, firm, corporation or association (other than agency or instrumentality of commonwealth) shall use words "Massachusetts State Fair" or any such words or phrases without written consent of commissioner of agriculture. (c. 110, §4B). Fines of up to $200 or imprisonment for up to one year or both may be imposed for violations of aforementioned sections. (c. 110, §26; c. 266, §71A).

Corporation shall not assume name of another corporation, firm, association or person organized or doing business in commonwealth without written permission; provided, however, that in case of corporation formed to act as insurance agent, broker or fire insurance adjuster, corporate name must receive written approval of commissioner of insurance. (c. 155, §9).

Registration.—Person who adopts and uses trademark in Massachusetts may file an application for registration of said mark with office of state secretary. Facsimile of mark in triplicate and filing fee, currently $50, must accompany application. (c. 110B, §2). Secretary will then issue Certificate of Registration, which is admissible in evidence in any action or judicial proceeding in commonwealth. (c. 110B, §4). Registration is effective for ten years and can be renewed for successive periods of ten years by filing renewal application within six months before date of expiration, accompanied by renewal fee, currently $50. (c. 110B, §5).

Assignments.—A mark and its registration are assignable with good will of business in which mark is used. Assignment must be by written instrument, which may be recorded with state secretary upon payment of fee, currently $50. Assignment of registration is void as against subsequent purchaser for value without notice unless recorded with secretary within three months of date of said assignment or prior to subsequent purchase. (c. 110B, §6). Registration, renewal and assignment fees are determined annually by secretary of administration. (c. 7, §3B).

Protection Afforded.—Registration of a mark is constructive notice of registrant's claim of ownership thereof and is prima facie evidence of registrant's exclusive right to use said mark in connection with goods or services specified in application for registration. (c. 110B, §4). However, registration of a mark will not adversely affect rights in common law which another party may have acquired in said mark at any time by good faith use thereof. (c. 110B, §14). Common law entitles tradename or service mark owner to injunction forbidding another from using tradename or service mark so similar as to mislead public. (398 Mass. 480, 498 N.E.2d 1044).

Infringement.—Subject to exception noted in previous subhead, any person who, without consent of registrant, uses a copy or colorable imitation of a registered mark in conjunction with sale or other distribution of goods or services within commonwealth will be liable to registrant in civil action. (c. 110B, §11). Registrant is not entitled to recover profits or damages absent proof that acts have been committed with knowledge that such mark is intended to be used to cause confusion or mistake or to deceive. (c. 110B, §11). In addition to damages, registrant can seek injunctive relief in Superior Court to restrain unauthorized use of mark. (c. 110B, §13). Likelihood of injury to business reputation or dilution of distinctive quality of mark is ground for injunctive relief notwithstanding absence of competition between parties or of confusion as to source of goods or services. (c. 110B, §12).

Tradenames.—A person conducting business in the commonwealth under any title other than the real name of the person conducting the same, or a partnership conducting business under any title not including the true surname of at least one partner, or a corporation conducting business under any other title than its true corporate name, must file with the clerk of every city or town where an office is maintained a certificate under oath stating the full name and residence of each person conducting such business and its address. (c. 110, §§5, 6). Such certificate must be executed under oath by each person whose name appears as conducting such business and signed by each such person in presence of city or town clerk or their designees or in presence of person authorized to take oaths. City or town clerk or person authorized to take such oaths may request person to produce evidence of his identity, and if such person does not produce evidence of his identity, notation of this fact shall be entered on face of certificate. (c 110, §5). Upon discontinuing or withdrawing from such business or change in information in file, it is necessary to file with clerk a sworn statement of withdrawal from such business or a statement otherwise correcting information on file. (c. 110, §5). If any business is conducted by trustees under written instrument, names of trustees with reference to instrument must be filed in like manner. (c. 110, §6).

TRADE SECRETS:

Crime of larceny has been extended to cover those who steal or with intent to defraud, obtain by false pretense, or who unlawfully and with intent to steal or embezzle, convert, secrete, unlawfully take, carry away, conceal or copy with intent to convert any trade secret of another, regardless of value, whether such trade secret is or is not in his possession at time of such conversion or secreting. Trade secret includes anything tangible or intangible or electrically kept or stored which constitutes, represents, evidences or records secret scientific, technical, merchandising, production or management information, design, process, procedure, formula, invention or improvement. Penalties include fine up to $25,000 and/or imprisonment. (c. 266, §30[4]).

Statute applies both to those who take and to those who knowingly receive or deal with such secrets. Broad injunctive relief available to aggrieved party where conversion is in violation of terms of written employment agreement. (c. 93, §42A). See also category Civil Actions and Procedure, topic Injunctions.

In addition to criminal sanctions, guilty party may be liable in tort for civil damages, and, in discretion of court, civil damages may be increased to twice amount of damages suffered. (c. 93, §42).

LEGAL PROFESSION

ATTORNEYS AND COUNSELORS:

SJC has denied petition for establishment of integrated bar. (321 Mass. 747, 74 N.E.2d 140). In 1974, however, SJC established Board of Bar Overseers, which is authorized to oversee attorney conduct and to recommend appropriate discipline. (365 Mass. 695, 699, 313 N.E.2d 561, SJC Rule 4:01, §5[3]). See subheads Annual Registration and Disbarment or Suspension, infra.

Massachusetts Rules of Professional Conduct based on ABA Model Rules of Professional Conduct, with modifications. (SJC Rule 3:07).

Jurisdiction over Admission.—SJC and Superior Court have jurisdiction over admission of attorneys. (c. 221, §37).

Eligibility.—U.S. citizen over 18 years of age may file petition with SJC or Superior Court to be examined for admission. All petitions referred to Board of Bar Examiners for report on applicant's character, acquirements and qualifications. Admission entitles attorney to practice in all courts of commonwealth. (c. 221, §§36-37, SJC Rule 3:01, §1.3).

Aliens permitted to file petition for admission only after making primary declaration to become U.S. citizen. (c. 221, §38A).

Registration as Law Student.—No requirement. SJC Rule 3:03, §1 and Local Rule 83.5.1(b)(1) of Rules of U.S. District Court for District of Mass. provide that senior law student enrolled in evidence or trial practice course may appear in certain enumerated cases under supervision of member of Massachusetts Bar with written approval of dean of accredited law school. SJC Rule 3:03, §8 and Local Rule 83.5.1(b)(5) also permit limited appearances by student who has begun next-to-last year and is currently participating in law school clinical instruction program. If appearance of senior law student is not permitted as of right under Rule 3:03, §§1 and 8, justice of SJC or appeals court may permit senior law student, provided student is qualified and supervised as specified in Rule, to appear on behalf of Commonwealth. (SJC Rule 3:03, §6). Enrollment in or completion of course in appellate practice may be substitute for trial practice or evidence course. (SJC Rule 3:03, §6). Appearing law students must certify that they are familiar with local rules and will abide by standards of professional conduct set out in SJC Rules 3:07 and 3:08. (SJC Rule 3:03, Local Rule 83.5.1[b][6]). Student must certify that client has been informed of student's status as law student and authorizes student to appear. (Local Rule 83.5.1[b][6]).

Educational Requirements.—To take bar examination, applicant must be graduate of public day high school or its equivalent, and must have completed work acceptable for college or university bachelor's degree or equivalent education, and must have been graduated from law school approved by ABA or authorized by Mass. statute. Provision made for foreign law school applicants. (SJC Rule 3:01, §3; c. 221, §36).

Petition for Admission.—Petition must be filed with Clerk of SJC accompanied by recommendation of Massachusetts attorney and fee of $200. (c. 221, §37; SJC Rule 3:01, §1). See subhead Admission Without Examination, infra.

Examination.—Petitioners are examined by Board of Bar Examiners twice yearly. Petitioner admitted upon recommendation by Bar Examiners as to moral character, acquirements, and qualifications. (c. 221, §37; SJC Rule 3:01, §§2,5).

Bar examination includes both state law and multi-state questions. Petitioner must also pass multistate professional responsibility examination. (SJC Rule 3:01, §3). Requirements are set forth in detail in regulations issued by Board of Bar Examiners.

Clerkship.—No requirement.

Admission Without Examination.—See SJC Rule 3:01, §6; c. 221, §§37,39. Attorney admitted in another state, district, or U.S. territory, may petition SJC for admission without regular examination, and Board of Bar Examiners may waive bar examination, if attorney complies with certain conditions, including: (a) Admitted in other jurisdiction for at least five years; (b) practiced or taught law in other jurisdiction so as to satisfy Board of Bar Examiners as to moral character and legal ability; (c) submits letters of recommendation for admission from three attorneys from Massachusetts or other jurisdiction in which applicant was admitted to bar or last resided; (d) satisfies educational requirements (see subhead Educational Requirements, supra); (e) passed multistate professional responsibility examination; (f) passed limited written examination in Massachusetts practice and procedure. To be admitted to Massachusetts bar, attorney admitted in foreign country must also comply with foregoing conditions, except that must also have principal residence in Massachusetts and must submit letters of recommendation from three members of bar of foreign jurisdiction and from two members of Massachusetts bar. Petition must be accompanied by fee of $500 (c. 227, §37) plus $200 for National Conference of Bar Examiners report.

See note at head of Digest as to 1998 legislation covered.

See Topical Index in front part of this volume.

MA – 54

ATTORNEYS AND COUNSELORS . . . *continued*

Admission Pro Hac Vice.—Member in good standing of bar of another state may appear in action, by permission of court, provided that such other state grants like privilege to Massachusetts lawyers. No requirement that foreign attorney must associate with Massachusetts attorney on matter. (c. 221, §46A). Local Rule 83.5.3(b) of Rules of U.S. District Court for District of Mass. requires certification by attorney seeking admission pro hac vice of good standing, of no pending disciplinary proceedings and of familiarity with local rules; and no appearance may be entered until application to appear has been granted, except attorney may file complaint or any paper necessary to prevent entry of default for failure to answer or otherwise plead if such complaint or other paper is accompanied by application to appear.

Licenses.—See subhead Annual Registration, infra.

Annual Registration.—Every attorney admitted to, or engaging in, practice of law in Massachusetts must register annually with Board of Bar Overseers, under penalty of suspension, supplying certain required information, and paying annual registration fee. (SJC Rules 4:02, 4:03.) Portion of funds so collected by Board of Bar Overseers is allocated to cost of attorney registration and disciplinary enforcement, and clients' security board, Massachusetts lawyers' assistance programs, and other purposes within Board of Bar Overseer's discretion and subject to Supreme Judicial Court approval. (SJC Rules 4:04-4:06). There are also registration requirements for individuals who engage in lobbying activities appearing before certain state agencies which affect attorneys. (c. 3, §§39-44 and 47, am'd St. 1995, c. 80).

Privileges.—No special provisions.

Disabilities.—No attorney shall become surety in any criminal or civil proceeding, except as endorser for costs, nor shall attorney for plaintiff in trustee process appear or act for party summoned as trustee. Except by leave of court, no attorney shall take part in conduct of trial in which he intends to appear as witness for his client. (Superior Court Rules 11, 12; Dist./Mun. Cts. Supp. Civ. Proc. Rule 113).

Liabilities.—No attorney on behalf of creditor shall collect or attempt to collect debt in unfair, deceptive, or unreasonable manner from one who has incurred debt primarily for personal, family or household purposes. (c. 93, §49; see regulations of attorney general). No attorney member of professional society or committee thereof shall be liable for damages for acts performed within scope of his duties as member, provided he acted in good faith. (c. 231, §85N). See also category Civil Actions and Procedure, topic Costs.

Compensation.—See SJC Rule 3:07(1.5) for detailed regulations governing fees. Lawyer may not charge illegal or clearly excessive fee. (SJC Rule 3:07[1.5]; 398 Mass. 18, 494 N.E.2d 1327). Factors that determine clearly excessive fee include: time and labor required; novelty, difficulty and skill required; likelihood that acceptance of employment precludes other employment; custom; amount involved and results obtained; time limitations imposed; nature of professional relationship with client; experience, reputation and ability of lawyer; whether fee fixed or contingent. (SJC Rule 3:07[1.5(a)]).

Contingent fees allowed except in divorce, alimony, support, property settlement or criminal matters. (SJC Rule 3:07[1.5(c)]). Contingent fee must be in writing, signed in duplicate by attorney and client, attorney must retain copy for seven years, and attorney must notify client at conclusion of matter in writing showing payments and methods. (SJC Rule 3:07[1.5(c)]). Contingent fee agreement must state (i) client's and lawyer's name and address, (ii) nature of legal matter, (iii) contingency upon which fee paid and any other fee obligation outside contingency, (iv) method fee determined, and (v) method other expenses deducted. (SJC Rule 3:07[1.5(c)]).

See also c. 231, §§6E-G, governing assessment of attorney's fees where court finds all or substantially all claims, defenses, setoffs, or counterclaims wholly insubstantial, frivolous, and not advanced in good faith.

See also c. 261, §§23, 26, only nominal attorney's fees included in customary statutory "costs". Attorney's fees, however, may be awarded under specific statutes. See e.g., c. 93A, §§9, 11 (recovery under consumer protection act).

Acting as Fiduciary.—Attorney acting as fiduciary, who charges compensation for his services, and whose gross annual income from all fiduciary services exceeds $25,000 for each of three next immediate preceding taxable years, is required to furnish to his customer certain information described in c. 203, §§4A, 4B.

Lien.—C. 221, §50 provides that attorney who is authorized by client to appear in any court action or in any state or federal department, board, or commission proceeding, shall have lien for his reasonable fees and expenses upon judgment, decree or order in his client's favor and upon proceeds derived therefrom. Statute provides for enforcement of lien. See also c. 221, §§50A, 50B. Breakdown of lawyer-client relationship serves as good cause for withdrawal, without waiver of attorney's lien. (24 Mass. App. 592, 511 N.E.2d 42).

Attorney Ethics.—Massachusetts Rules of Professional Conduct modeled after ABA Model Rules of Professional Conduct, with modifications. (SJC Rule 3:07).

Disbarment or Suspension.—SJC Rule 4:01 vests exclusive jurisdiction in SJC for discipline of any attorney admitted to, or engaging in practice of law in Massachusetts. Court-appointed 12 member Board of Bar Overseers is authorized to investigate conduct of any attorney within Court's jurisdiction, to conduct hearings, and to recommend appropriate discipline to Court pursuant to SJC Rules 4:01, 4:02, and 4:03, and Rules and Regulations of Board of Bar Overseers. Lawyers not required to report ethical violations of other lawyers. (SJC Rule 3:07 [8.3]). Collateral estoppel applies to bar discipline cases to same extent it applies in civil cases. (420 Mass. 6, 647 N.E.2d 1182). See also c. 221, §40, providing that SJC or Superior Court may assess damages and remove attorney from practice of law for deceit, malpractice or other gross misconduct. Disciplinary proceedings against attorney temporarily suspended from practice must be instituted within reasonable time after suspension, and must be given priority over other cases concerning attorneys not under suspension. (399 Mass. 431, 504 N.E.2d 652). Commonwealth recognizes reciprocal discipline rule. (407 Mass. 1010, 555 N.E.2d 233).

Unauthorized Practice.—C. 221, §41 provides for fines and imprisonment of one who practices law who has been removed from practice of law, or who has not been admitted to practice law, or who misrepresents his authority to represent persons in settling claims belonging to such persons. C. 221, §46 prohibits corporations (other than professional corporations authorized pursuant to c. 156A), and associations from practicing law or holding themselves out as being entitled to practice law.

Mandatory Continuing Legal Education.—No requirements.

Specialty Certification Requirement.—No requirements.

Professional Corporations.—Are authorized under c. 156A. Attorneys incorporating under c. 156A must also comply with provisions set forth in SJC Rule 3:06. See category Business Organizations, topic Corporations.

Limited Liability Companies.—Attorneys may form limited liability companies or partnerships under c. 156C or c. 108A. See category Business Organizations, topics Partnerships, subhead Limited Liability Partnerships; Limited Liability Companies. Attorneys registering as limited liability companies must also comply with SJC Rule 3:06.

Advertising.—Commonwealth adopted ABA Model Rules of Professional Conduct with modifications. (SJC Rule 3:07). Lawyer may not make false or misleading communication about lawyer or services. (SJC Rule 3:07[7.1]). Communication false or misleading if it contains material misrepresentation or omission, creates unjustified expectations, compares services with other lawyer's services, unless comparison factually substantiated. (SJC Rule 3:07[7.1]).

Lawyer may advertise, with certain restrictions, in public media not involving solicitation. (SJC Rule 3:07[7.2(a)]). Lawyer may not solicit prospective clients through coercion or harassment. (SJC Rule 3:07[7.3]). Solicitation defined and explained in Rule 7.3, §§(b)-(e).

MINERAL, WATER AND FISHING RIGHTS

MINES AND MINERALS:

Activities such as dredging, excavating, removing, filling, altering or polluting in coastal areas, in certain agricultural land and in wetlands are subject to regulation. (c. 21A, §14; c. 132A, §15; c. 184, §31 et seq.; c. 131, §§40, 40A; c. 252, §1 et seq.). Earth removal activities and excavation of sand, gravel and other materials may be subject to municipal regulation by ordinance or bylaws.

All coal mining operations are regulated by c. 21B.

The owner of mines or mineral deposits, which, on account of adjacent land belonging to other persons or occupied as a highway, cannot be worked in the ordinary manner without crossing such land or highway may construct roads, tunnels and railways thereto and when such construction is required by public convenience may take land of such other persons upon filing petition and bond with county commissioners if they find such improvements necessary. (c. 252, §§15-23). The sale of stock in mining companies is regulated. (c. 93, §15).

MORTGAGES

CHATTEL MORTGAGES:

Covered by Uniform Commercial Code. (c. 106, §§9-101 to 9-507).

Filing.—

Place of Filing.—Except with respect to fixtures, timber to be cut or minerals, including oil and gas, as to which filing is in registry of deeds where mortgage on real estate would be filed or recorded, filing is required in office of state secretary and in office of clerk of town or city where debtor resides or, if nonresident, has place of business. In case of filing with respect to consumer goods, farm equipment or farm products by farmer where debtor does not reside in commonwealth, local filing is required in office of clerk of town or city in which goods are kept. (c. 106, §9-401).

For central filing, address is: Secretary of Commonwealth of Massachusetts, 17th Floor, 1 Ashburton Place, Boston, Massachusetts 02108, Attn: Uniform Commercial Code Filing Section. Enclose postage-prepaid, self-addressed envelope for returns.

Fees.—(1) Financing statement, continuation statement or any amendment of either is set by filing officer, but if original financing statement or amendment thereof which is filed in registry of deeds is more than one page, fee is $10 ($20 for first four pages and $1 for each additional page in registry of deeds); (2) termination statement, fee is $5 ($10 for first four pages and $1 for each additional page in registry of deeds); (3) separate instrument of assignment, $10 ($10 for first four pages and $1 for each additional page in registry of deeds); (4) release of collateral, set by filing officer ($10 for first four pages and $1 for each additional page in registry of deeds); (5) information request (note, not available from register of deeds or assistant recorders of land court), $5; copies of filed statements, $2, and if statement consists of more than three pages, additional $1 for fourth and each succeeding page (75¢ per page for photostatic copies and $1 per page for all other copies in registry of deeds; $15 for copies certified by state secretary).

Forms.—Forms at end of this Digest are frequently used but have no official status. Printed forms are available. Modifications may be freely made as long as basic requirements of statute are met.

No official forms have been adopted with reference to the creation of a security interest. However, it is essential when creating a security interest that draftsman review c. 255, §§12C, 13I, 13J (Consumer Notes), c. 255B (Retail Installment Sales of Motor Vehicle Contracts), c. 255C (Insurance Premium Finance Agreements), c. 255D (Retail Installment Sale Agreements) and c. 93, §48 (form of notice of right of cancellation). In addition many agreements creating security interest will be subject to commonwealth's Truth-in-Lending Law. (c. 140D).

COLLATERAL SECURITY:

See category Debtor and Creditor, topic Pledges.

See note at head of Digest as to 1998 legislation covered.

See Topical Index in front part of this volume.

MA – 55

MORTGAGES OF PERSONAL PROPERTY:

See topic Chattel Mortgages.

MORTGAGES OF REAL PROPERTY:

Mortgage Brokers and Mortgage Lenders.—See category Business Regulation and Commerce, topic Brokers, subhead Mortgage Brokers.

Execution.—The usual form of mortgage is a deed upon "mortgage covenants" executed under seal, acknowledged, and recorded in all respects like an absolute conveyance, containing a condition subsequent and power of sale upon default. (c. 183, §§18-21). An absolute conveyance with a separate instrument of defeasance will also constitute a mortgage but will be treated as absolute conveyance as against any person other than maker of instrument of defeasance and his heirs and devisees and persons having actual notice of it unless it is recorded in registry of deeds for county or district where land affected is situated (c. 183, §53), and in equity absolute conveyance may be shown by parol evidence to have been intended as mortgage and will be so treated.

Discrimination.—Persons engaged in business of granting mortgage loans may not discriminate against any person, either in granting of such loan or in interest, rate, terms or duration of loan, because of race, color, religion, creed, national origin, sex, sexual orientation, children, ancestry, handicap or, subject to certain exceptions, age. (c. 151B, §4[3B]). No mortgagee doing business in Massachusetts may discriminate with respect to financing of acquisition of dwelling with indoor ambient formaldehyde level of not more than .10 ppm. (c. 167, §47). Arbitrary denial of residential mortgage loans for one to four family, owner-occupied dwellings based on location of property is forbidden. (c. 183, §64). No mortgagee may refuse to finance, or discriminate in terms of financing, based on presence of lead in paint or other materials. (c. 111, §199A[a]).

Restrictions apply as follows to loans of more than $1,500 secured by mortgage on real estate other than a first mortgage and assessed for not over $40,000 having a dwelling house for six or less separate households and used as a home by mortgagor: (a) maximum interest 1½% per month on unpaid principal balance of loan before default and for six months after default; (b) after six months of continuing default maximum interest 1% per month; (c) except where borrower in writing agrees to a different application of payments in cases where partial payments are made the interest shall be calculated to the time of payment, and such payment shall first be applied to interest and the balance to principal; (d) interest includes all sums paid by borrower to lender for interest, brokerage, commissions, services, extension of loan, forbearance to enforce payment, but does not include sums paid to lender for recording and foreclosure costs, charges for title examination and collection (c. 140, §90A); (e) various other detailed requirements are imposed (c. 140, §§90A-90E; c. 140D).

Conditions and restrictions may be imposed by commissioner of banks whenever any note secured by first lien on dwelling house of four or fewer separate households occupied or to be occupied in whole or in part by mortgagor provides for installment payments of principal or interest or both that will not amortize outstanding principal amount in full by maturity of such note and term of mortgage securing such note is for period not less than original or anticipated amortization period. Such conditions and restrictions shall include, but not be limited to, following: (1) Minimum term of note; (2) method by which rate of interest on renewed or extended note may be assigned; (3) maximum increase in rate of interest at renewal or extension of note; (4) provisions for decreases in rate of interest at renewal or extension of note as may be warranted by market conditions; (5) provisions for automatic renewal or extension of note at option of mortgagor; (6) requirements for advance notification and explanation of adjustment of rate of interest in connection with renewing or extending note, provided that such notification and explanation shall occur no less than 30 days prior to rate adjustment; (7) methods of disclosure to mortgagor of terms and conditions of loan as may be required under provisions of c. 140D. Notwithstanding any provision of law to contrary, commissioner may, by further conditions and restrictions, provide that rate of amortization may be varied, including utilizing period of negative amortization, in order to adjust rate of interest. These provisions summarized above do not apply to such transaction entered into by person, partnership, association, trust or corporation making five or fewer mortgage loans in calendar year; provided, however, that in computing number of mortgage loans there will be counted in loans of more than one partnership, association, trust or corporation, majority interest of which are owned or controlled directly or indirectly by same person or persons, partnerships, associations, trusts or corporations and including in loans of partnership, trust or company not incorporated loans of several members thereof; provided, further, that note exempt as described in this sentence shall contain following statement appearing conspicuously therein: THIS NOTE IS A CONTRACT FOR A SHORT-TERM LOAN. THIS LOAN IS PAYABLE IN FULL AT MATURITY. YOU MUST REPAY THE ENTIRE PRINCIPAL BALANCE OF THE LOAN AND UNPAID INTEREST WHEN DUE. THE LENDER IS UNDER NO OBLIGATION TO REFINANCE THE LOAN AT THAT TIME. YOU WILL, THEREFORE, BE REQUIRED TO MAKE PAYMENT OUT OF OTHER ASSETS YOU MAY OWN, OR WILL HAVE TO FIND A LENDER WILLING TO LEND YOU THE MONEY AT PREVAILING MARKET RATES, WHICH MAY BE CONSIDERABLY HIGHER THAN THE INTEREST RATE ON THIS LOAN. (c. 183, §60). Other disclosure requirements for first mortgage loans on owner-occupied one-to-four family residences contained in c. 184, §§17C, 17D and 209 C.M.R. 38.01-38.99 promulgated thereunder. Federal alternative mortgage regulation provided by P.L. 97-320, §804 does not apply. (1985, c. 224).

Until Dec. 31, 1997, loan fees, finder's fees, points or similar fees on mortgage loan on one-to-four-family owner-occupied dwelling shall not be charged except if fees or points previously disclosed in writing. (c. 183, §63). Effective Dec. 31, 1997, loan fees, finder's fees, points or similar fees on first mortgage loan on one-to four-family owner-occupied dwelling for originating and underwriting expenses limited by commissioner of banks. Mortgagees may be reimbursed for secondary marketing fees. (c. 183, §63). Mortgagee may revise mortgage terms per request of owner of equity of redemption on one- to four- family, owner-occupied residence, subject to certain restrictions regarding loaning or advancement of additional funds and applicable interest rate. (c. 183, §63A).

For time and form that loan proceeds must be transferred to mortgagor, see c. 183, §63B. Every application for a mortgage loan on real estate consisting of a dwelling

house with accommodations for four or less separate households and occupied or to be occupied in whole or in part by obligor on mortgage debt shall be made on a printed form which shall contain following two statements in type of at least two points larger than other type used on said application: (1) The responsibility of the attorney for the mortgagee is to protect the interest of the mortgagee; (2) The mortgagor may, at his own expense, engage an attorney of his own selection to represent his own interests in the transaction. (c. 184, §17B).

In addition to foregoing, every application and copy thereof must, if applicable, in type of at least same size as above required statements, disclose information relative to following: (a) Approximate expiration date of note; (b) rate of interest charged; (c) statement that as of expiration date of said note, mortgagee may demand payment of said note, may rewrite note by agreement at a greater or lesser rate of interest, or may, by agreement, allow payments to be made on said note at same, or a lesser, or a greater rate of interest. (c. 184, §17B).

Printed copy of above statements and information shall be given to mortgagor at time of making application. (c. 184, §17B).

Lenders must notify applicants, upon issuance of determination letter, of availability of any appraisal or other report obtained in connection with application for first mortgage loan and provide copy thereof without additional charge upon applicant's request, provided request is made within 30 days of notice. Mortgagee or appraiser shall not be liable for damages to applicant or to seller of such property on account of disclosure or contents of such report. (c. 184, §17C).

Lender must provide upon oral or written request good faith estimate of all "settlement services" as defined in 12 USC §2602. (c. 184, §17D[b]).

Lenders must also provide following upon applicant's request or at time application is provided, whichever is earlier: (a) Worksheet to enable applicant to calculate closing costs; (b) copy of HUD's pamphlet, "Settlement Costs"; (c) in case of certain variable rate first mortgage loans, copy of FHLBB's "Consumer Handbook on Adjustable Mortgages"; and (d) disclosure statement to aid prospective borrowers in understanding mortgage application process.

Within 21 days of receipt of application, mortgagee must notify applicant of any information which is needed to act on application. When mortgagee determines that application is complete, mortgagee must so notify applicant and notify applicant that he or she will be informed of mortgagee's decision within 30 days. Such notification shall include following legend in no smaller than 12-point boldface type: "IMPORTANT DISCLOSURE—PLEASE READ." (c. 184, §17D).

Disclosure of finance charges is required in accordance with Truth in Lending law, c. 140D. See category Business Regulation and Commerce, topic Interest, subhead "Truth in Lending" Law. Massachusetts has granted exemption for certain classes of credit transactions regulated by it pursuant to c. 140D. (c. 140D, §2). Disclosure information shall include full statement of closing costs to be incurred by customer which shall be presented before loan consummation or, if loan subject to Real Estate Settlement Procedures Act of 1974 (P.L. 93-533) and regulations issued thereunder (RESPA) before consummation or not later than three business days after receipt of customer's application, whichever is earlier. Good faith estimates of settlement costs required by RESPA may be substituted for itemization of amount financed.

Mortgagee who holds first mortgage on dwelling house of four or fewer units which is occupied in whole or in part by mortgagor and who requires advance payment of real estate taxes, must pay interest, to be determined by mortgagee, to mortgagor on amounts paid in advance. (c. 183, §61). Such mortgagee must also pay to city or town where mortgaged premises are located taxes due on or before due date to extent mortgagor has made advance payments of taxes to mortgagee. (c. 183, §62).

Title Report.—Mortgagee's attorney shall render certification of title on certain mortgages for not more than four family mortgagor-occupied dwellings. Such certification must include title examination which covers at least 50 years to warranty or quitclaim deed which on its face does not suggest defect. Certification must include statement that mortgagor holds good and sufficient record title to mortgaged premises free from all encumbrances and must enumerate exceptions thereto. Willful failure by attorney to render required certification to mortgagor constitutes unfair or deceptive act under c. 93A.(c. 93, §70). In case of registered land, title examination may start with present owner's certificate of title issued by Land Court, except bankruptcy indices and federal and state liens shall be examined. (c. 93, §70).

Recording.—An unrecorded mortgage is not valid against third parties having no actual knowledge thereof. (c. 183, §4). Mortgage on registered land is registered by filing deed and entering memorandum on owner's duplicate certificate. (c. 185, §§67, 68). No mortgagee may deliver documents for recording unless at time of delivery, net proceeds of loan transferred pursuant to c. 183, §63B.

Recording Fees.—As to recording generally, fees, etc., see category Documents and Records, topic Records.

Taxes.—For purposes of taxation the mortgagor and mortgagee are assessed for the value of their respective interests in the land, but tax is not invalidated by failure to assess the mortgagee, unless a sworn statement has been filed showing his interest. (c. 59, §§12-12F). If mortgagor fails to pay taxes, mortgagee may do so and add amount thereof to mortgage debt. (c. 60, §58). If separate assessments are made, and either mortgagor or mortgagee fails to pay, other may do so, and amount is added to or deducted from mortgage debt. (See c. 60, §59. Also see c. 60, §§38-39.) If person assessed has not previously applied for abatement of tax, mortgagee who has paid not less than one-half of tax may apply for abatement between Sept. 20 and Oct. 1 of year to which tax relates. (c. 59, §59).

Trust Deeds.—Trust deeds are valid, but seldom used except to secure issues of bonds.

Ownership of Mortgaged Property.—Except as against the mortgagee, the mortgagor is still deemed the owner of the premises. The mortgagee is in general, however, entitled to damages for injuries permanently affecting the value of the land. Thus where mortgaged land is taken on eminent domain both mortgagor and mortgagee may join in the petition for award of damages and the judgment on such petition shall apportion the damages according to their interests. (c. 79, §§32, 33).

MORTGAGES OF REAL PROPERTY . . . *continued*

Future Advances.—A mortgage may be written to cover future advances and will be binding as to third parties providing that statement to that effect is included in it, it is recorded and mortgagee is under obligation to make advances. (254 Mass. 282, 150 N.E. 293). Any sum or sums which shall be loaned by mortgagee to mortgagor at any time after recording of any mortgage of real estate, to be expended for paying for repairs, improvements, lead paint removal, or replacements to, fuel for, or for taxes or other municipal liens, charges or assessments on mortgaged premises, shall be equally secured with and have same priority as original indebtedness, to extent that aggregate amount outstanding at any time when added to balance due on original indebtedness shall not exceed amount originally secured by mortgage. (c. 183, §28A). Advances by mortgagee to consumer under open-end credit plan will be secured up to principal amount specified in mortgage as amount intended to be secured thereby. Priority shall apply to principal, interest and fees charged. (c. 183, §28B).

Late Charges.—No mortgagee secured by a first or subordinate lien on house of four or fewer separate households or on residential condominium unit occupied by mortgagor shall require mortgagor to pay penalty or late charge for any payment made within 15 days from date such payment is due. After period of 15 days late charge shall not exceed 3% of principal and interest overdue but not including amount of payment representing estimated tax payments required by mortgage note or deed. (c. 183, §59).

Prepayment.—If a mortgage note, secured by a first lien on a dwelling house of three or fewer separate households, occupied or to be occupied in whole or in part by mortgagor, is prepaid, any prepayment penalty may not exceed balance of first year's interest or three months interest whichever is less provided, however, that with respect to any such mortgage loan issued by F.H.A., mortgagor may be required to reimburse mortgagee to full amount of any charges, premiums or fees required by F.H.A. to be paid by mortgagee upon payment of such note before date fixed for payment. However, if anticipatory payment is for purpose of refinancing loan in a financial institution and takes place within 36 months from date of note an additional payment not in excess of three months interest may be charged. (c. 183, §56). If prepayment is result of eminent domain taking pre-payment penalty is not enforceable but this does not apply to mortgage notes executed prior to Aug. 13, 1970. (c. 183, §57).

Property Insurance.—Mortgagees granting more than five mortgage loans per year must accept preliminary memorandum of insurance or "binder" at closing, provided insurance contract for at least one year is issued within 30 days of closing (c. 183, §65), and may not require insurance in excess of replacement cost of buildings on mortgaged premises (c. 183, §66).

Priorities are determined in accordance with priority of recording.

Subordination Agreements.—A mortgagee may agree to subordinate his mortgage in whole or in part to another lien.

Assignment.—A mortgage is assigned by instrument in writing and under seal, acknowledged and recorded. (c. 183, §§1A, 4, 6C, 28). See categories Business Regulation and Commerce, topic Frauds, Statute of and Documents and Records, topic Seals.

Release.—An unrecorded assignment is not good against one subsequently taking a release from the mortgagee without notice, but may be good on the ground of laches against a subsequent assignee who does not obtain possession of the note or bond secured by the mortgage.

Any part of the mortgaged premises may be released without impairing the mortgage as to the balance.

Discharge.—A mortgage on registered land may be discharged by the mortgagee in person on the registration book in same manner as mortgage on unregistered land may be discharged by entry on record book at registry of deeds, and discharge shall be attested by assistant recorder. (c. 185, §69).

Satisfaction.—One of two or more joint holders of mortgages may discharge it by written acknowledgment of payment or satisfaction or by deed of release duly acknowledged and recorded. (c. 183, §54). Recordation of discharge duly executed and acknowledged constitutes discharge and release of lien created by mortgage. (c. 183, §54B).

Refusal to discharge mortgage after full performance of condition after 45 days creates liability in damages to owner. (c. 183, §55). Upon failure to provide release or written acknowledgment of payment, attorney's affidavit of payment may be recorded as discharge. (c. 183, §55).

Insurance.—See category Insurance, topic Insurance Companies, subhead Coercion.

Foreclosure.—A mortgage may be foreclosed after breach of condition by writ of entry in which the court renders a conditional judgment for possession, unless payment of the amount due or performance of the condition is made within two months. Three years peaceable possession under such judgment bars equity of redemption. (c. 244, §§1, 3-8, am'd 1991, c. 157). This method is seldom used.

Mortgagee may also make open and peaceable entry to foreclose, and foreclosure will become absolute in three years thereafter if certificate, sworn to by two witnesses, or memorandum on mortgage deed signed by mortgagor or person claiming under him, is made and recorded. (c. 244, §§1-2, am'd 1991, c. 157). In case of registered land, mortgagee must similarly file with Land Court. After foreclosure complete, mortgagee may petition for new certificate. (c. 185, §70, am'd 1991, c. 157).

In proceeding in equity for authority to foreclose mortgage, brought because of Federal Soldiers' and Sailors' Civil Relief Act of 1940, as amended, it is sufficient service if copy of notice designated in statute is recorded in each registry and clerk's office where mortgage is recorded before return day or as court directs published once not less than 21 days before return day in newspaper designated by court and mailed to each defendant by registered mail not less than 14 days before return day; and recorded copy of court's order authorizing foreclosure and of its approval thereof is conclusive evidence of compliance with such Act, so far as court may determine, as against all persons except interested parties of record prior to recording of notice unless they were named as defendants and had notice of proceeding. (1943, c. 57, §§1-3, as am'd by 1945, c. 120, §1, as further am'd by 1959, c. 105, §§1-2, as further am'd by 1982, c. 127, §1, as further am'd by P.L. 102-12 as further am'd by 1990, c. 496 as further am'd by 1998, c. 142).

Sales.—The usual mode of foreclosure is by sale under a power in the mortgage. (c. 244, §§11-15). With respect to limitation of actions, see topic Limitation of Actions, subhead Real Actions. Such sale must be in conformity with the power, and notice thereof must be published once a week for three weeks in a newspaper, if any, published in city or town where land is situated, or in newspaper with general circulation in town where land lies or, if none is so published, in county, first publication to be at least 21 days before sale. Notice thereof must also be sent by registered mail to owner or owners of record of equity of redemption as of 30 days prior to date of sale, said notice to be mailed 14 days prior to date of sale to said owner or owners to address set forth in registered land records, if land is then registered or, in case of unregistered land, to last address of owner or owners of equity of redemption appearing on records of holder of mortgage, if any, or if none, to address of owner or owners as given on his deed or on petition for probate by which he acquired title, if any, or if in either case no address appears, then to address to which tax collector last sent tax bill for mortgaged premises to be sold, or if no tax bill has been sent for last preceding three years, then to address of any of parcels of property in name of said owner of record which are to be sold under power of sale. (c. 244, §14). There is also provision for notice of sale to persons holding interest in property junior to mortgage being foreclosed as of 30 days prior to date of sale. Said notice to be mailed at least 14 days prior to date of sale. (c. 244, §14). Form of notice of sale provided by statute, but other forms may be used. After sale, person selling must cause copy of notice and affidavit of his acts under power to be recorded. (c. 244, §15). Deed of sale is deemed to convey premises sold subject to, and with benefit of, all restrictions, easements, improvements, liens or incumbrances, but no purchaser at sale need complete it if there are incumbrances, other than those named in mortgage and notice of sale, which are not stated at sale and included in auctioneer's bargain. (c. 244, §14). Any balance of proceeds after paying debt and costs is payable to mortgagor or those claiming under him. (c. 244, §36). Proper execution of power of sale absolutely bars equity of redemption at foreclosure auction. (c. 244, §18). No transfer by mortgagor impairs power of sale. (c. 244, §17). Mortgagee or any person acting for him may in absence of any provision to contrary purchase at foreclosure sale. (c. 183, §25). 1985 U.S. Bankruptcy Court decision held that mortgage foreclosure sale conducted in compliance with Massachusetts law, may be fraudulent conveyance under Bankruptcy Act if sale price is less than fair market value and decision suggests that appraisal of property, advertisement in real estate section of local newspaper and mailed notice to anyone who has expressed interest in property and real estate brokers within limited radius of property are required in addition to requirements under Massachusetts law for foreclosure sale. (55 B.R. 163). However, 1994 U.S. Supreme Court decision effectively overturned 1985 Bankruptcy Court decision by holding that when interpreting 11 U.S.C. §548 (Bankruptcy Code), reasonably equivalent value for foreclosed property is price received in fact from sale conducted in accordance with all of state's foreclosure laws. (511 U.S. 531). It is frequent practice as safety precaution to foreclose both through power of sale and through entry.

Deficiency Judgments.—If the proceeds of the sale do not pay off the mortgage note, the mortgagor is liable for any deficiency if prior to foreclosure a prescribed statutory notice of intention to foreclose has been mailed, postage prepaid, by registered mail, return receipt requested, not less than 21 days before date of sale and prescribed statutory affidavit has been signed within 30 days after sale. Statute of limitations is two years after date of foreclosure sale or two years after maturity of note, whichever date is later. (c. 244, §17A, 17B).

Moratorium.—No provision.

Redemption.—A mortgagor or a person claiming or holding under him may after breach of condition redeem the land mortgaged, unless the mortgagee or person claiming or holding under him has obtained possession of the land for breach of condition and has continued that possession for three years, or unless the land has been sold pursuant to a power of sale contained in the mortgage deed. (c. 244, §18). Land is sold when memorandum of sale is executed at auction. (181 Mass. 49, 62 N.E. 984). Prior to expiration of three years limited for redemption, and before or after entry for breach of condition, and before sale pursuant to power contained in mortgage, person entitled to redeem may pay or tender to mortgagee whole amount then due and payable on mortgage, performing or tendering performance of every other condition contained therein, and if there has been any action to recover land, paying or tendering costs of such action; or such person may commence suit for redemption offering to pay such amount as shall be found due from him or to perform such other conditions as case may require. (c. 244, §§19, 21-34). If person entitled to redeem makes such tender and mortgagee does not accept same mortgagor may within one year after tender commence suit for redemption, then paying to clerk of court amount tendered. (c. 244, §21).

If the mortgagee has had possession, he must account for rents and profits, and must be allowed all amounts expended in reasonable repairs and improvements, all lawful taxes, and assessments paid and all other necessary expenses in the care and management of the land. Balance, if due from mortgagee, shall be deducted from mortgage debt. If due to mortgagee, balance shall be added to debt and paid. (c. 244, §20).

Recovery of judgment for any part of the debt, after a foreclosure of a mortgage not containing a power of sale, on the ground that the value of the land mortgaged at the time of foreclosure was less than the amount due, opens the foreclosure, and the person entitled may redeem the land by suit for redemption brought within one year after recovery of such judgment, despite expiration of three year possession period. (c. 244, §35).

Reverse mortgage loans (loans proceeds of which are advanced in installments) authorized on one to four family residences owned and occupied by person 60 or more years old. Loan limited to 80% of value and term may not exceed ten years. Borrower must have completed home equity conversion counseling program approved by executive office of elder affairs. Borrower shall not be bound for seven days after loan commitment is made and shall sign statement acknowledging full disclosure by lender of all loan contingencies and terms including interest fixed at origination and ability to prepay without penalty. (c. 167E, §2[B], ¶14A). (See full text of ¶14A for complete

MORTGAGES OF REAL PROPERTY.... *continued*
disclosure requirements.) Mortgagee may add additional terms pursuant to 12 USC §1715z to obtain federal insurance for such loans.

Forms are set forth in Appendix to c, 183. Every mortgage and assignment of mortgage shall contain address of mortgagee or assignee (c. 183, §6C), and every discharge of mortgage shall contain street address of mortgaged property, volume and page or document number of mortgage and name of mortgagor; however, failure to include any such information shall not affect validity of instrument. (c. 183, §54). Statutory short form of mortgage is as follows:

Forms

Mortgage Deed.—
...... of ......, ... County, ... for consideration paid, grant to ...... of . ..... with mortgage covenants, to secure the payment of ..... dollars in ..... years with ..... per cent interest per annum, payable semi-annually, as provided in ..... note of even date, the land in . . . .
. . . . (description and encumbrances, if any)
This mortgage is upon the statutory condition, for any breach of which the mortgagee shall have the statutory power of sale.
Witness . . . . . hand and seal this . . . . . . day of . . . .
. . . .
(Here add acknowledgment.)   (Seal.)

Co-operative Bank Mortgage.—
...... of ......, ... County, Massachusetts ..... for consideration paid, grant to ...... Co-operative Bank, situated in ..... County, Massachusetts, with mortgage covenants, to secure the payment of ..... dollars, and interest and fines ...... as provided in ...... note of even date, the land in . . . .
. . . .
(description and encumbrances, if any)
. . . . . hereby transfer and pledge to the said mortgagee shares in the ..... series of its capital stock as collateral security for the performance of the conditions of this mortgage, and ..... said note upon which shares said sum of ..... dollars has been advanced to . . . . . by the mortgagee. The monthly payments under this mortgage are . . . . . dollars. In the event of an assignment of this mortgage, interest on the unpaid balance of the principal shall be at the rate of . . . . . per cent per annum.
This mortgage is upon the statutory co-operative bank mortgage condition, for any breach of which the mortgagee shall have the statutory co-operative bank power of sale.
Witness . . . . . hand and seal this . . . . . . day of . . . .
. . . .
(Here add acknowledgment.)   (Seal.)

The construction of the words "mortgage covenants" is set forth in c. 183, §19. The "statutory condition," which may be incorporated by reference, is set forth in c. 183, §20. The "statutory power of sale," which also may be incorporated by reference, is set forth in c. 183, §21.

The statutory form of partial release of mortgage is as follows:
the holder of a mortgage by . . . . to . . . . dated . . . . recorded with . . . . Deeds, book . . . ., page . . . ., for consideration paid, release to . . . . . . all interest acquired under said mortgage in the following described portion of the mortgaged premises:
                                                          (description)
Witness . . . . hand and seal this . . . . day of . . . .
(Here add acknowledgment).   (Seal).

The statutory form of assignment of mortgage is as follows:
holder of a mortgage from . . . . to . . . . dated . . . . recorded with . . . . Deeds, book . . . ., page . . . ., assign said mortgage and the note and claim secured thereby to . . . .
Witness . . . . hand and seal this . . . . day of . . . .
(Here add acknowledgment).   (Seal).

The statutory form of discharge of mortgage is as follows:
holder of a mortgage from . . . . to . . . . dated . . . . recorded with . . . . Deeds, book . . . ., page . . . ., acknowledged satisfaction of the same.
Witness . . . . hand and seal this . . . . day of . . . .
(Here add acknowledgment).   (Seal).

Other forms are set forth in the appendix to c. 183. In each case the instrument should give a reference to the book and page where the mortgage is recorded, should be acknowledged, and should be under seal. See category Documents and Records, topic Seals.

Chattel Mortgages.—See topic Chattel Mortgages.

Uniform Commercial Code adopted. See category Business Regulation and Commerce, topic Commercial Code.

PROPERTY

ABSENTEES:

Care of Property.—If one having property in Massachusetts has disappeared or absconded from the place where he was last known to be, and has no agent in Massachusetts, and it is not known where he is, or if such person has so disappeared without providing for his spouse or minor children dependent upon him for support, and it is not known where he is, or if it is known that he is without commonwealth, anyone who would be entitled to administer upon his estate, if he were deceased, or, if there is none such, then any suitable person, including such spouse, or someone in behalf of such spouse or minor children, may file petition in Probate Court for county where any such property is, stating name, age, occupation and last known residence or address of

such absentee, stating facts of disappearance, names and residences of other persons of whom inquiry may be made and schedule of property, real and personal, and its location, and asking for receiver. State treasurer must be made party to petition and given notice of subsequent proceedings. (c. 200, §1). After notice by registry or registry district recording or filing (as to real property), publication, posting and mailing (c. 200, §§2, 3, 4), receiver may be appointed (c. 200, §5). After receiver's bond has been approved, receiver shall take possession of all property of absentee within common-wealth and shall file schedule of such property (c. 200, §6) and upon court order such receiver may take possession of additional property, collect debts due absentee, sell, lease and invest property, and pay charges incurred in support of absentee's spouse and minor children and also such debts as may be proved against absentee. Court may make orders for disposition of property and proceeds in possession of receiver. (c. 200, §§7, 9-10).

Distribution.—Seven years after disappearance or, if receiver not appointed within six years, one year after appointment of receiver, absentee's interest in property ceases and it must be distributed as though absentee had then died intestate. If absentee or legal representative appears before distribution complete, court may order other distribution. (c. 200, §13).

A tax equivalent to that which would have been imposed had the absentee died intestate within the state is due and payable on such distribution. (§13).

Escheat.—Property (including dividends, bank deposits and legacies) unclaimed for three years and dividends or distributions upon liquidation of domestic corporation or other legal entity with transferable shares, which remain unclaimed for one year after final distribution to shareholders, must be reported and turned over to commonwealth which holds same subject to right in owner to recover same. (c. 200A). Unclaimed money held by municipality may revert to its general treasury. (c. 200A, §9A).

Process Agent.—Individual not inhabitant of Massachusetts, or partnership of such individuals, who has usual place of business or engages in construction in Massachusetts must file with state secretary written power of attorney appointing citizen-resident to be attorney for service of process and reciting that service of lawful process on such attorney is of same force and validity as service on individual or partnership. In absence of power of attorney, service may be made on state secretary who must mail notice of action to defendant's last known address. (c. 227, §5). Other nonresident doing business in Massachusetts must file with clerk of each city or town where he does business statement setting forth full name, address, place of business, and trade name and appointing city or town clerk agent for service of process. In absence of statement, service may be made on city or town clerk with mailed copy to defendant's last known address. (c. 227, §5A).

As to appointment of agent by foreign corporation, see category Civil Actions and Procedure, topic Process, subhead Agents for Service of Process. As to appointment of agent by nonresident executor or administrator, see category Estates and Trusts, topic Executors and Administrators, subhead Eligibility and Competency.

ADVERSE POSSESSION:

Character of Possession.—Open, notorious and uninterrupted possession of premises under claim of title. No right or title may be acquired in registered land by adverse possession, implied necessity or prescription. (c. 185, §53).

Duration of Possession.—Continuous adverse possession for more than 20 years, by operation of law invests with title to estate, subject to usual extensions in favor of reversioners, remaindermen and persons under disability. See category Civil Actions and Procedure, topic Limitation of Actions, subhead Real Actions.

Easements.—Easement of light and air cannot be acquired by use. (c. 187, §1). Easement of direct sunlight may be acquired by express grant or covenant or by solar access permit. (c. 187, §1A). Other easements cannot be acquired by adverse use or enjoyment unless such use or enjoyment is continued uninterruptedly for 20 years. (c. 187, §2).

Disabilities.—See category Civil Actions and Procedure, topic Limitation of Actions.

Notice of Intention to Prevent Easement by Adverse Use.—If a person apprehends that an easement in or over his land may be acquired by use or otherwise he may give public notice of his intention to prevent the acquisition of such easement by causing a copy of such notice to be posted in a conspicuous place upon the premises for six successive days. Such posting will prevent the acquisition of such easement by use for any length of time thereafter. Particular person may be prevented from acquiring such easement by causing such notice to be served on such person by means used for service of summons in civil action. Certificate of such posting or service by officer qualified to serve civil process, made on original notice and recorded with it within three months after posting or service is conclusive evidence thereof. (c. 187, §3).

CONVEYANCES:

See topic Deeds; category Documents and Records, topic Records. See also category Environment, topic Environmental Regulation regarding necessity of inspection of property with septic systems before conveyance. In 1998, potential movement toward unified state-wide system.

CURTESY:

See generally c. 189. Curtesy has been abolished in Massachusetts, but surviving husband given same dower rights as surviving wife. (c. 189, §1). See topic Dower.

DEEDS:

See topic Real Property for types of estates.

Execution.—No instrument purporting to affect interest in land shall be void because it is not sealed or does not recite seal. (c. 183, §1A). (See category Documents and Records, topic Seals.) Deed executed and delivered by person, or by attorney of person having authority, shall, subject to recording requirements for notice, be sufficient without any other act or ceremony to convey land. (c. 183, §1). Acknowledgment is, in general, not necessary for validity of deed, but acknowledgment by one or more

DEEDS . . . *continued*

grantors or attorney executing deed, or certificate of proof of execution, is necessary for recording. (c. 183, §29). Full name, residence and post office address of grantee and street address of granted premises must be endorsed on each deed, as well as recital of amount of full consideration in dollars or nature of other consideration but failure to include address will not affect validity of document. Full consideration means total price for conveyance without deduction for liens or encumbrances. (c. 183, §§6, 6B). Decree for separate support of Probate Court may direct that one party to proceeding convey interest in real estate to second party. In such case, decree itself may take place of deed and operate to vest title in other party if party so directed fails to comply with order. (c. 209, §32D). Judgment for alimony made in proceeding for divorce directing that deed, conveyance or release of any real estate be made will also operate to vest title if judgment has not been complied with at time that divorce judgment becomes final and judgment thereafter recorded. (c. 208, §34A). See category Documents and Records, topics Acknowledgments, Records. For conveyances of property in which homestead estate exists see category Debtor and Creditor, topic Homesteads. Dower and curtesy rights need not be specifically released in deed. See topics Dower, Curtesy.

Recording.—Conveyances of estates in fee simple, fee tail or for life, certain leases, or proper notices thereof (see topic Landlord and Tenant), mortgages and assignments of mortgages of real estate are among those instruments which have no effect, except as against grantor or lessor, his privies or heirs or devisees, or persons having actual notice thereof, unless recorded (or in case of registered land, registered), in registry of deeds for county or district in which land to which it relates is situated. (c. 183, §4). Deeds presented for recording or registration must be accompanied by form containing such information as commissioner of revenue may require in order to facilitate valuation of property for tax purposes. (c. 36, §24B). See also category Documents and Records, topic Records.

Recording Fees.—As to recording generally, fees, etc., and as to requirements for recording of real estate purchase and sale agreement, see category Documents and Records, topic Records, subheads Requisites for Recording; Recording Fees.

Operation and Effect.—No special provisions.

Taxes.—See category Taxation, topic Real Estate Conveyance Tax.

Forms.—Technical words of inheritance are not necessary to convey a fee. (c. 183, §13). "Grant" is a sufficient word of conveyance but implies no covenant. (c. 183, §12). No witnesses are necessary. (c. 183, §1).

Forms

Statutory short forms of deeds (c. 183, Appendix) are as follows:
Warranty Deed.—
. . . . . of . . . . , ... County, ... for consideration of . . . . dollars paid, grant to . . . . . of . . . . . with warranty covenants . . . . . the land in . . . .
. . . .
(description and encumbrances, if any)
Witness . . . . . hand and seal this . . . . . day of . . . . . .
. . . .
(Here add acknowledgment.)   (Seal.)
————————

Quitclaim Deed.—
. . . . . of . . . . , ... County, ... for consideration of . . . . dollars paid, grant to . . . . . of . . . . . with quitclaim covenants . . . . . the land in . . . .
. . . .
(description and encumbrances, if any)
Witness . . . . . hand and seal this . . . . . day of . . . . . .
. . . .
(Here add acknowledgment.)   (Seal.)
————————

Deed of Executor, Administrator, Trustee, Guardian, Conservator, Receiver or Commissioner.—
. . . . . executor of the will of . . . . . administrator of the estate of . . . . . trustee under . . . . . guardian of . . . . . conservator of . . . . . receiver of the estate of . . . . . commissioner by the power conferred by . . . . ., and every other power, for . . . . . dollars paid, grant to . . . . . the land in . . . . . (description) . . . . . .
Witness . . . . . hand and seal this . . . . . day of . . . .
. . . .
(Here add acknowledgment.)   (Seal.)
————————

Release.—
. . . . . of . . . . . County, ... for consideration of . . . . . dollars paid, release to . . . . . of . . . . . the land in . . . .
. . . .
(description)
Witness . . . . . hand and seal this . . . . . day of . . . . . .
. . . .
(Here add acknowledgment.)   (Seal.)
————————

Failure to Disclose Encumbrances.—A grantor is liable by way of penalty for failure to disclose encumbrances of which he has knowledge before the consideration is paid. (c. 266, §80).

Conveyance by Attorney.—See topic Powers of Attorney.

DEEDS OF TRUST:

See category Mortgages, topic Mortgages of Real Property.

DOWER:

See generally c. 189. All citations, unless otherwise indicated, refer to said chapter.
Certain limited dower and curtesy rights (merged and together called dower) remain but must be claimed by filing claim therefor in registry of probate within six months after approval of executor's or administrator's bond. Dower is limited to real estate owned by deceased spouse at time of death and all encumbrances take precedence over dower rights. Probate Court may assign dower, and tenant by dower is entitled to possession and profits of undivided one third of deceased spouse's real estate until assignment is made. (§1). Wild lands not used with farm or dwelling are not subject to dower (§3), nor equitable interests (192 Mass. 5, 78 N.E. 301), nor assets of revocable intevivos trust. (390 Mass. 864, 460 N.E.2d 572).

Release.—Spouse may be barred of dower by jointure settled before marriage with his or her assent (§7) or by pecuniary provision in lieu of dower made with his or her assent (§8).

Limitations.—After ten years from recording conveyance, spouse of conveying party may not claim dower unless prior notice recorded identifying conveyance and dower claim. (§16).

Election.—See category Estates and Trusts, topics Descent and Distribution, subhead Election, and Wills, subhead Dower.

ESCHEAT:

See topic Absentees, subhead Escheat; category Estates and Trusts, topic Descent and Distribution, subhead Escheat.

LANDLORD AND TENANT:

Uniform Commercial Code Art. 2A adopted. (c. 106, §2A-101 et seq.).

Kinds of Tenancy.—Tenancy for life, tenancy of years, tenancy at will and tenancy at sufferance are recognized. Tenancy from year to year is not recognized.

Leases.—An unwritten lease creates only an estate at will. (c. 183, §3). Lessor who has agreed orally to execute a lease and obtains lessee's signature, must, despite any purported waiver, deliver signed copy of lease within 30 days. Violations punishable by fine up to $300. (c. 186, §15[D]). Lease is properly under seal, but need not be under seal. (322 Mass. 670, 79 N.E.2d 288). There are no requirements for witnesses. Lease must be acknowledged before it may be recorded. No clause in lease of residential property may waive lessor's notice requirements for nonpayment of rent (c. 186, §15A) or allow lessor to enter premises except to inspect, make repairs or show property to prospective tenant, purchaser, mortgagee or their agents. Lessor may, however, enter such premises in accordance with court order or if premises appear to have been abandoned by lessee, or to inspect premises, within last 30 days of tenancy or after either party has given notice to other of intention to terminate tenancy, premises for purpose of determining amount of damage, if any, to premises which would be cause for deduction from any security deposit held by lessor. (c. 186, §15B).

Residential Tenant's Payments and Security Deposit.—Detailed regulations govern security deposits and advance payments of rents for residential property, including provision that lessor may not require payment in excess of following: Rent for first full month of occupancy, rent for last full month of occupancy calculated at same rate as first month, security deposit equal to first month's rent and, purchase or installation cost for key and lock. Nor may lessor demand at any time subsequent to commencement of tenancy rent in excess of current month's rent or security deposit in excess of statutory limit. Lessor must hold deposits and advance payments of rents in interest-bearing account, and pay lessee interest of 5% per year at end of each year (if held more than one year). Lessor must also provide certain detailed information regarding condition of premises and account information for deposits and advance payments. Failure of lessor to comply may result in award of triple damages plus court costs and reasonable attorney's fees. These provisions do not apply to vacation or recreational rentals of 100 days duration or less. (c. 186, §15B).

Recording.—Lease for term of more than seven years is not valid, except as against grantor, his successors, or persons with actual notice thereof, unless lease or proper notice thereof is recorded in registry of deeds (c. 183, §4), or if registered land, registered with land court (c. 185, §71). Lease for less than seven years with option to renew, which, if exercised, would cause lease to extend for more than seven years, must be recorded or notice of such lease recorded pursuant to c. 184, §4, to be effective against third parties without actual notice. (162 Mass. 473, 39 N.E. 280). Lease which provides that it shall continue on year to year basis until lessee gives prescribed notice must be recorded. (323 Mass. 310, 81 N.E.2d 821).

Rent.—A tenant at sufferance is liable to pay rent for such time as he occupies or detains the premises. (c. 186, §3). No interest can be charged under provision in lease for failure to pay rent until rent is over 30 days due. (c. 186, §15B). Massachusetts rejects common law rule that tenant's obligation to pay rent is totally independent of any of landlord's obligations. Tenant's covenant to pay rent is dependent on landlord's implied warranty of habitability; upon breach thereof by landlord, tenant may terminate lease with no further obligation to pay rent or may withhold rent pursuant to procedures in c. 239, §8A, and may raise landlord's breach as defense to action for eviction for nonpayment of rent. (363 Mass. 184, 293 N.E.2d 831). See also supra, subhead Residential Tenant's Payments and Security Deposit.

Residential Lease Tax Escalation Provisions.—Tax escalation clause in residential lease is against public policy and void unless provision sets forth: (1) That tenant shall be obligated to pay only his pro rata share of increased tax, (2) exact percentage of any increase which tenant shall pay and (3) that if landlord obtains abatement of tax, proportionate share of abatement, less reasonable attorney's fees, shall be refunded to tenant. If tenant pays more than pro rata share, excess must be refunded by landlord with interest of 5% per annum. (c. 186, §15C). See also supra, subhead Residential Tenant's Payments and Security Deposit.

Rent Control.—Massachusetts Rent Control Prohibition Act provides that no city or town may enact, maintain, or enforce rent control, except any city or town may adopt rent control where compliance by owner is voluntary and uncoerced. (c. 40P, §4[a]). Such regulations, if adopted, may not regulate occupancy, services, evictions, condo conversions, nor apply to any rental unit that is owned by person or entity owning less than ten units or that has fair market value rent exceeding $400 (c. 40P, §4[b]); and city or town must compensate owner for difference between unit's fair market value rent and unit's controlled rent (c. 40P, §4[c]).

Lien.—A landlord (other than an innkeeper) has no lien on the property of the tenant.

LANDLORD AND TENANT . . . *continued*

Termination of Tenancy.—Estates at will may be determined by either party by three months notice in writing or, if rent is payable at periods less than three months, by notice equal to interval between payments, or 30 days, whichever is longer. (c. 186, §12). No dispossession of dwelling may be made where lease terminated by operation of law or by act of landlord unless written notice received by tenant and interval between days of rent payments or 30 days, whichever is longer, has expired thereafter. But tenancy at will of property occupied for dwelling purposes shall not be terminated by operation of law by conveyance, transfer, or leasing of premises by owners or landlord. (c. 186, §13). In case of neglect or refusal by a tenant at will to pay rent due, his tenancy may be terminated by 14 days notice to quit, in writing, in form prescribed by statute, unless tenant tenders full amount of rent due within ten days of receipt thereof and has not received another similar notice within 12 months next preceding receipt of such notice. (c. 186, §12).

Provisions terminating tenancy if tenant shall have children who shall occupy premises are void. (c. 186, §16).

Written lease of premises for dwelling purposes may be terminated for nonpayment of rent upon 14 days written notice to quit unless tenant tenders rent, interest and costs on or before date answer due in landlord's action to recover possession (c. 186, §11), or, in case of written lease of premises for other than dwelling, landlord may also terminate in accordance with lease provisions (c. 186, §11A). If termination of non-dwelling lease by statutory notice, tenant may cure by tendering rent, interest and costs on or before date that answer is due in landlord's action to recover possession. (c. 186, §11A).

Reprisals Against Tenants.—Landlord of residential property who threatens or takes reprisals against tenant for seeking enforcement of tenant's rights, reporting landlord's violations of law, or organizing or joining tenants' union or similar organization shall be liable for damages not less than one month's rent or more than three month's rent, or actual damages sustained, whichever is greater, and costs of suit, including reasonable attorney's fees. Receipt of notice of termination, increase in rent, or substantial alteration in terms of tenancy within six months after tenant's action creates rebuttable presumption that such notice is reprisal against tenant. Waiver of above is void. (c. 186, §18). Attempted illegal reprisal also affords defense to action for summary process. (c. 239, §2A).

Holding Over.—Landlord may bring summary process proceedings to evict tenant if tenant holds over unlawfully. (c. 239, §1).

Dispossession.—Evictions are prohibited except through judicial process. (c. 184, §18). Summary process for possession of land is available to a lessor if lessee or person holding under him holds possession without right after determination of lease by its own limitation or by notice to quit or otherwise. (c. 239, §1). Recovery of possession before determination of lease by its own limitation is regulated by c. 239, §1A. Execution may be stayed for up to 12 months (c. 239, §9), except with respect to evictions for nonpayment of rent or because of tenant's fault. Rent arrearages may be recovered in summary process actions. If court finds dwelling premises are in violation of minimum standards for human habitation and advance notice of withholding rent has been given to landlord, and conditions may endanger or impair health or safety of tenants, residential tenants are presumed to have defense to eviction. Other claims based on condition of premises or services or equipment may also prevent recovery of possession. Court may order rent paid into court or receiver appointed to take charge of rents and remedy condition. If owner or agents knew of code violations, then no notice as aforesaid need be given provided such knowledge existed before arrearage in rent occurred. (c. 239, §8A). See subheads Nuisances; and Unsafe Conditions in Rental Property, infra. Landlords may recover possession only through civil remedies, as tenants holding over after alleged termination of term of occupancy cannot be arrested for criminal trespass. (c. 266, §120). If tenant is evicted without court order, tenant has option to recover possession or terminate lease, and landlord is liable for three times tenant's damages or for three months' rent, plus attorney's fees. (c. 186, §15F). For procedures applicable to residential care and services licensed, funded or operated by department of mental health, in effect from 7/1/96 to 6/30/2001, see 1995, c. 38, §308.

Discrimination.—See topic Real Property, subhead Discrimination; category Employment, topic Labor Relations.

Nuisances.—Regulated by c. 111, §122, et seq. If board of health determines that building is unfit for human habitation, or is or may become nuisance or cause of sickness or accident, owner or occupant may be ordered to clean premises, or comply with state sanitary code or rules of local board of health. Copy of order is served on mortgagees of record. If owner or occupant refuses, board of health may cause premises to be cleaned at owner's or occupant's expense, may remove occupant forcibly and close up premises, or may issue written notice to landlord requiring conditions to be remedied. Board of health may remedy conditions by petition in equity, and expenses incurred may be charged against owner of property as debt. (c. 111, §127B).

If residential buildings fall below standards of fitness for human habitation established under state sanitary code, or by board of health, any affected tenant or board of health may file petition with district court which states that premises have been inspected and found to violate sanitary code, and that condition may endanger health and was not caused by tenant. Certified copy of report is admissible in any proceeding as prima facie evidence. Process then issues to owner and hearing is held at which public health report is evidence. (c. 111, §127C, E).

If court finds facts as alleged, it may order petitioner to pay to clerk, in lieu of rent, amount equal to fair value of use and occupation of premises less any abatement due to violation, said amount to be used to effectuate removal of violation. Petitioner may bring substantially same action in Superior Court, which may grant injunctive relief or appoint receiver. (c. 111, §§127A-J).

Affected tenant may also petition district court without stating that premises have been found by inspection agency to violate such standards by stating facts indicating likely violation, that conditions not substantially caused by tenant and that unanswered request for inspection was made to appropriate agency 24 hours before filing. (c. 111, §127C).

Cities or towns may remove or demolish burnt, dangerous or dilapidated buildings from property and cost thereof may constitute a debt due city or town. (c. 139, §3A).

Unsafe Conditions in Rental Property.—Landlord of real estate other than owner-occupied two or three family dwelling, upon notice from tenant by registered or certified mail of unsafe condition not caused by tenant, must exercise reasonable care to correct condition. Tenant or guest injured by failure to correct condition shall have right of action in tort. No notice need be given for unsafe condition in areas not under tenant's control. Notice of code violation from a governmental agency is satisfactory notice. This provision cannot be waived in lease. (c. 186, §19). Landlord is precluded from raising as a defense in an action brought by tenant who has been injured by a defect in a common area that said defect existed at time of letting property if said defect was at time of injury a violation of building code. (c. 186, §15E). If tenants' health, safety and well-being are endangered by owner's violation of sanitary code or other provision, tenants, after certification of violation by board of health, other enforcement agency or a court, notice to owner in writing and owner's failure to commence repairs five days after receipt of such notice and failure to substantially complete repairs within 14 days after such receipt, may repair defects constituting violation and withhold costs of such repairs from rent up to four months' rent in any twelve month period. Except in certain circumstances, this provision cannot be waived in lease. (c. 111, §127L). For court action to correct sanitary code violations, see c. 111, §§127A-J. Tenant may assert breach of warranty of habitability as partial or complete defense to landlord's claim for rent. (363 Mass. 184, 293 N.E. 2d 831).

Distress.—There is no distress of rent in this commonwealth.

Agreements with Respect to Furnishing Heat, Light or Water.—The lessor of any dwelling or manufactured home (other than motel) who is required by law or contract to furnish heat, light, water, hot water, power, gas, elevator service, telephone service, janitor service, refrigeration service, is subject to fine or imprisonment for intentional failure to furnish same, or for interference with quiet enjoyment, or for attempting to regain possession by force without benefit of judicial process. Violators liable for actual and consequential damages, or three months' rent, whichever greater, court costs, and attorneys' fees. Setoff provision may apply. (c. 186, §14). This provision may not be waived.

Lease for More Than One Hundred Years.—A lease for 100 years or more, so long as 50 years remain unexpired, is considered an estate in fee simple for all purposes. (c. 186, §1).

Uniform Residential Landlord and Tenant Act not adopted.

Prohibited Provisions.—Certain provisions of leases and rental agreements indemnifying lessor against liability to lessee or tenant for any omission, fault, negligence or other misconduct of the lessor are against public policy and void. (c. 186, §15). Provisions of residential leases or rental agreements whereby tenant waives right to trial by jury in litigation with landlord or agrees that no action or failure to act by landlord constitutes constructive eviction are against public policy and void. (c. 186, §15F).

Fixtures placed on the premises by a life tenant may be removed within a reasonable time after the termination of his estate. (c. 184, §12).

Identification of Landlord.—Landlord of any residential property not occupied by landlord and without resident manager or agent, shall post notice not less than 20 square inches in size in location visible to all tenants bearing landlord's name, address and telephone number. If nonresident manager or agent is employed, his name, address and telephone number must also be provided. If building is owned by corporation, name, address and telephone number of its president shall be posted and if owned by trust or partnership, name, address and telephone number of managing trustee or partner shall be posted. Fine of $50 for violation. Each day that violation continues is separate offense. (c. 143, §3S).

Manufactured Housing Communities.—Defined as any tract with three or more manufactured homes for dwelling purposes. (c. 140, §32F). Governed generally by c. 140, §§32A-R. Owner of mobile home park must be licensed. Tenants in mobile home parks have been extended some of protection afforded tenants in residential real estate. (c. 140, §§32F-R).

Unfair or Deceptive Acts or Practices.—Broadly defined by c. 93A, §2. Applies to landlords and real estate brokers. For remedies see c. 93A. Attorney General has promulgated regulations under c. 93A which, in substance, construe violations of tenant protection laws to be unfair and deceptive conduct. (940 CMR 3.00 et seq.). For specific regulations governing landlord-tenant relationships, see 940 CMR 3.17.

LEASES:

See topic Landlord and Tenant.

PERPETUITIES:

Common law rule against perpetuities superseded by c. 184A, Uniform Statutory Rule Against Perpetuities except as to any limitations valid prior to Jan. 1, 1955. See category Courts and Legislature, topic Statutes, subhead Uniform Acts. Present 30-year limitation retained with regard to exercise of option in gross or non-vested easement in gross, contingent commencement of lease term, fee simple determinable in land, and fee simple in land subject to right of entry for condition broken. (c. 184A, §§5, 7). Certain options in gross held by government or certain other public entities must be exercised or become vested within 50 years. (c. 184A, §5[d]).

For rule as to income accumulations, see category Estates and Trusts, topic Trusts, subhead Accumulations.

PERSONAL PROPERTY:

No statute on tenancy by entireties in personal property but SJC has stated that tenancies by entirety exist with reference to personal property. (293 Mass. 67, 199 N.E. 383).

POWERS OF ATTORNEY:

Uniform Durable Power of Attorney Act adopted 1981 as c. 201B.

Attorneys in Fact.—No special form is required for letters of attorney, but letters of attorney for conveyances of real estate should be acknowledged (and under seal), and

See note at head of Digest as to 1998 legislation covered.

See Topical Index in front part of this volume.

POWERS OF ATTORNEY . . . *continued*
may be recorded in same manner as deeds. (c. 183, §§29, 32). But see topic Deeds, subhead Execution; category Documents and Records, topic Seals, subhead Effect of Seal.

REAL PROPERTY:

Estates of tenancy in common, joint tenancy and tenancy by the entirety are recognized. Conveyance or devise to two or more persons (except mortgage or conveyance or devise in trust) creates tenancy in common unless instrument states that they shall take jointly or as joint tenants or it appears from tenor of instrument that it was intended to create joint tenancy. (c. 184, §7). Conveyance or devise after Aug. 30, 1979 to two persons as tenants by entirety, who are not married to each other, creates joint tenancy and not tenancy in common. (c. 184, §7).

Estates or interests in land created without instruments in writing signed by the grantor or his attorneys are at will. (c. 183, §3).

A term of 100 years or more, so long as 50 years thereof remain unexpired, is regarded as an estate in fee simple for all purposes. (c. 186, §1).

Real estate may be transferred by person to himself jointly with another person or to himself and his spouse as tenants by entirety. (c. 184, §8).

Valid instrument affecting interest in land not void for lack of seal or failure to recite seal. (c. 183, §1A).

Conveyance of estate in fee simple, fee tail or for life, lease for more than seven years from making thereof, or assignment of rents or profits not valid against anyone but grantor or lessor and persons with actual notice, unless official copy, or, where applicable, notice of lease or notice of assignment of rents or profits recorded in registry of deeds (c. 183, §4), or, if registered land, registered in land court (c. 185, §§64, 71).

Offer to purchase real estate which contemplates execution of later purchase/sale agreement may be binding. (44 Mass. App. Ct. 274, 690 N.E.2d 460).

Rule in Shelley's Case has been abolished. (c. 184, §5).

Conveyances between husband and wife are valid to same extent as if parties were single. (c. 209, §3).

Doctrine of worthier title has been abolished. (c. 184, §§33A-33B).

Foreign Conveyances or Encumbrances.—See category Documents and Records, topic Records.

Condominiums are recognized as real estate and are governed by detailed statutory provisions. Building designed for office purposes may be established as condominium. (See generally c. 183A.) Real estate time shares are also governed by detailed statutory provisions. (c. 183B). Towns and cities are authorized to pass condominium conversion control laws. (1983, c. 527, §§1-5D, 7-8).

Lis Pendens.—Proceedings affecting title to land or use and occupation of buildings have no effect against third persons without actual notice thereof until memorandum of notice of such proceedings is recorded in registry of deeds for district (c. 184, §15) or in case of registered land, registered (c. 185, §86). If subject matter of action constitutes claim of right to title to real property or use and occupation thereof, justice of court may endorse said finding on memorandum. No register of deeds shall accept such memorandum for recording without such endorsement and affidavit of notice given. Ex parte proceeding available subject to right to dissolve. (c. 184, §15). Excepted proceedings and notice requirements are listed in statute. (c. 184, §15). After final disposition, certificate of judgment, decree, discontinuance, dismissal or other final disposition must be recorded (c. 184, §§16, 17), or registered (c. 185, §§86, 87) within 60 days to be effective against third persons having no actual notice. See category Civil Actions and Procedure, topic Judgments.

Restrictions.—No restriction enforceable unless of actual and substantial benefit to dominant estate. (c. 184, §§26-30). Obsolete restrictions or restrictions inequitable to enforce are unenforceable except by award of damages. (c. 184, §30). Restrictions otherwise unlimited as to time are limited by statute to 30 years after date of deed or other instrument, or date of probate of will, creating them, except in cases of gifts or devises for public, charitable or religious purposes and except for those contained in deed, grant or gift of commonwealth or existing on July 16, 1887 or to those having benefits of c. 184, §32. (c. 184, §23). C. 184, §§26-30 not applicable to restrictions in leases, mortgages and other security agreements, certain restrictions in orders of takings by commonwealth, and certain conservation, preservation and affordable housing restrictions. (c. 184, §26). Restrictions imposed after Dec. 31, 1961 enforceable only by party (or its successor) to instrument imposing restriction which states that restriction is for its benefit, or by owner of interest in benefited land. Such restrictions expire after 30 or 50 years, depending on date of instrument imposing restriction, unless notice filed before end of term. (c. 184, §§27, 28).

Discrimination against person seeking to buy or rent publicly assisted or multiple dwelling or contiguously located housing or other covered accommodations or commercial space forbidden if due to person's race, religious creed, color, sexual orientation, sex, age, ancestry, national origin, marital status, being veteran or member of armed services, deaf, blind, or having any other handicap. (c. 151B, §4[6,7,8,]). Term "handicap" does not include current, illegal use of controlled substances. (c. 151B, §4[1]). State must demonstrate compelling interest to enforce c. 151B, §4(6) when unmarried cohabitants refused rental based on landlord's religious beliefs. (418 Mass. 316, 636 N.E.2d 233). Unlawful to advertise housing accommodations stating preference for any of above conditions or for or against children, recipients of public assistance, or sexual orientation other than that involving minor children as sex object. (c. 151B, §4[7B]). Provision in instrument relating to real property which restricts conveyance, encumbrance, occupancy, or lease to individuals of specified race, color, religion, sex, or national origin is void. Any condition which limits use or occupancy of real property on basis of race, color, religion, sex or national origin is void except for certain real property held by religious organizations. (c. 184, §23B).

Rent control of residential properties prohibited except where voluntary by owner and city or town reimburses owner for difference between fair market value rent and controlled rent. (c. 40P, §§1-5).

Blockbusting is prohibited. See c. 151B, §§1, 3(13), 4(13) (general definitions and prohibitions); c. 112, §87AAA (sanctions against real estate brokers).

Taxes.—See category Taxation, topic Property Taxes.

See also topics Curtesy, Deeds, Dower, Landlord and Tenant; categories Civil Actions and Procedure, topic Partition; Debtor and Creditor, topic Homesteads; Documents and Records, topic Records; Family, topic Husband and Wife; Mortgages, topic Mortgages of Real Property.

Tort Liability.—Common law distinction between licensees and invitees has been abandoned in favor of duty of reasonable care owed by occupier of land to all lawful visitors (363 Mass. 693, 297 N.E.2d 43) and to child trespassers (378 Mass. 177, 390 N.E.2d 716).

Building Code.—State has building code which supersedes any less stringent requirements of local codes (c. 143, §§93-100). Copies are available, upon payment of fee, from State Bookstore, State House, Room 116, Boston, Massachusetts 02133.

Zoning.—Zoning bylaws and ordinances are enacted by cities and towns pursuant to Zoning Act, c. 40A, and St. 1956, c. 665 (Boston only).

TRUST DEEDS:

See category Mortgages, topic Mortgages of Real Property.

TAXATION

ADMINISTRATION:

Department of revenue is revenue agency of Massachusetts, located at 100 Cambridge Street, Boston, MA 02204, tel. 617-727-4545, and is composed of divisions of account management, audit, processing, operations and local services, child support enforcement, compliance, collections, problem resolution, taxpayers service, legal, forms, and information services, each headed by deputy commissioner. General administrative provisions with respect to various state taxes administered and collected by commissioner have been consolidated and appear in c. 62C. General administrative provisions relative to supervision by commissioner of local taxation appear in c. 58. Dept. of revenue regulations appear in 830 CMR.

Local taxation is dealt with in cc. 59 and 60.

Penalties.—Various penalty provisions set forth in c. 62C apply to enforcement of taxation generally. Such provisions are made expressly applicable, insofar as pertinent and consistent, to (among others) taxes imposed by cc. 62-65C (income, withholding, corporation excise [income], gasoline, cigarette, stamps, special fuels, room occupancy, sales, use, inheritance, and estate taxes). (c. 62C, §2). Such general penalty provisions include: Interest accruing after July 1, 1983 (federal rate before July 1, 1983) and before Jan. 1, 1993 at 18% per annum added to taxes not paid on or before statutory due date computed from such date until taxes are paid (c. 62C, §32); beginning Jan. 1, 1993 interest is at federal short-term rate under IRC §6621(b) plus 4%, compounded daily (c. 62C, §32); for failure to file return with commissioner, penalty added to tax equal to 1% of amount of tax required to be shown on return per month or part thereof during which failure continues, up to 25% of tax amount, but commissioner, for good and sufficient cause, may waive or abate such additional penalty tax (c. 62C, §33); for wilfully attempting to evade or defeat any tax in any manner, various penalties dependent upon manner employed and type of taxpayer (c. 62C, §73); for refusing or failing to file return or to correct inaccurate or insufficient return, or for filing return with intent to evade tax, within 30 days after notification by commissioner of such failure, inaccuracy or insufficiency, commissioner may determine tax due and may assess tax at up to twice amount determined after 30 days notice to taxpayer (c. 62C, §28); for nonpayment of any check for any tax, interest, penalty, fee or other charge, additional penalty equal to 2% of check, if $500 or more, and lesser of $10 or amount of check, if under $500, although commissioner has discretion to abate penalty (c. 62C, §35); revocation of license to conduct profession or business under certain circumstances (c. 62C, §§47A, 49A). Beginning Jan. 1, 1993, interest on late payment penalties accrues at federal short-term rate under IRC §6621(b) plus 4%, compounded daily from 31st day following notice of tax due; interest on late filing penalties accrues at same rate from due date of return. (c. 63C, §§32, 33). Penalties or additions to tax will be abated or waived if attributed to erroneous written advice given by revenue department employee and reasonably relied upon by taxpayer in response to written inquiry by taxpayer. (c. 62C, §36B).

Other significant penalties which apply to only certain taxes include:

Local Taxes.—In case of failure to file annual return of personal property no abatement of tax assessed can be obtained unless applicant shows reasonable excuse for delay or unless such tax exceeds by 50% amount which would have been assessed if return had been filed when due, and in such case only excess over such 50% can be abated. (c. 59, §61).

Delinquent real estate and personal property taxes bear interest at rate of 14% per annum (c. 59, §57), except that no interest is due if tax bill is not sent until after due date, provided tax is paid within 30 days after bill is first sent.

Persons not paying property taxes when due are liable for costs of collection. See subhead Local Taxation, catchlines Collection, and Tax Levy and Sale, supra. Penalty for tendering insufficient funds check to pay property taxes is greater of $25 or 1% of amount due. (c. 60, §57A).

Income Tax.—In case of failure to file by nonresident, commissioner may assess tax based on estimate of gross income from sources within Massachusetts, without allowance for deductions or exemptions, and with penalties and interest. (c. 62C, §26[e]).

Withholding.—Employer failing to withhold and pay over income tax, including responsible officers or employees of employer corporation, is personally liable for amount which should have been withheld, with interest and penalties. (c. 62B, §§5, 6).

Employee who makes statement under c. 62B, §4 (in furnishing employer with withholding exemption certificate) which, without reasonable basis, results in decrease in amount deducted or withheld, is subject to penalty of $500. (c. 62B, §11A).

See note at head of Digest as to 1998 legislation covered.

See Topical Index in front part of this volume.

MA – 61

ADMINISTRATION . . . *continued*

Estimated Tax.—There is additional charge accruing at federal short-term rate under IRC §6621(b) plus 4%, compounded daily, for period of underpayment of required installments. Required annual payment is lesser of 80% (66²/₃% for farmers and fishermen) of tax for year or 100% of preceding full year's tax, except no additional charge if: (1) Tax is less than $200, (2) in preceding full taxable year taxpayer was inhabitant of commonwealth and had no tax liability, (3) commissioner determines unusual circumstances, or (4) taxpayer over 61 or disabled and had cause for underpayment. (c. 62B, §14).

Estate Tax.—Interest at annual rate four percentage points higher than federal short-term rate is imposed on taxes not paid when due (c. 62C, §32), but commissioner may in his discretion extend time for payment with interest (c. 65C, §10). From July 1, 1983 through Dec. 31, 1992, interest was instead calculated at fixed rate of 18% per annum. If underpayment is due to fraud, penalty equal to 50% of underpayment is added in lieu of penalty under c. 62C, §33. (c. 65C, §13).

Stamp Tax.—Fine of not less than $500 nor more than $1,000 and/or imprisonment for not more than one year may be imposed for falsely or fraudulently affixing or removing stamps, or for altering or removing cancellation of stamps. (c. 64D, §§7, 8). Fraudulent use of stamps without effective cancellation is punishable by fine of not less than $200 nor more than $500. (c. 64D, §9).

Gasoline, etc. Taxes.—Violation of c. 64A is punishable by fine of not more than $1,000 and/or by imprisonment for not more than one year. (c. 64A, §11). Certain violations of c. 64E are punishable by fine of not more than $100. Others punishable by fine of not more than $1,000 and/or by imprisonment for not more than one year. (c. 64E, §§2, 11).

Cigarette Tax.—Except as otherwise provided in §10, violation of c. 64C or filing of false return, affidavit or statement is punishable by fine of not more than $1,000 and/or by imprisonment for not more than one year. (c. 64C, §10).

Controlled Substance Tax.—Violation of c. 64K punishable by penalty equal to 100% of tax and fine up to $10,000 and/or imprisonment not more than five years. (c. 64K, §9).

Employment Security Tax.—In event of failure by employer to pay amounts when due, interest will be charged from due date at 12% per annum (calendar 1983), or greater of 12% or rate established under c. 62, §13, currently 18% (calendar 1984 and following) will be charged from due date or, in lieu of such interest, penalty of $5 per day may be imposed for not more than number of days of default. If employer fails to file any report of wages or contributions within 15 days of written demand by commissioner, commissioner may assess penalty equal to 10% of contributions due, but not less than $35 nor more than $1,000 for each such failure to file. (c. 151A, §15).

Any employer, or any officer or agent of employer, who knowingly makes false statement or representation to avoid or reduce any contribution shall be guilty of felony and punishable by fine of not less than $10,000 nor more than $50,000 and/or imprisonment for not more than five years. Any such person who knowingly fails or refuses to pay any benefit or contribution, or to furnish any report or information required by commissioner, or makes any deduction from wages to pay any contribution, or who attempts to coerce any individual to waive any rights under c. 151A, is punishable by fine of not less than $2,500 nor more than $10,000 and/or by imprisonment for not more than one year. Each such failure, or refusal, to pay each such deduction from wages and each attempt to coerce, shall constitute separate and distinct offense and any other violation of c. 151A or of order, rule or regulation of commissioner for which no other punishment provided shall be punished by fine of not more than $100 for first offense, and for any subsequent offense within two years of offense, punishable by fine of not less than $200 and not more than $500 and/or by imprisonment for not more than two years. (c. 151A, §47). Any person convicted of violation of any provision of c. 151A or of any order, rule or regulation of director for which punishment is not otherwise provided is punishable by fine of not more than $100 for first offense and, for any offense within two years after conviction for like offense, by fine of not less than $100 nor more than $500, and/or by imprisonment for not more than two years. (c. 151A, §47).

Person knowingly making false statement to obtain or increase benefits is subject either to disqualification (at discretion of commissioner) or fine of between $100 and $1,000 and/or imprisonment of up to six months. (c. 151A, §§25[a], 47). If employer fails to report claimant's base period wages within seven days of date of request by commissioner, director will establish claimant's rights on basis of claimant's own statement of wages, supplemented by such other information as may be available to commissioner. (430 CMR §5.04[3]).

Sales and Use Taxes.—Representation by vendor that tax will be absorbed or refunded is punishable by fine of up to $100 for each offense. (c. 64H, §23; c. 64I, §24).

Motor Vehicle Excise Tax.—Owners neglecting to pay excise tax pay 12% per year interest on tax from time tax payable and may not renew or exchange car registration or driver's license. (c. 60A, §§2, 2A).

Poll tax repealed.

Reciprocal Enforcement of Tax Liabilities.—Tax liabilities due commonwealth or any subdivision may be enforced in courts of other states, and other states may bring similar suits in Massachusetts courts to enforce tax liabilities. (c. 58, §28C).

Failure to Pay Money Received.—Any person who, in connection with preparation or filing of tax return for another, or payment of any tax, receives money from such other person to be paid to discharge tax liability and wilfully fails to pay it over to commissioner is guilty of felony and punishable by fine of not more than $100,000, or $500,000 in case of corporation, and/or imprisonment for not more than three years, together with costs of prosecution. (c. 62C, §73).

Liens.—In addition to liens for local taxes on real estate (see catchline Lien under subhead Local Taxation, supra), lien for unpaid personal income, corporation excise, bank excise, insurance company, utility, certain corporations selling liquor, gasoline, sales, use, cigarette, estate, realty transfer and room occupancy taxes arises at time of assessment and terminates not later than six years thereafter. (c. 62C, §50). See c. 62C, §55A for property of individual taxpayers which is exempt from levy. See also c. 36, §24; c. 185, §§46, 78, 80.

ALCOHOLIC BEVERAGES TAX:

Excise tax on sale of alcoholic beverages in commonwealth, see c. 138, §21.

An income tax of 57% of gross receipts is imposed upon corporations (not subject to corporate excise), associations or organizations licensed to sell alcoholic beverages. (c. 63A).

BUSINESS TAXES:

Franchise Taxes.—See category Business Organizations, topic Corporations.

Employment security tax is imposed on employers, as defined, at a fixed rate of payroll, particular rate depending on benefit payment experience of particular employer compared with benefit payment experience in commonwealth generally. (c. 151A, §14). Workforce training contribution of .075% of overall payroll required. (c. 151, §14L). Tax is imposed with respect to total remuneration for employment, but not over greater of $6,000 a year for each employee or amount specified as "wages" under FUTA. (c. 151A, §14). Tax is payable in such manner and at such times as commissioner of department of employment and training requires. (c. 151A, §13). Tax for each calendar quarter must be paid to commissioner on or before last day of month following such quarter. There is no tax on employees. Employers not subject to tax on amounts paid to independent contractors or to certain types of workers. (c. 151A, §§2, 4A, 6, 6A, 8). Nonprofit organizations and governmental employers may elect to reimburse state for benefits paid rather than pay contributions under §14. (c. 151A, §14A).

Room Occupancy Tax.—Tax of 5% of rent is imposed on occupancy, for 90 consecutive days or less, in hotels, motels, bed and breakfast establishments with over three rooms and lodging houses, of rooms designed and normally used for sleeping and living purposes. Exemptions include rooms at federal, state, municipal, charitable, educational or religious institutions, convalescent homes, summer camps, and occupancy where rent is less than $15 per day. Reimbursement is collected from occupant. Returns and payment are due on 20th of each month for preceding month. (c. 64G; c. 62C, §16). Rate reflects 14% surtax. (1969, c. 546, §22). Local excise tax up to 4% (4.5% in Boston) of rent is also collectible by commissioner if rent exceeds $15 per day for room in hotel, lodging house, motel or bed and breakfast establishment within city or town accepting c. 64G, §3A, effective first day of calendar quarter following 30 days after acceptance or first day of such later calendar quarter as city or town may designate. (c. 64G, §3A, 1997, c. 152, §22). Additional 2.75% excise for each occupancy in Boston, Springfield, Cambridge, and Worcester. (1997, c. 152, §9).

CIGARETTE TAX:

See c. 64C. Excise tax imposed on sale of cigarettes in commonwealth at rate of 25¹/₂ mills, plus any amount of federal excise less than 8 mills, per cigarette. Notwithstanding preceding, tax of 15% of price paid for smoking tobacco assessed. (c. 64C, §§6, 7). Portion of tax credited to Health Protection Fund, Health Care Access Fund, and Local Aid Fund. (c. 64C, §§7C, 28[a], [b]).

ESTATE TAX:

Estate tax is imposed under c. 65A and, with respect to estates of decedents dying on or after Jan. 1, 1976, also under c. 65C. For estates of resident decedents dying on or after Jan. 1, 1997, estate tax under c. 65C will be in amount equal to Federal credit for state death tax purposes, determined at date of death and adjusted for such taxes payable in other jurisdictions. For estates of nonresident decedents dying on or after said date, such tax will be in proportion which value of Massachusetts real and tangible personal property bears to total Federal gross estate. (c. 65C, §2A).

Definitions.—For purposes of c. 65C, Code means Federal Internal Revenue Code, as am'd and in effect on Jan. 1, 1975 (thus Massachusetts did not incorporate important amendments of various IRC sections referred to infra enacted by 1976 Tax Reform Act, and subsequent federal tax acts); Federal gross estate means gross estate as defined under Code, except three-year rule of former §2035 and former inclusion of ¹/₂ joint tenancy are retained; Massachusetts adjusted gross estate means Massachusetts gross estate less deductions allowable in computing Massachusetts taxable estate pursuant to §§2053 and 2054 of Code; Massachusetts gross estate means federal gross estate, whether or not filing of federal estate tax return is required, less value of real and tangible personal property with situs outside commonwealth and plus, for estates of those dying on or after Jan. 1, 1986, value of any property in which decedent had income interest for life and value of any property for which deduction was allowed for Massachusetts estate tax purposes with respect to transfer of property to decedent; Massachusetts net estate means Massachusetts gross estate less, to extent allowable in computing Massachusetts taxable estate, deductions for funeral expenses, claims against estate and unpaid mortgages on, or any indebtedness in respect of, property where value of decedent's interest therein, undiminished by such mortgage or indebtedness, is included in value of Massachusetts gross estate; Massachusetts taxable estate means Massachusetts gross estate less certain exemptions and deductions allowable under c. 65C, §3; and resident means person domiciled in commonwealth. (c. 65C, §1).

Tax and Rates.—Tax at following rates is imposed on transfer of Massachusetts taxable estate of deceased resident dying on or before Dec. 31, 1996: if Massachusetts taxable estate is not over $50,000, 5% thereof; if over $50,000 but not over $100,000, $2,500 plus 7% of excess over $50,000; if over $100,000 but not over $200,000, $6,000 plus 9% of excess over $100,000; if over $200,000 but not over $400,000, $15,000 plus 10% of excess over $200,000; if over $400,000 but not over $600,000, $35,000 plus 11% of excess over $400,000; if over $600,000 but not over $800,000, $57,000 plus 12% of excess over $600,000; if over $800,000 but not over $1,000,000, $81,000 plus 13% of excess over $800,000; if over $1,000,000 but not over $2,000,000, $107,000 plus 14% of excess over $1,000,000; if over $2,000,000 but not over $4,000,000, $247,000 plus 15% of excess over $2,000,000; if over $4,000,000, $547,000 plus 16% of excess over $4,000,000; provided that such tax is not to be greater than 20% of amount by which Massachusetts net estate exceeds amount of exemption noted in following paragraph. (c. 65C, §2[a]). If such tax is exceeded by maximum credit for state death taxes allowable to estate of resident or nonresident against federal estate tax,

See note at head of Digest as to 1998 legislation covered.

See Topical Index in front part of this volume.

MA – 62

ESTATE TAX ... *continued*
computed according to rate schedule of §2011 of Code based on Massachusetts taxable estate, such excess is added to such tax. (c. 65C, §2[b]).

Exemptions and Deductions.—For estates of decedents dying during 1993, exemption is equal to Massachusetts net estate for such estates of $300,000 or less; similar exemption for estates of $400,000 or less of decedents dying during 1994; $500,000 or less of decedents dying during 1995; $600,000 or less of decedents dying during 1996. Exemption shall not exceed smallest federal taxable estate that absorbs allowable federal credit under IRC §2010. (c. 65C, §3[a]). If Massachusetts net estate exceeds amount of exemption, no exemption will apply, except for purposes of exemption referenced immediately above regarding federal taxable estate. (c. 65C, §3[a]). In addition, deductions allowable in computing Massachusetts taxable estate consist of deductions or portions thereof, other than exemption of §2052 of Code, allowable in determining federal taxable estate and attributable to property in Massachusetts gross estate; provided that, with respect to estates of decedents dying on or before June 30, 1994, deduction for property passing to surviving spouse is not to exceed 50% of Massachusetts adjusted gross estate. (c. 65C, §3[a]). Also see c. 65C, §3(a) for exemptions and deductions regarding estate of decedent dying on or after July 1, 1994. No deduction allowed for interest unless paid or accrued within three years of date of return. Waiver of right to claim deduction for federal estate tax purposes is considered waiver of right for Massachusetts estate tax purposes. (c. 65C, §3).

Qualified Terminable Interest Property.—No part of such property will be treated as passing to any person other than surviving spouse for purposes of §2056 of Code as long as total deduction for property passing to spouse, with respect to estates of decedents dying on or before June 30, 1994, does not exceed 50% of Massachusetts gross estate. For estates of decedents dying on or after July 1, 1994, deduction of terminable interest property will not be limited by IRC 2056(c). (c. 65C, §3A).

Generation Skipping Tax.—Effective July 1, 1983, tax imposed on every generation-skipping transfer in which either original transferor is Massachusetts resident or property transferred includes real or personal property in Mass. on date of transfer. Tax equals amount allowable as credit for state death taxes under IRC 2602 as in effect on Dec. 31, 1981. (c. 65C, §4A). It is unclear whether 1986 repeal of IRC 2602 effectively repealed tax imposed by c. 65C, §4A.

Nonresidents.—Transfer of real and tangible personal property of deceased nonresident, if such property were includable in Massachusetts gross estate had decedent been resident, is taxed in accordance with above. Tax is amount which bears same ratio to tax which would have been due had decedent been resident as value of all such property, diminished by any mortgage or lien thereon, bears to value of decedent's Massachusetts gross estate, diminished by any mortgage or lien thereon, determined as if decedent had been resident. (c. 65C, §4). Provision is made to assure payment to decedent's domiciliary state of any inheritance, succession, transfer, estate or other death taxes due to that state (c. 65C, §21[b]), provided such state has reciprocal provision (c. 65C, §21). Foreign executor of nonresident decedent may obtain license to sell real estate under court order if c. 202, §32 provisions are satisfied.

Valuation of property in Massachusetts gross estate is as of date of death, but if alternate valuation under §2032 is used for federal return, Massachusetts estate is similarly valued. If no federal estate tax payable, whether or not return is filed, §2032 date may be elected for Massachusetts return. Value of less than absolute interest in property determined in accordance with §2031. Farm real property may be valued as in §2032A. (c. 65C, §5).

Executor; Returns.—Tax is to be paid by executor, which term in c. 65C means executor or administrator, or if none appointed, qualified and acting within commonwealth, any person in actual or constructive possession of decedent's property. Probate Court may authorize, in same manner as for payment of debts, executor to sell so much of property as will enable payments of tax. (c. 65C, §6[a]). For death before Jan. 1, 1997, no executor's final account is to be allowed by Probate Court unless and until executor files therein certificate of commissioner showing that tax has been paid, payment has been secured as permitted or no tax is due. (c. 65C, §6[b]). For deaths on or after Jan. 1, 1997, certificate of commissioner not required. (c. 65C, §6). If executor makes written application, accompanied by copy of final determination of federal estate tax liability, to commissioner for determination of tax and discharge from personal liability therefor, commissioner, as soon as possible, and in any event within one year after making of application or, if such is made before return is filed, within one year after return is filed, is to notify executor of amount of tax, upon payment of which executor is to be discharged of personal liability for any deficiency in tax thereafter found due and is to be entitled to receipt or writing showing such. (c. 65C, §7). For decedent dying on or before Dec. 31, 1996, and Massachusetts gross estate exceeds exemption under c. 65C, §3(a), or for decedent dying after Dec. 31, 1996, if estate is liable for any tax under c. 65C, executor is to make return with respect to tax imposed by c. 65C within nine months after date of death. (c. 62C, §17[a]). If executor is unable to make complete return as to part of federal gross estate, he is to include in his return description of such part and name of every person holding legal or beneficial interest therein, who, upon notice from commissioner, is in like manner to make return as to such part. (c. 62C, §17[b]). Every person liable for tax or collection thereof is to keep records, render statements, make returns and comply with rules and regulations as commissioner may from time to time prescribe. (c. 65C, §8). For good cause commissioner may grant reasonable extension of time for filing return, but only if tentative return is filed prior to date tax is to be paid and amount equal to reasonably estimated tax due is paid on or before such date. Failure to pay 80% of tax due on or before such date voids extension and return is subject to late return penalty. Such penalty may be abated by commissioner in whole or part for good and sufficient cause. (c. 62C, §19). Penalty determinations made under c. 62C, §33.

Due Date; Extensions; Postponement.—Tax is due and payable by person liable at expiration of nine months from date of death. Return must be filed in cases where Massachusetts gross estate exceeds amount of exemption in c. 65C, §3(a). (c. 62C, §§17[a], 32). Commissioner may extend time for payment of tax for reasonable period not to exceed six months or, if he finds payment of any part thereof on due date would result in undue hardship, for reasonable period not to exceed three years from date fixed for payment. If extension is granted, commissioner may require deposit with State Treasurer of bonds or negotiable obligations of commonwealth or U.S. in amount as he may from time to time deem necessary to adequately secure payment or giving of bond to state treasurer in amount and with sureties as he deems necessary, conditional upon payment in accordance with terms of extension. (c. 65C, §10[a]). If value of reversionary or remainder interest in property is included in gross estate, payment of part of tax attributable thereto may, at executor's election, be postponed until six months after termination of precedent interest, which postponed amount shall then be payable with interest thereon at 8% per annum from original due date until paid. Such postponement is to be under regulations prescribed by commissioner and upon condition that person liable give bond to state treasurer in amount and with sureties as commissioner deems necessary, conditioned as prescribed. (c. 65C, §10[b]).

Assessment.—Tax is deemed to be assessed at lesser of amount shown as due on return or any amendment, correction or supplement thereof or at amount properly due, and at later of time when return is filed or required to be filed. (c. 62C, §26[a]). If commissioner determines that full tax has not been or is not deemed to be assessed, he may within three years of later of date return was filed or was required to be filed assess same with interest as prescribed to date payment of deficiency assessment is required to be paid, first giving notice of his intention to person to be assessed, which person or his representative may within 30 days after date of notification confer with commissioner or his representative. After such 30 days, commissioner is to assess tax remaining due or portion thereof he believes has not been theretofore assessed. Failure of receipt of such notice does not affect validity of tax. (c. 62C, §26[b]). In case of arithmetical, clerical or other obvious error on face of return, commissioner may assess deficiency without giving prior notice. (c. 62C, §26[c]). In case of false or fraudulent return filed with intent to evade tax or failure to file return, commissioner may make assessment at any time, without notice of intention, determining tax due according to best information and belief. (c. 62C, §26[d]). If executor omits items from gross estate includible therein exceeding 25% of gross estate stated in return, tax may be assessed any time within six years after return is filed, but no such item is considered omitted if disclosed in return or attached statement in manner adequate to apprise commissioner of nature and amount thereof. (c. 62C, §26[f]). If any underpayment of tax required to be shown on return is due to fraud, there is to be added tax of 50% of such underpayment, such underpayment meaning deficiency assessed as above described in connection with which notice of intention is required, except that tax shown on return is to be taken into account only if such return was filed before last day prescribed for filing with extensions. If such penalty is assessed, no penalty under c. 62C, §33 is to be assessed with respect to same underpayment. (c. 65C, §13).

Lien, etc.—Unless paid, tax is lien for ten years from date of death upon Massachusetts gross estate, except that such part thereof used for payment of charges against estate and expenses of administration, allowed by Probate Court having jurisdiction, is to be divested of such lien. (c. 65C, §14[a]). For deaths on or after Jan. 1, 1997, affidavit of executor stating that gross estate of deceased does not require federal estate tax filing releases lien. (c. 65C, §14[a]). If tax is not paid when due, spouse, transferee, trustee, surviving tenant, person in possession of real or personal property by reason of exercise, nonexercise or release of power of appointment, or beneficiary, who receives or has on date of decedent's death, real or personal property included in Massachusetts gross estate, to extent of value of such property on such date of death, is to be personally liable for tax. Real property conveyed prior to decedent's death by recorded deed not disclosing intent that it take effect at or after death, and personal property transferred by, or by transferee of, such persons to bona fide purchaser, mortgagee or pledgee, for adequate and full consideration in money or money's worth is divested of such lien and lien then attaches to all property of such transferor, except any part transferred to bona fide purchaser, mortgagee, or pledgee for adequate and full consideration in money or money's worth. (c. 65C, §14[b]). Such lien is not to be valid with respect to any of certain securities as against any mortgagee, pledgee or purchaser thereof, for adequate and full consideration in money or money's worth, or if at time of such mortgage, pledge or purchase such mortgagee, pledgee or purchaser is without notice or knowledge of existence of such lien. Such security means any bond, debenture, note or certificate or other evidence of indebtedness, issued by any corporation, including one issued by government or political subdivision thereof, with interest coupons or in registered form, share of stock, voting trust certificate, or any certificate of interest or participation in, certificate of deposit or receipt for, temporary or interim certificate for, or warrant or right to subscribe to or purchase any of foregoing; negotiable instrument; or money. (c. 65C, §14[c]).

Commissioner may release or partially discharge any such lien with respect to all or part of property subject thereto if satisfied collection of tax will not be jeopardized thereby, certificate as to which is to be held conclusive that lien on property covered by certificate is extinguished. (c. 65C, §14[d]). Such lien is to cease to attach to personal property after same is sold or disposed of for value by person lawfully entitled to make such sale or disposition, provided that such lien is thereupon to attach to proceeds or other property acquired in substitution therefor. License or decree authorizing sale of real estate of resident decedent or of any property of nonresident decedent subject to such lien must affirmatively state that lien has been released or discharged, and before license is issued or decree entered authorizing sale of real estate of resident or any property of nonresident decedent subject to such lien, probate court records must show that commissioner has released or discharged such lien with respect to such property. (c. 65C, §14[e]). Election under c. 65C, §5(c) for qualified farm property will create lien in favor of commonwealth for adjusted tax difference under §2032A of Code, as in effect on Jan. 1, 1985. (c. 65C, §14[f]).

Transferee's Liability.—Amount of liability, at law or equity, of transferee of decedent's property in respect of tax is, except as follows, to be assessed, collected and paid in same manner and subject to same provisions and limitations as in case of tax with respect to which liability was incurred, whether such liability is as to tax shown on return or deficiency in tax. (c. 65C, §15[a]). Period of limitations for assessment of any such liability of subsequent transferee is to be, in case of liability of initial transferee,

See note at head of Digest as to 1998 legislation covered.

See Topical Index in front part of this volume.

MA – 63

ESTATE TAX . . . *continued*
within one year after expiration of period of limitations for assessment against transferor and, in case of liability of transferee, within one year after expiration of such period against preceding transferee, but not more than three years after expiration of such period against initial transferor; except that if, before expiration of such period, court proceeding for collection of tax or liability in respect thereof has been begun against initial transferor or last preceding transferee, respectively, then such period is to expire one year after return of execution. (c. 65C, §15[b]). Absent notice of fiduciary relationship as described in c. 65C, §16, any notice of such liability is to be sufficient if addressed in name of decedent or other person subject to liability and mailed to his last known address. (c. 65C, §15[c]). Transferee in this catchline includes donee, heir, legatee, devisee and his distributee, and any person described in c. 65C, §14(b), who is personally liable for any part of tax. (c. 65C, §15[d]).

Fiduciary Relationship.—Upon notice to commissioner that person is acting as executor, such person is to assume powers, rights, duties and privileges of executor in respect of tax until notice is given such person is no longer so acting. (c. 65C, §16[a]). Upon notice to commissioner that person is acting in fiduciary capacity for person subject to liability described in catchline Transferee's Liability, supra, fiduciary is to assume on behalf of such person powers, rights, duties and privileges of such person as so described, except that liability is to be collected from estate of such person, until notice is given that fiduciary capacity has terminated. (c. 65C, §16[b]).

Collection.—Commissioner is to have for collection of tax all powers and remedies provided by c. 60 for collection of taxes on personal estate by collectors of taxes of towns, and may recover any tax in action of contract in name of commonwealth. (c. 62C, §§46, 47). Tax is to be collected within six years of assessment or prior to expiration of period of collection agreed upon in writing by commissioner and taxpayer before expiration of six-year period, including subsequent extensions, or before any release of levy under c. 62C, §64 after six-year period. If any question relative to tax is pending before any agency or court at end of above period, commissioner's right to collect is to continue until one year after final determination of such question. (c. 62C, §65).

Abatement and Appeal.—Person aggrieved by tax assessment may apply in writing to, on form approved by, commissioner for abatement thereof at any time within later of three years after due date, two years from date tax was assessed or deemed assessed, or one year after payment thereof. Commissioner required to grant applicant hearing thereon if requested on application. If commissioner finds tax excessive or illegal, he must abate tax, in whole or part, and if tax has been paid, state treasurer, upon certification of commissioner, must repay amount of abatement with interest as prescribed. (c. 62C, §§37, 40). Person aggrieved by refusal of commissioner to abate tax, in whole or part, may appeal therefrom within 60 days after date of notice of commissioner's decision or within six months after time when application for abatement is deemed denied as provided in c. 58A, §6 by filing petition with, if appeal is from commissioner's determination of value of asset of estate, clerk of appellate tax board or, if appeal is from any other matter, clerk of appellate tax board or Probate Court having jurisdiction of decedent's estate. If board or court on hearing finds person making appeal was entitled to abatement, it is to make abatement as it sees fit, and if tax has been paid, state treasurer, upon presentation to him of notice of decision of board or court, is to repay petitioner amount of abatement with interest thereon computed in accordance with c. 62C, §40. (c. 62C, §39). To facilitate collection commissioner may make installment payment agreements. (c. 62C, §37B).

Regulations issued by commissioner pursuant to c. 14, §6 for interpretation or enforcement of provisions set forth in c. 62C, §2 are to conform so far as commissioner may deem practicable to regulations relating to U.S. estate tax laws. (c. 62C, §3).

Penalties are imposed for certain wilful attempts to evade or defeat tax or payment thereof, certain wilful failures to pay tax, make return or supply information and certain wilful false, fraudulent or improper acts. (c. 65C, §§26-28).

C. 65A Estate Tax.—Tax is imposed on transfer of estate of every resident in amount by which 80% of estate tax payable to U.S. under Federal Revenue Act of 1926 exceeds aggregate amount of all estate, inheritance, legacy and succession taxes actually paid to several states of U.S. in respect to any property owned by such decedent or subject to such taxes as part of or in connection with his estate. Similar tax is provided to absorb any credit which may be allowed under any future federal revenue act. Tax is also imposed on transfer of real property or tangible personal property in commonwealth of every resident of U.S., who was not resident of commonwealth at time of death, and upon transfer of all property, both real and personal, within commonwealth of every person who at time of death was not resident of U.S. Amount of such tax shall be equal to such proportion of amount by which credit allowable under applicable federal revenue act for estate, inheritance, legacy and succession taxes actually paid to several states exceeds amount actually so paid for such taxes, exclusive of estate taxes based upon difference between such credit and other estate taxes and inheritance, legacy and succession taxes, as value of property in commonwealth bears to value of entire estate, subject to estate tax under applicable federal revenue act. (c. 65A, §1). Tax imposed by c. 65A due and payable 12 months after death of decedent. If not paid when due, interest accrues pursuant to c. 62C, §32, however, commissioner may extend time for good cause.

Apportionment.—As to apportionment among recipients and beneficiaries of estate of resident decedent of estate tax under c. 65C or c. 65A or any estate tax law of U.S., see c. 65A, §5.

EXCISE TAXES:

Automobile Excise Tax.—See category Transportation, topic Motor Vehicles.

Watercraft Excise Tax.—See c. 60B. City or town where vessel is habitually moored or docked or principally situated is required to levy excise of $10 per $1,000 of valuation. (c. 60B, §2). Payment of tax exempts owner from any other tax thereon. (c. 60B, §2[d]).

GASOLINE AND SPECIAL FUELS TAXES:

Gasoline, Diesel and Other Combustible Motor Fuels Taxes.—For per gallon tax see c. 64A, §1 (gasoline); c. 64E, §4 (other fuels). Twenty-one cent per gallon minimum tax on gasoline and other motor fuels, no minimum tax on liquefied gas. Special restrictions and taxes are imposed upon persons bringing such gasoline and motor fuel into state. (c. 64F). Diesel motor fuel tax is imposed upon user and it is unlawful to operate diesel powered vehicle, except certain noncommercial vehicles, without first securing user's license from commissioner. (c. 64E, §2). Under certain circumstances nonhighway users may be entitled to refund of taxes paid on fuel consumed on farm. (c. 64A, §§7, 7A; c. 64E, §5). Distributors may sell tax free to other distributors in state or for export from commonwealth. (c. 64A, §8A).

Aviation fuel is taxed at 7.5% of average price or 10¢ per gallon whichever is higher (not applicable to aircraft fuel as defined in c. 64J, §1). (c. 64A, §1).

GENERATION SKIPPING TAX:

See topic Estate Tax, subhead Generation Skipping Tax.

GIFT TAX:

None.

INCOME TAX:

Taxation of incomes is dealt with in c. 62. Taxable entities include by definition certain estates, fiduciaries, partnerships, associations, trusts and corporate trusts. (c. 62, §§1, 8, 9, 10, 13, 17).

Shareholders of S corporation are subject to tax on their individual distributive share of corporation's income and may take their pro rata share of deductions and losses incurred by corporation, as provided by c. 62 and IRC §1361 et seq. (c. 62, §17A).

Residents.—Starting point for computation of tax is gross income as determined under Internal Revenue Code (IRC) as amended on Jan. 1, 1998, and in effect that taxable year, except that reference in c. 62 to IRC §§162(a), 274(n) shall refer to IRC as amended. (c. 62, §1). Following are then added to gross income: Interest on governmental obligations excluded under IRC 103 other than interest on certain obligations issued by commonwealth or political subdivisions thereof or certain agencies or instrumentalities of either; earned income from foreign sources excluded under IRC 911; certain contributions for annuity contracts excluded under IRC 403(b); and amounts excluded under IRC Subchapter S for federal S corporations subject to taxation under c. 62 as corporate trusts. (c. 62, §2[a]). Items then subtracted from federal gross income are: Interest on obligations of U.S. exempt from state income taxation to extent included in federal gross income and certain exempt-interest dividends received from regulated investment company qualified under IRC 851; amounts included under Subchapter S for federal S corporations subject to taxation under c. 62 as corporate trusts (c. 62, §2[a][2][B]); income received from fiduciary which is taxable to fiduciary; dividends received from corporate trust to extent exempt from tax under c. 62, §8; income from any contributory annuity, pension, endowment, or retirement fund of U.S. or commonwealth or any political subdivision thereof to which employee has contributed; and income from annuity, stock bonus, pension, profit-sharing or deferred payment plans or contracts described in IRC 403(b) or 404 or individual retirement accounts or annuities or retirement bonds described in IRC 408 or 409 to limit of aggregate amount contributed and previously included in Massachusetts gross income; any amount included as federal gross income under IRC 408A (Roth IRA) or education individual retirement account under IRC 530 subject to tax only to extent taxed under IRC (c. 62, §5); gain from sale of principle residence excluded from gross income to same extent as IRC 121 (c. 62, §2); income received from royalties or from sale, lease or other transfer of patent approved by commissioner of energy resources and relating to energy conservation or alternative energy development; social security benefits included in federal gross income under IRC 86. (c. 62, §2[a]).

For taxable years beginning before Jan. 1, 1996, resulting amount, known as Massachusetts gross income, is, except as indicated below, divided into Part A gross income: (interest and dividends [other than interest and dividends from deposits in banks or certain similar institutions located in commonwealth, including accounts of $100,000 or more (406 Mass. 92, 546 N.E.2d 157), and other than interest on loans made by pawnbrokers] and capital gain net income) and Part B gross income: all other Massachusetts gross income. (c. 62, §2[b]). For taxable years beginning on or after Jan. 1, 1996, Massachusetts gross income is, except as indicated below, divided into Part A gross income: (interest and dividends [other than interest and dividends from deposits in banks or certain similar institutions located in commonwealth, including accounts of $100,000 or more (406 Mass. 92, 546 N.E.2d 157), and other than interest on loans made by pawnbrokers] and capital gain net income), Part C gross income: capital gain income (see list of class B-G capital gain income, below), and Part B gross income: all other Massachusetts gross income. (c. 62, §2[b]). Massachusetts adjusted gross income is sum of Part A adjusted gross income and Part B adjusted gross income. (c. 62, §2[g]). For taxable years beginning on or after Jan. 1, 1996, Massachusetts adjusted gross income is sum of Part A adjusted gross income, Part B adjusted gross income and Part C adjusted gross income. (c. 62, §2[i]). For taxable years commencing on or after Jan. 1, 1989 and before Jan. 1, 1991, Part B taxable income shall not include unemployment compensation, alimony, Massachusetts bank interest, rental income, pension and annuity income or IRA/Keogh distributions and income from these sources shall be Part C taxable income. (1989, c. 287, §§18, 19, am'd 1990, c. 121). For taxable years commencing on or after Jan. 1, 1991, Part C income is eliminated and becomes part of Part B income.

Part A adjusted gross income is determined by deducting from Part A gross income following: (1) Excess of deductions allowed under c. 62, §2(d) over Part B gross income, but not in excess of Part A gross income "effectively connected" with active conduct of trade or business; (2) smaller of net capital loss or $1,000 is applied against interest and dividends (with one year carryover for excess); (3) deduction not to exceed 50% of net capital gain computed after reduction, if any, taken under (1) above. (c. 62, §2[c]). For taxable years beginning before Jan. 1, 1996, Part A adjusted gross income is determined by deducting from Part A gross income and including following class of

See note at head of Digest as to 1998 legislation covered.

See Topical Index in front part of this volume.

INCOME TAX. . . *continued*
gain income: (1) Excess of deductions allowed under c. 62, §2(d) over part B gross income, but not in excess of Part A gross income "effectively connected" with active conduct of trade or business; (2) losses from sale or exchange of capital assets held one year or less, provided losses exceeding Part A gross income must be loss in succeeding taxable years; (3) deduction of 50% of gain income from sale or exchange of property under IRC 408(m)(2), and held for more than one year, after reduction by any losses in (2) above. (c. 62, §2[c]).

Part A taxable income is determined by deducting from Part A adjusted gross income following: That portion of Part A adjusted gross income of fiduciaries which is payable to or accumulated for nonresidents to extent such income would not be taxable if received by nonresident; that portion of Part A adjusted gross income of trustees, executors or administrators which is payable to or irrevocably set aside for charitable purposes; and excess of exemptions allowed by c. 62, §3, B over Part B adjusted gross income less deductions allowed by c. 62, §3, B, (a). (c. 62, §3, A).

Part B adjusted gross income is Part B gross income less deductions allowed by IRC 62 and 404, without regard to IRC 265 and less expenses for travel, transportation incurred by outside salesmen if taxpayer itemizes and expenses are allowed under IRC 67(a). (To claim expenses if joint federal return is filed, joint Mass. return required.) However, following deductions are not allowed: (see c. 62, §2[a]); deductions allowed to life tenants and income beneficiaries insofar as such deductions are allowed to trust or estate subject to taxation under c. 62; any deduction relating to income not includable in Massachusetts gross income; any net operating loss deduction allowed by IRC 172; in case of individual who is employee within meaning of IRC 401(c)(1), deductions allowed by IRC 404 to extent attributable to contributions made on behalf of such individual; deduction allowed by IRC 1379(b)(3); deductions for individual retirement savings allowed by IRC 219; deduction allowed by IRC 402(e)(3) relating to ordinary income portion of lump sum distribution; deduction for forfeitures due to premature withdrawals under IRC 165 to extent that income represented by forfeiture was not included in Massachusetts gross income; deduction allowed by IRC 162(h) for expenses of state legislators traveling away from home; deductions from federal S corporations treated as corporate trusts under c. 62; and deduction allowed by IRC 164(f); for taxable years beginning on or after Jan. 1, 1996, deduction for expenses relating to influencing legislation, participation in political activities, legislative matters, or activities involving executive branch officials in attempts to influence officials; deduction allowed by IRC 62(a)(3). (c. 62, §2[d]).

Part B taxable income is determined by deducting from Part B adjusted gross income following: (see c. 62, §3 B[a]-[c]). That portion of Part B adjusted gross income of fiduciaries which is payable to or accumulated for nonresidents to extent such income would not be taxable if received by a nonresident; that portion of Part B adjusted gross income of trustees, executors, or administrators which is payable to or irrevocably set aside for charitable purposes; taxes paid under F.I.C.A. or Federal Railroad Retirement Act; amounts deducted from wages as contributions to an annuity, pension, endowment or retirement fund of U.S. government, commonwealth or any political subdivision thereof (but in no event shall aggregate of otherwise allowable deductions for these taxes and amounts attributable to any one taxpayer exceed $2,000); income from any contributory annuity, pension, endowment or retirement fund of U.S. government, commonwealth or any political subdivision thereof, to which employee has contributed; income from contributory annuity, pension, endowment or retirement fund of any other state or political subdivision, provided such state grants reciprocal privilege; $100 of interest and dividends in case of single person or married person filing separately, or $200 in case of married persons filing joint return; amount equal to employment-related expenses allowed in determining dependent care credit under IRC; 10% of cost of renovating abandoned building in economic opportunity area; and, if no such deduction for dependent care is claimed and if taxpayer maintains household which includes one or more dependents under age of 12, $600, provided that if such taxpayer is married, such deduction shall be allowed only if such taxpayer and his spouse file joint return for taxable year; in case of individual or husband and wife who pay rent for principal place of residence located in Massachusetts, 50% of such rent but no more than $2,500. (c. 62, §3B[a]).

For taxable years beginning on or after Jan. 1, 1996, Part C gross income is capital gain income comprised of following classes: Class B gain which equals gains from sale or exchange of capital assets held for more than one year but less than or equal to two years; Class C gain which equals sale or exchange of capital assets held for more than two years but less than or equal to three years; Class D gain which equals gains from sale or exchange of capital assets held for more than three years but less than or equal to four years; Class E gain which equals gains from sale or exchange of capital assets held for more than four years but less than or equal to five years; Class F gain which equals gains from sale or exchange of capital assets held for more than five years but less than or equal to six years; Class G gain which equals gains from sale or exchange of capital assets held for more than six years. (c. 62, §2[b][3]).

Part C adjusted gross income shall be Part C gross income comprised of following classes as adjusted: Class B net gain which equals excess of Class B gains over losses from sale or exchange of capital assets held for more than one year but less than or equal to two years; Class B net loss which equals excess of losses from sale or exchange of capital assets held for more than one year but less than or equal to two years over Class B gains; Class C net gain which equals excess of Class C gains over losses from sale or exchange of capital assets held for more than two years but less than or equal to three years; Class C net loss which equals excess of losses from sale or exchange of capital assets held for more than two years but less than or equal to three years over Class C gains; Class D net gain which equals excess of Class D gains over losses from sale or exchange of capital assets held for more than three years but less than or equal to four years; Class D net loss which equals excess of losses from sale or exchange of capital assets held for more than three years but less than or equal to four years over Class D gains; Class E net gain which equals Class E gains over losses from sale or exchange of capital assets held for more than four years but less than or equal to five years; Class E net loss which equals excess of losses from sale or exchange of capital assets held for more than four years but less than or equal to five years over Class E gains; Class F net gain which equals Class F gains over losses from sale or exchange of capital assets held for more than five years but less than or equal to six years; Class F net loss which equals excess of losses from sale or exchange of capital assets held for more than five years but less than or equal to six years over Class F gains; Class G net gain which equals Class F gains over losses from sale or exchange of capital assets held for more than six years; Class G net loss which equals excess of losses from sale or exchange of capital assets held for more than six years over Class G gains. (c. 62, §2[e]).

For taxable years beginning before Jan. 1, 1996, Part C taxable income is Part C adjusted gross income less deductions and exemptions allowable under Part C of c. 62, §3. (c. 62, §2[h]). In determining Part C taxable income, Part C adjusted gross income shall be reduced by following deductions and exemptions: Net amount of Part C adjusted gross income of trustees; (1) of other fiduciaries subject to tax under §9 or 10 as payable to or accumulated for persons not in commonwealth to extent such income not subject to tax under §5A if received by nonresident; (2) of executors or administrators pursuant to terms of instrument governing estate or trust currently payable to or irrevocably set aside for public charitable purposes, or for benefit of charitable organization. (c. 62, §3C).

For taxable years beginning after Jan. 1, 1998 short term capital gain, short term capital loss, long term capital gain, long term capital loss, net short term capital gain, net short term capital loss, net long term capital gain, net long term capital loss have same meaning provided in IRC 1222 as amended and in effect for taxable year. (c. 62, §1). Amount of gain or loss on sale, exchange, or other disposition of property determined under c. 62, §6F.

Exemptions allowed under §3C equal amount by which total exemptions allowable under §3B exceed Part B adjusted gross income less deductions allowable under §§3B(a) and 3A adjusted gross income less deductions allowable under §3A(a). No exemption allowed to married person filing separate return. (c. 62, §3C).

For taxable years beginning on or after Jan. 1, 1996, tax on Part C taxable income is sum of following: Class B net gain or net loss multiplied by 5% rate; Class C net gain or net loss multiplied by 4% rate; Class D net gain or net loss multiplied by 3% rate; Class E net gain or net loss multiplied by 2% rate; Class F net gain or net loss multiplied by 1% rate; Class G net gain or net loss multiplied by 0% rate. (c. 62, §4[c]).

Personal exemptions are allowed as follows: For single persons or married filing separately—$4,400 personal exemption, additional $2,200 for blind taxpayer, and $700 additional exemption for taxpayers age 65 or over; for married filing jointly—$8,800 personal exemption, $2,200 for each spouse who is blind, $700 additional exemption for each spouse age 65 or over and $1,000 for each dependent; for head of household—$6,800. (c. 62, §3, B).

Exemptions are allowed for medical expenses allowed under IRC 213 if individual itemizes deductions on his federal income tax return, files joint state tax return if he files joint federal return, and for adoption fees in excess of 3% of Part B adjusted income (c. 62, §3B[b]). For part-time residents exemptions are allocated in proportion that Massachusetts gross income bears to amount which would have been Massachusetts gross income if resident for entire year. (c. 62, §3B[c]).

Deductions are allocated first to Part B income, then to Part C income, including any Part B net loss, except that deduction under c. 62, §3B(a)(6) is applied only to Massachusetts bank interest, and deductions relating to rental income from real estate are applied first against Part C income. Any resulting Part B or Part C net loss may be applied against other class. Exemptions are allocated first to Part B income, then to Part C income, then to Part A income. (c. 62, §§2 and 3, am'd 1989, c. 287, §19).

For taxable years beginning on or after Jan. 1, 1989 and before Jan. 1, 1990, Part A taxable income is taxed at rate of 10%; Part B taxable income is taxed at rate of 5.375%; and Part C taxable income is taxed at rate of 5%. For taxable years beginning on or after Jan. 1, 1990 and before Jan. 1, 1991, Part A taxable income is taxed at rate of 12%; Part B taxable income is taxed at rate of 5.95% for 1990, 6.25% for 1991 and 5.95% thereafter; and Part C taxable income is taxed at rate of 5.95%. (c. 62, §4; 1989, c. 287, §19, am'd 1990, c. 121, §§83, 106, 114). For taxable years beginning before Jan. 1, 1995, no tax may be imposed which reduces Massachusetts adjusted gross income below $8,000 for individuals and $12,000 for married couple filing jointly. (c. 62, §5). For taxable years beginning on or after Jan. 1, 1995, no tax may be imposed reducing Massachusetts adjusted gross income below $8,000 for individuals and $7,600 plus deductions allowed under c. 62, §3 ([B][b][A-B]), for person filing as head of household or for husband and wife filing joint return. (c. 62, §5). Personal income tax return must be filed by person having Massachusetts adjusted gross income in excess of $8,000. (c. 62C, §6).

For taxable years beginning Jan. 1, 1998 Part A taxable income consisting of capital gains is taxed at rate of 12%; Part A taxable income consisting of interest and dividends taxed at rate of 5.95%. (c. 62, §4).

Subject to certain limitations, credits against taxes imposed are granted: (1) To residents of commonwealth for taxes due to any other state, territory, or possession of U.S., or to Canada, on account of Massachusetts gross income, subject to restrictions (c. 62, §6[a]); (2) to any owner of residential premises who pays for containment or abatement of any paint, plaster, or other accessible materials containing dangerous levels of lead, credit in amount of lesser of cost of such treatment or $1,500 per dwelling unit, and excess credit allowed to carry forward seven years (c. 62, §6[e]); (3) to owners credit for 5% of cost of property used in "certified project" in economic opportunity area (defined in c. 23A, §3A) if property would qualify for §31A credit if purchased by eligible corporation, but credit cannot exceed 50% of tax liability; and (4) to owners or tenants of residential property occupying same as principal residence for installation of renewable energy sources, credit in amount of lesser of 15% of cost or $1,000 and excess credit allowed to carry forward three years. (c. 62, §6[d]).

Report of change in federal taxable income is required, together with payment of any additional Massachusetts tax due, within one year of receipt of notice of final determination of federal tax. (c. 62C, §30).

Innocent spouses may be relieved of liability on joint return in certain circumstances. (c. 62C, §84, effective July 1, 1993).

Any person may contribute to Massachusetts U.S. Olympic Fund. (c. 62, §6G).

Abatement.—Application for abatement of tax must be filed within three years from last day for filing return or within two years after tax is assessed or deemed assessed or

See note at head of Digest as to 1998 legislation covered.

See Topical Index in front part of this volume.

MA – 65

INCOME TAX ... *continued*

within one year after date that tax was paid, whichever occurs later. (c. 62C, §37). Taxpayer may also apply for abatement of Massachusetts tax within one year of notice of final determination of taxpayer's federal income tax. (c. 62C, §30). Abatement applications and other forms subject to due dates filed with tax commissioner presumed delivered on postmark date. (c. 62C, §33A). Applications not acted on by commissioner for six months are, in absence of applicant's written consent within such period to later action, deemed denied. (c. 58A, §6). Petitioner has 60 days from date of notice of commissioner's decision in which to claim appeal to appellate tax board. (c. 62C, §39). No abatement will be granted unless tax return has been filed. (c. 62C, §38). In general, interest accruing before Jan. 1, 1993 on refund of taxes abated is at 18%; thereafter, interest accrues at federal short-term rate under IRC §6621(b) plus 4%, compounded daily. (c. 62C, §40). Abatements for certain exempt persons and property may increase annually not exceeding Consumer Price Index cost of living increase. (c. 59, §5[cl.1, 17, 17C, 17C¹/₂, 17D]).

Low Income Families.—Tax relief provisions for low income families contained in c. 62, §§1-5, 5A, 6, 8, 10, 17.

Nonresidents.—Amount of Part A taxable income, Part B taxable income and Part C taxable income of any nonresident derived with respect to items of gross income from sources within commonwealth is taxed according to provisions summarized above. However, only those deductions which are attributable to items included in Massachusetts gross income will be allowed. Items of gross income from sources within commonwealth are items of gross income "derived from or effectively connected" with any trade or business, including employment in commonwealth, participation in any lottery or wagering in commonwealth or ownership of any real or tangible personal property in commonwealth. (c. 62, §5A). Nonresident who is shareholder of S corporation (as defined under IRC §1361, and subject to tax under c. 63) shall be subject to tax on his distributive share of income. (c. 62, §17A[b]).

Miscellaneous.—For special provisions as to corporate trusts, see c. 62, §8. For special provisions as to installment sales, see c. 62, §63. For special provisions as to income from partnerships, see c. 62, §17 and c. 62C, §7. For special provisions as to pooled income funds, charitable remainder annuity trusts, and charitable remainder unitrusts, see c. 62 §11A and §11B. For special provisions as to common trust funds, see c. 62, §17(e).

For taxation of income of corporations, see category Business Organizations, topic Corporations, subhead Taxation.

For excise tax on insurance premiums, see category Insurance, topic Insurance Companies, subhead Excise Taxes.

Trust Income.—For special provisions relating to income from trust estates, see c. 62, §§9-16.

If grantor or another person is treated as owner of any part of trust assets under IRC 671-8, income, deductions and credits against tax which are attributable to such part are not taken into account in calculating taxable income of trust but are taken into account in calculating taxable income of grantor or such other person under c. 62. (c. 62, §10[e]). Trustee must file information return and disclose person(s) so treated and amounts of income, deductions and credits allocable to such person(s). (c. 62, §10[f]). Trustees having control of income payments to such person(s) not resident in state must deduct and withhold income tax at applicable rate. (c. 62, §10; c. 62C, §31A).

Withholding of Tax.—
Wages Subject to Withholding.—Employers are required to deduct income tax from all wages subject to tax. (c. 62B). Wages defined as in IRC 3401(a) plus periodic payments and nonperiodic distributions as defined in IRC 3405(a)(b) which are subject to federal withholding. (c. 62B, §1). Definitions in Federal Internal Revenue Code are adopted for employer (IRC 3401[d]), and employee (IRC, 3401[c]), except that full-time students engaged in seasonal or temporary employment, whose estimated annual income does not exceed $2,000, are not subject to tax withholding (c. 62B, §1). Wages not subject to withholding must be reported by employer annually to commissioner. (c, 62C, §8).

Employer, including any responsible officer or employee, who fails properly to withhold and pay to commissioner amounts required to be withheld and so paid is personally liable for amounts not withheld and paid. (c. 62B, §5).

Employer who fails upon notice to withhold income tax, or pay over to commissioner amounts withheld, on income of employees is subjected to fine of not less than $100 nor more than $5,000 and/or imprisonment of up to one year. (c. 62B, §7). Individual who decreases withholding by making statement on withholding certificate without reasonable basis subject to penalty of $500 in addition to any criminal penalties. (c. 62B, §11A).

Withholding Tables.—Taxes are withheld in accordance with tables prepared by commissioner. (c. 62B, §2).

Withholding Deduction and Exemption Certificates.—Every employee is required to furnish employer signed withholding deduction certificate showing number of dependency deductions claimed. (c. 62B, §4).

Time for Filing Returns and Payment of Tax.—Employers are required to file returns and pay taxes withheld in manner prescribed in regulations prepared by commissioner. Such regulations must generally conform to regulations promulgated under sections of IRC applicable to withholding of federal income taxes. Employer must furnish statement as to tax withheld (similar to federal W-2 form), to each employee by Jan. 31 of succeeding year, or within 30 days after final payment of wages on termination of employment before close of year. (c. 62B, §5). Individual return (Form 1, 1-NR, or ABC) due by Apr. 15 (with six-month automatic extension period), with payment of tax. (c. 62A, §6[a]; 830 CMR 62C.19.1[5]). In general, interest accruing before Jan. 1, 1993 on late payment is at 18% per annum, plus penalty of ¹/₂% per month up to 25%, with additional penalty for failure to file return equal to 1% of tax per month up to 25% with additional penalty for failure to show amount of tax required to be shown on return equal to ¹/₂% per month up to 25% of tax not shown, if such tax not paid within 30 days following notice of tax due. Beginning Jan. 1, 1993, interest on late payments accrues at federal short-term rate under IRC §6621(b) plus 4%, compounded daily; interest on late

payment penalties accrues from 31st day following notice of tax due; interest on late filing penalties accrues on due date of return. (c. 62C, §§32, 33). Commissioner must abate or waive any portion of any penalty or addition to tax attributable to erroneous written advice furnished to taxpayer by department of revenue provided that it was reasonably relied on by taxpayer and penalty or addition to tax did not result from inadequate or inaccurate information provided by taxpayer. (c. 62C, §36B).

Declarations of Estimated Tax.—
Requirements for Filing.—Declarations of estimated tax are required from taxpayer who expects to receive taxable income, other than wages subject to withholding, for which estimated tax is over $200. (c. 62B, §13). For declarations by corporations, see category Business Organizations, topic Corporations, subhead Taxation—Declaration of Estimated Tax. In general, interest accruing before Jan. 1, 1993 on underpayment of tax is at 18% per annum; thereafter, interest accrues at federal short-term rate under IRC 6621(b) plus 4%, compounded daily. (c. 62C, §32). Required annual payment of estimated taxes is lesser of 80% (66²/₃% for farmer or fisherman) of tax for year or 100% preceeding full year's tax. (c. 62B, §14).

Time for Filing of Estimates.—Estimated tax, less estimated amount of tax to be withheld, must be paid in four equal installments on Apr. 15, June 15, Sept. 15 and Jan. 15. (c. 62B, §14). Taxpayer whose estimated gross income from farming or fishing is at least two-thirds his total gross income may file return and pay tax on or before Mar. 1 of following taxable year and avoid addition to tax for underpayment. (c. 62B, §14).

INHERITANCE TAX:

Inheritance tax is dealt with in c. 65.
Massachusetts has adopted Uniform Interstate Arbitration of Death Taxes Act and Uniform Interstate Compromise of Death Taxes Act. (c. 65B, §§1-7).
Caveat.—By 1975, c. 684, §97, c. 65 is suspended for estates of decedents dying on or after Jan. 1, 1976, and remains in force and effect only for estates of decedents dying prior thereto except for certain future interests in property of estates of such decedents dying so prior. See subhead Estate Tax, infra for tax on estates of decedents dying on or after Jan. 1, 1976.

MARIJUANA AND CONTROLLED SUBSTANCES TAX:

Controlled Substance Tax.—See c. 64K. Varying rate tax imposed on marijuana and controlled substances held in violation of Massachusetts law.

PROPERTY TAXES:

Taxes upon real estate and tangible personalty are assessed and collected by cities and towns in state independently. Assessment based on fair cash valuation (c. 59, §38) is by board of assessors, elected or appointed locally (c. 41, §§1, 4A). County taxes are apportioned by county commissioners among cities and towns in several counties, respectively, and share of each city and town is included by it in assessment of city or town taxes. (c. 35, §31).

Taxable Property.—All real and personal property situated in Massachusetts and all personal property of Massachusetts inhabitants wherever situated is taxable unless expressly exempt. (c. 59, §2).

Exemptions.—Property exempt from taxation includes property owned by U.S. or Massachusetts (c. 59, §5, cls. 1 & 2), unless excluded by, e.g., c. 59, §2B; personal property owned by, and real property owned and occupied by, certain charitable organizations (c. 59, §5, cl. 3); certain property of horticultural and agricultural societies, veteran, fraternal or retirement associations, annuity, pension or endowment associations and religious organizations (c. 59, §5, cls. 4-11); certain agricultural and horticultural land taxed under c. 61A (c. 59, §5, cl. 49); certain real property owned by economic development corporation organized as nonprofit corporation under c. 180 (c. 59, §5, cl. 46); certain corporate personal property (taxed under corporate excise tax) (c. 59, §5, cl. 16); certain limited liability company property (c. 59, §5, cl. 16A); certain mobile homes (c. 59, §5, cl. 36); certain personal property of mechanics, farmers and fishermen (c. 59, §5, cl. 20); motor vehicles subject to excise tax thereon (c. 59, §5, cl. 35); water and air pollution control facilities (excluding hazardous waste facilities used principally for treatment of waste produced by others) (c. 59, §5, cl. 44); solar or wind powered devices for supplying energy (exemption limited to period of 20 years from installation) (c. 59, §5, cl. 45); 10% of value of certain commercial property occupied by certain small businesses (c. 59, §5I); and certain alterations or improvements to residential real estate provided alterations are necessary to provide housing to person who is at least 60 years of age (c. 59, §5, cl. 50). Partial exemptions for real estate are available to certain needy surviving spouses and minor children, veterans and their surviving spouses and parents, surviving spouses and minor children of policemen and firemen killed in line of duty; real property owned and occupied by blind persons or persons over 70 with limited income or estate, and who meet residency requirements. (c. 59, §5, cls. 17-18, 22-22E, 42, 43, 37, 37A, 41, 41B, 41C). Real property tax on residence owned and occupied by certain persons over 65 may be deferred under certain conditions until death under agreement with assessors with interest charged at 8% on deferred amounts. (c. 59, §5, cl. 41A).

Assessment.—Real estate is assessed to owner of record title on Jan. 1, or, if authorized by commissioner, to person in possession on Jan. 1. Commissioner may also authorize assessment of any present interest to owner of such interest on Jan. 1. Also, whenever commissioner deems it proper he may authorize in writing assessment of taxes upon real property to persons unknown. In cluster development or planned unit development, assessment on common land may be allocated to assessment on each individual lot. (c. 59, §11). Commissioner may also authorize in writing assessment, not later than June 20 of tax year, or 90 days after date on which tax bills are mailed, whichever is later, of any real or personal property which has been unintentionally omitted from annual assessment. (c. 59, §75). For taxation of mortgaged real estate, see topic Mortgages of Real Property. Agricultural lands may be assessed at worth for agricultural purposes only but any property so assessed shall be subject to lien for special conveyance tax imposed on certain sales and changes of use. (c. 61A). Qualifying recreational land will be assessed at no more than 25% of fair cash value upon

PROPERTY TAXES ... *continued*

application by owner to local board of assessors. (c. 61B). Special conveyance tax assessed for sale within ten years of initial recreational classification (c. 61B, §7) or if land ceases to qualify as recreational land within ten years (c. 61B, §8). Real estate subject to permanent conservation restriction must be assessed as separate parcel. (c. 59, §11). Municipality which accepts c. 59, §57C may give notice of preliminary tax by July 1 of each year, tax to be paid in two installments on Aug. 1 and Nov. 1. (c. 59, §57C). Municipality may only give notice after July 1 upon approval by commissioner of revenue, tax to be paid in two installments; 30 days after mailing of notice and Nov. 1. (c. 59, §57C).

Owners of certain real property improved in assessed value over 50% by new construction pay pro rated tax from occupancy permit date to end of fiscal year. (c. 59, §2C).

Amendment to Constitution permits property to be classified according to use and taxed at different percentages. Home rule system authorizes each municipality to establish, within specified limits, its own classification system. (c. 40, §56). Classes are residential, commercial, industrial and open space. (c. 59, §§2A, 38). With multiple use property, percentage value must be allocated to each classification. (c. 59, §2A[b]). Residential property which is used by taxpayer as principal residence may be given special exemption not exceeding 20% of average of assessed values of such property. (c. 59, §5C). Classification cannot start until 100% valuation has been completed and certified by state. (c. 59, §2A[c]). Municipalities so certified must use new method. (c. 59, §2A[b]).

Real property owned by government but used for other than public purposes shall be assessed and taxed to user, lessee or occupant. (c. 59, §2B).

Grantee of land sold by federal or state government or instrumentality pays pro rata amount in lieu of real estate taxes that would have been due if real estate owned by grantee on Jan. 1 of year of sale and, if sale between Jan. 1 and June 30, Jan. 1 of preceding year. (c. 59, §2C).

Generally, tangible personal property (certain ships and vessels excepted) is assessed to owner in place where it is situated on Jan. 1. Certain personal property is assessed at place where owner resides on Jan. 1. (c. 59, §18). Personal property mortgaged or pledged is assessed to owner or mortgagee or pledgee in actual physical possession on Jan. 1. (c. 59, §19). Before executor or administrator is appointed, personal property of deceased is assessed to "estate" and after appointment executor or administrator is liable therefor. (c. 59, §18).

Local Tax Levy Limitation.—Total local taxes assessed may not exceed 2½% of full and fair cash valuation of property in municipality in any fiscal year or, in municipality in which total local taxes assessed do not exceed this limit, 102½% of maximum limit in prior year plus (a) amount equal to prior year tax rate times assessed valuation of property taxed for first time plus (b) any override approved by majority vote of voters. (c. 59, §21C). Corresponding limit of 2½% in increase by commonwealth, any county, district or other governmental entity, except regional school, water and sewerage districts, legally authorized to assess costs, charges or fees upon municipalities in costs, charges or fees assessed over total assessed in prior year. (c. 59, §20A). Local authority may add water and sewage debt charges to residential property tax assessments, regardless of property tax cap provisions. (c. 59, §21C[n]).

Returns.—All persons are called upon to make return of property held by them subject to taxation on Jan. 1. Return must be filed with assessors before date fixed by them, and in case of property held for literary, temperance, benevolent, charitable, educational, or scientific purposes, before Mar. 1, unless extended. (c. 59, §29). With certain qualifications, filing of such list is made condition precedent to abatement of tax on personal property. Abatement of tax on real estate may be obtained even if list has not been filed provided sufficient description of real estate is included in application for abatement. (c. 59, §§29, 61). In event of failure to file return, assessors ascertain as nearly as possible particulars of real and personal estate, and estimate value according to their best information and belief. (c. 59, §36).

Review of Assessment (Abatement).—As to filing of return being condition precedent to securing abatement, see supra, subhead Returns.

For abatement purposes, person acquiring title to realty after Jan. 1 is treated as person upon whom tax has been assessed. (c. 59, §59).

Abatement of assessment of property for more than its fair cash value or for improper classification may be obtained by application to assessors on or before last day of payment of first installment of actual bill. (c. 59, §59). Applications not acted upon for three months are, in absence of applicant's written consent within such period to later action, deemed denied. (c. 59, §64). Appeal from decision of assessors to county commissioners or to Appellate Tax Board may be taken by formal or informal procedure within three months after receiving notice of decision or within three months after presumed denial as aforesaid if: (1) Tax is on personal property and at least one half of tax has been paid, or (2) tax is on real property, at least one-half of tax has been paid (without accrual of interest), and taxpayer petitions Board on inability to pay remaining tax. (c. 59, §§64, 65B). While appeal pending, assessors can increase or reduce assessment. (c. 58A, §7). Taxes abated are refunded with interest at 8%, computed from time of payment or due date, whichever is later. (c. 59, §69). In certain circumstances Board may extend time for filing appeal. (c. 59, §65C). From any decision of Board there may be appeal on questions of law to Appeals Court, MRAP will govern such appeal. (c. 58A, §13).

Abatement of up to $200 available to qualifying senior citizens for increase in residential property tax attributable to water and sewage charges. (c. 59, §5, cl. 52).

Payment.—Tax bills are payable July 1. (c. 59, §57). Betterment assessments, water rates, annual sewer use charges, and one-half of real estate and personal property taxes bear interest at 14% computed from Oct. 1 if unpaid by Nov. 1. Remaining half of such real estate and personal property tax bears interest at 14% computed from Apr. 1 if unpaid by May 1. (c. 59, §57). City or town may assess additional 14% interest on unpaid real estate or personal property taxes not over $50. (c. 59, §§57A, 57B). City or town may allow 3% property tax discount for early tax payment. (c. 59, §58).

Collection.—Taxes may be collected, if payment is not made in 14 days after demand and after issuance of warrant to collect and warrant to distrain or commit, by distress or

by seizure and sale without unnecessary delay of goods, certain necessary articles, however, being exempt (c. 60, §§24-28), or by arrest and imprisonment (c. 60, §§29-34); person so imprisoned may request examination by court having authority to examine debtors under supplementary proceedings relative to his ability to pay; if found unable to pay such tax he may be discharged (c. 60, §31). Failure to receive demand does not invalidate any tax or collection proceedings therefor. (c. 60, §16). Owner located outside commonwealth must appoint agent. (c. 59, §57D). Remedies for property taking by city or town for tax payment failure set forth in c. 59, §57D. In town or city adopting c. 59, §57D provisions, owner of record must sign affidavit of address in preliminary real estate and personal property tax notice. (c. 59, §57D). Demand for payment must be made upon mortgagee if he gives written notice to collector that he holds mortgage on land. (c. 60, §38). Collector of taxes may also bring suit for collection in his own name. (c. 60, §35). In addition to tax due, collector may require payment of specified costs of collection. (c. 60, §15).

Lien.—Property owner may avoid lien on property for betterment assessment by paying assessment upon receipt of notice indicating assessment amount. (c. 80, §12). Taxes assessed on real estate are lien thereon from Jan. 1 in year of assessment. Lien ceases after three years and six months from end of fiscal year which taxes were assessed. (c. 60, §37). If sale or taking cannot be legally made while lien is in force, it may be extended. (c. 60, §37). City or town adopting property owner information requirements in c. 59, §57D may use remedies in §57D for taking property for failure to pay taxes. (c. 59, §57D).

Tax Levy and Sale.—Taxes on real estate with all incidental costs and expenses may be levied, if not paid within 14 days after demand made either on owner or person occupying estate, by sale of smallest undivided part of real estate which will suffice to discharge taxes and charges, or of whole, if necessary (c. 60, §43), or by taking of whole real estate by city or town, in which case instrument of taking must be recorded within 60 days (c. 60, §§53-55). After city or town has taken or purchased real estate for payment of taxes, and even though it has assigned its tax title, lien of city or town, for subsequently assessed taxes continues and on redemption or foreclosure of redemption, such taxes must be paid as part of terms of redemption. (c. 60, §61). Before making such sale or taking, collector must give notice by publication and posting in two or more convenient places 14 days before sale or taking, giving substantially accurate description of property, amount of tax, and names of all owners known to collector. (c. 60, §§40-42, 53). Property taken in accordance with these provisions may be held for collection of rents and income from property, such income to be applied to delinquent tax account. (c. 60, §53). Property so taken may be sold to highest bidder at public auction, provided sum paid is not less than that necessary for redemption. (c. 60, §52). Collector upon sale executes deed to purchaser, which must be recorded within 60 days, and if so recorded is prima facie evidence of all facts essential to its validity. (c. 60, §45). Sale may be adjourned. If after one or more adjournments no suitable bid is made, land may be purchased by collector for city or town. (c. 60, §48). Municipality may, under certain circumstances, assign, transfer, or sell municipality's right to receive payments owed by taxpayer through public sale or public auction. (c. 60, §2C).

Redemption.—Any person having interest in land taken or sold for taxes, or his heirs or assigns, may redeem it at any time prior to filing of petition for foreclosure, if land has been taken or purchased by town and has not been assigned, by paying or tendering to treasurer amount of tax title account and interest at 16% per annum plus lawful charges; or by paying or tendering to treasurer installments not less, in each case except last, than 25% of tax with all charges and interest, to be applied toward redemption, until tax title account is paid or tendered in full, but each payment or tender must include all intervening costs, charges, fees and interest. Treasurer on accepting any payment may once extend, not exceeding one year, time during which foreclosure proceedings may not be instituted. Redemption may also be effected by paying or tendering to purchaser, other than town, or to town's assignee, or to their respective representatives or assigns, at any time prior to filing of foreclosure petition, if purchaser is other than town, original sum, intervening taxes, costs, interest, or, if purchaser is assignee of tax title from town, amount stated in instrument of assignment with interest at 6½% from date of assignment, and in each case not more than $3 legal fees and recording fee for tax deed or evidence of taking; such payment (with $1 additional) may be made to treasurer. (c. 60, §62). Purchaser acquires no right of possession until right of redemption is foreclosed. (c. 60, §45). Within specified time after sale or taking of land for taxes whoever then holds title may bring petition for foreclosure of all rights of redemption but any person claiming interest may appear in proceedings and in discretion of court be permitted to redeem by payment of amount above recited together with costs of proceeding and such counsel fee as court deems reasonable. (c. 60, §§65-70). Land Court has exclusive jurisdiction of all such petitions for foreclosure subject to review of questions of law by Supreme Judicial Court. (c. 60, §§64-73). Land Court also has jurisdiction in equity as to redemption in all cases of taking or sale of land for nonpayment of taxes, if relief is sought before foreclosure proceedings have been begun. (c. 60, §§76-76A).

Right of redemption of land of low value may be foreclosed by sale without court proceeding. (c. 60, §79).

REAL ESTATE CONVEYANCE TAX:

Real Estate Conveyance Tax in amount of $2 is levied on all conveyances of real estate effective June 30, 1997, when consideration of interest or property conveyed, exclusive of value of any lien or encumbrance, remaining thereon at time of sale, exceeds $100 and does not exceed $500, and $2 for each additional $500 or part thereof. Effective from July 1, 1992 through Jan. 4, 1993, rate was $1.14. Effective until June 30, 1992, rate was $2. No tax is imposed on mortgages or conveyances to which U.S. or commonwealth is party. Tax is imposed on seller. (c. 64D). Rates reflect 14% surtax. (1969, c. 546, §23).

SALES AND USE TAXES:

Sales Tax.—See, generally, c. 64H. Tax is imposed upon retailers at rate of 5% of gross receipts from Massachusetts sales of tangible personal property (including meals) and telecommunications services. (c. 64H, §2, am'd 1991, c. 4). Tax on retail sale of

SALES AND USE TAXES . . . *continued*

motor vehicle paid by purchaser to registrar of motor vehicles. (c. 64H, §3, am'd 1991, c. 4). Vendors are entitled to reimbursement from purchaser. (c. 64H, §3).

Exemptions (§6, am'd 1991, c. 4) include: (1) sales which commonwealth prohibited from taxing under federal constitution or laws; (2) interstate sales where vendor is obligated to deliver to purchaser outside commonwealth; (3) casual or isolated sales (but for casual or isolated sales of motor vehicles or trailers or any such sale of boat or airplane see subhead Use Tax, infra); (4) sales to U.S., Massachusetts, or their political subdivisions and agencies; (5) sales for use in their exempt activities to charities, etc., which are exempt under IRC 501(c)(3) and which have received sales tax exemption certificate from commissioner; (6) sales of gasoline, certain special fuels and liquor (all of which are subject to other excise taxes); (7) food for human consumption (except restaurant meals), school, hospital, etc. meals; (8) utility services used for residences; (9) residential heating and aircraft fuels (but see next paragraph); railroad fuels; (10) clothing up to sale price of $175; (11) prescription medicines, prosthetic devices, insulin and insulin syringes, kidney dialysis machines, life sustaining resuscitators, incubators, heart pacemakers, hospital bed for home use; (12) newspapers, magazines; (13) books required for instructional purposes in educational institutions, books for religious worship, publications by charities; (14) motion picture films for commercial exhibition; (15) certain funeral items; (16) vessels or barges of at least 50 tons capacity manufactured in Massachusetts or vessels used in commercial fishing; (17) agricultural items; (18) containers; (19) ingredients of and machinery used to manufacture tangible personal property for sale or for use in agriculture, commercial fishing and certain other commercial activities including production of animals for health research and testing; (20) truck-mounted concrete mixers; (21) vending machine sales under $1; (22) U.S. flag; (23) fire and ambulance equipment sold to volunteer nonprofit fire and ambulance companies; (24) solar, wind-powered or heat pump equipment used in Mass. principal residence; (25) molds, etc. used exclusively in manufacture of cast metal products for sale; (26) printed material printed to special order in Massachusetts and delivered to interstate carrier, mailing house or post office for delivery or mailing to purchaser outside Massachusetts; (27) sales of specified materials by typographers, compositors and color separators for use in preparing printed matter or folding boxes to be sold; (28) rental charges for refuse containers placed on customer's premises by waste service firms; (29) sales of scientific equipment or apparatus as defined in IRC 170(e)(4) by manufacturer free of charge to nonprofit educational or other specified institutions in Massachusetts; (30) sales of building materials and supplies for use in certain public works or charitable structures; (31) sales of motor vehicles to handicapped persons; (32) sales of certain medical supplies necessitated by colostomy or ileostomy; (33) sales of buses to certain common carriers; (34) meals furnished by hospitals, nursing homes, boarding homes for aged, churches or synagogues, persons transporting passengers for hire, certain organizations for elderly or handicapped, certain schools or related programs; and (35) sales of tangible personal property purchased with federal food stamps, if not otherwise exempt under c. 64H. Trade-in allowance given by dealer in case of motor vehicle, trailer, boat, snowmobile, recreation vehicle, or aircraft is excluded in computing tax. (c. 64H, §§26, 27A; c. 64I, §27). Person who purchases property to use in manner which exempts it from tax under c. 64H may give exempt use certificate to vendor. Similarly, person who purchases for resale may give resale certificate to vendor. These certificates relieve vendor from liability to collect tax; otherwise all of vendor's sales are presumed to be taxable. (c. 64H, §8).

Purchasers of aircraft fuel subject to excise tax of greater of 5% of average price or 5¢ per gallon (collected by vendor who pays to commissioner) on all fuel sold or used in any city or town accepting c. 64J, effective first day of calendar quarter following 30 days after acceptance or first day of such later calendar quarter as city or town may designate. (c. 64J).

Vendors required to register each place of business in Massachusetts. (c. 62C, §67; c. 64H, §7). Vendors must file returns and pay tax by 20th day of each month for preceding month. Returns may be for such other period as commissioner may determine. (c. 62C, §16[h]). Representing that tax will be absorbed by vendor is prohibited. (c. 64H, §23). Any nonresident who engages in business in commonwealth as condition precedent to and by engaging in business in commonwealth, is deemed to appoint state secretary his agent for service of process under c. 64H. Such service shall be sufficient service upon person, provided that notice of service and copy of process is sent by registered mail to person's last known address. (c. 64H, §32).

Promoters who rent space for four or more flea markets or other retail shows per year required to file notice at least ten days before show and file report with commissioner 20 days after end of calendar month in which show was held and to require each exhibitor to be registered under §67 as vendor. (c. 62C, §§1, 8A, 34, 67A).

For abatement, see c. 62C §§37, 40.

Sales Tax on Services.—Telecommunications services are subject to 5% tax on gross receipts if call originates from, is received in or charged to address in Massachusetts. Exemption for residential main telephone service under $30 per month. (830 CMR 64H.1.6[5]). Convention Center Fund requires surcharges for parking, certain sightseeing activities, and car rental in Boston. (1997, c. 152, §§8, 9). No other services are currently subject to sales tax. (c. 64H, §§1, 2, am'd 1991, c. 4).

Use Tax.—See generally c. 64I. Tax of 5% of sales price is imposed upon storage, use or other consumption in Massachusetts of tangible personal property. (c. 64I, §2). Excluded are sales upon which sales tax is imposed, sales which are exempt from sales tax (except that tax applies to motor vehicle or trailer unless purchaser is vendor's spouse, parent, brother, sister, or child), and sales on which purchaser has paid tax to another state, provided that if tax in other state is at lower rate than in Massachusetts, tax must be paid to extent of difference in rates in the two states. (c. 64I, §7). Provisions for filing returns and paying tax are parallel to those under sales tax. For abatement, see c. 62C, §§37, 40.

STAMP TAX:

See topic Real Estate Conveyance Tax.

TRANSPORTATION

MOTOR VEHICLES:

General Supervision.—Exercised by Registry of Motor Vehicles, 100 Nashua Street, Boston, MA 02114.

Vehicle License.—Vehicle registration required annually, including trailer. (c. 90, §§1, 2, 6, 7, 9, 33). Registry of motor vehicles issues vehicle registrations with staggered expiration dates but registration expires immediately upon transfer of ownership of vehicle. (c. 90, §2). Transferor of motor vehicle must remove all visible evidence of registration from motor vehicle. (c. 90, §2B). One number plate is required on rear of vehicle and, if two plates are issued, one in front. (c. 90, §6). There are special provisions for registration of antique motor vehicles, certain farm motor vehicles and for registration of motor vehicles owned by minors. (c. 90, §§6A, 2A, 5). Registration of heavy vehicle may be refused absent proof of payment of federal heavy vehicle tax. (c. 90, §1A).

Every applicant for registration of motor vehicle is required to appoint registrar of motor vehicles his attorney upon whom may be served any process growing out of any accident or collision in which he or his agent may be involved while operating motor vehicle within commonwealth during period of registration. (c. 90, §3D). Registration of motor vehicles and display of number plates not required for 30 days for vehicles having registrations and displaying plates issued by armed forces of U.S. in foreign countries. (c. 90, §9B). Former prisoners of war, members of Legion of Valor, or Purple Heart medal recipients may have distinctive license plates. (c. 90, §2). Plates bearing official U.S. Olympic Committee emblem may be purchased for $25 plus registraton fee. (c. 90, §2).

Licensing of operators of commercial motor vehicles regulated by Uniform Operation of Motor Vehicles Act adopted as c. 90F.

Registration of motor vehicles, including fleet vehicles, authorized on apportionment or allocation basis under International Registration Plan. (c. 90, §2).

Commencing with 1993 model year vehicles, vehicles not meeting motor emission standards may not be registered. (c. 90, §2; c. 111, §142K).

Registrar may withhold title, registration, license or plate if any fee not duly paid. (c. 90, §33).

Upon final determination of child support delinquency from dept. of revenue, registrar must suspend or prohibit issuance or renewal of license. (c. 90, §22).

Disabled Persons.—Certain special privileges are accorded to disabled and handicapped persons and to disabled veterans. (c. 90, §2).

Operator's License.—Required. Obtainable from registrar by any person 18 years of age or over who passes examination. Licenses have staggered expiration dates from one to five years. (c. 90, §§8, 10).

Licenses issued by registrar are subject to regulations establishing classifications of motor vehicles. (c. 90, §8).

Junior operator's license may be obtained by person between 16 1/2 and 18 if he has successfully completed approved driver education and training course, held valid learner's permit for no less than six months without permit suspension, maintained driving record free of surchargeable incidents, and has not been convicted of violating alcohol or drug-related laws. (c. 90, §8). Holders of junior operator's license may only operate motor vehicle under certain conditions. (c. 90, §8).

Learner's permits may be obtained by person 16 years or older. Holders of learner's permits may only operate motor vehicle under certain conditions. (c. 90, §8B).

Special license required to operate school bus. (c. 90, §§8A, 8A1/2).

Member of armed forces on active duty may operate motor vehicle if licensed in state where he is domiciled or, if returning from duty outside U.S., for maximum of 45 days after his return with license issued by armed forces in foreign country. (c. 90, §10). Persons against whom default or arrest warrant is outstanding may not obtain license. (c. 90, §22H).

Titles.—Massachusetts is certificate of title state. (c. 90D). Every owner of vehicle for which certificate of title has been issued must, if transferring ownership, execute assignment including actual odometer reading and warranty of title to transferee and cause certificate and warranty to be mailed or delivered to transferee or registrar. (c. 90D, §15[a]).

Sales.—Title to vehicle transferred by seller executing and delivering assignment and warranty of title to purchaser in space provided on certificate of title. Promptly thereafter, purchaser must file application for new certificate with registrar. (c. 90D, §15[b]).

Retail installment sales of motor vehicles are regulated by c. 255B. Retail installment contract must be in writing and contain certain terms and specified language. (c. 255B, §9).

Massachusetts has adopted "Lemon Law" relating to sales or lease of motor vehicles. (c. 90, §7N1/2). Law applies to motor vehicles not used for habitation or business and sold after Jan. 1, 1984. (c. 90, §7N1/2[1]). Manufacturer, its agent or authorized dealer of motor vehicle must effect repairs which are necessary to conform motor vehicle to any applicable express or implied warranty within reasonable number of attempts. (c. 90, §7N1/2[3]). Term of protection under law runs from day of delivery for period of one year or for 15,000 miles whichever is shorter and extends to any original buyer or subsequent transferee of motor vehicle who takes title during duration of any express or implied warranty. (c. 90, §7N1/2[1]). Manufacturer must accept return of motor vehicle with nonconformity and, at consumer's option, refund full contract price or replace vehicle with one acceptable to consumer if nonconformity is not cured after three or more attempts or 22 business days of use have been lost due to repair. (c. 90, §71/2[4]).

Revocation and Suspension.—Registrar may, after notice and hearing, revoke or suspend license or registration when he has reason to believe that holder is incompetent to operate motor vehicle or is driving improperly. (c. 90, §22[b]). He may revoke license if person is convicted of violation or there is adjudication that person is delinquent child. (c. 266, §139). He may revoke or suspend license or registration for 30 days without hearing when he has reason to believe that holder will constitute immediate threat to public safety. (c. 90, §22[a]). Registrar may suspend license: for up to seven days for permitting littering from vehicle (c. 90, §22G); for failing to appear in

MOTOR VEHICLES . . . *continued*
court in response to summons for automobile law violation after 30 days written notice by registrar of intent to revoke (c. 90C, §3[6][a]); for failing to satisfy judgment in motor vehicle case (c. 90, §22A); or of habitual traffic offender (c. 90, §22F). License may also be suspended or revoked for various criminal violations. (c.90, §24 and c. 266, §28). Registrar may revoke operator's license, registration, title, plate, or other item issued by registrar when operator fails to duly pay fine or penalty imposed by magistrate or court. (c. 90C, §3A[6][b]). Motor vehicle violation convictions in other states or countries given same effect for purposes of suspension or revocation as if violation occurred in commonwealth. Revocation or suspension of license in another state or country bar to license or grounds for revocation of license. (c. 90, §22[c]). License may be suspended or revoked for convictions in states party to interstate compact. (c. 90, §30B). License shall be suspended for 90 days if prosecution makes prima facie showing at arraignment that operator was operating motor vehicle while percentage, by weight, of alcohol in his blood was ten one-hundredths or more. (c. 90, §24N).

Registrar shall suspend license for 120 days without hearing of operator who refuses to submit to blood test by physician or nurse when officer has reason to believe that person has been operating vehicle under influence of intoxicating liquors provided that operator is afforded opportunity to have his own physician perform another test. (c. 90, §§24[1][e][f]). However, refusal to take test is not admissible in evidence in criminal or civil proceedings. Anyone who operates motor vehicle while under influence of intoxicating liquor, marijuana, narcotic drugs, depressants or stimulants may be fined and/or imprisoned. (c. 90, §24[a]). Anyone who, while under influence of intoxicating liquor, marijuana, narcotic drugs, depressants, or other stimulant substances, recklessly or negligently operates motor vehicle so that lives or safety of public might be endangered, and by such operation causes serious bodily injury shall be punished by imprisonment of not less than six months. (c. 90, §24L).

Liens.—There is lien in favor of public garage owners upon automobiles placed with them with owner's consent. (c. 255, §25). Creation of security interest in vehicles is governed by statute. (c. 90D, §§21-25).

Identification Marks.—There are criminal penalties for altering or defacing identification marks. (c. 266, §139). Buyer may require seller to remove material advertising seller placed on vehicle without buyer's prior written consent. (c. 90, §7R½).

Operation Prohibited.—By person whose license has been suspended or revoked or who is not licensed to operate or who is intoxicated. (c. 90, §§8, 10, 24). All persons operating motor vehicle are required to have on their person or in vehicle operator's license and registration certificate for vehicle. Dealers, manufacturers, repairmen, owner-repairmen, farmers and dealers in boats and boat trailers need not carry registrations. Rental cars must provide photostats of registration certificate accompanying rental agreement. (c. 90, §11). No unregistered or improperly equipped motor vehicle may be operated. (c. 90, §9).

Size and Weight Limits.—Regulated by c. 90, §§7P, 19, 19A, 19C-19E, 19I, 19J.

Lights and Equipment Required.—Regulated by c. 90, §§7-7E, 7G-7K, 7M, 7O, 7Q, 9A, 9D. Special requirements for school buses. (c. 90 §§7B-7D½).

Mandatory Seat Belt Law.—Children under five years and children weighing 40 pounds or less must be secured by child passenger restraint. Children between five and 12 years must wear safety belt. (c. 90, §7AA).

Inspection.—All motor vehicles must undergo safety and emissions test annually in accordance with rules promulgated by registrar. (c. 90, §7A). Semi-annual inspection for school buses. (c. 90, §7A). Failure to comply carries fine of $50. (c. 90, §20).

Snowmobiles and certain other recreation vehicles are regulated by statute. (c. 90B, §§20, 21-29). Certain safety features are required and noise levels are regulated. (c. 90B, §24). Such vehicles may not be operated on or immediately adjacent to public way. (c. 90B, §25). Protective headgear must be worn. (c. 90B, §26). Trespassing on private land, whether posted or not, by means of snowmobiles or other powered vehicles, is punished by fine of not more than $250. (c. 266, §121A).

Motorized bicycles or mopeds are permitted and are not defined as motor vehicles, but operator must possess valid license or learner's permit. (c. 90, §§1, 1B-1D and 8B).

Accidents.—Operator of motor vehicle involved in accident must submit written report on form approved by registrar within five days of accident, if accident caused injuries to persons or property damage in excess of $1,000. Report must be submitted to registrar with copy to police department having jurisdiction over place where accident occurred. (c. 90, §26). Operator of vehicle involved in accident resulting in any injury to any persons or property must stop and make known his name and residence and registration number of vehicle. (c. 90, §24[2][a]).

Liability of Owner.—Ownership is prima facie evidence of responsibility for acts of operator. Nonresponsibility must be pleaded as affirmative defense. (c. 231, §85A).

Guests.—Liability of owner or operator for injury to guest in car is not restricted by statute, and passenger in exercise of due care may recover upon proof that operator was guilty of ordinary negligence resulting in injuries or damages. (c. 231, §85L).

No-fault Insurance.—Massachusetts has adopted "No-fault" insurance as to personal injury. (c. 90, §34A). Motorists must carry these coverages as well as $20,000/$40,000 bodily injury liability coverage and $5,000 property damage liability coverage as prerequisite to registration of vehicle in Massachusetts. (c. 90, §§34A, 34M, 34O).

"No-fault" personal injury coverage applies only to accidents occurring within commonwealth, and exemption from tort liability is similarly restricted. (c. 90, §34A). Coverage for property damage is not geographically restricted. (See c. 90, §34O.)

Person injured by insured vehicle may recover most of his out-of-pocket losses due to bodily injury from insurer of vehicle up to a limit of at least $8,000, but not more than $2,000 if injured person covered by other insurance without necessity of establishing negligence on part of anyone, and, in most cases, despite fact that such person might have nonintentionally caused or contributed to his injury. Insurers may exclude person from personal injury protection if such person's conduct contributed to his injury in any of following ways: (1) Operating under alcohol or drugs; (2) committing felony or seeking to avoid arrest; (3) operating vehicle with intent to injure himself or others. Authorized operators and occupants, other than passenger for hire in case of taxicab, but including guests, and pedestrians are covered as well as named insured unless such person is entitled to benefits under Workers' Compensation Act, c. 152. Up to limit, insured may collect all reasonable and necessary medical expenses incurred within two years of accident, 75% of his average weekly wage or salary lost less any amount due under wage continuation program, and if such insured is unemployed at time of injury, he is entitled to recovery for loss by reason of diminution of earning capacity without regard to 75% limitation. (c. 90, §34A). Policyholder may elect deduction applicable to himself alone or to himself and members of his household in amount of $100, $250, $500, $1,000, $2,000, $4,000 or $8,000. (c. 90, §34M).

Recovery for pain and suffering is allowed only if reasonable and necessary medical expenses exceed $2,000, or if injury causes death, loss of body member, sight or hearing, or disfigurement, or consists of a fracture. (c. 231, §6D).

Every owner, registrant, operator or occupant of a vehicle covered by a "No-fault" policy, and any other legally responsible person, is exempt from tort liability for bodily injury or the like caused in such capacity within commonwealth, to extent that injured party is, or would be but for deduction, entitled to personal injury protection benefits under "No-fault" policy. (c. 90, §34M). There is no exemption from tort liability for or as against out-of-state driver not covered by "No-fault" type policy, and he may sue or be sued. Massachusetts insured injured by such out-of-state driver is covered by his "No-fault" policy unless he recovers damages from out-of-state party. (c. 90, §34M). In any case, an action may be brought to recover: (1) Balance of medical expenses, 75% of lost earnings, and/or diminution in earning capacity, over the $2,000 personal injury protection limit; (2) future medical expenses to be incurred more than two years after accident; (3) for wrongful death; (4) for 25% of lost wages not covered by "No-fault" policy; and (5) for pain and suffering subject to conditions previously discussed. (c. 90, §34A).

Each Massachusetts insured is required to carry property damage liability insurance for damages to property of others. "No-fault" tort liability exemption for property damage has been abolished. Insured may select for insured's own vehicle full collision coverage without regard to fault (with basic $500 deductible) or limited collision coverage, which provides benefits in four specific classes of accidents, so long as insured's comparative negligence does not exceed 50%. (c. 90, §34O). Such insurance must provide that benefits will not be payable if loss of or damage to insured vehicle occurs when operator of vehicle is household member other than insured who is not listed as operator on policy and if listed, would be classified as inexperienced driver or would subject policy to increased premiums under safe driver insurance plan established under c. 175, §113B. (c. 90, §34O). Strict provisions for auto repair shops must be met before insurance companies must pay them for accident repairs. (c. 90, §34O). Payment may be made directly to insured under plan approved by commissioner; if made to repair shop, must not exceed approved appraisal. (c. 90, §34O). Auto repair shops must be registered. (c. 100A, §2).

No company issuing a "No-fault" policy may require a medical examination of applicant. (c. 175, §113N).

Compulsory Uninsured Motorists Coverage.—Massachusetts insured must obtain coverage against injury or death from accident involving uninsured motorist. (c. 175, §113L). Provision which excludes coverage for automobiles owned and regularly used but not listed is invalid. (400 Mass. 259, 508 N.E.2d 845). Exclusion of coverage for accidents and losses occurring outside USA and Canada is valid. (402 Mass. 810, 525 N.E.2d 651).

Transfer of Compulsory Insurance.—Under certain circumstances, insurance coverage on transferred motor vehicle is continued in force and covers newly acquired motor vehicle for two registry business days. (c. 175, §113A[6]).

Safe Driver Insurance Plan.—In classifying risks for insurance premium fixing purposes, commissioner is to establish safe driver insurance plan providing premium adjustments based on at-fault accidents, convictions of moving violations, filing of four or more comprehensive claims totalling $2,000 or more under certain circumstances, previous driving experience in other states, assignments to driver alcohol education program with credits for safe drivers and premium reductions for incorporation of certain safety features. (c. 175, §113B). In addition, commissioner shall determine whether insurance companies utilize adequate programs to control costs and expenses, in accordance with standards determined or approved by commissioner. (c. 175, §113B).

Death or Insolvency of Owner.—Compulsory insurance, unless cancelled, continues in effect until policy's expiration date following death or insolvency of owner and covers legal representative of estate. (c. 175, §113A[6]).

Insurance.—See generally c. 175, §§113A-P and c. 175E, and see subheads No-fault Insurance, Safe Driver Insurance Plan, Compulsory Uninsured Motorists Coverage, and Death or Insolvency of Owner, supra.

Foreign Vehicles (c. 90, §3), owner of which has fully complied with registration laws of state or country of registration, may be operated in Massachusetts for not exceeding aggregate of 30 days in one year without registration, provided state or country of registration grants similar privileges to residents of Massachusetts. It may be operated beyond 30-day aggregate limit without registration provided owner maintains liability insurance, if state or country of registration affords similar privileges to residents of Massachusetts. Failure to have, on person or in vehicle, policy or certificate thereof, creates presumption in damage cases and is prima facie evidence in other cases that no insurance was in force. Registrar may suspend or revoke rights of nonresident for cause. (c. 90, §3).

Nonresident students enrolled in Massachusetts school or college who operate vehicle in Massachusetts registered in another state for more than 30 days in aggregate between Sept. 1 of any year and Aug. 31 of following year are required to file report form with police department of city or town where school or college is located and decal must be displayed on window of vehicle. (c. 90, §3).

Nonresident Operators.—Foreign owner or employee may operate his own foreign vehicle in state without operator's license if he has complied with home state licensing requirements and has evidence of such compliance on his person. Nonresident may

See note at head of Digest as to 1998 legislation covered.

See Topical Index in front part of this volume.

MOTOR VEHICLES ... continued

operate any private vehicle registered in commonwealth and any commercial vehicle engaged in interstate commerce, without local operator's license, if he has complied with home state requirements and has evidence of compliance on his person, and if home state grants substantially similar privileges to residents of Massachusetts and requires substantially as high standards of fitness. (c. 90, §10).

Action Against Nonresidents.—Operation by nonresident of motor vehicle or trailer upon public way, or private way if entrance thereto was made from way, or in any place to which public has right of access in commonwealth is deemed equivalent to appointment of registrar as attorney upon whom may be served process in any action growing out of any accident involving nonresident while operating motor vehicle on such way or in such place. (c. 90, §3A). Service on registrar with required fee is sufficient service provided copy of process is sent to defendant by registered mail or is served by officer qualified to serve like process in state where defendant is found. (c. 90, §3A).

Motor Vehicle Carriers.—Regulated by Department of Public Utilities, 100 Cambridge Street, Boston, Massachusetts 02202.

Carriage of Passengers.—(c. 159A). Vehicles must be licensed in every city or town in which they operate (c. 159A, §1); common carriers must deposit with state treasurer bond to indemnify passengers for negligent or unlawful injury to person or property (c. 159A, §6); must have certificate from department of public utilities declaring after public hearing that public convenience and necessity require such operation (c. 159A, §7); must also have permit from department of public utilities issued only after inspection of vehicles and conformity of same to regulations as to construction, equipment, etc. (c. 159A, §8).

Carriage of Property.—(c. 159B). A common carrier, defined to include any person who directly or by his agent or under a lease or any other arrangement, or by arrangement with any other common carrier, transports property for general public for compensation on ways (c. 159B, §2), must have certificate from department of public utilities issued on finding, after public hearing, that applicant is fit, willing and able properly to perform service proposed and to conform to all lawful requirements, and that proposed service is or will be required by present or future public convenience and necessity (c. 159B, §3). Fee for application determined annually by secretary of administration, currently $100. (c. 159A, §3). Must also pay tariff filing fee of $15 and decal fee of $20. Such carrier must also file with department schedules of rates, and rates in effect from time to time must be strictly adhered to. Department may, after hearing, allow, disallow or alter any filed or existing rates and may prescribe just and reasonable rates. (c. 159B, §6).

A contract carrier, defined to include any person not within the definition of common carrier who, under special and individual contracts, directly or by agent or under a lease or any other arrangement, transports property for compensation on ways, must have permit from department issued on finding, after hearing, that applicant is fit, willing and able properly to perform the service proposed, and that the proposed operation will be consistent with public interest, safety and welfare of the public on the ways, preservation and maintenance of the ways and proper regulation of common carriers using same. Fee for application is determined annually by secretary of administration, currently $100. Must also pay tariff filing fee of $15 and decal fee of $20. Such carrier must also file with department copies of all transportation contracts and department may require it to file schedules of minimum charges and may, after hearing, prescribe such charges as may be necessary or desirable in the public interest. No such carrier may make less than established minimum charge. (c. 159B, §4).

There are special provisions relating to agricultural carriers and private carriers which are defined in c. 159B, §§2, 3, 6.

Diesel Powered Motor Vehicles.—For special licensing provisions see category Taxation, topic Gasoline and Special Fuels Taxes, subhead Gasoline, Diesel and Other Combustible Motor Fuels Taxes.

Motor Vehicle Taxes.—Automobiles and trailers are excepted from the general property tax and, with certain exceptions, subjected to a special excise tax based upon fixed percentage of list price, decreasing to 10% in fifth and succeeding years following designated year of manufacture. Rate of tax is uniform throughout state and $25 per $1,000 of valuation is maximum rate. Excise tax does not apply to motor vehicle owned and registered by former prisoner of war who is defined as any regularly appointed, enrolled, enlisted or inducted member of military forces of U.S. who was captured and incarcerated by enemy of U.S. during armed conflict. (c. 60A, §1). Registrar of Motor Vehicles may refuse to renew operator's license and registration of anyone failing to pay motor vehicle excise tax. (c. 60A, §2A). Interest on late payment at 12% annual rate must be paid. (c. 60A, §2).

Gasoline Tax.—See category Taxation, topic Gasoline and Special Fuels Taxes, subhead Gasoline, Diesel and Other Combustible Motor Fuels Taxes.

Dealers.—Business practices between dealers and public and franchises and selling agreements between motor vehicle manufacturers, distributors and dealers are regulated. (c. 93B). Persons defrauded by tampering with odometers can recover in tort three times actual damages sustained or $1,500 whichever is greater, plus costs and reasonable attorney fees. Criminal penalties are fines between $500 and $1,000 or imprisonment. (c. 266, §§141-141A). Advertised price of motor vehicles must include freight, handling, and other charges, exclusive of taxes. (c. 93B, §5A). See also subhead Sales, supra, and category Business Regulation and Commerce, topics Consumer Protection, Sales.

Rental.—Lessee must show lessor that he is duly licensed. (c. 90, §32C). Persons in business of leasing and renting motor vehicles must be licensed as sellers of second hand motor vehicles. (c. 140, §57). Right to operate subject to suspension for certain violations. (c. 90, §3).

Actions Against Parking Facilities.—Disclaimers and exclusions of liability on parking receipts do not constitute defense in tort or contract actions. (c. 231, §85M).

Bicycles.—Bicycle traffic patterns and required safety equipment are now regulated in much the same manner as those of motor vehicles. (c. 85, §11B). Accommodations for bicycle and pedestrian traffic must be considered in planning public ways. (c. 90E, §2A).

Motor boats and recreational vehicles regulated under c. 90B. Motor boats, other than those owned by governments or agencies, ship's lifeboats and marine documented vessels, required to be numbered and to display numbers (§§2, 3) with penalties for falsifying, removal or defacing (§§4A, 4B, 14). Certain lights, signalling, safety equipment required. (§§5, 5A). Certain dangerous operations prohibited (§8) with penalties of fine up to $500 ($1,000 if death ensues) or imprisonment up to six months (one year if death ensues) or both (§14). Operation of jet skis limited. (§9A). Director of division of law enforcement of department of fisheries, wildlife and environmental law enforcement empowered to establish speed limits, revoke numbers and otherwise enforce chapter with other state and local police and enforcement officers also empowered to enforce chapter. (§§11, 12). Recreational vehicles also required to be registered (§22), to have certain lights and equipment and to meet certain noise levels (§24). Dangerous operations prohibited (§26) with small fine ($20-$100) for violations (§34). Enforcement as for motorboats. (§32). Person refusing to produce identification or certificate of vessel upon request by officer will be fined $100. (§38).

Motor Vehicle Theft.—In addition to fine up to $15,000 or imprisonment up to 15 years in state prison or up to 2½ years in jail or both (c. 266, §28), thief of, committer of malicious damage to or receiver of stolen motor vehicle also subject to restitution of damages or financial loss (c. 276, §92A).

Abandoned Motor Vehicles.—Whoever abandons motor vehicle upon any way, or upon property other than his own without owner's consent, subject to fine of $250 for first abandonment and $500 for each subsequent abandonment, loss of driver's license up to three months, denial of right to register motor vehicle for one year. (c. 90, §22B). Special statute (1988, c. 212) applies to abandonments in Boston.

Towing.—Police or fire department personnel may tow illegally parked vehicles without being subject to penalties for improper removal of vehicles. (c. 89, §7A).

RAILROADS:

See category Business Regulation and Commerce, topic Carriers.

See note at head of Digest as to 1998 legislation covered.

See Topical Index in front part of this volume.

COMMERCIAL CODE FORMS

See also categories Business Regulation and Commerce, topic Commercial Code; Mortgages, topic Chattel Mortgages.

Financing Statement—Form UCC 1.—

This FINANCING STATEMENT is presented to a filing officer
for filing pursuant to the Uniform Commercial Code.

4. ☐ Filed for record in the real estate records.	5. ☐ Debtor is a Transmitting Utility.	6. No. of Additional Sheets Presented:
1. Debtor(s) (Last Name First) and address(es)	2. Secured Party(ies) and address(es)	3. For Filing Officer (Date, Time, Number, and Filing Office)

7. This financing statement covers the following types (or items) of property:

☐ Products of Collateral are also covered.

. . . .

. . . .

Signature(s) of Debtor
(Or Assignor)   Signature(s) of Secured Party
(Or Assignee)

Continuation, etc. Statement—Form UCC 3.—

This FINANCING STATEMENT is presented to a filing officer for a filing pursuant to the Uniform Commercial Code.

4. ☐ Filed for record in the real estate records.	5. ☐ Debtor is a Transmitting Utility.	6. No. of Additional Sheets Presented:
1. Debtor(s) (Last Name First) and address(es)	2. Secured Party(ies) and address(es)	3. For Filing Officer (Date, Time, Number, and Filing Office)

7. This statement refers to original Financing Statement No. _____ filed (date) _____ with _____

8. ☐ A. Continuation   The original Financing Statement bearing the above file number is still effective.

☐ B. Termination   The Secured Party of record no longer claims a security interest under the Financing Statement bearing the above file number.

☐ C. Release   From the Collateral described in the Financing Statement bearing the above file number, the Secured Party of record releases the following:

☐ D. Assignment   The Secured Party of record has assigned the Secured Party's rights in the property described below under the Financing Statement bearing the above file number to the Assignee whose name and address are shown below:

☐ E. Amendment   The Financing Statement bearing the above file number is amended as set forth below: (Signature of Debtor and Secured Party is Required)

☐ F. Other

By . . . .

Signature(s) of Debtor(s)
(only on amendment)   Signature(s) of Secured party(ies)

MICHIGAN LAW DIGEST REVISER

Miller, Canfield, Paddock and Stone, P.L.C.
150 West Jefferson, Suite 2500
Detroit, Michigan 48226
Telephone: 313-963-6420
Fax: 313-496-7500
Internet: http://www.millercanfield.com

Reviser Profile

Miller, Canfield, Paddock and Stone traces its history to 1852 when Sidney Davy Miller (1830-1904) opened a practice on Detroit's Jefferson Avenue. Today Miller Canfield is one of the largest law firms in Michigan and one of the nation's leading firms in its specialty areas. We have grown to a legal staff of 250 attorneys and over 50 legal assistants.

Our offices in Michigan are located in Ann Arbor, Bloomfield Hills, Detroit, Grand Rapids, Howell, Kalamazoo, Lansing, and Monroe. We also have offices in New York City and Washington, D.C. with affiliated offices in Pensacola, Florida, and Gdańsk, Katowice, and Warsaw, Poland. Our offices in Poland enable us to serve clients throughout Eastern Europe.

Our practice areas are organized into the following practice groups: Bankruptcy/Workout, Business Services, Employee Benefits, Environmental, Estate Planning, Federal Taxation, Finance and Development, Health Care, Intellectual Property, International Business, Labor and Employment, Product Liability/Tort Litigation, Commercial Litigation, Dispute Resolution, State/Local Taxation, Public Law and Bond Counsel.

We represent individuals in their personal and business concerns, trusts and estates, publicly traded companies, and many start-up, small, and medium sized businesses. Clients also include public bodies such as the state of Michigan and many of its agencies, authorities and universities, cities, counties, townships, school and community college districts, and special authorities throughout Michigan and in other states. We represent many nonprofit, tax-exempt institutions, such as hospitals, charitable corporations, and professional associations.

The Firm's areas of concentration are: Accounting Litigation, Administrative, Admiralty/Maritime, Antidumping, Antitrust, Appellate Practice, Banking, Bankruptcy & Reorganization, Commercial Transactions, Computer, Condemnation, Condominiums & Cooperatives, Construction Litigation, Corporate, Domestic Relations, Education, Emerging Business, Environmental, Estate Planning & Administration, Foundations & Nonprofit Organizations, Franchising, Health Care & Hospital, Immigration, Insurance, Intellectual Property, International Law, International Trade & Customs, Labor & Employment, Libel & Slander Litigation, Licensing & High-Technology, Litigation & Alternative Dispute Resolution, Litigation Management, Mergers & Acquisitions, Municipal & Governmental Law, Nuclear Power Plant Litigation, Oil & Gas, Pension, Profit-sharing & Employee Benefits, Product Liability Consulting & Defense, Professional Malpractice Consulting & Defense, Public Law, Real Estate Development & Investment, Securities (Corporate & Municipal), Securities Litigation, State, Municipal, School & Public Finance including Bond Counsel, Taxation, Tax-exempt Financing, Telecommunications, Toxic Torts Litigation, Transportation, Utilities, Zoning.

MICHIGAN LAW DIGEST

(The following is a list of all Categories and Topics, including cross-references, covered in this Digest.)

MICHIGAN LAW DIGEST

Revised for 1999 edition by

MILLER, CANFIELD, PADDOCK and STONE, P.L.C. of the Detroit, Ann Arbor, Bloomfield Hills, Grand Rapids, Howell, Kalamazoo, Lansing, Monroe, Michigan; Pensacola and St. Petersburg, Florida, New York, New York, Washington, D. C. and Gdańsk, Katowice and Warsaw, Poland Bars.

(Unless otherwise noted, section references are to Michigan Compiled Laws Annotated (abbreviated MCLA, herein) and Michigan Statutes Annotated (abbreviated MSA, herein); recent Public Acts are cited by year and act number. "Rule" indicates Michigan Court Rules of 1985, effective Mar. 1, 1985 as am'd. Parallel citations to the North Western Reporter begin with 41 Mich.)

Note.—Legislature not finally adjourned at time of going to press. Public Acts of 1998 through Act No. 44 included.

INTRODUCTION

GOVERNMENT AND LEGAL SYSTEM:

The State of Michigan is a constituent state of the United States of America. For further discussion of the U.S. federal system, see Introduction to the Federal Government of the United States at the beginning of this volume. A great many laws are promulgated by the federal government of the United States and are not reflected in the topics below. See the Introduction to this volume for references to the federal law topics covered.

Like all but one of the United States, Michigan has a common law legal system, with roots in English common law. For information on the courts and legislature of Michigan, see Category Courts and Legislature.

HOLIDAYS:

Holidays are: Jan. 1, 3d Mon. in Jan., Feb. 12, 3d Mon. in Feb., last Mon. of May, July 4, 1st Mon. in Sept., 2d Mon. in Oct., Nov. 11, 4th Thur. in Nov. and Dec. 25. Saturdays are half-holidays from noon to midnight. (MCLA §435.101; MSA §18.861).

Holiday Falling on Sunday.—Next day is a holiday. (MCLA §435.102; MSA §18.862).

Transactions on Holiday.—Provision that conveyance of real property or any contract, except contract of marriage, made on Sun. is absolutely void (MCLA §435.11-.13; MSA §18.850) was repealed, effective June 23, 1974 by 1974, No. 171.

OFFICE HOURS AND TIME ZONE:

Michigan is in the Eastern (GMT −05:00) time zone. Office hours are generally from 9 a.m. to 5 p.m.

BUSINESS ORGANIZATIONS

AGENCY:

Common law rules govern. See category Property, topic Powers of Attorney.

ASSOCIATIONS:

Persons may associate together without incorporation for any purpose not prohibited by law or public policy. Unless engaged in business for profit, such associations are not partnerships. (74 Mich. 269, 41 N.W. 921). Most fraternal, benevolent, religious, patriotic, agricultural, recreational, social and similar associations now incorporate under acts providing simplified procedure and small fees. (MCLA §§450-.691-.696; 453.1-458, 460, 458.521-.536; MSA §§21.321-.326, 21.361-21.1970, 21.2001-.2016). Michigan Nonprofit Corporation Act applies to several types of associations formed for nonprofit purposes. (MCLA §450.2123; MSA §21.197[123]).

Formation.—No formalities are prescribed by statute except if association is incorporated. Articles of agreement adopted by members are enforced as contract. (74 Mich. 269, 41 N.W. 921).

Rights and Powers.—Associations not covered by statutes referred to in introductory paragraph generally do not appear to have rights or powers as entities apart from members. See, e., 213 Mich. 642, 182 N.W. 22; 295 Mich. 547, 295 N.W. 259.

Liabilities.—Members who act or authorize acts on behalf of association are liable individually. (111 Mich. 108, 69 N.W. 147).

Actions.—Class action under Rule 3.501 is presumably appropriate procedure where suit by or against all members is impracticable.

Dissolution is by agreement. Upon dissolution property of association belongs to members jointly, subject to conditions of their articles of agreement. (103 Mich. 307, 61 N.W. 501).

Professional Associations.—See topic Corporations, subhead Professional Corporations.

CORPORATIONS:

Business Corporation Act (MCLA §450.1101 et seq.; MSA §21.200[101] et seq.) adopted, effective Jan. 1, 1973, governing all corporations except insurance, surety, savings and loan associations, fraternal benefit societies, railroad, bridge and tunnel companies, union depot companies and banking corporations. Unless otherwise provided in, or inconsistent with, Act under which such corporation is or has been formed, this Act applies to deposit and security companies, summer resort associations, brine pipeline companies, telegraph companies, telephone companies, safety and collateral deposit companies, canal, river and harbor improvement companies, cemetery, burial and cremation associations, railroad, bridge, and tunnel companies and agricultural and horticultural fair societies. Such entities may not, however, be incorporated under this Act. (MCLA §450.1123; MSA §21.200[123]).

General Supervision.—Department of Consumer and Industry Services (Department) Lansing, has general supervision of corporations. (MCLA §450.1105[1]; MSA §21.200[105][1]).

Purposes.—Corporation may be formed for any lawful purpose. (MCLA §450.1251; MSA §21.200 [251]). Use of so-called "all purposes clause" permitted. (MCLA §450.1202[b]; MSA §21.200[202][b]).

Name.—Corporate name of domestic corporation must contain word "corporation," "company," "incorporated," or "limited" or shall contain one of following abbreviations: "corp.," "co.," "inc.," or "ltd.". (MCLA §450.1211; MSA §21.200[211]). Corporate name shall not suggest purpose other than as permitted in articles of incorporation and shall be distinguished from name of any other domestic or qualified foreign corporation, limited liability company, or limited partnership or any name reserved, registered or assumed by any of same. (MCLA §450.1212; MSA §21.200[212]). Compliance with this section does not create substantive rights in use of name. (MCLA §450.1212[3]; MSA §21.200[212]). Corporation (other than registered bank holding company) may not use name which implies that it is banking corporation, insurance or surety company or trust company and shall not use words "bank," "industrial bank," "deposit," "surety," "security," "trust" or "trust company." (MCLA §450.1213; MSA §21.200[213]). "Co-operative" or "Co-op" may only be used by cooperative corporations. (MCLA §450.99; MSA §21.100). Corporation may file assumed name certificate and may do business under such assumed name. (MCLA §450.1217; MSA §21.200[217]). Corporation surviving merger may use name of any entity participating in merger by transferring assumed name in merger agreement if certificate on file prior to merger or providing for use of assumed name in merger agreement without transfer. (MCLA §§450.1217, .1707, .1712, .1724; MSA §§21.200[217], [707], [712], [724]). See also category Intellectual Property, topic Trademarks and Tradenames, subhead Tradenames.

Corporate name may be reserved by filing application with administrator. Reservation expires at end of sixth full calendar month following month in which application filed. Reservation of name may be transferred by filing notice, executed by applicant and stating name of transferee. (MCLA §450.1215; MSA §21.200[215]). Fee is $10. (MCLA §450.2060; MSA §21.200[1060]). No separate procedure for name clearance available.

Term of Corporate Existence.—Corporate term is perpetual unless limited period is fixed by articles. (MCLA §§450.1261, 405.1202[h]; MSA §§21.200[261], 21.200[202][h]). Corporation may extend term by amendment to articles. (MCLA §450.1602; MSA §21.200[602]). Corporation whose term has expired may renew corporate existence pursuant to statutory procedure. (MCLA §450.1815; MSA §21.200[815]).

Incorporators.—One or more persons may become incorporators of corporation by signing in ink and filing articles of incorporation therefor. (MCLA §450.1201; MSA §21.200[201]). Such "person" may be individual, partnership, domestic or foreign corporation, or any other association, corporation, trust or legal entity. (MCLA §450.1108[2]; MSA §21.200[108][2]). There are no requirements as to citizenship or residence of incorporators.

Articles of Incorporation shall contain: (a) Name of corporation; (b) purposes for which corporation is formed; (c) aggregate number of shares, and par value, if any, which corporation has authority to issue; (d) if shares divided into classes or series, designation of such classes and series, number of shares in each class and series, and statement of relative rights, preferences and limitations of shares of each class and series; (e) if any class of shares is to be divided into series, statement of authority vested in board to divide such class of shares into series and to determine or change designation, number of shares, relative rights, preferences and limitations of series; (f) street address and mailing address, if different, of corporation's initial registered office and name of corporation's initial resident agent; (g) names and addresses of incorporators; and (h) duration of corporation if other than perpetual. (MCLA §450.1202; MSA §21.200[202]). Articles may contain statutory language regarding compromise, arrangement or reorganization. (MCLA §450.1204; MSA §21.200[204]). Articles may also contain any provision not inconsistent with Act or another state statute, including provision for management of business and conduct of affairs of corporation, or creating, defining, limiting, or regulating powers of corporation, its directors and shareholders, or class of shareholders (MCLA §450.1209[a]; MSA §21.200[209(a)]) and provision eliminating or limiting director's liability to corporation or its shareholders for monetary damages for any action or failure to take action, with limited exceptions.

Filing of Articles.—Original of articles must be forwarded for filing to Corporation, Securities and Land Development Bureau of Department, either by hand at 6546 Mercantile Way, Lansing, MI 48910 or by mail at P.O. Box 30054, Lansing, MI 489090-7554, or by facsimile (after approval of application) at (517) 334-8048. (MCLA §450.1131; MSA §21.200[131]).

Incorporation Tax or Fee.—Domestic profit corporation, cooperative association and domestic regulated investment company shall pay to Department organization and admission fee of $50 for first 60,000 authorized shares and $30 for each additional 20,000 authorized shares or portion thereof, up to maximum fee of $5,000 for first 10,000,000 authorized shares. Fee is $30 for each 20,000 authorized shares or portion

See note at head of Digest as to 1998 legislation covered.

See Topical Index in front part of this volume.

CORPORATIONS . . . *continued*
thereof in excess of 10,000,000 shares up to maximum of $200,000 for such initial filing. Similar fees are payable upon increase in capital stock. Initial admission franchise fee of foreign profit corporation and foreign regulated investment company is $50 and authorized capital stock in amount of 60,000 shares shall be deemed initially attributable to state at time of admission. Number of authorized shares attributable to state is determined by multiplying total number of authorized shares by most recent apportionment percentage used in computation of tax required by single business tax act. (MCLA §§208.1-145; MSA §§7.558[1]-[145]). If business activity confined solely to state, all authorized shares are considered attributable to state. Foreign profit corporation filing amended application shall pay therewith additional fee for additional authorized shares attributable to state comparable to domestic corporations. (MCLA §450.2062, .2021; MSA §21.200[1062], [1021]).

Nonprofit corporations pay franchise fee of $10. (MCLA §450.3061; MSA §21.200[2061]).

Filing Fees.—Filing fees for various corporate documents established by statute. (MCLA §450.2060; MSA §21.200[1060]).

License to Do Business.—Certificate of authority is issued to foreign corporation upon compliance with statute. (MCLA §§450.2002, 450.2011, 450.2015-.2016; MSA §§21.200[1002], 21.200[1011], 21.200[1015]-[1016]).

Organization.—Before or after filing of articles, majority of incorporators, at meeting or by written instrument, shall select board and may adopt bylaws. On or after filing date of articles, any member of board may call first meeting of board upon not less than three days notice by mail to each director. Majority of directors constitutes quorum for first meeting of board. At first meeting, board may adopt bylaws, elect officers and transact such other business as may come before meeting. (MCLA §450.1223; MSA §21.200[223]).

Paid in Capital Requirements.—No minimum capital requirement established by statute.

Amendment of Articles.—Corporation may amend articles if amendment contains only such provisions as might lawfully be contained in original articles filed at time of amendment. Corporation may amend articles to become nonprofit corporation by adopting restated articles containing only provisions authorized by Nonprofit Corporation Act. (MCLA §450.1601; MSA §21.200[601]). Types of amendments, but without limitation, are listed by statute. (MCLA §450.1602; MSA §21.200[602]). Amendment of articles shall be by majority vote of shareholders upon notice of meeting setting forth proposed amendment, except for certain specified amendments, which may be made by board action unless prohibited by articles. (MCLA §450.1611, .1301a, .1302[d]; MSA §21.200[611], [301a], [302(5)]). Prior to first meeting of board, incorporators may amend articles. (MCLA §§450.1611[1], 450.1631[1]; MSA §§21.200[611][1], 21.200[631][1]). Amendment becomes effective upon filing thereof with Department, together with fees and documents required by law. (MCLA §450.1131; MSA §21.200[131]).

Increase or Decrease of Authorized Capital Stock.—Corporation may amend articles to increase or decrease number of shares or shares of any class or series of any class in same manner as any other amendment to articles. (MCLA §450.1602; MSA §21.200[602]). For additional franchise fees payable on increase in authorized stock and on increase in proportion of foreign corporation's authorized stock attributable to state, see subhead Incorporation Tax or Fee, supra.

Bylaws.—Initial bylaws of corporation shall be adopted by incorporators, shareholders or board. Shareholders or board may amend or repeal bylaws or adopt new bylaws unless power to do so is reserved exclusively to shareholders by articles or bylaws. Shareholders may prescribe in articles or bylaws that any bylaw made by them shall not be altered or repealed by board. Bylaws may contain any provision for regulation and management of affairs of corporation not inconsistent with law or articles. (MCLA §450.1231; MSA §21.200[231]).

Stock.—May be divided into classes having such designations and such relative voting, dividend, liquidation and other rights, preferences and limitations as stated in articles and consistent with act. If articles so provide, class of shares may be divided into series, with such relative rights and preferences as prescribed by articles. (MCLA §450.1301, .1302; MSA §21.200[301], [302]). When provided in articles, corporation may issue shares convertible, at option of holder or corporation or on happening of specified event, into shares of any class or series of any class or into bonds. (MCLA §450.1303; MSA §21.200[303]).

Stock Certificates.—Shareholders are entitled to certificates signed by chairperson of board, vice-chairman of board, president or vice-president which may be sealed with corporate seal or facsimile thereof, stating number, class, series, if any, name of person to whom issued, statement that corporation is formed under laws of this state. Signatures of officers may be facsimiles. Certificate representing shares issued by corporation authorized to issue shares of more than one class shall set forth required legend on face or back. Existence of restrictions on transfer under §§473 and 488, if any, must be noted conspicuously on face or back of certificate for shares issued, and certificates representing previously issued shares must be replaced with certificates in conformance with §488 if applicable. (MCLA §§450.1473, .1488; MSA §§21.200[473], [488]). Unless prohibited by articles or bylaws, board may authorize shares without certificates. (MCLA §450.1336; MSA §21.200[336]). If issuing uncertificated shares, corporation must send shareholders written information statement containing information that would be required to be noted on shares' face or back, if certificated, including, if applicable, information regarding authorization of shares of more than one class, transfer restrictions under §472, and shareholder agreements under §488. (MCLA §§450.1331, 450.1332; MSA §§21.200[331], 21.200[332]).

Issuance of Stock.—Shares may be issued for consideration fixed by board unless articles reserve right to shareholders. Consideration for issuance of shares may be paid, in whole or in part, in tangible or intangible property or benefit to corporation including cash, promissory notes, services performed, contracts for services to be performed, or other securities of corporation. Judgment of board is conclusive insofar as nature and amount of consideration relates to whether shares are validly issued, fully paid and nonassessable. (MCLA §450.1314; MSA §21.200[314]). Unless otherwise provided in articles or agreement between corporation and shareholders, corporation may issue unissued shares, including security convertible into or carrying right to subscribe for or acquire shares, without first offering them to existing shareholders. (MCLA §450.1343; MSA §21.200[343]).

Transfer of Stock.—Governed by Uniform Commercial Code. (MCLA §§440.8301-.8406; MSA §§19.8301-.8406).

Uniform Securities Ownership by Minors Act not adopted.

Uniform Simplification of Fiduciary Security Transfers Act adopted. (MCLA §§441.101-.112; MSA §§19.356[1]-[12]).

Uniform Commercial Code adopted. (MCLA §§440.1101-440.9994; MSA §§19.1101-19.9994). See category Business Regulation and Commerce, topic Commercial Code. Michigan has not adopted Revised Art. 8—Investment Securities.

Stock Transfer Tax.—None.

Stockholders.—See subheads Stock Certificates, Issuance of Stock, supra and Stockholders' Meetings, Voting, Voting Trusts, Books and Records, Appraisal, infra, for voting rights, preemptive rights, rights to stockholders' list, rights to examine books and records, appraisal rights, and other rights of stockholders.

Stockholders Actions.—Shareholder may bring action in circuit court of county in which corporation's principal place of business or registered office is located, to establish that acts of directors or those in control of corporation are illegal, fraudulent or willfully unfair and oppressive to corporation or shareholder. If shareholder establishes grounds for relief, court may make order or grant relief it considers appropriate, including but not limited to relief specified in statute. Such action shall not be brought by shareholder whose shares are listed on national securities exchange or regularly traded in market maintained by one or more members of national or affiliated securities association. (MCLA §450.1489; MSA §21.200 [489]). Shareholder may not commence or maintain derivative proceeding unless he was shareholder at time act or omission complained of occurred or became shareholder through transfer by operation of law from one who was shareholder at time; he fairly and adequately represents interests of corporation in enforcing right of corporation; and he continues to be shareholder until time of judgment, unless failure to continue to be shareholder is result of corporation action taken after derivative proceeding was commenced and former shareholder did not acquiesce to such action. (MCLA §450.1492a; MSA §21.200 [491a]). Shareholder may not commence derivative proceeding until written demand has been made upon corporation to take suitable action and 90 days have expired from date of demand, unless shareholder has earlier been notified that demand has been rejected or unless irreparable injury to corporation would result by waiting for 90-day period to expire. (MCLA §450.1493a; MSA §21.200[493a]). Court shall dismiss derivative proceeding if, on motion by corporation, court finds that one of groups specified has made determination in good faith after conducting reasonable investigation that proceeding is not in best interests of corporation. Burden of proof is on corporation or plaintiff, depending on which of specified groups determined proceeding was not in best interests of corporation. (MCLA §450.1495; MSA §21.200[495]. See category Civil Actions and Procedure, topic Costs, for securities for expenses statute.

Stockholders' Liabilities.—Except as provided in articles, shareholder not personally liable for acts or debts of corporation except by reason of his own acts or conduct. (MCLA §450.1317; MSA §21.200 [317]).

Stockholders' Meetings.—Meetings of shareholders may be held at place within or without state as provided in bylaws. In absence of such provision, meetings shall be held at registered office or such other place as determined by board. (MCLA §450.1401; MSA §21.200[401]). Unless otherwise restricted by articles or bylaws shareholder may participate by conference telephone or similar equipment if all participants are advised of equipment and names of all participants. (MCLA §450.1405; MSA §21.200 [405]). Unless greater or lesser quorum is provided in articles, bylaws adopted by shareholders or incorporators or Act, shares entitled to cast majority of votes at meeting constitute quorum at meeting. When holders of class or series are entitled to vote separately on item of business, same provision applies to determine presence of quorum of such class or series. (MCLA §450.1415; MSA §21.200[415]). Unless otherwise provided in Act, written notice of time, place and purpose of meeting of shareholders shall be given not less than ten nor more than 60 days before meeting, either personally or by mail, to each shareholder of record entitled to vote at meeting. Unless corporation has securities registered under §12 of Securities Exchange Act of 1934, 15 U.S.C. 78(1), notice of purpose shall include notice of shareholder proposals which are intended to be presented by shareholders who have given corporation notice of their intention to submit such proposals at meeting. Reasonable procedures for submission of proposals prior to meeting may be established in bylaws. (MCLA §450.1404; MSA §21.200[404]). Determination of shareholders entitled to notice of, and to vote at meeting shall be made in conformance with §412(1). (MCLA §450.1412[1]; MSA §21.200[412(1)]). Officer or agent having charge of stock transfer books shall make and certify complete list of shareholders entitled to vote at shareholders' meeting, and such list must be produced at time and place of meeting for inspection by any shareholder during meeting. (MCLA §450.1413; MSA §21.200[413]). Each meeting of shareholders shall be presided over by chair who will establish rules of conduct for meeting and for closing polls for shareholder voting. Rules and conduct of meeting must be fair to shareholders. (MCLA §450.1406; MSA §21.200[406]).

Stockholder Action Without Meeting.—Articles may provide that any action required or permitted by Act to be taken at annual or special meeting of shareholders may be taken without meeting, without prior notice and without vote, if consents in writing, setting forth actions so taken and bearing date of signature of each shareholder are signed by holders of outstanding stock having not less than minimum number of votes necessary to authorize or take such action at meeting at which all shares entitled

CORPORATIONS . . . *continued*

to vote thereon were present and voted. Within 60 days after record date for determining shareholders entitled to consent or dissent to action, written consents dated not more than ten days before record date and signed by requisite number of shareholders must be delivered to corporation. Notice of taking of corporate action without meeting by less than unanimous written consent shall be given to shareholders who would have been entitled to notice if action had been taken at meeting. Any action required or permitted by Act to be taken at annual or special meeting of shareholders may be taken without meeting without prior notice and without vote, if all shareholders entitled to vote thereon consent thereto in writing. (MCLA §450.1407; MSA §21.200[407]).

Voting.—Unless articles provide otherwise, voting for directors is not cumulative. (MCLA §450.1451; MSA §21.200[451]). Shares held by fiduciary may be voted by him without transfer of shares into his name. (MCLA §450.1445; MSA §21.200[445]). Pledgee may not vote shares until they have been transferred into his name. (MCLA §450.1444; MSA §21.200[444]). Corporation may, in articles, confer voting rights upon bondholders. (MCLA §450.1391; MSA §21.200[391]). Proxy is valid for three years unless otherwise provided therein. (MCLA §450.1421; MSA §21.200[421]). Shareholder may grant proxy, without limitation, by executing writing or by transmitting or authorizing transmission of telegram, cablegram or other means of electronic transmission. (MCLA §452.1421; MSA §21.200[421]). Proxy is revocable unless entitled "irrevocable proxy", stating it is irrevocable, and holder thereof falls within one of statutory classes. (MCLA §450.1422, .1423; MSA §21.200[422], [423]).

Voting trusts for periods up to ten years are authorized. (MCLA §450.1466; MSA §21.200[466]).

Directors.—Business and affairs of corporation are managed by board, except as otherwise provided in Act or articles. (MCLA §450.1501; MSA §21.200[501]). Articles or shareholder agreements may eliminate or restrict discretion of board and otherwise govern exercise of corporate powers of management or relationship among shareholders, directors, and corporation. Such article or agreement is not grounds for imposing personal liability even if it results in failure to follow corporate formalities. Such article or agreement is only effective so long as security is not listed on national exchange or regularly traded in market maintained by one or more members of national or affiliated securities association. (MCLA §450.1488; MSA §21.200[488]). Director need not be shareholder unless articles or bylaws require. Articles or bylaws may prescribe qualifications for directors. (MCLA §450.1501; MSA §21.200[501]). Board shall consist of one or more members, with number of directors to be fixed by bylaws, unless established in articles. (MCLA §450.1505; MSA §21.200[505]). Directors are elected annually, unless provision in articles or bylaws adopted by shareholders or incorporators permits classification of election of directors. (MCLA §§450.1505[2], 450.1506; MSA §21.200[505][2], 21.200[506]). If board elected by shareholders voting as single class, vacancies on board may be filled by majority of remaining directors, unless right to fill vacancy is reserved to shareholders by articles. (MCLA §450.1515[1]; MSA §21.200[515][1]). Vacancies in class of directors elected by particular class or series of shareholders may be filled by majority of such class of directors. (MCLA §450.1515[2]; MSA §21.200[515][2]). Unless otherwise provided by articles, vacancies in class of directors elected by particular class or series of shareholders may be filled by majority of such class of directors or holders of shares of such class. (MCLA §§450.1515[2], .1515a; MSA §§21.200[515][2], [515a]). Shareholders or board may designate one or more directors as independent director. Independent director may receive reasonable compensation in addition to compensation received by directors generally as determined by board or shareholders and reimbursements for expenses reasonably related to service as independent director. (MCLA §450.1505; MSA §21.200[505]). Directors may be removed, with or without cause, by vote of holders of majority of shares entitled to vote at election of directors, unless articles provide that directors may be removed only for cause or that higher vote required for removal without cause. (MCLA §450.1511; MSA §21.200[511]).

Directors' meetings may be held in or outside state. Regular meeting may be held with or without notice as prescribed in bylaws. Special meeting shall be held upon notice as provided in bylaws. Attendance or participation of director at meeting constitutes waiver of notice thereof, unless upon arrival, director objects to meeting or transaction of business and does not vote in favor of any action taken at meeting. (MCLA §450.1521; MSA §21.200[521]). Majority of members of board constitutes quorum unless articles or bylaws provide for larger or smaller number. Vote of majority of members present at meeting at which quorum is present constitutes action of board, unless vote of larger number is required by Act, articles or bylaws. (MCLA §450.1523; MSA §21.200[523]).

Directors' Action Without Meeting.—Directors may act by unanimous written consent without meeting, unless prohibited by articles or bylaws. (MCLA §450.1525; MSA §21.200[525]).

Powers and Duties of Directors.—Powers of corporation are exercised by board unless otherwise provided in Act or articles. (MCLA §450.1501; MSA §21.200[501]). Board may designate one or more committees, which shall serve at pleasure of board, unless otherwise provided in articles or bylaws. (MCLA §450.1527; MSA §21.200[527]). Unless otherwise provided in articles or bylaws, officers shall be elected or appointed by board. (MCLA §450.1531; MSA §21.200[531]). Officers may be removed by board with or without cause, unless officer is elected by shareholders, in which case such officer may be removed with or without cause only by vote of shareholders. (MCLA §450.1535; MSA §21.200[535]). Transaction in which director is determined to have interest shall not, because of interest, be enjoined, set aside, or give rise to award of damages or other sanctions, if such director establishes any of following: (a) transaction was fair to corporation when entered into; (b) material facts of transaction and director's interest were disclosed or known to board, board committee or independent directors, and board, committee or independent directors authorized, approved or ratified transaction; (c) material facts of transaction and director's interest were disclosed or known to shareholders and they authorized, approved or ratified transaction. Transaction is authorized, approved or ratified if it received affirmative vote of majority of directors or committee members who had no interest in transaction though less than quorum or all independent directors who had no interest. Presence of, or vote cast by, director with interest does not affect validity of action taken. Transaction is authorized, approved or ratified by shareholders if it receives majority of votes cast by holders of shares who did not have interest in transaction and majority of such shares constitutes quorum for purpose of taking such action. Board may establish reasonable compensation of directors for services as directors without shareholder approval unless required by articles, bylaws or specific provisions of Act. (MCLA §450.1545a; MSA §21.200[545a]). Corporation may lend money to, or guaranty obligation of, or otherwise assist officer or employee of corporation or its subsidiary, including officer or employee who is director, when in judgment of board, loan, guaranty or assistance may reasonably be expected to benefit corporation or is pursuant to plan authorizing loans, guarantees, or assistance, which plan will benefit corporation as reasonably determined by board. Loan, guaranty or assistance may be with or without interest, and may be unsecured, or secured in such manner as board approves. (MCLA §450.1548; MSA §21.200[548]). Corporation shall have power to indemnify person who is party or has threatened to be made party to any threatened, pending or completed litigation by reason of fact that he is or was director, officer, employee or agent of corporation, so long as statutory conditions are met. Provision in articles or bylaws, resolution of board or shareholders, or agreement making indemnification mandatory also makes advancement of expenses mandatory unless specifically otherwise stated. (MCLA §§450.1561, .1562, .1563, .1564a, .1564b, .1564c, .1565; MSA §§21.200[561], [562], [563], [564a], [564b], [564c], [565]). Corporation shall have power to purchase and maintain insurance on behalf of any person who is or was a director, officer, partner, trustee, employee or agent of corporation. Such insurance may be purchased from insurer owned by corporation but only if articles contain provision eliminating or limiting liability of director and only if it insures director to extent it could indemnify director. (MCLA §450.1567; MSA §21.200[567]).

Liabilities of Directors.—Directors shall discharge duties of position in good faith and with that degree of diligence, care and skill which an ordinarily prudent person in like position would exercise under similar circumstances and in manner director reasonably believes to be in best interests of corporation. In discharging duties, director entitled, when acting in good faith, to rely on information, opinions, reports or statements, including financial statements and other financial data prepared or presented by (a) directors, officers or employees of corporation, or of business organization under joint or common control, whom director or officer reasonably believes to be reliable and competent in matters presented; (b) legal counsel, public accountants, engineers or others as to matters such director or officer reasonably believes are within such person's professional or expert competence; or (c) board committee of which such director or officer is not member if he or she reasonably believes committee merits confidence. Action against director for failure to perform duties imposed above shall be commenced within three years after cause of action accrues or within two years after time when cause of action is discovered or should reasonably have been discovered, whichever sooner occurs. (MCLA §450.1541a; MSA§21.200[541a]). See subhead Books and Records, infra. Directors who vote for, or concur in, any of following corporate actions are jointly and severally liable to corporation for benefit of its creditors or shareholders to extent of legally recoverable injuries suffered by such persons as a result of such action, but not to exceed difference between amount paid or distributed and amount that could lawfully have been paid or distributed: (a) Declaration of share dividend or other distribution to shareholders contrary to Act or contrary to articles; (b) distribution to shareholders during or after dissolution of corporation without paying or providing for debts, obligations and liabilities of corporation as required by Act; (c) making of loan to officer, director or employee of corporation or subsidiary contrary to Act. Director is not liable, however, if he has complied with §541a of Act. (MCLA §450.1551; MSA §21.200[551]). Director against whom claim is successfully asserted under §551 is entitled to contribution from other directors who voted for, or concurred in, action upon which claim is asserted. (MCLA §450.1552; MSA §21.200[552]). Director who is present at meeting at which corporate action referred to in §551 is taken is presumed to have concurred in action unless his dissent is entered in minutes or unless he files written dissent with secretary of meeting before or promptly after adjournment. Director who is absent from such meeting is presumed to have concurred in action unless he files his dissent with secretary of corporation within reasonable time after he has knowledge of action. (MCLA §450.1553; MSA §21.200[553]). Any action against director or shareholder for recovery under §551 shall be commenced within three years after cause of action accrues. Any action under §552 shall be commenced within three years after payment by director to corporation. (MCLA §450.1554; MSA §21.200[554]). Articles may contain provision eliminating or limiting director's liability for monetary damages for any action or failure to take action, with limited exceptions. (MCLA §450.1209[c]; MSA §21.200[2.09][c]).

Officers of Corporation.—Shall consist of president, secretary, treasurer, and if desired, chairman of board, one or more vice-presidents, and such other officers as may be prescribed by bylaws or determined by board. Two or more offices may be held by same person, but officers shall not execute, acknowledge or verify instrument in more than one capacity if instrument is required by law, articles or bylaws to be executed, acknowledged or verified by two or more officers. Officer has such authority and shall perform such duties in management of corporation as may be provided in bylaws, or determined by resolution of board not inconsistent with bylaws. (MCLA §450.1531; MSA §21.200[531]). Officer elected or appointed by board may be removed by board with or without cause. Officer elected by shareholders may be removed, with or without cause, only by vote of shareholders. (MCLA §450.1535; MSA §21.200[535]).

Liabilities of Officers.—Liabilities of officers are same as liabilities of directors, except that no limitation on availability of monetary damages against officer is authorized by statute. See subhead Liabilities of Directors, supra.

Indemnification of Directors and Officers.—See subhead Powers and Duties of Directors, supra.

See note at head of Digest as to 1998 legislation covered.

See Topical Index in front part of this volume.

CORPORATIONS . . . *continued*

Principal Office and Resident Agent.—Each domestic corporation and each foreign corporation authorized to transact business in state shall have and continuously maintain in this state: (a) Registered office which may be same as place of business; (b) resident agent which agent may be individual resident in this state whose business office or residence is identical with registered office, domestic corporation or foreign corporation authorized to transact business in state and having business office identical with such registered office. (MCLA §450.1241; MSA §21.200[241]).

General Powers of Corporations.—Corporation, subject to any limitation provided in Act, in any other statute of Michigan, or in its articles, shall have power in furtherance of its corporate purposes to do broad range of activities specified in Act. (MCLA §450.1261; MSA §21.200[261]). Act by corporation, otherwise lawful, is not invalid because corporation was without capacity or power to do act. However, lack of capacity or power may be asserted in any of following circumstances: (a) action by shareholder against corporation to enjoin action, (b) action by or in right of corporation to procure judgment in its favor against incumbent or former officer or director for loss or damage due to his unauthorized act, or (c) action or special proceeding by attorney general to dissolve corporation or enjoin it from transacting unauthorized business. (MCLA §450.1271; MSA §21.200[271]).

Distributions.—Unless distribution would be contrary to any restriction in articles, board may authorize corporation to make distributions to shareholders except if after giving effect to distribution, corporation would not be able to pay its debts as they become due in usual course of business, or corporation's total assets would be less than sum of its total liabilities plus, unless articles permit otherwise, amount needed, if corporation dissolved at time of distribution, to satisfy preferential rights upon dissolution. (MCLA §450.1345; MSA §21.200[345]). Share dividend may be issued pro rata without consideration unless articles provide otherwise, except shares of one class or series may not be issued as share dividend to holders of different class or series unless either articles so authorize, holders of class or series to be issued approve issuance by majority vote, or there are no outstanding shares of class or series to be issued. (MCLA §450.341a; MSA §21.200[341a]). Determination of shareholders' entitlement to dividend or distribution shall be made in accordance with MCLA §450.1412(3); MSA §21.200(412[3]).

Unclaimed Dividends.—See category Property, topic Absentees, subhead Escheat.

Sale or Transfer of Corporate Assets.—Sale, lease, exchange of all or substantially all corporate property and assets in usual and regular course of business as conducted by corporation, and mortgage or pledge of any or all corporate property and assets whether or not in usual and regular course of business, may be made upon such terms and conditions and for such consideration as authorized by board. Unless articles otherwise provide, approval of shareholders is not required. Corporation may, without further shareholder approval, sell, lease, exchange or otherwise dispose of all, or substantially all, of its property and assets following shareholder approval of dissolution if either of two conditions are satisfied. Corporation may, without shareholder approval, transfer any or all of its property and assets to any entity wholly owned by corporation, whether or not in usual and regular course of business. (MCLA §450.1751; MSA §21.200[751]). Subject to foregoing exceptions sale, lease, exchange of all or substantially all corporate property and assets, with or without goodwill, if not in usual and regular course of business as conducted by corporation may be made upon such terms and conditions and for such consideration in accordance with following. Board must recommend proposed transactions to shareholders unless board determines existence of conflict of interest or other special circumstances and communicates same to shareholders with proposal. Proposal must be submitted for approval at meeting of shareholders. Notice of meeting must be given to all shareholders of record not less than 20 days before meeting. Notice must contain summary of principal terms of proposed transaction and inform those shareholders who have right to dissent that they may do so and be paid fair value of their shares. At meeting, shareholders may authorize transaction and fix or authorize board to fix any term or condition thereof and consideration to be received by corporation. Authorization requires affirmative vote of majority of outstanding shares entitled to vote thereon, and if class or series is entitled to vote as class, affirmative vote of majority of outstanding shares of each such class or series. Notwithstanding authorization by shareholders, board may abandon transaction subject to rights of third parties under contracts, without further action or approval by shareholders. Sale, lease, exchange or other disposition of all, or substantially all, of property of entity whose majority of shares or beneficial interests are owned by second corporation shall also be treated as disposition by second corporation of its pro rata share of property and assets of entity for purposes of Act. Transaction that constitutes distribution to shareholders is governed by §345 of Act rather than provisions governing disposition of assets. (MCLA §450.1753; MSA §21.200[753]).

Books and Records.—Corporation must keep books and records of account and minutes of proceedings of shareholders, board, and executive committee, if any, and such books and records may be kept outside of this state unless otherwise provided in bylaws. Corporation must keep at its registered office, or at office of its transfer agent in or outside state, records containing names and addresses of all shareholders, number, class and series of shares held by each and dates when each became holders of record. Any books, records, or minutes may be in written form or in any other form capable of being converted into written form within reasonable time. If not in written form, corporation must convert any such record into written form without charge upon written request of person entitled to inspect them. (MCLA §450.1485; MSA §21.200[485]). Upon written request, corporation must mail to shareholder its balance sheet as at end of preceding fiscal year; its statement of income for such fiscal year; and, if prepared by corporation, its statement of source and application of funds for such fiscal year. Shareholder of record may examine, for any proper purpose, in person or by agent or attorney, during usual business hours, corporation's stock ledger, list of shareholders and other books and records if shareholder gives corporation written demand describing with reasonable particularity purpose and records which shareholder desires to inspect and records are directly connected with purpose. If corporation does not permit inspection within five business days after receipt of demand which satisfies requirements, or imposes unreasonable conditions upon inspection, shareholder may apply to circuit court to compel inspection in accordance with provisions of Act. Director may examine corporation's books and records for purpose reasonably related to position as director. Director may apply to circuit court to compel inspection. If court orders inspection of records demanded by either shareholder or director, court must order corporation to pay shareholder's or director's costs including reasonable attorney fees, incurred to obtain order unless corporation proves it failed to permit inspection in good faith based on reasonable basis. Right to inspect records includes right to copy and make extracts and if reasonable, right to require corporation to supply copies. (MCLA §§440.1485, .1487; MSA §§21.200[485], [487]).

Reports.—Domestic corporations must make annual financial report and distribute such report to each shareholder within four months after end of fiscal year. Report must include information specified in section. (MCLA §450.1901; MSA §21.200[901]). Each domestic and foreign corporation subject to Act must file report with chief officer of Department no later than May 15 of each year. Such report must be on approved form and must contain information specified in section. (MCLA §450.1911; MSA §21.200[911]). Report must be filed in duplicate together with $15 filing fee. Original of report shall be open to reasonable inspection by public promptly after filing. (MCLA §450.1915; MSA §21.200[915]). Penalties provided by statute for failure to file report or for filing report containing false statements. (MCLA §§450.1921, .1922, .1924, .1931, .1932; MSA §§21.200[921], [922], [924], [931], [932]). All foreign and domestic nonprofit corporations except medical care and hospital service corporations must file annual report with Department of Commerce on or before Oct. 1st and pay filing fee of $10. Such report must be on approved form and contain information specified in section. (MCLA §450.2911; MSA §21.197[911]).

Corporate Bonds or Mortgages.—See subhead General Powers of Corporations, supra. Articles may confer on bondholders rights to inspect corporate books and records and to vote for directors and on any other matters on which articles permit shareholders to vote. Articles may grant to board power to confer such voting or inspection rights under terms of any bonds. Signatures of officers upon a bond may be facsimiles. (MCLA §450.1391; MSA §21.200[391]).

Merger.—Two or more domestic corporations may merge into one corporation pursuant to approved plan. Board of each corporation shall adopt plan of merger setting forth information specified in §701. (MCLA §450.1701; MSA §21.200[701]). Corporation may acquire all outstanding shares of one or more classes or series of another corporation pursuant to approved plan setting forth information specified in §702 adopted by board of each corporation. (MCLA §450.1702; MSA §21.200[702]). Plan adopted by board of each constituent corporation must be submitted for approval at meeting of shareholders. Notice of meeting must be given to each shareholder of record, whether or not entitled to vote at meeting, within time and in manner specified for giving of notice of meetings of shareholders. Notice must include copy of or summary of plan and statement that copy is available upon request, statement informing those shareholders who have right to dissent of such right and that they have right to be paid fair value of their shares. At meeting, vote of shareholders must be taken on proposed plan, and plan shall be approved upon receiving affirmative vote of majority of outstanding shares entitled to vote thereon, and if class or series is entitled to vote thereon as class, affirmative vote of majority of outstanding shares of each such series or class. Class or series of shares is entitled to vote as class if plan contains provision which, if contained in proposed amendment to articles, would entitle class or series of shares to vote as class. Class or series is not entitled to vote as class in case of merger, sole purpose of which is to change corporation's jurisdiction of incorporation. (MCLA §450.1703[a]; MSA §21.200[703][a]). Unless required by articles, vote of shareholders of corporation surviving merger is not necessary to authorize merger if both of following conditions are satisfied: (1) Plan does not amend articles of surviving corporation; and (2) each share of stock of surviving corporation outstanding immediately before merger becomes effective shall remain as identical share of surviving corporation and either of following are not satisfied: (1) Securities to be issued or delivered in acquisition are, or may be converted into, shares of surviving corporation or (2) common stock to be issued or delivered plus common stock initially issuable upon conversion or exchange of any other securities to be issued or delivered under plan will exceed 100% of number of common shares outstanding immediately prior to merger plus number of common shares, if any, initially issuable upon conversion or exchange of any other securities then outstanding. (MCLA §§450.1703[a], 450.1754; MSA §§24.200[703][a], 201.200[754]). Domestic corporation which has not commenced business, not issued shares, and not elected board may merge by unanimous consent of incorporators. (MCLA §450.1706; MSA §21.200 [706]). After approval of plan, certificate of merger or share exchange must be executed and filed on behalf of each corporation. Certificate must set forth information specified in Act. Certificate shall become effective at time filed, unless subsequent effective time is set forth in document. (MCLA §450.1707; MSA §21.200[707]).

Domestic corporation owning at least 90% of outstanding shares of each class of another domestic corporation may merge such corporation into itself, or may merge itself, or itself and any such subsidiary into another subsidiary without approval of shareholders of any of corporations except approval by shareholders of subsidiary must be obtained if its articles require approval of merger by affirmative vote of holders of more than percentage of shares of any class or series of such corporation then owned by parent corporation; and approval of shareholders of parent must be obtained when its articles require shareholder approval of merger; or pursuant to MCLA §450.1703(a); MSA §21.200(703)(a), when plan contains provision which would amend articles of parent corporation, or subsidiary is to be surviving corporation. Board of parent corporation must approve plan setting forth matters required by statute. Approval by board of subsidiary is not required. If parent owns less than 100% of outstanding shares of any constituent subsidiary, it must mail promptly after filing of certificate of merger summary of plan to each minority shareholder of any constituent subsidiary, unless waived in writing. Parent corporation must also comply with provisions of Act regarding dissenters' rights. (MCLA §§450.1711-.1713; MSA §§21.200[711]-[713]). Certificate of merger shall be executed and filed on behalf of parent corporation and set forth information specified in this section. Certificate shall

See note at head of Digest as to 1998 legislation covered.

See Topical Index in front part of this volume.

MI – 4

CORPORATIONS . . . *continued*
become effective at time filed unless subsequent effective time is set forth in document. (MCLA §450.1712; MSA §21.200[712]).

Foreign and domestic corporations may be merged if permitted by laws of jurisdiction where each foreign corporation is organized. Domestic corporation must comply with Act with respect to merger of domestic corporations and foreign corporation must comply with laws of jurisdiction where it is organized. If surviving or new corporation is to be governed by laws of jurisdiction other than Michigan, it must comply with provisions of this Act with respect to foreign corporations if it is to transact business in state. Such corporation is liable, and subject to service of process in proceeding in Michigan for enforcement of obligation of domestic corporation which is party to merger and in proceeding for enforcement of right of dissenting shareholder of any such domestic corporation against surviving or new corporation. Foreign and domestic corporations may be merged as provided in MCLA §450.1711, MSA §21.200(711), if permitted by laws of jurisdiction where foreign corporation is organized, but if parent is foreign corporation, notwithstanding laws of its jurisdiction of incorporation, it must mail summary of plan to each minority shareholder of record of each subsidiary, unless waived in writing, and also inform any shareholder who has right to dissent of such right and that he may be paid fair value of his shares. If foreign corporation is authorized to do business in state it must also file amended application to do business or information statement evidencing event. (MCLA §450.1735, .1736; MSA §21.200[735], [736]). Any time before effective date of certificate of merger or share exchange, such merger or share exchange may be abandoned subject to contractual rights, if any, without shareholder action, in accordance with plan or if none, in manner determined by board or share exchange. If certificate of merger has been filed, corporation shall file certificate of abandonment within ten days after abandonment, but not later than proposed effective date. (MCLA §450.1741; MSA §21.200[741]). Fee to chief officer of Department of Commerce for examining, filing and copying any certificate of merger is $50; for filing certificate by surviving foreign corporation that merger has become effective under laws of jurisdiction of foreign corporation which was party to merger with Michigan corporation, $10; for examining, filing and copying any certificate of abandonment, $10. (MCLA §450.2060; MSA §21.200[1060]).

One or more domestic corporations may merge with one or more business organizations (domestic or foreign limited liability company, general or limited partnership, or any other type of business enterprise) provided that board of each domestic corporation adopts plan of merger in conformance with §736(4). (MCLA §450.1736[4]; MSA §21.200[736(4)]). Adopted plan shall be submitted for approval to meeting of shareholders as provided in §703(2). (MCLA §450.1703[2]; MSA §21.200[703(2)]). After approval, certificate of merger shall be filed and executed in conformance with §736(7). (MCLA §450.736[7]; MSA §21.200[736(7)]). Such certificate shall be effective when filed. Once effective and specified events take place, surviving entity is liable and subject to service for enforcement of obligation of domestic corporation that is party to merger and for enforcement of dissenting shareholder rights.

Share Exchange.—Corporation may acquire all outstanding shares of one or more classes or series of another corporation pursuant to plan of share exchange. Procedure for adoption and consummation is equivalent to that with respect to merger. (MCLA §450.1702; MSA §21.200[702]).

Certain business combinations and transactions involving Michigan corporation require approval by not less than 90% of votes of each class of stock entitled to be voted, and at least 2/3 of votes of each class of stock entitled to vote other than voting shares beneficially owned by interested shareholder (shareholder owning directly or indirectly 10% or more of voting power of corporation or affiliate of corporation who at any time within prior two years owned such voting power) and any affiliate of interested shareholder. (MCLA §450.1780; MSA §21.200 [780]).

Transactions covered are any merger, or share exchange which alters contract rights of shareholders set forth in articles, or which changes or converts outstanding shares of corporation with those of any interested shareholder or affiliate; any sale, lease, transfer or other disposition of property, not in ordinary course of business to interested shareholder or affiliate within 12 month period, book value of which is more than 10% of net worth; issuance or transfer of equity security of corporation with market value more than 5% of total market value of outstanding shares to any interested shareholder or affiliate, except pursuant to exercise of rights or warrants offered pro rata to all voting shareholders or other method affording proportionate treatment; liquidation or dissolution in which any interested shareholder or affiliate will receive other than cash, reclassification, reverse stock split or reorganization which has effect of increasing by 5% or more proportionate amount of any class of equity securities of corporation or any subsidiary owned by any interested shareholder or affiliate. (MCLA §450.1776; MSA §21.200[776]).

Special voting requirements will not apply: (i) If consideration paid shareholders meets certain tests as to amount and type; and after interested shareholder became interested shareholder, there has been no reduction of regular dividends and interested shareholder has received no loans, guarantees or other financial assistance from corporation and has not acquired additional shares of corporation since becoming interested shareholder, except for shares acquired as part of same transaction by which shareholder became interested shareholder and there has been five years between date of becoming interested shareholder and date business combination is consummated; (ii) if directors have approved transaction with particular interested shareholder prior to time first became interested shareholder; and (iii) to corporation having existing interested shareholder on May 29, 1984 unless directors elect by resolution to be subject to special voting requirements; or (iv) unless articles provide otherwise, to corporation having fewer than 100 beneficial owners of stock, to registered investment company, or to corporation whose shareholders amend articles after May 29, 1984 by vote of not less than 90% of each class of stock entitled to vote and not less than 2/3 of each class held by persons other than interested shareholders. (MCLA §§450.1781-.1784; MSA §§21.200[781]-[784]).

Tender Offers.—Effective Apr. 1, 1988, control share acquisitions are regulated by MCLA §§450.1790 et seq.; MSA §§21.200(791) et seq.

Dissolution.—Dissolution without court action may be accomplished in following ways:

(1) Automatic Dissolution by Expiration of Corporate Term.—Certificate of dissolution not required. (MCLA §§450.1801[a], .1831[a]; MSA §§21.200[801][a], [831][a]). Corporation whose term has expired may renew corporate existence, if proceeding asking for court supervision is not pending, by board resolution followed by proper notice to each shareholder entitled to vote and affirmative vote on proposed renewal by holders of majority of outstanding shares of corporation or of each class or series of such shares if such class or series is entitled to vote thereon as a class. Certificate of renewal shall be filed setting forth name of corporation, date and place of shareholders' meeting at which renewal was approved, statement that renewal was approved by requisite vote of directors and shareholders and duration of corporation if other than perpetual. Upon such filing, corporate existence becomes effective, and corporation may again transact business. Renewal does not relieve corporation of any penalty or liability accrued against it under any law of state. Administrator may require adoption of different corporate name in accordance with act. (MCLA §§450.1815, .1817; MSA §§21.200[815], [817]).

(2) Dissolution by Consent of Majority of Shareholders.—Board may propose dissolution. Dissolution must be recommended unless board determines conflict of interest or other special circumstances and such is communicated to shareholder. After proper notice to shareholders, upon resolution of holders of majority of outstanding shares entitled to vote thereon (or majority of each class if entitled to vote thereon as a class), certificate of dissolution is executed and filed, stating name of corporation, date, place of shareholders' meeting at which dissolution was approved, and statement that dissolution was approved by requisite vote of shareholders and directors. (MCLA §§450.1801[c], .1804; MSA §§21.200[801][c], [804]).

Upon filing of certificate, revocation of dissolution proceedings becomes effective, and corporation may again transact business. Revocation of dissolution does not relieve corporation of any penalty or liability accrued against it under any state law. If during period of dissolution, corporate name or confusingly similar name has been assigned to another corporation, administrator may require adoption of different name upon filing of certificate of revocation of dissolution. (MCLA §450.1817; MSA §21.200[817]).

(3) Dissolution by shareholder agreement under §488 is effected by executing and filing certificate of dissolution on behalf of corporation, stating corporation's name and that it is dissolved pursuant to §488. (MCLA §450.1805; MSA §21.200[805]).

Dissolution proceedings commenced pursuant to (2) or (3) above may be revoked before complete distribution of assets, if proceeding requesting court supervision is not pending, by filing certificate of revocation executed, in person or by proxy, by all shareholders. (MCLA §450.1811; MSA §21.200[811]).

(4) Dissolution Before Beginning Business.—Majority of directors or incorporators file certificate stating name of corporation, that corporation has not commenced business and has issued no shares, and has no debts or other liabilities, and has received no payments on subscriptions to its shares, or, if it has received payments, has returned them to those entitled thereto, less any part thereof disbursed for expenses, and that majority of incorporators or directors have elected that corporation be dissolved. (MCLA §450.1803; MSA §21.200[803]).

In all of above, where filing certificate of dissolution is necessary, fee therefor is $10. (MCLA §450.2060[g]; MSA §21.200[1060][g]). Clearance from Department of Revenue is required as to sales and use tax, intangibles tax, business activities tax, as well as any privilege taxes before certificate of dissolution is issued by Administrator.

(5) Dissolution for Failure to File Annual Report or Pay Privilege Fee.—Neglect or refusal by domestic corporation to file any annual report or pay fees as required for two consecutive years results in automatic dissolution. Such failure by foreign corporation for one year results in revocation of corporation's certificate of authority unless default is corrected within 90 days after notice of default is mailed to corporation at its registered office in Michigan and at its headquarters by administrator. Domestic corporation dissolved, or foreign corporation whose certificate of authority has been revoked, for failure to file annual reports, may renew its corporate existence or certificate of authority by filing reports and paying fees for any years not filed or paid, together with prescribed penalties. Upon compliance with foregoing, all rights of corporation are same as if dissolution or expiration of term had not occurred, and all contracts entered and rights acquired during interval are valid and enforceable. (MCLA §§450.1801[f], .1831[d], .1922, .1925, .2041, .2042; MSA §§21.200[801][f], [831][d], [922], [925], [1041], [1042]).

(6) Dissolution of Nonprofit Corporation, Foundation or Trustee Corporation.—If corporate purpose is to hold property for charitable purposes other than religious purposes dissolution may be had only with 45 days prior notice to Attorney General absent court proceedings for dissolution, with his consent. (MCLA §§450.251-53; MSA §§21.290[1]-[3]).

Dissolution with court supervision may be accomplished in following ways:

(1) Dissolution on Insolvency or for Benefit of Stockholders.—Dissolution under court supervision may be had on petition of majority of directors setting forth that corporation is in danger of insolvency or that dissolution is deemed beneficial to stockholders. All stockholders and creditors are made defendants. (MCLA §600.3501; MSA §27A.3501). Information to appear in complaint is specified. (Rule 3.611). Process may be served as in ordinary case, or court may order hearing on 30 days notice mailed to all creditors and stockholders. (Rule 3.611). Where appropriate, court dissolves corporation and appoints receiver. (MCLA §600.3505; MSA §27A.3505).

(2) Dissolution by Court having Jurisdiction of Receivership or Bankruptcy Proceedings.—Corporation whose assets have been wholly disposed of under court order in receivership or bankruptcy proceedings may be summarily dissolved by order of court having jurisdiction of proceedings. Copy of order shall be filed by clerk of court with administrator. (MCLA §450.1801[2]; MSA §21.200[801][2]).

(3) Dissolution by Attorney General's Action.—Dissolution is based upon attorney general's showing that corporation has procured its organization through fraud, repeatedly and wilfully exceeded its lawful authority, or repeatedly and wilfully conducted its business in an unlawful manner. In addition, attorney general may bring suit for

See note at head of Digest as to 1998 legislation covered.

See Topical Index in front part of this volume.

MI – 5

CORPORATIONS . . . *continued*
dissolution, revocation, or forfeiture based upon any other statutory or common law action. (MCLA §450.1821; MSA §21.200[821]).

(4) Dissolution by Directors' or Shareholders' Action Where Corporation Unable to Function.—One or more directors or shareholders entitled to vote may bring action for dissolution alleging that (a) management (directors or shareholders pursuant to §463[1]) is unable to agree by requisite vote on material matters respecting management of corporation's affairs, or shareholders are so divided in voting power that they have failed to elect successors to any director whose term has expired or would have expired upon election and qualification of his successor, and (b) that as result of condition stated above, corporation is unable to function effectively in best interests of its creditors and shareholders. (MCLA §450.1823; MSA §21.200[823]).

In (2), (3) and (4) above, action must be brought in circuit court of county in which principal place of business or registered office of corporation is located.

(5) Dissolution on Expiration of Term.—Where term of manufacturing, mining or smelting corporation has expired and further term allowed by law for winding up has expired or will expire without completion of any other proceeding, any stockholder or creditor may apply to court for winding up and disposition of assets. (MCLA §600.3520; MSA §27A.3520). Rule 3.612 sets forth procedure to be followed.

Provisions Applicable to Dissolution Effected in any Manner.—Except as court may otherwise direct, dissolved corporation shall continue its corporate existence solely for purpose of winding up its affairs by collecting its assets, selling assets not to be distributed in kind to its shareholders, paying its debts and other liabilities, and doing all other acts incident to liquidation of its business. (MCLA §450.1833; MSA §21.200[833]). Directors are not deemed to be trustees of corporation's assets during this period, and are held to same standard of conduct as before dissolution (MCLA §450.1834; MSA §21.200[834]; see also MCLA §450.1541a; MSA §21.200[541a]). Title to corporation assets remains in corporation until transferred in corporate name. Dissolution does not change provisions relating to quorum or voting requirements for directors or shareholders nor provisions regarding election, appointment, resignation or removal of, or filing vacancies among, directors or officers, nor provisions regarding amendment or repeal of bylaws or adoption of new bylaws. Shares may be transferred, corporation may sue and be sued in its corporate name, process issuing by and against corporation as if dissolution had not occurred. Action brought against corporation before its dissolution does not abate because of dissolution. (MCLA §450.1834; MSA §21.200[834]).

Dissolved corporation may give written notice of dissolution to existing claimants who have claims or rights against corporation, whether claim is liquidated or unliquidated, but does not include contingent liability based on event occurring after dissolution. Notice must describe information to be included in claim, specify deadline for making claim which may not be less than six months from effective date of notice and state that claim will be barred if not received by deadline. Claim rejected by written notice by dissolved corporation barred if proceeding to enforce not commenced within 90 days of rejection. (MCLA §450.1841a; MSA §21.200[841a]).

After dissolution, corporation may publish notice of dissolution and request persons with claims to present them in writing within one year after publication date. Notice shall be published once in newspaper of general circulation in county in which principal office of corporation is located, or if none, location of registered office. (MCLA §450.1842a; MSA §21.200[842a]). Claimant who does not present corporation with claim is barred unless claimant brings proceedings against corporation, with certain exceptions.

After dissolution in any manner, corporation, a creditor, or shareholder may apply at any time to circuit court of county in which principal place of business or registered office is located for judgment that affairs of corporation and liquidation of its assets continue under supervision of court. For good cause shown, court may permit creditor who has not filed his claim or commenced action on a rejected claim within required time limits to file such claim or commence such action within such time as court directs. (MCLA §450.1851; MSA §21.200[851]).

Assets remaining after payment of, or provision for claims against, corporation shall be distributed in cash or kind or both to shareholders according to their respective rights and interests in accordance with Act. (MCLA §450.1855a; MSA §21.200[855a]).

Insolvency and Receivers.—Court is authorized to appoint receiver where execution issued upon judgment is returned unsatisfied in whole or in part and upon final judgment court can direct fair distribution of property of corporation and proceeds thereof to creditors of corporation. (MCLA §600.3610; MSA §27A.3610). Insolvency alone does not ordinarily justify appointment of receiver and dissolution of corporation (305 Mich. 580, 9 N.W.2d 849), but cf. 201 Mich. 1, 166 N.W. 948. Receiver may properly be appointed on undisputed averment of insolvency and showing of danger of misappropriation or waste of assets. (55 Mich. 387, 21 N.W. 375).

See subhead Dissolution, supra.

Close Corporations.—There is no separate chapter set aside for close corporations. Rather, special provisions for such corporations are included at appropriate points throughout Act. Among these provisions are sections dealing with: incorporation by one incorporator, board of directors with fewer than three members, optional high-vote or high-quorum requirements, relaxed formalities including management by shareholders, stock transfer restrictions, shareholder agreements, deadlock, dissolution, and arbitration. See appropriate subheads, supra, for detail.

Appraisal.—Shareholder is entitled to dissent from and obtain payment of fair value of shares in event, subject to certain exceptions, of: (a) consummation of plan of merger or share if shareholder approval is required, (b) consummation of sale or exchange of substantially all of property of corporation other than in usual and regular course of business, if shareholder is entitled to vote thereon, (c) certain amendments to articles of incorporation, (d) action taken pursuant to shareholder vote to extent articles, bylaws or resolutions of directors provide for dissenter's rights, (e) approval of control share acquisition. Unless otherwise provided in articles, bylaws or board resolution shareholder may not dissent from (a) corporate action set forth in (a) to (e) above as to shares listed on national securities exchange or designated as National Market System Security on interdealer quotation system by National Association of Securities Dealers, (b) consummation of plan of merger or share exchange or sale of substantially all of assets not in usual course of business in which shareholders receive cash or shares meeting criteria set forth above or any combination thereof, (c) amendment to articles giving rise to right to dissent conducted pursuant to plan of dissolution meeting certain criteria and providing for distribution of substantially all assets within one year of transaction.

Shareholder wishing to assert dissenter's rights must deliver to corporation before proposal is submitted to vote of shareholders written notice of intent to demand payment if proposed action is effectuated and must not vote shares in favor of or consent to proposed action. Within ten days after shareholders' authorize action corporation shall give dissenters' notice to objecting shareholders containing specified information and form of payout dividend. Shareholder receiving such dissenters' notice must demand payment, certify he acquired shares prior to specified date, and deposit share certificates in accordance with notice. Unless corporation elects to withhold payment for after-acquired shares in accordance with §771, within seven days after proposed corporate action is taken or upon receipt of payment demand (whichever is later), corporation must pay each dissenter who fulfilled statutory requirements amount equal to corporation's estimate of fair value of shares plus accrued interest. Payment must be accompanied by specified financial information.

If dissenting shareholder demands different amount and demand remains unsettled, corporation within 60 days or dissenting shareholder within 30 days thereafter must file action to determine fair value of their shares and accrued interest. Final order in action shall determine fair value of shares of each dissenting shareholder and require corporation to pay amount by which fair value plus interest exceeds any amount paid by corporation, or amount equal to fair value plus accrued interest of after-acquired shares for which corporation elected to withhold payment to dissenting shareholders as well as such interest as court finds equitable. Costs and expenses are determined by court and generally assessed against corporation unless dissenting shareholders acted not in good faith. (MCLA §§450.1761-.1774; MSA §§21.200[761]-[774]).

Foreign Corporations.—Certificate of authority to do business in state is required. (MCLA §450.2011; MSA §21.200[1011]). To procure certificate, corporation must file copy of articles and good standing certificate from state of incorporation. (MCLA §450.2016; MSA §21.200[1016]). Application, which must be accompanied by filing and franchise fees, is made on form provided by department stating name of corporation and jurisdiction and date of incorporation, duration of corporation, street address of main business office, address of registered office in state and name of resident agent, statement of character of business and authorization to transact same in state of incorporation, and such other facts as may be required. (MCLA §450.2015; MSA §21.1200[1015]). For calculation of franchise and filing fees, see MCLA §§450.2060, .2062; MSA §§21.200(1010), (1062). Authority to transact business continues until surrendered, suspended or revoked, so long as annual franchise fees paid. (MCLA §§450.2016, .2062; MSA §§21.200[1016], [1062]). Amended application must be filed and additional franchise fees paid upon increase in number of authorised shares attributable (using Single Business Tax apportionment percentage) to this state. (MCLA §450.2062; MSA §21.200, [1062]).

Foreign corporation cannot use courts to enforce obligation if doing business in Michigan and has not qualified. (MCLA §450.2051; MSA §21.200 [1051]). For penalties on corporations doing business in state without authority, see MCLA §450.2055; MSA §21.200[1055]). If permitted by its charter, foreign corporation may acquire real property in Michigan by purchase or otherwise and hold or dispose of same. (25 Mich. 214). Foreign corporation may acquire, hold and dispose of real estate without certificate, provided in so doing it is not carrying on its business. (251 Mich. 602, 232 N.W. 367).

See subheads Reports, Incorporation Tax or Fee, and Filing Fees, supra, and Franchise Tax, infra.

Surrender of Authority.—Withdrawal is effected by filing with administrator an application for withdrawal stating name of corporation and state of incorporation and statement that corporation is not transacting business in state and surrenders authority to do so. (MCLA §450.2031; MSA §21.200[1031]). Filing fee is $10. (MCLA §450.2060; MSA §21.200[1060]).

Taxation of Corporate Property.—Rules for taxation of corporate property are similar to rules for taxation of individual. See category Taxation, topic Property (Ad Valorem) Taxes, subheads Taxable Situs, Rate. Residence of corporation for tax purposes is where office stated in articles is located except, if principal office is elsewhere, latter shall be deemed its residence. If no principal office in state, then residence is where corporation or agent transacts business. (MCLA §211.11; MSA §7.11).

Taxation of Corporate Stock.—See category Taxation, topic Intangible Personal Property Tax.

Franchise Tax.—Effective May 14, 1977, corporate franchise tax statute (MCLA §§450.304-.309a; MSA §§21.205-.210[1]) is repealed. Final levy of franchise tax was on May 15, 1976. (1975, No. 230).

See category Taxation, topic Business Taxes, subhead Single Business Tax.

Professional Corporations.—Persons rendering personal service to public requiring license or other legal authorization are permitted to form professional corporation under specified conditions. (MCLA §450.221; MSA §21.315[1]; MCLA §450.222; MSA §21.315[2]; MCLA §450.224; MSA §21.315[4]; MCLA §450.228; MSA §21.315[8]; MCLA §450.229; MSA §21.315[9]; MCLA §450.230; MSA §21.315[10]; MCLA §450.231; MSA §21.315[11]; MCLA §450.234; MSA §21.315[14]). See topic Partnerships, subhead Partnership Associations.

Limited Liability Companies.—See topic Limited Liability Companies.

Deeds.—See category Property, topic Deeds.

Model Non-Profit Corporation Act not adopted.

For various taxes affecting corporations, see category Taxation, topic Business Taxes.

See note at head of Digest as to 1998 legislation covered.

See Topical Index in front part of this volume.

MI – 6

JOINT STOCK COMPANIES:

No statutory provisions.

Professional Corporations.—See topic Corporations, subhead Professional Corporations.

LIMITED LIABILITY COMPANIES:

Michigan Limited Liability Company Act ("Act") effective June 1, 1993 as amended effective July 1, 1997, permits formation of limited liability company ("LLC"). (MCLA §§450.4101 et seq.; MSA §§21.198[4101] et seq.). Act was amended by P.A. 52, 1997 to remove "bullet-proof" qualities of Act and increase flexibility.

Tax Treatment.—Generally, Michigan LLC with two or more members should be treated as partnership for federal tax purposes upon compliance with applicable IRS regulations and one member LLC should be treated as sole proprietorship.

General Supervision.—Department of Consumer and Industry Services (herein "Department"), Lansing, has general supervision of LLCs. (MCLA §450.4102; MSA §21.198[4102]).

Formation.—One or more persons may form LLC by filing executed articles of organization ("Articles") with Department. (MCLA §450.4202; MSA §21.198[4202]).

Articles Requirements.—Articles must be filed with Department along with appropriate fees. Articles must contain (a) name; (b) purposes; (c) street address of registered office and name of registered agent (mailing address if different); (d) statement, if applicable, that LLC will be managed by managers; and (e) other desired provisions not inconsistent with Act. Duration will be perpetual unless otherwise stated in Articles. (MCLA §§450.4201, .4202, .4203; MSA §§21.198[4201], [4202], [4203]).

Purpose.—LLCs may be organized for any lawful business purpose including providing professional services. (MCLA §§450.4201, .4901; MSA §§21.198[4201], [4901]).

Name.—LLC's name must include designation "limited liability company" or abbreviations "L.L.C." or "L.C." (with or without periods) and may not imply LLC is organized for purpose not stated in Articles. LLC's name must be distinguishable from names of other entities and trade or assumed names as filed, registered or reserved with Department. (MCLA §450.4204; MSA §21.198[4204]). Name may be reserved by submitting application and filing fee to Department. (MCLA §§450.4205, .5101; MSA §§21.198[4205], [5101]).

Maximum Duration.—Articles must state duration if other than perpetual. There is no limit on duration. (MCLA §450.4203; MSA §21.198[4203]).

Registered Office and Resident Agent.—Each domestic LLC and foreign LLC authorized to transact business must maintain registered office and resident agent. Resident agent may be domestic corporation or LLC or foreign corporation or LLC authorized to do business in Michigan. (MCLA §450.4207; MSA §21.198[4207]). Information kept at registered office must include (a) names and addresses of each member and manager; (b) copy of Articles and any amendments; (c) federal, state and local tax returns for last three years; (d) financial statements for last three years; (e) copies of any operating agreements; and (f) records indicating members' voting rights. (MCLA §450.4213; MSA §21.198[4213]).

Reports.—LLC must file annual statement containing name and address of resident agent in Michigan. Annual statement must be filed no later than Feb. 15 each year. No annual statement is required in following year if LLC is formed after Sept. 30th of previous year. (MCLA §450.4207; MSA §21.198[4207]).

Amending or Correcting Articles.—LLC may amend its Articles if amendment contains only such provisions as might lawfully be contained in original Articles at time of amendment. (MCLA §450.4601; MSA §21.198[4601]). Amendment becomes effective upon filing thereof with Department, together with fees and documents required by law. (MCLA §450.4104; MSA §21.198[4104]). Amendments to Articles must be signed and state (a) name of LLC; (b) filing date of original Articles; (c) entire Articles or sections being amended; and (d) that amendment has been approved by unanimous vote of members entitled to vote unless LLC's operating agreement authorizes amendment by majority vote of members entitled to vote. (MCLA §450.4603; MSA §21.198[4603]). Articles must be amended if change occurs in LLC's (a) name; (b) purpose; (c) method of management; (d) maximum duration; or (e) statement in Articles has become false or erroneous. (MCLA §450.4602; MSA §21.198[4602]).

Powers.—LLC has all powers necessary or convenient, including all powers granted to general business corporations, subject to limitations of its Articles, Act and any other statute of State of Michigan. (MCLA §450.4201; MSA §21.198[4201]).

Limited Liability.—Except as otherwise provided by law or in operating agreement, no member and/or manager of LLC is personally liable for acts, debts, or obligations of company. (MCLA §450.4501; MSA §21.198[4501]).

Management.—Unless Articles provide for management by managers, LLC is to be managed by members, who then are imbued with all rights and responsibilities of managers. (MCLA §450.4401; MSA §21.198[4401]). Articles may provide for management by one or more managers who may also be members. (MCLA §450.4402; MSA §21.198[4402]). Unless otherwise provided in operating agreement, managers are elected or removed by majority of members. Managers may be removed with or without cause unless operating agreement provides otherwise. (MCLA §450.4403; MSA §21.198[4403]). Unless otherwise provided in operating agreement, if LLC has more than one manager, management decisions are by majority vote of all managers with each manager having one vote. (MCLA §450.4405; MSA §21.198[4405]). Each manager is agent with authority to bind LLC for transactions in ordinary course of business. LLC is not bound by manager's transaction with third party who has knowledge of manager's lack of authority. (MCLA §450.4406; MSA §21.198[4406]). If Articles delegate management of LLC to managers, Articles will be deemed notice to third parties that only managers can bind LLC. (MCLA §450.4402; MSA §21.198[4402]).

Managers have duty to act in good faith, with ordinary care and in LLC's best interests. Managers may reasonably rely on (a) one or more members, managers or employees of LLC; (b) professional advisors to LLC; and (c) committees comprised of other managers. (MCLA §450.4404; MSA §21.198[4404]).

Operating agreement or contract may limit aspects of manager's liability and provide for indemnification of managers for judgments, settlements, penalties, fines or expenses for acts or omissions as manager. LLC may not limit liability of manager for (a) receipt of improper financial benefit; (b) knowing violation of law; or (c) approval of distributions in violation of operating agreement or Act. (MCLA §450.4408; MSA §21.198[4408]).

Member Contribution.—Members may contribute any tangible or intangible property or benefit to LLC including cash, property, services or promissory notes. (MCLA §450.4301; MSA §21.198[4301]). Promise to contribute is not enforceable unless it is in writing and signed by member. Member failing to make agreed contribution is obligated at option of LLC to contribute agreed amount in cash. Member's obligation to make agreed contribution may be compromised only as provided in operating agreement or by unanimous consent of members. Creditor may under certain circumstances enforce member's obligation to make capital contribution. (MCLA §450.4302; MSA §21.198[4302]).

Distributions of cash or other assets are allocated in equal shares to members unless operating agreement provides otherwise. (MCLA §450.4303; MSA §21.198[4303]). Distributions are not allowed if, after distribution (a) LLC would be unable to pay its debts as they become due; or (b) if LLC's total assets would be less than sum of LLC's total liabilities plus (unless operating agreement provides otherwise) amount that would be needed, if LLC were to be dissolved at time of distribution, to satisfy any preferential rights on dissolution superior to member or members receiving distribution. (MCLA §450.4307; MSA §21.198[4307]). Member or manager who votes for or member who receives improper distribution is personally liable for amount of improper distribution that exceeds amount that could have been properly distributed for two years after distribution. (MCLA §450.4308; MSA §21.198[4308]).

Member's Interest and Assignment of Interest.—Member's ownership interest in LLC is personal property, and member has no interest in specific assets of LLC. (MCLA §450.4504; MSA §21.198[4504]). Unless operating agreement provides otherwise, member's interest in LLC is assignable. Assignment of member's interest does not automatically entitle assignee to all rights and privileges held by assignor. Generally, assignment of member's interest only transfers assignor's right to share of LLC's distributions. Member ceases to be member upon assignment of member's entire membership interest. (MCLA §450.4505; MSA §21.198[4505]). Grant of security interest in member's membership interest does not cause member to lose membership, unless otherwise provided in operating agreement. (MCLA §450.4508; MSA §21.198[4508]).

Unless otherwise provided in operating agreement, assignee may become member (a) only if members unanimously consent; (b) in any manner provided in operating agreement; or (c) in accordance with terms of agreement between member and LLC in case of one-member LLC. (MCLA §450.4506; MSA §21.198[4506]).

Inspection of Records.—Member or member's designated representative may, at member's expense and upon reasonable written request, inspect and copy any of LLC's records during normal business hours at location where records are kept. Members may also obtain upon written request (a) copies of LLC's most recent financial statements and tax returns; (b) complete information regarding current business and financial condition of LLC; and (c) any other information as is "just and reasonable" regarding affairs of LLC. Member also has right to formal accounting if provided in operating agreement or if such formal accounting is just and reasonable. (MCLA §450.4503; MSA §21.198[4503]).

Derivative Action.—Member may sue on behalf of LLC only if all of following are met: (a) member is unable to cause LLC to sue on its own behalf; (b) member made written demand requesting that LLC sue on its own behalf; (c) member has not been notified within 90 days that demand has been rejected or LLC would suffer irreparable injury by waiting 90 days; (d) member is member at time of suit and was member at time of alleged wrong or is assignee of member who was; (e) member fairly and adequately represents interests of LLC; and (f) member continues to be member until time of judgment, unless no longer member as result of action by LLC to which former member did not acquiesce. (MCLA §450.4510; MSA §21.198[4510]). Upon termination of derivative proceeding, court may order one of following: (a) plaintiff to pay any of defendant's reasonable expenses, including reasonable attorney fees, if proceeding was commenced or maintained in bad faith or without reasonable cause; or (b) LLC to pay plaintiff's reasonable expenses, including reasonable attorney fees, if proceeding resulted in substantial benefit to company. Court will direct plaintiff to account to LLC for any proceeds received by plaintiff in excess of expenses awarded by court (this provision does not apply to judgment rendered for benefit of injured member only and recovery was limited to loss or damage sustained by such member). (MCLA §450.4514; MSA §21.198[4514]).

Action by Minority Member.—Member may bring action in circuit court to establish that acts of managers or members in control of LLC are illegal, fraudulent, or willfully unfair and oppressive to LLC or member. Relief may include: (a) dissolution or liquidation, (b) cancellation or alteration of provision in Articles or operating agreement, (c) direction, alteration or prohibition of act of LLC, members or managers, (d) purchase of members' interest in LLC at fair value, or (e) damages to LLC or member. (MCLA §450.4515; MSA §21.198[4515]).

Expulsion.—Operating agreement can provide for expulsion of member upon occurrence of specified events. (MCLA §450.4509; MSA §21.198[4509]).

Withdrawal.—Except as provided in operating agreement, member may not withdraw from LLC. If operating agreement allows for withdrawal, withdrawing member will receive fair market value for his membership interest in LLC as of date of withdrawal, unless otherwise provided in LLC's operating agreement. (MCLA §§450.4305, .4509; MSA §§21.198[4305]), [4509]).

See note at head of Digest as to 1998 legislation covered.

See Topical Index in front part of this volume.

MI – 7

LIMITED LIABILITY COMPANIES . . . *continued*

Voting.—Unless otherwise provided in operating agreement, each member is entitled to one vote. Operating agreement may provide that certain members or groups have limited or no voting rights. Members have statutory right to vote on (a) dissolution of LLC; (b) merger of LLC; and (c) amendment to Articles. Transactions in which manager has interest must be approved by members unless it is preapproved by operating agreement or connected with dissolution. Articles may provide other voting rights. (MCLA §450.4502; MSA §21.198[4502]).

Conversion of Partnership.—General partnership or limited partnership may be converted to LLC by filing Articles and Certificate of Conversion with Department. All property rights of converting partnership are thereafter vested in converted LLC.

Merger.—LLC may merge with any other business entity pursuant to plan of merger. (MCLA §450.4701; MSA §21.198[4701]). Plan of merger must be approved by unanimous consent of members of each merging LLC, unless operating agreement provides for less than unanimous consent. If operating agreement provides for approval by less than unanimous consent, dissenting members have right to withdraw and receive fair market value interest of their membership on date of withdrawal. (MCLA §450.4702; MSA §21.198[4702]). Upon consummation of merger, resulting entity succeeds to all rights and obligations of merged entities. (MCLA §450.4704; MSA §21.198[4704]).

Dissolution and Winding Up.—LLC is dissolved upon: (a) time specified in Articles or operating agreement; (b) happening of event specified in Articles or operating agreement; (c) unanimous consent of members; or (d) upon judicial degree. (MCLA §450.4801; MSA §21.198[4801]). Members that have not wrongfully dissolved LLC may wind up LLC's affairs. (MCLA §450.4805; MSA §21.198[4805]). Upon winding up, LLC's assets are distributed in following order: (a) to creditors of LLC, including members who are creditors; (b) unless otherwise provided in operating agreement, to members and former members to satisfy claims for declared distributions or payments upon withdrawal; (c) unless otherwise provided in operating agreement, remaining assets to members and former members in accordance with their membership interests. Before any asset distributions are made, LLC must file tax returns and pay any tax obligation. (MCLA §450.4808; MSA §21.198[4808]). Upon commencement of winding up, LLC must file certificate of dissolution with Department setting forth (a) name of LLC; (b) reason for dissolution; and (c) effective date of dissolution. (MCLA §450.4804; MSA §21.198[4804]).

Foreign LLC Qualification.—Foreign LLC must file application for certificate of authority to transact business with Department containing: (a) LLC's name and name under which it proposes to transact business; (b) jurisdiction and date of LLC's organization; (c) name and address of its resident agent; (d) consent for appointment of Department as agent to accept service of process if no registered agent is appointed, or agent's authority is revoked, agent resigns or agent cannot be found or served; (e) name and address of member or manager to whom copies of any process served may be sent; (f) address of office in foreign jurisdiction or its principal place of business; and (g) other appropriate information. (MCLA §450.5002; MSA §21.198[5002]). Foreign LLC will not be denied registration in Michigan based on any difference between laws of LLC's state of organization and Michigan law. Foreign LLC's internal affairs are governed by laws of its state of organization. (MCLA §450.5001; MSA §21.198[5001]). Certain listed activities do not constitute transacting business in Michigan. (MCLA §450.5008; MSA §21.198[5008]). Foreign LLC cannot use courts of this state to enforce obligations if it is doing business in Michigan and has not qualified to transact business in Michigan. (MCLA §450.5007; MSA §21.198[5007]).

Filing fees for various LLC documents established by statute. (MCLA §450.5101; MSA §21.198[5101]).

Professional Limited Liability Company.—Persons rendering personal service to public requiring license or other legal authorization are permitted to form professional LLCs under specified conditions. (MCLA §§450.4901-.4910; MSA §§21.198[4901]-[4910]).

PARTNERSHIPS:

Uniform Partnership Act adopted. (MCLA §§449.1 et seq.; MSA §§20.1 et seq.).

Variations from Official Text.—Partners may consist of husband and wife. (MCLA §449.6; MSA §20.6). See also subhead Limited Liability Partnership.

Formation.—Partnership certificates for general partnerships must be filed with county clerk, setting forth name and residence of partners, place of business and name and style of the firm. Partnership not complying cannot sue in any court until after compliance. When place of business is changed or partnership goes out of business, certificate so stating must be filed. Renewal certificate required every five years. (MCLA §§449.101-.106; MSA §§20.111-.118). Certificate of limited partnership must be filed with Department of Consumer and Industry Services. (MCLA §449.1201; MSA §20.1201).

Name.—See category Intellectual Property, topic Trademarks and Tradenames.

Limited Partnership.—Revised Uniform Limited Partnership Act (1976) (without 1985 amendments) (MCLA §§449.1101 et seq.; MSA §§20.1101 et seq.) adopted with numerous variations, including: (1) "administrator" replaces "Secretary of State" throughout; "administrator" means chief officer of Michigan Department of Consumer and Industry Services or designee thereof (MCLA §449.1101; MSA §20.1101); (2) name may not contain words "corporation", "incorporated", or any abbreviation thereof or imply purpose other than that stated in certificate of limited partnership (MCLA §449.1102; MSA §20.1102); (3) adds section permitting transaction of business under assumed name if certificate filed (MCLA §449.1104; MSA §20.1104); (4) adds section permitting limited partnership to agree in writing to pay interest in excess of legal rate but not in excess of criminal usury rate (MCLA §449.1109; MSA §20.1109); (5) adds section authorizing merger with foreign or domestic limited partnership or with corporation, limited liability company, general partnership, or other business organization (MCLA §449.1210; MSA 20.1210); (6) judicial dissolution on application of partner permitted only when acts of general partners are illegal, fraudulent, or wilfully unfair and oppressive to such partner (MCLA §449.1802; MSA §20.1802); (7) adds section authorizing Attorney General to bring action for dissolution upon specified grounds (MCLA §449.1803; MSA §20.1803); and (8) adds section enumerating activities not constituting transaction of business in state by foreign limited partnership (MCLA §449.1909; MSA §20.1909).

Limited Liability Partnership.—Uniform Partnership Act permits partnership to register as limited liability partnership by filing prescribed form with Department of Consumer and Industry Services and paying fee; annual renewal required. (MCLA §449.44; MSA §20.44). Last words or letters of name must be "limited liability partnership", "L.L.P.", or "LLP". (MCLA §449.45; MSA §20.45). Except for taxes, partner of registered limited liability partnership not liable for partnership liabilities arising (through tort, contract, or otherwise) from negligence, wrongful acts, omissions, misconduct, or malpractice committed by another partner or by employee or agent of partnership, but provision does not affect liability for partner's own acts or those of person under partner's direct supervision and control. (MCLA §449.46; MSA §20.46). Foreign limited liability partnership may not conduct business in Michigan until registered with Department of Consumer and Industry Services; annual renewal required. (MCLA §449.47; MSA §20.47).

Out-of-State Partnerships.—See subheads Limited Partnership and Limited Liability Partnership, supra.

Partnership Associations.—Three or more persons may form partnership association by contributing capital thereto and filing articles of association with Secretary of State and County Clerk. Members are not individually liable for obligations of partnership association except liabilities for labor. "Limited" must be last word of name and must be affixed on outside of every place of business and used whenever name written; omission of "limited" makes members liable for indebtedness, damage, or liability arising therefrom. (MCLA §§449.301-.351; MSA §§20.91-.107).

BUSINESS REGULATION AND COMMERCE

BANKS AND BANKING:

Uniform Commercial Code adopted. (MCLA §440.1101 et seq.; MSA §19.1101 et seq.). See topic Commercial Code.

Regulated by Banking Code of 1969. (MCLA §487.301 et seq.; MSA §23.710[1] et seq.).

Financial Institutions Bureau under a Commissioner and deputies, has jurisdiction over banks, industrial banks, trust companies and safe and collateral deposit companies. (MCLA §§487.305-.311; MSA §23.710[5]-[11]).

Stockholders.—A list of stockholders must be filed with Commission on demand. (MCLA §487.394; MSA §23.710[94]) . Bank has lien on its shares, with power of sale, for indebtedness of stockholders (MCLA §487.377; MSA §23.710[77]), but note Uniform Commercial Code MCLA §440.8103; MSA §19.8103 which requires liens be noted on certificate. Stockholders other than holders of preferred stock may be assessed in case of impairment of capital and their stock sold to satisfy assessment, but there is no longer any double liability of stockholders. (MCLA §487.501; MSA §23.710[201]). Stockholders may vote only in person or by proxy, except that they may enter into a voting trust agreement approved by Commissioner. (MCLA §487.391; MSA §23.710[91]).

Fiduciary Powers.—Commissioner may grant trust or fiduciary powers. Fiduciary assets must be segregated and separate books kept. Bank with trust powers may contract with another bank to carry on trust services in its name. Current funds must be deposited in another banking institution or secured by a pledge of government securities except to extent insured by federal deposit insurance corporation. Grant of fiduciary powers is subject to Commissioner's discretion, including his judgment as to sufficiency of capital and surplus of bank. Without regard to capital, bank may be permitted to exercise limited fiduciary powers to act only as executor, administrator and guardian or as trustee of testamentary trusts. Banks receiving trust funds may invest them in same manner as individual trustees unless otherwise specified in agreement. (MCLA §§487.481-.486; MSA §§23.710[181]-[186]).

Deposits.—Interest cannot be paid by state banks on demand deposits unless such is permitted national banking associations and commissioner, by appropriate rule, permits state banks to pay such interest at same rate and in same manner. (MCLA §487.493; MSA §23.710[193]).

Deposits by or in name of minor are held for his exclusive right and benefit and are payable to person in whose name deposit was made. (MCLA §487.701; MSA §23.301). Deposit made in trust for another without written notice to bank of existence and terms of trust may be paid to persons for whom deposit was made in event of trustee's death, except that if deposit exceeds $5,000 and such person is under 18, deposit may be paid only to his legally appointed guardian and if deposit is less than $5,000 and person is under 18, deposit may be paid to person if person is married, parent, or person with care and custody of minor child under court order and with whom child resides. (MCLA §487.702; MSA §23.302).

Deposit made in names of two or more persons payable to either or survivor together with any additions thereto made by any of persons becomes property of such persons as joint tenants and, prior to bank's receipt of written notice not to pay deposit in accordance with its terms, such deposit and additions may be paid to any one of said persons or to survivor or survivors after death of one of them. Making deposit in such form, absent fraud or unique undue influence, is prima facie evidence of intention of depositors to vest title in survivor or survivors. (MCLA §487.703; MSA §23.303). Creation of joint account creates presumption, rebuttable by competent evidence to contrary, of ownership by survivor. (320 Mich. 195, 30 N.W.2d 834). Also, statutory joint accounts may be created in names of two persons. Statute prescribes form of contract, which governs who owns and may withdraw funds during life of both or if

See note at head of Digest as to 1998 legislation covered.

See Topical Index in front part of this volume.

MI – 8

BANKS AND BANKING . . . *continued*

either dies first, who owns funds if both die simultaneously and who may revoke contract. (MCLA §§487.711 et seq.; MSA §§23.295[1] et seq.).

Uniform Commercial Code governs effect of stop payment orders, forged or altered instruments and delay in presentment.

Unclaimed Deposits.—Uniform Unclaimed Property Act adopted. (MCLA §567.221 et seq.; MSA §26.1055[1] et seq.). Except as provided in Act, property held, issued or owing in ordinary course of business and remaining unclaimed for five years after becoming payable or distributable is presumed abandoned. (MCLA §567.223; MSA §26.1055[3]). Banks, trust companies and other banking organizations must report annually to state treasurer all property in its possession presumed abandoned. (MCLA §567.238; MSA 26.1055[18]). Not less than 60 days or more than 365 days prior to report, notice to apparent owner of property presumed abandoned must be given if address is known, claim is not barred by statute of limitations and value is $50 or more or, if holder filing report is reporting at least 25,000 properties over $50, value is $100 or more.

See category Property, topic Absentees.

Collections.—Uniform Commercial Code governs. (MCLA §§440.4101-.4504; MSA §19.4101-.4504). Substantially all 1990 conforming Amendments to U.C.C. Art. 4 were adopted effective Sept. 30, 1993.

Loans.—As to interest, see topic Interest.

Uniform Common Trust Fund Act (with additions and variations) in effect; Official Amendment not adopted. (MCLA §§555.101-.113; MSA §§23.1141-.1153).

Foreign Banks.—Non-U.S. banks authorized to obtain certificate of authority to conduct business in Michigan, but not authorized to solicit or accept deposits from citizens or residents of U.S. or exercise trust powers. (MCLA §§487.441-.446; MSA §§23.710[141]-[146]). See categories Estates and Trusts, topic Executors and Administrators; Family, topic Guardian and Ward.

BILLS AND NOTES:

Uniform Commercial Code adopted. (MCLA §440.1101 et seq.; MSA §19.1101 et seq.). See topic Commercial Code. 1990 Official Amendments to Art. III and conforming Amendments to Art. IV Adopted. (Public Act 130, effective Sept. 30, 1993). For other options and deviations from U.C.C., see topic Commercial Code.

Days of grace are no longer recognized.

Fraudulent Issuance.—It is a felony to make, draw or utter, with intent to defraud, checks, drafts or orders without an account or credit on which the item is drawn. (MCLA §750.131a; MSA§28.326[1]). It is a felony or misdemeanor depending on size of check and number of offenses to make, draw, utter or deliver, with intent to defraud, checks, drafts or orders knowing that maker or drawer has insufficient funds in or credit with bank or other depository for payment thereof, or having insufficient funds when presentation for payment is made to drawee. (MCLA §750.131; MSA §28.326).

Usury is no defense against holder in due course, unless he has actual notice. (MCLA §438.5; MSA §19.3).

Judgment notes are unknown in this state and suit is necessary before any note or other negotiable instrument before levy can be made. Judgment by confession may be had only on a warrant of authority in a proper instrument distinct from bond, contract or other evidence of the demand for which judgment was confessed. (MCLA §600.2906; MSA §27A.2906).

Attorney Fees.—Provision for reasonable attorney fee (in relation to work performed and expenses incurred) is enforceable. (241 Mich. 52; 216 N.W. 405). Stipulated attorney fee is not enforceable (39 Mich. 137) even though valid in state where note executed (184 Mich. 148, 150 N.W. 847).

BILLS OF LADING:

See topic Carriers.

BILLS OF SALE:

See topic Sales.

BLUE SKY LAW:

See topic Securities.

BROKERS:

Uniform Commercial Code adopted. (MCLA §440.1101 et seq.; MSA §19.1101 et seq.). See topic Commercial Code.

Michigan Department of Commerce, Bureau of Occupational and Professional Regulation regulates real estate brokers and salesmen, former including real estate appraisers, real estate mortgage brokers, building job brokers, rental brokers, business chance brokers and others whose principal vocation is sale of real estate. (MCLA §§339.2501-.2518; MSA §§18.425[2501]-[2518]).

Licenses.—Department of Commerce, Bureau of Occupational and Professional Regulation examines and licenses real estate brokers and salespersons. (MCLA §§339.2504-.2506; MSA §§18.425[2504]-[2506]). License fees: Broker $20 and annual renewal $18; associate broker $20 and annual renewal $18; salesperson $10 and annual renewal $13. (MCLA §338.2237; MSA §3.30[37]). One broker's license may be issued to firm to be used by certain individuals designated as principals and this license shall not be transferable, but associate broker's license issued to non-principal may be transferred. Licensee may be nonresident, provided he maintains place of business in this state and files irrevocable consent to service of process on Department. Issuance and, after hearing, revocation of license is discretionary with Department. Sales of promotional nature of property outside state must be submitted to Department for investigation. (MCLA §§339.2501-.2518; MSA §§18.425[2501]-[2518]). Written

disclosure of party represented by broker is required. (MCLA §339.2518; MSA §18.425[2518]).

Real Estate Brokers.—See subhead Licenses, supra.

BULK SALES:

See category Debtor and Creditor, topic Fraudulent Sales and Conveyances.

CARRIERS:

Uniform Commercial Code adopted. (MCLA §440.1101 et seq.; MSA §19.1101 et seq.). See topic Commercial Code.

Public Service Commission has general supervision of common carriers (MCLA §460.1 et seq.; MSA §22.13[1] et seq.) except that Michigan Department of Transportation has general supervision of railroads and railroad, bridge and tunnel companies regulated by Michigan Railroad Code of 1993 (MCLA §462.101-.451; MSA §22.1263[101]-[451]); railroad companies are also subject to Michigan Business Corporation Act (MCLA §450.1101 et seq.; MSA §21.200[101] et seq.) unless inconsistent with Michigan Railroad Code of 1993 or act under which formed (MCLA §462.205; MSA §22.1263[205]). Provisions described under subheads Rates, Discrimination and Limiting Liability, catchline Freight infra do not apply to railroad, bridge or tunnel companies regulated by Michigan Railroad Code of 1993. (MCLA §462.2a; MSA §22.21a). See MCLA §462.249; MSA §22.1263(249) for provisions regulating railroad, bridge and tunnel company use charges.

Rates between points within state are required to be just and reasonable. (MCLA §462.4; MSA §22.23). Schedule of all rates must be filed with commission and kept open to inspection in each depot and office, and may not be changed without notice to commission. (MCLA §462.10; MSA §22.29). Provision is made for hearing and adjudication by commission of complaint that rates are unreasonable or discriminatory. (MCLA §§462.22-.27; MSA §§22.41-.46).

Discrimination is unlawful as to rates or service, and subjects carrier to criminal penalty and double damages in civil suit. (MCLA §462.15-.19; MSA §22.34-.38).

Limiting Liability.—

Freight.—Uniform Commercial Code adopted. (MCLA §440.1101 et seq., see especially §§7103, 7309, 1205, 1102; MSA §§19.7103, 7309, 1205, 1102). No limitation or change of common law liability by contract or otherwise as to negligent acts of agents and servants. (MCLA §462.40; MSA §22.58). No contract or receipt may exempt intrastate common carrier from liability for damage caused by it or any other common carrier to whom property delivered or over whose lines property passes. (MCLA §462.7; MSA §22.26).

Passengers.—Contract exempting common carrier in that capacity from liability to full fare passenger for negligence of self or employees void as against public policy. (151 Mich. 260, 115 N.W. 43). Carrier can limit liability by stipulations which are just and reasonable (212 Mich. 259, 180 N.W. 361) and called to attention of passenger and assented to by him (205 Mich. 278, 171 N.W. 423).

Bills of Lading.—Uniform Commercial Code governs. (MCLA §§440.7101-.7603; MSA §§19.7101-.7603). Optional language in §7-403 U.C.C. omitted. (MCLA §440.7403; MSA §19.7403). Criminal penalty provisions of Uniform Bills of Lading Act have been retained. (MCLA §482.44-.50; MSA §22.1164-.1170). For other options and deviations from U.C.C., see topic Commercial Code.

Liens.—Uniform Commercial Code governs. (MCLA §440.7307-.7308).

COMMERCIAL CODE:

Uniform Commercial Code adopted, effective Jan. 1, 1964. (MCLA §440.1101 et seq.; MSA §19.1101 et seq.). Michigan has adopted new Article 2A (Leases) effective Sept. 30, 1992, 1990 Revision of Article 3 (Negotiable Instruments), 1990 Amendments to Article 4 (Bank Deposits and Collections), new Article 4A (Funds Transfers) effective June 25, 1992, 1977 Revision to Article 8 (Investment Securities) and 1972 Revision to Article 9 (Secured Transactions). Section numbers of Michigan act generally correspond with those of 1972 Official Text, printed in Uniform and Model Acts section, except that Michigan omits hyphen between first and second digits. Thus §3-501 of 1972 Official Text corresponds with §3501 of Michigan act. (MCLA §440.3501; MSA §19.3501).

Material variations from 1972 Official Text, and options or alternatives adopted, are as follows (citations are to U.C.C. 1972 Official Text and to sections of MCLA §§440.1101 et seq.; MSA §§19.1101 et seq.).

§1-108 U.C.C. is omitted.

§1-109 U.C.C. is omitted.

§1-207 U.C.C. (MCLA §440.1207; MSA §19.1207) adopted. A subsection (2) which states: "Subsection (1) does not apply to an accord and satisfaction."

§1-209 U.C.C. (MCLA §440.1209; MSA §19.1209)—(optional section) adopted.

§2-313b added extending period of express warranty by number of days between date goods delivered to merchant or warrantor for warranteed repairs and date purchaser notified that repairs completed, days between date repairs attempted at purchaser's premises until repairs completed, and days preceding beginning of repairs after merchant or warrantor receives notice from purchaser that goods inoperative; applies only if total number of days exceeds either ten days or 10% of warranty period. (MCLA §440.2313b; MSA §19.2313[2]).

§2-316(3) U.C.C. (MCLA §440.2316[3]; MSA §19.2316[3]) adds subsection (d) providing that there is no implied warranty that cattle, hogs, or sheep are free from disease if seller shows all state and federal animal health law has been satisfied.

§2-326 U.C.C. (MCLA §440.2326; MSA §19.2326) adds subsection (5) providing that work of fine art delivered to art dealer for sale, or exhibition and sale, to public on commission, is not subject to claims of art dealer's creditors.

§2A-103(1)(e) U.C.C. (MCLA §§440.1201[37]; MSA §19.1201[37])—optional words adopted ($25,000).

§2A-104(3) U.C.C. (MCLA §440.2804[3]; MSA §19.2A104[3])—Subsection provides, "Failure to comply with any applicable statute has only the effect specified in the statute."

See note at head of Digest as to 1998 legislation covered.

See Topical Index in front part of this volume.

COMMERCIAL CODE... *continued*

§2A-216 U.C.C. (MCLA §440.2866; MSA §19.2A216)—Alternative A adopted.

§3-312 U.C.C. (MCLA §440.3312; MSA §19.3312) adds new definitional section regarding lost, destroyed or stolen cashier's checks, teller's checks or certified checks.

§4-104(1) U.C.C. (MCLA §440.4104[1][a]; MSA §19.4104[1][a])—"deposit or credit" deleted and "depositor credit" inserted.

§4-104(9) U.C.C. (MCLA §440.4104[1][i]; MSA §19.4104[1][i])—"4a" deleted and "2a" inserted.

§4-104(c)(3) U.C.C. (MCLA §440.4104[3]; MSA §19.4104[3])—list includes "Draft" which is defined in §3-104.

§4-106 U.C.C. (MCLA §440.4106; MSA §19.4106)—Alternative B adopted.

§4-301(d)(1) U.C.C. (MCLA §440.301[4][a]; MSA §19.4301[4][a])—"clearing-house" preceding "rules" deleted and "its" inserted.

§§4-405, 4-501, 4-502, 4-503 and 4-504 of 1990 Conforming Amendments to Art. IV not adopted.

§5-112 U.C.C. (MCLA §440.5112; MSA §19.5112)—optional language in last sentence of subsection (1) adopted.

§5-114 U.C.C. (MCLA §440.5114; MSA §19.5114)—optional subsections (4) and (5) adopted.

§6-102(3) U.C.C. (MCLA §440.6102[3]; MSA §19.6102[3])—Specifically includes restaurant, cafe, tavern, hotel, club, school, hospital, other establishment that dispenses food, or any enterprise that manufactures what it sells.

§6-104 U.C.C. (MCLA §440.6104; MSA §19.6104)—blank in subsection 1(c) is filled with phrase "Secretary of State."

§6-106 U.C.C.—not adopted.

§6-107(2)(e) U.C.C.—not adopted.

§6-108(3)(c) U.C.C.—not adopted.

§6-109(2) U.C.C.—not adopted.

§7-204(4) U.C.C.—not adopted.

§7-403(1)(b) U.C.C.—optional language not adopted.

§9-203(4) U.C.C. (MCLA §440.9203[4]; MSA §19.9203[4])—Blank filled in with references to MCLA §§493.1-.26; MSA §§23.667(1)-(26) (act regulating business of making loans up to $3,000); MCLA §§566.301, .302; MSA §19.415(1), (2); and MCLA §§492.101-.138; MSA §§23.628(1)-(38) (both acts regulating installment sales of motor vehicles).

§9-301(2) U.C.C. (MCLA §440.9301[2]; MSA §19.9301[2])—Michigan act permits secured party 20 days to file with respect to purchase money security interests.

§9-302(1)(d) U.C.C. (MCLA §440.9302[1][d]; MSA §19.9302[1][d])—Michigan act follows Official Text except that language concerning motor vehicles is expanded to include mobile homes and certain watercraft.

§9-302(3)(b) U.C.C. (MCLA §440.9302[3][b]; MSA §19.9302[3][b])—Michigan act fills in blank with references to MCLA §257.216; MSA §9.1916 (motor vehicles subject to registration); MCLA §281.1220; MSA §18.1288(20) (certain watercraft); MCLA §125.2330a; MSA §19.855(130a) (motor homes); and any other Michigan statute requiring certificate of title.

Michigan act adds subsections (4)-(7) to U.C.C. 9-307, effective Jan. 1, 1986. Debtor shall upon request of security holder provide list of potential buyers. Debtor may then only sell to those buyers. Security holder may notify only those buyers of its security interest. Upon receipt of notice buyers must pay for purchases by check to seller and security holder jointly. (MCLA §440.9307[4]-[7]; MSA §19.9307 [4]-[7]).

Michigan act gives priority to purchase money security interest retained by seller of farm produce over conflicting security interests if perfected within 20 days of debtor receiving collateral, except for perfected security interest in crops for new value given to enable debtor to produce crops. (MCLA §440.9312[4]; MSA §19.9312[4]).

§9-401(1) U.C.C. (MCLA §440.9401[1]; MSA §19.9401[1])—Michigan act elects second alternative subsection (1); blanks in subsection (1)(a) filled in "register of deeds."

§9-401(3) U.C.C. (MCLA §440.9401[3]; MSA §19.9401[3])—Alternative subsection (3) not elected in Michigan.

§9-402(1) U.C.C. (MCLA §440.9402[1]; MSA §19.9402[1])—Michigan act inserts, after first comma in first sentence, "in printed or typewritten form,".

§9-402(1) U.C.C. (MCLA §440.9402[1]; MSA §19.9402[1])—Michigan Act adds statement that financing statement shall include debtor's tax identification number with certain exceptions.

§9-402(7) U.C.C. (MCLA §440.9402[7]; MSA §19.9402[7])—Michigan act omits "after the change" in second sentence and substitutes "after the debtor notifies the secured party in writing of the change."

Michigan act also adds subsections (9) and (10) to U.C.C. §9-402 providing, respectively, for recording of financing statements (and related continuation statements, termination statements, amendments and assignments) in real estate records notwithstanding failure to comply with formal requisites for documents to be recorded under real estate law (MCLA §565.47; MSA §26.563), and for noting thereon by register of deeds date and time of recording and liber and page (MCLA §§440.9402[9], [10]; MSA §§19.9402[9], [10]).

Michigan act also adds subsections (11) and (12) to U.C.C. §9-402 providing for register of deeds' entering such financing statements and related documents, in order received, in entry book where real estate mortgages entered (subsection [11]) and indexing such financing statements and related documents by debtor's name and name of record owner of real property (subsection [12]). (MCLA §§440.9402[11], [12]; MSA §§19.9402[11], [12]).

Michigan Act also adds subsections (13), (14) and (15) to U.C.C. §9-402 providing that beginning Sept. 1, 1988, all original filings of security interest or financing statement shall contain debtor's tax identification number, subject to certain exemptions. (MCLA §§440.9402 [13], [14], [15]; MSA §§19.9402 [13], [14], [15]).

§9-403(2) U.C.C. (MCLA §440.9403[2]; MSA §19.9403[2])—Michigan act inserts "within 6 months" between "filed" and "prior to the lapse" in second sentence.

§9-403(3) U.C.C. (MCLA §440.9403[3]; MSA §19.9403[3])—In second sentence Michigan act inserts "and where the original financing statement describes real property, by liber and page of recording thereof" after "by file number." After second

sentence, Michigan Act inserts sentence "A continuation statement also may, but is not required to, include the debtor's tax identification number."

§9-403(4) U.C.C. (MCLA §440.9403[4]; MSA §19.9403[4])—Reference in first sentence to subsection (7) is changed to subsection (8) in Michigan act.

§9-403(6) and (7) U.C.C. (MCLA §§440.9403[7], [8]; MSA §§19.9403[7], [8])—Subsections (6) and (7) are renumbered (7) and (8) respectively; subsection (8) of Michigan version adds "or covers crops grown or to be grown" after reference to U.C.C. §9-103(5).

§9-404(1) U.C.C. (MCLA §440.9404[1]; MSA §19.9404[1])—Blank is filled in with "the effective date of this 1978 amendatory act" (Jan. 1, 1979); termination statement for financing statement describing real property must include liber and page where recorded; termination statement for original filing made before July 1, 1976, with officer other than Secretary of State may be sent directly to debtor; $100 liability described in official text applies only if secured party fails to file termination statement within 20 days after demand.

§9-405(2) U.C.C. (MCLA §440.9405[2]; MSA §19.9405[2])—Assignment of rights under financing statement describing real property must show liber and page where recorded; Michigan act adds "or covering crops grown or to be grown," after reference to §9-103(5) in fourth sentence; fee for filing assignment is $3 if in standard form (otherwise $6) plus $3 for each name more than one required to be indexed.

§9-407 U.C.C. (MCLA §440.9407; MSA §19.9407)—Michigan act adopts (optional).

§9-410 U.C.C. (MCLA §440.9410; MSA §19.9410)—Michigan acts adds §9-410 permitting Secretary of State to establish microfilm service for bulk sale of filed documents.

§10-101 U.C.C.—Appears as MCLA §440.9991; MSA §19.9991. Act effective on Jan. 1, 1964.

§10-102(1) U.C.C.—Appears as MCLA §440.9992; MSA §19.9992.

§10-102(2) U.C.C.—Appears as MCLA §440.9993; MSA §19.9993.

§10-103 U.C.C.—Michigan has not adopted this section.

§10-104 U.C.C. (MCLA §440.9994; MSA §19.9994)—subsection 2 omitted.

§11-102 U.C.C. (MCLA §440.11102; MSA §19.11102)—Official Text not enacted; section instead provides that continuation statement (signed by debtor and secured party) may be filed between Jan. 1, 1979 and July 1, 1979 electing application of Michigan version of 1972 Official Amendments—otherwise transactions entered into before Jan. 1, 1979 governed by act as in effect prior to amendment.

§§11-103 through 11-108 not enacted in Michigan.

Permanent Editorial Board's Recommendations for Amendment and for Optional Amendment of Uniform Commercial Code of 1966 were not enacted.

1972 Official Amendments.—Adopted effective Jan. 1, 1979.

1973 Official Amendment to §8-102 adopted, except for minor changes in wording. (MCLA §440.8102[3]; MSA §19.8102[3]).

1977 Official Amendments to Art. VIII adopted, effective Apr. 24, 1987.

1990 Official Amendments to Art. III and conforming Amendments to Art. IV adopted, effective Sept. 30, 1993.

Forms.—See end of this Digest.

See also topics: Banks and Banking, Bills and Notes, Brokers, Carriers, Contracts, Factors, Frauds, Statute of, Sales, Securities, Warehousemen; categories Business Organizations, topic Corporations; Civil Actions and Procedure, topic Limitation of Actions; Debtor and Creditor, topics Assignments, Fraudulent Sales and Conveyances, Liens, Pledges; Documents and Records, topics Records, Seals; Mortgages, topic Chattel Mortgages.

CONDITIONAL SALES:

See topic Sales.

CONSIGNMENTS:

See topic Factors.

CONSUMER CREDIT:

Consumer Credit Code not adopted.

CONSUMER PROTECTION:

Consumer Protection Act.—Effective Apr. 1, 1977, consumer protection act adopted. Prohibited practices include: using deceptive representations or causing confusion as to source, sponsorship, approval, certification, geographic origin, condition, quality, style, model, grade, supply, date of delivery or price of goods; disparaging goods, services, business or reputation of others by misleading representation; misrepresenting need for part, replacement or repair; causing probability of confusion as to authority of salesperson, terms of credit or extent of warranty; using coercion or duress in connection with sale; and misrepresenting or omitting to state facts material to transaction. Enforcement is by action for declaratory or injunctive relief or for damages by attorney general, prosecuting attorney or private citizen. (MCLA §§445.901-.922; MSA §§19.418[1]-.418[22]).

Debt Collection Practices.—Collection agency prohibited from committing certain acts when attempting to collect debt allegedly owed or due to another. Remedies include actual and statutory damages and equitable relief. (MCLA §§339.901-.920; MSA §§18.425[901]-.425[920]). Regulated person who is not collection agency prohibited from committing certain acts when attempting to collect debt. Remedies include injunction, actual and statutory damages and cease and desist order issued by attorney general. (MCLA §§445.251-.258; MSA §§19.658[1]-.658[8]).

Deceptive advertising prohibited by statute. Prohibition includes untrue claims, misleading statements, over-statement of available supply, failure to state that products are defective or "seconds." Exemption provided for media disseminating such advertising without knowledge of falsity. Remedies include injunction in action by Attorney

CONSUMER PROTECTION . . . continued

General and civil penalty to State in amount not more than $1,000 for first offense, and $5,000 for subsequent offense. (MCLA §§445.356-.362; MSA §§19.853[6]-.853[24]).

Home improvement contracts must comply with statute regarding size of type and certain required provisions. Copy of contract must be delivered to buyer. Contract must grant right of cancellation to buyer by written notice given no later than 5:00 p.m. on next business day following date of execution. Contract may not contain waiver of defenses by buyer, liquidated damages to seller and certain other provisions. Finance charge in contract may not exceed $8 per $100 per annum, except that if prevailing interest rate at two successive auctions on 26-week U.S. treasury bills at time of contract exceeds 8%, finance charge on contracts entered before Dec. 31, 1987 may be equivalent to 16.5% interest per annum on unpaid balance; minimum finance charge of $12 permitted. Holder of contract is subject to all defenses of buyer. Remedies include criminal penalty, injunction in action by Attorney General or prosecuting attorney and civil penalty not exceeding $1,000 for violation of injunction. (MCLA §§445.1101-.1431; MSA §§19.417[101]-[431]).

Home Solicitation Sales.—On home solicitation sales involving more than $25, statute provides that buyer may cancel contract by written notice given before midnight of third business day following sale. Home solicitation sale contract must give notice of aforesaid right of cancellation. Seller seeking to collect under home solicitation sale contract must prove compliance with statute. (MCLA §§445.111-.117; MSA §§19.416[201]-[207]).

Lemon Law.—Manufacturer or motor vehicle dealer must repair defective new motor vehicle if consumer notified manufacturer or dealer during term of manufacturer's express warranty or within one year of date vehicle was delivered to original consumer, whichever is later. If defect continues to exist after reasonable number of repairs, within 30 days manufacturer has option to either replace vehicle with vehicle which is acceptable to consumer or accept return of vehicle in exchange for refund. (MCLA §§257.1401-.1410; MSA §§9.2705[1]-.2705[10]).

Mortgage lending practices regulated by statute. Credit granting institutions may not deny loan applications or vary contract terms due to racial or ethnic characteristics or trends in neighborhood or based on age of building (though condition and useful life may be considered) except on basis of written criteria uniformly applied to all neighborhoods in metropolitan statistical area or county. Minimum mortgage amount may not be more than $10,000 ($1,000 for home improvement loan). Written statement of reasons for denial of application or variance of terms is required. Credit granting institutions must make available pamphlet containing general criteria for approving loans, which must include consideration of credit eligibility of applicant, value of proposed security and factors known to institution potentially mitigating physical decline of neighborhood. Institutions must post written notice (in statutory form) disclosing rights of applicants under Act and must file reports with Commissioner of Financial Institutions Bureau of Department of Commerce. Person injured by violation has right of action for up to $2,000 or actual damages plus reasonable attorney fees (whichever is greater). (MCLA §§445.1601-.1614; MSA §§23.1125[1]-.1125[14]). Due-on-sale clauses and blended rate mortgages regulated by MCLA §§445.1621-1624; MSA §§23.1125(21)-.1125(26a).

Plain Language.—No "Plain Language" statute.

Retail Installment Sales.—See topic Sales, subhead Retail Credit Sales.

Uniform Deceptive Trade Practices Act not adopted. See subhead Consumer Protection Act, supra.

Unsolicited merchandise may not be sent to recipient as offer for sale. Recipient may refuse delivery thereof or may keep or dispose of such merchandise without obligation to seller. (MCLA §445.131; MSA §19.416[51]).

CONTRACTS:

Uniform Commercial Code adopted. (MCLA §§440.1101 et seq., MSA §§19.1101 et seq.). See topic Commercial Code; categories Documents and Records, topic Seals; Family, topic Infants; and Introduction, topic Holidays, subhead Transactions on Holiday.

FACTORS:

No factors act. Uniform Commercial Code adopted. (MCLA §§440.1101-.9994; MSA §§19.1101-.9994). See topic Commercial Code.

License Requirements.—Commission merchants in farm produce must be licensed. (MCLA §445.332 et seq.; MSA §19.672 et seq.).

Liens.—No statutory provision for factors' liens as such.

Consignment Agreements.—No special statutory provision for filing or recording of consignment agreements. See topic Commercial Code; see also U.C.C. §9-102.

FRANCHISES:

Uniform Franchise and Business Opportunities Act not adopted. Michigan Franchise Investment Law (MCLA §§445.1501-.1546; MSA §§19.854[1]-.854[46]) adopted, effective in 1974, governs offer, sale and purchase of franchises, and prohibits fraudulent practices relating to franchises. Department of Attorney General has general supervision of franchises. (MCLA §445.1502; MSA §19.854[2][a]).

Franchise is contract express or implied, oral or written, between two or more persons in which franchisee is (1) granted right to engage in business of offer, sale or distribution of goods or services under marketing plan substantially prescribed by franchisor, (2) granted right to engage in business of offer, sale or distribution of goods or services substantially associated with franchisor's trademark, service mark, advertising or other commercial symbol designating franchisor and (3) required to pay franchise fee either directly or indirectly. (MCLA §445.1502; MSA §19.854[2]).

Registration.—Franchisee must file annual notice with department and pay $250 fee prior to offering or selling franchise in state. (MCLA §445.1507a; MSA §19.854[7a]). Department will notify franchisor in writing of date by which notice

must be filed and penalties for failure to file, within 60 days of date franchisor required to file notice. Failure of department to notify franchisor does not relieve franchisor from requirement of complying with all provisions of Act. (MCLA §445.1507a, .1540; MSA §19.854[7a],[40]).

Disclosure.—Franchise must not be sold without furnishing prospective franchisee with disclosure statement naming franchisor, name under which franchisor does or intends to conduct business and other significant business and financial information and delivering to prospective franchisee copy of all proposed agreements relating to sale and notice as to prohibition of certain provisions sometimes found in franchise agreement at least ten business days prior to earlier of execution of agreement or receipt of consideration. (MCLA §445.1508; MSA §19.854[8]).

Exemptions.—Offer and sale of franchise exempt from registration and disclosure requirements include those: (1) by executor, administrator, sheriff, marshall, receiver, trustee in bankruptcy, guardian or conservator; (2) to bank, savings institution, insurance company, investment company or other financial institution, or to broker-dealer in which purchaser is acting for itself as fiduciary or in some fiduciary capacity; (3) in which franchise fee does not exceed $500; (4) in which franchisee not domiciliary of state and business of franchise will not be conducted in state; (5) isolated sale of franchise for franchisee's own account if franchisee provides purchaser full access to books and records related to franchise; (6) to existing franchisee who has actively operated franchise for last 18 months and purchases for investment, not for resale and (7) in which franchisee is currently in established business of franchise, person directly responsible for operation or management of franchise has been engaged in business of franchise for two or more years and franchisee and franchisor have reasonable grounds to believe that at consummation of sale, franchisee's gross sales (dollar value) will not exceed 20% of franchisee's gross sales (dollar volume) from franchisee's combined business operations. (MCLA §445.1506; MSA §19.854[6]).

Prohibited Practices.—Act prohibits employing any means to defraud, making any untrue statement or omission of material fact or engaging in any act which operates as fraud or deceit upon any person. Franchise shall not be offered if sale of franchise business involves illegal activities, or if person convicted of certain felony offenses, subject to administrative order or has judgment entered against him involving illegal offering of franchises or securities and department finds that person creates unreasonable risk to prospective franchisees, if franchise offering is subject of permanent or temporary injunction under federal or state law, or if franchisor has failed to pay proper fee. Pyramid or chain promotions illegal and against public policy. (MCLA §§445.1505, .1513, .1523, .1525, .1528; MSA §§19.854[5], [13], [25], [28]).

Damages.—Franchisee can rescind sale or recover from franchisor damages, with interest at 12% per year and reasonable attorney fees and court costs, subject to certain limitations. Franchisor who offers or sells franchise and does not comply with annual notice requirements is liable to franchisee for damages caused by noncompliance. (MCLA §445.1527(a), .1531; MSA §19.854[7a], [31]).

Limitation of Actions.—Action to enforce civil or criminal liability under act must be commenced within four years after act or transaction constituting violation. (MCLA §445.1527[a], 1533; MSA §19.854[7a][33]).

Penalties.—Person who violates act can be fined not more than $10,000 or imprisoned for not more than seven years, or both. (MCLA §445.1538; MSA §19.854[38]).

FRAUDS, STATUTE OF:

Uniform Commercial Code adopted. (MCLA §§440.1101-.9994; MSA §§19.1101-.9994). See topic Commercial Code.

In the following cases, every agreement, contract, or promise is void unless made in writing and signed by party to be charged: Agreement not to be performed in one year; special promise to answer for debt, default, or misdoings debt of another; contract for sale of lands or leasing for longer than one year; agreement made upon consideration of marriage except mutual promises to marry; special promise by personal representative to answer damages out of his own estate; agreement to pay commission for sale of interest in real estate; assignment of things in action; agreement or promise of cure relating to medical care or treatment; and commitment of financial institution to make loan or extend credit, modify or permit delay in repayment or performance, or waive provision of loan or other financial accommodation. (MCLA §§566.106, .132; MSA §§26.906, .922).

Contracts of Sale.—Uniform Commercial Code requires writing signed by party to be charged, or his authorized agent or broker, to enforce contract for sale of goods for $500 or more, and written contract is not enforceable beyond quantity of goods shown in writing. Between merchants, written confirmation of contract is sufficient to enforce contract against recipient of confirmation, although not signed by recipient, if recipient has reason to know contents of confirmation and fails to give written objection to its contents within ten days after it is received. Requirement of writing is not necessary: (i) in certain cases where goods are specially manufactured; (ii) if contract is admitted by party against whom enforcement is sought in court proceedings; (iii) if goods were received and accepted; or (iv) if payment was made and accepted. (MCLA §440.2201; MSA §26.910).

Part Performance.—Statute does not abridge power of chancery court to enforce specifically a contract for an interest in land which has been partly performed. (MCLA §566.110; MSA §26.910). For sale of goods see subhead Contracts of Sale, supra.

INTEREST:

Legal rate is 5%, subject to exceptions. (MCLA §438.31 et seq.; MSA §19.15[1] et seq.).

Maximum rate, permitted by written agreement and subject to exceptions, is 7%. (MCLA §438.31 et seq.; MSA §19.15[1] et seq.).

Judgments.—For complaints filed before June 1, 1980, judgments bear interest from date of filing complaint at 6% until June 1, 1980, and 12% thereafter, or, if founded on written instrument, at rate therein provided, if legal, but not exceeding, subsequent to date judgment is entered, 7% until June 1, 1980, and 13% thereafter. For

INTEREST . . . *continued*

complaints filed on or after June 1, 1980, but before Jan. 1, 1987, judgments bear interest at rate of 12%, or if founded on written instrument having higher interest rate, at rate therein provided, but rate shall not exceed 13% after date judgment is entered. For complaints filed on or after Jan. 1, 1987, interest accrues from date of filing complaint at rate certified by state treasurer semiannually as 1% plus average rate on five-year U.S. Treasury Notes, with interest calculated on entire amount of money judgment, including attorney fees and other costs, but amount of interest is retained by plaintiff, and not paid to plaintiff's attorney. For complaints filed on or after Oct. 1, 1986, interest is not allowed on "future damages," defined as personal injury damages accruing after damage findings are made. In tort cases, written settlement offer meeting certain conditions may affect foregoing. In medical malpractice cases, failure of party to allow access to medical records can affect effective time for calculation of interest charges. (MCLA §600.6013, .6301; MSA §27A.6013, .6301).

Open accounts do not bear interest in absence of agreement. (53 Mich. 421, 19 N.W. 127; 145 Mich. 37, 108 N.W. 498).

Partial payments are applied first to interest accrued to date and balance to principal. (187 Mich. 526, 153 N.W. 786).

Provision for compound interest on delinquent interest is permitted at rate agreed to in writing not exceeding 10% per annum or 7% per annum in absence of written agreement (MCLA §438.101; MSA §19.21), but only simple interest is allowed after maturity (41 Mich. 533, 2 N.W. 665).

Interest on Accrued Interest.—After interest has accrued, new promise to pay interest on it is permitted. (263 Mich. 609, 249 N.W. 10).

Regulated lenders are defined as Depository Institutions (defined as banks, savings and loan associations, savings banks, or credit unions, chartered under state or federal law which maintain principal office or branch in Michigan), sellers under Motor Vehicle Sales Finance Act or under Home Improvement Finance Act, secondary mortgage lenders, licensees under Regulatory Loan Act, and licensees under Consumer Financial Services Act, and licensees under Credit Card Arrangements Act. They may charge, collect and receive any rate of interest or finance charge for loan or credit sale not in excess of 25% per annum. (MCLA §445.1854; MSA §23.1300[54]).

Small Loans.—Licensee under Regulatory Loan Act may charge on loan not exceeding regulatory loan ceilings interest not exceeding 25% per annum. Loan processing fee not in excess of 2% of principal up to $40 may be charged. $5 handling fee may be charged for dishonored check or similar instrument. (MCLA §493.13; MSA §23.667[13]).

Security Broker Loans.—Interest charged on debit balances in customer accounts payable on demand and secured by stocks or bonds not subject to usury limitations. (MCLA §438.31c; MSA §19.15[1c]).

Credit Card Loans and Certain Installment Loans.—Depository Institutions (see subhead Regulated Lenders, supra) may charge, collect, and receive any rate of interest or finance charge for extensions of credit to cardholder of credit card or charge card issued by depository institution. (MCLA §445.1854; MSA §23.1300[54]). Prior to effectiveness of Credit Reform Act, banks may charge interest up to 12.83% per annum on unpaid balance (16.5% on auto loans made on or before Dec. 31, 1993), plus service charge of $1 per $50 but not to exceed $15, on loan for period not to exceed 84 months and 32 days which is repayable in uniform installments. (MCLA §§487.491-.492; MSA §§23.710[191]-[192]). See subhead Loans Secured by Real Estate, infra.

Credit Union Loans.—Interest rates on loans made by credit union may not exceed 25% per annum regardless of whether loan specifies term to maturity or is made pursuant to line of credit, credit card or other similar agreement. (MCLA §490.14; MSA §23.494).

Expenses.—Depository Institutions (see subhead Regulated Lenders, supra) may charge, collect and receive from borrower or buyer all fees and charges that are agreed to or accepted by borrower or buyer including those relating to making, closing, processing, disbursing, extending, committing to extend, readjusting, renewing, collecting payments upon, or otherwise servicing extension of credit or any occurrence or transaction related to extension of credit, but such fees and charges may not be excessive. Subject to exceptions in specific authorizing legislation (see e.g. subhead Small Loans, supra) sellers under Motor Vehicle Sales Finance Act or under Home Improvement Finance Act, secondary mortgage lenders, licensees under Regulatory Loan Act, licensees under Consumer Financial Services Act, or licensees under Credit Card Arrangements Act may charge processing fee for disbursing, extending, readjusting, or renewing extension of credit, which fee shall not exceed 2% of amount of credit extended. (MCLA §§445.1856-1857; MSA §§23.1300[56]-[57]).

Certain Bank and Insurance Company Loan Expenses.—Reasonable, actual expenses of lending by banks, insurance companies and lenders approved as mortgagees under National Housing Act (12 USC §§1701-1750g) or regulated by federal agency incurred in making, closing, extending, or renewing loans may be reimbursed by borrower to lender without same standing as part of interest paid. Inspection charges imposed by local units of government may not be charged to borrower. These provisions do not apply to Federal or State Savings and Loan organizations. (MCLA §§438.31a, .31b; MSA §§19.15 [1a], [1b]).

Motor Vehicles.—Motor Vehicles Sales Finance Act (MCLA §§492.102 et seq.; MSA §23.626[1] et seq.) provides that licensee may charge finance charge that does not exceed rate permitted by Credit Reform Act (MCLA §492.118; MSA §23.626[18]). Credit Reform Act provides that finance charge may not exceed 25%. (MCLA §445.1854; MSA §23.1300[54]).

Usury involves loss of all interest (MCLA §438.32 et seq.; MSA §19.15[2] et seq.), and loss of entire loan under Regulatory Loan Act (MCLA §493.13, .19; MSA §23.667[13], [19]). Usury cannot be pleaded against holder in due course of negotiable instrument (MCLA §438.5; MSA §19.3) nor by corporation if corporation agreed

to interest in writing (MCLA §450.1275; MSA §21.200[275]). Usury provisions inapplicable to loans by banks, insurance carriers and finance subsidiaries of manufacturers to "business entities," defined by statute to include any corporation, trust, estate, partnership, cooperative or association, or natural person submitting sworn statement as to type of business in which such person is engaged in which borrowed funds are to be used; other persons extending credit to "business entities" may agree in writing to rate not exceeding 25%. (MCLA §438.61; MSA §19.15[71]). Debtor cannot recover usurious payments if debt is completely satisfied, but if debt is partially outstanding, all interest charged (not just usurious portion) will be applied to principal. (297 Mich. 315, 297 N.W. 505). Usury statute does not apply to obligations whose issue and interest rate have been approved by Michigan Public Service Commission or Securities Bureau of Department of Commerce (MCLA §438.31; MSA §19.15[1]) nor to Federal Housing Administration-insured obligations (MCLA §§487.751-.752; MSA §§23.181-.182) nor to interest charged by trust forming part of stock bonus, pension or profit sharing plan which satisfies requirements of Internal Revenue Code §401(a) on loan to participating employee or beneficiary of trust (MCLA §438.31c; MSA §19.15[1c]). Defense of usury can be waived by nonprofit corporation. (MCLA §§438.31d, 450.1275; MSA §§19.15[1d], 21.200[275]). Person who knowingly charges or receives interest at rate exceeding 25% simple interest per annum is guilty of criminal usury unless otherwise permitted to charge such rate and is subject to imprisonment for up to five years and/or fine of up to $10,000. (MCLA §438.41; MSA §19.15[51]).

Loans Secured by Real Estate.—Notes, bonds or other evidences of indebtedness primarily secured by first lien against real estate, or land lease if tenant owns majority interest in improvements thereon, and land contracts may bear interest at rate greater than that specified in usury statute so long as statutory provisions (which include requirement that lender be approved mortgagee under National Housing Act, 12 USC §§1701-1750g or regulated by state, or by federal agency which is authorized by state or federal law to make such loans) are observed (such provisions do not apply if amount is $100,000 or more and property is not single family residence). (MCLA §438.31c; MSA §19.15[1][C]). Maximum rate on such loans and land contracts made by others is 11%. (MCLA §438.31c; MSA §19.15[1c]). Banks may charge up to 15% on real estate loans where primary security is not first lien. (MCLA §487.494; MSA §23.710[194]). Licensed secondary mortgage lender may charge up to 25% computed by actuarial method. (MCLA §493.71; MSA §26.568[21]). Indebtedness secured by lien on mobile home retained by seller in other than retail installment transaction may bear interest not exceeding 11%. (MCLA §438.31c[8]; MSA §19.15[1c][8]).

For finance charge limits in certain cases, see topic Sales, subhead Retail Credit Sales.

LICENSES, BUSINESS AND PROFESSIONAL:

The license laws of State are voluminous and cover great variety of callings, vocations, and businesses some of which are described in Occupational Code. (MCLA §339 et seq.; MSA §18.925[101] et seq.). In some cases licenses are issued by Bureau of Occupational and Professional Regulation, in others by political subdivision where licensed business is to be carried on. Office of Commercial Services in Department of Commerce provides information and assists in obtaining permits for most business undertakings. (MCLA §§445.11-.24; MSA §§3.541[101]-[114]).

Commercial Travelers.—No license required in upper peninsula of State for commercial traveler unless also a hawker, peddler or pawnbroker in which case license from Township may be required. (MCLA §446.101; MSA §19.571).

Cities have considerable latitude under charters and home rule acts as to licensing various occupations, such as pawnbrokers, junk dealers, peddlers, etc.

Special licenses to war veterans are provided for residents of State. (MCLA §35.441; MSA §4.1241).

Collection Agencies.—Persons engaged in collecting accounts for others or soliciting accounts for collection (except attorneys, justices of the peace, fiduciaries, banks and trust companies) must obtain license and post bond with department of licensing and regulation unless activity in State is limited to interstate communication. (MCLA §339.901 et seq.; MSA §18.425[901] et seq.).

MONOPOLIES, RESTRAINT OF TRADE AND COMPETITION:

Contract, combination or conspiracy between two or more persons in restraint of, or to monopolize, trade or commerce in geographical area of actual or potential competition is unlawful. Monopoly or attempted monopoly for purpose of excluding or limiting competition or controlling, fixing or maintaining prices, is unlawful. (MCLA §§445.771-.788; MSA §§28.70[1]-.70[18]).

Unfair Trade Practices.—Certain practices including improper and misleading use of words in connection with sales of goods are unlawful and various penalties are imposed for commission of such practices. (MCLA §§445.101-.109; MSA §§28.79[1]-.79[10]). Unfair methods of competition or deception in insurance business are prohibited. (MCLA §§500.2001-.2093; MSA §§24.12001-.12093). Such methods or practices include: charging different rate for same coverage based on sex, marital status, age, residence, location of risk, disability, or lawful occupation of risk unless rate differential is based on sound actuarial principles, reasonable classification system, and is related to actual or credible loss statistic. (MCLA §500.2020[c]; MSA §24.12020).

Resale Price Agreements.—See category Intellectual Property, topic Trademarks and Tradenames.

NEGOTIABLE INSTRUMENTS:

See topic Bills and Notes.

RESTRAINT OF TRADE:

See topic Monopolies, Restraint of Trade and Competition.

SALES:

Uniform Commercial Code adopted. (MCLA §§440.1101 et seq.; MSA §§19.1101 et seq.). See topic Commercial Code.

See note at head of Digest as to 1998 legislation covered.

See Topical Index in front part of this volume.

SALES . . . *continued*

Contracts of Sale.—Governed by Uniform Commercial Code. (MCLA §§440.1101 et seq.; MSA §§19.1101 et seq.). (See topic Frauds, Statute of.) No statutory requirement as to type size in printed contracts except as indicated in category Transportation, topic Motor Vehicles, subhead Installment Sale. For requirements as to size and weight of paper in secured transactions, see category Mortgages, topic Chattel Mortgages, subhead Requisites of Instrument.

Bills of Sale.—No statutory provision.

Conditions or Warranties.—Governed by Uniform Commercial Code. (MCLA §§440.1101 et seq.; MSA §§19.1101 et seq.).

Product Liability.—Breach of warranty, express or implied, is a ground of recovery for product-caused injury. (MCLA §440.2714; MSA §19.2714). (See this topic, subhead Conditions or Warranties, and see also topic Commercial Code.) Privity no longer required in action on implied warranty (353 Mich. 120, 90 N.W.2d 873), and might not be required in action on express warranty (512 F.2d 1294, cf. 276 F.2d 254). These rules may conflict with Uniform Commercial Code. (MCLA §§440.1101 et seq.; MSA §§19.1101 et seq., see especially MCLA §440.2318; MSA §19.2318).

Transfer of Title.—Governed by Uniform Commercial Code. (MCLA §§440.1101 et seq.; MSA §§19.1101 et seq.).

Delivery.—Governed by Uniform Commercial Code. (MCLA §§440.1101 et seq.; MSA §§19.1101 et seq.).

Stoppage in Transitu.—Governed by Uniform Commercial Code. (MCLA §§440.1101 et seq.; MSA §§19.1101 et seq.).

Remedies of Seller.—Governed by Uniform Commercial Code. (MCLA §§440.1101 et seq.; MSA §§19.1101 et seq.).

Remedies of Buyer.—Governed by Uniform Commercial Code. (MCLA §§440.1101 et seq.; MSA §§19.1101 et seq.).

Conditional Sales.—Governed by Uniform Commercial Code. (MCLA §§440.1101 et seq.; MSA §§19.1101 et seq.). No statutory requirement as to type size in printed contracts except as indicated in category Transportation, topic Motor Vehicles, subhead Installment Sale. For requirements as to size and weight of paper in secured transactions, see category Mortgages, topic Chattel Mortgages, subhead Requisites of Instrument.

Where sale on title retaining contract or chattel mortgage of any accessory, equipment, additional or replacement part is made to owner of motor vehicle, contract is void as against subsequent purchaser of motor vehicle or as against person who subsequently lends money on motor vehicle unless recorded on certificate of title to motor vehicle. (MCLA §§566.251-.253; MSA §§9.1495-.1497).

Retail Credit Sales.—Retail Installment Sales Act governs time sales of tangible personalty and certain services purchased for personal household or family use. Act sets type size, requires agreement to bear certain notices, sets out statement of price components, permits assertion of defenses against assignee and limits finance charge to $12 per $100 on first $500 principal balance, $10 per $100 on excess. Provisions in agreement for confession of judgment, acceleration of maturity without default, or not to assert defenses, not permitted. Holder of contract is subject to all defenses of buyer. (MCLA §§445.851-.872; MSA §§19.416 [101]-[122]).

Home Solicitation sales are regulated by statute providing right of revocation within three days under certain circumstances. (MCLA §§445.111-.117; MSA §§19.416[201]-[207]).

Home Improvement Finance Act regulates contracts for sale of goods and services to improve residential dwellings. Act providing for form of contract, limitation of finance charge, assertion of defenses against assignee and prohibitions with respect to certain practices incident to sale. (MCLA §§445.1101-.1431; MSA §§19.417[101]-.417[431]).

Bulk Sales.—See category Debtor and Creditor, topic Fraudulent Sales and Conveyances.

Sales of Motor Vehicles.—See category Transportation, topic Motor Vehicles. See also supra this topic, subhead Conditional Sales.

SECURITIES:

Uniform Securities Act, as am'd, adopted. (MCLA §451.501 et seq.; MSA §19.776[101] et seq.). Section numbers of Michigan Act generally correspond with those of Uniform Securities Act printed in Uniform and Model Acts section. Citations below which do not contain MCLA and MSA designations are from Uniform Act.

Supervision.—Administrator is Corporation, Securities and Land Development Bureau of Michigan Department of Consumer & Industry Services. (MCLA §451.806[a]; MSA §19.776 [406][a]). Address: 6546 Mercantile Way, P.O. Box 30222, Lansing, Michigan 48909.

Regulatory Powers of Supervisory Authority.—Under MCLA §451.808; MSA §19.776(408), Administrator may issue cease and desist order, as well as seek injunction. Optional §406(c) of Uniform Act omitted; joint investigations and inspections with other agencies or self-regulatory bodies authorized. (MCLA §451.806[c]; MSA §19.776[406][c]). Last sentence of §411(a) of Uniform Act omitted. (MCLA §451.811[a]; MSA §19.776[411][a]).

Prerequisites to Sales or Offerings.—Except to extent preempted by Federal law pursuant to National Securities Markets Improvements Act of 1996, unlawful without securities registration, unless security or transaction exempt under Michigan Act. (MCLA §451.701; MSA §19.776[301]).

Prerequisites to Transacting Business.—Michigan Act requires registration of commodity issuers, as well as broker-dealers, agents and investment advisers. (MCLA §451.601; MSA §19.776[201]). Requirements for registration of investment advisers now partially preempted by Federal law pursuant to National Securities Markets Improvements Act of 1996.

Securities to Which Act Applicable and Other Definitions.—"Security" includes contract where (1) person furnishes capital to issuer; (2) portion is subjected to risks of enterprise; (3) furnishing capital induced by representations of issuer, promoter or affiliates causing reasonable understanding that benefit will accrue to person as result of operation of enterprise; (4) person does not intend to be actively involved in management of enterprise; and (5) promoter or its affiliates anticipate gain as result of capital. (MCLA §451.801[1]; MSA §19.776[401][1]). Antifraud provisions cover conduct concerning commodities, as well as securities (MCLA §§451.501, .502[a]; .503, .810[a][2]; MSA §§19.776[101], [102][a], [103], [410][a][2]), and activities relating to commodity contracts covered in definitions of "agent", "broker-dealer" and "investment adviser". (MCLA §§451.801[b], [c], [f]; MSA §§19.776 [401][b], [c], [f]). "Commodity" includes goods defined as commodities in Commodity Futures Trading Act of 1974 and other goods commonly classed as commodities in trade (MCLA §451.801[n]; MSA §19.776[401][n]); "commodity contract" also defined (in MCLA §451.801[o]; MSA §19.776[401][o]). "Agent" does not include individual who represents issuer effecting transaction in security exempted under clauses (1)—(5), (9) or (10) of MCLA §451.802(a); MSA §19.766(402)(a). (MCLA §451.801[b]; MSA §19.776[401][b]). "Agent" also does not include officer or general partner of issuer whose securities are registered if no remuneration is paid or given and person acting solely as finder if registered under Michigan Act or acting in transaction exempt under MCLA §451.802(b)(19); MSA §19.776(402)(b)(19), and Administrator may also exclude others from definition of "agent" by rule or order. (MCLA §451.801[b]; MSA §19.776[401][b]). Michigan Act also excludes from definition of "broker-dealer" person acting solely as finder if registered under Michigan Act or acting in transaction exempt under MCLA §451.802(b)(19); MSA §19.776(402)(b)(19). (MCLA §451.801[c]; MSA §19.776[401][c]). "Investment adviser" includes finder; geologist and geophysicist are added to professional exclusions and also excluded are agent acting on behalf of broker-dealer where services solely incidental to broker-dealer business and, under certain conditions, trustee or adviser of trustee whose custody of assets is pursuant to judicial or trust indenture appointment or agreement. (MCLA §451.801[f]; MSA §19.776[401][f]). "Issuer" includes owner of any part of oil, gas or mining leases or payments out of production who creates and sells certificates of interest and participation therein and, for commodity contracts, person operating or performing clearing or certain other functions concerning commodity contracts trading market. (MCLA §451.801[g][2]; MSA §19.776[401][g][2]). "Nonissuer" definition provides sale is for benefit of issuer if: (1) sale is for benefit of director, executive officer, person holding similar status or 10% shareholder; (2) sale, together with all sales for benefit of issuer within six months other than pursuant to registration or exemption order, exceeds 1% of class outstanding; and (3) securities not of class designated by Administrator as eligible for trading in Michigan. (MCLA §451.801[b]; MSA §19.776[401][b]). "Sale", "sell", "offer" and "offer to sell" extend to commodity contracts, as well as securities. (MCLA §451.801[j]; MSA §19.776[401][j]). "Promoter" is person who takes initiative in founding and organizing issuer's business or enterprise or who in connection therewith receives 10% or more of proceeds of sale of any class of securities or 10% or more of equity interest after offering complete, unless received solely as underwriting commission in offering registered under Michigan Act or solely in consideration of property or legal or accounting services. (MCLA §451.801[q]; MSA §19.776[401][q]). "Commission" covers payment or promise or commitment to pay consideration for offering or selling, but excludes real estate commission commensurate with fees paid in area if paid to licensed real estate broker solely for real estate services rendered and payment to lawyer or accountant in connection with advice to client with whom there is established professional relationship if disclosure of payment and interest of professional in transaction, issuer or affiliate made in writing to client before sale. (MCLA §451.801[r], MSA §19.776[401][r]). "Direct or indirect compensation or remuneration" includes payment, receipt or use of proceeds or of securities or goods at less than amount paid by public, real estate commission, or other advantageous payment or arrangement to or with promoter, general partner, officer, director, person with similar status or affiliate of any of foregoing. (MCLA §451.801[s]; MSA §19.776[401][s]). "Affiliate" means person directly or indirectly controlling, controlled by or under common control with specified person. (MCLA §451.801[t]; MSA §19.776[401][t]). "Finder" means person who, for consideration, participates in offer, sale or purchase of securities or commodities by referring potential purchaser or seller but does not include person acting solely in transaction exempted by MCLA §452.802(b)(19); MSA §19.776(402)(b)(19), or person exempted by rule or order of Administrator. (MCLA §451.801[u]; MSA §19.776[401][u]).

Exempt Securities.—§402(a)(5) of Uniform Act omitted. §402(a)(7)(A) and §402(a)(7)(C) of Uniform Act omitted. Michigan version of §402(a)(1) "government securities" exemption also exempts any guarantee or other obligation made in connection therewith. (MCLA §451.802[a][1]; MSA §19.776[402][a][1]). §402(a)(7)(D) of Uniform Act expanded to include equipment trust certificate or equipment note or bond based on chattel mortgage, lease or conditional sale of cars, motive power, or other rolling stock mortgages, leased or sold or furnished for use of or upon railroads, other common carriers, public utilities or public utility holding companies, or equipment notes or bonds where ownership or title of equipment is pledged or retained in accordance with laws of U.S., any state, Canada or any Canadian province, to secure payment of such equipment trust certificates, bonds or notes. (MCLA §451.802[a][6][B]; MSA §19.776[402][a][6][B]). Michigan version of §402(a)(8) "stock exchange" exemption limited to New York and American exchanges. (MCLA §451.802[a][7]; MSA §19.776[402][a][7]). However, MCLA §451.802(a)(12); MSA §19.776(402)(a)(12) provides comparable exemption for NASDAQ national market system (subject to denial, revocation or decertification by Administrator). Uniform Act exempts securities of nonprofit issuers, but Michigan Act exempts only where total issue is $250,000 or less and all sold to bona fide members of issuer without commission or consulting fee, or (1) offering circular and $50 fee are filed at least ten days before offer or sale and exemption is not disallowed; (2) no commission or consulting fee is paid except to registered broker-dealer; and (3) sales are made only through registered broker-dealers or persons exempted from being "agents" by Administrator (who may by rule or order withdraw or further condition exemption or waive [1] and

See note at head of Digest as to 1998 legislation covered.

See Topical Index in front part of this volume.

SECURITIES . . . *continued*
[2] above). (MCLA §451.802[a][8]; MSA §19.776[402][a][8]). Under Michigan version of §402(a)(10) exemption, commercial paper must be: (1) prime quality and negotiable, (2) sold in amount of at least $25,000 to any one purchaser, (3) obligation to pay cash at fixed rate within nine months of issuance, and (4) sold through registered broker-dealer or institution whose securities are exempted under subdivision (a)(3); only nonautomatic renewals are exempted. (MCLA §451.802[a][9]; MSA §19.776[402][a][9]). No notice to Administrator required to exempt investment contracts or options under employee plan. (MCLA §451.802[a][10]; MSA §19.776[402][a][10]). Under certain conditions, Michigan Act also exempts securities issued by issuer registered as open-end management investment company or unit investment trust under §8 of Investment Company Act of 1940. (MCLA §451.802[a][11]; MSA §19.776[402][a][11]).

Exempt Transactions.—Michigan version of §402(b)(1) exempts isolated nonissuer transactions and, with respect to certificate of interest or participation in oil, gas or mining title or lease or payment out of production, applies only if involving no offer or sale by promoter. (MCLA §451.802[b][1]; MSA §19.776[402][b][1]). §402(b)(2) changed to exempt only nonissuer distribution of outstanding security whose issuer (and any predecessor) has gross operating revenue in each of immediately preceding five years and of at least $500,000 in at least three such years, and only if security meets certain other tests. (MCLA §451.802[b][2]; MSA §19.776[402][b][2]). §402(b)(5) exemption applies only if not one of series of transactions in related or adjacent properties or if involves offer or sale to financial institution. (MCLA §451.802[b][5]; MSA §19.776[402][b][5]). Michigan version of §402(b)(8) exemption covers offers and sale to Treasurer of State; no catch-all, however, for "other institutional buyer". (MCLA §451.802[b][8]; MSA §19.776[402][b][8]). Limited offering exemption applies if all of following satisfied: (A) issuer exercises reasonable care to see purchasers do not resell in violation of state and federal securities laws; (B) there is no general advertising or solicitation; (C) no commissions paid, except to registered broker-dealer (who must report to Administrator) and commissions disclosed in writing to offerees; and (D) each sale satisfies all conditions of one of following: (1) sales to no more than ten promoters, persons to be actively engaged in issuer's management or as attorneys or accountants to issuer, or relatives thereof, in 12-month period if all purchase with investment intent and/or to no more than 15 persons whose principal business is line of business to which offering relates and who are qualified by experience to evaluate risks, (2) sales to no more than 15 persons in Michigan in 12-month period if all offerees given, at least 48 hours before sale, offering circular (contents of which are specified), (3) sales to no more than 35 persons in Michigan in 12-month period if exemption application and offering circular filed ($100 fee), Administrator enters order granting exemption, and offering circular given to each purchaser at least 48 hours before sale, (4) sales by person other than issuer to no more than ten persons pursuant to no more than 15 offers in Michigan in 12 months if not part of distribution, or (5) sales to person seller has reasonable grounds to believe meets one of following conditions: (i) business entity with net income from operations after taxes over $100,000 in last year, or net worth over $1,000,000 and after purchase less than 10% of assets invested in securities of issuer, or (ii) individual who after purchase has more than $50,000 invested in securities of issuer, has either income before taxes over $100,000 and is capable of bearing economic risk or net worth over $1,000,000 and has such knowledge and experience that he is able to evaluate risks or has retained attorney, accountant or registered investment adviser. Sales under various subsections of (D) may be combined; rules are given for counting purchasers and offerees. (MCLA §451.802[b][9]; MSA §19.776[402][9]). Up to ten sales may be made under preorganization exemption (for corporate issuers only) if no commission paid, no advertising used without Administrator's approval and seller reasonably believes all Michigan purchasers (other than institutional investors) are buying for investment. (MCLA §451.802[b][10]; MSA §19.776[402][b][10]). Exemption for offers and sales to existing security holders is limited to 25 sales in 12 months (except for sales of underlying security to holders of convertible securities or warrants) and conditioned upon no payment of commission (other than stand-by commission), unless issuer files offering materials and pays $100 fee at least 20 days before first offer. (MCLA §451.802[b][11]; MSA §19.776[b][11]). (*Note:* Foregoing exemption affected by Federal preemption.) Offer, sale or issuance of securities pursuant to investment contract or option exempt under MCLA §451.802(a)(10); MSA §19.776(402)(a)(10) also is exempted. (MCLA §451.802[b][13]; MSA §19.776[402][b][13]). Michigan Act also exempts: offer or sale of security (as contemplated under Small Business Investment Act of 1958) to Small Business Administration, by small business concern to small business investment company, or by small business investment company to small business concern as condition to providing equity capital or loan (MCLA §451.802[b][14]; MSA §19.776[402][b][14]); offer or sale of security by Michigan nonprofit development corporation if purpose is to promote or assist growth of business in area in which it operates (MCLA §451.802[b][15]; MSA §19.776[402][b][15]); distribution by co-operative corporation of its securities to its patrons as patronage refund or return (MCLA 451.802[b][16]; MSA §19.776[402][b][16]); any nonissuer transaction through broker-dealer when security is of same class designated by Administrator as eligible for public trading ($100 fee for requesting designation order) (MCLA §451.802[b][17]; MSA §19.776[402][b][17]) (*Note:* Foregoing exemption affected by Federal preemption.); sale of stock of Michigan professional service corporation (MCLA §451.802[b][18]; MSA §19.776[402][b][18]); transaction incident to class vote by shareholders on merger, consolidation, reclassification of securities or sale of corporate assets (MCLA §451.802[b][19]; MSA §19.776[402][b][19]); any transaction Administrator exempts by order (MCLA §451.802[b][20]; MSA §19.776[402][b][20]); and any transaction pursuant to uniform limited offering exemption filing ($100 filing fee). (MCLA §451.802[b][21]; MSA §19.776[402][b][21]). (*Note:* Foregoing exemption affected by Federal preemption.)

Registration of Securities.—Small corporate offering registration (SCOR) procedures adopted. (MCLA §451.704a; MSA §19.776[304a]).

Exemptions from Broker-Dealer, Investment Adviser, Other Professional Registration.—§201(d)(3) of Uniform Act expanded to exempt from investment adviser registration persons whose only clients in Michigan are investment companies, insurance companies, banks or trust companies (MCLA §451.601[d][3]; MSA §19.776[201][d][3]) or are individuals who access person's services through 1-900 or 1-800 telephone number and services are generic and not customized or specific to individual and would not otherwise be considered offering of investment advice (MCLA §451.601[d][4]; MSA §19.776[201][d][4]). For offers and sales of mortgage loans, person licensed or registered as mortgage broker, lender, or servicer under Mortgage Brokers, Lenders, and Servicers Licensing Act (codified at MCLA §445.1651 et seq.; MSA §23.1125[51] et seq.) exempt from broker-dealer registration, and employees of such person acting in such capacity exempt from agent registration. (MCLA §451.601[i]; MSA §19.776[201][i]). Broker-dealer, agent, commodity issuer registration not required for person engaged in commodities business whose transactions meet specified conditions. (MCLA §451.601[f]; MSA §19.776[201][f]). County treasurer acting pursuant to authority under Local Government Investment Pool Act (codified at MCLA §129.141 et seq.; MSA §5.707[41] et seq.) excluded from investment adviser definition (MCLA §451.801[f]; MSA §19.77[401][f]) and exempt from all other registration requirements (MCLA §451.601[h]; MSA §19.776[201][h]).

Registration of Broker-Dealers, Investment Advisers, Other Professionals.—Unless member of national securities exchange, broker-dealer may be required by rule or order to register "principal" in charge of management, financial affairs or compliance. (MCLA §451.601[c]; MSA §19.776[201][c]). MCLA §451.602(a)(4); MSA §19.776(202)(a)(4) requires application to contain information with respect to any injunction or administrative order or conviction of misdemeanor, not only those dealing with securities or securities business. Under MCLA §451.602(a); MSA §19.776(202)(a), registration of broker-dealer does not automatically constitute registration of agent who is partner, officer, director, etc., of registered broker-dealer. MCLA §451.602(b); MSA §19.776(202)(b) provides for initial filing fee and annual fee of $250 for broker-dealer, $30 for principal, $250 for commodity issuer and $30 for agent; for $100 filing fee for registration of successor; for $30 fee if agent transfers to other broker-dealer. Under MCLA §451.602(d); MSA §19.776(202)(d), Administrator may prescribe minimum capital and ratio between net capital and aggregate indebtedness.

Bonds.—Under MCLA §451.602(e); MSA §19.776(202)(e), Administrator may by rule require posting of bond (or other security) of $100,000 by broker-dealer, commodity issuer, principal, agent or investment adviser, unless net capital exceeds $100,000. Fidelity bonds also may be required of broker-dealer or investment adviser by Administrator. (MCLA §451.602[f]; MSA §19.776[201][f]).

Denial, Revocation, Suspension or Cancellation of Registration of Broker-Dealer or Other Professional.—No requirement that violation or noncompliance be "wilful" under MCLA §401.604(a)(1)(B); MSA §19.776(204)(a)(1)(B). No ten year limitation under MCLA §451.604(a)(1)(C); MSA §19.776(204)(a)(1)(C). Michigan version of §204(a)(2)(F) omits Uniform Act exception, adds, in case of individual, order of SEC barring association with broker-dealer or investment adviser or equivalent order of Commodities Futures Trading Commission or order suspending or expelling from membership in national securities exchange or association, and also adds association (or association by partner, officer, director or principal) with broker-dealer liquidated under Securities Investor Protection Act of 1970 unless association terminated at least 12 months before litigation begun thereunder or unless factual matters established. (MCLA §451.604[a][1][F]; MSA §19.776[204][a][1][F]). Also, no five year limitation on entry of order by state securities administrator or SEC as grounds for revocation under MCLA §451.604(a)(1)(F); MSA §19.776(204)(a)(1)(F). MCLA §§451.604(a)(1)(J)-(Z); MSA §§19.776(204)(a)(1)(J-Z) substituted for §§204(a)(2)(J)-(K) as follows: (J) delaying unreasonably delivery of securities or commodities to extent delivery in registrant's control; (K) representing, without basis, that securities will be listed or application for listing will be made; (L) improperly inducing excessive trading (or trading beyond resources) in customer's account with intent to produce profits in disregard of customer's best interests; (M) recommending transaction without reasonable grounds to believe suitable; (N) recommending speculative low priced securities without knowledge, or in disregard, of customer's other holdings, financial situation, objectives and ability to bear risk; (O) executing transaction for customer without authority; (P) executing transactions for customer pursuant to general discretionary authority not evidenced in writing; (Q) acting on agency basis, without disclosure, for both seller and purchaser; (R) charging excessive commission when acting on agency basis, or selling at excessive markup when acting on principal basis; (S) entering into transaction with customer at price not reasonably related to market price; (T) extending credit to customer in violation of Securities Exchange Act of 1934 or regulations of Federal Reserve Board; (U) employing manipulative or deceptive device in connection with purchase or sale; (V) selling to or purchasing from customer without disclosing that it is market maker, or holds substantial market position, in security; (W) borrowing money from customer while registered as agent or investment adviser; (X) making unauthorized use of customer's funds, or hypothecating customer's securities without having lien thereon unless with prior written consent; (Y) while registered as agent, effecting transactions not recorded on records of employer broker-dealer; and (Z) operating account under fictitious name. Censure is additional available remedy. Sentence following §204(a)(2) omitted.

Advertisements.—Administrator may by rule or order require filing and acceptance prior to use of any prospectus, pamphlet, circular, form letter, advertisement, or other sales literature or advertising communication addressed or intended for distribution to prospective investors, including clients or prospective clients of investment adviser, unless security, commodity contract or transaction is exempt by MCLA §451.602(a)(1)-(7); MSA §19.776(202)(a)(1)-(7). (MCLA §451.803; MSA §19.776[403]). Partially preempted by National Securities Markets Improvement Act of 1996.

Civil Liabilities.—Reference to §305(h) omitted, and reference to §305(f) added, under MCLA §451.810(a)(1); MSA §19.776(410)(a)(1).

Subdivision Offerings.—Model Land Sales Practices Act adopted, with substantial modifications. (MCLA §565.801 et seq.; MSA §26.1286[1] et seq.).

See note at head of Digest as to 1998 legislation covered.

See Topical Index in front part of this volume.

MI – 14

SECURITIES . . . *continued*

Franchising, Pyramid Sales, Etc.—Regulated under Franchise Investment Law. (MCLA §445.1501 et seq.; MSA §19.854[1] et seq.). See topic Franchises.

Uniform Simplification of Fiduciary Security Transfers Act adopted. (MCLA §441.101 et seq.; MSA §19.356[1] et seq.). Governs, rather than Commercial Code, where statutes inconsistent. (MCLA §440.9994[2]; MSA §19.9994[2]).

STATUTE OF FRAUDS:

See topic Frauds, Statute of.

TRUST RECEIPT SECURITY:

See category Debtor and Creditor, topic Pledges.

WAREHOUSEMEN:

Uniform Commercial Code adopted. (MCLA §440.1101 et seq.; MSA §19.1101 et seq.). See topic Commercial Code.

Warehousemen are required to keep records of all property deposited, dates of deposit and names and address of owners of property. (MCLA §444.7; MSA §19.497). Separate provisions exist with respect to storage of farm produce, meat products and various other commodities. (MCLA §§285.61-.82, §§444.101-.109; MSA §§12.119[1]-[22], §§19.521-.529).

Bonds.—Warehousemen of farm produce must give bond, running to department of agriculture, with sufficient surety and conditioned upon faithful performance of duties. Amount of bond varies with warehouse capacity. (MCLA §285.67a; MSA §12.119[7]).

Licenses.—Warehousemen of farm produce must secure license annually from director of state department of agriculture. (MCLA §285.65; MSA §12.119[5]).

Warehouse Receipts.—Governed by Uniform Commercial Code. (MCLA §440.1101 et seq.; MSA §19.1101 et seq.).

Lien.—Governed by Uniform Commercial Code. (MCLA §440.1101 et seq.; MSA §19.1101 et seq.).

CITIZENSHIP

ALIENS:

Aliens do not have franchise (Const. Art. II, §1), but, if conditions are met, may act in representative capacity under appointment of probate court. (MCLA §§700.116[d], .531; MSA §§27.5116[d], .5531).

Property.—Aliens who are residents of this state enjoy same rights and privileges in property as citizens of this state. (Const. Art. X, §6). Any alien may acquire and hold lands, or any right thereto or interest therein, by purchase, devise or descent, and may convey, mortgage and devise the same, and if he dies intestate, the same descends to his heirs in same manner as if he were a native citizen of this state, or of the U.S. (MCLA §§554.135-.136; MSA §§26.1105-.1106).

CIVIL ACTIONS AND PROCEDURE

ACCORD AND SATISFACTION:

The principle is recognized and enforced as at common law. Accord and satisfaction is founded upon consideration, and consideration may take any form which would be held to constitute good consideration for any other agreement. Part payment of past due, liquidated and undisputed debt does not bar action for balance (330 Mich. 353, 47 N.W.2d 643), unless discharge in writing is signed by creditor. (MCLA §566.1; MSA §26.978[1]). An agreement to change or modify, or to discharge in whole or in part any contract where there is absence of consideration is not valid unless in writing and signed by party against whom it is sought to enforce the change, modification, or discharge. (MCLA §566.1; MSA §26.978[1]).

Uniform Commercial Code adopted. (MCLA §440.1101 et seq.; MSA §19.1101 et seq.). See category Business Regulation and Commerce, topic Commercial Code.

Compromise.—In general, compromise is governed by same principles as accord and satisfaction, stated supra.

Pleading.—Accord and satisfaction is an affirmative defense which must be pleaded. (Rule 2.111[F][3][a]).

ACTIONS:

Equity.—Procedural distinctions between law and equity are abolished. (Rule 2.101).

Forms of Action.—There is one form of action, known as a civil action. (Rule 2.101).

Conditions Precedent.—See topic Limitation of Actions, subhead Claim Against State.

Commencement.—See topics Process, Pleading.

Parties.—Actions must be brought in name of real party in interest, but personal representative, guardian, conservator, trustee, party who has contracted for benefit of another or person authorized by statute may sue in own name without joining party for whose benefit action is brought. (Rule 2.201[B]). Assignee for collection is real party in interest (269 Mich. 608, 257 N.W. 751). Infants sue by next friend or guardian of estate. (Rule 2.201[E]). Married women sue and are sued as if sole. (MCLA §600.2001; MSA §27A.2001).

Necessary parties are those whose presence is essential to permit court to render complete relief, although where jurisdiction over all such parties cannot be obtained court may proceed and grant such relief to parties as will prevent failure of justice. Reasons for omitting necessary parties must be pleaded. (Rule 2.205).

Parties may join as plaintiffs or be joined as defendants if right to relief is asserted jointly, severally as arising out of same transaction or series of transactions and there is common question of law or fact, or if convenient administration of justice will be promoted. Court may order separate trials. (Rule 2.206). Misjoinder of parties is not ground for dismissal, and parties may be added or dropped at any stage. (Rule 2.207). Class actions are permitted. (Rule 3.501). Uniform Class Actions Act not adopted. Third party defendant may be joined by timely filed third party complaint and otherwise by leave granted on motion with notice to all parties. (Rule 2.204).

Intervention.—Permitted as of right upon timely application when statute so provides, by stipulation of all parties or when applicant claims interest relating to property or transaction which is subject of action and is so situated that disposition of action may impair or impede applicant's ability to protect that interest; permitted in court's discretion when statute gives conditional right to intervene, or when applicant's claim or defense and main action have question of law or fact in common. (Rule 2.209).

Interpleader.—Persons having claims against plaintiff may be joined as defendants and required to interplead when plaintiff may be exposed to double or multiple liability. Court may order property or funds as to which plaintiff admits liability be deposited with court, or secured by bond, and may order plaintiff discharged from liability with respect thereto prior to determination of rights of claimants. Court may enjoin other actions. (Rule 3.603).

Joinder of Causes of Action.—All claims arising out of same transaction or occurrence must be pleaded in same action, but failure to object to misjoinder or nonjoinder of claims in pleading, by motion or at pretrial waives joinder rules and judgment merges only claims actually litigated. Party may join as many claims either legal or equitable as he may have against opposing party. Counterclaim or cross-claim must be filed with answer or as amendment to answer. Counterclaim may, but need not, diminish or defeat recovery sought; and may exceed in amount or be different in kind than that sought by opposing party. Cross-claim may be asserted against co-party arising out of subject matter of original action or of counterclaim therein or relating to any property which is subject of original action. (Rule 2.203).

Consolidation of Actions.—Court may order consolidation of pending actions involving substantial and controlling common question of law or fact. (Rule 2.505[A]).

Severance of Actions.—Court may order separate trial of any claim, cross-claim, counterclaim or third party claim, or of any separate issue. (Rule 2.505[B]).

Stay of Proceedings.—No injunction may be granted in one action to stay proceedings in another action pending in any court in which the relief may be sought. (Rule 3.310[E]). Court shall adjourn proceeding when attorney acting for party dies, is removed or suspended, or ceases to act as such, and party entitled to 28 days' notice to obtain new attorney or advise court of intention to appear on own behalf. (Rule 2.503[F]).

Abatement and Revival.—All actions and claims survive death. (MCLA §600.2921; MSA §27A.2921). If a party dies, court orders substitution of proper parties on motion made by his successors or representatives or by any party. Unless motion for substitution made within 91 days of filing of statement of fact of death, action must be dismissed as to deceased party unless showing of no prejudice to any other party of allowing later substitution. (Rule 2.202). See also category Estates and Trusts, topic Executors and Administrators.

Prohibited Actions.—Alienation of affections, criminal conversation, seduction of person 18 or more years old, breach of contract to marry. (MCLA §600.2901; MSA §27A.2901),

Limitation of.—See topic Limitation of Actions.

Small Claims.—See category Courts and Legislature, topic Courts.

Termination of Actions.—Question once decided by judgment on merits is final. (242 Mich. 234, 218 N.W. 783).

Administration.—See category Estates and Trusts, topic Executors and Administrators.

Direct Actions Against Insurer.—See category Transportation, topic Motor Vehicles, subhead Direct Actions.

APPEAL AND ERROR:

Appeals are governed by Rules and Revised Judicature Act. (MCLA §600.101 et seq., MSA §27A.101 et seq.).

From Circuit Court.—Review is by appeal to Court of Appeals pursuant to Rules 7.201-.219.

How Taken.—For appeal of right (Rule 7.204) appellant files claim of appeal with trial court and pays $25 appeal fee, files any appeal bond required by statute, files stay bond if stay is desired and secures trial court's approval thereof, serves on opposite party copy of claim of appeal and any bond which has been filed, and files with trial court proof of service and stenographer's or attorney's certificate that transcript has been ordered if transcript exists. Claim of appeal and proof of service thereof, with copy of judgment or order appealed from, copy of stenographer's or attorney's certificate that transcript has been ordered, copy of bond, and copy of trial court docket or calendar entries, are filed with Court of Appeals, with $250 entry fee, immediately after filing with trial court. Within 28 days thereafter docketing statement must be filed. Form and contents of claim of appeal are specified by Rule 7.204(D).

Application for leave to appeal (Rule 7.205) is filed with Court of Appeals, with entry fee, copies of order or judgment appealed from, copies of transcripts designated by Rule 7.205(B)(4), proof of service on all parties and other documents specified by rule. Application for leave to appeal must set forth reasons and grounds for appeal. No oral argument on application for leave to appeal. Form and content of application for leave to appeal are specified by Rule 7.205(B). Effective Nov. 1, 1995, application for leave to appeal which is more than 12 months after entry of order appealed from may not be granted. Limited exceptions are provided for criminal appeals. (Rule 7.205[F][3]). Criminal defendant may appeal judgment based on plea of guilty or nolo contendere only by application for leave to appeal. (MCLA §600.308[2][d]; MSA

See note at head of Digest as to 1998 legislation covered.

See Topical Index in front part of this volume.

APPEAL AND ERROR . . . *continued*
§27A.308[2][d]). If leave to appeal is granted, appeal then proceeds as appeal as of right. (Rule 7.205[D]).

Time for Taking.—Not later than 21 days after entry of judgment or order appealed from, or within 21 days after entry of order denying motion for new trial or rehearing or motion for other post judgment relief if such motion is made and served within original 21 day period or within further time allowed by trial court during such original 21 day period. (Rule 7.204[A]). If claim of appeal is filed late it must be filed as application for leave to appeal. (Rule 7.205[F]).

Appeal Bond.—Not required unless made condition of appeal by particular statute authorizing appeal or unless ordered by trial court or Court of Appeals. (Rule 7.204[E][3]).

Stay of Proceedings.—Appeal does not act as stay unless trial court or Court of Appeals orders otherwise. (Rule 7.209). No execution issues nor can other enforcement proceedings be taken until expiration of time for taking appeal. (Rule 7.101[H]). Rule 2.614 provides automatic stay, unless otherwise provided by court or rule for 21 days after entry of judgment. If motion for new trial, to alter or amend judgment, for judgment n.o.v., or to amend findings or for additional findings, is filed and served within such 21 days, no execution issues nor can other enforcement proceedings be taken until 21 days after entry of order on such motion unless court orders otherwise on motion for good cause shown. However, temporary restraining orders, preliminary injunctions, injunctive relief included in final judgment, interlocutory orders in receivership actions, and orders prior to judgment concerning custody, control and management of property, for temporary alimony, support or custody of minor children and expenses in divorce suits are not stayed unless court so orders on motion for good cause. (Rule 2.614). Further stay requires bond conditioned for prosecution of appeal, performance of judgment or order of appellate court, performance of judgment or order appealed from if appeal is dismissed or discontinued, payment of any damages to appellee from stay in appeals from foreclosure of mortgage or land contract or in cases involving possession of land, and performance of any other act specified in statute authorizing appeal as condition of appeal bond. (Rule 7.209).

Extent of Review.—In actions of an equitable nature both facts and law are reviewed. At law only questions of law are reviewed, and preponderance of evidence or lack of evidence on material fact question may be reviewed only if called to attention of trial court during trial or on motion for new trial. (152 Mich. 486, 116 N.W. 390).

Character of Hearing.—Review based on record. (Rule 7.210). Appellant and appellee must request oral argument if oral argument is desired. (Rule 7.212[C][1]).

Judgment or Order on Appeal.—Court of Appeals may reverse, affirm, remand with instructions, order new trial, give any judgment and make any order which ought to have been given or made, and make such orders and grant such relief as case may require.

Interlocutory orders of circuit court are appealable only upon leave granted by Court of Appeals. Within time limited for appeal as of right, appellant must file with Court of Appeals and serve on opposite party application for leave to appeal, setting forth reasons and grounds, including facts showing how appellant would suffer substantial harm by awaiting final judgment before taking appeal. (Rule 7.205). For procedures for application for leave to appeal see this subhead, catchline How Taken, supra.

From Court of Appeals.—Governed by Rules 7.301-7.318.

Appeals may be taken to Supreme Court only upon application and leave granted, upon a showing of meritorious basis of appeal and any one of following grounds: (1) Issue involves substantial question as to validity of legislative act; (2) issue has significant public interest and case is by or against state, agency or subdivision thereof or officer thereof acting in official capacity; (3) issue involves legal principles of major significance to state's jurisprudence; (4) in appeal before decision by Court of Appeals, delay likely to cause substantial harm; (5) in appeal from decision of Court of Appeals, decision clearly erroneous and will cause material injustice, or conflicts with Supreme Court decision or decision of Court of Appeals; or (6) in appeal from Attorney Discipline Board, decision is erroneous and will cause material injustice. (Rule 7.302[B]).

How Taken.—Appellant files with Supreme Court application for leave to appeal containing concise statement of material proceedings and facts, accompanied by supporting brief and copy of opinion or findings of trial court and, where Court of Appeals has ruled, by copy of decision of Court of Appeals and $200 fee. Precise contents of application are specified in Rule 7.302(A). Application is noticed for hearing in Supreme Court as motion. Copies of application and brief must also be filed in Court of Appeals and served on opposing party and proof of service is filed in Supreme Court. No oral argument on application for leave to appeal. If leave is granted, appeal is limited to issues raised in application for leave to appeal unless otherwise ordered by Supreme Court. (Rule 7.302[F]).

Time for Taking.—Application for leave to appeal prior to decision of Court of Appeals must be filed in Supreme Court within 28 days after filing of claim of appeal in Court of Appeals, or in case of appeals by leave, within 28 days after filing of application for leave to appeal to Court of Appeals or granting of such application, whichever is later. (Rule 7.302[C]).

Application for leave to appeal a decision of Court of Appeals must be filed within 21 days after the decision or within 21 days after denial of an application for rehearing timely filed. (Rule 7.302[C]).

Appeal Bond.—No requirement beyond bond imposed in connection with appeal to Court of Appeals.

Stay of Proceedings.—Stay bond filed on appeal to Court of Appeals operates to stay proceedings pending decision of Supreme Court unless otherwise ordered by court. Appeal to Supreme Court does not operate as stay in absence of such stay bond or stay entered by trial court or Court of Appeals. (Rules 7.209 and 7.302[G]).

Extent of Review.—In actions of an equitable nature both facts and law are reviewed. At law only questions of law are reviewed, and preponderance of evidence or lack of evidence on material fact question may be reviewed only if called to attention of trial court during trial or on motion for new trial. (152 Mich. 486, 116 N.W. 390).

Character of Hearing.—Review based on record. Appellant and appellee must request oral argument if oral argument desired. (Rule 7.312).

Judgment or Order on Appeal.—Supreme Court may reverse, affirm, remand with instructions, order new trial, give any judgment and make any order which ought to have been given or made, and make such orders and grant such relief as case may require. (Rule 7.316[A]).

Interlocutory orders of Court of Appeals may be made subject of application for leave to appeal to Supreme Court in same manner and on same grounds as final orders.

From Probate Courts.—Final orders in adoption proceedings, condemnation proceedings under Drain Code or specified final orders affecting rights of interested person in certain estates, trusts, or conservatorships are appealable as of right to Court of Appeals. (Rule 5.801[B]; MCLA §600.861; MSA §27A.861). Other orders may be appealed to Circuit Court (Rule 5.801[C]); or, with certification of issues by probate judge, to Court of Appeals (Rule 5.801[F]). Circuit Court judgment on appeal may be appealed by application to Court of Appeals. (MCLA §600.863; MSA §27A.863). Appeal fee paid to circuit court is $100.

From Municipal Courts and District Courts.—Appeals in civil cases from District Courts are to Circuit Court in county where judgment is rendered. Appeals from final judgments are as of right except for judgments based on pleas of guilty or nolo contendere which are by application. All others are by application for leave. Appeal fee is $100. (MCLA §600.8342; MSA §27A.8342[5]; Rule 7.101, 7.102).

Procedure on Appeal to Circuit Court.—

How Taken.—Appellant files claim of appeal and other specified papers with circuit court, claim of appeal, appeal bond and other specified papers with lower court and pays required fees, serves copies of claim of appeal and other specified papers on appellee and files proof of service with lower court and circuit court. (Rule 7.101). Lower court transmits to circuit court all original papers in file, including list of docket entries. (Rule 7.101). Application to Circuit Court for order allowing appeal is necessary (1) when no appeal of right exists, or (2) when time for taking appeal has expired. (Rule 7.103).

Time for Taking.—All steps by appellant must be taken within 21 days after entry of judgment or order of probate court, and within 21 days after entry of judgment or order denying motion for new trial or denying motion for judgment N.O.V. of lower court other than probate. When order of circuit court allowing appeal is required, motion for such order must be filed within same period as claim of appeal in appeals as of right, except where time for appeal has expired and showing is made by affidavit that delay was not due to lack of diligence. (Rules 7.101, 7.103).

Appeal Bond.—Must be filed with claim of appeal or order allowing appeal. Bond is not less than $200 and, except in appeals from probate court, not less than one and one-quarter the amount of judgment or claim allowed if appeal is by person against whom a claim has been asserted. In judgments for possession of land, penalty is governed by Rule 4.201(N). Bond must be executed by appellant and one or more sufficient sureties. (Rule 7.101).

Stay of Proceedings.—Filing of appeal bond operates as stay of all further proceedings in lower court. No execution issues nor can other enforcement proceedings be taken until expiration of time for appeal unless court otherwise orders on motion for good cause shown. (Rule 7.101). Order of probate court removing fiduciary appointing temporary personal representative, temporary guardian or temporary conservator, granting new trial or rehearing, granting allowance to spouse or children of decedent, granting permission to sue on fiduciary's bond, or suspending fiduciary and appointing special fiduciary is not stayed pending appeal unless ordered by court for good cause shown.

Extent of Review.—See catchline Character of Hearing, infra.

Character of Hearing.—Except for appeals from probate court, proceeding in Circuit Court is trial de novo. (Rule 7.102[C]). Review on appeal from probate court is based on record and is not de novo. (Rule 5.802[B]).

Judgment or Order on Appeal.—Circuit court may render any judgment or make any order which should have been rendered or made in lower court, and may grant such other relief as may be required. (Rule 7.102[C]).

From Worker's Compensation Commission.—Award of hearing referee is reviewed by Appeal Board, with presentation of additional testimony if leave is granted, by filing claim for review within 30 days. Both facts and law are reviewed by Appeal Board. Upon leave to appeal granted, on application within 30 days after award by Appeal Board, questions of law are reviewed by Court of Appeals. (MCLA §§418.851, .859a, .861; MSA §17.237[851], [859a], [861]).

From Employment Security Board of Review.—Any judgment may be appealed to Circuit Court. Appellant files claim of appeal with Circuit Court with-in 30 days after mailing to him of copy of decision of Appeal Board; serves copy of claim of appeal on Appeal Board and on all interested parties and files proof of service. Board of Review has 42 days to file certified copy of record with Circuit Court and appeal is heard on this record. (Rule 7.104[B]).

From Other State Agencies.—Governed primarily by statute affecting particular agency. If statute provides for appeal of any kind to Supreme Court, appeal now goes to Court of Appeals on leave granted. (Rule 7.203[B][3]). Where statute governing agency provides for appeal to Circuit Court or makes no provision for appeal, appeal is to Circuit Court in county of appellant's residence or of Ingham County, in same manner as other appeals to Circuit Court except appeal bond not required. (MCLA §600.631; MSA §27A.631; Rule 7.104).

BONDS:

Bonds required or permitted to be given in civil proceedings differ with respect to amount, sureties, justification of sureties, approval by court or other officer, procedure to attack sufficiency, and method of enforcement. Statutes relating to particular proceeding must be consulted. See also Rule 3.604 for provisions generally applicable to bonds given under Rules and Revised Judicature Act.

Substantial compliance with statutory form is sufficient and defective bond may be amended nunc pro tunc. (MCLA §600.2601; MSA §27A.2601). Change of parties does

See note at head of Digest as to 1998 legislation covered.

See Topical Index in front part of this volume.

BONDS . . . *continued*
not impair bond. (MCLA §600.2641; MSA §27A.2641). All bonds are recorded by clerk of court (MCLA §50.101; MSA §5.841), and his record or certified copy is evidence (MCLA §50.103; MSA §5.843).

Cash deposit may be substituted for bond in any civil cause, and check certified by bank in U.S., or U.S. or satisfactory municipal bond negotiable by delivery, may be deposited in lieu of cash. (MCLA §600.2631; MSA §27A.2631).

Sureties.—Surety company authorized to do business in state may be substituted for any one or more sureties required on any bond unless statute expressly provides otherwise. (MCLA §600.2621; MSA §27A.2621).

Enforcement.—In every action where bond or other security for costs, supersedeas, or other purposes has been posted, judgment may be entered against surety or security on motion. (Rule 3.604[I]). Other bonds are enforced by action on bond. (MCLA §600.2923; MSA §27A.2923).

CERTIORARI:

Supplanted by order of superintending control, which may be issued in appropriate circumstances by Supreme Court (Const., art VI, §4; MCLA §600.219; MSA §27A.219; Rule 3.302[C]), Court of Appeals (Const., Art. VI, §10; Rule 3.302[D]) and Circuit Courts (Const., art. VI, §13; Rule 3.302[D]). For other means of review see topic Appeal and Error.

CHARITABLE IMMUNITY:

See topic Damages.

COMMISSIONS TO TAKE TESTIMONY:

See topic Depositions and Discovery.

COSTS:

Policy is to limit costs to a moderate sum, and executory agreement for costs in excess of prescribed allowances is void. (39 Mich. 137).

Supreme Court.—Costs usually are awarded to prevailing party, except where public question is involved, or both parties prevail in part. Costs include appeal and entry fees, expense of transcript, of other documents reprinted as provided in Rules and of any stay bond. (Rules 7.219, 7.318; MCLA §600.2441; MSA §27A.2441).

Court of Appeals.—Prevailing party may recover necessary expense of transcript and of copies thereof, together with other documents required by Rules, cost of any stay bond, and fees paid to clerk, unless otherwise ordered by court. (Rule 7.219).

Circuit Court and District Court.—Prevailing party recovers costs except when express provision for costs is made in statute or rule, or unless court otherwise directs. (Rule 2.625). Costs are fees of officers and witnesses, some disbursements incident to trial, including bond premiums, and attorney fees authorized by statute or court rule, which are generally nominal. Cost of transcript is taxable only if transcript is desired for purpose of motion for new trial or to prepare record for appeal. (MCLA §600.2405; MSA §27A.2405, MCLA §600.2543; MSA §27A.2543; MCLA §600.8375; MSA §27A.8375).

Security for Costs.—Any party asserting claim in action may be required to give bond for costs on motion of defendant when such action appears reasonable and proper to court. (Rule 2.109).

Liability of Attorney.—Sanctions for frivolous claims or defenses may include payment of costs as well as attorney fees by party and/or by attorney for party. (MCLA §600.2591; MSA §27A.2591; Rule 2.114[E] and [F]). Supreme Court and Court of Appeals may impose costs on attorney for violation of rules. (Rule 7.219[I]).

DAMAGES:

Common law generally governs compensatory damages. Exemplary damages in excess of pecuniary loss are allowed, as compensation to plaintiff, where plaintiff is victim of tortious conduct on part of defendant. (409 Mich. 401, 295 N.W.2d 50).

Charitable immunity abrogated. (361 Mich. 1, 105 N.W.2d 1).

Sovereign immunity abrogated as to motor vehicle or aircraft negligence actions against state. (MCLA §600.6475; MSA §27A.6475).

Comparative Negligence Rule.—Doctrine of comparative negligence recognized in state. (405 Mich. 638, 275 N.W.2d 511).

Contribution.—Provided for by statute in certain instances (MCLA §600.2925[a]; MSA §927A.2925[1]) as well as by common law. See category Estates and Trusts, topic Death, subhead Action for Death.

No-Fault Insurance.—See category Transportation, topic Motor Vehicles.

Restaurant owner or employee is not liable for damages for good faith attempt to remove food lodged in individual's throat unless grossly negligent. (MCLA §691.1522; MSA §14.16[102]).

Donor of food to charitable organization for distribution to needy and organization which distributes such food are not liable for damages to recipient due to condition of food, subject to certain conditions. (MCLA §691.1572 and .1573; MSA §14.17[72] and [73]).

DEPOSITIONS AND DISCOVERY:

After commencement of an action, any party may take the deposition of any person, including a party, by deposition upon oral examination. (Rule 2.306[A]).

Uniform Foreign Depositions Act repealed.

Within State for Use Within State.—Depositions or parts thereof are admissible at trial, on hearing of motion, or in interlocutory proceeding only as provided in Rules of Evidence. (Rule 2.308[A]). Rule of Evidence 804 provides hearsay exception for deposition testimony of witness who is unavailable for trial if party against whom testimony is offered at trial, or in civil action, predecessor in interest, had opportunity and similar motive to develop deposition testimony by direct, cross, or redirect examination. Rule of Evidence 803(18) provides hearsay exception (availability of declarant immaterial) for deposition testimony of expert witness.

Within State for Use Elsewhere.—Uniform Foreign Depositions Act has been repealed. See also subhead Compelling Attendance of Witnesses, infra.

Outside of State for Use Within State.—See subhead Within State for Use Within State, supra, and subhead Compelling Attendance of Witnesses, infra.

De Bene Esse.—See subhead Within State for Use Within State, supra.

Perpetuating Testimony.—Provision is made for perpetuating testimony for use as evidence in suits not yet commenced, upon application to court of record showing necessity and persons interested, so far as known, and upon notice to expected adverse parties. (Rule 2.303[A]).

Before Whom Taken.—

Within the United States.—Depositions to be taken before: (1) Any person authorized to administer oaths by laws of this state or U.S. or of place where examination is held, or (2) any person appointed by court in which action is pending, or (3) any person upon whom parties agree by stipulation in writing. (Rule 2.304[A]).

In Foreign Countries.—Depositions to be taken: (1) On notice, before person authorized to administer oaths at place of examination under law there or U.S.; (2) before person commissioned by court; or (3) pursuant to letter rogatory. (Rule 2.304[B]).

Disqualification.—No deposition can be taken before relative or employee or attorney of any party or relative or employee of such attorney or person financially interested in action unless parties so agree in writing or on record. (Rule 2.304[C]).

Notice of Taking.—Party desiring to take deposition on oral examination must give reasonable written notice to every other party stating time and place and name and address of each person to be examined. (Rule 2.306[B]).

Party desiring to take deposition on written interrogatories serves them on every other party with notice stating name and address of person who is to answer interrogatories and name or descriptive title and address of person before whom deposition is to be taken. Cross-interrogatories, redirect interrogatories and recross-interrogatories may be served by respective parties. Party taking deposition delivers copy of notice or stipulation and copies of all interrogatories to person designated to take responses, who then takes testimony of witness in response to the interrogatories. (Rule 2.307).

Commissions.—See subheads Before Whom Taken, supra, and Compelling Attendance of Witnesses, infra.

Compelling Attendance of Witnesses.—

Where action is pending or anticipated in this state, clerk of court in county in which deposition is to be taken or in which action is pending issues subpoenas on request. Service of notice of taking of deposition of party, or director, trustee, officer or employee of corporate party on party or party's attorney is sufficient; subpoena need not be issued. Subpoena may command production of books, papers or tangible things which constitute or contain evidence related to matters within scope of permissible examination (see infra, subhead Examination of Witnesses), but in that event Rule 2.302 concerning protective orders is applicable and court on prompt motion may quash or modify subpoena if it is unreasonable or oppressive or require advancement of reasonable cost of producing books, papers or tangible things. (Rule 2.305[A]).

Deponent may be required to attend examination only in county where he resides or is employed or transacts his business in person, or any other convenient place fixed by order of court. Court may order nonresident plaintiff or officer or managing agent thereof to appear in this state or elsewhere upon just terms, including payment by defendant of travel expenses. On showing that deposition of nonresident defendant cannot be taken in state of his residence, court may order such defendant or officer or managing agent thereof to appear in this state or elsewhere upon just terms, including payment by plaintiff of travel expenses. (Rule 2.305[C]).

When place of examination is in another state, territory or country, party desiring to take deposition may petition any court thereof for subpoena or equivalent process. (Rule 2.305[D]).

Where action is pending in another state, territory or country, any officer or person authorized by laws of another state, territory or country to take any deposition in this state, with or without a commission, in any action pending in a court of that state, territory or country may petition court of record in county in which deponent resides or is employed or transacts his business in person or is found for subpoena to compel giving of testimony by him. Court may hear and act upon petition with or without notice, as it directs. (Rule 2.305[E]).

Examination of Witnesses.—Deponent may be examined and cross-examined regarding any matter not privileged and relevant to subject matter of action, whether it relates to claim or defense of examining party or any other party, including existence, description, nature, custody, condition and location of any books, documents or tangible things and identity and location of persons having knowledge of relevant facts. It is not ground for objection that information sought will be inadmissible at trial if information sought appears reasonably calculated to lead to discovery of admissible evidence. Parties may stipulate for examination regarding any matter. (Rule 2.302[B], [F]). On motion of party or deponent court may limit or forbid or terminate examination or otherwise protect party or witness. (Rules 2.302[C], 2.306[D]).

Return.—When deposition is transcribed, person conducting examination or stenographer certifies on deposition that witness was duly sworn and that deposition is true record of testimony given by witness. When one of parties requests filing, person conducting examination seals deposition in envelope indorsed with title of action and marked "Deposition of (name of witness)", promptly files it personally or by mail with court in which action is pending, and gives prompt notice of filing to all other parties. (Rule 2.306[F]).

Form.—See supra, subhead Return. Title of action is customarily indorsed on cover or first page of deposition together with indication of date, time and place of taking.

Discovery.—After commencement of action in state circuit court (where jurisdictional amount in controversy must exceed $10,000), parties may obtain discovery

See note at head of Digest as to 1998 legislation covered.

See Topical Index in front part of this volume.

MI – 17

DEPOSITIONS AND DISCOVERY . . . *continued*
through depositions, interrogatories, requests for production of documents and things and entry on land for inspection and other purposes. (Rule 2.302[A][1]). No discovery is allowed in state district court (amount in controversy is $10,000 or less) prior to judgment except by leave of court or stipulation of parties. (Rule 2.302[A][2]). No discovery is permitted at any time in small claims division of state district court or in civil infraction actions. (Rule 2.302[A][3]). Parties may also obtain on good cause shown and notice to person to be examined and all other parties order for examination of party or person under legal control of party when physical or mental condition of that person is in controversy. (Rule 2.311[A]).

Demand for Admission of Facts.—Parties may serve on other parties requests for admission whose truth shall be deemed conclusively admitted unless written answer or objection to request is served within 28 days. (Rule 2.312[A], [B][1], [D]). Matter as to which request for admission pertains may be statement or opinion of fact or application of law to fact, including genuineness of documents described in request, copies of which must be served with request unless previously furnished. (Rule 2.312[A]). Answers must admit truth of matter requested, specifically deny matter, or state in detail reasons why matter cannot be truthfully admitted or denied. (Rule 2.312[B][2]). Lack of knowledge or information is not reason for failure to admit or deny unless party answering states that it has made reasonable inquiry and information known or readily obtainable is insufficient to enable party to admit or deny. (Rule 2.312[B][2]). Denial must fairly meet substance of request and, when good faith so requires, answering party must specify those parts of request that are admitted and those parts that are denied. (Rule 2.312[B][2]). Answers may be amended by leave of court for good cause shown. (Rule 2.312[D][1]). Reasons must be given for objections but it is not sufficient to object that matter as to which admission has been requested presents genuine issue for trial. (Rule 2.312[B][4]). Requesting party may recover expenses incurred in proving genuineness of document or truth of matter which has been denied unless court finds that request was previously held objectionable, admission sought was of no substantial importance, party failing to admit had reasonable grounds to believe it might prevail on requested matter, or there was other good reason for failure to admit. (Rule 2.313[C]).

Interrogatories may, without leave of court, be served on plaintiff after commencement of action and on defendant with or after service of complaint on that defendant. (Rule 2.309[A]). Within 28 days of service, each interrogatory must be answered separately and under oath unless objected to for specific stated reasons. (Rule 2.309[B]). It is not ground for objection that information sought will be inadmissible at trial if information sought appears reasonably calculated to lead to discovery of admissible evidence. (Rule 2.302[B][1]). Party answering interrogatories has option to produce business records from which answer to interrogatory may be derived providing burden of deriving answer is substantially same for party serving interrogatory as for party served and business records are specified in sufficient detail to enable interrogating party to identify records from which answer may be derived. (Rule 2.309[E]). Answer to interrogatory may be used to extent permitted by rules of evidence. (Rule 2.309[D][3]).

Requests for Production of Documents and Things and for Entry onto Land for Inspection and Other Purposes.—Parties may without leave of court serve on other parties requests to inspect and copy specifically designated documents, requests to inspect and copy, test or sample tangible things, and requests to enter designated land or other property for inspection and other purposes. (Rule 2.310[B]). Parties may also without leave of court serve such requests on nonparties. (Rule 2.310[C]). Parties and nonparties have 28 days within which to serve written response to such requests stating that requested inspection will be permitted as requested or stating reasons for objection to requested inspection. (Rule 2.310[B][2], [C]). Documents shall be produced as they are kept in usual course of business or labeled to correspond to categories of request. (Rule 2.310[B][2], [C]).

EVIDENCE:

Witnesses.—No person excluded for interest, marital or other relationship to party or conviction of crime. (MCLA §600.2158; MSA §27A.2158). Child under ten may testify without oath if judge satisfied as to appreciation of obligation to speak truth. (MCLA §600.2163; MSA §27A.2163). Parties may be witnesses. (MCLA §600.2159; MSA §27A.2159).

See also topic Depositions and Discovery.

Privileged Communications.—Privilege attaches to information given by client to certified public accountant or public accountant in connection with audit, or to information derived or resulting therefrom (MCLA §339.732; MSA §18.425[732]), to communications by client to attorney in professional capacity (230 Mich. 444, 202 N.W. 959), to confessions to priests or ministers of gospel (MCLA §600.2156; MSA §27A.2156), to information acquired by physicians or surgeons in professional capacity if necessary to enable them to prescribe or act (MCLA §600.2157; MSA §27A.2157), to information transmitted between victim and sexual assault or domestic violence counsel (MCLA §600.2157a; MSA §27A.2157a), to communications from students or other juveniles to school executives, teachers, etc. and school records of students' behavior (MCLA §600.2165; MSA §27A.2165), and to information acquired by certified psychologists from persons consulting them which was necessary for rendering of professional services (MCLA §313.18237; MSA §14.15[18237]). Beneficiary of life insurance policy may waive physician patient privilege of deceased patient to document claim for benefits. (MCLA §600.2157; MSA §27A.2157).

Husband and Wife.—Communications made by one spouse to other during marriage are privileged. (MCLA §600.2162; MSA §27A.2162). Husband or wife cannot testify as to adultery by other; and cannot testify for or against other without other's consent except in suits for divorce, prosecutions for bigamy or illegal marriage or for crimes against children of either or both, cases arising from desertion, abandonment, nonsupport, or personal wrong or injury to other, or where title to separate property of either or his or her grantee denied by other. (MCLA §600.2162; MSA §27A.2162). Person may seek personal protection order restraining or enjoining conduct of spouse. (MCLA §600.2950; MSA §27A.2950).

Uniform Act to Secure Attendance of Witnesses From Without a State in Criminal Cases in effect. (MCLA §§767.91-.95; MSA §§28.1023[191]-.1025[195].

Uniform Rendition of Prisoners as Witnesses in Criminal Proceedings Act in effect. (MCLA §§780.111-.120; MSA §§28.1287[1]-.1287[10]).

Communications or Transactions with Persons Since Deceased or Incompetent.—Party cannot testify as to matters equally within knowledge of a "person incapable of testifying" in an action brought by or against a person incapable of testifying, unless some material portion of his testimony is supported by corroborating evidence. "Person incapable of testifying" includes any individual who is incapable of testifying by reason of death or incompetency and his heirs, representatives or assigns, and any individual or corporation whose agent, having such knowledge, is incapable of testifying. Evidence of acts and habits of person incapable of testifying is admissible to show improbability of claims of adverse party. (MCLA §600.2166; MSA §27A.2166).

Self-Incrimination.—No person can be compelled in any criminal case to be a witness against himself. (Const. Art. I, §17). Defendant may only at his own request be deemed a competent witness, and neglect to testify creates no presumption against defendant and court must not permit reference to or comment upon such neglect. (MCLA §600.2159; MSA §27A.2159). A witness is not required to give any answer which will have tendency to accuse himself of any crime or misdemeanor. (MCLA §600.2154; MSA §27A.2154).

Compelling Attendance.—See topic Depositions and Discovery.

Uniform Photographic Copies of Business and Public Records of Evidence Act adopted. (MCLA §600.2148; MSA §27A.2148).

INJUNCTIONS:

Procedure is governed principally by Rule 3.310. In general, Michigan practice is similar to Federal practice under Fed. R. Civ. P. 65. See topic Pleading.

Jurisdiction to issue injunctions is given to circuit courts. (MCLA §600.601; MSA §27A.601).

Prerequisites.—Granting of injunctions is within discretion of court. Standards are matter of common law.

Procedure.—Injunctions must be prayed for specifically in complaint (Rule 2.111[B]) or by motion (Rule 2.119[A]) and may be ordered only after hearing on motion or order to show cause. Trial of action may be consolidated with hearing on motion. (Rule 3.310[A][2]). Order granting injunction or restraining order must state reasons for its issuance, must be specific, and must describe acts restrained. (Rule 3.310[C]). See also subhead Temporary Restraining Order, infra.

Bond may be required in amount Court deems proper (Rule 3.310[D]), subject to objection procedure (Rule 3.310[D][3]and 3.604). Where required it must be filed before injunction will issue. (Rule 3.310[D]).

Temporary Restraining Order.—Restraining orders may be granted without notice pending hearing on motion or order to show cause upon clear showing by affidavit or verified complaint that otherwise immediate and irreparable damage or physical injury will result to applicant. (Rule 3.310[B]). Temporary restraining order granted without notice must state date and time of issuance, describe injury, why it is irreparable, and why order was issued without notice; and must set date for hearing on whether preliminary injunction should issue. (Rule 3.310[B][2]) Temporary restraining order expires by its terms within 14 days, unless extended by Court for good cause shown or by consent of enjoined party (except in domestic relations cases). (Rule 3.310[B][3]).

JUDGMENTS:

Judgments by Confession.—Judgment may be entered in circuit court on confession signed by attorney though no suit is pending, but authority to confess must be in instrument separate from obligation evidencing demand; authority must be produced to officer signing judgment, and is filed with clerk of court in which judgment is entered. (MCLA §600.2906; MSA §27A.2906).

Judgments by Consent.—A consent judgment is usually regarded as a judgment of parties rather than of court, and oral agreement outside court can be sufficient. (330 Mich. 295, 47 N.W.2d 616). As a general rule consent judgment will not be vacated or set aside without consent of parties in absence of claim that consent was not voluntarily given. (338 Mich. 679, 62 N.W.2d 634).

Judgments on Pleadings.—See subhead Summary Judgments, infra.

Summary Judgments.—Either party may move for summary judgment at any time on ground that court lacks subject matter jurisdiction; that other party has failed to state claim upon which relief can be granted, that other party has failed to state valid defense, or that except as to amount of damages there is no genuine issue as to any material fact. In latter case, supporting affidavits must be filed and other party may file opposing affidavits. Such affidavits, together with pleadings, depositions, admissions and documentary evidence are considered by court at hearing. Court may permit amendment of pleadings. If summary judgment is denied or if judgment rendered does not dispose of action, court may ascertain what material facts are without substantial controversy. (Rule 2.116).

Declaratory judgments are provided for in cases where actual controversies exist. (Rule 2.605).

Default Judgments.—In circuit court default may be entered for failure to plead or otherwise defend as required by Rules upon filing of affidavit showing such facts. Nonmilitary affidavit required by law must be filed in all cases where defendant failed to appear. (Rule 2.603). Rules allow clerk to enter judgment for sum certain if defaulted party has failed to appear and is not infant or incompetent; in other cases party entitled to judgment by default must apply to court, giving notice if defendant has appeared in action. (Rule 2.603). In practice application to court in all cases is often required. Court may conduct hearings, permit trial by jury or take other action including taking account, determining amount of damages or by investigating any other matter. (Rule 2.603).

See note at head of Digest as to 1998 legislation covered.

See Topical Index in front part of this volume.

MI – 18

JUDGMENTS . . . *continued*

Offer of Judgment.—Party may, until 28 days before trial, offer to allow judgment to be taken against him for all or part of claim, plus costs and interest then accrued. To accept adverse party must serve notice within 21 days after service of offer. Failure to respond constitutes rejection. Counteroffers may be accepted or rejected in same manner. If offer is rejected, and if offeree does not obtain judgment more favorable than rejected offer or if offer and counteroffer were made and rejected better than average of offers, offeree must pay actual costs incurred in prosecution or defense of action. (Rule 2.405).

Vacation or Modification.—Default regularly entered and based on personal service may be set aside as prescribed in Rule 2.612 (clerical mistakes, inadvertence, excusable neglect, etc.) or as prescribed in Rule 2.603(D) upon showing good cause supported by affidavit showing meritorious defense made within 21 days of entry of default judgment. (Rule 2.603[D]). Court is limited in power to set aside decrees in tax proceedings. (MCLA §211.70; MSA §7.115). Defendant over whom personal jurisdiction was necessary and acquired but who did not in fact have knowledge of pendency of action may enter appearance within one year after final judgment and court may relieve defendant from judgment upon showing of just cause and lack of prejudice to third parties on payment of costs or other conditions deemed just. (Rule 2.612[B]).

Lien.—Judgment as such imposes no lien. Judgments are a lien upon personal property after execution and levy (MCLA §600.6012; MSA §27A.6012), but not on real estate as to subsequent bona fide conveyances until notice of levy has been recorded in office of Register of Deeds in county where premises are situated (MCLA §600.6051; MSA §27A.6051), except judgments on workmen's compensation awards (MCLA §418.821; MSA §17.239[321]).

Revival.—Action for new judgment may be brought within ten years after rendered by Court of record of state, U.S. or of another state, within six years after rendered by Court not of record. New judgment is enforceable for same periods. (MCLA §600.5809; MSA §27A.5809).

Assignment.—No provision in statutes or Rules.

Satisfaction.—Judgment may be shown satisfied of record in whole or in part by: (1) filing satisfaction with clerk signed and acknowledged by parties or their attorneys of record in whose favor judgment was rendered, or (2) in case of money judgment only, payment to clerk of judgment, interest, and costs, or (3) filing motion with clerk for entry of order finding judgment satisfied. In latter case court hears proofs. (Rule 2.620).

Form of Satisfaction

State of Michigan, County of . . . . . ., ss.

. . . .

vs. In . . . . Court

. . . .

. . . . acknowledge satisfaction of a judgment rendered on the . . . . . day of . . . . . ., A.D. . . . . . ., in the above entitled cause in favor of . . . . the above named . . . . . . against . . . . the above named . . . . for . . . . . . Dollars, damages, and . . . . . . costs.

Dated . . . . . ., A.D. . . . .

Actions.—Actions founded upon judgments or decrees including an action for a new judgment must be brought within ten years from rendition of judgment by Court of record of this state, U.S. or another state and within six years after rendered by Court not of record. (MCLA §600.5809; MSA §27A.5809).

Foreign Judgments.—Where foreign courts had jurisdiction of person and subject matter, their judgments are conclusive upon Michigan courts. (108 Mich. 170, 66 N.W. 1095). A judgment may be entered upon a properly certified transcript of justice of the peace of a foreign jurisdiction. (46 Mich. 320, 9 N.W. 432).

Final foreign judgments granting or denying recovery of money, or support in matrimonial or family matters, but not including judgment for taxes, fine or penalty, are conclusive unless: tribunal not impartial or lack of due process including lack of sufficient time to defend; no personal or subject matter jurisdiction; fraudulently obtained; against public policy; conflict with other final judgment; agreement to settle disputes in other manner; seriously inconvenient forum if personal service. (MCLA §§691.1151-.1159; MSA §27.955[1]-[91]).

Foreign final decrees for alimony, where party was served with process within the jurisdiction may be sued on in an action at law. (MCLA §552.121; MSA §25.141).

Uniform Enforcement of Foreign Judgments Act not adopted.

Uniform Foreign Money Judgments Recognition Act adopted. (MCLA §§691.1151-.1159; MSA §27.955[1]-[9]).

LIMITATION OF ACTIONS:

Uniform Commercial Code adopted. (MCLA §§440.1101-.11102; MSA §§19.1101-.11102). See category Business Regulation and Commerce, topic Commercial Code.

Actions must be commenced within the following periods after they accrue:

Real Property Actions.—Action to recover land or possession of land, within five years if defendant claims under deed by fiduciary, by sheriff or other ministerial officer under order of court of this state, or by sheriff upon mortgage foreclosure sale; within ten years if defendant claims under tax deed of officer of this state or United States; within 15 years after probate of will in this state if defendant claims under devise in such will; otherwise within 15 years. (MCLA §600.5801; MSA §27A.5801). Action to foreclose mortgage, within 15 years after maturity or last payment. (MCLA §600.5803; MSA §27A.5803). Action to foreclose mechanic's lien, see category Debtor and Creditor, topic Liens, subhead Mechanic's and Construction Liens.

Actions to Recover Damages for Injury to Person or Property.—

One Year.—Libel or slander. (MCLA §600.5805; MSA §27A.5805).

Two Years.—Assault; battery; false imprisonment; malicious prosecution; malpractice; misconduct or neglect of office by sheriff or his deputies; negligence or misconduct of constable (two years after expiration of year for which constable was elected). (MCLA §600.5805; MSA §27A.5805).

Three Years.—Products liability action; all actions to recover damages for death of person, or injuries to persons and property, and where no shorter limitation period is specified. (MCLA §600.5805; MSA §27A.5805).

Six Years.—Action charging defective or unsafe condition of improvement to real property against licensed architect, professional engineer, land surveyor or contractor (limitation period commencing after first occupancy, use or acceptance of improvement) (alternative limitation period, one year from discovery of defect or when defect should have been discovered); action charging negligence of licensed land surveyor (limitation period commencing after delivery of survey). (MCLA §600.5839; MSA §27A.5839).

Actions to Recover Damages or Sums Due for Breach of Contract, or To Enforce Specific Performance of Contract.—

Two Years.—Action charging any surety for costs; action on bond or recognizance given on appeal from court in this state; action on constable's bond (two years after expiration of year for which constable was elected). (MCLA §600.5807; MSA §27A.5807).

Four Years.—Action charging any surety on any bond of any executor, administrator or guardian (four years after discharge of such fiduciary). (MCLA §600.5807; MSA §27A.5807). Action for breach of contract for sale of goods governed by Uniform Commercial Code. (MCLA §440.2725; MSA §19.2725).

Six Years.—All other such actions except those referred to immediately below under subhead Ten Years. (MCLA §600.5807; MSA §27A.5807).

Ten Years.—Action on bond of public officer; action founded on covenants in deeds and mortgages of real estate; action on bond, note, or other like instrument which is direct or indirect obligation of or issued by this state or any county, city, village, township, school district, special assessment district, or other public or quasi-public corporation in this state. (MCLA §600.5807; MSA §27A.5807).

Actions to Enforce Noncontractual Money Obligations.—

Six Months.—Action under bulk sales provisions of Uniform Commercial Code. (MCLA §440.6111; MSA §19.6111). (Period runs from transfer of possession or, if transfer concealed, from time of discovery of transfer).

Two Years.—Action for recovery of any penalty or forfeiture based on any penal statute brought in name of people of this state. (MCLA §600.5809; MSA §27A.5809).

Six Years.—Action founded on judgment or decree rendered in any court not of record in this state, or any other state from time of rendition of judgment. (MCLA §600.5809; MSA §27A.5809).

Ten Years.—Action founded on judgment or decree rendered in any court of record of United States, this state, or any other state (ten years from time of rendition of judgment). (MCLA §600.5809; MSA §27A.5809).

Common Carriers.—Actions by or against common carriers for charges or overcharges arising out of intrastate transportation must be brought within two years. (MCLA §600.5811; MSA §27A.5811).

Credit Service Organization.—Actions by or against Credit Service Organization must be brought within four years after date of execution of contract for services to which action relates. (MCLA §445.1824; MSA §23.1300[4]).

Insurance and Surety Companies.—Actions by or against insurance or surety companies including lenders for violations of State Insurance Code must be brought within five years after occurrence of violation. (MCLA §500.1243; MSA §24.11243).

Products Liability.—Period of limitations for products liability action (action based on any theory for death or injury to person or damage to property caused by faulty product) is three years, but if product has been in use for ten years or more, plaintiff is required to prove prima facie case without benefit of any presumption. (MCLA §§600.2945-.2949, .5805; MSA §§27A.2945-.2949, 5805).

Personal Actions Not Specifically Provided For.—Six years, (MCLA §600.5813; MSA §27A.5813).

Accrual of Claims.—Except as otherwise expressly provided, limitations run from time claim accrues. (MCLA §600.5827; MSA §27A.5827). Times when various claims accrue are specified at MCLA §§600.5829-.5838; MSA §§27A.5829-.5838. In cases not covered by these sections, claim accrues at time wrong was done regardless of time when damage results. (MCLA §600.5827, MSA §27A.5827). In personal injury case, claim does not accrue until all elements of cause of action can be alleged in complaint. (388 Mich. 146; 200 N. W. 2d 70). Uniform Commercial Code governs accrual of actions for breach of contract for sale of goods. (MCLA §440.2725; MSA §19.2725).

Disabilities of Plaintiff.—Where person first entitled to make claim is under 18 years of age or insane at time claim accrues, that person or those claiming under that person has one year after disability is removed by death or otherwise to bring action although period of limitations has otherwise run. (MCLA §600.5851; MSA §27A.5851). Where individual dies prior to or within 30 days after period of limitations runs, claim may be brought any time within two years after letters testamentary or letters of administration are granted despite running of applicable limitations period. (MCLA §600.5852; MSA 27A.5852).

Absence of Concealment of Defendant.—Where defendant fraudulently conceals existence of claim or identity of person liable for claim, action may be commenced within two years after plaintiff discovers or should have discovered existence of claim or identity of person who is liable for claim. (MCLA §600.5855; MSA §27A.5855).

Foreign Causes of Action.—Where cause of action accrued outside of State in favor of resident of State statute of limitations of Michigan applies. All other claims accruing outside State must be commenced within State period of limitation or statute of limitations of other state.

Malpractice Claims.—Claim of malpractice against member of state licensed profession or one who holds self out to be member of state licensed profession, accrues at

See note at head of Digest as to 1998 legislation covered.

See Topical Index in front part of this volume.

MI – 19

LIMITATION OF ACTIONS... *continued*

time person discontinues treating or serving plaintiff in professional or pseudo professional capacity as to matters out of which claim for malpractice arose, regardless of when plaintiff discovers or otherwise has knowledge of claim, except that medical malpractice claims against person or entity who or which holds itself out to be licensed health care professional, facility or agency, or employee or agent of such facility or agency, accrue at time of act or omission which is basis for claim. (MCLA §600.5838[a]; MSA §27A.5838[A]). Malpractice claim must be brought within two years after claim accrues or within six months after plaintiff discovers or should have discovered claim. Claim may not be brought more than six years after date of act or omission which is basis for claim, except where discovery of existence of claim was prevented by fraud, foreign object was left in patient's body or claim involves injury to reproductive system. (MCLA §600.5838; MSA §27A.5838). Claims accruing to person 13 years of age or less must be brought on or before person's 15th birthday. (MCLA §600.5851; MSA §27A.5851. Medical malpractice defendant must receive 182 days' prior written notice of action, during which statute of limitations is tolled. (MCLA §§600.2912b, .5856; MSA §§27A.2912[2], .5856).

Limitations Not Applicable.—Neither limitations nor laches apply to actions by state for recovery of land. However, person who could have asserted claim to title by adverse possession for more than 15 years is entitled to seek any other equitable relief in action to determine title to land. Limitations do not apply to actions by municipal corporations for recovery of possession of public highways or other public ground, nor to actions brought by this state or its political subdivisions for recovery of costs of care and treatment in state institutions. (MCLA §600.5821; MSA §27A.5821).

Counterclaims.—Provisions of limitations chapter do not bar counterclaims to extent of plaintiff's claim unless counterclaim was barred at time plaintiff's claim accrued. (MCLA §600.5823; MSA §27A.5823).

New Actions.—Statutes of limitation are tolled when complaint is filed and copy of summons and complaint are served on defendant, or when jurisdiction over defendant is otherwise acquired, or when complaint is filed and copy of summons and complaint are placed in officer's hands, in good faith, for immediate service, but in latter case statute is tolled no longer than 90 days. (MCLA §600.5856; MSA §27A.5856). See subhead Malpractice Claims, supra.

Disabilities of Plaintiff.—Where person entitled to action is under 18 years, insane or imprisoned at time his claim accrues, he or those claiming under him must bring action within one year after disability is removed. Disability must exist at time claim accrues, and successive disabilities cannot be tacked. (MCLA §600.5851; MSA §27A.5851). Disability due to war is recognized in certain instances. (MCLA §600.5854; MSA §27A.5854).

Absence or Concealment of Defendant.—If defendant is outside state at time claim accrues against him, period of limitation only begins to run when he enters this state unless means of service of process sufficient to vest jurisdiction in Michigan court was available to plaintiff With same qualification, running of time after accrual of claim is interrupted by any and all absences from state in excess of two months at a time. (MCLA §600.5853; MSA §27A.5853). As to concealment of defendant, see subhead Fraudulent Concealment, infra.

Death.—If a person dies before period of limitations has run or within 30 days thereafter, action which survives by law may be commenced by personal representative within two years after letters of authority are issued, except that all actions against an estate must be commenced within three years after period of limitations has run. (MCLA §600.5852; MSA §27A.5852).

Fraudulent Concealment.—If a person who is or may be liable fraudulently conceals existence of claim or identity of any person who is liable, action may be commenced within two years after plaintiff discovers or should have discovered existence of claim or identity of person liable, though action would otherwise be barred by period of limitations. (MCLA §600.5855; MSA §27A.5855).

Interruption of Statutory Period.—No statutory provision for any circumstances, occurring before statutory period has run, which fix a new date from which the entire period runs. See subheads New Actions, Disabilities of Plaintiff, Absence or Concealment of Defendant, Death, supra.

Revival of Barred Claims.—Express or implied contracts may be revived by acknowledgment or promise in writing signed by party to be charged. (MCLA §600.5866; MSA §27A.5866). Payment on debt may remove bar if made with intention to recognize entire debt. (327 Mich. 101, 41 N.W. 2d 338). Endorsement of payment by creditor is not admissible to prove payment to bar statute. (MCLA §600.5865; MSA §27A.5865).

Joint Obligors.—One or more of several joint obligors does not lose benefits of running of statute by reason of tolling of statute as against another joint obligor. (MCLA §600.5825; MSA §27A.5825).

Contractual Limitations.—Parties to contract may stipulate for a reasonable period of limitation shorter than the statutory period (281 Mich. 532, 275 N.W. 238), except in life insurance policies (MCLA §§500.100 et seq.; MSA §§24.1100 et seq.).

Foreign Causes of Action.—Period of limitation applicable to claim accruing outside this state, including right of action created by statute, is that prescribed by law of place where claim accrued or by law of this state, whichever bars claim, except that where claim is in favor of Michigan resident, Michigan statute of limitations applies. (MCLA §600.5861; MSA §27A.5861; am'd 1978, No. 542).

Pleading.—Bar of statute must be pleaded by answer (Rule 2.111), or raised by motion to dismiss (Rule 2.116[B], [C]).

Claim Against State.—Claim against state may not be maintained in Court of Claims unless claim or notice of intention to file claim is filed with clerk of that court within six months if claim is for property damage or personal injuries and otherwise within one year. (MCLA §600.6431; MSA §27A.6431).

PARTITION:

Persons holding lands as joint tenants or tenants in common may have partition thereof. (MCLA §600.3304; MSA §27A.3304). Action may be maintained by any person who has an estate in possession of lands of which partition is sought but not by anyone who has only an estate in remainder or reversion. (MCLA §600.3308; MSA §27A.3308).

Jurisdiction and Venue.—Circuit courts have jurisdiction. (MCLA §600.3301; MSA §27A.3301). County in which land or any part thereof is situated is proper county to bring action. (MCLA §600.1605; MSA §27A.1605).

Proceedings.—If court is satisfied that partition can be made without prejudice to owners it appoints disinterested person as partition commissioner to make partition. (Rules 3.401, .402).

Partition in Kind or Sale.—If partition in kind cannot be made without prejudice to owners, court may order public sale by circuit court commissioner and division of proceeds according to respective interests of parties. (MCLA §600.3332; MSA §27A.3332; Rule 3.403).

Probate court has jurisdiction to partition property assigned by decree in probate proceedings to beneficiaries in common and undivided. Such partition may be ordered on petition of any person interested on proper notice and hearing. (MCLA §§700.196-.214; MSA §§27.5196-.5214).

The court may fix the minimum price at which real property which cannot be partitioned may be sold. (MCLA §§600.3332, 700.208; MSA §§27A.3332, 27.5208).

Where a trust provides for sale, without limitation on power of alienation nor restriction as to time of division, trustee may divide the trust estate without court order where all consent, or with authority of court if all interested do not consent. (MCLA §§600.3360-.3372; MSA §§27A.3360-.3372).

PLEADING:

Pleading is codified and greatly simplified by Rules 1.101-2.119. Procedural distinctions between law and equity have been abolished. See also topics Actions, Process.

Pleadings Permitted.—Complaint, answer, reply, counterclaim and cross-claim, answer to cross-claim, third-party complaint, third-party answer, reply to third-party answer. (Rules 2.110[A], [B]; 2.113[A], 2.119[A]).

Complaint, Counterclaim, Cross-Claim, Third-Party Claim.—Sets forth facts upon which pleader relies with such specific averments as are necessary reasonably to inform adverse party, and demand for judgment for relief sought, and if for money, the amount thereof if sum certain. If claim is not for sum certain, specific amount of money need not be stated, but allegations must be included to show that claim is within court's jurisdiction. Relief in the alternative or of several different types may be demanded. (Rule 2.111[B]). All claims against opposing party arising out of subject matter of action must be joined. (Rule 2.203[A]).

Answer.—Pleader may assert as many defenses legal or equitable or both as he may have. Defenses not stated are waived. Averments of adverse party must be explicitly admitted or denied unless party lacks knowledge as to truth or falsity of allegation, and substance of matters relied upon to support denials must be set forth. Affirmative defenses must be set forth in separate sections. (Rule 2.111[C]-[F]). Execution of written instrument is admitted if not denied under oath. (Rule 2.112[E]).

Counterclaim or Set-Off.—May or may not diminish or defeat recovery sought by adverse party; may claim relief exceeding in amount or different in kind from that sought by adverse party (Rule 2.203[C]); may set forth as many legal or equitable claims as pleader may have (Rule 2.203[A], [B], [D], [F]).

Reply.—Reply is permitted although not required except where answer expressly demands it or where there is a denominated counter-claim. (Rule 2.110[A], [B], [C]).

Demurrer.—Demurrers are abolished, and all matters formerly raised by demurrer are now raised by motion to dismiss, to strike, or for summary judgment. (Rules 2.115, 2.116[C]-[I]).

Amended or Supplemental Pleadings.—Party may amend pleading once as matter of course within 14 days after responsive pleading is served, or if his pleading did not require responsive pleading and action has not been placed on trial calendar, he may amend it within 14 days after it is served on opposing party. Otherwise, pleading may be amended only by leave of court or by written consent of adverse party. (Rule 2.118[A]). Upon motion and just terms, court may permit supplemental pleading setting forth transactions or events since date of pleading sought to be supplemented. (Rule 2.118[E]). Amendments to conform to evidence may be made upon motion during or after trial, but when evidence is objected to at trial on ground not within issues made by pleadings, amendment is not allowed unless court is satisfied admission of evidence will not prejudice objecting party, and continuance may be granted. (Rule 2.118[C]).

Affidavits of Merit and Defense.—Either party may file affidavits in support of claim or defense in connection with motion for summary disposition, which replaces former motion to dismiss and motion for summary judgment. If it appears from affidavits and other submissions that judgment as matter of law is appropriate, court will enter judgment for moving party or may, in proper circumstances, enter judgment for opposing party. Court may order immediate trial of disputed questions of fact. (Rule 2.116[B]-[J]).

Bills of Particulars.—No requirement for bill of particulars as such. Any party may move for more definite statement before filing responsive pleading, pointing out defects complained of and details desired. (Rule 2.115[A]).

Verification.—Except when specifically provided by rule, pleadings need not be verified. (Rule 2.114[A], [B]). None of the ordinary pleadings such as complaint, answer, etc. requires verification.

Service.—Except for original service of complaint and summons, pleadings are served on party represented by attorney by service on the attorney, which may be by mail to his last known business address or by delivery to him personally or by leaving

PLEADING . . . *continued*

copy at his office with his clerk or some person in charge, or if no one is in charge or present, in some conspicuous place therein. If office is closed or attorney has no office, copy may be left at his usual place of abode with some person of suitable age and discretion residing therein. When party prosecutes or defends in person, service on him is by delivery of copy to him or by mailing copy to him at his address as stated in his pleadings. (Rule 2.107[B], [C]).

Filing.—Pleadings are filed with clerk of court except that judge may permit filing with him. (Rule 2.107[G]).

Time.—Answer must be served and filed within 21 days after personal service of summons and complaint in this state, within 28 days after service when summons and complaint are personally served outside this state or are required to be sent by registered mail addressed to defendant. When service is made by publication, court allows reasonable time for answer or other action, but not less than 28 days after publication is completed. Answer to cross-claim or counterclaim served on party or his attorney, and reply to a pleading requiring or permitting reply and so served, must be filed and served within 21 days after service. (Rule 2.108[A]).

Motion which raises defense or objection to a pleading must be filed within time for responsive pleading, or if no responsive pleading is required, within 21 days after service of pleading to which it is directed. (Rule 2.108[B]). Except for motions which may be heard ex parte, motion and notice of hearing together with any affidavits must be served on adverse party not later than nine, if mailed, or seven, if delivered, to party or attorney, days before time specified for hearing. Any response must be served at least five, if mailed, or three, if delivered to attorney or party, days before hearing. (Rule 2.119[C]).

In computing time periods, day of act, event or default after which designated period begins to run is excluded and last day of period is included unless it is Saturday, Sunday or legal holiday, in which event period runs until end of next day which is not Saturday, Sunday or holiday. (Rules 1.108; 2.108[E]).

Proof of Claims.—In action on open account or account stated, if plaintiff or someone in his behalf makes an affidavit of amount due over and above all legal counterclaims and attaches a copy of the account, and serves copy of affidavit and account on defendant with copy of complaint or with process by which action is commenced, such affidavit is prima facie evidence of the indebtedness unless defendant files affidavit denying same. Similar procedure is available to a counterclaiming defendant. Affidavit is deemed sufficient if made within ten days next preceding issuance of writ or filing of complaint or answer. (MCLA §600.2145; MSA §27A.2145). No special form of affidavit is preferred by local usage.

Frivolous claims are governed by MCLA §600.2591; MSA §27A.2591; Rules 2.114(E), (F), 2.625(A). If court determines civil action or defense frivolous, court will award prevailing party costs and fees incurred with such action, including court costs and reasonable attorney fees, and such costs and fees will be assessed against non-prevailing party and attorney.

Small Claims.—See category Courts and Legislature, topic Courts.

PRACTICE:

Practice is regulated by Revised Judicature Act of 1961 (MCLA §600.101 et seq.; MSA §27A.101 et seq.), effective Jan. 1, 1963 (cited herein "RJA"), and the Rules.

Discovery.—Party may obtain discovery of any matter not privileged which is admissible under rules of evidence governing trials and relevant to subject matter involved in action, including existence, description, nature, custody and location of any books, documents, or other tangible things and identity and location of persons having knowledge of discoverable matter. (Rule 2.302). After commencement of action, any party may take testimony of any person, including party, by deposition upon oral examination or written questions for purpose of discovery or for use as evidence or for both purposes. (Rule 2.306[A]). Party may also take discovery by written interrogatories on another party (Rule 2.309) or by request for production of documents for inspection and copying or photographing to another party or third parties (Rule 2.310).

Demand for Admission of Facts.—After commencement of action any party may serve on any other party written demand for admission of genuineness of any relevant document or of truth of any relevant matters of fact or application of law to fact. If admission is refused and genuineness of document or truth of matter of fact is thereafter proved, party so refusing may be required to pay reasonable expenses and attorney fees of other party in making such proof, unless court finds there were good reasons for refusal or that admissions sought were of no substantial importance. (Rules 2.312[A]-[C], 2.313[C]).

Direct Actions Against Insurer.—See category Transportation, topic Motor Vehicles, subhead Direct Actions.

Small Claims.—See category Courts and Legislature, topic Courts.

See also topics Actions, Appeal and Error, Depositions and Discovery, Injunctions, Judgments, Pleading, Process; category Debtor and Creditor, topics Attachment, Executions, Garnishment.

PROCESS:

Fee for commencement of action or filing application for extraordinary writ, except writ of habeas corpus, is $80 until Oct. 1, 1996; $90 until Oct. 1, 1997 and $100 thereafter. (MCLA §600.2529; MSA §27A.2529).

All civil actions are commenced by filing a complaint. (MCLA §600.1901; MSA §27A.1901). Upon complaint being filed clerk issues summons. (MCLA §600.1905; MSA §27A.1905).

General Requisites.—Summons must be accompanied by copy of complaint and must be under seal of court, contain name of court, names of parties, name of court clerk, be directed to defendant or defendants and state name and address of plaintiff's attorney, if any, otherwise plaintiff's address. (MCLA §600.1905; MSA §27A.1905). Summons must state time within which defendant must answer or take such other

action as may be permitted by law and shall notify defendant failure to do so will result in judgment against him. With personal service made within state defendant has 21 days, or if service is made outside state or when summons and complaint are required by rules to be sent to defendant by registered mail, 28 days, within which to answer complaint or take such other action as is permitted by law. (Rule 2.108). If service is made by publication court shall allow reasonable time, but not less than 28 days after publication is completed, within which to answer. (Rule 2.108). Form of summons is specified in Rule 105.

By Whom Issued.—Process is issued by clerk of court. (MCLA §600.1905; MSA §27A.1905).

Who May Serve.—Process in civil actions may be served by any person of suitable age and discretion who is not a party nor an officer of a corporate party unless process is to be personally served upon a person in a governmental institution, hospital or home, in which case process shall be served by person in charge of such institution or by member of his staff. (MCLA §600.1908; MSA §27A.1908).

Personal Service on Individual.—Effective by leaving summons and a copy of complaint with defendant personally (MCLA §600.1912; MSA §27A.1912) or upon his agent authorized by written appointment (MCLA §600.1930; MSA §27A.1930), or upon a nonresident individual by service of summons and a copy of the complaint upon such agent, employee, representative, salesman or servant of defendant as is found within state, and by sending a summons and a copy of the complaint to defendant at his last known address by registered mail (MCLA §600.1913[1][a]; MSA §27A.1913[1][a]; Rule 2.105[A]).

Personal Service on Infant.—Process may be served on infant as if of age, or by leaving summons and a copy of complaint with person having care and control of him with whom he resides, or with his legal guardian. (MCLA §600.1913[1][b]; MSA §27A.1913[1][b]; Rule 2.105[B][2]).

Personal Service on Incompetent Person.—Process may be served on incompetent person as if competent or if person has been judicially declared incompetent and a guardian has been appointed, by leaving summons and a copy of complaint with guardian. (MCLA §600.1913[1][c]; MSA §27A.1913[1][c]). If incompetent is inmate of governmental institution, hospital or home, process must be served by person in charge of such institution or by some member of his staff (MCLA §600.1908[2]; MSA §27A.1908[2]) and copy of complaint must be mailed to attorney general (MCLA §600.1913[2]; MSA §27A.1913[2]; Rule 2.105[B][3]).

Personal Service on Partnership.—Process is served on partnership or limited partnership by leaving summons and copy of complaint with any general partner or by leaving summons and copy of complaint with a person in charge of partnership office or place of business and sending a summons and copy of complaint by registered mail to any general partner's usual place of abode or last known address. (MCLA §600.1917; MSA §27A.1917; Rule 2.105[C]).

Personal Service on Association.—Process is served on partnership association (joint stock company) or unincorporated voluntary association by leaving summons and copy of complaint with any officer, director, trustee, agent or person in charge of an office or business establishment, and sending a summons and copy of complaint by registered mail to any office of the partnership association or unincorporated voluntary association, or if none, to a member of such association other than person with whom summons and complaint was left. (MCLA §600.1923; MSA §27A.1923; Rule 2.105[E]).

Personal Service on Domestic and Foreign Corporations.—Service of process upon a corporation, whether domestic or foreign, may be made by leaving summons and copy of complaint with any officer or, except with a defendant insurance company, the resident agent, or by leaving summons and copy of complaint with any director, trustee or person in charge of any office or business establishment and sending a summons and copy of complaint by registered mail to principal office of corporation. (MCLA §600.1920[1] and [2]; MSA §27A.1920[1] and [2]). If corporation has ceased to do business by inaction or by expiration of its corporate term, service may be made by leaving summons and copy of complaint with any of the persons who have been the last presiding officer, president, cashier, secretary, or treasurer of such corporation. (MCLA §600.1920[3]; MSA §27A.1920[3]). If corporation has failed to appoint and maintain a resident agent or if corporation has ceased to do business by inaction or by expiration of its corporate term, service may be made by mailing summons and copy of complaint by registered mail to the corporation or an officer and to Michigan Corporation and Securities Commission. (MCLA §600.1920[4]; MSA §27A.1920[4]). In case where a defendant is a foreign insurance company, two summonses and a copy of the complaint must be delivered or sent by registered mail to office of Commissioner of Insurance. (MCLA §600.1920; MSA §27A.1920; Rule 2.105[D]).

Personal Service on Individual Doing Business Under Assumed Name.—Effective by serving such individual (MCLA §600.1918; MSA §27A.1918) or by leaving summons and copy of complaint with person in charge of office or business establishment of such individual and sending a summons and copy of complaint by registered mail addressed to such individual at his usual place of abode or last known address. (Rule 2.105[B][4]).

Personal Service Outside of State.—There is no territorial limitation on range of process and persons who are subject to jurisdiction of Michigan, by reason of prescribed contacts, ties or relations, may be served anywhere. (Rule 2.105[J]). Thus any person who has consented to jurisdiction, any individual domiciled in Michigan, any corporation incorporated under Michigan law or carrying on a continuous and systematic part of its general business within Michigan, and any partnership, limited partnership, partnership association or unincorporated voluntary association formed under Michigan law or carrying on a continuous and systematic part of its general business within Michigan, has submitted to general jurisdiction of Michigan courts and personal service upon any such party outside Michigan has same force and effect as service in Michigan. (MCLA §§600.701, .711, .721 and .731; MSA §§27A.701, .711, .721 and 731). Any nonresident individual, corporation, partnership, limited partnership, partnership association, unincorporated voluntary association or the agent of any of the

PROCESS . . . *continued*

foregoing who: (1) Transacts any business in Michigan, (2) does any act, or causes any act to be done, or consequence to occur, in Michigan resulting in a tort, (3) owns, uses or possesses any real or tangible personal property situated in Michigan, (4) contracts to insure any person, property or risk located in Michigan at time of contracting, (5) enters into a contract for services to be rendered or materials to be furnished in Michigan, or (6) with respect to a nonresident individual, acts as director, manager, trustee or other officer of any domestic corporation or any foreign corporation having its principal place of business in Michigan, consents to the limited jurisdiction of Michigan courts with respect to actions arising out of any such relationships and personal service outside Michigan has same force and effect with respect to such actions as service in Michigan. (MCLA §§600.705, .715, .725, .735; MSA §§27A.705, .715, .725, .735).

Service by mail, standing alone, will not give court jurisdiction over an absent defendant, but as indicated above and below there are several situations where service by registered mail is necessary, in conjunction with personal service on a specified representative of defendant or service by publication, to confer personal jurisdiction of the court over defendant. Nonresident filing assumed name certificate with county clerk must also file consent to service of process on county clerk; plaintiff serves county clerk and notifies defendant by certified mail. (MCLA §445.3; MSA §19.825).

Substituted Service.—See various subheads supra relating to personal service.

Service by Publication.—In all civil actions in which personal jurisdiction is not required, court may order defendant to answer or take such other action permitted by law upon the filing by plaintiff, his attorney, or an agent having knowledge of the facts, of an affidavit, dated within ten days from entry of order, showing (1) Defendant resides outside state, or (2) whereabouts of defendant and his residence are unknown, or (3) summons has been returned showing service cannot be made in county where action is pending. Every affidavit must state defendant's address, or last known address, or that no address is known. Where present address or name of a defendant is not known, affidavit must set forth facts showing diligent inquiry. Order shall contain name of court, names of parties, directions as to when and where to answer or take other action permitted by law, statement of nature of proceeding and statement of effect of failure to take indicated steps. If order is not served upon defendant personally or by registered mail, return receipt, at least 20 days before time prescribed for answer, order must be published in a newspaper at least once each week for four consecutive weeks, or such further time as court shall direct, and a copy of the order must be sent by registered mail to defendant at his last known address, if known to plaintiff, on or before date of second publication. (MCLA §§600.1940, .1945, .1947, .1950 and .1951; MSA §§27A.1940, .1945, .1947, .1950 and .1951; Rule 2.106).

Long Arm Statute.—See subhead Personal Service Outside of State, supra.

Service on Unknown Defendants.—See subhead Service by Publication, supra.

Nonresident Motorist.—See category Transportation, topic Motor Vehicles.

Attachment.—A writ of attachment may only issue after filing of complaint. (Rule 3.103[A]). If return of writ of attachment shows that property has been attached but no defendant personally served, plaintiff must obtain order of court for defendant to appear and answer and publish order for four consecutive weeks and send copy of order to defendant, registered mail, at his last known address if known to plaintiff. Such notice does not give personal jurisdiction over defendant. (Rule 3.103[E]).

Garnishment.—After filing complaint in contract action or after any judgment, writ of garnishment may issue and may be served by any person not a party to the action or an officer of a corporate party. In case of garnishment prior to judgment, summons, copy of complaint and writ of garnishment must also be served upon principal defendant, either personally, by publication as outlined in subhead Service by Publication above, or upon his attorney. In all cases duty is imposed upon garnishee to notify principal defendant of garnishment. Garnishee has 15 days after service of writ to file disclosure touching upon his liability, if any, to principal defendant. (Rules 3.101, 3.102).

Proof of service may be made by (1) Written acknowledgment of the summons, (2) certificate of sheriff, deputy sheriff, medical examiner, bailiff, constable or deputy of such officers if such officer held office in county where issued, or (3) affidavit of person making service other than officers described above. (MCLA §600.1910; MSA §27A.1910).

Inferior Courts.—Process of circuit court commissioners and of justice, municipal, district and common pleas courts is extensively regulated by statute and rules adopted by such courts.

Uniform Interstate and International Procedure Act in effect. (MCLA §§600.1852, 600.2114a, 600.2118a; MSA §§27A.1852, 27A.2114[1], 27A.2118[1]).

REPLEVIN:

Civil action may be brought to recover any goods or chattels unlawfully taken or detained and to recover damages. (MCLA §600.2920; MSA §27A.2920).

Proceedings.—Plaintiff or someone on his behalf files claim and delivery complaint containing description of property claimed, its estimated value, whether it is part of divisible property, nature of claim and basis for judgment requested. Estimate of value serves to fix amount of bond and cannot be used as evidence or admission of value. (Rule 3.105[C]). Plaintiff may move for possession pending judgment. If granted, court may order sheriff to seize property. Plaintiff is required to furnish penalty bond of not less than $100 and at least double value of property as stated in plaintiff's complaint. Upon court order, sheriff seizes property, keeps it in secure place for five days, and then, upon receipt of his fees and expenses, delivers property to plaintiff. (Rule 3.105[E]-[G]).

Repossession.—Court may condition defendant's continued possession on penalty bond payable to plaintiff of not less than $100 and at least double value of property as stated in plaintiff's complaint. (Rule 3.105[E]).

Claims of Third Persons.—No specific provision in pertinent statute (MCLA §600.2920; MSA §27A.2920) or Rule 3.105 governing claim and delivery. See topic Actions, subhead Intervention.

Judgment or Order.—Court orders property delivered to person entitled to possession, and also awards damages sustained by the unlawful taking or detention. (MCLA §600.2920; MSA §27A.2920; Rule 3.105).

SEQUESTRATION:

When execution against domestic corporation is returned unsatisfied in whole or in part, judgment creditor or his representative may petition circuit court for appointment of a receiver and for sequestration of stock, property and things in action and effects of such corporation. (MCLA §600.3610; MSA §27A.3610).

In case of judgment against absent, concealed or nonresident defendant, performance of judgment may be compelled by sequestration of real and personal estate of defendant or of specific estate or effects demanded by complaint. Upon plaintiff's giving security, in sum directed by court, court may deliver specific estate or effects to plaintiff or may satisfy judgment out of estate or effects sequestered. (MCLA §600.6092; MSA §27A.6092).

Property constituting proceeds or instrumentality of crime may be seized and subjected to forfeiture. Seized property of crime victim shall be promptly returned. Information in seized computer or computer information storage device shall be copied immediately and provided to Court. (MCLA §§600.4702-.4703a; MSA §§27A.4702-.4703a).

See also category Debtor and Creditor, topics Attachment, Executions, Garnishment, Receivers.

SERVICE:

See topic Process.

STAY OF EXECUTION:

See topic Appeal and Error; category Debtor and Creditor, topic Executions.

SUBMISSION OF CONTROVERSY:

No statutory provisions.

VENUE:

Venue is not jurisdictional. (MCLA §§600.1601, .1651; MSA §§27A.1601, .1651). General rule, subject to numerous exceptions, is that action may be brought in county where any defendant resides, has place of business, conducts business or in which registered office of any defendant corporation is located or, if no defendant meets any such criteria, in county where any plaintiff resides, has place of business or in which registered office of any plaintiff corporation is located. (MCLA §600.1621; MSA §27A.1621). Actions, other than contract actions, real actions, actions for recovery of tangible personal property, actions against governmental units, and actions on probate bonds, may also be brought in county where cause of action or any part thereof arose. (MCLA §600.1627; MSA §27A.1627).

Real Action.—Actions (1) To recover real property, or an estate or interest therein, or for the determination in any form of right or interest therein, (2) to partition real property, and (3) to foreclose lien or mortgage on real property may be brought in county where subject of such action, or any part thereof, is situated. (MCLA §600.1605; MSA §27A.1605).

Action for Recovery of Tangible Personal Property.—County in which subject of action or any part thereof is situated is proper. (MCLA §600.1605; MSA §27A.1605).

Against Transportation Line.—Action must be brought where cause of action arose or in county of plaintiff's residence, if line or route traverses either county where cause of action arose or county of plaintiff's residence. Otherwise action may be brought in any county in which defendant has its principal place of business or owns, operates or leases a line or route. (MCLA §600.1635; MSA §27A.1635).

Against Governmental Units.—Any county where governmental unit exercises or may exercise its governmental authority is proper county to bring suit unless cause of action arose in county of its principal office, in which case suit must be brought in such county. (MCLA §600.1615; MSA §27A.1615).

Tort Action.—Action must be brought in county where cause of action arose and where any defendant resides, has place of business, conducts business or where registered office of any defendant corporation is located or, if no county meets such criteria, in county where cause of action arose and where any plaintiff resides, has place of business, conducts business or where registered office of any corporate plaintiff is located or, if no county meets such criteria, in county determined to be proper according to general venue rule. For product liability actions, corporation conducts business where its products are sold at retail. (MCLA §600.1629; MSA §27A.1629).

Probate of foreign will may take place in any county where testator left property affected by the will. (MCLA §600.2936; MSA §27A.2936).

On Bond Filed in Probate Court.—Action may be commenced in county where bond is filed. (MCLA §600.1611; MSA §27A.1611).

Attachment.—County where some of the property is situated is proper county of venue. (MCLA §600.4021; MSA §27A.4021).

Garnishment.—County which would be proper county of venue as designated in MCLA §600.1601 et seq.; MSA §27A.1601 et seq. (being the chapter covered by this topic) against garnishee defendant is proper county of venue if: (1) County is designated in MCLA §600.1601 et seq.; MSA §27A.1601 et seq. as proper county of venue for principal defendant, or (2) there is no common proper county of venue against principal and garnishee defendant, or (3) personal jurisdiction cannot be obtained over principal defendant. (MCLA §600.4025; MSA §27A.4025).

See note at head of Digest as to 1998 legislation covered.

See Topical Index in front part of this volume.

VENUE ... *continued*

Changes.—If action is brought in county of improper venue, case may be tried therein, unless defendant moves for change of venue before or at time defendant files answer, when case will be transferred to county of proper venue. Defendant may also move for change of venue after answer if court is satisfied that facts to support motion were not and could not be known to defendant until 14 days prior to motion. Each circuit court upon good cause shown may change the venue in any civil cause pending therein. (Rule 2.221). Motion for change of venue based on hardship or inconvenience may be granted. (Rule 2.222; MCLA §600.1629[2]; MSA §27A.1629[2]).

COURTS AND LEGISLATURE

COURTS:

United States District Courts.—
Eastern District.—Clerk's office: Detroit 48226.
Fee for filing complaint, $150.
Northern Division is composed of following counties: Alcona, Alpena, Arenac, Bay, Cheboygan, Clare, Crawford, Gladwin, Gratiot, Huron, Iosco, Isabella, Midland, Montmorency, Ogemaw, Oscoda, Otsego, Presque Isle, Roscommon, Saginaw and Tuscola.
Court sits at Bay City.
Southern Division is composed of following counties: Genesee, Jackson, Lapeer, Lenawee, Livingston, Macomb, Monroe, Oakland, St. Clair, Sanilac, Shiawassee, Washtenaw and Wayne.
Court sits at Ann Arbor, Detroit, Flint, Port Huron.
Western District.—Clerk's office: Grand Rapids 49502.
Fee for filing complaint, $150.
Northern Division is composed of following counties: Alger, Baraga, Chippewa, Delta, Dickinson, Gogebic, Houghton, Iron, Keweenaw, Luce, Mackinac, Marquette, Menominee, Ontonagon and Schoolcraft.
Court sits at Marquette, Sault Ste. Marie.
Southern Division is composed of following counties: Allegan, Antrim, Barry, Benzie, Berrien, Branch, Calhoun, Cass, Charlevoix, Clinton, Eaton, Emmet, Grand Traverse, Hillsdale, Ingham, Ionia, Kalamazoo, Kalkaska, Kent, Lake, Leelanau, Manistee, Mason, Mecosta, Missaukee, Montcalm, Muskegon, Newaygo, Oceana, Osceola, Ottawa, St. Joseph, Van Buren and Wexford.
Court sits at Grand Rapids, Kalamazoo, Lansing.

Michigan State Supreme Court.—Court sits at Lansing. Jurisdiction includes: (1) review of Judicial Tenure Commission orders (Rule 9.223-.226); (2) review by appeal of case pending in Court of Appeals or after decision by Court of Appeals (Rule 7.302); (3) review by appeal of final order of Attorney Discipline Board (Rule 9.122); (4) rendering of advisory opinion authorized by Const. art. 3, §8; (5) response to certified question (Rule 7.305); (6) superintending control over lower court or tribunal (Rule 7.304); and (7) other jurisdiction as provided by constitution or law (Rule 7.301).

Michigan State Court of Appeals.—Court of appeals has jurisdiction over appeals from all final judgments of circuit courts, court of claims and recorder's court, orders of probate court from which appeal of right may be taken and on leave to appeal granted by court as to final judgments from all lower courts. (MCLA §600.308; MSA §27A.308).
Court sits in divisions of three judges each except as otherwise directed by Supreme Court. Divisions sit in Detroit, Lansing, and Grand Rapids.

Circuit Courts.—Circuit courts for respective counties (83) have original jurisdiction in all cases of equitable nature and cases in law involving over $25,000 (MCLA §600.8301; MSA §27A.8301), appellate jurisdiction over district courts, probate courts (except as to final orders dealing with trusts, estates, adoption proceedings and condemnation cases, which are appealable as of right to Court of Appeals, MCLA §600.861; MSA §27A.861), certain state agencies, and general criminal jurisdiction for matters other than misdemeanors and ordinance and charter violations (MCLA §§600.601-631; MSA §§27A.601-.631).

Court of Claims.—Court of Claims has exclusive jurisdiction of all claims and demands, liquidated and unliquidated, ex contractu and ex delicto, against state and any of its departments, commissions, boards, institutions, arms or agencies, except where jurisdiction is conferred by statute on circuit court. Court will not entertain claims on which there is adequate remedy in federal court. Trial and appellate practice follows circuit court rules. Court holds not less than four sessions a year in Lansing. Judges of Thirtieth Circuit sit as judges of court of claims. (MCLA §§600.6401-.6475; MSA §§27A.6401-.6475). It is court of record. (MCLA §600.1416; MSA §27A.1416). No claim may be maintained against state unless written notice of intent filed within six months if claim is for property damage or personal injuries, and otherwise within one year. (MCLA §600.6431; MSA §27A.6431).

Probate Courts.—There are one or more judges of probate in each county or district, having exclusive jurisdiction of all matters relating to estates of deceased persons, trust administration and appointment of guardians or conservators for minors and incompetent adults. It has concurrent jurisdiction of matters ancillary to settlement of estate of decedent, ward or trust. (MCLA §§600.801-.899, 700.21-.22; MSA §§27.801-.899, 27.5021-.5022). It is court of record. (MCLA §600.801; MSA §27A.801).

Justice Courts.—Justice Courts are abolished as of Jan. 1, 1969. (MCLA §§600.8101-.9928; MSA §§27A.8101-.9928).

District Courts.—In each district in state except those cities which elect to retain their present municipal courts, District Courts have exclusive jurisdiction in civil actions where amount involved is not more than $25,000 (MCLA §600.8301; MSA §27A.8301) jurisdiction of all misdemeanors punishable by fine or imprisonment not exceeding one year, or both, and ordinance and charter violations, and jurisdiction over preliminary examinations in all felony cases, including fixing of bail and accepting bond (MCLA §600.8311; MSA §27A.8311). District court has no jurisdiction in suits for injunctions, divorce, or other actions historically equitable in nature except as otherwise provided by law. (MCLA §600.8315; MSA §27A.8315). Appeals shall be to circuit court for county in which judgment is rendered. Appeals from final judgments are as of right, and other appeals are by application. Appeals to Court of Appeals from judgments of circuit court on appeal from district court are by application. (MCLA §600.8342; MSA §27A.8342). Small claims division is established in each district as a division of district court. District court judges sit as judges of small claims division. Jurisdiction of small claims division is confined to cases for recovery of money, not exceeding $1,750. (MCLA §600.8401; MSA §27A.8401). Hearings are conducted in informal manner as to do substantial justice between parties. Attorneys may not participate in filing, prosecution, or defense except in their own behalf. Nor may any collection agency or employee thereof or any other person beside plaintiff and defendant so take part in litigation. Corporations may appear by full time employee who is not attorney at law. Either plaintiff or defendant may demand that cause be removed to district court. Acceptance of trial in small claims division is deemed waiver of right to counsel, right to trial by jury, and any right of appeal. Actions for libel, fraud, intentional torts and slander may not be instituted in small claims division nor shall state or any political subdivision of state or any governmental agency be party to any such action. Prevailing party is entitled to his costs. District court magistrate may arraign and sentence upon pleas of guilty or nolo contendere and issue warrants and fix bail in certain instances. (MCLA §600.8511; MSA §27A.8511).

Small Claims Courts.—See subhead District Courts, supra.

LEGISLATURE:

Regular sessions are convened on second Wed. in Jan. of each year at 12 noon. (Const., Art. IV, §13).

Special or Extraordinary Sessions.—Governor may convene legislature on extraordinary occasions. (Const., Art. V, §15).

Initiative and Referendum are both provided for. (Const., Art. II, §9).

Lobbyists.—MCLA §§4.411-.431; MSA §§4.1704(1)-(21).

REPORTS:

Official reports of Michigan Supreme Court are: Harrington's Chancery, 1 vol., Walker's Chancery, 1 vol., Douglass, 2 vols., and Michigan Reports from vol. 1 to date. Michigan decisions are also reported in Northwestern Reporter. Official report of Michigan Court of Appeals is Michigan Appeals Reports from Vol. 1 to date.

Digests are: Michigan Digest (Callaghan & Co., 1941), Michigan Civil Jurisprudence (Callaghan & Co., 1957), Michigan Criminal Law and Procedure (Callaghan & Co., 1953), Michigan Digest (West Publishing Co., 1932), Michigan Digest 2d (West Publishing Co., 1990) and Michigan Law and Practice (West Publishing Co., 1959), all kept current with pocket parts.

STATUTES:

Michigan Legislative Council prepares official compilations. (MCLA §8.41; MSA §2.243[1]). Latest is Michigan Compiled Laws of 1979. Public acts and joint resolutions are published and acts are assigned compilation numbers after each session of legislature. (MCLA §§8.21-.23; MSA §§2.221-.223). Callaghan publishes Michigan Statutes Annotated, and West publishes Michigan Compiled Laws Annotated, both of which are frequently brought up to date by pocket parts; neither has official status, but both are frequently cited by courts.

Uniform Acts recommended by National Conference of Commissioners on Uniform State Laws (NCCUSL) which have been adopted are: Aircraft Financial Responsibility (1955); Anatomical Gift (1968 Act) (1969); Arbitration (1961); Attendance of Witnesses From Without a State In Criminal Proceedings, Act to Secure (1970); Child Custody Jurisdiction (1975); Code of Military Justice (1980); †Commercial Code (1962); †Common Trust Fund (1941); Controlled Substances (1971); Criminal Extradition (1937); Determination of Death (1992); Disposition of Community Property Rights at Death (1975); Division of Income for Tax Purposes (1969); †Durable Power of Attorney (1978); Estate Tax Apportionment (1958 Act) (1963); Evidence, Rules of (1978); Federal Lien Registration (1983); Foreign Money Judgments Recognition (1967); Fraudulent Conveyance (1919); Gifts to Minors (1956 Act) (1959); Guardianship and Protective Proceedings (1978); Interstate and International Procedure (1967); Interstate Arbitration of Death Taxes (1956); Interstate Compromise of Death Taxes (1956); Interstate Family Support (1992 Act); Limited Partnership (1976 Act) (1982); Management of Institutional Funds (1976); Military Justice, Code of (1980); Nonprobate Transfers on Death (1996); Partnership (1914 Act) (1917); Photographic Copies of Business and Public Records as Evidence (1961); Principal and Income (1962 Act) (1966); Probate Code (1969 Act) (1978); Reciprocal Enforcement of Support (1968 Act) (1968); Reciprocal Transfer Tax (1929); Recognition of Acknowledgments (1969); Rendition of Accused Persons (1968); Rendition of Prisoners As Witnesses in Criminal Proceedings (1967); †Securities (1956 Act) (1964); Simplification of Fiduciary Security Transfers (1959); Simultaneous Death (1940 Act) (1941); State Administrative Procedure (1952); State Antitrust (1984); Statutory Rule Against Perpetuities (1988); Supervision of Trustees for Charitable Purposes (1961); Testamentary Additions to Trust (1960 Act) (1962); TOD Security Registration (1996); Transboundary Pollution Reciprocal Access (1988); Trustees' Powers (1978); Unclaimed Property (1995); Vendor and Purchaser Risk (1941).
For text of NCCUSL Uniform Acts falling within the scope of the Martindale-Hubbell Law Digests see Uniform and Model Acts section.
† Adopted with significant variations or modifications. See appropriate topics as to Acts within scope of Digests volume.

Uniform Acts not recommended by NCCUSL which have been adopted are: Uniform Act on Fresh Pursuit (1937); Uniform Budgetary and Accounting Act (1968); Uniform Condemnation Procedures Act (1980).

See note at head of Digest as to 1998 legislation covered.

See Topical Index in front part of this volume.

UNIFORM LAWS:

For list of Uniform Acts in force in this state see topic Statutes. For text of Uniform Acts within the scope of the Martindale-Hubbell Law Digests see Uniform and Model Acts section.

CRIMINAL LAW

BAIL:

See topic Criminal Law.

CRIMINAL LAW:

Criminal offenses are governed generally by MCLA §§750.1 et seq.; MSA §§28.191 et seq. Criminal procedures are governed generally by MCLA §§760.1 et seq.; MSA §§28.841 et seq. Michigan criminal proceedings also operate under Michigan Rules of Evidence of 1978, including amendments, and Michigan Court Rules of 1985, including amendments.

Indictment or Information.—Accused usually is brought to trial on information filed by prosecuting attorney, but may be brought to trial on indictment by grand jury. (MCLA §§767.1 et seq.; MSA §§28.941 et seq.).

Bail is allowed to all persons except following when proof of violation is evident or presumption is great: person has been convicted within 15 years of two or more violent felonies, person is charged with violent felony committed while on bail, person is charged with treason or murder or person is charged with criminal sexual conduct in first degree, armed robbery or kidnapping with intent to extort money or other value unless court finds clear and convincing evidence that that person is not likely to flee. (Const. Art. 1, §15; MCLA §765.1 et seq.; MSA §§28.888 et seq.). Standards for determining amount of bail are found at MCLA §765.6; MSA §28.893.

Uniform Controlled Substances Act is in effect. (MCLA §§333.7101-.7545; MSA §§14.15[7101-7545]).

Uniform Act to Secure Attendance of Witnesses from Without a State in Criminal Proceedings Act is in effect. (MCLA §§767.91-.95; MSA §§28.1023 [191-95]).

Uniform Criminal Extradition Act is in effect. (MCLA §§780.1-.31; MSA §§28.1285[1-31]).

Uniform Rendition of Accused Persons Act is in effect. (MCLA §§780.41-.45; MSA §§28.1287[51-55]).

Uniform Act on Fresh Pursuit is in effect. (MCLA §§780.101-.108; MSA §§28.1286[1-8]).

Uniform Rendition of Prisoners as Witnesses in Criminal Proceedings Act is in effect. (MCLA §§780.111-.120; MSA §§28.1287[1-10]).

Revised Uniform Reciprocal Enforcement of Support Act is in effect. (MCLA §§780.151-.183; MSA §§25.225[1-24]).

DEBTOR AND CREDITOR

ASSIGNMENTS:

Uniform Commercial Code adopted. (MCLA §§440.1101 et seq.; MSA §§19.1101 et seq.). See category Business Regulation and Commerce, topic Commercial Code. In general choses in action including certain tort claims (36 Mich. 318) (but not claims for fraud [190 Mich. 478, 157 N.W. 282], but see 365 Mich. 552, 114 N.W. 2d 154 [1962] [concurring opinion]) are assignable. Also assignable are contingent rights under existing contract (222 Mich. 664, 193 N.W. 235), and future rents of real property owned by assignor (133 Mich. 617, 95 N.W. 710; for limitations in connection with mortgages, see category Mortgages, topic Mortgages of Real Property, subhead Rents and Profits). Claims for worker's disability compensation (MCLA §418.821; MSA §17.237[821]), unemployment compensation (MCLA §421.30; MSA §17.532), old age and dependent children benefits (MCLA §400.63; MSA §16.463) and alimony (146 Mich. 298, 109 N.W. 425) are not assignable. Mere possibility of future rights, not coupled with interest or contract, is not assignable (57 Mich. 97, 23 N.W. 600), nor is expected interest in living ancestor's estate without consent of ancestor (181 Mich. 438, 148 N.W. 225). Neither income nor principal of spendthrift trust is assignable. (425 Mich. 364, 389 N.W. 2d 696).

Instrument Transferring Title.—Uniform Commercial Code adopted. (MCLA §§440.1101 et seq.; MSA §§19.1101 et seq.). See category Business Regulation and Commerce, topic Commercial Code. In transactions not governed by U.C.C., instrument transferring title must be in writing (MCLA §§566.132, .222; MSA §§26.922, .972) but need not be witnessed or acknowledged.

Filing.—Uniform Commercial Code adopted. (MCLA §§440.1101 et seq.; MSA §§19.1101 et seq.). See category Business Regulation and Commerce, topic Commercial Code. Assignments in transactions not governed by U.C.C., need not be filed or recorded.

Recording.—See subhead Filing, supra.

Notice.—Uniform Commercial Code adopted. (MCLA §§440.1101 et seq.; MSA §§19.1101 et seq.). See category Business Regulation and Commerce, topic Commercial Code. In transactions not governed by U.C.C., notice to debtor is not required to make assignment binding as between assignor and assignee. (163 Mich. 408, 128 N.W. 926). A debtor with notice of assignment is liable to assignee if he makes payment to assignor. (253 Mich. 548, 235 N.W. 249).

Effect.—Uniform Commercial Code adopted. (MCLA §§440.1101 et seq.; MSA §§19.1101 et seq.). See category Business Regulation and Commerce, topic Commercial Code. In transactions not governed by U.C.C., assignee of nonnegotiable chose in action takes only rights of assignor (49 Mich. 104, 13 N.W. 377), and subject to defenses existing at time of assignment, but not to latent equities (256 Mich. 441, 240 N.W. 44).

Assignment of wages is valid (36 Mich. 436) except where: (1) given as security to person licensed to engage in business of making loans of $3,000 or less (MCLA §493.17; MSA §23.667[17]); or (2) included in retail installment contract or retail charge agreement (MCLA §445.864; MSA §19.416[114]).

ATTACHMENT:

Actions in Which Allowed.—Attachment is available in both contract and tort actions. (MCLA §600.4001; MSA §27A.4001; Rule 3.103). Small claims court is proper forum for claims up to $1,750. (MCLA §600.8401; MSA §27A.8401).

Courts Which May Issue Writ.—Circuit court (MCLA §600.4001; MSA §27A.4001; Rule 3.103), district and municipal courts (MCLA §600.8306; MSA §27A.8306).

In Whose Favor Writ May Issue.—Any person, including nonresident or foreign corporation. (Rule 3.103).

Against Whom Writ May Issue.—Circuit courts have power to issue attachments with respect to any interest in things which are subject to judicial jurisdiction of state and belonging to person against whom claim is asserted. (MCLA §600.4001; MSA §27A.4001).

Claims on Which Writ May Issue.—All claims, matured or unmatured. (MCLA §600.4001; MSA §27A.4001).

Grounds.—In action to obtain original judgment, sole ground for prejudgment attachment against property located in state is that defendant is subject to judicial jurisdiction of state but cannot be served with process after diligent effort. In action brought on foreign judgment, alternative grounds for prejudgment attachment are: (i) defendant is not subject to judicial jurisdiction of state, or (ii) defendant is subject to jurisdiction of state but cannot be served with process after diligent effort. (MCLA §600.4001; MSA §27A.4001; Rule 3.103). Attachment will not issue from small claims division prior to judgment. (MCLA §600.8409; MSA §27A.8409).

Proceedings to Obtain.—After commencing action by filing ex parte motion requesting writ, supported by affidavit showing defendant is indebted to plaintiff in stated amount in excess of all setoffs; defendant is subject to judicial jurisdiction of State; and after diligent effort plaintiff cannot serve defendant with process. In tort action affidavit must describe injury claimed and state that affiant believes in good faith that defendant is liable to plaintiff in stated amount. In action on foreign judgment affidavit must show that defendant is indebted to plaintiff on foreign judgment in stated amount in excess of all setoffs and that defendant is not subject to judicial jurisdiction of State or that after diligent effort plaintiff cannot serve defendant with process. On issuance of writ order may specify further steps, if any, which plaintiff must take to notify defendant of action and attachment. (Rule 3.103).

Attachment Bond.—Plaintiff is not required to furnish bond. (See supra, subhead Proceedings to Obtain.)

Levy.—Sheriff attaches so much of defendant's property not exempt from execution, wherever found within county, as will satisfy plaintiff's demand and costs. Where property seized within county is not sufficient, officer seizes other property anywhere within state. Realty and interests therein are seized by officer's deposit of certified copy of writ including description of realty with register of deeds for county in which realty located. Shares of stock or interest of stockholder in domestic corporation are seized in manner provided for seizure of such property on execution. (See topic Executions.) (Rule 3.103).

Indemnity.—No provision for levying officer to require indemnity.

Lien.—Attachment binds goods and chattels from time they were attached. Attachment of realty constitutes lien from time when certified copy of attachment including description of realty is deposited in office of register of deeds in county where realty is situated. (MCLA §600-.4035; MSA §27A.4035).

Priorities.—Where one or more attachments or executions are issued against same debtor or his property, attachment or execution first delivered to officer has preference, except that if there has been levy and sale of goods or chattels before a levy under first attachment or execution, levy on such goods or chattels under first attachment or execution is not permitted. (MCLA §600.6007; MSA §27A.6007).

Unrecorded land mortgage has priority over subsequent attachment levy though attaching creditor had no notice of such mortgage when attachment was commenced. (130 Mich. 127, 89 N.W. 720).

Release of Property.—Attachment may be dissolved upon posting of bond. (MCLA §600.4045; MSA §27A.4045). Except in action on foreign judgment, defendant may obtain dissolution of attachment by submitting to jurisdiction of court. Defendant, or person who owns, possesses, or has interest in attached property may move for dissolution of attachment by proving: (i) defendant was not subject to jurisdiction of state, or (ii) attached property was exempt from attachment. Court may dissolve attachment for any other sufficient reason. Attachment is dissolved if action is dismissed or judgment is entered for defendant. (Rule 3.103).

Sale.—Where attached property consists of animals or is perishable, court may order sale and proceeds are brought into court to abide court's order. (Rule 3.103).

Third Party Claims.—See subhead Vacation or Modification, infra.

Vacation or Modification.—Any person whose property is attached or who is in possession of or has an interest in property attached may apply to circuit judge or circuit court commissioner of county where writ issued for dissolution of the attachment. Plaintiff is notified and hearing is held. If attachment found invalid, it is dissolved and property is returned to defendant. Defendant may be required to submit himself to personal jurisdiction of court prior to granting of dissolution order. (Rule 3.103).

CREDITORS' SUITS:

Judgment creditor, on motion in original action or in a separate action, may compel discovery of assets, prevent transfer of assets, obtain satisfaction of judgment out of property not exempt from execution, and procure appointment of receiver. Return of

---

CREDITORS' SUITS . . . *continued*
execution unsatisfied is not necessary prerequisite. (MCLA §600.6104; MSA §27A.6104). Persons having property of judgment debtor or indebted to him may also be required to appear for examination and produce books and records. (MCLA §600.6110; MSA §27A.6110). Upon request to appear for examination, third party is and judgment debtor may be restrained from transferring debtor's property. (MCLA §§600.6116, 6119; MSA §§27A.6116, 6119). Court may order judgment debtor to make installment payments. (MCLA §600.6107; MSA §27A.6107). Judgment creditor may also obtain any other relief formerly available by creditor's bill under MCLA §§606.4, 634.1 et seq.; MSA §§27.545, 27.2171 et seq. now repealed. (Rule 2.621).

EXECUTIONS:

Execution may be issued on judgment of court of record against realty or personalty. (MCLA §600.6001; MSA §27A.6001).

Kinds of Execution.—Except as otherwise provided by law, execution may be made against all personalty of judgment debtor liable to execution at common law (MCLA §600.6017; MSA §27A.6017) and against all realty interests of judgment debtor except tenancies at will. (MCLA §600.6018; MSA 27A.6018). Execution may also be made against body of judgment debtor. (See subhead Body Execution, infra.)

Exemptions.—See topic Exemptions.

Time for Issuance.—Writs issue immediately on judgments of courts of record unless stayed. (MCLA §600.6001 et seq.; MSA §27A.6001 et seq.).

Lien.—No lien before levy. (MCLA §600.6012; MSA §27A.6012).

Levy must be made before return day of the writ and may be made on the goods and chattels of the debtor or, in court of record, on his real estate if sufficient personalty is not found. (MCLA §600.6004; MSA §27A.6004).

Levy on real estate must be an act capable of being proved and clearly identified when it is done. (25 Mich. 381). The property levied on is bound from the time of levy (MCLA §600.6012; MSA §27A.6012), but no levy on real estate is valid against subsequent bona fide purchasers until a notice of levy is recorded in office of register of deeds for county where the premises are situated. (MCLA §600.6051; MSA §27A.6051). Lien acquired by execution is, from recording of such notice, valid also against all prior grantees and mortgagees of whose claims party interested has not actual or constructive notice. (MCLA §600.6051; MSA §27A.6051). Levy on real estate ceases to be a lien after five years from time of levy if property not sold thereunder within five years. (MCLA §600.6051; MSA §27A.6051).

Levy on Personalty.—The statute does not prescribe mode of levy in courts of record, but it is held that a levy on personalty must be made by manual seizure or such assertion of control as can be made effectual, and must be so made as to identify or give means of identifying property levied on. (42 Mich. 75, 3 N.W. 262).

Levy on Corporate Stock.—The corporate officer who is appointed to keep record of stockholders is required, upon exhibition to him of the execution, to give the officer a certificate of the number of shares or amount of interest held by judgment debtor. (MCLA §600.6037; MSA §27A.6037). The officer making the levy must leave a certified copy of the execution with the clerk, treasurer, cashier, or agent of the corporation, if there be any such officer, and if not, then with any officer or person who has at the time the custody of the books and papers of the corporation within the state, but no levy on shares of stock for which a certificate is outstanding is valid until such certificate is actually seized by the officer making the levy, or its transfer by the holder be enjoined or restrained. (MCLA §600.6037; MSA §27A.6037). The court from which the execution issued has full power upon motion, without notice, to make an order restraining the transfer of any such shares of stock, and upon service of a certified copy of such order the same is fully effectual. (MCLA §600.6037; MSA §27A.6037). A certified copy of the execution and return must, within 14 days after sale, be left with the corporate officer charged with keeping records of stock transfers, and the purchaser is thereupon entitled to a certificate or certificates of the shares bought by him, upon paying necessary transfer fees. (MCLA §600.6037; MSA §27A.6037).

Return.—Execution from court of record is returnable in not less than 20 nor more than 90 days. (MCLA §600.6002; MSA §27A.6002).

Stay.—Twenty-one days stay is given ex parte in circuit court, and in its discretion court, in addition, may stay execution pending disposition of motion for relief from judgment on certain grounds specified in Rule 2.612. Thereafter stay may be obtained upon filing bond for purposes of appeal. (Rule 2.614[A]). If more than 21 days stay is desired, bond must be given in amount designated by, and with sufficient sureties approved by, trial judge. (Rule 7.209).

Priorities.—Preference must be given to execution first delivered to officer, except that goods levied on and sold before levy under first execution may not be levied on by virtue of the first execution. (MCLA §600.6007; MSA §27A.6007).

Claims of Third Persons.—No statutory provisions except as indicated in subhead Priorities, supra.

Satisfaction.—When lands sold on execution are redeemed, or when any judgment is paid where record shows a levy, officer making sale or person receiving money has duty to discharge levy or judgment from records of register of deeds. (MCLA §600.6070; MSA §27A.6070).

Sales.—In case of personal property, sale is made, after setting out exemptions, on ten days notice in case of execution from court of record. (MCLA §600.6031; MSA §27A.6031). In case of real estate, sale is made after advertising for six weeks. (MCLA §600.6052; MSA §27A.6052).

Redemption.—There is no redemption after sale of personal property.

Where real estate is sold on execution, debtor and his underclaimants have one year (MCLA §600.6062; MSA §27A.6062), and his judgment creditor, 15 months, in which to redeem, if not redeemed by the owner, his heirs, or assigns. (MCLA §600.6063; MSA §27A.6063).

Supplementary Proceedings.—Proceedings may be taken permitting examination of judgment debtor and other persons and the enjoining of any conveyance of debtor's property. A receiver may be appointed with usual powers. See topic Creditors' Suits.

Body Execution.—In court of record judgment creditor may procure debtor's arrest or imprisonment on civil process only on showing that debtor has property which he fraudulently conceals or unjustly refuses to apply to judgment, or that debtor is about to remove his property out of jurisdiction of court in which suit was brought with intent to defraud his creditor, or has disposed or is about to dispose of some or all of his property with intent to defraud his creditor, and that execution has been made and returned against all property of debtor in that county and such property is not sufficient to satisfy judgment. Warrant must issue within 30 days from return of execution. (MCLA §§600.6075-6076; MSA §§27A.6075-6076). Judgment creditor must pay prisoner's board in advance. (MCLA §600.6082; MSA §27A.6082).

EXEMPTIONS:

Following property is exempt from execution, attachment and garnishment, except in case of any lien excluded from exemption by law. (MCLA §600.4031; MSA §27A.4031, MCLA §600.6023; MSA §27A.6023, MCLA §600.7267; MSA §27A.7267).

(1) Family pictures, arms required to be kept by law, all wearing apparel, and provisions and fuel for householder and his family for six months; (2) all household goods, furniture, utensils, books and appliances, not exceeding $1,000 in value; (3) pew in church and lot or tomb in cemetery; (4) to each householder, ten sheep, two cows, five swine, 100 hens, five roosters and sufficient hay or grain to keep same for six months; (5) tools, materials, stock, apparatus, vehicle, horses or other things to enable person to carry on his principal profession, trade, occupation or business, not exceeding $1,000 in value; (6) certain disability insurance benefits, except where recovery is sought for necessities contracted for after accrual of such benefits; (7) shares held by a householder in certain mutual building and loan associations to $1,000 at par value, except where debtor has a homestead exempted under general laws of this state; (8) a homestead (see topic Homesteads); (9) equity of redemption in mortgaged premises where judgment upon which execution was issued was based on the mortgage debt; (10) homestead of family after death of owner during minority of children; (11) individual retirement account including Roth IRA. IRA exemption does not apply to amounts contributed within 120 days of filing for bankruptcy or to extent such funds are subject to order of court pursuant to judgment of divorce or separate maintenance, order of court concerning child support, or contributions to IRA in excess of amount deductible under §408 of Internal Revenue Code.

No execution may issue upon a judgment against any township, village, city or the trustees or common council or officers thereof where the action was prosecuted by or against them in their name of office, any body or board having charge or control of any state institution, any school district, or any county or its board of supervisors or any county officer in an action prosecuted by or against him in his name of office. (MCLA §600.6021; MSA §27A.6021).

Substitution.—No statutory provision.

Debts Against Which Exemptions Not Allowed.—Exemption provisions do not exempt any real estate from taxation or sale for taxes. (MCLA §600.6024; MSA §27A.6024). No specific piece of property, real or personal, is exempt from execution issued on judgment for purchase money for the same property, and any sale of such property after commencement of action for purchase price and filing by plaintiff of required notice with register of deeds is null and void against such an execution. (MCLA §600.6024; MSA §27A.6024).

Waiver of Exemption.—Personal property exemption may be waived expressly or by conduct from which waiver may be implied. (255 Mich. 595, 238 N. W. 192).

Necessity of Claiming Exemption.—Officer levying execution makes inventory of so much of debtor's property as is sufficient to cover amount of exemptions and satisfy execution and causes appraisal to be made; debtor then selects items or amount of property exempt from execution, or on his failure to do so within ten days selection is made by officer. (MCLA §600.6025; MSA §27A.6025, MCLA §600.6026; MSA §27A.6026).

Earnings.—See topic Garnishment, subhead Earnings.

Insurance.—Life insurance contract may exempt proceeds of policy from execution or liability to any creditor of insured. (MCLA §500.4054; MSA §24.14054).

Homestead Exemption.—See topic Homesteads.

FRAUDULENT SALES AND CONVEYANCES:

Uniform Commercial Code adopted. (MCLA §§440.1101-.9994; MSA §§19.1101-.9994). See category Business Regulation and Commerce, topic Commercial Code.

Uniform Fraudulent Conveyance Act has been adopted. (MCLA §566.11 et seq.; MSA §26.881 et seq.). Uniform Fraudulent Conveyance Act inapplicable to distributions governed by Michigan Business Corporations Act. (MCLA §450.1122[3]; MSA §21.200[122][3]).

Conveyance made by person who is or will be rendered insolvent is fraudulent as to creditors, without regard to intent. (MCLA §566.14; MSA §26.884).

Conveyance made without fair consideration when person is, or is about to, engage in business, for whom property remaining in his hands is unreasonably small capital, is fraudulent as to creditors, without regard to intent. (MCLA §566.15; MSA §20.885).

Conveyance made without fair consideration when person making it intends or believes that he will incur debts beyond his ability to pay is fraudulent. (MCLA §566.16; MSA §26.886).

Conveyance made with actual intent to hinder, delay, or defraud creditors is fraudulent. (MCLA §566.17; MSA §26.887).

Every conveyance or assignment, in writing or otherwise, of any valuable interest in property whatsoever, made with intent to hinder, delay or defraud the creditors of the maker thereof, or any other person, of their lawful dues, and every bond or other instrument given, or suit commenced, decree or judgment suffered with like intent as

See note at head of Digest as to 1998 legislation covered.

See Topical Index in front part of this volume.

MI – 25

FRAUDULENT SALES AND CONVEYANCES . . . *continued*
against any person defrauded is void. (MCLA §566.221; MSA §26.971). Question of fraudulent intent is one of fact. (MCLA §566.224; MSA §26.974).

All deeds of gifts, gifts, transfers or assignments verbal or written of personal property or things in action made in trust for person making same are void as against all creditors. (MCLA §566.131; MSA §26.921).

Remedies.—As against all but purchaser for value without knowledge of fraud and his assigns, creditor with matured claim may attach or levy on property conveyed, or set aside conveyance or annul any obligation incurred. (MCLA §566.19; MSA §26.889). If creditor's claim is not matured, court may restrain disposition of property, appoint receiver, set aside conveyance, annul any obligation incurred, or make any other order required by circumstances. (MCLA §566.20; MSA §26.890).

Bulk Sales.—Governed by Uniform Commercial Code. (MCLA §§440.6101-.6111; MSA §§19.6101-.6111). U.C.C. §6-102(3) specifically includes restaurant, cafe, tavern, hotel, club, school, hospital, other establishment that dispenses food, or any enterprise that manufactures what it sells. (MCLA §440.6102[3]; MSA §19.6102[3]). U.C.C. §6-106 and related subsections 6-107(2)(e), 6-108(3)(c) and 6-109(2) are omitted. MCLA §440.6106; MSA §19.6106 adds different §6-106, providing that any taxing unit having right to assess personal property tax against property which is subject of bulk transfer is deemed creditor whether or not amount of tax has been determined. For other options and deviations from U.C.C., see category Business Regulation and Commerce, topic Commercial Code.

GARNISHMENT:

After personal action arising upon contract has been commenced in court of record or after any judgment from court of record or any transcript of a judgment filed in court of record, garnishment proceedings may be instituted. (Rules 3.101; 3.102). Prejudgment garnishment is available in action to obtain original judgment only if: (i) defendant is indebted to plaintiff on contract in stated amount in excess of all setoffs; (ii) defendant is subject to jurisdiction of state; and (iii) after diligent effort plaintiff cannot serve defendant with process. Prejudgment garnishment is available in action on foreign judgment, whether or not defendant is subject to jurisdiction of state, only if: (i) defendant is indebted to plaintiff foreign judgment in stated amount in excess of all setoffs; and (ii) defendant is not subject to jurisdiction of state, or after diligent effort plaintiff cannot serve defendant with process. (MCLA §600.4011; MSA §27A.4011; Rule 3.102).

Property Which May Be Reached.—Garnishee may be held liable to plaintiff for any or all of the following:
(1) All tangible or intangible property of principal defendant in his possession or control at time of service of writ on him, unless property is represented by negotiable document of title held by bona fide purchaser for value other than principal defendant; (2) all negotiable documents of title and all goods represented by negotiable documents of title belonging to defendant when documents of title are in possession of garnishee at time of service of writ on him; (3) all corporate share certificates in his possession or control at time of service of writ on him belonging to principal defendant; (4) except as to debts evidenced by negotiable instruments, all debts owing by garnishee to principal defendant at time of service of writ on garnishee, whether or not they are due; (5) all debts owing by garnishee evidenced by negotiable instruments held or owned by principal defendant at time of service of garnishment writ on principal defendant, which instruments are brought before court prior to their negotiation to bona fide purchaser for value; (6) all judgments in favor of principal defendant against garnishee in force at time of service of writ on garnishee; (7) all tangible or intangible personal property of principal defendant which at time of service of writ on garnishee the garnishee holds by conveyance, transfer or title void as to principal defendant's creditors, whether or not principal defendant could maintain action therefor against garnishee; (8) value of all tangible or intangible property of principal defendant which prior to service of writ on garnishee the garnishee received or held by conveyance, transfer or title void as to principal defendant's creditors, whether or not principal defendant could maintain action therefor against garnishee, and any contingent right on a claim against garnishee in favor of principal defendant at time of service of writ on garnishee; and (9) portion of defendant's earnings that are not protected from garnishment by law under 15 USC §1673. (Rules 3.101; 3.102).

Garnishment before judgment of indebtedness for labor performed by principal defendant or of property held or obligation owed by state or governmental unit of state is not permitted. (MCLA §600.4011; MSA §27A.4011).

Jurisdiction.—Personal property belonging to person against whom claim is asserted but in possession or control of third person is subject to garnishment if third person is subject to judicial jurisdiction of state and personal property is within state. Obligation owed to person against whom claim is asserted is subject to garnishment if obligor is subject to judicial jurisdiction of state whether or not state has jurisdiction over person against whom claim is asserted. (MCLA §600.4011; MSA §27A.4011; Rule 3.102).

Proceedings to Obtain.—Plaintiffs seeking writ of garnishment after judgment has been rendered must file affidavit stating: (1) judgment has been entered against defendant which remains unsatisfied; (2) amount of judgment, and amount remaining unpaid; and (3) affiant believes that named person has defendant's property or is indebted to, defendant. (Rule 3.101[D]). In actions to obtain original judgment plaintiffs seeking writ of garnishment before entry of judgment must file motion supported by affidavit showing that: (1) defendant is subject to jurisdiction of state; (2) defendant is indebted to plaintiff on contract in stated amount in excess of setoffs; (3) after diligent effort plaintiff cannot serve defendant with process; and (4) affiant believes that named person has property of, or is indebted to defendant. (Rule 3.102[B]). In actions on foreign judgment, plaintiffs' prejudgment garnishment affidavit must state: (1) defendant is indebted to plaintiff on foreign judgment in stated amount in excess of setoffs; (2) defendant is not subject to jurisdiction of state, or after diligent effort plaintiff cannot serve defendant with process; and (3) affiant believes that named person has property of, or is indebted to, defendant. (Rule 3.102[A][3][b]).

Answer of Garnishee.—Garnishee files disclosure under oath within 14 days after service, revealing any liability to principal defendant. Except as to claims for unliquidated damages for wrongs or injuries, garnishee may claim setoff. (Rule 3.101[H]). If garnishee fails to make disclosure or do other required act within time limits specified, default may be taken against him as in other civil actions. (Rule 3.101[S]). Upon order of court, garnishee may be required to pay indebtedness to plaintiff or deliver property to court clerk or otherwise secure delivery of property and receive receipt in complete discharge to extent of indebtedness paid or property delivered or secured. (Rule 3.101[E]).

Practice.—If plaintiff is not satisfied with disclosure, he may within 14 days after service of disclosure serve written interrogatories or demand for oral examination on garnishee, and discovery rules apply. Claims adverse to those of plaintiff or defendant may be litigated by interpleader or third-party defendant procedures as appropriate. (Rule 3.101[L]).

If writ is served after judgment, issue of garnishee's liability is brought to trial as set forth below. If writ is served before judgment, plaintiff proceeds to perfect judgment against principal defendant. If he fails to proceed in timely manner, garnishee or other interested party may move to discontinue garnishment proceedings. Plaintiff's failure to recover judgment against principal defendant or satisfaction of judgment thus recovered constitutes dismissal of all proceedings against garnishee. Issue of garnishee's liability stands for trial after judgment has been entered against principal defendant, except that if principal defendant moves for new trial or appeals after entry of judgment against him, issue of garnishee's liability is tried after disposition of motion or appeal. (Rule 3.101[M]).

Affidavit for writ stands as complaint and disclosure and answers to any written interrogatories and transcript of any oral examination stand as garnishee's answer, and garnishee's liability to plaintiff is tried on issues thus framed. Judgment for plaintiff to extent of garnishee's admissions may be entered on motion after notice to garnishee; otherwise issues are tried as in other civil actions. Jury trial demand must be filed within seven days after filing of disclosure, answers to interrogatories, or transcript of examination. If it is determined that garnishee is indebted to principal defendant but time for payment has not arrived, no judgment is taken until after time of maturity, which is stated in verdict or finding. (Rule 3.101[M]).

Special rules and procedures apply to postjudgment garnishment of state and interception of tax refunds. (MCLA §§600.4061, .4061a; MSA §§27A.4061, .4061[a]).

Adverse Claims.—See subhead Practice, supra.

Judgment.—Judgment may be entered against garnishee for payment of money or delivery of property as facts warrant. Money judgment against garnishee may be no greater than unpaid judgment, costs and interest. Judgment for specific property is enforced only to extent necessary to satisfy judgment against principal defendant. Judgment acquits and discharges garnishee from all demands by principal defendant for all moneys paid or property delivered in satisfaction of judgment. If garnishee is chargeable for specific property and refuses to expose it for levy of execution, court after show cause hearing may order execution against garnishee in amount not to exceed double value of the specific chargeable property. (Rule 3.101[O]).

Installment Judgment; Stay.—Where court has entered order for payment of any judgment in installments, issuance of writ of garnishment for work and labor is stayed during period defendant complies with such order. (MCLA §600.6215; MSA §27A.6215; Rule 3.101[U]).

Earnings.—Former exemption (MCLA §600.7511; MSA §27A.7511) repealed (1974, No. 297; see 415 F. Supp. 170). However, plaintiff is entitled to only those earnings that are not protected by law under 15 USC §1673.

Exemption of Money Owing for Milk or Cream.—Money owing a principal defendant on account of any milk or cream produced on his farm or farms is exempt from garnishment proceedings up to 40%. (MCLA §600.4031; MSA §27A.4031).

HOMESTEADS:

Any resident is entitled to hold a homestead exempt from execution, attachment or garnishment while such homestead is owned and occupied by him. (MCLA §§600.4031, .6023; MSA §§27A.4031, .6023).

Limitation of value is $3,500. (MCLA §600.6023; MSA §27A.6023).

Limitation of area is one lot in a city, village or recorded town plat, or forty acres in the country. (MCLA §600.6023; MSA §27A.6023). "Lot" is one or more platted lots improved as single parcel. (141 Mich. 545, 104, N.W. 980).

Debts or Liabilities against Which Exemption Not Available.—No exemption allowed as to any mortgage on homestead, lawfully obtained, except that such mortgage is not valid without signature of married judgment debtor's wife unless mortgage is given to secure payment of purchase money or portion thereof or mortgage is recorded for 25 years without filing of notice of claim of invalidity. (MCLA §600.6023; MSA §27A.6023). Under language of former statute exemption was not available against one who gave credit to provide homestead (308 Mich. 24, 13 N.W.2d 193), or owner of trust funds misappropriated to provide homestead (277 Mich. 505, 269 N.W. 577).

Designation of Homestead.—Occupancy by debtor is notice to all of homestead rights (304 Mich. 450, 8 N.W.2d 133), and no further notice or selection is necessary (271 Mich. 79, 259 N.W. 871).

Claim of Exemption.—If area occupied exceeds limitation, officer levying execution notifies debtor to select homestead, and in default of such selection, officer makes selection. (MCLA §600.6026; MSA §27A.6026).

Value in Excess of Exemption.—If jury of six appraises premises at value in excess of exemption and land cannot be divided, debtor has 60 days to pay excess over exemption of amount due on execution. In default of payment premises are offered for sale. (MCLA §600.6027; MSA §27A.6027).

Waiver of Exemption.—There is no specific statutory provision for waiver, although waiver is mentioned. (MCLA §600.6033; MSA §27A.6033).

HOMESTEADS . . . *continued*

Loss of Exemption.—Intention of debtor determines whether homestead has been abandoned. (213 Mich. 95, 181 N.W. 177).

Alienation or Encumbrance.—Alienation by married man requires wife's signature either to bar dower (MCLA §557.201; MSA §26.216[1]), or to convey entireties property (MCLA §557.203; MSA §26.216[3]). Encumbrance by married man, except purchase money mortgage, is invalid without signature of wife unless mortgage is recorded for 25 years without filing of notice of claim of invalidity. (MCLA §600.6023; MSA §27A.6023).

Proceeds of Sale.—If highest bid does not exceed exemption, no sale is made. If highest bid exceeds exemption, excess is applied on execution and amount of exemption is paid to debtor. Amount paid to debtor is exempt from execution for one year. (MCLA §600.6027, .6059; MSA §27A.6027, .6059).

Rights of Surviving Spouse and Family.—Exemption continues after death during minority of any children. If homestead owner dies leaving surviving spouse but no children, exemption continues and surviving spouse receives rents and profits before remarriage unless surviving spouse owns homestead in own right. (MCLA §§600.4031, .6023; MSA §§27A.4031, .6023). Surviving spouse is also entitled (without election against will) to homestead allowance of $10,000 and exempt property of $3,500 if spouse domiciled in Michigan. If there is no surviving spouse, minor children may qualify. Homestead allowance is charged against distributive share of estate. (MCLA §§700.285, .286; MSA §§27.5285, .5286).

See also categories Family, topic Husband and Wife; Property, topics Curtesy, Dower, Real Property.

JUDGMENT NOTES:

See category Business Regulation and Commerce, topic Bills and Notes.

LIENS:

Uniform Commercial Code adopted. (MCLA §§440.1101-.11102; MSA §§19.1101-.9994). See category Business Regulation and Commerce, topic Commercial Code.

Lien for wages on all property of employer is given to certain miners (MCLA §§570.194, .201, .251; MSA §§26.410, .421, .423) and suppliers of labor and material to oil and gas pipeline owners or lessees. Lien for wages on products of their labor is given to employees of loggers or processors of forest products. (MCLA §426.1; MSA §18.211). Former lien for wages of employees of railroads repealed by P.A. 1993, No. 354.

Lien for charges is given to mechanics, artisans or tradesmen for constructing in whole or in part or altering, fitting or repairing chattels or for caring or keeping of animals. Lien may be foreclosed by public sale after nine months possession and 30 days notice of time and place of sale and amount claimed, sent by registered mail to last known address of owner or bailor. (MCLA §§570.185-.187; MSA §§26.401-.403). Lien for charges is also given to horseshoers (MCLA §570.351; MSA §18.281), threshers, pressers and hullers (MCLA §570.331; MSA §12.11), owners of stallions for services (MCLA §287.210; MSA §12.560), garage keepers, including keepers of aircraft (MCLA §§570.301-.303; MSA §§9.1711-.1713), aircraft repair station operators (MCLA §259.205; MSA §10.305), and cleaners and dyers (MCLA §570.211; MSA §26.411[1]). Owner of self-service storage facility also given lien for charges upon all personal property stored at facility. Enforceable by public sale after 30 days notice. (MCLA §570.521 et seq.; MSA §26.411[21] et seq.). Molder has lien on any mold or form in its possession for amount due from customer. (MCLA §445.618; MSA §19.838[5]).

Liens on watercraft of more than five tons burthen are given for supplies, provisions, labor, wharfage, anchorage, dock hire, insurance, bottomry, salvage, towage, lighterage, violation of contracts of affreightment or carriage and personal injury or property damage caused by negligence. (MCLA §570.401 et seq.; MSA §26.341 et seq.).

Waiver, Loss or Extinguishment.—Lienholder's acts inconsistent with existence of lien may waive it by implication. (36 Mich. 358). Lien is waived by acquiescence in third person's taking possession on execution without notifying takers of adverse claim. (41 Mich. 505, 2 N.W. 895). Possessory lien is usually waived by voluntary parting with possession. (60 Mich. 61, 26 N.W. 832).

Enforcement.—Unless power of sale is given by statute or agreement, common law or other possessory lien gives lienor mere right to retain possession until claim is satisfied. (118 Mich. 162, 76 N.W. 371). Burden of proving lien rests on person claiming it. (319 Mich. 277, 29 N.W.2d 691).

Common Law Liens.—Many other liens are recognized as at common law.

Mechanic's and Construction Liens.—Contractors, subcontractors, suppliers of materials or equipment and laborers who provide improvements (including surveying, engineering, and architectural planning, construction management, clearing, demolishing, excavating, filling, building, erecting, constructing, altering, repairing, ornamenting, landscaping, paving, leasing equipment, or affixing fixture or material) to real estate pursuant to contract are entitled to lien for amount due. (MCLA §570.1107; MSA §26.316[107]).

Property Subject to Lien.—Lien covers entire interest of owner or lessee who contracted for improvement (including any subsequently acquired interest), to interest of owner who subordinated interest to mortgage for improvement and to interest of owner who required improvement. Where person contracting for improvement had no legal title, lien attaches to improvement. (MCLA §570.1107; MSA §26.316[107]). Special rules apply to condominiums. (MCLA §570.1126; MSA §26.316[126]). If owner or lessee has paid contractor or subcontractor who failed to pay person claiming lien, lien does not attach to residential structure, and claimant may collect from Homeowner Construction Lien Recovery Fund maintained by Department of Licensing and Regulation. (MCLA §§570.1201-.1203; MSA §§26.316[201]-[203]).

Limitation of Amount.—Total of liens is limited to amount which owner or lessee agreed to pay person with whom owner or lessee contracted for improvement. (MCLA §570.1107; MSA §26.316[107]). Maximum payable from Homeowner Construction Lien Recovery Fund is $75,000 per residential structure. (MCLA §570.1204; MSA §26.316[204]).

Notice of Commencement.—Before beginning of physical improvement, contracting owner or lessee must record "notice of commencement" in statutory form with county register of deeds; in case of residential structure, notice of commencement need not be recorded but must be furnished to each contractor who requests same. Notice of commencement (with attached blank form of "notice of furnishing") must be furnished by owner, lessee, "designee" of owner or lessee named in notice of commencement or contractor (or by subcontractor who has received same) within ten days after mailing by certified mail of written request by subcontractor, supplier or laborer. Notice of commencement must be kept posted in conspicuous place on site during improvement. Failure to record or furnish notice of commencement extends time within which lien claimant may furnish notice of furnishing until 20 days (in case of subcontractor or supplier) or 30 days (in case of laborer) after notice of commencement is recorded or furnished. (MCLA §570.1108; MSA §26.316[108]). Where property is residential structure, contractor, subcontractor, supplier or laborer must request owner or lessee to provide notice of commencement, and certain additional protections are given owner or lessee. (MCLA §570.1108a; MSA §26.316[108a]).

Notice of Furnishing.—Within 20 days after first labor or material is furnished (for subcontractor or supplier), 30 days after wages were due but not paid (for laborer), or by fifth day of second month following month in which fringe benefits or withholdings were due but not paid (for laborer), claimant other than contractor must provide "notice of furnishing" in statutory form to "designee" and general contractor named in notice of commencement by personal service or certified mail. Failure to provide notice of furnishing does not defeat lien of claimant other than laborer, but amount is reduced by payments made to contractor for work or materials furnished before service of notice of furnishing if paid pursuant to contractor's sworn statement. Failure of laborer to furnish notice of furnishing defeats lien. (MCLA §570.1109; MSA §26.316[109]).

Contractor's sworn statement in statutory form must be furnished by contractor to owner or lessee when payment is due or requested or when owner or lessee demands sworn statement. Subcontractor must furnish sworn statement on demand. Owner or lessee may withhold from amount due contractor or subcontractor amounts shown by sworn statement or notices of furnishing to be due subcontractors, suppliers and laborers and pay them directly. Claim of subcontractor, supplier or laborer may be avoided in reliance on sworn statement unless notice of furnishing has been served. Failure to furnish sworn statement does not invalidate lien of contractor or subcontractor, but lien may not be enforced until sworn statement is furnished. (MCLA §570.1110; MSA §26.316[110]).

Claim of Lien.—Right to lien terminates unless, within 90 days after claimant's last furnishing of labor or material, "claim of lien" in statutory form is recorded with county register of deeds. Claim of lien must be served on designee named in notice of commencement within 15 days after recording, and proof of service of notice of furnishing by subcontractor, supplier or laborer must be attached to claim of lien; service may be personal or by certified mail. (MCLA §570.1111; MSA §26.316[111]).

Duration.—Lien may not be enforced unless foreclosure proceeding is brought within one year after date of recording claim of lien. (MCLA §570 .1117; MSA §26.316[117]).

Waiver of Lien.—Waiver of lien obtained as part of construction contract is invalid except to extent payment made. Claimant who receives full payment is required to provide full waiver of lien, and partial waiver for partial payment must be given if requested. Statutory forms of waiver are provided. (MCLA §570.1115; MSA §26.316[115]).

Enforcement of lien is by foreclosure proceeding in circuit court for county where property is located and filing notice of lis pendens with county register of deeds. Plaintiff must join each person with interest in property which would be impaired by foreclosure. Contract claim may be joined in same action. (MCLA §570.1117; MSA §26.316[117]). Court may order foreclosure sale and may appoint receiver; lien may also be ordered satisfied out of rents, profits and income from property. (MCLA §§570.1121, .1122; MSA §§26.316[121], [122]).

Priorities.—All construction liens are of equal priority. Lien has priority over all other interests or encumbrances recorded after actual physical improvements. Mortgage or other encumbrance or interest recorded before actual physical improvement has priority over construction lien, but mortgage priority does not cover advances made after actual physical improvement unless made pursuant to sworn statement of contractor and waivers of lien from contractor and all subcontractors and suppliers who provided notices of furnishing. Lien of any claimant not set forth on sworn statement on which advance was made is subordinate to mortgage unless claimant, before advance, had provided notice of furnishing or filed claim of Lien. Advance made after service of notice of furnishing or filing of claim of lien is subordinate to lien unless, before advance, mortgagee receives unconditional waiver of lien from claimant for full amount due as of date of waiver and waiver is dated within 30 days before advance. (MCLA §570.1119; MSA §26.316[119]).

Redemption from foreclosure sale may be made by paying amount set forth in judgment of foreclosure (which may include taxes and insurance premiums due for redemption period) within period fixed by court, which may not exceed four months. (MCLA §570.1121; MSA §26.316[121]).

Public Works.—Contractor must give bond for payment of subcontractors, laborers and materialmen. (MCLA §§570.101-.105; MSA §§26.321-.325). Separate statutes govern contracts of state highway commissioner (MCLA §250.62; MSA §9.902) and other public contracts exceeding $50,000 (MCLA §§129.201-.211; MSA §5.232[1]-[11]).

Attachment Lien.—See topic Attachment.

Attorney's Lien.—See category Legal Profession, topic Attorneys and Counselors.

Carrier's Lien.—See category Business Regulation and Commerce, topic Carriers.

Execution Lien.—See topic Executions.

Judgment Lien.—See category Civil Actions and Procedure, topic Judgments.

See note at head of Digest as to 1998 legislation covered.

See Topical Index in front part of this volume.

MI – 27

LIENS . . . *continued*

Landlord's Lien.—See category Property, topic Landlord and Tenant.

Liens on Exempt Property.—See topic Exemptions.

Liens on Homestead.—See topic Homesteads.

Motor Vehicle Liens.—See category Transportation, topic Motor Vehicles.

Real Estate Mortgage Lien.—See category Mortgages, topic Mortgages of Real Property.

Tax Lien.—Uniform Federal Tax Lien Registration Act enacted. (MCLA §§211.661-.668; MSA §7.753[1]-[8]). State tax items are also recorded with register of deeds of county in which property is situated. (MCLA §§211.681-.687; MSA §7.753[51]-[57]). See category Taxation, topic Administration as to state tax liens generally.

MECHANICS' LIENS:

See topic Liens.

PLEDGES:

Uniform Commercial Code adopted. (MCLA §§440.1101 et seq.; MSA §§19.1101 et seq.). See category Business Regulation and Commerce, topic Commercial Code.

Remedies of Pledgee.—Governed by Uniform Commercial Code. (MCLA §§440.9101-.9507; MSA §§19.9101-.9507).

RECEIVERS:

Receivers are appointed by the courts in many proceedings under various statutes, to wind up corporations of all kinds organized under different statutes and under general equitable powers (MCLA §600.2926; MSA §27A.2926); also in garnishment proceedings, in proceedings against judgment debtors, in partition, to collect alimony from husband's estate, to enforce mechanic's liens, and other like cases.

Provision is made for personal receivership for persons owing obligations, the assignment of wages to clerk of designated court and payment of obligations to creditors; garnishment of wages pending payment is prohibited. Act does not affect rights of secured creditors or debts or obligations incurred after filing of petition by employee. (MCLA §§600.5301-.5371; MSA §§27A.5301-.5371).

Jurisdiction.—Circuit court in exercise of its equitable powers may appoint receivers in cases pending where appointment is allowed by law. (MCLA §600.2926; MSA §27A.2926). Particular statutes set forth various jurisdictional requirements.

Proceedings.—Appointment of receiver, unless otherwise specifically provided by statute, must be ancillary to a pending case. (37 F. 286).

Eligibility and Competency.—Receiver's eligibility and competency, unless otherwise specifically provided, is determined by discretion of court; however, receiver interested in a suit may be appointed only by consent of all parties concerned. (43 Mich. 292, 5 N.W. 627).

Qualification.—Unless otherwise specifically provided, court determines amount and conditions of receiver's bond. (MCLA §600.2926; MSA §27A.2926).

Powers and Duties.—Powers of receivers depend on statutes under which their appointment is made and orders by which they are appointed. (MCLA §600.2926; MSA §27A.2926). Receivers of banks and trust companies may borrow money. (MCLA §487.552; MSA §23.710[252]).

Compensation.—Compensation is generally provided and is determined by court in its discretion. (333 Mich. 513, 53 N.W.2d 356).

Discharge.—Court may terminate any receivership whenever termination appears to be in best interest of parties. (MCLA §600.2926; MSA §27A.2926).

REDEMPTION:

See topics Executions, Liens; categories Mortgages, topic Mortgages of Real Property; Taxation, topic Property (Ad Valorem) Taxes, subhead Redemption.

SUPPLEMENTARY PROCEEDINGS:

See topic Executions.

USURY:

See category Business Regulation and Commerce, topic Interest.

DISPUTE RESOLUTION

ALTERNATIVE DISPUTE RESOLUTION:

Mandatory Dispute Resolution.—

Mediation in Circuit Court.—Court may submit to mediation any civil action in which relief sought is primarily money damages or division of property. Mediation panels are composed of three persons selected in accordance with Rule 2.404. Typical mediation fee for each party is $75 per party. At least 14 days before hearing, each party must file with mediation clerk three copies of concise summary setting forth that party's factual and legal position on issues presented by action. Within 14 days after hearing, panel will make evaluation and notify attorney for each party of its evaluation in writing. Each party must file written acceptance or rejection of panel's evaluation with mediation clerk within 28 days after service of panel's evaluation. In mediations involving multiple parties, party accepting all of awards may make that acceptance conditional upon other parties' acceptance of all or some of awards. Failure to file written acceptance or rejection within 28 days constitutes rejection. If all parties accept panel's evaluation, judgment will be entered in that amount, unless amount of award is paid within 28 days after notification of acceptances, in which event court shall dismiss action with prejudice. Judgment or dismissal shall be deemed to dispose of all claims in action and includes all fees, costs, and interest to date entered. If party has rejected evaluation and action proceeds to verdict, that party must pay opposing party's actual costs unless verdict is more favorable to rejecting party than mediation evaluation. Verdict is considered more favorable to defendant if it is more than 10% below evaluation, and is considered more favorable to plaintiff if it is more than 10% above evaluation. Actual costs include those costs taxable in any civil action and reasonable attorney fee based on reasonable hourly or daily rate as determined by trial judge for services necessitated by rejection of mediation evaluation. Costs should not be awarded if mediation award was not unanimous. (Rule 2.403).

Medical Malpractice Action.—Medical malpractice cases are mediated in substantially same way as provided in Rule 2.403 (see catchline Mediation in Circuit Court, supra), however, few special rules for mediation apply in these cases. Mediation panel consists of five mediators. Plaintiff and defendant each designate health care professional to serve on panel with three other mediators selected pursuant to Rule 2.404. Health care professional selected for mediation panel may not be called as witness at trial. If panel determines that action or defense is frivolous as to any party and action proceeds to trial, party who has been determined to have frivolous action or defense must post cash or surety bond in amount of $5,000 for each party against whom action or defense was determined to be frivolous. If judgment is entered against party who posted bond, bond shall be used to pay all reasonable costs incurred by other parties and any costs allowed by law or court rule, including court costs and reasonable attorney fees. (MCLA §§600.4901-.4923; MSA §§27A.4901-.4923).

Tort Actions.—Mediation of tort cases is mandatory except where court on motion for good cause shown finds that mediation of action would be inappropriate. Bond requirement for actions or defenses which are deemed frivolous in medical malpractice actions also applies to tort actions. (MCLA §§600.4951-.4969; MSA §§27A.4951-.4969).

Mediation in Probate Court.—Court may submit to mediation one or more requests for relief in any contested proceeding. Rule 2.403 applies to extent feasible, except sanctions must not be awarded unless subject matter of mediation involves money damages or division of property. (Rule 5.403).

Mediation in U.S. District Court for Eastern District of Michigan.—Procedure in Eastern District of Michigan is substantially same as procedure utilized by state circuit courts under Rule 2.403. Sixth Circuit has held that attorney fees are not permissible sanction under this Rule. (865 F.2d 88). However, nothing precludes parties from stipulating to award of attorney fees as potential sanction. (E.D. Local Rule 16.3). One noteworthy distinction between Rule 2.403 and E.D. Local Rule 16.3 is that latter requires mediation panel to allocate damages between claims subject to federal income tax and claims not subject to federal income tax when parties make such request. (E.D. Local Rule 16.3 [f][4]). No such provision exists under Michigan rule.

Mediation in U.S. District Court for Western District of Michigan.—Western District of Michigan favors alternative dispute resolution whenever parties and court agree it may help resolve case. Court will consider alternative methods proposed by parties in addition to those specifically provided for by local rules. Western District of Michigan utilizes several forms of mediation: "Michigan Mediation" as provided in state circuit courts under Rule 2.403, voluntary facilitative mediation, and early neutral evaluation.

"Michigan Mediation" in Western District of Michigan is substantially similar to mediation under Rule 2.403 with few exceptions. Sanctions against party who rejects panel's evaluation and does not improve its position include only those costs and fees taxable in any civil action and mediation fees paid to panel. Parties may stipulate in writing before mediation award is tendered that court may also tax reasonable attorney's fees incurred from date of rejection. Medical malpractice actions and tort actions in which subject-matter jurisdiction is based solely on diversity of citizenship and for which rule of decision is supplied by Michigan law shall be ordered to mandatory mediation under MCLA §§600.4901-.4923; MSA §§27A.4901-.4923 and MCLA §§600.4951-.4969; MSA §§27A.4951-.4969, respectively. Sanctions apply. (W.D. Local Civil Rule 16.5).

Voluntary Facilitative Mediation is flexible, nonbinding dispute resolution process in which impartial third party, mediator, facilitates negotiations among parties to help them reach settlement. If district or magistrate judge is satisfied that selection of facilitative mediation is purely voluntary and is agreed to by all parties, judge will incorporate their selection in case management order and instruct parties to jointly select mediator within ten days. Parties choose one mediator from list of court certified mediators. Format for session is developed by parties and mediator and may involve more than one session. If settlement is reached, mediator helps parties draft settlement agreement along with stipulation and proposed order to dismiss, which is then filed with court. If settlement is not reached, parties have seven days to inform mediator whether they desire to continue with mediation process. Information disclosed during any mediation session is not disclosed to any other party without consent of party disclosing information. All mediation proceedings are deemed compromise negotiations within meaning of Fed. R. of Evid. 408. (W.D. Local Civil Rule 16.3). Early neutral evaluation is flexible, nonbinding dispute resolution process in which experienced neutral attorney (evaluator) meets with parties early in case to evaluate its strengths and weaknesses and value it may have, and to attempt to negotiate settlement. Parties jointly select neutral evaluator, attorney with five or more years of practice experience who has general peer recognition for his or her expertise. Judge may select evaluator, if parties are unable to agree. Evaluator is paid his or her normal hourly rate, receiving 50% from defendant(s) and 50% from plaintiff(s). Evaluator and parties develop format of session(s). Each party may make oral presentation (through counsel or otherwise) of its position. Evaluator assesses relative strengths and weaknesses of parties' positions and explains reasoning in support of assessment. At session's conclusion, evaluator determines whether some form of follow-up to session would contribute to case-development process or to settlement. If settlement is reached, evaluator helps parties draft settlement agreement. If no settlement is reached, parties have seven days to inform evaluator whether they wish to continue with evaluation process. Evaluator's report to court only indicates who participated and whether any issues were narrowed or settlement reached. (W.D. Local Civil Rule 16.4).

See note at head of Digest as to 1998 legislation covered.

See Topical Index in front part of this volume.

MI – 28

ALTERNATIVE DISPUTE RESOLUTION...*continued*

Court-Annexed Arbitration in Western District of Michigan.—W.D. Local Civil Rule 16.6 governs referral of certain actions to arbitration as authorized by c. 28, U.S. Code. All civil actions seeking only money damages in amount not in excess of $100,000, exclusive of punitive damages, interests, costs, and attorney fees, are subject to this Rule. At least ten business days prior to hearing, summary or brief of factual and legal positions, together with copies or photographs of all documents on questions of liability and damages shall be marked for identification and submitted to arbitrator and opposing counsel. Each party shall be allowed maximum of 2¹/₂ hours for presentation of its case. Party may cause transcript or recording to be made of proceedings at its expense. Arbitrator shall announce award to parties not more than ten days following close of hearing. Award shall state clearly and concisely name or names of prevailing party or parties and party or parties against which it is rendered, and precise amount of money and other relief awarded. Unless all parties have consented to arbitration, amount of award may not exceed $100,000. Party may file and serve written demand for trial de novo withing 30 days of filing of award. Clerk shall enter judgment on award in accordance with Rule 58, Federal Rules of Civil Procedure, immediately upon expiration of time for requesting trial de novo, unless trial de novo has been timely requested. In any trial de novo conducted after arbitration conducted with consent of all parties, court may assess opposing parties' costs under 28 U.S.C. §1920 and reasonable attorney's fees against party demanding trial de novo if such party fails to obtain judgment in court which is substantially more favorable to such party than arbitration award, and court determines that party's conduct in seeking trial de novo was in bad faith. (W.D. Local Civil Rule 16.6).

Summary Bench Trials, Summary Jury Trials, and Mini-Hearings in Western District of Michigan.—By stipulation of parties with approval of court, on motion by party with notice to opposing parties or on court's motion, case may be selected for summary jury trial, summary bench trial, or mini-hearing. Summary jury trial is abbreviated proceeding during which parties' attorneys summarize their cases before six-person jury. Unless parties stipulate otherwise, verdict is advisory only. Summary bench trial is abbreviated proceeding during which parties' attorneys summarize their cases before judge or magistrate judge. Unless parties stipulate otherwise, verdict is advisory only. Mini-hearing is abbreviated proceeding in which attorneys for corporate parties present their positions to parties' senior officials or to impartial experts to attempt to settle dispute. Parties may fashion procedure which they feel is appropriate. On proper motion, however, court may prescribe certain procedures and time limits. (W.D. Local Civil Rule 16.7).

Custody Action.—When custody of minor is contested, both parties may agree to mediation under MCLA §552.513; MSA §25.176(13) and office of Friend of the Court shall provide, either directly or by contract, domestic relations mediation to assist parties in settling voluntarily dispute concerning child custody or visitation that arises from domestic relations matter. Parties shall not be required to meet with domestic relations mediator.

Court Rule Mediation of Domestic Relations Disputes.—Rule 3.216 permits court to submit any pending divorce, separate maintenance, or annulment proceeding, but not custody or visitation issues, to mediation under this rule. Court may not submit any domestic relations dispute to mediation until disputes over custody of minor children have been resolved. Party may object to mediation on grounds that value of marital estate does not justify expense of mediation, discovery has not been substantially completed, there is outstanding custody issue, or other good cause. Mediation is conducted by one mediator, who is either selected by parties or who is selected by mediation clerk in accordance with procedure provided by Rule 3.216(E)(3). Mediator selected under 3.216(E)(3) must meet qualifications as set forth in Rule 3.216(F). Mediator's fees are based on reasonable hourly rate, commensurate with mediator's experience and usual charges for services performed.

If parties fail to negotiate settlement, mediator must prepare report on unresolved issues, along with mediator's recommendations on resolution. If both parties accept mediator's recommendations in their entirety, recommendations are incorporated into judgment which is entered as other settlements are entered. If mediator's recommendations are not accepted by both parties in their entirety, case proceeds to trial. If either party demands trial on all issues, even portion of mediator's recommendations which was accepted by both parties may be tried. Court may not sanction party for rejecting mediator's recommendation. Mediator may not inform court of rejecting party's or parties' identity.

Once parties stipulate to mediation, stipulation becomes enforceable. (Marvin v. Marvin, 203 Mich. App. 154, 511 N.W.2d 708 [1993]).

Community Dispute Resolution Act.—This Act provides for community dispute resolution centers which are funded in part by state and administered by state court administrator. Parties to dispute may participate by mutual agreement and form or technique utilized shall also be by mutual agreement of parties. Courts may refer parties to civil action to community dispute resolution center, but shall not require parties to settle through any process utilized at center. (MCLA §§691.1551-.1564; MSA §§27.15[51]-[64]).

Arbitration.—See topic Arbitration and Award.

Voluntary Dispute Resolution.—Parties to civil action in state court may avail themselves by mutual consent of any of mandatory dispute resolution techniques provided under state statutes and/or rules described above. Similarly, parties to civil action in federal court may avail themselves by mutual consent of any of mandatory dispute resolution techniques provided under local rules of district in which case lies.

Dissolution of Marriage.—See category Family, topic Divorce.

ARBITRATION AND AWARD:

Uniform Act adopted. (MCLA §§600.5001-.5035; MSA §§27A.5001-.5035). Existing dispute which might be subject of civil action may be submitted to arbitration by agreement in writing, and parties except infants and persons of unsound mind, may agree to entry of judgment on award in circuit court. Statute does not apply to collective contracts between employers and employees or associations of employees, nor to claims to fee or life estate in realty (except as provided in Condominium Act,

MCLA §§559.101-.275, MSA §§26.50[101]-.50[275]), but does cover controversies over claims to interest for term of years in real estate and over partition or boundaries of lands or admeasurement of dower (MCLA §§600.5001, .5005; MSA §§27A.5001, .5005).

Form and Requisites of Submission.—See introductory paragraph and subhead Contracts to Arbitrate Future Disputes, infra.

Contracts to Arbitrate Future Disputes.—Provision in written contract to settle by arbitration under MCLA §§600.5001-.5035; MSA §§27A.5001-.5035 a controversy thereafter arising between parties to the contract with relation thereto, in which it is agreed that circuit court may enter judgment on award, is valid and irrevocable except on grounds, at law or equity, which exist for rescission or revocation of any contract, and stands as submission of any controversy under contract not expressly excluded from arbitration. (MCLA §600.5001; MSA §27A.5001).

Rescission.—Neither party can revoke any agreement or submission made as provided in statute without consent of other party. If either party fails to appear before arbitrators after due notice, arbitrators may proceed on evidence of other party. (MCLA §600.5011; MSA §27A.5011). Court may order parties to proceed with arbitration, or may stay arbitration commenced or threatened on showing that there is no agreement to arbitrate, but not because claim in issue lacks merit or good faith. (Rule 3.602).

Powers of Arbitrators.—Witnesses and documents may be subpoenaed in manner authorized by Court Rules to appear before arbitrators. Arbitrators may permit deposition to be taken, for use as evidence, of witness who cannot be subpoenaed or is unable to attend hearing. Majority of arbitrators may determine any question and render final award unless concurrence of all arbitrators is expressly required in submission. Arbitrators appoint time and place for hearing and may adjourn hearing from time to time. Arbitrators have power to administer oaths to witnesses. (Rule 3.602).

Award and Enforcement Thereof.—Award may be confirmed by motion on filing with clerk of designated court within one year. Award may be vacated where procured by corruption or fraud, where partiality of arbitrator appointed as neutral or misconduct of any arbitrator is shown, when arbitrators exceeded their powers, where arbitrators refused to postpone hearing on sufficient cause shown or refused to hear material evidence or so conducted hearing as to prejudice rights of a party. Fact that relief exceeded that which could or would be granted by court of law or equity is not ground for vacating or refusing to confirm award. Court may modify or correct award. (Rule 3.602).

Judgment on Award.—Court may render judgment on award as corrected, confirmed or modified; costs are taxed as in civil actions, and execution issues as in other cases. (Rule 3.602).

Revocability of Agreement at Common Law.—Agreements not conforming to statute may be sustained as agreements for common-law arbitration (236 Mich. 425, 210 N.W. 488), but are revocable by either party before award unless (1) contract makes arbitration a condition precedent, express or implied, to bringing action or (2) contract is for construction or installation and person named or to be selected is charged with interpreting plans or specifications or estimating quantity or quality of work or materials in order to fix compensation of contractor or damages for default or defective performance (257 Mich. 670, 241 N.W. 807).

DOCUMENTS AND RECORDS

ACKNOWLEDGMENTS:

Uniform Recognition of Acknowledgments Act has been adopted. (MCLA §§565.261-.269; MSA §26.607[1]-[9]).

Acknowledgments may be taken by the following officers:

Within State.—Judge, clerk of court of record or notary public. (MCLA §§565.8, 600.1440; MSA §§26.527, 27A.1440).

Outside State but Within U.S. and Possessions.—Notary public or any other person authorized to perform notarial acts in place in which act is performed or any judge, clerk or deputy clerk of any court of record upon presentation of satisfactory evidence, such as picture identification (MCLA §§565.262; MSA §26.607[2]); and in addition, as to deeds, any master in chancery, justice of peace or other person authorized by laws of such place to take acknowledgments of deeds (MCLA §565.9; MSA §26.528).

Outside U.S.—Any officer of foreign service of U.S., consular agent or any other person authorized by regulations of U.S. Department of State to perform notarial acts in place in which act is performed, notary public or any other person authorized to perform notarial acts in place in which act is performed, or any judge, clerk, or deputy clerk of any court of record upon presentation of satisfactory evidence, such as picture identification (MCLA §565.262; MSA §26.607[2]); and in addition, as to deeds, any minister plenipotentiary, minister extraordinary, minister resident, chargé d'affairs, commissioner, or consul of U.S. appointed to reside there (MCLA §565.11; MSA §26.530). See also infra, subhead Persons in or with U.S. Armed Forces.

Persons in or with U.S. Armed Forces.—Commissioned officer in active service with U.S. armed forces and any other person authorized by regulation of U.S. armed forces may perform notarial acts for merchant seaman of U.S., member of armed forces of U.S., any other person serving with or accompanying armed forces of U.S. or dependent of any of foregoing. (MCLA §§565.262, 600.1440; MSA §§26.607[2], 27A.1440).

General Requirements as to Taking.—An officer who is interested cannot act. (132 Mich. 513, 93 N.W. 1067). See also infra, subhead Forms.

General Requirements of Certificate.—Notary must state when his commission expires, commissioned name and county in which authorized to officiate. (MCLA §55.221; MSA §5.1061). Person taking acknowledgment must certify that person acknowledging appeared before him and acknowledged he executed instrument and

ACKNOWLEDGMENTS . . . *continued*

either was known to him or that he had satisfactory evidence that person acknowledging was person named in and who executed instrument (MCLA §565.264; MSA §26.607[4]), all of which is imported by words "acknowledged before me" (MCLA §565.266; MSA §26,607[6]). Satisfactory evidence requires (1) sworn word of credible witness known by notary and who personally knows signer or (2) current identification card or document bearing signer's photograph and signature. (Act No. 5 of Public Acts of 1997). See also infra, subhead Forms.

Married Women.—Acknowledgment taken as if sole. (MCLA §§565.13, .281; MSA §26.531, .611).

Attorneys in Fact.—See infra, subhead Forms.

Corporations.—No special requirements. See infra, subhead Forms.

Foreign Acknowledgments.—Uniform Recognition of Acknowledgments Act has been adopted. (MCLA §§565.261-.269; MSA §§26.607[1]-[9]).

Effect of Acknowledgment.—Acknowledgment confers presumption of validity and genuineness of written instrument, and entitles it to be read in evidence, except notes, bills and wills. (MCLA §600.2131; MSA §27A.2131).

Compelling Acknowledgment.—Provision is made for compelling acknowledgment by resident of instrument affecting title to real estate. (MCLA §§565.16-.23, .46; MSA §§26.534-.541, .562).

Proof by Subscribing Witness.—Unacknowledged instruments affecting title to real estate may be proved by subscribing witness where party who executed instrument is dead or out of state and by proof of handwriting of grantor and any subscribing witness where subscribing witnesses are dead or out of state. (MCLA §§565.14-.15, .46; MSA §§26.532-.533, .562).

Authentication.—Acknowledgment taken within state is sufficiently authenticated for local purposes by hand of officer taking it. For purposes outside state, clerk of county in which officer is appointed certifies to official capacity and genuineness of signature under seal of circuit court. Fee varies by county.

Signature, rank or title, and serial number, if any, of notary public, of judge, clerk or deputy clerk of court of record, of officer of foreign service of U.S., consular agent, or other person authorized by regulation of U.S. State Department, or of commissioned officer in active service with U.S. armed forces or other person authorized by regulation of armed forces are sufficient proof of authority of such person (other than person authorized by laws or regulations of foreign country) to act, and further proof of authority is not required. Proof of authority of person authorized to take acknowledgments by laws or regulations of foreign country is provided by any of following: (a) Certification by foreign service officer of U.S. resident in country or diplomatic or consular officer of country resident in U.S. that person is authorized to act; (b) affixing official seal of person taking acknowledgment to document; or (c) appearance of title and indication of authority of person either in digest of foreign law or in list customarily used as source of such information. As to any other person acting outside of state, sufficient proof of authority exists if clerk of court of record in place in which notarial act is performed certifies to official character of person and authority to act. (MCLA §§565.262-.263; MSA §§26.607[2]-[3]).

Forms.—Following statutory short forms are provided for but use of other forms is not precluded (MCLA §565.267; MSA §26.607[7]):

For individual acting in own right:
State of _____
County of _____
The foregoing instrument was acknowledged before me this (date) by (name of person acknowledged).
(Signature of person taking acknowledgment)
(Title or rank)
(Serial number, if any)

For corporation:
State of _____
County of _____
The foregoing instrument was acknowledged before me this (date) by (name of officer or agent, title of officer or agent) of (name of corporation acknowledging) a (state or place of incorporation) corporation on behalf of the corporation.
(Signature of person taking acknowledgment)
(Title or rank)
(Serial number, if any)

For partnership:
State of _____
County of _____
The foregoing instrument was acknowledged before me this (date) by (name of acknowledging partner or agent), partner (or agent) on behalf of (name of partnership), a partnership.
(Signature of person taking acknowledgment)
(Title or rank)
(Serial number, if any)

For individual acting as principal by attorney in fact:
State of _____
County of _____
The foregoing instrument was acknowledged before me this (date) by (name of attorney in fact) as attorney in fact on behalf of (name of principal).
(Signature of person taking acknowledgment)
(Title or rank)
(Serial number, if any)

By public officer, trustee, or personal representative:
State of _____
County of _____
The foregoing instrument was acknowledged before me this (date) by (name and title of position).
(Signature of person taking acknowledgment)
(Title or rank)
(Serial number, if any)

Alternative to Acknowledgment or Proof.—See topic Affidavits, subhead Alternative to Affidavit.

Validating Acts.—Deeds of real estate executed within this state acknowledged before any county clerk or clerk of any circuit court, on any day prior to Sept. 18, 1903, and acknowledgment thereof, and, if recorded, record thereof are valid for all purposes so far as such acknowledgment and record are concerned. (MCLA §565.8; MSA §26.527).

AFFIDAVITS:

Within the state an affidavit may in general be taken before any justice, judge or clerk of any court of record, circuit court commissioner or notary public. (MCLA §600.1440; MSA §27A.1440).

Affidavit of a person residing in another state may be taken before any notary public, commissioner or justice of peace authorized by laws of such state to administer oaths therein. Signature of such notary public or justice of peace and fact that at time of taking of such affidavit person before whom same was taken was such notary public or justice of peace, must be certified by clerk of any court of record in county where such affidavit was taken, under seal of said court. (MCLA §600.2102; MSA §27A.2102).

Affidavit of a person residing in a foreign country must be authenticated by certification of consul or consul general of United States, or his deputy, there resident, that it was taken and subscribed before him, specifying time and place, with consular seal attached, or by certification of same facts by some judge of a court with seal. The genuineness of judge's signature, the existence of the court, and that judge is a member, must be certified by its clerk under seal. (MCLA §600.2102; MSA §27A.2102).

Affidavit of a person serving in or with U. S. armed forces (including civilian employee of armed forces and dependent of service man or of civilian employee), whether serving in or outside of U.S. territorial limits, may be taken before any commissioned officer in active service. Place of taking need not be shown. Officer certifies that affiant is known or satisfactorily proven to be serving in or with armed forces and that he is a commissioned officer of stated rank, and designates command to which he is attached. (MCLA §600.1440; MSA §27A.1440).

General Requirements as to Administration.—An officer may be disqualified to take an affidavit by reason of interest, but small or indirect interest does not suffice. (261 Mich. 483, 246 N.W. 193).

General Requirements of Jurat.—Notaries public must legibly type, print or stamp on each affidavit given or taken by them date upon which their commissions expire and commissioned names, and must state county in which they are authorized to act. (MCLA §55.221; MSA §5.1061).

Use of Affidavits.—Affidavits are not admissible as evidence in court proceedings, except recorded affidavits as to parties to instruments affecting title to real estate, adverse possession, boundaries, etc. (MCLA §§565.451-.453; MSA §§26.731-.733).

Form.—No statutory form of jurat. Form in common use is:

Form

Subscribed and sworn to before me this . . . . . . day of . . . . . . , 19. . . . . (Notary's signature) . . . . Notary public . . . . . . County, Michigan (or Notary public, ... County, Michigan, acting in . . . . County, Michigan)

Alternative to Affidavit.—Petition, inventory, accounting, proof of claim, or proof of service filed with Probate Court need not be verified, acknowledged, or made on oath if person signing instrument states immediately above date and his signature: "I declare under the penalties of perjury that this — was examined by me and that the contents thereof are true to the best of my information, knowledge and belief." Provision does not apply to nominations of guardians by minors. (MCLA §600.852, MSA §27A.852).Verification of pleading does not require jurat if it contains following signed and dated statement: "I declare that the statements above are true to the best of my information and belief." (Rule 2.114[A][2][a]). There is no other provision for alternatives to acknowledgments or affidavits.

NOTARIES PUBLIC:

Qualification.—Must be 18 years of age and must take oath of office and file same with county clerk (MCLA §§55.107, .109; MSA §§5.1041, .1043); must give bond in sum of $10,000 to be approved by county clerk (MCLA §55.110; MSA §5.1044).

Authentication.—See topic Acknowledgments, subhead Authentication.

Seal.—No duty to provide or use seal but notary customarily does so.

Powers and Duties.—Authorized to take proof and acknowledgment of deeds, administer oaths, take affidavits, demand acceptance of foreign and inland bills of exchange and promissory notes and to protest same for nonacceptance and nonpayment and to exercise such other powers and duties as by the laws, commercial usages of this state or any other state or country may be performed by notaries public. (MCLA §§55.112; MSA §5.1046).

Territorial Extent of Powers.—May act as such anywhere in state (MCLA §55.117; MSA §5.1051), but when acting outside county for which appointed must so indicate (MCLA §55.221; MSA §5.1061), customarily as follows: "Notary Public . . . . . . County, acting in . . . . . . County."

See note at head of Digest as to 1998 legislation covered.

See Topical Index in front part of this volume.

NOTARIES PUBLIC . . . *continued*

Expiration of Commission.—Must state date upon which commission expires in connection with official signature. (MCLA §55.221; MSA §5.1061).

Fees.—Fees vary with notarial act performed. (MCLA §55.117; MSA §5.1051; MCLA §600.2564; MSA §27A.2564).

Commissioners of Deeds.—May take acknowledgments of deeds executed in other states. (MCLA §565.9; MSA §26.528).

Officers of U.S. Armed Forces.—No statutory provisions conferring general notarial powers. Commissioned officer, if authorized to perform notarial acts where performed, may perform such acts for specified persons outside State for use in State. (MCLA §565.262; MSA §26.607[2]). See topic Acknowledgments.

RECORDS:

County registers of deeds have charge of records relating to property.

Uniform Commercial Code adopted. (MCLA §440.1101 et seq.; MSA §19.1101 et seq.). See category Business Regulation and Commerce, topic Commercial Code.

Recordable Instruments.—Every conveyance of real estate which is not recorded is void against subsequent purchasers in good faith and for a valuable consideration. (MCLA §565.29; MSA §26.547). Conveyance includes every instrument in writing by which any estate or interest in real estate is created, aliened, mortgaged or assigned; or by which title to any real estate may be affected except wills, leases for a term not exceeding three years, and executory contracts for sale or purchase of lands. Purchaser includes encumbrancer. (MCLA §§565.34-.35; MSA §§26.551, .552).

Uniform Commercial Code (MCLA §440.1101 et seq.; MSA §19.1101 et seq.) governs recording of security interest in personal property. See categories Business Regulation and Commerce, topic Commercial Code, and Mortgages, topic Chattel Mortgages, and subhead Filing under Commercial Code, infra.

Place of Recording.—Mortgages, deeds and other conveyances of real property or interest or estate therein are recorded in office of register of deeds of county where land lies. (MCLA §565.23; MSA §26.541). *For list of Counties and County Seats see first page for this state in Volume containing Practice Profiles Section.* As to security interest in personalty, see category Mortgages, topic Chattel Mortgages, and subhead Filing under Commercial Code, infra.

Filing Under Commercial Code.—If collateral is equipment used in farming operations or farm products or accounts or general intangibles arising from or relating to sale of farm products by a farmer, or consumer goods, or goods which are fixtures or are to become fixtures, filing is with register of deeds in county where land lies or debtor's residence. (MCLA §440.9401[a], [b]; MSA §19.9401[a], [b]). If collateral is a vehicle for which certificate of title is required, or an accessory, and not inventory held for sale, filing is with secretary of state and title application showing security interest must also be filed with secretary of state. (MCLA §§440.9302[4], .9401[1][c]; MSA §§19.9302[4], .9401[1][c]). In all other situations filing is with the secretary of state. (MCLA §§440.9401[1][c]; MSA §19.9401[1][c]). As to filing fees, see category Mortgages, topic Chattel Mortgages, subhead Filing.

Requisites for Recording.—In order that a deed, mortgage, power of attorney, etc., may be recorded, the following requirements must be met: (a) The instrument must be signed by the grantor or grantors (MCLA §565.1; MSA §26.521), and two witnesses (MCLA §565.8; MSA §26.527), but if executed without the state may be executed in accordance with laws of place of execution (MCLA §§565.9-.11; MSA §§26.528-.530). (b) The instrument must be properly acknowledged before an officer authorized to take acknowledgments (see topic Acknowledgments). (c) Names of parties executing instrument, witnesses and officer taking acknowledgment must be accurately and legibly printed, typed or stamped beneath respective signatures, address of each person executing instrument must be printed, typewritten or stamped on face, and instrument must contain name and business address of person who drafted it. (MCLA §§565.201-.203; MSA §§26.1221-.1223). (d) Deed or mortgage must show whether male grantors are married or single. (MCLA §565.221; MSA §26.581). (e) Deed must show post office address of each grantee legibly printed, typewritten or stamped. (MCLA §565.201; MSA §26.1221). (f) The instrument, if executed within this state after Apr. 1, 1997, must not be printed or typewritten in type smaller than 10 point, and paper must not be larger than 8½ x 14 inches nor smaller than 8½ x 11 inches or of less than 20 pound weight, and must have margin of unprinted space at least 2½ inches at top of first page and at least ½ inch on all remaining sides of each page. Register of deeds shall not record instrument which purports to evidence more than one recordable event. (MCLA §565.201; MSA §26.1221 [inapplicable where other statutory provisions conflict]). (g) Warranty deed, land contract or plat must include or have attached certificate of attorney general or county treasurer that all taxes due for five years preceding date of instrument have been paid and certificate of city, village or township treasurer that tax titles, tax certificates, etc., for five years preceding date of instrument, held by city, village or township, have been redeemed. (MCLA §211.135; MSA §7.194). (h) Instrument purporting to convey interest of survivor in land held jointly or by entireties cannot be recorded until proof of death of person indicated by such instrument to be deceased has been recorded. (MCLA §565.48; MSA §26.564). These provisions do not apply to security interests in personalty, as to which see categories Business Regulation and Commerce, topic Commercial Code and Mortgages, topic Chattel Mortgages. No written instrument on which stamp tax is imposed (see category Taxation, topic Real Estate Stamp and Transfer Taxes, subhead Stamp Tax) may be recorded unless stamps have been affixed and, where instrument does not disclose total consideration, affidavit stating value of property transferred. If instrument is not subject to stamp tax, reason for exemption is required to be stated on its face. (MCLA §§207.501-.513; MSA §§7.456[1]-.456[13]).

Recording fee is, effective July 1, 1984, $5 for first page; $2 for each additional page; additional $1 per page for each additional instrument assigned or discharged where any document assigns or discharges more than one instrument. Beginning Jan. 1, 1991, additional $2 fee for recording instruments, with certain exceptions. (MCLA §600.2567; MSA §27A.2567). Fee for recording notice of tax lien on personalty is $1, as is fee for tax lien discharge or subordination. (MCLA §211.685; MSA §7.753[55]).

For filing fees in connection with personal property under Uniform Commercial Code, see category Mortgages, topic Chattel Mortgages, subhead Filing.

Foreign Conveyances or Encumbrances.—Foreign conveyances or encumbrances are acceptable for recording, when executed and acknowledged without state, if executed and acknowledged in accordance with laws of place of execution. (MCLA §§565.9-.11; MSA §§26.528-.530). See category Property, topic Real Property, subhead Foreign Conveyances or Encumbrances.

Effect of Record.—Every conveyance of real estate which is not recorded is void against subsequent purchasers in good faith and for a valuable consideration. (MCLA §565.29; MSA §26.547). Copies, records, reproductions, replacements, transcripts or certified copies of recorded instruments are treated as originals for purposes of admissibility. (MCLA §§600.2137-.2138; MSA §§27A.2137-.2138).

Torrens Act not adopted.

Transfer of Decedent's Title.—In order to provide record evidence that the real estate of a resident decedent has passed to his devisees or heirs, there must be filed for record, in the office of the register of deeds of each county in which any such real estate is situated: (a) In case of testacy, a copy of the will certified by the judge who admitted it to probate; or (b) in case of intestacy, a certified copy of the order of distribution. In case of a nonresident decedent, ancillary administration must be had in this state and like papers filed for record in the register's office.

Vital Statistics.—All births, deaths, adoptions, marriages and divorces are recorded by State Department of Health, Lansing, Michigan 48913. (MCLA §§333.2815-.2876, 551.109; MSA §§14.15[2815]-[2876], 25.40). Births and deaths are recorded locally by registrar, usually health officer in larger cities and city, village or township clerk elsewhere. (MCLA §333.2815; MSA §14.15[2815]). Marriages are recorded locally by county clerk. (MCLA §551.103; MSA §25.33). Certificates of birth, death, marriage and divorce may be obtained at Michigan Department of Public Health, 3423 N. Logan St./Martin Luther King Jr. Blvd., Lansing 48914, c/o Vital Records. Fees are $13 for record search, including one copy or certified copy, $4 for each additional copy and $4 for each additional year searched. (MCLA §§333.2881-.2891; MSA §§14.15[2881]-[2891]).

Establishing Birth Records.—Unrecorded birth in Michigan may be recorded with State Department of Public Health subject to evidentiary requirements described by department. When department finds minimum documentation not to have been submitted or questions adequacy of documentation, applicant has right to appeal to probate court of county of residence or birth. Any birth outside continental U.S. of child born to parents, one or both of whom were residents of state at time of birth, and while one or both were in military or government service of U.S. may be registered with department if satisfactory evidence as to birth is shown by original or certified copy of birth certificate and, if in foreign language, accompanied by certified translation and affidavit from one or both parents setting forth that one or both were Michigan residents and were in military or government service of U.S. If either or both parents are dead, affidavits from credible persons with knowledge of facts may be submitted. (MCLA §§333.2827-.2828; MSA §§1415 [2827]-[2828]). Records of births so established are admissible in all courts and proceedings. (MCLA §§333.2827-.2831; MSA §§14.15[2827]-[2831]). When foreign born children are adopted by Michigan residents and facts of birth cannot be documented, probate court may determine facts and file delayed registration of birth with Department of Public Health. (MCLA §326.38; MSA §14.278).

SEALS:

Uniform Commercial Code adopted. (MCLA §§440.1101 et seq.; MSA §§19.1101 et seq.).

Seal is not required on any instrument affecting real estate executed by individual, partnership or corporation. (MCLA §§565.241-.242; MSA §§26.595-.596). No bond, deed of conveyance or other contract is invalid for want of seal or scroll. (MCLA §600.1401; MSA §27A.1401).

Except as to official seals, when a seal is desired on any instrument the word "Seal" or the letters "L. S." or a scroll or other device may be used in place thereof by any person or by a corporation having no corporate seal. (MCLA §565.39, .231; .232; MSA §§26.556, .591, .592).

Corporate Seals.—A corporation may have a seal and may alter same at its pleasure. The corporate seal is presumptive evidence of valid corporate authority and lawful execution of the instrument (MCLA §600.2142; MSA §27A.2142), but is not necessary (105 Mich. 300, 63 N.W. 205).

Effect of Seal.—A seal is only presumptive evidence of consideration. (MCLA §600.2139; MSA §27A.2139).

VITAL STATISTICS:

See topic Records.

EMPLOYMENT

LABOR RELATIONS:

All executive and administrative (non-legislative and nonjudicial) powers, duties and functions with respect to labor matters are vested in Department of Labor. (MCLA §16.104; MSA §3.29[4]). Head of Department of Labor is Director of Labor. (MCLA §16.476; MSA §3.29[376]).

Hours of Labor.—For hours of labor of minors under 18, see subhead Child Labor, infra.

Wages.—Minimum hourly wage is $4.75 beginning May 1, 1997 and $5.15 beginning Sept. 1, 1997. (MCLA §408.384; MSA §17.255[4]). Employer may pay new employee who is less than 20 years old training hourly wage of $4.25 for first 90 days of employment, in lieu of regular mandated minimum wage. Employer may not displace or reduce hours of employee merely to hire individual at lower training wage.

See note at head of Digest as to 1998 legislation covered.

See Topical Index in front part of this volume.

MI – 31

LABOR RELATIONS . . . *continued*

(MCLA §408.384b; MSA §17.255[4b]). Employer may petition state director of Department of Consumer and Industry Services to request permission to pay apprentices, learners, and persons with physical or mental disabilities who are clearly unable to meet normal production standards rate lower than regular mandated minimum wage. (MCLA §408.387; MSA §17.255[7]). "Tipped" employees may be paid $2.65 per hour, as long as (i) employee receives tips in course of employment, (ii) tips (on per hour basis) equal or exceed difference between $2.65 and regular mandated minimum wage, (iii) employee declares tips for FICA purposes, and (iv) employer informs employee of provisions of this statute. (MCLA §408.387a; MSA §17.255[7a]). Time and one-half must be paid for employment in excess of 40 hours per week with certain exceptions, including executives, professionals (including teachers), elected officials or political appointees, employees of recreational establishments closed at least five months per year, certain agricultural employees, and employees not subject to minimum wage. (MCLA §408.384a; MSA §17.255[4a]). In lieu of monetary overtime compensation, employers may choose to provide employees who would otherwise be entitled to time-and-a-half for overtime hours with compensatory time off at rate of 1½ hours for each hour of overtime worked. If employer has adopted such plan (or agreed to same as part of collective bargaining agreement), choice of whether to receive monetary compensation or compensatory time off for overtime hours worked rests solely with employee; it is civil infraction for employer to assign overtime based on its preference for employee who accepts compensatory time in lieu of pay or to directly or indirectly influence through intimidation, coercion, or threats employee's decision. Employees may not accrue more than 240 hours of compensatory time. Employers must allow employees with compensatory time to use time in whatever manner employee sees fit, unless use of time for period requested by employee will unduly disrupt operations of employer. Employee with accrued compensatory time may request to be paid in cash for that time, in lieu of actually taking time off work. Upon receipt of request, employers must compensate employee within 30 days of request for time at rate not less than employee's regular rate at time employee performed overtime work which led to accumulation of compensatory time. If employer decides to terminate its compensatory time off plan, it must give employees at least 60 days' notice. (MCLA §408.384a; MSA §17.255[4a]). Wages paid by contractors and subcontractors on state public works jobs must be equal to prevailing rates in job locality as determined by Director of Labor. (MCLA §§408.551-.558; MSA §§17.256[1]-[8]). No lien for wages, except for employees of railroads (MCLA §462.431; MSA §22.1263[431]) which right ended on Jan. 14, 1994 by implication from statute, corporations engaged in mining minerals in Upper Peninsula (MCLA §570.194; MSA §26.410), corporation engaged in mining coal, shale or clay (MCLA §570.201; MSA §26.421), and processors of forest products (MCLA §426.1; MSA §18.211). Wages for first 15 days of calendar month must be paid by first of following month, and wages for 16th and remaining days of calendar month must be paid by 15th of following month; weekly or bi-weekly pay schedules are permitted if payday occurs on or before 14th day after end of work period for which paid; monthly pay schedules are permitted if all wages for calendar month paid by first of following month. Employees engaged in hand harvesting of crops shall be paid all wages within two days following work week in which wages were earned, unless otherwise agreed in writing. (MCLA §408.472; MSA §17.277[2]). Employee quitting or discharged must be paid all wages earned as soon as amount can be determined with due diligence; as to employees engaged in hand harvesting of crops not later than three days after employee's voluntary termination of employment. Does not apply to contract employee who quits or is discharged and wages cannot be determined until termination of contract. In such case, employee to be paid all wages as nearly as can be estimated, with final payment to be made at termination of contract. (MCLA §408.475; MSA §17.277[5]). Wages must be paid in U.S. currency or by negotiable check or draft payable on presentation without discount in U.S. funds. Employer shall not deposit employee's wages in depositary institution without free written consent of employee. (MCLA §408.476; MSA §17.277[6]). Deductions other than those permitted or required by law or collective bargaining agreement shall not be taken without employee's full, free, and written consent, obtained without intimidation or fear of discharge for refusal to permit deduction. Overpayments of wages or fringe benefits may be deducted from employee's paycheck without written consent of employee if done so within six months of overpayment, if following conditions are met: (1) overpayment results from error or miscalculation; (2) by employer, its agent, or representative thereof; (3) employer provides written notice of deduction at least one pay period prior to deduction; (4) deduction does not exceed 15% of employee's gross wages in pay period in which deduction is taken; (5) deduction is made after all other deductions required or permitted by law or collective bargaining agreement, and after any employee-authorized deduction; and (6) deduction does not reduce employee's wages to below greater of state or federal minimum wage law. Employee aggrieved by this section may file complaint with department of labor within 12 months of violation. (MCLA §408.477; MSA §17.277[7]). Partial exemption from garnishment, see category Debtor and Creditor, topic Garnishment. Assignment of wages, see category Debtor and Creditor, topic Assignments.

Commissioned sales representatives must be paid final commissions within 45 days of termination or in accordance with contract between parties. (MCLA §600.2961; MSA §27A.2961).

Child Labor.—Regulated by Youth Employment Standards Act. (MCLA §§409.101-.124; MSA §§17.731[1]-[24]). Minor (person under 18 years of age) may not be employed in occupation which is hazardous to health or contrary to standards established by Department of Labor. Minimum age for employment of minors is 14 (11 for golf caddies, and 13 for persons employed in farming operations). (MCLA §409.103; MSA §17.731[3]). Minor may not be employed until employer obtains copy of work permit issued by school district where minor resides or where place of employment located. (MCLA §409.104; MSA §17.731[4]). Minor 16 years old or older may not be employed for more than six days in one week, nor longer than weekly average of eight hours per day or 48 hours per week, nor more than ten hours per day, nor between hours of 10:30 p.m. and 6 a.m., nor (if minor is in school) for more than combined school and work week of 48 hours, though during school vacation period or when minor is not enrolled in school, minor may be employed until 11:30 p.m.; with written parental consent, employer engaged in cleaning, sorting, or packaging fruits or vegetables may employ minor for periods greater than set forth above if minor is employed not more than 11 hours per day, not more than 62 hours in one week for not more than four weeks, not between hours of 2 a.m. and 5:30 a.m., and, if minor is student, such period of greater employment occurs when school is not in session. Minor may not be employed more than five hours continuously without at least 30 minutes rest period; rest period of less than 30 minutes not considered to interrupt continuous work. Employer must post copy of statutory hour restrictions on premises. Employer shall keep for at least one year at place where minor is employed adequate time record of hours minor works including daily starting and ending times. (MCLA §§409.110-.113; MSA §§17.731[10]-[13]). Minor may not be employed in occupation involving cash transaction after 8:00 p.m. or sunset, whichever is earlier, unless adult is present. (MCLA §409.112a; MSA §17.731[12a]). Work permit may not be issued authorizing employment of minor 16 years old or over in part of establishment where alcoholic beverages are manufactured, bottled, consumed or sold unless sale of other goods constitutes at least 50% of gross receipts; 14 and 15 year old minors may obtain work permits for employment in establishments where alcoholic beverages are sold at retail if sale of other goods constitutes at least 50% of gross receipts, but may not be employed in that part of establishment where alcoholic beverages consumed or sold for consumption on premises. (MCLA §409.115; MSA §17.731[15]). Act does not prohibit employment or minor in performance by performing arts organization if approval obtained from Department of Labor. (MCLA §409.114; MSA §17.731[14]). Act does not apply to or prohibit employment of minor: Age 16 or older who has completed high school graduation requirements; age 17 or older who has passed general educational development test; who is emancipated; student age 14 or older if written agreement between employer and board of education; in domestic work at private residence; in distributing or selling newspapers, magazines, political or advertising matter; in shoe shining; as members of youth organizations for citizenship training and character building if not to replace employees in occupations for which workers ordinarily paid; in business owned and operated by parent or guardian; in farm work if not in violation of Department of Labor standard; or by school, academy or college where student minor age 14 or older is enrolled. (MCLA §§409.116-.119; MSA §§17.731[16]-[19]).

Female Labor.—Discrimination between sexes in wages for similar work is misdemeanor. (MCLA §750.556; MSA §28.824).

Labor Unions.—Right to organize and bargain collectively is recognized. (MCLA §423.8; MSA §17.454[8]). No "right to work" statute.

Labor Disputes.—Employer may not interfere with employees' right to self-organization, initiate, dominate or interfere with formation or administration of labor union, discriminate against union members to discourage membership, or support company union. (MCLA §423.16; MSA §17.454[17]). Pursuit of work may not be hindered by mass picketing, intimidation, interference with entrance or egress from place of employment, or obstruction of public ways. Residence picketing is prohibited. (MCLA §423.9f; MSA §17.454[10.5]). Sitdown strike is prohibited. (MCLA §423.15; MSA §17.454[16]). Strike or lockout requires ten days notice to employment relations commission (30 days in case of public utility or hospital) and good faith participation in mediation. (MCLA §423.9; MSA §17.454[9]). Employment of professional strikebreakers or solicitation for employees without advising in the solicitation that they are replacements for striking or locked out employees is misdemeanor. (MCLA §§423.251-.254; MSA §§17.456[1]-[4]). Public employee, including public school employee, may not strike and public school employer may not institute lock-out. Public employee, upon request, is entitled to determination of whether employee actions violated non-strike provision before public employer may discharge or discipline employee for such actions. (P.A. 112 of 1994). Statutory requirement of majority vote of employees before strike (MCLA §423.9; MSA §17.454[9]) held to invade field preempted by Congress (339 U. S. 56, 94L.Ed. 663).

Civil Rights Act prohibits discrimination in employment because of race, color, religion, national origin, sex, age, marital status, familial status, height or weight. Commission is empowered to issue cease and desist order, and circuit court may enforce such orders. (MCLA §§37.2101 et seq.; MSA §§3.548[101] et seq.). Discrimination in employment because of handicap is also prohibited; same enforcement procedures apply. With exceptions, employer must accommodate handicapped individual unless accommodation would impose hardship. (MCLA §§37.1101 et seq.; MSA §§3.550[101] et seq.). Policy requiring arbitration of civil rights claims included in employee handbook which contains contract disclaimer is not enforceable. (Heurtebise v. Reliable Business Computers, 425 Mich. 405; 550 N.W. 2nd 243 [1996]).

Occupational Safety and Health.—Federal occupational safety and health act provides for state preemption where state plan is at least as effective as Federal. Michigan Safety and Health Act (MIDSHA) took effect Jan. 1, 1975. (MCLA §408.1001 et seq.; MSA §17.50[1] et seq.). MIDSHA incorporates federal standards. Primary responsibility for administering MIDSHA is with Michigan Department of Consumer and Industry Services. (Exec. Or. No. 1996-2).

Worker's Compensation Act abolishes defenses of contributory negligence (unless wilful), fellow servants' negligence and assumption of risk. (MCLA §418.141; MSA §17.237[141]).

Compensation Bureau has jurisdiction of all controversies. (MCLA §418.201; MSA §17.237[201]).

Employers Subject to Act.—All employers (including limited liability companies and partnerships) are subject to Act except those who regularly employ less than three persons, no one of whom has worked regularly 35 or more hours per week for 13 weeks during preceding year. Employers of domestic servants and of farm laborers are exempt as to employees if working less than 35 hours per week for 13 weeks or longer during preceding year. Employers of real estate salespersons on commission basis who do not claim salesperson as employee for tax purposes are also exempt. All public employers are subject to Act. (MCLA §§418.115-.118, .121, 151; MSA §17.237[115]-[119], [121], [151]).

LABOR RELATIONS . . . *continued*

Liability for Compensation.—If employee receives personal injury arising out of and in course of employment, not due to intentional and wilful misconduct, which incapacitates him for at least one week, employer is liable for medical care, weekly compensation during partial or total disability in amount and for length of time fixed by Act and if death results, for expenses of last illness and burial and indemnity to dependents as fixed by Act. (MCLA §§418.301-.305-.315, .345; MSA §§17.237[301]-[305]-[315], [345]).

Rate of compensation for death is 80% of deceased employee's average weekly wages or 80% of after-tax average weekly wages (whichever is greater) for period of 500 weeks from date of death with maximum payments varying with number of dependents. Period may be extended for minor dependents. (MCLA §418.321; MSA §17.237[352]). Limitation of 52 weeks of compensation payable to vocationally handicapped person. (MCLA §418.921; MSA §17.237[921]). Last sickness and burial allowance up to $1,500 is allotted. (MCLA §418.345; MSA §17.237[345]).

Recipients of payments are those wholly dependent on employee for support, with dependency conclusively presumed with certain relations. (MCLA §418.331; MSA §17.237[331]).

Rate of compensation for total disability is 66⅔% of employee's average weekly wages or 80% of after-tax average weekly wages (whichever is greater) for presumed period of 800 weeks up to maximum weekly amount which varies with number of dependents. (MCLA §418.351; MSA §17.237[351]).

Benefits under Act are reduced by amounts received under worker's compensation law of another state, 50% of old-age benefits under Social Security Act, and specified portions of disability insurance and pension benefits received by employee. (MCLA §§418.354, .846; MSA §§17.237[354], [846]).

Occupational Diseases.—Personal injury includes occupational disease, defined as any disease or disability due to causes and conditions characteristic of and peculiar to employer's business which arises out of and in course of employment. (MCLA §418.401; MSA §17.237[401]).

Liability to Employees of Independent Contractor.—Employer subject to Act is liable for compensation to employees of independent contractor who is not subject to Act or fails to comply with provision for insuring payment of compensation, subject to indemnity by independent contractor. (MCLA §418.171; MSA §17.237[171]).

Insurance of Payment.—Employer subject to Act must insure payment of compensation by adopting with approval of Compensation Bureau either of following methods: (a) Self-insurance, or (b) insurance by employer's liability company authorized to take such risks in Michigan. (MCLA §418.611; MSA §17.237[611]).

Claim for Compensation.—Proceeding for compensation will not be maintained unless oral or written claim is made to employer, or written claim is made to Compensation Bureau within two years after injury or death or, in case of physical or mental incapacity, within two years from time employee is not incapacitated from making claim. Employee must give employer notice of injury within 90 days after injury or after employee knew or should have known of injury; failure to give this notice is excused unless employer can prove he was prejudiced. Claim is not valid unless made within two years after later of date of injury, date disability manifests itself or last day of employment with employer against whom claim is made. Payment of compensation under Act shall not be made for any period of time earlier than two years prior to date on which employee filed hearing application with worker's compensation bureau, except payment for nursing or attendant care shall not be made for any period earlier than one year prior to date of such application. (MCLA §418.381; MSA §17.237 [381]).

Records and Reports.—Employer must record all injuries to employees which cause death or disability, and report to Bureau as required by rule. (MCLA §418.805; MSA §17.237[805]). Employer is also obligated to report to state Department of Consumer and Industry Services within eight hours of fatality or any hospitalization of three or more employees suffering injury from same accident or illness from exposure to same health hazard associated with their employment. (MCLA §408.1061; MSA §17.50[61]).

Waiver of Assignment of Compensation.—Employee may not waive right to compensation nor assign it nor is it subject to attachment or garnishment. Assignment valid if to insurance company, HMO or medical care or hospital services company. (MCLA §§418.815-.821; MSA §§17.237[815]-[821]).

Settlements must be approved by worker's compensation magistrate. (MCLA §418.835; MSA §17.237[835]).

Unemployment Compensation.—Unemployed individuals available for and seeking work are eligible for weekly benefit payments from state unemployment compensation fund. (MCLA §421.28; MSA §17.530). Amount of weekly benefit is (a) for benefit years beginning before July 1, 1997, 67% of individual's after tax weekly wage, but shall not exceed $300 per week; and (b) for benefit years beginning on or after Jan. 1, 1996, but before July 1, 1997, 67% of individual's after tax weekly wage, but shall not exceed $300 per week. For benefit years beginning after July 1, 1997, individual's weekly benefit rate shall be 4.1% of individual's wages paid in calendar quarter of year in which individual was paid highest total wages, plus $6 per dependent up to five dependents, where individual claims dependent(s) at time of filing for benefits but shall not exceed $300 per week. Amount of benefits individual is entitled to obtained by multiplying weekly benefit rate by ¾ of number of credit weeks earned in employment. Maximum amount of benefits payable to individual shall not exceed 26 times individual's weekly benefit rate. Number of weeks of benefits payable to individual is calculated by taking 40% of individual's base wages and dividing result by individual's weekly benefit rate (shall not exceed 26 weeks of benefits, nor be less than 14 weeks of benefits, payable in full benefit year). Employee of seasonal workforce may apply to commission for designation as seasonal employer 20 days before beginning of season. Designation is conclusive evidence that claimant is not entitled to benefits based on seasonal employment unless unemployment occurs during normal seasonal work period. Seasonal employment does not include employment in construction industry. Outstanding child support obligations shall be deducted and withheld from individual's benefits and forwarded to appropriate state of local child support enforcement agency. (MCLA §421.27; MSA §17.529). Individual is disqualified from receiving benefits if he or she left work voluntarily without good cause attributable to employer or employing unit; was fired for certain types of on-the-job misconduct (including intoxication, drug abuse, theft, strike or other concerted action contrary to existing bargaining agreement, destruction of property and assault and battery); undertook retaliatory misconduct upon learning of discharge; failed to accept suitable work when available; was absent for reason of certain convictions and incarceration or failed to give notice to temporary help firm that job assignment was completed and later sought unemployment benefits. Work not considered suitable is position (1) opened because of labor dispute, (2) remuneration, hours and condition of which are substantially less favorable than that normally prevailing or (3) where acceptance by individual is conditioned upon joining or refraining from joining labor organization. Requalification is possible, but benefit amount is reduced. (MCLA §421.29; MSA §17.531). Benefit received to which employee is not entitled will be deducted from employees subsequent state tax refund. (MCLA §§205.30a and 421.62; MSA §§7.657[30a] and 17.566). See also category Taxation, topic Unemployment Compensation Tax.

Commission sales representatives must be paid final commissions within 45 days of termination or in accordance with contract. (MCLA §600.2961; MSA §27A.2961).

WORKERS' COMPENSATION LAW:

See topic Labor Relations.

ENVIRONMENT

ENVIRONMENTAL REGULATION:

General Supervision.—Pursuant to Executive Order 1995-18, effective Oct. 1, 1995, Michigan Department of Environmental Quality (MDEQ) was created and certain duties and responsibilities formerly administered by Michigan Department of Natural Resources (MDNR) were transferred to MDEQ. MDEQ is composed of following divisions: Air Quality, Environmental Response, Environmental Assistance, Surface Water, Storage Tank, Waste Management, Office of Administrative Hearings, Office of the Great Lakes, Coordinator of Environmental Education, Environmental Education Advisory Committee, Environmental Investigations Unit of the Law Enforcement Division, Geological Survey Division, and Lands and Water Division.

Programs retained by MDNR include hunting and fishing, litigation response, parks and recreation, some law enforcement duties, forestry management, farmland and open space, and state fair.

Environmental Code.—Michigan's environmental statutory law has been incorporated into single environmental code, Natural Resources and Environmental Protection Act of 1994 (Public Act 451 of 1994) MCLA §324.101 et seq.; MSA 13A.101 et seq. ("NREPA"). Following represent most of primary parts of NREPA:

Department of Natural Resources: General Powers and Duty, MCLA §324.501, et seq.; MSA §13A.501 et seq.; Michigan Environmental Protection Act, MCLA §324.1701, et seq.; MSA §13A.1701, et seq.; Water Resource Protection, MCLA §324.3101, et seq.; MSA §13A.3101 et seq.; Air Pollution Control, MCLA §324.5501, et seq.; MSA §13A.5501 et seq.; Pesticide Control, MCLA §324.8301, et seq.; MSA §13A.8301 et seq.; Hazardous Waste Management, MCLA §324.11101, et seq.; MSA §13A.11101 et seq.; Solid Waste Management, MCLA §324.11501, et seq.; MSA §13A.11501 et seq.; Liquid Industrial Waste, MCLA §324.12101, et seq.; MSA §13A.12101 et seq.; Environmental Remediation, MCLA §324.20101, et seq.; MSA §13A.20101 et seq.; Underground Storage Tank Regulations, MCLA §324.21101, et seq.; MSA §13A.21101 et seq.; Leaking Underground Storage Tanks, MCLA §324.21301, et seq.; MSA §13A.21301 et seq.; Underground Storage Tank Financial Assurance, MCLA §324.21501, et seq.; MSA §13A.21501 et seq.; Soil Erosion and Sedimentation Control, MCLA §324.9101, et seq.; MSA §13A.9101, et seq.; Inland Lakes and Streams, MCLA §3224.30101, et seq.; MSA §13A.30101, et seq.; Shorelands Protection and Management, MCLA §324.32301, et seq.; MSA §13A.32301, et seq.; Wetlands Protection, MCLA §324.30301, et seq.; MSA §13A.30301, et seq.; Sand Dune Protection and Management, MCLA §324.35301, et seq.; MSA §13A.35301, et seq.; Farmland and Open Space Preservation, MCLA §324.36101, et seq.; MSA §13A.36101, et seq.; Endangered Species Protection, MCLA §324.36501, et seq.; MSA §13A.36501, et seq.

Michigan Environmental Protection Act (Part 17).—(MCLA §§324.1701—.1706; MSA §§13A.1701—.1706). Part 17 grants standing to any person to bring action for protection of air, water, and other natural resources and public trusts therein from pollution, impairment or destruction. It generally authorizes court to grant declaratory or equitable relief and to impose conditions upon defendant to protect environment. It also prohibits administrative actions which authorize conduct that may pollute, impair, or destroy environment as long as feasible and prudent alternatives exist.

Environmental Audit and Immunity (Part 148).—(MCLA §§324.14801—.14810; MSA §§13A.14801—.14810). Part 148 became effective Mar. 18, 1996. Subject to certain requirements and exceptions, Part 148 provides that voluntary environmental compliance audits are privileged and confidential, are not subject to discovery in civil, criminal and/or administrative lawsuits and are not admissible in such actions. Primary requirement for privilege is that appropriate action be taken to correct any noncompliance item within reasonable amount of time after it is identified. Part 148 also provides, subject to certain requirements and exceptions, that person is immune from specific civil and criminal penalties if person voluntarily discloses noncompliance item found in environmental audit and promptly corrects noncompliance item, provided MDEQ was notified prior to commencement of audit.

Hazardous Waste Management (Part 111).—(MCLA §§324.11101-.11152; MSA §§13A.11101-.11152). Part 111 provides for "cradle to grave" regulation of hazardous waste. This Part regulates generation, transportation, treatment, storage, and disposal of hazardous waste and provides for licensing of treatment, storage and disposal

See note at head of Digest as to 1998 legislation covered.

See Topical Index in front part of this volume.

MI – 33

ENVIRONMENTAL REGULATION... *continued*
facilities ("TSDF"). It requires treatment, storage, or disposal at approved TSDFs, and establishes manifest system to track hazardous waste. Part 111 was patterned after Resources Conservation and Recovery Act (RCRA), 42 USC 6901-6987.

Michigan has received from U.S. EPA authorization to implement Part 111 and its regulations in lieu of RCRA for most but not all aspects of Michigan hazardous waste management program. Michigan program is administered by MDEQ Waste Management Division. As with RCRA, Part 111 prescribes remedies and penalties for violation of its terms.

Water Resources Protection (Part 31).—(MCLA §§324.3101-.3119, MSA §§13A.3101-.3119). Part 31 is primary statute dealing with water pollution control and regulation of discharges into "waters of the state" and contents of such discharges. "Waters of the state" are broadly defined to include ground waters, lakes, rivers, streams, all other water courses and waters within confines of state and also Great Lakes bordering state. Part 31 authorizes regulation of use of water courses and flood plains, including occupation of or construction on flood plains, in stream beds and channels of streams and pollution of surface or underground waters and provides for establishment of standards and requirements for permits. Part 31 requires persons discharging waste to have permits, which may contain conditions; requires entities discharging liquid waste to surface or ground water other than through public sanitation to have facilities under control and supervision of persons certified by MDNR and requires annual reports containing specified information from those discharging waste water into waters of state or sewer systems.

Solid Waste Management (Part 115).—(MCLA §§324.11501-.11549; MSA §§13A.11501-.11549). Part 115 is intended to foster and encourage environmentally sound solid waste disposal methods that will maximize utilization of valuable resources and encourage resource conservation. It defines solid waste to include garbage, rubbish, ashes, incinerator ash, incinerator residue, street cleanings, municipal and industrial sludges, solid commercial and solid industrial waste, and animal waste. Solid waste does not include human body waste, medical waste, organic waste generated in production of livestock and poultry, liquid wastes, certain ferrous or nonferrous scrap, certain slag, or slag products, source or site separated materials and number of other substances including waste regulated by other statutes, as well as inert material. Construction permits are required for all new solid waste disposal facilities and operating licenses are required for all solid waste disposal facilities or areas. Exemptions from permit and licensing requirements are provided for certain transfer facilities and incinerators. Solid waste hauler must comply with requirements relating to vehicle transportation of solid waste and must deliver all waste to licensed facility. Landfill owners and operators must provide for closure and post-closure care and must provide financial assurance to cover related costs.

Wetland Protection (Part 303).—(MCLA §§324.30301-.303223; MSA §§13A.30301-.30323). Under Part 303 "wetlands" means land characterized by presence of water at frequency and duration sufficient to support, and which under normal circumstances does support, wetland vegetation or aquatic life and is commonly referred to as bog, swamp or marsh and which are contiguous to Great Lake or Lake St. Clair, an inland lake or pond, or river or stream. Definition also includes noncontiguous wetlands that are more than five acres in size and noncontiguous areas less than five acres if MDEQ determines that protection of area is essential to preservation of State's natural resources. Unless permit is obtained, person is prohibited from (1) depositing fill material in wetland; (2) dredging or removing soil or minerals from wetland; (3) constructing, operating or maintaining any use or development in wetland; or (4) draining surface water from wetland. State wetland permit applications may be obtained from local or district offices of MDEQ. Violations of Act can result in $10,000 per day civil fines. Permit will not be issued unless it can be shown that unacceptable disruption of aquatic resources will not occur and that either proposed activity is primarily dependent on being located in wetland, or feasible and prudent alternative does not exist. MDEQ must consider nine general criteria in reviewing applications to determine whether proposed activity is in public interest. MDEQ may hold public hearing on wetland permit application or may approve or disapprove of application without public hearing. MDEQ administers federal wetlands program under agreements which permit EPA and Corps. of Engineers to intervene in state permitting decisions in certain circumstances.

Environmental Remediation (Part 201).—(MCLA §§324.20101-.20141, et seq.; MSA §§13A.20101-.20141). Part 201 is state environmental cleanup statute and establishes liability for response activity costs at sites of environmental contamination, cleanup standards, liability standards and defenses. Liability is imposed on persons who were owners and operators prior to June 5, 1995, if they are "responsible for an activity causing a release or threat of release". Persons becoming owners or operators of contaminated property after June 5, 1995, must follow certain steps to acquire contaminated property (including property with underground storage tanks regulated under Part 213) without thereby incurring liability. Part 201 establishes cleanup standards and procedures, creates reporting and disclosure requirements, establishes defenses and exemptions to liability and provides for identification, risk assessment, and priority evaluation of sites of environmental contamination and provides for fines and penalties. It establishes obligations for all owners and operators of contaminated property, regardless of liability for cleanup and provides state and private parties right of access to contaminated property. Part 201 also establishes right of state to seek recovery of state cleanup costs and natural resources damages.

Underground Storage Tank Regulations (Part 211).—(MCLA §§324.21101-.21113; MSA §§13A.21101-.21113). Part 211 regulates certain underground storage tank (UST) systems. Types of tanks excluded from definition of UST system include: (1) farm or residential tanks of 1,100 gallons or less that are used for storing motor fuel for noncommercial purposes; (2) tanks used for storing heating oil for use on premises; (3) septic tanks; (4) any tank having capacity of 110 gallons or less; and (5) any tank that contains de minimis concentration of regulated substances. Owner of UST system must register and annually renew registration with MDEQ. UST owners or operators are required to file installation registration form with Storage Tank

Division of MDEQ at least 45 days before installing new UST system. If there is suspected or confirmed release from UST system, owner or operator of UST system must notify MDEQ within 24 hours. Person who installs or removes UST system must maintain pollution liability insurance with limits of not less than $1,000,000 per occurrence.

Leaking Underground Storage Tank (Part 213).—(MCLA §§324.21301-.21331; MSA §§13A.21301-.21331). Amended Mar. 6, 1996 to adopt same liability scheme as Part 201. (See subhead Environmental Remediation [Part 201], supra). Strict liability is imposed on owners and operators who were such prior to Mar. 6, 1996 if they are "responsible for an activity causing a release or threat of release". Following Mar. 6, 1996, persons becoming owners or operators of contaminated property attributable to UST release must follow certain steps as provided in Part 201 to acquire property without incurring liability. Adopts risk-based corrective action approach to cleanups. All remedial work must be performed by "qualified UST consultant", who must be on list approved by MDEQ. Also includes schedule of civil penalties for failure to submit reports on time and provides civil and criminal penalties for submitting false information or committing other fraud.

Underground Storage Tank Financial Assurance (Part 215).—(MCLA §§324.21501-.21551; MSA §§13A.21501-.21551). Part 215 provides fund for reimbursing owners or operators of petroleum USTs for costs incurred to remediate contamination as result of release. Reimbursement operates on copayment scheme where owner or operator pays 10% of each remediation-related invoice up to maximum of $15,000 for first release from UST system. Owner or operator is responsible for 30% of each invoice up to $45,000 for second release from UST system. Reimbursement is not available for third release. *Note:* Part 215 fund was declared insolvent on Mar. 31, 1995 and program is no longer available for new claims where invoices or request for indemnification were received after 5:00 p.m., June 29, 1995. Legislature extended collection of regulatory fee so that such claims submitted through June 29, 1995 will be reimbursed.

Michigan Air Pollution Control (Part 55).—(MCLA §§324.5501-.5542; MSA §§13A.5501-.5542). Part 55, with Federal Clean Air Act (42 USC 7401, et seq.), and regulations promulgated thereunder, provide regulatory framework for air emissions in Michigan. State air emission permitting program meets federal standards. Part 55 requires that permit be obtained before any installation, construction, reconstruction, relocation or alteration to any source of emission, including any process, fuel burning, refuse burning or control equipment. Numerous exemptions from permitting requirements are included in applicable regulations. Program to control toxic air substances administered through permitting process limits emissions and prohibits ambient impacts above initial threshold screening level or risk screening level as necessary to protect public health. Regulations implementing Renewable Operating Permit Program as required by Clean Air Act amendments of 1990 have been conditionally approved by EPA; startup, shutdown, and malfunction rules have been challenged.

Enforcement.—For most environmental statutes, enforcement rests with MDEQ. For air pollution control and abatement, MDEQ may conduct investigations; enter and inspect facilities, records, and equipment and take samples; seek administrative orders compelling compliance; and may initiate civil actions for fines, injunctions, and natural resource damage; initiate criminal prosecutions (MCLA §324.5526; MSA §13A.5526; MCLA §324.20137; MSA §13A.20137); and also may issue emergency orders to restrain activities creating imminent and substantial endangerment (MCLA §324.5518; MSA §13A.5518). MDEQ and its agents have right of entry to inspect or investigate conditions relating to pollution and obstruction of floodways. (MCLA §324.3105; MSA §13A.3105). MDEQ has authority to investigate matters relating to discharge and stage characteristics of streams and to promulgate regulations to prevent harm or interference with such characteristics. (MCLA §324.3107; MSA §13A.3107). For wetlands, MDEQ may hold public hearing on wetland permit application or may approve or disapprove application without public hearing. (MCLA §752.903; MSA §28.603[3]). Injunctive action may be brought in civil court by any person to restrain pollution of air, water or other natural resources. (MCLA §324.1701; MSA §13A.1701).

Penalties.—For violations of antipollution statutes, penalties are as follows: (1) For violation of air pollution statute, administrative penalties up to $10,000 per day per violation; civil penalties up to $10,000 per day per violation; and/or criminal penalties, including incarceration and fines up to $250,000, depending on violation (MCLA §§324.5529-.5532; MSA §§13A.5529-.5532); (2) for violation of water pollution statutes, civil fine of not less than $2,500 nor more than $25,000 per day of violation; felony fine for intentional violations not less than $2,500 nor more than $25,000, plus $25,000 per day ($50,000 for repeat offenders); if violation poses substantial danger to public health, safety, or welfare, additional fine of not less than $500,000 or not more than $5,000,000 (civil), or additional fine of not less than $1,000,000 and five years' imprisonment (criminal); misdemeanor fines of not more than $2,500 per day (MCLA §§324.3115, .3115a; MSA §§13A.3115, .3115a); (3) for violation of antilittering law, fine or imprisonment; (4) for violation of hazardous waste management, civil fine of not more than $25,000 per day for violation of permit; for misdemeanor fine of not more than $25,000 per day and/or one year imprisonment ($50,000 and two years for repeat offender); for intentionally posing threat to human life, fine of up to $250,000 and/or five years' imprisonment (for private entity, fine up to $1,000,000) (MCLA §324.11151; MSA §13A.11151); (5) for violation of solid waste management act civil penalty of up to $10,000 per day and violation of rule promulgated under act is misdemeanor subject to fine of $1,000 and up to six months in prison (MCLA §§324.11546, .11549; MSA §§13A.11546, .11549); (6) for wetlands, civil fine of $10,000 per day for violation of act (MCLA §324.30316; MSA §13A.30316); for violation under Part 201, fines and/or imprisonment depending on violation (MCLA §324.201; MSA §13A.201); (7) owners/operators of USTs are subject to civil penalty for failure to submit reports on time, and civil and criminal penalties for submitting false information or committing other fraud of up to $50,000 and five years' imprisonment (MCLA §324.21313a; MSA §13A.21313a and MCLA §324.21324; MSA §13A.21324).

See note at head of Digest as to 1998 legislation covered.

See Topical Index in front part of this volume.

ENVIRONMENTAL REGULATION . . . *continued*

Permits required for numerous activities which may damage environment. Exceptions and exemptions are as provided by statute. See subheads supra.

Uniform Transboundary Pollution Reciprocal Access Act adopted. (MCLA §§3.871-.880; MSA §§14.58[201]-14.58]210]).

ESTATES AND TRUSTS

ADMINISTRATION:

See topic Executors and Administrators.

ALLOWANCES:

See topic Executors and Administrators.

CLAIMS:

See topic Executors and Administrators; category Civil Actions and Procedure, topic Pleading.

DEATH:

Uniform Determination of Death Act adopted. (MCLA §§333.1031-.1034; MSA §§14.15[1031]-.15[1034]). Adds §3 providing that physician or registered nurse has authority to pronounce death of person. Medical facility may determine which of its personnel may pronounce death in facility.

Property of person absent and unheard of for seven years may be administered as though he were dead. If no claim is made by absent person or any person claiming to have succeeded to his rights within three years of qualification of fiduciary, conclusive presumption arises that absent person died seven years from date of disappearance. On sufficient showing that person died or may be presumed to have died in disaster, despite absence or inability to identify remains, probate judge may find fact and date of death and order issuance of death certificate (MCLA §333.2845; MSA §14.15[2845]), upon which administration of estate may be founded without waiting seven years (MCLA §700.492; MSA §27.5492).

Death Certificate.—See category Documents and Records, topic Records, subhead Vital Statistics.

Written finding of presumed death pursuant to federal Missing Persons Act (50 U. S. C. A. 1001 et seq.) is prima facie evidence of death (MCLA §720.501; MSA §27.966[1]).

Survivorship.—Uniform Simultaneous Death Act has been adopted. (MCLA §§720.101-.108; MSA §27.3178[621]-[628]).

Action for death lies under Wrongful Death Act. (MCLA §600.2922; MSA §27A.2922). Action is brought by personal representative. Recovery limited to certain relatives and devisees under will. Damages are reasonable medical, hospital, funeral and burial expenses for which estate is liable, reasonable compensation for pain and suffering of deceased while conscious, and loss to surviving spouse and next-of-kin. Trial court allocates amount of judgment representing loss to surviving spouse and next-of-kin and proportion to each. Probate court settles claims where no action brought in another court and distributes proceeds in both cases. (MCLA §§700.221-.222; MSA §§27.5221-.5222). Action must be brought within one to three years depending on cause of action. (MCLA §600.5805; MSA §27A.5805). There is no statutory limitation of amount recoverable.

Uniform Anatomical Gift Act.—See topic Wills, subhead Uniform Anatomical Gift Act.

Living Wills.—See topic Wills, subhead Living Wills.

DECEDENT'S ESTATES:

See topics Executors and Administrators, Descent and Distribution, and Wills.

DESCENT AND DISTRIBUTION:

All property of intestate decedent in excess of share of surviving spouse, or all if there be no surviving spouse, descends and is distributed as follows, each class of which member is living taking to exclusion of subsequent classes: (1) Issue, equally if all of same degree, otherwise according to right of representation; (2) parents, or surviving parent; (3) brothers and sisters and children of deceased brothers and sisters, equally if all of same degree, otherwise by right of representation; (4) grandparents or issue of grandparents (one-half maternal kindred, one-half paternal kindred, if no takers on one side then all to other), issue take equally if of same degree, more remote degrees are excluded; if no survivor known or determinable, to state by escheat. (MCLA §700.106; MSA §27.5106).

Surviving Spouse.—Portion of surviving spouse is as follows: If decedent left no issue nor parent, entire intestate estate; if no issue, but at least one parent, first $60,000, plus one-half of balance; if issue, all of whom are also issue of surviving spouse, first $60,000, plus one-half of balance; if issue, one or more of whom are not issue of surviving spouse, one-half of intestate estate. (MCLA §700.105; MSA §27.5105).

Surviving spouses are also entitled to certain allowances. See topic Executors and Administrators, subheads Priorities and Allowances.

Right of spouse to intestate share may be waived by written agreement made before or after marriage. (MCLA §700.291; MSA §27.5291).

Surviving spouse does not include: (1) One who obtains or consents to judgment of divorce, even if not recognized as valid in this state; (2) one who following defective decree of divorce, participates in marriage ceremony with third person; (3) one who at time of decedent's death is living in bigamous relationship; (4) one who was party to valid proceeding concluded by order purporting to terminate all marital property rights, or who voluntarily entered into valid written contract specifically settling all marital property rights. Such persons shall not inherit or take estate, right or interest whatever by way of inheritance, dower, allowance or otherwise. (MCLA §§700.141, .185; MSA §§27.5141, .5185).

Half blood kindred inherit as if they were of whole blood. (MCLA §700.109; MSA §27.5109).

Posthumous Children or Other Issue.—Considered as living at death of parent. (MCLA §700.109; MSA §27.5109).

Illegitimate child inherits from mother and mother's kindred as though legitimate. Such child inherits from father if: (1) father joins with mother and acknowledges that child is his child by completing acknowledgment as prescribed in Acknowledgment of Parentage Act; (2) father joins with mother in written request for correction of certificate of birth substituting record of birth as legitimate; (3) father establishes mutually acknowledged relationship of parent and child with such child before age 18 and continued until terminated by death of either; or (4) man has been determined to be father of child and order of filiation establishing paternity has been entered pursuant to Paternity Act, MCLA §§722.711-.730; MSA §§27.5711-.5730. (MCLA §700.111; MSA §27.5111). Property of illegitimate passes in accordance with laws of intestacy except that father and his kindred shall not be considered as relatives unless child might have inherited from father as provided above. (MCLA §700.111; MSA §27.5111).

Adopted Children.—See category Family, topic Adoption.

Determination of Heirship.—Probate Court may determine heirs and devisees in any matter before court. Any interested party may file petition for such determination and court shall schedule hearing on such petition upon notice of all interested parties. (MCLA §700.183; MSA §27.5183).

Advancements.—Property given by testator during lifetime to devisee shall be treated as satisfaction in whole or part of devise if will provides for deduction of lifetime gift. (MCLA §700.139; MSA §27.5139). Property given during lifetime to heir by person dying intestate treated as advancement only if declared to be advancement in contemporaneous writing by decedent or acknowledged to be advancement in writing by heir. (MCLA §700.111a; MSA §27.5111[1]).

Election.—Surviving spouse of Michigan decedent dying testate has right to elect (1) to abide by will; (2) to take one-half sum that would have passed to spouse had testator died intestate, reduced by one-half value of property otherwise passing to surviving spouse, or (3) if widow that she will take her dower right. Fiduciary shall serve surviving spouse notice of right to election prior to date for presentment of claims and surviving spouse shall elect within 60 days after date for presentment of claims or within 60 days after filing of proof of service of inventory on surviving spouse, whichever is later. If decedent died intestate leaving widow, widow may elect to take (1) intestate share, or (2) dower within same time periods. (MCLA §700.282; MSA §27.5282). See topic Wills.

Disclaimer of Legacy.—See topic Wills.

Escheat.—If decedent left neither surviving spouse nor kindred, entire estate escheats to state, subject to being recovered by heirs at any time. (MCLA §§700.106, 567.1-.75; MSA §§27.5106, 26.1011-.1053[65]).

See also topic Executors and Administrators.

ESTATES:

See category Property, topic Real Property.

EXECUTORS AND ADMINISTRATORS:

Probate court in each county has jurisdiction of settlement of estates of all deceased persons dying residents of this state or leaving any estate in this state to be administered. (MCLA §700.21; MSA §27.5021). If decedent at death was resident of this state, probate court of county of residence is proper forum; if decedent at death not resident of this state, probate court of county where property located is proper forum. (MCLA §§700.114, .145; MSA §§27.5114, .5145). Where two or more county probate courts are proper forum, first to take cognizance of estate has and retains jurisdiction for all probate proceedings in state. (MCLA §700.114; MSA §27.5114).

Preferences in Right to Administer.—For testate estates personal representatives named in will are appointed if competent; if persons named are not competent, or refuse to accept trust or to file bond, court appoints any one of beneficiaries named in will or person who would be entitled to administer if estate was intestate estate. (MCLA §700.514; MSA §27.5514).

For intestate estates, court will appoint one of following persons, if competent, in following order of right: Surviving spouse or person requested by such spouse, heir of decedent by degree of kinship or person requested by such heir, public administrator or interested person as court deems proper. (MCLA §700.116; MSA §27.5116).

Eligibility and Competency.—Since personal representative of estate is at all times amenable to process issued out of courts of this state, preference will be given to suitable and competent parties who are residents of this state and citizens of U.S. Nonresidents may qualify to serve as follows: Bank or trust company authorized to do business in state; guardian of resident minor and will of surviving parent nominates; nonresident who consents to service of process by resident agent. (MCLA §700.531; MSA §27.5531). Minor may not act, but if named in will as executor, will be appointed upon attaining majority and filing bond. (MCLA §700.163; MSA §27.5163). Creditor may not act as personal representative in intestate estate. (MCLA §700.116; MSA §27.5116). Judge other than municipal court judge may not act as fiduciary except for estates of immediate family. (MCLA §700.582; MSA §27.5582).

Qualification.—Prior to execution of his trust fiduciary, except in independent probate proceedings, must file bond approved by and running to court in such amount as court requires, condition of bond being proper administration of estate, including collection of all property, filing timely inventory, paying debts, accounting annually and performing all orders of court directed to him. (MCLA §700.502; MSA §27.5502). Deposit of collateral acceptable to court in lieu of bond is permitted. (MCLA §700.507; MSA §27.5507). Bond or acceptable collateral must be filed within 15 days

EXECUTORS AND ADMINISTRATORS . . . *continued*
of appointment (MCLA §700.507; MSA §27.5507) and secures all interested persons (MCLA §700.508; MSA §27.5508). In independent proceedings, providing statutory requirements are met, fiduciary may serve without bond unless will otherwise provides. (MCLA §§700.306-313; MSA §§27.5306-.5313).

Exemption from Bond.—Every executor and administrator must file bond or deposit acceptable collateral (MCLA §§700.502, .507; MSA §§27.5502, .5507), except that trust companies existing under state financial institutions act may on court approval substitute for bond their deposit with state treasurer (MCLA §700.507; MSA §27.5507), and except as provided with respect to independent probate proceedings (MCLA §§700.306-.313; MSA §§27.5306-.5313).

Issuance of Letters.—Upon presentation and approval of bond or satisfactory commencement of independent proceedings, court issues letters stating in substance duties of fiduciary and his authority to then act on behalf of estate. (MCLA §700.533; MSA §27.5533 and MCLA §700.312; MSA §27.5312). Upon request of interested persons, court will certify to proper issuance of letters which makes same prima facie evidence of facts set out in letters and eligible for recording. (MCLA §§700.536, .537; MSA §§27.5536, .5537).

Removal.—Fiduciary may be removed if he resides out of state, neglects to render accounts and settle estate or absconds or becomes incapacitated or otherwise unsuitable to discharge his responsibilities. (MCLA §700.574; MSA §27.5574). Fiduciary may be allowed to resign whenever his personal interests conflict with interest of estate or for another reason deemed appropriate by court. (MCLA §700.574; MSA §27.5574).

Special Kinds of Administration.—When court deems it expedient temporary personal representative may be appointed to collect and take charge of estate pending appointment of personal representative. (MCLA §700.174; MSA §27.5174). Temporary personal representative on court order may commence actions and sell perishable and other real or personal property of estate. (MCLA §700.175; MSA §27.5175).

If personal representative of estate dies or is by order of court removed or allowed to resign, or estate is closed without full administration, court shall appoint successor personal representative. (MCLA §700.577; MSA §27.5577).

Public Administrator.—Appointment authorized by statute when deemed appropriate by court; when no known heirs or no spouse or heir entitled to distributive share within U.S.; when such spouse or heir exists but no petition for administration is made within 30 days of death or if needed to make necessary burial arrangements and conserve estate of decedent. (MCLA §700.116; MSA §27.5116).

Inventory and Appraisal.—Fiduciary must file inventory within 60 days of appointment. (MCLA §700.605; MSA §27.5605). Inventory shall list each asset and its fair market value at date of death and shall include statement of any liens or encumbrances. If value of property is subject to reasonable doubt, personal representative may employ one or more qualified, disinterested appraisers to assist in such valuation. (MCLA §700.605; MSA §27.5605).

General Powers and Duties.—Fiduciary has right and duty to take possession of all assets of estate and to collect rents and profits (MCLA §700.601; MSA §27.5601 and MCLA §700.334; MSA §27.5334) and in support thereof may initiate proceedings in probate court for discovery of assets concealed, embezzled or conveyed away (MCLA §700.607; MSA §27.5607). Following collection of assets fiduciary has duty to protect estate from unlawful demands and settle estate promptly. (MCLA §700.544; MSA §27.544). During administration fiduciary must keep funds reasonably invested in investments authorized by statute (MCLA §555.201; MSA §26.85) unless otherwise provided by will or by court order (MCLA §700.561; MSA §27.5561).

Business of decedent may be continued by fiduciary on court order (MCLA §700.546; MSA §27.5546) or pursuant to authorization under will or pursuant to continuation agreement (MCLA §700.552; MSA §27.5552).

Fiduciary may mortgage or pledge estate assets only with court order and for limited purposes. (MCLA §700.665; MSA §27.5665). Real property of estate may be leased by fiduciary upon court order, including oil and gas leases. (MCLA §700.671; MSA §27.5671).

Notice of Appointment.—Notice of required hearing must be given to interested persons on all petitions for appointment of personal representative. (MCLA §700.172; MSA §27.5172). Notice may be given: (i) By personal service at least seven days prior to hearing, or (ii) by publication together with notice by registered or certified mail to all known interested persons 14 days prior to hearing, or (iii) by registered, certified, or first class mail, in manner above described, where all interested persons are known. (MCLA §§600.854, 700.31; MSA §27.5031). If any heirs-at-law are residents of a foreign country, written notice must be sent by mail to consul of the foreign country at least 60 days prior to hearing. (MCLA §700.180; MSA §27.5180). In independent probate proceedings, hearing is not required, however, Notice of Appointment and other documents, including copy of will and petition for independent probate, must be served upon interested parties within ten days of appointment. (MCLA §200.315; MSA §27.5315).

Notice to Creditors.—Upon appointment fiduciary must publish notice to creditors to present claims within four months after publication. Any known creditor i.e. one who has demanded payment from estate or decedent or one whose existence was reasonably ascertainable by investigation of decendent's available records for two years immediately preceding death and mail following death, is entitled to direct notice during four month period. If learned of within less than 30 days before expiration of such period such creditor is entitled to direct notice within 30 days of becoming known. (MCLA §700.703; MSA §27.5703). Once estate closed it may not be reopened for purpose of filing claim. (MCLA §700.593; MSA §27.5593).

Presentation of Claims.—Claims against estate, fiduciary and heirs are barred unless claimant complies with statutory requirements. (MCLA §700.710; MSA §27.5710). Claimant shall present claim either by (a) delivering to fiduciary written statement of claim containing specified information or (b) commencing proceeding to obtain payment in court of proper jurisdiction. (MCLA §700.712; MSA §27.5712).

Contingent and unliquidated claims are treated in same manner as other claims. (MCLA §§700.710,.733; MSA §§27.5710,.5733).

Secured claims need not be proved to protect security but must be proved to obtain deficiency. (56 Mich. 15, 22 N.W. 185).

Proof of Claims.—See subhead Presentation of Claims, supra.

Approval or Rejection of Claims.—Fiduciary may mail notice disallowing claim in whole or in part within 63 days after time for original presentation of claims. Failure to mail notice of disallowance constitutes allowance of claim. Court may upon petition allow timely filed claim in whole or in part. (MCLA §700.717; MSA §27.5717). Proceeding on claim must be commenced within 63 days of mailing notice of disallowance. (MCLA §700.712; MSA §27.5712).

Payment of Claims.—Upon expiration of four months from date of publication of notice fiduciary shall proceed to pay all claims allowed after making provision for various allowances, exemptions, costs of administration and unbarred or appealed claims. (MCLA §700.720; MSA §27.5720). If assets of estate are insufficient to satisfy all claims payment is to be made in accordance with MCLA §700.715; MSA §27.5715. Claims bear interest computed pursuant to MCLA §600.6013; MSA §27A.6013. See subheads Approval or Rejection of Claims and Presentation of Claims, supra.

Priorities.—Charges against estate shall be paid in following order of priority (MCLA §700.192; MSA §27.5192): (a) Expenses of administration; (b) funeral and burial expenses; (c) family allowance for spouse and minor children; (d) homestead provisions for spouse and minor children; (e) allowances for spouse and minor children; (f) claims allowed against estate as follows: (i) costs and expenses of administration, (ii) funeral and burial expenses, (iii) debts and taxes with priority under federal law, (iv) expenses of last illness, (v) debts and taxes with priority under law of State, (vi) all other claims. (MCLA §§700.192,.715; MSA §§27.5192,.5715).

Sales.—Personal property of estate may be sold by fiduciary at private sale without license from court for not less than inventory value, or if personalty has a market value definitely ascertainable because of quotations or listing on an exchange, then for market value. Order of court is required for sale of personalty specifically bequeathed and for all sales of personalty at a price less than current market value. (MCLA §700.631; MSA §27.5631).

Where real property of estate was subject of a contract to convey existing at time of death, fiduciary without court order may give deed upon full payment of contract price and on petition of purchaser to court may be compelled to do so. (MCLA §700.672; MSA §27.5672).

Except with power of sale in will, fiduciary may sell real estate with confirmation of court under following circumstances: (a) Personal estate insufficient to pay debts and expenses of administration; (b) personal estate sufficient, but it is in best interests of all persons interested to sell in lieu of disposing of personal estate; (c) when it appears necessary to preserve estate or prevent sacrifice thereof or to carry out provisions of will; (d) when devise by will is effectual to pass or charge real estate and personal estate insufficient to pay devise, together with debts and expenses; (e) when two or more persons are recipients and it is in best interests of all such persons to sell realty for purposes of distribution, provided it is agreed to in writing by persons owning majority interest in such real estate. (MCLA §700.635; MSA §27.5635).

Fiduciary may sell real estate if all of following occur: (a) He has authority to sell as defined above; (b) he reported sale in writing to court for confirmation and had hearing thereon; (c) he gave notice of such hearing to all parties in interest; (d) he filed and had approved bond required by court; (e) he obtained order from court confirming sale and directing giving of deed or other conveyance pursuant to sale. (MCLA §700.634; MSA §27.5634). Sale price must be payable on one of following terms: (a) For cash; (b) not less than one-third cash down with five-year mortgage or note; (c) executory contract with 20% down with five years to pay, may however provide if 50% of purchase price is paid, fiduciary may deed over land and take back five-year mortgage for remainder; after diligent effort by fiduciary to sell under above terms, he may sell upon terms he deems best for estate, ward or beneficiary. (MCLA §700.641; MSA §27.5641). Fiduciary is prohibited from purchasing either directly or indirectly. (MCLA §700.642; MSA §27.5642).

Actions by Representative.—All actions and claims survive death. (MCLA §600.2921; MSA §27A.2921). In pending actions fiduciary may be substituted. (Rule 2.202).

Actions against Representative.—See subhead Presentation of Claims, supra for procedure with respect to actions against estate arising from debts and obligations of decedent. Issues of liability between estate and personal representative may be determined in proceeding for accounting, surcharge or indemnification. (MCLA §700.726; MSA §27.5726).

Allowances.—Surviving spouse domiciled in Michigan and minor children decedent was obliged to support are entitled to reasonable family allowance during progress of administration, up to distribution or year whichever is earlier. In solvent estates, court may extend allowances beyond year on showing of necessity, but such payments will be treated as advances. (MCLA §700.287; MSA §27.5287).

Quarantine.—Surviving spouse may remain in dwelling house of spouse for one year after death or until share of surviving spouse is assigned, whichever is earlier without liability for rent. (MCLA §700.288; MSA §27.5288).

Intermediate Accountings.—Except in independent probate proceedings fiduciary must account annually, or oftener if court directs. (MCLA §700.563; MSA §27.5563).

Final Accounting and Settlement.—Final account must be rendered on closing date, which must occur as promptly as possible unless court extends time for good cause. (MCLA §700.563; MSA §27.5563). Following filing of each account, including intermediate accounts, hearing date is set unless court determines that assets and income are insufficient to justify expense, in which case hearing is deferred until final account. Notice of hearing to interested persons is required. Order allowing account is res judicata except for fraud. (MCLA §700.564; MSA §27.5564). Petition to compel settlement may be filed by any person beneficially interested or surety on bond.

EXECUTORS AND ADMINISTRATORS . . . *continued*
(MCLA §700.572; MSA §27.5572). Summary procedures may be used in certain independent proceedings. (MCLA §§700.325-326; MSA §§27.5325-5326).

Consent Settlement.—No statutory provision for settlement of accounts other than by hearing and order of court. In practice accounts are commonly presented to court with written consents to allowance of account and waiver of notice of hearing by interested persons.

Distribution.—Following payment of or provision for prior charges, court by order assigns residue of estate to persons entitled to same by law. (MCLA §700.192; MSA §27.5192). Order for distribution specifies by name and proportion persons entitled to estate property, and following 30 days after order named persons have right to demand and recover their shares unless appeal filed. (MCLA §700.193; MSA §27.5193). Person entitled to estate property may petition for delivery of same after payment of debts and other charges or before if he provides security for payment of his just proportion of prior charges. (MCLA §700.194; MSA §27.5194). Pecuniary bequests may be satisfied in kind with property valued as of distribution date in absence of contrary direction in will. (MCLA §§700.215-.216; MSA §§27.5215-.5216).

Distribution if Abroad.—When devisees are residents of foreign country, foreign consul for such country shall be notified, unless devisee files waiver of notice with court. (MCLA §700.180; MSA §27.5180). Where it appears distributee would not have benefit or use or control of property due him, court may order deposit of same with county treasurer for benefit of distributee. (MCLA §700.591; MSA §27.5591).

Liabilities.—Fiduciary is liable to interested persons for loss arising out of his embezzlement, commingling of estate funds with his own, negligent handling of estate, willful and wanton mishandling, self-dealing, failure to account or terminate when estate is ready for termination and for any misfeasance or other breach of duty. (MCLA §700.544; MSA §27.5544).

Compensation of Representatives.—Fiduciaries shall be allowed reasonable expenses and also reasonable compensation for services as approved by court. (MCLA §700.541; MSA §27.5541).

When Administration Unnecessary.—Special provision is made for summary administration of estates consisting of property of value not more than aggregate of all allowances and exemptions and for distribution without administration of estates consisting of property of less than $15,000 in value. (MCLA §§700.101-.102; MSA §§27.5101-.5102). Title to one or more vehicles whose value does not exceed $60,000 may be transferred by affidavit of surviving spouse or heirs where decedent left no other property requiring administration. (MCLA §257.236; MSA §9.1936).

Small Estates.—See subhead When Administration Unnecessary, supra.

Foreign Executors or Administrators.—Generally foreign representative has no rights to either real or personal property in state and ancillary administration necessary to release mortgage or to perfect title to real property in heirs or devisees. (194 Mich. 670, 161 N.W. 847; 55 Mich. 568, 22 N.W. 41). Foreign fiduciary may be qualified by filing bond and thereafter, with regard to property of nonresident decedent in Michigan, will have same powers and duties as local personal representative. (MCLA §700.236; MSA §27.5236). Bank accounts and intangible personalty, including securities which are held by bank or trust company can be released to foreign fiduciary upon affidavit and order of appointing court. (MCLA §700.236; MSA §27.5236).

Unsupervised Administration.—Procedures are available for appointment of independent personal representative, who may administer estate of decedent with minimal court supervision. (MCLA §700.301 et seq.; MSA §27.5301 et seq.). Independent personal representative has extensive powers to deal with assets of estate, but may upon petition of himself or any interested party be subjected to court supervision as to part or all of estate proceedings. (MCLA §§700.334-.351; MSA §27.5334-.5351). Independent proceedings are concluded by filing closing statement and either approval by court or elapsing of one year from date of filing. (MCLA §700.357; MSA §27.5357).

Uniform Anatomical Gift Act.—See topic Wills.

Uniform Fiduciaries Act not adopted.

Uniform Principal and Income Act.—Revised version adopted with local variations respecting bonds. (MCLA §§555.56-.63; MSA §26.79[6-13]).

Uniform Simplification of Fiduciary Security Transfers Act adopted. (MCLA §§441.101-.112; MSA §§19.356[1-12]).

Registration of Securities in Beneficiary Form Act adopted. (MCLA §§451.471-.481).

PROOF OF CLAIMS:

See topic Executors and Administrators; category Civil Actions and Procedure, topic Pleading.

TRUSTS:

Kinds.—Uses and trusts of land are abolished and legal title vests in beneficiary (MCLA §555.1; MSA §26.51), except where trustee has duties of management or discretion, and trust is created (1) to sell for benefit of creditors, (2) to sell, mortgage or lease for the benefit of legatees or to satisfy any charge on the land, (3) to receive rents and profits and apply them to use of any person for life or shorter term, (4) to receive rents and profits and accumulate them for benefit of married woman, (5) for beneficial interest of any person where fully expressed and clearly defined on face of instrument creating trust (MCLA §555.11; MSA §26.61). Resulting trusts of land are not recognized (MCLA §555.7; MSA §26.57), except in favor of creditors where fraudulent intent is not disproved (MCLA §555.8; MSA §26.58). Equity will imply a trust to relieve against fraud. (MCLA §§555.6, .9; MSA §§26.56, .59). Trust of personal property may be created for any purpose.

Spendthrift trust for income beneficiary is valid (255 Mich. 275, 238 N.W. 284), except that creditors may reach excess income not required for education and support

of beneficiary of a trust to receive the rents and profits of land where no valid direction for accumulation is given (MCLA §555.13; MSA §26.63).

Charitable trust does not fail for lack of trustee or uncertainty of object or beneficiaries or because it creates a perpetuity. (MCLA §554.351; MSA §26.1191).

Creation.—Trusts may be created inter vivos or by will. Trust of land must be declared in writing (9 Mich. 358) and unless declared in conveyance to trustee it is void as to trustee's subsequent creditors without notice and good faith purchasers (MCLA §555.20; MSA §26.70). Trust of personal property may be created by parol. (274 Mich. 484, 265 N.W. 441).

If controversy arises respecting inter vivos irrevocable trust, circuit court can approve compromise and bind all interests. (MCLA §555.81 et seq.; MSA §26.80[1] et seq.).

Appointment of Trustee.—Settlor of inter vivos trust names trustee. If testator names trustee, probate court must appoint person named, provided he qualifies. (156 Mich. 301, 120 N.W. 811). If trustee is not named, or is unable to serve, probate court will appoint trustee. (MCLA §700.805; MSA §27.5805).

Registration of trust by trustee with probate court is required except: (a) Testamentary trust, (b) trust under living trust agreement in existence before July 1, 1979, and (c) trust containing terms to exempt it from registration. (MCLA §700.801; MSA §27.5801).

Eligibility and Competency.—Person acting as fiduciary is at all times amenable to process issued by court, therefore resident of Michigan and citizen of U.S. who is suitable and competent is given preference. Nonresidents may be appointed. (MCLA §700.531; MSA §27.5531).

Qualification.—Testamentary trustee may be required to file bond. (MCLA §700.502; MSA §27.5502).

Removal of Trustee.—Equity has power to remove trustee upon proof of insolvency, incapacity, neglect, misconduct or violation of trust. (265 Mich. 358, 251 N.W. 555). If trustee resides outside state, neglects to render an account to court after due notice, absconds, becomes incapacitated, or is otherwise unsuitable or incapable to discharge trust, probate court has power of removal. (MCLA §700.574; MSA §27.5574).

General Powers and Duties of Trustee.—Powers and duties of trustee are determined largely by trust instrument. Inherent duty is to exercise honesty, good faith and reasonable diligence in preserving trust estate and executing trust purpose (265 Mich. 358, 251 N.W. 555), and to keep beneficiaries advised (52 Mich. 174, 17 N.W. 784). Trustee is commanded to keep trust estate invested (MCLA §555.201; MSA §26.85), and has inherent power to do whatever is necessary to preserve trust estate (274 Mich. 225, 264 N.W. 351), such as payment of liens, taxes and insurance premiums, or employment of attorney, or settlement of claim against estate (199 Mich. 88, 165 N.W. 643). He may not continue business venture of settlor or testator without express authority or court order. (275 Mich. 237, 266 N.W. 332). Remedy of trustee or beneficiary in absence of express authority is application to court for instructions. (255 Mich. 173, 237 N.W. 535). Trustees of trusts for charitable purposes must furnish copies of trust documents, inventories, periodic written reports, and copies of accounts or petitions for distribution to state Attorney General, who has general supervision over such trusts including power to make rules and regulations. (MCLA §14.251; MSA §26.1200[1]).

Trustees of trusts having a charitable beneficiary are subject to Charitable Trustees Powers Act which prohibits certain conduct and grants enforcement and supervisory power to attorney general. (MCLA §§14.271-.287; MSA §26.1200[21]-[37]).

Revised Probate Code enumerates certain powers granted inter vivos trustees and testamentary trustees who elect to proceed on unsupervised basis. (MCLA §700.821 et seq.; MSA §27.5821 et seq.).

Gift to Surviving Spouse.—See topic Wills, subhead Gift to Surviving Spouse.

Sales of trust assets are void unless authorized by power of sale or court order, except as to purchasers for value without notice of trust. (189 Mich. 566, 155 N.W. 599). Inter vivos trustees and unsupervised testamentary trustees may sell assets under statutory authority. (MCLA §700.822; MSA §27.5822).

Investments.—Prudent man rule has been adopted. Only investments expressly prohibited are securities or property purchased by trustee from himself, or if corporate, from itself or affiliate (MCLA §555.201; MSA §26.85). Trustee is under duty to use special skills if possessed or represented as possessed. (MCLA §700.813; MSA §27.5813).

Securities in Name of Nominee.—A corporate sole trustee, or a corporate co-trustee with consent of co-fiduciary, may hold registrable securities in name of nominee employed by corporation without mention of the trust on the certificates evidencing securities, unless trust instrument otherwise provides, but corporate trustee must retain possession of certificates in nominee form and maintain records showing real interest in certificates. (MCLA §§555.441, .443; MSA §§21.313[1], [3]).

Bequests and Devises to Inter Vivos Trusts.—See topic Wills.

Accounting.—Testamentary trustee accounts to probate court annually, or oftener if so ordered. (MCLA §700.563; MSA §27.5563). Trustee under living trust must account when requested (277 Mich. 505, 269 N.W. 577), and may apply to probate court for judicial settlement of account when desired (MCLA §700.805; MSA §27.5805).

Compensation.—Trustee is entitled to expenses and reasonable compensation for his services. (MCLA §700.541; MSA §27.5541). No schedule is fixed.

Discharge.—A trustee can be discharged by: (1) Extinction of the trust, (2) completion of duties, (3) means prescribed by declaration of trust, (4) consent of all beneficiaries, if have capacity to contract, (5) order of court upon finding grounds for removal (MCLA §§555.26, 700.574; MSA §§26.76, 27.5574), or (6) upon order of court accepting resignation. (MCLA §§555.25, 700.574; MSA §§26.75, 27.5574).

Uniform Common Trust Fund Act (with additions and variations) in effect; Official Amendment not adopted. (MCLA §§555.101-.113; MSA §§23.1141-.1153).

See note at head of Digest as to 1998 legislation covered.

See Topical Index in front part of this volume.

TRUSTS . . . *continued*

Revised Uniform Principal and Income Act.—Adopted with local variation respecting bonds. (MCLA §§555.5 et seq.; MSA §§26.79 et seq.).

Gifts to Minors.—See category Family, topic Infants.

Uniform Fiduciaries Act not adopted.

Uniform Simplification of Fiduciary Security Transfers Actadopted. (MCLA §§441.101-.112; MSA §§19.356[1]-[12]).

Uniform Supervision of Trustees for Charitable Purposes Act in effect. (MCLA §§14.251-.266; MSA §§26.1200[1]-.1200[16]).

Accumulations.—See category Property, topic Perpetuities.

Perpetuities.—See category Property, topic Perpetuities.

Pour Over Trusts.—See topic Wills, subhead Bequests and Devises to Inter Vivos Trusts.

Powers of Appointment.—Form, validity, rights under and manner of exercise of both general and special powers of appointment for real and personal property governed by statute. (MCLA §556.111 et seq. MSA §26.155[101] et seq.)

Release of Powers of Appointment.—Accomplished with or without consideration by written instrument signed by donee. (MCLA §556.118; MSA §26.155[108]).

WILLS:

Any person of sound mind and who has attained age of 18 years including married women, may make a will. (MCLA §700.121; MSA §27.5121).

Testamentary Disposition.—Except as provided in subhead Election, infra, no limitation is imposed on right to dispose of property by will.

Execution.—All wills, except holographic (see subhead Holographic Wills, infra), must be in writing, signed by testator or by some person in his presence expressly directed, and execution or acknowledgment of execution witnessed by two witnesses in presence of testator. Usual but not required to show residences of witnesses. (MCLA §700.122; MSA §27.5122).

Attestation Clause.—Usual but not required.

Form

On this . . . . . day of . . . . . ., 19. . . ., the above-named testator, ..., of the City of . . . ., County of . . . ., State of Michigan, in our sight and presence subscribed the foregoing instrument consisting of . . . . . . pages, including this page, and declared the same to be his Last Will and Testament, and we thereupon, at his request and in his sight and presence and in the sight and presence of each other have hereunto subscribed our names as attesting witnesses. (Witnesses sign).

Holographic wills are valid if dated, testator's signature appears at end of will and material provisions are in testator's handwriting. (MCLA §700.123; MSA §27.5123).

Nuncupative wills are not recognized.

Self-proved Wills.—No provision.

Revocation.—Wills may be revoked in whole or in part by subsequent will, by destruction of instrument with intention of revoking, or if after execution of will testator is divorced or marriage annulled, all provisions relating to former spouse are revoked and such property shall pass as if former spouse predeceased. Remarriage to former spouse revives such provisions. Any other change in circumstances does not revoke will. (MCLA §700.124; MSA §27.5124).

Revival.—When subsequent will revokes prior will, presumption upon revocation of subsequent will is prior remains revoked unless contrary intent of testator is evident from circumstances and/or declarations. If revocation of subsequent will is by third will, prior will is revived only by intent expressed in third will. (MCLA §700.125; MSA §27.5125).

Testamentary Gifts to Subscribing Witnesses.—Witness who is interested may not take under will unless there are two other competent witnesses, except that if the excluded beneficiary was also an heir, he will take so much of devise or bequest to him as does not exceed his intestate share. (MCLA §700.122; MSA §27.5122).

Bequests and Devises to Inter Vivos Trusts.—Uniform Testamentary Additions to Trusts Act adopted (MCLA §555.461 et seq.; MSA §26.78[1] et seq.) with modification of §2 to make act effective as to all wills regardless of when will executed, but no existing final judgment is to be affected. Pecuniary bequests or transfers in trust of a pecuniary amount may be satisfied in kind with property valued as of distribution date in absence of contrary direction in will. (MCLA §700.215; MSA §27.5215).

Testamentary Guardians.—See category Family, topic Guardian and Ward.

Probate.—Will must be proved in probate court. (MCLA §700.144; MSA §27.5144). Petition for probate is filed in county of testator's domicile. (MCLA §700.145; MSA §27.5145). Notice of hearing on petition, unless waived in writing, must be given to heirs, devisees and legatees by publication and mail 14 days before hearing, or seven days if personal service used. (MCLA §700.154; MSA §27.5154; Rules 5.105-.108). If person does not appear to object to admission of will, court may admit will without testimony, if will appears proper on its face. (MCLA §700.147; MSA §27.5147).

Contest.—Objections to admission of will to probate must be filed in writing prior to hearing for admission in probate court. (MCLA §700.148; MSA §27.5148). Appeal to Court of Appeals must be filed within 21 days of order of probate court. (Rule 7.204). Filing of objections not prerequisite to appeal. (MCLA §700.148; MSA §27.5148). In absence of appeal, judgment admitting will to probate is res judicata and not subject to collateral attack. (300 Mich. 575, 2 N.W.2d 509). Settlement of will contest governed by statute and requires court approval. See subhead Adjustment of Controversies Concerning Wills, infra.

Adjustment of Controversies Concerning Wills.—Subject to rights of creditors and taxing authorities, competent interested parties may agree among themselves to alter interests to which they are entitled under will or intestacy, in writing executed by all parties affected by its provisions. Transfer of asset pursuant to settlement, whether by such agreement or by other provisions of law, shall be treated for inheritance tax purposes as transfer to person receiving asset and not as transfer from that person named in will. Fiduciary of estate shall abide by terms of such settlement. (MCLA §700.191; MSA §27.5191). In cases where will contains charitable gift not to particular person or institution, settlement in circuit court is contemplated by statute and Attorney General is a necessary party. (MCLA §§14.251 et seq.; MSA §§26.1200 et seq.).

Legacies.—No specific statutory provisions as to time for payment or ademption. Payment may be compelled upon petition of that person entitled to such, while interest is awarded to pecuniary devisee after one year has elapsed since first appointment of personal representative. (MCLA §§700.166-.167; MSA §§27.5166-.5167). Ademption of general devise is matter of intention at time donor makes gift. (303 Mich. 103, 5 N.W.2d 672). Specific devises are adeemed if testator does not own property at death or same does not exist, subject to specific devisees' right to: (a) Any balance of purchase price together with security interest owing from purchaser to testator at death by reason of sale; (b) any proceeds unpaid at death on fire or casualty insurance on property, unless property is restored; (c) any amount of condemnation award unpaid at death; (d) property owned by testator at death as result of foreclosure of security for specifically devised obligation or property obtained in lieu of foreclosure. (MCLA §700.136; MSA §27.5136).

Unclaimed Legacies.—Deposited by fiduciary with county treasurer on order of court. (MCLA §700.584; MSA §27.5584). As to escheat see category Property, topic Absentees, subhead Escheat. See also topic Executors and Administrators, subhead Distribution if Abroad, and category Property, topic Absentees, subhead Beneficiary of Estate.

Disclaimer of Legacy.—MCLA §§554.501-.520; MSA §§26.1236(1)-(20) which apply to interests in property prior to June 1, 1996 make provision for disclaimer by heir, next of kin, devisee, legatee or other person similarly situated of interest in testamentary or non-testamentary instruments or powers of appointment. The Disclaimer of Property Interests Act, (MCLA §§554.871-.883; MSA §§26.1236[871]-[883]) which applies to interests in property effective June 1, 1996 conforms Michigan law to federal tax laws.

Lapse.—If devisee who predeceased testator was lineal descendant of testator's grandparents, his issue take unless will provides otherwise. (MCLA §700.134; MSA §27.5134).

Children.—Child omitted from will by accident or mistake takes share to which entitled in case of intestacy (MCLA §700.127; MSA §27.5127) as does also child born after execution of will unless will negatives intention to provide for such child (MCLA §700.127; MSA §27.5127).

Election.—Surviving spouse may (if widow) elect dower right or to take under will or to take as follows: One-half of sum or share that would have passed to spouse by intestacy, reduced by one-half of value of all property derived from decedent by any means other than testator intestate succession, including gifts within two years of death, property transferred subject to retained power which makes such property subject to federal taxes, and transfer via joint ownership, insurance or similar means. Surviving spouse must exercise election within 60 days after date for presentment of claims or within 60 days after proof of service of inventory on surviving spouse is filed, whichever is later. (MCLA §700.282; MSA §27.5282). Surviving spouse does not have right to elect against will if spouse: (a) Was wilfully absent from decedent; (b) deserted decedent; (c) neglected or refused to provide support for decedent if so required by law. (MCLA §700.290; MSA §27.5290). Election right and right to inherit may be waived by either spouse by written agreement before or after marriage. (MCLA §700.291; MSA §27.5291).

Gift to Surviving Spouse.—Surviving spouse omitted from will by accident or mistake takes share to which entitled in case of intestacy, as does spouse married after execution of will unless omission was intentional or testator provided for spouse by transfers outside of will. (MCLA §700.126; MSA §27.5126). Pecuniary bequest under will or trust agreement, unless instrument otherwise provides, may be satisfied with assets selected by fiduciary having aggregate value on date of distribution amounting to no less than and, to extent practicable, no more than amount of bequest as stated in formula in governing instrument. (MCLA §700.215; MSA §27.5215).

Contribution.—No statutory provision for contribution. Election held to have effect only of reducing testate property and will operates to pass balance in accordance with its terms (271 Mich. 627, 261 N.W. 98), except electing spouse may not receive legacy under will (250 Mich. 117, 229 N.W. 414).

Foreign Executed Wills.—Will is valid if executed in compliance with laws of Michigan or with law of place of execution or with law of place of domicile at time of execution or of death. (MCLA §700.151; MSA §27.5151).

Foreign Probated Wills.—Will of nonresident which has been admitted to probate outside state may be admitted to probate in any county where decedent left real or personal property upon presentation of authenticated copy of will and of record admitting will to probate outside state. (MCLA §700.152; MSA §27.5152).

Simultaneous Death.—See topic Death, subhead Survivorship.

Testamentary Trusts.—See topic Trusts.

Uniform Anatomical Gift Act.—Adopted. MCLA §§333.10101-.10109; MSA §§14.15 (1011)-.15(10204) adds provision for removal of eye or physical part thereof by licensed physician or person certified by state medical school in absence of donor or donee designated physician.

Living Wills.—Person 18 years or older of sound mind at time of designation may designate person 18 years or older as patient advocate to exercise powers with respect to care, custody and medical treatment decisions. Designation must be in writing signed in presence of two witnesses and be made part of patient's medical record

WILLS . . . *continued*

before implementation. Patient advocate must accept designation in writing. (MCLA §700.496; MSA §27.5496).

FAMILY

ADOPTION:

Consent Required.—Written consent required from: (a) Parents of adoptee unless (i) parental rights have been terminated by court order, (ii) adoptee has been released by parents for adoption to child placing agency or Department of Social Services, (iii) guardian has been appointed for adoptee, (iv) guardian has been appointed for that parent, (v) adoptee is not related to adopter within fifth degree of affinity or consanguinity, or (vi) parent having legal custody of adoptee is married to adopter; (b) Department of Social Services or child placing agency to whom adoptee permanently committed by court order or released by parents; (c) court having permanent custody of adoptee; (d) guardian of adoptee, if any; (e) guardian of parent; (f) child placing agency of another state or country which has authority to consent; and (g) adoptee if over 14 years old. Adult must consent to own adoption, and no other consent required. Guardian may not execute consent unless authority of court which appointed guardian obtained. Inability to obtain consent may be overcome by motion if arbitrary or capricious withholding is established by clear and convincing evidence. (MCLA §§710.43-.45; MSA §§27.3178 [555.43]-[555.44]).

Conditions Precedent.—Court (family division) directs full investigation unless waived as result of 12 month or longer foster care placement. (MCLA §710.46; MSA §27.3178[555.46]). Not later than 14 days after receipt of report of investigation, court orders termination of parental rights. (MCLA §710.51; MSA §27.3178[555.51]). Order of adoption entered six months following formal placement, but court may extend or shorten period. (MCLA §710.56; MSA §27.3178[555.56]).

Jurisdiction.—Court of county in which petitioner resides or adoptee is found. (MCLA §710.24; MSA §27.3178[555.24]).

Venue.—Court of county in which petitioner resides or adoptee is found. (MCLA §710.24; MSA §27.3178[555.24]).

Petition.—Person (and if married, wife or husband of such person) desiring to adopt child or adult, with or without change of name, files verified petition with probate court of county where petitioner resides or adoptee is found. Petition must state: (1) Name, date and place of birth and place of residence of petitioner, including maiden name of adopting mother, (2) name, date and place of birth and place of residence of adoptee, (3) relationship, if any, of petitioner to adoptee, (4) full name of adoptee after adoption, (5) description of property, if any, of adoptee, (6) names and addresses of parents of adoptee unless parental rights have been terminated by court of competent jurisdiction, and (7) name and address of guardian, if any, of adoptee. (MCLA §710.24; MSA §27.3178[555.24]). Concurrent with or subsequent to filing of petition, petitioner, Department of Social Services employee or agent of court, or child placing agency, as appropriate, must file required documentation. (MCLA §710.26; MSA §27.3178[555.26]).

Proceedings.—See subhead Conditions Precedent, supra.

Decree.—Decree entered after waiting period described under subhead Conditions Precedent, supra.

Name.—If decree provides for change of adoptee's name, such change of name effective upon entry of decree. (MCLA §710.60; MSA §27.3178[555.60]).

Effect of Adoption.—Upon entry of decree adopting parents occupy in law all rights and obligations of natural parents. Upon entry of such decree, adoptee becomes heir at law of adopting parents without distinction of any kind from natural heirs at law. Adoptee is not heir at law of natural parents unless interest vests before entry of adoption decree. (MCLA §710.60; MSA §27.3178[555.60]).

Setting Aside Adoption.—Adoption decree may be set aside on petition filed within 21 days after entry of decree. (MCLA §710.64; MSA §27.3178[555.64]). Appeal is to court of appeals within 21 days after entry of decree appealed from or after petition for rehearing denied. (MCLA §710.65; MSA §27.3178[555.65]).

ALIMONY:

See topic Divorce.

COMMUNITY PROPERTY:

See topic Husband and Wife.

DIVORCE:

Governed by MCLA §552 et seq.; MSA §25.81 et seq. and Rules 721-731.

Sole statutory ground for absolute divorce is breakdown of marriage relationship to extent that objects of matrimony have been destroyed and there remains no reasonable likelihood that marriage can be preserved. (MCLA §552.6; MSA §25.86).

Ground for separate maintenance is same as for divorce. (MCLA §552.7; MSA §25.87).

Residence Requirements.—Plaintiff or defendant must have resided in this state for 180 days immediately preceding filing of complaint. One spouse must have resided in county where suit is filed for ten days immediately preceding filing. (MCLA §552.9; MSA §25.89). Absent voluntary appearance, except where defendant is citizen of (or born in) country other than U.S.; parties have minor child(ren); and evidence exists based upon which court could conclude minor child(ren) are at risk of being removed from U.S. by defendant (MCLA §552.9[c]; MSA §25.89[2]), defendant must be domiciled in state at time suit if filed or at time cause for divorce arose, unless brought in by publication or personally served with process in this state or personally served with copy of order for appearance and publication within this state or elsewhere. (MCLA §§552.9, 552.9a; MSA §§25.89, 25.89[1], see category Civil Actions and Procedure,

topic Process). When cause for divorce occurred outside Michigan, one party must have resided in state for one year immediately preceding filing. (MCLA §552.9e; MSA §25.89[5]). See category Civil Actions and Procedure, topic Process.

Jurisdiction.—If residence requirements are satisfied, circuit court of county where parties, or one of them, resides has jurisdiction to issue divorce decree. (MCLA §§552.6, .9; MSA §§25.86, .89).

Venue.—No specific venue provisions.

Process.—If there are children under 18, copies of all process, pleadings and other papers must be served on friend of court and copy of summons must be served on prosecuting attorney. (Rule 3.203[1]). When there are children under 17, statute requires service of copy of summons on prosecuting attorney or on friend of court in counties having population of 500,000 or more which have a friend of court. (MCLA §552.45; MSA §25.121).

Whenever order for appearance is served outside Michigan proof of service must be made by affidavit of person serving same, made before justice of peace or notary public, and when such affidavit is made outside this state it must bear certificate of clerk of court of record certifying to official character of justice or notary and genuineness of his signature. (MCLA §552.9a; MSA §25.89[1]).

Pleading.—Action is commenced by filing of complaint. Statute requires every complaint to state names and ages of all children. (MCLA §552.45; MSA §25.121). Rule 3.206 specifies certain information to appear in complaint in all cases and in statement to friend of court where there are children under 18 or application for temporary or permanent support money or alimony is made. (Rule 3.206). Respondent may answer complaint without oath or affirmation. (MCLA §552.11; MSA §25.91).

Practice.—Proofs cannot be taken until 60 days after filing of complaint (except where cause for divorce is desertion), and not until six months after filing where there are dependent children under 18 (unless upon petition compelling necessity is shown). (MCLA §552.9f; MSA §25.89[6]).

Final decree is entered on determination that plaintiff is entitled to divorce.

Temporary Alimony.—Pending divorce proceedings temporary alimony may be ordered by court. (MCLA §552.13; MSA §25.93; Rule 3.206[C]).

Allowance for Prosecution or Defense of Suit.—Upon request of either party, court may order adverse party to pay requesting party's expenses in prosecuting or defending suit. (Rule 3.206[A]; MCLA §552.13; MSA §25.93).

Permanent Alimony.—Upon every divorce, court may award either party permanent alimony. (MCLA §552.23; MSA §25.103). On petition of either party, court may revise and alter decree respecting amount of alimony or payment thereof. (MCLA §§552.17, 28; MSA §§25.97, 106). Award of alimony may be terminated by court as of date party receiving alimony remarries unless contrary agreement specifically stated in divorce judgment. (MCLA §552.13[2]; MSA §25.93[2]).

Division of Property of Spouses.—Determined in decree. Court may restore to either party whole, or such parts it deems just and reasonable, of real and personal estate that came to either party by reason of marriage or award value thereof to be paid by either party in money. (MCLA §552.19; MSA §25.99). If estate and effects awarded to either party are insufficient for suitable support and maintenance of either party and children of marriage committed to care and custody of either party, court may further award to either party such part of real and personal estate of either party as it deems just and reasonable considering ability, character and situation of parties and all other circumstances. (MCLA §552.23; MSA §25.103). Husband and wife owning realty as joint tenants or as tenants by entirety become tenants in common unless otherwise determined by decree. (MCLA §552.102; MSA §25.132).

If party contributed to acquisition or improvement of spouse's property, court may award such party all of such property or equitable portion thereof. (MCLA §552.401; MSA §25.136).

Change of Wife's Name.—Court in divorce decree may, on wife's petition, restore her birth name or legal surname or allow her to adopt another surname if change not sought with fraudulent or evil intent. (MCLA §552.391; MSA §25.181).

Custody of Children.—On application of either party or friend of court, court may provide for custody of minor children during pendency of suit (MCLA §552.15; MSA §25.95) and upon divorce awards custody to one of parents (MCLA §552.16; MSA §25.96) or to third party until child attains age 18 (MCLA §552.17a; MSA §25.97[1]). Court may waive jurisdiction of children under 17 to probate court. (MCLA §§552.15, .16; MSA §§25.95-.96). Uniform Child Custody Jurisdiction Act in effect. (MCLA §§600.651-.673; MSA §§27A.651-.673).

Allowance for Support of Children.—Pending divorce proceedings support for minor children may be ordered by court (Rule 3.206[B]; MCLA §552.15; MSA §25.95), and upon divorce, court may order allowance for children to be paid by either party (MCLA §552.23; MSA §25.103). Court may order support for child after child reaches age of 18. Motion for support must be filed before child reaches age 19¹/₂. (MCLA §552.16a; MSA §25.96a). Enforcement of support and visitation orders provided for in MCLA §552.601 et seq. Support may include medical, dental, health care, child care or educational expenses. (MCLA §552.452). Upon petition of either party court may alter decree concerning maintenance of children. (MCLA §§552.17, .28; MSA §§25.97, .106).

Dower.—See category Property, topic Dower, subhead Divorce.

Remarriage.—No restrictions on marriage of divorced persons.

Foreign Divorces.—No statutory provisions barring recognition of foreign divorces. Foreign alimony decree will be enforced if defendant was present in court or was personally served with process within jurisdiction of foreign court. (MCLA §552.121; MSA §25.141).

Separation Agreements.—No statutory provision.

Annulment of Marriage.—See topic Marriage.

Antenuptial Contracts.—See topic Husband and Wife.

See note at head of Digest as to 1998 legislation covered.

See Topical Index in front part of this volume.

GUARDIAN AND WARD:

Probate courts appoint and have general jurisdiction of guardians of person and guardians of estate of minors and legally incapacitated persons resident or having any property within state. (MCLA §§700.401, .424, .424a, .427, .443, .444, .461; MSA §§27.5401, .5424, .5427, .5443, .5444, .5461). Guardians of estates are termed "conservators". Without appointing conservator, court may authorize, direct or ratify any transaction except making of will. (MCLA §§700.468, .469; MSA §§27.5468, .5469).

Selection of Guardian.—Parent may nominate guardian or conservator by will; spouse of legally incapacitated person may so appoint guardian. (MCLA §§700.422, .424, .441, .470; MSA §§27.5422, .5424, .5441, .5470). Minor above age 14 may nominate his own guardian or conservator. (MCLA §§700.423, .426, .470; MSA §§27.5423, .5426, .5470).

Eligibility and Competency.—Guardian must be resident or bank or trust company authorized to do business in state, except that nonresident may qualify as appointed guardian of person of resident minor if will of surviving parent makes such nomination. (MCLA §700.531[2][b]; MSA §27.5531[2][b]). Foreign state appointment under will of nonresident recognized. (MCLA §700.441; MSA §27.5441). Conservator or like fiduciary appointed in jurisdiction where protected person resides has priority for appointment as conservator. (MCLA §700.470; MSA §27.5470). Judge other than municipal court judge may not act as fiduciary except for estates of immediate family. (MCLA §700.582; MSA §27.5582).

Appointment of guardian or conservator is evidenced by certificate verifying issuance of letters of authority. (MCLA §700.535; MSA §27.5535). Letters of conservatorship evidence transfer of all assets to conservator. (MCLA §700.481; MSA §27.5481).

Qualification.—Guardian qualifies by filing acceptance of appointment. (MCLA §§700.421, .445; MSA §§27.5421, .5445). Court may require conservator to furnish bond. (MCLA §700.471; MSA §27.5471).

Powers and Duties.—Guardian has care and custody of person of his ward and supervision of education if minor; if no conservator appointed, guardian may receive money or personal property for support of ward. (MCLA §§700.403, .431, .455; MSA §§27.5403, .5431, .5455). Conservator has investment powers of trustee, discretion to retain or sell assets, and other enumerated powers to act with respect to property or affairs of protected person to same extent as if he were property owner, including implementation of known estate plan. Conservator also has parental rights of guardian if protected person is unmarried minor without parent or guardian. (MCLA §700.484-.488; MSA §§27.5484-.5488). Transactions of conservator affected by conflict of interest are voidable, but third party acting in good faith is protected without inquiring into propriety of conservator's exercise of power. (MCLA §§700.482, .483; MSA §§27.5482, .5483). Court may expand or limit conservator's powers. (MCLA §700.486; MSA §27.5486).

Investments.—See subhead Powers and Duties, supra.

Securities in Name of Nominee.—Conservator may so hold securities but is liable for acts of nominee. (MCLA §700.484[3][p]; MSA §27.5484[3][p]).

Real Estate.—Guardian has no authority with respect to real estate. Conservator holds title to all ward's property as trustee and may deal with real estate without obtaining court authorization or confirmation. (MCLA §§700.480, .484; MSA §27.5480, .5484).

Liabilities of Guardian.—Guardian or conservator is liable as any other fiduciary for loss of estate or other breach of duty. (MCLA §§700.477, .544; MSA §§27.5477, .5544). Guardian authorized to give medical consent and not liable for negligence or acts of third person unless such consent by parent would be illegal. (MCLA §700.431; MSA §27.5431). Conservator liable on contract only if failed to disclose capacity and identify estate, and in tort only if personally at fault. (MCLA §700.489; MSA §27.5489).

Accounts.—Guardian must report to court condition of ward and estate subject to guardian's control, as ordered by court on petition of interested person; account of funds received and expended must be given to conservator if one appointed. (MCLA §§700.431, .455; MSA §§27.5431, .5455). Conservator must file inventory under oath within 60 days of appointment, account periodically to court as court directs, account to court upon resignation or removal, and to court or ward upon termination of disability or minority. (MCLA §§700.478, .479; MSA §27.5478, .5479).

Termination of Guardianship.—Guardianship of minor terminates upon minor's death, adoption, marriage or attainment of majority. (MCLA §700.433; MSA §27.5433). Court may terminate guardianship or conservatorship when need for such protection shown to have ceased. (MCLA §§700.424c, .446, .490; MSA §§27.5424c, .5446, .5490).

Gifts to Minors.—See topic Infants.

Uniform Fiduciaries Act not adopted.

Uniform Simplification of Fiduciary Security Transfers Act adopted. (MCLA §441.101-.112; MSA §19.356[1]-[12]).

Insane Persons.—Provisions for guardianship of legally incapacitated persons apply to person unable to manage or protect his property or person because of mental incompetency or retardation, or chronic use of drugs or alcohol. (MCLA §700.8; MSA §27.5008).

Foreign Guardians.—Conservator or like fiduciary appointed in foreign state for nonresident ward may collect property of ward by presenting proof of appointment and affidavit that no protective proceeding pending in Michigan and that foreign conservator entitled to receive property. (MCLA §700.491; MSA §27.5491). See also subhead Eligibility and Competency, supra.

HUSBAND AND WIFE:

Marriage confers rights and imposes duties as at common law, except as to property. (26 Mich. 105). Loss of consortium by personal injury recoverable in action by wife

(359 Mich. 33, 101 N.W.2d 227), reversing earlier rule denying recovery in action by either spouse. Loss of wife's services is element of damages in suit by husband. (295 Mich. 611, 295 N.W. 333).

Disabilities of married women have been removed with respect to their capacity to enter into contract. (MCLA §557.23; MSA §26.165[3]).

Separate Property.—Property owned by husband or wife before marriage or thereafter acquired, except joint property (see subhead Joint Property, infra), is his or her separate property, with right to manage and dispose of it alone, except that husband's real estate is subject to dower. (MCLA §§557.21, .201, .202; MSA §§26.165[1], .216[1], .216[2]). Separate property of either spouse is not liable for debts of other. (MCLA §§557.21, .24; MSA §§26.165[1], .165[4]).

Joint Property.—Property held by entireties, or in such manner that neither husband or wife individually has separate property interest, constitutes separate property of husband and wife, as distinguished from community property. (MCLA §557.203; MSA §26.216[3]). Married woman may enter into written contract jointly or severally with another person. (MCLA §557.27; MSA §26.165[7]). Unless otherwise expressly provided, real property conveyed to husband and wife is deemed to be held by entireties (221 Mich. 515, 191 N.W. 213), and personal property in form of stocks, bonds, debentures, notes, mortgages and other evidences of indebtedness payable or endorsed or assigned to husband and wife, is deemed to be held jointly with right of survivorship with same incidents as real estate held by entireties (MCLA §557.151; MSA §26.211), but presumption does not extend to bank deposits (260 Mich. 246, 244 N.W. 462), land contracts (279 Mich. 598, 273 N.W. 282), insurance or other simple contracts (54 F.2d 5).

Contracts.—Married woman may enter into contract with respect to her separate property (MCLA §557.24; MSA §26.165[4]) or carry on business for her own account (238 Mich. 189, 213 N.W. 163), and may contract directly with her husband (37 Mich. 563), including partnership with him (MCLA §449.6; MSA §20.6; 304 Mich. 668; 8 N.W.2d 873). Husband is not liable for breach of contract entered into by wife relating to her separate property unless he acted as surety, cosigner or guarantor. (MCLA §557.24; MSA §26.165[4]). Married woman may act as surety for obligation of another, including her husband, and judgment on same may be satisfied out of her separate property whether or not contract of suretyship benefits or concerns that separate property. (MCLA §557.25; MSA §26.165[5]). Married woman may enter into written contract pledging or assigning her separate property as security for, or personally guaranteeing, debt of another (including her husband), and judgment on same may be satisfied out of her separate property whether or not separate property derives benefit from pledge, assignment or guarantee. (MCLA §557.26; MSA §26.165[6]).

Antenuptial Contracts.—Contract relating to property made between persons in contemplation of marriage remains in force after marriage. (MCLA §557.28; MSA §26.165[8]).

Agency.—Either spouse may act as agent or attorney in fact for the other. There is no presumption of husband's authority to act for wife (298 Mich. 721, 299 N.W. 780), but in contracting for family necessaries wife is presumed to act for husband (26 Mich. 179).

Conveyance or Encumbrance of Property.—To convey or encumber property held by entireties husband and wife must join in same instrument. (200 Mich. 328, 166 N.W. 886). Husband need not join in deed of wife's separate property. Dower is barred by wife's joining in husband's conveyance, or may be barred by separate instrument expressing intent to bar dower. (MCLA §558.13; MSA §26.229).

Actions.—Actions may be brought by and against married woman as if she were unmarried. (MCLA §600.2001; MSA §27A.2001). Action for tort of wife cannot be brought against husband or husband and wife jointly unless circumstances were such as to render both liable. (MCLA §600.2005; MSA §27A.2005). No statutory prohibition of action by one spouse against another, but common law disability may still exist. (See 117 Mich. 80, 75 N.W. 287; 288 Mich. 669, 286 N.W. 120.)

Desertion and Nonsupport.—Spouse is liable criminally for desertion and nonsupport. (MCLA §750.161; MSA §28.358).

Revised Uniform Reciprocal Enforcement of Support Act (as am'd) has been adopted. (MCLA §780.151 et seq.; MSA §25.225[1] et seq.). Among material differences from uniform text are: (1) Jurisdiction is vested in circuit court of county of petitioner's residence or in which valid prior and existing support order has been issued when proceedings initiated in Michigan, or if proceedings initiated in another state and valid support order has been issued, venue rests in county in which order issued, in county where obligor resides or is found (MCLA §780.160; MSA §25.225[10]); (2) prosecuting attorney has duty to represent petitioner upon request of State Department of Social Services, although petitioner may have private counsel at own expense (MCLA §780.160a; MSA §25.225[10a]); (3) significant differences from §14 (MCLA §780.170; MSA §25.225[20]); (4) jurisdiction is on original petition, without need for amended petition, where respondent is located in another county of the state (MCLA §780.163a; MSA §25.225[13a]); (5) privilege of husband-wife communications is not retained (MCLA §780.169; MSA §25.225[19]); (6) severability provision is omitted. Civil enforcement by circuit courts. (MCLA §780.153 et seq.; MSA §25.225[3] et seq.).

Community Property.—Statute establishing community property system (MCLA §§557.201-.220; MSA §26.216[1]-[20]) has been repealed, with very limited protection of rights acquired prior to May 10, 1948, when the repealing act became effective (MCLA §§557.251-.254; MSA §§26.216[21]-[24]). Uniform Disposition of Community Property Rights At Death Act in effect. (MCLA §§557.261-.271; MSA §§26.216[51]—.216[61]).

INFANTS:

Age of majority, 18 for both sexes effective Jan. 1, 1972. Prior thereto, age of majority was 21. (MCLA §§722.51-.55; MSA §§25.244[51]-[55]). Children under 17 may be fingerprinted upon written authorization of parent. (MCLA §§722.771 et seq.; MSA §25.248[50] et seq.).

See note at head of Digest as to 1998 legislation covered.

See Topical Index in front part of this volume.

INFANTS . . . *continued*

Emancipation.—Marriage releases infant from parental control. (MCLA §551.251; MSA §25.61).

Disabilities.—Infant lacks capacity to convey, or contract except for necessaries, but is liable for his torts. (293 Mich. 148, 291 N.W. 255). Parents of minor under 18 living with parents are liable up to $2,500 for wilful or malicious destruction of property or injury to person by minor. (MCLA §600.2913; MSA §27A.2913). Infant of 16 is bound by his contract for life or disability insurance, but not for note given for premium. (MCLA §500.2205; MSA §24.12205). Infant of 18 can receive and give discharge for life insurance or endowment benefits not exceeding $2,000 in any one year if contract or agreement specifies direct payment to minor. (MCLA §500.2206; MSA §24.12206).

Support by Parents.—Parents have joint and several obligations to support minor which may be enforced by minor, relative, guardian or government. (MCLA §722.3; MSA §25.244[3]). Support may include medical, dental, health care, child care and educational expenses. (MCLA §722.3).

Ratification of Contracts.—Infant's contract is voidable, unless it could not possibly be for his benefit, in which case it is void. (31 Mich. 182). Infant cannot disaffirm executed contract during minority. (268 Mich. 317, 256 N.W. 449). If he disaffirms on attaining majority, he must restore what remains in his possession of the consideration received. (183 Mich. 157, 149 N.W. 985). If he has received the benefit of the contract, he must disaffirm with reasonable promptness after attaining majority. (75 Mich. 204, 42 N.W. 805). He ratifies the contract by continuing to perform it after majority, or by any acknowledgment or act indicating an intention to be bound, but is not estopped merely by silence. (109 Mich. 640, 67 N.W. 908). Infant may not disaffirm contract for goods or loan if it appears at trial that he wilfully misrepresented his age and seller had no actual knowledge of his actual age, and if such misrepresentation was made in a separate instrument signed by him and dated or is admitted in open court. (MCLA §600.1403; MSA §27A.1403).

Actions.—Infants begin suit by next friend or guardian of estate and defend suits by guardians of estate, if any, otherwise by guardians ad litem. These are appointed by court on motion. Infants over 14 years of age may make their own selection. (MCLA §700.423; MSA §27.5423).

Next friend or guardian ad litem not required in divorce suit by or against infant. (MCLA §551.251; MSA §25.61).

Adoption.—See topic Adoption.

Uniform Child Custody Jurisdiction Act in effect. (MCLA §§600.651-.673; MSA §§27A.651-.673).

Uniform Gifts to Minors Act in effect; 1966 Amendments adopted. (MCLA §554.451 et seq.; MSA §27.3178[241.21] et seq.). Age of majority under Act is 18.

Uniform Securities Ownership by Minors Act not adopted.

Termination of Parental Rights.—If child remains in foster care in temporary custody of court following review hearing or permanency planning hearing, child may be placed in permanent custody of court if court finds by clear and convincing evidence any one of following: (1) Child has been deserted; (2) child or sibling of child suffered physical injury or physical or sexual abuse; (3) 182 or more days after issuance of order in proceeding brought against parent by juvenile division of probate court, court finds that conditions which led to adjudication still exist and likely to continue; (4) parent fails to provide proper care or custody for child and conditions likely to continue; (5) parent imprisoned for period that child will be deprived of normal home for more than two years and conditions likely to continue; (6) parental rights to one or more siblings of child terminated due to serious and chronic neglect or physical or sexual abuse, and prior attempts to rehabilitate parents failed. (MCLA §712A.19b).

MARRIAGE:

Age of consent, males and females, 16 (MCLA §551.103; MSA §25.33); marriage of female under 16 is void (MCLA §551.51; MSA §25.21) unless performed pursuant to MCLA §551.201; MSA §25.51.

Consent Required.—Consent of one parent or legal guardian is required where either party is under 18 years of age. Consent must be written and must be acknowledged in presence of county clerk or before notary public or other officer authorized to administer oaths. (MCLA §551.103; MSA §25.33).

Medical Examination.—Requirement for medical examination prior to marriage repealed. Applicant for marriage license must show certificate evidencing receipt of required HIV counseling. (MCLA §333.5119; MSA §14.15[5119]).

License.—License is required, issued by clerk of county where either party resides, or of county where ceremony to be performed where both parties nonresidents. (MCLA §551.101; MSA §25.31). Application may be made by either party, who is required in practice to appear before clerk in person. (MCLA §551.103; MSA §25.33). Three days must elapse between application and issuance of license unless probate judge authorizes immediate issuance of license. (MCLA §551.103a; MSA §25.34). Probate judge can issue secret license under certain circumstances to protect reputation. (MCLA §551.201; MSA §25.51).

Waiting Period.—None, except for three days between application and issuance of license. (MCLA §551.103a; MSA §25.34).

Ceremonial Marriage.—Ceremony may be performed by district court judge or magistrate (in his own district), judge of probate or municipal court (in his own county), mayor (in his own city), county clerk of county of more than 2,000,000 (in his own county), judge of federal court, minister of gospel who is pastor of church or continues to preach, or nonresident minister of gospel authorized to perform ceremony in own state. (MCLA §551.7; MSA §25.7). Clergyman or magistrate performing marriage must certify on license, time and place of marriage, name and residence of two witnesses, and sign his own name in certification that marriage has been performed by him. (MCLA §551.104; MSA §25.35).

Reports of Marriages.—Clergyman or magistrate performing marriage returns original to county clerk who issued license within ten days after ceremony (MCLA §551.104; MSA §25.35), who must file same and report to State Health Commissioner. (MCLA §551.103; MSA §25.33).

Record.—See category Documents and Records, topic Records, subhead Vital Statistics.

Common Law Marriages.—Cannot be effectuated after Jan. 1, 1957. (MCLA §551.2; MSA §25.2). As to local recognition of common law marriages outside this state, see subhead Foreign Marriages, infra.

Proxy marriages are not authorized.

Marriages by written contract are not authorized.

Prohibited Marriages.—Between first cousins or persons in nearer degrees of relationship or to specified relations of spouses; of insane persons, idiots, and persons with certain infectious diseases (MCLA §551.3-.6; MSA §25.3-.6); and marriage to female under 16 (MCLA §551.51; MSA §25.21) unless performed pursuant to MCLA §551.201; MSA §25.51.

Foreign Marriages.—Marriage valid where contracted is valid in Michigan although it would be invalid if contracted here, unless contrary to public policy. (239 Mich. 455, 214 N.W. 428; 31 Mich. 126). *Note*: Effective 6/26/96, marriage of same sex individuals are not valid. (MCLA §551.271; MSA §25.121).

Annulment.—Court may annul invalid marriage in proceeding for that purpose. (MCLA §552.3; MSA §25.83). If parties under age of consent at time of marriage and separated permanently before reaching that age, or consent of party obtained by force or fraud (MCLA §552.2; MSA §25.82), marriage void without decree. Except as cohabitation after age of consent affirms marriage, there is no specific statutory limitation on time for bringing action to avoid marriage for nonage. (MCLA §552.34; MSA §25.110)

Antenuptial Contracts.—See topic Husband and Wife.

MARRIED WOMEN:

See topics Husband and Wife, Marriage; categories Civil Actions and Procedure, topic Evidence, subhead Witnesses; Debtor and Creditor, topic Homesteads; Documents and Records, topic Acknowledgments; Estates and Trusts, topics Executors and Administrators, Wills; Property, topic Dower.

INSURANCE

INSURANCE COMPANIES:

Regulated by Insurance Code of 1956. (MCLA §500.100 et seq.; MSA §24.1100 et seq.).

Supervision.—Commissioner of Insurance has general supervision over all insurance and surety companies and their agents and has power to revoke licenses for cause. (MCLA §§500.200, .436; MSA §§24.1200, .1436).

Policies.—Policy provisions and features are extensively regulated by statute, as follows: Insurance contracts in general (MCLA §§500.2204-.2264; MSA §§24.12205-.12260); life insurance (MCLA §§500.4000, .4073; MSA §§24.14000, .14073); industrial life insurance (MCLA §§500.4200-.4244; MSA §§24.14200-.14244); group life insurance (MCLA §§500.4400-.4454; MSA §§24.14400-.14454); fire insurance (MCLA §§500.2804-.2866; MSA §24.12804-.12866); casualty insurance (MCLA §§500.3004-.3037; MSA §§24.13004-.13037); disability insurance (MCLA §§500.3400-.3475; MSA §§24.13400-.13475, certain sections held unconstitutional at 572 F. Supp. 943); group, blanket, and family expense disability insurance (MCLA §§500.3600-.3650; MSA §24.13600-.13650, certain sections held unconstitutional at 572 F. Supp. 943); credit life and credit health and accident insurance (MCLA §§550.601-.624; MSA §24.568[1]-[24]). No basic policy form of contract may be used until filed with and approved by Commissioner. (MCLA §500.2236; MSA §24.12236).

Rates.—Surety and fidelity, casualty, liability, automobile, worker's compensation, title, malpractice, reciprocal, and personal property floater rates are regulated by MCLA §§500.2400-.2484; MSA §§24.12400-.12484. Reinsurance, disability and aircraft rates are expressly excepted from regulation under these sections.

Fire, earthquake, lightning, wind and water, bombardment, explosion, burglary, theft, navigation, transit or transportation, personal property floater, precious stones, bridge, tunnel, pier, wharf, etc., automobile (limited), and inland navigation and transportation rates are regulated by MCLA §§500.2600-.2674; MSA §24.12600-.12674. Reinsurance and marine (as distinguished from inland marine) rates are expressly excepted from regulation under these sections.

Any insurer to which both rate regulatory chapters are applicable must file with Commissioner a designation as to which rate regulatory chapter shall apply to it. (MCLA §500.2401[4]; MSA §24.12401[4]).

Discrimination.—Discrimination in rates on life policy or annuity between individuals of the same class and equal life expectancy, or in rates on accident or health policy between individuals of the same class and essentially the same hazard, is defined as unfair competition (MCLA §§500.2019, .2020; MSA §§24.12019-.12020), which may be subject of cease and desist order issued by Commissioner (MCLA §§500.2038-.2041; MSA §§24.12038-.12041).

Cancellation.—Grounds for cancellation of policies of automobile liability insurance regulated by statute. (MCLA §500.3220; MSA §24.13220).

Rebates on life policies or annuities or accident and health policies are defined as unfair competition (MCLA §500.2024; MSA §24.12024), which may be subject of cease and desist order issued by Commissioner (MCLA §§500.2038-.2041; MSA §§24.12038-.12041). Rebates on all types of insurance are forbidden, and violation results in revocation of certificate of authority or license. (MCLA §500.2066; MSA §24.12066). Criminal penalties are also provided. (MCLA §500.2069; MSA §24.12069).

See note at head of Digest as to 1998 legislation covered.

See Topical Index in front part of this volume.

INSURANCE COMPANIES . . . *continued*

Liens.—No statutory provisions.

Annual statements must be filed with Commissioner on or before Mar. 1 of each year, unless extension not exceeding 30 days is granted for good cause shown. (MCLA §500.438; MSA §24.1438).

Investments are regulated by statute. (MCLA §§500.901-.947; MSA §24.1901-.1947).

Stock Ownership in Federal Loan Agencies.—When a federal agency to loan money on real estate mortgages is established, but requires membership or ownership of capital stock in such agency, domestic insurer may carry necessary amount of stock. (MCLA §500.916; MSA §24.1916).

Mergers and acquisitions by domestic insurers and their affiliates are extensively regulated by statute. (MCLA §§500.1301-.1379; MSA §§24.11301-.11379).

Agents and solicitors are subject to examination and continuing education requirements (MCLA §§500.1204, .1205, .1214; MSA §§24.11204, .11205, .11212), for which $10 fee is charged, and annual license fees, $5 for agents and $10 for solicitors (MCLA §500.240; MSA §24.1240).

Foreign Companies.—No foreign insurance company may do business in Michigan if its corporate purposes exceed those permitted Michigan companies. Foreign insurer which has been licensed to transact business of life insurance in State continuously since Jan. 21, 1921 may continue to transact kinds of insurance business which it was authorized to transact in State immediately before Jan. 21, 1941. For purpose of obtaining admission or renewal of authority, foreign insurer may by proper corporate action limit its powers as to Michigan business. (MCLA §500.406; MSA §24.1406). Foreign insurer must file with Commissioner of Insurance application accompanied by certified copies of its charter and by-laws, together with sworn statement of its business affairs up to any date required by Commissioner and any other information which Commissioner may demand. (MCLA §500.424; MSA §24.1424). If such application is approved, Commissioner issues his certificate of authority to applicant, which remains in force until terminated by insurer or revoked by Commissioner. (MCLA §500.435; MSA §24.1435).

Capital and Assets.—Every foreign company must have as much capital and assets as are required of domestic companies. (MCLA §500.404; MSA §24.1404).

Supervision.—Commissioner has powers of supervision and examination over foreign insurance companies to the same extent as over domestic companies. (MCLA §500.222; MSA §24.1222).

Process Agent.—Every foreign company, as a condition precedent to doing business in this state, must file with the Commissioner its irrevocable written stipulation that any legal process affecting the company, served on the Commissioner or his deputies, shall have the same effect as if personally served upon the company. The fee for service on the Commissioner is $5, payable at time of service. The appointment remains in force as long as any liability remains within Michigan. (MCLA §500.456; MSA §24.1456). In cases of false advertising within state by foreign insurer, transaction of any insurance business with residents of state constitutes Commissioner agent of foreign insurer for service of charges, notices and process. (MCLA §500.2093; MSA §24.12093).

Agents and solicitors must be licensed. (MCLA §500.1201; MSA §24.11201). Detailed licensing procedure provided by statute. (MCLA §§500.1204-.1214; MSA §§24.11204-.11214). With few statutory exceptions, only agent may solicit insurance or bind coverage. (MCLA §500.1201; MSA §24.11201). Solicitors must be resident. (MCLA §500.1202; MSA §24.11202).

Deposits.—No domestic foreign or alien insurer may transact business within state until deposits specified by statute have been made with state treasurer. (MCLA §500.411; MSA §24.1411). Any alien insurance company must have on deposit with State Treasurer of Michigan, or some other state officer of U.S., or trustees for benefit of policyholders resident in U.S., cash or securities in which such company is authorized to invest in amount not less than amount of liabilities of insurer in U.S. (MCLA §500.411; MSA §24.1411).

Revocation of Authority.—Commissioner may suspend, revoke or limit certificate of authority of an insurer upon a finding of certain enumerated statutory conditions. (MCLA §500.436; MSA §24.1436).

Retaliatory Law.—Michigan imposes on companies of other states which treat foreign companies less liberally than does Michigan the same taxes, fees, penalties, requirements as to deposits and other burdens that such states impose on Michigan companies. (MCLA §500.476a; MSA §24.1476[1]).

Privilege tax on domestic insurers, imposed by MCLA §§500.448-.449, MSA §§24.1448-.1449, was repealed, effective July 2, 1976. (1975, No. 232). See category Taxation, topic Business Taxes, subhead Single Business Tax.

Premium tax on foreign insurers imposed by MCLA §500.440, MSA §24.1440, was repealed effective Dec. 28, 1987. See category Taxation, topic Business Taxes, subhead Single Business Tax.

Direct Actions Against Insurer.—See category Transportation, topic Motor Vehicles, subhead Direct Actions.

No-Fault Insurance.—See category Transportation, topic Motor Vehicles.

Plain Language.—See category Business Regulation and Commerce, topic Consumer Protection.

SURETY AND GUARANTY COMPANIES:

Organization.—Regulated under Insurance Code of 1956 (MCLA §500.100 et seq.; MSA §24.1100 et seq.), which requires at least 13 incorporators, a capital stock of at least $250,000, and deposit of approved securities of value of at least $300,000 with State Treasurer (MCLA §§500.408-.411, .5006; MSA §§24.1408-.1411, .15006).

Rights and Powers.—Authorized surety company may take place of all sureties required by law in any proceeding, civil or criminal, or before any public officer or body. (MCLA §550.101; MSA §24.241).

Foreign Companies.—May be admitted to do business in state if authorized under laws of state of incorporation and under charter to perform specified functions of surety or guarantor. Must have assets in excess of liabilities, which include capital stock, debts and a premium reserve of 50% of the annual premiums on all outstanding obligations; must furnish sworn statement of financial condition; must have paid up, unimpaired capital of $250,000 and $200,000 in dividend paying or interest bearing stocks or securities created under the laws of its state or of the United States, or of good, solvent, dividend paying corporations, or in first mortgages on real estate worth double the amount loaned, which must be at or above par in value and be deposited with state officers of not more than two states where company does business, for benefit of holders of company's obligations; must appoint agent for service of process. (MCLA §550.103; MSA §24.243).

INTELLECTUAL PROPERTY

TRADEMARKS AND TRADENAMES:

Any individual, firm, partnership, corporation, association, union or other organization may adopt and use a trademark in this state. (MCLA §429.31; MSA §18.638[21]).

What May Be Used.—Any word, name, symbol, device or combination thereof adopted and used to identify and distinguish goods or services constitutes trademark or service mark. (MCLA §429.31; MSA §18.638[21]). Mark cannot be registered if it: (a) consists of immoral, deceptive or scandalous matter, (b) may disparage or falsely suggest connection with persons, living or dead, institutions, beliefs or national symbols, (c) consists of or comprises flag, coat of arms or other insignia of United States, any foreign nation, or any state or municipality, (d) consists of or comprises name, signature or portrait of any living person except with his written consent, (e) is merely descriptive or deceptively misdescriptive or primarily geographically descriptive or primarily merely surname (although this subsection [e] will not prevent registration of mark which has actually become distinctive), or (f) so resembles trademark registered in Michigan or trademark or tradename previously used in Michigan and not abandoned, as to be likely to cause confusion or mistake or to deceive (MCLA §429.32; MSA §18.638[22]).

Registration.—Application for registration of trademark may be filed with director of commerce on form furnished by him, accompanied by two specimens or facsimiles of trademark. Fee $50. (MCLA §429.33; MSA §18.638[23]). Registration is according to general classes of goods and services. (MCLA §429.40; MSA §18.638[30]). Registration is effective for ten years and may be renewed for successive ten-year periods upon application filed within six months prior to expiration. Renewal fee $25. (MCLA §429.35; MSA §18.638[25]).

Assignment.—A trademark and its registration are assignable with good will of business in which trademark is used or that part of good will of business connected with use of trademark. Assignment must be in writing and may be recorded with director of commerce. Fee $15. (MCLA §429.36; MSA §18.638[26]).

Protection Afforded.—Registrant is protected against subsequent registration of same or similar trademark likely to deceive or to cause confusion or mistake when applied to goods of subsequent applicant. (MCLA §429.32[f]; MSA §18.638[22][f]). See also subhead Infringement, infra.

Infringement.—Owner of registered trademark may enjoin infringement and recover damages suffered by him or profits derived by infringer, except that in certain circumstances damages and profits cannot be recovered unless acts of infringement were committed with knowledge that confusion, mistake or deception would result. (MCLA §429.42; MSA §§18.638[31]-[32]). Knowing and wilful forgery or counterfeiting of trademarks and other stamps with intent to deceive or defraud is misdemeanor. (MCLA §750.263; MSA §28.474). Common law rights and remedies are not affected by the act. (MCLA §429.44; MSA §18.638[34]).

Resale Price Agreements.—Statute authorizing resale price agreements repealed effective Mar. 31, 1976. (1975, No. 211).

Tradenames.—Any person, partnership or trust or other entity operating under an assumed name must execute, acknowledge and file with clerk of county where business is located a certificate identifying person operating under assumed name including full name and current address. (MCLA §445.1; MSA §19.821). One failing to file certificate when required is guilty of misdemeanor and cannot bring action on contracts made by him under assumed name until compliance with requirement. (MCLA §445.5; MSA §19.827).

TRADE SECRETS:

Uniform Trade Secrets Act has not been adopted.

Misappropriation of trade secrets is civilly actionable and will support monetary and injunctive relief. In general, trade secret is any formula, pattern, device or compilation of information which is used in business and which gives owner business advantage over competitors, and which has been kept secret by owner. In determining whether something is trade secret, courts consider extent to which it is known within relevant business; extent to which it is known by employees and others outside business; extent of measures taken to guard its secrecy; value of information to owner and competitors; amount of effort or money expended in developing alleged secret; and ease or difficulty with which it could be properly acquired or duplicated by others. (Hayes-Albion Corp v. Kuberski, 421 Mich 170; 364 N.W.2d 654).

Theft, embezzlement or copying of trade secret with intent to appropriate or to deprive owner of control over trade secret is criminal misdemeanor. (MCLA §§752.771-.773; MSA §§28.643[51]-[53]).

Trade secrets may also be exempted from disclosure by public body under Michigan Freedom of Information Act, if provided voluntarily, upon promise of confidentiality, to agency or public body for use in developing governmental policy. (MCLA §15.243[1][g]; MSA §4.1801[13][1][g]).

Trade secrets may also be afforded special protection to maintain confidentiality during investigations or proceedings taken in connection with Occupational Safety and

See note at head of Digest as to 1998 legislation covered.

See Topical Index in front part of this volume.

MI – 42

TRADE SECRETS . . . *continued*
Health Act (MCLA §408.1063; MSA §17.50[63]); Dept. of Public Health's oversight of occupational diseases (MCLA §333.5613; MSA §14.15[5613]); Commissioner of Insurance's administration of Nonprofit Health Care Corporation Reform Act (MCLA §550.1604; MSA §22.660[604]); and Department of Natural Resources regulation of hazardous wastes (MCLA §324.11129; MSA §13A.11129).

LEGAL PROFESSION

ATTORNEYS AND COUNSELORS:

All attorneys are members of State Bar of Michigan (integrated) organized under Supreme Court rules. (MCLA §600.901; MSA §27A.901).

It is not necessary to file a warrant of attorney to authorize an attorney to appear in court for either party to an action.

Jurisdiction Over Admissions.—Applicants certified by board of law examiners are admitted on motion by Supreme Court or any circuit court. (MCLA §600.910; MSA §27A.910).

Eligibility.—To be qualified for admission, good moral character, age of 18 years, residency in U.S. or territories, required general and legal education, fitness and ability and intention in good faith to practice or teach must be proven to law examiners. (MCLA §600.934, .937; MSA §27A.934, .937).

Registration as law student not required.

Educational Requirements.—Completion of two years of study entitling applicant to admission to junior class of accredited college in state authorized to confer collegiate degrees and graduation from a reputable and qualified law school in U.S. or territories. (MCLA §600.937, .940; MSA §§27A.937, .940).

Petition for Admission.—Applicants are admitted upon issuance of certificate of qualification by board of law examiners and on motion made in open court. (MCLA §§600.910, .925; MSA §§27A.910, .925; Rule 16, Supreme Court Rules Concerning the State Bar of Michigan).

Examination.—Board of law examiners conducts examination usually in early spring and late summer of each year. Fee of not more than $175 for examination, $100 for reexamination or recertification, or $400 for admission without examination is charged. (MCLA §600.931; MSA §27A.931).

Multi-state bar examination is utilized. (MCLA §900.934; MSA §27A.934). No additional local bar examination requirements. State accepts transfer of multi-state scores from other jurisdictions for test administered within three years immediately preceding multi-state bar examination in Michigan for which person would otherwise sit. Transfer of scores accepted only if person otherwise meets all requirements for admission to Michigan State Bar, person earns passing grades on examination, and state or territory from which person wishes score to be transferred accords reciprocal right to elect to use score achieved on multi-state examination administered in Michigan. (MCLA §600.934; MSA §27A.934).

Clerkship is not required.

Admission Without Examination.—An attorney admitted to practice in highest court of, and engaged in actual practice or teaching of law in, another state for three of the five years next preceding application may be admitted without examination if approved as to character and education by board of law examiners. Legal practice in armed services qualifies as actual practice. (MCLA §600.946; MSA §27A.946).

Admission Pro Hac Vice.—Practicing attorney from another state may be admitted on motion to try a certain case. (MCLA §600.916; MSA §27A.916). No statutory provision for association with local attorney.

Licenses.—Any active member of State Bar of Michigan is licensed to practice. (MCLA §600.901; MSA §27A.901). Annual dues for active members are $260, except dues for member admitted between Apr. 1 and Sept. 30 are $130 for fiscal year of admission. (Rule 4, Supreme Court Rules Concerning the State Bar of Michigan).

Privileges.—Members of state bar officers of courts of Michigan, have exclusive right to designate themselves "attorneys and counselors" or "attorneys at law" or "lawyers" (MCLA §600.901; MSA §27A.901), may practice law before any Michigan court and have exclusive privilege to become judges of courts of record (Const., Art. VI, §19).

Disabilities.—Practicing attorney cannot become surety or post bond for client in criminal or civil matter, except fiduciary's bond of $100 or less filed in probate court. (MCLA §600.2665; MSA §27A.2665).

Liabilities.—An attorney has duty to exercise reasonable skill, fidelity and care in the discharge of his professional tasks (37 Mich. 14), and is liable to his client for negligent performance of duties (132 Mich. 294, 93 N.W. 617). See category Civil Actions and Procedure, topic Costs.

Compensation.—Compensation is left to express or implied agreement of parties subject to regulation by Supreme Court. (MCLA §600.919; MSA §27A.919; MRPC 1.5). No requirement for filing contingent fee agreement.

Lien.—An attorney has general lien on all moneys and papers of his client which have come into his possession. (56 Mich. 135, 22 N.W. 222). He has also lien on judgment he recovers for his client (40 Mich. 218), although he cannot prevent his client from settling or discontinuing suit (103 Mich. 190, 61 N.W. 343). However, where other party has notice that attorney is to receive a certain per cent of recovery for his services, he should retain sufficient money to pay plaintiff's attorney his share. (73 Mich. 256, 41 N.W. 269).

Attorney Ethics.—American Bar Association Model Rules of Professional Conduct adopted with modification. (MRPC 1.0 et seq.).

Disbarment or Suspension.—Governed by rules of Supreme Court. (MCLA §600.904, .910; MSA §27A.904). See Supreme Court Rules Concerning the State Bar of Michigan.

Unauthorized Practice.—Persons not regularly licensed and authorized are prohibited from practicing law in Michigan. (MCLA §600.916; MSA §27A.916; Rule 16, Supreme Court Rules Concerning the State Bar of Michigan).

Mandatory continuing legal education requirement for newly admitted lawyers was discontinued by order rescinding Rule 17, Supreme Court Rules Concerning the State Bar of Michigan effective Apr. 1, 1994, with direction that requirement applicable to all attorneys shall be reconsidered.

Specialty certification requirements are not required.

Professional Association (or Corporation).—See category Business Organizations, topic Corporations, subhead Professional Corporations.

MINERAL, WATER AND FISHING RIGHTS

MINES AND MINERALS:

Coal mines are supervised and inspected by department of natural resources. (MCLA §324.63533 et seq.; MSA §13A.63533 et seq.). Copper and iron mines are supervised and inspected by inspector of mines elected in each county where such mines are situated and working. (MCLA §425.101; MSA §17.311).

Operation of Mines.—See subhead Safeguarding of Employees, infra.

Safeguarding of Employees.—Inspector of copper and iron mines has authority to condemn any such mine where employees are in danger from any cause. (MCLA §425.108; MSA §17.318).

Inspection of Mines.—See subhead Safeguarding of Employees, supra.

Oil and Gas.—Director of Department of Natural Resources is supervisor of oil and gas wells. (MCLA §324.61505; MSA §13A.61505). Permit is required to drill or deepen wells, including key wells for secondary recovery. (MCLA §324.61525; MSA §13A.61525). Supervisor may require filing of drilling log, well samples and drilling and production reports, which are confidential for 90 days. (MCLA §324.61506; MSA §13A.61506).

Spacing of wells (MCLA §324.61506; MSA §13A.61506) and production to prevent waste (MCLA §324.61513; MSA §13A.61513) are regulated. If oil wells and test holes are not cased, plugged or repaired in accordance with statute or regulations, commissioner may do so at owner's expense. (MCLA §324.61519; MSA §13A.61514). In certain circumstances commissioner may order unit operation of unit area. (MCLA §324.61704; MSA §13A.61704).

All unpatented overflowed lands, made lands, and lake bottom lands belonging to or held in trust for state are subject to lease for removal of oil and gas. State Department of Natural Resources is empowered to enter into such leases. (MCLA §324.33936; MSA §13A.33936). Exploration for, development, production, handling or use, of oil or gas under any such lease is subject to jurisdiction and control of supervisor of wells. (MCLA §324.33937; MSA §13A.33937). Covenants may be implied in oil and gas leases whether such leases contain special covenants or not. (MCLA §565.5; MSA §26.524). Any interested lessee may file petition with supervisor of wells requesting order for unit operation of pool. (MCLA §324.61703; MSA §13A.61703). However, no lessee is chargeable with more than amount of unit expense charged to his interest pursuant to plan of unitization. (MCLA §324.61719; MSA §13A.61719).

Taxes.—Severance tax of 5% of gross cash market value of total production of gas and 6.6% of gross market value of oil is reported and paid monthly (MCLA §§205.301-.315; MSA §§7.351-.365), plus fee not to exceed 1% of gross cash market value to cover regulation costs of oil and gas wells (MCLA §324.61524; MSA §13A.61524).

Low grade iron ore, low grade iron ore mining property and rights to minerals are subject to specific tax in lieu of certain other taxes. (MCLA §§211.621-.625; MSA §§13.157[1]-.157[5]). Underground beneficiated iron ore, underground agglomerated iron ore and related property are also subject to specific tax. (MCLA §§207.271-.279; MSA §§13.158[1]-.158[9]).

Mechanic's liens on oil and gas properties. See category Debtor and Creditor, topic Liens, subhead Mechanic's and Construction Liens.

MORTGAGES

CHATTEL MORTGAGES:

Uniform Commercial Code adopted with 1972 Official Amendments. (MCLA §440.1101 et seq.; MSA §19.1101 et seq.). See category Business Regulation and Commerce, topic Commercial Code.

What May be Mortgaged.—Uniform Commercial Code governs all consensual security interests in personal property and fixtures, and any sale of accounts or chattel paper (MCLA §440.9102; MSA §19.9102), except excluded transactions (MCLA §440.9104; MSA §19.9104), and ordinary building materials incorporated into improvement on land (MCLA §440.9313[2]; MSA §19.9313[2]).

After-acquired Property.—Governed by Uniform Commercial Code. (MCLA §§440.9204, .9108; MSA §§19.9204, .9108).

Floating Stock.—Governed by Uniform Commercial Code. (MCLA §440.9204; MSA §19.9204).

Future Advances.—Governed by Uniform Commercial Code. (MCLA §440.9204; MSA §19.9204).

Requisites of Instrument.—Uniform Commercial Code governs form of security agreements (MCLA §§440.9201, .9203; MSA §§19.9201, .9203) and of financing statements (MCLA §440.9402; MSA §19.9402).

Execution of Instrument.—See subhead Requisites of Instrument, supra.

Filing.—Uniform Commercial Code governs. (MCLA §§440.9103, .9302, .9304, .9313, .9401-.9410; MSA §§19.9103, .9302, .9304, .9313, .9401-.9410).

See note at head of Digest as to 1998 legislation covered.

See Topical Index in front part of this volume.

CHATTEL MORTGAGES . . . *continued*

Michigan act follows U.C.C. §9-302(1)(d) except that language concerning motor vehicles is expanded to include mobile homes and certain watercraft. (MCLA §440.9302[1][d]; MSA §19.9302[1][d]).

In U.C.C. §9-302(3)(b), Michigan act fills in blank with references to MCLA §257.216; MSA §9.1916 (motor vehicles subject to registration); MCLA §324.8032; MSA §13A.80320 (certain watercraft); MCLA §125.2330; MSA §19.855(130) (mobile homes); and any other Michigan statute requiring certificate of title. (MCLA §440.9302[3][b]; MSA §19.9302[3][b]).

Michigan act elects second alternative subsection (1) of U.C.C. §9-401; blanks in subsection (1)(a) filled in "register of deeds." (MCLA §440.9401[1]; MSA §19.9401[1]).

Alternative subsection (3) of U.C.C. §9-401 not elected in Michigan. (MCLA §440.9401[3]; MSA §19.9401[3]).

In U.C.C. §9-402(1), Michigan act inserts, after first comma in first sentence, "in printed or typewritten form,". (MCLA §440.9402[1]; MSA §19.9402[1]). Michigan Act adds statement that financing statement may include debtor's tax identification number. (MCLA §440.9402[1]; MSA §19.9402[1]).

In second sentence of U.C.C. §9-402(7), Michigan act omits "after the change" and substitutes "after the debtor notifies the secured party in writing of the change." (MCLA §440.9402[7]; MSA §19.9402[7]).

Michigan act also adds subsections (9) and (10) to U.C.C. §9-402 providing, respectively, for recording of financing statements (and related continuation statements, termination statements, amendments and assignments) in real estate records notwithstanding failure to comply with formal requisites for documents to be recorded under real estate law (MCLA §565.47; MSA §26.563), and for noting thereon by register of deeds date and time of recording and liber and page (MCLA §§440.9402[9], [10]; MSA §§19.9402[9], [10]).

Michigan act also adds subsections (11) and (12) to U.C.C. §9-402 providing for register of deeds entering such financing statements and related documents, in order received, in entry book where real estate mortgages entered (subsection [11]) and indexing such financing statements and related documents by debtor's name and name of record owner of real property (subsection [12]). (MCLA §§440.9402[11], [12]; MSA §§19.9402[11], [12]).

Michigan Act also adds subsections (13), (14) and (15) to U.C.C. §9-402 providing that beginning Sept. 1, 1988, all original filings of security interest or financing statement shall contain debtor's tax identification number, subject to certain exceptions. (MCLA §440.9402[13], [14], [15]; MSA §§19.9402[13], [14], [15]).

In U.C.C. §9-403(2), Michigan act inserts "within 6 months" between "filed" and "prior to the lapse" in second sentence. (MCLA §440.9403[2]; MSA §19.9403[2]).

In second sentence of U.C.C. §9-403(3), Michigan act inserts "and where the original financing statement describes real property, by liber and page of recording thereof" after "by file number." After second sentence, Michigan Act inserts sentence "A continuation statement also may, but is not required to, include the debtor's tax identification number." (MCLA §440.9403[3]; MSA §19.9403[3]).

Reference in first sentence of U.C.C. §9-403(4) to subsection (7) is changed to subsection (8) in Michigan act. (MCLA §440.9403[4]; MSA §19.9403[4]).

Fee for filing original financing statement, continuation statement, amendment or assignment is: $3 for filing with Secretary of State if on standard form (otherwise $6), $6 for filing with register of deeds if to be recorded in real estate records and if on standard form ($6 plus $2 per page over two pages if not on standard form), and $3 for all other filings with register of deeds. (MCLA §440.9403[5]; MSA §19.9403[5]). Additional fee of $3 for each name more than one required to be indexed. (MCLA §440.9403[6]; MSA §19.9403[6]).

Subsections (6) and (7) of U.C.C. §9-403 are renumbered (7) and (8) respectively. (MCLA §440.9403[7],[8]; MSA §19.9403[7],[8]).

Blank in U.C.C. §9-404(1) is filled in with "the effective date of this 1978 amendatory act" (Jan. 1, 1979); termination statement for financing statement describing real property must include liber and page where recorded; termination statement for original filing made before July 1, 1976, with officer other than Secretary of State may be sent directly to debtor; $100 liability described in official text applies only if secured party fails to file termination statement within 20 days after demand. (MCLA §440.9404[1]; MSA §19.9404[1]).

Fee for filing termination statement is $1 (whether or not in standard form) plus $1 for each additional name indexed, but no fee charged for termination statement relating to financing statement filed after June 30, 1976, unless filing was with register of deeds for recording on real property records, in which case fee is $3 for first page and $2 for each additional page. (MCLA §440.9404[3]; MSA §19.9404[3]).

Fee for filing financing statement showing assignment is $3 if in standard form (otherwise $6) plus $3 for each name more than one required to be indexed. (MCLA §440.9405[1]; MSA §19.9405[1]).

Assignment of rights under financing statement describing real property must show liber and page where recorded; fee for filing assignment is $3 if in standard form (otherwise $6) plus $3 for each name more than one required to be indexed. (MCLA §440.9405[2]; MSA §19.9405[2]).

Fee for filing statement of release is $3 if in standard form (otherwise $6) plus $3 for each name more than one required to be indexed. (MCLA §440.9406; MSA §19.9406).

Michigan act adopts optional U.C.C. §9-407; fee is $3 for certificate if requested on standard form (otherwise $6), $1 per page for copies of filed financing statements and assignments and $25 for expedited service by Secretary of State. (MCLA §440.9407; MSA §19.9407).

Michigan act adds §9-410 permitting Secretary of State to establish microfilm service for bulk sale of filed documents. Fee is $50 or actual cost, whichever greater. (MCLA §440.9410; MSA §19.9410).

Removal of Property by Mortgagor.—Governed by Uniform Commercial Code. (MCLA §440.9401; MSA §19.9401). Wrongful removal of mortgaged property to another state is criminal offense. (MCLA §§750.177-.178; MSA §§28.374-.375).

Sale of Property by Mortgagor.—Governed by Uniform Commercial Code. (MCLA §§440.9306, .9307, .9311; MSA §§19.9306, .9307, .9311).

Concealment or Destruction of Property by Mortgagor.—Embezzlement, concealment or disposition with intent to injure or defraud a mortgagee, lessor, vendor or their respective assigns is criminal offense. (MCLA §750.177; MSA §28.374).

Foreclosure by Court Proceedings.—Governed by Uniform Commercial Code. (MCLA §§440.9501-.9507; MSA §§19.9501-.9507). For appropriate judicial procedure to effect repossession, see category Civil Actions and Procedure, topic Replevin.

Sale by Mortgagee.—See subhead Foreclosure by Court Proceedings, supra.

Redemption.—Governed by Uniform Commercial Code. (MCLA §440.9506; MSA §19.9506).

Foreign Mortgages.—Governed by Uniform Commercial Code. (MCLA §§440.9103, .9401; MSA §§19.9103, .9401).

Taxation.—No specific provision. See category Taxation, topic Intangible Personal Property Tax.

Motor Vehicles.—For special provisions concerning installment sales of motor vehicles and liens thereon, see category Transportation, topic Motor Vehicles, subheads Installment Sale and Liens.

Forms.—Forms at end of this Digest have been approved by Secretary of State, printed by him on 8½" x 11" paper, and are available upon request. Two copies should be submitted to Secretary of State. Secretary of State will accept typed versions of Financing Statement and Continuation Statement without additional fee. For convenience in handling, Secretary of State would prefer to have typewritten statements on paper 11" high by 8.5" wide. If not in this form, Financing Statements are nonetheless acceptable. For filing fees for standard and nonstandard forms, see subhead Filing, supra.

COLLATERAL SECURITY:

See category Debtor and Creditor, topic Pledges.

MORTGAGES OF PERSONAL PROPERTY:

See topic Chattel Mortgages.

MORTGAGES OF REAL PROPERTY:

Mortgage creates a lien only and confers no title until foreclosure sale (302 Mich. 666, 5 N.W.2d 524), and, except as provided by statute (see subhead Rents and Profits, infra), no right to possession or to rents and profits until expiration of period of redemption (MCLA §600.2932[2]; MSA §27A.2932[2]; 278 Mich. 457, 270 N.W. 748). Although absolute in form a deed given to secure payment of a debt may be construed as an equitable mortgage (324 Mich. 583; 37 N.W.2d 558), even though intended conditional defeasance rests only in parol (289 Mich. 577; 286 N.W. 835).

Where mortgage provides for escrow of taxes, insurance or cost of improvements, mortgagee must account annually to mortgagor on status of escrow fund. (MCLA §§565.161-.162; MSA §§26.575[1]-.575[2]).

Execution.—Requirements are same as for deed. See categories Documents and Records, topic Records; Property, topic Deeds.

Recording is not necessary to validity as between parties, but unless recorded in county where land lies, mortgage is void as against subsequent purchaser or mortgagee in good faith for value whose conveyance or mortgage is first recorded. (MCLA §565.29; MSA §26.547). Also see category Documents and Records, topic Records.

Recording Fees.—See category Documents and Records, topic Records.

Taxes.—See category Taxation, topic Taxes, subhead Intangible Personal Property Tax.

Trust deeds are not in common use.

Trust Mortgage.—Mortgage may be made to a trustee to secure payment of bonds or other obligations. Trust indenture defines rights of bondholders and duties and powers of trustee with respect to default, foreclosure, purchase at foreclosure sale, and management and disposition of foreclosed property. Court may authorize trustee to purchase at foreclosure sale, manage and sell property. (MCLA §§451.402 et seq.; MSA §§27.1282 et seq.; MCLA §600.3170; MSA §27A.3170). Personnel and activities of bondholders protective committees are regulated by Corporation and Securities Commission. (MCLA §451.302 et seq.; MSA §27.1292 et seq.).

Rents and Profits.—Statutory provisions authorize assignment of rents and profits of mortgaged property, enforceable upon default and prior to expiration of redemption period in connection with mortgages of certain commercial or industrial property (MCLA §554.231 et seq.; MSA §26.1137[1] et seq.; 362 Mich. 114, 106 N.W.2d 515) and certain trust mortgages (MCLA §554.211 et seq.; MSA §26.1131 et seq.).

Future Advances.—Mortgage may cover future advances, subject to intervening rights of third persons. (253 Mich. 557, 235 N.W. 252). See subhead Priorities, infra.

Priorities of mortgages depend on order of recording, except as expressly subordinated (249 Mich. 89, 227 N.W. 674), or affected by notice (280 Mich. 335, 273 N.W. 589), estopped (262 Mich. 394, 247 N.W. 702), or equities in favor of purchase-money mortgagee (253 Mich. 51, 234 N.W. 113). Future Advance statute enacted effective Apr. 1, 1991. Future advance mortgage securing future advance has priority with respect to such future advance as if future advance made at time future advance mortgage recorded after Apr. 1, 1991 except to extent priority governed by construction lien act or tax lien act. (MCLA §§565.901-.906; MSA §§26.977 [901]-.977[906]). Priority statute does not apply to residential future advance mortgages unless mortgage contains statement as to its maximum principal amount and statement that "This is a future advance mortgage", both set forth in conspicuous manner on first page of mortgage or amendment. (MCLA §565.903a; MSA §26.977[903a]).

Subordination Agreements.—Priority of mortgage may be waived in writing on mortgage or by separate instrument witnessed and acknowledged as deed, and when

---

See note at head of Digest as to 1998 legislation covered.

See Topical Index in front part of this volume.

MORTGAGES OF REAL PROPERTY . . . *continued*
recorded is notice to all persons dealing with mortgage (MCLA §565.391; MSA §26.701).

Assignment.—Provision is made for recording assignments of mortgages, but record is not notice to mortgagor. (MCLA §565.33; MSA §26.550). Assignment of mortgage is nullity unless accompanied by assignment of debt secured by mortgage. (302 Mich. 666, 5 N.W.2d 524). Assignment of mortgage note carries equitable ownership of mortgage. (276 Mich. 267, 267 N.W. 829).

Duration of Lien.—Mortgage considered discharged of record unless renewed within 30 years from due date by recorded extension agreement or affidavit of owner showing amount unpaid (MCLA §565.382; MSA §26.692); and may not be foreclosed by advertisement (284 Mich. 417, 279 N.W. 884).

Release.—Part of mortgaged property may be released from lien of mortgage. Mortgage may incorporate clause providing for such part release on agreed terms and such clause runs with land. (244 Mich. 403, 221 N.W. 322).

Satisfaction.—Mortgage discharged of record upon presentation to register of deeds of certificate of circuit judge, mortgagee or his personal representative or assignee certifying mortgage paid, satisfied and/or discharged. (MCLA §565.42; MSA §26.559).

Foreclosure by Court Action.—Mortgage may be foreclosed by action in circuit court, in which case court may order sale after six months from filing of complaint, property being sold by circuit court commissioner or other person appointed by court at public auction to highest bidder. (MCLA §§600.3101-.3130; MSA §§27A.3101-.3130). Mortgagor and those claiming under him have six months from time of sale within which to redeem. (MCLA §600.3140; MSA §27A.3140). See also subhead Deficiency Judgments, infra.

Foreclosure by Advertisement.—If mortgage contains power of sale, it may be foreclosed by advertisement by publishing notice for four successive weeks, at least once a week, in a newspaper of county, that mortgage will be foreclosed by sale of premises. If foreclosing party is not original mortgagee, record must include all assignments made. Within 15 days after first publication of notice, copy thereof must be posted on premises. Sale must be at public auction to highest bidder. Mortgagor or those claiming under him have one year after time of such sale within which to redeem, except: (1) redemption period is six months in case of mortgage executed on or after Jan. 1, 1965 on commercial or industrial property or multi-family residential property exceeding four units, or in case of mortgage executed on or after Jan. 1, 1965 on residential property not exceeding four units and not more than three acres in size where amount claimed due at date of foreclosure notice is more than two-thirds of original indebtedness secured; (2) redemption period is three months in case of mortgage on residential property not exceeding four units and not more than three acres in size if amount claimed due at date of foreclosure notice is more than two-thirds of original indebtedness secured and property is abandoned. (MCLA §§600.3201-.3280; MSA §§27A.3201-.3280).

Sales.—See subheads Foreclosure by Court Action, and Foreclosure by Advertisement, supra.

Deficiency Judgments.—Foreclosure is the only remedy of mortgagee unless mortgage or separate instrument contains a promise to pay sum secured. (MCLA §565.6; MSA §26.525). On foreclosure by court action, judgment determines personal liability, if any, and execution issues for deficiency established on sale, but court may fix minimum price for which property may be sold. (MCLA §§600.3150-.3155; MSA §§27A.3150-.3155). On foreclosure by advertisement action lies for deficiency against those personally liable, but defendant may plead that sale was for less than true value, and judgment is only for difference between mortgage debt and true value. (MCLA §600.3280; MSA §27A.3280).

Moratorium.—None in effect.

Redemption.—For redemption periods see subheads Foreclosure by Court Action, and Foreclosure by Advertisement, supra. Mortgagor, any person lawfully claiming under him, or his personal representative may redeem during period by paying to purchaser at foreclosure sale, his personal representative or assignee or to register of deeds, amount bid at sale plus interest, fee of $5 and, where added by affidavits conforming to statutory requirements, certain sums advanced by mortgagee after foreclosure sale in payment of property taxes and insurance premiums. (MCLA §§600.3140, .3145, .3240; MSA §§27A.3140, .3145, .3240).

Forms.—Following forms are in common use:

Forms

Mortgage:

This Mortgage, Made the . . . . . . day of . . . . . . in the year 19. . . ., by . . . . . . mortgagor . . . ., whose address is . . . . . ., unto . . . . . . mortgagee . . . ., whose address is . . . ., Witnesseth, That the said mortgagor . . . ., in consideration of the sum of . . . . . . dollars, the receipt of which is acknowledged, and for the purpose of securing the repayment of the said sum, with interest, as herein after provided, and the performance of the covenants hereinafter contained, hereby mortgage . . . . and warrant . . . . unto the said mortgagee, ... heirs and assigns, the lands, premises and property situated in the . . . . . . of . . . . . . County of . . . . . . and State of Michigan, described as follows, to wit: . . . . . . Together with the tenements, hereditaments and appurtenances thereof.

And the said . . . . . . mortgagor . . . . for . . . .self. . . ., ...heirs, executors and administrators, hereby covenant. . . . with the said mortgagee . . . ., ... legal representatives and assigns, as follows:

First. Said mortgagor . . . . will pay to the said mortgagee . . . ., ... legal representatives and assigns, the said sum of . . . . . . dollars . . . . . . with interest thereon at the rate of . . . .% per annum, payable semi-annually, on the first days of . . . . . . and . . . . . . of each year, until the full payment of said principal sum, according to the terms of . . . . . . bearing even date herewith, executed by . . . . . . to the said mortgagee . . . ., and will pay interest at the rate of . . . .% per annum, semi-annually, upon all overdue interest or principal from the time of its maturity.

Second. The said mortgagor . . . ., within forty days after the same become due and payable, will pay all taxes and assessments which shall be levied upon the said lands, or upon the interest or estate in said lands created or represented by this mortgage, or by said indebtedness, whether levied against the said mortgagor . . . ., ... legal representatives or assigns, or otherwise; and, also, the said mortgagor . . . ., within forty days after the same become due and payable, will pay all taxes and assessments which shall be levied on account of this mortgage or the indebtedness secured thereby; provided, however, that the total amount so paid for taxes on said mortgage or indebtedness, together with the interest payable on said indebtedness, shall not exceed 7% per annum; and said mortgagor . . . . hereby waive . . . . any and all claim or right against said mortgagee . . . ., ... legal representatives or assigns, to any payment or rebate on, or offset against, the interest or principal of said mortgage debt by reason of the payment of any of the aforesaid taxes or assessments.

Third. The said mortgagor . . . . will also keep all buildings erected and to be erected upon said lands insured against loss and damage by fire, with insurers, and to an amount, approved by the mortgagee . . . . as a further security to said mortgage debt, and assign and deliver to the mortgagee. . . . all insurance upon said property.

Fourth. If said mortgagor . . . . make . . . . default in the payment of any of the aforesaid taxes or assessments, or in procuring and maintaining insurance, as above covenanted, said mortgagee . . . ., ... legal representatives or assigns, may pay such taxes and effect such insurance, and the sums so paid shall be a further lien on said premises under this mortgage, payable forthwith, with interest at the rate of . . . .% per annum.

Fifth. Should default be made in the payment of said principal, or interest, or taxes, or insurance premiums, or any part thereof, when the same are payable as above provided, and should the same, or any part thereof, remain unpaid for the period of thirty days, then the aforesaid principal sum, with all arrearages of interest, taxes and insurance premiums, shall, at the option of said mortgagee . . . ., ... legal representatives and assigns, become payable immediately thereafter, although the period above limited for the payment thereof shall not then have expired, anything hereinbefore contained to the contrary thereof in anywise notwithstanding.

Sixth. Said mortgagor . . . . shall pay to said mortgagee . . . ., ... legal representatives and assigns, the sum of . . . . . . dollars as a reasonable attorney's fee, in addition to all other legal costs, as often as any proceeding is taken in equity to foreclose this mortgage for default in any of its covenants, which sum shall be an additional lien on said premises.

Seventh. All the aforesaid covenants shall run with the land.

Eighth. Upon default being made in any of the aforesaid covenants, the said mortgagee . . . ., ... legal representatives and assigns, are hereby authorized and empowered to grant, bargain and sell, release and convey the said premises, property and appurtenances, at public vendue, and to execute and deliver to the purchasers at such sale good and sufficient deeds of conveyance in law, pursuant to the statute in such case made and provided, rendering any surplus moneys, after payment of the moneys due hereon, the attorney fee provided by law, and the costs and charges of such vendue and sale, to the said mortgagor . . . ., ... heirs, legal representatives and assigns.

In Witness Whereof, The said mortgagor . . . . ha. . . . hereunto set . . . . . . hand . . . . and seal . . . . the day and year first above written.

Signed, sealed and delivered in presence of . . . .(L. S.)
. . . .(L. S.)

. . . .
. . . .

(Acknowledgment).
(name and address of draftsman)

Assignment of Mortgage: Know All Men By These Presents, That . . . . . ., whose address is . . . . . ., part . . . . of the first part, for and in consideration of the sum of . . . . . Dollars, lawful money of the United States of America, to . . . . . . in hand paid by . . . . . ., whose address is . . . . . ., part . . . . of the second part, the receipt whereof is hereby acknowledged, ha . . . . sold, assigned and transferred, and hereby do. . . . sell, assign and transfer to the said part . . . . of the second part, all the right, title, and interest of the said part . . . . of the first part in and to a certain Real Estate Mortgage dated the . . . . . . day of . . . . . . in the year nineteen hundred . . . . . . made by . . . . . . to . . . . . . and recorded in the Register's Office of the County of . . . . . ., State of Michigan, in Liber . . . . of Mortgages, on page . . . .

Signed, sealed, and delivered the . . . . day of . . . . . A. D. . . . .

. . . .(L. S.).
. . . .(L. S.).

In presence of
. . . .
. . . .

(Acknowledgment).
(name and address of draftsman)

Release of Part of Mortgaged Premises: This Indenture, made this . . . . . . day of . . . . . in the year one thousand nine hundred and . . . . . . Between . . . . . ., whose address is . . . . . ., part . . . . of the first part, and . . . . . ., whose address is . . . . . ., part . . . . of the second part; Witnesseth:

Whereas, ... by indenture of mortgage, bearing date the . . . . . . day of . . . . . . one thousand nine hundred and . . . . . . for the consideration therein mentioned and to secure the payment of the money therein specified, did convey certain lands and tenements of which the lands hereinafter described are part, unto . . . . . ., which said mortgage was recorded in the office of the Register of Deeds, for the County of . . . . . ., State of Michigan, in Liber . . . . of mortgages, at page . . . . . .,

And whereas, the said part . . . . of the first part, at the request of the said part . . . . of the second part, ha . . . . agreed to give up and surrender the lands hereinafter

See note at head of Digest as to 1998 legislation covered.

See Topical Index in front part of this volume.

MI – 45

MORTGAGES OF REAL PROPERTY . . . *continued*

described, unto the said part. . . . of the second part, and to hold and retain the residue of the mortgaged lands as security for the money remaining due on said mortgage.

Now this indenture witnesseth that the said part . . . . of the first part, in pursuance of the said agreement, and in consideration of . . . . . . dollars, to . . . . . . duly paid at the time of the ensealing and delivery of these presents, the receipt whereof is hereby acknowledged ha . . . . granted, released, quit-claimed, and set over, and by these presents do . . . . grant, release, quit-claim and set over, unto the said part . . . . of the second part, all that part of the said mortgaged lands situated and being in the . . . . . . of . . . . . County of . . . . . and State of Michigan, described as follows, to wit: . . . . .

Together with the hereditaments and appurtenances thereunto belonging, and all the right, title and interest of the said part . . . . of the first part, of, in and to the same, to the intent that the lands and tenements hereby conveyed may be discharged from the said mortgage, and that the rest of the lands in the said mortgage specified may remain to the said part . . . . of the first part.

To have and to hold, the lands and premises hereby released and conveyed, to the said part. . . . of the second part, ... heirs and assigns, to . . . . . . their only proper use, benefit and behoof, forever, free, clear, and discharged of and from all lien and claim, under and by virtue of the indenture of mortgage aforesaid.

In Witness Whereof, the said part . . . . of the first part, ha . . . . hereunto set . . . . . . hand . . . . and seal . . . . the day and year first above written.

. . . .(L.S.).

. . . .(L.S.).

Signed, Sealed and Delivered
in presence of
. . . .
. . . .
(Acknowledgment).
(name and address of draftsman)

Discharge of Mortgage: Know All Men By These Presents, That . . . . . ., whose address is . . . . ., in the . . . . . . of . . . . . and State of . . . . . Do hereby certify, That a certain Indenture of Mortgage bearing date the . . . . . day of . . . . . A. D. . . . . . . made and executed by . . . . . of the first part to . . . . . of the second part, and recorded in the Register's Office for the County of . . . . . and State of . . . . . . in Liber . . . . . of Mortgages, on Page . . . . . . on the . . . . . day of . . . . . A. D. . . . . . . is fully paid, satisfied and discharged.

In Witness Whereof, ... have hereunto set . . . . . hand . . . . and . . . . . . the . . . . . . day of . . . . . . A. D. . . . .

. . . .(L. S.).

Signed, Sealed and Delivered
in presence of
. . . .
. . . .
(Acknowledgment).
(name and address of draftsman)

Chattel Mortgages.—See topic Chattel Mortgages.

PROPERTY

ABSENTEES:

Care of Property.—When person is absent from usual abode and whereabouts unknown for more than three months, temporary personal representative may be appointed to preserve estate until death or survival is determined. (MCLA §700.492[7]; MSA §27.5492[7]).

Distribution of Property.—When person is absent from last known abode for seven years, whereabouts unknown and no tidings received, his estate may be administered on statutory notice as estate of deceased person, but property cannot be sold or distributed for three years except to pay taxes, expenses, liens or insurance, to prevent depreciation, to support spouse and minor children or to discharge obligations contracted before disappearance, unless distributee gives surety bond. If disappeared person, or person claiming to have succeeded to rights of disappeared person by reason of his death after commencement of seven-year period, does not petition for vacation of proceedings within three years after qualification of personal representative disappeared person is presumed to have died at end of seven-year period, and estate is distributed and bonds given on prior distribution cancelled. (MCLA §§700.4, .492; MSA §§27.5004, .5492).

Beneficiary of Estate.—Where court determines that disappeared person is apparent beneficiary of estate of deceased person, and absence has continued for five years, share he would take if alive cannot be distributed until 18 months after decedent's death. After statutory notice, if no claim is made to disappeared person's share, distribution is made as though disappeared person predeceased decedent. (MCLA §700.493; MSA §27.5493).

Process Agent.—Service of process may be made upon any defendant by leaving summons and copy of complaint with agent authorized by written appointment to receive service of process. (MCLA §600.1930; MSA §27A.1930; Rule 2.105). See also category Civil Actions and Procedure, topic Process.

Escheat.—Prior statute has been repealed and Uniform Unclaimed Property Act, MCLA §567.221, MSA §26.1055(1) is adopted, effective Mar. 28, 1996. Act provides that property is, in general, presumed abandoned if it remains unclaimed for more than five years (shorter time frames are involved for utility deposits and certain insurance policy proceeds, etc.). New statute imposes reporting duties on persons holding abandoned property. (MCLA §567.238, MSA §26.1055[18]). State receives control of abandoned property and has duties to publish and ultimately sell at public sale abandoned property and, except as otherwise provided in Act, deposit into general fund of Michigan funds received from sale. (MCLA §567.244, MSA §26.1055[24]).

See category Business Regulation and Commerce, topic Banks and Banking, subhead Unclaimed Deposits, and category Estates and Trusts, topic Wills, subhead Unclaimed Legacies.

For other matters relating to absentees, see categories Business Regulation and Commerce, topic Securities; Civil Actions and Procedure, topics Partition, Process; Estates and Trusts, topics Death, Descent and Distribution, subhead Escheat.

ADVERSE POSSESSION:

Title to land may be acquired by adverse possession and such title is marketable. (112 Mich. 452, 70 N.W. 1038). Careful purchasers stipulate for title marketable in fact and of record. Title by adverse possession is not marketable of record unless established by decree quieting title. (325 Mich. 625, 39 N.W.2d 204).

Character of Possession.—Possession must be actual, continuous, visible, notorious, distinct and hostile (not permissive) throughout the statutory period. Adverse claimant need not show color of title, but if he enters without claim of title, his possession does not become adverse until he asserts title, as by exercising acts of ownership. (311 Mich. 567, 19 N.W.2d 101). Nature of acts necessary to constitute adverse possession depends upon character of premises. (305 Mich. 137, 9 N.W.2d 35).

Duration of Possession.—Title is established by showing adverse possession for 15 years. If claimant enters under color of title by tax deed, statutory period is ten years; if under color of title by deed made upon sale by personal representative, guardian or testamentary trustee or by ministerial officer under court order or decree, five years. (MCLA §600.5801; MSA §27A.5801). Claimant may tack periods of adverse possession by predecessors in privity and privity may be shown by parol transfer. (315 Mich. 598, 24 N.W.2d 414).

Easements.—Easement may be acquired by adverse use for 15 years. Requirements are the same as for acquisition of title by adverse possession, except that use need not be exclusive, provided right does not depend upon a like right in others. (240 Mich. 327, 215 N.W. 331).

Disabilities.—Period of limitation does not run against legal titleholder during his minority or insanity. (MCLA §600.5851; MSA §27A.5851).

Public Grounds.—Title cannot be acquired by adverse possession to public ways or grounds of municipal corporations. (MCLA §600.5821; MSA §27A.5821).

CONVEYANCES:

See topic Deeds.

CURTESY:

Abolished. (MCLA §§557.1-.5; MSA §§26.161-.164; 15 Mich. 60; 30 Mich. 422).

DEEDS:

An instrument, whatever its form or mode of execution, that passes a present interest vesting from the date of execution, is a deed. (145 Mich. 563, 108 N.W. 985).

Execution.—Signature and delivery are sufficient between parties and others with notice. (244 Mich. 403, 221 N.W. 322). Requirement of seal has been abolished. (MCLA §565.241; MSA §26.595). Two witnesses and acknowledgment are usual, and necessary to entitle instrument to be recorded. (MCLA §565.8; MSA §26.527). For circumstances in which spouse must join, see category Family, topic Husband and Wife, subhead Conveyance or Encumbrance of Property; category Debtor and Creditor, topic Homesteads, subhead Alienation or Encumbrance. For other recording requirements, see category Documents and Records, topic Records. See also topic Real Property.

Recording.—Unrecorded deed is void against subsequent purchaser in good faith (without notice) for a valuable consideration who records first. (MCLA §565.29; MSA §26.547). Deeds are recorded in office of the register of deeds of county where the land lies. (MCLA §565.23; MSA §26.541). Unless true consideration stated (or in case of gift, proper value) affidavit of value required in order to record. See category Documents and Records, topic Records.

Recording Fees.—See category Documents and Records, topic Records.

Operation and Effect.—No covenant implied in any conveyance of real estate, except oil and gas leases, whether containing special covenants or not (MCLA §565.5; MSA §26.524), except that statutory form warranty deed implies covenants of seisin, right to convey, quiet possession, freedom from incumbrances and to warrant and defend title (MCLA §565.151; MSA §26.571).

Taxes.—For tax on real estate transfers see category Taxation, topic Real Estate Stamp and Transfer Taxes.

Forms (Statutory).—

Forms

Warranty Deed.—"A. B. conveys and warrants to C. D. (here describe the premises) for the sum of (here insert the consideration)," to be dated, signed, sealed and acknowledged by grantor. (MCLA §565.151; MSA §26.571).

Quit Claim Deed.—"A. B. quit claims to C. D. (here describe the premises) for the sum of (here insert the consideration)," to be dated, signed, sealed and acknowledged by grantor. (MCLA §565.152; MSA §26.572).

DEEDS OF TRUST:

See category Mortgages, topic Mortgages of Real Property.

DOWER:

Dower is the widow's right to the use for life of one-third of all estate of inheritance of which her husband was seized during marriage. (MCLA §558.1; MSA §26.221).

See note at head of Digest as to 1998 legislation covered.

See Topical Index in front part of this volume.

DOWER . . . *continued*

Such estates aliened by a resident husband during marriage are subject to dower at his death as of the value at date of alienation. (MCLA §558.7; MSA §26.227).

Dower right will not prevail against a purchase money mortgage given by the husband. (MCLA §558.4; MSA §26.224).

Nonresident wife is not entitled to dower in lands conveyed by her husband, but only those of which he died seized. (MCLA §558.21; MSA §26.237).

Release.—A wife may contract with her husband for release of dower. (MCLA §558.13; MSA §26.229).

Bar.—A wife may bar her dower right by joining in husband's deed, by joining with husband in subsequent deed, or by direct conveyance to husband or grantee (MCLA §558.13; MSA §26.229), or by an antenuptial jointure (MCLA §558.14; MSA §26.230), or pecuniary agreement (MCLA §558.16; MSA §26.232), assented to in lieu of dower (MCLA §558.15; MSA §26.231). Dower of incompetent wife may be barred by proceeding in circuit court wherein cash value of dower interest is determined and paid to guardian other than husband. (MCLA §600.2931; MSA §27A.2931).

Divorce.—Judgments of divorce and judgments of separate maintenance must include in decree provision in lieu of dower of wife in property of husband, which is in full satisfaction of all claims wife may have in any property husband owns or may thereafter own. (MCLA §552.101; MSA §25.131). In case of failure of husband to pay allowance so decreed, court may award execution for collection of same or may sequester his real and personal estate or may appoint receiver thereof. (MCLA §552.27; MSA §25.105).

Election between dower and: distributive share of husband's estate, see category Estates and Trusts, topic Descent and Distribution; testamentary provision, see category Estates and Trusts, topic Wills, subhead Election.

ESCHEAT:

See topic Absentees, subhead Escheat; categories Business Regulation and Commerce, topic Banks and Banking, subhead Unclaimed Deposits; Estates and Trusts, topics Descent and Distribution, subhead Escheat; Wills, subhead Unclaimed Legacies.

LANDLORD AND TENANT:

Rights and liabilities generally are contractual in nature and have sources in both statutes and common law.

Uniform Residential Landlord and Tenant Act not adopted.

Kinds of Tenancy.—Law recognizes tenancies for years, from year to year, by sufferance and at will, including periodic tenancies at will.

Leases.—Leases for longer than one year are void unless in writing signed by party by whom lease is to be made or by person authorized in writing. (MCLA §566.108; MSA §26.908). Generally leases are viewed as contracts needing certainty. (195 Mich. 181, 161 N.W. 838). Modification does not need consideration if there is a writing signed by party against whom modification is sought. (MCLA §566.1; MSA §26.978[1]). Seal is not necessary for validity or recording. (MCLA §565.241; MSA §26.595). Witnesses and acknowledgment are not necessary to validity. (337 Mich. 344, 60 N.W.2d 298). All residential leases by law include covenant of landlord of fitness of premises for use and covenant to make reasonable repairs; for leases of one year or more such covenants can be modified by agreement. (MCLA §554.139; MSA §26.1109). Provisions of rental agreements covering residential premises are subject to detailed statutory regulations under Truth in Renting Act. (MCLA §§554.631-.641; MSA §§26.1138[31]-[41]).

Recording.—Lease for more than three years is conveyance subject to recording laws. (MCLA §565.35; MSA §26.552). (See category Documents and Records, topic Records.) Possession of tenant under lease for three years or less is notice to world of his interest. (204 Mich. 66, 170 N.W. 29).

Taxes.—Unless agreement to contrary, tenant may pay taxes and deduct amount from rent. (MCLA §211.53; MSA §7.97).

Rent.—Unless agreement to contrary, rent not due until end of rental period (55 Mich. 468, 21 N.W. 894), and payment by notes does not satisfy obligation (265 Mich. 252, 251 N.W. 404). Amount of rent may be left to future determination by landlord (214 Mich. 607, 183 N.W. 36), by lessee (342 Mich. 92, 68 N.W.2d 771), or by arbitration (126 F.2d 936).

Lien.—Parties to lease can contract for landlord's lien on tenant's property, but lien attaches only to property contemplated by agreement (49 Mich. 33, 12 N.W. 899), and not until tenant is in default (27 Mich. 529). Landlord has equitable lien on amounts owing insolvent tenant from sub-tenant, superior to claims of tenant's creditors. (270 Mich. 218, 258 N.W. 252).

Termination of Tenancy.—Seven days notice is required to terminate tenancy for nonpayment of rent. One month's notice is required to terminate tenancy by sufferance or at will. Periodic tenancy at will, where rent is payable at periods of less than three months, may be terminated at any time by notice equal to interval between periods. Tenancy from year to year may be terminated at any time by one year's notice. (MCLA §554.134; MSA §26.1104). No notice is required to terminate tenancy upon expiration of specified term. (183 Mich. 62, 148 N.W. 749).

In absence of an agreement to contrary, tenant may terminate lease where building has become untenantable without fault or neglect on his part. (MCLA §554.201; MSA §26.1121).

Holding Over.—Landlord may elect to treat tenant as trespasser or as tenant. (194 Mich. 276, 160 N.W. 554). Holdover tenant is not tenant at will unless he holds over by express or implied consent of landlord (40 Mich. 283), although in case of delay in eviction tenant may be by sufferance and entitled to statutory notice. (251 Mich. 512, 232 N.W. 178).

Dispossession.—Summary proceedings lie to recover possession on termination of tenancy or estate and upon certain other occurrences. (MCLA §600.5714; MSA §27A.5714). Summons must issue within prescribed time limits (MCLA §600.5735; MSA §27A.5735), and writ of restitution issues ten days after judgment unless judgment is appealed or unless judgment is based on nonpayment of money and defendant pays amount found due and costs. (MCLA §600.5744; MSA §27A.5744). If court determines that dispossession is sought by landlord as penalty for tenant reporting health or similar violation or for asserting rights under lease or under law, landlord will be denied relief. (MCLA §600.5720; MSA §27A.5720).

Discrimination on the basis of race, color, religion, sex, height, weight, age, marital status or national origin in housing is unlawful, except for certain owner occupied dwellings. (MCLA §§37.2101-.2804; MSA §§3.548[101]-[804]).

LEASES:

See topic Landlord and Tenant.

PERPETUITIES:

Uniform Statutory Rule Against Perpetuities.—Common law rule against perpetuities, MCLA §554.51; MSA §26.49(1), which applied to all conveyances and testamentary dispositions of real property made after Sept. 22, 1949 and/or personal estate whenever made, superseded by Uniform Statutory Rule Against Perpetuities, effective Dec. 27, 1988. (MCLA §§554.71-78; MSA §§26.48[1]-[8]). Uniform act does not apply to non-vested property interests created between Sept. 23, 1949 and Dec. 27, 1988. (MCLA §§554.51-.53, 554.76; MSA §§26.49[1]-[3], 26.48[6]).

If conveyance or testamentary disposition of real estate was made prior to Sept. 22, 1949, absolute power of alienation could not be suspended for a longer period than two lives in being, except that a contingent remainder in fee might be created to take effect upon termination of prior remainder during minority of persons to whom prior remainder was limited (MCLA §§554.15-.16; MSA §§26.15-.16); successive life estates might be limited only to persons in being, and remainder limited on more than two life estates takes effect on death of first two life tenants (MCLA §554.17; MSA §26.17).

Accumulations.—With respect to rents and profits of real estate under deeds or other instruments executed and delivered prior to Sept. 18, 1952, or under wills of persons dying prior to Sept. 18, 1952, accumulation may be directed only during minority of persons in being at creation of estate out of which rents and profits or income are to arise, and if to commence after creation of such estate, accumulation must commence within time permitted for vesting of estates (MCLA §554.37; MSA §26.37); and if directed for a longer time than minority of persons intended to be benefited, or longer than 33 years after death of testator, accumulation is void as to time beyond such minority or 33 years (MCLA §554.38; MSA §26.38). Other accumulations are permitted for lives in being plus 21 years.

Subsequent to Sept. 18, 1952 accumulations of all types are permitted for lives in being plus 21 years. (P.A. 1952, Nos. 6, 7).

Rules against perpetuities, suspension of power of alienation and accumulations do not apply to gifts or trusts for religious, educational, benevolent, charitable or public welfare purposes (MCLA §§554.351, .381; MSA §§26.1191, .1201), or to trusts created by employers for benefit of employees to pay pensions or disability or death benefits or to share profits or provide stock bonuses (MCLA §555.301; MSA §26.82[1]).

Possibilities of reverter and rights of entry on condition subsequent are unenforceable if specified condition does not occur within 30 years after terminable possessory interest was created or by Mar. 29, 1969 whichever is later, except rights of termination may be preserved by recording of written notice, within a period not less than 25 nor more than 30 years after creation of terminable interest or prior to Mar. 29, 1969, whichever is later. Restriction does not apply to leases, interests where contingency must occur within perpetuities period, terminable interests held for public or charitable, etc., purposes, or interest created in conveyance from U.S. (MCLA §§554.61-.65; MSA §§26.49[11]-.49[15]).

PERSONAL PROPERTY:

In absence of statutory prohibition, common law recognizes joint tenancy in personal property with rights of survivorship. Although occasionally referred to as tenancy by the entirety (297 Mich. 513, 298 N.W. 116), it is unclear whether such tenancy possesses all attributes (e.g., immunity from partition) enjoyed by tenancies by the entirety in real property. Joint tenancy with rights of survivorship has been found in bank accounts, contents of safety deposit boxes and securities. However, intent to create such a tenancy must be clearly shown by agreement of tenants.

POWERS OF ATTORNEY:

Attorneys in Fact.—No formalities of execution are requisite to validity between parties of power of attorney, but power to convey or encumber real estate should be executed with same formalities as deed to enable it to be recorded. (MCLA §565.36; MSA §26.553). See category Documents and Records, topic Records. Recorded power can be revoked only by recording instrument of revocation in same office. (MCLA §565.37; MSA §26.554). No special form is preferred by local usage.

Formalities.—See subhead Attorneys in Fact, supra.

Revocation.—See subhead Attorneys in Fact, supra.

Uniform Durable Power of Attorney Act (§§1-5) adopted with variations and modifications (MCLA §§700.495-.497; MSA §§27.5495-.5497).

Members of Armed Forces.—Authority to act as agent for person in armed forces or on duty therewith or in civilian connection with operations of armed forces, outside continental U.S., is not terminated by death of principal until actual notice comes to agent. Affidavit of agent, in absence of fraud, is proof of lack of notice and is conclusive proof of non-revocation or non-termination of power at such time. Affidavit is recordable when authenticated for record if power itself is recordable. No report or listing of "missing" or "missing in action" etc. constitutes actual notice of death of principal. (MCLA §35.501; MSA §4.1455).

See note at head of Digest as to 1998 legislation covered.

See Topical Index in front part of this volume.

MI – 47

REAL PROPERTY:

Estates in respect to the number and connection of their owners are divided into estates in severalty, in joint tenancy, and in common. All grants and devises of lands made to two or more persons, except such as are made in trust, or to executors or to husband and wife, and mortgages, are construed to create estates in common and not in joint tenancy unless expressly declared to be in joint tenancy. A joint tenancy between husband and wife is tenancy by entirety, and a conveyance to husband and wife creates such an estate, with its common law incidents. (MCLA §§554.43-.45; MSA §§26.43-.45).

One spouse cannot sever tenancy by entirety (200 Mich. 328, 166 N.W. 886), except by conveyance to the other spouse (MCLA §557.101; MSA §26.201). Other joint tenancy is severed by conveyance by one tenant (290 Mich. 143, 287 N.W. 411), but right of survivorship cannot be destroyed if expressly declared in conveyance creating joint tenancy (434 Mich. 271, 454 N.W. 2d 85).

Discrimination on basis of race, color, religion, sex, height, weight, age, marital status, familial status, or national origin in housing is unlawful, except for certain owner occupied dwellings. (MCLA §§37.2101-.2804; MSA §§3.548[101]-[804]).

For limitation on possibilities of reverter and right of entry on condition broken, see topic Perpetuities.

Rule in Shelley's Case.—Abolished. (MCLA §554.28; MSA §26.28).

Foreign Conveyances or Encumbrances.—When any deed or other instrument affecting title to land is executed and acknowledged in compliance with law of state where executed and has been recorded in county where property situated, such record or certified transcript thereof is prima facie evidence of due execution. (MCLA §565.9,-10; MSA §26.528, .529).

Condominiums.—Extensively regulated by MCLA §§559.101-.275; MSA §§26.50(101)-(275).

Land Contracts.—Land in Michigan is often sold on land contract, under which vendee acquires possession of the premises and an equitable title thereto, while legal title remains in vendor as security for vendee's performance of the contract. On death of vendee his interest passes to his heirs as real property (224 Mich. 365, 194 N.W. 996), but vendor's interest is personal property and passes to his executor or administrator on his death (129 Mich. 117, 88 N.W. 384). Specific performance is the common equitable remedy to enforce such contracts. Land contracts in general use usually contain a provision that, on breach of any term thereof by vendee, vendor may declare the contract forfeited and repossess himself of the premises. After forfeiture, proceedings before district or municipal court lie to enforce delivery of possession unless vendee makes voluntary surrender. (MCLA §600.5701 et seq.; MSA §27A.5701 et seq.). Writ of restitution issues ten days after entry of judgment for possession unless judgment is based on forfeiture of executory contract for purchase of premises. (MCLA §600.5744; MSA §27A.5744). Vendor may also sue at law for delinquent payments. (159 Mich. 160, 123 N.W. 539). Stamp tax imposed on land contracts; see category Taxation, topic Real Estate Stamp and Transfer Taxes, subhead Stamp Tax. Uniform Statutory Rule Against Perpetuities (with 1990 amendments) in effect. (MCLA §§554.71-.78; MSA §§26.48[1]-.48[8]). Uniform Vendor and Purchaser Risk Act adopted. (MCLA §§565.701-.703; MSA §§26.676[1]-.676[3]).

See also topics Curtesy, Deeds, Dower, Landlord and Tenant; categories Civil Actions and Procedure, topic Partition; Debtor and Creditor, topic Homesteads; Documents and Records, topic Records; Family, topic Husband and Wife; Mortgages, topic Mortgages of Real Property.

TRUST DEEDS:

See category Mortgages, topic Mortgages of Real Property.

TAXATION

ADMINISTRATION:

State Taxes.—In general, following taxes are imposed and/or administered by State of Michigan: Sales tax (Const., art. IX, §8; MCLA §205.51; MSA §7.521); use tax (Const., art. IX, §8; MCLA §205.93; MSA §7.553[3]); cigarette tax (MCLA §205.507; MSA §7.411[1]); liquor tax (MCLA §436.16a; MSA §18.987[1]); fuel taxes (MCLA §§207.101, et seq.; 207.253; MSA §§7.291, et seq., 9.1098[3]; MCLA §207.181, et seq.; MSA §7.318[1]; MCLA §281.509; MSA §3.534[9]; MCLA §259.303; MSA §10.303); unemployment compensation tax (MCLA §421.1, et seq.; MSA §17.501, et seq.); single business tax (MCLA §208.31; MSA §7.558[31]); income tax (MCLA §206.51; MSA §7.557[151]); estate tax (MCLA §205.223; MSA §7.584); employee withholding tax (MCLA §206.351; MSA §7.557[1351]).

Appeal of State (Non-Property) Tax Assessments.—Person may appeal contested portion of assessment, decision or order to Tax Tribunal within 35 days, or to Court of Claims within 90 days after assessment, decision or order. Uncontested portion must be paid as prerequisite to appeal. In appeal to Court of Claims, taxpayer must first pay tax, including applicable penalties and interest, under protest and claim refund as part of appeal. Appeal by right may be taken from decision of Tax Tribunal or Court of Claims to Court of Appeals.

State Tax Liens and Levies.—If Department of Treasury files lien pursuant to Revenue Act against property or rights of property under state Tax Lien Registration Act (MCLA §§211.681 to 211.687; MSA §§7.753[51] to 7.753[57]) and tax liability is satisfied, Department must file release within 20 days after tax liability is satisfied and funds applied to taxpayer's account. If Department files lien and determines that taxpayer named on recorded lien does not have any interest in properties owned by another person, upon request, Department shall file certificate of nonattachment with all due haste but not more than five business days after Department determines that lien is recorded against property to which state does not have lien interest. (MCLA §205.29a[1] and [2]; MSA §7.657[29a][1] and [2]). If Department issues and serves warrant or warrant-notice of levy upon person to levy on property to satisfy tax liability and Department determines tax liability has been satisfied, Department must serve release of levy within ten business days after tax liability is satisfied and funds applied to taxpayer's account. If warrant or warrant-notice levy is issued and served on property which is not property subject to levy, Department must serve release of levy with all due haste but not more than five business days after Department determines that property is not subject to levy. (MCLA §205.29a[3] and [4]; MSA §7.657[29a][3] and [4]).

Department must reimburse person for any fees paid to Department, bank, or other financial institution as result of erroneous recording or filing of lien or erroneous issuance and service of warrant or warrant-notice levy. (MCLA §205.29a[5]; MSA §7.657[29a][5]). If Department receives money to satisfy tax liability or information which would cancel tax liability and subsequently erroneously files lien or issues and serves warrant or warrant-notice of levy, upon request, Department, with all due haste but not more than five business days after it determines lien erroneously filed or warrant or warrant-notice was erroneously issued, shall file certificate of withdrawal of lien or release of levy. (MCLA §205.29a[6] and [7]; MSA §7.657[29a][6] and [7]).

Local Taxes.—In general, following taxes are imposed and/or administered by local governmental units: real and personal property taxes (MCLA §211.1, et seq.; MSA §7.1, et seq.); intangible personal property tax (MCLA §§205.131-.132; MSA §§7.556[1]-[2]); stamp tax (MCLA §207.501, et seq.; MSA §7.456[1], et seq.); real estate transfer tax (MCLA §207.522; MSA §7.456[22]).

Appeal of Local Tax Assessments.—See topic Property (Ad Valorem) Taxes, subhead Appeal of Property Tax Assessments.

Penalties.—For State taxes, in general, see topic Business Taxes, subhead Single Business Tax, catchline Penalties. For locally assessed taxes, see topic Property (Ad Valorem) Taxes, subhead Collection.

Interstate Cooperation.—Adopted Uniform Division of Income for Tax Purposes Act (also known as Multistate Tax Compact), effective July 1, 1970. (MCLA §§205.581-.589; MSA §§4.146[101]-[109]).

ALCOHOLIC BEVERAGE TAXES:

Liquor Tax.—Wine tax imposed by MCLA §436.16a; MSA §18.987(1). Beer tax imposed by MCLA §436.40; MSA §18.1011. Tax on spirits with alcoholic content of 21% or more imposed by MCLA §§436.121-.125, 141-148; MSA §§18.1030(11)-(15), 7.559(41)-(48).

BUSINESS TAXES:

Business Receipts Tax.—Repealed.

Single Business Tax.—Single Business Tax Act is administered by Revenue Division of Department of Treasury.

Rates.—Tax of 2.30% is imposed on adjusted tax base of every person with business activity that is allocated or apportioned to state. (MCLA §208.31; MSA §7.558[31]). "Adjusted tax base" means tax base allocated or apportioned to state under rules and exemptions set forth below. "Person" means individual, firm, bank, financial institution, limited partnership, copartnership, partnership, joint venture, association, corporation, receiver, estate, trust or other group or combination acting as unit. (MCLA §208.6; MSA §7.558[6]). "Business activity" means transfer of legal or equitable title to or rental of property, whether real, personal or mixed, or performance of services, or combination thereof, made, engaged in or caused to be made or engaged in within state, whether intrastate, interstate or foreign commerce, with object of direct or indirect gain, benefit or advantage, to taxpayer or others; does not include services rendered by employee to taxpayer, services as director of corporation or casual transaction. (MCLA §208.3; MSA §7.558[3]).

Computation of Tax Base.—Tax base is "business income" (defined as federal taxable income for corporation and that part of federal taxable income derived from business activity for other taxpayers including, for partnerships, payments and items of income and expense attributable to business activity of partnership and separately reported to partners), before apportionment or allocation, subject to following adjustments: (1) Add gross interest income and dividends on obligations or securities of states other than Michigan in same amount as excluded from federal taxable income, less related expenses not deducted under I.R.C. §§265 and 291; (2) add all taxes on or measured by net income and tax imposed by this Act to extent such taxes were deducted in computing federal taxable income; (3) add, to extent deducted in computing federal taxable income, (i) net operating loss carryback or carryforward, (ii) capital loss carryback or carryforward, (iii) deduction for depreciation, amortization or immediate or accelerated write-off relating to cost of tangible assets, (iv) dividends paid or accrued except those representing reduction of insurance premiums, (v) any deduction or exclusion by taxpayer due to its classification as domestic international sales corporation, western hemisphere trade corporation, China trade act corporation or like special classification purpose of which is to reduce or postpone federal income tax liability, but not applicable to provisions of I.R.C. §§805, 809, and 815(c)(2), (vi) all interest except amounts paid, credited or reserved by insurance companies as necessary to fulfill policy and contract liability requirements of I.R.C. §§805 and 809, (vii) all royalties, with certain exceptions, and (viii) any deduction for rent attributable to lease back under I.R.C. §168(f)(8); (4) add compensation, defined under MCLA §208.4; MSA §5.778(4) as all wages, salaries, fees, bonuses, commissions, or other payments during taxable year on behalf of or for benefit of employees, officers or directors of taxpayers and subject to or exempt from withholding under I.R.C. §3401 excluding, for tax years after Dec. 31, 1994, workers compensation, FICA and FUTA payments; (5) add capital gains related to business activity of individuals to extent excluded in computing federal taxable income; (6) deduct, to extent included in computing federal taxable income, (i) dividends received or deemed received including foreign dividend gross-up provided for in I.R.C., (ii) all interest except amounts paid, credited or reserved by insurance companies as necessary to fulfill policy and contract liability requirements of I.R.C. §§805 and 809, (iii) all royalties, with certain exceptions, and (iv) rent attributable to lease under I.R.C. §168(f)(8); (7) deduct any capital loss not deducted in computing federal taxable income; (8) to extent included in federal taxable income, add loss or subtract gain from tax base attributable to

BUSINESS TAXES...*continued*

another entity whose business activities are taxable under Act or would be taxable under Act if business activities were within state. (MCLA §208.9; MSA §7.558[9]). Tax base of financial organization is sum of federal taxable income and adjustments made in MCLA §208.9, MSA §7.558(9) except subsections (4)(f) and 7(b) thereof, but financial organization which is regulated investment company not subject to adjustments made in MCLA §208.9 subsections 9(2), 4(d) and 7(a). (MCLA §208.21; MSA §7.558[2]). Tax base and adjusted tax base of insurance company, for tax year after 1988, is product of .25 times insurance company's adjusted receipts as apportioned. "Adjusted receipts" defined in MCLA §208.22a(4); MSA 7.558(22a). Insurance company's tax base and adjusted tax base is not adjusted under MCLA §208.23; MSA §7.558(23) or MCLA §208.23b; MSA 7.558(23b). SBT for insurance company is in lieu of all other privilege or franchise fees or taxes imposed by any other law of State, except taxes on real and personal property and taxes under MCLA §500.1200 et seq.; MSA 24.11200. (MCLA §208.22; MSA §7.558[22]). Tax base of nonprofit persons not required to pay federal income taxes shall be sum of net additions specified in MCLA §§208.9, .23, MSA §§7.558(9), (23), less deductions specified in those sections. (MCLA §208.20; MSA 7.558[20]).

Apportionment and Allocation of Tax Base.—For taxpayer whose business activities are confined solely to state, except taxpayers whose business activities consist of transportation services, entire tax base is allocated to state. (MCLA §208.40; MSA §7.558[40]). For tax years prior to Dec. 31, 1988 for taxpayer whose business activities are taxable both within and without state, tax base, other than tax base derived principally from transportation, financial or insurance carrier services or specifically allocated, is apportioned to state by multiplying tax base by apportionment factor determined by dividing by three sum of 25% of property and payroll factors and 50% of sales factor. (MCLA §§208.41-.49; MSA §§7.558[41]-[49]). For tax years after Dec. 31, 1998, tax base is apportioned by multiplying tax base by percentage, which is sum of all of following percentages: (a) property factor multiplied by 5%; (b) payroll factor multiplied by 5%; (c) sales factor multiplied by 90%. For tax years after Dec. 31, 1998 if MCLA §208.23(e); MSA §7.558(23)(e) is not in effect, all of tax base is apportioned to this state by multiplying tax base by percentage, which is sum of all of following percentages: (a) property factor multiplied by 15%; (b) payroll factor multiplied by 15%; (c) sales factor multiplied by 70%. (MCLA §208.45a; MSA §7.558[45a]). For tax years before Jan. 1, 1991, tax base is apportioned to this state by multiplying tax base by fraction, numerator of which is property factor plus payroll factor plus sales factor, and denominator of which is three. For tax years after Dec. 31, 1990 and before Jan. 1, 1993, all of tax base is apportioned to state by multiplying tax base by percentage, which is sum of following percentages: (a) property factor multiplied by 30%; (b) payroll factor multiplied by 30%; (c) sales factor multiplied by 40%. This apportionment formula does not apply for tax year in which deduction under MCLA §208.23(c); MSA §7.558(23)(c), is not allowed. For tax years after Dec. 31, 1992 and before Jan. 1, 1997 and for years after Dec. 31, 1996 and before Jan. 1, 1998 if MCLA §208.23(e); MSA §7.558(23)(e) is not in effect, tax base is apportioned to state by multiplying tax base by percentage, which is sum of all of following percentages: (a) property factor multiplied by 25%; (b) payroll factor multiplied by 25%; (c) sales factor multiplied by 50%. Except as provided in subsections (4) and (7) of MCLA §208.45; MSA §7.558(45) and for tax years after Dec. 31, 1996 and before Jan. 1, 1999, tax base is apportioned to this state by multiplying tax base by percentage, which is sum of all of following percentages: (a) property factor multiplied by 10%; (b) payroll factor multiplied by 10%; (c) sales factor multiplied by 80%. For tax years after Dec. 31, 1997 and before Jan. 1, 1998 if MCLA §208.23(e); MSA §7.558(23)(e) is not in effect, tax base is apportioned to this state by multiplying tax base by percentage, which is sum of all of following percentages: (a) property factor multiplied by 20%; (b) payroll factor multiplied by 20%; (c) sales factor multiplied by 60%. (MCLA §208.45; MSA §7.558[45]). Special allocation formula provided by statute for taxpayers whose business activities consist of transportation services. (MCLA §208.57; MSA §5.778[57]).

Adjustments to Tax Base.—After allocation as described above, tax base is adjusted as follows: (1) (a) for tax years before Mar. 31, 1991 deduct cost, including fabrication and installation, paid or accrued in taxable year, of tangible assets of type eligible for depreciation, amortization or accelerated capital cost recovery for federal income tax purposes; this deduction shall be multiplied by apportionment factor, (b) for tax years before Mar. 31, 1991, deduct cost as defined in MCLA §208.23; MSA §7.558(23), provided assets are physically located in Michigan, (c) for tax years after Sept. 30, 1989 but before Jan. 1, 1997, for tangible assets located in and out of state, deduct cost, as defined in MCLA §208.23; MSA §7.558(23); deduction shall be multiplied by apportionment factor, (d) for tax years after Dec. 31, 1996, deduct cost, as defined in MCLA §208.23; MSA §7.558(23), provided assets are physically located in state for use in business activity in state and are not mobile tangible assets; deduction shall be multiplied by apportionment factor, (e) for tax years after Dec. 31, 1996, deduct cost, as defined in MCLA §208.23; MSA §7.558(23), of mobile tangible assets; deduction shall be multiplied by apportionment factor, (f) for tangible assets, other than mobile tangible assets, purchased or acquired for use outside of state in tax year after Dec. 31, 1996 and physically located in state after assets are purchased or acquired for use in business activity, deduct federal basis used for determining gain or loss as of date tangible assets were physically located in state for use in business activity plus cost of fabrication and installation of tangible assets in state; deduction shall be multiplied by apportionment factor, (g) for non-mobile tangible assets physically located in this state and for years after Dec. 31, 1996, deduction under MCLA §208.23(c) permitted if taxpayer meets certain criteria, such as taxpayer being headquartered in state, taxpayer's sales at retail of prescriptions are more than 2% and less than 10% of total sales, and more than 50% of taxpayer's total sales is comprised of retail sales of all of following: fresh, frozen or processed food, household products, prescriptions, health and beauty care products, cosmetics, pet products, carbonated beverages and beer, wine or liquor, (h) for tax years after Dec. 31, 1996 and for all other assets, except mobile tangible assets, deduct cost, including fabrication and installation, paid or accrued in taxable year of tangible assets eligible for depreciation, amortization, or accelerated capital cost recovery for federal income tax purposes; deduction shall be

multiplied by apportionment factor (MCLA §208.23; MSA §7.558[23]); (2) add gross proceeds from sale of tangible assets defined as above minus gain or plus loss from sale as reflected in federal taxable income and minus gain from sale added to tax base in MCLA §208.9(6), MSA §7.558(9)(6); this deduction shall be multiplied by apportionment factor; (3) deduct available business loss, defined as negative amount after allocation or apportionment as described above and adjustments provided in (1)-(3) above; loss can be carried forward to next ten taxable years in succession; (4) deduct unused net operating loss carryforward from state corporate income tax, but only for taxable years ending on or before Dec. 31, 1980. (MCLA §208.23; MSA §7.558[23]). Special adjustments are provided for taxpayers whose adjusted tax bases exceed 50% of gross receipts apportioned or allocated to state. (MCLA §208.31; MSA §7.558[31]).

Exemptions.—Exempt from tax imposed by Act are following: (1) For tax years beginning in 1990, first $42,000; for tax years beginning in 1991, first $43,000; for tax years beginning in 1992, first $44,000 and for tax years after 1992, first $45,000 of tax base of every person (special exemption provided for subchapter S corporations and professional corporations) which is increased by $12,000 for each partner or shareholder of subchapter S or professional corporation in excess of one, who is full time employee owning 10% of business and earning at least $12,000; (2) U.S., this and other states and agencies, political subdivisions and enterprises of each; (3) person who is exempt from federal income tax pursuant to provisions of I.R.C., and for tax years after Dec. 31, 1995 partnership, L.L.C., joint venture, general or limited partnership, unincorporated association, or other group or entity acting as unit if activities are exclusively related to charitable, educational or other exempt purpose, and if all partners or members of group or entity are exempt under I.R.C., except: (i) organization included under I.R.C. §§501(c)(12) or 501 (c)(16), (ii) organization exempt under I.R.C. §501(c)(4), which would be exempt under I.R.C., §501(c)(12) but for its failure to meet requirements in I.R.C. §501(c)(12) that 85% or more of its income must consist of amounts collected from its members, (iii) adjusted tax base attributable to activities giving rise to unrelated taxable business income of exempt person; (4) before Aug. 3, 1987, foreign or alien insurance company subject to premium tax imposed by law, but this exemption does not apply to tax base derived from business activity other than insurance carrier services; (5) that portion of payroll of domestic insurers or marketing corporation that constitutes insurance sales commissions paid to employees and salaries of employees primarily concerned with adjustment of claims (except certain marketing corporations not controlled by domestic insurers); (6) beginning Aug. 3, 1987, and before being apportioned, first $130,000,000 of disability insurance premiums, other than credit insurance and disability income insurance premiums, of each insurer subject to tax under this act, which exemption shall be reduced by $2 for each $1 by which insurer's gross premiums from insurance carrier services in this state and outside state exceed $180,000,000; (7) nonprofit cooperative housing corporation; (8) portion of tax base attributable to production of agricultural goods by person whose primary activity is production of such goods; (9) certain farmer's cooperative corporations. (MCLA §208.35; MSA §7.558[35]).

Credits.—Partial credit allowed against tax for certain charitable contributions, public utility taxes and child care services provided employees. (MCLA §§208.38, .39, .39a; MSA §7.558 [38], [39], [39a]). Partial credit for wages paid "qualified summer youth employee" (as defined in I.R.C. §51[d][12]) from May 1 to Sept. 15, 1983. (MCLA §208.36a; MSA §7.558[36a]). Certain taxpayers granted percentage credit against tax liability. Percentage credit equals 100% minus percentage computed by dividing adjusted business income by 45% of tax base, subject to certain maximum limits and reductions. (MCLA §208.36; MSA §7.558[36]). Unincorporated taxpayers and those electing subchapter S provisions are granted additional credit against tax calculated after credit provided in §36 of act. Additional credit is 20% of tax liability if business income is $20,000 or less, 15% of tax liability if business income is more than $20,000 but less than $40,000, or 10% of tax liability if business is $40,000 or more. (MCLA §208.37; MSA §7.558[37]). Credit is granted for authorized business under Michigan Economic Growth Authority Act (MCLA §207.801 et seq.; MSA §3.540[801] et seq.), for tax years beginning after Dec. 31, 1994 and for period not to exceed 20 years (MCLA §208.37c; MSA §7.558[37c] and MCLA §208.37d; MSA §7.558[37d]). Credit granted for tax liability attributable to qualified business activity as defined in enterprise zone act (MCLA §§125.2101 et seq., 208.37a; MSA §§3.540[301] et seq., 7.558[37a]) and to high technology activity (MCLA §208.37b; MSA §7.558[37b]). Certain employers granted credit against tax liability equal to increased federal unemployment taxes paid due to reduction of credits under I.R.C. §§3302(a) and (b) because of application of I.R.C. §3302(c)(2) in state as limited by I.R.C. §3302(f). (MCLA §208.38a; MSA §7.558[38a]). Carriers and employers subject to workers' disability compensation statute granted credit against tax liability for certain compensation supplements paid after Mar. 31, 1984. Credit must be claimed against estimated tax payments made. (MCLA §208.38b; MSA §7.558[38b]). For tax years 1997 to 2000, qualified taxpayer can claim credit equal to 10% of cost of eligible investment paid or accrued (as defined in MCLA §208.38[d][8]; MSA §7.558[38d][8]), for maximum amount not exceeding $1,000,000. (MCLA §208.38d; MSA §7.558[38d]). Credit for taxpayers training apprentices as defined in MCLA §208.38e(5); MSA §7.558(38e), equal to 50% or 100% of qualified expenses defined in MCLA §208.38e(5)(d), for maximum amount not to exceed $2,000 for each apprentice trained by taxpayer. (MCLA §208.38e: MSA §7.558[38e]).

Returns and Payments.—Estimated return and quarterly payment of tax required of taxpayer who reasonably expects liability for tax to exceed $600 or adjustments under MCLA §208.23; MSA §7.558(23) to exceed $100,000. For calendar year taxpayers, due dates are Apr. 30, July 31, Oct. 31 and Jan. 31. Fiscal year taxpayers use appropriately adjusted dates. (MCLA §208.71; MSA §7.558[71]). Final return shall be filed by last day of fourth month after close of taxpayer's tax year. Commissioner may extend date for filing annual return on application by taxpayer and showing of good cause. Tentative return must be timely filed and payment of estimated tax must be timely made. Interest on unpaid tax is 9% per annum. Interest provision applies to underpayment of estimated tax. Person whose gross receipts are less than $100,000 for tax years after Dec. 31, 1991 and before Jan. 1, 1994, $137,500 for tax years before Dec. 31, 1993 and before Jan. 1, 1995, or $250,000 for tax years after Dec. 31, 1994,

See note at head of Digest as to 1998 legislation covered.

See Topical Index in front part of this volume.

BUSINESS TAXES . . . *continued*

need not file return or pay tax. Affiliated group must combine gross receipts for purpose of calculating threshold. (MCLA §208.73; MSA §7.558[73]).

Penalties.—Interest rate on deficiency or excessive claim for credit is current monthly interest rate of one percentage point above adjusted prime rate per annum from time tax was due until paid. If deficiency or excessive claim is due to negligence, but without intent to defraud, there is penalty of $10 or 10% of total amount of deficiency, whichever is greater, plus monthly interest of one percentage point above adjusted prime rate. Penalty becomes due and payable after notice and informal conference. If taxpayer can show that deficiency or excess claim for credit was due to reasonable cause, department will waive penalty. No penalty will be imposed after June 30, 1994, unless and until department submits for public hearing, pursuant to administrative procedures act, rule defining what constitutes reasonable cause for waiver, with illustrative examples provided. If any part of deficiency or excessive claim is due to intentional disregard, but without intent to defraud, penalty of $25 or 25% of total amount of deficiency, whichever is greater, plus interest shall be added. If any part of deficiency or excessive claim is due to fraudulent intent to evade tax or to obtain refund, there is penalty of 100% of deficiency plus interest. (MCLA §205.23; MSA §7.657[23]). If taxpayer fails to file return or pay tax, penalty is 5% of tax due per month, to maximum of 50%, plus monthly interest of one percentage point above adjusted prime rate. (MCLA §205.24; MSA §7.657[24]).

Penalty for failure to file information return or other informational report is $10 per day for each day for each separate failure or refusal to $400 maximum. (MCLA §205.24; MSA §7.657[24]).

Franchise Taxes.—See category Business Organizations, topic Corporations, subhead Incorporation Tax or Fee.

Insurance Company Taxes.—See category Insurance, topic Insurance Companies.

CIGARETTE TAX:

Imposed by MCLA §205.507; MSA §7.411(7). See also Const. art IX, §36.

ESTATE TAX:

Michigan has estate and generation skipping tax effective for persons who died after Sept. 30, 1993 or to generation skipping transfer that occurs after Sept. 30, 1993. (MCLA §205.223; MSA §7.584). Former inheritance tax applies to estates of decedents dying prior to effective date of new provisions. (MCLA §205.223; MSA §7.584). Probate court has exclusive jurisdiction of court proceedings concerning this act. (MCLA §205.246[1]; MSA §7.591[16][1]).

Tax is imposed upon transfer of estate of every person who at time of death was resident of this state. Tax is equal to maximum allowable federal credit under Internal Revenue Code for estate, inheritance, legacy, and succession taxes paid to states. This tax is reduced by amount of all estate, inheritance, legacy, and succession taxes paid to states other than Michigan. This amount shall not exceed amount equal to proportional share of that maximum allowable federal credit that gross value of all real and tangible personal property located in states other than this state bears to gross value of all property included in decedent's gross estate wherever located. (MCLA §205.232[1]; MSA §7.591[2][1]).

Tax is imposed upon transfer of property located in this state of every person who at time of death was not resident of this state. Tax is amount equal to proportional share of maximum allowable federal credit under Internal Revenue Code for estate, inheritance, legacy, and succession taxes paid to states, that gross value of all real and tangible personal property located in this state bears to gross value of all property included in decedent's gross estate wherever located. (MCLA §205.232[2]); MSA §7.591[2][2]).

Generation-skipping tax is imposed upon every generation-skipping transfer in which original transferor is resident of this state at date of transfer made by original transferor. Tax is equal to maximum allowable federal credit under Internal Revenue Code for state generation-skipping transfer taxes paid to states. This tax is reduced by amount of all generation-skipping transfer taxes paid to states other than this state, which amount shall not exceed amount equal to proportional share of that maximum allowable federal credit that gross value of all transferred real and tangible personal property subject to generation-skipping transfer taxes located in states other than this state bears to gross value of all transferred property subject to generation-skipping taxes wherever located. (MCLA §205.233[1]; MSA §7.591[3][1]).

Generation-skipping tax is imposed upon every generation-skipping transfer in which original transferor is not resident of this state at date of transfer by original transferor but in which property transferred includes real and tangible personal property located in this state. Tax is amount equal to proportional share of maximum allowable federal credit under Internal Revenue Code for state generation-skipping transfer taxes paid to states that gross value of all transferred real and tangible personal property subject to generation-skipping transfer taxes located in this state bears to gross value of all transferred property subject to generation-skipping transfer taxes wherever located. (MCLA §205.233[2]); MSA §7.591[3][2]).

Personal representative of every estate required to file federal return shall file return with Department of Treasury on or before last day prescribed by law for filing federal return. Department of Treasury may waive this requirement. Department of Treasury shall extend time for filing return if time for filing federal return is extended. (MCLA §§205.1-.3, 205.237; MSA §§7.657[1]-[31]; 7.591[7]).

Return and Payment.—Tax is due and payable on or before last day prescribed by law for paying corresponding federal transfer taxes pursuant to federal return excluding extensions and shall be paid to Department of Treasury. Department of Treasury shall extend time for payment of tax or any part of tax if time for paying federal transfer tax is extended. Interest on underpayments is determined periodically. Interest is payable on refunds. Interest rate on refunds and underpayments floats. Penalty can also be assessed based upon negligence, intentional disregard of law, fraud and failure to file. Criminal liability can also attach. (MCLA §§205.1-.31, .237; MSA §§7.591[7], .657[1]-.657[31]). Upon payment of tax, Department of Treasury shall issue to personal representative receipts in triplicate, each of which is sufficient evidence of payment and entitles personal representative to be credited and allowed that amount by probate court having jurisdiction. If personal representative files complete return and makes written application to Department of Treasury for determination of amount of tax and discharge from personal liability for tax, Department of Treasury as soon as possible, but not later than one year after receipt of application, shall notify personal representative of amount of tax. Upon payment of tax, personal representative is discharged from personal liability for any additional tax found to be due and is entitled to receive receipt in writing showing discharge. However, discharge does not operate to release gross estate of lien of any additional tax subsequently found to be due while title to gross estate remains in personal representative or in heirs, devisees, or distributees. If after discharge is given title to any portion of gross estate has passed to bona fide purchaser for value, that portion of gross estate is not subject to lien or any claim or demand for tax. (MCLA §205.241; MSA §7.591[11]).

If, as result of audit, there is increase or decrease in amount of federal transfer tax, amended return shall be filed showing all changes made in original return and amount of increase or decrease in federal transfer tax within 60 days after final determination if there is increase in amount owed state, or within one year after final determination if there is refund owed by state. (MCLA §205.238[1]; MSA §7.591[8][1]).

Claim for Refund.—Must be made within one year from date of final determination of federal tax. Determination is considered to have become final on date of Internal Revenue Service closing letter or date of receipt of refund of federal tax, whichever is later. (MCLA §205.238[2]; MSA §7.591[8][2]).

Tax may not be refunded pursuant to any allegation that decedent was resident of another state unless this state is party to compromise agreement between decedent's transferee and other state or unless this state is allowed to intervene as party in any action in other state in which residency of decedent is at issue. MCLA §205.238[3]); MSA §7.591[8][3]).

Interest on refunds accrues from 45 days after date tax was paid or due date of tax excluding extensions, whichever is later. (MCLA §205.240[2]); MSA §7.591[10][2]).

Apportionment—Tax due shall be apportioned as provided by Uniform Estate Tax Apportionment Act. (MCLA §§205.242, 720.11 et seq.; MSA §§7.591[12], 27.3178[167.101] et seq.).

Lien.—Imposed upon gross estate of decedent until paid in full. Any part of gross estate used for payment of claims against estate and expenses of administration is divested of any lien for taxes. Any part of gross estate, other than real estate, of resident decedent transferred to bona fide purchaser, mortgagee, or pledgee for adequate and full consideration in money or money's worth is divested of lien, and lien shall then attach to consideration received for property from purchaser, mortgagee, or pledgee. Any real estate that is part of gross estate of decedent transferred to bona fide purchaser or mortgagee shall be divested of lien, lien shall attach to consideration received for real property, and department shall issue waiver releasing property from lien if one of following applies: (a) transfer of real estate is necessary for payment of claims against estate and expenses of administration even though other assets are then available for sale or mortgage. (b) Department of Treasury is satisfied that no tax liability exists or that tax liability has been fully discharged or provided for. (c) Except when Department of Treasury has filed notice of tax lien with county in which real estate is located, there is made partial payment of amount equal to either of following, whichever is applicable: (i) If transfer occurs before due date for filing of return including extensions, 8% of net cash proceeds payable at closing to seller in cash of sale or to mortgagor in case of mortgage; (ii) if transfer occurs after due date for filing of return including extensions, 16% of net cash proceeds payable at closing to seller in case of sale or to mortgagor in case of mortgage, or amount of unpaid tax as reflected on return filed with Department of Treasury, whichever is less. (d) Seller, purchaser, or mortgagee makes partial payment of amount determined to be sufficient to ensure payment of tax. (e) Seller, purchaser, or mortgagee makes partial payment of amount determined by probate court to be sufficient to ensure payment of tax. (f) Seller or mortgagor is person who holds real property as surviving joint tenant or tenant by entireties. (MCLA §205.243; MSA §7.591[13]).

Rights and Liabilities of Personal Representatives.—If personal representative makes distribution of any of property subject to transfer tax under this act to heirs, next of kin, distributees, legatees, or devisees without having paid or secured tax due or without having obtained release of property from lien of tax, personal representative becomes personally liable for tax, accrued penalties, and interest due state, or as much of tax, penalties, and interest that remains due and unpaid, to full extent of full value of any property belonging to person or estate that comes in personal representative's possession, custody, or control as required by law. (MCLA §205.244; MSA §7.591[14]).

Every personal representative has same right and power to take possession of or sell, convey, and dispose of real estate as assets of estate for payment of tax imposed by the Act as personal representative has for payment of debts of decedent. (MCLA §205.245; MSA §7.591[15]).

Appeals.—Personal representative or any person who is in actual or constructive possession of any property included in gross estate of decedent who is aggrieved by decision of Department of Treasury may appeal that decision by petitioning probate court. (MCLA §205.246[2]; MSA §7.591[16][2]).

Non-liability.—If it appears that estate is not subject to any tax under this Act, Department of Treasury shall issue to personal representative or to heirs, devisees, or distributees of decedent certificate in writing to that effect, showing non-liability to tax. Certificate of non-liability has same force and effect as receipt showing payment. Certificate of non-liability shall be in form recordable with register of deeds and admissible in evidence in same manner as receipts showing payment of taxes. (MCLA §205.250; MSA §7.591[20]).

Tax shall not be imposed in respect of personal property, except tangible personal property having actual situs in this state, if one of following applies: (a) transferor at time of transfer was resident of state or territory of U.S., or of any foreign country, that at time of transfer did not impose transfer tax or death tax of any character in

ESTATE TAX... *continued*
respect of personal property of residents of this state, except tangible personal property having actual situs in that state or territory or foreign country. (b) If laws of state, territory, or country of residence of transferor at time of transfer contained reciprocal exemption provision under which nonresidents were exempted from transfer taxes or death taxes of every character in respect of personal property, except tangible personal property having actual situs in that state, territory, or country, provided state, territory, or country of residence of nonresidents allowed similar exemption to residents of state, territory, or country of residence of transferor. For purposes of this section, District of Columbia and possessions of U.S. are considered territories of U.S. As used in this section, "foreign country" and "country" mean both any foreign country and any political subdivision of that country, and either of them of which transferor was domiciled at time of his or her death. For purposes of this section, "tangible personal property" is construed to exclude all property common classified as intangible personal property, such as deposits in banks, mortgages, debts, receivables, shares of stock, bonds, notes, credits, evidences of interest in property, evidences of debt, and like incorporeal personal property. (MCLA §205.253; MSA §7.591[23]).

Administration.—Taxes imposed shall be administered by Revenue Division of Department of Treasury. (MCLA §205.254; MSA §7.591[24]).

Disputes among states as to decedent's domicile for death tax purposes may be settled by arbitration if any executor or taxing official so elects, except that any executor may reject arbitration. Michigan Commissioner of Revenue may enter into agreement with executors and taxing officials of other states for settlement of all death taxes. (MCLA §§205.601 et seq.; MSA §§7.592[1] et seq.).

FEDERAL TAX LIENS:

See category Debtor and Creditor, topic Liens.

GASOLINE AND FUEL TAXES:

Gasoline Tax.—See subhead Fuel Taxes, infra.

Fuel Taxes.—Gasoline (MCLA §§207.101 et seq., 207.253; MSA §§7.291 et seq., 9.1098[3]), diesel motor fuel (MCLA §207.121 et seq.; MSA §7.316[1] et seq.), and liquefied petroleum gas (MCLA §§207.151, .253; MSA §§7.317[1], 9.1098[3]) taxes are imposed. See also MCLA §207.181 et seq.; MSA §7.318(1). Marine fuel tax is imposed by MCLA §324.71102, MSA §13A.71102. Aircraft fuel tax imposed by MCLA §259.303; MSA §10.303. Wholesale distributors of gasoline are taxed by MCLA §207.108; MSA §7.298.

GENERATION SKIPPING TAX:

See topic Estate Tax.

GIFT TAX:

None; but see topic Estate Tax.

INCOME TAX:

Income Tax Act is administered by Revenue Division of Department of Treasury.

Rates.—For individuals, trusts and estates is 4.6% before May 1, 1994, and 4.4% after Apr. 30, 1994. (MCLA §206.51; MSA §7.557[151]. Income tax on corporations and financial institutions replaced by Single Business Tax. See topic Business Taxes, subhead Single Business Tax. (MCLA §§208.1-108.145; MSA §§7.558[1]-[145]).

Taxable Income of Individuals.—Determined by (1) Subtracting from federal adjusted gross income: (a) Personal exemptions of $2,100 per year for each personal or dependency exemption allowed on federal return plus additional $900 exemption for person who is paraplegic, quadriplegic, deaf, over 65 years old or hemiplegic (prorated for periods of less than 12 months); for each tax year after 1997 personal exemption is adjusted by multiplying exemption for tax year beginning in 1997 by fraction, numerator of which is U.S. C.P.I. for prior tax year, and denominator of which is U.S. C.P.I. for 1995-1996 State fiscal year. Resultant product (rounded to nearest $100) is personal exemption for tax year; (b) income from obligations of federal government which states are prohibited from taxing and included in federal adjusted gross income; (c) compensation including retirement benefits for service in Armed Forces; (d) alimony, separate maintenance payments and principal sums payable in installments to extent deductible on federal return; (e) all retirement or pension benefits from public retirement system of State (or other state with income tax laws giving reciprocal deduction) or political subdivision, and such retirement or pension benefits from any other retirement or pension system as shall not exceed $3,500 ($7,000 on joint return) for 1997 tax year, and for tax years after 1997, ($15,000 on joint return); and for tax years after 1997, and senior citizens, such amount reduced by deduction taken for interest, dividends, and capital gains not to exceed $3,500 for single return and $7,000 for joint return for 1997 tax year, and for tax years after 1997, $7,500 for single return and $15,000 for joint return pursuant to MCLA §206.30c; MSA §7.557(130c). Retirement or pension benefits include, for example, qualified pension trusts and annuity plans, Keogh or HR 10 plans, individual retirement accounts, employee annuities or tax-sheltered annuities, 401k plans attributable to employee or employer contributions, plans of U.S., state governments other than State, political subdivisions, agencies or instrumentalities of State, plans maintained by church, all other unqualified pension plans that prescribe eligibility for retirement and predetermine contributions and benefits if distributions are from pension trust, and retirement or pension benefits received by surviving spouse (does not include surviving child) if benefits qualified for deduction prior to decedent's death. Retirement or pension benefits do not include, for example, deferred compensation plans, premature distributions or payments received as incentive to retire early, unless distributions are from pension trust; (f) political contributions but not in excess of $50 ($100 on joint return); (g) wages not deductible under I.R.C. §280C; (h) payments under advanced tuition payment contract under Michigan Education Trust Act; (i) for tax years after Sept. 30, 1994 and before 1997, senior citizen may deduct, to extent included in adjusted gross income, interest and dividends received not to exceed $1,000 for single return or $2,000 for joint return; however, for tax years before 1997, no deduction if taxpayer has taken deduction for retirement benefits; for tax years after 1996, senior citizen may deduct interest, dividends and capital gains received not to exceed $3,500 for single return and $7,000 for joint return for 1997 tax year, and $7,500 for single return and $15,000 for joint return for tax years after 1997; for tax years after 1996, maximum amounts shall be reduced by amount of deduction claimed for retirement benefits; (j) if included in federal adjusted gross income, deduct state and city income tax refunds and state income tax credits received; and (k) for 1998 and subsequent tax years, deduct amounts paid under Child Care Act of 1997, MCLA §206.30d; MSA §7.557(130d). (2) adding to federal adjusted gross income: (a) gross interest from obligations of states other than Michigan; (b) losses on sale or exchange of obligations of federal government, income of which state is prohibited from taxing to extent that loss is deducted to compute adjusted gross income; (c) income taxes to extent deducted to compute federal adjusted gross income; (d) amount of deduction under I.R.C. §221 (e) amount paid by State to repay outstanding principal on loan taken by taxpayer for advance tuition payment under Michigan Education Trust Act, on which taxpayer defaulted; and (3) adding to or subtracting from federal adjusted gross income: (a) shares of estate or trust income according to statutory rule; (b) adjustment to income derived from source attribution rules provided by statute; and (c) adjustment to income from recomputation of prior years' income. (MCLA §206.30; MSA §7.557[130]).

Attribution of income.—Governed by rules modeled after provisions of Uniform Division of Income for Tax Purposes Act. Net rents and royalties from real property located in this state are allocable to state; net rents and royalties from tangible personal property are allocable to state if, and to extent that, property is utilized in state. Net rents and royalties from tangible personal property are allocable to state, in their entirety and regardless of extent of utilization, in case of resident taxpayer or taxpayer having commercial domicile in state, unless taxpayer is organized under laws of, or taxable in state in which property is utilized. (MCLA §206.111; MSA §7.557[1111]). "Commercial domicile" is defined as principal place from which trade or business of taxpayer is managed. Computation of extent of "utilization" is determined by formula. (MCLA §206.6; MSA §7.557[106]). Capital gains and losses from sales or exchanges of real property located in state are allocable to state. Capital gains and losses from sales or exchanges of tangible personal property are allocable to state if (a) property had situs in state at time of sale; or (b) taxpayer is resident of state or has commercial domicile in state, provided taxpayer is not taxable in state in which property had situs. Capital gains and losses on sales or exchanges of intangible personal property are allocable to state if taxpayer is resident of state or is commercially domiciled in state. (MCLA §206.112; MSA §7.557[1112]). Interest and dividends are allocable to state if taxpayer is resident of state or has commercial domicile in state. (MCLA §206.113; MSA §7.557[1113]). Patent and copyright royalties are allocable to state (1) if and to extent patent or copyright is utilized in state, or (2) if and to extent that patent or copyright is utilized by taxpayer in state in which taxpayer is not taxable and taxpayer's commercial domicile is in Michigan. (MCLA §206.114; MSA §7.557[1114]). When taxpayer has income from business activity (other than rendering purely personal services by individual) both within and without state, he may allocate income. (MCLA §206.103; MSA §7.557[1103]). All business income, other than income from providing transportation services, is apportioned by formula. (MCLA §206.115; MSA §7.557[1115]). In case of nonresidents other than corporations, taxable income is allocable to state to extent it is earned, received, or acquired (a) for rendition of personal services performed principally in Michigan, (b) as distributive share of net profits of unincorporated business, profession or enterprise resulting from work done, services rendered and other business activities conducted in Michigan, except as allocated to another state, and, for tax years after 1996, State lottery prizes. (MCLA §206.110; MSA §7.557[1110]).

Credits.—Act allows credits against tax as follows: (1) For resident individual, trust or estate, tax imposed by another state or Canadian province on income derived from sources without state and subject to tax in another state or Canadian province (MCLA §206.255; MSA §7.557[1255]); (2) partial credit for income tax paid to state cities according to statutory formula (MCLA §§206.257, .481; MSA §§7.557[1257], [1481]); and (3) partial credit for property taxes paid on homestead or portion of rent paid therefor (MCLA §206.501 et seq.; MSA §7.557 [1501] et seq.). Credit allowed equal to 50% of charitable contributions to state or municipalities (of certain art works), public libraries, public broadcast station (as defined in 47 U.S.C. §397) not affiliated with institution of higher education, institutions of higher learning, Michigan Colleges Foundation, and to approved nonprofit corporation, fund, foundation, trust, or association for benefit of institution of higher learning; limit for resident estate or trust is lesser of 10% of tax or $5,000; limit for other taxpayers is lesser of 20% of tax or $100 ($200 for husband and wife filing joint return). (MCLA §206.260; MSA §7.557[1260]). Partial credit allowed for 1983-1991 tax years for cost of solar, wind, or water energy conversion device installed in taxpayer's residence or building owned and rented or leased as residence and located in Michigan. (MCLA §206.262; MSA §7.557[1262]). Variable (depending on number of exemptions and income level) credit allowed for heating fuel costs for homestead. (MCLA §§206.527, .527a; MSA §§7.557[1527], [1527a]). Credit in amount equal to 3.3% of amount contributed to medical care savings account. (MCLA §206.264; MSA §7.557[1264]). For tax years beginning in 1995, resident taxpayer with household income of $200,000 or less, can claim credit equal to 4% of all fees and tuition paid for student to qualified institution of higher learning, not to exceed $250 for each student, for maximum of four years. (MCLA §206.274; MSA §7.557[1274]).

Exemptions.—Provided for persons exempt from federal income tax, except unrelated taxable business income of exempt person as determined under internal revenue code. (MCLA §206.201, MSA §7.557 [1201]).

Estimated Tax.—Every calendar-year individual who is required to file declaration and pay estimated taxes for federal income tax purposes must do likewise for Michigan income tax purposes when his annual Michigan income tax reasonably can be expected to exceed amount withheld minus allowable credits by more than $100. (MCLA §206.301; MSA §7.557[1301]).

See note at head of Digest as to 1998 legislation covered.

See Topical Index in front part of this volume.

MI – 51

INCOME TAX . . . *continued*

Penalties.—See topic Business Taxes, subhead Single Business Tax, catchline Penalties.

Returns and Payments.—Every person, corporation and financial institution which is required to file federal income tax return and whose adjusted gross income exceeds his personal exemptions must file Michigan income tax return with Michigan State Department of Treasury by 15th day of fourth month following close of taxable year (Apr. 15 for calendar year taxpayers), under penalties for failure to file. (MCLA §§206.311, .315; MSA §§7.557[1311], [1315]).

For tax years beginning in 1997, taxpayers with taxable income of less than $100 (or $200 if joint return) and who have filed withholding exemption certificate, may elect to pay income tax without filing Michigan income tax returns. This election is called "No-Form Payment Option". (MCLA §206.51a; MSA §7.557[15(a)]).

Withholding.—Required of every employer who is required to withhold federal income taxes from employee's compensation based on State Tax Commission's Tables. (MCLA §206.351; MSA §7.557[1351]).

Uniform City Income Tax.—No village may impose any income tax. City income taxes must follow statutory uniform city income tax ordinance. Tax imposed on all income of resident. For nonresident, salaries, wages, profits and capital gains are taxed when result of activities within city. Rate is 1% on corporations and resident individuals, 1/2% on nonresidents, except that: (1) In cities of more than 1,000,000 population (currently only Detroit) rate may be not more than 2% on corporations, 3% on resident individuals and 1 1/2% on nonresidents, but not to exceed 1/2 of tax rate imposed on resident individuals, and (2) in cities of less than 1,000,000 population levying property taxes above certain levels and meeting other requirements, rate may be not more than 2% on corporations, 2% on resident individuals and 1% on nonresidents. Members of Armed Forces are exempt from tax on wages. (MCLA §141.501 et seq.; MSA §5.3194[1] et seq.).

City of Detroit Income Tax.—Applies to wages and salaries of all individual residents and all individual nonresidents for services rendered in Detroit; to net profits of all resident owners of unincorporated businesses, professions or other activities; to net profits of nonresident owners of unincorporated businesses, professions, and other activities as result of activities conducted in Detroit; and to net profits of all corporations doing business in Detroit as result of activities conducted in Detroit, whether or not corporation has office or place of business in Detroit. Rate limit is 2% on corporations, 3% on resident individuals, 1 1/2% on nonresidents, but not to exceed 1/2 of tax rate imposed on resident individuals. (MCLA §141.501 et seq.; MSA §5.3194[1] et seq.).

INTANGIBLE PERSONAL PROPERTY TAX:

Repealed effective for years after 1997.

MISCELLANEOUS SPECIFIC TAXES:

There is specific tax on railroad, union station, telephone, telegraph, sleeping car, express, car loaning, stock car, refrigerator car and fast freight line companies. (MCLA §207.4 et seq.; MSA §7.254 et seq.). Tax is based upon average rate of property tax throughout state.

Severance tax of 5% on gas and 6.6% on oil is imposed. (MCLA §205.301 et seq.; MSA §7.351 et seq.).

Iron ore property is subject to specific tax measured by shipments where ore is agglomerated or beneficiated locally. Tax is in lieu of all ad valorem taxes. (MCLA §207.271 et seq.; MSA §13.158[1]).

PROPERTY (AD VALOREM) TAXES:

Taxable Situs.—All real property within state and all personal property within state or belonging to inhabitant of state, except personal property permanently invested in business in another state, is subject to taxation under the general property tax act unless expressly exempted. (MCLA §211.1 et seq.; MSA §7.1 et seq.). Personal property in possession of person using same in business for profit is deemed property of such person. (MCLA §211.14; MSA §7.14). Intangible personal property is exempt from ad valorem taxes except computer software, which is taxable under MCLA §211.9d; MSA §7.9d. (MCLA §211.9e; MSA §7.9[5]).

Exemptions.—

Real Property.—There are numerous exemptions. For example, such property of U.S.; (MCLA §211.7; MSA §7.7) of Michigan; of political subdivisions used for public purposes: of nonprofit theater, library, benevolent, charitable, educational and scientific institutions and organizations devoted exclusively to fostering development of literature, music, painting or sculpture; charitable homes or fraternal societies; of boy and girl scout organizations and similar associations; nonprofit clinics and hospitals (but not physicians' residences); houses of public worship, parsonages of religious societies used as such, and burial grounds; homestead property of indigent persons (not corporations); of nonprofit charitable institution that is leased, loaned or otherwise made available to another nonprofit charitable institution, nonprofit hospital, or nonprofit educational institution (MCLA §211.70; MSA §7.7[41]); for taxes levied after 1996, in renaissance zone (MCLA §211.7ff; MSA §7.7[4cc]); housing owned and operated by nonprofit corporation or associations or by State or political subdivisions, for occupancy or use solely by elderly or disabled families (MCLA §211.7d; MSA §7.7[4a]); of certain railroad and communication companies which pay specific tax (see infra, subhead Miscellaneous Specific Taxes); of agricultural society used exclusively for fair purposes; landing areas of certain airports; public parks; of certain school districts, community colleges and other state supported educational institutions; of parent cooperative preschools; of municipal water authorities (MCLA §§211.7b-.7aa; MSA §§7.7[1a]-7.7[4w]); nursery stock seasonal protection units (but not land on which they are located), (MCLA §§211.7bb; MSA §§7.7[4bb]); solar, wind or water energy conversion devices; certain commercial housing facilities (but special commercial housing facilities tax equal to one-half of normal tax is imposed, which may be waived as to new facilities [MCLA §207.606(2); MSA §7.792(6)(2)]), high technology and industrial facilities for which exemption certificate granted, but not land on which situated; certain water pollution control facilities so long as certificate therefor is in effect (MCLA §323.354; MSA §7.793[54]); certain air pollution facilities so long as certificate of exemption in effect (MCLA §336.4; MSA §7.793[4]). Special treatment is accorded homesteads of certain veterans and their unremarried widows. (MCLA §211.7b; MSA §7.7[2]). Private forest reservations properly maintained are exempt except to value of $1 per acre. (MCLA §320.281; MSA §13.211). Commercial forest preserve is exempt but subject to specific tax and to yield tax. (MCLA §320.305 et seq.; MSA §13.225 et seq.). Trees, shrubs, vines growing on agricultural land exempt. (MCLA §211.7e; MSA §7.7[4b]). Metallic ores are exempt until mining begins, but not more than ten years. (MCLA §211.24; MSA §7.24). Special treatment is accorded plants beneficiating low-grade ores. (MCLA §211.622; MSA §13.157[2]).

Exempt real property is subject to tax as though owned by lessee or user when leased, loaned or otherwise made available to and used for profit by private individual, association or corporation, except (a) where use is by way of concession at public airport, park, market, or similar property available to general public, (b) property of any state-supported educational institution and federal property for which payments are made in lieu of taxes; (c) property used in conjunction with county fair, community fair, 4-H, or State fair, or in conjunction with special event for which lessee pays fee to county, community, 4-H or State fair; (d) property used by lessee in such manner that city or township receives revenue under §17 of horse racing law of 1995, (MCLA §§431.301-336; MSA §§18.966[301]-[336]); and (e) real property located in renaissance zone. (MCLA §211.181; MSA §7.7[5]).

Homestead property is exempt from tax levied by local school district for school operating purposes. Owner of property must claim homestead exemption by filing affidavit. Status of property as homestead is determined on date affidavit is filed. Affidavit must be filed on or before May 1 with local tax collecting unit. (MCLA §211.7cc[1]-[2]; MSA §7.7[4z][1]-[2]). To qualify as homestead, property must be owned and occupied as principal residence by owner of property on date affidavit is signed. Principal residence means one place where person has fixed and permanent home to which, whenever absent, intends to return. Homestead includes any portion of principal residence that is rented or leased so long as that portion is less than 50% of total square footage of living space. It also includes life care facility and property owned by cooperative housing corporation and occupied by tenant stockholders. "Person", for purposes of defining owner of homestead, means individual, partnership, corporation, limited liability company, association, or other legal entity. "Owner" means person who owns, in whole or in part, property or who is purchasing under land contract, or who owns property as result of being beneficiary of will or trust or as result of intestate succession, or who owns or is purchasing dwelling on leased land, or person who holds life lease in property previously sold or transferred to another, or grantor who has placed property in revocable trust or qualified personal residence trust. (MCLA §211.7dd[b]; MSA §7.7[4aa][b]). "Qualified Agricultural Property" is also exempt from tax levied by local school district for school operating purposes. (See MCLA §211.7ee; MSA §7.7[4bb].) Upon receipt of affidavit by local assessor, property is exempt through 1998 tax year or until Dec. 31 of year property is transferred or owner rescinds exemption claim. Owner of homestead property must file new exemption claim on same property in 1999 and every four years thereafter. Owner must file recision of exemption claim within 90 days after property is no longer used as homestead on form prescribed by department of treasury. Penalty for failure to file recision form is $5 per day, up to maximum of $200. If assessor disputes owner's homestead exemption claim, assessor must notify owner and department in writing of reason for denial and notify owner that denial may be appealed to department of treasury within 35 days after date of notice. Department of treasury determines whether property is homestead. Owner and/or assessor may appeal final decision of department to residential and small claims division of Michigan Tax Tribunal within 35 days of that decision. Payment of amount of tax in dispute is not required before appeal to department of treasury or Tax Tribunal. (MCLA §211.7cc[1]-[9], [13]; MSA §7.7[cc][1]-[9], [13] and MCLA §211.7dd; MSA §7.7[4aa]). Owner who owned and occupied homestead on May 1 for which tax exemption was not on tax roll may file appeal with July board of review in year for which exemption was claimed or immediately succeeding year or with Dec. board of review in year for which exemption was claimed or immediately succeeding year. If appeal of denial of exemption claim is received not later than five days prior to date of Dec. board of review, Dec. board of review shall be convened and appeal considered pursuant to MCLA §211.53b; MSA §7.97(2). (MCLA §211.7cc[13]; MSA §7.7[4z][13]). If homestead part of unit in multiple-unit dwelling or dwelling unit in multiple-purpose structure, owner can claim exemption for only that portion of total taxable value of property used as homestead of that owner. (MCLA §211.7cc[10]; MSA §7.7[4z]). Person who falsely or fraudulently, or aids or abets another to falsely or fraudulently claim exemption under §7cc, or person who fails to rescind homestead exemption when required, is guilty of misdemeanor punishable by one year imprisonment, fine of not more than $5,000, or up to 1,500 hours of public service, or both. In addition, person who knowingly swears or verifies affidavit claiming any exemption under §7cc that contains false or fraudulent statement, is guilty of perjury, misdemeanor. (MCLA §211.120; MSA §7.174).

When property is transferred and county register of deeds records transfer of ownership, register must notify local assessor of transfer. (MCLA §211.7cc[11]; MSA §7.7[4z][11]). Exemption affidavit and recision forms are made available by department of treasury; preparer of closing statements for sale of property must provide affidavit and recision forms to buyer and seller at closing, and if requested, file same with local assessor. (MCLA §211.7cc[12]; MSA §7.7[4z][12]).

Personal Property.—Exemptions of personal property include such property of nonprofit theater, library, benevolent, charitable, educational and scientific institutions and organizations devoted exclusively to fostering development of literature, music, painting or sculpture regularly available to public as whole incorporated under Michigan laws; charitable homes of fraternal societies; libraries not operated for gain; patriotic or religious organizations; scout organizations, 4-H clubs and similar associations; Indians not citizens; pensions receivable from U.S.; all personal property owned and used by householder, such as customary furniture, fixtures, provisions, fuel and

See note at head of Digest as to 1998 legislation covered.

See Topical Index in front part of this volume.

PROPERTY (AD VALOREM) TAXES . . . *continued*
other similar equipment, except where held as inventory for sale; household furnishings of fraternities, sororities, and student cooperatives up to $5,000 per household; mechanic's tools up to $500 per mechanic; fire fighting equipment; property used by householder in business, in his dwelling or in one other location in his residence locality up to $500; property actually used in agricultural operations and farm implements held for sale or resale by retail servicing dealers for use in agricultural production; products (except alcoholic beverages) located in public warehouse, U.S. customs port of entry bonded warehouse, dock or port facility on Dec. 31 of each year, if in transit to destinations out of state; personal property of bank or trust company organized under Michigan law, national bank or incorporated bank holding company; processed or unprocessed farm products (except alcoholic beverages) ultimately to be used as human or animal food and regularly stored in public warehouse, dock or port facility, sugar in solid or liquid form produced from sugar beets and dried beet pulp and molasses, when owned or held by processors; personal property of parent cooperative preschool; equipment used exclusively in wood harvesting; liquified petroleum gas tanks used to store liquified petroleum gas for residential or agricultural property use located on residential or agricultural property; water conditioning systems used for residential dwellings. (MCLA §211.9; MSA §7.9), various commodities or property on which specific taxes have been paid, i.e., grain, gasoline (MCLA §207.113; MSA §7.303), low grade iron ore under development (MCLA §211.624; MSA §13.157[4]), oil and gas rights (MCLA §205.315; MSA §7.365), and motor vehicles and vessels (MCLA §§207.51, 207.51a; MSA §§7.281, 7.281[1]); personal property of credit unions (MCLA §490.22; MSA §23.502); intangibles, which are separately taxed (MCLA §205.132; MSA §7.556[2]; see infra, subhead Intangible Personal Property Tax); certain air pollution control facilities so long as certificate of exemption is in effect (MCLA §336.4; MSA §7.793[4]); certain computer software (MCLA §211.9d).

Also, all special tools are exempt from taxation. "Special tools" means those manufacturing requisites, such as dies, jigs, fixtures, molds, patterns, gauges, or other tools, as defined by state tax commission, that are held for use and not for sale in ordinary course of business. Special tools are not exempt if value of special tools is included in valuation of inventory purchased for sale. (MCLA §211.9b; MSA §7.9[2]).

Effective with 1976 tax year, inventory property, excluding personal property under lease, is exempt from tax. (MCLA §211.9c; MSA §7.9[3]).

Rate.—Constitution limits total amount of general ad valorem taxes imposed upon real and tangible personal property for all purposes in any one year to 15 mills per dollar of assessed value, as finally equalized, except taxes imposed: (1) For payment of principal and interest on bonds or other evidences of indebtedness, (2) for payment of assessments or contract obligations in anticipation of which bonds are issued, (3) taxes imposed on which the limitations are provided by charter or general law. This limitation may be increased by a majority of qualified electors within a county, acting through initiative procedures, adopting a fixed division of millage among a county, its townships and school districts which is not to exceed 18 mills on each dollar of assessed valuation. This limitation may also be increased, for a period not exceeding 20 years at any one time, to an aggregate of not more than 50 mills on each dollar of assessed valuation, by a majority of the qualified electors of any taxing district. (Const., art. IX, §6).

Aggregate rate is determined by adding rates levied by various assessing districts in which property is assessed, and consequently varies in different districts.

Assessment.—Annual assessment of all taxable property is made by supervisors of townships or by other assessing officer if provided for in village or city charter (MCLA §211.10, MSA §7.10), to be completed by 1st Mon. in Mar. (MCLA §211.24; MSA §7.24). Assessment to be made on basis of 50% of true cash value. Legislature shall provide for general ad valorem taxation of real and tangible personal property not exempt by law except for taxes levied for school operating purposes. For taxes levied in 1995 and each year thereafter, taxable value of each parcel of property is lesser of following: (a) property's current state equalized value or (b) property's taxable value in immediately preceding year, minus any losses, multiplied by lesser of 1.05 or inflation rate, plus value of all additions. For taxes levied in 1995, property's taxable value in immediately preceding year is property's state equalized value in 1994. "Losses" and "additions" are defined in MCLA §211.34d(b) and (h); MSA §7.52(4)(b) and (h). When ownership of parcel of property is transferred, property is assessed at applicable proportion of current true cash value. (Const., art. IX, §3; MCLA §211.27; MSA §7.27). Upon transfer of property after 1994, property's taxable value for year following transfer is property's state equalized valuation for year following transfer. (MCLA §211.27a; MSA §7.27a). Transfer of ownership means conveyance of title to or present interest in property, including beneficial use of property, value of which is substantially equal to value of fee interest. MCLA §211.27a(6); MSA §7.27a(6) provides list of what constitutes transfer of ownership and includes following: (a) conveyance by deed or land contract; (b) conveyance to trust after Dec. 31, 1994, except if sole present beneficiaries are settlor or settlor's spouse, or both; (c) conveyance by distribution from trust, except if distributee is sole beneficiary or spouse of sole present beneficiary, or both; (d) change in sole present beneficiaries of trust, except change that adds or substitutes spouse of sole present beneficiary; (e) conveyance by distribution under will or by intestate succession, except if distributee is decedent's spouse; (f) conveyance by lease if total duration of lease is more than 35 years or lease grants lessee bargain purchase option (which means right to purchase property at termination of lease for not more than 80% of property's projected true cash value); (g) conveyance of ownership interest in corporation, partnership, sole proprietorship, limited liability company or partnership, or other legal entity if ownership interest conveyed is more than 50% of corporation, partnership, or other legal entity; (h) transfer of property held as tenancy in common; (i) conveyance of ownership interest in cooperative housing corporation, excepting portion not subject to ownership interest conveyed. MCLA §211.27a(7); MSA §7.27a(7) provides list of what does not constitute transfer of ownership including (a) transfer of property between spouses or from decedent to surviving spouse; (b) transfer from husband, wife, or husband and wife creating or disjoining tenancy by entireties in grantors or grantor and his or her spouse; (c) transfer subject to life estate or life lease retained by transferee, until termination of life estate or life lease; (d) transfer through foreclosure or forfeiture of recorded instrument, or through deed or conveyance in lieu of foreclosure or forfeiture, until mortgagee or land contract vendor subsequently transfers property (mortgagee must transfer property within one year of expiration of applicable redemption period); (e) transfer by redemption by person to whom taxes are assessed of property previously sold for delinquent taxes; (f) conveyance to trust if sole present beneficiary of trust is settlor or settlor's spouse, or both; (g) transfer pursuant to judgment or order of court ordering transfer, unless specific monetary consideration is specified or ordered by court for transfer; (h) transfer creating or terminating joint tenancy between two or more persons if at least one person is original owner of property when joint tenancy was initially created and, if property is held as joint tenancy at time of conveyance, at least one person was joint tenant when tenancy was initially created and that person has remained joint tenant since that date (person is original owner of property owned by that person's spouse); (i) transfer for security or assignment or discharge of security interest; (j) transfer of real property or other ownership interests among members of affiliated group, which means one or more corporations connected by stock ownership to common parent corporation. If requested by state tax commission, corporation must, within 45 days, furnish proof that transfer meets requirements, otherwise subject to $200 fine; (k) normal public trading of shares of stock or other ownership interest that, over any period of time, cumulatively represent more than 50% of total ownership interest in corporation or other legal entity and are traded in multiple transactions involving unrelated individuals, institutions, or other legal entities; (l) transfer of real property or other ownership interest among corporations, partnerships, limited liability companies, limited liability partnerships, or other legal entities if entities involved are commonly controlled. If requested by state tax commission, proof that transfer meets requirements must be provided within 45 days, otherwise subject to $200 fine; (m) direct or indirect transfer of real property or other ownership interest resulting from transaction that qualifies as tax-free reorganization under §368 of Internal Revenue Code of 1986, 26 USC 368. If requested by state tax commission, proof that transfer meets requirements must be provided within 45 days, otherwise subject to $200 fines.

MCLA §211.27a(8); MSA §7.27a(8) requires register of deeds to notify assessing officer not less than once each month of any recorded transaction involving ownership of property. Unless notification is provided under subsection (6) or (7) of MCLA §211.27a, buyer, grantee, or other transferee of property must notify assessing officer of transfer of ownership of property within 45 days of transfer, on form prescribed by state tax commission which states parties to transfer, date of transfer, actual consideration for transfer, and property's parcel identification number or legal description. Failure to notify assessor of transfer will result in adjustment to taxable value, penalty of $5 per day, up to maximum of $200, any additional taxes which would be due, and interest and penalties assessed from date tax would have been originally levied. (MCLA §211.27b; MSA §7.27b). If taxable value is increased, buyer, grantee or transferee may appeal increase to tax tribunal within 35 days of receiving notice of increase. Appeal limited to issue of whether transfer of ownership occurred and correcting arithmetic errors. Dispute regarding valuation of property not permitted. (MCLA §211.276[6]; MSA §7.27[b][6]). Taxable status of persons and personal property is determined as of Dec. 31. (MCLA §§211.2, .13; MSA §§7.2, .13). County Board of Supervisors equalizes assessments as between taxing districts in county on Tues. following 2d Mon. in April. (MCLA §§209.1-.8; MSA §§7.601-.608). State Board of Equalization equalizes assessments between counties on 2d Mon. in May (MCLA §209.1; MSA §7.601) and value so determined appears on rolls and tax statements (MCLA §211.24[b]; MSA §7.24[2]). County Tax Allocation Board determines maximum tax rate for each taxing District according to relative needs so as not to exceed constitutional tax rate limitation. (MCLA §§211.205-.217; MSA §§7.65-.77).

Assessing officer can require any person who is believed to have possession of personal property to make and sign written statement identifying all personal property owned by person or held for use of another. Assessing officer may require same for real property, if deemed necessary. (MCLA §211.18; MSA §7.18). Any person, member of firm, or officer of corporation who willfully neglects/refuses to make out and deliver statement, or falsely answers or refuses to answer questions concerning property under his or her control, is guilty of misdemeanor punishable by not less than 30 days to six months imprisonment, and/or fine of $100 to $1,000, or both. (MCLA §211.21; MSA §7.21). If assessing officer, State Tax Commission or county equalization director is satisfied that statement is incorrect, or cannot be obtained, assessing officer, State Tax Commission or county equalization director may examine, under oath, any person believed to have knowledge of amount or value of any property owned, held, or controlled by person neglecting or refusing to be examined or to furnish statement required under §18. Assessing officer is authorized to assess to person, firm or corporation subject to assessment amount of real and personal property assessing officer considers reasonable and just. (MCLA §211.22; MSA §7.22).

Review of Assessment.—Board of Review meets on 1st Tues. after 1st Mon. in Mar. to review taxable status of persons and property, and on following Mon. and Tues. to hear complaints of any person whose property is assessed and review valuations. (MCLA §§211.29-.30; MSA §§7.29-.30). Board of Review also meets in July and Dec. at which time clerical errors or mutual mistakes of fact can be reviewed and corrected (MCLA §211.53b; MSA §7.91[1]), and in some cases claims for homestead exemptions and/or exemptions for qualified agricultural property (MCLA §205.735; MSA §7.650[35]). Prior to delivery of tax roll to proper officer for collection of taxes but not later than 1st Mon. in May, assessment rolls are subject to inspection by State Tax Commission. (MCLA §211.152; MSA §7.210).

Appeal of Property Tax Assessments.—Tax Tribunal has exclusive and original jurisdiction over proceedings for direct review of final decision, finding, ruling, determination, or order of agency relating to assessment, valuation, rates, special assessments, allocation, or equalization, under property tax laws, and over proceedings for refund or redetermination of tax under property tax laws. (MCLA §205.731; MSA§7.650[31]). Proceedings before Tax Tribunal are original and independent and are considered de novo. For assessment disputes as to valuation of property or claims

See note at head of Digest as to 1998 legislation covered.

See Topical Index in front part of this volume.

MI – 53

PROPERTY (AD VALOREM) TAXES . . . *continued*
for exemption (excepting where July or Dec. board of review has authority to determine claims for exemption for qualified agricultural property or homestead property by Department of Treasury), assessment must be protested to local board of review before Tribunal acquires jurisdiction, except as provided in MCLA §205.737(5) and (7); MSA §7.650 (37)(5) and (7). For special assessment dispute, special assessment must be protested at hearing held for confirming special assessment roll before Tribunal acquires jurisdiction. (MCLA §205.735[1]; MSA §7.650[35]). Jurisdiction of Tribunal in assessment dispute is invoked by party in interest, as petitioner, by filing petition on or before June 30th of tax year involved. In all other matters, jurisdiction is invoked by filing petition within 30 days after final decision, ruling, determination, or order. Appeal of contested tax bill must be made within 60 days after mailing by treasurer and appeal is limited solely to correcting arithmetic errors or mistakes, not valuation or exemption disputes, or property's equalized value. (MCLA §205.735[2]; MSA §7.650[35][2]). In assessment disputes, Tribunal shall determine property's taxable value pursuant to MCLA §211.27a; MSA §7.27(1), and property's state equalized value. (MCLA §205.737[1] and [2]; MSA §7.650[37][1] and [2]). Petitioner has burden of proving true cash value of property and assessing agency has burden of proving average level of assessment. (MCLA §205.737[3]; MSA §7.650[37][3]). Before Tribunal issues its decision on original petition, taxpayer may add subsequent tax years by filing motion to amend petition to add subsequent tax years on or before June 30th of each tax year involved. Prior protest to local board of review is not required. (MCLA §205.737[4]; MSA §7.650[37][4]). If exemption is claimed, subsequent motions to amend are not required. (MCLA §205.737[5][a]; MSA §7.650[37][5][a]). Residential property and small claims division of Tribunal has jurisdiction over proceedings in which residential property (meaning homestead or other residential or agricultural real property including less than four rental units) is involved, for nonresidential property if amount of that property's taxable value or state equalized value in dispute is not more than $100,000, and in non-property matters, if amount of tax in dispute is $6,000 or less. (MCLA §205.762; MSA §7.650[62]). Formal record of proceeding is not required. Within 14 days after hearing referee issues decision or order, by leave of Tribunal and for good cause shown, party may request rehearing by Tribunal member. Rehearing is not limited to evidence presented before hearing referee. Hearing is held in county where property is located or in contiguous county. Appellant is not required to travel more than 100 miles from location of property to hearing site, except for rehearing which is held at site determined by Tribunal. (MCLA §205.762[3] and [4]; MSA §7.650[62][3] and [4]). Appeal to Court of Appeals from Tax Tribunal lies only for fraud, error of law or adoption of wrong principles. (Const, Art. VI, §28). Excessive taxes paid by clerical error or mutual mistake recoverable if action commenced in Tax Tribunal within three years of payment. (MCLA §211.53a; MSA §7.91[1]).

Payment.—See subhead Collection, infra.

Collection.—Taxes apportioned to an assessment district are assessed according and in proportion to valuations entered in assessment roll (MCLA §211.39; MSA §7.80), and tax roll is delivered to collection officer on or before day taxes become lien (MCLA §211.43; MSA §7.84). On Dec. 31 (or on date fixed by charter of cities which collect own taxes) real property tax becomes lien on property assessed, and personal property tax becomes paramount lien on all personal property of person assessed (MCLA §211.40; MSA §7.81). Collecting officer mails statements to each taxpayer at his last known address in tax roll, but failure to send statement or non-receipt by taxpayer does not prejudice right to collect tax. (MCLA §211.44; MSA §7.87). Collecting officer may distrain on any personal property to collect real or personal property tax, and may sue to collect personal property tax. (MCLA §211.47; MSA §7.91). He may also make jeopardy assessments of personal property taxes, accelerating due date and imposition of lien. (MCLA §211.691; MSA §7.51[1]).

Collection fee of 1% is added to taxes paid before Feb. 15 following assessment; additional 3% may be added to last day of Feb.; additional 4% county property tax administration fee and interest on tax at rate of 1% per month shall be added after last day of Feb. and before settlement with county treasurer.

Governing body of local property tax collecting unit may waive all or part of administration fees, or late penalty charges, or both. (MCLA §211.44; MSA §7.87). On Mar. 1, collecting officer returns delinquent taxes to county treasurer and thereafter payment of taxes to county treasurer must be accompanied by collection fee of 4% plus interest at 1% (1.25% for: [a] Taxes becoming delinquent Mar. 1, 1981 through Feb. 28, 1983 in counties with population of more than 1,500,000 and [b] 1981 taxes becoming delinquent on or before Mar. 1, 1982 in all other counties) per month or fraction thereof from Mar. 1, plus $10 per description if paid after Oct. 1. (MCLA §§211.59, .89; MSA §§7.103, .144).

In some cities state and county taxes are collected as above and separate machinery is maintained by city for collection, sale and redemption of city taxes. (MCLA §211.107; MSA §7.161; and see city charters).

Lien.—Notwithstanding any provision in city or village charter to contrary, all taxes become debt due to township, city, village or county on tax day, Dec. 31. Amounts assessed for state, county, village or township real property taxes become lien on real property on Dec. 1, on day provided for by city or village charter, or on day provided for in MCLA §211.40a; MSA §7.8(a). Notwithstanding any provision of city or village charters to contrary, all personal property taxes levied or assessed are first, prior and superior lien, on all personal property of persons assessed and lien continues until paid. Transfer of personal property does not divest or destroy lien, except where personal property is actually sold in regular course of retail trade. (MCLA §211.40; MSA §7.81).

Treasurer may designate tax day, Dec. 31, as lien date by filing affidavit with register of deeds for county in which real or personal property is located, attesting that one or more of following events have occurred: (a) Owner or person assessed has filed for Title 11 bankruptcy (11 U.S.C. 101 to 1330); (b) secured lender has brought foreclosure action or action to enforce interest secured by real or personal property assessed; (c) for personal property only, owner or person assessed has liquidated or is attempting to liquidate personal property assessed; (d) real or personal property assessed is subject to receivership under state or federal law; (e) owner or person assessed has assigned real or personal property for benefit of creditors; (f) real or personal property has been seized or purchased by federal, state or local authorities; (g) judicial action has been commenced that may impair ability of taxing authority to collect any taxes due in absence of lien on real or personal property assessed. (MCLA §211.40a[a]; MSA §7.8[a]). Affidavit must include all of following: (a) Year for which taxes due were levied; (b) date on which taxes due were assessed; (c) name of owner or person assessed as identified on tax roll; (d) tax identification number of real or personal property assessed. (MCLA §211.40a[2]; MSA §7.8[a][2]).

Sale.—Delinquent lands are sold for taxes on first Tuesday in May of each year. Sale covers taxes assessed in third year preceding sale and all prior years. On sale, collection fee of 4%, $10 for expenses and interest at 1.25% (1.5% for: [a] Taxes becoming delinquent Mar. 1, 1981 through Feb. 28, 1983 in counties with population of more than 1,500,000 and [b] 1981 taxes becoming delinquent on or before Mar. 1, 1982 in all other counties) per month from date of delinquency are added. (MCLA §§211.60, .89; MSA §§7.104, .144).

State Treasurer petitions Circuit Court of each county to foreclose tax lien. Petition, including each description, is published for three successive weeks and posted and persons to whom taxes are assessed are notified by first class mail, address correction requested at least 30 days before date of sale. Interested persons may appear and contest validity of tax on filing written objection and serving State Treasurer, prosecutor and taxing unit involved. If disputed tax is held valid payment in escrow to county treasurer within ten days is condition precedent to appeal. Decree is made at least ten days before sale. Each parcel is offered separately and sold to person who will pay tax, etc., and take smallest undivided fee simple interest (or entire parcel if no one will take less) subject to taxes assessed subsequently to those for which sold. Bids must be paid within 24 hours. Certificate of sale is issued to purchaser. Unsold parcels are bid off to state. County treasurer files report of sale, which stands confirmed unless objections are filed within eight days, and after confirmation no sale is set aside except on petition within one year after notice of sale showing that tax was paid of land exempt. (MCLA §211.61 et seq.; MSA §7.105 et seq.).

Redemption.—Any person owning any interest in land sold for taxes may redeem by payment to county treasurer or department of treasury, before first Tues. in May of year following sale, of amount for which land was sold with interest at 1.25% (1.5% for: [a] Taxes becoming delinquent Mar. 1, 1981 through Feb. 28, 1983 in counties with population of more than 1,500,000 and [b] 1981 taxes becoming delinquent on or before Mar. 1, 1982 in all other counties) per month. (MCLA §§211.74, .89; MSA §§7.120, .144). See also infra, subhead Perfection of Tax Title. Redemption period on property deeded to State is extended until owners of recorded property interest are notified of show cause hearing. After expiration of redemption period, title to property vests in State on first Tues. in Nov., and may be redeemed up to 30 days after show cause hearing, by paying taxes due, plus additional 50% of tax on which foreclosure was made. (MCLA §211.131e; MSA §7.190[3]).

Perfection of Tax Title.—After expiration of redemption period State Treasurer issues tax deed on application of holder of certificate of sale. (MCLA §211.72; MSA §7.117). No right to possession accrues under tax deed until six months after filing with county clerk of return by sheriff of personal service of notice of right to reconveyance on person with interest in property either in fee, for life, or for years; mortgages; assignee of undischarged mortgage; lienholders of record; executor, administrator, trustee or guardian; and persons in possession. (MCLA §211.141; MSA §7.199). Provision is made for substituted service by mail or publication on nonresidents and persons who cannot be located. (MCLA §211.140 et seq.; MSA §7.198 et seq.). Rights under tax, deed expire if notice is not given within five years after tax deed is available. (MCLA §211.73a; MSA §7.119). Any person having any estate in land is entitled to redeem within six months from proof of service of such notice by payment of amount of tax sale plus 50%, service fees and $5 per description, and is entitled to release and quitclaim if redemption is made after issuance of tax deed. (MCLA §211.141; MSA §7.199). If tax title is avoided for illegality of tax, purchaser may obtain refund with 6% interest from State Treasurer (MCLA §211.73; MSA §7.118), and if purchaser commences suit to quiet title under tax deed, and title is held invalid for any reason other than illegality of tax, he will have lien on land, with 7% interest, which may be foreclosed as mortgage in same proceeding (MCLA §211.72; MSA §7.117).

REAL ESTATE STAMP AND TRANSFER TAXES:

Stamp Tax.—There is imposed a state documentary stamp tax of 55¢ (in counties with less than 2,000,000 population) or up to 75¢(as determined by county board of commissioners in counties with 2,000,000 or more population) per each $500 fair market value on instruments of transfer and contracts for transfer of real property. Tax is imposed on transferor. Excepted from tax are transfers where value is less than $100, instruments evidencing contracts not to be wholly performed in state, instruments which state is prohibited from taxing under U.S. law and instruments which evidence security interests and leases, interests assessed as personalty, underground gas storage, certain instruments in which U.S., State, or any political subdivision or municipality thereof is grantee, grantor, guarantor or insurer, certain conveyances involving creation or disjoinder of tenancies by entireties, certain judgments making or ordering transfers, certain instruments used to straighten boundary lines, certain instruments (such as quitclaim deeds) used to confirm titles already vested in grantees, certain land contracts, instruments transferring mineral rights and interests and certain instruments creating joint tenancies. (MCLA §207.501 et seq.; MSA §7.456[1]et seq.).

Real Estate Transfer Tax.—After Jan. 1, 1995, in addition to all other taxes, including stamp tax, as to which see subhead Stamp Tax, supra, there is tax upon following written instruments when instrument is recorded: contracts for sale or exchange of property or any interest in property or any combination of sales or exchanges or any assignment or transfer of property or any interest in property; and deeds or instruments of conveyance of property or any interest in property, for consideration. (MCLA §207.522[a][b]; MSA §7.456[22][a][b]). Seller or grantor of property

See note at head of Digest as to 1998 legislation covered.

See Topical Index in front part of this volume.

MI – 54

REAL ESTATE STAMP AND TRANSFER TAXES . . . *continued*
is liable for tax. (MCLA §207.523; MSA §7.456[23]). If property is located within this State, but written instrument is executed outside of this State, transfer tax is imposed. (MCLA §207.524; MSA §7.456[24]). Tax is levied at rate of $3.75 for each $500 or fraction of $500 of total value of property being transferred. (MCLA §207.525; MSA §7.456[25]). Written instrument must state on its face total value of real property being transferred unless affidavit is attached to written instrument declaring total value of property. Form of affidavit shall be prescribed by Department of Treasury. If sale or transfer is of combination of real and personal property, is imposed only upon transfer of real property if values of real and personal property are stated separately on face of written instrument or if affidavit is attached to written instrument setting forth respective values of real and personal property. (MCLA §207.525[2]; MSA §7.456[25][2]). Instruments and transfers of real property which are exempt from real estate transfer tax are set forth in MCLA §207.526; MSA §7.456[25(2)], and include following: (a) Conveyance of property value of consideration of which is less than $100; (b) contract of transfer that is not to be performed wholly within state only to extent written instrument includes land lying outside of state; (c) written instrument that state is prohibited from taxing under U.S. constitution or federal statutes; (d) instrument given as security or assignment or discharge of security interest; (e) instrument evidencing lease, including oil and gas lease, or transfer of leasehold interest; (f) instrument evidencing interest that is assessable as personal property; (g) instrument evidencing transfer of right and interest for underground gas storage purposes; (h)(i) instrument in which grantor is U.S., State, or political subdivision, (ii) instrument given in foreclosure or in lieu of foreclosure of loan made, guaranteed, or insured by U.S., State, or political subdivision, (iii) instrument given to U.S, State, or one of their officers acting in official capacity as grantee, pursuant to terms or guarantee or insurance of loan guaranteed or insured by grantee; (i) conveyance from husband or wife or to husband and wife creating or disjoining tenancy by entireties in grantors or grantor and his or her spouse; (j) conveyance from mother or father to son or daughter or stepchild or adopted child; (k) conveyance from grandmother or grandfather to grandchild or stepgrandchild or adopted grandchild; (l) judgment or order of court of record making or ordering transfer, unless specific monetary consideration is specified or ordered by court for transfer; (m) instrument used to straighten boundary lines if no monetary consideration is given; (n) instrument to confirm title already vested in grantee, including quitclaim deed to correct flaw in title; (o) land contract in which legal title does not pass to grantee until total consideration specified in contract has been paid; (p) instrument evidencing transfer of mineral rights and interests; (q) instrument creating joint tenancy between two or more persons if at least one of persons already owns property; (r) transfer made pursuant to bona fide sales agreement made before date this tax is imposed under §§3 and 4 (MCLA §§207.523-.526; MSA §§7.456 [23]-[26]) if sales agreement cannot be withdrawn or altered, or contains fixed price not subject to change or modification. However, sales agreement for residential construction may be adjusted up to 15% to reflect changes in construction specifications; (s) instrument evidencing contract or transfer of property to person sufficiently related to transferor to be considered single employer with transferor under §414(b) or (c) of Internal Revenue Code of 1986, as amended; (t) instrument conveying interest in homestead property for which homestead exemption is claimed under school code of 1976, Act No. 451 of Public Acts of 1976 (being MCLA §§380.1-.1852), or State education tax, Act No. 331 of Public Acts of 1993 (being MCLA §§211.901-.906), if State equalized value of that homestead property is equal to or lesser than State equalized value on date of purchase or on date of acquisition by seller or transferor for that same interest in property. If after homestead exemption is claimed, sale or transfer of homestead property is found by treasurer to be at value other than true cash value, then penalty equal to 20% of tax will be assessed to seller or transferor in addition to transfer tax due; (u) instrument transferring interest in property pursuant to foreclosure of mortgage, including deed in lieu of foreclosure. Exemption does not apply to subsequent transfer of foreclosed property by entity that foreclosed. (MCLA §207.526[u]; MSA §7.456[26][u]); (v) conveyance or transfer of property to receiver, administrator or trustee in bankruptcy or insolvency proceeding. (MCLA §207.527; MSA §7.456[27]).

Payment of transfer tax must be evidenced by affixing of documentary stamp or stamps to each written instrument subject to tax imposed by person making, executing, issuing, or delivering written instrument. Documentary stamps may be purchased only in county in which property is located. (MCLA §207.528[1]; MSA §7.456[28(1)]). Treasurer may prescribe alternate means for county treasurer to evidence payment of tax. (MCLA §207.529; MSA §7.456[29]). Tax is collected by county treasurer and is deposited with treasurer. (MCLA §207.530; MSA §7.456[30]). Written instrument that is evidence of indebtedness or of contract right is subject to transfer tax only to extent of new consideration given for property. Written instrument that is given to supplement, reform or correct prior written instrument is subject to real estate transfer tax only to extent of new consideration given for property. (MCLA §207.532[1]; MSA §7.456[32(1)]). Tax is payable only once on transfer. Instrument is exempt by reason of prior payment or partial payment of tax on another written instrument executed as part of same transaction. Statement to that effect and date of payment must be set forth. (MCLA §207.532[2]; MSA §7.456[32(2)]). No written instrument subject to real estate transfer tax will be recorded in office of register of deeds of any county unless documentary stamps have been purchased at time of presentation by party liable for tax (seller or grantor of property). Stamps must be affixed to face of instrument before recording unless person specifically requests that instrument be recorded before stamps are affixed. If so requested, stamps may be affixed to reverse side of written instrument. (MCLA §207.533[1]; MSA §7.456[33(1)]). Any person who violates any one of prohibited acts in MCLA §207.534(1); MSA §7.456(34[1]), is guilty of misdemeanor, punishable by imprisonment for not more than one year or fined not more than $500 or both. (MCLA §207.534[2]; MSA §7.456[34(2)]).

SALES AND USE TAXES:

Sales Tax.—Levied on all persons within state engaged in the business of making sales at retail, including conditional sales and installment lease sales, and computer software offered for general sale to public or software modified or adopted to user's needs or equipment by seller if software is available for sale either from seller or software on as is basis or as end product without modification or adaptation but excluding isolated transactions. Sale at retail means transfer for consideration of tangible personal property in ordinary course of business for any purpose other than resale in form of tangible property or demonstration. Sale at retail does not include commercial advertising element if commercial advertising element is used to create or develop print, radio, television, or other advertisement, commercial advertising element is discarded or returned to provider after advertising message is completed, and commercial advertising element is custom developed by provider for purchaser. Commercial advertising element means negative or positive photographic image, audiotape or videotape master, layout, manuscript, writing of copy, design, artwork, illustration, retouching, and mechanical or keyline instructions. Sale at retail includes audiotape or videotape reproductions. Tangible property includes electricity, gas and steam. Tax is 6% of gross proceeds less credits for returned goods or refund less allowance for use made for motor vehicle returned under MCLA §257.1401-.1410; MSA §9.2705(1)-(10), as certified by manufacturer. (Const. art IX, §8; MCLA §§205.51, .52, .54; MSA §§7.521, .522, .524). Seller may add tax to price charged if he states it separately. (MCLA §205.73; MSA §7.544). Sale for residential use of electricity, natural or artificial gas, or home heating fuels is exempt from sales tax at additional rate of 2%, i.e. 4% sales tax applies. (MCLA §205.54n; MSA §7.527[14]).

Exempt are sales: (1) to United States or its agencies, instrumentalities or wholly owned corporations, American Red Cross, and State of Michigan or its departments, institutions or political subdivisions; (2) to parent cooperative preschools and to nonprofit educational institutions, nonprofit hospitals and nonprofit homes for children and aged persons so long as activities of such entity are carried on for benefit of public at large; (3) to churches; (4) of food to students by nonprofit educational institutions; (5) of tangible personal property affixed to and made part of real estate of nonprofit hospital or nonprofit housing; (6) of commercial vessels of 500 tons or more produced on special order and of fuel and stores for such vessels engaged in interstate commerce; (7) for agricultural production except property for human consumption or property which becomes part of real estate; (8) for industrial processing except: (a) property which becomes part of real estate, (b) services performed on property owned by others, which do not alter character of property, (c) office furniture and supplies, (d) receiving and storage of certain raw materials, (e) vehicles titled and licensed for use on public highways and (f) preparation of food and beverages by retailer for retail sale; (9) of newspapers, periodicals and copyrighted motion picture films; (10) for use or consumption in commercial radio or television transmission; (11) of hearing aids, contact lenses, eyeglasses or devices to replace part of human body or used to assist disabled person if prescribed by appropriate professional; (12) ambulance or fire department vehicles not for resale to Michigan nonprofit corporations; (13) for use or consumption in rendition of service use or consumption of which is subject to use tax, except exemption is limited to personal property located on premises of subscriber and to central office equipment or wireless equipment, directly used in transmitting, receiving, switching, or monitoring 2-way interactive communication (excluding cable or wireless facilities); (14) second class mail publications; (15) text books sold by public or nonpublic school to students in kindergarten through twelfth grade; (16) of prescription drugs for human use or food for human consumption, except prepared food intended for immediate consumption, excluding, however, milk, juices, non-carbonated beverages, fresh fruit, candy, nuts, chewing gum, bakery products, cookies, crackers, and chips sold from vending machine or vendor of mobile facility, of deposits on returnable containers, of food or other property purchased with federal food stamps, or of certain fruit or vegetable seeds or plants; (17) sales of tangible personal property purchased and installed as component part of water pollution control facility; (18) sales of subsurface irrigation pipe if used in production of agricultural products as business enterprise; (19) gross proceeds from out-of-state usage and from sale of qualified truck or trailer, purchased after Dec. 31, 1996 and before May 1, 1999, by interstate motor carrier and used in interstate commerce. (MCLA §§205.51, .54-.54g; MSA §§7.521, .524-.525[17]). Sales of certain air pollution equipment are also exempt if covered by certificate of exemption. (MCLA §336.4; MSA §7.793[4]). Deduction allowed for "bad debts" beginning Jan. 1, 1984. (MCLA §205.54i; MSA §7.525[9]). Also exempt are sales for use in qualified business activities as defined in enterprise zone act (MCLA §125.2101 et seq., 205.54j; MSA §§3.540[301] et seq., 7.525[10]), and sales to business certified by Department of Treasury as engaged in high technology activity (MCLA §205.541; MSA §7.525[12]).

Sales of tangible personal property not for resale are excluded from gross proceeds used for computation of sales tax, if made to following: (a) health, welfare, educational, cultural arts, charitable, or nonprofit benevolent organization that has been issued exemption ruling letter signed by administrator of sales, use, and withholding tax division of department of treasury. Exemption letter to each of these organizations will be reissued after effective date of this provision, Dec. 31, 1994, unless organization fails to meet requirements which originally entitled it to exemption; (b) organization not operated for profit and exempt from federal income tax under §501(c)(3) or 501(c)(4) of Internal Revenue Code. Exemptions do not apply to sales of tangible personal property and sales of vehicles licensed for use on public highways, that are not used primarily to carry out purpose of exempt organization as stated in its bylaws or articles of incorporation. At time of transfer of personal property, exempt organization shall do one of following: (a) present exemption ruling letter, (b) present signed statement, on form approved by department, stating that property is to be used or consumed in connection with operation of exempt entity and that organization qualifies as exempt organization. Transferee must provide transferor copy of federal exemption letter. Exemption ruling letter and signed statement with copy of federal exemption letter shall be accepted by all courts as prima facia evidence of exemption. Statement shall provide that if claim for exemption is disallowed, transferee shall reimburse transferor for amount of tax. (MCLA §205.54n; MSA §7.525[14]).

School, church, hospital, parent cooperative preschool, or nonprofit organization with tax exempt status under MCLA §§205.54n(1)(a) or (1)(b); MSA §§7.525(14a)(a) or (14a)(b), with aggregate sales at retail in calendar year of less than $5,000 and not operating for profit, may exclude from gross proceeds sales of tangible personal property for fund-raising purposes. Club, association, auxiliary, or other organization

See note at head of Digest as to 1998 legislation covered.

See Topical Index in front part of this volume.

MI – 55

SALES AND USE TAXES . . . *continued*
affiliated with school, church, hospital, parent cooperative preschool, or exempt nonprofit organization is not considered separate person for purposes of this exemption for fund raising. (MCLA §205.540; MSA §7.525[15]). MCLA §§205.54n and 540; MSA §§7.525(14) and (15) are effective for all sales at retail occurring after Dec. 31, 1994.

Persons engaged in taxable business are required to obtain license (fee $1 per year) and to report and pay tax monthly. (MCLA §§205.53, .56; MSA §§7.523, .527). Taxpayer required to keep specified records. Taxpayer may use blanket exemption certificates on form prescribed by Department that covers all exempt transfers between taxpayer and buyer for period of three years, or less if agreed to by buyer and seller. (MCLA §205.67; MSA §7.567).

Penalties are same as those for Single Business Tax discussed in topic Business Taxes, subhead Single Business Tax. (MCLA §205.59; MSA §7.530). Provision made for hearing before Department of Revenue if requested within 30 days following notice of intent to assess. (MCLA §205.21; MSA §7.657[21]). Department's decision subject to review on appeal to Michigan Tax Tribunal within 35 days or suit for refund can be instituted in Court of Claims within 90 days. (MCLA §205.22; MSA §7.657[22]).

Tax, including interest and penalties, is personal obligation and prior lien on all taxpayer's property, and failure to obtain license or pay tax is ground for injunction against doing business. (MCLA §§205.29, .66; MSA §§7.657[29], .537). Refusal to make return or making false return with fraudulent intent misdemeanor. (MCLA §205.74; MSA §7.545).

Use tax.—Levied on all persons using, storing or consuming tangible property or using certain services within state. Tax is 6% of price paid for use, storage or consumption less certain credits for timely payment. (Const. art IX, §8; MCLA §§205.93, .94f; MSA §§7.555[3], [4f]). Seller must collect tax. (MCLA §205.95; MSA §7.555[5]). Seller and consumer are liable until tax is paid. (MCLA §§205.97, .99; MSA §§7.555[7], [9]). Use means exercise of right or power over tangible personal property incident to ownership of that property including transfer of property in transaction where possession is given. (MCLA §205.92[b]; MSA §7.555[2][b]). Storage means keeping or retaining property in this state for any purpose after property loses its interstate character. (MCLA §205.92[c]; MSA §7.555[c]). Tangible personal property includes computer software offered for general use by public or software modified or adopted to user's needs or equipment by seller, only if software is available from seller on "as-is" basis or as end product without modification or adaption. It does not include computer software originally designed for exclusive use and special needs of purchaser. (MCLA §205.92[k]; MSA §7.555[2][k]). Tangible personal property does not include commercial advertising element. It does include audiotape or videotape reproductions. (MCLA §205.92[1]; MSA §7.555[2][1]). See subhead Sales Tax, supra.

Unless licensed under sales tax act, persons engaged in business of selling tangible property for storage, use or other consumption within state are required to register agents and places of business within state. (MCLA §205.95; MSA §7.555[5]). Users, unless tax was paid to seller, and sellers who collect use tax, are required to report and pay tax monthly. Corporate officer responsible for making returns and payment on behalf of corporation is personally liable for tax. (MCLA §205.96; MSA §7.555[6]). Penalty for failure to file is 5% of tax per month, to maximum of 50%, plus interest per month at one percentage point above adjusted prime rate. Penalty for negligent disregard is 10% of tax plus interest as above; penalty for fraud is 100% of tax plus interest as above. (MCLA §§205.23-.24; MSA §§7.657[23]-[24]).

Exempt from tax are: Property sold at retail to consumer where sales tax paid on sale; property as to which tax would be unconstitutional; property purchased for resale or demonstration purposes (limited in case of new car dealer) and driver education vehicles, and promotional merchandise transferred pursuant to redemption offer to person outside State and packaging material for use in fulfilling redemption offer or rebate to person outside State; property brought into state temporarily by nonresident (except when used in state in nontransitory business activity for more than 15 days); property on which sales or use tax at least as great has been paid in another state: certain property sold for use in purchaser's agricultural business (if purchaser signs statement to such effect); certain property sold to industrial processor; after Dec. 31, 1989, computers used in operating industrial processing equipment; property or services sold to U.S. (or agency, instrumentality or wholly-owned corporation thereof). American Red Cross or state (or its political subdivisions); property or services sold or donated by manufacturer, wholesaler, or retailer to parent cooperative preschools or to schools, hospitals, homes for children or aged and other benevolent institutions operated by church, fraternal or veteran's organization or Michigan nonprofit corporation; property or services sold or donated by manufacturer, wholesaler, or retailer to church (except where used in commercial activities and except licensed motor vehicles other than passenger van or bus with seating capacity of ten or more used primarily for transporting persons for religious purposes); commercial, special order vessels of 500 tons or more and supplies and repairs for such vessels engaged in interstate commerce; property to be structural part of real estate of nonprofit hospital or certain tax-exempt nonprofit housing projects; property obtained outside state where purchase price or actual value is less than $10 during calendar month; certain newspapers and periodicals, and copyrighted films; property purchased by commercial radio or television station for use as part of film, tape or recording for resale or transmission; automobile purchased out of state by resident member of U.S. military if sales tax paid in other state; certain vehicles purchased for removal from state under special registration; machinery and equipment for use or consumption in rendering any combination of services, except exemption is limited to personal property located on premises of subscriber and to central office equipment or wireless equipment, directly used in transmitting, receiving, switching or monitoring 2-way interactive communication (excluding cable or wireless facilities); prescription hearing aids, eyeglasses, certain contact lenses and other equipment for disabled persons; water delivered through mains or in tanks in quantities of at least 500 gallons: certain equipment for use in telephone, telegraph and similar services; vehicles used by nonprofit ambulance or fire department corporation; sales of certain water pollution control equipment covered by certificate of exemption; storage, use or consumption of aircraft owned or used by domestic passenger air carrier; property purchased by persons licensed to operate commercial radio or television station when property used in origination or integration of sources of material for transmission; purchase of new motor vehicle before Jan. 1, 1993, if qualifies for special 90 day registration under Motor Vehicle Code and vehicle purchased through country which Department of Treasury determines provides similar exemption for new motor vehicles to be removed from such country. (MCLA §205.94; MSA §7.555[4]); prescription drugs or food for human consumption (Const. art IX, §8), deposits on returnable containers, food or other property purchased with federal food stamps, or certain fruit or vegetables or plants (MCLA §205.94d; MSA §7.555[4d]); certain air pollution control equipment covered by certificate of exemption (MCLA §336.4; MSA §7.793[4]); until Dec. 31, 1996, parts and materials (other than shop equipment or fuel) affixed to aircraft owned or used by domestic air carrier that is any of following: (a) aircraft purchased after Dec. 31, 1992 for use solely in commercial transport of air cargo; (b) aircraft purchased after June 30, 1994 that is used solely in commercial transport of passengers; (c) aircraft purchased after Dec. 31, 1994 that has maximum takeoff weight of 12,500 pounds and designed for passenger seating of more than 30 seats and used solely in commercial transport of passengers (MCLA §205.94k; MSA §7.555[4k]); aircraft of domestic air carrier as defined purchased after specified dates and engaged in commerce as defined (MCLA §205.94[x][y][z]; MSA §7.555[4][x][y][z]). Also exempt are transfers to or purchases by spouse, mother, father, brother, sister, child, stepparent, stepchild, stepbrother, stepsister, grandparent, grandchild, legal ward, or legally appointed guardian of transferor. (MCLA §205.93; MSA §7.555[3]).

Exemptions for certain health and welfare organizations are comparable to those set forth under subhead Sales Tax, supra.

UNEMPLOYMENT COMPENSATION TAX:

Unemployment compensation tax is imposed on all employers employing one or more individuals during some portion of at least 20 weeks during calendar year or paying remuneration of $1,000 or more for employment during calendar year, period, all employers employing ten or more individuals for some portion of day in at least 20 weeks during calendar year in agricultural service or paying remuneration in cash of $20,000 or more to employees performing agricultural service during such period and on all employers subject to Title IX of Federal Social Security Act having employees engaged in Michigan employment.

Rate is 5.4% of pay roll during first two years of liability, and thereafter may be increased or decreased depending on unemployment record of employer and condition of unemployment fund balance. In lieu of tax, governmental and nonprofit employers may elect to reimburse unemployment fund for benefits paid which are attributable to service with such employers. Special rates apply to construction employers.

There is no tax on payment to any individual in excess of maximum amount subject to Federal Unemployment Tax Act (26 USC §3301-§3311) during any year. There is no tax on employees and agreement of employee to pay all or any portion of employer's contribution is invalid.

Employers' contributions are payable to Michigan Employment Security Commission semi-annually, or for such shorter periods (not less than 28 days) as Commission may prescribe by regulation. Reports must be filed on such forms and at such times as Commission prescribes. (MCLA §421.1 et seq.; MSA §17.501 et seq.).

TRANSPORTATION

MOTOR VEHICLES:

Michigan Vehicle Code (MCLA §§257.1-.923; MSA §§9.1801-.2623) is administered by Secretary of State, Lansing, Michigan 48913.

Vehicle License.—With limited exceptions, every motor vehicle, pickup camper, trailer coach, trailer, semi-trailer and pole-trailer driven or moved on highway is required to be registered with Secretary of State (MCLA §§257.216, .236a, .217, .238; MSA §§9.1916, 9.1936[1], 9.1938), and to display one registration plate (MCLA §§257.224, .225, .255; MSA §§9.1924, 9.1925, 9.1955). Plates are issued by Secretary of State. (MCLA §§257.201, .224; MSA §§9.1901, .1924). Registration and plates expire on last day of Feb. (commercial vehicles other than pickup trucks and vans owned by individuals and trailers), Mar. 31 (motorcycles), date assigned by Secretary of State (vehicles owned by businesses, corporations, or owners other than individuals), and owner's birthday (other vehicles). (MCLA §257.226; MSA §9.1926). No exemption for members of Armed Forces.

Operator's License.—Every person who drives a motor vehicle on a highway must be licensed by Secretary of State as operator or chauffeur. (MCLA §257.301; MSA §9.2001). Operator's license expires on operator's birthday in fourth year following date of issuance and chauffeur's first license expires on operator's next birthday. Subsequent chauffeur's licenses expire on operator's birthday in fourth year following date of issuance. Two-year license may be issued to persons convicted of certain violations. First license issued to person under age 20½ expires on 21st birthday of licensee. (MCLA §§257.314, 257.811; MSA §§9.2014, 9.2511). Neither operator's nor chauffeur's license may be issued to one under age 18. Restricted license can be issued to anyone at least age 14 years, nine months. MCLA §§257.303, .308 and 310e; MSA §§9.2003, .2008 and .2010[5]). Certain off-road recreational vehicles may be operated by persons between ages 10 and 16 only if operator is supervised by someone 18 years of age, is on land owned by parent or guardian, and possesses safety certificate issued by Dept. of Natural Resources. (MCLA §324.81129; MSA §13A.81129). Any member of Armed Forces when furnished driver's permit and when operating official motor vehicle in service of Armed Forces is exempt from licensing requirements. (MCLA §257.302; MSA §9.2002). Operator's license is not issued to any person under 18 who has not passed approved driver education course unless licensed for one year in another jurisdiction (MCLA §257.811; MSA §9.2511), except restricted licenses (MCLA §257.312; MSA §9.2012) and temporary instruction permits (MCLA §257.306; MSA §9.2006).

See note at head of Digest as to 1998 legislation covered.

See Topical Index in front part of this volume.

MI – 56

MOTOR VEHICLES . . . *continued*

Titles.—Application for certificate of title must contain name and address of owner; description of vehicle including make, body style, year or model, engine and serial or vehicle number, weight and odometer mileage; and statement of applicant's title and names and addresses of holders of any security interest in vehicle and in any accessory, in order of their priority. Rebuilt, salvage, scrap or comparable certificate of title issued by another state must be reissued by Secretary of State. (MCLA §257.217; MSA §9.1917). See subhead Sales, infra.

Sales.—Seller must endorse and acknowledge assignment to purchaser, with statement of all security interests in vehicle or accessories, on reverse side of certificate of title. (MCLA §257.233; MSA §9.1933). Purchaser, unless he is a dealer, must present such certificate to Secretary of State with required fees and new certificate will be issued. (MCLA §257.234; MSA §9.1934). Seller may retain plates for transfer to another vehicle upon application and payment of required fees. (MCLA §257.233; MSA §9.1933). Buyer must present certificate of title to Secretary of State so that new certificate of title and registration certificate may be issued. (MCLA §257.254; MSA §9.1934). Party transferring title to any motor vehicle must furnish transferee written statement setting forth: odometer reading at time of transfer, date of transfer, transferor's name and address; transferee's name and address; make, model, body type, year, and vehicle identification number, and, statement that to best of knowledge of transferor odometer reflects actual mileage, or if transferor knows that it reflects mileage in excess of mechanical limit, statement to that effect, or if transferor knows odometer reading is not accurate, statement that it does not reflect actual mileage and should not be relied upon including notice alerting transferor that discrepancy exists. Foregoing statement not required for vehicles: with rating over 16,000 pounds, which are not self-propelled, which are ten or more years old or which are being transferred from manufacturer to dealer. Civil and criminal sanctions provided by statute. (MCLA §257.233a; MSA §9.1933[1]). New motor vehicle dealer must disclose in writing to purchaser any damage sustained by vehicle after manufacture. Disclosure not required for damages to glass, tires, wheels, bumpers, audio equipment, in-dash components or components in living quarters of motor home, not affecting its operation as vehicle, if replaced with manufacturer's parts and materials. (MCLA §257.233b; MSA §9.1933[2]). Where security interest created or reserved at time of transfer, see subhead Liens, infra.

Installment Sale.—Contracts for sale of motor vehicle payable in two or more installments are extensively regulated by MCLA §§492.101-.141; MSA §§23.628(1)-.628(41) as to form of contract, finance charge, and other matters. Sellers and persons who purchase, discount or lend on the security of motor vehicle paper are required to be licensed. Contract must state nature and amount of all items entering into time balance, payment schedule, collateral security, buyer's rights with respect to prepayment and reinstatement after default, and seller's rights with respect to default charges and repossession. Buyer must acknowledge in writing receipt of copy of contract and receive certificate evidencing insurance placed by seller at buyer's expense. Finance charges may not exceed amounts permitted by Credit Reform Act. (MCLA §§445.1851-.1864; MSA §§23.1300[51]-[64]). See category Business Regulation and Commerce, topic Interest.

Liens.—Governed by Uniform Commercial Code. (MCLA §§440.1101 et seq.; MSA §§19.1101 et seq.). See categories Business Regulation and Commerce, topic Commercial Code; Mortgages, topic Chattel Mortgages. Application for registration and certificate of title must show all liens. (MCLA §257.217; MSA §9.1917). Certificate of title must show all liens. (MCLA §257.222; MSA §9.1922). Title certificate is returned to owner of vehicle after notation of all security interests is made on such certificate by Secretary of State. (MCLA §§257.222, .234, .238; MSA §§9.1922, .1934, .1938). See category Business Regulation and Commerce, topic Sales, subhead Conditional Sales for liens on motor vehicle accessories and equipment sold on title retaining contract.

Identification Marks.—Any person who without intent to mislead, conceals or misrepresents identity of motor vehicle by removing or defacing manufacturer's serial number or engine or motor number, or by replacing any part of vehicle bearing serial number or motor number with new part on which proper number has not been stamped, is guilty of misdemeanor. Such acts with intent to mislead constitute felony. (MCLA §750.415; MSA §28.647).

Odometer Alteration.—Any person who alters or allows odometer to be altered is guilty of felony. (MCLA §257.233a; MSA §9.1933[1]).

Operation prohibited by habitual violator of laws relating to operation of vehicle under influence of alcohol or controlled substances, habitually reckless driver (two convictions of reckless driving within seven years), habitual criminal (two convictions of felony), any person convicted of negligent homicide, manslaughter or murder resulting from operation of motor vehicle, persons suffering from mental or physical disability such as to impair control of motor vehicle or who are unable to understand signs in English or to pass knowledge, skill, or ability test administered by Secretary of State, or any person whose license has been suspended or revoked. (MCLA §257.303; MSA §9.2003).

Size and Weight Limits.—Regulated by MCLA §§257.716-.725; MSA §§9.2416-.2425.

Equipment Required.—Regulated by MCLA §§257.683-.714b; MSA §§9.2383-.2414(2).

Seatbelts.—All front seat occupants must wear safety belt. Children under age 4 must have safety belt or child restraint system. Children between four and 16 must wear seatbelt unless seatbelts are in use and child is not in front seat unless vehicle is truck with no rear seat. Seatbelt requirements do not apply to certain classes of vehicles, including commercial vehicles making frequent stops. Failure to wear safety belt may reduce civil damage recovery by no more than 5%. (MCLA §257.710e; MSA §9.2410[5]).

Lights Required.—Regulated by MCLA §§257.684-.703; MSA §§9.2383-.2404.

Inspection.—Any uniformed police officer for reasonable cause may stop vehicle and inspect equipment. (MCLA §§257.715-.715a; MSA §§9.2415-.2415a).

Traffic Regulations.—Traffic signs, signals and markings regulated by MCLA §§257.608-.616; MSA §§9.2308-.2316. Speed restrictions regulated by MCLA §§257.672-.633; MSA §§9.2327-.2353. Overtaking and passing regulated by MCLA §§257.634-.645; MSA §§9.2334-.2345. Turning and starting regulated by MCLA §§257.647-.648; MSA §§9.2347-.2348. Right-of-way regulated by MCLA §§257.649-.655; MSA §§9.2349-.2355. Operation of bicycles, motorcycles and toy vehicles regulated by MCLA §§257.656-.662; MSA §§9.2356-.2362. Street cars and safety zones regulated by MCLA §§257.663-.666; MSA §§9.2363-.2366. Special stops regulated by MCLA §§257.667-.671; MSA §§9.2367-.2371. Stopping, standing and parking regulated by MCLA §§257.672-.675d; MSA §§9.2372-.2375d.

Accidents.—The driver of any vehicle involved in an accident must stop, give occupants of other car his name and address, registration number of his vehicle, and name and address of owner, and exhibit operator's license; and if personal injury has resulted, render reasonable assistance in securing medical aid or transportation. Leasing agency not liable at common law for damages for injuries to persons or property resulting from operation of vehicle leased to person for more than 30 day period. (MCLA §§257.617-.619; MSA §§9.2317-.2319.) If other vehicle or property damaged and owner or operator cannot be located, driver must report to most convenient police officer. (MCLA §§257.620-.621; MSA §§9.2320-.2321).

Liability of Owner.—Owner is liable for any injury occasioned by negligent operation of vehicle, if driven with his express or implied consent, which is presumed if driven by close relative or immediate member of family. Leasing agency not liable at common law for damages for injuries to persons or property resulting from operation of vehicle leased to person for more than 30 day period. (MCLA §257.401; MSA §9.2101).

Guests.—Michigan guest passenger statute, enacted in 1929 limited liability of owner or operator for injury to guest to cases involving gross negligence or wilful misconduct declared unconstitutional (394 Mich. 655, 232 N.W.2d 636). Negligence of driver is not imputed to passenger in action against third party. (313 Mich. 218, 21 N.W.2d 105).

Proof of Financial Responsibility.—If any judgment is not satisfied within 30 days, license and registration of judgment debtor, or privileges of nonresident, are suspended until judgment is satisfied and proof of financial responsibility furnished in form of certificate of insurance, bond, or deposit of money or securities with Secretary of State. (MCLA §§257.511-.528; MSA §§9.2211-.2228).

Insurance.—See subhead No-Fault Insurance, infra.

No-Fault Insurance.—So-called "no-fault" insurance statute adopted, requiring security for payment of benefits to be provided. Complex statutory regulation governs amount and type of recovery as well as procedure. Tort liability is preserved in cases of death, serious impairment of body function or permanent serious disfigurement. (MCLA §§500.3101 et seq.; MSA §24.13101 et seq.).

Foreign Vehicles.—Nonresident owner of foreign vehicle may operate or permit operation of vehicle within state without registering same, if vehicle is registered in and displays registration certificate and plates issued in place of residence of owner, but only for ten days if vehicle operated for transportation of persons for compensation and owner obtains temporary permit, only for 90 days if vehicle is pleasure vehicle, and not at all without registering same if owner operates vehicle in connection with business carried on in state. (MCLA §257.243; MSA §9.1943).

Nonresident Operators.—See subhead Foreign Vehicles, supra.

Actions Against Nonresidents.—Service of summons may be made on Secretary of State as agent of nonresident in any action growing out of operation of vehicle within state by nonresident, or of vehicle owned by nonresident with his consent. (MCLA §257.403; MSA §9.2103).

Direct Actions.—Action against insurer by injured person not allowed. (MCLA §500.3030; MSA §24.13030).

Motor Vehicle Carriers.—Subject to certain exemptions (MCLA §479.2; MSA §22.567), transportation of property by motor vehicle for hire upon and over public highways of state is subject to supervision and regulation by Michigan Public Service Commission. (MCLA §475.2; MSA §22.532). No change may be made in any rate except on notice to commission and public, and commission may investigate and pass upon reasonableness of rates. (MCLA §479.6a; MSA §22.571[1]). Common motor carriers must obtain certificate of authority. (MCLA §476.1; MSA §22.534). Contract motor carriers must obtain permit. (MCLA §477.1; MSA §22.548). Motor carriers of passengers, not operated by municipalities, require Certificate of Authority from state transportation department under Motor Bus Transportation Act. (MCLA §474.101 et seq.; MSA §9.1675[1] et seq.).

Motor Vehicle Taxes.—Registration fee imposed at time of registering motor vehicle. (MCLA §257.801; MSA §9.2501). Additional tax imposed upon common and contract carriers. (MCLA §§478.1-.8; MSA §§22.560-.565). Specific weight tax imposed upon public transportation vehicles and city and suburban buses in lieu of taxes imposed under MCLA §257.801; MSA §9.2501. (MCLA §§257.971-.972; MSA §§7.370[1]-.370[2]).

Gasoline Tax.—See category Taxation, topic Gasoline and Fuel Taxes.

Lemon Law.—See category Business Regulation and Commerce, topic Consumer Protection.

RAILROADS:

See category Business Regulation and Commerce, topic Carriers.

See note at head of Digest as to 1998 legislation covered.

See Topical Index in front part of this volume.

COMMERCIAL CODE FORMS

See also category Business Regulation and Commerce, topic Commercial Code; Mortgages, topic Chattel Mortgages.

Financing Statement.—UCC-1.

This FINANCING STATEMENT is presented for filing pursuant to the Michigan Uniform Commercial Code.	(Please Type All Information)	FOR FILING OFFICER (Date, Time, Number, and Filing Officer)

1. Debtor(s) (Last Name First, If Individual) & Address(es)	Soc. Security #/Tax ID #	DO NOT WRITE IN THIS SPACE

Address

City	State	Zip Code

Debtor(s) (Last name First, if Individual & Address(es)

Address

City	State	Zip Code

2. If Filing without debtor signature,

Item a, b, c, or d must be marked [X].

a. [ ] Collateral was already subject to the security interest in another state when it was brought into Michigan, or when the Debtor's location changed to Michigan;
b. [ ] Collateral is proceeds of the original collateral in which a security interest was perfected;
c. [ ] A previous filing covering the collateral has lapsed (Prev. Filing # _____);
d. [ ] The filing covers collateral acquired after a change of name identity, or corporate structure of Debtor (MCLA 440.9402(2) & (7)) FROM:_____

(Prev. Filing # _____).

3. Secured Party(ies) and Address(es)

Secured Party #	5. No. of Add'l Sheets	6. State Account No.

7. (Mark [X] if applicable):

[ ] Products of collateral are also covered.
[ ] The debtor is a transmitting utility as defined in MCLA 440.9105 (1)(o).

4. MAIL ACKNOWLEDGEMENT COPY TO:

8. Assignee(s) (If any) and Address(es)	Secured Party #

9. This financing statement covers the following types (or items) of property:

TERMINATION STATEMENT: This Statement of Termination is presented to a Filing Officer for filing pursuant to the Uniform Commercial Code. The Secured Party no longer claims a security interest under the financing statement bearing the file number shown above. (Secured Party will receive an acknowledgement of termination only if this form is filed in duplicate (photocopy) with the filing officer.)

Dated_____ , 19 _____   By: _____

Signature(s) of Secured Party(ies) or Assignee(s) of Record - *Not valid until signed*

IF YOU WISH THE ACKNOWLEDGEMENT COPY TO MAILED TO AN ADDRESS OTHER THAN THE SECURED PARTY SHOWN IN ITEM 3, PROVIDE COMPLETE MAILING INFORMATION IN ITEM 4.   UCC-1

SECRETARY OF STATE COPY-ACKNOWLEDGEMENT

See note at head of Digest as to 1998 legislation covered.

See Topical Index in front part of this volume.

Financing Statement.—UCC-3.

UCC 3 - STATE OF MICHIGAN

This FINANCING STATEMENT is presented for filing
pursuant to the Michigan Uniform Commercial Code.   (Please Type All Information)

FOR FILING OFFICER
(Date, Time, Number, and Filing Officer)

1. Debtor(s) (Last Name First, If Individual) & Address(es)   *Soc. Security #/Tax ID #*

DO NOT WRITE IN THIS SPACE

2. Secured Party(ies) & Address(es)   *Secured Party #*

4. No. of Add'l Sheets	*5. State Account No.*

3. MAIL ACKNOWLEDGEMENT COPY TO:

6. THIS STATEMENT REFERS TO THE
ORIGINAL FINANCING STATEMENT BEARING
THE FOLLOWING:

Sec. of State File Number _____

Reg. of Deeds File Number _____

Liber _____ Page _____

7. [ ]   AMENDMENT - The Financing Statement bearing the file number(s) shown in Item 6 is amended as set forth in Item 13 below.

8. [ ]   ASSIGNMENT - All of Secured Party's right under the Financing Statement bearing the file number shown in Item 6 has been assigned to the assignee whose name and address appears in Item 13 below.

9. [ ]   PARTIAL ASSIGNMENT - A portion of the Secured Party's right under the Financing Statement bearing the file number shown in Item 6 to the property described in Item 13 below has been assigned to the assignee whose name and address appears in Item 13.

10. [ ]   CONTINUATION - The original Financing Statement bearing the file number shown in Item 6 is still effective. A CONTINUATION CANNOT BE FILED MORE THAN SIX MONTHS PRIOR TO EXPIRATION DATE.

11. [ ]   PARTIAL RELEASE - The Secured Party(ies) release(s) the following collateral described in Item 13 below from the original Financing Statement bearing the file number as shown in Item 6.

12. [ ]   TERMINATION - The Secured Party(ies) of record no longer claim(s) a security interest under the Financing Statement bearing the file number shown in Item 6.

13.

X _____

Signature(s) of Debtor(s)

X _____

Signature(s) of Secured Party(ies) or Assignee(s) of Record

X _____

Signature(s) of Debtor(s)

X _____

Signature(s) of Secured Party(ies) or Assignee(s) of Record

IF YOU WISH THE ACKNOWLEDGEMENT COPY TO MAILED TO AN ADDRESS OTHER THAN THE SECURED PARTY SHOWN IN ITEM 2, PROVIDE COMPLETE MAILING INFORMATION IN ITEM 3.

FILING OFFICER COPY

See note at head of Digest as to 1998 legislation covered.

See Topical Index in front part of this volume.

MINNESOTA LAW DIGEST REVISER

Faegre & Benson LLP
90 South Seventh Street
Minneapolis, Minnesota 55402-3901
Firm Telephone: 612-336-3000
Firm Fax: 612-336-3026
E-Mail Contact: rhentges@faegre.com

Reviser Profile

Faegre & Benson offers clients more than 290 lawyers in a full range of practice groups, with experience handling legal matters throughout the United States, as well as Europe and Asia. The firm maintains offices in Minneapolis, Denver, Des Moines, and Frankfurt, Germany, and offers on-site English legal services in London through its multi-national partnership, Faegre Benson Hobson Audley.

Established in Minneapolis in 1886 as Cobb & Wheelwright, the firm evolved with the region, serving as a legal partner for growing firms in retailing, banking, manufacturing, and mass media. Today, the firm continues to serve both established and emerging companies, including the region's largest merchant, largest bank, largest newspaper, and a wide range of national and international companies in such industries as medical devices, technology and software, health care, securities, agri-business, and construction.

When *American Lawyer* magazine surveyed four hundred corporate counsel and asked them to rate the law firms they had used in the past two years, Faegre & Benson was ranked among the top firms in the United States in nine of the eleven categories: bankruptcy and workouts, corporate, employment, environmental, insurance, intellectual property, litigation, mergers and acquisition, and tax. Nationwide, only six firms were ranked in more categories than Faegre & Benson.

The firm offers a wide range of sophisticated practice areas:

Litigation: Faegre & Benson has one of the largest litigation practices in the region, with experience in litigating matters at every level of the state and federal court systems, including the United States Supreme Court. The firm regularly litigates in construction, product liability, intellectual property, toxic torts, franchise and dealer disputes, employment law, insurance, antitrust, bankruptcy, contract and other commercial litigation.

Corporate: The firm regularly handles multi-billion-dollar mergers and acquisitions for leading regional and national companies. The firm has also provided legal counsel in connection with hundreds of public debt and equity offerings in the United States and Europe.

Banking: The firm has represented large and small financial institutions for over 75 years, including Norwest Bank and its affiliates, as well as one of the region's largest thrifts and a diverse group of banks and holding companies.

Construction: Faegre & Benson lawyers have represented owners, developers, engineers, architects, sureties and material suppliers in disputes venued in more than twenty-five states, totaling hundreds of millions of dollars.

Employee Benefits: Faegre & Benson has one of the largest groups of lawyers in the nation working in employee benefits law. The proficiency of the firm in employee benefits, ERISA and executive compensation matters has attracted clients from across the country.

Environmental: Lawyers in Faegre & Benson's environmental practice regularly represent clients in litigation and administrative proceedings, including Superfund actions, waste management, toxic tort litigation and the defense of criminal environmental claims.

Government Relations: The firm's government relations lawyers work to correct client issues by consulting with officials, drafting legislation, rules and regulations, and advancing these proposals through appropriate governmental bodies.

Health: Faegre & Benson's health law practitioners represent some of the Midwest region's leading health care providers, HMO's and PPOs, providing a cross-disciplinary perspective on the unique problems of health service enterprises.

Intellectual Property: Faegre & Benson counsels clients on strategies for protecting their intellectual property; prepares and prosecutes patent applications; handles trademark applications, oppositions and cancellations in the United States Patent and Trademark Office; and assists clients with licensing and copyright matters.

International: The firm counsels domestic companies on the legal, financial, tax and regulatory matters affecting business operations in the international market and represents foreign businesses in connection with trading and investment in the United States.

Labor and Employment: The firm advises private and public employers on issues in the workplace and represents employers in all types of employment-related litigation.

Media and Entertainment: The firm regularly counsels national media and entertainment clients. Faegre & Benson lawyers have been at the cutting edge of First Amendment theory in several cases which reached the United States Supreme Court.

Nonprofit Organizations: Faegre & Benson represents a diverse group of nonprofit organizations, including many of the region's best known churches, museums, orchestras, schools, and foundations.

Public Finance: During the last 35 years, Faegre & Benson has served as bond counsel for more than 350 communities and agencies for bond issues totaling several billion dollars.

Real Estate: Lawyers at the firm are experienced in handling the complex transactional details of commercial real estate, including construction agreements, leases, eminent domain, zoning, land use, and title claim issues.

Tax: Faegre & Benson provides tax counseling in connection with business and financial transactions of major publicly held corporations, partnerships, family businesses, and individuals.

Trusts and Estate Planning: Faegre & Benson provides estate planning and administration services to clients seeking to conserve and manage personal or family assets, including closely-held businesses.

MINNESOTA LAW DIGEST

(The following is a list of all Categories and Topics, including cross-references, covered in this Digest.)

MINNESOTA LAW DIGEST

Revised for 1999 edition by

FAEGRE & BENSON LLP, of the Minneapolis Bar.

(Citations, unless otherwise indicated, are to Minnesota Statutes 1996 which are numbered according to a decimal system by which figures preceding decimal point indicate chapters and those following indicate sections. Session Laws are cited by year and chapter number. Prefix RCP refers to Rules of Civil Procedure for the District Courts. Prefix CAP refers to Rules of Appellate Procedure. Rules for all courts appear in Appendix to Minnesota Statutes. Parallel citations to the North Western Reporter begin with 26 Minn. Official reporter discontinued following 312 Minn.)

Note: Legislature was adjourned at time of going to press. This revision incorporates 1997 Second and Third Special Session, 1998 Session Laws and 1998 Special Session.

INTRODUCTION

GOVERNMENT AND LEGAL SYSTEM:

The State of Minnesota is a constituent state of the United States of America. For further discussion of the U.S. federal system, see Introduction to the Federal Government of the United States at the beginning of this volume. A great many laws are promulgated by the federal government of the United States and are not reflected in the topics below. See the Introduction to this volume for references to the federal law topics covered.

Like all but one of the United States, Minnesota has a common law legal system, with roots in English common law. For information on the courts and legislature of Minnesota, see category Courts and Legislature.

HOLIDAYS:

Legal holidays are: New Year's Day, Jan. 1; Martin Luther King Jr.'s Birthday, 3d Mon. in Jan.; Washington's and Lincoln's Birthday, 3d Mon. in Feb.; Memorial Day, last Mon. in May; Independence Day, July 4; Labor Day, 1st Mon. in Sept.; Columbus Day, 2d Mon. in Oct.; Veterans Day, Nov. 11; Thanksgiving Day, 4th Thurs. in Nov.; and Christmas Day, Dec. 25. If Jan. 1, July 4, Nov. 11 or Dec. 25 falls on Sun., following day is holiday; if on Sat., then preceding day is holiday. (645.44).

Uniform Commercial Code adopted. See category Business Regulation and Commerce, topic Commercial Code.

Legality of Transactions on Holiday.—Acknowledgment (41 Minn. 269, 43 N. W. 7) or publication of summons (50 Minn. 457, 52 N. W. 915) on holiday is valid, but no civil process may be served thereon (645.44).

OFFICE HOURS AND TIME ZONE:

Minnesota is in the Central Standard (GMT −06:00) time zone. Office hours are generally from 9 a.m. to 5 p.m.

BUSINESS ORGANIZATIONS

AGENCY:

Common law rules generally apply.

Exclusive agency does not prevent principal from acting. (41 Minn. 535, 43 N.W. 569).

Adoption of act by one not previously authorized constitutes agency for similar act; but not for dissimilar act. (38 Minn. 66, 35 N.W. 568). Knowledge acquired in employment in no way connected with agency is not notice to principal (47 Minn. 352, 50 N.W. 240) unless such knowledge actually present in agent's mind while acting for principal (46 Minn. 298, 49 N.W. 129).

Disclosure of principal pending transaction relieves agent from liability. (38 Minn. 79, 35 N.W. 575; 61 Minn. 277, 63 N.W. 734). Agent liable unless he discloses principal. (59 Minn. 476, 61 N.W. 448).

ASSOCIATIONS:

Two or more persons transacting business as associates under common name may be sued by such name, and judgment binds joint property of all associates as though all had been named defendants. (540.15). No other general statutes except as to service of process. See category Civil Actions and Procedure, topic Process.

Religious associations are governed by c. 315.

Professional Associations.—See topic Corporations, subhead Professional Firms.

CORPORATIONS:

General.—Legislature can create only by general laws and not by special charter. Cannot amend, renew, extend or explain charter by special law. (Const., art. 12, §1). New business corporation act generally effective July 1, 1981. (c. 302A). Replaces business corporation act of 1933 (c. 301), which in turn replaced prior statutes (c. 300). Corporations formed under c. 300 became subject to c. 301 unless they elected otherwise prior to May 1, 1935. Any corporation formed for business purposes under c. 300 that has not subsequently become governed by c. 301 may elect to become governed by c. 302A. All business corporations in existence on or formed after Jan. 1, 1984 (except nonelecting corporations under c. 300) are governed by c. 302A. (302A.021).

Nonprofit Corporations.—New nonprofit corporation act was enacted in 1989. (c. 317A). As of Jan. 1, 1991, all nonprofit corporations even if incorporated under c. 317 or another statute, are governed by c. 317A. (317A.021). Acts apply to nonprofit corporations generally except cemeteries, cooperatives, certain religious corporations and certain others. (317A.051). Initial registration with Secretary of State is required between Jan. 1 and Dec. 31, 1990. Failure to file initial registration causes loss of good standing. (317A.821). Annual registration is required thereafter. (317A.823).

An act for organization and operation of development corporations adopted in 1957. (301.71-.84).

Act governing professional corporations was enacted in 1973. (c. 319A). Minnesota Professional Firms Act adopted 1997. (c. 319B). See infra subhead Professional Firms.

Purposes.—Corporation may be formed for any business purpose or purposes, unless some other statute requires incorporation for any of those purposes under different law. Unless otherwise provided in its articles, corporation has general business purposes. (302A.101).

Corporate name must contain word "corporation," "incorporated," "limited" or abbreviation of one of those words, or contain word "company" or abbreviation "Co." if that word or abbreviation not immediately preceded by "and" or "&." Name must be distinguishable upon records in office of Secretary of State from name of any other domestic corporation, limited partnership, limited liability partnership and limited liability company whether profit or nonprofit or foreign corporation, limited partnership, limited liability partnership or limited liability company authorized to do business in state. Secretary of State has authority to determine what is or is not "distinguishable" name. Applicant may obtain use of name that is same as or not distinguishable from another corporation, limited partnership, limited liability partnership or limited liability company by filing written consent, court decree of prior right, or certificate of inability to locate corporation, limited partnership or limited liability company formed or registered more than three years previously. Person doing business in state may contest subsequent registration of name. (302A.115). Procedure established for reservation of corporate name for unlimited number of 12-month periods. (302A.117).

Term of corporate existence of corporation under c. 302A is perpetual unless limited in articles. (302A.161). For renewal of term of c. 302A corporations whose articles limit their duration, see 302A.801. Term can be renewed after expiration and relates back to date of expiration. (302A.801, .805). For extension of term of nonprofit and like corporations, see 317A.801. For renewal of c. 300 corporations, see 300.13.

Incorporators.—One or more natural persons of full age may form business corporation. No statutory requirements as to citizenship or residence of incorporators. (302A.105).

Articles of incorporation must be signed by one or more incorporators; must state corporate name, address of registered office, aggregate number of shares corporation has authority to issue and name and address of each incorporator. (302A.111). Certain statutory provisions govern corporation unless modified in articles or, in certain instances, either in articles or bylaws. Checklist of these statutory provisions that may be modified only in articles, or either in articles or bylaws, and certain other optional provisions is set forth in 302A.111. Articles may establish or authorize board of directors to issue more than one class or series of shares. (302A.401). Liability of directors for certain breaches of fiduciary duty may be limited in articles. (302A.251). Board of directors has statutory authority, subject to any restrictions in articles, to issue securities, rights to purchase securities, to establish relative rights and preferences of different classes and series (302A.401) and to authorize distributions (302A.551).

Filing of Articles.—Articles effective and corporate existence begins when articles are filed with Secretary of State, together with payment of fees. (302A.153).

Filing Fees.—Filing fee of $35 paid to Secretary of State for filing any instrument required to be filed under c. 302A. (302A.011, subd. 11). For merger, additional fee of $25. (302A.153).

Total fees payable to Secretary of State for filing original articles under c. 302A are $135, including $100 incorporation fee and $35 filing fee. (302A.153).

Filing fees to be paid by c. 300 corporation to Secretary of State are: For filing original articles, $100; for filing any other instrument required by c. 300, $35. For merger, additional fee of $25. Not applicable to cooperative associations or corporations organized without capital stock and not for pecuniary profit. (300.49).

Additional $20 fee is charged for expedited over-the-counter filings with Secretary of State.

Notice of Incorporation—Publication not required.

Paid-in Capital Requirement.—There is no paid-in capital requirement under c. 302A.

Amendment of articles so as to include, modify or omit any provision which could have been lawfully included in, modified or omitted from original articles, or so as to extend corporate duration, may be adopted at any meeting of shareholders or by written action of all shareholders. (302A.131). Amendments proposed either by resolution approved by majority vote of directors or by shareholders owning 3% or more of shares entitled to vote may be submitted to vote at next regular or special shareholders meeting for which notice has not been but still can be timely given. Written notice to shareholders stating substance of proposed amendment required at least ten days prior to meeting or shorter time provided in articles or by-laws. Same or substantially same amendment proposed by shareholders need not be submitted to more than one shareholders' meeting during 15-month period. Proposed amendment is adopted when

See note at head of Digest as to 1998 legislation covered.

See Topical Index in front part of this volume.

CORPORATIONS . . . *continued*
approved by affirmative vote of shareholders required by 302A.437. However, in case of closely held corporation, if articles provide for specified proportion or number equal to or larger than majority, or if, in case of closely held corporation, proposed amendment seeks to provide for specified proportion or number equal to or larger than majority needed to transact specified type of business at meeting, proposed amendment must receive larger of vote necessary to transact that type of business prior to, or vote necessary to transact that type of business after, amendment becomes effective. For corporation other than closely held corporations, if articles provide for larger proportion or number to transact specified type of business at meeting, affirmative vote of that larger proportion or number is necessary to amend articles to decrease proportion or number. (302A.135). Capital stock may be increased or decreased by amendment of articles. Class voting is required if amendment would: (1) Increase or decrease aggregate number of authorized shares of class or series; (2) effect exchange, reclassification or cancellation of all or part of class or series; (3) effect exchange or create right of exchange of all or any part of shares of another class or series for shares of class or series; (4) change rights and preferences of class or series; (5) change shares of class or series into same or different number of shares of another class or series; (6) create new class or series having prior and superior preference or increase rights and preferences or number of authorized shares of class or series having prior or superior rights and preferences; (7) divide class into series and determine or authorize board to determine rights and preferences of each series; (8) limit or deny existing preemptive rights of class or series; or (9) cancel or otherwise effect distributions on shares of class or series that have accrued but not been declared. (302A.137). Amendments which have effect of denying, limiting or modifying right to cumulative voting or, if shareholders are entitled to cumulative voting, preemptive rights are not adopted if votes of proportion of voting power sufficient to elect director at election of entire board under cumulative voting are cast against amendment. (302A.215, 302A.413). Amendment effective upon filing with Secretary of State of articles of amendment signed by person authorized by c. 302A, articles, by-laws or duly adopted resolution, or upon such later date within 30 days after filing if amendment so provides. $35 filing fee. (302A.139, .153). Shareholder objecting to proposed amendment that materially and adversely affects rights or preferences of his shares in that it: (1) Alters or abolishes preferential right of shares; (2) creates, alters or abolishes right in respect of redemption of shares, including provision respecting sinking fund for redemption of shares; (3) alters or abolishes preemptive right to acquire shares, securities other than shares or rights to purchase shares or securities other than shares; or (4) excludes or limits right of shareholder to vote on matter, or to cumulate votes, except as right may be excluded or limited through authorization or issuance of securities of existing or new class or series with similar or different voting rights or termination of applicability of control share acquisition provisions (see subhead Control Share Acquisitions, infra), has right to dissent and obtain payment of fair value of shares by filing with corporation before vote on amendment written notice of intent to demand fair value of shares. If amendment approved, corporation must supply form of demand with instructions for use by dissenting shareholder. Appraisal procedure provided if corporation and dissenting shareholder cannot agree on value of shares. Corporation must forward payment of amount it determines to be fair value of shares, plus interest, pending appraisal. (302A.471, .473).

Increase or Decrease of Authorized Capital Stock.—See supra, subhead Amendment of Articles.

By-laws.—Corporation may, but need not, have by-laws. Board of directors may adopt, amend or repeal by-laws unless power reserved by articles to shareholders, subject to power of shareholders to adopt, amend or repeal by-laws adopted, amended or repealed by board. However, board of directors cannot make or alter any by-law fixing shareholder quorum, prescribing procedures for removal or replacement of directors or fixing their qualifications, classifications, term of office, or number, except that board may make or alter any by-law to increase their number. (302A.181).

Stock.—Articles may establish, or authorize board to establish, more than one class or series. Unless so established by board or specifically provided in articles, all shares are one class and one series, are common shares entitled to vote and having equal rights and preferences in all matters not otherwise provided by board and have 1¢ par value solely for tax purposes. Board of directors explicitly granted power to authorize issuance of shares and to fix rights and preferences attached to such shares, subject to any restrictions in articles. (302A.401).

Stock Certificates.—Shares may be either certificated or uncertificated. Certificates must state on their face: (1) Name of corporation; (2) statement that corporation is incorporated under Minnesota law; (3) name of person to whom issued; (4) number, class and designation of series, if any, that certificate represents. Certificate representing shares issued by corporation authorized to issue more than one class or series must state on face or back, or must state corporation will furnish upon request and without charge, full statement of designations, preferences, limitations and relative rights, so far as they have been determined, and authority of board of directors to so determine relative rights and preferences of subsequent classes or series. Each certificate must be signed by agent or officer authorized by articles or by-laws to sign certificates, or, in absence of such authorization, by officer. (302A.417). Such signatures may be facsimiles. (302A.011, Subd. 30).

Issuance of Stock.—Subject to any restrictions in articles, shares may be issued for any consideration, including money or other tangible or intangible property received or to be received by corporation under written agreement or services rendered or to be rendered to corporation under written agreement if authorized by resolution approved by affirmative vote of directors required by 302A.237 or, if provided for in articles, approved by affirmative vote of shareholders required by 302A.437. Price in money or other consideration, or minimum price or general formula or method by which price will be determined must be established. No consideration needed for exchange or conversion of corporation's shares or for share dividends, divisions, or combinations. Corporation may issue shares only upon receipt of consideration in full or with unanimous consent of shareholders. Consideration in form of promissory note, check or written agreement to transfer property or render services in future fully paid when note, check or written agreement is delivered to corporation. Directors or shareholders who are present and entitled to vote and who intentionally or without reasonable investigation fail to vote against approving issuance for consideration unfair to corporation are jointly and severally liable to shareholders who did not consent to extent of damages. Directors or shareholders present and entitled to vote who fail to vote against issuance knowing full consideration has not been paid are jointly and severally liable for difference between agreed consideration and consideration actually received by corporation if shares issued in violation of statute. Original shareholder and any transferee or successor in interest acquiring shares with knowledge of such violation also liable to same extent. Liability of pledgees limited to assets held as security. Any person found liable may sue any or all other persons found liable for contribution. Two year statute of limitations. (302A.405).

Transfer of Stock.—Uniform Commercial Code adopted. (c. 336). See category Business Regulation and Commerce, topic Commercial Code.

Subsection (2), §10-104 in 1962 Official Text adopted.

Uniform Securities Ownership by Minors Act not adopted.

Uniform Simplification of Fiduciary Security Transfers Act adopted. (520.21-31).

As to fixing record date for stock ownership, see infra, subhead Shareholders' Meetings.

Stock Transfer Tax.—None.

Shareholders' Inspection Rights.—Corporation required to keep at principal executive office, or if principal executive office out of state, to make available within ten days of shareholder demand, records of all proceedings of shareholders and directors for last three years, articles as amended, by-laws as amended, reports to shareholders within last three years, names and business addresses of directors and principal officers, voting trust agreements, shareholder control agreements and certain financial statements and contracts. Corporation also required to keep shareholder register at principal executive office or another place within U.S. named by board. Shareholders of corporation not publicly held given absolute right upon written demand to inspect and copy all documents required to be kept at such location and share register without showing "proper purpose within ten days after receipt by an officer of the written demand." Any other corporate records may be examined and copied by such shareholders upon written demand only upon showing of "proper purpose." Shareholders of "publicly held corporation" have, upon written demand stating purpose with reasonable particularity, acknowledged or verified, right to examine and copy corporation's share register and other corporate records reasonably related to stated purpose upon demonstrating stated purpose to be "proper purpose". Shareholder can only use records for "proper purpose" and corporation may obtain protective order or other relief as necessary. Corporation may obtain protective order from court in state permitting corporation to withhold portions of records of board for reasonable period of time, not to exceed 12 months, to prevent premature disclosure of confidential information which would be likely to cause competitive injury to corporation. Protective order may be renewed for successive 12 month periods, in total not exceeding 36 months. (302A.461). Corporation must prepare annual financial statements on basis of accounting methods reasonable in circumstances within 180 days after close of corporation's fiscal year and furnish such financial statements within ten days after written request by shareholder. (302A.463).

Shareholders' Liabilities.—Double liability of shareholders abolished, except as to certain banks. For liability of shareholders of banks and trust companies, see category Business Regulation and Commerce, topic Banks and Banking.

As to liability of shareholders where stock issued for inadequate consideration or less than full consideration, see supra, subhead Issuance of Stock. As to liability of shareholders receiving unlawful dividends or distributions, see infra, subhead Distributions.

Shareholders' Meetings.—Regular meetings may be held on annual or less frequent periodic basis but need not be held unless required by articles, by -laws or by demand of shareholder. If regular meeting not held during 15-month period, shareholders holding 3% of shares entitled to vote may demand regular meeting by sending written notice of demand to chief executive or chief financial officer. Within 30 days of receipt of demand, board must cause regular meeting to be called and held on notice no later than 90 days after receipt of demand, or if board fails to do so, shareholders making demand may call meeting by giving notice required by 302A.435. Regular meetings to be held on day and at time and place fixed by, or in manner authorized by, articles or by-laws, except for meetings called by or at demand of shareholders which must be held in county where principal executive office of corporation located. (302A.431). Special meetings may be called for any purpose at any time by chief executive officer, chief financial officer, two or more directors, any person authorized by articles or by-laws to call special meeting or, except for special meeting to facilitate business combination, shareholders holding 10% or more of shares entitled to vote. Shareholders holding 25% or more of shares entitled to vote may call special meeting to facilitate business combination. Procedure for demand of special meeting by shareholders similar to demand for regular meeting. (302A.433). Written notice specifying date, time and place, and purpose of special meeting or if otherwise required by articles, by-laws or law, must be given in accordance with statutory provisions. Waiver of notice effective whether given before, at or after meeting, and whether given in writing, orally or by attendance. Attendance constitutes waiver, unless objection made at beginning of meeting because meeting not lawfully convened or before vote on item because item may not lawfully be considered and objecting shareholder does not participate in consideration of item at meeting. (302A.435). Unless articles or by-laws specify larger or smaller proportion or number, holders of majority of voting power of shares entitled to vote are quorum for transaction of business. If quorum is present when meeting is convened, meeting may continue even though shareholder's withdrawal leaves less than quorum. (302A.443). Bylaws of closely held corporation may allow shareholder attendance at regular or special meetings by any means of communication that allows all shareholders to simultaneously hear each other. Participation by electronic communications also constitutes presence in person, or by proxy if proxy requirements are otherwise met, for quorum and waiver of notice purposes.

See note at head of Digest as to 1998 legislation covered.

See Topical Index in front part of this volume.

MN – 2

CORPORATIONS . . . *continued*
(302A.436). Except as required by law or in articles, shareholders take action by affirmative vote of greater of majority of voting power of (1) shares present and entitled to vote on that item of business, or (2) minimum number entitled to vote that would constitute quorum. In certain situations class voting may also be required. (302A.437). Any action required or permitted to be taken at meeting may be taken without meeting by written action signed by all shareholders entitled to vote on action. Such action is effective on date of last signature unless different effective time is provided in written action. (302A.441).

Voting.—Unless articles or terms of shares provide otherwise, each shareholder has one vote per share. Board may fix date not more than 60 days before date of meeting for determination of holders of shares entitled to notice of and to vote at meeting. When date is so fixed, only holders on that date are entitled to notice and permitted to vote. Unless corporation receives written notice to contrary, shares held jointly may be voted by any one of joint owners. When shareholder votes without signifying how many shares voted, all shares deemed voted. Articles may give or prescribe manner of giving creditor, security holder or other person right to vote. Board may establish procedure for treating beneficial owners as shareholders. (302A.445). Unless articles expressly provide that there shall be no cumulative voting, shareholders may cumulate their votes for election of directors if any shareholder gives written notice of intent to cumulate votes to any officer before meeting or to presiding officer at meeting at any time before vote. (302A.215). Specific rules regarding voting of shares by organizations and legal representatives. (302A.447). Shareholder may cast vote in person or through written proxy filed with officer of corporation at or before meeting. Written proxy may be signed by shareholder or authorized by electronic transmission. If shareholder gives proxy authority to vote on less than all items of business to be conducted at meeting, shareholder is considered present only with respect to those items. Proxy rules permit joint owner to appoint proxy unless another joint owner notifies corporation denying authority of first joint owner to appoint proxy or appoints different proxy, and permit corporation to accept votes of proxy without determining that vote is within authority of proxy. (302A.449). Special proxy rules with respect to control share acquisition, see infra, subhead Control Share Acquisitions.

Voting trusts may be entered into pursuant to written agreement for period not to exceed 15 years, except that if agreement is made in connection with indebtedness of corporation voting trust may extend until indebtedness is discharged. Unless otherwise specified therein, such voting trust may be terminated at any time by beneficial owners of majority of voting power of shares held by trustee. Copy of agreement must be filed with corporation. (302A.453).

Shareholder Voting Agreements.—Written agreement among shareholders or subscribers for shares, relating to voting of shares, is valid and specifically enforceable by and against parties. Agreement may override proxy rules and is not subject to voting trust provisions. (302A.455).

Shareholder Control Agreements.—Written agreement among shareholders and subscribers for shares relating to control of any phase of business and affairs of corporation, its liquidation and dissolution or relations among shareholders of or subscribers to shares is valid and specifically enforceable if it is signed by all persons who are then shareholders and subscribers. Copy of agreement must be filed with corporation. (302A.457).

Directors.—Corporation's business and affairs are to be managed by or under direction of board of directors, subject to any shareholder control agreement and power of holders of shares entitled to vote for directors to take by unanimous vote any action required or permitted by board. First board may be named in articles or elected by incorporators or shareholders. (302A.201). Board shall consist of one or more directors, number of whom shall be fixed by or in manner provided in articles or by-laws. Number of directors may be increased or decreased, subject to statutory limitations on removal of directors, by amendment to or in manner provided by articles or by-laws. (302A.203). Directors must be natural persons. Method of election and other qualifications may be imposed by or in manner provided in articles or by-laws. (302A.205). Directors may hold office for indefinite term, but any director serving indefinite term or whose term will expire within six months of regular shareholder meeting must stand for reelection at such meeting. (302A.207, .431). Fixed terms may be provided for in articles or by-laws but shall not exceed five years. (302A.207). Unless different rules for filling vacancies are provided in articles or by-laws, vacancies resulting from death, resignation, removal or disqualification may be filled by majority vote of remaining directors, even though less than quorum; vacancies resulting from newly created directorships may be filled by majority vote of directors serving at time of increase. (302A.225).

Directors' meetings may be held at such place within or without state as board may select or, if board fails to select place for board meeting, at principal executive office of corporation unless articles or by-laws provide otherwise. Meetings may be called by any director by giving ten days written notice or such shorter or longer notice as articles or by-laws may require. (302A.231). Except where articles or statute require affirmative vote of larger proportion or number, board acts by affirmative vote of greater of (1) majority of directors present at time of action or (2) majority of minimum proportion or number of directors that would constitute quorum. (302A.237). Quorum is majority unless larger or smaller proportion or number provided in articles or by-laws. (302A.235).

Directors authorized to give advance written consent or opposition to proposal to be acted upon at board meeting at which director will be absent if articles or by-laws so provide and proposal acted upon at meeting is substantially same or has substantially same effect as proposal to which absent director consented or opposed. Such consent or opposition does not constitute presence for purpose of quorum. (302A.233). Action required or permitted to be taken at board meeting may be taken by written action signed by all directors. If action need not be approved by shareholders and articles so provide, directors may act by written action taken by number of directors that would be required to take such action at meeting of board at which all directors were present. Written notice of such action must be given immediately to all directors. (302A.239). Presence at board meeting deemed to be assent to action taken thereat unless director registers dissent as provided in statute or is prohibited from voting because of conflict. (302A.251).

Committees.—Board may establish by affirmative vote of majority of board committees having authority of board in management of corporation to extent provided in resolution establishing committee. Committee may include special litigation committee consisting of one or more independent directors or other independent persons. Committee members may be appointed by affirmative vote of majority of directors present and need not be directors. (302A.241).

Liabilities of Directors.—Directors must act in good faith, in manner they reasonably believe to be in best interests of corporation and with care ordinarily prudent person in like position would exercise in similar circumstances. Directors who so perform their duties are not liable by reason of being or having been director. Director is entitled to rely on information, opinions and reports or statements of certain persons, such as counsel, public accountants, committees and other persons director reasonably believes to be reliable and competent. With certain exceptions, liability of directors for certain breaches of fiduciary duty may be limited in articles. (302A.251). As to liabilities of directors where unfair, or less than full consideration has been paid, see supra, subhead Issuance of Stock, or where directors authorize illegal dividend or distribution, see infra, subhead Distributions.

Registered Office.—Every corporation must maintain an office in the state known as its registered office, which can be changed by action of directors, without amending articles. Filing with Secretary of State required. (302A.121, .123).

Officers.—Corporation required to have one or more persons exercising functions of chief executive officer and chief financial officer. (302A.301). Duties of each specified by law unless articles, by-laws or board resolution provide otherwise. (302A.305). Board may elect or appoint other officers in manner specified by articles, by-laws or board resolution. (302A.311). Any offices may be held or exercised by same person. (302A.315). Officers are to discharge duties in good faith, in manner they reasonably believe to be in best interests of corporation and with care ordinarily prudent person in like position would exercise under similar circumstances. (302A.361).

Powers.—Unless limited by any other applicable statute of state, corporation has perpetual duration and has broad powers to: Sue and be sued; own and dispose of real and personal property; trade in securities and obligations of domestic and foreign governments and instrumentalities; make contracts, incur liabilities and secure any of its obligations; make investments; hold real and personal property as security; make donations irrespective of corporate benefit for public welfare; pay pensions, retirement allowances and compensation for past services and establish employee or incentive benefit plans; participate in promotion, organization, ownership, management and operation that participating corporation would have power to conduct by itself; provide life insurance and other insurance for officers, directors, employees and agents or on life of shareholder for purpose of acquiring shares at death; conduct business under assumed names; and may have and exercise all other powers necessary or convenient to effect any or all business purposes for which corporation is incorporated. Corporation may, but need not, have corporate seal. (302A.161).

Loans, Guarantees, Suretyship.—Corporation may lend money to, guarantee obligation of or otherwise assist any person if transaction is approved by majority of directors present and (1) is in usual and regular course of business, (2) is with or for benefit of related corporation or organization in which corporation has financial interest, business relationship or power to make donations or (3) is approved by holders of two-thirds of voting power of shares other than those held by interested person or by holders of all outstanding shares.

Corporation may lend money to, guarantee obligation of, or otherwise assist officer or other employee of corporation or subsidiary, including one who is director, whenever majority of directors present determines loan, guaranty or assistance may reasonably be expected to benefit corporation. May be with or without interest and secured or unsecured. (302A.501). Corporation may make advances for expenses, without director vote, to directors, officers and employees. (302A.505).

As to restrictions on ownership of real property by corporations having alien stockholders, see category Citizenship, topic Aliens.

As to conveyances by corporations, see category Property, topic Deeds.

Distributions.—Corporation may make distributions (defined as direct or indirect transfers of money or other property, other than own shares, or incurrence or issuance of indebtedness by corporation to shareholders, including cash dividends, distributions in liquidation, redemptions, purchases or other share acquisitions) provided that corporation will be able to pay debts in ordinary course of business after making such distribution. Such determination shall be made by board of directors in compliance with statutory standard of conduct (good faith, in manner director reasonably believes in best interests of corporation, and with care of ordinarily prudent person in like position under similar circumstances) on basis of financial information prepared in accordance with accounting methods or fair valuation or other method reasonable in circumstances. Effect of distribution in connection with purchase, redemption, or other acquisition of shares to be measured as of date on which money or other property transferred, or on date indebtedness payable in installments or otherwise is incurred, or on date shareholder ceases to be shareholder, whichever is earliest. Effect of other distributions measured as of date of authorization if payment within 120 days of authorization; as of date of payment if more than 120 days. (302A.251, .551). Shareholder liability for unlawful distribution only to extent distribution exceeded amount which properly could have been paid. (302A.557). Directors not liable if determination made in compliance with statutory standard of conduct on basis described above and only liable to extent distribution exceeded amount which properly could have been paid. Director may seek contribution from all other liable parties. Two year statute of limitations. (302A.559).

Share Dividends, Divisions or Combinations.—Shares may be issued pro rata to shareholders, or to shareholders of one or more classes or series, to effect share dividends, or divisions or combinations, provided no shares of any class or series

See note at head of Digest as to 1998 legislation covered.

See Topical Index in front part of this volume.

MN – 3

CORPORATIONS ... *continued*

which are then outstanding shall be issued to holders of another class or series (except in exchange for or in conversion of outstanding shares of other class or series) unless articles expressly provide for such issuance or issuance is approved by majority of voting power of all shares of same class or series. (302A.405). If share division or combination adversely affects rights and preferences of outstanding shares, or if percentage of unissued shares after division or combination exceeds percentage before, articles of amendment must be adopted by board and shareholders. Otherwise, board may effect share dividend, division or combination without shareholder approval. (302A.402).

Disposal of Assets.—Corporation may, by affirmative vote of majority of directors present, and without shareholder approval sell, lease, transfer or otherwise dispose of all or substantially all of corporate assets in usual and regular course of its business, grant security interest in part or all of its assets, whether or not in usual and regular course of its business, or transfer any or all of its property to corporation all shares of which are owned by corporation. Board of directors may sell, lease, transfer or otherwise dispose of all or substantially all of corporate assets, including good will, not in usual and regular course of its business, when and as authorized by written consent of all shareholders or by vote of holders of majority, or greater proportion as articles may require, of shares entitled to vote. (302A.661). Shareholders dissenting from transfer of assets may demand in writing before vote payment of fair value for shares unless net proceeds are to be distributed in accordance with respective interests of shareholders within one year after date of disposition. (302A.471). For procedure for demand, payment and appraisal rights, see supra, subhead Amendment of Articles. For provisions regarding disposition of assets with 10% or more shareholders, see subhead Business Combinations, infra.

Books and Records.—Corporation must keep share register at its principal executive office or another place within U.S. named by board. Other records to be kept at principal executive office, and if office out of state, must be made available at registered office within ten days of demand by shareholder. For corporations other than "publicly held" corporations, proper purpose no longer required to examine certain records. For provisions regarding documents to be maintained, see supra, subhead Shareholders' Inspection Rights. (302A.461).

Merger or Exchange.—Two or more corporations or corporation and limited liability company may merge, resulting in single corporation, or limited liability company with or without business purpose, pursuant to plan of merger. Shares of one or more classes or series of corporation may be exchanged for shares or other securities of same or different class of one or more other corporations or money other than property pursuant to plan of exchange. (302A.601). Plan of merger or exchange must contain: (1) Names of constituent organizations proposing to merge or participate in exchange; (2) in case of merger, name of surviving organization; (3) in case of exchange, name of acquiring corporation; (4) terms and conditions of proposed merger or exchange; (5) in case of merger, manner and basis of converting ownership interests of constituent organizations into securities of surviving or any other organization or into money or other property; (6) in case of exchange, manner and basis of exchanging shares to be acquired for securities of acquiring organization or any other organization or converting into money or other property; (7) in case of merger, statement of any amendments to articles of surviving organization; and (8) any other provisions deemed necessary or desirable. (302A.611). Unless otherwise provided in articles, plan of merger must be approved by majority of directors present and by majority vote of shareholders, except no shareholder approval of plan of merger by shareholders of surviving corporation required if articles of such corporation will not be amended, shareholders thereof will hold same number of shares with identical rights thereafter, and number of new shares entitled to vote or new participating shares thereafter will not exceed 20% of number of shares entitled to vote or participating shares, respectively, immediately before transaction. Unless otherwise provided in articles, plan of exchange must be approved by majority of directors present and by majority vote of shareholders of corporation whose shares will be acquired. Shareholders not entitled to vote as class solely because all classes of shares are to be canceled if appraisal rights available. If shareholder approval required, plan or short description must be submitted to shareholders as part of notice of meeting. (302A.613). Articles of merger or exchange filed with Secretary of State must include plan of merger or exchange and statement that plan was approved by each constituent organization pursuant to c. 302A and be signed on behalf of each constituent organization. (302A.615). Merger of 90% direct or indirect subsidiaries into parent or into other 90% direct or indirect subsidiaries or of parent into 90% direct or indirect subsidiary by action of board of directors of parent without vote of shareholders of parent or any subsidiary authorized. (302A.621). Specific provisions for abandonment of merger or exchange. (302A.631). Shareholders dissenting from merger or exchange may demand in writing before vote payment of fair value for shares. (302A.471). For procedure for demand, payment and appraisal rights, see supra, subhead Amendment of Articles. Merger or exchange effective when articles are filed with Secretary of State or on later date or at later time specified in articles of merger or exchange. (302A.641). For provisions regarding mergers or exchanges with 10% or more shareholders, see subhead Business Combinations, infra.

Control Share Acquisitions.—Unless otherwise provided in articles or by-laws approved by shareholders, information statement and shareholder approval generally required in order to vote any shares acquired of 302A corporation with at least 100 shareholders (and, in some cases, 50 shareholders) if, subject to certain specific exceptions, acquisition would result in new range of beneficial ownership of at least 20% but less than 33⅓%, at least 33⅓% but less than or equal to 50% or over 50%. (302A.011, .671). Proxies in control share acquisition must be solicited separately from offer to purchase or solicitation of offer to sell. (302A.449).

Business Combinations.—Unless otherwise provided in articles or by-laws before corporation becomes publicly held or elects to become subject to regulation under statute, or unless board adopts by-laws prior to Sept. 1, 1987, electing out, "business combinations" with "interested shareholders" of publicly held corporation are prohibited for period of four years following interested shareholder's share acquisition date.

Corporations which are not publicly held, but have 100 or more shareholders (or if election is made to be issuing public corporation prior to Jan. 1, 1998, 50 or more) may elect to become subject to regulation under statute. (302A.673). Interested shareholder is any person (other than issuing public corporation or employee benefit, savings or stock ownership plan) which is: (1) Beneficial owner, directly or indirectly, of 10% or more of voting power of outstanding shares entitled to vote or (2) affiliate or associate of issuing public corporation which was 10% or more shareholder during preceding four years. Business combinations include: (1) Mergers, statutory exchanges of shares or other securities and certain dispositions of assets of corporation or its subsidiaries involving interested shareholder (or its affiliates or associates), (2) certain issuances of stock by corporation or its subsidiaries to interested shareholder (or its affiliates or associates), (3) liquidations, dissolutions or reincorporations of corporation proposed by or on behalf of interested shareholder (or any affiliate or associate), (4) certain reclassifications, recapitalizations and transactions between corporation and its subsidiaries that have effect of increasing proportionate share of outstanding shares entitled to vote owned by interested shareholder (or any affiliate or associate), and (5) any receipt by interested shareholder (or any affiliate or associate) of any loans, guarantees, pledges or other financial assistance or any tax credits or tax advantages from corporation or any subsidiary. (302A.011). Not applicable to any business combination with interested shareholder who would have been interested shareholder on June 1, 1987 had section then been in effect or to transactions with persons who were interested shareholders before corporation became subject to regulation under statute and who are specified as being exempt in articles or in by-laws adopted by shareholders. (302A.673).

Takeover Offers.—Offerer may not acquire by any means shares of publicly held corporation within two years following last purchase of shares of that class pursuant to takeover offer, unless acquisition is approved by disinterested directors before takeover offer, or shareholder is afforded reasonable opportunity to dispose of shares to offeror upon substantially equivalent terms as those provided in earlier takeover offer. (302A.675).

Dissolution.—Corporation may be wound up and dissolved either voluntarily or involuntarily. Voluntary proceedings may be conducted either out of court or subject to supervision of court; involuntary proceedings must be subject to supervision of court. Incorporators or directors may dissolve corporation prior to issuance of shares. (302A.711). Shareholders may dissolve corporation by majority vote of holders of all shares entitled to vote. (302A.721). Involuntary dissolution authorized under various circumstances, including by shareholder action in event directors are deadlocked in management of corporation, directors or those in control of corporation have acted fraudulently or illegally toward one or more shareholders in their capacities as shareholders or directors, or as officers or employees of closely held corporation, or in manner unfairly prejudicial toward one or more shareholders in their capacities as shareholders or directors of corporation that is not publicly held corporation, or as officers or employees of closely held corporation, shareholders are so divided they fail to elect successors to directors for two consecutive regular meetings, or assets are misapplied or wasted. (302A.751). Resolution of dissolution no longer needs to be filed with Secretary of State; need only file notice of intent to dissolve. (302A.723). Officers or directors wind up corporation. Trustee eliminated. (302A.725). Alternative systems, depending on whether notice to creditors and claimants in connection with dissolution is given, established. (302A.727). Provision for revocation of dissolution. (302A.731). Articles of dissolution required to be filed with Secretary of State after expiration of certain time periods or occurrence of certain events. (302A.727, .7291). Court supervised voluntary and involuntary dissolution procedures almost identical. (302A.741 et seq.).

Close Corporations.—Court may grant dissolution or such other equitable relief it deems just and reasonable under circumstances when it is established that directors or those in control of corporation have acted fraudulently or illegally toward one or more shareholders in their capacities as shareholders, directors or as officers or employees of closely held corporation or in manner unfairly prejudicial toward one or more shareholders in their capacities as shareholders or directors of corporation that is not publicly held corporation, or as officers or employees of corporation that is closely held corporation. (302A.751). Closely held corporation is corporation with not more than 35 shareholders. (302A.011). Court may also order sale by plaintiff or defendant of all shares of closely held corporation to corporation or moving shareholder. In considering whether to order equitable relief, court is to take into consideration duty all shareholders owe one another and reasonable expectations of all shareholders as they exist at inception and develop through course of relationship. Written agreements among shareholders and corporation are presumed to reflect parties' reasonable expectations concerning matters dealt with in agreements. (302A.751).

Shareholders may assume management functions, either by unanimous vote or unanimous shareholder control agreement. (302A.201). See supra, subhead Directors.

Appraisal.—See subheads Amendment of Articles, Disposal of Assets and Merger or Exchange, supra. Corporation may in articles, by-laws or by board resolution also grant dissenting shareholders appraisal rights with respect to any action taken pursuant to shareholder vote. (302A.471).

Foreign Corporations.—All foreign corporations doing business in state (except insurance companies as defined in 60A.02 and banking or trust association acting as executor, administrator, trustee, guardian or conservator under 303.25) are required to comply with provisions of foreign corporations act. (c. 303). No foreign corporation may transact business in state that only bank, trust company or savings, building and loan association can transact in Minnesota except as provided in 303.25. (303.04). Making of contract to be performed in Minnesota or commission of tort in Minnesota against resident of Minnesota constitutes appointment of Secretary of State as agent for service of process in action or proceeding arising therefrom. (303.13). See also category Business Regulation and Commerce, topic Banks and Banking, subhead Foreign Corporations.

See Non-Profit Corporation Act with respect to foreign nonprofit corporations doing business in Minnesota. (5.25; c. 317A).

CORPORATIONS . . . *continued*

Certificate of Authority.—Foreign corporation must hold certificate of authority to transact business in the state. Such certificates are issued by Secretary of State on application made on forms prescribed and furnished by Secretary of State, executed by president, vice-president, secretary or assistant secretary of corporation, and delivered to Secretary of State with certificate of existence from filing officer of state, province or country of incorporation. Following activities do not constitute transacting business in state: Maintaining, defending or settling any action; holding meetings and carrying on internal affairs of corporation; maintaining bank accounts; maintaining offices or agencies relating to its securities; holding title to or managing real or personal property as executor or administrator of estate, trustee, or guardian or conservator of person or estate or both; participating in or creating loans, mortgages or security interests in real or personal property; collecting its debts; conducting isolated transaction completed in 30 days and not part of repeated number of like transactions. (303.03, .06, .08). 303.03 does not establish standards for those activities that may subject foreign corporation to taxation under 290.015 and to reporting requirements of 290.371.

Fees.—Initial license fee of $150 must be paid to State Treasurer at time of making application. Annual license fee to accompany annual report due between Jan. 1 and May 15. Fee is $20 per $100,000 or fraction thereof of Minnesota taxable net income for most recent fiscal year prior to payment. Minimum $40. (303.07). Fee for other filings with Secretary of State, $50. (303.21).

Registered Office and Agent.—Each foreign corporation authorized to transact business in the state must have registered office which may, but need not be, same as its place of business in the state, and registered agent (individual or corporate) whose business office is identical with registered office. (303.10).

Foreign corporation is subject to service of process upon its registered agent. If such registered agent cannot be found at registered office, if no registered agent has been appointed, if corporation has withdrawn from state, or if its certificate of authority has been revoked or cancelled, service may be made on Secretary of State, except that if corporation's application for withdrawal has been approved, service may be made on Secretary of State only when based on liability of corporation incurred within state or arising out of business done in state prior to issuance of certificate of withdrawal. (5.25; 303.13, .16).

Notice of change of registered agent or office and notices of change of name, dissolution or merger into another corporation must be filed with Secretary of State. Registered agent may resign by filing written notice with Secretary of State, including statement that signed copy of notice has been given or mailed to foreign corporation at its principal office in jurisdiction where organized. (303.10, .11).

Annual Report.—Between Jan. 15 and May 15 of each year, every qualified corporation must make and file with Secretary of State an annual report for previous calendar year on forms prescribed by Secretary of State. Report to set forth name of corporation and state or country of incorporation, address of registered office and name of registered agent, statement of corporate taxable net income as stated on Minnesota income tax return that was due in previous year, and annual license fee required. Divulgence of particulars with reference to net taxable income forbidden. (303.14).

Revocation of Certificate.—Certificate of authority may be revoked by Secretary of State if corporation fails to pay any fee due, to maintain registered agent, to file certificates of merger or name change or to file annual report. (303.17). There is provision for reinstatement by application after revocation or cancellation of certificate. (303.19).

Surrender of Authority.—Corporation desiring to withdraw from the state must file application for withdrawal setting forth: (1) Name and state of incorporation; (2) that it has no property in the state and has ceased to transact business therein; (3) that its board of directors has duly determined to surrender its authority to do business in the state; (4) that it revokes authority of its registered agent to accept service of process; (5) address to which Secretary of State may mail process against corporation served on Secretary; (6) that it will pay any additional license fees properly found to be due; (7) any additional information required or demanded by Secretary of State for determination of additional license fees. Application must be executed by same officers who would be required for application for certificate, except that application may be made by receiver or trustee if corporation is in hands of receiver or trustee. On payment of all fees, Secretary of State shall issue and record certificate of withdrawal. (303.16).

Effect of Failure to Obtain Certificate of Authority.—No foreign corporation transacting business in the State can maintain action in any state court until it has first obtained certificate of authority. Nor can successor or assignee of such corporation, except holder in due course of negotiable instrument or assignee without actual notice of violation (who cannot recover more than purchase price), maintain any action in state court arising out of transaction of business in the state by such corporation until such corporation or its successor has obtained certificate. But failure to obtain certificate of authority does not impair validity of any contract or act of corporation and does not prevent it from defending any court action. Any foreign corporation transacting business in the state without certificate of authority becomes liable to forfeit to state penalty not exceeding $1,000 and additional penalty not exceeding $100 for each month or fraction thereof during which it continues to transact business without certificate, penalties being collected by action in name of state brought by Attorney General. (303.20).

Professional Firms.—Minnesota Professional Firms Act adopted 1997. (c. 319B). Existing professional corporations governed by c. 319A will be governed by c. 319B beginning Jan. 1, 1999 and may elect to be governed by c. 319B before that date. Requires foreign and Minnesota firms that furnish professional services within Minnesota to elect to operate under c. 319B unless no Minnesota statute, Minnesota rule, or tenet of Minnesota common law requires firm to make election in order to furnish professional services or precludes firm from furnishing professional services in absence of election. (319B.03, 319B.04). Professional services include services provided by physicians, physician assistants, attorneys, accountants, chiropractors, optometrists, podiatrists, psychologists, dentists, nurses, architects, engineers, surveyors, landscape architects, geoscientists, interior designers, pharmacists, and veterinarians. (319B.02).

Franchise Tax.—There is no annual franchise tax on corporations.

Income tax on corporations, see category Taxation, topic Income Tax.

Deeds.—See category Property, topic Deeds.

Model Non-Profit Corporation Act not adopted. See supra this topic, subhead General.

Limited Liability Companies.—See topic Limited Liability Companies.

JOINT STOCK COMPANIES:

Few statutory provisions governing joint stock companies. Declarations of trust and business trusts are governed by c. 318.

All cooperative associations are governed by c. 308.

Purposes.—Business trust can transact any business except insurance (except title insurance), banking, or surety business. (318.01).

Formation.—Business trust can be organized by two or more natural persons or two or more corporations (including national banks and qualified foreign corporations). (318.01). Instrument under which trust is organized must be filed with Secretary of State before business is transacted and must include name and address of agent for service of process (filing fee $150), and amendments must also be so filed (filing fee $50). Any such association is business trust, not partnership, joint-stock association, agency, or other relation. Business trust is also known as common-law trust and Massachusetts trust for doing business. (318.02).

Rights, Powers and Liabilities.—Business trust has power to continue perpetually; to sue and be sued; to use seal (but failure to use shall not affect validity of any instrument); to do any acts necessary and incidental to transaction of its business or expedient for attainment of its purposes; and to acquire, sell, hold, encumber, transfer and otherwise deal in real and personal property. No personal liability for any obligation of business trust attaches to beneficial owners or trustees thereof. (318.02).

Business trusts are subject to registration with Securities Division (318.03) and to regulation, if engaged in insurance business, by Insurance Division (318.04).

Dissolution.—No statutory provisions.

Professional Corporations.—See topic Corporations, subhead Professional Firms.

LIMITED LIABILITY COMPANIES:

General.—Minnesota limited liability company act effective Jan. 1, 1993. (c. 322B). Most of Act is based on Minnesota business corporation act. (c. 302A). Significant distinctions from corporation act are summarized as follows:

Terminology.—Shareholders, directors and officers under corporation act are called members, governors and managers, respectively. (322B.30, 322B.606, 322B.67). Ownership interests are defined as membership interests. (322B.30). Membership interests are divided between governance rights and financial rights. (322B.03). Articles of incorporation and bylaws are articles of organization and operating agreement. (322B.115, 322B.603). Other terms similarly changed.

Name.—Company name must contain words "limited liability company" or abbreviation "LLC" or in case of professional limited liability company, "limited liability company" or "professional limited liability company" or abbreviations "LLC", "PLC" or "PLLC" and must not contain words "corporation" or "incorporated" or abbreviation of those words. (322B.12).

Two Member Requirement Eliminated.—Company must have one or more members. (322B.11).

Limited Term of Existence.—Term of 30 years unless articles of organization expressly authorize shorter or longer period of duration, which may be perpetual. (322B.115).

Articles of Organization.—Articles must be filed with Secretary of State, and must state company name, address of registered office, name and address of each organizer, statement of period of existence if different from 30-year period set forth in 322B.20, subd. 2. (322B.115, 322B.17). Company existence begins upon filing articles with Secretary of State together with payment of fees. (322B.175).

Amendment of Articles.—Member objecting to proposed amendment in that it (1) changes member's right to resign or retire, (2) establishes or changes conditions for or consequences of expulsion, (3) changes statement that was required in articles regarding power of remaining members power to avoid dissolution, or (4) changes statement that was required in articles regarding power of members to enter into business continuation agreement, if statement was required under law when articles executed, has right to dissent from, and obtain payment for fair value of member's membership interests. (322B.383). Other amendments giving rise to dissenters' rights substantially similar to those giving rise to dissenters' rights under corporate act. See topic Corporations, subhead Amendment of Articles. Dissenters' rights, with certain exceptions, may be waived in member control agreement. (322B.37).

Filing Fees.—Filing fee of $35 paid to Secretary of State for filing any instrument required to be filed under c. 322B. (322B.03). For merger, additional fee of $25. (322B.175). Total fees payable for filing original articles under c. 322B are $135, including $100 organization fee and $35 filing fee. (322B.175).

Membership Interests.—Member's membership interest personal property. Member has no interest in specific company property, which is property of company itself. (322B.30). Membership interests must (1) be one class, without series, unless articles establish or authorize board of governors to establish more than one class or series, (2) be ordinary membership interests entitled to vote in proportion to value of members' respective contributions, with equal rights and preferences in matters not otherwise provided for by board, unless articles fix relative rights and preferences of classes and series, and (3) share profits and losses and receive distributions in proportion to value of contributions. (322B.40). Subject to restrictions in articles, board may establish classes or series by resolution setting forth designation of class or series and fixing relative rights and preferences. Rights and preferences may be made dependent upon facts ascertainable outside articles or resolution establishing class or series, and may

LIMITED LIABILITY COMPANIES . . . *continued*

incorporate by reference terms of agreements entered into by company in connection with establishment of class or series, if company retains copy of agreement incorporated by reference. Name of company and certified text of resolution must be filed with Secretary of State before acceptance of contributions or, if members have received notice before acceptance of contributions of creation of membership interests not set forth in articles, within one year after acceptance. Resolution is effective upon filing with Secretary of State or if not required to be filed before acceptance of contributions, on date of adoption by governors. (322B.40). Upon member's request, company shall state in writing member's membership interest, including rights to vote, to share in profits, losses and distributions, restrictions on assignments of financial and governance rights and any assignment of member's rights other than security interest then in effect. (322B.30). Act restricts transfer of governance rights and, unless limited, permits transfer of financial rights making up membership interests. (322B.31, 322B.313).

Contributions may be accepted only when authorized by board, subject to restrictions in articles. Contributions may be made by paying money or transferring property interest to company or by rendering services to or for benefit of company, or pursuant to signed written obligation to any of foregoing. Contribution not effective until board of governors accepts contribution and in acceptance describes contribution including terms of any future performance and states value accorded to contribution, and contribution and its accorded value are both reflected in company's required records. Provisions regarding valuation of contribution are similar to those governing valuation of consideration received by corporation for issuance of stock, but do not address member liability for mistaken valuation. (322B.40). See topic Corporations, subhead Issuance of Stock. Board must restate value of all old contributions reflected in its required records when accepting new contribution. Specified restatement method required unless articles otherwise provide. (322B.41).

Distributions.—Unless otherwise provided in articles or by board if authorized, distributions must be allocated in proportion to value of contributions of members reflected in required records. (322B.50). Except as provided in articles, member is entitled to receive distributions before company's termination only as specified in operating agreement or by board action. (322B.51). At time member becomes entitled to receive distribution, member has status and rights of creditor of company with respect to distribution. (322B.53). Other provisions regarding distributions substantially similar to those governing corporations. See subhead Distributions, supra.

Transfer of Membership Interests.—Transfer of financial rights, governance rights or entire membership interest effective against company only when assignee's name, address, and nature and extent of assignment are reflected in company's required records. Security interest in such interest or rights effective according to Minnesota uniform commercial code. (322B.316). Statement of membership interest available upon member demand is not certificated security or negotiable instrument under commercial code and may not serve to transfer membership interest. (322B.30). For security interest purposes, membership interest and governance and financial rights are each to be characterized as general intangibles subject to exceptions in 336.8-103(c), under commercial code. (322B.30).

Assignment of Financial Rights.—Member's financial rights arising out of membership interest transferable in whole or in part. Assignee only entitled to receive member's share of profits and losses and distributions to extent assigned. Assignment of financial rights does not dissolve company or entitle assignee to become member, to exercise governance rights, to receive any notices or to cause dissolution. Assignment may not allow assignee to control member's exercise of governance rights. (322B.31). Voting agreement or proxy may not be used to circumvent prohibition. (322B.363, 322B.366). Additional written restriction on assignment of financial rights may be enforced against owner of restricted financial rights or successor or transferee if not manifestly unreasonable and noted conspicuously in company's required records. Restrictions may be included in articles or operating agreement, by member resolution or agreement or written action of members or among them and company. Restriction not binding with respect to financial rights reflected in required records before adoption of restriction, unless owners of such financial rights are parties to agreement or voted in favor of restriction. Restriction ineffective against person without knowledge of restriction, unless restriction noted conspicuously in required records. Assignee entitled to rely on statement of membership interest issued by company. (322B.31).

Assignment of Governance Rights.—Member may assign governance rights to another member without any other member's consent. Unless articles or member control agreement provide for written consent by fewer than all members, any other assignment of governance rights effective only by unanimous written consent of all other members. Security interest may be granted in entire membership interest or governance rights without consent, but secured party may take or assign ownership of governance rights only upon requisite approval of other members. Upon effective assignment of governance rights (other than security interest) assignee becomes member. If assignor does not retain any governance rights, assignor ceases to be member, and other members' consent to assignment constitutes dissolution avoidance consent if consent required for dissolution avoidance is not greater than consent for assignment. Assignee liable for assignor's obligations to make contributions, and for illegal distributions made to assignor, in proportion to interest assigned except to extent such liability was unknown to assignee or could not be ascertained from required records. Assignor remains liable. If attempted assignment of governance rights is ineffective for failure to obtain required consent, attempted assignment is ineffective in its entirety and any accompanying assignment of financial rights is void. (322B.313). Additional restrictions on assignment of governance rights permitted as permitted for financial rights. (322B.313, 322B.31). Secured party may enforce security interest in member's full membership interest or governance rights without consent of member whose interest or rights are subject to security interest. (322B.313).

Termination of Membership.—Unless otherwise provided in articles, member may not be expelled. Member always has power, if not right, to terminate membership at

any time by resigning or retiring, but such member has no power to transfer membership interest except as provided in Act. (322B.306). Resignation or retirement causes dissolution unless dissolution is avoided in accordance with Act or articles or member control agreement otherwise provide. (322B.306, 322B.80). If dissolution is avoided, then terminated member loses governance rights and is deemed assignee of financial rights owned before termination; if dissolution is not avoided, terminated member retains and may continue to exercise financial and governance rights. If dissolution avoidance consent is obtained, member who wrongfully retires or resigns is liable to company to extent damaged. (322B.306). If business is continued under business continuation agreement made prior to dissolution, member has dissenters' rights which can not be waived, but such rights are limited. (322B.873).

Required Records and Rights of Inspection.—Required records include current list of each member and each assignee of financial rights (other than secured party) together with description of rights assigned, copies of required financial statements and tax returns for three years and member control agreements, statements of all contributions accepted by company and all contribution and contribution allowance agreements, and explanation of any restatement of value made by company. (322B.373). Other required records are similar to those required to be kept by corporations. See subhead Shareholders' Inspection Rights, under topic Corporations. Member has absolute right to examine and copy all required records, and right to examine and copy other company records if member demonstrates a purpose reasonably related to interest as a member. (322B.373). Other provisions regarding records and inspection similar to those governing corporations. See topic Corporations, subhead Shareholders' Inspection Rights.

Members' Liabilities.—Member, governor, manager, or other agent of company not personally liable for obligations of company on account of status. Minnesota case law on piercing corporate veil expressly applicable to limited liability companies. Limited liability survives dissolution and termination of company. (322B.303). Provisions regarding member liability for unlawful distributions substantially similar to those governing corporations. (322B.56). See subhead Distributions, supra, also topic Corporations, subhead Distributions.

Voting.—Unless otherwise provided in articles or by board pursuant to authorization in articles, members have voting power in proportion to value of their contributions as reflected in required records. Articles may give or prescribe manner of nonmember voting rights, but no prescription may have effect of transferring voting rights of assignor of financial rights to assignee of such rights. (322B.356). Other provisions regarding voting are substantially similar to those governing corporations. See topic Corporations, subhead Voting, supra.

Member Voting Agreement.—Assignee of member's financial rights may not be party to voting agreement unless also member. Voting agreement may not relate to dissolution avoidance consent, consent to assignment of membership interest or assignment of rights under contribution or contribution allowance agreement. (322B.366). Other provisions regarding voting agreements are substantially similar to those governing corporations. See topic Corporations, subhead Shareholder Voting Agreements.

Member Control Agreement.—Written agreement signed by all members relating to control, liquidation or dissolution and termination of company, or relations among members, or to any phase of company's affairs is valid. Agreement may contain any provision required by Act to be in articles or operating agreement other than minimum information required to be in articles. Agreement may allocate to members authority ordinarily exercised by board and allocate to board authority ordinarily exercised by members, or structure governance of company in any agreed fashion. (322B.37). Agreement may waive member's dissenters' rights other than rights to dissent from business continuation agreement. (322B.37, 322B.873). Agreement enforceable by parties and binding upon only parties and those persons having knowledge of existence of agreement. Agreement, specifically enforceable. (322B.37).

Merger or Exchange.—Act does not provide for short form merger of substantially wholly-owned subsidiary. Other provisions regarding merger or exchange are substantially similar to those governing corporations. (322B.70). See topic Corporations, subhead Merger or Exchange.

Control Share Acquisitions, Business Combinations and Takeover Offers.—Act has no provisions analogous to those of corporation act dealing with control share acquisitions, business combinations or takeover offers. See topic Corporations, subheads Control Share Acquisitions, Business Combinations and Takeover Offers.

Dissolution.—Limited liability company dissolves when period fixed in articles for duration expires and upon occurrence of any event that terminates continued membership of member, including death, retirement, resignation, redemption of membership interest, assignment of all governance rights, buy-out, expulsion, bankruptcy, dissolution of member, merger in which company is not surviving corporation or exchange in which company is not acquiring corporation. Business is not dissolved and may be continued (1) if there is at least one remaining member by consent of all remaining members within 90 days after termination of continued membership or (2) if membership of last or sole member terminates and legal representative of that member causes company to admit at least one member. (322B.80). Business may also be continued after dissolution under business continuation agreement. (322B.03). If business is continued under business continuation agreement, member has dissenters' rights, subject to certain limitations, which can not be waived in member control agreement. (322B.873). Other dissolution procedures are substantially similar to those governing corporations. See topic Corporations, subhead Dissolution.

Foreign Limited Liability Companies.—Before transacting business in Minnesota, foreign limited liability company must obtain certificate of authority. Information required in application for certificate set forth in Act. Fee of $185 for application includes $150 initial license fee and $35 filing fee. (322B.91). Certificate of authority effective from date application is filed accompanied by requisite fees. (322B.915). Foreign limited liability company holding valid Minnesota certificate of authority has no greater rights and privileges than Minnesota company and may not exercise any

LIMITED LIABILITY COMPANIES . . . *continued*
power or purpose forbidden by law in Minnesota. (322B.90). Procedures and conditions for amendment, withdrawal and revocation of certificate set forth in Act. (322B.92, 322B.93, 322B.935). Foreign limited liability company transacting business in state may not maintain action, suit, or proceeding in state court until it possesses certificate of authority, but failure to obtain certificate of authority does not impair validity of any contract or act of foreign company or prevent it from defending any proceeding in state court. Transacting business in state without certificate constitutes appointment of Secretary of State as agent for service of process. Fees and penalties payable for transaction of business without certificate set forth in Act. (322B.94). Following activities do not constitute transacting business: (1) maintaining, defending, or settling any proceeding, (2) holding meetings of its members or carrying on other internal activities, (3) maintaining bank accounts, (4) maintaining offices, agencies, trustees or depositories for transfer, exchange, and registration of or with respect to company's own securities, (5) selling through independent contractors, (6) soliciting or obtaining orders requiring acceptance outside state, (7) creating or acquiring indebtedness, mortgages, and security interests, (8) securing or collecting debts or enforcing mortgages and security interests, (9) holding, protecting, renting, maintaining and operating real or personal property in state so acquired, (10) selling or transferring title to property in state, (11) conducting isolated transaction that is completed within 30 days and that is not part of course of repeated transactions. Ownership of income-producing property, other than exempt property constitutes transacting business in state. List of excluded activities not exhaustive. Provision has no effect on personal jurisdiction and does not apply in determining contracts or activities subjecting foreign company to service of process, taxation or regulation under any other state law. (322B.945).

PARTNERSHIPS:

Uniform Partnership Act adopted. (c. 323). Uniform Partnership Act (1994) adopted in 1997, effective Jan. 1, 1999, and repealing Uniform Partnership Act effective Jan. 1, 2002. (c. 323A). 1976 Uniform Limited Partnership Act adopted for limited partnerships formed after Dec. 31, 1980. (c. 322A). Limited partnership existing on Jan. 1, 1981 is subject to prior Uniform Limited Partnership Act (c. 322) unless it elects to come under provisions of c. 322A (322A.86). General partnership may become limited liability partnership for renewable one-year periods by registering with secretary of state. (323.44). Limited partnership may become limited liability limited partnership. (322A.88).

Filing of Certificate.—General partnership must file certificate with Secretary of State setting forth names of members, unless all names appear in firm name. (333.01).

Limited partnership must file certificate with Secretary of State. Fee, $60. Each original or annual renewal registration as limited liability partnership must be accompanied by $135 filing fee. (322A.11, .16).

BUSINESS REGULATION AND COMMERCE

BANKS AND BANKING:

Uniform Commercial Code adopted. (c. 336). See topic Commercial Code. Revised Art. 3 and conforming amendments to Arts. 1 and 4 adopted.

Supervision.—Department of Commerce supervises banks, savings banks, trust companies and other financial institutions under state laws. Commissioner of Commerce is in charge.

Liability of Stockholders.—Personal liability of stockholders of banks and trust companies abolished. (48.03).

Powers.—Bank cannot make loan or discount on security of its shares nor be purchaser or holder thereof unless necessary to prevent loss on debt previously contracted in good faith, and within six months after acquisition bank must sell or dispose of same at public or private sale. (48.23).

Bank may be authorized to transact trust business if it has $500,000 capital and surplus (48.44), provided it has deposited required securities with State Treasurer and filed receipt therefor with Commissioner of Commerce. Maximum deposit $1,000,000. (46.34, 48.37).

Branch banking restricted. (48.34). Bank, with permission of Commissioner, may establish and maintain detached facilities provided such facilities are located within municipality in which applicant bank's principal office is located; or within 5,000 feet of its principal office measured in straight line from closest points of closest structures involved; or within any municipality in which no bank is located at time of application; or in municipality of more than 10,000 persons, or if detached facility is located in municipality of 10,000 persons or less, as determined by Commissioner from latest available data from state demographer, or for municipalities located in seven county metropolitan area from Metropolitan Council, and all banks having principal office in municipality have consented in writing to establishment of facility. (47.52). Detached facility must not be closer than 50 feet to detached facility operated by any other bank and must not be closer than 100 feet to principal office of any other bank, measured in same manner previously described. This requirement inapplicable if proximity to detached facility or bank is waived in writing by other bank and filed with application to establish detached facility. (47.52). Bank whose home state is Minnesota may establish detached facility within 30 miles from its principal office in states of Iowa, North Dakota, South Dakota and/or Wisconsin, provided that law of any such host state permits such branch under conditions substantially similar to those imposed by Minnesota law and there exists cooperative agreement between regulators of Minnesota and of such host state. (47.52). Number of facilities, distance limitations, geographic and consent restrictions inapplicable if state bank applies to Commissioner pursuant to 47.51 to 47.56 and 49.35 to 49.41, to acquire another state bank or national banking association and its detached facilities through merger, consolidation or purchase of assets and assumption of liabilities and to operate them as detached facilities of successor bank. (49.34).

Interstate Banking.—An out-of-state bank holding company may acquire control of existing Minnesota bank provided that such bank has been in existence for at least five years and that out-of-state holding company files application to Commissioner of Commerce, subject to Commissioner's disapproval. (48.93, 48.92). Interstate branching by merger under §102 of Riegle-Neal Interstate Banking and Branching Efficiency Act of 1994, permitted according to Minn. Stat. §49.411. With approval of Commissioner of Commerce, Minnesota bank may establish, maintain and operate one or more branches outside Minnesota as result of interstate merger in which Minnesota bank is resulting bank. Out of state banks may merge with Minnesota banks, and resulting out of state bank may maintain and operate Minnesota branches of such Minnesota banks, subject to conditions and filing requirements of §49.411. If such merger results in out of state bank's acquisition of Minnesota bank or all or substantially all of its branches, such Minnesota bank shall have been in continuous operation for at least five years. (49.411).

See also topic Interest.

Interstate Contracts of Deposit and Withdrawals.—Provided Commissioner has been given notice and has not objected within 30 days, state bank, savings bank, savings association, or credit union or national banking association, federal savings association or federal credit union having its main office in this state ("Customer Institution") may contract with another such financial institution ("Service Institution") to grant Service Institution authority to render services to Customer Institution's depositors, borrowers or other customers. "Services" means accepting and receiving deposits, honoring and paying withdrawals, issuing money orders, cashiers' checks, and travelers' checks or similar instruments, cashing checks or drafts, receiving loan payments, receiving or delivering cash and instruments and securities and disbursing loan proceeds by machine. Service Institution is not considered branch of Customer Institution. (47.78).

Deposits.—Bank may not accept deposits in excess of 30 times amount of capital stock and actual surplus. (48.27). Deposits by or in name of minor are held for exclusive right and benefit of minor free from lien or control of any person except creditors and can be paid to minor without liability upon bank until conservator or guardian appointed for minor has delivered certificate of appointment to bank. (48.30). Part 1, Art. VI (Multi-Party Accounts) of Uniform Probate Code adopted with modifications. (524.6-201–524.6-214). Banks must offer to Minnesota resident savings account to promote thrift that has no service charge if account has average monthly balance of more than $50. (47.76). Banks generally must give account holder 30 days notice before closing deposit account or transferring funds from one deposit account to another. (47.77).

Unclaimed Deposits.—See subhead Revised Uniform Disposition of Unclaimed Property Act, infra.

Revised Uniform Disposition of Unclaimed Property Act adopted with modifications. Period after which property presumed abandoned reduced from seven to three years in many cases. (345.31-.60).

Savings banks may invest deposits in authorized securities. (50.14). Savings banks may establish negotiable order of withdrawal accounts. (50.175).

Trust Companies.—Trust companies are organized and supervised as are banks in general. May act as fiduciary. (48A.07).

Common trust fund may be created by trust company or bank with trust powers. (48A.07, subd. 6[g]).

Uniform Common Trust Fund Act not adopted.

Industrial Banks.—Industrial loan and thrift companies are organized and supervised as are banks in general. Such companies are forbidden to carry demand banking accounts, or to act as trustee, guardian, or administrator. (53.05).

Foreign Corporations.—No foreign corporation may transact, in the state, business which only a bank, trust company or savings association can transact in state. (303.04). However, foreign trust association may act as trustee, executor, administrator, guardian or conservator if laws of state in which association maintains its principal office accord like privilege to Minnesota corporate fiduciaries, such association appoints Secretary of State as its attorney for service of process and bond filed or deposit of securities made, unless deed of trust dispenses with requirement of security. (303.25).

BILLS AND NOTES:

Uniform Commercial Code adopted. (c. 336). See topic Commercial Code.
Revised Art. 3 and conforming amendments to Arts. 1 and 4 adopted.
See topic Commercial Code.

Special Provisions.—Note or check for gambling debt is void as between parties and as to all persons except those holding in good faith and without knowledge of illegality of consideration and except in connection with parimutuel betting, state lottery or Indian Gaming Regulatory Act, 25 U.S.C. §2701 et seq. or lawful gambling activities permitted under c. 349. (541.21).

Issuance of worthless check, see 609.535.

Rate of damages collectible on duly protested commercial paper payable without U.S., 10% upon contents thereof, with interest on contents computed from date of protest; said amount of contents, damages and interest to be in full of all damages, charges and expenses. (334.10). In case of inland paper, 5% damages, with interest provided in instrument, together with costs and charges of protest. (334.11).

Writing Requirement.—Agreement to extend credit is not enforceable unless in writing that expresses consideration, sets forth relevant terms and conditions and is signed by creditor and debtor. (513.33).

See note at head of Digest as to 1998 legislation covered.

See Topical Index in front part of this volume.

MN – 7

BILLS AND NOTES . . . *continued*

Judgment Notes.—Not used in Minnesota because of one year statute of limitations (541.09) and because certain additional instruments required. See category Civil Actions and Procedure, topic Judgments, subhead Confession of Judgment.

Collection of attorney fee clauses are enforceable. (58 Minn. 561, 60 N.W. 668). See also topic Sales.

BILLS OF LADING:

See topic Carriers.

BILLS OF SALE:

See topic Sales.

BLUE SKY LAW:

See topic Securities.

BROKERS:

Uniform Commercial Code adopted. (c. 336). See topic Commercial Code.

Brokers must furnish every customer or principal with written statement of any transaction executed for him, failure to do so being prima facie evidence of irregularity. (624.70).

Licenses.—Brokers must be licensed annually by Commissioner of Commerce. (80A.01-.31).

Real estate brokers, salespersons and closing agents licensed by Commissioner of Commerce. Licenses good for 24 months, until June 30 of expiration year. (82.20). Fees: $150 for each individual brokers license, $100 for renewal; $70 for initial salesperson's license, $40 for renewal; $85 for each initial real estate closing agent license, $60 for renewal; $150 for initial corporation, limited liability company, or partnership license, $100 for renewal; $75 for education, research and recovery fund, $50 for renewal; $20 for each transfer; $50 for license reinstatement and $20 for reactivating corporation, limited liability company, or partnership license without land. Applicant for salesperson's license must complete 30-hour course, approved by Commissioner before sitting for licensing examination. Applicant for salesperson's license must also complete additional 60 hours of instruction approved by Commissioner, which includes three hours of instruction on fair housing laws and two hours of instruction on agency representation and disclosure, before applying to Commissioner for license. Every salesperson must complete additional 30 hours of instruction approved by Commissioner within one year of initial licensure. Application for and obtainment of salesperson's license is required within one year of successful completion of examination or applicant will be required to repeat initial 30 hour course and examination before application for license is accepted. All salespersons and all brokers are required to complete 30 hours of continuing real estate education each 24-month licensing period after initial annual license renewal date, 15 hours of which must be completed during first 12 months. (82.22). Application for broker's license must be accompanied by proof applicant has had minimum of two years actual experience, within five-year period prior to application, as licensed real estate salesperson in Minnesota or in another state having comparable requirement, or is, in Commissioner's opinion, similarly qualified by reason of education or practical experience. Applicant for broker's license must have completed educational requirements of applicant for salesperson's license. Applicant for limited broker's license pursuant to 82.20(13) is not required to have minimum of two years of actual experience as real estate salesperson in order to obtain limited broker's license to act as principal only. (82.22). Applicant for closing agent's license must complete eight hour course approved by Commissioner. (82.22).

BULK SALES:

See category Debtor and Creditor, topic Fraudulent Sales and Conveyances.

CARRIERS:

Uniform Commercial Code adopted. (c. 336). See topic Commercial Code.

Express and railway companies are under general supervision of Commissioner of Transportation and Transportation Regulation Board. (cc. 174A, 218).

Carrier may only charge for services at rate set forth in published schedules, and discrimination and preferences by carrier are forbidden except in case of transportation for governmental units, fairs, and in religious, educational, charitable and other specified cases. (218.021).

Liability.—See topic Commercial Code.

Bills of Lading.—See topic Commercial Code.

Carrier cannot waive provisions of bill of lading. (149 Minn. 467, 184 N.W. 35).

Liens.—Carrier has lien for transportation or warehousing charges when not acting as carrier or warehouseman under Art. 7 of Uniform Commercial Code. (514.18, .19). If charges not paid within 90 days, goods may be sold at public sale, if notice thereof sent to owner. If goods to be sold are motor vehicles, 45 days written notice to all secured creditors listed on certificate of title of motor vehicles registered in Minnesota is required, or lien is ineffective against such creditors. (514.20-.22). See topic Commercial Code.

Unclaimed Property.—Personal baggage in possession of carrier of passengers unclaimed within 30 days and other property in possession of any common carrier for 60 days after notice to consignee may be put in storage and, if not claimed within 12 months, may be sold on three weeks published notice, or, if perishable or subject to decay, may be sold upon ten days notice if not removed in 30 days; if in state of decay, goods may be summarily sold by order of any judge of county or municipal district court after inspection and without notice; proceeds go to county treasurer. (345.09-.13). Unclaimed goods in hands of consignee or bailee may be sold after a year on 60 days notice and, after deducting costs and freight or storage due, proceeds

go to county treasurer. (345.01-.06). Owner may obtain proceeds from treasurer within five years after such sale if he furnishes satisfactory proof. (345.07).

Motor Vehicle Carriers.—See category Transportation, topic Motor Vehicles.

COMMERCIAL CODE:

Uniform Commercial Code adopted. (c. 336). Sections of Minnesota Statutes corresponding to Official Text are preceded by 336 and decimal point. Thus Code §1-201 is Minn. Stat. 336.1-201.

For text of 1962 Official Text, 1972 Official Amendments, 1977 Official Amendments, 1987 Official Amendments, 1990 Official Amendments, 1994 Official Amendments and 1995 Official Amendments; see Uniform and Model Acts section.

1972 Official Amendments adopted.

1977 Official Amendments adopted.

1987 Official Amendments adopted.

1990 Official Amendments adopted.

1994 Official Amendments adopted as follows: (a) Amendments to Arts. 1, 4, 5, 9 and 10 conforming to 1994 Revision of Art. 8 and Revised Art. 8 (1994 Revision), adopted effective Jan. 1, 1996, except: §§8-509(d) was omitted. (b) 1994 Amendments to UCC adopted to extent corrections therein were not previously adopted except: (i) changes to §9.206 were not adopted; and (ii) reference to "Leases" added to §9-203(1) and 9-302(1) were not adopted. 1995 Official Amendments adopted.

Laws of Minn. 1986, c. 444, §1, removed gender-specific references applicable to human beings throughout Minnesota statutes by adopting by reference proposed amendments prepared by Revisor of Statutes; amendments do not change substance of statutes amended.

Laws of Minnesota 1990, c. 171, Art. 2, repealed bulk sales provisions formerly found in Minn. Stat. 1990, §§336.6-101 through 336.6-111.

Laws of Minnesota 1992, c. 565 adopted revised Art. 3 and conforming amendments to Art. 1 and Art. 4. Laws of Minnesota 1992, c. 525 adopted Farm Product Statutory Liens Act. See summary following notes to Art. 9. Laws of Minnesota 1997, c. 11 adopted revised Art. 5 and confirming amendments to Art. 1, Art. 2 and Art. 9. Laws of Minnesota 1997, c. 137 amending §§336.9-403, 336.9-404 and 336A.04 subd. 4.

Variations from 1962 Official Text, 1972 Official Amendments, 1977 Official Amendments and Optional Provisions, 1987 Official Amendments, 1990 Official Amendments, 1994 Official Amendments, 1995 Official Amendments revised Art. 3 and conforming amendments to Art. 1 and Art. 4 adopted, are as follows:

Term "chapter" substituted for "Act" throughout.

§1-101—sentence added explaining numbering of sections.

§1-102—subsection (6) added stating that nothing in Code authorizes branch banking.

§1-105—subsection (2) Alternative A adopted.

§1-209—1966 Official Optional Amendment enacted.

§2-107—"of subsection (1)" inserted after "provisions" in subsection (3).

§2-318—1966 Official Optional Amendment Alternative C enacted; last 15 words omitted.

§2-403—subsection (4) Alternative A adopted.

§2-702—1966 Official Amendment not enacted.

§2-725—words added to following subsection (4): "The limitations of this section do not apply to actions for the breach of any contract for sale of a grain storage structure or other goods that are incorporated into an improvement to real property, except equipment and machinery. These actions are subject only to the statute of limitations set forth in section 541.051.

This section does not apply to claims against sellers of goods for damages to property caused by the goods where the property that is damaged is not the goods and the sale is not a sale between parties who are each merchants in goods of the kind."

§2A-104—1990 Official Amendment not enacted.

§2A-517—"that is not a consumer lease" omitted after "finance lease" in subsection (2).

§2A-524—1990 Official Amendment not enacted.

§2A-529—words "In addition to any other recovery permitted by this article or other law, the lessor may recover from the lessee an amount that will fully compensate the lessor for any loss of or damage to the lessor's residual interest in the goods caused by the default of the lessee." inserted after subsection (5).

§3-206—Subsection (g) added reading "Nothing in this section prohibits or limits the effectiveness of a restrictive endorsement made under Section 256.9831, subdivision 3."

§4-104(3)—definition of "Banking Day" excludes Sats., Suns., and holidays.

§4-106—Alternative B adopted.

§5-114—optional subsections (4) and (5) adopted.

Article 6—Alternative A adopted (repealing bulk sales article).

§7-204—subsection (4) omitted.

§7-209—1966 Official Amendment enacted.

§7-403—optional words in subsection (1)(b) omitted.

§8-102—1973 Official Amendment adopted.

§8-103—Subsection (c) modified and expanded to read as follows: "An interest in a partnership or limited liability company is a general intangible and is not a security or a financial asset, except as follows: (1) an interest in a partnership or limited liability company is a security and is not a general intangible if it is dealt in or traded on a securities exchange or in a securities market, its terms expressly provide that it is a security governed by this article, or it is an investment company security; (2) an interest in a partnership or limited liability company is a financial asset and is not a general intangible if it is held in a securities account."

§8-603—Dates specified. Period of "four months after the effective date" in second sentence of Subsection (b) changed to read "the period through December 31, 1996, so long as the security interest could have remained perfected under the law in effect on

---

See note at head of Digest as to 1998 legislation covered.

See Topical Index in front part of this volume.

COMMERCIAL CODE... *continued*

December 31, 1995, if that law continued in effect after December 31, 1995," and phrase "within that period" in said sentence changed to read "during the one-year period from January 1, 1996 to December 31, 1996."

§9-104—"such as Ship Mortgage Act, 1920," added after "United States".

§9-105(1)—Sentence "Any person filing a financing statement under this article and under authority of the provisions of Minnesota Statutes 1974, Sections 300.111 through 300.115 shall be deemed a " 'transmitting utility' hereunder" added to subsection (1)(n).

§9-105(2)—reference to definition of "Motor vehicle" added in subsection (2).

§9-106—" 'contract right':" added to heading after " 'account';". Words "to payment" omitted before "earned" in last sentence.

§9-203—blanks in subsection (2) were filled in as follows: "Minnesota Statutes, Sec. 48.153 to 48.157; Chapters 52, 53 and 56; and Sections 168.66 to 168.77; 222.13 to 222.16 and 334.01 to 334.06."

§9-301(2)—Period of "20" days substituted for time period of "10" days.

§9-302(1)(b)—Period of "20" days substituted for time period of "10" days.

§9-302(3)—Subsection (3)(b) divided into subsections (3)(b)(i) and (3)(b)(ii) after words "the following statutes of this state;" with "subsection (3)(b)(i) commencing with "Sections 168A.01 to 168A.31 and Sections 222 to 242;" followed by qualifying text "but during . . . . ." and subsection (3)(b)(ii) reading "Sections 300.11 to 300.115." without qualification.

§9-302(4)—Last sentence was modified to read: "A security interest perfected by compliance with such a statute or treaty is governed by this article in all respects not inconsistent with the provisions of the statute or treaty under which it was perfected, provided that this article shall not be deemed inconsistent if it provides for a more extensive duration of effectiveness."

§9-306(3), (3)(c) and (4)(d)(ii)—Periods of "20" days substituted for time periods of "10" days.

§9-307(1)—Modified by deleting phrase: "other than a person buying farm products from a person engaged in farming operations".

§9-312(4)—Period of "20" days substituted for time period of "10" days.

§9-318—"the" added before the word "assignor" in subsection (1)(a). Commas omitted before and after "and notwithstanding . . . . . assignment" in the first sentence of subsection (2).

§9-401—Second Alternative Subsection (1) adopted with substantial changes. Subsection (1) reads as follows:

"(a) When the collateral is consumer goods, or motor vehicles which are not covered by a certificate of title, then in the office of the county recorder in the county of the debtor's residence if the debtor is an individual who is a resident of this state but if the debtor is an individual who is not a resident of this state or is a corporation, partnership or other organization then in the office of the secretary of state;

(b) When the collateral is equipment to be used in farming operations, or farm products, or accounts or general intangibles arising from or relating to the sale of farm products by a farmer, or crops growing or to be grown, then in the office of the county recorder in the county of the debtor's residence if the debtor is an individual or organization with residence in this state, but if the debtor is not a resident of this state, then in the office of the secretary of state;

(c) When the collateral is timber to be cut or is minerals or the like (including oil and gas) or accounts subject to subsection (5) of section 336.9-103, or when the financing statement is filed as a fixture filing (section 336.9-313) and the collateral is goods which are or are to become fixtures, then in the office where a mortgage on the real estate would be filed or recorded;

(d) In all other cases, in the office of the secretary of state."

Subsection (3) substantially changed to read as follows:

"A filing which is made in the proper place in this state continues effective even though the debtor's residence in this state or the use of the collateral, whichever controlled the original filing, is thereafter changed."

Subsection (5) substantially revised to read as follows:

"(5) Notwithstanding the preceding subsections, the proper place to file in order to perfect a security interest in collateral, including fixtures, of a transmitting utility is the office of the secretary of state. Such a filing shall not be deemed a separate filing from the filings required by other laws, if applicable, set forth in subsection (3) of section 336.9-302. This filing constitutes a fixture filing (section 336.9-313) as to the collateral described therein which is or is to become fixtures."

A Subsection (7) added to define "motor vehicle" as follows:

" 'Motor vehicle' means any device propelled or drawn by any power other than muscular power in, upon, or by which any person or property is or may be transported or drawn upon a highway, excepting building and road construction equipment and vehicles that are inventory of licensed dealers."

§9-402(1)—"name" substituted for "names" in first sentence and "and the name of the record owner thereof and the crop years that are covered by the financing statement" added at end of third sentence. Debtors' social security or tax identification number required.

§9-402(2)—"within one year" added after word "lapsed" at end of subsection (c); "or" added at end of subsection (d), and following optional subsections added:

"(e) a lien filed pursuant to Minnesota Statutes, Chapter 514; or

(f) collateral which is subject to a filed judgment."

§9-402(2a)—Section added providing that, except for documents filed under §9-402(2)(e) and (f), reason for omitting a debtor's signature must be stated on front of financing statement.

§9-402(3)—"Debtors' Social Security Number or I.R.S. Tax Identification Number" added below address line of form; "and the name of the record owner thereof" added after "real estate" in paragraph 2 of the form.

§9-402(4)—Following language added after first sentence:

"If the sole purpose of the amendment is to change the name or address of the secured party, only the secured party need sign the amendment. A writing is sufficient if it sets forth the name and address of the debtor and secured party as

those items appear on the original financing statement or the most recently filed amendment, the file number and date of filing of the financing statement."

§9-402(5)—optional language included and the following added:

"No description of the real estate or the name of the record owner thereof is required for a fixture filing where the debtor is a transmitting utility. Notwithstanding the foregoing a general description of the real estate is sufficient for a fixture filing where a railroad is the record owner of the real estate on which the fixtures are or are to be located; and for the purposes of this subsection, the requirement of a general description is satisfied if the fixture filing (1) identifies the section, township and range numbers of the county in which the land is located; (2) identifies the quarter-quarter of the section that the land is located in; (3) indicates the name of the record owner of the real estate; and (4) states the street address of the real estate if one exists."

§9-402(6)—"and" omitted prior to "(b)" and "(c)".

§9-402(7)—"the" added before "names of partners" in first sentence; ", and gives the social security number of the debtor, or, in the case of a debtor doing business other than as an individual, the Internal Revenue Service taxpayer identification number of the debtor." added before "partners" in first sentence.

§9-402(8)—"amendment, continuation, assignment, release, or termination" added after "A financing statement". New sentence added: "The omission or any inaccuracy in stating the debtor's social security or federal tax identification number, is not, standing alone, a seriously misleading error."

§9-403(2)—The third sentence, which reads "if a security interest perfected by filing exists at the time insolvency proceedings are commenced by or against the debtor, the security interest remains perfected until termination of the insolvency proceedings and thereafter for a period of 60 days or until expiration of the five-year period, whichever occurs later," is omitted.

§9-403(3)—Following language inserted after "secured party" in second sentence: "set forth the name, social security number or other tax identification number of the debtor, and address of the debtor and secured party as those items appear on the original financing statement or the most recently filed amendment,". Following language is omitted from the sixth sentence, "microfilm or other photographic record" and the following language is added in its place, "copy in a format which meets archival standards." Following language is omitted from the seventh sentence, "by physical annexation of financing statements to continuation statements or other related filings, or by other means."

§9-403(4)—"microfilm or other photographic" and "thereof" omitted from first sentence, "in a format that meets archival standards" added in place of "thereof" in first sentence, "and" omitted following "number" in second sentence, and ", and the social security number or other tax identification number of the debtor given in the statement" added at end of second sentence.

§9-403(5)—"The secretary of state shall prescribe uniform forms for statements and samples thereof shall be furnished to all filing officers in the state. Uniform fee for filing and indexing and for stamping copy furnished by secured party to show date and place of filing:

"(a) for an original financing statement or statement of continuation on a standard form prescribed by the secretary of state, is $15 for up to two debtor names and $15 for each additional name thereafter;

(b) for an original financing statement or statement of continuation that is not on a standard form prescribed by the secretary of state, is $20 for up to two debtor names and $20 for each additional name thereafter;

(c) for an amendment on a standard form prescribed by the secretary of state that does not add debtor names, is $15;

(d) for an amendment that is not on a standard form prescribed by the secretary of state and that does not add a debtor name, is $20;

(e) for an amendment on a standard form prescribed by the secretary of state that adds more than one debtor name, is $15 per debtor name; and

(f) for an amendment that is not on a standard form prescribed by the secretary of state that adds more than one debtor names, is $20 per debtor name.

In no case will a filing officer accept more than four additional pages per financing statement for filing in the uniform commercial code records.

The secretary of state shall adopt rules for filing, amendment, continuation, termination, removal, and destruction of financing statements."

§9-403(7)—"for filing offices other than the secretary of state," inserted before "where indexing" in first sentence. Following sentence is added:

A subsection (8) added reading as follows:

"The fees provided for in this article shall supersede the fees for similar services otherwise provided for by law except in the case of security interests filed in connection with a certificate of title on a motor vehicle."

§9-404(1)—"which shall be identified by file number" deleted from end of first sentence and following new sentence added in substitution:

"The termination statement must set forth the name and address of the debtor and secured party as those items appear on the original financing statement or the most recently filed amendment; identify the original financing statement by file number and filing date; and be signed by the secured party."

§9-404(2)—Omit "microfilm or other photographic" and add "in a format that meets archival standards" after the first "statement" in the first sentence.

§9-404(3)—Subsection substantially revised to read as follows:

"(3) There shall be no fee collected for the filing of a termination if the termination statement is in the standard form prescribed by the secretary of state. The fee for filing a termination statement on a form that is not the standard form prescribed by the secretary of state is $5. If the original financing statement was subject to subsection (5) of section 336.9-402, the fee prescribed by section 357.18, subdivision 1, clause (1) is also required."

§9-405(1)—Last sentence revised to read as follows:

"The uniform fee for filing, indexing, and furnishing filing data for a financing statement so indicating an assignment shall be the same as the fee prescribed in section 336.9-403, clause (5)."

§9-405(2)—First two sentences revised to read as follows:

See note at head of Digest as to 1998 legislation covered.

See Topical Index in front part of this volume.

COMMERCIAL CODE... *continued*

"A secured party of record may record an assignment of all or a part of the secured party's rights under a financing statement. The assignment must be filed in the place where the original financing statement was filed. The assignment must be signed by the secured party of record. The assignment must state: (1) the name and address of the secured party of record and the debtor as those items appear on the original financing statement or the most recently filed amendment, (2) the file number and the date of filing of the financing statement, (3) the name and address of the assignee, and (4) a description of the collateral assigned. A copy of the assignment is sufficient if it complies with the preceding sentence." The word "separate" is omitted from the third sentence. The second to the last sentence is revised to read as follows:

"The uniform fee for filing, indexing and furnishing filing data about such a statement of assignment shall be $15 for up to two debtor names and $15 for each additional name thereafter if the statement is in the standard form prescribed by the secretary of state. If the statement is in a form that is not the standard form prescribed by the secretary of state, the fee is $20 for up to two debtor names and $20 for each additional name thereafter. In each case where the original financing statement was subject to subsection 5 of section 336.9-402, the fee prescribed by section 357.18, subd. 1, clause (1), is also required."

§9-406—Second sentence revised to read as follows:

"The statement of release is sufficient if it contains a description of the collateral being released, the name and address of the debtor and secured party as those items appear on the original financing statement or the most recently filed amendment, and identifies the original financing statement by file number and filing date. The words "and shall note the same upon the margin of index of the filing of the financing statement" are deleted. Last sentence revised to read as follows:

"The uniform fee for filing and noting such a statement of release shall be $15 if the statement is the standard form prescribed by the secretary of state. If the statement is not on the standard form prescribed by the secretary of state, the fee is $20. If the original financing statement was subject to subsection 5 of section 336.9-402, the fee prescribed by section 357.18, subdivision 1, clause (1), is also required."

§9-407—Optional provision included with clause (1) revised to read as follows:

"(1) If the person filing any financing statement, termination statement, statement of assignment, or statement of release, furnishes the filing officer the statewide computerized uniform commercial code copy thereof, the filing officer shall upon request note upon the copy the file number and date and hour of the filing of the original and deliver or send the copy to such person.

(2) Upon request of any person, the filing officer shall conduct a search of a file for any active financing statements naming a particular debtor. The filing officer shall report the findings as of the date and hour of the search by issuing:

(a) a certificate listing the file number, date, and hour of each filing and the names and addresses of each secured party;

(b) photocopies of those original documents on file and located in the office of the filing officer; or,

(c) upon request, both the certificate and the photocopies referred to in (b).

The uniform fee for conducting the search and for preparing a certificate shall be $15 if the request is in the standard form prescribed by the secretary of state. This uniform fee shall include up to ten photocopies of original documents. If the request for information is made on a form other than the standard form prescribed by the secretary of state, the fee shall be $20 and shall include up to ten photocopies of original documents. Another fee, at the same rate, shall also be charged for conducting a search and preparing a certificate showing federal and state tax liens on file with the filing officer naming a particular debtor. There shall be an additional fee of $1 per page for photocopy of each financing statement or tax lien prepared in excess of the first ten.

Notwithstanding the fees set in this section, a natural person who is the subject of data must, upon the person's request, be shown the data without charge, and upon request be provided with photocopies of the data upon payment of no more than the actual cost of making the copies." Notwithstanding section 13.49, a filing officer may include social security number information in a report of the findings following a search of the statewide computerized uniform commercial code database or the state and federal tax liens on file with the filing officer. A filing officer may also include social security number information on a photocopy of an original document on file whether provided in response to a request for information or in response to a request made pursuant to section 13.03."

§9-410—added section providing for destruction of lapsed statements after one year and termination statements after three years.

§9-411 added to read:

"(a) The secretary of state shall develop and implement a statewide computerized filing system to accumulate and disseminate information relative to lien statements, financing statements, state and federal tax lien notices, and other uniform commercial code documents. The computerized filing system must allow information to be entered and retrieved from the computerized filing system by county recorders, the Department of Revenue, the Department of Jobs and Training, and the Internal Revenue Service.

(b) County recorders shall enter information relative to lien statements, financing statements, state and federal tax lien notices, and other uniform commercial code documents filed in their offices into a central data base maintained by the secretary of state. The information must be entered under the rules of the secretary of state. This requirement does not apply to tax lien notices filed under Sections 268.161, subdivision 1, paragraph (b), clause (2); 270.69, subdivision 2, paragraph (b), clause (2); and 278.488, subdivision 1, but does apply to entry of the date and time of receipt and county recorder's file number of those notices.

(c) The secretary of state may allow private parties to have electronic-view-only access to the computerized filing system and other computerized records maintained by the Secretary of State on a fee basis. If the computerized filing system allows a form of electronic access to information regarding the obligations of debtors, the access must be available 24 hours a day, every day of the year.

Notwithstanding section 13.49, private parties who have electronic-view-only access to computerized records may view the social security number information about a debtor that is of record.

(d) The secretary of state shall adopt rules to implement the computerized filing system. The rules must:

(1) allow filings to be made at the offices of all county recorders and the secretary of state's office as required by section 336.9-401;

(2) establish a central data base for all information relating to liens and security interests that are filed at the offices of county recorders and the secretary of state;

(3) provide procedures for entering data into a central data base;

(4) allow the offices of all county recorders and the secretary of state's office to add, modify, and delete information in the central data base as required by the uniform commercial code;

(5) allow the offices of all county recorders and the secretary of state's office to have access to the central data base for review and search capabilities;

(6) allow the offices of all county recorders to have electronic-view-only access to records on file with the Secretary of State;

(7) require the secretary of state to maintain the central data base;

(8) provide security and protection of all information in the central data base and monitor the central data base to ensure that unauthorized entry is not allowed;

(9) require standardized information for entry into the central data base;

(10) prescribe an identification procedure for debtors and secured parties that will enhance lien and financing statement searches; and

(11) prescribe a procedure for phasing-in or converting from the existing filing system to a computerized filing system.

(e) The Secretary of State, county recorder's, and their employers and agents shall not be liable for any loss or damages arising from errors in or omissions from information entered into the computerized filing system as a result of the electronic transmission of tax lien notices under sections 268.161, subdivision 1, paragraph (b), clause (2); 270.69, subdivision 2, paragraph (b), clause (2); 272.483 and 272.488, subdivisions 1 and 3."

§9-412 added to read:

"The state, the secretary of state, counties, county recorders, and their employees and agents are immune from liability that occurs as a result of errors in or omissions from information provided from the computerized filing system."

§9-413 added to read in part:

"(b) The filing officer with whom a financing statement, amendment, assignment, statement of release or continuation statement is filed, or to whom a request for search is made, shall collect the filing fee and forward $5 of that fee as a surcharge on each filing or search. Surcharge amounts shall be collected quarterly by the secretary of state from each county recorder. The secretary of state shall send each county recorder an invoice at the end of each fiscal quarter and each county recorder shall forward payment to the secretary of state within 30 days of the date of the invoice. The surcharge does not apply to a search request made by a natural person who is the subject of the data to be searched except when a certificate is requested as a part of the search.

(c) The surcharge amounts received from county recorders and the surcharge amounts collected by the secretary of state's office must be deposited in the state treasury and credited to the uniform commercial code account.

(d) Fees that are not expressly set by statute but are charged by the secretary of state to offset the costs of providing a service under sections 336.9-411 to 336.9-413 must be deposited in the state treasury and credited to the uniform commercial code account.

(e) Fees that are not expressly set by statute but are charged by the secretary of state to offset the costs of providing information contained in the computerized records maintained by the secretary of state must be deposited in the state treasury and credited to the uniform commercial code account.

(f) Money in the uniform commercial code account is continuously appropriated to the secretary of state to implement and maintain the computerized uniform commercial code filing system under section 336.9-411 and to provide electronic-view-only access to other computerized records maintained by the secretary of state."

§9-501—subsections (6) and (7) are repealed on July 1, 1997, but until such time these sections are added to read as follows:

"(6) A person may not begin to enforce a security interest in collateral that is agricultural property subject to sections 583.20 to 583.32 that has secured a debt of more than $5,000 unless: a mediation notice under subsection (7) is served on the debtor after a condition of default has occurred in the security agreement and a copy served on the director; and the debtor and creditor have completed mediation under sections 583.20 to 583.32; or as otherwise allowed under sections 583.20 to 583.32.

(7) A mediation notice under subsection (6) must contain the following notice with the blanks properly filled in:

"TO: . . . . (Name of Debtor) . . . .

YOU HAVE DEFAULTED ON THE . . . . (Debt in Default) . . . . SECURED BY AGRICULTURAL PROPERTY DESCRIBED AS . . . . (Reasonable Description of Agricultural Property Collateral) . . . .

AS A SECURED PARTY, ... (Name of Secured Party) . . . . INTENDS TO ENFORCE THE SECURITY AGREEMENT AGAINST THE AGRICULTURAL PROPERTY DESCRIBED ABOVE BY REPOSSESSING, FORECLOSING ON, OR OBTAINING A COURT JUDGMENT AGAINST THE PROPERTY.

YOU HAVE THE RIGHT TO HAVE THE DEBT REVIEWED FOR MEDIATION. IF YOU REQUEST MEDIATION, A DEBT THAT IS IN DEFAULT WILL BE MEDIATED ONLY ONCE. IF YOU DO NOT REQUEST MEDIATION, THIS DEBT WILL NOT BE SUBJECT TO FUTURE MEDIATION IF THE SECURED PARTY ENFORCES THE DEBT.

IF YOU PARTICIPATE IN MEDIATION, THE DIRECTOR OF THE AGRICULTURAL EXTENSION SERVICE WILL PROVIDE AN ORIENTATION MEETING AND A FINANCIAL ANALYST TO HELP YOU TO PREPARE FINANCIAL INFORMATION. IF YOU DECIDE TO PARTICIPATE IN MEDIATION, IT WILL BE

COMMERCIAL CODE . . . *continued*
TO YOUR ADVANTAGE TO ASSEMBLE YOUR FARM FINANCE AND OPERATION RECORDS AND TO CONTACT A COUNTY EXTENSION OFFICE AS SOON AS POSSIBLE. MEDIATION WILL ATTEMPT TO ARRIVE AT AN AGREEMENT FOR HANDLING FUTURE FINANCIAL RELATIONS.

TO HAVE THE DEBT REVIEWED FOR MEDIATION YOU MUST FILE A MEDIATION REQUEST WITH THE DIRECTOR WITHIN 14 DAYS AFTER YOU RECEIVE THIS NOTICE. THE MEDIATION REQUEST FORM IS AVAILABLE AT ANY COUNTY RECORDER'S OR COUNTY EXTENSION OFFICE.

FROM: . . . . (Name and address of Secured Party) . . . ."

§9-502—"contract rights," inserted after "accounts" in second sentence.

§9-508—section added reading as follows:

"Any secured party desiring to perpetuate the evidence of any sale made under the terms of any security agreement may within ten days after such a sale file in the appropriate office for the filing of a financing statement covering the goods sold a report of the proceedings of the sale, specifying the property sold and that returned, if any, the amount received, the name of the purchaser, an itemized statement of all costs and expenses, the amount applied on the obligation secured, and the amount, if any, returned to the debtor. The report shall be made by the person conducting the sale and verified by the person conducting the sale and verified or, if he be an officer, certified by him. An affidavit or officer's certificate of the service or posting of notice of the sale, executed by the person who served or posted the notice of sale, may be filed with the report of the proceedings of the sale. When such a report, affidavit, or certificate has been filed, it is prima facie evidence of the facts therein stated."

§10-101—[expired].

§10-104—subsection (2) adopted.

§10-105—similar to §10-101 of Official Text.

Farm Product Statutory Liens.—§§336A.01-.16 establish computerized system for filing financing statements and lien notices against farm products. Effective financing statement must comply with other requirements of 336.9-402 and in addition must contain following statements: "THIS EFFECTIVE FINANCING STATEMENT . . . . WILL . . . . WILL NOT BE TERMINATED WITHIN 30 DAYS OF THE DATE ON WHICH THE OBLIGATION(S) IT SECURES NO LONGER EXIST." "THE INFORMATION CONTAINED IN THIS EFFECTIVE FINANCING STATEMENT WILL BE SENT TO FARM PRODUCT BUYERS REGISTERED IN MINNESOTA. SALE OF FARM PRODUCTS TO THOSE BUYERS MAY RESULT IN A CHECK BEING ISSUED PAYABLE JOINTLY TO BOTH THE SELLER AND THE SECURED PARTY." Effective financing statement (1) must set forth any payment obligations imposed on buyer, commission merchant, or selling agent as condition for waiver or release of farm products statutory lien, (2) may not be combined with Uniform Commercial Code financing statement form, and (3) remains effective for five years. Fee for filing and indexing standard form for lien notice, effective financing statement, or continuation statement, and stamping date and place of filing on copy of filed document furnished by filing party is $15 for up to two debtor names and $15 for each additional name thereafter; fee may not be charged for filing termination statement filed within 30 days after satisfaction of lien or security interest, otherwise fee is $10. (§336A.04, Subd. 3). Fee to conduct search of computerized filing system for effective financing statements or lien notices and statements of continuation and to issue certificate, is $15 per debtor name if request is in standard form, or $20 otherwise. (§336A.09 Subd. 2). Filing under c. 336A does not affect perfection or priority of security interests filed under Uniform Commercial Code or farm products statutory lien filed in accordance with provisions of law under which it was created. (§336A.05). Farm product dealers may register with Secretary of State to receive master lists of notices of security interests in farm products or farm products statutory liens. Registration must be made on annual calendar year basis. §336A.11. Buyer in ordinary course of business who buys farm products from seller engaged in farming operations takes free of farm products statutory lien applicable to purchased farm products even though farm products statutory lien is perfected and buyer knows lien exists unless lienholder has perfected farm products statutory lien and (1) buyer has failed to register with Secretary of State as provided in §336A.11, or (2) buyer has registered with Secretary of State, buyer receives notice from Secretary of State specifying that seller and farm products being sold are subject to lien notice, and buyer fails to secure waiver or release of farm products statutory lien specified in lien notice by making payment, satisfying obligation, or otherwise. §336A.15. Commission merchant or selling agent who sells farm products for others is not subject to farm products statutory lien even though farm products statutory lien is perfected and commission merchant or selling agent knows lien exists unless lienholder has perfected farm product statutory lien and (1) commission agent or selling agent has failed to register with Secretary of State as provided in §336A.11 or (2) commission merchant or selling agent has registered with Secretary of State as provided in §336A.11, commission merchant or selling agent receives notice from Secretary of State specifying that seller and farm products being sold are subject to lien notice, and commission merchant or selling agent fails to secure waiver or release of farm product statutory lien specified in lien notice by making payment, satisfying obligation, or otherwise.

Forms.—Pursuant to 336.9-403(5), Secretary of State has prescribed standard forms for financing statements (UCC-1), continuation and termination statements (UCC-3), and requests for information or copies (UCC-11). Other forms complying with statutory requirements may be used. For forms, see end of this Digest.

See also topics: Banks and Banking, Bills and Notes, Brokers, Carriers, Contracts, Factors, Frauds, Statute of, Sales, Securities, Warehousemen; categories Business Organizations, topic Corporations; Civil Actions and Procedure, topic Limitation of Actions; Debtor and Creditor, topics Assignments, Fraudulent Sales and Conveyances, Liens, Pledges; Documents and Records, topics Records, Seals; Mortgages, topic Chattel Mortgages; Transportation, topic Motor Vehicles.

CONDITIONAL SALES:

See topic Sales.

CONSIGNMENTS:

See topic Factors.

CONSUMER PROTECTION:

See topics Interest and Sales.

Deceptive Practices.—Uniform Deceptive Trade Practices Act adopted. (325D.43-48).

Fraud, Misrepresentation.—Act, use or employment by any person of any fraud, false pretense, false promise, misrepresentation, misleading statement or deceptive practice, with intent that others rely thereon in connection with sale of objects, wares, goods, commodities, intangibles, real estate, loans or services ("merchandise") and of solicitation for payment of money for merchandise not yet ordered or services not yet performed and not yet ordered enjoinable by Attorney General or county attorney. (325F.68-70).

Advertising.—Untrue, deceptive or misleading advertisement is misdemeanor. (325F.67). Advertising and marketing materials relating to legal gambling must be sufficiently clear to prevent deception and must not overstate attributes or benefits of participating in legal gambling. (325E.42).

Credit Cards.—No person liable for use of unsolicited credit cards for which they or family member derive no benefit unless accepted. (325G.03). Liability from unauthorized use of credit card limited to $50 provided notice of unauthorized charges given within 60 days of receipt of bill. (325G.04). Credit card issuers required to respond to requests for explanations. (325G.05). Unfair discriminatory practice to discriminate in extension of personal or commercial credit or in requirements for obtaining credit because of race, color, creed, religion, disability, national origin, sex, sexual orientation, or marital status. (363.03 subd. 8). Woman who is issued credit card may direct that card be issued in her current or former surname. (325G.041; 363.03 subd. 8).

Check Cashing.—Person cannot require as condition to accepting check that person presenting check provide credit card number. (325F.981).

Warranties.—All consumer sales are accompanied by implied warranties of merchantability and fitness unless disclaimed prior to sale by conspicuous prescribed language. Seller may limit damages or remedies for breach. (325G.18). Express warranties arising out of a consumer sale of new goods may not disclaim implied warranties of merchantability or fitness. (325G.19). Statutory warranties apply to sales of new residential construction and home improvements. (c. 327A). Warranty of merchantability, fitness, and conformance with applicable law implied in every sale of new manufactured home and cannot be disclaimed. (327B.02). Manufacturer must replace farm tractor or refund purchase price if tractor fails to conform to express warranty after four attempts at repair or 60 business days out of service. (325F.6651-59). Statutory minimum one year warranty applies to every sale of assistive devices intended to increase, maintain or improve functional capabilities of individuals with disabilities. Manufacturer must provide replacement device if repair lasts more than ten working days or device has been brought in for repair of same problem on two previous occasions. (325G.203-08).

Lemon Law.—Manufacturer of passenger motor vehicle under applicable express manufacturer's warranty must replace new motor vehicle or refund purchase price if: (1) Same nonconformity has been subject to repair four or more times within applicable express warranty term or during two years following date of original delivery of new motor vehicle to consumer, whichever is earlier date, but nonconformity continues to exist, or (2) vehicle is out of service because of repair for cumulative total of 30 or more business days during express warranty term or during two-year period, whichever is earlier date. (325F.665). If manufacturer offers replacement vehicle, consumer has option of rejecting replacement vehicle and requiring manufacturer to provide refund. (325F.665). Consumer who leases vehicle has same rights under 325F.665 as consumer purchasing new vehicle, except that if manufacturer must accept return of consumer's leased vehicle, then consumer lessee is entitled only to refund and consumer's written lease with lessor must be terminated. Refund to include full amount actually paid by consumer on written lease, including all additional charges if actually paid by consumer, less reasonable allowance for consumer's use. (325F.665). With respect to used motor vehicles, dealer required to give express warranty as specified in statute with exception of certain enumerated vehicles. (325F.662).

Odometers.—Tampering with odometers to lower mileage prohibited. Operating vehicle with disconnected or malfunctioning odometer with intent to defraud prohibited. In conjunction with sale of vehicle, seller must disclose true mileage or that true mileage unknown if odometer not accurate. (325E.13-.16).

Returned Merchandise Refunds.—Retail sellers required to give cash refund for acceptable returned merchandise unless seller posts clear and conspicuous written notice, in boldface type of minimum size of 14 points, of other policy in store. (325F.80).

Retail Credit Sales.—In consumer credit sale, seller or lessor may not take negotiable instrument other than check as evidence of obligation. Holder is not in good faith if negotiable instrument taken with notice of violation of foregoing. (325G.16).

No contract or obligation relating to consumer credit sale may contain any provision by which: consumer agrees not to assert against assignee any claim or defense arising out of transaction; in absence of default, holder may accelerate maturity without cause; power of attorney to confess judgment or assignment of wages is given; authority is given to enter consumer's premises unlawfully or commit breach of peace in repossession of goods; consumer waives right of action for illegal act committed in collection of payments or repossession of goods; or consumer relieves seller from any liability for any legal remedy against seller in connection with contract or obligation. (325G.16).

Assignee of contract or obligation relating to consumer credit sale is subject to all claims and defenses of consumer against seller arising from sale, notwithstanding any agreement to contrary. Assignee's liability, however, may not exceed amount owing assignee when claim or defense is asserted against assignee. Rights of consumer under

See note at head of Digest as to 1998 legislation covered.

See Topical Index in front part of this volume.

MN – 11

CONSUMER PROTECTION . . . *continued*
foregoing may only be asserted as a matter of defense to or set off against claim by assignee. (325G.16).

Consumer credit sale includes bailment, lease or terminable bailment or lease where bailee or lessee agrees to pay sum for use equivalent to or greater than aggregate value of goods and bailee or lessee has option to become owner upon compliance with agreement for no other or nominal consideration. Bailor or lessor in such transaction has security interest only. Contracts in form of terminable bailment or lease of goods relating to consumer credit sales must specify whether goods are new or used. (325G.15-.16).

If seller or lender repossesses or voluntarily accepts personal property in which it has security interest arising out of consumer credit transaction of $3,000 or less, subject to periodic adjustment by Commissioner of Commerce, buyer is not personally liable. Seller or lender has no repossession right or right to levy or execute on goods subject to security interest if it obtains judgment in circumstances where it has no right to deficiency judgment if it had elected to repossess. (325G.21-.22).

Referral Sales.—Referral and chain referral selling prohibited. Sales or lease agreements violating prohibition are unenforceable and buyer or lessee has option to rescind and obtain restitution or retain goods delivered and benefit of services performed without further obligation to pay. (325F.69).

Home Solicitation Sales.—Buyer has right to cancel home solicitation sale in excess of $25 until midnight of 3rd business day after sale by written notice of cancellation. Seller must furnish specified forms to buyer. Notice of cancellation need not take particular form; sufficient if buyer expresses in writing intent not to be bound by home solicitation sale. (325G.06-.11).

Unsolicited Goods.—Receipt of such goods deemed unconditional gift from sender. (325G.01).

Personal Solicitation Sales.—Seller of goods or services primarily for personal, family or household purposes, except nonprofit organization, who contacts buyer by telephone or in person other than at seller's place of business must first disclose seller's name, name of firm or organization represented, identity of goods or services and that seller wishes to demonstrate or sell same. When initial contact in person, seller must show identification card. (325G.12-.14). Use of automatic dialing announcing telephone device prohibited unless recipient has knowingly or voluntarily requested, consented to, permitted, or authorized receipt of message or message is immediately preceded by live operator who obtains recipient's consent before message is delivered; not applicable to recipients with whom caller has current business or personal relationship. (325E.27). Automatic dialing-announcing device must be designed so it disconnects within ten seconds after recipient ends call. (325E.28). When message is immediately preceded by live operator, operator must first disclose name of business or organization for which message is being made, purpose of message, identity or kinds of goods or services message is promoting, and, if applicable, fact message intends to solicit payment or commitment of funds. (325E.29). Commercial telephone solicitation prohibited before 9 a.m. or after 9 p.m. unless caller has current business or personal relationship. (325E.30).

Phone Services.—Phone service subscriber is not responsible for information service charges (including 1-900 calls) for calls made by minor or vulnerable adult unless call expressly authorized. It is fraudulent misrepresentation to advise subscriber otherwise. Charges for information services must be listed separately from other phone charges. (325F.692).

Prize Notices.—Statute sets forth extensive disclosure requirements associated with prize notices including retail value of prize and person's odds of receiving prize and requires that prize be awarded within 30 days after sponsor has represented that person has been awarded prize. (325F.755).

Videotape Sellers and Service Providers.—With certain exceptions, statute prohibits videotape sellers and service providers from disclosing information about their customers. (325I.01-.03). Videotapes and similar audiovisual material must have closed or open captioning if released after 6/1/97 and more than 500 copies are produced, or if it is produced by government entity for educational purposes. (3251.05).

Membership Cancellation.—Person who enters contract to become member of health club, social referral club or buying club can cancel contract within three days after entered. (325G.24). Same is also true with respect to membership travel contracts. (325G.50).

Plain Language.—

Consumer Contracts.—All contracts with consumer entered after July 1, 1983, including contracts transferring or authorizing security interest in personal property and residential leases (excluding contracts above $50,000, contracts mortgaging real property or to obtain money to buy or refinance real property, contracts where sale of personal property is only incidental to sale of realty, contracts involving securities transactions with broker-dealer registered with Securities and Exchange Commission, and contracts involving commodities with commission merchant registered with Commodities Futures Trading Commission) must be written in clear and coherent manner using words with common and everyday meanings and must be appropriately divided and captioned. Court may reform contract if violation substantially confused consumer to consumer's financial detriment. Consumer may recover actual damages for violation, but violation not defense to action on contract. Good faith and reasonable effort to comply is defense to action for violation. Contracts may be submitted to attorney general for certification of compliance. (325G.29-.37).

Insurance Policies.—Readability standards prescribed for all private passenger vehicle and homeowner's insurance policies or contracts issued, renewed or amended after July 1, 1979; all life and accident and health policies, HMO and nonprofit health service corporation contracts, and fraternal beneficiary association certificates issued, renewed or amended after July 1, 1980; and other policies after July 1, 1981. Covered policies to be filed with Commissioner of Insurance prior to issuance. (c. 72C).

Deficiency Judgments.—Seller or lender who repossesses or accepts surrender of goods in which it has security interest arising out of consumer credit transaction cannot obtain deficiency judgment if amount of credit extended was $3,000 or less. (325G.21-.22).

CONTRACTS:

Uniform Commercial Code adopted. (c. 336). See topic Commercial Code; categories Documents and Records, topic Seals; Family, topic Infants.

FACTORS:

Uniform Commercial Code adopted. (c. 336). See topic Commercial Code.

Grain buyers must obtain license and file bond and annual financial statements with Commissioner of Agriculture and must observe specified terms and procedures for grain purchases. Buying grain without license is misdemeanor. (223.15-.22).

FRANCHISES:

Franchise Law.—80C.01 et seq.

Uniform Franchise and Business Opportunities Act not adopted.

Supervision.—Commissioner of Commerce, Minnesota Department of Commerce.

Regulatory Powers of Supervising Authority.—Broad powers of investigation and revocation of registration. (80C.12).

Registration.—Unlawful to offer or sell franchise unless registered or exempt. (80C.02). Application for registration made by filing with Commissioner public offering statement accompanied by fee of $400. Public offering statement must contain certain specified information. (80C.04, 80C.05, 80C.06).

Exemptions.—Registration not required for following if method of offer or sale is not used for purpose of evading 80C.03 et seq.: (1) Offer or sale of franchise owned by franchisee, or of entire area franchise owned by subfranchisor if sale is not effected by or through franchisor; provided no more than one sale of franchise or area franchise during any 12 month period; (2) transaction by executor, administrator, sheriff, receiver, trustee in bankruptcy, guardian or conservator; (3) offer or sale to banking organization, financial organization or life insurance corporation (as defined in 345.31); (4) securities currently registered in Minnesota pursuant to 80A; (5) offer or sale of franchise, not including area franchise, provided (a) no more than one sale during any 12 month period, (b) no advertising or general solicitation, (c) franchisor deposits all franchise fees in escrow account in bank located in Minnesota until all obligations of franchisor to be performed prior to opening of franchise have been performed, and (d) required notice given to Commissioner; (6) offer or sale of fractional franchise; (7) transaction which Commissioner by rule or order exempts; and (8) offer or sale to resident of foreign state, territory or country who is neither domiciled or actually present in Minnesota, if franchise business is not to be operated in Minnesota, and if sale of franchise is not in violation of law of foreign state, territory or country concerned. (80C.03).

Annual report accompanied by $200 fee required within 120 days after fiscal year of registrant. (80C.08).

Unfair Practices.—Statutory provisions governing termination or cancellation, failure to review and withholding consent to transfer. Commissioner has broad power to adopt rules defining unfair or inequitable practices prohibited by statute. (80C.14).

Special provisions applicable to motor fuel franchises (80C.145) and burglar alarm franchises (80C.30).

FRAUDS, STATUTE OF:

Uniform Commercial Code adopted. (c. 336). See topic Commercial Code.

No action may be maintained upon any of following agreements unless some note or memorandum thereof, expressing consideration, is in writing subscribed by party to be charged therewith: (1) Agreements not to be performed within year from making; (2) special promise to answer for debt, default or doings of another; (3) every agreement, promise, or undertaking made upon consideration of marriage, except mutual promises to marry; (4) every agreement, promise, or undertaking to pay debt, which has been discharged by bankruptcy or insolvency proceeding; (5) every grant or assignment of any existing trust in goods or things in action (513.01; 513.03). Consideration must be expressed with reasonable clearness. (65 Minn. 104, 67 N.W. 802). See topic Commercial Code.

No estate or interest in lands, other than leases for term not exceeding one year, nor any trust or power over or concerning lands or relating thereto, may be created, granted, assigned, surrendered, or declared, unless by act or operation of law, or unless in writing, subscribed by parties creating, granting, assigning, surrendering, or declaring same, or by their lawful agents thereunto authorized in writing. (513.04). Rule is not applicable to disposition of real estate by will or to creation or extinguishment of trust by implication or operation of law. (513.04). Every contract for leasing of lands for longer period than one year, or for sale of lands or any interest therein, is void unless contract or some note or memorandum thereof, expressing consideration, is in writing subscribed by party by whom lease or sale is to be made, or by his lawful agent thereunto authorize by writing. (513.05). Where made by an agent such contract is not entitled to record unless authority of agent is also recorded. (513.05). This includes contract for sale of standing timber. (142 Minn. 89, 170 N.W. 920). Agreement extending time of payment for manual labor relating to cutting, hauling, banking or driving logs is void unless signed by party to be charged therewith, and promissory note for payment of agreed compensation, with interest is delivered to laborer. (513.07).

Credit Agreement.—Debtor may not maintain action on credit agreement unless it is in writing, expresses consideration, sets forth terms and conditions and is signed by creditor and debtor. (513.33). "Credit agreement" is agreement to lend or forbear repayment of money, goods or things in action, to otherwise extend credit, or to make any other financial accommodation. (513.33).

Cohabitation.—Contract between man and woman living together in Minnesota out of wedlock, or contemplating doing so, is enforceable as to terms concerning property

FRAUDS, STATUTE OF . . . *continued*
and financial relation of parties only if contract is in writing, signed by parties and enforcement is sought after termination of relationship. (513.075; 513.076).

Part Performance.—In all cases where there has been part performance, equity may compel specific performance of agreements without regard to statute of frauds. (513.06). Sufficient part performance, generally, where party had been induced to change party's situation to such extent that party cannot be placed in status quo, or compensated in money. (132 Minn. 86, 155 N.W. 1054). Lessee who occupies land without written lease cannot invoke statute of frauds to avoid its obligations to lessor. (446 N.W.2d 690). See topic Commercial Code.

INTEREST:

Legal rate is 6%. (334.01).

Judgments.—Interest rate for each year determined on or before Dec. 20 of prior year by state Court Administrator based on secondary market yield for most recent month on one year U.S. treasury bills, rounded to nearest 1%. (549.09). Statutory rate is 5% for 1996.

Maximum Rate.—Written contract may provide for any rate up to and including 8%. Contract must bear same rate after maturity as before, and provision increasing rate after maturity, unless no interest stipulated for before maturity, works forfeiture of all interest. Contracts for loans of $100,000 or more and contracts entered into on or after Dec. 31, 1974 for certain loans or forbearances between current and former participants in, and beneficiaries of, ERISA plans, and such plans, are exempt from limitation. (334.01). State banks and savings associations, national banks, and state or federally chartered savings banks, savings and loan associations and credit unions doing business in state may charge on any loan or discount made upon any note, bill or other evidence of debt except extensions of open-end credit pursuant to 48.185, interest at rate not more than 4½% above discount rate (including surcharge) on 90 day commercial paper at Ninth District Federal Reserve Bank. (48.195). State banks, savings associations and industrial loan and thrifts and national banks and federal savings associations with their home office in Minnesota may charge finance charge on any loan at annual percentage rate of up to 21.75% (various amounts greater than 21.75% for certain small loans; 18% for open-end credit pursuant to credit card) computed on 365 day year and in accordance with Truth in Lending Act regulations plus certain specified charges. (48.194, 47.59, 53.04). State credit union may charge up to 1% per month on unpaid balance or amount allowed by 48.195 at time loan is made, if greater. (52.14). Banks, savings banks and savings associations organized under Minnesota or Federal law with main office in Minnesota may also make loans secured by savings or time deposit accounts owned by borrower at 2% over rate of interest payable on said account. (334.012).

Insurance premium finance companies may not contract for or receive finance charge in excess of 5% above discount rate on 90 day commercial paper at Ninth District Federal Reserve Bank. (59A.09).

Brokers and dealers registered under Securities Exchange Act are exempt from state usury laws in respect of interest imposed on debit balances in their customers' demand margin accounts secured by securities or bonds. (334.19).

Mortgage Loans.—Banks, savings associations and certain other defined lenders may make loans, mortgages, credit sales or advances, secured by first liens on residential real property (or by first liens on residential manufactured house or on stock in residential cooperative housing corporation) without any limitation on rate or amount of interest, discount points, or other charges if such loans are made after June 2, 1981. (47.204).

Banks, savings associations and other specified financial institutions may make following mortgage loans without regard to any state restrictions on interest: (1) FHA-insured mortgage loans, (2) VA-guaranteed mortgage loans, (3) Farmers Home Administration insured or guaranteed loans, (4) such loans as would be eligible for purchase by FNMA or FHLMC, and (5) such loans as are authorized by Office of Thrift Supervision or Comptroller of Currency. (47.20-.21).

Contract for deed vendors may charge interest on contracts for deeds, and any lender may make conventional or cooperative apartment loans at rate not exceeding FNMA posted yield on 30-year mortgage commitments for delivery within 60 days on standard conventional fixed-rate mortgages published in Wall Street Journal for last business day of second preceding month plus four percentage points. "Conventional loan" is loan less than $100,000 secured by mortgage on real estate containing one or more residential units or upon which it is intended that one or more residential units will be constructed. "Cooperative apartment loan" is loan less than $100,000 secured by security interest on shares of stock or membership certificate issued to stockholder or member by cooperative apartment corporation. (47.20[4a]).

Precomputed loans must provide for refund of precomputed finance charge if loan is paid in full one month or more before final installment due date.

Small Loans.—Licensee under Regulated Loan Act (c. 56) may charge interest on loan with principal amount of up to greater of $100,000 or 15% of Minnesota corporate licensee's capital stock and surplus reserves not exceeding greater of 21¾% per year on unpaid balance of principal amount. (56.002, 56.131). Licensee under Industrial Loan and Thrift Company Act (c. 53) may charge rates and impose terms and conditions permitted licensees under Regulated Loan Act on loans up to greater of $100,000 or 15% of industrial loan and thrift's capital stock and surplus (but in no event shall any loan cause loans to person primarily liable to exceed 20% of industrial loan and thrift capital stock and surplus), and may charge 21¾% (or such greater amount including such fees and charges as provided by 47.59). (53.04, 53.05).

Bank may make certain installment loans not over $35,000 ($25,000 for savings bank, savings association or federal savings association) and charge greater of 12% on unpaid principal balance or 4½% above discount rate (including surcharge) on 90 day commercial paper at Ninth District Federal Reserve Bank. (48.153, 48.195). Banks, state savings banks and savings associations, and any federally chartered savings and loan associations may also extend credit through open-end loan account arrangement and impose finance charge of up to equivalent of annual percentage rate of 18%, computed on 365 day year and in accordance with Truth in Lending Act (15 U.S.C. §1601 et seq. and 12 C.F.R. 226) and may impose annual bank credit card charge of $50 (48.185).

Usury.—Contract for greater rate of interest than statute permits is void except as to holder in due course (other than contracts for deed, cooperative apartment loans, loans by certain financial institutions including banks, savings associations and credit unions, and instruments taken or received, in accordance with and in reliance on any statute). (47.20, 48.196, 334.03). In computation of interest upon any bond, note or other instrument or agreement, interest may not be compounded, but any contract to pay interest, not usurious, upon interest overdue, shall not be construed to be usury. Agreement extending maturity date of contract, note or instrument and providing for increased rate of interest after original maturity date is not usurious if increased rate of interest does not exceed 8%. Contracts for loans of $100,000 or more exempt from limitation. (334.01). Time price exception to usury law recognized in some circumstances. (283 Minn. 437, 168 N.W.2d 667; but see 402 N.W.2d 235 and 518 N.W.2d 544).

If instrument void, court may declare it void, enjoin all proceedings thereon and order its cancellation and surrender. (334.05).

Payor of usurious interest, or its representative, may recover from receiver or its representative, full interest or premium paid, with costs, provided action brought within two years. (334.02). Penalty on contract for deed or cooperative apartment loan is five times usurious portion of interest plus attorney fees. (47.20). Usurious rate by certain financial institutions including banks, savings and loan associations and credit unions results in forfeiture of all interest, and payor may recover twice amount of interest paid provided action brought within two years. (48.196).

Not usury: clerical error in computation; one-twelfth of 8% for every 30 days; payment of interest in advance for one year, not exceeding 8%; purchase of negotiable mercantile paper, bona fide before maturity, and no intent to evade statute, or where purchase not a part of original usurious transaction. (334.03).

Corporations and limited partnerships are forbidden to interpose defense of usury. (334.021). State banks, savings associations and industrial loan and thrifts and national banks and federal savings associations with home offices in Minnesota may charge "organization" including corporation and all partnerships, any agreed upon interest rate and other charges. (47.59).

Consumer Credit.—Usury provisions notwithstanding, seller may impose finance charge on outstanding unpaid balance under open end credit plan of up to 1½% per month (1⅓% per month in case of oil company with national sales above $10,000,000,000) computed on average daily balance during each monthly billing cycle, excluding sales made during billing cycle. Minimum finance charge of 50¢ per month permissible. (334.16). Seller forfeits three times finance charge imposed for intentional violation. (334.18).

Motor Vehicle and Mobile Home Installment Sales.—See category Transportation, topic Motor Vehicles, subhead Sales.

LICENSES, BUSINESS AND PROFESSIONAL:

Licenses are required for a large number of businesses and occupations.

Commercial travelers do not need licenses.

Collection agency must obtain license from consumer services section of department of commerce and must annually file bond for $20,000. Bond may be reduced to not less than $5,000 for agency collecting less than $30,000 in previous year. (332.33-.34). "Collection agency" does not include persons whose activities are confined to and directly related to operation of business other than that of collection agency. (332.32).

MONOPOLIES, RESTRAINT OF TRADE AND COMPETITION:

Contract, combination, or conspiracy between two or more persons in unreasonable restraint of trade or commerce is unlawful. (325D.51). Establishment, maintenance, or use of, or any attempt to establish, maintain, or use monopoly power for purpose of affecting competition or controlling, fixing, or maintaining prices is also unlawful. (325D.52). Certain price fixing, production control, allocation of markets, collusive bidding and concerted refusals to deal deemed unlawful. (325D.53). Nonprofit labor, electrical, agricultural or horticultural organizations instituted for purpose of mutual help exempt. (325D.55).

Violators subject to civil penalty of not more than $50,000; $100,000 for failure to comply with final judgment or decree. Willful violation of 325D.53 is felony. (325D.56). Treble damages recoverable. (325D.57). Injunctive relief available. (325D.58). Noncompliance with final judgment or decree can result in forfeiture of charter and privilege to do business. (325D.60).

Action for violation must be commenced within four years of date cause of action arose, except that if proceedings commenced by Attorney General, action may be commenced within one year after termination of such proceedings, if later. (325D.64).

Also following specific prohibitions: Unlawful discrimination in sale or purchase of grain in different localities for purpose of creating monopoly (235.10) or in sale of petroleum (325D.67); combinations or agreements to control price or restrict competition in adoption or sale of schoolbooks (127.21); combinations to monopolize markets for food products (325D.68).

Unfair trade practices and unlawful geographic discrimination in production, manufacture or distribution of commodities, goods, wares and merchandise in general use for purpose or with effect of injuring competitor or destroying competition are prohibited and provision is made for injunctive relief. Commodities, goods, wares, etc., may not be sold, offered or advertised for sale at less than cost, nor given away, offered or advertised to be given away, for purpose or with effect of injuring competitors. (325D.01 et seq.).

Unlawful to advertise or claim that sale is at wholesale, that seller is wholesaler or that price is wholesale or reduced when not so in fact; also to misrepresent quality, ingredients or origin of merchandise or for employer to sell to employees merchandise

MONOPOLIES, RESTRAINT OF TRADE AND COMPETITION *. . . continued* not regularly handled by employer. (325D.09 et seq.). Restraints on termination of sales representatives. (325E.37).

NEGOTIABLE INSTRUMENTS:

See topic Bills and Notes.

RESTRAINT OF TRADE:

See topic Monopolies, Restraint of Trade and Competition.

SALES:

Uniform Commercial Code adopted. (c. 336). See topic Commercial Code.

Bills of Sale.—No statutory provisions.

Contracts of Sale.—No statutory limitations as to type size in printed contracts.

Conditional Sales.—See topic Commercial Code. Special provisions relating to contracts for conditional sale of railway equipment or rolling stock. (222.15-.17). See also category Transportation, topic Motor Vehicles, subhead Sales.

Bulk Sales.—See category Debtor and Creditor, topic Fraudulent Sales and Conveyances.

Sales of Motor Vehicles.—See category Transportation, topic Motor Vehicles.

Product Liability.—See topic Commercial Code. Court adoption of rule of strict tort liability. (278 Minn. 322, 154 N.W.2d 488).

Consumer Sales.—See topics Consumer Protection and Interest.

SECURITIES:

Blue Sky Law.—80A.01 et seq.

Supervision.—Commissioner of Commerce, Minnesota Department of Commerce.

Regulatory Powers of Supervising Authority.—Broad powers of denial, suspension, investigation and revocation of registration. (80A.20, 80A.13).

Registration.—Unlawful to offer or sell any security in state unless registered, exempt or federal covered security. (80A.08).

By Notification.—Permitted in case of certain nonprofit organizations. (80A.09).

By Coordination.—Permitted in case of any security for which registration statement has been filed under Securities Act of 1933. (80A.10).

By Qualification.—Any security may be registered by this method. (80A.11).

Fees.—Registration or notice filing fee is minimum of $100 plus $1/10$ of 1% of maximum aggregate offering price of securities offered in state. Maximum fee, $300. Fee of $100 for every initial filing of federal covered security, plus additional fee of 1/20 of 1% of maximum aggregate offering price of securities offered in state if filing made in connection with redeemable securities issued by open end management company or unit investment trust. No maximum fee. If filing in connection with Federal covered security under §18(b)(2) of Securities Act of 1933, additional fee of $1/10$ of 1% of maximum aggregate offering price up to maximum fee of $300. Fee for amendment to registration, $25, plus percent fee in certain cases. Annual report fee, $100. Fee for written opinion of Commissioner, $50. (80A.28).

Securities exempt from registration requirements are: (1) Issued or guaranteed by U.S., any state, any political subdivision of state or any agency or corporate or other instrumentality of foregoing, but not including securities sold pursuant to §106(a)(1) or (2) of Secondary Mortgage Market Enhancement Act of 1984 or payable solely from payments to be received in respect of property or money used under a lease, sale, or loan arrangement by or for a nongovernmental industrial or commercial enterprise; (2) issued or guaranteed by Canada, any Canadian province, any political subdivision of such province, any agency or corporate or other instrumentality of foregoing, but not including revenue obligation payable solely from payments under lease, sale or loan arrangement by or for non-governmental industrial or commercial enterprise; (3) issued and representing interest in or debt of, or guaranteed by, national or state bank, savings institution or trust company; (4) issued or guaranteed by federal savings institution or by similar organization organized under laws of any state and authorized to do business in Minnesota; (5) issued or guaranteed by certain credit unions; (6) listed or approved for listing on New York Stock Exchange, American Stock Exchange, Midwest Stock Exchange, Pacific Stock Exchange or Chicago Board Options Exchange; or other security of equal or senior rank of same issuer; security called for by subscription rights or warrants so listed or approved; or warrant or right to purchase or subscribe to any of foregoing; provided that this exemption does not apply to second tier listings of any exchanges; (7) certain commercial paper maturing within nine months from date of issue and not advertised in media or by direct mailing; (8) interest in employee savings, stock purchase, pension, profit sharing or similar benefit plan, or self-employed person's retirement plan; (9) issued or guaranteed by railroad, other common carrier or public utility subject to federal regulation regarding issuance or guarantee of its securities; (10) interests in certain common trust or collective investment funds of bank or trust company or in certain separate accounts of insurance companies; (11) issued by certain entities with net income over $1,000,000 in four of last five years including most recent year, class of registered securities under 1934 Act, and no material default in last seven years on securities, debts or long-term leases, and if other than preferred stock, securities meet voting and dispersion tests; (12) certificate of indebtedness sold or issued, and any savings account or savings deposit issued, by industrial loan and thrift company, except certificate pledged as security for contemporaneous loan; (13) security designated or approved for designation upon notice of issuance on NASDAQ/National Market System; other security of same issuer of senior or substantially senior rank; security called for by subscription rights or warrants so designated or approved; warrant or right to purchase or subscribe to any of securities referred to in this section, provided that National Market System provides commissioner with notice of any material change in definition requirements. (80A.15).

Transactions exempt from registration requirements are: (1) Sales if (a) no person makes more than ten sales (exclusive of sales pursuant to clause [b]) of same issuer in 12 months, provided that if seller is issuer, seller reasonably believes buyers are purchasing for investment and securities not advertised to general public by newspaper or other publications of general circulation, radio, television, electronic means or similar communications media, or through program of general solicitation by mail or telephone; or (b) no issuer makes more than 25 sales (exclusive of sales pursuant to clause [a]) during any 12 consecutive months, provided issuer meets conditions in clause (a), makes required filing with Commissioner and pays only reasonable and customary commissions to licensed broker-dealers; (2) nonissuer distributions of outstanding securities of issuers listed in certain manuals and meeting certain requirements; (3) execution of certain orders by broker-dealer pursuant to unsolicited offer; (4) single nonissuer sale of bonds or notes secured by mortgage if sold to single purchaser in single sale; (5) judicial sale; (6) certain sales by pledgees; (7) sale to bank, savings institution, trust company, insurance company, investment company as defined in Investment Company Act of 1940, or other financial institution or institutional buyer, or to broker-dealer; (8) sales pursuant to Rule 505 or 506 of SEC Regulation D (ULOE exemption); (9) offer, but not sale, of security for which registration statement has been filed under Minnesota Blue Sky Law; (10) certain sales by cooperatives; (11) certain sales in connection with corporate acquisition or reorganization if required notice has been given to Commissioner; (12) transactions between issuer and underwriter or among underwriters; (13) certain distributions by corporation to its own security holders; (14) sales of issuer's securities by affiliates of issuer if registration statement for securities of same class is in effect and sales are exempt by rule or order of Commissioner; (15) certain transactions with existing shareholders if required notice has been given to Commissioner; (16) nonissuer sales of any security, including revenue bonds, issued by State of Minnesota or any of its political or governmental subdivisions, municipalities, governmental agencies or instrumentalities; (17) any transaction exempted by rule or order of Commissioner; (18) certain sales of securities issued in connection with employee's stock purchase, savings, option, profit sharing, pension, or similar employee benefit plan, subject to specified condition; (19) sales of certain securities of issuer that is pooled income fund, charitable remainder trust or charitable lead trust; (20) sales by qualified charities or charitable gift annuities if issuer meets net worth and other requirements. (80A.15).

Licenses.—Following must obtain licenses annually; Broker-dealers, fee $200; agents, fee $50; investment advisors, fee $100. (80A.04, 80A.28). Notice filings required for federal covered advisers, fee $100. (80A.05, 80A.28).

Corporate Take-overs.—Regulated by c. 80B. Any person who proposes to offer to acquire equity securities from resident of Minnesota required to register with Commissioner prior to offer if after acquisition of securities pursuant to offer such person would: Beneficially own more than 10% of equity securities of issuer of publicly-traded equity securities (a) which (1) has its principal place of business or its principal executive office located in Minnesota or (2) owns or controls assets located within Minnesota which have fair market value of at least $1,000,000 and (b) which (1) has more than 10% of its beneficial or record equity shareholders in Minnesota, (2) has more than 10% of its equity securities owned beneficially or of record by residents in Minnesota, or (3) has more than 1,000 beneficial or record equity shareholders resident in Minnesota (provided that such person beneficially owned less than 10% prior to commencement of offer). (80B.01, .03). Filing fee, $250. (80B.08). See category Business Organizations, topic Corporations, subheads Control Share Acquisitions; Business Combinations.

Franchises.—See topic Franchises. (80C.01 et seq.).

Uniform Commercial Code adopted. (c. 336). See topic Commercial Code.

Uniform Simplification of Fiduciary Security Transfers Act adopted. (520.21-.31).

Uniform Securities Ownership by Minors Act not adopted.

STATUTE OF FRAUDS:

See topic Frauds, Statute of.

TRUST RECEIPT SECURITY:

See topic Commercial Code; category Debtor and Creditor, topic Pledges.

WAREHOUSEMEN:

Uniform Commercial Code adopted. (c. 336). See topic Commercial Code. Variations from 1962 Official Text and optional provisions adopted include:
(1) §7-204—Subsection (4) omitted.
(2) §7-403—Optional words in subsection (1) (b) omitted.
(3) For additional variations see topic Commercial Code.

Licenses.—Warehousemen must be licensed by Minnesota Department of Agriculture. (231.16; 232.22; 233.08).

Bailment v. Sale.—Delivery of grain to warehousemen for storage, even though mixed with other grain or shipped or removed, is bailment and not sale. (235.07).

Bond.—Warehousemen must be bonded or provide such other forms of security in such amount as Minnesota Department of Agriculture may require. (232.13, 231.17).

Lien.—Minnesota has adopted UCC provisions creating lien for warehouse operators. (336.7-209; 336.7-210). See topic Commercial Code. In addition, one storing property as bailee but not as warehouseman under Art. 7 of Uniform Commercial Code has possessory lien while property in bailee's possession. Nonpossessory lien can be achieved by filing notice of lien. Place of filing and enforcement of nonpossessory lien governed by Uniform Commercial Code. (514.18, .19).

CITIZENSHIP

ALIENS:

Property.—Alien, except permanent resident alien who actually resides in U.S. at least six months in every 12-month period, cannot acquire directly or indirectly

ALIENS . . . *continued*
agricultural real estate or any interest therein within state, except by devise, inheritance, as security for indebtedness or by enforcement of lien, or unless alien is citizen of foreign country whose rights to hold land are secured by treaty, or unless land used for transportation purposes or mining or mineral processing operations or unless tract is 40 acres or less for pipeline facilities. Land acquired by alien through collection of debt or lien must be disposed of within three years. Permanent resident alien owning such land must file report each Jan. with commissioner of agriculture. (500.221).

Corporations.—Statutory limitation on agricultural real estate ownership by alien individual applies to corporations, and other business entities 20% or more owned by aliens other than permanent residents. (500.221).

CIVIL ACTIONS AND PROCEDURE

ACCORD AND SATISFACTION:

Compromise with Joint Debtor.—Creditor may discharge one joint debtor without impairing liability of other joint debtors. Discharge has effect of payment by discharged party of his equal share of debt, and must be pleaded in action by creditor against other joint debtors. Discharge does not defeat other joint debtors' right of contribution. (548.21).

Part payment of debt operates to extinguish the whole when accepted as payment in full by creditor. Immaterial whether claim out of which debt grew was disputed or not. (203 Minn. 567, 282 N.W. 459).

Pleading.—Accord and satisfaction must be pleaded as affirmative defense. (RCP 8.03).

See also category Business Regulation and Commerce, topic Commercial Code.

ACTIONS:

Federal Rules form basis of Rules of Civil Procedure. (See topics Practice, Process.) There is one form of action for enforcement or protection of private rights, styled a civil action. (RCP 2).

Equity.—Distinctions between actions at law and suits in equity have been abolished as well as forms of all such actions.

Conditions Precedent.—In action in tort against state, notice of claim must be presented to proper official. (3.736). See 342 N.W.2d 632, 382 N.W.2d 518 (state notice provision is not condition precedent and held nonjurisdictional but failure of notice is defense if state prejudiced). In action in tort against municipalities or other political subdivisions, notice of claim must be presented to proper governing body. (466.05). See 277 N.W.2d 30, 356 N.W.2d 655 (statute requiring notice of claim as condition precedent to action and requiring commencement of action within one year after notice held unconstitutional).

See also topic Limitation of Actions, subhead Action Against Governmental Units and category Property, topic Real Property, subhead Actions.

Commencement.—Action in district court is commenced by serving summons upon defendant, by receiving acknowledgment of service from defendant if service made by mail, or by delivering summons for service to sheriff in county where defendant resides if summons is served, or first publication made within 60 days thereafter. (RCP 3.01). District court summons must be subscribed by plaintiff or his attorney, give address within state where the subscriber can be served, state time for answer, and notify defendant that failure to answer will result in judgment by default. (RCP 4.01). Complaint must be served with summons except when service is by publication. (RCP 3.02). Summons may be served by sheriff or any person not less than 18 years of age and not party to action. (RCP 4.02). See topic Process.

Parties.—Action must be prosecuted in name of real party in interest, except in cases of executor or administrator, guardian, bailee, trustee of express trust, party who has contracted for benefit of another, or person authorized by statute. (RCP 17.01). Plaintiff's full correct name must be given, defendant's should be, but when not known and so stated, defendant may be sued by any name, and right name inserted by amendment. (RCP 9.08).

Rules as to joinder of parties follow Federal Rules 19 through 21 except last sentence of 19(a) omitted. (RCP 19-21). Rule as to class actions follows Federal Rules 23, 23.1 and 23.2, except in stockholder derivative actions no requirement of verification or allegation that suit is not collusive to confer jurisdiction. (RCP 23.06).

Two or more persons associating or doing business under common name may sue or be sued under such name. If sued, summons may be served on one or more or agent. Judgment benefits or binds all persons acting jointly. (540.15, .151).

Third Party Practice.—See topic Pleading.

Class Actions.—Uniform Class Actions Act not adopted.

Interpleader.—Federal Rule 22 followed except paragraph (2) omitted and state rule adds express authorization for discharge of defendant asserting interpleader if defendant admits being subject to liability.

Intervention.—Federal Rule 24 followed except provision for intervention pursuant to federal statute omitted and provision requiring notification of Attorney General of Minnesota when constitutionality of act of Minnesota legislature challenged is substituted for parallel provision in Federal Rule. Notice must state that in absence of objections within 30 days, intervention shall be deemed accomplished. (RCP 24).

Joinder of Causes.—Federal Rule 18 followed. (RCP 18.01).

Consolidation and Severance of Actions.—Court may order separate trials of claims or issues, joint hearings or trials, or consolidation of actions.

Stay of Proceedings.—Stay of execution or proceedings to enforce judgment may be ordered in discretion of court and on such conditions for security as are proper, pending certain motions. (RCP 62.01).

Abatement of action does not result from death, incompetency, disability or transfer of interest, if cause of action continues or survives. (RCP 25).

Cause of action for personal injury dies with death of injured person although there is cause of action for death (see category Estates and Trusts, topic Death). All other causes of action, whether or not in contract, survive death of either party. (573.01).

Nonresident Individual or Foreign Corporation.—See topic Costs.

Limitation of.—See topic Limitation of Actions.

Small Claims.—See category Courts and Legislature, topic Courts.

Direct Action Against Insurer.—See category Transportation, topic Motor Vehicles, subhead Direct Actions.

APPEAL AND ERROR:

From Probate Court.—Appeal to Court of Appeals from probate court allowed from order allowing or refusing probate of wills, appointing or refusing to appoint or remove representative, authorizing or refusing to authorize sale, mortgage or lease of real estate, directing or refusing to direct conveyance or lease of real estate under contract, allowing or disallowing claims or counterclaims of over $100, setting apart property or making allowances or refusing to do so, determining or transferring venue or refusing to do so, directing or refusing to direct payment of bequest or distributive share (when over $100), allowing or disallowing accounts (when over $100), adjudging person in contempt, vacating or refusing to vacate previous appealable order, etc., because of fraud, misrepresentation, surprise or excusable inadvertence or neglect, determining or confirming distribution or any order of general protection, order under 576.142, granting or denying restoration to capacity, directing or refusing to direct payment of representative's or attorneys' fees, extending time for settlement of estate beyond five years from date of representative's appointment, from order, etc. relating to or affecting estate taxes, and from judgment or decree of partial or final distribution. (525.71). Appeal may be taken by any person aggrieved within 30 days after service of notice of filing order, judgment or decree appealed from. If notice of filing not served, appeal must be taken within six months from date of filing judgment, order or decree. (525.712).

From Municipal Court.—Appeals allowed to Court of Appeals under same procedures as from other trial courts as specified in Rules of Appellate Procedure. (488A.01[14]; 488A.18[14]).

From County Court.—Appeal to Court of Appeals permitted. Appeal in civil case under same procedure as appeal from district courts. (487.191; CAP 104.01).

From District Court.—Appeal from district court to Court of Appeals may be taken from judgment entered in district court, from order granting, refusing, dissolving or refusing to dissolve an injunction, from order vacating or sustaining an attachment, from order refusing new trial, or granting new trial if district court expressly states therein, or in attached memorandum, that order is based exclusively upon errors of law occurring at trial, and upon no other ground, from order that, in effect, determines action and prevents judgment, from final order or judgment made in proceedings supplementary to execution, from final order or judgment affecting substantial right in administrative or other special proceeding, except as otherwise provided by statute, or, if trial court certifies that question presented is important and doubtful, from order denying motion to dismiss for failure to state claim upon which relief can be granted or denying motion for summary judgment. (CAP 103.03). Appeal must be taken directly to Supreme Court in legislative or statewide election contests or in criminal cases where defendant has been convicted of first degree murder. (209.09; 209.10; 590.06). Appeal from judgment must be taken within 90 days after entry thereof and from order within 30 days after service of written notice of filing thereof by adverse party unless different time is provided by law. Time for appeal from partial judgment disposing of less than all multiple claims or affecting less than all of multiple parties within 90 days of entry of judgment if trial court makes express determination that there is no just reason for delay and expressly directs entry of final judgment, otherwise time for such appeal runs from date of entry of final judgment which adjudicates all remaining claims and rights and liabilities of remaining parties. (CAP 104.01).

Appeal Bond.—Appellant must file bond or undertaking for costs in amount of at least $500 or deposit that sum with clerk of court. Bond may be waived by written consent of respondent filed with clerk of trial court, or by motion to trial court. (CAP 107).

Stay of Proceedings.—Where appeal is from money judgment, in order to stay execution, bond must be in amount approved by court conditioned on payment of judgment and damages if judgment affirmed or if appeal is dismissed. (CAP 108.01[3]). Where appeal is from order, proceedings may be stayed by supersedeas bond conditioned on payment of costs and consequential damages of appeal, and satisfaction of any order or judgment given by appellate court. (CAP 108.01[2]). Where appeal is from judgment directing assignment or delivery of documents or personal property, proceedings may be stayed by supersedeas bond conditioned on obedience to order or judgment of appellate court. (CAP 108.01[4]). Where appeal is from judgment directing sale or delivery of possession of real property, proceedings may be stayed by supersedeas bond conditioned on payment of value of use and occupation of property and on undertaking not to commit or suffer commission of any waste on property during pendency of appeal. (CAP 108.01[5]). In all other cases, filing of appeal bond shall stay proceedings. (CAP 108.01[6]).

Death of Party During Appeal.—Representative may be substituted. (CAP 143.02).

Judgment or Order on Appeal.—On appeal from judgment or order, appellate court may reverse, affirm or modify judgment or order, or take other action as justice requires. (CAP 103.04).

Review by Supreme Court.—Review of decisions of Court of Appeals is discretionary with Supreme Court. Party seeking review must petition Supreme Court within 30 days of filing of Court of Appeals' decision. (CAP 117). Party also may seek accelerated review of case pending in Court of Appeals by petition to Supreme Court if case is of such imperative public importance as to justify deviation from normal appellate procedure and to require immediate determination in Supreme Court. (CAP 118).

See note at head of Digest as to 1998 legislation covered.

See Topical Index in front part of this volume.

MN – 15

BONDS:

Bonds required or permitted to be made for security of the state, or any department thereof, or any other organization, must be signed by two or more sureties, who shall be residents and freeholders of state and, who must justify bond is at least double amount of penalty of such bond. Sureties may be accepted in discretion of approving body, for part only of penalty, and may justify in separate and different sums; but aggregate liability of sureties shall in all cases be not less than that required by law if each surety had justified in full amount. Any fiduciary required by law to give bond as such may include as part of lawful expenses actual sum paid for such suretyship; subject to limitations. (574.01, .17, .19).

Surety companies may be sureties on bonds, but no corporation can be accepted or approved as such unless it holds certificate of Commissioner of Commerce showing that it is authorized to contract as such. (574.15).

Enforcement.—Before action can be brought on bond, leave must be obtained from district court where action is triable by production of copy of bond and affidavit showing delinquency. (574.25).

Contractor's bonds for public work, see category Debtor and Creditor, topic Liens, subhead Mechanics' Liens on Real Property.

See also topic Costs.

CERTIORARI:

Direct review of administrative determinations is available as matter of right where provided by statute. Writs of certiorari in district court and Administrative Procedure Act also provide broad scope of appellate review of administrative determinations. Review by Court of Appeals of decisions of Commissioner of Jobs and Training and other decisions reviewable by certiorari and review of decisions appealable pursuant to Administrative Procedure Act may be had by securing issuance of writ of certiorari within 30 days after date of mailing of notice of decision sought to be reviewed unless applicable statute prescribes different time period. Procedure to secure writ is by petition to Court of Appeals. (CAP 115). Review by Supreme Court of decisions of Workers' Compensation Court of Appeals, decisions of Tax Court, and other decisions reviewable by certiorari may be had by securing issuance of writ of certiorari within 30 days after party applying for writ was served with written notice of decision sought to be reviewed unless applicable statute prescribes different time period. Petition and proposed writ are presented to clerk of appellate courts. (CAP 116).

CHARITABLE IMMUNITY:

See topic Damages.

COMMISSIONS TO TAKE TESTIMONY:

See topic Depositions and Discovery.

COSTS:

In appellate courts, unless otherwise ordered, costs are allowed: to prevailing party in judgment on merits, $300; on dismissal, $10. (549.02[2]; CAP 139.01). In addition, disbursements necessarily paid or incurred by prevailing party must be allowed unless otherwise ordered by court. (CAP 139.02). In district court for action to recover money only on judgment for over $100, entitled to $200. In all other actions, except as otherwise provided, $200. Defendant entitled to $200 if judgment or dismissal. To prevailing party: $5.50 for cost of filing satisfaction of judgment. (549.02[1]). Varies in municipal courts. Plaintiff is entitled to double costs in action for wages. (549.03). In every action in district court, prevailing party is allowed reasonable disbursements paid or incurred. (549.04). Special rule applies in fourth judicial district. (549.05).

Taxation of Costs.—In appellate courts, costs and disbursements are taxed by Clerk of Appellate Courts upon five days notice served and filed by prevailing party and inserted in judgment; failure to tax within 15 days after filing of decision or order constitutes waiver (CAP 139.03); objections to be served and filed within five days after service of notice of taxation (CAP 139.04). In district court, costs and disbursements may be taxed by court administrator upon two days' notice by either party and inserted in judgment; disbursements must be stated in detail, verified by affidavit and filed with court and copy must be served with notice; party may object in writing to any item and appeal will be heard by court on eight days notice. (RCP 54.04).

Security for Costs.—Nonresident plaintiff, individual or corporation, must, before service of summons, file with court administrator bond for at least $75, conditioned for payment of all costs and expenses adjudged against plaintiff. This applies to defendant who appeals to district court, but does not apply to action for wages or personal service. (549.18).

DAMAGES:

As general rule common law prevails as to damages, but statutory exceptions.

Charitable Immunity.—Doctrine of charitable immunity rejected. (122 Minn. 10, 141 N.W. 837).

Comparative fault rule adopted. (604.01).

Death.—See category Estates and Trusts, topic Death, subhead Action for Death.

No-Fault Insurance.—See category Transportation, topic Motor Vehicles.

Sovereign Immunity.—Doctrine abolished prospectively by state tort claims act as to state (3.736) and by municipal torts claims act as to municipalities and other political subdivisions (466.01 et seq.) except for discretionary duties and particular immunities granted by statute (3.736, 466.03); however, workers' compensation immunity held unconstitutional and repealed (376 N.W.2d 422). Abolishment of doctrine does not waive defense of judicial or legislative immunity except to extent liability insurance procured. (3.736[1]). State liable for acts or omissions of employees while acting within scope of office or employment, or of peace officers not acting on behalf of private employer and acting in good faith, under circumstances where private person would be liable, whether rising out of governmental or proprietary function. (3.736[1]). Municipalities or other subdivisions liable for their torts and those of their officers, employees and agents acting within scope of employment or duties whether acting out of governmental or proprietary function. (466.02). Indemnification of state and municipal officers and employees under certain circumstances. Statutory notice of claim requirements exist in both state and municipal tort claims acts. (3.736[5], 466.05). State notice provision is not condition precedent and held nonjurisdictional but failure of notice is defense if state prejudiced. (342 N.W.2d 632). Municipal notice provision is condition precedent and requires commencement of action within one year after notice; condition precedent and one-year requirement both held unconstitutional, but failure of notice is defense if municipality prejudiced. (356 N.W.2d 655; 382 N.W.2d 518). Recovery limited to specific dollar amount except to extent liability exceeds limits (3.736; 466.06), and then only to extent that valid and collectible insurance exceeds those limits and covers claim recoverable against state or municipality (3.736, 466.06); recovery of punitive damages from employees and officers possible (297 N.W.2d 152), against which municipality must defend and indemnify officers and employees provided that officer or employee was acting in performance of duties of position and was not guilty of malfeasance in office, willful neglect of duty, or bad faith (466.07). Municipality shall indemnify for punitive damages, provided officer or employee was (1) acting in performance of duties of position; and (2) was not guilty of malfeasance, willful neglect or bad faith. Procurement of liability insurance constitutes waiver of limits of governmental liability to extent of policy coverage. (3.736, 466.06). Governmental units also may be liable under other statutes, including state environmental response and liability act (115B.04), state environmental rights law (116B.10), wrongful death statute (573.02), civil damage act (340A.801), state civil rights statute (363.03), and federal civil rights statutes.

DECLARATORY JUDGMENTS:

See topic Judgments.

DEPOSITIONS AND DISCOVERY:

Practice with reference to depositions, interrogatories, physical and mental examinations, production of documents and requests for admission in district court follow Federal Rules 26-37 except as noted. (RCP 26-37).

Unless otherwise ordered by court or agreed to by parties, officer taking deposition shall send deposition to party taking deposition, who shall be identified on record. (RCP 30.06).

Form

State of . . . ., County of . . . ., Be it known that I took the forgoing deposition of . . . .; that I was then and there a . . . .; that, by virtue thereof I was duly authorized to administer an oath; that the witness, before testifying, was by me first duly sworn to tell the truth, the whole truth, and nothing but the truth relative to the above cause; that I am not related to any of the parties hereto nor an employee, nor interested in the outcome of the action. Witness my hand and seal this . . . . day of . . . ., 19. . . .

Depositions of employee, as well as officer, of party may be used. (RCP 30.02[f]; 32.01[b]).

Interrogatories to parties are limited to 50 unless more permitted by court for good cause shown. (RCP 33.01[a]). Answers due within 30 days after service; expansion of time for answer allowed by court for good cause shown except that defendant may serve answers or objections within 45 days after service of summons and complaint. (RCP 33.01[b]). Objections shall be stated with particularity; party proposing interrogatories may at anytime move to compel answers to interrogatories or to determine objections. (RCP 33.01[c]). Answers to interrogatories shall first set out question; interrogatories to state, corporation, partnership or association shall be answered by officer or managing agent. (RCP 33.01[d]).

Physical, mental and blood examinations of agents of party, as well as agent of party and person under control of party, may be taken for good cause shown upon motion with notice. (RCP 35.01). Automatic waiver of medical privilege is provided upon party's voluntarily placing in controversy mental, physical or blood condition of himself, decedent, or person under his control. (RCP 35.03). Following waiver, medical reports concerning waiving party and conclusions therein, shall be furnished ten days after written request. (RCP 35.04).

Compelling Attendance and Testimony of Witnesses.—

Within State for Use Within State.—Witness may be subpoenaed upon proof of service of notice to take deposition. (RCP 45.04[a]). Use of subpoena other than in connection with duly noticed deposition, hearing or trial is abuse of process. (RCP 45.01[b]). Nonparty resident may be required to attend examination only in county where he resides or is employed or transacts business in person or at place fixed by court order; nonresident may be required to attend in any county. (RCP 45.04[c]). Subpoena may be served by sheriff, deputy or any other person not a party. (RCP 45.03). Subpoena of nonparty witness testifying as to profession, business or trade must advise witness of right to receive reasonable compensation for time and expenses. (RCP 45.01[c], RCP 45.06). Party serving subpoena must arrange for reasonable compensation before deposition. (RCP 45.06). Failure to obey subpoena without adequate excuse is contempt of court. (588.01, subd. 3[8], RCP 45.07).

Within State for Use Elsewhere.—Any witness may be compelled to give deposition in any case pending in court of another state or country. Resident may be required to attend examination only in county where he resides or is employed or transacts business in person or at place fixed by court order; nonresident may be required to attend in any county. Clerk of any district court of state may issue subpoena for witness to appear based on proof of service of notice to take deposition. (RCP 45.04). Disobedience of subpoena duly served is contempt of court. (588.01, subd. 3[8], RCP 45.07).

Outside of State for Use within State.—May be taken before officer authorized to administer oaths by laws of U.S. or of place where examination is held, or before person appointed by court in which action is pending. (RCP 28.01).

DEPOSITIONS AND DISCOVERY . . . *continued*

Return should be in following form:

Form

State of . . . . . ., County of . . . . . ., Be it known that I took the foregoing deposition of . . . . . .; that I was then and there a . . . . . .; that, by virtue thereof I was duly authorized to administer an oath; that, the witness, before testifying, was by me first duly sworn to tell the truth, the whole truth, and nothing but the truth relative to the above cause; that, I am not related to any of the parties hereto nor an employee, nor interested in the outcome of the action. Witness my hand and seal this . . . . . . day of . . . . . ., 19. . . .

EQUITY:

See topics Actions, Pleading.

EVIDENCE:

Witnesses.—All persons may testify unless they are of unsound mind or intoxicated so as to lack capacity to remember facts or to relate them truthfully. Child under ten years of age is competent unless court finds lack of capacity to remember or relate facts truthfully. Child may describe or relate events in language appropriate to child of that age. In cases involving physical abuse or crimes of violence against testifying child or any other person, child less than 12 years of age, may testify in room other than courtroom, televised by closed-circuit equipment, or by videotape in courtroom for later showing to jury. Court may order defendant removed so not seen or heard by child. Attorneys for parties may be present with child in child protection, dissolution and custody proceedings. (595.02).

See also topic Depositions and Discovery.

Privileged communications are protected in cases of: attorney or his employee and client; minister and confessor or person seeking religious or spiritual advice; physician, surgeon, dentist, registered nurse, chiropractor or psychologist and patient, except in certain cases relating to abuse or neglect of minor; witness to documents or communications made during course of mediation pursuant to mediation agreement; public officers when public interest would suffer; parent and minor child in case of communications made in confidence by minor to parent except in certain intra-familial civil and criminal proceedings; sexual assault counselor and victim except where court determines good cause exists to order disclosure in proceeding for neglect or termination of parental rights; licensed chemical dependency counselors and persons consulting them, except in certain cases relating to contemplation or on-going commission of crime or in certain cases to charges against counselor. Interpreter for person handicapped in communication may not disclose otherwise privileged communication. (595.02).

Communications between husband and wife are privileged, but privilege does not apply to action or proceeding by one against other, nor to action or proceeding for crime committed by one against other or against child under care of either spouse, nor to criminal action for homicide where date of marriage of defendant is subsequent to date of offense, nor to any action for nonsupport, neglect, dependency or termination of parental rights. (595.02).

Communications with Persons Since Deceased or Insane.—Witness not precluded from giving evidence of or concerning conversations with or admissions of deceased or insane party merely because witness is party or has interest. (Deadman's Statute superseded.) (R. Evid. 617).

News Media.—Persons engaged in gathering, procuring, compiling, editing or publishing information for dissemination to public may not be required to disclose source or unpublished information which would tend to identify source. (595.023). Disclosure may be required on application to district court in certain circumstances. (595.024).

Self-incrimination.—In criminal proceeding (including grand jury proceeding), paternity proceeding, or proceeding in juvenile court, if it appears that person may be entitled to refuse to answer or produce evidence, prosecuting attorney may make written request for order that person answer or produce evidence, and judge may, after notice and hearing, so order if not contrary to public policy and not likely to expose witness to prosecution in other state or federal courts. After complying and if it would have been privileged, no testimony or information compelled under order and no information directly or indirectly derived from such testimony or information may be used against witness in any criminal case, except that witness may be prosecuted for perjury, false swearing or contempt with regard to his/her response to order. In any other proceeding where it is provided by law that witness not excused from giving incriminating testimony, witness must testify and use immunity provided, except for perjury. (609.09).

INJUNCTIONS:

No provisions governing issuance of permanent injunction; general equitable principles apply.

Injunction will not lie to restrain nonresident from prosecuting action. (134 Minn. 455, 159 N.W. 1084). Where plaintiff is entitled to injunction at time of commencement of action, it will be granted although defendant may have discontinued acts complained of. (115 Minn. 116, 131 N.W. 1075).

Federal Rules form basis of Rules of Civil Procedure. (See topic Practice.) RCP 65 establishes procedure for granting restraining orders and temporary injunctions.

Jurisdiction to issue injunctions rests with district court. (484.03).

Temporary Injunctions.—Temporary restraining order may be granted without oral or written notice if it appears by affidavit or verified complaint that immediate and irreparable injury would result to applicant before hearing and efforts have been made to give notice to adverse party or no such notice should be required. (RCP 65.01). Temporary injunction may be granted following hearing if it appears by affidavit, deposition testimony, or oral testimony in court that sufficient grounds exist therefor. (RCP 65.02). In general, temporary injunction will be dissolved where sworn answer sets forth specific facts which show allegations of complaint are not true, but this is not absolute rule. (55 Minn. 482, 57 N.W. 208). Temporary writ may be granted although permanent one is not asked for. (55 Minn. 482, 57 N.W. 208).

Procedure.—Temporary injunction is only granted on motion or order to show cause, but temporary restraining order may be issued ex parte. (RCP 65.01, 65.02). Five days notice (excluding Sats., Suns. and holidays) required on motion; three additional days required if served by mail. (RCP 6.01, 6.04, 6.05). Injunction may be granted, suspended, modified or restored during pendency of appeal upon such terms as to bond or otherwise as established by court. (RCP 62.02).

Bonds.—Court will ordinarily require bond or other form of security before temporary injunction will issue. (RCP 65.03). Bond of not less than $2,000 is required before restraining order will issue, except in execution, replevin, harassment proceedings, orders for protection in domestic abuse proceedings or marriage dissolution action. (Minn. Gen. R. Prac. 135). Remedy on bond is exclusive. Counsel fees necessarily incurred in procuring dissolution may be recovered on bond. (43 Minn. 507, 45 N.W. 1134).

JUDGMENTS:

Federal Rules form basis of Rules of Civil Procedure. See topic Practice.

Confession of judgment for money due or to become due or to secure against contingent liability of defendant may be entered upon filing with court administrator statement signed and verified by defendant authorizing entry of judgment for specified sum, stating facts out of which debt arose and showing that sum confessed is justly due or to become due. Judgment may be entered on plea of confession signed by attorney together with instrument signed by debtor authorizing such confession but such instrument must be distinct from that containing evidence of demand for which judgment is confessed. (548.22, .23). No provision for confession of judgment or power of attorney therefor in any retail installment contract, or separate agreement relating thereto, is valid or enforceable (168.71), and no consumer credit sales contract shall give power of attorney to confess judgment (325G.16).

Declaratory Judgments.—Uniform Declaratory Judgments Act adopted. (c. 555).

Default Judgments.—If defendant fails to answer or move within 20 days after service of summons and complaint, judgment may be entered by default. (RCP 12.01, 55.01).

Entry.—In case of default judgment in district court, in a money action on contract, court administrator enters judgment on request of plaintiff and affidavit; in other actions, court determines relief to be granted and orders court administrator to enter judgment accordingly. (RCP 55.01).

Docketing.—No judgment, except for taxes, shall be docketed until judgment creditor, or his agent or attorney, has filed with court administrator affidavit stating full name, occupation, place of residence and post office address of judgment debtor. In incorporated places of over 5,000, street number of both judgment debtor's residence and place of business must be added. (548.09, 487.23).

Lien.—Except as to judgments for support and maintenance (548.091), every judgment requiring payment of money is docketed by court administrator upon its entry (548.09, 487.23). From time of such docketing, it becomes lien on all debtor's real estate in county, then owned or thereafter acquired, for ten years after date of entry of judgment, but is not lien on registered land until filed as set out below. (548.09, 487.23). Judgment in district court may be made similar lien on real property in any other county by filing transcript with court administrator of district court of that county, who must docket same. (548.09). Judgment becomes lien on registered land only if person claiming lien files with registrar certified copy of judgment and statement containing description of land and proper reference to certificate of title. (508.63, 508A.63).

Judgment in U.S. District Court for District of Minnesota may be made a lien on real estate of debtor in any county by filing transcript in office of court administrator of state district court for that county. (548.11).

Assignment.—Every assignment of judgment must be in writing, signed and acknowledged, except written notice is sufficient for assignment of support and maintenance rights. To be valid against subsequent purchasers or creditors assignment must be filed with court administrator and docketed. (548.13).

Satisfaction.—Judgment is deemed satisfied when there is filed with court administrator: (1) Execution satisfied; (2) certificate of satisfaction signed and acknowledged by judgment creditor or by his attorney, unless attorney's authority has been revoked and entry of revocation made on register, attorney's authority being good only for six years after entry of judgment, certificate of satisfaction to be filed within ten days after satisfaction or within 30 days of payment by noncertified funds; (3) court order made on motion directing satisfaction to be entered; or (4) where judgment has been docketed elsewhere, copy of any of foregoing documents certified to by court administrator where original entry made. Court administrator thereupon enters such satisfaction in judgment roll and on docket. (548.15). Judgment debtor may pay court administrator if he cannot find creditor upon filing affidavit to that effect. (548.17). Obligor under judgment for support and maintenance may pay court administrator if he cannot find obligee or obligee refuses to receive payment upon filing affidavit to that effect. (548.17).

Foreign Judgments.—To create lien on real property or permit issuance of execution, suit must be brought and judgment obtained from court of this state. Judgment recovered in sister state is entitled to full faith and credit in this state. Such judgment is admissible in evidence when authenticated by attestation of court administrator under seal (28 U.S.C.A. §1738; 599.11); judgment of justice of peace in sister state must be certified by justice with certificate of magistracy thereon and signed and authenticated under seal by court administrator of a court of record in county where rendered (599.24).

Uniform Enforcement of Foreign Judgments Act adopted. (548.26-.33).

See note at head of Digest as to 1998 legislation covered.

See Topical Index in front part of this volume.

MN – 17

JUDGMENTS . . . *continued*

Judgment Renewal.—Child support judgments may be renewed by service of notice upon debtor, and filing notice and proof of service with court administrator. (548.091).

Judgment for Child Support.—Unpaid child support installment becomes judgment by operation of law on date it is due. To docket judgment statement identifying or copy of original judgment, affidavit of default, and affidavit of service of notice of entry of judgment must be filed with court administrator.

LIMITATION OF ACTIONS:

Uniform Commercial Code adopted. (c. 336). See category Business Regulation and Commerce, topic Commercial Code.

Action is barred unless commenced within following period after cause of action accrues:

Fifteen Years.—For recovery of real estate (541.02) or foreclosure of real estate mortgage (541.03). Time for foreclosure of mortgage not extended by nonresidence, partial payment after maturity of debt or extension of time of payment unless such extension in writing and recorded in same office as mortgage within limitation period of 15 years. (541.03).

Ten Years.—On judgment or decree of court of record of U.S. or any state or territory. (541.04).

Six Years.—Unless otherwise prescribed by Uniform Commercial Code: Contract or other obligation express or implied as to which no other limitation is expressly prescribed; liability created by statute except penalty or forfeiture or where shorter period is prescribed by 541.07; trespass upon real estate; taking, detaining or injuring personal property, and actions for specific recovery thereof; criminal conversation, or injury to person or rights of another not arising on contract and not hereinafter enumerated; relief on ground of fraud; to enforce trust or compel accounting, where trustee neglects to discharge trust or has repudiated it or claims to have fully performed same; against surety on bond of any public officer after expiration of term of office; for damages caused by dam used for commercial purpose. (541.05). For personal injury based on sexual abuse, cause of action accrues upon knowledge of injury caused by sexual abuse. (541.073). See category Business Regulation and Commerce, topic Commercial Code.

Action seeking to recover for personal injuries based upon allegations of negligence is governed by six-year statute of limitations. (209 Minn. 330, 296 N.W. 176).

Five Years.—Actions for civil racketeering under 609.911. (541.074).

Four Years.—Actions arising under Sales Article of Uniform Commercial Code. (336.2-725). See category Business Regulation and Commerce, topic Commercial Code. Action based on strict liability and arising from manufacture, sale, use or consumption of product. (541.05).

Three Years.—Against sheriff, coroner or constable as such official. (541.06). Proceeding to impose penalty or forfeiture for environmental damages. (541.075). See subhead Two Years, infra, as to certain actions for recovery of wages, overtime, damages, fees or penalties. See category Estates and Trusts, topic Death, as to statute of limitations for wrongful death action.

Two Years.—Unless otherwise prescribed by Uniform Commercial Code: For libel, slander, assault, battery, false imprisonment or other tort resulting in personal injury (but see subhead Six Years, supra as to personal injuries based on allegations of negligence); malpractice actions against physicians, surgeons, dentists, occupational therapists, other health care professionals, and veterinarians as defined in §156, hospitals, sanatoriums, for malpractice, error, mistake or failure to cure whether based on contract or tort, provided counterclaim may be pleaded as defense to any action for services brought by physician, surgeon, dentist, occupational therapist or other health care professional or veterinarian, hospital or sanitorium after limitations herein described, notwithstanding it is barred by provisions of this chapter, if it was property of party pleading it at time it became barred and was not barred at time claim sued on originated, but no judgment thereof except for costs can be rendered in favor of party so pleading it (541.074 and 541.075); for damages caused by dam used for other than commercial purposes; against master for breach of indenture of apprenticeship, limitation running from expiration of term of service; actions for recovery of wages, overtime, damages, fees or penalties accruing under any federal or state law respecting same, except that if employer fails to submit payroll records upon request of department of labor and industry or nonpayment is willful, limitation is three years; for damages caused by establishment of or change in street or highway grade; for damage to property resulting from application (but not manufacture or sale) of pesticide. (541.07). See category Business Regulation and Commerce, topic Commercial Code.

One Year.—On instrument authorizing confession of judgment and on foreign judgment or decree or judgment or decree of federal court entered by confession under warrant of attorney or other instrument authorizing such confession. (541.09).

Real Property Improvements.—Unless fraud or breach of certain statutory or written warranties involved, action for damages for injury to real or personal property, or for injury or death, arising from defective and unsafe condition of improvement to real property barred after two years of discovery of injury (or, in case of action for contribution or indemnity, after accrual of cause of action) against person performing or furnishing design, planning, supervision, materials, construction or observation of construction, except no action may be brought more than ten years after substantial completion of construction. Cause of action accrues upon discovery of injury or, in case of indemnity and contribution, upon payment of final judgment, arbitration award or settlement. Limitation not applicable to action for damages from negligence in maintenance, operation or inspection of real property improvement against owner or person in possession or to action by manufacturer or supplier of equipment or machinery installed upon real property. If action accrues in ninth or tenth year after substantial completion of construction, action may be brought within two years after date action accrues. Actions based on breach of certain statutory (327a.02) and express written warranties to be brought within two years of discovery of breach (541.051).

Land Surveys.—Unless fraud involved, no action for damages for error in land survey (or for contribution or indemnity) may be brought against person performing survey more than two years after discovery of error, nor in any event more than ten years after survey date. If action arises during ninth or tenth year after survey date, action for damages may be brought within two years after date action arises, but in no event may action be brought more than 12 years after date of survey. (541.052).

Time.—Action to recover balance due on mutual, open and current account, where reciprocal demands have been made between parties, accrues from date of last item proved on either side. (541.10).

Asbestos.—Action to recover for removal of asbestos from building, location or correction of other problems related to asbestos in building, or for reimbursement for correction of removal of asbestos problem is not barred from any other limitation period if begun before July 1, 1990. (541.22).

Disabilities.—Any of following grounds of disability existing at time when cause of action accrued or arising during period of limitation suspends running of period of limitation until disability is removed; that plaintiff is under age 18, or insane, or is alien and subject or citizen of country at war with U.S., or when beginning of action is stayed by injunction or by statutory prohibition. Time cannot be extended more than five years by any disability, except infancy, nor for more than one year after disability ceases. When two or more disabilities co-exist, suspension continues to run until all are removed. When cause of action alleges malpractice against health care provider, disability that plaintiff is under 18 suspends limitation period until disability is removed, but suspension shall not extend for more than seven years, or for more than one year after disability ceases. (541.15).

Absence.—When defendant is absent from state and not subject to process under Minnesota law when cause of action accrues or if he departs after its accrual and resides out of state, time of his absence is not counted. (541.13).

Foreign Causes of Action.—When action accrues in another state or in foreign country, and by laws thereof action cannot be maintained there because of lapse of time, action probably not thereby barred in Minnesota. (302 Minn. 359; 225 N.W.2d 238), but issue uncertain due to repeal of 541.14.

Revival of Barred Debt.—Debt barred by limitations may be revived and full period started running again by part payment of principal or interest or by signed written acknowledgment or new promise signed by party to be charged; but oral acknowledgment or new promise will not have this effect. (541.17).

Contractual Limitations.—In absence of special legislation affecting limitations of particular actions, parties may, by stipulation in their contract, reduce time for bringing suit thereon below period fixed by general statute of limitation, provided time be not unreasonably short. (248 Minn. 383; 80 N.W.2d 612).

Pleading.—Statute must be pleaded or raised on motion before answer to be available as a defense. (RCP 8.03).

Action Against Governmental Units.—Notice of tort claim against state must be presented within 180 days to attorney general and any state employee from whom claimant seeks compensation; special provisions apply for wrongful death claims and claims against University of Minnesota. Actual notice received by state or insurer complies with notice requirements. (3.736, subd. 5). Tort actions brought against state also governed by applicable limitation period. (3.736, subd. 11). Notice of claim against state requirement is not condition precedent to action and held nonjurisdictional but failure of notice is defense if state prejudiced. (342 N.W.2d 632). Notice of tort claim against municipalities or other political subdivisions must be presented within 180 days to governing body and special provisions apply for wrongful death claims. Actual notice received by governing body or insurer complies with notice requirements. (466.05) Notice of claim apparently is non-jurisdictional. (356 N.W.2d 655).

See also category Employment, topic Labor Relations, subhead Workers' Compensation Act.

PARTITION:

When two or more persons are interested either as joint tenants or as tenants in common, in realty in which one or more have an estate of inheritance, or for life or for years, an action may be brought by one or more such persons, against the others for partition thereof, according to respective rights and interests of parties interested therein, or for sale of such property, or a part thereof, if it appears that a partition cannot be had without great prejudice to owners. When title is established, court shall render judgment that partition be made accordingly, and shall appoint three referees to make partition and to set off shares of persons interested as determined by judgment. (c. 558). Orders and interlocutory judgments are appealable. (558.215).

PLEADING:

Pleading in district court actions governed by Rules of Civil Procedure which generally follow Federal Rules of Civil Procedure. (RCP 7-16). Pleadings for unliquidated claims for relief in excess of $50,000 may not specify amount but shall merely state that recovery of reasonable damages in amount greater than $50,000 is sought. (544.36).

Proof of Claims.—No special requirements with respect to proof of claims sent from other jurisdictions for collection. However, nonresident plaintiff or foreign corporation must post security cost bond of $75. (549.18).

Small Claims.—See category Courts and Legislature, topic Courts.

Frivolous claims may be penalized pursuant to both statute and court rule. (549.21; RCP 11). All pleadings must contain acknowledgment that party may be sanctioned for asserting frivolous claims or defenses. (549.21).

PRACTICE:

Proceedings in civil actions in district court and in county court with concurrent jurisdiction regulated by Rules of Civil Procedure adopted by Supreme Court pursuant

See note at head of Digest as to 1998 legislation covered.

See Topical Index in front part of this volume.

PRACTICE . . . *continued*
to enabling act. (480.051-.058). All other proceedings in county court and all proceedings in municipal court governed by virtually identical Rules of Civil Procedure adopted by Supreme Court. Rules are generally patterned after Federal Rules of Civil Procedure. District, county and municipal courts also may adopt practice rules not in conflict with rules promulgated by Supreme Court. (480.055). Also excepted are certain statutory proceedings, so far as they are inconsistent, including marriage dissolution, mechanics' liens, wrongful death, partition of real estate, tax proceedings, proceedings relating to trusts, registration of title to lands, eminent domain, adoption and change of name. (RCP 81.01).

Direct Actions Against Insurer.—See category Transportation, topic Motor Vehicles, subhead Direct Actions.

Small Claims.—See category Courts and Legislature, topic Courts.

See also topics Actions, Appeal and Error, Depositions and Discovery, Injunctions, Judgments, Pleading, Process; category Debtor and Creditor, topics Attachment, Executions, Garnishment.

PROCESS:

Federal Rules form the basis of Rules of Civil Procedure. See topics Actions, Practice.

Who May Serve.—Summons may be served by sheriff or any person at least 18 years of age not party to action. (RCP 4.02).

Personal service on individual is made by delivering copy to individual personally, or by leaving copy at individual's usual place of abode with resident of suitable age and discretion or according to statutory appointments or designations. If individual confined to state institution, must also serve chief executive officer thereof. If individual under 14, must also serve parent; if no parent in state, then resident guardian, if known; if none, person having control of individual or with whom individual resides or by whom individual is employed. (RCP 4.03[a]).

Personal service on partnership or association is made by delivering copy to member or managing agent, or according to statutory appointments or designations. (RCP 4.03[b]).

Personal service on unions, groups or associations is made by delivering copy to officer or managing agent of association, or in case of union or association having property or members outside of state and engaging in activities in state, except union subject to federal Railway Labor Act, by filing process, notice or demand with Secretary of State along with $35 fee, provided that notice of service and copy of process be sent by mail within ten days to union or association at its last known address. (5.25, 540.151-.153).

Personal service on domestic or foreign corporation is made by delivering copy to officer or managing agent or authorized or designated statutory agent pursuant to statutory provision for manner of service. May serve express or transportation corporation by delivering copy to ticket, freight or soliciting agent in county where action brought, or, if foreign corporation and no agent in such county, to agent anywhere in state. (RCP 4.03[c]). If private domestic corporation has no officer at registered office in state upon whom service can be made, of which return of sheriff or affidavit of private person not party is conclusive evidence, process may be served by depositing two copies and $35 fee with Secretary of State. (5.25, 543.08).

If foreign corporation authorized to transact business in state fails to appoint or maintain in state registered agent on whom service may be had, or if such registered agent cannot be found at its registered office in state, or if corporation has withdrawn from state or its certificate of authority has been revoked or cancelled, service may be made by delivering to Secretary of State two copies of process and fee of $50, provided that where corporation has withdrawn, service may be made only when based upon liability or obligation incurred in state or arising from business done in state prior to withdrawal. When summons so served on Secretary of State, corporation has 30 days from date of mailing by Secretary to corporation within which to answer. If foreign corporation makes contract with state resident to be performed in whole or part in state or commits tort in whole or part in state against state resident, service may be made by delivering to Secretary of State two copies of process and fee of $50, and corporation has 30 days from date of mailing by Secretary within which to answer. (5.25, 303.13).

Personal service on foreign insurance company may be made by copy of process with Commissioner of Commerce, but such service is not effective unless plaintiff sends Notice of Service and copy of process to defendant via certified mail at defendant's last known address and plaintiff files Affidavit of Compliance on or before return day of process, if any, or within further time as court allows. (45.028).

Personal Service Outside the State.—Minnesota court with subject matter jurisdiction has personal jurisdiction over foreign corporation or nonresident individual who: (1) Owns, uses or possesses property in state, (2) transacts any business in state, (3) commits act in state causing injury or property damage, or (4) commits act outside state causing injury or property damage in state unless Minnesota has no substantial interest in providing forum, or jurisdiction would violate fairness and substantial justice or cause of action lies in defamation or privacy. Process may be served personally outside state on any such nonresident in actions arising out of above enumerated activities within state. (543.19).

Service by publication may be made when (1) defendant is resident individual having departed from the state with intent to defraud creditors or to avoid service or remains concealed within state with like intent, (2) plaintiff has acquired lien upon property within state by attachment or garnishment and defendant is nonresident individual, foreign corporation, partnership or association, or resident individual who has departed from the state or cannot be found therein, (3) action is for marriage dissolution or separate maintenance and court has ordered that service be made by publication, (4) subject of action is real or personal property within state in or upon which defendant has or claims lien or interest, or relief demanded consists wholly or partly in excluding him from any such interest or lien, or (5) action is to foreclose mortgage or to enforce lien on real estate within state. Service is made by three weeks published notice after filing complaint and affidavit stating one of above cases and that defendant is not resident or cannot be found and that copy of summons has been mailed to defendant's residence or that residence is unknown. Service of summons deemed complete 21 days after first publication. Personal service outside state, proved by affidavit of server, has same effect as published notice. (RCP 4.04). If title to, interest in, or lien upon real property is involved, notice must contain description of real property and statement of object of action. (RCP 4.041). If defendant appears within ten days after completion of service by publication, copy of complaint must be served on him or his attorney within five days of appearance and defendant has at least ten days to answer. (RCP 4.042). If no actual notice, defendant may defend before judgment, upon application to court for sufficient cause, and, except in marriage dissolution action, on such terms as may be just at any time within one year after judgment. (RCP 4.043).

Nonresident Motorist.—See category Transportation, topic Motor Vehicles, subhead Action Against Nonresident.

Service on Process Agent.—Nonresident person or corporation owning or claiming any interest or lien in or upon lands in state may file with Secretary of State written agreement duly executed and acknowledged as deed (see category Property, topic Deeds) appointing resident agent to accept service of summons or process in any action or proceeding concerning such interest therein or lien thereon commenced in any court of state, except actions or proceedings for collection of taxes, and consenting to service of process or summons upon agent therein designated. Service shall be made on such agent and is in respects valid and binding upon principal. No service by publication can be made upon principal while agency is unrevoked. It may be revoked at any time, but not so as to affect any service previously made. (557.01; RCP 4.044).

Long Arm Statute.—See subhead Personal Service Outside the State, supra.

REPLEVIN:

Claimant of personal property may obtain possession prior to final judgment after notice to respondent and hearing. Recovery prior to notice and hearing authorized in certain circumstances. (565.21 et seq.).

Proceedings.—Claimant seeking to recover property after service of summons and complaint but before final judgment is to proceed by motion, accompanied by affidavit which states: (1) Particular property sought to be recovered, (2) facts giving rise to claimant's right to possession, (3) facts showing respondent wrongfully detaining property, (4) if property is security, date and amount of original obligation, amount paid and amount now owing, (5) if breach of contract other than debt, contractual provision and related facts, and (6) good faith estimate of current market value. Motion, affidavit and notice of hearing served on respondent in same manner as summons in civil action in district court, or if respondent has appeared in action, in same manner as pleadings subsequent to summons. (565.23). Notice of hearing, signed by claimant or attorney, to be in following form:

NOTICE OF HEARING

TO: [the Respondent]

A hearing will be held on the . . . . day of . . . ., 19. . . , at . . . . o'clock, . . . M., [place] to determine whether the sheriff shall remove from your possession and deliver to [claimant] (hereinafter "claimant") the following property:

[list property]

You have a right to appear at this hearing on your own behalf or with an attorney. You will have the opportunity to present defenses to the claimant's claims and to state reasons why the property described above should not be taken.

If the court determines that the claimant has a right to have possession of the property while this lawsuit is pending, you may nevertheless keep the property until the lawsuit is decided if you file with the court a surety bond in the amount of $. . . . . . . [In amount computed pursuant to section 565.25]. This amount is [1¼ times the claimant's estimate of the value of the property] [1½ times the claimant's claim against you]. If you believe the [value of the property] [amount of the claim] is overstated, you may ask the court to lower it.

If you do not appear at the hearing, the court has authority to issue an order directing that the above described property be immediately taken from your possession. (565.23).

If at hearing claimant shows probability of success and complies with bonding requirements of 565.25, court orders seizure unless respondent shows defense to merits of claimant's claim, defense is fair basis for litigation, and defense would, if established at hearing on merits, entitle respondent to retain property; that respondent's interests cannot be adequately protected by claimant's bond if property is delivered to claimant prior to final decision on merits; and respondent would suffer substantially greater harm than harm to claimant if property not seized. If seizure refused, court shall issue order protecting claimant's rights to extent possible, including part payment of debt or bond by respondent. (565.23).

Recovery Prior to Notice and Hearing.—Court may order prehearing seizure upon claimant's motion and affidavit if it finds: (1) Good faith effort to inform respondent of motion for prehearing seizure or such information would endanger ability to recover property, (2) claimant has shown probability of success on merits, (3) respondent about to remove property from state, conceal, damage or dispose of it, or other circumstances that will cause irreparable harm to claimant, and (4) claimant cannot be protected by order other than prehearing seizure. (565.24). If seizure refused, court may issue order protecting claimant's interest pending notice and hearing. If seizure ordered, court to set hearing at earliest practicable time. Respondent shall be served, in manner prescribed for personal service of summons or by court order calculated to provide actual notice, with copy of order for prehearing seizure, all other pleadings, and notice of post-seizure hearing, signed by claimant or attorney, in following form:

NOTICE OF HEARING

Court action has been taken which affects the following property:

[list property]

See note at head of Digest as to 1998 legislation covered.

See Topical Index in front part of this volume.

REPLEVIN . . . *continued*

[Claimant] (hereinafter "claimant") has claimed that claimant is entitled to this property and that claimant's interest in this property would have been harmed unless this court took immediate action.

You have a right to challenge claimant's claims at a hearing before a judge. This hearing has been scheduled for the . . . . day of . . . . . . , 19. . . , at . . . . . . o'clock . . . M., at [place] . . . . After this hearing the judge will decide, what should be done with the property pending a final decision on claimant's claim.

If court later finds motion for prehearing seizure made in bad faith, respondent may be awarded actual damages incurred by seizure. (565.24).

Repossession.—Claimant shall file bond, cash, cashier's or certified check prior to seizure in amount 1¹⁄₂ times fair market value of property seized. Respondent may retain or regain possession by filing bond in amount of lesser of 1¹⁄₄ times fair market value of property or 1¹⁄₂ times claimant's claim. Current fair market value of property presumed as stated in affidavit unless court determines otherwise. (565.25). Order of seizure may be stayed up to three days for respondent to post bond. (565.23). Costs of regaining possession borne by respondent except where property seized before hearing ordered returned to respondent. (565.25).

Court may allow respondent to retain or regain possession of property without filing bond and may stay claimant's action for reasonable time, not more than six months, if: (1) Respondent is unable to make required payments due to unforeseen economic circumstances beyond respondent's control, (2) respondent is dependent on use of property to earn living, (3) respondent insures property for fair market value, (4) respondent makes periodic payments to claimant representing depreciation in market value of property while respondent retains possession, in amount and during times determined by court, and (5) respondent makes periodic payments to claimant representing value of use of property or costs to claimant of lost opportunity to use property, in amount and during times determined by court. (565.25, .251).

Claims of Third Persons.—Party claiming interest in property or transaction which is subject of action may intervene by right if action may impair or impede ability to protect interest, or may, at court's discretion, be permitted to intervene if its claim or defense shares common question of fact or law with main action, and intervention would not unduly delay or prejudice rights of original parties. Intervention accomplished by filing and serving notice of intervention, accompanied by pleading, and motion to intervene. (RCP 24).

Judgment or order may include damages claimed in complaint or answer which prevailing party has sustained by reason of detention, or taking and withholding, of property. (546.23).

SEQUESTRATION:

Sequestration of property of corporation may be ordered where execution is returned unsatisfied. See category Debtor and Creditor, topic Receivers.

SERVICE:

See topic Process.

STAY OF EXECUTION:

See topic Appeal and Error; category Debtor and Creditor, topic Executions.

SUBMISSION OF CONTROVERSY:

Parties to controversy which might be subject of civil action may, without action, agree upon case containing facts on which controversy depends, and, upon affidavit that controversy is real and proceedings in good faith, submit same to any court which would have jurisdiction if an action had been brought, and such court can determine controversy and enter judgment. (548.24).

VENUE:

Subject to exceptions noted below, every action tried in county where begun. (542.01). Actions relating to recovery of real estate, foreclosure of mortgage or lien thereon, partition thereof, determination of form of estate or interest therein and for injuries to land within the state, must be tried in county of situs. (542.02). Actions on cost bonds of nonresidents—where bond filed. (542.05). Replevin—only where personal property taken, or where situated. (542.06). Otherwise, county in which one or more defendants reside when action began or in which cause of action or some part thereof arose. (542.09). Actions for recovery of wages or money due for manual labor may be brought in county where labor was performed. (542.08).

Change of Venue.—As matter of right: When county designated in complaint is not proper county. To effect change, defendant must, within 20 days after summons is served, serve demand accompanied by affidavit reciting residence at time action commenced, date of service of summons, and stating that cause of action did not arise where suit started, on plaintiff's attorney. On filing this with proof of service thereon with court administrator in county where action originally begun within 30 days, unless cause of action or some part thereof arose in county where action begun, venue automatically changed. Where several defendants reside in different counties, and where county designated in complaint is not county where cause of action or some part thereof arose, majority of defendants demanding change governs, or if numbers are equal, in nearest county. (542.10).

By order of court: (1) Upon written consent of parties; (2) where party made defendant for purpose of preventing change of venue; (3) where impossible to get impartial trial where venue is laid; (4) for convenience of witnesses and ends of justice. (542.11). Where judge of district court under disability or has interest or bias, another judge assigned. (RCP 63).

Action for recovery of wages due, if brought in county where work performed, can only be changed by written consent of plaintiff. (542.08). Auto vehicle cases, if

brought in county where action arose or where majority of defendants reside, can only be changed by written consent of plaintiff or court order. (542.095).

Domestic corporation other than public service corporation is considered as residing where it has an office, resident agent or place of business. (542.09).

COURTS AND LEGISLATURE

COURTS:

United States District Court.—Clerk's office: St. Paul 55101; Minneapolis 55401; Duluth 55802. Judges maintain chambers in Minneapolis and Saint Paul. Cases emanating from first, second, third, fourth and sixth divisions are assigned to either third or fourth division based on location of chambers of judge to whom case is assigned. Cases emanating from fifth division are assigned to fifth division. Files are maintained in division to which case is assigned. Papers relative to any case may be filed in any office of clerk of court. (Local Rule 83.11).

There are six divisions of United States District Court for Minnesota.

Fee for filing complaint in each division is $150.

First Division is composed of following counties: Dodge, Fillmore, Houston, Mower, Olmsted, Steele, Wabasha, Winona.

Division seat is at Winona.

Second Division is composed of following counties: Blue Earth, Brown, Cottonwood, Faribault, Freeborn, Jackson, Lac qui Parle, LeSueur, Lincoln, Lyon, Martin, Murray, Nicollet, Nobles, Pipestone, Redwood, Rock, Sibley, Waseca, Watonwan, Yellow Medicine.

Division seat is at Mankato.

Third Division is composed of following counties: Chisago, Dakota, Goodhue, Ramsey, Rice, Scott, Washington.

Division seat is at Saint Paul.

Fourth Division is composed of following counties: Anoka, Carver, Chippewa, Hennepin, Isanti, Kandiyohi, McLeod, Meeker, Renville, Sherburne, Swift, Wright.

Division seat is at Minneapolis.

Fifth Division is composed of following counties: Aitkin, Benton, Carlton, Cass, Cook, Crow Wing, Itasca, Kanabec, Koochiching, Lake, Mille Lacs, Morrison, Pine, St. Louis.

Division seat is at Duluth.

Sixth Division is composed of following counties: Becker, Beltrami, Big Stone, Clay, Clearwater, Douglas, Grant, Hubbard, Kittson, Lake of the Woods, Mahnomen, Marshall, Norman, Otter Tail, Pennington, Polk, Pope, Red Lake, Roseau, Stearns, Stevens, Todd, Traverse, Wadena, Wilkin.

Division seat is at Fergus Falls.

Supreme Court of Minnesota.—

Jurisdiction.—Original jurisdiction in cases prescribed by 480.04, such as writs of error, certiorari, mandamus, prohibition, quo warranto, etc. Court is always open for issuance and return of such writs and for hearing and determination of all matters involved therein. Appellate jurisdiction in all cases. (Const., art. 6, §2).

Court sits at St. Paul.

Court of Appeals.—Court of appeals, intermediate appellate court, established effective Aug. 1, 1983. Court has appellate jurisdiction over interlocutory decisions, and other matters, pursuant to provisions of appellate procedure rules and over final decisions of trial courts except decisions of conciliation courts, decisions in legislative or statewide election contests, and decisions involving first-degree murder convictions. Court also has jurisdiction over appeals from administrative agencies in contested cases pursuant to 14.63 to 14.69, review of administrative rules pursuant to 14.44 and 14.55, and appeals from decisions of Commissioner of Economic Security pursuant to 268.11. Court also has jurisdiction to issue writs of certiorari to all agencies, public corporations and public officials except Tax Court and Workers' Compensation Court of Appeals. (Const., Art. 6, §2; 480A.06).

Court of appeals consists of six judges appointed Nov. 1, 1983, and six judges appointed Apr. 1, 1984. (480A.01). One judgeship added in 1987. Decisions are by three-member panels with rotating memberships. Decisions must be issued within 90 days following later of oral argument or final submission of briefs, whichever is later. Chief justice or chief judge may waive 90-day limitation if good cause is shown. Court of appeals may publish only those decisions that: (1) Establish new rule of law; (2) overrule previous court of appeals decision not reviewed by supreme court; (3) provide important procedural guidelines in interpreting statutes or administrative rules; (4) involve significant legal issue; or (5) significantly aid in administration of justice. (480A.08[3]). Statement of decision without written opinion of Court of Appeals must not be officially published and must not be officially cited except as law of case, res judicata or collateral estoppel. (480A.08[3]). Chambers located in St. Paul. Court may sit in each judicial district. (480A.05, 480A.09).

District Courts of Minnesota.—Original jurisdiction in all civil and criminal actions, in all special proceedings not specially cognizable in another tribunal, and in all other cases in which jurisdiction specifically conferred by law. In addition, also have such appellate jurisdiction as is prescribed by law. (484.01; Const., art. 6, §3). Power to issue writs of injunction, ne exeat, certiorari, habeas corpus, mandamus, quo warranto, abatement of nuisance and all other writs, processes and orders necessary to complete exercise of jurisdiction. (484.03).

Districts.—

First Judicial District: Counties of Carver, Dakota, Goodhue, Le Sueur, McLeod, Scott, and Sibley.

Second Judicial District: County of Ramsey.

Third Judicial District: Counties of Dodge, Fillmore, Freeborn, Houston, Mower, Olmsted, Rice, Steele, Wabasha, Waseca, and Winona.

Fourth Judicial District: County of Hennepin.

Fifth Judicial District: Counties of Blue Earth, Brown, Cottonwood, Faribault, Jackson, Lincoln, Lyon, Martin, Murray, Nicollet, Nobles, Pipestone, Redwood, Rock, and Watonwan.

See note at head of Digest as to 1998 legislation covered.

See Topical Index in front part of this volume.

COURTS... *continued*

Sixth Judicial District: Counties of Carlton, Cook, Lake, and St. Louis.

Seventh Judicial District: Counties of Becker, Benton, Clay, Douglas, Mille Lacs, Morrison, Otter Tail, Stearns, Todd, and Wadena.

Eighth Judicial District: Counties of Big Stone, Chippewa, Grant, Kandiyohi, Lac qui Parle, Meeker, Pope, Renville, Stevens, Swift, Traverse, Wilkin, Yellow Medicine.

Ninth Judicial District: Counties of Aitkin, Beltrami, Cass, Clearwater, Crow Wing, Hubbard, Itasca, Kittson, Koochiching, Lake of the Woods, Mahnomen, Marshall, Norman, Pennington, Polk, Red Lake, and Roseau.

Tenth Judicial District: Counties of Anoka, Chisago, Isanti, Kanabec, Pine, Sherburne, Washington, and Wright.

Place of Sitting.—

Aitkin County: Ninth District; court sits at Aitkin.

Anoka County: Tenth District; court sits at Anoka.

Becker County: Seventh District; court sits at Detroit Lakes.

Beltrami County: Ninth District; court sits at Bemidji.

Benton County: Seventh District; court sits at Foley.

Big Stone County: Eighth District; court sits at Ortonville.

Blue Earth County: Fifth District; court sits at Mankato.

Brown County: Fifth District; court sits at New Ulm.

Carlton County: Sixth District; court sits at Carlton.

Carver County: First District; court sits at Chaska.

Cass County: Ninth District; court sits at Walker.

Chippewa County: Eighth District; court sits at Montevideo.

Chisago County: Tenth District; court sits at Center City.

Clay County: Seventh District; court sits as Moorhead.

Clearwater County: Ninth District; court sits at Bagley.

Cook County: Sixth District; court sits at Grand Marais.

Cottonwood County: Fifth District; court sits at Windom.

Crow Wing County: Ninth District; court sits at Brainerd.

Dakota County: First District; court sits at Hastings.

Dodge County: Third District; court sits at Mantorville.

Douglas County: Seventh District; court sits at Alexandria.

Faribault County: Fifth District; court sits at Blue Earth.

Fillmore County: Third District; court sits at Preston.

Freeborn County: Third District; court sits at Albert Lea.

Goodhue County: First District; court sits at Red Wing.

Grant County: Eighth District; court sits at Elbow Lake.

Hennepin County: Fourth District; court sits at Minneapolis.

Houston County: Third District; court sits at Caledonia.

Hubbard County: Ninth District; court sits at Park Rapids.

Isanti County: Tenth District; court sits at Cambridge.

Itasca County: Ninth District; court sits at Grand Rapids.

Jackson County: Fifth District; court sits at Jackson.

Kanabec County: Tenth District; court sits at Mora.

Kandiyohi County: Eighth District; court sits at Willmar.

Kittson County: Ninth District; court sits at Hallock.

Koochiching County: Ninth District; court sits at International Falls.

Lac qui Parle County: Eighth District; court sits at Madison.

Lake County: Sixth District; court sits at Two Harbors.

Lake of the Woods County: Ninth District; court sits at Baudette.

LeSueur County: First District; court sits at LeCenter.

Lincoln County: Fifth District; court sits at Ivanhoe.

Lyon County: Fifth District; court sits at Marshall.

Mahnomen County: Ninth District court sits at Mahnomen.

Marshall County: Ninth District; court sits at Warren.

Martin County: Fifth District; court sits at Fairmount.

McLeod County: First District; court sits at Glencoe.

Meeker County: Eighth District; court sits at Litchfield.

Mille Lacs County: Seventh District; court sits at Milaca.

Morrison County: Seventh District; court sits at Little Falls.

Mower County: Third District; court sits at Austin.

Murray County: Fifth District; court sits at Slayton.

Nicollet County: Fifth District; court sits at St. Peter.

Nobles County: Fifth District; court sits at Worthington.

Norman County: Ninth District; court sits at Ada.

Olmsted County: Third District; court sits at Rochester.

Otter Tail County: Seventh District; court sits at Fergus Falls.

Pennington County: Ninth District; court sits at Thief River Falls.

Pine County: Tenth District; court sits at Pine City.

Pipestone County: Fifth District; court sits at Pipestone.

Polk County: Ninth District; court sits at Crookston.

Pope County: Eighth District; court sits at Glenwood.

Ramsey County: Second District; court sits at St. Paul.

Red Lake County: Ninth District; court sits at Red Lake Falls.

Redwood County: Fifth District; court sits at Redwood Falls.

Renville County: Eighth District; court sits at Olivia.

Rice County: Third District; court sits at Faribault.

Rock County: Fifth District; court sits at Luverne.

Roseau County: Ninth District; court sits at Roseau.

St. Louis County: Sixth District; terms at Duluth, terms at Virginia, terms at Hibbing.

Scott County: First District; court sits at Shakopee.

Sherburne County: Tenth District; court sits at Elk River.

Sibley County: First District; court sits at Gaylord.

Stearns County: Seventh District; court sits at St. Cloud.

Steele County: Third District; court sits at Owatonna.

Stevens County: Eighth District; court sits at Morris.

Swift County: Eighth District; court sits at Benson.

Todd County: Seventh District; court sits at Long Prairie.

Traverse County: Eighth District; court sits at Wheaton.

Wabasha County: Third District; court sits at Wabasha.

Wadena County: Seventh District; court sits at Wadena.

Waseca County: Third District; court sits at Waseca.

Washington County: Tenth District; court sits at Stillwater.

Watonwan County: Fifth District; court sits at St. James.

Wilkin County: Eighth District; court sits at Breckenridge.

Winona County: Third District; court sits at Winona.

Wright County: Tenth District; court sits at Buffalo.

Yellow Medicine County: Eighth District; court sits at Granite Falls.

County Courts.—Except in Hennepin and Ramsey Counties, probate courts are also county courts. (487.01). Municipal courts and magistrate courts existing pursuant to municipal charter or ordinance in counties having county courts have been abolished. (487.191). Justice courts also abolished. (487.35).

County court has exclusive original jurisdiction over administration of estates of deceased persons, guardianship and incompetency proceedings, proceedings for management of property of persons who have disappeared and jurisdiction of juvenile court. (487.14). County court also has jurisdiction over all minor criminal and civil cases formerly residing in municipal courts other than municipal courts in Hennepin and Ramsey Counties plus gross misdemeanors. (487.16). Jurisdictional limit $15,000, exclusive of interest and costs, except for cases involving real estate. (487.15). Appeals are taken to Court of Appeals. (480A.06).

County court contains a probate division, a family court division and a civil and criminal division. Within civil and criminal division there is conciliation court and may be traffic and ordinance violations bureau. (487.27).

Following are combined probate and county court districts comprised of indicated counties: Kittson, Roseau and Lake of the Woods; Marshall, Red Lake and Pennington; Norman and Mahnomen; Cass and Hubbard; Wadena and Todd; Mille Lacs and Kanabec; Big Stone and Traverse; Grant and Douglas; Lincoln and Lyon; Rock and Nobles; Dodge and Olmsted; Lake and Cook; Pine, Isanti and Chisago; Sherburne, Benton and Stearns. Combined county court districts may be separated into single county courts by supreme court. (487.01).

Probate courts are also county courts, except in Hennepin and Ramsey Counties where district courts are also probate courts. Probate division of county court hears cases involving administration of estates of deceased persons, persons under guardianship, and proceedings for administration of trust estates. (484.011, 487.01, 487.27). See subhead County Courts, supra.

Municipal courts merged into county court system, except in Hennepin and Ramsey Counties which are governed by separate statutes. (487.01 et seq.; 488A.01 et seq.). See subhead County Courts, supra.

Conciliation courts may hear civil claims up to $7,500. (491A.01 et seq.). Procedure is very informal and customarily without attorneys.

Alternative Dispute Resolution.—Pilot project under way in Second and Fourth Judicial Districts (Hennepin and Ramsey Counties) to utilize various forms of nonbinding alternative dispute resolution in litigation involving amounts in excess of $7,500. (484.74).

Small Claims Court.—See subhead Conciliation Courts, supra.

LEGISLATURE:

Meets in regular session every year at times prescribed by law. Governor may call special sessions. (Const., art. 4, §12). No provision for initiative or referendum. Lobbyist registration required and lobbying activities regulated. (c. 10A).

REPORTS:

Minnesota Reports cover from 1850 to 1977. Decisions from 1850-1874 reported both in Minnesota Reports, volumes 1-20, and in Gilfillan Edition, volumes 1-20. Minnesota decisions are now officially reported in Northwestern Reporter 2nd.

Digests are Dunnell Minnesota Digest and West's Minnesota Digest.

STATUTES:

Minnesota Statutes 1994 constitutes latest official compilation of state statutes.

Uniform Acts which have been adopted are: Anatomical Gift (1969, 1985); Arbitration (1957, 1981); Attendance of Witnesses from Without a State in Criminal Proceedings (1935, 1985); Business Records as Evidence (1939); Certification of Questions of Law (1973, 1983); Child Custody Jurisdiction (1977, 1979); Code of Military Justice (1963, 1983); Commercial Code (1965, 1987); Condominium (1980, 1985); Conservation Easement (1985); †Controlled Substances (1971, 1987); Criminal Extradition (1939, 1985); Deceptive Trade Practices (1973, 1987); Declaratory Judgments (1933, 1943); Determination of Death (1989); Disposition of Unclaimed Property, Revised (1969, 1985); Division of Income for Tax Purposes (1983); Duties to Disabled Persons (1973); Enforcement of Foreign Judgments (1977, 1983); Evidence, Rules of (1977, 1987); Federal Lien Registration, Revised (1979, 1985); Fiduciaries (1945, 1961); Foreign Money-Judgment Recognition (1985); Fraudulent Transfer (1987); Fresh Pursuit (1939); International Wills (1978); †Interstate Arbitration of Death Taxes (1951, 1978); Interstate Compromise of Death Taxes (1951, 1978); Interstate Family Support (1994); Jury Selection and Service (1977, 1987); Land Sales Practices (1973, 1985); Limited Partnership (1919, 1976); 1976 Limited Partnership (1980, 1987); Management of Institutional Funds (1973, 1987); Mandatory Disposition of Detainers (1967, 1985); Motor Vehicle Certificate of Title and Anti-Theft (1971, 1985); Notarial Acts (1985); †Parentage (1980, 1985); Partnership (1921, 1984); Photographic Copies of Business and Public Records as Evidence (1951, 1953); Post-Conviction Procedure (1967, 1983); Principal and Income, Revised (1969); Probate Code (part) (1974, 1985); Prudent Investor (1996); †Securities (1973, 1987); Simplification of Fiduciary

See note at head of Digest as to 1998 legislation covered.

See Topical Index in front part of this volume.

STATUTES . . . *continued*
Security Transfers (1961); Simultaneous Death (1943); Statutory Rule Against Perpetuities (1987); Testamentary Additions to Trusts (1963, 1975); Trade Secrets (1980, 1987); Transfer of Dependents (1955); Transfers to Minors (1985, 1987).

For text of Uniform Acts falling within scope of Martindale-Hubbell Law Digests, see Uniform and Model Acts section.

† Adopted with significant variations or modifications. See appropriate topics.

UNIFORM LAWS:

For a list of Uniform Acts in force in this state see topic Statutes. For text of Uniform Acts within the scope of the Martindale-Hubbell Law Digests see Uniform and Model Acts section.

CRIMINAL LAW

BAIL:

See topic Criminal Law.

CRIMINAL LAW:

Criminal Code and Code of Criminal Procedure are contained in 609-643. Rules of Criminal Procedures adopted under M.S. 480.059; 49 M.S.A.R. Cr.P. 1-36. Revised Criminal Code adopted. (c. 609).

Indictment or Information.—Offenses punishable by life imprisonment prosecuted by indictment. Other offenses may be prosecuted by indictment or complaint. Misdemeanors and gross misdemeanors may also be prosecuted by tab charge. (RCP 17.01).

Bail.—Person charged with crime has right to reasonable bail in order to assure appearance in court. Rule provides that accused shall be ordered released pending trial on his personal recognizance, on order to appear, or on unsecured appearance bond in specified amount, unless it is determined that such release will be inimical of public safety or will not reasonably assure appearance of person. (RCP 6.02). Maximum cash bail that may be required for misdemeanor or gross misdemeanor violation offense is double highest cash fine that may be imposed for that offense (629.471[1]); however, for motor vehicle accidents (169.09), operating motor vehicle under influence of alcohol or controlled substance (169.121), aggravated violations of operating motor vehicle while under influence of alcohol or controlled substances (169.129), fourth-degree assault against firefighters or emergency medical personnel (609.2231[2]), fleeing peace officer in motor vehicle (609.487), and bringing stolen goods into state (609.525), maximum cash bail is quadruple highest cash fine that can be imposed (629.471[2]). For domestic abuse (518B.01), fifth-degree assault (609.224), and domestic assault (609.2242), maximum cash bail is six times highest paid fine that can be imposed (629.471[3]).

Interstate Compact for Supervision of Parolees and Probationers adopted. (243.16).

Uniform Criminal Extradition Act adopted. (629.01-.291).

Uniform Act to Secure Attendance of Witnesses from Without State in Criminal Proceedings adopted. (634.06-.09).

Uniform Act on Fresh Pursuit adopted. (626.65-72).

DEBTOR AND CREDITOR

ASSIGNMENTS:

Uniform Commercial Code adopted. (c. 336). See also category Business Regulation and Commerce, topic Commercial Code.

All causes of action which survive to personal representative of decedent are assignable. (150 Minn. 476, 185 N.W. 656).

Fire department service pensions (424.02; 424.27; 424A.02) and police pensions (423.39, 423.61, 423.813) are not assignable. Claim for personal tort, before judgment, is not assignable. (53 Minn. 249, 54 N.W. 1108). Vendor's lien on real estate is generally not assignable (44 Minn. 482, 47 N.W. 53), but vendor's interest in payments on contract for deed can be assigned. If assigned for security, perfection should be made as though interest were in both real and personal property. (784 F.2d 883).

Partial assignment is valid, but all parties interested must be joined in an action by assignee, so that whole controversy may be determined in one suit. (55 Minn. 122, 56 N.W. 586).

Effect.—Assignee of a thing in action takes subject to all defenses and setoffs existing at time of notice to debtor of assignment (540.03) unless party with setoff rights acknowledges assignment (439 N.W.2d 53). This rule is not applicable to bona fide purchaser of negotiable instrument. See category Business Regulation and Commerce, topic Commercial Code.

Assignment of Wages.—Any assignment of wages or salaries to be earned more than 60 days from date of assignment is void, except assignment of wages or salaries in excess of first $1,500 per month for less than five years and except that employee may, by written contract, authorize employer to make payroll deductions to pay union dues, insurance premiums, group annuities or contributions to credit unions or community chest fund, or Minnesota benefit association, federally or state registered political action committee, or participation in employee stock purchase or savings plan, for periods longer than 60 days. (181.06).

No valid action can be maintained on assignment of unearned wages unless written notice and copy of assignment is given employer within three days after assignment and his consent obtained. (181.04, .05). When unearned wages are assigned as security for loan of less than $200, employer must consent thereto and assignment and consent must be filed with clerk of court at assignor's residence or at place of employment of nonresident. Spouse must give written consent to any assignment of unearned wages by married person. (181.07).

Officials and employees of state or any political subdivision of state may assign salary or wages to same extent as may employees of private employers. (181.063). See category Civil Actions and Procedure, topic Judgments.

ATTACHMENT:

All property not exempt from execution under judgment demanded in civil action (see topic Exemptions) may be subject to attachment. (570.01).

Actions in Which Allowed.—Order for attachment is available as proceeding ancillary to any civil action for recovery of money. (570.01).

In Whose Favor Order May Issue.—Any claimant, including nonresident or foreign corporation, may obtain attachment. (570.011).

Claims on Which Attachment Ordered.—Not necessary that claim sued on be payable in state.

Who May Issue Order.—Only judge of court in county in which civil action is pending may issue order. (570.01).

Grounds.—Attachment intended to provide security for satisfaction of judgment allowed only when: (1) Respondent, with intent to delay or defraud creditors, has assigned, secreted or disposed of nonexempt property or is about to do so; (2) respondent, with intent to delay or defraud creditors, has removed nonexempt property from state or is about to do so; (3) respondent has converted or is about to convert nonexempt property into money or credit for purpose of placing such property beyond reach of creditors; (4) respondent has committed intentional fraud forming basis for civil action; (5) respondent has been convicted of felony forming basis for civil action; or (6) when respondent has violated law of this state respecting unfair discriminatory, and other unlawful practices in business, commerce, or trade, including but not limited to any of statutes specifically enumerated in §8.31, subd. 1. Attachment which acquires quasi-in-rem jurisdiction is allowed to extent consistent with due process of law. (570.02).

Proceedings to Obtain.—Absent extraordinary circumstances warranting securing of property prior to hearing, claimant seeking order of attachment must proceed by motion accompanied by affidavit setting forth: (1) Basis and amount of civil action claim; and (2) facts constituting grounds for attachment. Respondent must also be served with notice of hearing setting forth specific information found in statute, including notice of exemption. To succeed, claimant must demonstrate probability of success on merits, grounds for attachment, risk of uncollectability of any subsequently awarded judgment, and absence of any non-frivolous defense or counterclaim which cannot be adequately protected by claimant's bond. (570.026).

Preliminary Attachment Order.—Where extraordinary circumstances exist, claimant may make written application for prehearing preliminary attachment order. Application must be accompanied by affidavit setting forth: (1) Basis and amount of civil action claim; (2) facts constituting grounds for attachment; and (3) good faith estimate of harm to respondent if preliminary attachment order is issued.

Preliminary attachment order will be issued only where: (1) Claimant has made good faith effort to notify respondent of application or has demonstrated that notice would endanger collectability of any subsequently awarded judgment; (2) claimant has demonstrated probability of success on merits; (3) claimant has demonstrated grounds for attachment; and (4) extraordinary circumstances prevent claimant's interests from being protected in another way pending hearing. (570.025).

Bond.—In any proceeding for order of attachment, claimant must either provide bond for at least $500 or deposit cash, letter of credit, cashier's check or certified check with court. (570.041).

Levy made by officer as in case of execution and must be done within 90 days of date of order. In case of real estate, certified copy of order and of return of attachment with description of real estate filed with county recorder or registrar of titles if registered property, where land situated, and copy served on respondent. This creates lien on real estate at time of filing. Perishable property must be sold. (570.061).

Release of Property.—Any party may obtain vacation of attachment order or release of property before entry of judgment upon bond or other condition as ordered by court. Attachment expires on demand of respondent or upon discretion of sheriff where: (1) Summons and complaint delivered to sheriff for service and such service not obtained within 60 days after issuance of order for attachment; (2) judgment is entered in favor of respondent; (3) claimant fails to obtain judgment within three years after issuance of order for attachment; or (4) property subject to attachment is not applied to judgment within six months after judgment becomes final and nonappealable. (570.131).

Attachment of real estate is released by filing with county recorder or registrar of titles if registered property, certified copy of order vacating attachment or of final judgment for respondent or of satisfaction of judgment for claimant; certificate of satisfaction or discharge of attachment executed and acknowledged by claimant or his attorney; or deed of release of attached premises. (570.11).

CREDITORS' SUITS:

No statutory provisions.

EXECUTIONS:

District Court.—May be issued immediately upon entry of judgment, unless stayed or enjoined, or at any time within ten years. (550.01). There are two kinds of executions, one for delivery of possession of real or personal property, other against property of judgment debtor. (550.03). Writ of execution expires 180 days after issuance. (550.051). Alias execution may issue. (29 Minn. 87, 12 N.W. 145). All property, real and personal, equitable as well as legal estates (45 Minn. 341, 48 N.W. 187) may be levied on and sold (550.10). If against joint debtors, judgment is joint in form and levied on all joint property and on separate property of person served with summons and complaint. (550.04[4]). If judgment requires performance of any act other than payment of money or delivery of property, certified copy of judgment is served and compliance enforced by court. (550.02). Thirty days after judgment is docketed,

EXECUTIONS . . . *continued*
judgment creditor may request district court to order judgment debtor to mail to judgment creditor information as to judgment debtor's assets, etc. Judgment debtor's failure to comply is contempt of court. (550.011).

Exemptions.—See topic Exemptions.

Stay of Execution.—
District Court.—Six month stay by filing with clerk bond in double amount of judgment plus interest, approved by court, within ten days of entry of judgment in recovery of money only. (550.36). For amount of interest, see category Business Regulation and Commerce, topic Interest, subhead Judgments.

Attorney's Summary Executions.—After obtaining writ of execution under 550.04, attorney for judgment creditor may execute money judgment by levying on indebtedness owed to judgment debtor by third party, including financial institutions, employers, etc. (551.01; 551.05; 551.06). No more than $5,000 may be recovered by single summary execution. (551.01). Procedure for summary execution is set forth in 551.04.

Levy.—No formal levy on real estate is necessary. (127 Minn. 203, 149 N.W. 199). Personal property capable of manual delivery is levied on by officer taking it into his custody. (550.12). Levy may be made on bulky articles by filing certified copy of execution in appropriate filing office under Uniform Commercial Code. (550.13; UCC 336.9-401). See category Business Regulation and Commerce, topic Commercial Code.

Other personal property not capable of manual delivery is levied on by leaving copy of execution and notice specifying property levied on with person holding same or, in case of debt, with judgment debtor, or in case of stock, or interest in stock of corporation with its president, secretary, treasurer, cashier, officer or managing agent. (550.135[2]). In case of judgment debt from money owed judgment debtor by third party, levy may be made by sheriff through service of writ of execution on third-party by registered or certified letter of personal service. (550.135[3]).

Return.— In case of partial or full satisfaction, return of writ must be made to court administrator originally issuing writ with duplicate to court administrator of officer's county. (550.051[2]).

Third Party Claims.—See category Civil Actions and Procedure, topic Replevin.

Sale.—Ten days posted notice of sale, giving time and place, is necessary prerequisite to sale of personal property; six weeks posted and published notice in case of real estate, together with description thereof. (550.18). Notice of sale must be served on judgment debtor, if he is resident of county, at or before time notice posted. (550.19).

Sale must take place where property situated, and, if personal property, it must be in view. Must be sold in parcels such as are likely to bring highest price, and no more may be sold than necessary. (550.20). Where real estate is sold, officer making sale executes and gives to purchaser certificate describing execution, property, date of sale, name of purchaser, price paid, and time allowed for redemption. If recorded, it operates as conveyance when time for redemption expires. (550.22).

Redemption.—No redemption of personal property or of leasehold having less than two years' unexpired term. Real estate may be redeemed by judgment debtor, heirs or assigns, or by creditor having lien, legal or equitable, subsequent to that on which sale made (550.24); debtor or his heirs or assigns are allowed one year; creditors redeem in order of their respective liens, first creditor within five days after debtor's time expires, and each succeeding creditor within five days after time allowed all prior lien holders. Notice of intention to redeem must be filed within year of date of sale with court administrator where judgment entered. (550.25). Creditor of deceased debtor may redeem. (550.30-550.35.). During year of redemption, purchaser may pay overdue taxes, insurance premiums or interest or installments due on prior mortgage, and sum so paid, proven by affidavit of purchaser or his attorney or agent, filed with county recorder or registrar of titles, copy of which must be given sheriff at least ten days before expiration of year, becomes part of sum required to redeem. (582.03).

Supplementary Proceedings.—When execution returned unsatisfied in whole or part, judgment creditor entitled to order from judge of district court where debtor resides ordering debtor to appear before judge or referee to be examined as to his assets. (575.02). Judge may then order any property discovered in course of examination not exempt to be applied towards satisfying judgment. (575.05).

EXEMPTIONS:

Reasonable amount of property shall be exempt from seizure or sale for payment of any debt or liability. Amount of exemptions shall be determined by law. Exempt property liable to seizure and sale for any debts accrued for work done or materials furnished on construction, repair or improvement of that property. (Const., Art. 1, §12).

Only natural persons who are actual residents can obtain most exemptions available. (550.37).

General exemptions are: Family Bible, library and musical instruments; seat or pew in place of worship; lot in burial ground; all wearing apparel, one watch, utensils and foodstuffs; household furniture, household appliances, phonographs, radio and television receivers of debtor and family not exceeding $7,650 in value; one motor vehicle to extent of value not exceeding $3,400, or not exceeding $34,000 if motor vehicle has been modified, at cost of not less than $2,550, to accommodate physical disability of disabled persons; farm machines and implements used by debtor engaged principally in farming, livestock, farm produce and standing crops not exceeding $13,000 in value; tools, implements, machines, instruments, office furniture, stock in trade and library reasonably necessary in debtor's trade, business or profession, not exceeding $8,500 in value; provided that total farm and business property selected for exemption by debtor cannot exceed $13,000. (550.37).

Special Exemptions.—Other exemptions are:
Libraries, etc.—Library and philosophical and chemical or other apparatus belonging to, and used for instruction of youth in, any university, college or seminary or school indiscriminately open to public. (550.37).

Claims, Insurance, etc.—Money from claims for destruction of or damage to exempt property; life insurance payment to spouse or child on life of deceased spouse or parent, not exceeding $34,000 plus $8,500 for each dependent of surviving spouse or child. Aggregate interest not exceeding $6,800 in accrued dividend, interest or loan value of unmatured life insurance contract owned by debtor under which insured is debtor or individual of whom debtor is dependent. Right to receive payment or payments received under stock bonus, pension, profit sharing, annuity, individual retirement account or annuity, simplified employee pension, or similar plan on account of illness, disability, death, age or length of service, to extent exempt under ERISA or up to present value of $51,000 and additional amounts to extent reasonably necessary for support of debtor or dependent. All money, relief or other benefits payable to or to be rendered by any police, fire, beneficiary or fraternal benefit association to any person entitled to assistance therefrom or to any certificate holder thereof or beneficiary under any such certificate. Net amount payable under accident or disability insurance policies or under accident or disability clauses attached to life insurance policies. (550.37, .39).

Mobile home actually inhabited as a home by debtor. (550.37).

Veterans compensation, including pension, bonus, adjusted compensation, allotment or other benefit paid by State of Minnesota or U.S. (550.38).

Damages.—All claims for damages recoverable by reason of a levy on or sale under execution of exempt personal property or by reason of the wrongful taking or detention of such property and any judgment for such damages. (550.37).

All relief based on need. (550.37).

Rights of action for injuries to person of debtor or relative whether or not resulting in death and insurance proceeds therefor. (550.37; 550.39).

Substitution.—No provision permitting a debtor to hold other property or money exempt in lieu of articles specifically exempted but not owned by him.

Bankruptcy.—Federal bankruptcy exemptions available. Married persons filing petitions in bankruptcy both required to elect either state exemptions or exemptions under federal Bankruptcy Code. Applies to joint petitions and any individual petition filed within three years after petition by other spouse. (550.371).

Debts Against Which Exemptions Not Allowed.—No property is exempt in action for purchase money therefor. Certain personal property not exempt from pawnbroker's possessory lien. (550.37).

Earnings.—Earnings of debtor within 30 days prior to court's ordering satisfaction of judgment in supplementary proceeding exempt if earnings shown to be necessary for family support (575.05); 75% of disposable earnings of debtor or amount of wages equal to 40 times federal minimum hourly wage times number of weeks in pay period, whichever is greater, is exempt (550.37, 550.136, 571.922). Varying limitations apply to judgments for child support. (550.136). Wages of welfare recipient exempt. Wages of person returning to private employment or farming from relief or from state correctional institution exempt for six months. Earnings of minor child or any child support paid to any debtor not liable in action by reason of any debt not contracted for special benefit of child. (550.37). See also topic Garnishment.

Waiver of Exemption.—Exemption of wages and certain personal property may not be waived except that exemption for personal property may be waived as to purchase money security interests. Debtor with personal property above $7,200 exemption may select exemption in writing from itemized list of property at time loan made and give nonpurchase money security interest in excess. Other exemptions may be waived only by statement signed and dated by debtor at time of execution of contract surrendering exemption, adjacent to list of property, and in following form: "I understand that some or all of the above property is normally protected by law from the claims of creditors, and I voluntarily give up my right to that protection for the above listed property with respect to claims arising out of this contract." (550.37).

Homestead Exemption.—See topic Homesteads.

Certain Exemptions Held Unconstitutional Under Minnesota Constitution.—Exemption for police and fire departments, beneficiary and fraternal benefit associations (402 N.W.2d 551); exemption for musical instructors (76 B.R. 683); exemption for personal injury damages (119 B.R. 685) as to special damages (138 B.R. 943); exemption for certain retirement accounts (529 N.W. 2d 335).

FORECLOSURE:

See topic Liens; category Mortgages, topic Mortgages of Real Property.

FRAUDULENT SALES AND CONVEYANCES:

Uniform Commercial Code adopted. (c. 336). See category Business Regulation and Commerce, topic Commercial Code.

Uniform Fraudulent Transfer Act adopted. (513.41-.51).

Transfers in Trust.—Transfers of real or personal property by debtor to third party to be held in trust for use of debtor, void as against existing or subsequent creditors. (99 Minn. 301, 109 N.W. 242). See category Business Regulation and Commerce, topic Commercial Code.

Remedies of Creditors.—When, during pendency of action, defendant threatens to dispose of property with intent to defraud creditors, they may obtain injunction. (RCP 65) or possession of property (565.24). Remedies under Minnesota UFTA available to creditors only; not available to debtors. (122 B.R. 89).

In all cases where rights of creditors in good faith come in question, husband held to have notice of wife's contracts and debts and wife held to have notice of husband's contracts and debts as fully as if a party to transactions. (519.06).

Bulk Sales.—Art. 6 of Uniform Commercial Code repealed 1991. Art. 6 of Uniform Commercial Code continues to be effective for pre-1991 transactions. See category Business Regulation and Commerce, topic Commercial Code for pre-1991 variations to Art. 6.

Conveyance of Real Property.—Conveyance of estate or interest in lands, or rents or profits thereof, or any charge on same, made or created with intent to defraud

See note at head of Digest as to 1998 legislation covered.

See Topical Index in front part of this volume.

MN – 23

FRAUDULENT SALES AND CONVEYANCES . . . *continued*
purchasers for valuable consideration is void as against such purchaser. (513.08). However, conveyance or charge is not fraudulent as against subsequent purchaser with actual or constructive notice of charge or conveyance at time of purchase, when grantee or beneficiary of charge or conveyance was privy to intended fraud. (513.08). Conveyance or charge of estate or interest in land, containing any provision for revocation, determination or alteration of such estate or interest, or any part thereof, at will of grantor, is void, as against subsequent purchasers from such grantor for valuable consideration. (513.09).

GARNISHMENT:

Garnishment is permitted in all actions on contract, or in tort, for recovery of money.

Property Not Attachable.—(1) Any indebtedness, money, or other property due to debtor, unless at time of garnishment summons same is due absolutely or does not depend upon any contingency; (2) any judgment in favor of debtor against garnishee, if garnishee or garnishee's property is liable on execution levy upon judgment; (3) any debt owed by garnishee to debtor for which any negotiable instrument has been issued or endorsed by garnishee; (4) any indebtedness, money, or other property due to debtor where debtor is bank, savings bank, trust company, credit union, savings association, or industrial loan and thrift companies with deposit liabilities; (5) any indebtedness, money, or other property due to debtor with cumulative value of less than $10; and (6) any disposable earnings, indebtedness, money, or property that is exempt under Minnesota or federal law. (571.73, Subd. 4).

Property Which May Be Attached.—(1) All unpaid nonexempt disposable earnings owed or to be owed by garnishee and earned or to be earned by debtor within pay period in which garnishment summons is served and within all subsequent pay periods whose paydays occur within 70 days after date of service of garnishment summons; (2) all other nonexempt indebtedness, money or other property due or belonging to debtor and owing by garnishee or in possession or under control of garnishee at time of service of garnishment summons, whether or not same has become payable; and, (3) all other nonexempt intangible or tangible personal property of debtor in possession or under control of garnishee at time of service of garnishment summons, including property of any kind due from or in hands of executor, administrator, personal representative, receiver, or trustee, and all written evidences of indebtedness whether or not negotiable or not yet underdue or overdue; and (4) for garnishment on judgment for child support by county, all unpaid nonexempt disposable earnings owed to or to be owed by garnishee and earned or to be earned by debtor within pay period in which summons is served and written all subsequent pay periods until judgment is satisfied. (571.73, Subd. 3). Entire deposit in joint and several bank accounts subject to garnishment. (233 Minn. 467, 47 N.W.2d 194).

Salary or wages of any official or employee of a county, town, city, village or school district, or any department thereof, is subject to garnishment. (571.77).

As to exemptions, see topic Exemptions.

Procedure.—As ancillary proceeding to civil action for recovery of money, creditor may issue garnishment summons after entry of judgment, before entry of judgment if 40 days have elapsed since service of summons and complaint upon debtor when default judgment could be entered or before entry of judgment if it appears to court that (1) debtor has assigned, secreted, or disposed of, or is about to assign, secrete, or dispose of, any of debtor's nonexempt property, with intent to delay or defraud any of debtor's creditors; (2) debtor has removed, or is about to remove, any of debtor's nonexempt property from state, with intent to delay or defraud any of debtor's creditors; (3) debtor has converted or is about to convert any of debtor's nonexempt property into money or credits, for purpose of placing property beyond reach of any of debtor's creditors; (4) debtor has committed intentional fraud giving rise to claim upon which civil action is brought; (5) debtor has committed any act or omission, for which debtor has been convicted of felony, giving rise to claim upon which civil action is brought; or (6) purpose of garnishment is to establish quasi in rem jurisdiction and (i) debtor is resident individual having left state with intent to defraud creditors, or to avoid service, or, (ii) judgment had previously been obtained in another state consistent with due process, or (iii) claim in civil action is directly related to and arises from property sought to be attached, or (iv) no forum is available to obtain personal judgment against debtor in U.S. or elsewhere; or (7) creditor has been unable to serve upon debtor summons and complaint in civil action because debtor has been inaccessible due to residence and employment in building where access is restricted. (571.71, 571.93). Prejudgment garnishment is available either before notice and hearing (571.931) or after notice and hearing (571.932).

To enforce claim asserted in civil action, garnishment summons may be issued by creditor and served upon garnishee in same manner as other summons in that court of record, except that service may not be made by publication. Service of garnishment summons on garnishee may also be made by certified mail, return receipt requested. Effective date of service by certified mail is time of receipt by garnishee. Garnishment summons must state that garnishee must serve written disclosure and answers to all interrogatories within 20 days after service, but must not require disclosure of any property of debtor in garnishee's possession in excess of 110% of amount of unpaid claim. (571.72).

Creditor liable to debtor in amount of $100, plus actual damages, plus reasonable attorneys' fees and costs for serving garnishment prior to entry of judgment in main action, except where permitted. Judgment creditor may also be liable to debtor for damages, costs and attorneys' fees for actions taken in bad faith and in violation of certain statutory provisions. (571.90). Garnishee must be paid $15 fee, and, if required to appear for oral examination, regular witness fees. (571.76). Any party to garnishment proceeding may obtain ex parte order requiring oral disclosure upon filing affidavit showing upon information and belief that oral examination of garnishee would provide complete disclosure of relevant facts. (571.75).

Notice to Debtor.—Copy of garnishment summons and all other papers served upon garnishee must be served by mail on judgment debtor not later than five days after service on garnishee. (571.72; Subd. 4).

Intervention.—Other claimants may intervene. (571.83).

Answer of Garnishee.—Garnishee shall serve on both creditor and debtor, within 20 days after service of garnishment summons, written disclosure of garnishee's indebtedness, money, or other property owing to debtor. However, if garnishment is on earnings and debtor has garnishable earnings, garnishee shall serve disclosure and earnings disclosure worksheet within ten days after last payday to occur within 70 days after date of service of garnishment summons. Amount of garnishee's disclosure need not exceed 110% of amount of creditor's claim that remains unpaid, after subtracting total of setoffs, defenses, exemptions, ownership claims, or other interests. Answers to garnishment disclosure form may be served personally or by first class mail. (571.75).

Default by Garnishee.—If garnishee fails to make required disclosure, upon motion supported by affidavit, court may render judgment against garnishee for amount not exceeding creditor's claim against debtor or 110% of amount claimed in garnishment summons, whichever is smaller. For good cause shown, court may remove such default. (571.82).

No Discharge from Employment.—No employer may discharge or otherwise discipline any employee by reason of fact that employee's earnings are subjected to garnishment. (571.927).

Judgment against garnishee must be for amount due judgment debtor or so much thereof as is necessary to satisfy judgment creditor's judgment against judgment debtor, but not to exceed 110% of amount claimed in garnishee summons. (571.82). If garnishee's disclosure denies indebtedness to debtor or that any of judgment debtor's property is in garnishee's possession, disclosure operates as full discharge at end of 20 days from date of service of disclosure in absence of further proceedings. (571.79). Garnishee is not discharged if interested person serves motion within 20 days of service of disclosure or if creditor moves for leave to file supplemental complaint against garnishee and court vacates discharge. (571.80).

Discharge of Garnishment.—Garnishment lapses and garnishee discharged after expiration of 270 days from service of garnishment summons, if served before entry of judgment, or 180 days if served after entry of judgment. (571.79).

HOMESTEADS:

House owned and occupied by debtor as debtor's dwelling place, together with land on which situated, is exempt from seizure or sale under legal process on account of any debt not lawfully charged thereon in writing, except such as are incurred for work and materials furnished in construction, repair, or improvement of such homestead, or for services performed by laborers and servants thereon. (510.01; Const., art. I, §12). Homestead application is limited to 1/2 acre in area if in city (otherwise 160 acres) and to $200,000 in value (unless used primarily for agricultural purposes; then $500,000). (510.02).

Person may create homestead by actual residence thereon and defeat subsequent judgment (41 Minn. 227, 43 N. W. 52); but not prior judgment which is a lien thereon. Right extends to dwelling on land owned by another (510.04).

Limitation of Value.—None.

Limitation of Area.—1/2 acre within laid out or platted portion of city; 160 acres elsewhere. (510.02).

Exemption is not available against claim for unpaid purchase price of homestead. (507.03). See also first paragraph of this topic.

Alienation or Encumbrance.—Sale or mortgage of homestead requires signatures of both husband and wife, including signature by spouse's duly appointed attorney-in-fact, except in case of purchase money mortgage, conveyance between spouses creating joint tenancy, or severance of joint tenancy. (507.02).

Proceeds of sale or of insurance claim on homestead property are exempt for one year from judgments and debts from which homestead was exempt except that proceeds of sale are not exempt from judgment or debt for court-ordered child support or maintenance obligation in arrears. (510.07).

Waiver or Loss.—Exemption may be lost by abandonment or by deed or mortgage signed by both husband and wife, if claimant is married. Probably cannot be waived except by instrument in writing signed by both husband and wife creating specific charge on homestead. (See 510.01.)

Loss of Exemption by Abandonment.—Owner deemed to have abandoned when he removes from homestead and ceases to occupy same for more than six consecutive months, unless within that time he files with county recorder of county notice, subscribed and acknowledged as required for deed, describing land and stating that he claims it as his homestead. Exemption cannot continue for longer than five years after filing such notice unless, during portion of such time, homestead is occupied as actual dwelling place by owner or his family. (510.07).

Rights of Surviving Spouse and Children.—Right of exemption exists in favor of surviving spouse and minor children as against debts of all of them not secured thereon, also in favor of spouse and minor children when other spouse absconds from state or deserts family. (510.06). Surviving spouse must occupy property as homestead to prevent sale for own debts. (50 Minn. 264, 52 N.W. 862). Homestead of widow limited to lands actually occupied by her husband as such. (54 Minn. 190, 55 N.W. 960). See also infra, subhead Descent.

Descent.—Where decedent leaves surviving spouse, homestead (including mobile home which is family residence) descends free from any testamentary or other disposition thereof to which such spouse has not consented in writing or by election to take under will as follows: (1) if there is no surviving descendant of decedent, to spouse; (2) if there are surviving descendants of decedent, then to spouse for life and remainder in equal shares to decedent's descendants by representation. (524.2-402). Where there is no surviving spouse and homestead is not disposed of by will, it descends same as other real estate. (524.2-402). Homestead is subject to claims for state hospital care, unless claim is limited by Commissioner of Human Services. (246.53; 510.05; 524.2-402). If there is no surviving spouse homestead is subject to medical assistance

See note at head of Digest as to 1998 legislation covered.

See Topical Index in front part of this volume.

MN – 24

HOMESTEADS . . . *continued*

claims for total amount of assistance rendered to decedent and previously deceased spouse. Decedents homestead is subject to medical assistance claims for total amount of assistance previously rendered or being rendered to surviving spouse. (265B.45[1b]). Heirs and devisees are entitled to apply for waiver of claim based on value or undue hardship. (256B.15, 510.05, 525.145). Homestead passing to spouse, children or issue of deceased children exempt from other debts of decedent which were not charges against homestead. Homestead passing otherwise is subject to expenses of administration, funeral expenses, expenses of last illness, taxes, and debts. (524.2-402). For purposes of 524.2-402, except as to omitted spouses, surviving spouse is deemed to consent to any testamentary or other disposition of homestead to which spouse has not previously consented in writing unless spouse files petition asserting homestead rights. (525.145). See categories Business Regulation and Commerce, topic Commercial Code; Estates and Trusts, topic Descent and Distribution; Mortgages, topic Mortgages of Real Property.

JUDGMENT NOTES:

See categories Business Regulation and Commerce, topic Bills and Notes; Civil Actions and Procedure, topic Judgments, subhead Confession of Judgment.

LEVY:

See topics Attachment, Executions.

LIENS:

Uniform Commercial Code adopted. (c. 336). See category Business Regulation and Commerce, topic Commercial Code.

Revised Uniform Federal Lien Registration Act adopted. Amendments adopted. (272.479 et seq.).

General Lien Provisions.—Lien claims are assignable and assignee may file claims. (514.73; 58 Minn. 455, 60 N.W. 23). Note given for debt does not discharge lien unless obligation by its terms so provides, or unless time of payment thereof is extended beyond time fixed by law for enforcing lien. (514.75).

Carriers, warehousemen, etc., have lien on personal property in possession and right of detainer for transporting property but not as carrier under Art. 7 of Uniform Commercial Code; keeping or storing property as bailee but not as warehouse operator under Art. 7 of Uniform Commercial Code; care of domestic animals; use and storage of molds and patterns in possession of fabricator belonging to customer for balance due from customer for fabrication work; making, altering, repairing or expending any labor, skill or material on any article of personal property; towing and storing motor vehicles at request of law enforcement officer. (514.18, 514.19). Services must be at request of owner or legal possessor of property. (514.18). Liens secure all lawful charges paid by lienholders to third person, price and value of lienholder's care, storage or contribution and all reasonable disbursements from detention or sale of property. (514.18, 19). Lien is enforced by public sale if sum secured by lien not paid within 90 days after it becomes due. (514.20-.22). See also category Business Regulation and Commerce, topics Carriers, subhead Liens (concerning 45 days written notice before sale of motor vehicle), Commercial Code.

Self-service storage lien attaches upon default in favor of owner of self-service storage facility against personal property stored under rental agreement at facility for rent, labor and other charges specified in rental agreement. (514.972, subd. 1). Lien is perfected by possession and extends to proceeds of stored personal property. (514.972, subd. 1). No lien arises if owner holds security deposit sufficient to cover rents and other charges at time of alleged default. (514.972, subd. 3). Enforcement is pursuant to Uniform Commercial Code procedure for warehouse operators. (514.973; 336.7-210). Rental agreement must include disclosure of owner's lien rights. (514.975).

Motor Vehicle Lien.—See category Transportation, topic Motor Vehicles, subhead Liens.

Logs and timber liens for services in connection with cutting, loading, peeling, etc. Lien generally ceases unless statement filed within 30 days after termination of labor or service and filing shall continue lien for 90 more days unless action is commenced for its enforcement. Lien enforced by attachment of and levy on property. (514.40-.58).

Wage lien on property of employer in favor of employee for wages earned within prior six months, equal to greater of $1,000 or five weeks net wages, but not more than $3,000. Has priority over any attachment or execution levied on such property; also preferred to mortgages, judgments and other liens attaching after beginning of work for which wages earned. May not be waived by agreement with employer. Enforced by sale of employer's property. (514.59-.61).

Agricultural production input liens exist for suppliers of agricultural chemicals, seeds, petroleum products and feed used in producing crops or raising livestock. (514.950-.959). Priority of liens governed mainly by Uniform Commercial Code except that supplier's perfected lien may achieve priority over lender's earlier perfected security interest if supplier sends lien-notification statement to lender and lender does not respond within ten calendar days. (514.952). Lien is perfected by filing lien-notification statement by six months after last date production input was furnished. (514.956). Place of filing and enforcement of lien governed by Uniform Commercial Code. (514.956-.958; 336.9-401). See category Business Regulation and Commerce, topic Commercial Code.

The Minnesota Wholesale Produce Dealers Act, c. 27, provides that produce and products of produce of wholesale produce dealer are held in trust for benefit of unpaid sellers of perishable fruits and vegetables, milk and cream and products manufactured from milk and cream, and poultry and poultry products. (27.01 et seq.). To benefit from trust, unpaid sellers must file beneficiary's notice with wholesale produce dealer, Commissioner of Agriculture and in appropriate filing office under 336.9-401 as if trust were security interest. Notice must be filed within 40 days after due date for

payment to seller or 40 days after payment instrument to seller is dishonored, whichever is later. Unpaid seller's interest in trust assets is paramount to all other liens, security interests and encumbrances in trust assets. (27.138).

Planting crop owner's lien exists if planting crop owner's property right to harvest crops is involuntarily terminated before crops are harvested, then person or entity with property right to harvest crops is liable to planting crop owner for crop value. (557.12). Lien may be satisfied by allowing planting crop owner to harvest crop or by compensation for crop value. Lien is perfected by filing financing statement within 90 days after planting crop owner's right to harvest crop is terminated. Place of filing and enforcement of lien governed by Uniform Commercial Code. (557.12[5]; 336.9-401; 336.9-501). If lien is satisfied by allowing harvest of crops by planting crop owner, person or entity with right to harvest crops has lien on crop for fair market rental value of property where crops were grown which attaches to crops and crop products. (557.12[4]). See category Business Regulation and Commerce, topic Commercial Code.

Lien for service of male animals on offspring of such animals for price or value of its service. (514.62, 63). Place of filing governed by Uniform Commercial Code. (514.63; 336.9-401). See category Business Regulation and Commerce, topic Commercial Code.

Processing farm products lien exists on certain farm products of farmer in favor of person performing certain processing services in connection therewith. Prior to all other liens and encumbrances except those given to purchase seed from which grain grown. (514.65). Lien preserved by filing within 15 days after service completed. Place of filing and enforcement of lien governed by Uniform Commercial Code. (514.66; 336.9-401). See category Business Regulation and Commerce, topic Commercial Code.

Agricultural landlord lien exists in favor of person or entity that leases property for agricultural production for unpaid rent on crops produced on property in crop year and on crop products and their proceeds. (514.960). Prior to all other liens. Lien perfected by filing lien statement within 30 days after crops become growing crops. Place of filing and enforcement of lien governed by Uniform Commercial Code. (336.9-401, 336.9-501). See category Business Regulation and Commerce, topic Commercial Code.

Environmental lien against real property exists for state cleanup action expenses. (514.671-.676). Lien attaches when state: (1) Incurs cleanup costs and (2) serves and files required notices. Environmental lien notice may not be filed by commissioner until (a) agency board for cleanup action expenses, Petroleum Tank Release Compensation Board, persons who would be included in §514.672, subd. 1, and each record owner and mortgagee of real property are notified in writing of intention to file lien notice and (b) within 30 days of receiving such notice, persons who would be included in §514.672, subd. 1, receive notice and opportunity to appear and appropriate board approves filing. (514.672, .673). Lien is subject to rights of any other interest holder whose interest was perfected prior to filing of environmental lien notice in appropriate real property records. (514.672). Enforcement is by foreclosure in manner provided for judgment liens. (514.674; 550).

Governmental services lien exists for governmental services. No recording necessary to obtain first lien. (514.67).

Hospital charges lien for hospital care on all causes of action accruing to person who received care, or legal representative of person, on account of injuries which necessitated care. Filing with clerk of district court within ten days after person discharged necessary to perfect lien. (514.68-.72).

Mechanics' Liens on Real Property.—Given to all who contribute to improvement of real estate by performing engineering or land surveying services or performing labor, services and skill, or furnishing skill, material or machinery for any land or structure thereon when ordered expressly or impliedly by owner, agent or trustee, or vendee. (514.01). Homestead included. (Const., art. I, §12). Architects may have lien. (52 Minn. 522, 54 N.W. 746).

Mechanic's liens on real property extends to lines of railway, telephone, and similar projects, and to mines. (514.04; 514.17).

One who bona fide furnishes material to be used on premises, though not actually delivered to or used thereon, is entitled to lien. (159 Minn. 116, 198 N.W. 406).

Notice contained in statute advising owner of certain rights must either be included in contract between owner and contractor (copy of which contract must be given to owner) or, if there is no written contract, such notice must be prepared and delivered separately by contractors and subcontractors to owner, except in case of improvement to residential property with more than four family units or improvements to nonagricultural and wholly or partially nonresidential property with more than 5,000 square feet of floor space. (514.011).

Lien attaches when first item of material or labor is furnished for beginning of improvement, though plans may have been prepared some time earlier. (514.05; 134 Minn. 156, 158 N.W. 918).

Trade fixtures, not attached to building so as to become an accessory thereto or so as to legally constitute part of realty, are not lienable. (159 Minn. 182, 198 N.W. 424).

Preventing Lien.—Any person with interest in real property who has not authorized improvements to property may protect that person's interest from liens by giving notice in writing by personal service or by certified mail to last known address (service is complete upon mailing) to proposed lienors within five days after first information of labor or material furnished or keeping such notice posted in a conspicuous place on land or improvement thereon that it has not authorized improvements. (514.06).

Priorities.—As between mortgage (including mortgage to secure future advances if payment of advances obligatory) and mechanics' lien, mortgage has priority if lienholder had actual notice of mortgage if mortgage recorded before lien attaches, even though advances thereunder are made later. (134 Minn. 156, 158 N.W. 918). As to priority of mortgage and lien, and classes of same, see 54 Minn. 486, 56 N.W. 131, as modified by 514.05. Mortgage securing revolving line of credit, whether or not advances are obligations, is effective notice to all parties from time mortgage is

---

LIENS . . . *continued*

recorded as to all advances and readvances, provided mortgage states maximum line of credit. (507.325; 508.555).

Lien statement must be filed in writing, verified, with county recorder or, if registered land, with registrar of titles within 120 days from doing last of work or furnishing last item or lien ceases. (514.08).

Foreclosure.—Lienor commencing action to foreclose must make all other lienors defendants. No other action to foreclose may be commenced for enforcement of any lien arising from same improvement but all lienholders must answer in original action. Lienor not made party may intervene. Lien must be enforced, by action, or by answer in action started by another lienor, within one year after last item of labor or materials furnished. (514.11, .12). Single judgment is rendered, and property is sold, subject to rights of all persons which are paramount to such liens and to owner's one-year right of redemption.

Period allowed for redemption runs from date of confirmation of sale. (167 Minn. 208, 208 N.W. 654).

Public Works.—Unless amount of contract is $10,000 or less, contractor for public work must give a performance bond conditioned for payment of all claims and saving obligee harmless from all costs and charges on account of work and must give a payment bond for use and benefit of all persons doing work or furnishing skill, tools, machinery or materials or insurance premiums or equipment or supplies or taxes engaged under or performing the contract. (574.26, subd. 2). Any claim on payment bond by person furnishing labor or materials must be made by such person within 120 days after completion, delivery or provision by person of its last item of labor or materials for public work by serving written notice specifying nature and amount of claim and date of last item. (574.31). Provision has also been made for giving of security in lieu of payment and performance bond with approval of Commissioner of Administration where amount of contract not in excess of $5,000. (574.261). In connection with forestry development projects, Commissioner of Natural Resources may require performance or payment bonds or bid deposits. Person required to file such bond or bid deposits may deposit securities in lieu thereof. (574.263-.264).

Mechanic's Lien on Watercraft.—Lien on every boat or vessel in navigating waters of Minnesota for all debts contracted by master, owner, agent, or consignee thereof on account of supplies to or work done on boat; for all sums due for anchorage or wharfage of boat within Minnesota; for all injuries done to person or property by boat; and for all damages or demands accruing from breach of any contract of affreightment, etc. (579.01). Action against boat commenced by filing complaint in district court of county where boat is located. Upon filing of complaint, warrant shall be issued directing sheriff to seize boat. (579.02). if lienholder obtains judgment against boat, sheriff shall sell boat. (579.04). All actions against boat must be commenced within one year after cause of action accrues. (579.08).

Mechanics' Lien on Aircraft.—Nonpossessory lien for work done or materials furnished given to all who make, alter, repair or otherwise enhance value of any aircraft at request of owner or legal possessor and who give up possession of aircraft. (514.221). Lien must be filed within 90 days after performing work or furnishing materials and does not become effective until date of filing. Place of filing and enforcement of lien governed by Uniform Commercial Code except that foreclosure must be instituted within one year of date of filing and lien is subject to rights of purchaser who acquired aircraft prior to filing and without knowledge or notice of lien claimant's services. (514.221).

Shoeing Animals.—Every person who shall shoe animals shall have lien on animal for reasonable charge of shoeing. (514.23-.34).

Lien for Launderers.—Lien on any article for amount due on same for repairing, altering, dyeing, cleaning, pressing or laundering article. (514.77-.79).

Veterinarian's Emergency Services Lien.—Lien for value of emergency services in excess of $25 on animals which received services if services cost more than $25. Lien terminating 180 days after services performed, if no lien statement is filed, or one year after lien is filed, if no action to enforce lien has been initiated. (514.92-.94).

Agricultural Producer's Lien.—Person who produces agricultural commodity has lien for contract price or fair market value of agricultural commodity produced by person and delivered to buyer with exceptions. (514.945).

MECHANICS' LIENS:

See topic Liens.

PLEDGES:

Uniform Commercial Code adopted. (c. 336). See category Business Regulation and Commerce, topic Commercial Code. Revised Art. 8 and conforming amendments to Art. 9 adopted. See category Business Regulation and Commerce, topic Commercial Code.

Pledgor's interest in property is subject to execution. (550.16).

Redemption.—No provision for redemption from foreclosure sale of pledged personal property.

RECEIVERS:

When May be Appointed.—Whenever any execution on judgment against corporation is returned unsatisfied, upon complaint of creditor, court may sequester corporation's property and appoint receiver to dispose of same in following order: (1) Expenses of receivership; (2) debts due State of Minnesota and U.S.; (3) taxes and assessments; (4) claims for injuries to employees entitled to workers' compensation, where corporation carried no insurance; (5) claims for wages and fringe benefits earned within prior three months; (6) other claims duly proved and allowed. (316.05).

In proceeding for dissolution of corporation, court may appoint receiver, before or after full hearing, to collect and preserve assets and, subject to court order, to continue business and sell, lease, transfer or dispose of assets. (302A.753). Receiver may sue

and defend in all courts. (302A.755). Receiver may be natural person, domestic corporation or foreign corporation authorized to transact business in state. (302A.755).

Receivers may be appointed over affairs of insolvent banks or insurance companies or in connection with an injunction against them for violation of their charter. (316.12, 13). Also to enforce mechanics' liens (514.16) or payment of maintenance or support (518.24); or in supplementary proceedings (575.05). See also category Mortgages, topic Mortgages of Real Property.

In addition to above special cases, receiver may be appointed in general: (1) Before judgment, on application of any party to action who can show right to property which is subject of action and that said property or its rents and profits are in danger of loss or material impairment; (2) by or after judgment, pending appeal, or upon return of execution unsatisfied; (3) on dissolution of corporation, or where it is insolvent or has forfeited corporate rights, and in like cases of property of foreign corporations within state; (4) in such other cases as are authorized by law or existing practice (576.01), including cases of certain absentees (576.04). Receiver shall be appointed upon foreclosure of certain non-homestead and non-agricultural mortgages if certain mortgage covenants breached. (576.01).

Receivers may be appointed by consent. (134 Minn. 422, 159 N.W. 948).

Eligibility.—Except by consent of parties interested, no person who has been stockholder, director, or officer of corporation during preceding year may be appointed receiver of such corporation. (Rule 137.02, Minnesota General Rules of Practice for District Courts).

Notice.—Receivers may only be appointed upon notice to interested parties except in an emergency. (Rule 137.02, Minnesota General Rules of Practice for District Courts).

Bonds.—Every receiver must give bond in such amount as court may require, with sureties approved by it. (302A.755, 316.11). Cost thereof is lawful expense and may be so included. (574.19).

Actions Against Receivers.—When property is in custody of receiver, leave of court must be obtained before suit can be brought against him, except in connection with any act or transaction in carrying on business connected with such property. (540.14).

REDEMPTION:

See topics Executions, Liens; categories Mortgages, topic Mortgages of Real Property; Taxation, topic Property Taxes, subhead Redemption.

SUPPLEMENTARY PROCEEDINGS:

See topic Executions.

TRUSTEE PROCESS:

See topic Garnishment.

USURY:

See category Business Regulation and Commerce, topic Interest.

DISPUTE RESOLUTION

ALTERNATIVE DISPUTE RESOLUTION:

Mandatory Dispute Resolution.—State of Minnesota instituted pilot program for Second and Fourth Judicial Districts in which courts could order parties in all civil litigation with amount in excess of $7,500 in controversy to submit to nonbinding alternative dispute resolution. Alternatives include private trials, neutral expert fact-finding, mediation, minitrials and other forms of alternative dispute resolution. (484.74). Where more than $50,000 in controversy, court may appoint special magistrate for binding proceedings with consent and agreement of all parties. (484.74 subd. 2a).

State of Minnesota has authorized majority of judges in any judicial district to establish system of mandatory nonbinding arbitration on district-by-district basis for disposition of any civil action, with exception of matters relating to guardianship, conservatorship, civil commitment, matters within juvenile court jurisdiction involving children in need of protection or services or delinquency, matters involving termination of parental rights under §§260.221 to 260.245 or matters arising under §§518B.01 (domestic abuse), 626.557 (reporting of maltreatment of vulnerable adults) or 144.651 to 144.652 (patient bill of rights). (484.73).

Alternative Dispute Resolution.—Effective June 1, 1991, State of Minnesota directed supreme court to establish statewide alternative dispute resolution program for resolution of all civil cases filed with courts. Except for matters involving family law, rules require use of nonbinding alternative dispute resolution processes in all civil cases, except for good cause shown to presiding judge. Methods provided in rules include arbitration, private trials, neutral expert fact-finding, mediation, minitrials, consensual special magistrates including retired judges and qualified attorneys to serve as special magistrates for binding proceedings with right of appeal. All of these methods must be nonbinding unless agreed upon by parties. Alternative dispute resolution may not be required in guardianship, conservatorship, civil commitment matters; proceedings in juvenile court, including matters involving termination of parental rights under §§260.221 to 260.245 or matters arising under §§518B.01 (domestic abuse), 626.557 (reporting of maltreatment of vulnerable adults) or 144.651 and 144.652 (patient bill of rights). (484.76). In medical malpractice cases, all parties must unanimously agree before alternative dispute resolution begins. (604.11). Also see topic Arbitration and Award.

Minnesota General Rules of Practice for District Courts 114.01-.14 are rules for mandatory alternative dispute resolution in state district courts. In addition to exception set forth in Minn. Stat. §§484.74 and 484.76, these rules do not apply to following cases: (a) Conciliation court actions and conciliation court appeals where no jury trial is demanded; (b) family court matters governed by Minn.Gen.R. Prac. 301 through

---

ALTERNATIVE DISPUTE RESOLUTION . . . *continued*

312; (c) public assistance appeals under Minn.Stat. §256.045, subd. 7; (d) unlawful detainer actions pursuant to Minn.Stat. §§556.01, et seq.; (e) implied consent proceedings pursuant to Minn.Stat. §169.123; (f) juvenile court proceedings; (g) civil commitment proceedings subject to Special Rules of Procedure governing proceedings under Minnesota Commitment Act of 1982; (h) probate court proceedings; (i) periodic trust accountings pursuant to Minn.Gen.R.Prac. 417; (j) proceedings under Minn.Stat. §609.748 relating to harassment restraining orders; (k) proceedings for registration of land titles pursuant to Minn.Stat. c. 508; (l) election contests pursuant to Minn.Stat. c. 209; (m) applications to compel or stay arbitration under Minn.Stat. c. 572. However, court may invoke procedures of this rule in any action where not otherwise required.

ARBITRATION AND AWARD:

Uniform Arbitration Act adopted. (572.08-.30).

Mandatory Arbitration.—If labor dispute cannot be settled by negotiation between charitable hospital employers and their employees, either party may petition for mediation pursuant to Minn.Stat. §§179.01-179.17, insofar as not inconsistent with Minn. Stat. §§179.35-179.39. If dispute is not settled within ten days after submission to mediation, unsettled issues concerning terms and conditions of employment and other issues concerning union security will, upon service of written notice by either party upon other party and director of mediation services, be submitted to determination of board of arbitrators whose determination will be final and binding. (179.38).

DOCUMENTS AND RECORDS

ACKNOWLEDGMENTS:

May be taken and certified by following officers:

Within State.—Uniform Law on Notarial Acts adopted. (358.41 et seq.). Ex officio notaries subject to following area limitations; member of legislature while resident in district in which elected; clerk or recorder of city or town; and court commissioners, county recorders, and county auditors, and their deputies, and county commissioners, all within their respective counties; peace officers licensed under §626.845 for purpose of administering oaths upon information submitted to establish probable cause to any judge or judicial officer under Rules of Criminal Procedure. (358.15). Fee is legal fee allowed other officers for like services for acknowledgment by notary public. (357.17).

Outside State but Within United States.—Uniform Law on Notarial Acts adopted. (358.41 et seq.).

Outside the United States.—Uniform Law on Notarial Acts adopted. (358.41 et seq.).

Persons in or with U.S. Armed Forces.—Uniform Law on Notarial Acts adopted. (358.41 et seq.). However, acknowledgment may be taken by commissioned officer on active duty in military service of U.S. (358.43 et seq.).

General Requirements of Certificate.—A notary taking an acknowledgment must print or stamp his name in addition to signing and must endorse on certificate, after his signature and disconnected from his seal, a statement of date when his commission expires, except when expiration date is shown on seal. However, absence of typed or printed name of notary does not invalidate acknowledgment. (359.05). Notary seal may be affixed by means of stamp which prints seal in prescribed form. (359.03).

Married Persons.—Separate acknowledgment of each spouse is not required. Where husband and wife join in acknowledgment, they must be described in certificate as husband and wife. Where their acknowledgments are taken before different officers or same officer at different times, each must be described as spouse of other. (358.14).

Effect of Acknowledgment.—All acknowledged instruments, other than promissory notes, bills of exchange, and wills, are admissible into evidence in all courts without other proof of execution. (600.14). Acknowledgment made in representative capacity for and on behalf of corporation, partnership, trust, or other entity and certified according to c. 358 is prima facie evidence that instrument was executed and delivered with proper authority. (358.50).

Authentication.—Uniform Law on Notarial Acts adopted. (358.41 et seq.). Commission of notary recorded in court administrator's office of district court of notary's county of residence. Commission of nonresident notary recorded in court administrator's office of district court of Minnesota county that borders county in which nonresident notary resides. (359.061). Official character of other persons taking acknowledgments will be certified by Secretary of State; fee not statutory but usually $5.

Forms.—Uniform Law on Notarial Acts adopted. (358.41 et seq.).

Alternative to Acknowledgment or Proof.—No statutory provision.

AFFIDAVITS:

As to what officers may administer oaths, see topic Acknowledgments.

General Requirements of Jurat.—After signature of notary public, disconnected from seal, there must be indorsed unless expiration date is shown on seal, words: My commission expires . . . . . ., 19. . . . . (359.03; 359.05).

Use of Affidavit.—Oaths and affidavits out of the state taken before any officer authorized to administer oaths, and certified by a clerk of a court of record, may be used on any motion or read in any argument in the state. (600.09).

If taken out of state before notary public or commissioner for Minnesota, no certificate by court administrator required. (600.09).

Form.—After title of action state:

Form

Affidavit of A.B.

State of . . . . . ., County of . . . . . . ss.

. . . . ., being first duly sworn on oath, deposes and says: That he resides at . . . . . . in the State of . . . . . . that his business is that of . . . . . . (here insert affiant's statement).

Further affiant saith not.

. . . . . .

Subscribed and sworn to before me this . . . . . . day of . . . . . ., 19 . . . ., at . . . . . . State of . . . . . .

Notary Public (or other officer),

. . . . . . County,

State of . . . . . .

Alternative to Affidavit.—No statutory provision.

NOTARIES PUBLIC:

Appointment and commission by Commissioner of Commerce on behalf of Governor with advice and consent of Senate, for fee of $40. All commissions are issued for period of five years unless sooner removed by Governor, District Court or Commissioner of Commerce. (359.01, 02).

Powers and Duties.—Notaries have power throughout state to administer oaths, take and certify depositions, acknowledgments of deeds, mortgages, liens, powers of attorney and other instruments, in writing, and receive, make out and record notarial protests. Acts void unless authenticated by seal; signature to be followed by printed name of notary and, if expiration date is not shown on seal, date of expiration of commission. Absence of typed or printed name of notary does not invalidate acknowledgment. Notary seal may be affixed by means of stamp which prints seal in prescribed form. (359.03).

May compel attendance of and punish witnesses for refusing to testify on taking of depositions as provided by statute or court rule. (359.11).

Certificate of Authority.—See topic Acknowledgments, subhead Authentication.

RECORDS:

Uniform Commercial Code adopted. (c. 336). See category Business Regulation and Commerce, topic Commercial Code.

Recording Act.—Every conveyance of real estate, including mortgages (507.01), not recorded in office of county recorder of county where land is situated, is void as against subsequent recorded conveyances of land to bona fide purchasers, including quit claim deeds, and as against subsequent judgments and attachments obtained against record owner (507.34). *For list of counties and county seats see first page for this state in Volume containing Practice Profiles Section.* Recording constitutes notice to parties, except that recording an assignment of mortgage is not notice to mortgagor so as to invalidate payments made by him to mortgagee. (507.32)

Notice imparted by recorded instrument not impaired by defects in attestation, acknowledgment, or certification of acknowledgment of instrument. (507.251).

Instruments affecting standing timber, stone, ores, minerals, etc., may be recorded. (507.36).

For requirements to entitle instrument to record, see categories Mortgages, topic Mortgages of Real Property; Property, topic Deeds.

Conveyancing instruments executed after Jan. 1, 1970, affecting title to, interest in or lien on real estate must include name and address of person or corporation drafting same in order to be recorded by county recorder or registered by registrar of titles. Does not apply to decree, order, judgment or writ of any court, will or death certificate, nor any instrument executed or acknowledged outside state. (507.091).

Form

This instrument was drafted by . . . . (name), ... (address).

Recording fees currently chargeable by county recorder: $1 per page, minimum $15, except for documents containing multiple assignments, partial releases or satisfactions, which are charged $10 for each document number or book and page cited. (357.18). Charge of $15 ($20 if request not made on standard form) for UCC search, additional $10 for nonconforming documents. Charge of $15 for search of federal and state tax liens. Surcharge of $5 per search. Surcharge of $5 for each UCC filing with county recorder not applicable to search request made by natural person who is subject of search data and who requests to see data; if such person requests photocopy of data, photocopy charge not to be more than actual cost of copies. (336.9-407; 336.9-413). For fees payable to registrar of titles, see 508.82.

Filing under Commercial Code.—Financing statement should be filed as follows: (a) When collateral is consumer goods, or motor vehicles which are not covered by certificate of title, then in office of county recorder in county of debtor's residence if debtor is individual who is resident of state but if debtor is individual who is not resident of state or is corporation, partnership or other organization, then in office of Secretary of State; (b) when collateral is equipment to be used in farming operations, or farm products, or accounts or general intangibles arising from or relating to sale of farm products by farmer, or crops growing or to be grown, then in office of county recorder in county of debtor's residence if debtor is individual or organization with residence in this state, but if debtor is not resident of this state, then in office of Secretary of State; (c) when collateral is timber to be cut or is minerals or like or certain accounts or is goods which at time security interest attaches are or are to become fixtures, then in office of county recorder in county where real estate concerned is located; (d) in all other cases, in office of Secretary of State. (336.9-401). Mailing address of Secretary of State is Secretary of State, UCC Division, 180 State Office Building, St. Paul, MN 55155. Filing fee is $15 for up to two debtor names if submitted on prescribed form (otherwise $20 for up to two debtor names) plus, in either case, additional $5 if financing statement covers timber to be cut or minerals or like (including oil and gas), or accounts resulting from sale thereof at wellhead or minehead, or is filed as fixture filing. Surcharge of $5 for each UCC filing or search. (336.9-413).

See note at head of Digest as to 1998 legislation covered.

See Topical Index in front part of this volume.

RECORDS . . . *continued*

Torrens Act.—Registration of title in any county in the state is optional. (c. 508). Application for registration may be made by owner of land or by one with power of disposal, guardian, corporation by officer or agent, partnership by one or more of its partners, executor or administrator, one having title by adverse possession, municipal corporation or the state. (508.03, .07, .08).

Application must be signed and verified (508.05), setting forth name, and address of applicant or agent of applicant and agency relationship, marital status including full name and address of spouse, if any, whether applicant is or is not 18 years of age and any prior divorces, any legal incapacity, description of land, applicant's estate or interest therein, those claiming interests therein, occupants thereof, if any, recorded or unrecorded liens or incumbrances thereon, including addresses of those claiming interests, that requested determination terminating or modifying described interest, together with reason for relief requested, description of any other defects in applicants title and reason for curing defects. (508.06). Nonresident applicant must file agreement executed and acknowledged, appointing resident agent. (508.07).

Application must be addressed to district court of county where land is situated (508.10) and filed with court administrator (508.11). Title is referred to examiner of titles; if he finds it proper for registration, or if applicant wishes to proceed when finding is adverse to him, summons is ordered by court joining all parties as defendants who appear to have any interest in land. (508.12, 15). Summons served on all parties named as interested, giving them 20 days to answer; served on the state by delivering a copy to Attorney General or deputy or assistant Attorney General; on nonresidents by mailing; on parties unknown by three weeks published notice. (508.16). Anyone claiming an interest in land may answer. (508.17).

On hearing, court may enter default judgment, dismissal, or decree confirming title in applicant forever, quieting same. (508.17-.23). Decree may be reopened within 60 days (508.26); after six months, it cannot be attacked in any way, unless fraud is shown. (508.28; 99 Minn. 197, 108 N.W. 945). Appeals from decrees are provided for. (508.29). Registration runs with land. (508.24).

Certificates of title are issued by registrar of titles. (508.34-.39). Owner of registered land may plat and subdivide, mortgage, convey, and lease by any form of deed, mortgage, lease, etc., entry being made on certificate. (508.46-.48). Any interest not entered on certificate is invalid as against bona fide purchasers except: (1) Claims of U.S.; (2) liens of real property taxes or special assessments; (3) lease for less than three years if actual occupancy; (4) rights of public highways; (5) right to appeal or contest application; (6) rights of person in possession under deed or contract for deed from owner; (7) mechanic's liens rights. (508.25).

Registered land is subject to same incidents as unregistered land, such as those growing out of marriage relation, levy, attachment on mesne process, etc., but no title adverse to registered owner can be acquired by prescription or adverse possession. (508.02).

Certificate of Possessory Title.—County commissioners of any county may authorize registration of possessory title to real estate in county pursuant to c. 508A. Procedure is voluntary, is intended for uncontested titles, and permits registration of title without initial court adjudication. Procedure available to any person who is record owner of land, provided that person is in actual or constructive possession. (508A.01, 03). No title in derogation of rights of registered owner can be acquired by prescription or adverse possession after certificate of possessory title issued. (508A.02).

Application for certificate filed with examiner of titles must set forth name and address of applicant or agent of applicant and agency relationship, marital status including full name and address of spouse, if any, whether applicant is or is not 18 years of age, and prior divorces and any legal incapacity, describe land and applicant's interest in it, disclose all persons shown of record or known to claim any right or interest in land, all occupants of land and any recorded or unrecorded liens or encumbrances, and state facts supporting applicant's claim to possessory estate. (508A.06). Examiner prepares written report based on application, abstract of title and public records. Notices of registration are mailed by examiner to any person listed by examiner as having right, title, estate, lien or interest in land pursuant to address list and materials provided by applicant. (508A.13).

At least 20 days after mailing of notice, examiner issues written directive to registrar of titles that first certificate be issued, subject to exceptions listed in 508A.25, all outstanding interests stated in examiner's report and rights of persons in possession or which would be disclosed by survey. Upon determining from continued abstract and public records that applicant is record owner, examiner issues supplemental directive. (508A.22). Actions affecting possession or title to land and founded upon any instrument, event or transaction occurring before entry of first certificate which is not set out in separate memorial on certificate or saved by 508A.25(1)-(5) and (8) is barred unless action commenced and notice of lis pendens registered within five years after examiner's supplemental directive. (508A.17). Appeals are provided for. (508A.29).

Special procedures prescribed for transactions involving land following issuance of certificate of possessory title, including duplicate certificates, conveyances, mortgages, judgments, leases, trusts, liens, attachments, death of owner, subsequent adverse claims, agencies and eminent domain. (508A.40, .421-.73). Owner of land covered by certificate of possessory title may convey, mortgage, lease, charge or otherwise deal with land same as if it had not been registered. Voluntary instrument of conveyance, other than will or lease not exceeding three years, operates only as contract between parties and as authority to make registration. Act of registration is operative act to convey or affect land. (508A.47).

After expiration of five years from date of examiner's supplemental directive, owner may file with registrar of titles for changeover from certificate of possessory title to certificate of title. Changeover occurs automatically upon filing of any instrument transferring title from registered owner after five-year period. Owner of certificate of possessory title may commence registration proceeding under c. 508 at any time. (508A.85).

For registrar's fees, see 508A.82.

Transfer of Decedent's Title.—In case of land which is not registered, transfer to heir at law or devisee is shown of record by filing certified copy of will, if any, certified copy of order of distribution, if any, and personal representative's deed or certified copy of decree of distribution with county recorder of county in which land is situated. In case of registered land, new certificate of title is issued to heir at law or devisee upon filing certified copy of will, if any, certified copy of order of distribution, if any, and personal representative's deed or final decree of distribution with registrar of titles of county in which land is situated. Registrar cancels decedent's certificate of title and issues new certificate to person entitled thereto. (508.68, 69).

Vital Statistics.—Reports of births and deaths must be filed with state registrar or local registrar (144.215); reports of deaths must be filed with local registrar (144.221); marriage reports with court administrator of district court (517.10). Birth and death certificates available from Minnesota Department of Health, 717 Delaware Street S. E., Minneapolis, MN 55440. Fee for certified copy of birth and death certificates $11 per copy.

Establishing Birth Records.—Any person born in state, if no record of his birth exists, may petition appropriate court for order directing issuance of certificate. (144.217).

SEALS:

Uniform Commercial Code adopted. (c. 336). See category Business Regulation and Commerce, topic Commercial Code.

Use of private seals in written instruments is abolished. (358.01).

Corporation has power to adopt and use corporate seal, but failure to affix seal does not affect validity of any instrument, document or act. (301.09, 302A.163). See category Business Organizations, topic Corporations, subhead Powers.

TORRENS ACT:

See topic Records.

VITAL STATISTICS:

See topic Records.

EMPLOYMENT

EMPLOYER AND EMPLOYEE:

See topic Labor Relations.

LABOR RELATIONS:

Department of Labor and Industry has general jurisdiction over labor matters. (175.001-.007).

Unlawful to persuade workers to change their employment by means of representations known to be false. (181.64). Employers recruiting employees to relocate to work in "food processing industry" must give detailed written disclosure in English and Spanish of terms and conditions of employment. (181.635). Unlawful for employer to require employee or applicant to pay cost of medical examination or other records required as condition of employment. (181.61). Unlawful for employer or agent by direct or indirect coercion to request or require polygraph or other test of honesty of employee or prospective employee. (181.75). Lawful for employer to test employee or job applicants for drugs and alcohol pursuant to written policy if use and conduct of test conforms to statutory requirements. (181.93 et seq.).

Status of Employment.—Minnesota generally follows employment at will rule. (266 N.W. 872). However, personnel handbook can give rise to contract of employment (333 N.W.2d 622), and employees may recover damages for adverse action by employer resulting from employees' whistle-blowing activities (181.932, 181.935). Employer must give notice to employees of right to written statement of truthful reason for termination. (181.934). Statements must be provided within five working days of request and may not be made subject of libel, slander, or defamation claim. (181.933). Employee has right to review, obtain copy of, and challenge accuracy of information in employer's personnel records. (181.960-.966).

Wages and commissions earned and unpaid at time of discharge of employee by one employing labor in state become immediately due and payable on demand of employee, whether employed by day, hour, week, month or piece. (181.13). When employee quits, wages and commissions earned and unpaid are due and payable on first regularly scheduled payday following final day of employment, unless collective bargaining agreement has other provision. If first payday is within five days after final day of work, payment may be delayed until second regularly scheduled payday, but not more than 20 days from final day of work. However, wages of migrant workers become due and payable within five days of quit. Wages not paid within required time become immediately payable on demand of employee. (181.14). Employer in default if payment not made (or post marked, if employee requests mailing) within 24 hours after demand. Employee may charge and collect wages at rate agreed upon in contract of employment for such period not exceeding 15 days after expiration of 24 hours, as long as employer is in default. (181.13, 181.14). However, where discharged or resigning employee was entrusted with money or property, employer has ten calendar days following termination to audit and adjust accounts before wages and commissions become due. Payment to be made at usual place of payment unless employee requests payment by mail. (181.14). Commissioned salesperson who is independent contractor to be paid promptly on demand commissions due for services or merchandise which has been delivered to and accepted by customer by final day of employment. Payment to be made in three working days if salesperson discharged or resigned with at least five days written notice, and in six working days after resignation without such prior notice. Penalty for nonprompt payment equals 1/15 of unpaid amount per day of delay up to 15 days. (181.145). It is unlawful for any employer other than public service corporation to pay salary or wages by non-negotiable time check or order. (181.02). Public service corporations must pay their employees at least semi-monthly. (181.08). Wages of persons employed in transitory work requiring change of abode must be paid at least every 15 days and within 24 hours after termination of employment, whether

See note at head of Digest as to 1998 legislation covered.

See Topical Index in front part of this volume.

MN – 28

LABOR RELATIONS . . . *continued*
by discharge or by quitting. (181.10 et seq.). All employers must pay wages at least once every 30 days on regular payday designated in advance. (181.101).

At end of each pay period, employer must provide earnings statement including employee's name, hourly rate of pay (if applicable), total hours worked (unless exempt from minimum wage and overtime laws), total gross pay, list of deductions, net pay, last day of pay period, and legal name of employer (and operating name, if different). (181.032).

If no personal representative has been appointed for deceased employee, employer must, on request, pay to surviving spouse wages due decedent, not exceeding $10,000. (181.58).

Employer with annual gross volume of sale or business greater than $500,000 and which is covered by Minn. Fair Labor Standards Act must pay minimum wage of $5.15 per hour. Smaller employer must pay minimum wage of $4.90 per hour. However, during first 90 days of employment, employer of any size may pay employee under age 20 wage of $4.25 per hour. Gratuities may not be applied toward minimum wage. (177.24).

Overtime pay for work in excess of 48 hours in workweek (177.25) required by Minnesota Fair Labor Standards Act (177.21-.35). Employee must be allowed adequate time off from work every four hours to use nearest convenient restroom. (177.253). Employee working eight or more consecutive hours must be given sufficient time to eat meal, but meal break may be unpaid time. (177.245).

Employee has right to be absent from work for purposes of voting during morning of day of election without penalty or deduction from salary or wages. (204C.04). Individual selected to serve as election judge may, upon 20 days written notice, be absent from work without penalty other than deduction from pay for amounts paid for serving as election judge. (204B.195).

Employer Liabilities.—Any employer found by commissioner to have violated specified statutes regarding wages, hours or other employment conditions is liable for back pay, compensatory damages, additional equal amount in liquidated damages, civil penalty of up to $1,000 for each repeated or willful violation, and reimbursement of department and attorney general for litigation or hearing costs, and may be ordered to cease and desist from violations. (177.27). Commissioner's order becomes final if employer fails to respond within 15 calendar days. (177.27). Employee aggrieved by violation may bring civil action to recover civil penalties or damages provided in statute violated, compensatory damages, other appropriate relief, and attorneys fees, costs and disbursements. (177.27; 181.171).

Assignment of wages, see category Debtor and Creditor, topic Assignments.

Employee Benefits.—Employer employing ten or more state residents that provides plan or policy of health coverage to employees must make available to employees in state "qualified" plan of health coverage containing benefits specified by statute. (c. 62E). Statute held preempted by ERISA by U.S. Dist. Ct. (490 F.Supp. 931 [1980]). Patient Protection Act prohibits "gag" rules, requires disclosure to employees of certain information regarding managed care arrangements, and regulates resolution of benefits claims, access to emergency services and specialty care, and changes of providers. (62J.695, et seq.).

Child Labor.—Employer required to have proof of age of any minor employee. (181A.06). No minor under age of 14 may be employed, except in agricultural operations, or as actor, model, performer, or newspaper carrier. (181A.04; 181A.07). Minor under age of 16 may work only between 7:00 a.m. and 9:00 p.m., with limit of eight hours in 24 hour period and 40 hours per week. Minors under age of 18 may be restricted by rule from working in occupations which are hazardous or detrimental to their well-being. (181A.04). Minor under age of 16 may work during school hours only pursuant to employment certificate issued by school district, which employer is required to return to issuing officer upon termination of employment. (181A.04; 181A.05). High school students under age of 18 cannot work after 11:00 p.m. on evening before school day or before 5:00 a.m. on school day. (181A.04[6]). Note from student's parent or guardian can extend permissible working hours by one half-hour. (181A.04[6]). Regulations and exemptions administered by Commissioner of Department of Labor and Industry. (181A.07; 181A.09). Fines imposed on employers for violations, violations are misdemeanors, single violation resulting in minor's death or substantial bodily harm and repeated violations are gross misdemeanors. (181A.12).

Female Labor.—Wage discrimination based on sex prohibited under equal pay for equal work law. (181.66-.71). Employer must provide reasonable unpaid break time each day, and room or other location close to work area, for employee who needs to express breast milk for her infant child. (181.939).

Discrimination in employment based on race, color, religion, national origin, sex (including sexual harassment), marital status, status with regard to public assistance, membership activity in local anti-discrimination agency, disability, sexual orientation or age (over age of majority) prohibited by Human Rights Act. (363.01 et seq.). Mandatory retirement based on age also regulated by 181.81 et seq. Reprisal against employee for not contributing to charity or community organization prohibited. (181.937). Employer may not refuse to hire applicant or discipline or discharge employee for use of lawful consumable products off employer's premises during nonworking hours. (181.938).

Employee Leaves of Absence.—Employer of more than 20 persons must grant to employee who has been employed on at least half-time basis for at least 12 consecutive months, immediately preceding request, six weeks unpaid leave in conjunction with birth or adoption of child, must allow such employee to use personal sick leave benefits (but not salary continuation or disability benefits) for absences due to illness or injury of employee's child, and must allow up to 40 hours of paid leave for bone marrow donation. All employers must grant employees employed on at least half-time basis up to 16 hours of leave during any 12-month period to attend school conferences and school related activities. (181.940-.945).

Migrant Labor.—Employers of more than five recruited migrant laborers must provide health care insurance during period of employment or for illness or injury incurred during employment in accordance with regulations of Commissioner of Economic Security. (181.73). Wages become due and payable to migrant worker within 24 hours after discharge and within five days after quitting. (181.13; 181.14).

Labor Unions.—Employees have right to organize and bargain collectively and employers are forbidden to interfere in these activities. (179.10). Representatives chosen by majority of employees are exclusive collective bargaining representatives. (179.16). Director of mediation services, upon request of any party, may certify bargaining unit. (179.16).

No employer need negotiate with another union as long as valid collective bargaining agreement with union certified by director of mediation services or N.L.R.B. as accredited bargaining representative is in effect. (179.135). Employer may recover damages against third party for strike or boycott called to prevent accredited representative from acting. (179.28). Right to work law not adopted.

Labor Disputes.—Union seeking to negotiate or change contract and employer seeking to change contract must give notice to other party of such intention; if no settlement is reached within ten days after service of said notice, notice of strike or lockout may be served on director of mediation services and other party, and strike or lockout may not be commenced for ten days thereafter. Director is directed to take steps to effect settlement. (179.06). Where dispute affects public interest, Governor may appoint fact-finding commission and strikes and lockouts are prohibited for additional 30 days. (179.07). Where jurisdictional strike or picketing exists, director must notify Governor, who may appoint referee, and after such appointment, strike, boycott or picketing illegal. (179.083). Injunctions and restraining orders in labor disputes limited. (185.01-.18).

Strikes and lockouts by charitable hospitals and their employees are unlawful. (179.35 et seq.). Above restrictions not applicable to employer in interstate commerce, at least where activity is arguably subject to federal supervision. (236 Minn. 303, 53 N.W.2d 36; 370 U.S. 173).

Unfair labor practices are unlawful acts and may be enjoined unless employer in interstate commerce. (179.14).

Unfair labor practices by employees or unions are: (1) strikes in violation of collective bargaining agreement or in violation of collective bargaining agreement or in violation of notice provisions, set forth above, (2) seizing or occupying property during dispute, (3) for less than a majority of pickets to be employees of picketed business, (4) for more than one person to picket an entrance where no strike in progress, (5) to interfere with motor vehicle when neither its owner nor its driver is a party to strike, (6) to intimidate a person in an effort to make him join or refrain from joining a union or strike, (7) to call a strike unless majority of employees by secret ballot approve, (8) to interfere with agricultural producer, processor or marketer so as to bring pressure on another producer (179.11), (9) secondary boycotts (179.41 et seq.), (10) to interfere with use of public roads or obstruct entrance to any place of business (179.13).

Unfair labor practices by employers are: (1) to institute a lockout in violation of collective bargaining contract or notice provisions set forth above, (2) to encourage or discourage union membership by discrimination unless so provided by valid contract, (3) to discharge or discriminate against employee because of his activities under this Act, (4) to spy on union, (5) to blacklist, (6) to hire employee of another if such employee is paid less than wage agreed to be paid by hirer under existing union contract for same grade of work, (7) to willfully and knowingly utilize professional strike-breaker to replace employees involved in strike or lockout within state, or (8) grant or offer to grant permanent replacement status to persons performing bargaining unit work during lockout or during strike authorized by representative of employees. (179.12).

Public Employees.—Public Employment Labor Relations Act (c. 179A) provides binding arbitration of labor disputes (179A.16). Employees (other than persons defined as essential employees) may strike under specified circumstances. (179A.18, .19).

Action for Death.—Action against railroad for death of employee must be begun within two years. (219.83).

Employers' Liability Act.—When employer is a railroad, defense of contributory negligence is a bar only proportionately to amount of such contributory negligence. Defense of contributory negligence is abolished where employer violated statute enacted for safety of employees. Defense of assumption of risk is entirely abolished. Fellow servant rule also abolished. (219.77-.80).

Unemployment Compensation.—

Reemployment Insurance.—To be entitled to benefits individual must register for work at employment office, submit claim, have sufficient wage credits within base period to establish valid claim, be able and available for and actively seek work, wait one week during which eligible for benefits, and participate in reemployment services if determined to be likely to exhaust regular benefits. Ineligible if secondary school student, incarcerated, on voluntary leave of absence (excluding vacation shutdowns), performing 32 or more hours per week of employment, self-employment or volunteer work, or during suspension for 30 days or less for misconduct. (268.07, .085). Individuals who receive lump sum termination, severance or dismissal payments are not eligible for benefits for period following last day equal to lump sum divided by individual's regular weekly pay, but no more than four weeks plus one-half of any additional weeks. No deduction for jury duty pay. (268.085). Disqualification or offset also provided for vacation pay, certain workers' compensation payments, pension payments and certain Social Security benefits. Special rates provided for school employees or contractors, professional athletes, aliens, seasonal employees and business owners. (268.08). Disqualifications for voluntary quit (exceptions apply for former employees who resign subsequent employment), discharge for misconduct or gross misconduct, failure to apply for or accept suitable work (including reemployment), or participation in strike. (268.095). Weekly benefit amount is higher of (1) 50% of individuals average weekly wage during base period up to maximum of 66⅔% of state's average weekly wage, or (2) 50% of individual's average during higher quarter up to maximum of 50% of state's average weekly wage of $331, whichever is higher. Benefits are payable up to amount equal to ⅓ of individual's total base period wage

See note at head of Digest as to 1998 legislation covered.

See Topical Index in front part of this volume.

MN – 29

LABOR RELATIONS . . . *continued*

credits rounded to next lower dollar, not to exceed 26 times individual's weekly benefit amount. (268.07). Benefits due and unpaid at claimant's death may be paid to personal representative of claimant's estate, or, if none, to surviving spouse, children or parents. (268.087). Successful bidder on nonresidential construction or repair project who fails to provide unemployment or workers' compensation coverage required by state law is liable to any injured party for damages, attorneys fees and costs. Unsuccessful bidders presumed to be damaged in amount equal to projected profit. Violation is also misdemeanor. (181.721).

Workers' Compensation Act.—Workers' compensation is under control of Commissioner of Labor and Industry who supervises Division of Workers' Compensation within Department of Labor and Industry. (c. 175). Appellate tribunal for workers' compensation is Workers' Compensation Court of Appeals. (175A.01).

Employees of common carriers by railroad in interstate or foreign commerce, certain household workers, executive officers of certain closely held corporations and owners of family farms and family farm corporations and their spouses, parents and children, casual employees, independent contractors, persons covered under Domestic Volunteer Service Act of 1973, and managers and certain members of limited liability companies and certain of their relatives are not within Act. (176.041). Owners and certain officers of businesses or farms and their immediate relatives, employers of farm labor and household workers, managers of small limited liability companies, and employers of independent contractors may come under Act by purchase of valid compensation insurance policy covering such persons. (176.012, 051).

Compensation is provided, according to schedule of rates, for personal injury or death caused by accident in course of employment, unless injury intentionally self-inflicted or caused by drunkenness or occurred while participating in voluntary recreational programs sponsored by employer. Compensation is payable at regular wage periods during disability. (176.021, 101, 111). Benefits once awarded are adjusted periodically for changes in statewide average weekly wage. (176.645).

No agreement is binding which gives employee less than law allows him (176.021). Minors come within Act. (176.091, 101). Employers must insure unless they show ability to make payments. (176.181).

Where a person other than employer is liable for injury and is insured or self-insured and where both employer and such third person were engaged in furtherance of common enterprise or in accomplishment of same or related purposes on premises, employee has option of proceeding at law against third person for damages or against employer for compensation, but not against both; if he elects to sue such third person for damages, amount he can recover is limited by provisions of Compensation Act. If he elects to take compensation, employer has right of indemnity or subrogation against third person. In other situations where third person is liable, employee, employer or attorney general may proceed at law against him notwithstanding payment by employer or special compensation fund of compensation. If judgment is obtained, proceeds allocated between employee and employer or special compensation fund in accordance with statutory formula from compensation payable. Co-employee not liable unless injury resulted from gross negligence or was intentionally inflicted by co-employee. Settlement between third person and employee not valid unless prior notice of intent to settle given to employer. Settlement between employee or dependents and third person void as against employer's right of subrogation or indemnity for compensation paid. Copy of complaint and notice of trial or note of issue in action by employee or dependents against third party must be served on employer or insurer. Employer has lien on any judgment in such action. (176.061).

Where dispute arises between two or more employers or insurers as to liability for compensation, Commissioner, compensation judge, or court may direct either to pay up to limits of applicable coverage pending determination of liability and on determination must order party liable to reimburse any other party for payments made, with interest at 12% per annum, and award reasonable attorney's fees to claimant. Where dispute exists, payments may be made from special compensation fund, by health insurance carrier or by commissioner of public welfare, and on determination party liable must reimburse payments made, with interest at 12% per annum. Provision made for mandatory arbitration of such disputes in certain circumstances. (176.191).

Employee must sue within three years after notice to Commissioner of accident and within six years after accident. In case of death, dependents may bring suit within three years after notice to Commissioner and within six years after injury, unless compensation was paid for injury from which death resulted, which extends limitation to three years from notice and six years from death. In case of persons under physical or mental disability, limitation is extended for three years from date of removal of disability. In case of injury caused by radiation or other occupational disease, limitation is three years after employee has knowledge of cause of injury and injury has resulted in disability. (176.151).

Act applies to employee regularly performing primary employment duties in state who is injured while temporarily out of state in course of employment. Resident who is transferred outside U.S. as employee of Minnesota employer is presumed to be temporarily employed outside of state. Act does not apply to employee hired to or regularly performing primary employment duties out of state who is injured in state if employer has provided workers' compensation coverage for such injury under laws of any other state unless employee regularly resides and regularly performs part of employment duties in state. (176.041).

If employer is nonresident or foreign corporation on which service cannot be made, action may be brought in district court and garnishment or attachment is permitted. (176.295). Petition filed with Commissioner in disputed case referred for settlement conference within 60 days or administrative conference or hearing. If no settlement, summary decision may be issued, which is final unless formal hearing is requested. (176.291, 305). Where issue joined in district court action, court may try without jury or refer matter for hearing before compensation judge. (176.301). Appeals are to Workers' Compensation Court of Appeals, except for Commissioner's decisions which may be heard de novo in some other proceeding. (c. 175A, 176.421, .442). Decisions reviewable by Supreme Court upon certiorari. (176.471).

Claims for compensation are not assignable. (176.175).

Occupational diseases are "personal injuries" within Act. (176.66).

Occupational Safety and Health.—Regulated by c. 182. Employers are required to provide training programs for employees exposed to hazardous substances. Covered employers in industries designated by Commissioner of Labor and Industry must establish written workplace accident and injury reduction program. (182.653). Employees may demand access to information about hazardous substances in workplace and have right to refuse in good faith to work under conditions reasonably believed to present imminent danger of death or serious physical harm. (182.654). Employee, union or other person who knowingly discloses or receives information regarding hazardous substance which has been registered as trade secret is subject to statutory penalties and civil liabilities for theft of trade secrets. (182.668).

WORKERS' COMPENSATION LAW:

See topic Labor Relations.

ENVIRONMENT

ENVIRONMENTAL REGULATION:

General Supervision.—Pollution Control Agency. (c. 116).

Prohibited Acts of Pollution.—Pollution Control Agency has broad powers to establish standards and regulations relating to discharge of sewage, industrial wastes and other wastes into waters, including limitations on nutrients in cleaning agents and water conditioners, air contamination and pollution, acid deposition, noise pollution, hazardous wastes, leaking underground storage tanks, industrial wastes, and waste disposal and land pollution. Violation is public nuisance. (115.071).

Enforcement.—Provisions of law and Agency regulations or standards may be enforced by injunction, action to compel performance, or other appropriate action. (115.071). Pollution Control Agency director and county board that adopts ordinances with cooperation of Pollution Control Agency may issue orders requiring hazardous waste violations be corrected and may administratively access penalty of up to $10,000 for all violations. (116.072). Attorney General or County Attorney must bring action on request of Pollution Control Agency. Agency may issue emergency order without a hearing, or Attorney General may obtain temporary restraining order. (116.11). Any person, corporation, organization or other entity may maintain civil action in district court for declaratory or equitable relief in name of state for protection of air, water, land, or other natural or historical resources from pollution, impairment or destruction against any person violating any environmental quality regulation or standard of Pollution Control Agency, Department of Natural Resources, Department of Health or Department of Agriculture. (116B.03). Pollution Control Agency may take steps to determine whether real property has been site of release or threatened release of hazardous substance, and may clean up such hazardous waste sites. (115B.17). Persons responsible for hazardous waste and petroleum contamination sites are strictly liable, jointly and severally, for costs of clean up. (115B.04, 115C.04).

Penalties.—Violation, except as follows, is misdemeanor. Civil penalties and other remedies also provided. (115.071).

Permits.—Agency may, after public hearing, grant variances from requirements of its rules to avoid undue hardship. Local government unit authorized to exercise administrative powers may, after public hearing, grant variances from pollution control regulations adopted by it. (114C; 116.07). Permit of Agency required for construction of all sewage and industrial waste disposal systems (Minn R. 7080.0030) and emission and air contaminant treatment facilities and waste collection, transportation, storage, processing or disposal systems (116.081). Except for construction of buildings worth less than $500,000, building or construction permits may not be issued for industrial or commercial buildings employing more than 12 persons unless sewage or industrial waste originating in such buildings will be discharged into disposal system for which Agency permit has been granted, unless Agency has cause not to apply requirement. (115.03). Environmental impact statements required by regulation for certain projects. (Minn. R. 4410.4400). Routing permit required from Environmental Quality Board, after public hearings, for constructing pipelines for transportation of hazardous liquids. (116I.015). Commissioner of Public Safety, through Director of Pipeline Safety, must establish minimum safety standards for transportation of gas and pipeline facilities. (299J.01-.18). Criminal actions, civil penalties and action to compel performance brought by Attorney General at request of Commissioner in name of state, or other appropriate actions, are remedies for failing to report emergency release from pipeline (299J.07; 299J.16), or disposing of pipeline after emergency release (299J.15).

Liability for Hazardous Wastes.—Persons responsible are strictly liable for death, personal injury, disease or economic loss resulting from hazardous wastes. (115B.05). Whether responsible persons are jointly or severally liable depends upon application of applicable statutory and common law. (115B.055).

Liability for Leaking Underground and Above-ground Storage Tanks.—Persons responsible are strictly liable for costs of corrective action taken by MPCA. (115C.04).

ESTATES AND TRUSTS

ADMINISTRATION:

See topic Executors and Administrators.

ADVANCEMENTS:

See topic Descent and Distribution.

ALLOWANCES:

See topic Executors and Administrators.

CLAIMS:

See topic Descent and Distribution; category Civil Actions and Procedure, topic Pleading.

DEATH:

Anyone not heard from in four years, whose absence is not satisfactorily explained, is presumed dead. (576.141).

Finding made pursuant to Federal Missing Persons Act is prima facie evidence of death. (600.24 et seq.).

Survivorship.—Uniform Simultaneous Death Act adopted, with certain modifications. (524.2-702). Effective for estates of decedents dying after Dec. 31, 1986, person who fails to survive decedent by 120 hours is deemed to have predeceased decedent. (524.2-104).

Action for death by wrongful act or omission may be brought by trustee appointed by court having jurisdiction of action on petition of surviving spouse or next of kin. Recovery is for benefit of surviving spouse and next of kin, proportionate to pecuniary loss suffered as a result of death. Maximum recovery not limited by statute. Punitive damages may be awarded. With exceptions, action must be commenced within three years after death and within six years after act or omission causing death. Where action commenced by decedent, before his death, for injury of which he died, such action may be continued by trustee, and rules governing actions begun by such trustee apply. Action for special damages arising from injury may be brought by trustee when injured person dies from unrelated cause. (573.02). See also category Employment, topic Labor Relations.

Death certificate may be obtained from State Registrar of Vital Statistics, local registrar or clerk of district court. (144.213, .214, .221). See category Documents and Records, topic Records, subhead Vital Statistics.

DECEDENTS' ESTATES:

See topics Descent and Distribution, Executors and Administrators, Wills; category Debtor and Creditor, topic Homesteads.

DESCENT AND DISTRIBUTION:

See also topic Executors and Administrators.

For estates of decedents dying before Jan. 1, 1996, subject to allowance provided for surviving spouse or minor children and to payment of expenses of administration, expenses of last illness and funeral, taxes and debts, all real estate of intestate decedent, except cemetery lot and homestead (as to which see category Debtor and Creditor, topic Homesteads) and all personal estate of such decedent passes as follows: surviving spouse takes entire estate if intestate left no issue surviving. If all of surviving issue are also issue of surviving spouse, surviving spouse takes first $70,000 plus one-half of balance of intestate estate. If one or more surviving issue are not issue of surviving spouse, surviving spouse takes one-half of intestate estate. Excess of such real and personal estate over share of such surviving spouse, descends and is distributed as follows, each class of which a member is living taking to exclusion of subsequent classes:

(1) Children and/or issue of deceased children; (2) parents or surviving parent; (3) brothers, sisters and/or issue of deceased brothers or sisters; (4) next of kin of equal degree, except that those claiming through nearest ancestor take to exclusion of others of equal degree claiming through more remote ancestor. Degrees of kinship computed according to civil law rules (for estates of decedents dying before Jan. 1, 1987, see 525.13 et seq.).

Issue of deceased children take per stirpes even though there be no surviving child. Members of class (3) take equally if all of same degree of kindred to decedent, otherwise estate is divided into as many shares as there are living heirs in nearest degrees of kinship and deceased persons in same degree who left issue then surviving. In class (3), each living heir of nearest degree receives one share and issue of each deceased person of same degree take one share per stirpes.

Effective Jan. 1, 1996, law of descent and distribution revised as follows. Partial or full disinheritance by will allowed. Intestate share of disinherited heir passes as if heir had disclaimed. (524.2-101). Spouse receives entire estate if (i) there are no surviving descendants of decedent or (ii) all of decedent's surviving descendants are also issue of spouse and there is no other surviving descendant of surviving spouse. (524.2-102). If there are surviving descendants of decedent who are not descendants of spouse or there are surviving descendants of spouse who are not descendants of decedent, surviving spouse receives first $150,000 plus one-half of balance. Portion not passing to spouse passes as follows, each class of which there is living member taking to exclusion of subsequent classes: (1) surviving descendants by right of representation (per stirpes); (2) parents or surviving parent; (3) descendants of parents or either of them by right of representation (per stirpes); (4) grandparents or their descendants, with maternal grandparents or their descendants taking one-half and paternal grandparents or their descendants taking one-half, with descendants taking by right of representation (per capita); or if no grandparents or descendants to grandparents on either maternal or paternal side, other side takes entire estate in manner previously described; (5) next of kin in equal degree, except that those claiming through nearest ancestor take to exclusion of those claiming through more remote ancestor. Degrees of kinship computed according to civil law.

Survivorship by 120 Hours.—Effective for estates of decedents dying after Dec. 31, 1986, person who fails to survive decedent by 120 hours is deemed to have predeceased decedent for purposes of intestate distribution. (524.2-104).

Half-blood kindred inherit equally with those of whole blood of same degree, except that for estates of decedents dying before Jan. 1, 1987 where inheritance came to intestate by descent, devise or bequest from ancestor those not of blood of such ancestor are excluded. (524.2-107; for estates of decedents dying before Jan. 1, 1987, see 525.17).

Posthumous child inherits as though born in parent's lifetime, provided such child lives 120 hours or more after birth. (524.2-108; for estates of decedents dying before Jan. 1, 1987, see 515.171).

Illegitimate child inherits from his parents, regardless of marital status of parents. (524.114[2]). Parent and child relationship may be established by Parentage Act, §§257.51 and 257.74.

Adopted Children.—See category Family, topic Adoption.

Advancements.—§2-110 of Uniform Probate Code adopted with modifications. (524.2-109).

Determination of Descent.—Provision is made for proceedings to determine descent of real or personal property or any interest therein where former owner has been dead for more than three years and there has been no probate of will or grant of administration. (525.31 et seq.).

Escheat.—If decedent leaves no surviving spouse nor kindred, his estate escheats to the state. (524.2-105; for estates of decedents dying before Jan. 1, 1987, see 525.161). In event of erroneous escheat funds will be returned by state upon application to court. (525.84 et seq.).

References to Intestacy Laws.—Wills or other instruments executed before Jan. 1, 1996, directing distribution according to intestacy law deemed to refer to laws in effect before that date unless will or other instrument directs otherwise. (524.2-115).

Elective Share.—For estates of decedents dying after Dec. 31, 1986, elective share provisions of Uniform Probate Code, with certain modifications to augmented estate, will apply. (524.2-201 et seq.).

Family Allowances.—Surviving spouse is entitled to either life estate in homestead (if decedent was survived by issue) or whole of homestead (if decedent was not survived by issue) free of any transfer to which spouse has not consented in writing. (524.2-402). Notwithstanding any will, surviving spouse is allowed: (1) Wearing apparel, furniture and household goods and other personal property up to $10,000 in value, and (2) one automobile, without regard to value. If there is no surviving spouse, children receive property described in clause (1), except that where it appears from decedent's will child was omitted intentionally, child is not entitled to rights conferred by clause (1). Rights of adult children are subject to claims against decedent's estate for certain forms of financial assistance and to costs and expenses of administration, reasonable funeral expenses and debts and taxes with preference under Federal law. (524.2-403[f]). For estate of decedents dying after July 31, 1988, if decedent is survived by child who is not child of surviving spouse (or is adult and has different parent than decedent's minor children), selection of personal property by spouse or minor children is subject to right of decedent's child not entitled to allowance to receive certain tangible personal property which court determines has sentimental value to that child, with appropriate charges to such child's share of estate. (525.152). Spouse and children constituting family of decedent receive maintenance in monthly installments not to exceed $1,500 for 12 months if estate is insolvent or 18 months if estate is solvent. (524.2-404). All family allowances described above are excluded in computing elective share. For decedents dying after Dec. 31, 1986, elections with respect to homestead and other family allowances are separate from elective share, so spouse may take elective share of augmented estate and take homestead under will. (524.2-211[f]; 524.2-403[e]).

ELECTION:

See topic Wills.

ESTATES:

See category Property, topic Real Property.

EXECUTORS AND ADMINISTRATORS:

Original jurisdiction for administration of estates of deceased person provided by legislature. (Const., art. 6, §11). Probate jurisdiction is in probate court which is county court in all counties except Hennepin and Ramsey where probate court is division of district court. (484.011). Combined probate and county court districts are Kittson, Roseau and Lake of the Woods; Marshall, Red Lake and Pennington; Norman and Mahnomen; Cass and Hubbard; Wadena and Todd; Mille Lacs and Kanabec; Big Stone and Traverse; Grant and Douglas; Lincoln and Lyon; Rock and Nobles; Dodge and Olmsted; Lake and Cook; Pine, Isanti and Chisago; Sherburne, Benton and Stearns. (487.01).

Uniform Probate Code adopted (524.1-101 et seq.) with modifications. Portions of prior probate code in c. 525, have been retained.

Summary Proceedings.—If decedent's property has been destroyed, abandoned, lost or rendered valueless, or if there be no property except such as has been recovered for death by wrongful act, or such as is exempt from all debts and charges in court, or such as may be appropriated for payment of allowances to spouse and children, expenses of administration, funeral expenses, expenses of last illness and debts having preference under laws of U.S. and taxes, representative by order of court may pay same in order named and court may summarily determine heirs, legatees and devisees in its order of distribution or final decree assigning to them their share of property. (524.3-1203).

If court determines that there is no need for appointment of representative and that administration should be closed summarily for reason that all property in estate is exempt from debts and charges in court, final decree may be entered assigning such property to persons entitled thereto pursuant to terms of will or pursuant to law of intestate succession, as case may be. (524.3-1203).

Summary distribution of property in kind may be made in payment of allowances to spouse and children, funeral expenses, expenses of last illness and debts having preference under laws of U.S. and taxes when property so assigned exhausts estate assets. In all summary proceedings where no representative appointed, court may require petitioner to file corporate surety bond in amount fixed by court. (52.3-1203).

If estate will not be exhausted in payment of priority items listed above, estate may be summarily closed and distributed to proper persons if gross probate estate, exclusive of exempt homestead, is not in excess of $30,000. If closing and distribution is pursuant to will, hearing on formal probate of will must be held before decree shall

EXECUTORS AND ADMINISTRATORS . . . *continued*
issue. Showing of payment of priority items and bond required of representative or petitioner. (524.3-1203).

If value of entire probate estate, less liens or encumbrances, is less than $20,000 ($10,000 prior to Jan. 1, 1996), personal property may be collected by affidavit of person entitled to receive property if 30 days have elapsed since death and no administration commenced. (524.3-1201). Person collecting is required to pay over property to others with higher priority. Person collecting by affidavit must be successor to decedent or state or county agency collecting claim for medical assistance.

Action by Foreign Representative.—Any foreign representative may prosecute an action in state in his representative capacity if he has filed authenticated copy of his appointment with probate court of county in which action is commenced. (573.05).

Part 1, Art. VI (Multiple-Party Accounts) of Uniform Probate Code adopted. (524.6-201-214). Several modifications have been enacted, effective Aug. 1, 1985. (524.6-201 et seq.).

Uniform Anatomical Gift Act adopted. (525.921-95). Minor with written consent of parent or legal guardian, may make anatomical gift. (525.9211).

Uniform Fiduciaries Act, with exception of §§3-6 thereof, adopted. (520.01-.13).

Uniform Principal and Income Act adopted. (501B.59-.76).

Uniform Simplification of Fiduciary Security Transfers Act adopted. (520.21-.31). (Specifically saved from repeal by U.C.C., see 336.10-104.)

Uniform Testamentary Additions to Trusts Act adopted. (524.2-511).

Uniform Transfer on Death Security Registration Act adopted effective June 1, 1992. (524.6-301 et seq.).

FIDUCIARIES:

See topics Executors and Administrators, Trusts; category Family, topic Guardian and Ward.

INTESTACY:

See topic Descent and Distribution.

LIVING WILLS:

See topic Wills, subhead Living Wills—(Health Care Declarations).

PROOF OF CLAIMS:

See topic Executors and Administrators; category Civil Actions and Procedure, topic Pleading.

TRUSTS:

Statutory trust law recodified as c. 501B in 1989 effective Jan. 1, 1990. Statutory references are first to law prior to Jan. 1, 1990 then to law effective Jan. 1, 1990.

Except as authorized by statute and by law, uses and trusts are abolished. Active trust may be created for lawful purpose. (501.01; 501B.01, .02).

Minnesota Trustees Powers Act permits will or instrument creating inter vivos trust to incorporate by reference all or a portion of powers of trustee enumerated therein. (501.64-.67, 501B.79-.82).

Payment of Consideration by Third Person.—If transfer of property is made to one person and purchase price is paid by another, resulting trust is presumed to arise in favor of person by whom purchase price is paid, except: (1) if person by whom purchase price is paid manifests contrary intention, no resulting trust is presumed to arise; (2) if transferee is spouse, child or other natural object of bounty of payor, gift in favor of transferee is presumed and no resulting trust is presumed and (3) if transfer is made to accomplish illegal purpose, no resulting trust is presumed to arise unless it is needed to prevent unjust enrichment of transferee. (501B.07).

Qualification.—Trustees may apply to confirm appointment and obtain specifications as to manner of qualification in district court of county wherein they reside or have place of business or of county wherein will is being probated which thereafter has jurisdiction of trust as proceeding in rem. (501.33 et seq.; 501B.16 et seq.). In case of trust holding real property, such application may be made in district court of county in which real property is situated. (501B.17). Confirmed trustees must file inventory upon appointment and at least annually and may petition court at any time for instruction as to administration or construction of trust. (501.33 et seq.; 501B.16 et seq.).

Uniform Probate Code adopted in part (524.2-101 et seq.) with modifications.

Trust created prior to 1990, (except trust forming part of disability, medical or other employee welfare plan or part of stock bonus, pension or profitsharing trust for exclusive benefit of employees or members of employee organization) shall not continue for a period longer than life or lives of specified persons in being at time of its creation, and for 21 years after death of survivor of them, and that free alienation of legal estate by trustee shall not be suspended for period exceeding limit prescribed by statute relating to perpetuities (501.11) (see 191 Minn. 143, 253 N.W. 365; Uniform Statutory Rule Against Perpetuities adopted, effective Jan. 1, 1992; without reference to limitation on duration of trusts). Effective Jan. 1, 1990 (for trusts created before or after such date), power of alienation of property held in trust may not be suspended for more than 21 years. Future interest in real or personal property not held in trust is void if it would suspend power of alienation for period longer than lives in being plus 21 years. (501B.09). Not applicable to trusts if beneficial interests are evidenced by or constitute securities. (501B.09). Effective Jan. 1, 1990, income may be accumulated in trust for period of up to lives in being plus 21 years. (500.17, subd. 2). Effective Jan. 1, 1990, no statutory limitation on duration of trusts. See category Property, topic Perpetuities.

In case where express trust is created but not contained or declared in conveyance to trustees, such conveyance shall be deemed absolute as against subsequent creditors of trustees without notice of trust and as against bona fide purchasers for value from trustees. (501.21; 501B.05).

When purposes for which an express trust is created cease, estate of trustee shall also cease. (501.40). If purposes for which active express trust is created have been accomplished, or become impossible of accomplishment or illegal, trust shall terminate. (501B.03). If trust terms provide for successor trustee and method of qualification, title to assets rests on qualification. If no successor provided, district court appoints. (501B.08).

Distributions to Beneficiaries.—Effective May 15, 1993, trustee may not participate in exercise of power to distribute (1) to trustee as beneficiary unless power is limited by ascertainable standard related to trustee's health, maintenance, support or education, or (2) to any other person in discharge of trustee's support or other obligations. (501B.14). If trustee is disqualified, other trustees may act. Unless trust instrument specifically provides otherwise, by reference to section, prohibition applies to all trusts whenever created except (1) trustee who has unlimited non-fiduciary lifetime or testamentary power to appoint to trustee or trustee's estate, (2) trustee of trust created before May 15, 1993, if entire trust would be included in trustee's gross estate without regard to power, (3) trustee of trust created before May 15, 1993, if trust would not be included in trustee's gross estate even with power, (4) trustee of trust created before May 15, 1993, if trust would be subjected to generation skipping transfer tax by virtue of trustee not having power, and (5) trustee of trust irrevocable on May 15, 1993, if there is only one trustee.

Charitable Trusts.—Trust may be created for charitable, benevolent, educational, religious or other public use and shall not be void for indefiniteness or uncertainty or object or beneficiaries or because of a violation of rule against perpetuities, but shall not be construed to prevent or limit free alienation of title to any part of estate by trustee in administration thereof. Court may direct administration thereof. Court may direct administration of trust so as to carry out its general purposes if it is indefinite, impractical, inexpedient, etc. (501.12; 501B.31).

Trustees of private foundations, charitable trusts and split-interest trusts and corporations which are private foundations prohibited from activities which would result in federal excise taxes for failure to distribute investment income, self-dealing, retention of excess business holdings, investments which jeopardize exempt purposes, and making of taxable expenditure; provided, that foregoing is inapplicable if court determines that application would be contrary to terms of governing instrument and that such instrument may not be changed to comply. (501.115; 501B.32).

Most charitable trusts, including incorporated charitable foundations, are required to file registration statement and annual information with Attorney General. Failure to register and file annual information constitutes breach of trust. Attorney General has broad investigatory powers over charitable trusts and must receive notice of all court proceedings involving charitable trusts. (501B.33 et seq.).

Investments.—Effective Jan. 1, 1997, Uniform Prudent Investor Act adopted with modifications. (501B.151). Prudent investor rule is default rule which may be expanded, restricted, eliminated or otherwise altered by provisions of trust. (501B.151, subd. 1).

Trustee shall invest and manage trust assets as prudent investor would, by considering purposes, terms, distribution requirements, and other circumstances of trust. (501B.151, subd. 2). Trustee shall diversify investments of trust unless trustee reasonably determines that, because of special circumstances, purposes of trust are better served without diversifying. (501B.151, subd. 3).

Securities in Name of Nominee.—Statutory authority for allowing corporate fiduciary to hold securities in name of nominee. (48.74).

Common trust fund may be created by trust company or banks with trust powers. (48A.07, subd. 6[g]).

Deeds to Trustees; Recording.—Instrument affecting title to real estate in the state granting any interest to any person, as trustee, which is recorded in office of county recorder or filed with registrar of titles but which does not set forth powers of trustee and beneficiary of such trust, does not give notice to any person of rights of any beneficiary under such trust in said real estate. (507.35).

Certificate of Trust.—Grantor or trustee may execute certificate of trust setting forth less than all of trust provisions. Certificate must include (1) name of trust if one is given, (2) date of trust instrument, (3) name of each grantor, (4) name of each original trustee, (5) name and address of each trustee empowered to act at time of certificate, (6) statement that "the trustees are authorized by the instrument to sell, convey, pledge, mortgage, lease or transfer title to any interest in real or personal property, except as limited by the following: (if none, so indicate)", (7) any other trust provisions grantors or trustees include, and (8) statement as to whether trust has been terminated or revoked. (501B.56). Certificate may be recorded in real estate records. When recorded or presented, certificate serves to document existence of trust, identity of trustees, trustees' powers, and other matters contained in certificate. Until certificate is amended or full trust instrument is recorded or presented, certificate is prima facie proof of matters contained in it and any party may rely on its continued effectiveness.

Trust Provisions Tied to Public Assistance.—For trusts created after July 1, 1992, trust provision which provides for suspension, termination, limitation or diversion of trust principal or income upon beneficiary applying for or becoming eligible for public assistance is unenforceable as against public policy. (501 B.89). Person other than beneficiary, beneficiary's spouse or person obligated to pay beneficiary sum under settlement or judgment may create supplemental needs trust for person with disability at time trust is created. Supplemental needs trust may limit expenditures to those for living expenses and basic needs which are not provided by public assistance. Limitation will cease to be enforceable if beneficiary becomes resident after age 64 in state institution or nursing home for six months or more and there is no reasonable expectation that beneficiary will be discharged. Supplemental needs trust created on or after Aug. 11, 1993, for person with disability is enforceable. (501B.89[3]).

Uniform Anatomical Gift Act adopted. (525.921-.9224). Effective Aug. 1, 1985, minor, with written consent of both parents, guardian, or parent or parents with legal custody, may make anatomical gift. (525.9211 et seq.).

See note at head of Digest as to 1998 legislation covered.

See Topical Index in front part of this volume.

MN – 32

TRUSTS . . . *continued*

Uniform Fiduciaries Act, with exception of §§3-6 thereof, adopted. (520.01-.13).

Uniform Gifts to Minors Act adopted (527.01-.11); replaced by Uniform Transfers to Minors Act, effective Jan. 1, 1986 (527.01-11).

Uniform Principal and Income Act adopted. (501.48-.63; 501B.59-.76).

Uniform Prudent Investor Act adopted, effective Jan. 1, 1997. (501B.151).

Uniform Simplification of Fiduciary Security Transfer Actadopted. (520.21-.31). (Specifically saved from repeal by U.C.C., see 336.10-104).

Uniform Testamentary Additions to Trusts Act adopted. (524.2-511).

Uniform Transfers to Minors Act adopted, effective Jan. 1, 1986. (527.01-.11).

Uniform Statutory Rule Against Perpetuities adopted, effective Jan. 1, 1990. (501A.01).

Uniform Trustees' Accounting Act not adopted.

Accumulations.—No statutory restriction on accumulations of income from personalty. Accumulations of rents and profits from real estate permitted to same extent and for same period as accumulations of income from personalty, and reasonable sums set aside for depreciation and depletion not deemed an accumulation. (500.17). See category Property, topic Perpetuities.

Perpetuities.—See category Property, topic Perpetuities.

Pour Over Trusts.—See topic Wills, subhead Bequests and Devises to Inter Vivos Trusts.

WILLS:

Any person 18 years of age who is of sound mind may make will. (524.2-501). Coverture is not disability.

Execution.—Will must be in writing, signed by testator or in testator's name by some other person in his presence and at his direction and shall be signed by at least two persons each of whom signed within reasonable time after witnessing signing or testator's acknowledgment of signature or of will. (524.2-502). Signature on self-proving affidavit is considered affixed to will if necessary to prove due execution. (524.2-504).

Attestation Clause.—Customary to attach to will certificate reciting that will was signed, declared and published by testator as last will and testament in presence of witnesses and witnessed by them at request of testator and that they in presence of testator and of each other attest and subscribe certificate.

Who May Witness.—Any person generally competent to be witness may act as witness to will and will is not invalid because will is signed by interested witness. (524.2-505).

Holographic wills are not recognized.

Self-Proved Wills.—Attested will may at time of its execution or at any subsequent date be made self-provided, by acknowledgment thereof by testator and affidavits of witnesses, each made before officer authorized to administer oaths under laws of this state, or under laws of state where execution occurs, and evidenced by officer's certificate, under official seal, attached or annexed to will in form and content substantially as follows (524.2-504):

THE STATE OF . . . .
COUNTY OF . . . .

We, ... , ... , and . . . . the testator and the witnesses, respectively, whose names are signed to the attached or foregoing instrument, being first duly sworn, do hereby declare to the undersigned authority that the testator signed and executed the instrument as the testator's last will, that the testator signed it willingly or directed another to sign it for the testator, that it was executed as a free and voluntary act for the purposes therein expressed, and that each of the witnesses, in the presence and hearing of the testator, signed the will as witnesses, and that to the best of their knowledge the testator was at the time 18 or more years of age, of sound mind and under no constraint or undue influence.

. . . .
Testator

. . . .
Witness

. . . .
Witness

Subscribed, sworn to and acknowledged before me by . . . . , the testator, and subscribed and sworn to before me by . . . . and . . . . , witnesses, this . . . . . . day of . . . . , ...
(SEAL)

Signed . . . .
(Official capacity of officer)

Living Wills—(Health Care Declarations).—Effective Aug. 1, 1998, competent adult may execute Health Care Directive, whereby preferences and instructions regarding health care may be indicated and health care agent may be designated to make health care decisions on behalf of declarant. (145C.02).

Health Care Declaration (see 145B) and Health Care Power of Attorney in conformance with 145C executed prior to Aug. 1, 1998 are still effective. Declaration executed after Aug. 1, 1989 and prior to Aug. 1, 1998 must be substantially in form prescribed by statute. (145B.04). Form set out at 145B.04.

Directive must be signed by declarant and either by two witnesses (neither of whom is named as proxy) or notary public. (145C.03).

Declaration may be revoked by declarant at any time. (145C.09). Declaration executed in another state may be recognized if it complies with requirements of law of jurisdiction where executed or Minnesota law. Notwithstanding, however, assisted suicide not allowed. (145B.16).

Deposit of Wills.—Wills may be deposited with any court and are sealed. During lifetime may be delivered only to maker or on his order in writing. (524.2-515). (Prior law required two witnesses to written order to deliver will and some courts may require witnesses.) Conservator or guardian may be allowed to examine will. Fee for depositing will is $5. (357.021).

Effect.—Every devise of land, unless contrary appears from will, conveys testator's whole interest therein subject to liens and encumbrances thereon. (525.21).

Revocation.—Will or any part thereof is revoked by subsequent will which revokes prior will or part expressly or by inconsistency or will may be revoked by being burned, torn, canceled, obliterated, or destroyed, with intent and for purpose of revoking it by testator or by another person in his presence and by his direction. (524.2-507).

Divorce, dissolution or annulment of marriage (but not decree of separation) revokes any disposition or appointment of property to former spouse, any general or special power or appointment conferred and any nomination as personal representative, trustee or guardian of former spouse unless will expressly provides otherwise. Property passes as if former spouse failed to survive decedent. Will provisions are revived by testator's remarriage to former spouse. No other change of circumstances revokes will. (524.2-804).

Bequests and Devises to Inter Vivos Trusts.—Uniform Testamentary Additions to Trusts Act adopted. (524.2-511).

Separate Writing.—Any writing in existence when will is executed may be incorporated by reference if sufficiently identified. (524.2-510). Will may refer to written statement or list to dispose of items of tangible personal property not otherwise specifically disposed of by will, other than money, evidences of indebtedness, documents of title, and securities, and property used in trade or business. Statement may be prepared or altered after execution of will. (524.2-513).

Testamentary Guardians.—See category Family, topic Guardian and Ward.

Probate.—Uniform Probate Code adopted with modifications. (524.1-101 et seq.).

As to jurisdiction and venue in probate proceedings, see topic Executors and Administrators.

In proceeding for informal probate, will which appears to have required signatures and which contains attestation clause showing that requirements of execution have been met is probated without further proof. (524.3-303[c]). Some courts may require proof of due execution. In formal testacy proceeding execution of will can be proved by affidavit or testimony of one attesting witness. In contested case execution of will which is not self-proved must be established by testimony of at least one attesting witnesses, if within state and competent and able to testify. Due execution of will may be proved by other evidence. (524.3-406).

Legacies.—Bear interest at legal rate one year after first appointment of personal representative. (524.3-904).

Unclaimed Assets.—Any assets which have not been distributed because distributee cannot be found or refuses to accept same or cannot be distributed for any other good and sufficient reason may, upon direction of court, be deposited with county treasurer, with right to reclaim within 21 years after deposit. (524.3-914).

Lapse.—If devisee (legatee) is grandparent or lineal descendant of grandparent of testator and is dead at time of execution of will or fails to survive testator, issue of deceased devisee who survived testator take in place of deceased devisee. If all of same degree they take equally, but if of unequal degree those of more remote degree take by representation. Applies to class gifts except devise to "issue", "decedents", "heirs of the body", "heirs", "next of kin", "relatives" or "family." Words of survivorship such as "if he survives me" or devise to "my children who survive me" override statute. Alternate devise overrides statute only if expressly designated devisee is entitled to take. (524.2-603).

Children.—If testator omits to provide for any children born after will is executed, these take same shares of estate which they would have taken in case of intestacy, unless (1) it appears from will that omission was intentional, (2) testator devised substantially all of estate to other parent of omitted child, and other parent survives, (3) testator provides for omitted child outside will and statements of testator on amount of such other transfers shows intent that they be in lieu of testamentary provision, or testator had children living when will was executed and omitted such children. If testator had children living when will executed and devises property to one or more of them, omitted after-born child takes share of property so devised as if included equally with devisees children under will. (524.2-302).

Spouse's Elective Share.—For decedents dying after Dec. 31, 1986 and before Jan. 1, 1996, augmented estate elective share provisions of Uniform Probate Code (pre-1990 version) adopted with modifications, including following: (1) homestead is never included in augmented estate regardless of disposition (see topic Descent and Distribution, subhead Family Allowances); (2) for outright gifts, only gifts of more than $30,000 to one donee within one year before death are included; (3) proceeds of life insurance paid to someone other than surviving spouse are included to extent attributable to premiums paid by decedent during marriage; (4) annuities, retirement plan benefits and disability compensation (but excluding social security and tier 1 railroad retirement benefits) paid to someone other than surviving spouse are included to extent attributable to premiums or contributions by decedent during marriage; (5) life insurance annuities, and retirement benefits payable to spouse attributable to premiums or contributions by decedent. Contributions made by decedent's employer, partner or partnership are deemed made by decedent. (524.2-201 through .2-207).

Effective for decedents dying after Dec. 31, 1995, UPC augmented estate elective share provisions (1990) adopted with modifications. Augmented estate includes decedent's probate estate; nonprobate transfers to others (including property subject to general power of appointment, decedent's interest in property held with right of survivorship, life insurance proceeds if decedent owned policy, annuities under which decedent was primary annuitant, retirement plans); property transferred during marriage if (i) decedent retained income from property, (ii) decedent created general power of appointment exercisable by decedent alone or with another person or exercisable by non-adverse party, (iii) transfers of property during two years prior to death if transfer is

See note at head of Digest as to 1998 legislation covered.

See Topical Index in front part of this volume.

WILLS . . . *continued*

of interest that would have caused inclusion of non-probate property or to extent that amount transferred exceeds $10,000 per year to any donee. Surviving spouse's property and transfers are also included in augmented estate (and are considered as having passed to surviving spouse in determining whether surviving spouse is entitled to additional amounts from decedent's probate estate or non-probate property beneficiaries). Elective share is graduated depending on length of marriage, starting at 3% for marriage of one to two years and increasing to 50% for marriage of 15 years or more. Minimum supplemental amount of $50,000 is provided regardless of percentage elective share provided. (524.2-201-214).

Foreign Executed Wills.—Written will is valid if executed in compliance with Minnesota law, or with law at time of execution of place where will was executed, or of place where at time of execution or at time of death testator is domiciled, has place of abode or is national. (524.2-506). Uniform International Wills Act adopted. (524.2-1001 et seq.).

Foreign Probated Wills.—Authenticated copy of will probated in another jurisdiction may be probated here. (524.3-301[2]; 524.3-402[a]). Uniform International Wills Act adopted. (524.2-1001 et seq.).

Ancillary Probate.—If no probate or application or petition therefor is pending in Minnesota, domiciliary foreign personal representative may file with court in county in which property belonging to decedent is located: (1) Certified or authenticated copy of his appointment and bond, if any, and (2) notice of his intention to exercise as to assets in Minnesota, all powers of local personal representative and to maintain actions and proceedings in Minnesota Clerk of court shall thereupon publish, at expense of estate, required notice once a week for two consecutive weeks in legal newspaper in county. (524.4-204). Sixty days from filing domiciliary foreign personal representative may exercise all powers of personal representative over assets in Minnesota, and maintain any actions or proceedings in Minnesota If resident creditor files written objection within 60-day period personal representative cannot exercise powers. (524.4-205). Any application or petition for local administration terminates power of foreign personal representative but he may be allowed to exercise limited powers to preserve estate. (524.4-206).

Simultaneous Death.—See topic Death, subhead Survivorship.

Testamentary Trust.—See topic Trusts.

Family Allowances.—See topic Descent and Distribution.

FAMILY

ADOPTION:

Any person who has resided in the state more than one year, unless length of residence waived, may adopt any child or adult. (259.22).

Consent required of parents unless parent of child does not appear on child's birth certificate, has not substantially supported child, was not married to natural mother within 325 days before or ten days after child's birth, is not openly living with child or mother, has not been adjudicated child's parent, and has not evidenced intent to retain parental rights or unless parent has abandoned child or has been deprived of custody of child by divorce, juvenile court, or adoption decree; guardian, if any; if none of preceding parties exist, Commissioner of Human Services, or agency having authority to place child for adoption, if any; and consent of child over 14. Birth parent who intends to grant consent to adoption must give notice to other birth parent, if such parent's consent is also required. Notice must be given prior to or within 72 hours following placement of child. Birth parent who receives such notice shall have 60 days to respond, or shall be deemed to have granted consent. If unmarried parent who consents to adoption of child is under 18, consent of parent's parents or guardian or, if none, consent of Commissioner also required. If adoptee an adult, only his written consent required. All consents must be in writing, executed before two competent witnesses and acknowledged, and contain notice of right to withdraw consent, which is statutorily prescribed. (259.24, .26). Consent must be given no earlier than 72 hours after birth and no later than 60 days after placement. (259.24[2a]). Consent executed and acknowledged outside of state, either in accordance with law of state or law of place where executed, is valid. (259.24, .26). If, after execution of consent and agreement, child is diagnosed with mental or psychological condition that may present substantial barrier to adoption, agency is to make reasonable efforts to give notice of such condition to consenting party. If child is not adopted within two years after consent and agreement are executed, agency must notify consenting parent and request parent to take custody of child or to file petition for termination of parental rights; such notice to be provided in personal and confidential manner. (259.25[1]). Parent who has consented and agreed to adoption, upon request to agency, must be informed whether child has been adopted. (259.25[1]). Birth parents' social and medical history provided to adoptive parents. (259.43).

Conditions Precedent.—Investigation and report by Commissioner of Human Services; three months residence in proposed home. Both conditions may be waived by court. Prior to investigation, agency must give individuals statutorily prescribed written notice that upon adopting child, adoptive parents assume all rights and responsibilities of birth parents, including financial support and caring for health, emotional and behavioral problems and, except for subsidized adoptions under 259.67, adoptive parents are not eligible for state or federal subsidies besides those birth parent would be eligible to receive. (259.35). Individual who takes guardianship of foreign-born child for purpose of adopting must, upon taking guardianship from child's country of origin, assume all rights and responsibilities of birth and adoptive parents. (Id.). Minnesota agency that refers individuals to foreign agency or individual country for adopting child located in that country must provide in writing, at time of making referral: (1) Name of foreign governmental authority that licenses or regulates adoption agency or individual; (2) current director's name; (3) whether foreign country requires legal adoption to take place in that country before child is removed; and (4) statutorily required notice under 259.35(i) regarding parental responsibilities. (259.35[2]). Court shall submit adoption

petition to adoption agency if child has been committed to guardianship of such agency, or if child has been placed in petitioner's home by direct placement. If adopting parent is stepparent, to County Social Services Agency, and agency or welfare department must investigate and report. (259.53). No petition for adoption filed unless child placed by Commissioner or licensed agency, except when child over 14 years, adoption by related party pursuant to 245A.02(13), child placed under laws of another state while child and petitioner reside there, or prohibition against private placement waived by court. (259.22). Prospective adoptive parents may request and receive summary report on their suitability as adoptive parents at conclusion of agency's study. Summary must be used only for purposes mutually agreed upon by agency and prospective adoptive parents; summary must not identify sources of information outside agency or information about any child to be adopted. (259.53[3a]). Contents of all reports and records of Commissioner, county welfare board, or agency on suitability of proposed adoptive home and child to each other must not be directly or indirectly disclosed to any person other than Commissioner or judge having jurisdiction in manner, except judge, upon request, must disclose to party of proceeding or party's counsel any portion of report that relates solely to suitability of proposed adoptive parents. Judge may withhold identity of individuals providing information in report or record. Agency with custody of report or record must be permitted to present reasons for or against judge disclosing identities of individuals providing information. (259.27[3(b)]). Except in adoption by related party pursuant to 245A.02(13), adoption study by licensed child-placing agency must be completed before child is placed with prospective adoptive parents. (259.41). Study, which must include at least one in-home visit, to include medical and social history, assessment of potential parenting skills, financial ability to support child, and awareness of adoption issues, including where appropriate, interracial, cross-cultural and special needs adoptions. (259.41).

Court is to award adoption if in best interests of child. (259.57[1]). Court is to give preference first to relatives of child, next to friend with whom child has resided or had significant contact. Placement may not be denied or delayed based on race or ethnic heritage. When possible and in siblings' best interests, siblings to be placed together. Court to honor genetic parents request for same religious background but only within same racial or ethnic heritage of child. (259.57[2]). Adoption and foster care provisions must be construed consistently with Indian Child Welfare Act. (25 U.S.C. 1901-1963).

Direct adoptive placement allowed only with custody order from Court prior to placement with prospective adoptive parents. (259.47). Order must specify that birth parents have right to custody until any consent becomes irrevocable. Adoptive parents must have health insurance and must file affidavit of intent to remain resident for at least three months. Counseling and legal counsel must be made available to birth parents at expense of prospective adoptive parents. (259.47).

Party to Interstate Compact On The Placement of Children. (257.40).

Jurisdiction of adoption proceedings is in juvenile court. (259.23).

Venue of adoption proceedings is county of residence of adopting parents. If adopting parents acquire a new residence in another county, proceedings may be transferred to such county. (259.23).

Petition should set forth name, age, residence, and marital status of petitioner; when and from what person or agency physical custody of child acquired; date, county, and state of child's birth; name of child's parents and guardian; name of child; name to be given if change is desired; description and value of child's property; that petitioner desires to adopt child and that such adoption is in best interest of child. (259.23). If adoption by stepparent, parent who is stepparent's spouse is not required to join petition. (259.21[7]).

Proceedings.—Parent's consent may be withdrawn by written notice provided received by agency to which child surrendered within ten working days of execution of consent. Consent irrevocable thereafter except on court order after written findings that consent obtained by fraud. (259.24). Adoptive parents and child to be parties to proceedings. No presumption favoring natural parents allowed. Proceedings to be confidential. (259.24, .25).

Name may be changed to name of adopting parents. (259.57).

Effect of Adoption.—Adopter and adoptee sustain legal relation of natural parent and legitimate child with all rights and duties thereof, including right of inheritance. Adoption terminates legal relationship between child and natural parents, including right of inheritance, except that adoption by stepparent does not affect relationship between child and natural parent who is spouse of stepparent. If one parent dies and child is adopted by stepparent who is spouse of surviving parent, rights of inheritance of child or issue from or through deceased parent which exist at parent's death not affected by adoption. (259.59).

Death or Terminal Illness Notification.—Adoption agency must inform parents who adopt child on or after Aug. 1, 1987, that they must notify agency if child dies. (259.27). Agency must inform adoptive parents that adoptive parents of adopted child under 19 or adopted person age 19 or older may maintain current address on file with agency and indicate desire to be notified if agency receives information on genetic parent's death. Agency must inform genetic parents who are entitled to notice under 259.49 that agency will notify them of child's death and cause of death, if known, provided genetic parents desire notice and maintain current addresses on file with agency. (259.27). Genetic parents entitled to notice under 259.49 may designate individuals to notify agency if genetic parent dies, and agency receiving such information will share it with adoptive parents, if adopted person is under 19, or adopted person age 19 or older who has indicated desire of knowing of genetic parent's death and files current address with agency. (259.27). Notices of death must be provided by agency through personal, confidential contact, not by mail. (259.27). Adoptive parents whose child was adopted through out-of-state agency must, if child dies, notify agency of death. (259.27). Adoption agency must inform adoptive parents and genetic parents of child adopted on or after Aug. 1, 1987, that genetic parents, adopted parents of adopted person under age 19 or adopted person age 19 or older may request to be notified if genetic parent or child is terminally ill. Agency must notify other parties if request is received and, that upon their request, agency will share information regarding terminal illness with adoptive, or genetic parents, or adopted person age 19 or older. (259.27).

See note at head of Digest as to 1998 legislation covered.

See Topical Index in front part of this volume.

ADOPTION . . . *continued*

Setting Aside Adoption.—Adoptive parents may not terminate rights to adopted child for reasons that would not apply to birth parents seeking termination of parental rights. (260.221[2]).

ALIMONY:

See topic Dissolution of Marriage.

COMMUNITY PROPERTY:

System does not obtain in Minnesota.

DESERTION:

See topic Husband and Wife.

DISSOLUTION OF MARRIAGE:

Subject governed by c. 518.

Grounds for Dissolution of Marriage.—Dissolution of marriage may be granted upon showing of irretrievable breakdown of marriage relationship. Defenses abolished. (518.06).

Separation.—Legal separation may be granted upon showing that one or both parties need legal separation. If one or both parties petition for legal separation and neither party contests separation nor petitions for dissolution, court shall grant legal separation. (518.06).

Residence Requirements.—One party must have resided in, been domiciliary of, or been member of armed forces stationed in state 180 days immediately preceding filing of petition. (518.07).

Jurisdiction of proceedings for dissolution and legal separation is in district and county courts. (518.06).

Venue must be in county where either spouse resides. If neither party is resident, proceeding may be brought in county where either party domiciled. If neither party resident or domiciled in state and jurisdiction based on member of armed services being stationed in state for more than 180 days, proceeding may be brought in county where member stationed. (518.09).

Process.—Unless proceeding brought by both parties, respondent must be served personally. When service is outside state it may be proved by affidavit of person making same. When made outside U. S., it may be proved by affidavit of person making same taken before and certified by any U. S. diplomatic representative or his authorized deputies or before officer authorized to administer oath with certificate of officer of court of record of country where affidavit is taken as to identity and authority of officer taking same. If personal service cannot be made, court may order service by alternate means, determined by court on application. (518.11; RCP 4.04).

Pleading.—Petition for dissolution of marriage or legal separation must state name (and any prior name) and address of petitioner; social security number of petitioner if child support or spousal maintenance will be addressed; place and date of marriage; name (and any prior name) and, if known, address of respondent; social security number of respondent if child support or spousal maintenance will be addressed; name (and any prior name), age and date of birth of each living minor or dependent child born before marriage or born or adopted during marriage and reference to and expected date of birth of child of parties conceived during marriage but not born; state whether or not separate proceeding for dissolution, legal separation or custody is pending in any court; allege that one or both parties satisfy residence requirements; allege irretrievable breakdown in marriage relationship or, in proceeding for legal separation, allege need for separation; state any temporary or permanent maintenance, child support, child custody, disposition of property, attorneys' fees, costs and disbursement applied for, without setting forth amounts and state whether order for protection under c. 518B or similar law of another state governs parties or minor child of parties, is in effect and if so, jurisdiction where entered. (518.10). Fee for filing action for marriage dissolution, same as other civil matters—$122, plus local library fees. (357.021).

Practice.—Respondent has 30 days to answer petition. In case of service by publication, period runs from date of last publication. No answer required to counter petition. (518.12). If respondent fails to appear, court may hear matter as default. (518.13). Proposed findings of fact, conclusions of law, order for judgment, and judgment and decree must be submitted to court and may be filed without hearing in following circumstances: (1) there are no minor children, parties have stipulated, or 20 days have elapsed since time for answer has elapsed and service of petition is proved; or (2) where there are minor children, parties have signed and acknowledged stipulation and both parties are represented by counsel. (518.13). Rules of Civil Procedure applicable to dissolution proceedings to extent not inconsistent with c. 518. (RCP 81.01).

Decree.—Decree of dissolution entered on finding that irretrievable breakdown exists. Decree is final when entered, subject to right to appeal. (518.13, .145). Court may relieve party from some judgments and decrees, orders or proceedings under c. 518 for specified reasons.

Maintenance.—Court may, in its discretion, direct payment of temporary maintenance and support money (including reasonable attorney's fees and costs) pending suit. (518.131, .14, .62). In dissolution proceedings, court may make award of payments from future income of one spouse for support of other. (518.54 et seq.). Order for maintenance must provide for biennial cost-of-living adjustment in amount to be paid and must specify date for adjustments to become effective. (518.641). Court may reach, by order, property of nonresident defendant in divorce proceedings to secure maintenance. (58 Minn. 279, 59 N.W. 1017). Court may appoint trustees of maintenance or support (518.61), or sequester obligor's property to pay it. All counties are required to participate in administrative process for obtaining, modifying and enforcing child and medical support orders. (518.551). Order for maintenance or support may be modified. Motion for modification may be decided without evidentiary hearing.

Division of Property of Spouses.—Marital property system of distribution generally applies. Upon dissolution, court may make such disposition of marital property as is just and equitable without regard to marital misconduct. If court finds that either spouse's resources or property, including spouse's share of marital property, are so inadequate as to work unfair hardship, court may also apportion to spouse up to one-half of nonmarital property except property excluded by valid antenuptial contract. (518.58). All property, including vested public or private pension plan benefits or rights, acquired during marriage is presumed to be marital property unless shown to be nonmarital property. Nonmarital property is any property which is acquired as gift, bequest, devise or inheritance made by third party to one but not both spouses, is acquired before marriage, is acquired in exchange for or is increase on nonmarital property, is acquired after date of valuation, or is excluded by valid antenuptial contract. (518.54). Court may compensate party to dissolution for disposal of assets during or in contemplation of proceedings by other party if disposal not for necessities or in usual course of business. (518.58).

Change of Name.—In final decree of dissolution or legal separation, court will change party's name to any other name party requests, unless it finds intent to defraud or mislead. (518.27).

Custody and maintenance of children, both before and after decree, is in discretion of court, subject to statutory guidelines and cost-of-living adjustments for child support. (518.551). Child support obligation not terminated by death of obligor. (518.64[4]). Order may be later modified based on changed income, changed needs of child, receipt of public assistance, change in cost of living, extraordinary medical expenses of child not provided for under 518.171 or addition, elimination, substantial increase or decrease in work-related or education-related child care expenses where prior award unfair or unreasonable. If application of child support guidelines in 518.551 applied to current circumstances produces amount that is at least 20% and at least $50 per month higher or lower than current award, current award is rebuttably presumed unreasonable and unfair. (518.64). If obligor is member of licensed occupation subject to licensing board and is in arrears, court may order licensing board to conduct hearing to consider license suspension. Attorney obligor in arrears may be referred to lawyers professional responsibility board. (518.551)[12]. Driver's license may be suspended and lien placed on motor vehicle for obligor in arrears. (518.551[13], [14]). Request by either or both parties establishes rebuttable presumption joint custody is in child's best interest unless domestic abuse has occurred between parents. (518.17). For child's best interest, court to consider: (1) Parent's or parents' wishes as to custody; (2) if child of sufficient age, child's reasonable preference; (3) child's primary caretaker; (4) relationship of each parent and child; (5) interactions and interrelationships of child, parents, siblings and others who may significantly affect child's best interests; (6) child's adjustment to home, school, community; (7) length of time child has lived in stable, satisfactory environment and desirability of maintaining continuity; (8) permanence, as family unit, of existing or proposed custodial home; (9) mental and physical health of all involved; (10) capacity of parties to give child love, affection and guidance, and to continue educating and raising child in child's culture, religion or creed; (11) child's cultural background; (12) effect on child of abuser's actions if related to domestic abuse that has occurred between parents or between parent and another; (13) disposition of each parent to encourage and permit contact by other parent; and (14) evidence of false allegations of child abuse. (518.17). Primary caretaker factor may not be used to establish presumption. (518.17). Court may order mediation of child custody or visitation with mediator appointed by family court. (518.619). Court must appoint guardian ad litem when it believes child is victim of domestic abuse or neglect. (518.165). In subsequent custody proceedings, court may consider, but is not bound by, finding that domestic abuse has occurred between parties. Court must grant specified rights pertaining to records and information about minor children. (518.17).

Uniform Child Custody Jurisdiction Act adopted. (c. 518A).

Uniform Interstate Family Support Act adopted. (c. 518C).

Remarriage immediately after decree of dissolution becomes final is permitted. (517.03, 518.145).

Annulment of Marriage.—See topic Marriage.

DIVORCE:

See topic Dissolution of Marriage.

GUARDIAN AND WARD:

Subject is governed by 525.539, et seq. "Guardian" is person appointed by court to exercise all of powers and duties designated in 525.56 for care of ward, ward's estate or both. "Conservator" is person appointed by court to exercise some, but not all, of such powers for care of conservatee, conservatee's estate, or both. (525.539).

Guardianship and Conservatorship of Adults.—Court may appoint one or more persons suitable and competent to discharge trust as guardian of person or estate or both, or as conservator of person or estate or both, of any incapacitated person. "Incapacitated person" means any adult person impaired and lacking sufficient understanding or capacity to make or communicate responsible decisions and who has demonstrated deficits in behavior which evidence inability to meet needs for medical care, nutrition, clothing, shelter or safety, or to manage property. Guardian or conservator of estate may be appointed voluntarily upon person's petition or written consent if court is satisfied of need thereof, or involuntarily upon court's determination that: (1) Person is unable to manage property and affairs effectively, (2) property will be dissipated unless proper management is provided, or funds are needed for support, care and welfare of person or dependents, and (3) guardian or conservator is necessary to adequately protect estate or financial affairs. (525.54). Court must appoint attorney to represent proposed ward or conservatee in initial proceedings unless counsel provided by proposed ward or conservatee or others, or in meeting with court visitor, proposed ward or conservatee waives counsel. (525.5501). Does not apply in Eighth Judicial District. (525.5501). Fees for attorney to be paid from ward or conservatee's assets, or by county if ward or conservatee indigent. $20 surcharge imposed on all probate and guardianship petitions and applications to pay expenses. (525.5501).

See note at head of Digest as to 1998 legislation covered.

See Topical Index in front part of this volume.

GUARDIAN AND WARD . . . *continued*

Nonresident may be appointed if able to maintain current understanding of ward's or conservatee's physical and mental status and needs. (525.544[2]).

Protective Arrangements.—Instead of appointing guardian or conservator, court may: (a) Authorize, direct or ratify any transaction necessary or desirable to achieve any security, service or care arrangement meeting needs of protected person (including payment, delivery, deposit or retention of funds or property; sale, mortgage, lease or other transfer of property; entry into annuity contract, contract for life care, deposit contract or contract for training and education; or addition to or establishment of suitable trust), or (b) authorize, direct or ratify contract, trust or transaction relating to protected person's financial affairs or involving his estate. (525.54, subd. 7).

Appointment.—Any person may petition for appointment of guardian or conservator or for protective order for any person believed to be subject to guardianship or conservatorship. Petition of adult person for appointment of guardian or conservator of own person or estate has priority over petition of any other person. (525.541).

Effect of Appointment.—After filing of petition for guardianship or conservatorship, notice of lis pendens may be filed with county recorder of any county in which ward or conservatee owns real estate and, if ward or conservatee resident of state, in county of residence. If guardian or conservator appointed on petition and, in case of conservatorship, if conservatorship order removes or restricts conservatee's right to transfer property or to contract, all contracts except for necessaries and all transfers of real or personal property made by ward or conservatee after such filing and before termination of guardianship or conservatorship are void. (525.543). Appointment of conservator does not deprive conservatee of right to vote. Appointment of guardian is evidence of incompetency of ward. Appointment of conservator is not evidence of incompetency of conservatee. (525.54).

Bond.—Guardian or conservator must file bond in such amount as court may direct. If no personal property, court may waive bond requirement. However, if any personal property is subsequently received, guardian or conservator must immediately file report thereof. (525.551, subd. 6).

Powers and Duties.—Guardian of person has all powers and duties listed in 525.56, subd. 3. Conservator of person has some, but not all, of such powers, as determined by court. Guardian of estate has all powers and duties listed in 525.56, subd. 4. Conservator of estate has some, but not all, of such powers, as determined by court. General guardian or conservator of estate must pay for support, maintenance and education of ward or conservatee in accordance with his station in life and value of estate; pay ward's or conservatee's debts and charges incurred for support, maintenance and education of ward's or conservatee's spouse and children; and possess and manage estate, including collecting all debts and claims in favor of ward or conservatee, representing ward or conservatee in any court proceedings, and investing in authorized securities all funds not currently needed for debts and charges. On court order, may sell, exchange or purchase inherited undivided interest in real estate. (525.56).

Investments.—Authorized securities. See 525.56, subd. 4.

Accounting.—Unless expressly waived or modified by court, every guardian or conservator of estate must annually file verified account covering period from date of appointment or last account. Copy of annual account must be given to ward or conservatee unless waived by court. Ward or conservatee must also be given annual notice of right to petition for restoration to capacity, discharge of guardian or conservator, or modification of orders of guardianship or conservatorship, unless waived by court. On termination of guardianship or conservatorship, verified final account must be filed. (525.58).

Annual Report.—Unless expressly waived by court, every guardian or conservator of person must annually within 30 days of anniversary of appointment file report under oath containing good faith evaluation of following information regarding ward or conservatee for preceding year: (1) Changes in medical condition, (2) changes in living conditions, (3) changes in mental and emotional condition, (4) listing of hospitalizations, (5) if ward or conservatee is institutionalized, evaluation of care and treatment received. (525.58).

Special Guardians or Conservators.—On showing of necessity or expediency, court may, with at least 24 hours prior notice, which may be waived upon showing that immediate and reasonably foreseeable harm will result from 24 hour delay, appoint special guardian or conservator of person or estate or both. Such special guardian or conservator has only powers necessary to provide for demonstrated needs of ward of conservatee, as granted by court. No appeal from order appointing or refusing to appoint special guardian or conservator. (525.591).

Termination.—Guardianship or conservatorship of adult ward or conservatee terminates on death or restoration of capacity. Whenever there is no further need for guardianship or conservatorship, court may terminate same on such notice as it may direct. (525.60).

Restoration to Capacity.—Any adult person under guardianship or conservatorship, his guardian or conservator, or any other person may petition court in which he was so adjudicated that he be restored to capacity or that guardianship be transferred to conservatorship or to modify guardianship or conservatorship. On filing of such petition, court fixes time and place for hearing thereof and on suitable proof being made, will adjudge him restored to capacity. (525.61).

Guardianship and Conservatorship of Minors.—Person becomes guardian of minor by acceptance of testamentary appointment or appointment by court. Guardianship status continues until terminated without regard to location of guardian and minor ward. (525.615).

Minor of 14 or more years may prevent parent's testamentary appointment from becoming effective or may cause previously accepted appointment to terminate by filing written objections to appointment before or within 30 days after acceptance. Objection does not preclude appointment by court in proper proceeding. (525.616).

Orphans.—Juvenile court may order guardianship of orphan if no other appointment made or petition filed. Guardian has legal custody of ward but guardianship under 260.242 does not include guardianship of orphan's estate. (260.242).

Powers and Duties.—Guardian of minor has powers and responsibilities of custodial parent plus powers and duties in 525.619. (525.619).

Termination.—Guardian's authority and responsibility terminates on death, resignation or removal of guardian, or on minor's death, adoption, marriage or attainment of majority. Liability for prior acts and obligation to account for funds and assets of ward continue until discharged by court. (525.6192).

Facility of Payment or Delivery.—Any person (other than personal representative subject to 524.3-915, clause [b]) under duty to pay or deliver money or personal property to minor may perform duty, in amounts of $5,000 or less per annum, by paying or delivering money or property to: (1) Minor if age 16 or married; (2) person having care or custody of minor; (3) guardian of minor; (4) financial institution by depositing in name of minor and giving notice of deposit to minor. Does not apply if person has actual knowledge that conservator has been appointed or proceedings for appointment of conservator of minor's estate are pending. (525.6196). Court may order guardian or conservator to pay up to $2,000 to parent, custodian or custodial institution for benefit, support, maintenance, and education of minor, or may direct investment in name of minor. (525.6197).

Protective Proceedings.—Upon petition and after notice and hearing, court may appoint conservator for minor or make other protective order. Conservator shall file bond in such amount as court directs. (525.6198).

Delegation of Power by Parent or Guardian.—Parent or guardian of minor or incapacitated person may delegate by properly executed power of attorney any powers regarding care, custody or property of minor or ward, except power to consent to marriage or adoption of minor ward. Such delegation may be made for period not exceeding six months. (524.5-505).

Mortgages and Leases.—Governed by 525.62 to 525.705. "Lease" means lease for one or more years. (525.62).

Preexisting Guardianships and Conservatorships.—Guardians and conservators under law prior to Oct. 1, 1981 have all powers and duties of 525.56, subd. 3, as to person, and 525.56, subd. 4, as to estate, unless restricted by existing court order, until restricted or changed by court order.

Gifts to Minors.—See topic Infants.

Uniform Fiduciaries Act, with exception of §§3-6 thereof, adopted. (520.01-.13).

Uniform Simplification of Fiduciary Security Transfers Act adopted. (520.21-.31). (Specifically saved from repeal by U.C.C., see 336.10-104).

HUSBAND AND WIFE:

Married woman retains same legal existence and personality after marriage as before. (519.01).

Separate Property.—Married woman may hold any property, real or personal, as her separate property. (519.02).

Contracts.—Married woman may make any contract which she could make if unmarried, and is bound thereby, except that every conveyance and contract for sale of her real estate or any interest therein is subject to provisions of 507.02. (519.03. See infra, subhead Conveyances).

Wife may contract with her husband as with third person, except that no contract between them relative to real estate of either or any interest therein is valid, other than as provided in §500.19, subdivisions 4 and 5. (519.06).

Actions.—Married woman may sue in courts of law or equity for protection of her reputation, person, property or any natural right, and it is not necessary that husband be joined as party to action by or against his wife. (519.01). Wife may sue her husband, or vice versa, in her own name in any form of action to enforce any right affecting her property. (64 Minn. 381, 67 N.W. 206; 183 Minn. 306, 236 N.W. 455). Interspousal immunity abolished as complete defense to tort actions. (285 Minn. 366, 173 N.W.2d 416).

Agency.—Either spouse may act as attorney in fact for the other, except that no power of attorney or other authority from one to the other to convey real estate or any interest therein, other than conveyance creating joint tenancy, is valid, except that power of attorney executed on or after Jan. 1, 1996, may include power to convey real estate. (519.06).

Conveyances.—Husband and wife by their joint deed may convey real estate of either. Either spouse may, by separate deed, convey any real estate owned by him or her, except homestead (see category Debtor and Creditor, topic Homesteads), subject to statutory right of other spouse therein (see category Estates and Trusts, topic Descent and Distribution) and either may by separate conveyance relinquish rights in real estate so conveyed by the other. Subject to foregoing, either may separately appoint an attorney (including spouse after Jan. 1, 1996) to sell or convey any real estate owned by him or her, or join in any conveyance made by or for the other. (507.02).

Minor husband or wife has legal capacity to join in conveyance of real estate owned by his or her spouse if not incapacitated for some reason other than his or her minor age. (507.02).

Conveyance by one spouse may be binding on the other where afterwards adopted and confirmed by latter. (131 Minn. 299, 154 N.W. 1086).

Married person may dispose of real estate, except homestead, if spouse is incapacitated, with consent of guardian obtained after authorization of probate court when letters of guardianship are filed in county recorder's office where property is located, and may obtain judgment to dispose of real estate in case of desertion for more than one year. (507.04; 519.07).

Liabilities.—Neither spouse is liable for debts of other, except for necessaries furnished to other spouse. Husband and wife living together are jointly and severally liable for all necessary household articles and supplies furnished to and used by family. (519.05).

Antenuptial Contracts.—Man and woman of legal age may enter into antenuptial contract prior to day of solemnization of marriage provided there is full and fair disclosure of earnings and property of each party and parties have opportunity to consult legal counsel of own choice. Contract may determine rights of each party in nonmarital property upon dissolution of marriage, legal separation or death. Contract must be in

See note at head of Digest as to 1998 legislation covered.

See Topical Index in front part of this volume.

HUSBAND AND WIFE... *continued*

writing executed by parties personally in presence of two witnesses, and acknowledged by parties before any officer authorized to administer oaths. Contract affecting rights to real property may be recorded with county recorder, and is void against subsequent purchaser in good faith if not so recorded. Contract is prima facie proof of all matters acknowledged therein. (519.11). Postnuptial agreement allowed if in conformity with antenuptial requirements, each spouse is represented by separate counsel, and each spouse has title to assets of at least $1,200,000. (519.11[1a]). Postnuptial agreement not effective in dissolution within two years of execution.

Desertion and Nonsupport.—Intentional failure to provide care and support to spouse in necessitous circumstances or child is misdemeanor; such failure, or failure to provide care and support of pregnant wife, for period of in excess of 90 days, but not more than 180 days is gross misdemeanor and may be sentenced to up to one year of prison or $3,000 fine or both. Such failure for period of over 180 days is felony. (609.375). Deserted spouse may sue and defend in absent spouse's name, and have same powers and rights in action as he might have had. (540.09).

Uniform Interstate Family Support Act adopted. (c. 518C).

Community property system does not apply in Minnesota.

INFANTS:

Age of majority is 18 for both sexes (645.451), but minority of married man or woman does not affect his or her capacity to join in conveyance of real estate owned by his or her spouse. (507.02).

Validity of Contracts and Conveyances.—Infant is liable for his necessaries (56 Minn. 365, 57 N.W. 934) but all his contracts other than for necessaries are voidable and subject to disaffirmance by him (56 Minn. 365, 59 N.W. 992; 26 Minn. 389, 4 N.W. 695; 35 Minn. 488, 29 N.W. 201).

Conveyance made by infant is binding until disaffirmed by some positive act when infant reaches majority or reasonable time thereafter. (31 Minn. 468, 18 N.W. 283).

Actions.—In district court, infant may be represented by general guardian ad litem appointed by court at instance of infant if 14, otherwise by general guardian, relative or friend, or, after default, by plaintiff. Must be resident and must file consent and bond. (RCP 17.02). Action for injury to infant may be brought by parent, general guardian, or guardian ad litem. No settlement or compromise of such action is valid unless approved by court in which action is pending. Parent must file bond before receiving money in settlement or compromise or satisfaction of judgment. In lieu of bond, court may order property so received invested in U.S. securities or invested in savings account or certificate or annuity or other form of structured settlement, with evidence of such investment filed with clerk of court. Money so invested may be released to minor or minor's guardian only by court. (540.08).

Termination of Parental Rights.—Juvenile court may, upon petition, terminate parental rights with written consent of parent or with finding of abandonment, neglect, failure to support, palpable unfitness or other conduct inconsistent with parental obligations. If child has resided out of parent's home under court order for more than one year following determination of neglect, parent has failed to comply with orders and reasonable case plan to correct conditions, and efforts have been made by social service agency to reunite family, presumption attaches that reasonable efforts to correct neglect have failed and parental rights may be terminated. (260.221, .231). Presumption of unfitness attaches if child is found to be in need of protection because of abandonment, sexual abuse, or lack of food, clothing, shelter, education or medical care, and parent has had parental rights terminated with respect to other children during preceding three years. (260.221). With termination of parental rights all privileges, duties, and obligations, including rights of control and visitation, are ended. (260.241).

Delegation of Parental Powers.—Parent or guardian may delegate powers concerning care, custody or property of minor child for period of up to six months by power of attorney. (524.5-505). As of July 1, 1996, parent may delegate powers to another by Designated Caregiver Agreement. (257A.01-09). Agreement must be in writing and signed by all custodial caregivers, caregivers with court-ordered visitation rights, designated caregivers and alternate designated caregivers, with signatures notarized. Agreement is effective for up to four years after execution. Designated caregiver may act when no parent with physical custody is able to care for child. Designated caregiver exercising custody is exempt from foster care licensing, but must notify local social service agency, adult siblings and grandparents if child has been in designated caregiver's home for 30 days. Parent who has executed designated caregiver agreement may have symbol on driver's license indicating that designated caregiver has been appointed. (171.07). Fee is $3.50. Minnesota Department of Public Safety is to maintain records of designated parent agreements and may release information to law enforcement agencies.

Uniform Transfers to Minors Act adopted, effective Jan. 1, 1986. (527.21-.44). Age of majority under Act is 21.

Uniform Securities Ownership by Minors Act not adopted.

Uniform Parentage Act adopted with variations. See topic Marriage. (257.51-.74).

Adoption.—See topic Adoption.

MARRIAGE:

Age of consent: 18 for both males and females or 16 if with consent of parents, guardian or court and approval of judge of juvenile court of county of residence or, if judge of juvenile court is absent from county without having assigned another probate judge to act in judge's stead, by court commissioner or any district court judge in county. (517.02).

Marriage of any infant under age of consent is voidable. (518.02).

Marriage between persons of same sex prohibited. (c. 517; 291 Minn. 310, 191 N.W.2d 185).

Marriage license must be obtained from clerk of district court of any county, and marriage need not take place in county where license obtained. (517.07). Application

for license may be made by either party, who must appear in person, and must be made at least five days previous to issuance, unless in case of emergency, etc., when authorized by district. $70 fee. (517.08).

Waiting Period.—See supra, subhead Marriage License.

Ceremonial marriage may be solemnized by any clerk of court, any judge of court of record, retired judge of court of record, former court commissioner who is employed by court system or acting pursuant to order of chief judge of district, administrators of state schools for deaf and blind, or ordained minister of any religious denomination. (517.04). Solemnization practices of certain religious groups and American Indians recognized. (517.18). Minister's credentials of ordination must first be filed with clerk of district court of some county in state. (517.05). Lack of authority of person performing ceremony does not invalidate marriage if parties in good faith believed him to have necessary authority. (517.01).

No particular form required except that parties must contract in presence of authorized persons and at least two witnesses. (517.09).

Solemnizing marriage illegally or willfully making false certificate is misdemeanor. (517.14).

Illegitimate (Out of Wedlock) Children.—Parent and child relationship not dependent on marital status of parents. Parentage act establishes procedures for determining paternity, custody and visitation rights. (257.51-.74). Statistical presumption of paternity if likelihood of paternity, calculated with prior probability of no more than 50%, is 99% or greater and may be overcome only by clear and convincing evidence. (257.62, subd. 5).

Record.—See category Documents and Records, topic Records, subhead Vital Statistics.

Reports of Marriage.—Person solemnizing marriage must file certificate of marriage with district court clerk in county in which license issued within five days after ceremony. (517.10).

Common law marriages contracted on or before April 26, 1941, recognized (122 Minn. 407, 142 N.W. 593; 151 Minn. 72, 186 N.W. 126), but marriage contracted since that date void unless requirements hereinbefore stated complied with (517.01). Validity of marriage normally determined by law of jurisdiction where contracted and if valid there, valid in Minnesota unless it violates strong public policy. (239 Minn. 27, 57 N.W.2d 628). Strong public policy against common law marriage but court will recognize marriage if couple takes up residence and establishes elements of common law marriage in state which recognizes such marriages. (277 N.W.2d 653).

Proxy Marriages.—No statutory authorization.

Prohibited Marriages.—Persons related as ancestor and descendant, brother and sister, uncle and niece, aunt and nephew or first cousins may not intermarry; mentally retarded under guardianship or conservatorship may marry with permission of Commissioner of Human Services. (517.03). Marriages within prohibited degrees and bigamous marriages are absolutely void. (518.01).

See also topic Dissolution of Marriage and infra, subhead Annulment of Marriage.

Annulment of Marriage.—Where either party incapable of assenting through want of age or lack of capacity to consent not known to other party, or because of influence of drugs or consent obtained by force or fraud and there is no subsequent voluntary cohabitation, injured party may obtain annulment dating from time of adjudication. (518.02).

Remarriage immediately after dissolution of marriage or decree annulling marriage is permitted. (518.03, 518.145).

MARRIED WOMEN:

See topics Husband and Wife, Infants, Marriage; categories Civil Actions and Procedure, topic Evidence, subhead Witnesses; Debtor and Creditor, topic Homesteads; Documents and Records, topic Acknowledgments; Estates and Trusts, topics Executors and Administrators, Wills; Property, topic Dower.

INSURANCE

INSURANCE COMPANIES:

General supervision of insurance business is under Commissioner of Commerce.

Regulated by cc. 59A through 79A.

Standard Valuation Law (Guertin Act) adopted. (61A.25).

Deposit Requirements.—No company except farmers' mutual, or real estate title insurance companies can do business in state unless it has on deposit with Commissioner of Commerce securities in amount of $200,000 until July 1, 1986, $300,000 until July 1, 1987, $400,000 until July 1, 1988, and $500,000 on or after July 1, 1988 or one-half applicable financial requirement set forth in 60A.07, whichever is less. Commissioner may require special deposit by individual foreign insurer for protection of Minnesota policyholders or claimants. (60A.10).

Rates.—Rates and supporting information for casualty, fidelity, surety, guaranty bonds and allied lines, fire, title insurance and inland marine insurance on risk or operations in Minnesota, must be filed with Commissioner of Commerce before they become effective. (70A.02, 70A.06). Hearing may be held whenever rate change filed that would result in 25% or more increase in 12-month period over existing rates. Rate effective unless hearing finds rate is excessive. (70A.06, subd. 1a).

Policies.—Statutes regulate life insurance (cc. 61A, 61B), accident and health insurance (c. 62A), credit life and accident and health insurance (c. 62B), nonprofit health service plan corporations (c. 62C), health maintenance organizations (c. 62D), provision of health insurance to low-income persons (62J), small employer health benefits (62L), medical malpractice insurance (c. 62F), nonprofit legal service plans (c. 62G), joint self-insurance employee health plans (c. 62H), fraternal benefit societies (c. 64B), fire and related insurance (c. 65A), homeowner's insurance (65A.27 et seq.), automobile insurance (c. 65B), title insurance (c. 68A) workers' compensation insurance (c. 79,

INSURANCE COMPANIES .... *continued*

worker's compensation self-insurance (c. 79A) and health care utilization review services (62M). Readability of policies is regulated by c. 72C. See category Business Regulation and Commerce, topic Consumer Protection, subhead Plain Language.

Discrimination.—Unfair discrimination between individuals of same class on basis of disability in life or accident and health insurance policies, or applications therefor, prohibited unless claims experience and actuarial projections establish substantial differences in class rates. "Redlining" by issuers of homeowner's insurance coverage prohibited. Discrimination on basis of sex or marital status prohibited. Automobile insurer may not use employment status, status as tenant, previous failure to have automobile policy in force (unless policy was required by law) or prior claims for benefits (if applicant was less than 50% negligent) as underwriting standard or guideline or reason to deny coverage or charge differential rates. (72A.20). Discrimination prohibited in automobile insurance policies between persons of same class, on account of race, on account of physical handicap compensated for by training or equipment, or on account of marital dissolution. (65B.13).

Rebates prohibited. (72A.20).

Reinsurance.—Company other than life must not reinsure without filing sworn report with Commissioner. (60A.09).

Assumption transactions by life insurance companies regulated. Assumption agreements must be filed with Commissioner and must provide that original insurer remains liable to insured if assuming insurer is unable to fulfill its obligations unless policyholder consents in writing to release original insurer and consent form has been approved by Commissioner. (60A.09).

Mutual companies organized after April 1931 may not be licensed to write policies covering injuries in course of employment, health, fidelity, boilers, glass, burglary, water, theft, forgery, domestic animals, automobile, liability, attorneys fees, malpractice or elevators, or all risks for personal property, and valuable documents except upon compliance with special conditions. (60A.06, 66A.08).

Agents must be licensed by Commissioner of Commerce. (60K.02).

Foreign companies are admitted upon compliance with following requirements: (1) Depositing with Commissioner of Commerce certified copy of charter, by-laws and statement of financial condition and business; (2) furnishing Commissioner proof of authority to transact proposed business and that its assets, number of risks, reserve and other securities and guaranties for protection of policyholders, creditors and the public, comply with those required of like domestic companies; (3) appointing Commissioner of Commerce its agent for service of process as long as any liability exists in the state; (4) appointing as its agents residents of the state and obtaining from Commissioner license to transact business; (5) establishing financial requirements based on lines of business it is licensed to write in state of incorporation. (60A.19). For filing fees and annual report fees, see 60A.14.

Retaliatory law provides that whenever laws of any other state, territory, or country prohibit or do not provide for organization of or licensing in such state, territory or country of a class or kind of insurance companies or associations organized under laws of this state, then companies or associations of same kind or class of such other state, territory or country shall not be licensed to do business in this state. (60A.07, subd. 9).

Premium tax in amount of 2% of annual premiums levied on all domestic and foreign insurance companies on installment basis in lieu of all other taxes except those on real property within state. Premiums received under medical assistance, general assistance medical care, Minnesota-Care program, and Minnesota Comprehensive Health Insurance Plan are not subject to tax. Health maintenance organizations and nonprofit health service organizations are subject to tax of 1% of premiums. Health Maintenance Organizations, community integrated service networks, and nonprofit health service corporations that meet cost containment goals under §62J.04 for 1998 are exempt from payment of premium tax on premiums paid after Mar. 30, 1999 and before Jan. 1, 2000. Insurance company may offset against its premium tax liability to state amounts paid pursuant to assessments made for insolvencies occurring after July 31, 1994 under 60C.01 to 60C.22 as prescribed by statute. (60A.15).

No-Fault Insurance.—See category Transportation, topic Motor Vehicles.

Direct Actions Against Insurer.—See category Transportation, topic Motor Vehicles, subhead Direct Actions.

Uniform Insurers Liquidation Act not adopted.

SURETY AND GUARANTY COMPANIES:

Domestic or foreign corporation, holding certificate of Commissioner of Insurance of this state to effect that it appears to his satisfaction that corporation has complied with requirements of statute, may become surety on any bond, recognizance, obligation, stipulation or undertaking required by law in all actions, proceedings, municipal and other cases where same may be required with one surety or two or more sureties. (574.15).

Bonding Charges.—Any receiver, assignee, trustee, committee, guardian, executor or administrator or other fiduciary required by law to give bond may include as his lawful expense the charges therefor of surety company so qualified, not exceeding $10 per annum when amount of bond is not over $1,000, and not more than 1% per annum on excess. In all actions or proceedings party entitled to recover costs may include therein such reasonable sum as may have been paid such company for executing or guaranteeing bond or undertaking therein. (574.19).

INTELLECTUAL PROPERTY

TRADEMARKS AND TRADENAMES:

Trademarks and Service Marks.—Any person who adopts and uses trademark or service mark in state may file for registration of mark. (333.20). Fee, $50, payable to Secretary of State. (333.20). Each application to be on forms furnished by Secretary of

State; signed and verified by applicant, member of firm or an officer of corporation or association, or by manager of limited liability company and accompanied by single specimen or facsimile of such mark. (333.20). Upon acceptance by Secretary of State, certificate of registration will be issued. (333.21).

What May Not Be Used.—Trademark or service mark will not be registered if it (1) comprises immoral, deceptive or scandalous matter; (2) may disparage or falsely suggests connection with person, institution, belief or national symbol; (3) comprises flag or insignia of U.S. or any state or municipality, or any foreign nation; (4) comprises name, signature or portrait of living person without their consent; (5) is merely descriptive of goods or services unless distinctive; (6) is primarily geographically descriptive; (7) is primarily surname; or (8) so resembles registered mark or corporate or limited partnership name as to be likely to cause confusion. (333.19).

Duration and Renewal.—Registration is effective for ten year period with renewals permitted for successive ten year terms upon application within six months prior to end of term on forms furnished by Secretary of State, provided mark is then used by applicant and that there are no intervening rights. Renewal fee $25. Notice of expiration and necessity for renewal given registrant by Secretary of State. (333.22).

Assignment.—Conveyance or assignment of mark must be in writing and will be recorded by Secretary of State and new certificate issued to assignee for remainder of registration term. Recordation fee $15. Assignment will be void against subsequent purchaser for value without notice unless recorded with Secretary of State within three months of assignment or prior to subsequent purchase. (333.23).

Cancellation of Marks.—Secretary of State shall cancel registration: (a) For failure to renew mark; (b) upon request by registrant; or (c) in compliance with order of district court. (333.25).

Infringement and Remedies.—Civil action by owner of registered mark may be maintained against any person who, without consent of owner, uses such mark or confusingly or deceptively similar mark in connection with rendering of services or selling, offering to sell, or advertising any goods or services, or who counterfeits, reproduces, copies or imitates such mark and applies same to labels, advertisements, etc. (333.28). District court may grant injunction to restrain infringement and may require defendant pay damages or profits to registrant. (333.29). Recovery of damages or profits not allowed for acts of infringer in reproducing, counterfeiting, copying or imitating labels, advertisements, etc., unless committed with knowledge that such mark was intended to be used to cause confusion or mistake or to deceive. (333.28). Attorney's fees may be awarded. (333.29).

Common Law Marks.—Person's rights in mark acquired in good faith at any time at common law not affected by statutes, except that such person's rights against registrant of same or confusingly similar mark are limited to (a) areas of his use prior to registration date, and (b) areas in which mark had become known prior to registration date. (333.30).

Counterfeiting Trademarks a Misdemeanor.—Receptacles for beverages, cream, butter or ice cream with name, mark or other device thereon may also be registered. (509.01). Fee, $10. (509.01). Improper use by others is misdemeanor. (509.02).

Tradenames.—No business can be carried on under tradename unless registered with secretary of state, giving names and addresses of all those conducting business and unless published notice thereof is given. (333.01). Assumed or fictitious name must not intentionally misrepresent geographic origin or location of business. (333.01). Filing fee, $25. (333.055). Tradenames cannot include words denoting part of U.S. government such as "Army", "Navy", etc. (333.17). Tradename must not include corporation, incorporated, limited, chartered, professional cooperative, association, limited partnership, limited liability company, limited liability partnership, or professional limited liability partnership unless entity registering tradename could use these terms. (333.01). Assumed name not distinguishable from corporate limited liability company, limited liability partnership, cooperative or limited partnership name (or registered trade or service mark) in use or reserved in state by another not registered without written consent, court decree of prior right or affidavit of nonuser. Certificate effective for ten year period. Tradenames on file as of July 1, 1978 expired July 31, 1979, unless renewed. Renewal fee $25. (333.055). If any business that has failed to file tradename commences civil action in state court, action stayed until certificate filed and defendant entitled to $250 abatement or costs. Plaintiff entitled to $250 costs where any such business defends against civil action. (333.06). See also category Business Organizations, topic Partnerships.

Dilution.—Likelihood of injury to business reputation or of dilution of distinctive quality of mark or tradename shall be grounds for injunctive relief. (325D.165).

TRADE SECRETS:

Uniform Trade Secrets Act adopted. (325C.01 et seq.). Actual or threatened misappropriation may be enjoined. (325C.02). In exceptional circumstances injunction may condition future use upon payment of reasonable royalty for no longer than period of time for which use could have been prohibited. (325C.02). Except where monetary recovery would be inequitable, damages can be recovered for misappropriation. Damages can include both actual loss and unjust enrichment. (325C.03). Court may award damages in amount up to twice damages otherwise awardable for willful and malicious misappropriation. (325C.03). Action for misappropriation must be brought within three years after misappropriation is discovered or by reasonable diligence should have been discovered. (325C.06).

LEGAL PROFESSION

ATTORNEYS AND COUNSELORS:

The state bar is not integrated.

Jurisdiction over admission is vested in Supreme Court. (480.05). Current rules for admission are as amended through Dec. 15, 1997.

See note at head of Digest as to 1998 legislation covered.

See Topical Index in front part of this volume.

ATTORNEYS AND COUNSELORS ... *continued*

Eligibility.—Applicant for admission to bar must be 18 years of age, of good character and fitness, reside in state or maintain office in state, or designate Clerk of Appellate Courts as agent for service of process for all purposes.

Registration as Law Student.—No registration required.

Educational Requirements.—Applicant must have graduated with J.D. or L.L.B. from ABA-approved law school. Certificate of graduation, or of fulfillment of all requirements for graduation with graduation occurring within 120 days following examination, must be filed at least 30 days prior to examination.

Application for admission is to State Board of Law Examiners.

Examinations are held in Feb. and July of each year. Fee is $300, plus $325 if applicant will have been admitted in another jurisdiction for more than six months by date of next exam. Application deadlines are Oct. 15 for Feb. exam and Mar. 15 for July exam. Late filing fee is $150, but no applications accepted after Dec. 15 for Feb. exam or May 15 for July exam. State exam consists of Multi-State Bar Exam plus additional questions, and applicants must also have passed Multi-State Professional Responsibility Exam. Applicant who fails exam may retake at any regular exam date in next two years upon application before 15th day of second month preceding exam and payment of fee of $300. Applicant failing three times may take further exam only after submitting study plan approved by Director of State Board of Law Examiners at least 30 days prior to application.

Admission Without Examination.—Attorneys admitted in other states may, in discretion of Supreme Court, be admitted without examination: (1) After, as principal occupation, being actively engaged in practice of law (including judicial service, legal service with government, in military, or as corporate counsel or trust officer, or teaching full-time in approved law school) for at least five of previous seven years, or (2) if applicant passed written exam in other state within prior two years which included Multi-State Bar Exam on which applicant received scaled score of 145 or above. Applicant must meet age, good moral character and education requirements, and must have passed Multi-State Professional Responsibility Exam. Admission fee $625. Any applicant who was unsuccessful on Minnesota Exam may be eligible for admission without examination if licensed elsewhere and eligible by practice or by test score subsequent to failing Minnesota Exam.

Admission Pro Hac Vice.—Foreign attorneys may, in court's discretion, try or participate in trial or proceedings. (481.02).

Limited Practice.—Limited license to practice law available to individual admitted in another jurisdiction who is associated with legal services program in Minnesota. Admission fee $50.

Temporary License.—Applicant who has practiced law full-time for at least five of past seven years may receive 12-month license to practice in state solely for designated employer which is single corporation (or its subsidiaries), association, business or governmental entity engaged in business other than practice of law or provision of legal services. Fee is $825.

Powers.—Attorney may bind client at any stage of action or proceeding by agreement made in open court or in presence of clerk and entered in minutes by such clerk or made in writing and signed by such attorney. (481.08; 39 Minn. 355, 40 N.W. 262).

Attorneys may receive money claimed by client in action or special proceeding during its pendency, and within six years after judgment, upon payment thereof, may discharge claim or acknowledge satisfaction of judgment. (481.08). May, while authority to enforce and collect judgment continues, act for client in protecting and retaining same, and notice of proceedings affecting same must be served on attorney. (23 Minn. 518). But all such authority ceases on substitution of another attorney. May be required to produce authority to appear for client. (481.09). Attorney has no implied authority to compromise client's cause of action. (111 Minn. 183, 126 N.W. 731).

Compensation.—Upon petition of interested person, court may review reasonableness of compensation of attorney employed by personal representative in administration of estate. (524.3-721).

Substitution of Attorney for Nonresident.—In case attorney for nonresident ceases to act as such, other party may file with court administrator notice requiring substitution; and if nonresident fails to appoint new attorney or to appear in person within 30 days, nonresident is not entitled to notice of any subsequent proceeding. (481.12).

Lien.—Attorney has lien for compensation on cause of action from time of service of summons therein and upon judgment in action subordinate to rights of litigants; and, after filing notice of lien claim, on property wherever situated held by a third person in which client has an interest. (481.13). Lien is assignable (31 Minn. 201, 17 N.W. 337), and superior to claim of creditor in execution levied on judgment (39 Minn. 373, 40 N.W. 254).

Disbarment, etc.—As to grounds for disbarment, removal or suspension, see 481.15. Procedures specified in Rules on Lawyers Professional Responsibility adopted by Supreme Court.

Unauthorized Practice.—No person or association, except members of the bar, and no corporation (except an attorney's professional corporation organized under c. 319A) through its officers or employees may appear in any court of record to maintain or defend an action except in behalf of himself or itself or in certain cases involving rental property used for residential purposes and certain matters in conciliation court. Sole shareholder of corporation may appear on behalf of corporation. (481.02; 491A.02, Subd. 4).

Professional Associations.—See category Business Organizations, topic Corporations, subhead Professional Firms.

Registration of Attorneys.—Annual registration fee is $207 for attorneys admitted to practice more than three years, lesser fee for certain other classifications of attorneys. Penalty for nonpayment is automatic suspension of authorization to practice law in state.

Continuing Legal Education.—Every three years attorney must complete minimum of 45 hours of course work (of which three hours shall be devoted to legal ethics and two hours to eliminating bias), either as student or as lecturer, in continuing legal education in courses approved by State Board of Continuing Legal Education.

Attorney Ethics.—State Supreme Court has adopted American Bar Association Model Rules of Professional Conduct with modification. (Minnesota Rules of Professional Conduct).

MINERAL, WATER AND FISHING RIGHTS

MINES AND MINERALS:

Commissioner of Natural Resources has charge and control of minerals of state. (84.027).

State lands may be leased from the state for mining purposes, and prospecting permits may be issued. (c. 93).

Inspection.—There is an inspector of mines appointed by board of commissioners in every county where there are five mines or more in operation. Inspector has duty of visiting each mine at least once every 90 days and may do so more often. (c. 180).

Plural Ownership of Mineral Lands.—Where lands containing ore are owned by plurality of owners, owners of interest of one half or more may bring action in district court of county where lands situated, and court may authorize them to open mines upon filing sufficient bond for proper performance. They must account to court for their operations. Non-operating owners may enter lands to verify accounts at any time and are entitled to pro-rata share of profits. They may continue operation if work is abandoned. No liens, save judgment liens, can attach to such properties during operation. These sections apply only to output of workings of land, not lands themselves. (c. 560).

Filing of Severed Mineral Interests.—Owners of severed mineral interests where mineral interest is owned separately from fee title to surface of property upon or beneath which mineral interest exists, must file verified statement within one year after acquiring such mineral interests in office of county recorder or Registrar of Titles. (93.52). Failure to file results in forfeiture of mineral interests to state. (93.55).

Iron ore taxes and production taxes on certain other minerals imposed. (c. 298).

MORTGAGES

CHATTEL MORTGAGES:

Uniform Commercial Code adopted. (c. 336). For variations from 1962 Official Text see category Business Regulation and Commerce, topic Commercial Code.

Forms.—Secretary of State has prescribed uniform forms (see end of this Digest) for use in connection with filing under Uniform Commercial Code. (336.9-403). See category Business Regulation and Commerce, topic Commercial Code.

COLLATERAL SECURITY:

See category Debtor and Creditor, topic Pledges.

MORTGAGES OF PERSONAL PROPERTY:

See topic Chattel Mortgages.

MORTGAGES OF REAL PROPERTY:

Mortgage operates to create lien only, and is not conveyance enabling mortgagee to recover property without foreclosure, but statute provides that mortgagor may assign rents and profits from mortgaged real estate as additional security provided that mortgage (1) was executed subsequent to Aug. 1, 1977; (2) secures principal amount of $100,000 or more, or is lien upon residential property containing four or more dwelling units; and (3) is not lien upon property, homesteaded as agricultural, or residential property containing four or fewer dwelling units where at least one is homestead property. Any assignment of rents or profits from residential property of four or fewer units, however, may be enforced only against non-homestead portion. (559.17).

Deed absolute on its face may be proved a mortgage. (137 Minn. 450, 163 N.W. 746).

Execution.—Mortgage must be executed and acknowledged like deed (507.01, .24) and, in order to be entitled to record, name and address of draftsperson must appear on document with original signatures of notary public and executing party. (507.24). Lock-in agreements for interest rate or discount points must be written, and terms and conditions must be disclosed. Penalties for violation and unreasonable delay in processing loan application. (47.206).

Mortgage made outside of the state must be executed and proved in same manner as deed so made. See category Property, topic Deeds.

Recording.—Mortgages are recorded in office of county recorder, or registrar of titles if land is registered land, of county where real estate is located, and if not, are void as against subsequent bona fide purchasers or mortgagees recording their conveyances, or attaching or judgment creditors. (507.34).

Mortgages or deeds of trust covering easements or other less-than-fee-simple interests in real property securing debt of oil or gas pipeline company are filed with secretary of state. (300.115).

Recording Fees and Prerequisites.—See category Documents and Records, topic Records.

Taxes.—Mortgage registration tax is 23¢ on each $100 or fraction thereof of principal amount secured, excluding indeterminate amounts advanced to protect property or mortgage. (287.05). In Hennepin County, mortgage registration tax is 24¢ on each $100 or fraction thereof of principal amount secured. Additional $5 fee, on mortgages subject to mortgage registration tax and deeds subject to deed tax, collected in Anoka, Carver, Dakota, Douglas, Hennepin, Kandiyohi, Ramsey, Scott, Waseca, Washington, Winona, and Wright counties. (40A.152). If part of land is situate outside of Minnesota, tax is

MORTGAGES OF REAL PROPERTY . . . *continued*
based on value of land in Minnesota in proportion to value of whole. (287.05). Tax paid on maximum line of credit if revolving line of credit. (287.05). Tax is payable to county treasurer of county where land is situate. (287.08). No mortgage registration tax is due on contract for deed regardless of date of contract or whether contract was filed. (287.05).

Trust deeds are seldom used in place of mortgages.

Future Advances.—Mortgage may secure obligatory or voluntary future advances to be made by mortgagee from time to time after execution. However, priority of first mortgage will not extend to voluntary advances made by first mortgagee with notice of subsequent mortgage. (134 Minn. 156, 158 N.W. 918).

Reverse mortgage loans authorized. (47.58).

Graduated payment mortgages authorized. (47.201).

Priorities.—Mortgage first recorded has priority unless taken with actual notice of earlier mortgage. (54 Minn. 486, 56 N.W. 131).

Assignment.—Recording of assignment of mortgage is not of itself notice to mortgagor, his heirs or personal representatives so as to invalidate payment made by them or either of them to mortgagee. (507.32). But where debt is not due, maker cannot pay payee and defeat recovery by bona fide indorsee. (29 Minn. 177, 12 N.W. 517).

Release.—Mortgagee may release either personal liability or real security; release of one does not affect the other. (13 Minn. 301, 13 Gil. 278).

Conveyance of Mortgaged Premises by Mortgagor.—Purchaser of mortgaged premises becomes personally liable for mortgage debt by assuming and agreeing to pay it only if mortgagor was personally liable therefor. (117 Minn. 267, 135 N.W. 746).

Conveyance of premises by mortgagor to mortgagee raises no presumption that it was given as further security. (559.18).

Rights of Junior Mortgagee.—Junior mortgagee may pay overdue taxes or insurance premiums or unpaid installments due on prior lien and make debt part of his own. (580.29).

Satisfaction.—Mortgage may be discharged by filing for record certificate of its satisfaction executed and acknowledged by mortgagee, his representatives or assigns, in manner of conveyance. (507.40). Upon written request, good and valid satisfaction of mortgage in recordable form must be delivered to any party paying full and final balance of mortgage indebtedness; such delivery must be in hand or by certified mail postmarked within 45 days of receipt of request to holder of any interest of record in said mortgage and within 45 days of payment of all sums due thereon. Noncomplying lender liable for $500 civil penalty plus actual damages. (47.208).

Foreclosure.—

By advertisement: Where mortgage contains power of sale it may be foreclosed by advertisement. (580.01). Prerequisites for foreclosure are: (1) Default in condition of mortgage by which power to sell becomes operative; (2) no action is pending on debt; (3) mortgage and assignments thereof recorded (580.02); (4) six weeks published notice required (580.03); and (5) service of such notice, as with civil summons, on one in possession of premises, at least four weeks before sale. Notice must specify: (1) Names of mortgagor, mortgagee, and assignee and original principal amount secured by mortgage; (2) date of mortgage, when and where recorded or, if registered land, when and where registered; (3) amount claimed to be due and taxes paid by mortgagee; (4) description of premises; (5) time and place of sale; (6) time allowed by law for redemption by mortgagor; (7) if foreclosing party wishes to preserve right to reduce redemption period after first publication of notice, notice must state in capital letters that time allowed for redemption may be reduced (580.04); and (8) name of each mortgagor released from mortgage (580.04, 580.045). Where attorney forecloses, his authority must appear by power of attorney executed and recorded in same manner as conveyance. (580.05).

By action: Foreclosure by action is conducted like any ordinary civil suit (581.01), judgment being entered for amount due and ordering sale of premises except as provided for in c. 581. Certified transcript of judgment is authority to sheriff to make sale. (581.03). State may be made party if it has or claims mortgage or other lien. (582.13).

Mortgage may be foreclosed for failure to pay any installment of principal or interest. (580.09).

Receiver may be appointed to collect rents and apply same on taxes and repairs where mortgagor is committing waste and is insolvent, provided that security is inadequate. Second mortgagee may secure appointment of receiver when interest on first mortgage is unpaid. (151 Minn. 181, 186 N.W. 299). Statutory authorization for receiver if assignment of rents or other conditions satisfied. (559.17, 576.01).

If owner or junior lienor pays actual amount of default with interest disbursements, and greater of $150 or one half of authorized attorney's fees before sale, foreclosure action is dismissed. (580.30).

Strict foreclosure may be ordered when just or appropriate, but final decree cannot be made until one year after judgment. (581.12).

Attorney's fees are regulated by statute, depending on amount of mortgage debt. (582.01).

Mandatory Mediation.—

Notice of Right to Mediation.—Any creditor seeking to enforce debt of more than $5,000 against agricultural property (except "agriculturally related business"), including personal and real property, whether action is mortgage foreclosure, contract for deed termination, attachment, seizure, repossession, replevin, levy or execution, must serve personal notice on debtor after default in security agreement in statutory form of right to mediate debt through local agricultural extension service office. (336.9-501; 550.365; 559.209; 582.039; 583). These statutes do not apply to debtor who owns and leases less than 60 acres if debtor has less than $20,000 in gross sales in preceding year, or other debts specifically exempted in statute. (583.24). Notice must also be served on director of agricultural extension service. (582.039).

Request for Mediation.—Debtor has 14 days after receiving notice to request mediation by filing request form with agricultural extension service. (583.26). Request form must state all known creditors. (583.26). All time periods applicable to collection proceedings are suspended once meditation is initiated until 90 days after date debtor files mediation notice. (583.26). Creditor may begin proceedings sooner if mediator's affidavit is received stating debtor is not acting in good faith or five days after parties reach written agreement which has not been rescinded. (583.26). If mediation is not requested within 14 days, no mediation is required and creditor may proceed to exercise rights. (583.26). Once mediation request has been filed, agricultural extension service must provide orientation meeting at least five days before initial mediation meeting, and financial analyst to review and, if necessary, prepare debtor's financial records before initial mediation meeting. (583.26).

Notice of Initial Mediation Meeting.—Within ten days after receiving mediation request, director of agricultural extension service must send first mediation meeting notice to debtor and all known creditors with debts secured by agricultural property and all known unsecured creditors that are necessary for debtor's farm operation. (583.26). Proposed mediators may be vetoed by creditors and debtor; creditors and debtor may jointly choose professional mediator. (583.26). First mediation meeting must be held within 20 days of mediation meeting notice. (583.26).

Mediation period may last up to 60 days from date of first meeting. (583.26). Creditor with security interest in farm machinery has lien for rental value of farm machinery during mediation. (514.661). Contract for deed vendor has lien for reasonable rental value of property during mediation. (559.2091). Disputes as to market value are resolved by appraiser. (583.27).

Other Creditors.—Any creditor who has been notified by director of mediation meeting and does not object to agreement is bound by it. (583.26). After mediation agreement is reached, mediator must notify all creditors who have filed claim forms, and those creditors may file written objections within ten days after receiving notice. (583.28). Mediator has ten days after receiving objection to meet with debtors and creditors to attempt to work out new agreement. (583.28).

Failure to Mediate in Good Faith.—All parties (creditors and debtor) must mediate in good faith. (583.27). If mediator files affidavit with director and parties that creditor did not mediate in good faith, and debtor requests court supervised mediation, court must require further mediation for up to 60 days. (583.27). If court finds that creditor did not participate in mediation in good faith, court can further suspend creditor's remedies for additional period of 180 days. (583.27). Debtor who does not participate in good faith may be ineligible for mediation. (583.27).

Crop Rights on Foreclosed Land.—Where planting crop owner's right to harvest crops is involuntarily terminated before crops are harvested, person buying or leasing property must satisfy planting crop owner's lien by either compensating him for crop value or by allowing him to enter property and harvest crops and charging him fair market rental value of property for remainder of growing period. (557.12). If new owner or lessor of property does not notify planting crop owner within 30 days after taking over that he may harvest crop, then that new owner or lessor must compensate planting crop owner for crop value. (557.12). Planting crop owner may perfect lien for crop value by filing financing statement covering crop and crop products within 90 days after his right to harvest is terminated, and also by filing lien, in nature of mechanic's lien, against real estate within 120 days after crop was harvested or, if not harvested, 12 months after crop was planted. (557.12). New owner or lessor who permits planting crop owner to harvest also has lien against crops and crop products for fair market rental value of land. (557.12). Lien may be perfected by filing financing statement. (557.12). Judgments for debts on agricultural property owed by farmer/debtor may not be executed upon real or personal property after three years from date judgment was entered. (550.366). See category Debtor and Creditor, topic Liens, subheads Planting Crop Owner's Lien and Agricultural Landlord Lien.

Sales.—Land must be sold in separate tracts (580.08), unless, where foreclosure is by action, court orders sale of whole tract as most beneficial to interests of parties (581.04). Debtor has right to separate sale of designated homestead property (unless property cannot be divided without material injury); whenever real property is sold on execution and mortgage foreclosures, statutorily prescribed notice, in ten point capitalized letters, must set forth debtor's right to designate part of real property as homestead, to have designated homestead portion sold separately, and to redeem separately each portion of property; applies to all foreclosures or executions commenced on or after July 1, 1987. Notice is not to be published. (550.175, 582.041, 582.042). Upon objection to homestead designation, executing creditor is entitled to court-approved designation of homestead and/or court determination of value. (550.175). If court determines that value of claimed designation exceeds amount of homestead exemption, court shall order sale of entire property. (550.175). Debtor is then paid amount of homestead exemption out of proceeds. (550.175). Balance is applied to execution. (550.175). Sale under foreclosure by advertisement may be postponed by executing party, from time to time, by inserting notice in newspaper in which original advertisement was published and continuing until sale. (580.07). Where foreclosure is by action, postponement is by court order.

Right of First Refusal.—State or federal agency (other than commissioner of agriculture pursuant to security program), limited partnership or corporate owner of farmland (other than family farm corporation or authorized farm corporation) may not lease or sell agricultural land or farm homestead that was acquired by enforcing debt against agricultural land or farm homestead (including by accepting deed in lieu of foreclosure or cancellation) before offering or making good faith effort to offer land for sale or lease to immediately preceding prior owner at price no higher than highest price offered by proposed buyer or lessee. (500.245). Only family farm, family farm corporation or family farm partnership can be immediately preceding owner. (500.245). Selling or leasing property to third party is prima facie evidence that price is acceptable to seller or lessor. (500.245). Form of notice of offer is statutorily prescribed. (500.245). Notice must be personally delivered (with signed receipt) or sent by certified mail (with signed receipt) to immediately preceding owner's last known address. Notice must give informal description of property, as well as terms of proposed sale or lease to third party, and deadline for meeting proposed offer. (500.245). Copy of proposed purchase agreement or lease with third party must be included with notice, along with affidavit by seller or lessor that purchase agreement or lease is true, accurate and made in good faith. Notice must inform immediately preceding owner that three-year statute of limitations on actions for damages (other than fraud) accrues on date conveyance is recorded.

MORTGAGES OF REAL PROPERTY . . . *continued*
(500.245). Identity of third party may, at lessor's discretion, be deleted from purchase agreement or lease. (500.245). Offer to immediately preceding owner must be same cash price from third party which is acceptable to seller or lessor or, for time-price offer by third party, either same time-price terms or equivalent cash offer. (500.245). Prior owner has ten days after exercising right to lease or buy to fully perform according to terms of offer, including paying amounts due. Prior owner may elect to purchase or lease entire property or contiguous and compact portion of property. (500.245). If prior owner does not accept offer, or does not perform obligations of offer within ten days after acceptance, seller may sell and lessor may lease to third party in accordance with their lease or purchase agreement. (500.245). Seller or lessor may record prima facie evidence of termination of right of first refusal in form of affidavit stating that identical offer was made to former owner; time period for exercising right to buy has expired, former owner did not exercise its right to buy or exercised its right to buy but did not perform within ten days; and offer to former owner has terminated. (500.245). Former owner's rights under 500.245 may not be extinguished or limited by express statement in deed in lieu of foreclosure, deed in lieu of termination of contract for deed, instrument conveying rights to state or federal agency, instrument curing title defects, or deed to vendee of former owner. Other than as stated above, former owner's right to lease or purchase agricultural land under 500.245(6) may not be assigned or transferred other than to family members or by inheritance. (500.245). Right of first refusal must be exercised within 15 days (for leases) or 65 days (for sales) of receipt of offer. (500.245). Law applies for ten years after acquiring title if property was acquired before May 1, 1988, but only five years if acquired on or after May 1, 1988. (500.245). Offer to lease to immediately preceding owner is required only until immediately preceding owner fails to accept offer to lease property or property is sold; offer to sell to immediately preceding former owner is required until property is sold. (500.245).

Mortgagee or his representative may purchase at foreclosure sale. (580.11; 581.05). Surplus goes to mortgagor. (580.10; 581.06).

Where sale is by advertisement, officer making sale makes and delivers to purchaser certificate of sale containing description of mortgage and land, price paid, time and place of sale, name of purchaser, and time for redemption, provided that if certificate states five week redemption period and longer redemption period was stated in notice, certified copy of court order authorizing reduction of redemption period must be attached to certificate. (580.12). Certificate which states five week redemption period must be recorded within ten days after sale; any other certificate must be recorded within 20 days thereafter; in either case, certificate operates as conveyance of land after expiration of time of redemption. Certificates may not contain times for redemption less than those required by applicable statutes. (580.12). Within ten days after recording certificate of sale, affidavit of costs paid must be filed with county recorder. (580.17). Action to set aside sale because of certain defects, including defective notice, must be commenced within five years (excluding disabilities) thereafter (580.20); for defects other than those so specified, limitation period is 15 years (580.21). There are numerous curative acts, however.

When sale is by order of court, upon report of sale, court may grant order confirming it or may order new sale (581.08), and clerk enters satisfaction of judgment to extent of sum bid for premises, less expenses and costs. (581.09). If sale is confirmed, sheriff executes certificate of sale, to be recorded within 20 days. (581.08).

Deficiency.—In cases of foreclosure by advertisement, where amount realized is less than amount due on mortgage, independent action may be brought for deficiency unless statutory redemption period is six months or five weeks. (582.30). Amount is entered in full satisfaction of judgment unless deficiency is allowed under 582.30, in which event balance of judgment remaining unpaid may be executed and satisfied in same manner as personal judgment against mortgagor. (581.09). In cases of foreclosure involving mortgages on agricultural production property entered into after Mar. 21, 1986, deficiency judgment and determination of fair market value of property must be filed, if at all, within 90 days after foreclosure sale; for mortgages on such property entered into before Mar. 22, 1986, procedure is same except that deficiency judgment may not be executed until Mar. 22, 1987 (582.30); in either case, amount of deficiency judgment is difference between amount owed and fair market value as determined by jury (582.30); limit on execution of all deficiency judgments or personal judgments is three years (582.30). Creditor enforcing agricultural mortgage may obtain either personal judgment or foreclosure on mortgage and deficiency judgment, if allowed. (582.31).

Redemption.—Mortgagor may redeem within six months after sale if foreclosure was by advertisement, or within six months after confirmation of sale if foreclosure was by action, by paying sum for which premises were sold, with interest as provided by mortgage, not to exceed 8% if foreclosed by action, and 6% if not so provided, and additional cost. Mortgagor has 12 months to redeem if: (1) mortgage was executed prior to July 1, 1967; (2) amount owing on date of notice of foreclosure sale is less than two-thirds of original principal amount secured by mortgage; (3) mortgage was executed prior to July 1, 1987, and mortgaged premises exceeded ten acres on date of execution of mortgage; (4) mortgage was executed prior to Aug. 1, 1984, and mortgage premises exceed ten acres, do not exceed 40 acres, and were in agricultural use on date of execution of mortgage; (5) mortgaged premises, as of date of execution of mortgage, exceeded 40 acres; or (6) mortgage was executed on or after Aug. 1, 1984, and mortgaged premises exceed ten acres, do not exceed 40 acres, and were in agricultural use on date of execution of mortgage. Affidavit by mortgagor and certificate signed by county assessor stating mortgaged premises are not in agricultural use may be recorded against mortgaged premises as prima facie evidence of facts therein alleged. (580.23; 581.10). Redemption period is reduced to two months if mortgagor and mortgagee have agreed to voluntary foreclosure. (582.32). Purchaser at sale has same rights with respect to overdue taxes, insurance premiums or interest or installments on prior mortgage as purchaser at execution. (582.03. See category Debtor and Creditor, topic Executions.) Owner or junior lienor may reinstate mortgage by paying all amounts actually due prior to foreclosure sale. (580.30). Amount actually due refers only to delinquent payments, not to accelerated balance after default. (293 Minn. 44, 196 N.W.2d 473).

Creditor having lien on premises may redeem within five days after redemption period has expired if he files notice of intention during redemption period with county recorder or registrar of titles if property is registered. Creditors redeem in order of priority (from senior to junior) with each creditor getting successive five-day redemption period. (580.24; 581.10). Creditor of estate of decedent may redeem lands of decedent. (550.30). One desiring to redeem must offer money necessary and proof of right to redeem. Documents must be recorded within 24 hours. (580.25). He is then entitled to certificate of redemption executed in manner of conveyance, containing name of one redeeming, amount paid, description of sale from which redemption is made and of property, and statement of claim upon which redemption made. This must be filed within four days with county recorder or registrar of titles if property is registered. (580.26). If time for redemption will expire during pendency of action to set aside mortgage as fraudulent or void, right to redeem may be preserved (although action ultimately fails) by deposit with sheriff of amount for which premises sold with interest to date of deposit, together with bond conditioned to pay interest which may accrue, sheriff being directed to retain money and bond until final judgment (580.28).

Until time for redemption expires mortgagor, is entitled to possession of premises and rents and profits therefrom. (135 Minn. 443, 161 N.W. 165).

Redemption of Homesteads.—Debtor has right to separate redemption of homestead property from remaining property. (550.175). If sheriff receives homestead property designation to which executing creditor does not object or which court approves, sheriff must offer and sell designated homestead property separately from other property. (550.175). Debtor may then redeem designated homestead or remaining property, or both, separately. (550.175).

Forms.—Following are forms of mortgage, and assignment, satisfaction and partial release thereof by individuals and corporations:

Forms

Short Form of Mortgage (507.15).—

This statutory mortgage, made this . . . . . . day of . . . ., 19. . . ., between (give name and address) mortgagor, and (give name and address) mortgagee,

Witnesseth, that to secure the payment of (give description of indebtedness and instruments evidencing same), the mortgagor, hereby mortgages to the mortgagee (give description of premises "subject to" any incumbrances thereon).

And (. . . . . ., one of) the mortgagor covenants with the mortgagee the following statutory covenants: 1. To warrant the title to the premises. 2. To pay the indebtedness as herein provided. 3. To pay all taxes. 4. To keep the buildings insured against fire for $. . . . . ., and against (give other hazards insured against and amount of such other insurance) for the protection of the mortgagee. 5. That the premises shall be kept in repair and no waste shall be committed. 6. That the whole of the principal sum shall become due after default in the payment of any installment of principal or interest, or of any tax, or in the performance of any other covenant, at the option of the mortgagee.

If default be made in any payment or covenant herein, the mortgagee shall have the statutory power of sale, and on foreclosure may retain statutory costs and attorney's fees.

In witness whereof the mortgagor has duly executed this mortgage. (Or use other testimonium clause. Add signatures, acknowledgment and draftsperson identity.)

Assignment by Individual.—

KNOW ALL MEN BY THESE PRESENTS, That . . . . . ., part . . . . of the first part, in consideration of the sum of . . . . . . dollars, in hand paid by . . . . . ., part . . . . of the second part, receipt whereof is hereby acknowledged, do . . . . hereby sell, assign, transfer, and set over, to said part . . . . of the second part, ... and assigns, that certain mortgage executed by . . . . . . as mortgagor . . . . to . . . . . . as mortgagee . . . ., bearing date the . . . . . . day of . . . . . ., 19. . . ., filed for record in the office of the Register of Deeds (Registrar of Titles) of . . . . . . County, Minnesota, on . . . . . ., 19. . . ., and recorded in Book . . . . . . of Mortgages, page . . . ., as Document No. . . . . . together with all right and interest in the land therein described, and in the note . . . . and obligations therein specified, and to the debt thereby secured; and do . . . . hereby constitute and appoint said part . . . . of the second part . . . . . . attorney . . . . irrevocable to collect and receive said debt, and to foreclose, enforce, and satisfy said mortgage the same as the assignor might or could have done were these presents not executed, but at the cost and expense of second part . . . . and do . . . . hereby covenant with said part . . . . of the second part, ... and assigns, that there is still due and unpaid of the debt secured by said mortgage the sum of . . . . . . dollars, with interest thereon at . . . . . . per cent per annum from the . . . . . . day of . . . . . ., 19. . . ., and that first part . . . . ha . . . . good right to sell, assign, and transfer the same.

In Testimony Whereof, the said part . . . . of the first part ha . . . . hereunto set . . . . . . hand . . . . this . . . . . . day of . . . . . ., 19. . . . .

(Add signatures, acknowledgment and draftsperson identity.)

Assignment by Corporation.—

KNOW ALL MEN BY THESE PRESENTS, That . . . . . ., a corporation duly organized and existing under the laws of the State of . . . . . ., party of the first part, in consideration of the sum of . . . . . . dollars, in hand paid by . . . . . ., part . . . . of the second part, receipt whereof is hereby acknowledged, does hereby sell, assign, transfer, and set over, to said part . . . . of the second part, ... and assigns, that certain mortgage executed by . . . . . . as mortgagor . . . . to . . . . . . as mortgagee . . . ., bearing date the . . . . . . day of . . . . . ., 19. . . ., filed for record in the office of the Register of Deeds (Registrar of Titles) of the County of . . . . . . and State of Minnesota, on the . . . . . . day of . . . . . ., 19. . . ., as Document No. . . . . . . together with all right and interest in the land therein described, and in the note . . . . and obligations therein specified, and to the debt thereby secured; and hereby constitutes and appoints said part . . . . of the second part . . . . . . its attorney . . . . irrevocable to collect and receive said debt, and to foreclose, enforce, and satisfy said mortgage the same as it might or could have done were these presents not executed, but at the cost and expense of second part . . . ., and does hereby covenant with said part . . . . of the second part, ... and assigns, that there is still due and unpaid of the debt secured by said mortgage the sum of . . . . . . dollars, with interest thereon at . . . . . . per cent per annum from the . . . . . . day of . . . . . ., 19. . . ., and that it has good right to sell, assign, and transfer the same.

See note at head of Digest as to 1998 legislation covered.

See Topical Index in front part of this volume.

MN – 41

MORTGAGES OF REAL PROPERTY . . . *continued*

In Testimony Whereof, the said first party has caused these presents to be executed in its corporate name by its . . . . . . President and its . . . . . . and its corporate seal to be hereunto affixed this . . . . . ., day of . . . . . ., 19. . . . .
        (Add signatures, acknowledgment and draftsperson identity.)

Satisfaction by Individual.—

KNOW ALL MEN BY THESE PRESENTS, That a certain Indenture of Mortgage now owned by the undersigned, bearing date the . . . . . . day of . . . . . ., 19. . . ., made and executed by . . . . . ., as mortgagor . . . ., to . . . . ., as mortgagee . . . ., and recorded in the office of the Register of Deeds (Registrar of Titles) in and for the County of . . . . . . and State of Minnesota, on the . . . . . . day of . . . . . ., 19. . . ., as Document No. . . . . . ., is, with the indebtedness thereby secured, fully paid and satisfied. And the Register of Deeds (Registrar of Titles) of said County is hereby authorized and directed to discharge the same upon the record thereof, according to the statute in such case provided.

In Testimony Whereof, the undersigned ha. . . . hereunto set . . . . . hand . . . . this . . . . . . day of . . . . . ., 19. . . . .
        (Add signatures, acknowledgment and draftsperson identity.)

Satisfaction by Corporation.—

KNOW ALL MEN BY THESE PRESENTS, That a certain Indenture of Mortgage, now owned by the undersigned, a corporation existing under the laws of the State of . . . . . ., bearing date the . . . . . . day of . . . . . ., 19. . . ., made and executed by . . . . . ., as mortgagor . . . ., to . . . . . ., as mortgagee . . . ., and recorded in the Office of the Register of Deeds (Registrar of Titles) in and for the County of . . . . . . and State of Minnesota, on the . . . . . . day of . . . . . ., 19. . . ., as Document No. . . . . . ., is, with the indebtedness thereby secured, fully paid and satisfied. And the Register of Deeds (Registrar of Titles) of said County is hereby authorized and directed to discharge the same upon the record thereof, according to the statute in such case provided.

In Testimony Whereof, the said corporation has caused these presents to be executed in its corporate name by its . . . . . . President and its . . . . . and its corporate seal to be hereunto affixed this . . . . . . day of . . . . . ., 19. . . . .
[Seal] (Add signatures, acknowledgment and draftsperson identity.)

Partial Release by Individual.—

KNOW ALL MEN BY THESE PRESENTS, That the undersigned owner of the mortgage hereinafter described, for a valuable consideration, receipt whereof is hereby acknowledged, do . . . . hereby forever discharge and release the tract . . . . of land lying and being in the County of . . . . . ., State of Minnesota, described as follows, to wit: . . . . from all claims and liens of and under that certain mortgage, dated the . . . . . . day of . . . . . ., 19. . . ., executed by . . . . . . as mortgagor . . . ., to . . . . . ., as mortgagee . . . ., filed for record in the office of the Register of Deeds (Registrar of Titles) in and for said county on the . . . . . . day of . . . . . ., 19. . . ., as Document No. . . . . . ., page . . . . . ., covering the above described and other land.

In Testimony Whereof, the undersigned ha . . . . hereunto set . . . . . hand . . . . this . . . . . . day of . . . . . ., 19. . . . .
        (Add signatures, acknowledgment and draftsperson identity.)

Partial Release by Corporation.—

KNOW ALL MEN BY THESE PRESENTS, That the undersigned, a corporation under the laws of the State of . . . . . ., owner of the mortgage hereinafter described, for a valuable consideration, receipt whereof is hereby acknowledged, does forever discharge and release the tract . . . . of land lying and being in the County of . . . . . ., State of Minnesota, described as follows, to wit: . . . . from all claims and liens of and under that certain mortgage, dated the . . . . . . day of . . . . . ., 19. . . ., executed by . . . . . . as mortgagor . . . . ., to . . . . . ., as mortgagee . . . . ., filed for record in the office of the Register of Deeds (Registrar of Titles) of . . . . . . County, Minnesota, on . . . . . ., 19. . . ., as Document No. . . . . . ., covering the above described and other land.

In Testimony Whereof, the said corporation has caused these presents to be executed in its corporate name by its . . . . . . President, and its . . . . . . and its corporate seal to be hereunto affixed this . . . . . . day of . . . . . ., 19. . . . .
        (Add signatures, acknowledgment and draftsperson identity.)

For other Uniform Conveyancing Blanks, see c. 507.

Chattel Mortgages.—See topic Chattel Mortgages.

PROPERTY

ABSENTEES:

Care of Property.—Property situated within or without state of anyone who has disappeared or absconded from place where last known to be and who has no agent in state and whose whereabouts is unknown, or who leaves dependents, may be taken possession of by court and put into hands of receiver upon three weeks published and posted notice, copy of notice being mailed to absentee at his last known address and to all persons who claim interest in property. If absentee does not return within four years, court may enter order establishing death as matter of law and ordering distribution of property under probate proceedings. (576.04-16).

Beneficiary under insurance policy on absentee's life who is absentee's spouse, child or other dependent, and who has no other source of adequate support, may petition court for order directing periodic advance payments by insurer. Payments by insurer under order discharge it from liability on policy to extent of amounts paid. (576.121-123).

Process Agent.—Any nonresident owning or claiming any interest in lands within state may appoint resident agent for service, except in tax matters, by filing written designation with Secretary of State. (557.01). See also category Civil Actions and Procedure, topic Process.

Escheat.—See category Estates and Trusts, topics Descent and Distribution, subhead Escheat, Wills, subhead Unclaimed Assets.

Revised Uniform Disposition of Unclaimed Property Act adopted with modifications. Period after which property presumed abandoned reduced to three years in many cases. (345.31-.60).

ADVERSE POSSESSION:

Title to any real estate, except registered land (508.02) or public streets, parks, etc. and public or private cemeteries (541.01), may be acquired by adverse possession.

Duration of Possession.—Action for recovery of real estate or possession thereof cannot be maintained unless plaintiff, his ancestor, predecessor or grantor was seized or possessed of premises in question within 15 years before beginning of action. (541.02).

Easements, by analogy, may be acquired by prescription after 15 years continuous adverse use. (36 Minn. 273, 30 N.W. 886).

Disabilities.—See category Civil Actions and Procedure, topic Limitation of Actions.

CONVEYANCES:

See topic Deeds.

CURTESY:

Abolished. For statutory interest in lieu of curtesy see category Estates and Trusts, topic Descent and Distribution.

DEEDS:

See topic Real Property for types of estates.

Execution.—To entitle deed to record, must be executed and acknowledged. (507.24). Instrument must contain original signatures of parties and notary public. (507.24). See categories Debtor and Creditor, topic Homesteads, subhead Alienation or Encumbrance; Documents and Records, topic Acknowledgments; Family, topic Husband and Wife, subhead Conveyances.

Recording.—Deed executed as aforesaid may be recorded in office of county recorder, or registrar of titles if land is registered land, of county where land is situated. (507.24).

Unrecorded deed is void as against subsequent purchaser in good faith for valuable consideration whose deed is first duly recorded, as against any attachment levied on property, and as against any judgment lawfully obtained against person in whose name title to property appears of record obtained prior to recording of such deed. (507.34).

No deed or contract for deed or mortgage may be recorded unless name and address of person who or corporation which drafted instrument is printed, typewritten, stamped or written in legible manner thereon. (507.091). Following form accepted: "This instrument was drafted by . . . . (name) . . . . (address)."

No deed or contract for deed can be recorded until name and address of taxpayer to whom future tax statements are to be sent is indicated on instrument. (507.092). Contract for deed must be recorded within four months after execution or penalty of 2% of principal amount of contract debt is imposed as lien on property. (507.235).

Before deed or other instrument conveying land can be recorded, county auditor of county wherein land is situated must certify that there are no delinquent taxes on land to be conveyed or that taxes have been paid by sale where land has been sold or assigned to a purchaser for taxes. (272.12).

Deed or other instrument must also contain statement of grantor or grantee, or successor in interest, setting forth amount of realty transfer tax due or that it is exempt from tax. Certificate of value by grantor, grantee or legal agent must be filed in county when deed presented for recording and must state full actual consideration and financing terms and conditions of sale and tax classification of property. Items and value of personal property transferred with real property must be listed and deducted from sale price. (272.115, 287.241).

Recording Fees and Prerequisites.—See category Documents and Records, topic Records.

Restrictions against alienation to any class on account of religious faith, creed, race, or color cannot be given effect. (507.18).

Duty to Disclose Incumbrances.—When real property is conveyed or mortgaged, grantor must make known nature and existence of any known incumbrances, by exception in deed or otherwise. (507.20). Any conveyance containing covenant against incumbrances when incumbrance, known or not, appears of record, imposes upon grantor liability for all damages sustained in removing same. (507.21).

Corporation authorized to hold real estate may convey same by agent appointed by resolution of its directors for that purpose, copy of which, certified by clerk or secretary of such corporation, may be recorded in office of county recorder of county where land to which such vote relates is situated. (507.05). Corporate seal need not be affixed to deed or other conveyancing instrument to permit its recording.

Conveyance made outside of state may be executed in accordance with Minnesota law or laws or place of execution. (507.24).

Contract for Deed.—When default is made in conditions of any contract for conveyance of real estate or any interest therein that gives seller right to terminate it, written notice of termination must be given, served in same manner as summons in civil action, notwithstanding any contract provisions to contrary. General rule is that unexercised option conveys no interest in real estate and therefore need not be cancelled pursuant to 559.21. (310 Minn. 256, 246 N.W.2d 170). Contracts executed before Aug. 2, 1976 may be terminated within 30 days specified notice and opportunity to cure (559.21); contracts executed before May 1, 1980 may be terminated with 30 days specified notice and opportunity to cure if purchaser has paid less than 30% of purchase price paid, 45 days specified notice and opportunity to cure if 30% to less than 50% has been paid or 60 days specified notice and opportunity to cure if more than 50% paid (559.21); contracts executed before Aug. 1, 1985 may be terminated with 30 days specified notice and opportunity to cure if less than 10% paid, 60 days specified notice and opportunity to

DEEDS . . . *continued*
cure if more than 10% and less than 25% has been paid or 90 days specified notice and opportunity to cure if 25% or more paid (559.21); contracts executed after July 31, 1985 may be terminated with 60 days notice, except for earnest money contracts, purchase agreements and options exercised subject to 559.21, which may be terminated on 30 days notice unless by their terms they provide for longer termination period. (559.21). Notice must state amount required for purchaser to cure default, that purchaser may be eligible for extension of time in bold type, capitalized letters, or other form quickly and easily distinguishable from rest of notice, and address to which payment pursuant to notice may be sent. (559.21).

Taxes.—Realty transfer tax at rate of $1.65 for consideration of $500 or less (including no consideration and transfers pursuant to mergers, consolidations and reorganizations) plus $1.65 for each additional $500 or fraction of that amount is imposed on each deed, instrument, or writing conveying real estate after June 30, 1987, exclusive of value of lien or encumbrance remaining, but including value of personal property located on real property and including purchase of tax-forfeited lands. (287.21). Tax does not apply to mortgages, leases, executory contracts for deed, plats, deeds for cemetery lots, deeds for distribution by personal representatives, wills, instruments where U.S. or agency or instrumentality thereof is grantor, assignor, transferror, conveyor, grantee or assignee, any deed to or from co-owners partitioning undivided interests in property, any deed relating to exchange of school fund lands, any referee's or sheriff's certificate of sale from foreclosure sale or certificate of redemption therefrom issued to redeeming mortgagor, any deed or instrument which grants, creates, modifies or cancels easement, any deed or instrument between parties to marital dissolution, or on consideration paid for improvement in new residential construction, if deed tax on such consideration has been paid before first residential owners take possession of improvement. (287.22-287.221). No mortgage registry tax imposed to record contract for deed. (287.05). Additional $5 fee, on mortgages subject to mortgage registration tax and deeds subject to deed tax, collected in Anoka, Carver, Dakota, Hennepin, Ramsey, Scott, Waseca, Washington, Winona, and Wright counties. (40A.152). See category Mortgages, topic Mortgages of Real Property, subhead Taxes.

Forms

Warranty deed (short form): A. B., grantor, of (here insert the place of residence), for and in consideration of (here insert the consideration), conveys and warrants to C. D., grantee, of (here insert place of residence), the following described real estate in the County of . . . . . . in the State of Minnesota: (here describe the premises). Dated this . . . . . . day of . . . . . ., 19 . . . .
(Add signatures, acknowledgment and draft person identity.)

Above form covenants as to lawful seizing in fee simple and right to convey, against incumbrances, for quiet possession, and that grantor will defend title. (507.07).

Quit-claim deed (short form): A. B., grantor, of (here insert the place of residence), for the consideration of (here insert the consideration), conveys and quitclaims to C. D., the grantee, of (here insert the place of residence), all interest in the following described real estate in the county of . . . ., in the state of Minnesota: (here describe the premises).
Dated this . . . . . . day of . . . . . ., 19. . . .
(Add signatures, acknowledgment and draft person identity.)

Above form conveys interest of grantor, but does not extend to after acquired title unless expressly provided. (507.07).

For Uniform Conveyancing Blanks, see appendix following c. 507.

DEEDS OF TRUST:

See category Mortgages, topic Mortgages of Real Property.

DOWER:

Abolished. (519.09). For statutory interest in lieu of dower, see category Estates and Trusts, topic Descent and Distribution.

ESCHEAT:

See topic Absentees; category Estates and Trusts, topics Descent and Distribution, subhead Escheat, Wills, subhead Unclaimed Assets.

LANDLORD AND TENANT:

Leases.—Lease for one year or less need not be in writing; for more than one year, must be in writing (513.04); for more than three years, must be executed like deed (8 Minn. 524, 8 Gil. 467) and recorded in order to be valid against third persons without actual notice (507.01, .34). However, possession under unrecorded lease puts third persons on inquiry as to tenant's rights. (4 Minn. 282, 4 Gil. 201; 182 Minn. 244, 234 N.W. 320). Landlord is not obligated to be reasonable in consenting to assignment or sublet of lease which contains anti-assignment clause or which provides only that tenant must secure landlord's consent. (353 N.W.2d 198; 339 N.W.2d 901).

Rent.—If premises be destroyed without any fault or neglect on tenant's part or injured by elements or any other cause so as to become untenantable or unfit for occupancy, tenant is not liable for rent thereafter, unless otherwise expressly provided in writing. (504.05). Tenant may continue to occupy after building is repaired. (39 Minn. 385, 40 N.W. 361). To relieve himself from paying future rent, however, he must surrender premises within reasonable time. (47 Minn. 462, 50 N.W. 601). Burden on tenant to prove destruction or injury. (56 Minn. 1, 57 N.W. 157).

Liens.—No statutory provisions for landlord's liens except in connection with unlawful detainer proceedings. See infra, subhead Dispossession.

Where tenant is compelled to pay taxes which should have been paid by landlord, he may file notice with county recorder where land is located, giving amount and date of payment and description of land, which procedure will give him lien on land. (272.45). See category Debtor and Creditor, topic Liens, subheads Agricultural Landlord Lien and Planting Crop Owner's Lien.

Termination of Tenancy.—Estates at will may be determined by either party, by three months notice in writing given to other party; and when rent is payable at period of less than three months, time of such notice is sufficient if it is equal to interval between times of payment, and in all case of neglect or refusal to pay rent due on lease at will, 14 days notice to quit, given in writing by landlord, is sufficient to determine lease. (504.06).

Tenancy from year to year exists as at common law, except that notice must be given in writing at least three months prior to end of second and subsequent years. (47 Minn. 1, 49 N.W. 327). Automatic renewal provisions in year-to-year residential leases are restricted in that landlord must serve notice on tenant, either in person or by certified mail at least 15 and not more than 30 days before time which tenant must give notice of termination. (504.21). Where there is tenancy from month to month, lease may be determined by month's notice by either landlord or tenant (50 Minn. 139, 52 N.W. 390), but notice served on first of rental month does not terminate tenancy with end of that month (187 Minn. 497, 245 N.W. 825).

No surrender of lands leased for more than one year unless made in writing except by act or operation of law (513.04), which occurs when acts of tenant are equivalent to abandoning premises, and of landlord resuming possession thereof (56 Minn. 93, 57 N.W. 329). Landlord of residential property must refund any damage deposit within three weeks after termination of tenancy or five days after tenant leaves building or dwelling due to legal condemnation of same, and receipt of tenant's mailing address or delivery instructions, simple, noncompounded interest at 3% per annum until May 1, 1999, and at 4% per annum thereafter, or furnish written statements indicating reasons for withholding deposit. Failure of landlord to comply with 504.20 results in double damages, plus possible punitive damages up to $200. (504.20).

Holding Over.—Person holding over after end of lease after due notice to quit, or contrary to covenants or conditions of agreement, may be evicted. (566.03). Holding over and retaining possession of urban lands does not create tenancy longer than shortest interval between times for payment of rents under expired lease. (504.07).

Dispossession.—Where person holds over after sale of lands on execution of judgment, or after mortgage foreclosure and expiration of applicable time for redemption, or after termination of contract to convey, and expiration of applicable time for redemption provided that such tenant has received at least one months written notice of termination of tenancy, or when tenant holds over after termination of lease or after breach of its condition, or after rent is unpaid, or if tenant at will holds over after notice to quit, landlord may recover possession of premises in quasi criminal action of forcible entry and unlawful detainer. (566.03).

Action is brought by filing complaint describing premises, stating facts authorizing recovery, and praying for restitution thereof and if available, full name and date of birth of person against whom complaint is made. Summons is thereupon issued, commanding defendant to appear not less than seven nor more than 14 days from date of service. (566.05). Service is made as with ordinary summons (complaint must be attached). If defendant cannot be found in county and no person actually occupies premises described in complaint (if nonresidential premises), or if service has been attempted at least twice on different days, with at least one of attempts made between 6:00 and 10:00 p.m. (if residential premises), and plaintiff or attorney files affidavit stating that: (1) Defendant cannot be found or is not believed to be in state and (2) copy of summons has been mailed to defendant's last known address, then service may be made by posting summons in conspicuous place on premises for at least one week. (566.06). Trial may in all cases be continued up to maximum of six days within discretion of court. Either party may demand jury trial. (566.07). If court or jury finds for plaintiff, court shall order restitution of premises and tax costs for plaintiff. In most cases, restitution may be stayed up to seven days upon showing of substantial hardship except if unlawful detainer action was drug-related or on basis that tenant was causing nuisance or endangering safety of other residents. (566.09). Writ delayed 24 hours if defendant announces intent to appeal, except if case involves holdover tenant. (566.11). If appeal taken within ten days, further proceedings stayed upon filing of cost bond and supersedeas bond (RCP 103.01; 566.12), except in action on lease against tenant holding over in which plaintiff posts bond to pay damages if judgment reversed (566.12). If defendant fails to move out within 24 hours after service of writ on him, he may be removed by officer, and plaintiff will have lien for his costs on goods of defendant on premises, enforceable after 60 days by public sale. (566.17).

It is a defense to action for recovery of premises following termination of tenancy by notice to quit if alleged termination was intended as penalty for tenant's attempt to enforce rights under lease or good faith reporting of violation of health, safety, housing or building laws, or in case of nonpayment of rent, that rent was increased or services decreased as penalty for such lawful acts by tenant. (566.03, 566.28). Tenant under residential lease may also assert affirmative defense that landlord has violated statutory covenants (504.18) of lease (298 Minn. 54, 213 N.W.2d 339). As general rule, any effort by landlord to dispossess tenant other than by use of judicial process is unlawful. (264 N.W.2d 145). Landlord may also be liable for treble damages and attorney's fees, and guilty of misdemeanor, if landlord unlawfully removes tenant from possession or interrupts utility services to demised premises. (504.25, 504.255).

Reentry.—Where landlord has subsisting right of reentry for failure of tenant to pay rent, he may bring action to recover possession of property, and such action is equivalent to demand for land and reentry. If tenant, or successor in interest, when sued for restitution of premises because of nonpayment of rent, tenders amount due with interest and costs and $5 attorney fee before restitution granted, lessee may recover possession and hold property according to original lease terms (unless another action is pending alleging lessee's material violation of lease). If tenant is unable to pay interest and costs, landlord may pay these amounts and be restored to possession by stay of writ of restitution. Landlord and tenant may agree in writing to partial payment of rent in arrears without waiving landlord's right to recover possession of process for nonpayment of rent. (504.02). Where term for more than 20 years landlord cannot evict for nonpayment of rent until after 30 days notice to tenant and all creditors and those claiming interest in property. After eviction tenant can redeem within six months if he offers to pay amount due with interest and costs. If landlord recovers possession by action, certified copy of judgment must be filed with county recorder in county where

---

See note at head of Digest as to 1998 legislation covered.

See Topical Index in front part of this volume.

MN – 43

LANDLORD AND TENANT . . . *continued*

land situated (or registrar of titles if land is registered); if possession recovered by abandonment or surrender, affidavit setting forth such facts must be similarly filed. (504.02).

Distress.—Common law distress for rent has been abolished. (504.01).

Uniform Residential Landlord and Tenant Act not adopted.

LEASES:

See topic Landlord and Tenant.

PERPETUITIES:

Uniform Statutory Rule Against Perpetuities adopted, effective Aug. 1, 1990. (c. 501A).

Where accumulation permitted by will or other instrument, income from personal property and rents and profits from real estate may be accumulated for period during which power of alienation may be suspended by future interests in real or personal property not held in trust. Where authorization in instrument permits longer period, void only as to excess period. (500.17). See category Estates and Trusts, topic Trusts.

PERSONAL PROPERTY:

Tenancy by entirety does not exist. (43 Minn. 398, 45 N.W. 710).

POWERS OF ATTORNEY:

Attorneys in Fact.—Governed, generally by c. 523. Durable power of attorney surviving disability or incapacity of principal provided for. (523.07,.08). Powers of attorney to register real estate or to convey registered real estate must be recorded with county registrar. (508.72, 508A.72).

Statutory Short Form Power Attorney.—Statutory form, incorporating by reference powers set out in statute, provided by statute. (523.23, .24). Form effective Aug. 1, 1992, which must be reproduced exactly, is as follows:

Form

STATUTORY SHORT FORM POWER OF ATTORNEY
MINNESOTA STATUTES, SECTION 523.23

IMPORTANT NOTICE: The powers granted by this document are broad and sweeping. They are defined in Minnesota Statutes, section 523.24. If you have any questions about these powers, obtain competent advice. This power of attorney may be revoked by you if you wish to do so. This power of attorney is automatically terminated if it is to your spouse and proceedings are commenced for dissolution, legal separation, or annulment of your marriage. This power of attorney authorizes, but does not require, the attorney-in-fact to act for you.

PRINCIPAL
(Name and Address of Person Granting the Power)

_____

_____

_____

ATTORNEY(S)-IN-FACT (Name and Address)	SUCCESSOR ATTORNEY(S)-IN-FACT (Optional)
	To act if any named attorney-in-fact dies, resigns, or is otherwise unable to serve.
_____	(Name and address)
	First Successor
_____	
_____	_____
_____	_____
	Second Successor
_____	
_____	_____
	_____

NOTICE: If more than one attorney-in-fact is designated, make a check or "x" on the line in front of one of the following statements:

__ Each attorney-in-fact may independently exercise the powers granted.
__ All attorneys-in-fact must jointly exercise the powers granted.

EXPIRATION DATE
(Optional)
_____
Use Specific Month Day
Year Only

I, (the above-named Principal) hereby appoint the above named Attorney(s)-in-Fact to act as my attorney(s)-in-fact:

FIRST: To act for me in any way that I could act with respect to the following matters, as each of them is defined in Minnesota Statutes, section 523.24:

(To grant to the attorney-in-fact any of the following powers, make a check or "x" on the line in front of each power being granted. You may, but need not, cross out each power not granted. Failure to make a check or "x" on the line in front of the power will have the effect of deleting the power unless the line in front of the power of (N) is checked or x-ed.)

Check or "x"

__ (A)   real property transactions;
I choose to limit this power to real property in _____ County, Minnesota, described as follows: (Use legal description. Do not use street address.)
(If more space is needed, continue on the back or on an attachment.)

__(B) tangible personal property transactions;
__(C) bond, share, and commodity transactions;
__(D) banking transactions;
__(E) business operating transactions;
__(F) insurance transactions;
__(G) beneficiary transactions;
__(H) gift transactions;
__(I) fiduciary transactions;
__(J) claims and litigation;
__(K) family maintenance;
__(L) benefits from military service
__(M) records, reports, and statements;
__(N) all of the powers listed in (A) through (M) above and all other matters.

SECOND: (You must indicate below whether or not this power of attorney will be effective if you become incapacitated or incompetent. Make a check or "x" on the line if front of the statement that expresses your intent.)
__ This power of attorney shall continue to be effective if I become incapacitated or incompetent.
__ This power of attorney shall not be effective if I become incapacitated or incompetent.

THIRD: (You must indicate below whether or not this power of attorney authorizes the attorney-in-fact to transfer your property to the attorney-in-fact. Make a check or "x" on the line in front of the statement that expresses your intent.)
__ This power of attorney authorizes the attorney-in-fact to transfer my property to the attorney-in-fact.
__ This power of attorney does not authorize the attorney-in-fact to transfer my property to the attorney-in-fact.

FOURTH: (You may indicate below whether or not the attorney-in-fact is required to make an accounting. Make a check or "x" on the line in front of the statement that expresses your intent.)
__ My attorney-in-fact need not render an accounting unless I request it or the accounting is otherwise required by Minnesota Statutes, section 523.21.
__ My attorney-in-fact must render _____ (Monthly, Quarterly, Annual) accountings to me at _____ (Name and Address) during my lifetime, and a final accounting to the personal representative of my estate, if any is appointed, after my death.

IN WITNESS WHEREOF I have hereunto signed my name this _____ day of _____ . (Insert Date).

_____
Signature of Principal
(Acknowledgement of Principal)

STATE OF _____
COUNTY OF _____ } ss.
The foregoing instrument was acknowledged before me this _____ day of/ __, ____, by _____ (Insert Date and Name of Principal).

_____

_____
(Signature of Notary Public or other Official)

This instrument was drafted by:
_____
_____
_____

_____
Specimen Signature of Attorney(s)-in-Fact
(Notarization not required)

_____

_____

_____

Powers of attorney validly created pursuant to: (1) Common law, (2) law of another state or country, or (3) law of Minnesota as it existed prior to enactment of c. 523, if power of attorney executed before Aug. 1, 1984, are also validly executed for purposes of c. 523. Powers of attorney executed from Aug. 1, 1984 to July 31, 1992, using statutory form in effect during that period continue to be valid. (523.02). Third party refusing to accept authority of attorney in fact acting pursuant to statutory short form power of attorney accompanied by required affidavits of nontermination is liable to principal absent actual notice of termination. (523.20).

Formalities.—Power of attorney is validly executed when dated and signed by principal and, in case of signature on behalf of principal, by another, or by mark, acknowledged by notary public. (523.01). Expiration date in power of attorney must contain specific month, day and year; otherwise it has no effect. (523.075). Power of attorney affecting real estate must be recorded in every county where any of lands lie. (507.24). Power of attorney to convey real estate must be acknowledged like deed to be entitled to record. (507.24). See topic Deeds; category Family, topic Husband and Wife, subhead Conveyances.

Revocation.—Executed power may be revoked only by written instrument signed by principal and, in case of signature on behalf of principal, by another, or by mark, acknowledged before notary public. (523.11). Power terminates upon death of principal or upon expiration of time period specified in power if such period ends prior to death of principal or, in case of power of attorney to spouse of principal, upon commencement of proceedings for dissolution, separation, or annulment of principal's marriage. (523.09).

Durable Power of Attorney for Health Care.—Any competent person may designate another to make health care decisions in event principal is unable, in judgment of attending physician, to make or communicate such decisions. (c. 145C). Agent has personal, but not legal, duty to act. (145C.07). Suggested (not required) form is set out

POWERS OF ATTORNEY . . . *continued*

in 145C.16. Power of Attorney may be signed by principal or at principal's direction, dated, and either witnessed by two witnesses or acknowledged before notary public. (145C.03). Health care providers or their employees ineligible to act as agent unless individual related to principal by blood, marriage, registered domestic partnership, or adoption, or reason for appointment clearly set forth in directive.

Living Wills.—See category Estates and Trusts, topic Wills.

REAL PROPERTY:

Estates in land are divided into estates of inheritance (fee simple), and estates for life, for years, at will, and by sufferance. (500.01). Grant or devise to two or more persons creates tenancy in common unless expressly declared to be in joint tenancy. Requirement for unity of time, title, interest and possession to create joint tenancy abolished. Estates in severalty are also recognized. (500.19). Estates by entirety are not recognized.

Expectant estates, including contingent rights of re-entry for breach of conditions subsequent and possibilities of reverter, are descendible, devisable and alienable in same manner as estates in possession. Covenants, conditions, restrictions or extensions thereof in grant, devise or conveyance which are, or become merely nominal may be wholly disregarded. (500.16, 20).

Rule in Shelley's Case and Doctrine of Worthier Title abolished. (500.14).

Actions.—No action affecting possession of or title to real estate, founded on an instrument or transaction more than 40 years old, can be brought unless notice of claim describing real estate and instrument or transaction on which claim is founded is filed with county recorder or registrar of titles of county where real estate is located within 40 years after execution or occurrence. (541.023).

Foreign Conveyances or Encumbrances.—Real property may be conveyed or mortgaged by instrument executed outside of the state, provided execution according to laws of place where made be shown in prescribed manner.

Condominiums.—Uniform Condominium Act adopted. (c. 515A). Condominiums created prior to Aug. 1, 1980 also subject to prior act (c. 515) in some cases (515A.1-102). Plats required to be filed for condominiums recording declarations or amendments after July 31, 1986. (515A.2-105; 515A.2-115). Plat must contain certification by registered professional land surveyor or registered professional architect as to parts of plat each has prepared. (515A.2-110).

See topics Curtesy, Deeds, Dower, Landlord and Tenant; categories Civil Actions and Procedure, topic Partition; Debtor and Creditor, topic Homesteads; Documents and Records, topic Records; Family, topic Husband and Wife; Mortgages, topic Mortgages of Real Property.

TRUST DEEDS:

See category Mortgages, topic Mortgages of Real Property.

TAXATION

ADMINISTRATION:

Commissioner of Revenue has general supervision over administration of tax laws. (270.01).

Appeals.—An appeal lies from tax judgment as from judgment in ordinary civil action. (279.21). Notice of appeal must be served on county attorney. (23 Minn. 299).

Payment by Lienor.—Mortgagee or other lienor may pay taxes, interest, penalties and costs, and amount so paid constitutes additional lien on land and is collectible with, as part of and in same manner as amount secured by original lien. (272.44).

Penalties.—Whoever intentionally makes any statement required or authorized by law to be made as basis of imposing, reducing, or abating any tax or assessment, as to any material matter which he knows is false, may be sentenced to imprisonment for not more than one year or to payment of fine of not more than $3,000, or both. (609.41). For substantial understatement of tax, penalty is amount equal to 20% of underpayment attributable to understatement. For negligence or intentional disregard of rules and regulations without fraudulent intent, penalty is 10%. Late filing and payment penalties apply. Penalty is imposed for failure to report to Commissioner change or correction to person's federal return equal to 10% of amount of any underpayment of Minnesota tax attributable to federal change. (289A.60). Certain state licenses may not be issued or renewed if applicant owes delinquent taxes of $500 or more. (326.20).

Gasoline Tax.—If tax not paid when due, penalty of 1% per day accrued for first ten days of delinquency; thereafter tax, fees and penalty bear interest at rate to be adjusted annually based on average prime rate in previous six month period ended Sept. 30. (270.75, 296.15). Taxpayers violating gasoline tax laws, or making false statement in any gasoline report, record or sales ticket are guilty of gross misdemeanors. (296A.23).

Gross Earnings Tax.—Upon failure to pay tax within time for payment, specific penalty of 5% added; thereafter, tax and penalty bear interest at rate to be adjusted annually thereafter based on average prime rate in previous Sept. Upon failure to file required return, penalty of 5% is added. If pattern of repeated failure to timely file or pay and notice given to taxpayer, penalty of 25% is added. Additional penalty equal to 50% of tax due imposed on taxpayer who, with intent to evade tax, fails to file return or files false or fraudulent return. (294.03). (Above penalties apply to taxpayers subject to tax under either c. 294 or c. 295.)

Liquor Tax.—Penalties imposed by 297C.03 and .05.

Unemployment Compensation Tax.—Late taxes accumulate interest at rate of 1½% per month or any part thereof. Failure to submit contribution reports is penalized by greater of $25 or 1½% of accrued taxes covered by report, for each month of delinquency. Failure to file wage report is penalized by ½% of total wages paid, but no penalty may be less than $25. Penalties for failure to submit are in addition to interest and other applicable penalties. (268.044, .057). Any officer, director, or any employee of corporation or any manager, governor, member, or employee of limited liability company which is employer and who is responsible for filing reports or paying taxes

and who willfully fails to do so, and any personal representative of estate or fiduciary who voluntarily distributes assets without reserving sufficient amount, is personally liable for unpaid taxes, interest and penalties. (268.063). Any partner of limited liability partnership shall be jointly and severally liable for contributions or reimbursement, including interest, penalties and costs, in event employer does not pay such liability. (268.063).

For penalty and interest provisions affecting other taxes, see subhead involving specific tax, supra.

ALCOHOLIC BEVERAGE TAXES:

Liquor tax imposed by c. 297C.

ESTATE TAX:

For estates of decedents dying after Dec. 31, 1985, Minnesota has adopted pure "pick-up" tax based solely on federal credit for state death taxes. Tax is proportion of maximum federal credit equal to proportion of Minnesota gross estate to federal gross estate. For residents, tax is not less than federal credit reduced by taxes paid to other states. (291.03).

Determination and Collection.—Personal representative must file return of estate taxes with Commissioner of Revenue within nine months after death where decedent has interest in property with situs in Minnesota and federal gross estate in excess of federal unified credit equivalent. Return to be accompanied by copy of federal estate tax return. (291.09).

Taxes take effect at death and are due and payable nine months thereafter. (289A.20). Estate which is granted extension to pay federal tax under I.R.C. §6161 or 6166, and owes Minnesota tax of at least $5,000, may pay Minnesota tax at same time. Installment election must be made within nine months after death. (289A.30). Failure to pay installment when due, unless due to reasonable cause, makes entire tax and accrued interest payable in 90 days. (289A.30). Interest on tax not timely paid subject to annual rate adjustment, except rate on amounts taxpayer elects to pay and timely pays in installments is rate in effect nine months following date of death. (289A.55). For tax not paid when due, penalty of 3% of unpaid tax imposed for each 30 days (or portion thereof) tax is late up to maximum of 24%. If taxpayer fails to make and file return, following penalties are added to tax: 3% if failure to file is for no more than 30 days, plus 5% for each additional 30 days or fraction thereof, but such penalty not to exceed 23% of tax due. (289A.60). Maximum combined late filing and late payment penalty (except minimum late filing penalty) is 38% of tax not paid. Penalty of 50% imposed for failure to file or filing false or fraudulent return, failure or filing is with intent to evade tax. (289A.60). Persons who fail to report federal estate tax changes to Commissioner of Revenue are subject to addition to tax equal to 10% of underpayment of Minnesota tax attributable to federal change. (289A.38; 289A.60).

For estates of decedents dying after Dec. 31, 1985, deferred payment provisions generally conform to federal rules.

Prior Law.—In case of death prior to Jan. 1, 1980, estate tax in addition to inheritance tax imposed to obtain benefit of credit allowed under present federal revenue act, to be assessed in amount computed by Commissioner of Revenue and due 12 months after death of decedent, provided that in case of a nonresident decedent, amount of tax is in same proportion in tax on estates of residents as value of taxable property to value of entire estate subject to federal estate tax. (291.34).

Lien.—Prior lien for inheritance tax repealed. Any prior liens outstanding on Dec. 31, 1983 expire on that date.

Apportionment.—Minnesota estate tax and generation-skipping tax apportioned among beneficiaries unless will or other instrument provides otherwise. (524.3-916).

Interstate Co-operation.—Statutory procedure for determination of death taxes where decedent's domicile is disputed, see 291.41-.47.

GAMBLING TAX:

Gambling tax imposed by c. 349.

Pari-mutuel licenses are taxed at rate of 1% on total bets each racing day, and they are taxed 6% on amounts withheld from pari-mutuel pools which exceed $12,000,000 annually. (240.15).

All legal gambling (except tipboards purchased after 1988 and pull tabs purchased after 1987) is taxed at rate of 9.5% of gross receipts less prizes paid, unless entry is exempt from licensing requirements. This tax is in lieu of sales tax. Pull tabs and tipboards not sold to Indian gaming entities or to tax exempt organizations are taxed at distributor level at rate of 1.9% of face value. Sales taxes imposed on retail sales of pull tabs and tipboards are based on sale price less this tax. Combined receipts are also taxed if they exceed $500,000.

GASOLINE TAX:

Gasoline tax imposed by 296A.01 et seq.

GIFT TAX:

Repealed for gifts made after Dec. 31, 1979.

For gifts prior to Jan. 1, 1980, tax imposed by c. 292, on transfers by gift of property having situs in state.

GROSS EARNINGS TAX:

In general, insurance companies are subject to 2% tax on gross premiums less return premiums, other than premiums under children's health plan, health right plan, and Minnesota comprehensive health insurance plan. (60A.15). For 1997, 1998 and 1999 health maintenance organizations and nonprofit health service corporations are subject to 1% tax on gross premiums less return premiums paid. (60A.15). 2% tax is imposed (and is payable through estimated tax payments) on gross revenues of hospitals, surgical care centers, health care providers, pharmacies, and wholesale drug distributors, and on

---

See note at head of Digest as to 1998 legislation covered.

See Topical Index in front part of this volume.

GROSS EARNINGS TAX ... continued

price paid by person who receives prescription drugs for resale or use in Minnesota (other than from wholesale drug distributor). (295.52).

INCOME TAX:

Income tax is imposed by c. 290.

Tax applies to net income of every resident individual and to income assignable or apportionable to state of every nonresident individual, trust, estate, or corporation. (290.014, .02, .03). Exempt from this tax are corporations, individuals, estates or trusts engaged in mining or producing iron ore if subject to occupation tax. Also exempt are certain insurance companies domiciled in states or countries outside of Minnesota which impose on and does not exempt Minnesota insurance companies from retaliatory taxes or other charges for doing business in other jurisdictions, and certain town and farmers' mutual insurance companies and mutual property and casualty insurance companies. Organizations exempt from income tax under Internal Revenue Code are also exempt to same extent from state tax, but such organizations are subject to tax on unrelated business income defined under Internal Revenue Code. Commissioner may examine or investigate entity claiming exemption under this section or Internal Revenue Code, and may revoke exemption for violation of federal law regardless of whether such action has been taken under federal law. (290.05). S corporations are not subject to tax except to extent corporation recognizes income for federal income tax purposes; S corporations are subject to minimum fee (below). (290.014, 290.9725-9729). Nonresident entertainers (including athletes and public speakers) are subject to withholding tax of 2% of total compensation, and such compensation is exempt from income tax. No withholding on compensation paid to public speakers if less than $2,000 or constitutes speaker's expenses. (290.9201).

Persons other than resident individuals, conducting trade or business outside Minnesota are subject to tax if any income is assignable or apportionable to Minnesota. Activities creating jurisdiction to tax include: (1) Having business location in this state, (2) having employees, representatives, or independent contractors in this state, (3) owning or leasing real or tangible personal property in Minnesota; and (4) obtaining or regularly soliciting business from within Minnesota, including: (a) selling products or services received in Minnesota, (b) selling services performed outside Minnesota if benefits are consumed in Minnesota, (c) transacting business with Minnesota customers involving intangible property whose income flows from within Minnesota, (d) leasing tangible personal property in Minnesota, (e) selling or leasing personal property in Minnesota, and (f) if financial institution, receiving deposits from Minnesota customers. (290.015). Income derived from certain farm operations by corporation is assigned to Minnesota. Report disclosing business activities must be filed in certain cases if tax returns not filed and corporation not qualified to do business. Failure to file may preclude use of Minnesota courts. (290.371).

Net income of nonresident individual is taxable to extent: (1) It consists of compensation for labor or personal services performed within this state, (2) it is derived from tangible property having sites in this state, or (3) it is derived from business carried on within this state. (290.17, .191). Special allocation rules apply to nonresident athletes and entertainers. (290.17[2][a][2]). Certain pension and profit-sharing income of nonresident excluded even though services were performed within state. (290.032, 290.17[2][a][3]).

Taxable income includes income from all sources except those expressly exempted, less certain specified deductions.

In general, Income Tax Act follows income tax provisions of Internal Revenue Code of 1986, as subsequently amended. Net income means federal income subject to certain modifications. (290.01[19]). Taxable net income means net income for resident individuals, apportioned net income for nonresident individuals, and part of net income allocable to Minnesota by assignment or apportioned to Minnesota for all other taxpayers including insurance companies. (290.01[22]). Corporations are allowed 80% dividends received deduction if recipient owns at least 20% of payor's stock, by vote and value, and remaining 20% if dividends received are from affiliated corporation and dividend is eliminated under IRS regulations, and 70% if recipient owns less than 20% of payor's stock, by vote or value, but only if payor's stock is not in stock in trade of recipient or property held by recipient primarily for sale in true ordinary course, and only if recipient's business is not principally holding of stock and collection of income therefrom. (290.21). 80% of royalties, fees and other like income from certain foreign sources are excludable by certain corporations. (290.01). Corporations are required to modify federal accelerated cost recovery for property placed in service before Jan. 1, 1988. (290.01[19e]).

Net operating losses of individuals, estates, or trusts may be carried back and carried over in same manner as for federal purposes. Corporations are only allowed net operating loss carryover for 15 years. Insurance companies may take net operating loss or operations loss deduction. (290.095).

Rates applicable to individuals, estates and trusts are graduated to maximum rate of 8.5%. (290.06). Alternative minimum tax imposed at 7% rate. (290.091).

Withholding is required by every employer making payment of any wages taxable by Minnesota. Unemployment compensation benefits are to be subject to withholding unless recipient timely notifies Commissioner otherwise. Eight percent of Minnesota lottery winnings are to be withheld. (290.92). If amount assignable to Minnesota is at least $1,000, partnerships generally must withhold from shares paid or credited to nonresident partners based on their distributive shares (lien may arise on amounts otherwise exempt from withholding) and S corporations generally must withhold from nonresident shareholders based on their share of income. (290.92). For contracts exceeding $100,000, withholding required at 8% from payments to nonresident persons or foreign corporations to perform construction work in Minnesota as surety to guarantee payment of taxes, subject to exception if contractor gives bond or has fully complied with tax laws for preceding three years. (290.9705).

Tax credits available include dependent care credit (290.067), working family credit (290.0671), job creation and property tax credits (290.06) and credit for taxes paid to another state by residents (including pro rata portion of taxes deemed paid by member

of limited liability company to another state) and certain corporations and refunds for contributions to candidates and political parties (290.06). Corporations (other than S corporations) are allowed credit equal to 5% of first $2,000,000, and 2.5% of remainder of certain increases in research and experimental expenditures incurred in Minnesota, but not more than liability for tax. (290.068).

Inflation Adjustments.—In general, annual inflation adjustments provided for tax rate brackets and tax credits and standard deductions. (290.06).

Rate for corporations is 9.8% plus minimum fee (below). (290.06). In case of income derived from business carried on within and without state, statute prescribes formulae for determining portion deemed subject to tax on basis of sales (70%), property (15%) and payroll (15%). (290.191). For certain mail order businesses, property and payroll at distribution center outside of Minnesota are disregarded if sole activity is filling orders and no solicitation occurs at distribution center. (290.191). Multistate compact enacted with modifications. (290.171). Commissioner may require or permit combined reporting by affiliated corporations engaged in unitary business. (290.34). Foreign corporations not includible on combined report. Special rules apply to possessions companies and to certain domestic corporations with primarily foreign operations. (290.17). Alternative minimum tax equals excess of 5.8% of Minnesota alternative minimum taxable income (less certain credits) over regular tax imposed under 290.06, subd. 1. (290.0921).

Partnerships are not taxed generally, but are subject to minimum fee (below); distributive shares are taxed to individual partners. (290.31). Limited liability company formed in Minnesota or under similar laws of another state, which is considered partnership for federal income tax purposes, is considered partnership for Minnesota income tax purposes and its members must be considered to be partners. (290.01). Minnesota Department of Revenue recognizes "check the box" elections made for Federal purposes except for foreign entities with single "C" corporation owners that elect to be disregarded.

Minimum fee imposed on corporations, S corporations and partnerships (other than one that derives 80% of its income from farming) to maximum of $5,000 depending on entity's total Minnesota property, payroll and sales or receipts.

Accounting periods are same as under Federal Income Tax law. (290.07). Returns are required if taxpayer is required to file federal return under §6012 of Internal Revenue Code (289A.08), including exempt organizations subject to tax on unrelated business income. Corporations that obtained any business from within Minnesota must file notice of business activities report even if no income tax return required. (290.371). Information returns are required of partnerships, certain regulated investment companies, and, to extent required by §6041 of Internal Revenue Code, of persons, corporations or cooperatives making certain payments in any taxable year to any person or corporation on account of rents, royalties, interest, dividends or wages, etc. (289A.12). Information returns must be furnished to recipient by Jan. 31 and duplicate filed with Commissioner by Feb. 28. (289A.12). Returns are due Apr. 15, or 15th day of fourth month after close of fiscal year, except that returns of corporations must be filed on or before Mar. 15 or 15th day of third month after close of fiscal year. (289A.18). Extensions of time are available when, in Commissioner's judgment, good cause exists. Maximum extension period is six months (seven months for corporations), and tentative return with payment may be required on regular due date. (289A.19).

Payment.—Tax is payable to Commissioner at time of return. (289A.20). Estimated tax payments required if tax exceeds $500. (289A.25 and 289A.26).

Penalties.—Tax not paid when due, or within 30 days after final determination of appeal to Tax Court, is subject to penalty of 3% of amount remaining unpaid for first 30 days and 3% for each additional 30 days, up to maximum of 24%. If taxpayer fails to make and file return, following penalties are added to tax: 3% if failure is for not more than 30 days, plus 5% for each additional 30 days or fraction thereof, but such penalty not to exceed 23% of tax due. Combined failure-to-pay and failure-to-file penalties generally limited to 38% of tax. (289A.60). Sum of delinquent tax plus penalties bears interest at rate to be adjusted annually based on average prime rate in previous six month period ended Sept. 30. (289A.55; 270.75). If taxpayer with intent to evade tax fails to file return or files false or fraudulent return, penalty of 50% of any tax remaining due is imposed. Negligence penalty of 10% imposed. (289A.60). Any taxpayer who knowingly fails to make and file return is also guilty of gross misdemeanor, and any taxpayer who willfully makes and subscribes any return which he knows to be false as to any material matter or who willfully attempts to evade tax is guilty of felony. (289A.63). Penalty for substantial understatement of tax equal to 20% of amount of underpayment attributable to understatement. (289A.60). Employers who fail to withhold taxes are subject to same penalties as above. (289A.60, 270.75). Penalty for failure to file information returns is $50 for each failure, not to exceed $25,000 during any calendar year, unless failure is due to reasonable cause and not willful neglect. (289A.12). Employee who furnishes withholding exemption certificate or residency affidavit to employer containing materially incorrect statement subject to $500 penalty for each such instance. (289A.60). Persons who fail to report federal income tax changes to Commissioner of Revenue are subject to addition to tax equal to 10% of underpayment of Minnesota tax attributable to federal change. (289A.38; 289A.60). Commissioner of Revenue may abate penalties upon showing of reasonable cause, subject to approval of Attorney General if abatement exceeds $5,000, and may abate tax if taxpayer agrees to perform uncompensated public service work for State or nonprofit organization. (270.07).

INHERITANCE TAX:

Repealed for estates of decedents dying after Dec. 31, 1979.

IRON ORE TAXES:

See category Mineral, Water and Fishing Rights, topic Mines and Minerals.

MONEY AND CREDITS TAX:

Money and credits tax repealed.

See note at head of Digest as to 1998 legislation covered.

See Topical Index in front part of this volume.

MORTGAGE REGISTRATION TAX:

See category Mortgages, topic Mortgages of Real Property.

PROPERTY TAXES:

Taxable Property.—All real and personal property is subject to taxation unless exempted (272.01).

Exemptions.—Public burying grounds, public schoolhouses, public hospitals, academies, colleges, etc., churches and church property, institutions of purely public charity, public property used exclusively for public purposes, personal property used primarily to control air, land or water pollution, to extent so used, and real property used primarily to control air, water and land pollution as part of agricultural operation or as part of electric generation system, wetlands, native prairie, property used to provide emergency shelter for victims of domestic abuse, property owned by certain senior citizens' groups, property used primarily for production of hydroelectric or hydromechanical power on site owned by state or local government unit, property used as direct satellite broadcasting facility or fixed satellite regional or national program service facility, facility used to produce distilled spirituous liquors, liqueurs, cordials, or liquors designated as specialties regardless of alcoholic content but not including ethyl alcohol, property owned by private, nonprofit corporation and used primarily to generate and distribute hot water to heat buildings, certain state lands leased from department of natural resources, certain property of volunteer fire departments, certain property under management of housing redevelopment authority or public housing agency and certain property that is leased to school districts. All personal property is exempt except personal property used in electric generating, transmission, or distribution systems; pipeline systems for transporting or distributing water, gas or petroleum products; railroad docks and wharves; improvements on land owned by U.S.; certain leasehold interests; manufactured homes and sectional structures; and certain flight property. Taxpayers claiming certain exemptions must file statement of exemption with assessor (or with Commissioner, if pollution control property) on or before Feb. 1 of year for which exemption is claimed. (272.025).

Assessment.—Real estate is listed and at least one-fourth of parcels listed shall be appraised each year with reference to their value on Jan. 2 preceding assessment, and real property becoming taxable in any intervening year is listed with reference to its value on Jan. 2 of that year. Personal property is listed and assessed annually, with reference to its value on Jan. 2. Real property owned by State of Minnesota containing iron ore and leased after Jan. 2 is assessed with reference to value of ore removed prior to next Jan. 2. (273.01).

There are municipal, county, and state boards of equalization or review. (274.01).

Real and personal property subject to general ad valorem property taxation is classified for purposes of assessment. Tax capacity of property is based on sliding or fixed scale and depends on its market value and classification. (273.13).

Review of Assessment.—Taxpayer claiming unequal or unfair assessment of personal property real property, or that tax thereon is illegal, or that property is exempt, may contest same by filing petition in district court or tax court before Mar. 31 of year in which tax is payable. Notwithstanding general Mar. 31 date, whenever exempt status, valuation, or classification of real or personal property is changed other than by abatement or court proceeding, and owner is not given notice of change until after Jan. 31 (or after July 1 in some cases), person has 60 days from date of mailing notice to appeal change. (278.01 et seq.). If proceeding instituted by such filing is not completed before May 16 (in case of real and personal property), or Oct. 16 (in case of real property) of year in which tax is payable, partial payment of tax is due unless excused by court. (278.03).

Lien and Payment.—Tax on real estate is lien thereon from year in which property is assessed; as between grantor and grantee from first Mon. in Jan. following (272.31); and can be paid on or after first business day in Mar. (276.01). Tax on real estate and personal property tax assessed against improvements to leased property becomes delinquent if not paid prior to May 16 or 21 days after postmark date on envelope containing property tax statement, whichever is later, of year during which such tax is payable, except that tax in excess of $50 levied against any tract or lot not delinquent if at least one-half is paid prior to May 16 or 21 days after postmark date, whichever is later, and remainder prior to Oct. 16. Delinquent tax payable by May 16 or 21 days after postmark date, whichever is later, generally bears penalty of 4% (2% on homestead property) until May 31 and 8% (4% on homestead property) on June 1, which accrues on June 1 or 21 days after postmark date, whichever is later, plus 1% on first day of each month thereafter beginning July 1 up to and including Oct. 1. Delinquent tax payable by Oct. 16 bears penalty as of that date of 4% (2% on homestead property) and additional penalty of 4% on Nov. 1 and 4% (2% on homestead property) on Dec. 1. If first half becomes delinquent same may be paid with penalties without any further penalty attaching to second half if latter is paid before Oct. 16. (279.01). Rate of interest on property taxes levied in 1979 and prior years is 6% through 1982. Rate on such taxes beginning in 1983 and for taxes levied in 1980 and subsequent years is based on secondary market yield on one year U.S. treasury bills in Nov. prior to each calendar year. For property taxes levied in 1980 and prior years, interest is calculated on prorated monthly basis from second Mon. in May following year in which taxes became due. For taxes levied in 1981 and subsequent years, calculation is on prorated monthly basis from Jan. 1 following year in which taxes became due. Interest on delinquent property taxes, penalties, and costs unpaid on or after Jan. 1, 1991, shall be payable at per annum rate determined in 270.75, subd. 5 (adjusted prime rate charged by banks, rounded to nearest full percent), but in no case less than 10% or greater than 14%. Such interest shall be doubled if taxpayer owns one or more parcels of property for which delinquent taxes thereon after Jan. 1, 1992, exceed specified amount of local school district's taxes. (279.03, 549.09).

Tax on personal property, except manufactured homes and sectional structures, becomes due on first Mon. in Jan. following levy, and delinquent on May 16 or 21 days after postmark date of tax statement, whichever is later, when 8% penalty is added, except that half shall not be delinquent if paid before May 16 or 21 days after postmark date whichever is later, and balance is paid before Oct. 16. Personal property taxes assessed upon improvements to certain real property become delinquent on May 16 or 21 days after postmark date of tax statement, whichever is later, but if such tax exceeds $50, one-half may be paid before May 16 and balance is paid before Oct. 16 without penalty. (277.01). Tax (including penalties, interest, fees, and costs) assessed after Jan. 1, 1992 on personal property or manufactured homes is lien on all real and personal property in Minnesota of taxpayer which arises on Jan. 2 of year in which tax is due and continues until paid. (277.20). Such assessed tax may be collected by county treasurer within five years after date assessed or within ten years (plus any renewal period) if notice of lien is filed. (277.20; 277.21). Notice and demand is generally required before levy is made. (277.21). County treasurer may direct county sheriff to execute levy on any nonexempt property subject to lien. (277.21). Tax lien arising on personal property prior to Jan. 1, 1992 is perpetual lien on all personal property of taxpayer assessed from Jan. 2 of year assessed and sheriff may detain personal property subject to lien to satisfy all taxes. (272.50).

Tax Sales.—Tax delinquent lands are bid in for state on second Mon. in May following delinquency, to be held by state until redemption or forfeiture. (280.001 et seq.).

Redemption.—Any person claiming interest in land bid in for state may redeem same. (281.01). Except for certain abandoned or vacant property, period of redemption for lands within incorporated area bid in for state is three years from date of sale unless lands are certain homestead lands, agricultural lands or seasonal recreational lands, for which period is five years. (281.17). Period of redemption for lands in specified targeted neighborhoods sold to state is one year (three years for homesteaded lands). Five week redemption period applies to certain abandoned or vacant property. (281.17). Period of redemption for all lands constituting mixed municipal solid waste disposal facility that is qualified facility is one year from date of sale. Period of redemption for all other lands sold to state is five years from date of sale, except that for non-homestead agricultural land, such period is two years if owner also owns one or more parcels of property for which delinquent taxes thereon exceed specified amount of local school district's taxes. (281.17). Right to redeem expires 60 days after filing proof of service of notice of expiration of period of redemption. Such notice may be issued and served not earlier than 60 days before expiration of period of redemption. (281.21, 23). Amount required to redeem is amount for which land was bid in plus subsequent delinquent taxes, penalties, costs and interest. (281.02). Unless this amount is paid before expiration of time allowed within which to redeem, absolute title vests in state. (281.18).

Deed Transfer Tax.—See category Property, topic Deeds.

Contamination Tax.—Effective for taxes assessed in 1994 and payable in 1995, contamination tax imposed on real property to extent its property tax value reduced by contamination. Tax payable at same time and in same manner as property tax. In general, tax rate is property tax rate, but rate reduced if owner and operator are not "responsible persons" with respect to contamination and if response action plan or asbestos abatement plan is being implemented. (270.91 et. seq.)

REVISED UNIFORM FEDERAL LIEN REGISTRATION ACT:

Revised Uniform Federal Lien Registration Act adopted. Amendments adopted. (272.479 et seq.).

SALES AND USE TAXES:

Sales Tax.—Sales tax of 6.5% (subject to county option prior to July 1, 1995 to rescind 0.5%) of gross receipts of sales at retail made by any person in state, except that: (1) Rate for sales of farm machinery and aquaculture production equipment is 2.0% for sales after June 30, 1998 and before July 1, 1999, and 1.0% for sales after June 30, 1999 and before July 1, 2000. There will be no sales tax imposed on sales after June 30, 2000; (2) rate for sales of intoxicating liquor and nonintoxicating malt liquor is 9.0%; and (3) sales of manufactured homes used for residential purposes are taxed on 65% of dealer's cost of home, and new and used park trailers are taxed on 65% of sales price. (297A.02). Rental motor vehicle tax of 6.2% of sales price is imposed on rentals of cars, vans, and pickup trucks (but not hearses, limousines used for funerals or van designed or adapted primarily for transporting property), provided such rentals are not longer than 28 days. Such tax is to be collected like sales taxes. (297A.135). There is also 3% fee imposed on such rentals.

Taxable Transactions.—Sale and purchase includes (but is not limited to): (1) Any transfer of title or possession of tangible personal property and leasing or granting license to use or consume such property (other than manufactured homes used for residential purposes for continuous period of 30 days or more) for consideration of money, exchange or barter; (2) production, fabrication, printing or processing of tangible personal property for consumers who furnish materials used in same; (3) furnishing, preparing or serving of food, meals or drinks (excluding hospitals, sanatoriums, nursing or senior citizens homes, meals and lunches served at public and private schools, universities or colleges); (4) admissions to places of amusement, recreational areas, or athletic events and access to use of amusement devices, tanning facilities, reducing salons, steam baths, Turkish baths, massage parlors, health clubs, spas, or athletic facilities; (5) furnishing of lodging and related services by hotel, rooming house, tourist court, motel or trailer camp and license to use real property for 30 days or more (other than renting or leasing); (6) furnishing of utilities or certain telephone service, but excluding residential water and sewer services and natural gas fuel which propels certain vehicles; (7) furnishing of cable television services; (8) furnishing of parking services; (9) furnishing of following services: laundry; dry cleaning; repairing, altering or storing clothes; linen service; certain cleaning services; car washes; rustproofing; undercoating and towing of motor vehicles; detective agencies; security, burglar and fire alarm services; armored cars; pet grooming; certain lawn and landscaping services (other than installing shrubbery, plants, sod, trees, bushes, etc.); and mixed municipal solid waste management services (but not to collect and manage recyclable materials) massages (unless medically required); paid lodging, board and care services for animals in kennels, etc. (but not veterinary and horse boarding services); (10) transfer of computer software (excluding custom computer programs); (11) granting of membership in club, association, or other organization providing sports and athletic facilities to its members. (297A.01).

See note at head of Digest as to 1998 legislation covered.

See Topical Index in front part of this volume.

MN – 47

SALES AND USE TAXES ... *continued*

Exemption for gross receipts from: (1) Sale of food products except candy or soft drinks; (2) prescribed drugs and medicine, including insulin, prescription glasses, therapeutic and prosthetic devices, and aspirin and patient medical supplies purchased by health care facilities or providers such as bandages and non-prescription drugs; (3) sale, storage, use or consumption of property prohibited from taxation by state or federal constitution or federal laws; (4) sale of tangible personal property in interstate commerce; (5) sale of packing materials used to ship household goods out of state; (6) sale, storage, use or consumption of petroleum products where other nonrefundable state tax has been paid; (7) sale of clothing and wearing apparel with enumerated exceptions including jewelry, furs, perfumes, suitcases, and wallets; (8) sale, storage, use or consumption of materials used or consumed in agricultural or industrial production of personal property ultimately intended for retail sale, except for fuel used to mix concrete; (9) sale, storage, use or consumption of tangible personal property used or consumed producing any publication issued at least every three months and advertising and property used or consumed in such publications; (10) sales, including sales in which title is retained by seller or vendor, to U.S., its agencies and instrumentalities, to certain state schools and universities, and to state political subdivisions if acquired for their school districts, hospitals, nursing homes, libraries, and ambulance operations, and road maintenance and solid waste services (except not sales of vehicles), and sales to libraries; (11) certain isolated or occasional sales (not including sales of tangible personal property primarily used in trade or business unless nontaxable under Internal Revenue Code or sale is between members of affiliated group, sale of farm machinery, is farm auction sale, or is of substantially all assets of trade or business); (12) sale of airflight equipment, and storage, use or other consumption of such property by airline companies taxed under other state law; (13) sale of and storage, use or other consumption of mill liners, grinding rods and grinding balls consumed in producing taconite by persons taxed under other state law; (14) sales to charitable, religious or educational organizations, if property is used in performance of charitable, religious or educational functions, and sales to certain senior citizens organizations; (15) sales of caskets and burial vaults; (16) sales of automobiles and certain building materials to disabled veterans; (17) sale to licensed dealer of aircraft for which commercial use permit has been issued if dealer resells aircraft while permit is in effect; (18) textbooks; (19) advertising material to be used outside state; (20) residential heating fuels; (21) sale or use of tickets or admissions to arts events by tax-exempt organization or municipal board that promotes cultural and arts activities; (22) sale to, or storage, use or consumption by, certain tax-exempt veterans organizations of tangible personal property used for charitable, civic, educational, or nonprofit purposes; (23) sale of sanitary napkins, tampons or similar items; (24) sale of manufactured home to be used for residential purposes, unless sale is first retail sale in state; (25) sale of equipment for processing solid or hazardous waste at resource recovery facility; (26) sales of repair or replacement parts for farm machinery (except tires); (27) sales of tickets or admissions to regular season school games, events and activities; (28) motor vehicles subject to motor vehicle excise tax; (29) gross receipts from sale of tangible personal property purchased with food stamps and food purchased under Special Supplemental Food Program for women, infants and children, to extent required by federal law; (30) certain WATS line services; (31) YMCA, YWCA and JCC fees; (32) sales of used motor oil; (33) sales of cross country ski passes; (34) sales of state fair tickets; (35) sales of bullet-proof vests; (36) sales of capital equipment; (37) sales of chair lifts, ramps and elevators if authorized by physician; (38) sales of lubricants and repair parts for ships used principally in interstate or foreign commerce and vessels of at least three tons; (39) sale of wine for sacramental purposes if purchased from nonprofit religious organizations or from holder of sacramental wine license; (40) automatic fire-safety sprinkler systems; (41) wind energy conversion systems, photovoltaic devices, certain air cooling equipment; (42) parts and accessories used to make handicapped vehicles accessible; (43) materials to construct certain satellite broadcasting facilities; (44) pollution control equipment purchased by steel reprocessing firms; (45) sales of special tooling; (46) first $5,000 from sales of certain used farm tires; (47) construction materials used in constructive new corrugated recycling facilities; (48) sale of firefighters personal protective equipment; (49) sale of horses including racehorses and sales of certain materials used in breeding, raising and keeping horses; (50) personal computers and related software sold by schools to students if required by school; (51) sale of used farm machinery and, after June 30, 2000, sale of new farm machinery; (52) sale of construction materials used in constructing improvement to state convention center located in city outside of Minneapolis-St. Paul metropolitan area, Minneapolis Convention Center, St. Paul River Centre, Long Lake Conservation Center, Earl Brown Heritage Center, cooperatively owned soybean oilseed processing plant; sale of construction materials used in constructing indoor ice arena used for youth activities and which receives certain grant or public financing; and sale of wastewater treatment equipment to political subdivisions. (297A.25). Sales for fundraising purposes by certain nonprofit groups are exempt. (297A.256). Sales of lottery tickets exempt. (297A.259). Sales of certain airflight equipment to airline companies are exempt. (297A.25).

Collection.—Seller must obtain permit from Commissioner of Revenue to collect tax from purchaser. (297A.04 et seq.). Seller has burden of proof that any sale is not subject to tax, but exemption certificate will conclusively relieve retailer from collecting tax if taken in good faith. (297A.09, .10). Amounts collected as sales taxes are state funds that must be reported on return and are not subject to refund absent proof that such amounts have been refunded or credited to purchaser by seller. (297A.023).

Penalties.—Upon failure to pay tax within time for payment (generally on or before 20th day of month following sale or 25th day of month following sale if electronic funds transfer is required of retailer), penalty of 5% for first 30 days and 5% for each additional 30 days, up to maximum of 15% is added. Upon any failure to file required return, penalty is 5%. If pattern of repeated failure to timely file or pay and notice given to taxpayer, penalty of 25% is added. Upon failure to pay by electronic transfer after notice given to taxpayer, penalty of 5%, unless taxpayer pays by other means amount due at least three business days before due date. Additional penalty, equal to 50% of tax, imposed on person willfully either failing to file return or filing false or fraudulent return or otherwise willfully attempting to defeat or evade such tax, and such person is

guilty of gross misdemeanor, or felony if amount of tax involved exceeds $300. Negligence penalty of 10% imposed. Penalty is imposed for failure to timely report to Commissioner change or correction to person's federal return equal to 10% of amount of any underpayment of Minnesota tax attributable to federal change. (289A.60). Tax not timely paid, plus amount of any penalty, bears interest at rate to be adjusted annually based on average prime rate in previous six month period ended Sept. 30. (270.75). Commissioner of Revenue has power to abate penalties, if failure to file or to pay tax is due to reasonable cause, subject to approval of Attorney General if amount exceeds $5,000, and has power to abate tax if taxpayer agrees to perform uncompensated public service work for State or nonprofit organization. (270.07).

Use Tax.—Use tax of 6.5% (subject to county option to rescind 0.5%) of sales price of sales at retail, except that rate of 4.5% of sales price applies to special tooling and rate of 2.5% of sales price applies to farm machinery. Motor vehicles taxed at fair market value at time of transport into state if acquired more than three months prior thereto. (297A.14). Credit given for sales tax paid on sale of such property in another state. (297A.24). De minimis exemption for purchases made by individual for personal use (including gifts), total of which does not exceed $770 per year. (297A.14).

STAMP TAX:

No documentary stamp tax.

TRANSPORTATION TAXES:

Motor Vehicle Tax.—See category Transportation, topic Motor Vehicles.

Taxes on Aircraft and Scheduled Airline Flight Property.—See category Transportation, topic Motor Vehicles.

UNEMPLOYMENT COMPENSATION TAX:

Unemployment compensation tax is imposed on employer for each calendar year that employer paid wages to employees in covered employment, except for certain governmental units and nonprofit corporations. Tax rate is sum of employer's experience rating plus minimum tax of from $1/10$ of 1% to $6/10$ of 1% of covered payroll, depending on state unemployment compensation fund balance. Additional solvency assessment is possible if state fund balance is too low. Special rates apply to new employers and employers in construction industry. Taxable wage base is 60% of state's average annual wage in second previous calendar year. Exemptions similar to those under Federal Act. Returns must be made and tax paid quarterly to Department of Economic Security. (268.03 et seq.).

TRANSPORTATION

MOTOR VEHICLES:

General supervision in Motor Vehicles Division of Department of Public Safety, State Highway Building, St. Paul, Mn. 55155.

Vehicle license required annually. Number plates must be displayed front and rear, unless vehicle is motorcycle, etc., trailer or semitrailer (rear only) or truck-tractor, road-tractor or farm truck (front only). (169.79). It is unlawful to cover any numerical, letter or state of origin, including clear material that affects visibility or reflectivity. Registration and taxation provisions not applicable to motor vehicle operated by nonresident owner in military service if: (1) such motor vehicle is registered in and licensed by state of owner's residence and such vehicle is used only for personal transportation, or (2) for period of up to 30 days, such motor vehicle is owned and operated by person in military service, and vehicle is registered with and has plates of Armed Forces of U.S. in foreign country. (168.04). Vehicle registered in other jurisdiction must be registered in state within 60 days after date owner becomes resident of state, or if 60th day occurs after 15th of month, by end of such month. (168.012[8]).

Operator's license required. (171.02). Persons under 16 years of age may not be licensed, nor may persons under 18 years of age unless application is approved by parent, spouse of parent having custody or guardian having custody or if applicant has no living parent or guardian, by employer, and person has successfully completed approved course in driver education. (171.04). Restricted farm work license and motorized bicycle license or permit may be issued to person 15 years of age upon completion of safety course and examination. (171.041, 171.02). Limited license may be issued after appropriate waiting period by Commissioner to drivers whose licenses have been suspended or revoked if: (1) Driver's livelihood or attendance at chemical dependency treatment or counseling program depends upon use of driver's license; (2) use of driver's license by homemaker is necessary to prevent substantial disruption of education, medical, or nutritional needs of homemaker's family; or (3) attendance at post-secondary institution of education by enrolled student of that institution depends upon use of driver's license. (171.30).

Drivers' licenses classified according to types of vehicles which may be driven by holder. Class D license valid for all single two axle vehicles under 26,000 pounds, farm trucks, and certain emergency vehicles. Holders may tow vehicles if combination of vehicles has gross vehicle weight of 26,000 pounds or less. Other vehicles require either Class A, B or C license for which special qualifications must be met. (171.02).

Person possessing valid license issued by other state or province or by U.S. military authorities may operate motor vehicle for period of not more than 60 days after becoming resident before obtaining state license. (171.03).

Operation Prohibited.—By person under influence of alcohol or narcotics or both or whose blood alcohol content is .10% or more. If two or more tests within two year period show alcohol concentration of .07% or more, driver may be required to have chemical use assessment. (169.121). When sentenced for driving while under influence of alcohol or controlled substance, court must impose $125 chemical dependency assessment charge. (169.121[5a]). If second driving while under influence of alcohol or controlled substance conviction is within five years of first conviction or convicted of driving while intoxicated two or more times within ten years of first conviction, court must order person to submit to level of care recommended in chemical use assessment report. (169.121[3b]). Motor vehicle used in commission of third impaired driving

MOTOR VEHICLES . . . *continued*
conviction or license revocation within five year period, or fourth conviction or license revocation within 15 year period, is subject to forfeiture. (169.1217). Person charged with operating motor vehicle within ten years of first of three convictions for impaired driving, or any time after person's fourth conviction, may be released from confinement without posting maximum bail only under special conditions. (169.121[lc]).

Size and Weight Limits.—Regulated by 169.80-.88.

Equipment Required.—Regulated by 169.01, 169.19, 169.223, 169.47-.75, 169.974.

Lights Required.—Regulated by 169.48-.66, .75.

Traffic Regulations.—See c. 169.

Accidents.—Driver must stop, give assistance if necessary, give name, address, date of birth and registration number; show license and provide name and address of insurance carrier on request; notify local police officers, state patrol or sheriff if accident involves immediately demonstrable bodily injury to or death of person; and forward written report to Commissioner of Public Safety within ten days if accident involves bodily injury to or death of person or $1,000 property damage. Violation subjects driver to criminal penalties unless left to take person with immediately demonstrable bodily injury to emergency medical care. (169.09).

Liability of Owner.—Owner is liable for any injury or damage resulting from operation of his car with his express or implied consent, operator being deemed his agent. (170.54).

Guests.—No restriction of liability for injury to a gratuitous guest.

Insurance.—Insurance required to cover basic economic loss, residual liability up to $30,000 per individual and $60,000 per occurrence, and $10,000 property damage. Uninsured and underinsured motorist coverage also required. (65B.48, .49). Personal automobile insurance policies issued or renewed in Minnesota after Aug. 1, 1987, must cover rental of private passenger vehicles, pick-up trucks and vans unless rental is principally for business use or rented on monthly or longer basis. (65B.49[5a]). When motor vehicle is rented or leased in Minnesota, rental contract must contain statutorily prescribed notice that personal automobile insurance policy issued in Minnesota must cover rental of motor vehicle unless rental is principally for business use or rented on monthly or longer basis. No collision damage waiver or other insurance offered as part of, or in conjunction with, rental of motor vehicle may be sold unless person renting vehicle provides written acknowledgment that such protection notice has been read and understood. (65B.49[5a(f)]).

No-Fault Insurance.—No-fault insurance adopted effective Jan. 1, 1975. (65B.41 et seq.). Provides for basic economic loss benefits to every person suffering loss from injury arising out of maintenance or use of a motor vehicle or as result of pedestrian being struck by motorcycle for accidents in state and, if accident occurs in other state, U.S. possession or Canada, to insureds, certain drivers and occupants of secured vehicles and their dependents. Geographic coverage may be extended to other areas if expressly stated in policy. (65B.46). Negligence action may be brought for economic loss not covered by certain benefit limitations. (65B.51). No person may recover damages in negligence cause of action for noneconomic detriment unless medical expenses exceed $4,000 or injury results in permanent disfigurement or injury, death or disability for 60 days or more. (65B.51[3]). Mandatory no-fault motor vehicle claims arbitration for all cases in which claim is in amount of $10,000 or less at commencement of arbitration for no-fault benefits or comprehensive collision damage coverage. (65B.525).

Tests for Intoxication.—Operator of motor vehicle deemed to consent to test of blood, breath, or urine for purpose of determining presence of alcohol or controlled substance. Person has right to consult attorney so long as it does not unreasonably delay administration of test and to have additional tests made by person of his own choosing. (169.123[2][3]). Evidence of refusal to take test is admissible in prosecution. (169.121[2]). Peace officers, with probable cause to believe there is impairment by controlled substance, may require person to take blood or urine test in addition to breath test if reason to believe impairment caused by substance not subject to testing by breath test. Action may be taken against person refusing to take blood test or urine test only if alternative (blood test or urine test) was offered. (169.123[2a]).

Title.—Uniform Motor Vehicle Certificate of Title and Anti-Theft Act adopted. (168A.01-.31). Owner must obtain certificate of title for motor vehicles and manufactured homes. (168A.02). Application made to Registrar of Motor Vehicles on prescribed form. (168A.04). Certain vehicles exempt. (168A.03).

Sales.—Uniform Motor Vehicle Certificate of Title and Anti-Theft Act adopted. (168A.01-.31). After Oct. 1, 1972, transfer, other than by creation of security interest, is effected by execution of assignment and warranty of title to transferee in space provided on certificate at time of delivery of vehicle. Certificate and assignment must be delivered to transferee. Transferee must apply for new certificate in space provided on old certificate and mail or deliver old certificate to Registrar within ten days of transfer. If security interest is reserved or created at time of transfer, notification of security interest delivered or mailed to secured party. Except for purchases by dealers and as between parties, transfers are ineffective without compliance with transfer procedures. (168A.10). Special procedures applicable to dealers. (168A.11).

Motor Vehicle Retail Installment Sales Act (168.66-.77) covers all motor vehicle retail installment sales contracts which are defined to include sales of motor vehicles primarily for personal, family or household use and not for resale in which title or lien is retained by seller for security purposes, including certain bailment and lease arrangements, mortgages and conditional sales contracts, and retail installment sales of mobile homes. (168.66, 72). Contracts must be written and signed by buyer and seller. Copy of contract must be furnished buyer at time of execution. (168.71[a][1]). Cash price may not include documentary fee or document administration fee more than $25 for services rendered on behalf of retail buyer in preparing, handling and processing documents relating to motor vehicle and retail sale closing. (168.66[9]). Provisions in contracts for confession of judgment are invalid. Contracts may provide for collection charge of 5% or $5 (whichever less) for installment not less than ten days delinquent and for attorney's fees of not more than 15% of due and payable amount of contract. (168.71[a]). Contracts must contain: (1) Cash sale price; (2) total amount and kind of down payment; (3) difference between cash sale price and down payment; (4) charges for insurance and other benefits and specifications thereof; (5) principal balance; (6) finance charges; and (7) total of payments payable and number, amount and dates of installments, or disclosures that satisfy Federal Truth in Lending Act in effect as of time of contract, whether or not act applies to transaction. (168.71[b]).

Finance charges must be computed on principal balance and not exceed: (1) 18% per annum on current or past year's model vehicle; (2) 19.75% per annum on two or three years past model vehicles; (3) 23.25% per annum on all other vehicles. (168.72[1a]). Contracts may be interest bearing or pre-computed and fixed rate or variable rate. (168.72[1b]).

If insurance charge is made, policy or certificate containing pertinent information as to premium, coverage, terms etc. must be furnished buyer within 30 days after execution of contract. (168.71[c]).

Upon written request holder of contract must give buyer written statement of dates and amounts of unpaid installments. Written receipt must be given for any cash payment. (168.71[a],[5]). Contracts may be paid in full at any time without penalty, and buyer must receive refund credit equal to actuarial method under 168.73, less $15, after date prepayment is made, which may be deducted from refund so calculated. (168.73).

Effective Jan. 1, 1988, if precomputed contract extended, deferred or renewed, service fee of not more than $5 may be charged plus total additional charge not exceeding simple interest annual percentage rate under original retail installment contract calculated on respective descending balances computed from date of such extension, deferment or renewal. (168.74).

Sales finance companies engaged in purchase of contracts and retail sellers who create and hold contracts other than certain licensed financial institutions, must have license from Commissioner of Banks. Annual license fee is $150 for principal place of business and $75 for each branch. (168.67). Buyer may recover amount of whole contract and attorneys' fees for intentional failure to comply with Act or greater of triple amount of excess time differential or $50, plus attorneys' fees for nonwillful failure to comply. (168.75).

Uniform Commercial Code adopted. (c. 336). See category Business Regulation and Commerce, topic Commercial Code.

Warranties.—See category Business Regulation and Commerce, topic Consumer Protection, subhead Warranties.

Liens.—Uniform Motor Vehicle Certificate of Title and Anti-Theft Act adopted. (168A.01-.31). Exclusive means of perfecting security interest is by delivery to department of existing certificate of title, if any, application for certificate of title containing name and address of secured party, date of security agreement, and required fee. (168A.17[2]). Validity of security interest created in another state generally governed by law of that jurisdiction unless parties understood that vehicle would be kept in this state and vehicle was brought into this state within 30 days. (168A.17). Security interest perfected in another jurisdiction remains perfected if secured party appears on certificate of title issued in that state; otherwise security interest must be perfected in this state within four months. (168A.17). See category Business Regulation and Commerce, topic Commercial Code.

Identification Marks.—Alteration of registration numbers or identification marks on motor vehicles and certain farm machinery prohibited. (168.36[3]). Alteration of odometer prohibited and mileage disclosure required. (325E.13-.16).

Foreign vehicles registered in home state or country and displaying license plates required by laws of home state or country may operate in this state, if laws of home state or country grant like privileges and exemptions to vehicles owned by residents of Minnesota and registered in this state and if reciprocity agreement has been made by responsible officials. Nonresidents carrying on business in this state and operating motor vehicles in intrastate commerce therein, or temporarily residing in this state while employed on same job for six months or more, are subject to same requirements as residents. (168.181). Special registration and reciprocity provisions applicable to transport vehicles. (168.187).

Nonresident operator who is at least 15 years old and who has in his possession valid driver's license issued by his home state or country may operate motor vehicle in this state. Nonresident who is at least 18 and whose home state or country does not require license may operate motor vehicle in this state for not more than 90 days in any calendar year, if motor vehicle so operated is currently registered in his home state or country. (171.03).

Action against nonresident, or resident absent from the state six months continuously after accident, arising out of operation of car may be commenced by service of process on Commissioner of Public Safety, provided notice of such service and copy of process are mailed by plaintiff, within ten days, to defendant at his last known address. Driving car or permitting it to be driven in state is acceptance of this provision. (170.55).

Direct Actions.—Not authorized. (262 Minn. 509, 115 N.W.2d 266).

Motor vehicle carriers regulated by Commissioner of Transportation and Transportation Regulation Board. Must file tariffs of rates and charges, annual reports, etc. Must obtain permit or certificate of public convenience and necessity. Must file certificate of insurance evidencing bond or insurance or other form of satisfactory security. Must report accidents involving hazardous material. Applies to foreign vehicles, subject to reciprocal agreements with other jurisdictions. Interstate carriers must register with Commissioner. (221.011 et seq.).

Motor Vehicle Tax.—In lieu of all other taxes (except such wheelage taxes as municipalities may impose and gross earnings taxes), motor vehicles using public highways are subject to annual tax as follows: Passenger vehicles according to base value, minimum tax $25; buses and commuter vans according to weight and seating capacity; trucks, tractors, trailers and semi-trailers, classified by use and in the main taxed on basis of value or gross weight; recreational vehicles according to gross weight. Tax is reduced periodically for above types of vehicles based on age of vehicle. Annual tax of $10 on motorcycles, $6 on motorized bicycles. (168.013).

See note at head of Digest as to 1998 legislation covered.

See Topical Index in front part of this volume.

MOTOR VEHICLES . . . continued

Vehicles exempt from motor vehicle tax: Public vehicles, farm tractors, farm trailers, highway construction equipment, motorized saws, corn shellers, etc., motorized golf carts, motor vehicles not operated on highways, mobile homes, snowmobiles (regulated by 84.81 et seq.) and vehicles owned and used by foreign power. (168.012).

Motor Vehicle Excise Tax.—Excise tax at rate equal to 6% imposed on purchase price of any motor vehicle purchased or acquired, either inside or outside state, which is required to be registered in state, except $10 for passenger automobile ten years old or older, registered in Minnesota other than as classic car and not designated as above-market vehicle (resale value of $3,000 or more) by Registrar of Motor Vehicles. (c. 297B). Certain purchasers exempt. Purchases by nonresidents exempt if purchases occurred more than 60 days prior to date of moving residence to state. (297B.03).

Tax on Aircraft.—All private nonscheduled aircraft are subject to tax, in lieu of all other taxes, of 1% of value with minimum of greater of $50 or 25% of tax on base price. Base price value is determined by manufacturer's list price or list price of comparable aircraft. Ten per cent depreciation is allowed second year after manufacture and 15% each year thereafter. (360.531). Tax is July 1 of each year. (360.61). Noncommercial

aircraft of nonresidents using Minnesota air space or airports are not subject to tax unless in use in Minnesota for more than 60 days in any year. Aircraft of nonresident grounded at airport for major repairs not considered as using airport. Nonresident owner of aircraft used for air show or exposition must obtain temporary permit costing $25 for valid for up to three days. Annual fee for hot air balloon is $25. (360.55). Manufacturers of aircraft sold in Minnesota must, before Aug. 1 of each year, file with Commissioner of Transportation sworn statement showing various models manufactured and retail list price of each model. Must also file form of complete specifications of construction of each model. Statements covering new prices and models must be filed whenever changes occur. (360.57).

Tax on scheduled airline flight property is based on formula giving equal consideration to tonnage, equated plane hours and revenue ton miles flown in Minnesota as compared to total of these factors over airline's entire system. (270.071-.079).

Gasoline Tax.—See category Taxation, topic Gasoline Tax.

RAILROADS:

See category Business Regulation and Commerce, topic Carriers.

COMMERCIAL CODE FORMS

See also categories Business Regulation and Commerce, topic Commercial Code and Mortgages, topic Chattel Mortgages.

Following are official UCC-1, UCC-2, UCC-3, UCC-11 and UCC-12 forms:

STATE OF MINNESOTA UCC-1
FINANCING STATEMENT

For
Filing
Officer

This statement is presented for filing pursuant to *Minnesota Uniform Commercial Code Minnesota Statutes*
Chapter 336.9-402   (Type in Black Ink)

1. Individual Debtor - Last Name	First Name	Middle I.

Social Security #	Mailing Address		

City	State	Zip Code

2. Individual Debtor - Last Name	First Name	Middle I.

Social Security #	Mailing Address		

City	State	Zip Code

3. Business Debtor - Name

Fed. ID #	Mailing Address

City	State	Zip Code

4. Secured Party Name	5. Assignee of Secured Party

Mailing Address	Mailing Address

City	State	Zip Code	City	State	Zip Code

6. This financing statement covers the following types or items of property. (If crops are covered describe the real estate and list the name of record owner.)

_____ Debtor is a transmitting utility
as defined by Minnesota Statutes Chapter 336.9-105

RETURN ACKNOWLEDGEMENT COPY TO:
(name and address)

Debtor's Signature
(Required in Most Cases see instructions)

Debtor's Signature

Secured Party's Signature

Please do not type outside the bracketed area.
(06920819 Rev. 5/93) Standard Form Approved by Secretary of State

---

See note at head of Digest as to 1998 legislation covered.

See Topical Index in front part of this volume.

MINNESOTA - UCC 2

FIXTURE FINANCING STATEMENT

**STATE OF MINNESOTA
UCC FIXTURE FINANCING STATEMENT**

This statement is present for filing in Real Estate records under Minnesota Statutes Chapter 336.9-401 subdivision 1, paragraph c.

This fixture financing statement is made this _____ day of _____, 19__ between
DEBTOR(s): _____ of _____

                             NAMES   MAILING ADDRESS

of the County of _____ of the State of _____ Zip _____

and SECURED PARTY: _____ of _____ of

                                  NAME   MAILING ADDRESS

the State of _____ Zip _____ .

This Fixture Financing Statement Covers The Following Fixture(s):

. . . . . on land lying and being in the County of _____ and State of Minnesota, described as follows, to-wit:

Record owner of above described real estate if other than debtors:

State of _____

County of _____

The foregoing instrument was acknowledged before me this _____ day of _____ 19__ by _____

Drafted by: _____

_____

_____

                                 _____
                                 SIGNATURE OF DEBTOR

_____

                                 SIGNATURE OF PERSON TAKING ACKNOWLEDGMENT

                                        notary stamp or seal

See note at head of Digest as to 1998 legislation covered.

See Topical Index in front part of this volume.

STATE OF MINNESOTA
SATISFACTION OF FIXTURE FINANCING STATEMENT

This satisfaction is presented for filing in Real Estate records under
Minnesota Statutes Chapter 336.9-401 subdivision 1, paragraph c.

Date: _____ , 19 ____

That certain Fixture Financing Statement owned by the undersigned, dated _____ 19___, executed by _____ _____ as debtor(s) to

_____

_____ as secured party

and filed for record _____ , 19___, as Document Number _____

(or in Book _____ of _____ Page _____ , in the Office of the County Recorder)

(Registrar of Titles) of _____ County, Minnesota with its indebtedness is hereby satisfied.

STATE OF MINNESOTA

COUNTY OF _____

The foregoing instrument was acknowledged before me this _____ day of _____ 19 ____

by _____

_____

Drafted by: _____   _____

_____   SIGNATURE OF PERSON TAKING ACKNOWLEDGMENT

_____

notary stamp or seal

**STANDARD FORM
STATE OF MINNESOTA
UCC-3 STATEMENT OF
CONTINUATION, ASSIGNMENT, RELEASE, ETC.**

| For |
| Filing |
| Officer |

This statement is presented for filing pursuant to *Minnesota Uniform Commercial Code Minnesota Statutes Chapter 336.9-402* (Type in Black Ink)

1. Original Financing Statement No.	Original File Date

2. DEBTOR (Name and Address)	3. SECURED PARTY (Name and Address)	

The financing statement described above is changed to show a(n): (Please one function per form with the exception of amendment)

☐ 4. CONTINUATION the original financing statement bearing the file number shown above is continued for an additional 5 years. The original statement is still effective.

☐ 5. AMENDMENT the original financing statement bearing the file number shown above is amended as described in BOX 10. See instruction 5 on the reverse side for additional information.

☐ 6. TOTAL ASSIGNMENT all of the secured party's rights under the original financing statement have been assigned to the assignee whose name and address appear in BOX 10.

☐ 7. PARTIAL ASSIGNMENT some of the secured party's rights have been assigned to the Assignee whose name and address appear in BOX 10. A description of the collateral subject to the assignment must also be given.

☐ 8. PARTIAL RELEASE the secured party releases the collateral described in BOX 10 but retains a security interest in the original financing statement bearing the file number shown above.

☐ 9. TERMINATION the secured party of record no longer claims a security interest under the financing statement bearing the file number shown above.

10.

RETURN ACKNOWLEDGMENT COPY TO:
(name and address)

Debtor Signature

Secured Party   Date

Please do not type outside the bracketed area.

amend819 Rev. 5/93

Approved by Secretary of State of Minnesota

STATE OF MINNESOTA
UCC-11 REQUEST FOR INFORMATION OR COPIES
FROM UCC STATEWIDE DATABASE

| For |
| Filing |
| Officer |

This statement is presented for filing pursuant to *Minnesota Uniform Commercial Code, Minnesota Statutes*
Section 336.9-407   (Type in Black Ink)

OPTIONS (choose one)

☐ **Information listing only** (includes computer printout of statewide UCC filings showing all debtor names and addresses, secured party names and addresses, filing information and description of subsequent filings).

☐ **Copies only** (includes a computer printout of statewide UCC filings showing the file number, the file date, the place of filing and copies of the UCC documents that are filed in the filing office where the request was processed).

☐ **Combination information and copies** (includes computer printout as described in information option and copies of the UCC documents that are filed in the filing office where the request was processed).

FILING OFFICER please furnish certificate showing any presently effective financing statements as of:

☐ date of processing   ☐ from _____ to date of processing

1. Individual Debtor Last Name		First Name	Middle I.
Social Security #	Mailing Address		
City		State	Zip Code

2. Individual Debtor Last Name		First Name	Middle I.
Social Security #	Mailing Address		
City		State	Zip Code

3. Business Debtor Name			
Fed. ID #	Mailing Address		
City		State	Zip Code

RETURN REQUESTED INFORMATION TO:
(name and address)

_____
Signature of Requesting Party

( )
_____
Telephone Number

Please do not type outside the bracketed area
(06920913 Rev 5/93)

Approved by Secretary of State

STATE OF MINNESOTA
UCC-12 REQUEST FOR TAX LIEN INFORMATION OR COPIES

| | For Filing Officer |

This statement is presented pursuant to *Minnesota Statutes Sections 269.69, 272.479 and 336.9-407.*   (Type in Black Ink)
OPTIONS (choose one) SEARCH IS OF RECORDS OF SINGLE FILING OFFICE ONLY.

☐ **Information listing only** (includes computer printout of state and federal tax liens showing all taxpayer names and addresses, government entity, filing information and description of subsequent filings).

☐ **Copies only** (includes a computer printout of state and federal tax liens showing the file number, the file date and copies of the tax liens that are filed in the filing office where the request was processed).

☐ **Combination information and copies** (includes computer printout as described in information option and copies of the tax liens that are filed in the filing office where the request was processed).

FILING OFFICER please furnish certificate showing any presently effective tax liens as of:

☐ date of processing   ☐ from _____ to date of processing

1. Individual Taxpayer Last Name	First Name	Middle I.

Social Security #	Mailing Address

City	State	Zip Code

2. Individual Debtor Last Name	First Name	Middle I.

Social Security #	Mailing Address

City	State	Zip Code

3. Business Taxpayer Name

Fed. ID #	Mailing Address

City	State	Zip Code

RETURN REQUESTED INFORMATION TO:
(name and address)

_____
Signature of Requesting Party

(   ) _____
Telephone Number

Please do not type outside the bracketed area
(12921988 Rev 5/93)

Approved by Secretary of State

MISSISSIPPI LAW DIGEST REVISER

Watkins & Eager PLLC
The Emporium Building
Suite 300
400 East Capitol Street
Jackson, Mississippi 39201
Mailing Address: P.O. Box 650
Jackson, Mississippi 39205
Telephone: 601-948-6470
Fax: 601-354-3623

Reviser Profile

History: Watkins & Eager, PLLC is a full-service diversified law firm. Its proud heritage began in 1895 when William Hamilton Watkins became the twentieth lawyer at the Jackson bar. The influential career of Will Watkins spanned sixty-four years during which he argued over twenty-five cases before the Supreme Court of the United States. Pat H. Eager, Jr. joined Will Watkins in 1916 and practiced with the firm until his death in 1970; Pat Eager was recognized as a premier trial lawyer who served as president of the International Association of Defense Counsel (1943-44) and who was Mississippi's initial invitee into the American College of Trial Lawyers. For several decades the image of the firm was heavily influenced by two of Will Watkins' children. Elizabeth Watkins Hulen, an outstanding appellate advocate, was the first woman in Mississippi history to argue before the Supreme Court of the United States. Thomas H. Watkins earned a national reputation in the representation of corporate and governmental clients. Many others have contributed and continue to contribute to the growth and progress of the firm which now enjoys an extensive corporate and business practice in addition to its broad trial and appellate practice.

Practice Areas: The firm's areas of practice include Arbitration and Mediation, Civil Litigation (Appellate, Commercial and Business, Lender Liability, Products Liability, Professional Malpractice, First Amendment, Securities, Tort and General), Antitrust, Banking, Finance, Corporate, Bankruptcy, Probate, Real Estate, Taxation, Estate and Trust, Employment, Insurance, Oil and Gas, and Environmental. The client base includes major manufacturers, employers, contractors, oil and gas producers and refiners, banks and financial institutions, cable television operators, institutions of higher learning, investors, telecommunications providers, insurers and governmental entities on the federal, state, county and municipal levels.

Size: Watkins & Eager is comprised of thirty-six members and twelve associates, along with one former senior member serving of counsel. The firm has graduates in law from the University of Mississippi, Mississippi College, Florida State University, New York University, Tulane University, University of California Hastings College, University of Florida, University of Virginia, and Vanderbilt University. Orderly growth is expected. The staff is composed of an investigator, legal assistants, administrators, secretaries and others necessary to the successful operation of a full-service firm.

Significant Distinctions: The firm is proud of the achievements and qualifications of its lawyers. Members of the firm serve by invitation as Fellows of the American College of Trial Lawyers, the American Academy of Appellate Lawyers, the American College of Trust and Estate Counsel, and the American College of Labor and Employment Lawyers. Several members of the firm are active in The Defense Research Institute, including P. N. (Nick) Harkins who currently serves as Second Vice President and is slated to become President in 2001. Charles Clark, an active member of the firm, is the retired Chief Judge of the United States Court of Appeals for the Fifth Circuit practicing primarily in the areas of arbitration, mediation and appellate advocacy.

In-house professional endeavors are required in addition to mandatory continuing legal education. Participation in the State Bar pro bono program is encouraged.

MISSISSIPPI LAW DIGEST REVISER

Watkins & Eager PLLC

The Emporium Building

Suite 300

400 East Capitol Street

Jackson, Mississippi 39201

Mailing Address: P.O. Box 650

Jackson, Mississippi 39205

Telephone: 601-948-6470

Fax: 601-354-3623

Reviser Profile

MISSISSIPPI LAW DIGEST

(The following is a list of all Categories and Topics, including cross-references, covered in this Digest.)

MISSISSIPPI LAW DIGEST

Revised for 1999 edition by

WATKINS & EAGER PLLC, of the Jackson Bar.

(Citations, unless otherwise indicated, refer to Mississippi Code of 1972 and latest cumulative supplement. "MRCP" refers to Mississippi Rules of Civil Procedure. Parallel citations to the Southern Reporter begin with 64 Miss. See also category Courts and Legislature, topic Reports.)

Note: 1998 legislation includes session laws through c. 598.

INTRODUCTION

GOVERNMENT AND LEGAL SYSTEM:

The State of Mississippi is a constituent state of the United States of America. For further discussion of the U.S. federal system, see Introduction to the Federal Government of the United States at the beginning of this volume. A great many laws are promulgated by the federal government of the United States and are not reflected in the topics below. See the Introduction to this volume for references to the federal law topics covered.

Like all but one of the United States, Mississippi has a common law legal system, with roots in English common law. For information on the courts and legislature of Mississippi, see category Courts and Legislature.

HOLIDAYS:

Mississippi State holidays are: Jan. 1, 3d Mon. in Jan., 3d Mon. in Feb., last Mon. in Apr., last Mon. in May, July 4, 1st Mon. in Sept., Nov. 11, Thanksgiving Day, Dec. 25 and Mon. following any legal holiday falling on Sun. (3-3-7). County offices shall observe state legal holidays. (25-1-99). Board of supervisors can declare offices closed on those holidays created by executive order of Governor. (25-1-99).

Holiday Falling on Sun.—When holiday falls on Sun., courthouse may close on immediately succeeding Mon. (25-1-99).

Holiday Falling on Sat.—When holiday falls on Sat., courthouse may be closed on immediately preceding Fri. (25-1-99).

Legality of Transactions on Saturday, Sunday or Holiday.—Sun. closure law (97-23-63) repealed effective July 1, 1986.

OFFICE HOURS AND TIME ZONE:

Mississippi is in the Central (GMT-06:00) time zone. Office hours are generally from 9 a.m. to 5 p.m.

BUSINESS ORGANIZATIONS

AGENCY:

The relation is, in general, in accordance with the common law. An agent may make oath for a principal in any proceeding. (11-1-3). See category Property, topic Powers of Attorney.

ASSOCIATIONS:

No general statutory provisions; however, numerous statutes control specific type of association. Religious societies (79-11-31 to 79-11-47); Agricultural Associations (79-17-1, et seq.); Agricultural Co-Operative Marketing Associations (79-19-1, et seq.); Aquatic Product Marketing Associations (79-21-1, et seq.); Mississippi Limited Liability Company Act (79-29-101, et seq.). Provisions governing foreign limited liability companies. (79-29-1001 et seq.).

Formation.—See specific type of association.

Rights and Powers.—See specific type of association.

Liabilities.—See specific type of association.

Actions.—Unincorporated associations, while strictly not partnerships, partake of their nature and should sue and be sued in form usual in such cases. Representative suits, however, are allowed.

Dissolution.—Courts of equity have jurisdiction over bills for dissolution and appointment of receivers of such associations, and as general rule those who are members at that time are entitled to proportionate share of property.

Professional Associations.—Mississippi Limited Liability Company Act (79-29-101, et seq.), enacted in 1994, became effective July 1, 1994. Art. 9 of Act provides for formation of professional limited liability companies. (79-29-901 et seq.). One or more individuals, duly and properly licensed to render same or related types of professional services may form professional limited liability company. See also topic Corporations, subhead Professional Corporation.

CORPORATIONS:

Mississippi Business Corporation Act (79-4-1.01 et seq.), enacted 1987, is substantially same as Revised Model Business Corporation Act (1984). (For text of Revised Model Act, see Uniform and Model Acts section.) Mississippi Business Corporation Act became effective Jan. 1, 1988. Mississippi Professional Corporation Act became effective July 1, 1995.

Substantive deviations by Mississippi Act from Revised Model Act are set forth below. Section number listed is section number of Revised Model Act.

§1.20(d)   add "or if electronically transmitted, it must be in a format that can be retrieved or reproduced by the Secretary of State in typewritten or printed form."

§1.20(g)   "A document required or permitted to be filed under this chapter which contains a copy of a signature, however made, is acceptable for filing."

§1.20(i)   "Delivery may be made by electronic transmission if, to the extent and in the manner permitted by the Secretary of State."

§1.20(j)   correct filing fee, franchise tax, license fee, or penalty must be paid when document is delivered to Office of Secretary of State.

§1.22(a)   Add as 1.22(a)(27): "Application for certificate of existence or authorization $25.00."

Add as 1.22(a)(28): "Any other document required or permitted to be filed by Section 79-4-101, et seq. $25.00."

§1.23(c)   Add as 1.23(c): "Notwithstanding subsections (a) and (b) of this section, any document that has a delayed effective time and date shall not become effective if, prior to the effective time and date, a statement of withdrawal is filed with the Secretary of State."

§1.40(5)   "Delivery" means any method of delivery used in conventional commercial practice, including delivery by hand, mail, commercial delivery and electronic transmission.

§1.40(8)   "Electronic transmission" means any process of communication not directly involving physical transfer of paper that is suitable for retention, retrieval and reproduction of information by recipient.

§1.40(24)   "Signature" includes any manual, facsimile, conformed or electronic signature.

§2.02   Amended effective Jan. 1, 1997.

§2.02(a)(2)   Add "and any information concerning the authorized shares as required by Section 79-4-6.01." to end of sentence.

§2.02(b)(2)(v)   omitted

§2.02(d)   Add as 2.02(d): "For the purposes of this section, a 'director' shall include any person vested with the discretion or powers of a director under Section 79-4-7.32."

§4.02(a)   Delete "120" to "180".

§6.25(c)   Add "or the corporation must furnish the shareholder this information on request in writing and without charge." to first sentence. Delete second sentence.

§7.02(a)(2)   Add to beginning of sentence: "Unless the articles of incorporation provide otherwise,". A special meeting of shareholders will be held if shareholders having at least 10% of all votes to be cast on an issue make written demand. Written demand for meeting may be revoked by writing to that effect if received prior to corporation's receipt of demands sufficient in number to require holding special meeting.

§7.22   Allows electronic filings by shareholders of proxies and votes.

§7.28   In 7.28(b), substitute "shall" for "do not"; in 7.28(c), delete "[all]"; delete 7.28(d).

§8.04   Substitute "Each Class" for "A Class" in final sentence.

§8.24   Amended effective Jan. 1, 1997.

§8.30(d)   Redesignate as 8.30 (e) and add as 8.30 (d) following: "For purposes of this section, a director, in determining what he reasonably believes to be in the best interests of the corporation, shall consider the interests of the corporation's shareholders and, in his discretion, may consider any of the following:

(1) The interests of the corporation's employees, suppliers, creditors and customers;

(2) The economy of the state and nation;

(3) Community and societal considerations;

(4) The long-term as well as short-term interests of the corporation and its shareholders, including the possibility that these interests may be best served by the continued independence of the corporation."

§8.31   Repealed in 1990

§8.32   omitted

§8.33(b)(2)   Substitute "section 79-4-1.01 et seq." for "section 6.40".

§8.33(c)   substitute "(c)" for "e".

See note at head of Digest as to 1998 legislation covered.

See Topical Index in front part of this volume.

CORPORATIONS . . . *continued*

§8.43(a)   Delete "its board of directors" and "the board of directors provides that" from third sentence and insert "it" in place of "its board of directors".

§8.43(b)   Add "and any officer or assistant officer, if appointed by another officer, may likewise be removed by such officer." to end of sentence.

§§8-50-8.59   Amended effective Jan. 1, 1997.

§8.58(a)   Delete 8.58(a) and substitute: "Unless the articles of incorporation or bylaws provide otherwise, any authorization of indemnification in the articles of incorporation or bylaws shall not be deemed to prevent the corporation from providing the indemnity permitted or mandated by this subarticle."

§8.58(b)   Redesignate as 8.58(c) and add as 8.58(b) following: "Any corporation shall have power to make any further indemnity, including advance of expenses, to and to enter contracts of indemnity with any director, officer, employee or agent that may be authorized by the articles of incorporation or any bylaw made by the shareholders or any resolution adopted, before or after the event, by the shareholders, except an indemnity against his gross negligence or willful misconduct. Unless the articles of incorporation, or any such bylaw or resolution provide otherwise, any determination as to any further indemnity shall be made in accordance with subsection (b) of Section 79-4-8.55. Each such indemnity may continue as to a person who has ceased to have the capacity referred to above and may inure to the benefit of the heirs, executors and administrators of such person."

§10.04(e)   Add as 10.04(e): "The provisions of subsections (a)(1) and (a)(7) shall not apply to preferred stock issued by a public utility subject to the provisions of the Public Utility Holding Company Act, 15 United States Code, Section 79, et seq., where the issuance of its securities is regulated by an agency of the United States."

§13.02(b)   Redesignate as 13.02(c) and add as 13.02(b) following: "Nothing in subsection (a) (4) shall entitle a shareholder of a corporation to dissent and obtain payment for his shares as a result of an amendment of the articles of incorporation exclusively for the purpose of either (i) making such corporation subject to application of the Mississippi Control Share Act, or (ii) making such act inapplicable to a control share acquisition of such corporation."

§14.04(d)   Add to beginning of sentence: "Unless a delayed effective date is specified,".

§14.07(c)   End of first sentence before colon reads: "within the lesser of five (5) years after the publication date of the newspaper notice, or any other applicable limitations period established by applicable law;".

§14.21(a)   Add "except that such determination may be served by 1st class mail" at end of sentence.

§14.21(b)   Add "except that such certificate may be served by 1st class mail" to end of sentence.

§14.22(a)   Change "two years" to "five years".

§14.31(a)   Delete first sentence. Delete word "other" from second sentence of §14.31(a).

§14.34(i)   Add as 14.34(i): "Nothing contained in this section shall diminish the inherent equity powers of the court to fashion alternative remedies to judicial dissolution."

§15.01(d)   Add as 15.01(d): "A foreign corporation which is a partner or member of any general partnership, limited partnership (other than a limited partner), joint venture, syndicate, pool or other association of any kind, whether or not such foreign corporation shares with or delegates to others control of such entity, which entity is transacting business in this state, is hereby declared to be transacting business in this state."

§15.02(d)   Fill in blanks with "$10.00" and "$1,000.00" respectively.

§15.31(a)   Add "except that such determination may be served by 1st class mail" to end of sentence.

§15.31(b)   Add "except that such certificate may be served by 1st class mail" to end of sentence.

§15.32   Delete 15.32 and substitute: "(a) A foreign corporation whose certificate of authority is administratively revoked under Section 79-4-15.31 may apply to the Secretary of State for reinstatement within five (5) years after the effective date of such revocation. The application must:

(1) Recite the name of the corporation and the effective date of the administrative revocation;

(2) State that the ground or grounds for revocation either did not exist or have been eliminated;

(3) State that the corporation's name satisfies the requirements of Section 79-4-4.01; and

(4) Contain a certificate from the Mississippi State Tax Commission reciting that the corporation has properly filed all reports and paid all taxes and penalties required by revenue laws of this state.

(b) If the Secretary of State determines that the application contains the information required by subsection (a) and that the information is correct, he shall reinstate the certificate of authority, prepare a certificate that recites his determination and the effective date of reinstatement, file the original of the certificate, and serve a copy on the corporation under Section 79-4-5.04.

(c) When the reinstatement is effective, it relates back to and takes effect as of the effective date of the administrative revocation and the corporation resumes carrying on its business as if the administrative revocation had never occurred."

§15.33   Add as 15.33: "(a) If the Secretary of State denies a foreign corporation's application for reinstatement following administrative revocation, he shall serve the corporation under Section 79-4-5.04, Mississippi Code of 1972, with a written communication that explains the reason or reasons for denial.

(b) The corporation may appeal the denial of reinstatement to the Chancery Court of the First Judicial District of Minds County within thirty (30) days after service of the communication of denial is perfected. The corporation appeals by petitioning the court to set aside the revocation and attaching to the petition copies of the Secretary of State's communication of denial.

(c) The court may summarily order the Secretary of State to reinstate the revoked corporation or may take other action the court considers appropriate.

(d) The court's final decision may be appealed as in other civil proceedings."

§16.02(a)   Add to beginning of sentence, "subject to section 79-4-16.03(c)".

§16.22(a)   Add: "within sixty (60) days of each anniversary date of its incorporation with respect to a domestic corporation or its authorization to transact business in this state with respect to a foreign corporation, or such other date as may be established by the Secretary of State [see Editor's Note below]," after "shall deliver" and before "to the Secretary of State".

§16.22(c)   Omitted.

§16.22(d)   Redesignate as 16.22(c).

§16.22   *Note.* The Secretary of State has determined that the 1994 annual reports shall continue to be delivered to the Secretary of State between Jan. 1 and Apr. 1, 1994.

§17.05   Omitted.

§17.06   Omitted.

General Supervision.—Secretary of State, Business Services Division, P.O. Box 136, Jackson, MS 39205-0136.

Purposes.—(§3.01).

Name.—(§4.01).

Term of Corporate Existence.—Perpetual, unless its articles of incorporation provide otherwise. (§3.02).

Incorporators.—(§2.01).

Certificate or Articles of Incorporation.—Must set forth: (a) corporate name; (b) number of shares authorized to issue and information as to shares issued; (c) street address of registered office and name of registered agent; (d) name and address of each incorporator. (§2.02[a]). May set forth: (a) names and addresses of initial directors; (b) purposes, management, and powers of corporation; (c) any provision allowed or required to be set forth in bylaws; (d) provision limiting directors' liability; (e) provision requiring corporation to indemnify director. (§2.02[b]).

Filing of Certificate or Articles.—With Secretary of State. (§§2.01, 2.02).

Incorporation Tax or Fee.—See subhead Filing Fees, infra.

Filing Fees.—References are to Revised Model Business Corporation Act.
§1.22(a)(1), (5), (6), (10)-(12), (16), (20), (26): $50.
§1.22(a)(2)-(4), (13), (14), (21), (25), (27), (28): $25.
§1.22(a)(7), (8): $10.
§1.22(a)(23): $100.
§1.22(a)(8): not to exceed $1,000.
§1.22(a)(19): $500.
§1.22(a)(9), (15), (17), (18), (22), (24): no fee
§1.22(b): $25.
§1.22(c)(1): $1 per page for copying.
§1.22(c)(2): $10.

License to Do Business.—(§2.03).

Organization.—(§2.05).

Amendment of Certificate or Articles.—(§10.01, et seq.).

By-laws.—(§2.06).

Stock.—(§6.01, et seq.).

CORPORATIONS ... *continued*

Stock Certificates.—(§6.25).

Issuance of Stock.—(§6.21).

Transfer of Stock.—(§6.27).

Uniform Simplification of Fiduciary Security Transfers Actadopted (91-11-1, et seq.) and saved from repeal by Uniform Commercial Code (75-10-104[2]).

Shareholder.—(§7.01, et seq.).

Shareholder's Actions.—(§7.40).

Shareholder's Liabilities.—(§6.22).

Shareholder's Meetings.—(§7.01, et seq.).

Voting Trusts.—(§7.30).

Directors.—(§8.01, et seq.).

Directors' Meetings.—(§8.20, et seq.).

Powers and Duties of Directors.—(§8.01[b]).

Liabilities of Directors.—(§8.30, et seq.).

Officers.—(§8.40, et seq.).

Liabilities of Officers.—(§8.42).

Indemnification of Directors and Officers.—(§8.50, et seq.).

Registered Office and Registered Agent.—(§5.01, et seq.).

General Power of Corporations.—(§3.02).

Dividends.—(§§6.23 and 6.40).

Unclaimed Dividends.—See category Property, topic Absentees, subhead Escheat.

Sale or Transfer of Corporate Assets.—(§12.01, et seq.).

Books and Records.—(§16.01, et seq.).

Reports.—Required reports: When corporation indemnifies director, and when corporation issues shares for promissory notes or future services. (§16.21; see §16.20 et seq.).

Corporate Bonds and Mortgages.—Uniform Simplification of Fiduciary Security Transfers Act adopted and saved from repeal by Uniform Commercial Code. (75-10-104[2]).

Merger and Consolidation.—(§11.01, et seq.).

Share Exchanges or Acquisition.—(§11.02).

Dissolution.—(§14.01, et seq.).

Insolvency and Receivers.—(§14.32).

Foreign Corporations.—(§15.01, et seq.). Foreign business trusts separately regulated. (79-16-1).

Taxation of Corporate Property.—Rules are the same as for taxation of individual property. (27-35-31).

Taxation of Corporate Stock.—Stock of corporation is exempt from taxation. (27-35-31).

Franchise Tax.—Franchise tax, in addition to all other taxes, is imposed by 27-13-1 et seq. Tax is imposed upon every corporation, association or joint stock company at rate of $2.50 for each $1,000 or fraction thereof of value of capital used, invested or employed within this state during preceding calendar or fiscal year. (27-13-5 thru -9). Tax is measured by combined issued and outstanding capital stock, paid-in capital, surplus and retained earnings. (27-13-9). Minimum tax is $25. (27-13-5 thru -9). Book value is accepted as prima facie correct as to true capital. (27-13-11). Corporations and organizations exempt from tax listed in 27-13-63.

Where organization does business within and without this state, value of capital is determined by computing ratio between (1) real and tangible personal property owned in this state and gross receipts from business carried on in this state and (2) total real and tangible personal property owned and gross receipts wherever located and from wherever received; and applying said ratio to total capital stock, surplus, undivided profits and true reserves. Determined capital in this state, however, cannot be less than assessed value of real estate and tangible personal property in this state for year preceding year in which return is due. (27-13-13).

Return must be filed with and tax paid to Commissioner, who is Chairman of State Tax Commission, on or before 15th day of third month following close of annual accounting period. (27-13-17). Penalties are prescribed for failure to pay tax. (27-13-23, 27-13-25).

Payment of tax is condition precedent to continued corporate existence of a domestic corporation or continuance of right of foreign corporation to do business in this state. Certificate of dissolution or withdrawal in case of corporations admitted to do business must be withheld until commissioner notifies Secretary of State that franchise tax has been paid unless corporation is not subject to tax. (27-13-53).

Upon failure of a corporation to pay its franchise tax, State Tax Commission may suspend right of such organization to perform as a corporation or to do business in state. Such organization must be notified of such suspension. Commissioner must notify Secretary of State in writing of such suspension and Secretary of State must make a notation on margin of his record of such suspension. (27-13-27). Such suspension can be set aside within 12 months of its original imposition. After expiration of said 12 month period without suspension being set aside corporation is without right to exercise its power and is considered as nonexistent. Disposition of its assets follows general law. (27-13-43).

Professional Corporation.—Mississippi Professional Corporation Act became effective July 1, 1995. One or more adult residents of Mississippi, properly licensed under laws of Mississippi to render same or related types of professional services may associate to form corporation pursuant to Mississippi Business Corporation Act. (79-9-5). Professional services include, but are not limited to, personal services rendered by certified public accountants, dentists, architects, veterinarians, osteopaths, physicians,

surgeons and attorneys. (79-9-3). See also topic Associations, subhead Professional Associations.

Deeds.—See category Property, topic Deeds.

Model Non-Profit Corporation Act.—Mississippi adopted version of 1986 Revised Model Nonprofit Corporation Act with variations. (79-11-101 et seq.).

Limited Liability Companies.—See topic Limited Liability Companies. (79-29-101 et seq.).

JOINT STOCK COMPANIES:

Joint stock companies do not appear to be recognized in Mississippi. In instances where this term is used it appears that corporations are meant. Mississippi Constitution includes joint stock companies in its definition of "corporations". (Miss. Const. Art. 7, §199).

Massachusetts Trusts.—Registration of foreign business trusts. (§79-16-1 et seq.).

Professional Associations or Corporations.—See topic Corporations, subhead Professional Corporation.

LIMITED LIABILITY COMPANIES:

The "Mississippi Limited Liability Company Act" became effective on July 1, 1994. (79-29-101 et seq.). Act contains many sections similar to sections of Mississippi Business Corporation Act and, with respect to professional limited liability companies, contains many sections similar to Mississippi Professional Corporation Law. Selected provisions of Act are summarized as follows:

Limited Liability Companies ("LLCs").—
General Supervision.—(§79-29-102).
Formation.—To form LLC certificate of formation must be executed and filed with Secretary of State setting forth required information. (79-29-201). Certificate of formation may be amended by filing certificate of amendment with Secretary of State (79-29-202); restated certificate (§79-29-203).
Purposes.—A LLC may be formed to carry on any lawful business, purpose or activity subject, however, to provisions of its certificate of formation and to any other laws governing or limiting conduct of particular business or activity. (79-29-108).
Name of each LLC must contain words "limited liability company" or abbreviation "L.L.C." or "LLC" and may contain name of member or manager. Name may not contain prohibited words or abbreviations or combinations thereof. (79-29-104).
Articles of Organization.—Members of LLC may enter into limited liability company agreement to regulate or establish affairs of limited liability company, conduct of its business and relation of its members. (§79-29-306).
Filing Articles of Organization.—There is no requirement to file limited liability company agreement. Only certificate of formation must be filed with Secretary of State. (§§79-29-202, 79-29-207).
Registered Office of Registered Agent.—Each LLC must continuously maintain registered office which may be same as any of its places of business and registered agent for service of process. (§79-29-106).
Management of LLC is vested in its members unless certificate of formation provides for management of LLC by manager(s). Certificate of formation may limit powers of manager(s) (79-29-302); agency power of members and managers (79-29-303).
Managers.—If certificate of formation vests management in manager(s) no member, acting solely in member capacity, is agent of LLC and every manager is agent of LLC for purpose of its business and affairs. (79-29-303). Managers need not be residents of Mississippi or members of LLC unless certificate of formation or LLC agreement so requires. Certificate of formation or LLC agreement may prescribe other qualifications for managers. Unless otherwise provided in certificate of formation or LLC agreement managers are elected by members. (79-29-401). Manager must comply with prescribed standards of conduct. (79-29-402).
Dissolution occurs and affairs must be wound up at time specified in certificate of formation or upon occurrence of events specified in certificate of formation or LLC agreement or upon written consent of all members or such lesser number as provided in certificate of formation or upon entry of decree of judicial dissolution. Also, if LLC were formed on or before June 30, 1998, then LLC is dissolved upon event of dissociation unless continued by remaining members within 90 days following occurrence of event of dissociation. For those LLCs formed on or after July 1, 1998 or those previously formed which file certificate of amendment, then (LLC is dissolved) upon event of dissociation of majority of remaining members or is otherwise provided in certificate of formation or agreement consent to do so. (79-29-801). Judicial dissolution may occur when it is not reasonably practical to carry on business in conformity with certificate of formation or LLC agreement or managers or members in control have been guilty of or have knowingly countenanced persistent and pervasive fraud or abuse of authority or persistent unfairness toward any member or LLC property is being misapplied or wasted by such persons. (79-29-802).
Filing Fees.—Fees charged by Secretary of State are (1) reservation of LLC name, $25; (2) change of address of registered agent, $25; (3) resignation of registered agent, $5; (4) certificate of formation, $50; (5) amendment to certificate of formation, $50; (6) certificate of dissolution, $25; (7) certificate of cancellation, $25; (8) restated certificate of formation or amended and restated certificate of formation, $25; (9) certificate of withdrawal, $25; (10) application for registration of foreign LLC, $250; (11) certificate correcting application for registration of foreign LLC, $50; (12) certificate of cancellation of registration of foreign LLC, $25; and (13) any other document required or permitted to be filed, $25. (79-29-1203).

PARTNERSHIPS:

Uniform Partnership Act adopted (79-12-1 et seq.) with following material variations (section number listed is section number of Uniform Act):

§4(5)—Phrase "except as provided in Section 8(4)" added.
§7(5)—Add as §7(5): "Operation of a mineral property under a joint operating agreement does not of itself establish a partnership."

PARTNERSHIPS . . . *continued*

§8(4)—Following sentence added: "This subsection (4) shall apply to all conveyances to a partnership in the partnership name heretofore made, provided, however, any person having a cause of action, because of such conveyance as of April 1, 1977, may commence suit on such cause of action within one (1) year of said date, unless such cause of action be sooner barred by existing law, and not afterwards."

§10(6) Add as §10(6): "Nothing in this section shall be deemed to modify the statutes of limitations for lands."

§15 changed to read: "All partners are liable jointly and severally for *all* debts and obligations of the partnership including those under Sections 13 and 14."

§16(3) Add as §16(3): "A representation that a person is an 'associate' or a 'nonpartner member' of a partnership is not a representation that he is a partner in the partnership."

§18(2) Add as §18(2): "By written agreement, the partners may establish various classes of partners (such as 'senior partners,' 'junior partners,' 'managing partners' and others) and may provide for their varying rights and duties in relation to the partnership."

§18(3) Add as §18(3): "By written agreement, the partners may establish various classes of nonpartner employees (such as 'associates,' 'nonpartner members' and others) and may provide for their varying rights and duties in relation to the partnership."

§28(1)—Phrase "(or of any other owner of an interest in the partnership)" added after "partner".

§29(2)—Provision for limited liability partnerships.

§29(4) changed "a" to "any", "preceding" to "proceeding" and substituted "any debt, obligation or liability" for "the obligations arising out of the acts, omissions, negligence, wrongful acts, malpractice or misconduct".

§31(4)—Phrase "unless the agreement provides otherwise" added.

§32(a)—Substitute "mentally incompetent" for "lunatic."

§38(2)(c)(ii)—added phrase: "and to be indemnified against all existing liabilities of the partnership."

Formation.—(§§6,7, and 18).

Name.—Mississippi does not require registration of partnership name.

Rights and Liabilities of Partners Inter Se.—(§§18, 20, 21 and 22).

Rights and Liabilities of Partners as to Third Parties.—(§§9-15).

Dissolution.—(§§29-40).

Administration of Partnership Property.—(§§38 and 40).

Limited Partnership.—Governed by Mississippi Limited Partnership Act (79-14-101 et seq.) which is enactment of Revised Uniform Limited Partnership Act (1976) (with 1985 amendments) ("ULPA") effective Jan. 1, 1988, with following exceptions (section number listed is section number of ULPA):

Definitions.—"Person" defined more broadly than in ULPA to include governmental entities and "any other legal or commercial entity", including those in representative capacities. (§101[11]).

Name.—"Limited Partnership" may be abbreviated "L.P." (§102[1]). Reservation of name by Secretary of State lasts 180 days. (§103[b]). Prohibited words are "bank", "banker", "bankers", "banking", "trust company", "insurance", "trust", "corporation", "incorporated", or words of similar import. (§102[4]).

Office and Registered Agent.—Registered agent's change of address governed by nonuniform provisions; properly executed address change constitutes amendment to certificate of limited partnership. (§104[b]). Registered agent's resignation governed by nonuniform provision; resignation effective 90 days after compliance with provision. (§104[c]).

Record Keeping.—Tax returns, partnership agreements, and financial statements to be preserved six years. (§105).

Indemnification.—Nonuniform provision allows partnership, in agreement, to indemnify any partner or other person against any claim; absence of such agreement does not preclude such indemnification. (§108).

Formation and Certificates.—Addresses in certificate must include both street and mailing address. (§201). Addition to ULPA provides that duly certified copy of certificate of limited partnership is conclusive of its formation and prima facie evidence of its existence. (§201[c]).

Amendment required upon change of name or address of partnership or registered agent. (§202[c][4], [5], [6]). ULPA §202(f) not adopted. Nonuniform section adds 30-day grace period to correct false statements in certificates. (§207[b]). Nonuniform section allows for restatement and/or integration of all provisions of certificate into single "Restated Certificate"; distinguishes "Amended and Restated Certificate". (§210).

Merger and Consolidation.—Nonuniform section governs merger and consolidation of limited partnerships. (§211).

Dissolution and Cancellation.—Nonuniform section requires certificate of dissolution to be filed upon dissolution and commencement of winding up or whenever there are no limited partners. Cancellation certificate filed upon completion of winding up. (§203).

Liability to Third Parties.—Add word "endorsing" after "guaranteeing" and add "or providing collateral for the limited partnership" to ULPA §303(b)(3). Add word "assignment" between "mortgage" and "pledge" and substitute "or granting of a security interest in any asset or assets of the limited partnership" for portion after "transfer of" in Uniform Act §303(b)(6)(ii). Add "renewal, refinancing, payment or other discharge" after "incurrence" and delete "other than . . . business" from §303(b)(6)(iii). Add nonuniform §303(b)(8), "Serving on [audit committee or committee functioning thereas]." ULPA §303(b)(8) designated as §303(b)(9).

Information.—ULPA §305 regarding limited partner's right to information modified as follows: Purpose of request must reasonably relate to requester's interest as limited partner. Written partnership agreement may impose reasonable standards upon such right to information. (§305[a][2]). Court may enforce duty to provide information, and may award expenses incurred in action obtaining enforcement. (§305[b] and [c]). Waiver of rights provided by §305 is unenforceable. (§305[d]).

Voting; Classes of Limited and General Partnership.—Uniform Act §302 modified and designated §302(b). Partnership agreement granting right to vote may control notice (and waiver thereof) of meeting to vote, action without meeting, proxy and quorum requirements, other matters. (§302[c]). Partnership agreement may provide for different classes and groups of limited partners, and future creation thereof. (§302[a]). Same rules applied to voting and classes of general partners by nonuniform §405.

Addition of General Partners.—Substitute "specific written consent of each partner" for "written consent of every partner" in ULPA §401.

Finance.—Add "to the same extent as the partnership could pursuant to this section" to end of last sentence of ULPA §501(c). Partnership agreement may specify penalties or consequences to which partner's interest shall be subjected for his failure to meet obligation to make contribution. Nonuniform section provides nonrestrictive list of such penalties, consequences. (§502[d]).

Withdrawal of General Partner.—ULPA §402 adopted as §402(a), adding "or has entered against him an order for relief in any bankruptcy or insolvency proceeding" after "insolvent" in ULPA §402(4)(iii). Nonuniform §402(b) provides that until amended certificate filed, one who ceases to be general partner still deemed such as to third parties doing business with partnership and reasonably believing him to be general partner. §602 of ULPA adopted as §602(a), amended as follows: (1) Recovery by partnership restricted to cases of withdrawal violating partnership agreement; (2) certain early withdrawal constitutes breach unless otherwise provided, (3) offset remedy provided in ULPA is "in addition to any other remedies." Nonuniform §602(b) describes rights of one who ceases to be general partner pursuant to §402.

Withdrawal of Limited Partner.—For limited partnership formed on or after July 1, 1998, or those previously formed which file on certificate of amendment, revised language provides that "a limited partner may withdraw from a limited partnership at the time or upon the occurrence of events specified in writing in the partnership agreement." All previous provisions were deleted except as applied to limited partnership formed on or before June 30, 1998.

Distribution.—Add "limited" between "withdrawing" and "partner" in ULPA §604. Add "subject to §§607 and 804 of this Act," to beginning of ULPA §606. Add "and liabilities as to which recourse of creditors is limited to specific property of the limited partnership" between "interests" and "exceed," and add "provided that the fair value of any property that is subject to a liability as to which recourse of creditors is so limited shall be included in the limited partnership assets only to the extent that the fair value of the property exceeds this liability" to end of ULPA §607. Add "which were in existence at the date of receipt of the return of contribution and have not been subsequently discharged" to end of ULPA §608(a).

Assignment of Partnership Interests.—Add "a partner has no interest in specific limited partnership property" as second sentence to ULPA §701. Change third sentence of ULPA §702 to "An assignment entitles the assignee, to the extent assigned, to share in such profits and losses, to receive such distribution or distributions, and to receive such allocation of income, gain, loss, deduction, credit or similar item to which the assignor would have been entitled." Add "and which could not be ascertained from the partnership agreement kept pursuant to Section 105 of this act" to end of last sentence of ULPA §704(b). Substitute "Sections 207 and 402 of this act and Articles 5 and 6 of this Act" for "Sections 207 and 502" in ULPA §704(c).

Dissolution.—Partnership agreement may allow dissolution by agreement of less than all partners. (§801[3]). Nonuniform §802 provides that persistent fraud, abuse, or unfairness toward any partner, or misapplication or waste of partnership property by general partners, constitute additional grounds for judicial dissolution. (§802[b]). ULPA §803 adopted as §803(a), with additional provision for court to appoint liquidating receiver or trustee. Nonuniform section provides various enumerated powers to persons winding up partnership's affairs, and entitles limited partners winding up affairs to reasonable compensation therefor. (§803[b][c]). Add "(whether by payment or by establishment of reserves)" between "partnership" and "other" in ULPA §804(1).

Foreign Limited Partnerships.—Substitute "mailing and street address" for "business address" in ULPA §902(6) and for "address" in §902(7). Add "as provided in Section 1104 of this Act" between "fees" and "have" in ULPA §903(a). Name may include abbreviation "L.P." instead of "limited partnership". (§904). §905 adds fee to amendment certificate requirements. Add "or such other person as may be authorized to do so under the laws of the state under which the foreign limited partnership is organized" to end of first sentence in ULPA §906.

Derivative Actions.—Add as second sentence to §1004, "If those proceeds are insufficient to reimburse plaintiff's reasonable expenses, the court may direct that any such award of plaintiff's expenses, or a portion thereof, be paid by the limited partnership."

Filing Fees.—$25 for reservation of partnership name, change of registered agent's address, certificate of dissolution, certificate of cancellation, restated certificate of limited partnership or amended and restated certificate of limited partnership, certificate of withdrawal, and certificate of cancellation of registration of foreign limited partnership. $5 for resignation of registered agent. $50 for certificate of limited partnership, amendment to certificate of limited partnership, and certificate correcting application for registration of foreign limited partnership. $250 for application for registration of foreign limited partnership. (§1104).

Out-of-State Partnerships.—Registration requirements for foreign limited liability partnerships. (79-31-1 et seq.).

BUSINESS REGULATION AND COMMERCE

BANKS AND BANKING:

Uniform Commercial Code adopted, effective Mar. 31, 1968. See topic Commercial Code.

See note at head of Digest as to 1998 legislation covered.

See Topical Index in front part of this volume.

BANKS AND BANKING . . . continued

Regulated by State Board of Banking Review and Department of Banking and Finance. Banking Act is found at 81-3-1, et seq. Provisions relating to banking found in 81-5-1, et seq. Savings Association law is found at 81-12-1 et seq. Credit unions governed by 81-13-1 et seq. Savings Bank law is found at 81-14-1 et seq. Provisions relating to banks and other institutions engaging in trust business found in 81-27-1.001 et seq.

Stockholders.—Stockholder is individually liable, for benefit of depositors, to extent of par value of his stock in addition to his stock, unless bank was open for business on Apr. 2, 1934, or was organized thereafter, and is a member of the Federal Deposit Insurance Corporation or any similar agency established by U.S. laws. (81-5-27).

Holders of preferred stock are not individually liable for debts, contracts or engagements of bank or liable to assessment to restore impairment of capital. (81-5-23).

Deposits.—Joint deposits may be received and paid out to either depositor, whether or not the other is living. Intention that title vest in survivor is presumed if deposit is made under certain terms. (81-5-63). Deposits of minors or persons under disability may be received and paid out on their checks. (81-5-59).

Deposit not exceeding $7,500 may be paid to nearest relative of deceased depositor without necessity of administration. (81-5-63).

Unclaimed Deposits.—Escheat in accordance with Uniform Disposition of Unclaimed Property Act, adopted with minor variations. Time period for presumption of abandonment decreased from seven years to five years. (89-12-1, et seq.). See category Property, topic Absentees, subhead Escheat.

Checks may be paid in currency or valid exchange.

Collections.—Uniform Commercial Code adopted, effective Mar. 31, 1968. (75-1-101 et seq.).

Trust Companies.—Bank may: Receive money or real or personal property in trust; execute trusts committed to it by any person, corporation or court of record; act as agent for investment of money, management of property or issuance, registration, transfer or countersigning stocks, bonds or other evidences of indebtedness of any corporation, association, municipality, state, county or public authority; act as executor, administrator, guardian of infant or insane person, agent or attorney in fact, commissioner for sale of real or personal property, assignee, receiver, trustee in mortgage or bond issue or in any fiduciary capacity authorized by law; accept trust funds and other property on agreed terms and pay or deliver same to owners or beneficiaries according to terms of trust agreement; execute bond for protection of any trust or trust estate being administered by it. These powers may be exercised by bank previously doing business under state laws, without amendment of charter, after obtaining written consent of Commissioner. (81-5-33).

Banks may accept accounts in name of administrator, executor, guardian or other fiduciary and accounts payable at death governed by statute. (81-5-34).

Assets held in fiduciary capacity must be segregated from general assets and separate books and records kept in regard thereto. Trust funds held awaiting investment or distribution must be carried in separate account and not used in bank's business unless bank has set aside in trust department bonds of U. S. or State of Mississippi or subdivision thereof market value of which must always be not less than 10% in excess of trust funds exclusive of funds insured by FDIC. (81-5-33).

Bank may not invest trust funds in securities purchased from itself except under Uniform Common Trust Fund Act, or lend trust funds to any director, officer or employee. (81-5-33).

Trust department may not receive deposits subject to check or items for collection. (81-5-33).

Provisions governing multistate, state and limited liability trust institutions found in 81-27-1.001 et seq.

Uniform Trustees' Powers Act adopted. (91-9-103 et seq.).

Uniform Common Trust Fund Act in effect. (81-5-37).

Bank Holding Companies.—Operation of multibank holding companies permitted under certain restrictions. Bank holding company is prohibited from acquiring stock of bank in Mississippi if it would control banks in Mississippi having more than 25% of total deposits of all offices in state of commercial banks, savings banks, savings and loans, and credit unions. (81-7-19).

Branch Banking.—Branching de novo and by merger permitted under certain restrictions. (81-7-8). Interstate Bank Branching Act to be codified as new chapter within Title 81.

Foreign Banks.—Foreign banking corporations or foreign mutual savings banks not organized under the laws of this state may maintain bank accounts, hold mortgages on real property, collect debts, hold securities, sue or be sued within the state and service of process may be performed by service upon any custodian or agent appointed within the state. If no such agent has been appointed, then the Secretary of State is appointed as the duly authorized agent of nonresident banking corporations. Venue of any legal action must be in the county of the residence of the plaintiff except where land is involved and then venue must be in county in which land is located. (81-5-41; 81-5-43). As to right of foreign bank or trust company to act as executor, administrator, guardian or trustee see categories Estates and Trusts, topics Executors and Administrators, Trusts; and category Family, topic Guardian and Ward.

State banking board approval required for bank organized under laws of foreign country to transact business in state, upon approval such foreign bank subject to state banking laws; limited to transactions clearly related to foreign business and financing international commerce; unable to exercise fiduciary power and unable to receive deposits but may maintain for account of others credit balances incidental to international transactions. Application fee minimum $2,500, maximum $10,000. (81-5-40).

BILLS AND NOTES:

Uniform Commercial Code adopted, effective Mar. 31, 1968. (75-1-101). See topic Commercial Code.

Special Requirements.—Form of negotiable instruments. (75-3-104).

Judgment Notes.—Authority in notes to confess judgment is prohibited. (11-7-187).

Attorney Fees.—Cost of collection and attorney fee clauses are enforceable. (67 Miss. 60, 6 So. 615).

Special Defenses.—Enforcement of instruments. (75-3-302, 75-3-305, 75-3-306, 75-3-308). See topic Consumer Protection.

BILLS OF LADING:

See topic Carriers.

BILLS OF SALE:

See topic Sales.

BLUE SKY LAW:

See topic Securities.

BROKERS:

A privilege tax license is required of a broker before commencing business. No statutory lien is provided for.

Uniform Commercial Code adopted, effective Mar. 31, 1968. See topic Commercial Code.

Licenses.—Licensing requirements contained in 81-19-1 et seq. Commissioner of Banking and Consumer Finance regulates brokers. (81-19-17). License application fee is $300. (81-19-9). Surety bond in amount of $25,000 is required. (81-19-9). Separate license required for each business location of broker. (81-19-13). Agreements to find and obtain consumer loan for borrower must be in writing. (81-19-21). Certain activities are prohibited, violation of which constitute felony. (81-19-23).

Bond.—Surety bond in amount of $25,000 is required. (81-19-9).

Real Estate Brokers.—Licensing requirements contained in 73-35-1 et seq. Mississippi Real Estate Commission regulates brokers. (73-35-5). Brokers must be U.S. citizens at least 21 years old legally domiciled at time of application and satisfy education, exam and experience requirements. (73-35-7). License application fee is $100. Separate fees apply to salespersons and other activities. (73-35-17). Nonresident broker must be licensed broker in another state, affiliated with Mississippi broker or apply for Mississippi broker's license and maintain office in Mississippi. (73-35-8). Limitations apply to brokerage activities by partnerships, corporations and associations. (73-35-7).

BULK SALES:

See topic Commercial Code; also category Debtor and Creditor, topic Fraudulent Sales and Conveyances.

CARRIERS:

Public Service Commission has supervision of common carriers. (77-1-1 et seq.). *Note:* §§77-1-1 through 77-1-49 shall be repealed as of Dec. 31, 2002. Mississippi Department of Transportation enforces railroad laws, except rates. (65-1-2). Uniform Commercial Code adopted. (75-1-101, et seq.). See topic Commercial Code.

Licenses.—Permits generally required for all carriers. (77-7-49 to 77-7-61).

Rebates are unlawful, as are free or reduced rate passes. (77-9-15).

Each railroad operating in state pays pro rata share of $201,000 per year based on miles of track. (77-9-493).

Rates.—Common carrier must furnish list of tariffs to Public Service Commission. Commission shall revise, fix and regulate all tariffs not subject to exclusive congressional regulation. Interstate rates are advisory only. Factors to be considered when fixing rates. (77-7-221).

Discrimination.—Rate discrimination is prohibited. (77-7-311).

Limiting Liability.—Carrier who issues bill of lading whether negotiable or not must exercise reasonable care. Damages may be limited to value stated in documents. No limitation applies to conversion for carrier's own use. (75-7-309).

Bills of Lading.—Provisions and obligations found at 75-7-101, et seq.

Liens.—Carrier has lien on goods covered by bill of lading for subsequent storage and transportation charges and for unnecessary expenses. Lien is effective against consignor or other person entitled to goods. (75-7-307).

COMMERCIAL CODE:

Uniform Commercial Code adopted and found at 75-1-101 et seq. of Mississippi Code. 1962 Official Text adopted effective Apr. 1, 1978. (75-11-101). Section numbers are same as in 1962 Official Text. Article 9 section numbers are same as in 1972 Official Text.

Material variations and alternatives adopted from 1972 Official Text, as amended, (found in Uniform and Model Acts section) are as follows:

§1-105(1)—Law of Mississippi to always govern rights and duties of parties in regard to disclaimers of implied warranties of merchantability or fitness or necessity for privity of contract to maintain action for breach of said warranties notwithstanding agreement of parties to contrary.

§1-209—1966 Official Optional Amendment not enacted.

§2-314(1)—Phrase "Unless excluded or modified (Section 2-316)" is omitted.

§2-314(3)—Phrase "Unless excluded or modified (Section 2-316)" is omitted.

§2-314(4)—Added new subsection providing that there is no implied warranty that certain livestock are free from sickness or disease at time of sale. Allows disclaimers or express disclaimer or express modification of any implied warranties of merchantability and fitness for particular purpose or any limitation of remedies for breach of

COMMERCIAL CODE . . . *continued*
warranties concerning computer hardware, software, and services sold between merchants.

§2-314(5)—Added computer exclusion. See §2-314(1).

§2-315—Phrase "Unless excluded or modified under the next section" is omitted. Added new sentence providing that there is no implied warranty that certain livestock are free from sickness or disease at time of sale.

§2-315.1—Added new section limiting exclusion or modification of warranties to consumers.

§2-316—Omitted. There shall be no limitation of remedies or disclaimer of liability as to any implied warranty of merchantability or fitness for particular purpose.

§2-318—1966 Official Optional Amendment Alternative A adopted. (See 11-7-20.)

§2-615(a)—Inserted between "(c)," and "is" is following language: "or failure to take delivery as provided for under the contract on the part of a buyer who complies with paragraph (d),".

§2-615(d)—Following is added as paragraph (d): "The buyer must notify the seller seasonably that there will be a delay or total inability to take delivery, and where practicable, state the contingency which has occurred causing such delay or inability."

§2-617—New section adopted as follows: "**Force Majeure.**—Deliveries may be suspended by either party in case of Act of God, war, riots, fire, explosion, flood, strike, lockout, injunction, inability to obtain fuel, power, raw materials, labor, containers, or transportation facilities, accident, breakage of machinery or apparatus, national defense requirements, or any cause beyond the control of such party, preventing the manufacture, shipment, acceptance, or consumption of a shipment of the goods or of a material upon which the manufacture of the goods is dependent. If, because of any such circumstance, seller is unable to supply the total demand for the goods, seller may allocate its available supply among itself and all of its customers, including those not under contract, in an equitable manner. Such deliveries so suspended shall be cancelled without liability, but the contract shall otherwise remain unaffected."

§2-702(3)—Words "or lien creditor" deleted.

§2-719—Following has been added: "(4) Any limitation of remedies which would deprive the buyer of a remedy to which he may be entitled for breach of an implied warranty of merchantability or fitness for a particular purpose shall be prohibited." Provisions of §2-719(4) do not apply to computer hardware, software, and services sold between merchants.

§2-725(1)—Six year limitations period for breach of contract. Second sentence in subsection is deleted. Privity of contract not requirement for maintaining action for personal injury, property damage or economic loss in negligence, strict liability, breach of warranty, or action brought under UCC.

§2A-101—Art. 2A adopted, effective July 1, 1994, except as noted. Gender neutral language not adopted. "Articles" are referred to as "Chapters."

§2A-103(1)(e)—Optional language adopted; figure $25,000.00 inserted.

§2A-103(G)—Definition of finance lease expanded.

§2A-104(1)(a)—Text reads "Certificate of title statute of this state, including but not limited to, those pertaining to motor vehicles in Chapter 21, Title 63, Mississippi Code of 1972." §2A-201(1)(a)—Words "One Thousand Dollars" are inserted before figure, which is placed in parentheses, i.e., ($1,000.00).

§2A-209(4)—Lessee retains rights against supplier under agreement.

§2A-214—Not adopted.

§2A-216—Alternate A adopted.

§2A-303—Substantially altered.

§2A-307(2)(c)—Perfection before lease became enforceable.

§2A-311—Priority subject to subordination.

§2A-407(3)—Validity of lease terms which make lessee's promises irrevocable and independent of acceptance not affected.

§2A-508(1)(d)—Exercise any other right or pursue any other remedy in lease.

§2A-517(2) & (3)—Lessee may revoke acceptance of lot or commercial unit if lessor defaults under lease and default substantially impairs value of lot or unit; and lessee may revoke lot or commercial unit because of default of lessor if lease so provides.

§2A-523(1)(f), (2), & (3)(a) & (b)—Lessor may exercise rights and remedies provided in lease; incidental damages allowed under certain conditions.

§2A-532—Lessor's rights to residual interests.

§3-101 et seq.—1990 Revision of Art. 3 adopted, effective Jan. 1, 1993.

§3-204(a)—Provision added at end of subsection providing for blanket endorsement of instruments representing student loans and loans insured by U.S. Secretary of Education.

§3-415(a)—1993 Amendment, adding subsection (e) to those subsections to which subsection (a) is subject to, not adopted.

§4-106(b)—Alternate B is adopted.

§4A-101 et seq.—Art. 4A adopted, effective July 1, 1991.

§5-114(4)—Not adopted.

§5-114(5)—Not adopted.

§6-101 et seq.—Art. 6 repealed, effective July 1, 1995.

§7-204(4)—Not adopted.

§7-209—1966 Official Amendment not enacted.

§7-403(1)(b)—Optional language not adopted.

§9-105(h)—Goods defined so as to include farm raised fish and marine vessels.

§9-203(4)—Local statutes are referred to as follows: "Sections 75-67-101—75-67-135, inclusive, Mississippi Code of 1972, known as the 'Small Loan Regulatory Act'; Sections 75-67-201—75-67-243 inclusive, Mississippi Code of 1972, known as 'The Small Loan Privilege Tax Act'; Sections 75-67-1—75-67-39, inclusive, Mississippi Code of 1972, sometimes referred to as Pawnbrokers Act; Sections 63-19-1—63-19-55, inclusive, Mississippi Code of 1972, known as 'The Motor Vehicle Sales Finance Act'."

§9-301(2)—Purchase money secured party has 20 days to perfect security interest after debtor receives possession of collateral. (1986, c. 343).

§9-302(3)(b)—"§63-21-1 et seq." inserted in blank.

§9-302(5)—Following language is adopted: "The filing of a financing statement pursuant to this chapter, whether before or after the effective date of this provision, is the exclusive method of perfecting a security interest in instruments evidencing student loans, including loans that are insured by the United States Secretary of Education under 20 U.S.C.A. 1071, et seq., as amended, or by a state or non-profit private institution or organization with which the United States Secretary of Education has an agreement under 20 U.S.C.A. 1078(b), as amended; in other respects such security interest is subject to this chapter as if such security interest were a security interest in general intangibles. The provisions of this chapter providing for security interests prevail over the possession, negotiation and assignment provisions of Chapter 3 of this title as each provision affects the rights of a secured party in instruments evidencing student loans, and the rights of a secured party in instruments evidencing student loans perfected in accordance with this subsection are prior to the rights of a holder, owner or transferee of any instrument evidencing the right to receive payment under student loans."

§9-307(4)—Following is adopted as subsection (4): "Notwithstanding subsection (1) of this section, a secured party may not enforce a security interest in farm products against a buyer, commission merchant or selling agent who purchases or sells farm products in the ordinary course of business from or for a person engaged in farming operations unless the secured party has complied with the regulations issued by the Secretary of State under 75-9-319, or unless the buyer, commission merchant or selling agent has received from the secured party or seller written notice of the security interest which complies with the requirements of Section 1324 of the Food Security Act of 1985, as now enacted or as hereafter may be amended."

§9-312(4)—Purchase money security interest in collateral other than inventory has priority if perfected at time debtor receives possession of collateral or within 20 days thereafter.

§9-313(4)—New subsection (a) added and remaining subsections redesignated, effective July 1, 1992. Section (a) reads as follows: "The security interest is a purchase money security interest, the interest of the encumbrancer or owner arises before the goods become fixtures, the security interest is perfected by a fixture filing before the goods become fixtures or within twenty (20) days thereafter, and the debtor has an interest of record in the real estate or is in possession of the real estate; or"

§9-313(9)—Following language is adopted: "(a) Subject to provisions in subsections (4) and (5) of this section, but notwithstanding any contrary provision of the law of this state, a security interest in fixtures or goods that become fixtures shall not have priority over the conflicting interest of an encumbrancer or owner of real estate whose interest has been perfected under real estate law prior to the perfection of a security interest in fixtures against the real estate.

"(b) For the purposes of this section a security interest in fixtures is perfected against the real estate only when the filing or recording of an instrument, with respect to such security interests, constitutes constructive notice of such interest under the laws of this state, other than this chapter, which are applicable to the filing or recording of real estate mortgages and deeds of trust; provided, however, that no provision of this chapter nor of any other law of this state shall be construed to require that an instrument filed to perfect a security interest in fixtures shall have the signatures of the parties acknowledged or proved as required by Section 89-3-1, Mississippi Code of 1972."

"(c) Subject to the contrary provisions in subsections (4) and (5) of this section, but notwithstanding any contrary provision of the law of this state, no party having a security interest in fixtures which is subordinate to the interest of an encumbrancer or owner of real estate who is not the debtor, may remove his collateral from the real estate without the written permission of such encumbrancer or owner of the real estate."

§9-401(1)—Third alternative adopted. When collateral is farm products, security interest must also be filed in office of Secretary of State. Non-code subsection (c) added, effective July 1, 1995, reading as follows: " 'c' When the collateral is a sailboat or other vessel required to be numbered pursuant to Section 59-21-1 et seq., or an inboard or outboard motor used for the propulsion of vessels required to be so numbered, then in the office of the chancery clerk in the county of the debtor's residence and in the office of the Secretary of State."

§9-401(2)—Following language is included: "Except as provided in section 9-313,".

§9-401(3)—Following language is included: "Except as provided in section 9-313,".

§9-401(7)—Following is adopted as subsection (7): "For purposes of this section, in those counties having two (2) judicial districts, each such district shall be considered a separate county."

§9-402(5)—Bracketed provisions adopted. Add "or record lessee" to end of last sentence. Following sentence is added: "No provision of this chapter nor of any other law of this state shall be construed to require that an instrument filed to perfect a security interest under this subsection shall have the signatures of the parties acknowledged or proved as required by §89-3-1 of Mississippi Code of 1972."

§9-403(4)—Following sentence added: "Also, for indexing purposes, a continuation statement shall be treated as a financing statement by the filing officer and indexed in the same manner as financing statements."

§9-403(5)—Insert following in blanks in order listed: $5; $10; $2; $5; $2.

§9-403(6)—Sentence added, reading: "A financing statement covering a mobile home, other than a mobile home constituting inventory, remains effective, if it so states, until a termination statement is filed."

§9-404(1)—"April 1, 1978" inserted in blank.

§9-404(3)—Insert following in blanks in order listed: $5; $10; $2.

§9-405(1)—Insert following in blanks in order listed: $5; $10; $2; $5; $10; $2.

§9-406—Insert following in blanks in order listed: $5; $10; $2.

§9-407—Adopted. Requests under subsection (2) must be in writing and accompanied by $5 if on standard form or $10 if otherwise. Additional fee of $2 to be paid by requesting party for each financing statement listed on filing officer's certificate. $2 inserted in last blank in subsection (2).

§9-407(7)—Optional language adopted.

See note at head of Digest as to 1998 legislation covered.

See Topical Index in front part of this volume.

COMMERCIAL CODE . . . *continued*

§9-409—New section added as follows: "The Secretary of State shall prescribe and adopt the types of forms coming within the framework and meeting the requirements of the Uniform Commercial Code, for all filings to be made in his and other filing offices of this state. The use of nonstandard forms necessitates special handling by the filing officers, and a party submitting a filing on a nonstandard form shall be liable for costs incurred by special handling in the sum of five dollars ($5.00) payable to the filing officer concerned, in addition to the regular filing fee for the filing submitted on a nonstandard form."

§9-410—New section added as follows: "The Secretary of State may prepare a cumulative list of filings made in his office each day and furnish such list to any person requesting same, with the cost of its preparation and delivery to be charged to the requesting party and payable to the secretary of state at the time and in the manner agreed upon between the parties; provided, however, failure by the requesting party to pay as agreed may result in his suspension from receipt of further lists."

§10-101—Effective date Mar. 31, 1968.

§10-102—Several statutes specifically repealed.

§10-104(1)—Adopted.

§10-104(2)—Adopted with the blank filled in as follows: "Sections 5359-31 to 5359-43, inclusive, of Chapter 4, Title 21, Mississippi Code of 1942, Recompiled, cited as the Uniform Act for Simplification of Fiduciary Security Transfers." [§§91-11-1 to 91-11-21, Mississippi Code of 1972].

§§11-101 to 11-108—Transition provisions adopted.

1972 Official Amendments.—Adopted.

1973 Official Amendment.—Adopted.

1977 Official Amendments.—Adopted.

1989 Official Amendments.—Adopted.

1990—Adopted 1990 Revision of Art. 3, 1990 Amendments to Art. 4, new Art. 4A (Funds Transfers), 1977 Revision of Art. 8 and 1972 Revision of Art. 9.

1996—Adopted 1995 Revision of Art. 5.

Filing Fees.—See category Documents and Records, topic Records, subhead Filing Under Commercial Code.

See also topics: Banks and Banking, Bills and Notes, Brokers, Carriers, Contracts, Factors, Frauds, Statute of, Sales, Securities, Warehousemen; categories Business Organizations, topic Corporations; Civil Actions and Procedure, topic Limitation of Actions; Debtor and Creditor, topics Assignments, Fraudulent Sales and Conveyances, Liens, Pledges; Documents and Records, topics Records, Seals; Mortgages, topic Chattel Mortgages.

CONDITIONAL SALES:

See topic Sales.

CONSIGNMENTS:

See topic Factors.

CONSUMER PROTECTION:

Unfair Methods of Competition and Unfair or Deceptive Acts in Conduct of Trade.—Office of Consumer Protection established in office of Attorney General. Attorney General may bring action for temporary or permanent injunction in name of State against person who has engaged in any prohibited practice. Unfair methods of competition and unfair or deceptive acts or practices in conduct of trade or commerce defined as: passing off goods or services as those of another; misrepresentation of source, sponsorship, approval or certification of goods or services; misrepresentation of affiliation, connection or association with, or certification by another; misrepresentation of designations of geographic origin in connection with goods or services; representing that goods or services have sponsorship, approval, characteristics, ingredients, uses, benefits or quantities they do not have or that person has sponsorship, approval, status, affiliation, or connection he does not have; representing goods are original or new if they are reconditioned, reclaimed, used or secondhand; representing that goods or services are of particular standard, quality, or grade, or that goods are of particular style or model, if they are of another; disparaging goods, services, or business of another by false or misleading representation of fact; advertising goods or services with intent not to sell them as advertised; advertising goods or services with intent not to supply reasonably expectable public demand, unless advertisement discloses limitation of quantity; making false statements of fact concerning reasons for, existence of, or amounts of price reductions. Court may order restoration of money or property acquired by practice prohibited by Act. Civil penalty of not more than $5,000 per violation for violation of terms of injunction. Civil penalty of not more than $500 per violation for willfully using prohibited practice. District and county attorneys within their jurisdictions also have duty to enforce Act plus duty to assist Attorney General upon request. Provision also made for suits by persons suffering loss as result of use of prohibited practices. Loss may be asserted by setoff or counterclaim. Person may recover reasonable attorney's fees. (75-24-1 et seq.).

Door-to-Door Sales.—Buyer has three days to cancel home solicitation consumer credit sale. (75-66-1 et seq.). Uniform Deceptive Trade Practices Act not adopted.

Franchise and Pyramid Sales.—Franchise companies must not represent to prospective franchise participants as to amount of past or future earnings unless representations of amount are of a substantial number of participants in same area and accurately reflect earnings of those having circumstances similar to those of prospective participants. Grantor of franchise must give 90 day notice prior to termination of franchise agreement.

Pyramid sales schemes are prohibited and sales contracts for participations in such schemes are void. (75-24-51 et seq.).

Rental-Purchase Agreement Act requires numerous disclosures by lessor to consumers as well as certain provisions in rental-purchase agreements. It also requires certain disclosures in advertisements for rental-purchase agreements. (75-24-151 et seq.).

"Unsolicited goods" statute enacted. (75-65-101).

Lemon Law.—Motor Vehicle Warranty Enforcement Act adopted. (63-17-151 et seq.). Vehicle Service Contracts are regulated. (83-65-101 thru 83-65-129).

Plain Language.—No "plain language" statute.

CONTRACTS:

Provision in construction contract indemnifying person against own negligence is void and unenforceable. (31-5-41).

Department of Finance and Administration must approve all architectural or engineering service contracts entered into by state entity. (31-11-3).

See topics Consumer Protection, Frauds, Statute of; categories Documents and Records, topic Seals; Family, topic Infants.

Uniform Commercial Code adopted, effective Mar. 31, 1968. See topic Commercial Code.

FACTORS:

If a person shall transact business as a trader, or otherwise, with the addition of the words "agent," "factor," "and company," or "and Co." or like words, and fail to disclose the name of his principal or partner by a sign in letters easy to be read, placed conspicuously at the house where such business is transacted, or if any person shall transact business in his own name without any such addition, all the property, stock, money and choses in action used or occupied in such business shall, as to the creditors of any such person, be liable for his debts, and be in all respects treated in favor of his creditors as his property. This shall not apply to vending machine or container plainly designated as the property of another. (15-3-7).

It is a criminal offense for a factor or consignee fraudulently to pledge merchandise or documents entrusted to him as security for money borrowed, or fraudulently to dispose of or apply to his own use money or property received from the sale or other disposition of such merchandise or documents. (97-23-19).

Uniform Commercial Code adopted, effective Mar. 31, 1968. See topic Commercial Code.

License Requirements.—See topic Commercial Code.

Liens.—See topic Commercial Code.

Consignment Agreements.—See topic Commercial Code.

FRANCHISES:

Franchise companies must not represent to prospective franchise participants amount of past or predicted earnings unless past or predicted earnings are of substantial number of participants in area and reflect average earnings under similar circumstances. (75-24-55).

Franchises cannot be cancelled without 90 days notice in writing. (75-24-53).

Municipalities cannot grant exclusive franchises for use of public places without compensation or for more than 25 years. (21-27-1).

Uniform Franchise and Business Opportunities Act not adopted.

FRAUDS, STATUTE OF:

An action may not be brought whereby to charge a defendant or other party:

(A) Upon any special promise to answer for the debt or default or miscarriage of another; (B) upon any agreement made upon consideration of marriage, mutual promises to marry excepted; (C) upon any contract for the sale of lands, tenements or hereditaments, or the making of any lease thereof for a longer term than one year; (D) upon any agreement which is not to be performed within the space of 15 months from the making thereof; or (E) upon any special promise by an executor or administrator to answer any debt or damage out of his own estate, unless in each of said cases the promise or agreement upon which such action may be brought, or some note or memorandum thereof, is in writing, and signed by the party to be charged therewith, or some person by him or her thereunto lawfully authorized. (15-3-1). For writing requirements for lease contracts see UCC Art. 2A Leases 75-2A-201 et seq.

Contracts of Sale.—Contract for sale of personal property not including goods, securities, or security agreements which exceeds $5,000 must be in writing, state price, reasonably identify subject matter, and contain signature of party against whom enforcement is sought. (75-1-206). Contracts for sale of goods for price of $500 or more must be in writing and signed by party against whom enforcement is sought. (75-2-201).

Part Performance.—Mississippi does not recognize part performance acceptance in contracts for sale of land. (Reid v. Home, 187 So.2d 907 [Miss. 1977]).

Uniform Commercial Code adopted, effective Mar. 31, 1968. See topic Commercial Code.

INTEREST:

Maximum Rate.—Legal rate 8% (75-17-1[1]); contract rate: Yield not to exceed greater of 10% or 5% per annum above discount rate on 90-day notes at Federal Reserve Bank, excluding surcharge (75-17-1[2]). On contracts and obligations exceeding $2,500, partnerships, joint ventures, religious societies, unincorporated associations and corporations (profit or nonprofit) can pay up to greater of 15% or 5% per annum above discount rate on 90-day note at Federal Reserve Bank. (75-17-1[3]).

Residential real property loan or mortgage rate: Yield may not exceed greater of 10% per annum or 5% per annum above index of market yields of Monthly Twenty-Year Constant Maturity Index of Long-Term U.S. Government Bond Yields. (75-17-1[4]). Borrower and lender may contract for any finance charge agreed to in writing if principal balance to be repaid originally exceeds $2,000.

Retail seller or lender or issuer of credit card may charge finance charge of maximum of 1¾% per month on revolving charge agreement. (75-17-19). Credit card

See note at head of Digest as to 1998 legislation covered.

See Topical Index in front part of this volume.

INTEREST . . . *continued*

issuer may charge annual fee of up to $12. Any issuer charging annual fee may receive no more than 1½% per month interest on account. (75-17-19). No financing charges until one month after first billing statement date or purchases charged. (75-17-19).

Late payment charge up to statutory limit is not interest. (81-12-167).

Judgments and decrees founded on any sale or contract bear interest at rate of debt on which judgment was rendered. Other judgments bear interest at per annum rate set by judge from date determined by judge to be fair but not prior to filing of complaint. (75-17-7).

Open Accounts.—Retail seller or lender or issuer of credit card may charge finance charge of maximum of 1¾% per month on revolving charge agreement. (75-17-19). Credit card issuer may charge annual fee of up to $12. Any issuer charging annual fee may receive no more than 1½% per month interest on account. (75-17-19). No financing charges until one month after first billing statement date or purchases charged. (75-17-19).

Retail seller may charge following finance charges for closed end credit sales of goods, tangible property or services, made other than under revolving charge agreement: 24% on portion of balance up to $2,500; and 21% on balance over $2,500. (75-17-19). Interest in excess of lawful rates may be received on any debt under which principal balance to be repaid shall originally exceed: $125,000 from July 1, 1986 through June 30, 1987; $75,000 from July 1, 1987 through June 30, 1988; $25,000 from July 1, 1988 through June 30, 1994; $2,000 after June 30, 1994. As to such debts, any assertion of claim or defense of usury is invalid. (75-17-1[5]).

Small Loans.—Notwithstanding above rates, licensees under Small Loan Regulatory Law (75-67-101 et seq.) and Small Loan Privilege Tax Law (75-67-201 et seq.), may charge following maximum finance charges: 36% on amount up through $1,000; 33% on amount between $1,000 and $2,500; 24% on amount between $2,500 and $5,000; and 14% on amount greater than $5,000. However, above rates for amounts up to $1,000 may be increased by number of percentage points by which discount rate, excluding surcharge, on 90-day notes at Federal Reserve Bank, exceeds 8%; for amounts above $1,000, rates may be increased by number of percentage points by which same discount rate exceeds 10%. (75-17-21). Lender entitled to rely upon most recent discount rate announced by Commissioner of Banking and Consumer Finance. (75-17-33). As alternative, licensee may contract for and receive yield up to 18% on loans of at least $25,000. Closing fee limited to lesser of $50 or 2% of total payments due on loan. (75-17-21). Late payment charges limited; not considered finance charges. (75-17-27).

Special finance charge rates for mobile homes. (75-17-23).

Finance charge defined. (75-17-25).

Maximum percentages for prepayment penalties on real estate loans. (75-17-31).

Special finance charge rates for motor vehicles. (63-19-43).

See also topic Banks and Banking.

Usury forfeits all interest and finance charge; and if rate exceeds maximum authorized by law by more than 100%, any amount paid, principal or interest, may be recovered. (75-67-119). However, finance charges contracted for or received prior to July 1, 1974, shall not be unlawful if finance charge conforms to provisions of c. 564, Laws of 1974, or other law then in effect. (75-17-17). Person willfully collecting finance charges in excess of maximum permitted guilty of misdemeanor and subject to fine of not more than $1,000. (75-67-119). Each account on which excess finance charge collected constitutes separate offense. (75-17-13).

LICENSES, BUSINESS AND PROFESSIONAL:

A privilege license varying as to the character of the business and the amount invested is required in almost all instances.

Commercial Travelers.—License required for catching and transporting of certain fish for commercial purposes in coastal or territorial water under regulations of Mississippi Department of Marine Resources. Fees and regulations specified in 49-15-29. Athletic agents must register with Secretary of State before contacting Mississippi NCAA athlete. Fees and regulations specified in statute. (73-41-3 thru -23).

Collection Agencies.—No legislation. See generally 97-9-1, 19-3-41 and 27-17-1.

MONOPOLIES, RESTRAINT OF TRADE AND COMPETITION:

A trust or combine is a combination, contract, understanding or agreement, expressed or implied, between two or more persons, corporations, or firms, or associations of persons, or between one or more of either with one or more of the others: (a) to restrain trade; (b) to limit, increase or reduce price of commodity; (c) to limit, increase or reduce production or output of commodity; (d) to hinder competition in production, importation, manufacture, transportation, sale or purchase of commodity; (e) to engross or forestall commodity; (f) to issue, own or hold certificate of stock of any trust or combine; (g) to place control to any extent, of business or proceeds or earnings thereof, contrary to spirit and meaning of this chapter, in power of trustees, by whatever name called; (h) to enable or empower any other persons than themselves, their proper officers, agents and employees to dictate or control management of business; or (i) to unite or pool interests in importation, manufacture, production, transportation, or price of commodity; and is inimical to public welfare, unlawful and criminal conspiracy. (75-21-1).

Unfair Trade Practices.—Any corporation, domestic or foreign, or individual, partnership, or association of persons whatsoever, who shall: (a) Restrain, or attempt to restrain the freedom of trade or production; (b) monopolize or attempt to monopolize the production, control or sale of any commodity, or the prosecution, management or control of any kind, class or description of business; (c) engross or forestall, or attempt to engross or forestall any commodity; (d) destroy or attempt to destroy competition in manufacture or sale of commodity, by selling or offering same for sale at lower price at one place in this state than another, differences of freights and other necessary expenses of sale and delivery considered; or (e) destroy or attempt to destroy competition by rendering any service or manipulating, handling or storing any commodity for less price in one locality than in another, differences in necessary

expenses of carrying on business considered; shall be deemed and held trust and combine, and shall be liable to penalties, fines, forfeitures, etc. (75-21-3).

Any corporation, individual, partnership, or association of persons who, with intent to impede competitive sale of liquified gases or appliances therefor, or who accomplishes this result regardless of intent, by purchasing, or offering to purchase, such appliances of any consumer and obtaining exclusive right to serve or make sales to said consumer shall be deemed a trust or combine within meaning of section 75-21-3. (75-57-63).

NEGOTIABLE INSTRUMENTS:

See topic Bills and Notes.

RESTRAINT OF TRADE:

See topic Monopolies, Restraint of Trade and Competition.

SALES:

Uniform Commercial Code adopted. (75-1-101 thru 75-11-108). See topic Commercial Code.

Contracts of Sale.—See topic Frauds, Statute of.

Bills of Sale.—See topic Commercial Code.

Product Liability.—No manufacturer or seller shall be liable for damages caused by product (except for commercial damages to product itself) if claimant does not prove by preponderance of evidence: (i) product was defective (manufacturing, warning, design, or express warranty, as defined); (ii) defective condition rendered product unreasonably dangerous; and (iii) defective condition proximately caused damages. Special provisions address inherent characteristics, failure to warn, assumption of risk, open and obvious, and design defect. Provides for manufacturer's indemnification of seller in certain circumstances, provided notice is given within 30 days. Common law defenses remain. Lack of privity is no defense. (11-1-63).

Retail Credit Sales.—No special restrictions. See topics Interest and Consumer Protection.

Consumer Protection.—See topic Consumer Protection.

Bulk Sales.—See topic Commercial Code.

Sales of Motor Vehicles.—See category Transportation, topic Motor Vehicles.

International Sales of Goods.—See Part VI, Selected International Conventions.

SECURITIES:

Uniform Securities Act substantially adopted, cited as "Mississippi Securities Act." (75-71-101, et seq.).

Uniform Commercial Code adopted. (75-1-101 et seq.). See topic Commercial Code.

Supervision.—Secretary of State, P.O. Box 136, Jackson, MS 39205-0136; tel. (601) 359-1350. (75-71-107).

Regulatory Powers of Supervising Authority.—Secretary of State may make, amend and rescind rules and regulations not contrary to law. (75-71-107). Secretary of State also has enforcement powers, including authority to issue cease and desist orders and impose administrative penalties of up to $25,000. (75-71-715).

Prerequisites to Sales or Offerings.—Registration of all securities required unless exempt or federal covered security. (75-71-401).

Securities to Which Act Applicable.—Substantially follows Uniform Securities Act. (75-71-105[1]). Includes interests in limited partnerships.

Exempt Securities.—Substantially follows Uniform Securities Act. (75-71-201). Exempt securities include: securities issued or guaranteed by foreign governments with which U.S. maintains diplomatic relations, unless Secretary of State orders otherwise (75-71-201[2]); securities issued by and representing interest in, or debt of, insurance company (75-71-201[5]); securities of Mississippi cooperatives (75-71-201[12]); and any sales of oil, gas and mineral leases (75-71-201[13]).

Exempt Transactions.—Substantially follows Uniform Securities Act. (75-71-203). Exempt sales of securities during 12 month period to fewer than 11 persons, whether residents or nonresidents. (75-71-205[9]). Exempts offers or sales of preorganization certificate or subscription to 35 or fewer subscribers if no commission paid for solicitation. (75-71-205[10]). Secretary of State may exempt other transactions by rule or order. (75-71-205[13]).

Registration of Securities.—Registration required of all securities unless exempt or federal covered security. (75-71-409). Minimum fee is $150; maximum fee is $1,000.

Registration by Notification.—No provision.

Registration by Coordination.—Registration statement requirements identical to Uniform Securities Act. (75-71-405). Prospectus containing information designated by Secretary of State must be sent to purchaser before sale. (75-71-405[d]).

Filing of Federal Covered Securities.—Secretary of State may require filing of federal registration statement for security covered under §18(b)(2) of Securities Act of 1933 prior to initial offer of security in Mississippi. (75-71-408[1][a]). After initial offer, all amendments to federal registration statement must be filed with Secretary of State. (75-71-408[1][b]). Secretary of State may suspend offer and sale of federal covered security (except security covered under §18[b][1] of Securities Act of 1933) if in public interest and there is failure to comply with conditions of 75-71-408. (75-71-408[4]).

Registration of Dealers.—Substantially follows Uniform Securities Act. Registration required for all broker-dealers and agents (75-71-301) and investment advisers (75-71-303). Uniform Act's exception for investment advisers whose only clients are investment companies omitted. (75-71-303[a]). Federal covered advisers must file SEC filings with Secretary of State. (75-71-307). Registration fees set by Secretary of State.

See note at head of Digest as to 1998 legislation covered.

See Topical Index in front part of this volume.

SECURITIES . . . *continued*

(75-71-313). Secretary of State may establish minimum capital requirements for broker-dealers and minimum financial requirements for investment advisers. (75-71-317). Registration procedure substantially follows Uniform Act. (75-7-307). Post-registration requirements also follow Uniform Act, except record-keeping requirements for broker-dealers may not exceed those of §15 of Securities Exchange Act of 1934 and record-keeping requirements for investment advisers may not exceed those of §222 of Investment Advisers Act of 1940. (75-71-333[a]). Grounds for denial of registration set forth in §75-71-321 and substantiallly same as Uniform Act, except that §204(a)(2)(f) is omitted. Secretary of State may summarily suspend registration pending determination of application. (75-71-325).

Brokers and Agents.—See subhead Registration of Dealers, supra.

Licenses.—See subhead Registraton of Dealers, supra.

Bonds.—Secretary of State may require broker-dealers, agents and investment advisers to post surety bonds in amounts up to $30,000. (75-71-319).

Civil Liability.—Results from offer or sale of security in violation of Act or condition imposed by Secretary of State. (75-71-717[a][1]). Also results from offer or sale by use of false written oral communication. (75-71-717[a][2]). Buyer may recover consideration paid, 8% interest, and reasonable attorneys' fees, less income received from security. Seller may avoid liability by making written offer to repurchase security for sales price plus 6% interest. (75-71-717[b]).

Criminal Liability.—Willful violations punishable by maximum fine of $25,000 and/or imprisonment for five years. (75-71-735).

Tender Offers.—Regulated by Mississippi Business Tender Offer Law of 1980. (75-72-101 et seq.). Nonexempt tender offers require filing of disclosure statement with Secretary of State. (75-72-105). Fraudulent, deceptive or manipulative acts in connection with tender offer prohibited. (75-72-109).

Franchising, Pyramid Sales, Etc.—Pyramid sales schemes prohibited. (75-24-51 et seq.).

Uniform Simplification of Fiduciary Security Transfers Act adopted (91-11-1 et seq.) and saved from repeal by Uniform Commercial Code (75-10-104[2]).

Uniform TOD (Transfer on Death) Security Registration Act adopted, effective Mar. 24, 1997. (1997, c. 413).

STATUTE OF FRAUDS:

See topic Frauds, Statute of.

TRUST RECEIPT SECURITY:

See category Debtor and Creditor, topic Pledges.

WAREHOUSEMEN:

Uniform Commercial Code adopted. (75-7-101, et seq.). See topic Commercial Code.

Bonds.—Where goods are stored under statute requiring bond, receipt issued has effect of warehouse receipt. (75-7-201). Farm warehouses. (75-43-35, 75-44-35, 75-7-201).

Licenses.—Application for license must be filed with Mississippi Department of Agriculture and Commerce. (75-43-3).

CITIZENSHIP

ALIENS:

Provisions for income tax on nonresidents found at 27-7-23; aliens prohibited from labor management functions (71-1-49); provisions for unemployment compensation for aliens (71-5-511); worker's compensation benefits available under certain circumstances (71-3-27).

Property.—Resident aliens may acquire, hold, dispose of and transmit by descent lands, as citizens of state may. Nonresident aliens are not permitted to acquire or hold lands. They are allowed to take lien, on land, to secure debt, and may purchase, at sale made to enforce payment, but are not then permitted to hold land longer than 20 years. Nonresident aliens may acquire up to 320 acres of land for industrial development and five acres for residential purposes. However, former citizens who became aliens by marriage may inherit and hold lands and citizens of Syria or Lebanon may inherit from citizens of this state. (89-1-23). Land may escheat under certain circumstances. (89-1-23, 29-1-75). Provisions for quo warranto when lands acquired or held illegally found in 11-39-1.

CIVIL ACTIONS AND PROCEDURE

ACCORD AND SATISFACTION:

A creditor may settle or compromise with a joint debtor without releasing the co-debtors for the amount remaining due and unpaid, except that the full amount of the ratable share of the released debtor is credited on the debt even though he paid less than such amount. All obligations are joint and several so far as remedies are concerned. (85-5-1, 85-5-3). See topic Judgments.

Compromise.—Governor on advice of attorney general or state tax collector may compromise any doubtful claims of state or other governmental subdivisions. (31-19-29).

Pleading.—The defense must be pleaded affirmatively in answer.

ACTIONS:

Mississippi Rules of Civil Procedure promulgated by Mississippi Supreme Court based on Federal Rules of Civil Procedure with certain exceptions. See topic Practice.

Equity.—The distinction between law and equity is rigidly observed. Actions brought in wrong court are transferred.

Forms of Action.—There is but one form of action known as "civil action". (MRCP 2).

Conditions Precedent.—No conditions precedent are imposed for civil actions generally.

Commencement.—Civil action is commenced by filing complaint with court. (MRCP 3). See topics Pleading; Process.

Parties.—Rules 19, 20 and 21 of FRCP effective except for changes in matters not relevant to state practice. (MRCP 19, 20, 21).

Class Actions.—Rule 23 of FRCP omitted from MRCP. For rules regarding class actions, see 263 So.2d 764.

Intervention.—Rule 24 of FRCP effective except for changes in matters not relevant to state practice. (MRCP 24).

Interpleader.—Rule 22 of FRCP effective except for changes in matters not relevant to state practice. (MRCP 22).

Third Party Practice.—Rule 14 of MRCP provides for third party practice only by permission of court for good cause shown.

Joinder and Splitting of Causes of Action.—Rules 18 and 21 of FRCP effective. (MRCP 18).

Consolidation of Actions.—Rule 42(a) FRCP effective. (MRCP 42[a]).

Severance of Actions.—Rule 42(b) FRCP effective, except right of jury trial refers to §31 of Miss. Const.

Stay of Proceedings.—Rule 62 FRCP effective, except for changes in matters not relevant to state practice and subsection (e) omitted. (MRCP 62).

Abatement and Revival.—Where injuries produce death and party injured could have recovered damages if death had not occurred, cause of action survives to heirs. Suit can be brought by personal representative or persons entitled under statute to recover. Only one suit can be brought. (11-7-13).

Executors and administrators may commence and prosecute any personal action at law or in equity which testator or intestate might have commenced and prosecuted. They are, also, liable to be sued in any court in any personal action which could have been maintained against deceased. (91-7-233).

Action for trespass against deceased person can be maintained against his executor or administrator, but vindictive damages not allowed. Action must be brought within one year after notice to creditors. (91-7-235).

Cause of action survives against executor, administrator, receiver, trustee or any other selected or appointed representative in event of death or inability of nonresident to act. (13-3-57).

For definition of personal actions which survive, see 186 Miss. 850, 192 So. 45. Rule 25 FRCP effective, except subsection (d)(2) omitted and subsection (a)(1) is clear dismissal without prejudice. (MRCP 25). See also category Estates and Trusts, topic Executors and Administrators.

Limitation of.—See topic Limitation of Actions.

Small Claims.—See category Courts and Legislature, topic Courts.

Termination of Actions.—Plaintiff may voluntarily dismiss action by filing notice of dismissal before answer or motion for summary judgment. Thereafter, voluntary dismissal only permitted by stipulation of dismissal or by court order. Court may dismiss cases on which there has been no action for one year after notice to parties from clerk. (MRCP 41).

Prohibited Actions.—See topic Damages, catchline Sovereign Immunity.

Administration.—See category Estates and Trusts, topic Executors and Administrators.

Direct Actions Against Insurer.—Not permitted. See category Transportation, topic Motor Vehicles, subhead Direct Actions.

APPEAL AND ERROR:

Appeal lies for review of judgments of all inferior courts. Appeals lie as follows:

From Chancery and Circuit Courts.—Appeal to Supreme Court lies from all final judgments of chancery and circuit courts in civil cases, except those entered by default. (11-51-3).

Interlocutory appeal permitted under certain limited circumstances. (Miss. Sup. Ct. R. 5). Petition for permission to file interlocutory appeal must be filed within 14 days after entry of order with proof of service. (Miss. Sup. Ct. R. 5). Appeal to Supreme Court made by filing of notice of appeal with Clerk of Court where judgment, order or decree is entered. (Miss. Sup. Ct. R. 3,4).

Notice of appeal to Supreme Court must be filed within 30 days of date of entry of judgment, order or decree but when post-trial motions are filed, notice of appeal must be filed within 30 days of denial of motion. For infants or persons of unsound mind, time begins to run after removal of disability except when guardian ad litem is appointed for infant or person of unsound mind, such appeal must be taken within two years. (Miss. Sup. Ct. R. 4).

Record on appeal consists of those portions of papers and exhibits filed in trial court and transcript of proceedings that respective attorneys designate in writing. (Miss. Sup. Ct. R. 10). Record shall include certified copy of docket entries in all cases. Docket fee for civil and criminal case is $100. (25-7-3).

From County Court.—Appeal from law side lies to circuit court and from equity side to chancery court. (11-51-79). Appeal must be taken and bond given within ten days from entry of final judgment, but county judge may extend time to not exceeding 60 days. (11-51-79).

APPEAL AND ERROR . . . *continued*

From Justice Court.—Appeal lies to county court in county having such court and in other counties to circuit court. (11-51-85). In all cases where appeal without bond, from judgment of justice court, is desired, written demand for appeal must be filed within time allowed for such appeal. (11-51-103).

In other civil justice court cases appeal may be had by filing and giving bond within ten days. Bond must be for double amount involved and costs accrued or likely to accrue but not less than $100. Impoverished defendant may appeal upon affidavit stating inability to give bond or other security, but such appeal does not operate as supersedeas. (11-51-85).

From Special Court of Eminent Domain.—Appeals lie directly to Supreme Court. (11-27-29). Appeal made by giving notice within ten days from date of judgment or final order entered to court reporter to transcribe record as taken and by prepaying all costs adjudged against plaintiff. Notice to court reporter and payment of costs shall be as is otherwise required by law for appeals to Supreme Court. Plaintiff shall deposit sum or good and sufficient surety bond, acceptable to clerk, equal to double amount of judgment. (11-27-29).

From Youth Court.—Appeals directly to Supreme Court from final order or decree taken by filing written notice of intention to appeal with youth court clerk within ten days after rendition of such final order or decree. Costs in youth court and filing fee in Supreme Court shall be paid as is otherwise required by law for appeal to Supreme Court. If appeal with supersedeas is desired, it is first presented to youth court, and if refused, such orders shall be reviewed by Supreme Court. (43-21-651).

Court of Appeals has jurisdiction over appeals assigned by Supreme Court. Court of Appeals has no independent jurisdiction. (9-4-3). Review by Supreme Court is only by certiorari. (9-4-3).

Time Allowed for Decision.—Court of Appeals must issue decision in every case heard before Court of Appeals within 270 days after final briefs have been filed with Court.

Supreme Court must issue decision in every case within its original jurisdiction within 270 days after final briefs have been filed with Court. Supreme Court must issue decision in every case received on certiorari from Court of Appeals within 180 days after final briefs have been filed with Court. (9-4-3).

Appeal bond not accepted except in case of supersedeas. Appellant required to prepay all costs in lower court including costs of transcript, preparation of record and $100 prescribed by 25-7-3. (11-51-29; 11-3-45).

Stay of Proceeding.—In appeals from chancery courts and in circuit courts, stay of proceeding may be had, by filing bond, in penal sum of 125% of amount of decree or judgment appealed from or value of property or matter in controversy. Amount of bond may be reduced upon good cause shown at hearing in court from which appeal taken. (Miss. Sup. Ct. R. 8).

An appeal never vacates a judgment or decree. (11-51-3).

State, a county, city, town or village, or officials representing same, incorporated charitable or educational institutions maintained by state; incorporated instrumentalities owned by U.S., and former employees, directors and officials of penitentiary, Penitentiary Board or insane hospitals, sued individually for tortious acts committed while serving in said capacity may appeal without bond and such appeal may operate as a supersedeas. (11-51-101).

Extent of Review.—Review by Supreme Court may concern law and/or fact questions. (Miss. S. Ct. R. 14).

Character of Hearing.—Appeal of case from justice court is trial de novo. (11-51-91).

Appeal from county court to circuit or chancery court considered solely on record made in county court. (11-51-79).

Appeal from circuit or chancery court to Mississippi Supreme Court considered on record designated by parties and briefs of parties. (Miss. S. Ct. R. 10 and 28).

BONDS:

The use of, or failure to use a seal, by a private person, will not affect the bond, or in any way vary the rights of the parties to it. All bonds in legal proceedings shall be valid, without a seal.

Any bond, or undertaking of any kind, in a legal proceeding, or for the performance of public contract, or the faithful discharge of any duty, shall inure to the person to whom it is designed by law, as a security, and be subject to judgment in his favor, no matter to whom it is made payable, nor what is its amount, nor how it is conditioned.

Sureties.—Any company with capital of not less than $250,000, incorporated anywhere in U.S. for purpose of transacting business as surety which surety in compliance with requirements of 83-27-1, et seq. may be accepted as surety upon bond of any person, officer, or corporation required by laws of state to execute bonds. (83-27-1). Justification of sureties is not required except on official bond of county officer.

Enforcement.—When person bound as surety on any writing for payment of money, which shall remain unpaid by principal debtor, after maturity, surety shall pay or tender to creditor amount due thereon. Creditor shall then assign such writing to surety. (87-5-3). Surety becomes subrogated to all rights of party in whose favor security is given. (87-5-5, 9).

Where bond is not for any specified sum, it binds the parties executing it for the full amount for which such bond might have been required. The same provisions are applicable to official bonds.

CERTIORARI:

Jurisdiction.—Generally, Circuit Courts have jurisdiction by appeal (writ of certiorari) over administrative agencies. (11-51-93 to 11-51-97). Also Supreme Court may grant review of Court of Appeals decision by writ of certiori. (MRAP 17, 9-4-3).

Grounds.—Same as grounds for appeal. See topic Appeal and Error.

Proceedings.—Certiorari must be made by petition to Circuit Court within six months after ruling, supported by affidavit, with bond to be approved by clerk and judge for good cause shown. (11-51-93, 95).

Review.—All cases decided by justice court judge may within six months thereafter, on good cause shown by petition supported by affidavit, be removed to circuit court of county by writ of certiorari, which will operate as supersedeas, party in all cases filing bond with surety to be approved by judge or clerk of circuit court. Court is confined to examination of questions of law arising or appearing on face of record and proceeding. (11-51-93).

Like proceedings may be had to review the judgment of all tribunals inferior to the circuit court whether an appeal is provided by the law sought to be reviewed or not. (11-51-95).

CHARITABLE IMMUNITY:

Doctrine of charitable immunity abolished. (126 So. 465, 55 So.2d 142). See also topic Damages.

COSTS:

Generally, cost deposit shall be made with filing of complaint by plaintiff in amount required by local rule; or may be required of plaintiff upon motion within 60 days of clerk or any party. (MRCP 3). In cases not expressly embraced by statute or rule, court may order costs at its discretion. (11-53-55).

Security for costs may be given by recognizance entered into in open court, by written undertaking endorsed on or filed with papers in cause, or by deposit with clerk of cash or certified check.

State entities (state, county, city, town, village, state board, or officer of same suing in official capacity) not required to pay or give security for costs. (11-53-13).

Poor persons may sue without security for costs upon prescribed affidavit. (11-53-17, 11-53-19, 11-53-21).

Award of costs: want of prosecution (11-53-21); stale cases (11-53-25); liability of successful party for certain costs (11-53-31); certain cases (assault, assault and battery, libel and slander, recovery of less than $10) (11-53-33); chancery (11-53-35); class suits (11-53-37); executors and administrators (11-53-41, 11-53-43); next friend of infant (11-53-45); cases of setoff (11-53-49); appeals from justices of peace (11-53-51); cases of certiorari and appeals from inferior tribunals (11-53-53).

When paid: bill of costs made out and filed by clerk when cause determined (11-53-65); not payable until bill produced (11-53-67); not due until suit ended (11-53-69); taxation of costs accrued on trial before justice of peace or inferior tribunal or court (11-53-71).

Execution for bills not paid made out by clerk and executed and returned by sheriff or other proper officer of county where party resides (11-53-73); bill of costs appended to execution (11-53-75).

Liability of Attorney.—None provided by statute.

DAMAGES:

Common law generally prevails as to compensatory damages. Punitive damages can be awarded only if claimant proves by clear and convincing evidence that defendant acted with actual malice, gross negligence which evidences willful, wanton or reckless disregard for safety of others, or committed actual fraud. (11-1-65).

Comparative Negligence Rule.—In actions involving personal injuries, death, or injury to property, contributory negligence does not bar recovery, but damages must be diminished in proportion to amount of negligence attributable to person injured, or owner of property, or person having control over property. (11-7-15).

Charitable Immunity.—Doctrine of charitable immunity abolished. (126 So. 465, 55 So.2d 142).

Sovereign Immunity.—Governmental immunity partially waived from and after July 1, 1993 as to state and from and after Oct. 1, 1993 as to subdivisions. All claims arising after prescribed dates are limited to graduated amount not to exceed $500,000 for claims accruing after July 1, 2001. No award for punitive damages, prejudgment interest or attorney's fees unless attorney's fee specifically authorized by law. Claims accruing before July 1, 1993 as to state and Oct. 1, 1993 as to subdivisions governed by case law existing before Pruett v. Rosedale, 421 So.2d 1046 and by prior immunity statutory law. (11-46-1 et seq.). (*Note:*This provision held unconstitutional on 8/31/92 in Presley v. Highway Comm'n, 608 So.2d 1288.) Under pre-Pruett law, sovereign immunity waived under certain circumstances. See applicable case law and 11-46-1, et seq. for detailed analysis.

No-Fault Insurance.—See category Transportation, topic Motor Vehicles, subhead No-Fault Insurance.

Uniform Contribution Among Tortfeasors Act (Revised).—Under certain circumstances, contribution between fellow joint tortfeasors allowed. (85-5-7).

See category Estates and Trusts, topic Death, subhead Actions for Death.

DEPOSITIONS AND DISCOVERY:

Right to take depositions and discovery exists in Mississippi. Depositions are generally governed by Mississippi Rules of Civil Procedure, based on Federal Rules of Civil Procedure with minor variations. (MRCP 30). See topic Practice.

Under Mississippi rules, parties may obtain discovery regarding any matter, not privileged, which is relevant to issues raised by claims or defenses of any party, by one or more of following methods: depositions upon oral examination or written questions; written interrogatories; production of documents or things or permission to enter upon land or other property, for inspection and other purposes; and requests for admission. (MRCP 26).

Uniform Foreign Depositions Act not adopted.

Within State for Use within State.—Federal Rules of Civil Procedure adopted with minor variations. (MRCP 30).

See note at head of Digest as to 1998 legislation covered.

See Topical Index in front part of this volume.

DEPOSITIONS AND DISCOVERY . . . continued

Within State for Use Elsewhere.—Person desiring to take depositions may produce proof of service of notice to take deposition to clerk of court for county in which deposition is to be taken. Such proof of service constitutes sufficient authorization for clerk to issue subpoena. (MRCP 45).

Outside of State for Use within State.—Federal Rules of Civil Procedure adopted with minor variations. (MRCP 28, 30). See subhead Before Whom Taken, infra. Uniform Foreign Deposition Act has not been adopted.

De Bene Esse.—Federal Rules of Civil Procedure adopted with minor variations. (MRCP 27). See subhead Perpetuating Testimony, infra.

Perpetuating Testimony.—Federal Rules of Civil Procedure adopted with minor variations. (MRCP 27).

Before Whom Taken.—Federal Rules of Civil Procedure adopted with minor variations. (MRCP 28).

Commissions.—See subhead Before Whom Taken, supra.

Compelling Attendance of Witnesses.—Attendance of witnesses may be compelled by subpoena in accordance with MRCP 45. (MRCP 30). Resident of State of Mississippi may be required to attend examination only in county in which he resides or is employed or transacts his business in person, or at such other convenient place as is fixed by order of court. Nonresident subpoenaed within state may be required to attend only in county in which he is served, or at place within state not more than 40 miles from place of service, or at such other convenient place as fixed by order of court. (MRCP 45[d]). Failure by any person without adequate excuse to obey subpoena served upon him may be deemed contempt of court from which subpoena issued. (MRCP 45[f]).

Examination of Witnesses.—Federal Rules of Civil Procedure adopted with minor variations. (MRCP 30).

Return.—Stenographic reporter shall certify, under penalty of perjury, on transcript that witness was sworn in his presence and that transcript is true record of testimony given by witness. When deposition is taken by other than stenographic means, person transcribing it shall certify, under penalty of perjury, on transcript that he heard witness sworn on recording and that transcript is correct writing of recording. Deposition so certified shall be considered prima facie evidence of witness' testimony. (MRCP 30[f]). If all or part of deposition is filed with court, party making filing shall give prompt notice to all parties. (MRCP 30[f]).

Form.—All depositions shall be made on 8¹/₂" by 11" paper. (MRCP 7[c]). Format for all depositions shall comply with Guidelines for Court Reporters as provided in Mississippi Supreme Court Rule 11.

Discovery.—Right to obtain discovery exists in Mississippi. Discovery is governed by Mississippi Rules of Civil Procedure, based on Federal Rules of Civil Procedure with minor variations. (MRCP 26-37).

Demand for Admission of Facts.—Federal Rules of Civil Procedure adopted with no material variations. (MRCP 36).

Interrogatories.—Federal Rules of Civil Procedure adopted with no material variations. Leave of court is required to serve in excess of 30 interrogatories. (MRCP 33).

EVIDENCE:

Witnesses.—Every person is competent to be witness except (1) if spouse is party, other spouse is not competent without consent of both, (2) person convicted of perjury or subornation of perjury, even though pardoned or punished for same, (3) court appointed appraiser in eminent domain proceeding. (Mississippi Rule of Evidence 601).

Privileged Communications.—
Governed by Miss. R. Ev. 502-505.

Lawyer-Client.—(MRE 502). Lawyer-client is governed by MRE 502. Client may claim privilege to refuse to disclose and to prevent any other person from disclosing confidential communications made for purpose of rendering professional legal services. There is no privilege for communications made in furtherance of crime or fraud, communications relevant to breach of duty by lawyer to client or by client to lawyer; communications relevant to matter of common interest to joint clients, communications relevant to issue between parties who claim through same deceased client, or to communications relevant to issue concerning attested document to which lawyer is attesting witness.

Physician and Psychotherapist-Patient.—(MRE 503). Physician and psychotherapist-patient privilege is governed by MRE 503. Patient may claim privilege to refuse to disclose or allow disclosure of information derived by physician by virtue of his professional relationship or confidential communications made for purpose of diagnosis or treatment. There is no privilege in proceedings for hospitalization, examinations by order of court, issues relevant to breach of duty. Filing of action against professional for services rendered is waiver of privilege only to extent pleadings but in issue any aspect of patient's physical, mental or emotional condition.

Husband-Wife.—(MRE 504). Husband-wife privilege is governed by MRE 504. Person has privilege to prevent spouse, or former spouse, from testifying regarding communications made privately between spouses which are not intended for disclosure to any other person. There is no privilege if one spouse is charged with crime against other, child of either, or person residing in household of either.

Priest-Penitent.—(MRE 505). Priest-penitent privilege is governed by MRE 505. Person has privilege to refuse to disclose and prevent disclosure of confidential communications (those made privately and not intended for further disclosure) by person to clergyman in his professional character as spiritual adviser.

Husband and wife may be introduced by each other to testify in criminal and civil cases, and are competent witnesses in their own behalf, as against each other, in all controversies between them. Either spouse is competent and may be compelled to testify against other in criminal prosecution of husband or wife for criminal act against child, contribution to neglect or delinquency of child, desertion or nonsupport of child under age 16, or abandonment of child, but in all other instances where either is named

litigant, other shall not be competent as witness and not required to answer interrogatories or to make discovery without consent of both. (MRE 601).

Communications or Transactions With Persons Since Deceased or Incompetent.—These communications are governed by MRE 804. If declarant is now deceased, following are not excluded by hearsay rule: (1) former testimony, (2) statements under belief of impending death, (3) statements against interest, (4) statements of personal or family history, (5) any other statement having equivalent circumstantial guarantees of trustworthiness.

Self-Incrimination.—Protection against self-incrimination is provided by Mississippi Constitution §26 and 5th Amendment to U.S. Constitution. See topic Depositions and Discovery.

Compelling Attendance—See topic Depositions and Discovery.

INJUNCTIONS:

Both prohibitory and mandatory injunctions are available under Mississippi law. (11-13-1 et seq.).

FRCP 65 forms basis of governing procedural rule. (MRCP 65). See topic Practice.

Jurisdiction.—Both circuit and chancery courts have jurisdiction to grant injunctive relief; county and justice courts do not have original power to issue injunctions, but county court may hear and act upon application for injunction when directed to do so by circuit or chancery court. (9-9-23).

Prerequisites.—Injunction will not be granted unless judge or chancellor is satisfied of equity of plaintiff's position and of truth of allegations of complaint. (11-13-1).

Procedure.—FRCP 65 adopted without material variation. (MRCP 65).

Bond.—FRCP 65(c) forms basis of rule; no security required of State of Mississippi or of officer or agency thereof or, in court's discretion, in domestic relations actions. (MRCP 65[c]). Surety is given in form of bond, stipulation or other undertaking. (MRCP 65.1). MRCP 65.1 addresses court's jurisdiction over surety and proceedings against sureties.

Temporary Injunctions.—Temporary restraining orders and preliminary injunctions available on same basis as that provided by FRCP 65. (MRCP 65).

JUDGMENTS:

Judgments are final on the date of entry, unless set aside during the court term. The minutes must be duly signed. Procedural rules based on FRCP. (MRCP 54 et seq.). See topic Practice.

Circuit clerk of court must, within 20 days after adjournment of term, enroll all final judgments rendered at that term, in order in which they were entered on minutes. (11-7-189). Abstract of such judgments certified by clerk of court where rendered can be enrolled in office of circuit clerk in other counties. (11-7-195). Chancery clerk must within ten days after expiration of term furnish abstract of any decrees for money to circuit clerk and circuit clerk must forthwith enroll same as and with same effect as judgments of circuit court. (9-5-159).

Judgments by Confession.—Person indebted to another on promise or agreement within jurisdiction of circuit court may sign written confession of judgment in clerk's office of circuit court. To accomplish this creditor must file in clerk's office statement under oath that debtor is justly indebted to him in amount of $. . . . . as follows (setting out copy of written contract, indorsement or open account, as case may be), and that same remains due and unpaid, and that said sum is not due or claimed under fraudulent or usurious consideration.

The evidence of the debt (if in writing) or a copy of the open account must also be filed; and the debtor must sign, before the clerk, an acknowledgment written upon or annexed to such statement, to the following effect:

Form

"I do hereby acknowledge myself indebted to the said . . . . . . in the sum of . . . . . . dollars, which includes interest up to the first day of the next term of the said circuit court, and I give my consent for judgment to be rendered against me in favor of said . . . . . ., at the next term of the said circuit court, for said amount and all legal costs accruing thereon, with stay of execution (if any) until (as may be agreed upon)."

"Taken and acknowledged the . . . . . day of . . . . . . A. D. . . . . ., before me. . . . ., clerk." (11-7-181).

Confessed judgment becomes final at end of next succeeding term if called up for order by creditor. (11-7-183).

Judgments on Pleadings.—FRCP 12(c) forms basis of procedural rule; if matters outside pleadings not presented and motion sustained, party opposing motion granted 30 days leave to amend. (MRCP 12[c], 15[a]).

Summary Judgments.—FRCP 56 forms basis of procedural rule; if motion for summary judgment denied, costs will be awarded to prevailing party, and attorneys' fees may be awarded where motion found to have been brought without reasonable cause. (MRCP 56).

Declaratory Judgments.—Actions for declaratory judgments may be brought in courts of record within their respective jurisdictions for purpose of having rights and duties under contracts or statutes construed or having declaration of status or rights regarding trust or estate made. Contract may be construed either before or after breach. Procedure governing such actions is same as that provided for other civil actions. (MRCP 57).

Default Judgments.—FRCP 55 forms basis of procedural rule; default judgment can be entered only upon application to court. (MRCP 55). Default judgment cannot be taken against State. (11-45-3).

Offer of Judgment.—FRCP 68 forms basis of rule; offer must be more than 15 days prior to trial date. (MRCP 68).

Vacation or Modification.—FRCP 59 adopted without material variation. (MRCP 59). FRCP 60 forms basis of procedural rule governing relief from judgments; Rule

JUDGMENTS . . . *continued*
provides for relief from judgment on ground of "accident or mistake" where federal rule speaks of "mistake, inadvertence, surprise, or excusable neglect," suggesting continuation of state's stricter rule as to setting aside of default judgments (197 Miss. 353, 20 So.2d 697); motion based on fraud, accident or mistake, or newly discovered evidence must be made within six months of entry of judgment (MRCP 60).

Lien.—When enrolled in the office of the clerk of the circuit court, a judgment is a lien on all the judgment debtor's real and tangible personal property within county, except that where there are two judicial districts in county lien extends only to property within district in which judgment is enrolled. (11-7-191). Lien may be extended to property in any other county or district by filing certified abstract of judgment in office of clerk of circuit court of county or district in which property is located. (11-7-195).

Growing crops are not subject to the lien of a judgment. (11-7-199).

Duration of Lien.—A judgment or decree, including judgment or decree in favor of state or subdivision or municipal corporation, is not lien on property of defendant for more than seven years from rendition of judgment or decree unless action is brought thereon before expiration of that time or in case judgment in favor of state or any subdivision or municipal corporation entity refiles notice of lien. (15-1-51). Time during which execution is stayed or enjoined by supersedeas, injunction or other process, shall not be computed as any part of period. (15-1-47).

Priority of judgment liens is according to the order of enrollment. (11-7-191).

Suit on a judgment preserves lien as to creditors and subsequent purchasers without notice only if a notation thereof is made on the judgment roll within six months after the expiration of seven years from the time of the rendition of such judgment. (89-5-19).

Revival.—Judgments may be revived only by the institution of suit thereon within seven years from the date of the judgment or decree. (15-1-47).

Assignment.—See category Debtor and Creditor, topic Assignments.

Satisfaction.—Judgments are satisfied in whole or part by circuit clerk by entry of notice of satisfaction under proper heading in book entitled "Judgment Roll" on his subscribing entry. (11-7-189).

Actions.—See category Debtor and Creditor, topic Executions.

Foreign Judgments.—A judgment or decree rendered in any court of U.S. becomes a lien in any county in this state when abstract thereof certified by clerk of court where rendered is filed with circuit clerk. After filing in any county of this state, judgment may be enrolled in other counties as may local judgment. (11-7-195). Judgments of foreign country are admissible in evidence when certified under hand and seal of officer having custody of records and authenticated by certificate of any public minister, secretary of legation or consul of U.S. that officer certifying such copy is proper custodian of records and that his attestation is in due form. (13-1-101).

Revised Uniform Enforcement of Foreign Judgments Act adopted. (11-7-301 et seq.).

LIMITATION OF ACTIONS:

Actions must be brought within following periods after respective causes of action accrue or as otherwise provided in statute:

Twenty Years: For payment on public bond after maturity date of bond. (31-19-33).

Ten years: To recover real property (15-1-7); on trust not cognizable by court of common law and not otherwise provided for (15-1-39).

Seven years: On domestic judgment (15-1-47); on judgment of sister state or foreign court of record, unless person against whom rendered was a resident of this state when action was commenced, in which case action on judgment must be commenced within three years after rendition thereof (15-1-45).

Six years: To recover for breach of contract of sale under UCC (75-2-725); for personal injury or property damage due to construction deficiencies (wrongful death actions excepted) (15-1-41); and for tax evasion (27-3-79[3]).

Five years: Against guardian or his sureties after ward becomes 21. (15-1-27).

Four years: Against executor or administrator. (15-1-25).

Three years: To recover possession of personal property; on unwritten contract (except contract of employment [15-1-29]) or open account or account stated not acknowledged in writing (15-1-29); all actions for which no other period presented and for latent injury or disease, following discovery (15-1-49); suits to recover taxes paid or to collect taxes (27-65-49); for violation of Business Tender Offer Act of 1980 (75-72-119).

Two years: To recover property sold by order of chancery court where sale was in good faith and purchase money was paid or property partited in kind or sold for partition where purchase money is paid (15-1-37); action against physician, osteopath, dentist, hospital, nurse, pharmacist, optometrist, chiropractor or podiatrist for injury or wrongful death arising out of course of medical and/or surgical treatment must be brought within two years of date of act, omission or neglect shall or with reasonable diligence might have been first known or discovered (certain disabilities excepted) but no more than seven years after alleged wrongful act (15-1-36).

One year: For libel, slander, assault, battery, maiming, false imprisonment, malicious arrest or menace or failure to employ and claims under 42 U.S.C. §1983 (15-1-35); for penalty or forfeiture under penal statute (15-1-33); to recover on unwritten contract of employment (15-1-29); to recover on installment note or series of three or more notes secured by mortgage, trust deed, lien or other instrument, time running from date of foreclosure or sale of pledged property (15-1-23); actions against state or political subdivisions (11-46-11).

Six months: Actions under bulk transfer provisions of UCC. (75-6-111).

Uniform Commercial Code adopted, effective Mar. 31, 1968. (75-1-101, et seq.). See category Business Regulation and Commerce, topic Commercial Code.

No limitation: To enforce payment of note, bill or evidence of debt issued by bank or moneyed corporation. (15-1-79).

Actions Not Specifically Provided For.—Must be commenced within three years after accrual of cause of action. (15-1-49).

New Actions.—If duly commenced action is abated or otherwise defeated, under certain circumstances, plaintiff may commence new action for same cause of action within one year after abatement of original suit. (15-1-69).

Foreign Causes of Action.—When cause of action has accrued outside this state, and by laws of place outside this state where such cause of action has accrued action thereon cannot be maintained by reason of lapse of time, then no action thereon shall be maintained in this state; however where such cause of action has accrued in favor of resident of this state, this state's law or limitation period shall apply. (15-1-65).

Disabilities of Plaintiff.—If any person entitled to bring personal action is, at time at which cause of action accrues, under disability of infancy or unsoundness of mind, he/she may bring action within limitation period prescribed for type of cause of action involved, after disability is removed, but saving may never extend longer than 21 years. (15-1-59). For purposes of medical malpractice actions only, disability of minority/infancy shall be removed at age six. (15-1-36). When legal title to property or right of action is in executor, administrator or other trustee, time during which statute runs against such trustee is computed against person beneficially interested in such property or right in action, although such person may be under disability and within saving provision of statute. (15-1-53).

Absence or Concealment of Defendant.—Where person against whom cause of action accrues is absent from state at time of such accrual or thereafter departs from state, time during which he is absent is not counted. (15-1-63). However, if plaintiff can obtain process on nonresident defendant under long arm statute, plaintiff will not be entitled to tolling of statute during defendant's absence from state. (362 So.2d 1253).

Interruption of Statutory Period.—In contract actions, new promise in writing, under certain circumstances, may be construed new contract thereby starting again running of applicable limitation period. (15-1-73).

Revival of Barred Claims.—Once claim is barred by running of limitation period it generally cannot be revived. However, see commencement of new action (15-1-69); construction and improvements to real property (15-1-41); survival of actions against executor (91-7-235); and removal of remedy by legislature (Miss. Const. 97).

Contractual Limitations.—Period of limitation may not be changed by contract between parties and any attempted change by any contract or stipulation is void. (15-1-5).

Pleading.—Statute of Limitations as defense to cause of action, must be specially pleaded. (MRCP 8[c]).

PARTITION:

Partition of land held by adult joint tenants, tenants in common and coparceners may be made by agreement in writing, signed by parties. (11-21-1).

Any joint tenant, tenant in common, or coparcener, whether adult or infant, having an estate in possession or right of possession, and not in reversion or remainder, may procure a partition of said property by instituting proceedings for the partition of the land, or for a sale thereof. (11-21-3, 11-21-5).

Jurisdiction and Venue.—Partition suits are brought in the Chancery Court of the county in which the lands, or some part thereof, are situated; or, if the lands be held by devise or descent, the division may be ordered by the Chancery Court of the county in which the will was probated or letters of administration granted, although none of the lands be in that county. (11-21-3).

Proceedings.—Partition of property is a special statutory proceeding.

All persons in interest must be made parties, except remaindermen or reversioners, if any. In partition action involving only surface of land, it is not necessary to join mineral interest owners unless they also have surface interest. Infant or non compos mentis may be defendant or can be complainant, suing by guardian, if any, or next friend. (11-21-5).

Proceedings for partition are instituted and conducted as other suits in chancery, or county or justice court within jurisdictional limits. (11-21-7; 11-21-73).

All questions of title and all equities between tenants in common may be disposed of in proceeding, as well as equities and claims of encumbrances. (11-21-9).

Partition in Kind.—Partition in kind may be made by the court itself, or by master appointed by court. (11-21-11).

Owelty may be decreed by the court, either with or without a report of master. (11-21-13).

If partition is by master, same may be had either by assigning shares, or allotment of shares by ballot. Written report of master must be confirmed by court. (11-21-15—11-21-25).

Partition by Sale.—Partition is usually in kind but the court may order sale of the land, or any part thereof, for partition of the proceeds, if it is found that this will better promote the interest of all parties, or that an equal division in kind cannot be made. The court may appoint master to make sale. (11-21-11, 11-21-27).

PLEADING:

Mississippi Rules of Civil Procedure, based on Federal Rules of Civil Procedure, govern rules of pleading. (MRCP 1, 7-16). See topic Practice.

Pleadings Permitted.—Pleadings permitted are same as FRCP 7(a). (MRCP 7[a]). Pleadings permitted include complaint and answer; reply to counterclaim; answer to cross-claim; third-party complaint and third-party answer.

Complaint.—Same as FRCP 8(a), less jurisdiction allegations. (MRCP 8[a]). Complaint for medical malpractice shall not specify amount of damages claimed but shall only state that damages claimed satisfy jurisdictional amount requirement. (11-1-59).

Answer.—Same as FRCP 8(b), (c), (d) and 12(b). (MRCP 8[b], [c], [d]; 12[b]).

Counterclaim or Set-Off.—Similar to FRCP 13 except counterclaim is not compulsory if insurer is defending opponent's claim. (MRCP 13[a]). "State of Mississippi"

PLEADING . . . *continued*
substituted for "United States" in FRCP 13(d). (MRCP 13[d]). Counterclaim for medical malpractice, same as for complaint.

Reply.—Allowed as in FRCP 7(a). (MRCP 7[a]).

Demurrer.—Abolished. (MRCP 7[d]).

Amended or Supplemental Pleadings.—Similar to FRCP 15. (MRCP 15).

Affidavits of Merit.—Affidavits in support of motions shall be served with motion. (MRCP 6[d]).

Affidavits of Defense.—Affidavits in support of motions shall be served with motion. (MRCP 6[d]).

Bills of Particulars.—FRCP 12(e) adopted. (MRCP 12[e]).

Verification.—Similar to FRCP 11 with additional sanctions. (MRCP 11).

Service.—Similar to FRCP 5(a) with minor variations. (MRCP 5[a]).

Filing.—Similar to FRCP 3, 5(d), (e) with minor variations. Filing shall be made with clerk of court, except judge may permit papers to be filed with him, in which event he shall note thereon filing date and transmit papers to office of clerk. (MRCP 5[e]).

Time.—Defendant allowed 30 days to serve answer after service and plaintiff 30 days to reply to counterclaim after service of answer. (MRCP 12[a]). Thirty days allowed to serve response to third party complaint (MRCP 14[a]) or to crossclaim (MRCP 12[a]).

Proof of Claims.—No special provisions except to extent rule as to affidavit of merits (see subhead Affidavits of Merit, supra) may apply.

Small Claims.—See category Courts and Legislature, topic Courts.

PRACTICE:

Mississippi Rules of Civil Procedure are drafted and adopted by Supreme Court of Mississippi, not by state legislature. Federal Rules of Civil Procedure form bases for Mississippi Rules of Civil Procedure, which govern civil practice in circuit, chancery and county courts. 1993 Amendments to Federal Rules have not been incorporated.

In justice courts, suits are triable on fixed return days, no less than one nor more than two terms per month, and are triable after five days personal service on the defendant.

Pretrial Conference.—Similar to FRCP 16 except mandatory upon motion of all parties. Scope is broader than FRCP 16. (MRCP 16).

Discovery.—Federal Rules of Civil Procedure adopted with no material variations, except there is no provision for physical or mental examinations. (MRCP 26-37). 1993 Amendments to FRCP 26 not incorporated.

Direct Actions Against Insurer.—See category Transportation, topic Motor Vehicles, subhead Direct Actions.

Small Claims.—See category Courts and Legislature, topic Courts.

PROCESS:

Process is called summons. FRCP is basis for state procedure. (MRCP 4). Procedures for service of process in Justice Courts. (13-3-5, - 83). Procedures for service of process in certain enumerated chancery court matters. (MRCP 81[d]).

General Requisites.—Summons must be dated, signed and sealed, must have name of court, parties and plaintiff's attorney, must be directed to defendant, must state time within which defendant shall appear and defend and notify about default for failure to appear and defend, and must be served with complaint. (MRCP 4).

By Whom Issued.—Summons shall be issued by clerk. (MRCP 4).

Who May Serve.—Under prescribed circumstances service may be made by any person 18 years or older who is not party, by sheriff of county where defendant resides or is found, by mail or by publication.

Personal Service on Individual.—Deliver to defendant or agent authorized by law or appointment to receive, or if cannot serve defendant or agent, leave at defendant's usual place of abode with spouse or family member 16 years or older who will accept and mail copy to defendant at place where left summons. (MRCP 4[d]).

Personal Service on Infant.—Deliver to mother, father or legal guardian or person having care of unmarried infant or with whom he lives or if none available deliver to court appointed guardian ad litem if infant is under 12 years of age. If infant is 12 years or older deliver copy to infant too. (MRCP 4[d]).

Personal Service on Incompetent Person.—If not judicially confined, deliver to incompetent and incompetent's guardian or conservator or if there is none, then to person with whom incompetent lives. If judicially confined, deliver to incompetent and to incompetent's guardian, but if none, then to court appointed guardian ad litem. (MRCP 4[d]).

Personal Service on Partnership.—Deliver to officer, managing or general agent, or to agent authorized by appointment or by law to receive. (MRCP 4[d]).

Personal Service on Domestic Corporation.—Deliver to officer, managing or general agent or to agent authorized by appointment or by law to receive. (MRCP 4[d]).

Personal Service on Association.—Deliver to officer, managing or general agent, or to agent authorized by appointment or by law to receive. (MRCP 4[d]).

Personal Service on Joint Stock Company.—Deliver to officer, managing or general agent, or to agent authorized by appointment or by law to receive. (MRCP 4[d]).

Personal Service on Foreign Corporation.—Deliver to officer, managing or general agent, or to agent authorized by appointment or by law to receive. (MRCP 4[d]).

Personal Service Outside State.—In addition to other methods authorized by MRCP 4, may serve person by certified mail, return receipt requested, and where defendant is natural person, marked restricted delivery. (MRCP 4.[c]).

Service by Mail.—Upon adult, infant, incompetent, or domestic or foreign corporation, partnership, or other unincorporated association, by mailing first-class with two copies of notice and acknowledgment, and return envelope, postage prepaid addressed to sender. (MRCP 4[c]).

Substituted Service.—Substitute service is provided by statute in certain instances in addition to above provisions. Service in actions against foreign insurance companies or corporations may be made upon insurance commissioner. (11-11-7; 83-5-11). Service on nonresident obligors in actions on contractor's bonds may be made upon insurance commissioner as in actions against foreign insurance companies. (85-7-195). Service in actions against foreign corporations that have withdrawn from state may be made upon Secretary of State. (79-4-15-.20).

Service by Publication.—Can be used in any proceeding in Chancery Court or in any other court where authorized by statute when defendant is nonresident or cannot be found after diligent search and inquiry. Upon filing of sworn complaint, petition or affidavit, clerk prepares summons and delivers to plaintiff for publication. Publish once a week for three consecutive weeks in newspaper in county where action is pending or if there is no newspaper, post notice on courthouse door and publish in newspaper of adjoining county or at seat of government of state. Must file proof of publication. Defendant has 30 days from date of first publication to appear and defend. If address known, must mail copy to address. Unknown heirs as defendants served by publication as are nonresident defendants. Unknown parties in interest may be made parties by publication. (MRCP 4[c]).

Long Arm Statute.—Service shall be made in accordance with methods authorized by Rule 4. (13-3-57). See subhead Personal Service Outside State, supra.

Proof of Service.—Server must make return promptly and within time which defendant must respond to process.

Person, other than sheriff, making service must make return by affidavit. Return for service by mail is acknowledgment. Return for service by mail outside state is return receipt or envelope marked "refused". (MRCP 4[f]).

Nonresident Motorist.—See category Transportation, topic Motor Vehicles.

REPLEVIN:

An owner of personalty, who is entitled to immediate possession thereof, can replevy property if it is wrongfully detained by another and institute an action in replevin for determination of rights to property. Property which has been seized under execution or attachment cannot be replevied.

Proceedings.—Governed by 11-37-101 et seq. Replevin under bond held unconstitutional. (710 F. Supp. 180).

Jurisdiction and Venue.—Action of replevin may be instituted in circuit or county court of county, or justice court of district where either defendant or property may be found. Process may issue to other counties or districts.

Pleadings.—An action in replevin is begun by sworn complaint of individual, his agent or attorney showing: (1) A description of personal property; (2) value thereof, each article being separately valued; (3) that plaintiff is entitled to immediate possession thereof; (4) that property is in possession of defendant; and (5) that defendant wrongfully took and detains, or wrongfully detains property.

Issuance of Writ and Summons.—Upon presentation of complaint, Supreme Court, chancery court, county court, circuit court judge, justice court judge or other duly elected judge may issue order directing clerk of such court to issue writ of replevin for seizure of property and summons defendant to appear to determine rights as to seized property, or issue a fiat directing clerk to issue summons to require defendant to appear to determine rights as to certain described property.

Return of Writ.—Writ is returnable to proper circuit or county court where value of property, as alleged, exceeds jurisdictional amount of justice court; otherwise to proper circuit, county, or justice court. Writs may be made returnable to proper court of another county where property located.

Hearing.—All replevin actions, whether by writ or summons may be heard in term time or in vacation, provided defendant has at least five days process. With such process, court having proper jurisdiction may proceed to final determination of rights of parties to possession of property. Replevin actions are preference cases and shall be heard at earliest possible date, and without jury unless requested by one of parties.

Bond of Plaintiff.—If plaintiff requests writ of replevin for seizure of property, he must post replevin bond with sufficient sureties in double value of property conditioned to pay any damages from wrongful seizure of property.

Writ of Replevin.—Writ of replevin shall command proper officer to take possession of property described and after two days deliver it to plaintiff unless bonded by defendant and summons defendant to appear in court to answer to replevin action.

Repossession.—Defendant has right within two days from seizure of property, to have property restored to him pending judgment, by giving bond to plaintiff with sufficient sureties in double value of property conditioned that property will be forthcoming to satisfy judgment.

Claims of Third Persons.—If third person claims to be owner of property or entitled to its possession, he may intervene in suit and make oath of his claim. After trial of replevin action, an issue is made up between successful party and claimant, and trial shall be held to determine rights as between them.

Judgment or Order.—Judgment shall be for possession of property, or value thereof, and also for damages for taking or detention. If judgment be for defendant, judgment shall be for restoration of property, if it be had, or for value thereof, and damages for wrongful suing out of writ. (11-37-127, 11-37-129).

SEQUESTRATION:

Generally sequestration is governed by 11-29-1 thru 11-29-13. Complainant is required to make affidavit showing that he has cause to believe, and does believe, that there is danger of removal of property involved in suit beyond limits of state, or its concealment in state so as to be beyond possession of court, or of its transfer so as to defeat rights of complainant, and that such removal, concealment or transfer is about to occur, and moreover, must give bond with sufficient sureties to be approved in double amount of indebtedness claimed. Defendant has five days from date of seizure within

---

See note at head of Digest as to 1998 legislation covered.

See Topical Index in front part of this volume.

SEQUESTRATION . . . *continued*
which to give bond and obtain possession of property. If neither party has given bond for possession of property within ten days, property must be sold, if liable to waste or decay or if subject to extraordinary expense in preserving same. (11-29-1—11-29-13). (Sequestration procedure found unconstitutional, 475 F. Supp. 204.)

SUBMISSION OF CONTROVERSY:
No statutory provisions.

VENUE:
Under general statute, venue is in county where defendant or any one of several defendants may be found or where cause of action accrues. (11-5-1, 11-11-3). Where several claims or parties are joined, venue governed by MRCP 82.

Actions Affecting Land.—All local actions must be brought in county where land is situated. (11-5-1, 11-11-3).

Actions Against Domestic Corporations.—Venue of action against domestic corporation is county in which it is domiciled or in which cause of action arose. (11-11-3).

Actions Against Executors, Administrators or Guardians.—Venue for nonresidents appointed in this state in county of their appointment; publication of summons made as provided for absent and nonresident defendants. Venue for residents in county or judicial district of their appointment. (11-11-9).

Actions Against Foreign Corporations.—Foreign corporation qualified to do business in the state is, as regards venue, in same position as a domestic corporation (157 Miss. 626, 128 So. 887) and on transitory cause of action must be sued where cause of action accrued or perhaps (certainly where cause of action accrued out of the state) in county where it has a place of business and process agent (see 79-1-25; 178 So. 83).

Actions Against Insurance Companies.—Venue of action against insurance company, groups of insurance companies or an insurance association, is generally county where loss occurred or, in case of life policy, where beneficiary resides, and process may be served in any county. However, suit against domestic corporation may also be brought in county of principal place of business and suit against foreign corporation may be brought in county where service can be had on an agent or on Insurance Commissioner provided such county is one where either loss occurred or insured resided. (11-11-7; 169 Miss. 634, 152 So. 874).

Actions Against Public Utilities.—Suit against railroad or other public utility corporation may be brought in county where cause of action accrued, where defendant has its principal place of business or in county where plaintiff resided at time cause of action accrued. (11-11-5).

Actions Against Nonresidents.—Nonresident defendant (except corporation qualified to do business in state and having a process agent) may be sued where cause of action accrued or where plaintiff resides or is domiciled and process may be served in any county. (11-11-11, 13-3-57—13-3-63. See 152 Miss. 874, 120 So. 184; 169 Miss. 634, 152 So. 872). See also topic Actions.

Actions Against Nonresident Motorists.—Where a nonresident operating a motor vehicle on the highways of the State is involved in an accident or collision, upon suit where service of process is upon the Secretary of State, the venue thereof shall be either in the county where the cause of action accrued or in the county where the plaintiff resides. (13-3-57, 11-11-11).

Action Against State and Political Subdivision.—Action against state, venue is in county where action arose or in Hinds County. Action against subdivision, venue is in county where principal office of subdivision located.

Actions by Inmates of any Training School, Penitentiary, Prison, Jail or Hospital.—Application for writ of habeas corpus shall be made to Judge or Chancellor of district in which imprisoned, absent showing of good cause to contrary; however, petition by inmate of training school or hospital claiming denial of constitutional right shall be filed in county from which committed. (11-43-9).

Paternity Action.—Defendant may be sued in county where mother or child resides or where defendant is present or has property but defendant has 30 days to remove to county of his residence or domicile. (93-9-17).

Change of Venue.—Where objection to improper venue is made, action is transferred to proper venue. (MRCP 82).

Contract Provisions.—For example, 564 So.2d 36.

COURTS AND LEGISLATURE

COURTS:

United States District Courts.—
Northern District.—Clerk's office: Oxford 38655.
Eastern Division sits at Aberdeen and is composed of following counties: Alcorn, Attala, Chickasaw, Choctaw, Clay, Itawamba, Lee, Lowndes, Monroe, Oktibbeha, Prentiss, Tishomingo and Winston.
Western Division sits at Oxford and is composed of following counties: Benton, Calhoun, Grenada, Lafayette, Marshall, Montgomery, Pontotoc, Tippah, Union, Webster and Yalobusha.
Delta Division sits at Clarksdale and is composed of following counties: Bolivar, Coahoma, De Soto, Panola, Quitman, Tallahatchie, Tate, and Tunica.
Greenville Division sits at Greenville and is composed of following counties: Carroll, Humphreys, Leflore, Sunflower, and Washington.
Southern District.—Clerk's office: Jackson 39201.
Jackson Division sits at Jackson and is composed of following counties: Amite, Copiah, Franklin, Hinds, Holmes, Leake, Lincoln, Madison, Pike, Rankin, Scott, Simpson and Smith.
Eastern Division sits at Meridian and is composed of following counties: Clarke, Jasper, Kemper, Lauderdale, Neshoba, Newton, Noxubee and Wayne.

Western Division sits at Vicksburg and, if accommodations are provided at no cost to U.S., at Natchez. Jurisdiction consists of following counties: Adams, Claiborne, Issaquena, Jefferson, Sharkey, Warren, Wilkinson and Yazoo.
Southern Division sits at Biloxi and is composed of following counties: George, Hancock, Harrison, Jackson, Pearl River and Stone.
Hattiesburg Division sits at Hattiesburg and is composed of following counties: Covington, Forrest, Greene, Jefferson Davis, Jones, Lamar, Lawrence, Marion, Perry and Walthall.

Supreme Court (State).—Mississippi Supreme Court is court of last resort within state. Its jurisdiction is appellate with original jurisdiction over certain proceedings involving public utility rates. (9-3-9). Court sits at Jackson. (9-3-3). Clerk's office at Carroll Gartin Justice Bldg., P.O. Box 249, Jackson, MS, 39205-0249.

Court of Appeals (State).—Mississippi Court of Appeals' jurisdiction is limited to those matters assigned to it by Supreme Court. Decisions of Court of Appeals are final and not subject to review by Mississippi Supreme Court, except by writ of certiorari. (9-4-3).
Court sits in Jackson. (9-4-11). Clerk's office at 656 N. State St., Jackson, MS, 39201.

Circuit Courts.—State is divided into 22 circuit court districts. Court sits in terms at various county seats. Each county has circuit clerk. Circuit Court has original jurisdiction in all actions when principal of amount in controversy exceeds $200, and of all other actions arising under constitution and laws of this state which are not exclusively cognizable in some other court. (9-7-81). It also has appellate jurisdiction as prescribed by law, and also has jurisdiction of all cases transferred to it by Chancery Court or remanded to it by Supreme Court. (9-7-83). Appeals are taken directly to Mississippi Supreme Court.
Place of Sitting and location of clerk's office.
Adams County: Sixth Circuit; court sits at Natchez.
Alcorn County: First Circuit; court sits at Corinth.
Amite County: Sixth Circuit; court sits at Liberty.
Attala County: Fifth Circuit; court sits at Kosciusko.
Benton County: Third Circuit; court sits at Ashland.
Bolivar County: Eleventh Circuit, First District; court sits at Rosedale.
Bolivar County: Eleventh Circuit, Second District; court sits at Cleveland.
Calhoun County: Third Circuit; court sits at Pittsboro.
Carroll County: Fifth Circuit, First District; court sits at Carrollton.
Carroll County: Fifth Circuit, Second District; court sits at Vaiden.
Chickasaw County: Third Circuit, First District; court sits at Houston.
Chickasaw County: Third Circuit, Second District; court sits at Okolona.
Choctaw County: Fifth Circuit; court sits at Ackerman.
Claiborne County: Twenty-Second Circuit; court sits at Port Gibson.
Clarke County: Tenth Circuit; court sits at Quitman.
Clay County: Sixteenth Circuit; court sits at West Point.
Coahoma County: Eleventh Circuit; court sits at Clarksdale.
Copiah County: Twenty-Second Circuit; court sits at Hazlehurst.
Covington County: Thirteenth District; court sits at Collins.
De Soto County: Seventeenth Circuit; court sits at Hernando.
Forrest County: Twelfth Circuit; court sits at Hattiesburg.
Franklin County: Sixth Circuit; court sits at Meadville.
George County: Nineteenth Circuit; court sits at Lucedale.
Greene County: Nineteenth Circuit; court sits at Leakesville.
Grenada County: Fifth Circuit; court sits at Grenada.
Hancock County: Second Circuit; court sits at Bay St. Louis.
Harrison County: Second Circuit, First District; court sits at Gulfport.
Harrison County: Second Circuit, Second District; court sits at Biloxi.
Hinds County: Seventh Circuit, First District; court sits at Jackson.
Hinds County: Seventh Circuit, Second District; court sits at Raymond.
Holmes County: Twenty-First Circuit; court sits at Lexington.
Humphreys County: Twenty-First District; court sits at Belzoni.
Issaquena County: Ninth Circuit; court sits at Mayersville.
Itawamba County: First Circuit; court sits at Fulton.
Jackson County: Nineteenth Circuit; court sits at Pascagoula.
Jasper County: Thirteenth Circuit, First District; court sits at Paulding.
Jasper County: Thirteenth Circuit, Second District; court sits at Bay Springs.
Jefferson County: Twenty-Second Circuit; court sits at Fayette.
Jefferson Davis County: Fifteenth Circuit; court sits at Prentiss.
Jones County: Eighteenth Circuit, First District; court sits at Ellisville.
Jones County: Eighteenth Circuit, Second District; court sits at Laurel.
Kemper County: Tenth Circuit; court sits at DeKalb.
Lafayette County: Third Circuit; court sits at Oxford.
Lamar County: Fifteenth Circuit; court sits at Purvis.
Lauderdale County: Tenth Circuit; court sits at Meridian.
Lawrence County: Fifteenth Circuit; court sits at Monticello.
Leake County: Eighth Circuit; court sits at Carthage.
Lee County: First Circuit; court sits at Tupelo.
Leflore County: Fourth Circuit; court sits at Greenwood.
Lincoln County: Fourteenth Circuit; court sits at Brookhaven.
Lowndes County: Sixteenth Circuit; court sits at Columbus.
Madison County: Twentieth Circuit; court sits at Canton.
Marion County: Fifteenth Circuit; court sits at Columbia.
Marshall County: Third Circuit; court sits at Holly Springs.
Monroe County: First Circuit; court sits at Aberdeen.
Montgomery County: Fifth Circuit; court sits at Winona.
Neshoba County: Eighth Circuit; court sits at Philadelphia.
Newton County: Eighth Circuit; court sits at Decatur.
Noxubee County: Sixteenth Circuit; court sits at Macon.
Oktibbeha County: Sixteenth Circuit; court sits at Starkville.
Panola County: Seventeenth Circuit, First District; court sits at Sardis.

COURTS ... *continued*

Panola County: Seventeenth Circuit, Second District; court sits at Batesville.
Pearl River County: Fifteenth Circuit; court sits at Poplarville.
Perry County: Twelfth Circuit; court sits at New Augusta.
Pike County: Fourteenth Circuit; court sits at Magnolia.
Pontotoc County: First Circuit; court sits at Pontotoc.
Prentiss County: First Circuit; court sits at Booneville.
Quitman County: Eleventh Circuit; court sits at Marks.
Rankin County: Twentieth Circuit; court sits at Brandon.
Scott County: Eighth Circuit; court sits at Forest.
Sharkey County: Ninth Circuit; court sits at Rolling Fork.
Simpson County: Thirteenth Circuit; court sits at Mendenhall.
Smith County: Thirteenth Circuit; court sits at Raleigh.
Stone County: Second Circuit; court sits at Wiggins.
Sunflower County: Fourth Circuit; court sits at Indianola.
Tallahatchie County: Seventeenth Circuit, First District; court sits at Charleston.
Tallahatchie County: Seventeenth Circuit, Second District; court sits at Sumner.
Tate County: Seventeenth Circuit; court sits at Senatobia.
Tippah County: Third Circuit; court sits at Ripley.
Tishomingo County: First Circuit; court sits at Iuka.
Tunica County: Eleventh Circuit; court sits at Tunica.
Union County: Third Circuit; court sits at New Albany.
Walthall County: Fourteenth Circuit; court sits at Tylertown.
Warren County: Ninth Circuit; court sits at Vicksburg.
Washington County: Fourth Circuit; court sits at Greenville.
Wayne County: Tenth Circuit; court sits at Waynesboro.
Webster County: Fifth Circuit; court sits at Walthall.
Wilkinson County: Sixth Circuit; court sits at Woodville.
Winston County: Fifth Circuit; court sits at Louisville.
Yalobusha County: Seventeenth Circuit, First District; court sits at Coffeeville.
Yalobusha County: Seventeenth Circuit, Second District; court sits at Water Valley.
Yazoo County: Twenty-First Circuit; court sits at Yazoo City.

Chancery Courts.—State is divided into 20 chancery court districts. Court sits at least twice each year at various county seats. (9-5-3). Chancery Court has jurisdiction over all matters in equity; divorce and alimony; matters testamentary and of administration; minor's business; and cases of idiocy, lunacy and persons of unsound mind. (Const. Art. VI, §159). Court also has jurisdiction over matters transferred to it by Circuit Court or remanded to it by Mississippi Supreme Court. (9-5-81). Appeals are taken directly from Chancery Court to Supreme Court.

Place of Sitting.—
Adams County: Seventeenth District; court sits at Natchez.
Alcorn County: First District; court sits at Corinth.
Amite County: Fourth District; court sits at Liberty.
Attala County: Sixth District; court sits at Kosciusko.
Benton County: Eighteenth District; court sits at Ashland.
Bolivar County: Seventh District, First Division; court sits at Rosedale.
Bolivar County: Seventh District, Second Division; court sits at Cleveland.
Calhoun County: Eighteenth District; court sits at Pittsboro.
Carroll County: Sixth District, First Division; court sits at Carrollton.
Carroll County: Sixth District, Second Division; court sits at Vaiden.
Chickasaw County: Fourteenth District, First Division; court sits at Houston.
Chickasaw County: Fourteenth District, Second Division; court sits at Okolona.
Choctaw County: Sixth District; court sits at Ackerman.
Claiborne County: Seventeenth District; court sits at Port Gibson.
Clarke County: Twelfth District; court sits at Quitman.
Clay County: Fourteenth District; court sits at West Point.
Coahoma County: Seventh District; court sits at Clarksdale.
Copiah County: Fifteenth District; court sits at Hazlehurst.
Covington County: Thirteenth District; court sits at Collins.
De Soto County: Third District; court sits at Hernando.
Forrest County: Tenth District; court sits at Hattiesburg.
Franklin County: Fourth District; court sits at Meadville.
George County: Sixteenth District; court sits at Lucedale.
Greene County: Sixteenth District; court sits at Leakesville.
Grenada County: Third District; court sits at Grenada.
Hancock County: Eighth District; court sits at Bay St. Louis.
Harrison County: Eighth District, First Division; court sits at Gulfport. Second Division; court sits at Biloxi.
Hinds County: Fifth District, First Division; court sits at Jackson.
Hinds County: Fifth District, Second Division; court sits at Raymond.
Holmes County: Eleventh District; court sits at Lexington.
Humphreys County: Ninth District; court sits at Belzoni.
Issaquena County: Ninth District; court sits at Mayersville.
Itawamba County: First District; court sits at Fulton.
Jackson County: Sixteenth District; court sits at Pascagoula.
Jasper County: Second District, First Division; court sits at Paulding.
Jasper County: Second District, Second Division; court sits at Bay Springs.
Jefferson County: Seventeenth District; court sits at Fayette.
Jefferson Davis County: Thirteenth District; court sits at Prentiss.
Jones County: Nineteenth District, First Division; court sits at Ellisville.
Jones County: Nineteenth District, Second Division; court sits at Laurel.
Kemper County: Sixth District; court sits at De Kalb.
Lafayette County: Eighteenth District; court sits at Oxford.
Lamar County: Tenth District; court sits at Purvis.
Lauderdale County: Twelfth District; court sits at Meridian.
Lawrence County: Thirteenth District; court sits at Monticello.
Leake County: Eleventh District; court sits at Carthage.
Lee County: First District; court sits at Tupelo.
Leflore County: Seventh District; court sits at Greenwood.

Lincoln County: Fifteenth District; court sits at Brookhaven.
Lowndes County: Fourteenth District; court sits at Columbus.
Madison County: Eleventh District; court sits at Canton.
Marion County: Tenth District; court sits at Columbia.
Marshall County: Eighteenth District; court sits at Holly Springs.
Monroe County: First District; court sits at Aberdeen.
Montgomery County: Third District; court sits at Winona.
Neshoba County: Sixth District; court sits at Philadelphia.
Newton County: Second District; court sits at Decatur.
Noxubee County: Fourteenth District; court sits at Macon.
Oktibbeha County: Fourteenth District; court sits at Starkville.
Panola County: Third District, First Division; court sits at Sardis.
Panola County: Third District, Second Division; court sits at Batesville.
Pearl River County: Tenth District; court sits at Poplarville.
Perry County: Tenth District; court sits at New Augusta.
Pike County: Fourth District; court sits at Magnolia.
Pontotoc County: First District; court sits at Pontotoc.
Prentiss County: First District; court sits at Booneville.
Quitman County: Seventh District; court sits at Marks.
Rankin County: Twentieth District; court sits at Brandon.
Scott County: Second District; court sits at Forest.
Sharkey County: Ninth District; court sits at Rolling Fork.
Simpson County: Thirteenth District; court sits at Mendenhall.
Smith County: Thirteenth District; court sits at Raleigh.
Stone County: Eighth District; court sits at Wiggins.
Sunflower County: Ninth District; court sits at Indianola.
Tallahatchie County: Seventh District, First Division; court sits at Charleston.
Tallahatchie County: Seventh District, Second Division; court sits at Sumner.
Tate County: Third District; court sits at Senatobia.
Tippah County: Eighteenth District; court sits at Ripley.
Tishomingo County: First District; court sits at Iuka.
Tunica County: Seventh District; court sits at Tunica.
Union County: First District; court sits at New Albany.
Walthall County: Fourth District; court sits at Tylertown.
Warren County: Ninth District; court sits at Vicksburg.
Washington County: Ninth District; court sits at Greenville.
Wayne County: Nineteenth District; court sits at Waynesboro.
Webster County: Fourteenth District; court sits at Walthall.
Wilkinson County: Seventeenth District; court sits at Woodville.
Winston County: Sixth District; court sits at Louisville.
Yalobusha County: Third District, First Division; court sits at Coffeeville.
Yalobusha County: Third District, Second Division; court sits at Water Valley.
Yazoo County: Eleventh District; court sits at Yazoo City.

County Courts exist in some counties (see listing below). (9-9-1). County court has jurisdiction concurrent with justice court in all matters civil and criminal in which justice court has jurisdiction; concurrent with circuit and chancery courts in all matters of law and equity, wherein amount of value of thing in controversy does not exceed $75,000; concurrent with circuit court in all misdemeanors; exclusive jurisdiction in eminent domain, partition of personal property, and actions of unlawful entry and detainer. (9-9-21).

Courts and places of sitting:
Adams County: court sits at Natchez.
Bolivar County: First District; court sits at Rosedale. Second District; court sits at Cleveland.
Coahoma County; court sits at Clarksdale.
DeSoto County; court sits at Hernando.
Forrest County; courts sits at Hattiesburg.
Harrison County: court sits at Gulfport and Biloxi.
Hinds County: First District; court sits at Jackson. Second District; court sits at Raymond.
Jackson County; court sits at Pascagoula.
Jones County: First District; court sits at Ellisville. Second District; court sits at Laurel.
Lauderdale County; court sits at Meridian.
Lee County; court sits at Tupelo.
Leflore County; court sits at Greenwood.
Lowndes County; court sits at Columbus.
Madison County; court sits at Canton.
Pike County; court sits at McComb.
Rankin County; court sits at Brandon.
Warren County; court sits at Vicksburg.
Washington County; court sits at Greenville.
Yazoo County; court sits at Yazoo City.

Small Claims Courts.—
Justice Courts.—Each county has at least one justice court judge, required to sit at least once a month in his courtroom designated by county. (9-11-2, 9-11-5). Justice court judges have jurisdiction for collection of debts of every kind where principal amount sued for does not exceed $2,500. (9-11-9). For county seat locations, see subhead Circuit Courts, supra.

LEGISLATURE:
Regular session convenes annually on Tues. after first Mon. in Jan., for period limited to 125 calendar days every fourth year and 90 calendar days every other year. Session may be extended by resolution and required vote. (Const. Art. 4, §36).

Special or Extraordinary Sessions.—Governor has power to convene special session of legislature when, in his judgment, public interest requires it; Governor shall state by public proclamation matters to be considered in special session. (Miss. Const. Art. 5, §121).

Initiative and Referendum.—Neither provided for.

See note at head of Digest as to 1998 legislation covered.

See Topical Index in front part of this volume.

LEGISLATURE . . . *continued*

Lobbyists.—Regulated by 5-8-1, et seq. and by 97-7-57.

REPORTS:

Official reporter for decisions of Mississippi Supreme Court through 1966 is "Mississippi Reports", consisting of volumes 1 through 254, but early volumes are frequently cited by names of reporters, as follows: Walker, one volume; Howard, seven volumes; Smedes and Marshall, fourteen volumes. Mississippi cases since 1886 are also reported in Southern Reporter. For decisions reported after 1966, official reporter is "Southern Reporter—Mississippi Cases" (West Pub. Co.). (7-3-11, 7-3-13). Selected opinions of Court of Appeals may also be published. (Miss. R. App. P. 35-B).

Unofficial Reports.—None.

Digests.—Mississippi Digest (West Pub. Co.), supplemented by pocket parts, digests all Mississippi cases and federal cases arising in Mississippi. There are also Mississippi Digest (4 vols.) published in 1911, and Supplement (1 vol.) published in 1920, by Bobbs-Merrill Co.

STATUTES:

Latest official compilation of statutes is Mississippi Code of 1972, Annotated, effective after Nov. 1, 1973. Laws enacted subsequently are compiled according to legislative session in "General Laws of Mississippi" published by Secretary of State. Code volumes are supplemented by pocket parts and updated as needed.

Uniform Acts which have been adopted are: Anatomical Gift (1970, last am'd 1980); Attendance of Witnesses From Without a State in Criminal Proceedings, Act to Secure (1938); Business Corporation, Revised (1984); Child Custody Jurisdiction (1982); Commercial Code (1966); Common Trust Fund (1950); Conservation Easement (1986, last am'd 1988); Controlled Substances (1971, last am'd 1998); Determination of Death (1981); Disclaimer of Property Interests (1994); Disposition of Unclaimed Property (1982, last am'd 1997); Durable Power of Attorney (1994); Enforcement of Foreign Judgments (1984, last am'd 1985); Estate Tax Apportionment (1995); Federal Lien Registration (1989); Health-Care Decisions (1998); Interstate Family Support (1997); Jury Selection and Service (1974); Limited Partnership (1987, last am'd 1995); Minor Student Capacity to Borrow (1970); Motor Vehicle Certificate of Title and Anti-Theft (1968, last am'd 1997); Partnership (1914 Act); Paternity, Mississippi Uniform Law on (1962, last am'd 1997); Principal and Income (1966); Securities (1981, last am'd 1990); Simplification of Fiduciary Security Transfers (1960); Simultaneous Death (1956); State Administrative Procedure (1976, last am'd 1995); Testamentary Additions to Trusts (1958); Trade Secrets (1990); Transfers to Minors (1994); Trustees' Powers (1966, last am'd 1994).

Uniform Commercial Code enacted, effective Mar. 31, 1968. See category Business Regulation and Commerce, topic Commercial Code.

For text of Uniform Acts falling within the scope of the Martindale-Hubbell Law Digests see Uniform and Model Acts section.

CRIMINAL LAW

CRIMINAL LAW:

Crimes are governed by Title 97, 1972 Code. Criminal procedure is governed by Title 99, 1972 Code and Uniform Criminal Rules of Circuit Court Practice.

Indictment.—Criminal proceeding in felony initiated by returning and presentment of indictment by 12 grand jurors. (99-7-9, 99-7-11).

Bail.—Where proof is evident or presumption great, preconviction bail may be denied in capital cases, and also in cases with potential sentences of at least 20 years if defendant is special danger to community or his appearance cannot be assured. (Miss. Const. Art. III, §29). After conviction of felony, except those crimes listed in 99-35-115(1), and pending appeal, bail is matter of right unless court denies bail if special danger exists. In cases of treason, murder, rape, arson, burglary or robbery no bail of right is available unless court in exercise of greatest caution orders otherwise. (99-35-115).

DEBTOR AND CREDITOR

ASSIGNMENTS:

Uniform Commercial Code adopted. (75-1-101 thru 75-11-108). See category Business Regulation and Commerce, topic Commercial Code.

Instrument Transferring Title.—No general provision exists, however, specific requirements exist in some circumstances. In such action defenses against assignor which existed prior to notice to defendant of assignment are available. Generally, choses in action are assignable. (11-7-3). For acknowledgments and witness requirements, see generally 25-33-1 to 25-33-23 and 89-3-1 to 89-3-15.

Filing.—Assignment for benefit of creditors where property assigned $100,000 shall file petition relating to same under requirements of 85-1-1. Sale of chose in action made after suit filed shall be signed, acknowledged and filed with papers of court. (11-7-7). Certain liens which are assignable shall exist without writing and without recording between parties, unless otherwise expressly provided by statutes. (85-7-261). Assignments of indebtedness secured by mortgage, deed of trust, or other lien of record shall be entered on margin of record or assignments shall be acknowledged and filed for record. (89-5-17). Specific statutory provisions relate to various forms of assignments, need for recording same, and effect thereof.

Assignment of Wages.—Employer is not bound by assignment or pledge of wages unless copy thereof is served on him before delivery of goods or consummation of contract and he consents in writing to be bound thereby. (71-1-45).

ATTACHMENT:

Mississippi's chancery attachment statutes and statutory scheme for attachment at law were held unconstitutional. (444 F.Supp. 925). Mississippi attachment in chancery statutes were amended in 1980 to comply with procedural due process requirements. Through 1998 legislative session, Mississippi's attachment at law statutes have not been amended to comport with due process requirements. Therefore, it is advised that statutory scheme providing for attachment at law not be utilized in collection efforts until such time as it is amended. See generally 11-33-1 et seq.

Actions in Which Allowed.—Attachment in chancery permitted upon demands for legal or equitable indebtedness for damages for breach of contract or tort. (11-31-1). Attachment at law lies in all actions founded on any indebtedness, on damage claim for breach of contract or on penal statutes. (11-33-1). Exemptions exist. (71-1-43, 85-3-1 to 85-3-51).

Courts Which May Issue Writ.—Attachment writ in chancery issued by chancery court. (11-31-1). Attachment writ at law issued by supreme court judge, circuit judge, chancellor, clerk of circuit or chancery court or deputy of such clerk, or any justice court judge or mayor of any city, town or village (11-33-9, 11-33-19) and made returnable to circuit court or justice court (11-33-17).

In Whose Favor Writ May Issue.—Nonresidents, including foreign corporations, as well as citizens, can obtain writs of attachment. (19 Miss.[11 S&M] 53; 19 Miss.[11 S&M] 58; 147 Miss. 369, 112 So. 7).

Against Whom Writ May Issue.—Attachment writ in chancery, against any nonresident, absent or absconding debtor who has lands and tenements in state or against any such debtor and persons in this state who have effects or are indebted to such nonresident, absent or absconding debtor. (11-31-1). Attachment writ at law, against resident and nonresident debtors. (11-33-1, 11-33-7); joint debtors (11-33-3); partners (11-33-5); or nonresidents jointly indebted (11-33-7).

Claims on Which Writ May Issue.—It is not necessary in order to warrant attachment that claim sued on should be payable in this state. In some cases attachment may issue on unmatured claim. See infra, subhead Grounds.

Grounds.—Attachment in chancery, if ability to recover claim is endangered or impeded if attachment is not issued. (11-31-2). Attachment at law, if defendant: (1) is foreign corporation or nonresident of state; (2) has removed or is about to remove himself or property out of state; (3) so absconds or conceals himself that he cannot be served with summons; (4) contracted debt or incurred obligation in conducting business of water craft in some navigable waters of state; (5) has property or rights in action which he conceals and unjustly refuses to apply to payment of his debts; (6) has assigned or disposed of, or is about to assign or dispose of his property or rights in action, or some part thereof with intent to defraud his creditors; (7) has converted or is about to convert his property into money or evidences of debt with intent to place it beyond reach of his creditors; (8) fraudulently contracted debt or incurred obligations for which suit has been or is about to be brought; (9) is buying, selling or dealing in futures, directly or indirectly, or has done so within six months; (10) is in default as principal for public money, due state, county or municipality; (11) is banker, banking company or corporation, and received deposits, knowing at time that he or it was insolvent, or has made false or fraudulent statements as to his or its financial condition; (12) has judgment lien for nonpayment of support under Title 93 enrolled against him. (11-33-9).

Attachment will lie on ground that defendant is foreign corporation, even though it be domesticated in Mississippi. (181 Miss. 223, 177 So. 653).

Creditor may obtain attachment for debt not due by making affidavit to any of six of aforementioned 11 grounds of attachment, or that he has just cause to suspect and verily believes that his debtor will remove himself or his effects out of state before debt will become payable, with intent to hinder, delay or defraud his creditors, or has done so with such intent, leaving property in this state. (11-33-35).

Proceedings to Obtain.—Attachment in chancery; upon filing of bill of complaint, complainant may apply for order of attachment by presenting to chancellor bill and affidavit including following: (1) statement that action is one described in 11-31-1 and is brought against defendant described in said section; (2) detailed statement of facts and grounds which entitle complainant to order of attachment, which shall include statement of specific reasons why complainant's ability to recover amount of his claim may be endangered or impeded if order of attachment is not issued; (3) statement of amount plaintiff seeks to recover; (4) statement that complainant has no information or belief that claim is discharged or stayed in proceeding under Federal Bankruptcy Act; (5) description of property to be attached under writ of attachment and statement that complainant is informed and believes that such property is not exempt from attachment or seizure under 85-3-1; and (6) listing of other persons known to complainant to have interest in property sought to be attached, together with description of that interest. (11-31-2[1]).

Chancellor may issue order of attachment after examining affidavit only if: (1) complainant's ability to recover amount of his claim may be significantly impaired unless order is issued; (2) affidavit establishes prima facie case of complainant's right to recover against defendant; (3) complainant gives security satisfactory to court to abide further orders of court and to protect defendant from injury should action of attachment be judicially determined to have been wrongfully brought. (11-31-2[2]). Attachment at law, creditor or his agent must make affidavit to amount of his demand and to one or more of stated grounds for attachment at law. (11-33-4).

Attachment Bond.—Attachment in chancery, security is posted pursuant to court order. (11-31-2). Attachment at law, bond must be approved by officer issuing writ and must be double amount claimed. (11-33-11). Bond executed by agent or attorney of attaching creditors. (11-33-13). Amendment of bond. (11-33-15).

Levy.—In attachment in chancery (11-31-3, 11-31-5) and at law (11-33-23) attachment is levied on all nonexempt personal and real property.

Indemnity.—If officer who is required to levy attachment is in doubt as to ownership of property to be levied on, he may require indemnity bond in double value of such property. (13-3-157).

See note at head of Digest as to 1998 legislation covered.

See Topical Index in front part of this volume.

ATTACHMENT . . . *continued*

Lien.—Attachments constitute liens on all property in order in which they are levied. (11-33-23).

Priorities.—Attachment first levied has priority.

Release of Property.—Attachment in chancery, by immediate post-seizure hearing or by giving security of 125% of value of property attached or 125% of amount of claim, whichever is less. (11-31-2). Attachment at law, personal property may be replevied by giving bond, with good securities, payable to plaintiff in double value of property. (11-33-45).

Sale.—Where perishable property attached and not replevied officer holding same may sell property in manner property sold under execution. (11-33-71). Party to suit upon ten days notice may apply for order directing officer having custody of property to sell same, and upon sale proceeds are held by such officer pending result of suit. (11-33-73).

Third Party Claims.—All provisions of law in relation to third parties claiming property levied on shall extend and apply to claimants of property levied on by virtue of writs of attachment. (11-33-69).

Vacation or Modification.—No statutory provision.

CREDITORS' SUITS:

A suit in equity will lie on behalf of the creditors of which the chancery court has jurisdiction.

EXECUTIONS:

In courts of record, execution shall issue after adjournment of court for term at which judgment is rendered and upon request and at cost of owner of judgment. (13-3-111). In justice courts execution may not issue until ten days after rendition of judgment, unless party recovering judgment shall make and file affidavit that he believes he will be in danger of losing his debt or demand by such delay, in which case execution shall issue immediately; but other party shall not be deprived of his right of appeal within time prescribed. (11-9-131). See category Civil Actions and Procedure, topic Practice.

Kinds of Execution.—Types of execution governed by statute. There are procedures to enforce chancery decrees for money (11-5-81, et seq.); and other general garnishment procedures to enforce judgments (11-31-1 to 11-35-61).

Exemptions.—See topic Exemptions.

Time for Issuance.—See introductory paragraph under this topic.

Stay.—Judgment of justice court must be stayed by justice where debtor, within ten days after judgment, procures responsible person to appear before justice, and in writing, entered on justice's docket and signed by person so appearing, consents to become surety for payment. Period of stay is 30 days from date of judgment where judgment is not over $50 and 60 days where amount is larger. In case of nonpayment at expiration of stay execution issues against principal and sureties, or either, for principal, interest and costs. Debtor obtaining stay in this manner waives errors in judgment and abandons right of appeal or certiorari. (11-9-139). See category Civil Actions and Procedure, topic Appeal and Error.

Lien.—Writ of execution, where there is no judgment lien, shall bind defendant's property only from time of levy. (13-3-139).

Levy.—Where there is no judgment lien executions bind the property only from time of levy, and the first delivered is first levied and is the first satisfied. Officers are required to mark the hour of their receipt of the execution, and must levy in the order of receipt. (13-3-139). Execution cannot be levied on growing crops (13-3-137); landlord has priority lien on tenant's personal property, other than merchandise sold in normal course of business, to secure payment of rent, whether or not due (89-7-51).

Return.—Executions are returnable on the first day of the next term of court after the rendition of the judgment, provided 15 days elapse between such issuance and return, and, if not, on first day of term next thereafter. (13-3-113).

Priorities.—If there are two or more executions against the same person, that which was first delivered shall be first levied and satisfied. (13-3-139).

Claims of Third Persons.—When a person not a party to the execution claims to be the owner of or to have a lien on any personal property levied on, such person may make affidavit as to his right or title to the property and enter into bond payable to the plaintiff in the execution, with one or more sufficient sureties, in a penalty double the value of the property claimed, or in double the amount of the execution if that be less than the value of the property, conditioned for the prosecution of his claim. Upon the making of the affidavit and bond, the officer holding the execution must deliver the property to the claimant. The affidavit may be filed without the giving of the bond, in which event the property is not delivered to the claimant, but is sold or held by the officer. (11-23-7). Further proceedings are stayed until final decision of claim. (11-23-9).

Satisfaction.—No specific time period provided by statute upon expiration of which satisfaction is presumed.

Sale.—All sales of property under execution shall commence not sooner than 11:00 A. M., nor continue later than 4:00 P. M. All such sales shall be made by auction to highest bidder for cash, and only so much of property levied on shall be sold as will satisfy execution and costs. (13-3-169).

Redemption.—No period of redemption is provided by statute.

Supplementary Proceedings.—Upon written motion and order of court judgment creditor may examine judgment debtor and compel production of books, papers and other documents to aid in satisfaction of judgment over $100. (13-1-261). MRCP 69 provides supplementary procedure.

Body Execution.—No statutory procedure regarding satisfaction of damages or debt. However, attachment may be issued for nonappearing subpoenaed witness. (13-3-103). See also 99-9-15 and MRCP 45 for general treatment.

EXEMPTIONS:

Every debtor is entitled to these exemptions from seizure: $10,000 in tangible property selected by debtor, insurance proceeds on exempt real or personal property and proceeds of sale of such exempt property, income from disability insurance, certain stock bonus, pension, profit-sharing, annuity, or similar plans or contracts on account of illness, disability, death, age or length of service (as necessary to support debtor and dependents), and property subject to enforcement or collection of civil or criminal contempt orders, except orders or judgments for payment of alimony, separate maintenance and child support actions. (85-3-1).

Substitution.—Tangible property of any kind is subject to $10,000 exemption. (85-3-1). Debtor may select which property is exempt to which he has right of selection. (85-3-3).

Debts Against Which Exemptions Not Allowed.—Personal property exemption is not available against claim for taxes or for purchase price thereof.

Waiver of Exemption.—A general waiver of exemptions in advance is not enforceable (see 89 Miss. 360, 42 So. 174); but exemption of specific property may be waived by contract creating a lien thereon and any exemption may be waived by failure to claim it.

Necessity of Claiming Exemption.—See subhead Waiver of Exemption, supra.

Earnings.—Wages, salaries and compensation of resident workers are exempt for 30 days after service of attachment or garnishment writ. Thereafter, maximum subject to seizure is lesser of 25% of worker's disposable income each week or amount based upon formula incorporating federal minimum wage. (85-3-4).

FRAUDULENT SALES AND CONVEYANCES:

All fraudulent conveyances, whether by gift, grant or conveyance, are void. A pretended loan of chattels remaining in the possession of any person for three years, without demand therefor shall be taken, as to the creditors and purchasers of the person so remaining in possession, to be fraudulent, unless said loan was in writing, and acknowledged and filed for record. (15-3-3).

See category Business Regulation and Commerce, topic Monopolies, Restraint of Trade and Competition.

Uniform Commercial Code adopted, effective Mar. 31, 1968. See category Business Regulation and Commerce, topic Commercial Code.

Uniform Fraudulent Conveyance Act not adopted.

Remedies.—Creditor may treat conveyance as if never made. (Thomason v. Neeley, 50 Miss. 310).

Bulk Sales.—UCC Art. 6 Bulk Transfers repealed. See category Business Regulation and Commerce, topic Commercial Code.

GARNISHMENT:

The right to subject money or property of debtor in possession of third persons to claims against the debtor by garnishment is controlled by 11-35-1 thru 11-35-61.

Property Which May Be Reached.—All property in garnishee's hands belonging to defendant. Wages, salary and other compensation are exempt for 30 days after service of writ of garnishment. Thereafter, exemptions apply to percentages of earnings. (11-35-23; 85-3-4). Certain property is exempt from garnishment. See topic Exemptions.

Jurisdiction.—The clerk of court where judgment or decree was obtained by the creditor may issue writs of garnishment directed to sheriff or proper officer. (11-35-1, 11-35-3).

Proceedings to Obtain.—Writ issues on suggestion in writing by judgment creditor or attaching creditor that property of judgment debtor can be reached by garnishment. (11-35-1, 11-35-3). Bond is not required.

Answer of Garnishee.—Any garnishee duly summoned must answer on oath in writing whether or not he is indebted to the defendant, or was so indebted at the time of the service of the writ, or has since been indebted to the defendant, and, if so, in what amount and whether due or not and when to become due, and how debt is evidenced and what interest it bears; also, what effects of defendant he has or had at time of service of writ on him, or has since in his possession or under his control; also, whether he knows or believes that any other person is indebted to defendant and, if so, who, and in what amount and where such person resides; also, whether he knows of or believes that any other person has effects of defendant in his possession or under his control and, if so, who and where he resides. If garnishee is indebted to defendant for wages, salary or other compensation, he must answer on oath whether defendant is employee of garnishee, and if so, time interval between pay periods of defendant, including specific day paid. (11-35-25).

Garnishee may plead that judgment under which writ was issued is void and, if plea is sustained, no judgment can be rendered against him. (11-35-39).

Answers in the circuit or the chancery court are due on the first day of the return term; in the justice court, answer is due by noon on return day of writ. (11-35-27).

Practice.—After the issuance of the writ of garnishment and due service thereof, a failure to answer on the return term subjects garnishee to liability for full amount of the demand against the defendant and costs; garnishee, however, may by later filing sworn declaration in court showing property and effects in his possession belonging to debtor and his indebtedness to debtor, if any, limit his liability to extent of such property or money held by him. (11-35-31). But no judgment can be rendered against state, a county, a municipality or any state institution, board, commission, or authority, for default in failing to make answer to a writ. (11-35-13).

See note at head of Digest as to 1998 legislation covered.

See Topical Index in front part of this volume.

GARNISHMENT . . . *continued*

Either plaintiff or defendant may controvert the answer of the garnishee in writing, specifying in what particular they believe the answer is incorrect and thereupon an issue is made up and tried upon the correctness of the answer. (11-35-45, 11-35-47).

Adverse Claims.—If garnishee, by his answer or by affidavit, shows that he has been notified that any third person claims title to or interest in debt, or property, subject to writ, court suspends all further proceedings and summons issues for person or persons so claiming debt or property to appear and contest with plaintiff right to such money, debt or property. Or such third person, of his motion, can appear and claim debt or property, and issue is joined and tried and determined as other issues. (11-35-41, 11-35-43).

Judgment.—If the garnishee admits indebtedness to or possession of effects of defendant and same has not been delivered to sheriff, judgment is rendered against him in favor of plaintiff for amount of debt admitted or for property, or value thereof, admitted to be in his possession, but judgment may not exceed plaintiff's demand. (11-35-29).

If issue is found against garnishee, judgment is rendered against him in amount of debt or any money or property in his hands in favor of plaintiff as necessary to satisfy his judgment or claim against defendant, or in favor of defendant if judgment of plaintiff has been satisfied, or for so much thereof as may remain after satisfying said judgment. (11-35-51).

Garnishee can surrender to the sheriff any property, except wages, salaries or other compensation, in his hands belonging to defendant and officer is to dispose of property either as if levied on by execution or by writ of attachment. (11-35-23). If garnishee is indebted or shall become indebted to defendant for wages, salary or other compensation during first 30 days after service of writ of garnishment, garnishee shall pay over to defendant all of such indebtedness. Thereafter, garnishee shall retain and writ shall bind non-exempt percentage of disposable earnings as provided by 85-3-4 for such period of time as is necessary to accumulate sum equal to amount shown on writ as due court. Unless otherwise directed by court, garnishee shall then make one payment into court of amount due, except that at least one payment per year shall be made of all sums accumulated preceding year. (11-35-23).

HOMESTEADS:

Persons entitled to homestead exemption include every citizen of state, male or female, who is householder. (85-3-21, et seq.). But husband or wife, widower or widow, over 60 years of age, who has been entitled to exemption, shall not be deprived because of not residing therein. (85-3-21, 23).

Limitation of Value.—Land and buildings owned and used as residence may be exempted to extent of $75,000 (85-3-21, et seq.).

Limitation of Area.—Quantity of land which may be held exempt may not exceed 160 acres. (85-3-21). Ownership of property for purposes of claiming exemption now includes school lands leased for ten years or more and 20 year renewable lease of lands held in fee by Pearl River Valley Water Supply District when person claiming occupies property and pays taxes thereon. (27-33-17). Also included is land leased for ten years or more from fraternal or benevolent organization. (27-33-17). Dwelling and eligible land under lease of ten or more years from fraternal or benevolent organization actually occupied as dwelling may be claimed. (27-33-19). Condominium units constructed in accordance with 89-9-1, et seq. and actually occupied in accordance with above provisions may constitute homestead. (27-33-19).

Debts or Liabilities Against Which Exemption Not Available.—Homestead exemption not available against taxes, properly executed deeds of trust or mortgages; claims for purchase price, claims for labor done on homestead or materials furnished therefor or claims forfeited recognizance or bail bonds.

Designation of Homestead.—Homestead exemption not available unless application made on or before first day of Apr., subject to 30 day extension where governor proclaims tax assessor's office so damaged that it is impossible to file. However, once valid claim for exemption, filed on or after Jan. 1, 1991, is on file with tax assessor's office reapplication for exemption is not required annually unless there has been change in property description, ownership, use or occupancy since Jan. 1 of preceding year. Property shall be described by parcel number, which clearly locates and identifies property and states acreage. Kind of title or ownership right held shall also be indicated along with book and page where deed, or other evidence of ownership, is of public record. (27-33-31). Unplatted land to be described sufficiently to clearly locate and identify same. (27-33-27). For form of declaration see 85-3-25.

Claim of Exemption.—For appeals see 27-33-55.

Waiver of Exemption.—The homestead exemption cannot be waived or released by an instrument which otherwise conveys no property.

Loss of Exemption.—Claimant shall be ineligible for exemption for failure to comply with income tax laws of state, for claiming to be resident of other state when assessed with income taxes in this state, for failure to comply with road and bridge privilege tax laws. (27-33-63).

Alienation or Encumbrance.—Both husband and wife must join in same conveyance or incumbrance of homestead whether title is in husband or wife, unless spouse of owner is insane; otherwise instrument is void. (89-1-29).

Proceeds of sale of homestead are exempt pending investment thereof in another homestead. Widow of homestead owner may occupy entire homestead rent free during her widowhood. See also categories Family, topic Husband and Wife; Property, topic Real Property.

Rights of Surviving Spouse and Family.—Where deceased person leaves widow or widower or other heirs-at-law entitled to inherit from deceased person, they shall be entitled to homestead exemption, whether or not declared by decedent during lifetime. (85-3-33).

See categories Family, topic Husband and Wife, subhead Conveyance or Encumbrance of Property; Property, topic Deeds, subhead Execution.

LIENS:

Uniform Commercial Code adopted, effective Mar. 31, 1968. (75-1-101 thru 75-11-108). See category Business Regulation and Commerce, topic Commercial Code.

Waiver, Loss or Extinguishment.—Any laborer, materialman or architect entitled to lien on amount due contractor, who falsely and knowingly files notice under 85-7-197 without just cause forfeits lien. (85-7-201).

Expiration Within Six Months.—Unless judicial enforcement proceedings are begun, following liens expire within six months: laborer's lien on lumber and timber (85-7-3); laborer's or materialman's lien on water craft (85-7-7).

Expiration Within 12 Months.—Unless judicial enforcement proceedings are begun, following liens expire within 12 months: lien of owner of stallion, jackass, or bull or foal or calf (85-7-5); laborer's, materialman's, architect's, surveyor's, engineer's, water well driller's, or contractor's lien on buildings, water wells, structures, fixtures, subdivided real property, etc. (85-7-131).

Enforcement.—

Liens on Crops, Advances, Lumber, Timber, Foals, Calves or Water Craft.—Person holding lien on crops, advances, lumber, timber, foals, calves or water craft, under §§85-7-1 through 85-7-9, may enforce it by making affidavit to any officer authorized to administer oaths in county where property is located, setting forth various required information, whereupon clerk or justice shall issue writ to proper officer, commanding seizure of property and summons of interested persons to appear in designated court and answer complaint. (85-7-31). Nonresident and unknown parties may be made parties and proceeded against as in case of suits by attachment. (85-7-33). Form for affidavit and writ is provided in 85-7-35 thru 85-7-39. Writ is returnable to justice of peace if principal of sum claimed does not exceed $200; otherwise, it is returnable to circuit court and affidavit must be filed, by officer who issued writ, in circuit court clerk's office on or before return day of writ. (85-7-41). Writs returnable to justice of peace may be made returnable at any time that provides parties in interest five days' notice before trial; writs returnable to circuit court may be executed at any time before first day of term, and cause is triable at such term. (85-7-43). Return to wrong court does not affect case. (85-7-45). Any interested person may give bond and replevy property; bond is handled as in like case in action of replevin; any bond given inures to benefit of person in whose favor judgment is given. (85-7-47). Any interested person may contest plaintiff's demand, on return day of writ or on any day before final judgment, by filing written statement under oath of his defense or claim; case will then be tried as other cases in court; form and content of judgment is specified. (85-7-49). Death of party does not abate suit or judgment. (85-7-53). For sale of steamboat or other water craft, officer shall levy on, advertise and sell it as for personal property too cumbersome to be moved; purchaser acquires it free from all prior encumbrances saving rights of those having concurrent liens under title 85, c. 7. (85-7-53).

Liens on Watches, Jewelry, Etc., Left Over 90 Days for Repairs, Etc.—Watches, jewelry, etc., left over 90 days for repair may be sold to pay reasonable or agreed charges, provided notice is given of proposed sale and amount owing. (85-7-75). Notice constitutes mailing by registered or certified mail, at least 30 days before sale, of letter with return address marked, to owner at address given at time of delivery of such articles. (85-7-75). If articles are not redeemed within 30 days, they may be sold at time and place specified in letter, either at public auction or by private sale; proceeds in excess of lien must be held for six months, after which they escheat to county. (85-7-77). All persons utilizing provisions of these sections must post in prominent places in their offices two notices containing specified language. (85-7-79).

Liens for Labor and Materials on Articles Constructed, Manufactured or Repaired.—Mechanic to whom price of labor or material employed in constructing, manufacturing or repairing articles is owed has right to retain possession of such articles until price is paid; if not paid within 30 days, he may commence suit in any court of competent jurisdiction; upon proof of value of labor and material employed, he shall be entitled to judgment with costs, special order for sale of property retained, and execution for residue. (85-7-101).

Liens for Price of Feeding, Grooming, Etc., on Horses, Mules, Cows, Etc.—Owner of every livery stable, sale stable, feed stable or public pasture to whom price of feeding, grooming, etc., is owed has right to retain possession of animal until price is paid; if not paid within ten days, he may commence suit before justice court where principal of amount does not exceed $200, or in circuit court if it exceeds that sum; upon proof of debt, he shall be entitled to judgment with costs, special order for sale of property retained, and execution for residue. (85-7-103). If lienholder loses possession to owner, he retains his lien and may enforce it as provided by 87-5-31 and 85-7-53. (87-7-105).

Liens for Price of Labor and Materials Used in Constructing, Manufacturing or Repairing Motor Vehicles.—Mechanic to whom price of labor or material employed in constructing, manufacturing or repairing motor vehicles titled under "The Mississippi Motor Vehicle Title Law" is owed has right to retain possession of motor vehicle until price is paid; if not paid within 30 days, he may notify, by certified mail, legal owner and holder of any lien of amount owed and provide opportunity for redemption. If property is not redeemed within five days after such mailing, he may commence suit in any court of competent jurisdiction; upon proof of value of labor and materials employed, he shall be entitled to judgment with costs, special order for sale of property retained, and execution for residue. Proceeds in excess of lien must be held for six months, after which they escheat to county. (85-7-107).

Liens for Price of Towing and Storing Motor Vehicles.—Towing company that has towed motor vehicle at request of owner or at direction of law enforcement officer or real property owner has right to retain possession of motor vehicle until reasonable price of towing and storage is paid; if not paid within 30 days from initial tow, towing company may notify, by certified mail, legal owner and lienholders of notice of sale of property. Towing company must allow owner ten days to redeem property. Following ten-day redemption period and notice of sale published for two consecutive weeks in newspaper having circulation in county where vehicle was towed, towing company may sell vehicle. Excess proceeds paid to chancery clerk if not reclaimed within six months by owner.

Liens of Owner for Rent on Personal Property in Self-Storage Facility.—For rental agreements entered into on or after July 1, 1988, no enforcement action may be taken by

See note at head of Digest as to 1998 legislation covered.

See Topical Index in front part of this volume.

MS – 18

LIENS . . . *continued*
owner of self-storage facility against occupant until occupant has been in default continuously for period of 14 days. During default period, occupant must be notified in writing by certified mail, return receipt requested, at his last known address. Notice must include specified information, including demand for payment within specified time not less than 14 days after date of notice. After expiration of time specified in notice, owner must publish or post advertisement of sale, as specified. Sale to highest bidder will take place not sooner than 15 days after publication or ten days before posting of advertisement. If no one purchases property, owner may otherwise dispose of it. Any sale or disposition must be held at self-storage facility or at nearest suitable place. (85-7-125). Redemption by satisfaction allowed; sale proceeds in excess of lien must be held for one year, after which escheat to state. (85-7-131).

Mechanics' Liens.—See subhead Mechanics' Liens, infra.

Liens on Clothing, Etc., Placed in Storage.—Clothing or household goods placed in storage by agreement following repair, cleaning, etc., and left over twelve months without reasonable or agreed charges having been paid may be sold to pay said charges, providing notice is given of the time and place of such sale. (85-7-225). Notice constitutes mailing of a letter with return address marked, to the address given at time of delivery of the articles, at least ten days before the sale. (85-7-227).

Mechanics' Liens.—Every building, water well, and any fixed machinery, and every boat, water craft, railroad or railroad embankment, and subdivided property, is liable for the debt contracted and owing for labor done or services of architects, engineers, surveyors, or contractors, or material furnished and such debt is a lien from the time of filing in most instances. (85-7-131—85-7-135). As to oil and gas wells, operator has lien upon interest of each nonoperator owner of interest in mineral leasehold estate for such nonoperator's proportionate part of labor, material and services rendered by operator or for operator's account in behalf of each nonoperator in drilling or other operation of such oil and gas well. (85-7-131).

Such lien exists only in favor of person employed or with whom contract to perform such labor or furnish such materials is made, and his assigns, when contract or employment is made by owner or by his agent, representative, guardian or tenant authorized either expressly or impliedly by owner. (85-7-135).

When contract is in writing it may be acknowledged and recorded as deeds and other instruments and filed with clerk of chancery court of county or district if county is divided into districts where land on which building stands is situated.

If building is in city lien extends to and covers entire lot of land on which it stands. If it is not in city, lien covers one acre of land on which same stands, if there is so much, to be selected by holder of lien. If structure is railroad or railroad embankment, lien extends to and covers entire roadbed and right of way, depots and other buildings used or connected therewith.

Such lien takes effect as to purchasers or encumbrances for valuable consideration, without notice thereof, only from time of commencing suit to enforce lien or from time of filing contract under which lien arose in office of clerk of chancery court. (85-7-131 thru 85-7-133).

Enforcement.—Any person entitled to benefit of such lien must commence his suit in county in which property, or some part thereof, is located, within 12 months after time when money became due and payable, and may not commence suit thereafter. (85-7-141). All parties having interest in controversy or claiming liens on same property shall be made parties; omitted parties may be added by amendment; and claims of several parties having liens on same property may be joined in same action. (85-7-143). Defendants must be summoned as in other actions by law; nonresident or absent defendants may be summoned by publication as in chancery; in default of appearance, same proceedings shall be had as if such defendant had been duly summoned and made default. (85-7-145). Defenses and counterclaims may be made by answer to petition, including any lien defendant claims upon property; trial shall be confined to issues presented in pleadings. (85-7-147).

Judgment may be rendered against defendant generally with costs as in other cases, and with reasonable attorney's fees, with special order for sale of property upon which lien exists for payment thereof, and execution issues as in other cases. (85-7-151).

Sale of land is made as in other cases under execution. (85-7-155).

Of Subcontractors and Laborers.—Where any contractor or master workman entitled to lien does not pay any person who has furnished materials used or amount due by him to any subcontractor therein, or wages of any laborer employed by him, any such person, subcontractor or laborer may give notice in writing to owner of amount due him and claim lien therefor. Thereupon amount that may be due upon day of service of such notice by such owner to contractor is bound in hands of such owner for payment in full, or if insufficient, then pro rata, of all amounts due such person, subcontractor or journeyman or laborer, who might lawfully have given such notice in writing to owner. If suit be brought against owner, he may pay into court amount due on contract and all interested parties be summoned into court to protect their rights, to contest demands of any and all claimants and court must cause issue to be made up and direct payment of amount found due. In case judgment is given against owner, such judgment is a lien from date of original notice and is enforced as other such liens. Owner is, in no event, liable for greater amount than amount contracted for with contractor. (85-7-181).

When any contractor constructing or repairing building enters into bond guaranteeing faithful performance of contract, such bond must be subject to additional obligation that such contractor shall pay for all labor or material under said contract and person furnishing labor or material shall participate pro-rata in any suit on said bond, subject to rights of obligee. (85-7-185). If no suit is brought by obligee within six months from final settlement of contract, any persons supplying labor and material have right of action on said bond. (85-7-187). Such suit must be brought within one year from final settlement, or abandonment thereof by contractor. (85-7-189). Only one suit can be brought on bond and any other person entitled to sue may intervene. (85-7-191).

No contractor or master workman may assign, transfer, or otherwise dispose of in any way, contract or proceeds thereof, to detriment or prejudice of subcontractor, except where bond provided in accordance with 85-7-185. (85-7-183).

Attachment Lien.—See topic Attachment.

Attorney's Lien.—See category Legal Profession, topic Attorneys and Counselors.

Collateral Security.—See topic Pledges.

Execution Lien.—See topic Executions.

Judgment Lien.—See category Civil Actions and Procedure, topic Judgments.

Landlord's Lien.—See category Property, topic Landlord and Tenant.

Liens on Exempt Property.—See topic Exemptions.

Liens on Homesteads.—See topic Homesteads.

Real Estate Mortgage Lien.—See category Mortgages, topic Mortgages of Real Property.

Tax Lien.—See category Taxation, topic Property (Ad Valorem) Taxes, subhead Lien.

PLEDGES:

Attachment of pledgor's interest in pledged property is permitted.

A pledge may be foreclosed by sale after default. There are no formal proceedings for sale prescribed, and if expressly allowed, pledgee may purchase.

Uniform Commercial Code adopted, effective Mar. 31, 1968. See category Business Regulation and Commerce, topic Commercial Code.

RECEIVERS:

Jurisdiction of receivers is in chancery court. Appointment or removal is by court in term time or chancellor in vacation. (11-5-151, MRCP 66). At least five days notice of application for appointment required unless immediate appointment necessary or good cause for dispensing with notice shown (11-5-153), in which cases bond required of applicant (11-5-155). Receiver required to give bond (11-5-159) and subject to orders and instructions of court and of chancellor in vacation (11-5-161).

DISPUTE RESOLUTION

ALTERNATIVE DISPUTE RESOLUTION:

Mandatory Dispute Resolution.—No statutes or court rules required.

Voluntary Dispute Resolution.—No systematic methods established. Completely voluntary and at initiative of and only by agreement of parties.

See topic Arbitration and Award.

ARBITRATION AND AWARD:

Existing disputes may be submitted to arbitration by parties by written instrument. (11-15-1, et seq.). Existing and future disputes may be submitted to arbitration by parties to construction contract by written agreement. (11-15-101, et seq.).

(Not subject to Uniform Arbitration Act, except as noted below.)

Form and Requisites of Submission.—All competent persons may, by instruments of writing, submit any existing controversy to one or more arbitrators. (11-15-1). Arbitrators must be sworn. (11-15-9). Award may be confirmed by court having jurisdiction of subject matter. (11-15-21). Pending suits and actions may be referred to person or persons appointed by litigants. Award of such arbitrators is returned to court and approved and entered of record, having same effect as final judgment or decree of court, and execution may issue thereon. (11-15-35). Court may vacate award because of procurement of award by corruption, fraud or undue means; corruption of arbitrators; misconduct of arbitrators; or arbitrators exceeding powers. (11-15-23).

Contracts to Arbitrate Future Disputes.—Parties to construction contracts may agree to submit existing or future controversies to arbitration. Arbitration provision waived if one party sues and other party fails to assert provision as defense within time required for answer to suit. Bidder on public construction contract may refuse without penalty to consent to arbitration provision in such contract. Otherwise, Uniform Arbitration Act governs, with exceptions noted below. (11-15-101 et seq.).

Sellers of plant seeds who affix prescribed label to their product may not be sued for seeds' failure until buyer proceeds with timely arbitration. Seed Arbitration Council inspects plants or crops, and issues opinion regarding validity of claim. Opinion is admissible evidence in subsequent legal actions. (69-3-19).

Rescission.—Revocality of submissions to arbitration of existing nonconstruction disputes is governed by common law.

Construction Contract: Agreement to arbitrate existing or future dispute under Construction Contract is irrevocable unless parties waive arbitration by dispute without assertion of arbitrality as defense of suit. (11-15-103).

Powers of Arbitrators.—

Construction Contract: Arbitrators may grant any remedy which is just, equitable, and consistent with agreement of parties which is subject of arbitration. (11-15-119). Arbitrators may modify award for reasons ennumerated in 11-15-135. (11-15-123).

Award and Enforcement Thereof.—As to nonconstruction arbitration, see subhead Form and Requisites of Submission, supra.

Construction Contract: Award may be confirmed, vacated, modified, or corrected by circuit of appropriate jurisdiction. (11-15-125, 11-15-133, 11-15-135). Judgment or decree of court is entered and enforced as any other judgment or decree. (11-15-137). Appeal from such judgment or decree may be had in same manner or with other judgments or decrees in civil action. (11-15-141).

Judgment on Award.—As to nonconstruction arbitration, see subhead Form and Requisites of Submission, supra.

As to construction contract arbitration, see subhead Award and Enforcement Thereof, supra.

Mandatory Arbitration.—State Highway Arbitration Board hears all disputes on contracts of $25,000 or less between State Highway Commission and contractors. (65-2-1 et seq.). (Not subject to Uniform Arbitration Act.)

See note at head of Digest as to 1998 legislation covered.

See Topical Index in front part of this volume.

MS – 19

DOCUMENTS AND RECORDS

ACKNOWLEDGMENTS:

Uniform Acknowledgments Act and other uniform laws regarding acknowledgments have not been adopted.

Within State.—Acknowledgment of instrument affecting real estate or personal property may be taken by any judge of U.S. court; any judge of Supreme Court; judge of circuit or county court or chancellor, or before any clerk of court of record or notary public who shall certify such acknowledgment or proof under seal of his office; or before any justice court judge or police justice or mayor of any city, town or village, or member of board of supervisors. (89-3-3). Notary public, justice court judges, circuit and chancery court clerks and assistant secretaries of state can acknowledge all instruments commonly proved by notaries. (25-33-11; 25-33-17). Fee, up to $1. (25-7-29).

In connection with claims of veterans of all wars, their heirs or dependents, against the United States, acknowledgments may be taken by a post service officer of any of nationally chartered veterans' organizations in state under seal of office of post. (35-3-7).

Outside State but Within United States.—Acknowledgment of instrument affecting real estate or personal property may be taken by justice of U.S. Supreme Court, or U.S. circuit or district judge, or any other U.S. judge, or any judge or justice of Supreme or superior court of state or territory or District of Columbia or possession of U.S., or land over which U.S. has sovereign power, or any justice of peace of such state, territory, etc., whose official character is certified under seal or court of record in jurisdiction, or commissioner residing in such jurisdiction and appointed by Governor of Mississippi to take acknowledgments and proof of conveyances, or notary public or clerk of court of record having seal of office in such jurisdiction. (89-3-9).

Outside the United States.—Acknowledgment of instrument affecting real estate or personal property may be taken by any court of record or mayor or chief magistrate of any city, borough or corporation of foreign country or before any commissioner for Mississippi residing in such country, or before any ambassador, foreign minister, secretary of legation, or consul of U.S. to foreign country, or before notary public or other person authorized by foreign country to take oaths or acknowledgments, but certificate must show that party or party and witness were identified before officer, and that party acknowledged execution of instrument, or that execution was duly proved by witness. (89-3-13).

Persons in or with U. S. Armed Forces.—Persons in U.S. military service, their husbands or wives, merchant seamen outside limits of U.S., and anyone outside U.S. under authority of government department or official in connection with war activities may acknowledge any instrument before any commissioned officer in active service of U.S. Armed Forces. A certificate indorsed upon, or attached to, instrument, which shows date of notarial act and which states in substance that person appeared before officer, acknowledged instrument as his act or made or signed instrument under oath is sufficient. Signature, rank and branch of service of commissioned officer appearing on certificate is prima facie evidence of authority of officer and that person making oath or acknowledgment is within act. (25-33-23). Any acknowledgments made before any commissioned officer in U.S. Armed Forces prior to Mar. 30, 1946, is validated. (89-3-5). See topic Notaries Public.

Married women acknowledge instrument affecting real estate and personal property, and their signatures are proved, as in case of other persons; privy examination not required. (89-3-7).

Attorneys in Fact.—No special provisions govern acknowledgments of attorneys in fact.

Corporations.—Officer of corporation signing instrument acknowledges execution of instrument as in other cases; or proof may be made thereof by witness. (89-1-21).

Foreign Acknowledgments.—See subhead Outside the United States, supra.

Effect of Acknowledgment.—Instruments are valid between the parties without acknowledgment but acknowledgment or proof by witness is necessary to entitle them to be admitted to record. (89-3-1). Requirement of authentication or identification as condition precedent to admissibility into evidence is satisfied by evidence sufficient to support finding that matter in question is what its proponent claims. (Miss. R. Evid. 901). Authenticity is taken as sufficiently established for purposes of admissibility without extrinsic evidence in certain instances. (Miss. R. Evid. 902). Testimony of subscribing witness is not necessary to authenticate writing unless required by laws of jurisdiction governing validity of writing. (Miss. R. Evid. 903).

Proof by Subscribing Witness.—One of subscribing witnesses may appear before any officer authorized to take acknowledgments and acknowledge that he saw party whose name is subscribed thereto, sign and deliver same, or that he heard party who signed same, acknowledge that he signed and delivered same, and that he, witness, subscribed his name as witness in presence of party who signed instrument. (89-3-7).

If the grantor and witness or witnesses of an instrument are dead, or absent, so that personal attendance of neither can be had, instrument may be established by oath of any person who, on examination, before officer qualified to take acknowledgments, can prove handwriting of deceased or absent witness, or when such proof cannot be had, then handwriting of grantor may be proved and officer before whom such proof is made, shall certify accordingly. (89-3-15).

Authentication.—No authentication of a certificate of acknowledgment taken outside state is necessary except where taken by a justice of peace, in which case his official character must be certified under seal of a court. In this state chancery clerk of each county is proper officer to certify to official character of officer taking an acknowledgment. Fee, 50¢. Secretary of State can also certify. Fee $2.

Forms

(a) For natural persons acting in their own right:
"STATE OF _____
COUNTY OF _____

Personally appeared before me, the undersigned authority in and for the said county and state, on this __ day of _____, 19__, within my jurisdiction, the within named ____ _____, who acknowledged that (he)(she)(they) executed the above and foregoing instrument.

_____(NOTARY PUBLIC)
My commission expires:
_____"
(Affix official seal, if applicable)

(b) For corporations:
"STATE OF _____
COUNTY OF _____

Personally appeared before me, the undersigned authority in and for the said county and state, on this ___ day of _____, 19___, within my jurisdiction, the within named _____, who acknowledged that (he)(she) is _____ of _____, a _____ corporation, and that for and on behalf of the said corporation, and as its act and deed (he)(she) executed the above and foregoing instrument, after first having been duly authorized by said corporation so to do.

_____(NOTARY PUBLIC)
My commission expires:
_____"
(Affix official seal, if applicable)

(c) For persons acting in representative capacities:
"STATE OF _____
COUNTY OF _____

Personally appeared before me, the undersigned authority in and for the said county and state, on this ___ day of _____, 19___, within my jurisdiction, the within named _____, who acknowledged that (he)(she) is _____ of _____ and that in said representative capacity (he)(she) executed the above and foregoing instrument, after first having been duly authorized so to do.

_____(Notary Public)
My commission expires:
(Affix official seal, if applicable)

(d) For proof of execution by a subscribing witness:
"STATE OF _____
COUNTY OF _____

Personally appeared before me, the undersigned authority in and for the said county and state, on this ___ day of _____, 19___, within my jurisdiction, CD, one of the subscribing witnesses to the above and foregoing instrument, who, being first duly sworn, states that (he)(she) saw the within (or above) named AB, whose name is subscribed thereto, sign and deliver the same to EF (or that (he)(she) heard AB acknowledge that (he)(she) signed and delivered the same to EF); and that the affiant subscribed (his)(her) name as witness thereto in the presence of AB.

_____(CD)

(NOTARY PUBLIC)
My commission expires:
_____"
(Affix official seal, if applicable)
(89-3-7)

Validating Acts.—Acknowledgments to deeds which have been recorded for 20 years or more are good without regard to form. (89-5-13).

Alternative to Acknowledgment or Proof.—No statutory provision.

AFFIDAVITS:

Affidavits may be taken before any judge of a court of record, court reporter of such court, clerk of such court, justice court judge, member of board of supervisors, notary public, master, mayor or police justice of city, town or village, clerk of municipality and any officer of any other state, or of U.S., authorized by laws thereof to administer oaths, judge of any court of record, or mayor or chief magistrate of any city, borough or corporation of foreign country. (11-1-1).

General Requirements as to Administration.—None except forms required in certain circumstances.

General Requirements of Jurat.—Every notary's seal shall have name of county of notary's residence with that of state and his/her own name on margin and words "notary public" across center. Official act shall be attested by seal of office. (25-33-3). On any acknowledgment notary in addition to official seal and signature shall include written or printed recital of date his/her commission expires. (25-33-13). For acknowledgment forms, see topic Acknowledgments.

Use of Affidavit.—No general provision; for use in summary judgment motion see MRCP 56.

Form.—None except forms required in certain circumstances.

Alternative to Affidavit.—No statutory provision.

NOTARIES PUBLIC:

Qualification.—Bond required in amount of $5,000. Each notary required to take oath. Notary qualified by filing oath and bond with Secretary of State. (25-33-1).

Authentication.—See topic Acknowledgments. (89-3-13).

Seal.—Regulation seal is prescribed. (25-33-3).

Powers and Duties.—Following powers may be exercised by every notary public: To administer oaths and affirmations in all matters incident to his notarial office; to receive proof or acknowledgment of all instruments of writing relating to commerce or navigation, such as bills of sale, bottomries, mortgages, and hypothecations of ships, vessels, or boats, charter-parties of affreightment, letters of attorney, and such other writings as

NOTARIES PUBLIC . . . *continued*
are commonly proved or acknowledged before notaries; to perform all other duties required of notaries by commercial usage; and to make declarations and certify the truth thereof, under his seal of office, concerning all matters done by him in virtue of his office. (25-33-9, 25-33-11).

Territorial Extent of Powers.—A notary may act throughout state. Notaries empowered to administer oaths for taking oral testimony within state at large. (25-33-9).

Expiration of Commission.—Notary public shall hold office for term of four years. (29-33-1). This expiration date must be affixed to jurat. (25-33-13).

Fees.—Fee for taking acknowledgment is 25¢; for affidavit or oath and seal, 50¢. (25-7-29, 25-7-33).

Officers of U.S. Armed Forces.—Second lieutenant or higher in army or marine corps, ensign or higher in navy or coast guard, or equivalent ranks of any other component part of U.S. Armed Forces. (25-33-23).

RECORDS:

Clerk of Chancery Court has charge of records relating to property. Uniform Commercial Code adopted. (75–1-101 thru 75-11-108).

Recordable Instruments.—Conveyances, marriage instruments affecting land, deeds of trusts, mortgages (89-5-3); written contracts in relation to land (89-5-7); copies of records filed in other states or foreign countries (89-5-9); land patents (89-5-11); assignments of debt (89-5-15); satisfactions of debt (89-5-21); cancellations of oil, gas, and mineral leases (89-5-23); substitutions of trustee (89-5-45).

Place of Recording.—Records are kept by clerk of chancery court for county in which land is located (89-5-1); where county is divided into two districts, each district is treated as separate county for purpose of land records (89-5-41). *For list of Counties and County Seats, see first page for this state in Volume containing Practice Profiles Section.*

Requisites for Recording.—Acknowledgment or proof necessary to recording, form, methods (89-3-1, et seq.); recording of certificate of acknowledgment or proof of conveyances (89-5-1); acknowledgment for deed recorded 20 years valid regardless of form of certificate (89-5-13).

Recording Fees.—Clerks of chancery court charge following fees: recording and indexing deeds, wills, leases, amendments, subordinations, liens, releases, cancellations, orders, decrees, oaths, etc., $6; recording deeds of trust, $10; recording and indexing oil and gas leases, etc., $12; recording and indexing oil and gas cancellations, assignments, etc., $5 first page, $2 each additional page. (25-7-9).

Foreign Conveyances or Encumbrances.—Copy of record of any instrument affecting property in this state duly recorded in another state or foreign country may be recorded in this state in same way and with like effect as if it had been executed and acknowledged in this state. (89-5-9).

Effect of Record.—Mississippi is race-notice jurisdiction. (89-5-1, -3).

Torrens Act.—Repealed in 1930.

Transfer of Decedent's Title.—Failure to record transfer of decedent's title does not affect validity of transfer as between decedent and his heirs, and as to all subsequent purchasers with notice or without valuable consideration. (89-5-3).

Filing Under Commercial Code.—For equipment used in farming operations, or accounts or general intangibles arising from or relating to sale of farm products by farmer, in office of chancery clerk in county of debtor's residence or, if debtor is nonresident, in office of chancery clerk in county where goods are kept. For consumer goods, in office of chancery clerk in county of debtors' residence or, if debtor is nonresident, in office of chancery clerk in county where goods are kept. For farm products, in office of chancery clerk in county of debtor"s residence or, if debtor is nonresident of this state, in office of chancery clerk in county where goods are kept; and in office of secretary of state. For crops growing or to be grown, in office of chancery clerk in county where land is located; and, if debtor is resident, in office of chancery clerk in county of debtor's residence; and in office of secretary of state. For timber to be cut or minerals or the like or accounts subject to §75-9-103(5) or financing statements filed as fixture filing where collateral is fixtures; in office where mortgage on real estate would be filed or recorded. In all other cases; in office of secretary of state and, if debtor has place of business in only one county, also in office of chancery clerk of such county, or, if debtor has no place of business in this state but is resident, also in office of chancery clerk of county in which he resides. (75-9-401).

Fee for filing financing statement, termination statement, statement of assignment or statement of release is $5 if on standard form, $10 if not, plus $2 for each extra listing. (75-9-403—75-9-406). Search fee for certificate showing presently effective financing statement is $5 if on standard form, $10 if not, plus $2 for each financing statement listed, and copies of listed financing statements available at $2 per page. (75-9-407).

Vital Statistics.—

Bureau of Vital Statistics is a part of State Board of Health (41-57-1), and reporting and registration of vital statistics is performed by rules and regulations formulated by Board of Health (41-57-7). State is divided into registration districts and local registrars are appointed in each district. Reports of births and deaths are made by local registrar to State Board of Health, Department of Vital Statistics. (41-57-5, 41-57-11).

All marriages must be registered with State Registrar of Vital Statistics. Circuit clerk of each county must, each month, forward to Bureau of Vital Statistics records of marriages reported to him during previous month. (41-57-48).

Establishing birth records is accomplished by completing forms furnished by Mississippi State Dept. of Health. Evidence required in proving date and place of birth, parentage and citizenship is affidavit of applicant corroborated by that of close relative and two or more of following: (1) Statement from Bureau of Census; (2) certified baptismal record; (3) statement from insurance company with respect to policies more than five years old; (4) affidavit of school authority with respect to school records; (5) authentic Bible records; (6) hospital records; (7) world war army discharges; (8) affidavit of physician who attended at time of birth; (9) birth certificates of children of applicant.

Fee for search, verification or certified copy of birth, death or marriage records is $5 and may be obtained from State Dept. of Health, P.O. Box 1700, Jackson, Miss. 39215-1700. Certain records unavailable to persons without legitimate tangible interest. (41-57-2).

SEALS:

The use of private seals is dispensed with, except as to corporations. Failure to use a seal or scroll, by a private person, in no manner affects a written instrument, nor does it vary the rights of the parties to it. Bonds in legal proceedings need not be under seal.

Uniform Commercial Code adopted. (75-1-101 thru 75-11-108). See category Business Regulation and Commerce, topic Commercial Code.

Corporate Seals.—Private seals not dispensed with as to corporations. (75-19-1).

Effect of Seal.—Seal has no effect. (75-19-5).

EMPLOYMENT

LABOR RELATIONS:

Generally the rules of the common law control the relationship of master and servant.

There are special statutory regulations of employer and employee in mills, canneries, workshops, factories or manufacturing establishments. Enforcement of the act is under the supervision of a state factory inspector who is appointed by the State Board of Health and special duties are placed on the sheriff where child labor is regulated. (71-1-1 thru -53). Mississippi is at-will employment state.

Provisions for trusts as a part of pension, disability, death-benefit or profit-sharing plans by an employer are permitted. (71-1-41).

Hours of labor in any mill, cannery, workshop, factory or manufacturing establishment (excluding railroads and other public service corporations and except where perishable agricultural products are being handled in season with adult male labor only) are limited as follows (71-1-21): (a) employees over 16: a maximum of ten hours per day, except in cases of emergency or where public necessity requires. Thirty minutes per day additional can be added at first of week if deducted last days of week; (b) employees under 16 and over 14: maximum of eight hours per day and 44 hours per week, not between the hours of 7:00 P. M. and 6:00 A. M.

Child Labor.—Children under 14 may not be employed or permitted to work in any mill, cannery, workshop, factory or manufacturing establishment (71-1-17); and no child under 16 years of age can work in such establishment except on proof that such child has complied with compulsory school attendance law (71-1-19, 71-1-17).

Such establishments employing child labor are subject to inspection by the county health officer and children are removed from such employment by sheriff upon request of such county health officer. (71-1-25).

Violation of the act by employer is a misdemeanor. (71-1-29).

Persuading, enticing or decoying any child under 18 years, being unmarried, away from parent with whom it resides, for purpose of employing such child without consent of parents, is misdemeanor. (97-5-7).

Female Labor.—No statutory regulation.

Discrimination against public employees on basis of race, color, religion, sex, national origin, age or handicap is prohibited. (25-9-149). No statutory regulation for private employees.

Wages.—There is no statute establishing minimum wages.

Employers engaged in manufacture, employing over 50 persons, and public service corporations, are required to pay their employees at least once every two weeks or twice each month. (71-1-35).

Discounting of trade checks by employers, or purchaser thereof, is prohibited and made a misdemeanor (71-1-37), and trade checks must be paid in cash on regular pay days or 25% damages allowed (71-1-39). See category Debtor and Creditor, topic Assignments for treatment of assignment of wages.

Labor Unions and Labor Disputes.—Right of persons to work shall not be denied on account of membership or nonmembership in labor union. (71-1-47). Person who has been convicted of certain felonies, or been member of Communist party, may not hold office or occupy bargaining position, or act as labor relations consultant until five years after conviction or release from imprisonment or termination of membership in said party. (71-1-49).

Workers' Compensation Act.—An act to establish a system of workers' compensation for industrial injuries has been adopted. (71-3-1 thru -119).

Administration.—The act is administered by Workers' Compensation Commission consisting of three members appointed by Governor with consent of Senate. Commission has powers of court of record for compelling attendance of witnesses, etc., including power to adopt rules and regulations, make or approve forms, investigate and determine claims for compensation, and make awards. (71-3-85).

The act is applicable to any employer, whether person, firm, association or corporation, including legal representatives of deceased employer or receiver or trustee of any such employer, that has in service five or more workers or operatives regularly in same business, or in or about same establishment, under any contract of hire, express or implied. (71-3-5). Independent contractors, including newspaper carrier boys, are not "employees." (71-3-3 amended following 80 So.2d 770). Public service corporations are included. (71-3-5). All offices, departments, agencies, bureaus, commissions, boards, institutions, hospitals, colleges, universities, airport authorities or other instrumentalities of state are within act after July 1, 1990. Counties and municipalities within act after Oct. 1, 1990. All political subdivisions within act after Oct. 1, 1993. (71-3-5).

Exemptions.—Nonprofit charitable, fraternal, cultural or religious corporations or associations; domestic servants; farmers and farm labor; purchasers of timber products

LABOR RELATIONS . . . *continued*
who are not liable for unemployment tax or harvesters and delivers of timber; handicapped persons employed in sheltered workshop programs; transportation and maritime employments, for which rule of liability is provided by laws of U.S. and direct buyer-seller or vendor-vendee relationship where there is no employer-employee relationship; proprietors, partners, or employees owning 15% of stock of corporation who agree in writing. (71-3-5).

Election to Come Within the Act.—Employers exempted from act may come within it by purchasing valid insurance, and no other act is required. (71-3-5).

State, county and municipal institutions, departments, or agencies may elect to come under act. (71-3-5).

A contractor is liable to employees of a subcontractor unless the subcontractor has secured such payment. (71-3-7; and see 80 So.2d 819).

Exclusive Liability.—The liability under the act of any employer who has complied therewith is in place of all other liability of such employer to the employee, his dependents and next-of-kin, or anyone otherwise entitled to recover damages at common law. (71-3-9).

Noncompliance by Employer.—If an employer fails to secure by insurance the payment of compensation as required by the act, an employee, or his representative in case of death, may elect whether to claim compensation under the act or to maintain an action at law for damages. In such an action employer may not plead as a defense negligence of a fellow servant, assumption of risk or contributory negligence. (71-3-9; 297 Miss. 305, 85 So.2d 926).

Injuries Covered.—Liability of an employer under act covers disability or accidental death of an employee arising out of and in course of employment regardless of fault as to cause of injury. Compensation for aggravation of preexisting handicap may be proportionately reduced by that proportion which such preexisting disease contributed to results following injury. It includes also injury caused by willful act of a third person directed against an employee because of his employment while so employed and working on job. Injury includes disability or death due to radiation exposure and occupational disease. Act does not cover injury occasioned by intoxication of employee or by willful intention of the employee to injure or kill himself or another. (71-3-7).

Insurance of Compensation.—No claim for compensation shall be maintained unless, within 30 days after occurrence of injury, actual notice of injury is provided to employer; limitation not applicable to minor or incompetent without guardian or authorized representative. (71-3-35). Limitations period begins to run when claimant is or should reasonably have been aware of incurrence of compensable injury. (586 So.2d 823).

Rates of Compensation for Injuries.—For claims arising on or after July 1, 1988, compensation for disability or death never exceeds 66²/₃% of state average weekly wage (as determined annually by Employment Security Commission) multiplied by 450 weeks. Minimum payment is $25 per week. (71-3-13). Employer is liable for all medical, surgical, nursing and hospital expenses for such period as nature of injury or process of recovery may require. (71-3-15). Compensation for total disability (permanent or temporary) is 66²/₃% of average weekly wages subject to maximum weekly benefit rate for not to exceed 450 weeks. For permanent partial disability, 66²/₃% of average weekly wages for varying number of weeks never to exceed 450, depending on type of injury. (71-3-17). Temporary partial disability, 66²/₃% of difference between injured employee's average weekly wage before injury and his wage-earning capacity after injury, never to exceed 450 weeks. (71-3-21).

Rates of Compensation for Death.—$250 to widow; reasonable funeral expenses not to exceed $2,000; payments to surviving wife or dependent husband of 35% of average wages of deceased during widowhood, or dependent widowerhood, and additional 10% of such wages for each child; if no surviving widow or dependent husband, 25% of such wages for each dependent child; if no surviving wife or dependent husband or child, or if amount payable thereto is less than 66²/₃% of average wages of deceased, then 15% of such wage for support of any grandchild, brother, sister, parent or grandparent if dependent upon deceased at time of injury; total weekly compensation payable to all beneficiaries never to exceed weekly benefits set up in act and never to be paid for longer than 450 weeks. (71-3-25). Minimum is $25 per week except in partial dependency cases. (71-3-13 and 71-3-25—71-3-29).

Dependency.—All questions of dependency are determined as of time of injury. A surviving wife or children are presumed wholly dependent. All other dependents are considered on the basis of total or partial dependency as the facts warrant. (71-3-25).

How Benefits Payable.—First installment of compensation due on 14th day after due notice of injury or death. Payable every 14 days. (71-3-37).

Lien.—Compensation is a lien on the assets of employer and insurer. (71-3-45).

Priorities.—Compensation is entitled to priority in distribution of funds in case of insolvency. (71-3-45).

Exemption.—Compensation or benefits payable under the act are exempt from all claims of creditors and from levy under execution or attachment. Exemption may, however, be waived. (71-3-43).

Assignment of compensation or benefits is not permitted. (71-3-43).

Waiver of Right.—No agreement by an employee to waive his right to compensation under act is valid. (71-3-41).

Hearings on claims are had before the Compensation Commission, which has full power and authority to determine all questions relating to payment of such claims. Details of practice and procedure in the adjudication of claims are determinable by published rules of Commission. Commission is not bound by common law or statutory rules of evidence or formal rules of procedure. Informal hearings may be had by one Commissioner, or designated representative of Commission, and his decision will be final unless within 20 days request or petition for review by full Commission is filed. (71-3-47, 71-3-55).

Appeals.—Final award of Commission is conclusive unless an appeal to the circuit court of the county in which the injury occurred is perfected within 30 days. Appeals are considered only upon the record. The circuit court reviews all questions of law and of fact. If affirmed, the matter is remanded to the Commission for enforcement; if reversed, the circuit court enters such judgment or award as the Commission should have entered. Appeals may be taken from the circuit court to the Supreme Court. (71-3-51).

Enforcement of Award.—When an employer is in default for 30 days (if payments secured) or ten days (if unsecured), any party in interest may file with circuit clerk in county in which injury occurred, or county in which employer has his principal place of business, certified copy of final decision of Commission awarding compensation. Thereupon judgment is entered in circuit court by clerk of said court in conformity with Commission's decision. Such judgment is entered in same manner and has same effect as though rendered in suit duly heard and determined by circuit court, except that no appeal may be taken therefrom, and court can vacate or modify such judgment to conform to any later awards or decisions of Commission. (71-3-49).

Compromise.—The Commission has the authority to compromise an award and make lump sum settlements. (71-3-29).

Rights of an employee against third parties are not affected by the act except that employer or insurer is subrogated to such rights to the extent of compensation paid under the act and is entitled to notice and opportunity to join in any action against third parties by an employee or his dependents. (71-3-71).

Double compensation and death benefits are payable if injured employee at time of injury is a minor under 18 years of age, employed, permitted or suffered to work in violation of any provision of labor laws. Employer alone and not insurance carrier is liable for this increased compensation or death benefits. Any provision in insurance policy undertaken to relieve employer from such increased liability is void. However, penalty shall not apply to students 14 years of age and over who are employed between school terms with parental consent nor to students 14 years of age and over who are employed in on-the-job training with parental consent as a part of a regular education program. (71-3-107).

Forms can be secured by addressing the Chairman of Workers' Compensation Commission at Jackson.

Occupational diseases are compensable if direct causal connection between work and disease. (71-3-7).

Employer's Liability Act.—No separate act.

Unemployment Compensation.—Available to unemployed individual who meets following requirements: (1) Has registered and reports to employment office, unless registration and reporting are oppressive or inconsistent with purposes of this chapter, and participates in reemployment services (if it is determined to be likely that claimant will exhaust regular benefits), (2) has made claim for benefits, (3) is able and available for work, (4) has been unemployed for one week, (5) has been paid wages for insured work equal to not less than 36 times his weekly benefit amount for weeks beginning on or before July 1, 1982 and not less than 40 times his weekly benefit for weeks thereafter and has been paid wages for insured work during two quarters of his base period. (71-5-511).

Weekly benefit amount shall be 1/26 of total wages for highest quarter of base period, but in no event less than $30 or more than $165 per week. If weekly benefit computes to less than minimum, individual is not entitled to benefits. (71-5-503).

ENVIRONMENT

ENVIRONMENTAL REGULATION:

General Supervision.—Miss. Department of Environmental Quality (49-2-5) and Miss. Department of Wildlife, Fisheries and Parks (49-1-1).

Permit Board reviews applications for issuing, modifying, revoking, or denying air and water pollution control permits, solid waste and hazardous waste permits. (49-17-28-29).

Commission on Environmental Quality promulgates rules and regulations to prevent, control and abate pollution. (49-17-17).

State Board of Health administers radiation protection program. (45-14-7).

State Board of Health enforces drinking water regulations. (41-26-5).

State Oil and Gas Board, subject to Commission on Environmental Quality's approval, regulates disposal of oil and gas well waste. (53-1-17).

Mississippi Commission on Natural Resources regulates surface coal mining and reclamation operations. (53-9-45).

Prohibited Acts of Pollution.—See Miss. Air and Water Pollution Control Law (49-17-1-43); Miss. Solid Waste Disposal Law (17-17-1-61); Underground Storage Tank Act of 1988 (49-17-401, et seq.) and Radioactive Waste Transportation Act (45-14-51, et seq.); Mississippi Safe Drinking Water Law (41-26-1, et seq.); Surface Coal Mining and Reclamation Law (53-9-1, et seq.).

Air.—Causing pollution of air of state or placing or causing to be placed wastes in locations likely to produce pollution; discharging wastes into air of state which reduce quality of air below standards established by Commission; and building, erecting, altering, replacing, using or operating equipment which will cause issuance of air contaminants without permit from board. (49-17-29).

Water.—Causing pollution of any waters of state or placing or causing to be placed wastes in a location where they are likely to cause pollution of any waters of state; and discharging any wastes into any waters of state which reduce quality of such waters below water quality standards established by Commission. (49-17-29).

Drinking Water.—Contamination of public water system; intentionally damaging any pipe or other part of public water system; discharge of sewage at any location that may come in contact with public water system intake. (41-26-15).

Hazardous Waste Disposal.—Miss. Department of Environmental Quality to adopt regulations for management of solid wastes, consistent with U.S. Environmental Protection Agency and U.S. Dept. of Transportation regulations. (49-2-7, 57-49-1 et seq.). Handling of exempted hazardous wastes alongside ordinary wastes governed by 17-17-15.

Solid Waste Disposal.—Burning of garbage (17-17-9), spillage while hauling (17-17-9), unauthorized dumps (17-17-17), use of salt domes or other geologic structures for disposal of radioactive waste (17-17-49), disposition of compost (17-17-215), waste tires (17-17-405 et seq.), lead acid batteries (17-17-429 et seq.). See generally 17-17-1 et seq. Dept. of Environmental Quality has jurisdiction over nuclear waste policy, activities, and siting. (57-49-1 et seq.).

See note at head of Digest as to 1998 legislation covered.

See Topical Index in front part of this volume.

MS – 22

ENVIRONMENTAL REGULATION . . . *continued*

Wastewater Disposal.—Individual on-site wastewater disposal systems cannot be constructed without first submitting notice of intent to State Dept. of Health and unless systems are designed and installed by certified installers and engineers and according to Board of Health and Commission of Environmental Quality regulations. (41-67-54, et seq.).

Enforcement.—

Waters, Streams, and Air.—Attorney General to bring and defend for Commission all cases arising in state courts under Act or regulations of Commission. All district attorneys and county prosecuting attorneys to assist Attorney General.

Commission establishes standards of air and water quality after conducting public hearings and publishing due notice of same. (49-17-19, 49-17-25).

Commission may cause a written complaint to be served upon alleged violator(s) when it believes a violation has occurred. Complaint must specify: (a) provision(s) of Act or regulation or order allegedly violated, (b) facts constituting alleged violation; and it specifies time more than ten days later when violator must appear before Commission. After hearing, Commission will enter order and may assess penalties. Any interested person may make written request for Commission hearing, and Commission may call special or regular hearing. (49-17-31-35).

In addition to all other remedies, any person or interested party aggrieved by any order of Commission may file a sworn petition with Commission stating grounds and reasons for complaint and requesting a hearing. Witnesses may be subpoenaed and examined under oath and evidence submitted at instance of petitioner and/or Commission. Petitioner may appeal to appropriate Chancery Court within 15 days after adjournment of meeting at which final order is issued by Commission by filing a surety bond with Executive Director of Commission in an amount of $100-$500, as fixed in Commission order. Appeals may be taken from Chancery Court to State Supreme Court as prescribed by law. (49-17-41).

Drinking Water.—Director may cause written complaint to be served upon alleged violator. Hearing is held and presiding official enters findings of fact and conclusions of law. (41-26-17). Petitioner or other interested person may appeal to Chancery Court within ten days of entry of order. Appeals may be taken from Chancery Court to Supreme Court. (41-26-21).

Penalties.—Any person who violates any provision of Solid Waste Disposal Law (17-17-1 et seq.), Mississippi Air and Water Pollution Control Law (49-17-1 et seq.) or rule or written order of Commission may be after hearing before Commission penalized not more than $25,000. Appeal may be taken from imposition of penalty to Chancery Court. To stay execution of penalty, bond must be given equal to double amount of penalty. Provisions of Laws, rules and orders can also be enforced by Commission instituting Chancery Court suit for injunction or other appropriate relief. Each day constitutes separate violation of Act. Person who causes pollution liable for immediate remedial and cleanup expense. (17-17-29, 49-17-43). Persons causing death of fish or other wildlife liable, in addition to above, to State for money reasonably necessary to restock waters or replenish wildlife as determined by Commission after consultation with Dept. (Commission) on Wildlife, Fisheries and Parks. Commission can recover these costs in civil action in circuit court. Unlawful to discharge pollutants in violation of 49-17-29 or violation of condition or limitation of permit or to introduce pollutants into publicly owned treatment works in violation of pretreatment or toxic effluent standards. Punishable by fine of $2,500 to $25,000 per day of violation. (49-17-43). Any person who violates any provision of Surface Coal Mining and Reclamation Law (53-9-1 et seq.) may be assessed penalty by Commission not to exceed $25,000 per violation (53-9-55). Any person who violates any provision of Safe Drinking Water Law (41-26-1, et seq.) may be assessed penalty by director of State Board of Health not to exceed $25,000 per violation (41-26-31).

Permits.—Permit Board (49-17-28) is exclusive administrative body to make decisions on permit issuance, denial, modification or revocation of air pollution control and water pollution control permits and permits required under Solid Waste Disposal Law of 1974. (17-17-1 et seq.). Permit Board shall take action on application within 180 days following its receipt. Permit Board may hold public hearings on its proposed action. Party aggrieved by Permit Board's action may file written request for formal hearing within 30 days. Upon conclusion of formal hearing, Permit Board's decision becomes final unless appealed to chancery court within 20 days. Bond is required to appeal. Permit Board may authorize Executive Director of Department of Environmental Quality to make decisions on permits. See generally 49-17-29.

Permit Board (49-17-28) also makes decisions on permit issuance and denial under Surface Coal Mining and Reclamation Law. (53-9-7[g]). Permits will not be issued for term to exceed five years, unless applicant demonstrates necessity. Permit is terminated unless operations are commenced within three years.

ESTATES AND TRUSTS

ADMINISTRATION:

See topic Executors and Administrators.

ADVANCEMENTS:

See topic Descent and Distribution.

ALLOWANCES:

See topic Executors and Administrators.

CLAIMS:

See topic Executors and Administrators.

DEATH:

Any person who absents himself from this state or conceals himself in the state for seven consecutive years without being heard of, is presumed to be dead. (13-1-23).

Survivorship.—Uniform Simultaneous Death Act adopted. (91-3-1, et seq.).

Actions for Death.—Action for death caused by wrongful or negligent act or omission or by such unsafe machinery or appliances, or impurity of foods, drugs, or other articles intended for human consumption, as would, if death had not ensued, entitle injured party to maintain action, survives to widow or children, or both, or to husband or father or mother, or sister, or brother. Same privilege is afforded adopting parent. Suit may be brought by personal representative for benefit of all concerned, or by any or all of persons entitled to benefit of recovery. But there can be but one suit, which inures to benefit of all concerned. (11-7-13). Statute does not prescribe elements of damages.

Action must be brought within six years after injury or, for latent injury, discovery, if cause of action accrued before July 1, 1989; three years if cause accrued thereafter. (15-1-49). No statutory limitation on amount of recovery. Death does not abate tort action. (91-7-237).

Death Certificate.—See category Documents and Records, topic Records, subhead Vital Statistics.

Uniform Anatomical Gift Act.—Uniform Act has not been adopted, but Anatomical Gift Law adopted, 1970. (41-39-31 et seq.).

Living Wills.—See topic Wills.

DECEDENTS' ESTATES:

See topics Executors and Administrators, Descent and Distribution, and Wills.

DESCENT AND DISTRIBUTION:

Descent of realty and distribution of personality governed by same rules.
See also topic Executors and Administrators.

Surviving spouse takes all if no children or descendants of children, otherwise a child's share. (91-1-7).

Other heirs take in following order: (1) Children and descendants of deceased children, per stirpes; (2) parents, brothers and sisters equally, issue of deceased brothers or sisters taking per stirpes; (3) grandparents and uncles and aunts per stirpes; (4) otherwise next of kin in equal degree, computed by the rules of the civil law. There is no representation among collaterals, except among descendants of brothers and sisters. (91-1-3).

Half Blood.—Kindred of the whole blood are preferred to kindred of the half blood of equal degree. (91-1-5).

Illegitimates inherit from and through mother and her kindred, and mother and her kindred through illegitimate, according to statutes of descent and distribution. Inheritance from and through father, and that by father and his kindred from and through illegitimate, is had where: (a) Natural parents have married before birth of illegitimate, (b) paternity or legitimacy has been adjudicated prior to intestate's death, or (c) paternity has been adjudicated after intestate's death by clear and convincing evidence if brought within earlier of one year after death or 90 days after first publication of notice to creditors. However, father and his kindred shall not inherit from or through illegitimate unless father has openly treated child as his and has not refused or neglected to support it. As between mother and her kindred and father and his kindred, neither shall inherit from other through illegitimate where illegitimate has predeceased intestate unmarried and without issue; however, where illegitimate dies unmarried and without issue and leaves estate including inheritance from mother or father, such portion of illegitimate's estate shall be inherited according to statutes of descent and distribution. (91-1-15).

Adopted Children.—See category Family, topic Adoption.

Determination of Heirship.—Any interested person may seek in the chancery court of the residence of an intestate deceased, or if a nonresident in the county in which he owned real estate, to decree the heirs at law of the deceased. (91-1-27). All heirs and next of kin must be made parties to the petition and summons to unknown heirs shall be published. Court, upon due proof, must in decree designate heirs of decedent and as such place them in possession of his estate. Such decree is evidence in all courts that persons therein named are sole heirs of decedent. (91-1-29). Such decree is binding on parties after two years from date thereof, saving to minors and persons of unsound mind right to reopen said cause within one year after attaining majority or being restored to sanity. Such decree is recordable in land deed records and certified copies may be recorded in any county. Such decree may not be assailed collaterally except for fraud. (91-1-31).

Advancements.—When any of the children of a person dying intestate, or their descendants have received from such intestate in his lifetime any real or personal estate by way of advancement, and choose to go into partition and distribution of the estate with the other parceners and distributors, such advancement must be brought into hotchpot, and such party so bringing into hotchpot is thereupon entitled to his or her proper portion of whole estate, real and personal. (91-1-17).

Election by surviving spouse between rights under intestacy law and testamentary provision, see topic Wills.

Escheat.—Entire estate escheats to state where there are no heirs capable of inheriting. (89-11-1). See topic Executors and Administrators.

Uniform Simultaneous Death Act adopted. (91-3-1 et seq.).

ELECTION:

See topic Wills.

ESTATES:

See category Property, topic Real Property.

EXECUTORS AND ADMINISTRATORS:

Jurisdiction of administration is in Chancery Court in county of decedent's residence; if he had no fixed place of residence in county where part of his real estate situated, or if

See note at head of Digest as to 1998 legislation covered.

See Topical Index in front part of this volume.

EXECUTORS AND ADMINISTRATORS . . . *continued*

he had no real estate in county where he died or if only personal property be disposed of where part of personal property located. (91-7-1).

Preferences in Right to Administer.—The executor named in any last will or testament, whether made in this state or out of it, and admitted to probate here, is entitled to letters testamentary thereon, if not legally disqualified. (91-7-35). Guardian, conservator or other fiduciary of person under legal disability may upon death of person intestate be granted letters of administration unless relative or other proper person applies within 30 days. (91-7-68).

The court appointing administrators prefers first the surviving husband or widow, and then such others as may be entitled to distribution, selecting among those in equal right the person or persons best calculated to manage the estate, or the court may, in its discretion, appoint a stranger or a trust company organized under the laws of this state if the kindred are incompetent. If some such person does not apply within 30 days from the death of an intestate, the court may grant administration to a creditor, or any other suitable person. (91-7-63).

Eligibility and Competency.—Any person, male or female, over age of 18 years, of sound mind, who has not been convicted of a felony, may qualify as executor, executrix, administrator or administratrix. (91-7-35; 91-7-37; 91-7-65). Married woman may act, as may also foreign corporation.

There is no statutory provision that a nonresident may not be appointed administrator of an intestate's estate, but the court usually appoints a resident by preference. See infra, subhead Foreign Executors or Administrators.

Qualification.—See supra, subhead Eligibility and Competency, and infra, subhead Exemption from Bond.

Exemption from Bond.—Administrator must give bond in penalty equal to value of personal estate, with condition for faithful application, unless chancellor waives or reduces bond when administrator is sole heir or when all heirs are competent and petition to waive or reduce bond. (91-7-67). Executor must give bond equal to full value of estate unless this is dispensed with by will. (91-7-41, 91-7-45). Surety company bond may be given and premium charged to estate. No state or national bank domiciled in this state shall be required to give bond. (81-5-35).

Issuance of Letters.—None.

Removal.—Executor or administrator may be removed on petition of any interested person for misconduct or disqualification. (91-7-85).

Special Kinds of Administration.—Temporary administrator may be appointed when appeal taken from grant of letters testamentary or of administration, when will contested or probate interrupted or unreasonably delayed or whenever necessary for care and preservation of estate. Powers may be special or general. (91-7-53).

Public Administrators.—County Administrator may be appointed when no person has applied for letters testamentary or of administration, after expiration of 60 days from death of such person, letters of administration shall be committed to county administrator who shall administer estate. County administrator may also be appointed temporary administrator in instances where temporary administrator may be appointed. (91-7-79).

Inventory and Appraisal.—Inventory must be filed by executor or administrator within 90 days after the grant of his letters. (91-7-93).

Goods, chattels and personal estate shall be appraised by three persons unless dispensed with by clerk for good cause shown. (91-7-109 et seq.).

General Powers and Duties.—Lands may be leased to pay debts. (91-7-225). Court may decree power to encumbered land. (91-7-215).

Notice to Creditors.—Executor or administrator must make a reasonable attempt to locate persons with claims against estate and mail them notice of 90 day period in which to have claims probated. Thereafter executor or administrator must publish notice to creditors once a week for three consecutive weeks in newspaper published in county. (91-7-145).

Presentation Claims.—Claims must be duly verified and filed with clerk of Chancery Court in which letters were granted within 90 days from date of first publication of notice or, where estate has been declared insolvent, at time fixed in published notice for examination of claims. Claims not filed within time allowed therefor are barred. (91-7-151).

Proof of Claims.—If claim is on judgment or decree, certified copy thereof must be filed; if it is evidenced by writing, such writing must be filed; if there is no written evidence, itemized account of claim signed by creditor must be filed. If claim is on promissory note or instrument executed by decedent, same may be withdrawn provided clerk of court first makes certified copy thereof to be retained in file, but personal representative of estate or any party in interest may, upon good cause being shown, inspect original. (91-7-149).

Form.—

Form for presenting an account is as follows:

Form

State of . . . . }
. . . . County. } ss

Personally appeared before me, ..., the undersigned authority in and for the jurisdiction aforesaid, ..., who being by me first duly sworn, say that the annexed . . . . . . for . . . . . . Dollars against the estate of . . . . . ., deceased, as stated, is just and correct, and owing from the deceased; that it is not usurious, and that neither . . . . . . the affiant nor any other person has received payment in whole or in part thereof, except such as is credited thereon, if any, and that security has not been received therefor except as stated, if any.

Probated and allowed for $ and registered this . . . . . . day of . . . . . . A.D. 19. . . .(91-7-149).

. . . .
(Official character)

Approval or Rejection of Claims.—Disputed claim may be referred to auditors, who return their findings, with evidence, to court, which may then allow or disallow claim. (91-7-165).

Priorities.—Expenses of decedent's last illness and funeral and administration expenses, including commissions, are first paid and other claims share ratably if assets are insufficient for full payment. (91-7-261).

Sales.—

Personal Property.—Court, or chancellor in vacation, may authorize private sale of personal property. (91-7-177). Executor or administrator, without court order, may sell for cash, either at public or private sale, perishable goods or chattels of decedent whether necessary for payment of debts or not. Executor or administrator may sell any personal property necessary for payment of debts, as long as appraised value is realized. (91-7-179). Executor or administrator, upon proper notice, may petition court for order of sale of personal property, if necessary for payment of debts or if no debts and in best interest of all parties; if court is satisfied that sale is necessary or proper, it may order sale of entire or part of personal estate. Public sale of property must be advertised in at least three public places within county, ten days prior to sale to highest bidder for either cash or credit, as court may direct. (91-7-183).

Confirmation.—Executor or administrator must report any sale of personal property at next term of court for confirmation, specifying time, place and amount of sale, name of purchaser and satisfy court that directions of order, if any, were followed. (91-7-185).

Creditors have right to petition court for sale of real and personal property of decedent for payment of debts. (91-7-195).

Real Property.—Upon petition of executor, administrator, legatees or distributees, court may authorize sale of real property in preference to personal property, where necessary and in best interest of legatees or distributees (91-7-187); or if personal property insufficient to pay debts, court may authorize sale of all or part of real property sufficient to pay debts upon petition of executor or administrator (91-7-191). Sale or lease requirements of real property set out in 91-7-197—91-7-207.

Actions by Representative.—No current tort for "Actions by Representative". Representative may commence and prosecute any personal action which deceased might have commenced and prosecuted. (91-7-233).

Actions Against Representative.—Presentation of claim is condition precedent to action thereon, except to enforce security. Right to sue on claim is suspended during 90 days allowed for filing and proof of claims and action must be brought within four years after expiration of said 90 days. (91-7-239; 15-1-25). Action pending against decedent at time of his death may be continued against executor or administrator if cause of action survives. (91-7-237).

Allowances.—Appraisers of the estate of a decedent may set apart to the widow and children, or to the widow if there are no children, or to the children if there is no widow, such personal property as is exempt. (91-7-117).

It is the duty of the appraisers to set apart out of the effects of the decedent for spouse and children, who are being supported by decedent, one year's provisions including such provisions as may be embraced in exempt property set apart, and if there are no provisions, appraisers may allow money for comfortable support of spouse and children for one year, and in addition sufficient sum of money to purchase necessary wearing apparel for spouse and such children and to pay tuition for children for one year. (91-7-135).

Widow's Quarantine.—None.

Intermediate Accountings.—Executor or administrator is required to file annual accounts. (91-7-277).

Final Accounting and Settlement.—Final account to be filed when estate has been fully administered. (91-7-291). Final account remains on file subject to inspection of any person interested; summons issues, or publication is made, to all parties interested as in other suits in Chancery Court to appear at term of court or before chancellor in vacation not less than 30 days after service of summons or completion of publication to show cause why final account of executor or administrator should not be allowed and approved. (91-7-295).

Consent Settlement.—Claims belonging to estate which are not readily collected, can be sold or compromised on proper petition and decree of authorization. Executor or administrator must report in writing all sales and compromises to next term of court. (91-7-229).

Distribution.—Personal property and land are to be distributed according to law regarding descent and distribution. (91-1-1, et seq.).

Distribution if Abroad.—No statutory provision.

Liabilities.—(27-9-37). If payment of debts occurs prior to satisfaction of state tax executor/administrator is personally liable for same.

Compensation of Representatives.—Court fixes in its discretion for executor or administrator. (91-7-299).

When Administration Unnecessary.—See subhead Small Estates, infra.

Small Estates.—No special procedures authorized except that in estates valued at less than $500, publication of notice to creditors dispensed with, but posting notice for 30 days required (91-7-147); when value of entire decedent's estate does not exceed $20,000, debtor of decedent may repay debt to decedent's successor, upon affidavit of successor as to certain facts (91-7-322). See topic Wills, subhead Probate.

Foreign Executors or Administrators.—Executors and administrators, qualified in other states or countries, may sue in the courts of this state, or may receive without suit, any property of or debts due to their testators or intestates, after filing in the office of the clerk of the chancery court of the county where there may be some person indebted to the decedent, or having some of his effects in possession, a certified copy of the record of the appointment and qualification of the executor or administrator according to the law of the state or country where he qualified, and a certificate of the officer before whom he is liable to account as such that he is there liable to account for the things sued for or received. (91-7-259). See topic Wills.

See note at head of Digest as to 1998 legislation covered.

See Topical Index in front part of this volume.

EXECUTORS AND ADMINISTRATORS . . . *continued*

Any foreign banking corporation, or banking association, or foreign trust corporation, authorized to act as executor or administrator of estates of decedents in the state where it has its principal office, may apply and so act in this state, if similar corporations domiciled in this state are so permitted to act in such other state. Appointment in writing of Secretary of State as agent for process is condition precedent. (81-5-43). See topic Trusts; category Family, topic Guardian and Ward.

Uniform Fiduciaries Act not adopted.

Revised Uniform Principal and Income Act adopted. (91-17-3 et seq.).

Uniform Simplification of Fiduciary Security Transfers Act adopted. (91-11-1, et seq.). Saved from repeal by Uniform Commercial Code (75-10-104[2]).

Uniform Anatomical Gift Act not adopted, but Anatomical Gift Law adopted. (41-39-31 et seq.). See topic Wills.

FIDUCIARIES:

See topics Executors and Administrators, and Trusts; also category Family, topic Guardian and Ward.

INTESTACY:

See topic Descent and Distribution.

LIVING WILLS:

See topic Wills.

PROOF OF CLAIMS:

See topic Executors and Administrators; also category Civil Actions and Procedure, topic Pleading.

TRUSTS:

Uniform Trustees' Powers Act adopted as "Uniform Trustees' Powers Law". (91-9-101).

Kinds.—Express, constructive and resulting trusts are recognized. (91-9-1; 205 Miss. 328, 38 So.2d 756).

Creation.—All trusts in land, unless constructive or implied, and all assignments or transfers thereof, must be created by instrument in writing, signed by creator and acknowledged and filed for record in the office of the clerk of the chancery court of the county where the land lies. (91-9-1, 91-9-3).

Appointment of Trustee.—No statutory provision.

Eligibility and Competency.—Any foreign trust corporation or association authorized to act as trustee under wills and voluntary trust agreements in the state where it has its principal office, may apply and so act in this state, if similar corporations domiciled in this state are so permitted to act in such other state. Appointment in writing of Secretary of State as agent for process is condition precedent. This law, however, has no application to trust agreements executed for the purpose of securing loans or guaranties thereof. (81-5-43). See also topic Executors and Administrators; category Family, topic Guardian and Ward.

Qualification.—No statutory provisions.

Removal of Trustee.—Majority of local beneficiaries of educational, charitable, or religious trust may file complaint in chancery court in county where any part of corpus of said trust is situated requesting discharge of trustee or trustees (91-9-303). Power of court in removal proceedings. (91-9-305).

General Powers and Duties of Trustees.—Trustee has power to perform, without court authorization, every act which prudent man would perform for purposes of trust, including but not limited to, specified powers. (91-9-105, 91-9-107). Powers generally. (91-9-9; 91-9-101 to 91-9-119).

Provisions protecting trust in certain instances from money judgment and creditors and reaffirming spend thrift trust doctrine found in 91-9-501 et seq.

Sales.—Assignments. (91-9-3). Assignment by fiduciary of securities. (91-11-7). Powers of trustees generally. (91-9-107).

Investments.—Fiduciary investments. (91-13-1 through 91-13-11). Powers of Trustee. (91-9-107). See category Family, topic Guardian and Ward.

Securities in Name of Nominee.—Power of trustee to hold security in name of nominee. (91-9-107[p]). Registration in name of fiduciary. (91-11-5).

Bequests and Devises to Inter Vivos Trusts.—See topic Wills.

Accounting.—Trustee resigning position governed by 91-9-206. Trustee required by law or by instrument creating trust to file accounting. (91-9-5).

Compensation.—Trustee conferred power to pay compensation of trustee. (91-9-107[t]).

Discharge of trustee governed by 91-9-205.

Uniform Common Trust Fund Act adopted. (81-5-37).

Revised Uniform Principal and Income Act.—adopted. (91-17-1 to 91-17-31).

Gifts to Minors.—Repealed, effective Jan. 1, 1995. (91-19-1 to 91-19-19).

Uniform Fiduciaries Act not adopted.

Uniform Simplification of Fiduciary Security Transfers Act adopted and saved from repeal by Uniform Commercial Code. (75-10-104[2]).

Accumulations.—No limitations provided. See category Property, topic Perpetuities.

Perpetuities.—See category Property, topic Perpetuities.

Pour Over Trusts.—See topic Wills, subhead Bequests and Devises to Inter Vivos Trusts.

Mississippi.—No statutory provisions.

WILLS:

Uniform Probate Code has not been adopted in Mississippi.

Every person 18 years of age, being of sound and disposing mind, may execute will. (91-5-1).

Testamentary Disposition.—Person with testamentary capacity may devise all estate he has in real and personal property of any description whatsoever. Mortmain statute limiting bequests to charitable, religious, educational institutions has been repealed.

Execution.—Every person 18 years of age or older may execute a will. Every will (except holographic or nuncupative) must be signed by testator or by some person in his presence and at his direction and attested by two or more credible witnesses in his presence. (91-5-1).

Attestation Clause.—If will not wholly written by testator, it shall be attested by two or more credible witnesses in presence of testator.

Holographic wills are recognized. No witnesses are required. (See 91-5-1.)

Nuncupative wills can be established only if made during last illness of testator at his or her residence of where he or she resided for ten days next preceding death, except where testator was taken sick away from home and died before returning. If value of estate exceeds $100, will must be proved by two witnesses that he called on some person present to take notice or bear testimony that such was his or her will. (91-5-15). Such will can be probated only after expiration of 14 days from date of death and only on summons issuing for widow, if any, and next of kin if resident in this state (91-5-17) and must be probated within six months from time of speaking of testamentary words unless words, or substance thereof, were reduced to writing within six days after spoken (91-5-19).

Revocation of a will can be effected only by testator destroying, canceling or obliterating the same or causing this to be done in his presence, or by a subsequent will, codicil or declaration in writing made and executed. (91-5-3).

Testamentary Gifts to Subscribing Witnesses.—Devise or bequest to subscribing witness is void if will cannot be proved without his testimony. But if such witness would have been entitled to share in estate if decedent had died interstate he may take such share up to, but not in excess of, amount of devise or bequest. (91-5-9).

Bequests and Devises to Inter Vivos Trusts.—Pour over trusts recognized. (91-5-11). Uniform Testamentary Additions to Trusts Act adopted. (91-5-11).

Testamentary Guardian.—See category Family, topic Guardian and Ward.

Probate.—Jurisdiction is in chancery court. (91-7-1). As to probate venue, see topic Executors and Administrators. Execution of will proved by one subscribing witness, if alive and competent or by proof of testator's handwriting if witnesses not available. (91-7-7). If no contest, affidavit of witness sufficient to prove will. (91-7-9). For holographic will or codicil affidavits of two disinterested persons necessary. (91-7-10).

Will executed by any member of U. S. Armed Forces during the Korean or any other war may be admitted to probate by chancery court of county in which testator lived when he became a member of such Armed Forces, on the affidavit of any reliable person sufficient to satisfy the chancellor that the testator is dead, that the writing propounded for probate was signed by testator as his last will, that affidavits of the subscribing witnesses cannot reasonably be obtained and that there is good reason for such will to be then probated. (91-7-15).

A photostatic copy of the original will is authorized to be used by an attesting witness who is a nonresident for certification purposes. (91-7-11).

Will may be probated as muniment of title only, by sworn petition of all beneficiaries and surviving spouse, without necessity of administration, if will devises real estate in state and if value of decedent's personal estate is not more than $10,000 (exclusive of real property) and all known personal and estate taxes are paid. (91-5-35).

Self-proved Wills.—No provisions.

Living Wills.—Persons 18 or older may authorize, in advance, withdrawal of life-sustaining mechanisms. (41-41-201 to 41-41-205).

Contest.—A will probated without notice may be contested by any person interested at any time within two years after probate, saving to infants or persons of unsound mind the period of two years to contest the will after the removal of their disabilities. (91-7-23).

Unclaimed Legacies.—See topic Descent and Distribution, subhead Escheat.

Lapse.—Where a legacy or devise is given to a child or other descendant of the testator, who dies before the testator leaving issue who survive the testator, such legacy or devise does not lapse, but the issue of the deceased legatee or devisee take as though the latter has survived the testator and died intestate and unmarried. (91-5-7).

Children living when a will is executed may be disinherited by mere failure to mention them therein. While provisions with respect to children born after execution of a will vary somewhat according to whether or not testator had children living when the will was executed, it may be stated generally that afterborn children, including posthumous children, not provided for by settlement and neither provided for nor disinherited by the will, but merely pretermitted, take the share of the estate which they would have taken in case of intestacy. (See 91-5-3, 91-5-5.)

Election.—Surviving spouse cannot be disinherited. If will does not make satisfactory provision for surviving spouse, latter may, at any time within 90 days after probate of will, file a renunciation and thereupon is entitled to share which he or she would have taken if decedent had died intestate, not to exceed one-half of estate. (91-5-25). If will makes no provision for surviving spouse, latter takes as though decedent had died intestate, not to exceed one-half of estate, and renunciation of will is not necessary. (91-5-27).

However, if surviving spouse have separate property equal in value to what would be his or her lawful portion of the deceased spouse's estate, the surviving spouse cannot renounce the will and take his or her portion of the estate. If the separate estate is not of equal value, the surviving spouse can have the deficiency made up to him or her, notwithstanding the will. If the separate property of the surviving spouse does not amount in value to one-fifth the amount to which he or she would be entitled, the

WILLS . . . *continued*

surviving spouse can renounce the provisions of a will and elect to take his or her entire lawful proportion. (91-5-29).

Contribution.—See subhead Election, supra.

Foreign Executed Wills.—Ancillary probate proceedings are not necessary, but such may be contested as original might have been if it had been executed in this state. Will executed outside of state but not probated elsewhere can be probated originally in this state in county where there is property affected thereby. (91-7-33).

Foreign Probated Wills.—See subhead Foreign Executed Wills, supra.

Simultaneous Death.—See topic Death, subhead Survivorship.

Testamentary Trusts.—See topic Trusts.

Uniform Anatomical Gift Act. —Not adopted. See "The Anatomical Gift Law" at 41-39-31, et seq.

FAMILY

ADOPTION:

Adoptions are controlled by 93-17-1 et seq. Any person may be adopted.

Any husband and wife jointly or any unmarried adult may adopt provided petitioner(s) have resided in Mississippi for 90 days preceding filing of petition. 90-day restriction does not apply where child is related to one of petitioners within third degree according to civil law. (93-17-3).

Consent Required.—Consent is required; otherwise personal process or by publication required. Child's consent, or personal service of process upon child, necessary where child is over 14 years of age. (93-17-5). No infant can be adopted when either parent, after having been summoned, appears and objects before decree is entered, unless court finds that objecting parent has abandoned or deserted infant or is mentally, morally, or otherwise unfit. Parents are not summoned and have no right to object to adoption if parental rights have been terminated under statutory procedure. (93-17-7). Statute prescribes grounds and procedure for terminating parental rights. (93-15-101 et seq.).

Conditions Precedent.—90 day residency requirement unless petitioner is related to child within third degree. (93-17-3). Final decree must not be entered before expiration of six months after entry of interlocutory decree, except where child is stepchild of petitioner or related by blood within third degree according to civil law, or in any case where chancellor determines six month waiting period not necessary. Also, when child has resided in home of petitioner before entry of interlocutory decree, court may shorten waiting period for such period of time. (93-17-13).

Jurisdiction.—The chancery court, or the chancellor in vacation, has jurisdiction of adoption proceedings. (93-17-1). Chancery, Family or county court sitting as youth court has jurisdiction of termination of parental rights proceedings. (93-15-105).

Venue.—Proceedings must be brought in the chancery court of the county in which the adopting petitioner or petitioners reside or in which child to be adopted resides or was born, or was found when it was abandoned or deserted, or where child shall have been surrendered by person authorized to do so. (93-17-3).

Petition.—Must be sworn to and must be accompanied by a doctor's certificate showing physical and mental condition of child to be adopted, and a sworn statement of all property, if any, owned by child. Chancellor may allow adoption of child with mental or physical defect if adopting parent or parents file affidavit acknowledging defect and stating that they desire to adopt child notwithstanding defect. (93-17-3). Child must join in petition by its next friend. (93-17-5). No reference is required as to marital status of child's natural parents; and no recital is to be made that child was born out of wedlock in any petition filed or decree entered upon consent.

Proceedings.—After filing petition and completion of process, and before entry of final decree, court may require investigation and report concerning whether child is proper subject for adoption, or whether petitioners are suitable parents, or other material facts. (93-17-11-12). All proceedings are confidential and must be held in closed court, except upon court order. (93-17-25). All pleadings and records are confidential and docket entries must not refer to names of natural parents or to child's original name, but clerk must keep separate confidential index showing such information and name of adopting parents and new name of child. (93-17-29, -31).

Decree.—The court may enter an interlocutory decree and can require further investigation and reports after its entry. (93-17-11-12). Reference to child in decree must be by child's new name, if name is to be changed; and decrees spread upon court's minutes must not disclose names of natural parents nor child's original name. (93-17-29). Statute requires certified copy of final decree to be furnished to Bureau of Vital Statistics, whereupon revised birth certificate must be issued. Statute further provides for Bureau to maintain centralized adoption records which include: medical and social history of birth parents and other family members; report of birth parent(s) medical examination(s) if within one year of petition and if available; report describing prenatal care and medical condition of child at birth, if available; and medical and social history of adoptee. (93-17-205). Original birth certificate can be obtained thereafter only upon court order or permission of birth parent or pursuant to Mississippi Adoption Confidentiality Act. (93-17-201-223).

Name.—Chancery court or Chancellor in vacation shall have jurisdiction to alter name of such person, to make legitimate any living offspring, and to decree said offspring to be heir of petitioner. (93-17-1).

Effect of Adoption.—The person adopted inherits from and through the adopting parents and from other children of adopting parents in accordance with the statutes of descent and distribution. The adopting parents and their other children inherit from person adopted. Except for inheritance by or from adopted person, adopting parents and adoptive kindred and adopted person are vested with all rights as if person had been born to adopting parents in lawful wedlock, including all rights under wrongful death

statute. (93-17-13). See category Estates and Trusts, topic Death, subhead Actions for Death.

The natural parents and natural kindred of person adopted cannot inherit by or through him or her, except as to a natural parent who is spouse of adopting parent. (93-17-13).

Setting Aside of Adoption.—No adoption proceedings can be set aside except for jurisdictional defects and for failure to bring proceedings in conformity with proper statutes, and no action can be brought to set aside any final decree of adoption except within six months after the entry of same. (93-17-17, -15).

DISSOLUTION OF MARRIAGE:

See topic Divorce.

DIVORCE:

This subject is governed by 93-5-1 et seq.

Grounds for Absolute Divorce.—Natural impotency; adultery (unless there was collusion or condonation); sentence to penitentiary (unless pardoned before being sent there); desertion for one year; habitual drunkenness; habitual excessive use of drugs; habitual cruel and inhuman treatment; insanity or idiocy at time of marriage (unknown to complaining party); prior marriage undissolved; pregnancy by person other than husband at time of marriage (unknown to husband); consanguinity within prohibited degrees; incurable insanity, if insane party has been under regular treatment and confined in an institution for preceding three years. (Examination by two qualified physicians and affidavits by them that patient is mentally disturbed is condition precedent.) (93-5-1).

Irreconcilable differences is alternative ground for divorce, but only on joint complaint or uncontested petition after process. Parties must make adequate provision for custody and maintenance of children and for settlement of property rights or if unable to agree must consent in writing to allow court to decide issues. Complaints for divorce on this ground must be filed 60 days before hearing. (93-5-2).

Grounds for Legal Separation.—There is no statutory provision for legal separation from bed and board. However, chancery court has inherent power to award separate maintenance and normal prerequisites are separation without substantial fault on wife's part and willful abandonment by husband with refusal to support. (616 So.2d 294, 527 So.2d 617, 210 Miss. 729, 50 So.2d 603).

Residence Requirements.—Divorce jurisdiction may be exercised only if one of parties has been actual bona fide resident of state for six months before commencement of suit. Court may not take jurisdiction if residence was acquired for purpose of securing divorce. (93-5-5).

Jurisdiction.—Chancery Court. (Miss. Const. Art 6, 159).

Venue.—If defendant is a resident, county in which defendant resides or may be found or county of residence of parties at time of separation if plaintiff still resident of such county; if defendant is nonresident or absent so that he cannot be served, county of plaintiff's residence. Complaint solely on ground of irreconcilable differences in county of residence of either party; where one party nonresident in county of resident party. (93-5-11).

Process.—No special rules. See Miss. R. Civ. P. 4. No divorce judgments by default. (93-5-7).

Pleading.—Numerous special pleading provisions set out in 93-5-7, including that in divorces other than on irreconcilable differences, plaintiff must verify that complaint is not filed by collusion and that cause(s) for divorce as stated are true. See also 93-5-11 re filing of complaints.

Judgment or Decree.—Final decree is entered immediately on determination of issues. Marital rights cease on decree of divorce from bonds of matrimony. (93-5-25, 93-5-27). Property jointly owned is not affected,—tenancy by entirety becomes joint tenancy. (336 So.2d 497).

Temporary Alimony.—May be allowed to either wife or husband. (93-5-27)

Allowance for Prosecution of Suit.—Suit money may be allowed to either wife or husband. (93-5-23).

Permanent Alimony.—May be allowed to either wife or husband and may be modified or terminated based on material change of circumstances. (93-5-23).

Division of Property of Spouses.—Not community property state. No equitable distribution statute—case law permits distribution of marital assets. (Ferguson v. Ferguson, 639 So.2d 921, [Miss. 1991]; Hemsley v. Hemsley, 639 So.2d 909, [Miss. 1994]).

Change of Wife's Name.—May petition for under 93-17-1.

Custody of Children.—Governed by 93-5-24. Court may make temporary or permanent orders as to custody and may modify such orders based on changed circumstances.

Allowance for Support of Children.—Chancery Court has discretion in making orders touching care, custody and maintenance of children, but where both parents have estate or income, court making orders for support of children must require that each parent contribute to support in proportion to ability. (93-5-23). Uniform Reciprocal Enforcement of Support Act adopted. (93-11-3 et seq.). Civil enforcement is by Chancery Court. Uniform Child Custody Jurisdiction Act adopted. (93-23-1 et seq.). Court Clerk may serve order for withholding upon obligor's employer or payor upon proper proof that notice of delinquency was properly served on obligor and obligor has not filed petition to stay service. (93-11-109).

Remarriage.—No statutory prohibition against remarriage, but in cases of adultery court may prohibit remarriage of guilty party and may remove such disability after one year on petition and satisfactory evidence of reformation. (93-5-25).

Foreign Divorces.—Mississippi courts will determine for themselves jurisdiction of foreign court and consequent validity of divorce, notwithstanding recitals in decree of jurisdictional fact of residence or domicile. (173 Miss. 44, 159 So. 112; 174 Miss. 643, 165 So. 414).

See note at head of Digest as to 1998 legislation covered.

See Topical Index in front part of this volume.

DIVORCE . . . *continued*

Separation agreements are recognized and may be incorporated into divorce decrees subject to court approval. (478 So.2d 258).

Antenuptial Contracts.—See topic Husband and Wife.

GUARDIAN AND WARD:

Creation of guardianship is within jurisdiction of Chancery Court. (9-5-81). Venue is proper in county of residence of minor ward (3-13-13), incompetent adult (93-13-121) or missing armed services person (93-13-161) or in county where property of out of state ward is located (93-13-181).

Selection of Guardian.—Any parent may, by instrument wholly written and signed by him or her, or attested by two or more credible witnesses not including person appointed guardian, if not so made, appoint some suitable person as guardian of motherless or fatherless child to take effect at parent's death. Bond, inventory and accounting can be waived with court approval. (93-13-7).

Eligibility and Competency.—Minor cannot be appointed guardian of another minor. (185 Miss. 242, 187 So.229 [1939]). Nonresidents, if competent, are eligible to serve as guardians. (93-13-181).

Appointment of Guardian.—Ward is any person under legal disability such as minority, idiocy, lunacy, unsound mind, alcoholism, addiction to drugs or felony conviction. (1-3-58). Chancery court of county of residence of ward who has estate, real or personal, may appoint guardian for him, giving preference in all cases to natural guardian or next of kin, unless applicant is manifestly unsuitable for discharge of duties, but court may allow minor who is over age of 14 years and under no legal disability except minority to select his guardian. Nonresident ward owning property in this state may have guardian appointed by court of county in which such property is located. If over 14, minor ward may make selection before clerk of court of record of county of his residence. (93-13-13).

Qualification.—Every guardian, unless bond is dispensed with, by will or writing, must enter into bond payable to state in such penalty and with such sureties as court may require. No bond necessary for part of estate deposited in any one or more fully insured banks, building and loan associations or savings and loan associations. (93-13-17). No state or national bank domiciled in this state shall be required to give bond. (81-5-35).

Inventory.—The guardian, within three months after appointment, must return to the court under oath a true and perfect inventory of the estate, both real and personal, and he must annually return an inventory under oath of increase of estate, if any. (93-13-33).

Powers and Duties.—Guardian is not entitled to custody of ward as against parent who is suitable therefor. (93-13-5). Chancery court, or chancellor in vacation, may fix sum to be expended for maintenance and education. (93-13-35). Guardian may be empowered to sell or compromise claims due their ward, on same proceedings and under same circumstances prescribed by 91-7-229 for sale or compromise by executor or administrator of claims belonging to estate of deceased person. (93-13-59). Sums of $10,000 or less owed to ward may be paid directly to ward or other person, upon approval of chancery court, without necessity of guardianship under certain conditions. (93-13-211).

Investments.—Investment by guardians is regulated by statute. (91-13-1—91-13-11). Guardian may contract for life insurance for benefit of ward on life of any person owning an estate in which minor will participate. (83-7-19). See also category Business Regulation and Commerce, topic Banks and Banking, subhead Uniform Common Trust Fund Act; also category Estates and Trusts, topic Trusts.

All laws regarding disposition of property by executors and administrators applicable to guardians. (93-13-38). With approval of court, guardian may establish estate plan for ward's estate. (93-13-38).

Securities in Name of Nominee.—See category Estates and Trusts, topic Trusts, subhead Securities in Name of Nominee.

Real Estate.—Sale of land of ward may be had on petition of guardian, summons issued for parents or parent or two adult kin within third degree of ward (or they may join in petition), and decree of chancery court, which designates chancery clerk or guardian to make conveyance and sign deed. (93-13-51). With approval of court, guardian may execute encumbrance upon real estate of ward. (93-13-47). Undivided interest in real property of ward worth less than $10,000 may be sold without necessity of guardianship upon petition and approval of chancery court. (93-13-217).

Liabilities of Guardian.—All actions against guardian and sureties on his bond, or either of them, by ward, shall be commenced within five years next after ward shall arrive at age of 21 years, and not after. (15-1-27).

Accounts.—Guardians must exhibit accounts at least once a year, and more often if required except chancellor, for good cause shown, in his discretion, when satisfied it is to best interest and welfare of ward, may dispense with annual accounts, except final account, if ward's estate does not exceed $3,000 and no future funds will be received except interest or welfare benefits or if ward's total assets are deposited in fully insured savings account to remain until further court order. (93-13-67).

Termination of Guardianship.—Guardianship ceases when ward reaches age of 21, or in court's discretion, when ward reaches age of 18 or when estate does not exceed $2,000 and guardian must then turn over to ward all of ward's property in his hands. (93-13-75).

Insane Persons.—Persons under disabilities of idiocy, lunacy, or unsound minds are defined as wards under 93-13-5, et seq. (1-3-58). Chancery court can appoint guardian for person adjudged of unsound mind on application of relative, friend, or any interested party, or upon court's own motion. (93-13-123, 93-13-125).

Where person has not been adjudged of unsound mind, guardian may be appointed if person (1) has been confined in public mental hospital in Mississippi for more than one year and still so confined; (2) is of unsound mind; (3) is mentally incapable of handling estate; (4) is incapable of responding to process. Relative or friend may swear to petition. (93-13-125).

Upon death of incompetent, estate is settled in same manner as other decedent estates.

Foreign Guardians.—When any ward resides out of this state, but has property here, and a guardian has been appointed in the state of his residence, such guardian is entitled to be appointed guardian by court of county in this state in which property is situated. (93-13-181). Any foreign banking or trust corporation or association authorized to act as guardian of minors or incompetent persons in the state where it has its principal office, may apply and so act in this state if similar corporations domiciled in this state are so permitted to act in such other state. Appointment in writing of Secretary of State as agent for process is condition precedent. (81-5-43). See category Estates and Trusts, topics Executors and Administrators, Trusts.

If such nonresident guardian desires to remove the personal property of his ward out of the state, he must present his petition for that purpose to the court of this state by which he was appointed and on making a settlement of his guardianship accounts, the court may make an order to that effect, but the guardian must first give bond with two sureties residing in this state for the full value of the ward's personal estate. (93-13-185).

A foreign guardian is entitled to sue for, receive and give a valid acquittance for property of ward on same terms on which executors and administrators, who have qualified in other states or countries, are authorized to sue and receive without suit, property or debts due to their testators or intestates. (93-13-183).

Gifts to Minors.—Court shall decree that property of ward be delivered to guardian. (93-13-31). See topic Infants.

Uniform Fiduciaries Act not adopted.

Uniform Simplification of Fiduciary Security Transfers Act adopted and saved from repeal by Uniform Commercial Code. (91-11-3 et seq.).

HUSBAND AND WIFE:

Marriage confers rights and imposes duties as at common law.

Disabilities of married women have been totally abrogated. (93-3-1).

Separate Property.—All property of a married woman, except the homestead, is her separate property. Husband's property, except homestead, free from any claim of wife. (93-3-1).

Contracts.—Husband and wife may contract with each other except so as to permit one to receive pay from the other for services. (93-3-7).

All transfers of realty or personal property and all leases of land between them must be signed, acknowledged and recorded to be valid as against third persons. (93-3-9).

Antenuptial Contracts.—If made "upon consideration of marriage", governed by Statute of Frauds and therefore required to be in writing and signed. (15-3-1).

Actions.—Husband and wife may sue each other. (93-3-3). Doctrine of interspousal immunity fully abrogated. (518 So.2d 1205).

Husband who appropriates for own use property of wife or income and profit of her property is debtor to wife and can be sued for same, but not after expiration of one year from receipt of such income or profit. If husband is permitted by wife to use income from her estate, or her estate, in support and maintenance of family, he is not chargeable therewith, nor liable to account therefor. (93-3-13).

Agency.—One spouse can act as agent or attorney-in-fact for the other.

A husband who rents the wife's plantation and farming implements and stock, or who carries on business in his own name or on his own account with wife's means will be determined to be acting as her agent in such business unless contract between husband and wife which changes this relationship be evidenced by writing, subscribed by both spouses, duly acknowledged and filed for recordation with chancery clerk of county where such business is done. (93-3-7).

Conveyance or Encumbrance of Property.—There is no necessity for joinder of one spouse in deed, mortgage, etc., of other except where homestead is involved. See category Debtor and Creditor, topic Homesteads.

Desertion and Nonsupport.—Spouses have right to maintenance and support and suits therefor are maintainable in chancery court of county in which defendant lives. (See 152 Miss. 201, 119 So. 299.)

Uniform Reciprocal Enforcement of Support Act (1952 version) is in effect. (93-11-3 et seq.). Civil enforcement by chancery court.

Community property system does not exist in Mississippi.

INFANTS:

All persons become of age at 21 years. Drinking age is 21. (67-3-53).

Emancipation.—No statutory provisions.

Disabilities of minority may be removed, either partially or generally, under statutory procedure in chancery court of county where minor resides. (93-19-1). Married minors are treated as adults in suits for divorce, separate maintenance and support, child custody, and other related claims. (93-19-11, 93-5-9). Minors, 18, 19 and 20 years old, can contract in matters related to personal property and can settle personal injury claims without guardianship appointment. (93-19-13; 394 So.2d 321). Disabilities of minority of married minors 18 years or over are removed for purpose of signing or executing instruments pertaining solely to homestead. (93-3-11). Minors 17 years or older can donate blood without parent's consent. (41-41-15). Physicians can provide family planning information and supplies to married minor, minor who is parent, minor with consent of parent or guardian, or minor referred by doctor, clergyman, family planning clinic, school or state agency. (41-42-7). Persons 18 years or older may enter into contracts for personal property and by contract or will donate body to medical science. (41-39-9, 41-39-35). Minor of 12 years or older may choose custodial parent if both parents are determined fit and proper for custody. (93-11-65).

Ratification of Contract.—To charge any person upon any promise made after full age to pay any debt contracted during infancy, or upon any ratification after full age of any promise or contract made during infancy, promise or ratification must be signed and in writing. (15-3-11).

See note at head of Digest as to 1998 legislation covered.

See Topical Index in front part of this volume.

MS – 27

INFANTS . . . *continued*

Actions.—The court appoints a guardian ad litem to represent the infant in all court proceedings where the minor is not represented by a legal guardian, except that a married minor may file or defend in his own name a suit involving marital rights. (9-5-89). Court may order blood test in paternity action. (93-9-21).

Support of Minor.—It is felony for any parent to desert, willfully neglect or refuse to provide for maintenance and support of his child or children while child is under age of 16 years. (97-5-3). See also subhead Allowance for Support of Children under topic Divorce.

Parental Responsibility.—Public school district entitled to recover up to $20,000 from parents of minor child (between ages of 6-18) who maliciously and wilfully damages or destroys school property. (37-11-53). Property owner entitled to recover up to $2,000 from parents of minor over age of ten and under age of 18 who maliciously and wilfully damages property of such owner; this action in addition to all other actions or rights of such owner. (93-13-2). Otherwise, no parental tort liability imposed (109 Miss. 691, 69 So. 685) unless parent authorizes or ratifies tort (134 Miss. 616, 99 So. 440) or unless parent has made it possible for child to cause injury and probable that child would do so (238 Miss. 156, 117 So.2d 795).

Adoption.—See topic Adoption.

Uniform Transfers to Minors Act adopted. (91-20-19).

MARRIAGE:

There is no statute prohibiting, under all circumstances, marriage of persons under a specified age.

Consent Required.—Where the male is under age of 17 or female is under age of 15, consent of parents or guardian of underaged party is necessary plus written waiver of minimum age requirements by court. (93-1-5).

Medical Examination.—Medical certificate dated within 30 days prior to application must be presented to clerk showing applicants free from syphilis as determined by blood tests performed in laboratory approved by State Board of Health.

License is required and is obtained by (a) sworn application of both parties to clerk of circuit court of any county in the state, provided that if female applicant is a Mississippi resident under the age of 21, application must be made to circuit clerk of county of her residence. Application must include names, ages and addresses of applicants, names and addresses of their parents, and if no parents, names and addresses of guardian or next of kin, the signatures of witnesses and any other data which may be required by law or State Board of Health. Male applicant must be at least 17 years of age and female at least 15 years of age, unless court in county where either of applicants resides waives minimum age requirements. No license can be issued when it appears to clerk that applicant is drunk, insane or imbecile. (93-1-5, 93-1-11).

The issuance of license may be contested by any interested party by filing written protest in the circuit or chancery court of county where application is filed. Provision is made for necessary parties, issuance of process and a hearing on such protest. (93-1-7).

However, failure to comply with any of the foregoing requirements does not affect validity of any marriage duly solemnized and followed by cohabitation (93-1-9) nor validity of common law marriages entered into prior to Apr. 5, 1956; but after said date, no marriage is valid unless license is obtained and ceremony performed (93-1-15). Affidavit showing age of both applicants must be made by either father, mother, guardian or next of kin and filed with clerk, unless both applicants appear in person before clerk and subscribe oath showing their ages. Further proof of age must be given clerk in form of birth certificate, baptismal record, Armed Services discharge, etc., or other official document evidencing age.

Waiting Period.—Application must remain on file, open to public, in clerk's office for three days, unless court in judicial district waives waiting period. Where either party appears to be under 21, clerk must immediately notify, by prepaid certified mail, father, mother, guardian or next of kin of both applicants at addresses shown.

Ceremonial Marriage.—Any ordained minister of gospel in good standing, any Rabbi or other spiritual leader of any religious body authorized by such body to perform ceremony and in good standing, any judge of Supreme Court, Court of Appeals, circuit court, chancery court or county court, justice court judges, and members of board of supervisors within their respective counties may perform ceremony. (93-1-17). Any marriage performed by mayor before Mar. 14, 1994 is valid if all other requirements of law are met and marriage would have been valid if performed by official authorized to solemnize rites of marriage.

Reports of Marriages.—Certificate of marriage signed by minister, judge, justice, or other person authorized to solemnize marriage shall be transmitted by such minister within three months to clerk who issued license. Exemplication thereof is evidence of marriage. (93-1-21).

Record.—See category Documents and Records, topic Records, subhead Vital Statistics.

Common law marriages were valid prior to Apr. 5, 1956. (93-1-15). If common law marriage is valid in state where celebrated then it will be recognized in Mississippi. (389 So.2d 1389).

Proxy Marriages.—Not authorized by statute.

Marriages by Written Contract.—Not authorized by statute.

Prohibited Marriages.—Between parent and child, grandparent and grandchild, stepmother and stepson, brother and sister (whole or half blood), aunt and nephew, first cousins and between persons of same gender. (93-1-1). Children of such marriages are not legitimate. (93-7-5).

Foreign Marriages.—Any attempt to evade 93-1-1 prohibiting certain marriages by marrying out of state and returning shall also be declared incestuous and void. (93-1-3). Same sex marriages from other states also not recognized.

Annulment.—All bigamous or incestuous marriages are void, and either party may obtain declaration of nullity. (93-7-1). Marriage may also be annulled for any of following causes existing at time of marriage: incurable impotency; insanity or idiocy; failure to procure valid license (provided there has been no subsequent cohabitation); marriage obtained by force or fraud, or where either party was incapable of consent because of age or understanding, or either party was physically incapable of entering into marriage state (provided there has been no ratification); or where wife was pregnant by one other than her husband (provided there has been no ratification). (93-7-3). Except for incestuous marriages, issue of void marriage is legitimate. (93-7-5 et seq.) and custody may be determined as in divorce (93-7-7). Venue in county where defendant resides, where marriage license issued, or where plaintiff resides if defendant nonresident. (93-7-9).

Antenuptial Contracts.—See topic Husband and Wife.

INSURANCE

INSURANCE COMPANIES:

Regulated by 83-1-1 et seq.

Supervised by Insurance Department headed by Commissioner of Insurance, 1804 Sillers Building, Jackson, MS 39201.

Rates for most types of property and casualty insurance are regulated by 83-2-1 et seq.

Annual statements must be filed with Commissioner of Insurance. (83-5-55).

Policies.—Life insurance policies are regulated by 83-7-1 et seq. Accident and sickness (health) insurance policies are regulated by 83-9-1 et seq. Automobile insurance policies are regulated by 83-11-1 et seq. Fire insurance policies are regulated by 83-13-1 et seq. Credit life and credit disability insurance policies are regulated by 83-53-1 et seq.

Discrimination.—Rating Bureau shall not recommend any rates for insurance upon property which discriminates unfairly in same territorial classification between risks in application of like charges and credits or which discriminates unfairly between risks of essentially same hazard and having substantially same degree of protection against fire. (83-3-23). Discrimination through fictitious grouping, except as to life, accident, health and hospitalization insurance, is prohibited. (83-5-27). Making or permitting any unfair discrimination between individuals of same class and equal expectation of life in rates charged for life insurance contract or life annuity or in dividends or benefits payable thereon, or in any other terms and conditions, is prohibited. Making or permitting any unfair discrimination between individuals of same class and of essentially same hazard in amount of premium, policy fees, or rates charged for any policy or contract of accident or health insurance or in benefits payable thereunder, or in any other terms and conditions of contract, or in any other manner whatsoever is prohibited. (83-5-35). No life insurance company doing business in Mississippi shall discriminate in favor of individuals of same class and equal expectation of life in amount of payments of premiums or rates charged, or in dividends or other benefits payable thereon, or in any terms and conditions of contract. (83-7-3).

Rebates are prohibited except as specified in insurance policy. (83-3-121). Unfair methods of competition and unfair and deceptive acts or practices are prohibited. (83-5-35). Rebates on life insurance policies are prohibited. (83-7-3).

Agents and Brokers.—Every person who solicits insurance on behalf of any insurance company or transmits application for, or policy of, insurance, or receives or delivers policy, or who examines or inspects any risk or receives or transmits any premiums, or does or performs any other act in making or consummation of any contract of insurance for or with insurance company, or who examines into or adjusts any loss for insurance company is held to be agent of company for which act is done or risk is taken, as to all duties and liabilities imposed by law. Term "agent" also includes all creditors whose officers, employees, or legal representatives authorized to act in any manner directly or indirectly in solicitation or negotiation for or procurement or making of contract of property insurance, under small loan insurance license, where coverage is written on collateral in which creditor has insurable interest. "Credit property insurance" means insurance on any personal property which protects creditors from damages to collateral for loan. (83-17-1). For discussion of when insurance broker is considered insurer's agent, see 240 Miss. 691, 128 So.2d 544.

An insurance agent is personally liable on all contracts of insurance unlawfully made by or through him for any company not authorized to do business in the state. (83-17-3).

Every agent of any insurance company authorized to do business in Mississippi shall be required to obtain from Insurance Commissioner continuous certificate under seal showing that company is licensed to do business in state and that he is agent of company and authorized to do business for it. (83-17-5).

Insurance agents and solicitors writing fire, allied lines, automobile, physical damage, casualty, liability, fidelity, surety, guaranty, inland marine, life, health or accident insurance, and annuity contracts are subject to examination by and must be licensed by and are under supervision of Insurance Commission. (83-21-15—83-21-27, 83-17-101 et seq., 83-17-201 et seq.).

Investments of capital, surplus and other funds are regulated by 83-19-51.

Process Agent.—Foreign insurance companies shall, in addition to appointing Commissioner of Insurance, appoint some resident as its agent for service of process. (83-21-1).

Foreign Insurance Companies.—In order to be admitted, foreign insurance company must have done business for at least two years in state of domicile (unless it is subsidiary or affiliate of company already licensed in this state). (83-21-3). It must deposit with Commissioner of Insurance certified copy of charter and statement of financial condition, sworn to by president and secretary or other proper officer; fee for filing, $1,000. (83-21-1). It must deposit with state treasurer securities in amount not less than $50,000 unless company furnishes certificate that it is maintaining deposit with state of domicile. (83-21-3). Company must satisfy Commission that it is legally organized, its capital or net assets are well invested and immediately available for paying losses in this state, and that it insures no single hazard for more than one-tenth of

See note at head of Digest as to 1998 legislation covered.

See Topical Index in front part of this volume.

MS – 28

INSURANCE COMPANIES . . . *continued*
its net assets. Company must comply with specified agent for process requirements. (83-21-1). Company shall not be admitted until it has secured Commissioner's certificate that it has complied with state laws and is authorized to make contracts. (83-21-1).

Foreign insurance company which is prohibited by its charter or by-law of its domicile from investing assets, other than capital stock, in bonds of this state may not be granted a license to transact business in this state. (83-21-9).

Revocation or Suspension of Certificate.—When the Insurance Commissioner determines that foreign insurance company is in unsound condition, or is informed by State Tax Commission that it is delinquent in state tax payments, or has failed to comply with law or to submit to examination, or perform any legal obligation in relation thereto, Commissioner must revoke or suspend its certificate of authority and cause notification thereof to be published and no new business can be done while such default or disability continues nor until authority to do business is restored by Commissioner. (83-1-29).

Resident Agents.—Foreign companies not authorized to transact business in this state, except life insurance companies, can only write or issue policies after risk has been approved in writing and countersigned by a resident agent; countersignature may be by facsimile in certain instances. Such agent must receive minimum of 50% of local agent's commission on business owned by resident of state and minimum of 20% on business located in state but owned by nonresident of state. Insurer subject to penalty of $100 or three times normal gross commission of policy, whichever is greater, for failure to pay prescribed countersigning fees. This does not apply to rolling stock of railroads or property in transit while in custody of common carrier. (83-17-21).

Process Agent.—Foreign insurance company, upon being admitted and authorized to do business in state, must, by a duly executed instrument filed with Commissioner of Insurance, constitute and appoint Commissioner its true and lawful attorney upon whom all process in any action or legal proceeding against it may be served as if served on company. Authority must continue in force irrevocably so long as any liability of company remains outstanding in state. Such company must also appoint as its agent or agents in state some resident other than Commissioner, which appointment must be in writing and filed with Insurance Commissioner and must authorize agent to acknowledge service of process for and on behalf of company, and such company must consent that service of process on this agent shall be as valid as if served upon company. (83-21-1).

When process is served upon the Commissioner of Insurance, he must immediately notify the company of such service by letter prepaid and directed to its secretary and must within two days after such service forward a copy of the process served on him to the designated official of the company; but failure of the Commissioner so to notify the company does not affect validity of such service. (83-5-11).

Nonresidents or Agents.—Commissioner is required to impose license fees and other conditions on nonresident agents or brokers whenever existing or future laws of other jurisdictions require the licensing of resident of this state as nonresident agent or broker. (83-21-15).

Taxes.—See subheads Premium Tax and Privilege Tax, infra.

Retaliatory Laws.—When home state or country requires, of Mississippi insurers or agents thereof, taxes, licenses, and other fees, in aggregate, and any fines, penalties, deposit requirements or other material obligations in excess of those required of insurers and their agents of such other state or country, like requirements are imposed on such company and its agents. (27-15-123).

Premium Tax.—In addition to license tax, foreign insurance companies are assessed with annual license or privilege tax of 3% of gross amount of premium receipts received from policies written in or covering risks located in this state, except foreign insurance companies providing service under state employees life and health insurance plan are not required to pay annual license or privilege tax on premiums collected for coverage under plan; but in determining amount of premiums, there are deducted premiums received for reinsurance from companies authorized to do business in this state, cash dividends paid in this state, cancellations and premiums returned; and mutual insurance companies (including interinsurance and reciprocal exchanges, but not including mutual life, accidental, health or industrial insurance companies) may deduct any refunds to policyholders other than for losses. "Premium" includes all fees collected and no deduction is allowed for agent's commission. Companies withdrawing from this state must pay tax as long as premiums are collected from policyholders in state. (27-15-103; 27-15-105).

In addition to license tax, domestic companies pay annual tax of 3% of gross amount of premiums collected on policies written in or covering risks located in state, except for premiums received or policies issued to fund retirement, thrift or deferred compensation plan qualified under §401, §403 or §457 of Federal Tax Code. (27-15-109). No premium tax levied on state employee life and health plans. (27-15-103; 27-15-109). Where domestic company pays additional premium tax under retaliatory laws of other states, total of such additional tax may be deducted from income tax due this state. (27-15-109). In addition to all other taxes authorized by law, insurance companies must pay license and privilege taxes imposed by 27-15-81 and 27-15-83, taxes imposed by 27-15-103 to 27-15-117, taxes imposed on annuities by 27-15-119, ad valorem taxes on real estate and tangible personal property, state income tax, sales tax levied on vendor with requirement of adding it to sales price and use tax levied on cost of tangible personal property purchased outside state for use in state. (27-15-115; 27-15-119). Reduction in insurance premium tax for qualifying Mississippi investments. (27-15-129). For imposition of premium retaliatory tax, see subhead Retaliatory Laws, supra.

Privilege Tax.—Insurance companies are required to pay license tax, ranging from $25 to $350. (27-15-83).

Uniform Insurers Liquidation Act not adopted. Insurers Rehabilitation and Liquidation Act governs, adopted 1991. (83-24-1, et seq.).

No-Fault Insurance.—See category Transportation, topic Motor Vehicles, subhead No-Fault Insurance.

Plain Language.—See category Business Regulation and Commerce, topic Consumer Protection.

SURETY AND GUARANTY COMPANIES:

A foreign surety and guaranty company must first procure a license before being permitted to do business in this state. It must have a paid-up capital of not less than $250,000, and at least $100,000 of this paid-up capital must be invested in solvent securities created by laws of United States, or of this state, or under the laws of the state in which the company is incorporated, or in other safe securities, the value of which shall be at, or above par, which shall be deposited with the proper officer in the state, under which the company is incorporated. (83-27-1 et seq.).

INTELLECTUAL PROPERTY

TRADEMARKS AND TRADENAMES:

Any individual, firm, partnership, corporation, association, union or other organization may acquire trademark. (75-25-1 and 75-25-5).

What May Be Used.—A registered trademark shall not consist of: (a) immoral, deceptive or scandalous matter; (b) matter which may disparage or falsely suggest connection with persons, living or dead, institutions, beliefs or national symbols, or bring them into contempt or disrepute; (c) flag, coat of arms or insignia of U.S., state, municipality or foreign nation, or simulation thereof; (d) name, signature or portrait of living individual without written consent; (e) deceptively descriptive mark or surname; (f) mark resembling mark registered in state to another; (g) mark resembling mark registered in U.S. Patent Office to another. (75-25-3).

Registration.—Any person who adopts or uses trademark may file application for registration on form provided in office of Secretary of State subject to limitations of Trademark Act. Following pertinent information is required on application: (a) Name and business address of applicant and if corporation, state of incorporation; (b) goods the mark is used in connection with and manner of use; (c) date trademark first used anywhere and date first used in this state; (d) statement that applicant is owner of trademark and has right to use of same and that no other person in this state uses mark resembling same or that might be mistaken for; (e) statement that no other person has registration of same or similar trademark in U.S. Patent Office and that applicant is owner of concurrent registration in U.S. Patent Office covering area which includes this state. Application must be signed and verified by proper persons and accompanied by specimen or facsimile of trademark in triplicate. Filing fee of $25 ($35 for nonresident) must accompany application payable to Secretary of State. (75-25-5).

Upon compliance with requirements of Act, Secretary of State issues a certificate of registration under his signature and seal of state showing above information and registration date. Any certificate of registration or certified copy thereof is admissible in evidence as competent proof of registration in any jurisdictional proceeding in this state. (75-25-7).

Provisions are made for cancellations and for classifications of types of trademarks. (75-25-15, 75-25-17).

Assignment.—Trademark and its registration with goodwill of business where used is assignable. Assignment instrument must be duly executed and recorded with Secretary of State upon payment of $25 filing fee. Assignee must be issued new certificate for remainder of term. (75-25-11).

Protection Afforded.—Registration is effective for term of ten years and renewal for like terms thereafter upon payment of filing fee of $25. (75-25-9). Owner of registered trademark is protected from unlawful manufacture, use, display or sale of any counterfeits or limitations. (75-25-23).

Infringement consists of use without consent of registrant of reproduction, counterfeit, copy of colorable limitation of registered mark in conjunction with sale or advertising of any goods where such use is likely to confuse or deceive as to origin or source of goods. Upon infringement of trademarks owner may proceed by suit to enjoin counterfeits or imitations in any court of competent jurisdiction and said court may require defendants to pay owner all profit derived by use and also damages for wrongful use of same and further require destruction of imitation. (75-25-21, 75-25-23).

Tradenames.—Distributors or sellers of economic poisons are required to place on the label the manufacturer's name and address and the name, brand or trademark under which the article is sold. (69-23-5, 7). There are no other requirements for registration of business names.

TRADE SECRETS:

Mississippi Uniform Trade Secrets Act.—Adopted, from and after July 1, 1990. (75-26-1 et seq.).

LEGAL PROFESSION

ATTORNEYS AND COUNSELORS:

Bar is integrated and active attorneys must be members of Mississippi Bar. (73-3-119).

Jurisdiction over Admissions.—Supreme Court of Mississippi is vested with jurisdiction to admit attorneys to practice of law. (73-3-2).

Eligibility.—Person applying for admission to bar in order to be eligible for examination for admission, shall be at least 21 years of age, of good moral character, and must have diploma or certificate from approved law school or must have received bachelor's degree from accredited college or credit for requirements of first three years of college work and completion of law school course from college with six-year pre-law and law course if applicant previously enrolled in law school more than ten years prior to date of application and applicant graduated prior to Nov. 1, 1984. Applicant who has begun law school or study under supervision of Mississippi lawyer prior to Nov. 1, 1979, must submit proof of completion of two years of college work. (73-3-2). Educational requirements both as to general education and legal education do not apply to any person who may have graduated from law school prior to Oct. 1, 1954. (73-3-31).

See note at head of Digest as to 1998 legislation covered.

See Topical Index in front part of this volume.

MS – 29

ATTORNEYS AND COUNSELORS . . . continued

Certain law students participating in law school legal internship programs or clinical legal education courses may be authorized to engage in limited practice under certain conditions receiving no compensation, but gaining academic credit towards law school requirements. (73-3-201, et seq.).

Registration as Law Student.—No such requirement.

Examination.—Applicant is examined in writing by Board of Bar Admissions. Board will set and collect examination and admission fees. Applicant may sit for examination after graduation or within 60 days prior to graduation from approved law school. Board shall conduct not less than two bar examinations each year.

Multi-State Bar Examination given; does not accept transfer of multi-state bar scores from other jurisdictions; additional local subjects tested: Commercial law (business associations and partnerships), federal statutes on judiciary and bankruptcy, constitutional law (Mississippi and U.S.), domestic relations, chancery practice, statutory law (statute of frauds, statute of limitations, workers' compensation), criminal law, evidence and pleading (circuit court), personal property and UCC, real property, ethics, federal procedure and torts.

Clerkship.—None required.

Admission Without Examination.—Not available.

Admission Pro Hac Vice.—Attorneys of other states, in good professional standing and of good moral character and familiar with the customs of legal profession in this state may appear and plead in any special cause before any court or administrative agency in this state provided attorney subject himself to jurisdiction of Board or Bar Admissions and consents to application of Mississippi law. But upon petition of two members of bar of this state, or upon its own initiative, State Board must investigate and may refuse such attorney privilege of continuing to appear or plead. (73-3-39).

Licenses.—Attorneys must pay enrollment fees not to exceed $160 annually to State Bar Association if admitted to practice for three years or more; $110 if admitted for more than one and less than three years; and $50 if admitted less than one year; and $50 if inactive. Dues optional for lawyers over 75 years old, and judges of various courts are exempt from dues. (73-3-123; 73-3-125).

Privileges.—None.

Disabilities.—None.

Liabilities.—None.

Compensation.—Board of Commissioners shall have no authority to regulate fees or charges of lawyers. (73-3-171).

Lien.—None.

Attorney Ethics.—Supreme Court adopted ABA Model Rules of Professional Conduct effective 7/1/87.

Disbarment or Suspension.—Attorneys practicing law in Mississippi subject to disciplinary jurisdiction of Mississippi Supreme Court and certain designated agencies consisting of board of commissioners, committee on complaints and complaint tribunals. Proceedings for disciplinary action initiated by written complaint sworn to by complaining party. Procedure for hearing complaints and penalties set out in 73-3-301, et seq. If suspended or disbarred, attorney cannot practice in state unless privilege restored. Attorney may petition Court for termination of suspension or reinstatement after designated interval. Conviction or plea of nolo contendere of designated offenses results in automatic suspension and initiation of disciplinary action. Act does not restrict or modify inherent right of courts of record to supervise bar as incident to their power to admit attorneys to practice. (73-3-143 et seq.).

Mandatory Continuing Education.—Attorneys practicing law in Mississippi are required to complete minimum of 12 hours of continuing legal education each year.

Unauthorized Practice.—It is a misdemeanor to practice law without first procuring a license.

Making or certifying to any abstract of title to real estate is to be engaged in practice of law, but abstract companies incorporated in this state may make abstracts or certify to titles where they act through some person or agent authorized under laws of Mississippi to practice law. Also, an abstract company chartered under laws of Mississippi, with a paid-up capital of $50,000 or more, may make or certify to abstracts through president, secretary or other principal officer of such company. (73-3-55).

Professional Association.—See category Business Organizations, topic Corporations, subhead Professional Corporation.

MINERAL, WATER AND FISHING RIGHTS

MINES AND MINERALS:

State Oil and Gas Supervisor is solely responsible for administration of offices of State Oil and Gas Board. (53-1-7).

Operation of Mines.—Drilling and production regulated (53-3-5); allowable production (53-3-9); surface mining and reclamation operations (53-5-1 et seq.); surface coal mining (53-9-1 et seq.).

Safeguarding of Employees.—See category Employment, topic Labor Relations.

Inspection of Mines.—Supervisor and employees have access to all oil and gas wells at all times. (53-1-33). Supervisor has authority to employ field inspectors. (53-1-9). Mississippi commission on natural resources may test or take sample material which affects or may affect emission of air contaminants. (49-17-21).

Oil and Gas.—Term "oil" includes any type of salvaged crude oil, which, after any treatment, becomes marketable. (53-1-71).

Taxes.—All non-producing mineral interests and leases created after June 10, 1946, are exempt from ad valorem taxation (27-31-73), but are subject to mineral documentary tax paid by attachment of documentary tax stamps to instrument prior to and as condition precedent to recordation of same (27-31-77). Amount of tax depends upon number of mineral acres or royalty acres conveyed or primary term of lease. (27-31-79). Non-producing mineral interests and mineral leases, created prior to June 10, 1946, may be exempted from ad valorem taxation after Jan. 1, 1947, by application for said exemption and attachment of documentary stamps to application. (27-31-75).

Privilege tax on producing or severing oil or gas for sale, profit or commercial use is: 6% of value at point of production. Rate is 3% on oil produced by enhanced oil recovery in which carbon dioxide is used provided carbon dioxide is transported by pipeline to oil well site. Rate is 3$\frac{1}{2}$% on occluded natural gas produced from coal seams for first five years of production if commercial production begins before July 1, 1993. (27-25-503,-703).

For payment of costs of administering conservation act there is levied and assessed against each barrel of oil produced and saved in state a charge not to exceed 35 mills on each barrel; also, against each 1,000 cubic feet of gas produced a charge not to exceed four mills per thousand cubic feet. Oil and Gas Board fixes amount of such charge and may from time to time change, reduce or increase amount thereof, within above limits. Collections are made by Oil and Gas Board. Persons owning interests in oil or gas produced are liable for such tax in proportion to their ownership at time of production. (53-1-73).

Exemptions.—Oil produced or under the ground on producing properties and producing oil equipment owned by the producer and all leases in production, including mineral rights in producing property, are exempt from ad valorem taxes. (27-25-523). Ad valorem taxation exemption now applies to all oil, gas and other petroleum products refined or to be refined in this state. (27-31-19). Equipment used to facilitate transportation in certain oil recovery projects is exempt except taxes for school district purposes. (27-31-102).

MORTGAGES

CHATTEL MORTGAGES:

Uniform Commercial Code adopted, effective Mar. 31, 1968. See category Business Regulation and Commerce, topic Commercial Code.

Filing.—See category Documents and Records, topic Records.

Taxation.—See category Taxation.

Forms.—See categories Business Regulation and Commerce, topic Commercial Code and Documents and Records, topic Records.

Renewal.—There is no limitation of time with respect to the lien of a chattel mortgage except the general statute of limitations applicable to written contracts. (See category Civil Actions and Procedure, topic Limitation of Actions.) To extend the lien beyond such time, renewal before period expires is necessary, and may be effected by endorsement on margin of record where mortgage is recorded or by filing renewal for record.

Motor Vehicles.—Chattel mortgages securing purchase price of motor vehicles are governed by 63-19-1 et seq. Persons or corporations in business of purchasing such retail installment contracts from sellers of motor vehicles must be licensed with the State Banking Department and sellers in business of holding such retail installment contracts involving motor vehicles aggregating in excess of $500,000 must secure such license. The form of a retail installment contract entered into between a retail buyer and a retail seller when retail buyer buys a motor vehicle from a retail seller at a time price payable in one or more deferred installments when title to or a lien upon vehicle is retained or taken by a retail seller from a retail buyer as security for the buyer's obligation is controlled by 63-19-31. Maximum finance charge for credit sale of motor vehicles (including commercial motor vehicles) graduated from 14% per year or, through June 30, 1986, up to 5% per year above discount rate on 90-day notes at Federal Reserve Bank, excluding surcharge, for new vehicles manufactured in same year or year prior to year in which sale made to 28.75% per year through June 30, 1986 and 26.75% thereafter for used vehicles manufactured more than four years prior to year in which sale made. (63-19-43). Violations of Act carry heavy penalties.

MORTGAGES OF PERSONAL PROPERTY:

See topic Chattel Mortgages and/or category Business Regulation and Commerce, topic Commercial Code.

MORTGAGES OF REAL PROPERTY:

Both mortgages and deeds of trust are valid in this state, but the former have been practically superseded by the latter.

The grantor is deemed the owner of the legal title, except as against the mortgagee or the trustee after the breach of condition of such mortgage or deed of trust.

The interest of the mortgagor may be sold under execution. (89-1-43).

Execution.—No seal is necessary. No witnesses are necessary. Instrument must be properly signed by parties owning property. Instrument is valid as between parties without acknowledgment. (201 Miss. 294, 30 So.2d 44). However, instrument must be properly acknowledged and filed for record to give notice to third parties. (89-5-1, 89-5-3).

Recording.—All deeds of trust and mortgages are void as to all creditors and subsequent purchasers for valuable consideration without notice, unless they are acknowledged and lodged for record with clerk of chancery court of county (district if county divided into districts) where land is located, but as between parties and their heirs, and as to all subsequent purchasers with notice or without valuable consideration, they are valid. (89-5-3, 89-5-1). Mortgage and deed of trust takes effect as to subsequent purchasers for valuable consideration without notice and as to all creditors only from time when it is delivered to clerk to be recorded. (89-5-5). Mortgage lien ceases after running of statute of limitations unless notice of renewal or extension is properly entered on margin of official record. (89-5-19).

See note at head of Digest as to 1998 legislation covered.

See Topical Index in front part of this volume.

MORTGAGES OF REAL PROPERTY . . . continued

Recording Fees.—See category Documents and Records, topic Records. Fee for recording deeds of trust is $10. Fee for sectional index entry per section or subdivision is $1. (25-7-9[c]).

Taxes.—Ad valorem taxes on real property become lien on Jan. 1 of each year and are entitled to preference over liens. (27-35-1). Mortgagees may redeem land that they have deeds of trust on by applying in writing to Chancery Clerk and following requirements of statute. (27-45-7). See category Taxation, topic Property (Ad Valorem) Taxes, subhead Redemption.

Trust Deeds.—Deed of Trust is commonly used to secure debts and it may be foreclosed by power of sale as well as through judicial foreclosure.

Future Advances.—Both future advance clause and dragnet clause are valid and enforceable but breadth of coverage is dependent on language of particular deed of trust. (434 So.2d 1351).

Priorities.—Priority of instruments. (89-5-5). Every mortgage given at time of purchase of real estate to secure payment of purchase money is entitled to preference over all judgments and other debts of mortgagor as to land purchased. (89-1-45). Any mortgage, deed of trust, judgment, materialman's lien, federal tax lien or similar lien recorded or enrolled prior to recording of deed of trust will generally have priority over such instrument.

Subordination Agreements.—No statutory restriction. Fee for recording. (25-7-9).

Assignment.—If indebtedness secured by mortgage or deed of trust is assigned, assignor shall be required by assignee to enter fact of assignment on margin of record of lien in chancery clerk's office, and assignment, in writing, duly acknowledged, can be filed for record. (89-5-15). Assignment of debt secured by deed of trust or mortgage shall be entered on margin of record of lien, or assignment shall be acknowledged and filed for record. (89-5-17).

Release.—No statutory provisions.

Satisfaction.—Payment of debt extinguishes mortgage or deed of trust and revests title in mortgagor as effectively as it conveyed. (89-1-49). When such payment has been made, mortgagee or assignee must enter satisfaction on margin of record which entry must be attested by clerk of court. In event mortgagee does not within one month after payment make such entry on record, he is liable to penalty of $50, which may be recovered by suit; and if, after request, he fails or refuses to make such acknowledgment of satisfaction, he becomes liable to party aggrieved, for any sum not exceeding mortgage money, to be recovered by action. (89-5-21).

Satisfaction can be entered by agent of mortgagee if authorization is duly acknowledged and recorded. (89-5-21).

Trustee in deed of trust may cancel same of record as effectually as cestui que trust may. (89-1-51).

Discharge.—No statutory provision.

Foreclosures.—Mortgages or deeds of trust can be foreclosed by proceedings in the chancery court or by sale in accordance with terms of instrument and statutes. (89-1-55).

Sales.—All lands comprising a single tract and wholly described by the subdivisions of the governmental surveys, sold under mortgages and deeds of trust, must be first offered in subdivisions not exceeding 160 acres or one-fourth section and then offered as an entirety, and the price bid for the latter controls only when it exceeds the aggregate of the bids for the subdivisions. (89-1-55).

Lands sold at public outcry under deeds of trust must be sold in the county in which the land is located or in the county of the residence of the grantor or one of the grantors, provided that where the land is situated in two or more counties, the parties may contract for a sale of the whole in any of the counties in which any part of land lies. (89-1-55).

Sale of land must be advertised for three consecutive weeks preceding the sale in a newspaper (13-3-31) published in county or counties in which any part of land lies, and also by posting one notice for same time, at courthouse of county where land is situated, which notice and publication must disclose name of original mortgagor or mortgagors, whose property is advertised for sale, regardless of any contract to contrary. Sale of land under deed of trust is not valid unless such sale is so advertised. (89-1-55).

A sale of land by a substituted trustee under a deed of trust is absolutely void unless the substitution appears of record in the office of the chancery clerk of the county where the land is situated and has actually been spread of record before the first publication or notice of sale has been posted or published. (89-5-45).

Deficiency Judgments.—No statutory restriction. Subject to "commercial reasonableness" standard. (566 So.2d 1218). Deficiency suit must be commenced within one year from date of foreclosure of property pledged as security note. (15-1-23).

Moratorium.—Procedure established for obtaining relief from inequitable mortgage foreclosure after President of U.S. has declared that emergency or major disaster exists in certain areas. (89-1-301).

Redemption.—There is no period of redemption after valid foreclosure sale under state law. (235 Miss. 162, 108 So.2d 546).

Form.—No prescribed form.

PROPERTY

ABSENTEES:

Absentee voting is governed by 23-15-449 and 23-15-621 to 23-15-755.

Care of Property.—No statutory provision save as to nonresident or unknown owners of mineral interests. See category Mineral, Water and Fishing Rights, topic Mines and Minerals.

Process Agent.—Foreign corporation transacting business in Mississippi must appoint agent for service of process. (79-4-15.07). Registered agents are appointed by filing required documents with secretary of state's office. (79-4-15.08). Appointment of agent by foreign corporation establishes agent for service of process on that corporation. (79-4-15.10[a]).

Escheat.—Escheat of unclaimed intangible personal property in accordance with provisions of Uniform Disposition of Unclaimed Property Act, adopted with minor variations. Time period for presumption of abandonment decreased from seven years to five years. (89-12-1 et seq.). See categories Business Regulation and Commerce, topic Banks and Banking, subhead Unclaimed Deposits; Estates and Trusts, topics Descent and Distribution, subhead Escheat, Wills.

ADVERSE POSSESSION:

Ten years actual and uninterrupted adverse possession of land by any person claiming to be the owner vests in the occupant or possessor a full and complete title. (15-1-7, 15-1-13).

Character of Possession.—Occupancy is not necessary to establish actual adverse possession. Possession by either claimant or tenant is sufficient. Cultivating, pasturing, cutting and selling of timber, and other acts of ownership and control can be sufficient—the extent of the necessary use varying according to the character of the land. Without color of title adverse possession does not extend beyond the land actually and continuously used; but color of title to a whole tract coupled with actual possession of part constitutes constructive possession of the whole.

Duration of Possession.—Period of ten years does not vary according to the character of land or according to the basis of claim of title, except in the case of claimants through tax sales. See category Taxation, topic Property (Ad Valorem) Taxes, subhead Suits to Recover, catchline Tax Titles.

Easements.—Can be acquired by ten years adverse possession.

Disabilities.—There is saving to infants and persons of unsound mind of right to sue and set aside title allegedly acquired by adverse possession within ten years after removal of such disability; but saving in favor of persons under disability of unsoundness of mind never extends beyond 31 years. (15-1-7, 15-1-13).

CURTESY:

Abolished. (93-3-5).

DEEDS:

Estate of inheritance or freehold, or for term of more than one year, in lands shall not be conveyed from one to another unless conveyance be declared by writing, signed and delivered. (89-1-3). See topic Real Property for types of estates.

Execution.—All conveyances of land must be in writing, signed and delivered. (89-1-3). Seals and scrolls are unnecessary except official seals. Absence of corporate seal does not affect validity of conveyance where executed by officer or authorized agent or attorney in fact, (89-1-21). A spouse need not join in the execution of a deed unless the property is the homestead. (89-1-29). All bodies politic, public corporations, and private corporations may convey lands. (89-1-21).

See topic Real Property; categories Debtor and Creditor, topic Homesteads, subhead Alienation or Encumbrance; Family, topic Husband and Wife, subhead Conveyance or Encumbrance of Property.

Recording.—In order to affect creditors and subsequent purchasers for value without actual notice, a deed must be acknowledged or proved and filed for record with clerk of chancery court of county (district if county divided into districts) where property is located. (89-5-1, 89-5-3). Priority of instruments controlled by date of filing for record. (89-5-5). See also category Documents and Records, topic Records.

Recording Fees.—Clerk's fee for recording deeds is $6, including indexing. Fee for sectional index entries per section or subdivision is $1 (25-7-9). See category Documents and Records, topic Records.

Operation and Effect.—Word "warrant" without restrictive words in conveyance has effect of embracing all of five covenants known to common law, to wit: seisin, power to sell, freedom from encumbrance, quiet enjoyment and warranty of title. (89-1-33).

Words "warrant specially," in conveyance, constitute covenant that grantor, his heirs and personal representatives, will forever warrant and defend title of property unto grantee and his heirs, representatives, and assigns, against claims of all persons claiming by, through, or under grantor. (89-1-35).

Words "grant," "bargain" and "sell" operate as express covenant that grantor was seized of estate, free from encumbrances made or suffered by grantor, and also for quiet enjoyment against grantor, unless limited by express words contained in conveyance. (89-1-41).

Conveyance without warranty operates to transfer title and possession of grantor as quitclaim and release. (89-1-37). Conveyance of quitclaim passes all of estate or interest of grantor in land conveyed and estops grantor and his heirs from asserting subsequently acquired adverse title to lands conveyed. (89-1-39).

Taxes.—See category Taxation, topic Real Estate Conveyance Tax.

Forms.—Conveyance of land may be in following form:

Form

"In consideration of (here stated), I convey and warrant unto . . . . . . the land described, [as described]. Witness my signature this . . . . . . day of . . . . . ., 19 . . . . ." If only a special warranty is intended add the word "specially" to the word "warrant" in the conveyance. (89-1-61).

DOWER:

Abolished. (93-3-5).

See note at head of Digest as to 1998 legislation covered.

See Topical Index in front part of this volume.

ESCHEAT:

See topic Absentees, subhead Escheat; categories Business Regulation and Commerce, topic Banks and Banking, subhead Unclaimed Deposits; Estates and Trusts, topics Descent and Distribution, subhead Escheat, Wills, subhead Unclaimed Legacies.

LANDLORD AND TENANT:

Kinds of Tenancy.—

Week-to-week.—If rental agreement does not define length of tenancy, it shall be week-to-week tenancy where tenant pays rent weekly and month-to-month tenancy in all other cases. (89-8-19).

Tenants in Common.—All conveyances will be construed to create tenancy in common and not joint tenancy or tenancy by entirety unless so designated by instrument. Tenancy by entirety and joint tenancy are permitted, but must be created by instrument of conveyance. (89-1-7).

Leases for more than one year must be in writing, signed and delivered, and in order to constitute notice to third persons must be recorded in office of chancery clerk of county (district if county divided into districts) in which property is situated. (15-3-1). Possession under unrecorded lease is, however, held to constitute notice. (120 Miss. 778, 83 So. 179).

Security Deposits.—Provisions governing payment, use, retention, return and lien status of security deposit for dwelling rental agreements covered by Residential Landlord and Tenant Act. (89-8-21).

Recording.—Race-Notice State. (89-5-3; 89-5-5). Conveyances of land shall be filed with clerk of chancery court of county in which lands are situated. (89-5-1).

Rent.—Provisions governing set off of rent for dwelling rental agreements covered by Residential Landlord and Tenant Act. (89-8-21).

Lien.—Landlord has right to lien on agricultural products of leased premises to secure payment of rent. (89-7-5). Landlord has right to lien on personal property in order to secure payment of rent if personal property is found on leased premises and is owned by lessee, except for merchandise sold in ordinary course of business. (89-7-51). Construction liens are allowed. (85-7-137).

Termination of Tenancy.—For dwelling rental agreement covered by Residential Landlord and Tenant Act, week to week tenancy and month to month tenancy may be terminated by written notice at least seven and 30 days, respectively, prior to termination date. (89-8-19). All other rental agreements require: two month's notice for year to year tenancy, one month's notice for $1/2$ or $1/4$ year tenancy and one week notice for month or week tenancy. (89-7-23). Joint tenancy or tenancy by entirety with right of survivorship can be terminated by deed of one spouse to other. (89-1-7).

Holding Over.—Tenant holding over after notice to vacate liable for double rent. (89-7-25).

Dispossession.—If one wrongfully possesses or converts rights in land to himself, complaining party may seek judgment from court. If judgment is in favor of plaintiff, warrant shall issue to sheriff which will command him to put plaintiff in possession of premises. Defendant shall pay costs of proceedings. (89-7-41). For unlawful entry and detainer see 11-25-23 and 11-25-113. Suit for ejectment may be maintained. (11-19-1). Tenant shall give notice to landlord if ejectment suit is filed against tenant. (11-19-9).

Distress or seizure can be made for rent or supplies that are due. Attachment may be executed for rental supplied on property of rentor, but property may not be removed from county where seizure was made. (89-7-85).

Uniform Residential Landlord and Tenant Act adopted in modified form in 1991. (89-8-1 et seq.).

PERPETUITIES:

Estates in fee tail are prohibited. Any person may make conveyance or devise of lands to succession of donees then living and upon death of last of said successors to any person or any heir. (89-1-15).

Accumulations.—The common law rules prevail; except that an investment trust or a trust of real or personal property, or both, created by an employer as part of a pension plan, disability or death benefit plan, or profit-sharing plan, for exclusive benefit of some or all employees, is exempt against perpetuities, restraints on alienation or suspension of the power of alienation, or the accumulation of income, where contributions to such trust are made by employer or employees, or both, and where purpose of trust is to distribute earnings and principal to employees. (79-15-21, 71-1-43). See also category Estates and Trusts, topic Trusts, subhead Accumulations.

PERSONAL PROPERTY:

Tenancy by entirety recognized. (89-1-7).

POWERS OF ATTORNEY:

Attorneys in Fact.—Such agency need not be created by writing save when within the terms of the Statute of Frauds. Thus powers of attorney granting authority to answer for the debt or default or miscarriage of another person, or authority to make a contract for the sale of lands, or the making of any lease thereof for a longer term than one year, must be in writing. (15-3-1). Conveyances of land, or contracts relating thereto, executed by an attorney in fact for his principal, and duly acknowledged and proved, have the same force and effect as if executed and acknowledged by the principal, and the same need not be formally executed in the name of principal. (87-3-3, 87-3-9).

Form.—Letter of attorney to transact any business need only express plainly the authority conferred. (87-3-7). Letters of attorney pertaining to conveyances of land may be filed in county where land is situated. (87-3-1). Before attorney-in-fact may execute land conveyance letters of attorney should be filed of record. (528 So.2d 800). Form to convey land suggested by 87-3-9 is as follows:

Form

Know all, that I, ..., of . . . . . . County, Mississippi, do hereby appoint . . . . . ., of . . . . . . County, my attorney in fact, with full power to sell and convey in fee simple, with general warranty (or without warranty, as the case may be) of title, that land situated in (describe it).

Witness my signature, the . . . . . . day of . . . . . ., A.D. . . . .

(Signature).

Formalities.—Before attorney-in-fact may execute land conveyance letters of attorney should be filed of record. (528 So.2d 800). Letters of attorney may be acknowledged or proved as conveyances of land are required to be and when so acknowledged or proved may be recorded in like manner. (87-3-1 and 89-5-1). See topic Deeds.

Revocation.—Letters of attorney duly recorded continue in force until revoked in writing or by death as to all persons who deal with the attorney in good faith without notice. Subsequent disability or incompetence of principal will not revoke authority of attorney-in-fact if power of attorney executed by principal contains language showing intent that power continue despite disability or incompetence. (87-3-15, 87-3-111). Any writing revoking letters of attorney may when acknowledged, as conveyances of land are acknowledged, be recorded in like manner and is effective from time of being filed for record in office in which letters revoked were recorded. (87-3-17).

Death of principal revokes the agency except as to one who, without notice of such death, in good faith and under circumstances repelling the imputation to him of fraud or negligence, deals with such agent, believing upon good reason that he is still such. (87-3-15).

Uniform Durable Power of Attorney Act.—Adopted. (87-3-101 et seq.). Uniform Probate Code not adopted.

Members of Armed Forces.—No specific provision.

REAL PROPERTY:

Any interest or claim to land may be conveyed to vest immediately or in the future by writing signed and delivered. Such writing transfers, according to its terms, the title of the person signing and delivering as fully and perfectly as if the same was transferred by feoffment with livery of seizin notwithstanding there may be an adverse possession thereof. (89-1-1).

There is statutory procedure for confirmation of tax titles and removing clouds upon titles. (11-17-1—11-17-37). Any person or corporation claiming an interest in real property from any county or municipality or political subdivision may confirm and quiet title to such property by proceedings in chancery court. (11-17-19).

Conveyance is deemed to carry fee simple unless limited by express words, or unless it clearly appears from instrument that less estate was intended. (89-1-5).

Condominiums.—May convey condominium granting separate interest in residential, commercial or industrial building. Plan of building must be filed with chancery clerk. Project owner must file declaration of restriction, and may provide for management of project by governing bodies. Real property divided for condominium use includes leasehold and any other estate in land recognized by law. (89-9-5, 89-9-7). See also category Debtor and Creditor, topic Homesteads.

Rule in Shelley's Case has been abolished. (89-1-9).

See also topics Deeds, Dower, Landlord and Tenant; categories Business Regulation and Commerce, topic Securities; Civil Actions and Procedure, topic Partition; Debtor and Creditor, topic Homesteads; Family, topic Husband and Wife; Mortgages, topic Mortgages of Real Property.

TAXATION

ADMINISTRATION:

Tax statutes may be found in Mississippi Code of 1972, Annotated, Title 27.

General supervision of tax matters is vested in State Tax Commission, Chairman of which is known as Tax Commissioner.

The Commission has full supervision of Income, Estate and Privilege Taxes; forms, waivers, etc., may be secured from the Commissioner in Jackson, Miss.

Penalties.—In addition to other penalties, any person who is eligible for brief "tax amnesty" program in 1986 and failed to pay delinquent taxes, as well as any person who wilfully attempted to avoid any taxes imposed by State Tax Commission, is guilty of felony. Maximum penalties include imprisonment up to five years and/or fines up to $100,000 for individual offenders or $500,000 for corporate offenders. (27-3-79).

Income Tax.—Any person knowingly making false return subject to ten years imprisonment. (27-7-87). Underpayment subjects taxpayer to additional assessment plus interest at rate of 1% per month from time due. (27-7-51). If any part of additional tax due is result of fraud penalty of 75% of underpayment attributable to fraud. (27-7-17). Failure to file return or to pay due tax will result in assessment of tax plus interest at rate of 5% if failure to pay is not for more than one month, with additional 5% for each month or fraction of month during which failure continues, not to exceed 25% of aggregate. (27-7-53).

Estate Tax.—Any person making false affidavits accompanying return subject to ten years imprisonment. (27-9-57).

Privilege Taxes.—Negligent failure to file return may result in imposition of 10% penalty of total taxes due. Penalty increases for each subsequent offense. If failure to file return is intentional with intent to evade law, penalty of 50% of total taxes due and interest of 1% per month is added. (27-65-39).

Lubricating Oil Tax.—Penalties set out in 27-57-21.

Private Railroads.—Penalty up to 10% of tax for failure to file required statements. (27-35-513).

As to real and personal property taxes see also subhead Sales, supra.

See also category Business Organizations, topic Corporations, subheads Taxation of Corporate Property, Taxation of Corporate Stock, Franchise Tax.

See note at head of Digest as to 1998 legislation covered.

See Topical Index in front part of this volume.

ESTATE TAX:

Imposed by 27-9-1 et seq. Tax equal to sum of following percentages of value of net estate is imposed upon transfer of net estate of every decedent, whether a resident or nonresident. Estate tax schedules conform to federal estate tax law. Phased-in tax schedules are in 27-9-5. Uniform Estate Tax Apportionment Act adopted. (1994, c. 348). Act does not apply to taxes due on account of death of decedents before Jan. 1, 1995.

Gross estate is determined by including value at time of decedent's death; or in alternative, whichever more nearly complies with method used on Federal Return as follows: (1) In case of property distributed, sold, exchanged, or otherwise disposed of, within six months after decedent's death such property shall be valued as of date of distribution, sale, exchange, or other disposition. (2) In case of property not distributed, sold, exchanged or otherwise disposed of, within six months after decedent's death such property shall be valued as of date six months after decedent's death. (3) Any interest or estate which is affected by mere lapse of time shall be included at its value as of time of death (instead of later date) with adjustment for any difference in its value as of later date not due to mere lapse of time. (27-9-7).

All property, tangible or intangible, shall be included as follows: (a) To extent of interest of deceased in all property in which decedent has an interest except that in case of a resident, gross estate shall not include real and tangible personal property located outside state, proceeds of annuity or other payment receivable by any beneficiary under military family protection plan, survivor benefit plan or other comparable plan under federal law and allowances due MIA of armed forces subsequently declared to be dead; and in case of nonresident gross estate shall not include tangible personal property even when located in Miss.; (b) to extent of any interest held jointly or as tenants in entirety with any other person, or in any bank or other institution, in their joint names, and payable to either or to survivor, except such part as may be shown to have never belonged to decedent, provided, however, if decedent and spouse were only owners of property or any interests held jointly or as tenants by entirety, it is assumed that each spouse contributed equally to acquisition, unless surviving spouse proves that his or her contribution was greater than one-half of cost; (c) to extent of any property passing under general power or appointment exercised by decedent by will, or by deed executed in contemplation of or intended to effect possession or enjoyment at or after death, except for bona fide sale for fair consideration in money or money's worth; (d) to extent of any interest in any trust created by decedent in contemplation of or intended to take effect in possession or enjoyment at or after his death, except in case of bona fide sale for fair consideration. Any transfer in nature of final disposition or distribution made within three years of death of decedent without any consideration is deemed prima facie to have been made in contemplation of death unless contrary is shown; (e) to extent of amount receivable by executor or administrator as insurance under policies taken out upon decedent's life, and to extent of amount receivable by all other beneficiaries under insurance policies taken out by decedent upon his own life; (f) as to any annuity other than annuity described in item (a), to extent only of decedent's contribution. (27-9-7).

Value of Farm and Closely Held Business Property.—Value of qualified real property located in state and owned by resident decedent where executor complies with 27-9-8 is determined by use under which it qualifies. (27-9-8).

Valuation Date.—See supra, catchline Gross Estate.

Deductions for Residents.—For the purpose of arriving at the value of a net estate, in case of a resident, the following may be deducted from the gross estate:

(1) Funeral expenses, administration expenses, claims against the estate, unpaid mortgages, losses during the existence of the estate caused by fires, storms, shipwreck, or other casualties, or from theft, when such losses are not compensated by insurance or otherwise, and such amounts actually and reasonably required for the support during settlement of those dependent upon the decedent, as are allowed by the laws of Mississippi, excluding, however, any income taxes upon income received after the death of decedent or any estate taxes.

(2) The value at the time of decedent's death of any property which can be identified as having been received by the decedent as a share in the estate of any person who died within two years prior to the death of the decedent, or which can be identified as having been acquired by the decedent in exchange for property so received, if an estate tax under Mississippi law was collected from such estate, and if such property is included in the decedent's gross estate.

(3) All bequests, legacies, devises or gifts made to the State of Mississippi, or any political subdivision thereof, for exclusive public purposes, or to the use of any corporation or association organized and operated exclusively for religious, charitable, scientific, literary or educational purposes, no part of the net earnings of which inures to the benefit of any private stockholder or individual, or to a trustee or trustees exclusively for such religious, charitable, scientific, literary or educational purposes. This deduction must be made in all cases when not prohibited by the Mississippi statute of mortmain, but same is limited to charities located within U.S. or its possessions. (27-9-9).

(4) Value of qualified terminable interest property. (27-9-10).

In determining value of net estate of resident, for estate tax purposes, further deduction of $120,666 for decedent dying in 1978; sum of $134,000 for decedent dying in 1979; sum of $147,333 for decedent dying in 1980; sum of $161,563 for decedent dying in 1981; sum of $175,625 for decedent dying in 1982 or thereafter prior to Oct. 1, 1988; sum of $400,000 for decedent dying on or after Oct. 1, 1988, but prior to Oct. 1, 1989; sum of $500,000 for decedent dying on or after Oct. 1, 1988 but prior to Oct. 1, 1990; and sum of $600,000 for decedent dying on or after Oct. 1, 1990, but prior to Jan. 1, 1998; sum of $625,000 in case of decedent dying in 1998; sum of $650,000 in case of decedent dying in 1999; sum of $675,000 in case of decedent dying in 2000 or 2001; sum of $700,000 in case of decedent dying in 2002 or 2003; sum of $850,000 in case of decedent dying in 2004; sum of $950,000 in case of decedent dying in 2005; and sum of $1,000,000 in case of decedent dying on or after Jan. 1, 2006. (27-9-11).

Deductions for Nonresidents.—The value of the taxable net estate of a nonresident is determined by deducting:

(1) From the value of that part of his gross estate which, at the time of death, is situated in Mississippi, that proportion of the deductions specified in subparagraphs (1), (2) and (4) above under catchline Deductions for Residents (27-9-9) that value of such part of gross estate situated in Mississippi bears to value of entire gross estate.

(2) An amount equal to the value of any property forming a part of the gross estate situated in Mississippi of any person who died within two years prior to death of decedent, which can be identified as such; but this exemption not allowed unless an estate tax has been paid on behalf of the estate of such prior decedent and is allowed only to the amount placed by the Commissioner on such property in determining the value of the gross estate of such prior decedent, and only to extent that value of such property is included in that part of decedent's gross estate which is situated in this state and which is not already deducted.

(3) The amount of all bequests, legacies, devises or transfers, except bona fide sales, in contemplation of or intended to take effect at or after death, to or for the use of the State of Mississippi, or a subdivision thereof, for exclusive public purposes, or to or for the use of any domestic religious, charitable or educational organization, so long as no part of the net earnings inures to the benefit of any private stockholder or individual, and provided that such bequests are not void under the statutes of mortmain. (27-9-15).

Executor of estate of a nonresident has option of paying on the proportion of the estate located in Mississippi, which said proportion bears to the entire estate wherever located, and taking the allowable deductions in the same proportions; or by paying upon the gross estate located in Mississippi without taking any deductions; but nonresident is not required to pay on any gross estate that is less than specific exemption provided in 27-9-11. (27-9-17).

Situs of Property.—All tangible property, real, personal or mixed, located within this state at the time of decedent's death shall be deemed property within this state and shall be reported unless otherwise exempt. (27-9-19). Intangible personal property of nonresidents of this state is exempt from estate taxes where laws of state of residence of decedent have a similar reciprocal provision. (27-9-13).

Returns.—Executor of estate of gross value exceeding amount of specific exemption provided in 27-9-11 must within 60 days after decedent's death, or within 60 days after qualifying as such, give written notice to Commissioner, showing name of decedent, date of death, name of attorney, probable value of gross estate and all transfers made by decedent within two years before his death. (27-9-21).

Executor must make return in all cases where gross estate exceeds amount of specific exemption provided in 27-9-11, within nine months after death of decedent, or in case of every nonresident when any part of gross estate is situated in Mississippi. If he is unable to make complete return as to any part of gross estate of decedent, he must include in his return description of such property, name of every person holding legal or beneficial interest therein, and upon notice, Commissioner may require such persons to make return as to such part of gross estate. (27-9-23). If no return is made after notice by Commissioner, penalties will be imposed. (27-9-45).

In event no administration is granted, or no return is filed, or if returns are false or incorrect, on some material facts, Commissioner, his deputy or agent, must make a return and Commissioner must assess tax thereon as provided by law. (27-9-25).

Lien.—Unless tax is paid in full, it is a lien for four years from date of filing return upon the decedent's gross estate, but where no return is filed it is a lien for ten years from due date of return. If Commissioner is satisfied that the tax liability of an estate has been fully discharged, he may issue a certificate or waiver releasing any or all property of the estate from such lien. The executor or administrator, who pays any unauthorized debts before paying this tax, may become personally liable for this tax. (27-9-35, 27-9-37).

Payment.—Tax is due and payable nine months after decedent's death, but where Commissioner finds undue hardship extension not to exceed six months in any one extension may be granted. Tax due upon qualified farm and closely held business property due at time Federal return due. Unpaid balances bear interest at 1/2 to 1% per month from due date until paid. (27-9-27). When tax is paid temporary receipt is issued, and Commissioner has four years to make any investigation desired. Should executor receive statement from Federal Government that all federal estate taxes have been paid, Commissioner may issue final receipt. (27-9-29).

Agreement as to Amount of Taxes.—For purpose of facilitating settlement and distribution, Commissioner, upon approval by Attorney General, on behalf of state, may agree upon amount of taxes at any time due or to become due, and payment in accordance with such agreement is full satisfaction of taxes to which agreement relates. (27-9-41).

Refunds.—Where it appears that an amount in excess of the true tax has been paid, such overpayment must be refunded by certificate of overpayment issued by the Commissioner to the State Auditor, which must be investigated and approved by the Attorney General, and the Auditor must issue his warrant on the Treasurer, which warrant must be paid out of any funds appropriated for that purpose. (27-9-49).

Enforcement of the act is by the State Tax Commissioner, at Jackson, who may make rules and regulations from time to time as he deems necessary. Copies of any rules and regulations, forms, receipts, discharges and certificates are obtained from Commissioner. (27-9-51).

Information Confidential.—It is unlawful for the members of the tax commission, or any deputy, agent, clerk, officer or employee, thereof, except in accordance with proper judicial order, to divulge or make known in any manner the value of any estate, or any particulars set forth or disclosed in any report or return. Any person violating this secrecy is guilty of a misdemeanor, and is subject to fine and/or imprisonment; and if offender be an officer or employee of state he is incapable of holding any public office in this state for a period of five years. Commissioner may, however, permit Commissioner of Internal Revenue of U.S., or of any state, by its proper officer, which is imposing a similar estate tax, to inspect estate tax return of any individual, or may furnish such officer an abstract of return for estate tax of any executor or administrator, or supply him with information concerning any item contained in any return disclosed by report of an executor or administrator; but such information may not be given unless U.S. or other state as case may be, grants substantially similar privileges to proper officer of this state charged with administration of estate tax law. (27-9-55, 27-9-57).

See note at head of Digest as to 1998 legislation covered.

See Topical Index in front part of this volume.

MS – 33

ESTATE TAX . . . *continued*

Final account of an executor may not be allowed until estate taxes have been paid. (27-9-41).

Duration of Tax.—The estate tax law is to be in effect as long as the Government of the United States retains federal estate tax in effect, and will be automatically repealed as and when the Government of the United States ceases to impose an estate tax. (27-9-59).

Apportionment Against Inter Vivos Dispositions.—No statutory provisions.

Interstate Cooperation.—No procedure for compromise of death taxes where decedent's domicile is disputed.

GASOLINE TAX:

Imposed by 27-55-1 et seq.; other motor fuel tax, 27-55-301 et seq.; lubricating oil tax, 27-57-1 et seq. (27-57-305, 311, 327, 329, 333, 335, 349, 355); other oils, 27-57-301 et seq.; liquefied compressed gas used as highway motor fuel, 27-59-1 et seq. Privilege tax imposed on motor fuels used over state highways by certain motor carriers, 27-61-3 et seq. (27-61-5, 27-61-9, 27-61-21). State tax commissioner responsible for administering and enforcing above taxes. (27-55-1, 27-55-53).

See category Transportation, topic Motor Vehicles, subhead Motor Vehicle Taxes.

GIFT TAX:

None.

INCOME TAX:

For each calendar year a tax is levied upon the net income (defined in 27-7-13) of every resident individual, corporation, association, trust or estate, in excess of certain credits provided for. (27-7-5). Every corporation subject to taxation shall file separate return except that affiliated corporations may elect or may be required in certain cases to file consolidated or combined return. (27-7-37).

Nonresidents.—In case of nonresident individuals, partnerships, trusts and estates, income from trade, business, or other commercial activity taxed to extent derived from such activity within this state. Taxable nonresident allowed personal deductions such as contributions to charitable organizations, medical expenses, taxes, interest and optional standard deduction in ratio that net income from sources within state bears to total net income from all sources of such taxable nonresident, computed as if such taxable nonresident were resident of Mississippi. (27-7-23).

Foreign Corporations and Other Organizations.—All business income of corporation allocated or apportioned as follows: (1) If business income of corporation is derived solely from property owned or business done in this state and corporation not taxable in another state, entire business income allocated to this state; (2) if business income of corporation is derived in part from property owned or business done in this state and in part from property owned or business done without this state and corporation is taxable both within and without this state, only that portion of business income attributable to property owned or business done within this state shall be allocated to this state. Income in like manner attributable to property owned or business done in another state shall be allocated to that state if taxable in that state. Business income derived from intangible property shall be treated as income from sources within this state if evidence of ownership of such property has acquired business, commercial or actual situs in this state. Business income derived from unitary multi-state activities which cannot be allocated to any state apportioned to this state by use of formula prescribed by commissioner. (27-7-23).

Deductions from Gross Income.—In arriving at net income, certain specified deductions can be taken or taxpayer may take optional standard deduction: Married individuals filing joint return $3,400 through calendar year 1997, $4,200 for calendar year 1998, and $4,600 for each calendar year thereafter; married individuals filing separate return $1,700 through calendar year 1997, $2,100 for calendar year 1998, and $2,300 for each calendar year thereafter; head of family $3,400; unmarried individual $2,300. (27-7-17). Gross income is defined in 27-7-15. Limitations on capital losses from sales or exchanges of capital assets provided for. (1991, c. 542). Employers may deduct contributions to plans or trusts for pension disability or related purposes. (27-7-17). Employee may deduct contributions to employees' pension trust, tax-sheltered annuity plan, authorized deferred compensation plan, self-employed retirement plan, individual retirement account (Roth or traditional IRA) or retirement bond provided plan meets IRS requirements. (27-7-16).

Exemptions are: Single individual $6,000; married individuals $9,500 through calendar year 1997, $10,000 for calendar year 1998, $11,000 for calendar year 1999, and $12,000 for each calendar year thereafter; head of family $9,500; $1,500 for each additional dependent; additional $1,500 for taxpayer or spouse over 65; additional $1,500 exemption for blind taxpayer or spouse; husband and wife filing combined returns may either designate one to take whole exemption or divide exemptions as they choose; husband and wife filing separate returns must equally divide exemptions. Nonresidents and part-year residents entitled to same exemptions as residents, but must prorate exemptions on basis of net income from Mississippi sources to total income. Married nonresident individual with spouse with independent income must file joint return; but where both spouses make income from Mississippi sources, they may file separate returns and divide exemptions. If one spouse resident and one not, treated as if both nonresidents. Exemption for estates, $600. Exemptions for trusts required to distribute current income, $300; all other trusts, $100. No specific exemptions for corporations, foundations, joint ventures or associations. (27-7-21). Earnings and principal of irrevocable trust forming part of a pension plan, stock bonus plan, disability or death benefit or profit-sharing plan of an employer for employees' exclusive benefit, are not taxable hereunder. Likewise exempted are trusts created under a retirement plan for which exemption has been provided under federal income tax. (27-7-27). Interest income on loans by foreign lenders other than insurance companies or foreign lenders qualified to do business in this state or which maintain office or place of business in this state secured by real estate located within state is exempt from state income tax. (27-7-23). Nonprofit mutual savings banks, religious, charitable, educational or scientific associations or institutions, labor organizations, chambers of commerce, civic leagues, nonprofit farming cooperatives, nonprofit electric power associations, and others, are exempt from state income tax. (27-7-29).

Rates applicable to income in excess of credits provided are: 3% on first $5,000 or part thereof; 4% on next $5,000; 5% on all taxable income in excess of $10,000. (27-7-5).

Payment.—Tax with interest, penalties, etc., is a personal debt of person liable to pay same. (27-7-7). Employers are required to deduct and withhold tax monthly.

Returns of individuals, estates, trusts and partnerships must be filed on or before 15th day of fourth month following close of fiscal year; or if return made on calendar year basis on or before Apr. 15. Returns of corporations must be filed on or before 15th day of third month following close of fiscal year; or if return filed on basis of calendar year on or before Mar. 15. Commissioner may grant reasonable extension of time where good cause shown or commissioner may automatically recognize extension authorized by IRS. (27-7-41).

Partners are liable for income tax only in their individual capacity, but if individual partners do not pay taxes on partnership income, then partnership and general partners are jointly and severally liable. (27-7-25). Partnership or S corporation must file income tax return annually. (27-7-29, 27-7-33).

Fiduciary must file income tax returns for individual, trusts or estate for whom he acts. (27-7-35).

Credit allowed individual resident taxpayers for taxes paid outside of state on business transacted or property held without state. (27-7-77). $1,000 credit per full-time employee allowed for any qualified business located in free enterprise zone. (27-7-22). Credit of 25% granted to employer sponsoring basic skills training or retraining programs through or approved by community college district in which employer is located. (57-23-25).

INHERITANCE TAX:

None. As to estate tax see topic Estate Tax.

LINT COTTON:

Subject to tax of one-fifth cent per pound by Mississippi Levee District.

MORTGAGE TAX:

None.

PROPERTY (AD VALOREM) TAXES:

Ad Valorem Tax Exemptions.—Following property is exempt from taxation: cemeteries; property of state or any subdivision thereof; property of units of Mississippi National Guard if not used for profit; property lawfully owned by religious society, ecclesiastical body, charitable society, historical or patriotic association, or garden or pilgrimage club not used for profit; property of college or institution for education of youths, provided land does not exceed 640 acres and provided institution is not commercial or trade school operated for profit; property used for operation of grammar school, junior high school, high school or private military school; property of fraternal or benevolent organization not used for profit; public school property; property of religious, charitable or benevolent organizations used for hospital purposes and nurses' homes; property of rural waterworks or sewage systems incorporated under 79-11-1; wearing apparel; jewelry to extent of $100 for each person; provisions on hand for family consumption; farm products for two years after harvesting (except tax on lint cotton by Mississippi Levee District) when owned by producer; lint cotton for five years and cottonseed, soybeans, oats, rice and wheat for one year regardless of ownership; guns and pistols; poultry; household furniture; cattle, oxen, sheep, goats, hogs, horses, mules and asses; farming implements; property of agricultural associations and fairs; libraries; pictures and works of art; tools of mechanics; state, county, municipal and school bonds; evidence of indebtedness issued by any church in state; notes and evidences of debt which bear a rate of interest not greater than maximum rate per annum applicable under law, and money loaned at rate not exceeding maximum rate per annum applicable under law; stocks and bonds of foreign corporations; property situated between Mississippi River and levee exempt from road taxes; money on deposit in banks; horse-drawn vehicles; boats and fishing equipment; materials used in construction or conversion of vessels; ships and drilling equipment while in possession of manufacturer, builder or converter for 12 months after completion of construction or conversion; 66⅔% of nuclear fuel and certain nuclear fuel by-products for generating electricity; leasehold interests in property belonging to state or certain political subdivisions thereof, which interests were created prior to July 1, 1984 and which had been exempted from ad valorem taxation prior to July 1, 1984; real or personal property used for housing or providing services to elderly, mentally impaired or disabled persons if not for profit corporation whose membership is appointed by religious society or ecclesiastical body. *Note:* This section was amended in 1998 to provide that watercraft used in connection with gaming operations are not exempt from ad valorem taxes. (27-31-1). Exemptions are permitted on trust funds created by employer as part of pension plan, disability or death-benefit or profit-sharing plan for benefit of employees. (71-1-43). Exemption in favor of charitable, religious, educational or civil institutions does not apply to lands, acquired by devise; such lands are taxable. (§270, Miss. Constitution of 1890). Property of little theatres, excepting motor vehicles, if nonprofit organizations, is exempt from ad valorem taxation. (27-31-5). Counties and municipalities have discretion to exempt from ad valorem taxation products owned by manufacturer, warehouse/distribution centers, research facilities, and other industries established by Department of Economic and Community Development located within their boundaries. (27-31-7, 27-31-101). Limited credits are permitted for any manufacturer, distributor, wholesale or retail merchant who pays to county, municipality, school district or any other taxing authority, ad valorem taxes imposed on commodities, products, goods, wares held for resale. (1994, c. 304, §1). Any single-family dwelling of which construction completed on or after Jan. 1, 1983 exempt from ad valorem taxation until first leased, rented, sold

See note at head of Digest as to 1998 legislation covered.

See Topical Index in front part of this volume.

MS – 34

PROPERTY (AD VALOREM) TAXES . . . *continued*
or occupied. (27-31-29). Municipalities given discretion to grant exemption from ad valorem taxes for new structures or improvements to or renovations of existing structures located in municipality's central business district for not more than ten years from completion date. (27-31-31). Private railroads are exempt from local ad valorem taxes but pay sum assessed by State Tax Commission. (27-35-515). Amount received from public employment retirement in excess of $6,000 is exempt. (25-11-129).

No exemptions granted solely for members of armed forces or veterans.

Homestead.—Resident head of family is allowed an exemption of homestead to extent of $7,500 from specified ad valorem taxes. If person has use and possession of home by divorce decree, that person is eligible for full exemption, regardless of whether property is jointly owned. (27-33-19). Head of family who is 65 or over or veteran with 100% service-connected disability or one classified as disabled under Federal Social Security Act exempt from all ad valorem taxes on homestead not in excess of $7,500. (27-33-3). Exemption is denied to one claiming immunity from, or not complying with, state income tax or road and privilege tax laws. (27-33-63).

New Enterprises.—Certain specified new advanced technology businesses, new factories and new enterprises of public utilities may, upon application, be exempted by county and municipal authorities from ad valorem taxation on tangible property used in or necessary to operation of service or industry, but not upon products or vehicles or trucks operating on Miss. highways. Ad valorem taxes for school district purposes are excepted from such exemption. Both county and municipal exemption may not exceed ten years from date of completion of new enterprise. (27-31-101). Exemptions for expansions and additions to such facilities are also obtainable within discretion of county and municipal authorities. (27-31-103, 27-31-105, 27-31-107).

New Structures and Renovations.—Authorities of municipalities with populations of more than 25,000 may, upon application, grant exemption from municipal ad valorem taxes, excluding those levied for school district purposes, to privately owned new structures and new renovations or improvements to existing structures lying within designated central business districts, where such construction, renovation or improvement is made pursuant to requirements of approved urban renewal projects. Such exemption shall in no event be granted for period of more than seven years. Authorities of counties containing such municipalities may similarly grant exemptions from county ad valorem taxes under same circumstances and restrictions. (17-21-5).

Nonprofit Industrial Corporations.—Certain unimproved real property owned by nonprofit industrial corporations, foundations or associations may be exempted by county and municipal authorities from ad valorem taxation. Such exemptions are granted on annual basis and may be terminated as to any year subsequent to their being granted. (17-21-1).

Timber.—All growing, standing timber is exempt from ad valorem tax, and exemption continues after severance while timber remains in unmanufactured condition and while title not in manufacturer or processor. (27-25-27).

Assessment.—Each person must render a verified list of his taxable property as of Jan. 1 of each year to tax assessor, who compiles his roll of both real and personal property. Land rolls and personal rolls are compiled annually. (27-35-47, 27-35-49). Board of Supervisors can by order declare current land assessment roll to be in force for one additional year. However, such roll is subject to objections and must be approved as new roll. (27-35-133). Board's assessment of county ad valorem taxes to be filed before Sept. 15, but if incomplete or not approved by Commission by following Feb. 1, Board may amend. (27-39-317). Tax assessor is authorized to assess persons or property escaping taxes for preceding years for period of seven years from date when right so to do first accrued. (27-35-155).

Assessment ratios for taxable property for ad valorem tax purposes are as follows: Class I real property, assessed at 10% of true value. Class II property, assessed at 15% of true value. Class III property, assessed at 15% of true value. Class IV and Class V property, assessed at 30% of true value. (27-35-4).

Review of Assessment.—Any person dissatisfied with assessment must present his objection in writing during month of July. Assessment will become final if no objection is made. (27-35-83, 27-35-87, 27-35-89, 27-35-93, 27-35-135).

An appeal lies from a tax assessment, if taken within ten days from the adjournment of the meeting at which a final decision was made, if a bond is given for double the amount in dispute, but in no case for less than $100. (11-51-77).

Payment.—Taxes generally are due on or before Feb. 1, but may be paid one-half on Feb. 1, one-fourth on May 1 and one-fourth on July 1. (27-41-1). Interest at 1% per month is charged on taxes not paid by Feb. 1. If Feb. 1 falls on weekend, tax is due on next business day. (27-41-9).

Collection.—Increases, penalties and interest accrued are recoverable as a part of the tax with respect to which they are imposed and constitute a debt due the state or municipality. (27-41-15, 27-75-3).

Lien.—Taxes assessed upon land become lien as of Jan. 1; personal property except motor vehicles and heavy duty equipment as of Mar. 1; taxes assessed on stock of goods or merchandise based on value of inventory on Jan. 1 of year or average monthly inventory during preceding 12 months from Jan. 1 of each year; tax lien attaches to all heavy duty equipment when brought into or situated in state. As to lands owned by state, which lands leased to private agricultural enterprises, tax lien attaches at time crop harvested. (27-35-1). The tax levied is a debt and may be recovered by action. See category Transportation, topic Motor Vehicles, subhead Motor Vehicle Taxes.

Enrolled Lien.—After accrual of tax liability, Commissioner may file certificate with circuit clerk for entry upon judgment roll, and same becomes judgment lien from the time of filing. (27-7-55,-57).

Tax lien is given preference over all judgments, executions, encumbrances, or liens, whensoever created. Taxes on stock of goods or merchandise are a lien regardless of changes in those items. (27-35-1).

Sales.—If real property taxes are not paid when due, auction sales of property are held on 1st Monday in Apr. and 3d Monday in Sept. of each year. (27-41-55). Property not bid on by any individual is struck off to state. Collector may enforce payment of personal property taxes by distress and sale. (27-41-15).

Tax-Forfeited Land Sold.—The Land Commissioner, with the approval of the Governor, may sell such land for such price as the Land Commissioner and the Attorney General may fix, taking into consideration the value of the land, but the minimum price for which it may be sold is $2 per acre. (29-1-33).

Holders of liens against land to be sold for taxes must be sent notice by certified mail. (27-43-5).

Presumption of Validity of Forfeited Tax Land Patent.—When forfeited tax land patent has been issued by the state for at least ten years and the patentee has paid the consideration fixed by the commission and all taxes accruing and payable subsequent to the issuance of patent, it is presumed that the patentee paid the valid, legal and adequate consideration therefor, complied with all the requirements of law and practiced no fraud upon the state, and that such patent is a valid and legal patent. The state is forever precluded from questioning the validity of such patent. (29-1-115).

Presumption of Lost Patent.—Where tax-forfeited land has been certified to the state for more than 25 years and there is no record that a patent issued, there arises a presumption that said land has been duly patented out of the state if taxes to the state and county have been paid on said land for each year for the past ten years. The Land Commissioner, with the consent of the Attorney General, is authorized to strike such sale under such condition, upon application by the one claiming title, and such striking operates as a disclaimer of any right, title or interest which the state has in such land. (29-1-113).

Suits to recover any privilege, income, franchise, or other excise tax, and applications for refund or credit, must be filed or made within three years after return filed, or assessment made, or tax paid, whichever is the earlier. Income tax limitation is six years where reported net income has been reduced by Bureau of Internal Revenue. (27-73-5).

Tax Titles.—Actual occupancy of land by tax purchaser for three years after two years from date of sale for taxes bars any suit to recover such land or assail title thereto because of any defect in sale or in steps leading up thereto, except that minors and persons of unsound mind may sue within two years after removal of disability. (15-1-15).

Removal of Cloud.—One claiming title to land under a tax sale may file suit to remove any clouds from such tax title, and may include as a defendant any political subdivision of the state having or asserting any evidence or claim of title adverse to such tax title. (11-17-31).

Action to cancel tax title of state or its patentees to land sold to state for taxes can be brought in Chancery Court, but must be brought within two years after time for redemption has expired, except where taxes were actually paid or owner is under disability. (15-1-17). This limitation has been held inapplicable where possession has not changed after tax sale. (182 Miss. 385, 182 So. 102; 188 Miss. 771, 196 So. 227).

Redemption.—Land sold for unpaid taxes may be redeemed within two years from date of sale, and person under disability has a like period after removal of disability, except that this saving to minors is only as to land inherited or acquired by will. (27-45-3).

In order to redeem, owner, lien holder or person interested must pay to chancery clerk amount of taxes for which land was sold with costs incident to sale, 5% damages on amount of taxes, interest on taxes and costs at 1% per month from date of sale, and all taxes and costs that have accrued since sale with interest from date such taxes accrued at 1½% per month. On such payment, clerk will execute release of claim or title of state or purchaser, which instrument may be recorded as deeds are recorded. (27-45-1, 27-45-3).

REAL ESTATE CONVEYANCE TAX:

None except where oil and gas interests involved. (27-25-501 et seq.).

STAMP TAX:

No requirement of documentary stamps on corporate stock or other instruments.

UNEMPLOYMENT COMPENSATION TAX:

Unemployment compensation tax, termed "contributions," is imposed on all employers who for some portion of a day in each of 20 different weeks in either current or preceding year employ or employed one or more individuals or paid $1,500 or more in wages in any calendar quarter after 12-31-71. (71-5-11). Statutory rate is 4%, 5.4% or 2.7% depending on certain conditions; but statute contemplates that rates may be based on benefit experience. (71-5-353). Employer must report all wages paid, but no tax is payable on compensation in excess of $6,000 to any employee during calendar year. Contributions must not be deducted from wages of employees, and no contribution is required of any employee. Contributions are payable to Mississippi Unemployment Compensation Commission which is charged with administration of law. By rule of Commission, contributions are payable quarterly on or before last day of Jan., Apr., July and Sept. following close of preceding quarter.

UNIFORM FEDERAL LIEN REGISTRATION ACT:

Adopted. (§85-8-1 et seq.).

USE TAX:

Compensating (or Use) Tax at rates imposed under 27-65-17, 27-65-19, 27-65-23, 27-65-25 for privilege of using, storing or consuming within this state, any article of tangible personal property, either purchased at retail, or acquired by gift, or extracted or produced or manufactured for use, by person so doing same. It applies to property acquired at casual or isolated sale, and including by-products used by manufacturer thereof, and tangible personal property withdrawn from stock for consumption by user within this state. Tax applies to persons receiving benefits for services rendered for which charge is made, including persons receiving benefits from services of cleaning, pressing, dyeing or laundering. Tax applies to any vehicle, operation of which requires payment of road and bridge privilege tax (license tag) and is computed on full delivered sales price of vehicle without any deduction for amount allowed for trade-in. Tax is not applicable on use, storage, or consumption of any tangible personal property or service

See note at head of Digest as to 1998 legislation covered.

See Topical Index in front part of this volume.

MS – 35

USE TAX ... *continued*

whereon sales tax has been paid or where subject is specifically exempt from sales tax, or where property is brought into state by individual nonresident for personal and temporary use; or on use, storage or consumption of literature, videotapes and slides used by religious institution, and on use of any tangible personal property purchased and first used in another state by religious institutions; or for use of motor vehicles or personal and household effects purchased by individual while bona fide nonresident, or on use of busses or common carriers paying 3% highway privilege license tax, or on rental of motion picture film by person paying state amusement tax or one operating television broadcasting station; or on use of natural gas owned and consumed by pipeline from its own lines as fuel to operate compressor stations and other facilities necessary to marketing of gas, or on charges or amounts paid for use if motor vehicles and equipment by common carriers which have no permanent situs in this state and which are used exclusively in interstate commerce. Mississippi tag for vehicle purchased by member of armed forces in another state while stationed there is not subject to tax. Tax is payable to Chairman of State Tax Commission before 20th day of succeeding month. (27-67-1 et seq.).

TRANSPORTATION

MOTOR VEHICLES:

Supervision.—Supervising authority is State Tax Commission, P.O. Box 960, Jackson, MS 39205.

Vehicle license required annually. Number plate must be displayed in rear only. Unlawful to deface, cover or obstruct license tag. (27-19-31). Fleets governed separately. (27-19-66). License tags are issued for five years. License decals are issued each intervening year. (27-19-31).

No exemption for members of armed forces.

Operator's license required for all operators except operators of motor vehicles of armed forces or road machinery and tractors and nonresidents (see infra, subhead Nonresident Operators). (63-1-5, 63-1-7). Separate endorsement or restricted motorcycle operator's license required for operators of motorcycles. (63-1-6). Learner's permit good for 60 days may be obtained upon payment of $1 fee. (63-1-21). Special provision applies for renewal of driver's license issued to certain persons going overseas. (63-1-49). Federal Commercial Motor Vehicle Safety Act of 1986 implemented as Miss. Commercial Driver's License Law. (63-1-73). License not issued to person under 16 years old, to persons under 18 years old who have not met certain education requirements, habitual drunkard or narcotic addict or person physically or mentally incapacitated. (63-1-9). Operator's license from any state may be deposited with arresting officer in lieu of other security to insure driver's appearance in court for offense against motor vehicle laws. (63-9-25). By operating vehicle on public road, operator gives his implied consent to breathalyzer test to determine alcohol content of blood. (63-11-5). Operator's license revoked upon conviction of certain offenses. (63-1-51). Person less than 21 but at least 17 years of age may be issued commercial driver's license which restricts him to driving commercial motor vehicles on intrastate highways only. (63-1-79).

Titles and Sales.—Certificate of title obtained from State Tax Commission for all motor vehicles manufactured or assembled after July 1, 1969 or subject of first sale for use after July 1, 1969; also required for motor vehicle sold by dealer after July 1, 1969; voluntary applications may be made for any model. (63-21-9). On sale, assignment and warranty of title must be executed on certificate and transferee apply for new certificate. (63-21-31). Seller furnishes buyer signed bill of sale, showing make, model, vehicle identification number, other identifying marks, seller's address, name and address of person from whom seller purchased. (63-17-1). Fee for recording, 50¢. Fee for purchasing certified copy, 50¢. (63-17-3).

Persons or corporations in business of purchasing retail installment contracts involving motor vehicles and retail sellers engaged in business of creating and holding retail installment contracts involving motor vehicles aggregating an amount in excess of $500,000 must secure a license from State Department of Banking and Consumer Finance. (63-19-1 et seq.). Maximum finance charge for credit sale of motor vehicles (including commercial motor vehicles), graduated from 18%, excluding surcharge, for new vehicle manufactured in same year or year prior to year in which sale occurred, to 28.75% per year for used vehicles manufactured more than four years prior to year in which sale made. (63-19-43). Violations of provisions of "The Motor Vehicle Sales Finance Law" result in severe penalties. (63-19-55).

Manufacturer's Sales.—Motor Vehicle Commission Act creates eight man commission to license manufacturers, distributors, factory representatives, wholesalers, dealers, salesmen and carry out prohibitions against impositions on dealers. Commission has rule making power to carry out Act subject to 30 days written notice of proposed rule to affected persons within or without State. (63-17-57, et seq.).

Specifically, no manufacturer or his agent can order dealers to: (a) Accept goods not voluntarily ordered; (b) order or accept any vehicles with any special features not included in list price; (c) order any goods for any person; or (d) contribute anything to any cooperative or advertising program. (63-17-73).

Act forbids: (a) Refusal to deliver vehicles covered by franchise agreement represented to be available for delivery; (b) coercion to enter agreement by threatening cancellation of franchise, exclusive of good faith notice of violation of terms of contract agreement; (c) termination of franchise of dealer without good cause; (d) discrimination between dealers on price of new vehicles or parts, excluding volume discounts if equally available; (e) restriction of reasonable changes in capital structure or sale of part dealers interest, except sale of franchise. (63-17-73).

Appropriate provision made for hearings on violations. Civil damages actions authorized by licensee suffering pecuniary loss because of willful failure to comply by other licensee. (63-17-51 et seq.).

Liens.—See categories Business Regulation and Commerce, topic Sales; Mortgages, topic Chattel Mortgages, subhead Motor Vehicles.

Identification Marks.—Misdemeanor to alter or remove serial numbers or other identification marks of maker or knowingly to deal with or possess car so altered. (63-17-11, 63-17-13).

Felony to change or mutilate any identification number on any motor vehicle or farm implement for purpose of depriving true owner of possession thereof, or to have knowledge of and fail to report such changing or mutilating.

Odometer.—Unlawful to alter or disconnect odometer or misrepresent actual mileage. (63-7-203).

Operation Prohibited.—By intoxicated person. By unlicensed person, except nonresident. By any person under influence of narcotic drugs. (63-1-7, 63-1-9). See infra, subhead Nonresident Operators.

Size and Weight Limits.—Regulated by 63-5-13—63-5-43, 63-5-49, 63-5-51, 27-19-89.

Equipment Required.—Regulated by 63-7-65, 63-7-55—63-7-59, 63-7-69—63-7-71, 63-7-63.

Seat Belts Required.—Operator and front-seat passenger must wear seat belts. Violation along with conviction of other offense constitutes misdemeanor. (63-2-7). No additional duty, standard of care or liability created between operator and passenger. Failure to provide and use seat belt not considered contributory or comparative negligence. Violation not entered on individual driving record. (§§63-2-1-,-3,-7).

Child Restraints.—Must be used for children under age of four. (63-7-301). Fine for violation. (63-7-309).

Lights Required.—Regulated by 63-7-11 et seq.

Inspection.—Annual inspection of all motor vehicles and display of certificate required. (63-13-5—63-13-11).

Traffic Regulations.—Regulated by 63-3-1 et seq.

Accidents.—Driver must stop, give assistance if necessary, give name, address and registration number of vehicle, exhibit operator's license and, where accident results in injury, death or property damage of $100 or more, he shall give notice to local authorities. If there is personal injury or damage of $250 or more, driver must file written report to Dept. of Public Safety within ten days. (63-3-401—63-3-411; 63-3-423). Report is confidential, except upon written request of involved person or his estate representative. (63-3-417). Any person who in good faith renders emergency care to injured person at accident is not liable for damages resulting from such acts. (63-3-405).

Liability of Owner.—Owner liable for negligence of others only when present in car or car operated by his servant or agent within scope of authority and duty.

Guests.—There is no statute restricting liability for injury to a guest.

Proof of Financial Responsibility.—Operator of every motor vehicle involved in accident in this state in which person is killed or injured or damage to property occurs in excess of $250 must within ten days report matter, in writing, to Department of Public Safety. Report must contain information to enable said Department to determine whether person responsible for accident has ability to respond in damages for liability. (63-15-9). If 20 days after receipt of said report, Department does not have satisfactory evidence that person is financially responsible, Department must determine amount of security which will be sufficient in its judgment to satisfy any judgment for damages resulting from such accident. (63-15-11).

If the person causing the accident is not financially responsible, Department must within 60 days after receipt of above report suspend licenses of each operator and all registrations of each owner, and, if operator is nonresident, privilege of operating motor vehicles within this state unless such operators or owners deposit security in sum determined by Department and notice of suspension must be sent. (63-15-11[2]). Person receiving notice has right to hearing, with right of appeal from hearing. (63-15-11[3]).

The above action does not apply under the following conditions: (1) if such operator or owner had in effect at the time of such accident a liability policy with respect to the motor vehicle involved in the accident; (2) if the operator of such motor vehicle had in effect at such time a liability policy with respect to the operation of the motor vehicle not owned by him; (3) if such operator or owner is, in the judgment of the Department, covered by any other form of liability insurance policy or bond of an authorized surety company; (4) to any person qualifying as self-insurer under Act; (5) to owner or operator of motor vehicle legally parked at time of accident; (6) to owner of vehicle if stolen at time of accident; or (7) to any person whom department has found in hearing is not reasonably probable to have judgment rendered against him in action arising out of accident. Insurance provided for must afford at least 10-20-5 coverage. (63-15-11[4]).

Further exceptions to requirements as to security and suspension are as follows: (1) Where there was no injury or damage caused to person or property of another; or (2) if prior to date of suspension there is satisfactory evidence filed with department that person otherwise due to file security has been finally adjudicated not liable or has executed acknowledged written agreement for payment of agreed amount in installments, on any injury or damage claim resulting from accident. (63-15-13).

Insurance.—Not specifically required if financially responsible.

Automobile liability, property or collision policies insuring single individual or husband and wife resident in Mississippi may not be canceled or denied renewal except under specified conditions.

Notice of cancellation of policy effective only if based on: (a) Nonpayment of premium; (b) suspension or revocation of driver's license of named insured or operator residing in same household during policy period or 180 days immediately preceding effective date; (c) failure to pay dues to or maintain membership in designated association when original issuance dependent on membership.

Restrictions on cancellation not to apply to any new policy in effect less than 60 days when notice of cancellation made. Inclusion of $100 deductible is not cancellation. Notice of cancellation not effective unless mailed to named insured 20 days before effective date of cancellation.

No insurer shall fail to renew a policy unless insured is given 30 days notice by mail at address shown on policy. This stipulation will not apply if: (a) Insurer has agreed to

See note at head of Digest as to 1998 legislation covered.

See Topical Index in front part of this volume.

MOTOR VEHICLES . . . *continued*

renew subject to unmet conditions; (b) insured has shown unwillingness to renew; (c) premiums are in arrears; or (d) failure to pay dues to association as in (c) above.

Notice of cancellation other than for nonpayment of premium should apprise named insured of possible eligibility for liability insurance under assigned risk. Notice of reason for cancellation must be forwarded within five days of request of named insured. No cause of action can arise for statements made in any written notice of cancellation, etc.

Persons desiring to contest reasons for cancellation or nonrenewal will, within seven working days after notice of cancellation, file written request for hearing and $15 fee with Commissioner stating basis for appeal. Upon seven days notice Commissioner to call hearing at conclusion of which he shall issue written findings.

If Commissioner or his designate finds for insured, he orders notice of cancellation rescinded; or if effective date has passed, orders policy reinstated. Such order operates retroactively for 20 days from date cancellation would otherwise have been effective and prospectively from date of order. Reinstatement by order does not extend expiration or anniversary date.

Within 60 days of decision either party may appeal to Chancery Court for trial de novo. (83-11-1 et seq.).

See subhead Proof of Financial Responsibility, supra.

No-Fault Insurance.—No statutes have been adopted.

Foreign Vehicles.—Owner of vehicle licensed in another state, not transporting persons or property for hire, must, within 30 days after entering state, make application for license to State Auditor, through county tax collector.

This requirement does not apply to privately owned vehicles used by resident of adjoining state who is tourist, out-of-town student or engaged in seasonal agricultural work. (27-19-63).

For operation of a commercial vehicle of two tons or more capacity, there is a flat privilege fee on a mileage basis. Before operating in state, privilege must be procured direct from State Auditor or by application to tax collector or inspection station of first county entered.

Noncompliance with Act carries penalties. (27-19-57, 27-19-63, 27-19-89, 27-19-131). Trip permits authorized on payment of privilege tax. (27-19-79).

Nonresident operators may operate in this state for not over 60 days without local license if (a) over 18 years of age and duly licensed by home state or country, or (b) home state or country does not require operator's license. (63-1-7).

Actions Against Nonresidents.—Acceptance by nonresident of privilege of operating motor vehicle in state is equivalent to appointment of Secretary of State as his attorney, on whom service of process or summons may be made in any action growing out of operation of vehicle in state. Service is made by delivery of copy to Secretary of State or his office and a copy is sent to defendant (or to personal representative of estate in event of nonresident's death) by registered mail, which, together with affidavit and return registry receipt, is equivalent to personal service. Also applies to anyone who is nonresident when action is commenced even though said person was resident at time action accrued. (13-3-63). See category Civil Actions and Procedure, topic Process.

Direct actions not permitted.

Motor vehicle carriers are regulated by Public Service Commission and must obtain license and certificate of public convenience and necessity. Vehicles transporting passengers must provide liability insurance with minimum limits of $100,000/$300,000/$25,000; and vehicles transporting property must provide liability insurance with minimum limits of $100,000/$300,000/$20,000 and $5,000 cargo liability up to three tons and $10,000 cargo liability for more than three tons. (77-7-83). Failure to comply with insurance requirements shall be cause for revocation or suspension of certificate or permit, or for imposition of fine not exceeding $1,000, or both. (77-7-93).

Motor vehicles operated for hire in any city or town must carry liability insurance with minimum limits of $10,000/$20,000/$10,000. (21-27-133).

Motor Vehicle Taxes.—Ad valorem tax, payable with license tag fee, is imposed upon motor vehicles. (29-19-48, 27-51-1 et seq.). Exemptions set forth 27-51-41.

Privilege tax is imposed on the operation of trailers and semitrailers upon state highways. (27-19-17).

Prorated refund may be obtained for unexpired part of annual privilege tax or annual permit if motor vehicle damaged to extent that it is unusable or if compressed gas carburation equipment removed. (27-59-35).

Highway privilege tax is levied annually upon each carrier of property with exception of carrier who is licensed outside the state and who transports harvesting equipment to and from a particular county in this state during a certain period. Rate is specified in a statutory schedule. (27-19-11). Highway privilege taxes for three, six or 12 mo. periods assessed at rate set forth in 27-19-11 on basis of 35%, 60%, 100% respectively. (27-19-64). Highway privilege tax is levied annually on common carriers. (27-19-7). No privilege tax imposed for vehicles owned by U.S. or Mississippi governments or their agencies. (27-19-27).

Gasoline Tax.—See category Taxation, topic Gasoline Tax.

Lemon Law.—See category Business Regulation and Commerce, topic Consumer Protection.

MISSOURI LAW DIGEST REVISER

Swanson, Midgley, Gangwere, Kitchin & McLarney, LLC.
Commerce Trust Building, Suite 1500
922 Walnut
Kansas City, Missouri 64106-1848
Telephone: 816-842-6100
Fax: 816-842-0013

Reviser Profile

Our Practice—Areas of Emphasis and Growth: Swanson Midgley is a full service law firm with a primary emphasis in litigation and business matters. In recent years, the firm has represented clients in a number of complex, multi-party litigation matters, including cases involving school desegregation, television antitrust, bankruptcy, securities fraud, business fraud, insurance and products liability, construction litigation, and RICO claims. As general counsel for The National Collegiate Athletic Association, the firm is involved in sports litigation across the country. For many years, Swanson Midgley has had a strong insurance defense practice, with particular emphasis on the field of life, health, and disability insurance law where it has represented many insurance clients for more than 50 years and the Prudential Insurance Company of America since before the turn of the century.

The firm's practice is complemented by subspecialties in municipal law, corporate and commercial law, bankruptcy, insolvency and reorganization, sports law, workers compensation, antitrust, tax, employee benefits, labor and employee relations, securities, real estate, estate planning and probate. This comprehensive approach to the practice of law coupled with the personal attention given to client matters has made Swanson Midgley particularly well suited to meet the needs of virtually any client.

Tradition: Swanson, Midgley, Gangwere, Kitchin & McLarney, LLC. is one of the oldest law firms in Kansas City. The firm was founded in 1886 by two graduates of the University of Michigan School of Law, Delbert J. Haff and Arba S. Van Valkenburgh. The firm's long and distinguished record of service to the community began in its earliest years. Mr. Haff, as legal counsel and then President of the Park Board of Kansas City, was instrumental in the creation of the City's much admired park and boulevard system. Mr. Van Valkenburgh served as the United States Attorney for the Western District of Missouri, and later as United States District and Circuit Judge. Today, the two Michigan graduates' firm consists of 20+ lawyers who utilize traditional talents and the latest technology to serve client needs.

Professional Development: Swanson Midgley believes strongly in continued professional study and career development. In addition to paying enrollment costs and expenses for lawyers to attend outside continuing legal education courses, the firm has an in-house continuing legal education program. Associates participate in a comprehensive trial practice program developed by the National Institute of Trial Advocacy. This program is conducted by members experienced in litigation. Members of the firm have co-authored several books. In addition, Swanson Midgley attorneys have contracted with West Publishing Company and other publishers to act as authors and consultants on legal texts, treatises and form books.

Service to the Community and the Bar: Members of Swanson Midgley have continued to serve their state and city with distinction. Two former members of the firm have served on the Missouri Supreme Court. Other members of the firm have served as presidents of the Kansas City Board of Education, as members of the Kansas City Board of Police Commissioners, and as the leaders of numerous civic, social and charitable organizations. A few recent examples of civic involvement include Mr. George Gangwere's Presidency of the Friends of the Zoo, Mr. Robert W. McKinley's leadership as President of the Men's Division of the Philharmonic, and Mr. Richard Bien's work as President of Kansas City Corporate Challenge.

The firm has also been well represented in national, state and local bar organizations. Mr. Richard Bien has served on several American Bar Association task forces and councils and is currently serving on the Board of Governors of The Missouri Bar. Mr. Roy Swanson, a member of the firm from 1927 until his death in 1985, was a past President of the Missouri Bar. Mr. John Black is also a past President and Mr. George Gangwere served on the Board of Governors. Mr. Swanson, Mr. Gangwere and Mr. Kenneth Midgley all served as Presidents of the Lawyers Association of Kansas City.

Management: Swanson Midgley is managed by a three-person executive committee. Through regular practice area group meetings, the firm monitors case management, attorney performance, client relationship and case disposition. The three managing members' activities are supplemented by the activities of five directors in charge of finance, marketing, human resources, professional services and long-range planning.

MISSOURI LAW DIGEST REVISER

Swanson, Midgley, Gangwere, Kitchin & McBratney, LLC.
Commerce Trust Building, Suite 1500
922 Walnut
Kansas City, Missouri 64106-1845
Telephone: 816-842-6100
Fax: 816-842-0013

Reviser Profile

MISSOURI LAW DIGEST

(The following is a list of all Categories and Topics, including cross-references, covered in this Digest.)

MISSOURI LAW DIGEST

Revised for 1999 edition by

SWANSON, MIDGLEY, GANGWERE, KITCHIN & McLARNEY, LLC., of the Kansas City Bar.

(References, unless otherwise noted, are to sections of Missouri Revised Statutes 1986 and 1993 Cumulative Supplement. "c." denotes chapter of statutes. "C.R." denotes section of Missouri Rules of Civil Procedure. Parallel citations to the South Western Reporter begin with 89 Mo. and 94 Mo. App., and end with 365 Mo. and 241 Mo. App., after which South Western Reporter is only reporter.)

Note: All acts of 1998 legislature included.

INTRODUCTION

GOVERNMENT AND LEGAL SYSTEM:

The State of Missouri is a constituent state of the United States of America. For further discussion of the U.S. federal system, see Introduction to the Federal Government of the United States at the beginning of this volume. A great many laws are promulgated by the federal government of the United States and are not reflected in the topics below. See the Introduction to this volume for references to the federal law topics covered.

Like all but one of the United States, Missouri has a common law legal system, with roots in English common law. For information on the courts and legislature of Missouri, see category Courts and Legislature.

HOLIDAYS:

Public holidays are Jan. 1, 3d Mon. in Jan., Feb. 12, 3d Mon. in Feb., May 8, last Mon. in May, July 4, 1st Mon. in Sept., 2d Mon. in Oct., Nov. 11, 4th Thurs. in Nov. and Dec. 25. When any such holiday falls on Sun., the Mon. next following shall be considered holiday. (9.010).

OFFICE HOURS AND TIME ZONE:

Missouri is in the Central (GMT −6:00) time zone. Office hours are generally from 9 a.m. to 5 p.m.

BUSINESS ORGANIZATIONS

AGENCY:

A principal is bound by the acts of his agent within the scope of his employment. Notice to agent is usually notice to principal. Undisclosed principal may sue or be sued, or the aggrieved party may elect to sue the agent.

ASSOCIATIONS:

No provision as to organization of unincorporated associations. See topic Corporations.

CORPORATIONS:

Special provisions are made for the following classes of corporations: railroad companies; motor carriers, contract haulers, and express companies; street railroads; telegraph and telephone companies; manufacturing and business companies; gas, electricity, and water companies; bridge companies; mutual savings funds; building and loan associations; co-operative companies; benevolent, religious, scientific, educational, and miscellaneous associations; booming and rafting companies; loan and investment companies; exposition companies; training schools for minors; police and firemen's relief associations; not-for-profit corporations; development finance corporations; farming corporations.

General supervision is vested in Secretary of State of Missouri, Jefferson City, Mo. 65101. (Const. Art IV, §14).

Purposes.—Corporations for profit, except those which are required to be organized exclusively under other provisions of law, may be organized under this chapter for any lawful purposes. (351.020).

Name must contain word "company," "corporation," "incorporated," "limited," or conclude with abbreviation of one of such words and may not include any word or phrase which indicates or implies that it is governmental agency and it must be distinguishable from name of any domestic corporation, foreign corporation, limited partnership, or limited liability company existing or authorized to transact business in Missouri or name exclusive right to which is reserved at time. If name is same, word must be added to make name distinguishable from name of such other corporation, limited liability company or limited partnership. (351.110). Secretary of state has adopted policy refusing common name unless nature of business included.

Availability.—Secretary of state in response to written or telephone request will advise if name is available. No fee is charged for service. However, availability is not unconditional unless reserved.

Reservation.—Name reserved by filing in office of secretary of state application to reserve specified corporate name executed by applicant and payment of $20 fee. Blank forms for reserving names are available from secretary of state. If name available for corporate use secretary of state must reserve same for exclusive use of applicant for period of 60 days. Right to exclusive use of reserved name may be transferred by filing in office of secretary of state notice of transfer executed by person for whom such name was reserved and specifying name and address of transferee. (351.115).

Incorporators.—One or more natural persons of age of 18 years, or more, may act as an incorporator. All of stock may be owned by one owner. (351.050).

Term of Corporate Existence.—Any number of years or perpetual. (351.055). If at time of expiration it held title in real estate or did not suspend its lawful business, charter may be revived within two years on payment of fee of $50. (351.542).

Articles of incorporation must set forth: (a) name of corporation; (b) address, including street and number, if any, of initial registered office in this state, and name of initial registered agent at such address; (c) aggregate number of shares which the corporation will have authority to issue, number of shares of each class, if any, that are to have a par value and par value of each share of each such class, number of shares of each class, if any, that are to be without par value and statement of preferences, qualifications, limitations, restrictions and special or relative rights, including convertible rights, if any, in respect of shares of each class; (d) extent, if any, to which preemptive right of shareholder to acquire additional shares is limited or denied; (e) name and place of residence of each incorporator; (f) either (i) number of directors to constitute first board of directors and statement to effect that thereafter number of directors shall be fixed by, or in manner provided in, bylaws of corporation, and that any changes shall be reported to secretary of state within 30 calendar days of such change, or (ii) number of directors to constitute board of directors, except that number of directors to constitute board of directors must be stated in articles of incorporation if corporation is to have less than three directors. Persons to constitute first board of directors may, but need not, be named; (g) term of existence, which may be any number of years or perpetual; (h) purposes for which corporation is formed; (i) any other provisions, not inconsistent with law, which incorporators may choose to insert. (351.055).

Execution and Filing of Articles.—Articles, in duplicate, signed and verified by incorporators, are delivered to office of Secretary of State of Missouri, Jefferson City, Mo. 65101. If approved, he files them when organization taxes or fees are paid, retains one copy as permanent record, issues certificate of incorporation, attaches same to other copy, and delivers them to incorporators. (351.060). Blank forms for articles of incorporation are available from secretary of state.

Form

Verification must be in form substantially as follows:

STATE OF . . . .
COUNTY OF . . . . } SS

I, ..., a notary public, do hereby certify that on the . . . . . day of . . . ., 19. . . . . ., personally appeared before me . . . . (and . . . .,) who being by me first duly sworn, (severally) declared that he is (they are) the person(s) who signed the foregoing document as incorporator(s), and that the statements therein contained are true.

. . . .
Notary Public

(NOTARIAL SEAL) (351.051).

Commencement of Business.—Corporate existence dates from time of filing its articles with Secretary of State. (351.075).

Certificate of Authority.—Certificate given by Secretary of State shall be taken by all courts of this state as evidence of corporate existence of such corporation. (351.075).

State fee for issuing certificate of incorporation is $50 for first $30,000 or less of capital stock, plus $5 for every additional $10,000. Fee on increase of capital stock is $5 for each $10,000 or fraction thereof. Dollar amount of authorized shares is par value thereof or, for no par value stock, $1 per share. In addition a $3 charge is assessed for an attested copy, which is automatically sent. (351.065).

As to qualification fee of foreign corporation, see infra, subhead Foreign Corporations.

Fees of Secretary of State are charged for most services. However, no charge is made for information relating to a corporation's registered agent.

Amendment of Articles.—At any time or times before corporation has received any payment for any shares, board of directors may adopt amendments to articles of incorporation by executing and verifying certificate of amendment. (351.090).

After corporation has received any payment for any shares, amendments to articles of incorporation must be made only in following manner: (a) Board of directors may adopt resolution setting forth proposed amendment and directing that it be submitted to vote at either annual or special meeting of shareholders except that proposed amendment need not be adopted by board of directors and may be directly submitted to any annual or special meeting of shareholders (351.090); (b) written or printed notice setting forth proposed amendment or summary thereof shall be given to each shareholder entitled to vote at such meeting (351.090) not less than ten nor more than 50 days before date of meeting, either personally or by mail (351.230). Attendance at meeting constitutes waiver of notice except where shareholder attends for express purpose of objecting to transaction of any business because meeting not lawfully called or convened. (351.230).

All amendments shall be adopted by a majority vote of all outstanding shares entitled to vote. However, if articles of incorporation or bylaws provide for cumulative voting in election of directors, number of directors shall not be decreased to less than three by amendment to articles of incorporation when number of shares voting against proposal for decrease would be sufficient to elect a director if such shares were voted cumulatively at election of three directors. (351.090).

Holders of outstanding shares of class shall be entitled to vote as class upon proposed amendment whether or not entitled to vote thereon by articles of incorporation if amendment would change aggregate number of authorized shares of class; change par

CORPORATIONS . . . *continued*
value of shares of class; create new class of shares with prior or superior rights; increase rights, preferences, or number of authorized shares of class of shares with prior or superior rights; or adversely alter or change powers, preferences, or special rights. Merger or consolidation not deemed to involve proposed amendment to articles of incorporation. (351.093).

Any number of amendments may be submitted to the shareholders and voted on by them at one meeting. (351.090).

Duplicate copies of certificate of amendment executed by majority of board of directors and verified by one of them with corporate seal affixed must be sent to Secretary of State with $20 fee. Certificate of amendment shall state name of corporation and original name if it has been changed, date of adoption of amendment by shareholders, amendment adopted, number of shares outstanding, number of shares entitled to vote on amendment or if shares of any class are entitled to vote as class number of shares of each class entitled to vote, number of shares voted for and against amendment, if amendment provides for exchange, reclassification or cancellation of issued shares or reduction of number of authorized shares of any class below issued shares, statement of manner in which it shall be effected, and if effective date of amendment is to be date other than date of filing, then effective date which may not be more than 90 days following filing date. (351.095).

Increase or Decrease of Authorized Capital Stock.—Reduction of stated capital of corporation, whether by retirement of reacquired shares or otherwise, may be made in following manner but nothing contained in this section is construed to forbid retirement of shares or reduction of stated capital in any other manner permitted by this chapter: (a) Board of directors may adopt resolution setting forth amount of proposed reduction and manner in which reduction shall be effected and directing that it be submitted to vote at either annual or special meeting of shareholders, except that it need not be adopted by board of directors and may be directly submitted to any annual or special meeting of shareholders; (b) written or printed notice stating that purpose or one of purposes of such meeting is to consider question of reducing stated capital of corporation must be given to each shareholder entitled to vote at such meeting (351.195) not less than ten nor more than 50 days before date of meeting, either personally or by mail (351.230); (c) at meeting vote of shareholders entitled to vote thereat must be taken on question of proposed reduction of stated capital which shall require for its adoption affirmative vote of holders of at least two-thirds of outstanding shares entitled to vote at meeting (351.195).

When reduction of stated capital has been approved as provided in this section statement must be executed in duplicate originals or original and a copy by corporation by president or vice president and verified by him and corporation's seal must be thereto affixed attested by secretary or assistant secretary which statement must set forth: (a) Name of corporation; (b) copy of resolution of shareholders approving such reduction; (c) total number of shares outstanding; (d) number of shares voted for and against such reduction respectively; (e) statement of manner in which reduction is effected and statement expressed in dollars of amount of stated capital and amount of paid-in surplus of corporation adjusted to give effect to reduction. Such statement must be delivered in duplicate to secretary of state. If secretary of state finds such statement conforms to law he must file same, retain original and return copy to corporation or its representative. Upon filing of statement in office of secretary of state reduction shall be effective. No reduction of stated capital may be made which would reduce stated capital represented by shares without par value having preferential right in assets of corporation in event of involuntary liquidation to amount less than aggregate preferential amount provided from time to time to be payable upon such shares in event of such involuntary liquidation. Surplus, if any, created by or arising out of reduction of stated capital of corporation is paid-in surplus. No distribution of assets to shareholders in connection with reduction of stated capital may be made out of stated capital unless assets of corporation remaining after reduction of stated capital are sufficient to pay any debts of corporation, payment of which shall not have been otherwise provided for. Shares retired under this or any other section shall become authorized and unissued shares of class to which they belong unless reissue thereof is prohibited by articles of incorporation in which case authorized shares of such class should be reduced to extent of shares so retired. (351.195). Preferential shares have additional requirements. (351.200).

Bylaws.—Shareholders have power to make, amend or repeal bylaws unless articles of incorporation vest such power in directors except original bylaws may be adopted by directors or if persons to constitute first board of directors are not named in articles of incorporation incorporators may adopt original bylaws by unanimous vote. (351.290). Bylaws may contain any provisions for regulation and management of affairs of corporation not inconsistent with law or articles of incorporation. (351.290).

Stock.—Shares may be issued with or without par value, and may be divided into one or more classes or one or more series within any class and such classes or series may have such voting powers or no voting powers and such preferences, rights, and restrictions as stated in articles of incorporation or in resolution approved by directors pursuant to authority expressly vested in directors by articles of incorporation. If corporation is authorized to issue more than one class of stock or more than one series of any class, voting powers, preferences, rights, and restrictions of each class or series must be set forth in full or summarized on stock certificate or statement that corporation will furnish complete information about voting powers, preferences, rights, and restrictions to stock holder free of charge must be on certificate. Issuing corporation must file certificate with secretary of state setting forth resolutions and number of shares of each class and series to which resolution applies if corporation issues shares or series of class of shares not provided in articles of incorporation but by resolution of board. (351.180). Corporations may issue options entitling holders to purchase shares of stock if provided in articles of incorporation or by resolution of board. (351.182).

Stock Certificates.—Unless otherwise provided in articles or by-laws, shares must be represented by certificates signed by president or vice-president and secretary or an assistant secretary or treasurer or an assistant treasurer and sealed with seal of corporation. Such seal may be facsimile, engraved or printed. Any or all of signatures may be facsimile. (351.295).

Every certificate for shares without par value must have plainly stated on its face the number of shares which it represents. No such certificate may express any par value or any rate of dividend to which such shares shall be entitled in terms of percentage of any par or other value. (351.295).

Issuance of Stock, Bonds, Etc.—Shares of stock, bonds or other obligations may be issued only for money paid, labor done, or property actually received. All fictitious issues or increases of stock or indebtedness are void, provided that no such issue or increase made for valid bone fide antecedent debts shall be deemed fictitious or void. (351.160).

Stock Books and Stock Transfers.—Every corporation must keep correct and complete books and records of account, including amount of assets, minutes of shareholder and board of director meetings, names and addresses of officers and it must keep at its registered office or principal place of business in this state, books in which must be recorded number of shares subscribed, names of owners of shares and number owned by them respectively, amount of shares paid, and transfers of shares, with dates of transfers. Stockholders must be afforded access to stock ownership record books at all proper times under such regulations as may be prescribed in bylaws and if any officer in charge of books shall refuse to permit examination by stockholder upon demand, he shall forfeit $250 for each offense. (351.215).

Board of directors may close transfer books for not exceeding 70 days preceding date of any meeting of shareholders or of dividend payment or for allotment of rights or effective date of change or conversion or exchange of shares. Alternative of record date provided. (351.250).

Uniform Commercial Code in force. See category Business Regulation and Commerce, topic Commercial Code.

Uniform Simplification of Fiduciary Security Transfers Act adopted. (403.250-.350, specifically saved from repeal by U.C.C., see 400.10-.102).

Stockholders or subscribers to shares are under no obligation to the corporation or its creditors except to pay to the corporation the full consideration for which such shares were, or were to be, issued. (351.275).

Tender Offers.—Offeror making take over bid to acquire control of Missouri corporation which has principal executive offices, significant business operations and at least 10% of owners of its voting stock in Missouri must file with commissioner of securities and deliver to target corporation registration statement which includes all details of take over bid. (409.500-.566).

Stockholders Actions.—Stockholders may enjoin ultra vires acts. (351.395). Courts will hear stockholder complaints in equity for accounting or other relief when there is no adequate remedy at law and complainant shows exhaustion of remedies within corporation. (40 S.W.2d 496).

Stockholder Liabilities.—Limited to amount originally subscribed on stock. (Const. Art. XI, §8).

Stockholders' meetings may be held either within or without Missouri as may be provided in the bylaws. In absence of such provision all meetings must be held at the registered office in this state. Annual meeting to elect directors on second Monday in Jan. unless bylaws fix another date. (351.225).

Voting.—Shareholders may vote in person or by proxy executed in writing by the shareholder or by his duly authorized attorney in fact. Unless articles of incorporation or bylaws provide otherwise, cumulative voting will be utilized. Proxies invalid 11 months after date unless otherwise provided therein. Shares belonging or hypothecated to corporation are not entitled to vote. (351.245). Person who knowingly falsifies proxy in material respect is guilty of infraction. (351.265).

Action Without Meeting.—Any action required to be taken or which may be taken at meeting of shareholders, may be taken without meeting if consents in writing setting forth action so taken, are signed by all shareholders entitled to vote. Such consents have same force as unanimous vote of shareholders at meeting duly held. (351.273).

Notice of Stockholders' Meetings.—Written or printed notice of each meeting of shareholders stating place, day and hour of meeting and, in case of special meeting, purpose of meeting, shall be given not less than ten days nor more than 70 days prior to meeting. Printed or written notice is sufficient if sent by mail to address of stockholder appearing upon corporation's books. (351.230).

If all stockholders sign waiver, the written, printed and published notice may be dispensed with. (351.655).

Voting Trusts.—Shareholders may create voting trust. (351.246).

Directors.—A corporation must have three or more directors, except may have one or two if number to constitute board of directors is stated in articles of incorporation. (351.310-.315). If first board of directors is not named in articles of incorporation incorporators may elect first board of directors by unanimous vote. (351.080). Elected at annual meeting of shareholders for terms of one or more years, not to exceed three, but there must be annual election for such proportion as number of years composing term bears to entire number of directors. (351.315). Unless articles of incorporation or bylaws otherwise provide, vacancies on board or new directorships may be filled by majority vote of remaining directors until next election of directors by stockholders except if shareholders elect directors by class pursuant to 351.315, director need not be presented for election until class which director elected is presented for election to shareholders. (351.320). At meeting called expressly for that purpose, directors may be removed in manner provided in this section. Such meeting must be held at registered or principal business office of corporation in this state or in city or county in this state in which principal business office is located. Unless articles of incorporation or bylaws provide otherwise, one or more or entire board of directors may be removed, with or without cause, by vote of holders of majority of shares then entitled to vote at election of directors. If articles of incorporation or bylaws provide for cumulative voting in election of directors, if less than entire board is to be removed, no one of directors may be removed if votes cast against his removal would be sufficient to elect him if then cumulatively voted at election of entire board of directors, or, if there be classes of directors, at election of class of directors of which he is part. Whenever holders of

See note at head of Digest as to 1998 legislation covered.

See Topical Index in front part of this volume.

MO – 2

CORPORATIONS . . . *continued*
shares of any class are entitled to elect one or more directors by provisions of articles of incorporation, provisions of this section shall apply, in respect of removal of director or directors so elected, to vote of holders of outstanding shares of that class and not to vote of outstanding shares as whole. (351.315). Impartial, provisional director may be appointed by court if even number of directors are equally divided to danger of corporation. (351.323).

Directors' meetings may be held within or without state as may be provided in articles of incorporation or by-laws. Members of board of directors or any committee designated by board of directors may participate in meeting by means of conference telephone or similar communications equipment whereby all participants can hear each other and participation in this manner constitutes presence in person. (351.335). Majority of full board is quorum unless greater number is required by articles of incorporation or bylaws. (351.325).

Voting.—If all directors severally or collectively consent in writing to any action to be taken by directors, such consents have same force as unanimous vote of directors at meeting duly held. (351.340).

Liabilities of Directors.—Directors are liable for debts during term of office to the extent of the dividends paid, for knowingly declaring and paying dividends except as permitted by statute, provided, that a director may rely in good faith upon the books of account and statements of the corporation prepared by any of its officials. (351.345).

However, a director may be indemnified by corporation against liabilities, expenses, counsel fees and costs reasonably incurred in connection with any action or claim in which he is made a party by reason of being a director, if he acted in good faith and in manner reasonably believed to be in or not opposed to best interests of corporation or, if criminal proceeding, had no reasonable cause to believe his conduct was unlawful unless action is brought in right of corporation. If action is brought in right of corporation, director may be indemnified by corporation if he acted in good faith and in manner he reasonably believed to be in or not opposed to best interests of corporation, unless he is adjudged liable for negligence or misconduct in performance of his duty in which case he can only be indemnified if court determines that he is reasonably entitled to indemnity. Unless ordered by court, indemnity must be voted by majority of quorum of directors who are not parties to action or, if not obtainable, or if disinterested directors so direct, by independent legal counsel of shareholders. Corporation may purchase liability insurance on behalf of its directors. (351.355).

Anti-Greenmail Law.—Missouri corporations which have principal executive offices, significant business operations and owners of at least 10% of their voting stock in Missouri may not enter into "business combinations" with "interested shareholders" (generally shareholders owning 20% or more of outstanding voting stock) unless: (1) "Business combination" is approved by board of directors before "interested shareholder" obtains enough shares to make him interested shareholder, (2) business combination is approved by majority of other voting shares at meeting which is held no sooner than five years after interested shareholder acquires number of shares required to be interested shareholder or (3) result of business combination is that other shareholders receive highest price per share paid by interested shareholder at time when he was owner of 5% or more of outstanding voting shares within five years before announcement of business combination or five years prior to becoming interested shareholder, whichever is higher. "Business combination" with interested shareholder is: (1) Merger, (2) sale or transfer of assets having value of at least 10% of assets of corporation, 10% of outstanding value of stock or 10% of corporation's net income, (3) issuing stock which has market value of at least 5% of all outstanding stock, (4) adopting plan of liquidation pursuant to agreement, (5) adopting plan of reclassification of securities or recapitalization pursuant to agreement which results in interested shareholder obtaining increase in shares of voting stock, or (6) entering into loans or providing other financial assistance. Provisions do not apply to corporations which have no voting stock registered with securities and exchange commission nor to certain other corporations which have elected not to be subject to this law. (351.459).

Executive Committee.—If bylaws so provide, board of directors, by resolution adopted by a majority of the whole board, may designate two or more directors to constitute an executive committee, which may, to extent provided in such resolution or in bylaws, exercise all authority of the board of directors. Designation of an executive committee does not relieve the directors of the responsibility imposed upon them by law. (351.330).

Officers.—Corporation shall have president and secretary, who shall be chosen by directors, and such other officers and agents as shall be prescribed by bylaws. Unless articles of incorporation or bylaws otherwise provide, any two or more offices may be held by same person. (351.360).

Registered Office.—Every corporation must maintain a registered office in Missouri, but this office need not be the same as its place of business. (351.370).

General powers of corporations are: (a) to have succession by corporate name for the period limited in articles of incorporation or perpetually where there is no limitation; (b) to sue and be sued, complain and defend in any court of law or equity; (c) to have and make use of corporate seal; (d) to purchase, take, receive, lease, or otherwise acquire, own, hold, improve, use and otherwise deal in, sell, convey, mortgage, pledge, lease, exchange, transfer and otherwise dispose of all or any part of its real or personal property, or any interest therein, or other assets, wherever situated; and to hold for any period of time, real estate acquired in payment of debt, by foreclosure or otherwise, or real estate exchanged therefor; (e) to be general or limited partner; (f) to purchase, receive, subscribe for or otherwise acquire and own, vote, mortgage, pledge or otherwise dispose of shares or other interest in or obligations of other domestic or foreign corporations, associations, partnerships or individuals, or direct or indirect obligations of U.S. or of any other government, state, territory, governmental district or municipality or of any instrumentality thereof; (g) to make contracts and guarantees and incur liabilities; to borrow money at such rates of interest as corporation may determine without regard to restrictions of any usury law of this state; to issue its notes, bonds, and other obligations; to issue notes or bonds secured or unsecured, which by their terms are convertible into shares of stock of any class, and to secure any of its obligations by mortgage, pledge, or deed of trust of all or any of its property, franchises and income; (h) to invest its surplus funds from time to time and to lend money and to take and hold real and personal property as security for payment of funds so invested or loaned; (i) to conduct its business within and without State and to exercise its powers in any other state or possession of U.S. or any foreign country; (j) to elect or appoint directors, officers and agents of corporation, define their duties and fix their compensation and to indemnify directors, officers and employees to extent and in manner permitted by law; (k) to make or alter bylaws not inconsistent with its articles of incorporation or with laws of this State; (l) to transact any lawful business in aid of U.S. in prosecution of war, to make donations to associations and organizations aiding in war activities and to lend money to state or federal government for war purposes; (m) to cease its corporate activities and surrender its corporate franchise; (n) to have and exercise all powers necessary or convenient to effect any or all of purposes for which corporation is formed; (o) to make contributions to any corporation organized for civic, charitable or benevolent purposes, community chest or community fund not operated or used for profit to its members. (351.385).

Dividends may be declared and paid, subject to the following limitations: (a) no dividends may be declared or paid when the payment thereof would reduce the net assets below the stated capital of the corporation (351.220); (b) dividends may be declared out of paid-in surplus if all accrued cumulative dividends on preferred classes of shares have been fully paid and the payment is identified as a liquidating dividend (351.210); (c) if a stock dividend of par value shares is declared, an amount of surplus equal to the aggregate par value of the shares to be issued as a dividend must be transferred to stated capital; (d) if a stock dividend of shares without par value is declared and such shares have preferential rights in the event of involuntary liquidation, such shares must be issued at their liquidation value, and there must be transferred to stated capital an amount of surplus equal to the aggregate preferential amount payable upon such shares in the event of involuntary liquidation; (e) if a stock dividend of shares without par value is declared, and none of the shares has preferential rights in the event of involuntary liquidation, such shares may be issued at a value fixed by the directors, and there must be transferred to stated capital an amount of surplus equal to the aggregate value so fixed of such shares.

A split-up or division of issued shares into a greater number of shares of the same class is not a share dividend.

No dividends may be paid contrary to any restrictions of the articles of incorporation. (351.220).

Registration.—Every corporation, foreign or domestic, except corporations exempt from taxation, shall file annual registration report simultaneously with franchise tax return or within 30 days of date of incorporation. Registration will state: (1) Corporate name; (2) registered agent and office in this state, giving street and number, or building and number, or both as case may require; (3) names and residence addresses of all its officers and directors; (4) mailing address of principal place of business or headquarters. Extension of time to file franchise tax does not extend due date of registration report. (351.120).

Fee for registering is $40 with additional fee of $15 for each 30 days late. Report must be filed and accepted within 90 days; failure to comply results in forfeiture. (351.125).

Reports.—Every corporation liable for annual franchise tax under 147.010 shall make report in writing showing financial condition of corporation at beginning of business on first day of its taxable year to Secretary of State annually on or before 15th day of fourth month of its taxable year. Report shall be signed by officer of corporation. (147.020).

Special reports as to financial condition may be required at any time.

If any corporation subject to provisions of this chapter shall fail or neglect to make report required by §§147.010 to 147.120 or pay its franchise taxes within 90 days after time required by §§147.010 to 147.120 (determined with regard to any extension of time for failing its franchise tax report or for payment of its franchise tax), such corporation, if organized under laws of this state, shall forfeit its certificate of incorporation or, if foreign corporation, shall forfeit its certificate of authority to engage in business in this state under provisions of §§351.484 and 351.486. (147.040[8]).

See also infra, subhead Annual Franchise Tax.

Increase of bonded indebtedness requires prior approval by board of directors, but vote or consent of shareholders not necessary unless required by articles of incorporation. (351.160).

Sale or Exchange of Corporate Assets.—Sale or exchange, other than by mortgage, deed of trust or pledge, of all or substantially all of property and assets of corporation not made in regular course of business must be approved at stockholders' meeting by vote of two-thirds of outstanding shares entitled to vote at such meeting. Dissenting stockholder who files written objection to sale at or prior to meeting may receive payment for fair value of his shares upon his written demand made within 20 days after vote is taken. (351.400-.405).

Control share acquisition procedure applicable where articles of incorporation or bylaws do not exempt corporation are addressed in §351.407.

Merger and Consolidation.—Any two or more domestic corporations, or foreign corporations, if permitted by states of organization, may merge into one of such corporations or consolidate into a new corporation. (351.410). Domestic corporation may merge or consolidate with one or more domestic or foreign limited partnerships, general partnerships, limited liability companies, trusts, business trusts, corporations, real estate investment trusts and other associations or business entities, at least one of which is not corporation. (351.461, 355.196). Such merger or consolidation must be approved by board of directors of each corporation and submitted to vote of stockholders at annual or special meeting. Plan of merger or consolidation must receive two-thirds vote of outstanding shares entitled to vote at such meeting. Dissenters' rights same as under subtopic Sale or Exchange of Corporate Assets, supra. (351.410-.455). If 90% or more of outstanding shares of corporation is owned by another corporation, parent corporation may merge subsidiary corporation into itself or merge itself into subsidiary corporation by resolution of directors with no vote of stockholders, except that where parent

See note at head of Digest as to 1998 legislation covered.

See Topical Index in front part of this volume.

MO – 3

CORPORATIONS . . . *continued*

corporation is not surviving corporation, two-thirds of outstanding shares of parent corporation entitled to vote must approve merger at meeting duly called and held. Owners of shares of subsidiary corporation other than parent corporation have dissenters' rights as described under subhead Sale or Exchange of Corporate Assets, supra. (351.447). Merger of domestic corporation with wholly owned subsidiary by resolution of directors with no vote of stockholders if in connection with holding company reorganization. (351.448).

Voluntary Dissolution.—(a) Majority of incorporators or initial directors of corporation that has not issued shares or has not commenced business may dissolve corporation by delivering to secretary of state for filing articles of dissolution that set forth: (1) Name of corporation; (2) date of its incorporation; (3) either that none of corporation's shares have been issued, or that corporation has not commenced business; (4) that no debt of corporation remains unpaid; (5) that net assets of corporation remaining after winding up have been distributed to shareholders, if shares were issued; and (6) that majority of incorporators or initial directors authorized dissolution. (351.462).

(b) Corporation's board of directors may propose dissolution for submission to shareholders. For proposal to dissolve to be adopted: (1) Board of directors must recommend dissolution to shareholders unless board of directors determines that because of conflict of interest or other special circumstances it should make no recommendation and communicates basis for its determination to shareholders; and (2) shareholders entitled to vote must approve proposal to dissolve as provided in subsection 5 of this section.

Board of directors may condition its submission of proposal for dissolution on any basis. (351.464).

Corporation shall notify each shareholder, whether or not entitled to vote, of proposed shareholders' meeting in accordance with §351.230. Notice must also state that purpose, or one of purposes, of meeting is to consider dissolving corporation.

Unless articles of incorporation or board of directors require greater vote, including vote by any class of stock or any series of stock, proposal to dissolve to be adopted must be approved by at least two-thirds of votes entitled to be cast on that proposal. (351.464).

(c) Corporation may be dissolved by written consent of holder of record of all of its outstanding shares entitled to vote on dissolution. (351.466).

(d) At any time after dissolution is authorized, corporation may dissolve by delivering to secretary of state for filing articles of dissolution setting forth: (1) Name of corporation; (2) date dissolution was authorized; (3) if dissolution was approved by shareholders: (A) number of votes entitled to be cast on proposal to dissolve, and (B) either total number of votes cast for and against dissolution and statement that number cast for dissolution was sufficient for approval or statement that dissolution was approved by written consent of all shareholders; and (4) if voting by any class of stock or any series of any class of stock was required, information required by subdivision (3) of this subsection must be separately provided for each class of stock or series thereof entitled to vote separately on plan to dissolve. Corporation is dissolved upon effective date of its articles of dissolution. (351.468).

Officers and directors of corporations dissolved before Aug. 28, 1990 are to act as trustees of corporation. Trustees may sue and be sued as trustees and will have joint and several liability to creditors and shareholders of corporation, to extent of corporation property. (351.526).

Dissolved corporation continues its corporate existence but may not carry on any business except that appropriate to wind up and liquidate its business and affairs. (351.476).

Claims against dissolved corporation must be filed later of 90 days after issuance of rejection notice of claim or statutory period of limitation for claim. (351.483).

Involuntary Dissolution.—Secretary of state may commence proceeding under 351.486 to dissolve corporation administratively. (351.484). Written notice shall be served on corporation if determination is made to dissolve corporation administratively. (351.486).

Close Corporations.—Missouri provides for close corporations. (351.755).

Qualification or Domestication.—Statutory close corporation is corporation whose articles of incorporation contain statement that corporation is statutory close corporation. (351.755).

Following statement shall appear conspicuously on each share certificate issued by statutory close corporation:

"The right to shareholders in a statutory close corporation may differ materially from the rights of shareholders in other corporations. Copies of the articles of incorporation and bylaws, shareholders' agreements, and other documents, any of which may restrict transfers and affect voting and other rights, may be obtained by a shareholder on written request to the corporation." (351.760).

Corporation having 50 or fewer shareholders may become statutory close corporation by amending its articles of incorporation to include above statement. Amendment shall be approved by holders of at least two-thirds of votes of each class or series of shares of corporation, voting as class or series, whether or not otherwise entitled to vote on amendments. If amendment is adopted, shareholder who voted against amendment is entitled to assert dissenters' rights under §§351.870 to 351.930. (351.755).

Corporate Powers.—All shareholders of statutory close corporation may agree in writing to regulate exercise of corporate powers and management of business and affairs of corporation or relationship among shareholders of corporation.

Agreement authorized by this section is effective although: (1) It eliminates board of directors; (2) it restricts discretion of powers of board of directors or authorizes director proxies or weighted voting rights; (3) its effect is to treat corporation as partnership; or (4) it creates relationship among shareholders or between shareholders and corporation that would otherwise be appropriate only among partners. (351.800).

Statutory close corporation may operate without board of directors if its articles of incorporation contain statement to that effect. (351.805).

Personal Liability.—Failure of statutory close corporation to observe usual corporate formalities or requirements relating to exercise of its corporate powers or management

of its business and affairs is not ground for imposing personal liability on shareholders for liabilities of corporation. (351.825).

Termination of Status.—Corporation that terminates its status as statutory close corporation is thereafter subject to all provisions of c. 351 other than §§351.750 to 351.865 or, if incorporated under c. 356, RSMo, to all provisions of that law.

Termination of statutory close corporation status does not affect any right of shareholder or of corporation under agreement or articles of incorporation unless §§351.750 to 351.865, c. 356, RSMo, or another law of this state invalidates right. (351.840).

Dissolution.—Articles of incorporation of statutory close corporation may authorize one or more shareholders, or holders of specified number of percentage of shares of any class or series, to dissolve corporation at will or upon occurrence of specified event or contingency. Shareholder or shareholders exercising this authority shall give written notice of intent to dissolve to all other shareholders. Thirty-one days after effective date of notice, corporation shall begin wind up and liquidate its business and affairs and file articles of dissolution under §§351.468 to 351.482.

Unless articles of incorporation provide otherwise, amendment to articles of incorporation to add, change, or delete authority to dissolve described above shall be approved by holders of all outstanding shares, whether or not otherwise entitled to vote on amendments, or if no shares have been issued, by all subscribers for shares, if any, or if none, by all incorporators. (351.845).

Transfer of Shares.—(1) Person desiring to transfer shares of statutory close corporation subject to transfer prohibition of §351.765 shall first offer them to corporation after obtaining offer to purchase shares for cash from third person who is eligible to purchase shares under subsection 2 of this section. Offer by third person must be in writing and state offeror's name and address, number and class, or series, of shares offered, offering price per share, and other terms of offer.

(2) Third person is eligible to purchase shares if: (a) He is eligible to become qualified shareholder under any federal or state tax statute corporation has adopted and he agrees in writing not to terminate his qualification without approval of remaining shareholders; and (b) his purchase of shares will not impose personal holding company tax or similar federal or state penalty tax on corporation. (351.770).

Appraisal.—See subheads Amendment of Articles, Sale or Exchange of Corporate Assets, Merger and Consolidation, supra.

Foreign Corporations.—(Provisions of the act as to foreign corporations do not apply to corporations whose right to do business in this state is controlled by some board, bureau or administrative agency of the state other than the Secretary of State; e.g., banking or insurance corporations.)

Name of Corporation.—Corporate name, including fictitious name, of foreign corporation must be distinguishable from: (1) Corporate name of corporation incorporated or authorized to transact business in this state; (2) corporate name reserved or previously registered; (3) fictitious name of another foreign corporation authorized to transact business in this state; (4) corporate name of not for profit corporation incorporated or authorized to transact business in this state; (5) partnership name of limited partnership or limited liability company formed pursuant to Missouri law; (6) partnership name reserved or registered under Uniform Limited Partnership Law; and (7) partnership name of foreign limited partnership or limited liability company authorized to transact business in this state or registered pursuant to provisions of Uniform Limited Partnership Law. (351.584). Exceptions: If other corporation consents to use in writing and submits to distinguishing its name with records of secretary of state; if its obtains court order allowing right to use name; if merged, formed by reorganization of other company; or acquired all or substantially all of assets of other corporation. (351.584[3, 4]).

Domestication Tax or Fee.—Such corporation shall be required to pay into state treasury fee of $150 for issuing certificate of authority to do business in this state. (351.576).

Change of Name.—If corporation changes its name to one that does not satisfy Missouri law, it may not transact business under changed name until it adopts name satisfying statutory requirements and obtains amended certificate of authority. (351.584[5]).

Executing Trusts.—Foreign corporation may not act as testamentary trustee (456.120) unless it qualifies under reciprocal corporate fiduciary act (362.600). See category Business Regulation and Commerce, topic Banks and Banking, subhead Foreign Banks.

Doing Business Without Authority.—Any foreign corporation doing business in Missouri which fails to comply with Missouri laws is subject to a fine of not less than $1,000 and is prohibited from maintaining any suit or action in the state courts on any demand arising while the requirements of the Missouri corporation laws have not been complied with. (351.574).

Registered Agents.—Each foreign corporation authorized to transact business in this state shall continuously maintain in this state: (1) Registered office that may be same as any of its places of businesses; and (2) registered agent, who may be: (a) individual who resides in this state and whose business office is identical with registered office, (b) domestic corporation or not for profit domestic corporation whose business office is identical with registered office, or (c) foreign corporation or foreign not-for-profit corporation authorized to transact business in this state whose business office is identical with registered office. (351.586).

Surrender of Authority.—Foreign corporation authorized to transact business in this state may not withdraw from this state until it obtains certificate of withdrawal from secretary of state. Foreign corporation authorized to transact business in this state may apply for certificate of withdrawal by delivering application, to secretary of state, which states: (1) Name of foreign corporation and name of state or country under whose laws it is incorporated; (2) that it is not transacting business in this state, and that it surrenders its authority to transact business in this state; (3) that it revokes authority of its registered agent to accept service on its behalf and appoints secretary of state as its agent for service of process in any proceeding based on cause of action arising during time it was authorized to transact business in this state; (4) mailing address to which secretary of state may mail copy of any process served on him; and (5) commitment to notify secretary of state in future of any change in its mailing address. (351.596).

Annual franchise tax of ¹/₂₀ of 1% of par value of outstanding stock and surplus, or portion thereof employed in state, is imposed on all corporations, whose stock value and

CORPORATIONS . . . *continued*
surplus exceeds $200,000 for non-par value corporations (147.010), except corporations not organized for profit, express and insurance companies paying annual tax on gross receipts in Missouri, banking institutions paying annual franchise fees imposed by 148.010 to 148.110, and electric and telephone corporations declared tax exempt organizations under §501(c) of Internal Revenue Code. (See categories Business Regulation and Commerce, topic Carriers; Insurance, topic Insurance Companies.) Annual report for purposes of this tax is required to be made annually on or before Apr. 15th to Secretary of State. (147.020). Tax is payable to Director of Revenue on or before 15th day of fourth month of corporation's taxable year. (147.030). If not paid by due date, penalty of 5% per month or fractional part thereof up to 25% maximum will be charged until tax paid. Interest at rate determined by 32.065 shall also be added. (147.120). Failure to file report or pay tax within 90 days of due date forfeits certificate of incorporation or certificate of authority.

Stock without par value is valued at $5 per share, or at actual value if that exceeds $5 per share, for purpose of computing organization or qualification tax or fees or franchise tax. (147.010).

Income Tax on Corporations.—See category Taxation, topic Income Tax.

Limited Liability Companies.—See topic Limited Liability Companies.

Professional Corporations.—One or more natural persons licensed in same profession in Missouri may incorporate and own stock in professional corporation to practice that same type of professional service by filing articles of incorporation with secretary of state except that if more than one type of professional service is permitted to be practiced by professional corporation then one or more natural persons still licensed to practice any of permitted professional services may act as incorporator and professional corporation may be incorporated to practice all professional services permitted to be practiced by one professional corporation. (356.041). Professions included: accountants; architects or engineers; attorneys; chiropodists-podiatrists; chiropractors; dentists; optometrists; osteopaths; psychologists; doctors of medicine; veterinarians; registered nurses; natural persons licensed as real estate salespersons; physical therapists. (356.021).

Missouri Non-Profit Corporation Act adopted. (c. 355).

See also categories Business Regulation and Commerce, topic Banks and Banking; Civil Actions and Procedure, topics Process, Venue; Debtor and Creditor, topic Attachment; Insurance, topics Insurance Companies, Surety and Guaranty Companies.

JOINT STOCK COMPANIES:

The term "corporation" includes all joint stock companies or associations having any powers or privileges not possessed by individuals or partnerships. (Const. Art. XI, §1). This does not make such companies corporations, nor require their incorporation. (288 Mo. 679, 233 S.W. 20).

Actions.—Such companies may sue and be sued. (276 Mo. 322, 208 S.W. 39). Voluntary unincorporated associations not given special powers or privileges by statutes cannot sue. (326 Mo. 617, 31 S.W.2d 803).

See also topic Corporations.

LIMITED LIABILITY COMPANIES:

Missouri Limited Liability Company Act created. (347.010).

Purposes.—Limited liability companies may be organized for any lawful purposes. (347.035).

Name.—Must contain word "limited company", "limited liability company", or abbreviation "L.C." or "L.L.C." and company must transact business under this name unless registered another name under which it transacts business or conspicuously discloses names as set forth in articles. Name must not contain word "association", "corporation", "incorporated", "limited partnership", "L.P.", "Ltd.", or abbreviation of such words or any word or phrase indicating it is organized for any purpose not stated in articles or that it is governmental agency. Name must be distinguishable from name of any corporation, limited liability company, limited partnership or other business entity organized, reserved or registered in Missouri, or licensed or registered in Missouri as foreign corporation, limited liability company or limited partnership, unless written consent is obtained from such other entity to use name and such other entity files with secretary of state documentation changing its name to name distinguishable from name of applying limited liability company or limited liability company files with secretary certified copy of final court decree establishing prior right to use name. (347.020).

Name reserved by filing with secretary of state application to reserve name executed by applicant. If name is available, secretary of state must reserve name for exclusive use of applicant for period of 60 days. Right to exclusive use of reserved name may be transferred by filing with secretary of state notice of transfer, executed by person for whom name was reserved and specifying name and address of transferee. (347.025). Fee to file reservation is $20. (347.179).

Registered Office and Agent.—Limited liability company must maintain registered office in Missouri. Registered office need not be its place of business. Limited liability company must maintain registered agent in Missouri for service of process. Agent may be either Missouri resident, whose business office is identical with registered office, or domestic or foreign corporation authorized to do business in Missouri, and whose business office is identical with registered office. (347.030).

Organizers.—Any person, whether or not member or manager, may form limited liability company by signing and filing articles of organization with secretary of state. (347.037).

Articles of organization must set forth: (a) name of limited liability company; (b) purposes for which company is formed; (c) address, including street number, if any, of registered office and name of registered agent at such address; (d) whether management of company is vested in one or more managers; (e) latest date on which company is to dissolve; (f) right, if any, of remaining members to continue business and affairs of company upon withdrawal of member; (g) name and address of each organizer; and (h) any other provision, not inconsistent with law, which are in operating agreement. (347.039).

Execution and Filing of Articles and Other Documents.—Initial articles of organization must be executed by organizer or organizers or person duly authorized under power of attorney. (347.047). Filing fee for original articles of organization is $100. (347.179). Amended or restated articles of organization, statement of change of registered agent or office, notice of merger or consolidation, notice of winding up, or articles of termination must be executed by authorized person, person authorized under operating agreement or person duly authorized under power of attorney. Articles, notices and documents required to be filed by limited liability company in hands of receiver, trustee or other court-appointed fiduciary must be filed by such fiduciary. (347.047).

Commencement of Business.—Limited liability company is formed when articles of organization are filed with secretary of state or at later date set forth in articles of incorporation, not to exceed 90 days from filing date. If articles of organization are not in conformance with filing provisions, secretary must return articles with statement as to nonconformity. (347.037).

Evidence of Organization.—Copy of articles of organization stamped "filed" and marked with filing date is conclusive evidence that limited liability company has been legally organized and formed. (347.037).

Amendment of Articles.—Articles of organization must be amended promptly, and not later than 60 days after occurrence of following events: (1) to reflect that management of company is vested in one or more managers, where such management had not previously been vested; (2) to reflect that management is no longer vested in one or more managers, where management had previously been vested in one or more managers; (3) to reflect name change of company; or (4) to reflect change in time set forth in articles for company to dissolve. Unless otherwise provided in operating agreement, articles of organization may be amended at any time and in any respect so long as articles of organization contain only those provisions as are contained in operating agreement at time of amendment. Articles of organization are amended by filing with secretary of state articles of amendment, which must set forth: (1) name of limited liability company; (2) date articles of amendment are filed, and if not to become effective until specified date after filing, date they are to become effective which must not be more than 90 days after filing date; (3) if filing of articles of amendment is necessitated by event, nature and date of event; (4) amendment to articles of organization; and (5) statement that amendment is authorized under operating agreement or is required to be filed. (347.041). Amendment fee is $20. (347.179).

Integration of Articles of Organization and Amendments.—Limited liability company may integrate into single instrument articles of organization and amendments thereto by filing with secretary of state "Restated Articles of Organization" stating that restated articles only reinstate and integrate and do not further amend articles previously filed, and there is no discrepancy between provisions. At same time as integrating, company may also further amend or supplement articles of organization by filing with secretary of state "Amended and Restated Articles of Organization". (347.043). Restatement fee is $20. (347.179).

Liability of Members and Managers and Authorized Persons.—Members and managers of limited liability company are not liable, solely by reason of being member or manager, under judgment, decree, or court order, or in any other manner, for debt, obligation or liability of limited liability company, whether arising in contract, tort or otherwise, or for acts or omissions of other member, manager, agent or employee of company. (347.057).

Liability Where Limited Liability Company Unauthorized.—Persons acting as limited liability company without authority and without good faith belief in authority are jointly and severally liable for debts and liabilities incurred. (347.059). Authorized person not liable for action taken with respect to duties under operating agreement, or failure to take such action, if performs duties in compliance with this section. (347.090).

Management.—Unless articles of organization provide management is vested in one or more managers, management is vested in members, who have authority to manage company affairs and make decisions, subject to provisions in operating agreement or provisions of this chapter restricting or enlarging management rights or responsibilities. If articles provide management is vested in one or more managers, such manager or managers have right to manage company affairs and make decisions to extent provided in operating agreement. Unless otherwise provided in operating agreement, must obtain consent of all members to change management from members to managers, or vice versa. Managers must be designated in operating agreement, or designated, appointed or elected by members in manner prescribed in operating agreement, and may be removed or replaced as provided in operating agreement. Managers need not be members of company or individuals, unless required by operating agreement. If operating agreement does not provide manner for designating, appointing, electing, removing or replacing managers, managers are designated, appointed, elected, removed or replaced by vote of majority of members and unless earlier removed or resigned, managers hold office until successors are designated, appointed or elected and qualified. (347.079).

Operating Agreement.—Members must adopt operating agreement. Operating agreement may contain any provision, not inconsistent with law, relating to conduct of business and affairs of company, its rights and powers, and rights, powers and duties of its members, managers, agents and employees. (347.081). Unless otherwise provided in operating agreement, must obtain approval or consent of all members to amend operating agreement. (347.081). Operating agreement is enforceable at law or in equity by member, to extent provided in law; except member's agreement or consent to continue business or affairs of company upon withdrawal of member is subject to specific performance, if otherwise available, only if: (1) approval or consent is set forth both in articles of organization and operating agreement; or (2) approval or consent is obtained after withdrawal of member. (347.081).

Voting.—Unless otherwise provided in operating agreement, action or vote which must be taken at meeting of managers or members, may be taken without meeting, if obtain written consent of all persons entitled to act or vote on matter.

LIMITED LIABILITY COMPANIES . . . *continued*

Distributions.—Limited liability company must make distributions of cash or other property to members before dissolution and winding up of affairs at times or upon events specified in operating agreement, or if operating agreement does not specify, at times approved by majority of authorized persons. (347.101). No distribution may be made to extent that after distribution: (1) company would not be able to pay debts as due in usual course of business; or (2) total assets would be less than sum of total liabilities plus, unless operating agreement provides otherwise, amount needed if company were to be dissolved at time of distribution to satisfy preferential rights of members whose rights to distributions are superior to rights of members receiving distribution, except that, liabilities to members or former members are excluded from determination. (347.110).

Assignments.—Interest of member in limited liability company is personal property, and except as provided in operating agreement, may be assigned in whole or part. Assignment of interest does not entitle assignee to participate in management or exercise member rights, unless member had power to grant assignee right to become member and assignee exercises power in compliance with conditions limiting exercise thereof. Unless otherwise provided in operating agreement, if assignee becomes member, assignor is not released from liability to company without written consent of all members. (347.115).

Conversion of Partnership to Limited Liability Company.—General or limited partnership may convert to limited liability company by filing articles of organization including: (1) name of former general or limited partnership; and (2) for limited partnership, date and place of filing certificate of limited partnership and application for registration as limited liability partnership, and (3) for general partnership, date of filing of fictitious name registration of partnership and application for registration as limited liability partnership. Conversion does not constitute dissolution of general or limited partnership prior to conversion. Duties, debts, liens, liabilities and rights of creditors against former partnership and its partners continues without impairment and attaches to limited liability company. Existing claim, action or proceeding pending by or against partnership or its partners may be prosecuted as if conversion had not occurred, or against limited liability company to same extent as if duties, debts, liens and liabilities had been incurred or contracted by it. Judgment against partnership constitutes lien against limited liability company and may be enforced against it. (347.125).

Merger and Consolidation.—Domestic limited liability company may merge or consolidate with one or more limited liability companies, and domestic or foreign limited liability company by agreement shall provide for surviving entity. Domestic limited liability company may merge or consolidate with one or more general partnerships or domestic or foreign limited partnerships, limited liability companies, trusts, business trusts, corporations, real estate investment trusts and other associations or business entities at least one of which is not limited liability company. (347.127). Must obtain approval or consent of all members, unless otherwise provided in operating agreement. (347.079). In case of merger or consolidation solely between two or more domestic limited liability companies and one or more foreign limited liability companies, surviving entity must file notice of merger or consolidation with secretary of state, executed by at least one authorized person of domestic limited liability company and one authorized agent, or equivalent, for other party who is duly authorized to execute such notice. (347.129). Filing fee for notice of merger or consolidation is $20. (347.179). If merger or consolidation is not consummated, domestic limited liability company must promptly file notice of abandonment of merger or consolidation. (347.179). Filing fee is $20. (347.129). Domestic limited liability company that is not survivor must file articles of termination, with effective date not later than effective date of merger or consolidation. (347.179). Filing fee is $20. (347.129). Merger or consolidation is effective at latter of: (1) date secretary files notice of merger or consolidation; or (2) date set forth in notice of merger or consolidation, not to exceed 90 days after notice accepted for filing. (347.131).

In case of merger or consolidation between one or more domestic corporations and one or more constituent entities at least one of which is not corporation, one or more domestic limited partnerships and one or more constituent entities at least one of which not limited partnership, or one or more domestic limited liability companies and one or more constituent entities at least one of which is not limited liability company, each constituent entity must enter into written agreement of merger or consolidation. (347.715). Agreement of merger or consolidation must be authorized, approved and certified. (347.720). Surviving entity must file two duplicate originals of agreement of merger or consolidation with secretary of state or, alternatively, articles of merger or consolidation. Merger or consolidation effective when filed by secretary of state, unless later date specified in agreement or articles, but date may not exceed 90 days after agreement or articles delivered to secretary. (347.725).

Dissolution.—Domestic limited liability company is dissolved upon: (1) happening of events specified in operating agreement; (2) written consent of all members; (3) except as provided in operating agreement, withdrawal of member, if majority, by number, of remaining members agree to dissolve within 90 days after withdrawal; (4) withdrawal of sole remaining member; (5) entry of decree of dissolution; or (6) fact that limited liability company is not surviving entity in merger or consolidation. As soon as possible after occurrence of events (1)-(4) above, company must file notice of winding up with secretary of state. (347.137). Filing fee is $20. (347.179). When all remaining property and assets have been distributed, articles of organization must be canceled by filing articles of termination. (347.045). Filing fee is $20. (347.179). Upon filing articles of termination, existence of limited liability company ceases, except for purposes of suits, other proceedings and appropriate action. (347.139).

Disposal of Known Claims.—Dissolved limited liability company may dispose of known claims, other than contingent liabilities or claims based on events occurring after effective date of dissolution, by providing written notification of dissolution any time after its effective date. Notice must: (1) describe information necessary for claim; (2) provide mailing address to send claim; (3) state deadline, which may not be fewer than 90 days from effective date of notice by which company must receive claim; (4) state that claim will be barred if not received by deadline. Notwithstanding contrary provisions of law, claim against limited liability company dissolved without fraudulent intent is barred if either: (1) claimant who was given written notice does not deliver claim by deadline; or (2) claimant whose claim was rejected does not commence proceeding to enforce claim within 120 days from effective date of rejection notice. (347.141).

Disposal of Unknown Claims.—Dissolved limited liability company may dispose of unknown claims by filing notice of winding up which must: (1) contain request that persons with claims present them in accordance with notice; (2) describe information necessary for claim and mailing address to send claim; and (3) state that claim will be barred unless proceeding to enforce claim is commenced within three years after publication of notice. Notwithstanding other provisions of law to contrary, if limited liability company dissolved without fraudulent intent files notice of winding up, claims of following claimants are barred unless proceeding to enforce claim is commenced within three years after filing of notice of winding up: (1) claimant who did not receive written notice; (2) claimant whose claim was timely sent to company but not acted on; (3) claimant whose claim is contingent or based on event occurring after effective date of dissolution. (347.141).

Involuntary Dissolution.—Limited liability company may be dissolved involuntarily be decree of circuit court of county of registered office, or if address unknown, in circuit court of Cole County, in action by attorney general if limited liability company: (1) procured articles of organization through fraud; (2) exceeded or abused authority conferred upon it; (3) carried on, conducted or transacted business in fraudulent or illegal manner; or (4) abused its powers contrary to public policy. On application by or for member, court may decree dissolution whenever not reasonably practicable to carry on business in conformity with operating agreement. (347.143).

Winding Up.—Unless otherwise provided in operating agreement, upon dissolution, members who have not wrongfully dissolved limited liability company, or legal representative of last surviving member, not bankrupt, have, if management vested in members, right to wind up company affairs; or if management vested in one or more managers, right to authorize such manager or managers to wind up company affairs or complete unfinished transactions, except that any member, his legal representative or assignee, upon cause, may obtain winding up by court. (347.147).

Liquidation.—Court has power to liquidate assets and business of limited liability company: (1) in creditor action, after dissolution, when claim has been reduced to judgment and execution returned unsatisfied and where limited liability company is insolvent; (2) upon application by limited liability company, or for cause shown by member, after dissolution to have liquidation continued under court supervision; (3) in action by attorney general after issuance of decree of dissolution; or (4) in action by member after issuance of decree of dissolution. (347.149).

Foreign limited liability company must register with secretary of state before transacting business in Missouri. Filing fee for registration and issuance of certificate to transact business is $100. (347.179). Must submit to secretary, in duplicate, application for registration as foreign limited liability company signed and acknowledged by member, manager or other authorized agent setting forth: (1) name of foreign limited liability company and, if different, name under which it proposes to register and transact business in Missouri; (2) jurisdiction in which it was formed and date of formation; (3) purpose of company or general character of business it proposes to transact in Missouri; (4) name and address of registered agent and registered office in Missouri; (5) statement that secretary is appointed as its agent if company fails to maintain registered agent in Missouri or if agent cannot be found or served with reasonable diligence; and (6) address of office required to be maintained in its jurisdiction of organization, or if not required, of principal office of foreign limited liability company. (347.153).

If application for registration conforms to law and requisite fees paid, secretary must: (1) endorse on original and duplicate copies of application word "Filed", and date of filing; (2) file original application; (3) issue certificate of registration to transact business in Missouri; and (4) return certificate and copy of application to person who filed or his representative. (347.155).

If statement in application for registration was or later becomes erroneous, foreign limited liability company must promptly file with secretary of state certificate of correction signed and acknowledged by manager, member or authorized agent. (347.159). Filing fee is $20. (347.179).

Foreign limited liability company transacting business in Missouri which fails to register or comply with statutory provisions is subject to fine not less than $1,000 and may not maintain action, legal or equitable, in Missouri court, whether in contract or tort, while requirements are not met. Failure to register in Missouri does not impair validity of contract or company act or prevent company from defending action in Missouri courts. Member of foreign limited liability company is not liable for debts, obligations or liabilities of company solely by reason of having transacted business in Missouri without registration. (347.163).

Cancellation.—Secretary of state may cancel or disapprove articles of organization if limited liability company fails to file required documents, fails to maintain registered agent, fails to pay required filing fees, uses fraud or deception in any filing or violates federal or state criminal laws. Secretary must provide written notice 30 days prior to cancellation specifying reasons. Company may appeal notice of proposed cancellation to circuit court of county of its registered office by filing petition with copy of articles of organization or other relevant documents and copy of proposed written cancellation. Petition must be filed within 30 days after notice of cancellation. Company may appeal from circuit court as in other civil actions. Secretary may rescind cancellation if: (1) company provides necessary documents and affidavits indicating correction of conditions prompting cancellation; or (2) company provides documentation or statements that company is not in violation of criminal code. (347.183).

Taxation.—Limited liability company and its authorized persons, or their equivalent, must withhold and pay taxes as imposed by law on basis consistent with company's classification as partnership or association under §7701, IRC (1986). Solely for purposes of cc. 143 and 144, RSMo., limited liability company and members shall be classified and treated on basis consistent with limited liability company's classification for federal income tax purposes. (347.187).

See note at head of Digest as to 1998 legislation covered.

See Topical Index in front part of this volume.

MO-6

PARTNERSHIPS:

Uniform Partnership Act adopted. (c. 358).

Liabilities of Partners.—General partners are jointly and severally liable for the debts of the partnership. (358.150).

Administration of Partnership Property.—In addition to Uniform Partnership Act provisions (U.P.A. Part V, §25, Part VI, §37; 358.250-.370), surviving partner(s) file a verified inventory of partnership assets and liabilities in probate court within 30 days after issuance of letters testamentary for estate of deceased partner (473.220). Surviving partner(s) may continue in possession of partnership estate, pay its debts, and settle its business, and shall account to deceased partner's personal representative upon order of probate court. (473.223). Probate court may order surviving partner(s) to give security (473.227), may commit surviving partner(s) to jail for failure to perform aforementioned duties, and may appoint a receiver for partnership estate (473.230).

Partnership Name.—See category Intellectual Property, topic Trademarks and Tradenames.

Limited Partnership.—Revised Uniform Act adopted, eff. 1/1/87 for new Missouri limited partnerships or for foreign limited partnerships doing business in Missouri on 1/1/87. (c. 359). Missouri limited partnerships formed prior to 1/1/87 must elect to comply with revised Act prior to 1/1/89 by filing new certificate of limited partnership or original certificate of limited partnership and designation of registered agent and office with secretary of state and paying $50 filing fee. (359.641).

Limited liability partnerships may be organized for any lawful purposes. No partner in registered limited liability partnership shall be liable for obligations chargeable to partnership. Registered limited liability partnership may sue and be sued in its own name. (358.150). For provisions applicable to registration of limited liability partnership see 358.440-.510.

See also topics Associations, Joint Stock Companies.

BUSINESS REGULATION AND COMMERCE

BANKS AND BANKING:

Uniform Commercial Code adopted. (c. 400). See also topic Commercial Code.

Supervision.—Division of Finance, in Department of Consumer Affairs Regulation and Licensing at Jefferson City, has charge of execution of laws relating to banks, trust companies, savings and safe deposit companies, and all banking business in this state, including incorporation and winding up of affairs of dissolved or insolvent banks, under management of Director of Finance. (c. 361; c. 362).

Director of Finance passes on all applications of banks to open branch offices. He may take charge of any bank: (1) When it refuses to submit its records and affairs to inspection; (2) when it is insolvent; (3) when its continuance in business will jeopardize its depositors or other indebtedness; (4) when any bank desires to have him take charge of its affairs. He may subsequently permit such bank to resume business, or may request the Attorney General to institute proceedings to procure dissolution of such bank. Director may, during his possession, compound doubtful claims of or against such bank, except deposit claims, and may sell or dispose of the property of such bank on order of the circuit court. He approves or rejects claims filed against bank, and may declare dividends on order of circuit court. (361.230-.300-.340-.350-.380-.470-.540 and -.570). For additional powers see 361.480.

Shares of stock shall be divided into shares having a par value. (362.055).

Any banking corporation, with consent of a majority of stockholders, may issue and sell preferred stock of one or more classes, with par value of not less than $20 nor more than $100, which stock will be invalid until 100% of par value thereof in lawful money of U.S. has been paid into treasury of issuing corporation. (362.075, 362.090).

Powers of Banks.—Banking corporations organized under laws of this state have general banking powers and may hold real estate conveyed to it in satisfaction of debts, and such as it may purchase at sales under judgments, decrees or liens held by it. Bank may exercise powers through subsidiary company. Real estate so acquired by any bank must be sold within ten years thereafter unless there is building thereon occupied by bank as office. Bank may purchase shares in Federal Deposit Insurance Corporation, offer financial consulting, provide securities brokerage services, purchase and sell investment securities, and establish mutual funds (362.105-.165), may purchase shares in small business investment companies (362.173), and may purchase and hold stock in corporations whose only purpose is to purchase or convey real property which bank or trust company itself could purchase (362.105).

Loans.—Various restrictions on amounts of loans depending on type, character of security, etc., are set out in the statutes. (362.170).

Fiduciary Powers.—Any bank, organized under laws of state and having paid-up capital of at least $50,000 in city of less than 10,000 population, $100,000 in city of from 10,000 to 50,000 population, or $200,000 in city of more than 50,000 population, may exercise all fiduciary powers granted to trust companies by laws of state. Director, on application and proper showing, must issue certificate showing that bank is entitled to exercise such powers, and thereupon such bank may use words "trust company" as part of corporate name. (362.115).

Deposits in name of depositor and another, payable to either or survivor, create joint tenancy (362.470) except a tenancy by entirety is created when husband and wife are named (758 S.W.2d 197). Payment to either, or survivor after death of one, releases bank prior to receipt by bank of written notice by one tenant not to pay. (362.470). Deposits in name of depositor and "pay on death to John Doe" shall, during depositor's lifetime be depositor's property and under his sole control. At depositor's death such account shall become property of person named as "pay on death" person. If there are more than one first named persons as depositor, they shall be joint tenants with right of survivorship. (362.471). Deposits by or for minor are payable to minor and such payment releases bank. (362.465).

Deposits by any person as trustee are payable upon check or order of such person bearing his signature and containing same words as deposit unless bank has further written notice of terms of trust. (362.480). Death of person making deposit as trustee of another, without further notice to bank of terms of trust, justifies payment to stated beneficiary. (362.475).

Unclaimed Deposits.—See category Property, topic Absentees, subhead Escheat.

Uniform Common Trust Fund Act and Official Amendment adopted. (362.580).

Investments in Name of Nominee.—Unless expressly forbidden by instruments, etc., setting up trust, any bank or trust company qualified to act as fiduciary may, if cofiduciaries consent, hold investments in name of nominee. Records must show true owner. (362.207).

Liens.—Bank has a lien for rent of safe deposit boxes, and on other personal property left in its keeping as bailee. (362.485).

Stop Payment Orders.—Governed by Commercial Code. (400.4-403, 404).

Collections.—See topic Commercial Code.

Savings and Loan Associations.—Regulated by statute. (c. 369).

Savings Banks.—Regulated by statute. (369.400-.445).

Credit Unions.—Regulated by statute. (c. 370).

Private Bankers.—New private banks may not be established. (362.015).

Foreign Banks.—Foreign banking corporation may be licensed by Director of Finance to do limited business in this state, on application showing compliance with the laws of state of its incorporation and authority to carry on such business, proof of its financial condition and nature of its business, and upon designating Director as its agent for service of process. There is a license fee of $250 per year. (362.430-.445).

Director of Finance determines eligibility of all foreign corporations applying for a license to do a banking business in this state, and if satisfied issues a license. He may revoke such license whenever he finds that such corporation, or any private banker, is carrying on business in an unauthorized or unsafe way. (362.450-.455).

Foreign banks or other corporations organized under laws of any state other than Missouri and national banking associations having their principal place of business in such state may act in any fiduciary capacity in Missouri, if so authorized to act in such other state, without being licensed to do banking business or qualifying as foreign corporation, if such other state permits Missouri banks or other corporations or national banking associations with principal place of business in Missouri and authorized to act in fiduciary capacity in Missouri, to act in such capacity either on appointment of agent for service of process in that state, or law of which provides that engagement in any acts in fiduciary capacity in that state is deemed to constitute appointment of state official for valid service of process, or substantially similar provision, provided certificate of reciprocity reciting eligibility to act in such fiduciary capacity is obtained from Missouri Director of Finance. (362.600).

Foreign banks, trust companies, and savings and loan associations may acquire indebtedness in Missouri secured by mortgage or deed of trust on real estate, with or without other security, and service, collect and enforce the same, without becoming licensed herein or doing business within the meaning of any law of this state. (362.423).

Regional Banking.—Bank holding companies in states adjoining Missouri may acquire control of Missouri bank or bank holding company if adjoining state has reciprocal legislation. (362.925).

See also categories Estates and Trusts, topic Executors and Administrators; Family, topic Guardian and Ward.

Taxation.—A tax of 7% measured by net income, minus certain credits, is imposed on national banking associations and state bank and trust companies in lieu of tax on bank shares and tangible and intangible personal property. (148.030). Apportionment formula is used for financial institution conducting business in other states. (148.097).

BILLS AND NOTES:

Uniform Commercial Code in force. See topic Commercial Code.

Judgment Notes.—Authority in a note to enter appearance and confess judgment is ineffectual, but does not invalidate note. (220 Mo. 717, 120 S.W. 36).

Attorney fee clauses are enforceable. (400.3-106[e]).

BILLS OF LADING:

See topic Carriers.

BILLS OF SALE:

See topic Sales.

BLUE SKY LAW:

See topic Securities.

BROKERS:

Real estate brokers are licensed by Missouri Real Estate Commission. License fees are set by commission. Applicant for license must submit to oral or written examination by Commission. Action brought by broker must allege broker was licensed. (339.010-.160). Residential mortgage brokers are licensed by Residential Mortgage Board. (408.653).

Uniform Commercial Code in force. See topic Commercial Code.

See also topics Securities, Factors; category Insurance, topic Insurance Companies.

BULK SALES:

See topic Commercial Code; category Debtor and Creditor, topic Fraudulent Sales and Conveyances.

See note at head of Digest as to 1998 legislation covered.

See Topical Index in front part of this volume.

CARRIERS:

Carriers are subject to provisions of act creating Public Service Commission, which has supervision of execution of the act and determines reasonableness of rates. (cc. 386 and 387).

Discrimination between long and short hauls, with certain exceptions, and pooling between carriers are forbidden. (389.320, 387.100).

Bills of Lading.—See topic Commercial Code.

Liens.—See topic Commercial Code.

Gross Receipts Tax on Express Companies.—Express companies must, on or before April 1 of each year, file with State Director of Revenue a report of receipts for the preceding calendar year and pay $2.50 on each $100 of gross receipts from business done within the state. Failure to file and pay tax by May 31 incurs penalty of $100 for each additional day and prevents doing business in state until filing and payment. (153.010-.020).

Uniform Commercial Code in force. See topic Commercial Code.

Motor Vehicle Carriers.—See category Transportation, topic Motor Vehicles.

COMMERCIAL CODE:

Uniform Commercial Code adopted. (c. 400). Section numbers of Missouri Revised Statutes generally correspond with those of 1962 Official Text, printed in Uniform and Model Acts section except that all parts are prefixed by chapter number and decimal point.

Material variations from 1962 Official Text, and options or alternatives adopted, are as follows:

Conforming amendments to Art.1 have been adopted to conform to Revised Art. 3 of Code.

1-201 (26) reads:

"A person 'notifies' or 'gives' a notice or notification to another by taking such steps as may be reasonably required to inform the other in ordinary course whether or not such other actually comes to know of it. A person 'receives' a notice or notification when

"(a) it comes to his attention, or

"(b) it is duly delivered at the place of business through which the contract was made or at any other place held out by him as the place of receipt of such communications; or

1-201(37) (1987 amendment) has been adopted to conform to Art. 2A of Code.

1-209—1966 Official Optional Amendment not enacted.

2-316(5) reads: "A seller is not liable for damages resulting from the lack of merchantability or fitness for a particular purpose of livestock he sells if the contract for the sale of the livestock does not contain a written statement as to a warranty of merchantability or fitness for a particular purpose of the livestock."

2-318—1966 Official Optional Amendment Alternative A enacted.

2-702—1966 Official Amendment enacted.

Art. 2A (1987) of Code has been adopted.

Art. 3 (1990 Revision) of Code has been adopted.

Art. 4 (1990 Revision) of Code has been adopted.

4-104(1)(c)—Banking day defined to exclude Sats., Suns. and legal holidays.

4-106—Alternative B of this section has been adopted.

Art. 4 (1989) of Code has been adopted.

Art. 5 (1995 Revision) of Code has been adopted.

5-112—Optional language in Code omitted.

5-114—Optional provisions (4) and (5) are omitted.

6-104(1)(c)—List to be filed in office of Recorder of Deeds of county in which transferor resides.

6-106—Whole section in UCC is deleted.

6-107—Part (e) is omitted from Missouri statutes.

6-108—Part (3)(c) is omitted from Missouri statutes.

6-109—Part (2) is omitted from Missouri statutes.

7-204(4)—New material is added to the Code after the words "impair or repeal . . . .".

400.7-204(4) reads:

"This section does not impair or repeal any existing statute of this state which imposes a higher responsibility upon the warehouseman or invalidates contractual limitations which would be permissible under this article."

7-209—1966 Official Amendment not enacted.

Art. 8 (1977 and 1994 Revisions) of Code have been adopted.

9-103 (1977 amendment) has been adopted to conform to revised Art. 8 of Code.

9-105 (1977 amendment) has been adopted to conform to revised Art. 8 of Code.

9-106—1966 Official Optional Amendment not enacted.

9-113 (1987 amendment) has been adopted to conform to Art. 2A of Code.

9-203 (1977 amendment) has been adopted to conform to revised Art. 8 of Code.

9-302 (1977 amendment) has been adopted to conform to revised Art. 8 of Code.

9-304 (1977 amendment) has been adopted to conform to revised Art. 8 of Code.

9-305 (1977 amendment) has been adopted to conform to revised Art. 8 of Code.

9-309 (1977 amendment) has been adopted to conform to revised Art. 8 of Code.

9-312 (1977 amendment) has been adopted to conform to revised Art. 8 of Code.

9-401—(1) is third alternative with "recorder of deeds" inserted in blanks in Code, and last two words of paragraph (b) changed to "for record, and any such filing shall be for record."

9-401—Part (3) is used and not Alternative (3) of Code.

9-403(3)—Filing fee is $6 for officially approved forms and is to be inserted in blank in Code. Uniform fee for filing forms of a size other than that officially approved by Secretary of State is $6, plus $1 per page for attachments.

9-407—Fee for certificate $8. Upon request copy of all financial statements and assignments furnished for $8 fee.

400.9-408 has been added and reads: "Notwithstanding any other provisions of this chapter, the following special provisions apply where a financing statement is required to be filed for record in the office where a mortgage on the real estate concerned would be filed for record.

"(1) Any amendment, continuation statement, termination statement, statement of assignment, or statement of release incidental to such a financing statement shall be filed for record in the same office where the original financing statement is recorded.

"(2) In addition to other requirements of this part of this chapter, every such statement incidental to such a financing statement shall refer to the original financing statement by book and page of the record thereof.

"(3) Such financing statements and such other statements incidental thereto shall be recorded in the real estate mortgage records, and shall be indexed as real estate mortgages. If any statement shows the name of a record owner of the real estate which is other than the name of the debtor or the secured party, the statement also shall be indexed in the mortgagor index according to the name of such record owner. Such financing statements and such other statements incidental, thereto are entitled to be recorded even though not proved or acknowledged and certified. Fees for recording and related services shall be the same as the fees authorized by law in the case of real estate mortgages.

"(4) The recorder of deeds shall not be liable for any loss resulting from failure of the recorder to record and index a financing statement or other statement incidental thereto as a mortgage on real estate unless it is clearly evident that such recording is desired, either by written instructions indorsed on the financing statement or other statement incidental thereto directing that it be recorded and indexed as a mortgage on real estate, by payment of the recording fee, or otherwise."

Other changes which were made but which are believed to be immaterial are:
(1) 1-109—This is deleted from the statutes.
(2) 7-403(1)(b)—Bracketed material in Code is omitted.

Forms.—See end of this Digest.

See also topics: Banks and Banking, Bills and Notes, Brokers, Carriers, Contracts, Factors, Frauds, Statute of, Sales, Securities, Warehousemen; categories Business Organizations, topic Corporations; Civil Actions and Procedure, topic Limitation of Actions; Debtor and Creditor, topics Assignments, Fraudulent Sales and Conveyances, Liens, Pledges; Documents and Records, topics Records, Seals; Mortgages, topic Chattel Mortgages.

CONDITIONAL SALES:

See topic Sales.

CONSIGNMENTS:

No legislation.

CONSUMER PROTECTION:

Unsolicited merchandise may be refused or deemed gift and be used or disposed of freely without any obligation to sender. (407.200).

Advertising.—Misdemeanor to recklessly make or cause to be made false or misleading statement in any advertisement addressed to public or to substantial number of persons. (570.160). Misdemeanor to advertise sale of property or services with purpose not to sell or provide property or services: (1) At price offered; (2) in quantity sufficient to meet reasonably expected public demand, unless quantity specified in advertisement; or (3) at all. (570.170).

Credit User Protection Law.—Regulates credit services organizations. (407.436).

Home Solicitation Sales.—Generally, buyer may cancel until midnight of third business day after day buyer signs agreement or offer to purchase. (407.705). If cancelled, seller within ten days must tender to buyer any payments, note or other evidences of indebtedness with "cancelled" stamped conspicuously on face. (407.715[1]). If down payment includes goods traded in, goods must be tendered in substantially as good condition as when received by seller or buyer may elect to recover amount equal to trade-in allowance stated in agreement. (407.715[2]). Buyer may retain and has lien on goods delivered to him by seller until seller complies with this section. (407.715[3]).

Lemon Law.—If manufacturer, through its authorized dealer or agent, cannot conform consumer's new motor vehicle to any express warranty by repairing or correcting condition which impairs use, market value or safety of vehicle after reasonable number of attempts, manufacturer must, at its option, either replace vehicle or refund full purchase price, less reasonable allowance for consumer's use of vehicle. (407.567). It is presumed that reasonable number of repair attempts have been taken if (1) same nonconformity has been subject to repair four or more times or (2) vehicle is out of service for cumulative total of 30 or more working days. (407.571). Consumer must give manufacturer written notice of need for repair, and manufacturer has ten calendar days to correct nonconformity. (407.573). Actions under this section must be brought within six months after expiration of warranty, or within 18 months following date of delivery of vehicle, whichever is earlier. (407.573[3]). If manufacturer has established informal dispute settlement procedure, consumer must utilize procedure, and actions must be brought within 90 days following final action of panel. (407.573[3]; 407.575). If consumer prevails, costs and attorney's fees are recoverable. (407.577).

Motor Vehicle Odometers.—Misdemeanor to advertise for sale, sell, install or have installed any device which causes odometer to register mileage other than true mileage driven. (407.516). Felony if, with intent to defraud, one disconnects, resets, or alters odometer of motor vehicle with intent to change indicated number of miles. (407.521). Misdemeanor if, with intent to defraud, one operates motor vehicle less than ten years old knowing that odometer is disconnected or not functioning. (407.526). If odometer incapable of registering same mileage as before repair or replacement, odometer must be adjusted to read zero with written notice attached to left door frame of vehicle by owner or agent specifying prior mileage and date odometer was repaired or replaced and no one may remove or alter notice. (407.531). Any person transferring ownership of motor vehicle must do so by assignment of title and must place mileage at time of transfer above signature of transferor. If true mileage is different from odometer reading or if true mileage is unknown, statement from transferor relating to all facts known

See note at head of Digest as to 1998 legislation covered.

See Topical Index in front part of this volume.

CONSUMER PROTECTION . . . *continued*

concerning true mileage must accompany assignment. (407.536). Civil, criminal, and injunctive remedies available. (407.511-.556).

Time-Share Plans.—Purchaser of time-share plan has five days to cancel. (407.620).

Plain Language.—No "plain language" statute.

Usury.—See topic Interest.

Uniform Commercial Code adopted. See topic Commercial Code.

Uniform Deceptive Trade Practices Act not adopted.

CONTRACTS:

See categories Documents and Records, topic Seals; Family, topic Infants.

Uniform Commercial Code in force. See topic Commercial Code.

FACTORS:

Liens.—See topic Commercial Code.

Uniform Commercial Code in force. See topic Commercial Code. See also topic Brokers; category Property, topic Powers of Attorney.

FRAUDS, STATUTE OF:

All leases, estates, interests of freehold or term of years, or any uncertain interest in realty, not in writing, have the force and effect of leases or estates at will only. (432.050). No lease, estate, interest, either of freehold or term of years, or any uncertain interest of, in, to or out of any lands, tenements or hereditaments can be assigned or granted unless in writing signed by the party assigning or granting the same or his lawful agents authorized by writing or by operation of law. (432.060).

No action shall be brought to charge any executor or administrator, upon any special promise to answer for any debt or damages out of his own estate, or to charge any person upon any special promise to answer for the debt, default or miscarriage of another person, or to charge any person upon any agreement made in consideration of marriage, or upon any contract made for the sale of lands, tenements, hereditaments, or an interest in or concerning them, or any lease thereof, for a longer time than one year, or upon any agreement that is not to be performed within one year from the making thereof, unless the agreement upon which the action shall be brought, or some memorandum or note thereof, shall be in writing and signed by the party to be charged therewith, or some other person by him thereto lawfully authorized, and no contract for the sale of lands made by an agent shall be binding upon the principal, unless such agent is authorized in writing to make said contract. (432.010).

Contracts of Sale.—Uniform Commercial Code in force. See topic Commercial Code.

Part Performance.—Court of equity will enforce verbal contract if plaintiff shows: (a) Performance of acts which are cogent evidence of existence of pleaded contract; (b) terms of verbal contract shown by clear, cogent, unequivocable and convincing testimony; (c) prove acts that are evidence of existence of pleaded contract were done in reliance on contract and that as result of acts positions of parties were so changed that to permit other parties to rely on statute of frauds would result in gross injustice. (429 S.W.2d 269).

Representations.—No action may be brought to charge any person upon or by reason of any representation or assurance made concerning the character, conduct, credit, ability, trade or dealings of any other person, unless such representation or assurance be made in writing and subscribed by the party to be charged thereby, or by some person thereunto by him lawfully authorized. (432.040).

See also categories Civil Actions and Procedure, topic Limitation of Actions; Estates and Trusts, topic Trusts; Family, topic Infants.

INTEREST:

Legal Rate.—9% in absence of agreement fixing rate. (408.020).

Maximum Rate.—No limit on interest allowable for loans to corporations, business loans of $5,000 or more, real estate loans other than residential real estate loans, loans of less than $5,000 secured by real estate used for agriculture, and loans of $5,000 or more secured solely by stock, bonds, bills of exchange, certificates of deposit, warehouse receipts, or bills of lading. (408.035). Other loans except certain small loans (see subhead Small Loans, infra) maximum interest 10% if agreed in writing except that where "market rate" (monthly index of long term U.S. Government Bond yields for second preceding calendar month prior to beginning of calendar quarter plus 3% rounded to nearest 1/10%) is greater than 10%, parties may agree in writing to rate of interest not exceeding "market rate." (408.030). "Market rate" determined by Director of Division of Finance on or before 20th day of last month of quarter for next quarter. (408.030).

In lieu of percentage rate of interest, parties may agree in writing to fee of $10 on any loan but no lender shall permit any borrower to be indebted to him on two or more contracts with result of contracting for or receiving fees exceeding that permitted by law. (408.031).

Judgments.—9% or higher lawful rate stipulated in contract sued on. (408.040).

In tort actions, if claimant has made demand for payment of claim or offer of settlement of claim, to party, parties or their representatives and amount of judgment or order exceeds demand for payment or offer of settlement, prejudgment interests, at rate of 9%, shall be calculated from date 60 days after demand or offer was made, or from date demand or offer was rejected without counteroffer whichever is earlier. (408.040).

Open Accounts.—9% from time demand of payment is made after same falls due. (408.020).

Small Loans.—Lender must register with Director of Finance, who may require bond in principal amount of $1,000. Registration fee of $300 (prorated for less than a year) until following June 30 and annually thereafter by June 30, payable to Director of Revenue. Separate certificate required for each office or place of business. If lender not subject to examination or required to make reports under city ordinances, report of business conducted during preceding calendar year must be filed with Director on or before Apr. 30 and Director may examine business at any time. Director issues regulations governing types and limits of insurance which may be sold in connection with loans, cost of which shall not exceed standard rates and insurer must be authorized to do business in Missouri. Registrant or employees may be licensed as insurance agent. Insurance premiums cannot be considered as interest, service charges or fees. Suspension or revocation of certificate only after ten days notice and hearing before Director and as to place of business where violation occurred. Violations by registered lenders or transacting such business without certificate are misdemeanors. Act not applicable to those subject to supervisory jurisdiction of Director or of Savings and Loan Supervisor under any other law. (367.100-.200).

On loans to corporations and loans not secured by real estate, nonprocessed farm products, livestock, farm machinery or crops, lender may contract for and receive interest at rates agreed to by parties. (408.100).

Interest cannot be discounted or deducted from principal or received at time loan is made, nor compounded. Repayment may be in consecutive monthly installments, none substantially greater than any preceding installment, but first installment may be payable any time within 45 days. Repayment may also be as parties agree, provided agreement allows for payment of simple interest at rates not to exceed those authorized by 408.100 and 408.200. (408.120).

Statement must be delivered to borrower at time loan is made showing name and address of lender, date of loan, schedule of installments or description thereof, type of security, principal amount, rate or amount of interest, prepayment privilege and if interest has been added to principal, that it is subject to following refund requirements if loan is prepaid in full month or more before final installment date. (408.130).

No further or other charge or amount whatsoever may be directly or indirectly charged, contracted for or received for interest, service charges or other fees as incident to extension of credit, except insurance premiums as provided in 367.100-.200, and except on loans for 30 days or longer which are other than "open end credit"; fee not to exceed 5% of principal amount loaned not to exceed $50, but no fee for extension, refinance, restructure or renewal unless investigation made on application for extension; lawful fees actually and necessarily paid out for filing, recording or releasing instruments securing loan; if contract so provides, charge for late payment on each installment in default not less than 15 days not exceeding 5% of installments due or $25, whichever is less, but minimum of $10; charges or premiums for insurance written in connection with loan against loss of or damage to property or against liability arising out of ownership or use of property; charges assessed for processing refused instrument plus handling fee of not more than $15; and if contract or promissory note, signed by borrower, provides for attorney fees, and if necessary to bring suit, attorney fees may not exceed 15% of amount due and payable under contract or promissory note. (408.140).

If excess interest on small loans is charged or received except as result of error, lender shall be barred from recovery of any interest on contract and upon demand return all interest received. (408.150).

False advertising regarding interest, charges, terms or conditions of loans prohibited. (408.160).

Lender must recompute amount of interest earned to date of prepayment on basis of same rate, or deduct from amount of interest contracted for proportion of such amount that sum of monthly balances prepaid bears to sum of all monthly balances of contract, but if prepaid at any time, buyer receives refund calculated by actuarial method. Lender shall not retain more interest than is actually earned if note or loan contract is prepaid. (408.170).

Provisions of 408.120-408.180-.200 do not apply where rate of interest is no more than 10% simple interest or law provides no limit to interest chargeable. (408.190).

Time charge schedule maximum amounts are: On principal balance up to and including $750 amount is 15%; on that part of principal balance over $750 and less than $1,000 amount is 12%; and on that part of principal balance over $1,000 and less than $7,500 amount is 10%; and on that part of principal balance of $7,500 and over, amount is whatever is agreed to by parties. (408.300).

Retail Credit Sales charges regulated by statute. (408.250-.370). See topic Sales, subhead Retail Credit Sales.

Usury invalidates any security interest in personal property or any lien thereon (408.070) but does not avoid debt (196 S.W.2d 442), and creditor may recover 9% interest instead of contract rate (408.060; 98 Mo. App. 382, 72 S.W. 132). See, however, as to small loans, subhead Small Loans, supra. Where usury has been collected, excess over legal rate is applied on principal or debtor may recover such excess with costs. Corporation cannot interpose defense of usury. (408.060).

LICENSES, BUSINESS AND PROFESSIONAL:

Licenses are required for a large number of businesses and occupations. Among these are accountants (c. 326), architects (c. 327), auctioneers (c. 343), audiologists (c. 345), bail bond agents (c. 374), barbers (c. 328), bingo operators and suppliers (313.005-.080), boat dealer (301.550-301.572), boxing and wrestling (c. 317), brokers and exchange dealers (c. 423), children's boarding homes and child-placing agencies (210.201-245), child care facility (c. 210), chiropodists (c. 330), chiropractors (c. 331), cosmetologists, hairdressers and manicurists (c. 329), dentists (c. 332), embalmers (c. 333), engineers (c. 327), geologists (256.456), hospitals (c. 197), insurance brokers (c. 375), interpreter for the deaf (161.409), liquor sales (c. 311), manufacturers (150.300-.370), marital and family therapists (337.700 to .739), meat plants (265.410), merchants (150.010-.290), midwives, physicians and surgeons (c. 334), motor fuel terminal storage (142.295), motor vehicle dealer (301.550-301.572), nurses (c. 335), nursing homes (c. 198), optometrists (c. 336), osteopaths (c. 334), pharmacists (c. 338), physical therapist (c. 334), plumbers (c. 341), podiatrist (c. 330), real estate agents and brokers (339.010, .060, .120), residential mortgage brokers (408.653), retail sales of, transportation of, or installation of equipment using liquified petroleum gas (323.060), sale and issue of checks, drafts and money orders by other than banks, trust companies, savings and loan associations or Federal government or its agencies (365.030), shows, circuses and

See note at head of Digest as to 1998 legislation covered.

See Topical Index in front part of this volume.

MO – 9

LICENSES, BUSINESS AND PROFESSIONAL . . . *continued*

amusements (c. 316), social worker (337.600-.639), speech language pathologists (c. 345), surveyors (c. 327), theatrical booking agency (289.100-.130), and veterinarians (c. 340).

Commercial travelers need not be licensed unless they are itinerant vendors or peddlers. An itinerant vendor is defined as one conducting a temporary or transient business of selling goods, wares and merchandise for not more than 120 days in a room, building or other structure for the exhibition and sale of goods, etc. (150.380). A peddler is defined as one who goes from place to place to sell patents, patent rights, patent or other medicines, lightning rods, goods, wares or merchandise, except pianos, organs, sewing machines, books, charts, maps and stationery, agricultural and horticultural products, including milk, butter, eggs and cheese. (150.470).

Hunting and Fishing.—Licenses are required for hunting and fishing and may be procured from Missouri Conservation Commission at Jefferson City, any county clerk or license collector of City of St. Louis. (Rules and Regulations of the Conservation Commission, §§8-18; per 252.002). Motorboat numbering required. (306.020-.080).

Collection Agencies.—No Legislation. Local laws prohibited. (Const. Art. III §40[4]).

See also topics Brokers, Factors, Securities, Warehousemen; categories Business Organizations, topic Corporations; Family, topic Marriage; Insurance, topic Insurance Companies; Legal Profession, topic Attorneys and Counselors; Transportation, topic Motor Vehicles.

MONOPOLIES, RESTRAINT OF TRADE AND COMPETITION:

§416.031 contains essentially same substantive prohibitions as §§1 and 2 of Sherman Act and §3 of Clayton Act, and is to be construed in harmony with ruling judicial interpretations of those federal statutes. (416.141). Person violating Sherman Act type provisions is guilty of misdemeanor, punishable by maximum of one year in county jail, fine up to $50,000 or both. (416.051). Attorney general is charged with both criminal and civil enforcement. (416.051). Persons injured by such acts may recover triple damages. (416.121). Statute of limitations for all actions is four years from date cause of action accrued. (416.131). Successful prosecution to final judgment by state in any civil or criminal action will be prima facie evidence against defendant in any action brought by another party within one year. (416.061).

Injunction.—Attorney general or person injured may institute action to enjoin unlawful practices. (416.121).

Missouri Motor Fuel Marketing Act.—Business cannot sell motor fuel below cost with intent to injure competition. Cannot sell at lower price than that offered to others at same distribution level. (416.615). Business engaged in commerce in motor fuel must publicly disclose transfer price to itself for distribution of motor fuel at another marketing level. (416.610). Violations subject to $1,000 to $5,000 civil penalty per day. (416.625). Attorney General enforces and may seek civil penalties and injunctions against below-cost sales. (416.630). Persons within relevant geographic area damaged by below-cost sales may sue for damages and injunctive relief. Treble damages and attorneys' fees authorized. (416.635).

NEGOTIABLE INSTRUMENTS:

See topic Bills and Notes.

RESTRAINT OF TRADE:

See topic Monopolies, Restraint of Trade and Competition.

SALES:

Bills of Sale.—Not required, but in sale of motor vehicle certificate of ownership must be assigned. See category Transportation, topic Motor Vehicles.

Product Liability.—Privity not required in action for injuries on implied warranty theory. (372 S.W.2d 41).

Products liability claim means that portion of plaintiff's damages claim is based on theory that defendant is strictly liable because: (1) Defendant, wherever situated in chain of commerce, transferred product in course of his business; and (2) product was used in manner reasonably anticipated; and (3) either or both of following: (a) product was then in defective condition unreasonably dangerous put to reasonably anticipated use, and plaintiff was damaged as direct result of such defective condition or as existed when product was sold, or (b) product was then unreasonably dangerous when put to reasonably anticipated use without knowledge of its characteristics, and plaintiff was damaged as direct result of product being sold without adequate warning. (537.760).

Defendant whose liability is based solely on his status as seller in stream of commerce may be dismissed from products liability claim if defendant provides affidavit that he is aware of no facts or circumstances upon which verdict might be reached against him, other than his status as seller in stream of commerce and there is no credible contradicting evidence. (537.762).

State of the art shall be plead as affirmative defense and shall be complete defense for action based on strict liability for failure to warn of dangerous condition of product. (537.764).

Pure comparative fault shall apply to products liability claims. (537.765).

Conditional Sales.—See topic Commercial Code.

Motor vehicle time sales subject to regulation similar to retail credit sales; persons in business of purchasing retail installment contracts involving motor vehicles regulated. (c. 365).

Uniform Commercial Code in force. See topic Commercial Code.

Retail credit sales involving tangible chattels or services thereon are regulated by statute as to contract content and execution, including written listing of price, downpayment, insurance, fees, time charge, balance and sales price before signing by buyer. Printing must be in eight point type with ten point notice. Limits are placed on insurance, collection charges, and time charges. Buyer must receive copy of contract

and may prepay in full before maturity. Exemptions for motor vehicles, nonprocessed farm products, livestock and money. (408.550). Credit may not be denied on basis of sex or marital status. (408.250-.370).

Retail Time Contract.—On balance of principal, on contracts payable in substantially equal successive monthly payments, in lieu of interest charge, retailer may collect per year time charge of $15 per $100 of first $750; $12 per $100 for amount over $750 but less than $1,000; and $10 per $100 for amount over $1,000 but less than $7,500; and charge will be as agreed by parties on portion over $7,500. For retail time contracts not providing for substantially equal successive monthly payments, in lieu of any other charge, retailer may collect minimum charge of $12 per contract. (408.300[1]).

Retail Charge Agreement.—On balance of principal, retailer may collect time charge per month of 16.7¢ per $10. (408.300).

Bulk Sales.—See topic Commercial Code.

See also topic Frauds, Statute of; categories Debtor and Creditor, topics Assignments, Executions, Fraudulent Sales and Conveyances, Liens, Pledges; Family, topic Guardian and Ward; Mortgages, topics Chattel Mortgages, Mortgages of Real Property; Property, topic Deeds; Taxation, topic Sales and Use Tax; Transportation, topic Motor Vehicles.

SECURITIES:

Uniform Securities Act adopted. (c. 409). Section numbers of Missouri Revised Statutes generally correspond with those of Official Text printed in Uniform and Model Acts section except that all articles are prefixed by chapter number and decimal point. Significant Missouri variations from Official Text are set forth below:

Registration Procedure.—§202(a), Immediately following §202(a)(5): Missouri does not require publication. §202(b), For broker-dealer or investment advisor, initial registration filing fee, $200; renewal registration filing fee $100. For agent, initial and renewal registration filing fee $50. No filing fee subject to refund. §202(d), Missouri uses net capital or minimum ratio between net capital and aggregate indebtedness. §202(e), Commissioner may require bonds of up to $25,000. No bond required where net capital exceeds $100,000. Missouri adds subsection (f) allowing commissioners to require fidelity bonds of up to $250,000 covering employees, general partners and officers.

Denial, Revocation, Suspension, Cancellation, and Withdrawal of Registration.—§204(a)(2)(J), Missouri adds requirement of keeping records required by this act or any commission rule or order. §204(b)(6), Missouri adds provision that no examination is required of those registered as broker-dealers or agents or who were general partners or officers of registered broker-dealers at time of adoption of Act who have been registered continuously since, §204(f), Missouri substitutes its own procedure.

Registration by Notification.—§302, Missouri deletes (a)(2) of Uniform Act. Missouri deletes (b)(6) of Uniform Act. §302(c), Registration statement becomes effective at 2 p.m. central time of second full business day after filing. (409.302[c]).

Registration by Coordination.—§303(b)(3), Missouri deletes "filed under the Securities Act of 1933." §303(c)(2), Registration statement must be on file 15 days. Missouri adds a subsection (d) which allows registration by coordination of securities for which a prospectus or offering circular is required by S.E.C. regulations.

Registration by Qualification.—§304(b)(17), Commissioner may require supporting information at applicant's expense.

Provisions Applicable to Registration Generally.—§305(b), Filing fee: $100. Registration fee: 1/20 of 1% of amount maximum aggregate offering price exceeds $100,000, total fee not to exceed $900. In case of withdrawal of registration statement or pre-effective stop order, commissioner retains filing fee. §305(f), Omitted by Missouri. §305(g), Missouri 409.305(f). Missouri adds requirement of deposit in escrow of securities to be issued to promoter, issued to a promoter within past three years, issued to promoter for consideration substantially different from public offering price within past ten years or issued to any person for consideration other than cash. §305(h), Missouri §409.305(g). §305(i), Missouri §409.305(h). Similar to Uniform Act §305(i) except Missouri omits second and third sentences of 305(i) of Uniform Act. §305(k) omitted and in its place §305(j) providing that registration statements involving securities of investment company or other similar securities involving continuous offering may request registration of indefinite amount of securities but for such securities annual report stating amount sold in fiscal year and payment of registration fee of 1/20th of 1% of amount sold in fiscal year required within 30 days after end of issuer's fiscal year but in no case shall fee exceed $3,000.

Denial, Suspension, and Revocation of Registration.—§306(a)(2)(E), Missouri also allows stop-order if any aspect of offering is substantially unfair, unjust, inequitable or oppressive, or if issuer's enterprise is based upon unsound business principles.

General Provisions.—§401(b), Agent includes a broker-dealer, a partner, officer or director of a broker-dealer, or a person occupying a similar status or performing similar functions. Partner, officer, or director of broker-dealer, however, is agent only if he otherwise comes within definition of agent under §401(b). In §401(b)(1) Missouri adds, as exempted transactions, §§402(a)(4), (6), (9), and security issuance by Missouri agricultural cooperatives. §401(c), Missouri: a broker-dealer may also be an agent. §401(1), Missouri adds contract or bond for sale of realty not situated in Missouri on deferred payment or installment plan.

Exemptions.—§402(a)(9), Commissioner must be notified in writing 30 days before security sold or offered under this subsection. §402(a)(12), adopted in Missouri under §409.402(a)(5). §402(b), Missouri does not exempt transactions in oil. §402(b)(3), Missouri omits an unsolicited order to buy. §§402(b)(9) and (10) Missouri omits these and the following are substituted:

§409.402(b)(9)—"[A]ny transaction by an issuer in a security of its own issue if immediately thereafter the total number of persons who are known to the issuer to have any direct or indirect record or beneficial interest in any of its securities (but not including persons with whom transactions have been exempted by paragraph [8] of this subsection) does not exceed twenty-five and if no commission or other remuneration is paid or given to anyone for procuring or soliciting the transaction;"

See note at head of Digest as to 1998 legislation covered.

See Topical Index in front part of this volume.

SECURITIES . . . continued

§409.402(b)(10)—"[A]ny transaction by an issuer in a security of its own issue if (A) during the twelve months' period ending immediately after such transaction the issuer will have made no more than fifteen transactions exempted by this paragraph (other than transactions also exempted by paragraphs [8] and [9]), and (B) the issuer reasonably believes that the buyer is purchasing for investment and the buyer so represents in writing and (C) no commission or other remuneration is paid or given to anyone for procuring or soliciting the sale; but the commissioner may by rule or order, as to any security or transaction or any type of security or transaction, withdraw or further condition this exemption, or increase or decrease the number of prior transactions permitted by clause (A) or waive the conditions in clauses (B) or (C) with or without the substitution of a limitation on remuneration;"

Missouri adds four sections as follows:

"§409.402(b)(13) any non-issuer transaction by a person who does not control, or who is not controlled by or under common control with, the issuer in a security which has been (and securities which are of the same class as securities of the same issuer which have been) either registered for sale under the laws of this state regulating the sale of securities or lawfully sold in this state as a security exempt from such registration;

"§409.402(b)(14) any non-issuer transaction in a security which at the time of such transaction would be eligible for registration by notification;

"§409.402(b)(15) any non-issuer transaction by a person who does not control, and is not controlled by or under common control with, the issuer if (i) the transactions is at a price reasonably related to the current market price, and (ii) the security is registered with the Securities and Exchange Commission under section 12 of the Securities Exchange Act of 1934 and the issuer files reports with the Securities and Exchange Commission pursuant to Section 13 of that act.

"§409.402(b)(16) any patronage distributions of an agricultural cooperative corporation received by a patron or member in the form of capital stock, revolving fund certificate, retain certificate, certificate of indebtedness, letter of advice or other written notice."

Missouri adds §402(c) permitting Commissioner to exempt from Sections 301 and 403 any other transaction not exempted in 402(b) and to withdraw or condition exemption in public interest.

§402(c), Missouri 409.402(d).

Missouri adds §409.402(e) providing Commissioner may by order after hearing deny or revoke any exemptions for security issued by agricultural cooperative corporation not qualifying under 402(a)(5).

§402(d) is Missouri 409.402(f).

§406(a), Act administered by commissioner of securities under secretary of state. §407(a)(1), Commissioner may also investigate to determine whether registration may be granted, denied or revoked. §407(d), Missouri §409.407(e).

Missouri inserts §409.408. Fraudulent practices, order prohibiting. (a) Commissioner may require additional information to support exemption. Right to sell such security or regulation of broker-dealer, agent or investment advisor may be suspended for failure to comply. (b) Commissioner may by order prohibit current or impending fraudulent or illegal practices.

§408, Missouri §409.409. §409, Missouri §409.410. §410, Missouri §409.411. §409.411(a), interest recoverable at 8%.

§411, Missouri §409.412. (a) Aggrieved party has remedy under Chapter 536, R.S.Mo.; (b) Missouri §409.412(d).

Missouri adds two sections: §409.412(b). Circuit Court of Cole County has jurisdiction in equity to review, modify, amend or annul any ruling, finding or order of Commissioner. §409.412(c). Parties aggrieved under §409.412(b) have right of appeal to Supreme Court.

§412, Missouri §409.413. Uniform §412(f) is Missouri §409.412(e).

§413, Missouri §409.414. (c), Commissioner may keep information secret. (e), Commissioner may charge up to $100 for interpretative opinions. Missouri adds subsection (f) dealing with evidence.

§414, Missouri §409.415. (c), Missouri adds proviso that an offer directed outside Missouri is considered for purposes of this section not made in Missouri if lawful in state to which directed.

§415, Not adopted in Missouri. §417, Not adopted in Missouri. §418(a), Not adopted in Missouri. §419, Not adopted in Missouri.

Uniform Simplification of Fiduciary Security Transfers Act adopted. (403.250-.350).

Uniform Commercial Code in force. See topic Commercial Code.

Uniform Securities Ownership by Minors Act not adopted.

See also category Business Organizations, topic Corporations.

STATUTE OF FRAUDS:

See topic Frauds, Statute of.

TRUST RECEIPT SECURITY:

Uniform Commercial Code in force. See topic Commercial Code; category Debtor and Creditor, topic Pledges.

WAREHOUSEMEN:

License and Bond.—Warehouseman doing business in cities of over 25,000 inhabitants and other than grain storage must procure license from circuit court of county, or circuit court of city of St. Louis, where warehouse is situated, and must file bond or legal liability insurance policy with clerk of such court in sum of $25,000. (415.010-.030).

Grain Warehouses.—Warehouses equipped for handling and storing grain (unless used exclusively for storage of grain grown by the owners or operators) are subject to Missouri Grain Warehouse Law. (c. 411). Must display sign at main entrance and on or about scale of warehouse notifying whether warehouse is licensed under state or federal warehouse laws. (411.778).

Lien.—See topic Commercial Code.

Warehouse Receipts.—See topic Commercial Code.

Warehousemen are prohibited from issuing receipts, or other vouchers for grain without having actually received same in store or on premises of warehouse. (411.451).

Uniform Commercial Code in force. See topic Commercial Code.

CITIZENSHIP

ALIENS:

Property.—Persons not citizens or residents of U.S. and corporations not created under laws of U.S. are prohibited from acquiring by grant, purchase, devise or descent tracts of agricultural land larger than five acres, and from holding leaseholds of ten or more years or beneficial interests in such tracts under contracts of sale or similar arrangements. These restrictions, however, do not apply to agricultural land located in counties which border state of Oklahoma which was owned prior to Jan. 1, 1995. No restrictions on ownership of personal property or other real estate. (442.560).

CIVIL ACTIONS AND PROCEDURE

ACCORD AND SATISFACTION:

Common law rules govern. Must be pleaded. (C.R. 55.08; 509.090).

Uniform Commercial Code in force. See category Business Regulation and Commerce, topic Commercial Code.

See also topic Judgments; category Mortgages, topic Mortgages of Real Property.

ACTIONS:

Federal Rules of Civil Procedure form basis of Civil Rules. (C.R. 41-90). See topic Practice.

There is but one form of action, known as a Civil Action. (C.R. 42.01; 506.040).

Equity.—There are no separate courts of law and equity, but the distinction between legal and equitable causes and principles is preserved. (506.010; C.R. 41.02).

Conditions Precedent.—None of general application.

Commencement.—See topic Process.

Parties.—Civil actions must be prosecuted in name of real party in interest, except in case of executors, administrators, guardians, trustees of express trusts, named party to contract for benefit of another or others expressly authorized by statute. (C.R. 52.01).

A person must be joined in action if: (1) In his absence complete relief cannot be accorded among those already parties; or (2) he claims an interest relating to subject of action and disposition of action in his absence may (a) impair or impede his ability to protect that interest or (b) leave any persons already parties subject to substantial risk of incurring double, multiple, or otherwise inconsistent obligations by reason of his claimed interest. If he has not been joined, court must order that he be made a party. If he should join as a plaintiff but refuses to do so he may be made a defendant. (C.R. 52.04).

If such person cannot be made a party, court must determine whether action should proceed among parties before it or should be dismissed, absent party being regarded as indispensable. (C.R. 52.04).

All persons asserting or having asserted against them any right jointly, severally or in the alternative arising from same occurrences or transactions may be joined as plaintiffs or defendants respectively, if any question of law or fact common to all will arise in the action. (C.R. 52.05).

Class Actions.—Federal rules obtain. (C.R. 52.08). Uniform Class Actions Act not adopted.

Intervention.—On timely application by motion accompanied by pleading stating claim or defense sought to be interposed, intervention must be allowed: (1) When a statute confers an unconditional right; (2) when applicant claims an interest relating to subject of action and disposition of action may impair or impede his ability to protect that interest, unless applicant's interest is adequately represented by existing parties. Intervention may be permitted: (1) When a statute confers a conditional right; (2) when applicant's claim or defense and main action have a common question of law or fact; or (3) when validity of constitutional provision, statute, regulation or ordinance is in question; court may notify legal officer of state or subdivision thereof. (C.R. 52.12).

Interpleader.—Persons having claims against the plaintiff may be joined as defendants and required to interplead when plaintiff may be exposed to double or multiple liability. Defendant exposed to similar liability may also obtain such interpleader. (C.R. 52.07).

Third Party Practice.—Federal rules obtain. (C.R. 52.11[a]). Additionally, if counterclaim is served against plaintiff, he may cause third party to be brought in under circumstances which under this rule would entitle defendant to do so. (C.R. 52.11[b]). Where third-party defendant is liable to plaintiff or anyone holding similar position or claim on which third-party plaintiff has been sued, execution by third-party plaintiff on judgment against third-party defendant limited to amount third-party plaintiff has paid on judgment obtained against him by obligee. (C.R. 52.11[c]).

Joinder of Causes of Action.—Plaintiff in petition or in reply setting forth counterclaim, or defendant in answer setting forth a counterclaim, may join either as independent or alternate claims as many claims, either legal or equitable or both, as he may have against an opposing party. (C.R. 55.06[a]).

Consolidation of Actions.—Whenever same plaintiff has several civil actions founded alone upon liquidated damages pending in same court against same defendant or several defendants court may in its discretion order such civil actions to be consolidated into one civil action. (C.R. 66.01[a]). When civil actions involving common

See note at head of Digest as to 1998 legislation covered.

See Topical Index in front part of this volume.

ACTIONS . . . *continued*
question of law or fact are pending before court it may order joint hearing or trial of any or all matters in issue in civil actions. (C.R. 66.01[b]). If injury not resulting in death is inflicted upon person of one spouse and cause of action therefor accrued to injured spouse and also to other spouse for loss of consortium or services or medical expenses they must be enforced in one action by both spouses if they have ever been co-parties in action or if notice is given. (C.R. 66.01[c]).

Splitting Causes of Action.—Single cause of action may not be split and adjudication of suit first filed on split cause of action is bar to second suit. (731 S.W.2d 859).

Severance and Separate Trial.—The court in furtherance of convenience or to avoid prejudice may order separate trial of any claim, cross-claim, counterclaim or third-party claim, or of any separate issue, or of any number of claims, cross-claims, counterclaims, third-party claims or issues. (C.R. 66.02).

Medical Malpractice.—Recovery in medical malpractice action from any one defendant is limited to $350,000 for noneconomic damages. Punitive damages can only be awarded if there was willful, wanton or malicious misconduct. Damages are divided into: (1) Past economic damages, (2) past noneconomic damages, (3) future medical damages, (4) future economic damages other than medical, and (5) future noneconomic damages. Future damages are expressed at present value. Past damages are payable in lump sum but any party may request that future damages be paid, in whole or in part, in periodic payments if total future damages exceed $100,000. Court may require judgment debtor to post security or purchase annuity adequate to assure full payment of future payments. If claimant dies before all future payments are made, obligation to make payments except for future medical payments continues. Obligation for future medical payments continues only until medical payments owing at death and due to injury for which damages were awarded are paid. (538.210-.220).

Plaintiff in medical malpractice action must file affidavit with courts stating that he has obtained written opinion of legally qualified health care provider that defendant failed to use such care as reasonably prudent or careful health care provider would have under similar circumstances and that such failure directly caused or directly contributed to damages claimed. Affidavit must include qualifications of affiant, and there must be separate affidavit for each defendent. Affidavits must be filed no later than 90 days after petition is filed or court may dismiss action without prejudice. (538.225).

In medical malpractice actions fault is apportioned among parties and persons released from liability, but defendants are only jointly liable with those defendants whose apportioned share of damages is equal to or less than such defendants. Claim of plaintiff against parties who were not released is reduced by amount of released person's equitable share of total obligation imposed by court pursuant to full apportion of fault as though there had been no release. (538.230).

Licensed physician, surgeon, registered professional nurse, licensed practical nurse or mobile emergency medical technician who renders emergency care without compensation at scene of emergency or accident not liable for civil damages other than those resulting from gross negligence or willful or wanton acts or omissions. (537.037).

Licensed physician, surgeon, registered professional nurse, licensed practical nurse or mobile emergency medical technician who renders emergency care without compensation to any minor involved in accident or in competitive sports or other emergencies at scene without first obtaining consent of parent or guardian shall not be liable for any civil damages other than for gross negligence or willful or wanton acts or omissions. (537.037).

Abatement and Revival.—Causes of action for injury to person or property survive death of either wrongdoer or injured party and may be brought against estate of deceased or by executor or administrator of injured party. (537.010, 537.020). If party becomes incompetent, court may, on motion, allow action to continue by or against his representative. (C.R. 52.13).

Limitation of.—See topic Limitation of Actions.

Criminal Conversation.—Cause of action abolished. (516-140).

Small Claims.—See category Courts and Legislature, topic Courts.

Direct Actions Against Insurer.—See category Transportation, topic Motor Vehicles.

See also topics Pleading, Practice; category Family, topic Infants.

APPEAL AND ERROR:

Appeal from associate circuit court lies to circuit court, and may be taken in person or by agent, by filing application for trial de novo with clerk serving associate circuit judge within ten days after judgment. (512.180-.190).

Bond.—Applicant, or some person for him, together with one or more solvent sureties, must, in order to stay execution, within ten days after judgment file bond in a sum sufficient to secure payment of judgment and costs, to be approved by associate circuit judge. (512.190).

Trial in circuit court on appeal from associate circuit court is anew. (512.270).

Judgment.—If judgment be affirmed, or be against the appellant, such judgment shall be rendered against appellant and his sureties. (512.320).

Appeal from probate division of circuit court lies to circuit court, upon filing of notice of appeal within ten days after judgment, and presentment of bond. (See subhead Appeal from Circuit Court, catchline Bond, infra.) (472.180-.210).

Appeal from circuit court lies to Supreme Court or to one of the courts of appeals, according to circuit from which appeal taken and subject matter of action or amount involved. (Const. 1945, art. V, Sec. 3; 477.040; 512.020). Notice of appeal must be filed within ten days after judgment or order appealed from becomes final. On motion and notice, appellate court, within six months from date of final judgment, may allow appeal on special order where merit shown and delay is not due to culpable negligence. (C.R. 81.04-.07).

Bond.—Appeal may be taken with or without bond, but does not operate as supersedeas where no bond given unless appellant is an executor, administrator, guardian, curator or municipality. Bond, when given, must be in amount fixed by court sufficient to cover whole amount of judgment unsatisfied, costs on appeal, interest and damages for delay, or if judgment is for property, the amount recovered for the use and detention, costs of action and appeal, interest, and damages for delay, conditioned to prosecute appeal, to perform judgment in case of affirmance or modification, and to pay all damages, interest and costs awarded by appellate court. Court may allow time not exceeding 20 days to file bond. (C.R. 81.09).

Docket Fee.—Appellate court docket fee of $50 must be deposited with clerk of trial court at time of filing appeal. (C.R. 81.04).

Appeal from Administrative Agencies.—Procedure for review of actions of any administrative officer or body is provided. (C.R. 100.01-.02; 536.021-.050-.063-.150). See also topic Certiorari.

BONDS:

See topics Appeal and Error, Injunctions, Costs, Replevin; categories Business Organizations, topic Corporations; Business Regulation and Commerce, topics Brokers, Securities; Debtor and Creditor, topics Attachment, Executions; Estates and Trusts, topic Executors and Administrators; Family, topic Guardian and Ward; Insurance, topic Surety and Guaranty Companies; Legal Profession, topic Attorneys and Counselors.

Sureties.—On bonds of all county officers, sureties must be residents of county. (107.010). No sheriff, collector, constable, county treasurer, attorney, clerk, judge or justice of any court of record, may be surety on any official bond. (107.020). Corporate surety with paid up capital of not less than $200,000 admitted to transact such business in Missouri may qualify on furnishing satisfactory evidence of solvency. (107.080-.090).

Enforcement.—Suits on official bonds or bonds executed to the state are brought by the Attorney General at the direction of the Governor in the name of the state. (107.150).

CERTIORARI:

Supreme Court or any of various courts of appeal (depending on jurisdictional grounds) and circuit courts may issue this writ to any inferior court and Supreme Court may also issue the writ to any court of appeals and finally determine the cause the same as on original appeal. (Const. 1945, art. V, §§4, 10).

See also topic Appeal and Error.

CHARITABLE IMMUNITY:

See topic Damages.

COMMISSIONS TO TAKE TESTIMONY:

See topic Depositions and Discovery.

COSTS:

Prevailing party recovers costs, except where different provision is made by law. (C.R. 77.01). In all civil and criminal cases, additional fee of $7 is assessed as costs. (476.053 and 514.015).

Allowances by the court are chargeable as costs.

When Due.—All court costs are payable prior to time service is rendered. (514.015). Court may require party to furnish security for contemplated costs. (C.R. 77.02).

Liability of Attorney.—If an attorney commences and fails to prosecute an action, or brings the wrong action and a non-suit is the consequence, the court may, in its discretion, enter judgment against the attorney for the full amount of the costs and damages in consequence thereof. (484.160).

Costs Where Settlement Proposed.—If defendant offers to settle matter more than ten days before trial by allowing judgment against him with costs and plaintiff refuses to accept offer and at trial obtains judgment which is not more favorable than offer of settlement, plaintiff shall not recover costs from time of offer but shall pay costs accrued after that time. (C.R. 77.04).

DAMAGES:

Common law generally prevails as to compensatory damages. Punitive damages are allowed where injuries are negligently caused and the negligence is of such an aggravated form or attended by such circumstances as to be wanton and reckless in character. Exemplary or punitive damages generally are not allowed in suits on contracts. (765 S.W.2d 646).

Sovereign immunity doctrine established except for suits for compensatory damages for injuries caused by negligent acts of public employees in operation of motor vehicles within course of their employment or injuries caused by condition of public entity's property if plaintiff establishes that property was in dangerous condition at time of injury, that injury directly resulted from dangerous condition, that dangerous condition created reasonably foreseeable risk of kind of injury which was incurred, and that either negligent or wrongful act of public entity employee within course of employment created dangerous condition or public entity had actual or constructive notice of dangerous condition in sufficient time prior to injury to have taken measures to protect against dangerous condition. (537.600). Any county, city, person, organization or agency or their employees who has charge of or benefits from free work performed as condition of probation cannot be sued for damages as result of injuries to those performing free work unless injuries are result of intentional tort or gross negligence. (559.021).

Charitable immunity doctrine abolished for tort actions arising after Nov. 10, 1969 (446 S.W. 2d 599), except that good faith donor of canned or perishable food, which is fit for human consumption and complies with all Mo. food and drug laws under c. 196, shall not be subject to criminal or civil liability arising from injury or death due to condition of food unless result of negligence, recklessness or intentional misconduct by donor.

Any officer or member of governing body of entity which operates under standards of §501(c) of Internal Revenue Code of 1986, who is not compensated for his services on salary or prorated equivalent basis, shall be immune from personal liability for any civil

DAMAGES . . . *continued*
damages arising from acts performed in his official capacity. Immunity shall extend only to such actions for which person would not otherwise be liable, but for his affiliation with entity. (537.117). Above does not apply to actions relating to improper health care under 538.205-538.230.

Volunteer of nonprofit organization or governmental entity is immune from personal liability for act or omission resulting in damage or injury to person intended to receive benefit from volunteer's service if volunteer acted in good faith, within scope of official functions and duties, and damage or injury was not caused by intentional or malicious conduct or by negligence of volunteer.

Treble Damages.—May be awarded in the following instances: waste committed by a tenant for life or years during his term of anything belonging to the tenement (537.420), and in any action for waste wantonly committed (537.490); trespass (537.340), unless defendant had probable cause to believe the land or the things taken, injured, or destroyed were his own (537.360); and in some other instances.

Punitive Damages.—All actions tried before jury involving punitive damages shall be conducted in bifurcated trial before same jury if requested by any party. (510.263).

Doctrines of remittitur and additur, based on trial judge's assessment of totality of surrounding circumstances, shall apply to punitive damage awards. Above does not apply to actions relating to improper health care under 538.205-538.230.

Double Damages.—May be awarded in the following instances: trustee selling property at auction under any writing securing payment of a debt charging a commission in excess of 2% on first $1,000 of amount of sale, 1% on sums over that and under $5,000 and 1/2 of 1% on all sums over $5,000 (443.360-.370); tenant for life or years or other person in possession under or by collusion with tenant, holding over after termination of term and after demand and notice in writing requiring possession by person entitled thereto, and any tenant giving notice in writing of his intention to quit at a specified time, who fails to deliver possession at such time, for the time he retains possession (441.080-.100); malicious or wanton damages or destruction of personal property (537.330); and in some other instances.

Collateral Source Rule.—If prior to trial defendant or his insurer or authorized representative, or any combination of them, pays all or any part of plaintiff's special damages, defendant may introduce evidence that some other person other than plaintiff has paid those amounts. Evidence shall not identify any person having made such payments. Such introduction of evidence shall constitute waiver of any right to credit against judgment pursuant to §490.710. (490.715). Above does not apply to actions relating to improper health care under 538.205-538.230.

Insurance.—Vexatious refusal of an insurance company to pay any loss under a policy authorizes the court or jury to allow plaintiff damages not to exceed 20% of first $1,500 of loss, and 10% of amount of loss in excess of $1,500 and reasonable attorney's fee. (375.420).

No-Fault Insurance.—Not adopted.

Comparative Negligence Rule.—Pure comparative fault. Damages assessed by jury before allocation of fault among parties. Court-adopted system same as that of Uniform Comparative Fault Act. (661 S.W.2d 11). See also category Estates and Trusts, topic Death, subhead Action for Death.

Joint and Several Liability.—In all tort actions for damages in which fault is not assessed to plaintiff, defendants shall be jointly and severally liable for amount of judgment rendered against such defendants. (537.067). Above does not apply to actions relating to improper health care under 538.205-538.230.

Uniform Contribution Among Tortfeasors Act not adopted.

Medical Malpractice.—See topic Actions, subhead Medical Malpractice.

DECLARATORY JUDGMENTS:

See topic Judgments.

DEPOSITIONS AND DISCOVERY:

A party to any suit pending in any court of this state may obtain the deposition of the adverse party or of any witness for discovery or evidence. (C.R. 57.03).

Uniform Foreign Depositions Act not adopted.

Outside of State for Use within State.—See subhead Before Whom Taken, infra.

Perpetuating Testimony.—Depositions may also be taken to perpetuate testimony. (C.R. 57.02).

Before Whom Taken.—Depositions may be taken by some one of the following officers (C.R. 57.05):

Within This State.—By some judge, justice, magistrate, notary public or clerk of any court having a seal, in vacation of court, mayor or chief officer of a city or town having a seal of office.

Without This State.—By some office out of this state appointed by authority of the laws of this state to take depositions, or by some consul or commercial or diplomatic representative of the United States, having a seal, or mayor or chief officer of any city, town or borough, having a seal of office, or by some judge, justice of the peace, or other judicial officer, or by some notary public, within the government where the witness may be found.

Special Commissioner.—Court may, in its discretion, appoint commissioner to take such depositions and fixing time and place thereof, and depositions must then be taken pursuant to said order. Such commissioner is empowered to hear and determine all objections to testimony, but on demand of party aggrieved must report his ruling excluding any evidence to court or judge forthwith or at close of depositions, for approval or reversal, continuing depositions for further proceedings if required. Commissioner shall be member of Missouri Bar. (C.R. 57.06).

Notice of time and place of taking depositions and witnesses to be examined must be delivered to adverse party or his attorney of record no less than seven days before taking of deposition. (C.R. 57.03). Deposition of witness may be taken in this state after giving of such notice without obtaining commission (C.R. 57.06), and deposition of witness may be taken in another state after giving of such notice and without obtaining commission if adverse party by written stipulation waives issuance of dedimus.

Under certain conditions, upon application to court in which suit is pending, or judge thereof in vacation, time for which notice is given may be shortened. (C.R. 57.03).

Examination of Witnesses.—Ordinarily depositions are taken, after due notice, by oral interrogatories, in shorthand and transcribed in the presence of the officer before whom depositions were taken. (C.R. 57.03[d]).

Only objections as to the form of questions or answers are waived, when not made at the time before the officer taking the deposition; all other objections may be made at trail. (C.R. 57.07). Refusal of adverse party to answer proper question in deposition is ground for striking his pleadings from the files. (491.180).

Compelling Attendance of Witnesses.—Every person, judge, or other officer of the state required to take depositions of witnesses pursuant to the foregoing sections of the statutes, or by virtue of any commission issuing out of any court of record in this or any other government, has power to issue subpoenas for witnesses to appear and testify, and to compel their attendance in the same manner and under like penalties as any court of record of this state. (C.R. 57.09). Party duly summoned, refusing to attend and testify, in addition to punishment for contempt, may have his pleadings stricken on motion. (491.180).

Forms.—Officers taking depositions must observe following forms and mode of proceeding, commencing thus:

Form

Depositions of witnesses, produced, sworn and examined on the . . . . day of . . . ., in the year of our Lord 19. . . ., between the hours of 8 o'clock in the forenoon and 6 o'clock in the afternoon of that day, at . . . . in the county of . . . . and State of . . . . before me (name the officer and style of office), in a certain cause now pending in the . . . court of the county of . . . ., in the State of Missouri between . . . ., plaintiff and . . . ., defendant, on the part of the plaintiff (or defendant).

(Here insert names of parties and attorneys appearing).

(Here insert name of witness), of lawful age, being produced, sworn and examined on the part of the . . . ., deposeth and saith (here insert the statement of the witness).

Every deposition must be recorded by reporter. (C.R. 57.03). When testimony is fully transcribed deposition must be submitted to witness for examination and read to or by him, unless such examination and reading are waived by witness and by parties. Any changes in form or substance which witness desires to make must be entered upon deposition by officer with statement of reasons given by witness for making them; original answers, changes, and reasons all being part of deposition. Deposition must then be signed by witness, unless parties by stipulation waive signing or witness is ill or cannot be found, or is dead or refuses to sign. If deposition is not signed by witness, officer must sign it and state on record reason for it not being signed by witness; and deposition may then be used as fully as though signed, unless on motion to suppress, court holds that reasons given for refusal to sign require rejection of deposition in whole or in part. (C.R. 57.03).

If any paper or exhibit is produced and proved, or referred to by the witness, it ought to be described in his deposition, or marked and referred to by the deponent, in such manner that it may be identified when the deposition is read; and all such papers and exhibits must be attached to and returned with the deposition. (C.R. 57.03).

The officer will annex at the foot of the deposition of each witness the following certificate:

Subscribed and sworn to before me, on the day, at the place, and within the hours first aforesaid. (Signature and title).

Then proceed with other depositions (if any) in the same form, annexing a like certificate to each. When all the witnesses who appear have been sworn and examined, and their depositions reduced to writing, subscribed and certified, as above, the officer will attach to the depositions all papers and exhibits proved or referred to in the examination, the commission and notice, with the following certificate indorsed thereon or attached thereto:

Form

"I (name of officer and style of office) within and for the . . . ., in the State of . . . ., do certify that in pursuance of the within (or annexed) commission and notice (or notice alone if commission has been waived), came before me at . . . ., in the county and State last aforesaid (insert names of the witnesses), who were by me severally sworn (or affirmed) to testify the whole truth of their knowledge touching the matter in controversy aforesaid; that they were examined, and their examination reduced to writing and subscribed by them, respectively, in my presence, on the day, between the hours, and at the place in that behalf first aforesaid, and their said depositions are now herewith returned." If the officer knows the residence of the witness, he will include the following in his certificate: And I further certify that said (here insert the names of the witnesses) are residents of said county of . . . ., in said State of . . . . Given at . . . ., in the county of . . . . and State of . . . ., this . . . . day of . . . ., 19. . . . . (Signature and title).

If the officer has no official seal, the return must be accompanied by a certificate of the official character of the officer taking the depositions, attested by the seal of the state of his residence or by the seal of some court of record within said state at the time when the depositions were taken, stating that such officer was duly commissioned as such.

It is advisable for the officer to note at the bottom of the depositions the amount of costs, and if paid, by which party.

The officer taking depositions is required to enclose, in a strong envelope, securely sealed, the depositions, papers and exhibits, commission, notice and certificates, and direct the same to the clerk of the court, noting on some convenient part of the envelope the style of the cause and contents, thus:

John Doe, plaintiff, against Richard Roe, defendant. Depositions for . . . .

The depositions must be begun on the day mentioned in the notice. If they cannot be completed on that day, the taking of them may be adjourned to the succeeding day, at

---

See note at head of Digest as to 1998 legislation covered.

See Topical Index in front part of this volume.

DEPOSITIONS AND DISCOVERY . . . *continued*

the same place and between the same hours. The person taking them should, in such case, make the following entry, closing the business for that day, viz.:

Not being able to complete the taking of said depositions, by reason that (here insert the reason), I adjourn the further taking of the same until tomorrow, then to be continued at the same place and between the same hours mentioned in the annexed notice. (Signature and title).

On the succeeding day, let the person taking the depositions commence as follows:

Pursuant to adjournment, as above stated, on the . . . . day of . . . ., 19. . . ., between the hours of . . . in the forenoon and . . . . in the afternoon, at the . . . ., I continued the taking of said depositions as follows, viz.:

(Here insert name), in continuation of his deposition, commenced yesterday on his oath further says, etc.

───────────

See also topic Evidence, subhead Witnesses; category Documents and Records, topic Affidavits.

EVIDENCE:

Uniform Business Records as Evidence Act adopted. (490.660-.692). In addition, all other parties must be served with copies of records and affidavit as follows:

THE STATE OF _____
COUNTY OF _____

AFFIDAVIT

Before me, the undersigned authority, personally appeared _____, who, being by me duly sworn, deposed as follows:

My name is _____, I am of sound mind, capable of making this affidavit, and personally acquainted with the facts herein stated:

I am the custodian of the records of _____ Attached hereto are _____ pages of records from _____ These _____ pages of records are kept by _____ in the regular course of business, and it was the regular course of business of _____ for an employee or representative of _____ with knowledge of the act, event, condition, opinion, or diagnosis recorded to make the record or to transmit information thereof to be included in such record; and the record was made at or near the time of the act, event, condition, opinion or diagnosis. The records attached hereto are the original or exact duplicates of the original, or, accurate reproductions of the original records as permitted by subsection 1 of section 362.413, RS Mo.

───────────
Affiant

In witness whereof I have hereunto subscribed by name and affixed my official seal this _____ day of _____, 19____.

_____   _____
(Signed)   (Seal)

(490.692, 362.413[4]).

Witnesses.—All persons are competent except those who are mentally incapacitated, and children under ten years old who appear incapable of receiving correct impressions or relating them truly. (491.060). Exception to ten year old rule is that if such child is alleged to be victim of offense under 565, 566 or 568 of R.S.Mo., then he is competent witness without qualification. Conviction of crime does not disqualify but may be shown to affect credibility. (491.050).

Child Victim Witness Protection Act allows limited videotape testimony for victims of abuse. (491.675 to 491.705).

See also topic Depositions and Discovery.

Privileged Communications.—Attorneys and physicians may not testify as to professional communications or matters unless privilege waived by client or patient. Information obtained by ministers, priests or rabbis in their capacity as spiritual advisors, counselors or consultants is exempt from testimony. (491.060).

Husband or wife may testify in civil actions brought by or against the other.

Where one party to contract or cause of action is dead or insane, prior relevant statements made by that party shall not be excluded as hearsay. (491.010).

Adverse parties may be compelled to testify. (491.030).

Self-incrimination.—Witness generally cannot be compelled to give self-incriminating testimony. (491.040). Circuit judge may issue order compelling witness to give self-incriminating testimony, but such testimony cannot be used as part of criminal prosecution against witness except for perjury, giving false or misleading statement, contempt committed in answering or failing to answer, or in producing or failing to produce evidence in accordance with order. (491.205).

See also topic Depositions and Discovery; category Documents and Records, topic Affidavits.

Uniform Act to Secure Attendance of Witnesses From Without a State in Criminal Proceedings adopted. (491.400-.450).

See also topic Depositions and Discovery.

INJUNCTIONS:

Injunctions will lie whenever any irreparable injury is being done or about to be done and the injured party has no adequate remedy at law. (526.030).

Jurisdiction.—Injunction may be granted by circuit judge, and if specially assigned or transferred to hear cause, or if there is no circuit judge present in county, by associate circuit judge. (526.010-.020).

Temporary Injunctions.—When it shall appear by the petition that the plaintiff is entitled to the relief demanded, and such relief consists in the restraining of some act of the defendant, which, during the litigation, would produce injury to the plaintiff, or if the defendant is threatening to do some act which would render a judgment ineffectual, a temporary injunction or restraining order may be granted. (526.050).

Bond.—No injunction or restraining order may issue, unless on final hearing, except in suits instituted by the state on its behalf, until the plaintiff shall have executed a sufficient bond in such sum as the court may direct to secure the amount or other matter

to be enjoined and all damages, costs or sums of money that shall be adjudged against him if the injunction be dissolved. (C.R. 92.02).

JUDGMENTS:

Judgments became final 15 days after entry, or upon disposition of motion for new trial which is deemed denied if not passed on within 90 days after filing. (C.R. 78.04, 78.06).

Summary judgment proceeding commenced by motion therefor with at least 10 days notice before hearing. Supporting affidavit may be used. If hearing shows no genuine issue on any material fact and party is entitled to judgment as matter of law, judgment must be entered. Judgment may be on liability only with damages to be tried. (C.R. 74.04).

Default.—Interlocutory judgments authorized for failure of defendant to file or serve a pleading. (C.R. 74.05). May be set aside for good cause within reasonable time not to exceed one year. (C.R. 74.05).

Judgment non pros. authorized for failure of plaintiff to file or serve a pleading. (511.050). May be set aside within 30 days after given for good cause. (C.R. 74.05).

Declaratory Judgments.—Uniform Act adopted. (C.R. 87.01-.11, 527.120).

Vacation or Modification.—Trial court may vacate, reopen, correct, amend or modify its judgment for good cause within 30 days from entry thereof. After filing notice of appeal and before filing transcript on appeal, court may, after expiration of 30-day period, vacate, amend or modify judgment upon stipulation of parties accompanied by withdrawal of appeal. (C.R. 75.01).

Lien.—Judgment or decree of any court of record except associate, small claims and municipal divisions of circuit courts, shall be liens on real estate of judgment debtor situate in county for which or in which court is held. (511.350[1]). Any such judgment or decree, on filing of and indexing of transcript thereof in circuit clerk's office of another county, becomes lien on real estate of judgment debtor situate in such other county. (511.424). Lien commences upon entry of judgment, and extends to then owned and after acquired realty. When two or more judgments are rendered at same term, as between judgment plaintiffs lien commences on last day of term. (511.360). Judgment rendered by associate circuit court is lien on real estate only after transcript of such judgment is filed in circuit clerk's office. (511.350[2]). Owner may redeem property prior to foreclosure by paying collector. (141.420). Owner may not redeem property from judgment if property is residential property adjudged vacant for six months or more prior to judgment. (141.520).

Revival.—At any time within ten years scire facias may be sued out to revive a judgment and lien. (C.R. 74.09).

Assignment.—Judgments may be assigned in writing, executed and acknowledged by assignors and filed with clerk of court where judgment entered. (C.R. 74.12).

Execution on a judgment may be had at any time within ten years. (516.350).

Foreign Judgments.—Uniform Enforcement of Foreign Judgments Act adopted. (C.R. 74.14). Uniform Foreign Country Money-Judgments Recognition Act adopted. (§§511.770 through .787; adopted under title shown.)

See also topic Appeal and Error; categories Business Regulation and Commerce, topic Interest; Debtor and Creditor, topics Executions, Liens.

LIMITATION OF ACTIONS:

Actions must be brought in the following periods:

Ten years: (1) An action which is brought on any instrument in writing, whether sealed or unsealed for the payment of money or property, except as hereinafter stated; (2) actions brought on any covenant of warranty contained in any deed of conveyance of land shall be brought within ten years next after there shall have been a final decision against the title of the covenantor in such deed, and actions on any covenant of seizin contained in any such deed shall be brought within ten years after the cause of such action shall accrue; (3) actions for relief not otherwise provided for. (516.110). Action on judgment is barred after ten years from date of rendition or revival. (516.350). Action for recovery of land must be commenced within ten years from time plaintiff, his ancestor, predecessor, grantor or other person under whom he claims was seized or possessed of the premises. (516.010). Any action against person whose sole connection with improvement is performing or furnishing design, planning or construction, including architectural, engineering or construction services to recover damages for personal injury, property damage or wrongful death arising out of defective or unsafe condition of any improvement to real property, including for contribution or indemnity must be commenced within ten years of date improvement is completed. (516.097).

Five years: (1) All actions upon contracts, obligations or liabilities, express or implied except those aforementioned and except where a different time is limited; (2) action upon a liability created by a statute other than a penalty or forfeiture; (3) action for trespass on or injury to real estate; (4) action for taking, detaining or injuring any goods or chattels, including actions for the recovery of specific personal property, or for any other injury to the person or rights of another, not arising on contract and not herein otherwise enumerated; (5) action for relief on the ground of fraud, the cause of action in such case to be deemed not to have accrued until the discovery by the aggrieved party, at any time within ten years, of the facts constituting the fraud. (516.120).

Four years: (1) Contracts of sale under U.C.C. U.C.C. §2-725 adopted. (400.2-725).

Three years: (1) Action against a sheriff, coroner or other officer upon a liability incurred by the doing of an act in his official capacity and in virtue of his office, or by the omission of any official duty, including the nonpayment of money collected upon an execution or otherwise; (2) action upon a statute for a penalty or forfeiture, where the action is given to the party aggrieved, or to such party and the state (516.130); (3) customer who fails to discover and report an unauthorized signature or any alteration on the face or back of the item or does not within three years from that time discover and report any unauthorized endorsement is precluded from asserting against the bank such unauthorized signature or endorsement or such alteration (400.4-406[4]); (4) actions for wrongful death (537.080).

───────────

LIMITATION OF ACTIONS . . . *continued*

Two years: (1) Action for libel, slander, assault, battery, false imprisonment, malicious prosecution or violation of 290.140 (service letter statute); (2) actions by employees for payment of minimum wages or overtime compensation, or for recovery of any amount under Fair Labor Standards Act (516.140); (3) actions against physicians, hospitals, dentists, registered or licensed practical nurses, optometrists, podiatrists, pharmacists, chiropractors, professional physical therapists, any entity providing health care services for damages for malpractice, error, or mistake, statute running from date of occurrence of negligence, except that minor under ten years has until his 12th birthday to sue, and where act is introducing and negligently permitting foreign object to remain within body of living person, action must be brought within two years of discovery or from date on which patient should have discovered, whichever is first, but action must be brought within ten years from date of act (516.105); (4) action for breach of covenant restricting land use (516.095).

Proceedings on bond of executor or administrator barred two years after discharge. (473.213).

See also category Estates and Trusts, topic Death, subhead Action for Death.

Six Months: Bulk sales—U.C.C. §6-111 adopted. (400.6-111).

See also category Estates and Trusts, topic Wills, subhead Will Contests.

When Time Begins to Run.—Except in actions for recovery of real property, limitation begins to run only upon ascertainment of the last item of damages resulting from the wrong done or breach of duty or contract. (516.100).

As to accrual of actions under Art. III of U.C.C., see U.C.C. §3-122. (400.3-122).

Disabilities.—Where the person in whose favor a cause of action accrues is an infant, insane or imprisoned on a criminal charge or under sentence of a criminal court for a term less than life, the statutory period does not begin to run until the disability is removed, but no action to recover real property or the possession thereof may be commenced later than 21 years after cause or action or right of entry accrued. (516.030, .170). If any person entitled to sue dies before statutory period expires, if such cause of action shall survive to his representatives, his executor or administrator may, after expiration of such time and within one year after such death, commence such action, but not after that period. (516.180).

Absence from the state of a party against whom a cause of action accrues while he is a resident of the state suspends the operation of the statute of limitations except for actions for the recovery of real property. (516.200).

Foreign Causes of Action.—Where a cause of action has become fully barred by the laws of the state or country in which it originated, it is barred in Missouri. (516.190).

Interruption of Statutory Period.—Part payment under circumstances not inconsistent with intent to pay balance tolls the running of the statutory period. (516.340; 239 Mo. App. 73, 188 S.W.2d 84).

Revival.—A debt may be revived by an acknowledgment or new promise in writing signed by the party to be charged, but not otherwise. (516.320). One joint debtor cannot revive the demand as against another joint debtor. (516.330).

Contractual limitations are not permitted. (431.030).

Pleading.—Limitations must be pleaded affirmatively by answer (C.R. 55.08), unless defect appears on face of petition in which case point may be raised on motion to dismiss.

Uniform Commercial Code in force. See category Business Regulation and Commerce, topic Commercial Code.

See also categories Business Regulation and Commerce, topic Monopolies, Restraint of Trade and Competition; Employment, topic Labor Relations; Mortgages, topic Mortgages of Real Property; Property, topic Adverse Possession.

PARTITION:

In all cases where lands, tenements, or hereditaments are held in joint tenancy or tenancy in common, including estates in fee, for life, or for years it shall be lawful for any one or more of parties interested therein, whether adults or minors, to file petition in circuit court of proper county, asking for partition, if same can be done without great prejudice to parties in interest, and if not, then for sale of premises and division of proceeds thereof among all parties according to their respective rights and interests. In case one or more of such parties, or share or quantity of interest of any of parties is unknown to petitioner, or such interest is uncertain or contingent, or ownership of inheritance is dependent upon executory devise or remainder shall be contingent, so that such parties cannot be named, it must be so stated in petition. (C.R. 96.01, .05).

Partition in Kind or Sale.—Commissioners are appointed to make the partition and if partition cannot be made without great prejudice to the owners the land is sold under order of the court and the proceeds divided (C.R. 96.12-.18-.29).

PLEADING:

Governed by Rules of Civil Procedure.

Pleadings Permitted.—Pleadings consist of petition, answer, reply if answer contains a counterclaim, answer to crossclaim if answer contains one, third party petition if leave given to summon person not an original party, and third party answer. No other pleading required except as court may order. (C.R. 55.01).

Frivolous Claims.—Signature of attorney or party constitutes certificate that pleading has been read, is well-grounded in fact, and is warranted by existing law or good faith argument for extension or reversal thereof. Sanctions may include expenses incurred by opposing parties and attorneys' fees. (C.R. 55.03).

General Rules of Pleading.—Technical forms are not required. Each averment must be simple, concise and direct. (C.R. 55.04). Pleading setting forth claim for relief must contain short and plain statement of facts supporting claim and demand for judgment. (C.R. 55.05, 509.050). If damages requested are money damages, no dollar figure shall be included except to determine proper jurisdictional authority, but prayer shall be for such damages which are fair and reasonable. (509.050). Relief in alternative or of several different types may be demanded. (509.050, C.R. 55.10).

As many claims, either legal or equitable or both, as may be had against an opposing party may be joined as either independent or alternate claims. (C.R. 55.06).

Averments of adverse parties must be admitted or denied. Defenses to each claim asserted must be stated in short and plain terms. Averment of lack of knowledge sufficient to form a belief as to truth of an allegation has effect of a denial. If in good faith denying only a part of an averment, specify so much as is true and deny the remainder. Make specific denials of designated averments or deny generally except such designated averments as are expressly admitted, unless intending to controvert all averments, in which case general denial may be made. (C.R. 55.07).

Matters constituting affirmative defenses or an avoidance must be set forth affirmatively. (C.R. 55.08). Averments to which a responsive pleading is required are admitted unless denied, except as to amount of damage. If reply is filed, whether required or not, all affirmative defenses in answer not denied are deemed admitted. If responsive pleading is not required and not filed, all averments are taken as denied or avoided. (C.R. 55.09).

Averments must be made in numbered paragraphs. Each claim founded on separate transaction or occurrence and each defense, other than denial, must be stated in a separate count or defense. (C.R. 55.11).

Statements in pleadings may be adopted by reference in same or other pleadings or motions. Exhibits to a pleading are a part thereof for all purposes. (C.R. 55.12). Items of special damage must be specifically stated. Amount of exemplary or punitive damages sought must be separately stated. (C.R. 55.19). In tort action, amount sought may not be stated except to determine proper jurisdiction, and prayer must be for such damages as are fair and reasonable. (C.R. 55.19).

Written instrument may be pleaded according to legal effect. It may also be recited at length or a copy attached as an exhibit, in which case execution is deemed confessed unless party charged specifically denies execution. (C.R. 55.23).

Amended or Supplemental Pleadings.—Pleadings may be amended any time before responsive pleading is filed, or if none required, within 20 days after it is served. Otherwise, only by leave of court or consent of adverse party. On motion and notice, supplemental pleadings setting forth occurrences since date of pleading may be permitted by court. (C.R. 55.33).

Time of Answering.—Thirty days after service of summons and petition; if served by mail, 30 days after return registered mail receipt is filed; if served by publication only, 45 days after first publication and notice. Answers to crossclaims or replies to counterclaims, 20 days after filing. (C.R. 55.25).

Small Claims.—See category Courts and Legislature, topic Courts.

PRACTICE:

Governed by Missouri Rules of Civil Procedure.

Discovery is obtained by written interrogatories (C.R. 56.01), motion to produce nonprivileged documents or objects (C.R. 58.01), motion for physical or mental examination of person (C.R. 60.01) and depositions (see topic Depositions and Discovery). Requests for admissions of facts and genuineness of documents authorized. (C.R. 59.01). Enforcement of discovery by parties provided. (510.060).

Direct Actions Against Insurer.—See category Transportation, topic Motor Vehicles.

Small Claims.—See category Courts and Legislature, topic Courts.

See also topics Actions, Appeal and Error, Depositions and Discovery, Injunctions, Judgments, Pleading, Process; category Debtor and Creditor, topics Attachment, Executions, Garnishment.

PROCESS:

(C.R. 53.01; 54.01-.03-.06-.12).

Civil action is commenced by filing a petition with court. (C.R. 53.01). See topic Pleading.

Form and Contents.—Summons in a civil action must contain name of court and parties, be directed to defendant and state name and address of plaintiff's attorney, if any, otherwise plaintiff's address, and time within which and place where defendant is required to appear and defend and it shall notify him that in case of his failure to do so, judgment by default shall be rendered against him for the relief demanded in petition. (C.R. 54.02).

By Whom Issued.—Clerk of court. (C.R. 54.01).

Who May Serve.—Must be by a sheriff, or his deputy, or in case sheriff in any cause is for any reason disqualified, then by coroner of county in which such process is to be served; or, for good cause shown, some person other than sheriff or coroner may be specially appointed by court in any cause, but such appointment is valid for service of process only for which such person was specially appointed. (C.R. 54.03, .05). Party may request that fees to special process server be awarded in any judgment entered in action. (506.140).

Sheriff Fees.—Service of summons, writ or other order of court $20 for each item; service of subpoena $10. (57.280).

Service in ordinary suits is made by delivering a copy of the petition and summons to defendant personally, or by leaving copies of same at his usual place of abode with some person of his family over 15 years of age, or by delivering copies of same to an agent authorized by law to receive service. (C.R. 54.13).

Service on a domestic or foreign corporation, partnership or unincorporated association is made by delivering a copy of summons and petition to an officer, partner or managing or general agent, or by leaving copies at any business office of defendant with person having charge thereof, or delivering same to any other agent authorized by appointment or required by law to receive service of process. (C.R. 54.13). Foreign corporation and foreign limited partnership is bound by provisions of 506.500 for personal service of process.

Service on a public, municipal, governmental or quasi-public corporation or body is made by delivering a copy of the summons and petition to the clerk of the

See note at head of Digest as to 1998 legislation covered.

See Topical Index in front part of this volume.

MO – 15

PROCESS . . . *continued*
county court in the case of a county, to the mayor or city clerk or city attorney in the case of a city, and to the chief executive officer in the case of any other public, municipal, governmental or quasi-public corporation or body. If there is, for the time being, no such officer as is specified by this subsection, court may designate appropriate officer to whom copies of summons and petition may be delivered in order to effect service. (C.R. 54.13).

Service on nonresident owner or operator of motor vehicle or watercraft in suit for damages. See category Transportation, topic Motor Vehicles.

Personal service outside state on party domiciled within state has same effect as if served within state and warrants general judgment. Party served has 30 days within which to appear. (C.R. 54.07, 55.25).

Outstate service is authorized in case of any person, whether or not a resident, firm, or corporation who in person or through an agent does any of following: (1) Transaction of any business within this state; (2) making of any contract within this state; (3) commission of a tortious act within this state; (4) ownership, use, or possession of any real estate situated in this state; (5) contracting to insure any person, property or risk located within this state at time of contracting; (6) engaging in act of sexual intercourse within this state with mother of child on or near probable period of conception of that child. (506.500; C.R. 54.06). Service may be made by personally serving defendant outside state or, in case of corporations, by serving managing officer or registered agent in any state. Process, copy or petition, and fees must be sent to court of record or court officer at place where defendant may be served. Process may be personally served by person authorized to serve process at that place. Affidavit of person serving process, stating time, manner, and place of service, must be returned to office of clerk or judge from which it issued. (506.510). Such service empowers court to render personal judgment. Default judgment may be entered 30 days after service and may only be set aside on showing timely and sufficient to set aside default judgment rendered on ordinary service of process within this state. (506.520).

Service by mail or publication and personal service outside the state is allowed in cases affecting a fund, will, trust estate, specific property or any interest therein, or any res or status within the jurisdiction of the court. (C.R. 54.12, 54.13 & 54.14).

Service by Mail.—Party desiring service by mail must file with the judge or clerk an affidavit, verified by oath of the party or of someone in his behalf, for an order for such service. The petition or affidavit must show why service cannot be had in ordinary manner and state name and address of party to be served by mail. The clerk shall serve a copy of summons and of petition by registered mail, addressed to defendant at address furnished by plaintiff, requesting a return receipt signed by addressee only. (C.R. 54.16).

Service by Publication.—Party desiring service by publication shall allege in his petition or affidavit, verified by oath of the party or of someone in his behalf, for an order of publication, why service cannot be had in the ordinary manner and give the last known address of defendant or state that the same is unknown. The judge or clerk must issue an order of publication of notice to the defendant, notifying him of commencement of the action, stating briefly the object and general nature thereof, and describing the property, if any, to be thereby affected. The notice must also contain the name of the court and the names of the parties, and state the name and address of plaintiff's attorney, if any, otherwise the plaintiff's address, and the time, at least 45 days after first publication, within which defendant is required to appear and defend, and must notify him that in case of his failure to do so, judgment by default will be rendered against him. Such notice must be published at least once each week for four successive weeks in some newspaper published in county where suit is instituted, if there be a paper published there, which plaintiff or his attorney of record may designate, if not, then in some paper published in this state, which court may designate as most likely to give notice to person to be notified. Within ten days after said order, the clerk must mail a copy of the notice to each defendant whose address has been stated. When one or more of defendants are unborn or the names of one or more defendants are unknown to plaintiff, he may so state in his petition or affidavit for order of publication, and the judge or clerk may issue an order of publication of notice to the unborn or unknown defendants, who may be sufficiently described as the heirs, grantees or successors of the person to whom the property to be affected was last known to have been transferred. Attorney to represent defaulting unborn or unknown defendants may be appointed. The court may require personal service in addition to publication. (C.R. 54.17).

Personal Service Outside the State.—Plaintiff may cause a copy of the petition, with a copy of the summons, to be delivered to each defendant residing or being without this state, and at any place within the United States or their territories summoning said defendant to appear and plead within 30 days after service upon said defendant; and if the defendant shall refuse to receive such copy of the petition and summons, and the offer of the officer to deliver same to him, such refusal shall be as effectual service as though such copies were actually delivered to such defendant. Such service may be made by any officer authorized by law to serve process in civil actions within the state or territory where such service is made, or by his deputy, and shall be proved by the affidavit of such officer, or deputy, stating the time and manner of such service, made before the clerk or judge of the court of which affiant is an officer. Such clerk or judge shall certify to the official character of the affiant, and to his authority to serve process in civil actions within the state or territory where such service was made. When such certificate is made by a clerk or judge of a court of record, the same shall be attested by the seal of such court, and when the same is made by a judge of a court not of record, the official character of such judge shall also be certified by the proper officer of the state, under his official seal. Any return of service, made and certified as above provided, shall be prima facie evidence of the facts stated in such return. If the plaintiff, or his attorney of record, shall allege in his verified petition, or at the time of filing same, or at any time thereafter shall make the affidavit required for service by publication, and shall file in said cause proof of service of process on any defendant or defendants, in conformity with the provisions of this paragraph, it shall not be necessary for such plaintiff to obtain the order for service by mail or by publication or to procure the publication provided in the rule. (C.R. 54.20; 54.21).

Long Arm Statute.—See subhead Outstate Service, supra.

REPLEVIN:

If a party claim the possession of specific personal property he may at the time of filing his complaint or at any time thereafter, before the rendition of judgment in the cause, request court order requiring defendant to deliver property specified to sheriff. (C.R. 99.01, .04).

Affidavit.—Plaintiff seeking to replevy property must file his affidavit or affidavit of some other person in his behalf showing: (1) Description of property; (2) facts showing party entitled to possession of property; (3) actual value thereof; (4) that it has not been seized under any legal process; and (5) that he will be in danger of losing property unless immediate possession is obtained or property is otherwise secured. (C.R. 99.03).

Bond.—On filing of such affidavit the writ of replevin is issued but before sheriff takes property plaintiff is required to give bond, with one or more sufficient sureties, for double value of property stated in affidavit. (C.R. 99.06).

Repossession.—Before or after delivery to plaintiff by sheriff defendant may retain or obtain redelivery of property by giving bond with one or more sufficient sureties in double value of property. (C.R. 99.07-.08).

Damages are recoverable for injuries to and detention of the property. (C.R. 99.12).

Claims of Third Persons.—No authority for intervention by third persons claiming adverse interests in the property. (69 Mo. App. 594).

SEQUESTRATION:

Sequestration of property may be ordered in the following cases: (1) For alimony or separate maintenance when defendant neglects to furnish security when ordered by court or defaults in payment of same (452.130); (2) in case of judgment for performance of act other than payment of money, when court deems such procedure necessary (511.340); (3) when execution for judgment creditor returned unsatisfied against state or municipal employee (525.310).

See also category Debtor and Creditor, topics Attachment, Executions, Garnishment, Receivers.

SERVICE:

See topic Process.

STAY OF EXECUTION:

See topic Appeal and Error; category Debtor and Creditor, topic Executions.

SUBMISSION OF CONTROVERSY:

Actual controversy may be submitted on an agreed statement of facts to any court of competent jurisdiction which may render judgment thereon as in an action. It must appear by affidavit that controversy is real and proceedings in good faith. (511.740).

See also category Dispute Resolution, topic Arbitration and Award.

VENUE:

Suits may be brought by summons either in county in which defendant resides (if he is Missouri resident) or in county wherein plaintiff resides, and defendant can be found; or, if there are several defendants (whether or not all are residents of state), in any county in which one of them resides; or when defendants are all nonresidents, in any county. Tort actions may also be brought in county where cause of action accrued. (508.010). If venue is in county that has two judicial circuits, venue in judicial circuit where factors exist, arose, occurred. (478.461).

Suits against municipal corporations may be brought only in county where seat of government is situated, except cities of over 400,000 may be sued in any county in which any part of the city is situated. (508.050).

Actions Affecting Property.—Actions for possession of real or personal property, or whereby title to real estate may be affected or for enforcement of lien of any special tax bill thereon must be brought in county where property or some part is situated. (508.020-.030).

Change of venue must be granted on agreement of parties (C.R. 51.02), and as matter of right in counties of 75,000 or less (C.R. 51.03), and may be granted for specified reasons (C.R. 51.04).

COURTS AND LEGISLATURE

COURTS:

United States District Courts.—

Eastern District.—Clerk's office; St. Louis 63101.

Northern Division is composed of following counties: Adair, Chariton, Clark, Knox, Lewis, Linn, Macon, Marion, Monroe, Pike, Ralls, Randolph, Schuyler, Scotland and Shelby.

Court sits at Hannibal.

Eastern Division is composed of following: City of St. Louis; counties of Audrain, Crawford, Dent, Franklin, Gasconade, Iron, Jefferson, Lincoln, Maries, Montgomery, Phelps, St. Charles, St. Francois, Ste. Genevieve, St. Louis, Warren and Washington.

Court sits at St. Louis.

Southeastern Division is composed of following counties: Bollinger, Butler, Cape Girardeau, Carter, Dunklin, Madison, Mississippi, New Madrid, Pemiscot, Perry, Reynolds, Ripley, Scott, Shannon, Stoddard and Wayne.

Court sits at Cape Girardeau.

Western District.—Clerk's office: Kansas City 64106.

Clerk's fee is $120.

Western Division is composed of following counties: Bates, Carroll, Cass, Clay, Henry, Jackson, Johnson, Lafayette, Ray, St. Clair and Saline.

Court sits at Kansas City.

Southwestern Division is composed of following counties: Barry, Barton, Jasper, Lawrence, McDonald, Newton, Stone and Vernon.

See note at head of Digest as to 1998 legislation covered.

See Topical Index in front part of this volume.

MO – 16

COURTS . . . *continued*

Court sits at Joplin.

Southern Division is composed of following counties: Cedar, Christian, Dade, Dallas, Douglas, Greene, Howell, Laclede, Oregon, Ozark, Polk, Pulaski, Taney, Texas, Webster and Wright.

Court sits at Springfield.

Central Division is composed of following counties: Benton, Boone, Callaway, Camden, Cole, Cooper, Hickory, Howard, Miller, Moniteau, Morgan, Osage and Pettis.

Court sits at Jefferson City.

St. Joseph Division is composed of following counties: Andrew, Atchison, Buchanan, Caldwell, Clinton, Daviess, DeKalb, Gentry, Grundy, Harrison, Holt, Livingston, Mercer, Nodaway, Platte, Putnam, Sullivan and Worth.

Court sits at St. Joseph.

Supreme Court of Missouri.—Supreme Court is composed of seven judges, has appellate and superintending jurisdiction over circuit and other courts of record, and has power to issue writs of habeas corpus, quo warranto, mandamus, certiorari, and other remedial writs. There are two divisions of this court of equal dignity.

Jurisdiction.—Supreme Court has exclusive appellate jurisdiction of cases involving: construction of federal or state constitution, federal treaties or statutes, or state revenue laws; authority exercised under Federal laws; title to state office; and offenses punishable by death or life imprisonment. (Const. Art. 5, §3). It has general superintending control over all inferior courts and may issue and determine original remedial writs.

Court sits at Jefferson City.

Court of Appeals.—Court of Appeals consists of three districts, Eastern, Western and Southern. (477.040). Court has appellate jurisdiction of all cases from Circuit Courts and inferior courts of record and control over those courts, except in those cases in which appeal lies directly to Supreme Court. (See subhead Supreme Court of Missouri, supra.) Court of Appeals has power to issue prerogative and remedial writs and to hear and determine cases in which such writs may be determined.

Eastern District.—Jurisdiction comprises City of St. Louis and Counties of Audrain, Cape Girardeau, Clark, Franklin, Jefferson, Gasconade, Knox, Lewis, Lincoln, Madison, Marion, Monroe, Montgomery, Osage, Perry, Pike, Ralls, St. Charles, St. Francois, Ste. Genevieve, St. Louis, Scotland, Shelby, Warren and Washington. (477.050).

Sessions.—In St. Louis.

Western District.—Jurisdiction comprises Counties of Adair, Andrew, Atchison, Bates, Benton, Boone, Buchanan, Caldwell, Callaway, Cass, Chariton, Clay, Clinton, Carroll, Cole, Cooper, Daviess, De Kalb, Gentry, Grundy, Henry, Holt, Howard, Harrison, Jackson, Johnson, Lafayette, Linn, Livingston, Macon, Mercer, Miller, Moniteau, Morgan, Nodaway, Platte, Putnam, Pettis, Randolph, Ray, Saline, Schuyler, Sullivan, Vernon and Worth. (477.070).

Sessions.—In Kansas City.

Southern District.—Jurisdiction comprises Counties of Barry, Barton, Bollinger, Butler, Camden, Carter, Cedar, Christian, Crawford, Dade, Dallas, Dent, Douglas, Dunklin, Greene, Hickory, Howell, Iron, Jasper, Laclede, Lawrence, McDonald, Maries, Mississippi, New Madrid, Newton, Oregon, Ozark, Pemiscot, Phelps, Polk, Pulaski, Reynolds, Ripley, Scott, Shannon, St. Clair, Stoddard, Stone, Taney, Texas, Wayne, Webster and Wright. (477.060).

Sessions.—In Springfield and Poplar Bluff. (477.220).

Circuit Courts.—

Jurisdiction.—Circuit Courts have original jurisdiction over all cases and matters, civil and criminal.

Juvenile Court Commissioners.—In each county of first class, having charter form of government, except counties having family court, majority of Circuit Judges, en banc, may appoint one or two persons having same qualifications as Circuit Judge, for term of four years to devote full time to such duties. In City of St. Louis one person may be so appointed. (211.023).

Place of Sitting.—

Adair County: Second Circuit; court sits at Kirksville.

Andrew County: Fifth Circuit; court sits at Savannah.

Atchison County: Fourth Circuit; court sits at Rock Port.

Audrain County: Twelfth Circuit; court sits at Mexico.

Barry County: Thirty-ninth Circuit; court sits at Cassville.

Barton County: Twenty-eighth Circuit; court sits at Lamar.

Bates County: Twenty-seventh Circuit; court sits at Butler.

Benton County: Thirtieth Circuit; court sits at Warsaw.

Bollinger County: Thirty-second Circuit; court sits at Marble Hill.

Boone County: Thirteenth Circuit; court sits at Columbia.

Buchanan County: Fifth Circuit; court sits at St. Joseph.

Butler County: Thirty-sixth Circuit; court sits at Poplar Bluff.

Caldwell County: Forty-third Circuit; court sits at Kingston.

Callaway County: Thirteenth Circuit; court sits at Fulton.

Camden County: Twenty-sixth Circuit; court sits at Camdenton.

Cape Girardeau County: Thirty-second Circuit; court sits at Cape Girardeau and Jackson.

Carroll County: Eighth Circuit; court sits at Carrollton.

Carter County: Thirty-seventh Circuit; court sits at Van Buren.

Cass County: Seventeenth Circuit; court sits at Harrisonville.

Cedar County: Twenty-eighth Circuit; court sits at Stockton.

Charlton County: Ninth Circuit; court sits at Keytesville.

Christian County: Thirty-eighth Circuit; court sits at Ozark.

Clark County: First Circuit; court sits at Kahoka.

Clay County: Seventh Circuit; court sits at Liberty.

Clinton County: Forty-third Circuit; court sits at Plattsburg.

Cole County: Nineteenth Circuit; court sits at Jefferson City.

Cooper County: Eighteenth Circuit; court sits at Boonville.

Crawford County: Forty-second Circuit; court sits at Steelville.

Dade County: Twenty-eighth Circuit; court sits at Greenfield.

Dallas County: Thirtieth Circuit; court sits at Buffalo.

Daviess County: Forty-third Circuit; court sits at Gallatin.

DeKalb County: Forty-third Circuit; court sits at Maysville.

Dent County: Forty-second Circuit; court sits at Salem.

Douglas County: Forty-fourth Circuit; court sits at Ava.

Dunklin County: Thirty-fifth Circuit; court sits at Kennett.

Franklin County: Twentieth Circuit; court sits at Union.

Gasconade County: Twentieth Circuit; court sits at Hermann.

Gentry County: Fourth Circuit; court sits at Albany.

Greene County: Thirty-first Circuit; court sits at Springfield.

Grundy County: Third Circuit; court sits at Trenton.

Harrison County: Third Circuit; court sits at Bethany.

Henry County: Twenty-seventh Circuit; court sits at Clinton.

Hickory County: Thirtieth Circuit; court sits at Hermitage.

Holt County: Fourth Circuit; court sits at Oregon.

Howard County: Fourteenth Circuit; court sits at Fayette.

Howell County: Thirty-seventh Circuit; court sits at West Plains.

Iron County: Forty-second Circuit; court sits at Ironton.

Jackson County (eastern portion): Forty-sixth Circuit; court sits at Independence.

Jackson County (western portion): Sixteenth Circuit; court sits at Kansas City.

Jasper County: Twenty-ninth Circuit; court sits at Carthage and Joplin.

Jefferson County: Twenty-third Circuit; court sits at Hillsboro.

Johnson County: Seventeenth Circuit; court sits at Warrensburg.

Knox County: Second Circuit; court sits at Edina.

Laclede County: Twenty-sixth Circuit; court sits at Lebanon.

Lafayette County: Fifteenth Circuit; court sits at Lexington and Higginsville.

Lawrence County: Thirty-ninth Circuit; court sits at Mt. Vernon.

Lewis County: Second Circuit; court sits at Monticello and Canton.

Lincoln County: Eleventh Circuit; court sits at Troy.

Linn County: Ninth Circuit; court sits at Lineus and Brookfield.

Livingston County: Forty-third Circuit; court sits at Chillicothe.

Macon County: Forty-first Circuit; court sits at Macon.

Madison County: Twenty-fourth Circuit; court sits at Fredericktown.

Maries County: Twenty-fifth Circuit; court sits at Vienna.

Marion County: Tenth Circuit; court sits at Palmyra.

McDonald County: Fortieth Circuit; court sits at Pineville.

Mercer County: Third Circuit; court sits at Princeton.

Miller County: Twenty-sixth Circuit; court sits at Tuscumbia.

Mississippi County: Thirty-third Circuit; court sits at Charleston.

Moniteau County: Twenty-sixth Circuit; court sits at California.

Monroe County: Tenth Circuit; court sits at Paris.

Montgomery County: Twelfth Circuit; court sits at Montgomery City.

Morgan County: Twenty-sixth Circuit; court sits at Versailles.

New Madrid County: Thirty-fourth Circuit; court sits at New Madrid.

Newton County: Fortieth Circuit; court sits at Neosho.

Nodaway County: Fourth Circuit; court sits at Maryville.

Oregon County: Thirty-seventh Circuit; court sits at Alton.

Osage County: Twentieth Circuit; court sits at Linn.

Ozark County: Forty-fourth Circuit; court sits at Gainesville.

Pemiscot County: Thirty-fourth Circuit; court sits at Caruthersville.

Perry County: Twenty-fourth Circuit; court sits at Perryville.

Pettis County: Eighteenth Circuit; court sits at Sedalia.

Phelps County: Twenty-fifth Circuit; court sits at Rolla.

Pike County: Eleventh Circuit; court sits at Bowling Green.

Platte County: Sixth Circuit; court sits at Platte City.

Polk County: Thirtieth Circuit; court sits at Bolivar.

Pulaski County: Twenty-fifth Circuit; court sits at Waynesville.

Putnam County: Third Circuit; court sits at Unionville.

Ralls County: Tenth Circuit; Court sits at New London.

Randolph County: Fourteenth Circuit; court sits at Huntsville and Moberly.

Ray County: Eighth Circuit; court sits at Richmond.

Reynolds County: Forty-second Circuit; court sits at Centerville.

Ripley County: Thirty-sixth Circuit; court sits at Doniphan.

St Charles County: Eleventh Circuit; court sits at St. Charles.

St. Clair County: Twenty-seventh Circuit; court sits at Osceola.

St. Francois County: Twenty-fourth Circuit; court sits at Farmington.

Ste. Genevieve County: Twenty-fourth Circuit; court sits at Ste. Genevieve.

St. Louis City: (See subhead Circuit Court of the City of St. Louis, infra).

St. Louis County: Twenty-first Circuit; court sits at Clayton.

Saline County: Fifteenth Circuit; court sits at Marshall.

Schuyler County: First Circuit; court sits at Lancaster.

Scotland County: First Circuit; court sits at Memphis.

Scott County: Thirty-third Circuit; court sits at Benton.

Shannon County: Thirty-seventh Circuit; court sits at Eminence.

Shelby County: Forty-first Circuit; court sits at Shelbyville.

Stoddard County: Thirty-fifth Circuit; court sits at Bloomington.

Stone County: Thirty-ninth Circuit; court sits at Galena.

Sullivan County: Ninth Circuit; court sits at Milan.

Taney County: Thirty-eighth Circuit; court sits at Forsyth.

Texas County: Twenty-fifth Circuit; court sits at Houston.

Vernon County: Twenty-eighth Circuit; court sits at Nevada.

Warren County: Twelfth Circuit; court sits at Warrenton.

Washington County: Twenty-third Circuit; court sits at Potosi.

Wayne County: Forty-second Circuit; court sits at Greenville.

Webster County: Thirtieth Circuit; court sits at Marshfield.

Worth County: Fourth Circuit; court sits at Grant City.

Wright County: Forty-fourth Circuit; court sits at Hartville.

Jackson County.—Jackson County is split for jurisdiction and venue purposes into "western portion", roughly encompassing Kansas City and Grandview, and "eastern portion".

See note at head of Digest as to 1998 legislation covered.

See Topical Index in front part of this volume.

COURTS . . . *continued*

Circuit Court of the City of St. Louis.—City of St. Louis, under a provision of present Constitution of this state, is a separate municipality, having no county organization, and is entirely distinct from County of St. Louis. It constitutes Twenty-second Judicial Circuit. Circuit court sits in separate divisions, as follows: one assignment division, eleven civil divisions, three domestic relations and juvenile divisions and three criminal divisions. Judges from time to time sit in general term to establish rules of court.

Courts of Record.—Supreme Court, Courts of Appeals, Circuit Courts, and Associate Circuit Courts are courts of record.

Family court is established in Circuit Courts of Boone, Callaway, Clay, Greene, Jackson, St. Louis Counties, City of St. Louis and other which choose. Family court has exclusive original jurisdiction over actions including but not limited to dissolution of marriage, legal separation, separate maintenance, child custody, adoption, juvenile proceedings, adult abuse and change of name. Additional $30 fee for cases filed in family court. (211.023).

Probate Division.—Probate Division of Circuit Court has jurisdiction over all matters pertaining to probate business, granting letters testamentary and of administration, appointment of guardians of minors and persons of unsound minds, settling accounts of executors, administrators, and guardians, and sale or leasing of lands by administrators, executors and guardians, construction of wills as incident to administration of estates, determination of heirship, administration of testamentary and inter vivos trusts, of mental incompetency proceedings, and of such other probate business as may be prescribed by law. (472.020).

Clerks.—Judge in most counties acts ex officio as his own clerk, but may appoint a separate clerk.

Associate Circuit Courts.—In counties of not more than 30,000 inhabitants, there is one associate circuit judge; in counties of more than 30,000 and less than 100,000 inhabitants there are two associate circuit judges. In counties of 100,000 inhabitants or more there are two associate circuit judges and one additional associate circuit judge for each additional 100,000 inhabitants or major fraction thereof. (478.320).

Suits may be instituted either by voluntary appearance and agreement of parties or by process (summons or attachment). No formal pleadings required but before process issued plaintiff must file statement of facts, or instrument, or statement of account which constitute claim suit is founded upon; if defendant has setoff or counterclaim he must do likewise before trial commenced. Trial procedure generally governed by circuit court usage and practice, and by c. 517. Executions returnable not less than 30 nor more than 90 days and are proceeded upon as executions from other courts of record. See c. 517 generally.

Jurisdictional limit is $25,000. (517.011).

Associate circuit courts have jurisdiction in actions for forcible entry and detainer and unlawful detainer. (534.060).

County Courts.—County courts have control and management of property belonging to county, power to purchase, lease and receive by donation any property for use of county, to sell and cause to be conveyed any real estate or personal property belonging to county, and to audit and settle all demands against county.

Small Claims Courts.—Each associate circuit judge must maintain separate "small claims" docket and must set aside and specify times that may be reasonable and necessary for hearing small claims. When acting as small claims court, associate circuit court has original jurisdiction of all civil cases whether tort or contract where amount in controversy does not exceed $3,000 in first-class counties exclusive of interest or costs. Parties may prosecute their claims and defenses without assistance of attorney. Corporations or unincorporated associations including labor unions may enter their appearance and be represented by officer or authorized employee. Except as otherwise provided in this act or by rule of Supreme Court, established structure, administration and procedure of associate circuit courts in their respective counties must prevail. Proceedings must be conducted in informal summary manner. Formal rules of evidence and procedure do not apply. Judge must assume affirmative duty to determine merits of claims and defenses of parties and may question parties and witnesses. No discovery permitted. Trial must be to judge sitting without jury. When associate circuit court is hearing small claims matters it is known as "small claims court".

If amount in controversy in action otherwise cognizable in associate circuit court exceeds $3,000 in first-class counties plaintiff may file and prosecute small claims action for recovery of money but he thereby waives his claim for any sum in excess of $3,000 in first-class counties in that or any subsequent proceeding involving same parties and issues. At any time up to ten days after service of process and before date of hearing defendant may file counterclaim which does not arise out of same transaction or occurrence as plaintiff's original claim. Pleading requirements for filing such counterclaim are same as those for filing original claim. At any time up to and including time of hearing defendant may raise counterclaim which grows out of same transaction or occurrence as plaintiff's original claim. If during course of hearing judge determines that defendant has counterclaim arising out of same transaction or occurrence as plaintiff's original claim, judge may question parties on counterclaim and render judgment on it as if it had been raised on initiative of defendant.

If amount of counterclaim exceeds by itself jurisdictional limit of small claims court, court shall have jurisdiction to hear both claim and counterclaim with consent of all parties to proceeding. Court must not accept consent of any party unless court has informed him he has right to consult attorney prior to giving or withholding consent. If all parties do not consent and if counterclaim grew out of same transaction or occurrence as plaintiff's original claim cause must be transferred by small claims court to associate circuit court or to another appropriate court of record. If one or more of parties does not consent and counterclaim does not grow out of same transaction or occurrence as original claim court must dismiss counterclaim without prejudice to its being heard separately in appropriate court. If one or both of parties does not consent and if counterclaim grew out of same transaction or occurrence as plaintiff's original claim and court determines amount or nature of counterclaim is not in good faith then court must dismiss counterclaim without prejudice.

No claim may be filed or prosecuted in small claims court by party who is assignee of claim or has filed more than eight other claims in Missouri small claims court during previous 12 months. At time of filing action plaintiff must sign statement so stating. However, defendant is not prohibited from filing or prosecuting counterclaim based on same transaction or occurrence.

No claim may be filed unless: (a) At least one defendant is resident of county in which court is located or at least one plaintiff is resident of county in which court is located and at least one defendant may be found in said county, or (b) facts giving rise to cause of action took place within county in which court is located.

Clerks under supervision of associate circuit judge must explain to litigants procedures and functions of small claims court and assist them in filling out all forms and necessary pleadings for presentation of their claim or counterclaim to court.

Action may be commenced by filing with clerk of court petition substantially similar to petition form provided in Act. Petition form must be provided by clerk free of charge to any person. Copy of complaint must be attached to summons. Filing fee is $10 unless claim is less than $100 then filing fee is $5. Plaintiff must pay cost of service in advance. Plaintiff must not be required to give security for costs. Court may in its discretion award fees and assess costs. Personal service of summons not required unless specifically requested by plaintiff upon showing that service by certified mail cannot be had. Service may be made by mailing copy of summons and complaint to defendant at his last known address by certified mail return receipt requested. Envelope and return receipt must be stamped with docket number of case. Receipt for certified mail must state name and address of addressee and date of mailing and must be attached to original summons. Return receipt when signed by addressee returned to court must be attached to original summons and if it shows delivery at least ten days before date of appearance constitutes proof of service. Clerk must note fact of service in permanent record.

Defendant must appear at time and place specified in summons and case must be tried on day set unless continued by court upon request of either party. No party entitled to more than one continuance except on showing of good cause and at discretion of judge. If defendant appears he need not file answer and allegations of complaint must be considered denied and defense may be provided as if specifically pleaded. If upon date for hearing defendant being duly summoned fails to appear, court may enter judgment for amount claimed. If plaintiff does not appear or if neither appears court may enter order dismissing action. Any action dismissed may not be brought in small claims court again but may be brought in appropriate associate circuit court using regular proceedings. If court finds small claims proceedings are being used by plaintiff or defendant for purpose of oppression or harassment it may issue order denying plaintiff or defendant use of small claims proceedings for up to one year.

No judgment is lien on real estate. Any person aggrieved by final judgment rendered except judgment by consent may appeal to circuit court as provided for appeals from associate circuit courts. (482.300-.365).

See also category Civil Actions and Procedure, topic Venue.

JUSTICES OF THE PEACE:

Abolished. See topic Courts, subhead Associate Circuit Courts.

LEGISLATURE:

Meets annually in January. (Const. Art. III, §20).

Special Sessions.—Governor may call special sessions. (Const. Art. IV, §9).

Initiative and referendum are provided for. (Const. Art. III, §§49-53).

Lobbyists.—Registration with clerk of house of representatives and secretary of senate and reports of money expended required. (105.470).

See also topic Statutes.

REPORTS:

Missouri Reports contain decisions of the Supreme Court; Missouri Appeal Reports contain decisions of the St. Louis, Kansas City and Springfield Courts of Appeals; both series numbered consecutively beginning with vol. 1. Missouri decisions are also reported in Southwestern Reporter, which is only Missouri decision reporter since end of publication of Missouri Reports (Vol. 365, 1957) and Missouri Appeal Reports (Vol. 241, 1956).

Digest.—Decisions are digested in Missouri Digest.

STATUTES:

Current official revision of statutes is Revised Statutes Missouri 1986. Missouri Revised Statutes Annotated is in general use, but not an official publication.

Uniform Acts which have been adopted are: Anatomical Gift (1969); Arbitration (1980); Business Records as Evidence (1949); Child Custody Jurisdiction Act (1978); Commercial Code (1963); Common Trust Fund (1955); Criminal Extradition (1953); Enforcement of Foreign Judgments (1951); Facsimile Signature of Public Officials (1959); Fiduciaries (1959); Foreign Money-Judgments Recognition (1984); Fraudulent Transfers (1992); Fresh Pursuit (1951); Individual Accident and Sickness Insurance (1959); Interstate Family Support (1996); Judicial Notice of Foreign Law (1949); Limited Partnership, Revised (1985); Mandatory Disposition of Detainer (1982); Parentage (1987); Partnership (1949); Reciprocal Enforcement of Support (1959); Securities (1967); Simplification of Fiduciary Security Transfers (1959); Simultaneous Death (1947); To Secure Attendance of Witnesses From Without a State In Criminal Proceedings (1959); Veterans' Guardianship (1947); Vital Statistics (1947).

Significant variations or modifications, if any, to adopted Uniform Acts appear in topics in which these acts are discussed.

For text of Uniform Acts falling within the scope of the Martindale-Hubbell Law Digests see Uniform and Model Acts section.

See note at head of Digest as to 1998 legislation covered.

See Topical Index in front part of this volume.

UNIFORM LAWS:

For list of Uniform Acts in force in this state see topic Statutes. For text of Uniform Acts within the scope of the Martindale-Hubbell Law Digests see Uniform and Model Acts section.

CRIMINAL LAW

BAIL:

See topic Criminal Law.

CRIMINAL LAW:

Criminal Code is included in Revised Statutes. Criminal proceedings are instituted by indictment or information.

Persons shall be bailable by sufficient sureties, except for capital offenses when proof is evident or presumption great. (Const. Art. I, §20). If defendant poses danger to victim, community or other person, court may increase bail, deny bail or impose special conditions. (595.209)

Sentencing Advisory Commission to establish system of recommended sentences. (588.019).

Any person or organization contracting with any person convicted and incarcerated for crime shall pay any money owing to convict into escrow account to division of worker's compensation and payable to any victim who has obtained money judgment against convict. (595.047).

Uniform Criminal Extradition Act (c. 548) and **Uniform Law to Secure Attendance of Witnesses From Without State** (491.400-.450) in effect.

DEBTOR AND CREDITOR

ASSIGNMENTS:

Causes of action ex delicto which are not personal and causes of action ex contractu are assignable.

Assignment of wages must be in writing, with correct date and amount thereof and names of persons owing the same. Assignment of unearned wages is void. (432.030).

Prior to release of any offender from imprisonment, assignment no greater than 10% of offender's income from any source shall be requested. Such assignment shall be valid no longer than five years. (217.829).

Assignment of Judgment.—See category Civil Actions and Procedure, topic Judgments.

Assignments of Accounts Receivable.—See category Business Regulation and Commerce, topic Commercial Code.

Uniform Commercial Code in force. See category Business Regulation and Commerce, topic Commercial Code.

ATTACHMENT:

An attachment may be had in any civil action in circuit or associate circuit court.

In Whose Favor Writ May Issue.—Any plaintiff, including a nonresident or foreign corporation, may obtain an attachment. (56 S.W.2d 28).

Claims on Which Writ May Issue.—It is not necessary that the claim sued on be payable within the state.

As to claims not due see infra, subhead Grounds.

As to limitations on right to attach or garnish wages, see topic Garnishment.

Grounds for attachment are that defendant: (1) Is not a resident of this state; (2) is a corporation whose chief office or place of business is out of this state; (3) conceals himself so that the ordinary process of law cannot be served upon him; (4) has absconded or absented himself from his usual place of abode in this state so that ordinary process of law cannot be served upon him; (5) is about to remove his property or effects out of state, with intent to defraud, hinder or delay creditors; (6) is about to remove out of state with intent to change his domicile; (7) has fraudulently conveyed or assigned his property or effects so as to hinder or delay his creditors; (8) has fraudulently concealed, removed or disposed of his property or effects so as to hinder or delay his creditors; (9) is about fraudulently to convey or assign his property or effects so as to hinder or delay his creditors; (10) is about fraudulently to conceal, remove or dispose of his property or effects so as to hinder or delay his creditors; or (11) that the cause of action accrued out of this state, and defendant has absconded or secretly removed his property or effects into this state; or (12) that the damages for which the action is brought arose from the commission of some felony or misdemeanor or the seduction of a female; or (13) that defendant has failed to pay the price or value of an article or thing delivered which by contract he was bound to pay upon delivery; or (14) that the debt sued for was fraudulently contracted on the part of defendant. Attachment may also be brought for rent due within one year in certain cases. Attachments may issue upon a demand not due in any of the cases above mentioned, except the first, second, third and fourth; but final judgment will not be rendered against the defendant until the demand matures. (521.010-020).

Proceedings to Obtain.—Plaintiff, or someone in his behalf, must make affidavit that plaintiff has just demand against defendant, that amount which affiant believes plaintiff ought to recover, after allowing all just claims and setoffs, is . . . . dollars, and that affiant has good reason to believe and does believe that one or more of grounds for attachment exists, specifying grounds upon which he intends to rely in language set forth above. (521.060). Plaintiff wishing to sue by attachment shall file with clerk of court where attachment is instituted petition of his cause and also affidavit and attachment bond (see subhead Attachment Bond, infra) if required and thereupon sue out original attachment against lands, tenements, goods, moneys effects and credits of defendant wherever he may be. (521.050).

Attachment Bond.—Bond must be given in double amount of debt, by plaintiff or some responsible person as principal and one or more sureties, except in suits instituted by state or county in its own behalf, and except where defendant is nonresident, in which cases no bond is required, but in latter case attachment is dissolved, on motion, upon defendant entering his appearance and filing his answer to merits unless plaintiff files bond within ten days. If attachment is set aside or dismissed, attaching creditor is liable on his bond for such damages as resulted from his levy and proceedings thereunder. (521.050-.070).

Levy.—Officer may seize, as attachable property evidences of debt of the defendant, as well as other property real, personal and mixed and also judgment debts; but no property or wages exempt from execution may be attached, except in case of nonresident or one who is about to move out of state. (521.240). Provisions of law governing attachments apply to proceedings before circuit judges and associate circuit judges in same manner except as may be specifically provided otherwise. (521.660).

Indemnity.—There is no statutory authority for the officer to require indemnity before levying.

Priorities.—Where same property is attached in several actions by different claimants, court shall determine priority, validity, good faith, and force and effect of different attachments, and may dissolve any attachment, wholly or partially, or make such other order as may be required. If writs have issued from different courts, all matters regarding attachments shall be determined by court out of which first writ was issued. (C.R. 85.18).

An attaching creditor is not a bona fide purchaser for value, but obtains only such rights as the debtor had in the property at the time and is postponed to other liens or claims on the property which became effective before the attachment. (112 Mo. 599, 20 S.W. 686).

Release of Property.—Owner of property may retain or regain possession of property levied on by filing sufficient bond approved by court, executed by owner of property as principal and one or more sureties, to claimant in amount equal to value of property, or amount of claim and costs, whichever is less. (C.R. 85.09).

Sale.—Court may order sale of attached personal property if property is likely to perish, is likely to depreciate in value to considerable extent, or keeping it will cause undue expense. (C.R. 85.23).

Third Party Claims.—Person claiming interest in property which has been attached may intervene in attachment proceedings. (C.R. 85.20).

Dissolution.—Attachments may be dissolved on motion made by owner of property at any time before final judgment. Claimant shall have burden of proving that attachment was properly granted. Attachment shall be dissolved at any time before final judgment when court finds: (1) Bond provided for in Rule 85.08 is inadequate and claimant fails to file sufficient bond, approved by court, within such time as court directs; (2) affidavit is insufficient and claimant fails to file sufficient affidavit, approved by court, within such time as court directs; (3) owner of property has entered his appearance in action and bond provided for in Rule 85.09 has been filed or approved; or (4) for any other reason writ of attachment should not have been issued. (C.R. 85.14).

See also topics Executions; Garnishment; Exemptions.

CREDITORS' SUITS:

All existing remedies at law, to which there is a possibility of resort must ordinarily be exhausted before a creditor's bill can be maintained. Insolvency of the debtor is usually a condition precedent, also. The general rule is there must be a judgment, execution and a return of nulla bona before this equitable relief is granted although exceptions exist where existence and amount of debt are admitted by debtor and where debtor is absent from state and not subject to ordinary processes of law within state. (135 S.W.2d 355).

See also topics Fraudulent Sales and Conveyances, Executions; category Estates and Trusts, topic Executors and Administrators.

EXECUTIONS:

Execution from court of record may issue to different counties at the same time. (C.R. 76.05-.06).

Exemptions.—See topic Exemptions.

Time for Issuance.—Execution from court of record may issue at any time within ten years after rendition of judgment (513.020), or revival, or part payment of such judgment when entered of record (516.350).

Execution on judgment of circuit court is not issued until time for filing motion for new trial has expired and if such motion is filed not until it is overruled.

Lien.—An execution is not a lien on personal property until levied thereon. (C.R. 76.07).

Levy.—Officer making levy on real property not subject to lien of judgment (see category Civil Actions and Procedure, topic Judgments) must file with recorder of deeds of county in which such real estate is situated, notice of such levy. (C.R. 76.07).

Defendant may select what property, real or personal, may be levied upon to satisfy execution, and if he gives to officer list of property so selected, sufficient to satisfy such execution, officer must levy on such property and no other, if in his opinion it is sufficient; if not, then upon such additional property as may be sufficient. (C.R. 76.09).

Sale of real and personal property taken in execution by an officer, must be held on the day advertised between hours of 9 A.M. and 5 P.M., and the highest bidder shall be the purchaser. (C.R. 76.18). Notice of sale of real estate must be published at least 20 days (C.R. 76.16), and of sale of personal property at least ten days, before day of sale (C.R. 76.13). Bill of sale may be secured from officer making execution sale on demand at time of sale. (C.R. 76.21).

Real Property.—When an execution is levied upon real estate, the officer levying the same must divide such property, if susceptible of division, and sell so much thereof as will be sufficient to satisfy such execution, unless the defendant in the execution desires

EXECUTIONS . . . continued

the whole of any tract or lot of land to be sold together, in which case it must be so sold. (C.R. 76.11).

Leases for an unexpired term of three years or more are subject to execution and sale as real property. (513.200).

Return.—Execution from a circuit court is returnable not less than 30 days nor more than 90 days after issuance. (C.R. 76.04).

Redemption.—There is no right of redemption of property sold at execution sale.

Stay.—Court out of which execution issued may, on verified petition setting forth good cause and after notice to opposite party, order execution stayed, provided sufficient bond or security to satisfy execution is furnished. (C.R. 76.25). As to stay pending review by higher court, see category Civil Actions and Procedure, topic Appeal and Error.

Claims of Third Persons.—Any person, except judgment debtor, claiming interest in property which has been levied upon may intervene by serving motion upon all parties affected thereby. Motion shall state grounds therefor, and be accompanied by pleading setting forth claim for which intervention is sought. (C.R. 76.10 and 52.12).

Supplementary Proceedings.—When execution is returned unsatisfied, judgment creditor may petition court which rendered judgment to enter order requiring debtor to appear and be examined concerning means of satisfying judgment. (C.R. 76.27).

See also topics Attachment, Exemptions; category Civil Actions and Procedure, topics Appeal and Error, Sequestration.

EXEMPTIONS:

Following property is exempt from attachment and execution to extent of any person's interest therein: (1) Household furnishings, goods and wearing apparel held primarily for personal, family, or household use, not exceeding $1,000 in value; (2) jewelry held primarily for personal, family or household use, not exceeding $1,000 in value; (3) any other property not exceeding $400 in value; (4) any implements, professional books or tools of trade, not exceeding $2,000 in value; (5) any motor vehicle not exceeding $1,000 in value; (6) any mobile home used as principal residence, not exceeding $1,000 in value; (7) any one or more unmatured life insurance contracts other than credit life insurance contract; (8) any accrued dividend or interest of any one or more unmatured life insurance contracts wherein insured is such person, not exceeding $5,000 less any amount of property transferred by insurance company to itself, not to be exempt from any claim for child support; (9) professionally prescribed health aids; (10) right to receive certain government benefits, alimony not exceeding $500 a month and payments made under certain pension and annuities plans unless subject to qualified domestic relations order under 414(p) of Internal Revenue Code, and money from certain qualified retirement plans; (11) right to receive payment for wrongful death claim. (513.430). Spendthrift trusts created for benefit of employees are exempt from attachment and execution prior to payment or delivery of trust earnings and principal. (456.072).

Substitution.—Head of family may select and hold exempt from execution any other property, real, personal or mixed, or debts and wages not exceeding in value amount of $850 plus $250 for each additional unmarried dependent child under 18, except 10% of any debt, income, salary or wages due such head of family. (513.440).

Debts Against Which Exemptions Not Allowed.—Personal property is subject to execution on a judgment against the purchaser for the purchase price thereof, and cannot be made exempt from such execution and judgment except in the hands of an innocent purchaser for value without notice of existence of prior claim for purchase money. (513.140). Nothing is exempt from attachment or execution on a judgment or decree for alimony or support and maintenance of children or from attachment or execution in proceeding by married woman for maintenance (452.140), or from execution against property of debtor who is about to leave state or for the payment of taxes due to the state or any city, town or county (513.465, 513.425), or against a claim for personal services of a house servant or common laborer, not exceeding $90, provided suit be instituted within six months after last service rendered (513.060; 513.470).

Exemptions must be claimed in order to be available.

Earnings.—Maximum part of earnings of individual for workweek subject to garnishment, after deduction of amounts required by law, may not exceed: (a) 25% or (b) 30 times current federal maximum hourly wage or (c) if employee head of family and resident of state 10%, whichever is less. Restrictions do not apply to any court order for support of any person, any court order under Chapter 13 of Bankruptcy Act or state or federal tax debt. (525.030[2]).

Homestead Exemptions.—See topic Homesteads.

See also topic Garnishment; categories Estates and Trusts, topic Executors and Administrators, subhead Allowances; Taxation, topic Property Taxes.

FORECLOSURE:

See topic Liens; category Mortgages, topic Mortgages of Real Property.

FRAUDULENT SALES AND CONVEYANCES:

Bulk Sales.—See category Business Regulation and Commerce, topic Commercial Code.

Uniform Commercial Code in force. See category Business Regulation and Commerce, topic Commercial Code.

Uniform Fraudulent Conveyance Act not adopted.

Uniform Fraudulent Transfers Act adopted. (428.005-.059).

See also topic Attachment.

GARNISHMENT:

Writs of attachment may be levied by garnishing a debtor of the defendant, as well as by levy upon property. All persons are subject to garnishment on attachment or execution who are named as garnishees in the writ, or have in their possession goods, moneys or effects of the defendant not actually seized by the officers, and all debtors of the defendant and such others as the plaintiff or his attorneys shall direct to be summoned as garnishees. (C.R. 90.02).

Property Which May Be Reached.—All goods, personal property, money, credits, bonds, bills, notes, checks, choses in action, or other effects of defendant in his possession or control between time notice is served and return date of writ of garnishment. (C.R. 90.01-.06).

Garnishee can discharge himself before final judgment by payment into court of sufficient money or property of defendant to satisfy debt and costs. (C.R. 90.07).

Garnishee must answer interrogatories filed by plaintiff. If he denies that he is indebted, issue can be made with him, which is tried in court as other causes. (C.R. 90.13).

Adverse Claims.—Adverse claimant may intervene in cause. (C.R. 90.15).

Exemptions from Garnishee Process.—No sheriff, constable, or other officer charged with the collection of money shall, prior to the return day of an execution or other process upon which the same may be made, be liable to be summoned as garnishee; nor shall any county collector, county treasurer, or municipal corporation, or any officer thereof, or any administrator or executor of an estate, prior to an order of distribution, or for payment of legacies or the allowance of a demand found to be due by his estate, be liable to be summoned as garnishee. (525.030).

Wages in excess of amount exempt (see topic Exemptions) are not subject to garnishment (525.030), and no wages shall be attached or garnished before personal service is had upon defendant, unless suit be brought in county where defendant resides or where debt was contracted and cause of action arose or accrued and in cities of over 100,000 population in city where defendant resides or debt was contracted and cause of action accrued, and petition or statement in such case and writ or summons of attachment or garnishment must affirmatively show place where defendant resides and place where debt is contracted and cause of action arose. Wages earned out of state and payable out of state are exempt from attachment or garnishment in all cases where cause of action arose or accrued out of state unless defendant is personally served with process. (C.R. 90.20).

See also topics Attachment; Exemptions; and Executions.

HOMESTEADS:

Head of family is entitled to hold exempt from attachment and execution homestead consisting of dwelling house and appurtenances and land used in connection therewith, together with rents, issues and products thereof, subject to limitation as to value. (513.475).

Limitation of value of homestead which may be held exempt is $8,000. (513.475).

Limitation of Area.—None.

Debts or Liabilities Against Which Exemption Not Available.—Homestead exemption is not available as against causes of action existing prior to time when title acquired by descent or devise vested or when deed to debtor was filed for record. (513.510).

Designation of homestead not necessary.

Loss of Exemption.—Abandonment of homestead if intent to abandon and external act by which that intention is carried into effect. (256 Mo. 501, 165 S.W. 1017).

Claim of Exemption.—Where value exceeds limitation housekeeper or head of family may choose part to which exemption shall apply. (513.480).

Alienation or Encumbrance.—Husband and wife jointly (but not husband alone) can sell, mortgage or alienate homestead. (513.475).

Proceeds of sale of homestead are exempt for a reasonable time pending investment in another homestead. (513.515).

See also category Family, topic Husband and Wife.

JUDGMENT NOTES:

See category Business Regulation and Commerce, topic Bills and Notes.

LEVY:

See topics Attachment, Executions.

LIENS:

The following are among the liens provided for by statute: architects, professional engineers, landscape architect and land surveyors (429.015), liens of inn and boarding-house keepers (419.060), liens of warehousemen (see category Business Regulation and Commerce, topic Commercial Code), mechanics' liens on realty (429.010), landscaper's lien on realty (429.560), factors' liens (see category Business Regulation and Commerce, topic Commercial Code), liens of contractors, laborers, and materialmen against railroads (429.440), liens for keeping and repairing vehicles, including motor vehicles (430.010-.082), for keeping or training animals (430.150), liens of hospitals (430.230), liens of common carriers (447.070), owners of self-storage facilities (415.415).

Mechanics' Liens on Real Property.—Every person who does work or performs labor or who furnishes any material, fixtures, engine, boiler or machinery for any building, erection or improvements upon land, or who repairs or furnishes landscaping goods or services pursuant to contract, may obtain lien on such land and improvements and lot, tract or parcel of land upon which same are situated to secure payment for his labor or materials, except that if such land and improvements are not within limits of any city, town or village, then such lien shall be also upon land to extent necessary to provide roadway for ingress to and egress from lot, tract or parcel of land upon which such building, erection or improvements are situated, not to exceed 40′ in width, to

LIENS . . . *continued*
nearest public road or highway. (429.010). This includes labor or material for any sidewalk, street, curb, sewer, water or other pipeline in front of, adjacent to, along or adjoining lot in town, city or village. (429.020). Contract provision which makes payment obligation contingent upon receipt of payment from any other party is not defense to mechanic's lien. (431.183).

Licensed or Leased Property.—Where contract is with lessee or licensee, lien attaches only to leasehold or license but not to the reversion. (429.070).

Notice.—Original contractor must provide person with whom contract is made before receiving any payment either at time of execution of contract, when material is delivered, work commenced or delivered with first invoice, following notice in ten-point bold type: "Notice to Owner: Failure of this contractor to pay those persons supplying material or services to complete this contract can result in the filing of a mechanic's lien on the property which is the subject of this contract pursuant to Chapter 429, RSMo. To avoid this result you must ask this contractor for 'Lien Waivers' from all persons supplying material or services for the work described in this contract. Failure to secure lien waivers may result in your paying for labor and material twice." Giving this notice is condition precedent to mechanic's lien in favor of contractor, and failure to give notice with intent to defraud is misdemeanor. Notice provision does not apply to new residence if buyer has lien protection through title insurance company. Every person, other than original contractor, must give written notice to owner or agent ten days before filing lien stating that he holds claim against specified property, amount, and from whom due. Proof of service required. (429.012, .100).

Owner.—Every person, including all cestui que trusts, for whose immediate enjoyment or benefit building, erection or improvement is made. (429.150). Mortgagee and holder of security interest not having immediate realization of any benefit conferred by improvements, not parties to contract and having no obligation to pay subcontractor's claims, are not owners entitled to ten days notice. (513 S.W.2d 365).

Filing.—Every original contractor every journeyman and every day laborer, and every other person seeking to obtain mechanic's lien must file with clerk of circuit court of proper county just and true account of lien demand due him or them after all just credits have been given, and true description of property, or so near as to identify same, upon which lien is intended to apply with name of owner or contractor, or both, if known to person filing lien, which shall, in all cases, be verified by oath of himself or some credible person for him within six months after indebtedness accrued. (429.080).

Owner Occupied Residential Property.—In case of improvements to owner occupied residential property of four units or less, no person other than original contractor who performs any work or furnishes any materials, fixtures, engine, boiler or machinery for any structure shall have lien unless owner of building pursuant to written contract has agreed to be liable for such costs in event costs are not paid. Consent shall be printed in ten point bold type and signed separately from contractor's notice required by 429.012 and shall state: CONSENT OF OWNER-CONSENT IS HEREBY GIVEN FOR FILING OF MECHANIC'S LIEN BY ANY PERSON WHO SUPPLIES MATERIALS OR SERVICES FOR THE WORK DESCRIBED IN THIS CONTRACT ON THE PROPERTY ON WHICH IT IS LOCATED IF THEY ARE NOT PAID. Original contractor must retain consent and furnish copy to any person performing work or supplying material upon their request. It shall be condition precedent to creation and validity of any lien by supplier or workman that copy of signed consent form be attached to claim of lien. (429.013).

Jurisdiction.—The circuit court has jurisdiction for the enforcement of such liens. (429.080). Associate circuit courts have jurisdiction to enforce mechanics' liens, as circuit court, when amount or balance claimed to be due does not exceed jurisdiction of magistrate courts in different counties in ordinary civil actions. (429.350).

Time Limitation.—Actions to enforce such liens must be commenced within six months after filing the lien. (429.170).

Parties.—All parties to the contract must and all others interested in the property may be made parties, but those not made parties will not be bound by the proceedings. (429.190).

Action in Equity.—Any and all liens provided for by statute may be adjudicated and the rights of all parties interested in the property against which the same is claimed may be determined and enforced in one action after the statement for such lien is filed in the office of the clerk of court or such action may be brought by any owner or lessee of the property or mortgagor or holder of any encumbrance thereon. Such action must be an equitable action for the purpose of determining the various claimants, and is for the purpose of marshaling, applying and distributing the proceeds of the sale of such property that may be ordered and decreed in said action. (429.270). All persons claiming any lien or encumbrance upon property and all persons having rights in or against it and all owners and lessees thereof to be affected thereby as disclosed by proper public records must be made parties in said action, and all parties are bound by proceedings, orders and judgments in said action. (429.280). This does not apply to instances where there is only one lien claimant. (429.330). Court may appoint referee to hear and report evidence and make conclusions and findings of fact and law therein and report to court. (429.320). After such equitable action is commenced, same is exclusive of all other remedies for enforcement of mechanics' liens. (429.290).

Public Works.—Contractor for public work of any kind to be performed for the state, county, town, township, school or road district must execute a bond to the state or such municipality, etc., for payment for material, lubricants, oil, and gasoline used in or consumed in construction of such work and for all labor performed in such work, whether by subcontractor or otherwise. (107.170).

Mechanics' Liens on Chattels.—Every person expending labor or material upon any chattel at the request of its owner, his authorized agent or lawful possessor thereof, in the amount of $25 or less shall have a lien upon such chattel from the date of the commencement of such expenditure for the contract price until possession of such chattel is voluntarily relinquished to such owner or authorized agent or one entitled to possession thereof. (430.080).

Enforcement.—Unless the chattel is redeemed within three months of the completion of such expenditure, or within three months of the date agreed upon for redemption, the lien may be enforced by a sale as provided in the statute. (430.090).

Notice of Sale.—Such sale shall be held only after not less than 20 days notice (1) by mailing a copy of the notice by registered mail if the address is known, to the owner for whom such expenditure was made, in which case a return receipt shall be evidence of due notice; (2) by not less than two publications in some newspaper of general circulation where the property was received and is to be sold, the last publication to be not less than 20 days prior to the date of sale; (3) if no newspaper be published within the county, then by posting five hand bills not less than 20 days prior to the date of sale in different places within the township, one of which shall be posted where the property was received and is to be sold. (430.100).

The form of notice by statute (430.100) must be substantially as follows:

Form

Notice is hereby given that on (insert date), a sale will be held at (insert place), to sell the following articles to enforce a lien existing under the laws of the State of Missouri against such articles for labor, services, skill or material expended upon such articles at the request of the following designated persons, unless such articles are redeemed prior to the date of said sale.

Name of Owner	Description of Article	Amount of Lien
. . . .	. . . .	. . . .
. . . .	. . . .	. . . .

. . . .
Name of Lienor

Notice of several liens may be combined in one publication. (430.100).

Sale and Proceeds Thereof.—If the chattel is not redeemed prior to the date of sale provided in the notice, the lienor may sell such articles on the date and at the place specified in the notice, and shall thereupon deposit with the county treasurer (or city treasurer in the City of St. Louis) the proceeds of the sale in excess of the charges for the expenditure of labor and material and the necessary expenses of advertising with a sworn statement containing (a) the name of the owner, (b) description of articles, (c) amount of lien, (d) sale price, (e) name of purchaser, (f) cost and manner of advertising, (g) amount paid to any prior lienholders. Proceeds shall be distributed in following order: (1) Seller's lien and expenses of advertising, (2) prior liens on chattel created by financing statement duly perfected. The treasurer shall credit such excess to the general revenue fund of the county, or the City of St. Louis, subject to the right of the owner or his representative to reclaim the same within three years of the date of such deposit after presentation of proper evidence of ownership and obtaining an order of the county court (or the Comptroller of the City of St. Louis) directed to said treasurer for the return of said excess deposit. (430.110).

Actions Against Lienor.—Any lienor failing or refusing to deliver to said treasurer such excess proceeds together with the sworn statement within 30 days after such sale shall be liable for double the excess proceeds of such sale, to be recovered in any court of competent jurisdiction. (430.120). Conformity to the requirements of the Act is a perpetual bar to any action against the lienor by any person for the recovery of such chattels or the value thereof or damages growing out of the failure of such person to receive such chattels. (430.130).

Application to Armed Services.—No provision of the Act applies to any member of the armed services of the United States until six months after his discharge from said service. (430.140).

Redemption.—There is no right of redemption from a sale in a proceeding foreclosing any of the liens hereinbefore mentioned (430.130); except chattels not exceeding $100 in value, which unless redeemed within one year of date agreed upon for redemption, are barred from recovery (430.135).

Mechanics' Lien on Motor Vehicles or Trailers.—Every person expending labor, services, skill or material upon any motor vehicle, boat or trailer at written request of its owner, authorized agent of owner, or person in lawful possession thereof, or who provides storage for motor vehicle or trailer at written request of its owner, authorized agent of owner or person in lawful possession thereof or at written request of peace officer, shall where maximum to be charged for labor, service, skill or material has been stated as part of written request and/or daily storage charge has been stated as part of written request, have lien upon chattel from date of commencement of such expenditure for actual value of expenditure until possession of chattel is voluntarily relinquished to owner, authorized agent or one entitled to possession thereof.

Enforcement.—If chattel is not redeemed within three months lienholder may apply to director of revenue for certificate of ownership, but in case of charges for storage and/or towing, after three months lienholder must notify owner and any known lienholders and if after 45 days after notification has been mailed chattel is not redeemed, then lienholder may apply to director of revenue for certificate of ownership. Such application must be accompanied by: (a) Original, conformed or photostatic copy of written request of owner or agent with maximum amount to be charged stated therein, (b) lienholder's affidavit that owner has defaulted on payment and payment is three months past due, (c) statement of actual value of expenditure and amount unpaid, (d) fee of $10.

Notice of Lien.—If director is satisfied with genuineness of application and supporting documents, he must notify by registered mail, postage prepaid, owner and lienholders of record, other than applicant, at their last known address that application has been made for lien title on chattel. Thirty days after such notification, if no lienholder or owner has redeemed chattel and application has not been withdrawn, and if owner or lienholder has informed director that he demands hearing and enforcement of lien as provided in §430.160, director must issue, in same manner as repossessed title is issued, certificate of ownership which must clearly be captioned "Lien Title."

Sale of Chattel.—Upon receipt of lien title, holder must within ten days begin proceedings to sell chattels as prescribed in §430.100. Provisions of §430.110 shall apply to disposition of proceeds and lienholder must be entitled to actual and necessary expenses incurred in obtaining lien title, but no person who is issued lien title shall be allowed any excess proceeds of sale. Charges for service and towing shall not exceed charges allowed in 304.155. (430.082).

Attachment Lien.—See topic Attachment.

See note at head of Digest as to 1998 legislation covered.

See Topical Index in front part of this volume.

MO – 21

LIENS . . . *continued*

Attorney's Lien.—See category Legal Profession, topic Attorneys and Counselors.

Collateral Security.—See topic Pledges.

Execution Lien.—See topic Executions.

Judgment Lien.—See category Civil Actions and Procedure, topic Judgments.

Landlord's Lien.—See category Property, topic Landlord and Tenant.

Real Estate Mortgage Lien.—See category Mortgages, topic Mortgages of Real Property.

Tax Lien.—See category Taxation, topic Property Taxes, subhead Lien.

Uniform Commercial Code in force. See category Business Regulation and Commerce, topic Commercial Code.

For other liens, see topics Attachment, Pledges; categories Business Regulation and Commerce, topics Banks and Banking, Commercial Code; Civil Actions and Procedure, topic Judgments; Legal Profession, topic Attorneys and Counselors; Mortgages, topic Mortgages of Real Property; Property, topic Landlord and Tenant; Taxation, topic Property Taxes, subhead Lien.

MECHANICS' LIENS:

See topic Liens.

PLEDGES:

Whenever any personal property is pledged or mortgaged to secure an indebtedness, action to foreclose is necessary for the enforcement of the lien, unless it is agreed in writing, that the property pledged may be sold or disposed of in some other manner. (400.9-501). In any action for enforcement of liens on personal property pledged to secure indebtedness, or to maintain or secure possession of property so pledged, proof that party holding, or claiming to hold, any such lien has received or exacted usurious interest renders pledge invalid and illegal. (408.070).

Uniform Commercial Code in force. See category Business Regulation and Commerce, topic Commercial Code.

See also category Mortgages, topic Chattel Mortgages.

RECEIVERS:

The circuit court, or any judge thereof in vacation, has power to appoint a receiver whenever such appointment shall be deemed necessary. (C.R. 68.02).

Bonds.—Receivers are required to give bonds. (C.R. 68.02).

Duties of a receiver are to keep and preserve any money or other thing deposited in court, or that may be subject of a tender, and to keep and preserve all property and protect any business or business interest entrusted to him, pending any legal or equitable proceeding concerning the same, subject to the order of court. (C.R. 68.02).

Compensation.—Court allows such sum for services as may be reasonable, and taxes same as costs to be paid as other costs in cause. (C.R. 68.02).

See also topic Executions.

REDEMPTION:

See topics Executions, Liens; categories Mortgages, topic Mortgages of Real Property; Taxation, topic Property Taxes, subhead Sales and Redemption.

SUPPLEMENTARY PROCEEDINGS:

See topic Executions.

TRUSTEE PROCESS:

See topic Garnishment.

USURY:

See category Business Regulation and Commerce, topic Interest.

DISPUTE RESOLUTION

ALTERNATIVE DISPUTE RESOLUTION:

Mandatory Dispute Resolution.—Uniform Arbitration Act adopted. (435.350-435.470).

Civil Justice Expense and Delay Reduction Plan adopted by U.S. District Court, Eastern District of Missouri to reform pretrial case management and litigation practices, reduce cost and delay. (U.S. Dist. E.D. Mo. Appendix). Civil cases randomly assigned to district and magistrate judges. (E.D. Mo. App. I). If assigned to district judge, parties may consent to trial before magistrate and district judge must approve before reassignment. (E.D. Mo. App. I). If assigned to magistrate judge, parties return signed form within 20 days after entry of appearance of last served party consenting or opting for reassignment to district judge. (E.D. Mo. App. I). If party includes filing of motion requiring immediate attention of district judge, case randomly assigned to district judge. (E.D. Mo. App. I). Differentiated case management system assigns civil case to one of five tracks based on objective factors. (E.D. Mo. App. II). Track 1 expedited cases in which disposition expected in 12 months with few parties, limited discovery, low monetary claims. (E.D. Mo. App. II). Track 2 standard cases in which disposition expected in 18 months with multiple parties, substantive legal and factual disputes, moderate discovery, significant damage claims. (E.D. Mo. App. II). Track 3 complex cases in which disposition expected in 24 months with numerous parties with diverse interests, complicated factual and legal issues, extensive discovery. (E.D. Mo. App. II). Track 4 administrative cases such as administrative appeals, social security cases, non-death penalty habeas corpus, bankruptcy appeals. (E.D. Mo. App. II). Track 5 pro se prisoner civil rights cases. (E.D. Mo. App. II). Parties file Track Information Sheet with complaint or first responsive pleading. (E.D. Mo. App. II). Mandatory disclosure in

F.R.C.P. 26(a)(1) not applicable to any civil case filed in Eastern District of Missouri except as otherwise agreed or ordered. (E.D. Mo. App. VI). Track assignment will determine discovery and disclosure. (E.D. Mo. App. IV). For Tracks 2 and 3, parties prepare joint proposed scheduling order within 30 days after defendants entry of appearance and after scheduling conference, Court enters case management scheduling order and may order referral to alternative dispute resolution. (E.D. Mo. App. IV). For Tracks 1 and 4, clerk issues binding scheduling order unless modified by judge. (E.D. Mo. App. IV). If mediation ordered, attendance of parties and counsel mandatory. (E.D. Mo. App. III). Moving party must notify clerk if any motion not decided within 60 days after submission. (E.D. Mo. App. IV).

U.S. District Court, Western District of Missouri has implemented experimental program known as Early Assessment Program (Program) as means to resolve disputes in faster, less costly manner. (U.S. Dist. W.D. Mo. Appendix). Cases excluded from Program are multi-district; social security appeals; bankruptcy appeals, habeas corpus; prisoner pro se; class actions; student loan. (W.D. Mo. App. IIA). One of every three cases filed assigned to participate in Program; one of every three cases assigned to group that may or may not elect to participate in Program; one of every three cases assigned to control group that is exempted from participation in Program unless specifically requested. (W.D. Mo. App. IIA). Requests to opt out made in writing to Administrator of Program within ten days of receiving notice. (W.D. Mo. App. IIC). Clerk provides copy of notice of case selection upon filing action and must be attached to summons. (W.D. Mo. App. IID). Within 20 days of filing, lawyer files certificate stating notice has been provided to each party. (W.D. Mo. App. IID). If service is waived or accepted, lawyer files within 20 days of waiver or acceptance, certificate stating lawyer mailed notice to each party that lawyer represents. (W.D. Mo. App. IID). Parties attend all Program sessions unless excused by Administrator and when party not natural person, person with settlement authority attends. (W.D. Mo. App. IV). All written and oral communications, not under oath, made in Program session are confidential and must not be disclosed. (W.D. Mo. App. VA). These communications must not be used for impeachment or in any future proceeding except by consent of parties. (W.D. Mo. App. VA). Any information made under oath may be used for impeachment purposes. (W.D. Mo. App. VC). No recording of Program session may be made. (W.D. Mo. App. VC). Program session held within 30 days after completion of responsive pleadings. (W.D. Mo. App. IIB). Administrator advises parties of various alternative dispute resolution options including mediation, nonbinding arbitration, early neutral evaluation, magistrate settlement, mini-trials, summary jury trials. (W.D. Mo. App. IIB). Administrator identifies areas of agreement and explores possibility of settling case. (W.D. Mo. App. IIB). Participants select ADR option or Administrator will select. (W.D. Mo. App. IIB). First session of ADR process held not later than 90 days after first Program session. (W.D. Mo. App. IIB). Failure to comply with attendance or settlement authority requirements subjects party to sanctions. (W.D. Mo. App. VIIA). Court may sanction failure to make good faith effort to participate in Program. (W.D. Mo. App. IX).

All civil actions in federal Western District court where money damages only are being sought that are not expected to exceed $100,000 are designated for compulsory arbitration. (U.S. Dist. Ct. R. W.D. Mo. 30). Unless otherwise agreed, arbitration hearing held before panel of three arbitrators. (W.D. Mo. 30). Arbitration award entered as judgment of Court unless party requests trial de novo within 30 days. (W.D. Mo. 30). If party receives less favorable award at trial de novo than arbitration award, party must pay arbitration fees. (W.D. Mo. 30). In practice, this arbitration requirement is effectively superseded by experimental Early Assessment Program. (W.D. Mo. App.).

Voluntary Dispute Resolution.—

Child Custody and Visitation.—Any judicial circuit may establish mediation program for child custody and visitation disputes whereby neutral mediator appointed by court assists parties to reach mutually acceptable agreement. (C.R. 88.02). Mediator of contested child custody must be attorney or one who possesses graduate degree in field of psychiatry, psychology, social work, counseling or other behavioral science substantially related to marriage and family relationships and must have at least 20 hours of child custody mediation training. (C.R. 88.05). Mediator in writing must advise parties of cost, does not represent parties, and should obtain independent legal advice. (C.R.88.05[a]). Mediated agreement is not binding until in writing and signed by parties and their attorneys, if any. (C.R. 88.05[c]). Termination of mediation can occur by any party after two hours or by mediator if continuation would cause harm or prejudice or agreement is unlikely. (C.R. 88.07).

Any judicial circuit court may establish early dispute resolution program to foster voluntary settlement. (C.R. 17.01). Notice of dispute resolution services provided at time action is filed or with summons and petition. (C.R. 17.03). Individuals providing early dispute resolution services must have training or experience including 16 hours of formal training for mediators. (C.R. 17.04). Early dispute resolution results are binding on parties to extent agreed upon. (C.R. 17.05). Early dispute resolution process regarded as settlement negotiations and settlement is enforceable or admissible in evidence if parties agree. (C.R. 17.07). Admissions, representations, or confidential communications made in dispute resolution process are inadmissible as evidence and not subject to discovery. (C.R. 17.06). No person can reveal to court why, who or what caused mediation to cease or result of mediation. (C.R. 17.06). Discovery may proceed while participating in early dispute resolution program. (C.R. 17.08).

ARBITRATION AND AWARD:

Uniform Arbitration Act adopted. (c. 435).

Effect of Contract Provision.—Written agreement to submit existing controversy to arbitration or provision in written contract, except insurance contract or contract of adhesion, to submit any future controversy to arbitration is valid and enforceable. Warranties against defects in construction of new houses and reinsurance contracts are not contracts of insurance or contracts of adhesion. (435.350).

Powers of Arbitrators.—Arbitrators have power to issue subpoenas and compel attendance of witnesses. (435.380).

Enforcement of Award.—When judgment entered on award, obedience may be enforced in same manner as to any other judgment or decree. (435.415).

See note at head of Digest as to 1998 legislation covered.

See Topical Index in front part of this volume.

ARBITRATION AND AWARD . . . *continued*
Mandatory Arbitration.—None.

DOCUMENTS AND RECORDS

ACKNOWLEDGMENTS:

May be taken by following officers, etc.:

Within state: Court having a seal or judge, justice or clerk of such court; notary public. (442.150). Maximum fee $2. (486.350).

Outside state but within United States: Notary public; state or federal court having a seal or clerk of such court; commissioner appointed by Governor of Missouri to take acknowledgments. (442.150; 486.100-.140).

Outside United States: Court of any state, kingdom or empire, having official seal; mayor or chief officer of any city or town having a seal; U.S. minister or consular officer; notary public having a seal. (442.150).

Married Women.—Husband and wife may convey real estate of wife and wife may relinquish dower in real estate of husband by their joint deed certified and acknowledged by both. No separate examination of wife required but she must be described as wife in acknowledgment. (442.030, 442.050, 442.210). See also categories Family, topic Husband and Wife; Property, topics Deeds, Dower.

Attorneys in Fact.—Instruments containing power must be acknowledged or proved, and certified in same manner as deeds of real estate. (442.360, 490.570).

Certificate must state act of acknowledgment and that person making same was personally known to one judge of court or officer granting certificate, which must conform to laws of this state. (442.210). If acknowledgment is taken by notary public, certificate must clearly and legibly, by means of rubber stamp, typewriting or printing, indicate notary's name, county of commission, and words "Notary Public", "State of Missouri", My Commission Expires . . . (Expiration date)". (486.280).

Seal of officer taking acknowledgment must be affixed.

Authentication.—Not necessary that seal or signature of notary of another state be authenticated by any other officer. Proper officer to certify to official character of notary of this state is Secretary of State, upon submission of written request, notarized document and $2 fee.

Evidence.—Written instruments conveying or affecting real estate, when acknowledged, may be read in evidence without further proof. (490.410).

Proof by Witnesses.—If a deed is attested by subscribing witnesses and not acknowledged by the grantor, proof of its execution may be made by the testimony of a subscribing witness or where all the subscribing witnesses are dead or cannot be produced, by evidence of the handwriting of the party, and of at least one subscribing witness, given by at least two credible witnesses to each signature. (442.260).

No proof by a subscribing witness may be taken unless such witness is personally known to one judge of the court, or the officer taking the proof, to be the person whose name is subscribed to the instrument as a witness thereto, or is proved to be such by at least two credible witnesses. (442.270).

No proof by evidence of handwriting may be taken unless the court or officer taking same is satisfied that all the subscribing witnesses to such instrument are dead or cannot be produced. (442.300).

Such proof may be taken by any one of the courts or officers named above as those authorized to take acknowledgments. (442.260-.320).

Alternative to Acknowledgment or Proof.—No statutory provision.

Forms.—The following are authorized and used:

Forms

Natural person: State of . . . ., County of . . . ., ss. On this . . . . day of . . . ., 19. . . ., before me personally appeared (here insert name or names and if grantor is married add "his wife" after her name), to me known to be the person (or persons) described in, and who executed the foregoing instrument, and acknowledged that (he or they) executed the same as his (or their) free act and deed.

In testimony whereof I have hereunto set my hand and affixed my official seal at my office in said county and state the day and year last above written.

My term expires . . . .

. . . ., Notary Public.

If grantor is single, added: And the said . . . . further declared . . . .self to be single and unmarried.

Attorney in fact: State of . . . ., County of . . . ., ss. On this . . . . day of . . . ., 19. . . ., before me personally appeared (here insert name), to me known to be the person who executed the foregoing instrument in behalf of (here insert name), and acknowledged that he executed the same as the free act and deed of said (here insert name). (Certificate as above).

Corporation or joint stock associations: State of . . . ., County of . . . ., ss. On this . . . . day of . . . ., 19. . . ., before me appeared (here insert name), to me personally known, who, being by me duly sworn (or affirmed), did say that he is the president (or other officer or agent of the corporation or association) of (describing the corporation or association), and that the seal affixed to said instrument is the corporate seal of said corporation (or association), and that said instrument was signed and sealed in behalf of said corporation (or association) by authority of its board of directors (or trustees), and said (here insert name) acknowledged said instrument to be the free act and deed of said corporation (or association). (Certificate as above).

If corporation or association has no corporate seal, omit "and that the seal affixed to said instrument is the corporate seal of said corporation (or association)" and add, at end of certificate, "and that said corporation (or association) has no corporate seal." (442.210).

Persons in or with U. S. Armed Forces.—Acknowledgment of person without state, in military service of United States on active duty, may be taken by any commissioned, other than warrant, officer on active duty in any of the Armed Forces of the U. S., and also that of spouse, if nature of instrument requires it. (442.160).

Form

With the Armed Forces of the United States at . . . . . . ss. On this . . . . . . day of . . . . ., A.D. 19. . . ., before me, a commissioned officer of the Armed Forces of the United States, on active duty therewith, personally appeared . . . . . ., a member of the Armed Forces of the United States, on active duty therewith, (and . . . . . . (his wife, her husband),) to me known to be the person . . . . . . described in and who executed the foregoing instrument, and acknowledged that . . . . . . executed the same as . . . . . . free act and deed. (The said . . . . . . declared . . . . . . to be single and unmarried.)

IN TESTIMONY WHEREOF, I have hereunto set my hand and grade (serial number, branch of service, and permanent mailing address).

(Signature)   (Serial Number)

. . . .
(Grade)   (Branch of Service: Army, Navy, etc.)

. . . .
(Permanent mailing address)

. . . .

See also topics Affidavits; categories Mortgages, topic Mortgages of Real Property; Property, topic Deeds.

AFFIDAVITS:

See topic Acknowledgments.

General Requirements as to Administration.—Affidavit may be made before notary public (486.250), court or judge, justice or clerk thereof, certified court reporter or certified shorthand reporter (492.010). If made before judge of another state, his official character must be certified under seal of clerk and if made before justice of peace of another state must be accompanied by certificate of official character and authority, that he had power to administer oaths when affidavit was taken, and that his signature is genuine, attested by seal of state or by certificate and seal of clerk of court of record. (490.530-.540).

Persons in Military Service.—Any commissioned officer, other than commissioned warrant officer, of any of Armed Forces of U.S., on active duty, may take affidavit of member of Armed Forces. (492.070).

Form

With the Armed Forces of the United States at . . . . ss. (Body of instrument). Subscribed and sworn to (affirmed) by . . . ., to me known to be a member of the Armed Forces of the United States, on active duty therewith, before me, a commissioned officer of the Armed Forces of the United States, on active duty therewith, this . . . . day of . . . . A.D. 19 . . .

(Signature)   (Serial Number)

. . . .
(Grade) (Branch of Service: Army, Navy, etc.)

. . . .
(Permanent Mailing Address)

. . . .

See also categories Civil Actions and Procedure, topics Depositions and Discovery, Evidence, subhead Witnesses; Estates and Trusts, topic Executors and Administrators.

Admissibility.—Affidavits generally are not admissible in evidence, but are admitted as prima facie proof of endorsements on negotiable instruments and the existence of partnerships, names of partners and general nature of partnership business. (490.510-.520).

Requirements of Jurat.—Expiration of notary's commission must be stated and officer's seal affixed.

Form

State of Missouri, County of . . . . . ., ss., John Doe of lawful age, being duly sworn on his oath says, etc.

. . . . Affiant.

Subscribed and sworn to before me this . . . . day of . . . ., 19. . . . .

. . . . Notary Public. (Seal).

My commission expires . . . .

Alternative to Affidavit.—Every document filed with probate court shall be signed by or on behalf of petitioner or claimant, and shall contain statement that it is made under oath or affirmation and that its representations are true and correct to best knowledge and belief of person signing, subject to penalties of making false affidavit or declaration. (472.080).

Form

State of Missouri, County of . . . ., the undersigned states that the above is made under oath or affirmation and that its representations are true and correct to the best of his knowledge and belief, subject to the penalties of making a false affidavit or declaration.

Signed . . . .

NOTARIES PUBLIC:

Qualification.—Notary must furnish $10,000 bond running to state with two sureties approved by clerk of county court or circuit court in City of St. Louis. (486.235).

Seal.—Notary must have and use seal reciting his name and words "Notary Seal," "Notary Public," and "State of Missouri." (486.285).

See note at head of Digest as to 1998 legislation covered.

See Topical Index in front part of this volume.

NOTARIES PUBLIC ... continued

Powers.—Notaries are empowered to: (1) Take acknowledgments, (2) administer oaths and affirmations, (3) certify that copy of document is true copy of another document, and (4) perform any other act permitted by law. (486.250).

Territorial Extent of Powers.—Notary's jurisdiction extends throughout State. (486.210).

Certificate.—Every notary certificate must indicate in printing, rubber stamp or typewriting exact name of notary, "Notary Public," "State of Missouri," and "My commission expires . . . . . (commission expiration date)". (486.280).

Certificate of Authority.—See topic Acknowledgments, subhead Authentication.

Records.—Notary must keep in a special book an exact record of all his official acts. (486.265).

Maximum fee for notarization of signature and recording thereof is $2. Fee for certification of facsimile document and recordation thereof is $2 for each sheet retained in notary file. Fee is $1 for all other notarial acts. (486.350).

Durable Power of Attorney.—See category Property, topic Powers of Attorney, subhead Durable Power of Attorney.

RECORDS:

The recorder of deeds in each county has charge of records relating to property.

Uniform Commercial Code adopted. (c. 400). See category Business Regulation and Commerce, topic Commercial Code.

Recordable Instruments.—It is the duty of recorder to record all deeds, mortgages, conveyances, deeds of trust, assignments, bonds, covenants, defeasances, or other writings of or concerning any lands and tenements, or goods and chattels, when proved or acknowledged according to law; papers and documents concerning land and tenements, or goods and chattels received from French or Spanish authorities at change of government, marriage contracts and marriage certificates, all official commissions and official bonds required to be recorded, and records of births when furnished. (59.330).

All deeds, mortgages, conveyances, deeds of trusts, assignments, bonds, covenants or defeasances, except supplemental indentures of utility companies and rural electric cooperatives, must contain legal description of land affected.

Restrictive covenants on property relating to race, color, religion or national origin in any instrument filed with recorder of deeds are void and unenforceable. (442.403).

It is also the duty of recorder to record any certified copy of any bankruptcy matter required to be filed by Act of Congress. (59.335).

All instruments affecting real estate, except supplemental indentures of utility companies and rural electric cooperatives, must contain legal description of lands and all deeds, except deeds of easement of right-of-way, must contain mailing address of grantee to be recorded. (59.330[1]).

In cities of over 400,000 population and in all counties of the first class no trustee's or mortgagee's deed under power of sale in foreclosure of any security instrument recorded prior to 1-1-86 may be recorded unless notes or other obligations for default in payment of which foreclosure was had or affidavit of owner as to loss thereof are produced to recorder. (443.390).

Place of Recording.—The recording in the case of real estate must be in the county where the land is situated. (442.380).

For List of Counties and County Seats see first page for this state in Volume containing Practice Profiles Section.

Indices are kept, showing names of grantor and grantee, date of instrument, date of filing for record and description of land. Separate indices are kept for instruments affecting personal property. (59.350-.440).

Requisites for Recording.—Size of print or type on any document to be recorded shall not be smaller than eight point and if any document to be recorded contains smaller than eight point it must be accompanied by exact typewritten copy which will be recorded contemporaneously with document. Document must be sufficiently legible to produce clear and legible reproduction or exact typewritten copy must accompany document and be recorded contemporaneously. Signatures on documents must have corresponding name typed, printed or stamped underneath signature. (59.310).

All deeds, mortgages, deeds of trust or other instruments conveying lands or tenements or goods and chattels must be acknowledged or approved to be recorded and all deeds, except deeds of easements or right of way conveying lands or tenements must contain mailing address of one of grantees. (59.330).

Recording Fees.—Fee for recording every deed or instrument, $5 for first page and $3 for each page thereafter; for recording plat or survey of a subdivision, $25 per page of drawings and calculations plus $5 per page of other material; for recording survey of one tract of land on one page, $5; copy of recorded instruments, $2 for first page and $1 per page thereafter; copy of plat or survey, $5 per page; certificate or seal, $1 when not recording an instrument. State user fee of $1 for all instruments conveying real estate; 25¢ fee for identifying each note to instrument when document is recorded that creates lien against real estate. (59.310). Additional user fees of $7 shall be charged for recording any instrument. (59.319).

Effect of Recording.—No instrument conveying or affecting the title to real estate is valid, except as between the parties and such as have actual notice, until deposited for record; thereafter notice is imparted to all persons. (442.390-.400).

Torrens system not adopted.

Transfer of Decedent's Title.—Whether decedent was a resident or a nonresident, administration in Missouri is necessary to free title from his debts, unless claims of creditors are barred by lapse of time. Probate court records should be included in abstracts of title and need not be recorded with recorder of deeds. To provide record evidence in case of testacy, a certified copy of the will must be recorded, within six months after probate, in office of recorder of deeds in each county in which real estate is situated (474.500) and it is customary to record also a certified copy of order admitting will to probate. In case of intestacy, unless the probate records include an affidavit

stating date of death and names of surviving spouse, if any, and heirs, such an affidavit must be recorded with recorder of deeds.

Uniform Commercial Code in force. See category Business Regulation and Commerce, topic Commercial Code.

Filing Under Commercial Code.—Most financing statements are filed with secretary of state and, if debtor has place of business in only one county in Missouri, also with recorder of deeds for that county. If debtor has no place of business in Missouri but lives in Missouri then financing statement is filed with recorder of deeds for county in which he resides as well as with secretary of state. If collateral is consumer goods, farm equipment, farm products or proceeds of sale of farm products by farmer or collateral is or will become fixture on real estate, financing statement is not filed with secretary of state but only in county of debtor's residence unless collateral is fixture in which case it is filed with recorder of deeds for county in which fixture will be located. If collateral is crops, financing statement is also filed in recorder's office of county where crops are growing or will be grown. (400.0-401). Filing fee $4 for officially approved forms. Fee for filing forms other than approved by Secretary of State $6. (400.9-401). See category Business Regulation and Commerce, topic Commercial Code.

Vital Statistics.—Reports of births and deaths must be filed with local registrar of vital statistics (193.085; 193.145); reports of marriages with recorder of deeds who issued license (451.150). Certified copy of birth or death certificate can be obtained from Registrar, Bureau of Vital Statistics, Division of Health, P.O. Box 570, Jefferson City, Missouri 65102, for fee of $10 payable to Department of Revenue. (193.265). Certified copy of marriage certificate can be obtained from Recorder of Deeds for fee of $2. (59.310).

Establishing Birth Records.—If birth certificate of person born in Missouri has not been filed within seven days after birth, birth certificate may be filed after that time as provided by regulations of Division of Health. Birth certificates registered more than one year after birth are made on forms provided by state Registrar of Vital Statistics and are marked "Delayed". If delayed birth certificate is rejected by state Registrar of Vital Statistics, affected individual may petition local Circuit Court for order establishing record of date and place of his birth and his parentage on forms provided by state Registrar of Vital Statistics. If court finds that person for whom delayed certificate of birth was born in Missouri, it shall make findings as to place and date of birth and parentage and shall issue order to establish certificate of birth. This order will be forwarded to state Registrar of Vital Statistics and shall constitute birth certificate. (193.105; 193.115).

SEALS:

Necessity of private seals is abolished, but seal (or scroll if corporation has no seal) is necessary to valid conveyance of real estate of corporation. (442.060).

Uniform Commercial Code in force. See category Business Regulation and Commerce, topic Commercial Code.

See also topics Acknowledgments, Affidavits.

TORRENS ACT:

Not adopted. See topic Records.

VITAL STATISTICS:

See topic Records.

EMPLOYMENT

EMPLOYER AND EMPLOYEE:

See topic Labor Relations.

LABOR RELATIONS:

The Industrial Commission of Missouri has general jurisdiction over labor matters. (286.060).

Hours of Labor.—Period of eight hours constitutes legal days work; providing parties may agree upon longer or shorter time. (290.010-.020). Workers in mill or plant engaged in mining, mechanical, chemical manufacturing or smelting business must work only eight of 24 hours unless otherwise consented to. Children under 16 must work no more than eight hours in a day nor three hours day when school is in session nor more than six days or 40 hours in any week nor before seven a.m. or after nine p.m. or seven p.m. when school is in session. (294.030). These requirements may be waived by director. (294.030).

Wages.—Corporations must pay wages as often as semi-monthly within 16 days of the close of each payroll period, except that executive, administrative, professional, sales and other employees on a commission basis in whole or in part, may be paid monthly, and at least once a month furnish to employees a statement showing total deductions for the period. Violation of this section is a misdemeanor. (290.080). Claims of employees for wages, not to exceed $100 and earned within three months next preceding demand, have priority of payment from the assets of a corporation in the hands of a receiver or assignee, except that they are not preferred over specific liens on property. (430.360).

Corporation which reduces wages without giving 30 days notice must pay to employee a penalty of $50. (290.100).

When an employee of a corporation is discharged, with or without cause, his unpaid wages are due on the date of such discharge, and he may request, in writing, that the money due him or a valid check be sent to any station or office where a regular agent is kept, and if payment does not reach such station or office within seven days from date of such request, the employee's wages continue until paid, but not for more than 60 days unless an action therefor be commenced within that time. (290.110).

No minimum wage provisions.

No lien for wages.

Assignments of Wages.—See category Debtor and Creditor, topic Assignments.

LABOR RELATIONS . . . *continued*

Lesser wage rates due to sex are prohibited. (290.400-.450).

Missouri Council of Women's Economic Development and Training is established, 11 members to be appointed by Governor, four appointed by General Assembly. Purposes of Council are to: (1) Promote and increase women's economic and employment opportunities, (2) promote occupational mobility of women workers, (3) promote access to jobs with higher skill and responsibility, (4) initiate programs to assist women in small business enterprises, (5) assure access of women to nontraditional skilled trades, (6) promote retraining programs for unemployed women, (7) apply for relevant federal and private grants, (8) conduct studies and programs in cooperation with government agencies relating to women's economic issues, (9) prepare state plan to identify and prioritize economic needs of women. (c. 186).

Child Labor.—Employment of children under age of 14 is prohibited, except in sale and distribution of newspapers, magazines and periodicals, which may be performed by children age 12 or older, and service for parent or guardian, or occasional work for others with consent of parent or guardian. (294.011-.021). Employment of children under age of 16 is strictly regulated. (294.024-.110). Employment of children in entertainment industry and in dangerous situations is also strictly regulated. (294.022).

Labor Unions.—Missouri has no "right to work" laws. Employees have right to organize and bargain collectively. (Const. 1945, Art. 1, §29).

Dismissal.—Statute declaring that employee of corporation discharged or voluntarily quitting (if employed at least 90 days) shall, upon written request, receive letter signed by superintendent or manager setting forth nature and character of service rendered and duration thereof and cause for quitting service (290.140) held not to be so vague as to be violation of due process when properly viewed as regulatory statute governing business activities (656 F.2d 323 [8th Cir. 1980]).

Discrimination.—Employers of more than six persons are prohibited from refusing to hire, discharging, or discriminating against employee because of race, creed, color, religion, national origin, sex, age (between 40 and 70), handicap, ancestry, or familial status as it relates to housing, except corporations and associations owned and operated by religious or sectarian groups. Labor organizations, lenders, sellers and renters of dwellings, owners of places of public accomodations and employment agencies similarly prohibited. Unlawful to refuse to permit handicapped person to reasonably modify dwelling. Multifamily dwellings built after 3/13/91 must be handicapped accessible. (213.040). Missouri commission on human rights acts on complaints, with appeal available to courts. (213.010-.126).

Fatal Accidents.—Division director of labor standards shall investigate all accidents which result in death, file written report, and make safety recommendations to employer. (286.147).

Workers' Compensation.—Workers' Compensation Act (c. 287), is administered by Division of Workers' Compensation of Department of Labor and Industrial Relations of State of Missouri (287.020), which may sue and be sued in its official name (287.590). Division may appoint administrative law judges, who must be duly licensed lawyers and may be discharged or removed only by Governor. Administrative law judges shall devote their whole time to duties of their office, and shall only have jurisdiction to hear and determine claims upon original hearings and shall have no jurisdiction upon any review hearing or by way of opening any prior award. (287.610).

To Whom Applicable.—Act applies to all employers employing over five employees. (287.030). Employee does not include owner or operator of motor vehicle leased or contracted with driver as for-hire common or contract carrier operating within commercial zone, or under certificate issued by transportation division or interstate commerce commission. (287.020). Act applies to minors even if employed in violation of law. (287.020). Act applies to all state employees, and Act applies to construction industry employers if have one or more employed. (287.020).

Act does not apply to employment of farm labor, qualified real estate agents and direct sellers; domestic servants in private home, including occasional laborers, and family chauffeurs; worker who is member of employer's family within third degree (by marriage) of affinity, employment of inmate confined in prison, penitentiary or jail or patient or resident in state mental health facility where labor is exclusively on behalf of custodial entity; volunteers of tax-exempt organizations; or persons providing services as adjudicators, sports officials or contest workers for interscholastic activities or similar amateur youth programs who are not otherwise employed by sponsoring entity, unless employer voluntarily elects to accept Act. (287.090).

Corporation may file with division notice of election to be exempt from Act, when there are only two corporate owners who are also its sole employees. (287.090).

Basis of Liability.—Employer is liable irrespective of negligence when injury is clearly work related. Injury must have arisen out of and in course of employment. Not compensable if work was mere triggering or precipitating factor. Employment must be substantial factor causing injury, injury followed as natural incident of work, employment fairly traceable as proximate cause, injury not due to hazard or risk unrelated to employment to which worker was exposed. Deterioration of body by aging not compensable, except where follows as incident of employment (287.020); not liable where injury intentionally inflicted by employee. Burden of proof of intentional self-inflicted injury is on party contesting claim. Not liable for stress unless work related and extraordinary and unusual (exception does not apply to firefighters). (287.120). Special rules as to hernia. (287.195).

Notice is proper when sent by registered or certified mail properly stamped and addressed to person or entity to whom given, at last known address in time to reach person or entity in time to act. (287.520).

Compensation.—For temporary total disability from injuries occurring on or after 9/28/83 but before 9/28/86, $66\frac{2}{3}\%$ of average weekly earnings (as defined in 287.250) but not more than 70% of state average weekly wage determined by Div. of Employment Security as of July 1 preceding injury per week for not more than 400 weeks; for disability from injuries occurring on or after 9/28/86 but before 8/28/90, $66\frac{2}{3}\%$ weekly earnings but not more than 75% of state average weekly wage as of July 1 preceding injury; for injuries occurring on or after 9/28/86 but before 8/28/90, $66\frac{2}{3}\%$ weekly earnings as of date of injury but not more than 75% of state average weekly wage; for injuries occurring on or after 8/28/90 but before 8/28/91, $66\frac{2}{3}\%$ weekly earnings as of date of injury but not more than 100% of state average weekly wage; for injuries occurring on or after 8/28/91, $66\frac{2}{3}\%$ weekly earnings as of date of injury but not to exceed 105% of state average weekly wage; minimum weekly compensation $40 for injuries occurring on or after 8/28/91. Compensation for temporary total disability shall not be paid for more than 400 weeks.

For temporary partial disability from injuries occurring on or after 9/28/83 but before 9/28/86, $66\frac{2}{3}\%$ of average earnings up to maximum of 70% of state average weekly wage as of July 1 preceding injury per week for not more than 100 weeks; for disability from injuries occurring on or after 8/28/86 but before 9/28/90, $66\frac{2}{3}\%$ of average earnings as of date of injury, not to exceed 75% of state average weekly wage as of July 1 preceding injury; for injuries occurring on or after 9/28/90 but before 9/28/91, $66\frac{2}{3}\%$ of injured employee's average weekly earnings, provided that compensation not exceed 100% of state average weekly wage; for injuries occurring on or after 9/28/91, $66\frac{2}{3}\%$ of injured employee's average weekly earnings, provided that compensation not exceed 105% of state average weekly wage. (287.180).

For permanent partial disability from injuries occurring on or after 9/28/83 but before 8/28/90, $66\frac{2}{3}\%$ of employee's average weekly earnings as of date of injury; but not more than 45% as of July 1st immediately preceding date of injury; for all injuries occurring on or after 9/28/91, weekly compensation shall be at least $40 per week; for all injuries occurring on or after 8/28/90 but before 8/28/91, $66\frac{2}{3}\%$ of employee's average weekly earnings as of date of injury, provided that weekly compensation does not exceed 50% of state average weekly wage; for all injuries occurring on or after 8/28/91 but before 8/28/92, $66\frac{2}{3}\%$ of employee's average weekly earnings as of date of injury, provided that weekly compensation does not exceed 52% of state average weekly wage; for all injuries occurring on or after 8/28/92, $66\frac{2}{3}\%$ of employee's average weekly earnings as of date of injury, provided that weekly compensation does not exceed 55% of state average weekly wage. (287.190).

If disability is due to severance or complete loss of use of members included in schedule of losses, benefits increase 10%. For permanent injuries other than those listed in schedule, compensation will be paid proportionate to relation which other injury bears, not to exceed 400 weeks. If employee's head, neck, hand or arm is permanently disfigured, additional compensation of up to 40 weeks can be awarded. Permanent partial disability is in addition to compensation for temporary total or temporary partial disability. (287.190).

For permanent partial disability from injuries occurring on or after 9/28/83 but before 9/28/86, $66\frac{2}{3}\%$ of average earnings but not more than 45% of state average weekly wage as of July 1 preceding injury for period of scheduled losses (from eight to 232 weeks depending on nature of injury); for disability from injuries occurring on or after 9/28/81, weekly minimum compensation $40. If disability is due to severance or complete loss of use, benefits increase 10%. If employee's head, neck, hand or arm is seriously and permanently disfigured, additional compensation of up to 40 weeks can be awarded. Permanent partial disability is in addition to compensation for temporary total or temporary partial disability. (287.190).

For permanent total disability occurring on or after 9/28/83 but before 9/28/86, $66\frac{2}{3}\%$ of average weekly earnings during year preceding injury but not more than 70% of state average weekly wages as of July 1 preceding injury for life; for disability from injuries occurring on or after 9/28/86 but before 8/28/90, $66\frac{2}{3}\%$ of average weekly earnings during year preceding injury but not more than 75% of state average weekly wage as of July 1 preceding injury for life; for disability from injuries occurring on or after 8/28/90 but before 8/28/91, $66\frac{2}{3}\%$ of average weekly earnings as of date of injury but not more than 100% of state average weekly wage; for injuries occurring on or after 8/28/91, $66\frac{2}{3}\%$ of average weekly earnings, not to exceed 105% of state average weekly wage. (287.200).

Compensation is payable as wages were prior to injury, but at least once every two weeks. None is payable for first three regular work days of disability unless disability lasts longer than 14 days. Late payments increased by interest at 10% per annum. If employee agrees in writing, employer may pay employee directly and be indemnified by insurer. Employer or insurer is reimbursed by employee if claim found non-compensable. (287.160).

On application of either party, award may be commuted by the Division under unusual circumstances. (287.530).

Employees may be required from time to time during disability to submit to examination. (287.210). Commission, division or judge may appoint qualified impartial physician to examine employee. (287.210).

Employer is required to provide medical, surgical, chiropractic and hospital treatment, including nursing, custodial, ambulance and medicine, reasonably required to cure and relieve effects of injury. Employee may select his own physician at his own expense and employer required to advance travel expenses, but not for more than 100 miles, for necessary medical treatment under certain conditions. Health care provider has duty to communicate fully with employee regarding injuries. (287.140). Referring physicians must disclose financial interests in referee. (287.140). When employer has provided compensation, and then terminates compensation, employer must notify employee of termination and reason. If employee disputes termination of benefits, employee may request hearing before division. Reasonable recovery cost awarded to prevailing party. (287.203).

No health care provider, other than one selected by employee at own expense, may attempt to collect fee for services rendered employee due to work-related injury or report to credit agency failure of employee to make payment, where injury covered under Act and such health care provider has received actual notice stating name of employer, insurer, employee, nature of injury and where claim filed. Health care provider may pursue employee for unpaid fee if injury determined non-compensable under Act. (287.140).

Failure of employer to comply with statutes regarding safety devices increases compensation 15%. Willful failure of employee to use such devices, or failure of employee to obey reasonable, posted safety rules, reduces compensation 15%. (287.120).

In third party action by employer under subrogation rights, recovery apportioned between employer and employee or his dependents. (287.150).

See note at head of Digest as to 1998 legislation covered.

See Topical Index in front part of this volume.

MO – 25

LABOR RELATIONS . . . *continued*

In case of accident with less than $500 medical costs and no lost employment time, employer must notify employee, in writing, of rights under Act. (287.380).

In all cases in which employer found to knowingly employ minor contrary to law, 50% additional compensation allowed. (287.250).

Death Benefits.—If injury causes death, employer must pay direct to person furnishing same reasonable burial expenses, not to exceed $5,000. Employer must also pay to total dependents of employee death benefit as follows: (a) If injury which caused death occurred on or after 9/28/83, but before 9/28/86, 66²/₃% of employee's average weekly earnings per week during year preceding injury but not more than 70% of state average weekly wage as of July 1 preceding injury per week; (b) if injury which caused death occurred on or after 9/28/86 but before 8/28/90, 66²/₃% of employee's average weekly wage per week during year preceding injury but not more than 75% of state average weekly wage as of July 1 preceding injury; (c) if injury which caused death occurred on or after 8/28/90 but before 8/28/91, 66²/₃% of employee's average weekly wages but not more than 100% of state average weekly wage; (d) if injury which caused death occurred on or after 8/28/91, 66²/₃% of employee's average weekly wage but not more than 105% of state average weekly wage; (e) if injury which caused death occurred on or after 9/28/81, weekly compensation shall in no event be less than $40 per week. If partial dependents and no total dependents, payment must be made to them proportionately. (287.240).

Second Injuries.— In cases of permanent disability where there has been previous disability, compensation computed on basis of average earnings at time of last injury. If employee has preexisting permanent partial disability of seriousness to constitute obstacle to employment and said disability, if as to whole body, equals at least 50 weeks of compensation, or if major extremity injury only equals at least 15% permanent partial disability, and employee receives subsequent compensable injury resulting in permanent partial disability so that degree of disability, in amount equaling at least that as described above, caused by combined disabilities is substantially greater than that which would have resulted from last injury, considered alone, and if employee is entitled to compensation because of combined disabilities, employer at time of last injury is liable only for degree of disability from last injury had there been no preexisting disability. Balance paid from second injury fund. In case of total and permanent disability, above minimum degrees of disability are inapplicable; employer liable only for disability resulting from last injury considered alone. Balance paid from second injury fund. (287.220).

Funds received by employer, or his dependents, through civil or other action, must be used to reimburse second injury fund for payments made to employee or dependents. (287.220).

If employee has more than one employer at time of compensable injury, employer for whom employee working at time of injury is only responsible for lost wages in that employment. Employee may file claim against second injury fund for lost wages attributable to other employment where injury did not occur, up to maximum weekly benefit less benefits paid by aforementioned employer. (287.220). In case of multiple employments, total average weekly wage equals sum of total average weekly wage for each employment employee is unable to return due to injury. (287.250). Records pertaining to second injury fund claims open to public. (287.220).

Limitations.—Injured party must notify employer within 30 days from injury unless good cause for failure to do so is shown (287.420), and, except for second injury fund claims, must file within two years after date of injury or death, or last payment made on account of injury or death; provided, however, that if report of injury or death was not filed by employer as required, claim may be filed within three years after date of injury, death or last payment made on account of injury or death. If suit at law or in admiralty or action under compensation laws of another state is filed within two years after filing by employer of report of injury or death, or where payments have been made, within two years of last payment, and recovery is denied on ground that person was employee subject to provisions of Missouri Workmen's Compensation Act, two year limitation for filing claim begins to run with termination or abandonment of such suit or proceeding. Claim against second injury fund must be filed within two years after date of injury or within one year after claim is filed against employer or insurer. (287.430-.440).

Review.—When parties are unable to agree as to compensation, hearing is held before Division through a referee, except hearing applications will not be considered until 14 days after received. (287.450-.460). Full Commission may review award (287.480), and appeal from decision of full Commission may be taken to appellate court. Appeal must be filed within 20 days of Commission's final decision. That court is bound by findings of fact within powers of Commission, hears no additional evidence, reviews only questions at law and may modify, remand for rehearing, set aside or reverse award only on one of following grounds: (1) That Commission acted without or in excess of its powers; (2) that award was procured by fraud; (3) that facts found by Commission do not support award; (4) that there was not sufficient competent evidence in record to warrant making of award. Appeals to circuit and appellate courts have precedence over all cases except election contests. (287.490).

False Claims.—Unlawful to knowingly present false or fraudulent claim for payment of benefits, knowingly present multiple claims for same occurrence with intent to defraud, purposefully present or participate in preparation of writing to support false or fraudulent claim, or knowingly assist, abet, solicit or conspire with person regarding above, knowingly make false or fraudulent claim for health care benefits, knowingly submit claim for health care benefits not used by, or on behalf of, claimant; knowingly present multiple claims for health care benefits with intent to defraud, knowingly make false or fraudulent material statement or representation to obtain or deny benefit, knowingly make false or fraudulent statement regarding entitlement to benefits with intent to discourage injured worker from making claim. Aforementioned false claims punishable as class A misdemeanor and liable for fine up to $10,000, or double value of fraud, whichever greater. (287.128).

Unlawful for insurance company or self-insurer to intentionally refuse to comply with legally indisputable compensation obligations, administer compensation obligations in dishonest manner or in manner to cause injury to public or person dealing with employer or insurer. Punishable same as above. (287.128).

Employer failing to insure liability under Act is guilty of class A misdemeanor and is liable to State for penalty of twice annual premium had employer been insured, or $25,000, whichever greater. (287.128).

Employer's Insurance.—Insurance must be carried by employer through some company authorized to insure such liability, or may be carried by employer himself or on group insurance basis when proof of ability to do so is shown. (287.280). Insurance carriers must provide comprehensive safety and loss control services to their insureds. Failure to provide such programs may result in combination of fines up to $10,000 or suspension or revocation of insurer's right to sell insurance. (287.123). Employees are not permitted to pay cost of insurance. (287.290). Employer must post special notice distributed by Division of Worker's Compensation. (287.127).

Employees Savings and Insurance.—Benefits from other sources are no bar to recovery under the act. (287.270).

Assignability of Compensation, etc.—Compensation is not assignable, nor subject to attachment, garnishment, execution, set-off or counterclaim. (287.260).

Settlements.—All compromises or settlements must be approved by administrative law judge or commission. (287.390). Claim for compensation may be reactivated after settlement only for payment of life threatening surgical procedures or if claimant requires use of new or modification of existing prosthetic device. (287.430). Mediation services provided at pretrial conference if division determines claim may be settled, or upon application by either party. Upon request of either party, person providing mediation services is disqualified from conducting evidentiary hearing. (287.460).

Occupational Diseases.—Included in workmen's compensation provisions. (287.110). For claims procedure and compensation see subhead Workers' Compensation, supra.

Occupational Disease defined as disease arising out of and in course of employment including loss of hearing in one or both ears due to prolonged exposure to harmful noise in employment and disability due to radioactive properties or to Roentgen rays or exposure to ionizing radiation. Employee with repetitive trauma injury who has worked for employer less than three months must file claim against prior employer where that employment is substantial cause of injury. (287.067).

Employers' Liability Act.—See subhead Workers' Compensation, supra.

Unemployment Compensation.—An insured worker, who has been paid within base period (worker who has been paid wages of at least $1,000 in at least one calendar quarter of base period) shall be eligible if: (1) He has registered for work and reports regularly to employment office; (2) he is able and available for (actively seeking) work; (3) he has reported to division office as directed by deputy; (4) prior to first week of benefits he has been partially or totally unemployed for one week; (5) he makes claim for benefits; and (6) he is participating in certain job search services (288.030-.040).

For what constitutes employer see 288.032.

Benefits are based on a formula which allows an insured worker 4¹/₂% of total weekly wage paid to him during that quarter of his base period in which his wages were highest, but not more than $130 for claims filed 1/1/86 to 1/1/88; or $140 for claim filed after 12/31/87 and before 1/1/89; or $160 for claims filed after 12/31/89 and before 1/1/91; or $170 for claims filed after 12/31/90 and before 1/1/92; or $180 for claims filed after 12/31/91 and before 1/1/93; or $170, $175, $180 for claims filed after 12/31/92 and before 1/1/98 depending upon percentage increase in contribution rates. For claims filed after 12/31/97, benefits are based upon formula which allows insured worker 4% of total weekly wage paid to him during that quarter of his base period in which his wages were highest, but not more than $205 for claims filed in calendar year 1998, $220 for claims filed in calendar year 1999, $235 for claims filed in calendar year 2000, and $250 for claims filed in calendar year 2001 or thereafter. (288.038).

See also category Debtor and Creditor, topic Assignments.

Smokers.—Unlawful to discharge or fail to hire worker because smoker or nonsmoker, as long as person complies with applicable workplace policy concerning smoking. (290.105).

WORKERS' COMPENSATION LAW:

See topic Labor Relations.

ENVIRONMENT

ENVIRONMENTAL REGULATION:

General Supervision.—Control over water pollution problems is vested in Clean Water Commission of State of Missouri, Jefferson City, Mo. 65101. (644.021-.026). Control over air pollution is vested in Air Conservation Commission. (643.040).

Prohibited Acts of Pollution.—It is unlawful to (1) cause pollution of any waters or to permit any water contaminant in location where it is reasonably certain to cause pollution of any waters; (2) discharge water contaminants which reduce quality of water below water quality standards of 644.006 to 644.141; (3) violate toxic material control regulations or to exceed effluent regulations; or (4) discharge radiological, chemical or high level radioactive waste. (644.051). Air pollution is presence in ambient air of one or more air contaminants in quantities, of characteristics and of a duration which directly and proximately cause or contribute to injury to human, plant, or animal life or health or to property or which unreasonably interfere with enjoyment of life or use of property. (643.020).

Treatment of Waste.—First class counties may establish one or more solid waste processing facilities and direct that all waste generated or located in county be disposed of there. (260.201). Treatment of infectious waste is regulated by 260.203.

Enforcement.—Water pollution provisions may be enforced by Clean Water Commission. After investigation and a public hearing, Board may institute legal proceedings. Also, prosecuting attorney of any county or State Attorney General may seek injunctive relief notwithstanding fact that no administrative hearing has been held. (644.076). Air Conservation Commission, after investigation and hearing, may institute civil action in any court of competent jurisdiction, through Attorney General of state.

See note at head of Digest as to 1998 legislation covered.

See Topical Index in front part of this volume.

MO – 26

ENVIRONMENTAL REGULATION . . . *continued*
Air Conservation Commission may establish motor vehicle emissions inspection program for any non-attainment area. (643.300-.355).

Specific requirements for release of petroleum, crude oil, natural gas, natural gas liquids, liquified natural gas, or synthetic gas usable for fuel by either intrastate or interstate facilities. (260.500).

No person engaged in business of waste clean-up of environmental hazards created by others, shall be liable for any damages arising from release or discharge of pollutant, resulting from such activity, in amount greater than $1,000,000 to any one person or $3,000,000 to all persons for single occurrence. (260.552).

No person shall be liable for removal costs or damages resulting from action or omissions consistent with National Contingency Plan or as directed by federal or state official with responsibility for oil spill response. (260.819). This provision does not apply to personal injuries, to responsible parties or to negligent or willful misconduct.

Owner/operator of underground storage tank that is not source of release will be reimbursed for all reasonable direct costs for testing and monitoring including third-party claims not to exceed $1,000,000 per occurrence. (319.107-.131). Petroleum Storage Tank Insurance Fund provides monies for cleanup of contamination caused by releases if owner applied or participating in fund by certain date. (319.129-.131).

No person shall haul for commercial profit, collect, process, or dispose of waste tires except as provided for in 260.270. Third violation of this section, and each subsequent violation, may be punishable by fine not to exceed $5,000, and any other penalties authorized by law.

Penalties.—Under Missouri Clean Water Law, Commission may seek penalty not less than $2,500 nor more than $25,000 per day of violation, or imprisonment for not more than one year, or both. Second and successive violations shall be punished by fine of not more than $50,000 per day of violation, or by imprisonment for not more than two years, or both. (644.076). Further, state or any subdivision thereof may bring action for actual damages sustained. (644.096). Under Air Pollution Act Commission may seek injunctive relief or fines of up to $10,000 per violation per day, or any combination thereof. No liability for violation caused by act of God, war, strike, riot or other catastrophe. (643.151).

Permits.—Permit must be obtained by any person seeking to build, erect, alter, operate, use or maintain any water contaminant or point source. No permits will be issued unless meets standards, rules or regulations promulgated pursuant to 644.006 to 644.141. (644.051). Air Conservation Commission may grant individual variances from air pollution standards whenever it is found that compliance would result in arbitrary and unreasonable taking of property without just compensation or in practical closing and elimination of any business, occupation or activity without sufficient corresponding benefit or advantage to people. However, no variance will be granted where effect will be to permit continuation of health hazard. Any variance granted will not relieve person receiving it from any liability imposed by other law for commission or maintenance of nuisance. Director shall act on petition within 30 days and make recommendation within 120 days or hearing may be requested under 643.100. (643.110).

Permit must be obtained from Department of Natural Resources before any person can operate solid waste management system or solid waste disposal area of solid waste management system. Before applying for permit to construct solid waste disposal area person or operator must request preliminary site investigation from Department of Natural Resources. Person or operator must further provide to Department of Natural Resources detailed surface and subsurface geologic and hydrologic investigation. (260.205).

Nuclear Energy.—Midwest Interstate Low-Level Radioactive Waste Compact adopted.

All-terrain Vehicles.—Limitations on operation found in 300.348 and 304.013.

ESTATES AND TRUSTS

ADMINISTRATION:

See topic Executors and Administrators.

ADVANCEMENTS:

See topic Descent and Distribution.

ALLOWANCES:

See topic Executors and Administrators.

CLAIMS:

See topic Executors and Administrators; category Civil Actions and Procedure, topic Pleading.

DEATH:

Any person who has resided in the state and goes therefrom and does not return thereto for five successive years, is presumed to be dead. (473.697; 490.620).

Survivorship.—Uniform Simultaneous Death Act has been adopted. (471.010-.080).

Action for Death.—When death results from any act, conduct, occurrence, transaction or circumstance which, if death not ensued, would have entitled decedent to recover damages, person who would have been liable had death not ensued shall be liable in action for damages brought by: (1) Spouse, children (natural or adopted, legitimate or illegitimate), father or mother of deceased (natural or adoptive); (2) brother or sister of deceased or their descendants if none of persons in (1) available; (3) plaintiff ad litem appointed by court having jurisdiction of cause of action upon application of person entitled to share in recovery if no person in (1) or (2) available. (537.080).

Damages unlimited but recovery for grief or bereavement prohibited. (537.090).

When recovery is by plaintiff ad litem, distribution of proceeds in accordance with laws of descent and distribution unless court otherwise directs. (537.095).

If two or more persons are entitled to maintain action any one may settle claim with approval of any Circuit Court or may maintain suit without joinder of any person provided claimant satisfies court that he had diligently attempted to notify all parties having cause of action. (537.095).

Action must be brought within three years of date of accrual. (537.100).

Death Certificate.—See category Documents and Records, topic Records, subhead Vital Statistics.

Durable Power of Attorney.—See category Property, topic Powers of Attorney.

Uniform Anatomical Gift Act.—See topic Wills.

Living Wills.—See topic Wills.

DECEDENTS' ESTATES:

See topics Descent and Distribution, Executors and Administrators, Wills; category Debtor and Creditor, topic Homesteads.

DESCENT AND DISTRIBUTION:

Subject to payment of claims and rights (see subhead Surviving Spouse, infra) of surviving spouse, all property as to which any decedent dies intestate descends and is distributed to one of the following classes, each class of which a member is living taking to exclusion of all subsequent classes: (1) Children and descendants of deceased children; (2) parents, brothers, sisters and descendants of deceased brothers and sisters; (3) grandparents, uncles, aunts and descendants of deceased uncles and aunts; (4) great grandparents and descendants and so on without end, the estate going to the nearest lineal ancestors and their children and descendants of deceased children of such ancestors, provided that collateral relatives more distant than ninth degree of kinship according to rules of civil law may not inherit. (474.010[2]).

If there be no children or their descendants, father, mother, brother nor sister, nor their descendants, husband or wife, nor any paternal or maternal kindred capable of inheriting, the estate goes to the kindred of the intestate's predeceased spouse in like course as though such spouse had survived the intestate and then died entitled to the estate. (474.010[3]).

Where all the descendants, ancestors or collaterals coming into partition are of equal degree of kin to the intestate they take per capita; otherwise they take per stirpes. (474.020).

Surviving spouse takes the entire estate if intestate left neither parent nor issue. If decedent left no issue but did leave one or both parents, or if decedent left issue all of whom are also issue of surviving spouse, surviving spouse takes first $20,000 of estate plus one-half balance. (474.010[1]). Surviving spouse takes one-half intestate estate if there are surviving issue who are not issue of surviving spouse. (474.010[1]). Premarital contracts whereby any estate, real or personal, is received effective after death of spouse and expressed to be in full discharge of all rights of inheritance or other statutory rights in estate, are valid. (474.120).

Gifts in fraud of marital rights shall at election of surviving spouse be treated as a testamentary disposition and recovered from donee or transferees without adequate consideration and applied to payment of spouse's share as in case of election to take against a will. (474.150).

In addition to the foregoing, either surviving spouse is entitled to certain specified articles and allowances for support. See topic Executors and Administrators, subhead Allowances.

Collaterals of the half blood take only one-half of the share which goes to collaterals of the whole blood in same degree or to ancestors. (474.040).

Posthumous children or descendants inherit as though born in decedent's lifetime, but no other persons inherit unless in being and capable of taking as heirs at time of intestate's death. (474.050).

Illegitimate children inherit and transmit inheritance on the part of the mother, but not the father unless natural parents participated in marriage ceremony even if attempted marriage is void or paternity is established by adjudication before death of father or by clear and convincing proof after death of father. (474.060-.070).

Adopted Children.—See category Family, topic Adoption.

Determination of Heirship.—Where person leaves property or any interest in property in this state and no administration has been commenced on estate of decedent in this state within one year after death of decedent, and if no written will has been presented for probate within time provided in 473.050, any person claiming interest in such property as heir or through heir may file petition in probate court to determine heirs of decedent and their respective interest as heirs. Petition must state: (a) Name, age, domicile, last residence address and fact and date of death of decedent; (b) names, relationship to decedent and residence addresses of heirs so far as known or can with reasonable diligence be ascertained; (c) names and residence addresses of heirs of decedent at decedent's death; (d) names and residence address of any persons claiming through heir of decedent when heir died after decedent; (e) particular description of property of decedent with respect to which determination is sought; and (f) net value of such property. Court must conduct hearing notice of which must be given to all persons known or believed to claim any interest in property as heir or through heir, persons who may at date of filing petition be shown by records of conveyances of county in which any real property described in petition is located to claim any interest therein through heirs of decedent and any unknown heirs. Notice must be given by publication by publishing once each week for four consecutive weeks last insertion of publication to be at least seven days before hearing. Notice must be given personally or by registered mail to every person whose address is known to petitioner. Upon hearing, court issues decree determining persons entitled to property and respective interest. Decree is conclusive evidence of facts determined against all parties. Certified copy of decree must be recorded at expense of petitioner in each county in which any real property described is situated. (473.663).

Advancements.—When any of the children of an intestate has received, in his lifetime, any real or personal estate, by way of advancement, it must be counted toward the advancee's intestate share, but excess not required to be refunded. Inter-vivos

See note at head of Digest as to 1998 legislation covered.

See Topical Index in front part of this volume.

MO – 27

DESCENT AND DISTRIBUTION... *continued*

transfers must be shown to be advancements rather than gifts. Value of advancement determined as of time advancee came into possession or enjoyment, or at death of intestate, whichever first occurs. (474.090).

Renunciation.—No statutory provision for renunciation by beneficiary.

Escheat.—If any person dies intestate seized of any real or personal property, leaving no heirs or representatives capable of inheriting same, or if upon final settlement of executor or administrator there is balance on hand belonging to some legatee or distributee who is nonresident who is not in situation to receive same and give discharge thereof, or who does not appear by himself or agent to claim and receive same, or under other specific situations enumerated by statute, such real and personal estate escheats and vests in state. (470.010, 474.010[4]). Money paid into state treasury may be claimed by person entitled thereto within 21 years thereafter. (470.040).

Uniform Probate Code not adopted.

See also topic Executors and Administrators; categories Citizenship, topic Aliens; Debtor and Creditor, topic Homesteads; Family, topic Adoption.

ELECTION:

See topic Wills; category Property, topic Dower.

ESTATES:

See category Property, topic Real Property.

EXECUTORS AND ADMINISTRATORS:

Jurisdiction over administration is in probate division of circuit court. (472.020).

Preferences in Right to Administer.—Surviving spouse has prior right to administer, and next right is in one or more distributees according to discretion of court. (473.110).

Durable Power of Attorney.—See category Property, topic Powers of Attorney.

Uniform Anatomical Gift Act adopted. (194.210-.290).

Uniform Fiduciaries Act adopted. (456.240-.350).

Uniform Principal and Income Act not adopted.

Uniform Simplification of Fiduciary Security Transfers Act adopted. (403.250-.350, specifically saved from repeal by U.C.C., see 400.10-.102).

Eligibility and Competency.—Following may not be appointed personal representatives: (1) Judge or clerk of any court or his deputy (unless decedent was spouse or relative in third degree of consanguinity or affinity); (2) person under 18 or of unsound mind; (3) person under legal disability because of commission of crime; (4) habitual drunkard; (5) foreign corporation, partnership or association except as provided in 362.600. See category Business Regulation and Commerce, topic Banks and Banking, subhead Foreign Banks; (6) personal representative of personal representative. (473.117).

Qualification.—Personal representative must give bond in amount fixed by judge or clerk. (473.157). Amount of bond may be reduced if fiduciary deposits certain securities with domestic trust company. Bond is not required of corporation licensed to transact trust business. (473.160).

Exemption from Bond.—Testator may exempt executor from bond unless court in its discretion requires it. (473.160).

Issuance of Letters.—Upon application verified by applicant stating: (a) Name, age, sex, domicile, residence address and date of decedent's death; (b) names, relationships and addresses of surviving spouse, heirs, devisees and legatees of decedent; (c) value of realty and personalty; (d) if decedent not domiciliary, location and value of land and personalty in state; (e) contents of will; (f) name and address of named executor; (g) if intestate, name, address and relationship of applicant to decedent; (h) name and address of applicant's attorney; (i) if letters issued he will make inventory, pay debts and legacies and perform other duties of administration; and (j) whether application is for supervised or independent administration. (473.017). Granted by probate court or clerk. (473.023).

Removal.—Grounds for include: unsound mind, conviction of felony, nonresidence or absence for four months, drunkard, failure to discharge official duties, waste or mismanage estate, failure to answer citation and attachment to make settlement. (473.140).

Special Kinds of Administration.—Administrator d.b.n. appointed where all executors or administrators die, resign or letters revoked and goods remain unadministered, or after final settlement and discharge unadministered asset or unpaid allowed claim remains or upon good cause shown. (473.147). Independent administration where will so provides or all interested parties agree. (473.780).

Public Administrator.—Where there is no surviving spouse or heir in state, or executor is absent or fails to qualify, and in certain other cases, public administrator must take charge and administer estate. (473.743).

Inventory must be filed by representative within 30 days after letters granted. (473.233).

Notice to Creditors.—Clerk of probate court upon issuance of letters testamentary or administration shall publish in newspaper published in county, notice of appointment of personal representative and notice to creditors to present claims within six months from date of first publication or within two months from date notice was mailed to creditor by personal representative, whichever is later. This six months does not extend limitation period that would bar claims one year after decedent's death, as provided in §473.444, or any other applicable limitation periods. Notice published weekly for four weeks. Clerk shall send copy by ordinary mail to each heir or devisee appearing on letters for application. (473.033).

Presentation of claims barred unless presented within six months after first publication of notice of granting of letters or within two months from date notice was actually mailed, whichever is later. (473.360; 473.033). Claims must be in writing, and verified by claimant or someone having knowledge of facts. If founded on written instrument, original or copy with all endorsements must be attached to claim. (473.380). If claim is secured, security must be described in claim papers. Failure to file within prescribed time does not deprive creditor of security but precludes recourse against general assets. (473.387).

Unmatured claim must be filed in prescribed time. Court may order payment at present value, or require representative to retain assets, or permit distribution if distributees give bond. (473.383)

Contingent claim must also be filed. Order thereon must state nature of contingency. Court may order representative to retain assets, or order bond of distributees, or permit distribution without regard to claim. In latter case distributees may be required to account to the extent of assets received by them. (473.390).

Creditor may bring claim against beneficiary of non-probate transfer if commenced within 18 months after decedent's death and personal representative fails to do so. (461.300).

Form.—(Proof of claim). Missouri has no statutory form for proof of claim. The following is a form in current use in one county, and generally acceptable.

Form

In the Probate Court of . . . . County, Missouri

at . . . .

State of Missouri, ...

County of . . . . } ss.   Estate Number . . . .

Claim Against Estate

In the estate of . . . .

. . . . deceased incompetent minor—

. . . . ,

Administrat— Execut— Guardian

                                         Address

Affidavit of Claimant

. . . ., being duly sworn, states on oath that there is due h. . . . from the estate of . . . . deceased, incompetent, minor—, the sum of $. . . . . . on account of . . . .

                                     (describe nature of claim)

An itemized statement of such claim showing dates and amounts is "is   *as" follows: is attached hereto:

*(strike words not applicable)

. . . .

**The claimant holds security for . . . . . claim as follows: . . . .

                  (If none, so state; otherwise describe)

Claimant states that to the best of h. . . . knowledge and belief . . . he has given credit to such estate for all payments and offsets to which it is entitled and that the balance claimed as above stated is justly due.

            . . . .

                 (claimant)

Subscribed and sworn to before me this . . . . day of . . . . . ., 19. . . . .

(Seal)

              Notary Public   Clerk

            By . . . .

                 Deputy Clerk

Notary commission expires

. . . . .Probate Court of

Service of all notices is waived.

Consent for immediate hearing is given.

Consent is given to judgment allowing claim for $. . . . . .

(If signed, strike any part not agreed to.)

            . . . .

            Administrat— Execut— Guardian

**As to manner of payment of secured claims see Secs. 473.287, 473.902, 473.387 and 474.540, RSMo. Date of first publication . . . . .; Claim allowed on . . . . . in the amount of $. . . . . and placed in Class . . . . . . Abstract of Claims Book . . . . ., Page . . . . .

            Judge, Commissioner, Clerk.

Notice of Filing Claim

To the . . . .

              administrator-rix executor-rix guardian

of the above named estate:

Take notice that the original claim, of which the above is a copy and on which is endorsed the date of filing, to-wit, the . . . . day of . . . . . ., 19. . . ., was filed in the Probate Court of . . . . County, Missouri, and that you have ten days from the service of this notice to file any offset or counterclaim which you may have against said claim. The time for hearing such claim is the . . . . day of . . . . ., 19. . . ., at . . . . . o'clock . . . .M.

           . . . .

                   Claimant

(Attach Affidavit of Service of Notice or
Sheriff's Return)

Action on Claims.—Court fixes date for hearing, not less than 20 days following notice unless shorter time is specially fixed. (473.413). Appeals may be taken within 30 days after ruling on claim. (472.180). Claims for expenses of administration may be approved at any settlement, whether paid or not, on application of representative or claimant, or in discretion of court. (473.403[3]). Court may approve compromise of claim or suit against estate. Compromise without prior or subsequent approval does not bind estate. (473.427).

EXECUTORS AND ADMINISTRATORS . . . *continued*

Payment of Claims.—Representative may pay claims (other than his own) without filing or court's allowance if paid or filed within six months after 1st publication of notice of letters granted. (473.403[2]). Persons interested may except to such allowances at final settlement. (473.403[2]). Payment is on order of classification (see subhead Priorities, infra) and no claim need be paid until all previous classes are satisfied. If assets inadequate to pay any class, claims in class are prorated. No claim need be paid prior to six months after publication of notice of letters unless refunding bond is given. Thereafter claims except those of seventh class are due, and draw interest. Six months thereafter all claims are due. If estate insolvent or unable to pay claims, court may make appropriate order. (473.430-.433). Representative is liable for failure to pay allowed claim when ordered. (473.573). Actions on bond must be brought within one year after discharge of representative. (473.213).

Priorities.—Order of payment of claims where estate is insufficient to pay all claims is by class as follows: (1) Costs; (2) expenses of administration; (3) exempt property, family and homestead allowances; (4) funeral expenses; (5) debts and taxes due U.S.; (6) expenses of last illness, wages of servants, cost of tombstone; (7) debts and taxes due State of Missouri or political subdivisions; (8) judgments against decedent in lifetime; and (9) all other claims. (473.397).

Actions.—There is no suspension of the right to sue the representative on claims against the estate. Action on a claim may be brought in circuit court within six months after 1st publication of notice of letters granted in lieu of filing claim in probate court, but if judgment is obtained in circuit court transcript thereof should be filed in probate court. (473.363-.370). Written notice to probate court of revival or institution of action within six months after first publication of letters necessary to recover against estate's assets. (473.360-.363-.367).

Settlements.—Supervised representative must make annual settlement on anniversary of grant of letters until administration is completed. (473.540). Independent representative files petition for order of complete settlement or statement of account within one year after appointment or as continued by court. (473.837, 473.840).

Compensation of representative is commission on personal property and proceeds of sale of realty. Minimum scale is specified in 473.153.

Allowances.—Widower or widow or unmarried minor children are entitled to keep, as his, her or their absolute property, family Bible and other books; one passenger motor vehicle; all wearing apparel of family; all household electrical appliances, musical and other amusement instruments; all household and kitchen furniture, appliances, utensils and implements, without regard to its value (474.250); and such sums of money, to exclusion of all debts, claims, charges, legacies and bequests, as court may deem reasonable for proper support of widower or widow and minor children, if any, for one year after death of spouse, in manner suited to his, her or their condition in life, taking into account condition of decedent's estate (474.260). In addition to above court must make homestead allowance, on application of surviving spouse or of guardian, conservator, or person having custody of persons of unmarried minor children, of amount not exceeding 50% of value of estate exclusive of exempt property and allowance for support and in no case more then $7,500, which may consist of money or property with right of selection, to be absolute property of surviving spouse, if any, otherwise of unmarried minor children in equal shares. If survived by married children or those of full age as well as unmarried minor children, but no spouse, amount as above determined is divided by number of all children, and shares of unmarried minors constitute homestead allowance. This allowance is exempt from all claims. It is charged against share to which recipient is entitled as distributee of estate but is not diminished if greater than distributive share. It is in lieu of all dower and homestead rights in land and is deemed waived if application therefor is not filed in ten days after expiration of time for filing claims, in which case there is no right to homestead or homestead allowance under any law of state. If surviving spouse selects property with value in excess of allowance, spouse may elect to pay difference or take undivided interest, or court may partition real estate. Court may order appraisal of property selected as homestead allowance; interested party may file written objections thereto within five days of appraisal; court may then order sale of such property. (474.290).

Intermediate Accountings.—For supervised administration, one year from grant of letters; annually thereafter until administration completed. (473.540).

Final Accounting and Settlement.—Six months and ten days after first publication of notice of letters granted or as soon thereafter as administration is completed; ten days after revocation of letters; upon application to resign. (473.540).

Distribution.—None compelled within six months of date of letters unless legacies are perishable or subject to injury. (473.610). After six months, if other distributees and claimants not prejudiced thereby, may distribute under order of court, which may order the return at any time before decree of final distribution and may require distributee to give security for such return. If distribution made without request for security, executor or administrator and sureties liable for loss to any party as a result. (473.613). If personal property susceptible to division in kind, court may order it partitioned. For partition in kind, court appoints three disinterested commissioners of no kin to the parties, whose report is subject to approval by the court. (473.640). If not to advantage of distributees to divide or to sell, on application of a majority, court shall order property delivered to such person as they designate, who shall collect all notes, accounts, and choses in action, dispose of all property to their best interest and distribute all moneys realized. Bond may be required in the discretion of the court. (473.643). If after distribution, refunding becomes necessary for the payment of debts, court will apportion the same according to the amount received, except that specific legacies shall not be required to be refunded unless residue insufficient. Court will enter judgment on application of executor or administrator in case of failure of legatee or distributee to refund amount apportioned to him. (473.637). Distribution to distributee may be made to distributee or to person holding power of attorney executed by distributee in accordance with law of place of execution, or to distributee's personal representative, guardian or conservator. (473.657).

Administration Dispensed With.—Probate court may refuse to grant letters at any time when estate of decedent is not greater than exempt property and allowance to surviving spouse or unmarried children or when personal estate does not exceed $15,000 and there is no surviving spouse or unmarried minor child whose claim has not been barred or any creditor may apply for refusal of letters by giving bond in sum not less than value of estate. (473.090).

When Administration Unnecessary.—See subhead Administration Dispensed With, supra.

Small Estates.—Distributees of estate consisting of personal property or real property or both have defeasible right to personal property and are entitled to real property thereof without awaiting granting of letters testamentary or administration if: (a) Value of estate, less liens and encumbrances, is less than $40,000, and (b) 30 days have elapsed since death of decedent and no application for letters or for administration or refusal of letters is pending or has been granted, and (c) file bond in amount not less than value of personal property, approved by court, conditioned upon payment of debts of decedent, including debts to State, expenses of funeral and upon compliance with further orders of probate court in relation to estate of decedent and conditioned that any property to which distributee is not entitled will be delivered to persons entitled thereto under law. Liability of sureties on bonds terminates unless proceedings against them are instituted within two years after bond is filed, except court can dispense filing of bond if it finds same unnecessary. Affidavit made by personal representative under will if presented for probate otherwise distributee entitled to receive decedent's property anytime 30 days after decedent's death and must include: (1) Decedent left no will or will was properly presented for probate, (2) unpaid debts, claims or demands against decedent or estate, all inheritance taxes due, if any, on property transfers involved have been or will be paid, (3) itemized description and valuation of property of decedent, (4) names and addresses of persons having possession of property, (5) names, addresses and relationship to decedent of persons entitled to and who will receive specific items of property, and (6) facts establishing right to specific items of property. Certificate of clerk must be annexed to or endorsed on affidavit and must show names, addresses of persons entitled to property under facts stated in affidavit, recite that will of decedent has been probated or that no will has been presented to court and that all inheritance taxes on property, if any due, have been paid. Copy of affidavit and certificate must be filed in office of probate clerk and copies furnished by clerk. (473.097).

Distributees may establish their right to succeed to real estate of decedent by filing copy of affidavit and certificate of clerk in office of recorder of deeds of each county where property is situated. When value of property in affidavit exceeds $15,000, notice to creditors must be published once a week for two consecutive weeks. Creditors notified claims barred one year after death of decedent. Creditor may request estate be opened for administration. Upon compliance with foregoing procedure, personal property and real estate involved shall not be taken in execution for any debts or claims against decedent, but such compliance has effect in establishing right of distributees to succeed to property as if complete administration was had; nothing herein affects right of secured creditors with respect to such property. Property of decedent must be liquidated by affiant necessary to pay debts of decedent. Affiant must distribute remaining property to persons identified in affidavit. (473.097).

Estates of Nonresidents.—Property, tangible or intangible, of a nonresident decedent which is located in Missouri is subject to original administration proceedings under the authority of this state solely, conducted as if the decedent were a resident. (473.668). The situs of stock certificates, bonds, negotiable instruments, insurance policies payable to an estate and similar instruments is declared to be in the state where located. The situs of other debts, rights and choses in action is where the debtor is found. (473.671). However, the following are not affected: (a) Methods of proving foreign wills or the admissibility of such wills to probate or to record; (b) the rights of a surviving spouse electing to accept or take against the will of a nonresident decedent, or the method of such election; (c) the right of a person to take as a pretermitted heir or otherwise against the will of a nonresident decedent; (d) the effect of divorce or the birth of a child as working or not working a revocation or partial revocation of the will of a nonresident; (e) the effect of the contest in another jurisdiction of the will of a nonresident decedent upon its validity in Missouri; (f) the applicability of any law in determining the validity of the execution of the will of a nonresident decedent; (g) the determination or the ultimate burden of estate or inheritance taxes imposed by reason of death of a nonresident decedent. (473.675[1]).

Real property of an intestate nonresident decedent descends according to the laws of this state, and his personal property devolves to his heirs or next of kin determined in accordance with the laws of the state or country of his domicile. (473.675[2]).

Support and family allowances to surviving spouses and unmarried minor children are governed by the more liberal (to them) of the laws of the decedent's domicile and the laws of this state, but the court of this state in making such allowance and in ruling on applications for orders of refusal of letters of administration shall take into account any allowance which may be made in other jurisdictions and satisfied from property therein. (473.675[3]).

Notwithstanding the requirements of this section that distributions during or at the conclusion of an administration shall be made as if the decedent were a resident, if the court finds that hardship to a foreign creditor would result therefrom or that the best interests of all persons having an interest in the estate would be forwarded by making a distribution to a foreign personal representative, the court may, in its discretion, order such distribution to the extent it finds necessary to avoid such hardship or to forward such interests. (473.675[4]).

If the aggregate of liabilities of the estate in all jurisdictions exceeds its aggregate assets, the court shall order distribution, as far as practicable, so that all the creditors of decedent's estate, here and elsewhere, may receive a share in proportion to their respective obligations, with regard being given to any preferential rights determined by the court. To this end, distribution to a foreign personal representative may be ordered if all creditors whose claims have been allowed in the administration in this state shall have received their just proportions that would be due to them if the whole of the estate of the decedent, wherever found, were divided among all creditors in proportion to their respective obligations, after applying Missouri law respecting preferences to different species of obligations, and if and to the extent that the court finds such preference to be equitable under all the circumstances of the particular case. (473.675[5]).

See note at head of Digest as to 1998 legislation covered.

See Topical Index in front part of this volume.

MO – 29

EXECUTORS AND ADMINISTRATORS . . . *continued*

If no local administration or application therefor in this state, domiciliary foreign personal representative may file authenticated copy of his appointment and any bond he has given with probate division of county in which property belonging to decedent is located. (473.676). Domiciliary foreign personal representative may than exercise all powers of local personal representative as to assets in this state. (473.677). Application or petition for local administration of estate terminates power of foreign personal representative but court may allow foreign personal representative to exercise limited powers to preserve estate. (473.678).

Personal representative appointed by court of decedent's domicile has priority over all other persons for appointment as local personal representative except different person nominated in decedent's will to be personal representative in this state and in state of domicile. (473.682). Domiciliary personal representative may nominate another, who shall have same priority as domiciliary personal representative. (473.682).

Foreign personal representative submits himself to jurisdiction of Missouri courts by: (1) filing authenticated copies of his appointment, (2) receiving payment of money or taking delivery of personal property, or (3) doing any act as personal representative in this state which would have given state jurisdiction over him as individual. Jurisdiction under (2) is limited to money or value of personal property collected. (473.685).

Foreign personal representative also subject to jurisdiction of Missouri courts to same extent that decedent was subject to such jurisdiction immediately prior to death. (473.687). Service of process on foreign personal representative by registered or certified mail addressed to last reasonably ascertainable address. (473.689). Foreign personal representative shall be allowed at least 30 days within which to appear or respond. (473.689).

Any person, firm or corporation upon whom no demand has been made by a personal representative or other person authorized by this state to collect a nonresident decedent's personal property may, at any time 60 days or more after his death, transfer, pay or deliver personal property of nonresident decedent to foreign personal representative, or, if none, to such other person as may be entitled thereto under laws of said foreign state, and shall not be liable for debts of or claims against nonresident decedent or his estate by reason of having made such transfer, payment or delivery. (473.691).

See also topics Wills; Descent and Distribution.

INTESTACY:

See topic Descent and Distribution.

TRUSTS:

Declarations of trust of any lands must be in writing, signed by the party declaring such trust, or by his last will in writing, except when trust arises or results by implication or construction of law, and all grants and assignments of any trust must be in writing, signed by party granting or assigning same, or by his last will in writing. (456.010).

Sales.—When trust terms manifest intention that trustee, of active or passive trust, shall have full legal ownership of trust property, exercise by trustee of express or implied power of sale or other transaction incident to administration of trust, shall bind trust. (456.020).

Trusts Void as to Creditors, etc.—Settlor may provide that interest of beneficiary may not be voluntarily or involuntarily transferred before payment of interest to beneficiary and such provision will prevent settlor's creditors from satisfying claims from trust except: (1) Where conveyance of assets to trust intended to hinder, delay or defraud creditors or purchasers; (2) to extent of settlor's beneficial interest in trust assets, if at time trust established or amended: (a) settlor was sole beneficiary of income or principal of trust or retains power to revoke trust, or (b) settlor was one of class of beneficiaries and retains right to receive specific portion of income or principal of trust determinable solely from provisions of trust instrument. This section does not apply to certain spendthrift trusts. (456.080).

Competency as Trustee.—A foreign corporation cannot act as testamentary trustee (456.120), except those organized under the laws of an adjoining or next adjoining state, and national banking associations having their principal places of business in adjoining or next adjoining state, laws of which permit Missouri corporation to act in fiduciary capacity there, if certificate of reciprocity is obtained from Director of Finance reciting its eligibility to act in such capacity (362.600). See category Business Regulation and Commerce, topic Banks and Banking, subhead Foreign Banks.

Substitute Trustee.—In case of death, resignation, inability, neglect, or refusal to act, of trustee under any deed of trust, will or other instrument to whom property has been conveyed for use of any person, circuit court of county in which property is situated is authorized to appoint substitute trustee upon affidavit presented by trustee, beneficiary or representative thereof. Unless all capable trust beneficiaries consent to proposed successor trustee in affidavit, notice and hearing on appointment of successor trustee is required. (456.190-.200).

Testamentary trusts are subject to control of Probate Court or Circuit Court, including requirement of bond of trustee and of accounting to court. If trustee is surviving spouse or certified trust company (362.115) or if will creating trust so directs, no bond shall be required (456.225).

Transfer or devise may be made by will or other instrument including designation of beneficiary under life insurance policy and not invalid because trust is amendable or revocable. Transfer can be made to name of trust or trustee of trust. (456.232).

Investments by fiduciaries are regulated by 362.550; 369.219-.254; and 475.190.

Investments in Name of Nominee.—Unless expressly forbidden by instruments, etc., setting up trust, any bank or trust company qualified to act as fiduciary may, if cofiduciaries consent, hold investments in name of nominee. Records must show true owner. (362.207).

Accounting.—Unless contrary to trust terms or waived in writing by adult competent beneficiary, trustee shall deliver written statement of accounts to each income beneficiary at least annually. (456.233). Uniform Trustee Accounting Act not adopted.

Delegation of Duties.—Unless otherwise prohibited by law or trust instrument, trustee cannot transfer office or delegate entire administration of trust to co-trustee or another person. (456.530).

Discretionary Distributions.—Unless trust instrument provides otherwise, donee of power (other than settlor acting as sole trustee) to make discretionary distributions of principal or income to or for benefit of himself is exercisable only for his health, education and support in his accustomed manner of living. (456.535). Power conferred upon two or more trustees, none of whom is settlor, to make discretionary distributions of principal or income to one of them cannot be exercised by such beneficiary but shall be exercised by trustees who are not so disqualified. (456.540).

Durable Power of Attorney.—See category Property, topic Powers of Attorney.

Multiple Trustees.—Any power in three or more trustees may be exercised by majority. Trustees not joining majority are not liable to beneficiaries or others for consequences of majority's action. Remaining co-trustees succeed to power, duties and authority of any co-trustees who cease to act. (456.540).

Uniform Fiduciaries Act adopted. (456.240-.350).

Uniform Principal and Income Act not adopted.

Uniform Simplification of Fiduciary Security Transfers Act adopted. (403.250-.350).

Uniform Common Trust Fund Act adopted. (362.580).

Spendthrift trusts are subject to claims of any wife, child or children of beneficiary for support and maintenance. (456.080).

Employee benefit trusts created as part of a stock bonus, pension, disability or death benefit, medical benefit plan, profit-sharing, or retirement plan, where contributions are made by either employers or employees or self-employed are not subject to rule against perpetuities and may exist for such time as necessary to accomplish purpose of plan. Accumulations of income in employee benefit trusts are also excepted from rule against perpetuities. (456.060-.070). See also category Property, topic Perpetuities.

Gifts to Minors.—See category Family, topic Infants.

Accumulations.—See subhead Employee Benefit Trusts, supra.

Perpetuities.—See category Property, topic Perpetuities.

Pour Over Trusts.—See topic Wills, subhead Bequests and Devises to Inter Vivos Trusts.

See also topic Executors and Administrators; categories Business Organizations, topic Corporations; Business Regulation and Commerce, topic Monopolies, Restraint of Trade and Competition; Family, topic Guardian and Ward; Mortgages, topic Mortgages of Real Property; Property, topic Perpetuities.

WILLS:

Testamentary Capacity.—Any person of sound mind 18 years of age or older may devise his real or personal property and may also devise whole or any part of his body to any college, university, licensed hospital or State Anatomical Board. (474.310).

Testamentary Disposition.—No limit on extent to which testator may dispose of property.

Execution.—Every will, except nuncupative, must be in writing, signed by the testator, or by some person by his direction in his presence, and must be attested by two or more competent witnesses subscribing their names to the will in the presence of the testator. (474.320).

Form.—Usual form of attestation clause is as follows:

Form

"Signed, sealed, published and declared by . . . ., the above named testator, as and for his last will and testament in the presence of us, who, at his request and in his presence and in the presence of each other have hereunto subscribed our names as witnesses this . . . . day of . . . . ."

Holographic Wills.—No statutory or judicial pronouncement on validity of handwritten wills.

Nuncupative will is valid only if made in imminent peril of death and death resulted therefrom, declared to be his will before two disinterested witnesses, reduced to writing by or under direction of a witness within 30 days, and submitted for probate within six months after death. It can dispose only of personal property of not more than $500, and neither revokes nor changes existing written will. (474.340).

Revocation.—Divorce revokes all provisions in favor of divorced spouse, effect being same as if such spouse had died at time of divorce. No other change in circumstances will revoke will or any part. (474.420).

Testamentary Gifts to Subscribing Witnesses.—No will invalid because attested by interested witness; but unless there are two other disinterested witnesses, such interested witness forfeits so much of provisions therein made for him as exceeds share of estate which would have descended or been distributed to him in case of intestacy. (474.330[2]).

Bequests and Devises to Inter Vivos Trusts valid. (353 S.W.2d 770). No decisions on effect of amendment of trust instrument subsequent to date of will.

Probate.—Will probated in county of deceased's domicile or, if nonresident, county where deceased left major part of real estate or, if no real estate, county where deceased left any other property. (473.010).

Testimony of two subscribing witnesses proves will. If one or both witnesses unavailable, will proved by witness who is available, if any, and proof of handwriting of other witness or witnesses, or such other competent evidence as is available. (473.053).

Commission may be issued to take attestation of witness if witness cannot attend court to prove will. (473.057).

Will must be presented for and admitted to probate within six months after date of publication of notice granting letters or within 30 days after commencement of action to establish or contest validity of will or where no notice then within one year after death.

See note at head of Digest as to 1998 legislation covered.

See Topical Index in front part of this volume.

WILLS . . . continued

Presented for means delivery of will or verified statement if will unavailable to probate court and affidavit or petition seeking to admit will to probate or authenticated copy of order in other state admitting will to probate. (473.050). Action to establish interest in estate by descent must be filed prior to expiration of objection period for final settlement. (473.070).

Will ineffective to prove title to or right to possession of real or personal property until admitted to probate. (473.087).

See also topic Executors and Administrators.

Self-proved Wills.—Will properly executed on its face with affidavit attesting to execution may be admitted to probate without witnesses appearing before court. (473.065, 474.337).

Self-proving affidavit as follows:

THE STATE OF . . . .

COUNTY OF . . . .

I, the undersigned, an officer authorized to administer oaths, certify that . . . ., the testator, and the witnesses, whose names are signed to the attached or foregoing instrument, having appeared together before me and having been first duly sworn, each then declared to me that the testator signed and executed the instrument as his last will, and that he had willingly signed or willingly directed another to sign for him, and that he executed it as his free and voluntary act for the purposes therein expressed; and that each of the witnesses, in the presence and hearing of the testator, signed the will as witness and that to the best of his knowledge the testator was at that time eighteen or more years of age, of sound mind, and under no constraint or undue influence.

IN WITNESS WHEREOF, I have hereunto subscribed my name and affixed my official seal this . . . . . day of . . . ., 19. . . . . . .

                      (Signed) . . . .

                                    (Official capacity of officer)

(SEAL)

Recording.—Where a will devises land a copy thereof must be recorded, within six months after probate, in office of recorder of deeds of each county where such land is situated. (474.500).

Will contests must be brought within six months after probate or rejection or first publication of letters, whichever is later. (473.083). Compromise of will contest is permitted with probate division approval. (473.084, 473.085).

Legacies are not payable until after six months after date of letters (unless perishable or subject to injury if retained six months). (473.610). Upon application of executor or administrator, or of distributee after six months, court may order delivery of any specific real or personal property if other distributees and claimants are not prejudiced thereby, subject to return, and security therefor may be required. (473.610-.613; and see subhead Distribution under topic Executors and Administrators). Legacies other than residuary and chattels bear interest rate equal to that allowed by law on money due upon order of court after one year from testator's death, unless court finds payment of legacy would jeopardize rights of others. If jeopardizing rights of others, court shall determine what rate of interest, if any, not exceeding rate allowed by law on money due upon order of court. Yield on specifically bequeathed securities belongs to legatee. (473.633).

Unclaimed Legacies.—See topic Descent and Distribution, subhead Escheat; also category Property, topic Absentees, subhead Escheat.

Lapse.—Where an estate is devised to a child or grandchild or other relative of the testator and such devisee shall die before the testator leaving lineal descendants, such descendants shall take the property as such devisee would have done in case he had survived the testator. (474.460).

Children not Provided for.—A testator is deemed to have died intestate as to children born or adopted after making last will (including posthumous) not named or provided for in his will unless it appears from will omission was intentional, or at time of will had child or children known to be living and devised substantially all of estate to child's other parent or child is provided for by transfer outside will with intent that transfer be in lieu of testamentary provision.

Election.—Surviving spouse electing to take against will receives in addition to exempt property and one year support allowance, one-half of the estate if no lineal descendants of testator, one-third otherwise both subject to payment of claims. (474.160). In determining spouse's share when there is election, all property is considered even if not subject to probate such as trust property, insurance, profit sharing plans, pension plans, and joint property. (474.163). Election may be made within ten days after expiration of time for contesting will, or 90 days after final determination of litigation re validity or construction of will, or existence of surviving issue, or any matter affecting amount of surviving spouse's share. (474.180).

Foreign Probated Wills.—Property of testate nonresident decedent may be devised by his last will if duly executed according to laws of this State, and his personal property may be bequeathed by his last will if duly executed according to laws of this State or State in which it was executed. (473.675[2]). Real property of intestate nonresident decedent descends according to laws of this state, and personal property devolves to heirs or next of kin determined in accordance with laws of state or country of his domicile. (473.675[2]).

Foreign Executed Wills.—Any person owning any real or personal estate in this state may devise or bequeath same by last will, executed and admitted to probate according to laws of this state or executed according to laws of this state and probated according to laws of this state or state or territory in which will is probated. (474.360). Authenticated copies of wills, probated in another state, and probate thereof, shall be recorded in same manner as wills executed and proved in this state, and shall be admitted in evidence in same manner and with like effect. (474.370). Any will admitted to probate in any state, territory or district of U.S. together with order admitting same to probate therein, authenticated according to acts of Congress, shall be admitted to

probate in this state in any county where real estate is affected thereby, or filed in office of recorder of deeds in such county. (474.380).

Testamentary Guardian.—See category Family, topic Guardian and Ward. Proceedings to obtain ancillary probate are the same as for residents of Missouri. See also topic Executors and Administrators, subhead Estates of Nonresidents.

Simultaneous Death.—See topic Death, subhead Survivorship.

Testamentary Trusts.—See topic Trusts.

Uniform Anatomical Gift Act adopted. (194.210-.295).

"Living wills", directing withholding or removal of death-prolonging procedures, authorized. (459.010-.055). Declarant must be 18 or over and competent. Living will must be in writing signed by declarant or another at his direction and in his presence, dated and, if not in declarant's own handwriting, must be witnessed by two persons at least 18 years of age, neither of whom signed document for declarant and at his direction. Statutory sample form: "Declaration. I have the primary right to make my own decisions concerning treatment that might unduly prolong the dying process. By this Declaration I express to my physician, family and friends my intent. If I should have a terminal condition it is my desire that my dying not be prolonged by administration of death-prolonging procedures. If my condition is terminal and I am unable to participate in decisions regarding my medical treatment, I direct my attending physician to withhold or withdraw medical procedures that merely prolong the dying process and are not necessary to my comfort or to alleviate pain. It is not my intent to authorize affirmative or deliberate acts or omissions to shorten my life rather only to permit the natural process of dying. Signed This _____ Day of _____ Signature _____ City, County, and State of Residence _____ The Declarant is known to me is 18 years of age or older, of sound mind and voluntarily signed this document in my presence. Witness _____ Address _____ Witness _____ Address _____ Revocation Provision: I hereby revoke the above Declaration. Signed _____ Date _____" (459.015).

See also topics Executors and Administrators, Descent and Distribution; category Taxation, topics Estate Tax, Inheritance Tax.

FAMILY

ADOPTION:

Interstate Adoption Assistance Compact enacted. (453.500). Division of Family Services may agree with another state's agency in emergencies. (210.622).

Jurisdiction and Venue.—Adoption is by petition to and decree of juvenile division of circuit court or family court in certain circuits of county in which person seeking to adopt resides, child sought to be adopted was born, child is located at time of filing of petition, or either birth person resides. (453.010). If child under continuing jurisdiction of court pursuant to c. 211, petition to juvenile division of circuit court having jurisdiction over child. (453.010).

Consent Required.—Where a person sought to be adopted is over 14 years of age, his written consent is required unless court finds he has not sufficient mental capacity to give the same. When under 18 years of age, written consent of mother; man who is either presumed father, has filed notice to claim paternity or acknowledgment of paternity, or has filed action to establish paternity; or child's current adoptive parents or other legally recognized mother and father (453.030) shall be required, except that consent of parent adjudged incompetent shall not be required nor of one who for period of six months immediately prior to filing of petition either wilfully abandoned or neglected to provide proper care and maintenance nor parent whose rights regarding child have been legally terminated nor parent who has waived necessity of consent. When identity of father is unknown, however, service shall be made by publication on "John Doe" as provided in 506.160.

Juvenile court may, upon application, if it appears wise, permit parent of child to waive necessity of his or her consent to future adoption of such child. Any consent or waiver shall be valid even though parent was under age of 18 years at time of execution and shall be irrevocable without leave of court having jurisdiction of child, given at hearing, notice of which has been given to all interested parties. Where person sought to be adopted is 18 years of age or older, his written consent alone is sufficient. (453.030-.060).

Conditions Precedent.—Person sought to be adopted, if a minor, must have been in the lawful and actual custody of person seeking to adopt him for at least nine months prior to entry of adoption decree. (453.080).

Petition.—Petition must state name, sex and place of birth of person sought to be adopted; name of his parents; and if person sought to be adopted is minor, fact that petitioner has ability to care for, maintain and educate person; and if it is desired to change name of person, new name of person. (453.020).

Proceedings.—There must be full investigation of mental, physical and hereditary background of both adoptee and adopter and assessment of adoptive parents and appropriate post-placement assessments and written report thereof must be submitted to court within 90 days of request for investigation. Court may waive it where child under 18 years of age is natural child of one petitioner and where all parents required to give consent do so. Foster parent or parents over 18 years of age having cared for child continuously 12 months or more and bonding has occurred as evidenced by positive interaction, may apply to agency for placement of child for adoption and if child eligible for adoption, agency must give preference and first consideration for adoptive placement to foster parents, but court has final determination of adoption. (453.070). Signed and verified accounting of any money or other consideration paid by or on behalf of petitioner in connection with placement or adoption. Court may decline to issue decree of adoption if it determines that payments were unreasonable or if petitioner fails to adequately report payments. (453.075).

Name.—The court may change the name of child according to the prayer of the petition. Clerk must send copy of entry of decree to State Bureau of Vital Statistics, which must change the birth records to conform. (453.080-.100; 193.125).

See note at head of Digest as to 1998 legislation covered.

See Topical Index in front part of this volume.

ADOPTION . . . *continued*

Effect of Adoption.—On adoption all legal relationships and all rights and duties between child and his natural parents, other than a natural parent who joins in the petition for adoption, cease and the child thereafter is deemed for every purpose the child of his parent or parents by adoption as fully as though born to him or them in lawful wedlock, except that for purposes of intestate succession adoption of child by spouse of natural parent has no effect on relationship between child and either natural parent. Adopter and adoptee inherit from each other same as natural parent and child, and child may inherit property limited expressly to heirs of body of such parent or parents. (453.090 and 474.060).

Special Needs Adoption.—Any person who legally adopts special needs child shall be eligible for tax credit of up to $10,000. (135.327). Any business entity providing funds to employee to enable that employee to legally adopt special needs child shall receive tax credit for up to $10,000. (135.327).

Adoption Records.—Adopted adults 21 or over may obtain physical description, nationality, religious background and medical history of their biological parent or siblings from child placement agency or juvenile court upon written request. In addition, in some circumstances adopted adult may obtain name, date of birth, place of birth and last known address of biological parent or sibling. Adopted adult requests this information in petition to court. If adoptive parents consent to request, court orders child placement agency or juvenile court having records of adoption and within three months juvenile court or child placement agency must make reasonable efforts to notify biological parents of request by adopted adult and inform biological parents of their right to file affidavit to have information disclosed to adopted adult. If biological parent cannot be located identifying information cannot be revealed. If biological parent is deceased and previously executed affirmative affidavit, information is released to adopted adult. If biological parent is deceased and has not previously executed affirmative affidavit, information can be released if court finds releasing information is necessary for health related purposes.

Adopted adults may also request identifying information concerning adult siblings following same procedure as for information concerning biological parents.

Biological parents may also follow same procedures as adopted adults to obtain identifying information. (453.121).

Division of Family Services maintains central registry by which biological parents and adopted adults may indicate their desire to contact each other. (453.121).

ALIMONY:

See topic Dissolution of Marriage.

COMMUNITY PROPERTY:

System does not obtain in Missouri.

DESERTION:

See topic Husband and Wife.

DISSOLUTION OF MARRIAGE:

Governed by c. 452.

Uniform Marriage and Divorce Act not adopted.

Grounds for Dissolution of Marriage.—Court finds no reasonable likelihood that marriage can be preserved and therefore marriage is irretrievably broken. (452.305).

Grounds for Legal Separation.—Same as for dissolutions. (452.305).

Residence Requirements.—Either party must be a resident or a member of armed services who has been stationed in state for 90 days next preceding commencement of proceeding. (452.305).

Jurisdiction.—Circuit Court or Family Court in certain circuits have jurisdiction in all cases of dissolution or maintenance.

Venue.—Proceedings shall be had in county where plaintiff resides, and proceedings may be directed, in first instance, in any other county in state where defendant resides. (452.300).

Pleading must be verified and allege marriage is irretrievably broken. (452.310). Arrangements as to custody and support of children, maintenance of spouse, date of marriage and place registered, residence, date of separation, names, ages of children and whether wife is pregnant must be included in petition. (452.310).

Decree becomes final as any other judgment. (452.360). See category Civil Actions and Procedure, topic Judgments.

Alimony.—Court may allow temporary maintenance to either party. (452.315). Provisions of any decree respecting maintenance or support may be modified only as to installments accruing subsequent to motion for modification and only upon showing of changed circumstances so substantial and continuing as to make terms unreasonable. Unless otherwise agreed in writing or expressly provided in decree, obligation to pay future maintenance is terminated upon death of either party or remarriage of recipient. (452.370).

Division of Property of Spouses.—See subhead Property Rights, infra.

Property Rights.—Court shall set apart to each spouse his property and shall divide marital property as Court deems just after considering relevant factors including: (1) Contribution of each spouse to acquisition of marital property, including contribution of spouse as homemaker; (2) value of nonmarital property set apart to each spouse; (3) economic circumstances of each spouse at time division of property is to become effective, including desirability of awarding family home or right to live therein for reasonable periods to spouse having custody of any children; (4) conduct of parties during marriage; and (5) custodial arrangements for minor children. (452.330).

Custody of Children.—Court makes such orders as are reasonable with respect to care, custody and maintenance of children. (452.375). Court must determine custody in accordance with best interests of child. Court may not give preference to either parent

solely because of parent's age, sex or financial status, nor because of age or sex of child. Prior to awarding custody, Court must consider joint custody to both parents. Court shall not grant custody to parent who has been found guilty of, or plead guilty to felony violation of c. 566, when child was victim, or violation of §568.020, when child was victim. (452.375). Grandparents denied visitation may request and Associate Circuit Court may order mediation with party in custody. (452.403).

Support of Children.—Both parents owe duty of support to child. Court determines support considering relevant factors including: (1) financial needs and resources of child; (2) financial resources and needs of parents; (3) standard of living child would have had but for dissolution; (4) physical, emotional and educational needs of child. Rebuttable presumption that child support guideline amount is correct. Child support terminates when child dies; marries; enters active military duty; becomes self-supporting; reaches age 18 unless incapacitated or enrolled in school or non-custodial parent is primary caregiver for 28 consecutive days or longer. (452.340). Maintenance or support modified only upon showing of substantial and continuing changed circumstances. (452.370).

Paternity.—Uniform Parentage Act adopted, (210.817).

Setting Aside Decree.—Court may, not later than 30 days after entry of judgment, of its own initiative, order a new trial, or reopen, correct or modify its judgment for good cause. (C.R. 75.01).

Remarriage.—No statutory restrictions on remarriage of divorced persons.

Annulment of Marriage.—See topics Marriage, Husband and Wife.

DIVORCE:

See topic Dissolution of Marriage.

GUARDIAN AND WARD:

Appointment of Guardian.—Any person may petition for himself or any other qualified person to be guardian of minor or incapacitated person, or conservator of estate of minor or disabled person, or both. (475.055-.065).

Natural Guardians.—A father and mother, with equal powers, or the survivor of them, are the natural guardians of their minor children, and have the custody and care of their persons, education, and of their estates if derived from parents. If no lawful father, then the mother. With respect to property derived from him, the parent may invest as is reasonable and prudent without court order. (475.025).

Curators.—When a minor is entitled to, or possessed, of an estate not derived from a living parent who is acting as natural guardian, the court must appoint another person as guardian of that part of the estate. (475.030). If the minor be over the age of 14 years, he may choose the guardian, subject to the approval of the court. (475.045).

Eligibility and Competency.—Any person at least 18 years of age, unless parent, may be appointed guardian of person or conservator of estate, or both, and need not reside within Missouri. Corporations, charitable organizations, social service agency and national banking associations may act if empowered by charter and authorized to act in Missouri except no corporation other than social service agency can be appointed guardian of incapacitated person. (475.055).

Qualification.—Before entering on duties of his office, conservator of estate must give bond, with sufficient surety, to be approved by court, in amount fixed by court. (475.100).

Powers and Duties.—A guardian of the person, whether natural or legal, is entitled to the custody, and control of the person of his ward, and the care of his education, and maintenance. (475.120). Conservator of estate has care and management of estate of minor or disabled person, subject to control by court. (475.130).

Real Estate.—Conservator may, by order of court, sell, encumber, lease or exchange any property of estate, when for care, education, treatment, habilitation, support and maintenance of protectee and his family. (475.200; 442.035).

Investments.—See 475.190.

Investments in Name of Nominee.—See category Estates and Trusts, topic Trusts.

Inventory.—Inventory and appraisement of protectee's estate must be made after conservator's appointment unless estate received by conservator from personal representative, or former conservator, already has been appraised. (475.145, 475.150).

Accounts.—Annual settlement required. (475.270). Final settlement required 60 days after all terminations of guardianship. (475.290).

Termination of Guardianship.—When minor ward becomes 18 years of age; upon marriage of ward; adjudication of competency of previously incompetent ward; revocation of letters; court's acceptance of guardian's or conservator's resignation; upon ward's or protectee's death; and upon expiration of order appointing guardian or upon court order terminating guardianship. (475.083; 475.285).

Control of Court.—The probate court directs the proper education, and maintenance of protectees and their families, according to their means, and from time to time may make necessary appropriations out of estate for that purpose. (475.125).

Incompetents.—On filing of information with probate court, and after notice and hearing, court may appoint guardian or conservator of person and estate, or separate conservator of estate. (475.075-.090). Interstate compact on mental health in effect. (630.810).

Settlement of Estate of Insane Persons.—No special procedure for settlement of estate of insane persons. Normal procedures are followed.

Veterans.—Uniform Veterans' Guardianship Act adopted. (475.380-.480).

Gifts to Minors.—See topic Infants.

Uniform Fiduciaries Act adopted. (456.240-.350).

Uniform Simplification of Fiduciary Security Transfers Act adopted. (403.250-.350).

See note at head of Digest as to 1998 legislation covered.

See Topical Index in front part of this volume.

GUARDIAN AND WARD...*continued*

Personal Custodian.—Legally competent adult may make revocable transfer of property to "personal custodian" to hold and administer for person as beneficiary of custodianship. Transferors may also transfer property to beneficiary by delivery to person designated by transferor as beneficiary's personal custodian. Creditors rights provisions do not create lien on specific property subject to non-probate transfer. (404.570). Custodianships under transfers to minors law may be continued into adulthood. On beneficiary's death, personal custodian may make distribution pursuant to beneficiary designation or transfer on death direction. (404.560). Custodianships may also be used by older adults as property management device. (404.420).

See also topic Infants.

HUSBAND AND WIFE:

Separate Property of Married Women.—A married woman may hold as her separate property any property, real or personal, owned by her at the time of marriage, thereafter acquired by gift, bequest, devise or descent or purchased with her separate money or means, anything due her as wages of her separate labor, any rights of action arising out of violation of her personal rights, and all income, increase and profits of any such property. Such property shall not be liable to be taken by any process of law for debts of her husband. (451.250).

Contracts.—A married woman may make contracts which will bind her personally and her separate property, may contract with her husband as with a third person and may sue or be sued by him. She may become bound as surety for her husband or any other person. (451.290).

Antenuptial Contracts.—All marriage contracts shall be in writing. (451.220).

Actions.—A married woman may sue or be sued without her husband being joined as a party. (451.290).

Conveyances.—A spouse should either join in or give acknowledged consent in writing to a conveyance of other's separate real property (474.150), unless marital rights have been released by prenuptial contract (474.120), but failure to join will not prevent loss of marital rights unless fraud is present (474.150; 327 S.W.2d 823). Also, difficulty in establishing separate character of property makes joinder advisable.

Right of Wife to Invoke Exemption and Homestead Laws.—A married woman may invoke all exemption and homestead laws for the protection of the personal and real property owned by the head of a family, except in cases where the husband has claimed such exemption and homestead rights for the protection of his own property. (451.290).

Liability of One Spouse for Debts of the Other.—The wife's property is not liable for the debts of her husband (451.250), except that the annual products of her real estate are liable for the husband's debts incurred for necessaries of the family or for labor or materials furnished on or for cultivation of such lands (451.260).

The husband's property, except such as may have been acquired from his wife, is not liable for debts or liabilities contracted or incurred by the wife before the marriage. (451.270).

Liability of Husband for Torts of Wife.—A husband is not liable for civil injuries caused by his wife, but she is solely responsible therefor, unless under the law he would be jointly responsible with her if the marriage did not exist. (537.040).

Desertion.—Where a husband, without good cause, abandons his wife and neglects to provide for her, the circuit court, on petition of the wife, may order her support and maintenance to be paid by the husband out of his property. (452.130).

Uniform Reciprocal Enforcement of Support Act (as amended) adopted and applies to cases filed by Missouri or received by Missouri prior to Jan. 1, 1997. (454.010-.360). In all other cases, the Uniform Interstate Family Support Act applies. (454.850-.980).

Community property system does not obtain in Missouri.

See also topics Marriage, Dissolution of Marriage; categories Civil Actions and Procedure, topic Evidence, subhead Witnesses; Debtor and Creditor, topic Homesteads; Estates and Trusts, topic Descent and Distribution; Property, topics Curtesy, Dower, Real Property.

INFANTS:

Minor is any person under 18 years of age as to contracts (431.055), ownership and conveyance of real estate (442.020), and party to suit (507.115), guardianship proceedings (475.055, 475.285) and for all purposes in connection with law of trusts and estates (475.010).

Disabilities.—Infants are subject to common law disabilities.

Veterans.—The disability of minority of any person not under the age of 18 otherwise eligible for guaranty of a loan pursuant to the Servicemen's Readjustment Act of 1944, and of the spouse of such person, is removed solely for the purposes of acquiring or encumbering or selling and conveying property and the incurring of indebtedness or obligations incidental thereto, or the refinancing thereof, and litigating or settling controversies arising therefrom, if all or part of the obligations be guaranteed by the Administrator of Veteran's Affairs pursuant to such Act, or the property covered by a loan so guaranteed, and such persons are denied the right to repudiate the written obligation so made on reaching the age of 21. (442.100).

Actions.—Infant sues by guardian or next friend appointed by court or officer thereof, and defends by guardian. (C.R. 52.02; see also 507.110-.220).

Parental Responsibility.—Parent or guardian, excluding foster parents, of unemancipated minor under 18 in their care and custody against whom judgment has been rendered for purposely marking upon, defacing or damaging any property or for intentionally causing personal injury to any individual shall be liable for payment of judgment up to $2,000 if parent or guardian joined as defendant in original action. (537.045). Judge may order parent or minor to work for owner of property or person injured in lieu of payment if all parties are in agreement. (537.045).

Ratification of Contracts.—Infant's contract may be ratified after attaining age 18 by acknowledgment in writing, part payment, disposal of part or all of property for

which debt was contracted or refusal to deliver such property to person to whom debt is due, if still under former infant's control on demand in writing. (431.060). As to instruments affecting real estate, if executed while under 18, may be disaffirmed within two years after disability removed by filing deed in office of recorder of deeds where land is situate. (442.080).

Joinder in Conveyance, etc.—Infant who is married may join with adult spouse in conveyance or encumbrance of such spouse's real estate. (442.040).

Uniform Gifts to Minors Act repealed. (L.1985, S.B. 35). Missouri Transfers to Minors Law is c. 404. (c. 404). Age of majority under Transfers to Minors Law is 21. (404.007).

Child Safety.—Every person except public carrier for hire must use child passenger restraint system when transporting child under four. (210.104).

Uniform Securities Ownership by Minors Act not adopted.

Uniform Child Custody Jurisdiction Act adopted. (452.440).

Life Insurance Benefits Payable Directly to Minor.—See category Insurance, topic Insurance Companies, subhead Life Policies.

Adoption.—See topic Adoption.

See also topics Guardian and Ward, Marriage, Adoption; categories Civil Actions and Procedure, topics Limitation of Actions, Process, Evidence, subhead Witnesses; Employment, topic Labor Relations; Estates and Trusts, topic Wills.

MARRIAGE:

Marriage is considered a civil contract to which consent of parties capable in law of contracting is essential. (451.010).

Minimum Age.—No license can be issued to a person under 15 years of age except on order of the circuit or associate circuit court. (451.090).

Consent Required.—No license may be issued for person under 18 years, except with written consent, duly signed and sworn to of his or her custodial parent or guardian. (451.090).

License must be obtained from recorder of deeds of any county (451.080), who is required to record same in special book. No requirement that divorced applicant for license present copy of decree. No length of residence or waiting period is required.

Serological Tests.—None required.

Ceremonial Marriage.—Marriages may be solemnized by any clergyman, active or retired, who is a U.S. citizen in good standing with any church or synagogue in this state or by any judge of court of record, other than municipal judge. Marriages may also be solemnized by religious society, religious institution, or religious organization of this state according to customs thereof when either party to marriage is member thereof. (451.100).

Marriage Certificate.—Person performing ceremony must issue a certificate setting forth the names and residence of the parties and the date of such marriage and the county from which the license issued and date of same. (451.110).

Record.—See category Documents and Records, topic Records, subhead Vital Statistics.

Common law marriages contracted after Mar. 31, 1921, are null and void. (451.040). Those contracted prior to that date are valid. (233 Mo. App. 900, 110 S.W.2d 845). Local recognition depends on law of state where marriage contracted apparently. (116 S.W. 432).

Proxy marriages are not authorized.

Marriage contracts by which any real or personal estate is secured or conveyed, or may be affected in law or equity, must be in writing, acknowledged by each of contracting parties or proved by a subscribing witness (451.220) and, to be effective as to third persons, who have no actual notice thereof, must be recorded in the county where the estate is situated (451.240).

Prohibited Marriages.—Between parents and children or ancestors and descendants of every degree, brothers and sisters of half as well as whole blood, uncles and nieces, aunts and nephews, first cousins, and between persons either of whom is insane, imbecile, or feebleminded; and such prohibition extends to persons born out of lawful wedlock as well as in lawful wedlock. All such marriages are absolutely void. (451.020).

Marriage is void where either party has a former living spouse, unless former marriage dissolved. (451.030).

Annulment.—Marriage may be annulled by suit in equity for causes existing at time of marriage, including duress, fraud and incapacity of either party. No statutory rules.

See also topics Husband and Wife, Dissolution of Marriage; categories Estates and Trusts, topic Descent and Distribution; Property, topics Curtesy, Dower.

MARRIED WOMEN:

See topics Husband and Wife, Marriage; categories Civil Actions and Procedure, topic Evidence, subhead Witnesses; Debtor and Creditor, topic Homesteads; Documents and Records, topic Acknowledgments; Estates and Trusts, topics Executors and Administrators, Wills; Property, topics Deeds, Dower.

INSURANCE

INSURANCE COMPANIES:

Regulated generally by Insurance Code. (cc. 375; 376; 379).

Supervision.—Director of Insurance, Division of Insurance, Jefferson City, Mo. 65101 has general supervision of all insurance companies and is charged with enforcement of all insurance laws. (374.010). Trade practices regulated. (375.930-.948).

Missouri Property and Casualty Insurance Association created to protect insureds from insolvency of insurers. (375.772).

See note at head of Digest as to 1998 legislation covered.

See Topical Index in front part of this volume.

INSURANCE COMPANIES . . . *continued*

Rates of insurance other than life are regulated. (379.315-.415).

Certificate of Authority.—No company or person may transact any insurance business in this state, unless it has first procured from superintendent of insurance department certificate authorizing it to do business, stating that requirements of insurance laws of this state have been complied with, which certificate must be renewed annually as of July 1 but remains in effect until renewed or refused. (c. 375).

Investments.—For authorized investments of domestic companies, see 376.300-.307. Foreign companies licensed in Missouri may invest in same manner as domestic companies, or as permitted by law of their respective domiciles (376.310), subject, however, to constitutional provisions as to holding of real estate (Const. Art. XI, §5). Investment in investment pools is allowed. (376.311, 379.080). Domestic companies' ownership of real estate is further regulated by statute. (375.300, 375.305, 375.330, 375.345; see also 376.303, 376.080).

Fire insurance companies can issue policies only in standard form approved by Insurance Commissioner (379.160), except where fire and casualty are combined in single policy (379.017), file rating plan (379.321), and may not give discriminating rebates or special rates (379.356). They may not deny that real property insured was worth amount of policy when issued. (379.140). Life and health insurers must meet risk based capital standards. (382.210).

Surplus Lines Insurance Law.—See 379.085.

Life Policies.—Any life insurance policy may restrict liability for death as result of suicide in event that insured dies within one year of date of issuance. (376.620).

Misrepresentations made in obtaining an insurance policy on the life of a citizen of this state are not deemed material and do not render the policy void, unless the matter misrepresented actually contributed to the contingency or event on which the policy becomes due and payable, and whether they so contributed is a question for the jury. (376.580). Defenses based on misrepresentations in obtaining life policies are not valid unless, at or before trial, insurer deposits in court, for benefit of plaintiff, the premiums received on such policies. (376.610).

Generally speaking, no life policy may be forfeited after the payment of three or more annual premiums, but extended insurance in an amount not less than the face of the policy minus indebtedness must be granted by applying three-fourths of net value of policy, less all indebtedness (or a greater value if granted in policy [333 Mo. 191, 61 S.W.2d 704]) to pay a net single premium (376.630). But this rule does not apply to fraternal insurance (210 Mo. App. 547, 243 S.W. 260) or to policies issued by assessment companies (51 S.W.2d 142). But see 376.670, providing generally that any specified paid-up nonforfeiture benefit must be granted unless insured elects another benefit.

No additional stipulated premium plan life insurance companies are permitted. (377.199).

Employer may insure lives of its directors, employees or retired employees with consent of insured. (376.531). Certain charitable institutions can own insurance policy on life of individual if that individual consents. (377.080).

Life, stipulated premium, industrial and prudential insurance companies cannot make or permit any distinction or discrimination between insureds of same class and life expectation, or allow rebates or special favors as inducement to insurance, and violation renders company liable to have its charter revoked. Agents so doing are guilty of misdemeanor. (376.500-.510).

Proceeds of insurance on husband's life, payable to wife, inure to her sole benefit, free of claims against husband's estate, provided that premiums were paid by her out of her own funds. (376.530). Proceeds of assessment and stipulated premium plan policies are free from claims of creditors of insured's estate or of beneficiary. (377.090, .330).

Life insurance benefits payable directly to minor 18 years or older due to death of his spouse may be paid by insurer without necessity of guardianship or other court proceeding, if proceeds do not exceed $10,000. (431.066).

Life Reserves and Valuation.—For required reserves and valuation of policies see 376.370-.380.

Viatical Settlements.—For viatical settlements, see 376.1100-.1141.

Group and Individual Policies Marketed with Illustrations.—Policies except: (1) variable life insurance; (2) individual and group annuity contracts; (3) credit life insurance; (4) policies written by companies with less than $25 million in annual direct life insurance premiums; (5) life insurance policies with no illustrated death benefits exceeding $10,000; (6) life insurance policies written on forms identified as marketed without illustration; shall include illustrations in conformance with 376.1500-.1527.

Accident and Health Policies.—Forms for group accident or health policies must be approved by Director of Division of Insurance. (376.405). Uniform Individual Accident and Sickness Insurance Law adopted. (376.770, 376.800). All individual and group health insurance policies providing coverage on unit basis issued by nonprofit corporations and all self-insured group benefit plans must provide for hospital treatment of alcoholism; however, individual health insurance contracts insuring specific individuals and their families are exempt. Valid health care service claims must be paid within 30 days of receipt by insurer of all documents reasonably needed to determine claim. (376.427). No individual or group insurance policy can discriminate against Medicaid eligible individuals. (376.818). No health insurer may cancel or deny coverage to any person because person is incarcerated. (595.047[1]).

Individual and group health insurance policies that provide maternity benefits must provide minimum inpatient care of 48 hours if natural delivery or 96 hours if cesarean delivery. (376.995).

Reserves are required on accident and health policies upon basis stated in 376.410, but this does not affect supplementary provisions of life policies. Reserves also required for prepaid dental plans. (354.710).

Motor vehicle insurance liability coverage must include vehicles loaned to insureds. (379.201).

Transfer of Insurance.—Insurer must notify insured before transferring policy to another insurer. Insurer has right to refuse. (382.210).

Vexatious refusal to pay loss authorizes award of damages not exceeding 20% of first $1,500 of loss and 10% of loss in excess of $1,500, and reasonable attorney's fee in addition to amount of loss and interest. (375.420).

Insurance brokers are examined, licensed and regulated by Director of Insurance. Biennial fee $100. (c. 375).

Insurance agencies must be licensed by Director of Insurance. Annual fee $100. (375.061). Owners, officers, managers or directors of agencies acting without authority are guilty of misdemeanor. (375.061). Agents must also be licensed by Director of Insurance. Biennial application fee $25. (375.018).

Multiple Employer Self-insured Health Plan.—Must have not less than 250 covered employees and be regulated by Director of Insurance. Annual license fee is equal to 2% of paid Missouri claims. (382.210).

Foreign Corporations.—Foreign insurance corporations must, before doing business in state, designate state director of insurance as agent for service of process, in form required by law, and his authority extends to all suits by residents and by nonresident beneficiaries or assignees on policies issued or liabilities incurred in Missouri. (375.906).

Foreign insurance companies admitted to transact business in state upon obtaining certificate of authority issued by director of insurance. (375.791). In order to secure certificate of authority must make application to director of insurance. Applications to state: (a) Name of company and state of incorporation; (b) date of incorporation and period of duration; (c) address of principal office in state of incorporation; (d) names of states and countries, if any, where admitted or qualified to do business; (e) kinds of insurance authorized to write in state of organization; (f) kind of insurance proposed to write in this state; (g) aggregate number of outstanding shares, if any, and par value thereof and amount of surplus as regards to policyholders; and (h) additional information as may be requested by Director of Insurance. (375.811).

Companies doing business in this state must file annual statements showing condition of affairs, maintain reserve, and make deposits similar to domestic insurance companies and transacting a similar kind of business. (375.891[1]). In lieu of such deposit or part thereof, company may file current certificate of any other state to effect that a like deposit or part thereof of insurer is being maintained in public custody pursuant to a law of that state for protection of insurer's policyholders or policyholders and creditors. If company writes more than one kind of insurance for which a deposit is otherwise required and deposit in another state is not less than aggregate amount of all such deposits so otherwise required in this state, commissioner shall accept single certificate relative to deposit in other state without specification of kind or kinds of insurance to which same relates. Director, when satisfied by such certificate deposit or part thereof was made and is held, shall accept it in lieu of requirement of subsection (1). (375.891[2]).

Every insurance company doing business in this state shall pay following fees to director of revenue: (1) Valuations of policies or other obligations of assurance, $1,000 for all ordinary forms of policies, and costs of computing special evaluation tables; (2) $50 for declaration on organization of each company; (3) $50 for statement and certified copy of charter of foreign companies; (4) $250 for filing annual statement of company doing business; (5) $10 for supplementary annual statement of any company doing business in state; (6) $50 for any other paper required to be filed with Director of Insurance; (7) $2 for each agent's copy of his company's certificate of authority to license; (8) $.20 for copies of papers, records and documents; (9) $10 for affixing seal of Office of Director of Insurance; and (10) $10 for accepting Service of Process upon Company. (374.230).

All insurance companies must deposit with Director of Insurance bonds or treasury notes issued or guaranteed by U.S., or bonds of this state, any school district of this state or bonds of any political subdivision of this state in following amounts: (1) If stock company, amount of minimum capital required of company to write lines of business it proposes; (2) if mutual company or reciprocal or interinsurance exchange, amount equal to amount required to be deposited by stock company transacting same kind of business; however, for mutual companies not to exceed amount of its policyholders' surplus. (379.098).

Foreign companies admitted to do business in the state may make contracts of insurance only by lawfully constituted and licensed agents. (375.901).

Foreign insurance companies not authorized under Missouri law, doing specified acts in this state by mail or otherwise, are deemed to have appointed Director of Insurance as agent for service of process. (375.256). Service of process may also be had in such cases on agents of insurer within state, but copy of petition and of summons with return thereon must be sent by registered mail, return receipt requested, within ten days to last address of insurance company. Forty-five days after service on Director of Insurance, default may be taken. (375.266-.276). Insurance company must furnish bond or certificate of authority to do business before pleading. Damages for vexatious refusal to pay authorized. (375.281, .296).

Retaliatory Law.—If the laws of another state or foreign country impose on foreign insurance companies any greater fees, taxes, deposits, etc., than the Missouri laws as to foreign insurance companies, then insurance companies of such state or country seeking to transact business in Missouri must pay all fees, taxes, etc., and do all of acts which, by the laws of the state or country in which said company was organized, are in excess of the fees, taxes, deposits, etc., required by the Missouri laws of foreign companies. (375.916).

Premium Tax.—All domestic companies (whether stock, mutual, associations, or reciprocal inter-insurance exchange, including life companies) and all foreign insurance companies or associations are taxed 2% per annum on direct premiums received, either in cash or notes, in this state and on account of business done in this state. (148.320-.370). Premium tax is subject to deduction of income, franchise and personal property taxes and of valuation, registration and examination fees paid under Missouri law in addition to other credits. (148.400). Returns must be made to Director of Insurance on or before Mar. 1 of each year for year ending on previous Dec. 31. (148.330, 148.350).

See note at head of Digest as to 1998 legislation covered.

See Topical Index in front part of this volume.

MO-34

INSURANCE COMPANIES . . . *continued*

Fire and casualty companies are credited with cancelled or returned premiums, and all companies with amounts returned to policyholders, including dividends. (148.340-.380-.390).

Excluded from premiums taxed are premiums received on policies issued in funding of pension, annuity, profit-sharing plan or individual retirement annuity, qualified or exempt under Federal Internal Revenue Code. (148.390).

Medical Malpractice Insurance.—Any physician or surgeon on staff of hospital in county of more than 75,000 must have at least $500,000 in medical malpractice insurance unless practice is exclusively in hospital and hospital's malpractice insurance covers them. (383.500).

Uniform Insurer's Liquidation Act adopted but applies only to proceedings instituted prior to 8/28/91. (375.950).

Direct Actions Against Insurer.—See category Transportation, topic Motor Vehicles, subhead Direct Actions.

SURETY AND GUARANTY COMPANIES:

Surety companies incorporated under laws of this, or any other, state or foreign government, may be accepted on bonds on production of evidence of solvency, satisfactory to court, judge, clerk, or officer authorized to approve same. (379.010, 107.080).

Capital Requirement.—In order to be so accepted, the company must have a paid up capital of not less than $800,000 ($200,000 if public works). (379.010, 107.080).

Law Governing.—Foreign surety companies are subject to the laws relating to insurance companies other than life insurance companies. (107.090).

See also topic Insurance Companies; categories Business Organizations, topic Corporations; Civil Actions and Procedure, topic Bonds.

INTELLECTUAL PROPERTY

TRADEMARKS AND TRADENAMES:

Any mechanic, manufacturer, association or union of workingmen or other persons may adopt a word, name, symbol or device as trademark by filing application, together with facsimile, for registration in office of Secretary of State. Fee for filing and registration, $50. No such label, trademark or form may be registered if it in any way resembles or would probably be mistaken for label or trademark already registered. Registration effective for ten years, renewal fee $10. Assignment or transfer fee, $50. (417.005-.031).

Penalties for fraudulent use. (417.051-.061).

Federal trademark may not be registered except by the owner.

Tradenames.—Person doing business under name other than his own true name must register same with Secretary of State within five days after beginning such business. (417.210) Fee $2. (417.220). Person failing to register guilty of misdemeanor. (417.230).

Limited Partnerships.—Must register with secretary of state on forms supplied by him within five days of engaging in business in Missouri. (417.215). Fee $2. (417.220).

TRADE SECRETS:

Missouri Uniform Trade Secrets Act provides injunctive, monetary, and punitive relief for actual or threatened misappropriation of trade secrets. (c. 417). Five-year statute of limitations is imposed.

LEGAL PROFESSION

ATTORNEYS AND COUNSELORS:

The state bar is integrated. The official name of the organization is The Missouri Bar.

Power to admit to practice is vested exclusively in Supreme Court. (484.040). Supreme Court rules on subject may be obtained from clerk.

Student Registration.—Applicant for registration must file with the Clerk of the Supreme Court a written application in prescribed form, and present proof of completion of 3/4ths of work acceptable for a bachelor degree granted for a 4-year period of study in residence at a principal college or university, within 90 days after commencing study of law. For good cause in particular case, later registration may be permitted. Registration fee of $10 ($15 for late registration) must be paid to Clerk. (Rule 8.04).

Eligibility.—Applicant for admission shall have: (1) Registered as law student or, if person is admitted to practice in highest court of another state, in lieu thereof, certificate of good standing from each state in which applicant is licensed; (2) graduated with L.L.B. or J.D. degree, or equivalent first degree in law, from law school approved by Section of Legal Education and Admissions to the Bar of American Bar Association; (3) filed application to take bar examination; and (4) received approval of Board of Law Examiners. Additionally, applicant who has been admitted to practice in highest court of another state but who does not have degree in law may, in discretion of Board of Law Examiners, be permitted to take bar examination upon: (a) furnishing character report from National Conference of Bar Examiners; (b) furnishing satisfactory evidence that applicant has been for at least five years: (i) lawfully engaged in full-time practice of law in jurisdiction or jurisdictions where applicant was admitted to practice, (ii) served full-time as lawyer with U.S. Government or its armed forces, or (iii) taught as full-time instructor in law school approved by Section of Legal Education and Admissions to the Bar of American Bar Association. (C.R. 8.03, 8.06, 8.07).

Admission Without Examination.—May be admitted without examination if: (a) Has for five of preceding ten years devoted substantial portion of lawyer's time to: (1) practice of law in jurisdiction or jurisdictions where lawyer was admitted to practice, or (2) service as lawyer with U.S. Government or its armed forces, or (3) teaching as instructor in law school approved by Section of Legal Education and Admissions to the Bar of American Bar Association; (b) is graduate of law school that at time of lawyer's graduation was approved by Section of Legal Education and Admissions to the Bar of American Bar Association; and (c) Has made application for such admission to clerk of this Court. Application consists of: (1) Application form setting out facts establishing above qualifications, including certificate establishing lawyer's satisfaction of requirement signed by judge of court of general jurisdiction in state in which applicant practiced, served or taught and affidavits of good moral character signed by two members of Bar of this state; (2) application form for character report then being used by National Conference of Bar Examiners; and (3) nonrefundable application fee of $300 plus then current fee of National Conference of Bar Examiners for preparation of character report.

Lawyer admitted pursuant to this Rule is required to meet Missouri continuing legal education requirements.

Admission without examination is not matter of right but will be granted only in those cases where public interest, considering character, education, extent and continuity of practice and ability of applicant, will be furthered by permitting such admission. (C.R. 8.10).

Application.—Applicant must file application with Clerk of Supreme Court: for July examination or before Apr. 15; for Feb. examination on or before Nov. 15, and pay Clerk fee of $150. (Rule 8.06). Application must be accompanied by affidavits from two attorneys admitted in Missouri that applicant is of good character. If applicant fails to pass examination he may at any time within one year, without further charge, be permitted to take second examination. Thereafter subsequent examinations require same fee as original examination. (Rule 8.09). Forms for application to take bar examination may be obtained from Clerk of Supreme Court, Post Office Box 150, Jefferson City, Missouri 65102.

Examination.—Examination given twice annually, first in Feb. or Mar. and again in June or July, at Jefferson City, Missouri by Board of Law Examiners of Missouri Bar. Two day examination consisting of essay questions on local law and Multi-State Bar Exam. All applicants must also pass Multi-State Professional Responsibility Exam. Multi-State Bar Exam scores may be transferred from another jurisdiction if taken within 19 months preceding examination, score is at least 128 and applicant passed bar exam in other state. (Regulations of Board of Law Examiners, promulgated under C.R. 8.08).

Admission Pro Hac Vice.—Any attorney, not a member of The Missouri Bar but member in good standing of bar of any court of record may be permitted to participate in a case in any court upon filing with his initial pleading statement identifying court of which he is member of bar and certifying that neither he nor any member of his firm is disqualified to appear in any such court, and designate member of The Missouri Bar having an office within Missouri as associate counsel. (Rule 9.01-.03).

Judge Advocates.—Member of bar of another state on active military duty in Missouri designated and assigned as a Judge Advocate by his branch of service and by legal officer of Missouri post of duty must be permitted to appear as attorney for active duty personnel or their dependents if unable to pay fee for services involved. (Rule 9.04).

License.—License issued by Supreme Court of Missouri required to practice law. (C.R. 8.08). Annual enrollment fee $135 except for persons licensed by examination less than three years before ($95) or persons licensed but not residing, practicing or employed in State. ($85). Fee paid to clerk of Supreme Court, Supreme Court Building, Jefferson City, Missouri 65101 by Jan. 31 of each year. $50 fine and $5 per month for delinquency. (C.R. 6.01).

Disabilities.—Attorney may not be surety on bond in probate proceeding or official bond. (473.180; 107.020).

Liabilities.—See category Civil Actions and Procedure, topic Costs.

Compensation of attorney is governed by agreement, express or implied, which is not restrained by law. (484.130).

Lien.—From commencement of action or service of answer containing counterclaim, attorney for party has lien upon his client's cause of action or counterclaim and upon written notice by attorney who has made fee agreement with client served on defendant that such agreement has been made and interest he has in cause of action agreement operates as lien upon proceeds realized from claim to extent attorney's portion thereof. (484.130-.140).

Division of Fees.—Attorney may not divide any fee or compensation received in practice of law with any person not a licensed attorney, or any firm not wholly composed of licensed attorneys, or any association or corporation. Any person, firm or corporation who receives part of such fees is guilty of a misdemeanor and is subject to fine of from $25 to $500 and costs, and is subject to be sued for treble amount so paid. (484.150).

Discipline.—Any attorney may be removed or suspended from practice if convicted of any criminal offense involving moral turpitude, or if he unlawfully retains his client's money or is guilty of any malpractice, fraud, deceit or misdemeanor whatsoever in his professional capacity; or if he shall have been removed, suspended or disbarred from practice in any other state or jurisdiction and shall fail to disclose such facts in his application for license. (484.190).

Attorney Ethics.—American Bar Association Rules of Professional Conduct have been adopted with modifications. (C.R. 4).

Mandatory Continuing Legal Education.—Each lawyer must complete and report at least 15 credit hours of accredited programs and activities. Not more than six credit hours may consist of self-study, videotape, audiotape, or other similar accredited programs or activities. Lawyer is not required to complete or report any credit hours in reporting year in which lawyer initially licensed to practice law in Missouri. Three credit hours, at least every three years, must be completed in programs devoted exclusively to professionalism, legal or judicial ethics, or malpractice. (C.R. 15.05).

Specialty Requirements.—No specialization permitted in bar.

Professional Corporations.—See category Business Organizations, topic Corporations, subhead Professional Corporations.

See note at head of Digest as to 1998 legislation covered.

See Topical Index in front part of this volume.

MO – 35

ATTORNEYS AND COUNSELORS . . . *continued*

See also category Civil Actions and Procedure, topics Costs, Evidence, subhead Witnesses.

MINERAL, WATER AND FISHING RIGHTS

MINES AND MINERALS:

The Division of Mine Inspection of the Department of Labor and Industrial Relations, with offices at Jefferson City, has general supervision of all mines and caves. (286.100-.110; c. 293).

Inspection.—The Director of Division of Mine Inspection of the Department of Labor and Industrial Relations is charged with duty of inspection for safety and health of employees in all mines. Twice yearly mine inspection required. Director must make annual report to Governor. Judicial enforcement of detailed rules is provided. (c. 293).

Regulations.—Hoisting and lowering of men is strictly regulated, applying only to mines employing more than 16 underground. (293.590).

Notices.—Owners of land or tenants under recorded leases, who permit other persons than employees to mine or prospect, must during the time such permission continues, keep a printed statement of the terms of such permission posted at the principal office of such owner or tenant, in the county where the lands lie or in a county contiguous thereto. (444.010).

Licensees are entitled to ore excavated, subject to payment of the royalty prescribed by the terms of the notice or where no notice is posted, the prevailing rate in the neighboring properties. (444.030).

Employees may not be worked more than eight hour day without consent. (293.050).

Operators.—Operators must file quarterly reports and pay fees. Operators may be required to make maps of mine. (293.030-.040).

See also category Employment, topic Labor Relations.

MORTGAGES

CHATTEL MORTGAGES:

Practically any kind of personal property may be subject to a chattel mortgage.

Uniform Commercial Code in force. See category Business Regulation and Commerce, topic Commercial Code.

After-acquired Property.—A chattel mortgage may cover property to be acquired by mortgagor after execution of the mortgage.

Floating Stock.—Chattel mortgage or deed of trust of stock in trade which remains in possession of mortgagor or grantor and from which sales by him are permitted, is fraudulent and void as against creditors and subsequent purchasers, unless the stock is sold in the usual course of business and the proceeds applied towards payment of the debt.

Execution.—See category Business Regulation and Commerce, topic Commercial Code.

Recording or Filing.—See category Business Regulation and Commerce, topic Commercial Code.

Duration of Lien.—See category Business Regulation and Commerce, topic Commercial Code.

Removal of Property.—There is no requirement of rerecording or refiling in case the property is moved within the state.

Liens on Motor Vehicle.—See category Transportation, topic Motor Vehicles.

Usury invalidates a chattel mortgage. See category Business Regulation and Commerce, topic Interest.

Mortgages on Unplanted Crops.—See category Business Regulation and Commerce, topic Commercial Code.

Assignments.—The transfer of a note secured by a chattel mortgage carries with it the mortgage.

Foreclosure.—See category Business Regulation and Commerce, topic Commercial Code.

Forms.—Secretary of State has prescribed standard forms of financing statement (UCC-1 and UCC-1A); change of financing statement (UCC-3); and request for information (UCC-11). Printed forms of security agreements are available from local stationers. For forms, see end of this Digest.

Redemption.—Chattel mortgages with powers of sale and all sales made by mortgagee or his personal representatives in pursuance thereof, are valid and foreclose all rights and equity of redemption of the property so sold. (443.290).

Foreign Mortgages.—A chattel mortgage duly executed and recorded in another state is valid against the mortgaged property after it is removed into this state, although the mortgage is not recorded here, unless the mortgagee consented to or acquiesced in the removal and the rights of innocent third persons have intervened. (205 Mo. App. 357, 224 S.W. 113).

See also category Debtor and Creditor, topics Pledges, Fraudulent Sales and Conveyances.

COLLATERAL SECURITY:

See category Debtor and Creditor, topic Pledges.

MORTGAGES OF PERSONAL PROPERTY:

See topic Chattel Mortgages.

MORTGAGES OF REAL PROPERTY:

Mortgages are executed and acknowledged as deeds. Lien theory obtains.

Recording.—In order to be valid against any person other than the parties thereto, who is without actual notice thereof, a mortgage must be recorded in the office of the recorder of deeds of the county in which the land is situated. (59.330, 442.380-.390).

Recording Fees.—See category Documents and Records, topic Records, subhead Recording Fees.

Trust Deeds.—The usual form of giving security on real property is by deed of trust. In deed of trust the property is conveyed to a trustee with power to sell and convey the property absolutely, if the debt which is usually evidenced by promissory notes is not paid according to the terms mentioned in the conveyance.

Future Advances.—Mortgages and deeds of trust may secure future advances made or incurred within ten years of execution of instrument, if such advances do not exceed face amount of instrument, which must be clearly stated thereon; except in case of advances made to protect security interest in real property or to complete improvement under construction loan contract. (443.055).

Competency of Trustee.—Nonresident individual or foreign corporation may not act as trustee in any security instrument affecting any property, real or personal in state unless instrument names as co-trustee individual citizen of state or domestic corporation. (443.350). However, corporation organized under laws of adjoining or next adjoining state or national banking association having its principal place of business in such state, laws of which permit Missouri corporation to act in fiduciary capacity there, may if qualified obtain certificate of reciprocity from Commissioner of Finance reciting its eligibility to act in such capacity without resident co-trustee. (362.600). See category Business Regulation and Commerce, topic Banks and Banking, subhead Foreign Banks.

Insurance.—Mortgage may be insured up to 97% of fair market value if buyer is low or moderate income or first-time buyer. (384.021[1]).

Assignment of note secured by mortgage carries the security with it and no assignment of mortgage is necessary.

Satisfaction or Release.—Mortgages and deeds of trust may be satisfied upon the margin of the record in the office of the recorder of deeds, or by deeds of release, which must be acknowledged in the same form as other deeds, but in both cases the notes must be presented to the recorder for cancellation, or proper affidavits made as to their payment and loss or destruction. (443.060). A partial release may be made by a deed of release or on the margin of the record on presentation to the recorder of deeds of the notes secured by the mortgage or deed of trust or accounting for them as in case of a full release. (443.090). Deed of release or acknowledgment of satisfaction of mortgage or deed of trust must be executed by mortgagee, cestui que trust or assignee, and it is not necessary for trustee to join therein. (443.060). Release of any security interest may be made by release deed by president, vice-president, secretary, treasurer or cashier of corporation. (443.150).

Release of record, containing defects in execution, acknowledgments, or recording, deemed valid after ten years. (443.185).

Special provisions are made for satisfaction of mortgages or deeds of trusts of public utility companies subject to regulation of the public service commission and of whole or partial release of mortgages or deeds of trust providing for issue of notes or bonds of $100,000 or more, without producing the bonds, notes or coupons. (443.080-.110).

Foreclosure under deeds of trust is generally without suit, by advertisement and sale in accordance with terms of the deed of trust in the county where the land is situated. Real estate conveyed in such deeds cannot be sold by the trustee without giving at least 20 days notice of sale. (443.310). Such notice must set forth the date and book and page of the record of the mortgage or deed of trust, the grantors, time, place and terms of sale and description of the property and must be given by advertisement inserted at least 20 times, and continued to the day of sale, in some daily newspaper, in counties having cities of 50,000 inhabitants or more; and in any other county such notice must be given by advertisement in some weekly newspaper published in such county for four successive issues, the last insertion to be not more than one week prior to sale, or in some daily, tri-weekly or semi-weekly paper, published in such county at least once a week for four successive weeks, the notice to appear on the same day of each week, and last insertion to be not more than one week prior to sale. If no newspaper in county, then in nearest one thereto in this state. Where any part of the property is in a city of 50,000 or more population, notice must be published in daily paper in such city, but where property wholly or partly within a city extending into two or more counties, notice must be in newspaper published in county in which property lies in manner provided for such county, notwithstanding it lies in a city of 50,000 inhabitants. (443.320). Trustee is granted one continuance of sale not to exceed seven days without additional notice by announcing continuance on day, time and place of sale. (443.355).

Limitations.—Foreclosure proceedings cannot be commenced after obligation secured is barred by limitations, nor in any event can foreclosure be had after 20 years from date last maturing obligation secured by instrument to be foreclosed is due according to face of such instrument, unless within such 20 years owner of debt or some one for him files affidavit or duly acknowledged instrument showing amount due and owing. (516.150). For deeds of trust and mortgages recorded after Jan. 1, 1979, if due date of last maturing obligation secured by instrument to be foreclosed upon does not appear on face of instrument, foreclosure proceedings cannot be commenced after 20 years from date of execution of instrument or if that date does not appear, from date of acknowledgment, and if that date does not appear, from date of secured obligation. (516.155).

Redemption.—All real estate sold by trustees in any deed of trust, according to the terms of said deed, without the deed of trust having been first foreclosed by judgment or decree of court, and which shall be bought in at sale by holder of debt or obligation, or by any other person for them, shall be subject to redemption by grantor in deed, or his heirs, devisees, executors, administrators, grantees or assigns, at any time within one year from date of sale upon payment of debt and interest or other obligation secured by deed of trust and to accrue thereon together with all sums paid by any holder thereof or purchaser at such sale or holder of rights of such purchaser for interest, principal or

MORTGAGES OF REAL PROPERTY . . . *continued*
prior incumbrances and for taxes and assessments and all legal charges and costs incurred in making sale. (443.410).

No party shall have the benefit of the above until he shall give security to the satisfaction of the circuit court for the payment of interest to accrue within such year, all interest which the purchaser or his representatives may pay on any prior encumbrance, and all interest to accrue thereon; costs of sale, taxes and assessments, with interest and costs thereon, together with interest at 6% on all such sums paid by purchaser or those claiming under him, and for all damages and waste that may be occasioned or permitted by the party giving such security or those claiming under him during such year unless said property is so redeemed. Notice in writing of intention so to redeem must be given at or within ten days before the sale to the person making or who is to make the sale, and such security furnished within 20 days after sale. If the circuit court is not in session, the clerk may take and approve the security. (443.420-.440). The equity of redemption may be foreclosed, if the debt secured by the mortgage or deed of trust amounts to $50 or more, by filing petition in office of clerk of circuit court against mortgagor and actual tenants or occupiers of said real estate, or persons in possession of personal property, setting forth substance of mortgage deed, and praying that judgment may be rendered for debt and damages and that equity of redemption may be foreclosed, and mortgaged property be sold to satisfy amount due. (443.190).

When the sale is fairly conducted and the property is not purchased by the cestui que trust, or his representative, no right to redeem exists. (481 S.W.2d 531).

Form.—Following form of deed of trust, with power of sale, may be used:

Form

This deed, made and entered into this . . . . day of . . ., 19. . . ., by and between . . . ., part. . . . of the first part, and . . . ., party of the second part, and . . . ., part. . . . of the third part,

Witnesseth: that the part. . . . of the first part, in consideration of the debt and trust herein after mentioned and created, and the sum of $1 to . . . . paid by the said party of the second part, the receipt of which is hereby acknowledged, do. . . . by these presents grant, bargain and sell, convey and confirm unto the said party of the second part the following described real estate situate in the county of . . . . in the State of Missouri: (insert description); and possession of said premises now delivered unto said party of the second part;

To have and to hold the same, with the appurtenances, to the said party of the second part, and to his successor hereinafter designated, and to the assigns of him and his successor, forever.

In trust however, for the following purposes: whereas, the said . . . ., did on the . . . . day of . . . ., 19. . . ., make and deliver to (insert statement of obligation secured):

And whereas, said part. . . . of the first part agree with said part. . . . of the third part and . . . ., endorsees or assignees of said promissory note . . . ., and each of them, to pay on demand all taxes and assessments, general and special, now existing against said lands and improvements, and to pay when due or within the time required by law, all taxes and assessments, general or special, hereafter levied or charged thereon or therefor, and also to keep the improvements upon said land constantly and satisfactorily insured until said note . . . . be paid, for the sum of at least . . . . dollars, and the policy or policies thereof constantly assigned or pledged and delivered to . . . ., for further securing the payment of said note. . . ., with power to demand, receive and collect any and all moneys becoming payable thereunder and the same to apply toward the paying of said note. . . ., unless otherwise paid, and also to keep said land and improvements thereon free from all statutory lien claims of every kind; and if any or either of said agreements be not performed as aforesaid, then said part. . . . of the third part, or . . . . said endorsees or assignees or any of them, may pay such taxes and assessments or any part thereof, and may effect such insurance for said purpose, paying the cost thereof, and may also pay the final judgment for any statutory lien, including all costs; and for the repayment of all moneys paid in the premises, with interest thereon from the time of payment at the rate of . . . .% per annum, these presents shall be security in like manner and with like effect as for the payment of said note. . . . .

Now, if the said note. . . . and the interest thereon be paid when due, and said agreements be faithfully performed as aforesaid, then these presents, including the lease hereinafter set forth shall be void, and the property hereinbefore conveyed shall be released at the cost of said part. . . . of the first part; but if default be made in the payment of said note. . . . or any part thereof or any of the interest thereon when due, or in the faithful performance of any or either of said agreements as aforesaid, then the whole of said note. . . . shall become due and be paid as hereinafter provided, and this deed shall remain in force, and the said party of the second part, or in case of his death, inability, refusal to act or absence from . . . . County, Missouri, when any advertisement and sale are to be made hereunder, then, whoever shall be sheriff of . . . ., County, Missouri, at the time when any such advertisement and sale are to be made (who shall thereupon for the purpose of that advertisement and sale succeed to the second party's title to said real estate and the trust herein created respecting the same), may proceed to sell the property hereinbefore described, and any and every part thereof, at public vendue, to the highest bidder, at the . . . . front door of the . . . . County Circuit Court House, in . . . ., in the County of . . . ., aforesaid, for cash, first giving twenty days public notice of the time, terms and place of sale, and of the property to be sold, by advertisement in some newspaper printed and published in . . . ., Missouri, and upon such sale shall execute and deliver a deed of conveyance of the property sold to the purchaser or purchasers thereof, and any statement or recital of fact in such deed in relation to the nonpayment of money hereby secured to be paid, existence of the indebtedness so secured, notice by advertisement, sale, receipt of money, and the happening of any of the aforesaid events whereby the sheriff may become successor as herein provided, shall be prima facie evidence of the truth of such statement or recital; and said trustee shall receive the proceeds of said sale out of which he shall pay, first the cost and expenses of executing this trust, including compensation to the trustee, for his services, and next to said third party or . . . . endorsees or assignees, upon the usual vouchers therefor, all moneys paid for insurance or taxes and judgments upon statutory liens, claims and interest thereon as hereinbefore provided for; and next all said note. . . . then due and unpaid; and next the principal of such of said notes as are not

then due when payment thereon shall be demanded, with interest up to the time of such payment, and if not enough therefor, then apply what remains; and the balance of such proceeds, if any, shall be paid to the said part. . . . of the first part or . . . . legal representatives.

And the said party of the second part covenants faithfully to perform the trust herein created.

And the said part. . . . of the second part, hereby lets said premises to said part. . . . of the first part until a sale be had under the foregoing provisions therefor, upon the following terms and conditions thereof, to wit:

The said part. . . . of the first part, and every and all persons claiming or possessing such premises, and any part thereof, by, through, or under . . . . shall or will pay rent therefor during said term at the rate of 1¢ per month, payable monthly upon demand and shall and will surrender peaceable possession of said premises, and any and every part thereof, sold under said provisions, to said party of the second part . . . . successors, assignees, or purchasers thereof under such sale, within ten days after making of such sale without notice or demand therefor.

In witness whereof, the said first part. . . . ha. . . . hereunto set . . . . hand . . . . the day and year first above written.

Executed in the presence of:

Chattel Mortgages.—See topic Chattel Mortgages.

PROPERTY

ABSENTEES:

Care of Property.—No statutory provisions other than for appointment of public administrator on order of probate division of circuit court to take possession of any estate to prevent its being injured, wasted, purloined or lost. (473.743).

Escheat.—Unclaimed dividends on assignment for benefit of creditors, unclaimed shares of proceeds of partition sale, property unclaimed on final settlement of an estate or of a receiver of company doing business in state and unclaimed refunds of premiums, rates, fares or charges deposited in any court or with custodian in connection with litigation escheat to state, subject to reclamation by persons entitled. (470.010-.050, 470.270-.350). Unclaimed deposits, dividends and interest of liquidated banks are held by Director of Finance, then escheat to state. (361.200).

See also category Estates and Trusts, topic Descent and Distribution.

Presumption of death of absentee, see category Estates and Trusts, topic Death.

Process Agent.—No provision for appointment by nonresident of agent for service of process, except in case of foreign corporations (see category Business Organizations, topic Corporations) and issuers of securities for sale in state (see category Business Regulation and Commerce, topic Securities) and personal representatives of decedent's estates. (473.117).

Service on Nonresidents.—See categories Civil Actions and Procedure, topic Process; Transportation, topic Motor Vehicles.

See also categories Business Organizations, topic Corporations; Civil Actions and Procedure, topics Costs, Limitation of Actions, Process, Venue; Debtor and Creditor, topic Attachment; Estates and Trusts, topics Executors and Administrators, Trusts; Family, topic Guardian and Ward.

ADVERSE POSSESSION:

Character of Possession.—Possession to defeat an action must be actual, open, hostile, exclusive and continuous under claim of ownership. (775 S.W.2d 568).

Duration and Disabilities.—Persons not under any disability are barred by ten years adverse possession; persons under disability (except dower claimant) have at least three years after removal of disability in which to bring action, but are barred in any event by 21 years adverse possession; dower is not barred until ten years after husband's death. (516.010-.030).

Persons having a claim against land in the lawful possession of another on any date, must bring his action to recover within one year from such date, if the person claiming or those under whom he claims have not had possession or paid taxes thereon for 30 years. (516.070).

Easement may be created or acquired by prescription. (753 S.W.2d 940).

CONVEYANCES:

See topic Deeds.

CURTESY:

Estate of "curtesy" is abolished, but the widower is given the same rights of inheritance, allowances, and exemptions as a widow has. (474.110-.250-.260-.290-.010). See topic Dower.

See also category Estates and Trusts, topic Descent and Distribution.

DEEDS:

See topic Real Property for types of estates.

Execution and Recording.—All deeds must be acknowledged before a proper officer, or proved as provided by statute, and recorded in the county in which the property conveyed is located in order to be effective as against third persons without actual notice. (442.130-.380-.400). No witness required if deed is acknowledged. Deed of individual does not require seal.

For circumstances in which spouse must join see category Debtor and Creditor, topic Homesteads; also category Family, topic Husband and Wife.

In cities of over 400,000 population, and in all counties of first class, no trustee's or mortgagee's deed may be recorded unless notes or other obligations for default in payment of which foreclosure was had, or affidavit of owner of notes as to loss thereof,

DEEDS . . . *continued*
are produced to recorder. (443.390). See also category Documents and Records, topic Records.

To qualify for recording, all deeds (except supplemental indentures of utility companies and rural electric cooperatives) must have legal description of lands and mailing address of at least one grantee. Failure to contain address does not affect deed's validity. (59.330[1]).

See also categories Debtor and Creditor, topic Homesteads, subhead Alienation or Encumbrance; Family, topic Husband and Wife, subhead Conveyances.

Operation and Effect.—Words "Grant, bargain and sell", unless restricted by express terms contained in such conveyances, mean grantor had indefeasible fee simple estate free of encumbrances by grantor or person under whom he claims. (442.420). Where grantor undertakes to convey fee simple estate and has not legal title at time of conveyance, but afterwards acquires it, estate subsequently acquired passes to grantee. (442.430).

Lands may be conveyed by attorney of owner, provided the power is acknowledged and recorded. (442.020). Married woman may convey her real estate or relinquish her dower by a power of attorney authorizing its conveyance, executed and acknowledged by her jointly with her husband like a deed. (442.050).

See also topic Real Property; categories Debtor and Creditor, topic Homesteads; Family, topic Husband and Wife.

Corporate deed must be executed in name of corporation, under corporate seal, and signed and acknowledged by president, presiding member, or trustee. Also, holder of any office thereof, the incumbent of which is generally or specifically authorized to convey by resolution of the governing board. (442.060).

Recording Fees.—See category Documents and Records, topic Records, subhead Recording Fees.

Forms.—Following may be used:

Forms

Warranty deed: This Indenture, Made on the . . . . day of . . . ., A. D., 19. . . ., by and between . . . . of the County of . . . ., State of . . . ., part. . . . of the first part, and . . . . of the County of . . . ., State of . . . ., part. . . . of the second part, Witnesseth. That the said part. . . . of the first part, in consideration of the sum of . . . . Dollars, to . . . . paid by said part. . . . of the second part (the receipt of which is hereby acknowledged), do. . . . by these presents, Grant, Bargain and Sell, Convey and Confirm unto the said part. . . . of the second part . . . . heirs and assigns, the following described lots, tracts or parcels of land lying, being and situate in the County of . . . . and State of Missouri, to-wit: . . . . To have and to hold the premises aforesaid with all and singular, the rights, privileges, appurtenances and immunities thereto belonging or in anywise appertaining unto the said part. . . . of the second part and unto . . . . heirs and assigns forever; the said . . . . hereby covenanting that . . . . lawfully seized of an indefeasible estate in fee of the premises herein conveyed; that . . . . has. . . . good right to convey the same; that the said premises are free and clear from any incumbrance done or suffered by . . . . or those under whom . . . . claim. . . .; and that . . . . will warrant and defend the title to the said premises unto the said part . . . . of the second part and unto . . . . heirs and assigns forever, against the lawful claims and demands of all persons whomsoever. In Witness Whereof, The said part. . . . of the first part ha. . . . hereunto set . . . . hand and seal. . . . the day and year above written . . . .(Seal).

Quit-claim deed: Same form as warranty deed except in following particulars. Omit words "grant, bargain, sell, convey and confirm" and substitute "remise, release and forever quit-claim." Omit warranty provision "the said . . . . hereby covenanting . . . . against the lawful claims and demands of all persons whomsoever" and substitute "so that neither the said part. . . . of the first part nor . . . . heirs, nor any other person or persons, for . . . . or in . . . . name or behalf, shall or will hereafter claim or demand any right or title to the aforesaid premises or any part thereof, but they and each of them shall, by these presents, be excluded and forever barred."

See also topic Powers of Attorney; categories Business Regulation and Commerce, topic Frauds, Statute of; Debtor and Creditor, topics Fraudulent Sales and Conveyances, Homesteads; Documents and Records, topic Acknowledgments; Family, topics Infants, Husband and Wife.

DEEDS OF TRUST:

See topic Deeds; category Mortgages, topic Mortgages of Real Property.

DOWER:

Estate of "dower" is abolished. (474.110). (For marital rights of widow in husband's estate, see category Estates and Trusts, topic Descent and Distribution, subhead Surviving Spouse.) Where land or any interest therein was conveyed between Jan. 1, 1900 and Jan. 1, 1935, spouse failing to join or spouse's heirs, personal representatives, devisees or grantees are barred unless suit brought before Oct. 9, 1953, or if right has not accrued by death, claimant or claimants must file with Recorder of Deeds sworn notice setting forth facts upon which claim rests, residence of claimants, and complete description of land affected, before Oct. 9, 1953, or claim is barred. (516.065).

Release.—The wife may release her marital rights in real estate by joining in a deed, acknowledged and certified, with her husband (442.030; 474.150) or by prenuptial contract (474.120).

Bar.—Abandonment of spouse without reasonable cause for one year next preceding death of husband, or dwelling in adultery with another bars marital rights unless reconciliation and resumption of cohabitation. (474.140).

Election.—For election between marital rights and testamentary provision, see category Estates and Trusts, topic Wills.

Surviving husband has same rights in wife's real estate as widow has in husband's real estate, including right of election. (See topic Curtesy.) But according to decisions, wife may defeat such rights as to her separate property by her conveyance without his joinder. See category Family, topic Husband and Wife.

See also category Estates and Trusts, topic Descent and Distribution.

ESCHEAT:

See topic Absentees, subhead Escheat; category Estates and Trusts, topic Descent and Distribution, subhead Escheat.

LANDLORD AND TENANT:

Municipalities' code enforcement agency or occupants of one-third or more of dwelling units within building may bring civil action alleging nuisance exists with respect to dwelling unit, building or premises. (441.510). If court finds nuisance exists, it may order rent be paid into court, allowing owner reasonable time to correct deficiencies, authorize owner to draw upon rents deposited in court to pay cost of necessary repairs upon presentation to court of original copy of invoice for work performed or materials purchased or appoint receiver to administer or collect rent and correct deficiencies. (441.570, .590). Tenant not obligated to rebuild or repair building destroyed by fire in absence of express agreement. (441.010). Illegal use of premises renders lease void and owner has same remedies for recovery as if tenant holding over his term. (441.020). Tenant at will, sufferance or term less than two years may not assign his term or interest without written consent of landlord, violate conditions of written lease or commit waste. (441.030). If owner fails to pay building's utility bills, utility or agents may have receiver appointed to collect rent and use rental revenues to continue utility service. (441.650).

Kinds of Tenancy.—At will, sufferance, month-to-month, and year-to-year.

Leases.—All leases not in writing create estate at will only (432.050) terminable by one month's notice in writing, except leases of real estate for agricultural purposes other than garden which create tenancies from month to month (441.060) and except that a parol lease for longer than one year followed by entry into possession and payment of rent is converted by law into a tenancy from year to year (31 Mo. 13; 201 S.W.2d 509) and except that leases of land upon which person owns and occupies mobile home are terminable not sooner than 60 days from date rent payment next comes due (441.060).

Security Deposits.—

(1) Landlord may not demand or receive security deposit in excess of two months' rent.

(2) Within 30 days after date of termination of tenancy, landlord shall: (a) Return full amount of security deposit; or (b) furnish to tenant written itemized list of damages for which security deposit or any portion thereof is withheld, along with balance of security deposit. Landlord shall have complied with this subsection by mailing such statement and any payment to last known address of tenant.

(3) Landlord may withhold from security deposit only such amounts as are reasonably necessary for following reasons: (a) To remedy tenant's default in payment of rent due to landlord, pursuant to rental agreement; (b) to restore dwelling unit to its condition at commencement of tenancy, ordinary wear and tear excepted; or (c) to compensate landlord for actual damages sustained as result of tenant's failure to give adequate notice to terminate tenancy pursuant to law or rental agreement; provided that landlord makes reasonable efforts to mitigate damages.

(4) Landlord shall give tenant or his representative reasonable notice in writing at his last known address or in person of date and time when landlord will inspect dwelling unit following termination of rental agreement to determine amount of security deposit to be withheld, and inspection shall be held at reasonable time. Tenant shall have right to be present at inspection of dwelling unit at time and date scheduled by landlord.

(5) If landlord wrongfully withholds all or any portion of security deposit in violation of this section, tenant shall recover as damages not more than twice amount wrongfully withheld. (535.300).

Recording.—There is no statute requiring leases to be recorded, but they may be recorded. Actual possession puts third persons on inquiry. (99 Mo. 459; 12 S.W. 287).

Rent.—Court, after hearing on claim that nuisance exists with respect to dwelling unit, building or premises may order rents paid to clerk of court until deficiencies have been remedied. (441.570).

Termination of Tenancy.—Tenancies at will or by sufferance or for less than one year require one month's notice in writing to person in possession requiring him to remove. (441.060). Tenancy from year-to-year requires 60 days written notice. (441.050). No notice required where term is to end at a certain time. (441.070).

Liens.—Landlord has superior lien (against which tenant entitled to no exemption) on crop of tenant raised on leased premises for money or supplies furnished to tenant to enable him to raise and harvest crops or subsist during tenancy, which is limited to 120 days after expiration of tenancy. In case of removal of property, lien continues for 15 days thereafter. (441.290). Landlord has also lien on crops for eight months after annual rent is due and payable. (441.280).

Attachment for Rent.—Landlord may attach tenant's property for rent if tenant intends or attempts to remove, or within 30 days has removed, the same from premises without paying rent, or when rent is due and unpaid after demand. (441.240).

Holding Over.—A tenant who holds over after the termination of the time for which lands or possessions were let to him, or who wrongfully and without force obtains and continues in possession of lands, and after demand made in writing for possession by the person having the legal right thereto, is guilty of unlawful detainer. (534.030). Suit may be brought in any associate circuit court of county (534.060), regardless of amount of rent involved (61 Mo. 253), and associate circuit judge may render judgment for possession and for double amount of rents and profits (441.100-.110). There are special provisions for appeals and changes of venue. (534.380).

If premises are leased in writing and the tenant holds over, extension or renewal of lease cannot be shown by oral evidence, but contract in writing required to give right to continue in possession. (441.120).

Dispossession.—Whenever rent has become due and payable and payment has been demanded, but not made, landlord or agent may file statement, verified by affidavit, in

LANDLORD AND TENANT . . . continued

any associate circuit court in county in which property lies, setting forth terms upon which property was rented, amount of rent actually due, that rent has been demanded, and that payment has not been made, and particular description of property leased or rented. (535.020). Judge thereupon issues his summons which shall be executed ten days before return date thereof. If return is that defendant is not found or has absconded or absented himself from his usual place of abode, judge shall order notices set up for ten days in one public place in county. On proof of notice by affidavit, case proceeds same as if there had been personal service. (535.030). If upon hearing it shall appear facts set forth are true, and tenant does not tender rent, with all costs, before judge, he shall render judgment that landlord recover possession of premises and amount of rent, with costs, provided amount of rent due does not exceed his jurisdiction. He shall then issue execution commanding officer to put landlord into immediate possession, and to make debt and costs out of goods and chattels of defendant, upon which execution officer shall deliver possession of property to landlord within five days from time of receiving said execution and proceed to collect debt and costs. If plaintiff so elects, plaintiff may sue for possession alone. (535.040).

See also category Mineral, Water and Fishing Rights, topic Mines and Minerals, subhead Notices.

Landlord-Tenant Courts.—Statute provides for establishment of landlord-tenant commissioners to hear initial disputes in St. Louis City and Jackson County. (H.B. 361).

Uniform Residential Landlord and Tenant Act not adopted.

LEASES:

See topic Landlord and Tenant.

PERPETUITIES:

Future contingent interests must vest within a life or lives in being and 21 years and ten months thereafter. (199 S.W.2d 344). The only exception to this rule is a trust of real or personal property, created as part of an employer-employee stock bonus, pension, disability or death benefit, profit-sharing, or retirement plan, where contributions are made by employers or employees or self-employed for the benefit of employees or self-employed. Such a trust may continue for such time as necessary to accomplish its purposes. (456.060).

Accumulations.—The income arising from any property held in trust as part of such an employees' benefit plan may be permitted to accumulate until the fund is sufficient to accomplish the purposes of the plan. (456.070). See also category Estates and Trusts, topic Trusts.

PERSONAL PROPERTY:

Tenancies by the entireties in personal property do exist. (637 S.W.2d 332).

POWERS OF ATTORNEY:

It is not necessary for agent to be authorized in writing to act for principal, except to contract for sale of lands. Contract for sale of lands made by agent is not binding upon principal unless such agent is authorized in writing to make such contract. (432.010). Every instrument containing power to convey real estate or to execute, as agent or attorney, any instrument conveying real estate or whereby real estate may be affected must be acknowledged or proved and certified and recorded like other written instruments conveying or affecting real estate. (442.360).

Durable Power of Attorney.—Authority granted by principal to attorney in fact in written power of attorney is not terminated in event principal becomes wholly or partially disabled or incapacitated or in event of uncertainty as to whether principal is dead or alive if power of attorney is denominated as "Durable Power of Attorney", is subscribed by principal, dated and acknowledged as prescribed by law for conveyances of real estate, and includes provision stating: "THIS IS A DURABLE POWER OF ATTORNEY AND THE AUTHORITY OF MY ATTORNEY IN FACT SHALL NOT TERMINATE IF I BECOME DISABLED OR INCAPACITATED OR IN THE EVENT OF LATER UNCERTAINTY AS TO WHETHER I AM DEAD OR ALIVE"; or "THIS IS A DURABLE POWER OF ATTORNEY AND THE AUTHORITY OF MY ATTORNEY IN FACT, WHEN EFFECTIVE, SHALL NOT TERMINATE OR BE VOID OR VOIDABLE IF I AM OR BECOME DISABLED OR INCAPACITATED OR IN THE EVENT OF LATER UNCERTAINTY AS TO WHETHER I AM DEAD OR ALIVE." (404.705).

Durable Power of Attorney for Health Care Act.—If patient wishes to confer on attorney in fact authority to direct health care provider to withhold or withdraw artificially supplied nutrition and hydration, patient shall specifically grant such authority in power of attorney. This limitation shall not be construed to require that artificially supplied nutrition and hydration be continued when, in medical judgment of attending physician, patient cannot tolerate it.

Before attorney in fact or physician may authorize withdrawal of nutrition or hydration which patient may ingest through artificial means, physician must: (1) Attempt to explain to patient intention to withdraw nutrition and hydration and consequences for patient and to provide opportunity for patient to refuse withdrawal of nutrition and hydration; or (2) insert in patient's file certification that patient is comatose or consistently in condition which makes it impossible for patient to understand intention to withdraw nutrition and hydration and consequences to patient. (404.805).

REAL PROPERTY:

Tenancy in severalty, tenancy in common, joint tenancy, tenancy by the entirety, homestead, and life estates are recognized.

Grant or devise to two or more persons (except executors, trustees or spouses) creates tenancy in common unless expressly declared to be in joint tenancy. (442.450).

Real estate may be conveyed by owner or owners to himself or themselves and others, or one or more of themselves and others, or to one or more or all of themselves, and the conveyance has the same effect as to whether it creates a joint tenancy, tenancy by the entireties, tenancy in common, tenancy in partnership, or a separate ownership,

as if it were granted by a stranger who owned the real estate to the persons named as grantees. (442.025).

Real property sold at tax sale subject to recorded covenants and easements. (140.722).

Rule in Shelley's case is abolished. (442.490; 474.470).

Condominium property law in effect. (448.1-101-.210). Time-sharing plans regulated. (407.630).

See also topics Curtesy, Deeds, Dower, Landlord and Tenant; categories Civil Actions and Procedure, topic Partition; Debtor and Creditor, topic Homesteads; Family, topic Husband and Wife; Mortgages, topic Mortgages of Real Property.

TRUST DEEDS:

See category Mortgages, topic Mortgages of Real Property.

TAXATION

ADMINISTRATION:

Department of Revenue.—A Department of Revenue, with certain prescribed powers and duties has been created. (32.028).

State Tax Commission likewise created. (138.190).

The Commission, between June 20 and the second Monday in July, annually, must equalize the valuation of real and tangible personal property among the several counties in the State by allocating the property in certain designated classifications. (138.390). The Commission must exercise general supervision over all the assessing officers in the State. (138.410). Taxpayers, under rules and regulations prescribed by Commission have right to appeal to it from local boards of equalization. (138.430).

Interstate Cooperation.—Multistate tax compact (32.200-32.260) provides for proration and allocation of state and local tax on income of business entities doing business in party states.

Penalties.—

Income Tax.—Upon conviction for false return or failure to file fine up to $10,000 or imprisonment from one to five years or both. (143.911-.941). Interest on extension of filing date is discretionary with director of revenue. (143.551). Failure to file without intent to evade, 5% penalty per month not to exceed 25%; 50% penalty for fraud. (143.741-.751).

Estate Tax.—Failure to file without intent to evade, 5% penalty; 50% penalty for fraud. (145.985).

Sales Tax.—Refusal by purchaser to pay is misdemeanor. (144.060). Fine up to $1,000; imprisonment up to one year. (560.016; 558.011). Seller failing to collect or remit, misdemeanor. (144.080). Delinquency interest set each Oct. at nearest full percentage point of prime rate. (144.170, 32.065). Failure to file return a misdemeanor. (144.510). No return or false return with intent to defraud, fine up to $10,000 or one to five years imprisonment or both. (144.480, .490). Fraud or evasion, penalty 25%. (144.500).

Use Tax.—Failure to make return, 5% penalty per month not to exceed 25%. (144.665). Fine up to $10,000 or imprisonment one to five years or both. (144.735). Fraud, 25% penalty. (144.675). Violations generally a misdemeanor. (144.745).

Gasoline Tax.—Filing false report, license cancelled. (142.120). Delinquency, 5% per calendar month, cumulative to 25% of total tax. (142.180). Failure to comply with statutory requirements misdemeanor, fine $100-$1,000; imprisonment six months or both. Same for persons using knowing that tax has not been paid. (142.340[1]). Failure to pay tax collected, embezzlement: imprisonment two to five years; fine $100-$1,000. (142.340[2]). False oath, misdemeanor: imprisonment up to one year; fine $50-$1,000 or both. (142.340[3]). Evasion of tax through exempt export distributor misdemeanor: fine $500-$10,000; imprisonment 30 days to one year. (142.340[4]). Various other penalties. (142.340[5 through 8]).

Cigarette Tax.—Violation shall be cause for revocation or suspension of cigarette sales license. Failure to affix tax stamps: penalty equal to 100% of tax plus tax with interest set each Oct. at nearest full percentage point of prime rate. Unstamped cigarettes are contraband, subject to confiscation. Counterfeiting, tampering with stamps, meters, false reports or entries in records a felony: imprisonment two to five years. Other violations not covered by specific criminal penalties are misdemeanor: fine up to $500; imprisonment up to one year or both. (149.025-.081).

Merchants' Tax.—Failure to pay taxes, forfeiture of license given to secure taxes, and judgment for double amount owing and costs. (150.230). Delinquency, penalty 1% per month plus 10% interest, not to exceed 10% per annum total. (150.235). False statement, forfeit license and a misdemeanor: fine $100-$500; imprisonment up to six months. (150.260).

Manufacturers' Tax.—See catchline Merchants' Tax, supra, same penalties.

Unemployment Compensation Tax.—Delinquency, interest 1/2% per month. (288.150). Failure to report and pay tax, penalty 10% of principal and interest; for fraud 25%. (288.160). Violations a misdemeanor: fine $50-$1,000; imprisonment up to six months; or both, for each offense; forfeit credits. (288.380).

Credit Institutions Tax.—Interest on extension of filing date, 1% per month from due date. (148.160). Nonpayment, 1% per month not exceeding 10% per annum. (148.180).

Building and Loan Associations and Savings and Loan Associations Tax.—Delinquency, same penalties as those imposed on tangible personalty. See catchline Tangible Personal Property Tax, infra. (148.180).

Tangible Personal Property Tax.—Failure to provide list of property by Mar. 1, results in penalty between $10 and $100 depending on amount of property owned. No penalty assessed for certain cases of unavoidable and non-willful neglect. (137.280). Refusal to certify list misdemeanor. (137.360). False list, double assessment and possible liability for perjury (137.285); with intent to defraud, misdemeanor (137.420).

AIRCRAFT TAX:

Tax imposed by c. 155.

See note at head of Digest as to 1998 legislation covered.

See Topical Index in front part of this volume.

CIGARETTE TAX:

Cigarette tax imposed by c. 149.

CORPORATE TAXES:

Franchise Taxes.—See category Business Organizations, topic Corporations.

Taxation of Banks.—See category Business Regulation and Commerce, topic Banks and Banking.

Gross receipts tax on express companies, see category Business Regulation and Commerce, topic Carriers.

Premium tax on insurance companies, see category Insurance, topic Insurance Companies.

Tax on Credit Institutions.—A tax of 7% of net income is imposed on credit institutions (exclusive of banks, trust companies, credit unions, insurance companies, mutual savings and loan associations, savings and loan associations, or real estate mortgage loan companies). Credit is given for all other taxes imposed by State of Missouri or any political subdivision thereof. Return is due on or before Apr. 15, annually except return for year in which franchise is received is due June 1 of following year. (148.120-.230).

Building and loan associations and savings and loan associations are taxed at annual rate of 7% of net income for preceding year. Apportionment formula is used for savings and loan associations conducting business in other states. Tax is payable to Director of Revenue on or before Apr. 15. (148.610-.710).

ESTATE TAX:

Equal to maximum credit for state death taxes on federal estate tax return. Extension of time to file federal estate tax results in similar extension for state tax. (c. 145).

Apportionment Against Inter Vivos Dispositions.—No statutory provision.

GASOLINE TAX:

Gasoline tax imposed by c. 142. An additional tax may be imposed by cities upon voter approval. (Const. 1945, Art. IV, §30[a]).

GENERATION-SKIPPING CREDIT TAX:

Tax imposed on generation skipping transfer equal to maximum credit for state death taxes allowed by Internal Revenue Code §2604. (145.995).

GIFT TAX:

None.

INCOME TAX:

Income tax is levied on all incomes with certain exceptions, exemptions and deductions. See also category Business Regulation and Commerce, topic Banks and Banking, subhead Taxation.

Tax applies to incomes of residents and nonresidents. Single residents with gross income of $1,200 or more and married couples with gross income of $2,400 or more, and single nonresidents with Missouri nonresident adjusted gross income of $600 or more must file returns. (143.481). Residents are taxed on Missouri taxable income of every resident (143.011); nonresidents on income from sources within state (143.041; 143.181); residents for only part of year are taxed as nonresidents (143.051). Tax on income of estates or any kind of property held in trust is assessed to executor, administrator, trustee or other fiduciary, if not returned to beneficiary, but where income is regularly distributed, rate of tax is based on amount of individual share distributed. (143.501; 143.351). Tax does not apply to trust or other unincorporated organization which by reason of its purposes and activities is exempt from Federal income tax. (143.321).

Resident Individual Income.—Adjusted gross income is Federal adjusted gross income plus any Federal income tax refund received for a prior year, interest on any non-Missouri governmental obligation reduced by amounts applicable to such interest that would have been deductible in computing taxable income of taxpayer except only for application of §265 of IRC if interest is at least $500; minus interest or dividends on obligations of U.S. and its territories and possessions or of any authority, commission or instrumentality of U.S. to extent exempt from Missouri income taxes under laws of U.S., reduced by any interest on indebtedness incurred to carry same and by any expenses incurred in production of interest or dividend income if expenses total at least $500 and only if said amounts have been deducted from Federal adjusted gross income or included in Missouri itemized deduction; portion of any gain from sale or other disposition of property having a higher adjusted basis to taxpayer for Missouri income tax purposes than for Federal income tax purposes; amount necessary to prevent taxation of any annuity or other amounted income or gain which was properly included in income or gain and was taxed under laws of Missouri for taxable year prior to 1/1/73; accumulation distributions from a trust to extent that same are included in Federal adjusted gross income; and a sum either added or subtracted for a taxpayer's share of Missouri fiduciary adjustment (143.351) and partner modification (143.411). (143.121). Adjusted gross income is reduced by: (1) Either Missouri standard deduction (143.131) or Missouri itemized deduction (143.141), (2) deduction for personal exemptions (143.151), (3) deduction for dependency exemptions (143.161), (4) deduction for Federal income taxes. For tax years beginning on or after Jan. 1, 1994, may only deduct for federal income tax liability maximum of $5,000 on single return, $10,000 on combined return. (143.171).

Nonresident Individual Income.—Includes that part of nonresident's federal adjusted gross income derived from income from sources within state as modified in same manner with respect to residents (143.121), but does not include compensation paid by U.S. for services in armed forces of U.S. performed by nonresident (143.181).

Personal exemptions are $1,200 for resident, $1,200 for spouse (143.151), $400 for each dependent (143.161), if entitled to such deductions for Federal income tax purposes. Additional $800 deduction for resident who qualifies as unmarried head of household or surviving spouse for Federal income tax purposes. (143.161).

Rates for Individuals.—Tax is always at a flat rate on entire income in excess of exemptions and credits, but such rate varies according to amount of Missouri taxable income as follows: Not over $1,000, 1½%; over $1,000 but not over $2,000, $15, plus 2% of excess over $1,000; over $2,000, but not over $3,000, $35, plus 2½% of excess over $2,000; over $3,000 but not over $4,000, $60, plus 3% of excess over $3,000; over $4,000 but not over $5,000, $90, plus 3½% of excess over $4,000; over $5,000 but not over $6,000, $125, plus 4% of excess over $5,000; over $6,000 but not over $7,000, $165, plus 4½% of excess over $6,000; over $7,000 but not over $8,000, $210, plus 5% of excess over $7,000; over $8,000 but not over $9,000, $260, plus 5½% of excess over $8,000; over $9,000 but not over $10,000, $315, plus 6% of excess over $9,000; over $10,000 but not over $20,000, $375, plus 6.5 of excess over $10,000; over $20,000 but not over $30,000, $1,025, plus 7% of excess over $20,000; over $30,000 but not over $40,000, $1,725, plus 7.5% of excess over $30,000; over $40,000, $2,475, plus 8% of excess over $40,000. (143.011).

Rates for Corporations, etc.—Corporations, joint stock companies and associations, organized or doing business in this state, are taxed as follows: if Missouri taxable income is: not over $100,000, 5% of the Missouri taxable income; over $100,000 but not over $300,000, $5,000 plus 6% of excess over $100,000; over $300,000 but not over $500,000, $17,000 plus 7% of excess over $300,000; over $500,000 but not over $1,000,000, $31,000 plus 8% of excess over $500,000; over $1,000,000, $71,000 plus 10% of excess over $1,000,000. (143.071; 143.431-.471).

Provision is made for allocating income to this state on interstate business not subject to segregation, and taxpayer may show taxable Missouri income by its own method of allocation if approved by the Director of Revenue. (143.451-.461).

Special provisions are made for apportioning income of railroad, bridge, telegraph and telephone companies, lines or property of which are partly within and partly without state. (143.441; 143.451).

Withholding.—Employers must withhold from the wages of each employee each pay period amount determined by Director of Revenue, constituting payment on account of employee's income tax. Withholding returns are filed by employer each quarter-month, month, quarter or year depending on amount withheld. (143.191, 143.211, 141.225).

Returns must be filed no later than 15th day of fourth month following close of taxpayer's taxable year except exempt organizations file on date set by Internal Revenue Code. (143.511).

Estimated tax declarations must be filed if individuals' estimated tax will be $100 or more. Declaration due Apr. 15, with necessary amendments quarterly thereafter. Pro rata payments or estimate due on Apr. 15 and quarterly thereafter. Fiscal year adjustments provided. (143.521-.541).

Information Returns.—Person, corporation, etc., making payment to another person of any fixed or determinable gains, profits or income of $1,200 or more to any single person or $100 or more in case of interest or dividends must make return thereof to Director of Revenue and person to whom such payment is made, on or before Feb. 28 of year following year in which such payments were made. (143.591).

Payment.—Tax is payable on or before date on which return is due (see supra, subhead Returns) and is delinquent on following day. (143.511).

INHERITANCE TAX:

None.

MANUFACTURERS' TAX:

Manufacturers are taxed on all raw materials, finished products, and tools, machinery and appliances used by them in the same manner and to the same extent as merchants are taxed. If the value of the above listed items is less than $1,000 no manufacturers' tax is imposed. (150.310-.370).

MERCHANTS' TAX:

Merchants must pay ad valorem tax on amount of all merchandise in their possession whether owned by them or consigned to them for sale on Jan. 1 of each year. Merchant is defined as every person, corporation, copartnership or association of persons, who shall deal in the selling of goods, wares and merchandise at any store, stand or place occupied for that purpose. Term merchant includes all merchants, commission merchants, grocers, manufacturers and dealers in drugs and medicine, except physicians for medicine used in their practice. Tax is equal to rate levied on real estate. Motor vehicle dealers are considered merchants but are not subject to ad valorem tax. (150.010-.290).

PROPERTY TAXES:

Assessment.—All property is classified as real property and tangible personal property. Real property is further subclassified into residential property, assessed at 19% of true value; agricultural property, assessed at 12%; and industrial property, assessed at 32%. (137.115). Assessment of personal property, except for grain, other crops, livestock, farm machinery, historic motor vehicles, aircraft 25 years or older and poultry, shall be at 33¹/₃% of its true value. (137.115).

For purposes of taxation assessor shall make list of all real and tangible personal property and may call residence or place of business of owner to obtain correct statement thereof assigned. Assessors in each county and city of St. Louis may send personal property assessment forms by mail. (137.115).

Exemptions.—Property of state, county and political subdivisions; religious, educational, charitable, agricultural and horticultural societies. (Const. Art. X, §6).

No exemption for members of armed services.

Review.—A person who thinks himself aggrieved may appeal to the county board of equalization (137.275, 138.060), and the owner of real property or tangible personal

PROPERTY TAXES . . . *continued*
property has the right of appeal from the local board of equalization under rules prescribed by the State Tax Commission (138.430-.470).

Lien.—Taxes on real property are liens thereon. (137.085).

Payment.—Taxes are delinquent Jan. 1. (140.010). If real estate taxes not paid before Jan. 1, penalty of 18% per year is imposed. If taxes which were delinquent for preceding year are paid prior to sale, penalty added may not exceed 2% per month. (140.100).

Collection.—County collector collects tax on tangible property and forwards to state division of taxation and collection. All other money payable to state must be sent directly to division of taxation and collection. (136.010).

Sales and Redemption.—Any person interested in or owner of land upon which there is lien for delinquent taxes may redeem land by paying original taxes with interest at rate of 18% plus costs and attorneys fees if suit has commenced. After delinquent tax sale of land, execution and recording of deed to purchaser shall not occur for two years during which time owner or any person having interest may redeem by paying amount of judgment, interest and costs. Deed executed by sheriff is prima facie evidence of title. Action for recovery of taxes must be commenced within five years from date of delinquency. (140.110; 140.160; 140.340; 141.010-.180).

REAL ESTATE CONVEYANCE TAX:

None.

SALES AND USE TAXES:

Sales and use tax (c. 144) of 4% is imposed on amount paid or charged on or for: (a) Retail sales in state of tangible personal property (if transaction involves exchange, fair market value of property exchanged, at time and place of exchange, is included in basis of tax); (b) admission and seating accommodations, or fees paid to or in any place of amusement, entertainment, recreation, game or athletic event; (c) electricity, electric current, water and gas; (d) service to telephone subscribers and equipment or services pertaining or incidental thereto; (e) services for transmission of messages by telegraph companies; (f) rooms, meals and drinks furnished at hotel, tavern, inn, restaurant, eating house, drug store, dining car, tourist cabin, tourist camp or other place in which rooms, meals or drinks are regularly served to public; (g) intrastate tickets by operator of railroad, sleeping car, dining car, express car, boat, airplane, and such busses and trucks as are licensed by Transportation Division of Department of Economic Development, engaged in transportation of persons for hire; (h) rental or lease of tangible personal property unless lessor paid sales tax thereon or property is exempt under 144.030. (Const. Art. IV, §43[a]; 144.020). On local option, some cities and counties impose additional sales taxes. (144.032).

When article on which Missouri sales or use tax has been paid is traded in and trade-in allowance is less than purchase price, sales tax computed only on difference. Where trade-in allowance exceeds purchase price, no sales or use tax is owed. Sale of motor vehicles by owner subject to same provision if replacement vehicle purchased or ordered from dealer within 90 days before or after sale. (144.025).

Sales to duly licensed physicians, dentists, optometrists and veterinarians, of tangible personal property used in practice of their professions are deemed to be for use or consumption and not for resale. (144.010).

Retail sales of food shall be taxed at rate of 1%. (144.014).

Brackets used for collection of tax are established by director of revenue. (144.285).

Vendor rendering periodic statements covering taxable purchases can use brackets or apply tax rate to total on statement. (144.285).

Sales Tax.—

Exemptions.—Motor fuel subject to excise or sales tax under another law of this state; fuel to be consumed in manufacturing or creating gas, power, steam, electrical current or in furnishing water to be sold ultimately at retail; feed, medications and vaccinations administered to livestock or poultry to be sold ultimately in processed form or otherwise at retail; grain to be converted into foodstuffs to be sold ultimately in processed form at retail; all sales of pesticides and bedding used in production of livestock or poultry for food or fiber; seed, limestone or fertilizer to be used for crops, which when harvested will be sold at retail or will be fed to livestock or poultry to be sold ultimately in processed form at retail; economic poisons which are to be used for spraying growing crops, fruit trees or orchards, the crop of which when harvested will be sold at retail or will be converted into foodstuffs, which are to be sold ultimately in processed form at retail; materials incorporated in new products; materials used in motor vehicles, watercraft, railroad rolling stock or aircraft used as common carriers; machinery replacing obsolete manufacturing machinery or for expansion of manufacturing plants and construction for such machinery; tangible personal property used solely for products sold to U.S.; sales of animals and poultry for breeding or feeding and sales of horses; newsprint for public newspapers; rental of films and records; common carrier pipeline pumping equipment; railroad rolling stock for use in transporting persons or property in interstate commerce; electrical energy used in actual primary manufacture, processing, compounding, mining or producing of product, or electrical energy used in actual secondary processing or fabricating of product, if total cost of electrical energy so used exceeds 10% of total cost of production, either primary or secondary, exclusive of cost of electrical energy so used; anodes which are used or consumed in manufacturing, processing, compounding, mining, producing or fabricating and which have useful life of less than one year; machinery, equipment, appliances and devices purchased or leased and used solely for purpose of preventing, abating or monitoring water and air pollution, and materials required for construction of such and so certified as such by director of department of natural resources; and tangible personal property purchased by rural water district; amounts paid to political subdivisions for admission or participation in any amusement, games or athletic events where individual making payment is actually participating in activity proceeds do not inure to private persons; sales of insulin and prosthetic or orthopedic devices including hearing aids and hearing aid supplies and prescription drugs; sales of aircraft to carriers for storage or use in interstate commerce; sales by income tax exempt summer theatre organization; ticket sales by benevolent, scientific and educational associations formed to promote progress and improvement in science and agriculture; sales to not-for-profit private secondary schools; sales of new or used farm machinery parts other than motor vehicles and fuel or electricity used to dry crops; water service, electricity, gas, wood, coal, and heating oil for domestic use; sales of handicraft items made by seller or his spouse if seller or spouse is at least 65 and total proceeds of such sales do not constitute majority of annual gross income of seller; federal excise tax on retail sales; sales of fuel delivered and consumed in operation of ships, barges or waterborne vessels used primarily in or for transportation of property, cargo or persons for hire on navigable rivers bordering or located in this state; computers and computer software purchased by certain entities headquartered in this state; sale at retail of certain types of electrical current to battery manufacturers; livestock sales when seller is grower, producer or feeder or in business of buying and selling livestock; sale of barges used primarily in transportation of property on interstate waterways. Also exempt are sales by or to: Religious and charitable organizations or institutions and elementary and secondary schools operated at public expense, in their religious, charitable or educational functions and activities; eleemosynary and penal institutions; industries of state; any institution of higher learning supported by public funds; state relief agencies in exercise of relief functions and activities; and admissions to museums, zoos and planetariums. (144.030-.046). Energy consumed in process of steelmaking is exempt from sales and use tax; 100% exempt in 1994; exemption reduced by 10% each year; exemption expires 2003. (144.036). Sale of light aircraft to nonresident purchaser exempt. (144.043). Purchase of materials for construction, repairs or remodeling of exempt organization's facilities are tax exempt. (144.062).

License issued at no cost by Director of Revenue required of all persons collecting sales tax, which license is prerequisite for obtaining city, county or state occupation license. License may be revoked for default in payment of sales tax, or bond required. Bond required for itinerant or temporary business. (144.083-.087).

Returns.—Return for each quarterly period of three months must be filed with and the tax paid to the Director of Revenue on or before the last day of month following each such quarterly period. (144.080). If deemed necessary to insure payment, or to facilitate collection of amount of taxes, or if revenue needs demand it, Director of Revenue may require returns and payment of amount of taxes for monthly or annual periods instead of calendar quarters. (144.090).

Where for either first or second month of quarter tax is more than $250 seller shall pay such amount by 20th day of next month and credit for amount paid allowed on quarterly return. Where amount of quarterly taxes is less than $45, seller shall be permitted to file return for calendar year only. (144.080).

Returns are not required on sales of motor vehicles where payment is made by purchaser to Director of Revenue when registering vehicle. See category Transportation, topic Motor Vehicles, subheads Sales Tax and Use Tax. (144.070).

Use Tax.—4% tax on storing, using or consuming tangible personal property in state. Exemptions include: (a) constitutional exemptions; (b) property taxed under sales taxes of this state; (c) property which would not be subject to sales taxes if sold in this state; (d) property taxed under other states' sales or use tax, except as less than 4%, in which case shall be taxed on difference; (e) property held for resale; (f) personal and household effects and farm machinery of nonresident coming into this state. Duty of collection is on vendor, but purchaser must file return if tax is not paid to vendor. Vendor must register with Director of Revenue, may be required to give bond, and must file return quarterly. Purchaser must file return if tax is not paid to vendor unless aggregate purchases subject to use tax are less than $2,000 in calendar year. (144.600-.748).

May impose local use tax at rate equal to local sales tax, 4% on motor vehicles. (144.440; 144.450). See category Transportation, topic Motor Vehicles.

STAMP TAX:

No requirement of stamps on corporate stock or other instruments.

UNEMPLOYMENT COMPENSATION TAX:

Unemployment compensation tax (termed "contributions") is imposed on every employer having one or more persons in partial or full daily employ in each of 20 different calendar weeks, whether or not weeks are consecutive, or on any unit which in any calendar quarter in either current or preceding year paid employment wages of $1,500 or more except in: Service of spouse or parent of employer; service of child under 21 years old for parent; agricultural labor; domestic service; service of children under 18 in delivery of newspapers or shopping news, not including delivery to distribution point; service of state or political subdivision or instrumentality thereof; service with respect to which unemployment compensation is payable under system established by Congress; service in employ of foreign government, or of wholly owned instrumentality of foreign government if such foreign government grants equivalent exemption with respect to similar service performed in its country by employees of U. S. Government and its instrumentalities; service under arrangement between division and agency administering other state or federal unemployment insurance law under which services of individual are performed entirely within jurisdiction of other state or federal agency; service for school, college or university in any calender quarter by enrolled student regularly attending classes if remuneration does not exceed $50, exclusive of board, room and tuition; service as insurance agent if sole remuneration is by commissions; service of local college club or local chapter of college fraternity or sorority; service of nonprofit religious, charitable, scientific, literary or educational organization, or for prevention of cruelty to children or animals, if nonprofit. Tax applies only to wages not in excess of $7,000 per year for 1988 through 1992, $7,500 per year for 1993, and $8,500 per year thereafter to any individual employee. Rates vary according to statutory classification. No tax is imposed on employees. Payment is due at such intervals, no less frequently than quarterly, and on such dates as may be fixed by regulation of Division of Employment Security of Department of Labor and Industrial Relations, which is charged with administration of Unemployment Compensation Law. (c. 288). Quarterly payments are due on or before last day of month following calendar quarter for which contributions are payable. Transient employers must post notice of registration of unemployment insurance. (285.234).

See note at head of Digest as to 1998 legislation covered.

See Topical Index in front part of this volume.

MO – 41

UNEMPLOYMENT COMPENSATION TAX . . . *continued*

See also categories Business Organizations, topic Corporations; Business Regulation and Commerce, topic Licenses, Business and Professional; Insurance, topic Insurance Companies; Transportation, topic Motor Vehicles.

TRANSPORTATION

MOTOR VEHICLES:

General supervision is in State Director of Revenue, Jefferson State Office Bldg., Jefferson City 65101.

Vehicle license required annually. Number plates must be displayed front and rear, or in rear if only one plate is issued and must be clearly visible at night. Plates are not transferable, but upon transfer of ownership or discontinuation of operation of original vehicle owner may register another vehicle under same number. (301.030, .140). Application must be accompanied by receipt showing applicant's previous year's personal property tax assessment has been paid, and if subject to Federal heavy vehicle use tax imposed by §4481 IRC, proof of payment, or that such tax is not owing. (301.025). No exemptions for members of Armed Forces. Annual inspection required by authorized station. (307.350). Stations may charge up to $7 for inspection, certificate and sticker, and up to $6 for trailer or motorcycle. (307.365).

Operator's license required. Not issued to person under 16 years of age as private operator, nor to person under 18 as chauffeur (302.060) or person under 21 as operator of school bus or common carrier vehicle, unless licensed as a chauffeur except that drivers of trucks of less than one ton manufacturer's rated capacity may be licensed as chauffeur if 18 years old (302.070). Temporary permit may be obtained between ages 15½ and 16. (302.020). Curfew between 12:00-5:00 a.m. for drivers between 16-18. (302.020). Active duty members of Armed Forces, no examination if renewal of license and prior license not suspended or revoked. (302.173).

As to nonresident operators, see subhead Nonresident Operators, infra.

Interstate Driver License Compact entered. (302.600-.605).

Municipal license taxes on motor vehicles are authorized within limits, also occupation taxes on business of transporting freight or passengers. (301.340).

Titles and Sales.—Owner must obtain certificate of ownership from Director of Revenue. (301.190). On transfer of ownership, seller must indorse on certificate an assignment with warranty of title and statement of all incumbrances and deliver same to buyer at time of delivery of vehicle. Buyer must present assigned certificate to Director of Revenue and thereupon new certificate is issued to him. Unlawful to buy or sell vehicle without assignment of certificate and such sale declared fraudulent and void. (301.210). Owner may request certificate of ownership in beneficiary form. (301.681). Certificate in name of husband and wife presumed to create estate by entirety, and on proof of death new certificate will be issued in name of survivor. (301.195).

See also infra, subheads Sales Tax and Use Tax. See also category Business Regulation and Commerce, topic Sales, subhead Motor Vehicle Time Sales.

Liens are not valid against subsequent transferees or lienholders who took without notice unless lien is perfected as required by law. Liens are perfected by delivery to director of revenue of (1) existing certificate of ownership, (2) application for certificate of ownership containing name and address of lienholder and date of his security agreement, and (3) required fee. Releases are sent to director of revenue for removal of lienholder's name and/or issuance of new certificate of ownership without lienholder's name. (301.600-.670).

Identification Marks.—Felony offense to remove, alter or deface manufacturer's number, motor number or other distinguishing mark, or knowingly to possess or deal with car so altered. (301.390-.400).

Operation Prohibited.—By persons under 16 (577.110), intoxicated persons, persons under influence of drugs (577.010), or persons whose licenses have been suspended or revoked in this state (302.200) including suspension or revocation under point system (302.302-.304).

It is a misdemeanor for any person to authorize or knowingly permit a motor vehicle owned by him or under his control to be operated on any highway by a person not authorized to operate such vehicle. (302.260).

Size and Weight Limits.—Regulated by 304.180-.190.

Equipment Required.—Regulated by 307.130-.196.

Seat belts are required to be worn by passengers in front seat and all drivers of cars manufactured after 1/1/68 except children under four. $10 fine. (307.178).

Children's car seats are required for children under four riding in front seat and car seats or seat belts are required for children under four in backseat. (210.104).

Lights Required.—Regulated by 307.020-.125.

Inspection.—Annual. (307.366). For certain non-attainment areas, emissions inspection required biannually and prior to sale or transfer. (643.300-.355).

Accidents.—Operator must stop and give his name, residence, including street number, motor vehicle number and chauffeur's or registered operator's number, if any, to opposite party or to police officer or to nearest policy station or judicial officer. (577.060). If injury or death or property damage to one car over $500 accident must be reported to police immediately if within city. (300.110).

Liability of owner for negligence of another person depends on agency. No statutory extension of liability.

Guests.—No statutory restriction of liability for injury to guest.

Mandatory Financial Responsibility.—Missouri drivers must maintain adequate financial responsibility. Motor vehicle liability insurance is principal method of meeting financial responsibility requirement, though law also permits certificates of deposit, surety bonds and self-insurance. Each owner certifies at vehicle's registration that he will maintain adequate financial responsibility. Insurance companies furnish insurance identification cards to be carried in cars. Department of Revenue is authorized to conduct verification samples. Driver's license and vehicle registrations of any person who does not maintain adequate financial responsibility can be suspended. (c. 303).

Insurance.—See subhead Mandatory Financial Responsibility, supra.

No-Fault Insurance not adopted.

Foreign vehicles, duly registered in home state or country and displaying number plate or plates issued by such state or country, may be operated in Missouri without local registration, but only to extent that home state or country grants similar exemption to Missouri vehicles. (301.271).

Nonresident Operators.—A nonresident at least 16 years old, who has in his immediate possession a valid operator's license issued to him in his home state or country, may operate a vehicle in Missouri, but only as a private operator. Nonresident at least 18 years old, who has in his immediate possession a valid chauffeur's license issued to him in his home state or country, may operate a vehicle in Missouri, either as chauffeur or as private operator, but may not accept employment as chauffeur from a resident of Missouri without Missouri license as chauffeur. Nonresident at least 18 years old, whose home state or country does not require licensing of operators, may operate a vehicle duly registered in his home state or country for not more than 60 days in any calendar year. (302.080).

Actions Against Nonresidents.—Nonresident owner of motor vehicle or trailer operating on Missouri highways is deemed to have appointed Secretary of State his agent on whom process may be served in any suit for damages growing out of such operation by himself or agent. Secretary of State must send notification of service by restricted registered mail to such defendant. (506.210, .240; C.R. 54.14-.19).

Direct Actions.—No direct action against insurer by injured party is allowed.

Dealers.—Motor vehicle and boat dealers must make monthly reports to Missouri Department of Revenue as to sales on or before 15th day of month in which sales reported. (301.280). Motor vehicles dealer, boat dealer, manufacturer and boat manufacturer must obtain license. (301.559). Dealers, except boat dealers, must have lot displaying one or more vehicles. Dealers, except wholesale dealers, must display sign carrying name and class of business. (301.560). Wholesale and public motor vehicle auctions are also subject to signage and licensure requirements. (301.559-.561).

Motor vehicle carriers are regulated by Public Service Commission. Common carriers must obtain certificate of public convenience and necessity and contract carriers a permit from the Public Service Commission. (390.051-.061). Must pay an annual license fee and file a liability insurance policy in such form as Commission may require to make compensation for injuries to person or property resulting from negligent operation, unless Commission satisfied of financial ability to act as self-insurer. (390.126-.136). Commission may enter into reciprocal contracts or agreements with other states relating to motor carriers. (386.220).

Vehicles exempted include, among others, private carriers and motor vehicles which are domiciled and licensed in another state and whose operations in this state are interstate in character and are limited exclusively to a municipality and its commercial zone. (390.030).

Commercial vehicles must display in a conspicuous place on both sides thereof: (1) the name of the owner; (2) the address from which such motor vehicle is operated; and (3) in addition to foregoing local commercial vehicles must display in conspicuous place word "local". (301.330). Registration fees and penalties regulated by 301.058. Commercial vehicles with non-expiring license plates pursuant to §301.277 may file supplemental application with Missouri Highway reciprocity commission and transfer plate to replacement commercial vehicle. (301.130).

Watercraft.—Service of process on nonresident owner or operator causing injury to persons or property in this state may be had in like manner to motor vehicles. See subhead Actions Against Nonresidents, supra. Person in charge of craft required to report injuries to sheriff of county within 24 hours. (506.330-.350). Motorboat numbering required. (306.020).

Outboard Motors.—The owner or the person responsible for an outboard motor kept within this State shall register it in office of director of revenue who shall issue certificate of title for same. (306.530).

Sales Tax.—Subject to certain exemptions, sales tax must be paid to the Director of Revenue at the time of obtaining a certificate of ownership; also applies to trailers. (144.070). See category Taxation, topic Sales and Use Tax, subhead Sales Tax.

Home Trailer Parking Rental Tax.—See category Taxation, topic Sales and Use Tax, subhead Use Tax.

Use Tax.—4% of entire purchase price on any motor vehicle or trailer required to be registered under laws of Missouri. Allowed credit for amount of sales or use tax previously paid in another state. Not applicable to vehicles on which Missouri sales tax paid, nor those registered and in good faith regularly operated in another state 90 days prior to registration in Missouri, nor those acquired by registered dealers for resale, nor those used in regular religious, charitable or eleemosynary functions, or acquired by gift, will, or inheritance if tax has been paid by donor or decedent, or those owned or used by the state or political subdivisions or public educational institutions, nor to farm tractors. (144.440; .450).

When motor vehicle or trailer on which Missouri sales or use tax has been paid is traded in on another vehicle or trailer subject to use tax and the difference between trade-in allowance and purchase price exceeds $500, use tax computed only on difference. Where purchaser of motor vehicle, trailer, boat or outboard motor receives rebate, tax computed only on portion of purchase price in excess of rebate. (144.025).

Gasoline Tax.—See category Taxation, topic Gasoline Tax.

RAILROADS:

See category Business Regulation and Commerce, topic Carriers.

See note at head of Digest as to 1998 legislation covered.

See Topical Index in front part of this volume.

MO – 42

COMMERCIAL CODE FORMS

See also categories Business Regulation and Commerce, topic Commercial Code; Mortgages, topic Chattel Mortgages.

Financing Statement—Form UCC-1.—

This FINANCING STATEMENT is presented to a Filing Officer for filing pursuant to the Uniform Commercial Code:	No. of Additional Sheets Presented:	Maturity Date 3. (Optional):
1. Debtor(s) (Last Name First) and Address(es):	2. Secured Party(ies): Name(s) and Address(es):	4. For Filing Officer: Time, Date, No., Filing Office

5. This Financing Statement Covers the Following Types (or Items) of Property:

☐ Proceeds— ☐ Products of the Collateral are Also Covered:

6. ☐ To be Recorded in Real Estate Mortgage Records

7. Description of Real Estate:

8. Name(s) of Record Owner(s): . . . .

10. This statement is filed without the debtor's signature to perfect a security interest in collateral (check ☒ if so)
☐ already subject to a security interest in another jurisdiction when it was brought into this state, or
☐ which is proceeds of the following described original collateral which was perfected:

9. Assignee(s) of Secured Party and Address(es)

By . . . .
Signature(s) of Debtor(s)

By . . . .
Signature(s) of Secured Party(ies)

Termination Statement.—An addendum to page 3 (acknowledgment) of Form UCC-1.—

TERMINATION STATEMENT: This Statement of Termination of Financing is presented to a Filing Officer for filing pursuant to the Uniform Commercial Code. The Secured Party certifies that the Secured Party no longer claims a security interest under the financing statement bearing the file number shown above.

(Pink Copy)

Date . . . . 19 . . .

By: . . . .
(Signature of Secured Party or Assignee of Record. Not Valid Until Signed.)

(3) FILING OFFICER COPY— ACKNOWLEDGMENT

Filing Officer is requested to note file number, date and hour of filing on this copy and return to the person filing, as an acknowledgment.

Continuation, etc. Statement—Form UCC-3.—

This STATEMENT is presented to a Filing Officer for filing pursuant to the Uniform Commercial Code:	No. of Additional Sheets Presented:	Maturity Date 3. (Optional):
1. Debtor(s) (Last Name First) and Address(es):	2. Secured Party(ies) Name(s) and Address(es):	4. For Filing Officer: Date, Time, No., Filing Office

5. This Statement Refers to Original Financing Statement No. . . . . . Filed (date) . . . . . . with . . . .

6. ☐ A. Continuation — The original Financing Statement bearing the above file number is still effective.
☐ B. Termination — The Secured Party of record no longer claims a security interest under the Financing Statement bearing the above file number.
☐ C. Release — From the Collateral described in the Financing Statement bearing the above file number, the Secured Party of record releases the following:
☐ D. Assignment — The Secured Party of record has assigned the Secured Party's rights in the property described below under the Financing Statement bearing the above file number to the Assignee whose name and address are shown below:
☐ E. Amendment — The Financing Statement bearing the above file number is amended as set forth below: (Signature of Debtor is required if Collateral is added.)

7. Description of Collateral:

8. Name(s) of Record Owner(s): . . . .

By . . . .
Signature(s) of Debtor(s)
(Only on Amendment)

By . . . .
Signature(s) of Secured Party(ies)

See note at head of Digest as to 1998 legislation covered.

See Topical Index in front part of this volume.

MONTANA LAW DIGEST REVISER

Crowley, Haughey, Hanson, Toole & Dietrich P.L.L.P.
500 Transwestern Plaza II
490 North 31st Street
P.O. Box 2529
Billings, Montana 59103-2529

Telephone: 406-252-3441

Fax: 406-256-8526; 406-256-0277; 406-259-4159

Email: crowley@crowleylaw.com

Helena, Montana Office: 100 North Park Avenue, Suite 300, P.O. Box 797, 59624.
Telephone: 406-449-4165. Fax: 406-449-5149

Williston, North Dakota Office: 113 East Broadway, P.O. Box 1206, 58802-1206.
Telephone: 701-572-2200. Fax: 701-572-7072.

Kalispell, Montana Office: 431 First Avenue West, P.O. Box 759, 59903-0759.
Telephone: 406-752-6644. Fax: 406-752-5108.

Reviser Profile

Background: Crowley, Haughey, Hanson, Toole & Dietrich P.L.L.P., which originated in 1895, is the largest law firm in Montana and its adjoining states of Wyoming, Idaho, North Dakota, and South Dakota. Clients are served from offices in Billings, Helena, Kalispell and Williston, North Dakota. The firm's 60 practicing attorneys have an active presence in the state and Northern Rockies region, representing a wide range of clients including national and international corporations as well as local businesses, farmers, and ranchers.

Areas of Practice: Because of its size and expanded service area, the firm offers efficient and specialized legal expertise in nearly all areas of law, and provides each client with prompt, personalized service of the highest caliber. The firm is organized into three separate areas of specialization. Lawyers in the litigation section specialize in general civil litigation, products liability, insurance defense, personal injury, professional malpractice, employment litigation, energy litigation, environmental litigation, foreclosures, lender liability, bankruptcy, workers' compensation, labor, construction, condemnation, RICO, and bad faith. Lawyers in the natural resources section are specialists in the law of oil and gas, mining, water, public land, environmental and Indian law. Lawyers in the commercial and tax section specialize in banking, health care and hospital law, real estate, land use and zoning, agriculture, corporations and other business entities, corporate finance, employment law, immigration, intellectual property, public finance, regulated industries, employee benefits and pension planning, tax, and probate and estate planning. Ten lawyers who handle the full range of environmental law problems recently authored a text of Environmental Law in Montana. The professional competence of numerous members of the firm has been recognized by their election as Fellows of the American College of Trial Lawyers, American College of Real Estate Lawyers, the American College of Trust and Estate Counsel, and the American College of Tax Counsel.

The client base of the firm includes banks, savings and loan associations, life and casualty insurance companies, utilities, energy and mining companies, manufacturing companies, railroads, farmers and ranchers, health care organizations, charitable organizations, small businesses and individuals, and both national and international companies doing business in the region.

Community and Professional Service: In addition to its ongoing commitment to providing the highest caliber of legal services, the firm has a long-standing tradition of leadership in professional and community organizations; members of the firm are very active in community affairs and voluntarily serve on boards and special committees of numerous civic and charitable organizations and foundations. W. J. Jameson served as president of the American Bar Association in 1953, president of the American Judicature Society from 1956 to 1957, and as the United States District Judge for Montana for over 30 years. W. J. Jameson, Arthur F. Lamey, Sr., Cale Crowley, Bruce R. Toole, George C. Dalthorp and Sherry Scheel Matteucci have served as presidents of the Montana Bar Association. James M. Haughey and Norman Hanson have served as presidents of the Rocky Mountain Mineral Law Foundation, and other members of the firm have been on its board of trustees. James M. Haughey is a past member of the Board of Visitors of the School of Law of the University of Montana.

Lawyers are members of the American Bar Association, the State Bar of Montana, North Dakota, and Wyoming and various County Bar Associations. Members of the firm actively participate in the Rocky Mountain Mineral Law Foundation, American Academy of Hospital Attorneys, American Agricultural Law Association, National Association of Bond Counsel, National Academy of Elder Law Attorneys, American Immigration Lawyers Association, American Society for Pharmacy Law, International Association of Defense Counsel, Federation of Insurance Counsel, Defense Research Institute, Montana Association of Defense Counsel, Association of Trial Lawyers of America, Montana Trial Lawyers Association, Wyoming Trial Lawyers Association, American Board of Trial Advocates, American Judicature Society, and Fellows of the American Bar Foundation.

The firm has played an important part in the state. James M. Haughey served in the Montana Legislature for ten years, being senate minority leader two of those years. Jack Ramirez served in the Montana House of Representatives for about ten years and was house minority leader for two years. Arthur F. Lamey, Sr. was an alternate United States delegate to the United Nations.

Management: Crowley, Haughey, Hanson, Toole & Dietrich P.L.L.P. is managed by a three-member Executive Committee. In addition, each department is chaired by one lawyer, and a Law Practice Committee addresses ethical and professionalism concerns.

MONTANA LAW DIGEST

(The following is a list of all Categories and Topics, including cross-references, covered in this Digest.)

MONTANA LAW DIGEST

Revised for 1999 edition by

CROWLEY, HAUGHEY, HANSON, TOOLE & DIETRICH P.L.L.P. of the Billings, Helena and Kalispell Bars.

(Unless otherwise indicated, citations refer to sections of Montana Code Annotated. See category Courts and Legislature, topic Statutes herein. "M.R.Ev." indicates Montana Rules of Evidence. Parallel citations to the Pacific Reporter begin with 4 Mont.)

Note: This Revision covers all legislation approved by the Governor through August 1997.

INTRODUCTION

GOVERNMENT AND LEGAL SYSTEM:

The State of Montana is a constituent state of the United States of America. For further discussion of the U.S. federal system, see Introduction to the Federal Government of the United States at the beginning of this volume. A great many laws are promulgated by the federal government of the United States and are not reflected in the topics below. See the Introduction to this volume for references to the federal law topics covered.

Like all but one of the United States, Montana has a common law legal system, with roots in English common law. For information on the courts and legislature of Montana, see category Courts and Legislature.

HOLIDAYS:

Legal holidays are: Suns.; Jan. 1; Memorial Day (last Mon. in May); Independence Day (July 4); Labor Day (1st Mon. in Sept.); Columbus Day (2nd Mon. in Oct.); Veterans Day (Nov. 11); Thanksgiving Day (4th Thur. in Nov.); Christmas Day (Dec. 25); state general election day; President's Day (3d Mon. in Feb.); and Martin Luther King Day (3d Mon. in Jan.). If any of above dates except Sun. fall on Sun., holiday is next Mon. All other days are business days. (1-1-216).

Act Due on Holiday.—Where day appointed by law or contract for performance of secular act falls on holiday or Sat., performance on next business day sufficient. (1-1-307).

Legality of Act Performed on Holiday.—Act performed or contract made on holiday valid.

OFFICE HOURS AND TIME ZONE:

Montana is in the Mountain (GMT −07:00) time zone. Office hours are generally from 8 a.m. to 5 p.m.

BUSINESS ORGANIZATIONS

AGENCY:

In general, common law rules apply. (28-10-101 to 28-10-802). Agent is one who represents another, called principal, in dealings with third persons. That representation is called agency. (28-10-101).

No consideration is necessary to make authority binding upon principal (28-10-202), and oral authorization is sufficient except for authority to enter into contract required by law to be in writing can only be by instrument in writing (28-10-203).

Authority expressed in general terms, however broad, does not authorize agent to act in his own name unless in usual course of business, to define scope of his agency, or to do any act which trustee is forbidden to do by Title 72, c. 34. (28-10-407).

Authority to Sell.—Authority to sell personal property includes authority to warrant title of principal and quantity and quality of property. (28-10-421). Authority to sell and convey real property includes authority to give usual covenants of warranty. (28-10-422). General agent to sell, with possession, has authority to receive purchase price. (28-10-423). Special agent to sell has authority to receive price on delivery but not afterwards. (28-10-423).

ASSOCIATIONS:

Allows any individual, partnership, limited liability partnership, corporation or other association to use assumed business name and provides for registration of name. (30-13-201 et seq.).

Any cooperative stocks or nonprofit nonstock agricultural association formed after July 1, 1921, may own and operate two or more cooperative enterprises in different parts of state.

Actions.—When two or more persons, associated in any business, transact such business under a common name, whether it comprises the names of such persons or not, they may be sued by such common name, the summons being served upon one or more of them, and the judgment in such action binds the joint property of all the associates in the same manner as if they had all been named as defendants and sued upon a joint liability. (25-5-104).

Professional Associations.—See topic Corporations, subhead Professional Corporations.

CORPORATIONS:

Note: Revised Model Business Corporation Act (hereinafter cited as Revised Act), prepared by Committee on Corporate Laws (Section of Corporation, Banking and Business Law) of American Bar Association, has been adopted, with variations, effective Jan. 1, 1992, and is known and cited as "Montana Business Corporation Act" (hereinafter cited as Act). (35-1-112 to 35-1-1312). Except where otherwise indicated, all references are to sections of Act. For text of Revised Model Business Corporation Act as well as Official Comments and Reporter's Annotations, see Model Business

Corporation Act Annotated (3d ed. 1994), as supplemented through 1996. Law as digested below relates only to material variations of Montana Act from Revised Act. Following sections of Revised Act have not been adopted: §§1.22, 2.04, 14.20 through 14.23 and 15.10.

General Supervision.—Secretary of State, State Capitol, Helena, Montana 59601, (406)444-3665. §1.30 of Revised Act adopted. (35-1-1307).

Definitions.—§1.40 of Revised Act adopted. (35-1-113).

Purposes.—§3.01 of Revised Act adopted, with modification specifically excluding incorporation under Act for purpose of banking or insurance. (35-1-114).

Name.—§§4.01 through 4.03 of Revised Act adopted. (35-1-308 to 35-1-311). Act also provides that name must be distinguishable from corporate name of domestic corporation that has dissolved within last 120 days and from any assumed business name, limited partnership name, limited liability company name registered with Secretary of State. (35-1-308). Availability of name, which must be "distinguishable" from other names reserved or in use (35-1-308), obtainable from Secretary of State by either correspondence or unofficially by telephone, without charge.

Term of Corporate Existence.—§3.02 of Revised Act adopted. (35-1-115).

Incorporators.—§2.01 of Revised Act adopted. (35-1-215).

Articles of Incorporation.—§2.02 of Revised Act adopted. (35-1-216). Articles must set forth corporate name, number of authorized shares, street address (and, if different, mailing address) of initial registered office, name of initial registered agent and name and address of each incorporator. In addition to required provisions, articles may also set forth names and addresses of initial directors, and include provisions (1) not inconsistent with law regarding purposes, management of affairs, powers of shareholders and directors, par value and imposition of personal liability on shareholders, (2) required or permitted to be set forth in bylaws, and (3) limiting directors' personal liability to corporation. (35-1-216). Articles must be signed by incorporator and may, but need not, be acknowledged. (35-1-217).

Filing of Articles.—§1.20 of Revised Act adopted. (35-1-217).

License Fees.—In addition to prescribed filing fee, Secretary of State shall charge and collect following license fees on authorized shares: $50 for 0 to 50,000 shares; $100 for 50,000 to 100,000 shares; $250 for 100,000 to 250,000 shares; $400 for 250,000 to 500,000 shares; $600 for 500,000 to 1,000,000 shares; and $1,000 for over 1,000,000 shares. (35-1-1207).

Filing Fees.—§1.22 of Revised Act not adopted. Secretary of State shall establish fees for filing documents and issuing certificates; fees must be reasonably related to costs of processing and preparing and providing services. (35-1-1206).

License to Do Business.—§2.03 of Revised Act adopted. Corporate existence begins when articles of incorporation filed, unless delayed effective date is specified. (35-1-220).

Organization.—§2.05 of Revised Act adopted. Organizational meeting held at call of majority of incorporators or of initial directors, if named in articles. (35-1-222).

Paid in Capital Requirements.—No provisions with respect to amount to be paid in on incorporation or before commencing business.

Amendment of Articles.—§§10.01 to 10.09 of Revised Act adopted. (35-1-225 to 35-1-233).

Amendment of Bylaws.—§§10.20 to 10.22 of Revised Act adopted. (35-1-234, 35-1-238, 35-1-239).

Increase or Decrease of Authorized Capital Stock.—See supra, subhead Amendment of Articles.

Shares.—§6.01 of Revised Act adopted, except for addition of new subsection (e) (35-1-618[5]) as follows: "When authorized by its articles of incorporation to do so, a corporation may issue bonds, debentures or other obligations convertible into shares of any class, in the amounts and on such terms and conditions that may be provided by resolutions of the board of directors." §§6.02 and 6.03 of Revised Act adopted. (35-1-619, 620).

Preemptive Rights.—§6.30 of Revised Act adopted. Under §6.30, preemptive rights not available unless expressly granted in articles. (35-1-535).

Stock Certificates.—§§6.04, 6.25 and 6.26 of Revised Act adopted. (35-1-621, 35-1-626, 627). Uncertificated shares permitted. Signatures may be facsimiles. (35-1-626). Scrip or certificates may be issued for fractional shares; if scrip, no voting rights or participation in assets or dividends unless provided therein. Scrip convertible to full shares. (35-1-621).

Issuance of Shares.—§§6.20 through 6.24 and §6.28 of Revised Act adopted. (35-1-622 to 35-1-625, 35-1-629; 35-1-534).

Shares Acquired by Corporation.—§§6.03 and 6.31 of Revised Act adopted. (35-1-620, 630). §6.03 is intended when read with §6.31 to abolish concept of "treasury shares." (35-1-620, 630, 35-1-712).

Transfer of Shares.—Uniform Commercial Code adopted. (Tit. 30). See category Business Regulation and Commerce, topic Commercial Code. §6.27 of Revised Act adopted. Certain stock transfer restrictions enforceable if restrictions noted conspicuously on certificate, or if holder has actual knowledge of restrictions. (35-1-628).

See note at head of Digest as to 1998 legislation covered.

See Topical Index in front part of this volume.

CORPORATIONS . . . *continued*

Uniform Securities Ownership by Minors Act not adopted.

Uniform Simplification of Fiduciary Security Transfers Act adopted. (30-10-401 to 411). *Caveat:* This act is not among those specifically repealed by U.C.C., but U.C.C. 10-104(2), specifically negating such repealer, is not present in Montana act. (30-1-111).

Share Transfer Tax.—None.

Shareholders.—Revised Act generally adopted. See specific subheads herein. If authorized by articles or bylaws, directors can adopt resolution to allow stockholder to certify that he holds shares for account of specified person. This specified person is then treated as owner of record of those shares. (35-1-526).

Shareholder Agreements.—Shareholders may agree to opt out of certain state law provisions set forth in statute. Agreement must be set forth in articles of incorporation or bylaws, or in separate written agreement (signed by all shareholders at time of agreement) subject to amendment only by all shareholders at time of amendment, and valid for ten years unless otherwise provided. (35-1-820).

Shareholders' Actions.—§§7.40 through 7.47 of Revised Act adopted (Derivative Proceedings). (35-1-541 to 35-1-548). §§13.01 to 13.03, 13.20 to 13.28, and 13.30 and 13.31 of Revised Act adopted (Dissenters' Rights). (35-1-826 to 35-1-839).

Shareholders' Liabilities.—§6.22 of Revised Act adopted. (35-1-534).

Shareholders' Meetings.—§§7.01 to 7.07 of Revised Act adopted, except that subsection has been added to §§7.01 and 7.02 permitting corporations with 50 or fewer shareholders to allow participation in meetings by telephone if provided in bylaws. (35-1-516 to 35-1-522).

Shareholder Voting.—§§7.20 to 7.28 of Revised Act adopted with several modifications. (35-1-523 to 35-1-531). In §7.20(d), all language after "corporation's expense" has been deleted and in its place, "and may provide recovery to a shareholder for costs (including reasonable attorneys fees)" has been inserted. (35-1-523). §7.21 has been modified to provide that shares acquired by corporation pursuant to §35-1-630 are not entitled to vote as long as they are owned by corporation. (35-1-524). §7.28 revised to provide mandatory right to vote cumulatively in all elections for directors unless denied by statement to that effect in articles. (35-1-531).

Proxies expire in 11 months unless otherwise provided in proxy. Proxy is revocable by shareholder unless appointment form states otherwise and appointment is coupled with one of following interests: pledgee, purchaser of shares, creditor who extends credit on consideration of proxy, employee of corporation whose employment contract requires proxy, or party to voting agreement. Proxy not revoked by death or incompetence unless written notice of death or adjudicated incompetence received before authority exercised. Irrevocable proxy becomes revocable when interest with which it is coupled is extinguished. Irrevocable proxy is revocable by purchaser who buys without notice of proxy, unless noted on certificates. Subsection (i) added to §7.22 of Revised Act prohibits sale of vote or proxy, except as otherwise provided. (35-1-525).

Voting Trusts and Agreements.—§§7.30 and 7.31 of Revised Act adopted. (35-1-532, 533).

Directors.—§§8.01 to 8.11 of Revised Act adopted, except new §8.08(c) (35-1-424[3]) as follows: "Any director or the entire board of directors may be removed only by a vote of the holders of two-thirds of the shares entitled to vote at an election of directors unless otherwise provided by the articles of incorporation or bylaws. If the shareholders have the right to cumulate their votes when electing directors and if less than the entire board is to be removed, a director may not be removed if the votes cast against the director's removal would be sufficient to elect him if cumulatively voted at an election of the entire board of directors or, if there are classes of directors, at an election of the class of directors of which the director is a part. If the corporation has fewer than 100 shareholders, the entire board of directors may be removed only by a vote of a majority of the shares then entitled to vote." (35-1-416, 417 and 35-1-419 to 35-1-427). §8.30 of Revised Act adopted, which imposes on directors standard of good faith and ordinary care. Directors entitled to rely on reports and advice of officers, committees, counsel, accountants and other professionals reasonably believed to be competent. Director deemed not acting in good faith if he has knowledge that would cause such reliance to be unwarranted. No liability on director who meets standard. (35-1-418).

Directors' Meetings and Action.—§§8.20 to 8.25 of Revised Act adopted, except new §8.20(c) (35-1-431[3] as follows: "If requested by a director, minutes of any regular or special meeting must be prepared and be distributed to each director." (35-1-431 to 35-1-435, 35-1-439).

Liabilities of Directors.—§8.33 of Revised Act adopted. Liability for unlawful distributions. (35-1-713).

Conflicts of Interest.—§§8.60 to 8.63 of Revised Act adopted. (35-1-461 to 35-1-464).

Indemnification.—§§8.50 to 8.58 of Revised Act adopted. (35-1-451 to 35-1-459).

Officers.—§§8.40 to 8.44 of Revised Act adopted. (35-1-441 to 35-1-445).

Principal Office.—§§5.01 and 5.02 of Revised Act adopted. (35-1-313, 314).

Resident Agent.—§§5.01 through 5.03 of Revised Act adopted. (35-1-313 to 35-1-315).

Service of Process.—35-1-316, which is not derived from Revised Act, provides for service of process on domestic corporation by delivering copy of summons and complaint (1) to officer or director; (2) to registered agent; (3) if sheriff shall make return that no person upon whom service may be made can be found in county, then to person in charge of any office of corporation; or (4) if suit is against corporation whose charter or right to do business in Montana has expired or been forfeited, to any one of persons who have become trustees for corporation and its shareholders. (Rule 4D[2][e]). In case of voluntary dissolution, "trustees" for corporation and its shareholders are those persons so designated in filing made with Secretary of State, or if no filing, directors and officers listed in annual report most recently filed with Secretary of State. In case of involuntary dissolution, "trustees" are persons designated as receivers or trustees by court or directors and officers listed in annual report most recently filed with Secretary of State. (35-1-316).

General Powers of Corporations.—§43.02 of Revised Act enacted with modifications of subsection (13) allowing donations for religious and war activities. (35-1-115).

Distributions.—§6.40 of Revised Act adopted. No distributions in excess of amount that would render corporation insolvent or reduce assets below sum of liabilities and liquidation preferences. (35-1-712).

Unclaimed Dividends.—See category Property, topic Absentees, subhead Escheat.

Sale or Transfer of Corporate Assets.—§§12.01 and 12.02 of Revised Act adopted, except subsection (h) (35-1-823[8]) has been added to §12.02, allowing majority shareholder approval, instead of two-thirds approval, if provided in initial articles, or articles amended by two-thirds vote. (35-1-822, 823). See also subhead Dissolution, infra.

Books and Records.—§§16.01 to 16.04 of Revised Act adopted (35-1-1106 to 35-1-1109), except for following modifications of §16.01: Added "or a location from which the records may be recovered within two business days" after "principal office" in subsection (e); and subsection (e)(5) provides that corporation keep only copy of "the financial statements available to shareholders for the past three years under §16.02." (35-1-1106).

Reports.—§§16.21 and 16.22 of Revised Act adopted. (35-1-1104, 1111). §16.20 of Revised Act not adopted. Corporation must provide any shareholder with financial statements upon written request. (35-1-1110).

Notice.—§1.41 of Revised Act adopted. (35-1-116).

Corporate Bonds or Mortgages.—§3.02 of Revised Act generally adopted. (35-1-115). See also subhead Stock Certificates, supra.

Share Exchange.—§§11.01 to 11.07 of Revised Act adopted (35-1-813 to 35-1-819), except subsection (j) (35-1-815[10]) has been added to §11.03, allowing majority shareholder approval, instead of two-thirds approval, if provided in initial articles, or articles amended by two-thirds vote. (35-1-815).

Dissolution.—§§14.01 to 14.07 of Revised Act adopted (35-1-931 to 35-1-937), except subsection (f) has been added to §14.02, allowing majority shareholder approval, instead of two-thirds approval, if provided in initial articles, or articles amended by two-thirds vote. (35-1-932). §§14.30 to 14.33 of Revised Act adopted (35-1-938, 35-1-940 to 35-1-942). §14.30A added allowing court in action for dissolution to make such order to grant such relief, other than dissolution as in its discretion it deems appropriate, including, without limitation, order: (1) canceling or altering any provision contained in articles, or amendment of articles, or in bylaws; (2) canceling, altering, or enjoining any resolution or other act of corporation; (3) directing or prohibiting any act of corporation or of shareholders, directors, officers or other persons party to action; or (4) providing for purchase at fair value of shares of any shareholder, either by corporation or by other shareholders. (35-1-939). Such relief may be granted as alternative to decree of dissolution or may be granted whenever circumstances of case are such that relief, but not dissolution, would be appropriate. (35-1-939). §14.40 of Revised Act adopted. (35-1-943). Added §35-1-944, not derived from Revised Act, which prohibits filing or entry of decree of involuntary dissolution until after state tax clearance certificate issued by Department of Revenue has been filed with court or Secretary of State, as part of original instrument affecting dissolution. Involuntary dissolution is by order of Secretary of State for reasons stated in §87 of Model Act, plus failure to remit required fees. (35-6-101 to 203).

Insolvency and Receivers.—See subhead Dissolution, supra.

Appraisal.—See subhead Dissolution, supra.

Transition Provisions of Act.—§17.01 to 17.05 of Revised Act adopted. Effective date of Act is Jan. 1, 1992.

Assessment of Stock.—Generally assessment of stock not permitted, unless permitted by statute, except that water companies, water users associations, and irrigation, canal, ditch and reservoir companies may levy assessment if their articles so provide; Act sets forth detailed provisions as to time and amounts of levy if articles do not so prescribe.

Unauthorized Assumption of Corporation Powers.—§2.04 of Revised Act not adopted. In lieu thereof, Act provides that all persons who assume to act as corporation without authority to do so shall be jointly and severally liable for all debts and liabilities incurred. (35-1-119).

Foreign Corporations.—Revised Act generally adopted. See specific subheads in this topic.

Admission.—§15.01 of Revised Act adopted, except property described in subsection (b)(9) must neither produce income nor be used in performance of corporate function. (35-1-1026[2][i]).

Effect of Certificate of Authority.—§15.05 of Revised Act adopted. (35-1-1030).

Name.—§15.06 of Revised Act adopted. (35-1-1031).

Application for Certificate of Authority.—§15.03 of Revised Act adopted, with addition of subsection (1)(g), which requires statement of purposes of corporation which it proposes to pursue in transaction of business in Montana. (35-1-1028).

Amended Certificate of Authority.—15.04 of Revised Act adopted. (35-1-1029).

Registered Office and Registered Agent.—§§15.07 to 15.09 of Revised Act adopted. (35-1-1032, 1033, and 1036).

Service of Process on Foreign Corporations.—§15.10 of Revised Act not adopted. Act provides for such service in manner provided by Montana Rules of Civil Procedure. (35-1-1034). See category Civil Actions and Procedure, topic Process.

Withdrawal.—§15.20 of Revised Act adopted except: new subsection (2)(f) added requiring application to set forth that all state taxes are paid, to be supported by tax clearance certificate; and new subsection (2)(g) added requiring application to set forth additional information deemed necessary for determination and assessment of unpaid fees and taxes. (35-1-1037).

See note at head of Digest as to 1998 legislation covered.

See Topical Index in front part of this volume.

MT – 2

CORPORATIONS . . . *continued*

Revocation of Certificate of Authority.—§§15.30 to 15.32 of Revised Act adopted. (35-1-1038 to 35-1-1040).

Transacting Business Without Certificate of Authority.—§15.02 of Revised Act adopted. (35-1-1027).

Annual Report.—See subhead Reports, supra.

License Tax.—See subhead License Tax, infra.

License Fees.—Act specifies initial license fee of $100 at time of filing certificate of authority application. (35-1-1207).

Taxation of Corporate Property.—Generally, corporate property is subject to same property taxes as property of individual. See category Taxation, topic Property Taxes.

Corporate property is assessed in the county where located (15-8-402), but franchises are taxed in the county where the principal place of business is located. (15-8-403). Property centrally assessed shall be assessed by Department of Revenue. (15-23-101 et seq.).

License Tax.—Every corporation, as defined in §5-31-101, MCA, "engaged in business" or "doing business" in Montana must annually pay license fee for privilege of carrying on business in State. (15-31-101). License fee is computed on corporation's total net income for taxable period. (15-31-112). Net income is defined in §15-31-113. (15-31-113-119). Tax rate is 6³/₄% unless taxpayer is filing water's edge election and rate is 7%. (15-31-121). Minimum tax is $50. (15-31-121). Alternative tax is available in certain situations (15-31-122) as are certain credits (15-31-123-137, 15-31-151-162). Small business corporations as defined in 15-31-201 are not subject to license tax. (15-31-202). Corporation having business activity within and without state must allocate and apportion its net income. (15-31-301-313).

Exemption.—Certain organizations are exempt from license tax. (15-31-102). New research and development corporation exempted from corporate income taxes for its first five taxable years. (15-31-103).

Returns and Payment.—Calendar year corporation must file return and pay tax with Department of Revenue on or before May 15; fiscal year corporation must file return and pay tax on or before 15th day of fifth month following close of fiscal year. (15-31-111). Taxable year shall be same as for federal income tax purposes. Department of Revenue shall be promptly notified of any change in taxable year. (15-31-112).

Penalties.—Corporation which refuses or neglects to file a return, or files a false or fraudulent return, is subject to penalty up to $5,000, and may be denied right to continue business in state. (15-31-543). Delinquent corporate license tax assessed interest at 12%. (15-31-510). Officer or employee of any corporation who, without fraudulent intent, fails to make or sign any return or supply information is subject to penalty up to $100. (15-31-543).

Additional license taxes are imposed on specific industries. See category Taxation, topic License Taxes.

Alternate Tax.—See subhead Alternate Tax, infra.

Estimated Tax Payment.—Each corporation shall make estimated tax payments if annual estimated tax is $5,000 or more. (15-31-502). Payment schedule same as federal. Underpayment penalty is 20% per year. (15-31-510).

Income Tax.—Corporate income tax is imposed (15-31-401 to 408) on all corporations not subject to license tax discussed supra, upon net income derived from sources within Montana. Income from sources within Montana includes income from tangible or intangible property located in or having a situs in Montana and income from and activities carried on in Montana, regardless whether carried on in intrastate or interstate or foreign commerce, but does not include interest earned on certain secured loans held by out-of-state financial institutions. (15-31-403). Tax rate is same as imposed under license tax. Other license tax provisions incorporated by reference. (15-31-406). There shall be offset against income tax equal in amount to any license tax imposed against corporation during same period. (15-31-404).

Alternate tax of ¹/₂% of gross sales in lieu of other taxes for sales corporations not owning or renting realty or tangible personalty in Montana whose gross volume of sales does not exceed $100,000, pursuant to Art. IV, §16 and §17 of Multi-State Tax Compact. (15-31-122).

Limitation of Actions.—Action to enforce provisions of c. 31 of title 15 must be brought within five years. (15-31-509).

Facsimile filing with Secretary of State is permitted. Date of Corporations failing to pay license tax assessed penalty of 10% unless failure due to reasonable cause; filing is date of receipt of facsimile copy.

Small business corporations, which are corporations doing business in Montana that have made valid election under Subchapter S of Internal Revenue Code of 1986 and that have not revoked such federal election or had it terminated, may elect to have earnings taxed solely through personal income tax of stockholders; changes regarding Subchapter S Corporations contained in 1976 federal Tax Reform Act incorporated. (15-31-201 to 209).

Qualifying corporations may take investment credit equal to 5% of federal investment credit. (15-30-162 and 15-31-123).

Domestic International Sales Corporations (DISC).—Corporations electing to be treated as DISC under federal Internal Revenue Code are exempt from corporate license tax; shareholders are taxed in same manner as under federal law. (15-31-102).

Close Corporations.—Model Statutory Close Corporation Supplement (hereinafter cited as "Model Supplement"), prepared by Committee on Corporate Laws (Section of Corporation, Banking and Business Law) of American Bar Association, has been adopted, with variances, effective Oct. 1, 1987, and is known and cited as "Montana Close Corporation Act". (35-9-101 to 35-9-504). See 49 Mont. L. Rev. 66. Amendments of Model Supplement have been made where necessary for proper cross-reference of Model Supplement to Act.

Definition and Election.—§3 of Model Supplement generally adopted except that close corporation is limited to 25 or fewer shareholders. (35-9-103). Articles of incorporation must contain statement that corporation is statutory close corporation. (35-9-103).

Existing Corporations.—§3 of Model Supplement generally adopted except that close corporation is limited to 25 or fewer shareholders. Existing corporation must amend articles of incorporation to include statement that corporation is statutory close corporation. Amendment must be approved by holders of at least two-thirds of votes of each class or series of shares, voting as separate groups, whether or not entitled to vote on amendments. Shareholders who voted against amendment are entitled to assert dissenters rights pursuant to 35-1-826 to 35-1-839. (35-9-103).

Share Transfer Restrictions.—§§10 through 17 of Model Supplement adopted. (35-9-201 to 35-9-208). Statutory notice must appear on each share. (35-9-201). Share transfer restrictions include general prohibition on share transfers, subject to certain statutory exceptions, except to extent otherwise provided by articles of incorporation (35-9-202); corporate right of first refusal (35-9-203); and compulsory purchase of shares after death of shareholder (35-9-205).

Shareholder Agreements.—§20 of Model Supplement adopted. (35-9-301).

Board of Directors.—§21 of Model Supplement adopted. Close corporation may operate without board of directors if its articles of incorporation contain statement to that effect. (35-9-302).

Bylaws.—§22 of Model Supplement adopted. Close corporation need not adopt bylaws if provision required by law to be contained in bylaws are contained in either articles of incorporation or shareholder agreement. (35-9-303).

Annual Meeting.—§23 of Model Supplement adopted. (35-9-304).

Limited Liability.—§25 of Model Supplement adopted. Failure to observe usual corporate formalities or requirements relating to exercise of its corporate powers or management of its business and affairs is not ground for imposing personal liability on shareholders. (35-9-306).

Reorganization and Dissolution.—§§30 to 33 of Model Supplement adopted. (35-9-401 to 35-9-404).

Shareholder Protection.—§§40 to 43 of Model Supplement adopted. (35-9-501 to 35-9-504).

Limited Liability Companies.—See topic Limited Liability Companies.

Religious Corporations.—Montana Religious Corporation Sole Act (Tit. 35, c. 3) provides special corporate form for religious denominations, societies, or churches to hold or manage their estate, properties, temporalities and business. (35-3-201). Where no specific provision applies, provisions of Non-Profit Corporation Act apply. (35-3-102).

Professional Corporations.—Model Professional Corporation Act, prepared by American Bar Association, has been adopted, with variances, effective Oct. 1, 1983, and is known and cited as "Montana Professional Corporation Act." (Tit. 35, c. 4). Following sections of Model Act have not been adopted: §§21, 23(2), 24, and 25.

Nonprofit Corporations.—Revised Model Non-Profit Corporation Act (1987) has been adopted with variations, effective Jan. 1, 1992. (Tit. 35, c. 2).

JOINT STOCK COMPANIES:

Joint stock companies or Massachusetts trusts may be formed for any lawful purpose.

Taxation.—Such associations are taxed as corporations. (15-31-101).

Qualification to do business in state, in same manner as foreign corporation, required of foreign joint stock company.

Actions.—Any association may be sued in its common name, summons being served on one or more of the associates. (25-5-104).

Professional Associations (or Corporations).—See topic Corporations, subhead Professional Corporations.

LIMITED LIABILITY COMPANIES:

Montana Limited Liability Company Act, effective Oct. 1, 1993. (35-8-101—35-8-1307). General supervision is in Secretary of State.

Name.—Must contain words "limited liability company" "limited company" or abbreviations "L.L.C.","L.C.","LLC", or "LC". "Limited" may be abbreviated as "Ltd.", and "company" as "Co." (35-8-103[1]). Name must be distinguishable on records of Secretary of State from other limited liability companies, business corporations, nonprofit corporations, general partnerships, and limited partnerships. (35-8-103[2]). Reservation of name is effective for nonrenewable 120-day period and is made by filing with Secretary of State. (35-8-104).

Formation of limited liability company may be by one or more persons by signing and filing articles of organization with Secretary of State. (35-8-201).

Purposes.—May be formed for any lawful purpose, except for purposes of banking or insurance. (35-8-106).

Powers are enumerated in 35-8-107 and are as follows: (i) sue, be sued, complain, and defend in all courts; (ii) transact business, carry on operations, and have and exercise powers granted by this section; (iii) make contracts and guarantees, incur liabilities, and borrow money; (iv) sell, lease, exchange, transfer, convey, mortgage, pledge, and otherwise dispose of its assets; (v) acquire by purchase or any other manner, take, receive, own, hold, improve, or otherwise deal with any interest in real or personal property, wherever located; (vi) issue notes, bonds, and other obligations and secure them by mortgage, deed of trust, or security interest of its assets; (vii) purchase, take, receive, subscribe for, or otherwise acquire, own, hold, vote, use, employ, sell, mortgage, loan, pledge, or otherwise dispose of and use and deal with stock or other interests and obligations of corporations, associations, partnerships, limited liability companies, business trusts and individuals; (viii) invest surplus funds, lend money in any manner that may be appropriate to enable it to carry on operations or fulfill purposes set forth in its articles of organization, and take and hold real and personal property as security for payment of funds loaned or invested; (ix) elect or appoint agents and define their duties and fix their compensation; (x) sell, convey, mortgage, pledge, lease, exchange, transfer, or otherwise dispose of all or any part of its property or assets; (xi) be promoter, stockholder, partner, member, associate, or

See note at head of Digest as to 1998 legislation covered.

See Topical Index in front part of this volume.

LIMITED LIABILITY COMPANIES . . . *continued*

agent of any corporation, partnership, limited liability company, joint venture, trust, or other enterprise; (xii) indemnify and hold harmless any member, agent, or employee from and against any claims and demands whatsoever, except in case of action or failure to act by member, agent, or employee that constitutes willful conduct or recklessness, and subject to standards and restrictions, if any, set forth in articles of organization or operating agreement; (xiii) cease its activities and dissolve; (xiv) pay pensions and establish pension plans, pension trusts, profit sharing plans, share bonus plans, share option plans and benefit or incentive plans for any of its current or former directors, officers, employees, or agents; (xv) make donations for public welfare or for charitable, religious, scientific, or educational purposes; and (xvi) do every other act not inconsistent with law that is appropriate to promote and further business and affairs of limited liability company.

Content of articles of organization is prescribed by 35-8-202 and includes name; duration; address of principal place of business and registered agent; form of management and description; if management by members, names and addresses of initial members; if manager, then name and address of initial manager; if professional limited liability company, type of services offered; and other provisions members elect to set out. It is not necessary to set out in articles any powers enumerated in act under 35-8-107. (35-8-202[2]). Articles of organization may be amended by filing articles of amendment with Secretary of State. Articles of amendment must set forth name of LLC, date articles were filed, and amendments. (35-8-203).

Articles of Organization.—Original and one duplicate copy filed with Secretary of State. Filing must include appropriate filing fees. (35-8-205).

License Fee.—In addition to fees for filing, copying, and services as set by Secretary of State (35-8-211), license fee of $50 is due at time of filing articles of organization and upon application for certificate of authority to transact business in Montana (35-8-212).

Certificate of Authority.—Foreign limited liability companies may not transact business in Montana until certificate of authority is obtained from Secretary of State. (35-8-1001[1]). The following do not constitute transacting business: (I) maintaining, defending, or settling any proceedings; (II) holding meetings or other internal affairs activities; (III) maintaining bank accounts; (IV) maintaining offices or agencies for exchange or registration of company's own securities; (V) selling through independent contractors; (VI) soliciting or obtaining orders, whether by mail or through employees or agents or otherwise, if orders require acceptance outside Montana before they become contracts; (VII) creating or acquiring indebtedness, mortgages, and security interests in real or personal property; (VIII) securing or collecting debts or enforcing mortgages and security interests in property securing debts; (IX) owning real or personal property that is acquired incident to activities described in subsection VIII if property is disposed of within five years after date of acquisition, does not produce income, or is not used in performance of function of limited liability company; (X) conducting isolated transaction that is completed within 30 days and is not transaction in course of repeated transactions of similar nature; or (XI) transacting business in interstate commerce. (35-8-1001[2]).

Registered office and registered agent must be maintained in state. (35-8-105). Same may be changed by delivering notice to Secretary of State as prescribed in 35-8-105(3).

Annual report must be filed pursuant to 35-8-208. Report must be filed between Jan. 1 and Apr. 15. (35-8-208).

Contributions to capital of members of cash, property, services rendered, or promissory note or other obligation to contribute cash or property or to perform services. (35-8-501). Member liable to company for written promise to contribute. (35-8-502).

Profits, losses and distributions are shared equally, based upon proportion of each member's interest, unless otherwise expressed in articles of organization or operating agreement. (35-8-503 and 601). Each member must also be repaid that member's capital contribution. (35-8-503).

Assignment of Interest.—Except as provided in articles of organization or operating agreement, membership interests are assignable in whole or in part, assignee receives full transferred rights and assignment does not dissolve limited liability company. (35-8-704). Assignment in and of itself, does not allow assignee to participate in management and affairs of LLC or to exercise any rights of member. (35-8-704).

Liability.—Person is not liable solely by reason of being member or manager, or both, under judgment, decree or court order, or in any other manner, for debt, obligation, or liability of limited liability company, whether arising in contract, tort, or otherwise, or for acts or omissions of any other member, manager, agent, or employee of limited liability company. Failure of limited liability company to observe usual company formalities or requirements relating to exercise of its company powers or management of its business is not ground for imposing personal liability. (35-8-304).

Events of Disassociation.—Party ceases to be member upon one of following events: (I) member withdraws by voluntary act; (II) member transfers member's entire interest; (III) member is removed as member, pursuant to 38-8-802(c) or pursuant to articles of organization or operating agreement in accordance with 35-8-802(d). (35-8-802).

Dissolution.—Limited liability company is dissolved upon: (I) occurrence of events or duration of time specified in articles of organization or operating agreement; (II) written consent of all members; (III) disassociation of member, unless limited liability company is continued by consent of all remaining members within 90 days following occurrence of event or as otherwise provided in articles of organization or operating agreement; or (IV) decree of judicial dissolution. (35-8-901). Secretary of State may involuntarily administratively dissolve company pursuant to 35-8-209.

Facsimile filing with Secretary of State is permitted. Date of filing is date of receipt of facsimile copy.

LIMITED PARTNERSHIPS:

Revised Uniform Limited Partnership Act (1976) with 1985 Amendments generally adopted (35-12-501 to 1404), except:

Certificate.—Need not include latest date upon which limited partnership is to dissolve. (35-12-601). One original and one copy of certificate of limited partnership and certificates of amendment, restatement or cancellation must be delivered to Secretary of State. (35-12-606).

Term of Certification.—Certification of limited partnership effective for five years from date of filing or renewal of certification. Certification cancelled by Secretary of State if application for renewal not filed within 90 day period prior to expiration date of certification. (35-12-610).

Renewal of Certification.—Certification may be renewed for additional five year terms. (35-12-610). Application for renewal of certification follows same requirements as original certificate set forth in 35-12-601. (35-12-611).

Facsimile filing with Secretary of State is permitted. Date of filing is date of receipt of facsimile copy.

Withdrawal of Limited Partner.—If partnership agreement does not specify time or events on happening of which limited partner may withdraw, limited partner may not withdraw prior to time of dissolution and winding up of limited partnership. (35-12-1003).

PARTNERSHIPS:

Revised Uniform Partnership Act adopted. (35-10-101 to 644).

Name.—Partnership may use assumed business name. (30-13-201). May file application with Secretary of State, who reserves name for 120 days, unless name is deceptively similar to name already registered. (30-13-211 and 30-13-203). Must file application with Secretary of State, who registers name unless name is deceptively similar to name already registered. (30-13-202 and 30-13-203). Registration is effective for five years from date of registration; can be renewed for additional five year terms upon application. (30-13-206). Filing Fees: Reservation $10, Registration $15, and Renewal $15.

Limited Liability Partnership.—Partnerships permitted to register with Secretary of State to become limited liability partnerships. (35-10-701 to 35-10-710).

Facsimile filing with Secretary of State is permitted. Date of filing is date of receipt of facsimile copy.

BUSINESS REGULATION AND COMMERCE

BANKS AND BANKING:

Regulated by 32-1-101 to 921. Uniform Commercial Code adopted. (Tit. 30). See topic Commercial Code.

Supervision.—Department of Commerce is statutorily required to exercise constant supervision over books and affairs of all banks doing business within state. Further, Department of Commerce is required to examine, at least once every 24 months, each bank or trust company and verify assets and liabilities as well as investigate character and value of assets to ascertain with reasonable certainty that values are correctly carried on books. Authorized examination by regulatory or insuring agency of U.S. may be accepted as examination of bank. (32-1-211).

Stockholders' Liability.—Stockholders of bank that is member of federal deposit insurance corporation are not liable for debts of bank. (32-1-552).

Deposits.—Uniform Commercial Code adopted. (Tit. 30). See topic Commercial Code.

Unclaimed Deposits.—Uniform Unclaimed Property Act adopted. Bank accounts are presumed abandoned after five years of no activity. (72-14-302). See category Property, topic Absentees, subhead Escheat.

Statements to depositors are not required by statute. There is no time limitation on actions brought to recover money or other property deposited except: Any action to question or set aside any stated or settled account must be brought within five years, and any action arising out of payment of forged or altered checks or note must be brought within three years from date of notification to depositor of payment or received check or note marked "paid". (27-2-213).

Lien of bank is a general one, dependent on possession, on all property in its hands for balance due from bank's customer in course of business. (71-3-1502).

Collections.—Uniform Commercial Code adopted. (Tit. 30). See topic Commercial Code.

Bad Checks.—See topic Bills and Notes.

Loans to a person, corporation or partnership, including loans to partnership and to members of partnership, may not exceed 20% of unimpaired capital and surplus. This limitation does not apply to certain loans, obligations or extensions of credit secured by obligations of U.S. having current market value of 100% of amount loaned; or secured or covered by guaranties, or by commitments or agreements to take over or to purchase them made by federal reserve bank or by U.S., certain political subdivisions of U.S., and other enumerated entities of U.S., exclusive of certain secured or guaranteed loans. In addition, limitation is not applicable to loans between banks when term of loan does not exceed two business days, loan is secured by pledged deposits in lending bank, or when loan is covered by guarantee or by commitments or agreements to take over or purchase loan made by agency or board of state of Montana authorized by law to provide such guarantees, commitments or agreements. (32-1-432).

Interest.—See topic Interest.

Private banks other than foreign capital depositories, are subject to Bank Act. (32-1-102).

See note at head of Digest as to 1998 legislation covered.

See Topical Index in front part of this volume.

BANKS AND BANKING . . . *continued*

Tax.—National and state banks are subject to corporation license tax. Foreign capital depository chartered under Montana law is not subject to corporation license tax until Oct. 1, 2012. (15-31-101). See category Business Organizations, topic Corporations, subhead License Tax.

Trust companies may be formed to receive money, perform trust duties, act as trustee and transfer property and buy and sell certain investments. (32-1-107).

Branch Banks.—Bank may establish and maintain branch bank at any place in Montana, with prior approval of Department of Commerce. Branch banks may, but are not required to, offer all services offered by bank. (32-1-372).

Consolidation.—Any two or more banks doing business within state may, with approval of Department of Commerce, consolidate or merge into one bank. Before consolidation becomes effective, it must be approved by shareholders of each merging bank by vote of not less than two-thirds of outstanding shares of each class of voting stock entitled to vote on merger proposal at meeting called to consider merger, as directed by Title 35, c. 1. (32-1-371).

Uniform Common Trust Fund Act adopted. (32-1-701 to 706). Montana Addition to §1 of Act. Bank or trust company qualified to act as fiduciary in this state, which is not member of federal reserve system, shall, in operation of common trust fund, comply with rules adopted by department of business regulation, and department may adopt rules it considers necessary and proper in premises.

Subsidiary trust companies permitted if affiliated with commercial bank. (32-1-801 to 808).

BILLS AND NOTES:

Uniform Commercial Code adopted. (Tit. 30). See topic Commercial Code.

Special Requirements.—There are no special requirements as to recitals in notes of particular kinds or based on particular considerations.

Judgment notes are not recognized. Provisions in contracts allowing another party to enter judgment by confession, or provisions in contracts appointing agent to confess judgment, accept service of process, or consent to entry of default are illegal and void. (28-2-709).

Attorney fee clauses are enforceable. (11 Mont. 285, 28 Pac. 291; 30 Mont. 111, 75 Pac. 953). Also, for contracts entered into after July 1, 1971, where one party has express right to recover attorney fees in event he prevails in action on contract, all parties thereto shall be deemed to have same right, and any party prevailing can recover his attorney fees from losing party. (28-3-704).

Bad Checks-Civil Remedy.—Payee may bring civil action against issuer of check dishonored for lack of funds or because issuer has no account with drawer. Payee must, however, make written demand for payment at least ten days before suit. Damages awarded must be amount equal to service charge (not greater than $30) plus greater of $100 or three times amount of check, but in no case may damages exceed value of check by more than $500. (27-1-717).

BILLS OF LADING:

See topic Carriers.

BILLS OF SALE:

See topic Sales.

BLUE SKY LAW:

See topic Securities.

BROKERS:

Uniform Commercial Code adopted. (Tit. 30). See topic Commercial Code.

Real Estate Brokers.—Regulated by 37-51-102 to 401. License required. (37-51-301).

BULK SALES:

Art. 6 of Uniform Commercial Code repealed.

CARRIERS:

Uniform Commercial Code adopted. (Tit. 30). See topic Commercial Code.

Public Service Commission has power to supervise and regulate carriers in so far as they are subject to state law. (69-1-102).

Duties.—Carrier of persons for pay must use utmost care and diligence and must exercise reasonable degree of skill. Carrier of property for pay must at least use ordinary care and diligence in performance of all his duties. Carrier of messages for pay must use greater care and diligence. (69-11-107). Carrier in sense is employee of both consignor and consignee, and as such he must comply with their directions. When these directions conflict, carrier must comply with those of consignor, except as to delivery of freight, as to which he must comply with directions of consignee, unless consignor has forbidden carrier to receive any directions from consignee not in accordance with his own. (69-11-402).

Delivery of Goods.—The carrier must deliver the property to the consignee as addressed in accordance with custom of place. If there is no usage to contrary, it must be delivered, in case of railway, at station nearest place to which it is addressed. In case of water carrier it may be delivered at wharf or suitable landing within reasonable distance of place to which it is addressed. In other cases it must be delivered to consignee or agent, personally, if either, after due diligence, can be found. If carrier is unable to make personal delivery of freight, he must give due notice to consignee, and keep same in safety, upon his responsibility as warehouseman until consignee has had reasonable time to remove it. If then it is not removed, carrier may relieve himself from responsibility by placing property in suitable place and notifying consignee. (69-11-404, 405).

Consignee is liable for freightage if he accepts the property with notice from consignor that consignee is to pay it. (69-11-406).

Limiting Liability.—Generally, the obligations of a carrier can be limited by special contract, but liability for gross negligence, fraud or wilful wrong cannot be limited (69-11-105) nor can it limit its liability for delay resulting from negligence (28 Mont. 297, 72 Pac. 642).

Bills of Lading.—Uniform Commercial Code governs. (Tit. 30). See topic Commercial Code.

Liens.—Uniform Commercial Code governs. (Tit. 30). See topic Commercial Code. Liens also exist on passenger's baggage for fare. (69-11-206).

Motor Vehicle Carriers.—See category Transportation, topic Motor Vehicles.

COMMERCIAL CODE:

Uniform Commercial Code adopted. (Tit. 30). Section numbers of Montana Code correspond with those of 1962 Official Text, except that prefix "30" is added. Thus 3-501 of 1962 Official Text corresponds with 30-3-501 of Montana Act.

Filing and Certification.—Montana Secretary of State announces following policy on fees, requests for certificates of information and copies:

Presentation for Filing.—Instruments must be properly completed, executed, and accompanied by precise fee. Noncomplying instruments will be returned with fee and notice of defect. Multiple instruments covered by single check for all fees will be returned if any one defective. No instrument or fee will be held in suspense file. No overpayment will be returned.

Filing fees are $7 per financing statement. Continuations and amendments are $5. No fee for termination.

Certificates of Information.—Each request for certificate of information on record must concern a specifically identified debtor, request summary of all effective financing and assignment statements on file as of a specific date and hour, and be accompanied by precise fee. Certificate of information on record will show all instruments on file, name and address of each secured party, and filing date and hour for each instrument. (9-407).

Copies.—Request for copies must identify filed instruments required. Fee is 50¢ per page. (9-407). Because precise fee cannot be predetermined, Secretary of State will accept blank check to be completed not in excess of stated amount with a request for copies or will bill in advance of furnishing copies. No UCC record information furnished by telephone.

Secretary of State may treat facsimile copy of document and signatures in same manner as original. If all other requirements are met, date of filing relates back to date of receipt of facsimile copy.

Variations appear in the following sections (Tit. 30 omitted before section numbers):

1-101—adds subsection (2) defining "code" as "Uniform Commercial Code".

1-105—adds "Letters of Credit," deletes "Bulk Transfers" from subsection (2).

1-110—adds Section 1-110, "Provision for transition."

1-111—adds Section 1-111, "Laws not repealed."

2-207(2)—adds words "or different" after word "additional".

2-316—Livestock exempt from implied warranties. No implied warranty that agricultural seed is disease free.

2-328—omitted. Codified as 11-502.

2-403(1)(d)—Substitutes "theft" for "larcenous".

2-403(3)—Substitutes "has been such as to constitute theft" for "have been such as to be larcenous".

2-702—1966 Official Amendment has been enacted.

2-711(2)(b)—substitutes "recover the goods" for "replevy the goods."

2-716(3)—substitutes "a right to maintain an action for the recovery of goods" for "a right of replevin for goods."

2A-103(1)(e)—inserts "$25,000."

2A-216—adopts Alternative A.

2A-507—in subsection (1), substitutes "at the time of the default" for "at the times specified in Sections 2A-519 and 2A-528."

Art. 6—Repealed 1991.

7-204—omits subsection 4.

7-209—1966 Official Amendment not enacted.

9-103—Montana did not adopt changes which conform this Section with Revised Art. 5; Montana did adopt 1994 Amendments to this Section.

9-104—adds subsection (13) excluding liquor in agency liquor store and (14) excluding letters of credit from Art. 9.

9-105—adopts 1995 amendments which conform Section to Revised Art. 5.

9-106—adopts 1995 amendments which conform Section to Revised Art. 5.

9-115—enacted in 1997.

9-116—enacted in 1997.

9-203—refers to unrepealed acts applying to same subject, to wit:

Title 32, Chapter 5 (Consumer Loans).

Title 31, Chapter 1, Part 2 (Retail Installment Sales).

Sections 81-8-301 to 305 (Relating to notices of security agreements, renewals, assignments and satisfactions covering livestock).

Title 61, Chapter 3 (Registration of Motor Vehicles).

Title 31, Chapter 1, Part 4 (Pawnbrokers and Junk Dealers).

Title 16, Chapters 1 through 6 (Alcohol).

9-401(1)—excepts financing statements filed under 9-409 from its provisions; centralized filing system for farm products, equipment, accounts and other intangibles to office of Secretary of State.

9-401(3) provides: "A filing which is made in the proper place in this state continues effective even though the debtor's residence or place of business or the location of

See note at head of Digest as to 1998 legislation covered.

See Topical Index in front part of this volume.

COMMERCIAL CODE . . . *continued*

the collateral or its use, whichever controlled the original filing, is thereafter changed."

9-402(2)—sets forth acceptable form for financing statements.

9-403(1)—Secretary of State may accept fax copy only if followed by original within five days.

9-403(2)—for insolvency, security interest remains perfected for 60 days after insolvency proceedings or end of five year period, whichever later.

9-403(3)—allows filing officer to remove statement from file after lapse if record is retained on microfilm or other photographic record.

9-403(5)—refers to subsection (12).

9-403(8)—provides for centralized and computerized filing system for farm products, etc.

9-403(11)—repealed.

9-403(12)—renumbered subsection (11).

9-403(13)—renumbered subsection (12); allows Secretary of State to set fees.

9-405(2)—First sentence excepts 9-409(2) from its provisions.

9-406—First sentence excepts 9-409(2) from its provisions.

9-407(2)—requires filing officer to disclose, upon request, information about individual debtors including financing statements and collateral. Imposes fee of 50¢/page for copies of financing statement.

9-407(3)—imposes fee for computer printout of specific debtor information.

9-407(4)—former subsection (4) repealed. New subsection (4) imposes obligation to ensure that centralized filing system conforms to federal law.

9-409 and 410 added, effective Feb. 26, 1965. Provides that place of filing financing statements of "transmitting utility" covering personal property or fixtures is in office of Secretary of State (9-409[1]); that if financing statement covers goods of transmitting utility which are or are to become fixtures, no real estate description required (9-409[2]); and that security interest in rolling stock of transmitting utility may be perfected either by filing with Secretary of State or as provided in §20(c) of Interstate Commerce Act (9-409[3]). Transmitting utility defined in 9-105(n).

9-411—added 1963. Requires filing officer to retain statements for eight years or lapse of original statement, whichever later.

9-412—added 1983. Allows consignor or lessor to file financing statements.

9-421—added 1985. Allows Secretary of State to adopt rules concerning agricultural lien filing.

9-423—added 1985. Liens on branded livestock must be filed with Department of Livestock; subsection 9-403 does not limit Department of Livestock's authority.

9-431—added 1989. Secretary of State may treat fax as original; imposes treble damages on those who file false document by fax.

9-432—added 1993. Filing officer may reject or remove improper or fraudulent liens; imposes treble damages on those who file improper or fraudulent lien.

9-504(3) and 9-505(2)—Notification of debtor with respect to sale of collateral is reasonable if sent by certified mail to debtor's most recent address.

9-511—added 1962. Attorney fees allowed in all foreclosure actions, notwithstanding agreements to contrary.

Article 11 not enacted. 1-110 is transition provision: transactions validly entered into before Jan. 1, 1965 remain valid. 1-111 adds that chapter on Documents of Title does not modify laws prescribing form or contents of documents of title or services or facilities to be afforded by bailees; but violation of such laws does not affect status of document of title otherwise complying with 1-201; and that "References to a 'branch' or 'separate office' of a bank" are not to be construed as amending banking laws relative to operation of branches or separate offices and that "This act does not repeal or modify" 30-11-504 (relating to auctioneer's memorandum of sale); 69-14-216 (claims against carriers for damage to livestock); or Title 18, c. 1, Part 4 (contract actions against state). See Title 30, c. 5 for 1997 comprehensive revisions concerning letters of credit. See Title 30, c. 8 for 1997 comprehensive revisions concerning investment securities.

In addition, the following options in the 1962 Official Text and Permanent Editorial Board's 1966 Recommendations for Optional Amendment have been exercised:

1-209—1966 Official Optional Amendment enacted.

2-318—1966 Official Optional Amendment not enacted.

4-106—optional language omitted.

4-202(1)(b)—optional clause adopted.

4-212—optional subsection (2) adopted.

5-112(1)—optional clause omitted (repealed 1997).

5-114—optional subsections (4) and (5) omitted (repealed 1997).

7-204—subsection (4) omitted.

7-403—optional clause omitted.

9-401—second alternative subsection (1) adopted.

9-401—alternative subsection (3) not adopted. See above for variation.

9-407—optional section adopted.

Blanks filled in 1962 Official Text:

9-401(1)(a)—"county clerk and recorder" inserted in each blank.

9-401(1)(c)—provides for filing in office of Secretary of State.

1972 Official Amendments.—Adopted in 1983, as follows:

1-105

1-201

2-107

5-116 (repealed 1997)

9-102 through 9-106

9-114

9-203 through 9-205

9-301

9-302—refers to Title 61, Chapter 3 (motor vehicle registration); Title 23, Chapter 2, parts 5 and 6 (boats and snowmobiles).

9-304—Paragraphs (1), (4) and (5) add "certified securities" to text.

9-305—Excludes "certificated securities".

9-306

9-308

9-312

9-313

9-318

9-401 through 9-407

9-501

9-502

9-504

9-505

1973 Official Amendments.—Adopted 1973.

1977 Official Amendments.—Adopted 1983, as follows:

1-201

5-114 (repealed 1997)

8-102 through 8-108 (repealed 1997)

8-201 through 8-208 (repealed 1997)

8-301 through 8-321 (repealed 1997)

8-401 through 8-408 (repealed 1997)

9-105

9-309

1990 Revised Article 3.—Adopted 1991, with variations to following Sections:

3-102

3-103

3-104

3-105

3-106

3-108

3-110

3-118

3-201

3-204

3-206

3-207

3-303

3-307

3-309

3-310

3-311

3-312—omitted.

3-404

3-405

3-406

3-407

3-412

3-413

3-414

3-415

3-416

3-417

3-418

3-419

3-420

3-501

3-502

3-504

3-603

3-605

1990 Amended Article 4.—Adopted 1991, with variations to following Sections:

4-102

4-104

4-106

4-110

4-202

4-205

4-209

4-212

4-215

4-216

4-301

4-302

4-303

4-401

4-403

4-406

Article 4A.—Adopted 1991, with variations to following Sections:

4A-205

4A-403

1995 Revised Article 5.—Adopted 1991, with variations to following Sections:

5-131

5-135

5-136

1994 Revised Article 8.—Adopted 1997, with variations to following Section:

8-603—omitted.

1994 Amendments to Article 9.—Art. 9 amended to conform to Revised Art. 8.

1995 Amendments to Article 9.—Art. 9 amended to conform to Revised Art. 5.

See note at head of Digest as to 1998 legislation covered.

See Topical Index in front part of this volume.

COMMERCIAL CODE . . . continued

Financing Statement.—See category Mortgages, topic Chattel Mortgages.

Leases.—Covered by Uniform Commercial Code—Leases. Parties are limited on ability to choose applicable law in consumer lease transactions. If jurisdiction chosen is different than where lessee resides at time lease agreement becomes enforceable or within 30 days thereafter, choice is void. (30-2A-106). Lease contract is not enforceable unless total payments are less than $1,000 or lease is in writing, signed by party against whom enforcement is sought or by that party's authorized agent, sufficient to show lease has been made, term, and goods leased. (30-2A-201). Agreement modifying lease needs no consideration to be binding. (30-2A-208). Express warranties may be created by lease. Such warranties extend to any natural person who is in family or household of lessee or who is guest in lessee's home, if it is reasonable to expect that such person may use, consume, or be affected by goods and who is injured by breach of warranty. (30-2A-216). Except in case of finance lease, risk of loss is retained by lessor. (30-2A-219). Perfected interest of lessor of fixtures has priority over conflicting interest of encumbrancer or owner of real estate if lease is purchase money lease and fixture filing is made within ten days or interest of lessor is perfected before interest of encumbrancer. (30-2A-309). Action for default under lease contract must be commenced within four years after cause of action accrued. (30-2A-506).

See also topics: Banks and Banking, Bills and Notes, Brokers, Carriers, Contracts, Factors, Frauds, Statute of, Sales, Securities, Warehousemen; categories Business Organizations, topic Corporations; Civil Actions and Procedure, topic Limitation of Actions; Debtor and Creditor, topics Assignments, Fraudulent Sales and Conveyances, Liens, Pledges; Documents and Records, topics Records, Seals; Mortgages, topic Chattel Mortgages; Transportation, topic Motor Vehicles.

CONDITIONAL SALES:

See topic Sales.

CONSIGNMENTS:

See topics Commercial Code, Factors.

CONSUMER PROTECTION:

See topics Interest, Sales.

Product Safety.—Comprehensive legislation designed to prevent sale or transfer of hazardous substances, including children's toys or articles. (50-30-101 to 50-30-307). Department of Public Health and Human Services charged with enforcement. Introduction or delivery for introduction of any misbranded or banned hazardous substance, or alteration or mutilation of any label on hazardous substance is prohibited. (50-30-301).

Montana Unfair Trade Practices and Consumer Protection Act of 1973 proscribes unfair methods of competition and unfair or deceptive acts or practices in conduct of any trade or commerce. (30-14-101 to 30-14-225).

Cooling-off period of three days provided buyer in commercial transaction of more than $25 occurring at residence of buyer and not: (1) Pursuant to preexisting revolving charge account, (2) pursuant to prior negotiations by buyer at place of business of seller, or (3) in which buyer may cancel under federal law. Seller must provide a return-addressed cancellation form. In event seller fails to return purchase price, buyer has right of action for price plus $100 penalty plus attorney's fees. Buyer has lien on goods. Buyer must tender goods in substantially same condition. (30-14-501 to 30-14-508).

Consumer reporting agencies defined as those who, for fee, assemble or evaluate credit information on consumers for reporting to third persons, are regulated by 31-3-101 to 31-3-153.

"Unsolicited goods" statute adopted. (70-3-104).

Plain Language.—Minimum language simplification standards are specified for insurance policies. (33-15-325). Consumer contracts must be written in language with common everyday meanings, appropriately divided and captioned, with readable type size using ink which contrasts with paper. These requirements do not apply to consumer contracts for value exceeding $50,000, consumer contracts for securities or commodities, insurance policy contracts, and when government agency is acting as seller, lessor or lendor. (30-14-1101 to 1113).

Motor Vehicle Warranty Remedy.—Consumer who notified manufacturer or its agent during warranty period that new motor vehicle does not conform to express warranties may expect warrantor to be liable for repairs or expenses of repairs regardless of expiration of warranty period after notification by consumer. (61-4-502). Arbitration procedure provided by Department of Commerce for consumer and manufacturer to resolve disputes over warranties. (61-4-515).

CONTRACTS:

Uniform Commercial Code adopted. (Tit. 30). See topic Commercial Code; categories Documents and Records, topic Seals; Family, topic Infants.

Good Faith and Fair Dealing.—Conduct required by implied covenant of good faith and fair dealing is honesty in fact and observance of reasonable commercial standards of fair dealing in trade. (28-1-211; but see 791 P.2d 767.)

FACTORS:

Uniform Commercial Code adopted. (Tit. 30). See topic Commercial Code and 30-11-601 through 607.

License Requirements.—None.

Liens.—Factor's lien is among security devices governed by Uniform Commercial Code. (30-9-102). Factor has general lien which is dependent upon possession, for all that is due him, upon articles of commercial value that are entrusted to him by same principal. (71-3-1501).

Consignment Agreements.—Uniform Commercial Code does not apply to consignments of fine art. (22-2-505).

FRANCHISES:

Montana has not adopted Uniform Franchise and Business Opportunities Act and has no special legislation addressing franchises. Farm Implement Dealership Agreements receive special protection (30-11-801 through 811) as do Alcoholic Beverage Distributors (16-3-201 through 244) and Motor Vehicle Dealers (61-4-101 through 61-4-141).

See topic Monopolies, Restraint of Trade and Competition.

FRAUDS, STATUTE OF:

Uniform Commercial Code adopted. (Tit. 30). See topic Commercial Code.

Following contracts are invalid unless same, or note or memorandum thereof, are in writing subscribed by party to be charged, or his agent: agreements not to be performed within a year; to answer for debt, default or miscarriage of another; in consideration of marriage, except mutual promise to marry, agreement authorizing or employing real estate agent or broker to purchase real estate for compensation or commission. (28-2-903).

Land.—Sale or lease for more than one year, of any interest therein, and, if subscribed by agent, latter's authority must be in writing. Also agreement authorizing agent or broker to buy or sell realty on commission. (28-2-903).

Contracts of Sale.—Governed by Uniform Commercial Code.

Part Performance.—Uniform Commercial Code adopted. See 30-2-201. Equitable doctrine of part performance to take case out of statute of frauds is recognized as to contracts for sale of real estate. (119 Mont. 45, 169 P.2d 722).

INTEREST:

Legal rate is generally 10%. (31-1-106).

Maximum rate permitted by written contract: Not to exceed greater of 15% or amount that is more than six percentage points per annum above prime rate of major New York banks as published in Wall Street Journal edition dated three business days prior to execution of agreement. (31-1-107).

Exemption.—Regulated lenders are exempt from all limitations on rate of interest and from operation of all usury statutes. (31-1-111, 112).

Judgments.—Interest rate 10% per annum. Interest on judgment involving contractual obligation that specifies interest rate must be paid at that rate. (25-9-205).

Open Accounts.—Unless otherwise agreed, interest runs from time of demand and, if none, from time suit begun. (29 Mont. 139, 74 P. 201).

Damages.—Interest is allowed on ascertained damages from date right to recover such damages accrued, unless law or act of creditor prevents payment. (27-1-211).

Computation of Time.—Interest for period less than one year is based upon 365 days equalling one year. (31-1-106[2]).

Small Loans.—Persons or corporations making small loans must be licensed under Consumer Loan Act. (32-5-101 to -506). Interest charges must be added to principal and not discounted. (32-5-301). Holder of supplementary license may make open-end loans. (32-5-501).

Usury.—Penalty for usury is forfeiture of double amount of interest received, reserved or charged. Where usurious interest paid, penalty may be recovered by payor, his heirs, executors, administrators or assigns by action brought within two years after payment. Written demand for return of interest paid a condition precedent to action. (31-1-108).

See also topic Sales.

LICENSES, BUSINESS AND PROFESSIONAL:

State licenses varying in amount are required of nearly every business and profession carried on or practiced in the state. City councils are authorized to license all industries, pursuits, professions and occupations (7-21-4101) but this power may be exercised only in aid of police regulations and to pay the cost of special police protection or supervision, and not for purpose of raising revenue (38 Mont. 369, 99 P. 1059). Lapsed professional or occupational license that is not renewed within three years of most recent renewal date automatically terminates. (37-1-141).

Itinerant Vendors.—A $15 annual license (7-21-2303) is required of every itinerant vendor retailing goods for future delivery to consumers, door to door, but license requirement does not apply to any vendor with commercial rating and permanent place of business in state. (7-21-2302).

License Taxes.—See category Taxation, topic License Taxes.

Collection Agencies.—No legislation.

MONOPOLIES, RESTRAINT OF TRADE AND COMPETITION:

Unfair trade practices including restraint of trade and unfair competition are unlawful. Department of Commerce enforces Montana Unfair Trade Practices and Consumer Protection Act. (30-14-101, et seq.). Certain practices in motion picture industry, such as blind bidding and payment of minimum guarantees on percentage pictures, are prohibited (30-14-301 to -308). Uniform Trade Secrets Act enacted. (30-14-401, et seq.).

Resale Price Agreements.—See category Intellectual Property, topic Trademarks and Tradenames.

NEGOTIABLE INSTRUMENTS:

See topic Bills and Notes.

RESTRAINT OF TRADE:

See topic Monopolies, Restraint of Trade and Competition.

See note at head of Digest as to 1998 legislation covered.

See Topical Index in front part of this volume.

SALES:

Uniform Commercial Code adopted. (Tit. 30). See topic Commercial Code.

Contracts of Sale.—Uniform Commercial Code governs. There is no statutory limitation of type size except as to retail installment contracts. (31-1-231). See infra, subhead Retail Installment Sales.

Consumer Protection.—See topic Consumer Protection.

Products Liability.—Uniform Commercial Code adopted. (Tit. 30). See topic Commercial Code. Restatement (2nd) Torts 402A substantially adopted by statute. (27-1-719 [1987]). Strict liability adopted by case law prior to 1987.

Sales of Motor Vehicles.—See category Transportation, topic Motor Vehicles.

Bulk Sales.—See topic Commercial Code.

Retail Installment Sales.—All contracts where buyer promises to pay sale price of goods or services in one or more deferred installments must be in writing and are governed by 31-1-201 to -243.

Contracts must contain specified information including notice to buyer of his rights, cash sale price, down payment, difference between sale price and down payment, amount included for insurance and official fees, principal balance, finance charge, time balance, number of installments and amount and due date of each. (31-1-231). Printed portions of contract, except instructions for completion, must be at least 8 point type and certain portions must be at least 10 point bold type, unless transaction is subject to federal Truth-In-Lending Act and seller complies with requirements of that law.

Blanks.—Contracts must not be signed which contain blank spaces to be filled in later, except for identification and due date of first installment of goods not yet delivered. (31-1-231).

Refund of insurance premium must be credited to final installment except to extent applied toward payment for similar insurance protecting interests of buyer and holder. (31-1-233).

Transfer of equity fee of not over $50 may be charged by holder if buyer transfers equity. (31-1-234).

Delinquency charge allowed plus attorney's fees, court costs, and actual expenses. Delinquency charge may not exceed $10. (31-1-235).

Finance charge shall be at rate agreed upon by retail seller and buyer. (31-1-241).

Prepayment by buyer entitles him to refund credit. (31-1-242).

Refinancing permitted. (31-1-243).

Satisfaction.—Upon payment in full and written demand by buyer, seller must acknowledge payment and release all security in goods. (31-1-236).

Licensing of Sales Finance Companies.—Persons in business of purchasing retail installment contracts must obtain license from Department of Commerce. Fee is $100 per place of business per year. (31-1-221).

Conditional Sales.—Uniform Commercial Code adopted. (Tit. 30). See topic Commercial Code.

SECURITIES:

The "Securities Act of Montana," 30-10-101 to 30-10-323, is substantial adoption of major provisions of Uniform Securities Act, but numerous changes have been made.

Uniform Commercial Code adopted. (Tit. 30). See topic Commercial Code.

Supervision.—State Auditor is Securities Commissioner, who supervises and controls administration of Act. (30-10-107). Commissioner's office is Room 270, Sam W. Mitchell Building, 126 North Sanders, Helena, Montana 59620.

Regulating Powers of Supervising Authority.—License is required for sale of securities. (30-10-201).

Prerequisites to Sales or Offerings.—All securities offered for sale must be registered under the Act, except exempt securities or securities sold in exempt transactions. (30-10-202).

Securities to Which Act Applicable.—"Securities" include notes, stocks, treasury stocks, bonds, commodity investment contracts, commodity options, debentures, evidences of indebtedness, certificates of interest or participation in any profit-sharing agreement, collateral-trust certificates, preorganization certificates or subscriptions, transferable shares, investment contracts, voting-trust certificates, certificates of deposit for security, certificates of interest or participation in oil, gas or mining titles or leases or in production payments, and in general, any interest or instrument commonly known as "security", any put, call, straddle, option, or privilege on any security, certificate of deposit, or group or index of securities, including any interest in security or based on value of security, or any certificate of interest in, temporary or interim certificate for, receipts for, guarantee of, and warrant or right to subscribe to or purchase any of foregoing. "Security" does not include any insurance or endowment policy or annuity contract under which insurance company promises to pay fixed sum of money either in lump sum or periodically for life or some other specified period. (30-10-103[22]). Definition of "security" under Montana law is identical to definition of "security" under federal law. (State v. Duncan, 181 Mont. 382, 593 P.2d 1026, 1031).

Exempt Securities.—The following are exempt from operation of Act: Securities issued or guaranteed by United States, any state or political subdivision thereof, except if security is payable solely from payments received in respect of property or money used under lease, sale or loan arrangement by or for non-governmental industrial or commercial enterprise, unless enterprise or security is within exceptions in statute; securities issued or guaranteed by Canada, any Canadian province or political subdivision thereof, or by any agency or corporate or other instrumentality of one or more of foregoing, or by any other foreign government with which U.S. maintains diplomatic relations if security is recognized as valid obligation by issuer or guarantor; securities issued by and representing interest in or debt of, or guaranteed by, any bank organized under federal law, or any bank, savings institution, or trust company organized under and regulated by laws of any state; securities issued by and representing interest in or debt of federal savings and loan associations or building and loan or similar associations organized under laws of any state and authorized to do business in this state; securities issued or guaranteed by federal or other credit unions, industrial loan or similar associations, organized and supervised under Montana laws; with certain limitations, securities issued or guaranteed by railroads and other common carriers, public utilities and holding companies; equipment trust certificates of equipment conditionally sold or leased to railroads or public utilities if other securities issued by them would be exempt; any security that meets all of following conditions: foreign issuer that has agent in U.S. for service of process, class of issuer's securities has been registered under §12 of Securities Act of 1934 for at least three years prior to issue, issuer has not defaulted in certain payments for seven years, consolidated net income of at least $1,000,000 in four of last five years, security to be issued (unless preferred) has voting rights, security to be issued (unless preferred) must have been owned within six months prior to offering by at least 1,200 persons, and there must be at least 750,000 shares outstanding with aggregate market value of at least $3,750,000; securities issued by organizations operated not for private profit and exclusively for religious, educational, benevolent, charitable, fraternal, social, athletic, or reformatory purposes ($50 fee and notification required); commercial paper arising from current transactions evidencing obligation to pay cash within nine months of date of issuance, renewals thereof likewise limited, or guarantees thereof, when such paper is sold to banks or insurance companies; investment contracts issued in connection with employee's stock purchase, savings, pension, profit sharing, or similar benefit plan; any security for which Commissioner determines by order that exemption would better serve purposes of 30-10-102 than would registration ($50 fee may be required); any security listed or approved for listing upon notice of issuance on New York, American, Pacific, Midwest, Philadelphia or Boston Stock Exchanges, Chicago board of options exchange, or any other stock exchange registered with Federal Securities and Exchange Commission and approved by Commissioner; any national market system security listed or approved for listing upon notice of issuance on national association of securities dealers automated quotation system or any other national quotation system approved by Commissioner; and any security issued by and representing interest in or debt of or guaranteed by any insurer organized and authorized to transact business under laws of any state. (30-10-104).

Exempt Transactions.—The following transactions are exempt from operation of Securities Act: any non-issuer isolated transaction; non-issuer distributions of outstanding securities by registered broker-dealer if certain conditions are fulfilled; non-issuer transaction through registered broker-dealer pursuant to unsolicited order or offer to buy; transaction between issuers and underwriters or between underwriters; transaction by executors, administrators, sheriffs, marshals, receivers, trustees in bankruptcy, guardians or conservators in performance of their official duties; transaction executed by bona fide pledgee without intention to evade Act; offer or sale to banks, savings institutions, trust companies, insurance companies, investment companies as defined in Investment Company Act of 1940, pension or profit-sharing trusts or other financial institution or institutional buyer or to broker-dealers; transaction pursuant to offers made in state to not more than ten persons in Montana during 12 consecutive months if seller reasonably believes buyers are purchasing for investment and no solicitation commission is paid; offer or sale of preorganization certificates or subscriptions if no commission for solicitation is paid, there are not over 25 subscribers, and no payments are made by any subscribers; transaction pursuant to offer to existing security holders of issuer if no commission for solicitation is paid, or if issuer files notice of terms of offer and Commissioner does not disallow; offer of security for which registration statements have been filed under Act and federal Securities Act of 1933 if no stop orders are pending or in effect; issuance of stock dividends if nothing of value is given by stockholders except surrender of right to cash dividend; transaction incident to right of conversion or statutory or judicially approved reclassification, recapitalization, reorganization, quasi-reorganization, stock split, reverse stock split, merger, consolidation or sale of assets; any transaction in compliance with such rules as Commissioner in his discretion may adopt to serve purposes of 30-10-102; transaction in securities of certified Montana capital company or certified Montana small business investment capital company, sale of commodity investment contract traded on commodities exchange recognized by Commissioner at time of sale; transaction within exclusive jurisdiction of commodities future trading commission as granted under Commodity Exchange Act; transaction involving purchase of precious metals which requires within seven days of payment physical delivery of precious metal to purchaser or depository as defined in statute; transaction involving commodity investment contract solely between persons engaged in producing, processing, using commercially, or handling as merchants each commodity subject to contract or any by-product of commodity; any offer or sale of security to employee of issuer, pursuant to stock ownership plan qualified under §401 of Internal Revenue Code of 1986; and, under certain circumstances, offer or sale of securities by cooperative association. Commissioner may in his discretion require that 30-10-201 through 30-10-207 apply to any or all transactional exemptions adopted by rule. (30-10-105).

Registration of Securities.—All securities must be registered either by notification, coordination or qualification, unless they are federal covered securities. (30-10-202). See 30-10-203, -204, -205 and -206 as to conditions and requirements under each method. Federal covered securities are securities that are covered under §18(b) of federal Securities Act of 1933.

Brokers and Agents.—All broker-dealers, salespersons, investment advisers and investment adviser representatives must be registered (except for exempt transactions). Registration is accomplished by application to Commissioner on forms prescribed by Commissioner and payment of prescribed fee. Registration must be renewed each Dec. 31 and is subject to revocation if in public interest or upon grounds specified in statute. Hearing will be granted upon request after denial or revocation of registration. (30-10-201). Unlawful for broker to employ any salesman who is not registered. (30-10-201[2]). Suspension or revocation of registration of any broker-dealer, salesman or investment advisor may result in fine of not more than $5,000. Appeal may be taken from imposition of fine. (30-10-201[18]).

Liabilities.—Criminal liability is imposed for violation of Act with maximum penalties of not more than $5,000 and imprisonment for not more than ten years, with mandatory imprisonment of not less than one year for persons previously convicted of

See note at head of Digest as to 1998 legislation covered.

See Topical Index in front part of this volume.

MT – 8

SECURITIES ... *continued*

felony involving securities. (30-10-306). Civil liability is imposed upon any person who offers or sells security in violation of Act or by means of fraud or misrepresentation, for repayment of consideration paid plus interest, costs and reasonable attorney's fee less amount of any income received on security, or for damages if purchaser no longer owns security. (30-10-307). Act limits damages in private actions to difference between purchase or sale price received by plaintiff for security and mean trading price of security during 90-day period beginning on date on which information connecting misstatement or omission is disseminated to public. However, if plaintiff sells or repurchases security before 90-day period (referenced above), plaintiff's damages may not exceed difference between purchase or sale price received by plaintiff for security and mean trading price during period beginning immediately after dissemination of information correcting misstatement or omission and ending on date on which plaintiff sells or repurchases security. (30-10-318). Act also provides "safe harbor" for forward looking statements under certain statutory criteria. (30-10-319).

Uniform Act for the Simplification of Fiduciary Security Transfers adopted. (30-10-401 to -411). *Caveat:* This act is not among those specifically repealed by U.C.C., but U.C.C. 10-104(2), specifically negating such repealer, is not present in Montana act. (30-1-111).

Uniform Securities Ownership by Minors Act not adopted.

STATUTE OF FRAUDS:

See topic Frauds, Statute of.

WAREHOUSEMEN:

Uniform Commercial Code adopted. (Tit. 30). See topic Commercial Code.
Agricultural Warehouse, Commodity Dealer, and Grain Standards Act enacted. (Tit. 80, c. 4).

CITIZENSHIP

ALIENS:

Every person within the jurisdiction of the state is entitled to its protection. (49-1-201). Rights of aliens are limited, however, in following respects:

Inheritance.—No person is disqualified to take as heir because he or person through whom he claims is or has been alien. (72-2-121). In estate where property does not vest in alien because of 72-2-121, personal representative must file report with attorney general within 30 days of filing inventory stating name, address and proportionate share of alien and value of estate. (72-2-215). (This provision is currently inconsistent with amended version of 72-2-121.)

Public Office and Suffrage.—Aliens cannot hold elective or appointive offices (Const. IV, 4) or vote (Const. IV, 2).

CIVIL ACTIONS AND PROCEDURE

ACCORD AND SATISFACTION:

Accord is an agreement to accept in extinction of obligation something different from or less than that to which person agreeing to accept is entitled. (28-1-1401). Though parties to accord are bound to execute it, original obligation is not extinguished until accord is fully executed. (28-1-1401).

See also category Business Regulation and Commerce, topic Commercial Code.

Satisfaction is acceptance by creditor of consideration of accord which extinguishes obligation. (28-1-1402).

Part performance of an obligation, either before or after breach, when expressly accepted in writing in satisfaction, extinguishes obligation. (28-1-1403).

Pleading.—Accord and satisfaction is affirmative defense that must be affirmatively pleaded. (Rule 8[c]).

ACTIONS:

Governed by Montana Rules of Civil Procedure patterned after Federal Rules of Civil Procedure. See topic Practice.

Equity.—No separate equity jurisdiction exists. (Mont. Constitution Art. VII, §§1-5). However, traditional equitable grounds must be shown for equitable relief.

Forms of Action.—There is only one form of action known as "Civil Action." (Rule 2).

Commencement.—See topics Process, Pleading.

Conditions Precedent.—Any individual, partnership, corporation or other association conducting or transacting business under assumed or fictitious name must register assumed name to maintain suit or action in courts of Montana. (30-13-215). Foreign corporation must be authorized to do business in state before it may maintain proceeding in any Montana court. (35-1-1027[1]).

Parties.—Actions are to be prosecuted in name of real party in interest, except that personal representative, guardian, bailee, trustee of express trust, party with whom or in whose name contract has been made for benefit of another, or party authorized by statute may sue in that person's own name without joining party for whose benefit action is brought. (Rule 17). Rule 17(b) differs from Federal Rule 17(b). Mont. R. Civ. P. 17(b) provides only that capacity to sue or be sued must be determined by appropriate statute.

Class Actions.—Uniform Class Actions Act not adopted. One or more members can sue or be sued if joinder impractical, common questions of law or fact exist, claims or defenses typical and members will fairly and adequately protect interests of class. (Rule 23). Rule 23(f) allows judge to require security for costs and charges which may

be awarded against representative party. Undertaking to be executed by two or more persons.

Necessary Joinder.—Person subject to service of process must be joined if (1) his presence necessary for complete relief for existing parties; or (2) he claims interest in subject of action and absence may impair his ability to protect interest or may expose existing parties to double, multiple, or inconsistent obligations. (Rule 19[a]). Rule 19(a) differs from Federal Rule 19(a) in that there is no provision precluding joinder if joinder will deprive court of jurisdiction over subject matter. Provision made for class actions. (Rule 23).

Permissive Joinder.—All persons asserting any right to relief arising out of same transaction or occurrence may join as plaintiffs, and all persons against whom any such right is asserted may be joined as defendants, if, in either case some question of law or fact common to all of them will arise in the action. (Rule 20[a]).

Intervention may be had as a matter of right upon timely application when (1) statute unconditionally permits; or (2) applicant claims interest in property or transaction which is subject of action and his interest may be impaired by action, unless applicant's interest is adequately represented by existing parties. (Rule 24[a]).

Permissive intervention may be had when a statute confers a conditional right to intervene, or when applicant's claim or defense and main action have question of law or fact in common. (Rule 24[b]).

Interpleader.—Persons having claims against plaintiff may be joined as defendants and required to interplead when plaintiff may be exposed to double or multiple liability. Defendants exposed to similar liability may obtain interpleader by cross-claim or counter-claim. (Rule 22).

Joinder of Claims.—Party may join as many claims, whether legal, equitable, or both, as he may have against opposing party. (Rule 18). Rule 18(b) adds to Federal Rule 18(b) that rule not applied to permit joinder of liability or indemnity insurance carrier, unless carrier is by law or contract directly liable to person injured or damaged.

Consolidation of Actions.—Actions involving common question of fact or law pending before court may be heard jointly in whole or in part, or they may be consolidated. (Rule 42[a]).

Severance of Actions.—Court may order separate trial of any claim or of any separate issue. (Rule 42[b]). Rule 42(b) does not refer to right to jury trial as Federal Rule 42(b) does.

Abatement and Revival.—Action, cause of action or defense does not abate by death or disability of party. (27-1-501). Where party dies while action by or against him is pending, and cause of action survives, court may order substitution of proper parties upon motion by deceased's successors or representatives. (Rule 25[a]). Rule 25(a) provides for reasonable time for substitution rather than 90 days of Federal Rule 25(a).

Limitation of.—See topic Limitation of Actions.

Small Claims.—See category Courts and Legislature, topic Courts.

Termination of Actions.—Plaintiff may dismiss action without order of court by filing notice of dismissal before adverse party serves answer or motion for summary judgment, or by filing stipulation of dismissal signed by all parties who have appeared. Such dismissal is without prejudice unless otherwise stated. (Rule 41[a]). Defendant may move for dismissal for failure to prosecute, failure to comply with the Montana Rules of Civil Procedure, or failure to comply with order of court. Such dismissal is adjudication upon merits unless otherwise specified by court. (Rule 41[b]). Upon motion of any interested party or court itself, action must be dismissed as to defendant if appearance not made within three years after commencement of action, or if summons not issued within one year, or if summons issued within one year is not served and return made and filed with clerk within three years. (Rule 41[e]). In Rule 41(a) dismissal is always without prejudice, no exception as in Federal Rule 41(a).

Tort actions against state are permitted in district court on any tort claim against governmental entity arising out of governmental or proprietary function of governmental entity or employees acting within scope of their employment except that state is not liable for damages suffered by person confined in correctional facility for criminal offense as result of employee's negligence. (2-9-101 to 2-9-318). Immunity from suit if acting in official duty: for legislative acts and omissions (2-9-111); judicial acts, and omissions (2-9-112); gubernatorial actions concerning legislation (2-9-113); local governmental entity and elected executive officer immune from suit for damages for lawful discharge of duties. Montana Constitution Art. II, §18 provides that state and all sub-entities shall have no immunity from suit for injury to person or property unless provided by statute passed by ⅔ vote of legislature. Tort claims against state first must be presented to department of administration and denied prior to filing in district court. Statute of limitations on claim is tolled 120 days. (2-9-301).

Administration.—See category Estates and Trusts, topic Executors and Administrators.

Direct Actions Against Insurer.—See category Transportation, topic Motor Vehicles, subhead Direct Action.

See also topic Damages.

APPEAL AND ERROR:

From Small Claims Court.—As of July 1, 1997, small claims court procedure in district court must conform to small claim's court procedure in justice court. Title 25, c. 34 governing small claims court in district court has been repealed and small claims courts in both district court and justice court are governed by Title 25, c. 35. Appeal from small claims division of district court or justice court may be taken to district court of county in which judgment was rendered. (25-35-803). Any such appeal is tried de novo. Appeals from small claims division of justice court are governed by 25-35-803. Trial is not de novo; appeal is limited to questions of law. (25-35-803[2]). Notice of Appeal must be filed within ten days of entry of judgment. (25-35-803).

APPEAL AND ERROR . . . *continued*

From Justice or City Court.—Appeal from justice or city court in civil action may be taken to district court within 30 days from date of judgment by filing notice of appeal with justice or judge and serving copy on adverse party or his attorney. (25-33-102). Appeal not permitted from judgment by default except on questions of law or abuse of discretion in setting aside or refusing to set aside judgment. (25-33-303). In all cases action is tried de novo in district court. (25-33-301). State may only appeal in cases provided for in 46-20-103. (46-17-311).

From District Court.—Appeals in civil cases to Supreme Court from district court and original proceedings in Supreme Court are governed by Montana Rules of Appellate Procedure (cited M.R.App.P.), effective Jan. 1, 1966, which are generally patterned after the Mar. 1964, Preliminary Draft of Proposed Uniform Rules of Federal Appellate Practice of Committee on Rules of Practice and Procedure of Judicial Conference of U.S. Appeal from district court to Supreme Court may be taken in following cases: (1) From final judgment in action commenced in district court, or brought into district court from another court or administrative body; (2) from following orders: granting new trial; refusing to permit action to be maintained as class action; granting or dissolving injunction; refusing to grant or dissolve injunction; dissolving or refusing to dissolve attachment; changing or refusing to change place of trial when county designated in complaint is not proper county; appointing or refusing to appoint receiver, or giving directions with respect to receivership, or refusing to vacate order appointing or affecting receiver; directing delivery, transfer, or surrender of property; from any special order made after final judgment; and from such interlocutory judgments or orders in actions for partition as determine rights and interests of respective parties and direct partition to be made; (3) from judgment or order granting or refusing to grant, revoking or refusing to revoke, letters testamentary, or of administration, or of guardianship; or admitting or refusing to admit will to probate, or against or in favor of validity of will, or revoking or refusing to revoke probate thereof; or against or in favor of setting apart property, or making allowance for widow or child; or against or in favor of directing partition, sale, or conveyance of real property, or settling account of executor, or administrator, or guardian; or refusing, allowing, directing distribution or partition of any estate, or any part thereof, or payment of debt, claim, legacy, or distributive share; or confirming or refusing to confirm report of appraiser setting apart homestead. (M.R.App.P. 1).

Time for Filing Notice of Appeal.—From small claims division of justice court, within ten days after entry of judgment. (25-35-803[1]). From justice or city court or small claims division of district court, within 30 days after rendition of judgment. (25-33-102). From district court, within 30 days from entry of default judgment or order, and 30 days from service of notice of entry of judgment. (M.R.App.P. 5[a][1]).

Time is 60 days where State of Montana or officer, agency or political subdivision thereof is party. (M.R.App.P. 5). If notice of entry of judgment is required under Mont. R. Civ. P. 77(d), time period does not begin to run until service of notice of entry of judgment. (Id.).

An appeal is taken from district court by filing notice of appeal in district court, which notice must specify party or parties appealing and shall designate judgment or order appealed from. (M.R.App.P. 4[a], [c]). Clerk of district court serves notice of filing of notice of appeal by mailing copy to each party or their counsel of record, and to clerk of Supreme Court. (M.R.App.P. 4). For appeals to district courts from lower courts, see 25-33-101 to 104 and 25-35-803.

Appeal bond or other security in amount it deems sufficient may be required by district court. (M.R.App.P. 6).

Upon appeal from justice court when judgment is for payment of money, undertaking on appeal may be in form of appeal bond or deposit of money bond in amount of judgment, including costs. (M. Justice Courts R.Civ.P. 24).

Stay of Proceedings.—Upon entry of judgment or order, party may apply to district court for stay of execution of judgment or order, which may be granted by court in its discretion. Upon service of notice of appeal, party may secure court's approval of supersedeas bond, which bond shall be conditioned for satisfaction of judgment or order in full, together with costs, interest and damages for delay. No stay permitted upon judgment or order which adjudges defendant guilty of usurping, intruding into, or unlawfully holding public office. No stay can be granted in mandamus or prohibition against tribunal, corporation, public officer, or board commanding certain acts to be done by such entities not requiring payment of money. (M.R.App.P. 7). Upon filing of judgment or order of Workers' Compensation Judge, party may apply to Workers' Compensation Judge, upon notice or ex parte, for stay of execution of judgment or order. Stay of execution may not extend for more than 30 days following Judge's disposition of post-trial motions.

Stay of execution on property in justice or city court may issue upon filing of undertaking or deposit. (25-33-204).

Extent of Review.—Supreme Court may, on appeal from judgment, review verdict or decision or any intermediate order excepted to, involving merits or necessarily affecting judgment, except order from which appeal might have been taken. (M.R.App.P. 2). On questions of fact, jury's verdict (32 Mont. 137, 79 Pac. 690) or trial court's findings (83 Mont. 214, 271 Pac. 433) are conclusive if supported by substantial evidence.

Judgment or Order on Appeal.—Supreme Court may affirm, reverse, or modify any judgment or order appealed from, and may direct proper judgment or order to be entered, or direct new trial or further proceedings to be had. (3-2-204).

Appeal by State.—In criminal cases, state may only appeal from judgment that results in: (a) dismissing case; (b) modifying or changing verdict; (c) granting new trial; (d) quashing arrest or search warrant; (e) suppressing evidence; (f) suppressing confession or admission; (g) granting or denying change of venue; or (h) imposing sentence that is contrary to law. (46-20-103).

BONDS:

All official bonds must be signed and executed by principal and two or more sureties or by principal and one or more surety companies. (2-9-504).

Enforcement.—Any official bond may be sued on by any person injured or aggrieved by any wrongful act of the principal. (2-9-527).

Sureties.—In all cases where a bond or an undertaking is required by law, the officer taking it must require the sureties to accompany it with an affidavit that they are residents and householders or freeholders within the state, and are each worth the sum specified in the undertaking, over and above all their just debts and liabilities, exclusive of property exempt from execution; but when the amount specified in the undertaking exceeds $3,000, and there are more than two sureties thereon, they may state in their affidavits that they are severally worth amounts less than that expressed in the undertaking, if the whole amount be equivalent to that of two sufficient sureties. (33-26-102).

Surety companies qualified to do business in state may furnish bonds, and need not justify. (33-26-101, 102).

CERTIORARI:

The writ of certiorari may be denominated a writ of review. (27-25-101).

Jurisdiction and Grounds.—Writ may be granted by Supreme Court and any justice of Supreme Court, in proceedings for contempt in district court. It may also be granted by Supreme Court or district court, or any judge thereof, when lower tribunal, board or officer has exceeded its jurisdiction, and there is no appeal or other adequate remedy. (27-25-102).

Proceedings.—Application must be made on affidavit. Court may grant writ with or without notice. (27-25-201).

Extent of Review.—Review upon this writ is limited to whether inferior tribunal, board or officer has regularly pursued its or his authority. (27-25-303).

CHARITABLE IMMUNITY:

See topic Damages.

COMMISSIONS TO TAKE TESTIMONY:

See topic Depositions and Discovery.

COSTS:

In certain actions costs and disbursements are allowed to the prevailing party as a matter of course, while in other actions costs may be allowed or not, and if allowed, may be apportioned between parties in discretion of court. No costs can be allowed in action for recovery of money or damages when plaintiff fails to recover more than $50, or in action to recover possession of personal property, when value of property is not more than $50. (25-10-101 to 25-10-103). Costs are allowed to plaintiff if plaintiff qualifies for award of attorney fees in actions for property damage arising out of ownership, use, or maintenance of motor vehicle, without regard to dollar limits. (25-10-101).

Costs are also in discretion of court when new trial is ordered or judgment is modified, and when application is made for postponement of trial. On appeal, costs are discretionary when new trial ordered or judgment is modified. In all other cases, successful party on appeal recovers costs. (25-10-104).

In an action prosecuted or defended by an executor, administrator or trustee, or any party authorized by statute, costs are chargeable only against the estate, fund or party represented, though they may become a personal charge as result of mismanagement or bad faith. (25-10-108).

Court has discretion to order party who unreasonably multiplies proceedings to personally satisfy costs, expenses and attorneys' fees incurred because of that conduct. (37-61-421).

New Action After Voluntary Dismissal.—Where plaintiff who has voluntarily dismissed action commences another action based on or including same claim, against same defendant, court may make order for payment of costs of previous action, and may stay pending action until order for payment is satisfied. (Mont.R.Civ.P. 41d).

Security for Costs.—When plaintiff resides out of state, security for costs may be required by an undertaking not exceeding $300. (25-10-601). In justice court, justice of peace may require security before issuing summons. (25-31-402).

Prepayment.—Each party, except governmental entity to civil action or poor persons as defined in 25-10-404, is required to pay fees fixed by law for performance of any service by officer, and no officer is bound to perform any service or duty unless fees are first paid or tendered, except when action is brought in forma pauperis. (25-10-403 to 25-10-405).

DAMAGES:

Common law generally prevails. Rules are set forth in 27-1-101 et seq. See also topic Pleading, subhead Complaint; category Estates and Trusts, topic Death, subhead Action for Death.

Comparative Negligence Rule adopted. (27-1-702). Joint tortfeasors are jointly and severally liable for any amount that may be awarded to claimant but each has right to contribution from any other person whose negligence may have contributed as proximate cause to injury complained of. (27-1-703). However, any party whose negligence is determined to be 50% or less of combined negligence of all joined as parties is severally liable only and is liable only for percentage of negligence attributable to him unless party acted in concert with others. (27-1-703). In any action based on negligence, defendant may assert as defense that damages of claimant were caused in full or in part by person with whom claimant has settled or who claimant has released from liability. (27-1-703). Defendant who alleges that person released by claimant or with whom claimant has settled is at fault in matter has burden of proving: (i) negligence of such person; (ii) any standard of applicable care to such person; and (iii) that negligence of person was contributing cause under applicable law to matter. (27-1-703). Defendant alleging that settled or released person is at fault in matter shall affirmatively plead settlement or release as defense in answer. (27-1-203). Defendant who gains actual knowledge of settled or released person after filing of answer may plead

DAMAGES ... *continued*

defense of settlement or release with reasonable promptness. (27-1-203). If defendant alleges that settled or released person is at fault in matter, defendant shall notify each such person. (27-1-203).

Doctrine of charitable immunity not abrogated by statute. However, federal district court imposed tort liability. (DC Mont., 193 F. Supp. 191).

Doctrine of interspousal tort immunity abrogated by case law.

Doctrine of sovereign immunity has been abolished by constitutional provision that state and local government entities shall have no immunity from suit for injury to a person or property for causes of action arising after July 1, 1973 unless specifically provided for by law. (Const. Art. II, §18). See topic Actions.

Voluntary payments to or on behalf of one sustaining injury to person or property by or on behalf of alleged tortfeasor shall not be construed as admission of fault or liability as to any claim arising out of occurrence, or as release or waiver of claim, and shall not be construed to reduce amount of damage pleaded or proved in any action arising out of occurrence. Upon final settlement parties are free to treat all voluntary partial payments as they may. In event of judgment greater than such payments, amounts shall be deductible as partial satisfaction of judgment. In event judgment is less than such payments, there shall be no right of action for recovery of excess paid. (26-1-703 et seq.).

Jury awards may be reduced for amounts paid or payable from collateral source. (27-1-308).

Emotional or mental distress damages prohibited in contract cases except in those cases involving physical injury to plaintiff. (27-1-310).

No-Fault Insurance.—See category Transportation, topic Motor Vehicles, subhead No-Fault Insurance.

Uniform Contribution Among Tortfeasors Act (Revised) not adopted.

DECLARATORY JUDGMENTS:

Uniform Act Adopted. (27-8-101 et seq.).

DEPOSITIONS AND DISCOVERY:

Federal Rules of Civil Procedure form basis for Montana Rules of Civil Procedure. See topic Practice.

Uniform Foreign Depositions Act not adopted.

Within State for Use Within State.—After service of process on any defendant, testimony of any person, whether party or not, may be taken by deposition (Rule 30a) before person authorized by laws of Montana to administer oaths (Rule 28a), on oral examination (Rule 30a) or written interrogatories (Rule 31a), for purpose of discovery, for use as evidence in action or for both purposes (Rule 32a). Regarding depositions taken outside state for use within, see subheads Outside of State for Use Within State; and Before Whom Taken, infra.

Within State for Use Elsewhere.—When deposition of person is to be taken in this state for use elsewhere, district court of county where witness is to be served, upon proof that notice of deposition has been served, may issue necessary subpoenas. (Rule 28d).

Outside of State for Use Within State.—Whenever deposition of any person is to be taken outside Montana for use within Montana, clerk or other equivalent officer of any court having jurisdiction at place where witness is served or deposition will be taken may issue necessary subpoenas or equivalent court instruments to compel attendance of witness upon proof that notice of deposition has been served or that parties have stipulated thereto. (Rule 28e). See subhead Before Whom Taken, infra.

Before Whom Taken.—If taken within territory subject to dominion of U.S., depositions may be taken before a person authorized to administer oaths by laws of Montana, U.S., place where examination is held, or before a person appointed by court in which action is pending, which persons shall have power to administer oaths. (Rule 28a). If taken in a foreign country, deposition may be taken before a person authorized to administer oaths in place of examination, before person commissioned by court, or pursuant to letters rogatory. (Rule 28b). No deposition may be taken before relative, employee, attorney or counsel of a party, or relative or employee of attorney or counsel, or one who is financially interested in action. (Rule 28c).

Compelling Attendance of Witnesses.—Federal Rule 45(d) adopted (Rule 45d), adding phrase "where the action is pending, or" following words "Clerk of the District Court" in 45(d)(1), and striking 40 mile limitation in 45(d)(2). Federal Rule 37, excluding paragraphs (e) and (f), adopted. (Rule 37).

Examination of Witnesses.—Examination and cross-examination proceed as at trial. (Rule 30c). Each deposition shall not last more than eight hours nor take place on more than one day without leave of court. (Rule 30[b][8]).

Interrogatories to Parties.—Federal Rule 33 adopted. (Rule 33). No party may serve more than 50 interrogatories in aggregate including subparts without leave of court.

Perpetuating Testimony.—Deposition to perpetuate testimony before action may be taken regarding any matter cognizable in district court of State of Montana. Proceeding is commenced by filing verified petition in district court of any expected adverse party. Notice of proceeding must be given as directed by court and must be personally served on persons named in petition as expected adverse parties. If adverse parties fail to appear within 20 days after service, attorney will be appointed to represent them and cross-examine deponent. Such deposition may at any time thereafter be used in trial in which petitioner or any successor in interest is party, or between any parties in trial in which it is material to establish facts which such testimony proves or tends to prove where witness giving deposition is unable to be present at trial. (Rule 27a). Depositions may also be taken pending appeal. (Rule 27b).

Commissioned officers in U. S. armed forces have power to take depositions in those cases where they may take acknowledgments or affidavits. (1-5-607). See category Documents and Records, topic Acknowledgments.

Form ordinarily used for authenticating depositions is as follows:

Form

(Title).

Pursuant to the Montana Rules of Civil Procedure, there appeared before me, A. B., a Notary Public for the State of Montana, residing at . . . . ., Montana, on the . . . . day of . . . ., 19 . . . ., at the courtroom of Department No. . . . ., ..., County Courthouse, ..., Montana, at the hour of . . . . . ., of said date, the within-named C. D., who being duly sworn by me was then and there interrogated by the said counsel of record, and the following proceedings were had, to-wit:

Certificate attached is usually in the following form:

STATE OF MONTANA   } ss.
County of . . . .

I, A. B., a Notary Public for the State of Montana, and an officer authorized by the laws of the State of Montana to administer oaths, DO HEREBY CERTIFY:

That the witness, C. D., was produced at the time and place noted on page . . . . hereof, and that there appeared at said time and place the attorneys named on page . . . . hereof;

That the witness was first by me duly sworn to testify the truth, the whole truth, and nothing but the truth; that thereupon and thereafter the said witness was examined orally by the aforenamed counsel; that his deposition was by me reduced to writing, and when completed was read by said deponent and corrected by him in any particular desired, and was then and there subscribed by said witness before a Notary Public for the State of Montana; that I am not counsel, attorney, or relative of any party, nor otherwise interested in the event of this suit; that the foregoing transcript is a full, true, and correct transcript of his testimony given at said time and place, and is now by me certified as such officer.

IN WITNESS WHEREOF, I have hereunto set my hand and affixed the seal of my office as such Notary Public this . . . . . . day of . . . . . ., 19 . . . .

. . . .
Notary Public for the State of
Montana
Residing at . . . .
Montana
My commission expires . . . .

EQUITY:

See topic Actions.

EVIDENCE:

See topics Depositions and Discovery, Damages.

Federal Rules of Evidence adopted with some changes. (Title 26, c. 10).

Witnesses.—Rule 601, Montana Rules for Evidence, abolishes all incompetencies of witnesses except as otherwise provided in Montana Rules of Evidence. (Rule 601 Montana Rules of Evidence). Witness is disqualified if she/he cannot express matter in manner understandable by judge or jury or if she/he is not capable of understanding duty to tell truth.

See also topic Depositions and Discovery.

Privileged Communications.—Attorneys at law (26-1-803), clergymen and priests (26-1-804), or licensed physicians, surgeons, or dentists in civil actions except as provided in Rule 35, Montana Rules of Civil Procedure (26-1-805), cannot testify as to matters communicated to them professionally without consent of person making such communication. Communications between psychologist and his client are placed on same basis as attorney-client communications. (26-1-807). Speech pathologists, audiologists cannot, without consent of client, be examined in civil action. (26-1-806). Teachers of psychology may not testify, in any civil action, as to observations of children without consent of parent. (26-1-808). School counselors, psychologists, nurses, and teachers may not testify as to student's confidential communications without consent of student and parent if student is minor. (26-1-809). Public official cannot be examined as to official confidence made to him when public interests would suffer by disclosure. (26-1-810). Media have privilege not to disclose sources. (26-1-902).

Husband and Wife.—Neither husband nor wife can testify for or against each other, except by the consent of the other, nor can either testify during or after marriage regarding any communication from one to other made during marriage without consent of other, at any time, but this rule does not apply to civil actions by one against other, or to criminal action for crime committed by one against other. (26-1-802; 46-16-212).

Physician and Patient.—Any physician who diagnoses physical or mental condition that, in physician's judgment, will significantly impair person's ability to safely operate motor vehicle may, if he chooses, report person's name and other information relevant to his condition to department of justice. Department shall then cause examination or investigation to be undertaken. (37-2-311; 61-5-207).

Physician's report may be introduced as evidence in any proceeding involving granting, suspension, or revocation of person's driver's license before division or court. In no other proceeding, criminal or civil, may report be used without patient's consent. (37-2-311).

Communications or Transactions with Persons Since Deceased.—Limitations against testimony regarding transactions or oral communications with persons since deceased abolished by Rule 601, Montana Rules of Evidence.

Self-Incrimination.—Witness need not answer question if answer will have tendency to subject him to punishment for felony; nor if answer will have direct tendency to degrade his character, unless answer be to very fact in issue. (26-2-302).

Compelling Attendance.—See topic Depositions and Discovery.

See note at head of Digest as to 1998 legislation covered.

See Topical Index in front part of this volume.

INJUNCTIONS:

Federal Rules of Civil Procedure have formed basis for procedural statutes. However, procedures for granting of restraining orders and temporary and permanent injunctions are outlined in other statutes. (Rule 65, Mont.R.Civ.P.).

Temporary restraining order may be granted either before or after answer until hearing and decision on application for preliminary injunction. (27-19-314). Temporary restraining order may be granted without notice to adverse party if affidavit or verified complaint show that delay would cause immediate and irreparable injury to applicant before adverse party could be heard and if written certification is given to court stating efforts, if any, made to give notice and reasons that notice should not be required. (27-19-315).

Preliminary injunction order may be granted when it appears that: (1) applicant is entitled to relief demanded, and such relief consists in restraining act or acts complained of; (2) continuance of act complained of during litigation would produce great or irreparable injury; (3) adverse party is doing, threatening to do or permitting to be done some act in violation of applicant's rights, respecting subject of action, and which tends to render judgment ineffectual; (4) adverse party is about to remove or dispose of adverse party's property, with intent to defraud applicant; (5) applicant, under provisions of 40-4-121 or Tit. 40, c. 15, alleges physical abuse by partner or family member. (27-19-201). Preliminary injunction order may be granted at any time before judgment after reasonable notice and hearing based upon affidavits or oral testimony. (27-19-301 and -303).

Final injunction may be granted to prevent the breach of an obligation existing in favor of the applicant where: (1) pecuniary compensation would not afford adequate relief; (2) it would be extremely difficult to ascertain amount of compensation which would afford adequate relief; (3) restraint is necessary to prevent multiplicity of judicial proceedings; or (4) obligation arises from trust. (27-19-102).

Jurisdiction to issue is vested in district court (3-5-302), and in Supreme Court pending appeal from order of district court refusing or dissolving injunction, or in original actions where state is party, public is interested, or rights of public are involved. (3-2-205).

Prerequisites and Procedure.—In action by citizens group where injury is to property or civil right of individuals, names and addresses of persons injured and statement of injury must appear in complaint. (27-19-104). Reasonable notice to adverse party required before issuance of injunction. (27-19-301).

Bond shall be required by court except in domestic disputes or in interest of justice. (27-19-306).

JUDGMENTS:

Federal Rules of Civil Procedure form the basis for procedural statutes. See topic Practice.

Judgments are final subject only to appeal.

Judgment by Confession.—(27-9-101 to -104). Judgment may be confessed, without action, by defendant filing verified statement authorizing entry of judgment against him for specified sum, stating concisely facts out of which liability or debt arose and showing that sum for which judgment is confessed is justly due or to become due. Confession of judgment for purpose of securing plaintiff against contingent liability must state facts constituting such liability and show that sum for which judgment is confessed does not exceed such liability. (27-9-101, -102).

Contract authorizing judgment by confession or creating agency to confess judgment, accept service of process, or consent to entry of default is void. (28-2-709).

Consent judgments as distinguished from judgments by confession are not provided for.

Judgment Notes.—See category Business Regulation and Commerce, topic Bills and Notes.

Judgments on Pleadings.—Federal Rule 12[c] adopted. (Rule 12[c], Mont.R.Civ.P.).

Summary Judgment.—Federal Rule 56 adopted. (Rule 56, Mont.R.Civ.P.).

Declaratory Judgments.—Uniform Declaratory Judgments Act adopted. (27-8-101 to -313).

Default Judgments.—Federal Rule 55 adopted except 55(e); addition to 55(b)(1) is requirement of personal service; additions to 55(c) are requirement of application, provision for stipulations between parties for extension of time, and provision that party making appearance before application shall not be considered in default as to that appearance. (Rule 55, Mont.R.Civ.P.).

Offer of Judgment.—Federal Rule 68 adopted. (Rule 68, Mont.R.Civ.P.).

Docketing.—Clerk must docket judgment immediately after entry. (25-9-301). Prevailing party must serve notice of entry of judgment within ten days after entry of judgment. (Rule 77[d]; 223 Mont. 113, 724 P.2d 704).

Vacation or Modification.—Federal Rule 60 adopted, with additional language added relating to time within which motion shall be made. (Rule 60[b], Mont.R.Civ.P.). For good cause shown court may set aside entry of default. (Rule 55[c], Mont.R.Civ.P.).

Lien.—A judgment is a lien from time of filing judgment with clerk of district court in which real property is located and on all which may be afterwards acquired by debtor, lien expiring in six years. (25-9-301, 25-31-914). Certified transcript filed with court clerk of another county extends lien to such county. (25-9-302).

Revival.—In all cases the judgment may be carried into effect after the expiration of six years by leave of court on motion or by judgment for that purpose, founded upon supplemental pleadings. (25-13-102).

Actions on judgments, either foreign or domestic, generally barred after ten years. (27-2-201).

Satisfaction.—Satisfaction may be entered in clerk's docket upon acknowledgment of satisfaction made in manner of acknowledgment of conveyance of real property by judgment creditor or by his endorsement on the face or on the margin of the record of the judgment or by his attorney. (25-9-311). Following form is suggested: (Title of Court and Cause)

Form

For and in consideration of the sum of \$. . . . . . to me paid by . . . . . ., the defendant in the above entitled action, full satisfaction is hereby acknowledged of a certain judgment rendered and entered in the above entitled court in said action on the . . . . . . day of . . . . . . in favor of . . . . . ., the plaintiff in said action, and against said defendant for the sum of \$. . . . . ., with interest thereon from . . . . . . at the rate of six per cent per annum until paid, together with said plaintiff's costs and disbursements, amounting to \$. . . . . ., and recorded in Book . . . . . . of Judgments at page . . . . And I hereby direct and authorize the clerk of said court to enter satisfaction of record of said judgment in the said action.

. . . . . .

(Acknowledgment)

See also topic Practice.

Foreign Judgments.—Judgment of court of record of U.S. (26-3-201) or of sister state (26-3-203) is same as that of domestic court, except that: (1) it can be enforced only by action brought within this state; (2) authority of guardian, executor or administrator cannot extend beyond jurisdiction vesting him with authority (26-3-203). Judgment of foreign court against specific thing is conclusive of title, and against person is presumptive evidence of right against such person which can be repelled only by lack of jurisdiction, notice to party, collusion, fraud, or clear mistake of law or fact. (26-3-205).

Uniform Foreign Money-Judgments Recognition Act adopted. (25-9-601 to -609).

Uniform Enforcement of Foreign Judgments Act adopted, but with changes to section on notice of filing. (25-9-501 to -508).

Uniform Foreign-Money Claims Act adopted. (25-9-701 to -715).

LIMITATION OF ACTIONS:

The periods prescribed for the commencement of actions are as follows:

Lifetime of Offender.—Action under 46-18-247(3) to enforce order of restitution by court may be commenced at any time during offender's lifetime. (27-2-201).

Within ten years: Action upon a judgment of any court of record (27-2-201); action for mesne profits of real estate (27-2-214); action sounding in tort arising from design supervision, inspection, or construction of improvement to realty (27-2-208); action to collect past due child support (27-2-201).

Within eight years: An action upon a contract, obligation, or liability founded upon an instrument in writing, sealed or unsealed. (27-2-202).

Within five years: An action for recovery of real property, provided plaintiff seize or possess property (70-19-401); actions upon contract, account or promise, not founded upon instrument in writing (27-2-202); actions upon judgments of court not of record (27-2-201); and actions for relief not otherwise provided for (27-2-231). In action upon open or running account, computation of time shall be from date of last item thereof. (27-2-302). Action to enforce statutory debt created by payment of public assistance, or, if fraud involved, within five years of discovery of fraud. (27-2-211). Action challenging creation of planning and zoning district. (76-2-101[4]).

Within four years: For breach of contract for sale of goods, Uniform Commercial Code governs. (30-2-725).

Within three years: Tort action for general and personal injury. (27-2-204). Action against sheriff or other officer in his official capacity (but see subhead Within One Year), actions to recover damages for death of one caused by wrongful act or neglect of another and action upon obligation or liability, not founded upon instrument in writing, other than contract or promise. (27-2-202 and 209). Action for medical and legal malpractice must be brought within three years after plaintiff discovers or should have discovered injury, but in no case later than five years from injury in medical case, ten years from date of act in legal malpractice case. (27-2-205 and 206). Limitation shall be tolled where doctor failed to disclose to plaintiff any act, error, or omission which is known or should have been known to such practitioner. (27-2-205). Limitations statute for medical malpractice applies to actions in tort or contract against physician, surgeon, dentist, registered nurse, nursing home or hospital administrator, dispensing optician, optometrist, licensed physical therapist, podiatrist, psychologist, osteopath, chiropractor, clinical laboratory bioanalyst, clinical laboratory technologist, pharmacist, veterinarian, licensed hospital or long-term care facility or licensed medical professional corporation. Limitations period for action for death or injury of minor under age of four on date of injury begins to run on minor's eighth birthday or death whichever occurs first. Actions to assess deficiencies in tax reported by special fuel users and dealers must be brought within three years, except in cases of fraudulent or negligent returns. (15-70-335). Actions to recover damages for injury suffered as result of childhood sexual abuse must be brought within three years after abusive act or after plaintiff discovers or reasonably should have discovered that injury was caused by abuse. (27-2-216).

Within two years: For a statutory penalty or forfeiture (27-2-211); action for libel, slander, assault and battery, false imprisonment or seduction (27-2-204); action for injury to or trespass on real or personal property; action for taking, detaining or injuring any goods or chattels including actions for specific recovery of personal property (27-2-207); action for relief on ground of fraud or mistake, although claim does not accrue until discovery of fraud or mistake (27-2-203); action for killing or injuring of stock by railroad company (27-2-207).

Within one year: An action against a sheriff or other officer for the escape of a prisoner arrested upon civil process, an action against a municipal corporation for damages caused by a mob, or an action by a municipal corporation for the violation of a city ordinance, an action against an officer or a de facto officer, to recover for goods, wares and merchandise, seized by such officer, or for damages done to person or property in making such seizure. (27-2-209 to 211). Claims against a city or town. (7-6-4301).

See note at head of Digest as to 1998 legislation covered.

See Topical Index in front part of this volume.

MT – 12

LIMITATION OF ACTIONS . . . *continued*

Within six months: An action for claims against county which have been rejected by county commissioner. (27-2-209[3]).

Actions not otherwise provided for must be brought within five years. (27-2-231).

Limitation of actions brought pursuant to Securities Act of Montana. (See 30-10-305, 307.)

New Actions.—New action permitted within one year of reversal or termination of action, if original action brought within statutory period, even though limitation period may have expired before new action brought, except for voluntary discontinuance or judgment on merits. (27-2-407).

Liens.—As to actions to foreclose various statutory liens, see category Debtor and Creditor, topic Liens.

Disability of Plaintiff.—If person is either minor or has been committed, time of disability is not part of time limit for commencing action. However, time limit cannot extend more than five years except in case of infancy. (27-2-401).

Absence of Defendant.—If, when cause of action accrues against person, he is out of state and cannot be served with process, action may be commenced within period of limitation after return to state, and if, after cause of action accrues, he departs from state, time of absence is not part of period of limitation. (27-2-402).

Death of Either Party.—If person entitled to bring action dies before expiration of time limited for commencement thereof and cause of action survives, action may be commenced by representatives after expiration of time and within one year from death. (27-2-404).

Foreign Cause of Action.—Except in case of unfairness, if claim is substantially based upon law of one other state, limitation period of that state applies; or upon law of more than one state, limitation period of one of those states applies. (27-2-503).

Acknowledgment of debt or partial payment of debt causes statute of limitations to begin running anew. Acknowledgment must be in writing and signed by debtor. (27-2-409).

Contractual Limitations.—Contractual provision limiting limitations period is void. (28-2-708; 91 Mont. 525, 9 P.2d 469).

Pleading.—Expiration of statute of limitations is affirmative defense and must be raised in first responsive pleading. (Rule 8[c]).

Paternity Actions.—40-6-108 et seq.

PARTITION:

Civil action may be brought for partition of real property held by joint tenants or tenants in common. Procedure regulated by statute. (70-29-101 to 70-29-330).

Jurisdiction is in district courts. (3-5-302).

Venue is in county in which property or any part thereof is located. (25-2-123).

Proceedings.—Person entitled to partition must set forth in complaint interests of all persons in property (70-29-103), and must name specified owners as parties (70-29-104). If no prejudice would result court must order a partition. (70-29-202).

Partition in Kind or Sale.—When property cannot be divided without great prejudice to owners, court may order sale under supervision of referees. (70-29-202). Sales of real property must be at public auction with public notice. (70-29-301).

PLEADING:

Federal Rules of Civil Procedure form basis for pleading rules of Montana Rules of Civil Procedure. (Rules 7 to 16).

Pleadings permitted are same as Fed. Rule 7(a). (Rule 7[a]). All motions to be signed per Rule 11. (Rule 11).

Complaint.—Same as Fed. Rule 8(a), less jurisdiction allegations. (Rule 8[a]). In action for personal injury or wrongful death, amount of claim may not be stated. (25-4-311). Defendant may request statement of amount of claim after action filed. (25-4-312).

Answer.—Same as Fed. Rules 8(b), (c), (d), and 12(b), except for omission of improper venue as defense which may be made by motion. (Rules 8[b], [c], [d], 12[d]). Subdivisions (i) through (iii) have been added to Rule 12(b) which specify time and manner for motions for change of place of trial.

Counterclaim or Set-Off.—Similar to Fed. Rule 13 except that reference to "state of Montana or any of its governmental subdivisions, agencies or officers" is substituted for "United States" in Rule 13(d). If action pending, need not plead compulsory counterclaim. (Rule 13).

Reply.—Allowed as in Fed. Rule 7(a). (Rule 7[a]).

Demurrer.—Abolished. (Rule 7[c]).

Amended or Supplemental Pleadings.—Similar to Fed. Rule 15. (Rule 15).

Motion for More Definite Statement.—Same as Fed. Rule 12(e). (Rule 12[e]).

Verification.—Similar to Fed. Rule 11. (Rule 11).

Service.—Fed. Rule 5(a) adopted except for seizure of property paragraph. (Rule 5a). Can perform service by mail. (Rule 4D).

Filing.—Similar to Fed. Rules 3, 5(d), and 5(e). Original of paper filed by facsimile must be filed within five business days. (Rules 3; 5[d]; 5[e]).

Time.—Twenty days for serving answer, answer to cross-claim, reply to counterclaim, and responsive pleading after order of court on motion unless otherwise ordered by court. (Rule 12a). No ten day provisions as in Fed. Rule 12(a). State has 40 days to answer. (Rule 12).

Proof of Claim.—No statutory provisions other than for claim against an estate. See category Estates and Trusts, topic Executors and Administrators, subhead Uniform Probate Code, catchline Claims. (72-3-803).

Small Claims.—See category Courts and Legislature, topic Courts.

Frivolous Claims.—Attorney who, in determination of Court, multiplies proceedings in any case unreasonably and vexatiously may be required by court to satisfy personally excess costs, expenses, and attorney fees reasonably incurred because of such conduct. (37-61-421).

PRACTICE:

Federal Rules of Civil Procedure form basis for Montana Rules of Civil Procedure. Practice before administrative agencies governed by Montana Administrative Procedure Act. (Tit. 2, c. 4).

Discovery.—See topic Depositions and Discovery. Federal Rules 35(a), 35(b)(1), 35(b)(3) adopted (Rule 35[a], 35[b][l], 35[b][3]); phrase "or may hold him in contempt of court, or both." added to end of last sentence of Federal Rule 35(b)(1). Rule 35(b)(2) expanded to provide for waiver of privilege upon commencement of action which places in issue mental or physical condition of party bringing action. Waiver is not applicable to mental or physical conditions not related to pending action.

Demand for Admission of Facts.—Federal Rules 36 and 37 adopted. (Rule 36 and 37).

Direct Actions Against Insurer.—See category Transportation, topic Motor Vehicles, subhead Direct Action.

Medical Malpractice.—No action may be filed prior to review by Medical Malpractice Panel. (Tit. 27, c. 6).

Small Claims.—See category Courts and Legislature, topic Courts.

See also topics Actions, Appeal and Error, Depositions and Discovery, Injunctions, Judgments, Pleading, Process; category Debtor and Creditor, topics Attachment, Executions, Garnishment.

PROCESS:

Governed by Montana Rules of Civil Procedure which are patterned after Federal Rules of Civil Procedure. Substantial changes were made in jurisdiction and process portions.

See also topic Practice.

Civil action is commenced by filing complaint. (Rule 3). Upon filing of complaint, Clerk of Court issues summons. (Rule 4C[1]).

General Requisites.—Summons must contain signature of clerk, seal of the court, name of court and parties, name and address of plaintiff's attorney, and must state time within which defendant is required to appear. It must be directed to defendant and notify him that if he fails to appear as directed judgment by default will be rendered against him. Additional information necessary in quiet title action. (Rule 4C[2]).

By Whom Issued.—Upon filing of complaint, clerk of court issues summons. (Rule 4C[1]).

Who May Serve.—Service of process within state may be made by Sheriff or Deputy of county where party served is found, by Constable authorized by law, or by any person over 18 and not party to action. (Rule 4D[1]). Service outside state to be made in manner provided for service within state. (Rule 4D[3]).

Registered Process Server.—Person other than sheriff, constable, coroner, elisor, other government employee acting in course of employment or licensed attorney who makes more than ten services of process within state during one calendar year shall file verified certificate of registration as process server with Clerk of District Court. (25-1-1101). Registered Process Server may act as levying officer under Title 25, c. 13. (25-1-1101).

Personal service on individual is made by delivering copy of summons and complaint to him personally or to an agent authorized by appointment or law to receive service of process. (If agent designated by statute, such further notice must be given as is required by statute). (Rule 4D[2][a]).

Personal service on minor over 14 made by delivering copy of summons and complaint to him personally and by leaving copies at his dwelling house with adult residing therein, or by delivering copies to agent authorized by appointment or by law to receive service. (Rule 4D[2][b]).

Personal Service on minor under 14 made by delivering copy of summons and complaint to guardian within state, and if he has no guardian, to father, mother or other person or agency having his care or control or with whom he resides, or if service cannot be made on any of them, as ordered by court. (Rule 4D[2][c]).

Personal service on incompetent person by delivering copy of summons and complaint to court appointed guardian residing in state. If there is no such guardian, court must appoint guardian ad litem. When party is alleged to be of unsound mind, but has not been so adjudged by a court, process may be served on him personally, and court may stay pending action against him upon learning that he is of unsound mind. (Rule 4D[2][d]).

Personal service on domestic or foreign corporation, partnership, or association made by delivering copy of summons and complaint to: (1) An officer, director, superintendent or managing or general agent, or partner, or associate for such entity, or by leaving at office or place of business of such entity within state with person in charge of such office; or (2) to any agent or attorney in fact authorized by appointment or law to receive service (such further notice as may be required by statute is also necessary); or (3) if sheriff can find no such person in county, service may be made by leaving copies at any office of such entity within state with person in charge of such office; or (4) if defendant is corporation which no longer has right to do business in state, by delivering copies to one of trustees of such corporation. (Rule 4D[2][e] and 35-1-316). Foreign entity must have place of business within state or be doing business herein either permanently or temporarily, or have been doing business herein either permanently or temporarily at time claim for relief accrued. (Rule 4D[2][e]).

Personal Service Outside the State.—Where service on any person cannot be made, with due diligence, personally within state, service may be made outside state in manner provided for service within state with same force and effect. Personal service outside

---

See note at head of Digest as to 1998 legislation covered.

See Topical Index in front part of this volume.

PROCESS . . . *continued*

state dispenses with necessity for following procedure for service by publication. (Rule 4D[3]).

Service by publication is permitted when subject of action is real or personal property in this state and defendant, known or unknown, has or claims lien or interest therein, or relief sought consists of excluding an interest of defendant therein; when action is to foreclose, redeem or satisfy a mortgage, claim or lien on property within state; in actions for divorce or annulment of marriage of Montana resident, or for modification of divorce decree; and when defendant has property in state which has been attached or garnished. (Rule 4D[5][a]). Status, property, or thing acted upon by defendant served by publication will be subject to decree, but such defendant will not be bound personally unless some ground for personal jurisdiction exists. (Rule 4D[5][b]). Summons must be published once a week for three successive weeks in a newspaper published in county in which action is pending (Rule 4D[5][d]). Copy of summons for publication and complaint must be mailed to defendant not later than ten days after first publication of summons unless affidavit for publication states that defendant's address is unknown. Special provisions are made for mailing to corporations. (Rule 4D[5][e]). First publication or personal service outside state must be made within 60 days after filing affidavit for publication. (Rule 4D[5][f]). Service by publication or personal service outside state is complete on date of last publication or date of personal service. (Rule 4D[5][g]).

Long Arm Statute.—See supra, subhead Personal Service Outside the State, and infra, subhead Service on Secretary of State.

Proof of Service.—If served by sheriff or other officer, his certificate; by any other person, his affidavit; by publication, affidavit of publisher of publication and mailing; or by written admission of defendant. (Rule 4D[8]). Affidavit of personal service by person other than sheriff or officer must state that person serving is of legal age, date and place of making service, and that person serving knew person served was person named in papers served and person intended to be served. (Rule 4D[9]).

Service on Secretary of State.—In actions against domestic corporations, or foreign corporations who have either qualified to do business in Montana or are otherwise subject to jurisdiction of this state, or national banking associations which through insolvency or lapse of charter have ceased to do business in Montana, where specified officers and agents cannot be found in Montana, personal service may be made upon Secretary of State; provided, that when service is made in actions and proceedings in which personal service of summons is not required to be made in order to obtain relief, service by publication must also be made. (Rule 4D[2][f]). In all other cases refer to detailed provisions in Rule 4D(6) for manner and method of serving Secretary of State.

Nonresident Motorist.—See category Transportation, topic Motor Vehicles.

REPLEVIN:

The common law action of replevin has been abolished in this state, and instead, the plaintiff in an action to recover possession of personal property may claim the same at the time of issuing summons, or before answer is made, according to the following procedure:

Proceedings.—An affidavit must be made by the plaintiff or some one in his behalf stating: (1) That the plaintiff is the owner of the property claimed, or is lawfully entitled to the possession thereof; (2) that the property is wrongfully detained by the defendant; (3) that the same has not been taken for a tax, assessment or fine, pursuant to statute, or seized under an execution or attachment against the property of the plaintiff, or if so seized, that it is exempt from execution; and (4) the actual value of the property. (27-17-201).

The plaintiff must also give to the defendant a written undertaking, executed by two or more sufficient sureties approved by the sheriff, to the effect that they are bound to the defendant, in double the value of the property, and for the return of the property to the defendant, if a return is adjudged, and for the payment of such sum as may be recovered against the plaintiff. The plaintiff may thereupon require the sheriff or constable where the property is claimed to take the same from the defendant. Judgment being given in favor of the plaintiff, and if the property has not been materially injured, and if return can be made, judgment will be for the return of the property, otherwise a money judgment will be rendered for the value of the property. (27-17-205, 303, 402, 403).

Sheriff cannot make seizure without court order which requires show cause hearing or proof that delay before hearing would impair remedy. (27-17-203).

Repossession by Defendant.—At any time before delivery of property to plaintiff, if defendant does not except to sureties of plaintiff, defendant by giving to sheriff written undertaking, may require return of property. Sureties may be required to justify, and sheriff is responsible for defendant's sureties until they justify and he may retain property until justification is complete or expressly waived. Qualification of sureties in claim and delivery action are same as in bail on order of arrest. (27-17-304 to 307).

Third Party Claims.—If third person claiming the property serves on sheriff an affidavit of his title, sheriff need not keep property or deliver it to plaintiff unless indemnified. (27-17-309).

Judgment must be in the alternative, for the return of the property or its value (69 Mont. 46, 220 Pac. 101), but if property has diminished in value, action may be maintained for its undiminished value or for damages for its detention (27-17-403).

SEQUESTRATION:

No statutory provision.

SERVICE:

See topic Process.

STAY OF EXECUTION:

See topic Appeal and Error; category Debtor and Creditor, topic Executions.

SUBMISSION OF CONTROVERSY:

Parties to a cause in difference which might be subject of a civil suit may, without action, agree on case containing facts of controversy and submit it to any court which would have jurisdiction if action brought. It must appear by affidavit that controversy is real and proceedings in good faith to determine rights of parties. Court must hear and render judgment as if action were pending. (27-7-101, 102). Judgment must be entered in judgment book without costs for any proceeding prior to trial, may be enforced as if rendered in action and is subject to appeal. (27-7-103, 104).

VENUE:

An action affecting the title to or any interest in real property must be brought in the county where all or part of property is situated. (25-2-123). Actions to recover penalty or forfeiture imposed by statute (25-2-124) or against public official (25-2-125) must be in county where cause arose. Actions against state must be brought in county in which claim arose or in Lewis and Clark County, or if action is by Montana resident, in county of his residence. (25-2-126). Actions upon contract must be brought in county of defendants' residence or county in which contract was to be performed. (25-2-121). Tort actions must be brought in county of defendants' residence or where tort was committed unless defendant is corporation incorporated in state outside of Montana, then proper place of trial is county where tort was committed, where plaintiff resides or where corporation's registered agent is located. (25-2-122; 133 Mont. 320, 323 P.2d 269). If tort is interrelated with claim for breach of contract, tort is deemed to be committed where contract is to be performed. (25-2-122). In all other cases, civil actions must be brought in county where defendants or any of them reside at commencement of action; or if none of defendants reside in Montana in contract action, in county in which contract was to be performed. (25-2-121). In tort action, if defendant is resident of state other than Montana, (1) county in which tort was committed; or (2) county in which plaintiff resides. (25-2-122, as am'd in 1997).

Change of Venue.—Change of venue is required when county designated in complaint is not proper, when there is reason to believe that impartial trial cannot be had therein; when convenience of witnesses and ends of justice would be promoted; or upon consent of all parties. (25-2-201, 25-2-202).

Contract Provisions.—Provision in agreement fixing venue enforceable. (25-2-202; 132 Mont. 243, 316 P.2d 788).

COURTS AND LEGISLATURE

COURTS:

United States District Court.—Montana, exclusive of Yellowstone Park, constitutes one judicial district.

Billings Division, comprised of Counties of Big Horn, Carbon, Carter, Custer, Daniels, Dawson, Fallon, Garfield, Golden Valley, McCone, Musselshell, Park, Petroleum, Phillips, Powder River, Prairie, Richland, Roosevelt, Rosebud, Sheridan, Stillwater, Sweetgrass, Treasure, Valley, Wheatland, Wibaux and Yellowstone, and Court shall be held in Billings Division at Courtroom in U. S. Courthouse, Billings, Montana.

Butte Division, comprised of Counties of Beaverhead, Deer Lodge, Gallatin, Madison and Silver Bow, and Court shall be held in Butte Division at Courtroom in Federal Building, Butte, Montana.

Great Falls Division, comprised of Counties of Blaine, Cascade, Choteau, Fergus, Glacier, Hill, Judith Basin, Liberty, Pondera, Teton and Toole, and Court shall be held in Great Falls Division at Courtroom in Post Office Building, Great Falls, Montana.

Helena Division, comprised of Counties of Broadwater, Jefferson, Lewis and Clark, Meagher and Powell, and Court shall be held in Helena Division at Courtroom in Federal Building, Helena, Montana.

Missoula Division, comprised of Counties of Flathead, Granite, Lake, Lincoln, Mineral, Missoula, Ravalli and Sanders, and Court shall be held in Missoula Division at Courtroom in Federal Building, Missoula, Montana.

Fees.—Fee for starting civil action is $150 which covers all appearances in action. Fee for habeas corpus proceeding is $5.

Supreme Court of Montana.—Supreme Court has appellate jurisdiction extending to all cases in law and equity.

Supreme Court sits at Helena.

District Courts.—District courts have civil, criminal, and probate jurisdiction. In criminal actions, they have jurisdiction in all cases amounting to a felony, and in misdemeanors not otherwise provided for. District courts have concurrent jurisdiction with justice courts in misdemeanors arising from same transaction as charged felony, resulting from reduction of felony charge, or included as lesser offense found by jury in felony case. (3-5-302). They have appellate jurisdiction from justices' and police courts within county. (3-5-303).

Districts.—

First District: Counties of Broadwater and Lewis and Clark.
Second District: County of Silver Bow.
Third District: Counties of Deer Lodge, Granite and Powell.
Fourth District: Counties of Mineral, Missoula and Ravalli.
Fifth District: Counties of Beaverhead, Jefferson and Madison.
Sixth District: Counties of Park and Sweet Grass.
Seventh District: Counties of Dawson, McCone, Prairie, Richland and Wibaux.
Eighth District: County of Cascade.
Ninth District: Counties of Glacier, Pondera, Teton and Toole.
Tenth District: Counties of Fergus, Judith Basin and Petroleum.
Eleventh District: County of Flathead.
Twelfth District: Counties of Chouteau, Hill and Liberty.
Thirteenth District: Counties of Big Horn, Carbon, Stillwater and Yellowstone.
Fourteenth District: Counties of Golden Valley, Meagher, Musselshell and Wheatland.
Fifteenth District: Counties of Daniels, Roosevelt and Sheridan.

See note at head of Digest as to 1998 legislation covered.

See Topical Index in front part of this volume.

COURTS . . . continued

Sixteenth District: Counties of Carter, Custer, Fallon, Garfield, Powder River, Rosebud and Treasure.

Seventeenth District: Counties of Blaine, Phillips and Valley.

Eighteenth District: County of Gallatin.

Nineteenth District: County of Lincoln.

Twentieth District: Counties of Lake and Sanders.

Locations of courts are as follows:

Beaverhead County; 5th District; Court sits at Dillon.

Big Horn County; 13th District; Court sits at Hardin.

Blaine County; 17th District; Court sits at Chinook.

Broadwater County; 1st District; Court sits at Townsend.

Carbon County; 13th District; Court sits at Red Lodge.

Carter County; 16th District; Court sits at Ekalaka.

Cascade County; 8th District; Court sits at Great Falls.

Chouteau County; 12th District; Court sits at Fort Benton.

Custer County; 16th District; Court sits at Miles City.

Daniels County; 15th District; Court sits at Scobey.

Dawson County; 7th District; Court sits at Glendive.

Deer Lodge County; 3rd District; Court sits at Anaconda.

Fallon County; 16th District; Court sits at Baker.

Fergus County; 10th District; Court sits at Lewistown.

Flathead County; 11th District; Court sits at Kalispell.

Gallatin County; 18th District; Court sits at Bozeman.

Garfield County; 16th District; Court sits at Jordan.

Glacier County; 9th District; Court sits at Cut Bank.

Golden Valley County; 14th District; Court sits at Ryegate.

Granite County; 3rd District; Court sits at Philipsburg.

Hill County; 12th District; Court sits at Havre.

Jefferson County; 5th District; Court sits at Boulder.

Judith Basin County; 10th District; Court sits at Stanford.

Lake County; 20th District; Court sits at Polson.

Lewis and Clark County; 1st District; Court sits at Helena.

Liberty County; 12th District; Court sits at Chester.

Lincoln County; 19th District; Court sits at Libby.

Madison County; 5th District; Court sits at Virginia City.

McCone County; 7th District; Court sits at Circle.

Meagher County; 14th District; Court sits at White Sulphur Springs.

Mineral County; 4th District; Court sits at Superior.

Missoula County; 4th District; Court sits at Missoula.

Musselshell County; 14th District; Court sits at Roundup.

Park County; 6th District; Court sits at Livingston.

Petroleum County; 10th District; Court sits at Winnett.

Phillips County; 17th District; Court sits at Malta.

Pondera County; 9th District; Court sits at Conrad.

Powder River County; 16th District; Court sits at Broadus.

Powell County; 3rd District; Court sits at Deer Lodge.

Prairie County; 7th District; Court sits at Terry.

Ravalli County; 4th District; Court sits at Hamilton.

Richland County; 7th District; Court sits at Sidney.

Roosevelt County; 15th District; Court sits at Wolf Point.

Rosebud County; 16th District; Court sits at Forsyth.

Sanders County; 20th District; Court sits at Thompson Falls.

Sheridan County; 15th District; Court sits at Plentywood.

Silver Bow County; 2nd District; Court sits at Butte.

Stillwater County; 13th District; Court sits at Columbus.

Sweet Grass County; 6th District; Court sits at Big Timber.

Teton County; 9th District; Court sits at Choteau.

Toole County; 9th District; Court sits at Shelby.

Treasure County; 16th District; Court sits at Hysham.

Valley County; 17th District; Court sits at Glasgow.

Wheatland County; 14th District; Court sits at Harlowton.

Wibaux County; 7th District; Court sits at Wibaux.

Yellowstone County; 13th District; Court sits at Billings.

Probate Courts.—There are no separate probate courts. Probate jurisdiction is exercised by district courts.

Justice of the Peace Courts.—

Jurisdiction.—At least one in each county, to be located at county seat; county given authority to add additional justice, if necessary; and city over 5,000 may request justice court. (3-10-101). Have civil jurisdiction where amount in controversy does not exceed $5,000, in following actions: (1) On contract for recovery of money only; (2) for damages for taking, detaining or injuring personal property, for injury to real property where issue of title or possession not raised, and for some injuries to person; (3) to recover possession of personal property; (4) for fine, penalty, or forfeiture given by statute or ordinance; (5) upon bonds or undertakings; (6) to take and enter judgment for recovery of money on confession (see topic Judgments) of defendant. (3-10-301). Also have civil jurisdiction to issue temporary restraining orders and orders of protection in domestic setting and in actions against sellers or distributors of cigarettes to minors. (3-10-301). Concurrent jurisdiction with district courts over unlawful detainer and forcible entry. (3-10-302). In criminal cases, jurisdiction of misdemeanors punishable by fine not more than $500, imprisonment not more than six months, or both; misdemeanor fish and game violations punishable by fine not more than $1,000 or imprisonment not more than six months, or both; concurrent with district court of misdemeanors punishable by fine exceeding $500 or imprisonment exceeding six months, or both; concurrent with district court of misdemeanor fish and game violations punishable by fine exceeding $1,000 or imprisonment exceeding six months, or both; and jurisdiction of all violations of Tit. 61, c. 10 (3-10-303), and misdemeanors arising from transaction where felony

charged, resulting from reduction of felony charge, or included as lesser offense found by jury in felony case (3-5-302).

Procedure.—Action is commenced by filing of complaint or copy of instrument with statement of amount due. (Rules 3 and 7A, Montana Justice and City Court Rules of Civil Procedure). Defendant must file written answer and serve same on plaintiff or his attorney within 20 days after service of summons. (25-31-406). Summons may be served by sheriff or constable of appropriate county in state, or any resident over 18 years and not party to suit. Rules for manner of service, return, and service by publication are similar to Rules of Civil Procedure for District Courts. (Rule 4D1, Montana Justice and City Court Rules of Civil Procedure).

Judgment.—Justice's court judgment creates no lien on lands of defendant unless transcript of original docket, certified by clerk of justice's court, is filed with Clerk of District Court. When so filed judgment is lien upon all real property of judgment debtor in such county. Lien continues for six years. (25-31-914).

City Court established in each city or town. (3-11-101). Concurrent jurisdiction with justice's court of all misdemeanors punishable by fine not more than $500 or imprisonment not more than six months or both. (3-11-102). Exclusive jurisdiction for: Enforcement of ordinance; collection of city taxes; money due to city when less than $5,000; recovery of city property under $5,000. (3-11-103). City Court abolished where Municipal Court established. (3-6-102).

Municipal Courts.—Cities of over 4,000 population may provide for municipal courts having concurrent jurisdiction with justices' courts, exclusive jurisdiction of same matters as city courts in other cities and towns, and concurrent jurisdiction with district courts in forcible entry and unlawful detainer. (3-6-101 and 3-6-103). Municipal courts are courts of record. (3-1-102).

Small Claims Courts.—Small claims courts have jurisdiction over all actions for recovery of money or specific personal property when amount claimed does not exceed $3,000, exclusive of costs, and defendant can be served within county where action is commenced. (25-35-502). District court may remove action to small claims court if amount in controversy does not exceed $3,000. (25-35-503). Proper venue for actions commenced in small claims court is same as that provided for by law for civil actions. (25-35-504). Party may not be represented by attorney unless all parties represented by attorney. Action commenced by executing sworn small claims complaint. Except for claims under 27-1-718, no party may file more than ten claims in any calendar year. (25-35-505). Pamphlets explaining procedure are given to plaintiff and copy of pamphlet must be attached to notice given defendant. (25-35-601). Defendant may remove action to justices' court within ten days of service of complaint, and failure to remove constitutes waiver of rights to trial by jury and to representation by counsel. (25-35-605). Defendant may assert counterclaim arising out of same transaction or occurrence. (25-35-606). Appeal may be made to district court following small claims court decision. (25-35-803). Upon removal to justice's court by defendant, or upon appeal, prevailing party may be granted attorney fees and reasonable costs. (25-35-806).

Judges Pro Tempore/Special Master.—Parties to civil action may stipulate in writing to have action tried before judge pro tempore or special master. Judge pro tempore or special master may also be appointed by district court judge to conduct preliminary, non-dispositive proceedings in criminal action. (3-5-113).

LEGISLATURE:

Const. V, 6 provides that legislature shall meet each odd-numbered year for not more than 90 legislative days, and permits any legislature to extend time limit on sessions for any subsequent legislature.

Special or Extraordinary Sessions.—Const. V, 6 provides that governor or majority of legislature may convene special session.

Initiative and Referendum.—Constitution provides for initiative and referendum except for appropriation of money. (Const. III, 4 and 5).

Legislative Council.—Twelve member group of legislators serving two year terms to study and review state government, propose legislation. (5-11-101 to 107). Legislative services division established. May establish functional organization within council. (5-11-112).

Lobbyists regulated by 5-7-101 to 305. Licenses required. Extensive reporting required by lobbyist and principal. (5-7-201, 5-7-208). Failure to comply with requirements of chapter gives rise to civil and criminal penalties. (5-7-305).

Expenditure Limitation.—Except in declared emergency, or pursuant to legislative declaration, legislature cannot appropriate for expenditures in excess of previous biennium plus growth factor based on personal income of Montana residents. (17-8-106).

REPORTS:

Decisions of Supreme Court are reported in Montana Reports and Pacific Reporter. Also published in State Reporter.

Digests are Montana Digest and Pacific Digest.

STATUTES:

Statutes of state are recodified as "Montana Code Annotated," formerly Revised Codes of Montana, 1947. Recodification completed Jan. 1, 1979. Montana Code Annotated (MCA) is reenactment and continuation of previous law. (1-11-103). Code Commissioner is responsible for republication, updating and supplementation. New printing of entire code after each biennial legislative session is contemplated.

MCA is arranged by Title, Chapter and Section. Citation to Title 1, Chapter 1, Section 1 would appear as 1-1-101, MCA.

Uniform Acts adopted are: Acknowledgment (1947); †Adoption (1957); Alcoholism and Intoxication Treatment (1975); Anatomical Gift (1969, adopted 1987 form of Act effective 1989); Arbitration (1985); Attendance of Witnesses From Without a State in Criminal Proceedings, Act to Secure (1937); Child Custody Jurisdiction (1977); Commercial Code (1963); †Common Trust Fund (1955) (adopted in Montana as "Common Trust Act"); Conflict of Laws-Limitations (1991); Controlled Substances (1973); Crime

See note at head of Digest as to 1998 legislation covered.

See Topical Index in front part of this volume.

STATUTES . . . *continued*

Victims' Reparations Act (1978); Criminal Extradition as Revised (1937): Declaratory Judgments (1935); Determination of Death (1983); Disposition of Community Property Rights at Death (1989); Division of Income for Tax Purposes Act (1969); Durable Power of Attorney (1974); Enforcement of Foreign Judgments (1989); Estate Tax Apportionment (1958 Act, 1975); Evidence, Rules of (1974 Act, 1977); Facsimile Signatures of Public Officials (1959); Federal Lien Registration (1967); Foreign-Money Claims (1993); Foreign Money-Judgments Recognition (1993); Fraudulent Transfer (1991); Guardianship and Protective Proceedings (1982); Health-Care Information (1987); International Wills (1991); Interstate Family Support (1969); † Land Sales Practices (1969); Revised Limited Partnership (1981); Machine Gun Act (1935); Management of Institutional Funds (1973); Marriage and Divorce (1975); Model Business Corporation (1991); Model Non-Profit Corporation (1991); Motor Vehicle Safety Responsibility (1951); Non-profit Corporation (1969); Notarial Acts (1993); Parentage (1975); Partnership, Revised (1993); Paternity (1963); Premarital Agreement (1987); Principal and Income, Revised (1983); Probate Code (1975); Reciprocal Enforcement of Support, 1968 Revision (1969); Residential Landlord and Tenant (1977); Rights of Terminally Ill Act (1989 version, 1985); † Securities (1961); Simplification of Fiduciary Security Transfers (1963); State Administrative Procedure (1971); Statutory Form Power of Attorney (1993); † Statutory Rule Against Perpetuities (1989); Testamentary Additions to Trust (1960 Act, 1959); Trade Secrets (1985); Transboundary Pollution Reciprocal Access (1983); Transfers to Minors (1985); Unclaimed Property (1981 Act).

Uniform Commercial Code adopted. (Tit. 30). See category Business Regulation and Commerce, topic Commercial Code.

For text of Uniform Acts falling within the scope of the Martindale-Hubbell Law Digests see Uniform and Model Acts section.

† Adopted with significant variations or modifications. See appropriate topics as to Acts within scope of Digests volume.

UNIFORM LAWS:

For list of Uniform Acts in force in this state see topic Statutes. For text of Uniform Acts within the scope of the Martindale-Hubbell Law Digests see Uniform and Model Acts section.

CRIMINAL LAW

BAIL:

See topic Criminal Law.

CRIMINAL LAW:

Substantive provisions of crimes and punishments appear in Tit. 45. These chapters include: (1) General Preliminary Provisions; (2) General Principles of Liability; (3) Justifiable Use of Force; (4) Inchoate Offenses; (5) Offenses Against the Person; (6) Offenses against Property; (7) Offenses against Public Administration; (8) Offenses against Public Order; (9) Dangerous Drugs; (10) Model Drug Paraphernalia Act. Tit. 46 covers code of criminal procedure, including following chapters: (1) General Provisions; (2) Jurisdiction; (3) Venue; (4) Investigative Procedures; (5) Search and Seizure; (6) Arrest; (7) Initial Appearance of Arrested Persons; (8) Right to Counsel; (9) Bail; (10) Preliminary Examination; (11) Commencement of Prosecution; (12) Arraignment of Defendant; (13) Pretrial Motions; (14) Mental Competency of Accused; (15) Production of Evidence; (16) Trial; (17) Lower Court Proceedings; (18) Sentence and Judgment; (19) Execution of Judgment; (20) Appeals; (21) Post-Conviction Hearing; (22) Habeas Corpus; (23) Probation, Parole, and Clemency; (24) Treatment of Victim and Witnesses (cc. 25 through 29 Reserved); (30) Uniform Criminal Extradition Act; (31) Interstate Agreement on Detainers. Offenses of criminal and negligent endangerment created. (45-5-207 and 45-5-208).

Indictment or Information.—All prosecutions of offenses charged in district court must be by indictment or information. (46-11-102[1]). Information is filed by county attorney. (46-11-201). Indictment may be found by eight of 11 grand jurors. (46-11-331). All prosecutions of other offenses must be by complaint. (46-11-102[2]).

Bail is permitted as matter of right, except where offense charged is punishable by death and proof of guilt is evident or presumption of guilt is great. (46-9-102).

Interstate Compact for Supervision of Parolees and Probationers adopted. (46-23-1101 to 46-23-1106).

Uniform Criminal Extradition Act adopted. (46-30-101 to 46-30-203). Person may be extradited without warrant provided in Uniform Act after hearing and presentation of copy of agreement to waive extradition or copy of warrant from other state. (46-30-228 and 46-30-229).

DEBTOR AND CREDITOR

ASSIGNMENTS:

Uniform Commercial Code adopted. (Tit. 30). See category Business Regulation and Commerce, topic Commercial Code. Property of any kind may be transferred (70-1-503) except mere possibility not coupled with interest (70-1-504). Chose in action arising out of violation of property right or out of obligation may be transferred. (70-2-102).

Instrument Transferring Title.—Uniform Commercial Code adopted. (Tit. 30). See category Business Regulation and Commerce, topic Commercial Code. With respect to transfers not governed by U.C.C., transfers may be made without writing except where writing is expressly required by statute. (70-1-506). Instrument need not be witnessed or acknowledged.

Filing.—Uniform Commercial Code adopted. (Tit. 30). See category Business Regulation and Commerce, topic Commerical Code. Assignments in transactions not governed by U.C.C. need not be filed or recorded.

Notice.—Uniform Commercial Code adopted. (Tit. 30). See category Business Regulation and Commerce, topic Commercial Code. In transactions not governed by U.C.C. notice to obligor not required.

Action by the assignee, in case of assignment of thing in action, is without prejudice to any set-off or other defense existing at time of, or before, notice of assignment; but this applies only to extent not otherwise provided for by U.C.C. (27-1-503).

Assignments of Wages.—Payments made in consideration for any sale or assignments of wages are deemed loans governed by the Consumer Loan Act. (32-5-101 to 32-5-406). (See 32-5-310[1]; 31-1-308.) (See category Business Regulation and Commerce, topic Interest.) Assignments of wages to licensee under Act must not exceed 10% of wages owing at time of notice to employer and thereafter to become owing. Assignments must be written and signed by borrower and spouse, if any. Notice to employer of assignment is required only in event debtor defaults. Honoring of assignment is at option of employer. (32-5-310, 32-5-310[2]). Assignments of wages other than those made to licensee under Act are subject to following restrictions: (1) Must be for fixed and definite part of all wages or salary theretofore earned (31-1-304); (2) wife or husband of married assignor must join in assignment, acknowledging same before notary or other authorized officer, other than assignee or person connected with him (31-1-306); (3) written notice with copy of assignment must be served on employer within one day after execution and filed in office of county clerk of county where assignor resides (31-1-307).

Wage Brokers.—Any person who accepts assignment of wages as security for loan is a wage broker (31-1-303), and must secure license from County Commissioners or City Council (31-1-301).

ATTACHMENT:

Actions in Which Allowed.—Any action upon a contract express or implied for the direct payment of money, where contract is not secured by mortgage or lien on real property, or is originally secured, where security has without act of plaintiff become valueless; also in action based upon statutory stockholders' liability. (27-18-101). Guaranty of loan in which only condition precedent to obligation of guarantor is default is unconditional contract for direct payment of money. (27-18-101[3]).

Courts Which May Issue Writ.—Both justice (27-18-1501) and district courts (27-18-205).

In Whose Favor Writ May Issue.—Any plaintiff (27-18-101, 102); no provision discriminating against nonresident plaintiffs.

Claims on Which Writ May Issue.—On unmatured claims, if it appears from plaintiff's affidavit that (1) defendant is about to leave the state with his property to defraud his creditors, or (2) that defendant is disposing of, or about to dispose of, property subject to execution to defraud his creditors. (27-18-203).

Grounds.—See supra, subhead Actions in Which Allowed.

Proceedings to Obtain.—Plaintiff must file affidavit stating: That defendant is indebted in specified amount on contract such as that described above; that attachment is not sought to hinder, delay or defraud any creditor of defendant; that facts exist which create reasonable belief defendant will leave Montana taking nonexempt property with him, is disposing or about to dispose of nonexempt property, or has power to dispose of, conceal or remove property subject to execution, or may suffer liens on such property. Affidavit must contain description and actual value of property to be attached. (27-18-202).

Writ is issued by court (27-18-205) or by justice of peace (27-18-1502) after receipt of affidavit, written undertaking and prima facie showing of right to and necessity for seizure. In case of personal property, must have show cause hearing with three days notice to defendant unless plaintiff shows in open court that delay caused by notice and hearing would seriously impair remedy sought. (27-18-205).

Attachment bond in double the amount claimed if amount is $1,000 or less, or equal to amount claimed if in excess of $1,000, but in no case in excess of $20,000, must be filed before writ issues. (27-18-204). Within 30 days after summons served defendant may except to sufficiency of sureties. Failure so to do is waiver of defects. (27-18-715). In justice court, bond must be for not less than $50, nor more than $300. (27-18-1502). Exception to sureties may be taken within two days. (27-18-1503).

Levy may be made on any property of defendant not exempt from execution (27-18-301) but chose in action for personal injuries cannot be attached (100 Mont. 496, 50 P.2d 249).

Real property is attached by filing a copy of writ, description of property, and notice of attachment with county clerk (27-18-402); personal property capable of manual delivery is attached by taking it into custody, except where in possession of third person (27-18-404); investment securities may be attached only by seizure (30-8-317, 27-18-409); corporate stocks or shares other than investment securities may be attached either by seizure or by leaving with president, secretary, cashier or managing agent of corporation, copy of writ and notice of attachment (27-18-409); debts or credits and personal property in possession of third person, by leaving copy of writ and notice of attachment with person owing debt or in possession or control of property (27-18-405); judgments by leaving with clerk of district court copy of writ and notice of attachment (27-18-408); interest in personal property belonging to estate of decedent, by serving personal representative with copy of writ and notice of attachment and filing copy with clerk of court in which estate is being administered (27-18-412).

Claim and Delivery Bond.—Plaintiff must submit written undertaking executed by two or more sureties for double value of property in order to attach property. (27-17-205).

Indemnity.—Attachment bond required for application to discharge attachment levied upon interest in partnership. (35-10-506). In event of third party claim, sheriff may require bond. (27-18-602).

Lien accrues at time of attachment and in order in which writs are levied. (27-18-307).

ATTACHMENT . . . *continued*

Priorities.—Levying officer must execute writs against same defendant in order in which officer receives them. (27-18-303).

Sale of property may be had prior to judgment on order of court, proceeds to be deposited in court. (27-18-802).

Release.—After appearance defendant may obtain release of attachment upon filing undertaking in amount to be fixed by court. (27-18-721, 722). If no proceedings have been taken for five years in action in which attachment was issued, defendant or record owner may apply to clerk of court for release. (27-18-732).

Discharge.—If it appears writ was improperly or illegally issued, it must be discharged. Court may permit amendment of affidavit or undertaking. (27-18-713).

Vacation or Modification.—Defendant has right to post-seizure hearing unless writ issued after show cause hearing. (27-18-701). If motion based on papers supporting writ, it must be made with or without notice as court sees proper; otherwise notice required. (27-18-726). Motion to vacate or modify may be made by defendant or any person acquiring interest in property after attachment. (27-18-725).

Third Party Claims.—If third party claims personal property by filing affidavit with sheriff, sheriff must deliver property to claimant unless plaintiff gives indemnity bond within ten days after notice. (27-18-602).

CREDITORS' SUITS:

No statute.

EXECUTIONS:

While rules are patterned after federal rules, executions are still governed by statute. (Rule 69). See category Civil Actions and Procedure, topic Judgments.

Judgments for money, possession of real or personal property, or arrest are enforced by writs of execution (25-13-201); judgments for sale of property, by orders of sale (25-13-202); and judgments requiring other acts, by serving certified copy of judgment on defendant or person required to obey judgment, and may be enforced by court (25-13-203).

Exemptions.—See topic Exemptions.

Time for Issuance of Writ of Execution.—Generally, any time within six years after entry of judgment (25-13-101) and thereafter by leave of court on motion or by judgment for that purpose founded on supplemental pleadings (25-13-102). Judgment for payment of child support may generally be issued within ten years after termination of support obligation or within ten years from entry of lump-sum judgment or order for support arrears. (25-13-101[2]).

Stay of Execution.—See category Civil Actions and Procedure, topic Appeal and Error.

Contents of Writ.—Writ must be issued in name of state of Montana, sealed, and subscribed by clerk of court; be directed to sheriff or levying officer; and refer to judgment and require sheriff or levying officer to act. (25-13-301). In executions amount must be computed as near as may be in dollars and cents. (25-13-301).

Execution Against Property of Judgment Debtor.—For writ against property of judgment debtor, sheriff or levying officer shall satisfy judgment plus interest from debtor's personal property, unless insufficient, then from debtor's real property. (25-13-304, 305).

The writ is executed by levying on sufficient property of the judgment debtor, collecting or selling his claims or other things in action, and selling such other real or personal property as may be necessary to satisfy the judgment. (25-13-402). Writ must be executed no later than 60 days after receipt by sheriff or levying officer. (25-13-402).

Levy.—Execution is levied in same manner as writ of attachment, except party requesting execution should provide bond covering costs incurred, if substantial. (25-13-403). (See topic Attachment.)

As to levy on mortgaged personal property, see category Mortgages, topic Chattel Mortgages.

Lien.—If judgment is lien upon debtor's real property, sheriff shall satisfy judgment from real property owned by debtor on day of judgment or after acquired by debtor, unless execution is to be issued in county other than where judgment recovered, then property owned when transcript was filed in that county. (25-13-305).

Return by officer must be not less than ten nor more than 60 days after his receipt of the writ. (25-13-404).

Priorities are the same as in case of attachment. (See topic Attachment.)

Claims of third persons are disposed of in same way as in case of attachment. (See topic Attachment.)

Property Subject to Execution.—Generally, all goods, chattels, money and other real and personal property or any interest in such property of judgment debtor is liable to execution. (25-13-501). (See topic Attachment.) Debts owed to judgment debtor may be paid to sheriff to satisfy execution. (25-13-502).

Property Exempt from Execution.—Generally following are exempt: prescribed health aids; benefits from federal social security or public assistance; veteran's benefits; disability benefits; health care benefits to extent used for health care; maintenance and child support; and burial plot. (25-13-608). However, veterans' and social security legislation benefits for remuneration for employment and disability benefits are not exempt if execution is for child support or maintenance to spouse or former spouse who is custodial parent of child from whom support is owed and judgment debtor is parent. See also 25-13-609 allowing for exemptions for personal property from specified categories with aggregate limit of $4,500, up to $1,200 in automobiles, up to $3,000 in professional books, and tools, and up to $4,000 in unmatured life insurance. (25-13-609).

Satisfaction.—No provision distinct from satisfaction of judgment. See category Civil Actions and Procedure, topic Judgments, subhead Satisfaction.

Sale.—Notice of sale is given by posting written notice in three public places, in the township or city where sale is to be held: (1) in case of perishable property, a reasonable time; (2) in case of other personal property, five to ten days and by publishing copy of notice at least one week before sale in newspaper of general circulation published in county, if there be one; (3) in case of real estate, 20 days, in both township or city where sale held and where property situated, and publication once a week for same period. (25-13-701). Sales are made at auction, to highest bidder between hours of 9 and 5 until sufficient property to satisfy judgment has been sold. (25-13-704).

Redemption.—Real property with estate greater than two year leasehold interest, sold on execution may be redeemed by debtor, debtor's spouse, his successor in interest, or lien holder at any time within one year from date of sale, on paying purchaser amount of his purchase, with interest at rate established by judgment up to time of redemption, and any taxes which purchaser may have paid thereon after purchase and interest thereon, plus reasonable maintenance and repair costs. If purchaser is creditor having prior lien to that of redemptioner, other than judgment under which purchase was made, amount of lien with interest must also be paid. After first redemption property may be successively redeemed, in 60 days after last redemption under like conditions. If judgment debtor redeems, effect of sale is terminated and he is restored to his estate. (25-13-801 to 809).

If the judgment debtor personally occupies premises as home for himself and family, he is entitled to remain in possession until the expiration of the period of redemption, but may be restrained from committing waste. (25-13-821). If tenant be in possession, purchaser is entitled to rents from time of sale. (25-13-822). For disposal of agricultural land see Title 25, c. 13, Part 9.

Supplementary Proceedings.—When an execution against property is returned unsatisfied, or before the return of execution, upon proof, by affidavit of a party, that any judgment debtor has property which he unjustly refuses to apply toward the satisfaction of the judgment, the court may, by an order, require the judgment debtor to appear at a specified time and place to answer concerning his property, and such proceeding extends to the application of such property to the satisfaction of the judgment. Instead of the order requiring the appearance of the debtor, the court may, upon affidavit that there is danger that the debtor is about to leave the state, order his arrest. No judgment debtor can be required to attend before a judge or referee out of the county in which he resides. (25-14-101, 102).

Supplementary proceedings are not applicable against corporations, as judgment debtors, but where the proceedings are against third parties indebted to the judgment debtor, such third parties, including a corporation, may be required to appear and answer. (25-14-104). Witnesses may be required to appear in like manner as in trial of original issue. (25-14-105).

After issuing an order for the appearance of the judgment debtor or third person, the court, may appoint receiver for property of judgment debtor. (25-14-201 to 205). At least two days' notice of application must be given personally to judgment debtor, unless judge is satisfied judgment debtor cannot be found in state. (25-14-201).

Body Execution.—Where judgment debtor unjustly refuses to apply property toward satisfaction he may be ordered to appear before judge or arrested. (25-14-102).

EXEMPTIONS:

Nonresident has no exemptions.

Resident is entitled to exemptions against execution provided by statute. (25-13-606).

Judgment debtor is entitled to exemption from execution of following: Professionally prescribed health aids, social security benefits, veteran's benefits, disability benefits, health care benefits to extent used for health care; maintenance and child support and burial plot. Veteran's benefits, social security benefits and disability benefits are not exempt if debt is for child support or maintenance to be paid to spouse or former spouse with custody of child for whom child support is owed. (25-13-608). Also exempt are judgment debtors' interest in personal property not to exceed $4,500 aggregate-value of any one item not to exceed $600; value in one car up to $1,200; $3,000 in materials necessary for trade or business; and judgment debtor's interest in any unmatured life insurance contracts owned by him not to exceed $4,000 in value. (25-13-609).

Property necessary to carry out government functions is exempt. (25-13-613).

Substitution.—There is no provision authorizing a debtor who does not own articles specifically exempted to hold other articles or money exempt in lieu thereof.

Bankruptcy.—Individual in any bankruptcy proceeding may not exempt from his estate, property specified in 11 U.S.C. 522(d) except that property exempt from execution of judgment, unemployment compensation and retirement benefits. (31-2-106).

Traceable proceeds from sale of exempt property or from lost or damaged exempt property is exempt for six months. (25-13-610[1]). Earnings, exempt under 25-13-614, that are traceable, remain exempt for 45 days. (25-13-610[2]).

Earnings of judgment debtor not subject to garnishment are exempt. Earnings subject to garnishment are not exempt but amount is limited as set forth in 25-13-614. Separate garnishment statutory limitations apply to judgments or orders for maintenance. (25-13-614). In any action where amount sued for is $10 or less, wages or earnings for personal services rendered within 30 days are exempt from attachment. (27-18-102).

Workers' compensation benefits are exempt from attachment or garnishment for debts (39-71-743) unless such payments are awarded for medical and hospital services (71-3-1118). Workers' compensation benefits may also be subject to garnishment or attachment for payment of child support. (39-71-743).

Silicosis benefits are exempt from execution, levy, garnishment, bankruptcy, insolvency law and other legal process. (39-73-110).

Waiver.—Personal property exemptions may be waived.

Identification of Exempt Property.—Where debtor owns more property of given class than law exempts; it is necessary to identify property to which claim attaches. (54 Mont. 524, 171 P. 1148).

Homestead Exemption.—See topic Homesteads. See also topic Garnishment.

See note at head of Digest as to 1998 legislation covered.

See Topical Index in front part of this volume.

FORECLOSURE:

See topic Liens; category Mortgages, topics Chattel Mortgages, Mortgages of Real Property.

FRAUDULENT SALES AND CONVEYANCES:

Uniform Fraudulent Transfer Act has been adopted. (31-2-326 to 342). Uniform Commercial Code adopted. (Tit. 30). See category Business Regulation and Commerce, topic Commercial Code.

Bulk Sales.—Governed by Uniform Commercial Code.

GARNISHMENT:

In general, garnishments are in all respects subject to same statutes as attachments. See topic Attachment.

Property Which May be Reached.—Debts, credits or other personal property in possession or control of another person. (27-18-405). Various exemptions are set forth for retirement benefits of certain employees, public assistance payments, and earnings of judgment debtors. See also topic Exemptions.

Jurisdiction.—District court has jurisdiction (27-18-205) as does justice court (27-18-1501).

Proceedings to Obtain.—The sheriff, on receiving information in writing from the plaintiff or his attorney that any person has in his possession or under his control any credits or personal property belonging to the defendant, or is indebted to him, shall serve a copy of the writ of attachment upon such person, and a notice that such credits or other property or debts are attached in pursuance of such writ. (27-18-405).

Liability of Garnishee.—Person so served will be liable to the plaintiff for the amount of such credits, property or debts until the attachment is discharged, unless they deliver same to sheriff. (27-18-407).

Answer of Garnishee.—Garnishee must, upon application of levying officer, furnish a statement of property of defendant held by garnishee. (27-18-502).

Appearance of Garnishee.—Such garnishee may also be required to appear in court or before a judge to answer as to his indebtedness to the defendant. (27-18-501).

Adverse Claims.—Third person claiming attached personal property must give sheriff notice and affidavit of claim. (27-18-602).

HOMESTEADS:

Exemption.—Homestead consists of dwelling house or mobile home, and all appurtenances, and land on which same is situated. (70-32-101). Claimant must be in actual residence on premises. (70-32-106). If borrower borrows money and encumbers real property that otherwise would qualify as homestead, lender shall require borrower to sign written statement acknowledging that real property is not exempt from execution as homestead because it may be subject to forced sale to satisfy mortgage. (70-32-221).

Limitation of value is $60,000. In any proceeding to determine value of such homestead, assessed valuation thereof is prima facie evidence of such value. (70-32-104).

Debts or Liabilities Against Which Exemptions Not Available.—The homestead is subject to execution or forced sale in following cases only: on debts secured by construction or vendor's liens; on mortgages executed by husband and wife or unmarried claimant; on mortgages executed and recorded before homestead declaration recorded. (70-32-202).

Designation of Homestead.—Person selecting homestead must execute and file for record declaration of homestead with county clerk of county where land is located. Premises described in declaration constitute homestead from time declaration is filed for record. (70-32-105 to 107).

Waiver prior to judgment or levy is permissible if specific and executed by claimant and spouse, if any. (70-32-301; 93 Mont. 11, 17 P.2d 62).

Abandonment, Conveyance or Encumbrance.—A homestead, once selected and recorded as such, cannot be abandoned, conveyed or encumbered except by written instrument executed and acknowledged by both husband and wife. (70-32-301, 302). See also category Mortgages, topic Mortgages of Real Property.

Proceeds of Sale.—Upon application of a judgment creditor who has levied, an order must be entered directing the sale of the homestead when the value thereof exceeds the amount of the exemption and the property cannot be divided. (70-32-210). After sale on execution against homestead, proceeds up to amount of exemption are paid to debtor and balance applied to satisfaction of judgment. (70-32-212). Money paid to debtor is entitled, for 18 months thereafter, to same protection against legal process and voluntary disposition of either spouse which law gives to homestead. (70-32-213).

Rights of Surviving Spouse and Children.—Surviving spouse is entitled to homestead allowance of $20,000. If there is no surviving spouse, allowance is divided between decedent's minor and dependent children. (72-2-412).

If estate is sufficient, specifically devised property may not be used to satisfy homestead allowance. Subject to this restriction, surviving spouse, guardians of minor children, children, or personal representative if above are unable, may select property of estate to satisfy homestead allowance. (72-2-415).

In case of death of a person entitled to a homestead without a homestead having been selected during decedent's lifetime, personal representative shall select a homestead for use of surviving spouse and minor children. (72-2-415).

LEVY:

See topics Attachment, Executions.

LIENS:

Uniform Commercial Code adopted. (Tit. 30). See category Business Regulation and Commerce, topic Commercial Code.

Person furnishing seed has lien on crop raised therefrom. (71-3-701). Verified notice showing kind, quantity and value of seed, person to whom furnished, and description of land on which used, must be filed with secretary of state within 90 days after seed is furnished. (71-3-703).

Hotel, boarding-house and lodging-house keepers have lien upon baggage or other property brought into hotel, inn, boarding or lodging-house by guest. (71-3-1401). After six months, owner may sell property at public auction after publication of notice once a week for two successive weeks. (71-3-1402, 71-3-1403).

Lien for Licenses.—All property held or used in any trade, occupation or profession is subject to lien for the amount of any state license, which may be enforced by county treasurer in manner provided for sales of personal property for taxes. (7-21-2104).

Mining partner has a lien on the partnership property for debts due creditors of the partnership and for any advances by him. (35-13-205). Lien exists notwithstanding partnership agreements to contrary.

Thresherman has lien on grain and other crops threshed. (71-3-801 to 808). Notice of intention to claim lien must be filed with secretary of state within 30 days after last service rendered. (71-3-802). Notice of lien must be sent to elevatorman or other private purchaser. (71-3-802). Action to foreclose lien must be begun within six months. (71-3-807).

Farm laborer has lien on crops raised during time services were performed. Lien cannot exceed $1,000, nor cover services extending over more than 60 days preceding filing. (71-3-401). Verified lien must be filed with secretary of state within 30 days after services are fully performed. (71-3-402). Action to foreclose lien must be commenced within 90 days, and notice of foreclosure must be given to all similar lienholders. (71-3-404, 405).

Agister's Lien.—Person who keeps, feeds, or pastures stock under express or implied contract has lien on stock for amount due. (71-3-1201). Person keeping personal property or rendering services also has lien for amount due. (71-3-1201). Upon nonpayment for 30 days, claimant may enforce lien by delivering to sheriff statement of amount of claim, description of property, and name of owner or of person requesting services. Upon receipt of statement, sheriff shall proceed to advertise and sell at public auction property sufficient to cover lien. Sale must be in accordance with 25-13-701 (1) (b). (71-3-1203). Crop or grain liens for spraying or dusting provided for in 71-3-901 et seq.

Logger has lien on lumber or timber of person for whom work done. (71-3-601 to 616).

Vendor of realty has lien for unpaid purchase price, except as against purchaser or encumbrancer in good faith and for value. (71-3-1301 to 1303).

Vendee of realty has special lien on realty for such part of the price paid as he may be entitled to recover in event of failure of consideration. (71-3-1302).

Servants and Employees.—In case of assignment by insolvent debtor or levy of attachment or execution, servants and employees have lien on assets for wages owed and for services rendered within four months preceding. (71-3-301, 31-2-205). They have similar priority in case of death of employer and in cases of execution or attachment. (71-3-302, 303). To enforce the lien, claimant must serve notice on sheriff or other officer executing writ against defendant. (71-3-303).

Physicians, nurses, physical therapists, occupational therapists, chiropractors, dentists, psychologists, licensed social workers, licensed professional counselors and hospitals, providing medical care to person injured through fault of another have lien on cause of action, any judgment obtained and money paid in satisfaction or settlement. (71-3-1114). Lien is subordinate to attorney's lien. (71-3-1114[3]). If injured person is insured or beneficiary of insurance contract, there is lien on proceeds or payment to value of services rendered. (71-3-1114[2]). Notice of lien is filed with Clerk of Court if action is commenced. (71-3-1116). Failure to recognize lien after notice results in liability for insurer. (71-3-1117). Notice is served on person and upon his insurer, if any. (71-3-1115). Provisions apply only to contracts of insurance for payment of determinable benefits upon determinable contingencies; life, group life and disability insurance, annuity contracts and benefits under qualified pension plan are excluded. Applicable to payments awarded for medical and hospital services under Worker's Compensation Act or Occupational Disease Act. (71-3-1118).

Construction Liens.—Person furnishing service or materials pursuant to real estate improvement contract may claim construction lien. (71-3-523). Lien extends to interest of contracting owner of real estate subject to provisions of 71-3-525. With certain exceptions, person who may claim construction lien shall give notice of right to claim lien to constructing owner in order to claim lien. Notice must be given within 20 days after service or materials are first furnished to contracting owner. (71-3-531). Notice of right to claim construction lien to regulated lender providing funds for services or materials must be given no later than 45 days after services or materials are first furnished. (71-3-531). Notice must be by certified mail or personal delivery in form specified by statute. (71-3-531). Contents of notice are set forth in statute. (71-3-532). Lien attaches only if filed not later than 90 days after final furnishing of services or materials or owner files notice of completion pursuant to 71-3-533. (71-3-535). Contents of lien statement must conform to statutory requirements. (71-3-536). Construction lien claimants who contribute to same real estate improvement project have equal priority, regardless of date of contribution or service and regardless of date notice is filed. (71-3-541). Construction liens attaching at different times have priority in order of attachment. (71-3-541). Liens take priority over subsequent interests, liens, mortgages or encumbrances, and over certain prior interests, liens, mortgages or encumbrances with certain limitations. (71-3-542). Contracting owner may substitute bond of $1^1/_2$ times amount of lien prior to commencement of action on lien. (71-3-551). Bond must be filed with Clerk of District Court. Lien must be discharged upon posting of bond. Lienholders shall then have right of action on bond in lieu of lien. (71-3-553). Action for foreclosure of lien must be begun within two years after filing of same. (71-3-562).

See note at head of Digest as to 1998 legislation covered.

See Topical Index in front part of this volume.

LIENS . . . *continued*

Public Works.—Contractor performing public work must furnish bond for faithful performance of contract and payment of all laborers, mechanics, subcontractors, materialmen, and persons supplying provisions, provender, material or supplies. Statute specifies notice to be given to public body and also provides for notice to contractors of furnishing provender, material or supplies to subcontractor. (18-2-201 to 208).

Common Expense.—When association of unit owners acting through manager provide services, labor or materials lawfully chargeable as common expenses shall have lien on individual unit and undivided interest in common elements provided statutory requirements are met. (70-23-607 to 608).

Oil Liens.—Laborers and material men have a lien for labor performed or materials, machinery or oil well supplies furnished in drilling and operating of oil or gas wells or construction of pipe lines if within six months a verified, itemized account of claim is filed with county clerk and recorder of county where wells or pipe lines are situated. (71-3-1002 to 1004). Such liens are enforced in same manner as construction liens. (71-3-1005). Priority is date of furnishing first labor or materials as against other encumbrances. All oil liens on same property are of equal standing. (71-3-1007). Property subject to lien may not be removed without consent of lienholder. (71-3-1010).

Oil and gas production damage mitigation account administered by Board of Oil and Gas Conservation has lien for costs of plugging and reclaiming oil and gas wells, plus interest accrued at rate of 10% per year, against all real and personal property in this state, owned in whole or in part, by responsible person. (82-11-164). Lien is valid until discharged. (82-11-164).

Attorney's fees are allowed to prevailing party in action to foreclose mechanic's, construction, materialman's, laborer's or oil lien, farm laborer's lien and liens for salaries and wages. (71-3-124).

Redemption.—Except as otherwise provided by Uniform Commercial Code, every person having an interest in property subject to lien has a right of redemption at any time after the claim is due and before the right of redemption is foreclosed. (71-3-117). Inferior lienor may be subrogated to benefits of superior lien if necessary for protection of his interest, upon satisfying the claims secured thereby. (71-3-118). Redemption is made by performing or offering to perform the act for the performance of which the lien is a security, and paying or offering to pay damages, if any, to which holder of lien is entitled for delay. (71-3-116).

Real property, except when the estate is less than leasehold of two years' unexpired term, is subject to redemption within one year after foreclosure sale. (25-13-801, 802).

Enforcement.—Where no special method of enforcement is provided, security interest may be foreclosed in same manner as real estate mortgage. (30-9-508).

Extinguishment.—Lien extinguished by sale of property to satisfy debt secured, or in case of personal property, lien extinguished by wrongful conversion of property by lienholder (71-3-121), by expiration of statute of limitations (71-3-122) or by voluntary restoration of property to owner where lien depends on possession (71-3-123).

Attachment Lien.—See topic Attachment.

Attorney's Lien.—See category Legal Profession, topic Attorneys and Counselors.

Carrier's Lien.—See category Business Regulation and Commerce, topic Carriers.

Collateral Security.—See topic Pledges.

Execution Lien.—See topic Executions.

Factor's Lien.—See category Business Regulation and Commerce, topic Factors.

Judgment Lien.—See category Civil Actions and Procedure, topic Judgments.

Landlord's Lien.—See category Property, topic Landlord and Tenant.

Liens on Exempt Property.—See topic Exemptions.

Liens on Homestead.—See topic Homesteads.

Real Estate Mortgage Lien.—See category Mortgages, topic Mortgages of Real Property.

Tax Lien.—See category Taxation, topics Inheritance Tax, subhead Lien, Property Taxes, subhead Lien.

MECHANICS' LIENS:

See topic Liens.

PLEDGES:

Uniform Commercial Code adopted. (Tit. 30). See category Business Regulation and Commerce, topic Commercial Code.

Lien of pledge is dependent on possession. (71-2-103).

Remedies of Pledgee.—Uniform Commercial Code adopted. (Tit. 30). See category Business Regulation and Commerce, topic Commercial Code.

Pawnbrokers' pledges are governed by special law prescribing conditions. (31-1-401 to 407).

Trust Receipts.—Uniform Commercial Code adopted. (Tit. 30). See category Business Regulation and Commerce, topic Commercial Code.

RECEIVERS:

A receiver may be appointed: (1) In an action by a vendor to vacate a fraudulent purchase of property, or by a creditor to subject any property or fund to his claim, or between partners or others jointly owning property, on application of any party interested, where it is shown that property or fund is in danger of being lost, wholly or in part; (2) in an action for foreclosure of a mortgage, where it appears that mortgagee is in danger of losing his security, wholly or in part, or that property is insufficient security for mortgage debt; (3) after judgment, to carry judgment into effect; (4) to preserve property during appeal (27-20-102); (5) in an action to enjoin violation of Consumer Loan Act (32-5-405); (6) in all other cases where receivers have heretofore been appointed by usages of courts of equity (27-20-102).

Jurisdiction to appoint is vested in district courts. (3-5-302).

Proceedings.—Generally, notice of application before judgment required. (27-20-201). Two days' notice must be given to judgment debtor before court will appoint receiver during proceedings in aid of execution. (25-14-201).

Eligibility and Competency.—No party, attorney or person interested in the action can be appointed without written consent of parties. (27-20-202).

Qualification.—Oath and bond, in amount fixed by judge, must be filed. (27-20-301).

Powers.—Under control of court, receiver has power to bring and defend actions, to take and keep possession of property, receive rents, collect or compromise debts, make transfers. (27-20-302).

REDEMPTION:

See topics Executions, Liens; categories Mortgages, topic Mortgages of Real Property; Taxation, topic Property Taxes, subhead Redemption.

SUPPLEMENTARY PROCEEDINGS:

See topic Executions.

USURY:

See category Business Regulation and Commerce, topic Interest.

DISPUTE RESOLUTION

ALTERNATIVE DISPUTE RESOLUTION:

Mandatory Dispute Resolution.—Some district courts have promulgated rules which allow court to order parties to participate in settlement conference.

Voluntary Dispute Resolution.—Some district courts have promulgated rules which allow any party to request court to convene settlement conference. See topic Arbitration and Award.

ARBITRATION AND AWARD:

Persons capable of contracting may submit to arbitration any controversy which might be subject of civil action between them, except in cases outlined below.

Uniform Arbitration Act, as modified, adopted effective Oct. 1, 1985. (27-5-111 to 324).

Form and Requisites of Submission.—Written agreement to submit existing controversy to arbitration is valid and enforceable except upon grounds that exist for revocation of contract. (27-5-114[1]).

Contracts to Arbitrate Future Disputes.—Written agreement to submit to arbitration future disputes is valid and enforceable except upon such grounds as exist at law or in equity for revocation of contract. (27-5-114[2]). Notice that contract is subject to arbitration must be typed in underlined capital letters on first page of contract or contract may not be subject to arbitration. (27-5-114[4]).

Power of Arbitrators.—Arbitrator appointed pursuant to agreement or by court has all powers permitted under agreement. Arbitrators shall appoint time and place for hearing, cause notice to be given all parties, adjourn or postpone hearing, hear evidence and make award. Majority of arbitrators at hearing may determine any question and render final judgment unless otherwise provided by agreement. (27-5-212 to 213).

Award and Enforcement Thereof.—Award must be in writing and signed by arbitrators. (27-5-216). District court may confirm, modify, correct or vacate award as provided by law. (27-5-311, 27-5-312, 27-5-313).

Judgment on Award.—Upon granting of order confirming, modifying or correcting award, judgment must be entered in conformity with order and enforced as any other judgment. (27-5-314).

Award may be set aside or modified by court on grounds of fraud, corruption, partiality, arbitrator exceeded powers, miscalculation, mistake, award of matter not submitted, or imperfection. (27-5-312, 27-5-313).

Exclusions.—Arbitration agreements not valid and enforceable in cases involving personal injury claims, agreements between insurers and insureds relating to policies or annuity contracts, workers' compensation claims, and any contract by individual for acquisition of real or personal property, services, or money or credit where total consideration to be paid or furnished by individual is $5,000 or less. (27-5-114).

DOCUMENTS AND RECORDS

ACKNOWLEDGMENTS:

Uniform Law on Notarial Acts adopted. (1-5-601 to 611).

May be taken by following persons:

Within State.—Notary public of this state; judge, clerk, or deputy clerk of any court of this state; any other person authorized to perform specific act by law of this state.

Outside State.—Notary public of that jurisdiction; judge, clerk, or deputy clerk of court of that jurisdiction; any other person authorized by law to perform specific act. (1-5-606).

Reciprocity of Notarial Acts.—Montana notarial officer may perform notarial act in bordering state if state recognizes officer's authority within state. Notarial act performed in Montana by notarial officer of bordering state has same effect as if act were performed by Montana notarial officer, provided that bordering state grants Montana's notarial officers similar authority within bordering state. (1-5-605).

Notarial Acts Under Federal Authority.—Has same effect under law of this state as if performed by notarial officer of this state if performed anywhere by following persons: judge, clerk, or deputy clerk of court; commissioned officer on active duty in

See note at head of Digest as to 1998 legislation covered.

See Topical Index in front part of this volume.

ACKNOWLEDGMENTS . . . *continued*

military service of U.S.; officer of foreign service or consular officer of U.S.; any other person authorized by federal law to perform notarial acts. (1-5-607).

Foreign Notarial Acts.—Has same effect under law of this state as if performed by notarial officer of this state if it is performed within jurisdiction of and under authority of foreign nation by any of following persons: notary public or notary; judge, clerk, or deputy clerk of court of record; any other person authorized by law of that jurisdiction to perform notarial acts. (1-5-608).

Requirements as to Taking Acknowledgment.—Officer shall determine, either from personal knowledge or from satisfactory evidence, that acknowledgor is person whose true signature is on instrument. (1-5-603).

Fee for taking acknowledgment is $1 for first signature and 50¢ for each additional signature. (1-5-418). Additional fees which may be charged by notaries in statutory list.

Effect of Acknowledgment.—Extrinsic evidence of authenticity as condition precedent to admissibility is not required for acknowledged documents. (M.R.Ev. 902[8]; 72 Mont. 345, 232 P. 90).

Alternatives to Acknowledgment or Proof.—Execution of instrument may be established by proof of handwriting of party and subscribing witness, if any, when parties and all subscribing witnesses are dead, are nonresidents, or residence or whereabouts of subscribing witness are unknown. (1-5-302).

Forms.—Following acknowledgment forms are authorized by 1-5-610:

(1) *For an acknowledgment in an individual capacity:*

State of . . . .

(County) of . . . .

        This instrument was acknowledged before me on (date), by (name(s) of persons(s)).

        _____

        (Signature of notarial officer)

(Seal, if any)   Title (and Rank)

        [My commission expires: . . . .]

(2) *For an acknowledgment in a representative capacity:*

State of . . . .

(County) of . . . .

        This instrument was acknowledged before me on (date) by (name(s) of person(s)) as (type of authority, e.g., officer, trustee, etc.) of (name of party on behalf of whom instrument was executed).

        _____

        (Signature of notarial officer)

(Seal, if any)   Title (and Rank)

        [My commission expires: . . . .]

Validating Acts.—Notwithstanding any defect, omission, or informality in execution or acknowledgment, instruments affecting real property recorded prior to Jan. 1, 1991 shall be deemed to impart after that date notice of their contents to subsequent purchasers and encumbrancers. (70-21-309). Similar validating acts in force for unacknowledged deeds executed prior to Jan. 1, 1983. (70-20-315). All instruments acknowledged on behalf of corporation prior to July 1, 1947, and certain subsequent dates, by any person duly authorized to execute instruments are validated as of those dates respectively. (Not recodified.)

AFFIDAVITS:

An affidavit to be used before any court, judge or officer of this state, may be taken:

Within the state, before any judge, clerk of any court, justice of peace, county clerk or notary public. (26-1-1003). For fee, see topic Acknowledgments.

Without the state but within the United States, before a commissioner appointed by the Governor of this state, a notary public or any judge or clerk of court of record having a seal. (26-1-1004).

In foreign country, before ambassador, minister, consul, vice-consul or consular agent of U. S. or before any judge of court of record having seal in such country. (26-1-1005).

General Requirements of Jurat.—A notary must authenticate all acts with notary public's official seal, adding to his signature words "Notary Public for the State of Montana, residing at . . . . " and expiration date of notary's commission. Notary public may not authorize notary's own signature. (1-5-416).

Authentication.—If taken before a judge of a court in another state or foreign country, the genuineness of the signature of the judge, the existence of the court, and the fact that such judge is a member thereof, must be certified by the clerk of the court under the seal thereof. (26-1-1006).

Use.—Affidavits may be used to verify a pleading or a paper in a special proceeding, to prove service of summons, notice or other paper in an action or special proceeding, to obtain a provisional remedy, examination of a witness, or a stay of proceedings, or upon a motion, and in any other cause expressly permitted by provisions of Code. (26-1-1002). Affidavits may be used and considered on motion for summary judgment as provided by Rule 56, M.R.Civ.P.

Form.—No statutory form exists. Following is usual:

Form

State of . . . . }

County of . . . . } ss.

. . . . . , being first duly sworn, deposes and says: (Insert statements as to necessary matters).

        _____

        (Signature of affiant).

Subscribed and sworn to before me this . . . . day of . . . ., 19. . . . .

(Signature and full official designation of officer, with date of expiration of commission and residence, city and state, of notary. Use official seal, if any).

Alternative to Affidavit.—Party may, at his option, affirm or declare instead of taking oath, by assenting when addressed in following form: "You do solemnly affirm (or declare), etc." (1-6-104).

NOTARIES PUBLIC:

Uniform Law on Notarial Acts enacted. (1-5-401 et seq.).

Qualification.—Bond in amount of $5,000 must be approved by, and oath must be filed with, Secretary of State. Upon approval, Secretary of State has discretion whether to issue commission.(1-5-405). Must be resident for one year preceding appointment and cannot be convicted felon. (1-5-402).

Authentication.—See topic Affidavits.

Seal must be provided by notary, which must show name, and which must be used to authenticate all official acts. (1-5-416).

Powers and Duties.—To take acknowledgments, take depositions and affidavits, and administer oaths and affirmations. Notary public may not notarize notary's own signature. (1-5-416).

Territorial Extent of Powers.—The jurisdiction of a notary extends throughout the state regardless of the notary's place of residence. (1-5-415).

Extraterritorial Extent of Powers.—Montana notary may perform notarial act in bordering state if state recognizes officer's authority within state. Notarial act performed in Montana by notarial officer of bordering state has same effect under Montana law as if act were performed by Montana notarial officer, provided that bordering state grants Montana's notarial officers similar authority within bordering state. (1-5-415 and 1-5-605).

Expiration of Commission.—Date must be added to signature in all cases and place of residence must be shown. (1-5-416).

Fees.—Affidavits, depositions, etc., $3.50 per page; acknowledgments, first signature, $1; each additional, 50¢; administering oath or affirmation, $1; certifying affidavit, $1. (1-5-418).

RECORDS:

Uniform Commercial Code adopted. (Tit. 30). See category Business Regulation and Commerce, topic Commercial Code.

Place of Recording.—Instruments relating to property which are entitled to recording are filed with county clerk and recorder of county where property is located. (7-4-2613). *For list of Counties and County Seats see first page for this state in Volume containing Practice Profiles Section.* See also category Property, topic Deeds, subhead Recording.

Recordable Instruments.—Any instrument or judgment affecting real property or interests appurtenant thereto. (70-21-201). Abstracts of such instruments may be recorded in lieu of original document. (7-4-2613). Recordable abstract of instrument, conveyance, or encumbrance must contain: (a) Names and addresses (street, city, state) of parties thereto; (b) description of real property affected; (c) statement that it is an abstract of another document; (d) short statement of effect of document abstracted, and (e) name and address of person who will provide a full and complete copy of document abstracted, without cost, upon request of any person. Abstract shall be executed and acknowledged or proved by all parties executing abstracted document. (70-21-101). Abstract of conveyance or encumbrance of real property acknowledged or proved, and certified and recorded as prescribed by law, shall have same effect for all purposes as if abstracted document had been acknowledged or proved, and certified and recorded as prescribed by law. (70-21-305).

Filing Under Commercial Code.—Place; Fees.—Financing Statements filed as follows: (a) When collateral is consumer goods, then in office of County Clerk and Recorder in county of debtor's residence or if debtor is not resident of Montana then in Office of County Clerk and Recorder in County where goods are kept; (b) when collateral is timber to be cut or minerals or the like (including oil and gas) or accounts subject to 30-9-103(5), or when financing statement is filed as fixture filing (30-9-313) and collateral is goods which are or will become fixtures, then in office where mortgage on real estate would be filed or recorded; (c) in all other cases, in office of Secretary of State, Helena, Montana. (30-9-401). Follows 1962 version of commercial code with 1972 amendments.

Fees.—Filing fees are $7 per financing statement. Continuations and amendments are $5. No fee for termination. AG-2 forms are $2 per document. Certificate may be obtained from filing officer showing whether any presently effective financing statement naming particular debtor or statement of assignment exists; fee is $7. Filing officer will furnish copy of filed financing statement or statement of assignment for fee of 50¢ per page.

See also category Business Regulation and Commerce, topic Commercial Code.

Requisites for Recording.—Judgments, decrees, and patents do not require acknowledgments. All other instruments do. (70-21-203, 205, 207). In case of deed, mortgage or assignment of mortgage, address of grantee, mortgagee or assignee must appear. (7-4-2618). In case of transfer of realty, a realty transfer certificate describing consideration paid or to be paid for property transferred must be prepared and presented to clerk and recorder before transfer instrument will be recorded. (15-7-301 to 311).

Recording Fees.—Recording fee is $6 per page or fraction thereof. (7-4-2631, 2632).

Effect of Record.—Recording is constructive notice to third persons. (70-21-302).

Torrens system or any similar system of land registration or title to land not adopted.

Transfer of Decedent's Title.—Uniform Probate Code adopted. (Tit. 72). Special procedures for property interests not requiring probate when termination results from death of person holding interest. (72-16-501 to 505).

See note at head of Digest as to 1998 legislation covered.

See Topical Index in front part of this volume.

RECORDS . . . *continued*

Vital Statistics.—Birth and death certificates must be filed with County Clerk and Recorder, who files copies with Division of Vital Statistics, Department of Public Health. (7-4-2613[4]). Clerks of court must file with Division certificates of marriage licenses issued, and of decrees of dissolution, annulment and adoption entered. (50-15-101 to 407). Department of Public Health must also be notified in certain instances of exposures to infectious disease. (50-16-701 to 705). Clerks of court must also file with Division of Vital Statistics report containing certain vital statistics relating to divorced parties. (50-15-302).

Certified copies of birth and death certificates are obtainable from local County Clerk and Recorder (fee, $5 and $3, respectively), or from Division of Vital Statistics, Department of Public Health, Helena, Montana 59601 (fee, $5 for either). (7-4-2631, 50-15-111). Certified copies of marriage certificates are obtainable from local clerk of court (fee, $2). Court orders are required for obtaining some information in vital statistics records, including information concerning illegitimacy of birth. (50-15-122).

Establishing Birth Records.—Delayed certificates are accepted for filing on submission or proof satisfactory to Division of Vital Statistics, which requires proof of birth by at least three documents of different origin, such as affidavits of attending physician, midwife or parents, baptismal or confirmation records, school census reports, insurance policies, etc. (50-15-204, 16.6.303 Administrative Rules of Montana). Person may petition district court for an order establishing date and place of birth and parentage. Order is entered after proof satisfactory to judge and copy thereof is filed with Division of Vital Statistics and county clerk. Division issues delayed certificate based on order. (50-15-121 et seq.).

SEALS:

Uniform Commercial Code adopted. (Tit. 30). See category Business Regulation and Commerce, topic Commercial Code.

No seal necessary, except in some official and corporate acts. (1-4-205). Stamp may be used as official seal. (1-4-202).

TORRENS ACT:

Not adopted.

VITAL STATISTICS:

See topic Records.

EMPLOYMENT

EMPLOYER AND EMPLOYEE:

See topic Labor Relations.

LABOR RELATIONS:

An employer is liable for all services properly rendered. An employer must indemnify his employee for all that he necessarily expends or loses in direct consequence of the discharge of his duties, or in his direct obedience to the directions of the employer, even though unlawful, if not known to be such by the employee at the time, but the employer is not bound to indemnify employee against the ordinary risks of the business for which he is employed. The employer must indemnify the employee for want of ordinary care. (39-2-101 to 39-3-706).

Labor law administered by Department of Labor and Industry. (39-1-102).

Wages.—Employer of labor must pay employees in lawful money of U.S. or checks on banks convertible into cash on demand for full face value. (39-3-204). Payment may be made by electronic funds transfer. (39-3-204). Employer who fails to pay employee or who violates any other provision of this part is guilty of misdemeanor. Penalty must also be assessed against and paid by employer to employee in amount not to exceed 110% of wages due and unpaid. (39-3-206). When employee separates from employ of any employer, all unpaid wages of employee are due and payable on next regular payday for pay period during which employee was separated from employment or 15 days from date of separation from employment, whichever occurs first, either through regular pay channels or by mail if requested by employee. Except when employee is discharged by reason of theft connected to employee's work, when employee is separated for cause or laid off from employment by employer, all unpaid wages of employee are due and payable immediately upon separation unless employer has written personnel policy governing employment that extends time for payment of final wages to employee's next regular payday for pay period or to within 15 days from separation, whichever occurs first. (39-3-205). Employer must furnish employee with statement of money deducted for income taxes, social security, or other reasons. (39-3-101).

In assignments, estates, attachment and similar liens, wages earned within four months have priority. (71-3-301 to 71-3-307).

Woman is entitled to equal pay with man for equivalent services. (39-3-104).

Minimum wage equals minimum hourly wage rate as provided under Federal Fair Labor Standards Act excluding value of tips received by employee and special provisions for training wage. (39-3-409). Minimum wage rate for business whose annual gross sales are $110,000 or less is $4 an hour. (39-3-409).

Employer prohibited from discriminating against employees who consume lawful products during nonworking hours. (39-2-313).

Assignment of wages; see category Debtor and Creditor, topic Assignments.

Child labor.—Provisions vary with type of job and age of child. (See 41-2-102 through 41-2-118.)

Hours of Labor.—Limitation of eight-hour day applies to certain occupations, excluding hydroelectric dam employees (39-4-101 to 39-4-112), including retail stores in towns having population of 2,500 or over (39-4-105) and restaurants (39-4-111).

Labor Unions.—Few statutory provisions with respect to collective bargaining or recognition in private sector. Montana Public Employees' Collective Bargaining Act

enacted. (39-31-101 to 39-31-409). Collective bargaining for nurses regulated by statute. (39-32-101 to 39-32-114). Limited right to work law prevents union interference with sole proprietor or partnership of not more than two, and their immediate family, where engaged in retail or amusement activity. (39-33-101 to 39-33-105).

Labor Disputes.—Injunction cannot be granted in labor dispute when same conditions would not warrant injunction if parties were not laborers or dispute did not involve labor. (27-19-103).

Wrongful Discharge.—Common law remedies eliminated. Statute provides that discharge is wrongful only if it was not for good cause after probationary period has passed, it was in retaliation for employee's refusal to violate public policy or for reporting violation of public policy, or employer violated express provisions of its own personnel policy. Employee may recover punitive damages if employee establishes by clear and convincing evidence that employer engaged in actual fraud or actual malice when discharging employee. (39-2-901 to 39-2-915).

Workmen's Compensation Act applies to all employers except household employment, casual employment, dependent family member for whom exemption may be claimed under Internal Revenue Code, sole proprietors or partners, members of L.L.C., real estate broker or salesperson, employment with railroad, employment as official at school amateur athletic event, newspaper carriers and freelance correspondents, cosmetologists, person employed by enrolled tribal member, jockeys, petroleum land professionals, officer of ditch company, ministers, employees covered by federal government, direct home sales people, and persons performing services for aid or sustenance only except air search and rescue volunteers. (39-71-401). Independent contractors are not covered. (39-71-120). Exemptions may be applied for. Employers are required to post signs giving notice of their coverage. (39-71-401).

Law in effect at time of injury is controlling. (Buckman v. Montana Deaconess Hosp., 730 P.2d 380). Given significant variation in procedural and substantive aspects of 1983, 1985, 1987, 1991, 1993, 1995 and 1997 Acts, careful attention to date of injury is required. Compensability and availability of wage and medical benefits must be determined with specific reference to version of Act in effect on date of injury.

The law is administered by Department of Labor and Industry.

Lump sum advance settlement may be made. (39-71-741).

Burial compensation up to $1,400 provided for. (39-71-725).

The employer may adopt one of three plans of compensation. Under plan one employer may make payments direct to employees as they become entitled to receive same under terms of act. To operate under this plan, employer must furnish satisfactory proof to department of his solvency and financial ability to pay compensation and benefits in act provided for. Under plan two employer may insure liability to pay compensation and benefits provided for by any insurance company authorized to transact business in state. Plan three is coverage by State Compensation Insurance Fund.

Act provides a schedule of payments for all classes of disability suffered by employee, medical benefits and rehabilitation benefits. (39-71-701 to 39-71-743, 39-71-1004, et seq.). Disability to be supported by objective medical findings. (39-71-407). Injured employee whose employer has elected to come under terms of act can only recover compensation provided for in Act. (39-71-412). Non-covered claims and intentional conduct give rise to independent civil action. Exclusive remedy provision does not apply to mental injuries without physical component. Where third party joins employer in civil suit, based upon express indemnity agreement, exclusive remedy provides complete defense for employer. Compensation may be reduced where worker also receives disability social security benefits. (39-71-701 and 702). Fund exists to compensate injured employee of uninsured employer. (39-71-502). Uninsured employee may elect to take under fund, bring action against employer, and/or pursue any other legal remedy. (39-71-508). Department of Labor and Industry may concurrently pursue criminal and civil actions against uninsured employer. (39-71-507). Employee may bring suit against employer for failure to enroll in compensation plan and recover compensation employee would have received had employer been enrolled. (39-71-515). Employee, uninsured employer, and beneficiaries may enter into liability settlement. (39-71-519). Contributory negligence (unless willful), assumption of risk and fellow servant rule are not defenses in such action. (39-71-509). Compensation for death payable to beneficiaries as defined in 39-71-116. (39-71-721). Obtaining any benefits fraudulently constitutes theft.

Claims are barred unless presented within 12 months, however, department may waive statute of limitation upon showing of latent injury or equitable estoppel. (39-71-601). Notice of claim for injuries not resulting in death must be served within 30 days. (39-71-603). Insurers must accept or deny claim within 30 days, and denials must be in writing. Insurers must notify each employer of all compensation benefits ongoing and charged to employer's account. (39-71-606). Biweekly compensation for temporary total disability shall be continuously paid until claimant is released by doctor, returns to work, or no longer suffers loss of earning capacity. Termination or reduction of biweekly compensation may be made only after 14 days written notice to claimant unless claimant returns to work. (39-71-609, 610). Insurer shall pay reasonable costs and attorney fees if: (1) Insurer denies liability or terminates benefits; (2) claim is later adjudged compensable; and (3) insurer's actions were unreasonable. (39-71-611).

Where injury results from act or omission of third person while employee is performing duties of employment, employee may collect compensation and also prosecute action against such third person (39-71-412), but employee can prosecute action against fellow servant or employer only for intentional or malicious acts or omissions (39-71-413). Employer or insurer is subrogated to extent of all compensation and benefits paid under Act if, after request by employee bringing action, insurer agrees to pay proportionate share of costs of action and attorneys' fees. Failure to so agree waives 50% of subrogation right. Insurer entitled to subrogation only if award is in excess after claimant is "made whole" through workers' compensation benefits and third party claim recovery. If employee fails to bring action within one year, employer or insurer may do so on behalf of employee or his representative. (39-71-414).

Occupational Disease Act applies to all diseases arising out of or contracted from and in course of employment. (39-72-305). Act applies to all employers and employees subject to Workmen's Compensation Act. (39-72-301). Last injurious exposure rule applies, with exceptions for pneumoconiosis. (39-72-303). Claimant must present claim

See note at head of Digest as to 1998 legislation covered.

See Topical Index in front part of this volume.

LABOR RELATIONS . . . *continued*

for benefits, in writing, within one year from date claimant knew or should have known of occupational disease. Department may waive claim time up to additional two years.

Schedule of payments for all classes of disability same as Workmen's Compensation Act provisions with exceptions for pneumoconiosis and retraining. (39-72-701). No compensation for partial disability. (30-72-703). When insurer denies liability, department shall direct claimant to member of medical panel for examination. (39-72-602). Second panel examination may be requested. Report of medical panel is prima facie evidence. (39-72-609). Claimant must prove proximate causation. (39-72-408). When payment has been unreasonably delayed or refused, worker's compensation judge may increase compensation benefits awarded by 20%.

Unemployment Insurance.—Benefits are payable to any individual, except athlete and illegal alien and when unemployment is result of strike (39-51-2305), who is or becomes unemployed, providing certain eligibility requirements are met. Individual may be required to participate in reemployment services. (39-51-2103 to 39-51-2110). Public school employees are ineligible for benefits between academic terms. (39-51-2108). Weekly benefit amounts vary from $12 to $1/26$ of total wages for insured work during calendar quarter of recipient's highest earnings. Limit on benefits is 60% of average weekly wage for all classes of similar employment (39-51-2201), with maximum number of weeks payable depending on amount of earning during base period (39-51-2204). Extended benefits available. (39-51-2501 to 2510). Recipient may be disqualified for extended benefits by failure to apply for or accept suitable work, or to return to customary occupation. (39-51-2508). Unemployment Insurance Act has been amended to conform with Federal Unemployment Tax Act.

For discussion of employer contributions, see category Taxation, topic Unemployment Compensation Tax.

WORKERS' COMPENSATION LAW:

See topic Labor Relations.

ENVIRONMENT

ENVIRONMENTAL REGULATION:

Const. Art. IX gives constitutional dimension to environmental protection. Legislature is directed to maintain and improve clean and healthful environment for present and future generations, to provide adequate remedies for protection of eco-systems and resources, and to provide effective reclamation standards. All water declared property of state for use of its people, subject to existing rights to use of waters for useful or beneficial purposes. Central administration of water rights required in addition to present system of local records. Legislature required to identify, acquire, and restore, enhance and preserve scenic, scientific, cultural and recreational areas and sites for use and enjoyment of people.

General Supervision.—Montana legislature enacted Environmental Policy Act (75-1-101 to 75-1-324) to encourage productive harmony between man and his environment, eliminate damage to biosphere, and enrich understanding of ecological systems and resources important to state. Act broadly directs all state agencies to administer laws in accordance with ecological principles; to utilize a systematic, interdepartmental approach in planning; and to include in every recommendation or report on proposals a detailed statement on environmental impact of proposal, any adverse effects, alternatives, and any irreversible commitments of resources. Environmental impact statements must include evaluation of regulatory restrictions on private property. (75-1-201). Environmental Quality Council consisting of 13 members is empowered to appoint an executive director qualified in environmental sciences and shall monitor environmental developments, prepare recommendations for legislation, conduct investigations and studies, review operating programs, and prepare recommendations for remedying existing deficiencies. (75-1-324). Council has authority to investigate and inspect all records of any state agency, board, or commission. (75-1-311). Council has subpoena power to compel attendance of witnesses at hearings and investigations. (75-1-312). Presently, supervision of individual control programs is vested in state agency having general supervisory power over particular industry or activity involved. See specific subheads, infra.

Air Pollution.—Clean Air Act of Montana (75-2-101 to 75-2-514), administered by Department of Environmental Quality, Cogswell Building, Helena, Montana 59601, with advice of Air Pollution Control Advisory Council, provides for departmental regulation of levels, concentrations, or quantities of emissions of various pollutants from any source necessary to prevent, abate, or control air pollution. (75-2-203). Standards for fluorides established through limitations on concentrations in forage grasses, hay, silage. (75-2-202). Enforcement by notice detailing corrective action or by requiring violator to appear and answer charges. Voluntary compliance encouraged. Action initiated under this section may include administrative civil penalty in lieu of criminal penalty of up to $10,000 for each day of violation, not to exceed $80,000. (75-2-401). Emergency procedure established. (75-2-402). Variances authorized. Hearing provided for. (75-2-212). Local air pollution control programs authorized (75-2-301 et seq.). Person who knowingly violates Clean Air Act or makes false report is guilty of criminal offense and faces maximum criminal penalties of $10,000 per offense and imprisonment not to exceed two years or both. (75-2-412). Each day of each violation constitutes separate violation. (75-2-412).

Public Health.—Proprietors of enclosed public places, including restaurants, stores, arenas, public transportation facilities, and other places, must designate non-smoking areas within establishment. (50-40-104). $25 fine for failure to comply. (50-40-109).

Water Pollution.—Comprehensive statute for prevention of water pollution (75-5-101 to 75-5-641), administered by Department of Environmental Quality, Cogswell Building, Helena, Montana 59601, proscribes contamination of state waters or placement of contaminants so as to indirectly infiltrate state waters and proscribes construction, modification, or operation of disposal system or outlets for discharge into state waters without permit; also proscribes construction of sewage lagoon less than 500 feet

from existing water well. (75-5-605). Permit application, modification, or suspension requires notice and opportunity for hearing. (75-5-403, -404). Department may require owner or operator of point source of pollution to monitor, record, and report discharge quantity and quality, and be subject to inspection by Department personnel. (75-5-602, -603). Hearing and judicial review provided for. (75-5-611, -641). Emergency procedure established permitting source endangering health, welfare, or livelihood to be immediately enjoined in District Court of any county in which defendant is located. (75-5-614, -622). Injunctive relief, suit for civil penalty, and criminal prosecution authorized. (75-5-614, -616, -631, -632). Any person may apply to Department protesting violation. Department shall investigate charge and, if investigation proves protest without reasonable cause, department may seek investigation costs from person making protest. (75-5-636). Violation of any rule, permit, effluent standard, or order shall be subject to civil penalty not to exceed $25,000 per day of violation. (75-5-631). Willful violation is criminal offense punishable by fine up to $25,000 per day of violation or one year imprisonment or both. Subsequent convictions up to $50,000 per day of violation or imprisonment for two years or both. (75-5-632). Responsible corporate officer included within definition of "person" for purposes of punitive provisions. (75-5-615[2]).

Mining.—Permit required prior to prospecting, exploration, or any operation for removal of a mineral. Requisite for permit is reclamation plan and performance bond.

Legislature declared purpose to allow exploration for and mining of minerals only while adequately providing for subsequent beneficial use of surface by reclamation. (82-4-301). Comprehensive legislative scheme requiring reclamation plan and bond prior to issuance of permit. Department of State Lands, 1625 Eleventh Avenue, Helena, Montana 59601, charged with environmental supervision of mineral exploration and operations. Montana has adopted regulation according to minerals. Coal and uranium are regulated by Montana Strip and Underground Mine Reclamation Act. (82-4-201 to 82-4-254). Sand, gravel, clay, scoria phosphate rock and bentonite removal regulated by Opencut Mining Act. (82-4-401 to 441). Hard rock and other minerals regulated by general statute for reclamation of mining lands. (82-4-301 to 82-4-362). Regulation of uranium solution extraction is vested in Department of Natural Resources and Conservation. (Formerly R.C.M. 50-1701 to 1704, temporarily not recodified.)

Strip and Underground Mine Reclamation Act, to reduce environmental impact of strip and underground mining and prospecting for strip mineable minerals, provides that all such operations be conducted under permits subject to comprehensive plan for surface reclamation and restoration and performance bond. (82-4-202). Five-year renewable permits issued by Department of State Lands prior to any strip or underground mining. Annual report must be filed stating progress with mining and reclamation, and revising operations schedule. Renewal upon application so long as compliance with requirements of Act and reclamation plan continues. (82-4-221). Permit contingent upon: detailed reclamation plan treating topography, vegetation and water; operation location; owners of record and any purchasers under contract for deed of surface within one-half mile of any part of affected area; mineral owners; existing permits; prior offenses or revocations, if any; meteorological data; test bore data; water drainage data; public notice by publication in newspaper of general circulation; and any other information Department may require by regulation. (82-4-222). Application fee, $100. Surety bond to State of Montana not less than $200 per acre, but at least $10,000. (82-4-223). Prospecting permit required for prospecting on land not covered by valid strip or underground mining permit. Prospecting permit application, $100. (82-4-226). Similar reclamation plan and bond required for prospecting permit. Core drilling locations must be specified, together with method to be used for sealing aquifers. Permit may not issue if damage likely to unique or historical characteristics or improvements specified in statute. (82-4-227). Statute specifies minimum operation requirements. (82-4-232). Suspension of all permits is remedy for noncompliance with any permit conditions. (82-4-251). Private party enforcement provided. (82-4-252). Right of action for water users affected by prospecting or strip and underground mining operations. (82-4-253). Civil penalty of $100 to $5,000 per day of violation provided. Failure to correct violation shall result in penalty of not less than $750 per day, up to 30 days, upon expiration of which other sanctions may be applied. Willful violation misdemeanor with fine of $500 to $10,000 or one year imprisonment or both. Each day of violation is separate offense. (82-4-254).

Strip and Underground Mine Siting Act.—All new strip and underground mines must obtain special permits. Permit necessary for preparation to open new strip or underground mine. Application fee $50. Bond of not less than $200 or more than $10,000 per acre to be determined by Board for preparatory work. Minimum amount of bond $5,000. Purpose to assure compliance with rules. Appeal provided for. (82-4-101 to -142).

Major Facility Siting Act.—Governs construction of power and energy conversion facilities within state. Requires certificate of environmental compatibility and public need prior to construction or operation. Detailed system for application and hearings provided by statute. Extensive list of items to be considered. (75-20-101 to -1205).

Opencut Mining Act, to reduce environmental impact of open cut mining, provides that any operator may contract with Department of State Lands to provide for restoration and reclamation of lands disturbed. (82-4-423). Statute specifies data required in application for contract. Application fee is $50. (82-4-432). Surety bond to State of Montana required in amount of $200 to $1,000 per acre. (82-4-433). Statute specifies reclamation standards. (82-4-434). Statute authorizes suit by or against state for contractual noncompliance. (82-4-423). Penalty of $100 to $1,000 per day for violations of Act, following service of notice of violation. (82-4-441).

Mining Lands Reclamation Act provides that no person shall engage in exploration for or development of mineral deposits within state without first obtaining a one-year permit renewable on 30 days application from Department of State Lands. (82-4-331). Department granted extensive rule making powers. (82-4-321). Exploration permit shall be issued to applicant who pays $5 fee, agrees to reclaim any surface area damages as required by Department and who is not otherwise in default of any other reclamation obligation. Exploration area must be disclosed. Disclosure of evacuation and prospecting techniques in disturbance of land is necessary. (82-4-332). Location certificate copy must be provided Department. Development permit shall be issued applicant who pays $25 fee, submits description of development area, provides suitable map or aerial

ENVIRONMENTAL REGULATION . . . *continued*

photos showing topographic, cultural and drainage features, submits statement of proposed development methods, estimate of acreage to be disturbed, and proposed reclamation plan. (82-4-335). Operators shall be required to file performance bond. (82-4-338).

Reclamation plan shall to extent possible be conducted simultaneously with production activities and shall be completed within two years of completion or abandonment of production. Other details of plan specified by statute. (82-4-336). Inspection allowed. (82-4-337). Surety bond to be in amount equal to estimated cost of reclamation (not less than $200 nor more than $2,500 per acre or fraction thereof), and shall be executed by a duly qualified surety. Cash deposits or other forms of surety may be filed in lieu of bond. (82-4-338). Annual report of activities required of permittee. (82-4-339). Small miners exempt if previously agreeing in writing not to pollute any stream, to protect human and animal life with bulkheads and covers, and to not disturb more than five acres. Failure to comply with agreement is misdemeanor punishable by a fine of $10 to $100. (82-4-305). Violation of provisions of Act, fine up to $1,000 and additional penalty in same amount for each day of continuing violation. Injunctive relief authorized. Also punishable by civil penalty. (82-4-361). Sample collectors exempted. (82-4-310). Notice of noncompliance by department and suspension of permits provided for. (82-4-362).

Special tax incentives and grants have been created for development of new energy conservation and alternative energy sources programs. (15-32-101 to -203, 90-4-101 to -106).

Montana Uniform Transboundary Pollution Reciprocal Access Act provides that party injured in reciprocating jurisdiction by pollution originating in Montana may bring cause of action in Montana. (75-16-101 et seq.).

Hard-Rock Mining Impact Board established to mediate between local governments and large-scale mineral developers to accommodate impact on local economies, prepayment of property taxes; and written guarantees to provide funds to localities toward services and facilities. (90-6-301 to -311; 15-16-201; 82-4-335).

Developer and local governments must formulate impact plan to assess effect of large influx of people in area of development. (90-6-307).

Nuclear Waste.—Disposing of large quantity of radioactive material (defined: 49 CFR 173.389[6]) in Montana is punishable by fine up to $5,000 and imprisonment of up to two years. (50-79-301 to -304). Northwest Interstate Compact on Low-Level Radioactive Waste Management adopted. (50-79-501).

Littering.—Person convicted of littering forfeits hunting or fishing license or camping permit for one year. (87-2-112).

Land Use Planning.—Subdivision development regulated by statute under Montana Subdivision and Platting Act. (76-3-101 to 76-4-1251).

Pesticides.—Montana Pesticides Act administered by Department of Agriculture, 1300 Block Cedar, Airport Way Bldg. W., Helena, Montana 59601. (80-8-101 to -306). Every pesticide distributed, sold, or offered for sale or transported intrastate must be registered with department, and renewed annually by manufacturer or formulator of pesticide. Detailed specifications set for registration. (80-8-201). It is prohibited to sell or transport intrastate unregistered pesticides, pesticides not labelled in accordance with statute, pesticides harmful to man without additional label information, certain specified pesticides unless decharacterized, or misbranded pesticides. (80-8-202). Sampling and analysis required. (80-8-302). Embargo remedy provided along with criminal and administrative sanctions for violation of embargo. (80-8-303). License required for commercial applicators (80-8-204), operators (80-8-206), and dealers after examination (80-8-207, -208). Annual license required for sale or delivery within state. (80-8-207). Report of loss or damage required. (80-8-301). Department given investigative and enforcement authority. (80-8-304). List of activities constituting violations of Act provided. (80-8-305). Penalties for violations provided. (80-8-306). Hearings and administration of Act in accordance with Administrative Procedure Act. (80-8-106). Fees collected for pesticide education programs must be expended for such purposes. (80-8-109).

Billboards.—Comprehensive regulation of outdoor advertising along primary and interstate highways. Exception for advertising cultural exhibits of nonprofit, historical, or arts organizations. (75-15-111, -113, -121). Regulation and permit system administered by Department of Highways, Sixth and Roberts, Highway Bldg., Helena, Montana 59601. (75-15-122). Standards established. (75-15-113). Violation misdemeanor. (75-15-134). Nonconforming advertising is deemed nuisance by statute. (75-15-133). State empowered to acquire nonconforming advertising for just compensation. But if certain violations (75-15-112, -132) removal without compensation authorized (75-15-123). Hearing and appeal procedures established. (75-15-131).

Antiquities.—Statute provides a method for identification, acquisition, restoration, conservation and administration of historic, scientific and cultural sites and objects in state. State Historic Preservation Office is responsible for surveying, identifying, and inventorying heritage properties in Montana. (22-3-423). State agencies must consult with Historic Preservation Office and adopt rules for preservation of antiquities. (22-3-424). No antiquities can be disturbed without antiquities permit issued by Historic Preservation Office. (22-3-432). State agencies must consult with Historic Preservation Office when environmental impact statement is prepared and must devise mitigation plan for protection of antiquities. (22-3-433).

Disasters.—Governor may authorize payment of claims against state during emergency or disaster. (10-3-311).

Water Resources.—Development plan for water resources, including hydroelectric power generation. State Department of Natural Resources can lease sites for hydroelectric power generation to any person qualified to do business in Montana, or agency can generate and sell power. (85-1-501 et seq.).

Environmental Cleanup and Responsibility.—Comprehensive Environmental Cleanup and Responsibility Act (75-10-701 et seq.) generally adopts and parallels certain provisions of Federal Comprehensive Environmental Response, Compensation, and Liability Act. Act vests Department of Environmental Quality with broad investigative powers (75-10-707); rule making authority (75-10-702); and authority to assess penalties of not more than $10,000 per day (75-10-711). Department is vested with authority to take remedial and emergency actions. (75-10-711, 75-10-712). Act imposes joint and several liability on certain persons for release or threatened release of hazardous or deleterious substance from facility. (75-10-715). Person who receives notice under 75-10-711, who is held jointly and severally liable under 75-10-715, or who initiates voluntary cleanup may bring private right of action. (75-10-724).

Voluntary Environmental Audit Act provides immunity from imposition of civil or administrative penalties to polluters who voluntarily identify and remedy violations of environmental laws. (House Bill 293, 55th Leg. Sess. [1997]).

ESTATES AND TRUSTS

ADMINISTRATION:

See topic Executors and Administrators.

ADVANCEMENTS:

See topic Descent and Distribution.

ALLOWANCES:

See topic Executors and Administrators.

CLAIMS:

See topic Executors and Administrators; category Civil Actions and Procedure, topic Pleading.

DEATH:

Death defined as either irreversible cessation of circulatory and respiratory functions or irreversible cessation of total brain function. (50-22-101).

Uniform Probate Code adopted except person must be absent and unheard from for five years to be presumed dead. (72-1-108). See topic Descent and Distribution.

Survivorship.—Uniform Probate Code adopted effective July 1, 1975. (72-2-114).

Action for Death.—Either parent may sue for death of minor child. Guardian may sue for death of minor ward. (27-1-512). Heirs or personal representatives may sue for death of person not minor. (27-1-513). Above actions must be commenced within three years. (27-2-204). There is no statutory limit on amount of recovery, but amount must be reasonable. (27-1-302).

Action for personal injuries survives death. (27-1-501). Statutes do not prescribe elements of damages.

See also category Civil Actions and Procedure, topic Pleading, subhead Complaint.

Death Certificates.—See category Documents and Records, topic Records, subhead Vital Statistics.

Uniform Anatomical Gift Act.—See topic Wills.

Living Wills.—See topic Wills, subhead Living Wills.

DECEDENTS' ESTATES:

See topics Descent and Distribution, Executors and Administrators, Wills; category Debtor and Creditor, topic Homesteads.

DESCENT AND DISTRIBUTION:

Uniform Probate Code adopted, including 1993 Official Amendments. (Tit. 72). Following are exceptions to Uniform Probate Code:

Surviving Spouse's Intestate Share.—(1)Entire estate to surviving spouse if no surviving descendant or parent of decedent, or if all of decedent's surviving descendants are also descendants of surviving spouse and there is no other descendant of surviving spouse who survives decedent; (2) first $200,000, plus 3/4 of any balance of intestate estate, if no descendant of decedent survives decedent but parent of decedent survives decedent; (3) first $150,000, plus 1/2 of any balance of intestate estate, if all of decedent's surviving descendants are also descendants of surviving spouse and surviving spouse has one or more surviving descendants who are not descendants of decedent; (4) first $100,000, plus 1/2 of any balance of intestate estate, if one or more of decedent's surviving descendants are not descendants of surviving spouse. (72-2-112).

Heirs Other Than Surviving Spouse.—If there is no surviving descendant, grandparent, or descendant of grandparent, entire estate goes to person of closest degree of kinship with decedent. If more than one person is of that closest degree, those persons share equally. However, if more than one person is of closest degree and they claim through different ancestors, those who claim through nearer ancestor shall receive to exclusion of those claiming through more remote ancestor. (72-2-113).

See also topic Executors and Administrators.

ESTATES:

See category Property, topic Real Property.

EXECUTORS AND ADMINISTRATORS:

Uniform Probate Code adopted, including 1993 Official Amendments, but Art. VII, Trust Administration, not adopted. Tit. 72 contains following exceptions to Uniform Probate Code:

Preferences and Right to Administer.—Custodial parent has priority over noncustodial parent for appointment of deceased child's estate. (72-3-502). Public administrator added to priority list after other heirs of decedent. (72-3-502). Objection to appointment may only be made in formal proceedings. (72-3-503). Upon such objection, priorities in 72-3-502 apply, except that court may appoint any qualified person in cases where estate inadequate to discharge unsecured debts; and court may appoint person acceptable to heirs having more than half share of estate if objection to appointment is to person whose priority is not determined by will. (72-3-502).

Public Administrator.—Public administrator is a county officer, elected for two years. It is public administrator's duty to take charge of estates of persons dying within his

See note at head of Digest as to 1998 legislation covered.

See Topical Index in front part of this volume.

EXECUTORS AND ADMINISTRATORS . . . *continued*
county in following cases: (1) When no administrator has been appointed and such estates are being wasted or lost; (2) estates of decedents without known heirs; (3) if ordered by court; (4) estates upon which court has granted him letters of administration. (72-15-102). When public administrator takes charge of estate by order of court, he must obtain letters of administration, in like manner and in like proceedings as letters of administration are granted to other persons. (72-15-103). Administrator must make out and return inventory of all estates taken into his possession and administer same. (72-15-201).

See also infra, catchline Small Estates.

General Powers and Duties of Personal Representative.—Personal representative may abandon or compromise claims only with consent of heirs, devisees, or court. In supervised proceeding, court approval required before personal representative can purchase, directly or indirectly, property from estate. All sales are to be fairly conducted and for best price obtainable. (72-3-613). §3-711 not adopted. See category Citizenship, topic Aliens, subhead Inheritance.

Notice; Method and Time of Giving.—§1-401 adopted except 72-1-301 provides if address, or identity of person is not known and cannot be ascertained with reasonable diligence, notice shall be given by publishing in weekly paper once a week for three consecutive weeks, and if in newspaper published more often than once a week, by publishing on at least three different days of publication with at least ten days from first to last day of publication, including first and last day. (72-1-301[1][c]).

Presentation of Claims.—All claims which arose before decedent's death must be presented within one year after decedent's death or within four months after date of first publication of notice. (72-3-803).

Claims must either be mailed to personal representative, return receipt requested, or filed with clerk of court. (72-3-804[1]).

Allowance of Claims.—§3-806 adopted.

Priorities.—If estate assets are insufficient, claims are paid in following order: (a) Costs and expenses of administration; (b) reasonable funeral expenses and reasonable and necessary medical and hospital expenses of last illness of decedent, including compensation of persons attending decedent; (c) federal estate and Montana state estate and inheritance taxes; (d) debt for current child support obligation and past-due support for decedent's children pursuant to support order as defined in 40-5-201; (e) debts with preference under federal and Montana law; (f) other federal and Montana state taxes; (g) all other claims. (72-3-807).

Actions Against Representative.—Generally, personal representative is not individually liable for contracts entered into in fiduciary capacity unless fails to identify representative capacity and estate in contract. Personal representative individually liable for obligations arising from ownership and control of estate or for torts committed during administration only if personally at fault. Nonetheless, claims based on contract or tort can be asserted against estate. (72-3-612).

Actions by Representative.—Under survival statute, personal representative may maintain separate action or cause of action which arose prior to decedent's death. (27-1-501). Representative may bring action for wrongful death of one not minor. (27-1-513). Either parent may bring action for child and guardian may bring action for ward. (27-1-512).

Inventory and Appraisement.—Must be mailed to Department of Revenue within time required for filing U.S. estate tax return plus any extensions granted by IRS. (72-3-607).

Sale, Lease or Mortgage of Property.—Property which is affected by death of decedent and on which inheritance, estate or death taxes are due is subject to lien of state until such taxes have been paid. (72-16-432). Lien shall survive for ten years. (72-16-432).

Allowances and exempt property provided for in 72-2-412 through 72-2-414 are included in computing exemptions from inheritance tax provided for in 72-16-313 and are not in addition to such inheritance tax exemptions. (72-16-314). Homestead allowance is set forth fully in 70-32-101 through 70-32-303 (see category Debtor and Creditor, topic Homesteads, see also 70-2-412), and personal representative shall select homestead if not selected before decedent's death. (72-2-415).

Compensation.—Personal representative is entitled to reasonable compensation, not to exceed 3% of first $40,000 of value of estate and 2% of value of estate in excess of $40,000. Court may allow additional compensation for extraordinary services. (72-3-631). Attorney engaged by personal representative shall not receive more than one and one-half times compensation allowable to personal representative. (72-3-633).

Small Estates.—Summary administrative procedures shall apply to estates which do not exceed $7,500 as well as those which do not exceed allowances. (72-3-1101, 72-3-1103).

Closing Estates.—Before final distribution, certificate from Department of Revenue or paid receipt from county treasurer, showing that inheritance tax has been paid, or agreement with Department for extension of time in which to pay tax has been reached must be filed with clerk of court. (72-3-1006). Supreme Court administrator required to notify district judge if estate is not closed within two years after appointment of personal representative. If after show cause hearing, judge determines that good cause does not exist for failure to close, judge may order closed, and personal representative and his attorney may lose right to fees. (72-3-1015). Before final closing, personal representative must either file accounting with court or deliver same to all interested persons. (72-3-1005).

Uniform Fiduciaries Act not adopted.

Revised Uniform Principal and Income Act adopted. (72-34-401 to 416).

Uniform Simplification of Fiduciary Security Transfers Act.—Adopted. (30-10-401 to 30-10-411). *Caveat:* This Act is not among those specifically repealed by U.C.C., but U.C.C. 10-104(2), specifically negating such a repealer, is not present in Montana Act. (30-1-111).

Uniform Anatomical Gift Act 1987 Form adopted. (72-17-101 to 72-17-312).

Uniform Disposition of Community Property Rights at Death Act adopted. (72-9-101 to 72-9-120).

INTESTACY:

See topic Descent and Distribution.

PROOF OF CLAIMS:

See topic Executors and Administrators; category Civil Actions and Procedure, topic Pleading.

TRUSTS:

Uniform Probate Code adopted (Tit. 72) but Article VII, Trust Administration, not adopted. Effective Oct. 1, 1989, Montana Trust Code, enacted as cc. 33 through 36 of Title 72, repealing cc. 20 through 23. Chapters 33 through 36 are applicable to all trusts regardless of when created unless court determines (1) application of trust code to trusts created prior to Sept. 30, 1989 would substantially interfere with rights of parties and other interested persons; or (2) application of trust code to proceedings concerning trusts commencing after Sept. 30, 1989 would substantially interfere with effective conduct of proceedings or rights of parties or other interested persons and in both cases prior law applies. (72-33-102).

Creation.—Trust may be created for any purpose that is not illegal or against public policy. (72-33-204). Trust is created only if trustor properly manifests intention to create trust. (72-33-202). Trust may be created by (1) declaration by owner of property that owner holds property as trustee; (2) transfer of property by owner during owner's lifetime to another person as trustee; (3) testamentary transfer of property by owner to another person as trustee; (4) exercise of power of appointment to another person as trustee; or (5) enforceable promise to create trust. (72-33-201). There must be trust property and beneficiary or trust instrument must grant power to trustee to select beneficiaries. (72-33-203; 72-33-206). Trust created for indefinite or general purpose is not invalid for that reason if it can be determined with reasonable certainty that particular use of trust property comes within that purpose. (72-33-205). Trust is not valid unless evidenced by one of following: (1) By written instrument signed by trustee or trustee's authorized agent; (2) by written instrument signed by trustor or trustor's authorized agent; or (3) by operation of law. (72-33-208).

Appointment of Trustee.—District court is authorized to appoint trustee whenever trust instrument provides no method for filling vacancy; however, filling position is in discretion of court. (72-33-621).

Removal.—District court may remove trustee for breach of trust; if trustee is insolvent or unfit to administer it; if there is hostility or lack of cooperation among co-trustees; trustee fails or declines to act; or other good cause. (72-33-618).

General Powers and Duties.—Uniform Trustees' Powers Act repealed. Trustee has duty to administer trusts. (72-34-101). In case of revocable trusts, trustee shall follow any written direction acceptable to trustee given by person having power to revoke trust or by person to whom trustor delegates right to direct trustee. (72-34-102). Trustee must administer trust solely in interest of beneficiaries (72-34-103); and avoid conflicts of interest (72-34-105); however, certain actions and transactions performed by trustees which are regulated financial institutions or their affiliates do not violate these two duties. (72-34-117). Trustee is under duty to deal impartially with beneficiaries. (72-34-104). Trustee must not knowingly become trustee of another trust adverse to interest of first trust. (72-34-106). Trustee shall take control and preserve trust property (72-34-107) and make trust property productive (72-34-108) and dispose of improper investments. (72-34-109). Trustee is obligated to keep trust property separate and identified. (72-34-110); enforce claims that are part of trust property (72-34-111); and defend actions that may result in loss to trust. (72-34-112). Trustee may not delegate to others performance of acts reasonably required to be performed personally. (72-34-113). Exercise of care, skill, prudence and diligence under circumstances then prevailing that prudent person would use is required of trustee; and such standard of care is unaltered by fact that trustee is compensated. (72-34-114—72-34-118). Trustee must apply full extent of trustee's skills. (72-34-115). Discretionary powers conferred upon trustee are to be exercised reasonably. (72-34-129). Absolute discretion conferred upon trustee is to be exercised in accordance with fiduciary principles and consistent with purposes of trust. (72-34-130).

Co-trustees must act unanimously to bind trust property unless trust instrument provides otherwise. (72-33-611). Power vested in three or more trustees may be exercised by majority of such trustees unless trust instrument provides otherwise. (72-33-611).

Investments.—Trustee has power to invest, including making those investments provided for in 30-1-420, MCA, in any kind of property, whether real, personal or mixed. (72-34-309).

Securities in Name of Nominee.—Trustee has power to hold securities in name of nominee or another form without disclosure of trust. (72-34-330).

Bequests and Devises to Inter Vivos Trusts.—See topic Wills, subhead Bequests and Devises to Inter Vivos Trusts.

What Constitutes Notice of Trust.—Where instrument of record vests title in person as trustee, but no terms or conditions of trust appear, use of such descriptive phrase does not charge purchaser with notice of limitations on trustee's authority to convey property. (70-21-307).

Accounting.—Trustee must mail itemized annual statement of all current receipts and disbursements of both principal and income to each beneficiary. (72-34-126). This annual report is not required if waived in trust instrument or waived by beneficiary. (72-34-127).

Discharge.—Trustee who has accepted trust may resign only by one of following methods: (a) as provided by trust instrument; (b) in case of revocable trust, with consent of person holding power to revoke trust; (c) in case of irrevocable trust, with consent of all of adult beneficiaries entitled to receive income or principal if trust were terminated at time consent is sought; or (d) pursuant to court order upon petition by trustee. (72-33-616). Trustee may be removed in accordance with trust instrument or by court on its own motion or on petition of co-trustee or beneficiary. Grounds for removal include: (a)

TRUSTS ... *continued*

breach of trust; (b) where trustee is insolvent or otherwise unfit; (c) hostility among co-trustees; (d) where trustee fails or declines to act; (e) or for other good cause. (72-33-618).

Actions.—Trustee of express trust may sue without joining beneficiaries. (Mont. R. Civ. Pro. 17[a]). Proceedings concerning trusts are governed by 72-35-101 to 508.

Compensation.—When trust instrument is silent upon subject of compensation, trustee is entitled to reasonable compensation. (72-33-627). In addition to other compensation to which trustee is entitled, trustee is entitled to make reasonable charge for services rendered in making temporary investments. (72-33-628). Trustee has equitable lien on trust property in amount of advances, with any interest, made for protection of trust, and for expenses, losses and liabilities sustained in administration of trust. (72-33-632).

Uniform Common Trust Fund Act adopted in Montana as "Uniform Common Trust Act". (32-1-701 to 708). Accumulation of income permitted, but may not extend beyond time permitted for vesting of future interests. (72-2-1001, et seq.).

Revised Uniform Principal and Income Act adopted. (72-34-401 to 416).

Gifts to Minors.—See category Family, topic Infants.

Uniform Fiduciaries Act not adopted.

Uniform Simplification of Fiduciary Security Transfers Act adopted. (30-10-401 to 411).

Uniform Statutory Rule Against Perpetuities adopted. (72-2-1001 to 1017).

Pour Over Trusts.—See topic Wills, subhead Bequests and Devises to Inter Vivos Trusts.

Revocation.—If all beneficiaries of irrevocable trust consent, they may compel modification or termination of trust upon petition to court. However, if continuance of trust is necessary to carry out material purpose of trust, beneficiaries may not modify or terminate trust unless court in its discretion determines that reason for modification or termination under circumstances outweighs interest in accomplishing material purpose of trust. (72-33-406). If trustor and all beneficiaries consent, they may compel modification or termination of irrevocable trust. (72-33-407). Unless trust is expressly made irrevocable, trust is revocable by trustor; however, this applies only when trustor is Montana domicile on date trust is created, when trust instrument is executed in Montana, or when trust instrument provides Montana law is to govern. (72-33-401).

Restrictions on Voluntary and Involuntary Transfers.—If trust instrument provides that beneficiary's interest is not transferable, whether voluntary or involuntary, beneficiary's income or right to principal distribution under trust may not be transferred and is not subject to enforcement of money judgment until paid to beneficiary, unless trustor is beneficiary of trust. (72-33-301 to 306).

Funeral Plan Trusts.—Prior to death, person may contract for prearranged funeral plan or related service. (72-37-101). Recipient of money under contract holds money in trust (72-37-101), and must deposit money in banking institution or invest it in stock of savings or building and loan association or in shares of credit union (72-37-102).

WILLS:

Uniform Probate Code adopted (Tit. 72) including 1993 Official Amendments, but Art. VII, Trust Administration, not adopted.

Testamentary gifts to a subscribing witness are valid. Interest no longer disqualifies person as witness, nor does it invalidate gift under will. (72-2-525).

Election.—Elective share statutes (72-2-221 to 230) provide surviving spouse increasing share of augmented estate depending on length of marriage. Maximum elective share amount is now 50% of augmented estate and is applicable when decedent and surviving spouse were married to each other for 15 years or more. Shorter marriage, smaller percentage of augmented estate to which surviving spouse is entitled. $50,000 supplemental elective-share amount is available in cases where surviving spouse's assets and other entitlements are below that figure. (72-2-221). Surviving spouse's homestead allowance, exempt property, and family allowance, if any, are not charged against but are in addition to elective share and supplemental elective-share amounts. (72-2-226). Election to take elective share must be made within nine months of decedent's death or six months after probate of will, whichever last expires. (72-2-225).

Execution.—Individual 18 years of age of sound mind may make will. (72-2-521). Will must be in writing, signed by testator or in testator's name by another in testator's conscious presence and at testator's direction and signed by at least two witnesses. (72-2-522). Even though document does not comply with these requirements, still valid as holographic will if signature and material portions of document in testator's handwriting. (72-2-522). Even if does not meet requirements under 72-2-522, if shown by clear and convincing evidence document was will, document to be treated as such. (72-2-523).

Handwriting Analysis.—72-12-401 governs procedure for petitioning for handwriting expert. Petition may be made by any party to proceeding. Out of state or out of county expert must be specified and court determines necessity and whether expert is qualified.

Living Wills.—Adult may prepare declaration instructing physician to withhold or withdraw life-sustaining procedures if adult is in terminal condition and is unable to participate in medical treatment decisions. Declaration may be revoked. Liability of physicians and health care providers who implement declaration is limited. Criminal penalties for failing to comply with declaration established. (50-9-101 to 206).

Will Contest—Mandatory Attorney Fees.—When will is contested, contesting party must pay defending party attorney fees and costs (as provided in 25-10-201) incurred in defending validity or probate of will if court finds that will is valid or confirms probate. If will is found to be invalid and probate is revoked, costs (as provided in 25-10-201), but not attorney fees, must be paid by party resisting revocation. (72-12-206).

Bequests and Devises to Inter Vivos Trusts.—§1 of Uniform Testamentary Additions to Trusts Act adopted as 72-2-531.

Testamentary Guardians.—See category Family, topic Guardian and Ward.

Simultaneous Death.—See topic Death, subhead Survivorship.

Testamentary Trusts.—See topic Trusts.

Uniform Anatomical Gift Act adopted. (72-17-101 to 312).

FAMILY

ADOPTION:

Montana Adoption Act enacted in 1997 and effective Oct. 1, 1997 except that §§19 through 26, 28 through 38, 60, 65, 67, 68, and 75 are effective Oct. 1, 1998. §§27, 59, 64, 66, 69, and 74 terminate Oct. 1, 1998. (42-1-101, et seq.). Child is legally free for adoption if (a) child does not have living parent; (b) parental rights have been statutorily terminated; or (c) parents, guardian, or department that has custody consents. No consent required from: individual whose parental relationship to child judicially terminated for unfitness, determined not to exist, or has waived parental rights; parent who has been judicially declared incompetent; individual not married to mother of child who executes notarized statement denying paternity or acknowledging paternity but denying interest in child; or personal representative of deceased parent's estate. (42-2-302).

Putative father to receive notice of termination of parental rights if putative father complies with requirements of putative father registry. (42-2-204).

Petition.—Must be filed in triplicate, notarized by petitioners and include specific information regarding petitioners and adopted child. (§126).

Relinquishment.—Parent who voluntarily relinquishes custody of child for purposes of adoption may do so if custody of child relinquished to department, licensed child placing agency, or prospective adopting parent and parties have agreed to custody in writing. (42-2-402). Child may be relinquished only 72 hours after child's birth and if parent has been counseled. (42-2-408). Parent may relinquish parental rights for adoption by stepparent or member of child's extended family so long as relinquishment is executed in accordance with 42-2-401 through 42-2-413. (42-4-301).

Minor parent may irrevocably relinquish child for adoption if minor parent is advised by attorney. (42-2-405). Legal fees charged by minor's attorney are allowable expense that may be paid by prospective adoptive parents.

Agencies.—Agency is public or nonprofit entity licensed by jurisdiction of U.S. to place children in adoption. (42-1-103).

Records.—Department of Public Health and Human Services issues substitute birth certificates showing adoptive parents as parents. (50-15-304).

Adoption of adult without consent of parents is permitted. (42-4-401).

Inheritance.—Adopted person is child of adopting parent or parents and not of natural parents except (1) adoption by spouse of natural parent has no effect on relationship between child and either natural parent or right of child or descendant to inherit from or through other natural parent and (2) neither natural parent (nor their kindred) can inherit from or through child unless that natural parent has openly treated child as parent's and has not refused to support child. (72-2-124.)

Fees.—Reasonable fees may be paid by adoptive parent for actual cost of services. (42-7-101). Person who knowingly offers, gives, solicits, accepts or agrees to accept from another anything of greater value than fees listed in statute commits offense of paying or charging excessive adoption process fees. May be fined up to $10,000. (42-7-105).

ALIMONY:

See topic Dissolution of Marriage.

COMMUNITY PROPERTY:

System not in force.

DESERTION:

See topics Dissolution of Marriage, Husband and Wife.

DISSOLUTION OF MARRIAGE:

Uniform Marriage and Divorce Act adopted in Montana. (40-1-101 et seq.).

Grounds for Dissolution.—District court shall enter decree of dissolution of marriage if it finds that marriage is irretrievably broken. Such findings must be supported by evidence that parties have not lived together for 180 days prior to proceeding or that serious marital discord adversely affects attitude of one of parties. (40-4-104[1]).

Grounds for Legal Separation.—Same as grounds for dissolution except one party must request legal separation and other party must not object. (40-4-104[2]).

Defenses.—Previously existing defenses (connivance, collusion, condonation or recrimination) are abolished. (40-4-105[4]).

Citizenship Requirement.—None.

Residence Requirement.—One of parties to marriage must have been domiciled in Montana or stationed in Montana while member of armed services for 90 days prior to proceedings. (40-4-104[1][a]).

Jurisdiction is vested in district courts. (3-5-302).

Venue is in county in which petitioner resides (25-2-118).

Process.—Same as in civil actions. Service may be by publication. (Rule 4[d][5][iii]).

Pleading.—Same as in civil actions. (Rule 7a). Petition for dissolution or legal separation must be verified and contain certain specific allegations enumerated in statute. (40-1-103, 40-4-103 and 40-4-105). Each party must serve on other party preliminary disclosure statement regarding assets and liabilities within 60 days of service of petition.

DISSOLUTION OF MARRIAGE . . . *continued*

Practice.—Decree may not be entered until 20 days after date of service of process as provided by Montana Rules of Civil Procedure. (40-4-105). Decree final when entered. (40-4-108).

Temporary maintenance order, injunction or restraining order may be issued by court providing for support and maintenance of party or child or to preclude civil disturbance, disposing of marital property, or removal of children from jurisdiction. Injunctive relief may also be sought without filing petition for dissolution of marriage or legal separation by filing verified petition under rules for preliminary injunctions found at 27-19-301. Stalking may also be enjoined under 40-4-121 and 40-15-101 et seq. Stalking is defined at 45-5-220. Spouses, former spouses, persons dating or in ongoing intimate relationship, and family members, may obtain restraining order for domestic abuse. (40-4-121, 45-5-206 and 40-15-101).

Hearing is necessary prior to judicial decree that marriage is irretrievably broken. (40-4-107).

Judgment.—If one party disputes that marriage is irretrievably broken, court can make a finding on that issue (as in cases where there is no dispute) or continue matter up to 60 days and suggest that parties receive counseling. Finding that marriage is irretrievably broken is a determination that there is no reasonable prospect of reconciliation. (40-4-107). Decree of dissolution of marriage or legal separation is final when entered, subject to appeal. After six months, court can, upon motion, convert decree of legal separation to dissolution (40-4-108[2]).

Registration of Decree.—Decrees of dissolution must be forwarded by clerk of court to Department of Public Health and Human Services, Helena, Montana 59601. (50-15-303).

Alimony and Allowances.—Court may grant maintenance order for either spouse without regard to marital misconduct if petitioning spouse lacks property sufficient for his needs and is unable to support himself through appropriate employment or interests of dependents preclude employment. (40-4-203). Court shall consider all relevant facts, including: (1) financial resources of party; (2) time necessary to acquire education or training; (3) standard of living during marriage; (4) duration of marriage; (5) age and physical and emotional condition of party; and (6) ability of spouse to provide maintenance. (40-4-203). Modifications may be made upon showing of written consent or changed circumstances so substantial as to make terms unconscionable. (40-4-208). When decree does not provide for maintenance or support, may be modified to so provide but only within two years of date of decree. Obligation ends upon remarriage of party receiving maintenance or death of either party. (40-4-208).

Division of Property of Spouses.—Special equity type system. Court shall equitably apportion property, and assets belonging to either or both, however, and whenever acquired and without regard to title or marital misconduct. Court shall consider duration of marriage and prior marriage; age, health, station and occupation, employability, etc. of parties; custodial provisions; whether maintenance is awarded; and opportunity of each party to future acquisition of assets. (40-4-202). Court shall consider contribution of spouse as homemaker. Court may protect children by setting aside separate fund for their welfare. (40-4-202). Decree may be modified for failure to disclose assets and liabilities. (40-4-208).

Change of Wife's Name.—Upon request by wife whose marriage is dissolved, court must order her maiden or former name restored. (40-4-108[4]).

Custody of Children.—Uniform Child Custody Jurisdiction Act adopted. (40-7-101 to 125). Court shall determine parenting plan according to best interests of child. (40-4-212). Interim parenting plan may be adopted before hearing. (40-4-213). After judicial interviews and investigations, hearing must be held. (40-4-214 to 216). Amendment of parenting plan is possible if it is in best interests of child or child is at least 14 years old and desires amendment. (40-4-219). Courts must address several factors when deciding parenting plan. (40-4-212).

Allowance for Support of Children.—Either or both parents may be liable for support of children without regard to marital misconduct; court must apply statutory standards and formula for calculating support obligation adopted by State Department of Health and Human Services. (40-4-204). Any support obligation established by court order or modification of court order including temporary orders and defaults is subject to mandatory income withholding under 40-5-315 and 40-5-411 unless court makes written exception in support order stating why it is not in best interests of child. (40-4-204, 40-6-116). Child Support Income Deduction Act provides for deduction of money directly from income of liable party while income still under employer's control. (40-5-301, et seq., 40-5-401, et seq.). Any judgment, decree or modification establishing child support must include medical support order as provided for under 40-5-801, et seq. When one parent has been ordered to provide health insurance coverage for child and that parent fails to provide coverage, Department of Health and Human Services shall give delinquent parent 30 days to provide proof of insurance. If parent fails to comply, Department will purchase insurance for benefit of child and recover costs of premium from parent through withholding (40-5-824). Additionally, tribunal may impose fine of $25 per day for noncompliance with medical support order. (40-5-821). Failure to enroll child in insurance plan under medical support order is also punishable by contempt. (40-5-208 and 40-5-226). Enforcement procedures apply to support orders from other states which have been registered in Montana. (40-5-184, 40-5-411). Also support orders are subject to administrative review and modification if order is not in conformance with guidelines. (40-4-204, 40-5-201, 40-5-226, 40-6-116). If support order makes exception to mandatory withholding, department may monitor support payments, and may begin immediate withholding if payments are delinquent. (40-5-304, 40-5-412, 40-5-414). State Department of Revenue may also establish procedure to offset against debtor's income tax refund any debt for child support accrued through written contract, court judgment or administrative order and in form of liquidated sum due and owing for support. (17-4-105[4]). Uniform Reciprocal Enforcement of Support Act and Uniform Interstate Family Support Act adopted. (40-5-101 et seq.).

Mediation.—Court may require parties to participate in mediation to settle parenting plan, child support, visitation, maintenance, or property dispute. Mediation proceedings are confidential and may not be used as evidence in action. (40-4-301 et seq.).

Separation Agreements.—Husband and wife may agree in writing to immediate separation and provide for support of either and of children. (40-2-303). Such agreements are binding on court when entering a decree of legal separation or dissolution of marriage unless it finds agreement unconscionable. (40-4-201).

Remarriage.—Either party may marry after decree of dissolution is entered and during pendency of appeal not challenging finding of court that marriage is irretrievably broken. (40-4-108).

Annulment of Marriage.—See topic Marriage.

DIVORCE:

See topic Dissolution of Marriage.

GUARDIAN AND WARD:

Uniform Probate Code adopted but Art. VII, Trust Administration, not adopted. Tit. 72 contains following exceptions to Uniform Probate Code:

Qualification.—Written notice of acceptance by guardian must be given to minor and to person having his care or a close adult relation. (72-5-211).

Petition.—Any interested person may file request for notice of guardianship proceeding. (72-5-318). Contents required for petition are specified. (72-5-319).

Termination of Guardianship.—Termination does not affect guardian's liability for prior acts nor responsibility to account for funds. (72-5-233).

Incapacitated Person.—Includes person impaired by mental or physical illness, chronic drug or alcohol use, or other cause to extent he is unable to make or communicate responsible decisions concerning his person or rational decisions regarding his need for treatment. (72-5-101). Incapacitated person or any person interested in his welfare, including county attorney, may petition for finding of incapacity. (72-5-315). Guardian may petition court for 72-hour evaluation of ward who refuses treatment; ward has right to counsel. (72-5-322).

Investments.—See category Estates and Trusts, topic Trusts.

Securities in Name of Nominee.—See category Estates and Trusts, topic Trusts, subhead Securities in Name of Nominee.

Gifts to Minors.—See topic Infants.

Uniform Fiduciaries Act not adopted.

HUSBAND AND WIFE:

Husband and wife shall support each other out of their property and labor, including nonmonetary support provided by spouse as homemaker. (40-2-102). Otherwise, neither has any interest in property of other, except that neither can be excluded from other's dwelling unless enjoined by court. (40-2-201). Spouse can be convicted of criminal offense of sexual intercourse without consent; spouse less than 16 years old will not be deemed incapable of consent for purposes of this section. (45-5-503; 45-5-501[1][b][iii]).

Uniform Premarital Agreement Act adopted. (40-2-601 through -610). Premarital agreement must be in writing and signed by both parties although it is enforceable without consideration. (40-2-604).

Disabilities of Married Women.—In general, disabilities have been removed. Woman may be personal representative, conservator, guardian or trustee, and may bind herself and estate she represents without consent of her husband. (40-2-108).

Separate Property.—Property of married person owned before or acquired after marriage is their separate property. (40-2-202). While neither husband nor wife as such is answerable for debts of other, necessaries for family and education of children are chargeable upon property of both. (40-2-106). Separate property of married person may be held for spouse's debts if creditors dealt in good faith without knowledge that property does not belong to spouse. (40-2-209[2]).

Contracts.—Married person may enter into any transaction, respecting property, which person might, if unmarried. Both husband and wife may contract with their spouse to same extent, subject to general rules applying to persons in confidential relations. (40-2-301).

Spouses cannot, however, alter their legal relation except as to property and to permit a separation and may make provisions for support of either spouse and any children. (40-2-303).

Actions.—Married person may sue and be sued in same manner as if he or she were single. (40-2-107). Person has cause of action against his spouse for damages caused by spouse's intentional tort against such person. (40-2-109).

Agency.—Either spouse may act as agent for the other. (40-2-301; 122 Mont. 201, 200 P.2d 251, 263).

Conveyance or Encumbrance of Property.—Wife may convey or encumber her separate property without consent of husband. (40-2-202). He may do same with his property. However, both must join in any conveyance or encumbrance of homestead. (70-32-301).

Nonsupport.—Person commits offense of nonsupport if he fails to provide support which he can provide and knows he is legally obligated to provide to his spouse, child, or other dependent. Aggravated nonsupport occurs if offender has left state to avoid duty of support or has previously been convicted of offense of nonsupport. Inability to pay may constitute defense. Nonsupport is punishable by fine up to $500 or imprisonment up to six months or both. Nonsupport under court or administrative order for six months or more shall be fined up to $5,000 or imprisoned up to two years. Aggravated nonsupport is punishable by fine of $50,000 or imprisonment up to ten years. (45-5-621).

Parent, guardian, or other person supervising welfare of a child less than 18 years old commits offense of endangering welfare of children if he knowingly endangers child's

See note at head of Digest as to 1998 legislation covered.

See Topical Index in front part of this volume.

MT – 26

HUSBAND AND WIFE... *continued*

welfare by violating duty of care, protection or support. Offense punishable by fine up to $500 or imprisonment up to six months or both. (45-5-622).

Married person is not liable for support of spouse's children by former marriage. (40-6-217).

Uniform Interstate Family Support Act adopted. (40-5-101).

Community property system does not exist.

Uniform Disposition of Community Property Rights at Death Act adopted. (72-9-101 to 72-9-120).

Partner or Family Member Assault—Purposely or knowingly causing bodily injury or causing reasonable apprehension of bodily injury or negligently causing bodily injury or with weapon during quarrel to family member including past or present members of household of any relationship. Person convicted shall be required to pay for and complete counseling assessment with focus on violence, dangerousness, and chemical dependency and must complete, in addition to assessment, minimum of 25 hours of counseling as well as being subject to fines and/or imprisonment. (45-5-206).

INFANTS:

Age of majority for both males and females is 18. (41-1-101; Const. II, 14). Only exception is that drinking age raised to 21. (16-6-305).

Emancipation.—Parental authority ceases upon marriage of child, appointment of guardian, or attaining majority. (40-6-234). Minor may give valid consent for health services if married or previously married, has had child, graduated from high school, emancipated, separated from parents and self-supporting, pregnant, afflicted with any communicable disease (including sexually transmitted disease and drug or alcohol abuse), or in need of emergency care. (41-1-402).

Disabilities.—Minor cannot give delegation of power. (41-1-301).

Contracts and Conveyances.—Minor may convey or contract to same extent as adult, subject to his power to disaffirm (41-1-302). Minor may disaffirm upon death or return of consideration before or within reasonable time after majority. However, for purchases made with credit card minor need not return consideration. (41-1-304). Contracts for necessaries cannot be disaffirmed (41-1-305); nor can those which are either expressly authorized by statute (for instance, marriage settlement [40-2-315]) or entered into when minor has been granted limited emancipation, including specific right to enter into contracts, under 41-3-406 or 41-3-408. (41-1-306). Minors have full legal capacity to contract to borrow money for education beyond high school. (41-1-303).

Torts.—Infant is civilly liable for his torts, but cannot be held for exemplary damages unless capable of knowing at the time that his act was wrongful. (41-1-201).

Parents are liable for willful or malicious damage to property caused by their children living with them under 18. (40-6-237). Recovery limited to actual damages not to exceed $2,500, costs, and attorney's fee not to exceed $100. (40-6-238).

Actions.—A minor may sue or be sued but must be represented either by general guardian or guardian ad litem. (41-1-202, Rule 17[c], Mont.R.Civ.P.).

Support of Minor.—Parents of child entitled to custody must give child support and education suitable to child's circumstances. (40-6-211). Support order is prima facie evidence of legal obligation to provide support. Nonsupport is crime. (45-5-621).

Uniform Transfers To Minors Act adopted. (72-26-501 to -506).

Uniform Securities Ownership by Minors Act not adopted.

Adoption.—See topic Adoption.

Uniform Parentage Act has been adopted. (40-6-101 to -135). Man is rebuttably presumed to be natural father of child born during or 300 days after termination of marriage or attempted marriage between such man and natural mother, or if he has taken child into his home and holds out child as his natural child, or if he files paternity acknowledgment form with department of public health and human services, or if blood test shows 95% or higher statistical probability of paternity. (40-6-105). Action may be brought to determine father and child relationship at any time (40-6-107 to -120) or mother and child relationship (40-6-121).

Parent-Child Legal Relationship Termination Act adopted. (41-3-601 to -612). Parental rights may be terminated if in best interests of child, when child is abused or neglected as defined in 41-3-102. Provides extensive criteria and procedures for termination of rights by court order following petition by county attorney and judicial finding of relinquishment, abandonment, or unfitness of parents, such as conviction of felony involving sexual intercourse, violent tendencies, alcoholism, or penal confinement. (41-3-609). Court order terminates all rights and obligations except right of child to inherit from parent. (41-3-611).

MARRIAGE:

Uniform Marriage and Divorce Act has been adopted in Montana. (40-1-101 et seq.).

Uniform Premarital Agreement Act has been adopted in Montana. (40-2-601 et seq.). Applies to agreements executed on or after Oct. 1, 1987.

Minimum Age and Consent Required.—Persons 18 years of age may marry without consent of parents. Persons under 18 and over 16 may marry with consent of parents or guardian and authorization of District Judge. (40-1-213).

Premarital Certificate of Medical Examination.—Each female applicant for license, unless exempted for medical reasons, must present premarital certificate of physician on official form stating that she has had standard serological test. Certificates of tests from other states having comparable laws and certificates from U.S. armed forces in proper form are acceptable. (40-1-203 to 40-1-208). To be acceptable, test must be performed by either (a) lab of Department of Public Health and Human Services; (b) lab approved by Department of Public Health and Human Services; (c) lab operated by another state; or (d) lab operated by U.S. Public Health Service or U.S. Armed Forces. (40-1-206).

License is required, obtained upon application by both residents to clerk of any district, or if both parties are nonresidents of state, from clerk of district court of county

where marriage is to be performed. If one of parties is nonresident of county where license is to issue, his part of application may be completed and sworn to before person authorized to accept such applications in county or state where he resides. (40-1-201). Form of application for marriage license shall be prescribed by director of Department of Health and Human Sciences. (40-1-107). Upon proper application, payment of marriage license fee of $30, satisfactory proof that both parties have attained age of 18 or have necessary approval, satisfactory proof that marriage is not prohibited and certificate of results of medical examination, clerk of district court shall issue license to marry and marriage certificate form. (40-1-202).

No Waiting Period.—License to marry is effective upon issuance, and expires 180 days thereafter. (40-1-212).

Ceremony may be performed by judge of court of record, public official so authorized, by mayor or city judge or justice of peace, or by any religious denomination, Indian nation or tribe or native group in accordance with their recognized mode of solemnization. (40-1-301[1]). Solemnization of marriage is not invalidated because person solemnizing was not legally qualified to do so, if parties believed he or she had right to solemnize. (40-1-301[3]).

Reports of Marriages.—Person solemnizing marriage must complete marriage certificate and forward it to clerk of district court. (40-1-301).

Record.—See category Documents and Records, topic Records, subhead Vital Statistics.

Common law marriages are recognized. (40-1-403; 101 Mont. 246, 53 P.2d 451). See also subhead Foreign Marriages, infra.

Proxy Marriages.—Party unable to be present at solemnization may authorize in writing a third person to act as proxy. Parties may petition district court for an order permitting marriage to be solemnized by proxy if person solemnizing marriage is not satisfied that absent party has consented and is unable to be present. (40-1-301[2] and 40-1-213[3]).

Marriages by Written Contract.—Persons may marry without solemnization by making declaration of marriage which must contain names, ages, and residences of parties, fact of marriage, names and addresses of parents, including maiden names, and that both parties are legally competent to marry. Parties must also secure required medical certificate and attach it to declaration. Declaration must be attested by two witnesses, formally acknowledged before clerk of court, filed with premarital certificate attached, and accompanied by $30 filing fee. (40-1-311).

Prohibited Marriages.—Void between ancestor and descendant; brother and sister of half as well as whole blood; niece and uncle; nephew and aunt; and first cousins. Any marriage entered into prior to dissolution of a prior marriage of one of parties is also void. (40-1-401). No provision preventing intermarriage of races.

Marriage Settlements.—All contracts for marriage settlements must be in writing and executed and acknowledged or proved in like manner as in case of a grant of land. (40-2-312). Failure to record has same effect as failing to record in case of grant of real property. (40-2-314).

Foreign Marriages.—All marriages contracted outside state that were valid at time of contracting or were subsequently validated by either law of place of contracting or domicile of parties are valid in Montana. (40-1-104).

Annulment.—Marriage may be declared invalid by decree of district court if it is entered into under following circumstances: (a) One of parties lacked capacity to consent at time of marriage due to mental incapacity, influence of alcohol, drugs or other incapacitating substance, or because of inducement to enter marriage by force, duress or fraud; (b) one party is unable to consummate marriage by sexual intercourse and other party did not know of such incapacity at time of solemnization; (c) party was under age of 16, or was 16 or 17 and did not have judicial approval or consent of parents or guardian; or (d) marriage is prohibited. (40-1-402[1]). Party who may seek a declaration of invalidity and time within which such declaration must be sought are prescribed in statute. (40-1-402[3]). Children born of a marriage declared invalid are legitimate. (40-1-402[4]). Under certain circumstances, court may make decree nonretroactive. (40-1-402[5]). Clerk of court shall give notice of declaration of invalidity. (40-1-402[6]).

Putative Spouse.—Any person cohabitating with another in good faith belief that he is lawfully married is putative spouse until he has knowledge that he is not legally married. Putative spouse acquires rights of legal spouse. (40-1-404).

MARRIED WOMEN:

See topics Husband and Wife, Marriage; categories Civil Actions and Procedure, topic Evidence, subhead Witnesses; Debtor and Creditor, topic Homesteads; Documents and Records, topic Acknowledgments; Estates and Trusts, topics Executors and Administrators, Wills; Property, topics Deeds, Dower.

PARENT AND CHILD:

See topic Infants.

INSURANCE

INSURANCE COMPANIES:

See category Business Regulation and Commerce, topic Consumer Protection, subhead Plain Language.

Surety companies are classified as "insurers" (33-1-201[6]) and are subject to Insurance Code. See also topic Surety and Guaranty Companies.

Insurance generally is regulated by Insurance Code. (33-1-101 to 33-35-307). Insurance Commissioner may impose fine not to exceed $25,000 for any violation of insurance code, except that fine imposed on agents or adjusters shall not exceed $5,000. (33-1-317).

INSURANCE COMPANIES . . . *continued*

Supervision.—State auditor is ex-officio Commissioner of Insurance. (2-15-1903). He is charged with enforcement and execution of insurance code and protection of insurance consumer. (33-1-311). He has power, inter alia, to make rules and regulations; to conduct examinations, investigations and hearings; and to impose fines for violations of regulations and Insurance Code. (33-1-311 to -318). Appeals from orders of commissioner, or with respect to matters to which he has refused hearing, may be taken to district court of Lewis and Clark County. (33-1-711; 33-16-113).

Rates.—Provisions dealing with rates are 33-16-101 to -225. Rating organization to pay annual fee of $100. (33-16-403).

Annual Statements must be filed by each authorized insurer with Commissioner on or before Mar. 1. (33-2-701).

Insurance Information and Privacy Protection Act.—Establishes standards and limitations on disclosure of information collected in connection with insurance transactions by insurers or insurance-support organizations. Provides procedure for access by private individuals to information gathered about them; penalties and equitable relief available. (33-19-101 to -409).

Policies.—Provisions relating to insurance contracts in general are found in 33-15-101 to -514. Provisions regulating particular types of insurance are: life and annuities, 33-20-101 to -401; group life, 33-20-1001 to -1213; disability, 33-22-101 to -311; long-term care, 33-22-1101 to -1121; credit life and disability, 33-21-101 to -207; property, 33-24-101 to -105; title, 33-25-104 to -403; surety, 33-26-101 to -107; surplus line, 33-2-301 to -326; medicare supplement insurance, 33-22-901 to -924. Minimal health insurance must be offered to those otherwise considered uninsurable. All insurers, insurance arrangements, societies and health service corporations must be members of Montana Comprehensive Health Association, which offers health coverage of last resort. Association is subject to insurance code regulations. Minimal coverage, details of association operations, and duties of association members are detailed in Comprehensive Health Association and Plan Part. (33-22-1501 to -1521).

Discrimination on basis of sex or marital status in issuance or operation of insurance policies or retirement plans is prohibited. (49-2-309).

Unlawful discrimination between individuals of same class and equal expectation of life is prohibited in rates charged or in dividends payable in any contract for life insurance, annuity, or disability policy. Insurer may not refuse to consider application for life or disability insurance on basis of genetic condition, developmental delay, or developmental disability. (33-18-206).

Special regulations pertaining to particular types of insurers are: domestic stock and mutual, 33-3-101 to -704; farm mutual, 33-4-101 to -511; benevolent associations, 33-6-101 to -405; reciprocal, 33-5-101 to -503; alien, 33-2-201 to -215; fraternal benefit societies, 33-7-101 to -533.

Trade practices in business of insurance are regulated by 33-18-101 to -1006. Some practices prohibited are: misrepresentation of terms of policy or financial condition of insurer, deceptive advertising, incomplete comparisons for purpose of inducing action by policy holders, boycott tending to result in restraint of insurance business, unfair discrimination between individuals or property of same class, directing insureds to specific companies for glass repair work, and rebate of premiums not specified in contract. Practices excepted from prohibition of rebates and discriminations are listed in 33-18-209.

No person who lends money or extends credit may require as condition precedent to loan or extension of credit or renewal thereof that person to whom loan is made or credit extended purchase insurance through particular agent or insurer, but this does not apply to credit life or credit accident and health insurance. (33-18-501). No insurance of any kind may be written by a licensee under the Consumer Loan Act (32-5-101 to -506) in connection with any loan of $300 or less (32-5-306). Agents may extend credit to policyholders in connection with insurance or servicing policies under certain requirements. (33-18-213).

Political contributions by insurer's are forbidden. (33-18-305).

Liens.—No provision allowing insurance company lien on policy.

Written notice of cancellation or refusal to renew of life and disability insurance policies to be given before cancellation of policies for nonpayment of premiums. (33-22-121, -122).

Insurance producers, solicitors and adjusters are regulated by 33-17-101 to -1207. Licenses for each are required. (33-17-201, -301). Applicants must be qualified as required by code. (33-17-211, -301). Continuing education for insurers is required. (33-17-1201 to -1207). Applicants for license as insurance producer or solicitor, with certain exceptions, must take written examination. (33-17-212). Commissioner may conduct examination or arrange for it to be conducted by testing service, which may recover cost of examination from applicant. (33-17-212). Commissioner may issue only nonresident license to person, partnership, or corporation otherwise qualified under insurance code but not resident of this state. (33-17-401). Adjuster's license fee is $15 per year. (33-2-708). For other fee amounts, see 33-2-708.

Process Agent.—All insurers applying for authority to transact insurance in this state must appoint the Commissioner their agent for service of process. (33-1-601, 33-2-315). Service is made by serving duplicate copies of process on commissioner and paying $10. (33-1-603).

Uniform Unauthorized Insurers Process Act has been adopted. (33-1-611 to 616).

Investments of domestic insurers are regulated by 33-2-801 to 851, foreign insurers by 33-2-852, farm mutual insurers by 33-4-403, and fraternal benefit societies by 33-7-408.

Foreign Insurance Companies.—Certificates of authority are required except as provided in 33-2-102. (33-2-101). Applications are made to Commissioner and must show name, location of home office (or principal office in U.S. if alien insurer), kinds of insurance to be transacted, date of organization or incorporation, form of organization, and domicile. (33-2-115). Insurers must file with Commissioner following: certified copy of corporate charter or articles of incorporation, or if mutual insurer, certified copy of bylaws, or if reciprocal insurer, certified copies of power of attorney of its attorney-in-fact and its subscribers' agreements; certified copy of financial statement as of Dec. 31 next preceding; certified copy of report of last examination made of insurer; appointment of Commissioner as attorney for service of process; certificate of supervisor of insurance of domicile or state of entry into U.S. that is it authorized to transact kind of business to be transacted in Montana; any certificate of deposit required by 33-2-111; specimen copies of policies to be offered with applicable rates; and, if alien insurer, copy of appointment and authority of its U.S. manager (33-2-115).

Compliance with reserve requirements set forth in 33-2-501 to -537 is required.

Filing fees are required as follows: application for certificate of authority, $600; annual continuation of certificate, $600; reinstatement of certificate, $25; original articles of incorporation, $20; amendment of articles, $25; by-laws or amendments thereto, $10; annual statement, $25 (other than as part of original application); appointment of resident agent or annual renewal thereof, $10. (33-2-708). Appointment of nonresident agent $10, renewal of appointment of agent is $10 each insurer. (33-2-708).

Restrictions on right to hold real property are found in 33-2-832.

Person acting as agent for insurers not authorized to transact business in state in violation of code are upon conviction thereof, guilty of a felony. (33-2-104). Unauthorized insurers may not sue in state to enforce rights arising out of insurance transactions in state. (33-2-105).

Foreign insurers may invest in Montana real property or securities secured thereby without certificate of authority. (33-2-103).

Retaliatory Laws.—Insurer, state or country of whose domicile requires of Montana insurers any taxes, licenses, and other fees, in aggregate, and any fines, penalties, deposit requirements or other obligations, prohibitions or restrictions in excess of those imposed by Montana upon similar insurers of such other state is subject to same requirements in Montana, except that this does not apply to any fees in conjunction with licensing of insurance agents, to personal income taxes, ad valorem property taxes, or to special purpose obligations in connection with particular kinds of insurance other than property insurance. (33-2-709; 33-17-401).

Premium Tax.—Insurers must file by Mar. 1 report showing total direct premium income and pay tax of 2¾% thereon. (33-2-705). Insurance premium finance companies are authorized and regulated. (33-14-101 to -307).

Filing and license fees are prescribed by 33-2-708. (For foreign insurers, see subhead Foreign Insurance Companies, supra.) Expenses of examinations by commissioner must be paid by person examined. (33-1-413).

Direct Actions Against Insurer.—Insured has independent cause of action against insurer for actual and exemplary damages caused by insurer's violation of trade practices act. Insurer may not be liable if it had reasonable basis in law or fact for contesting claim or amount of claim. Period prescribed for commencement of action against insurer by insured is two years from date of violation of 33-18-201. For third-party claimant period is one year from date of settlement or entry of judgment on underlying claim. (33-18-242).

Self-insurer may also be sued. (33-18-242). See also category Transportation, topic Motor Vehicles, subhead Direct Action.

Uniform Insurers Liquidation Act.—Not adopted.

No-Fault Insurance.—Not adopted.

Variable Contracts.—Life insurers may establish separate accounts to provide for variable life insurance policies and variable annuity contracts. (33-20-606).

Viatical Settlement Act.—Viatical Settlement Providers and Viatical Settlement Brokers must be licensed to do business in Montana. To obtain license one must be financially responsible and have good reputation as well as not being untrustworthy, incompetent, dishonest, engage in fraudulent conduct, or engage in practice of making unreasonable payments to policyholders. Viatical Settlement Providers and Brokers may not charge fees in excess of 2% of amount paid to policyholder. All viatical settlement contracts must be filed and approved by Commissioner of Insurance. Viatical settlement contracts must contain provision enabling policyholder to rescind contract within 30 days of contract execution or within 15 days of receiving viatical settlement proceeds, whichever is longer. Viatical Settlement Providers must file annual reports and make extensive disclosure to policyholders entering into viatical settlement contracts. Viatical Settlement Providers must obtain extensive consents, disclosures, and witnessed documents from and about policyholder before entering into viatical settlement contract. Licensees may not pay finder's fees, commissions or other compensation for referrals. Licensees may not sell any other type of insurance to policyholder. (33-20-1301).

SURETY AND GUARANTY COMPANIES:

Surety companies are classified as "insurers" (33-1-201[6]) and are subject to insurance code (Title 33 Montana Code Annotated). See topic Insurance Companies.

Rights and Powers.—Any corporation with paid-up capital of not less than $100,000 which is incorporated in Montana for purpose of making, guaranteeing or becoming surety upon bonds or undertakings, may become and shall be accepted as security or as sole and sufficient security. (33-26-101). For requisites of undertaking or bonds of individuals see 33-26-102. Surety insurer has power to become surety on bonds and undertakings subject to all rights and liabilities of private persons. (33-26-103). No foreign or other surety company is allowed to furnish bond for any state, county or city official where in addition to payment of reasonable premiums company indemnity or other security. (33-26-105).

Foreign Companies.—See topic Insurance Companies; category Business Organizations, topic Corporations.

Taxation.—See topic Insurance Companies.

See note at head of Digest as to 1998 legislation covered.

See Topical Index in front part of this volume.

INTELLECTUAL PROPERTY

TRADEMARKS AND TRADENAMES:

Definitions.—Trademark is any word, name, symbol, device, or any combination thereof adopted and used by person to identify goods made or sold by person and to distinguish them from goods made or sold by others. Trade name is word, name, symbol, device or combination thereof used by person to identify person's business, vocation, or occupation and to distinguish from businesses, vocations or occupations of others. Service mark is mark used in sale or advertising of services to identify services of one person and distinguish them from services of others.

Registration.—Application for registration of mark is made to Montana Secretary of State. (30-13-311). Registration of mark is effective for term of ten years and may be renewed for another ten-year period. (30-13-313). Filing Fees: Registration $20 and Renewal $20.

Assignment.—Any mark and registration may be assigned in conjunction with good will of business in which mark is used for remaining registration period. An assignment is void as against subsequent purchasers for valuable consideration without notice unless it is recorded with Montana Secretary of State within three months after date of assignment or prior to such subsequent purchase. (30-13-315). Filing Fee: Assignment $20.

Remedies.—Any owner of registered mark may proceed by suit to enjoin manufacture, use, display, or sale of any counterfeits or imitations of mark. (30-13-335). Owner of work may also seek injunctive relief for likelihood of injury to business reputation or dilution of work. (30-13-334).

Deceptive Business Practices.—Unlawful use of registered mark may lead to criminal liability. (45-6-318).

Common Law.—Nothing in statutes adversely affects rights or enforcement of rights in marks acquired at common law in good faith at any time. (30-13-336).

Trade Names.—See category Business Organizations, topic Partnerships.

TRADE SECRETS:

Montana has adopted Uniform Trade Secrets Act. (30-14-401).

Injunctive relief may be sought for actual or threatened misappropriation of trade secrets. (30-14-403). In exceptional circumstances, injunction may condition future use on payment of reasonable royalty for no longer than period of time for which use could have been prohibited. (30-14-403).

Damages—Complainant is entitled to damages for misappropriation, including actual loss and unjust enrichment caused by misappropriation, unless monetary recovery is inequitable due to material and prejudicial change of position prior to acquiring knowledge or reason to know of misappropriation. (30-14-404). Exemplary damages may also be awarded if willful and malicious misappropriation exists. (30-14-404).

Statute of Limitations.—Action of misappropriation must be brought within three years after misappropriation is discovered or by exercise of reasonable diligence should have been discovered. (30-14-407).

LEGAL PROFESSION

ATTORNEYS AND COUNSELORS:

Montana bar is integrated.

Jurisdiction over admission of attorneys is vested in Supreme Court. (37-61-101). Montana Supreme Court has appointed ad hoc Commission On Admission Rules Revision Committee to scrutinize admission process governing pro hac vice admissions and provisions permitting out-of-state attorneys to petition for admission without taking bar exam. Court is reviewing rules proposed by Commission.

Eligibility.—Any citizen or person who has bona fide declared intention to become citizen in manner required by law, who is of good moral character, and who possesses necessary qualifications of learning and ability is entitled to admission as attorney and counselor. (37-61-202; Mont. Const. Art. VII, §2 [Annotations containing rules for admission to Montana Bar]).

Registration as Law Student.—See rules for admission to Montana Bar, §§I, III, and VIII found in Annotations to Mont. Const. Art. VII, §2.

Educational Requirements.—Applicant must be graduate of accredited law school approved by Montana Supreme Court.

Examination.—Any applicant deemed foreign student applicant or student applicant must take and pass Montana bar examination. Any applicant deemed attorney applicant with less than five years of practice in another state, territory, or district must take and pass same bar examination as student applicant. Under existing rule, attorney applicant who has been admitted to practice of law in another state, territory, or district for five or more years may petition Supreme Court of Montana for abbreviated bar examination or waiver of examination. All applicants must obtain and complete State Bar of Montana application and questionnaire and affix affidavit and authorization and release. However, as of May 13, 1998, Montana Supreme Court has stayed any further consideration of petitions for admission on motion pending further order of Court. Court received comments through June 30, 1998, and will review rules proposed by Admissions Commission regarding admission by petition. These documents must be returned to State Bar Office by Mar. 1 along with $75 fee for student applicants and $150 fee for attorney. (Rules for Admission to Montana Bar §§1, 3, found at Annotations to Mont. Const. Art. VII, §2).

Examinations are conducted by State Board of Bar Examiners once a year commencing on summertime date when bar examination is given nationally, presently last Wed. of July. Examination includes Multi-State Bar Examination (one day) and essay questions (two days). Multi-State Bar Examination scores transferable if application made within two years of examination date. Applicants also must pass Multi-State Professional Responsibility Examination which is administered three times each year (Mar.,

Aug., and Nov.) at University of Montana Law School. (Rules for Admission to State Bar of Montana found at Annotations of Mont. Const. Art. VII, §2).

Fingerprints.—Department of Justice and other criminal justice agencies may accept fingerprints of applicants for admission to state bar, and shall exchange available state, multistate, local, federal, and other criminal history record information with state bar for licensing purposes. Rules for Admission to State Bar of Montana found at Annotations of Mont. Const. Art. VII, §2. (44-5-302[2]).

Clerkship.—Rules relating to clinical training as condition of admission to be promulgated.

Admission pro hac vice may be secured on motion of local attorney, but there is no requirement that local attorney be associated unless local court rules state otherwise. (37-61-208). Commission on Admission Rules Revision Committee has proposed new rules which Montana Supreme Court is reviewing for admission pro hac vice.

Licenses.—Annual license fee is $25 (37-61-211) which has been suspended for those in Armed Forces (10-1-605). No attorney shall practice in Montana until such attorney pays license tax for current fiscal year and obtains certificate. (37-61-214).

Change of Attorneys.—The attorney in an action or special proceeding may be changed at any time before or after final judgment: 1st, upon consent of client and attorney filed with clerk; 2d, upon order of court on application of client or attorney, after notice. When attorney dies, is removed or ceases to act, person whom such attorney represented must be, by written notice given by adverse party, required to appoint another or appear in person. (37-61-403 to 405).

Liabilities.—An attorney or counselor who is guilty of any deceit, or collusion, or consents to the same, with intent to deceive the court or a party, is guilty of a misdemeanor, and is liable to treble damages to the party injured. (37-61-406). Any attorney who wilfully delays his client's cause, with view to his own gain, or wilfully receives money or allowance for or on account of money which he has not laid out or become responsible for, is liable to party injured in treble damages, is guilty of misdemeanor and must be removed from office. (37-61-407, 409).

Compensation.—May be fixed by court in probate matters. (25-10-301). Fees are also regulated by division in workers' compensation cases. (39-71-613). Otherwise governed by agreement, express or implied, which is not restrained by law. (37-61-420). Compensation may be divided among attorneys. (37-61-408[2]). Where one party has express right to recover attorney fees in event he prevails in action on contract, all parties thereto shall be deemed to have same right, and any party prevailing can recover his attorney fees from loser. (28-3-704). In actions solely for property damages arising out of ownership, maintenance or use of motor vehicles, attorney fees awarded to plaintiff if plaintiff receives judgment equal to or greater than amount of damages claim in his last written offer prior to filing cause of action. (25-10-303).

Disabilities.—Attorney cannot become surety on any bond on recognizance of any sheriff, constable or coroner, or any appearance bond, or on any bond for payment of money into court without consent of judge of district court (37-61-419), cannot act as receiver in action in which he is interested, without consent of parties (27-20-202).

Champerty.—An attorney must not buy or be interested in buying a bond, promissory note, bill of exchange, book debt or other thing in action in order to bring action thereon. (37-61-408[1]).

Justice of the peace who is licensed attorney in Montana may practice law in Montana except that he or any partner, member, or associate may not represent party involved in case filed or tried in, or appealed from his court or any other justice court in his township. (3-1-602).

Lien.—Attorney has lien for compensation upon client's cause of action and proceeds thereof. (37-61-420).

Disbarment or Suspension.—Supreme Court has exclusive jurisdiction to disbar or suspend attorney. (37-61-301).

Unauthorized Practice.—Practicing law without license prohibited. (37-61-210).

Mandatory Continuing Legal Education.—Continuing legal education as requirement for engaging in practice of law is mandatory under rules and regulations for continued legal education. Each active member of Montana Bar shall complete minimum of 15 hours of approved continuing legal education activity during each year. (Rule 4[A]). Of those 15 hours, ten hours must be earned by attendance at live seminars approved by Board. Five credit hours may be earned by audio/video presentation, by writing and publishing law review article, by teaching and preparing written materials for approved activity, and by attending in-house courses offered by law firms, corporate legal departments, or similar entities. (Rule 4[A], 6[B], 7[B]). On or before Mar. 1 of each year, each attorney who is not exempt under Rule 4(B) shall file affidavit with Board reporting compliance with Rule 4 in previous year. (Rule 5). Exceptions to continuing legal education requirements for inactive members, lawmakers, and special circumstances constituting undue hardship are available. (Rule 4[B][1][4]). Accreditation of continuing legal activities, compliance, noncompliance and related matters are monitored by Board of Continuing Legal Education. (Rules 3, 6 and 7; see generally rules and regulations for continuing legal education found at Annotations of Mont. Const. Art. VII, §2).

Attorney-Client Privilege.—Attorney cannot, without consent of his client, be examined as to any communication made by client to him or his advice given to client in course of professional employment. Client cannot, except voluntarily, be examined as to any communication made by him to his attorney or advice given to him by his attorney. (26-1-803).

Specialty Certification Requirements.—None.

Professional Corporations.—See category Business Organizations, topic Corporations, subhead Professional Corporations.

Attorney Ethics.—Montana has adopted American Bar Association Model Rules of Professional Conduct with modification.

See note at head of Digest as to 1998 legislation covered.

See Topical Index in front part of this volume.

MINERAL, WATER AND FISHING RIGHTS

MINES AND MINERALS:

Permit.—Legislature declared purpose to allow exploration for and mining of minerals while adequately providing for subsequent beneficial use of surface by reclamation. Comprehensive legislative scheme has been enacted requiring a permit prior to prospecting, exploration, or operation of a mineral removal facility. For details concerning permit for each category of mineral regulation, see category Environment, topic Environmental Regulation, subhead Mining. Coal leases upon state-owned lands subject to approval and rules of State Board of Land Commissioners. (77-3-301 to 321).

Notice to Surface Owner.—All prospectors, miners, or others contemplating disturbance of surface other than by hand tools are required to ascertain ownership and possessory right of surface before beginning such disturbance. (82-2-302). Written approval must be acquired from persons controlling surface. Notice to surface owner must include map of proposed operations and plan for restoration in sufficient detail to permit surface owner to evaluate extent of disturbance contemplated. (82-2-303). Act exempts discovery pits on federal land excavated with hand tools. (82-2-304). Act exempts operations performed pursuant to prospecting permit, lease of a mineral interest, or other agreements authorizing such operations. (82-2-305). Violation is a misdemeanor. (82-2-306). Oil and gas developers required to give surface owners written notice of intent to begin drilling operations no more than 90 days and no fewer than ten days prior to commencing any activity on land surface, and required to compensate surface owners for damages caused by drilling and production operations. (82-10-503 and 504).

Location of Mining Claims.—Locators of mining claims on public domain of U.S. must, under U.S. law: (1) Post notice at point of discovery; (2) within 30 days mark location on ground so that its boundaries can be readily traced; and (3) within 60 days after posting notice, comply with Federal mining laws and record location in office of county clerk and recorder. (82-2-101 and 102). Locators must record all locations in office of clerk and recorder within 60 days after posting notice of location, otherwise there is prima facie presumption of intent to abandon. (82-2-102). Claims may be relocated or amended in certain circumstances. (82-2-105 to 114). Filing false or invalid claim with county clerk and recorder punishable by fine of $5,000, five years imprisonment, or both. (82-2-115).

Operation of Mines.—Montana law conforms and is equal to Federal Mine Safety and Health Act of 1977. As long as that Act is administered and enforced, Montana Department of Labor and Industry is not authorized to conduct inspections of those mines. (50-72-201 to 210).

Safeguarding Employees.—There is a comprehensive code of safety regulations for coal mines (Tit. 50, c. 73) and mines other than coal (Tit. 50, c. 72). Division of Workmen's Compensation, Department of Labor and Industry appoints mine inspectors (50-73-401) and supervises enforcement of safety regulations (50-73-402, et seq.). Department of Health and Environmental Sciences is authorized to make and enforce regulations with respect to unsanitary conditions and reporting of occupational diseases. (50-70-101 to 118).

Inspection of Mines.—Coal mines must be inspected at least quarterly. (50-73-406).

Oil, Gas and Coal—Defined.—Coal defined as combustible carbonaceous rock formed from compaction and induration of various plant remains. Coal does not include methane gas or any other natural gas that may be found in any coal formation, oil shale, or gilsonite. Gas defined as all natural gases and all other fluid hydrocarbons, including methane gas or any other natural gas found in any coal formation, as produced at wellhead and not defined as oil. Oil is defined as crude petroleum oil and other hydrocarbons, regardless of gravity, that are produced at wellhead in liquid form by ordinary production methods and that are not result of condensation of gas before or after it leaves reservoir.

Oil and Gas Administering Agency.—Board of Oil and Gas Conservation has duty of enforcing statutory regulations on oil and gas industry which include conservation laws defining and prohibiting waste of oil and gas and provisions for well spacing and drilling units, including compulsory pooling. (Tit. 82, c. 11). Violation of any Board rule or order is misdemeanor and also subjects violator to civil penalty of at least $75 and not more than $10,000 per day. (82-11-149). Board can order unitization with approval of parties. Powers of board are set forth with respect to unitization. (82-11-204 to 216).

Pooling and Spacing of Oil and Gas Wells.—Temporary and permanent spacing units may be established in interests of protecting correlative rights, preventing waste of oil and gas, and avoiding drilling of unnecessary wells. (82-11-201). Pools may be divided into different zones. (82-11-201[3]). Interests within spacing unit may be force-pooled by Board. (82-11-202). Penalties for nonjoinder by working interest owner and for nonjoinder by owner of oil and gas interest in spacing unit not subject to lease or other contract for development. (82-11-202[2][a][b] and [c]).

Mineral leases, including oil and gas leases, which have become forfeited, must be released of record by lessee within 60 days after forfeiture. (82-1-201). Lessee has 30 days to file release upon receiving written notice from lessor. (82-1-201). If not, lessor may bring action 20 days after demand for release, and recover damages, plus attorney's fees. (82-1-202, 203). Lessee who fails to remove expired lease from record is guilty of misdemeanor. (82-1-201).

Taxes.—Net proceeds tax is assessed by Department of Revenue against metal mines and royalty interests therein. (15-23-501 to 15-23-507). Metals mined are taxed on ad valorem basis. (15-23-802). There is also metalliferous mines license tax (15-37-101 to 117); and micaceous mineral mine license tax of 5¢ per ton mined (15-37-201 to 221).

Persons engaged in mining gold, silver, copper, lead or other metal or precious or semiprecious stones must pay annual license tax of $1 plus amount computed on gross value of products in preceding calendar year as follows: For concentrate shipped to smelter, mill, or reduction work first $250,000, 0%; more than $250,000, 1.81% of increment. For gold, silver, or any platinum group that is dore, bullion, or matte and that

is shipped to refinery, first $250,000, 0%; more than $250,000, 1.6% of increment. (15-37-103).

The surface ground of mines is taxed at its full value as are all improvements and machinery thereon, and the annual net proceeds of all mines are taxed like other personal property. Net proceeds of royalty interests are subject to the net proceeds tax and the amount of the tax may be withheld by the operator who, in addition to the royalty holder, is personally liable therefor. (15-23-501 to 523). Production of oil and natural gas is taxed on gross taxable value of production based on type of well and type of production according to schedules for working interest and nonworking interest owners. (15-36-304).

Privilege and license tax is imposed for purpose of defraying expense of enforcing laws concerning oil and gas conservation, and operator or producer of oil and gas shall pay assessment not to exceed ³/₁₀ of 1% of market value of petroleum originally produced, saved, marketed, or stored within state, or exported from state. Same rate on market value of each 10,000 cubic feet of natural gas. (82-11-131). Coal severance tax. (15-35-103, et seq.).

Certain royalties received by Montana Indian tribes are exempt. (15-36-309 and 15-38-121).

Resource Indemnity Trust Act provides for establishment of an investment fund in principal sum of $100,000,000, earnings from which shall be used to improve total environment and rectify damage to environment. (15-38-101 to 203). Severance tax to be paid by persons engaged in mining, extracting, or producing mineral resource in amount of $25 plus ¹/₂ of 1% of gross value of product in excess of $5,000, except for coal, which amount is $25 plus additional amount computed on gross value of product for coal produced in Montana during calendar year immediately preceding at rate of 0.4%. (15-38-104). Report of gross yield must be made on or before Mar. 31 for preceding year, together with other information required. (15-38-105). In event of failure to make report, Department of Revenue must estimate and assess tax from available information. (15-38-107).

Report to Department of Labor and Industry.—Employer in oil or mining industry, who owns less than one-half unencumbered fee being worked, must file with Commissioner, Department of Labor and Industry, and county clerk a verified list of names and addresses of persons interested in such operations and name of agent for service of process. Failure to file statement is a misdemeanor. (39-3-501, 502).

Bond for Payment of Wages.—Employer in oil or mining industry who fails to pay wages of employees may be required to give bond for payment of future wages. (39-3-510, 511).

Reclamation.—See subhead Permit, supra.

MORTGAGES

CHATTEL MORTGAGES:

Uniform Commercial Code adopted. (Tit. 30). See category Business Regulation and Commerce, topic Commercial Code.

What May be Mortgaged.—Uniform Commercial Code adopted. (Tit. 30). See category Business Regulation and Commerce, topic Commercial Code.

After-acquired Property.—Uniform Commercial Code adopted. (Tit. 30). See category Business Regulation and Commerce, topic Commercial Code.

Floating Stock.—Uniform Commercial Code adopted. (Tit. 30). See category Business Regulation and Commerce, topic Commercial Code.

Future Advances.—Uniform Commercial Code adopted. (Tit. 30). See category Business Regulation and Commerce, topic Commercial Code.

Requisites and Execution of Instrument.—Uniform Commercial Code adopted. (Tit. 30). See category Business Regulation and Commerce, topic Commercial Code.

Filing and Refiling.—Uniform Commercial Code adopted. (Tit. 30). Effective Jan. 1, 1965. See category Business Regulation and Commerce, topic Commercial Code, subhead Filing and Certification.

Removal or Sale of Property by Mortgagor.—Uniform Commercial Code adopted. (Tit. 30). See category Business Regulation and Commerce, topic Commercial Code.

Release.—Uniform Commercial Code adopted. (Tit. 30). See category Business Regulation and Commerce, topic Commercial Code.

Satisfaction or Discharge.—Uniform Commercial Code adopted. (Tit. 30). See category Business Regulation and Commerce, topic Commercial Code.

Foreclosure by Court Proceedings.—Security interests in personal property may be foreclosed in same manner as provided by law for foreclosure by action of mortgages upon real property. (30-9-508).

Foreign Mortgages.—Uniform Commercial Code adopted. (Tit. 30). See category Business Regulation and Commerce, topic Commercial Code.

Taxation.—Chattel mortgages are exempt from taxation. (15-6-204).

Forms.—

Financing Statement.—Form FS-1 is four page snap-apart preinserted carbon paper form. First two copies are sent to filing officer. First copy is filed alphabetically and numerically. Filing date, time, and office are inserted on second copy by filing officer and returned to Secured Party. In addition, this copy has termination statement at bottom of page, to be signed and filed when secured party no longer claims security interest in collateral covered by financing statement. Third and fourth copies are for Debtor and Secured Party, respectively.

Each page is 5" x 8" and has space for following information:

1. Debtor(s) (Name) and mailing address: (The debtor's social security number or tax identification number must be included.)
2. Secured Party(ies) Name and address:
3. Type of filing: ( ) commercial filing. ( ) agricultural filing. ( ) transmitting utility. ( ) informational filing.
4. For Filing Officer (Date, Time, Number and Filing Office):

See note at head of Digest as to 1998 legislation covered.

See Topical Index in front part of this volume.

CHATTEL MORTGAGES... *continued*

5. This Financing Statement covers the following types (or items) of collateral (If collateral is crops growing or to be grown or goods which are or are to become fixtures, also describe real estate concerned:
6. Name and address of Assignee of Secured Party:
7. Name and address of record owner or record lessee if real estate concerned:
8. Check if covered: ( ) Proceeds of collateral are also covered.
( ) Products of collateral are also covered. Number of additional sheets presented: . . . .
9. This statement is filed without Debtor's signature to perfect a security interest in collateral: ( ) already subject to a security interest in the state of . . . . when it was brought into this state, or ( ) which is proceeds of the original collateral described above in which a security interest was perfected. ( ) original Filing No. . . . . lapsed, collateral remains the same.
10. By: . . . . Signature(s) of Debtor(s)
11. By: . . . . Signature(s) of Secured Party(ies)

Financing statement may be filed before security agreement is made or security interest otherwise attaches. When statement covers crops growing or to be grown, statement must also contain description of real estate concerned. Financing statement may be amended by filing writing signed by both parties. This does not extend period of effectiveness of financing statement. Financing statement covering timber to be cut or minerals or the like, or financing statement filed as fixture filing must show that it covers this type of collateral, must recite that it is to be filed in real estate records, and must contain description of real estate sufficient if it were contained in mortgage of real estate to give constructive notice of mortgage. (30-9-402).

Statements of continuation, assignment, partial release, and termination Form FS-3 are also on four page snap-apart preinserted carbon paper form, with space for following:

1. Debtor(s) (Name) and mailing address:
2. Secured Party(ies) Name and address from Form FS-1 or latest FS-3:
3. Maturity Date (if any):
4. For Filing Officer (Date, Time, Number and Filing Office):
5. This statement refers to Original Financing Statement, File No.:   Date Filed:
6. CONTINUATION
( ) The original financing statement between the Secured Party and Debtor, bearing the File No. shown above is still effective.
7. TERMINATION
( ) The Secured Party certifies that it no longer claims a security interest.
8. PARTIAL RELEASE
( ) The Secured Party releases the collateral described below from the collateral described in the financing statement bearing the File No. shown above.
9. FULL ASSIGNMENT
( ) The Secured Party states that the Secured Party has assigned to the assignee whose name and address is shown below, Secured Party's rights under the financing statement bearing the File No. and filed on the date shown above in the collateral listed below:
10. PARTIAL ASSIGNMENT
( ) The Secured Party states that it has assigned to the assignee whose name and address is shown below, part of Secured Party's rights under the financing statement bearing the File No. and filed on the date shown above in the collateral listed below:
11. ( ) OTHER
12. Debtor(s) signature required if: new Debtor is added onto this Form, Debtor(s) name/address changed, collateral is added or changed on this Form, in compliance with the Federal Farm Bill Requirement):
13. By: . . . . (Signature(s) of Debtor(s))
14. By: . . . . (Signature of Secured Party)

Security Agreement.—Forms of security agreements employed in other states will be adequate for use in Montana provided minimum standards of Code are met.

Caveat: Montana has adopted a Retail Installment Sales Act (31-1-201 to 243) which may be applicable to financing arrangement contemplated. See category Business Regulation and Commerce, topic Sales, subhead Retail Installment Sales. See also category Business Regulation and Commerce, topic Interest, subhead Small Loans.

COLLATERAL SECURITY:

See category Debtor and Creditor, topic Pledges.

MORTGAGES OF PERSONAL PROPERTY:

See topic Chattel Mortgages.

MORTGAGES OF REAL PROPERTY:

Any interest in real property capable of being transferred may be mortgaged. (71-1-201). Mortgage is not deemed conveyance so as to enable owner of mortgage to recover possession of property without foreclosure and sale. (71-1-202). Lien of mortgage is eight years from maturity of debt with renewal possibility for eight additional years. (71-1-210).

Execution.—A mortgage must be executed with the same formalities as a deed. (71-1-203). Post office address of mortgagee must appear in the instrument to entitle it to be recorded. (7-4-2618).

Mortgage of Mortgagor's Home.—Mortgage of land personally occupied by mortgagor as his home cannot contain waiver of right to possession prior to foreclosure and during the year allowed for redemption. (71-1-229).

Recording.—In order to be effective against subsequent purchasers or incumbrancers in good faith without actual notice, a mortgage must be recorded in the office of the county clerk and recorder of the county where the land lies. (70-21-302, 303). Abstract of instrument may be recorded. (70-21-101, 70-21-305). See category Documents and Records, topic Records, subhead Recordable Instruments.

Recording Fees.—Recording fee is $6 per page or fraction thereof. (7-4-2631, 2632).

Taxes.—Mortgages are exempt from taxation. (15-6-204).

Mortgage or other encumbered real property is not exempt from execution as homestead if written acknowledgment to that effect is signed by borrower. (70-32-221).

Priorities.—Purchase-money mortgage takes priority over all other liens created against purchaser, subject to recording laws. (71-3-114). Liens otherwise equal have priority according to their time of creation. (71-3-113).

Future Advances.—Mortgage may cover future advances, which has priority just as if advanced at mortgage execution, if total amount of all contemplated future advances or total indebtedness that may be outstanding at any given time is stated in mortgage, not withstanding fact that from time to time during term of mortgage no indebtedness is due from mortgagor to mortgagee. Total amount of indebtedness that may be secured by mortgage may decrease or increase from time to time, but total principal amount of obligations secured at any one time may not exceed face amount stated in mortgage together with interest as provided in instrument secured by mortgage. (71-1-206).

Subordination agreement or waiver in favor of subsequent purchaser or encumbrancer may be executed by record holder of mortgage and recorded like mortgage. (71-1-208).

Assignment.—The assignment of the debt secured by mortgage carries with it security. (71-1-110). Assignment may be recorded in like manner as mortgage and record operates as legal notice to mortgagor and other persons, including subsequent purchasers and incumbrancers. Assignment must contain assignee's post office address in order to be recorded. (71-1-207).

Discharge by County Clerk when presented with certificate issued by mortgagee, personal representative, or assignee in proper form for recording specifying mortgage satisfied. (71-1-211).

Satisfaction.—Failure of mortgagee to deliver satisfaction on receipt of full payment subjects him to penalty of $100 plus actual damages. (71-1-212).

Trust Deeds.—Small Tract Financing Act of Montana provides for use of trust indentures for estates in real property not exceeding 30 acres to secure obligation with power of sale in trustee upon breach. Foreclosure may be by advertisement and sale or by judicial procedure as mortgage. (71-1-304). Trustee must be member of bar, bank, trust company, savings and loan association or title insurer or title insurance agent or agency authorized to do business in state under laws of state or U.S. (71-1-306). Trustee may foreclose by advertisement and sale upon default of grantor if trust deed is recorded with county clerk of county in which property is located, and if trustee or beneficiary has filed for record with said clerk notice of sale containing required information concerning nature of default and proposed sale. (71-1-313). Trustee must give notice of sale by mailing by registered or certified mail copy of recorded notice of sale at least 120 days prior to date of sale to grantor and other persons specified in statute, by posting copy of said notice in conspicuous place on property at least 20 days before sale, and by publishing said notice in county where property is situated once a week for three successive weeks, last publication to be at least 20 days prior to sale. Affidavit of compliance is to be recorded prior to sale. Any person including beneficiary but excluding trustee may bid at sale. Sale must be for cash. Trustee must execute deed to purchaser. (71-1-315). Purchaser is entitled to possession on tenth day after sale. (71-1-319).

Grantor or junior encumbrancer at any time prior to sale may pay amount due plus costs and trustee's and attorney's fees, not exceeding lesser of $1,000 or 1% of amount of principal and interest due on obligation at time of default, whereupon all proceedings must be discontinued and deed of trust reinstated. (71-1-312, 320).

Proceeds of sale must be applied to expenses of sale including reasonable trustee's and attorney's fees, obligations, and then surplus to the persons entitled thereto. Trustee may deposit surplus with county clerk. (71-1-316).

Debtor's obligation is extinguished by foreclosure by advertisement and sale and no deficiency judgment may be obtained. (71-1-317). Deficiency judgment may be obtained if trust deed is judicially foreclosed as mortgage. (71-1-305).

Small Tract Financing Act does not invalidate or preclude use of deeds of trust, trust deeds, or trust indentures, which are not executed in conformity with Act and such instruments are considered mortgages, subject to all laws relating to mortgages, and are considered constructive notice of contents to subsequent purchasers and encumbrancers from time filed of record. (71-1-321).

Foreclosure.—Real estate may be foreclosed by usual action in equity (71-1-222), or mortgage may give power of sale to mortgagee (71-1-111, 223).

Deficiency Judgment.—If the sale is made under a judgment of the court, and the proceeds are insufficient to pay the amount due, a judgment for the deficiency may be docketed, except in case of mortgage executed subsequent to Feb. 5, 1935, to vendor for balance of purchase price. (71-1-222, 232).

Attorney Fees.—Attorney's fees are allowed as part of the costs, where the mortgage or promissory note secured so provides. (71-1-234).

Redemption.—There is a right of redemption within one year after sale under a mortgage deed of trust, whether foreclosure is by suit or by exercise of a power of sale in the instrument, except trust deeds foreclosed by advertisement and sale pursuant to the terms of 71-1-301 to 320. Redemption is effected by same persons, on same terms and in same manner as in case of execution sale. (71-1-228). See category Debtor and Creditor, topic Executions.

Forms

Mortgage of real property may be made in the following form (71-1-204):

This mortgage, made the . . . . day of . . . ., in the year . . . ., by A. B., of . . . ., mortgagor, to C. D., of . . . ., mortgagee, witnesseth: That the mortgagor mortgages to the mortgagee (here describe the property), as security for the payment to him of . . . . dollars, on (or before) the . . . . day of . . . . in the year . . . ., with interest thereon (or as security for the payment of an obligation. describing it, etc.). (Signature and Acknowledgement)

See note at head of Digest as to 1998 legislation covered.

See Topical Index in front part of this volume.

MORTGAGES OF REAL PROPERTY . . . *continued*

Renewal Affidavit.—No statutory form is prescribed. The following is suggested:

State of Montana, County of . . . ., cc. . . . . being first duly sworn, deposes and says: That affiant is the mortgagee of/located at (address) (or heir, personal representative, successor or assignee of mortgagee as the case may be) named in that certain real estate mortgage dated . . . . from . . . . of (address) as mortgagor to . . . . as mortgagee covering (describe property), which mortgage was given to secure payment of that certain promissory note for the sum of $. . . . dated . . . . due . . . ., and which mortgage was duly filed for record in the office of the county clerk and recorder of . . . . county on . . . . where the same now appears of record in Book . . . . . of Mortgages at page . . . . thereof; that the amount of the debt secured by the mortgage still remaining unpaid is the sum of $. . . .; that affiant hereby renews the mortgage and that the mortgage is not renewed for the purpose of hindering, delaying of defrauding creditors of the same mortgagor or the owner of the land above described. Subscribed and sworn to, etc. (Signature and acknowledgment).

Assignment.—No statutory form is prescribed. Following form is suggested:

Know All Men By These Presents that . . . ., the part. . . . of the first part of (address), for and in consideration of the sum of $. . . . to . . . . in hand paid by . . . ., the part. . . . of the second part of (address), the receipt whereof is hereby acknowledged, do. . . . by these presents grant, bargain, sell, assign, transfer and set over unto the said part. . . . of the second part that certain indenture of mortgage bearing date the . . . . day of . . . ., made and executed by . . . . to . . . . and given to secure the payment of . . . ., which mortgage was filed for record in the office of the county clerk and recorder of . . . . County, State of Montana, at . . . . o'clock, ... M., where the same now appears of record in Book . . . . of Mortgages at page . . . . thereof, together with the notes or obligations therein described and the money due and to become due thereon, with interest (without recourse on part. . . . of the first part).

To Have and To Hold the same unto the said part. . . . of the second part, ... executors, administrators or assigns, subject only to the provisions in the said indenture of mortgage contained.

In Witness Whereof, etc. (Signature and acknowledgment).

In case of a second or subsequent assignment, care should be taken that previous assignments are recorded so that the assignor's ownership of the mortgage be apparent, and a recital of previous assignments might well be inserted.

Satisfaction.—No statutory form is prescribed. Following form is suggested:

Know All Men By These Presents that . . . . ., of . . . ., do . . . . . hereby certify and declare that a certain mortgage bearing date the . . . . . day of . . . ., made and executed by . . . ., the part . . . . . of the first part mentioned in said mortgage, to . . . ., the part. . . . . of the second part therein mentioned, and given to secure the payment of . . . ., and which mortgage was duly recorded in the office of the county clerk and recorder of . . . . County, State of Montana, on the . . . . day of . . . ., at . . . . . o'clock . . . . . M. in Book . . . . . of Mortgages at page . . . . ., together with the debt thereby secured, is fully paid, satisfied and discharged.

In Witness Whereof, etc. (Signature and acknowledgment).

In case of satisfaction by an assignee of the mortgage, care should be taken that all assignments are recorded so that it is apparent that person satisfying mortgage is owner thereof, and recital of assignments, showing such ownership, might well be inserted in form.

Chattel Mortgages.—See topic Chattel Mortgages.

PROPERTY

ABSENTEES:

There is no general statute affecting the rights and liabilities of nonresidents or absentees. Particular provisions other than those herein mentioned are digested under the following: categories Civil Actions and Procedure, topics Costs, Limitation of Actions; Process; Debtor and Creditor, topic Attachment; Estates and Trusts, topics Death, Executors and Administrators; Family, topics Guardian and Ward, Husband and Wife; Transportation, topic Motor Vehicles.

Care of Property.—Uniform Probate Code adopted (Tit. 72), except that absence period upon which presumption of death is based is reduced to five years (72-1-108[5]).

Escheat.—Uniform Unclaimed Property Act adopted (§§1-29) effective July 1, 1997 (70-9-801 et seq.). Title 70, c. 9, parts 1-3 have been repealed and replaced. Uniform Probate Code adopted. (Tit. 72).

When title to any property, either real or personal or mixed, fails for any reason including absence of heirs, title vests in state immediately upon death of owner. (72-14-102). Property administered by Department of Revenue. (70-9-809). Presumption of abandonment. (70-9-803). See also categories Business Regulation and Commerce, topic Banks and Banking, subhead Unclaimed Deposits; Estates and Trusts, topics Descent and Distribution, Wills.

ADVERSE POSSESSION:

A person may acquire title to real estate by adverse possession. (70-19-405, 407).

Character of Possession.—Where possession is assumed under claim of title founded on written instrument claimed to be a conveyance or a decree of a competent court, such possession is adverse. (70-19-407). In such case, possession is evidenced by: (1) Cultivation or improvement; (2) enclosure; (3) use for supply of fuel or fencing, timber for husbandry, pasturage or other ordinary uses. (70-19-408). Where possession is actual and continued, but not based on written instrument, possession is adverse (70-19-409), but such possession may be evidenced only by: (1) Enclosure or (2) cultivation or improvement (70-19-410).

Duration of possession is five continuous years. (70-19-411).

Taxes must have been paid during five year period by adverse possessor and his predecessors. (70-19-411).

Easements may be acquired by prescription in same manner as title to land is acquired by adverse possession. (70-19-405; 92 Mont. 227, 12 P.2d 273). However, no taxes need be paid to acquire easement by prescription. (89 Mont. 489, 300 Pac. 245).

Disabilities.—If one acquires title while a minor, committed under 53-21-127, or imprisoned for term less than life, period of limitation does not begin to run until death of titleholder or termination of disability. Action to receive real property must be commenced within period of five years after death or termination of disability. (70-19-413).

CONVEYANCES:

See topic Deeds.

CURTESY:

No right of curtesy. (72-2-122).

DEEDS:

An estate in real property, except an estate at will, or for a term not exceeding one year, can be transferred only by operation of law, or by an instrument in writing. (70-20-101[1]). See topic Real Property for types of estates.

Execution.—A deed must be signed, but no witnesses are necessary. Corporate deed should bear seal, although this is probably not essential. Deed must be proved by either subscribing witness or acknowledgment pursuant to Title 1, c. 5 (70-21-203) and show address of grantee to entitle it to record (7-4-2618), although these requirements do not affect its validity between parties. For circumstances in which spouse must join, see categories Debtor and Creditor, topic Homesteads, subhead Abandonment, Conveyance or Encumbrance; Family, topic Husband and Wife, subhead Conveyance or Encumbrance of Property.

Delivery.—A grant duly executed is presumed to have been delivered at its date, and it takes effect only upon delivery. It cannot be delivered conditionally, without discharging the conditions and thus rendering it absolute, except it be deposited by the grantor with a third person, to be delivered to the grantee on performance of the conditions, and on delivery by the depository it will take effect. A grant is constructively delivered in the following cases: (1) Where the instrument is, by agreement of the parties, understood to be delivered, and under circumstances entitling the grantee to immediate delivery; (2) where it is delivered to stranger for grantee, and his assent is shown, or may be presumed from circumstances. Redelivery of grant or canceling it does not operate to retransfer title. (70-1-506 through 70-1-512).

Recording.—In order to affect subsequent purchasers and mortgagees without actual notice, deed must be properly acknowledged or proved and certified and recorded in office of county clerk and recorder of county where land is situated. (70-21-302 and 304). Abstracts of conveyance may be recorded. (70-21-101). See category Documents and Records, topic Records, subhead Recordable Instruments.

Recording Fees.—Recording fee is $6 per page or fraction thereof when done by photographic or similar process. (7-4-2632). Certificate of recordation, $2. (7-4-2631). Filing and indexing fee is $5. (7-4-2631). See also category Documents and Records, topic Records.

Interpretation.—A grant is to be interpreted in favor of the grantee, but a reservation in a grant and a grant by a public officer to a private person are to be interpreted in favor of the grantor. (70-1-516). Fee simple is presumed to pass by grant, unless it appears that lesser estate was intended. (70-20-301).

Operation and Effect of Deed.—Where a person purports by proper instrument to grant real property in fee simple, and subsequently acquires any title or claim of title thereto, the same passes by operation of law to the grantee or his successors, except in case of a quitclaim deed. (70-20-302). Every grant of estate in realty is conclusive against grantor and against everyone afterwards claiming under him, except purchaser or incumbrancer in good faith, and for valuable consideration who acquires title or lien by instrument that is first duly recorded (70-20-303), but attachment will not prevail over prior unrecorded deed (84 Mont. 276, 275 Pac. 278).

The effect of a grant by an owner of an estate for years or life, purporting to convey a greater estate is to pass to the grantee all the estate which the grantor could lawfully transfer. (70-20-313).

Taxes.—See category Taxation.

Covenants Implied.—From the word "grant" in any conveyance which passes an estate of inheritance, the following covenants and none other, are implied: (1) That previous to the time of such conveyance, the grantor has not conveyed the same estate, or any right, title or interest therein to any person other than the grantee; (2) that such estate at the time of the execution of the conveyance is free from encumbrances. (70-20-304). However, agreement on part of seller of real property to give usual covenants binds him to insert in deed covenants of "seizin," "quiet enjoyment," "further assurance," "general warranty," and "against encumbrances." (30-11-109). Statute recites substance of covenants, and language may be incorporated by reference to 30-11-110. MCA, or set out in full.

Form.—Use of substantially following form is authorized (70-20-103):

Form

I, ..., in consideration of . . . . dollars now paid, grant to . . . . all the real property situated in . . . . county, State of Montana, bounded (or described) as follows: (insert description, or give descriptive name of land if it has such). Witness my hand this . . . . day of . . . ., 19. . . (Signature and acknowledgment).

Attorney in fact must subscribe his own name and his principal's when executing instrument transferring estate. (70-20-108).

See also categories Debtor and Creditor, topic Homesteads, subhead Abandonment, Conveyance or Encumbrance; Family, topic Husband and Wife, subhead Conveyance or Encumbrance of Property.

DEEDS OF TRUST:

See category Mortgages, topic Mortgages of Real Property.

DOWER:

Abolished. (72-2-122).

EMINENT DOMAIN:

When interest in real property, other than fee simple interest, which was acquired by right of eminent domain or for public purpose, is abandoned or purpose for which it was acquired is terminated, property reverts to original owner or successor in interest. (70-30-321, 322). Fee simple interest in real property acquired for public use may be sold at public auction if use is abandoned and original owner or successor in interest has option to purchase property for amount equal to amount bid at sale or, if no bid, appraised value of property. (70-30-321, 322).

ESCHEAT:

Escheated Estates Act.—(72-14-101 to 403). Whenever title to any real, personal or mixed property fails, title vests in state of Montana immediately upon death of owner and there is no presumption that owner died leaving heirs or next of kin. (72-14-102). Attorney general is advisor for all escheated property. (72-14-103). For procedure for state acquisition of escheated property see 72-14-201 to 210. Persons claiming property which is in hands of state treasurer must bring action in Lewis and Clark County, serving state treasurer, attorney general and director of revenue. (72-14-301). Action must typically be brought within five years from date on which money or property is received by state treasurer with several exceptions. (72-14-302).

See topic Absentees, subhead Escheat; categories Business Regulation and Commerce, topic Banks and Banking, subhead Unclaimed Deposits; Estates and Trusts, topics Descent and Distribution, Wills.

LANDLORD AND TENANT:

Every tenant who receives notice of any proceedings to recover real property occupied by him, or the possession of the same, must immediately inform his landlord of such notice; and if the notice is in writing, must deliver such writing to the landlord, and is responsible to the landlord for damage resulting from any omission to inform him of such notice. (70-26-104).

Uniform Residential Landlord and Tenant Act adopted as modified in Montana Residential Landlord and Tenant Act, effective July 1, 1977. (70-24-101 to 442). Sections omitted: 1.203; 2.101; 4.104(b). Significant variations from Uniform Act: excluded are rental agreements for non-city occupancies including hunting, fishing, or agricultural privileges (70-24-104); reasonable attorneys fees allowed in action on rental agreement notwithstanding any agreement to contrary. (70-24-442); landlord's maintenance must comply with housing codes in effect at time of original construction on units built after July 1, 1977 (70-24-303); tenants in one-, two- or three-family residence may agree to perform landlord's maintenance (70-24-303); landlord's rules substantially modifying tenant's bargain valid after seven days written notice in week-to-week tenancy, 30 days written notice in month-to-month tenancy (70-24-311); tenant may make repairs and deduct up to one month's rent if landlord fails to maintain premises (70-24-406); tenant may recover damages under 70-24-406(2) up to one month's rent for landlord's noncompliance with rental agreement or with 70-24-303 (70-24-407); special provisions apply to mobile home parks (70-24-436). Other variations contained in subheads Rent, and Termination of Tenancy, infra.

Kinds of Tenancy.—For life, years, from year to year, quarter to quarter, month to month, etc., for other indefinite and unascertained durations except estates at will. (70-15-202).

Leases for more than one year must be in writing (28-2-903) and must be acknowledged to be recorded (70-21-203). Validity of lease between parties not affected by absence of acknowledgment. For formal requirements, see topic Deeds.

Security Deposits.—Governed by 70-25-101 to 206. Security deposit can be used to cover damages to property, unpaid rent, cleaning expenses, utilities, penalties due under lease, and other money owed to landlord as defined by statute. (70-25-201). Before landlord can withhold security deposit he must provide tenant with list of damages and cleaning costs. (70-25-202). Tenant can recover security deposit if wrongfully withheld. (70-25-204, 205). Landlord must provide written statement of condition of premises and any damages given to previous tenant to charge security deposit to new tenant. (70-25-206). Waivers of statutory provisions are invalid. (70-25-103).

Recording.—Leases required to be in writing, unless recorded, are void as against subsequent purchasers or incumbrancers whose deeds or incumbrances are first recorded. (70-21-304). However, unrecorded lease is valid as to persons having notice thereof (70-21-102) and open and notorious possession of lessee is constructive notice of facts relating to his interest which reasonable inquiry would reveal (see 63 Mont. 38, 206 Pac 407).

Rent.—Periodic rent payable at landlord's address without demand at beginning of term; apportionable day-to-day. (70-24-201). After written notice and reasonable time tenant may make repairs to premises that cost less than one months rent and deduct same from rent. Tenant may terminate rental agreement after three days in case of emergency landlord fails to repair. (70-24-406). After notice to landlord and reasonable time tenant may deduct cost of essential services from rent if to be provided by landlord in rental agreement. (70-24-408).

Lien.—Landlord does not have lien on tenant's property, but may sell abandoned property after reasonable attempt to contact tenant or destroy it if value would be exceeded by storage cost. (70-24-430).

Termination of Tenancy.—Written notice to tenant stating noncompliance with rental agreement terminates tenancy within 14 days unless breach remedied. Notice of similar breach during next six months terminates tenancy within five days. Tenancy terminates three days following failure to pay rent after written warning and demand therefor. However, notice period for rental agreements involving tenants renting space

for mobile home is 15 days. (70-24-422). For breaches involving unauthorized pets or persons, lease will terminate after three days notice unless breach is remedied within that time. (70-24-422). Termination also effected by mutual consent; on seven day notice in week-to-week tenancy and 30 day notice in month-to-month tenancy; by destruction of property; by tenant acquiring title superior to landlord; or automatically following landlord's failure to comply with tenant's written demand for repairs. (70-24-406). Where hiring of real property is for unspecified term, notice of intention to terminate tenancy must be given at least one rent period, not exceeding 30 days, before termination. (70-26-205). Tenancy at will terminated by 30-day notice. (70-27-104). Treble damages may not be recovered for tenant's early termination of tenancy. (70-24-422).

Holding over renews lease for like term, not exceeding one month of rent payable monthly or in any case one year, if landlord accepts rent. (70-26-204).

Damages for Holding Over.—If tenant holds over after expiration of the term of his tenancy without landlord's consent and in bad faith, he is liable to landlord for three months rent or treble damages, whichever is greater. (70-24-429).

Dispossession.—Where tenancy has been terminated by notice or otherwise, or where tenant is in default in rent or other respects, landlord may evict him, first serving a three day notice. (70-27-108, 110). Action may be brought in either justice or district court. (70-27-101). Complaint must allege giving of required notice. (88 Mont. 162, 293 Pac. 315).

Distress.—No right of distraint.

LEASES:

See topic Landlord and Tenant.

PERPETUITIES:

Uniform Statutory Rule Against Perpetuities adopted (72-2-1001 to 72-2-1007) which provides nonvested property interest is invalid unless when interest is created, it is certain to vest or terminate no later than 21 years after death of individual then alive, or, interest either vests or terminates within 90 years after its creation.

PERSONAL PROPERTY:

Tenancy by entirety is not a permissible mode of ownership. (143 Mont. 183, 387 P.2d 907).

POWERS OF ATTORNEY:

Real Property.—Authority to buy, sell, lease (28-2-903) or mortgage (71-1-102) real property must be in writing. Attorney in fact must subscribe name of principal and his own name as attorney in fact. (70-20-108). Where attorney in fact releases mortgage, release must be accompanied by power of attorney if latter not already of record. (71-1-213).

Delegation of Powers.—Agent unless specially forbidden can delegate powers in following cases only: (1) When act to be done is purely mechanical; (2) when act is such agent himself cannot and subagent can lawfully perform it; (3) if it is the usage of the place to delegate such powers; (4) when such delegation is specially authorized by principal. (28-10-501).

Agency is terminated as to every person having notice of (1) Expiration of its term; (2) extinction of its subject; (3) death of agent; (4) renunciation of agency; (5) incapacity of agent to act. (28-10-801). Unless power of agent is coupled with interest in subject of agency it is terminated by revocation by principal, his death, or his incapacity to contract. (28-10-802).

Attorneys in Fact.—Power to convey real estate must be acknowledged like deeds (70-21-203) and may be recorded (70-21-201).

Recorded power of attorney can be revoked only by acknowledging and recording revocation in same office with original. (70-21-308).

Uniform Durable Power of Attorney Act adopted. (72-5-501 and 72-5-502).

Uniform Statutory Form Power of Attorney Act adopted. (72-31-201 to 72-31-238).

REAL PROPERTY:

Estates in real property, in respect to duration, are either: (1) Of inheritance or perpetual estates; (2) for life; (3) for years; (4) from year to year, quarter to quarter, month to month, week to week, day to day and other indefinite and unascertained durations of enjoyment whatsoever except estates or tenancies at will; or (5) at will. (70-15-202). Ownership of property by several persons is of either: (1) Joint interests; (2) partnership interests; or (3) interests in common (70-1-306). Every interest created in favor of several persons in their own right, including husband and wife, is an interest in common, unless acquired by them in partnership for partnership purposes or declared in its creation to be a joint interest. (70-1-314).

Rule in Shelley's Case has been abolished. (70-15-215).

Condominiums.—Unit Ownership Act adopted. (70-23-101 to 70-23-1002). Condominium filed after July 1, 1973, is deemed subdivision for purposes of regulation, approval and environmental impact. (76-4-102). See subhead Subdivided Land, catchline Montana Subdivision and Platting Act, infra.

Montana Timeshare Act.—Adopted. (37-53-101 to 37-53-506). Provides for registration of timeshare offerings (37-53-201, et seq.); regulation of advertising associated with timeshare offerings (37-53-214, 37-53-401, et seq.); licensure of timeshare brokers and salespersons (37-53-301, et seq.); disclosure to purchasers (37-53-304); and provides for both criminal and civil penalties for violations (37-53-307, 37-53-308, and 37-53-504 to 37-53-506).

Subdivided Land.—

Montana Subdivision and Platting Act (76-3-101 to 76-3-625), requires that land divided into two or more parcels, whether contiguous or not, any of which is less than

REAL PROPERTY . . . *continued*
160 acres which cannot be described as one-quarter aliquot part of U.S. Government section when parcels have been segregated from original tract (condominiums excepted) and cannot be described except by metes and bounds, must be surveyed and platted. This requirement does not apply to lands owned by state unless another parcel is created for residential purposes. Act is inapplicable to divisions created by court order, lien, mortgage, trust indenture, life estate reserved, lease for agricultural purposes; or if it creates cemetery lots, or an interest in gas, oil, minerals, or water severed from surface. Certain subdivisions are exempt from regulation under this part, but remain subject to survey requirements. (76-3-104, 76-3-201 to 76-3-209, 76-3-302, and 76-3-401 to 76-3-405). Before court orders division of land it shall notify and request written comment from local governing body. (76-3-201). Engineering plans, specifications, reports, and soil and ground water investigations required shall be prepared and filed by registered engineer, subject to regulations, with board of county commissioners or other planning board designated by commissioners. Transport, utilities, open space and recreation easements are to be considered. Environmental impact report is necessary but divisions of fewer than ten parcels and 20 acres may be exempted by planning board. Variances from strict compliance permitted to prevent hardship. (76-3-501 to 76-3-508). Public hearing required prior to preliminary approval. Fifteen days public notice required. Joint hearings on preliminary plat and annexation required when proposed subdivision is to be annexed to municipality. (76-3-605). Final plat to be submitted with certificate of abstractor showing interests of record and title insurance guaranteeing public's interest in dedicated land. (76-3-612). Preliminary plat must be accompanied by environmental impact assessment describing topography, surface water, ground water, vegetation, geology, soil suitability, and community impact, including education and bussing, road and maintenance, water, sewage, solid waste, police and fire protection. (76-3-603). Final plat cannot be approved without certification by county treasurer that there are no delinquent taxes on property. (76-3-611). Person who violates provision of Act or local regulations adopted pursuant thereto shall be guilty of misdemeanor punishable by fine of $100 to $500 or imprisonment up to three months or both. (76-3-105).

County clerk and recorder cannot accept for record a plat, nor may an owner dispose of any lot within a subdivision, erect a building providing or requiring water or sewage disposal facilities, or occupy any permanent building within subdivision until environmental impact statement has been prepared by developer, approval has been obtained from local planning board and health officer, and, when municipal water and sewage facilities will not be used, Department of Health and Environmental Sciences has approved plat and proposed plans and removed any existing sanitary restriction. (76-4-122). Condominium filed under Unit Ownership Act and camper and mobile home parks are deemed subdivision for purposes of Act. (76-4-102).

Subdivided land shall not be offered for sale or lease outside State of Montana until owner files a notice of intention with real estate commission setting forth information required by regulation and providing certain minimum protection for buyers. (76-4-1101 to 76-4-1117). Injunctive relief, civil and criminal penalties provided. (76-4-1115 to 76-4-1117).

See also topics: Deeds, Eminent Domain, Landlord and Tenant; categories Civil Actions and Procedure, topic Partition; Debtor and Creditor, topic Homesteads; Documents and Records, topic Records; Family, topic Husband and Wife; Mortgages, topic Mortgages of Real Property.

TAXATION

ADMINISTRATION:

Department of Revenue has general supervision of assessment and tax laws.

Credit for Taxes Paid Elsewhere.—In case of resident of Montana who died domiciled in Montana inheritance and estate taxes are credited with amount of any valid inheritance, estate, legacy or succession taxes actually paid to any other state or to any territory of U.S. or to District of Columbia. Credit cannot exceed tax on same property paid to Montana. (72-16-317).

Tax Moratorium.—Collection of income taxes due from persons serving in U. S. armed forces is deferred for period of service plus six months, if service impairs ability to pay. Any other tax obligation of person in such service may be suspended for like period by order of court on showing that military service impairs ability to pay. (15-30-313, 314).

Penalties and interest are as follows:

Property tax penalty is 2% of amount due. Interest is 5/6of 1% per month of tax due. (15-16-102). Moving mobile home on which tax is due is misdemeanor. (15-24-208).

Income Tax.—Penalty of 5% (minimum $5) of any balance of unpaid tax for failure to file return. Penalty of 10% (minimum $5) for failure to timely pay tax and interest at 9% per year. If failure to file return or pay tax is with intent to evade, penalty is 25% (minimum $25) and interest at 1% per month. Also, penalty of not more than $1,000 may be recovered from any individual, corporation, partnership, or officer, member or employee thereof, who with intent to evade any tax or requirement of this act fails to pay tax, file return, withholds information or supplies fraudulent information. Said individual is also guilty of misdemeanor, subject to $1,000 fine and/or imprisonment up to one year. (15-30-321). Deficiency penalty of 5% is also imposed on any additional assessment. (15-30-323).

Inheritance Tax.—If tax not paid within 18 months after death, interest is charged at 10% per year, from date of death, unless delay is unavoidable, then rate is 6%. (72-16-441).

Unemployment Compensation.—Contributions not paid on date on which they are due and payable are subject to penalty of 2% per month. All past due contributions bear interest at 1½% per month. (39-51-1301).

Withholding.—All withholding taxes unpaid on due date are subject to penalty of 2% per month for maximum penalty of 24%. All past due payments bear interest at rate of 1½% per month. (15-30-209).

Special corporation license taxes, discussed supra under subhead License Taxes, contain special penalty provisions.

See also category Business Organizations, topic Corporations, subheads Taxation of Corporate Property and License Tax.

BUSINESS TAXES:

Premium Tax.—See category Insurance, topic Insurance Companies.

ESTATE TAX:

Estate tax is imposed on all estates subject to tax under Internal Revenue Code and which have a taxable situs in Montana. Statute designed to be "pick-up" tax and capture full benefit of maximum state death tax credit allowable against federal estate tax. Where more than one tax situs is involved, statute provides for allocation of entire credit proportioned by fraction of estate with Montana situs. (72-16-901 to 912).

Apportionment Against Inter Vivos Dispositions.—Uniform Probate Code adopted. (Tit. 72).

Interstate Co-operation.—No procedure is available for compromise of death taxes where decedent's domicile is disputed.

GASOLINE TAX:

Montana imposes tax on gasoline in form of license tax on distributors for privilege of engaging in business in state. (15-70-201 to 236). "Special fuel" (diesel) distributors must be licensed and post security in order to do business in state. (15-70-341). Alcohol Tax Incentive and Administration Act of 1983 provides tax incentive of up to 30¢ per gallon for alcohol produced in Montana for mixture or production of gasohol. (15-70-501 to 527).

GIFT TAX:

None.

INCOME TAX:

Income tax is imposed on taxable income of individuals. Taxable income is defined as adjusted gross income less deductions and exemptions. (15-30-101[18]). For 1997 tax year, tax rates are as follows: 2% on first $1,000 or part thereof; 3% on next $1,000 or part thereof; 4% on next $2,000 or part thereof; 5% on next $2,000 or part thereof; 6% on next $2,000 or part thereof; 7% on next $2,000 or part thereof; 8% on next $4,000 or part thereof; 9% on next $6,000 or part thereof; 10% on next $15,000 or part thereof; and 11% in excess of $35,000. These brackets to be adjusted annually for inflation. (15-30-103). Specified deductions and exemptions allowed, including exemptions for single person, spouse and dependents, additional exemptions, for taxpayer or spouse if blind or aged 65 or more, and dependent child. (15-30-112, 114). Standard deduction of 20% of adjusted gross income allowed in lieu of specified deductions with 1997 maximum is $3,000. (15-30-122). Net operating loss deduction established. (15-30-117). Dividend and capital gain income from investment in small business investment companies is exempt. (15-33-106).

Adjusted gross income equals taxpayer's federal income tax adjusted gross income, with adjustments for, inter alia, tax refunds, interest on government obligations, and pension and annuity income. (15-30-111).

Nonresidents are taxed on income earned in state. After calculating tax imposed on nonresident's entire net income, tax due and payable is determined based on ratio of income earned in Montana to total income. (15-30-105). Alternate tax provided for certain corporations and individuals with gross sales of less than $100,000 in Montana. See category Business Organizations, topic Corporations, subhead Alternate Tax. (15-30-105).

Members of Military.—Salaries received by residents of Montana serving on active duty in armed services and who entered into active duty from Montana are exempt from state income tax. (15-30-116).

Fiduciaries are taxed at same rates as individuals. (15-30-143).

Investment Credit.—Individuals may take credit against taxes imposed by 15-30-103 for investment in qualified property equal to 5% of federal investment credit. Amount is limited to lower of taxpayer's tax liability or $500. (15-30-162).

Credit for Dependent Care Assistance.—Credit for 20% of amounts paid by employer for Dependent Care Assistance. (15-30-186). Credit may not exceed $1,250 of day care assistance paid to or on behalf of employee. (15-31-131).

Credit for Energy Conserving Expenditures.—Credit against tax in amount equal to lesser of $150 for residence ($300 for building not used as residence) or 5% of expenditure. (15-32-109). Additional credit against tax for installation of energy system using recognized nonfossil form of energy generation or low emission wood or biomass combustion devices. (15-32-201).

Credit for expenses incurred in care of elderly family members in amount of 30% of qualified elderly care expenses for taxpayers with less than $25,000 adjusted gross income. Taxpayers with greater than $25,000 adjusted gross income receive credit for greater of 20% of qualified elderly care expenses or 30% of qualified elderly care expenses less 1% for each $2,000 or fraction thereof by which adjusted gross income exceeds $25,000. (15-30-128).

Homestead Tax Credit.—Credit against income tax liability for persons age 62 or over for property taxes (or 15% of rent) paid on residence. (15-30-171 through 179).

Credit for Taxes to Other States.—Where same income is taxable in Montana and also in another state, limited credit on Montana tax may be allowed on tax paid to such other state. (15-30-124).

Who Must File.—Every single individual and every married individual not filing jointly with income of $1,500 and married individuals filing jointly with income in excess of $3,000 must file return with Department. Amounts referred to are increased by $1,480 as adjusted for inflation for each additional personal exemption allowed. (15-30-142).

See note at head of Digest as to 1998 legislation covered.

See Topical Index in front part of this volume.

MT – 34

INCOME TAX... *continued*

Returns must be filed with Department of Revenue, Helena, Montana, on or before Apr. 15 or 15th day of fourth month following close of fiscal year, except automatic four month extension is allowed provided proper extension application and applicant has paid 90% of current year's tax liability during course of tax year or 100% of previous year's tax liability. Applicant may request additional two-month extension which may be granted by Department upon showing a good cause. (15-30-144). Taxpayer must furnish copy of Federal Income Tax Return on request of Department. (15-30-304).

Declaration and Payment of Estimated Tax.—Every individual except farmers, ranchers, must file declaration of estimated tax by Apr. 15, and make installment payments of estimated tax if net income from sources other than wages, salaries and bonuses will equal or exceed net income from wages, salaries and bonuses subject to withholding. (15-30-241).

Withholding.—Employers making wage payments for employment must withhold tax on such wages according to tables prepared and issued by Department of Revenue. Employer whose liability for withholding during preceding 12 month period ending preceding June 30 ("lookback period") was $12,000 or greater, shall make return and payment on due date of federal income tax weekly withholding payment, shall file quarterly return on or before last day of Apr., July, Oct. and Jan., and shall file annual summary statement on each employee by Feb. 28. If liability during preceding lookback period was less than $12,000 but greater than $1,199, payments due monthly and shall file annual summary return. If employer's liability for lookback period was less than $1,200, employer must file return and make payment on annual basis by Feb. 28. Each employer shall provide to each employee summary form by Jan. 31. Excess tax withheld will be refunded to employee on timely filing of state income tax return. (15-30-201 to 209).

As to corporate license tax based on income see category Business Organizations, topic Corporations, subhead License Tax.

INHERITANCE TAX:

Inheritance tax is imposed and regulated by 72-16-101 to 805.

Taxable Transfers.—Subject to exemptions, an inheritance tax is imposed on the transfer of all property of a resident decedent and of all property of a nonresident decedent within the jurisdiction, when the transfer is: by will or intestate succession; in contemplation of, or intended to take effect at, or after, death; or right of survivor in property held as joint tenancy with right of survivorship. Insurance proceeds in excess of $250,000 are subject to inheritance tax. (72-16-304). Property shall be considered transferred if decedent at time of death has general power of appointment. (72-16-302). Certain conveyances made within three years of death are deemed made in contemplation of death. (72-16-301).

Rates are as follows: For property passing to lineal ancestors of decedent, 2% on first $25,000 remaining after subtracting exemptions from total value of property received; 4% on next $25,000 or part thereof (excess over $25,000 up to $50,000); 6% on next $50,000 or part thereof (excess over $50,000 up to $100,000); 8% on excess over $100,000. For property passing to brother or sister of descendant of brother or sister of decedent and to wife of son or husband of daughter of decedent, double rates for lineal descendants, for property passing to uncle, aunt or first cousin of decedent, three times rates for lineal descendants and for property passing to all others four times rates for lineal descendants. (72-16-321 and 322).

Exemptions for clear value of all property distributed or passing apply to spouse, child or lineal descendant of decedent, and to any stepchild; $7,000 of property transferred to lineal ancestors who have attained majority, $1,000 of property transferred to brother or sister of descendant of brother or sister of decedent or wife of son or husband of daughter of decedent. (72-16-313).

Total exemption is allowed for each transfer to: (1) State or local government unit within state for strictly county, city, town or municipal purposes; (2) any organization operated exclusively for religious, charitable, scientific, literary, or educational purposes, where no part of net earnings inures to benefit of any individual, and where no substantial part of organization's activities consists of attempts to influence legislation. To qualify for exemption, one of following conditions must also be met: (a) Group was organized solely for any of above purposes under laws of Montana or U.S.; (b) the transferred property is limited for use within Montana; or (c) where recipient group was organized or existing under laws of another state or foreign country, one of following conditions must exist: (i) that state or foreign country does not impose similar tax on transfers to similar organizations existing under laws of Montana; (ii) that state or foreign country has reciprocal provision for transfers to organizations existing under laws of another state or foreign country; or (iii) organization operates crippled children's hospital to which afflicted children of Montana are gratuitously admitted and property transferred is limited for use at such hospital. (72-16-312).

First $250,000 of insurance exempt, to be prorated in proportion to amount of insurance to be paid to each person. (72-16-304).

Personal property of nonresident decedent, except tangible personal property having actual situs in this state, is exempt if state or territory of decedent's residence imposes no tax on such property of Montana residents or provides for a reciprocal exemption for such property of nonresidents. (72-16-801).

Deductions allowed are: debts of decedent owing at date of death, expenses of funeral and last illness, state, county, municipal and federal taxes fixed in amount and owing by decedent at date of death, ordinary expenses of administration, including compensation of executors and administrators and their attorneys actually allowed and paid, federal estate taxes due or paid, and federal gift tax exclusion provided within §2503(b) IRS. Debts secured by decedent's joint interest in property on which decedent was jointly and severally liable, is deductible only to extent of $^1/_2$ or other proper fraction representing decedent's share of property. (72-16-308).

Determination of Tax.—Tax is determined by Income and Miscellaneous Tax Division of Department of Revenue after receipt from personal representative or other interested person of completed form of Application for Determination of Inheritance Tax, and Inventory and Appraisement form, and certified copy of will for testate death. Determination of tax is then mailed to applicant and clerk of appropriate district court. (72-16-401).

Joint Tenancies.—Where decedent was joint tenant, or held life estate, tax determined upon filing of verified application, copy of death certificate, and evidence of existence of joint tenancy or life estate. (72-16-501 to 505).

Appeal to district court of tax determination by Department of Revenue must be made within 60 days after determination is filed with clerk of court. (72-16-403). Appeal lies from district court as in other cases. (59 Mont. 220, 195 Pac. 1033).

Valuation is at clear market value as of time of death. (72-16-414). No allowances are made for contingencies, but if value is subsequently reduced by occurrence of contingent event, proportionate refund may be secured. (72-16-418). Alternate valuation of certain farm and business real property allowed under certain circumstances. (72-16-333).

Valuation of contingent or future estates is made by commissioner of insurance, on application of a district court, or of Department of Revenue. Mortality tables are used, with interest at 5%. (72-16-417).

Valuation date for inheritance taxes is date of death. (72-16-414). See also catchline Determination of Tax, supra.

Payment.—Tax is due at time of death, but may be paid at any time within 18 months after date of death before any penalty accrues. It is payable to State Department of Revenue or County Treasurer. On payment to County Treasurer, five receipts are issued, one filed in County Treasurer's office, and others distributed to clerk of district court, person paying tax, State Department of Revenue, and County Clerk and Recorder. (72-16-434).

A discount of 5% is allowed if tax is paid or deposited with county treasurer within 18 months after death. See also subhead Penalties and Interest, infra. (72-16-440).

State Department of Revenue may permit deferred payment of tax for not more than five years on request within 18 months of decedent's death. (72-16-438).

Application may be made for in-kind payment by transfer to state for payment of inheritance and estate taxes of objects, sites, and buildings of significant historical interest. (72-16-445 to 450).

Lien.—The tax is a lien on the property transferred for ten years from date of death. (72-16-432). Tax lien for inheritance and estate taxes may be perfected and executed upon as other tax liens are perfected and executed upon. (15-1-702, 72-16-432, 72-16-477, 478).

Liability for Tax.—Representatives of estates and beneficiaries are personally liable for the tax. Representatives must deduct or collect the tax before distribution, and are not permitted to deliver specific devises until taxes thereon are collected. Heirs or devisees of lands subjected to any charge must deduct tax on charge and pay it to estate representative. If devise is payable in money, for limited period, representative must retain tax on entire amount. When devise is not payable in money, representative must apply to court, when necessary, for apportionment of tax, and for further orders. Representatives may sell property to pay taxes, as in case of sale for payment of debts. (72-16-436).

If foreign executor or administrator transfers stocks or other securities in this state, subject to inheritance tax, tax must be paid to treasurer of proper county or state treasurer on transfer; otherwise corporation permitting such transfer becomes liable to pay tax. (72-16-701).

The attorney general may apply to the district court for a citation directing any person appearing to be liable for a tax, to show cause why the tax should not be paid. In case this procedure is inapplicable, attorney general may bring action to recover tax. (72-16-443).

Refunds are allowed in equitable proportions, when beneficiary is obliged to refund property received, to pay debts subsequently proved against estate. (72-16-442).

Forms, Information, etc.—Form of Application for Determination of Inheritance Tax, and Form of Inventory and Appraisement may be obtained either from Department of Revenue, Inheritance Tax Division, Helena, Montana 59601, or from clerk of district court. Consent to transfer stock obtained from Department of Revenue.

LICENSE TAXES:

General Corporation License Tax.—See category Business Organizations, topic Corporations.

License taxes are imposed on metal mines (15-37-101 to 226); cement or gypsum products manufacturers or importers (15-59-101 to 221); electrical energy producers (15-51-101 to 114); gasoline dealers (15-70-201 to 236); oil and gas producers (82-11-131); cigarette distributors (16-11-122); telephone companies (15-53-101 to 115); on sale of liquor and beer (16-1-401 to 411); public contractors (15-50-101 to 311). Public utility may apply for credit against certain license taxes if it makes energy conservation loans. (15-32-107).

MINING TAXES:

See category Mineral, Water and Fishing Rights, topic Mines and Minerals.

PROPERTY TAXES:

Property Subject to Taxation.—All property located in Montana is subject to taxation unless specifically exempted. (15-6-101).

Exemptions.—Following categories are generally exempt from taxation: (a) property of U.S., State of Montana, counties, cities, towns and school districts, nonprofit irrigation districts organized in Montana, municipal corporations, public libraries and rural fire districts, (b) property used for religious purposes, (c) property used exclusively for agricultural and horticultural societies, for educational purposes, and for nonprofit health care facilities, (d) property owned by nonprofit cemeteries, (e) property owned by public charities or leased from federal, state or local government entity if used for purely charitable purposes, (f) evidence of debt secured by mortgage, (g) nonprofit

PROPERTY TAXES . . . *continued*

public museums, art galleries, zoos, and observatories, (h) all household goods and furniture and wearing apparel, (i) certain truck covers or toppers, (j) bicycles used for personal transportation, (k) motor homes, travel trailers and campers, (l) all watercraft, (m) property owned by nonprofit corporation organized to furnish water to its members for other than irrigation of agricultural land, (n) rights of entry relating to oil, gas, coal and minerals reserved or received by conveyance (exclusive of leasehold interests), (o) property owned and used by nonprofit corporation for care of developmentally disabled, mentally ill or vocationally handicapped or for care of retired, aged or chronically ill, (p) farm buildings with value of less than $500 and farm implements and machinery with value less than $100, (q) property owned by nonprofit corporation organized to provide athletic training and practice for or competition in international sports and athletic events, (r) first $15,000 of hand-held tools used for construction of real property or repairing machinery and equipment, (s) harness, saddlery and other tack equipment, (t) title plant, (u) timber, (v) trailers and semitrailers with gross weight of 26,000 pounds or more and registered through proportioned registration agreement under 61-3-721, MCA, and (w) all motor vehicles registered under 61-3-456, MCA. (15-6-201). Freeport merchandise and business inventories. (15-6-202). Veterans' clubhouse and incompetent veterans' trust. (15-6-203). Moneys and credits. (15-6-204). State water conservation projects. (15-6-205). Certain irrigation and drainage facilities. (15-6-206). Certain agricultural products. (15-6-207). Certain mineral production. (15-6-208). Building and appurtenant land, not exceeding three acres owned by community services organization. (15-6-209). Certain disabled or deceased veterans' residences. (15-6-211). Down-hole equipment in oil and gas wells. (15-6-213). Certain motion picture and television commercial property brought into state for 180 consecutive days or less. (15-6-215). Improvements to commercial buildings made to assist disabled individuals. (15-6-216).

Classification of Property and Basis of Assessment.—Nature of property included in each class and taxable percentages are as follows: Class 1, 100% of annual net proceeds of mines and mining claims, except coal and metal mines. (15-6-131). Class 2, 3% of annual gross proceeds of metal mines.(15-6-132). Class 3, 3.86% of market value, determined by variable percentages based on income, of agricultural land defined within 15-7-202, certain nonproductive patented mining claims, and nonagricultural parcels of land exceeding 20 acres but not exceeding 160 acres. (15-6-133). Class 4, currently 3.86% but being reduced by .022% each year until rate is equal to or less than 2.78% of all land and improvements except those specifically included in another class, graduated schedule of taxation on first $100,000 of market value of any improvement on real property and appurtenant land not exceeding five acres owned or under contract for deed and actually occupied at least seven months of year as primary residential dwelling of any person whose total income from all sources including otherwise tax-exempt income of all types, but excluding social security income paid directly to nursing home, is not more than $15,000 for single person or $20,000 for married couple. 1.93% of market value of golf courses, including land and improvements. (15-6-134). Class 5, 3% of market value of all property used and owned by rural cooperative, electrical and telephone associations, air and water pollution control equipment, new industrial property, property used primarily for production of gasohol (during construction and first three years of operation), property owned by research and development firm and used for that purpose, and machinery and equipment used in electrolytic reduction facilities. (15-6-135). Class 6, 4% of market value of livestock and domestic animals (except household pets), items of personal property intended for lease in ordinary course of business if acquisition cost of property is less than $15,000 and is leased on hourly, daily or weekly basis by business whose primary income is from rental of property, and machinery and equipment used in canola seed oil processing facility. (15-6-136). Class 7, 8% of market value of property used and owned by persons or organizations involving furnishing telephone communications exclusively to rural areas or towns of less than 800 people; property owned by cooperative rural electrical and cooperative rural telephone associations serving less than 95% of electrical consumers or telephone users within incorporated limits of cities or towns; electric transformers, meters, electric light and power substation machinery, natural gas measuring and regulating station equipment owned by centrally assessed public utilities; machinery used to repair and maintain property. (15-6-137). Class 8, 7% of market value for tax year 1997 and 6% of market value for tax years beginning after Dec. 31, 1997, on agricultural implements and equipment; mining machinery, fixtures, equipment, tools and supplies except those included in Class 5; manufacturing machinery, fixtures, equipment, tools and supplies; except those included in Class 5; all goods and equipment intended for rent or lease; buses and trucks having rated capacity of more than one ton; furniture, fixtures, and equipment, except that which is specifically included in another class; X-ray, medical and dental equipment; citizens' band radios and mobile telephones; radio and television broadcasting and transmitting equipment; cable television systems; coal and ore haulers (exceeding 18,000 pounds per axle); theatre projectors and sound equipment, all other property not included in preceding classes, except property subject to fee in lieu of property tax. (15-6-138). Class 9, 12% of market value of centrally assessed electric power companies' allocations and for centrally assessed natural gas companies. (15-6-141). Class 10, forest lands, are taxed at rate of .79% of forest productivity value. (15-6-143). Class 12, certain railroad and airline property, is taxed at rate of 12% or percentage determined by formula, whichever is less. (15-6-145).

Assessment.—Department of Revenue has full charge of assessing all property subject to tax. (15-8-101). Department has revalued Class 3, 4 and 10 property as of 12/31/96 and all changes in value will be phased in at rate of 2% per year of total change in valuation. All other property must be revalued annually. (15-7-111). Assessments of all property, with certain exceptions, including motor vehicles assessed under 15-8-202, motor homes, watercraft, livestock, and mobile homes held by distributor or dealer as stock in trade, are made by Department between Jan. 1 and 2d Mon. in July. (15-8-201).

Review.—Assessments may be reviewed by county tax appeal board, consisting of three members appointed by county commissioners, which has power to reassess. (15-15-101 to 104). Appeal lies to State Tax Appeal Board consisting of three members appointed by governor. (15-2-101 to 306). Judicial review provided. (15-2-303).

Lien.—Taxes are lien on real estate as of Jan. 1 each year. (15-16-403). Personal property tax is lien on property taxed and also first lien on real estate for taxable value up to $10,000. Where taxes of personal property based on taxable value exceeds $10,000, personal property tax is first lien on real estate, unless owner of mortgage or other lien files notice with county assessor and county treasurer before tax lien attaches. Where owner has failed to pay taxes on real estate and personal property for one or more years, owner of mortgage on real estate may have property separately assessed and personal property tax does not become lien on real property. (15-16-402). Personal property taxes which are not lien on real property and other contractual obligations cancelled after five years payment delinquency. (15-16-701 to 704).

Collection.—Personal property taxes may be collected by suit (15-16-503) or by sale (15-16-119). County Treasurer in charge of collection.

Payment.—One-half of tax and special improvement assessments are payable on or before Nov. 30th, and the other half on or before May 31st. (15-16-102 to 103). See also topic Administration, subhead Penalties and Interest.

Sale.—On or before last Monday of each June, County Treasurer must publish notice of time and place of sale of all property on which delinquent taxes are a lien, together with statement of amount due. (15-17-122). Publication must be for three successive weeks. If no person pays delinquent taxes, including penalties, interest, and costs, on first day of tax sale, county is considered to be purchaser. (15-17-214).

Warrant of Distraint.—Department of Revenue may issue warrant for distraint ordering sheriff to levy on and sell real and personal property of delinquent taxpayers, for tax administered and collected by Department that is unpaid 30 days after due; 30 days notice required before issuance of warrant, unless emergency exists which would allow Department to proceed without waiting period. Procedures for review of tax liability (except inheritance, estate, or property tax liability) prior to execution of warrant filed with District Court (15-1-704); Department must provide notice of such right to taxpayer; and review process and any appeals must be completed prior to execution (15-1-704). Review process can be eschewed in emergency, but post-execution hearing must then be provided. Execution on warrant same as execution on any judgment. Warrant for distraint not exclusive remedy. (15-1-701 to 709).

Redemption.—Redemption of property tax lien acquired at tax sale or otherwise may be made by owner, or any person having interest in or lien on property, within 36 months from date of purchase or within 60 days following giving of required notice, whichever is later. (15-18-111 and 15-18-212). Time for redeeming property subdivided as residential or commercial lot upon which special improvement district or rural special improvement district assessments are delinquent is 24 months or within 60 days following giving of required notice. (15-18-111).

REAL ESTATE CONVEYANCE TAX:

None.

SALES AND USE TAXES:

Sales Tax.—No general sales tax. Specific sales taxes enacted in form of graduated tax on new cars, fee in lieu of tax on motor homes, travel trailers, snowmobiles, and campers. Tax of 18¢ per package of 20 cigarettes, or fraction thereof, sold or possessed in Montana (16-11-111) and 4% statewide bed tax on users of hotel, motel, and campground facilities (15-65-111). Defined resort area may also establish resort tax on defined luxury items, hotel services, restaurants, food store, bar, and lounge goods and services. (7-6-4461 to 4469).

Use Tax.—None.

STAMP TAX:

No requirement of documentary stamps on corporate stock or other instruments.

TRANSPORTATION TAXES:

Passenger Tramway Tax.—Imposed on gross receipts. (23-2-715).

UNEMPLOYMENT COMPENSATION TAX:

Unemployment compensation tax, in the form of "contributions," is imposed by 39-51-101 to 3207.

Contributions are required from every employer whose total annual payroll in current or preceding calendar year exceeds $1,000 or who has acquired business of another employer subject to Act. (39-51-202). Act does not, however, apply to agricultural labor except in certain situations, domestic service in private homes; service performed on vessel in navigable waters of U.S.; service in employ of son, daughter or spouse, under age 21 in employ of parent; service of U.S. or any other state or its political subdivision; or service with respect to which unemployment compensation is payable under system established by act of Congress where State Commission has agreed with U. S. agencies for reciprocal treatment; services of free-lance correspondent or newspaper carrier if person performing services or parent or guardian acknowledges person is not covered; services by real estate, securities and insurance salesperson paid solely on commission; service performed by student enrolled in and regularly attending classes at school, college or university; services performed by patient of hospital; services performed by cosmetologist or barber; casual labor not in employer's trade or business; employment of sole proprietors, working members of partnership, members of member-managed LLC, or partners of LLP; services of floor covering installer; and services performed by petroleum land professional. (39-51-204).

UNIFORM FEDERAL LIEN REGISTRATION ACT:

Uniform Federal Lien Registration Act enacted. (71-3-201 to 207).

See note at head of Digest as to 1998 legislation covered.

See Topical Index in front part of this volume.

TRANSPORTATION

MOTOR VEHICLES:

Following uniform acts adopted: Uniform Accident Reporting Act (61-7-101 to 118); Uniform Motor Vehicle Safety Responsibility Act (61-6-101 to 151). General supervision exercised by Registrar of Motor Vehicles, Deer Lodge, Montana 59722.

Vehicle registration required annually. (61-3-311). Vehicle includes automobile, truck, motorcycle, semi-trailer, trailer, and trailer-house. (61-1-102 and 61-1-103). Number plates must generally be displayed front and rear. (61-3-301). No exemption for members of Armed Forces.

Operator's License.—Drivers licenses are required. (61-5-102). Licenses expire on anniversary of date of birth of licensee eight years or less after date of issue until age 75, after that, every four years. (61-5-111). Nonresident must be licensed within 90 days of residence in state. (61-5-103). License may not be issued to any person under 16 unless (1) at least 15 years of age and has passed approved driver education course, or (2) at least 13 years old and can demonstrate individual hardship entitling individual to restricted license. (61-5-105). Member of Armed Forces exempt while driving U.S. government vehicle on official business. (61-5-104).

Titles.—Motor vehicle owner must file application for registration with county treasurer. (61-3-303). Division of Motor Vehicles, Department of Law Enforcement and Public Safety will then issue certificate of registration and certificate of ownership to owner. (61-3-322 and 61-3-202).

Sales.—Dealer transfers title to used vehicle by forwarding certificates of registration and owner to county treasurer and new vehicle by forwarding copy of temporary permit. (61-4-112; 61-4-111).

Motor vehicle manufacturer must make repairs necessary to bring motor vehicle into compliance with express warranties. If repairs unsuccessful, manufacturer must provide for replacement or refund. (61-4-503).

Liens.—Lien notice on Division approved form showing security interest has been created and financing statement must be filed with Division of Motor Vehicles, Department of Law Enforcement and Public Safety, Deer Lodge, Montana 59722, to be valid as against third parties. Copy of security agreement is sufficient as lien notice if it contains name and address of debtor and secured party, complete vehicle description, amount of lien, and is signed by debtor. (61-3-103). Financing statement may be omitted if security agreement meets formal requirements of financing statement. Security agreement must contain description of motor vehicle, including year, make, model and identification and motor number. Amount of security interest must also be shown. Security interests in motor vehicles held as inventory by dealer must be perfected in accordance with Tit. 30, c. 9. (61-3-103).

Identification Marks.—Crime to sell or offer for sale vehicle with original vehicle identification number altered or removed which is punishable by fine of $200 to $500 and jail term of 30 to 180 days. (61-3-604).

Operation prohibited by persons under influence of alcohol or other drugs. (61-8-401). "Under the influence" means that as result of taking into body alcohol, drugs, or any combination of alcohol or drugs, person's ability to safely operate motor vehicle has been diminished. (61-8-401). Every operator deemed to have given consent to chemical test for purpose of determining alcoholic content of blood or presence of drugs. (61-8-402). Inference of sobriety if 0.04 or less by weight. No inference if over 0.04 but less than 0.10 by weight. Rebuttable inference of intoxication if 0.10 by weight. (61-8-401). Absolute liability as provided in 45-2-104 will be imposed for violation of this section. (61-8-406).

Size and Weight Limits, Enforcement and Penalties.—Regulated by 61-10-101 to 148.

Equipment Required.—Regulated by 61-9-101 to 61-9-520.

Lights Required.—Regulated by 61-9-201 to 61-9-229.

Inspection.—Various officials may require submission to inspection, where reasonable cause to believe that vehicle is unsafe exists. (61-9-501 and 61-9-503).

Seat Belts Required.—No driver may operate motor vehicle upon highway of state of Montana unless each occupant of designated seating position is wearing properly adjusted and fastened seatbelt, subject to exceptions. (61-13-103). Violation does not affect driving record but subjects driver to $20 fine effective Jan. 1, 1988. (61-13-104). Evidence of compliance or failure to comply is not admissible in civil actions. Failure to comply does not constitute negligence. (61-13-106).

Accidents.—Driver must stop, render assistance, and give name, address and license number to person injured or other occupant or owner of property damaged. (61-7-105). Accident involving death, personal injury or property damage to any one person to apparent extent of $250 or more must be reported immediately to police chief, sheriff or highway patrol. (61-7-108). Unless accident was investigated and reported by law enforcement officer, written report of accident must be made within ten days if accident involved personal injury or death or where damage to property of any one person exceeds $400. (61-7-109). Parties to accident or their representatives may examine reports. (61-7-114).

Owner Liable.—For negligence of others only when car is operated by his servant or agent within the scope of his authority and duty. (61-6-201). Family purpose doctrine not recognized. (63 Mont. 488, 208 Pac. 924).

Liability for Operation by Minor.—Parent, custodian, guardian, or other person signing application of minor for driver's license liable for any negligence or wilful misconduct of minor, unless motor vehicle liability policy, as prescribed in Tit. 61, c. 6, is in effect. (61-5-108).

Offenses Committed by Persons Under 18.—Person under 18 convicted of offense under Title 61 shall not be punished by incarceration. Can be fined in same amount as if offense was committed by adult; revocation or suspension of license; and/or vehicle impoundment. (61-8-723).

Guests.—No limitation of liability of owner or operator for injury to guest, effective July 1, 1975. (1975, c. 236).

Proof of financial responsibility required under Motor-Vehicle Safety–Responsibility Act. (61-6-101 to 61-6-151).

Department, on receipt from clerk of court of certified copy of judgment, must suspend license, and nonresidence operating privilege of person against whom judgment rendered, unless judgment creditor consents in writing that judgment debtor be allowed license, or nonresidence operating privilege, in which event Department may allow same for six months and thereafter until consent is revoked. (61-6-122). Suspension continues until judgment is stayed, satisfied in full or in part as provided or for six years after entry of judgment. (61-6-123).

If Division revokes operator's license such license shall remain revoked until proof of financial responsibility is given. Such proof is also required for renewal of nonresidence operating privilege. (61-6-131).

A nonresident operator of motor vehicle not registered in Montana, may give proof of financial responsibility by filing with Division of Motor Vehicles a written certificate of an insurance carrier authorized to transact business in state in which motor vehicle is registered, provided insurance carrier executes a power of attorney authorizing Division to accept service of process in any action arising out of motor vehicle accident in this state and agrees in writing that policy shall be deemed to conform with laws of this state relating to terms of motor vehicle liability policies issued herein. (61-6-134).

Insurance.—Motor vehicle liability insurance is compulsory unless exemption applies or certificate of self-insurance is issued. (61-6-301). Proof of compliance with this requirement must be carried in motor vehicles. (61-6-302). Exemptions include government vehicles, vehicles for which adequate bond is posted, equipment driven only incidentally on highways, motorcycles, human or animal-powered vehicles and vehicle owned by nonresident if it is currently registered in owner's resident jurisdiction and he is in compliance with motor vehicle liability insurance requirements, if any, of that jurisdiction. (61-6-303). Insurance is prerequisite to operation of vehicle. (61-6-301). Penalties and suspension of vehicle registration and license plates provided. (61-6-304).

No-Fault Insurance.—Not adopted.

Foreign Vehicle.—Vehicle operated for profit or used by owner while engaged in gainful occupation, except vehicles part of interstate fleet otherwise registered and licensed in state, must secure special registration certificate and pay regular license fee. (61-3-701). Nonresidents employed temporarily in Montana must pay license fees quarterly. (15-24-301).

Nonresident operator is not required to obtain local operator's license.

Action against nonresident, arising out of highway accident, may be commenced by service on Secretary of State, who must mail copy of process to defendant and must notify defendant by registered or certified mail marked "Deliver to Addressee Only" and "Return Receipt Requested." The return receipt must be received by the Secretary of State. Defendant may also be served personally outside of state. (25-3-601, 602; Rule 4D[6]).

Direct action against insurer by injured person not allowed. (98 Mont. 31, 37 P.2d 565).

Motor Vehicle Carriers.—Regulated by Public Service Commission. Must have certificate of public convenience and necessity. Act does not apply, among other things, to vehicles used to transport employees engaged exclusively in construction or maintenance of highways or in logging or mining operations; or to operation of municipal or district transportation system. (69-12-102). Must file bond to indemnify passengers and others injured by operation. Act applies to interstate and international carriers as far as permitted by Federal Constitution, treaties and statutes, provided no showing of public convenience and necessity is required except as to intrastate transportation. (69-12-101 to 423). Authorizes reasonable inspections. (69-12-203). Special fuel users must display original or reproduced copy of their permit in vehicle except in certain circumstances. (15-70-302).

Motor Vehicle Taxes.—Registration fees imposed on all motor vehicles, trailers, semi-trailers, and dealers in motor vehicles and recreational vehicles (61-3-321). Additional fees imposed upon trucks, truck-tractors, trailers and semi-trailers, based upon maximum gross loaded weight, (61-10-201) with specified exemptions (61-10-214) upon motor trucks and trailers from other states operated in Montana upon itinerant basis (61-10-211); and upon new passenger motor vehicles, not otherwise assessed (61-4-102).

Multistate Highway Transportation Agreement adopted. (61-10-1101).

Gasoline Tax.—See category Taxation, topic Gasoline Tax.

RAILROADS:

See category Business Regulation and Commerce, topic Carriers.

See note at head of Digest as to 1998 legislation covered.

See Topical Index in front part of this volume.

NEBRASKA LAW DIGEST REVISER

Fraser Stryker Vaughn Meusey

Olson Boyer & Bloch, PC
500 Energy Plaza
409 South 17th Street
Omaha, NE 68102-2663
Telephone: 402-341-6000
Fax: 402-341-8290

Reviser Profile

History: Fraser, Stryker was founded in Omaha in 1898 by three graduates of Michigan Law School. The firm, continuously located in downtown Omaha, is the fourth largest in the city.

Specialty Areas: Fraser, Stryker offers expertise in virtually all areas of practice. In its early years, the firm was widely known for its expertise in litigation, utility and construction law. In recent decades it has experienced considerable growth in the following substantive areas: Banking; Bankruptcy; Coal and Natural Resources; Construction; Corporate and Commercial; Environmental; Estates and Estate Planning; General Practice; Hospital and Health Care; Labor and Employment Discrimination; Legislation; Litigation (including Commercial, Personal Injury, Toxic Tort and Professional Malpractice); Federal, State and Local Taxation; Real Estate; Technology; Telecommunications; and Utility Law. At least two partners and several associates devote their practice to or are substantively familiar with each practice area.

Client Base: In addition to representing many local and regional businesses and individuals, the firm is counsel to a large number of national companies who regularly or periodically require the services of Nebraska counsel (it also has a partner and an associate licensed to practice in Iowa). The firm has been general counsel to the public power utility serving eastern Nebraska since its inception, and for many years has been counsel to the largest auto and casualty insurer in the state. The firm is counsel to two major area hospitals, and provides labor counsel to management of over 100 businesses. For the past six years the firm has served as counsel to several major international telecommunications companies. The firm also offers specialty work on multi-state property tax matters to national companies.

Firm Philosophy: The firm's long standing policy has been to provide consistently excellent work in the shortest possible time and with the least expense to the client. It employs a full complement of support staff to provide the most efficient and economical service to its clients.

Significant Distinctions: Members of the firm are frequent lecturers at continuing legal education seminars and have published works in their specialty areas. One firm member is a Fellow in the International Society of Barristers and a past President of the Nebraska Association of Trial Lawyers; three are Fellows in the American College of Trial Lawyers. The firm is counsel to many community and civic organizations, including the United Way, Mid-America Council of the Boy Scouts of America, Omaha Community Playhouse and Omaha Zoological Society. Several firm members hold leadership positions in the local and state Bar Association.

NEBRASKA LAW DIGEST

(The following is a list of all Categories and Topics, including cross-references, covered in this Digest.)

NEBRASKA LAW DIGEST

Revised for 1999 edition by

FRASER STRYKER VAUGHN MEUSEY OLSON BOYER & BLOCH, PC, of the Omaha Bar.

(References are to sections of Revised Statutes of Nebraska, 1943, as reissued, 1997 Supplement, the Uniform Commercial Code volume and Laws of Nebraska, Ninety-fifth Legislature First Session. LB refers to legislative bills of 1998 session. Parallel citations to the North Western Reporter begin with 9 Neb. and 1 Neb. Unof.)

Note: This Revision incorporates the 1997 Acts passed by the Ninety-fifth Legislature Second Session and approved by the Governor.

INTRODUCTION

GOVERNMENT AND LEGAL SYSTEM:

The State of Nebraska is a constituent state of the United States of America. For further discussion of the U.S. federal system, see Introduction to the Federal Government of the United States at the beginning of this volume. A great many laws are promulgated by the federal government of the United States and are not reflected in the topics below. See the Introduction to this volume for references to the federal law topics covered.

Like all but one of the United States, Nebraska has a common law legal system, with roots in English common law. For information on the courts and legislature of Nebraska, see category Courts and Legislature.

HOLIDAYS:

Legal holidays are: Jan. 1; 3d Mon. in Jan.; 3d Mon. in Feb.; last Fri. in Apr.; last Mon. in May; July 4; 1st Mon. in Sept.; 2d Mon. in Oct.; Nov. 11 and federally recognized holiday therefor, or either of them; 4th Thurs. and Fri. in Nov.; Dec. 25. (62-301[1]). Bank may close on Sat. and Sat. is then treated as holiday for bank transactions. (62-301.01).

Holiday Falling on Sat.—All courts and their offices observe preceding Fri. as holiday. (25-2221).

Holiday Falling on Sun.—Next succeeding business day is holiday. (62-301[1]).

Federal Holiday.—If date different (except Vet. Day), Federal holiday observed. (62-301[1]).

Legality of Transactions on Holiday.—Transactions valid. (See 62-301.01.)

OFFICE HOURS AND TIME ZONE:

Nebraska is in the Central (GMT −06:00) time zone. Office hours are generally from 9 a.m. to 5 p.m.

BUSINESS ORGANIZATIONS

ASSOCIATIONS:

No statutory provision for organization in this state. Any association doing business in Nebraska, and not incorporated under Nebraska law, must record in office of county clerk of county where place of business of association is located certificate signed by each member, giving name of association, general nature of business, principal place and full name and residence of each member. (67-101). See category Intellectual Property, topic Trademarks and Tradenames.

Professional Associations.—See topic Corporations, subhead Professional Corporations.

Actions.—Unincorporated associations may sue and be sued by such usual name as such association may have assumed or be known by. (25-313 to 316).

CORPORATIONS:

Note: Model Business Corporation Act, prepared by Committee on Corporate Laws (Section of Corporation, Banking and Business Law of American Bar Association), has been adopted, with variances, effective 1963, and is known as "Business Corporation Act". For text of Model Act, see Uniform and Model Acts section. Law as digested below relates only to variances of Business Corporation Act from Model Act as revised through 1993, and contained in Uniform and Model Acts section. In addition none of subsequent amendments to Model Act have been adopted except where indicated. Most provisions of Revised 1993 Act adopted, operative on Jan. 1, 1996.

Sections Not Adopted.—§2(o); §54(j); §69; §80(c); §82(a)(6); §§94(a), (d) and (e); §108(a); §§110(f thru k); §116; §§119(f thru h); §121(a); §130; §131; §136; §137; §138; §140; §146.

General Supervision—Secretary of State, State Capitol Building, Lincoln. All questions and filings should be addressed to: Scott D. Moore, Secretary of State, Corporations Division, 2300 State Capitol Building, Lincoln, NE 68509, (402) 471-2554.

Purposes.—With some exceptions, corporations may be organized under this act for any lawful purpose. (21-2018). Different manner of organization prescribed for corporations for particular purposes. (c. 21, arts. 6, 13, 14, 17, 19, 22).

Name is not to be same as or deceptively similar to other corporation or trade name of any domestic corporation or foreign corporation authorized to do business. Shall contain word corporation, company, incorporation, or limited, or abbreviation of such words except corporation organized to conduct banking business. (21-2028). Affected corporation may acquiesce in use of name similar to its own by another corporation by filing consent with Secretary of State. (21-2028). Reserve available name by letter and $25 fee. (21-2005). Suggest call to Secretary of State.

Incorporators.—One or more natural persons of age of majority may act as incorporators, who have direction of company until directors are elected. (21-2017).

Filing and Recording of Articles.—Original and duplicate copy of articles, signed by all incorporators to be filed with Secretary of State. A duplicate copy, with Secretary of State stamp, is returned to incorporators and is to be recorded with clerk of county where registered office of corporation is located. Corporate existence begins upon filing and recording with Secretary of State. (21-2019). Articles need not be notarized or acknowledged.

Organization.—After corporate existence begins, majority of incorporators may call first shareholders meeting, on three days written notice for electing directors and adopting bylaws. Directors then hold meeting on at least one day written notice (21-2021).

Paid in Capital Requirements.—No required minimum. (21-2018).

Amendment of Articles of Incorporation.—Purposes, procedure and class voting generally same as Model Act, except unanimous consent of directors and shareholders obviates need for meeting or vote. (21-20,118). Amendment must be approved by holders of two-thirds outstanding stock of each class thereof. (21-20,118). If amendment adversely affects shareholder's rights he can dissent. (21-20,138). When amendment would change existing priority rights or provisions of outstanding class of shares, adversely affected shareholder may enjoin adoption on ground of fraud or unfairness unless proponents show amendment equitable. Incorporators may file amendments before acceptance of any subscription to stock. (21-20,120).

Filing.—Secretary of State not expressly required to find that amendments conform to law. Amended articles effective upon filing and recording original with Secretary of State. (21-20,121). Copy of amendment with Secretary of State stamp required to be filed in county clerk's office of county where registered office is located. (21-20,121).

Revision of Articles of Incorporation.—Amendment considered a revision upon compliance with 21-20,116.

Restatement of Articles of Incorporation.—Upon directors' resolution, filing with Secretary of State and payment of required fees, restated articles become effective. Secretary of State required to find restated articles conform to law. Duplicate copy of restated articles filed in county clerk's office of county where registered office is located. (21-20,122).

Reorganization.—Generally same as Model Act. In addition: If plan or reorganization has been approved by court decree articles of amendment shall be executed and acknowledged by person appointed by court, and include name of corporation, amendments approved by court, date of decree, title of court proceedings, and statement that such decree was entered by court having jurisdiction over reorganization pursuant to federal law. (21-20,123).

Bylaws.—Initial bylaws to be adopted by shareholders. Shareholders or directors may change bylaws, except directors may not amend or repeal bylaw which prohibits their so doing, or adopt bylaw requiring more than a majority of shareholders for a quorum or action at their meeting, except where articles of incorporation or the act establish higher percentage. (21-2022).

Stock.—Generally, same as Model Act. Sept. 1977 amendment to §23 of Model Act adopted. (21-2022). All stock except preferred, to be of equal par value. Shares may or may not be represented by certificates. (21-2035). Articles may limit voting rights for any class of stock. Voting stock shareholders have right to vote for directors. (21-2059). One vote is allowed for each share of stock. Stockholder may vote in person or by proxy and at election for directors may cumulate his vote. (21-2060). Cooperative and mutual companies may limit voting. (Const., Art. XII, §1). Shares not preferred as to dividends or liquidation distributions not to be designated preferred. Shares having such preference not to be designated as common. (21-2066).

Amount of Stated Capital.—Directors may increase stated capital by directing transfer of surplus. Directors may direct that transferred surplus is stated capital in respect of any designated class of shares.

Stockholders.—Shareholder obligation to corporation with respect to shares limited to payment of full consideration for shares.

Preemptive Rights.—None, unless in articles of incorporation. (21-2048).

Stockholders' Liabilities.—Generally same as Model Act. Ascertained corporate obligations to be satisfied out of corporate assets, then by original subscribers to extent subscriptions unpaid. This subscriber obligation follows stock. (21-2018).

Stockholders' Meetings.—Generally same as Model Act. (21-2051).

Action Without Meeting.—Unanimous, signed consent of shareholders has same effect as unanimous vote. (21-2057).

Voting List.—Generally same as Model Act, except no provision for failure to comply with §21-2029 and no provision for damage recoverable by shareholder (21-2031), and list must be available for inspection for two days prior to meeting after notice (21-2055).

Directors.—Generally same as Model Act. Number of directors shall be fixed by by-laws. Articles of incorporation may provide for staggering terms of directors by dividing total number of directors into two or three groups. (21-2080).

Removal.—At meeting of shareholders called for such purpose, majority of shareholders may remove any director with or without cause unless articles of incorporation provide otherwise. (21-2085).

See note at head of Digest as to 1998 legislation covered.

See Topical Index in front part of this volume.

CORPORATIONS . . . *continued*

Vacancies.—Unless articles of incorporation provide otherwise, vacancy may be filled by: (a) shareholders; (b) board of directors; (c) directors remaining in office if there is less than quorum. (21-2089).

Indemnification.—Corporation has power to indemnify directors. (21-2004[15]).

Directors' Meetings.—Generally same as Model Act. (21-2089).

Action without meeting permitted upon unanimous, written consent of directors. (21-2090).

Board or committee meetings may be by means of conference telephone or similar communications equipment. (21-2089).

Director's Dissent.—Nebraska Business Corporation Act amended to authorize certified mail as notice regarding director's dissent. (21-2093[4]).

Directors' Liabilities.—Generally same as Model Act. Director must exercise such care as ordinary prudent person in like position under similar circumstances. Directors voting for or assenting to loans to officer or director or loans secured by shares of corporation (except to prevent loss upon debt previously contracted) are jointly and severally liable for amount loaned until repayment. Officers are elected and removed as in Model Act. Directors present at meeting where action taken presumed to have assented to same unless written dissent filed or entered in minutes. Articles of incorporation may limit liability of outside director for breach of duty for certain acts. (21-2095).

Director's Liability, Nonprofit Corporations.—Noncompensated directors immune from civil liability for acts within scope of official capacity unless act is willful, wanton departure from duty.

Registered Office and Registered Agent.—Agent may be either resident individual or domestic or foreign corporation. (21-2031). Street address of its initial registered office and name and street address of its initial registered agent must be identical. (21-2031). Must use Secretary of State form for statement of change of agent of office. (21-2032). Duplicate of statement bearing Secretary of State filing date must be filed with clerk of county where corporation's registered office located. (21-2031). If statement changes location of registered office to another county, statement should be filed in both counties. (21-2034). *Caveat:* Failure to comply with 21-2034 can result in dissolution of corporation. Registered agent may transfer office from address in city to another in same city by filing acknowledged statement with Secretary of State. (21-2034).

Officers.—Any two or more offices may be held by same person. (21-2097).

Officers' Personal Liability.—Corporate officers not personally liable for unpaid corporate taxes. (21-2099).

General Powers of Corporation.—In addition to those enumerated in Model Act, corporation expressly empowered to enter into partnerships, joint ventures, syndicates, pools, associations and other arrangements for carrying out its purposes and to purchase liability insurance for directors, officers and employees and indemnify directors, officers and employees for expenses, fees and judgment under certain circumstances. (21-2025). Corporation may not make loans secured by its shares or loan to officers or directors. (21-2025). Corporations may guarantee obligations of others for corporate purposes.

Acquisition of own shares permitted to extent of unreserved and unrestricted surplus as defined in the act. (21-2025).

Dividends.—Generally same as Model Act.

Unclaimed Dividends.—See category Property, topic Absentees, subhead Escheat.

Sale or Transfer of Corporate Assets.—Directors may authorize sale of all or substantially all assets in regular course of business or mortgage of any or all assets whether or not in usual course of business. (21-20,136). Such a sale not in regular course of business must be authorized by holders of at least two-thirds of outstanding shares or each class thereof, but such mortgage does not need such authorization. (21-20,136). Each share entitled to vote whether or not articles of incorporation so provide. (21-2025).

Merger, Consolidation and Exchange.—Notice to be given to all shareholders must be written or printed. Plan to be approved in case of merger, consolidation or by acquired corporation or in case of exchange by at least ⅔ of outstanding shares of each class. (21-20,130). Each share entitled to vote whether or not it has such rights under articles of incorporation. (21-20,130). Copy of articles with Secretary of State's stamp to be filed with clerk of county where registered office of surviving, new or acquiring corporation located. (21-20,132).

Subsidiary may be merged without vote of shareholders if 90% owned by parent. (21-20,131).

Merger, consolidation or exchange effective upon effective date of merger or exchange. (21-20,133).

Surviving corporation's articles of incorporation deemed amended to extent changes stated in merger plan. (21-20,133).

Exchange of Stock.—Model Act provision adopted. (21-20,134).

Shareholders may dissent in writing to plan of merger, consolidation or sale of substantially all assets not in regular course of business, any plan of exchange in which corporation's shares are to be acquired, any amendment to articles of incorporation which materially and adversely affects rights of dissenting shareholders if it: (i) Alters or abolishes preferential right, (ii) creates, alters or abolishes redemption right, (iii) alters or abolishes preemptive right, or (iv) excludes right of shareholder to vote on any matter. (21-20,139). Shareholders required to dissent before vote at shareholders meeting. (21-20,140). If shareholder dissents he cannot attack validity of underlying transaction, unless action is unlawful or fraudulent. (21-20,138).

Payment for Shares.—Upon effectuation of plan corporation must pay shareholder fair value as determined by corporation. (21-20,138). If shareholder disagrees he must demand within 30 days additional payment of what he considers deficiency. (21-20,148). If corporation disagrees with shareholder demand, corporation requests court to determine fair value of shares. (21-20,149). If corporation fails to file suit within 60 days, shareholder shall be paid his demanded amount. (21-20,148).

Disposition of Shares.—To be treated as treasury shares or as prescribed in consolidation, merger, or exchange plan. (21-20,146).

Shareholders' Protection Act adopted. (21-2431). Act requires shareholder approval before shares of certain "issuing public corporations" possess voting rights on matters other than elections of directors. Issuing public corporation is Nebraska corporation with 100 shareholders or more, at least $10,000,000 of assets in Nebraska, or 10% or more of its shareholders reside in Nebraska or 10% or more of its shares owned by Nebraska residents; or foreign corporation with 100 or more shareholders, its principal executive offices in Nebraska, 10% or more of its shareholders reside in Nebraska or 10% or more of its shares owned by Nebraska residents, and at least 500 employees in Nebraska. Act also prohibits "business combinations" (i.e. mergers, consolidations, sales, leases, etc. of 10% or more of corporate assets or corporate shares, etc.) between issuing public corporations and shareholders owning 10% or more of issuing public corporation, for five year period.

Dissolution.—Generally same as Model Act.

Incorporators may file original and duplicate copy of articles of dissolution with Secretary of State if corporation has not commenced business or issued any shares. Duplicate copy, with Secretary of State stamp, and certificate of dissolution returned to incorporators to be recorded in county clerk's office in county where registered office of corporation is located. (21-20,153).

Corporation or shareholders may dissolve corporation. Holders of at least two-thirds of outstanding stock, or each class thereof, must approve dissolution. Each outstanding share entitled to vote whether or not articles of incorporation so provide. (21-20,152). Statement of intent to dissolve filed with Secretary of State and clerk of county where corporation's registered office located. (21-20,154). Dissolution not allowed until all occupation taxes due or assessable have been paid and report filed. (21-20,153). Articles of dissolution, stamped by Secretary of State must also be so filed. (21-20,153). Corporate existence ceases upon filing articles of dissolution with Secretary of State. (21-20,153). Statement of revocation of dissolution proceedings by corporation or shareholders with Secretary of State's stamp to be filed with clerk of county where corporation's registered office located. (21-20,154).

Involuntary dissolution effected by decree of District Court in an action filed by Attorney General when it is established that: (1) Corporation procured its articles of incorporation through fraud; or (2) corporation has continued to exceed or abuse the authority conferred upon it by law. (21-20,162). Other Model Act grounds not adopted.

Dissolution for Nonfiling of Report and Nonpayment of Tax.—Date of involuntary dissolution is Apr. 16 of years when report and tax due. (21-20,165).

District Court also has power to liquidate assets and business of a corporation upon action brought by shareholder or creditor on grounds enumerated in the act. (21-20,163). Court may appoint receiver. (21-20,164). Decree of dissolution to be filed with Secretary of State and clerk of county in which registered office located. (21-20,153[1]).

Publication of notice for three successive weeks in legal newspaper of general circulation near registered office of corporation required for incorporation, amendment, merger, consolidation, statement of intent to dissolve with consent, or statement of intent to dissolve by act of domestic corporation. (21-20,189).

Incorporation notice must show: (1) Corporate name for corporation; (2) number of shares corporation is authorized to issue; (3) street address of corporation's initial registered office and name of initial registered agent at that office; and (4) name and street address of each incorporator. (21-20,189[1]).

Amendment, merger or consolidation notice to include brief resume of plan.

Dissolution notice to include terms and conditions of dissolution, names and titles of persons who are to manage corporate affairs and distribute assets, and statement of assets and liabilities. (21-20,189[2]).

Proof of publication to be filed with Secretary of State and clerk of county where registered office is located. (21-20,189[3]).

Incorporation Fees.—Fees for filing certificate of incorporation with Secretary of State are graduated according to amount of capital stock, as follows: Not over $10,000, $60; over $10,000 but not over $25,000, $100; over $25,000 but not over $50,000, $150; over $50,000 but not over $75,000, $225; over $75,000 but not over $100,000, $300; plus $3 for each $1,000 in excess of $100,000. Fees are based on authorized capital stock, regardless of amount to be used in Nebraska. (21-2005: 33-101).

Filing and Recording Fees.—Other fees payable to Secretary of State are: For recording articles, amendments, revised or restated articles, changes of registered office or registered agent, merger or consolidation, statement of intent to dissolve, revocation of dissolution, $25 plus $5 per page; articles of dissolution, $45; application for certificate of authority, $130; any other document required or permitted to be filed by Business Corporation Act, $25. County clerk entitled to fee of $5 per page for filing articles. Copies of records $1 per page. $10 secretary certificate. (21-2005).

Payment for Stock.—Labor or property used to pay for stock may not be taken at a greater value than the actual value at time said labor was done or property delivered. (21-2040). All fictitious increases in stock shall be void. (21-2040).

Transfer of Stock.—Uniform Commercial Code adopted. See category Business Regulation and Commerce, topic Commercial Code. Uniform Fraudulent Transfer Act adopted. (36-701 to -711). See category Debtor and Creditor, topic Fraudulent Sales and Conveyances.

Uniform Simplification of Fiduciary Security Transfers Act adopted. (30-3301-3311).

Stock Transfer Tax.—None.

Reports.—See infra, subheads Foreign Corporations; Occupation Tax.

Bonds.—Corporation has power to issue bonds. (21-2025).

See note at head of Digest as to 1998 legislation covered.

See Topical Index in front part of this volume.

NE – 2

CORPORATIONS . . . *continued*

Forfeiture or Revocation of Charter.—Corporation shall be automatically dissolved for failure to pay occupation taxes on Apr. 16 of current year when tax becomes delinquent. (21-323).

Appraisal.—If shareholder and corporation disagree on fair value of stock of stockholders who dissented from merger, consolidation, exchange or sale of substantially all of property and assets of corporation, court will determine fair market value and may use appraisers. (21-20,149).

Close Corporations.—No special statutory provisions.

Foreign Corporations.—Generally same as Model Act. Foreign corporations not to do business in state without certificate of authority from Secretary of State. (21-20,170).

Doing Business.—Activities not constituting doing business for purposes of being required to secure certificate are those listed in Model Act plus, acting as foreign corporate trustee to extent authorized by 30-2805. (21-20,168).

Enumerated activities are not standards for amenability to service of process or liability for ad valorem taxes assessed against any real property or interest therein. (21-20,168). Requirements of Business Corporation Act do not apply to foreign or alien insurers. Instead, see c. 44 of Neb. Rev. Stats. (21-20,168).

Change of Name.—Corporation may do business 180 days under old name, then must change to a name available under the act or obtain consent of other, confusingly similar corporation or registered trade name; otherwise, certificate of authority will be suspended. (21-20,171). Amended certificate of authority must be obtained if name changed. (21-20,171).

Certificate of authority obtained after filing with Secretary of State application on forms provided by Secretary of State (21-20,170), and certificate of compliance less than 30 days old from state of incorporation (21-20,170).

Revocation of Certificate.—Secretary of State may revoke certificate on at least 30 days notice when corporation has failed to appoint and maintain registered agent, failed to file statement required when registered office changed or made a misrepresentation in any document filed pursuant to act. (21-20,179). Corporation shall be barred from doing business if annual report and occupation tax delinquent after Apr. 15 of current year when report and tax become delinquent. (21-325).

Registered office location may be changed from one address to another in same city, or village upon agent's filing statement with Secretary of State. (21-20,174).

Service of process on corporation's registered agent. (21-20,174).

Transacting Business Without Certificate of Authority.—Corporation and its corporate successors and assignees can institute but cannot maintain court action until certificate of authority obtained. (21-20,169; 276 N.W.2d 659). Maintenance of lawsuit does not alone constitute "transacting business". (21-20,169; 290 N.W.2d 199).

Reports.—Must be in writing as of Jan. 1 and forwarded to Secretary of State on or before Apr. 15. Report shall be for calendar year beginning Jan. 1. Annual fee is due and assessable on that date and delinquent if not paid on or before Apr. 15. (21-20,188; 21-301 or 21-304).

Foreign corporation may not take or hold real estate or any leasehold for more than five years (76-402) except real estate necessary for construction and operation of railroads, public utilities, common carriers, manufacturing or industrial establishments and incidental facilities or filling or bulk stations for petroleum products or real estate within corporate limits of a city or village or within three miles thereof (76-412 to 414). For violation of the law corporation shall be barred from doing business in state and land forfeited to state. (76-407). If state declares forfeiture it must pay full value of land to owner. (76-408). Foreign corporation may, however, acquire lien on real estate and foreclose said lien, and hold any land acquired thereunder for ten years. (76-411). May also own and operate oil and gas leases for not exceeding ten years and as long thereafter as oil, gas or other hydrocarbon substances can be produced in commercial quantities. (76-404). State alone can question title and good title may be conveyed by corporation before forfeiture has been declared by state. (115 Neb. 33; 211 N.W. 210).

Uniform Trade Secrets Act adopted. (87-501 to 87-507).

Taxation of Corporate Property.—For most corporations, same as individuals. See category Taxation, topic Corporate Tax.

Income Tax.—See category Taxation, topic Income Tax.

Occupation Tax.—Every domestic corporation organized for profit must file with Secretary of State, on or before Apr. 15 of each year, report signed by its president, vice-president, secretary or treasurer (21-301) (obtain forms from Secretary of State if registered agent fails to receive same in advance mailing) stating: (1) Name of corporation, (2) location of its registered office, (3) names of president, secretary, treasurer and directors with street address of each, (4) amount of paid up capital stock, (5) nature and kind of business in which corporation is engaged, (6) change or changes, if any, in above particulars made since last annual report (21-302). Annual occupation tax is due on Jan. 1 and delinquent Apr. 15 by every corporation for profit registered on Jan. 1, and payment must accompany report. (21-303). Minimum fee $13. (21-303). Upon failure to pay tax and file report, Secretary of State shall upon Apr. 16 of same year dissolve corporation for nonpayment of taxes. (21-313). Tax is computed on paid-up capital and rates can be obtained from Secretary of State at (402) 471-2554.

Foreign corporation must, on or before Apr. 15 of each year, file with Secretary of State, report signed by its president, vice-president, secretary, or treasurer (21-304), stating: (1) Name of corporation, (2) under laws of which state or country organized, (3) location of registered office in Nebraska, (4) mailing address of corporation's principal office, (5) names of president, secretary, treasurer and directors with street address of each, (6) nature and kind of business in which company is engaged, (7) value of property owned and used by company in Nebraska and where such property is situated, (8) change or changes, if any, in above matters made since last annual report. (21-305). If foreign corporation has domesticated, tax is same as on domestic corporation. (21-303). If foreign corporation is merely operating under a license to do business in this state, tax is measured by all property employed in conduct of its business in Nebraska and for purpose of computing tax, property consists of all real estate and

personal property employed in Nebraska by such foreign corporation in transaction of business. Tax is computed at double fees prescribed by 21-303 maximum of $15,000, same rate as for domestic corporations set out above and is payable to Secretary of State when filing report. (21-306).

Professional Corporations.—Persons rendering personal service which requires as a condition precedent the obtaining of a license such as certified public accountant, physician, real estate broker, and attorneys, may form professional corporation. (21-2201 to -2222). All shareholders, officers and directors must be licensed professional employees, with exception of secretary and assistant secretary who may be nonprofessional. (21-2216).

Deeds.—See category Property, topic Deeds.

Nebraska Non-Profit Corporation Act.—Act modeled after ABA's Revised Model Nonprofit Corporation Act with revisions. (21-1901 et seq.).

Limited Liability Companies.—See topic Limited Liability Companies.

JOINT STOCK COMPANIES:

No special legislation.

LIMITED LIABILITY COMPANIES:

Limited Liability Company Act (21-601) sets forth guidelines for establishment of limited liability companies. Limited liability companies may generally be formed for any lawful purpose other than banking or insurance. Articles must state name (including "Limited Liability Company" or L.L.C.), duration, purpose, address of its principal place of business, name and address of registered agent, total amount of cash contributed to capital and description of agreed value of property, total additional contributions to be made by members and when those contributions will be made, right, if any, of members to admit additional members, identification of management, and may state other provisions. Liability of members is limited to (1) difference between their contributions to capital as actually made and as stated in Articles of Organization as having been made and (2) for any unpaid contribution to capital which members agreed in Articles of Organization to make in future at time and on conditions stated in Articles of Organization. Members and manager of limited liability company shall not be liable under judgment, decree, or order of court or in any other manner for debt, obligation, or liability of limited liability company. Limited liability company shall be classified for state income tax purposes in same manner as it is classified for federal income tax purposes. Secretary of State charges and collects fee for filing original Articles of Organization based on capital of limited liability company.

PARTNERSHIPS:

Uniform Partnership Act adopted. (67-301 to -343).

Certificate.—Partners must record in office of county clerk where place of business is located a certificate signed by each member showing name of partnership, general nature of business, principal place of doing business and full name and residence of each member. (67-101).

On dissolution or change in partnership, a new certificate must be recorded, signed by each of the then members and former members, if any, showing (a) name of partnership and change therein, if any, (b) general nature of business and principal place of business and changes therein, if any, (c) the full name and residence of each member and the changes therein, if any, (d) any other changes since original certificate was filed. In addition to recording certificate, notice of dissolution or change must be published once in a legal newspaper published or in general circulation in each county where partnership had place of business and proof of publication must be filed with county clerk of each county. (67-102, 103).

Actions.—Partnership may sue or be sued in its usual name. (25-313).

Limited Partnership.—Revised Uniform Limited Partnership Act adopted Jan. 1, 1982, amended Mar. 13, 1990. (67-233 to -297). After Jan. 1, 1983 those limited partnerships existing prior to Jan. 1, 1982 must file certificate of limited partnership to continue to exist. (67-292). Business Corporation Act adopted. (21-21,201 et seq.).

BUSINESS REGULATION AND COMMERCE

BANKS AND BANKING:

Department of Banking and Finance, whose administrative officer is Director of Banking and Finance, has general supervision and control of banks and banking. (8-102 and -103; 8-101 et seq. designated Nebraska Banking Act by L.B. 1321).

General Powers, Duties and Liabilities.—Bank may hold real estate conveyed to it for debts and may purchase real estate at sale on judgments, decrees, deeds of trust or mortgages held by bank or upon its securities at amount not in excess of judgment and costs, but must sell same within five years, unless Department authorizes longer holding. (8-150).

Interest paid on deposits controlled by regulation of director of banking. Bank may secure deposits of trustee by pledge of assets or surety bond. (8-133).

Uniform Commercial Code in effect. See topic Commercial Code.

Uniform Common Trust Fund Act adopted. (24-601.01 and -601.02).

Par Collection of Checks.—All checks, except those sent as special collection items, must be paid at par. (8-153).

Delayed Deposit Services Licensing Act adopted. (45-901 et seq.).

Loan Limits.—Except within specific exceptions, no bank shall loan more than 25% of paid-up capital, surplus, and capital notes and debentures of bank to any single entity. (8-141).

See note at head of Digest as to 1998 legislation covered.

See Topical Index in front part of this volume.

BANKS AND BANKING . . . *continued*

Destruction of Records.—Most records other than ledger sheets showing unpaid balances in favor of depositors and corporation records relating to bank may be destroyed after six years. Photostatic or photographic copies may be used in evidence. (8-170).

Currency Transaction Reports.—All financial institutions must report currency transactions in excess of $10,000 to Nebraska State Patrol. (28-1439.01 §§11-17).

Unclaimed Deposits.—See category Property, topic Absentees, subhead Escheat.

Foreign Banks.—Foreign mortgage bank must be licensed with Department of Banking and Finance. (45-701 et seq.).

Accrual and Limitation of Actions.—Actions based on claims inconsistent with entry on books of bank accrue one year after date of entry and must be brought within five years from date of accrual. (8-173).

Stockholders' Liability.—Stockholders' double liability has been abolished.

Trust Companies.—Department of Banking has power to issue permits to and to supervise and regulate all trust companies. National banks authorized to act in fiduciary capacity may make deposits similar to those required of domestic companies, which are held and used the same as deposits made by domestic companies. (8-201 and -209; 8-201 et seq. designated Nebraska Trust Company Act by L.B. 1321).

Trust company has power to: Receive trust funds for investment for specific purposes as agreed; execute such trusts as may be committed to it; take, accept and hold by order of any court or by gift any real or personal property, care for or manage same and execute and perform any such trust; act as agent or attorney in fact; act either by itself or jointly with any natural person or persons as executor, administrator, guardian, conservator or trustee; loan money upon real estate and upon collateral security when collateral would be legal investment for said corporation; borrow money; execute and issue its notes payable at future date and to pledge its real estate, mortgages or other securities therefor (no loan may be made to any officer or director of corporation); issue and sell capital notes or debentures, with approval; buy, hold, own and sell securities issued or guaranteed by U.S. government or any agency or wholly owned corporation thereof, or with authority to borrow directly from U.S. Treasury, or any security secured by obligations of any state or political subdivision thereof which possesses general powers of taxation, stocks, warrants, bills of exchange, notes, mortgages, banker's acceptances, certificates of deposit in institutions insured by FDIC, and other investment securities, except stock or other securities of any corporation organized under article relating to trust companies; purchase, own and improve such real estate as it may be required to bid in under foreclosure or in payment of other debts; perform all acts and exercise all powers incident to or necessary for full exercise of rights granted. Trust company may not conduct banking business. (8-206). Commercial banks may be authorized to conduct trust business. (8-160). All trust business may be transferred from affiliated bank to trust company pursuant to order of County Court. (8-231). State trust company, with approval of two-thirds of its capital stock, may merge with state bank. (8-229). Each trust fund doing business under §§8-201 to 8-226 must obtain fidelity bond naming trust company as obligee. (8-205.01).

Interstate Trust Company Office Act adopted. (L.B. 1321). Nebraska state-chartered trust companies may maintain out-of-state branches with prior approval of Director of Banking and Finance. Provides requirements for establishment of Nebraska branch of out-of-state trust company. (L.B. 1321).

Private banking is prohibited. (8-114; 182 Neb. 164, 153 N.W.2d 743).

Joint Deposits.—Deposits in the name of two or more persons, payable to either or their survivor(s), may be paid to any such persons or their survivor(s) in due course of business. (30-2708 and -2709).

See also topic Commercial Code.

Multibank holding companies authorized in Nebraska in certain circumstances. (8-910). Auxiliary offices, automatic teller machines and point-of-sale terminals are also authorized. (8-157). See also Interstate Branching by Merger Act of 1997. (8-2101 to -2108).

Savings Associations.—Bank may acquire eligible savings association and convert it into auxiliary office of bank. (8-157; 8-1516). Savings and loan associations incorporated under laws of Nebraska have all rights, benefits, powers, and privileges as do federal savings and loan associations doing business in Nebraska. (8-355). Any state or federal savings association may apply for conversion to state bank. (L.B. 1321).

Nebraska Bank Holding Company Act of 1995 adopted. (8-908 et seq.). Out-of-state bank holding companies may not form or establish banks in Nebraska unless bank is formed to acquire all or most assets of bank chartered for five years. (8-911[2]). Out-of-state banks may not acquire state banks chartered for less than five years. (8-911[1]).

BILLS AND NOTES:

Uniform Commercial Code in effect. See topic Commercial Code.

Days of Grace.—Abolished. Neb. UCC no provision.

Patent Rights.—Negotiable instruments, consideration for which in whole or in part is right to make, use or vend a patented invention or one claimed to be patented, must have written or printed prominently and legibly across face thereof and above signature the words "Given for a patent right." Such instrument in hands of any purchaser or holder is subject to same defenses as in hands of original owner or holder, and any person who purchases or becomes holder of negotiable instrument, knowing it to have been given for such consideration holds it subject to such defenses although the required words are not on its face. (62-302; 84 Neb. 808, 122 N.W. 61).

Business College Notes.—Business college may not contract for or receive for tuition or scholarship negotiable note or negotiable contract, except it have printed in red ink prominently and legibly and in 24 point bold type diagonally across its face and above the signatures, "Negotiable note given for tuition," if note, or words, "Negotiable contract note given for tuition and scholarship," if contract, and unless copy of instrument is delivered to makers thereof at time of signing same. Business college shall not sell or dispose of such instrument prior to three days from entrance and personal registration of student. (62-303). Note or contract taken in violation of this foregoing provision is void. (62-305).

Judgment Notes.—No confession of judgment, power to confess judgment or to appear for maker may be given in note to industrial loan companies (8-447) or to bank on personal installment loan (8-823), nor power of any kind to installment loan licensee (45-143).

Attorney fee clauses are not enforceable. (90 Neb. 223, 133 N.W. 199).

BROKERS:

Uniform Commercial Code in effect. See topic Commercial Code.

Real estate brokers and salespersons must obtain licenses from State Real Estate Commission. (81–885.07). Fee payable by broker is set by Commission, but maximum fee is $300 for examination and application, $150 for license, $300 for nonresidents. Fee payable by salesperson is set by Commission: maximum fee is $300 for examination and application, $100 for license ($200 for nonresidents). (81–885.14). Reexamination fees are set by Commission, with maximum fee of $150. Each applicant for sales license must complete two courses in real estate subjects, approved by Commission, composed of not less than 60 class hours of study, or correspondence courses approved by Commission. Each two year period, every licensee shall complete 12 hours of continuing education. Broker or salesman must be 19 years old and must either be high school graduate or holder of certificate of equivalency. Special requirements have been established for nonresident brokers and salespersons. Obtaining nonresident broker's license shall constitute sufficient contact with this state for exercise of personal jurisdiction over licensee in any action arising out of licensee's activity in this state. (81-885.01 to -885.48).

Contract for broker's compensation for sale of real estate must be in writing, subscribed by owner, and must describe land and broker's compensation. (36-107). Promissory note made by vendor to real estate broker and accepted by broker in payment for commission is enforceable even if no written sales contract. (206 Neb. 753, 295 N.W.2d 106).

Insurance Brokers.—See category Insurance, topic Insurance Companies.

Loan Brokers.—Regulated by Department of Banking and Finance. (45-189 et seq.).

Security Brokers.—See topic Securities.

See also topic Commercial Code.

BULK SALES:

Bulk sales portion of Uniform Commercial Code has been repealed. See topic Commercial Code.

See also category Debtor and Creditor, topic Fraudulent Sales and Conveyances.

CARRIERS:

Uniform Commercial Code in effect. See topic Commercial Code.

Supervision of common carriers is lodged with Public Service Commission, which has power to regulate rates and services and exercise general control. (75-109).

Rates.—Legislature can fix maximum rates. (Const. Art. X, §4). Public Service Commission fixes both passenger and freight rates. (75-118). Printed schedule showing all rates must be kept by carrier for public inspection. (75-124).

Discrimination.—Prohibited. (75-126).

Bill of Lading.—Penalty for issuing false bill of lading with intention to defraud is fine or imprisonment up to 20 years. (28-603).

Limitation of liability by railroads is forbidden (Const., art. X, §4), but liability on interstate shipment may be limited to an agreed value on which rate is adjusted (226 U. S. 513).

Motor Vehicle Carriers.—See category Transportation, topic Motor Vehicles.

COMMERCIAL CODE:

Uniform Commercial Code (1962 text) has been adopted. Rights previously created are not affected. 1972 and 1977 Official Amendments adopted, with variations discussed below. 1986 Official Amendments not adopted. 1990 Revisions adopted. Code appears in a separate volume of the official statutes and is cited herein as Neb. UCC, sections numbered substantially same as U.C.C. Nebraska annotated act reissued in 1980.

Material Variations From 1962 Text and 1972 and 1977 Official Amendments.—

The following sections of the U.C.C. are omitted:
§3-122
§§6-101 to 6-111
§9-111.

Following sections of U.C.C. are modified as indicated:

§1-110 U.C.C. (Neb. U.C.C. 1-110)—provides that repeal of bulk sales provisions will not affect obligations arising thereunder prior to repeal.

§1-201 U.C.C. (Neb. UCC 1-201)—subsections (26)(a) and (b) enacted as subsections (26)(c) and (a), respectively; subsection (26)(b) relating to notice by publication added; subsection (37) redefines term "security interest;" including provision that security interest does not include consumer national purchase agreement.

§2-201 U.C.C. (Neb. UCC 2-201)—subsection (2)(b) provides that contracts between merchant, and buyer or seller of grain not merchant, are enforceable unless written notice of objection is given within ten days and all other requirements of section are met.

§3-113 U.C.C. (Neb. UCC 3-113)—subsection (9) now subject to exception as provided in §4-401(c).

§3-410 U.C.C. (Neb. UCC 3-410)—"continental" added before words "United States" in subsection (b).

See note at head of Digest as to 1998 legislation covered.

See Topical Index in front part of this volume.

COMMERCIAL CODE . . . *continued*

§3-504 U.C.C. (Neb. UCC 3-504)—"continental" added before words "United States" in subsection (4).

§4-106 U.C.C. (Neb. UCC 4-106)—bracketed language enacted; reference to Art. 3 omitted.

§4-202 U.C.C. (Neb. UCC 4-202)—bracketed language in subsection (1)(b) enacted.

§4-212 U.C.C. (Neb. UCC 4-212)—bracketed subsection (2) enacted.

§7-204 U.C.C. (Neb. UCC 7-204)—subsection (4) not enacted.

§7-210 U.C.C. (Neb. UCC 7-210)—subsection (2)(b) provides for personal or "registered" mail delivery of notice.

§7-403 U.C.C. (Neb. UCC 7-403)—bracketed language in subsection (1)(b) not enacted.

§8-102 U.C.C. (Neb. UCC 8-102)—subsection (2) provides " 'Proper Form' means regular on its face with regard to all formal matters." Subsections (2), (3), (4), (5), and (6) changed to (3), (4), (5), (6), and (7), respectively.

§8-208 U.C.C. (Neb. UCC 8-208)—subsection (1)(a) provides ". . . . . the certificated security or initial transaction statement is genuine and in proper form. . . . . ." Subsection (1)(c) omits the words ". . . . . in the form and . . . . ."

§8-306 U.C.C. (Neb. UCC 8-306)—subsection (3) includes a second sentence that a broker is not an intermediary within meaning of this subsection.

§8-308 U.C.C. (Neb. UCC 8-308)—subsection (8)(a) includes only a "successor" fiduciary.

§8-320 (Neb. U.C.C. 8-320)—subsection 6 requires clearing corporation to furnish to any issuer list disclosing names of persons who have securities of issuer.

§9-203 U.C.C. (Neb. UCC 9-203)—subsection (4) provides that transaction subject to Art. 9 is also subject to "the Credit Union Act, the Neb. Installment Sales Act and sections 8-401 to 8-417.01, 8-815 to 8-829, and 45-114 to -158, Reissue Revised Statutes of Nebraska, 1943, and amendments thereto." Subsection (5) states time when debtor has rights in certain collateral.

§9-206 U.C.C. (Neb. UCC 9-206)—references to "lessee" and "lessor" in subsection (1) not enacted.

§9-301 U.C.C. (Neb. UCC 9-301)—subsection (2) allows 20 (instead of ten) days after possession for filing purchase money security interest.

§9-303 U.C.C. (Neb. UCC 9-303)—subsection (1) provides that steps required for perfection are specified "in sections 9-115, 9-302, 9-304, 9-305 and 9-306." Subsection (7) provides that if future advances are made while a perfected security interest exists, the security interest will have the same priority for purposes of §9-303(5) and §9-115 with respect to the future advances as it does with respect to the first advance. (L.B. 1321).

§9-307 U.C.C. (Neb. UCC 9-307)—subsection (1) provides "a buyer of farm products may be subject to a security interest under sections 52-1301 to 52-1321." Subsection (3) provides that buyer ". . . takes free of a security interest to the extent that it secures future advances made after the secured party acquires knowledge of the purchase." Subsection (4) adds that no buyer may use offset ". . . to defeat a priority established by any lien or security interest."

§9-312 U.C.C. (Neb. UCC 9-312)—Subsection 4 mirrors 9-301(2) change to 20 days.

§9-401 U.C.C. (Neb. UCC 9-401)—Section title adds "change of residence or place of business"; removal of collateral. Generally adopts, with some variation, 1972 Amendments:

"(1) The proper place to file in order to perfect a security interest is as follows:

(a) When the collateral is timber to be cut or is minerals or the like (including oil and gas) or accounts subject to subsection (5) of section 9-103, or when the financing statement is filed as a fixture filing (section 9-313) and the collateral is goods which are or are to become fixtures, then in the office where a mortgage on the real estate would be filed or recorded.

(b) In all other cases, in the office of the Secretary of State.

(2) A filing which is made in good faith in the improper place or not in all of the places required by this section is nevertheless effective with regard to any collateral as to which the filing complied with the requirements of this article and is also effective with regard to collateral covered by the financing statement against any person who has knowledge of the contents of such financing statement.

(3) A filing which is made in the proper place in this state continues effective even though the debtor's residence or place of business or the location of the collateral or its use, whichever controlled the original filing, is thereafter changed. A debtor's residence is presumed to be the residence shown on the filing. The showing of an improper residence shall not affect the validity of the filing or the perfection of such filing.

(4) The rules stated in section 9-103 determine whether filing is necessary in this state.

(5) Notwithstanding the preceding subsections, and subject to subsection (3) of section 9-302, the proper place to file in order to perfect a security interest in collateral, including fixtures, of a transmitting utility is the office of the Secretary of State. This filing constitutes the fixture filing (section 9-313) as to the collateral described therein which is or is to become fixtures."

§9-402 U.C.C. (Neb. UCC 9-402)—substantially adopts 1972 Amendment with addition of subsection (1) reference to form prescribed by Secretary of State; subsection (1) provides that secured party can include social security number or federal tax identification number of secured party and debtor if such information is available. (L.B. 1321).

Carbon, photographic or electronic copy of security agreement or financing statement is sufficient if permitted by security agreement or if original (including electronic original) is filed in this state. (L.B. 1321).

§9-403 U.C.C. (Neb. UCC 9-403)—section title adds "uniform fees; fee distribution." Subsection (3) last two sentences not enacted; subsection (5)(a) provides uniform fee for ". . . an original filing statement, an amendment, a separate statement of assignment, a continuation statement, a partial release, or a full release . . ." is $6; there is no filing fee for termination statement, and uniform fee for each name more than one required to be indexed (includes tradenames) shall be $4. Subsection (5)(b) provides fee for filing "lien notification statement" shall be $6; uniform fee for each name more than one required to be indexed is $4; subsection (8) added, relating to nonapplicability of Neb. UCC 9-403(2) and (3) to mortgages or deeds of trust and/or supplements or amendments thereto covering real estate as well as personal property where such property constitutes portion of property used in carrying on business of public utility or gas or oil pipeline system. Subsections (9) and (10) added regarding distribution of filing fees collected.

§9-404 U.C.C. (Neb. UCC 9-404)—1972 Amendment not adopted: Subsection 1 requires separate signed statement of assignment to accompany termination statement, and complying with 9-405(2), with failure resulting in liability to debtor for loss and attorney's fees. Subsection 2 requires filing offices to make notation in index and to return stamped copy of any duplicate to secured party. Subsection (3) refers to 9-403(5) for fee.

§9-405 U.C.C. (Neb. UCC 9-405)—subsections (1) and (2) delete references to fees. Subsection (1) refers to 9-403(4) regarding filing officer's actions when assignment is noted on financing statement. Subsection (2) refers to 9-403(4) regarding filing officer's treatment of assignment by separate written statement. Subsection (3) provides that successor in interest of party of record is recognized as secured party of record without filing of assignment under this section. (L.B. 1321). Subsection (4) refers to 9-403(5) for fees.

§9-406 U.C.C. (Neb. U.C.C. 9-406)—written assignment must comply with 9-405(2) and (3) fees provided in 9-403(5), or reflect that person signing statement of release is successor of secured party of record. (L.B. 1321).

§9-407 U.C.C. (Neb. UCC 9-407) bracketed subsection (1) adopted.

Neb. UCC 9-408—provides that all instruments must be filed on paper no smaller than 8x5 inches and no larger than 8½x11 inches in size. $3 additional fee for off-size instruments. Attachments 50¢ per page for first five attachments.

§9-408 U.C.C. (Neb. UCC 9-409)—provides for 50¢ per page fee for filing of attachments to instruments. (L.B. 1321). Adopts §9-408 of 1972 official text as Neb. §9-409.

§9-410 U.C.C. (Neb. U.C.C. 9-410)—allows public access to filing information on computer.

§9-411 U.C.C. (Neb. U.C.C. 9-411)—provides mechanism for written and telephone inquiries regarding filings. No fee for personal inspection up to ten names a day; $1 per each additional name.

§9-412 U.C.C. (Neb. U.C.C. 9-412)—provides that financing statement or continuation statement filed before amendment will lose its priority if not filed with Secretary of State before Dec. 31, 1999. (L.B. 1321).

§9-413 to -415 U.C.C. (Neb. UCC 9-413 to -415)—express Legislative intent, transmittal of filing information to Secretary of State and development of centralized computer system.

§9-414 U.C.C. (Neb. UCC 9-414)—recording and indexing by Secretary of State of financing statements, assignments, continuation and termination statements, releases of collateral and liens. (L.B. 1321).

§9-420 U.C.C. (Neb. UCC 9-420)—provides for establishment of cash fund to be used for computer printers. Provides for furnishing of county clerks with computer hardware compatible with centralized computer system and fees for computerized information. (L.B. 1321).

§9-504 U.C.C. (Neb. UCC 9-504)—provides notice requirements for disposal of collateral; subsection (8) specifies that guarantors are entitled to notice.

(52-1601 to -1605)—provides for compilation of master lien list of non-U.C.C. liens to be distributed on quarterly basis with annual registration fee of $30. Fee is $200, $25 for microfiche. Buyer of farm products who is registered to receive list shall take free of any liens created under c. 52, arts. 2, 5, 9, 11, 12 or 14, if lien not on latest quarterly list or if buyer has not received written notices of lien.

§10-104 U.C.C. (Neb. UCC 10-104)—subsection (2) provides "This act does not repeal the Uniform Act for Simplification of Fiduciary Security Transfers (Sections 24-621 to 24-631) and transfers made under either act shall be valid and given the effect accorded under the act followed."

Permanent Editorial Board's Recommendations for Amendments.—

§2-702—1966 Official Amendment not enacted.

§3-501—1966 Official Amendment not enacted.

§7-209—1966 Official Amendment not enacted.

Optional Provisions.—

§1-209—1966 Official Optional Amendment not enacted.

§2-318—1966 Official Optional Amendment Alternative A enacted.

§3-121 U.C.C. (Neb. UCC 3-121)—Alternative B enacted.

§9-105—1966 Official Optional Amendment not enacted.

§9-106—1966 Official Optional Amendment not enacted.

1972 Official Amendments.—

§§1-105, 1-201, 2-107, 5-116, 9-102 to -106, 9-114, 9-203 to -205, 9-301 to -302, 9-304 to -308, 9-312 to -313, 9-318, 9-401 to -403, 9-405 to -408, 9-501 to -502, 9-504 to -505—Adopted.

Filing Fees.—$6 per debtor's name, $4 per each additional name, extra charge of $3 for items smaller than 5x8, or larger than 8½x11. Attachments 50¢ per page for first five pages of attachment. Filing made in Secretary of State's office, Lincoln, Neb., U.C.C. Division, after 1981, for previous filings check with clerk of county where property located. Assignments, $4 per assignee; releases, $6 per name; each additional name, $4. No fee for filing termination statements. Written information requests: $3 per debtor or trade name searched, additional $4 for certificate. Phone inquiries: $1 per debtor's name. Personal inspection: no charge for up to ten names per day; $1 per each additional name.

Forms.—See end of this Digest.

See also topics: Banks and Banking, Bills and Notes, Brokers, Carriers, Contracts, Factors, Frauds, Statute of, Sales, Securities, Warehousemen; categories Business Organizations, topic Corporations; Civil Actions and Procedure, topic Limitation of Actions; Debtor and Creditor, topics Assignments, Fraudulent Sales and Conveyances,

See note at head of Digest as to 1998 legislation covered.

See Topical Index in front part of this volume.

NE – 5

COMMERCIAL CODE... *continued*

Liens, Pledges; Documents and Records, topics Records, Seals; Mortgages, topic Chattel Mortgages; Transportation, topic Motor Vehicles.

CONSUMER PROTECTION:

Uniform Deceptive Trade Practices Act adopted with modifications, §§2(a)(12) and 7 not adopted. (87-301 to -306). Criminal penalties added for violation of Act. (87-303.08 to -303.09). Use of dialing announcing device for advertising purposes prohibited unless Public Service Commission permit obtained. (87-308). Unsolicited fax transmissions for advertising purposes prohibited. (87-302 and -307). Certain chains and pyramid sales are unlawful. (87-301 to -302). Loan broker activities regulated; advance fees prohibited. (45-189 to 193).

Consumer Rental Purchase Agreement Act adopted regulating terms of agreements. (69-2101 to -2119). Membership Campground Act adopted, prohibiting deceptive practices, requiring disclosure statements and registration of membership contracts. (76-2101 to -2121).

Home solicitation sales regulated. (69-1601 to -1607). Buyer's right of cancellation provided. (69-1603).

Unconscionable act by supplier in consumer transaction is unlawful. (87-303.01).

Consumer Default Procedures.—Creditor required to give ten days notice of default and debtor is given 20 days to cure. (45-1,106 to -1,107).

Unsolicited goods statute adopted. (69-2201).

Nebraska Drug Product Selection Act providing for sale of drugs by generic name. (71-5401 to -5408).

Motor Vehicle Service Contract Reimbursement Insurance Act.—See category Insurance, topic Insurance Companies.

Plain Language.—See category Insurance, topic Insurance Companies.
See also category Debtor and Creditor, topic Creditors' Suits.

Hospitals.—Medicaid residents: Require long-term care hospitals to meet conditions relating to retention of residents. (76-6023.01).

CONTRACTS:

Common law rules followed.

Uniform Commercial Code in effect. See topic Commercial Code. See also topic Consumer Protection; categories Dispute Resolution, topic Arbitration and Award; Documents and Records, topic Seals; Family, topic Infants.

FACTORS:

License Requirements.—None.

Liens.—See topic Commercial Code.

Consignment Agreements.—See topic Commercial Code.

FRANCHISES:

Uniform Franchise and Business Opportunities Act (1987) not adopted.

Franchise Practices Act adopted to define relationships and responsibilities of franchisors and franchisees in connection with franchise agreements. (87-401 to 87-410). Separate statutes control fuel franchises. (87-411 to 87-414).

Beer Distribution.—Distribution agreements between beer suppliers and beer wholesalers defined and regulated. (53-201 to 53-223).

FRAUDS, STATUTE OF:

See Neb. UCC 2-201, 1-206, 3-416, 8-319, 9-203. See topic Commercial Code.

Real Property.—No estate or interest in land other than lease for one year or less may be created, granted, assigned, surrendered or declared unless by operation of law or by deed of conveyance subscribed by parties creating same. (36-103). Contract for leasing for longer than one year, or for sale of land, is void unless contract or some note or memorandum thereof be in writing, signed by party by whom lease or sale to be made. (36-105). Auction of real estate without reserve is within statute. (208 Neb. 330, 303 N.W.2d 496).

Personal Property.—See topic Sales; category Mortgages, topic Chattel Mortgages. See Neb. UCC as above.

Contracts.—Following agreements are void unless some note or memorandum thereof in writing be subscribed by party to be charged: Agreement by its terms not to be performed within one year; special promise to answer for debt, default or misdoings of another person; agreement in consideration of marriage, except mutual promises to marry; special promise of executor or administrator to answer damages out of his own estate; agreement for repurchase of corporate stocks, bonds or other securities. (36-202).

Part Performance.—Common law applies.

INTEREST:

Maximum rate of 16% is valid on any loan or forbearance, if expressly agreed. (45-101.03). This limit does not apply to loans made by Department of Banking licensees or permittees; loans made to any corporation, partnership or trust, or to guarantor or surety thereof; when principal amount is $25,000 or more; loans guaranteed, sponsored, etc. by federal or state government; loans on securities as defined in 8-1101(13); interest charges made on open credit accounts; minimum charge of $10 per loan; loans made by state or federal savings and loan defined in 8-319(4); certain loans made primarily for business or agricultural purposes; loans under installment contracts for goods and services. (45-101.04). Variable rate loans permitted, on consumer goods loan ten days notice before increase required. (45-101.03). Amounts charged for actual filing and recording fees, or for premiums on credit life, sickness and accident insuring policies in regard to loan transactions, and fees agreed to by parties for loan service costs for exceeding authorized limits are not considered as interest. (8-821).

Legal rate is 12% through Aug. 31, 1983, then 6% commencing on Sept. 1, 1983, unless greater rate, not exceeding 16%, is contracted for. (45-102).

Judgments bear interest at 1% above bond equivalent yield, as published by U.S. Secretary of the Treasury of average accepted auction price for last auction of Treasury bills in effect on date of judgment, provided judgment interest rate is not provided by law or judgment interest rate agreed by contract. (45-103). Prejudgment interest allowed only in limited circumstances. (45-103.02).

Accounts that are unsettled bear 12% interest from date of billing unless paid within 30 days from date of billing. Settled accounts bear same rate but from day balance is agreed upon. (45-104).

Usury.—Contract for more than 16% is not void because of usury; however in any action principal, only, is recoverable. (45-105). Contract for payment of money in satisfaction of debt which prevents full discharge by paying same number of dollars in lawful money of U.S. as debtor originally contracted to pay, plus interest not in excess of maximum legal rate, is usurious. (45-109). In any action on such contract plaintiff's recovery is limited to same number of dollars contracted for at time original contract was made, plus interest not exceeding maximum legal rate and costs. (45-110).

Delinquent taxes draw interest at 14% from date due. (77-207).

Installment Loan Act inhibitory provisions apply to both licensed and nonlicensed lenders. (162 Neb. 11, 75 N.W.2d 122). Loan limit rates: Unpaid balance charges not to exceed 24% on unpaid principal on first $1,000 and 21% of remainder. (45-137).

Installment Sales Act of 1965; except for certain vehicles, fixed or variable annual percentage rate that is agreed to by parties, not to exceed 18%, except that minimum time-price differential of $10 may be charged on installment contract and $10 origination fee. (45-338). Installment sale defined. (45-335).

Consumer Rental Purchase Agreement Act adopted. (69-2101 to -2115).

Industrial loan and investment companies may receive on any loan charges not exceeding 19%; minimum charge of $10 approved. (8-435).

Registered banks and trust companies may, on loans initiated by credit cards contract for any amount agreed upon by parties. (8-820). On all other personal loans 19%. (8-820). Permitted to charge commercially reasonable fees for credit cards. (8-820).

Credit unions may lend at rates of interest not exceeding 18% on unpaid balance. (21-1773).

Building and loan associations may, on property improvement loans made under Title I of National Housing Act, as am'd, and unsecured loans authorized in §5C of Home Owners Act, as am'd, charge interest not exceeding lawful rate. (8-330).

Revolving Charge Accounts.—$1^3/_4$% per month on amounts less than $500; $1^1/_2$% per month on $500 or more. (45-207). No time price differential shall be assessed on account if payment of outstanding balance is received prior to beginning of next billing cycle under agreement.

LICENSES, BUSINESS AND PROFESSIONAL:

Statutes require licenses for numerous occupations.

Cities, towns and villages generally provide by ordinance for license fees by transients engaged in business within corporate limits and by permanent residents pursuing occupations regarded as affected with public interest.

Commercial Travelers.—No statute, but license required in some cities under city ordinance.

Installment Paper Purchasers.—It is unlawful, with certain exceptions, to engage in business of purchasing installment paper without having first obtained license from Department of Banking. (45-345). Such license may be renewed on or before Oct. 1 annually upon payment of fee of $150. (45-348). Licenses may be revoked by Department of Banking for enumerated grounds. (45-346). See topic Interest.

Private Correspondence School.—Permitted.

Collection Agencies.—Collection Agency Act adopted. (45-601 to -622). Collection agency required to secure license from Collection Agency Licensing Board. (45-601). May be retained by state agency, county, city or other political subdivision for debt collection. (45-623).

LIQUOR:

Legal drinking age, see category Family, topic Infants.

MONOPOLIES, RESTRAINT OF TRADE AND COMPETITION:

Every contract or combination in form of trust or conspiracy in restraint of trade or commerce is illegal. Violation is class IV felony. (59-801). Following are specifically prohibited: Discrimination in rates between different sections for purpose of destroying business of competitor (59-501); attempt to monopolize any part of trade or commerce in state (59-802); combinations to drive other persons out of business (59-805).

Violations of foregoing requirements generally subject offenders to fine or imprisonment or both (59-505, -802, -805, and -830) and liability to party injured for damages with attorney's fee (59-821). Corporate violator also forfeits right to do business. (59-508).

Musical Compositions.—Price charged different licensees must not be discriminatory. (59-1405).

School Books.—Contract with publisher who becomes party to combination in restraint of trade for purpose of raising price of school books becomes null and void at option of school board. (79-4,120).

MONOPOLIES, RESTRAINT OF TRADE AND COMPETITION . . . *continued*

Fair Trade Act.—Unconstitutional. (159 Neb. 703, 68 N.W.2d 608; modified, 160 Neb. 319, 68 N.W.2d 608; 202 Neb. 524, 276 N.W.2d 191).

SALES:

Uniform Commercial Code in effect. See topic Commercial Code.

Recording of bill of sale is not required by statute, but it may be recorded in office of county clerk; fee, $5 per page. (33-109).

Contracts of Sale.—No statutory limitation as to type size in printed contracts.

Consumer Protection.—See topic Consumer Protection. Uniform Deceptive Trade Practices Act adopted. (87-301-306).

Product Liability and Retail Credit Sales.—Manufacturer strictly liable in tort when it knowingly markets article without inspection and defect injures rightful user. (187 Neb. 428, 191 N.W.2d 601 [1971]). Strict liability in tort applicable to physical harm to property alone, without physical injury. (213 Neb. 782, 332 N.W.2d 39 [1983]).

Bulk Sales.—See topic Commercial Code; category Debtor and Creditor, topic Fraudulent Sales and Conveyances.

Sales of Motor Vehicles.—See category Transportation, topic Motor Vehicles.

SECURITIES:

Uniform Securities Act adopted. (8-1101 to 1123).
Uniform Commercial Code in effect. See topic Commercial Code.

Supervision.—Sales of Securities are regulated by Securities Act of Nebraska (8-1101 to -1123), enforcement of which is by Director of Banking and Finance, except regulations of securities issued by or representing interest of insurance companies enforced by Director of Insurance (8-1120).

Prerequisites to Sales or Offerings.—Unless securities are exempt (under 8-1110) or sold in exempt transactions (under 8-1111), sale of any security is unlawful unless registered by (a) Notification (under 8-1105), (b) coordination (under 8-1106) or (c) qualification (under 8-1107). (8-1104). (See subhead Registration of Securities, infra.)

Securities to Which Act Applicable.—Security is defined as any note, stock, treasury stock, bond, debenture, units of beneficial interest in real estate trust, evidence of indebtedness, certificate of interest or participation in any profit sharing agreement, collateral-trust certificate, preorganization certificate or subscription, transferable share, investment contract, voting trust certificate, certificate of deposit for security, certificate of interest or participation in oil, gas or mining title or lease or in payments out of production under such title or lease, or in general, any interest or instrument commonly known as security, or any certificate of interest or participation in, temporary or interim certificate for, guarantee of, or warrant or right to subscribe to or purchase, any of foregoing. (8-1101[13]).

Security does not include endowment or annuity contract of insurance company. (8-1101[13]).

Exempt Securities and Transactions.—Following securities are exempt from operation of Securities Act (8-1110): (1) Security, including revenue obligation issued or guaranteed by State of Nebraska, any political subdivision, or any agency or corporate or other instrumentality thereof or any certificate of deposit for any of foregoing; (2) security issued or guaranteed by government with which U.S. maintains diplomatic relations; (3) any security issued or guaranteed by any federal credit union, or any credit union, industrial loan, and investment company or similar association organized under Nebraska law; (4) any security issued or guaranteed by any railroad, other common carrier, public utility, or holding company which is: (a) Subject to jurisdiction of I.C.C., (b) registered holding company under Public Utility Holding Company Act of 1935 or subsidiary of such company within meaning of that act, (c) regulated by U.S., state, or municipal authority with regards to its rates and charges, or (d) regulated in respect of issuance or guarantee of security by governmental authority of U.S., any state, Canada, or any Canadian province; (5)(a) any security listed on Chicago Stock Exchange, Chicago Board Options Exchange, Tier I of the Pacific Stock Exchange, Tier I of the Philadelphia Stock Exchange, or any other stock exchange or market system approved by director, if, in each case, quotations have been available and public trading has taken place for such class of security prior to offer or sale of that security in reliance on exemption, (5)(b) issuer of any security which has been approved for listing or designation on notice of issuance on such exchanges or market systems, and for which no quotations have been available and no public trading has taken place for any of such issuer's securities, may rely upon exemption stated in subdivision (5)(a) of this section, if notice is filed with director, together with filing fee of $200, prior to first use of disclosure document covering such securities in this state; failure to file such notice in timely manner may be cured by director in his or her discretion, (5)(c) director may adopt rules and regulations which, after notice to such exchange or market system and opportunity to be heard, remove any such exchange or market system and opportunity to be heard, remove any such exchange or market system from exemption stated in subdivision (5)(a) of this section if director finds that listing requirements or market surveillance of such exchange or market system is such that continued availability of such exemption for such exchange or market system is not in public interest and that removal is necessary for protection of investors (8-1110); (6) any security meeting all of following conditions: (a) if issuer is not organized under laws of U.S. or state, it has authorized agent in U.S. for service, (b) class of issuer's securities if required to be and is registered under §12 of S.E.C. Act of 1934, and was registered for three years preceding offering date, (c) neither issuer or significant subsidiary has had material default during last seven years, or during issuer's existence if in existence less than seven years, in payment of principal, interest, dividends, or sinking fund installments on preferred stock or indebtedness for borrowed money or rentals under leases with terms of three or more years, (d) issuer has had consolidated net income, not taking into account extraordinary items and cumulative effect of accounting changes of at least $1,000,000 in four of its last five fiscal years, and if its offering is of interest-bearing securities issuer has had for its last fiscal year net income before taxes and depreciation, of at least one and one half times issuer's annual interest expense, (e) if offering is of other than preferred stock or shares, such securities have voting rights (at least as many votes as shares, and right to vote on as many general corporate decisions as holders of issuer's other outstanding stock or shares) except as otherwise required by law, (f) if offering is of stock or shares other than preferred stock or shares, such securities are owned beneficially or of record, on any date within six months prior to commencement of offering, by at least 1,200 persons, and on such date there are at least 750,000 such shares outstanding with aggregate market value of $3,750,000, based on average bid price for that day, (g) except that, if issuer of securities is finance company which has liquid assets of at least 105% of its liabilities, other than deferred income taxes, deferred investment tax credit, capital stock, and surplus, at end of its last five fiscal years, net income requirement of subdivision (h) of this section, before deduction for interest expense, shall be one and one-fourth times its annual interest expense. As used in this subdivision, finance company shall mean company engaged primarily in business of wholesale, retail, installment, mortgage, commercial, industrial, or consumer financing, banking, or factoring and liquid assets shall mean cash receivables payable on demand or not more than 12 years following close of company's last fiscal year, less applicable reserves and unearned income, and shall also mean readily marketable securities less applicable reserves and unearned income, and (i) except that, if any security is issued or guaranteed as to both principal and interest by international bank of which U.S. is member, such security shall be exempt from registration under this section; (7) any security issued by any person organized and operated not for private profit but exclusively for religious, educational, benevolent, charitable, fraternal, social, athletic, or reformatory purposes, or as chamber of commerce or trade or professional association; (8) any commercial paper which arises out of current transaction or proceeds of which have been or are to be used for current transactions (nine months) (8-1110).

Certain transactions are exempted, most patterned after federal law with others peculiar to Nebraska. See 8-1111. Of interest is exemption of any transaction pursuant to sale to not more than 15 persons in this state during any period of 12 consecutive months, if: (a) Seller reasonably believes that all buyers are purchasing for investment, (b) no commission or other remuneration is paid or given directly or indirectly for soliciting any prospective buyer, except to broker-dealer registered under The Securities Act of Nebraska, (c) notice generally describing terms of transaction and containing representation that conditions of this exemption are met is filed by seller with director within 30 days after first sale for which exemption is claimed, and (d) no solicitations are made by newspaper, radio, or television. Also transactional exemption is provided for any offer or sale of preorganization certificate or subscription if: (a) No commission or other remuneration is made or given directly or indirectly for soliciting any prospective subscriber, (b) number of subscribers does not exceed ten, and (c) no payment is made by any subscriber. Issuance of any investment contract in connection with employees stock purchase, savings, pension, profit sharing, or similar benefit plan is exempt under certain conditions. (8-1111). Federal limits on securities registration provided in Philanthropy Protection Act of 1995 do not apply in Nebraska. Nebraska retains authority to require or not require federal registration under Securities Act of Nebraska, or to have such registration requirements apply in all administrative and judicial actions. (L.B. 1180).

In any proceeding under this Act, burden of proving an exemption is upon person claiming it. (8-1111).

Registration of Securities.—Securities may be registered by: (1) Notification if (a) issuer or predecessor has been in continuous operation for five years and there has been no default during preceding three years in payment of principal, interest or dividends on any security with fixed maturity, interest or dividend provision and issuer and predecessor during past three fiscal years have had average net earnings equal to at least 5% of amount of securities without fixed maturity, interest or dividend provision outstanding on date of registration; (b) any security other than interest in oil, gas or mining has been registered under this Act or a predecessor Act, or security was originally issued pursuant to an exemption under provisions of this Act or a predecessor Act. (8-1105[1]); (2) Any security for which a registration statement was filed under Federal Securities Act of 1933 may be registered by coordination. (8-1106[1]); (3) Any security may be registered by qualification. (8-1107[1]).

In each mode of registration issuer must file a statement with Director setting forth information required by same. (8-1105, -1106 and -1107). Filing fee equal to 1/10 of 1% of aggregate offering price of securities offered, minimum $100. (8-1108[3]). Registration effective for one year or until sooner revoked. (8-1008[4]).

Regulatory Powers of Supervising Authority.—Director may make full investigation of registrations, possible violations or to aid in enforcement at applicant's expense. Director may take testimony, subpoena witnesses, and issue subpoena duces tecum. (8-1115).

Registering as broker-dealer, issuer-dealer, or investment adviser, or directly or indirectly offering security constitutes sufficient contact with state for exercise of personal jurisdiction. (8-1112).

Misrepresentation.—False or misleading statements, omissions, misrepresentation to buyer make person who makes same and those who directly or indirectly control or are employed by said person liable for damages of buyer. Person so charged sustains burden of proof that he did not know, and exercising reasonable care could not know of existence of facts on which liability is based. (8-1118).

Criminal Liability.—Willful violation of any provision of this Act is a criminal offense punishable by fine not more than $10,000 or imprisonment of not more than five years, or both. Action must be brought within five years. (8-1117).

Whenever it appears to Director that a violation of Act has occurred or is about to, he may seek injunction of such acts in any court of competent jurisdiction. (8-1116).

Tender Offers.—See category Business Organizations, topic Corporations.

Subdivision Offerings.—Subdivision property is not considered security; however sale of such property may only be made by broker upon application to Real Estate Commission and approval of Attorney General. Application fee is $100 plus $25 for each 100 lots. (81-885.33 to -885.55).

See note at head of Digest as to 1998 legislation covered.

See Topical Index in front part of this volume.

NE – 7

SECURITIES . . . *continued*

Uniform Simplification of Fiduciary Security Transfers Act repealed. (30-3301). Fiduciary security transfers governed by §8 Uniform Commercial Code.

Uniform Securities Ownership by Minors Act not adopted.

Shareholders Protection Act adopted. (21-2431 to 21-2453). See category Business Organizations, topic Corporations.

WAREHOUSEMEN:

Public Service Commission has general supervision of public warehouses.

Uniform Commercial Code in effect. Vol. 6, Neb. Rev. Stats. See topic Commercial Code.

Lien.—Uniform Commercial Code in effect. See topic Commercial Code.

Public Grain Warehouses.—Any grain elevator, mill, grist mill, building, or receptacle in which grain is held in storage for more than ten consecutive days, except those licensed under U.S. Warehouse Act, shall be licensed and regulated by Public Service Commission. License required for person to operate warehouse or act as warehouseman. (88-527). Such warehouses shall be inspected by Commission at least once every nine months. (88-527). Each applicant for license and each warehouse licensee shall annually file application with Commission in form prescribed by Commission to do business under Grain Warehouse Act and shall include report of audit or review prepared in accordance with generally accepted accounting principles by person who holds permit granted by Nebraska State Board of Public Accountancy and shall set forth location of warehouse, relation to railroad trackage, capacity, general plan and equipment, and ownership. (88-528). Annual license fee shall be charged by Commission, except as provided in 88-531, based on warehouse capacity. (88-529). Each license applicant must show sufficient net worth or equity to conform with financial requirements promulgated by Commission and file with Commission bond, irrevocable letter of credit, or certificate of deposit for benefit of all persons storing grain in warehouse. Bond is conditioned upon warehouse's carrying of insurance, delivery of grain upon surrender of warehouse receipt, and faithful performance of applicable law. (88-530). License shall expire 12 calendar months after issuance, but may be kept in continuous force by filing application for renewal which Commission can approve prior to termination date. (88-532). Notice of security filed with Commission and all warehouse storage, receiving, and load-out fees shall be posted in conspicuous place. (88-532).

No warehouse licensee shall increase storage capacity without approval of Commission and applicable revision in security and fees. (88-533).

Warehouse licensee shall, at time of delivery to or shipment from warehouse, issue lawful scale ticket to owner of grain containing all information prescribed by Commission. Scale ticket issued by warehouse licensee is prima facie evidence of holder's claim of title to goods described thereon. (88-535).

Public Service Commission may prescribe forms of warehouse receipts and fix storage rates. (88-536, 541).

Property, books, records, accounts, papers, and proceedings of every warehouse shall be subject to inspection by Commission at all times during business hours. (88-542).

Penalty for issuing receipt when grain not actually received subjects person to fine of not more than $10,000 or imprisonment for not more than five years, or both. (88-543).

At election of warehouseman, storage contracts may be terminated on application to Commission and upon good cause shown according to rules and regulations of Commission. Owner may terminate contract at any time by payment or tender of all legal charges and surrender of warehouse receipt, together with demand for delivery of such grain or notice to sell same. (88-544).

Penalty for violation of Public Grain Warehouse Act subjects persons to fine of not more than $10,000, or imprisonment for not more than five years, or both, in addition to any damages arising from such violation. (88-545).

Each warehouseman, at least once each calendar year and not later than one year from date of receipt of previous written notice, shall send written notice to each person storing grain, specifying type and amount of grain in storage, location of grain being stored, and current rate of storage. Any violation of this section is punishable by fine of not more than $10,000 or imprisonment for not more than five years, or both. (88-549).

Farm Warehouses.—Provisions regulating farm warehouses repealed. (77-2318).

Bonded and Licensed Storage Areas.—Freeport statute repealed 1982.

CITIZENSHIP

ALIENS:

Real Estate.—May acquire property in any city or village or within three miles thereof. (76-414). In addition thereto may acquire and hold property anywhere in state necessary for construction and operation of railroads, public utilities and common carriers, manufacturing or industrial establishments and facilities incidental thereto or for filling or bulk stations for handling petroleum products. (76-412 and -413). Cannot acquire other property or leasehold interest therein for more than five years except in satisfaction of lien thereon. Property so acquired must be sold within ten years after title is obtained or it will escheat to state. (76-411). Resident alien may acquire title by devise or descent and hold for not more than five years (76-405), and widow or heirs of alien who acquired title before Mar. 16, 1889, may hold for ten years. (76-403). Before expiration of such periods land must be sold to bona fide purchaser or it escheats to state. (76-403 and -405).

Alien owning land on Mar. 16, 1889, may dispose of same during his life time. (76-410).

Corporation organized to hold or holding real estate (except real estate which aliens or foreign corporations may hold under sections 76-412 to -414 and oil leases and oil production facilities which foreign corporations may acquire under section 76-

404) may not elect aliens as directors or trustees in number sufficient to constitute majority of board or as executive officers or managers, or have majority of capital stock owned by aliens (76-406), under penalty of provisions applicable to alien persons. Domestic corporations violating this provision are held to be alien and shall forfeit charter and be dissolved and foreign corporations forfeit right to do business in state. (76-407). State alone may question title; corporation may pass good title though real estate might have been subject to escheat. (115 Neb. 33, 211 N.W. 210).

Rights to take property by devise or succession controlled by 4-107 and 76-402, et seq.

CIVIL ACTIONS AND PROCEDURE

ACCORD AND SATISFACTION:

Pleading.—Must be specifically pleaded and proved. (222 Neb. 69, 382 N.W.2d 313).

See category Business Regulation and Commerce, topic Commercial Code.

ACTIONS:

Distinction between actions at law and suits in equity and forms of such actions and suits abolished; only one form recognized; called civil action. (25-101). Feigned issues abolished. (25-103).

Conditions Precedent.—None except for special actions. Forcible entry and detainer, three days notice to quit (24-571), cancellation of oil or gas leases, 20 days demand that lease be discharged of record (57-209).

How Commenced.—See topic Process.

Parties.—Real party in interest must prosecute. (25-301; 203 Neb. 727, 280 N.W.2d 53). Executor, administrator, guardian, trustee of express trust, person with whom contract made for another's benefit or person authorized by statute, may bring action without joining beneficiary; officer may sue and be sued in name authorized by law and official bonds may be sued on same way; assignee of choses in action assigned for collection may sue on any claim assigned in writing. (25-304). Unincorporated associations which engage in business, hold property or represent employees in collective bargaining in this state may sue or be sued under their usual names. (25-313). In actions for recovery of real or personal property, any person having interest in property may be made party on application to court. (25-324). All persons may join in one action as plaintiffs if they assert any right to relief jointly, severally, or alternatively arising out of same transaction or occurrence, or series thereof and if common question of law or fact will arise in action. (25-311; L.B. 234). Unknown claimants to real estate may be designated as "all persons having or claiming any interest in" real estate accurately described, followed by words "real names unknown." (25-321).

Intervention.—Permitted by any person claiming an interest in the matter in litigation. (25-328).

Third Party Practice.—After commencement of action, defendant as third party plaintiff may bring in a person not a party to action who is or may be liable to him for all or part of plaintiff's claim against him. Third party plaintiff must obtain leave of court by motion upon notice to all parties prior to filing third party petition. Third party defendant shall have all rights of defendant and may assert against plaintiff any defenses which third party plaintiff has to plaintiff's claim. Third party defendant may assert any claim against third party plaintiff arising out of transaction or occurrence that is subject matter of plaintiff's claim against third party plaintiff. Plaintiff may assert any claim against third party defendant arising out of transaction or occurrence that is subject matter of plaintiff's claim against third party plaintiff. Third party defendant or subsequent defendants may proceed under this section. Court on its own motion or motion of any party may move to strike third party claim or for its severance or separate trial. (25-331).

Interpleader.—Permitted by order of court upon affidavit of defendant. (25-325, and -326).

Joinder.—Party asserting claim for relief as original claim, counterclaim, cross claim, or third party claim may join as many claims as party has against opposing party. (25-701; L.B. 234). Need not obtain judgment against uninsured motorist as condition precedent to bringing suit against uninsured motorist coverage carrier. (209 Neb. 396, 308 N.W.2d 503).

Class Actions.—Permitted (25-319); unless members of class would have inconsistent interests (195 Neb. 170, 237 N.W.2d 86).

Splitting Causes of Action.—Common law rule prevails.

Consolidation.—Where causes of action might have been joined, actions in same court may be consolidated on motion of defendant, by order of court or judge in vacation. (25-703, and -704). No requirement of joinder. (207 Neb. 24, 295 N.W.2d 302).

Small Claims.—See category Courts and Legislature, topic Courts.

Termination.—Action may be dismissed without prejudice to future action: By plaintiff before final submission without prejudice to future action by plaintiff; by court, if plaintiff fails to appear, or for want of necessary parties or on application of some defendants where there are others whom plaintiff fails to diligently prosecute or for plaintiff's disobedience of order concerning proceedings in action. (25-601). Order sustaining demurrer is not final adjudication, plaintiff may dismiss as matter of right upon motion. (207 Neb. 425, 299 N.W.2d 435). If no counterclaim or setoff has been filed by opposite party, plaintiff in vacation may dismiss without prejudice, upon payment of costs. (25-602). Despite plaintiff's dismissal or failure to appear, defendant may proceed to trial on his counterclaim or setoff. (25-603).

Abatement and Revival.—In addition to causes which survive at common law, causes of action for mesne profits, for injury to real or personal estate, or for deceit or fraud survive and action may be brought notwithstanding the death of person entitled or liable to same. (25-1401). No action pending in any court abates by death of either

ACTIONS . . . *continued*

or both parties thereto, except libel, slander, malicious prosecution, assault, assault and battery or nuisance, all of which abate by death of defendant. (25-1402).

After death of one of the parties, if right of action survives against remaining parties, action may proceed against surviving parties (25-1403) or may be revived in name of proper representative of deceased (25-1405).

Limitation of.—See topic Limitation of Actions.

APPEAL AND ERROR:

Writs of error abolished in civil cases. (25-1930). Judgments of district courts in civil cases now come to Court of Appeals and/or Supreme Court by appeal. (25-1911 et seq.).

Appeals Lie: To Court of Appeals and/or Supreme Court from district court (24-1105 and -1106); Worker's Compensation Court (48-185); Juvenile Court (43-2,126), and in all actions by or against state (24-331); to district court from county courts except in matters arising under Nebraska Probate Code or involving adoption, inheritance tax, or domestic relations (25-1901; 25-2807), small claims court (24-527), and other tribunals, boards and officers exercising judicial functions and inferior to district court in jurisdiction, other than Juvenile Court (25-1901; 25-2807). Order of remittitur entered by district court in law action is deemed final order for purposes of appeal to Court of Appeals. (25-1936).

Method and Time.—

To Court of Appeals.—By filing in office of clerk of district court in which judgment was rendered within 30 days from rendition of judgment or overruling of motion for new trial, notice of appeal signed by appellant and depositing with said clerk $50 docketing fee. (25-1912 and -1913, 33-103). Motion for new trial not necessary for consideration of trial errors but is necessary for review of damages asserted as excessive or inadequate. (25-1912.01). Appellant must designate each specific document to be included in transcript prepared by clerk of court. (Rules of Supreme Court, R.4.A). Certified transcript containing judgment must be filed with clerk of Supreme Court within 30 days from filing notice of appeal. (25-1912). Case will be heard by Court of Appeals, unless case involves life imprisonment, death penalty or constitutionality of statute. Supreme Court hears all cases involving constitutionality of statute and life imprisonment or death penalty cases. Juvenile court's final order or judgment may be appealed to Court of Appeals. (43-2,106.01).

To Supreme Court—From Court of Appeals.—Party may file petition with Supreme Court to bypass review by Court of Appeals immediately upon filing of appeal. Party aggrieved by Court of Appeals decision may petition Supreme Court for review within 30 days of issuance of decision. Supreme Court may, on its own motion, remove case from consideration of Court of Appeals for decision by Supreme Court. (24–1106 and -1107).

To District Court—From County Court; Small Claims Court.—By filing with clerk of lower court, within 30 days after rendition of judgment, or making of final order complained of, notice of appeal and $59 docketing fee. (24-541.02 and -527, 33-106). Notice of appeal must be served upon all parties who have appeared in action or upon their attorney of record and proof of service must be filed with notice of appeal. (24-541.02).

Proceedings to reverse, vacate or modify judgment or final order must be commenced within 30 days after rendition of judgment or making of order, except that infant, mentally incompetent or person imprisoned has one year, exclusive of time of disability, within which to commence proceedings. (25-1931).

Appeal Bond.—On appeal from district court, appellant must file cost bond for $75 or deposit $75 in cash with clerk of district court within 30 days from rendition of judgment or making of order or overruling of motion for new trial, unless supersedeas bond has been given. (25-1914). No appeal bond required from state or any officer litigating in official capacity. (24-334).

On appeal from small claims court to district court appellant must file cost bond or undertaking with at least one surety approved by court, in amount of $50.

See Uniform Probate Code adopted as Nebraska Probate Code for appeal bond provision in probate matters.

Stay of Proceedings.—Appeal to appellate court does not stay proceedings unless supersedeas bond is filed within 30 days after rendition of judgment or making of order or overruling motion for new trial (25-1916), except that if judgment is for conveyance or other instrument, appellant may execute same, deposit it with clerk of court which renders judgment and no bond is then necessary (25-1917).

Perfecting appeal from lower court to district court does not operate as supersedeas, unless appellant within 30 days after rendition of judgment deposits with clerk of lower court cash bond or undertaking with at least one surety approved by court. No bond required for appeals under Nebraska Probate Code, Uniform Residential Landlord and Tenant Act. (24-541.03).

Supersedeas Bond.—In appeals from district court on money judgment, bond is for amount of judgment plus estimated costs, estimated interest pending appeal as fixed by trial court, is conditioned on prosecution of appeal without delay and payment of final judgment and costs. (25-1916). Special requirements are imposed in particular cases. (25-1907, -1908, -1916 and -1918).

Bond and sureties must be approved by court in which judgment was rendered or clerk thereof. (25-1908 and -1918). Cash may be deposited in lieu of bond. (25-1916).

In appeals from lower courts to district court involving money judgment, bond is for amount of judgment, costs, and estimated interest pending appeal. In cases involving judgment for possession of specified personal property, bond is at least double amount of property. (24-541.03).

Extent of Review.—Appeals to appellate court are tried on record from lower court; only errors appearing in record are considered. On questions of law, appellate court obligated to reach independent conclusion from that of trial court. In law actions, standard of review is that district court judgment will not be set aside on appeal unless it is clearly wrong and not supported by evidence. In equity actions, case is tried de novo on record, errors in law and fact are considered. (25-1925).

Appeals to district court from county court are reviewed for error appearing on record. (24-541.06).

Appeals to district court from small claims court are tried de novo without jury. (24-541.07).

Judgment on Appeal.—If judgment or final order shall be reversed either in whole or in part, in Court of Appeals or Supreme Court, courts shall proceed to render such judgment as court below should have rendered or remand cause to court below for such judgment. (25-1926 and -1315.03).

On appeals to district court from county court, district court shall render judgment, which may affirm, affirm but modify, or reverse judgment or final order of county court. If district court reverses, it may enter judgment in accordance with its findings, or remand case to county court for further proceedings consistent with judgment of district court. Within two days after decision of district court becomes final, clerk of district court shall issue mandate to clerk of county court. (24-541.06).

In appeals from small claims court to district court, district court shall vacate judgment of small claims court. (24-541.07).

Appeal Under Newly Enacted Laws.—When law does not prescribe appeal procedure, appeal to district court is same as appeal from county court in civil actions. Appeal from district court is same as appeal to supreme court in civil actions. (25-1937; 180 Neb. 121, 141 N.W.2d 768).

BONDS:

Surety on every undertaking, bond and recognizance provided for by code must be resident of Nebraska and have property liable to execution situated in county in which bond, etc., is to be given and filed worth at least double the sum to be secured beyond all liens and encumbrances thereon and his exemption. This provision does not apply to incorporated surety companies authorized to transact business in this state. Except in case of incorporated surety companies, where there are two or more sureties for same bond, etc., they must in aggregate have qualifications prescribed above. (25-2223).

All officers required to take security, undertakings, bonds and recognizances must require surety to make affidavit as to his qualifications. (25-2222).

Surety Company Bonds.—Whenever bond required with one surety or with two or more sureties, it is sufficient if executed alone by surety company, organized under laws of Nebraska, or of any state of United States, having paid up capital of not less than $100,000 and power under its charter to become surety in same manner and with same rights and liabilities as natural persons, but bond must be approved in each instance by proper officer. (11-123).

Disability as Surety.—No state or county officer or deputy may be security on bonds of any administrator, executor or other officer from whom by law bond is required. (11-114). See also category Legal Profession, topic Attorneys and Counselors.

Action on bond may be brought in county where any defendant resides, in county where cause of action arose, in county where transaction or some part of transaction occurred, or if all defendants are nonresidents of state, in any county. (25-403.01).

CERTIORARI:

Writ abolished in civil cases. (25-1930).

CHARITABLE IMMUNITY:

See topic Damages.

COSTS:

Awarded to prevailing party in actions for money judgments, or for recovery of specific real or personal property, but may be awarded, taxed and apportioned by court in its discretion in other actions. (25-1708 to -1711). District court may tax actual fees and expenses of jury trial demanded for frivolous or capricious reason. (25-1711).

Security for Costs.—Plaintiff not residing in county where action brought may be required to furnish security for costs or deposit cash with clerk. (25-1701). Partnership must give security for costs. (25-315). In all cases proper officer may require costs paid in advance or security given therefor. (33-120).

Liability of Attorney.—None.

DAMAGES:

Common law generally prevails as to compensatory damages. Punitive damages not generally allowed. Liquidated damages, if not in fact a penalty, may be allowed in proper cases. Only actual damages are imposed for unlawful restraint of trade. (59-821).

Comparative Negligence.—For causes of action accruing after Jan. 1, 1992, fault of plaintiff diminishes proportionately amount of award; if plaintiff's fault is equal to or greater than fault of all defendants, plaintiff cannot recover. (25-21,185).

Sovereign Immunity.—Cities and all other governmental subdivisions and local bodies of state are not immune from tort liability arising out of ownership, use and operation of motor vehicles. (183 Neb. 430, 160 N.W.2d 805). See State Tort Claims Act (81-8, 209 to -8, 235) and Political Subdivision Tort Claims Act (13-901 to -926). Limit of liability for political subdivisions $1,000,000 per person for claims arising from single occurrence and $5,000,000 for all claims arising from single occurrence. (13-926).

Charitable Immunity.—Abrogated. (180 Neb. 183, 141 N.W.2d 852).

See also category Estates and Trusts, topic Death, subhead Action for Death.

Hospital-Medical Liability Act.—University of Nebraska: to authorize establishment of risk-loss trusts; to provide for use of such trusts; to provide for applicability of certain laws; to provide requirements for certain risk-loss trusts; to provide duties for Director of Insurance; to harmonize provisions; and to repeal original sections. (44-2824 to -2855; 85-1126 and -1127).

See note at head of Digest as to 1998 legislation covered.

See Topical Index in front part of this volume.

DEPOSITIONS AND DISCOVERY:

Depositions may be taken by either party, upon oral examination, by videotape under certain circumstances, or written interrogatories, for discovery or as evidence, after action started and service had on defendant. Leave of court unnecessary unless notice of taking is served by plaintiff within 30 days after service of summons. (25-1242).

Statutory discovery rules repealed. Rules now promulgated by Nebraska Supreme Court. (25-1273.01). Copy of Nebraska Supreme Court Rules of Practice and Procedure may be obtained for $10 by writing Clerk of Supreme Court, 2413 State Capitol Building, Lincoln, NE 68509. Rules are similar to Federal Rules of Civil Procedure (pre-1993 Amendments) except as noted. See topic Practice.

Uniform Foreign Depositions Act not adopted.

Within State for Use Within State.—At trial, or hearing of motion, or interlocutory proceedings, deposition may be used against party present or represented at taking of deposition, or who had notice thereof, in accordance with any one of following: (1) Contradicting or impeaching testimony of deponent as witness; (2) deposition of officer, director, or managing agent of corporation, partnership or association, which is party, may be used by adverse party for any purpose; (3) deposition of witness, whether party or not, may be used for any purpose if court finds (a) witness dead, (b) witness is at greater distance than 100 miles from place of trial or hearing, or out of state, or beyond subpoena power of court, unless absence procured by party offering deposition, (c) witness aged, sick, infirm or imprisoned, (d) party offering deposition unable to procure attendance of witness by subpoena, (e) exceptional circumstances exist, (f) upon application and notice in interest of justice. (Rule 32).

Within State for Use Elsewhere.—Deposition may be taken within state for use elsewhere in same manner and by same process and proceedings as may be employed for purpose of taking testimony in proceedings pending in this state. District Court for county where deponent is found may make such orders as could be made in laws and rules of such foreign jurisdiction. (Rule 28[e]). Parties can stipulate to modify procedure for other methods of discovery. (Rule 29).

Outside of State For Use Within State.—See subheads Before Whom Taken; and Notice, infra.

Perpetuating Testimony.—Person desiring perpetuation of own or others' testimony may file verified petition in district court covering residence of expected adverse party showing (1) that action expected but presently unable to be brought, (2) subject matter of and petitioner's interest in expected action, (3) facts desired to be established and reason for perpetuating them, (4) names and addresses of expected adverse parties, (5) names and addresses of persons to be examined and substance of expected testimony, (6) prayer for authorization to take testimony. (Rule 27[a][1]). Notice, stating time and place petitioner will apply to court, together with copy of petition, must be served upon expected adverse party at least 20 days before date of hearing. Provision made for perpetuation of testimony after district court decision where appeal to be taken and testimony to be used in event of further proceedings in district court. (Rule 27[a][2]).

Before Whom Taken.—Within Nebraska depositions may be taken before judge or clerk of Supreme Court or District Court, county judge, associate county judge, notary public, or any person appointed by court in which action is pending. (Rule 28[a]).

Elsewhere in U.S. depositions may be taken before officer authorized to administer oaths by laws of U.S. or of place where examination is held, or before person appointed by court in which action is pending. (Rule 28[b]).

Notice.—Prior to taking deposition by oral examination reasonable notice in writing must be given to every other party to action. Notice must state time and place for taking deposition and name and address of each person to be examined. If subpoena duces tecum is to be served, notice must also contain list of materials to be produced. (Rule 30[b][1][A]). Notice must state manner in which testimony will be recorded and preserved. Rule 30 also provides for deposition by videotape. (Rule 30[b][8][A]).

When party against whom deposition is to be used is unknown, party may be notified of deposition by publication. Publication must be made in some newspaper printed in county where action is pending, if none, in state newspaper of general circulation in that county. Publication must contain same as written notice. Proof of publication set forth in 25-520. (Rules 30[b][1][B], 31).

By Stipulation.—If parties stipulate in writing deposition may be taken before any person, at any time or place, upon any notice, and in any manner; and when so taken may be used like other depositions. (Rule 29).

By Written Interrogatories.—Notice of examination by written interrogatory must be served upon every other party to action. Notice must state name and address of person who is to answer written questions and name and address of officer before whom deposition is to be taken. Within 30 days after notice and written interrogatories are served, any party may serve cross-questions upon all other parties. Ten days after cross-questions served redirect questions may be served. Ten days after redirect questions served party may serve recross-questions. (Rule 31[a] [2]).

Compelling Attendance of Witnesses.—A subpoena may be issued by any officer authorized to take depositions. (25-1225).

Examination of Witnesses.—After being placed under oath, witness may be examined on any nonprivileged, relevant matter, including matter reasonably calculated to lead to discovery of admissible evidence, and may be cross examined same as at trial except that court in which action pending upon motion and notice and good cause may limit scope, subject matter and persons present. Party taking deposition shall determine in what manner testimony is to be taken. Evidence objected to shall be taken subject to objections. (Rule 30).

Objections.—Objections for incompetency, irrelevancy or immateriality not waived by failure to make at time of deposition unless ground of objection is one which might have been obviated if presented at that time. Objections may be made at trial to receive deposition or part thereof for any reason requiring exclusion if witness present and testifying, except that errors in manner of taking depositions, qualifications of person recording deposition, in form of questions or answers, in oath, in conduct of party, or errors which might be obviated if promptly presented, are waived. Objections may be heard on motion of either party before trial. (Rules 30 and 31).

Return.—After certifying on deposition that witness duly sworn and that deposition is true record, unless otherwise directed by court, officer delivers original to party taking deposition, and files with clerk of court certificate setting forth to whom original was delivered, date it was delivered, and charges for deposition. (Rule 30[f]).

Form

The form ordinarily used is as follows:

Depositions of sundry witnesses taken before me (here insert the name of the magistrate and his official character as a justice of the peace, or notary public, etc.), within and for the county of . . . . . ., in the State of . . . . . ., on the . . . . day of . . . . . . in the year . . . . . ., between the hours of . . . . A. M. and . . . . P. M., at . . . . . . in said county, pursuant to the annexed notice (or agreement as the case may be), to be read in evidence in behalf of the (plaintiff or defendant as the case may be) in an action pending in . . . . . (naming the court), in which . . . . . . is plaintiff and . . . . . . is defendant.

A. B., of lawful age, being by me first duly examined, cautioned and solemnly sworn, as hereinafter certified (or affirmed), deposes and says as follows, viz: (Here write the deposition), and so on with all witnesses.

Depositions are closed with a certificate in this form:

I, A. B. (naming the official character of the magistrate according to the fact) do hereby certify that (naming all witnesses who have testified) were by me first severally duly sworn (or affirmed) to testify the truth, the whole truth and nothing but the truth and that the depositions by them respectively subscribed as above set forth, were reduced to writing by myself (or if by any other person, name him, and say by . . . . . ., who is not interested in the suit, in my presence, and) in the presence of the witnesses respectively, and were respectively subscribed by the said witnesses in my presence and were taken at the time and place in the annexed notice (or agreement) specified; that I am not counsel, attorney or related to either party or otherwise interested in the event of this suit. (If there be adjournments, add) and said depositions were commenced at the time in said notice specified and continued by adjournments from day to day as above stated.

In Testimony Whereof, I have hereunto set my hand and affixed my official seal, at . . . . . . in said county, the day and year last above written.

(Signature).

(Title of officer).

Form of endorsement for outside of envelope in which depositions are transmitted to clerk of the court:

In the . . . . . . Court of . . . . . . County, Nebraska.

. . . .
Plaintiff,
vs. — Deposition of (insert name of witness).
. . . .
Defendant.

Demand for Admission of Facts.—This follows Federal Rule by providing procedure for determining sufficiency of answers or objections, and controlling effect and withdrawal of admissions. (Neb. Disc. Rule 36).

Written Interrogatories.—33(a) differs from Federal Rules by imposing limit of 50 interrogatories upon any party, unless court permits more for good cause shown. 33(b) and 33(c) follow Federal Rules (pre-1993 Amendments). (Neb. Disc. Rule 33).

EVIDENCE:

Proposed Federal Rules of Evidence materially adopted as Nebraska Evidence Rules, Aug., 1975. (27-101 et seq.). Provision restricting use of evidence in sexual assault cases enacted in 1983. (28-321). See subhead Witnesses, infra; topic Depositions and Discovery.

Witnesses.—Every person of sound mind is competent to be witness. (27-601). See also topic Depositions and Discovery. Expert witnesses are entitled to reasonable fees.

Privileged Communications.—Communications between attorney, physician, surgeon, minister or priest, professional counselor (27-504), and client, etc., are privileged if occurring while rendering professional service (27-503 to -506).

Husband and wife may not testify concerning any communication made by one to the other during the time of marriage, whether called while that relation exists or afterwards. (27-505). During marriage privilege can be waived if both parties consent. (27-505).

Either spouse may be witness against other in action brought by husband or wife against third person relating to marriage relationship or interruption of same. Also, in any criminal case where crime charged is crime of violence, bigamy, incest or any crime committed by one against person or property of another or of child of either or in any criminal prosecution against husband for wife or child abandonment. (27-505). Either spouse is competent in any divorce proceedings brought against other. Except as stated, neither husband nor wife can be witness against other, except in certain criminal proceedings; but either may be witness for other in any criminal proceeding. (27-505).

"Dead-Man" Statute repealed.

Self-incrimination.—Witness is not excused from answering question on ground that he would subject himself to civil liability (25-1209), but cannot be compelled to answer when matter sought to be elicited would tend to render him criminally liable or to expose him to public ignominy, except that witness may be interrogated as to his previous conviction for felony but no other proof of such conviction is competent except record thereof (Art. 1, §12, Neb. Const.).

INJUNCTIONS:

Injunction may be final judgment in an action, or allowed as a provisional remedy and when so allowed shall be by order; writ of injunction abolished. (25-1062). Injunction may be granted at time of commencing action or any time afterwards before judgment by Supreme Court or any judge thereof or by district court or any judge thereof. (24-734; 25-1064). Order of injunction must be addressed to party enjoined, must state injunction and must be issued by clerk. (25-1068). It binds party from time he has notice thereof and undertaking required by applicant therefor is executed. (25-1070).

Temporary Injunctions.—Plaintiff or his agent must make affidavit showing right to a temporary restraining order which may be issued immediately with direction that reasonable notice be given to party restrained to appear and show cause why temporary injunction should not issue. (25-1064). On hearing of application for injunction each party may read affidavits. (25-1074). If injunction granted without notice defendant may apply for vacation or modification thereof at any time before trial. (25-1075).

Bonds.—Party obtaining injunction must give bond with one or more sufficient sureties approved by clerk of court granting injunction in amount to be fixed by court or judge allowing same, to secure party enjoined as to damage which he may sustain if final decision is that injunction should not have been granted, and no injunction, unless provided by special statute, is operative until bond is given. (25-1067). Additional security may be required by court on application of party enjoined. (25-1073).

If party enjoined disobeys injunction he may be punished by contempt and required to give security. (25-1072).

JUDGMENTS:

May be given for or against one or more of several plaintiffs or for or against one or more of several defendants; it may determine ultimate rights of parties on either side as between themselves, may grant to defendant any affirmative relief to which entitled. In action against several defendants, court in its discretion may render judgment against one or more of them, leaving action to proceed against others, whenever several judgment may be proper. (25-1302).

Judgments by Confession.—Any person indebted or against whom cause of action exists may personally appear in court of competent jurisdiction and with assent of creditor or person having such cause of action, confess judgment therefor, which must be entered accordingly. (25-1309). Creditor's assent presumed where judgment confessed for amount claimed in petition. (22 Neb. 235, 34 N.W. 367). Debt or cause of action must be briefly stated in judgment or in writing to be filed as pleadings in other actions. (25-1310). Confession operates as release of errors and judgment is enforceable as any other. (25-1311). Attorney must produce warrant of authority to confess judgment; original or copy must be filed with clerk of court. (25-1312).

Summary Judgments.—Permitted by any party, with or without supporting affidavits. (25-1130 and -1331). Motion must be served at least ten days prior to hearing. (25-1332). Usual standards apply for granting motion; may be rendered on issue of liability alone. (25-1332).

Declaratory Judgments.—Uniform Declaratory Judgments Act adopted. (25-21,149 to -21,155).

Judgment Notes.—See category Business Regulation and Commerce, topic Bills and Notes.

Default Judgments.—If defendant fails to file appropriate written response to petition within 30 days after service, district court may enter judgment for relief demanded in petition. In county court, default judgment may be entered 30 days after commencement of action. (25-2704; L.B. 234). Judgment by default shall not be different in kind from that demanded in petition. If only special damages are demanded judgment by default shall not exceed amount demanded in petition. (25-821 and -1308).

Offer of Judgment.—Defendant may offer in court to confess judgment for part of amount claimed or part of causes involved in action, and if plaintiff does not accept such offer and fails to recover more than was offered he must pay all costs incurred by defendant after offer. (25-906). Similar offer may be made in court before action is brought and if claimant, after notice of offer, does not accept same and afterwards commences action and does not recover more than amount offered he must pay all costs of action. (25-907).

Docketing.—All judgments and orders must be entered on journal of court. Complete record, unless such record or part thereof duly waived, must be made up by clerk, and signed by presiding judge. (25-1318 to -1321).

Lien.—Lands and tenements of debtor within county where judgment is entered are bound for satisfaction thereof from day on which judgment is rendered, if judgment was entered by district court. All other lands, as well as goods and chattels of debtor, are bound from time they are seized on execution. (25-1504).

Transcript of judgment of any district court in state may be filed in office of clerk of district court in any county and when entered on judgment record, is a lien on property of debtor in county where filed in same manner and under same conditions as in county where judgment rendered, and execution may be issued as on original judgment. (25-1303). Filing fee is $26; $5 per page, plus 50¢ per lot.

Transcript of any judgment or decree rendered in United States district court within state, may be filed in office of clerk of district court in any county, and, when entered on judgment record is a lien on property of debtor in county where filed in same manner and under same conditions as if such judgment or decree had been rendered by district court of such county. Lands and tenements of debtor within county where judgment entered are bound for satisfaction thereof from day on which judgment is rendered without filing of transcript. (25-1305).

Order reviving dormant judgment becomes lien on lands and tenements of judgment debtor only where entered on judgment record in same manner as original judgment. (25-1305).

Judgment for unpaid court costs ceases to be lien on realty unless action has been brought thereon within five years after last payment thereon, or five years after case becomes inactive or is closed by final judgment. (25-1716).

Judgment for fines and costs in criminal cases is a lien on all property of defendant within county from time of docketing case, and judgments upon forfeited recognizance are a like lien from time of forfeiture. (29-2407).

Revivor.—If either or both of the parties die after judgment, and before satisfaction thereof, their representatives may be made parties in manner prescribed for reviving actions before judgment. (25-1419). If execution not sued out within five years from date of judgment or if five years intervene between successive executions thereon, judgment and all taxable costs of action in which it was obtained become dormant and cease to operate as a lien. (25-1515). If judgment becomes dormant it may be revived, within ten years after dormancy, by motion and order of court on notice to adverse party. (25-1420).

Assignment.—Assignee of a judgment takes it subject to the then existing equities. (89 Neb. 445, 131 N.W. 960).

Satisfaction.—On payment, but not otherwise, attorney may discharge judgment claim and acknowledge satisfaction of judgment. (7-107). Judgment may be satisfied by proper notation on docket, signed by attorney or by separate instrument, for which no form is prescribed. (25-2210).

Uniform Enforcement of Foreign Judgments Act adopted. (25-1587 to -15,104).

LIMITATION OF ACTIONS:

See Neb. UCC including 2-725, 3-122, 4-406. See category Business Regulation and Commerce, topic Commercial Code.

Actions must be commenced within the following periods after respective causes of action accrue:

Ten years: To recover real estate or foreclose mortgage thereon (25-202, and see subhead When Cause of Action Accrues, infra as to accrual of cause of action to foreclose); statute of repose for product liability actions, from date when injury causing product was sold (25-224[2]); on official bond of executor, administrator, guardian, sheriff or other officer or on attachment or injunction bond or other bond required by statute (25-209).

Five years: On specialty or any agreement, contract or promise in writing, express or implied, or foreign judgment. Action on contract made pursuant to statute later held unconstitutional must be brought within one year from effective date of decision. Otherwise, action on invalid sales agreement must be commenced within one year after last payment. (25-204 and -205).

Four years: On contract not in writing, express or implied, on statutory liability other than forfeiture or penalty, for trespass on real property, for taking, detaining or injuring personal property or to recover possession thereof, for relief on ground of fraud (time running from discovery), for injury to right not arising under contract for which no other limitation fixed (25-206, -207, and -214); against surety on guardian's bond (time running from discharge of guardian and person out of state or under disability having five years from return or removal of disability) (25-210); for damages arising out of want or failure of consideration for contract or to recover money paid on contract consideration for which has failed in whole or in part (25-211); action for which no other period prescribed (25-212); action for breach of any contract for sale of goods (Neb. UCC 2-725); products liability actions (except one in 25-224[5]) (25-224); for unfair trade practice (87-303-10).

Three years: On liability, other than forfeiture or penalty, created by federal statute providing no period of limitation. Certain claims under probate code. (30-2408).

Two years: For malpractice (25-208); for death (30-810); action against the state (25-218).

Eighteen months: Action to recover collateral transferred to third party which was used as security for payment pursuant to written agreement covering farm products. (25-205[2]).

One year: For forcible entry and detainer or detainer only of real estate (25-203); for libel, slander, assault and battery, malicious prosecution or false imprisonment or for statutory penalty where no other limitation fixed (25-208); for fine for violation of laws applicable to cities of second class and villages (17-565).

Tort claim against state must be filed within two years with State Claims Board; suit must be filed within six months of final disposition by Board. (81-8,209 to -8,239). *Caveat:* Action against State must be commenced within two years from time claim arises. (25-218).

Tort claim against political subdivision must be filed within one year with governing body; suit must be filed within two years or six months of final disposition by governing body, whichever is later. (23-2416).

When cause of action accrues as regards subsequent purchaser and encumbrancers for value, cause of action for foreclosure of mortgage deemed to have accrued at last date of maturity of debt as stated in or ascertainable from record of such mortgage or in extension thereof duly executed and recorded and if no date of maturity be stated thereon or be ascertainable therefrom, not later than 20 years from date of mortgage. But if mortgage creditor, before mortgage is barred under this section, files in recorder's office mortgage or sworn copy or affidavit that mortgage is unpaid and still valid and subsisting lien, cause of action is not barred until expiration of ten years from such filing. Period of ten years not extended by nonresidence, legal disability, partial payment, acknowledgment of debt, or promise to pay. (25-202).

Action is deemed commenced on date petition is filed with court. If service is not obtained within six months, action dismissed without prejudice. (25-217).

Foreign Causes of Action.—Action barred by laws of any other state, territory or county is barred in this state, but not unless same would have been barred by provisions hereinbefore set forth had defendant been a resident of this state for the period prescribed. (25-215).

Disabilities of Plaintiff.—If person entitled to bring action, except for penalty or forfeiture or for recovery of title or possession of lands or foreclosure of mortgage thereon, be, at time action accrues within age of 20, with mental disorder or imprisoned,

See note at head of Digest as to 1998 legislation covered.

See Topical Index in front part of this volume.

NE – 11

LIMITATION OF ACTIONS . . . *continued*
he may bring action within respective times limited, after removal of disability. For recovery of title or possession of land or foreclosure of mortgage thereon such person is entitled to bring action within 20 years from accrual, but in no case longer than ten years after termination of disability. Absence from state, death or disability does not extend period within which such actions in rem are to be commenced by and against nonresident or his representative. (25-213).

Absence or Concealment of Defendant.—If when cause of action accrues against a person he is out of the state or has absconded or concealed himself time does not commence to run until he comes into state or while he is absconded or concealed. If after cause of action accrues, he departs from state or absconds or conceals himself, time of his absence or concealment is excluded in computing time within which action must be brought. (25-214).

Interruption of Statutory Period.—On part payment or written acknowledgment of debt, statute starts to run anew from date of payment or acknowledgment. (25-216).

Revival of Barred Debts.—In any case founded on contract, when any part of principal or interest has been voluntarily paid, or an acknowledgment of an existing liability, debt or claim or any promise to pay has been made in writing, an action may be brought in such case within the period prescribed for same, after such payment, acknowledgment or promise. (25-216).

Contractual limitations are not permitted. (171 Neb. 820, 108 N.W.2d 84).

See Neb. U.C.C. 2-725(1); parties may reduce period of limitation to not less than one year for breach of contract for sale.

Pleading Statute.—Defense must be pleaded by demurrer or answer or will be considered waived. (171 Neb. 820, 108 N.W.2d 84).

See also categories Business Regulation and Commerce, topic Commercial Code; Courts and Legislature, topic Courts; Estates and Trusts, topic Executors and Administrators.

PARTITION:

Tenants in common or joint tenants of estate in land, including mineral, oil and gas rights, may be compelled to make or suffer partition. (25-2170).

Jurisdiction is concurrent between district court and county court when amount in controversy is less than $15,000, but solely in district court when such amount exceeds $15,000. If county court's ward, jurisdiction is concurrent for any amount. (25-2706; 24-517).

Proceedings.—Petition must describe property and several estates of joint owners if known. (25-2170). If number of shares or interests is known, but owners are unknown or if there are or are supposed to be any interests which are unknown, contingent or doubtful, these facts must be set forth in petition with reasonable certainty. (25-2171). Encumbrancers may appear in action on owner's default. (25-21,109). Persons having contingent interests may be made parties. (25-21,110). Creditors having a general or specific lien upon all or any portion of the property may or may not be made parties at option of plaintiff. (25-2172). Each party appearing must exhibit his documentary proof of title, if he have any and must file same or copies thereof with clerk. (25-2177). Uncontradicted statements in petition and answers are taken as true. (25-2178). After all shares or interests have been settled, confirming judgment must be rendered directing partition to be made accordingly (25-2179), with appointment of referees not exceeding three in number, to make partition (25-2180). If referees conclude partition cannot be made without prejudice to owners, they must so report. (25-2181). Special allotment may be made under order of court. (25-2182).

Sale.—Court may order sale (25-2183), after referees have given security fixed by court or judge thereof (25-2184). Same notice must be given as on execution sale and sale must be conducted in same manner. (25-2185). Referees must make report to court. (25-2186). Encumbrances on land must be ascertained and paid or payment provided for by deposit in court. (25-2186 to 2192). If land is located in two or more counties sale may be held in county where any part is located. Place and terms of sale is fixed in court order.

If sale confirmed court orders referee or majority of referees to execute conveyance when purchase money is paid or secured. (25-2196). Such conveyance, recorded in county where premises are situated, is valid against all parties and subsequent purchasers. (25-2197).

If sale is disapproved, money and security must be returned. (25-2199).

Lien on one or more undivided interests remains a charge on proceeds of sale or property awarded debtor, but a due proportion of the costs is chargeable on such interest or interests and is paramount to all other liens. (25-2173).

PLEADING:

Rules of pleading formerly existing for civil actions abolished—forms of pleading and rules by which sufficiency to be determined are those prescribed by code. (25-802). Special rules apply to actions against political subdivisions. (23-2401 to -2420).

Pleadings permitted are petition of plaintiff, answer or demurrer of defendant, demurrer or reply of plaintiff, demurrer to reply by defendant, third-party complaint, counterclaim and cross-claim. (25-331; -803; -812, and -813).

General Requirements.—Every pleading in court of record must be subscribed by the party or his attorney. (25-823). If action, counterclaim or setoff is founded on account or on note, bill or other instrument as evidence of indebtedness, copy thereof must be attached to and filed with pleading except in action founded upon note issued to circulate as money; if not so attached and filed, reason thereof must be shown in pleading. (25-832). In pleading judgment or other determination of court or officer of special jurisdiction, sufficient to state that such judgment or determination was duly given or made. (25-835). In pleading performance of conditions precedent in contract, sufficient to state that party duly performed all conditions on his part. (25-836). In action, counterclaim, or setoff founded on account, promissory note, bill of exchange or other instrument for unconditional payment of money only, sufficient to give copy of account or instrument with all credits and indorsements thereon and to state that there is due on such account or instrument specified sum, which is claimed with interest. When others than makers of promissory note or acceptors of bill of exchange are parties necessary to state also kind of liability of several parties and facts which fix their liability. (25-837).

Petition must contain name of court and county in which action brought, names of parties plaintiff and defendant, statement of facts constituting cause of action in ordinary and concise language, without repetition, demand of relief. If money, amount of special damages must be pleaded; general damages shall not be pleaded. (25-804). Actions on account or negotiable instruments must include copy of document. (25-832). If interest thereon be claimed, time from which computed must also be stated. (25-804). Separate causes of action must be separately stated, and numbered. (25-805).

Answer must contain: (1) general or specific denial of all matters controverted; (2) a concise statement of new matter constituting a defense, counter-claim, or set-off. (25-811).

Setoff, Counterclaim and Cross-Claim.—Setoff can only be pleaded in action founded on contract and must be cause of action arising on contract or ascertained by court decision. (25-816). Counterclaim must be one existing in favor of defendant and against the plaintiff between whom a several judgment might be had in the action and arising out of the contract or transaction set forth in the petition as foundation of plaintiff's claim or connected with the subject of the action. (25-813). Defendant may cross-claim against any party who is or may be liable for all or part of plaintiff's claim against him. (25-812).

Third-Party Practice.—Defendant, as third-party plaintiff, may file third-party complaint against person who is or may be liable to him for all or part of plaintiff's claim against him. Third-party defendant may assert claim against plaintiff arising out of transaction or occurrence which is subject matter of plaintiff's claim. (25-331).

Reply.—Where answer contains new matter, plaintiff must reply to such new matter. (25-820; 132 Neb. 624, 273 N.W. 46).

Demurrer.—Defendant may demur to petition for: Lack of jurisdiction appearing on face of petition; lack of legal capacity to sue; another action pending between same parties for same cause; defect of parties plaintiff or defendant; improper joinder of causes of action; or failure to state facts sufficient to constitute cause of action. Demurrer should distinctly specify ground of objection. (25-806, -807).

Motions.—Redundant, scandalous or irrelevant matter may be stricken on motion and pleader may be required to make pleadings more definite and certain. (25-833).

Amendments and supplemental pleadings are allowed with some liberality, and variances which do not mislead or errors or defects which do not affect substantial rights are disregarded. (25-846 and -856).

Verification.—Pleadings of fact need not be verified. (25-824). All pleadings must be signed by party or his attorney. (25-823).

Service and Filing.—Except for service by publication, copy of petition is served with summons. Plaintiff shall give clerk sufficient copies at time of filing. (25-504.01). All subsequent filings must be served upon adverse party if pro se, or his attorney if represented, and original must be so certified.

Time for Serving or Filing.—Answer or demurrer of defendant must be filed within 30 days after service of summons and petition or completion of service by publication. Reply or demurrer of plaintiff must be filed within 15 days after filing of answer. (25-821). Court, or judge thereof in vacation, for good cause shown, may extend time on such terms as may be just. (25-822).

Preparation of Claim.—If claim is based on judgment rendered in foreign state, copy of judgment should be obtained and registered in any state court having jurisdiction. (25-1588 and -1589).

Small Claims.—See category Courts and Legislature, topic Courts.

PRACTICE:

Governed by Code of Civil Procedure and Rules promulgated by Nebraska Supreme Court.

Discovery rules are promulgated by Nebraska Supreme Court. (25-1273.01). These rules follow structure of pre-1993 Amendment discovery portion of Federal Rules, but content of Nebraska Rules is not always same. Federal rule numbers were retained for convenience. See topic Depositions and Discovery.

Physical or Mental Condition of Party.—Nebraska Rule follows Federal Rule, and establishes useful procedure for exchange of medical reports. Subdivision (b)(2) of Federal Rule is not used because 27-504 contains direct waiver of privilege. (Neb. Disc. Rule 35).

Demand for Admission of Facts.—This rule follows Federal Rule by providing procedure for determining sufficiency of answers or objections, and controlling effect and withdrawal of admissions. (Neb. Disc. Rule 36). See also topic Depositions and Discovery.

Written Interrogatories.—33(a) differs from Federal Rules by imposing limit of 50 interrogatories upon any party, unless court permits more for good cause shown. 33(b) and 33(c) follow Federal Rules. (Neb. Disc. Rule 33).

Direct Actions Against Insurer.—See category Transportation, topic Motor Vehicles, subhead Direct Actions.

Small Claims.—See category Courts and Legislature, topic Courts.

See also topics Actions, Appeal and Error, Depositions and Discovery, Injunctions, Judgments, Pleading, Process; category Debtor and Creditor, topics Attachment, Executions, Garnishment.

PROCESS:

Civil action must be commenced by filing petition in office of clerk of proper court. (25-501). Action deemed commenced on date petition is filed if proper service obtained within six months of filing. Action shall stand dismissed without prejudice as to any

See note at head of Digest as to 1998 legislation covered.

PROCESS . . . *continued*
defendant not served within six months from date of filing petition. (25-217). Plaintiff must file with clerk praecipe for summons stating name and address of each party to be served and manner of service for each party. (25-502.01).

Form and Requisites of Summons.—Summons shall be directed to defendant or defendants, and contain names of parties, and name and address of plaintiff's attorney or plaintiff. It shall notify defendant that written response must be filed with court within 30 days, or upon failure court may enter relief demanded. (25-503.01). Copy of petition shall be served with summons, except when by publication. Plaintiff shall deliver to clerk sufficient copies at time of filing. (25-504.01).

Issuance of Summons.—Summons is issued by clerk of proper court. (25-2204). Must be signed by clerk, with seal of court, and dated day issued. (25-2201).

Who May Serve.—Except when plaintiff elects service by certified mail, summons served by sheriff of county where service is made, person authorized by law, or person not party to action specially appointed by court. Service by certified mail made by plaintiff or attorney. (25-506.01). Some Nebraska sheriffs do not serve civil process from other states.

Personal Service.—Plaintiff may elect following methods: (1) Personal service by leaving summons with person to be served; (2) residence service by leaving summons at usual place of residence, with some person of suitable age and discretion residing therein; (3) certified mail service by (a) sending summons within ten days of issuance to defendant by certified mail and (b) filing proof of service with signed receipt attached. (25-505.01).

Personal service on partnership or limited partnership may be made by personal, residence, or certified mail service upon any partner except limited partner, or by certified mail to usual place of business, or left with employee at usual place of business. (25-512.01). When such organization does not have usual place of business in state, it is required to appoint agent upon which process may be served. (25-530.08). Unincorporated association is served in same manner as partnership. (25-513.01).

When defendant is minor under 14, he may be served by personal, residence, or certified mail service upon adult with whom minor resides and is minor's parent, guardian or person having care for minor. If none can be found, minor may be served by personal service. (25-508.01).

Summons against corporation may be served by personal, residence or certified mail service upon any officer, director, managing agent, or registered agent, or by leaving process at corporation's registered office, or by certified mail to registered office. (25-509.01).

Dissolved corporation may be served by personal, residence, or certified mail service upon appointed receiver, and if none, then upon any person who at time of dissolution was officer, director or managing agent or registered agent at time of last annual report. (25-511.02).

Summons against county, city, or village may be served by personal, residence or certified mail service upon chief executive or clerk. (25-510.02).

Any political subdivision defined in 13-903, other than county, city, or village, may be served by personal, residence, or certified mail service upon chief executive, clerk, secretary, or any other member of governing board or body, or by certified mail to principal office of subdivision. (13-905).

Service on Bus or Trucking Company.—See category Transportation, topic Motor Vehicles, subhead Motor Vehicle Carriers.

Where defendant is foreign corporation, service may be on registered or managing agent. (25-509.01).

Nonresident Motorist.—See category Transportation, topic Motor Vehicles.

Voluntary appearance is equivalent to service except that special appearance may be made for purpose of objecting to court's jurisdiction over defendant. (25-516.01).

Agent for Service.—Any person, association or corporation owning or claiming any interest in or lien upon real estate lying within state may file in office of register of deeds of county in which such real estate is located an appointment in writing of some resident of county upon whom process may be served in any action concerning such real estate to which such owner or claimant shall be made a party. (25-528). See also categories Business Organizations, topic Corporations; Business Regulation and Commerce, topic Securities; Insurance, topic Insurance Companies; Transportation, topic Motor Vehicles.

Service by publication may be made: (1) When such service is elsewhere provided for by statute or (2) when ordered by court. (25-518.01). Motion and affidavit must be filed that service cannot be made with reasonable diligence by any other method provided by statute. (25-517.02).

Publication must be made once each week for four consecutive weeks in newspaper printed in county where petition filed or if none, in newspaper printed in state of general circulation in that county. Must contain summary statement of object and prayer of petition, mention court wherein it is filed and notify person or persons thus to be served when they are required to answer. (25-519). Service by publication is complete when made in manner and for time above set forth, and is proved by affidavit of printer or his foreman or principal clerk or other person knowing same. (25-520). Party or his attorney may designate newspaper. (25-522).

Legal newspaper must be printed in English language, with bona fide circulation of at least 300 copies weekly, published within county 52 successive weeks prior to publication of notice and printed in whole or in part in office maintained at place of publication. (25-523).

Mailing of Publication Notice.—Party serving notice by publication must within five days after first publication mail a copy thereof to every party having a direct legal interest therein whose name and post office address is known to him. Registered or certified mail not required. Proof of mailing such notice must be made by affidavit within ten days after mailing. Affidavit must state that party and his attorney after diligent search and investigation were unable to ascertain the post office address of any parties other than those to whom notice mailed. Mailing of notice or notices may be waived in writing or by entering a voluntary appearance or by personal service. (25-520.01).

Service Without State.—Service without state may be made: (a) In manner prescribed for service within state; (b) in manner prescribed by law in state where service is to be made; (c) as directed by foreign authority in response to letters rogatory; or (d) as directed by court. Proof of service may be made by affidavit of individual who made service, or in manner prescribed by law, order pursuant to which service was made, or law of place in which service was made. (25-540).

Personal Service Outside State.—Court may exercise personal jurisdiction over person: (1) Who acts directly or by agent as to cause of action arising from person (a) transacting business in state, (b) contracting to supply services or things in state, (c) causing tortious injury by act or omission in state, (d) causing tortious injury by act or omission outside state if person regularly does or solicits business, engages in any persistent course of conduct, or derives substantial revenue from goods used or consumed, or services rendered in state, (e) having interest in, using, or possessing real property in this state, or (f) contracting to insure any person, property, or risk located within state at time of contracting; or (2) who has any other contact with or maintains any other relation to state to afford basis for exercise of personal jurisdiction consistent with constitution of U.S. (25-536).

Service on Less Than All Defendants.—If action is against two or more defendants and one or more, but not all, are served, plaintiff may proceed as follows: If action be against defendants jointly indebted on a contract, he may proceed against defendant served unless court otherwise directs; if action be against defendants severally liable, he may without prejudice to his rights against those not served proceed against defendants served as though they were the only defendants. (25-527).

Long Arm Statute.—See subhead Personal Service Outside State, supra.

Uniform Interstate and International Procedure Act.—Nebraska has not adopted this uniform act, although its long arm statute (see subhead Personal Service Outside State, supra) is patterned after it. (25-536).

REPLEVIN:

Plaintiff in action to recover possession of personal property may at commencement of suit or at any time before answer, request delivery of such property by replevin. (25-1093).

Grounds for replevin are plaintiff's right to immediate possession by virtue of ownership or some interest in specific personal property. (25-1094).

Jurisdiction.—Action may be brought in district, county, or municipal court with due regard to jurisdictional amount. See category Courts and Legislature, topic Courts.

Affidavit.—Before issuance of order of replevin, plaintiff, his agent or attorney, must file with clerk of court in which action is brought an affidavit showing: (1) Description of property claimed; (2) that plaintiff is owner of property or has special ownership or interest therein (stating facts in relation thereto), and that he is entitled to immediate possession of same; (3) that property is wrongfully detained by defendant; (4) that it was not taken in execution on any order or judgment against said plaintiff, or for payment of any fine, tax or amercement assessed against him, or by virtue of an order of delivery or any other mesne or final process issued against him, or that property was taken on execution of judgment or order other than an order of delivery in replevin and that same is exempt from such execution or attachment under laws of state. Attached to affidavit shall be specific request for delivery of property and issuance of order by court to that effect. (25-1093.01). On filing of affidavit, defendant with full knowledge of allegations and effect of plaintiff's request may agree that such delivery be had and execute voluntary waiver under oath of his rights to notice and hearing, in which event court shall order all further proceedings be suspended and property be delivered to plaintiff forthwith. If defendant does not so waive this right, court shall issue temporary order requiring defendant to hold property described, in condition it was at time of order until further order of court. Order shall give notice of hearing at which will be determined rights of possession pending final hearing and at which defendant must show cause why plaintiff should not get possession. Hearing shall be no sooner than seven days and no later than 14 days after service of notice. (25-1093.02). If filed at commencement of suit, notice shall accompany summons. (25-1093.03).

Order.—If court finds at hearing plaintiff is entitled to possession, order shall issue and be delivered to sheriff for service and return. Order for delivery will be executed by clerk of court after receipt of order of court that there is sufficient probability that plaintiff has receipt for such service. (25-1093.04 to -1094).

Execution of Order.—Order is executed by sheriff by taking property and serving copy of order on person detaining property, or leaving copy of order at his usual place of residence. (25-1097). Officer has property appraised (25-1099), and if plaintiff gives proper bond (see subhead Bond, infra) delivers property to plaintiff (25-1098).

Bond.—In order to secure delivery of property to him, plaintiff must give the officer bond for twice the appraised value thereof, conditioned that plaintiff shall duly prosecute action, pay all costs and damages which may be awarded against him and return property to defendant in case judgment for return of such property is rendered against him. (25-1098). Bond must be given within 24 hours from taking of property by officer; otherwise property is returned to defendant. (25-10,100). Defendant may except within 24 hours to sufficiency of sureties in which case they must justify. (25-10,101).

Repossession by Defendant.—If, before delivery to plaintiff, defendant executes within 24 hours from levy bond in double property's value, officer must return property. (25-1098).

Claims of Third Persons.—No special provision. All persons having any apparent interest may be made parties. (25-328).

Disposition of Cause.—If property has been delivered to plaintiff and plaintiff fails to prosecute his action, defendant may have jury impaneled to ascertain his right in property and possession thereof and if jury finds that said property was property of defendant at commencement of action, or that defendant was entitled to possession only at commencement of action, jury must assess damages for defendant, on which finding,

See note at head of Digest as to 1998 legislation covered.

See Topical Index in front part of this volume.

REPLEVIN . . . *continued*
together with costs, court renders judgment. (25-10,102). On issue joined and tried, jury must make findings as to ownership of property or right to possession thereof, and if judgment is rendered in favor of defendant, it must be in alternative for return of property or value thereof, in case return cannot be had, or value of possession of same and damages for withholding said property if defendant was entitled to possession only, together with costs of suit. (25-10,103 and -10,104). If verdict is for plaintiff, jury must assess damages for illegal detention of property and judgment for same together with costs of suit, must be rendered for plaintiff. (25-10,105). When property has not been taken or has been returned to defendant for want of bond, action may proceed as one for damages only. (25-10,106).

SEQUESTRATION:

No statutory provisions.

SUBMISSION OF CONTROVERSY:

Parties to a question which might be subject of civil action, may without action agree upon case containing facts in controversy and present submission of same to any court which would have jurisdiction if action had been brought. They must file affidavit that controversy is real and proceedings are in good faith to determine rights of parties. Court shall thereupon hear and determine same and render judgment as if action were pending. (25-903). Case, submission and judgment constitute complete record. (25-904). Judgment is with costs, may be enforced and is subject to reversal in same manner as if rendered in action, unless otherwise provided in submission. (25-905).

VENUE:

Real Property Actions.—All actions to recover damages for trespass upon or injury to real property must be brought only in county where such real estate or some part thereof is situated, except that such an action against a railroad company may be brought in any county where service of summons can be had. Action for recovery of real property or estate or interest therein, partition of real property, or sale of real property under mortgage or other encumbrance or charge, must be brought where subject of action is situated. If property be an entire tract or separate tracts situated in two or more counties action may be brought where any part thereof is situated, unless action is for recovery of possession, in which case if the property be an entire tract situated in two or more counties, action may be brought in either of such counties but if it consists of separate tracts in different counties, possession must be recovered by separate actions, each brought in county where real property is situated. (25-401, -402). Action for specific performance of contract for sale of real property may be brought in any county where any of defendants reside or, if all defendants are nonresidents, in county where real property or some part thereof is situated. (25-403).

Other Actions.—(1) County where defendant resides, (2) county where cause of action arose, (3) in county where transaction or some part of transaction occurred out of which cause of action arose, or (4) if all defendants are nonresidents of this state, in any county. (25-403.01). If venue improper, court may order attorney's fees paid upon transfer. (25-411).

Venue Definitions.—(1) Any private corporation organized under laws of this state and any foreign corporation authorized to transact business in this state is resident of any county in which it has its registered office or other office or is doing business. Foreign corporation not authorized to transact business in this state is not resident of this state. (2) Partnership sued in its firm name is resident of any county in which any partner resides or in which partnership has office or is doing business. If all partners are nonresidents of this state and partnership does not have office or do business in this state, partnership is not resident of this state. (3) Voluntary unincorporated association sued in its own name is resident of any county in which association has office or in which any officer of association resides. If it has no office in this state, voluntary unincorporated association is not resident of this state. (25-403.02).

Change of venue, on the usual grounds, is provided for. (25-410 to -412).

See also category Estates and Trusts, topic Executors and Administrators.

COURTS AND LEGISLATURE

COURTS:

United States District Court.—Clerk's office: 215 N. 17th St., #9000, Omaha, NE 68102.

Nebraska comprises one Federal District coterminous with State of Nebraska and is not subdivided into divisions for any purpose. Official name is U.S. District Court for District of Nebraska. Official station of clerk of court is Omaha. Deputy clerks are stationed at Omaha and Lincoln.

Civil cases may be filed in clerk's office either at Omaha or Lincoln.

Court sits at Omaha, at Lincoln, and at North Platte.

Place of trial of civil cases as between Omaha, Lincoln or North Platte, by requests, if all request identical place. Plaintiff, or removing party, files request with complaint or petition for removal. Defendant files request with first pleading. Plaintiff in removed action files request within ten days after notice of removal. Copies of requests must be served on all parties affected. If places requested are not identical, on notice and hearing, a judge will determine place where case shall be calendared for trial, with due consideration for convenience of litigants, witnesses and counsel. Changes in designation of place of trial may be sought by motion with reasons stated made before case is calendared for trial. In criminal cases government attorney endorses request on information or indictment, defendant requests in writing within ten days after giving bond or arrest, where no bond is given, and case is calendared in one of said three cities designated by defendant, unless government attorney files objection within ten days after defendant's request.

Deposits.—On institution of any civil suit $120 must be paid to clerk; on filing notice of appeal to Circuit Court of Appeals or U.S. Supreme Court $5 filing fee must be paid with $100 docket fee.

Bankruptcy Court.—Clerk's office, P.O. Box 428, Omaha 68101; 460 Federal Building, 100 Centennial Mall North, Lincoln 68508. C. 7, $175; c. 13, $160; c. 11, $800; c. 12, $200; c. 9 Municipality Adjustment Petition, $300. Judge may also require deposit to cover expenses before proceeding with case on matters raised by motion of opposing counsel, trustee or creditors' committee.

Supreme Court of Nebraska.—There are seven judges in Supreme Court, one of whom is chief justice. All sessions of court are held in Capitol Building at Lincoln and all judges reside in Lincoln although they originally resided in specific judicial districts with equal representation statewide.

Jurisdiction.—Supreme Court has original jurisdiction in cases relating to revenue, civil cases in which state is a party, mandamus actions, quo warranto and habeas corpus (Const. Art. V, §2) and has appellate jurisdiction in all civil and criminal actions appealed from district or appellate court. (24-204).

A majority of judges is necessary to constitute a quorum and opinions and judgments can be given by majority except in cases involving constitutionality of statute, in which concurrence of five judges is necessary to declare act unconstitutional. Court has power to appoint judges of district court to act as associate judges of Supreme Court and to divide court into two divisions of five judges each when associate judges are sitting with Supreme Court. When court is sitting in two divisions, four of judges are necessary to constitute a quorum or to render an opinion or decision. In all cases involving constitutionality of a statute and all appeals from conviction for homicide, Supreme Court sits without division.

Court sits at State Capitol (33-103), Lincoln.

Fees.—Docket entry $50, security for costs $75 or bond. (25-1914).

Court of Appeals.—Consists of six judges sitting in panels of three.

Jurisdiction.—All cases appealed from District Court except death penalty or life imprisonment cases and cases raising constitutionality of statute.

District Court.—District court has original jurisdiction in both chancery and common law, and has general jurisdiction over all matters except probate matters. District court also has appellate jurisdiction on appeals from county courts. On appeal, action is tried de novo on record.

Districts.—District court is divided into 12 districts, comprising counties as set out below. Court is held in each county at county seat thereof. (See list of counties and county seats at head of Nebraska Geographical Section, in volume containing list of Nebraska lawyers.)

First District. Counties of Saline, Jefferson, Gage, Thayer, Johnson, Pawnee, Nemaha, Fillmore, and Richardson.

Second District. Counties of Sarpy, Cass, and Otoe.

Third District. County of Lancaster.

Fourth District. County of Douglas.

Fifth District. Counties of Merrick, Platte, Colfax, Boone, Nance, Hamilton, Polk, York, Butler, Seward, and Saunders.

Sixth District. Counties of Dixon, Dakota, Cedar, Burt, Thurston, Dodge, and Washington.

Seventh District. Counties of Knox, Cuming, Antelope, Pierce, Wayne, Madison, and Stanton.

Eighth District. Counties of Cherry, Keya Paha, Brown, Rock, Blaine, Loup, Custer, Boyd, Holt, Garfield, Wheeler, Valley, Greeley, Sherman, and Howard.

Ninth District. Counties of Buffalo and Hall.

Tenth District. Counties of Adams, Clay, Phelps, Kearney, Harlan, Franklin, Webster, and Nuckolls.

Eleventh District. Counties of Hooker, Thomas, Arthur, McPherson, Logan, Keith, Perkins, Lincoln, Dawson, Chase, Hayes, Frontier, Gosper, Dundy, Hitchcock, Red Willow, and Furnas.

Twelfth District. Counties of Sioux, Dawes, Box Butte, Sheridan, Scotts Bluff, Morrill, Garden, Banner, Kimball, Cheyenne, Grant, and Deuel.

A clerk of district court for each county is located at county seat.

Fees.—Civil cases including appeals and domestic relations, $59, except dissolution of marriage, $84; transcribing record of judgment, $29.

County Courts.—County courts are courts of record and have exclusive original jurisdiction in all matters of probate and administration of estates of deceased persons and in proceedings to determine heirship, appointment of conservators and settlement of their accounts, supervision of testamentary trusts and juvenile matters in counties where there is no juvenile court. They have exclusive original jurisdiction in all matters relating to guardianship of person and in matters of adoption, except if separate juvenile court already has jurisdiction over child in need of guardian or child to be adopted; in that case, they have concurrent original jurisdiction with separate juvenile court. County courts have concurrent jurisdiction with District Court to involuntarily partition ward's interest in real estate and in paternity determinations as provided in §24-517 and §25-2740, respectively.

They also have jurisdiction, concurrently with district court in civil actions up to $15,000. County courts have concurrent original jurisdiction with district courts in any criminal matter classified as misdemeanor or for any infraction, and exclusive jurisdiction over city ordinance violations except in counties having municipal court. (24-517). County court certifies proceedings to district court of county in which action is pending (1) when pleadings or discovery proceedings indicate there is amount in controversy in excess of $15,000 or (2) when relief requested is exclusively within jurisdiction of district court.

Fees.—Generally set in accordance with respective value of estate involved.

Probate Courts.—There are no separate probate courts. Probate jurisdiction is exercised by county courts. (24-517).

Small Claims Court.—County and municipal courts have small claims department having jurisdiction in civil actions of any type when amount in controversy is less than $2,100, exclusive of interest and costs. (25-2802). Parties cannot be represented by attorneys, and must represent themselves except as provided in §25-2805. Corporation or association represented by officer or employee. Partnerships represented by partner or employee. No assigned claims can be filed. Setoff or counterclaim may be filed, if less

COURTS . . . *continued*

than $1,500, exclusive of interest and costs. If setoff or counterclaim exceeds such amount, entire case is transferred to regular county court. No prejudgment actions of attachment, garnishment, replevin, or other provisional remedy may be filed. All actions tried to court without jury. No formal pleadings, or rules of evidence, except for privileged communications. Default judgments may not be set aside but may only be appealed. Appeal may be made to district court. (25-2807).

Fees.—$9, plus service costs.

Juvenile Courts.—Separate juvenile court may be established in any county having population of 75,000 or more. Douglas, Lancaster and Sarpy Counties have established separate juvenile courts. These courts have exclusive original jurisdiction over: (1) Child under 18 years of age who is homeless, destitute, or without proper support through no fault of his parent, guardian, or custodian; (2) child under 18 who is: (i) abandoned, (ii) lacks proper care by reason of fault or habits of parent or guardian, (iii) whose parent, guardian or custodian neglects or refuses to provide proper or necessary subsistence, education or other care necessary for his health, morals or welfare, (iv) whose parent, guardian or custodian neglects or refuses to provide special care made necessary by child's mental condition or (v) who is in situation or engages in occupation which is dangerous to life, limb or injurious to his health and morals; (3) any child under 16 at time he violated any law of state or any city or village ordinance amounting to offense other than felony or traffic offense or parking violation; (4) any child under 18: (i) who by reason of being wayward or habitually disobedient, uncontrolled by his parent or guardian, (ii) who is habitually truant from school or home or (iii) who deports himself so as to injure or endanger seriously morals or health of himself or others; (5) parent, guardian or custodian who has custody of any child described above; (6) proceedings for termination of parental rights.

These courts have concurrent jurisdiction with district court as to: (1) Any child under 18 who has committed felony, (2) any child 16-17 who violated law amounting to offense other than felony or parking violation, and (3) any child under 16 at time he committed traffic offense. (43-245 et seq.). Where no separate juvenile court established, county court has exclusive jurisdiction. Separate juvenile courts are prohibited from appointing juvenile probation officers after Dec. 31, 1984. (43-247).

Juveniles; Jurisdiction of county court expanded to include jurisdiction over parents of detained juveniles to cause parents to pay support money to agency where juvenile is detained. (43-254 and -290).

Nebraska Worker's Compensation Court.—This court consists of seven judges appointed by Governor and has original jurisdiction to determine all controversies arising under Nebraska Worker's Compensation Law. (48-152). Hearings are held within county where accident occurred unless some other place is fixed by agreement of parties. (48-177). Claims for compensation will be barred unless filed within two years after accident or within two years of last compensation paid arising out of accident (48-137), or within two years after learning that compensable disability resulting from original accident (211 Neb. 704, 320 N.W.2d 111).

LEGISLATURE:

Legislature is a unicameral body. (Const., art. III, §1). Regular sessions are held each year commencing on 1st Wed. after 1st Mon. in Jan. Sessions shall not exceed 90 legislative days in odd numbered years and 60 legislative days in even numbered years unless extended by vote of not less than ⁴/₅ of all legislators. (Const., art. III, §10). Governor may call extra sessions. (Const., art. IV, §8). People have initiative and referendum. (Const., art. III, §§2, 3).

REPORTS:

Decisions of Supreme Court are officially reported in Nebraska Reports, and unofficially reported in Northwestern Reporter and Nebraska Supreme Court Journal. Decisions of Court of Appeals which are approved for publication by Supreme Court will appear in Nebraska Court of Appeals Reports and Northwestern Reporter.

Digests are: Nebraska Digest (West Publishing Company) consisting of 12 volumes and pocket supplement. Covers all Nebraska Reports, Nebraska cases in Northwestern Reporter and Nebraska cases reported in Federal Courts and the United States Supreme Court.

STATUTES:

Revised Statutes of Nebraska compiled in 1943. Supplements issued annually, Cumulative Supplements periodically. Session Laws published at close of each session of legislature. Statutes printed in volumes, updated from time to time in "Reissue" reprints. Current Reissues: Vols. 1 and 1A, 1991; Vols. 2 and 2A, 1989; Vols. 3, 3A and 3B, 1988; Vols. 4 and 4A, 1990; Vol. 5 and 5A, 1987; Uniform Commercial Code Vol. 6, 1980.

Uniform Acts are: Acknowledgments (1969); Anatomical Gift (1996); Arbitration (1997); Attendance of Witnesses from Without the State in Criminal Proceedings (1937); Business Corporation Act (1963); Child Custody Jurisdiction (1979); Commercial Code (Revised, 1972); Common Trust Fund (1953); Composite Reports as Evidence (1951); Construction Lien (1981); Controlled Substances (1974); Criminal Extradition (1935); Deceptive Trade Practices (1969); Declaratory Judgments (1929); Determination of Death (1992); Disposition of Unclaimed Property (1969); Divorce Recognition (1949); Durable Power of Attorney (1985); Enforcement of Foreign Judgments (1993) (with significant modifications); Federal Lien Registration (1988); Federal Rules of Evidence (1975); Foreign Executed Wills (1941); Fraudulent Transfer (1989); Fresh Pursuit (1937); Gifts to Minors (1957); Interstate Arbitration and Compromise of Death Taxes (1976); Interstate Family Support Act (1993); Judicial Notice of Foreign Law (1947); Limited Partnership (Revised, 1990); Military Justice (1969); Model Health Maintenance Organization Act (1978); Model Uniform Choice of Forum (1969); Out of State Parolee Supervision (1937); Partnership (1997); Photographic Copies of Business and Public Records as Evidence (1951); Premarital Agreement (1983); Principal and Income Act (1981); Probate Code (1977); Property (1941); Prudent Investor (1997); Reciprocal Enforcement of Support, Revised (1971); Reciprocal Transfer Tax

(1945); Recognition of Acknowledgments (1969); Regulating Traffic on Highways (1931); Rendition of Accused Persons (1969); Rendition of Prisoners as Witnesses in Criminal Proceedings (1969); Residential Landlord and Tenant Act (1973); Securities (1965); Simplification of Land Transfers Art. 5 (1982); Simultaneous Death (1947); State Administrative Procedure Act (Model) (1987); State Tax Lien Registration and Enforcement (1986); Statutory Rule Against Perpetuities (1989); Testamentary Additions to Trusts Act (1974); Trade Practices Act (1979); Trade Secrets (1988); Transfer to Minors (1992); Trustees' Powers Act (1980); Unauthorized Insurers (1969); Unfair Competition and Trade Practices (1973); Veteran's Guardianship (1929); Voting By New Residents in Presidential Elections (1963).

Uniform Commercial Code in effect. See category Business Regulation and Commerce, topic Commercial Code.

For text of Uniform Acts falling within the scope of the Martindale-Hubbell Law Digests see Uniform and Model Acts section.

CRIMINAL LAW

CRIMINAL LAW:

Nebraska Criminal Code covers all crimes and criminal procedure. (28-101 et seq., 29-101 et seq.). Persons accused of crime are brought to trial by indictment of grand jury (29-1416), or on information filed by prosecuting attorney (29-1601, 1602). Defendant has burden of proving insanity defense by preponderance of evidence. (29-2203).

Bail.—All persons are bailable by sufficient sureties, except on charge of treason, sexual offenses involving penetration by force or against will of victim, and murder where proof is evident or presumption great. (Const., art. I, §9).

Victims Reparation.—Criminal victims may seek reparations from Crime Victim's Reparations Committee. (81-1801).

Sex Offender Registration Act adopted. (28-320). Sex offenders of minors must register with officials.

Uniform Rendition of Accused Persons Act adopted. (29-3101).

Uniform Rendition of Prisoners as Witnesses in Criminal Proceedings Act adopted. (29-3201).

Uniform Deceptive Trade Practices Act adopted. (87-301 to -306).

Uniform Controlled Substances Act adopted in compliance with federal classification. (28-4,117).

Uniform Act for Out-of-State Parolee Supervision adopted. (29-2637).

DEBTOR AND CREDITOR

ASSIGNMENTS:

In general all choses in action except those of personal nature are assignable.

Accounts Receivable.—See category Business Regulation and Commerce, topic Commercial Code.

Instruments Transferring Title.—Assignment of mortgage, effect of (76-256); assignment of mineral rights (72-311).

Recording is not required except as to security interests. (Neb. UCC 9-405).

Effect.—Assignee of thing in action may maintain action in his own behalf (25-302), subject to setoff or defenses between original parties, except bona fide purchasers of negotiable paper (25-303, -818).

Enforcement.—Assigned claim cannot be filed in small claims court. (24-523).

Assignment of wages of head of family must be in writing and signed and acknowledged by both husband and wife. Spouse need not join in authorization for payroll deductions for purchase of Government bonds, contributions to charities, payment of dues, insurance, etc. Person withholding wages under void assignment is liable to injured party for expense of recovering same, including attorney's fees, and also guilty of misdemeanor. (36-213, -213.01).

Licensee under Installment and Chattel Loan Act may not take assignment of wages for more than amount of loan. All blanks in assignment must be filled in (45-142) and assignment must be signed personally by borrower (45-143); if borrower is married written consent of husband or wife must be obtained (45-144).

Liens.—Generally assignable, see specific topic headings; see also topic Liens.

Form.—No special form prescribed by law.

See also category Business Regulation and Commerce, topic Commercial Code.

ATTACHMENT:

Actions in Which Allowed.—Attachment may be allowed in any civil action for the recovery of money only. (25-1001 and -1002).

Courts Which May Issue Writ.—All courts having jurisdiction of civil cases. (25-1001, -1002).

Time for Issuance.—Attachment may issue at or after the commencement of an action. (25-1001).

In Whose Favor Writ May Issue.—Any plaintiff, in civil action, including nonresident or foreign corporation, may obtain attachment. (25-1001).

Claims on Which Writ May Issue.—Attachment may issue on either matured or unmatured claim. (25-1001 and -1049).

Grounds of attachment in action on matured claim are that defendant, or one of several defendants: (1) Has absconded with intent to defraud creditors; (2) has left county of his residence to avoid service of summons; (3) so conceals himself that summons cannot be served upon him; (4) is about to remove his property or part thereof out of county in which property is located with intent to defraud creditors; (5) is about to convert his property or part thereof into money for purpose of placing it beyond reach

---

See note at head of Digest as to 1998 legislation covered.

See Topical Index in front part of this volume.

ATTACHMENT . . . *continued*

of creditors; (6) has property or rights in action which he conceals; (7) has assigned, removed or disposed of or is about to dispose of property with intent to defraud creditors; (8) fraudulently contracted debt or incurred obligation for which suit is about to be or has been brought. (25-1001).

On claims not due grounds of attachment are that debtor: (1) Has sold or conveyed or otherwise disposed of property with fraudulent intent to cheat or defraud, hinder or delay creditors; (2) is about to make such sale, disposition or conveyance of his property with such fraudulent intent; (3) is about to remove property with intent or effect of cheating, defrauding, hindering or delaying creditors. (25-1049).

Proceedings to Obtain.—In order to obtain an attachment plaintiff must file an affidavit showing: (1) That facts set forth in plaintiff's petition state valid cause of action and amount plaintiff is entitled to recover are true; (2) describing existence and approximate value of defendant's property known to plaintiff to be subject to jurisdiction of court; and (3) stating specific facts demonstrating reasonable cause that one or more of grounds for attachment exist. (25-1002).

If claim sued on is not due an order is required from court in which action is brought or from judge thereof or county judge, and before attachment is allowed affidavit shall be presented demonstrating: (1) That plaintiff will possess valid cause against defendant when claim becomes due; (2) date when claim shall be due; (3) amount of claim; (4) description of existence and approximate value of defendant's property known to be within jurisdiction of court and not exempt from attachment; and (5) existence of at least one of grounds for attachment. (25-1050).

Bond.—Judge to whom affidavit is presented shall determine amount of bond, taking into account amount of probable damage suffered by defendant if property is wrongfully attached. (25-1003).

Issuance of Writ.—The writ is issued from the office of the clerk of the court in which the action was brought and directed to the sheriff.

Levy, Inventory and Appraisement.—Sheriff must make levy in presence of two residents of county and, with such residents, make and return an inventory and appraisement of property attached. Where real property is attached, sheriff must leave with occupant thereof, or if there is no occupant, in a conspicuous place thereon, a copy of the order. Accessible personal property is taken into sheriff's custody and held subject to order of court. (25-1004 to -1008).

Lien.—Order of attachment binds property attached from time of service. (25-1017).

Priorities.—If same officer has several attachments against same defendants he must serve them in order received, and each attachment is subject to all prior attachments. (25-1007).

Release or Discharge.—Defendant may obtain release of property attached by giving surety bond in appraised value thereof conditioned that such value and money shall be forthcoming to answer judgment (25-1009); or may obtain discharge of attachment by giving bond in amount of plaintiff's claim conditioned for performance of judgment rendered in action (25-1024).

Sale of property is by order of court as on execution. (25-1033).

Third Party Claims.—If personal property be claimed by any person other than defendant, officer must have validity of claim tried. (25-1036).

Vacation or Modification.—Defendant may at any time before judgment upon reasonable notice to plaintiff move to discharge an attachment as to whole or part of property. (25-1040). If attachment discharged by order, any party affected and excepting may appeal within time fixed by court or judge, on giving surety bond, conditioned for payment of all damage in consequence of appeal if attachment finally discharged. (25-1047).

In inferior courts rules for attachments are same as in district courts. (25-1042).

CREDITORS' SUITS:

If consumer is in default for at least ten days, creditor may give notice to consumer. Consumer then has 20 days to cure. If no cure, creditor may accelerate or take possession of collateral. (45-1,105).

If judgment debtor has no personal or real property subject to levy on execution sufficient to satisfy judgment, any interest he may have in any banking, turnpike, bridge, or other joint stock company or in any money, contract, claims or choses in action due or to become due, any judgment or decree or any money, goods or effects which he may have in possession of any person, body politic or corporate, may be subjected to payment of such judgment by proceedings in equity. (25-1564). Where execution is returned unsatisfied debtor may be examined before District Judge. (25-1565).

Claims upon debtor's estate which arose before death of decedent must be made within two months of notice by publication made by personal representative of debtor. (30-2485).

EXECUTIONS:

Money judgments are enforceable by execution. (25-1503). Execution may issue against property of judgment debtor and for delivery of possession of real property with damages for withholding same and costs. (25-1502).

Attachments.—See topic Attachment.

Exemptions.—See topic Exemptions.

Time for Issuance.—Execution may issue immediately after judgment, or on expiration of stay if any granted. (25-1513). Judgment becomes dormant after five years unless execution issued. (25-1515; 25-1542; 213 Neb. 243, 328 N.W.2d 759). Judgments may be kept alive indefinitely by issuance of executions at intervals of not more than five years. (213 Neb. 243, 328 N.W.2d 759).

Stay.—On all court judgments for recovery of money only (except judgment rendered on appeal or writ of error or for money received in fiduciary capacity or for breach of official duty) there may be stay if within 20 days from rendition of judgment defendant gives surety bond for payment of judgment, interest, and costs. Period of stay

is three months if judgment does not exceed $50; six months if it exceeds $50 but does not exceed $100; nine months if it exceeds $100. No stay for more than nine months after rendition of judgment. (25-1505 and -1507). No appeal allowed after stay taken and no stay granted on judgment against surety for stay of execution. (25-1509).

Levy.—Officer having execution must immediately levy on goods and chattels; if none found, he must endorse "No goods" on writ and forthwith levy on lands and tenements of debtor. (25-1518). If execution is for delivery of possession of real property, writ must require officer to deliver property, particularly describing it, to party entitled thereto and may require officer to satisfy any costs and damages recovered in same judgment out of goods and chattels, or if none, out of lands and tenements, of judgment debtor. (25-1581).

Return.—Execution from court of record is returnable as soon as practicable after writ has been served. (25-1543).

Claims of Third Persons.—Officer levying on goods claimed by third person must give written notice to court, stating names of plaintiff, defendant and claimant, and schedule of property claimed. Court shall immediately enter notice upon docket and determine right of claimant to property in controversy. (25-1521).

Sale.—On sale of personal property, four successive weeks notice must be given by advertisement once per week in newspaper printed in county or if none, by putting up advertisements in five public places in county, two in precinct where sale to be held. (25-1525). On execution sale of personal property officer delivers same to purchaser without court action.

On sale of land at least four successive weeks' notice must be given by advertisement printed once per week in newspaper printed in county, or if none, in newspaper of general circulation therein and by putting up advertisement on court house door and in five other public places in county, two in precinct where land lies. (25-1529). Prior to execution sale, party seeking confirmation of sale must inform debtor of homestead exemption procedure. Notice shall be made by certified mail at least ten days prior to hearing on confirmation. (25-1531). Posting notice unnecessary if notice was published. (7 Neb. 456). Sale is held at county court house or at door of house in which district court last held. (25-1536). Sale is subject to confirmation, which may be made conditional on such terms as may be just and equitable. (25-1531). If not confirmed new sale is held. If sale is postponed it must be readvertised. (64 Neb. 472, 90 N.W. 245). After confirmation selling officer makes deed to purchaser, conveying all interest of judgment debtor. (25-1532).

No appraisement required before sale of either real or personal property.

Redemption.—Owner of land sold on execution may redeem at any time before sale confirmed by paying into court amount of decree with interest and costs; if land sold to any person not party to suit, owner redeeming must pay to purchaser 12% interest on purchase price from date of sale to date of redemption, or deposit same with clerk of court where decree or judgment rendered. (25-1530).

Supplementary Proceedings.—Upon return of execution unsatisfied in whole or part, judgment debtor may be required to appear and answer concerning his property. (25-1565).

Person indebted to debtor may be similarly examined. (25-1569).

Judge may appoint receiver of property of judgment debtor and may also forbid transfer or disposition of property of judgment debtor not exempt, and any interference therewith. (25-1573).

Notice must be given to all parties affected of time and place of application for receiver (25-1082 and -1089), but if delay is hazardous to rights of any party, court or judge may direct sheriff to take temporary possession of property and appoint early day for hearing of application (25-1083).

Judge may order any property of judgment debtor, not exempt by law, to be applied toward satisfaction of judgment; however, greater of 85% of wages of heads of families and 75% of other wage earners or 30 times minimum hourly wage, on weekly basis is exempt from attachment, execution and garnishment. (25-1558).

Arrest of Debtor.—If judge is satisfied, by affidavit of party or otherwise, that there is danger of debtor leaving state or concealing himself to avoid examination, he may issue warrant for debtor's arrest. Warrant issuable only by county judge or judge of district court of county in which debtor resides or may be arrested. If on examination it appears there is danger of debtor leaving state and that he has property which he unjustly refuses to apply to judgment, he may be ordered to give bond in sum prescribed by judge with one or more sureties that from time to time he will attend for examination before judge or referee as directed; on default of bond, may be committed to county jail by warrant of judge as for contempt. (25-1566).

EXEMPTIONS:

Federal exemptions provided by 11 U.S.C. §522(d) rejected. (25-15,105).

Any resident is entitled to exemption of immediate personal possessions, necessary wearing apparel, interest, not exceeding $1,500 in household goods, of interest not exceeding $2,400 in tools or supplies for use in family's principal trade or business (25-1556), and also, in lieu of homestead (see topic Homesteads), to further exemption of $2,500 in personal property to be selected by him (25-1552).

Following property also exempt: Burial lots used exclusively for burial purposes, not for profit (12-517); burial grounds so recorded in county clerk's office (12-520); crypts, lots, tombs, niches, vaults, sold or contracted to be sold by mausoleum associations, if for sole purpose of interment, used or held for burial purposes only, not for profit (12-605); fire fighting equipment, except as against voluntary liens by bill of sale, or security agreement as defined in Art. 9 U.C.C. (35-105); property of public library (51-218).

Sales and Use Tax Exemptions. (77-2704). State Board of Agriculture exempt from sales tax. (77-2704).

Debts Against Which Exemptions Not Allowed.—Claim for wages of clerks, laborers or mechanics or money due from attorney to person for whom he received same. (25-1552). Personal and property taxes. (25-1555).

Waiver of Exemption.—No statute.

See note at head of Digest as to 1998 legislation covered.

See Topical Index in front part of this volume.

EXEMPTIONS . . . *continued*

Necessity of Claiming Exemption.—Debtor claiming exemptions in lieu of homestead exemptions must file request for hearing in county issuing writ of execution. (25-1516; 25-1552). Debtor must also file list of all property owned indicating all exempt property and its value. (25-1552).

Annuities or Insurance.—All proceeds, not exceeding $10,000 in loan value, cash surrender value and all and every benefit accruing under any annuity contract, or under any policy or certificate of life insurance payable to beneficiary other than estate of insured and under any accident or health insurance policy is exempt from all claims of creditors of insured and of beneficiary if related to insured by blood or marriage unless written assignment to contrary has been obtained by claimant. (44-371).

Pensions.—Every resident who was soldier, sailor or marine disabled in U.S. service has exemption of all pension money and of all property purchased and improved exclusively therewith, not exceeding $2,000. (25-1559). In bankruptcy and collection of money judgment, interest under stock bonus, pension, profit-sharing or similar contract payable on account of illness, disability, death, age, or length of service is exempt to extent reasonably necessary for support of debtor and dependents unless certain conditions exist. (25-1563.01).

Earnings.—Maximum part of aggregate disposable earnings of individual for any work week subject to garnishment not to exceed lesser of: (1) 25% of his disposable earnings that week; (2) amount by which his disposable earnings for that week exceed 30 times federal minimum hourly wage; or, (3) 15% of his disposable earnings that week if he is head of family. (25-1558). Foregoing exemptions do not apply to any court order for support of any persons, any court order of bankruptcy under Ch. 13 of The Bankruptcy Act, or any state or federal tax debt. (25-1558).

Suit or action on claim or debt against laborer, servant, clerk or employee of individual, firm or corporation engaged in interstate business may not be commenced or prosecuted for purpose of seizing, attaching or garnishing wages of such person earned within 60 days prior to commencement of proceeding. (25-1560). Nonresident cannot claim benefits of this section. (77 Neb. 857, 110 N.W. 547). Plaintiff bringing such action becomes liable for amount of debt with all costs, expenses and reasonable attorney's fee and also to fine not exceeding $200 and costs. (25-1563).

Homestead Exemption.—See topic Homesteads.

See also topic Garnishment; category Estates and Trusts, topic Executors and Administrators.

FRAUDULENT SALES AND CONVEYANCES:

Uniform Commercial Code in effect. See category Business Regulation and Commerce, topic Commercial Code.

Dual contracts between identical parties one of which is inflated to obtain loan on real property constitutes misdemeanor; punishable by fine of $100-$500 or jail of five to 30 days. (76-2,106 to -2,108).

Uniform Fraudulent Conveyance Act repealed. (36-601).

Uniform Fraudulent Transfer Act adopted. (36-701 to -712).

Bulk Sales.—Bulk sales provisions of U.C.C. repealed. See category Business Regulation and Commerce, topic Commercial Code.

GARNISHMENT:

Garnishment is allowed and procedure to obtain writ is similar to attachment, except garnishment of wages only after judgment. (25-1010). See topic Attachment.

Property Which May Be Reached.—Debts and property that cannot be reached directly by attachment may be reached by garnishment. See 25-1010.

Property exempt from garnishment includes: proceeds or interest from payments or settlements under Workers' Compensation Act (48-149), except for attorney's fee approved in writing by district court (48-108); fraternal insurance benefits (44-1072); certain wages; all proceeds, cash values and benefits accruing under any annuity contract, policy or certificate of life insurance payable upon death of insured to beneficiary other than estate of insured, or under any accident or health insurance policy, to extent of $10,000 (44-371) (see topic Exemptions).

Grounds.—For grounds for issuing writ, see topic Attachment.

Jurisdiction.—Any court in which a civil action is pending has jurisdiction.

Proceedings to Obtain.—To garnish before judgment, plaintiff must file affidavit containing necessary allegations of affidavit of attachment (see topic Attachment) and in addition: (1) That plaintiff has good reason to and does believe that any person, partnership, or corporation to be named, (2) within county where action is brought, (3) has property of defendant, describing same (4) in his possession, and (5) that cannot be levied upon by attachment. (25-1010).

Garnishment in Aid of Execution.—After judgment, creditor may file affidavit setting forth amount due on judgment, interest, and costs, and that he has good reason to believe a person has property of, or is indebted to, judgment debtor and have garnishment issued. Except when wages are involved, garnishee must hold all property and credits of defendant, to extent of amount set forth in summons, in possession at time of service of summons and interrogatories until further court order. When wages involved, garnishee must pay employee earnings exempted from garnishment, and hold earnings remaining after such payment until further order of court. Thereafter, service of order of garnishment and further proceedings will be had same as in garnishment before judgment. (25-1056). Garnishment may become continuing lien on nonexempt earnings of judgment debtor. (25-1056).

Practice.—Interrogatories are filed with affidavit. Summons, order of garnishment, interrogatories (in duplicate), notice to judgment debtor form, and request for hearing to be served upon garnishee. (25-1010 and 1011). Garnishee is required to answer under oath within ten days. (25-1010). Supreme Court shall promulgate uniform garnishment forms for future use. (25-1011). If garnishee answers that he has money or property, he may pay same into court and will be discharged. (25-1027). If garnishee fails to answer he is presumed to be indebted to defendant to full amount of plaintiff's claim and upon notice as directed by court judgment may be entered against him. (25-1028). Garnishee may be permitted to retain property upon giving bond. (25-1029). If garnishee's answer is unsatisfactory or he fails to comply with order of court by delivering property, plaintiff may file application within 20 days for determination of liability of garnishee. Trial is had upon application of determination of liability and garnishee's answer and judgment rendered as facts justify. If plaintiff fails to file application within 20 days garnishee is released and discharged. (25-1030; 1030.01 and -1030.02). Fee for issuance of writ of execution, restitution, garnishment, attachment, and examination in aid of execution is $5 each. (25-1031.02).

Adverse Claims.—Any person claiming the money or property in the hands of garnishee may intervene and set up his claim thereto. Defendant in original action may also set out facts showing property not liable for plaintiff's claim. (25-1030.03).

Judgment.—Final judgment deferred until determination of action against defendant. (25-1031).

Earnings in excess of amount exempt subject to garnishment. See topic Exemptions.

HOMESTEADS:

Every head of a family is entitled to hold, exempt from execution or forced sale, a homestead consisting of the dwelling house in which he resides and its appurtenances and land on which it is situated. (40-101).

Limitation of value of property which may be held exempt is $10,000. (40-101).

Limitation of area which may be held exempt is 160 acres in country or two lots in incorporated city or village. (40-101).

Debts or Liabilities Against Which Exemption Not Available.—Debts secured by mechanics', laborers' or vendors' liens on the premises or by mortgage on the premises executed and acknowledged by debtor and his or her spouse, if any. (40-103).

Designation of Homestead.—Homestead of married debtor may be selected from separate property of husband or, with consent of wife, from her separate property; homestead of unmarried head of family may be selected from any of his or her property. (40-102).

Filing of application required. (40-107).

Alternative Homestead.—If debtor's residence and ground on which it is situated, with five acres surrounding same, amount to more than homestead exemption, other land on which no buildings or residence stand may be selected as homestead. (40-110).

Claim of Exemption.—When execution for enforcement of judgment not within 40-103 is levied upon lands or tenements, head of family may apply to court for order determining whether exemption exists. (40-105). Application must contain: (1) Fact that execution has been levied upon property claimed as homestead, (2) name of judgment creditor, (3) facts giving rise to exemption, and (4) value of exemption. (40-106). Service of notice must be ten days before hearing. (40-107).

Waiver of Exemption.—No statute.

Loss of Exemption.—If homestead abandoned or if owner fails to claim exemption.

Alienation or Encumbrance.—Both husband and wife must execute and acknowledge a conveyance or mortgage of the homestead of a married person. Special provisions for mortgaging property where spouse is incompetent. (40-104).

Proceeds of Sale.—If land claimed as homestead exceeds in value the amount of homestead exemption and cannot be divided, court orders sale at which no bid will be received unless it exceeds $6,500 and proceeds of sale up to $6,500 are paid to claimant and excess applied to satisfaction of execution. (40-111 to -112). Money so paid to debtor is within homestead exemption for six months thereafter. (40-113).

Homestead may be sold and another homestead selected or purchased. In case of sale proceeds up to $6,500 (or in case sale is under lien as against which exemption is not available, excess proceeds over amount of lien, up to $6,500) are exempt for six months. (40-116).

Rights of Surviving Spouse.—Subject to Uniform Probate Code elections.

Taxation.—See category Taxation, topic Administration, subhead Exemptions.

See also category Estates and Trusts, topic Executors and Administrators.

LIENS:

See Neb. UCC including 4-504, 7-209, 7-307, 8-103. See category Business Regulation and Commerce, topic Commercial Code.

Common law lien of vendor of real estate for balance of purchase price is recognized. (29 Neb. 672, 44 N.W. 857; 49 Neb. 369, 68 N.W. 531).

Artisans.—Person who makes, alters, repairs or in any way enhances value of any vehicle, automobile, machinery, farm implement or tool, or shoes horse or mule at request or with consent of owner has lien on property, while in his possession, for reasonable or agreed charge for work done or material furnished and may retain property until charges are paid. (52-201).

Jewelers, silversmiths and watch and clock repairers have a lien on articles left with or given to them for repairs, parts or work thereon for cost of repairs, parts or work thereon and materials. (52-301).

Cleaners, Repairers, etc.—Persons altering, cleaning, repairing or pressing garments or household goods, or storing garments after 90 days, have lien for their reasonable or agreed charges, enforceable by sale after prescribed notice to owner. (52-801 to -806).

Physicians, nurses and hospitals have lien for services and professional treatment on sum awarded (except in workers' compensation cases) on judgment or settlement as damages for personal injuries. (52-401).

Owner or operator of threshing machine or corn sheller has lien on grain, seed or corn which he threshes, hulls or shells with such machine, for agreed price or reasonable charge. Lien must be evidenced by notice filed with county clerk where work done within 30 days thereafter. On sale, lien shifts to proceeds. If sale made with consent of lienor, lien is lost unless lienor notifies purchaser in writing, if sale made within 30 days after work done. Lien is foreclosed like secured transaction under UCC. (52-501).

See note at head of Digest as to 1998 legislation covered.

See Topical Index in front part of this volume.

LIENS . . . *continued*

Landlord's Lien.—Nebraska has adopted Uniform Residential Landlord and Tenant Act. (76-1401 to -1449). Purported lien or security interest on behalf of landlord in tenant's household goods is unenforceable and distraint for rent is abolished. (76-1434).

Owner or Keeper of Hotel, Restaurant, Apartment House, Tourist Camp, or Rooming House.—Statutes allowing landlord to seize and hold property without prior notice or hearing held unconstitutional by Nebraska Federal District Court in Dielen v. Levine, 344 F. Supp. 823. (D. Neb. 1972). Provisions repealed 1981.

Owner of land has agister's lien on stock running at large for damage done by them, enforceable by sale after statutory notice. (54-402 and -407).

Person caring for livestock under contract has lien thereon for contract price of feed and care, which may be foreclosed like secured transactions under U.C.C. Art. 9. Prior to removal of livestock, person entitled to lien must file affidavit with Secretary of State. (54-201).

Services of Stallion, etc.—Owner, lessee, agent or manager of stallion, jack or bull has lien on mare or cow served and on colt or calf gotten for reasonable value or agreed price of service. Lien foreclosed by delivery to sheriff or constable of true copy of lien certified by county clerk, with affidavit of lienor or agent or attorney having knowledge of facts stating amount due. (54-202; -204; and -205).

Mechanics' Liens.—See subhead Construction Lien *infra*.

Construction Lien.—Nebraska Construction Lien Act adopted. (52-125 to -159). Lien covers both structure and land. No consensual improvements lien permitted. (52-126). Act limits liability of owner-occupied residential real property to payments made to general contractors after notice by claimant. (52-136).

Notices and Recordings.—

(1) Notice of commencement defines priority of lien and serves to limit liability. (52-145). Form—"Notice of Commencement"—Be advised (owner's name) of (owner's address) has contracted to benefit (legal description), (contractor's name) shall provide (general description of project) to (erect or repair) premises. This notice shall last for duration of (date). (Must be signed by owner).

(2) Notice of lien liability required to past owner of residential owner-occupied property on notice. May be sent any time after contracting. (52-135). Form—"Notice of Lien Liability" (claimant's name and address) hereby gives notice of a right to assert a lien against (address/legal of property) for services or materials (specify) furnished in connection with improvements of said property under a contract with (name and address of contracting party) for the amount of ($ amount—actual or estimate).

"WARNING . . . . . If you did not contract with the person giving this notice, any future payments you make in connection with this project may subject you to double liability."

You are also instructed to provide notice to claimant upon the filing of any Notice of Termination of the Notice of Commencement.

(3) Notice of termination of notice of commencement must be filed at least 30 days before termination date and serves to limit period of exposure. Copies must be sent to all parties having requested notice, and published for three consecutive weeks once per week in paper of general circulation. (52-146).

(4) Lien.—Recorded in county of property location and set forth subjected real estate description, description or services or materials, name and address of: Claimant, person against whom lien is claimed and claimant's contractor, amount claimed and date of last furnishing by claimant. (52-147).

Time for Filing.—Lien must be filed within 120 days of last furnishing materials or services and attaches as of date of recording of notice of commencement, or if no recording of notice then earliest of filing lien, or visible commencement of improvements. (52-137).

Duration of Lien.—From commencement of labor or furnishing of material until two years after filing lien. (52-140).

Transfer of Lien.—May be assigned with proper notice or bond substituted by owner. (52-149). In case of subdivisions liens can be apportioned to owners of record affected.

Foreclosure of Lien.—By civil action or suit in equity in district court brought any time after lien is filed and before the expiration of lien. (52-155). Procedure is practically same as foreclosure of real estate mortgage.

Release of Lien.—On payment of debt lienholder is required to release lien either on margin of record or filing release in the same manner as releasing a real estate mortgage. (52-142).

Railroads and Utilities.—Covered by special statute. (52-115 to -117).

On public works, mechanics' liens are not recognized; officials must take from contractor bond in sum not less than contract price with one surety company, conditioned for payment of all laborers and mechanics, and suppliers of material and equipment. Bond must run to board awarding contract, and no contract may be made until bond is first taken. (52-118). Action on bond must be brought within one year from settlement of principal contract. (52-118.02).

Transportation of Oil Field Equipment.—Owner must file verified claim within four months after delivery of equipment with county clerk of county in which equipment was delivered and serve copy upon owner or agent. Claim must set out amount claimed, items thereof, name of owner, name of contractor, name of claimant and description of property. If equipment is removed from point of original delivery to another county, within 30 days after receipt of notice of such removal claimant may file copy of lien with county clerk of county to which property was removed. Action to foreclose lien must be instituted within two years. (57-303 and -304).

Electrical Power or Seed.—Lien on crops produced therefrom. (52-1201).

As to other liens mentioned in various topics of this digest, see topics Attachment, Pledges; categories Business Regulation and Commerce, topics Carriers, Factors, Warehousemen; Civil Actions and Procedure, topic Judgments; Mortgages, topics Chattel Mortgages, Mortgages of Real Property; Property, topic Landlord and Tenant; Taxation, topics Administration, subhead Uniform Federal Lien Registration Act; Inheritance Tax; Property Tax; Transportation, topic Motor Vehicles.

Foreclosure.—In addition to the remedies listed above under the respective liens, all liens may be foreclosed by a common law suit in equity.

Redemption.—There is no right of redemption as to personal property after foreclosure sale and as to real property after the sale is confirmed by the court. Property may be redeemed any time prior thereto by paying or tendering the amount of the lien, including interest and accrued costs. (25-1530).

See also category Business Regulation and Commerce, topic Commercial Code.

Uniform Federal Tax Lien Registration Act adopted. (52-1001 to -1007).

PLEDGES:

Uniform Commercial Code in effect. See category Business Regulation and Commerce, topic Commercial Code.

RECEIVERS:

May be appointed by district court: (1) In action by vendor to vacate fraudulent purchase of property or by creditor to subject property or funds to his claim or between partners, limited liability company members or others jointly owning or interested in any property or fund on application of any party to suit, when property or fund is in danger of being lost, removed or materially injured; (2) in mortgage foreclosure when there is danger of loss, removal or material injury or probable insufficiency to discharge debts; (3) after judgment or decree, to carry same into execution or to dispose of property according to decree or judgment or to preserve during pendency of appeal; (4) in all cases provided for by special statutes; (5) in all other cases where receivers have heretofore been appointed by usages of courts of equity. (25-1081).

Proceedings for Appointment.—Receiver may not be appointed except in a suit actually commenced and pending and after notice to all parties to be affected thereby of time and place of application, names of proposed receiver, proposed sureties of receiver and of applicants. Service may be made on the party or his attorney and must be at least five days before proposed hearing. (25-1082).

Applicant must give bond to cover damages if receiver is wrongfully appointed. (25-1084).

Eligibility and Competency.—Cannot be attorney for either party or interested in the action. (25-1086). A trust company organized under the laws of this state may act as receiver. (8-207).

Qualification.—Receiver must give bond for the faithful performance of his duties. (25-1084).

Powers and duties are fixed by the order of appointment or subsequent orders issued by the court. (25-1087).

Compensation.—If appointed to preserve property or continue a business, receiver may be compensated by a fixed salary or a lump sum allowance. If appointed to liquidate a business compensation is based on a percentage of the cash accounted for. (25-1092).

Discharge.—By order of court appointing receiver.

DISPUTE RESOLUTION

ALTERNATIVE DISPUTE RESOLUTION:

Mandatory Dispute Resolution.—Pre-dispute arbitration agreements unconstitutional. (369 N.W.2d 69).

Voluntary Dispute Resolution.—See topic Arbitration and Award.

ARBITRATION AND AWARD:

Uniform Arbitration Act adopted with changes. (25-2601 to 2622). Claim for worker's compensation not subject to Arbitration Act. (25-2602). Court shall appoint odd number of arbitrators. (25-2604). Notification may also be served by certified mail not less than ten days before hearing. (25-2606). Within 60 days court shall confirm award. (25-2612). Nothing in Act shall empower Commission of Industrial Relations to order that any party under its jurisdiction submit to, or contract to submit to, arbitration. (25-2618).

DOCUMENTS AND RECORDS

ACKNOWLEDGMENTS:

Uniform Recognition of Acknowledgments Act adopted. (64-201 to -210). Acknowledgments may be taken by following officers:

Within State: Judge or clerk of any court, U.S. Magistrate or notary public (76-217); deputy clerk of district or county court in name of his principal (84-809); Secretary of State, or his deputy on Secretary's appointment in Secretary's absence or disability (84-507, and -508); register of deeds or deputy appointed by him under authority of county board and who has given bond (23-1505); county clerk or his deputy, under seal of county (23-1307). Officer can take acknowledgment only within his territorial jurisdiction. (76-217). Fee, 50¢. See topic Notaries Public.

Outside State but Within U.S.: Court of record or clerk or other officer holding seal thereof; commissioner appointed by Governor of Nebraska; notary public. (76-219).

Outside U.S.: U.S. minister plenipotentiary, extraordinary or resident chargé d'affaires, commissioner, commercial agent or consul appointed to reside in country where taken; notary public under his seal. (76-226).

Notarial Powers of Officers in U.S. Armed Forces.—See topic Notaries Public.

General Requirements.—Officer must know, or have satisfactory evidence of, identity of person acknowledging. (76-234). He must endorse on instrument his certificate, signed by himself, setting forth matter required to be done, known or proved, and names of witnesses examined before him, with their places of residence and evidence given. (76-233).

ACKNOWLEDGMENTS . . . *continued*

Qualification to Take.—Person having direct pecuniary interest in conveyance is disqualified to take acknowledgments of grantors. However, shareholder, director, employee, agent or elected or appointed officer of savings and loan association, industrial loan and investment company, insurance company, and co-operative credit association or credit union, and shareholder, officer or director of bank and attorney or any employee or associate of such attorney, or employee of professional corporation authorized to practice law, and real estate broker or salesman or employee or associate of such broker may, if notary public, take acknowledgment on instruments running to or from such concern. (64-211, 212, 213, 215). Attorney may not take acknowledgment when he is interested party. (207 Neb. 44, 295 N.W.2d 711).

Effect.—Properly acknowledged deed entitled to be recorded and to be read in evidence without further proof. Acknowledgment may be rebutted. (76-235).

Proof by Affidavit.—If grantor dies before acknowledgment, or his attendance cannot be procured, or he refuses to acknowledge, proof of execution and delivery of deed may be made by any competent subscribing witness before any officer authorized to take acknowledgment. Witness must state on oath his residence, and that he set his name to deed as witness, knew grantor, and saw him sign or heard him acknowledge he had signed. Officer must be personally acquainted with subscribing witness or have satisfactory evidence of his identity. (76-228). If all subscribing witnesses are dead or out of state, execution of deed may be proved by proof of handwriting of grantor and of any subscribing witness. (76-231).

Authentication of acknowledgment taken outside of state not required if taken before notary public or other officer using official seal. In other cases there must be attached certificate of clerk of court of record or proper certifying officer of county, district or state within which acknowledgment was taken under seal of his office, showing official character of person taking acknowledgment and that certifying officer is acquainted with handwriting of such person and believes signature to be genuine and that instrument is executed according to laws of place where taken. (76-242).

Certificate of authority for local notaries costs $10 and may be obtained from Secretary of State, Notary Office, State Capitol, Lincoln, NE 68509.

Forms.—No particular form is mandatory by statute. Statute does authorize following (64-206):

Form
Individual acting in his own right:
State of . . . .
County of . . . .
The foregoing instrument was acknowledged before me this (date) by (name of person acknowledged).
    (Signature of Person Taking
    Acknowledgment)
    (Title or Rank)
    Serial Number, if any)

Corporation:
State of . . . .
County of . . . .
The foregoing instrument was acknowledged before me this (date) by (name of officer or agent, title of officer or agent) of (name of corporation acknowledging) a (state or place of incorporation) corporation, on behalf of the corporation.
    (Signature of Person Taking
    Acknowledgment)
    (Title or Rank)
    (Serial Number, if any)

Partnership:
State of . . . .
County of . . . .
The foregoing instrument was acknowledged before me this (date) by (name of acknowledging partner or agent), partner (or agent) on behalf of (name of partnership), a partnership.
    (Signature of Person Taking
    Acknowledgment)
    (Title or Rank)
    (Serial Number, if any)

Attorney in Fact:
State of . . . .
County of . . . .
The foregoing instrument was acknowledged before me this (date) by (name of attorney in fact) as attorney in fact on behalf of (name of principal).
    (Signature of Person Taking
    Acknowledgment)
    (Title or Rank)
    (Serial Number, if any)

Public Officer, trustee, or personal representative:
State of . . . .
County of . . . .
The foregoing instrument was acknowledged before me this (date) by (name and title of position).
    (Signature of Person Taking
    Acknowledgment)
    (Title or Rank)
    (Serial Number, if any)

Note.—For seal, see general requirements. (64-210).

Validating Acts.—Defective acknowledgments taken by army officers (76-227), and those in which seals are defective (76-217.01), or by shareholders and officers of certain corporations (64-213), have been validated.

Alternative to Acknowledgment or Proof.—No statutory provision.
See category Property, topic Deeds.

AFFIDAVITS:

May be made either within or without state before any person authorized to take depositions, including attorney for client making affidavit. (25-1245). See category Civil Actions and Procedure, topic Depositions and Discovery.

General Requirements as to Administration.—No statute.

Use.—Affidavits may be used to verify pleadings, prove service of summons, notice or other process, in action, to obtain provisional remedy, examination of a witness, stay of proceedings, upon motion and in any other case permitted by law. (25-1244).

Affidavit explaining or correcting apparent defect in chain of title to real estate may be recorded as instrument affecting real estate, and record is prima facie evidence of facts recited therein. (76-271, and -272).

Referee in partition proceedings may receive affidavits of parties interested. (25-2189).

Form

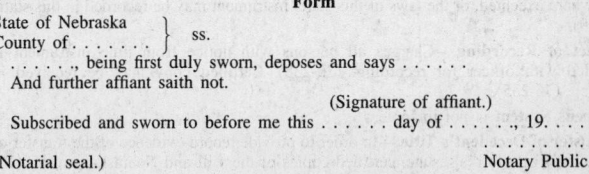

State of Nebraska ⎰
County of . . . . . . ⎰ ss.
. . . . . ., being first duly sworn, deposes and says . . . . . .
And further affiant saith not.
                        (Signature of affiant.)
Subscribed and sworn to before me this . . . . . . day of . . . . . ., 19. . . . .
                                        . . . .
(Notarial seal.)   Notary Public.

Alternative to Affidavit.—No statutory provision.

NOTARIES PUBLIC:

Must be resident of Nebraska and 19 years of age. (64-101). Must give bond in sum of $10,000. (64-102).

Authentication.—See topic Acknowledgments, subhead Authentication.

Seal.—Notary must have seal bearing words "State of Nebraska, General Notary" or "State of Nebraska General Notarial" and his name (64-210) and may show also date of expiration of his commission. All official acts must be authenticated by seal. (64-210).

Powers and Duties.—To administer oaths in all cases, take depositions, acknowledgments and proof of execution of deeds, mortgages, powers of attorney and other instruments in writing to be used or recorded in this or another state; to demand acceptance or payment of any foreign, inland or domestic bill of exchange, promissory note or other obligation in writing, and to protest same for nonacceptance or nonpayment, and give notice to endorsers, makers, drawers or acceptors of such demand or nonacceptance or nonpayment; to exercise and perform such other powers and duties as by law of nations, and according to commercial usage, or by laws of U.S., or of any other state or territory of U.S., or of any foreign government or country, may be exercised and performed by notaries public and over his signature and official seal to certify performance of such duties so exercised and performed. His certificate is presumptive evidence in all courts of this state as to facts therein certified. When notice or commission to take depositions has been deposited with notary, he may issue summons for witnesses and punish witnesses for neglect or refusal to testify when present by commitment to county jail for contempt and all sheriffs and constables within state must serve and return all process issued by notaries public in taking of depositions. (64-107, and -108).

Territorial Extent of Powers.—Notary may act throughout state. (64-102).

Expiration of Commission.—Must be stated in connection with notary's signature unless this date appears on his seal. (64-210).

Fees.—For each protest, $1; for recording protest, $2; for each notice of protest, $2; for taking affidavit, $2; for administering oath, $2; for taking deposition, $1 for each one hundred words; for certificate and seal, $5; for taking acknowledgment, $5. (33-133). Mileage at rate provided in 81-1174 - 81-1176 for state employees.

Certificate of Authority.—See topic Acknowledgments, subhead Authentication.

Officers of U.S. Armed Forces.—Authorized to perform all notarial acts. If instrument shows signature, rank and branch of service of officer, no further proof of authority required. (76-227).

RECORDS:

Uniform Commercial Code in effect. See category Business Regulation and Commerce, topic Commercial Code.

In counties having population of more than 20,000, and not more than 400,000 county clerk is ex officio register of deeds. If population of county which has separate office of register of deeds falls below 20,000 after establishing register of deeds or has separate office prior to July 10, 1990, and has population below 20,000, office of register of deeds shall continue. (32-518).

Recordable Instruments.—Deeds, mortgages, and all instruments affecting title to real property (76-238); copy of will with certificate of probate (76-248); articles of incorporation and appointment of resident agent (21-21,203); certificate of partnership (67-101).

Place of Recording.—Deeds, instruments affecting real property, and certified copy of will covering real property, in office of register of deeds of each county where said real estate or any portion thereof is located. (76-245). Certificate of incorporation must be filed with Secretary of State and county clerk of county where principal office is located. (21-21,203). Designation of registered office and agent of foreign corporation

RECORDS... *continued*
must be filed with Secretary of State and with register of deeds of county where registered office is located. (21-21,205). Notice of assignment of accounts receivable is filed with county clerk and controlled by Uniform Commercial Code.

For list of Counties and County Seats see first page for this state in Volume containing Practice Profiles Section.

Filing Under Commercial Code.—See category Business Regulation and Commerce, topic Commercial Code, subhead Material Variations from 1962 Text and 1972 and 1977 Official Amendments, §9-401; also subhead Filing Fees.

Requisites for Recording.—Deeds, mortgages, or instruments affecting real estate must be acknowledged or proved to be entitled to record. (76-241). Witness not required. Only originals will be recorded.

Recording Fees.—For recording deed, mortgage, release, recording and indexing will or decree in testate estate, proof of publication, or any other instrument, $5 per page plus 50¢ per lot or section. For certified copy, $1.50 for certification plus $1.50 per page. (33-109). For filing financing statement, continuation, amendment, separate assignment, or full or partial release, $6 plus $4 per additional name, 50¢ per lot, 50¢ per attachment, plus $3 additional if form is smaller than 5" x 8" or larger than 8½" x 11". No fee for termination statement. (Neb. U.C.C. 9-403).

Foreign Conveyances or Incumbrances.—If executed in accordance with laws of place where executed, or the laws of this state, instrument may be recorded in this state. (76-219).

Effect of Recording.—Charges all persons with notice from time instrument is deposited with officer for recording. (76-238). Certified copy may be received in evidence. (76-235).

Torrens System is not in force.

Transfer of Decedent's Title.—In order to provide record evidence of the transfer of a decedent's title to real estate, certified copies of the will and Nebraska probate (30-238) or, in case of intestacy, certified copy of death certificate and an inheritance tax determination order must be filed in office of register of deeds of each county in which such real estate is located.

Vital Statistics.—Department of Health has supervision of registration of vital events. (71-601). Fee for certified copy of record $9. (71-612). Records may be obtained from Bureau of Vital Statistics, P.O. Box 95007, Lincoln, Nebraska 68508.

Establishing Birth Record.—Any person born in Nebraska whose birth is not registered within one year of date of birth may file application for delayed registration of birth with Bureau of Vital Statistics. If birth occurred after 1905, applicant must pay $7 search fee. Applicant must be 18 years of age; however, application of minor may be made by father, mother, guardian or attendant at birth. Application must be accompanied by three independent supporting records which are specified in statute. Registrations not supported by minimum supporting evidence will be denied birth certificates. Denial may be appealed by petition to county court of Lancaster county, county of petitioner's residence or county in which birth is claimed to have occurred. If court finds from evidence that person was born in this state, it shall order delayed birth certificate issued. Department of Health shall charge $9 fee for each application submitted. (71-617.01 to 71-617.15). As to procedure in case of adopted child, see 71-626, 627.

Death Certificate.—Undertaker and physician last in attendance must execute certificate on form prepared by Department of Health showing cause of death, etc., and file same with Registrar where death occurred prior to burial or removal of the body from the county. (71-605). Where death occurred while in military service United States certificate may be recorded with Department of Health. (71-605.01). See also category Estates and Trusts, topic Death.

SEALS:

Uniform Commercial Code in effect. See category Business Regulation and Commerce, topic Commercial Code.

Private seals have been abolished and are not required on any instrument. (76-212). Corporation may adopt a seal. (21-21,201 et seq.).

Effect of Seal.—None. (76-212 and -213).

VITAL STATISTICS:

See topic Records.

EMPLOYMENT

LABOR RELATIONS:

Hours of Labor.—Any person, firm or corporation running assembly plant, workshop or mechanical establishment must provide 30 min. lunch break. (48-212).

Child between 14 and 16 may not work, without permit, after 10 P.M. Child under 14 may not work after 6 P.M. without permit. (48-310).

Wages.—Employer required to pay wages on regular days designated or agreed upon. Before paydays can be altered, 30 days notice must be given to employee. On termination of employment, wages due next regular payday or within two weeks, whichever is sooner. If wages not paid within 30 days of regular payday, employee may institute court proceeding. (48-1230).

For assignment of wages, see category Debtor and Creditor, topic Assignments.

Child Labor.—Child under 16 may not be employed in (1) service for wages or (2) be under contract for hire or (3) in any business service during hours when public schools are in session or (4) more than 48 hours in any one week, more than eight hours per day, nor before 6 a.m. or after 8 p.m. (48-302). Child under 16 may be employed on certificate approved by superintendent of schools. (48-302 and -303). No child under age of 16 may be employed in any work dangerous to life, limb, health or morals. (48-313). Employers who are parents or persons standing in loco parentis to child employee are exempted from certain child labor law requirements. (48-302.02).

Female Labor.—Unlawful to discriminate wage rate on basis of sex for comparable work. (48-1219 to -1227).

Labor Unions.—Closed shop prohibited. (Const. Art. XV, §§13-14-15; 48-217 to -219).

Unlawful for alien to be elected to or hold office in a labor or educational organization. (4-106).

Labor Disputes.—Legal picket must display sign with name of protesting organization. Interfering with legal picketing subjects person to fine of not more than $500 or imprisonment of not more than three months, or both. No statutory prohibition against issuing injunctions in labor disputes in proper cases. Unlawful picketing includes: (1) Use of threatening language toward worker or immediate family to (or attempt to) induce or influence employee to quit or refrain from seeking employment, or by communicating with person or immediate family for such purpose; (2) following or interrupting employee against will; (3) menacing, threatening, coercing, intimidating, or frightening in any manner; (4) committing assault on employee; (5) picketing or patrolling place of work or residence of employee or street, alley, road, highway, or any other place where employee may be and against his will. (28-1317, and -1318). Mass picketing prohibited. Mass picketing includes: (1) More than two pickets within 50 feet of entrance; (2) more than two pickets within 50 feet of other pickets; (3) pickets constitute obstacle to free ingress and egress. (28-1317 to 28-1320).

Court of Industrial Relations has jurisdiction of labor disputes involving public utilities, governmental services, or between labor organization and city of more than 5,000 or any city under civil service. (48-810). State Employees Collective Bargaining Act: (1) Recognizes right of state employees to organize for purpose of collective bargaining; (2) requires state employee be represented by exclusive bargaining agent to negotiate and enter agreements with chief negotiator of Division of Employee Relations. (81-1370). Act provides that state employees be divided into 12 units by occupation. (81-1373). Act provides for appointment of mediator mutually selected by parties if impasse is reached. (81-1381). Act prohibits unfair labor procedures and provides for appeal procedures. §48-810 et seq. amended to reflect adoption of Collective Bargaining Act. State or governmental subdivision cannot be compelled to enter employment contract with labor organization. (48-810.01).

Discrimination.—Unlawful employment practice to: (1) Fail or refuse to hire or to discharge any individual or to otherwise discriminate against any individual, because of race, color, religion, sex, age, disability, pregnancy, marital status, or national origin; (2) to limit, advertise, solicit, segregate, or classify employees because of race, color, religion, sex, age, disability, pregnancy, marital status, or national origin. (48-1001 to -1125). Employer includes state of Nebraska, governmental agencies and political subdivisions. Jurisdiction lodged with Equal Opportunity Commission. (48-1007).

Workers' Compensation Act (48-101 et seq.) applies to the State of Nebraska and every governmental agency created by it and to every employer having one or more employees in the regular trade, business, profession or vocation of such employer, except railroad companies engaged in interstate commerce and employers of household or domestic servants or farm laborers. (48-106).

It provides for compensation by: (1) Action at law; or (2) elective compensation. Employers and employees are presumed to accept terms of compensation schedule as outlined in statute, for injuries arising out of and in course of employment. It is not defense in Workers' Compensation proceeding: (a) That employee was negligent, unless negligence was wilful or that employee was intoxicated; (b) that injury was caused by negligence of a fellow employee; or (c) that employee assumed risks inherent in, or incidental to, or arising from failure of employer to provide and maintain safe premises and suitable appliances. (48-102). If employer does not carry policy of workers' compensation insurance or qualify as self-insurer, employer loses right to assert three defenses mentioned above in any negligence action later brought by employee. (48-103).

A special court, known as "Nebraska Workers' Compensation Court," has original jurisdiction to determine all controversies arising under Nebraska Workers' Compensation Laws. Court consists of seven judges. First hearing on any dispute is held before one member of court, who makes his findings and award. If either party is dissatisfied, trial de novo is held by court en banc. Appeal may be taken to Supreme Court. Appeals are given preference as to time of hearing. (48-152 to -191). See also category Courts and Legislature, topic Courts.

All claims against state shall be filed with Risk Manager of State Claims Board. There is Workers' Compensation Claim Fund established in state treasury to be administered by Risk Manager. (81-8,212).

Benefits are as follows:

Total Disability.—During total disability 66⅔% of wages received but not more than $265 per week; minimum benefit of $49 per week. (48-121.01).

Partial Disability.—66⅔% of the difference between wage received at time of injury and earning power thereafter but not more than $200 per week and for not more than 300 weeks after date of accident. If total disability precedes or follows partial disability number of weeks paid for total disability shall be deducted from 300 weeks maximum allowed for partial disability. (48-121).

Loss of Limb, etc.—In accordance with schedule. (48-121).

Death leaving one or more persons dependent 66⅔% of wage but not more than $245 (48-121.01) nor less than $49 per week, provided if wage is less than $49 per week, then full amount of wage. Payments to spouse, children and/or dependent blood relatives according to schedule. Payments not more than $245 (48-121.01) or less than $49 per week. Schedule complicated and interrelated. (48-122). Expenses of burial, not exceeding $6,000 are also paid to dependent or personal representative. (48-122). Nonresident alien dependents receive same as resident dependents except employer may commute future installments by paying lump sum. (48-138). Consul or his representatives shall be sole representative for adjusting and collecting compensation due alien dependent. (48-144).

Occupational diseases are within the Act. (48-101). Last injurious exposure rule followed.

Attorney fees will be added to award which is affirmed on rehearing or appeal if employer took appeal. (48-125).

See note at head of Digest as to 1998 legislation covered.

See Topical Index in front part of this volume.

NE – 20

LABOR RELATIONS . . . *continued*

Employers' Liability Act is included in Workers' Compensation Act.

As to employees of railroads and street railways, assumption of risk doctrine abolished (25-21,184), and contributory negligence does not bar recovery for injury, comparative negligence rule being adopted (25-21,185).

Unemployment Compensation.—Employment Security Law governs unemployment compensation. (48-601 to -671). Unemployment Compensation Fund administered by Commissioner of Labor. (48-617). Amount of weekly benefit payable to individual determined by reference to unemployment benefit table. (48-624). Unemployed individual eligible to receive benefits if individual: (1) has registered for work and continued to report for work at unemployment office; (2) has made claim for benefits; (3) is able to work, and is available to work; (4) has been unemployed for waiting period of one week; and, (5) has for any benefit year, beginning on or before Dec. 31, 1998, within base period, been paid total sum of wages for employment equal to not less than $1,200 of which at least $400 has been paid in each of two quarters in base period and for any benefit year, beginning on or after Jan. 1, 1999, within base period, been paid total sum of wages for employment equal to not less than $1,600, of which sum at least $800 has been paid in each of two quarters in base period, and subsequent to filing he has insured work in at least four weeks. (48-627; L.B. 225). Commissioner of Labor may require employer to submit quarterly wage reports. (48-612). Child support may be withheld from unemployment compensation. (48-647).

WORKERS' COMPENSATION LAW:

See topic Labor Relations.

ENVIRONMENT

ENVIRONMENTAL REGULATION:

General Supervision.—Environmental Control Council and Department of Environmental Quality. (81-1501, et seq., controlling environment of water, air and land).

Prohibited Acts of Pollution.—Discharging into air, land or water any pollutants or wastes which are below standards set by Council. Any of following acts done without first obtaining a permit: (a) Discharge of any pollutant into waters of state; (b) construction, installation, modification or operation of any disposal system or part thereof; (c) increase in volume or strength of any waste in excess of permissive discharge as specified, under any existing permit; (d) construction, installation or operation of any industrial, commercial, or other establishments or any extension or modification thereof or addition thereto, operation of which would cause an increase in discharge of waste into air, waters or land of State or would otherwise alter physical, chemical or biological properties of air, water or land of State in any manner not already lawfully authorized; (e) construction or use of any new outlet for discharge of any waste into air, waters or land of State; (f) construct and operate livestock waste control facility without first obtaining permit. (81-1506; L.B. 1209).

No person shall dispose of any refuse, garbage or rubbish at any place, except disposal area licensed as provided by Act. (81-1516).

It shall be unlawful for any property owner or person in lawful possession of property to allow accumulation of junk on property that is not purely agricultural in character to extent that such accumulation is a potential hazard to health.

Section 46-601 et seq. regulates use of ground water under Ground Water Management Act.

Low-Level Radioactive Waste Disposal Act governs disposal of low-level radioactive waste. (81-1578 to 81-15,116).

Wastewater Treatment Facilities Construction Assistance Act governs construction of sewage and wastewater treatment plants. (81-15,147 to -15,158).

Buffer Strip Act governs use of and government compensation for strips of vegetation used to intercept or trap field sediment, organics, pesticides, and other potential pollutants before they reach surface water. (L.B. 1126).

Wellhead Protection Area Act governs protection of underground water supplies from contaminants. (L.B. 1161).

Livestock Waste Management Act governs prevention and reduction of livestock pollutant discharge to state waters. (L.B. 1209).

Enforcement.—(81-1504). Department of Environmental Control shall be enforcing agency.

In all cases, Department shall make every effort to obtain voluntary compliance through warning, conference, or any other appropriate means prior to initiating enforcement proceedings. (81-1510).

Where a violation of Act is suspected, a notice may be served upon violator specifying provision violated, and including an order for corrective action. Such order shall become final unless, no later than 30 days after date notice and order are served, person named therein requests in writing a hearing before Director. Upon such request, Director shall hold a hearing. In lieu of an order, Director may require that alleged violator appear before Director for a hearing at a time and place as specified in notice to answer charges complained of. (81-1507).

Any duly authorized officer or representative of Department may at any reasonable time and with proper warrants enter and inspect any property for purpose of ascertaining state of compliance with this Act and rules and regulations in force pursuant thereto. Nothing in this section shall be construed to prevent prompt inspection without consent or appropriate warrant in acute and compelling emergency situations when there is neither sufficient time nor opportunity to obtain a search warrant. If requested, owner or operator of premises shall receive a report setting forth all facts found which relate to compliance status. (81-1511).

Department has exclusive general supervision over administration and enforcement of Act, and all rules, regulations and orders thereunder. (81-1504).

Penalties.—Any person who violates any provision of Environmental Protection Act, Integrated Solid Waste Management Act or Livestock Waste Management Act (Acts), by knowingly and willfully committing any of following offenses is guilty of Class IV felony: (a) violating any rule or regulation, permit, license or permit or license condition or regulation of: water pollution control law pursuant to National Pollutant Discharge Elimination System; air pollution control law; hazardous waste control law; mineral production, mineral exploration or injection control law; (b) making any false statement, representation or certification in any application, label, manifest, record, plan, or other document required to be filed or maintained by Acts, rules or regulations; (c) falsifying, tampering with or rendering inaccurate any monitoring device or method used or required for compliance with any permit or license or Acts or rules or regulations; or (d) transporting hazardous waste to unpermitted facility. (81-1508).

Any person who knowingly and willfully violates any solid waste control law or livestock control law or rule, regulation, permit, license, or permit or license condition or limitation shall be guilty of Class I misdemeanor. (81-1508). Any person who knowingly and willfully violates any other provision of Acts or rule or regulation adopted and promulgated pursuant to Acts shall be guilty of Class III misdemeanor. Each violation under this section (81-1508) shall be actionable. In case of continuing violation, each day shall constitute separate offense. Any person who knowingly and willfully violates this section shall be subject to personal liability. In assessing amount of any fine, court shall consider degree and extent of violation, size of operation, any economic benefit derived from noncompliance. Each day upon which such violation occurs shall constitute separate violation. Any person guilty of violation of Act which causes death to fish or wildlife, shall in addition to other penalties be liable to pay to state any sum reasonably necessary to restock fish, or replenish wildlife. In addition, injunction may be obtained pursuant to this Act on showing that some person or persons are violating or about to violate provisions of Act, and such injunction shall be granted without necessity of showing lack of adequate remedy at law. (81-1508).

Laws make it unlawful for any person: (a) To refuse right of entry and inspection to any authorized representative of department who is acting under provisions of permit issued by department; (b) to violate any air, water, or land quality standards, any emission or effluent standards or limitation, any permit or license condition or limitation, any order of director, or any monitoring, reporting, or record-keeping requirements pursuant to Acts, rules or regulations adopted and promulgated pursuant to Acts; (c) to make any false statement, representation, or certification in any application or other document required to be maintained by such acts, rules or regulations; (d) to falsify, tamper with, or render inaccurate any monitoring device or method used or required for compliance with permit or license or such acts, rules or regulations; or (e) violate any other provision or fail to perform any other duty imposed by such acts, rules or regulations. (81-1508). Each violation of 81-1508 or 81-1506 shall subject person to civil penalty of no more than $10,000 per day. In case of continuing violation each day shall constitute separate offense. Amount of penalty shall be based on degree and extent of violation, size of operation, and any economic benefit derived from noncompliance. (81-1508.01).

Permits.—All persons engaged or desiring to engage in operations which result or which may result in air, water or land pollution must secure a permit from Department of Environmental Control and must establish proof of financial responsibility prior to installation or operation or continued operation. (81-1505, -1506). Variance may be obtained. (81-1513).

ESTATES AND TRUSTS

ADMINISTRATION:

See topic Executors and Administrators.

Administration.—See topic Executors and Administrators.

Direct Action Against Insurers.—See category Transportation, topic Motor Vehicles, subhead Direct Actions.

DEATH:

Death is presumed in case of continued and unexplained absence from home for five years where person not heard of or from (30-2207), and may be presumed after shorter period where circumstances show exposure to danger probably resulting in death (96 Neb. 130, 147 N.W. 112; 18 Neb. 664, 26 N.W. 460). Estate of person domiciled in state so presumed dead may be administered by county court of domicile. (30-2210 and -2211).

Survivorship.—Uniform Simultaneous Death Act was adopted in 1947. (30-121 to -128). See topic Executors and Administrators. Heirs must survive decedent for 120 hours. (30-2304).

Action for Death.—Action lies for wrongful death, if commenced within two years thereafter. Must be brought by personal representative of decedent for exclusive benefit of widow, widower and next of kin. Recovery of settlement must be paid into court for payment and distribution to widow or widower and next of kin in proportion pecuniary loss suffered by each bears to total pecuniary loss suffered by all such persons. Claim may not be compromised without approval of court. (30-809 and -810). No statutory limitation of amount which may be recovered.

Death certificate may be obtained from Bureau of Vital Statistics, Dept. of Health, Lincoln Executive Building, 1003 "O" St., Lincoln, Neb. 68508. Fee, $7, unless requested by U.S. Veterans' Admin., in which case such certificate is provided free of charge. (71-612). Local deputies are appointed in some counties and copies may be obtained at same fee if death occurred in that county. See also category Documents and Records, topic Records, subhead Vital Statistics.

Uniform Anatomical Gift Act adopted. (77-4801—4820).

DESCENT AND DISTRIBUTION:

Uniform Probate Code adopted at 30-2201 et seq. See topic Executors and Administrators.

Escheat.—If decedent leaves no surviving spouse or kindred his real and personal property escheats to state. (30-2305).

Uniform Disposition of Unclaimed Property Act adopted. (69-1301 to -1329).

See note at head of Digest as to 1998 legislation covered.

See Topical Index in front part of this volume.

DESCENT AND DISTRIBUTION . . . *continued*

Personalty.—Can be passed by separate written list (30-2338), or collected and distributed by affidavit when value of net estate does not exceed $25,000. (30-24, 125).

Real Property.—Deed of distribution of real property must be recorded with register of deeds. (30-24, 105).

EXECUTORS AND ADMINISTRATORS:

Trustees.—Subject to Nebraska Trustees' Powers Act. (30-2819 to -2826).

Uniform Probate Code adopted, with modifications. (30-2201 to -2902).

Material Variances From Uniform Probate Code.—

§1-201. Definitional differences.

§1-401. Notice of any hearing, unless other specific notice requirements are provided, must be given by publication for three consecutive weeks with last publication at least three days before hearing and by mailing copy of notice to each interested person at least 14 days before hearing. (30-2220).

§2-301. Nebraska eliminates provisions relating to intentional omissions and transfers outside will, unless waived. (30-2320).

§2-404. Court may require notice before distribution of assets and satisfaction of family allowances. (30-2325).

§2-503. Holographic will, to be valid, must have indication of date; either written, or from extrinsic evidence; or be only writing. (30-2328).

§2-513. Requirement of indication of date; or from extrinsic evidence; or be only writing, or contain no inconsistency with any other like writing added to language list provisions. (30-2338).

§3-108. Will may be formally admitted to probate after three years from informal probate for purpose of proving it as document of title. (30-2408).

§3-301. Notice of informal probate must be given by newspaper publication for three weeks within 30 days thereof. (30-2415).

§3-307. Notice of appointment must be given by newspaper publication for three weeks within 30 days thereof. (30-2420).

§3-803. Time for filing claims under Nebraska Code is two months, rather than the four months of Uniform Probate Code; provision for late claims also included. (30-2485).

§3-906. If distribution is of real property, deed shall be recorded with register. (30-24,105).

§7-101. Registration of living trust is discretionary rather than mandatory. (30-2801).

Uniform Anatomical Gift Act adopted. (71-4801—4820).

Uniform Principal and Income Act not adopted, but see Nebraska Principal and Income Act. (30-3101 to -3115).

Uniform Fiduciaries Act not adopted.

Uniform Simplification of Fiduciary Security Transfers Act adopted. (24-621 to -631).

Uniform Simultaneous Death Act adopted. (30-121 to -128).

TRUSTS:

Uniform Probate Code adopted as Nebraska Probate Code at 30-2201 et seq. See topic Executors and Administrators.

There is no statute concerning creation of trusts or determination of rights of trustee and cestui que trust, except as same may come within provisions of statute of frauds or statutes concerning wills or conveyances; except for Trust Deeds Act relating to trust deeds held as security for performance of an obligation. (76-1001 to -1018).

Gifts to Minors.—See category Family, topic Infants.

Fiduciary Investments.—Unless otherwise authorized by the instrument creating the trust, trustees, executors, guardians and administrators, whether appointed by Nebraska court, or acting under other authority, having funds for investment, must invest same in investments nature of which prudent men would retain for their own account. (24-601).

Trust funds received by administrators, executors, trustees or guardians may be kept invested in the securities received by them unless otherwise ordered by court of appointment or unless instrument under which such trust was created directs change of investment, and they are not liable for any loss due to depreciation of such securities. (24-602 and -603).

Common trust funds permitted to be established by Bank and Trust Company for investment of fiduciary funds. (24-601.05).

Securities in Name of Nominee.—Trust securities may be registered either in name of trustee or nominee without words indicating the fiduciary capacity if certain requirements are met. (24-604 and -605).

Uniform Principal and Income Act not adopted.

Uniform Fiduciaries Act not adopted.

Uniform Simplification of Fiduciary Security Transfers Act adopted. (24-621 to -631).

Perpetuities.—See category Property, topic Perpetuities.

Employees' Trust Plans.—Trustee must be licensed to do business in Nebraska. (24-620).

Accounting.—Trustee shall keep beneficiaries reasonably informed of trust and its administration. Upon reasonable request, trustee must provide report. (30-2814).

WILLS:

Uniform Probate Code adopted as Nebraska Probate Code at 30-2201 et seq. See topic Executors and Administrators.

Probate.—County court has exclusive original jurisdiction in probate of wills. (Const., art. V, §16).

In all matters arising under Nebraska Probate Code, appeals shall be allowed as provided in Neb. Rev. Stat. §§24-541.01 to 24-541.10 and 24-551. (30-1601).

Contest.—There is no provision for contesting a will after it has been probated. If probate was obtained by fraud, the judgment could be attacked the same as any other judgment.

Evidence.—Uncontested will may be admitted into evidence in any court proceeding upon certification by clerk magistrate. (30-2402).

Recording.—Probated will affecting real estate may be recorded with register of deeds. (76-248).

Legacies are payable at time fixed by court for distribution (see topic Executors and Administrators) and do not bear interest.

Unclaimed legacies or sums due creditors are payable to county judge (24-560) who holds them for three years on behalf of legatee or creditor. If no claim is made within that time he notifies State Treasurer and pays such fund into permanent school fund on direction by state treasurer. (24-561 to -563).

Uniform Disposition of Unclaimed Property Act adopted. (69-1301 to -1329).

Uniform Anatomical Gift Act adopted. (77-4801 to -4820).

Living Wills.—No legislation.

FAMILY

ADOPTION:

Minor child may be adopted by any adult person and any adult child may be adopted by spouse of such child's parent. (43-101). If adopter is married, husband and wife must join in petition and jointly adopt said child, unless he or she is parent of child. (43-101). Adoption of American Indian children governed by Nebraska Indian Child Welfare Act. (43-1501).

Consent Required.—Of: (a) Minor if over 14 years of age or adult child of adopting person's spouse; (b) any district or separate juvenile court having jurisdiction of custody of minor by virtue of divorce proceedings; and (c) both parents, if living, of child born in lawful wedlock; or surviving parent of child born in lawful wedlock; or mother of child born out of wedlock unless alleged father files notice of intent to claim paternity with Department of Social Services within five days after birth of child, in which case natural father must consent. Consent of parent is not required if parent: (1) Has relinquished child for adoption by written instrument; (2) has abandoned child for six months next preceding filing of petition; (3) has been deprived of his parental right by any court of competent jurisdiction; or (4) is incapable of consenting. (43-104, -104.02). Where consent of both parents of child born in lawful wedlock is not required, consent may be given by: (1) Department of Social Services if minor has been committed to state home (Nebraska Center for Children and Youth) for dependent children (43-906); (2) licensed agency for placement of children to which child has been relinquished for adoption; or (3) guardian or guardian ad litem of minor, with approval of court having jurisdiction of guardianship. Substitute consent does not apply to biological father whose consent is not required. (43-105). Consent must be in writing, signed in presence of at least one witness and acknowledged before officer who may not also be witness. (43-106).

Specific consent requirements for adoption of foreign born children. (43-104.07).

Conditions Precedent.—(1) Adopted child must reside with adoptive parent for at least six months next preceding entry of decree of adoption, and where petition of adoption filed after Sept. 1, 1988; (2) copy of child's and biological parent's (if available) medical history filed with court; and (3) relinquishing parent signs affidavit acknowledging receipt and explanation of non-consent form. (43-109).

Notification of Father.—When child claimed born out of wedlock and biological mother contacts adoption agency or attorney to relinquish rights to child, or biological mother joins in petition for adoption filed by her husband, agency or attorney contacted must attempt to establish identity of biological father and inform biological father of right to execute relinquishment and consent to adoption or denial of rights. (43-104.08).

Proceedings.—Adopter must file signed and verified petition accompanied by required consent of adoption forms, affidavits regarding vital statistics of child, and completed replacement adoptive home study. Adoption decree not issued until six months after adoptive home study completed. (43-102). Members of armed forces in state for one year deemed resident of state and county where stationed. (43-102.01). Court thereupon fixes time for hearing and directs what notice, if any, shall be given. (43-103). County judge shall request Department of Social Services or placement agency to examine allegations and propriety of such adoption and report its findings; discretionary in adoption by stepparent. (43-107).

At hearing child, unless over age of 14, and adopting parents must appear in person before judge; court may accept affidavit of absent spouse who is in armed forces and it appears to court absent spouse will not be able to be present for one year because of his military assignment. (43-108).

Department or agency may charge reasonable fee to recover expenses in amount established by department or agency in rules and regulations. Department may waive fee if requesting party shows that fee would work undue financial hardship on party.

Fee for filing petition for adoption in county court is $18 if child was born in state, $7 if child was born out of state. Birth certificate $6 from State Department of Health.

Decree of adoption may not disclose that child was born out of wedlock. (43-109).

Name of adopted child may be changed by decree. (43-109).

Effect.—Adopted child and adopting parents bear all the legal relations and consequences of the natural relation of child and parent. (43-110). The natural parents of the adopted child are relieved from any further parental duties or responsibilities for such child and have no rights over such child or over his or her property by descent and distribution. (43-111).

Setting Aside Adoption.—Adoption conclusively presumed valid in all respects unless action challenging validity brought within two years. (43-116).

Special Needs Child.—Department of Social Services may make payments on behalf of child with special needs after legal completion of child's adoption. Child so adopted

---

See note at head of Digest as to 1998 legislation covered.

See Topical Index in front part of this volume.

ADOPTION . . . *continued*

shall have been child for whom adoption would not have been possible without financial aid. (43-117 and 43-118).

Access to Records.—Adopted child 25 years of age has access to names of relatives or to original birth certificate if consent form has been filed by relatives. (43-130, and -131).

DISSOLUTION OF MARRIAGE:

Divorce is called dissolution of marriage. Subject governed by 42-341 to 42-823.

Grounds for Dissolution of Marriage.—Finding by court that marriage is irretrievably broken. (42-361).

Legal Separation.—No statutory grounds are stated for decree of legal separation. Apparently within court's discretion. (42-347, -350, and -368).

Jurisdiction.—In District Court or County Court of county in which one of parties resides. (42-348).

Citizenship Requirements.—None.

Residence Requirements.—No action for dissolution can be brought unless at least one party has actually resided in state for one year prior to filing of petition, with bona fide intent of making state his permanent home, or unless marriage was solemnized in state and at least one party has resided in state from time of marriage. Persons serving in armed forces who have been continuously stationed at any military base or installation in Nebraska are deemed residents of Nebraska. (42-349).

Venue is in county where one of the parties resides. (42-348).

Process.—Respondent must be properly served with summons and copy of petition or enter appearance in case. (42-355). See topic Process.

Pleading.—Petition must contain (1) Name and address of petitioner and his attorney; (2) name and address of respondent, if known; (3) date and place of marriage; (4) name and date of birth of each child whose custody and welfare might be affected; (5) statement of whether petitioner is a party to any other action for divorce, separation or dissolution, and if so, where such action is pending; (6) statement of relief sought; and, (7) allegation that marriage is irretrievably broken. (42-353). Responsive pleading, if any, must be filed and served on petitioner within 30 days of service on respondent. (42-354). No final hearing or trial may be had until 60 days after service or entry of appearance. (42-363).

Decree is final when rendered. If appeal is instituted within 30 days after date decree is rendered, decree not final until proceedings are finally determined or one of parties dies. (42-372). Property settlements can provide for immediate waiver of rights to decedent's estate. (30-2316). Filing fee for dissolution of marriage action is $84.

Temporary Alimony.—Discretionary with court. (42-357).

Allowance for Prosecution of Suit.—Discretionary with court. (42-367).

Alimony.—Court may order payment of such alimony by one party to the other as is reasonable, having regard for circumstances of parties, etc.; reasonable security for payment may be required by court; except for amounts accrued prior to service of a petition to modify, orders of alimony can be modified or revoked on a showing of good cause, but where no alimony was provided for in original decree, such decree cannot be modified to award alimony. Except as otherwise agreed by parties or by court order, alimony terminates upon death of either party or remarriage of recipient. (42-365).

Division of Property of Spouses.—Generally, Nebraska falls into marital property category of property division. Court may include inherited property and retirement plans in marital estate. While criteria for reaching reasonable division award of alimony may overlap, the two serve different purposes and are to be considered separately. (42-365). Where dissolution or separation is decreed, parties can enter into written property settlement regarding support, maintenance and property as to themselves and any minor children. Agreement, except for terms relating to support and custody of minor children, is binding upon court unless it finds agreement is unconscionable. Unless agreement provides to contrary, it becomes part of decree. Terms of agreement can be enforced by all available remedies. Alimony may be ordered in addition to property settlement. Except for terms concerning custody and support of minor children, decree may preclude or limit modification of its terms. (42-366).

Change of Spouse's Name.—When pleading is filed pursuant to 42-353, 42-354 or 42-373, either petitioner or respondent may include request to restore his or her name. (42-380).

Custody and Support of Children.—Court may make suitable orders concerning custody and support of children and occupancy of either party's premises during pendency of suit and after final decree. (42-357). Custody shall be determined on basis of children's "best interests". Grandparent visitation rights provided for in certain instances. Court may order employer of parent-employee to withhold for support of minor child; Department of Social Services may apply to set off against debtor's income tax refund any debt owing for support of minor child. (42-364.01 et seq.). Support can be modified upon showing change of circumstance. (202 Neb. 345, 275 N.W.2d 287). Court may order, on its own motion or at request of party, genetic testing to determine paternity.

Lien of Judgment for Alimony and Child Support.—Same as other judgments except judgment for alimony ceases to be a lien upon property ten years from date of either entry of judgment, most recent payment or most recent execution, whichever date is latest; judgment for alimony or child support not lien after ten years after youngest child becomes of age or dies, or most recent execution, whichever is later, and such lien shall not be reinstated. (42-371; 157 Neb. 57, 58 N.W.2d 600). Delinquent child support payments draw interest at legal rate and such interest shall be computed as simple interest. (42-358.02). With approval of court rendering decree person to whom child was committed may execute partial or total release of child support judgment. (42-371). On application of person desiring release and upon notice to person having custody of child, court may release lien. (42-371). Upon application and notice, court may release

either general or specific property from alimony lien. (42-371). Judgment for child support does not abate upon death of judgment debtor.

Remarriage.—No restrictions after decree has become final.

Foreign Divorces.—Uniform Divorce Recognition Act adopted 1949. (42-341 to 42-344). Invalid if both parties were domiciled in Nebraska at divorce. (42-341).

Separation Agreements.—See subhead Division of Property of Spouses, supra.

Annulment of Marriage.—See topic Marriage.

Curative Act.—Divorce decrees entered prior to Aug. 27, 1951, conclusively presumed valid regardless of record or failure of record unless action is brought prior to Aug. 27, 1953, attacking validity. (42-345). Decrees entered after Aug. 27, 1951, conclusively presumed valid regardless of record or lack of record unless action brought within two years from entry of decree attacking validity. (42-346).

DIVORCE:

See topic Dissolution of Marriage.

GUARDIAN AND WARD:

Uniform Probate Code adopted with modifications. (30-2201 to -2902). Uniform Durable Power of Attorney Act adopted. (30-2664 to -2672).

County courts have exclusive original jurisdiction to appoint guardians and settle their accounts. (Const., art. V, §16; 24-517). Venue is in court of county in which minor resides or, in case of nonresident minor, of county where property is situated. (30-2609). Conflicts of venue and change of venue. (30-2212).

Selection of Guardian.—Surviving parent may appoint guardian by will. (30-2606). Where no such appointment guardian is selected by court, unless minor is over 14, in which case minor may select guardian subject to approval of court. (30-2610).

Eligibility and Competency.—Parents or surviving parent are natural guardians. (30-2608). Court may appoint as guardian any person whose appointment would be in best interests of minor. Court shall appoint person nominated by minor 14 or older, unless contrary to minors best interests. (30-2610).

Guardian or conservator may be required to give bond for faithful performance of duty. (30-2640).

Real Estate.—Generally under Uniform Probate Code property of ward, including real estate is subject to control of conservator rather than guardian. Guardian has limited power with court approval. (30-2613).

Listing for Taxation.—Guardian must list ward's personal property for taxation. (77-1201, -1229).

Investments.—Guardian or conservator may invest funds in securities in which he has no interest. (24-601). See category Estates and Trusts, topic Trusts.

Securities in Name of Nominee.—See category Estates and Trusts, topic Trusts, subhead Securities in Name of Nominee.

Use of Principal.—Under certain circumstances guardian of minor may, with approval of court, use principal for support and education of minor. (30-2613).

Gifts to Minors.—See topic Infants. Uniform Gifts to Minors Act adopted. (38-1001 to 38-1010).

Accounting and Settlement.—Guardian must, upon expiration of guardianship, settle account with court or ward and deliver and pay over effects then in his hands. (30-2613[1][d]).

Termination of Guardianship.—On minor's becoming of age, being adopted or married or dying; or death, resignation or removal of guardian (30-2614), or incompetent being adjudicated competent (30-2623), or death of guardian or ward (30-2622).

Uniform Veterans' Guardianship Act not adopted.

Insane Person.—Guardian appointed by county court on application of relative or friend of incompetent or any interested person after notice to incompetent. (30-2619). County court of county where nonresident incompetent owns property may also appoint guardian for nonresident. (30-2618). See Uniform Durable Power of Attorney Act. (30-2664 to -2672).

Temporary guardian may be appointed pending hearing on appointment of regular guardian. (30-2626).

Foreign Guardians.—No provision. However foreign conservator may act with all powers of local conservator after filing with court. (30-2661). See Uniform Durable Power of Attorney Act. (30-2664 et seq.).

Fees Payable to County Court.—Appointment of guardian or conservator, $25; consolidated appointment of both guardian and conservator, $25; successor guardian or conservator, $22; temporary guardian or temporary or special conservator, $25; protective order in absence of guardianship or conservatorship, $25. Only one fee assessed if more than one ward listed in petition for guardian or conservator. For each report filed, $5 while guardianship or conservatorship pending; appointment of custodian, $25. (33-126.02).

Uniform Child Custody Jurisdiction Act adopted. (43-1201 to -1225).

Uniform Fiduciaries Act not adopted.

Uniform Simplification of Fiduciary Security Transfers Act adopted. (24-621 to -631).

See also category Estates and Trusts, topic Executors and Administrators.

HUSBAND AND WIFE:

Separate Property of Married Women.—Property which woman owns at time of marriage and issue thereof and property which comes to her by descent, devise or gift of any person except her husband or which she acquires by purchase or otherwise, is her sole and separate property, and is not subject to disposal of her husband or liable for his debts; but all property of married woman, not exempt by law from sale on execution or

HUSBAND AND WIFE . . . *continued*

attachment, is liable for debts contracted for necessaries furnished her family after execution against husband has been returned unsatisfied. (42-201).

Any woman married out of state, if her husband afterwards becomes resident of the state, enjoys all rights as to property acquired by laws of any other state, territory or country or by virtue of any marriage contract or settlement made out of this state. (42-204). Nothing in statute invalidates any marriage settlement or contract. (42-205).

Contracts.—Married woman may bargain, sell and convey her real and personal property and enter into any contract concerning same, as freely as married man (42-202), but in order for her contract to bind her it must be made in reference to, or with intent to bind, her separate property, trade or business (121 Neb. 847, 238 N.W. 750). She may contract with her husband as with third person and may become bound as surety for her husband or any other person. She may carry on any trade or business and perform any labor or service on her own account and her earnings are her sole and separate property, to be used and invested by her in her own name. (42-203).

Antenuptial Contracts.—Uniform Premarital Agreement Act adopted. (42-1001 to -1011).

Torts.—A married woman is liable for her torts as though unmarried. (25-305).

Actions.—Married women may sue and be sued as if unmarried (25-305), and defend in own name; if sued with husband may also defend his right if he neglects to do so (25-306). One spouse can sue the other to enforce contract and property rights (9 Neb. 16, 2 N.W. 221; 72 Neb. 845, 101 N.W. 989); interspousal tort immunity abrogated (203 Neb. 537, 279 N.W.2d 382).

Agency.—Agency may be created by slight circumstances. (212 Neb. 826, 326 N.W.2d 179).

Conveyances of Real Estate.—If both husband and wife are residents of this state, each must join in a conveyance of the real estate of the other in order to cut off his or her statutory rights therein. (200 Neb. 672, 264 N.W.2d 865; see 40-103). Married woman who joins in conveyance of her husband's property for sole purpose of relinquishing her statutory rights therein is not bound by convenants in deed. (42-207; 109 Neb. 716, 192 N.W. 195).

Sale or Encumbrance of Household Goods.—Conveyance by way of mortgage or otherwise, or sale or transfer of household goods or any interest therein owned by husband and wife and used by them for their dwelling house, or purchased or held by them or either of them for use of family, is void unless executed and acknowledged by both spouses like real estate conveyance. Special provision is made, however, for conveyance or mortgage where one spouse is insane or incapable of executing instrument. (42-501).

Antenuptial Debts of Wife.—Property of husband is not liable for debts of wife contracted before marriage. (42-206).

Desertion and Nonsupport.—Any person who fails to provide support legally obligated to provide, on conviction is guilty of class II misdemeanor; if in violation of court order class IV felony. (28-706).

Enforcement of Child Support.—Court may at any time appoint an attorney to initiate contempt proceedings for failure of any party to pay permanent child support upon motion of any aggrieved party in cases where payments are more than 30 days in arrears. (42-358).

Uniform Interstate Family Support Act adopted. (42-701 to -751). Complies substantially with standard Act.

Uniform Divorce Recognition Act.—(42-341 to -344).

Community Property Law has been repealed.

See also topic Guardian and Ward; category Estates and Trusts, topic Executors and Administrators.

INFANTS:

Age of majority, 19 for both sexes. (43-2101).

Emancipation.—Marriage of male or female terminates minority. (43-2101).

Contracts.—Infant's indorsement of negotiable instrument passes property therein although infant incurs no liability thereon. Building and loan association stock may be subscribed for, held, transferred, surrendered, withdrawn or forfeited and payment thereon received and receipted for by any minor with same effect as adult, except that neither the infant nor his estate is bound on subscription to stock except to extent of payment actually made thereon. (8-318).

Infant may withdraw money from savings account. (8-135). Infants may have building and loan association accounts and withdraw funds therefrom. (8-318).

Ratification of Contracts.—Common law applies.

Earnings are property of wage earner, parent is only custodian.

Uniform Child Custody Jurisdiction Act adopted. (43-1201 to -1225).

Uniform Gifts to Minors Act adopted. Age of majority under Act is 19. (43-2201-2210).

Uniform Securities Ownership by Minors Act not adopted.

Actions.—Infant sues by guardian or next friend and defends by guardian ad litem. Dismissal of action by guardian or next friend must be by approval of court. (38-114; 25-307, -310).

Infant heir may maintain action for injury to real estate in time of his ancestor as well as in his own time, unless barred by statute of limitations. (25-2133).

Children under age of four or weighing less than 40 pounds must be restrained with appropriate child passenger restraint system while riding in vehicle driven by Nebraska resident. Also, safety belt restriction on children between four and five or over 40 pounds and under age five. (39-6,103.01).

Parents liable for willful and intentional infliction of personal injury or destruction of property by minor or unemancipated children limited to actual expenses, not to exceed $1,000 for each occurrence. (43-801).

Termination of Parental Rights.—Parental rights may be terminated when in best interest of juvenile and juvenile has been abandoned, neglected, parents unfit or upon conditions leading to juvenile court jurisdiction. (43-292). After termination, care of child may be awarded to State Department of Social Services; Department may consent to adoption. (43-293). See also topic Adoption, subhead Notification of Father.

Adoption.—See topic Adoption.

Foster care subject to periodic review. (43-1301 to -1318).

Legal age for consumption of alcohol is 21 years. (53-180).

MARRIAGE:

Age of consent: Males and females 17. (42-102).

Consent Required.—Where party is a minor, written consent under oath required from (1) either parent or parents, if living together, (2) parent having legal custody of minor if parents are separated, (3) surviving parent if one is dead, (4) guardian if both parents dead or guardian has actual custody of minor. Affidavit of person giving consent is sufficient proof of his authority to consent. (42-105).

License must be obtained from a Nebraska county clerk. License must be used within one year of issuance. (42-104). It is not necessary that either applicant appear in person before county clerk, but both applicants must sign application and swear to it before person authorized to take acknowledgments. Female applicant for license must file certificate stating female has immunological response to rubella unless applicant is over 50, surgically sterilized or has evidence of prior test confirming immunity.

Ceremony.—Marriage must be solemnized by authorized person, otherwise invalid. (42-104). Ceremony may be performed by any judge or minister of the Gospel authorized by usages of church to which he belongs. (42-108). Marriage according to rites and customs of religious society to which parties belong is valid. (42-115). No particular form of ceremony is required, but parties must declare that they take each other as husband and wife, and there must be two witnesses besides person performing ceremony. (42-109). Marriage not invalidated by lack of authority of person performing ceremony if consummated with full belief of either party that marriage was lawful. (42-114).

Report of marriage must be made to county clerk within 15 days after marriage. (42-108).

Record.—See category Documents and Records, topic Records, subhead Vital Statistics.

Common law marriages cannot be contracted in Nebraska since 1923. However, common law marriage validly contracted in another state is recognized. (161 Neb. 782, 74 N.W.2d 919).

Proxy Marriages.—If both parties to the marriage are members of a religious sect which recognizes proxy marriages and the ceremony is conducted in accordance with the rights and customs of the said sect, the marriage is presumably valid; but there is no authoritative decision on this point in Nebraska.

Marriages by Written Contract.—No statute.

Prohibited Marriages.—Marriage is void where: Either party has husband or wife living or has mental disorder at time of marriage; parties (born in or out of wedlock) related as parent and child, grandparent and grandchild, brother and sister (whole or half blood), first cousins of whole blood, uncle and niece or aunt and nephew. (42-103; 28-702). Person with venereal disease may not marry. (42-102). If such person does marry, marriage is voidable, not void. (144 Neb. 763, 14 N.W.2d 613).

Foreign marriage, valid where contracted, is valid in Nebraska. (42-117).

Affirmance.—If validity of marriage denied by either party, the other may file petition for affirmance. (42-120).

Annulment.—If marriage is solemnized when either party is under age of legal consent and they separate during such non-age and do not cohabit together afterwards or if consent of one of parties was obtained by force or fraud, and thereafter there is no voluntary cohabitation, marriage is voidable. (42-118). When marriage is supposed to be void or validity doubted either party may file petition for annulment in district court of county or county court where one party resides; proceedings same as in divorce cases. (42-119). Actions for annulment brought in same manner as actions for dissolution, except only residency requirement is that petitioner be actual resident of county in which petition is filed. (42-373). Grounds for annulment: (1) Marriage prohibited by law; (2) impotency; (3) bigamy; (4) mental illness or retardation; (5) force or fraud. (42-374). Petition may be filed by parent or next friend. Annulment cannot be had if parties freely cohabited after ground for annulment has terminated or become known to innocent party. (42-375). Children born of annulled marriage are legitimate unless otherwise decreed by court. (42-377). If court finds a party entered into marriage in good faith supposing other party to be capable of marrying, and marriage is declared a nullity, such fact is grounds for compensatory damages and award of costs and attorney fees. (42-378).

Time Within Which Annulment Action Must Be Commenced.—No special statute.

Antenuptial Contracts.—See topic Husband and Wife.

INSURANCE

INSURANCE COMPANIES:

Companies may be organized for practically all kinds of insurance. (44-201). They may be formed on stock or mutual or fraternal plans, or, with number of exceptions, on assessment plan. (44-202). Domestic company may perform any activity complementary or supplementary to its insurance business and may in certain circumstances act as trustee or fiduciary in administration of pension, profit-sharing and other benefit plans. (44-202). Mutual insurance company must maintain minimum surplus of at least $2,000,000. (44-219). All lines insurers must maintain minimum surplus of at least $2,000,000. (44-243).

See note at head of Digest as to 1998 legislation covered.

See Topical Index in front part of this volume.

INSURANCE COMPANIES . . . *continued*

Supervision.—Insurers Supervision, Rehabilitation and Liquidation Act adopted to protect interests of insureds, claimants, creditors and public. (44-4801 to -4861). Insurers Examination Act adopted to provide system for examining activities and financial condition of insurance companies. (44-5901-5910). Department of Insurance has general supervisory power and may adopt rules and regulations. It issues all certificates and licenses and must require domestic company to keep its books and records so as to verify annual statements. It must cause domestic company to be examined at least once every four years. It may engage services of independent agents if deemed necessary; costs to be paid by company being examined. It must cause foreign companies to be examined at least every five years and may require production of all books and papers. (44-101.01, -106). Director establishes specific standards for group or individual medicare supplement policies. (44-3604).

Policies.—Standard provisions are fixed by statute for: Fire insurance (44-501), life or endowment policies (44-503), and sickness and accident insurance (44-710). Protection required against uninsured and hit-and-run vehicles unless rejected by named insured. (60-577). No prerequisite that judgment first be obtained against uninsured motorist as condition precedent to bringing suit. (209 Neb. 396, 308 N.W.2d 503). Cancellation of sickness and accident insurance must be by registered mail. (44-710.04). No policy of group life insurance shall be delivered unless it is issued under 21-17,116, 44-1602 to-1606.01, 44-1615 or under policy issued to similar group which director of insurance deems subject to issuance of group life insurance policy. (44-1601).

Plain Language.—Nebraska Life, Sickness and Accident Insurance Policy Readibility Act. (44-3401 to -3408).

Prepaid Limited Health Service Organization Act adopted. (44-4701 to -4727).

Property and Casualty Insurance Data Reporting Act adopted. (44-4601 to -4607).

Rates.—Combination to control rates is prohibited and license of offending companies shall be revoked. (44-360). Property and Casualty Insurance Rate and Form Act adopted (44-5001 to -5039); fire, marine, and inland marine rates (44-1443 to -1486). Appeal in accordance with Administrative Procedure Act. (44-1485).

Rebates are forbidden. (44-361). Those in violation may be subject to penalties. (44-367).

Unfair practices are defined and prohibited. (44-1524, -1525, -1540, and -2143, 1994).

Reports.—On or before Mar. 1 of each year every company authorized to do business in state must file annual report on forms furnished by Department. (44-322). Fraternal beneficiary society must file report at same time (44-1097), also must provide valuation of certificates in force Dec. 31 previous.

No insurance company can transact business without certificate of authority from Department of Insurance. Certificate expires Apr. 30 and must be renewed annually. (44-303).

Agents and Brokers.—Insurance Producers Licensing Act (44-4001 to -4044) provides:

Agent soliciting application for insurance presumed representing insurer. (44-4004). Must be licensed, unless: (1) Strictly salaried clerical or administrative services; (2) person who secures and furnishes information for group life, enrolling individuals under such insurance plans or issuing certificates thereunder, or administering plans, if no commission paid, or (3) person administering employee benefit plan if person/employee is not compensated by insurance company. (44-4006).

Agent may qualify for resident license only if principal place of residence in state. (44-4007). Agent may qualify for license as nonresident if holds resident license in any state, territory or province of Canada. (44-4008). Reciprocity. (44-4009).

No person is eligible for life insurance broker's license unless first having been licensed as life and accident and health agent or broker in this or another state for three years. Must be licensed as personal and commercial lines agent in Nebraska or other state for three years prior to eligibility as casualty broker. Must be resident to become broker. (44-4012). Must be 19. (44-4017).

Application for license made to Director of Insurance and accompanied by fee established by Director subject to statutory limitations. (44-4019). Written exam required. (44-4020). Exam fee not exceeding $50. (44-4402). Re-examination can be required by director if lack of competence suspected. (44-4025).

Temporary license can be issued: (1) To surviving spouse, personal representative, legal guardian, employer of personal representative, or employee of deceased licensed agent; (2) to designee of licensed agent entering active service in armed forces; (3) in discretion of Director to agency required to be licensed; (4) in other circumstances which Director deems to be in public interest. (44-4036).

Agent is responsible in fiduciary capacity for funds received. (44-4038).

Each insurer must notify Director of appointment of agent within ten days of execution. Appointment valid if mailed to department within ten days of execution. Appointment shall be on Director's forms and insurer shall pay fee as established by director not to exceed $10. Notice of termination must be given Director within five days of termination. (44-4035).

Signature or countersignature is not required unless laws or regulations of another state require signature or countersignature by agent resident of that state on policy written by nonresident agent or broker of that state, in which case policy written by agent of that state who is nonresident in Nebraska must be signed or countersigned by Nebraska resident agent (44-4041). No policy deemed invalid due to absence of signature or countersignature.

Any license valid on operative date of Act expired Apr. 30, 1985. (44-4044).

Other Fees.—Filing of documents, papers, statements, etc., required by law upon entry of foreign or alien insurers or rating bureaus $300. Amendment to articles of incorporation, $20. Restated articles of incorporation, $20. Renewing certificate of authority, $100, unless domestic assessment association, doing business in less than 31 counties, then $20. (44-114[1]-[4]). Annual statement, $200. Certificate of valuation, deposit, compliance, or other certificate, $5. Filing reports required from unincorporated mutual associations, $5. Copying 50¢ per page. Review of documents for admission of foreign or domestic insurer, nonrefundable, $1,000. (44-114[7]-[11]).

Bond for license under §44-5503 (surplus lines) at least $100,000, depending on circumstances. (44-5504).

Investments.—Insurers Investment Act adopted. (44-5101 to -5154).

Foreign company shall file in office of Department of Insurance authenticated copies of articles of incorporation or charter and by-laws, including all amendments, with certificate of officer having custody of articles or charter, under seal of his office, that company is authorized under laws of state or country where incorporated to do business therein; certificate showing amount of capital stock and assets; and duly certified copy of last annual statement made in state or country where organized, and must furnish such other information as Department requires. (44-304). Capital funds must be invested in class of securities specified for domestic insurance corporation, except that Department of Insurance, in its discretion, may recognize as legal investments securities authorized by law of company's home state or country. (44-5104). Such company must have unimpaired capital stock, if stock company or unimpaired net assets, if mutual company, equal to minimum paid up capital or assets required for domestic company. Alien company must deposit with insurance department of some state of U.S. not less than $200,000 in approved securities for benefit of policyholders in U. S. (44-305).

Motor Club Services Act adopted to provide services to motorists, including insurance for injury or death. (44-3701 to -3721).

Nebraska Hospital-Medical Liability Act adopted to provide alternative method for determining malpractice claims. (44-2801 to -2855).

Nebraska Hospital and Physicians Mutual Insurance Association Act adopted. (44-2901 to -2918).

Process.—Procuring certificate of authority to do business in this state constitutes sufficient contact with state for exercise of personal jurisdiction over company. (44-135 and -1204).

Retaliatory statute authorizes the Department of Insurance, in case any state imposes on Nebraska companies requirements as to deposits, taxes, fines, penalties, license fees, loan, surrrender or nonforfeiture values to policy holders, certificates of solvency and good management, etc., in excess of gross requirements imposed by Nebraska on foreign companies generally, to impose the same requirements on companies of such state. (44-150 to -152).

Taxation.—Every insurance company, except fraternal benefit societies, transacting business in Nebraska shall on or before Mar. 1 of each year pay to Director 1% of gross amount of direct writing premiums received by it during preceding calendar year; except that: (1) For group sickness/accident rate is .5 of 1%, (2) for property/casualty, excluding individual sickness/accident, rate shall be 1%. Taxable premiums shall include premiums paid on lives of persons residing in this state whether or not insurance was written in Nebraska. (77-908).

If tax not paid, Director may revoke license. (77-911).

Surety and Guaranty Companies.—See topic Surety and Guaranty Companies.

SURETY AND GUARANTY COMPANIES:

These are classified as surety, mortgage guaranty or financial guaranty insurance companies, and are subject to same general provisions as regards incorporation, operation and supervision as other insurance companies. Department of Insurance has general supervision. (44-101.01).

Organization.—Five or more persons may form insurance corporation. Articles of incorporation must be approved by Dept. of Insurance before being filed in offices of Secretary of State and County Clerk. (44-205).

Rights and Powers.—Authorized surety company may execute any bond required in connection with any official proceeding, in lieu of two or more individual sureties.

Foreign companies may qualify in Nebraska upon filing copy of articles of incorporation, by-laws and a report with Department of Insurance and having same accepted by that department. Capital and surplus requirements must be met. (44-304 to 307).

Rates.—Department of Insurance has authority to investigate and fix maximum schedule of rates or premiums for various classes of bonds and undertakings issued and certify same to authorized companies. (44-387). Exacting a higher rate subjects officer, agent or company to fine or imprisonment or both. (44-390).

Taxation.—Surety companies are taxed the same as insurance companies. (See topic Insurance Companies.)

INTELLECTUAL PROPERTY

TRADEMARKS AND TRADENAMES:

Registration of Tradename.—Any person who adopts a tradename for use in this state may file in office of Secretary of State on a form furnished by Secretary of State an application for registration of tradename setting forth: (a) Name and street address of applicant for registration; and, if corporation, state of incorporation; (b) tradename sought to be registered; (c) general nature of business in fact conducted by applicant; (d) length of time during which tradename has been used in this state; (e) acknowledged signature of applicant; and (f) filing fee of $100. (87-210).

Tradename consisting of immoral, deceptive, or scandalous matter, misleading or so resembling tradename already registered in this state or name of corporation doing business within state, so as to be confusing or deceptive shall not be registered. (87-209).

Registration of tradename shall be effective for term of ten years, and within six months prior to expiration date of term registration may be renewed for successive ten year periods. Renewal fee is $100. Secretary of State shall notify registrants of necessity of renewal within year next preceding expiration of ten years from date of registration or of last renewal, by writing to registrant's last known address. (87-211).

TRADEMARKS AND TRADENAMES . . . *continued*

Any tradename so registered shall be assignable with goodwill of business. Assignment fee is $5. (87-212).

Violation in use of tradename subjects such violator to civil liability to registrant of tradename. (87-216).

Any person, not excepted by §87-210, who shall engage in or transact any business in state under trade name without registering such trade name shall be guilty of class V misdemeanor. (87-220).

Registration of Trademark.—Any person who adopts or uses a trademark in this state may file in office of Secretary of State, an application for registration of that trademark setting forth: (a) Name and street address of person applying for such registration; and, if corporation, state of incorporation; (b) goods in connection with which mark is used and mode or manner in which mark is used in connection with such goods and class in which such goods fall; (c) date when trademark was first used anywhere and date when it was first used in this state by applicant or his predecessor in business; and (d) statement that applicant is owner of trademark and that no other person has right to use such trademark in this state either in identical form thereof or in such near resemblance thereto as might be calculated to deceive or to be mistaken therefor. Application for trade-mark must have applicant's signature acknowledged and must be accompanied by specimen or facsimile of such trademark and filing fee of $100. (87-113 and -114).

Trademark, by which goods or services of any applicant for registration may be distinguished from goods and services of others shall not be registered if it consists of immoral, deceptive, scandalous, misleading matter, or so resembles a trademark already registered or used in this state so as to cause confusion or deception. (87-112).

Registration shall be effective for a term of ten years, and within six months prior to expiration of term registration may be renewed for successive ten year periods. Renewal fee is $100. Secretary of State shall notify registrants of necessity of renewal within year next preceding expiration of ten years from date of registration or of last renewal, by writing to registrant's last known address. (87-115).

Any trademark and its registration hereunder shall be assignable with goodwill of business in which trademark is used, or with that part of goodwill of business connected with use of and symbolized by trademark. Filing fee is $5. (87-116).

Violations in use of trademark subject such violator to civil liability to owner of registered trademark. (87-121).

Assignment.—Trademark (87-116) or tradename (87-212) is assignable with goodwill of business in which it is used.

Owner of farm, ranch or home may have name thereof recorded with county clerk of county where located (fee $5 per page), and thereupon no other farm, ranch or home in same county may use such name unless plain designating words are prefixed or affixed or both. Transfer of registration may also be recorded. (61-105).

Fair Trade Act unconstitutional. (159 Neb. 703, 68 N.W.2d 608).

Uniform Deceptive Trade Practices Act adopted. (87-301 et seq.). See category Business Regulation and Commerce, topic Consumer Protection.

TRADE SECRETS:

Nebraska has adopted Uniform Trade Secrets Act which makes illegal misappropriation or disclosure of trade secret. (87-501 et seq.). Statute of limitations is four years. (87-506).

LEGAL PROFESSION

ATTORNEYS AND COUNSELORS:

Integrated Bar.—Nebraska bar has been integrated under rules promulgated by Supreme Court. All practicing attorneys must be members of Nebraska State Bar Association, annual dues $102.50 for first five years and $205 thereafter; judicial active $205; inactive fee is $27, senior active (75 years old) is $41.

Jurisdiction over Admission.—Supreme Court has control over admission to practice (7-102) and has promulgated rules for admission.

Admission on Examination.—Examination is given twice annually by Commission appointed by Supreme Court. Application for admission must be made at least four weeks prior to examination. Applicant must be citizen of U.S., 21 years old, resident of Nebraska, of good moral character and hold LL.B. or J.D. degree from accredited law school. Examinations are held on day set for National Multi-state Bar Examination and day following each year. List of subjects to be covered by examination is published by Commission and includes use of Multi-State Exam and Nebraska law on Agency, Commercial Paper, Conflicts, Corporations, Equity, Family, Jurisdiction, Partnerships, Probate, Property, Practice, Professional Responsibility, Reg. Industry, Tax, Trusts & Wills. Multi-State scores of other states not accepted. Fee of $200 must accompany application. Applicants must also pass Multi-State Professional Responsibility Exam.

Registration as Law Student.—Not required.

Admission Without Examination.—Supreme Court may admit on motion, without examination, any practicing attorney upon proof of his having, at time of his admission in another state, qualifications equal to those presently required in this state or upon proof that he has practiced law at least five full years in another state. Fee, $300. (7-109).

Admission Pro Hac Vice.—Practicing attorneys admitted in other states may be admitted on motion and taking oath for appearance in a particular case if associate is a Nebraska practicing lawyer; not required to comply with this provision if from state whose laws permit practicing attorneys of other states to practice in their courts without association with local attorney. (7-103).

Powers.—May execute in name of client bond for an appeal, or any other paper necessary and proper for prosecution of suit already commenced; may bind client by agreement in respect to any proceeding within scope of proper duties and powers; may receive money claimed by client in action or proceedings, during pendency thereof or

afterward, unless previously discharged by client, and upon payment thereof, may discharge claim or acknowledge satisfaction of judgment. (7-107).

Disability as Surety.—Practicing attorney may not be taken as surety on any official bond or bond in any legal proceeding in district in which he resides. (11-114).

Liabilities.—See category Civil Actions and Procedure, topic Costs.

Ethics.—American Bar Association's Code of Professional Responsibility as in effect Mar., 1984, together with amendments and additions approved by Nebraska Supreme Court through July, 1990, adopted as standard for Nebraska Association.

Discipline.—Special committees are established for hearing complaints against attorneys. Disbarment proceedings are before Supreme Court under special rules of procedure. (Revised Rules of Supreme Court, Disciplinary Proceedings).

Mandatory Continuing Legal Education.—No requirement.

Speciality Certification Requirements.—None.

Professional Association.—See category Business Organizations, topic Corporations, subhead Professional Corporations.

MINERAL, WATER AND FISHING RIGHTS

MINES AND MINERALS:

State aid for coal and iron development (57-101) industries. All pipe lines are under jurisdiction of Public Service Commission. (75-501). Statute makes provision as to forfeiture of oil, gas and mineral leases. (57-201). Executors, guardians, etc., may grant easements for pipe lines by obtaining proper license from court. (57-401, 402). 77-802 provides for taxation of public services on basis of original cost of all property in tax subdivision to original cost of all property located in state.

Oil and Gas.—Adopted Petroleum Product Act. (66-1215 to -1224).

MORTGAGES

CHATTEL MORTGAGES:

Uniform Commercial Code in effect. See category Business Regulation and Commerce, topic Commercial Code.

What May be Mortgaged.—Uniform Commercial Code governs. (Neb. UCC 9-102). For exclusions see Neb. UCC 9-104.

After-acquired Property.—Uniform Commercial Code governs. (Neb. UCC 9-204).

Future Advances.—Uniform Commercial Code governs. (Neb. UCC 9-204).

Mortgage of Motor Vehicle.—See category Transportation, topic Motor Vehicles, subhead Liens.

Requisites of Instrument.—Uniform Commercial Code governs. (Neb. UCC 9-402).

Execution of Instrument.—May be executed by mortgagor's agent if authorized in writing. (Neb. UCC 1-201[35] and 1-201[39]).

Filing and Refiling.—
Necessity.—Uniform Commercial Code governs. (Neb. UCC 9-302). See category Business Regulation and Commerce, topic Commercial Code, subhead Optional Provisions.
Time for Filing.—Uniform Commercial Code governs. See category Business Regulation and Commerce, topic Commercial Code, subhead Material Variations From 1962 Text and 1972 and 1977 Official Amendments.
Place of Filing.—Uniform Commercial Code governs. (Neb. UCC 9-401). See category Business Regulation and Commerce, topic Commercial Code, subhead Material Variations From 1962 Text and 1972 and 1977 Official Amendments.
Fees.—Uniform Commercial Code governs. (Neb. UCC 9-403). See category Business Regulation and Commerce, topic Commercial Code, subhead Filing Fees.

Disposal or Removal of Property.—Uniform Commercial Code governs. (Neb. UCC 9-401).

Satisfaction.—Uniform Commercial Code governs.

Foreclosure by Court Proceeding.—By common law equity action in district court.

Foreclosure and Sale without Court Action.—Uniform Commercial Code governs. (Neb. UCC 9-503 et seq.).

Redemption.—Uniform Commercial Code governs. (Neb. UCC 9-506).

Foreign Mortgages.—Uniform Commercial Code governs. (Neb. UCC 9-103). See category Business Regulation and Commerce, topic Commercial Code, subhead Material Variations From 1962 Text and 1972 and 1977 Official Amendments.

Taxation.—No special statute.

Forms
For forms of Financing Statement, Termination Statement, and Statement of Continuation, Partial Release, Assignment, etc., see end of this Digest.
Security Agreement.—

SECURITY AGREEMENT

. . . .

DATE

. . . . , a resident of

NO. AND STREET   CITY

. . . .

COUNTY   STATE

(hereinafter called "DEBTOR"), for consideration grants to
Name:
Office Address:

CHATTEL MORTGAGES . . . *continued*

(hereinafter called "SECURED PARTY") a security interest in the following property and any and all additions, accessions and substitutions thereto or therefore (hereinafter called the "COLLATERAL"):

Mark if applicable ☐ (a) All of Debtor's inventory including all goods, merchandise, raw materials, goods in process, finished goods and all other tangible personal property now owned or hereafter acquired and held for sale or lease or furnished or to be furnished under contracts of service or used or consumed in Debtor's business (all hereinafter called the "Inventory"), and in contract rights with respect thereto and proceeds of both. Without limitation the term "Inventory" includes

Mark if applicable ☐ (b) All accounts, notes, drafts, chattel paper, acceptances and other forms of obligations and receivables now or hereafter received by or belonging to Debtor for goods sold by it or for services rendered by it, all guaranties and securities therefor, all right, title and interest of Debtor in the merchandise which gave rise thereto, including the right of stoppage in transit, and all rights of Debtor earned or yet to be earned under contracts to sell goods or render services and in the proceeds thereof.

The security interest granted hereby is to secure payment of the indebtedness evidenced by a certain promissory note of even date herewith payable to the Secured Party, or order, as follows: together with such additional sums as may hereafter be advanced to the Debtor or expended by the Secured Party or its assigns on behalf of the Debtor or his assigns for any purpose whatsoever and evidenced by notes, drafts, open account, or otherwise, with interest thereon at rates to be fixed at the time of advancing or expending such additional sums, provided, however, that the making of any such advances or expenditures shall be optional with Secured Party, or its assigns; and this security agreement shall secure the payment of any and all extensions or renewals and successive extensions or renewals of said note or notes, and of any indebtedness at any time owing to Secured Party, or its assigns, and shall further secure the payment of any and all indebtedness owing by Debtor to Secured Party, and for all of which this security agreement shall stand as a continuing security until paid (all of such indebtedness being referred to as the "Obligations"); and the Debtor agrees that the Secured Party, its successors or assigns, may apply any payments made on the Obligations secured hereby, at its option, on any of the notes or other indebtedness secured hereby.

DEBTOR EXPRESSLY WARRANTS AND COVENANTS:

1. That except for the security interest granted hereby Debtor is, or to the extent that this agreement states that the Collateral is to be acquired after the date hereof, will be, the owner of the Collateral free from any adverse lien, security interest or encumbrance; and that Debtor will defend the Collateral against all claims and demands of all persons at any time claiming the same or any interest therein.

Mark if applicable ☐ 2. Debtor is a duly organized and existing corporation under the laws of the State of . . . . and is duly qualified and in good standing in every other state in which it is doing business.

Mark if applicable ☐ 3. The execution, delivery and performance hereof are within Debtor's corporate powers, have been duly authorized, are not in contravention of law or the terms of Debtor's charter, by-laws, or other incorporation papers or of any indenture, agreement or undertaking to which Debtor is a party, or by which it is bound.

Mark if applicable ☐ 4. As to all accounts receivable, Debtor will from time to time, as requested by Secured Party give Secured Party a list of the accounts receivable existing at the time of the request and all accounts reported to the Secured Party will be good and valid accounts representing an undisputed bona fide indebtedness of the account debtor to Debtor for merchandise theretofore shipped or delivered pursuant to or in connection with a contract of sale or for services theretofore rendered by Debtor to or for said account debtor; there are and will be no set-offs or counter claims of any nature whatsoever against any such account; no agreement under which any deduction or discount may be claimed has been or will be made with the account debtor on any of such accounts except as reflected in the report furnished by Debtor; the Debtor will be lawful owner of all such accounts and will have good right to pledge, sell, assign and transfer the same and grant a security interest therein. None of such accounts has been or will be pledged, sold, assigned or transferred to any other person than Secured Party or in any way encumbered except to Secured Party and Debtor will warrant and defend all accounts against the lawful claims and demands of all persons.

5. Debtor will keep its records concerning accounts, contract rights and inventory at . . . . Debtor will at all reasonable times and from time to time allow Secured Party by or through any of its officers, agents, employees, attorneys, or accountants to examine and inspect the inventory and to examine, inspect and make extracts from Debtor's books and other records, and to arrange for verification of accounts receivable, under reasonable procedures directly with account debtor or by other methods. Debtor will furnish to Secured Party upon request all notes or other papers evidencing any accounts receivable and any guarantees, securities or other documents and information relating thereto.

Mark if applicable ☐ 6. So long as Secured Party does not request that the account debtors on the Collateral be notified of the assignment thereof to Secured Party, Debtor shall make collections of such accounts and turn over such proceeds to Secured Party weekly or at such longer intervals as the Secured Party may allow, together with a collection report in form satisfactory to Secured Party. Secured Party may at any time notify account debtors that the accounts have been assigned to Secured Party and shall be paid to Secured Party. Upon request of Secured Party at any time, Debtor will so notify such account debtors and will indicate on all billings to such account debtors that the accounts are payable to Secured Party. Any proceeds of accounts thereafter received by Debtor shall be turned over to the Secured Party daily in the exact form in which they are received.

7. To evidence Secured Party's rights hereunder Debtor will assign or endorse the Collateral or proceeds thereof to Secured Party as Secured Party may request. Secured Party shall have full power to collect, compromise, endorse, sell or otherwise deal with the Collateral or proceeds thereof in its own name or that of Debtor. Debtor shall pay to Secured Party on demand any and all expenses incurred or expended by Secured Party in the collection or attempted collection of Collateral and in protecting and enforcing the obligations and other rights of Secured Party hereunder.

Mark if applicable ☐ 8. With regard to inventory Debtor shall immediately notify Secured Party of any event causing loss or depreciation in the value of the inventory and the amount of such loss or depreciation. Debtor will deliver to Secured Party prior to the tenth day of each month a report in form satisfactory to Secured Party with respect to the next preceding month, showing opening inventory, inventory acquired, inventory sold and delivered, inventory sold and held for future delivery, inventory returned or repossessed, inventory used or consumed in Debtor's business and closing inventory.

Mark if applicable ☐ 9. Until default, Debtor may use the inventory in any lawful manner not inconsistent with this agreement or with the terms or conditions of any policy of insurance thereon and may also sell the inventory in the ordinary course of business. A sale in the ordinary course of business does not include a transfer in partial or total satisfaction of a debt. Debtor will report to Secured Party weekly, or at such longer intervals as Secured Party may allow, the sales of inventory for such week or longer period. All proceeds of inventory received by Debtor shall be turned over to Secured Party, together with the periodic report required above, unless Secured Party agrees that the proceeds for any period need not be turned over to it.

10. That no financing statement covering the Collateral or any proceeds thereof is on file in any public office and that at the request of Secured Party, Debtor will join with Secured Party in executing one or more financing statements pursuant to the Nebraska Uniform Commercial Code in form satisfactory to Secured Party and will pay the cost of filing such financing statement, this security agreement and any continuation or termination statement, in all public offices wherever filing is deemed by Secured Party to be necessary or desirable.

11. To pay all taxes and assessments of every nature which may be levied or assessed against the Collateral.

12. Not to permit or allow any adverse lien, security interest or encumbrance whatsoever upon the Collateral and not to permit the same to be attached or replevined.

13. At its option, Secured Party may discharge taxes, liens or security interests or other encumbrances at any time levied or placed on the Collateral and may pay for the repair of any damage or injury and may pay for the maintenance and preservation of the Collateral. Debtor agrees to reimburse Secured Party on demand for any payment made or expense incurred by Secured Party pursuant to the foregoing authorization. Until such reimbursement, the amount of any such payment, with interest at the rate of 9% per annum from date of payment until reimbursement, shall be added to the indebtedness owed by Debtor and shall be secured by this security agreement.

14. That Debtor will at Debtor's own expense forthwith insure the tangible Collateral in a reliable insurance company against loss or damage by fire, extended coverage and theft for an amount equal to the value of said Collateral, and keep the same so insured continuously until the full amount of said indebtedness is paid, with loss payable to Secured Party as its interest may appear, and that Debtor will on demand deliver said policies of insurance or furnish proof of such insurance to the Secured Party, and in case of loss, the Secured Party shall retain from the insurance money an amount equal to the total balance of said indebtedness remaining unpaid, whether according to the tenor and effect of any promissory note or notes evidencing such indebtedness the same is due or not. Should the Debtor fail or refuse to forthwith effect such insurance and deliver the policies or furnish proof of such insurance as aforesaid, or fail to keep the Collateral so insured continuously until the full amount of said indebtedness is paid, the Secured Party may at its option effect such insurance and the amount so paid for such insurance with interest at the rate of 9% per annum from date of payment until repaid shall be added to said indebtedness, and the same shall be secured by this security agreement.

15. Debtor will pay the reasonable attorney's fees of Secured Party and said Debtor will pay said Secured Party any and all costs and expenses incurred in recovering possession of the Collateral and incurred in enforcing this security agreement, and the same shall be secured by this security agreement.

16. That Debtor will not use the Collateral in violation of any applicable statutes, regulations or ordinances.

UNTIL DEFAULT Debtor may have possession of the Collateral and use it in any lawful manner not inconsistent with this agreement and not inconsistent with any policy of insurance thereon, and upon default Secured Party shall have the immediate right to the possession of the Collateral.

DEBTOR SHALL BE IN DEFAULT under this agreement upon the happening of any of the following events or conditions:

(a) default in the payment or performance of any obligation, covenant or liability contained or referred to herein or in any note evidencing the same;

(b) any warranty, representation or statement made or furnished to Secured Party by or on behalf of Debtor proves to have been false in any material respect when made or furnished;

(c) any event which results in the acceleration of the maturity of the indebtedness of Debtor to others under any indenture, agreement or undertaking;

(d) loss, theft, damage, destruction, sale (except as authorized in paragraph 9 hereof) or encumbrance to or of any of the Collateral, or the making of any levy, seizure or attachment thereof or thereon;

(e) death, dissolution, termination of existence, insolvency, business failure, appointment of a receiver of any part of the property of, assignment for the benefit of creditors by, or the commencement of any proceeding under any bankruptcy or insolvency laws by or against Debtor or any guarantor or surety for Debtor.

UPON SUCH DEFAULT and at any time thereafter, or if it deems itself insecure, Secured Party may declare all Obligations secured hereby immediately due and payable and shall have the remedies of a secured party under the Nebraska Uniform Commercial Code. Secured Party may require Debtor to assemble the Collateral and deliver or make it available to Secured Party at a place to be designated by Secured Party which is reasonably convenient to both parties. Unless the Collateral is perishable or threatens to decline speedily in value or is of a type customarily sold on a recognized market, Secured Party will give Debtor reasonable notice of the time and place of any public sale thereof or of the time after which any private sale or any other intended disposition thereof is to be made. The requirements of reasonable notice shall be met if such notice is mailed, postage prepaid, to the address of Debtor shown at the beginning of this agreement at least five days before the time of the sale or disposition.

CHATTEL MORTGAGES . . . *continued*

No waiver by Secured Party of any default shall operate as a waiver of any other default or of the same default on a future occasion. The taking of this security agreement shall not waive or impair any other security said Secured Party may have or hereafter acquire for the payment of the above indebtedness, nor shall the taking of any such additional security waive or impair this security agreement; but said Secured Party may resort to any security it may have in the order it may deem proper, and notwithstanding any collateral security, Secured Party shall retain its right of setoff against Debtor.

All rights of Secured Party hereunder shall inure to the benefit of its successors and assigns; and all promises and duties of Debtor shall bind his heirs, executors or administrators or his or its successors or assigns. If there be more than one Debtor, their liabilities hereunder shall be joint and several.

This agreement shall become effective when it is signed by Debtor.
Debtor:
By . . . .
. . . .

NAME   TITLE

See also category Business Regulation and Commerce, topic Commercial Code.

MORTGAGES OF PERSONAL PROPERTY:

See topic Chattel Mortgages; also category Business Regulation and Commerce, topic Commercial Code.

MORTGAGES OF REAL PROPERTY:

In absence of stipulation to contrary mortgagor of real estate retains legal title and right of possession. (76-276). Every deed which, by any other instrument in writing, appears to have been intended only as security by way of mortgage must be so considered. (76-251).

Execution.—Mortgage must be signed and acknowledged by grantor (76-211, 242); but mortgage not acknowledged, except as to a homestead, is good between the parties (50 Neb. 656, 70 N.W. 241). All consensual interests in real property which secure payment or performance of obligation should be denominated "Security Interest". (52-127[15]).

Recording.—Mortgage must be recorded in county in which real estate or part thereof is located and as to creditors and subsequent purchasers in good faith without notice takes effect only on delivery to register of deeds for record; but is valid between parties without record. (76-238, and -245).

Recording Fees.—$5 per page. (33-109). Indexing, 50¢ for each entry. (33-112).

Taxes.—None required on recording. Mortgage is treated as interest in real property and interests of mortgagor and mortgagee are assessed separately (77-1402), unless mortgage contains provision requiring mortgagor to pay the tax in which event both interests are assessed and taxed to mortgagor (77-1407).

Trust deeds as substitute for mortgage authorized by Nebraska Trust Deed Act. (76-1001 to -1018).

Trustee must be member of State Bar, licensed real estate broker of Nebraska, corporation authorized to conduct trust business in Nebraska, bank, building and loan association, savings and loan association, credit union, or title insurer authorized to do business in Nebraska. (76-1003). If expressly provided, trustee may have power of sale, or trust deed may be foreclosed as provided for mortgages, after execution of acknowledgment to beneficiary, that document executed is trust deed and not mortgage. (76-1005). Written notice by publication of sale must be given. (76-1007). Such sale of property must be made within period prescribed for commencement of action on obligation secured by trust deed. (76-1015). Transfer of any debt secured by trust deed operates as transfer of security therefor. (76-1016). Trust deed may be recorded. (76-1017).

Future Advances.—Any interest in real property capable of being transferred may be mortgaged to secure future advances necessary to protect security, and any future advances made at option of parties; provided, that at no time shall secured principal future advances, not including sums advanced to protect security, exceed total amount, or percentage of total amount stated in mortgage.

However, if any optional future advance is made under mortgage, after written notice of an intervening mortgage, lien or claim against property, or written notice of labor or material furnished on said property, or contracted to be so furnished, then amount so advanced shall be junior to any such mortgage, lien or claim. (76-238.01).

Subsequent advances under security agreement recorded before construction lien have priority if it is made under construction agreement and in payment of agreed improvements or to protect security interest. (52-139).

When Mortgage Effective.—As to creditors and subsequent purchasers in good faith and without notice mortgage becomes effective on delivery to register of deeds for recording (76-238); as to other persons from execution and delivery of mortgage.

Subordination Agreements.—No statute.

Assignment.—Recording of assignment of mortgage is not sufficient notice to mortgagor, his heirs or representatives, so as to invalidate subsequent payments to mortgagee. (76-256). "Due on sale" clauses are not restraints on alienations, nor are they against public policy. (206 Neb. 469, 293 N.W.2d 843).

Satisfaction.—Recorded mortgage discharged by register of deeds upon receipt of certificate executed by mortgagee, personal representative or assignee acknowledged, proved, or certified (see 76-216, 64-204, 76-236) specifying mortgage paid, satisfied, or discharged (76-253).

Release of part of property by senior mortgagee will, if made with notice of a junior mortgage, operate in favor of junior mortgagee as a satisfaction of senior mortgage to extent of value of property released. (58 Neb. 670, 79 N.W. 613).

Foreclosure.—Suit must be brought in district court of county where land or some part thereof is located. (25-401, and -2137). Court has power to decree sale of mortgaged premises or sufficient thereof to pay debts and costs of suit. Petition must state whether any proceedings have been had at law for recovery of debt and whether any part of debt has been paid. (25-2142). If judgment obtained in suit at law for any part of mortgage debt no proceeding for foreclosure unless return of execution shows that it is unsatisfied in whole or in part and that defendant has no property to satisfy execution, except mortgaged premises. (25-2143).

If petition is based on nonpayment of interest or installment of principal and other portions become due subsequently, petition must be dismissed upon defendant bringing into court at any time before decree of sale principal and interest due, with costs. (25-2148). If, after decree for sale, defendant brings into court principal and interest due, with costs, proceedings must be stayed but court must enter decree of foreclosure and sale to be enforced by further order of court upon subsequent default in payment of any installment of principal or interest. (25-2149). If defendant does not bring into court amount due with costs or if for any other cause a decree passes for complainant, court may direct reference to sheriff to ascertain and report situation of mortgaged premises or may determine same on oral or other testimony and if it appears same can be sold in parcels without injury to parties, decree must direct so much of mortgaged premises to be sold as will be sufficient to pay amount then due on mortgage, with costs, and such decree remains as security for any subsequent default (25-2150), on happening of which court may on petition or complaint direct sale of so much of mortgaged premises as will satisfy amount due, with costs, which proceedings may be had as often as default happens (25-2151). If court concludes sale of whole property will be most beneficial to parties, decree must be entered accordingly in first instance. (25-2152).

Clerk of district court, on satisfaction or payment of amount of decree, must forward to register of deeds certificate of satisfaction, on payment of $3, taxable as costs. (25-2154).

Order of sale stayed up to nine months after rendition of judgment, if mortgagor within 20 days after such rendition files with clerk of court written request for stay, otherwise order of sale may be issued immediately after expiration of 20 days. If maturity of mortgage on lot or residential property less than three acres is more than 20 years from filing of petition, then stay is three months and if such original maturity is more than ten years but not more than 20 years from date of filing then stay period is six months. (25-1506; 128 Neb. 415, 258 N.W. 873). Court of equity has power to relieve mortgagor from effect of operative acceleration clause when default results from unconscionable conduct by mortgagee. (203 Neb. 727, 280 N.W.2d 53).

Sales are made by sheriff or some other person authorized by court in county where premises or some part thereof located. (25-2144). Sheriff's deed vests in purchaser same estate that would have vested in mortgagee if equity had been foreclosed; deed is as valid as though executed by mortgagor and mortgagee. (25-2145). Proceeds applied to discharge of debt and costs and surplus, if any, brought into court for use of defendant or other person entitled thereto, subject to order of court. (25-2146).

Officer must give public notice of time and place of sale before sale, by publication once each week for four successive weeks in some newspaper printed in county or, if none, in newspaper of general circulation therein and by posting notice on court house door and in five other public places in county, two of which must be in precinct where lands lie. Sale made without such notice must be set aside on motion. (25-1529).

Officer making sale files a return with clerk of court, and if sale is approved court enters order confirming sale and directing officer to deed property to purchaser. Such deed conveys as good title as debtor could have made at time property became liable to judgment or at any time thereafter and is sufficient evidence of legality of sale. (25-1531, and -1533). Except in circumstances described in 40-103, party seeking confirmation of sale must provide debtor notice of homestead exemption procedure. Failure to provide such notice may result in setting aside of sale. (25-1531).

Deficiency judgment is not granted in foreclosure action. (25-2139).

After foreclosure petition has been filed and decree rendered thereon, no proceedings may be had at law for recovery of mortgage debt unless authorized by court. (25-2140). After exhausting remedy in equity, action at law may be brought for deficiency. (138 Neb. 518, 293 N.W. 424).

Redemption.—Owner may redeem at any time before sale is confirmed by paying into court the amount of the judgment with interest and costs to date or, if the property has been sold to some person other than plaintiff, by paying to the purchaser or into court for use of the purchaser, the purchase price with 12% interest thereon from date of sale to date of redemption. No redemption after sale confirmed. (25-1530).

Ordinary form is as follows:

Form

This indenture, made and executed this . . . . . . day of . . . . . ., A.D. . . . . . ., by and between . . . . . . party of the first part, and . . . . . . party of the second part, Witnesseth, that the said party of the first part, for and in consideration of . . . . . . Dollars, paid by said party of the second part, the receipt whereof is hereby acknowledged, has granted, bargained, sold and conveyed, and by these presents, does grant, bargain, sell and convey, unto said party of the second part, the following described real property, situate in the County of . . . . . . and State of Nebraska, to-wit: . . . . . . together with the tenements, hereditament and appurtenances to the same belonging, and all the estate, title, dower, right of homestead, claims and demands whatsoever of the said party of the first part of, in or to said premises or any part thereof; and said party of the first part does hereby covenant that said party of the first part is lawfully seized of said premises; that said premises are free from incumbrance . . . . . . and that said party of the first part will warrant and defend the title to said premises against the lawful claims and demands of all persons whomsoever . . . . . .

Provided always, and these presents are upon these conditions: Whereas, said party of the first part has executed and delivered to the said party of the second part . . . . . . promissory note . . . . . . and whereas, the party of the first part has agreed to keep the buildings, if any, upon said premises, insured in some company or companies approved by said party of the second part, for the sum of not less than . . . . . . dollars, and deliver to said party of the second part the policy or policies containing a clause with the loss payable to said party of the second part, or assigns, and has agreed to pay all taxes and

MORTGAGES OF REAL PROPERTY . . . *continued*
assessments against said premises before the same, by law, become delinquent, and has agreed that if said party of the first part does not provide such insurance, or fails to pay all taxes as aforesaid, then said party of the second part, or holder thereof, may pay such insurance and taxes, or either of them, and all amounts so paid by said party of the second part shall bear interest at the rate of 9% per annum from date of payment, and this mortgage shall stand as security therefor, and said sum may be added to the amount of the mortgage debt, and the same recovered as a part thereof. Now, if the said party of the first part shall well and truly pay or cause to be paid the said sum of money in said note. . . . mentioned, with interest thereon according to the tenor and effect of said note. . . . and shall keep said buildings insured as aforesaid, and shall keep all taxes and assessments paid, and shall duly keep, and perform all the other covenants and agreements herein contained, then these presents to be null and void. But if said sum of money or any part thereof, or any interest thereon, is not paid when the same is due, or if said buildings shall not be kept insured as aforesaid, or if the taxes and assessments against said premises are not paid at or before the time the same become by law delinquent, or if said party of the first part shall fail to keep and perform any covenants herein contained, the holder hereof shall have the option to declare the whole of said indebtedness due and payable at any time after such failure or default, and may maintain an action at law or equity to recover the same, and the commencement of such action shall be the only notice of the exercise of said option required.

And it is further provided and agreed that the said mortgagor shall and will pay all taxes levied upon this mortgage or the debt secured thereby, together with any other taxes or assessments which may be levied under the laws of Nebraska, against the said mortgagee or the legal holder of the said principal note. . . . on account of this indebtedness.

In Testimony Whereof, ... hereunto set . . . . . . hand. . . . the date above written.

. . . .

(Acknowledgment). . . . .

Form of Assignment.—Know All Men by These Presents: That . . . . . . of the first part, in consideration of the sum of . . . . . . Dollars to . . . . . . in hand paid by . . . . . . of the second part, receipt whereof is hereby acknowledged, have sold and by these presents do sell, assign and transfer unto the said part. . . . of the second part a certain indenture of mortgage bearing date the . . . . . . day of . . . . . . in the year 19. . . ., made by . . . . . . in favor of . . . . . . and conveying . . . . . . in . . . . . . county, in the state of . . . . . . and which mortgage was recorded in the records of said county on the . . . . . . day of . . . . . . in the year 19. . . . in book . . . . . . of mortgages on page . . . . . ., together with the notes or obligations therein described, without recourse or in any event or for any cause.

To Have and to Hold the same unto the said part. . . . of the second part, ... executors, administrators or assigns, subject only to the provisions in the said indenture of mortgage contained.

In Witness Whereof, ... have set . . . . . . hand. . . . and . . . . . . seal. . . . this . . . . . . day of . . . . . . in the year 19. . . . . .

. . . .

(Acknowledgment). . . . .

Form of Release.—In Consideration of the payment of the debt named therein. I hereby release the mortgage made by . . . . . . to . . . . . . on the following described property situate in the County of . . . . . . and State of Nebraska, to-wit: . . . . . . which was recorded on the . . . . . . day of . . . . . ., 19. . . ., in Book . . . . . . of Mortgages, at page . . . . . . of the mortgage records of . . . . . . County, Nebraska.

Witness my hand this . . . . . . day of . . . . . ., 19. . . . .

. . . .

(Acknowledgment). . . . .

PROPERTY

ABSENTEES:

Uniform Probate Code adopted. (30-2201 et seq.).

On partition, share of absent owner is retained or proceeds invested for his benefit. (25-21,111). Clerk receives same in official capacity. (134 Neb. 824, 279 N.W. 778).

Process Agent.—No statutory provision.

Escheat.—Individual alien and foreign corporations' real property escheats to state in some instances. (76-402, and 415, 4-107). Uniform Disposition of Unclaimed Property Act adopted. (69-1301 to 1329). See category Estates and Trusts, topics Descent and Distribution, subhead Escheat, Wills, subhead Unclaimed Legacies or Sums Due Creditors.

ADVERSE POSSESSION:

Character and Duration of Possession.—Persons in actual, continued, notorious and adverse possession under claim of ownership to land for ten years are vested with valid title (154 Neb. 221, 47 N.W.2d 504), except as against county, city, town, village, other municipal corporation, public power district, public irrigation district or natural resources district which may begin action any time for recovery of title or possession of any public road, street, alley or other public grounds or city or town lots (25-202).

Easements.—Hereditaments can be obtained by adverse possession. (25-202).

Disabilities.—Persons under disability may bring action within 20 years from date of accrual but in no event more than ten years after termination of disability. (25-213).

CURTESY:

Abolished. (30-104).

DEEDS:

See topic Real Property, for types of estates; also categories Debtor and Creditor, topic Homesteads, subhead Alienation or Encumbrance; Family, topic Husband and Wife, subhead Conveyances of Real Estate.

Execution.—Deed of real estate or any interest therein, except lease for one year or less, must be signed by grantor of lawful age, and must be acknowledged or proved and recorded. (76-211, -216, -228, and -237). However, deed without acknowledgment, except as to homestead, is valid between parties. (76 Neb. 335, 107 N.W. 580; 12 Neb. 152, 10 N.W. 545). Neither seal nor witness is necessary. There is no recital of consideration requirement. (76-214).

Corporate deed if signed by president or presiding officer of board of directors and acknowledged by such officer to be an act of corporation is prima facie a proper conveyance of corporation. (21-2077.01). May be executed by other persons if authorized by proper corporate action. Corporate seal unnecessary.

Deed by Agent.—Deed may be subscribed by agent authorized in writing. (36-409). Power of attorney must be proved or acknowledged to be entitled to record (76-204), but unacknowledged power is valid except as to conveyance of homestead (61 Neb. 537, 85 N.W. 565).

Foreign Deed.—Deed executed in any other state, territory or district of United States must be executed and acknowledged or proved, according to laws of such place or of this state (76-219). Deed of land situated in this state, executed in another state and acknowledged there before notary public presumed to have been executed according to laws of that state though not witnessed, and is entitled to be received in evidence in this state without other proof that grantors actually executed and delivered deed. (134 Neb. 33, 277 N.W. 785). Deed executed in foreign country may be executed according to its laws. (76-226).

After acquired interest passes under deed purporting to convey greater interest than grantor had, but not under quitclaim or special warranty deed. (76-209).

Uniform Property Act adopted. (76-101 to-123).

Recording.—Deed must be recorded in county where real estate or any part thereof is located in order to be effective as against creditors or of subsequent purchasers or incumbrancers from vendor (76-245), and as to such persons takes effect from delivery to register of deeds for record (76-238). Deeds must be acknowledged or proved to be entitled to record. (76-241). Witness not required. See also category Documents and Records, topic Records.

Statement to be Filed With Deed.—Grantee must file completed Property Tax Administrator's statement with deed. Effective Jan., 1986, statement must contain social security number of grantee, if living, or federal employer identification number. (76-214). Failure to complete and file is misdemeanor punishable by fine of $10 to $500. (76-215).

Recording Fee.—$5 per side of page (33-109); each entry of index 50¢ (33-112); certified copy of any recorded instrument $1.50 per page (33-109).

Taxes.—State documentary tax stamps on deeds at rate of $1.75 per $1,000 of actual consideration. Tax shall not apply to certain deeds. (76-902). Grantor pays tax. (76-901).

Forms.—No statutory forms. Bar Association promulgated forms are optional. Real estate transfer tax forms available from county recorder and are required at time of filing.

Forms

Warranty Deed.—Ordinary form is as follows:

Know All Men by These Presents, That . . . . . . and . . . . . ., husband and wife, in consideration of $. . . . in hand paid, do hereby grant, bargain, sell, convey and confirm unto . . . . . . the following described real estate situate in the county of . . . . . . and State of Nebraska, to-wit: . . . ., together with all the tenements, hereditaments and appurtenances to the same belonging and all the estate, title, dower, right of homestead, claim or demand whatsoever of the . . . . . . of, in, or to the same or any part thereof.

To Have and to Hold the above described premises, with the appurtenances, unto the said . . . . . . and to his heirs and assigns forever, and we, the said . . . . . ., for ourselves and our heirs, executors and administrators, do covenant with the said . . . . . . and with his heirs and assigns, that we are lawfully seized of said premises; that they are free from encumbrance except . . . . . .; that we have good right and lawful authority to sell the same and that we will and our heirs, executors and administrators shall warrant and defend the same unto the said . . . . . . and his heirs and assigns forever against the lawful claims of all persons whomsoever.

In Witness Whereof we have hereunto set our hands this . . . . . . day of . . . . . ., 19. . .

. . . .

(Acknowledgment). . . . .

Warranty Deed to Joint Tenants.—The following form may be used:

Know All Men by These Presents, That . . . . . . in consideration of . . . . . . Dollars, in hand paid, do hereby grant, bargain, sell, convey, and confirm unto . . . . . . as joint tenants, and not as tenants in common, the following described real estate, situated in the County of . . . . . . and State of Nebraska, to-wit: together with all the tenements, hereditaments, and appurtenances to the same belonging, and all the estate, title, dower, right of homestead, claim, or demand whatsoever of the said grantor . . . . . ., of, in, or to the same, or any part thereof.

It being the intention of all parties hereto, that in the event of the death of either of said grantees, the entire fee simple title to the real estate described herein shall vest in the surviving grantee.

To Have and to Hold the above described premises, with the appurtenances, unto the said grantees as Joint Tenants, and not as tenants in common, and to their assigns, or to the heirs and assigns of the survivor of them, forever, and . . . . . . the grantor . . . . . . named herein for . . . . . . and . . . . . . heirs, executors, and administrators, does covenant with the grantees named herein and with the assigns and with the heirs and assigns of

DEEDS . . . *continued*

the survivor of them, that . . . . . . lawfully seized of said premises; that they are free from incumbrance except as stated herein, and that . . . . . . the said grantor . . . . . . has good right and lawful authority to sell the same, and that . . . . . . will and . . . . . . heirs, executors, and administrators shall warrant and defend the same unto the grantees named herein and unto their assigns and unto their heirs and assigns of the survivor of them, forever, against the lawful claims of all persons whomsoever, excluding the exceptions named herein.

In Witness Whereof . . . . . have hereunto set . . . . . . hand . . . . . . this . . . . . . day of . . . . . ., A.D. . . . . . .

(Acknowledgment).   . . . .

Quitclaim Deed.—The following form may be used:

This Indenture, made this . . . . . . day of . . . . . ., in the year one thousand . . . . . . between . . . . . . of the first part, and . . . . . . of the second part, Witnesseth, that the said part . . . . . . of the first part, in consideration of the sum of . . . . . . Dollars, to . . . . . . duly paid, the receipt whereof is hereby acknowledged, ... granted, conveyed, remised, released and quitclaimed, and by these presents does grant, convey, remise, release, and forever quitclaim unto the said part . . . . . . of the second part, and to . . . . . . heirs and assigns forever, all . . . . . . right, title, interest, estate, claim, and demand, both at law and in equity, of, in and to the following described real estate, situate in . . . . . . County and State of Nebraska, to-wit; . . . . together with all and singular the hereditaments and appurtenances thereunto belonging; To Have and to Hold the above described premises unto the said . . . . . ., heirs and assigns.

In Witness Whereof, the said part . . . . . . of the first part ha . . . . . . hereunto set . . . . . hand the day and year first above written.

(Acknowledgment).   . . . .

DOWER:

Abolished. (30-104).

ESCHEAT:

See topic Absentees, subhead Escheat; categories Business Regulation and Commerce, topic Banks and Banking; Estates and Trusts, topics Descent and Distribution, subhead Escheat, Wills, subhead Unclaimed Legacies or Sums Due Creditors.

LANDLORD AND TENANT:

Uniform Residential Landlord and Tenant Act became effective July 1, 1975. Uniform Commercial Code Art. 2A adopted. (2A-101 to -532).

Kinds of Tenancy.—Unless rental agreement fixes a definite term, tenancy shall be week-to-week in case of roomer who pays weekly rent, and in all other cases month-to-month. (76-1414).

Lease Provisions.—Certain provisions in leases are unenforceable and knowing inclusion of such provisions may subject landlord to liability for actual damage to tenant. (76-1415).

Security Deposits.—Not to exceed one month's rent (except pet deposit), and may be applied to payment of rent and damages at termination of lease. Balance shall be returned to tenant within 14 days of demand. (76-1416).

Recording.—Leases executed the same as a deed may be recorded; but possession of tenant gives notice of his rights.

Lien.—For hotel, apartment house, tourist camp, or rooming house, see category Debtor and Creditor, topic Liens.

Termination of Tenancy.—If personal property is left after termination of lease, landlord must give written notice to tenant. (69-2303). If personal property has value greater than $250, landlord may notify tenant and charge storage fee or hold public sale. If personal property is less than $250, notice must inform tenant of landlord's right to keep, sell or dispose of property without further notice. (69-2301 to -2314).

Holding Over.—Landlord may bring action for possession and damages if willful and in bad faith. (76-1436).

Dispossession.—Action for possession may be filed in district or county court, and must contain: Facts entitling landlord to possession; reasonably accurate description of premises; compliance with notice provisions (76-1441). Summons must contain enumerated items, and may be served by anyone. Trial must not be less than ten nor more than 14 days after service. (76-1442).

Right of action for forcible entry and detainer remains, but is not applicable to premises covered by URLTA. (201 Neb. 91, 266 N.W.2d 222).

Forms.—Statutory form for writ of execution (25-21,230) is as follows:

Form

The State of Nebraska ⎫
. . . . County ⎬ ss.

To any Constable or Sheriff of . . . . . . County:

Whereas in a certain action for the forcible entry and detention, (or the forcible detention, as the case may be) of the following described premises, to wit: . . . . lately tried before the court, wherein . . . . . . was plaintiff, and . . . . . . was defendant, judgment was rendered on the . . . . . . day of . . . . . . A.D. . . . . . ., you therefore are hereby commanded to cause the defendant to be forthwith removed from said premises, and the said plaintiff to have restitution of the same; also that you levy of the goods and chattels of the said defendant, and make the costs aforesaid, and all accruing costs; and of this writ make legal service and due return.

Witness my hand this . . . . . . day of . . . . . ., A.D.

. . . .
                                    Clerk of County Court

PERPETUITIES:

No statutes. Common law rule prevails. (152 Neb. 753, 42 N.W.2d 802).

PERSONAL PROPERTY:

Tenancy by the entirety does not exist. (60 Neb. 663, 84 N.W. 92).

Some business and private personal property subject to state taxation. See category Taxation, topic Property Tax.

POWERS OF ATTORNEY:

Uniform Durable Power of Attorney Act adopted. (30-2664 to -2672).

Nebraska Short Form Act adopted. (49-1501-1561). Provides standard forms for power of attorney and other instruments.

Attorney in Fact.—Real estate may be conveyed under power of attorney. See topic Deeds.

See also category Estates and Trusts, topic Executors and Administrators.

REAL PROPERTY:

Tenancy in common and joint tenancy recognized. (76-118; 175 Neb. 883, 125 N.W.2d 68). Conclusive presumption of co-tenancy when present interest in real estate is conveyed to more than one person and grantees are named in disjunctive. (76-275.07). Estate in realty may be created to take effect at future date. (76-210). Estates tail (76-110; 104 Neb. 678, 178 N.W. 262), and estates by entirety (60 Neb. 663, 84 N.W. 92) not recognized.

Uniform Property Act adopted. (76-101 to -123).

Future Interests.—Rights of reentry and possibilities of reverter limited to 30 years. (76-107). Exceptions noted in 76-2, 104(5) and 248 Neb. 353, 535 N.W.2d 400.

Rule in Shelley's Case is abolished. (76-112).

Foreign Conveyances or Encumbrances.—Conveyances executed in another state may be executed and acknowledged or proved according to the laws of place where executed or of this state. (76-219). Conveyances executed in foreign countries may be executed according to the laws of said country. (76-226). See category Documents and Records, topic Acknowledgments.

Condominiums.—Uniform Condominium Act repealed.

Curative Acts.—Many conveyances that might otherwise be defective validated by curative acts. (76-258 to -275.07).

Restrictive Covenants.—Covenants restricting use of property are not favored in law and will be construed in manner permitting maximum unrestricted use of property. (206 Neb. 42, 291 N.W.2d 228).

Historical Properties.—Properties of historical interest or natural beauty may be protected by filing easement which runs with land. (76-2,111).

Virgin prairie land belonging to state or any political subdivision can be protected by declaring boundaries in recorded covenants binding upon subsequent purchasers. (76-2,111 and -2,112, effective July 1, 1983).

Marketable Title Act adopted 1947. Persons having unbroken chain of title through themselves, immediate or remote grantors recorded for more than 22 years deemed to have marketable title with certain exceptions. (76-288 to -298).

See also topics Curtesy, Deeds, Dower, Landlord and Tenant; categories Civil Actions and Procedure, topic Partition; Debtor and Creditor, topic Homesteads; Documents and Records, topic Records; Family, topic Husband and Wife; Mortgages, topic Mortgages of Real Property.

TAXATION

ADMINISTRATION:

Taxable Property.—Current state of taxation is unclear. At center of controversy is language of Art. VIII of State Constitution that taxes shall be levied by valuation uniformly and proportionately upon all tangible property and franchises. Various legislation has been challenged on this basis in Nebraska courts. See 238 Neb. 565, 471 N.W.2d 734; 237 Neb. 357, 466 N.W.2d 461; 229 Neb. 822, 428 N.W.2d 919; 229 Neb. 60, 425 N.W.2d 320; 226 Neb. 236, 411 N.W.2d 35; 885 F.2d 415; 238 Neb. 696, 472 N.W.2d 363; 237 Neb. 591, 467 N.W.2d 55. Taxes shall be levied by valuation uniformly and proportionately upon real property and franchises; tangible personal property shall be taxed at depreciated cost using same depreciation method with reasonable class lives, as determined by legislature, or shall be taxed by valuation uniformly and proportionately (allows Legislature to classify, exempt or tax personal property). Subsequent court decision has challenged legality of system of taxation passed by 1992 Legislature. (See 241 Neb. 106, 147, 486 N.W.2d 883 [1992].) §13-509 places depreciable business equipment and machinery, farm machinery, and breeding livestock on local tax rolls at net book value.

Exemptions.—Following property exempt: Property of state and its governmental subdivisions; property owned and used exclusively for agricultural and horticultural societies or for educational, religious, charitable or cemetery purposes, when not owned or used for financial gain or profit to either owner or user; household goods and personal effects when such property is not owned or used for financial gain or profit to either owner or user; increased value of land by reason of shade or ornamental trees planted along highway; tangible personal property which is not depreciable; business and agricultural inventory. (77-202). Any organization or society seeking tax exempt status on tangible personal property must apply to county assessor on or before Dec. 31 of year preceding year for which exemption is sought. Any organization or society which fails to file exemption application on or before Dec. 31 may apply on or before June 30 to County Assessor. Organization or society shall also file in writing request with County Board of Equalization for waiver. (77-202.01). Value of mobile home occupied or used by disabled or blind honorably discharged veteran exempt. (77-202.24).

ADMINISTRATION . . . *continued*

Exemption under §77-202.24 must be applied for on or before Apr. 1 of each year. (77-202.25).

Collection of most taxes is vested in County Treasurer. (77-1701 to -1767).

Reciprocity With Other States.—Any state of U.S. or any political subdivision thereof has right to sue in courts of State of Nebraska to recover any lawfully unpaid taxes which may be owing it, whether or not taxes have been reduced to judgment, when like right is accorded to State of Nebraska and its political subdivisions either by statute or granted as a matter of comity. (77-1774).

Penalties.—If County Assessor finds that taxpayer has failed to file a personal property tax return or has omitted property on a return filed, for current year or for three previous taxing periods, he must assess tax due plus a 50% penalty as to tax due on tangible property plus interest of 14% (45-104.01) on both tax and penalties until said amount is paid (77-1233.04).

For omitted returns or omitted personal property of deceased three years before his death, or any part thereof, consult 77-399.

Any person making false or fraudulent list of taxable property, or willfully failing or refusing to deliver to assessor a list of taxable property or who shall temporarily convert such property into property not taxable, to evade payment of taxes, shall be guilty of Class IV misdemeanor for any such offense committed before tax year 1993, and Class II misdemeanor for any such offense regarding tax year 1993 or thereafter. (77-1232).

If, before notice by any taxing official, return of tangible personal property filed or omitted property reported, penalty added is 10%. Interest on penalty shall be assessed from date of delinquency until paid. (77-1233.05).

Penalties and interest assessed under 77-1233.05 may be waived in total or in part by county assessor with approval of county board if omitted property or failure to return was result of innocent mistake. (77-1233.05).

See topics and subheads detailing particular taxes.

Interstate Co-operation.—Nebraska repealed Multistate Tax Compact in 1985.

Uniform Federal Lien Registration Act adopted. (52-1001 et seq.).

ALCOHOLIC BEVERAGES TAX:

Any manufacturer or wholesaler is taxed at rate of 23¢ per gallon on beer; 75¢ per gallon on wine containing not more than 14% and not less than $^5/_{10}$ of 1% of alcohol per volume; $1.35 per gallon on wines and other dilute alcoholic beverages containing more than 14% of alcohol by volume. (53-160 et seq.).

CIGARETTE TAX:

Imposed by 77-2601 et seq.

CONDOMINIUM TAX:

Condominium taxes and assessments, assessed to and collected on each individual condominium apartment, each of which should be carried on tax book as a separate taxable entity. No sale of a condominium building, as a whole, for delinquent taxes, will divest or affect title on individual units. Value of common areas determined by assessor and taxes apportioned against individual units. (76-823).

CORPORATE TAX:

Taxation of Corporations.—Corporate income tax is based on Nebraska taxable income: 4.25% on first $50,000 and 6.5% on taxable income over $50,000. When corporation operates in more than one state, Nebraska taxable income will be computed (beginning in 1992) by using sales-only formula. Percentage of sales occurring in Nebraska will be deemed to be percentage of total corporate income taxable in Nebraska. (77-2734.05 to 77-2734.16). For 1992, additional corporate occupation tax of $150 is levied on all corporations except §501(c)(3) corporations. Tax credits to businesses are available under Employment and Investment Growth Act (77-4101 et seq.) and under Employment Expansion and Investment Incentive Act (77-27,187 et seq.).

Credits applicable to larger corporations can be gained through agreement with Tax Commissioner. Proposal must include plan for either: (a) Investment in qualified property of at least $3,000,000 and addition of at least 30 new employees, or (b) minimum investment in qualified property, resulting in net gain in total value of tangible property in state of type subject to depreciation, amortization, or other recovery under Internal Revenue Code of 1986, of $20,000,000. Depending on proposal, credits and incentives may include: (1) Election to use sales-only formula for income computation in years prior to 1992; (2) exemption on various personal property; (3) refund of all sales and use taxes paid on qualifying investments; and (4) credit equal to 5% of compensation paid to either Nebraska employees or base-year employees plus credit for 10% of investment in qualified properties. (77-4104 and 4105). Certain transactions or activities are ineligible for credits. (See 77-4104.)

Smaller qualifying businesses may receive tax credits by adding two fulltime employees, and investing $75,000 in real or depreciable tangible personal property within Nebraska. Credit will be $1,500 for each new employee and $1,000 for each $75,000 of investment, except for qualifying taxpayers located within boundaries of enterprise zone pursuant to Enterprise Zone Act, amount of credit for such qualifying taxpayers shall be $4,500 for each new employee and $3,000 for each $75,000 of increased investment if at least 50% of new employees live within boundaries of zone; or $4,500 for each new employee residing within boundaries of zone, and $1,000 for each $75,000 of increased investment if less than 50% of new employees reside within such zone. This credit shall not exceed $75,000. (77-27,188). Amount of credit shall not exceed 50% of taxpayer's tax liability, except credits for enterprise zones which shall not exceed total tax liability reduced by all other nonrefundable credits. (77-27,188 to -27,188.01).

Financial Institutions State Franchise Tax.—See category Business Regulation and Commerce, topic Banks and Banking.

ESTATES TAX:

In addition to inheritance tax, an estate or excise tax is levied on the estate of every resident decedent based upon the state tax credit allowed by the Federal Estate Tax. In case of decedents dying after Aug. 16, 1954, estate tax is amount by which maximum credit allowable upon Federal Estate Tax exceeds aggregate amount of all estate, inheritance, legacy or succession taxes paid to any state, territory, District of Columbia or possession of U. S. in respect to any property included in gross estate. Estate tax is due and payable to State Treasurer within 12 months from date of death of decedent, and limitation of time in which tax return shall be open to inspection and examination is three years from date of filing same. Executors, administrators, trustees, grantees, donees, beneficiaries and surviving joint owners are liable for tax until it is paid and tax is lien on property subject thereto until paid except that no interest in any property passing from decedent to decedent's surviving spouse shall be subject to this lien. If tax is not paid when due, it draws interest at legal rate from due date. Interest on deficiency accrues beginning on date tax becomes payable. (77-2101.01 to -2102).

Valuation Date.—Value of assets is determined as of date of death; no optional date.

GASOLINE TAX:

Adopted Interstate Motor Carriers Base State Fuel Tax Compact Act. (66-1401 to -1415).

GENERATION SKIPPING TAX:

Apportionment Against Inter Vivos Disposition.—See: 77-2108.

GIFT TAX:

None; but inheritance tax applies to gifts made within three years of death.

GRAIN AND SEED TAX:

Grain and seed, if business or agricultural inventory, are exempt from personal property tax. (77-202).

INCOME TAX:

Returns are to be filed at or before time for filing federal return and payment made of any tax due. Declaration and payment of estimated tax are to be made at time for filing federal tax estimates, unless otherwise provided by regulation issued by Tax Commissioner. Authority to make regulations on other matters is also given. Extensive provisions deal with collection of tax deficiencies, making of refunds and imposition of penalties. Taxes unpaid after demand, together with interest and penalties, become a lien upon taxpayer's real estate or any interest therein, which lien is valid against a mortgagee, purchaser or judgment creditor, only after notice thereof has been filed with Register of Deeds of county where property of taxpayer is located. (77-2714 to -27,124). Nebraska is not member of Multistate Tax Compact (repealed, 1985).

Rates.—Beginning with tax years on or after Jan. 1, 1987, tax on income earned by residents and Nebraska-source income earned by nonresidents is based on Nebraska taxable income, calculated by making certain Nebraska adjustments to federal taxable income. Legislature sets rate of income tax which shall become effective Jan. 1 of succeeding year and remain in effect until changed. (77-2715.01). Tax rate is based on four-tier progressive schedule starting at rate of 2.2%, with top marginal rate of 6.4% for tax year starting Jan. 1, 1990, and starting at rate of 2.4%, with top marginal rate of 6.9% for tax years starting on and after Jan. 1, 1991. (77-2714 et seq.).

Special Provisions.—There are special provisions relating to trusts and estates and their beneficiaries, resident and nonresident, partnerships, determination of Nebraska income of nonresident individuals and of corporations subject to tax. Withholding from wages taxable under law is provided for. (77-2717 et seq.).

INHERITANCE TAX:

All property, including life insurance payable to executor or administrator, passing by will or intestate laws of state or by transfer made in contemplation of death or intended to take effect in possession or enjoyment after death of grantor is subject to an inheritance tax, based on clear market value. Interests passing to surviving spouse by will shall not be subject to tax. (77-2004). If joint property was acquired by gift from third person, only fractional part owned by deceased is included in his estate. (77-2001, and -2002).

Valuation Date.—Value of assets is determined as of date of death; no optional date. (117 Neb. 854, 223 N.W. 633).

Rates and exemptions for each beneficiary are:

(1) Transfer to father, mother, grandfather, grandmother, child or any lineal descendant, brother, sister, or any lineal descendant legally adopted, or to any person to whom deceased for not less than ten years stood in relation of parent. Exempt up to $10,000; 1% on excess. Also exempt is value of homestead allowance, exempt property, family maintenance allowance, statutory interest in real property and value of specific personal property vested in spouse under 30-103. Interest passing to surviving spouse by will or otherwise, shall not be subject to tax. (77-2004).

(2) Transfer to uncle, aunt, nephew, niece or lineal descendant of any of these: exempt up to $2,000; 6% on excess over $2,000 up to $60,000; 9% on excess over $60,000. (77-2005).

(3) All other transfers: exempt up to $500; 6% on excess over $500 up to $5,000; 9% on excess over $5,000 up to $10,000; 12% on excess over $10,000 up to $20,000; 15% on excess over $20,000 up to $50,000; 18% on excess over $50,000. Rates applied to clear market value of beneficial interests received. (77-2006).

Gifts to United States or any agency or instrumentality thereof, to the State of Nebraska or any sub-division, municipality or agency or instrumentality of the state or sub-division (77-2007.03) or to any religious, charitable or educational corporation or trustee of such corporation provided any one of the following conditions exist: (a) corporation is organized under the laws of the State of Nebraska or United States; (b) property to be used solely within the state; (c) corporation is organized under the laws of another state that has no similar tax or has a reciprocal provision for tax exemptions, are exempt (77-2007.04).

See note at head of Digest as to 1998 legislation covered.

See Topical Index in front part of this volume.

INHERITANCE TAX . . . . *continued*
Transfers.—

*Transfer of Securities of Nonresident Decedent.—*No statutory procedure for obtaining waiver of inheritance tax on transfer of securities owned by nonresident decedent.

Uniform Reciprocal Transfer Tax Act (see Part III of this volume for text) has been adopted pertaining to personal property (except tangible personal property having an actual situs in this state) of a nonresident decedent. (77-2007.01).

Assessment.—County court of county in which decedent resided or in which real property of nonresident decedent is located, has jurisdiction to determine all questions of assessment of said tax. (77-2027). Court may appraise the estate or appoint an appraiser, who sets time and place for hearing and gives interested parties notice thereof and at said time and place appraises all property of estate and reports to court. Clerk magistrate also has authority to appoint appraiser. Appraiser's fees and expenses are paid by county treasurer on certificate of county court out of money collected on said tax. (77-2019 to -2024). Any person dissatisfied with appraisement may appeal to Court of Appeals in same manner as appeal from district court to Court of Appeals. (77-2023). County court computes tax from appraisement and certifies same to county treasurer of proper county and when tax is paid county treasurer gives receipt therefor. (77-2022). In absence of probate of estate, proceedings for determination of tax may be instituted, by petition of county attorney or other person having legal interest in property (77-2018.02).

Lien.—Except as to bona fide purchasers for value without notice, tax is a lien for ten years from date of death if, within five years after amount of inheritance tax is finally ascertained and assessed by court having jurisdiction, action is brought for collection of tax. (77-2037).

Payment and Collection.—All taxes are due and payable 12 months from decedent's date of death and draw interest at legal rate from said date. (77-2010).

Executor or administrator may pay tax and deduct same from property of legatee or person entitled thereto and may sell property to raise funds for this purpose. (77-2011, -2013). If tax not paid, collection may be enforced by county treasurer in same manner as collection of other tax, or person from whom tax is due may be cited by county court to appear before court and show cause why tax is not paid. (77-2028, 2030).

Estates in Possession and Remainder.—If bequest, devise or transfer is in trust or otherwise for life or term with vested or contingent remainder over, the entire property is assessed and the tax allocated between beneficiaries in accordance with regulations of State Tax Commissioner. Where any interest is contingent a tax is computed on the highest possible rate and on happening of the contingency tax can be recomputed and surplus, if any, refunded. Tax is paid out of corpus and refund becomes a part of corpus. (77-2008 to -2008.02).

Application for forms, etc., should be made to State Tax Commissioner, Lincoln.

Application for information should be made to county judge in charge of particular estate.

Uniform Act on Interstate Arbitration and Compromise of Death Taxes adopted. (77-3301 to -3316).

INSURANCE TAX:

Taxation of Insurance and Surety Companies.—See category Insurance, topic Insurance Companies.

MARIJUANA AND CONTROLLED SUBSTANCES TAX:

77-4301 et seq. imposes and governs taxes on marijuana and other controlled substances held or acquired by dealer in violation of Nebraska law.

MECHANICAL AMUSEMENT DEVICE TAX:

See 77-3001 to -3011.

MOTOR VEHICLES TAX:

Motor vehicles are assessed separately. (See category Transportation, topic Motor Vehicles.) Tax situs of vehicle owned or used by student shall be place of student's residence. (77-1240). Member of Armed Forces of U.S. need not pay tax if such person has not established domicile in Nebraska. (77-1242.01).

MUSIC TAX:

Musical Compositions.—A tax of 3% of gross receipts from disposal of or licensing use of must be paid to Secretary of State before March 15 of each year. (59-1403).

OCCUPATION TAX:

Occupation tax on corporations, see category Business Organizations, topic Corporations.

PARI-MUTUEL TAX:

See 2-1208.01.

PROPERTY TAX:

Assessment.—General supervision of assessment of property taxes rests in County Assessor (appointed by Governor [77-363]) and State Board of Equalization consisting of Governor, Secretary of State, State Auditor, State Treasurer and Tax Commissioner. (77-501). Immediate assessment is made by County Assessor. (77-1311).

Real property is assessed annually on Jan. 1 at 12:01 A.M. (77-1301) on basis of actual value (77-201). Actual value is market value in ordinary course of trade, determined by (1) comparison with sales of property of known or recognized value, taking into account location, zoning, and current functional use; (2) earning capacity of property; and (3) reproduction cost less depreciation, among other things. (77-112). Agricultural land and horticultural land shall constitute separate and distinct class of property

for purposes of property taxation, valued at 80% of its actual value for agricultural or horticultural use pursuant to §§77-1359 to -1363. (77-1344; 77-1359 to -1363; L.B. 611). After Apr. 1 and on or before July 25, County Assessor shall report to County Board of Equalization any overvaluation or undervaluation of any real property. County Board of Equalization shall consider report in accordance with §77-1504. (77-1315). Mortgage on real property in state is treated as interest in real property and interests of mortgagor and mortgagee are assessed separately (77-1402), unless mortgage contains provision that mortgagor shall pay tax, in which event both interests are assessed and taxed to mortgagor or owner. (77-1407).

Tangible personal property is assessed annually on Jan. 1 at 12:01 A.M., which assessment shall be used as basis of taxation until next regular assessment. (77-1201). Tangible personal property, not including motor vehicles registered for highway operation, shall constitute separate and distinct class for purposes of property taxation, valued at net book value. (77-112). Tangible personal property transferred as gift or devise or as part of transaction which is not purchase shall be subject to taxation based upon date property was acquired by previous owner and at previous owner's adjusted basis. Motor vehicles constitute separate and distinct class, valued as in 77-1239 to 77-1241.01. (77-201). Every person of legal age and sound mind shall list and verify by statement of all personal property (except motor vehicles, grain, and seed) which he is required to list, either as owner, lessee or occupant in control thereof or as parent, guardian, trustee, personal representative, administrator, receiver, accounting officer, partner, limited liability company member, or agent, upon blanks furnished by county assessor and prescribed by Property Tax Administrator. (77-1201; 77-1229). Schedule must also be filed by corporation, partnership, manufacturer's agent, personal representative, administrator, receiver and holder of leased or escrowed property. (77-1201). Taxable tangible personal property shall be listed and assessed when it has acquired tax status. (77-1202). Place for listing determined by county board or Property Tax Administrator. (77-1216). Taxable tangible personal property brought into state or into one county from another county after 12:01 A.M. Jan. 1 and before July 1 taxable unless tax has been paid thereon in some other state. (77-1211). Where owner changes residence between Jan. 1 at 12:01 A.M. and July 1 property assessed where assessor first calls upon owner. (77-1212).

Decision of county assessor may be appealed to board of equalization, and then appealed de novo to district court within 20 days of notice of rejection in manner prescribed in 77-1510, 77-1511. (77-399).

Review of Assessment.—County board of equalization may meet between June 1 and July 25 to consider and correct current year's assessment of any real property which has been undervalued, overvalued, or omitted. Action of board may be protested within 30 days after mailing of notice. (77-1504). Appeals may be taken from County Board of Equalization to Tax Equalization and Review Commission in accordance with Tax Equalization and Review Commission Act. (77-1510). Commission equalizes valuations between counties. (77-505). Appeal may be taken from State Board of Equalization to Court of Appeals. (77-510).

Payment and Lien.—Real property taxes are payable to county treasurer on Dec. 31 next following levy. One-half of tax becomes delinquent on May 1 (Apr. 1 in all counties having population of more than 100,000 inhabitants) following and other half becomes delinquent on Sept. 1 (Aug. 1 in all counties having population of more than 100,000 inhabitants). (77-203, 204). Delinquent real property taxes draw interest at legal rate from date of delinquency. (77-207; 45-104.01). Taxes on real property are first lien thereon from Dec. 31 next following levy until paid or extinguished. (77-203).

Personal property taxes become due and payable on Nov. 1 next following date of levy. (77-205). One-half thereof becomes delinquent on Dec. 1 and the second half on July 1 next following date on which tax becomes due and payable. (77-206). Due date is accelerated in event of attempted sale, levy of attachment, or attempted removal from jurisdiction. (77-1214). Delinquent personal property taxes draw interest at legal rate from date of delinquency. (77-207; 45-104.01). Personal property taxes are first lien on all personal property of person to whom assessed, after Nov. 1 next following date of levy until paid. (77-205).

Tax Sales.—

*Real Property.—*All real property, on which there are delinquent taxes, is offered for sale on first Mon. of Mar. of each year by county treasurer. (77-1802). Treasurer must give notice by publication in some newspaper in counties having more than 250,000 inhabitants, once each week for three consecutive weeks, commencing first week in Feb., and by posting copy of said notice in his office. Notice must describe property and give amount of delinquent taxes due thereon. (77-1804).

Sales continue from day to day until all parcels have been offered for sale or sold. (77-1806). After such sale has closed, treasurer may sell land at private sale to any person who will pay amount of taxes, penalty and costs. (77-1814). A certificate known as "County Treasurer's Certificate of Tax Sale" is issued to purchaser, stating sum paid, description of property and when purchaser will be entitled to deed, if not redeemed. (77-1818 and -1819). Certificates are assignable. (77-1822).

Treasurer's deed cannot be issued until holder of certificate, at least three months before applying for deed, serves every person in possession and also all record owners and encumbrancers, if found in the county, with notice stating when such purchaser purchased land, description thereof, in whose name assessed, for what year taxed or specially assessed, and that after expiration of three months from date of service, deed will be applied for. (77-1831 and -1832). If address of owner or encumbrancer appears of record, notice may be sent by registered mail, otherwise if cannot be found in county, notice may be published for three consecutive weeks in newspaper published or in general circulation therein, first time not more than five months and last time not more than three months before time for redemption expires. (77-1832 to -1835). Deed must be applied for within six months after expiration of three years from date of sale. (77-1837). No action can be brought for recovery of real property sold for nonpayment of taxes after five years from execution and recording of treasurer's deed, unless owner is minor, mentally incompetent person or convict in penitentiary, in which case it must be brought within five years from removal of disability. (77-1855).

See note at head of Digest as to 1998 legislation covered.

See Topical Index in front part of this volume.

PROPERTY TAX . . . *continued*

If owner of tax sale certificate fails to demand deed or commence action for foreclosure within six months after expiration of three years from date of sale, certificate is cancelled by county treasurer. (77-1856).

Tangible Personal Property.—Delinquent personal taxes may be collected by distress warrant after Sept. 1 of year following levy, executed in same manner as execution on personal property. (77-1717; L.B. 306).

Redemption from Tax Sales.—Tax certificates may be redeemed at any time before delivery of deed by county treasurer by payment to the treasurer of sum mentioned in certificate with interest at 14% per annum (45-104.01) from date of purchase to redemption, together with all subsequent taxes paid by holder of certificate with interest thereon at same rate from date of payment to date of redemption, and treasurer must issue redemption certificate to person so redeeming (77-1824). There is absolute right of redemption for period of not less than two years from such sale and occupant must in all cases be served with personal notice before time of redemption expires. (Const., art. VIII, §3).

Foreclosure of Tax Lien.—Instead of applying for treasurer's deed, or if deed has been issued by surrendering same in court, holder of a tax certificate may foreclose tax lien by suit in district court brought within six months from expiration of three years from date of sale. (77-1902).

If any parcel of real estate is not sold at treasurer's sale for want of bidder, county board may order county attorney to foreclose tax lien by equity suit. If suit is based on tax certificate, confirmation may be had immediately after sheriff's sale; otherwise final confirmation may not be had for two years from sheriff's sale. All tax certificates owned by the plaintiff, even if they cover separate tracts owned by different people, may be included in one suit. All persons claiming any interest in the real estate may be joined; if owners are unknown or can not be found, action may proceed against the land itself, and service may be had in manner provided for service on unknown defendants. Attorney's fee of 10% of tax, interest, and costs may be taxed as a part of the costs and apportioned with other costs. Decree may order surplus from sale of one parcel to be applied on lien on another tract owned by same defendant if rights of third persons are not affected thereby. Court may order that only so much of the land owned by any defendant shall be sold as may be necessary to satisfy the lien on all the land owned by said defendant. Order of sale may issue twenty days after entry of decree. The property is sold as upon execution. If the purchaser is a private person, all subsequent taxes must be paid before confirmation, except that if a taxing unit has issued to it a tax sale certificate covering the subsequent taxes, upon production of such certificate in court the sale may be confirmed, even though the subsequent taxes have not been paid. (77-1901 to -1913).

Redemption from Tax Foreclosure.—Any party entitled to redeem may redeem at any time after decree of foreclosure and before final confirmation by paying to clerk of court the amount found due with interest and costs to date of redemption and, in addition thereto, where the land has been sold to a purchaser other than the plaintiff, interest on the purchase price at the rate of 14% per annum (45-104.01) from date of sale to date of redemption (77-1917).

RAILROAD TAX:

Railroad property is taxed as provided by 77-601 to -675.

REAL ESTATE CONVEYANCE TAX:

See subhead Stamp Tax, supra.

SALES AND USE TAXES:

Sales Tax.—Tax upon sales at retail, is applicable to sales of tangible personal property, utility services, temporary lodgings and admissions, with certain exceptions and exemptions. Rate set annually by Legislature as assisted by Nebraska Economic Forecasting Advisory Board. (77-2702 to -2713). Beginning July 1, 1998, and until July 1, 1999, the tax rate is 4.5%. Beginning July 1, 1999, the rate returns to 5%. (77-2701.02; L.B. 1104). Any purchaser of depreciable agricultural machinery or equipment purchased on or after Jan. 1, 1992, for use in commercial agriculture may apply for refund of all Nebraska sales or use taxes and all local option sales or use taxes paid thereon. (77-2708.01). Incorporated municipality may, by ordinance of its governing body, impose sales and use tax of 1/2 to 1½% if majority of electors have approved. (77-27,142 to -27,148).

Use tax at same rates applies with similar exemptions. Reporting and payment of tax is provided for monthly with 2½% deduction on first $3,000 remitted each month and 1/2% on all amounts in excess thereof, as reimbursement for cost of collecting tax. However, for each month from Oct. 1, 1991 to Sept. 30, 1992, such collectors shall withhold as reimbursement 3% of first $5,000 remitted each month and 1% of all amounts in excess thereof and for each month from Apr. 1, 1993 to Mar. 31, 1994 such collectors shall withhold ¾% of first $2,000 remitted each month and ¼% of all amounts in excess thereof. (77-2703[2][d]).

SPECIAL FUELS TAX:

All motor fuel suppliers, distributors, wholesalers, importers, and retailers licensed under Nebraska law shall furnish cash bond to state. (66-733 to -736).

STAMP TAX:

Stamp Tax.—$1.75 per $1,000 value on real estate transfers, but see subhead Exemptions, supra. (76-901 to -908).

UNEMPLOYMENT COMPENSATION TAX:

Unemployment compensation tax, in the form of "contributions," is imposed by 48-601 to -671.

Rate is such percentage of payroll as may be determined by Commissioner of Labor to be necessary to maintain required reserve. Reserve and rate of contribution are based on employer's entire payroll, without limitation as to amount paid to any individual. (48-649).

No contributions are required from employees and employer may not deduct his contributions from wages of employees.

Commissioner of State Department of Labor is charged with administration of the act and given authority to prescribe time and manner of payment of contributions. (48-648).

TRANSPORTATION

MOTOR VEHICLES:

Department of Motor Vehicles, State Capitol Building, Lincoln, Nebraska 68509, has general supervision of motor vehicles.

Vehicle license required, must show proof of financial responsibility to register vehicle (60-302; and -334), renewable annually, fee is $15 (60-329). Special licenses for dealers. (60-320; 60-334). On number plates issued to tax exempt vehicles, words tax exempt will appear on plate. (60-311.02). Salvage certificate of title not valid for registration purposes. (60-302). Number plates must be displayed front and rear. (60-323). New plates are issued every three years, beginning in 1984. Renewal tabs are issued in years when plates are not issued. (60-311). Members of armed forces may renew license without examination. (60-488). Message license plates permitted; fee is $30 annually. (60-311.10 to -311.12).

Operator's license issued by county treasurer (60-4,119) on application and examination by Director of Motor Vehicles (60-4, 113). Examination required if renewal application not made within 90 days before expiration date, except members of U.S. Armed Forces or spouses. (60-4,121). Application for replacement license because of change of name or address must be made within 60 days of change. (60-4, 120). Minimum age 16 years. To obtain license, any person under age of 18 must produce certified birth registration or notarized birth registration, must have possessed valid operator's permit for 12 months prior to application and must not have accumulated three or more points in the 12 months prior to application. (60-484; L.B. 320). Person 15 years or more may obtain learner's permit, may operate vehicle if accompanied by licensed operator who is at least 21. (60-4,123; L.B. 320). To obtain permit, applicant must successfully complete department-approved driver safety course. (L.B. 320). Nonresident individuals who serve in state on active duty as members of armed forces or who are considered full-time students are exempt from licensing requirements of Nebraska if duly licensed in state of residence. Any person who lives on farm and is 13-16 years of age may obtain farm permit. (60-4, 126). Nonresident individuals engaged in temporary agricultural employment in Nebraska, not to exceed 60 days, may be granted additional 30 day immunity if similar immunity is granted by state of his permanent residence. (60-488). All licenses expire on licensee's birthday in year in which age is divisible by four. (60-490). Licensee may waive written portion of exam if driving record is free of moving violations for four years. Must present abstract of record to examiner. To obtain record, mail $2 to Department of Motor Vehicles, Drivers Record Office, P.O. Box 94789, Lincoln, Nebraska 68509, and include date of birth, name, driver's license number and self-addressed stamped envelope. Allow two weeks. (60-4,122).

Titles.—Certificate of title is required, which is issued by county clerk where applicant resides. (60-105, and -106; 196 Neb. 595, 244 N.W.2d 209). Application for certificate of title must include statement that identification inspection has been conducted unless surrendered ownership document is Nebraska certificate of title, manufacturer's or importer's statement of origin, or vehicle is to be registered under 60-305.09. (60-106).

Sales.—Manufacturer or importer selling new car to dealer for resale must furnish dealer with a manufacturer's or importer's certificate. Any other seller must deliver to purchaser a certificate with proper assignment thereon, failing in which purchaser acquires no title. Within 30 days after delivery of motor vehicle, purchaser must apply for certificate of title, which is issued by county clerk on presentation of certificate duly assigned or bill of sale or other satisfactory proof of ownership. Such certificate may be cancelled by Department of Motor Vehicles if issued to wrong person, and vehicle may not be operated after cancellation. The act also covers commercial trailers, semi-trailers and cabin trailers. (60-101 to -117). Fee for issuing title certificate is $6. (60-115).

Liens.—Security agreement, conditional sale contract or other instrument intended to operate as lien on a motor vehicle must be accompanied by certificate of title or manufacturer's or importer's certificate, which must be retained by lienholder unless, in case of certificate of title, county clerk has made notation of lien on face thereof. When lien is discharged, holder must endorse cancellation on certificate over his signature and certificate may then be presented to county clerk who will note cancellation in his records. These provisions supersede other statutory provisions as to filing of security agreements, conditional sale contracts, etc., so far as motor vehicles are concerned. (60-110). No limitation on length of time lien continues.

Fee for noting lien on certificate is $3. (60-115). No fee for notation of release of lien. (60-110).

Uniform Commercial Code in effect. See category Business Regulation and Commerce, topic Commercial Code.

Identification Marks.—Person selling motor vehicle whose motor number or manufacturer's serial number has been altered or defaced is subject to fine up to $10,000 or imprisonment up to five years, or both. (60-116).

Odometer Alteration.—Unlawful; $100 minimum, $500 maximum fines. (60-132, 60-318, 28-106).

Operation Prohibited.—By person under 16 or intoxicated person or person under age of 21 who has consumed any alcohol. (60-6,211.01 to -6,211.04). However, outside of metropolitan cities and cities of primary and of first class, person between ages of 14 and 16 may obtain limited permits to drive to and from school by nearest way or may drive under personal supervision of parent or guardian. Also, person 15 years or more may obtain learner's permit, may operate vehicle if accompanied by licensed operator who is at least 21. (60-4,123; L.B. 320). Operating motor vehicle to avoid arrest can

See note at head of Digest as to 1998 legislation covered.

See Topical Index in front part of this volume.

NE – 33

MOTOR VEHICLES . . . *continued*

lead to order forbidding operator from driving motor vehicle for two years. (28-905). See also subhead Traffic Regulations, infra.

Size and Weight Limits.—Regulated by 60-6,288 to -6,294.

Tolerance.—Gross weight on which registration has been paid plus 1,000 lbs. (60-6,300). Fines of $25 for each 1,000 pounds or fraction thereof for overloading. (60-6,300).

Equipment Required.—Regulated by 60-6,226; 60-6,244—6,246; 60-6,262—6,263; 60-6,283-6,286. Studded snow tires permitted between Nov. 1 and Apr. 1. (60-6,250). See also subhead Seat Belts, infra; category Family, topic Infants.

Inspection.—Held unconstitutional and program abandoned July 1, 1982.

Lights.—Regulated by 60-6,219 to -6,225, and general provisions of Uniform Act.

Traffic Regulations.—Substantially all of provisions of Uniform Act Regulating Traffic on Highways has been adopted. (39-628.01). Driving while intoxicated law stiffened, and applied to liquor or drugs. First offense, mandatory minimum seven days imprisonment and $400 fine. Second offense 30 days and $500, subsequent offenses three months minimum, one year maximum sentence, $600 fine (L.B. 309). In addition, for first offense, court shall order person not to drive for six months and license revoked for same period; second offense within 12 years, one year loss of driving privilege with revocation of license for same; for three or more offenses prior to current conviction within past 12 years, 15 year loss of privilege and license revoked for same. (60-6,196—6,197; 60-6,205—6,208; 28-106; L.B. 309).

Helmet Requirement.—Person shall not operate or be passenger on motorcycle on any highway unless wearing approved protective helmet. Violators shall be fined $50. (60-6,278 to -6,282).

Towing Motor Vehicles.—Any transporter doing business in state may, in lieu of registering each vehicle transported, secure transporter's certificate and one transporter number plate from Department of Motor Vehicles. Fee, $10. Transporter plate or certificate may not be displayed upon work or service vehicle. Applicant shall keep record of each vehicle transported for three years. (60-320; 60-334).

Accidents.—Operator is required to stop and render reasonable assistance to injured parties. Must give name, address, registration number of vehicle and show operator's license. Penalty is fine not more than one year or $1,000 or both and revocation of driver's license. (60-696 to -698).

Insurance.—See subhead Proof of Financial Responsibility, infra.

Liability of owner for negligence of others is governed by common law generally. Owner is liable for injuries caused by automobile driven by servant between garage and place of employment, despite slight deviation from direct route. (143 Neb. 344, 9 N.W.2d 488). Owner and head of family who furnishes automobile for pleasure and convenience of family is liable for injury inflicted by car when driven by member of family with his express or implied consent (Family Purpose Doctrine). (238 Neb. 1, 468 N.W.2d 604).

Liability of Lessor.—Owner of leased truck, truck-tractor, or trailer is liable for injury or death resulting from operation thereof. (25-21,239).

Guests.—No liability for injury to guest including guest related to operator of car by marriage, or parent, grandparent, child, grandchild or sibling of operator, unless operator of car was intoxicated or guilty of gross negligence. (25-21,237). Statute is constitutional. (210 Neb. 272, 313 N.W.2d 688).

Proof of Financial Responsibility.—Motor-Vehicle Safety Responsibility Act has been adopted. Owner or operator of any motor vehicle involved in accident causing property damage to apparent extent in excess of $500 to that of each person or personal injury or death of any person must, within ten days, make written report of accident to Department of Motor Vehicles. (60-699). License and registration of residents and all operating privileges of nonresidents are suspended unless owner or operator: (1) Has insurance or bond in effect to cover $25,000 property damage, $25,000 for personal injury to or death of one person and $50,000 for two or more persons; (2) qualifies as self-insurer; (3) within 60 days deposits securities in such amount as Department may determine to satisfy any judgment growing out of accident; (4) within 60 days is released from liability by judgment of court or any judgment rendered is satisfied. Insurance must be written in company authorized to do business in Nebraska or if written outside state by company not authorized to do business in Nebraska company must execute acknowledgement that it shall be amenable to process issued by Nebraska court in any action upon policy. (60-509). Provision is made for reinstatement of license and registration on certain conditions. Penalties for various violations run up to $1,000 or one year imprisonment or both. (60-501 to -569).

Under Insured Motorist Insurance Coverage Act incorporated into Motor-Vehicle Safety Responsibility Act: Owner or operator of any motor vehicle must carry insurance to cover underinsured motorist liability in amount of: (1) $25,000 for one person for bodily injury, or death; (2) $50,000 for two or more persons. Insured may request additional coverage but not to exceed $100,000 per person or $300,000 per accident. Maximum liability of insurer is lesser of difference between limit of underinsured's coverage and amount paid to insured; or amount of damages sustained but unrecovered. Act does not apply if: (1) Insured in writing refuses coverage; (2) insured enters into settlement which adversely affects rights of insured; (3) injury caused by insured or family member; (4) statute of limitations has expired. (60-571 et seq.).

See also subhead Vehicle License, supra; category Insurance, topic Insurance Companies, subhead Policies.

No-Fault Insurance not adopted.

Foreign vehicle registered in home state and displaying license plates required by laws thereof may operate without license provided trucks, truck-tractors, semitrailers or buses must comply with regulations imposed on Nebraska trucks, truck-tractors, semitrailers or buses and pay same fees as are charged residents of Nebraska. (60-305.03).

Nonresident operator who has complied with license and registration requirements of home state may operate car in state without Nebraska operator's license for a period not exceeding 30 days. Privilege forfeited on conviction of violation of any motor vehicle law. (60-488).

Nonresident owner gainfully employed or present in Nebraska shall register his car after 30 days employment or presence, unless home state grants reciprocity. (60-305.01; to -305.03).

Action against nonresident arising out of operation of vehicle in state may be commenced under general provisions on service of process as they apply to all civil proceedings.

Nonresident Violator Compact of 1977 adopted. (60-4,100).

Direct actions against insurer by injured person not authorized by statute.

Motor Vehicle Carriers.—Public Service Commission has jurisdiction of intrastate commerce by motor vehicle and power to make rules covering method of operation, rates, accounting, employment, and other matters. Carrier must obtain certificate of public convenience and necessity before commencing operation. Carrier must charge published schedule of rates approved by the Commission and penalty is prescribed for rebating, discrimination or other violations of the rules of Commission or provisions of statute. (75-109).

License fees to foreign motor carriers are generally amount charged Nebraska residents. (60-305.03, 60-305.09).

There are special provisions with respect to shipment of livestock (54-145.01; 60-331; 86-502 to -503), and transportation of motor vehicle fuels (66-501 to -524).

Motor Vehicle Dealers License Board.—Persons or firms engaged in sale of or lease, for more than 60 days, motor vehicles in Nebraska, new or used, must be licensed by the Board. Application for license, in form prescribed by Board, must be submitted in writing, accompanied by proof of insurance. (60-1407; 60-1407.01). Board has power to deny, revoke or suspend license after hearing. (60-1413). Annual fees not to exceed: Dealers $200, salesmen $10, manufacturer $300, distributors $300, factory representatives $10, distributor representatives $10, finance companies $200, wrecker or salvage dealer $100, factory branch $100, motorcycle dealer $200, auction dealer $200, supplemental dealer's license $10. (60-1411.01).

Taxation.—Before license issued applicant must show payment of current tax on said vehicle or camper unit. (60-303, 60-1803; 60-334). Valuation fixed by Tax Commissioner. (77-1239). If motor vehicle transferred during year transferor is given refund for number of full months remaining in registration year if amount is $2 or more. (77-1240.03). Vehicle must be registered in county where vehicle is domiciled, or where bona fide business conducted. Every owner of vehicle required to be registered shall make application for registration to county treasurer of county in which vehicle has tax situs, as defined in §77-1238. (60-302). Fees are payable to County Treasurer where registered unless otherwise provided. (60-318; and -334). Municipalities have local option authority for vehicle flat fee tax. Armed Forces members need not pay tax provided they are not domiciled in Nebraska. (77-1242.01).

Gasoline Tax.—See category Taxation, topic Gasoline Tax.

Service on Unauthorized Foreign Manufacturers or Distributors of Motor Vehicles.—See category Civil Actions and Procedure, topic Process.

Seat Belts.—Required equipment in motor vehicles manufactured after 1973. Statute requires seat belt usage on all roadways. Violators are fined $25. (60-6,270; 60-6,265—6,266; 60-6,272).

See note at head of Digest as to 1998 legislation covered.

See Topical Index in front part of this volume.

COMMERCIAL CODE FORMS

See also categories Business Regulation and Commerce, topic Commercial Code; Mortgages, topic Chattel Mortgages.

Financing Statement.—Standard Form.

This FINANCING STATEMENT is presented to a Filing Officer for filing pursuant to the Uniform Commercial Code:	No. of Additional Sheets presented:	Maturity Date 3. (Optional):
1. Debtor(s) (Last Name First) and Address(es): Social Security No. _____	2. Secured Party(ies): Name(s) and Address(es): Federal I.D. No. _____	4. For Filing Officer: Time, Date, No., Filing Office

5. The Financing Statement Covers the Following Types (or Items) of Property:

☐ Proceeds—   ☐ Products of the Collateral are Also Covered:

6. ☐ To be Recorded in Real Estate Mortgage Records

7. Description of Real Estate:

8. Name(s) of Record Owner(s): _____

9. Assignee(s) of Secured Party and Address(es)

10. This statement is filed without the debtor's signature to perfect a security interest in collateral (check ☐ if so)   X
   ☐ already subject to a security interest in another jurisdiction when it was brought into this state, or
   ☐ which is proceeds of the following described original collateral which was perfected:

By _____
       Signature(s) of Debtor(s)

By _____
       Signature of Secured Party

(1) FILING OFFICER COPY

Termination Statement.—Addendum to page 3 of Financing Statement.

TERMINATION STATEMENT: This Statement of Termination of Financing is presented to a Filing Officer for filing pursuant to the Uniform Commercial Code. The Secured Party certifies that the Secured Party no longer claims a security interest under the financing statement bearing the file number shown above.

Date _____, 19____   By: _____

Signature of Secured Party

Filing Officer is requested to note file number, date and hour of filing on this copy and return to the person filing, as an acknowledgment.

(Signature of Secured Party or Assignee of Record.
Not Valid Until Signed.)

Statement of Continuation, Partial Release, Assignment, Etc.—Standard Form.

This **STATEMENT** is presented to a filing officer for filing pursuant to the Uniform Commercial Code:		3. Maturity date (if any).
1. Debtor(s) (Last Name First) and address(es)	2. Secured Party(ies) and address(es)	For Filing Officer (Date, Time, Number, and Filing Office)

4. This statement refers to original Financing Statement bearing File No. _____

Filed with _____ Date Filed _____, 19___

5. ☐ **Continuation.**   The original financing statement between the foregoing Debtor and Secured Party, bearing file number shown above, is still effective.

6. ☐ **Termination.**   Secured Party no longer claims a security interest under the financing statement bearing file number shown above.

7. ☐ **Assignment.**   The Secured Party's right under the financing statement bearing file number shown above to the property described in Item 10 have been assigned to the assignee whose name and address appears in Item 10.

8. ☐ **Amendment.**   Financing Statement bearing file number shown above is amended as set forth in Item 10.

9. ☐ **Release.**   Secured Party releases the collateral described in Item 10 from the financing statement bearing file number shown above.

10.

Number of additional Sheets presented: _____

by: _____   by: _____

Signature(s) of Debtor(s) (necessary only if Item 8 is applicable).   Signature(s) of Secured Party(ies)

See note at head of Digest as to 1998 legislation covered.

See Topical Index in front part of this volume.

NEVADA LAW DIGEST REVISER

Woodburn and Wedge
First Interstate Bank Building
One East First Street, Sixteenth Floor
P.O. Box 2311
Reno, Nevada 89505
Telephone: 702-688-3000
Fax: 702-688-3088

Reviser Profile

History: The firm was founded in 1917 by William Woodburn and is the oldest law firm in the State. In 1952, the law firm of Wedge and Blakey merged into our firm which has experienced a period of continuous growth by the addition of various lawyers with necessary expertise in the areas of the firm's practice. The firm presently consists of twenty-eight lawyers located in offices both in Reno and in Las Vegas.

Areas of Emphasis and Growth: The firm provides a full range of services for a variety of national and local clients. Our clients require services ranging from individual tax and estate planning, to business planning, corporate mergers, international gold loans, environmental matters and litigation. In order to service our clients, we have developed practice areas in Bankruptcy, Corporations, Litigation, Environmental Law, Mining, Natural Resources and Water Law, Real Property, Estate Planning and Taxation.

Client Base: Our firm's client base includes national manufacturing, mining, printing, financial and service industries, together with statewide and local businesses, individuals, churches and hospitals.

Firm Activities: Our firm encourages the involvement of its members and associates in professional organizations and involvement in civic functions as well as pro bono activities. All members of the firm are members of the American Bar Association, State Bar of Nevada and Washoe and/or Clark County Bar Association; various members are associated with both national and local professional organizations in their respective fields of expertise.

Management: Our firm is managed by an executive member who directly supervises an office manager. The executive manager reports to the firm's Board of Directors which monitors the economic and technical development of the firm and its growth.

Significant Distinctions: The firm was selected by the United States Air Force to represent it in acquiring water rights for a significant national project. The firm successfully defended a major recording corporation and a rock band in a landmark suit involving subliminal speech and free speech issues. The firm was selected to handle a major bank merger. Present and past members of the firm have served in numerous positions of distinction such as president of the State Bar, Chairman of the Republican National Committee, Chairman of the National Public Land Advisory Council, Democratic National Committeeman and as chairman of numerous local boards and commissions. Former members of the firm left the firm for appointments to the Ninth Circuit Court of Appeals, the Nevada Supreme Court and State District Court.

NEVADA LAW DIGEST

(The following is a list of all Categories and Topics, including cross-references, covered in this Digest.)

NEVADA LAW DIGEST

Revised for 1999 edition by

WOODBURN and WEDGE, of the Reno and Las Vegas Bars.

(Citations, unless otherwise indicated, refer to Nevada Revised Statutes. N.J.R.C.P. refers to the Nevada Justices' Court Rules of Civil Procedure. N.R.C.P. refers to The Nevada Rules of Civil Procedure. N.R.A.P. refers to The Nevada Rules of Appellate Procedure. 1995, c. refers to chapters of the laws of the State of Nevada passed at the 1995 Legislature. Parallel citations to the Pacific Reporter begin with 17 Nev.)

Note: This revision covers all Acts approved by the Governor through Oct. 1, 1997. The Nevada Legislature did not meet in 1998. See category Courts and topic Legislature.

INTRODUCTION

GOVERNMENT AND LEGAL SYSTEM:

The State of Nevada is a constituent state of the United States of America. For further discussion of the U.S. federal system, see Introduction to the Federal Government of the United States at the beginning of this volume. A great many laws are promulgated by the federal government of the United States and are not reflected in the topics below. See the Introduction to this volume for references to the federal law topics covered.

Like all but one of the United States, Nevada has a common law legal system, with roots in English common law. For information on the courts and legislature of Nevada, see category Courts and Legislature.

HOLIDAYS:

Following days are legal holidays for state and county government offices: Jan. 1, 3d Mon. in Jan., 3d Mon. in Feb., last Mon. in May, July 4, 1st Mon. in Sept., Oct. 31, Nov. 11, 4th Thurs. in Nov., Dec. 25 and any day that may be appointed by President except appointment of fourth Mon. in Oct. as Veterans' Day. (236.015). If Jan. 1, July 4, Oct. 31, Nov. 11, and Dec. 25 fall upon Sun., Mon. following shall be observed as legal holiday. (236.015). If Jan. 1, July 4, and Oct. 31, Nov. 11, Dec. 25 fall upon Sat., Fri. preceding shall be observed as legal holiday. (236.015). Sundays and all of preceding holidays are nonjudicial days and on such days, with certain exceptions, no judicial business may be done. (1.130).

When performance of any act fixed by law or contract falls upon holiday or nonjudicial day it may be performed on the next business day. (10.030).

OFFICE HOURS AND TIME ZONE:

Nevada is in the Pacific (GMT-08:00) time zone. Office hours are generally from 9 a.m. to 5 p.m.

BUSINESS ORGANIZATIONS

AGENCY:

The rights and liabilities of principal and agent with respect to each other are largely determined under common law rules. The Uniform Fiduciaries Act, covering particular phases of the relationship, has been adopted here. (162.010-162.140).

ASSOCIATIONS:

Five or more persons may form a cooperative association for purpose of transacting any lawful business. (81.180). Co-operative nonprofit associations may be formed by three or more persons, and have powers similar to those of private corporations. (81.010-81.160).

Formation.—Co-operative association must prepare articles of association, setting forth name, purpose, name of resident agent with street address for service of process and mailing address if different, term to exist, which may be perpetual, number, names and residences of directors, amount which each member is to pay as fee for membership and name and address of each person executing articles, which must be filed with Secretary of State together with certificate of acceptance of appointment executed by resident agent. (81.200).

Rights and Powers.—Has succession by associate name, in such name may sue and be sued, have seal, hold and convey real and personal property, as purposes of association may require, execute contracts necessary to purpose for which formed, borrow money and issue evidences of indebtedness. (81.220).

Liabilities.—Property of association is subject to judgment and execution. (81.260). By-laws must state amount of indebtedness which may be incurred (81.230), and no member is responsible for any of debts in excess of his proportion of such indebtedness (81.190).

Actions.—May sue and be sued by association name. (81.220).

Dissolution.—May be obtained in accordance with general corporate law contained in c. 78. (81.010).

Professional Associations.—May be formed by two or more persons authorized to perform any type of personal service that can legally be performed only pursuant to a license, certificate of registration, or other legal authorization. (89.010 et seq.). See also topic Corporations, subhead Professional Corporations.

CORPORATIONS:

Uniform Commercial Code has been adopted. (104.1101-104.9507). See category Business Regulation and Commerce, topic Commercial Code.

The present corporation law, digested here, is 78.010-91.340. Model Business Corporation Act has not been adopted.

Purposes.—Corporation may be formed for any lawful business or any legitimate object or purpose, except to carry on business of a trust company, savings and loan association, thrift company or banking corporation. Insurance and mutual fire insurance companies, surety companies, express companies and railroad companies, not infringing laws of another jurisdiction wherein the carrying on of business is contemplated, may be incorporated under the statute, and such corporations may conduct business within state on complying with other regulatory statutes. (78.020, 78.030).

Nonprofit corporations are governed by special act. (82.006-82.690).

Nonstock nonprofit corporations are provided for with specified rights and duties. Public utilities are not included unless they comply also with the special rules governing utilities. (81.410-81.660).

Corporate name must be distinguishable from names of all artificial persons registered under cc. 78, 78A, 80-82, 84, 86-89 whose name is on file; if name not so distinguishable, articles of incorporation shall be returned to incorporator, unless written consent of holder of reserved or registered name is obtained. (78.039). Name appearing to be that of natural person and containing given name or initials must not be used as corporate name except with additional word or words such as "Incorporated," "Limited," "Inc.," "Ltd.," "Company," "Co.," "Corporation," "Corp.," or other word which identifies it as not being natural person. (78.035).

The words "trust" or "bank" cannot be used in corporate name unless corporation proposes to carry on banking or trust company business either exclusively or in connection with bank or savings and loan. (78.045).

Words "engineer," "engineered," "engineering," "professional engineer" or "licensed engineer" cannot be used in corporate name unless state board of engineers certifies that principals of corporation are registered, or that corporation is exempt from NRS 625.520, or corporation has publicly traded securities and is regulated by Securities Exchange Act of 1934 and does not engage in practice of professional engineering. (78.045).

Name can be cleared through Secretary of State at no cost and without application for reservation. Name is reserved upon application, for 90 days during which use by another requires consent of reserving party. (78.040). Fee is $20. (78.785).

Term of Corporate Existence.—Unless otherwise specified in articles, has perpetual existence. (78.060).

Incorporators.—One or more persons may establish corporation. No statutory requirements that they be residents of state or subscribers of stock. (78.030).

Articles of Incorporation.—Articles of incorporation must contain:

1. Name of corporation. For requirements as to name, see subhead Corporate Name, supra.

2. Name of person or corporation designated as resident agent and street address where process can be served and mailing address if different from street address.

3. Number of shares authorized to issue and if more than one class or series is authorized, classes, series, and number of shares of each authorized, unless articles authorize Board to determine by resolution classes, series, and numbers of each class or series.

4. Whether members of governing board shall be called directors or trustees, their number (not less than three unless articles provide for less than three initial stockholders), and names and post office or street addresses, either residence or business, of first board. Also any desired provision as to changing number of directors.

5. Name and post office or street address, either residence or business, of each incorporator executing articles. (78.035).

Limitation of Liability.—Articles may provide provision limiting personal liability of director or officers to corporation and stockholders for breach of fiduciary duty except for acts or omissions involving intentional misconduct, fraud or knowing violation of law or unlawful payment of distributions. (78.037).

Execution and Filing of Articles.—Articles must be executed, acknowledged and filed in office of Secretary of State together with certificate of acceptance of appointment executed by resident agent. (78.030).

Secretary of State will return articles to incorporator that propose name not distinguishable from name of artificial person registered under cc. 78, 78A, 80-82, 84, 86-89 whose name is on file, unless written consent of holder of reserved or registered name is obtained. (78.039).

Secretary of State may not file certificate or articles of corporation organized to do insurance business without approval of Insurance Commissioner, any articles of corporation where "trust" or "bank" is used in name without approval of commissioner of financial institutions, nor articles where word "engineer" or similar words used without approval of state board of professional engineers and land surveyors. (78.045). See topic Insurance Companies.

Filing Fees.—For articles of incorporation or subsequent filing which authorizes increase in stock:

$25,000 or less	$125
Over $25,000 and not over $75,000	$175
Over $75,000 and not over $200,000	$225
Over $200,000 and not over $500,000	$325

See note at head of Digest as to 1998 legislation covered.

See Topical Index in front part of this volume.

CORPORATIONS . . . *continued*

Over $500,000 and not over $1,000,000 . . . . $425

Over $1,000,000 for the first $1,000,000 . . . . $425
and for each additional $500,000 or fraction thereof $225.

Maximum fee that may be charged is $25,000.

Value of shares for fee purposes is: (1) if only shares of a par value are provided for, the aggregate par value of all shares; (2) if only shares without par value are provided for, the product obtained by multiplying the number of shares by $1; (3) if shares with and without par value are provided for, aggregate par value of shares with par value plus product of number of shares without par value multiplied by $1. Consideration or value prescribed for shares without par value can not be used to determine filing fees. Corporate shares worth par value less than 1/10 of 1¢ are treated as having par value of 1/10 of 1¢ for calculating fees. (78.760).

Fees are payable on the filing in office of Secretary of State. (78.755-78.760).

Existence of the corporation commences when articles and certificate of acceptance executed by resident agent are filed in office of Secretary of State, fees paid and certificate of incorporation is issued by that officer; filing of articles does not, by itself, constitute commencement of business of corporation. (78.050).

A copy of certificate or articles of incorporation, certified by Secretary of State under official seal, or of the copy thereof filed with any county clerk, or microfilmed by clerk, under county seal, certified by clerk, must be received as prima facie evidence of facts therein stated and of existence and due incorporation of such corporation. (78.055).

Organization.—Organization meeting is usually held by directors named in articles of incorporation.

Paid In Capital Requirements.—There is no provision requiring any capital to be paid in before commencing business.

Amendment of Articles of Incorporation.—Any changes in articles of incorporation may be made by amendment, except that provision which it would have been unlawful or improper to insert in original articles cannot be inserted therein by amendment. (78.385). Amendment is effected by resolution passed by board of directors declaring such amendment advisable and calling meeting of stockholders, specifically stating purpose is to take action thereon. If at such meeting majority in interest of stockholders having voting power vote in favor of such amendment and no greater number is required by articles, corporation must make by hands of president or vice-president, certificate accordingly, setting forth such amendment or articles as amended, and vote by which such amendment was adopted, which certificate, executed and acknowledged before officer authorized to take acknowledgments of deeds, must be filed in office of Secretary of State. Amendment becomes effective when filed with Secretary of State. If amendment would change any preference or right of one or more classes of stock, holders of such stock are, unless articles provide otherwise, entitled to vote as class on such amendment, even though not given voting power by articles, and majority vote of such class is necessary to pass amendment. (78.390).

Before any stock in corporation has been issued two thirds of incorporators or two thirds of board of directors may make, acknowledge and file amended articles. (78.380).

Increase or decrease of authorized stock may be effected by amendment of articles of incorporation, provided such amendment conforms to 78.035 and 78.037. (78.385).

Unless articles otherwise provide corporation may change number of shares of class or series of its authorized stock by increasing or decreasing number of authorized shares of class and series and correspondingly increasing and decreasing number of issued and outstanding shares of each stockholder by resolution adopted by board of directors without stockholder approval, except where proposal to increase or decrease number of authorized shares provides that only money will be paid or script issued to stockholders who before increase or decrease held 10% or more of outstanding shares of affected class or series and would otherwise be entitled to receive fractions of shares in exchange for cancellation of their outstanding shares must be approved by majority, or greater number if required by articles, of affected class and series. (78.207). Any such proposal which includes provisions that only money will be paid or script issued to stockholder who before increase or decrease held 1% or more of outstanding shares of affected class or series and would otherwise be entitled to receive fraction of share in exchange for cancellation of all of their outstanding shares allows affected stockholder to dissent pursuant to 78.207.

Unless increase or decrease of number of authorized shares is accomplished by action that otherwise requires amendment to articles of incorporation, such amendment not necessary; change is effective after filing statutory certificate with Secretary of State; however, if proposal would alter or change any preference or other right given to any class or series of shares, proposal must be approved by majority vote of affected class or series regardless of restrictions on their voting power. (78.207).

By-laws.—Corporation may make by-laws not inconsistent with the constitution or laws of the United States or of the state. (78.060). Subject to by-laws adopted by stockholders, directors may make them. (78.120).

Seal.—Use of seal or stamp on any corporate document not necessary. (78.065).

Stock.—Corporation must prescribe class, series and number of shares of each which corporation is authorized to issue in articles; if more than one class or series authorized articles must prescribe, or vest authority in Board to prescribe, class, series and number of each and voting powers, designations, preferences, limitations, restrictions and relative rights of each, and distinguishing designation for each class or series. Unless articles provide otherwise, no stock issued as fully paid up may ever be assessed, and articles cannot be amended in this matter. If more than one class of stock authorized voting powers, designations, preferences, limitations, restrictions and relative rights must be summarized on certificate, or informational statement may be sent setting forth office of corporation where shareholder may obtain, without cost, statement of voting powers, designations, preferences, limitations, restrictions and relative rights of various classes. (78.195).

Stock Certificates.—Stockholder is entitled to certificate signed by designated officers or agents unless corporation provides for issuance of uncertified shares, in which case corporation must send shareholder statement containing information required on certificate and must thereafter confirm annually. Stock issued by transfer agent may bear facsimile of signature of officers or agents lithographed or printed thereon. (78.235).

Issuance of Stock.—Board may authorize shares to be issued for any consideration consisting of property or benefit to corporation provided Board has determined that consideration to be received is adequate, which determination is conclusive in absence of actual fraud when corporation receives authorized consideration, shares issued are fully paid and non-assessable. (78.211).

Shareholders do not have preemptive right to acquire stock except to extent articles so provide. (78.265). Preemptive right does not exist to acquire: (1) Shares issued to directors, officers, or employees pursuant to approval of majority vote, (2) shares sold for consideration other than cash, (3) shares issued at same time, or as part of same offering in which, shareholder claiming preemptive right acquired his, or (4) shares, treasury shares or securities convertible into shares, if shares or those into which convertible securities may be converted are upon issuance registered pursuant to 15 USC §781. Holders of preferred or limited shares not entitled to preemptive rights, and holders of common without voting rights not entitled to preemptive rights of shares of common with voting rights. Holders of common have preemptive right to shares of preferred or limited class unless convertible into shares of common. (78.265).

Transfer of Stock.—Restriction on transfer or registration of transfer of stock may be imposed either by articles of incorporation, bylaws, or agreement among shareholders, or between shareholders and corporation. Restriction must be noted on stock certificate or contained in statement of information required by 78.235. (78.242). Uniform Commercial Code adopted. See category Business Regulation and Commerce, topic Commercial Code.

Uniform Simplification of Fiduciary Security Transfers Act adopted. (162.150).

Uniform Commercial Code—Investment Securities adopted. (104.8101-104.8511).

Uniform Commercial Code adopted. (104.1101-104.9507). See category Business Regulation and Commerce, topic Commercial Code.

Stock Transfer Tax.—None.

Stockholders' Liabilities.—Unless articles provide otherwise, no stockholder is liable for debts or liabilities of corporation. Purchaser of shares only liable to pay consideration for which share authorized to be issued or specified in written subscription agreement. (78.225).

Stockholders' meetings may be held either within or without state as directed in articles of incorporation or by-laws. (78.310). There must be written notice signed by president or vice-president or secretary or assistant-secretary, given personally or by mail to each stockholder not less than ten nor more than 60 days before meeting. Articles of incorporation or by-laws may require publication of notice also. Any stockholder may waive notice by writing signed by him or his attorney before or after meeting. Unless articles or bylaws provide otherwise, whenever any shareholder to whom notice of two consecutive annual meetings and all notices of meetings between those two consecutive meetings, or all or at least two payments sent by first class mail of dividends or interest on securities have been addressed to him at his address shown on corporate records but have been returned undeliverable, giving of further notice is not required. (78.370). Unless otherwise provided in articles, closing date for record ownership may be fixed by directors not more than 60 days prior to meeting. (78.350).

Unless c. 78, articles or by-laws otherwise provide: (a) majority of voting power in person or proxy constitutes quorum and stockholder action is approved, other than election of directors, if number of votes in favor of action exceeds opposition; (b) any action that could be taken at meeting may be taken without meeting if written consent signed by stockholders holding at least majority, or larger proportion if required, of voting power; and (c) stockholders may participate at meeting by telephone conference or similar method of communication by which all participants can hear each other, such participation constitutes presence in person at meeting. (78.320).

Stockholders' Derivative Suit.—As to security for costs, see category Civil Actions and Procedure, topic Costs.

Voting may be cumulative only when articles of incorporation or amendment so provide, and then only if written notice is given president or secretary at least 48 hours before meeting date if at least ten day notice had been provided, otherwise not less than 24 hours before meeting. (78.360). Voting may be by proxy, including one limited to designated matters, appointed by written instrument. (78.355).

Voting trusts may be created for period not exceeding 15 years but may be extended by written agreement. Agreement must be in writing and duplicate copy thereof must be filed in registered office of corporation. Stock placed in such trust must be cancelled and new certificates issued to voting trustees and it must appear that stock is issued pursuant to agreement. Shareholders, by written agreement for period not exceeding 15 years, may agree that their stock must be voted pursuant to provisions of agreement, as they may subsequently agree, or in accordance with agreed upon procedure. (78.365).

Directors.—Business must be managed by board, all of whom must be natural persons who are at least 18. Corporation must have at least one director but may provide for other number, variable number within fixed maximum and minimum, and for manner of increasing or decreasing directors. Directors need not be residents of Nevada nor stockholders, unless articles provide otherwise. (78.115). At least one-fourth of them must be elected annually. (78.330). Articles may provide that voting power of individual directors or classes may be greater or less than that of other individual directors or classes. (78.330). Vacancy in board may be filled by remaining directors, unless otherwise required by articles. (78.335).

A director or directors may resign effective at close of meeting and such directors may participate in election of successors. (78.335) President need not be director. (78.130).

Directors' meetings may be held within or without the state. (78.310). A majority then in office is necessary for quorum unless articles or by-laws otherwise provide. (78.315).

Unless restricted by articles of incorporation or by-laws, any action required or permitted to be taken at any meeting of board of directors or committee thereof may be

CORPORATIONS . . . *continued*

taken without a meeting if all members give written consent. (78.315). Unless otherwise restricted by articles of incorporation, members of board of directors can participate in meeting of such board by telephone conference or similar communication method by which all persons participating in meeting can hear each other. Such participation constitutes presence. (78.315).

Duties of Directors.—Directors have full control of corporation and may make by-laws. (78.120). Directors must exercise powers in good faith with view to best interest of corporation. May rely on information, opinions and reports prepared or presented by other directors, officers or employees reasonably believed to be reliable and competent, counsel, accountants or others reasonably believed to be within his or her competence, or committee of directors on matters which it is reasonably believed to merit confidence. (78.138).

Liabilities of Directors.—Liable for willful or grossly negligent wrongful declaration of distributions. (78.300).

Officers.—Every corporation must have a president, a secretary, and a treasurer. May also have vice-presidents, assistant secretaries, assistant treasurers, etc. No requirement that officers be directors. Any person may hold two or more offices. All officers must be natural persons. (78.130).

Insurance.—Corporation may purchase and maintain insurance, or other arrangements, for director, officer, employee or agent for liability asserted and expenses incurred in that capacity whether or not corporation has authority to indemnify such person. (78.752). In absence of fraud, decision of board as to such insurance is conclusive; insurance is not void or voidable and any director approving it, even if beneficiary, is not subject to personal liability for such approval. (78.752).

Registered Office.—Every corporation, domestic or foreign, to do business in state, must have resident agent except during any period of vacancy. (78.090, 80.060).

Resident Agent.—Corporation must designate a resident agent who has street address for service of process. (78.090).

Address of resident agent is registered office of corporation. Within 60 days after filing articles corporation must file list of officers and directors and designation of resident agent. Designation of resident agent must be filed with Secretary of State. (78.090; 80.060; 14.020).

Resident agent can terminate his capacity by filing a duly acknowledged and signed statement to that effect with Secretary of State together with acknowledged statement of corporation appointing successor resident agent. If no corporate statement appoints successor, resident agent must give written notice to any officer of corporation other than resident agent; within 30 days thereafter corporation must file certificate of acceptance executed by new resident agent. (78.097; 80.070).

Powers.—Corporation has power to: have succession by its corporate name until dissolved, sue and be sued; make contracts and adopt and use a common seal or stamp; hold, purchase and convey real and personal property, and mortgage or lease same with its franchises, including power to take same by devise or bequest; appoint officers and agents as corporation requires; make bylaws for management of its affairs, transfer of its stock, transaction of business and calling and holding of meetings; wind up and dissolve itself, and unless articles otherwise provide, engage in any lawful activity. Use of seal or stamp by corporation on any corporate documents is not necessary. (78.060-78.065).

Subject to any limitations contained in the articles, it has also power to: borrow money and contract debts; issue bonds, promissory notes, bills of exchange, debentures and obligations, secured or unsecured; guarantee, purchase, hold, take, obtain, receive, subscribe for, own, use, dispose of, sell, exchange, lease, lend, assign, mortgage, pledge or otherwise deal in bonds, obligations or securities issued by any person, government, governmental agency or political subdivision and to exercise all rights of ownership including right to vote; purchase, hold, sell and transfer shares of its own stock; conduct business and to have offices, hold and dispose of property in any of states and in foreign countries; make donations for public welfare, enter into any relationship with another person; do all things incidental to those enumerated in its articles. (78.070).

Distributions.—Except as otherwise provided in articles, Board may authorize and corporation may make distributions to shareholders, provided that no distribution can be made if, after giving it effect, corporation would not be able to pay its debts as they become due in usual course of business, or corporations total assets would be less than sum of its liabilities plus amount needed if corporation was dissolved to satisfy preferential rights on dissolution of those shareholders whose preferential rights are superior to those receiving distribution. (78.288).

Unclaimed Dividends.—Dividend declared by corporation escheats to state when stockholder (either an individual, or corporation, whose charter has expired and right to dividend has passed to successor) fails to claim it within seven years from date of declaration. (78.292). See category Property, topic Absentees, subhead Escheat.

Books and Records.—Every corporation shall keep at its registered office certified copy of its articles of incorporation, its by-laws, and stock ledger or duplicate stock ledger revised annually, of all stockholders alphabetically arranged, showing their places of residence and number of shares held by each. Stock ledger must be open daily during business hours for inspection by designated stockholders, and they may make extracts therefrom. In lieu of such stock ledger, corporation may keep at its principal office statement designating name of custodian of stock ledger, with complete post office address. Corporation incurs penalty of $25 per day for noncompliance. (78.105).

Financial Records.—Any stockholder owning 15% of issued and outstanding shares of corporation, including subchapter S corporation, is entitled to inspect books of account and financial records of corporation, to make extracts therefrom, and conduct an audit of such records upon furnishing an affidavit that such inspection is desired solely in relation to his interest as a stockholder. This law does not apply to any corporation listed and traded on any stock exchange or any corporation that furnishes its stockholders a detailed, annual financial statement. (78.257).

Reports.—Domestic corporations, foreign corporations, and all nonprofit corporations doing business in state must file with Secretary of State, before first day of second month after filing articles of incorporation, or copy thereof in case of foreign corporation, list on form furnished by Secretary of State containing name of corporation, file number of corporation, names and titles of required officers and all directors with their addresses certified by officer of corporation. On or before last day of month in which anniversary date of incorporation occurs domestic corporation must file on form furnished by Secretary of State similar list, or certification that no changes have occurred; foreign corporation must file such list and designation plus any amendments to its articles which change its name or increase its capitalization. Filing fee of $85 for domestic, $85 for foreign corporations, $15 for nonprofit corporations, must accompany required reports. Canceled check for filing fee received by corporation constitutes certificate authorizing it to transact business within this state for one year. (78.150-78.165; 80.110-80.140).

Foreign corporation, in addition to above-described reports, must publish each year not later than month of Mar. statement of its last calendar year's business in two numbers or issues of newspaper published in this state. If fiscal year is other than calendar year, statement must be published not later than end of third month following close of fiscal year. Any foreign corporation that fails to publish statement liable for penalty of $100 for each month statement not published. (80.190).

Failure to make required filings and pay fee within time fixed results in penalty of $15 for domestic or foreign corporations, $5 for nonprofit corporations. Foreign corporation forfeits right to transact any business in state if filing fee and penalty not paid before first day of ninth month following month filing fee was required. (80.150). Secretary of State shall notify, by letter to resident agent, each corporation in default. Immediately after first day of ninth month following month filing was required, corporation's charter is revoked and right to transact business in State is forfeited; Secretary of State shall compile list of such corporations and shall notify each corporation. (78.175, 80.160).

Reinstatement.—Secretary of State may reinstate any corporation on payment of filing fee, reinstatement fee, and penalties, except if charter has remained revoked for five consecutive years it cannot be reinstated. (78.180, 80.150, 80.170).

Merger and exchange, acquiring all outstanding shares of one or more classes or series of another corporation permitted. (92A.110). Plan of merger of exchange must set forth in writing name, address, place of organization, and governing law of each entity; terms and conditions of exchanging shares or other interests; and may set forth other provisions. (92A.110). After adopting plan, Board of each corporation to merger and Board whose shares will be acquired in exchange, must submit plan for shareholders' approval (78.453); but action by shareholder of survivor not required for merger if articles of survivor are not different, shareholders would hold same number with identical rights, designations, preferences and limitations after merger, number of voting or participating shares after merger plus voting or participating shares after merger plus voting on participating shares issued as result of merger not exceed 20% of total number of voting or participating shares of survivor outstanding immediately before merger (92A.130). Simplified procedure for parent corporation owning at least 90% of outstanding shares of each class of subsidiary. (92A.180). After plan effective, surviving or acquiring entity must file articles of merger or exchange with Secretary of State. (92A.200).

Foreign entity may merge or enter into exchange agreement with domestic entity; provided in case of merger, it is permitted by law of foreign entity, if in case of exchange where acquired interests are of domestic entity, regardless of law of foreign acquiring entity provided both entities comply with act. Surviving foreign entity to merger and acquiring foreign entity in exchange must appoint Secretary of State as agent for service of process to enforce dissenters' rights. (92A.190).

Shareholders may dissent and obtain fair value of shares in event of merger or exchange (92A.380); but if stock listed on national securities exchange or held by at least 2,000 shareholders, no such right exists (92A.390).

Dissolution.—Board of directors may adopt resolution approving dissolution if corporation has not issued stock; if corporation has issued stock must recommend dissolution and submit to stockholder vote for approval; if dissolution approved certificate setting that fact and list of names and addresses of corporations, officers and directors must be filed with Secretary of State. (78.580).

The effect of a dissolution or forfeiture of charter is to permit corporation to function with limited rights and for limited purposes; does not impair any claims available to or against it, its directors, officers or stockholders, arising before dissolution and commenced within two years. (78.585).

Receiver.—Where corporation is insolvent or certain other circumstances exist, court may appoint receiver to manage affairs of corporation and, if necessary, to wind up its business. (78.630; 78.635; 78.650).

Close Corporations.—May be formed provided all issued stock held by not more than 30 shareholders, stock subject to restrictions on transfer, and corporation makes no public offering of stock. (78A.020). Stock certificates of close corporation must contain statutory statement concerning shareholders rights. (78A.040). Shares in close corporation may not be transferred except as permitted by certificate of incorporation, bylaws, shareholders agreement, or voting trust agreement. (78A.050). Close corporation may operate without board of directors if certificate of incorporation so provides. (78A.090). Any written agreement of shareholders, or provision in certificate of incorporation or bylaws relating to any phase of affairs of corporation is not invalid on ground that it is attempt to treat corporation as partnership. (78A.080). Certificate of incorporation may include provision granting any shareholder or percentage of shareholders option to dissolve corporation at will or upon occurrence of specified event or contingency. (78A.160).

Appraisal.—If merger or exchange requires stockholders' vote notice of meeting must advise of dissenters' rights, if no stockholders' vote required, corporation must provide written notice of dissenters' rights in accordance with 92A.410 and 92A.430. If meeting required dissenting stockholder must deliver written notice of intent to demand payment before vote taken and not vote shares in favor of action (92A.420); if no meeting required shareholder receiving statutory notice of dissenters' rights must demand payment and deposit certificates in accordance with notice (92A.440). Corporation must then pay what it determines to be fair value of shares, plus interest (92A.460);

See note at head of Digest as to 1998 legislation covered.

See Topical Index in front part of this volume.

CORPORATIONS . . . *continued*
dissenter may notify corporation, in writing, of shareholder's own estimate of fair value, plus interest, and demand payment (92A.480); corporation must commence action within 60 days after receiving demand if matter remains unsettled and court may appoint appraisers to recommend decision of fair value (92A.490 and 92A.500).

Foreign Corporations.—Every foreign corporation before doing business in this state must file with Secretary of State: (1) Certificate of corporate existence issued not more than 90 days before date of filing by authorized officer of jurisdiction of its incorporation setting forth filing of documents related to articles of incorporation, or governmental acts or other authority by which corporation created; (2) certificate of acceptance of appointment executed by its resident agent, who must be resident or corporation with registered office in Nevada, which must contain complete address of resident agent; (3) acknowledged statement by officer of corporation setting forth: (a) authorized stock, number of par value shares and their par value, number of no par value shares, as of date not earlier than six months prior to filing, and (b) general description of corporate purposes. Secretary of State will not file documents if name is same or deceptively similar to name of corporation or limited partnership formed in this state, foreign corporation or limited partnership authorized to do business in this state or name reserved for corporation or limited partnership.

Foreign corporation not qualified cannot commence, maintain or defend lawsuit in state however can commence proceeding seeking extraordinary remedy pursuant to NRS c. 31 provided corporation qualifies within 45 days thereafter (80.210), and tardy compliance not sufficient (93 Nev. 270, 563 P.2d 582).

Filing fees for foreign corporations are same as incorporation fees of domestic corporations, but in no case will the amount exceed $25,000 for initial filing or $25,000 for filing certificate increasing authorized capital stock. (80.050). See subhead Filing Fees, supra.

Real Property.—A nonresident corporation has power to take, hold and enjoy real property on same terms and conditions as residents. (111.055). Foreign corporations owning property must appoint and keep a resident agent in state. (80.060).

Doing Business.—Following does not constitute doing business in this state: maintaining or defending any proceeding, holding board or shareholder meetings, maintaining bank accounts, maintaining offices for transfer, exchange and registration of corporation's own securities, making sales through independent contractors, soliciting orders outside state and accepting them outside state and shipping goods into state, creating or acquiring indebtedness, mortgages and security interstate in real or personal property, securing or collecting debts or enforcing mortgages and security interests in property securing debts, owning real or personal property, isolated transactions not completed within 30 days, production of motion pictures, transacting business as out of state depository institution pursuant to NRS Title 56 and transacting business in interstate commerce. Foreign corporation not doing business within meaning of this statute does not have to qualify with 80.010-80.220, c. 652B, or Titles 55 and 56 of NRS unless maintains office in state for transaction of business, or solicits or accepts deposits in this state. (80.015).

Withdrawal.—Any foreign corporation may surrender its right to do business in this state by filing with Secretary of State notice of its purpose to do so duly authorized by resolution of its board of directors and executed under corporate seal, and paying required fee of $30 provided corporation's right to do business had not previously been forfeited. (80.200, 80.050).

For other matters relating to foreign corporations, see supra, subheads Registered Office; Resident Agent; Books and Records; Reports; Merger and Exchange.

Fictitious Name.—No action may be commenced or maintained by corporation conducting, carrying on, or transacting business under assumed or fictitious name or designation which does not show real name of corporation upon or on account of any contract made or transaction had under such fictitious name, nor upon or on account of any cause of action arising or growing out of business so carried on, unless a certificate signed by an officer of corporation, and acknowledged before some officer authorized to take acknowledgments of conveyances of real property, is filed with county clerk of each county in which business is being carried on. (602.010–602.090).

Taxation.—No annual franchise tax. Corporations are taxed on their property in county where located, the same as individuals. Foreign corporations regularly doing business here are similarly taxed.

There is no corporation income tax.

Professional corporations may be formed to provide any type of personal service which may legally be performed only pursuant to a license, certificate of registration or other legal authorization. Must file annual statements with Secretary of State and pay fee of $30. (89.010–89.100).

See also topic Associations, subhead Professional Associations.

Deeds.—See category Property, topic Deeds.

Model Non-Profit Corporation Act not adopted. See subhead Purposes, supra.

Limited Liability Company.—See topic Limited Liability Companies.

JOINT STOCK COMPANIES:

There are no statutes concerning the organization of companies, except corporations and partnerships. The common law concerning joint stock companies prevails. See also topic Associations.

Professional Associations.—See topic Associations, subhead Professional Associations; topic Corporations, subhead Professional Corporations.

LIMITED LIABILITY COMPANIES:

One or more persons may form by signing, verifying and filing articles of organization and certificate of acceptance signed by resident agent (86.151), provided last words of name contain words limited, or ltd. liability company (86.171). Articles must set forth name, name and business address of resident agent, name and P.O. Box or street address of each organizer executing articles; if company managed by manager name and address of manager or if company managed by members name and address of members. Articles may include any other provision which members elect for regulation of internal affairs of company. (86.161).

Operation.—Must maintain office, which may be different from place of business, which is business office of resident agent where its records maintained. (86.231). Unless otherwise provided by operating agreement, limited liability company shall keep: current separate list of name and address of each member and manager, copy of filed articles of organization and any amendments, copies of effective operating agreements. (86.241).

Liability.—Unless otherwise provided in articles or agreement signed by person charged, no member or manager is individually liable for debts or liabilities of company (86.371); however persons who assume to act as such company without authority are jointly and severally liable for all debts and liabilities of company (86.361). Statutory provisions exist for company to indemnify managers, members, employees and agents (86.411-86.451), and for maintaining insurance for such persons (86.461-86.481).

Dissolution.—Company must be dissolved and its affairs wound up at time specified in articles, on occurrence of event specified in operating agreement or by unanimous written agreement of members. (86.491).

PARTNERSHIPS:

Uniform Partnership Act adopted with modifications. (87.010-87.430).

Name.—The names and places of residence of all the partners must be filed in the proper county or counties (see category Intellectual Property, topic Trademarks and Tradenames), and upon every change in membership, within a month thereafter, a new certificate must be filed containing the required information. (602.040).

Limited Partnership.—Revised Uniform Limited Partnership Act with 1985 Amendments has been adopted. (88.315 et seq.). In addition to maintaining specified office and designation of resident agent, such agent must file certificate setting forth street address where process may be served, with Secretary of State. Agent must notify Secretary of State if address changes; if office containing records changes, general partner must notify Secretary of State. (88.330). If agent dies, resigns or moves from state, Secretary of State must be advised and successor agent appointed. (88.332). Also, limited partnership must file with Secretary of State annual lists certified by general partners as to partnership name, file number of limited partnership, names and addresses of general partners, or if no changes since previous list certification to that effect, with fee of $85. (88.395).

Fees.—Secretary of State will charge for filing certificate of limited partnership or registering foreign limited partnership, $125, amendment or restated certificate, $75, reinstated certificate, $50, annual list and designation of resident agent, $85, certificate for change of location of resident agent's office or designation of new resident agent $15. Fee for reservation of name, $20. (88.415).

Mining Partnership.—See category Mineral, Water and Fishing Rights, topic Mines and Minerals.

BUSINESS REGULATION AND COMMERCE

BANKS AND BANKING:

Regulated by 657.010-668.115; even though banks incorporated under earlier statutes.

Uniform Commercial Code adopted. (104.1101-104.9507). See topic Commercial Code.

General Supervision.—Commissioner of financial institutions as chief of division of financial institutions of Dept. of Commerce supervises banking activities.

Branch banks are permitted. Principal office and parent bank must be within this State. (660.015).

Loans and Discounts.—Bank may lend money on chattels, personal security or mortgage on real estate (662.015), but may not make loan or discount on security of shares of its own stock or member's interest, or be purchaser or holder of such shares or interests unless such security or purchase is necessary to prevent loss on debt previously contracted in good faith, or has been approved by commissioner and such stock or interest must be sold or disposed of within two years after its acquisition unless commissioner authorized otherwise. (662.125).

Liabilities of Directors, Officers, etc.—Any director, manager, officer, or other person who knowingly and intentionally participates in violations of state laws relating to banks is liable for damages which bank or its stockholders, members, depositors or creditors suffer in consequence thereof. (661.195). Director, officer or employee cannot become endorser or surety on any obligation to bank. (668.025). They may not receive deposits after bank is known to be insolvent or in failing circumstances or give creditor any unfair preference. (668.045). Violation makes such person guilty of felony and responsible for losses. (668.045).

Stock and Stockholders.—Shares of stock are deemed personal property. A full and correct list of names and places of residence of stockholders must be kept. Stockholders are not liable to assessment on stock except for purpose of repairing impaired capital. (661.085).

Where capital of bank is impaired, commissioner of financial institutions must notify bank to make impairment good with a time fixed, not more than three months from date after notice. Thereupon directors may declare assessment on stock or managers shall make assessment on members. If impairment is not made good within three months, commissioner may take possession of business until its affairs are finally liquidated. (661.085). Bank has prior lien on stock or interest for assessment and stock of delinquent stockholder or interest of member may be sold to meet same. (661.185).

Deposits and Withdrawals.—Banking division of financial institutions may authorize any bank for good cause shown to restrict for limited period percentage of withdrawals from all accounts. (664.015).

See note at head of Digest as to 1998 legislation covered.

See Topical Index in front part of this volume.

NV – 4

BANKS AND BANKING . . . *continued*

Joint bank accounts are recognized by Nevada law (100.085), but clear proof of creation of such account is required by courts, tendency being to limit rather than extend application of theory of joint tenancy (62 Nev. 41, 140 P.2d 566).

Deposits in trust are permitted. On death of trustee this deposit may be paid to person for whom deposit was made. (663.025).

Unclaimed Deposits.—Uniform Disposition of Unclaimed Property Act has been adopted. (120A.010 et seq.). Demand, savings, matured time deposits or other certificate of deposit with banking organization escheat in five years. (120A.160).

Checks.—Uniform Commercial Code adopted. See topic Commercial Code.

Making or passing check with fraudulent intent is misdemeanor unless check is in amount of $250 or more, is subject to imprisonment and/or fine. Anyone having been previously convicted of this misdemeanor three times, in this or any other state, is guilty of Category D Felony. (205.130).

Demand Notes.—Uniform Commercial Code adopted. See topic Commercial Code.

Collections.—Uniform Commercial Code adopted. See topic Commercial Code.

Investments.—Governed by 662.046-662.205.

Emergency Closing.—Governor may direct closing of any or all banks for definite periods when public interest requires. (223.140).

Trust Companies.—Bank may, by so stating in articles of incorporation, conduct a trust company business in connection with banking business, or it may be organized for trust company business only. Such bank may act as trustee under any mortgage or bond, accept and execute municipal or corporate or individual trust not inconsistent with law, act under appointment of court as guardian, administrator, receiver or trustee, act as executor or trustee under any will, as resident agent for foreign (except insurance) corporations, or as fiscal agent for any state, municipality, or corporation. (662.235).

See also category Estates and Trusts, topic Trusts, subhead Trust Companies.

Uniform Common Trust Fund Act adopted. (164.070-164.120).

Savings Banks.—Bank may carry on savings bank business under certain restrictions. (662.215).

Building, savings and loan associations are formed under special statute which regulates branch offices, activities of officers, directors, employees and capital stockholders, investments and borrowing, shares, surpluses and dividends, appraisals, loans and withdrawals, etc. (673.001-673.850). Commissioner of financial institutions shall supervise domestic and foreign associations doing business within state. (673.040).

Federal associations may be converted into domestic. (673.650-673.740).

BILLS AND NOTES:

Uniform Commercial Code adopted. (104.1101-104.9507). See topic Commercial Code.

Collection of attorney fee clauses are enforceable though no statutory authority exists.

Judgment Notes.—The status of judgment notes in Nevada is questionable, there having been no Supreme Court decision as to the effect of the usual judgment note.

BILLS OF LADING:

See topic Carriers.

BILLS OF SALE:

No statute.

BLUE SKY LAW:

See topic Securities.

BROKERS:

Uniform Commercial Code adopted. (104.1101-104.9507). See topic Commercial Code.

Real Estate Brokers and Salesmen.—Must be licensed and are regulated by real estate division of department of commerce. (645.001-645.850). Statutory definitions of "broker," "broker-salesman," and "salesman" are broad. (645.030-645.040). Applicant cannot have had real estate license revoked within ten years prior to date of application, by any state. (645.330). Applicant to be licensed as broker must be actively engaged as full-time licensed broker-salesman or salesman in Nevada, or as full-time licensed broker, broker-salesman, or salesman in another state or District of Columbia, for at least two or four years immediately prior to issuance of Nevada broker's license and must submit statement required by division. (645.330). Applicants must submit verified application on forms furnished by real estate division of department of commerce. (645.350). All applicants must pass written examination held by real estate division at least bimonthly. (645.450-645.480). Broker or salesman cannot recover commission without alleging and proving possession of license. (645.270). Cities, towns, and counties may require a license for revenue purposes only. (645.550).

Insurance Brokers.—See category Insurance, topic Insurance Companies.

BULK SALES:

See topic Commercial Code.

CARRIERS:

Jurisdiction over carriers and their rates is in Public Service Commission, subject to judicial review. (704.010; 704.020).

Uniform Commercial Code adopted. (104.1101-104.9507). See topic Commercial Code.

Schedules of rates must be filed and adhered to and rates are subject to regulation by Commission. (704.040-704.110, 704.210).

Bills of Lading.—Uniform Commercial Code adopted. See topic Commercial Code.

Railroad Corporations.—Railroad corporations may be formed under general corporation law. (78.020).

Corporate powers of railroads extend to operation of motor-vehicle transportation. (78.075).

Railroad may sell or lease property or franchises. (705.080).

Licenses.—Any common carrier, before commencing any intrastate business, must procure certificate of public convenience from Public Service Commission. (704.330).

Motor Vehicle Carriers.—See category Transportation, topic Motor Vehicles.

COMMERCIAL CODE:

Uniform Commercial Code adopted.

Contained in Nevada Revised Statutes 104.1101-104.9507. Section numbers follow Uniform Commercial Code Official Text section numbers, but prefixed by "104.". Dashes in U.C.C. Official Text are omitted and in some cases (e.g., 104.4105) numbers have been substituted for letters in subsections. Thus, U.C.C. §1-101 becomes NRS 104.1101. For 1962 Official Text of Uniform Commercial Code and Amendments see Uniform and Model Acts section.

1966 Official Amendments to §§2-702, 3-501, 7-209 not adopted.

1966 Optional Amendments to §§1-209, 9-105, 9-106 not adopted. Optional Amendment to §2-318 adopted in form of Alternative A.

1972 Official Amendments adopted, effective July 1, 1975.

1973 Official Amendment adopted.

1977 Official Amendments adopted.

1989 Optional Amendments adopted repealing Article 6-Bulk Transfers; adopting revised Article 6-Bulk Sales in form of Alternative A, and Article 4A-Funds Transfers.

1990 Amendments adopted providing for new Art. 2A-Leases, revision of Art. 3-Negotiable Instruments and amendments to Art. 4-Bank Deposits and Collections.

1994 Revised Art. 8-Investment Securities adopted.

1995 Revised Art. 5-Letters of Credit adopted.

Material Variations from 1962 Text.—
104.1105: 1972 Amendment enacted.
104.1109: Omitted.
104.1110: (Added Section): "Provision for Transition."
104.2107: 1972 Amendment enacted, 1989 Amendment Revised Article 6 in form of Alternative A enacted.
104.2318: Alternative A-1966 Optional Official Amendment enacted.
104.4105: Adds subsection 7: "Each branch or separate office of a bank shall be deemed a separate bank for the purpose of the definitions of this section."
104.4106: Rewritten: "A branch or separate office of a bank is a separate bank for the purpose of computing the time within which and determining the place at or to which action may be taken or notices or orders shall be given under this article and under article 3, and the receipt of any notice or order by, or the knowledge of, one branch or separate office of a bank is not actual or constructive notice to or knowledge of any other branch or separate office of the same bank and does not impair the right of such other branch or separate office to be a holder in due course of an item."
104.4204: Adds subsections 2(d) and (e): "(d) Any item to any Federal Reserve bank; and (e) Any item to any other bank or agency thereof. Items may be sent to the place of business of, or to any place designated by, those to whom items may be sent under paragraphs (a), (b), (c), (d) or (e)." Subsection 3 omitted.
104.4211: Adds to subsection 1 subparagraphs (e) and (f): "(e) Credit on the books of any Federal Reserve bank or of any bank designated as a depositary by the collection bank; or (f) Money."
104.4212: Omits subsection 2. Adds subsection 7: "The right to obtain refund is not affected by: (a) Prior use of the credit given for the item; or (b) Failure by any bank to exercise ordinary care with respect to the item except to the extent of the bank's liability therefor."
104.4213: Paragraph 1(c) omitted: Paragraphs 1(b) and 1(d) rewritten: "(b) Settled for the item without having a right to revoke settlement under statute, clearing house rule, agreement or reservation thereof; or (d) Settled for the item having a right to revoke the settlement under statute, clearing house rule, agreement or reservation thereof, and failed to revoke the settlement in the time and manner permitted under such right."
104.4303: Rewritten following the word "served" in subsection 1: "* * * and the bank does not have a reasonable time to act thereon before, or the setoff is exercised after, the happening of any of the following:
"(a) The bank has accepted or certified the item;
"(b) The bank has paid the item in cash;
"(c) The bank has settled for the item without having a right to revoke the settlement under statute, clearing house rule, agreement or reservation thereof:
"(d) The cutoff hour (NRS 104.4107) or the close of the banking day if no cutoff hour is fixed of the day on which the bank received the item;
"(e) The bank has become accountable for the amount of the item under paragraph (d) of subsection 1 of NRS 104.4213 and NRS 104.4302 dealing with the payor bank's responsibility for late return of items; or
"(f) The item has been deposited or received for deposit for credit in an account of a customer with the payor bank.
"2. Subject to the provisions of subsection 1 items may be accepted, paid, certified or charged to the indicated account of its customer in any order convenient to the bank and before or after its regular banking hours. A bank is under no obligation to determine the time of day an item is received and without liability may withhold the amount thereof pending a determination of the effect, consequence or priority of any knowledge, notice, stop-order or legal process concerning the same, or interplead such amount and the claimants thereto."

See note at head of Digest as to 1998 legislation covered.

See Topical Index in front part of this volume.

COMMERCIAL CODE ... *continued*

104.4401: Adds following the word "overdraft" in subsection 1: "* * * and in such event recover or obtain refund of the amount of the overdraft."

104.4403: Rewritten: "1. A customer, or any customer if there is more than one, or any person authorized to sign checks or make withdrawals thereon, may stop payment of any item payable for or drawn against such customer's or customer's account, but the bank may disregard the same unless the order is in writing, is signed by such customer or authorized person, describes with certainty the item on which payment is to be stopped, and is received by the bank in such time and in such manner as to afford the bank a reasonable opportunity to act on it prior to the happening of any of the events described in NRS 104.4303.

"2. An order may by disregarded by the bank 6 months after receipt unless renewed in writing.

"3. The bank is liable to its customer for the actual loss incurred by him resulting from the payment of an item contrary to a binding stop payment order, not exceeding the amount of the item unless the bank is guilty of negligence. The burden of establishing the fact and amount of loss resulting from the payment of an item contrary to a binding stop payment order is on the customer."

104.4405: Subsection 2 rewritten: "2. Even with knowledge of the death of a customer or of any person authorized to sign checks or make withdrawals a bank may, for 10 days after the date of death, pay or certify checks drawn by the decedent on or prior to that date unless the bank has received notice of an adverse claim supported by a court order or by a surety bond acceptable to it which need not exceed double the amount claimed."

Subsections 3 and 4 added: "3. Even with knowledge of the incompetence of a customer, whether adjudicated or not, a bank may, if the item would have been effective prior to such incompetence, accept, pay, collect and account for the proceeds of any item drawn by any other customer or person authorized by such other customer, unless the bank has received notice of an adverse claim supported by a court order or by a surety bond acceptable to it which need not exceed double the amount claimed.

"4. A bank may refuse to pay a check, draft or other order for the withdrawal of money from an account, whether commercial or savings, if it believes or receives an affidavit stating that the person drawing, endorsing or presenting the instrument is or was at the time of signing, endorsing or presenting it so under the influence of liquor or drugs or so mentally or physically disabled as to raise doubt whether such person is or was competent to transact business. No damages shall be awarded in any action against the bank, or its officers or other employees, for refusing in good faith to pay any such instrument for that reason or in relying upon such affidavit."

104.4406: Subsection 4 rewritten following the word "item"; "* * * or any unauthorized endorsement, and if the bank so requests exhibit the item to the bank for inspection, is precluded from asserting against the bank such unauthorized signature or endorsement or such alteration."

104.5116: 1972 Amendment adopted, adding after paragraph (c) in subsection 2: "As used in paragraphs (b) and (c) of this subsection, the word 'issuer' includes any confirming bank."

104.7106: (Added Section): "This article does not repeal or modify any laws prescribing the form or contents of documents of title or the services or facilities to be afforded by bailees, or otherwise regulating bailees' businesses in respects not specifically dealt with in this article; but the fact that such laws are violated does not affect the status of a document of title which otherwise complies with the definition of a document of title (NRS 104.1201)."

104.7403: Optional language included.

104.8102: 1973 Amendment enacted.

104.901–104.905: Transition provisions for 1972 Amendments. Correspond to official sections:

  104.901: §11–104
  104.902: §11–105
  104.903: §11–106, subsections 1, 2, and 4.
  104.904: §11–107
  104.905: §11–108

1972 Amended Text in effect for Article 9 with following options and alternatives exercised and revisions made:

104.9106: Language from 1966 Optional Amendment adopted but modified to provide that rights to payment under charter or other contract involving use of vessel are accounts.

104.9312: Omits subsection 2.

104.9401: Paragraphs (a) and (b) of third alternative version of subsection 1 adopted. In Paragraph (a) words "county recorder" are inserted in blank spaces. In paragraph (a) words defining "farm collateral" are omitted. In paragraph (b) phrase "except as otherwise provided in subsection 5" is added at beginning. Paragraph (c) reads simply "In all other cases, in the Office of the Secretary of State."

Reference to NRS 704.205 is substituted for "office of the Secretary of State" in subsection 5.

Optional Section 6 is adopted.

104.9402: Instead of "the statement must also contain a description of the real estate concerned" following "grown" in subsection 1, NRS uses "and if the debtor does not have an interest of record in the real estate, the financing statement must show the name of a record owner."

Optional language in subsections 3 and 5 is adopted.

104.9403: Revised language in subsection 4 following "name of the debtor" reads: ". . . and the name of the record owner of the real property as given in the financing statement. The filing officer shall also note in the indexes. . . ."

Optional language in subsections 5 and 7 adopted.

104.9404: "Secretary of State" added.
104.9405: "Secretary of State" added.
104.9406: "Secretary of State" added.
104.9407: Optional section adopted.

Article 10 omitted. See 104.1110, 104.7106 and 104.8108.

Filing.—See category Documents and Records, topic Records, subhead Filing Under Commercial Code.

Forms.—See end of this Digest.

See also topics: Banks and Banking, Bills and Notes, Brokers, Carriers, Contracts, Factors, Frauds, Statute of, Sales, Securities, Warehousemen; categories Business Organizations, topic Corporations; Civil Actions and Procedure, topic Limitation of Actions; Debtor and Creditor, topics Assignments, Fraudulent Sales and Conveyances, Liens, Pledges; Documents and Records, topics Records, Seals; Mortgages, topic Chattel Mortgages.

CONDITIONAL SALES:

See topic Sales.

CONSIGNMENTS:

See topic Factors.

CONSUMER PROTECTION:

Revised Uniform Deceptive Trade Practices Act has been adopted with significant variations. (598.360–598.640).

Consumer affairs division of department of business and industry investigates deceptive trade practices (598.510) which are enumerated by statute (598.410) and may apply to courts for temporary restraining orders or injunctions, for return of money or property to deceived person, and for commencement of criminal proceedings (598.540). Penalties up to $10,000 for each violation are possible, and willful violation is misdemeanor, if within past ten years, second violation gross misdemeanor, third violation felony. (598.640). Suspension of right to conduct business or dissolution of corporation possible. (598.005).

Attorney General may commence action if he has reason to believe deceptive trade practice is occurring, provides notice thereof to commissioner, and appropriate action not completed within 30 days. (598.512).

Consumer's advocate for customers of public utilities may represent public interest and any class of customers in any proceedings. (228.390).

Civil action for consumer fraud may be brought by any person who is victim of deceptive trade practice enumerated by statute, or of misleading or inaccurate advertising or breach of statutory warranty by vehicle dealer or rebuilder, or of unlawful misrepresentation, deceit, or fraud in sale of land. This action is not action upon any underlying contract. (41.600).

Retention of Unsolicited Merchandise.—Person who receives merchandise offered for sale but not ordered by him, orally or in writing, may consider such to be an unconditional gift, except when merchandise is sent by mistake or as substitute in response to order for other goods, or is sent by mistake to member of subscription-type plan, or is delivered by mistake to person other than person who ordered goods, or has been ordered by another to be delivered directly to recipient. (598.090).

Credit and Credit Reporting.—Discrimination by creditor against credit applicant with respect to any aspect of credit transaction because of applicant's sex or marital status is unlawful. (598B.100). Creditor must consider combined income of husband and wife for purpose of extending credit to married couple. (598B.110). If husband and wife separately apply for and obtain credit, their credit accounts cannot be combined for purposes of determining finance charges or loan ceilings. (598B.120). For violations, court may grant injunctive relief, damages, or both. (598B.170).

Credit reporting agency must identify separately in its reports, credit histories of any person, person's spouse, and joint accounts of person and spouse, to extent information is available. (598B.130).

Advertising.—Any use or publication of a statement known or which should be known to be false, deceptive or misleading to induce purchase, lease, or sale of any property or services is unlawful (207.171) with civil and criminal penalties (207.174, 207.175).

Door-To-Door Sales.—Seller commits deceptive sales practice unless he identifies himself and purpose of call immediately, or if he offers investment and makes misrepresentations or charges fee for advice concerning investment and fails to disclose he is selling product or is licensed relating to service he is providing. (598.412). Buyer entering door-to-door contract for goods or services exceeding $25 in price may rescind in writing within three business days. (598.230). Seller must furnish written copy of contract which informs buyer of his right to cancel (598.240) and includes a detachable "Notice of Cancellation" for buyer's use (598.250). Seller may assess penalty for cancellation of 5% of price, $15, or any down payment, whichever is lesser amount. (598.260).

Deceptive trade practice occurs when one in course of business knowingly passes off goods or services as those of another, makes false representations as to source of goods, or affiliation or association with another, uses deceptive representations of geographic origin of goods, makes false representations as to ingredients, uses or benefits of goods or services, represents goods as new when in fact they are not, represents goods or services of particular quality knowing they are not, disparages goods of another by false or misleading statements, advertises goods or services with intent not to sell as advertised or to supply reasonable expected demand unless limited supply is disclosed, advertises under guise to obtain sales personnel when purpose is to sell product to applicant, makes false or misleading statements as to price (598.410); when one in course and scope of business employs "bait and switch" advertising consisting of offer to sell goods or services which seller may not intend to sell accompanied by refusal to show goods advertised, disparagement of advertised goods or services, requiring other sales or undisclosed conditions to be met before advertised sale, refusing to take orders within reasonable time period, showing defective goods impractical for advertised purposes, or accepting deposit and switching purchase order to higher priced goods or services (598.411); or when one in course of business knowingly fails to identify water damaged goods, solicits by telephone or door-to-door unless seller identifies himself and who he represents within first one-half minute, knowingly misstate that services or repairs are needed, fails to make delivery within reasonable period

---

See note at head of Digest as to 1998 legislation covered.

See Topical Index in front part of this volume.

CONSUMER PROTECTION . . . continued

of time, advertises opportunity for investment unless strict compliance with statute, notifies person as part of advertising plan he has won prize but to receive it he must purchase or rent goods or services, or fails to inform customers that refunds or exchanges are not allowed (598.412). Violation of deceptive trade practice may result in penalty not more than $10,000 for each violation and criminal penalties for violator or its officers or managing agents. (598.640).

Pyramid promotional sales and endless chain distributions constitute deceptive trade practice. (598.110).

Motor vehicle repairs are regulated. Person authorizing repairs to motor vehicle must be given upon request, written estimate of total charge including costs of labor and any necessary parts or accessories. (598.705). No charge may be made exceeding estimate by 20% or $40, whichever is less, without consent of person authorizing repairs. (598.710).

Mobile home manufacture and sale are regulated. (489.021-489.491).

Plain Language.—No "plain language" statute enacted.
See also topic Interest; category Insurance, topic Insurance Companies.

CONTRACTS:

Uniform Commercial Code has been adopted. (104.1101-104.9507). See topic Commercial Code.

There are no statutory provisions modifying the common law of contracts. See also categories Documents and Records, topic Seals; Family, topic Infants.

FACTORS:

Uniform Commercial Code adopted. (104.1101-104.9507). See topic Commercial Code.

No other statutory provision. Common law governs.

FRANCHISES:

Manufacturer, distributor or factory may not require dealer to agree to jurisdiction or venue or tribunal in which controversy arising under franchise agreement may or may not be submitted for resolution, may not prohibit dealer from bringing action in any forum allowed by Nevada, may not require dealer to waive right to jury trial and may not terminate or refuse transfer of franchise, or controlling interest in dealership because dealer prior to Oct. 1, 1997 established additional franchise to sell other new vehicles, or after that date unreasonably prevent dealer from establishing additional franchise to sell or service other makes of new vehicles in same facility. (482.3638).

Uniform Franchise and Business Opportunities Act has not been adopted.

FRAUDS, STATUTE OF:

Every conveyance of any interest in land (except a lease for one year or less) and every trust or power over or concerning lands must be in writing expressing the consideration and signed by the grantor or his lawful agent. (111.205-111.210).

Every agreement which, by its terms, is not to be performed within one year from the making thereof, every special promise to answer for the debt, default or miscarriage of another, every promise or undertaking made on consideration of marriage, except mutual promises to marry, every promise or commitment to loan money or extend credit of at least $100,000 made by one in business of lending money or extending credit, and every promise or commitment to pay fee of $1,000 or more for obtaining loan or extension of credit are void unless in writing, expressing consideration and subscribed by party to be charged therewith. (111.220).

Uniform Commercial Code adopted. (104.1101-104.9507). See topic Commercial Code.

Contracts of Sale.—See topic Commercial Code.

Grants and assignments of existing trusts in realty and personalty are void unless in writing subscribed by the maker or his lawfully authorized agent. (111.235).

Part Performance.—Nothing in the statute abridges the power of the courts to compel specific performance of agreements in cases of part performance of such agreements. (111.015).

INTEREST:

Legal rate when no express written contract is 12%. (99.040). In absence of express contract providing otherwise, open account bears interest only from time when balance due is ascertained. (99.040).

Maximum Rate.—Parties may agree for payment of any rate of interest and for compounding interest on money due on any contract. (99.050).

Judgments.—Where no rate of interest is provided by contract or specified in judgment, judgment draws interest from service of summons and complaint until satisfied at rate equal to prime rate at largest bank in Nevada ascertained by commissioner of financial institutions. (17.130).

Usury.—Parties may agree for payment of any rate of interest and for compounding interest on money due on any contract. (99.050).

Thrift companies are licensed and regulated by department of commerce which shall require licensee insured by FDIC to comply with any reserves and limits imposed by that insurer. (677.230, 677.620). Statutory limitations on amount of unsecured and secured loans licensee can make. (677.770). Loans may be secured by real or personal property regardless of location or nature of property. (677.780). Licensee may lend at any rate of interest and subject to any charge as parties agree. (677.730).

Time Price Differential.—On purchase of goods at retail by conditional sales contract, finance charge, and any other fee, expense, or charge may be any amount agreed upon by parties. (97.195).

LICENSES, BUSINESS AND PROFESSIONAL:

Many businesses, occupations and activities are deemed to be affected with a public interest sufficient to require or justify licensing them. For example, recent legislation deals with some phase of licensing the following: accountants (628.380); architects (623.010-623.360); chiropodists (635.010-635.180); chiropractors (634.010-634.230); contractors (624.010-624.360); child care facilities (432A.010-432A.280); debt adjusters (676.110-676.210); dentists (631.015-631.400); employment agencies (611.020-611.320); escrow agents (645A.020-645A.040); farmers' markets (244.336-244.338; 268.091-268.093); hearing aid specialists (637A.010-637A.360); hospital pharmaceutical technicians (639.2325); livestock auctioneers (573.020); manufacturers or wholesalers of drugs and medicines (639.100); mobile home dealers, manufacturers and rebuilders (489.301-489.441); mortgage companies (645B.020-645B.050); nurses (632.030-632.500); optometrists (636.010-636.420); pharmacists (639.100-639.2122); practice of traditional Oriental medicine (634A.010-634A.240); private detectives (648.060-648.149); taxidermists (502.370); and wholesale liquor dealers (369.180).

Retail merchants must procure a license, upon a showing (1) whether the applicant is engaged in business under a fictitious name, and if so whether he has complied with the fictitious name statute (see category Intellectual Property, topic Trademarks and Tradenames); and (2) whether there was any change in the business during the preceding calendar year, and if so whether there was a compliance with the bulk sales law (see category Debtor and Creditor, topic Fraudulent Sales and Conveyances). (364.110).

Games.—The operation of gambling games and devices is licensed by the state and county, the license fees in general varying according to the number of games and devices operated. (463.010-463.480).

Collection agents (except attorneys and individuals employed by them at regular wages as collectors, banks, nonprofit cooperative corporations, abstract companies doing an escrow business) duly licensed real estate agents and out of state collection agencies must be licensed by commissioner of financial institutions and must give bond for $25,000, running to State of Nevada, conditioned to account for all collections in accordance with agreement with customer and to comply with all requirements of present or future statutes on subject. Within three months after issuance of license, and semiannually thereafter, commissioner shall determine appropriate amount of bond and may increase amount required in accordance with NRS 649.105. Managers must obtain certificate from, and employees handling money or making contact with public must register with, Superintendent. (649.075-649.165).

License expires July 1 following issuance and must be renewed annually. It is not transferable and must be framed and hung in place of business. (649.245; 649.315). Change in business location must receive prior written approval from commissioner. (649.325). License is revocable by commissioner after complaint under oath and hearing. (649.385; 649.395). Collecting without license is misdemeanor. (649.435).

Bond must be that of a surety company authorized to do business in Nevada. It covers all matters placed with licensee during term of license or renewal. Action on bond must be brought within two years after revocation of license. (649.115).

MONOPOLIES, RESTRAINT OF TRADE AND COMPETITION:

Unfair Trade Practices.—Nevada Unfair Trade Practice Act prohibits bid rigging and other price fixing, tying arrangements, and agreements between competitors to divide markets or to allocate customers. (598A.060). Act does not apply to labor, agricultural and horticultural organizations organized for self-help and not for profit; or to religious or charitable activities of nonprofit organizations established exclusively for such purposes; or to conduct expressly authorized or approved by federal or state statute or local ordinance, excepting ordinances relating to community antenna television companies, or otherwise regulated by federal, state, or local agency; or to restrictive covenants which are part of contract of sale of business and carry reasonable time limitation, or which are part of commercial shopping center lease. (598A.040).

Attorney general and district attorneys, as he permits or directs, enforce Act, investigate suspected violations, and bring suit for injunctive relief against threatened damage and for civil and criminal penalties for determined violations. (598A.070). Individual violator is liable for damages, fine and/or imprisonment. (598A.280). Corporation, partnership, or other legal entity is liable for acts of officers, directors, or representatives. (598A.230). Dissolution of domestic corporation or other entity may be ordered. Privilege to conduct business of domestic or foreign corporation or association may be suspended. (598A.180; 598A.190).

Under Act: (1) Civil action for any violation to recover actual damages and secure other relief, may be brought by attorney general as parens patriae of Nevada residents, or as representative of class or classes of persons within state; or as parens patriae with respect to damages sustained by general economy of state or political subdivision (598A.160); (2) attorney general may sue person engaging in activities prohibited and recover amount not exceeding 5% of gross income from sale of commodities or services by such person in each year in which prohibited activities occurred (598A.170); (3) person injured or threatened with violation has civil action for treble damages or injunctive relief (598A.210); (4) state or political subdivision injured in business or property by any violation has action for treble damages (598A.200).

Costs and attorney fees are recoverable to prevailing plaintiff. (598A.200; 598A.210).

Limitation of actions: Four years after cause of action accrues under Act, or if action based on conspiracy, within four years after plaintiff discovered, or should have, facts relief upon to prove conspiracy. Private damages action or action by state as parens patriae, or as class representative, must be brought within one year after conclusion of any damages action brought by state or political subdivision for injury to its property or for violations, if second action is based in whole or in part on same matter as first. (598A.220).

Franchise Agreements.—

Alcoholic Beverages.—Franchises between liquor suppliers and wholesalers are regulated. (598.290-598.350). Discrimination between wholesalers as to franchise terms and termination of franchise without cause are prohibited. (598.330). Wholesaler has action for damages. (598.340). Proof of good faith action and for good cause is complete defense. (598.350).

See note at head of Digest as to 1998 legislation covered.

See Topical Index in front part of this volume.

MONOPOLIES, RESTRAINT OF TRADE AND COMPETITION . . . *continued*

Person wholesaling or importing alcoholic beverages cannot retail alcoholic beverages, except federally bonded winery. Investment in business of importing, wholesaling, or retailing alcoholic beverages by person in business of manufacturing, blending or bottling alcoholic beverages is limited. (598.355).

Petroleum Products.—Relationship between refiners of products and wholesale distributors and retailers (service station operator pursuant to franchise with refiner or wholesale distributor) is regulated. (598.650—598.680). As of July 1, 1987, refiner may not commence direct operation of service station or sale of vehicle fuel at station; as of July 1, 1988, refiner may not engage in direct operation of more than 15 service stations in this state. (598.677). Refiner cannot fail to act in good faith in performing or complying with franchise or contract with wholesale distributor, or use undue influence to induce retailer to surrender any right contained in franchise. (598.679). Refiner cannot change any of restrictions on business activities of retailer during term of franchise that are not related to sale of petroleum products, unreasonably reduce or curtail supply of petroleum products, or place unreasonable restrictions on business of retailer that are not related to sale of petroleum products or on any business activities of wholesale distributor. (598.655) Refiner cannot fail to renew franchise of retailer without compensation at fair going business value if: (1) Investment was entered into with reasonable and prudent business judgment for purpose of fulfilling franchise, and (2) failure to renew not done in good faith.

With exceptions, refiner may not terminate or cancel agreement without first giving written notice to retailer or wholesale distributor specifying matters of noncompliance and allowing retailer or wholesale distributor 30 days to comply. (598.655). Refiner cannot fail to renew without giving 30 days notice of intention not to renew or specifying changes in contract to which renewal is subject. (598.665) Failure of refiner to serve notice as required constitutes grant of 45-day option to wholesale distributor or retailer to renew franchise for one year on existing terms. (598.670).

Retailer, wholesale distributor or refiner has action for damages and/or injunctive relief for violation of franchise agreement. (598.680).

Resale Price Agreements.—See category Intellectual Property, topic Trademarks and Tradenames.

NEGOTIABLE INSTRUMENTS:

See topic Bills and Notes.

RESTRAINT OF TRADE:

See topic Monopolies, Restraint of Trade and Competition.

SALES:

Uniform Commercial Code adopted. (104.1101-104.9507). See topic Commercial Code.

Contracts of Sale.—Except as to retail installment sales there is no statutory provision as to size of type in printed contracts. Retail installment sale contracts must be in a size equal to 8-point type. (97.165).

Bills of Sale.—There is no statutory provision for bills of sale and recording them has no effect.

Product Liability.—Uniform Commercial Code adopted, 1966 Optional Amendment 2-318 on third party beneficiaries of warranties adopted in form Alternative A. For text, see Part III of this Volume.

Privity required before liability can be based on implied warranties of fitness or merchantable quality under previous statute, U.S.A. Privity held not to exist between seller and buyer's employee. (79 Nev. 241, 382 P.2d 399).

Court adoption of rule of strict tort liability. (86 Nev. 408, 470 P.2d 135).

Conditional Sales.—See topic Commercial Code.

See also category Transportation, topic Motor Vehicles, subhead Titles, Sales and Liens.

Retail Credit Sales.—Upon purchase of goods at retail by conditional sales contract amount of finance charge and any other fee, expense, or charge may be amount agreed upon by parties. (97.195). See topic Interest, subhead Time Price Differential.

Bulk Sales.—See topic Commercial Code.

Lease Option Agreements.—Lease of personal property primarily for personal, family or household purposes with option to purchase must contain statutory disclosures (598.2803, 598.2804) and cannot contain confession of judgment, negotiable instrument, security interest, assignment of wages, waiver of defenses, or provision authorizing lessor to commit breech of peace to repossess (598.28055). If lessee has paid less than 2/3 of total price and voluntarily surrenders property to lessor, lessor may reinstate agreement within 21 days after property is returned, if paid more than 2/3 may reinstate within 45 days. (598.2806). Not apply to lease option agreements for business, commercial or agricultural purposes, agreement made with any governmental agency, lease incidental to lease of real property and lease of motor vehicle. (598.28035).

Consumer Protection.—See topic Consumer Protection.

SECURITIES:

Uniform Securities Act (1985) has been adopted. (90.211-90.860). Act administered by Secretary of State and administrator of securities division of office of Secretary of State. (90.710).

Fees.—Applicant for license must pay following annual license fees: Broker-dealer $150, sales representative $55, investment advisor $150, and representative of investment advisor $55. Administrator may by regulation require licensing of branch offices and impose license and annual fee. (90.360). Filing fee for registration statement is 1/10 of 1% of maximum aggregate offering price but not less than $350 nor more than $2,500; if registration statement is thereafter amended, filing fee for amendment is three times fee otherwise payable. (90.500). Open end management company, face amount certificate company or unit investment trust may register indefinite amount of securities by paying filing fee of $500 and within 60 days after its fiscal year during which

statement is effective fee of $2,000 or file report specifying sales and pay fee of 1/10 of 1% of total sales price of securities sold in this state which shall not be less than $350 nor more than $2,500. (90.500).

Uniform Commercial Code adopted. (104.1101-104.9507). See topic Commercial Code.

Uniform Simplification of Fiduciary Security Transfers Act adopted. (162.150). Corporation registering security in name of one described as fiduciary not bound to inquire into existence or extent of fiduciary relationship, and may assume that relationship continues until written notice to contrary (162.170); and may transfer security pursuant to assignment without inquiry. (162.180).

Uniform Securities Ownership by Minors Act not adopted.

See also topic Consumer Protection.

STATUTE OF FRAUDS:

See topic Frauds, Statute of.

TRUST RECEIPT SECURITY:

See topic Commercial Code.

WAREHOUSEMEN:

Uniform Commercial Code adopted. (104.1101-104.9507). See topic Commercial Code.

Permits required for storage of household goods and effects. (712.040).

CITIZENSHIP

ALIENS:

Except where a taking by descent or inheritance, any nonresident alien person, including a corporation, may take, hold, and enjoy real property or an interest therein to same extent as a resident citizen or domestic corporation. (111.055). The right of a nonresident alien to take by descent or inheritance real or personal property depends upon existence of a reciprocal right accorded to U. S. citizens by country which he inhabits or of which he is a citizen. (134.230).

CIVIL ACTIONS AND PROCEDURE

ACCORD AND SATISFACTION:

Common law rules apply. (48 Nev. 430, 233 Pac. 530).

Pleading.—An accord and satisfaction must be specially pleaded. (48 Nev. 430, 233 Pac. 530; N.R.C.P. 8[c]).

Uniform Commercial Code adopted (104.1101-104.9507). See category Business Regulation and Commerce, topic Commercial Code.

ACTIONS:

There is but one form of action. Law and equity may be administered in same action, but distinction between law and equity is preserved. Federal Rules of Civil Procedure form basis for procedural statute. (N.R.C.P. 1-86). See topic Practice. Uniform Contribution Among Tortfeasors Act adopted. (17.225-17.305).

Commencement.—A civil action is commenced by filing a complaint with the court. (N.R.C.P. 3).

Parties.—Every action must be prosecuted in name of real party in interest, except that an executor or administrator, a guardian, a bailee, a trustee of an express trust (including a person with whom or in whose name a contract is made for benefit of another) or a person expressly authorized by statute may sue without joining with him person for whose benefit action is prosecuted. (N.R.C.P. 17a).

Permissive Joinder.—All persons may join as plaintiffs if they assert right to relief, or as defendants if there is asserted against them a right to relief, jointly, severally or in the alternative in respect of or arising out of the same transaction, occurrence, or series of transactions or occurrences and if any question of law or fact common to all will arise in the action. (N.R.C.P. 20).

Necessary Joinder.—Persons having a joint interest must be made parties and joined on the same side as plaintiffs or defendants if person is subject to service of process and joinder will not deprive court of subject matter jurisdiction. One who should but refuses to be plaintiff may be made defendant or involuntary plaintiff. (N.R.C.P. 19).

Tort action against present or former officer or employee of state or any political subdivision, independent contractor who provides medical services for department of prisons, or state legislator arising out of act or omission within scope of his public employment must name state or appropriate political subdivision as party defendant. (41.0337).

Class Actions.—One or more members of a class may sue or be sued on behalf of all if class so numerous that joinder of all members impracticable; there are questions of law or fact common to all; claims or defenses of representative parties are typical of claims or defenses of all; and representative parties will fairly and adequately protect interests of all. (N.R.C.P. 23).

Derivative Actions.—Complaint must be verified, allege plaintiff was member at time of complained transaction, and allege with particularity plaintiff's efforts to obtain desired action and reason for failure to obtain action or not making effort. Such action cannot be maintained if plaintiff does not fairly and adequately represent interests of other members. Action cannot be dismissed or compromised without court approval and notice to other members. (N.R.C.P. 23.1).

Intervention.—As of right intervention may be had upon application (1) when statute confers unconditional right to intervene; (2) when applicant claims interest relating to property or transaction which is subject of action and he is so situated that

ACTIONS . . . *continued*

disposition of action may impair his ability to protect that interest, unless his interest is adequately represented by existing parties. Permissive intervention may be had upon application (1) when statute confers conditional right to intervene; (2) when applicant's claim or defense and main action have a question of law or fact in common. (N.R.C.P. 24).

Interpleader.—Persons having claims against plaintiff may be joined as defendants and required to interplead when plaintiff may be exposed to double liability. Defendant exposed to similar liability may obtain interpleader by cross-claim or counterclaim. (N.R.C.P. 22).

Third Party Practice.—Defendants, and plaintiffs facing counterclaims, may cause to be made parties, persons liable to them for any part of claim against them. If third-party complaint not filed within ten days of serving original answer, third-party plaintiff must obtain leave to make service. Third-party defendants may raise defenses and counterclaims against plaintiff and third-party plaintiff in same manner as original defendant and is subject to claim of plaintiff arising out of transaction or occurrence that is subject matter or plaintiff's claim. (N.R.C.P. 14).

Joinder of Claims.—Party asserting claim to relief as an original claim, counterclaim, crossclaim, or third-party claim, may join, either as independent or alternative claims, as many claims, legal or equitable, as he has against an opposing party. (N.R.C.P. 18a).

Joinder of Remedies.—Whenever a claim is one heretofore cognizable only after another claim has been prosecuted to a conclusion, the two claims may be joined. (N.R.C.P. 18b).

Consolidation.—When actions involving a common question of law or fact are pending court may order (1) a joint hearing on any or all matters in issue; or (2) consolidation of all actions; or (3) may make such order as may tend to avoid unnecessary costs or delays. (N.R.C.P. 42a).

Separate Trials.—Court may, in furtherance of convenience or to avoid prejudice, or when separate trials will be conducive to expedition and economy, order a separate trial of any claim, cross-claim, counterclaim, or third party claim, or of any separate issue or of any number of claims, cross-claims, counterclaims, third party claims, or issues, always preserving inviolate right of trial by jury. (N.R.C.P. 42b).

Substitution of Parties.—If party dies and claim is not thereby extinguished, court, upon application made 90 days after notice of death is on record (unless reasonable excuse for delay be shown) may order substitution. If party becomes incompetent, upon motion action may be continued by or against representative. If there is transfer of interest, action may continue against original parties unless court, on motion, directs substitution. (N.R.C.P. 25).

Stay of Proceedings.—On demand or motion of either party, a trial or proceeding may be stayed pending an appeal of an order granting or refusing to grant a motion to change place of trial of an action or proceeding. (N.R.A.P. 3A[b][4]).

Abatement.—No cause of action lost by reason of death of any person, but may be maintained by or against executor or administrator. (41.085).

An action for a wrong does not abate by the death of any party after verdict has been rendered, but proceeds in same manner as cases where cause of action survives by law. (12.100).

Termination of Action.—Voluntary dismissal may be had by plaintiff without order of court (1) by notice filed before answer or motion for judgment; or (2) by stipulation signed by all appearing parties. Involuntary dismissal may be had (1) on motion of defendant for failure to prosecute; or (2) after plaintiff has completed his evidence, defendant may without waiving his right to present evidence, move for dismissal on the ground that upon the facts and the law, plaintiff has no right to relief.

Dismissal for want of prosecution is mandatory after five years, discretionary after two years from date of commencement of suit. (N.R.C.P. 41).

Prohibited Actions.—No action may be brought for alienation of affections or breach of promise to marry (41.380), or for criminal conversation that accrued after July 1, 1979 (41.380).

Limitation of.—See topic Limitation of Actions.

Small Claims.—See category Courts and Legislature, topic Courts.

Direct Actions Against Insurer.—See category Transportation, topic Motor Vehicles, subhead Direct Actions.

Against State or Political Subdivision.—See topic Damages, subhead Sovereign Immunity.

Conditions Precedent.—No tort action can be brought unless claim filed within two years from accrual of cause of action with state board of examiners or governing body of political subdivision. (41.036). Also claim based on conduct of immune contractor, employee or officer of political subdivision must be filed with political subdivision before complaint filed. (41.039).

Arbitration.—If claim for relief filed in District Court arises in Nevada, and amount in issue does not exceed $25,000, all civil actions filed for damages must be submitted to nonbinding arbitration pursuant to Supreme Court Rules. (38.250). Following actions are excluded from this requirement: class, equity, title to real property, probate, declaratory relief, divorce or domestic relations, relief based on extraordinary writs, judicial review of administrative decisions, those where parties have by agreement submitted controversy to arbitration or other alternative dispute resolution, and appeals from courts of limited jurisdiction. (38.255).

APPEAL AND ERROR:

Controlled by Nevada Rules of Appellate Procedure (N.R.A.P. 1-48).

Appeal to Supreme Court may be taken from final judgment of district court from order granting or refusing new trial and from certain orders before and after judgment. Appeal may be taken without first moving for new trial. (N.R.A.P. 3A).

How Taken.—Appeal is taken by filing with district court a notice of appeal within 30 days from service of written notice of entry of the judgment appealed from. (N.R.A.P. 4). A cost bond of $250 must be filed with notice of appeal. (N.R.A.P. 7). Record on appeal must be docketed with Supreme Court within 40 days from date of filing notice of appeal. (N.R.A.P. 11[a]).

Extent of Review.—Supreme Court reviews errors of law and sufficiency of evidence. (N.R.A.P. 3A[a]). May require attendance of counsel and parties at settlement conference in civil appeals. (N.R.A.P. 16).

Appeal to district court may be taken from a justice's court on any appealable judgment or order in a civil action. (N.J.R.C.P. 72[a]). Appeals from justice's courts are governed by N.J.R.C.P. 72-76.

How Taken.—By filing a notice of appeal with justice's court. (N.J.R.C.P. 73[a]). Notice must specify parties taking appeal; judgment or order of part thereof appealed from; whether taken on questions of law or fact or both; court appealed to. Notice shall be mailed to all parties except appealing parties. (N.J.R.C.P. 73[b]).

Justice certifies to district court a copy of his docket, all papers in case, notice of appeal and undertaking. (N.J.R.C.P. 75[g]).

Time for Taking.—Appeal must be taken within 30 days after notice of entry of judgment. (N.J.R.C.P. 73[a]).

Appeal Bond.—Undertaking of $100 for costs must be given. (N.J.R.C.P. 73[c]).

Stay of Proceeding.—If stay is desired, undertaking in double amount of judgment is required. (N.J.R.C.P. 73[d]).

Extent of Review.—May be on questions either of law or fact. If taken on questions of law only, appellant must, within ten days from rendition of judgment, file with justice a statement containing errors relied on and so much of evidence as explains grounds. (N.J.R.C.P. 75[d]).

Character of Hearing.—Where appeal is on law and facts there is no statement, but a trial de novo is had in district court. (N.J.R.C.P. 75[l]).

BONDS:

Bonds in civil actions or for fiduciaries require two sureties worth sum equal in amount to penalty. When bonds are for $3,000 or over there may be more than two sureties, each qualifying for less than the penalty, but all aggregating at least two sufficient sureties. (20.010). Bond is presented to clerk of court in which action is pending for approval before filing. (20.050). Approval may be refused if power of attorney in fact covering agent signing bond is not on file with clerk. (20.050).

Bondsmen on official bonds must be residents of state and freeholders or householders therein. (282.140).

Surety companies after qualifying to do business in Nevada may become sole sureties, but all surety company bonds, where statute so requires or where given in civil actions, must be approved by court, judge, clerk or deputy. (20.030).

Sureties may be required to justify before proper officer and if examination does not show them to be worth amount specified over debts and liabilities and property exempt from execution new bond is required. (20.010, 20.020).

In condemnation proceeding by state to occupy property in advance of compensation payment, no bond is required but only pledged public faith and credit of state, or state may deposit with clerk an amount equal to value of premises plus damages as appraised by state (37.100); no bond, undertaking or security is required of state, or any county, city, town or officer thereof in his official capacity which is a party to an action (20.040).

Form.—N.R.S. 20.015 provides that undertaking may be in substantially following form:

Form

State of Nevada

County of . . . .

In the . . . . court . . . . (state title of the action). Whereas the above named . . . . desires to give an undertaking for . . . . (state purpose) as provided by NRS . . . . Now, therefore, we the undersigned sureties, do hereby obligate ourselves, jointly and severally to . . . . (name the obligee) under the provisions of NRS . . . . in the sum of $. . . . .

Dated this . . . . day of . . . . , A. D. 19 . . . . .

. . . .
(Signature of Principal)

. . . .
(Signature of Sureties)

CERTIORARI:

A writ of certiorari may be granted by the Supreme or district court when an inferior tribunal, board or officer exercising judicial functions has exceeded its or his jurisdiction and there is no appeal or other plain, speedy and adequate remedy. (34.020).

Jurisdiction.—Both Supreme Court and district court have jurisdiction to issue writ to inferior tribunal or board or officer exercising judicial function. (34.020).

Grounds.—Granted in all cases when an inferior tribunal, board, or officer, exercising judicial functions, has exceeded its or his jurisdiction and there is no appeal or other plain, speedy and adequate remedy. (34.020).

Proceedings.—Application made on affidavit and court may require notice to adverse party, or grant order to show cause why it should not be allowed, or grant writ without further notice. (34.030, 34.040-34.140).

Review.—The review may not extend, further than to determine whether the tribunal, board or officer has regularly pursued its or his authority. (34.090).

Where, on appeal from justice's or municipal court, district court has passed on constitutionality of statute or ordinance, writ may be granted for review by Supreme Court of question of constitutionality. (34.020).

See note at head of Digest as to 1998 legislation covered.

See Topical Index in front part of this volume.

CHARITABLE IMMUNITY:

See topic Damages.

COMMISSIONS TO TAKE TESTIMONY:

See topic Depositions and Discovery.

COSTS:

Costs must be allowed to prevailing party in actions to recover real property, or possessory right thereto, to recover personal property in excess of $2,500, in actions for damages exceeding $2,500, in special proceedings, except those conducted pursuant to 306.040, and in actions involving title or boundaries to real estate, or legality of any tax, assessment, or municipal fine. All other cases are left to discretion of court. (18.010–18.060, 69.020). Attorney fees are allowed as costs in justice court (69.030) and in district court when authorized by statute or to prevailing party who has not recovered more than $20,000, or without regard to recovery sought when court finds claim or defense was brought without reasonable ground or to harass prevailing party, however, limitations in district court do not apply to actions arising out of written instrument or agreement which entitles prevailing party to award of reasonable attorneys fees (18.010).

See also category Business Regulation and Commerce, topic Monopolies, Restraint of Trade and Competition.

Security for Costs.—Nonresident plaintiff may be compelled to give security for costs in sum of $500 with two sufficient sureties (18.130) or by bond of qualified surety company (691B.020), provided demand therefor is made within time limited for answering complaint (18.130). In justice court, security required is $100, but increase may be ordered. (69.010). Plaintiff in shareholders' derivative action may be required by court to give security for costs upon finding that there is no reasonable possibility that suit will benefit corporation or that moving party, if other than corporation, did not participate in transaction complained of in any capacity. (41.520).

DAMAGES:

Common law generally prevails as to compensatory damages. In actions for breach of obligation not arising from contract, where proven by clear and convincing evidence that if defendant is guilty of oppression, fraud or malice, express or implied, plaintiff, in addition to actual damages, may recover punitive damages not to exceed three times compensatory damages, if such damages exceed $100,000, or if compensatory damages are less, not to exceed $300,000. This cap on punitive damages does not apply to actions for defective product, bad faith actions against insurer, actions for violation of law prohibiting discriminatory housing practices, actions for injury caused by emissions, disposal or spilling of toxic or hazardous waste or material, or actions for defamation. If punitive damages are claimed pursuant to this section, and trier of fact concludes they should be assessed, subsequent proceeding before same trier of fact must be conducted. (42.005). In action for breach of obligation where defendant caused injury by operation of vehicle in violation of 484.379 or 484.3795 after willfully using alcohol or another substance knowing that he would thereafter operate vehicle, plaintiff in addition to compensatory damages, may recover punitive damages without any limitation as to amount and without any subsequent proceeding. (42.010). Person suffering injury as proximate result of perjury or subornation of perjury committed by another, convicted for same, may recover actual damages and any punitive damages which facts warrant. (41.365). Owner may bring civil action for treble damages against knowing receiver of stolen property. (41.580). Any person rendering emergency care or assistance gratuitously and in good faith cannot be held civilly liable for any act or omission not amounting to gross negligence, except when act or omission of licensed physician or nurse occurs in licensed health facility and relative to person with whom there is preexisting relationship as patient. Person licensed under NRS c. 630.632 or 633 who renders emergency care or obstetrical care during labor or delivery not liable for civil damages if care rendered in good faith, doesn't amount to gross negligence or willful or wanton conduct, provider had not previously provided care for woman, and damages are reasonably related to woman's lack of prenatal care. Person who completed course in cardiopulmonary resuscitation and course in basic emergency care of persons in cardiac arrest and directed by instructions of agency that provides emergency medical service who in good faith renders cardiopulmonary resuscitation not liable for civil damages if care does not amount to gross negligence. Person who completed course in basic emergency care of persons in cardiac arrest and completed training in use of automatic external defibrillator and who renders emergency care involving use of external defibrillator, and person's employer, not liable for civil damages if care does not amount to gross negligence. (41.500, 41.505). Doctrine of charitable immunity prevails, based not upon trust theory but rather beneficiary theory. (51 Nev. 372, 277 Pac. 798).

See also category Estates and Trusts, topics Death, subhead Action for Death; Monopolies, Restraint of Trade and Competition.

No-Fault Insurance.—See category Transportation, topic Motor Vehicles, subhead No-Fault Insurance.

Comparative Negligence Rule.—Contributory negligence of plaintiff does not bar recovery for damages for death, injury to person or property if his negligence was not greater than negligence of defendant. Damages allowed are diminished in proportion to amount of plaintiff's negligence. If defendant settles with plaintiff before judgment, neither comparative negligence of that defendant nor amount of settlement is admissible, but judge deducts amount of settlement from verdict. (41.141).

Medical Malpractice.—In medical malpractice action, amount of damages, if any, awarded must be reduced by amount of any prior payment made by or on behalf of provider to injured person or claimant to meet reasonable expenses of medical care, other essential goods and services, or reasonable living expenses except amount so reduced must not include any amount for which there is right of subrogation to rights of claimant, if right exercised by serving notice of lien on claimant before settlement or entry of judgment. (42.020).

Sovereign Immunity.—State, its agencies and political subdivisions waive immunity from liability and action unless otherwise provided by statute. (41.031). No waiver of action brought based on act or omission of officer, employee, or independent contractor who provides medical service for department of prisons, exercising due care in execution of statute or regulation or performance or failure to perform discretionary duty (41.032), except owner of property may commence action to recover actual damages caused by arbitrary or unlawful action which imposes limitations or conditions on use of property in excess of that authorized by ordinance or regulation (278A.0233). No waiver of action brought based on failure to inspect or failure to discover hazard regardless of whether inspection made (41.033), or act or omission of member or employee of Nevada National Guard while engaging in training or duty (41.0333). No action can be brought against police chief, sheriff or chief of fire department based solely on act or omission of officer, deputy or fireman. Fire department or law enforcement agency not liable for negligence of its employees or volunteers unless person made specific representation to another who relied on it to his detriment, or conduct of person affirmatively caused harm. Award of damages in tort action limited to $50,000 and may not include punitive damages. (41.035).

DECLARATORY JUDGMENTS:

See topic Judgments.

DEPOSITIONS AND DISCOVERY:

Federal Rules of Civil Procedure, as am'd in 1970, form basis for procedural statute. (N.R.C.P. 26-37). See topic Practice.

Any party may take deposition of any person, including a party, upon oral examination or written questions for purpose of discovery or use as evidence. (N.R.C.P. 30, 31).

Prerequisite To Discovery—Case Conference Report.—Within 30 days after service of answer, and not more than 180 days thereafter, attorneys must meet and (1) exchange all documents, reasonably available, used to support pleadings, (2) request from other party all documents discoverable, (3) identify all tangible things within scope of Rule 26(b) and arrange for inspection or testing, (4) request to inspect, test or sample tangible things in custody of other party, (5) exchange written list of persons with knowledge of relevant facts, (6) propose plan and schedule of discovery, (7) discuss settlement and use of alternative dispute resolution and (8) discuss other matters that may resolve controversy. Thirty days thereafter joint case conference report must be filed. Any time there-after court may direct attorneys and parties to appear before court or discovery commissioner for dispute resolution conference. In complex litigation, court may on motion and for good cause shown waive these requirements. (NRCP 16.1).

Uniform Foreign Depositions Act adopted. (53.050-53.070).

Leave of Court.—After filing joint case conference report or entry of order waiving compliance with Rule 16.1 leave not necessary; but must be obtained if notice of taking is served by plaintiff within 30 days after such commencement unless defendant has sought discovery. (N.R.C.P. 30).

Action Pending Elsewhere.—Any party may take deposition of any person within this state as if such action were pending within this state. (53.060).

Within State for Use within State.—Unless otherwise indicated, rules under this topic apply.

Within State for Use Elsewhere.—See subheads Action Pending Elsewhere, supra, and Foreign Depositions, infra.

Outside of State for Use within State.—Same as Federal Rule 30, as am'd in 1970.

Before Action.—One who desires to perpetuate his testimony or that of another may file a verified petition in the district court of the county where the expected adverse party may reside. Petition must show (1) petitioner expects to be party but is presently unable to bring action; (2) subject of expected action and his interest therein; (3) facts he desires to establish and reasons for desiring to perpetuate testimony; (4) names or description, and addresses of persons he expects will be adverse parties; (5) names and addresses of persons to be examined and substance of testimony expected; (6) a request for an order authorizing the taking of the deposition for the purpose of perpetuating testimony. Notice, and a copy of the petition, must be served at least 20 days before hearing on expected adverse parties, which notice must state that petitioner will apply at stated time and place for order sought. (N.R.C.P. 27).

Pending Appeal.—If appeal has been taken, or if time has not expired, district court may allow perpetuation of testimony for use in event of further proceedings. Application and notice as if action were pending in district court, except that notice must show (1) names and addresses of persons to be examined and the substance of testimony; (2) reasons for perpetuating testimony. (N.R.C.P. 27).

Before Whom Taken.—Within the United States, before an officer authorized to administer oaths by laws of the United States or of place of examination, or before a person appointed by the court in which action is pending. (N.R.C.P. 28).

In Foreign Countries.—On notice before: (1) Person authorized to administer oaths in foreign country; or (2) such person or officer as may be appointed by commission. (N.R.C.P. 28).

Stipulation.—Unless court orders otherwise, parties may by written stipulation agree to take a deposition before any person, at any time or place, upon any notice and in any manner; and parties may also modify procedures provided by N.R.C.P. for other methods of discovery, except stipulations extending time provided in Rules 33, 34 and 36. (N.R.C.P. 29).

On Oral Examination.—Party desiring to take deposition must give at least 15 days written notice to every other party, stating time and place and names and addresses of persons to be examined. If subpoena duces tecum is to be served on person to be examined, designation of materials to be produced must be attached to or included in notice. Court may enlarge or shorten time, parties may stipulate or court may order that deposition be recorded by other than stenographic means, and on showing that examination is being conducted in bad faith or to unreasonably annoy, embarrass or oppress,

DEPOSITIONS AND DISCOVERY . . . *continued*

court may order termination of examination or limit scope and manner as provided by Rule 26(c). Party may in his notice name corporation, partnership, association or governmental agency and designate matters on which examination is requested; organization must then designate person or persons who will testify as to matters known or reasonably available to organization. Notice may be accompanied by Rule 34 Request For Production but Rule 34 procedure must apply. Telephonic depositions allowed. (N.R.C.P. 30).

On Written Questions.—Party desiring to take deposition on written questions must serve them on every party not in default with notice of name and address of person to answer and name or descriptive title of officer. Within 30 days party served may serve cross-questions; within ten days thereafter recross questions may be served. Copy of notice and all questions must be delivered by party taking deposition to officer who must promptly proceed as in case of oral examination, to take deposition, prepare, certify, file or mail deposition to clerk for filing. Notice of filing must be given promptly to all parties by one taking deposition. (N.R.C.P. 31).

Record of Examination.—Officer must put witness on oath, testimony must be taken stenographically and transcribed unless court, upon motion, orders otherwise or parties agree otherwise which must designate person before whom deposition is to be taken, manner of recording, preserving and filing deposition, and may include other necessary matters. All objections made at time of examination to qualifications of officer, manner of taking, evidence presented, conduct of any party, and any other objection to proceeding must be noted by officer. Evidence objected to must be taken subjective to objection. Testimony shall be transcribed if requested by one of parties. Instead of participating in oral examination, parties may serve written questions in sealed envelope on party taking deposition who shall transmit them to officer who shall propound them to witness and record answers. (N.R.C.P. 30).

Termination and Limiting Examination.—At any time during taking, on motion of any party or deponent and upon showing that examination is being conducted in bad faith or unreasonably annoys, embarrasses or oppresses deponent or a party, court where action is pending may order officer to cease forthwith or may limit scope and manner as stated above in case of oral examination. If so terminated, examination must be resumed only on order of court in which action is pending. Witness may not be instructed to refuse to answer question except on ground of privilege. (N.R.C.P. 30).

Signing and Certification.—After deposition transcribed officer must notify witness and parties in attendance that original transcript is available for signing and reading within 30 days (unless waived by parties). If not signed by witness within 30 days of its submission of notice to him, officer must sign and state on record reason. Officer must certify on deposition that witness was duly sworn and that deposition is true record of testimony. He must securely seal deposition, endorse with title of action, and mark "Deposition of . . . . . ." and send it to party who took deposition. (N.R.C.P. 30).

Scope of Examination.—Unless otherwise ordered by court, deponent may be examined regarding any matter, not privileged, which is relevant, including insurance agreements. (N.R.C.P. 26).

Compelling Attendance of Witnesses.—At request of party, subpoena issued by clerk under a seal of court; if for production of documentary evidence, subpoena is signed and sealed, but otherwise left in blank to be filled in before service by requesting party. Served by sheriff, deputy, or disinterested party over 18 years of age. Failure to obey deemed contempt. Person to whom subpoena is directed may, within ten days after service, object in writing to subpoena, whereupon requesting party has burden of obtaining court order. (N.R.C.P. 45).

Use of Deposition.—So far as admissible deposition may be used (1) against any party who was present or had notice to contradict or impeach; (2) by adverse party for any purpose; (3) if court finds that witness is dead or out of State or at greater distance than 100 miles from place of trial or hearing, unable to testify because of age, sickness, infirmity or imprisonment, or party is unable to procure attendance by subpoena; or in exceptional circumstances in the interest of justice. If only part of deposition offered in evidence by party, other party can compel introductions of other parts. (N.R.C.P. 32).

Interrogatories to parties may be served on adverse party after commencement of action and without leave provided joint case conference report has been filed or order entered waiving compliance with Rule 16.1. Party upon whom served must serve copy of answers or objections within 30 days, except that defendant may service answers or objections within 45 days after service of summons and complaint on him. Party to whom interrogatory directed has option to produce business records under certain circumstances. Number limited to 40 interrogatories without prior stipulation or order. (N.R.C.P. 33).

Discovery.—A party may, without leave of court, provided joint case conference report has been filed or order entered waiving compliance with Rule 16.1 request any other party to produce and permit inspection or copying of designated documents, papers, books, accounts, letters, photographs, objects, tangible things which constitute or contain evidence or may request permission to enter upon land for inspection, etc. Party upon whom request is made must serve response, permitting discovery or objecting, within 30 days of request, except that defendant may serve response within 45 days after service of summons and complaint on that defendant. (N.R.C.P. 34).

Physical and Mental Examination.—If physical or mental condition of a party or person in custody or under control of a party is in controversy, court may, provided joint case conference report has been filed or order entered waiving compliance with Rule 16.1, order him to submit to examination by disinterested and impartial physician. (N.R.C.P. 35).

Admission of Facts.—Provided joint case conference report has been filed or order entered waiving compliance with Rule 16.1 party may serve on another party written request for admission of truth of any matters within scope of Rule 26(b) that relate to statements or opinions of fact or application of law to fact, including genuineness of any document described in request. Party served must answer or object within period designated (30 days, except that defendant may answer or object within 45 days after

service of summons and complaint), or matter will be admitted. No more than 40 requests for admissions can be served without prior stipulation or order. (N.R.C.P. 36).

Foreign Depositions.—Uniform Act adopted. (53.050-53.070).

Perpetuating Testimony.—See subhead Use of Deposition, supra.

Commissions.—See subheads Before Whom Taken, Foreign Depositions, and Outside of State for Use within State, supra.

Forms.—Following may be used:

Forms

In the . . . . . Judicial District Court of the State of Nevada in and for the County of . . . . .

JOHN DOE,
    Plaintiff,
      vs.   } Deposition of . . . .
RICHARD ROE,
    Defendant.

Be it Remembered, that pursuant to (oral, or written, stipulation of counsel) (the annexed notice) in the above-entitled action, and under the provisions of the Nevada Rules of Civil Procedure, the deposition of . . . . . ., a witness in said action, was taken before me, ..., a Notary Public in and for the County of . . . . . ., State of . . . . . ., at the offices of . . . . . ., in the City of . . . . . ., County of . . . . . ., State of . . . . . ., on the . . . . . . day of . . . . . ., 19 . . . ., commencing at the hour of . . . . M. of said day.

That the said witness was first duly sworn by me to tell the truth, the whole truth, and nothing but the truth, in the testimony he was about to give in the above-entitled matter and, thereupon, while said witness was under oath I (counsel) propounded to him the (oral) (written) interrogatories (attached to said notice) and he gave the following answers to them, respectively:

(If deposition is an oral interrogatories, insert transcript of proceedings. If on written interrogatories, insert questions and answers, numbering each question and answer correspondingly.)

(After the deposition is taken, the interrogatories and answers should be signed by the witness unless signature is waived.)

The Notary Public should then certify as to the time, place and manner of taking the deposition, as follows:

STATE OF NEVADA
COUNTY OF . . . . } ss.

I, ..., a Notary Public in and for the County of . . . . . ., State of . . . . . ., duly commissioned, qualified and acting, hereby certify that the deposition of . . . . . ., a witness in the above-entitled action, was taken before me at the offices of . . . . . ., in the City of . . . . . ., County of . . . . . ., State of . . . . . ., on the . . . . . . day of . . . . . ., 19 . . . ., commencing at the hour of . . . . . . .M. of said day;

That before the taking of said deposition, said witness was first duly sworn by me to testify to the truth, the whole truth and nothing but the truth; that thereupon, and while said witness was under oath, said witness was examined upon (oral) (written) interrogatories (attached to said notice) propounded to him by me (counsel), and said witness made answers thereto; that said interrogatories and said answers thereto, and the proceedings had at the taking of said deposition, were caused by me to be reduced to writing; that the foregoing record of said deposition is a full, true and correct transcription of all of said interrogatories so propounded and of all of said answers made by the said witness thereto, and of all of said proceedings had on said day, in the order in which said interrogatories, answers and proceedings were made;

That, when completed, said deposition was read by (to) said witness and corrected by him in every particular he desired, and was thereupon subscribed by him in my presence (that by stipulation the reading, correcting and signing of said deposition by said witness were expressly waived);

That I am not an attorney or counsel for, or related to or employed by, any of the parties to the said action in which this deposition was taken, and that I am not a relative or employee of any attorney or counsel employed by the parties hereto, and am not financially interested in said action.

In Witness Whereof, I have hereunto set my hand and affixed my notarial seal at the City of . . . . . ., County of . . . . . ., State of . . . . . ., this . . . . . . day of . . . . . ., 19 . . . .

(Seal)

                   Notary Public in and for the County of
                   . . . . . ., State of . . . . . .
                   _____

EQUITY:

See topic Actions.

EVIDENCE:

Witnesses.—Every person is competent to be a witness except a person may not testify to a matter unless he has personal knowledge of it or states an opinion as expert. (50.015; 50.025). Interpreter must be appointed at public expense for handicapped person who is witness in criminal proceeding. (50.050). Judge and jurors of trial may not testify at that trial. (50.055; 50.065).

See also topic Depositions and Discovery.

Privileged Communications.—Client of an attorney or accountant has a privilege to refuse to disclose, and to prevent any other person from disclosing, confidential communications (1) between himself or his representative and his attorney or accountant, (2) between his attorney or accountant and representative of attorney or accountant, and (3) made for purpose of facilitating rendition of professional services to client by him or his attorney or accountant to an attorney or accountant representing another in a matter of common interest. (49.035-49.205). Patient of a doctor, dentist, osteopath, or psychiatric social worker has privilege to refuse to disclose and to prevent others from disclosing confidential communications among himself, his doctor or persons participating in diagnosis or treatment, including members of patient's family. No such privilege exists

---

See note at head of Digest as to 1998 legislation covered.

See Topical Index in front part of this volume.

EVIDENCE . . . *continued*

for communications relevant to proceedings to hospitalize for mental illness, or made in course of court ordered examination, or written medical or hospital records relevant to condition of patient in any proceeding in which condition is element of claim or defense, or if services of physician are sought or obtained to aid or enable person to commit fraud or any unlawful act in violation of NRS c. 616 or 617 which person knows or should know is fraudulent or unlawful, or in certain statutory proceedings concerning controlling communicable diseases. (49.215-49.245). Member of organized hospital committee and committee of organizations providing emergency medical services having duties to evaluate and improve care and review committees of medical and dental societies cannot be compelled to testify concerning meetings, and proceedings of such meetings not subject to discovery, however no privilege exists as to statement by one in attendance who is party, person requesting staff privileges, or proceedings concerning action against insurance carrier alleging bad faith failure to settle. (49.265). Clergyman may not be examined as witness to any confession made to him in professional capacity unless confessor consents. (49.255). Public officer may not be examined as to communications made to him in official confidence if public interest would suffer. (49.285). No reporter, former reporter or editorial employee of press or employee of radio or television station may be required to disclose, in any legal proceedings or investigation, published or unpublished information obtained or prepared by such person in his professional communications capacity or source of any information. (49.275). Certified school counselor cannot be examined as witness concerning pupil's communications in counseling in any civil or criminal action to which pupil is party, unless crime punishable by death or life imprisonment is involved. (49.290). Pupil's communications to licensed teacher during counseling concerning possession or use of drugs or alcohol are privileged. (49.291). No privilege exists in child abuse or neglect cases except attorney who acquires knowledge of conduct from client and clergyman who acquires knowledge from offender during confession. (432B.220).

Husband and Wife.—A husband or wife cannot be examined as a witness, the one against the other, without that other's consent, as to any communication made during marriage except in civil action by one against other; or proceeding to commit or place spouse or property under control of third party; or proceeding to establish competence; or proceeding in juvenile or family court; or criminal action involving charges against spouse for bigamy or incest, or crime relating to abandonment of child or nonsupport; or criminal proceedings that took place before marriage; or crime against other's person or property; or crime involving neglect of wife or child (49.295); but when one spouse has been adjudged insane other may testify, while such insanity adjudication continues, to any fact which transpired before or during insanity (49.295-49.305).

Communications or Transactions with Persons Since Deceased.—Personal representative of deceased client of an attorney or accountant may claim privilege and prevent disclosure, except as to a communication relevant to an issue between parties who claim through same deceased client. (49.105-49.115, 49.195-49.205). Personal representative of deceased patient may prevent doctor's disclosure. (49.235-49.245).

Self-Incrimination.—Prohibited by Nev. Const. Art. I, §8.

Compelling Attendance.—Witnesses served with subpoenas are compelled to appear and remain until testimony is closed. Person present may be compelled to testify as if subpoenaed to appear. (50.165).

INJUNCTIONS:

Federal Rules of Civil Procedure form the basis for procedural statute. (N.R.C.P. 1-86). See topic Practice.

An injunction may be granted; when it appears that the plaintiff is entitled to the relief demanded, and such relief consists wholly or in part in restraining the commission or continuance of the act complained of either for a limited time or perpetually; when it appears that the commission or continuance of some act during the litigation would produce great or irreparable injury to the plaintiff; when during the litigation it appears that the defendant is doing or threatens or is about to do or procure or permit the doing of some act in violation of plaintiff's rights respecting the subject of the action and tending to render the judgment ineffectual. (33.010).

Preliminary Notice.—None issued without notice to adverse party.

Temporary Injunction or Restraining Order.—Will not be granted without notice to adverse party, unless it appears that irreparable injury will result to applicant before notice and a hearing can be had and applicant's attorney certifies to court efforts made, if any, to give notice. Period covered by said order may not exceed 15 days, but court in its discretion may renew for a like period. Such orders are filed with county clerk and a hearing must be set at earliest possible moment, and adverse party may demand such a hearing on two days notice. No notice is necessary in divorce, alimony, separate maintenance or child custody suits. (N.R.C.P. 65).

Security.—No restraining order or preliminary injunction may issue without the giving by applicant of security in such form as court deems proper for payment of damages to any party who is found to be wrongfully restrained. No such security is required of the state or its officer or agency, nor in any divorce, alimony, separate maintenance or child custody suit. The surety on such a bond submits himself to the jurisdiction of the court and irrevocably appoints the clerk as his agent upon whom any papers affecting his liability on the bond may be served. (N.R.C.P. 65.1).

JUDGMENTS:

Federal Rules of Civil Procedure form the basis of the procedural statute. (N. R.C.P. 1-86). See topic Practice.

Judgment includes a decree and any appealable order.

Judgment on Pleadings.—After pleadings are closed any party may move for judgment. If matters outside pleadings are presented and not excluded, motion must be as one for summary judgment. (N.R.C.P. 12c).

Summary Judgment.—A party seeking relief may at any time after 20 days from commencement of action or after service of motion for summary judgment by adverse party, move with or without supporting affidavits for summary judgment. Party against whom relief is claimed may so move at any time. Motion must be served at least ten days for hearing. (N.R.C.P. 56).

Default Judgment.—When plaintiff's claim is for sum certain or for a sum which can by computation be made certain and defendant has been personally served in this state, clerk upon request must enter judgment for amount due and costs. In all other cases party entitled must apply to court. (N.R.C.P. 55).

Declaratory Judgments.—Uniform Act adopted but modified. (30.010-30.160).

Vacation or Modification.—On motion and upon such terms as are just, made within reasonable time, usually six months, court may relieve a party from judgment. (N.R.C.P. 60).

Offer of Judgment.—At a time more than ten days before trial, one defending a claim may serve upon the adverse party offer to allow judgment as specified in offer with costs then accrued. If offer accepted within ten days judgment will be entered by the clerk upon receiving notice of acceptance. If not accepted and judgment is obtained by the offeree which is not more favorable than the offer, the offeree may not recover costs nor attorney's fees. When liability of one party determined by verdict or judgment, but amount of liability remains to be determined, party adjudged liable may make offer of judgment if served within ten days prior to commencement of hearing to determine amount of liability. (N.R.C.P. 68).

Statute provides any party may serve written offer of judgment at any time more than ten days before trial. If offer accepted judgment is to be entered; if not accepted before trial or within 30 days after made it is deemed withdrawn. If party to whom offer made fails to obtain more favorable judgment, he cannot recover costs, attorney's fees or interest on judgment for period between service of process and entry of judgment and must pay offeror's taxable costs incurred from date action commenced and may have to pay costs of services of expert witnesses, interest on judgment and attorney's fees from time of offer. (17.115).

Judgment by confession may be entered without action, either for money due or to become due or to secure any person against contingent liability on behalf of the defendant, or both. (17.090).

Authorization for such a judgment must be by a statement in writing, signed and verified by defendant, and must authorize entry of a judgment for a specified sum. If confession of judgment is for money due or to become due, the facts out of which liability arose must be stated concisely, and it must appear that sum confessed is justly due or to become due. if purpose of confessing judgment is to secure plaintiff against a contingent liability, facts constituting liability must be stated concisely, and it must appear that sum confessed does not exceed liability. (17.100).

Entry of Judgment.—Statement is filed with clerk of court in which judgment is to be entered, and clerk indorses upon it, and enters in judgment book, a judgment for amount confessed with $24 costs. Judgment and affidavit, with judgment indorsed, constitute judgment roll. (17.110).

In any judgment, interest on the verdict or decision must be entered, and the clerk must insert a computation of costs in the copies and docket of judgment. (17.130; 17.190).

Lien.—District court judgment or judgment of court of U.S. in and for District of Nevada may be made a lien on other real property of defendant by filing transcript of original docket or abstract or copy of any judgment or decree, certified by clerk of court, with county recorder of county in which such real property is located. Lien continues for six years from date of original docketing, excluding any time during which execution of judgment is suspended by appeal or action of court or defendant and is continued each time judgment is renewed unless judgment is for arrearages of child support payments in which lien continues until judgment is satisfied. (17.150). There is no lien on personal property until levy of execution thereon.

Justice's Judgments.—A judgment rendered in a justice court does not create a lien upon lands unless an abstract thereof is filed in the office of the recorder of the county in which the lands are situated. When so recorded it becomes a lien for six years. (68.040).

Assignment.—The common law rule as to assignment of judgment prevails.

Satisfaction.—A satisfaction of judgment may be entered in the clerk's docket if execution returned satisfied and if acknowledgment of satisfaction filed with clerk, acknowledged as conveyance of real property by judgment creditor, or by attorney, unless revocation of his authority is previously filed. Whenever judgment is satisfied it is duty of party or attorney to give such acknowledgment and party who has satisfied judgment may move court to compel it or to order clerk to enter satisfaction in docket of judgment. (17.200).

Form of Satisfaction.—No statutory form. The following is suggested:

Form

(Title of court and cause).

For and in consideration of the sum of . . . . dollars ($ . .), current lawful money of the United States, to me paid by . . . ., the defendant in the above-entitled action, full satisfaction is hereby acknowledged of a certain judgment rendered and entered in said . . . . Court in the said action, on the . . . . day of . . . ., 19 . ., in favor of . . . ., the plaintiff in said action, and against the said defendant, for the sum of . . . . dollars ($ . .), current lawful money of the United States, with interest thereon from the . . . . day of . . . ., 19 . ., at the rate of . . . . per cent per annum until paid, together with said plaintiff's costs and disbursements, amounting to the sum of . . . . dollars ($ . .), and recorded in book of judgments, at page . . . . . And I hereby authorize and direct the clerk of said Court to enter satisfaction of record of said judgment in said action.

(Acknowledgment). . . . . . .

Foreign Judgments.—Authentication or identification is a condition precedent to admissibility and is satisfied by evidence that matter in question is what its proponent claims. (52.015). Evidence that a writing authorized by law to be recorded or filed and in fact recorded and filed in a public office is from public office where items of this nature are kept is sufficient to authenticate document. (52.085).

See note at head of Digest as to 1998 legislation covered.

See Topical Index in front part of this volume.

NV – 12

JUDGMENTS . . . *continued*

Document purporting to be executed or attested in his official capacity by a person authorized by laws of foreign country to make such execution is presumed authentic if accompanied by final certification as to genuineness of signature and official position of executing person or any foreign official whose certificate of genuineness and official position is involved. Final certification may be made by a secretary of embassy or legation, consul general, consul, vice-consul or consular agent of U. S., or a diplomatic or consular official of foreign country assigned to U. S. If reasonable opportunity is given to all parties to investigate authenticity of official document, court may treat it as presumptively authentic without final certification. (52.115).

Copy of an official record is presumed authentic if it is certified as correct by custodian or other person authorized to make certification. (52.125).

Uniform Enforcement of Foreign Judgments Act has been adopted. (17.330-17.400).

LIMITATION OF ACTIONS:

Uniform Commercial Code adopted. (104.1101-104.9507). See category Business Regulation and Commerce, topic Commercial Code.

Legal proceedings must be brought in the following times:

Within six years: Action on judgment or decree of court within U.S. or renewal thereof, or on contract, obligation or liability evidenced by writing, sealed or unsealed, not limited by specific statute. (11.190). See also subhead Within Four Years, infra. No action may be commenced against designer or builder of improvements on real property for faulty design or construction or for personal injury or wrongful death caused by deficiency apparent by reasonable inspection more than six years after substantial completion of such improvements. (11.205).

Within five years: Actions to recover real property or the possession or rents or profits thereof, except as hereinafter stated. (11.030-11.180). Victim, person against whom crime has been committed or killed or injured as direct result of crime or surviving spouse, parent or child of such person, may commence action that arises from commission of felony against felon within five years after felon becomes entitled to receive compensation for any book, articles, movies, interviews substantially related to felony perpetrated against victim; however if limitation period has otherwise expired liability of felon limited to compensation received. (217.007).

Within four years: (1) Actions upon accounts; (2) actions upon contracts, obligations or liabilities not founded upon instruments in writing. (11.190). Statute commences to run from date of last transaction or last item charged, or last credit given; and whenever any payment on principal or interest has been or shall be made upon an existing contract, whether it be a bill of exchange, promissory note or other evidence of indebtedness, if such payment be made after the same shall have become due, the limitation shall commence from the time the last payment was made. Where there are reciprocal charges statute runs from last item on either side. (11.200, 11.210); (3) actions for breach of contracts of sale under Uniform Commercial Code. (104.2725); (4) malpractice action, after date of injury, or two years after plaintiff discovers, or should have, injury, whichever occurs first, in action against professional health care provider for negligence, rendering professional services without consent, or for error or omission in such provider's practice; however, statute is tolled during period action is pending before medical malpractice screening panel. (41A.097); (5) malpractice actions against attorneys and veterinarians measured from time plaintiff sustained damage or within two years after plaintiff discovered or should have discovered facts constituting cause of action, whichever occurs earlier (11.207); (6) action under Nevada Unfair Trade Practice Act, after cause of action accrues, or if action based on conspiracy, within four years after plaintiff discovered, or should have, facts relied upon to prove conspiracy (598A.220); (7) malpractice action against accountant measured from completion of performance of service or date of initial issuance of report or within two years after plaintiff discovered or should have discovered facts constituting cause of action, whichever occurs earlier (11.2075).

See further category Business Regulation and Commerce, topic Monopolies, Restraint of Trade and Competition.

The four year limitation applies also to actions for any relief not otherwise specified. (11.190-11.220).

Within three years: (1) Upon a liability created by statute other than a penalty or forfeiture; (2) for waste or trespass on real property; (3) for taking, detaining or injuring goods and chattels; (4) an action for relief upon the ground of fraud, time running from discovery; (5) action by financial institution against borrower who makes false statement or conceals material fact for purpose of obtaining loan (11.190); (6) action to recover real estate sold by guardian, time running from termination of guardianship; (7) action to recover real estate sold by executor or administrator in probate proceedings, time running from sale (11.260; 11.270); (8) action against corporate directors on statutory liability, time running from discovery (11.380).

Within two years: (1) Against sheriff, coroner or constable for official misconduct; (2) upon statute for penalty or forfeiture; (3) for libel, slander, assault, battery, false imprisonment or seduction; (4) action against sheriff, or other officer, for escape of prisoner arrested or imprisoned on civil process; (5) action to recover damages for injury to person or for death of person by wrongful act or neglect of another (11.190); (6) after plaintiff discovers, or should have, injury due to negligence, rendering services without consent, or error or omission by professional health care provider (41A.097); (7) upon action to recover mining claim or possession thereof (11.060).

Within one year: (1) Action against de facto officer to recover personal property seized in supposed official capacity, or its value; (2) action for damages to person or property in such seizure, or for money paid him under protest or seized by him; (3) actions or claims against state or political subdivision rejected by governing body (11.190); (4) actions under Nevada Equal Credit Opportunity Law (598B.180).

Three months from date of payment of last installment when property owner taxpayer sues tax department and commission for excessive assessment. (361.420).

One Hundred Eighty Days.—Action for restoration of rights by person injured by unfair employment practice. Tolled during pendency of complaint before commission. (613.430).

Ninety Days.—Actions to recover fees paid by motor convoy carriers. (706.581).

Twenty-five Days.—Actions seeking judicial review of orders of governing bodies concerning planning or zoning. (278.027).

Within fourteen days if no recount is demanded or within five days after recount completed, proceedings must be begun to contest any election. (293.413).

Stay of Action.—Time during which commencement of action is stayed by injunction or statutory prohibition is no part of limitation period. (11.350).

Disability of Plaintiff.—If person entitled to sue for recovery or possession of real property is, when title first descends or accrues, a minor, insane or imprisoned for a criminal offense for a term less than life, action may be commenced within two years after removal of the disability or within two years after the death of such person while still under disability. If the action be to recover real estate sold by a guardian or by an executor or administrator in probate proceedings, it must be commenced within one year after disability is removed. (11.180; 11.280).

If person entitled to bring action other than for recovery of real property is, when cause of action accrues, infant, insane or in custody of state, if placed in such care while less than 18 years of age, except when person imprisoned, paroled or on probation, time of such disability is no part of time limited for commencing action. (11.250).

Parent, guardian, or legal custodian of any minor child is responsible for prosecuting medical malpractice action on behalf of child. If parent, guardian, or legal custodian fails to commence action on behalf of minor child within time of limitation, child is not permitted to bring action on same alleged injury upon removal of his legal disability, except that in case of brain damage or birth defect, period of limitation is extended until child attains ten years of age, and in case of sterility, period of limitation is extended until two years after child discovers injury. (41A.097).

Action to recover damages for injury arising from sexual abuse of plaintiff which occurred when plaintiff was less than 18 years of age must be commenced within three years after plaintiff reaches 18 years of age, or discovers or should have discovered that injury was caused by sexual abuse, whichever occurred later. (11.215).

Death of Party.—
Prospective Plaintiff.—If a person entitled to bring an action dies before expiration of the time limited for commencement thereof, and the cause of action survives, action may be commenced by his personal representatives within one year after his death. (11.310).

Prospective Defendant.—If a person against whom an action might be brought dies before expiration of the time limited for commencement thereof and cause of action survives, action may be brought against his executor or administrator within one year after issuance of letters, provided the claim has been properly presented and the final account of the representative has not been filed. (11.310). If such person dies outside of the state, action may be brought within one year after issuance of letters within the state. (11.320).

Absence of defendant from the state suspends the running of the statute. (11.300).

Foreign cause of action is barred if barred in state or country where it arose, unless it is in favor of a citizen of Nevada who has held it since its accrual. (11.020).

Contractual Limitations.—No statutory prohibition.

Pleading.—Facts showing bar must be pleaded, as an affirmative defense. (N.R.C.P. 8).

Acknowledgment of debt or cause of action is not evidence of a new or continuing contract, sufficient to take the case out of the operation of the statute unless it is in writing, signed by the party to be charged thereby. (11.390).

Revival of Barred Claims.—Only written promise signed by the party is sufficient evidence of a new or continuing contract to take case out of operation of statute, except whenever part payment made time runs from date of last payment. (11.390, 11.200).

PARTITION:

Any one of several persons holding possession of real estate as joint tenants or in common, in which they have an estate of inheritance or for life, or lives, or years, may bring suit for partition and sale of property, or part of it, if partition cannot be had without prejudice to owners or if owners consent to sale. When impracticable or inconvenient to make complete partition among all parties, court may determine shares held by original co-tenants and cause partition to be made as if such original co-tenants were sole parties in interest, and partition separately each share or portion so ascertained and allotted between those claiming under original tenant, or may allow them to remain tenants in common thereof if they desire. (39.010).

Proceedings.—The complaint must set forth the interests of all persons in the property. (39.020).

Lienholders of record must be brought in as parties, or a referee will be appointed to ascertain and report the extent of their interests. (39.100-39.110).

Lienholders not of record need not be made parties. (39.030).

Notice of lis pendens must be filed by plaintiff immediately after filing complaint. (39.040).

Summons must be directed to all interested parties. (39.050).

Unknown parties may be served by publication and court may appoint attorney to represent. (39.060).

The answer must specify defendants' interests, and the nature and amount of any liens they claim. (39.070).

Partition in Kind or Sale.—If partition in kind cannot be made without great prejudice to owners, or if owners consent, sale may be ordered. Otherwise partition must be ordered and master appointed to make partition. (39.120).

Partition among heirs, devisees, and legatees of a decedent's real or personal estate may be had on a petition filed at any time before the decree of distribution. (152.010-152.170). When real property cannot be divided without prejudice or inconvenience to

See note at head of Digest as to 1998 legislation covered.

See Topical Index in front part of this volume.

PARTITION . . . *continued*

the owners, it may be assigned to one of them who will accept and pay the others a just price or furnish adequate security; and this may be done where a tract is of greater value than any party's share in the estate and cannot be divided without injury. (152.150).

A sale may be ordered on recommendation of the commissioners, where the property cannot be divided fairly. Such a sale must be conducted, reported on and confirmed, in the same manner as sales by an executor or administrator pursuant to court order. (152.110). See category Estates and Trusts, topic Executors and Administrators.

PLEADING:

Governed by N.R.C.P. 7 et seq.; patterned largely on Federal Rules.

Pleadings Permitted.—There must be a complaint and an answer; reply to counterclaim; answer to cross-claim; a third party complaint if leave is given; third party answer. (N.R.C.P. 7).

Complaint or any pleading which sets forth a claim for relief must contain a short and plain statement of claim. (N.R.C.P. 8).

Defenses and Objections.—

When Presented.—Defendant must serve his answer within 20 days after service of summons is complete. An answer to a cross-claim must be served within 20 days after service; reply to a counterclaim in an answer must be served within 20 days after service of answer. (N.R.C.P. 12).

How Presented.—Every defense to a claim for relief must be asserted in a responsive pleading, if one is required, except that the following may, at pleader's option, be made by motion: (1) lack of jurisdiction over subject-matter; (2) lack of jurisdiction over person; (3) insufficiency of process; (4) insufficiency of service of process; (5) failure to state a claim on which relief can be granted; and (6) failure to join an indispensable party.

Counterclaim.—Pleading must state as a counterclaim any claim pleader has against the opposing party if it arises out of transaction or occurrence that is the subject-matter of opposing party's claim if it does not require the presence of a third party of whom the court cannot acquire jurisdiction. Pleading may state as a counterclaim any claim against an opposing party not arising out of the same transaction or occurrence that is the subject-matter of the opposing party's claim. (N.R.C.P. 13).

Cross-Claim.—A pleading may state as a cross-claim any claim by one party against a co-party arising out of transaction or occurrence that is subject of original action or of a counterclaim, or relating to any property that is subject-matter of original action. (N.R.C.P. 13).

Frivolous Claims.—Signature of attorney or party on pleading constitutes certificate that pleading has been read, that it is well grounded in fact and is warranted by existing law or good faith agreement for extension, modification or reversal of existing law, and that it is not interposed for any improper purpose. (NRCP 11). If pleading is signed in violation of Rule 11, court shall impose sanctions upon person who signed it, represented party, or both. (N.R.C.P. 11).

Demurrer is abolished. (N.R.C.P. 7).

Verification is not required unless specifically provided by rule. Pleading of a party who is represented must be signed by one attorney in his individual name, plus his address, and if not so represented, by party. (N.R.C.P. 11).

Amendments.—Any pleading may be amended once as of course before time for responsive pleading has expired. Further amendment allowed in discretion of court. (N.R.C.P. 15).

Service and Filing.—All pleadings are served on adverse party or attorney and filed with clerk of court. (N.R.C.P. 5).

Form.—Appendix to Rules sets forth forms intended for illustration only and to indicate the simplicity and brevity of statement which the rules contemplate.

Time to answer in justice's court is five days if served in township or city in which action brought, ten days when served elsewhere in same county and twenty days if served outside of county. (N.J.R.C.P. 12).

Proof of Claims.—Claims sent for collection should be accompanied by a fully itemized bill and the following information should be given: Is creditor a corporation? If so in what state incorporated? If a partnership, what are full names of partners? If doing business under a fictitious name who compose the association and has it complied with the laws of its own state as to fictitious names? In order to avoid demand for bond as nonresident plaintiff it is better to send blank assignment of claim. If creditor is corporation, title of executing officer should appear and seal be affixed. Instructions for immediate attachment are futile unless affidavit is sent, fully complying with attachment statute. (See category Debtor and Creditor, topic Attachment.)

Affidavits cannot be made upon information and belief. Attachment bond should also be arranged.

The general rules governing this subject are those of the common law. (58 Nev. 433, 82 P.2d 746; 42 Nev. 378, 178 Pac. 23).

Small Claims.—See category Courts and Legislature, topic Courts.

PRACTICE:

Federal Rules of Civil Procedure form the basis for the procedural statute. (N.R.C.P. 1-86).

Direct Action Against Insurer.—See category Transportation, topic Motor Vehicles, subhead Direct Actions.

Small Claims.—See category Courts and Legislature, topic Courts.

See topics Actions, Appeal and Error, Depositions and Discovery, Injunctions, Judgments, Pleading, Process; category Debtor and Creditor, topics Attachment, Executions, Garnishment.

PROCESS:

Federal Rules of Civil Procedure form the basis for procedural statue. (N.R.C.P. 1-86). See topics Pleading, Practice.

By Whom Issued.—The summons is issued and signed by the clerk under seal of the court and delivered to plaintiff or counsel who is responsible for service. (N.R.C.P. 4).

Who May Serve.—The summons may be served by the sheriff of the county where the defendant is found, or his deputy, or by any citizen of the United States over 18 years of age.

Service outside of the United States may be made (after an order of publication) by a citizen of the United States, or a resident of the country, territory, colony, or province wherein the defendant is found, who is over 18 years of age. (N.R.C.P. 4).

Time Limitation on Service.—If summons and complaint not served on defendant within 120 days after filing of complaint and party seeking service cannot show good cause, action shall be dismissed as to that defendant without prejudice. (N.R.C.P. 4[i]).

Personal service on an individual is made by delivering a copy of the summons, attached to a copy of the complaint, to the defendant personally. (N.R.C.P. 4 and 5).

Personal service on an infant under 14 years of age, residing in the state, is made by delivering the above described copies to the infant personally, and to his father, mother, or guardian within the state, if any, otherwise to the person having the care or custody of the child, or with whom the child resides or by whom the child is employed. (N.R.C.P. 4).

Personal service on an incompetent residing in the state, and judicially declared to be such, is made by delivering the copies to the incompetent and also to his guardian. (N.R.C.P. 4).

Personal Service on Partnership.—Personal service on nonresident partnership doing business and having a managing or business agent, cashier, or secretary within state can be made on such agent, cashier, or secretary, or on an agent designated for service of process, as required by law. In event no such agent is designated, service is made on Secretary of State or Deputy Secretary of State, as provided by law. (N.R.C.P. 4[d]).

Service on Domestic Corporation.—If defendant be a Nevada corporation, service must be made on president or other head of corporation, secretary, cashier, managing agent or resident agent. Service can be made upon resident agent by leaving copy with person of suitable age and discretion at address shown on certificate filed with Secretary of State. (78.090). If such service cannot be made, defendant may file affidavit setting forth facts, and service may then be made by delivering copy of summons attached to certified copy of complaint, to Secretary of State or his deputy and posting copy in office of clerk of court in which action is brought. Thereafter, if it appears from affidavit that there is a last known address of a known officer outside state, plaintiff must send, by registered mail, to such officer at such address a copy of summons and certified copy of complaint. Defendant has 20 days after service on Secretary of State and posting (or after mailing as above stated) in which to answer. (N.R.C.P. 4).

Service on Foreign Corporation or Nonresident Joint Stock Company or Association.—If defendant be a foreign corporation or a nonresident joint stock company, or association, doing business or owning property within state, process may be served on its resident managing or business agent, cashier or secretary (N.R.C.P. 4), or on its duly appointed resident agent, or if none of the above, on Secretary of State or Deputy Secretary of State. (14.020-14.030). Service can be made upon resident agent by leaving copy with person of suitable age and discretion at address shown on certificate of acceptance filed with Secretary of State. (14.020). Service on Secretary of State must include citation to statute and $10 fee, and affidavit of diligence showing that service cannot otherwise be made, and if such affidavit shows last known address of corporation or any officer thereof copy of summons and certified copy of complaint must be sent by registered mail to corporation or such officer. (14.020; 14.030).

Any nonresident company, firm, partnership, corporation or association producing or otherwise supplying directly or indirectly products to be sold, distributed or used within state may be served with process in any action for damages for injury to person or property resulting from such distribution, sale or use within state by delivering a copy of process to secretary of state and mailing by registered mail with return receipt to last known address of company a copy of summons and certified copy of complaint. Defendant is allowed 40 days after date of service to answer or plead. This is an additional means of service and does not invalidate any other service. (14.080).

Service on a city, town or county is made by delivering process to mayor, president of council or trustees or other head of legislative department or chairman of board of commissioners. (N.R.C.P. 4).

Service on nonresident in action arising out of automobile accident, see category Transportation, topic Motor Vehicles.

Service by Publication.—Service on nonresident or absent defendant may be made by publication in a newspaper, on affidavit and an order of the court or judge. If residence of a nonresident defendant is known, certified copy of complaint and copy of summons must be mailed to him in addition to publication. Personal service out of the state is equivalent to publication. Personal service out of the state must be shown by affidavit of person making it. (N.R.C.P. 4).

See also supra, subhead Who May Serve.

In an action relating to property in this state (real or personal), in which the defendant (individual or corporate) claims a lien or interest (actual or contingent), or in which a part of the relief demanded consists in excluding the defendant from any interest therein, service by publication may be had as above stated, in case of nonresidence, absence, or concealment of the defendant. (N.R.C.P. 4).

Long Arm Statute.—Court in this state may exercise jurisdiction over party in civil action on any basis not inconsistent with Nevada or U.S. Constitution. Personal service of summons on party outside state is sufficient to confer jurisdiction over party served if service is made by delivering copy of summons and complaint to party served in manner provided by statute or rule for service on person within this state.

See note at head of Digest as to 1998 legislation covered.

See Topical Index in front part of this volume.

REPLEVIN:

Replevin is also known in Nevada as "Claim and Delivery."

Plaintiff in an action to recover personal property, except property subject to proceeding for forfeiture by law enforcement agency used in certain crimes or proceeds of crime, may at time of issuing summons, or at any time before answer, claim delivery of such property to him. (31.840).

Proceedings by Plaintiff.—Where delivery is claimed, an affidavit shall be made by plaintiff, or by some one in his behalf and filed with court, showing: (1) that plaintiff is owner of property claimed (particularly describing it), or is lawfully entitled to possession thereof; (2) that property is wrongfully detained by defendant; (3) alleged cause of detention thereof according to his best knowledge, information, and belief; (4) that same has not been taken for a tax, assessment, or fine, pursuant to a statute, or seized under an execution or an attachment against property of plaintiff, or, if so seized that it is exempt by statute; and, (5) actual value of property. (31.850).

If affidavit meets requirements, court will issue an order to defendant to show cause why property should not be taken from him and delivered to plaintiff. (31.853). Hearing is held to determine who, with reasonable probability, is entitled to possession pending final adjudication. Following finding for plaintiff, writ of possession may be issued if plaintiff files written undertaking executed by two or more sufficient sureties, approved by court, to effect they are bound to defendant in double value of property for return of property to defendant if return thereof is ordered. If plaintiff is reasonably believed to be secured party, no undertaking will be required. (31.863).

Writ of possession may issue prior to a hearing if plaintiff establishes that: (1) Defendant gained possession by criminal act; (2) property consists of negotiable instruments or credit cards; or (3) property is perishable or in immediate danger of destruction, concealment, removal from state, or sale. A written undertaking is also required. (31.856).

Writ of possession describes property and its location, directs sheriff to seize and retain it, and advises defendant of his right to except to sureties or file a written undertaking for redelivery of property. Written undertaking filed by plaintiff must be attached to writ. Sheriff must forthwith take property described in writ, if it be in possession of defendant or his agent, and retain it in his custody. He must also without delay serve on defendant copy of writ and undertaking. (31.866-31.870).

Proceedings by Defendant.—Defendant may within two days after service of such copy give notice to sheriff that he excepts to sufficiency of the sureties. If he fails to do so, he is deemed to have waived all objection to them. If defendant excepts to sureties they must justify before court. Sheriff is responsible for sufficiency of sureties until objection to them is waived or until they are justified. If defendant excepts to sureties, he cannot reclaim property. (31.880).

If defendant does not except to sureties, he may at any time, before delivery of property to plaintiff, require return thereof, upon filing with court and serving plaintiff with a written undertaking, approved by court and executed by two or more sufficient sureties, to effect they are bound in double value of property, for delivery thereof to plaintiff, if such delivery be adjudged and for payment to him of such sum as may for any cause be recovered against defendant. (31.890).

Claims of Third Parties.—If such return of property is not so required within five days after serving writ of possession and undertaking upon defendant, it must be delivered to plaintiff unless property is claimed by some other person than defendant or his agent, and such person makes an affidavit of his title thereto, or right to possession thereof, stating grounds of such title or right, and files affidavit with court and serves a copy upon sheriff, in which instance sheriff is not bound to keep property or deliver it to plaintiff, unless plaintiff on demand of sheriff or his agent, indemnifies sheriff against such claim by an undertaking, by two sufficient sureties or surety company, accompanied by their affidavits that they are worth double value of property, as specified in affidavit, over and above their debts and liabilities, exclusive of property exempt from execution, and are freeholders, or householders in county. No claim to such property by any other person than defendant or his agent shall be valid against sheriff unless so made. (31.940).

Sheriff's Return.—Sheriff must file writ of possession and undertaking with his proceedings thereon with clerk of court in which action is pending, within 20 days after taking property mentioned therein. (31.950).

Judgment may be for the property or, if return cannot be held, then for its value, together with damages. (17.120).

SEQUESTRATION:

Available only in matrimonial (see category Family, topic Divorce) and equitable actions.

SERVICE:

See topic Process.

STAY OF EXECUTION:

See topic Appeal and Error; category Debtor and Creditor, topic Executions.

SUBMISSION OF CONTROVERSY:

Nevada laws do not provide for submitting a controversy to a court on an agreed statement, except through the medium of arbitration on a question of law. See category Dispute Resolution, topic Arbitration and Award.

VENUE:

Except as otherwise specially provided, the residence of the defendant or any of the defendants determines the county in which the action must be tried. If no defendant resides in the state or no residence therein is known to plaintiff, the action may be tried in any county which plaintiff may designate. If a defendant is about to leave the state, the action may be tried in any county where either of the parties resides or can be served, subject to the power of the court to change the place of trial under prescribed rules. (13.040).

Location of Real Property.—Actions to recover real property or for injuries thereto, to recover an interest therein, for partition, or for foreclosure of a mortgage, must be tried in county where property, or part thereof, is situated. Action to foreclose mortgage on property in different counties may be tried in either county, except that if plaintiff applies for an injunction pending the action, it must be tried in the county in which the defendant, or a majority of defendants, reside at the commencement of the action. (13.010).

Place Where Cause Arose.—Action to recover a penalty or forfeiture imposed by statute must be tried in the county where the cause arose, except that when it arose on a lake, river or other stream situated in two or more counties, action may be brought in any county bordering thereon and opposite the place where the offense was committed. Action against a public official or person especially appointed to execute his duties, for an act done in virtue of his office, or against a person who by his command or in his aid does anything touching the duties of such official, must be tried in county where cause arose. Any tort action against State or its agencies may also be brought in Carson City. (13.020).

Actions against a county may be commenced in the judicial district court embracing said county, provided, that actions between counties must be commenced in a court in any county not a party. (13.030).

Place Where Obligation Is to Be Performed.—Where one has contracted to perform an obligation at a particular place outside of the county in which he resides, an action on such contract must be commenced in the county in which he resides or in the county in which the obligation is to be performed. The county in which the obligation is incurred is deemed to be the county in which it is to be performed unless there is a special contract to the contrary. (13.010).

Venue in Divorce Actions.—See category Family, topic Divorce.

Change of Venue.—A defendant is entitled to a change of place of trial upon timely and sufficient application, where the county designated in the complaint is not the proper county, or there is reason to believe that an impartial trial cannot be had therein, or the convenience of witnesses and the ends of justice will be promoted by the change. (13.050; 43 Nev. 182, 183 Pac. 391). This rule applies to divorce actions. (53 Nev. 228, 297 Pac. 504).

Justice Court Actions.—If there is no court for township or city in which defendant resides, in any township or city of county in which defendant resides; in cases of injury to person or property in township or city where injury was committed or defendant resides; actions to recover personal property or value thereof or damages for taking or detaining same, in township or city in which property may be found or was taken, or in which defendant resides; when defendant is a nonresident of the county, in any township or city where he may be found; when defendant is a nonresident of state, in any township or city in the state; when a contract is to be performed at a particular place, in the township or city where it is to be performed, and the township or city in which it was incurred is deemed the place of performance, unless there is a special contract to the contrary; when parties voluntarily appear and plead without summons, in any township or city in the state; in all other cases, in the township or city in which defendant or one of several defendants resides. (66.010-66.070).

Contract Provisions.—See subhead Place Where Obligation Is to Be Performed, supra.

COURTS AND LEGISLATURE

COURTS:

United States District Court.—Clerk's office: Reno 89502, Las Vegas 89101.

Fee for filing complaint, $126.

Court sits at Reno or Las Vegas according to the convenience of parties, witnesses and counsel.

Supreme Court of Nevada.—Supreme Court consists of five justices, and senior justice in commission is chief justice. Three justices constitute a quorum to transact business and concurrence of three justices who heard argument is necessary to pronounce judgment. (2.140).

Clerk's office: Carson City 89701.

Jurisdiction.—Court has appellate jurisdiction in all cases arising in district courts; also in all other civil cases not included in general subdivision of law and equity; and also in all questions of law in criminal charges amounting to felony, and also to issue common law writs of mandamus, certiorari, prohibition, quo warranto, and habeas corpus, and writs necessary to complete exercise of its appellate jurisdiction; writs of habeas corpus may be issued by any one of justices, returnable before justice issuing or before court or before any district court or judge. (Const. Art. 6, §4; 2.090).

District Courts of Nevada.—

Jurisdiction.—These are courts of general jurisdiction, and have original jurisdiction in all cases in equity and in all cases at law, except those in which exclusive jurisdiction is conferred upon justices' or other inferior courts. District court has appellate jurisdiction in cases arising in justices', municipal or other inferior courts. Counties whose population exceeds 100,000 have family court as division of district court which has exclusive jurisdiction of proceedings brought pursuant to cc. 31A, 62, 123, 125, 125A, 125B, 126, 127, 128, 129, 130, 159, 425, or 432B of NRS, specified actions concerning minors and approving withdrawal of life sustaining procedures except if child is subject to jurisdiction of Indian tribe. (Const. Art. 6, §6; 4.370; 3.223).

Districts.—

First District.—Counties: Carson City and Storey.

Second District.—Washoe County.

Third District.—Counties: Churchill and Lyon.

Fourth District.—Elko County.

Fifth District.—Counties: Esmeralda, Mineral and Nye.

See note at head of Digest as to 1998 legislation covered.

See Topical Index in front part of this volume.

COURTS . . . *continued*

Sixth District.—Counties: Lander, Humboldt and Pershing.

Seventh District.—Eureka, White Pine and Lincoln Counties.

Eighth District.—Clark County

Ninth District.—Counties: Douglas County.

(3.010).

Locations.—District courts sit at respective county seats of counties within districts. Clerks' offices are likewise so located.

Probate Courts.—Probate jurisdiction is exercised by district courts sitting in probate. (Const. Art. 6, §6; 136.010).

Juvenile Courts.—District courts exercise exclusive original jurisdiction over children under 18 years, and adults incidental thereto, in proceedings concerning child within county in need of supervision and care or rehabilitation, has committed delinquent act, or needs commitment to mental institution (62.040; 62.043) except if child is subject to jurisdiction of Indian tribe. Delinquent act does not include murder or other related offense arising out of same facts, sexual assault or attempt with force or violence used or threatened or any offense involving use or threatened use of firearm if child was 16 years of age or over and had been previously adjudged delinquent for act that would have been felony if committed by adult. (62.040). District court may transfer case to justices' courts or municipal courts to try juvenile charged with minor traffic violation. (62.040).

Justices' Courts.—Justices' courts have jurisdiction, within their respective townships, of actions at law and suits on mechanics' liens, when amount of demand, or value of property, does not exceed $7,500, in criminal misdemeanor cases, and except in counties whose population exceeds 100,000, orders for protection against domestic violence. (4.370).

Procedure.—Justice's Courts Rules of Civil Procedure.

Municipal courts may be established by legislature in incorporated towns or cities. Jurisdiction is over violations of city ordinances, vagrancy, minor public offenses, and civil actions involving city where amount in controversy does not exceed $2,500. (5.050).

Small Claims Court.—Justice courts have jurisdiction in cases for recovery of money where sum does not exceed $3,500 and defendant is resident of, is employed in, or does business in, township, in which action is maintained. (73.010). No attachment or garnishment shall issue before judgment including garnishment in aid of execution. (73.020). No attorney fees allowable in small claim actions except in civil shoplifting actions. (73.040).

LEGISLATURE:

Meets biennially in January, of odd numbered years. Governor may call special sessions. (Const. Art. 4).

Initiative and referendum are provided for. (Const. Art. 19; 295.015-295.220).

REPORTS:

Nevada Reports, beginning with volume one, contain Supreme Court decisions. Nevada decisions are also reported in Pacific Reporter, beginning 1883 with volume 17 of Nevada Reports.

Digests.—Nevada Digest, published by Bancroft Whitney Company, 1912, in one volume, digests cases in Nevada Reports, volumes 1 to 32 inclusive and contains annotations of cases in volumes 1 to 30 inclusive.

Revised Laws 1919 (being Revised Laws, Volume 3) contain, in addition to statutes, a digest of Nevada Reports, volumes 33 to 40 inclusive. Compiled Laws 1929 contains a digest of volumes 33 to 51.

Nevada Digest, published by Legislative Counsel Bureau, Carson City, Nevada, in 1965, in looseleaf form so it can be updated as needed.

All Nevada Supreme Court decisions are digested in Pacific Digest.

STATUTES:

Latest compilation is Nevada Revised Statutes of 1957, a loose-leaf type code which is supplemented after each legislative session by reprinting or adding.

Uniform Acts which have been adopted are: Act on Rights of Terminally Ill (1991); Anatomical Gift (1969); Arbitration (1969); Attendance of Witnesses from Without State in Criminal Proceedings, Act to Secure (1967); Child Custody Jurisdiction (1969); †Commercial Code (1965; 1973); Common Interest Ownership Act (1991); Common Trust Fund (1955); †Contribution Among Tortfeasors (1973); Revised Controlled Substances (1991); †Criminal Extradition (1967); †Declaratory Judgments (1929); Determination of Death (1985); Disposition of Unclaimed Property (1979); Enforcement of Foreign Judgments (1979); Facsimile Signatures of Public Officials (1963); †Federal Tax Lien Registration (1967); †Fiduciaries (1923); Foreign Depositions (1921); Foreign Executed Wills (1915); Fraudulent Transfer (1987); Illegitimacy (1923); Insurers Liquidation (1971); Interparty Agreements (1927); Interstate Fresh Pursuit (1967); Interstate Arbitration of Death Taxes (1987); Interstate Compromise of Death Taxes (1987); Joint Obligations (1927); Revised Limited Partnership (1976 Act with 1985 Amendments) (1985); Military Justice Code (1967); Motor Vehicle Drivers' License (1969); Notarial Acts (1993); †Out-of-State Parolee Supervision (1967); †Partnership (1931); Post-Conviction Procedure (1967); Premarital Agreement (1989); Principal and Income, Revised (1969); Reciprocal Enforcement of Support Act, Revised (1969); Securities (1985); Simplification of Fiduciary Security Transfers (1959); Simultaneous Death (1949); Statutory Rule Against Perpetuities (1987); Testamentary Additions to Trust (1967); Trade Secrets (1987); †Transfers to Minors (1985, 1991); Trustees' Accounting (1941 and 1955); †Trusts (1941); Unclaimed Property (1981); Vendor and Purchaser Risk (1987); Veterans' Guardianship (1929).

Uniform Commercial Code adopted. (104.1101-104.9507). See category Business Regulation and Commerce, topic Commercial Code.

For text of Uniform Acts falling within the scope of the Martindale-Hubbell Law Digests see Uniform and Model Acts section.

† Adopted with significant variations or modifications, or subsequently amended. (See appropriate topics.)

UNIFORM LAWS:

For list of Uniform Acts in force in this state see topic Statutes. For text of Uniform Acts within the scope of the Martindale-Hubbell Law Digests see Uniform and Model Acts section.

CRIMINAL LAW

BAIL:

See topic Criminal Law.

CRIMINAL LAW:

Chapters 193 to 208 of the Nevada Revised Statutes contain most of the law relating to crimes. Criminal procedure is largely found in Chapters 169 to 179A.

Indictment, Information or Complaint.—Prosecutions are by indictment of grand jury filed in district court except for offenses tried in justices' courts, arising in militia, or in connection with removal of a civil officer (see 172.015; 172.035), and by information filed by district attorney after preliminary examination before justice of the peace or other examining officer (see 173.035). In cases of criminal proceedings in justices' courts, procedure is governed by Ch. 189 and Title 14 of NRS. (185.015).

Bail.—Before conviction, all offenses are bailable except in capital cases in which proof is evident or presumption great, or felony committed while released on bail or on probation or parole for different offense without court order. In some instances persons charged with misdemeanors may be released without bail. (178.484—178.4853). Bail is allowable pending review unless it appears that appeal is frivolous or taken for delay. (178.488).

Interstate Compact for Supervision of Parolees and Probationers adopted. (213.185).

Uniform Criminal Extradition Act adopted. (179.177-179.235).

Uniform Desertion and Nonsupport Act adopted. (201.020-201.080).

Uniform Act on Interstate Fresh Pursuit adopted. (171.154-171.164).

Uniform Act on Intrastate Fresh Pursuit adopted. (171.166-171.176).

Uniform Controlled Substances Act (1990) adopted. (453.011-453.361).

Uniform Act for Out-of-State Parolee Supervision adopted. (213.180-213.210).

Uniform Act To Secure the Attendance of Witnesses From Without a State in Criminal Proceedings adopted. (174.395-174.445).

Interstate Compact on Juveniles adopted. (214.010-214.060).

Interstate Corrections Compact adopted. (215A.010-215A.060).

DEBTOR AND CREDITOR

ASSIGNMENTS:

Uniform Commercial Code adopted, effective Mar. 1, 1967. See category Business Regulation and Commerce, topic Commercial Code.

Assignments which would be good at common law, are good in Nevada.

Except as provided in U.C.C., where assignment is of a thing in action, an action by assignee is without prejudice to any set-off or other defense, existing at time of, or before notice of, assignment; but this does not apply to a negotiable promissory note, or bill of exchange, transferred in good faith, and for value before maturity. (12.010).

Assignment of wages, salary or earnings by person against whom unsatisfied judgment for debt exists in this state is prima facie evidence of fraud, and is void as against judgment creditor. (608.170).

See also category Estates and Trusts, topic Death, subhead Action for Death.

ATTACHMENT:

Actions in Which Allowed and Grounds.—

With Notice and Hearing: (1) Action upon a judgment or contract, for direct payment of money which is not secured by mortgage, lien or pledge upon real or personal property situated in this state, or if so secured, when such security has been rendered valueless or insufficient without act of plaintiff or person to whom security was given. If security has depreciated without such act, attachment lies for excess of debt over value of security; (2) action in which one or more of grounds with or without notice exists; (3) action where court finds that extraordinary circumstances exist making it improbable for plaintiff to reach property of defendant by execution after judgment. (31.013).

Without notice to defendant, in following actions only: (1) Against a defendant not residing in this state. Domestic and foreign corporations qualified to do business in this state are deemed residents; (2) upon a foreign judgment for direct payment of money; (3) for recovery of value of personal property which has been taken or converted by defendant without consent of owner; (4) where defendant is about to remove his money or property from this state and defendant's remaining property will be insufficient to satisfy plaintiff's claim. (5) where defendant is about to give, assign, hypothecate, pledge, dispose of or conceal his money or property, or any part, if that remaining is insufficient to satisfy plaintiff's claim; (6) for recovery of money or property obtained through embezzlement, forgery, larceny or extortion; (7) one brought under Uniform Fraudulent Conveyances Act; (8) one by state, or a political subdivision, brought under Uniform Reciprocal Enforcement of Support Act; (9) one where jurisdiction can be obtained only by attachment of defendant's property. (31.017).

Courts Which May Issue Writ.—District court and justice court. (31.010, 71.090).

Time for Issuance of Writ.—The plaintiff at the time of issuing the summons, or at any time afterwards, may have the property of the defendant attached as security for the

ATTACHMENT . . . *continued*
satisfaction of any judgment that may be recovered, unless the defendant give security to pay such judgment. (31.010).

In Whose Favor Writ May Issue.—There is no provision excluding nonresidents or foreign corporations from the right to obtain attachment.

Claims on Which Writ May Issue.—There is no provision requiring that the contract or obligation sued on should be made or payable within this state. Neither is there any provision which authorizes issuance of the writ on any unmatured claim. A writ may issue for a foreign judgment for direct payment of money. (31.017).

Proceedings to Obtain.—Application for writ of attachment must be accompanied by affidavit by or on behalf of plaintiff showing nature of claim and that same is valid; stating amount which affiant believes plaintiff is entitled to recover; describing in reasonable and clear detail all facts which show existence of grounds for attachment without notice or with notice and hearing; describing in reasonable detail money or property sought to be attached, its location, value, and any exemption from execution; naming all third persons upon whom writ of garnishment will be served; and including copy of any foreign judgment. (31.020).

Court will order clerk to issue writ of attachment without notice to defendant if plaintiff's affidavit and any additional evidence meet these elements and it determines that ground for attachment without notice exists. (31.022).

If application seeks a writ of attachment after notice and hearing and affidavit sets forth items required, court will issue an order to defendant to show cause why order for attachment should not be issued. Upon hearing held by court without jury, writ of attachment will be issued if court determines from all evidence that plaintiff's claim is probably valid or defendant fails to appear. (31.024).

Attachment Bond.—Plaintiff must give a written undertaking with two or more sureties in a sum not less than amount claimed by plaintiff or value of property to be attached, whichever is less, for payment of costs and damages, including attorney's fees, should defendant recover judgment or attachment be discharged. Defendant may except to sufficiency of sureties, and if they fail to justify, writ must be vacated. (31.030).

The sureties to the undertaking must be residents and householders or freeholders within this state, and worth double the amount specified in the undertaking, over and above all debts and liabilities, exclusive of property exempt from execution. (31.030). The undertaking may also be made by a surety company authorized to do business in this state. Surety company bonds must be approved by the judge, clerk, or deputy clerk. The plaintiff may also deposit cash in lieu of a bond. (20.030).

Examination as to Property or Debts.—The defendant, or any person owing him, may be cited to appear before the court, judge, or justice cited to appear before the court, judge, or justice of the peace and be examined on oath as to property of defendant or debts owing to him. (31.100).

Levy.—Stocks, debts and any property not exempt from execution may be attached provided judgment creditor or sheriff also serves statutory notice of execution and procedure for claiming exempt property (31.045): (1) Real property by filing copy of writ with county recorder, with description of property attached, and by leaving copy of writ with occupant, or if not occupied by posting copy conspicuously on premises; (2) personal property by taking it into custody and if directed by plaintiff using authorized carrier to tow it to authorized facility, or by placing keeper in charge of going business where such property is located, during which period defendant may continue to operate business if all sales are for cash and proceeds given to keeper; (3) debts, credits and other personal property in possession or under control of persons other than defendant by service of writ of garnishment. (31.050-31.060).

Indemnity.—Sheriff or constable may demand indemnity if third party claim is made. (31.070). Plaintiff must deposit with sheriff amount sufficient to pay expenses of taking, transporting and keeping personal property for 30 days. (31.065).

Lien of attachment on real property is conclusively presumed discharged after ten years. (108.250).

Release of Property.—Where amount sought to be released is less than demand of writ, court or judge, upon application of defendant and notice to plaintiff, may discharge attachment in whole or in part, upon defendant giving bond in amount sought to be released. Where amount sought equals or exceeds demand of writ, defendant may discharge attachment by giving bond in amount of judgment which may be recovered in favor of plaintiff, or demand of writ, whichever is less. On like application writ may be discharged if improperly or improvidently issued, if properly levied on is exempt from execution or necessary and required by defendant for support and maintenance of himself and family, or if levy excessive. Property may also be released upon written stipulation by plaintiff and defendant. (31.180-31.220).

Sale.—Perishable property may be sold by officer on reasonable posted notice and attached debts and credits collected if possible without suit. (31.120). Court or judge may order attached property sold as under execution if beneficial to parties. (31.130). If plaintiff recovers judgment attached property is sold under execution. (31.140).

Third Party Claims.—If verified third party claim is filed with attaching officer, he must release property unless, within seven days after written demand, plaintiff gives undertaking in double value of property. Plaintiff or third party claimant is entitled to trial of title before court within ten days after filing of claim, on seven days notice to claimant. (31.070).

Mortgaged Personal Property.—Uniform Commercial Code adopted. (104.1101-104.9507).

CREDITORS' SUITS:

No statutory provision.

EXECUTIONS:

Money judgments and those requiring delivery of real or personal property are enforced by execution; where any other act is required a certified copy of the judgment is delivered to the party affected or to the officer required to execute. (21.050).

Exemptions.—See topic Exemptions.

Time for Issuance.—Execution may issue at any time before judgment expires except enforcement of judgment for child support which may be commenced at any time (21.010), unless stayed by supersedeas bond (17.150).

Death of Party.—Execution may issue after plaintiff's death upon application of personal representative or successor in interest. It may issue after defendant's death only upon judgment for recovery of real or personal property. (21.060).

To Whom Issued.—Execution may issue from the district court to the sheriff of any specified county in the state. (21.070).

Writ is issued by clerk under seal of court and directed to sheriff, or by a justice of the peace and directed to constable or sheriff; if it is against property, must require satisfaction from personal property or if insufficient, real property. If it is against debtor's property in hands of third persons, must require satisfaction from that property. If it is issued on judgment payable in specified kind of money or currency, must require satisfaction in that kind of money or currency. If it is for delivery of real or personal property, it must direct him to deliver it to party entitled, and to satisfy costs, etc., out of defendant's personal property. If it is against person of debtor, it must direct him to arrest debtor and detain him in jail until judgment is satisfied or legally discharged. (21.020). If personal property levied on under writ of execution belongs to going business and judgment debtor consents, sheriff must place keeper in charge of such property for at least two days. During such period judgment debtor may continue to operate business if all sales are for cash and proceeds are given to keeper for purpose of execution. (21.118).

Effect of Issuance.—Mere issuance of an execution does not affect any property of the defendant; a levy is necessary for this purpose. (21.080).

Levy.—See supra, subhead Writ.

Return.—An execution must be returnable not less than ten nor more than 60 days after its receipt by sheriff. (21.040).

Stay may be granted by district court in its discretion after entry of judgment or on motion for new trial with conditions of security or on an appeal by filing supersedeas bond. (N.R.C.P. 62).

In justice court, justice may stay execution for ten days. (70.010). No express requirement of bond.

Notice of sale under execution after sheriff has served statutory Notice of Writ of Execution and copy of Writ is given in case of perishable property by posting notice in three public places in township or city where sale is to take place, for such time as may be reasonable, considering character and condition of property. (21.130).

In case of other personal property, by posting a notice of the time and place of sale in three public places not less than five nor more than ten days, and in case of a sale on an execution out of a district court, by publication of the notice in a newspaper, if there by one in the county, at least twice, the first publication being not less than ten days before date of sale. (21.130).

In case of sale of real property, by personal service upon each judgment debtor, or by registered mail to last known address of each, and by posting a notice for 20 days successively in three public places in township or city where property is situated, and also where property is to be sold; also by publishing copy three times, once a week for three successive weeks, in newspaper if there by one in county, provided that where judgment is for less than $500, notice may be given by posting only in three public places in county. (21.130).

Mode and Conditions of Sale.—All execution sales must be made at auction to the highest bidder. Only so much of the property of the judgment debtor as is necessary to satisfy the judgment, costs and expenses of the sale may be sold. The judgment debtor may direct the order in which the property shall be sold. (21.150, 21.110).

Redemption.—Real property sold under execution may be redeemed by judgment debtor, his successor or a creditor having a judgment or mortgage lien subsequent to that under which property was sold, such creditors being called redemptioners. (21.200).

Time, Mode and Effect.—Redemption may be made, within one year after sale, by paying price of sale with interest at 1% per month from time of sale until redemption and also any taxes, assessments or payments toward liens created prior to purchase, paid by purchaser, with interest. If purchaser be a creditor holding a lien prior to that of redemptioner (other than judgment under which purchase was made) amount of such lien and interest must also be paid. If property is redeemed by redemptioner, judgment debtor or another redemptioner may redeem within 60 days thereafter by paying amount paid on previous redemption plus 2% and also any taxes or assessments, with interest, paid by prior redemptioner and also amount, with interest, of any lien prior to his own held by such prior redemptioner, buy judgment under which property was sold need not be paid as prior lien. Such redemptions may be continued, each within 60 days after preceding redemption. When debtor redeems, his estate is restored. Where redemptioners redeem, last redemptioner is entitled to deed after 60 days but not before one year from sale, judgment debtor having full year to redeem. Where there is no redemption, purchaser is entitled to deed after one year from sale. (21.210-21.220).

Any person redeeming may deduct from amount to be paid the amount of rents and profits received or claimed by purchaser or prior redemptioner. (21.250).

Third Party Claims.—Procedure in case of attachment (see topic Attachment) is applicable. (21.120).

Supplementary Proceedings.—Upon return of execution unsatisfied, the creditor may have an order requiring judgment debtor to appear and answer concerning his property; but he may not be required to appear outside county of residence. (21.270). Judgment debtor may also be required to so appear and answer, before return of execution, upon proof that he has property that he unjustly refuses to apply in satisfaction of judgment. Execution proceedings may thereupon be had against property. Upon

---

See note at head of Digest as to 1998 legislation covered.

See Topical Index in front part of this volume.

NV – 17

EXECUTIONS . . . *continued*

affidavit that there is danger of debtor absconding he may be arrested and required to give security to attend from time to time before judge, and that he will not in meantime dispose of his property. In default of such security he may be committed to prison. (21.280). Persons indebted to judgment debtor may be also required to appear and answer concerning such indebtedness, and witnesses may be required to appear and testify in such proceedings. (21.300-21.310).

Order.—The judge may order property of or debts due to the judgment debtor to be applied on the execution, if not exempt. (21.320. See topic Exemptions.) In case of an adverse claim to such property or debts by the third party, the judge may authorize a suit to be brought to test his right, and may enjoin any transfer of the property. (21.330).

Body Execution.—See supra, subhead Writ.

EXEMPTIONS:

There are numerous exemptions from execution of personal property, usually limited as to value. (21.090).

Other exemptions are: corpus and income of spendthrift trust or any trust created by, or corpus of which proceeded from, any person other than judgment debtor or beneficiary (21.080); all monies, benefits, privileges and immunities growing out of life insurance, to extent that annual premium does not exceed $1,000, qualified I.R.A.'s and pension or profit sharing plan not to exceed $500,000; all moneys paid for support and maintenance of child or former spouse. (21.090).

Substitution.—There is no provision for holding money or other property in lieu of articles of personalty specifically exempted but not owned by the debtor.

Debts Against Which Exemptions Not Allowed.—Exemption is not available against taxes, claims for purchase money or valid liens. (21.090).

Earnings of a debtor are exempt to extent of greater of 75% of disposable earnings for any pay period, or amount by which his disposable earnings for each week of such period exceed 30 times minimum hourly wage prescribed by §6(a)(1) of Federal Labor Standards Act of 1938. This exemption does not apply to court orders for support of any person, any order of court of bankruptcy, or of any debt due for any state or federal tax. "Disposable earnings" means that part of earnings remaining after deductions withheld as required by law. (21.090).

Homestead Exemptions.—See topic Homesteads.

FORECLOSURE:

See topic Liens; category Mortgages, topic Mortgages of Real Property.

FRAUDULENT SALES AND CONVEYANCES:

Uniform Commercial Code adopted. (104.1101-104.9507). See category Business Regulation and Commerce, topic Commercial Code.

Uniform Fraudulent Transfer Act adopted. (112.010-112.130).

Criminal Liability.—Every person who is a party to any fraudulent conveyance of lands or chattels or any right issuing out of the same or any fraudulent concealment, removal or destruction thereof is guilty of a gross misdemeanor. (205.330).

Bulk Sales.—Uniform Commercial Code adopted. See category Business Regulation and Commerce, topic Commercial Code.

GARNISHMENT:

At time of order directing writ of attachment to issue, or at any time thereafter, court may order that writ of garnishment issue as security for any judgment plaintiff may recover. (31.240). No writ of garnishment in aid of attachment may issue except on order of court. Plaintiff's application must be made by affidavit in which affiant expresses a belief garnishee is defendant's employer or is indebted to or has property belonging to defendant which is not exempt from execution. If garnishee is state, writ must be served on state controller. Grounds and procedure are identical to those for writ of attachment. (31.249).

Property Which May Be Reached.—Under writ plaintiff may attach money, credits, effects, debts, choses in action and other personal property of defendant in possession or under control of any third person as garnishee. (31.240). Debts and credits, due or to become due, and items in process of collection unless item is returned unpaid from bank or savings and loan association, moneys collected by peace officers and clerks of court, and moneys held by executors or administrators may be reached. (31.291-31.292). If garnishee answers that he is defendant's employer writ continues for 120 days or until amount demanded is satisfied, whichever first occurs. (31.296).

Answer of Garnishee.—The garnishee, upon payment to him of $5, is required to answer under oath what property effects, etc., he has in his possession belonging to the defendants, and whether he is in any manner indebted to the defendants. (31.270; 31.290).

Failure of Garnishee to Answer.—If garnishee fails to answer, court may enter judgment for defendant for use of plaintiff against garnishee for value of amount specified in writ. Notice must be given to each defendant before such judgment is given. (31.320).

Interpleader.—When the answer of the garnishee discloses that any person other than the defendant claims the indebtedness or property in his hands, the court may order such claimant to be interpleaded, giving notice to all parties. (31.350).

Judgment.—If the garnishee has property in his possession, the court may enter judgment that the garnishee deliver it to the sheriff, and if the plaintiff recover judgment, that the property so delivered be sold as upon execution. If the garnishee answers that he is indebted to the defendant, and if the plaintiff recovers judgment, the court must enter judgment in favor of the defendant for the use of the plaintiff against the garnishee, for the amount of the indebtedness, not greater than is necessary to satisfy judgment of plaintiff. (31.300).

Judgment against a garnishee acquits him from all demands by the defendant for all goods, effects and credits paid, delivered or accounted for by the garnishee by force of such judgment. (31.370).

Execution Against Garnishee.—When judgment is rendered against any garnishee and it appears that the debt from him to the defendant is not yet due, execution may not issue until the debt becomes due. (31.390).

Wages due at time of garnishment and not exempt (see topic Exemptions) may be garnisheed. (31.295).

HOMESTEADS:

See also categories Family, topic Husband and Wife; Property, topics Curtesy, Dower; Real Property.

Head of a family in this state, if a husband and a wife or single person claiming homestead, are entitled to a homestead exempted from execution. Trustee may claim homestead for settlor or beneficiaries if person for whom claim made resides on property. (115.010; 115.020).

Property Which May Be Claimed.—A homestead may be set aside from either community property or separate property. Homestead not extinguished where underlying property placed in trust for individuals who declared it. (115.020).

Dwelling house, including mobile home, may be exempt, though situated on land not owned by occupant $125,000 of equity limit. (21.090).

Limitation of value which may be held exempt is $125,000 of equity in property unless allodial title has been established and not relinquished in which case exemption extends to all equity in dwelling, appurtenances, and land on which it is located. Allodial title is issued by State Treasurer on application of owner of single-family dwelling free and clear of all encumbrances and prepayment of all future property tax liability for that dwelling in accordance with formula set forth in 361.900. (115.010).

Limitation of Area.—None.

Exemption is not available against claims for purchase price, mechanics' or laborers' liens or mortgages or deeds of trust executed thereon, liens to which prior consent was given through acceptance of property subject to recorded declaration of restriction, deed restriction, restrictive covenant or equitable servitude, including assessment lien of unit owners association. (115.010; 115.040). Mortgage or deed of trust must be executed, and consent to lien given, by both husband and wife when that relationship exists. (115.040).

Designation of Homestead.—Declaration of homestead must be recorded in county recorder's office in county where homestead is situated. If homestead is declared from separate property of either spouse, when marriage relationship exists, both must join in declaration. (115.020-115.030).

Waiver of Exemption.—Homestead may be waived by written abandonment, signed, acknowledged and recorded or by conveyance or mortgage executed by husband and wife, head of family, or single person claiming homestead. (115.040).

Alienation or Encumbrance.—No mortgage or conveyance of homestead valid if made to secure loan or indebtedness on property unless executed by husband and wife, when that relationship exists, and acknowledged separately by wife apart from husband. (115.040). Any mortgage or conveyance of a homestead whether declared or not must be by joint consent of husband and wife. (123.230).

Proceeds of Sale.—If homestead is sold under execution, proceeds up to $125,000 of equity in property are exempt. Statute does not provide for any exemption of proceeds of voluntary sale. (115.050).

Rights of Surviving Spouse and Family.—Exemption from execution upon homestead declared as community property by husband and wife continues until death of surviving spouse. If homestead is separate property, exemption continues until death of spouse deemed to own separate property as to debts existing at time of death but ceases as to any subsequent debt of survivor. Exemption of homestead declared property of single person continues against certain qualified individuals who continue to reside on homestead. If two unrelated persons have claimed homestead of single parcel exemption continues as to debt of decedent and other declarant until death of last declarant if declarant continues to reside on property unless otherwise provided in premarital agreement. (115.060). If no homestead had been selected, probate court, on own motion or on application shall set apart homestead. (146.020).

JUDGMENT NOTES:

See category Business Regulation and Commerce, topic Bills and Notes.

LEVY:

See topics Attachment, Executions.

LIENS:

Uniform Commercial Code adopted. (104.1101-104.9507). See category Business Regulation and Commerce, topic Commercial Code.

All common law liens exist, with common law remedies thereon.

Agistor's Lien.—Person who boards animals has a lien which can be foreclosed by public sale of the animals after compliance with certain notice provisions. (108.540-108.570).

Persons working for wages have certain liens. See category Employment, topic Labor Relations.

Jewelers.—Liens are given for labor and materials in repairing watches, clocks and jewelry. (108.370).

Innkeepers' liens have been extended to owners of furnished or unfurnished apartment houses and bungalow courts. See category Property, topic Landlord and Tenant, subhead Lien.

Hospital Liens.—Reasonable value of hospitalization allowed as a lien against amounts recovered as damages for personal injuries. (108.590-108.660).

LIENS . . . *continued*

Enforcement.—Justices of the peace have concurrent jurisdiction with district courts to enforce the liens above mentioned when the amount claimed does not exceed $7,500. (4.370).

Motor Vehicle Liens.—Vehicle dealers, garages, repair men, mobile or manufactured home dealers, and landlords have special lien, not dependent on possession, inferior to any existing conditional sale contract. Lien can be enforced by auction sale of vehicle or home after written notice of lien has been served, written notice of sale sent registered mail to owner and interested persons at least ten and not more than 30 days before sale and publication of notice of sale for three consecutive weeks setting forth time which cannot be less than 22 days after first publication, and place of sale. Misrepresentation or fraud in creating lien is misdemeanor. (108.270-108.360).

Mechanics' Liens.—Every person who performs labor or furnishes material of value of $500 or more in or for construction, alteration, or repair of any structure or mine has lien thereon for unpaid balance agreed upon if parties entered into written contract, or in absence of written contract amount equal to fair market value of labor or materials, including reasonable overhead and profit. If license required for work, only licensed contractor, or employee, or one who furnishes materials to project may have lien. (108.222).

Person who at request of an owner of lot or tract of land grades, plants, landscapes or otherwise improves land or street adjoining it has lien on it. (108.223).

Foundrymen, boiler makers and persons performing labor or furnishing material for the construction, maintenance or operation of a mill, factory or hoist are entitled to a similar lien. (108.240).

Extent and Priority of Lien.—Land on which any structure stands and a convenient space around it is subject to lien in like manner as structure. Such liens are preferred to any mortgage, encumbrance placed on property after structure was commenced or work thereon begun; or to any mortgage or encumbrance unrecorded at time when structure was commenced or work thereon begun. (108.224-108.225).

Nonresponsibility Notice.—Any improvement made with knowledge of owner or other interested person is deemed made at his request unless, within three days after knowledge of construction or intended construction, he files a notice of nonresponsibility with county recorder of county where land or building is situated. (108.234).

Lien Claim.—Every person other than one who performs only labor who claims benefit of mechanics lien statutes must within 31 days after first delivery of material, or performance of work or services under his contract deliver in person or by certified mail notice to owner or reputed owner of property that such person has supplied materials or performed work or services. Said notice must give general description of material, work or services and anticipated total value. If said notice is not given, no lien for materials furnished or for work or services performed except labor may be perfected. (108.2394). Every person claiming a lien must record his notice of lien within 90 days after completion of his contract, delivery of material by him or performance of his labor. In event owner records a notice of completion, then notice of lien must be recorded within 40 days thereafter. Lien claim must be verified by oath of claimant or some person on his behalf and be filed in county recorder's office of county where property is situated and in addition within 30 days after recording must be served on owner in person, or prescribed substituted service effected. Person who knowingly makes false statement in recording notice of lien guilty of gross misdemeanor. (108.226-108.227).

Duration of Lien.—No lien binds property for more than six months unless suit is commenced to enforce lien within that time after lien is filed, unless time is extended by written instrument prior to expiration of the six months period. Such written extension binds only persons signing it and second extension may not be given. In no case shall extension be given one year beyond recording of lien. (108.233).

Enforcement of Lien.—Any number of persons claiming liens against the same property may join in same action or after lien claims are filed they may be assigned to one for purpose of collection or separate actions by lien claimants may be consolidated. The court must allow as part of costs, reasonable attorney's fees for foreclosing and may allow as costs interest and money paid for recording lien. (108.237).

Mechanics' liens may be enforced in any court of competent jurisdiction. Those not exceeding $7,500 may be foreclosed in justice's court. (4.370). All others must be foreclosed in district court. (108.239).

Sale and Redemption.—Sale is made by sheriff as upon executions. Redemption statute applies. See topic Executions. If claim is not satisfied by sale, claimant has personal judgment for residue against party liable therefor. (108.239).

The lienee may apply to have lien discharged, on reasonable notice and posting an undertaking equal to one and a half times amount of lien. (108.2391).

Public improvements are not subject to mechanics' liens, but where the contract price of a public building or other public improvement exceeds $20,000, contractor must give performance bond and payment bond, each not less than 50% of contract amount. No action may be brought unless party who has furnished labor or materials gives written notice describing nature of his claim to principal, obligee and surety within 90 days after he finished performing, and commences action within one year after work ceased. Where claims exceed amount of bond, claims are prorated and to that end all actions are consolidated. (339.015-339.065).

Attachment Lien.—See topic Attachment.

Attorney's Lien.—See category Legal Profession, topic Attorneys and Counselors.

Collateral Security.—See topic Pledges.

Execution Lien.—See topic Executions.

Landlord's Lien.—See category Property, topic Landlord and Tenant.

Liens on Exempt Property.—See topic Exemptions.

Liens on Homestead.—See topic Homesteads.

Real Estate Mortgage Lien.—See category Mortgages, topic Mortgages of Real Property.

Tax Lien.—See category Taxation, topic Property Taxes.

MECHANICS' LIENS:

See topic Liens.

PLEDGES:

Remedies of Pledgee.—Our "one action" statute (40.430), dealing specifically with mortgage or lien, does not apply to pledges, and a pledgee may proceed personally against the pledgor for the whole debt without selling the pledge. (58 Nev. 261, 75 P.2d 992).

The business of a pawnbroker is regulated by statute, with special reference to keeping records of transactions. (646.010-646.060).

Uniform Commercial Code adopted. (104.1101-104.9507). See category Business Regulation and Commerce, topic Commercial Code.

RECEIVERS:

Receivers may be appointed by district court in which action pending or judge thereof:

1. In an action by a vendor to vacate a fraudulent purchase of property, or by a creditor to subject any property or fund to his claim, or between partners or others, jointly owning or interested in any property or fund, on application of the plaintiff, or of any party whose right to or interest in the property or fund, or the proceeds thereof, is probable, and where it is shown that the property or fund is in danger of being lost, removed, or materially injured;

2. In an action by a mortgagee for the foreclosure of his mortgage and sale of the mortgaged property, where it appears that the mortgaged property is in danger of being lost, removed, or materially injured, or that the condition of the mortgage has not been performed, and that the property is probably insufficient to discharge the mortgage debt;

3. After judgment, to carry the judgment into effect;

4. After judgment, to dispose of the property according to the judgment, or to preserve it during the pendency of an appeal or in proceedings in aid of execution, where an execution has been returned unsatisfied, or when the judgment debtor refuses to apply his property in satisfaction of the judgment;

5. In the cases when a corporation has been dissolved, or is insolvent; or in imminent danger of insolvency, or has forfeited its corporate rights;

6. In all other cases where receivers have heretofore been appointed by the usages of the courts of equity. (32.010).

In connection with injunction proceedings a receiver may be appointed for an insolvent or failing corporation. (78.635). See 49 Nev. 145, 241 Pac. 317.

Powers and duties of a receiver of an insolvent corporation are outlined in law regarding private corporations. (78.720, 78.627).

Compensation.—Receivers are paid a reasonable compensation for their services. (78.705).

See also category Property, topic Absentees, subhead Escheat.

REDEMPTION:

See topics Executions, Liens; categories Mortgages, topic Mortgages of Real Property; Taxation, topic Property Taxes, subhead Redemption.

SUPPLEMENTARY PROCEEDINGS:

See topic Executions.

TRUSTEE PROCESS:

See topic Garnishment.

USURY:

See category Business Regulation and Commerce, topic Interest.

DISPUTE RESOLUTION

ARBITRATION AND AWARD:

Uniform Arbitration Act adopted. (38.015 et seq.).

DOCUMENTS AND RECORDS

ACKNOWLEDGMENTS:

Uniform Law on Notarial Acts adopted. (240.161-240.168).

Acknowledgments may be taken by the following officers:

Within State.—Judge or clerk of court; justice of peace; notary public of this state; or other person authorized to perform specific act by law of this state or federal authority. (240.1635; 247.060, 111.265).

Without State but Within United States.—Notary public of that jurisdiction, judge or clerk of court of that jurisdiction, or any other person authorized by law of that jurisdiction to perform notarial acts or under federal authority. (240.164).

Federal Authority.—If performed anywhere by following under Federal authority: judge or clerk of court, commissioned officer on active duty in U.S. Military service, foreign service officer or consular officer of U.S., or any other person authorized by federal law to perform notarial acts. (240.1645).

Without U.S.—If performed within jurisdiction of and under authority of foreign nation, its constituent units or multi-national or international organization by: notary public or notary, judge or clerk of court of record, or any other person authorized by law of that jurisdiction to perform notarial acts. (240.165).

General Requirements.—Notarial act must be evidenced by certificate signed and dated by notarial officer. Certificate must include identification of jurisdiction in which act is performed, title of office of notarial officer, and may include official stamp or seal.

See note at head of Digest as to 1998 legislation covered.

See Topical Index in front part of this volume.

ACKNOWLEDGMENTS ... *continued*

If officer is notary public must include date of expiration, if any, of office; if officer is commissioned officer on active duty in U.S. military, must include officer's rank. (240.1645).

In taking acknowledgment notary public must determine from personal knowledge or identification on oath of credible witness personally known to notary, or identified on basis of identification document that person making acknowledgment is person whose signature is on instrument. (240.071).

Married Women.—No special requirements. As to necessity of acknowledgement by married woman of instrument affecting real property, see category Family, topic Husband and Wife.

Effect.—Acknowledgment entitles an instrument affecting real estate to be recorded provided instrument includes grantee's mailing address and assessor's parcel number, if any (111.312, 111.310) and imparts notice of its contents (111.320). Certificate of acknowledgment may be rebutted. (111.340).

Proof by a subscribing witness has same effect as acknowledgment. (111.115).

Authentication.—No authentication as to official character or genuineness of signature of officer taking acknowledgment to be used within the state is required, except as to justices of the peace, as above stated. It is imperative that notary attach his stamp. There is no statute providing for authentication of acknowledgments taken within the state for use elsewhere; in practice such authentications are made by county clerks, usual fee $1. (111.265).

Forms of acknowledgment and proof are as follows, substantial compliance therewith being sufficient:

Forms
Acknowledgment by person, corporation or partnership (111.270):
Following certificate is sufficient for acknowledgement in representative capacity: State of Nevada, County of . . . .—ss. This instrument was acknowledged before me on . . . (date) by . . . . (name(s) of person(s)) as . . . . (type of authority, e.g., officer, trustee, etc.) of . . . . (name of party on behalf of whom instrument was executed) . . . . (signature) (stamp).

Following certificate is sufficient for verification upon oath or affirmation: State of Nevada, County of . . . .—ss. Signed and sworn to (or affirmed) before me on . . . . (date) by . . . . (name(s) of person(s) making statement. (signature) (stamp).

Following certificate is sufficient for witnessing or attesting signature: State of Nevada, County of . . . .—ss. Signed or attested before me on . . . . (date) by . . . . (name(s) of person(s). (signature) (stamp).

Following certificate is sufficient for attesting copy of document: State of Nevada, County of . . . .—ss. I certify that this is a true and correct copy of a document in the possession of . . . . Dated . . . . (signature) (stamp).
Proof by subscribing witness (111.115-111.130):
State of . . . ., county of . . . .—ss. On this . . . . day of . . . ., A.D. . . . ., before me, ..., a notary public, (or judge or other officer as the case may be) in and for said county of . . . ., personally appeared A.B., known to me to be the same person who is described in and who executed the within instrument as subscribing witness thereto, and who being by me first duly sworn, deposes and says: That on the . . . . . . day of . . . . . ., A. D. . . . . ., he was personally acquainted with C. D., the person described in and who executed the within instrument; that on said last-named day he saw the said C. D. execute the said instrument, that the said C. D., whose name is subscribed to said instrument as a party thereto, is the person who executed the same; that he executed the same freely and voluntarily and for the uses and purposes therein mentioned; that affiant thereupon signed the same as subscribing witness thereto. Witness my official stamp at . . . . . in said county, the day and year in this certificate first above written.

. . . .
(signature) (stamp).

Alternative to Acknowledgment or Proof.—No statutory provision.

Fees.—Notary, $2 first signature of each signer; $1 each additional and agreed upon traveling fees. (240.100).

AFFIDAVITS:

Within State.—Affidavit to be used before any court, judge or officer of this state may be taken before judge or clerk of any court, or any justice of peace or notary public in state. (53.-010).

Without State but in United States.—Affidavit taken in another state or territory of United States must be taken before commissioner appointed by Governor of this state to take affidavits and depositions in such other state or territory, or before any notary public or judge of a court of record having seal. (53.020).

Foreign Country.—Affidavit in foreign country must be taken before ambassador, minister, consul, vice-consul or consular agent of United States, judge of court of record with seal attached, notary public or other person authorized by laws of such country to administer oaths. If taken before court that has no seal such fact must be certified by judge or clerk. (53.040).

General Requirements as to Administration.—No statute.

General Requirements of Jurat.—When taken before judge of court outside of this state, but within U. S., genuineness of signature of the judge, existence of court, and that such judge is a member thereof, must be certified by clerk of court under the seal thereof. (53.030).

Where affidavit is taken before a notary public, his stamp must be affixed. (240.040).

Use of Affidavit.—Affidavits may be used in court in ex parte proceedings, in support of motions, to prove service of process, and for purpose of setting aside process on motion. Affidavit or declaration of qualified person or expert as to presence or identity of alcohol or controlled substance is admissible in criminal trial in certain cases.

Defendant who demands expert is responsible for witness' expenses if convicted. (50.325). Grand jury investigating charge for purpose of presentment or indictment may receive similar affidavit or declaration from expert in lieu of personal testimony or deposition as to presence or identity of alcohol or controlled substance and may receive affidavit of owner, possessor or occupant of property. (172.135).

Form.—The usual form of heading and jurat or certificate is as follows:

Form
State of . . . ., county of . . . . ss. . . . ., being first duly sworn deposes and says: (then follows statement of facts, followed by signature of affiant). Subscribed and sworn to before me this . . . . day of . . . ., (giving correct date) adding officer's signature, office, and seal or stamp.

If affidavits are taken out of the United States, then they are headed in the country and correct subdivision thereof.

Alternative to Affidavit.—No statutory provision.

NOTARIES PUBLIC:

Qualification.—Appointed by Secretary of State; may appoint resident of adjoining state under certain statutory restrictions. (240.010). Notary must pay secretary $35, take official oath, and execute bond for $10,000, to be filed with county clerk. Bond and oath are filed and recorded in county clerk's office, thereafter Secretary of State issues certificate of appointment. Court reporter who has registration certificate pursuant to NRS 656.180 may apply for appointment as notary public with limited powers to administer oath or affirmation without bond. (240.030).

Authentication.—See topic Acknowledgments, subhead Authentication.

Seal.—No seal required. Stamp required gives name, number of certificate of appointment, phrase "Notary Public, State of Nevada" and date appointment expires. If notary public is resident of adjoining state appointed by Secretary of State, stamp must include word "nonresident". (240.040).

Powers and Duties.—Notary may, during normal business hours, perform notarial acts in lawful transactions for person who requests act and tenders fee. (240.060). However, notary cannot perform any notarial act if he executed or is named in instrument, or will receive any consideration from transaction relating to instrument or pleading in excess of his authorized fees, or is related to person whose signature he is notarizing. (240.065). Notary must not influence person concerning transaction involving notarial act, certify instrument containing known false statements, perform any act as notary with intent to deceive, promote any product or service if his appointment as notary is used in promotional statement, certify copies of birth, death or marriage certificate or divorce decree, or allow another to use notary's stamp or sign notary's name in notarial capacity. (240.075).

Liabilities.—Notary is liable on bond for damages caused by misconduct or negligence; employer of notary public liable for damages caused by misconduct of notary acting within scope of employment at that time and employer consented to misconduct. Revocation or suspension of appointment and statutory fines for willful neglect or violation of duty. (240.150).

Territorial Extent of Powers.—Functions may be performed anywhere in state. (240.020).

Expiration of Appointment.—Notary's stamp gives date of expiration. (240.040).

Fees.—For taking acknowledgment first signature of each signer $2, additional signatures of each signer $1, for administering oath or affirmation $1, for certified copy $1, for each signature on jurat $2 plus any agreed upon travel fees. 25¢. (240.100).

Commissioners of Deeds.—Commissioner has power to administer oaths, take and certify depositions and affidavits, and take and certify acknowledgments of recorded instruments. (240.-210).

RECORDS:

Uniform Commercial Code adopted. (104.1101-104.9507). See category Business Regulation and Commerce, topic Commercial Code.

Any instrument concerning real property must, in order to constitute notice to third persons, be acknowledged and recorded with the recorder of the county in which the property is situated, or, for instrument filed by public utility in office of Secretary of State to extent permitted by 105.010-105.080, and conveyance or incumbrance of real estate is void as against subsequent bona fide purchaser or incumbrancer for value whose deed or other instrument is first recorded. (111.315-111.325). *For list of Counties and County Seats see first page for this state in Volume containing Practice Profiles Section.* Unrecorded instruments are, however, good as between parties thereto. (111.315). All instruments filed for recordation must have names of signers typed or printed thereon. (247.190). All instruments conveying real property, or agreeing to do so must contain grantee's mailing address and assessors parcel number of property. (111.312).

An instrument filed, but not for recordation, as permitted by law, imparts constructive notice to all persons of its contents. (247.190).

Filing and recording fees are charged and collected by county recorders according to following uniform fee schedule: Recording any document, first page, $7, each additional page, $1; recording each portion of a document which must be separately indexed, after first indexing, $3; copying any record, for each page, $1; certifying, including certificate and seal, first seal, $3, each additional seal, $1, certified copy or abstract of marriage certificate, $7. (247.305).

Foreign Conveyances or Encumbrances.—See category Property, topic Real Property.

Stamp Tax.—See category Taxation, topic Real Estate Conveyance Tax.

Filing Under Commercial Code.—Place of filing financing statement or security agreement is Office of County Recorder; and, in certain instances, Office of Secretary of

RECORDS . . . *continued*

State, U.C.C. Division, Capitol Complex, Carson City, Nevada 89710. See U.C.C. §9-401, third alternative subsection 1 as modified. (104.9401).

Fees.—Filing, indexing and furnishing filing data for original or continuation statement, on form conforming to standard prescribed by Secretary of State shall be $15, and in all other cases $20; filing and indexing termination statement, filing, indexing and furnishing filing data for financing statement indicating an assignment, filing, indexing and furnishing filing data about separate statement of assignment, filing and noting statement of release, are all $15 on prescribed form of Secretary of State and $20 in other cases; any attachment to document additional $1 per page. If termination statement includes additional debtor, increase fee $1 per additional debtor (104.9403-104.9406); certification of filing officer showing effective financing statement naming particular debtor, $15 on form prescribed by Secretary of State otherwise $20, copy of filing financing statement or statement of assignment, and payment of statutory fees for copies (104.9407).

Torrens Act has not been adopted.

Transfer of Decedent's Title to Real Estate.—Whether decedent be resident or nonresident, his estate must be administered in Nevada and a certified copy of decree of final distribution recorded in office of recorder of county where property situated. Where property is held in joint tenancy, or as community property with right of survivorship, survivor takes without administration. Usually recording of death certificate or certified copy in county wherein property is located is sufficient. (40.470). If question of identify of decedent arises simple proceeding for termination of life estate is used. (40.460).

Vital Statistics.—Birth and death certificates must be filed with local health officer, who must make and keep a copy and register same and transmit original to State Board of Health, Carson City, which keeps and registers same. Certified copies are prima facie evidence. (440.010-440.780). Certified copies of certificates of birth or death may be obtained from Registrar of Vital Statistics, Health Division, Department of Human Resources, 201 S. Fall, Carson City 89701, at fees set by statute. (440.700).

Procurement or possession of birth certificate of another for purpose of establishing false identity is prohibited. (440.765).

Marriage certificates are recorded in office of recorder of county from which license was issued. (122.130). Copies may be obtained from county recorder for $1 for each page. Certified copies or abstracts of marriage certificates cost $7. (247.305).

Record of each marriage is also filed with state registrar. (440.595). District courts file report with state registrar for each divorce and annulment granted. (440.605).

Establishing Birth Record.—Any person who desires to establish the date and place of his birth and his parentage may file, in the district court of the county in which he has been a resident for at least six months, a verified petition reciting the facts and accompanied by his finger print chart and a small recent photograph of himself. Action must be entitled "In the Matter of the Parental Relation of . . . . and . . . .". Notice of action must be served in accordance with N.R.C.P. upon person whose parentage it is sought to establish and each known or alleged parent. Court can compel State Registrar of Vital Statistics to examine any relevant data. After hearing, and if proof be satisfactory, court issues decree establishing facts, which is prima facie evidence thereof, and copies of which must be filed with State Health Officer and in office of county clerk in county in which decree was rendered. No fee may be charged by county clerk (who is ex-officio clerk of district court). (41.210-41.260).

Proof of Public Writings.—A judicial or official record and all records of State of Nevada and political subdivisions may be proved by a microfilm or photostatic copy, duly certified. (52.125, 52.265).

SEALS:

Private seals are not necessary to validity of any instrument. (52.315).

Effect of Seal.—No effect.

Uniform Commercial Code adopted. (104.1101-104.9507). See category Business Regulation and Commerce, topic Commercial Code.

TORRENS ACT:

None.

VITAL STATISTICS:

See topic Records.

EMPLOYMENT

EMPLOYER AND EMPLOYEE:

See topic Labor Relations.

LABOR RELATIONS:

Labor Commissioner must enforce all labor laws whose enforcement is not otherwise provided for. (607.160). Labor Commissioner or other designated agent of employees may take assignments of wage or commission claims and bring single action against any one employer on any number of such assigned claims. (607.175).

Every employer must furnish safe and healthful employment and guard life, health, and safety of his employees in accordance with standards of Department of Industrial Relations. (618.005-618.720).

Hours of Labor.—Except for situations of one employee, and for employees under collective bargaining agreement, all employees must be granted meal period of at least a half hour and two ten-minute rest periods over continuous eight-hour working period. Rest periods are counted as hours worked. (608.019).

No child under 16 years of age may be employed more than 48 hours in one week or more than eight hours in any one day, except in domestic or farm work or employment as performer in motion picture. (609.240).

See also category Mineral, Water and Fishing Rights, topic Mines and Minerals.

Wages.—All wages are due and payable semimonthly, unless by agreement paid more frequently. Discharged employee is entitled to wages immediately and employee who resigns or quits is entitled to wages no later than day he would have been regularly paid or seven days after resignation, whichever is earliest. (608.030). If employer fails to pay within three days after wages of discharged employee become due or on day wages due employee who resigns, wage continues at same rate until paid or 30 days, whichever is less. Employee who secretes or absents himself, or refuses to accept wages tendered is not entitled to payment during such time as he secretes or absents himself. Every employer must establish and maintain regular pay days and post and maintain notices thereof in at least two conspicuous places. (608.020-608.080).

Any check or writing issued as evidence of an indebtedness for wages due must be negotiable. In event of nonpayment, holder in due course stands in same position as payee had with respect to unpaid wage claim. Employer who knowingly issues negotiable instrument for wages for which there are insufficient funds to pay must reimburse employee for any penalty or charge incurred. (608.130).

Minimum wages for employees in private employment: $3.35 per hour, but labor commissioner may prescribe increases in accordance with federal law; minor must receive at least 85% of minimum for persons 18 years or older. Provisions do not apply to casual babysitters, live-in domestic service employees, salespersons who work on commission basis, some agricultural employees, and taxicab and limousine drivers specified severely handicapped persons. (608.250).

Employee suing for wages and recovering is entitled to attorney's fees in addition to wages, penalties and costs, if at least five days before bringing suit he made written demand for a sum not exceeding the amount found due him. (608.140).

Public building contracts of state or any political subdivision thereof including projects financed from public money must provide that workers be paid prevailing wage in their locality. (338.020). "Wages" includes fringe benefits. (338.010).

Deductions from Wages.—An employer may retain dues, rates or assessments for hospital association, or for other institutions maintained for benefit of employees, or poll tax, or deductions which may be authorized by law from wages. (608.110). But employer is prohibited from collecting any hospital fees unless there is hospital actually furnished. (613.180).

Liens and Priorities.—In case employer assigns property to pay debts, employees have a preferred claim for wages up to $600 for services within 90 days before assignment. In case of attachment, execution and similar writs against employer's property such claims are preferred to other debts. (100.010-100.030). When corporation becomes insolvent employees have lien for three months' wages not exceeding $1,000. (78.720). On death of employer, employee has preferred claim for services rendered within three months before death, ranking next after administration and funeral expenses and family allowance debts having preference under U.S. laws, and moneys owed to department of human resources resulting from payment of benefits. (150.220).

Every employee also has the same rights as are accorded under mechanics' lien act or NRS 108.221 to 108.2395, inclusive. (608.050).

Discharge.—An employee may not be discharged or disciplined on information of special agent in matter which involves question of integrity or honesty of employee or violation of rules without a hearing and an opportunity to face his accuser. (613.160).

Discrimination with respect to hiring, discharging, compensation, or conditions of employment because of race, color, religion, sex, age, disability or national origin is unlawful employment practice. (613.330).

It is unlawful to discriminate on basis of sex in paying unequal wages to employees performing equal work. (608.017).

Discrimination is prohibited employment practice under Local Government Employee-Management Relations Act. (288.270).

Collective bargaining by employees is authorized (614.090), and violation of Act results in a misdemeanor (614.110).

Labor organization representing gaming casino employees must file with gaming control board list of officers and others in policymaking and other functional roles as designated. Persons listed must supply board with specified information including organizational and occupational history. (463A.030). Pursuant to statutory procedure, board may disqualify for cause person from function as listed. (463A.040).

Local Government Employee-Management Relations Act recognizes right of local government employees to organize and bargain collectively (288.010-288.280), enumerates mandatory bargaining subjects and subjects excluded from bargaining (288.150).

See also subhead Union Membership, infra.

Labor Disputes.—Governor may, no request of either party to controversy, use his best efforts to settle same, either personally or by a commission appointed for the purpose. Such disputes may, on agreement of parties, be settled by arbitration. (614.010-614.080).

Union Membership.—It is unlawful for any person, firm or corporation to enter into a contract by terms of which an employee of such person, firm or corporation, as a condition for obtaining or continuing employment, shall be required to become or continue a member of any labor organization. (613.230-613.300).

Employment Frauds.—It is unlawful for any person to influence or engage workmen to change from one place to another in this state, or bring workmen to this state through means of deceptive representations, false advertising or false pretenses concerning the kind and character of work to be done, compensation paid, sanitary conditions, existence or non-existence of a strike, or trouble pending between employer and employee, and violations result in gross misdemeanors. (631.010-631.030).

Child Labor.—Person employing, or parent allowing employment of, child under 14 years of age in store, factory, mine or other inside labor not associated with farm or housework must have written permission from district court. (609. 220). No child under 16 years of age may be employed more than 48 hours in one week or more than eight hours in any one day, except in domestic or farm work or employment as performer in motion picture. (609.240).

See note at head of Digest as to 1998 legislation covered.

See Topical Index in front part of this volume.

NV – 21

LABOR RELATIONS . . . *continued*

Minors under 16 years of age are forbidden employment in designated industries, and labor commissioner determines other employment injurious to health or morals or minors. (609.190-609.200).

Railroads are liable to employees or personal representatives for benefit of surviving widow, husband, children, parents or dependents of employee for injury or death resulting in whole or in part from negligence of any officer, agent, or employee of railroad or by reason of any defect or insufficiency due to employer's negligence. Contributory negligence is not a bar to action, but comparative negligence doctrine applies to diminish damages. Contributory negligence is no defense where violation by employer of any state or federal statute enacted for safety of employees contributed to accident. Assumption of risk is not a defense. Occurrence of accident is presumptive evidence of negligence. Contract to exempt from liability under this statute is void. Receivers or other persons or corporations charged with duty of management and operation of business are included in the act. Action must be brought within two years from accrual of cause of action. (705.260-705.340).

Workmen's Compensation Act.—This is known as State Industrial Insurance System. It is applicable to practically every relation of master and servant. It is compulsory upon state, county and municipal corporations and upon school districts, also upon every contractor, sub-contractor and employee of same. (616.055-616.087; 616.275-616.280). It extends to employer with single employee. (616.285).

Employers wishing to accept Act may either pay monthly premiums or obtain certificate as self-insured employer. Requirements for self-insured status are listed in NRS 616.291.

If an employer fails to accept the provisions of the act he is deemed to have rejected the same and in case of injury to an employee is deprived of various common law defenses, which make non-acceptance of the act hazardous. If employer fails to provide or maintain compensation, manager may order immediate cessation of all business operations until performance. (616.629). If employer fails to provide mandatory coverage, employee who suffers accident or injury may elect coverage by filing claim for compensation from system, written notice to division and irrevocable assignment to division of right to be subrogated to employee's rights pursuant to 616.560. (616.377).

An employee is presumed to have accepted the benefits of the act unless he gives written notice of rejection to his employer, administrator and insurer. Where employee rejects, employer, if under act, may plead practically all common law defenses. Employee who rejects coverage may rescind at any time upon written notice to employer, administrator and insurer. (616.315).

The act makes employers responsible for such medical, surgical, hospital and certain other treatment as may be reasonably required at the time of the injury to an employee and within six months thereafter, but by paying certain additional premium he can be insured by the act against this liability. (616.515).

The act provides stated compensation for death and for various injuries. (616.570-616.628). As to employment outside state such compensation is exclusive and calls for complete release of liability. (616.520). If employment is exclusively in another state that requires coverage, laws of that state control. (616.260).

Pamphlet copy of Act can be secured from Nevada Industrial Commission, 515 E. Musser, Carson City, Nevada 89701.

Nevada Occupational Diseases Act provides a complete program for compensating an employee who is disabled because of an occupational disease arising out of and in the course of the employment, or his dependents in case of death. The administration of the Act is committed to Department of Industrial Relations, in conjunction with, but not as part of State Industrial Insurance System. (617.010-617.500). If employer fails to provide mandatory occupational disease coverage, employee who contracts occupational disease may elect coverage by filing claim for compensation from system, written notice to division and irrevocable assignment to system of his right of action against uninsured employer, division of right to be subrogated to employee's rights pursuant to 616.560. (616.377).

Unemployment Compensation.—Unemployed person eligible if administrator finds that he has registered for work at, and reports to, office of division, has made claim for benefits pursuant to statutes, is able to work and is available for work, and has, during base period, been paid wages equal to or exceeding one and one-half times his total wages for highest quarter of base period, or in each of at least three of four quarters of base period. Also unemployed person determined to likely exhaust regular benefits and need services to assist in reemployment may be eligible for benefits for any week if he participates in those services. (612.375). Claimant not eligible if he voluntarily leaves last work without good cause unless he left unsuitable employment to enter training approved by 19 USC §2296 (612.380); discharged from his last work for misconduct connected with his work (612.385); has failed without good cause to apply for available suitable work or to accept suitable work when offered (612.390); when his unemployment is due to labor dispute at establishment where he was last employed (612.395); has received benefits under any other unemployment compensation law (612.400); received wages or severance pay for that week (612.420); is on paid vacation (612.425); or has made false statement or failed to disclose material fact for purpose of causing benefit to be paid or increased (612.445).

Rates Generally.—Weekly benefit equal to 1/25th of total wages during quarter when total wages were highest, but in no case less than $16 or more than 50% of average weekly wage (excluding tips) of workers employed subject to provisions of c. 612 as reported for preceding calendar year. (612.340-612.345). Standard rate of employer contribution is 2.95%. (612.540).

Extended unemployment benefits are provided. (612.377; 612.3786).

WORKERS' COMPENSATION LAW:

See topic Labor Relations.

ENVIRONMENT

ENVIRONMENTAL REGULATION:

General Supervision.—State Environmental Commission adopts rules and regulations in accordance with Nevada Water Pollution Control Law. (445.201). Department of Conservation and Natural Resources is state water pollution control agency for all purposes of federal water pollution control legislation. (445.211). Department has final authority in administration of water pollution prevention, abatement and control. (445.344). Department of Conservation and Natural Resources is air pollution control agency for purposes of federal acts. (445.456). Department issues orders to implement state air pollution laws. (445.473). State Environmental Commission establishes air quality standards and emission control requirements and requires registration of air pollution sources. (445.461). If federal regulations of indirect sources of air contaminants effective after Jan. 17, 1977, authority of state agency to review new indirect sources may be exercised only to enforce those regulations or to extent federal act requires enforcement by state. (445.493).

Public Service Commission, subject to review of State Environmental Commission, has general supervision of environmental aspects of location and construction of all utility lines and associated facilities. (704.820-704.900).

State environmental commission develops statewide solid waste management system plan and approves local plans required of every municipal governing body.

State Department of Conservation and Natural Resources is State Agency for purposes of Federal Resource Conservation and Recovery Act of 1976. (444.590).

Respective boards of county commissioners may regulate, control or prohibit excessive noise. (444.440-440.620).

Department of Motor Vehicles and Public Safety regulates noise emission from vehicles. (484.6101). State environmental commission regulates standards for exhaust emissions, fuel evaporative emissions and visible smoke emissions from mobile internal combustion engines, but standards pertaining to motor vehicles must have prior approval of Dept. of Motor Vehicles and Public Safety. (445.620). It establishes rules regarding approval, installation and maintenance of pollution control devices. (445.630).

Certain populated counties control emissions from motor vehicles by compulsory inspection programs for diesel fueled vehicles being reregistered or registered and used motor vehicles being registered to new owner. (455.630, 445.635).

Department of Agriculture regulates use of pesticides. (586.230). Person retailing restricted use pesticide must be registered (586.406), and person using must be certified (555.280-555.300).

State Conservation Commission directs conservation, protection and controlled development of renewable natural resources. (548.010-548.550).

Forest practices and logging are regulated by division of forestry of state Department of Conservation and Natural Resources. (528.010-528.140).

Hazardous waste storage, transportation and disposal are regulated by State Department of Conservation and Natural Resources. (444.700—444.778). State Board of Health regulates possession, transfer and disposal of radioactive material. (459.201—459.370).

Prohibited Acts of Pollution.—

Water.—Persons may not discharge any pollutant into any waters of state or any treatment works, inject fluids through well into any waters of state, discharge from any point source pollutant or inject fluids through well that could be carried into waters of state by any means, or allow such to remain in place where pollutant or fluids could be carried into waters of state by any means except as authorized by permit. (445.221). Persons may not violate standards established by State Environmental Commission or Department of Conservation and Natural Resources. (445.224).

Air.—No person shall discharge into atmosphere any substance, except water vapor and water droplets, which violates air quality standards established by State Environmental Commission. (445.411, 445.461). All governmental sources of air contaminants must comply with local and state pollution laws, regulations and ordinances with limited statutory exceptions. (445.586). Motor vehicles must comply with state or federal law concerning motor vehicle pollution control devices. (484.644).

Regulations may also be promulgated by supervisory departments or boards.

Enforcement.—

Water.—State Environmental Commission and Department of Conservation and Natural Resources may require person injecting wells discharging pollutants to install monitoring equipment, sample discharges, maintain records and make reports on such discharges. (445.307). Department may enter any premises violating regulations, inspect records and monitoring equipment, and sample discharges. (445.304). Department is authorized upon discovery of violation or imminent violation to prescribe corrective action, commence civil action for fine or injunction, or seek criminal indictment or information through attorney general. (445.274).

Commission hears appeals on department action on permits.

Any person planning construction of any treatment works must obtain permit from department. (445.261).

Air.—Authorized representative of department may enter and inspect any property at which an air contaminant source is located or being constructed. (445.476). State Environmental Commission may require person responsible for source of air contaminant to apply for and obtain operating permit for source. (445.491).

Department Director has power to serve notice on persons responsible for violating air and water pollution laws. Notice may include order to take corrective action.

Commission regulates warnings and emergency standards when imminent and substantial danger to health exists due to ar pollution. (445.571).

Any peace officer may enforce State Environmental Commission's regulations on engine pollution standards. (445.710).

Solid Waste.—State Department of Conservation and Natural Resources or solid waste management authority may bring action in court to enjoin violation of solid waste laws or its regulations. (444.600).

See note at head of Digest as to 1998 legislation covered.

See Topical Index in front part of this volume.

ENVIRONMENTAL REGULATION ... *continued*

Actions for declaratory and equitable relief may be commenced by resident of state where any pollution violation is alleged to have occurred, if such resident has first given 30 days written notice of his intention to file suit. (41.540-41.570).

Penalties.—

Water.—Violation of terms of permit is gross misdemeanor or treated as violation of hazardous waste permit, whichever is greater. (445.334). Permit is also subject to revocation or suspension. (445.271). Violation or aiding and abetting violation of Nevada Water Pollution Control Law, or any regulation or permit issued under it, is subject to civil penalty of up to $25,000 per day plus actual damages and expenses for correction. (445.331). One who intentionally or with criminal negligence violates regulations is guilty of gross misdemeanor punishable by fine up to $25,000 for each day of violation or by imprisonment up to one year, or both; second violation is Category D Felony punishable by imprisonment of one to four years and fine up to $5,000. (445.334). Knowing false representation on any required document or tampering with monitoring devices is gross misdemeanor punishable by fine up to $10,000 or imprisonment up to one year, or both. (445.337).

Air.—Violators of air pollution control law may be subject to administrative fine of up to $10,000 for each day of violation. Lesser violations subject to administrative fine not exceeding $500. (445.601). Violation of motor vehicle pollution control regulations is misdemeanor. (445.710).

Solid Waste.—Person violating state board of health regulation or local ordinance guilty of misdemeanor. (444.610).

Permits.—

Water.—Department of Conservation and Natural Resources may grant renewable permits for fixed terms up to five years which must specify appropriate quantitative limitations of authorized discharges or injection of fluid through well. (445.227). No permit may be granted to discharge or inject fluid through well of any radiological, chemical or biological warfare agent or high-level radioactive waste, to discharge material which would substantially impair anchorage and navigation, to discharge material inconsistently with area waste treatment plan or with commission regulations. (445.224). Permits to discharge radioactive, or hazardous waste can be obtained (445.287), but applicant must deposit security to assure compliance with terms and conditions (445.294). Department may grant, deny or waive certification of applicant if federal license or permit is required. (445.284).

Air.—State environmental commission may require operating permits for any source of air contaminant. (445.491). Owner or operator of source of air contaminant or person desiring to establish such source may apply to commission for variance from regulations. (445.506).

Utilities.—Person, other than local government, must obtain permit from public service commission before commencing to construct utility facility in state. (704.865).

ESTATES AND TRUSTS

ADMINISTRATION:

See topic Executors and Administrators.

ADVANCEMENTS:

See topic Descent and Distribution.

ALLOWANCES:

See topic Executors and Administrators.

CLAIMS:

See topic Executors and Administrators; category Civil Actions and Procedure, topic Pleading.

DEATH:

There is a disputable presumption that a person not heard from for three years is dead. (47.250).

Death Certificate.—See category Documents and Records, topic Records, subhead Vital Statistics.

Uniform Anatomical Gift Act adopted with amendments. (451.500-451.585). Hospitals must establish policies to identify potential donors, and at or near time of death of donor obtain necessary consent. (451.577).

Survivorship.—Uniform Simultaneous Death Act adopted. (135.010-135.090).

As to survival of action or cause of action notwithstanding death of party, see category Civil Actions and Procedure, topic Actions.

Action for death may be brought by guardian of deceased ward or by heirs or personal representatives of decedent (12.090; 41.085) provided same is commenced within two years after death (11.190). In action by heirs, may recover damages for grief, loss of support, companionship, consortium and decedent's pain and suffering which damages are not liable for decedent's debts. In action by personal representative, may recover as special damages, expenses decedent incurred and any penalties, including punitive damages, decedent would have recovered if he lived, which damages are liable for decedent's debts unless otherwise exempt. Personal representative of person insured under life insurance policy may recover all damages resulting from act that constitutes unfair practice pursuant to 686A.310. In action against personal representative, may recover any damages that would have been awarded if decedent lived, except punitive damages. (41.085, 41.100).

Right to Die.—See topic Wills, subhead Living Wills.

See also topic Executors and Administrators, subhead Special Administrator; categories Civil Actions and Procedure, topic Actions, subhead Abatement; Employment, topic Labor Relations, subhead Workmen's Compensation Act.

DECEDENTS' ESTATES:

See topics Descent and Distribution, Executors and Administrators, Wills; category Debtor and Creditor, topic Homesteads.

DESCENT AND DISTRIBUTION:

See also topic Executors and Administrators.

In absence of limitation by marriage contract, separate real and personal estate of an intestate decedent, or if there is a surviving spouse the excess over the share of such spouse, descends and is distributed as follows, each class of which a member is living taking to the exclusion of subsequent classes: (1) Child or children and descendants of deceased children, equally if all of the same degree and otherwise according to right of representation; (2) parents equally or all to surviving parent; (3) brothers and sisters and children of deceased brothers and sisters according to right of representation; (4) next of kin of equal degree except that those claiming through the nearest ancestor take to the exclusion of those of equal degree claiming through a more remote ancestor. (134.030-134.110). No person convicted of murder of decedent is entitled to succeed to any portion of estate. (134.007).

If decedent left more than one child or one child and issue of one or more deceased children, and a child dies unmarried and before attaining majority, the share of such child descends to the other children and issue of deceased children, equally if all of the same degree and otherwise according to the right of representation. (134.080).

Surviving spouse takes the following share of the separate estate, real and personal, of the deceased spouse: (1) One-third if decedent left more than one child, one child and descendants of one or more deceased children or descendants of two or more deceased children; (2) one-half if decedent left one child, descendants of one child, parent or parents, brother or sister, or child or children of deceased brother or sister; (3) all if decedent left none of the aforementioned relatives. (134.040-134-050). As to disposition of community property see category Family, topic Husband and Wife.

Posthumous children are considered as living at death of parent. (134.140).

Illegitimate Child.—Obligation of parent is enforceable against his estate in such amount as court may determine. (126.-281).

Adopted Children.—See category Family, topic Adoption.

Advancements are regarded as part of the estate for purposes of distribution, and must be taken by the heir receiving the same as or towards his share. But no gift is deemed an advancement unless so expressed in the gift or charged in writing by the decedent as an advancement or acknowledged in writing by the heir to be such. (151.120-151.130).

Community Property.—As to disposition thereof in case of death of either spouse, see category Family, topic Husband and Wife.

Petition for Distribution.—The executor or administrator, the heirs, assignees, etc., may petition for their share of estate after three months from issuance of letters, on giving bond to secure creditors unless court dispenses with same (151.010), or when final account is settled (151.080). Customary procedure is for executor or administrator to petition for distribution in connection with final account.

Escheat.—In absence of heirs, property escheats to the state, but after-discovered heir may sue for property or proceeds within six years. In case of an infant or person of unsound mind, suit may be brought within five years after removal of the disability. (134.120, 154.120).

ESTATES:

See category Property, topic Real Property.

EXECUTORS AND ADMINISTRATORS:

District courts have exclusive jurisdiction of administration. Wills may be proved and letters testamentary or of administration granted in county in which decedent resided at time of death, and court of such county has exclusive jurisdiction. Estate of nonresident may be administered in any county where part of estate may be, and court to which application first made has exclusive jurisdiction. (136.010).

Preferences in Right to Administer.—Right to administration of intestate estate is in following order: (1) Surviving spouse; (2) children; (3) father or mother; (4) brother or sister; (5) grandchildren; (6) any kindred entitled to share in estate; (7) creditors; (8) public administrator; (9) other kindred within fourth degree; (10) any other person legally competent. (139.040). If anyone above is Nevada resident, he has right to appointment, and if he nominates Nevada resident for appointment, nominee's priority is same as that of nominator. (139.040). As among persons having equal right to administer relatives of whole blood are preferred to those of half blood (139.060), or court may, in its discretion, grant letters to one or more of such persons (139.070). Persons in each class have right to nominate others to be appointed in their stead. (139.050). Partner of decedent may not be appointed if anyone objects. (139.030).

When letters of administration have been granted to any person other than surviving husband or wife, child, father, mother, brother or sister of an intestate, any one of them may obtain revocation of the letters by a petition praying revocation and that letters be issued to him or her. (139.140).

Competency.—Woman (married or unmarried) may act as executor or administrator. (138.020, 138.030, 139.010, 139.020). Minor cannot act, nor can one who has been convicted of felony or adjudged by court incompetent because of drunkenness, improvidence or want of integrity or understanding, nor can one not a resident of Nevada act as an administrator. (138.020; 139.010). Any person interested may contest application for letters on ground of incompetency of applicant, by filing written opposition, or may assert his own right and pray for letters. (138.060, 139.110).

No organization other than domestic organization having its principal place of business in this state or is depository institution authorized to operate in this state or national banking association having its principal place of business in this state may be appointed executor, to act as fiduciary unless it associates as co-fiduciary bank whose principal place of business is in this state or national bank or trust company organized under laws

See note at head of Digest as to 1998 legislation covered.

See Topical Index in front part of this volume.

EXECUTORS AND ADMINISTRATORS . . . *continued*
of and has principal place of business in another state which allows reciprocity is authorized by its charter to act as fiduciary, and appoints Secretary of State as its attorney for service of process. (662.245).

Foreign bank cannot act as executor unless it associates as co-executor Nevada bank, but may appoint substitute executor, without association, provided appointee is Nevada resident. (138.020).

Administrator c. t. a. may be appointed where executors fall or refuse to act. (138.020). Executor of deceased executor may not administer estate of first testator but administrator c.t.a. must be appointed. (138.070). Administrator c.t.a. has same powers as conferred upon executor by law; otherwise, no discretionary powers. (138.090). On probate of foreign will, executor named therein may nominate administrator c.t.a. (136.260).

Special administrator may be appointed to collect, take charge of and preserve estate where there is delay in granting letters, where letters have been granted irregularly, where no petition for letters is filed, or in any other proper case. (140.010). He must give such bond as court may direct. (140.030). Appointment of special administrator to prosecute right of action for wrongful death of decedent is valid in Nevada, even though right of action is not an asset of estate. Bringing of action is not part of administration of estate and proceeds realized are held for benefit of persons entitled thereto. (83 Nev. 208, 427 P.2d 383).

Public administrator may apply for letters on estate subject to administration in his county where heirs or next of kin named in statute do not petition therefor. (139.040).

Issuance of Letters.—Letters of administration are issued to applicant on petition, after notice and hearing (139.090-139.100), upon proof of death and intestacy (139.120). Letters testamentary are issued upon probate of will. (138.010). Before letters issue, executor or administrator must file with county clerk written statement containing his name and permanent address at which process may be served. (143.190).

Removal.—Executor or administrator may be removed for: failure to furnish sufficient bond (142.100); failure to file inventory (144.080); failure to render account (150.080); absconding or concealing himself (150.140); or waste, conversion, fraud, neglect, unreasonable delay, or incompetence to act (141.090).

Oath and Bond.—Requirement of bond for executor or administrator is discretionary with court. No bond required of banking corporation or trust company doing business in state unless court requires. Any person with interest in estate exceeding $10,000 may demand bond. Amount of bond is to be value of personal property plus one year income from all property, unless will provides otherwise, or court so orders. (142.010-142.020).

Exemption from Bond.—Bond may be required despite provisions of will. (142.070).

Inventory.—Within 60 days after his appointment, executor or administrator must file an inventory and appraisement. (140.010). Executor or administrator may engage disinterested appraisers. Where no reasonable doubt as to value of assets such as money, bank deposits, securities, bonds, or life insurance policies, executor or administrator must file verified record of value in lieu of appraisement. (144.020). Inventory must include all of estate of deceased wherever situated; statement of all debts, partnerships and other interests; also what portion of estate is community property and separate property. (144.040).

Powers, Duties and Liabilities.—Executor or administrator has right of possession of assets, is entitled to rents and profits of real estate until estate settled or real estate given to heirs by court order and must make necessary repairs (143.020); must collect debts due decedent (143.030); without court's approval: may place estate funds in U.S. treasury notes, bills, or bonds, negotiable commercial paper not exceeding 180 days maturity, bankers' acceptances, savings accounts, or as authorized by law or a will (143.175); with court's approval; may compromise with debtor unable to pay in full, in cases where estate is benefited, and may extend, renew or modify terms of any obligation owing to decedent (143.140); may hold stock in name of nominee without mention thereof in stock certificate or registration book if his records show such holding and nominee has signed a statement showing true interest of administrator or executor, but he is personally liable for any loss resulting from act of nominee with regard to the stock (143.187); may convey real property covered by decedent's written contract, either on judgment in suit against him and persons interested in estate or on order in estate matter after report and proof of contract and performance by vendee (149.110); with court's approval may borrow money and mortgage real property (149.010-149.050), sell property in general (148.010-148.160), personal property (148.170-148.210), real property (148.220-148.320), and mining property (148.360-148.400); and lease property (149.060-149.100); is not liable for debts uncollected without his fault and cannot profit by increase of estate and is not chargeable with loss without his fault (150.070); and cannot directly or indirectly purchase property of estate (143.170). Business of decedent may be continued by fiduciary on court order. (143.050).

Executor or administrator must close estate within 18 months after appointment. If claim against estate in litigation, or amount of federal estate tax has not been determined, court on petition shall order certain amount of assets be returned and remainder of estate be distributed. If contest of will or proceeding to determine heirship pending, court may order partial distribution or for good cause order that entire estate be retained. (143.037). Executor or administrator of estate not closed must file explanation with court within six months of appointment if no federal estate tax return required, within 15 months if federal return required and court must set hearing to determine if reasonable diligence has been used in administration of estate. (143.035).

Notice to Creditors.—An executor or administrator must, publish and mail notice to creditors whose names are readily ascertainable. (147.010). Notice by publication must be in newspaper published in county where probate pending or, if none, in paper of general circulation; publication must occur on three dates and, if paper published more than once a week, must be more than ten days between first and last dates of publication. In addition, as soon as practical after appointment, copy of notice must be mailed to creditors whose names and addresses are readily ascertainable and to State Welfare Administrator. Notice must advise creditors to file claims within 90 days after mailing or first publication. (155.020).

Where summary administration has been ordered, notice to creditors must be given in accordance with 155.020, above; however, claims must be filed within 60 days after mailing or first publication of notice. (145.050, 145.060).

Presentation of Claims.—Unless a claim is filed as required in the notice to creditors it is absolutely barred, unless it is made satisfactorily to appear, by affidavit, that claimant had no notice, in which case it may be filed any time before filing of final account. (145.060, 147.040).

Secured claim need not be filed to protect security, but must be filed in order to protect excess over security, which excess, if any, ranks with general claims against estate. (25 Nev. 378.60 Pac. 834).

Claim on which action was pending when decedent died must be presented. (147.100).

Proof of Claims.—Every claim filed of $250 or more must be supported by affidavit of claimant that amount is justly due, or if claim is not yet due, that amount is just demand and will be due on . . . . day of . . . . . , that no payments have been made thereon which are not credited, that there are no offsets to same to knowledge of claimant or other affiant. Every claim filed with clerk must contain mailing address of claimant and any written notice mailed by executor or administrator to claimant is proper notice. When affidavit is made by any other person than claimant, reasons why it is not made by claimant must be set forth in affidavit. Oath may be taken before any person authorized to administer oaths. Amount of interest must be computed and included in statement of claim and rate determined. Court may for good cause shown, allow defective affidavit to be corrected or amended on application any time before final account. (147.070).

When claim is founded on written instrument, original need not be filed, but copy with all indorsements may be attached to claim filed. (147.080).

If mortgagor dies, mortgagee must file the original mortgage or a certified copy from record, attached to claim, and in absence thereof right to deficiency judgment is deemed waived. (147.080).

Approval or Rejection of Claims.—Within 15 days after time for filing claims has expired, executor or administrator must either pass on same, and allow or reject or file notice of allowance or rejection, and within five days after said 15 days, he must present all allowed claims to district judge for his approval or rejection. Refusal or neglect of executor or administrator to endorse allowance or rejection on claim or a failure to file notice is deemed rejection, but claim may nevertheless be allowed by executor or administrator at any time before final accounting. (147.110).

Payment of Claims.—Claims which are approved by the judge rank as acknowledged debts of the estate and are paid in due course of administration. (147.120). Payment may be enforced by petition to the court.

Executor or administrator must pay expenses of funeral and last illness, family allowance, money owed to Dept. of Human Resources as result of payments for Medicaid, and wage claims as soon as funds are available, but may retain sufficient for expenses of administration; executor or administrator may, without court approval, pay debts of $500 or less if proper claim filed, debt is due and estate is solvent; executor or administrator need not pay other debts until ordered by court. (150.230).

Claims bear interest from date of filing at rate equal to prime rate at largest bank in Nevada as ascertained by commissioner of financial institutions unless different rate is applicable.(147.220).

Amount of unmatured claim is paid into court to await maturity. (150.250).

Priorities.—Charges against estates are payable in the following order: (1) Funeral expenses; (2) expenses of last illness; (3) family allowance; (4) debts having preference by laws of the United States; (5) money owed to Department of Human Resources resulting from payment of benefits for Medicaid; (6) wages up to $600 for services within 120 days of death; (7) judgments and mortgages in order of their date, mortgage preference extending only to proceeds of mortgaged property; (8) all other demands. (150.220). If secured claim exceeds security, creditor prorates with other creditors as to excess. If estate is insolvent, creditors of each class must be paid in full before creditors of any subsequent class receive anything, and creditors of same class are paid pro rata if assets are insufficient to pay all in full. (150.240).

Compromise of Claims.—After time for filing claims, executor or administrator may with court approval, compromise any claim. (147.180).

Sales.—Perishable property, property liable to depreciate and personal property necessary for family allowances may be sold by representative without notice. (148.170). Stocks and bonds may be sold without confirmation on order of court. (148.180). Sale as directed by will may be made with or without notice as executor determines. (148.080). Personal property may be sold without notice in summary administration. (148.190).

Sales may be made when necessary to pay debts, legacies, family allowances or expenses or when for best interest of estate, and there is no preference between real and personal property. Sale may be either public or private. (148.010-148.050). Sale of personalty must be after ten days published notice. (148.190). Notice of time and place of sale of real property must be published in newspaper published in county in which land or some portion thereof lies (or if there be none so published in such paper as court or judge may direct) for two weeks (three publications, one week apart) before day of sale, or, in case of private sale, before day on or after which sale is to be made. Where inventoried value of property does not exceed $500, publication may be dispensed with by posting notice of time and place of sale for two weeks in three of most public places in county in which land or some portion thereof lies. (148.220-148.240).

If real estate is sold on credit, the representative must take a note or notes for the unpaid purchase money secured by mortgage or deed of trust on the property; if the purchaser defaults the court may vacate the confirmation of the sale and order a resale. (148.290-148.300).

Allowances.—Widow and/or minor children may remain in homestead and possess wearing apparel, provisions and household furniture, and are entitled to reasonable provision for support. After inventory return, court may set apart homestead and exempt

See note at head of Digest as to 1998 legislation covered.

See Topical Index in front part of this volume.

NV – 24

EXECUTORS AND ADMINISTRATORS . . . *continued*
personal property for widow and/or minors, and it is not subject to administration. If property set apart is insufficient for support, a further allowance may be made, but is estate is insolvent this may not continue more than one year after granting of letters. (146.010-146.030).

Actions.—The right to sue on any claim against the estate is suspended until such claim has been filed and rejected or deemed rejected because of failure to act thereon (147.150), except that action may be brought to enforce a secured claim against the security without filing a claim provided the complaint waives all recourse against other property of the estate (147.150).

If claim is rejected, executor or administrator must immediately notify holder, who must bring suit within 60 days thereafter, whether or not claim is due, or, if claim filed by Welfare Division of Dept. of Human Resources, file petition for summary proceeding within 20 days thereafter, failing in which claim is forever barred. (147.130). If claim on which action was pending when decedent died is rejected, executor or administrator may be substituted as defendant. (147.100). Actions against estates of decedents are within exclusive original jurisdiction of district courts, regardless of amount involved. (Const. Art. 6, §6; 4.370).

Executor or administrator may sue or be sued to recover property, to quiet title and on decedent's contracts. He may sue for waste, destruction. taking or conversion of goods of decedent and for trespass and may be sued for similar acts of decedent. (143.060).

Fraudulent Conveyances.—In case of deficiency of assets, an executor or administrator may sue to recover property (real or personal) fraudulently conveyed by decedent. Property recovered may be sold for benefit of creditors. (143.150).

Accounting and Settlement.—Executor or administrator must file first account within 30 days after judge has acted on claims; intermediate accounts when deemed advisable or directed by court; and final account when estate is ready to be closed. (150.080, 150.090). All interested persons must be given notice of hearing of petition for final distribution, individually by mail to persons entitled, including Administrator of Welfare Division of Dept. of Human Resources, and to public by publication once weekly for two weeks before hearing. (151.090, 155.020). Where property is undelivered executor or administrator must render annual account. (151.200).

Distribution.—It is customary to file petition for distribution with final account, but after three months from issuance of letters any heir, devisee or legatee may petition for his share of the estate. If, on hearing after notice, it appears that estate is little indebted and that petition may be granted without injury to creditors, it may be granted on petitioner giving bond for his proportionate share of debts. (151.010, 151.040).

Distribution if Abroad.—No statutory provision as to distribution of funds payable to a distributee to whom payment is not feasible except that estate escheats to state where no distributee capable of inheriting. (154.010).

Community property may, or may not, be subject to administration in ordinary manner according to the circumstances. (See category Family, topic Husband and Wife.)

When Administration Unnecessary.—See subhead Small Estates, infra.

Small Estates.—Provision is made for summary administration of estates not exceeding $200,000 (145.010-145.100) and for dispensing with administration where estate does not exceed $50,000 (146.070). Order for summary administration dispenses with regular proceedings and notices except for notice of petition for probate and issuance of letters, notice to creditors which must be both mailed and published, and notice for application of attorney's fees and provides for inventory and appraisal or record of value. Notice is given by publication, or as otherwise ordered by court when publication cost exceeds $25. (145.050). Creditors must file claims with clerk within 60 days after mailing or first publication. Executor or administrator must act on claims within ten days thereafter. (145.060).

Proceedings to set aside estate without administration are originated by verified petition describing decedent's property, estimating value, listing liens and recorded encumbrances, stating known debts of decedent, and identifying heirs, devisees and legatees. Petitioner must give notice by registered or certified mail to heirs, devisees and legatees. (145.070).

Compensation of administrator, and of executor unless specific compensation is provided by the will, is at following rates on estate accounted for: 4% on first $15,000, 3% on next $85,000 and 2% on excess over 100,000. If there are two or more executors or administrators, compensation is apportioned. (150.020). Further allowances for extraordinary services such as management, sales, litigation and services concerning realty may be made by court. (150.030). Contracts for compensation higher than that allowed by statute are void. (150.040).

Claim against executor is not affected by his being named as such in the will, but his commissions must be applied on his debt to the estate. (144.050).

Attorney's Fees.—Attorney for executor or administrator in charge of decedent's estate is entitled to reasonable compensation paid out of estate, in amount agreed to by attorney and executor or administrator, or in absence of agreement, set by court. (150.060).

Foreign executors or administrators have no power over the decedent's estate in Nevada. See also topic Wills, subhead Foreign Probated Wills.

Uniform Fiduciaries Act adopted. (162.010-162.140).

Uniform Principal and Income Act (Revised) adopted. (164.140 et seq.).

Uniform Simplification of Fiduciary Security Transfers Act adopted (162.150-162.250) and not repealed by Uniform Commercial Code (104.8108).

Uniform Anatomical Gift Act adopted with amendments. (451.500-451.585).

INTESTACY:

See topic Descent and Distribution.

PROOF OF CLAIMS:

See topic Executors and Administrators; category Civil Actions and Procedure, topic Pleading.

TRUSTS:

May be created by will, by operation of law or by deed or conveyance in writing subscribed by trustor or his lawful agent authorized in writing. (111.205). Certain powers of trustee may be incorporated by reference to statute. (163.260). District court has jurisdiction over confirmation of trustee on petition and thereafter over administration. (164.010-164.040). Upon motion of trustee with concurrence of beneficiaries, district court having jurisdiction may transfer supervision of trust to another judicial district in state, or to any court outside state which accepts jurisdiction over trust, when it appears desirable to parties concerned. (164.130).

Testamentary Trusts.—The district court retains a limited jurisdiction over trusts created by will, including life estates and estates for years to be administered by fiduciaries after decree of distribution, for the purposes of settlement of the trustee's accounts and distribution of the residue under the terms of the trust. The trustee or fiduciary may petition the court for instructions from time to time, upon giving the notice prescribed for similar proceedings taken by executors or administrators prior to final distribution. (153.020-153.040).

Spendthrift trusts are authorized and regulated. (166.010-166.160).

Trust Companies.—A domestic corporation formed under the banking act with trust company powers may act as trustee. (662.235). Domestic bank, authorized depository institution, national banking association whose principal place of business is in this state, or national bank or banking corporation organized under laws and has its principal place of business in another state that allows reciprocity, and is authorized by its charter to act as fiduciary, and appoints Secretary of State as its agent for service of process may act as fiduciary. Nonresident bank may act as trustee if it associates as cofiduciary with domestic bank. (662.245).

Trust companies not engaged in banking business regulated in detail. (669.010 et seq.).

Uniform Principal and Income Act (Revised) adopted. (164.140-164.370).

Uniform Fiduciaries Act adopted excluding §3. (162.010-162.140).

Uniform Simplification of Fiduciary Security Transfers Act adopted. (162.150). See category Business Regulation and Commerce, topic Securities.

Uniform Trusts Act adopted (163.010-163.210), with following variations: §2 is omitted; §§6 and 7 are modified by adding, at the end of each "of a trustee, except with the approval of the district court having jurisdiction of the trust estate and of the accounting thereof." Also, §6 is amended to permit banks and corporate trustees to sell certain securities to themselves as fiduciaries. (163.060).

Investments.—In the management and investment of trust property, a trustee is required only to exercise the judgment which persons of ordinary intelligence use in managing their own affairs with a view to probable safety. Subject to express limitation in the trust instrument, investment may be made in any kind of property, including corporate bonds, debentures, and stocks, preferred and common. Propriety of investment decision determined by what trustee knew or should have known at time of decision about nature and expected performance of investment attributes of portfolio, general economy, and needs and objectives of beneficiaries at time of decision. In determining any liability for performance of investment consideration given to performance of particular investment and portfolio as whole. (164.050). Trust funds may be invested in bonds of federal agencies. (164.065).

Securities in Name of Nominee.—A fiduciary may hold stock in the name of a nominee if all records, accounts and reports of trustee clearly show the ownership and the facts of its holding and nominee has deposited with trustee a signed statement showing the trust ownership. Trustee is personally liable for loss resulting from acts of the nominee. (163.090).

Accounting.—Uniform Trustees' Accounting Act adopted (165.010-165.250), with provision that trustee of a nontestamentary trust must annually furnish each beneficiary entitled to receive income under trust and surety on trustee's bond with account of trust (165.135).

Actions.—Trustee of express trust may sue without joining beneficiary. (N.R.C.P. 17[a]). Court may allow costs out of trust fund or against trustee personally for mismanagement or bad faith in action or defense. (18.090).

Compensation of trustees is fixed by the court. (153.070).

Accumulations.—There are no statutory limitations on accumulations of income.

Perpetuities.—See topic Wills; category Property, topic Perpetuities.

Pour Over Trusts.—See topic Wills, subhead Bequests and Devises to Inter Vivos Trusts.

Gifts to Minors.—See category Family, topic Infants.

WILLS:

Every person over 18 years of age, of sound mind may dispose of his or her estate by will. Married women may dispose of both their separate property and interest in the community property. (133.020-133.030). Certain powers of fiduciaries may be incorporated by reference to statutes. (163.260).

Testamentary Disposition.—There are no limitations on power to dispose of property except such as result from husband's right to manage and deal with community property after death of wife and from rights of family of decedent with respect to homestead (see category Debtor and Creditor, topic Homesteads) and personal property exempt from execution. (133.020-133.030).

Execution.—No will except a holographic or nuncupative will is valid unless it is in writing, signed by the testator or by some person in his presence and by his express direction, and attested by two competent witnesses subscribing their names to the will in the presence of the testator. There is no required statutory form of attestation clause. (133.040).

Testator or executor may request a self-proving affidavit from any or all attesting witnesses, executed within or without the state, before any person qualified to administer oaths, written on will or attached thereto in following form:

See note at head of Digest as to 1998 legislation covered.

See Topical Index in front part of this volume.

NV – 25

WILLS . . . *continued*

Form

STATE OF . . . . } ss.
COUNTY OF . . . . }

(Date) . . . .

Then and there personally appeared the within named . . . . and . . . ., who, being duly sworn, depose and say: That they witnessed the execution of the within will of the within named testator, ...; that said testator subscribed said will and declared the same to be his last will and testament in their presence; that they thereafter subscribed the same as witnesses in the presence of said testator and in the presence of each other and at the request of said testator; that the said testator at the time of the execution of said will appeared to them to be of full age and of sound mind and memory, and that they make this affidavit at the request of said testator.

. . . .
. . . .

Subscribed and sworn to before me this . . . . day of . . . ., 19. . .

. . . . (Stamp)
Notary Public (133.050).

Nuncupative Wills.—A nuncupative or verbal will is valid if the estate bequeathed does not exceed in value $1,000, if proved by the testimony of two witnesses who were present at the making thereof, if the testator at the making of the same bid some one present bear witness that such was his will, during his last sickness. It must be proved within six months, and the substance reduced to writing, within 30 days after testamentary words were spoken. (133.100, 136.080).

Holographic Wills.—Property may be disposed of and taken under wills entirely written, dated and signed by the hand of the testator. Such wills shall be valid and have full effect for the purpose for which they are intended. A holographic will is subject to no other form than that it be written entirely by the hand of the testator himself. It may be made in or out of this state, and need not be witnessed. It may be proved in same manner as other private writings. (133.030, 133.090, 136.190).

Revocation.—A will may be revoked by burning, tearing, cancellation, or obliteration with the intention of effecting a revocation, or by the due execution of another will or codicil, or by implication of law from changes in the testator's condition or circumstances. (133.120).

If a person marries after making a will, and the spouse survives the maker, the will is revoked as to the spouse, unless the latter is provided for in the marriage contract or the will, or is mentioned in the will in such a way as to show an intention not to make provision; and no other evidence may be received to rebut the presumption of revocation. (133.110).

Revival.—If after making a will the testor executes a second one, the destruction, canceling, or revocation of the second does not revive the first, unless a contrary intention appears from terms of revocation, or unless after such revocation first is duly reexecuted. (133.130).

Gifts to a subscribing witness are void unless there are two other competent witnesses to the will, but a mere charge on estate for payment of debts does not prevent a creditor from being a competent witness. (133.060-133.070).

Probate and Contest.—Will may be proved in the district court of the county in which the testator resided at the time of his death. May be contested prior to and subsequent to probate. (137.010-137.130).

Self-proved Wills.—See subhead Execution, supra.

Foreign Probated Wills.—Uniform Foreign Executed Wills Act (133.080) has been adopted. When copy of certified probated will filed in clerk's office with petition for letters, notice of hearing will be given and proceedings will be same as if original will had been probated. (136.270). Presentation for probate may be made by nominee of executor. (136.260). Ancillary probate is only recognized method of establishing title under a foreign probated will.

Bequests and Devises to Inter Vivos Trusts.—Uniform Testamentary Additions to Trusts Act adopted. Any devise or bequest subject to Nevada law may be made by will to existing trust established by testator if trust is identified in will and its terms are set forth in a written instrument executed before or concurrently with execution of will. No gift is invalid because trust is amendable or revocable, but termination of trust before death of testator causes gift to lapse. (163.220-163.250).

Legacies.—Court directs payment of legacies when all liabilities of the estate have been paid. (150.280). Legatees may petition for their share of estate after three months from issuance of letters, on giving bond to secure creditors (151.010), or when final account is settled (151.080-151.100). There is no provision for interest on legacies.

Unclaimed Legacies.—Estates escheat to the state when any person dies within the state and leaves no heirs, representatives, devisees or legatees capable of inheriting or holding the estate. (154.010).

Lapse.—A devise or bequest to a child or other relation of the testator, when the devisee or legatee dies before the testator, leaving lineal descendants, does not lapse, but the descendants take the estate in the same manner as the devisee or legatee would have taken had he survived, in the absence of a contrary provision in the will. (133.200).

Children.—Where will omits to provide for any child of testator or for issue of any deceased child, it shall be presumed that omission was intentional. Should court find that omission was unintentional, such child or issue of any deceased child shall have same share in estate of testator as if he or she had died intestate. (133.170). Children born after making of will shall receive intestate share unless contrary intent is expressed in will. (133.160).

Election.—The surviving spouse has no right of election to take under the intestacy law and against the will.

Divorced Spouse.—Divorce or annulment of marriage of testator revokes every devise, legacy, or interest given to testator's former spouse by will executed before decree unless separate property agreement or former will is approved by court in divorce proceedings. (133.115).

Simultaneous Death.—See topic Death, subhead Survivorship.

Testamentary Trusts.—See topic Trusts.

Uniform Anatomical Gift Act adopted with changes. (451.500-451.585).

Living Wills.—Adult person may voluntarily execute declaration in same manner as will is executed, except witnesses cannot be attending physician or related to declarant, directing that when he is in terminal condition and becomes comatose or incapable of communicating with attending physicians, life sustaining procedures be withheld or withdrawn. (449.600).

FAMILY

ADOPTION:

Any adult person who is ten years older than person adopted (127.020) and who has resided within this state during six months prior to granting adoption (127.060) may adopt a minor. Petition for adoption of child who currently resides in home of petitioners may be filed after child has lived in home for 30 days (127.110), however, no order or decree of adoption may be made until after child has lived for six months in petitioner's home (127.150). If petitioner is married other spouse must join in petition. (127.030). Adoption of younger adults by adults permitted by agreement approved by decree of adoption of district court of county where either person resides. (127.190).

Consent Required.—Consent of minor child is required if over 14 years of age. (127.020). Written consent of minor's parents or living parent or guardian is necessary. (127.040). Consent must be in writing and acknowledged by person consenting. (127.040). Parental consent is unnecessary if parent has been incurably insane for two years (127.040) or when parental rights have been terminated by order of court (127.090).

Adoption of adults by adults requires only consent of spouses, if capable, of adopting and to be adopted adults. (127.200).

No consent is valid unless it is in writing, signed by persons consenting, acknowledged in form required for conveyances, contains names of persons to whom consent is given, attested by two competent disinterested witnesses who may sign affidavits showing due execution in form prescribed by statute, one of which must be social worker as defined if neither petitioner nor spouse related to child within third degree of consanguinity, and true copy of such consent is delivered to division of child and family services of department of human resources ("division"). (127.053-127.057).

Relinquishments.—Specified agencies may accept relinquishments for adoption from parent or guardian and give the consent thereto. (127.050). Relinquishment must be in writing and acknowledged by person relinquishing and such writing is generally irrevocable. (127.040; 127.080). Relinquishment by minor parent is irrevocable upon coming of age. (127.080).

Petition.—Two or more brothers and sisters may be adopted in one petition. (127.060). The district court of any county is a proper court in which to make application. The petition is filed in duplicate with the county clerk, who transmits copy of petition to division for investigation unless petitioner, or spouse of petitioner, and child are related within third degree of consanguinity where court may waive such investigation which order waiving investigation must be sent to welfare division by petitioners within seven days after entry. (127.120). Division or designated agency must submit report within 30 days after receipt of copy of petition or before child lived in home of petitioners for six months, whichever is later, but if court is dissatisfied with it independent investigation may be ordered. (127.120). Any placement for adoption may be terminated by mutual consent of petitioners and adoption agency, or order of district court on application of agency when agency feels placement is detrimental to interests of child. (127.051).

Petition for adoption of child who currently resides in home may be filed at any time after child has lived in petitioner's home for 30 days. (127.110).

Contents of petition must include: Full names, age, and length of residency within state of petitioners, age of child and length of time child has lived in petitioner's home, proposed adoptive parent or parents, desire or not to have name of child changed, desire to establish parent and child relationship, and sworn representation that proposed adoptive parents are fit and proper persons for such relationship, have complied with requirements of law, have financial ability to care for and support child, and whether child is Indian child. (127.110).

Petition for adoption of adults by adults filed in district court of county where either resides. Court may require investigation by division. Petition prays for approval of adoption agreement. (127.210).

Hearings.—The hearings and agencies' reports are confidential. (127.140).

Appeal.—An appeal lies to the Supreme Court. (127.180).

Decree or Order.—The effect of the decree or order of adoption is to vest in the parties the same legal rights as though the child were the natural child of the adoptive parents. There is a complete severance of legal ties between the natural parent or parents and their next of kin. (127.160).

Effect of Adoption.—Upon adoption child becomes legal child of adopting parents and they become legal parents with rights and duties of natural parents of legitimate child.

Adopted child inherits from adoptive parents or relative the same as though he were legitimate. If child dies intestate, adoptive parents and relatives inherit his estate. After adoption, natural parents of adopted child are relieved of parental responsibility and have no rights over adopted child or property. Adopted child will not inherit from natural parents or kindred nor does he owe them any legal duty. (127.160).

See note at head of Digest as to 1998 legislation covered.

See Topical Index in front part of this volume.

NV – 26

ALIMONY:

See topic Divorce.

COMMUNITY PROPERTY:

See topic Husband and Wife.

DESERTION:

See topics Divorce, Husband and Wife.

DIVORCE:

Grounds for Absolute Divorce.—(1) Insanity existing for two years prior to commencement of action; (2) spouses living separate, apart and without cohabitation for one year; (3) incompatibility. (125.010).

Legal Separation.—There is no provision for divorce a mensa et thoro. As to separate maintenance see topic Husband and Wife.

Residence Requirements.—Unless the cause of action accrued within the county where the action is brought while both plaintiff and defendant were actually domiciled therein, no court has jurisdiction to grant a divorce unless either plaintiff or defendant has been a resident of the state for not less than six weeks preceding the commencement of the action. (125.020).

Mere intention to make residence in Nevada is insufficient. There must also be actual, physical presence within the state for the required time (10.020), corroborated by credible local witness (54.010).

Jurisdiction of matrimonial actions is in the district courts. (125.020).

Venue is county in which cause for divorce accrued, or in which defendant resides or is found, or in which plaintiff resides, or in which parties last cohabited, or in any county if plaintiff has resided within state for six weeks. (125.020. See 56 Nev. 467, 56 P.2d 147).

Change of Venue.—See category Civil Actions and Procedure, topic Venue.

Process.—Personal service of summons and a copy of complaint is made upon defendant in person within state when he can be there found; or, when defendant cannot be served personally, then by publication of summons for period of four weeks in newspaper to be designated by court in its order and also by mailing to defendant at his place of residence, a copy of summons and complaint. Personal service upon defendant wherever he may be outside of state, is equivalent to publication of summons and mailing a copy of summons and complaint. (N.R.C.P. 4).

Appearance of the defendant by attorney or in person is the equivalent of personal service of the summons within the state. (N.R.C.P. 12).

Where a default decree has been entered, the defendant may thereafter, on written consent of plaintiff, enter a general appearance in the action with the same effect as if entered before trial. Thereupon court may make modified decree showing such general appearance and enter same nunc pro tunc as of date of original decree. Parties may stipulate for further modification of decree. (N.R.C.P. 60).

Pleading.—The complaint of the plaintiff or the cross-complaint or counterclaim of the defendant must be verified and may state cause or causes for divorce upon which party or parties rely, in words of statute. (125.020-125-030).

Defendant has 20 days after completion of publication and mailing or personal service without the state in which to answer. (N.R.C.P. 4).

Bills of Particulars.—Where the grounds for divorce are pleaded in the words of the statute, either party, after appearance of the defendant and upon five days written demand therefor, is entitled to a bill of particulars stating in detail the facts, dates, times and occasions upon which the plaintiff or the defendant relies for cause of action, and either party may, upon motion, be required to furnish in writing a further bill of particulars upon good cause shown. Such bill or bills of particulars need not be filed, and if filed may be withdrawn upon the written consent of the parties. (125.030).

Trial.—The judge of the court determines all questions of law and fact. (125.070).

The court must, upon demand of either party, direct that the trial and issue or issues of fact joined therein be private, and upon such direction all persons, except the officers of the court, the parties, and their witnesses and counsel, must be excluded from the court or chambers wherein the action is tried. (125.080).

Where divorce is sought on the ground of insanity, the court must require corroborative evidence of the insanity of the defendant at the time of the trial. (125.010).

There is no provision for delay between the commencement of a divorce action and disposition thereof once the matter reaches issue.

Application for decree by default may be by affidavit, unless court requires testimony, that supports application and corroborates residence. If property settlement agreement, it must be identified in, and attached to, affidavit. Affidavit must be on personal knowledge, contain admissible evidence, give factual support to each allegation, and establish competency of affiant to testify. (125.123).

Judgment or decree of divorce is final. (125.130). There is no interlocutory decree. No divorce binding on parties may be attacked by third parties. (125.185).

Where it appears to court that grounds for divorce exist, court in its discretion may grant divorce to either party. (125.120).

Judgment Roll and Other Papers.—The papers and pleadings which constitute or will make up the judgment roll in an action for divorce are open to public inspection in the clerk's office. But all other papers, records, proceedings and evidence, including exhibits and transcript of the testimony must, upon the written request of either party to the action, filed with the clerk, be sealed and may not be open to inspection except to the parties or their attorneys, or when required as evidence in another action or proceeding. (125.110).

Support of Insane Spouse.—A decree of divorce granted on ground of insanity does not relieve plaintiff from contributing to support and maintenance of defendant and plaintiff may be required to give bond therefor in amount fixed by court. (125.010).

Temporary Alimony and Suit Money.—Court may require either spouse to pay other such sum necessary to provide temporary maintenance for other party or temporary support for children of parties, or to enable other party to carry on or defend divorce suit. Court may make necessary order affecting property of either spouse or both. (125.040).

Allowance for Provision of Suit.—Reasonable attorneys' fees may be awarded to either party if such fees are an issue under pleadings, whether or not application for suit money has been made. (125.150).

Permanent alimony may be granted to wife, or to husband unless premarital agreement provides otherwise. Unless otherwise decreed, alimony ceases on death of either party or remarriage of spouse to whom alimony was to be paid. (125.150).

Court may modify alimony decree or agreement upon a showing of changed circumstances whether or not modification jurisdiction was expressly retained on all decrees after July 1, 1975. Court cannot modify decree or agreement with respect to payments already accrued at the time of motion for modification. (125.150).

Arrearage default may warrant order for arrears, with costs and reasonable attorney's fees. (125.180).

Division of Property of Spouses.—Nevada is community property jurisdiction. Property rights are determined by court, which may make such disposition of community property or joint tenancy property as appears equitable (125.150) and may also set apart such portion of husband's property for wife's support, or wife's property for husband's support, or property of either spouse for support of their children as shall be deemed just and equitable (125.150). Division of interest in, or entitlement to pension or retirement benefit provided by Public Employees Retirement System is determined pursuant to 125.155.

Agreements settling property rights are favorably considered and usually approved. Property settlement agreement, made when divorce suit is pending or immediately contemplated, is not invalidated by a provision therein that it shall become effective only in event of divorce. If such contract is introduced as exhibit in a divorce action and is adopted, approved or ratified by the court, it has same force as if copied into the decree or attached thereto by reference. (123.080). To avoid merger in decree, decree should specifically provide that agreement is not merged but shall survive. (80 Nev. 386, 395 P.2d 321).

Effect on Will.—See category Estates and Trusts, topic Wills, subhead Divorced Spouse.

Change of wife's name to any former name she has legally borne may be ordered. (125.130).

Custody of Children.—Court determines matters relating to custody and support of children and at any time during minority of children may order changes of custody or support where it appears to their best interests even if divorce obtained by default. Sole consideration for court is best interests of child and there is presumption that joint custody is in best interest of child. (125.134; 125.140).

Agreements with respect to custody and support of children are favorably considered and usually approved.

Remarriage.—No restrictions.

Annulment of Marriage.—See topic Marriage.

Uniform Premarital Agreement Act adopted. (123A.010—123A.100). See topic Husband and Wife.

GUARDIAN AND WARD:

When necessary or convenient guardians of the person and estate, or either, of minors may be appointed.

Selection of Guardian.—Court shall appoint qualified person who is most suitable and is willing to serve giving consideration to: request of parent contained in will or other written instrument; request by minor 14 years of age or older; relationship by blood or marriage of proposed guardian. (159.061).

Rights of Parents to Appointment.—Parents, if qualified and suitable, shall be preferred over all others. (159.061).

Who May Apply for Appointment.—Proposed ward, governmental agency, nonprofit corporation or any concerned person may petition for appointment of guardian. (159.044).

Jurisdiction for appointment of guardian is in any court having jurisdiction of persons and estates of minors. (159.035).

Venue is in county where minor resides, or any county in which any property of minor is located if minor does not reside in this state, or county in which minor is physically present. (159.037).

Notice of hearing must be given by serving citation on spouse and adult children of incompetent, upon any person or institution having custody and control of incompetent, and incompetent. If proposed ward is minor, service shall be made upon his parents. Guardian may be appointed without court issuing citation if: Petitioner is parent seeking appointment of guardian for minor child who is in lawful custody of petitioner; if minor is 14 years of age or older petition must be accompanied by written consent of minor, or minor consents in open court; petitioner is foreign guardian of nonresident minor and petition is accompanied by authenticated copy of record of appointment and evidence of existing authority of foreign guardian. (159.047-159.049).

Qualification.—Person is not qualified to serve as a guardian who is: an incompetent, a minor, a person who has been convicted of a felony, a person suspended for misconduct or disbarred from practice of law during period of suspension or disbarment, a nonresident of this state who has not associated as co-guardian resident or banking corporation whose principal place of business is in this state, and caused appointment to be filed in guardianship proceeding. Before entering upon his duties as guardian, every guardian must execute and file bond with sufficient surety in amount to be determined by court. If banking corporation is appointed guardian of estate of ward, no bond shall be required unless specifically required by court. No bond shall be required if there are

GUARDIAN AND WARD . . . *continued*
no assets of ward. If person is appointed in will to be guardian and will provides that no bond is to be required, court may direct letters of guardianship to issue to person on his taking and subscribing oath of office and filing his name and address in proceeding. Every guardian shall take and subscribe official oath and file in guardianship proceeding his name, residence, and post office address. (159.059-159.073).

Inventory.—Guardian must file verified inventory of all property which comes to his possession or knowledge within 60 days after date of appointment and if any further property comes into his possession must file a verified supplemental inventory within 30 days. (159.085).

Powers and Duties.—Guardian of person has care, custody, and control of person and shall perform duties necessary for proper care, maintenance, education and support of ward. Guardian of estate shall protect, preserve, manage, and dispose of estate of ward according to law and for best interest of ward. Estate of ward shall be applied for proper care, maintenance, education, and support of ward and any person to whom ward owes a legal duty of support. Guardian of person and estate has authority and shall perform duties set forth above. (159.079).

Investments.—Investments may be made upon petition to court for an order authorizing investment. (159.113, 159.117).

Securities in Name of Nominee.—Guardian may hold stock in name of nominee if all records, accounts, and reports of guardian clearly show ownership and facts of its holding and nominee has deposited with guardian a signed statement showing trust ownership. Guardian is personally liable for loss resulting from acts of nominee. (159.101). See category Estates and Trusts, topic Trusts, subhead Securities in Name of Nominee.

Sale of Realty.—Real or personal property of estate may be sold by guardian in same manner as property of estate of decedent. (159.127; 159.132; 159.134). (See category Estates and Trusts, topic Executors and Administrators, subhead Sales.)

Sale of Personalty.—See subhead Sale of Realty, supra.

Liability of Guardian for Acts of Ward.—Guardian and minor ward are jointly and severally liable for injury or death to person, or injury to private or public property resulting from ward's act of willful misconduct. Liability of guardian cannot exceed $100,000. (41.470). See also topic Infants; category Transportation, topic Motor Vehicles.

Accounts.—Guardian must account annually or at such other times as court may order and ward may entitled to examine vouchers of payments made of his behalf. (159.177).

Termination of Guardianship.—Guardianship terminates when minor reaches age of majority under law of minor's domicile; on death of ward; or upon order of court, if guardianship is no longer necessary. (159.191). Age of majority is 18 years; court may declare minor who is at least 16 years of age emancipated under certain conditions. (129.010).

Compensation.—Guardian may be allowed expenses and reasonable compensation. (159.183).

Incompetent Persons.—Guardian for insane or mentally incompetent person may be appointed in similar manner and with like authority as guardian for minor. (159.035).

Foreign Guardians.—Where nonresident has a foreign guardian and no guardian has been appointed in this state, and person in this state is indebted to such nonresident, or he has property within this state capable of removal and not subject to a mortgage, pledge, lien, or other encumbrance restricting removal of property from this state, person in possession of property may deliver it, or person indebted may pay such debt, to foreign guardian. Delivery of payment constitutes a release and discharge with respect to such property of debt. Foreign guardian may be required by court to post bond in same manner as required of resident guardian and may enter orders necessary to protect secured creditors of ward and unsecured creditors of ward who are residents of this state. (159.203).

Temporary Appointment of Guardians for Minors.—Temporary guardian may be appointed for a minor by written instrument executed by parent or parents having legal custody. Any competent adult person residing in this state may be appointed. Instrument shall contain provision for its expiration on a date not more than six months after date of execution unless renewed by acknowledged writing prior to its expiration date. Absent such provision, instrument shall expire by operation of law six months after its execution. Appointment may be terminated at any time by an instrument in writing signed by either parent having legal custody of minor or by any order of a court of competent jurisdiction appointing a guardian. (159.205).

Uniform Veterans' Guardianship Act adopted. (160.010-160.190).

Guardian ad Litem.—See topic Infants.

Gifts to Minors.—See topic Infants.

Uniform Fiduciaries Act adopted. (162.010-162.140).

Uniform Simplification of Fiduciary Security Transfers Act adopted. (162.150-162.250).

HUSBAND AND WIFE:

The unity of husband and wife, and the rule that the residence of the husband is that of the wife unless, having ground for divorce she establishes a separate residence, are recognized by our courts. No action may be brought for alienation of affections or for criminal conversation that accrued after July 1, 1979. (41.380). Husband and wife cannot by agreement alter their legal relations, except as to property, and except that they may agree to immediate separation; and such agreement is not invalid because made conditional on procuring of contemplated divorce. (123.080).

Marriage Contracts.—All marriage contracts or settlements must be in writing and acknowledged or proved in same manner as deeds. (123.270). If contract affects real property, it must be recorded in office of county recorder where property located (123.280) which provides notice to all persons of contents of contract (123.290). No such contract valid as to any real property, except as between parties, until it is recorded. (123.300).

Uniform Premarital Agreement Act adopted. (123A.010-123A.100).

Tenancy of Property.—Real or personal property may be held by husband and wife in joint tenancy, tenancy in common, or as community property. (123.030).

Separate Property.—All property of each spouse owned before marriage, and all acquired afterward by gift, bequest, devise or descent, or by an award for personal injury damages, with rents, issues and profits thereof, is separate property of that spouse. (123.130). If husband and wife are living separate, earnings of minor children unless relinquished, are separate property of spouse with custody, or with whom children are living. (123.180). Written authority by one spouse to other to appropriate spouse's earnings to his own use is deemed gift and separate property. (123.190).

If married person is a resident of Nevada, an inventory of separate property, exclusive of money, duly acknowledged or proved, may be recorded in county of residence. If real property situated in another county is included in a recorded inventory, inventory must also be recorded in such other county. (123.140). Failure to file inventory for record, or omission from inventory, is prima facie evidence, as between such married person and good faith purchaser from other spouse, that property omitted or not filed is not separate property of such person. (123.160).

Contracts.—Husband and wife may contract with each other, and either or both may contract with a third person, to the same extent as if they were unmarried, subject to general rules governing persons in a confidential relationship. (123.070).

Debts and Obligations to Support.—Neither separate property of a spouse nor his share of community property is liable for debts of other spouse contracted before marriage. (123.050).

Where husband does not furnish necessaries to wife, any other person may do so and recover from husband. Separate property of husband is liable for cost of necessaries if community property is insufficient. (123.090).

Husband or wife abandoned by spouse is not liable for support of abandoning spouse until such spouse offers to return, unless abandonment was justified by misconduct of abandoned spouse. (123.100). Where there is no community property or separate property of husband, wife must support infirm husband from her separate property. (123.110).

Revised Uniform Reciprocal Enforcement of Support Act adopted. (130.010).

Conveyance or Encumbrance of Property.—Either spouse may, without consent of other spouse, convey, charge, encumber or otherwise in any manner dispose of his separate property. (123.170).

Actions.—Husband and wife may sue jointly on all causes belonging to either or both of them, except when action is for personal injuries, injured spouse is a necessary party; and when action is for compensation for services rendered, spouse having rendered services is a necessary party. (12.020).

If husband and wife are sued together, either or both may defend, and if either neglects to defend, other may defend for both. (12.030).

When suit is joint, damages must be segregated. If action is for personal injuries, damages for injuries, pain and suffering belong to injured spouse as separate property; damages for loss of comfort and society belong to spouse who suffers such loss; damages for loss of services and for medical and hospital expenses belong to spouses as community property. If action is for injury to property, damages to separate property belong to spouse owning injured property; damages to community property belong to spouses as community property. (123.121).

Desertion.—Uniform Desertion and Non-Support Act adopted. (201.020-201.080).

Separate Maintenance.—When either has been deserted for 90 days or has any cause for divorce against other, he may maintain separate maintenance action for his support and that of children. Each has much the same summary remedies as in divorce cases. (125.190-125.280).

Community Property.—All property acquired after marriage, by either husband or wife, except that acquired by gift, devise, bequest or descent, or an award for personal injury damages, with rents, issues and profits thereof, unless otherwise provided by written agreement between spouses, effective only as between them, or by a decree of separate maintenance or by other decree or written agreement, or, in case of spouse's own earnings, by written authorization from other spouse for earnings spouse to appropriate same to his own use. (123.130, 123.220).

Either spouse, acting alone, may control community property, with a like power of disposition as acting spouse has over his separate property, except that neither spouse may devise or bequeath by will more than one-half community property; neither spouse may give community property without other's consent, express or implied; community real property can be conveyed or encumbered only by an instrument executed and acknowledged by both spouses; transaction of purchase or execution of contract to purchase community real property must be joined in by both spouses; both spouses must join in a contract of sale of, or in execution of an agreement creating, a security interest, other than a purchase money security interest in community household goods, furnishings, or appliances; and neither spouse may acquire, purchase, sell, convey or encumber assets, including real property and goodwill, of a business where both spouses participate in its management without consent of other. (123.230). Husband or wife may give written power of attorney to other to sell, convey or encumber any property held as community property; except neither may devise more than one-half of community property, make gift of community property without consent of other, or sell, convey or encumber community real property unless both execute and acknowledge instrument. (123.230).

On death of either husband or wife, an undivided one-half interest in community property is property of surviving spouse and such person's sole separate property, except that no person convicted of murder of decedent may succeed to any portion of estate. Remaining interest is subject to testamentary disposition of decedent and in absence thereof, goes to surviving spouse, and is only portion subject to administration under probate laws. (123.250).

See note at head of Digest as to 1998 legislation covered.

See Topical Index in front part of this volume.

INFANTS:

Males and females under age of 18 are infants unless 16 or older and are emancipated by court. (129.010).

Emancipation of infants, at least 16 years of age, may be ordered by District Court in county of minor's residence. (129.080). If court enters decree of emancipation, it removes all disabilities of minor that may affect incurring indebtedness or contractual obligations, litigation and settlement, acquiring, encumbering or conveying property, consenting to medical, dental or psychiatric care, enrolling in school, and establishing own residence. (129.130).

Disabilities.—In cases specified by statute, certain infants may enter into contract for insurance. (687B.070).

Minors are prohibited from purchasing or consuming alcoholic beverages or possessing same in public (202.020) or loitering in saloons (202.030) if under age of 21 years, and, if under age of 18 years, from purchasing cigarettes (202.010). Person who contributes to delinquency or improper dependency of child may be punishable by fine or imprisonment or both or directed to perform fixed periods of work for benefit of community. (193.150; 201.080-201.110).

Ratification or repudiation of contracts after attaining majority is governed by common law rules, there being no statute on the subject.

Actions.—Where an infant is a party to an action he must appear by general guardian or by guardian ad litem appointed by the court in which the action is prosecuted or by a judge thereof. (12.050; NRCP 17).

Rights and liabilities of Parents.—Governed by the common law.

Willful misconduct of a minor child resulting in injury or death to another person or in property damage is imputed to parents or guardian. Joint and several liability of parents or guardian with minor cannot exceed $10,000. (41.470). Also, see category Transportation, topic Motor Vehicles.

Uniform Gifts to Minors Act repealed; Uniform Transfers to Minors Act adopted. (167.010-167.110). Age of majority under Act is 18. (167.020).

Uniform Securities Ownership by Minors Act not adopted.

Adoption.—See topic Adoption.

MARRIAGE:

Marriage is a civil contract to which the consent of the parties, capable in law of contracting, is essential. (122.010).

Who May Marry.—Male and female person, both at least 18 years old, may marry (122.020), provided marriage does not violate any of statutory prohibitions (see infra, subhead Prohibited Marriages). Person, at least 16 but less than 18 years old, may marry only with consent of either parent, or legal guardian. (122.020). Persons under 16 years need authorization by district court in addition to consent from either parent or guardian. (122.025).

Consent Required.—Persons under 18 must have consent of either parent or guardian. Such consent must be given personally to clerk when license is applied for or certified by parent or guardian attested by two witnesses, one of whom must appear and swear that he saw parent or guardian subscribe same or heard him acknowledge same, or in writing subscribed to and acknowledged before person authorized to administer oaths. (122.040). Persons under 16 also need authorization by District Court. (122.025).

Marriage license must be obtained from the county clerk of any county by either of the prospective parties, who must appear and apply in person; license expires one year after date of issuance. (122.040).

Time and Place of Marriage.—Marriage may take place immediately after issuance of license and may be solemnized in any county. (122.040-122.080).

Who May Solemnize Marriage.—Ministers of the gospel, duly licensed, and holding a valid certificate of permission from county clerk of county in which they reside (122.062-122.073). Supreme and district court judges and justices of the peace and municipal judges subject to statutory restrictions may solemnize marriages. (122.080). Temporary replacements for licensed ministers, duly certified, may solemnize marriages for period up to 90 days. (122.062). Military chaplain assigned in this state may solemnize marriage upon obtaining certificate of permission from county clerk. (122.062).

A person who undertakes to join others in marriage, knowing that he is not lawfully authorized to do so or that there is a legal impediment to the marriage, is guilty of a misdemeanor. (122.260).

However, a marriage solemnized by a person professing to be entitled to perform the ceremony is valid if consummated with full belief on part of the persons married that they are lawfully married. (122.090).

Marriage Ceremony.—There is no particular form of solemnization, except that the parties must declare, in the presence of the person performing the ceremony, that they take each other as husband and wife. One witness is necessary. (122.110).

Other Marriages.—Marriage solemnized among people called Friends or Quakers, or members of Indian tribes, according to their own form and practices, are valid in Nevada. (122.150, 122.160, 122.170).

Marriage Certificate and Record.—After marriage solemnized, person doing so must give couple being married marriage certificate in statutory form. Person who solemnizes marriage must make record thereof within ten days and deliver same to recorder of deeds of county where such license was issued. Certificate must be filed and recorded by county recorder. Person solemnizing marriage, who fails to deliver such certificate within time, or recorder who fails to record copy of certificate, is guilty of misdemeanor and punishable by fine and imprisonment. (122.120; 122.130).

The making of a false certificate of marriage or pretended marriage is a gross misdemeanor. (122.250).

Record.—See category Documents and Records, topic Records, subhead Vital Statistics.

Certificate as Evidence.—The original certificate of marriage or certified copy of record or abstract thereof is presumptive evidence of marriage. (122.030).

Common law marriages are prohibited. (122.010).
Local Recognition of Out of State.—No statutory provision.

Proxy Marriages.—No statute authorizing.

Marriages by Written Contract.—No statute authorizing.

Prohibited Marriages.—Persons who are nearer of kin than second cousins, or cousins of the halfblood, may not intermarry. (122.020).

Marriages prohibited by law on account of consanguinity between the parties, or on account of either of them having a wife or husband then living, are void without decree of divorce, annulment or other legal proceedings. Such void marriages do not bar prosecution for bigamy. (125.290).

Legitimacy of Children.—Marriage of parents of illegitimate children legitimizes children. (122.140). Issue of a marriage deemed null in law are legitimate. (125.410).

Foreign Marriages.—No statute, except as to Quaker marriages (see subhead Other Marriages, supra) and presumption in annulment suits (see infra, subhead Annulment of Marriage).

Annulment of Marriage.—

Venue.—Annulment may be obtained by complaint under oath to any district court within state if marriage contracted within state. If marriage contracted without state, annulment may be obtained by complaint to any district court within state if plaintiff shall have resided within state for six weeks before suit is brought. If plaintiff shall have not resided in state for six weeks, then by complaint to court of county in which defendant shall reside or county in which plaintiff shall reside if it is county in which parties last cohabited. (125.370).

Residence Requirement in Case of Foreign Marriage.—No court in Nevada has authority to annul any marriage performed, contracted or entered into out of Nevada unless one of parties has resided in state for six weeks before filing the complaint. (125.370).

Grounds.—Annulment may be granted where marriage was induced by fraud or either party was incapable of assenting for want of age or understanding and consent required of parents, guardian, or court was not obtained and there has been no subsequent cohabitation, or where there is ground for annulling or declaring void a contract in a court of equity. (125.300-125.350).

Limitation.—Suit to annul marriage on ground of underage and lack of consent must be brought within one year after attainment of age of consent. (125.320). See supra, subhead Who May Marry.

Process.—In a suit for annulment of marriage, process is served in the same manner as in actions at law, and the courts have the same power upon a substituted or constructive service of process to annul such marriage and regulate and determine the status of the parties as they would have had if process had been personally served. (125.400).

Presumption as to Foreign Law.—In any suit for annulment of marriage in any wise affected by the law of another state, it must be presumed that the law of such other state is the same as the law of Nevada, unless and until the law of such other state is alleged and proved. (125.420).

Regulating Status of Parties.—As an action for annulment of a marriage is in rem, the court may, in addition to annulling the marriage or declaring it void, regulate and determine the status of the parties. (125.390).

Cohabitation as Precluding Annulment.—A marriage may not be annulled if cohabitation is continued after attainment of legal age, restoration to sanity, or acquisition of knowledge of fraud. (125.310-125.340).

Legitimacy of children of the marriage is not affected by annulment on the ground of nonage of either or both of the parties to the marriage. (125.410).

Effect on Will.—See category Estates and Trusts, topic Wills, subhead Divorced Spouse.

MARRIED WOMEN:

See topics Husband and Wife, Marriage; categories Civil Actions and Procedure, topic Evidence, subhead Witnesses; Debtor and Creditor, topic Homesteads; Documents and Records, topic Acknowledgments; Estates and Trusts, topics Executors and Administrators, Wills; Property, topic Dower.

INSURANCE

INSURANCE COMPANIES:

Regulated by Nevada Insurance Code. Insurance commissioner and advocate for insurance customers of department of insurance enforce insurance laws. (232.805-232.835). Insurers issuing health or life policies or annuity contracts must be members of Nevada Life and Health Insurance Guaranty Association which acts to protect persons specified in statute against insolvent insurers. (686C.020; 686C.100).

Rates and rate service organizations are regulated by statute. (686B.010-686B.250).

Annual statements must be filed with Insurance Commissioner on or before Mar. 1. (680A.270).

Policies.—Statutes regulating particular policies are: life insurance and annuity contracts (688A.010-688A.410), group life insurance (688B.010-688B.180), health insurance (689A.010-689A.380), group and blanket health insurance (689B.010-689B.110), credit life and health insurance (690A.010-690A.140), casualty insurance (690B.010-692A.011), property insurance (691A.010), surety insurance (691B.010-691B.030), title insurance (692A.230), fraternal benefit societies (695A.010-695A.580), nonprofit hospital, medical and dental service corporations (695B.010-695B.320), motor clubs (696A.010-696A.360).

Insurer cannot cancel, refuse to renew or increase premium on policy of motor vehicle insurance covering private cars or commercial vehicles as result of claims made to which insured not at fault. (687B.385).

See note at head of Digest as to 1998 legislation covered.

See Topical Index in front part of this volume.

INSURANCE COMPANIES . . . *continued*

Discrimination.—Unfair discrimination between individuals of same class and equal life expectancy prohibited in life insurance and life annuity contracts; between individuals of same class and essentially same hazard prohibited in health insurance contracts; between persons legally qualified to provide particular services prohibited in health insurance contracts (686A.100); between insureds or property having like characteristics in premiums or rates, benefits, or other terms, in property, casualty, surety or title insurance (686A.130).

Rebates are prohibited with certain exceptions. (686A.110-686A.120).

Misrepresentation or false advertising of policies, or engaging in unfair claims settlement practice, enumerated in statute, is punishable by administrative fine and/or suspension or revocation of license. (686A.020-686A.310).

Agents, Solicitors and Brokers.—Policies may be written only through legally authorized agents, solicitors, or brokers licensed by commissioner. (683A.090). Agents must be bona fide residents of, and reside within, state, with limited statutory exceptions. (683A.130). Nonresident broker or agent must pass a written examination, except where a reciprocity arrangement exists. (683A.170; 683A.190).

Every resident agent or broker must maintain office in state. (683A.380). Agent or broker must keep records of all insurance business transacted for three years after expiration of policy. (683A.390).

Process Agent.—Every insurer must appoint Commissioner as attorney for service of process. (680A.250). Every nonresident agent or broker shall appoint Commissioner as attorney upon whom process may be served, and must file with Commissioner agreement to appear pursuant to notice of hearing, show cause order or subpoena issued by Commissioner. (683A.350).

Investments.—Insurance companies may invest in certain securities enumerated by statute. (682A.010-682A.290). Domestic insurers may organize or acquire subsidiaries, or invest in subsidiaries. (692C.130).

Foreign Insurance Companies.—Foreign insurer to be authorized to transact insurance in state must maintain required reserves, be authorized to transact such business in its domiciliary state or country, and not be in arrears to this state for any sums due it. If insurance protects from liability from ownership use or maintenance of vehicle, insurer must comply with 485.314 and demonstrate compliance to Department of Vehicles and Public Safety. (680A.080). Foreign insurer must hold a substituting certificate of authority from Commissioner authorizing it to transact insurance business in this state. (680A.060). No foreign insurer owned or controlled in whole or substantial party by any government or government agency can transact insurance business in Nevada. (680A.090). General corporation laws do not apply to certified foreign insurers which do not solicit or accept deposits in this state, except provision for publication of annual statement and registering with Secretary of State and paying $50 fee. (680A.230). Service of process against foreign insurer is made only upon Commissioner. (680A.250).

Investment Requirements.—Investment portfolio of a foreign insurer may be as permitted by laws of its domicile if of a quality substantially equal to that required under Nevada Insurance Code for similar funds of like domestic insurers. (682A.290).

Insurance holding company law only authorizes domestic insurers to organize or acquire subsidiaries, or to invest in subsidiaries. (692C.130).

Retaliatory Laws.—Commissioner may issue a license to a nonresident agent or broker if he is licensed in another state or province and under laws of that state or province a Nevada resident is not prohibited from acting as a nonresident agent or broker. (683A.340).

Premium Tax.—Each insurer and property bondsman must, on or before Mar. 15 of each year, file with department of taxation report showing total income derived from premiums written and other income (680B.030), and pay tax of 3.5% upon net premiums and net consideration received. (680B.027).

Fee Schedule.—Commissioner must collect in advance miscellaneous charges. Some of charges are as follows: For filing power of attorney, $5; for issuance and annual continuation of any one kind of insurance, $283; for two kinds of insurance, $578; filing charter documents, $10; filing annual statement, $25; for issuing following licenses, fees are: original resident and qualified nonresident agent's license, $78; resident agent's appointment, $5; temporary license, $10; other nonresident agent's license, $138; nonresident agent's appointment, $25; resident and qualified nonresident broker, $78; other nonresident broker, $258; surplus lines broker, $78; solicitors, $78; managing general agents, $78; adjusters, $78; associate adjusters, $78; motor vehicle physical damage appraisers, $78; each insurance vending machine, $78; licenses and renewals for title agents and escrow officers, $78. (680B.010). Cities, towns and counties may require additional license fees. (680B.020).

Direct Actions Against Insurer.—See category Transportation, topic Motor Vehicles, subhead Direct Actions.

No-Fault Insurance.—See category Transportation, topic Motor Vehicles, subhead No-Fault Insurance.

SURETY AND GUARANTY COMPANIES:

Surety Companies may be formed under the laws regarding private corporations. (78.020).

Surety Bonds.—See category Civil Actions and Procedure, topic Bonds.

INTELLECTUAL PROPERTY

TRADEMARKS AND TRADENAMES:

Any person who adopts or uses mark in this state may file in Secretary of State's office, on designated form, application for registration of that mark (fee $50). Registration of mark is effective for five years and may be renewed within six months prior to expiration (fee $25) (600.340-600.360). It is unlawful to imitate or use such label, trademark, form of advertising, name or seal without authorization and imitation may be

enjoined with judgment for damages, costs and accounting for profits. Violation is also misdemeanor. (600.420-600.450).

Assignment.—No statutory provision, common law applicable.

Fixing Resale Price.—Fair Trade Act (599.010-599.070) repealed. Common law governs.

Tradenames.—Every person doing business in this state under assumed or fictitious name which does not disclose real name of each person owning interest therein must file with county clerk of each county where business is conducted a certificate showing such real name or names and places of residence. (602.010, 602.020). No person may use fictitious name which includes "Corporation" or like designation unless such person is corporation. (602.017). Such certificate must be filed also where there is change in membership of co-partnership. (See category Business Organizations, topic Partnerships.)

Fee for filing with county clerk certificate of doing business under fictitious name $10.

Assignment.—No statutory provision, common law applicable.

Persons violating this requirement, or their assignees, cannot commence or maintain an action on any transaction or cause arising out of the business illegally conducted until they file the requisite certificate before commencement of action. (602.070). Such violation also constitutes a misdemeanor. (602.090).

For limitation on use of surnames by limited partnership, see 88.060, 88.320.

LEGAL PROFESSION

ATTORNEYS AND COUNSELORS:

"The State Bar of Nevada" is incorporated and is under the exclusive jurisdiction and control of Supreme Court. It is governed by rules adopted by Supreme Court. (7,275). It is an integrated bar. (Sup. Ct. Rule 77).

Jurisdiction over Admission.—Admission is by Supreme Court upon recommendation of Board of Examiners of State Bar of Nevada. (Sup. Ct. Rule 49).

Educational Requirements.—Applicant for admission must have completed three years of college and received a degree of Bachelor of Laws, or its equivalent, from an American Bar Association approved law school. (Sup. Ct. Rule 51).

Registration as Law Student.—No requirement.

Fees.—Before application is further considered, applicant must pay to treasurer of State Bar of Nevada $150, or $250 if previously admitted to practice in another jurisdiction; except an applicant who, within two years, as a resident of Nevada, has been admitted to practice in another jurisdiction must pay $150. (Sup. Ct. Rule 54). Applicant admitted must pay an additional $25 before receiving license. (7.030). Annual membership fee for active members in practice more than five years $150; for active members in practice less than five years $125; judges serving full time in judicial office not engaged in private practice $150; inactive members $25. (Sup. Ct. Rule 98).

Petition for Admission.—Applicants must, before Mar. 1 preceding date for examination, file with Secretary of State Bar, on forms furnished by him, affidavit in triplicate stating: (a) When and where applicant was born, various places of his residence, and giving at least two references in each place in which he has resided since attaining age of 21 years and for the five years immediately preceding filing of application; (b) whether or not he has been engaged in business at any time; and, if so, when, where and kind of business; (c) names and post office addresses of all persons by whom applicant has been employed, for a period of ten years immediately preceding his application; (d) applicant's general and legal education, what schools he has attended, length of time in attendance at each, and whether or not he is a graduate of any school or schools; (e) whether or not applicant has ever applied to any entity for admission to practice law; if so, when and where, and results thereof; (f) if a naturalized citizen, when and where naturalized; (g) how long applicant has resided in Nevada and whether he is a bona fide resident; (h) whether or not applicant has ever been arrested; if so, when and where, nature of crime and disposition of charge, complaint, indictment of information; (i) marital status of applicant; if married, name of spouse, date and place of marriage, and number and names of children, if any; if divorced, name of former spouse, date and court granting decree; (j) whether applicant has ever been admitted to practice law in any jurisdiction, and if so whether his status as attorney has been terminated giving full particulars. Applicant who has so practiced must present also: (1) Certificate of clerk of court in state in which he last practiced, certifying that he is a member in good standing of bar of that state or district, and that no disbarment or other proceedings affecting his standing as an attorney are pending and undisposed of before court; (2) letter from secretary of local bar association of city or county in which he last resided (or, in case there be no local bar association, from Secretary of State Bar Association), certifying to his good moral character; (3) letter of recommendation from the judge of court of record before which he last practiced; (4) such other evidence of good moral character and fitness as may be required by court; and (5) such other evidence as may be required by board of bar examiners; (k) whether or not applicant is, or ever has been, a member of Communist Party or an organization supporting or advocating support of communism, giving full particulars. Applicants must arrange to be fingerprinted by police or sheriff's office on a form provided by state bar and attach it to application. (Sup. Ct. Rules 52-53).

Examination.—Applicants for license to practice as attorneys and counselors will be examined annually by Board of Bar Examiners, at places fixed by order of Board.

Examination will consist of Multistate Bar Examination and separate written bar examination held for three days during July to coincide with July date set by National Conference of Bar Examiners for Multistate Bar Examination. Two days immediately preceding or following Multistate Bar Examination date board of bar examiners will give separate written examination which must embrace ten specified subjects; and may include also questions on five enumerated optional subjects. (Sup. Ct. Rules 64-66). Transfer of Multi-State Bar Examination scores from another jurisdiction not accepted.

Clerkship.—No requirement.

ATTORNEYS AND COUNSELORS . . . *continued*

Admission Without Examination.—All applicants must take an examination.

Admission Pro Hac Vice.—Nonresident attorney, even though admitted to practice in Nevada, may practice in Nevada only when associated with Nevada attorney who resides in Nevada and is personally present at all proceedings. Nonresident attorney must also file application on form approved by State Bar, file and serve all counsel and State Bar, pay $100 filing fee to State Bar and set application for hearing; nonresident attorney may not practice until application approved by court. (Sup. Ct. Rule 42).

License.—See subhead Fees, supra.

Liabilities.—No statute.

Compensation.—The compensation of an attorney and counselor for his services is governed by agreement, express or implied, which is not restrained by law. (18.010). See also category Estates and Trusts, topic Executors and Administrators, subhead Attorney's Fees.

Lien.—Attorney has lien on any claim or demand placed in his hands by client for suit or collection, or upon which suit or other action instituted, for amount of agreed upon fee or if no agreement, for reasonable fee for services rendered. Lien attaches to verdict, judgment or decree entered and to money or property recovered from time of service of statutory notices. (18.015).

Attorney Ethics.—American Bar Association Model Rules of Professional Conduct adopted. (Sup. Ct. Rule 150 et seq.).

Disbarment or Suspension.—Board of Governors of State Bar has power, after hearing, to discipline members, or to recommend to Supreme Court disbarment, suspension, or fine. Decisions of Board are reviewable by Supreme Court of state. (Sup. Ct. Rules 105, 111-112).

Unauthorized Practice.—It is unlawful to practice unless one is an active member of the state bar. (Sup. Ct. Rule 77).

Professional Association.—See category Business Organizations, topic Associations, subhead Professional Associations.

MINERAL, WATER AND FISHING RIGHTS

MINES AND MINERALS:

Bureau of mines and geology has been established and placed under direction of regents of University of Nevada and community college system and director appointed by them. (514.010-514.080).

Safeguarding of Employees.—Department of Industrial Relations may adopt any regulations for mine health and safety consistent with Federal Mine Safety and Health Act, 30 U. S. C. 801 et seq. (513.131). Whenever serious accident occurs, operator must immediately notify mines inspector and must preserve conditions to facilitate determination of accident's cause. (512.220). Operator who violates health or safety standard is guilty of gross misdemeanor. (512.270).

Persons employed or working in underground mines or underground workings must not be employed more than eight hours in any 24-hour period except in emergencies or in event no qualified employee is available for relief. Persons employed in smelters, mills, open mines, plaster or cement mills, or working on or about surface workings of underground mines must not be employed more than eight hours in any 24-hour period except in emergencies or when working person voluntarily agrees to greater hours. (608.200-608.240).

Portal to Portal Time.—Time occupied in getting to place of work and back again or for meals is not included in eight hours. (608.200).

Inspection of Mines.—Department of Industrial Relations has authority to inspect without advance notice all mines, surface structures and equipment used in mining, smelters, mills, and underground workings. At least once a year, inspector or designee must inspect and investigate all mines which inspector determines require inspection. Mine worker or worker representative with reasonable grounds to believe imminent danger or violation of health or safety standard may obtain inspection by giving notice to Department of Industrial Relations of danger or violation. (512.200).

Maliciously removing or altering a boundary mark is a public offense proportionate to value of loss resulting therefrom, but not less than a misdemeanor. (206.220).

A mortgagee of a mining claim may preserve it by doing the acts his mortgagor could do to prevent a forfeiture. (111.050).

Lode Locations.—Any U. S. citizen or anyone who has made declaration of intention to become a citizen, who discovers a vein or lode, may locate a lode claim by erecting a monument at place of discovery and posting thereon a notice of location. Boundaries must be marked within 60 days after posting location notice and two maps of claim must be filed with county recorder within 90 days. Within 90 days after posting location notice, claim must be recorded with county recorder by filing duplicate location certificates. (517.010-517.080).

Placer Claims.—Location of placers must be made by posting notice of location, marking boundaries, recording notice of location and two maps of claim with county recorder. (517.090-517.110).

Mill Site.—Proprietor of mine or mining claim or owner of mill or reduction works may locate five acres of non-mineral land as mill site by posting notice of location, marking boundaries, and recording notice of location and two maps of claim with county recorder. (517.120-517.140).

Tunnel rights may be located by posting notice of location, marking boundaries and recording notice and maps as in other cases. (517.150-517.180).

All Locations.—Locater of lode or placer claim or claim for mill site or tunnel right must post separate notice of location and record separate certificate of location for each location; if either includes more than one location, void as to all others. (517.195). Fee

of $1.50 per claim must accompany each filing. (517.185). Division of minerals must prescribe forms for documents to be recorded and adopt regulations concerning maps. (513.075).

Oil and Gas.—Production of oil and gas is regulated by statute with view to conservation, under supervision of division of mineral resources of Department of Conservation and Natural Resources. (522.010-522.150).

Pipe lines transporting crude oil or petroleum are declared to be common carriers and placed under the jurisdiction of Public Utilities Commission. (708.010-708.140).

Sale and distribution of petroleum and its products are regulated by statute, and standard specifications prescribed for products sold as "gasoline." (590.010-590.330).

Mining Partnerships.—Express agreement not necessary. Profits and losses shared pro rata. Each member has lien. Gravel worked by is property of partnership. Not dissolved by sale of interest. Purchaser takes subject to liens. Part of partners cannot bind by writing. Majority govern. (520.160-520.260).

Taxation.—Mines and mining claims, when not patented, are not taxed, the proceeds and royalties only being taxable. (362.100-362.240). If proceeds of unpatented mine are uncollectible in executive director's opinion, upon approval of county commissioners, district attorney and Nevada Tax Commission, department may remove name and amount from its tax records. (362.175). Patented mines may be assessed at not less than $500, in addition to tax on net proceeds, except when $100 in labor has actually been performed thereon during year. (Const., Art. X, §1). Department of taxation determines and assesses net proceeds of operating mines; appraises and assesses smelters, mills, and other facilities, and all machinery, equipment, and improvements used in connection with mining or related operations. Every operator and recipient of royalties must file verified report of claimed net proceeds with department on or before Feb. 1 of each year. (362.100-362.110). For deductible items and determining gross yield, see 362.120. Royalty payments do not include fixed and periodic rental or other compensation not related to extent of use, or fixed and periodic minimum royalty covering period when mine not in production. (362.105).

Exploration of Patented Claims Forfeited for Nonpayment of Taxes.—When a patented mine or claim has become property of county for nonpayment of amount of one year's taxes, plus penalties and costs, county commissioners may, without charge, and provided mine or claim has been property of county for less than one year, grant permit to explore it for period of six months, with privilege of purchase at expiration thereof. When mine or claim is property of county for more than one year, any U.S. citizen may file with board of county commissioners of such county to have such mine or claim advertised for sale to highest bidder. (517.390-517.460).

Printed pamphlets of mining laws may be secured without charge from Inspector of Mines, 515 E. Musser, Carson City 89701.

MORTGAGES

CHATTEL MORTGAGES:

Uniform Commercial Code adopted. (104.1101-104.9507). See category Business Regulation and Commerce, topic Commercial Code.

See also category Transportation, topic Motor Vehicles, subhead Titles, Sales and Liens.

What May Be Mortgaged.—See category Business Regulation and Commerce, topic Commercial Code.

Requisites of Instrument.—See category Business Regulation and Commerce, topic Commercial Code.

Execution of Instrument.—See category Business Regulation and Commerce, topic Commercial Code.

Filing.—See category Documents and Records, topic Records, subhead Filing Under Commercial Code.

Real estate mortgage and chattel mortgage may be included in one instrument and recorded in a special book provided instrument complies with statutory requirements (see category Documents and Records, topic Acknowledgments). (247.180).

Refiling or Extension.—See category Business Regulation and Commerce, topic Commercial Code.

Duration of Lien.—See category Business Regulation and Commerce, topic Commercial Code.

Removal of Property by Mortgagor.—See category Business Regulation and Commerce, topic Commercial Code.

Fraudulent Intent.—Mortgagor who removes mortgaged property from county in which mortgaged with intent to hinder, delay or defraud mortgagee is guilty of gross misdemeanor. (205.335).

Assignment or Discharge.—See category Business Regulation and Commerce, topic Commercial Code.

Foreclosure.—See category Business Regulation and Commerce, topic Commercial Code.

Redemption.—See category Business Regulation and Commerce, topic Commercial Code.

Forms.—See end of this Digest.

COLLATERAL SECURITY:

See category Debtor and Creditor, topic Pledges.

MORTGAGES OF PERSONAL PROPERTY:

See topic Chattel Mortgages.

See note at head of Digest as to 1998 legislation covered.

See Topical Index in front part of this volume.

MORTGAGES OF REAL PROPERTY:

Property of all kinds may be mortgaged, including mining claims and possessory claims to public lands as well as estates for years. (111.010; 106.195; 106.200). Mortgage is not alienation, but mere security for debt, and though absolute in form does not give mortgagee right of possession. (40.050; 23 Nev. 134, 43 Pac. 916; ; 54 Nev. 388, 19 P.2d 769).

Execution.—A mortgage is within the provisions of statute dealing with conveyances, and must be executed in the manner of a conveyance. (111.010; 55 Nev. 350, 34 P.2d 1076). See category Property, topic Deeds. No seal is required. (52.315).

Recording.—Mortgages must be recorded in the county where the property is situated or, for instrument filed by public utility, in office of Secretary of State to extent permitted by 105.010-105.080, and such record imports notice to all persons. If not so recorded, mortgage is void as against subsequent purchaser or mortgagee in good faith and for valuable consideration whose deed or mortgage is first recorded. (111.320; 111.325). As to recording fees, see category Documents and Records, topic Records.

Real and personal property may be included in the same mortgage, which is recorded in special book. (247.180).

Future Advances.—Mortgage may cover future advances. (106.025).

Assignment or Subordination.—An assignment of a mortgage of real property or of the beneficial interest under a deed of trust, or a copy thereof certified by a notary public or other officer authorized to take acknowledgment, may be recorded, and record operates as constructive notice of contents of instrument from date of recordation. Same rule applies to any instrument by which a mortgage, deed of trust, lien on or interest in real or personal property is subordinated or waived as to priority. (106.210-106.220).

A mortgage may be assigned by an entry on the margin of the record, signed by the mortgagee, his personal representative, or assignee. (106.260).

Discharge and Satisfaction.—Upon full performance of the conditions of the mortgage, whether or not there has been a breach, the mortgagor is entitled to a certificate of discharge, duly acknowledged and recorded. A properly executed entry of satisfaction on the margin of the record likewise discharges the mortgage. (106.260-106.290).

Partial release may be executed and acknowledged by mortgagee and recorded. It should describe the mortgage, its place of record and the land released from lien. (106.260-106.270).

Foreclosure.—Except as provided in U.C.C. (c. 104) or when real collateral is environmentally impaired if estimated clean up and remedial costs exceeds 10% of indebtedness secured by collateral there is but one action for foreclosure of mortgage, which must be by suit in district court. Judgment and decree must direct sale of property by sheriff to pay mortgage debt and costs and expenses. Sale must be made by sheriff in same manner as sales upon execution. (40.430-40.450; 40.512). Notice of lis pendens must be filed in recorder's office of county where suit commenced. (14.010). Priority of distribution of proceeds of foreclosure sale are: (a) Payment of expenses of taking possession and protecting property, costs and fees of sale including trustees fees, taxes, costs of title insurance, and if provided in lien, any advances, and attorney fees and expenses; (b) satisfaction of obligation being enforced by sale; (c) satisfaction of obligations secured by junior liens in order or priority, and (d) balance, if any, to debtor. Junior lien holders must submit proof of obligation within 15 days or demand by person conducting sale, or will waive any right to proceeds. (40.462). If there be surplus from proceeds of sale, it may be paid to person entitled to it. (40.440). If there be deficiency, judgment creditor or beneficiary of deed of trust, within three months from date of foreclosure sale or trustee's sale held pursuant to NRS 107.080, and after hearing to determine fair market value of property sold as of date of foreclosure sale or trustee's sale, shall be awarded deficiency judgment. Deficiency judgment must not exceed lesser of difference between fair market value of property at time of sale with interest from date of sale and amount of secured indebtedness, or difference between sale price and amount of indebtedness. (40.451-40.459).

No moratorium on mortgage foreclosures.

Obligation of guarantor on note secured by deed of trust not within scope of one action rule. (91 Nev. 396, 536, P.2d 487). Upon full satisfaction by guarantor or other surety on note secured by deed of trust, payor is entitled to assignment of security and can enforce all remedies against mortgagor or grantor of deed of trust (40.475); upon partial satisfaction, payor has lien in proceeds of indebtedness to extent of payment (40.485).

Redemption.—Property sold under foreclosure of mortgage may be redeemed within same times, by same persons and in same manner as property sold under execution. (21.210-21.220). See category Debtor and Creditor, topic Executions.

Deeds of Trust.—Any estate in real property, including an estate for years, may be transferred in trust to secure performance of obligation for payment of any debt. (107.020). Power of sale is conferred upon trustee. After breach beneficiary must record notice of such breach and of his election to cause sale to be made and mail copy of notice to grantor and to person who holds record title as of date notice is recorded at their respective addresses; and not less than three months must thereafter elapse before noticing of such sale. Grantor or successor in interest or anyone else who has subordinate lien of record on property has period of 35 days following filing of notice of breach in which to make good his deficiency in performance or payment. If acceleration is permitted by note secured by deed of trust, such acceleration shall not occur if deficiency in performance or payment is made good and cost of recording such notice is paid within 35 days following recording of such notice. Notice of time and place of sale must be given after expiration of three month period and in manner and for time not less than required by law for sale of real property upon execution. Notices must be given to grantor and person who holds record title as of date of notice of default; however any person who is or may be liable for any debt secured by lien on property who recorded request for notice must also be given notice. Statute particularly describes various covenants of grantor commonly used in deeds of trust and provides that they may be incorporated in deed of trust merely by reference to them by covenant numbers as contained in act; any assumption fee must be set forth in deed of trust at time of execution. (107.030-107.160).

There is no equity or right of redemption after a sale made under the power of sale contained in such trust deeds. (107.080).

Persons with an interest evidenced by recorded instrument in real property subject to trust deed or any other person who is or may be liable for any debt secured by lien on property may file request for notice of default or sale under deed of trust on real property at county recorder's office of county where property is located. Request should identify deed of trust by stating names of parties, date recorded, and volume and page number and state name and address of those requesting it. Person authorized to record notice of default must send copy to whoever requested it within ten days of recordation. Person authorized to make sale must send notice of sale to those who requested it 20 days before sale. (107.090).

Deficiency Judgments.—See subhead Foreclosure, supra.

Form.—The following is the briefest form of mortgage:

Form

This indenture, made this . . day of . . by and between . . mortgagor, and . . mortgagee, witnesseth: That the mortgagor for and in consideration of the sum of $. . in hand paid by the mortgagee, receipt of which is hereby acknowledged, does by these presents grant, bargain, sell, convey and confirm unto the mortgagee; his heirs (or if it is a corporation, its successors) and assigns forever, all that certain real property situate, lying and being in (put in name of city, county, etc.), State of Nevada, described as follows, to-wit (insert description). Together with all and singular the tenements, hereditaments and appurtenances thereunto belonging or in any wise appertaining, and the reversion and reversions, remainder and remainders, rents, issues and profits thereof.

Nevertheless this conveyance is intended as a mortgage to secure the payment of all sums which are or may hereafter in any manner become due or owing from the mortgagor to the mortgagee, and particularly the payment of a certain promissory note, which note is in the words and figures following to-wit: (Insert copy of note). In witness whereof, mortgagor has hereunto set his hand and seal the day and year first above written.

. . . . (Seal).

Add acknowledgment.

In addition, it is customary to insert in a mortgage provisions that it is to secure any additional sums loaned by mortgagee to mortgagor, provisions concerning insurance on the premises, for payment of taxes by mortgagor, right of mortgagee to compromise adverse claims, fixing rate of interest on sums advanced over and above original indebtedness, provisions for right of mortgagor to take possession or have receiver appointed therefor in event of default and starting suit to foreclose, statement that all covenants bind, heirs, representatives and assigns of mortgagor and mortgagee, warranties of title, covenants against waste, and similar provisions for protection of parties in accordance with the idea of person drawing the mortgage.

Most such covenants are contained in a statute and can be incorporated in mortgage or deed of trust by reference to statute and number of covenant. (106.010-106.050; 107.030-107.050).

Master form mortgages or deeds of trust can also be incorporated by reference to county where it is recorded, date it was recorded, book or volume and first page of record in recorder's office where located, and by paragraph numbers that definitely identify provisions incorporated. (111.353).

There are no statutory forms for assignment, satisfaction or partial release of mortgage. Any form which particularly describes the object is sufficient.

Chattel Mortgages.—See category Business Regulation and Commerce, topic Commercial Code.

PROPERTY

ABSENTEES:

Unknown Heirs.—In actions involving title to real property where names and residences of a decedent's heir are unknown to plaintiff, such heirs may be described as the unknown heirs of such decedent with name, last place of residence, and any further available identification of decedent. Upon trial, proof must be given of diligent search to ascertain the names and residences of heirs, and that same remain unknown to plaintiff. (12.120).

See also category Estates and Trusts, topic Death.

In probate proceedings, court may appoint attorney to represent absent heirs, devisees or legatees unless absent party retains own counsel. (136.200; 150.180, 152.040).

Care of Property.—When property is assigned or distributed to a person who cannot be found, or to a minor or incompetent person who has no legal guardian, the money may be deposited in name of such person with county treasurer, who is liable on his official bond therefor. (151.170). If such nonresident is a minor, or insane or incompetent, distribution may be made to the legally appointed foreign guardian of such person. (151.180). If estate remains unclaimed for one year, it may be sold by order of the court and the proceeds paid to county treasurer. (151.190).

Process Agent.—There is statutory provision for appointment of an agent for service of process upon resident agent for foreign corporation, upon Secretary of State in absence of such resident agent and upon Director of Department of Motor Vehicles under Nonresident Motor Vehicle Statute.

See category Civil Actions and Procedure, topic Process; also category Transportation, topic Motor Vehicles.

Escheat.—In any receivership a dividend unclaimed for five years reverts to general fund of estate and is applied, in order, to pay: (1) Costs of administration, and (2) creditors not previously paid in full. If expense of paying either costs or creditors is deemed too great to warrant such distribution, money escheats to state. (32.020).

See also categories Business Regulation and Commerce, topic Banks and Banking, subhead Unclaimed Deposits; Estates and Trusts, topics Descent and Distribution, subhead Escheat, Wills, subhead Unclaimed Legacies.

See note at head of Digest as to 1998 legislation covered.

See Topical Index in front part of this volume.

ADVERSE POSSESSION:

Possession is presumed to be in holder of legal title, and possession of another is presumed to be subordinate to the legal title until adverse elements are made to appear. (11.100). Possession of tenant is presumed to be possession of landlord. (11.160).

Character of Possession.—Where occupant's possession is under a written instrument, it is sufficient that the land has been usually cultivated or improved, or protected by a substantial enclosure, or where not enclosed has been used for supply of fuel or fencing timber, husbandry, pasturage or ordinary uses of occupants. Where a known farm or single lot is partly improved, the portion not cleared or enclosed, according to the usual course and custom of the adjoining country, is deemed occupied for the same time as the part improved and cultivated. (11.120). Where premises consist of a tract divided into lots, possession of one lot is not deemed possession of any other lot of the same tract. (11.110).

Where the occupant's claim is not founded upon a written instrument, only the premises actually occupied are deemed held adversely (11.130), and the property must have been protected by a substantial enclosure or cultivated or improved in accordance with the usual and ordinary methods of husbandry (11.140).

Payment of Taxes.—In all cases, whether occupant's possession is or is not under a written instrument, occupant or his predecessors must have paid or tendered all state, county and municipal taxes on property for five years immediately preceding action. (11.150).

Duration of Possession.—Five years adverse possession is sufficient to defeat recovery by another (11.070-11.080); two years for mining property (11.060). Fifteen years of adverse possession is necessary for possessor to bring action to remove cloud upon title to real property unless cloud was created by possessor in which case possession must be for ten years. (40.090).

Easements.—Five years adverse user is sufficient. (11.070-11.180; 19 Nev. 69, 6 Pac. 437).

Disabilities.—Where the owner is under age of majority, insane, or imprisoned, there is no adverse possession for the period of disability if it existed at the time title first accrued to him, and he may bring action to recover property within two years after removal of the disability (11.180), but where the property has been sold by a guardian, executor or administrator, he has only one year (11.280).

CONVEYANCES:

See topic Deeds.

CURTESY:

Abolished by 123.020.

DEEDS:

See also topic Real Property; categories Debtor and Creditor, topic Homesteads; Family, topic Husband and Wife.

Execution.—Conveyances of land or of any estate or interest therein may be made by deed, signed by the grantor, if of lawful age, or by his lawful agent or attorney, and acknowledged or proved. (111.105, 111.240). For circumstances in which spouse might join see category Family, topic Husband and Wife.

A deed does not need to be witnessed. A seal is not necessary; however, it is better practice to place a seal on a corporate deed. (52.085, 52.315).

Delivery.—A deed does not take effect until delivered. To be effective, the delivery must place the deed beyond the control of the grantor. (51 Nev. 437, 279 Pac. 32).

Recording.—When properly acknowledged, a deed is entitled to be recorded in the office of any county recorder in this state (111.310) provided it contains grantee's mailing address and assessor's parcel number, if any (111.312). For recording fees, see category Documents and Records, topic Records.

A conveyance of or agreement to convey real estate is valid and binding between the parties without any recording, but in order to operate as notice to third persons it must be recorded in the office of the recorder of the county in which the real estate is situated or, for instrument filed by public utility, in office of Secretary of State per 1995 c. 352, §§2-9, and if not so recorded it is void as against subsequent purchaser in good faith and for valuable consideration whose conveyance is first recorded. (111.315-111.325). See also category Documents and Records, topics Notaries Public, Records.

Power of attorney to convey real estate must be executed, acknowledged and recorded like a deed in order to be effective. (111.330).

Effect.—The words "grant, bargain and sell" warrant that grantor has not suffered any encumbrance or transfer of title prior to the execution of the conveyance. (111.170). Special warranties may be inserted.

Deeds (except quitclaim) convey after acquired title as well as present title. (111.160). Deeds to two or more grantees convey a tenancy in common unless they expressly state that title is to be held by joint tenancy. (111.060).

Taxes.—See category Taxation, topic Real Estate Conveyance Tax.

Form.—The following may be used:

Form

This indenture, made this . . . . day of . . . ., 19. . . ., between . . . . of the county of . . . ., party of the first part, and . . . . of the county of . . . ., party of the second part. Witnesseth: That said party of the first part, for and in consideration of the sum of . . . . dollars to him in hand paid by said party of the second part, the receipt whereof is hereby acknowledged, does by these presents grant, bargain and sell unto said party of the second part, his heirs and assigns forever, all that certain lot, piece or parcel of land situate, lying and being in the county of . . . ., state of . . . ., and more particularly described as follows, to wit: . . . . . Together with all and singular the tenements, hereditaments and appurtenances thereunto belonging or in anywise appertaining, and the reversion and reversions, remainder and remainders, rents, issues and profits thereof. To have and to hold, all and singular the said premises together with the appurtenances unto said party of the second part, and to his heirs and assigns forever. In witness whereof, the party of the first part has hereunto set his hand and seal the day and year first above written.

In a quitclaim deed, the conveying words are "remise, release and forever quitclaim."

In a joint tenancy deed, the conveyance should run to "the said parties of the second part and the survivor of them," and the same words should be used in the habendum clause.

DEEDS OF TRUST:

See category Mortgages, topic Mortgages of Real Property.

DOWER:

Abolished by 123.020.

ESCHEAT:

See topic Absentees, subhead Escheat; categories Business Organizations, topic Corporations, subhead Unclaimed Dividends; Business Regulation and Commerce, topic Banks and Banking, subhead Unclaimed Deposits; Estates and Trusts, topics Descent and Distribution, subhead Escheat, Wills, subhead Unclaimed Legacies.

LANDLORD AND TENANT:

Statutory provisions govern rights, liabilities, obligations and remedies under rental agreement for dwelling unit (118A et seq.) and mobile homes (18B et seq.). Landlord must deliver premises to tenant at commencement of rental term in habitable condition. (118A.280). In absence of good faith agreement to contrary, landlord must maintain dwelling unit in habitable condition. (118A.290).

Uniform Commercial Code Art. 2A adopted. (c. 104A).

Rent.—Rent may be increased only upon 45 days' written notice, or in case of tenancy of less than one month, 15 days in advance of first rental payment to be increased. (118A.300). Landlord may not demand or receive security (including last month's rent, cleaning or repair deposit) which total amount exceeds three months' periodic rent. (118A.240).

Leases.—Written rental agreements must be signed by landlord and tenant, or their agents, and must contain certain specified provisions as to duration, rent, manner and time of payment, occupancy by children or pets (guide, hearing, or helping animals for physically disabled person may not be excluded, 118.105), services included with unit, extra fees, deposits, late charges, charges for returned checks, inspection rights of landlord, listing of persons or number of persons to occupy unit, responsibility for utility charges, and inventory of premises (118A.200, 118A.210). Leases for more than one year must be in writing. (111.210). Lease may not exceed following terms: Agricultural or grazing land, 25 years; other real property, 99 years. Lease for longer period is void as to excess. (111.200).

Notices.—At or before commencement of tenancy, landlord, or agent, must disclose to tenant names and addresses of manager, owner and person authorized to accept service of notices, demands and process regarding premises. Service upon manager is deemed service upon landlord. (118A.260; 118A.270).

Termination.—If landlord fails to comply with rental agreement or fails to maintain dwelling unit in habitable condition, tenant shall deliver written notice to landlord specifying acts and omissions constituting breach. If landlord fails to remedy breach, or make reasonable effort to do so, within 14 days tenant may terminate rental agreement and recover actual damages unless condition complained of was caused by his act. If landlord breaches rental agreement or fails to maintain premises in habitable condition, and reasonable cost of compliance is less than greater of $100 or one month's rent, tenant may notify landlord of his intention to correct condition at landlord's expense. If landlord fails to correct condition within 14 days after notice, tenant may correct condition and deduct cost of work from his rent, upon submission of itemized statement to landlord. (118A.350, 118A.360). Tenant may also terminate agreement under certain circumstances if landlord fails to deliver possession (118A.370), fails to provide essential services, including heat, air conditioning, water, electricity, etc. (118A.380), unlawfully removes or blocks tenant from premises (118A.390) or if premises are damaged or destroyed by fire or casualty (118A.400). Landlord may terminate for any breach of rental obligation or statutory obligation, but tenant must be given notice and five days to remedy breach. If tenant's breach can be remedied by repair, replacement of damaged item or cleaning, and tenant fails so to do within 14 days after written notice, landlord may enter unit, complete work and bill tenant for work so done on next periodic rent. (118A.430, 118A.440).

Landlord may not terminate in retaliation for any exercise by tenant of rights granted in rental agreement or by statute. (118A.510).

Abandonment of Dwelling Unit.—If tenant abandons, landlord must store tenant's property for 30 days, after which tenant's property may be sold. Landlord must notify or attempt to notify tenant of his intent to dispose of property 14 days before intended sale. (118A.450, 118A.460).

Other Abandonment.—If tenant abandons property before expiration of term, lease terminates when tenant provides notice of intent to abandon and landlord accepts surrender of property, landlord re-rents property, and property is deemed to be abandoned. (118.185). Property is deemed to be abandoned if landlord, believing tenant has abandoned property and tenant is in default of payment of rent, serves tenant with notice and within five days thereafter tenant fails to pay rent due and to provide landlord with written notice setting forth intent not to abandon and address where tenant may be served with process. (118.195).

Lien.—Landlord's lien or security interest in tenant's household goods must be created by attachment or garnishment. (118A.520).

Distress.—Distraint for rent is abolished. (118A.520).

See note at head of Digest as to 1998 legislation covered.

See Topical Index in front part of this volume.

LANDLORD AND TENANT . . . *continued*

Summary Proceedings.—Summary dispossession of tenant is by unlawful detainer proceedings. Tenant of real property or mobile home for term less than life is guilty of unlawful detainer when having leased: (1) Real property or mobile home for indefinite time with periodic rent, if he continues in possession after five days' notice for tenancy at will, seven days' notice for weekly tenancy and 30 days' notice for all other periodic tenancies, (2) dwelling unit defined in 118A if he continues in possession after expiration of its term and expiration of notice of seven days for weekly tenancies and 30 days for all others or five days' notice of breach by tenant of obligations under 118A, (3) mobile home lot defined in 118B if he continues in possession after advance notice of five days if termination due to tenant's conduct constituting nuisance, ten days if termination due to failure to pay rent or service fees, 90 days if termination due to change of land use by landlord, 45 days if termination for any other reason. (40.250-40.255).

Tenant of real property or mobile home for term less than life also guilty of unlawful detainer if: (1) Continues in possession after default in payment of rent and written notice requiring rent or surrender of premises not complied with for five days, or in case of mobile home lot ten days (40.2512), (2) assigns or sublets contrary to lease terms, commits waste, conducts unlawful business, or maintains any nuisance, or violates certain statutes involving controlled substances on leased premises, and continues in possession after service of three days' notice to quit (40.2514), or (3) continues in possession after failure to perform any term of lease or agreement (other than specified above) after service of five days' written notice requiring performance of term or surrender of property (40.2516).

When tenant is guilty of unlawful detainer, landlord is entitled to summary eviction procedures, except that written notice to surrender premises must be given to tenant, which notice advises tenant of his right to contest action by filing affidavit with Justice of Peace that he is not guilty of unlawful detainer. (40.250). If tenant timely files affidavit that he has tendered payment or paid rent, landlord, after receipt of conformed copy of filed affidavit cannot provide for nonadmittance of tenant to premises by locking or otherwise. If tenant disputes costs claimed by landlord, may file motion with court which conducts hearing within ten days to determine costs, if any, and order release of tenant's property. (40.253). Landlord utilizing summary eviction procedures must submit affidavit to Justice of Peace containing: (1) Date tenancy commenced, its term, and copy of rental agreement; (2) date when tenancy allegedly terminated; (3) date when unlawful occupancy commenced along with supporting facts; (4) date when written notice was given; (5) statement that claim for relief was authorized by law. (40.250). Summary eviction procedures are also available when tenant of any dwelling, apartment, mobile home or commercial premises with periodic rent reserved by month or any shorter period is in default in payment of such rent. Landlord must follow substantially same procedure as outlined for summary eviction in unlawful detainer cases. (40.253).

Court may issue temporary writ of restitution, pendente lite, on application after defendant has been given opportunity to be heard, and upon filing of sufficient bond. (40.300).

If verdict, or court finding, is in favor of plaintiff judgment is entered for restitution of premises, and if case be for unlawful detainer, after failure to perform any condition of lease or agreement or after default in rent, judgment forfeits lease or agreement. Judgment must also cover damages occasioned by forcible entry or forcible or unlawful detainer, waste and unpaid rent. Judgment in forcible entry or forcible or unlawful detainer must include rent due and treble damages. Where case is for unlawful detainer after default in rent and lease has not by its terms expired execution is stayed for five days after entry of judgment, during which tenant, subtenant, or other party interested may pay judgment and estate be restored. If no such payment made judgment and possession of premises. In all other cases judgment may be enforced immediately. (40.360).

Public Housing Authorities and Landlords.—Summary statutory procedure for eviction if tenant or person residing with tenant is convicted of certain offenses regarding controlled substances. (315.031, 315.041, 315.051).

Remedies of tenant against subtenant to obtain possession of premises are much same as remedies of original lessor to obtain possession from his lessee. (40.270).

LEASES:

See topic Landlord and Tenant.

PERPETUITIES:

No perpetuities are allowed except for charitable purposes. (Const., Art. XV, §4).

PERSONAL PROPERTY:

There are no tenancies by entireties. See 123.010 and 123.220, which apply community property law to all property except enumerated cases.

POWERS OF ATTORNEY:

Every power of attorney designed to affect an interest in real estate must be acknowledged, or proved and certified, and recorded, in the same manner as conveyances generally. (111.330).

The revocation of a recorded power of attorney can be effected only by depositing the revocation in the office in which the instrument containing the power is recorded. (111.330).

Revocation.—Written power of attorney that contains words that it is not affected by disability of principal, or becomes effective upon such disability, or similar words, may be exercised as provided in power notwithstanding principal's later disability, incapacity or uncertainty of his death; all acts done by attorney bind principal, guardian, heirs, devisees and personal representative as if principal were alive, competent and not disabled. If guardian thereafter appointed for principal, attorney in fact shall account to guardian who shall have same power principal had to revoke, suspend or terminate power of attorney. (111.460).

Death, disability or incompetence of principal who executed power of attorney other than pursuant to N.R.S. 111.460 does not terminate agency as to attorney in fact or other person who, without actual knowledge of death, disability or incompetence, acts in good faith under power of attorney. Affidavit executed by attorney in fact stating that at time of acting pursuant to power he did not have actual knowledge of revocation or termination by death, disability or incompetence is, in absence of fraud or bad faith, conclusive proof of nonrevocation of power at that time. (111.470).

REAL PROPERTY:

In Nevada, real estate may be held in joint tenancy (111.065), tenancy in common (111.060-111.064), as community property of husband and wife (123.030), and/or in condominium (117.010). Tenancy by entirety is not mentioned in statute but seems to be abolished by implication.

Tenancy in common is created by a grant or devise to two or more persons, other than executors and trustee, unless the instrument expressly declares the estate granted or devised to be a joint tenancy. (111.060).

Joint tenancy may be created without the intervention of a third person or "straw man." (111.065).

Foreign Conveyances or Encumbrances.—See category Documents and Records, topic Acknowledgments.

Soliciting Land Sales.—Board of county commissioners and governing body of an incorporated city may license and regulate solicitation of customers for land sales. (599A.050). Regulations for solicitation and advertisement of subdivision sales are provided by statute. (119.010-119.340). Any concealment or misrepresentation of a material fact, or false or deceptive statement, or failure to disclose obligations connected with any free benefit offered to customers, or contacting any person to attend a sales presentation without first disclosing purpose is a misdemeanor. (599A.060).

Condominiums are allowed if plan is recorded in county where located which describes surface of land, diagrams floor plans of buildings in order to identify each unit, and contains consent of record owners and holders of security interests to recordation of such plan. Rule against perpetuities and rule against unreasonable restraints on alienation do not defeat provisions of NRS 117 relating to condominiums. (See generally 117.101-117.110.) Time share estates are regulated. (119A.010—119A.700).

Planned unit developments are regulated. (278A.010-278A.540).

Uniform Common Ownership Act adopted. (116.1101-116.4120).

Rule in Shelley's Case does not obtain in this state. (111.070).

Rule Against Perpetuities.—Uniform Statutory Rule Against Perpetuities adopted. (111.103).

See also topics Curtesy, Deeds, Dower, Landlord and Tenant; categories Civil Actions and Procedure, topic Partition; Debtor and Creditor, topic Homesteads; Family, topic Husband and Wife; Mortgages, topic Mortgages of Real Property.

TRUST DEEDS:

See category Mortgages, topic Mortgages of Real Property.

TAXATION

ADMINISTRATION:

Department of taxation headed by tax commission with seven members has general supervision and control over entire state revenue system. (360.200). Department has original power of appraisal and assessment of property. (360.210). Chief administrative officer of department is director appointed by governor. (360.120).

Poll Tax.—None.

Penalties.—

All Taxes.—Department, if not satisfied with amount of tax to be paid state or if person fails to file return, may determine amount due; if any part of deficiency is due to negligence or intentional disregard of statute or rules, 10% penalty is added; if due to fraud or intent to evade payment for tax or fee assessed by Department of Taxation, 25% penalty is added or, if tax imposed pursuant to NRS c. 372 or 374 for storage, sale, use or consumption of vehicle, vessel or aircraft, three times amount of determination is added. Taxpayer may petition for redetermination 30 days after service of determination. Determination becomes final 30 days after served with notice of determination, or if petition for redetermination filed after 30 days notice of redetermination unless appeal filed with Tax Commission, than 30 days after Commission's order. All determinations due and payable when they become final; penalty of 10% of amount of determination, exclusive of interest, is added if not paid when due, together with interest at 1.5% per month. (360.300-360.415). If department believes collection of tax would be jeopardized by delay, it determines amount to be collected, serves notice; amount specified in notice must be paid within ten days unless petition for redetermination is filed, otherwise penalties and interest added to amount of determination. (360.412-360.416). Unless different penalty or rate specifically provided, failure to pay tax imposed by NRS cc. 362, 365, 369, 370, 372, 373 or 374, fee in 482.313 or 590.700-590.920, or business license tax imposed by NRS c. 364A when required results in penalty of 10% of amount of tax owned in addition to tax, plus interest at 1.5% per month. (360.417).

Property Taxes.—4% of installment on first quarter delinquency, 5% of two installments on second quarter delinquency, 6% of three installments on third quarter delinquency, 7% of total tax on fourth quarter delinquency. (361.483). See also subhead Collection and Sale, supra.

Sales and Use Taxes.—Retailer who fails to furnish required information or who renders false or fraudulent return is guilty of misdemeanor subject to a fine not exceeding $500 for each offense. (372.755). Any person required to make, sign or verify any report who makes any false or fraudulent return with intent to defeat or evade the determination of an amount due required by law to be made, shall for each offense be fined not less than $300 nor more than $5,000, or may be imprisoned for not exceeding one year or be subject to both. (372.760). Any violation of Sales and Use Tax statutes

ADMINISTRATION . . . *continued*

except as otherwise provided is misdemeanor. (372.765). Any person who fails to pay any tax to state within time required shall pay a penalty of 10% of tax in addition to tax plus interest at rate of 1.5% per month. (372.505).

Cigarette Tax.—It is unlawful for any person with intent to defraud state to alter or counterfeit any license permit stamp for cigarettes or to have any such forged stamp in his possession or to affix to any package of cigarettes a stamp or cigarette tax meter impression which has been removed from any other package of cigarettes or possession of cigarettes for sale which do not bear indicia of state tax. First violation is misdemeanor and subsequent offenses are Category D Felony punishable by one to four years imprisonment and fine up to $5,000. (370.380). All other violations of Cigarette Tax Act constitute gross misdemeanors. (370.390).

Gasoline Tax.—Unlawful for anyone to violate any gasoline tax statutes. (365.570, 365.580). Taxes to be paid before 25th of each month; if not paid before 25th of next month penalty as provided above. (365.340).

Unemployment Compensation.—Violation of any provision of statutes relating to unemployment compensation is misdemeanor. Any person failing to make reports as required by law must pay a forfeit of $5 for each report. In addition if such report is more than ten days delinquent such person must pay interest upon wages subject to contributions involved in such report of one-tenth of 1% for each month thereafter until such report has been filed. (612.735, 612.740).

Tax forms may be obtained from Department of Taxation, 1100 E. William, Carson City 89701.

ALCOHOLIC BEVERAGE TAXES:

Intoxicating liquor tax imposed by 369.330-369.380 et seq.

BUSINESS TAXES:

Business Tax.—Tax imposed on privilege of conducting business which must be paid quarterly based on total number of fulltime employees of previous quarter. (364A.140). No business may be conducted without obtaining business license issued by Department of Taxation; application for license must be made on form prescribed by department, set forth name and location of business, declare estimated number of employees and be accompanied by $25 fee. (364A.130).

Taxation of Insurance Companies.—See category Insurance, topic Insurance Companies.

Taxation of Mines and Mining Claims.—See category Mineral, Water and Fishing Rights, topic Mines and Minerals.

Taxation of Bank Stock.—See category Business Regulation and Commerce, topic Banks and Banking.

CASINO ENTERTAINMENT TAX:

Imposed by 463.401-463.406.

CIGARETTE TAX:

Imposed by 370.010-370.430.

ESTATE TAX:

Tax imposed on transfer of taxable estate of resident decedent in amount of maximum credit allowable against federal estate tax for payment of state death taxes. (375A.100). Legislature cannot increase this tax due to Nevada Constitution Art. 10, §4.

Apportionment Against Inter Vivos Dispositions.—Provided for by 150.290 through .390.

GASOLINE AND SPECIAL FUELS TAXES:

Gasoline tax imposed by 365.170-365.210.

Special fuel tax on fuels other than gasoline imposed by 366.190-366.210.

GIFT TAX:

None.

INCOME TAX:

None.

INHERITANCE TAX:

None.

PROPERTY TAXES:

Taxable Property.—All property of every kind and nature within this state is subject to taxation, except that which is specifically exempted by Constitution or statute. (361.045). Where certain exempt real or personal property is leased to person in connection with business conducted for profit, or such property is leased or loaned to person as residence, taxes will be assessed to lessee in same manner as taxes assessed to owners of real property, except property located within or on limits of public airport, park, market or fairground or any property owned by public airport, unless property not located on public airport and is leased or made available for any purposes other than public airport, payments are made on federal property in lieu of taxes, property belongs to state-supported school, property is leased under Taylor Grazing Act, U.S. Forest Service, or Bureau of Reclamation, property is made available to public employee or officer incident to employment, personage, or property owned by charitable or religious corporation used as residence by person in connection with carrying out activities of organization, low cost housing owned by government, occasional rental of meeting rooms, and exempt property providing day care by nonprofit organization. (361.157; 361.159).

Various political subdivisions submit budgets to tax commission for approval and upon adjustment it certifies the combined tax rate for state and local areas. (361.455; 361.4547). Rate statutorily limited to $3.64 on each $100 of assessed valuation in all counties unless Nevada Tax Commission determines that local government's financial condition is in state of "severe financial emergency" at which time additional taxes may be imposed per 354.685 and 354.695 and rate constitutionally limited to 5¢ on each $1 of assessed valuation (Const. Art. 10).

Exemptions.—The following property is exempt from taxation: All public property within state; property owned by Nevada Rural Housing Authority; personal property held for sale by merchant or manufacturer, and tangible personal property purchased by businesses to be consumed during operation of business, livestock, bees, boats, slide-in campers and camper shells; pipe and other agricultural equipment used to convey water for irrigation of legal crops; property of nonprofit private schools; unpatented mining claims (proceeds taxable); volunteer fire departments; property of Nevada Heritage Association used for association functions; churches, parsonages, etc., used for religious worship, with their furniture; funds, furniture, etc., of Elks, Eagles, Knights of Pythias, Knights of Columbus, Masons, Odd Fellows, Lahontan and National Audubon Societies, Defenders of Wildlife, or other charitable or benevolent organization or society, used for benevolent purposes or noncommercial amateur theatrical corporations, not exceeding $5,000 to any one society; real estate and fixtures of above organizations exempt from taxation; cemeteries set apart for public use when no charge is made for burial therein; property of widows and orphan children residing in community, not exceeding $1,000; property of blind, not over $3,000; funds, furniture, buildings, fixtures, and lots on which situated, owned by and used for organizational purposes of post or unit of national organization of ex-service men or women; property of Nevada resident honorably discharged from U.S. Armed Forces after active duty during specified dates, not over $1,000; severely disabled veterans up to $10,000; real property of University of Nevada or Nevada Southern University fraternity or sorority; all property leased or rented to University and Community College System of Nevada at less than 10% fair market rental or lease value; land, buildings and equipment used by Y.M.C.A., Y.W.C.A., Red Cross, Salvation Army, and Girl and Boy Scouts and Sierra Arts Foundation, not to exceed $5,000 each, and not including property rented for valuable consideration for non-membership purposes, or otherwise used for income purposes unless rent or other consideration is paid or given to tax exempt 501(c)(3) organization; land and improvements acquired by Nature Conservancy held for ultimate acquisition by state or other governmental association or nonprofit cooperative corporation; all property of water users' nonprofit association or nonprofit cooperative corporation; property used to control air or water pollution unless such property produces net profit to owner or net reduction of operating costs; percentage of all property of business found by Commission on Economic Development to have as primary purpose conservation of energy or substitution of alternative sources of energy. (361.050-361.159). Resident senior citizen, 62 years old on first day of assessment year, who has owned home since July 1 immediately preceding filing of claim and whose household income is under $21,500, may claim allowance against property taxes on his home according to schedule provided in statute. (361.833). Senior citizen with same qualifications who rents is entitled to comparable percentage discount. (361.835). All claims for tax exemption on real property must be filed by June 15; once initial claim filed by exempt organization not required to file annual claims if property remains exempt. (361.155).

Personal property in transit through state and that stored in warehouse within state for final distribution or resale outside Nevada is expressly excluded from taxation. (361.160-361.185).

The annual levy for state and county taxes is made by county commissioners immediately after commission certifies combined tax rate and lien attaches on July 1 of year for which taxes are levied. (361.445-361.470). Personal property taxes are lien on all property in county and on real property in other counties from time certified copy of unpaid tax is filed for record with county recorder. (361.450).

Assessment.—All taxes are assessed by county assessors each year. (361.260). Assessment is based upon 35% of taxable value of property. (361.225). County assessor with county and state boards of equalization determine taxable value using factors enumerated by statute. (361.227).

Agricultural real property and open space real property is assessed upon application at 35% of taxable value for agricultural use and open space use respectively, with notification to owner of agricultural use or open space use assessment with notation that deferred taxes will become due when parcel converted to higher use. (361A.130, 361.220). Fiscal year when property converted to higher use becomes base year and deferred taxes for previous years of deferred taxes and penalties calculated pursuant to statutory formula become lien on property. (361A.280).

State tax commission establishes valuations of property of an interstate or intercounty nature (361.320) and of all land and mobile homes (361.325). County assessor must appraise property applying factors adopted and approved by tax commission, and reappraise all property at least once every five years thereafter using same standards. (361.260). Whenever property is appraised or reappraised, assessor must deliver or mail written notice, on or before Jan. 1 of fiscal year in which appraisal or reappraisal is made, to owner of property stating its assessed valuation as determined. (361.300).

Property tax appraiser employed by state or political subdivision must be certified by department. (361.221).

Payment.—Taxes on net proceeds of minerals extracted are due on or before May 10 of year certificate indicating amount due is received. (362.130-362.150). Annual taxes on migratory property are payable to assessor immediately upon being assessed if owner owns no realty in county. (361.505). Real property taxes are payable in four equal installments on or before third Mon. in July, and first Mon. in Oct., Jan., Mar. (361.480).

Prepayment of All Property Taxes.—Owner of single-family dwelling, free and clear of all encumbrances except unpaid assessments for public improvement may apply to county assessor to establish allodial title; upon application, state treasurer determines amount of money required to be paid that would be adequate to pay all future tax liability of property for life expectancy of youngest titleholder; and upon payment of that amount, state treasurer issues certificate of allodial title to property. (361.900).

See note at head of Digest as to 1998 legislation covered.

See Topical Index in front part of this volume.

PROPERTY TAXES . . . continued

Certificate transmitted to assessor, who shall collect no further taxes from allodial titleholder, and state treasurer shall pay all amounts due for taxes even if there is deficiency based on treasurer's determination of amount due. (361.905). Allodial title valid as long as homeowner continues to own residence unless he chooses to relinquish allodial title and receive refund of moneys paid to establish title pursuant to 361.915. (361.910).

Collection and Sale.—In all cases where taxes are delinquent county tax receiver, after giving prescribed notice, must issue to county treasurer certificate authorizing him to hold property as trustee until it is redeemed or time for redemption has expired, property being assessable to treasurer during such period. (361.565-361.575). At expiration thereof treasurer, upon order of county commissioners and after giving prescribed notice, must sell property for taxes, costs, penalties, and interest (which is added for such period at rate of 10% per annum). Before deed is delivered it must be recorded at purchaser's expense, and with it must be furnished affidavits showing that all required proceedings have been taken. Such deed is primary evidence of regularity of proceedings. (361.585-361.595).

Where the net amount of the delinquent tax exceeds $3,000, suit must be brought by the district attorney of the county in which it was assessed and the tax collected by prescribed proceedings, unless sooner paid by the delinquent. (361.625-361.730).

Redemption.—Real estate held by county treasurer for delinquent taxes may be redeemed by owner at any time within two years, by paying taxes, penalties and costs, with 10% per annum interest (361.570), and right of redemption continues after expiration of two year period until such time as county treasurer gives public notice of sale (361.585).

Tax Liens.—Property taxes constitute perpetual lien against property assessed until such taxes, penalty charges, and interest are paid. Lien for taxes on personal property attaches to real property assessed against property assessment is filed with county recorder in county in which real property is situated. (361.450).

Uniform Federal Tax Lien Registration Act adopted in Nevada. (108.825-108.837). Federal tax liens on real property recorded in county where property located, and liens on personal property recorded in county where taxpayer resides or with Secretary of State if taxpayer is corporation or partnership having principal executive officer in state. (108.825-108.837). County shall charge its standard fee for recording and Secretary of State shall charge $20. (108.833).

Corporations are taxed on their property in county where property is located. There is no franchise tax or income tax on corporations.

REAL ESTATE CONVEYANCE TAX:

County recorder computes and collects tax of 65¢ for each $500 of value of any lands, except unpatented mines or mining claims, transferred to another person if consideration paid exceeds $100. Each deed evidencing transfer of title subject to tax must have a signed form attached declaring amount of documentary transfer tax due and whether tax was computed on full value of property conveyed or on full value less liens and encumbrances remaining thereon at time of transfer; and county recorder must collect amount of tax due. Statutory exemptions contained in 375.090. Certain counties may by ordinance impose tax on transfer of real property. (375.010-375.110).

SALES AND USE TAXES:

Sales tax at rate of 2% of sale price and city-county relief tax is imposed on retail sales of tangible personal property to be passed on to purchaser insofar as possible. (372.105; 377.040). Separate tax of 2.25% imposed on gross receipts of retail sales of all tangible personal property within county. Known as Local School Support Tax Law. (374.010, et seq.). Constitutionality of School Support Tax upheld in 83 Nev. 266, 428 P.2d 371.

Use tax at rate of 2% of sales price is imposed on storage, use or other consumption in state of tangible personal property purchased from a retailer on or after July 1, 1955. (372.185). Separate tax of 2.5% is imposed on storage, use or other consumption of tangible personal property purchased on or after July 1, 1967, as part of Local School Support Tax, supra. (374.190). Among exemptions applicable to both taxes are: property subject to proceeds of mines tax, motor vehicle fuels, animal food products, animal feeds, seeds and plants, horses, fertilizers, containers and labels, gas, electricity, water and heating fuels, newspapers and periodicals, prosthetic devices, medicines, aircraft, aircraft engines; in addition, property shipped out of state, sales to U.S. or Nevada governments or their agencies, nonprofit organizations created for religious, charitable or educational purposes and common carriers for use in business are exempt from sales tax, and property sold under sales tax liability or property for subsequent export out of Nevada are exempt from use tax. (372.260-372.350).

Monthly returns must be filed with Nevada Tax Commission. (372.355-372.395).

STAMP TAX:

See topics Cigarette Tax, Real Estate Conveyance Tax.

UNEMPLOYMENT COMPENSATION TAX:

Employers within Act must pay, without deduction from wages, 2.95% of wages or such rate or proportion thereof as administrator of Employment Security Division may fix under prescribed rules of classification and .05% of wages paid into special revenue fund administrated by Executive Director for employment of claimants (612.602; 612.535; 612.540).

Act applies to all employers of one or more individuals who have payroll of $225 or more for any calendar year, including with some exceptions, agricultural labor, domestic services in private home, and employment by state or political subdivision, but not including service in crew of foreign vessel on navigable waters of U.S.; service in employ of son, daughter or spouse; service of child under 18 years old in employ of father or mother; service in employ of Federal Government or any state or of any instrumentality or political subdivision of either, with certain limitations and exceptions; service for various religious, charitable, scientific and similar organizations; service

with respect to which unemployment compensation is payable under act of Congress; service of person under 18 years old in delivery or distribution of newspapers, except for subsequent distribution; service by licensed real estate salesman or broker employed by another broker if paid solely by commission; service by lessee engaged in mining. (612.055-612.142).

UNIFORM FEDERAL TAX LIEN REGISTRATION ACT:

See topic Property Taxes, subhead Tax Liens, catchline Uniform Federal Tax Lien Registration Act.

TRANSPORTATION

MOTOR VEHICLES:

Motor vehicle law is administered by Department of Motor Vehicles and Public Safety and Nevada Highway Patrol, a division thereof, 555 Wright Way, Carson City 89701. (481.015-481.180).

Vehicle license is required annually. Registration card must be carried and number plates displayed in front and rear. (482.255, 482.275).

No exemption for members of armed forces.

Operator's License.—Uniform Motor Vehicle Drivers' License Act adopted. (482.010-483.630).

Under certain circumstances, department may refuse to issue license or revoke existing license. (483.250; 483.460).

Driver's License Compact requiring exchange of records of motor vehicle violations with party states adopted. (482.640-483.690).

Members of armed forces when operating a vehicle in service of armed forces are exempt from license. (483.240).

Identification Marks.—Destruction or alteration of motor number, identification number, or other identification mark of part of motor vehicle placed on it by manufacturer is gross misdemeanor. (482.553). Knowingly to operate vehicle with altered identification mark or distinguishing number required for registration or with part with altered identification number or mark placed on it by manufacturer is misdemeanor. (482.255; 482.545).

Titles, Sales and Liens.—Department of Motor Vehicles and Public Safety with whom every vehicle is registered, issues certificate of ownership which must disclose both name and address of owner and legal owner and odometer reading by seller. (482.245). If security interest is taken or retained by seller of vehicle, such information must appear on certificate of ownership. (See 482.428.) Registration fee is $33 for auto, $33 for truck under certain weight, and additional fee of $6 for transfer of registration; to reinstate registration of vehicle suspended pursuant to 485.317, fee of $250 if owner failed to have insurance, or fee of $50 if owner allowed insurance coverage to expire without first cancelling registration for vehicle. (482.-480). Notice of sale of repossessed vehicles, see 482.516. Repossessed vehicle must be sold in commercially reasonable manner. (482.5163). See also category Debtor and Creditor, topic Liens.

Operation Prohibited.—Driving while intoxicated or under influence of liquor or stimulating or stupefying drugs. (484.379). Drinking liquor in moving vehicle. (484.378). Any person who drives or is in actual physical control of vehicle upon highways, or on premises to which public has access, is deemed to have given consent to evidentiary test for alcoholic or drug content of his blood, urine, or breath. (484.383).

Size and Weight Limits.—Regulated by 484.737-484.775. Multistate Highway Transportation Agreement enacted. (481A.010-481A.020).

Equipment Required.—Regulated by 484.541-484.646. Unlawful to drive passenger car unless it is equipped with seat belts; driver and front seat passenger of car weighing less than 6,000 pounds must wear belt or be subject to fine. Failure to do so however is not moving traffic violation, may not be considered as negligence in civil or criminal action, and may not be considered misuse or abuse of product in any action for damages for injury resulting from manufacture, sale or use of product. (484.641). Motorcycle operator and passenger must wear protective headgear and if motorcycle not equipped with windscreen, glasses or face shields. (486.231).

Lights Required.—Regulated by 484.543-484.591.

Inspection.—Peace officers and department vehicle safety inspectors, with reasonable grounds, may require driver to submit vehicle to inspection and appropriate tests. Department may establish vehicle inspection centers to inspect tires and brakes on certain vehicles intended to be registered. (484.695).

Traffic Regulations.—Rules of road, 484.251-484.513.

Accidents.—Driver must stop, give assistance if necessary, give name and address of owner, passengers and driver and license numbers if demanded, and report accident to nearest police station if in city, otherwise to sheriff. (484.219; 484.223). When unoccupied vehicle is struck must get name of owner or license number and make similar report. When accident results in damage to fixtures or other property legally upon or adjacent to highway, driver must attempt to locate and notify owner and make similar report. (484.225). Driver of vehicle involved in accident on highway or premises to which public has access, causing death or bodily injury or apparent property damage of $750 or more, must file written report of accident with department within ten days. No report required if accident investigated by law enforcement officer whose report contains name and address of insurance company with coverage, number of each policy and dates when coverage begins and ends. (484.229). If any person is injured in accident, driver of colliding vehicle is subject to fine and imprisonment if he fails to stop and give assistance. (484.219). Causing death or substantial bodily injury to another while under influence of alcohol or drugs is felony; if defendant transporting child under 15 years of age, at time, court must consider such aggravating factor in determining sentence. (484.3795).

Liability of Owner.—Negligence or willful misconduct of operator of motor vehicle driven with express or implied permission of owner is imputed to owner for all purposes

See note at head of Digest as to 1998 legislation covered.

See Topical Index in front part of this volume.

MOTOR VEHICLES . . . *continued*

of civil damages where operator is wife, husband, son, daughter, father, mother, brother, sister, or other immediate member of owner's family. (41.440-41.460).

Abandonment of Vehicle.—Registered owner of any vehicle abandoned on public property responsible for cost of removal and disposition. (487.220).

Liability for Acts of Minors.—Negligence or willful misconduct of minor under 18 years operating motor vehicle resulting in injury or death to another person or property damage is imputed to person who signed minor's application for license. (483.300; 486.101). Such person or parent or guardian is relieved of liability where he files verified written request to Driver's License Division of Department that minor's license be cancelled. (483.310; 486.111).

Guests.—There is no limitation on liability for injury to guest. (91 Nev. 506, 538 P.2d 574; 1977, c. 149).

Insurance.—See subhead Security Following Accident, infra.

No-Fault Insurance.—Nevada's No-Fault Act (698.010 et seq.) was repealed effective Jan. 1, 1980.

Security Following Accident.—Accident report must be filed within ten days if injury or property damage exceeding $750 unless accident investigated by law enforcement officer whose report contains name and address of insurance company with coverage, number of each policy and dates when coverage begins and ends. (484.229). Department is required to suspend his license and registration privileges of owner, and to see that adequate security is furnished, unless full protection is assured injured or damaged third person under liability policy or bond, or arrangement has been made for satisfying claims. (485.190-485.300). Owner or operator has right to hearing before any suspension. (485.191).

Foreign vehicle, duly licensed in home state, may be operated by nonresident without local license until current nonresident registration expires, provided plates issued by home state are displayed. (482.385). If foreign vehicle is furnished to resident of Nevada for his continued use, it must be registered in Nevada within 30 days. (482.385). If owner becomes resident he must register vehicle in this state within 30 days or at time he obtains driver's license, whichever is earlier. (482.385). Nonresident carrier for hire must comply with law governing motor vehicle carriers, unless laws of his state grant reciprocal rights to Nevada carriers, in which case only nonresident permit is required. (482.390).

Nonresident Operators.—No restrictions.

Actions Against Nonresidents.—Use of highway by any person, either as principal, master, agent or servant, is equivalent to appointment of Director of Department of Motor Vehicles and Public Safety as his attorney on whom process may be served in action growing out of such use or resulting in damage or loss to person or property while using public highway. Process so served is equivalent to personal service on motorist, provided notice of such service and copy of process are forthwith sent, by registered mail to defendant at address supplied in his accident report, if any, and if not at best address available to plaintiff, and return receipt signed by defendant or by United States Postal Service stating that defendant refused to accept delivery, or could not be located or that address was insufficient and plaintiff's affidavit of compliance with requirements are appended to original process and filed in action. Personal service of such notice and copy of process on defendant outside state is equivalent of mailing and may be proved by affidavit appended to original process and filed. Court may order such continuances as may be necessary to give defendant reasonable opportunity to defend. (14.070).

Direct Actions.—Direct action by injured person against insurer not allowed.

Motor vehicle carriers are licensed by Department. (706.186). Transportation services authority regulates licensing (706.481-706.631) and rates (706.311-706.371). All carriers licensed (706.491) and "fully regulated common motor carriers" must have certificate of public convenience and necessity (706.386). Every fully regulated carrier and operator of tow car must file, as authority requires, liability insurance policy or certificate or bond of surety. (706.291). All fully regulated carriers and brokers keep detailed accounts of business transacted and render them to commission upon request and file annual report to commission by May 15 in form and detail prescribed by regulation. (703.191, 703.193).

Taxicabs are regulated in detail by c. 706.

Intrastate carriers must furnish such information as authority may request. (706.266).

Motor Vehicle Taxes.—Annual tax imposed on privilege of operating vehicle on public highways is 4¢ on each $1 valuation. (371.030, 371.040). Valuation based upon 35% of manufacturer's suggested retail price or of retail price to original purchaser where determinable except for buses and certain trucks and trailers. (371.050). Depreciation allowances set forth in 371.060. Tax collected by Department. (371.120).

Gasoline Tax.—See category Taxation, topic Gasoline and Special Fuels Taxes.

RAILROADS:

See category Business Regulation and Commerce, topic Carriers.

See note at head of Digest as to 1998 legislation covered.

See Topical Index in front part of this volume.

COMMERCIAL CODE FORMS

See also categories Business Regulation and Commerce, topic Commercial Code; Mortgages, topic Chattel Mortgages.
There is no single form of security agreement currently in widespread use in Nevada. Following security agreement form has been used by local lending institutions. Forms UCC-1, UCC-2, and UCC-3 supplied by Department of State of Nevada.

Vehicle Security Agreement and Note   No. . . . .

$. . . . . Nevada . . . . , 19. . . . .
For value received, I promise to pay in lawful money of the United States of America to the order of . . . .
. . . . at its . . . . Branch in this city the principal sum of
. . . . Dollars on demand, if no demand is made then in instalments as
follows: . . . . Dollars ($. . . . .) or more on the . . . .
day of . . . . , 19. . . . . . and . . . . Dollars ($. . . . .) or more on the . . . . .
. . . . day of each and every . . . . thereafter until the . . . . day of . . . .
. . . . , 19. . . . . , on which said date the entire balance of principal then unpaid shall become due and payable.

If default be made in the payment when due of any part or instalment of principal or interest, or in the event any act by or against the undersigned is deemed by the Bank in good faith to impair the prospect of payment, then the whole sum of principal and interest shall become immediately due and payable at the option of the holder of this note, without notice.

In the event that I shall fail to make any payment herein provided for, at the time when the same becomes due under the provisions hereof, and said payment shall become overdue for a period in excess of 10 days, I promise to pay an "Accounting Service Charge" of five cents (5¢) for each dollar so overdue, for the purpose of defraying the expense of following up and handling the said delinquent payment, but not to exceed five dollars ($5.00) in respect to any one such late payment.

In addition thereto I promise to pay reasonable attorney's fees and costs incurred in the collection of this note or any part hereof without suit, or in the event of suit such additional sum as attorneys' fees as the court may adjudge reasonable. For the purpose of attachment or levy of execution, this note shall be payable wherever I may be situated, at the option of the holder.
(1) . . . .   (2) . . . .
Including charge fee for: If a charge for life insurance is made the person whose life is
                    Life $ . . . .   to be insured should sign line (1).
                    Disability $ . . . .

Security Agreement

This AGREEMENT, made this . . . . day of . . . . , 19. . . . . . by . . . .
. . . .
of . . . ., County of . . . . , State of Nevada,
hereinafter designated as DEBTOR, to . . . . , having its principal
place of business in the City of Reno, County of Washoe, State of Nevada, hereinafter designed as SECURED PARTY.
WITNESSETH: Debtor hereby transfers and conveys to Secured Party a security interest in that certain vehicle described as
follows:

Year	New or Used	Make Trade Name	No. Cyl.	Equipment: Std. Sports, Deluxe, Etc.	Type of Body	Model No. or Letter	Manufacturer's ID No.

now and to be permanently located in the City of . . . ., County of . . . .
State of Nevada, together with all equipment, parts, appliances and appurtenances now or hereafter to be placed thereon, all of which shall become a component part thereof and included under the terms of this agreement, as security for the payment by Debtor of a promissory note hereinafter referred to as note in the original amount of . . . . Dollars ($. . . . .), dated the . . . . day of . . . .
. . ., 19. . . . . , in accordance with its terms and executed by Debtor and payable to Secured Party, and for the payment of any other sum now, or hereafter owing from Debtor to Secured Party; provided, however, that the maximum amount to be secured hereby and remaining unpaid at any one time shall not exceed twice the original amount of the note, above described. The Debtor hereby promises to pay said note and all other money obligations according to their tenor, and to perform all agreements as in said note and hereinafter in this agreement stated, according to their terms, all payments to be made in lawful money of the United States of America.

All extensions and renewals of said note, or any part thereof, advances thereunder and all costs of litigation, collection (including attorney's fees or other costs expended or incurred in connection with the discovering, locating or taking possession of said vehicle) and any and all costs of returning said vehicle to the location above referred to (including costs of repairing, rehabilitating or storing said vehicle) together with an Accounting Service Charge of five cents (5¢) per dollar ($1.00 minimum) of any monthly instalment not paid when due are all likewise secured hereby.

Each person signing this agreement, other than the bank, is a debtor; and the obligations of all debtors are joint and several.

By . . . .

. . . .
                            TITLE

. . . .
                    BRANCH ADDRESS

Debtor incorporates and acknowledges the terms and conditions on the reverse side hereof as a part of this agreement.

DEBTOR DECLARES THAT HE HAS READ THIS AGREEMENT AND UNDERSTANDS THE EFFECT AND PURPORT THEREOF.

. . . .
                            DEBTOR

. . . .
                            DEBTOR

. . . .
                            ADDRESS

. . . .
                            ADDRESS

See note at head of Digest as to 1998 legislation covered.

See Topical Index in front part of this volume.

Reverse Side.—   TERMS AND CONDITIONS

The terms and conditions of this agreement are as follows:

(1) Debtor hereby warrants that he is the sole owner of the vehicle described herein and that there are no liens or encumbrances or adverse claims of any kind whatever thereon or on any part thereof.

(2) Debtor agrees that he will neither use or permit said vehicle to be used for any unlawful purpose; that he will register, use, operate and control the same in accordance with all statutes, ordinances and regulations relating to the registration, use, operation and control of said vehicle.

(3) Debtor will not, nor will he attempt to, assign, pledge, encumber, hypothecate or otherwise dispose of said vehicle or any part thereof, during the terms of said note and this agreement, nor will he remove said vehicle or permit the same to be removed from the county where said vehicle is permanently located, as set forth herein for any period in excess of ten (10) days, without the prior written consent of Secured Party.

(4) The Debtor agrees forthwith to properly register said vehicle and procure and keep a license therefor from the State in which this Security Agreement is executed and to immediately report the license number thereof to the Secured Party, and to have the license and certificate of legal ownership show the Secured Party herein, or its assigns, as the legal owner of said vehicle, during the term of this Security Agreement and that said certificate of legal ownership shall be delivered to and held by Secured Party during the existence of this Security Agreement, and until the Secured Party shall have been paid in full and until this Security Agreement has been satisfied in full.

(5) Debtor agrees to exhibit said vehicle to Secured Party upon demand and to keep said vehicle in as good as condition and repair as it now is, ordinary wear and tear excepted and to promptly pay all taxes levied or assessed thereon and all liens which may attach thereto. Service of any notice upon Debtor may be made by deposit in the United States mail, postage prepaid, directed to Debtor at his address set forth herein.

(6) Debtor agrees to take out, pay for and keep in full force and effect a policy or policies of insurance, in form satisfactory to Secured Party and issued by an insurance carrier approved by Secured Party (covering both Secured and Debtor), for the hazards of fire, theft and total or partial destruction, and such additional hazards as may be mutually agreed upon by Debtor and Secured Party. The loss under every such policy shall be paid first to the Secured Party or its assigns up to the amount of the obligation secured, and the balance, if any, to the Debtor; said policy to be in the possession of the Secured Party until satisfaction of all obligations secured by this agreement. In the event that Debtor should for any reason fail to take out said insurance or pay for the same, the Secured Party may, at the cost and expense of the Debtor, take out and pay for such insurance, and any sums advanced therefor shall be added to the balance of said note and secured by this agreement. Any sums received upon cancellation of any policy may be applied by Secured Party upon the then remaining balance of any obligation secured hereby.

(7) Should Secured Party make any advance or advances or spend any money for the protection or preservation of its security, or should there accrue or be due any collection costs or other obligations arising under this agreement, such advance or advances, together with such collection costs or other obligations arising under this agreement and unpaid shall be added to the unpaid balance of said note and shall be secured hereby, and the Secured Party shall have the right upon the receipt of any instalment or payment due under the terms of said note and this agreement to apply the same, first in satisfaction of any collection costs or other moneys advanced by Secured Party hereunder; second, to the satisfaction of any unpaid interest, and third, the balance of said instalment or instalments in payment of principal. Should there be a deficiency in the amount of any instalment or payment after the payment of said costs as in this agreement provided, such deficiency shall be payable forthwith, and the failure on the part of the Debtor to pay or satisfy same shall accelerate for immediate payment the entire unpaid balance of said obligation, including all advances made and collection costs and interest accrued, and Secured Party may exercise such right or rights as are reserved to Secured Party under the terms of this agreement or permitted by law.

(8) Should Debtor fail to make payment of any part of the principal or interest as provided in said note, or if any breach be made of any obligation or promise of the Debtor herein contained or secured, or if Debtor shall abandon said vehicle, or regardless of any other default, if said vehicle be attached or bankruptcy proceedings be instituted by or against Debtor, then the whole principal sum unpaid upon said note with interest accrued thereon, and all other sums of money due or unpaid at the time of said default, and interest thereon, or advanced under the terms of this agreement, or secured hereby, and the interest thereon, shall immediately become due and payable at the option of Secured Party, without notice to Debtor, and it may at once proceed to foreclose this agreement according to law, or it may, as its option, and it is hereby empowered so to do, enter upon the premises where the said vehicle may be and take possession thereof; and remove and sell and dispose of the same at public or private sale without any previous demand of performance or notice to Debtor of any such sale whatsoever, notice of sale and demand of performance and every other notice or demand whatsoever being hereby expressly waived by Debtor to the extent that such notice and or demand may be waived by law, and from the proceeds of sale retain all costs and charges incurred by it in the said taking or sale, including reasonable attorney's fee incurred; also all sums due on said note under any provisions thereof, or advanced under the terms of this agreement, and interest thereon or due or owing to Secured Party under any provisions of this agreement, or secured hereby, with interest thereon, and any surplus of such proceeds remaining shall be paid to Debtor or whomever may be lawfully entitled to receive the same; if there be a deficit, Debtor agrees immediately to pay the same to Secured Party.

Secured Party, or its agent, may bid and purchase at any sale made under this agreement.

(9) Debtor further agrees that if from any cause there shall be a substantial decrease in the value of said property, Secured Party shall have the option of demanding of Debtor further security in order to offset said decrease in value, and upon the failure of Debtor to give additional security, Secured Party may proceed in the same manner as herein provided in case of any other default.

(10) This agreement shall bind and inure to the benefit of parties hereto and their executors, administrators, heirs and assigns.

It is further specifically agreed that the taking of any action by Secured Party shall not be deemed to be an election of that action, but rather, the rights and privileges and options granted to Secured Party under the terms of this agreement shall be deemed cumulative, and not alternative.

Time is declared to be the essence of said note and this agreement with respect to the performance of the covenants and obligations set forth herein and it is further specifically agreed that no waiver by Secured Party of any breach or default of or by the Debtor, whether under the terms of the aforesaid note, or of this agreement, shall be deemed a waiver of any breach or default thereafter occurring.

See note at head of Digest as to 1998 legislation covered.

See Topical Index in front part of this volume.

This FINANCING STATEMENT is presented for filing pursuant to the Nevada Uniform Commercial Code

1. DEBTOR (Last Name First)		1A. Social Security or Federal Tax No.	
1B. MAILING ADDRESS	1C. City, State		1D. Zip Code
1E. RESIDENCE ADDRESS (If an Individual and Different Than 1B)	1F. City, State		1G. Zip Code
2. ADDITIONAL DEBTOR (If Any) (Last Name First)		2A. Social Security or Federal Tax No.	
2B. MAILING ADDRESS	2C. City, State		2D. Zip Code
2E. RESIDENCE ADDRESS (If an Individual and Different Than 2B)	2F. City, State		2G. Zip Code
3. DEBTOR(S) TRADE NAME OR STYLE (If Any)		3A. Federal Tax Number	
4. ADDRESS OF DEBTOR(S) CHIEF PLACE OF BUSINESS (If Any)	4A. City, State		4B. Zip Code

5. SECURED PARTY
   Name
   Mailing Address
   City   State   Zip   Code

5A. Social Security No., Federal Tax No. or Bank Transit and A.B.A. No.

6. ASSIGNEE OF SECURED PARTY (If Any)
   Name
   Mailing Address
   City   State   Zip   Code

6A. Social Security No., Federal Tax No. or Bank Transit and A.B.A. No.

7. This FINANCING STATEMENT covers the following types or items of property (if crops or timber, include description of real property on which growing or to be grown and name of record owner of such real estate, if fixtures, include description of real property to which affixed or to be affixed and name of record owner of such real estate; if oil, gas or minerals, include description of real property from which to be extracted.

7A. _____   7C. $ _____
       Signature of Record Owner   Maximum Amount of Indebtedness to
                                               be Secured at Any One Time (Optional)

7B. _____
       (Type) Record Owner of Real Property.

8. Check ☒ If Applicable	A ☐ Proceeds of collateral are also covered	B ☐ Products of collateral are also covered	C ☐ Proceeds of above described original collateral in which a security interest was perfected	D ☐ Collateral was brought into this State subject to security interest in another jurisdiction

9. Check ☒ If Applicable	☐ Debtor is a "Transmitting Utility" in Accordance with NRS 704.205 and NRS 104.9403

10. _____
            (Date) _____ 19 ____

By: _____
       Signature(s) of Debtor(s)   (Title)

By: _____
       Signature(s) of Secured Party(ies)   (Title)

12. This Space for Use of Filing Officer
    (Date, Time, File Number and Filing Officer)

11.   *Return Copy to*

NAME
ADDRESS
CITY,
STATE
AND ZIP

(1) FILING OFFICER COPY-ALPHABETICAL Uniform Commercial Code-Form
UCC-1 (Rev. 7-77)

Approved by the
Nevada
Secretary of the State

FILING FEES
SEE INSTRUCTIONS

See note at head of Digest as to 1998 legislation covered.

See Topical Index in front part of this volume.

This STATEMENT is presented for filing pursuant to the Nevada Uniform Commercial Code

1. File No. of Orig. Financing Statement	1A. Date of Filing of Orig. Financing Statement	1B. Date of Orig. Financing Statement	1C. Place of Filing Orig. Financing Statement

2. DEBTOR (Last Name First)		2A. Social Security or Federal Tax No.	
2B. MAILING ADDRESS		2C. City, State	2D. Zip Code

3. ADDITIONAL DEBTOR (If Any) (Last Name First)		3A. Social Security or Federal Tax No.	
3B. MAILING ADDRESS		3C. City, State	3D. Zip Code

4. SECURED PARTY
   Name
   Mailing Address
   City   State   Zip Code

4A. Social Security No., Fed. Tax No. or Bank Transit and A.B.A. No.

5. ASSIGNEE OF SECURED PARTY (If Any)
   Name
   Mailing Address
   City   State   Zip Code

5A. Social Security No., Fed. Tax No. or Bank Transit and A.B.A. No.

6. A ☐ CONTINUATION—The original Financing Statement between the foregoing Debtor and Secured Party bearing the file number and date shown above is continued. If collateral is crops or timber, fixtures, or oil, gas or minerals check here ☐ and insert description of real property on which growing or to be grown or to which affixed or to be affixed or from which to be extracted in Item 7 below. If crops or fixtures, also insert name of record owner of real estate. Effective if submitted within 6 months of expiration date.

   B ☐ RELEASE—From the collateral described in the Financing Statement bearing the file number shown above, the Secured Party releases the collateral described in Item 7 below. Release does not terminate debt.

   C ☐ ASSIGNMENT—The Secured Party certifies that the Secured Party has assigned to the Assignee above named, all the Secured Party's rights under the Financing Statement bearing the file number shown above in the collateral described in Item 7 below.

   D ☐ TERMINATION—The Secured Party certifies that the Secured Party no longer claims a security interest under the Financing Statement bearing the file number shown above.

   E ☐ AMENDMENT—The Financing Statement bearing the file number shown above is amended as set forth in Item 7 below. (Signature of Debtor and Secured Party required on all amendments.)

   F ☐ OTHER (May be used for change of address.)

7.

THIS SPACE FOR USE OF FILING OFFICER

8.
        (Date) _____ 19 ____

By: _____
    Signature(s) of Debtor(s)   (Title)

By: _____
    Signature(s) of Secured Party(ies)   (Title)

9. This Space for Use of Filing Officer
   (Date, Time, Filing Officer)

11.   *Return Copy to*

NAME
ADDRESS
CITY,
STATE
AND ZIP

(1) FILING OFFICER COPY-ALPHABETICAL Uniform Commercial Code-Form N-UCC-2 (Rev. 7-77)

Approved by the
Nevada
Secretary of State

FILING FEE
SEE INSTRUCTIONS

See note at head of Digest as to 1998 legislation covered.

See Topical Index in front part of this volume.

NEW HAMPSHIRE LAW DIGEST REVISER

Wadleigh, Starr & Peters
95 Market Street
Manchester, New Hampshire 03101
Telephone: 603-669-4140
Fax: 603-669-6018
Email: fdesk@wspdc.com

Reviser Profile

History: The firm was founded in Manchester, New Hampshire in 1899 by David Taggart and George Bingham. It has maintained its offices in downtown Manchester, New Hampshire since that time.

Areas of Concentration: Historically, Wadleigh, Starr & Peters has been one of the major litigation firms in the state of New Hampshire, providing representation in virtually every area of civil litigation, including professional malpractice, products liability, construction, environmental, commercial and insurance defense. The firm also contains one of this state's most established commercial and real estate practices which provides comprehensive services to a wide variety of clients, including financial institutions, developers, general contractors, corporations, as well as individuals. Additionally, the firm's practice includes industrial, commercial, and residential real estate law; tax, corporate, commercial, labor, constitutional, municipal, hospital and banking law, including creditor's representation in bankruptcy and reorganization procedures. The firm also maintains a busy practice in probate matters, including wills, estates and guardianships.

Representative Clients: The firm has provided representation either directly or through insurance carriers for most U. S. major manufacturers. The firm has represented Johns-Manville Corporation in asbestos litigation, G. D. Searle & Company in IUD and birth control cases, E. R. Squibb and Sons, Inc. in D. E. S. cases, Cone Mills Corporation and Better Fabrics Testing Bureau, Inc. in fabric flammability cases, and AVCO and Delta Airlines in plane crash litigation. The firm has also defended other product liability cases for Ford Motor Company, American Motors Corporation, and many other equipment manufacturers. The firm has represented most hospitals in the state and many physicians and other professionals in professional liability cases.

In the commercial and real estate area, the firm serves as counsel to a number of institutional lenders such as the Fleet Bank-NH, Concord Savings Bank, Dime Savings Bank of New York, FSB, Shawmut Bank, N.A., Bank of New Hampshire, Colonial Mortgage, Inc., First Deposit National Bank and First National Bank of Boston. The firm's clients also include New England Development, Bailey Distributing Corporation and Corriveau-Routhier, Inc.

The firm also represents a number of municipalities and school districts along with many local businesses.

Significant Distinctions: The firm has a tradition of public service dating back to one of the founders, George Bingham, who served as both a Justice of the New Hampshire Supreme Court and a Judge of the United States Circuit Court of Appeals between 1913 and 1934. Other members of the firm have served with distinction as Judges in the New Hampshire court system, Attorneys General of the state of New Hampshire and members of the United States Congress.

NEW HAMPSHIRE LAW DIGEST

(The following is a list of all Categories and Topics, including cross-references, covered in this Digest.)

NEW HAMPSHIRE LAW DIGEST

Revised for 1999 edition by

WADLEIGH, STARR & PETERS, of the Manchester Bar.

(Citations, unless otherwise indicated, refer to New Hampshire Revised Statutes Annotated, 1955, which are kept up to date by cumulative pocket supplements. Session laws are cited by year and chapter number. Parallel citations to the Atlantic Reporter begin with 64 N. H.)

All session laws passed by the 1998 Legislature have been included or considered.

INTRODUCTION

GOVERNMENT AND LEGAL SYSTEM:

The State of New Hampshire is a constituent state of the United States of America. For further discussion of the U.S. federal system, see Introduction to the Federal Government of the United States at the beginning of this volume. A great many laws are promulgated by the federal government of the United States and are not reflected in the topics below. See the Introduction to this volume for references to the federal law topics covered.

Like all but one of the United States, New Hampshire has a common law legal system, with roots in English common law. For information on the courts and legislature of New Hampshire, see category Courts and Legislature.

HOLIDAYS:

Legal holidays are: Jan. 1; 3d Mon. in Jan.; 3d Mon. in Feb.; last Mon. in May; July 4; 1st Mon. in Sept.; 2d Mon. in Oct.; election day; Nov. 11; Thanksgiving Day; Dec. 25. (c. 288, §1).

Holiday Falling on Sunday.—Following day is observed as holiday.

Holiday Falling on Saturday.—No effect.

Legality of Transactions on Saturday, Sunday or Holiday is not governed by statute, but statute prohibits any person from doing secular work, business or labor, to disturbance of others, on Sunday, except works of necessity or mercy. (c. 332-D, §1).

OFFICE HOURS AND TIME ZONE:

New Hampshire is in the Eastern Standard (GMT −05:00) time zone. Office hours are generally from 9 a.m. to 5 p.m.

BUSINESS ORGANIZATIONS

AGENCY:

Common law rules govern except that any bank specified in c. 384, §29 doing business in this state may continue to recognize power of an attorney-in-fact authorized in writing to make withdrawals either in whole or in part from account of a depositor, whether minor or adult, until it receives written notice or is on actual notice of revocation of his authority or has received notice of death, adjudication of incompetency or appointment of guardian (c. 384, §39). Relationship between real estate licensees and their clients and consumers governed by c. 331-A.

As to conveyance by attorney, see category Property, topic Deeds.

ASSOCIATIONS:

No statutory provisions except as to religious societies (c. 306), proprietors of meeting houses (c. 307), proprietors of common lands (c. 303), cooperative marketing and rural electrification associations (c. 301) and consumers' cooperative associations (c. 301-A). Common law rules as to unincorporated associations apply. Association may register name, insignia, etc. with office of secretary of state. (c. 302, §2). Associations doing business in New Hampshire shall register trade name of business with secretary of state. (c. 349, §1).

Professional Associations.—See topic Corporations, subhead Professional Corporations.

CORPORATIONS:

Note: Model Business Corporation Act, prepared by Committee on Corporate Laws (Section of Corporation, Banking and Business Law of American Bar Association), has been adopted, with variances as set forth below, and is known as "New Hampshire Business Corporation Act". (c. 293-A, §1.01). See Uniform and Model Acts section for Model Business Corporation Act. New Hampshire has not adopted amendments of Sept. 24, 1977, Sept. 23, 1978, and June 20, 1980. It has, however, adopted amendments of Jan. 14, 1978. New Hampshire has not adopted 1984 Revised Model Act.

General Supervision.—Secretary of State, Corporations Division, State House Annex, Concord, New Hampshire 03301.

Purposes.—Corporations may be organized for purpose of carrying on any lawful business except banking, construction and maintenance of railroads, business of making contracts for payment of money at fixed date or upon happening of some contingency, or business of trust, surety, indemnity, or safe deposit company. (c. 293-A, §3.01).

Name.—Corporate name shall contain word "corporation," "incorporated" or "limited," or abbreviation thereof. Corporate name shall not be same as name of any domestic corporation, foreign corporation authorized to transact business in state, reserved name or agency or instrumentality of U.S. or New Hampshire or subdivision thereof, or name of proprietorship, partnership or association registered as tradename in New Hampshire. (c. 293-A, §4.01). Name may be reserved for period of 120 days for fee of $15. Informal name clearance may be obtained through Secretary of State's Office. (c. 293-A, §§1.22, 4.02).

Articles of Incorporation.—In addition to requirements of Model Business Corporation Act, principal purpose of corporation may also be set forth in its articles of incorporation. (c. 293-A, §2.02).

Filing of Articles of Incorporation.—Articles of incorporation should be filed with Secretary of State's Office. Incorporators must also file statement with Insurance Commissioner, 169 Manchester Street, Concord, New Hampshire 03301, that stock issued by corporation has either been registered or is exempt from registration, and whether stock will be offered for sale, within terms of c. 421-B (see category Business Regulation and Commerce, topic Securities), and Insurance Commissioner must certify that these requirements have been complied with. (c. 421-B, §13).

Filing Fees.—Fee for filing articles of incorporation is $35, and $50 for addendum pursuant to c. 421-B. (c. 293-A, §1.22).

Stock certificates must be signed by either chairman or vice-chairman or president or vice-president of corporation and secretary or assistant secretary of corporation, or treasurer or assistant treasurer of corporation.

Uniform Simplification of Fiduciary Security Transfers Act.—Not adopted. Uniform Commercial Code adopted. See category Business Regulation and Commerce, topic Commercial Code.

Tender Offers.—See category Business Regulation and Commerce, topic Securities.

Directors.—Cumulative voting for directors not required.

Officers.—New Hampshire does not require corporate vice-president. New Hampshire corporation has officers described in its by-laws. Same individual may simultaneously hold more than one office. (c. 293-A, §8.40).

Resident Agent.—See subhead Officers, supra.

Foreign Corporations.—Law governing foreign corporations also applies to Massachusetts trusts and Business trusts. (c. 293-A, §15.01). Foreign corporations are subject to trustee process in New Hampshire. (c. 293-A, §15.10). Application for certificate of authority to do business in State must set forth name of corporation, its place of incorporation, its date of incorporation, period of its duration, address of its principal office, address of its registered office in state, name of its registered agent in state, names and addresses of directors and officers of corporation. (c. 293-A, §15.03). Completed application must also be delivered with certificate of existence. Fee for application for certificate of authority is $35. Foreign corporations must also file statement required of domestic corporations from Insurance Commissioner, and file certification from Insurance Commissioner that c. 421-B has been complied with along with $50 fee (see subhead Filing of Articles of Incorporation, supra).

Taxation of Corporate Property.—Taxable property of corporations and property taxable to corporations shall be taxed to corporation by its corporate name, in town in which it is located, except where other provision is made. (c. 73:3). See generally category Taxation, topic Property Taxes, subhead General Property Tax.

Professional Corporations.—New Hampshire has adopted Professional Corporations Supplement to Model Business Corporation Act. (c. 294-A). Professional corporations may be incorporated for purpose of rendering professional services. "Professional services" are services that may lawfully be rendered only by certified public accountants, public accountants, architects, attorneys, podiatrists, chiropractors, dentists, pharmacists, professional engineers, land surveyors, registered professional nurses, optometrists, physicians and surgeons, physician assistants, psychologists, veterinarians, and all other professionals licensed, registered, certified, or otherwise authorized and permitted to practice independently under specified statutory provision and which may not lawfully be rendered by corporation organized under laws governing business corporations. New Hampshire has adopted Alternate 1 to §11(d), imposing no greater personal liability on shareholder of professional corporation than that imposed on shareholder of corporation under Business Corporation Act (c. 294-A, §17, IV). New Hampshire did not adopt §§23, 24, 25 and 26 of Professional Corporations Supplement.

Deeds.—See category Property, topic Deeds.

Model Non-Profit Corporations Act.—Not adopted.

Limited Liability Companies.—See topic Limited Liability Companies.

JOINT STOCK COMPANIES:

No statutory provisions.

Professional Corporations.—See topic Corporations.

LIMITED LIABILITY COMPANIES:

Effective July 1, 1993, may be formed by delivery of certificate of formation to secretary of state. (c. 304-C, §12,I). Certificate must state name (including "limited liability company" or "L.L.C.") (c. 304-C, §3,I); nature of primary business; name and address of registered agent; date of dissolution; identification of management; any other matters members decide to include (c. 304-C, §12,II). No member or manager of L.L.C. is personally liable for L.L.C's obligations merely by being member or manager. (c. 304-C, §25).

See note at head of Digest as to 1998 legislation covered.

See Topical Index in front part of this volume.

PARTNERSHIPS:

Uniform Partnership Act adopted with modifications. (c. 304-A).

Limited Partnership.—Uniform Act has been adopted. (c. 304-B). Foreign partnerships must be registered with Secretary of State. (c. 305-A). Partnership includes registered limited liability partnership. (c. 304-A, §6). Registration requirements set forth at c. 304-A, §§44-55.

BUSINESS REGULATION AND COMMERCE

BANKS AND BANKING:

Uniform Commercial Code has been adopted. See topic Commercial Code.

Regulated by N. H. RSA Chapters 383 through 397.

Stock must be divided into shares of not less than $1 each. (c. 392, §25). Stock may not be issued until the par value thereof, together with a surplus of 20% of such par value, has been paid in cash. (c. 392, §21).

Deposits.—Deposits in trust for another are, upon death of trustee payable to person for whom deposit was made, including a minor, where no notice of existence and terms of a legal and valid trust have been given in writing to bank. (c. 384-D, §1). Joint accounts, upon death of either, are payable to survivor. (c. 384, §28). Written consent of state tax commission is required for transfers of stock or other assets in joint names of decedent and other person unless surviving joint tenant stands in relation of husband, wife, father, mother, lineal descendant or adopted child to deceased joint tenant. (c. 86, §73).

Unclaimed Deposits.—Accounts in savings banks which have been inactive for 15 years shall be reported to state treasurer. After publication of notice by state treasurer, if no claim made within 15 years, property escheats to state. (c. 471-A).

See also category Property, topic Absentees, subhead Escheat.

Loans.—First mortgage loans by savings banks on real estate in New Hampshire or within any state contiguous to New Hampshire may not exceed 75% of value of mortgaged real estate except that a loan may be made which exceeds 75% but not 90% if real estate contains a dwelling unit of not more than four families and if note secured by mortgage is payable within period of 40 years. In determining whether any loan exceeds authorized percentage of value of real estate no consideration shall be given to (1) that portion of obligation which is guaranteed by Administrator of Veterans' Affairs under Title III of Servicemen's Readjustment Act of 1945, as amended from time to time or (2) an obligation wholly guaranteed under such Title, nor shall any bank be restricted to above authorized percentages on a loan secured by property which borrower is purchasing from bank. (c. 387, §4).

First mortgage loans by savings banks on real estate outside New Hampshire and states contiguous thereto may not exceed 75% of value of mortgaged real estate, unless loan is further secured by guarantee satisfactory to commissioner, in which case it shall not exceed 90% of value of said real estate. In determining whether or not any loan exceeds above specified percentages, no consideration is given to that portion of obligation which is guaranteed by Administrator of Veterans' Affairs under Title III of Servicemen's Readjustment Act of 1944, as amended, and to any obligation wholly guaranteed under such Title. (c. 387, §4).

Collections.—Upon repayment, lenders shall mark loan documents "paid in full" or "cancelled" and return or provide to borrower within reasonable time. (cc. 399-A, §5; 397-A, §5; 398-A, §2; 384, §16-g). Uniform Commercial Code applies. (c. 382-A).

Common Trust Funds.—Uniform Common Trust Fund Act adopted. (c. 391).

Investments.—Investments of savings banks are governed by c. 387 as amended.

Fiduciary Powers.—Any trust company or similar corporation incorporated under laws of New Hampshire or any national bank duly authorized and located within New Hampshire may be appointed trustee or executor, subject to same conditions and requirements as individuals. Foreign banks and trust companies may be similarly appointed trustee or executor provided laws of state in which such trust company is incorporated or in which such national bank has its principal place of business allow banks and trust companies incorporated or located in New Hampshire to be appointed trustees or executors in that state. (c. 390, §13).

Savings banks, incorporation is governed by c. 386-A. Minimum capital requirement is $250,000. (c. 386-A, §21).

Trust companies, formation is governed by c. 392. Minimum capital requirement is $250,000. (c. 392, §25).

Verification of Deposits.—Savings banks, trust companies, cooperative banks and building and loan associations shall conduct verification of deposits and due books as required by commissioner. (c. 386, §21).

Mutual savings banks, limitations on conversions. (cc. 386, §§59-63, 386-B).

Mutual holding company, governed by c. 386-B, §8.

Building and loan associations are under the supervision of the Bank Commissioner. (c. 393). No foreign building and loan association may do business in this state. (c. 393, §44).

Credit unions are under the supervision of the Bank Commissioner. (c. 394-B).

Private banking is prohibited. (c. 384, §24).

Taxation.—See category Taxation, topic Business Taxes.

Mortgage Bankers and Brokers.—Licenses required. (c. 398-A; c. 397-A).

Deceptive or misleading advertisement is prohibited. (c. 397-A, §14-a).

Mortgage servicing companies, regulated by Bank Commissioner under c. 397-B. Registration must be filed annually before Aug. 31. (c. 397-B, §4). Requirements for escrow accounts. (c. 397-B, §5).

Fees and interest rates must be disclosed. (cc. 397-A, §16; 398-A, §2).

Interstate Acquisitions.—Authorizes establishment of new New Hampshire banks and acquisition of New Hampshire banks or bank holding companies by out-of-state bank or bank holding company. Includes or merges with opt-out provision by New Hampshire banks and bank holding companies. (c. 384, §44 et seq.).

BILLS AND NOTES:

Uniform Commercial Code applies. (c. 382-A). See topic Commercial Code.

Judgment Notes.—Judgment notes are authorized and process for judgment does not destroy negotiability. (c. 382-A, §3-104 [a][3][ii]).

Attorney Fees.—(§3-104[a]). Attorney fees not recoverable in action on retail installment contract or extension of credit where goods purchased or loan proceeds are used primarily for personal, household or family purposes unless contract or evidence of indebtedness also provides: (1) That retail buyer, borrower or debtor shall be awarded attorney's fees if (a) he prevails in suit brought by retail seller or lender or (b) he prevails in action brought against seller or lender; and (2) that if buyer, borrower or debtor successfully asserts partial defense or set-off, recoupment or counterclaim, court may withhold from seller or lender entire amount or such portion of attorney fees as court considers equitable. (c. 361-C).

Special Defenses.—See subhead Uniform Commercial Code, supra.

BILLS OF LADING:

See topic Carriers.

BILLS OF SALE:

See topic Sales.

BLUE SKY LAW:

See topic Securities.

BROKERS:

Uniform Commercial Code has been adopted. See topic Commercial Code.

Real Estate Brokers.—No person can act as a real estate broker or real estate salesman without obtaining a license from Real Estate Commission. (c. 331-A, §3). Nonresidents may be licensed provided they file irrevocable consent that legal actions may be filed against them in this state. (c. 331-A, §22). Nonresident whose license is under revocation or suspension in another state shall not be granted license in this state. (c. 331-A, §23). Reasonable fees may be charged for original broker's license and for each annual renewal. (c. 331-A, §24).

Mortgage Brokers—Any person who engages in business of brokering first mortgage loans secured by state-located real property must obtain license from banking department. (c. 397-A, §3). Brokers with principal place of business outside of state must designate in-state agent for service of process. (c. 397-A, §6). Each licensee must file annual report with banking department concerning operations for preceding year. (c. 397-A, §13).

As to security brokers, see topic Securities.

BULK SALES:

See topic Commercial Code and category Debtor and Creditor, topic Fraudulent Sales and Conveyances.

CARRIERS:

Uniform Commercial Code has been adopted. See topic Commercial Code.

Common carriers are supervised by the Public Service Commission and Commissioner of Transportation. (c. 365, §§1, 22).

Rates for freight and passengers are subject to regulation by the Public Service Commission. (c. 378, §7). Rate schedules must be published. (c. 378, §1).

Limiting Liability.—Liability of railroad for personal baggage lost or damaged in transit is limited to $100 unless notice given of value in excess of that amount and extra charge paid. (c. 377, §14).

Bills of Lading.—Uniform Commercial Code applies. (c. 382-A).

Note: The criminal provisions of the Uniform Bills of Lading and Warehouse Receipts Acts remain in force, despite repeal of the balance of those acts. (c. 335, §§50-55).

Motor Vehicle Carriers.—See category Transportation, topic Motor Vehicles.

COMMERCIAL CODE:

Uniform Commercial Code has been adopted, and became effective July 1, 1961. (c. 382-A).

Material Variations from 1962 Text.—See topics Bills and Notes, Sales, Securities.

New Provision: §2-329—Covers express warranties given by manufacturers. Concerns time within which manufacturers must provide replacement warranted parts, how long manufacturer must keep warranted parts available, requirements for warranty service, and penalties for failure to comply with law. See topic Sales.

Optional Provisions:

Art. 2A on leases adopted (eff. 1/1/94).

Revised Art. 3 adopted (eff. 1/1/94).

Revised Art. 4 adopted (eff. 1/1/94).

Art. 4A on funds transfers adopted (eff. 1/1/94).

§ 5-112, U.C.C.—Optional subsections 4 and 5 omitted, subsection 1 modified.

§ 5-114, U.C.C.—Optional Subsections 4 and 5 omitted.

Art. 6 of U.C.C. on bulk sales repealed (eff. 1/1/94).

§ 7-204, U.C.C.—optional subsection 4 omitted.

§ 7-403 (1) (b), U.C.C.—optional language omitted.

See note at head of Digest as to 1998 legislation covered.

See Topical Index in front part of this volume.

COMMERCIAL CODE . . . *continued*

Revised Art. 8 adopted (eff. 7/24/87). Replace by 1994 Revisions in their entirety (eff. 1/1/99).

§9-203, U.C.C.—defer to cc. 398, 398-A, 399-A, 399-B, 399-C and 399-D.

Permanent Editorial Board's Recommendations for Amendments.—

§2-702, 1966 Official Amendment not enacted.

§3-501, 1966 Official Amendment not enacted.

§7-209, 1966 Official Amendment not enacted.

Permanent Editorial Board's Recommendations for Optional Amendments.—

§1-209, 1966 Official Optional Amendment not enacted.

§2-318, 1966 Official Optional Amendment not enacted.

1972 Official Amendments.—Adopted.

Filing.—

§ 9-401, U.C.C.—Third alternative subsection (1) adopted.

§9-404, U.C.C.—Insert July 1, 1980.

§ 9-404 (3), U.C.C.—word "Uniform" omitted.

§§9-405, (1), (2), 9-406, U.C.C.—fees outlined in c. 478:17-g.

§9-407, (2), U.C.C.—Insert $5, $7 and $.75 respectively.

§ 9-407, U.C.C.—optional provision adopted; word "Uniform" omitted.

Forms.—See end of this Digest.

See also topics: Banks and Banking, Bills and Notes, Brokers, Carriers, Contracts, Factors, Frauds, Statute of, Sales, Securities, Warehousemen; categories Business Organizations, topic Corporations; Civil Actions and Procedure, topic Limitation of Actions; Debtor and Creditor, topics Assignments, Fraudulent Sales and Conveyances, Liens, Pledges; Documents and Records, topics Records, Seals; Mortgages, topic Chattel Mortgages.

CONDITIONAL SALES:

See topic Sales.

CONSIGNMENTS:

See topic Factors.

CONSUMER PROTECTION:

Consumer Fraud.—It is unlawful to use any unfair method of competition or any unfair or deceptive act or practice in conduct of any trade or commerce, including: passing off goods or services as those of another, causing likelihood of confusion or of misunderstanding as to source, sponsorship, approval or certification of goods or services, causing likelihood of confusion or of misunderstanding as to affiliation, connection or association with, or certification by, another, using deceptive representations or designations of geographic origin in connection with goods or services, representing that goods or services have sponsorship, approval, characteristics, ingredients, uses, benefits, or quantities that they do not have or that a person has a sponsorship, approval, status, affiliation, or connection that he does not have, representing that goods are original or new if they are deteriorated, altered, reconditioned, reclaimed, used or secondhand, representing that goods or services are of a particular standard, quality, or grade, or that goods are of a particular style or model, if they are of another, disparaging goods, services, or business of another by false or misleading representation of fact, advertising goods or services with intent not to sell them as advertised, advertising goods or services with intent not to supply reasonably expectable public demand, unless advertisement discloses a limitation of quantity, failing to disclose legal name or street address of business under c. 361-B:2-a, making false or misleading statements of fact concerning reasons for, existence of, or amounts of price reductions, and conducting going out of business sales other than name implies, or which last more than 60 days, or which are held more than once every two years by same owner of business. (c. 358-A, §2). Consumer Protection and Antitrust Bureau of Department of Justice investigates and prosecutes complaints. (c. 358-A, §4). Private and class actions are allowed. (c. 358, §§10, 10a). Interstate commerce exemption repealed. (c. 358-A, §3, II).

Retail installment sale agreements arising from door-to-door solicitation may be cancelled by buyer before midnight of third day after buyer has signed agreement. All contracts must contain language to this effect. If seller has made no effort to recover his property after 90 days following sale, goods become property of buyer without further obligation. (c. 361-B).

Consumer credit reporting regulated by c. 359-B. Obsolete information may not be reported. Consumer has right to receive copy of report, sources of information, list of persons receiving report and nature and substance of all information in full (except medical). Consumer may file statement as to any disputed item which must be provided with reports.

Land Sales Disclosure Act requires registration with Attorney General's Office (Department of Justice) of all residential subdivisions of more than 15 lots and all time sharing subdivisions prior to all offerings. (c. 356-A).

Condominium Act requires registration with Attorney General's Office (Department of Justice) of all residential condominiums of more than ten units and all time sharing condominiums prior to all offerings. (c. 356-B).

Protection of Tenants in Conversion of Rental Property.—(c. 356-C).

"Unsolicited goods" statute adopted. (c. 339, §2-a).

Chain distributor schemes whereby person is sold license or right to solicit or recruit one or more additional persons who are also sold such license or right are prohibited. (c. 358-B).

Collection Practices.—Unfair, deceptive and unreasonable debt collection practices against consumers are prohibited. (c. 358-C).

Health Clubs, Rental Referral Agencies and Buying Clubs regulated. (c. 358-H, I, J).

Plain Language.—No "Plain Language Statute".

Exclusion or Modification of Warranties.—Sellers are restricted in their ability to exclude or modify warranties in sale of consumer goods. (c. 382–A, §2–316[4]).

Ureaformaldehyde Foam Insulation.—Manufacture and sale in new homes prohibited. (c. 339-A, §9). Warnings of use in existing homes required. (c. 339-A, §11).

See category Transportation, topic Motor Vehicles, subhead Sales; also topic Sales, this category.

CONTRACTS:

Common Law rules apply. Uniform Commercial Code adopted. See topic Commercial Code. (c. 382-A).

See also categories Documents and Records, topic Seals; Family, topic Infants.

FACTORS:

Uniform Commercial Code adopted. (c. 382-A). See topic Commercial Code.

License Requirements.—None.

FRANCHISES:

Franchising is governed by Distributorship Disclosure Act unless by order Attorney General exempts distributorship from provisions of Distributorship Disclosure Act. (c. 358-E). No person may offer or sell distributorship without first registering with Attorney General. (c. 358-E, §§2, 3). Each prospective distributor must be provided with disclosure statement seven days prior to execution of agreement. (c. 358-E, §4).

FRAUDS, STATUTE OF:

Uniform Commercial Code has been adopted. (c. 382-A). See topic Commercial Code.

No action can be maintained on a contract for the sale of land or on a promise by an administrator or executor to pay out of his own estate, nor to hold one for the debt, default or miscarriage of another, nor on an agreement in consideration of marriage, nor on any contract not to be performed within one year, unless there is a note or memoranda of the same in writing signed by the party to be charged or by his agent duly authorized. (c. 506, §§1-2). Power of attorney to convey real estate must be in writing, signed and acknowledged. (c. 477, §9).

Part Performance.—The doctrine that part performance takes a case out of the Statute of Frauds is an equitable doctrine, and at law a party cannot maintain an action upon a parol contract to convey land to him, even when he has performed it on his part. (55 N. H. 471, 475). However, in equity a part performance of a parol agreement for the sale of land will take it out of the statute. Note that payment of purchase money is not such part performance as will have this effect. (67 N. H. 389, 390, 32 A. 154). If, in addition to payment of purchase price, purchaser under verbal contract has entered into possession, with assent of other party, and made improvements, specific performance may be decreed. (35 N. H. 235, 254).

Contracts of sale of goods for a price of $500 or more must be in writing set forth in Uniform Commercial Code. (c. 382-A).

Guarantee Written On Commercial Paper.—Uniform Commercial Code applies. (c. 382-A, §3-416).

INTEREST:

Interest may be at any rate, but is computed at 10% unless a different rate is expressly stipulated in writing. Annual rate of interest on judgments, determined by state treasurer, is prevailing discount rate of interest on 52-week U.S. Treasury bills at last auction preceding last day of Sept. of prior year, plus two percentage points, rounded to nearest tenth of a percentage point. (c. 336, §1).

Judgments.—In any action on a debt or account stated or where liquidated damages are sought, interest runs from time of institution of suit. (c. 524, §1-a). In all other civil proceedings at law or in equity in which a verdict is rendered or a finding is made for pecuniary damages, whether for personal injuries, wrongful death, for consequential damages, for damages to property, business or reputation or for any other type of loss for which damages are recognized there is added forthwith by clerk of court to damages interest from date of writ or filing of petition. (c. 524, §1-c).

Small Loans.—No person, partnership or corporation shall engage in business of making loans up to amount of $10,000 without securing license from bank commissioner. Interest on open and closed end loans $10,000 and under governed by c. 399-A, §3.

Home Mortgage Loans.—On loans secured by second mortgage on real property occupied in whole or in part as home by obligor, interest shall be at rate agreed upon; however, following sixth month of any period in which loan has been in continuous default, not more than 1¹/₂% per month on any unpaid balance. (c. 398-A, §2).

Usury.—There is no general usury law, but see subheads, supra.

LICENSES, BUSINESS AND PROFESSIONAL:

Licenses are required before persons can engage in practically any businesses for which licenses are usually required, and are granted by state and local authorities. See Title XXX Occupations and Professions cc. 309A-332F.

The provisions of the act requiring licenses of hawkers and peddlers do not apply to any person selling the products of his own labor or the labor of his family and the product of his own farm or the one which he tills. (c. 320, §3).

Itinerant vendors must obtain both state and local licenses and are subject to stringent regulations. (c. 321, §§1, 4, 11). The provisions requiring licenses of itinerant vendors do not apply to sales made to dealers by commercial travelers or selling agents. (c. 321, §3).

Marriage Licenses.—See category Family, topic Marriage, subhead New Requirements.

See note at head of Digest as to 1998 legislation covered.

See Topical Index in front part of this volume.

MONOPOLIES, RESTRAINT OF TRADE AND COMPETITION:

Every contract, combination or conspiracy in restraint of trade is unlawful. (c. 356, §2-I). Establishment, maintenance or use of monopoly power or any attempt to establish, maintain or use monopoly power over trade or commerce for purpose of affecting competition or controlling, fixing or maintaining prices is unlawful. (c. 356, §3). Local government exempt from liability from land use planning, zoning and solid waste disposal. (c. 149-M, §21).

Restraints Prohibited.—Contracts, combinations or conspiracies are unlawful which have purpose or effect of: Fixing, controlling or maintaining prices, rates, quotations or fees in any part of trade or commerce; fixing, maintaining, controlling, limiting, or discontinuing production, manufacture, mining, sale or distribution of any commodity or service; allocating or dividing customers or markets in any part of trade or commerce; refusing to deal, or coercing, persuading or inducing any person to refuse to deal with another person; or fixing or controlling price quotation of any bid for public or private contract, submitting sham or complementary bids or controlling submission of bids including refusals to bid. (c. 556, §2-II).

NEGOTIABLE INSTRUMENTS:

See topic Bills and Notes.

RESTRAINT OF TRADE:

See topic Monopolies, Restraint of Trade and Competition.

SALES:

Uniform Commercial Code has been adopted. See topic Commercial Code.

Bills of Sale.—No statutory form is prescribed.

Bulk Sales.—See topic Commercial Code; and category Debtor and Creditor, topic Fraudulent Sales and Conveyances.

Conditional Sales.—Uniform Commercial Code applies. See topic Commercial Code. No statutory limitation exists as to type size in printed contracts.

Consumer Protections.—See topic Consumer Protection; and category Debtor and Creditor, topic Fraudulent Sales and Conveyances.

Contracts of Sale.—No statutory limitation exists as to type size in printed contracts.

Product Liability.—Governed by general principles of common law tort liability and U.C.C., where applicable (c. 382-A, §§2-313 to 2-315). Restatement of Torts 2d, §402A adopted. (Buttrick v. Lessard, 110 N.H. 36, 260 A.2d 111 [1969]).

Breach of warranty actions under UCC 2-313, 2-314, 2-315, are limited to four years from when breach of warranty occurs. (c. 382-A, §2-725).

Requirement of privity has been substantially abolished by revision of UCC 2-318 which requires only that plaintiff be a person whom manufacturer, seller or supplier might reasonably have expected to use, consume or be affected by goods. (c. 382-A, §2-318). Labeling of hazardous substances is required. (c. 339-A). Donors of food for charitable purposes are, under certain circumstances exempt from liability for all but gross negligence, recklessness or intentional conduct when harm results from ingestion. (c. 508, §15).

Retail Credit Sales.—Any person in the business of extending credit must provide a written statement to borrower or purchaser clearly setting forth finance charges. (c. 399-B, §2). See topic Interest. Repossession of goods by seller requires retroactive allocation of payments received under contract to purchases in same proportion as original cash prices bear to one another. Down-payment must be allocated in its entirety to related purchase. Allocation report must be given to buyer and buyer has 15 day right to cure. (c. 399-B, §6).

SECURITIES:

Uniform Securities Act adopted. (c. 421-B).

Uniform Commercial Code in effect. See topic Commercial Code.

Supervision.—Sales of Securities are regulated by Uniform Securities Act, c. 421-B, which is enforced by Secretary of State, State of New Hampshire, Concord, New Hampshire.

Exempt Securities.—Following securities are exempted from registration requirements of Act (c. 421-B, §17): (A) Securities issued or guaranteed by U.S., any state, any political subdivision of state or any agency or corporate or other instrumentality of one of foregoing, but industrial development bonds and industrial revenue bonds are not exempt; (B) securities issued by any foreign government with which U.S. currently maintains diplomatic relations, if security is recognized as valid obligation by issuer or guarantor; (C) any security issued by or representing interest in or debt of, or guaranteed by, any bank organized under laws of U.S., or any bank, savings institution, or trust company organized under laws of any state; (D) any security issued by and representing interest in or debt of, or guaranteed by, any federal savings and loan association, or any building and loan or similar association organized under laws of any state and authorized to do business in New Hampshire; (E) any security issued or guaranteed by any federal credit union or any credit union or similar association organized under laws of New Hampshire; (F) any security listed or approved for listing upon notice of issuance on New York Stock Exchange, American Stock Exchange, Boston Stock Exchange, Chicago Board Options Exchange, NASDAQ/NMS or securities designated by Federal Reserve System as "O.T.C. Margin Stocks"; (G) any commercial paper arising from current transaction or proceeds of which have been or are to be used for current transactions, and that evidences obligation to pay cash within nine months of date of issuance, or any guarantee of such paper or of any renewal not advertised for sale to general public; (H) any interest in any employees savings, stock purchase, pension, profit sharing or similar benefit plan, or self-employed persons retirement plan; (I) any security issued or guaranteed by any railroad, other common carrier or public utility subject to regulation by governmental authority of U.S. with respect to issuance or guarantee of securities; (J) any interest in common trust fund or similar fund maintained by state bank or trust company organized and operating under laws of New Hampshire, or of national bank, for collective investment and reinvestment and reinvestment of funds contributed to such common trust fund or similar fund by bank or trust company in its capacity as trustee, executor, administrator, or guardian; (K) any security meeting all of following conditions: if issuer is not organized under laws of U.S. or this state, it has appointed duly authorized agent in U.S. for service of process and prospectus sets forth that agent's name and address; class of issuer's securities is registered under §12 of Securities and Exchange Act of 1934 and has been so registered for three years immediately preceding offering date; neither issuer nor significant subsidiary has had material default during last seven years of principal, interest, dividend or sinking fund installment on preferred stock or indebtedness for borrowed money, or rentals under leases with terms of three years or more; issuer has had consolidated net income of at least $1,000,000 in four of last five fiscal years including last fiscal year and, if offering is of interest bearing securities, has had net income in its last fiscal year of at least one and one half times issuer's annual interest expense; if offering is of stock or shares other than preferred stock or shares, securities have voting rights including right to have at least as many votes per share and right to vote on at least as many general corporate decisions as each of issuer's outstanding classes; and, if offering is of stock or shares, other than preferred, securities are owned beneficially or of record, on any date within six months prior to offering, by at least 1,200 people, and on that date there are at least 750,000 such shares outstanding with aggregate market value of at least $3,750,000; (L) any certificate of indebtedness sold or issued for investment other than certificate of indebtedness pledged as security for loan made contemporaneously by industrial loan and thrift company; (M) any security issued by any person organized and operated not for private profit but exclusively for charitable purposes, or as chamber of commerce or trade or professional association; (N) any security designated by rule or order by secretary of state after finding that designation is consistent with purposes fairly intended by policy and provisions of this title.

Exempt Transactions.—Following transactions are exempt from registration requirements of Act (c. 421-B, §17): (A) Any isolated sales, but no person shall make more than five sales in total of securities of same issuer in all jurisdictions combined pursuant to this exemption other than those designated in subsection 17 I(h), II(g), II(l) and II(p)(1) during any 12-month period provided that in case of sales by issuer, seller reasonably believes that all buyers purchasing for investment; (B) any non-issuer distribution of outstanding security other than common stock rated in top three categories of Moody's, Fitch's or Standard & Poor's Security Manuals if: any of these manuals contains names of issuer's officers and directors, balance sheet of issuer of date not more than 18 months prior to sale and profit and loss statement for fiscal year preceding, and issuer or its predecessor has been in active business operation for five-year period preceding date of sale, and if security has fixed maturity or fixed interest or dividend provision, issuer has not defaulted in payment of principal, interest or dividends on any such securities within three preceding fiscal years; (C) execution of any orders by licensed broker-dealer for purchase or sale of any security pursuant to unsolicited offer to purchase or sell so long as broker-dealer has no direct material interest in sale or distribution and receives no compensation from any source other than purchaser and seller; (D) any non-issuer sale of notes or bonds secured by mortgage lien if entire mortgage, together with all notes or bonds secured thereby, is sold to single purchaser at single sale; (E) any judicial sale, exchange or issuance of securities made pursuant to court order; (F) sale by pledge holder of security pledged in good faith as collateral for bona fide debt; (G) any offer or sale to bank, savings institution, trust company, insurance company, investment company, pension or profit-sharing trust, venture capital company operating small business investment company under Small Business Investment Act of 1958, or other financial institution, or to broker-dealer; (H) any sale by issuer to such number of persons as when aggregated with number of persons to whom sales have been made pursuant to subparagraph (a) or (k) or contract shall not exceed five persons in state during any period of 12 consecutive months whether of not purchaser is then present in state; (I) any offer, but not sale, of security for which registration statement has been filed under both this chapter and Securities Act of 1933, if no stop order is in effect and no public proceeding or examination is pending under either Act; (J) offer and sale by cooperative association organized under laws of New Hampshire of its securities when such securities are offered only to its members, or when purchase of such securities is necessary or incidental to establishing membership in such associations, or when securities are issued as patronage dividends; (K) any offer or sale of securities if, after giving effect to sale, aggregate number of holders of all of issuer's securities does not exceed ten or higher number approved by secretary of state by rule or order, provided no commission or other remuneration has been paid and no advertising circulated and all sales are consummated within 60 days after date of incorporation or formation of issuer; (L) issuance and delivery of any securities of one corporation to another in exchange for acquisition of all or substantially all of assets of such other corporation, or in connection with consolidation or merger of such corporation; (M) any transaction between issuer or other person on whose behalf offering is made and underwriter or among underwriters; (N) distribution by corporation of its securities as stock dividend, stock split or reverse stock split; (O) offer or sale of securities by affiliate of issuer if registration statement is in effect with respect to such securities and such offer has been exempted from registration by Secretary of State; (P) any transaction pursuant to offer to existing security holders of issuer where securities held were issued for value if no commission or other remuneration is paid or given directly or indirectly for soliciting any New Hampshire shareholder, or issuer first files notice specifying terms of offer and Secretary of State does not disallow exemption within next ten full business days; (Q) any offers or sales made pursuant to c. 384, §§44-54 governing acquisition of NH banks or bank holding companies by out of state banks; (R) offers and sales that are made in accordance with limited offering transactional exemption adopted by Secretary of State; (S) transaction made by issuer-member of qualified designated matching service; (T) any security designated by rule or order by secretary of state after finding that designation is consistent with purposes fairly intended by policy and provisions of this title.

See note at head of Digest as to 1998 legislation covered.

See Topical Index in front part of this volume.

NH – 4

SECURITIES . . . *continued*

Registration of Securities.—Securities may be registered by notification, coordination or qualification. Industrial development bonds, industrial revenue bonds and any securities issued by person or organization exclusively for social, religious, educational, benevolent, fraternal, charitable, reformatory, athletic, chamber of commerce, trade, industrial development or professional association purposes and not for pecuniary gain, may be registered by notification. Securities for which registration has been filed under Securities Act of 1933 may be registered by coordination. Registration statement filed by coordination must be accompanied by two copies of latest form of prospectus and any other documents required by Secretary of State. Registration statement becomes automatically effective at moment federal registration statement becomes effective so long as no stop order is in effect and no proceeding pending, registration statement has been on file with Secretary of State for at least 20 days, and statement of maximum and minimum proposed offering prices and maximum underwriting discounts and commissions has been on file for two full business days. (RSA 421-B:11-14).

Any security may be registered by qualification. Security registered by qualification must contain information required by §305 of Uniform Securities Act and any other information required by Secretary of State. (RSA 421-B:14).

Licenses.—All licenses for agents, broker-dealers, investment advisers and issuer dealers expire every year on Dec. 31. (RSA 421-B:6).

Bonds.—Licensed broker-dealers, agents and investment advisors may be required to post surety bonds in amount equal to at least $25,000. (RSA 421-B:7).

Postlicensing Provisions.—Each broker-dealer doing business in New Hampshire must within 60 days of close of fiscal year, file with Secretary of State document showing its financial statement, changes in management, changes in ownership and any significant changes in method of doing business in preceding fiscal year. Secretary of State may require at any reasonable time any other statements, reports or information from persons subject to this Act. (RSA 421-B:8).

Secretary of State must examine each domestic broker-dealer and domestic branches of foreign broker-dealers at least once every two years. This examination shall consist of review of affairs, transactions, accounts, records, documents and assets of each licensed broker-dealer as to any matter relevant to its financial affairs or obligations or any other fact relative to its business methods, management and its dealings with clients. (RSA 421-B:9).

Tender Offers.—RSA 421-A requires filing of registration statements prior to any takeover bid with respect to equity securities of any New Hampshire corporation or corporation having its principal place of business or principal executive office within State.

Uniform Simplification of Fiduciary Security Transfers Act not adopted. Uniform Commercial Code adopted.

STATUTE OF FRAUDS:

See topic Frauds, Statute of.

TRUST RECEIPT SECURITY:

See category Debtor and Creditor, topic Pledges.

WAREHOUSEMEN:

Any person, firm or corporation having a place of business in the state, who keeps or maintains for hire a warehouse for the storage of goods, wares and merchandise, is defined to be a public warehouseman. A public warehouseman must obtain an annual license from the Secretary of State upon payment of a license fee of $50. (c. 348, §1). Licensee must give bond to state for faithful performance of duties. Suit on bond may be brought in name of state. (c. 348, §§2, 3).

Warehousemen must give bailor negotiable receipt for property so stored unless such person requests that receipt be stamped "nonnegotiable". (c. 348, §5).

Uniform Commercial Code has been adopted. See topic Commercial Code.

Note: Criminal provisions of Uniform Bills of Lading and Warehouse Receipts Acts remain in force, despite repeal of balance of those acts. (c. 335, §§50-55).

Warehouse Receipts.—Warehouse receipts and other documents of title and the rights, duties and liabilities of warehousemen are covered by the Uniform Commercial Code. (c. 382-A).

A public warehouseman, who has in storage any property for which a storage charge is at least one year overdue, may sell the same by public auction, after notice in writing to the person in whose name it is stored that such property will be sold at a time and place specified in the notice unless the amount due for storage, the advances made thereon and the expenses of advertising and sale are paid before the sale is made. From the proceeds he may retain said storage charges, advances made and expenses of advertising and sale. (c. 348, §15).

Cold storage warehouses are specially licensed by the State Department of Health and Human Services, Division of Public Health Services, and specially regulated. (c. 145, §§1, 2).

CITIZENSHIP

ALIENS:

Aliens in general have same rights as citizens. Where state of war exists or is imminent, registration of alien enemies may be required by Governor. (c. 114, §1).

Property.—Resident alien may take, purchase, hold, convey or devise real estate, and it may descend in the same manner as in the case of a citizen. (c. 477, §20). If the wife of an alien has resided in this state six months successively, separate from her husband, she may acquire and hold real and personal estate and convey it the same as if she were sole and unmarried and she may have the exclusive care, custody and guardianship of her minor children living with her in the state. (c. 460, §12).

CIVIL ACTIONS AND PROCEDURE

ACCORD AND SATISFACTION:

No statutory provisions. The payment and acceptance as in full of something less than or different from what might legally be claimed under a liquidated or unliquidated obligation is a defense to an action for the balance. (74 N.H. 358, 68 A. 325, reaffirmed at 107 N.H. 321, 221 A.2d 236).

See category Business Regulation and Commerce, topic Commercial Code.

ACTIONS:

The common law actions are in use, modified by statutes.

Special writs in common use are: Replevin (c. 536-A); scire facias (c. 543, §1); habeas corpus (c. 534, §§1, 8); mandamus and quo warranto (c. 491, §7).

Equity.—Distinction between law and equity is still maintained, but both are administered by the same court. (c. 491, §7; c. 498, §1).

Class Actions.—Superior court determines whether class action is to be maintained. (Superior Court Rule 27-A).

Conditions Precedent.—Notice of claim against governmental unit must be sent by registered mail to clerk of unit within 60 days after injury specifying date, time and location, provided that in any case where lack of written notice, actual knowledge or reasonable opportunity to obtain knowledge of any injury within said 60 day period is alleged by governmental unit, burden of proof shall be on governmental unit to show that it was substantially prejudiced thereby. (c. 507-B, §7).

Commencement.—Actions at law are begun by summons. Equity actions are commenced by petition. (c. 509, §4). See topic Process.

Summary Judgment.—See topic Judgments.

Parties.—Writs against unknown defendants may be issued in fictitious name and later amended. (c. 509, §7). No abatement may be had for non-joinder (c. 514, §10) or misjoinder (c. 514, §13) of parties and such errors may be cured by amendment (c.514, §9).

Interpleader.—Depositaries of personal property may interplead. (c. 543, §1). The State of New Hampshire is authorized to enter into interpleader compacts with other states which provide that personal jurisdiction may be obtained over foreign parties in interpleader actions. (c. 5A).

Abatement.—Proceedings will not be abated because of a mistake, where the person or case may be rightly understood by the court, nor through any defect in form only. (c. 514, §8). No action abates by death of a party if the cause survives. In case of death the court may at any time before the end of 12 months (Belkner v. Preston, 115 N.H. 15, 332 A.2d 168) after death of plaintiff or grant of administration on estate of defendant allow action to continue by or against personal representatives (c. 556, §10). When one of two or more plaintiffs or defendants dies, and the right of action survives, the action may be prosecuted by or against the surviving parties, such death being suggested on the record. (c. 514, §12).

Survival.—Actions for tort for physical injuries to the person and all other actions and causes of action existing in favor of or against a deceased person, except those for recovery of penalties and forfeitures of money under penal statutes, survive, and may be prosecuted or defended by decedent's executor or administrator. (c. 556, §§9, 15). There is six years statute of limitations on new actions for personal injury. (c. 556, §11).

Tender.—At any time before the return day of the writ, the defendant may tender to the attorney who brought the action the amount of the debt with interest and costs, and such tender bars any further proceedings in the case. (c. 515, §1).

Small Claims.—See topic Practice; category Courts and Legislature, topic Courts.

Prohibited Action.—For breach of promise to marry. (c. 508, §11). Liability of governmental unit for personal injury or property damage arising out of ownership, occupation, maintenance, or operation of public sidewalks, streets and highways is limited as provided in c. 231, §§90-93, and liability of any governmental unit with respect to publicly owned airport runways and taxiways is limited as provided in c. 422. (c. 507-B, §2). Liability of municipality or school district operating facility for purpose of skateboarding, rollerblading or rollerskiing is limited. (c 507-B, §11). Liability of municipality for hazards caused by snow, ice or other inclement weather is limited. (c. 507-B, §2).

Limitation of.—See topic Limitation of Actions.

Administration.—See category Estates and Trusts, topic Executors and Administrators.

Direct Actions Against Insurer.—See category Transportation, topic Motor Vehicles, subhead Direct Actions.

APPEAL AND ERROR:

From Probate Courts.—Appeals of questions of law may be taken to Supreme Court from all decisions of probate court in accordance with rules of Supreme Court. (c. 567-A, §1). Appeals from decisions of commissioners of insolvent estates are governed by c. 558. Filing of appeal shall stay all proceedings pending determination by Supreme Court. (c. 567-A, §7). Supreme Court may reverse, affirm or remand case for further proceedings. (c. 567-A, §8).

From District or Municipal Court.—In civil cases, questions of law may be transferred to Supreme Court in same manner as from Superior Court. (c. 502-A, §17-a; c. 502, §24). In criminal cases, appeal may be taken to Superior Court except in cases in district courts served by regional jury trial courts. (c. 502-A, §12-a; c. 599, §1). Recognizance with sufficient sureties, up to $2,000, may be required. (c. 599, §2).

From Superior Court.—Appeal from Superior Court decision on merits may be made to Supreme Court which may, in its discretion, decline to accept any appeal. (Sup. Ct. R. 7). Interlocutory appeals prior to decision on merits may be made from

See note at head of Digest as to 1998 legislation covered.

See Topical Index in front part of this volume.

APPEAL AND ERROR . . . *continued*

lower court ruling (Sup. Ct. R. 8) or prior to lower court ruling (Sup. Ct. R. 9). Supreme Court may, in its discretion, decline to accept any interlocutory appeal. (Sup. Ct. R. 8 and 9).

From Administrative Agencies and Commissions.—Appeals from orders of any administrative agency or commission may be taken to Supreme Court. (c. 541, §6; Sup. Ct. R. 10). Appealing party must file Motion for Rehearing with agency or commission from whose decision appeal is sought. (c. 541, §3). No new or additional evidence may be presented in Supreme Court, but upon good cause, Supreme Court may remand case for further proceedings. (c. 541, §14).

Writs of Error.—The Supreme Court has authority to issue writs of error. (c. 490, §4). Writs of error may be sued out within three years after judgment, and not afterward unless allowed by the court for sufficient cause, upon petition and notice. (c. 508, §7).

Stay of Execution.—Since questions of law are generally transferred to the Supreme Court prior to the entry of judgment, without bond, the necessity of staying execution rarely arises. Injunctions may, however, issue for cause shown against levying an execution which has issued. (c. 527, §17). There is no provision requiring the giving of a supersedeas bond in such a case.

BONDS:

Common law rules apply.

CERTIORARI:

Supreme Court has jurisdiction to issue writs of certiorari. (c. 490, §4).

CHARITABLE IMMUNITY:

See topic Damages.

COMMISSIONS TO TAKE TESTIMONY:

See topic Depositions and Discovery.

COSTS:

In all actions or petitions in superior court costs are allowed to prevailing party for certain expenses including: service or publication, entry, parties' travel, witness attendance fee and travel, expense of view, printing of reserved case or transcript. (c. 525, §§13, 14, 14-a).

Security for Costs.—Writs must be indorsed by the plaintiff or his agent or attorney if he is a resident of the state. If a nonresident, writ must be indorsed by some responsible resident (usually the attorney who brings suit) and indorser becomes liable for costs. (c. 509, §§8, 9)

DAMAGES:

Common law generally prevails as to compensatory damages, although it has been stated that liberal damages may be awarded in cases where malice, wantonness, or willful indignity in causing the injury are present. (112 N.H. 71, 73, 289 A.2d 66). In any action for personal injury, damages awarded may include compensation for noneconomic loss, but such damages shall in no case exceed $875,000. (c. 508, §4-d, I). This limitation has, however, been held unconstitutional. (134 N.H. 50).

The following schedule of punitive damages is provided for willful trespass and conversion: forest products and mill logs, up to ten times value thereof (c. 539, §§1-3-a); fences, three times value thereof (c. 539, §3); stone, ore, gravel, clay, sand, turf or mold, three times the value thereof and not more than $15 (c. 539, §4); property of an electric utility, actual damage and costs incurred by utility plus attorney's fees. (c. 539, §7).

Doctrine of charitable immunity abrogated. (105 N.H. 53; 193 A.2d 788).

Exemplary damages may be recovered against a defendant who files a plea of title in a landlord and tenant action if judgment is subsequently recovered against him. (c. 540, §23).

Comparative Negligence.—Contributory negligence not a bar to recovery if plaintiff's negligence not greater than defendant's. Damages reduced in proportion to negligence of plaintiff. If more than one defendant, damages proportioned in accordance with their negligence. Adopted 1969. In all actions, damages are apportioned among parties. (c. 507, §7-e). Rule of contribution among tortfeasors adopted as of July 1, 1986. (c. 507, §7-f; see also c. 507, §7-g, h, i).

See also category Estates and Trusts, topic Death, subhead Actions for Death.

DECLARATORY JUDGMENTS:

See topic Judgments.

DEPOSITIONS AND DISCOVERY:

See also topic Practice.

Depositions de bene esse may be and are freely taken.

Uniform Foreign Depositions Act adopted. Effective Jan. 1, 1998. (c. 517-A).

Within State for Use Within State.—Depositions in all cases generally are taken by agreement but may be taken by notice and subpoena. (c. 517, §4; c. 516, §4). Statute relative to taking and use of depositions (c. 517, §1) has been repealed in favor of N.H. Rules of Evidence. Respondent in criminal case may take deposition of any person in his defense and may use same at trial of case whenever in discretion of court, such use is deemed necessary for promotion of justice. However, no party in criminal case in which victim, at time of offense, was under 16, shall take deposition of victim or of any witness who was under 16 at time of offense (c. 517, §13), unless court, upon motion of party or victim, authorizes taking of videotape deposition on grounds that child will suffer emotional or mental strain from testifying in court or that

further delay will impair child's ability to recall and relate facts. Videotape deposition of witness under 13 in criminal case will generally be taken. (c. 517, §13-a).

No person may write the testimony of a witness, or act as magistrate in taking the same, who would be disqualified to act as juror on the trial of the cause, for any reason except exemption from service as a juror. (c. 517, §3).

Within the State for Use Elsewhere.—Commissioners or other persons appointed by courts of record of other states may take depositions here. (c. 517, §18).

Outside of State for Use Within State.—Any commissioner appointed under the laws of the state to take depositions in other states, any judge or justice of the peace or notary public in any other state or country, may take the deposition. (c. 517, §2). A justice of the superior court, either in term time or vacation, may appoint any suitable person to take depositions outside the state. (c. 517, §15; 123 N.H. 570, 467 A.2d 202).

Deposition in perpetual remembrance of any fact may be taken before a court of record, or before two justices of the peace, one of whom shall be of the quorum. (c. 518, §1). A person desiring to take such deposition must present his petition to the court or justices in writing, under oath, briefly setting forth his interest in the subject, and the facts to which the desired testimony relates, the names and residences of all persons supposed to be interested therein, or, if the fact be so, that the names or residences of such persons are unknown, and the names of the witnesses proposed to be examined. (c. 518, §2). Notice must be given by the court or justices to such interested parties in the manner provided for the taking of ordinary depositions, which notice must contain or be annexed to a copy of the petition for the taking of the depositions. (c. 518, §3). If the name or residence of a party interested is unknown the notice must be published three weeks successively, beginning at least eight weeks before the time of taking, in some newspaper printed in Concord, and in some newspaper printed in the county, and, if the deposition relates to land, a like notice must be posted in some public place in the shire town of the county in which the land lies. (c. 518, §5). Caption and manner of taking are the same as in ordinary depositions (c. 518, §6). If the depositions relate to real estate, or to any transaction connected therewith, the petition, depositions, certificate, notice and evidence of service must within 90 days from the taking thereof, be recorded in the registry of deeds of the county where the estate lies; and the depositions taken in any other case may be so recorded. (c. 518, §8).

Depositions in perpetual remembrance may be used in the trial of any cause wherein the matters concerning which they were taken are drawn in question; and in case they shall be lost or out of the possession and control of the party desiring to use them a copy of the record thereof may be used. (c. 518, §9).

Compelling Attendance of Witnesses.—Any New Hampshire justice or notary can summons witnesses to appear before himself or any other justice or notary to give depositions in any matter or cause in which the same may be lawfully taken. (c. 516, §4). If a person so summoned neglects to attend or to give his attendance so long as may be necessary for the purpose for which he was summoned, or refuses to testify or to give his deposition if required, having no reasonable excuses therefor, he shall be liable to the party aggrieved for all damages sustained thereby. (c. 516, §6). In addition the justice or notary before whom he has been summoned may find him guilty of violation (carrying penalty up to $100; c. 651, §2, IVa) and may order him to pay costs. (c. 516, §7).

Commissioners or other persons appointed by foreign courts have the same powers of procuring the attendance of witnesses, and of requiring the production of papers as have local justices of the peace within this state. (c. 517, §18).

Commissioners appointed by New Hampshire courts to take depositions elsewhere for use here have all the powers conferred by the laws of other states, territories and foreign countries upon commissioners or other persons authorized to take depositions in such other states, territories and foreign countries for use in causes pending in this state. (c. 517, §17).

Notice Required.—The party proposing to take a deposition must cause a notice in writing, signed by a justice or notary, stating the day, hour and place of taking the same, to be delivered to the adverse party, or one of them, or to be left at his abode, if either of such parties resides in this state, and within 20 miles of the place of taking, or of the party taking the same, a reasonable time before the taking thereof. (c. 517, §4). No notice to the adverse party of the taking of depositions is deemed reasonable unless served three days, exclusive of the day of service and the day of caption, before the day on which they are to be taken: and when the adverse party lives more than ten miles from the place of caption, one day more must be allowed for every additional 20 miles. However, 20 days notice is deemed reasonable in all cases, unless otherwise ordered by the court. (Superior Court Rule 38). No deposition shall be taken within 20 days after service of action, except by agreement or by leave of court for good cause shown. (Superior Court Rule 38).

Where the statute requires notice of the taking of depositions to be given to the adverse party, it may be served on such party, or on attorney of record of such party. In cases where action is in name of nominal party, and writ or docket discloses real party in interest, service must be made on party in interest, or on attorney of record of such party. Service may be given by mail or in hand. (Superior Court Rule 40).

If the adverse party resides out of the state, or more than 20 miles from the place of caption, or from the party proposing to take the deposition, a like notice, given to the agent or attorney of such adverse party or left at his abode, is sufficient. No person may be deemed an agent or attorney for this purpose unless he has indorsed the writ in the cause, or has appeared for his principal before the court, justice, referees or arbitrators, where the action is pending, or has given notice in writing that he is such attorney or agent. (c. 517, §§5-6).

Time Limit.—No deposition taken after the Monday next preceding first day of term shall be used in any trial, unless deponent is witness, except for good cause shown and upon such terms as court may order. (Superior Court Rule 37).

Manner of Taking.—Interrogatories shall be put by attorneys and interrogatories and answers shall be taken in shorthand or other form of verbatim reporting approved by court and transcribed by a competent stenographer agreed upon by parties or their

DEPOSITIONS AND DISCOVERY . . . . *continued*

attorneys present at deposition. In absence of such agreement, stenographer shall be designated by court. Failure to object in writing to stenographer in advance of taking of deposition shall be deemed agreement to stenographer recording testimony. (Superior Court Rule 41).

No deposition, as transcribed, shall be changed or altered, but any alleged errors may be set forth in separate document attached to original and copies. (Superior Court Rule 41).

Magistrate shall cause to be noted any objection to any interrogatory or answer without deciding its competency. If complaint is made of interference with any witness, magistrate shall cause such complaint to be noted and shall certify correctness or incorrectness thereof in caption. (Superior Court Rule 41).

Parties can and usually do agree that deposition may be taken by stenographer in shorthand and later transcribed. Court may allow as costs whole or any part of expense thereof, as justice may require. (c. 517, §20). Deponent must sign his deposition and make oath to its truth. (c. 517, §7).

Caption.—The magistrate taking the deposition must certify the oath of the deponent, with the time and place of taking the deposition, the case and court in which it is to be used, that the adverse party was or was not present, was or was not notified, and that he did or did not object. (c. 517, §8).

Return.—The deposition must be sealed up by the magistrate, directed to the court or justice before whom it is to be used, with a brief description of the case, and so delivered into court, (c. 517, §10). If the adverse party did not attend, there must be annexed to the deposition a copy of the notice left with the adverse party, his agent or attorney, with a return of service written thereon, stating the time when the notice was left. (c. 517, §9). It is customary for parties to agree at the time of the deposition that all formalities of filing shall be waived. Upon motion, court may order filing of depositions, and, upon failure to comply with such order, court may take such action as justice may require. (Superior Court Rule 41).

Forms

The usual form of notice to take depositions is as follows:

State of New Hampshire, ... ss.

To . . . . . .

You are hereby notified that one or more depositions will be taken before a justice of the peace, at the office of . . . . . in . . . . . . in said County of . . . . .on the . . . . . . day of . . . . . ., 19. . . ., at . . . . . of the clock in the . . .noon to be used in an action to be heard and tried at the Superior Court to be holden at . . . . . . in said County of . . . . . . on the . . . . . . Tuesday of . . . . . ., 19. . . ., in which plea . . . . . . and . . . . . . of . . . . . . in . . . . . . County of . . . . . . is . . . . . . Dated at . . . . . the . . . . . . day of . . . . ., 19. . . . .

Justice of the Peace.

The usual form of deposition is:

I, ... of . . . . . . in the County of . . . . . . and State of . . . . . . on oath depose and say in answer to the following interrogatories: (insert questions and answers. (Add signature of deponent).

The caption is usually in the following form and should be annexed to the deposition:

State of . . . . }

County of . . . . } ss

Personally appeared before me, the subscriber, a (state magistrate's title), the within named A. B., at the office of . . . . . in . . . . . . in said County, on the . . . . . . day of . . . . . ., 19. . . ., and made solemn oath that the within deposition by him subscribed contains the truth, the whole truth and nothing but the truth relative to the cause for which it was taken. The said deposition is taken at the request of C. D., of . . . . . ., to be used at the . . . . . . Court of the State of New Hampshire to be held at . . . . . . in and for the County of . . . . . . on the . . . . . . day of . . . . . . next, in a plea wherein . . . . . . of . . . . . . is plaintiff and the said C. D. is defendant; and the taking of the same was begun at . . . . . . o'clock in the forenoon, on the first mentioned day, and continued until the whole was completed.

The said . . . . . being duly notified was (or was not) present, and did not object.

(Signature and title).

Any waiver by the parties of formalities as to the manner of taking the deposition, or of formalities with respect to notice, caption, or filing, should be stated in the caption.

When the deposition is filed it should be accompanied by a statement as follows:

To the . . . . . . Court of the State of New Hampshire:

Enclosed is a deposition to be used in an action in which . . . . . . is plaintiff, and . . . . . . is defendant, taken and sealed by

(Signature and official title).

EQUITY:

See topic Actions.

EVIDENCE:

See topic Depositions and Discovery.

Witnesses.—No person interested as party or otherwise in the result of an action is excluded or excused from testifying on that account (c. 516, §22) except as hereinafter stated.

Privileged Communications.—There is no statutory privilege as to communications to attorneys; however, confidential physician-patient communications are placed by statute "on the same basis as those provided by law between attorney and client" (c. 329, §26) as are communications between certified psychologists and their clients (c. 330A, §19). Priest-penitent privilege is also recognized. (c. 516, §35). Confidential communications between victims of sexual assault or domestic abuse and their counselors and third persons present to assist communication with victim are privileged. (c. 173-C, §2).

Death or Incompetency of Party to Transaction.—In action by indorsee or assignee of bill of exchange, promissory note or mortgage, against original party thereto, defendant may not testify in his own behalf if either of original parties to such bill, note or mortgage, is dead or insane, unless plaintiff testifies or offers testimony of original party thereto. (c. 516, §26).

See also topic Depositions and Discovery.

INJUNCTIONS:

The superior court has jurisdiction to issue injunctions whenever the same are necessary to prevent fraud or injustice (c. 498, §2), and it is specifically provided that injunctions may issue in certain enumerated cases (c. 207, §§43, 44).

Temporary Restraining Order; Notice; Hearing; Duration.—Temporary restraining order may be granted only by justice of superior court without written or oral notice to adverse party or his attorney only if it clearly appears from specific facts, shown by affidavit or by verified petition, that, immediate and irreparable injury, loss or damage will result to applicant before adverse party or his attorney can be heard in opposition. Every temporary restraining order, which is granted without notice, shall be endorsed with date and hour of issuance, shall define injury and state why it is irreparable and why order was granted without notice, and shall expire by its terms within such time after issuance, not to exceed ten days, as court fixes, unless, within time so fixed, order, for good cause shown, is extended for like period, or unless party, against whom order is directed, consents that it may be extended for longer period. In case temporary restraining order is granted without notice, application for preliminary injunction shall be set down for hearing at earliest possible time, and in any event within ten days, and, when matter comes on for hearing, party, who obtained temporary restraining order, shall proceed with application for preliminary injunction, and if he does not do so, court shall dissolve temporary restraining order. On two day's notice to party who obtained temporary restraining order without notice, or on such shorter notice to that party as court may prescribe, adverse party may appear and move its dissolution or modification, and, in that event, court shall proceed to hear and determine such motion as expeditiously as ends of justice require. (Superior Court Rule 161[a]).

Preliminary Injunction.—No preliminary injunction shall be issued without notice to adverse party and they shall only be issued by Justice of Superior Court. (Superior Court Rule 161[b]).

Bond.—Whenever an injunction is issued without notice to, or appearance by, the adverse party (except in marital cases), the party at whose request it is issued, ordinarily shall, and in any case may, be required to give bond with sufficient sureties, conditioned to pay and satisfy all such damages as may be occasioned to the adverse party by reason of the injunction, in case it shall appear that the injunction was improper. (Superior Court Rule 163).

See also topic Practice.

JUDGMENTS:

Interest.—See category Business Regulation and Commerce, topic Interest.

Summary Judgment.—In any action a party may move for summary judgment as to all or part of any claim, counter-claim or cross-claim. Motion shall be supported by affidavit and unless counter-affidavits are filed within 30 days and show a genuine issue, judgment shall be entered. (c. 491, §8-a).

Judgment by Default.—If a defendant neglects to enter his appearance within the first seven days after the return day, he is defaulted, and judgment is entered accordingly; and no such default can be stricken off, except by agreement or order of court upon notice and affidavit of defense. (Superior Court Rule 14).

Declaratory Judgments.—Any person claiming a present legal or equitable right or title may maintain a petition against any person claiming adversely to such right or title, to determine the question between the parties, and the judgment or decree of the court thereon is conclusive. (c. 491, §22). District court has concurrent authority with superior court, but defendant has right to remove action to superior court if claim exceeds $1,500. (c. 491, §22). Probate court has exclusive jurisdiction over claim arising under its subject matter jurisdiction authority in c. 547 and c. 552, §7. Authority to determine insurance coverage is given to U.S. District Court in appropriate cases. (c. 491, §22-c).

Lien.—No lien is created by the entry of a judgment, but if property was attached when suit was commenced, attachment lien continues for 60 days on personal property and six years on real estate from rendering of judgment. (c. 511, §55). All real estate liens recorded prior to Jan. 1, 1976 will expire on Jan. 1, 1988 unless properly renewed prior to that date. (c. 511, §55, III).

Revised Uniform Enforcement of Foreign Judgments Act adopted. Effective June 6, 1994. (c. 524-A).

See also topic Practice.

LIMITATION OF ACTIONS:

Uniform Commercial Code enacted. See category Business Regulation and Commerce, topic Commercial Code.

Actions must be brought within the following periods after the respective causes of action accrue:

Twenty Years.—Actions for the recovery of real estate (c. 508, §2); actions of debt upon judgments, recognizances and contracts under seal (c. 508, §5); actions on notes secured by mortgage of real estate (c. 508, §6).

Eight Years—Actions for injuries resulting from creation of improvement to real property must be commenced within eight years after substantial completion of improvement. (c. 508, §§4-6, I).

Six Years.—Whenever execution is returned, satisfied in whole or in part by extent or levy upon estate or property not liable to be taken upon execution, action of debt may be brought upon judgment, within six years after extent or levy, for amount equitably due and costs of levying. (c. 507, §4). If action of tort is not commenced prior to death of party, one may be brought within six years after said death, subject to c. 508. (c. 556, §11).

LIMITATION OF ACTIONS . . . *continued*

Four Years.—Actions for breach of any contract for sale must be commenced within four years after the cause of action has accrued (c. 382-A, §2-725); actions against governmental units for personal injuries or property damage arising out of ownership, occupation, maintenance or operation of certain premises and motor vehicles (c. 507-B, §7).

Three Years.—All personal actions except where otherwise specified. (c. 508, §4).

Two Years.—Writs of scire facias on bonds given in discharge of attachments (c. 511, §42); all suits or prosecutions founded upon any penal statute for penalties or forfeitures, time running from commission of offense (c. 616, §9); certain personal injury actions against ski area operators (c. 225-A, §25, IV).

Whenever one has a claim against the estate of a deceased person which has not been prosecuted within the time limited by law, such person may apply to superior court having subject matter jurisdiction over nature of claim, by petition setting forth all facts; and if court shall be of opinion that justice and equity require it, and that claimant is not chargeable with culpable neglect in not bringing or prosecuting his suit within time limited by law, it may extend time for filing and prosecuting claim; however no such extension or judgment entered upon claim shall affect any payments or compromises made before beginning of proceedings. (c. 556, §28).

If no administration shall have been granted upon the estate of a deceased person within two years from the date of death, no creditor of the deceased shall thereafter be entitled to maintain any action or proceeding in any court to appropriate the real estate or interests therein of which the deceased died seized, to the payment or satisfaction in whole or in part of his claim against the estate. (c. 556, §29).

One Year.—Writs of scire facias for costs against a person who has endorsed a writ (c. 509, §§9-10); writs of scire facias in civil proceedings, time running from final judgment against principal (c. 532, §8); actions by and against estates of decedents not already barred by statute of limitations, time running from death of decedent (c. 556, §7); action in contribution, after judgment or payment or agreement to pay disproportionate share (c. 507, §7-g).

Six Months.—If a fire insurance company notifies its assured that it intends to insist upon this provision, action by the assured on a fire insurance policy will be barred unless a writ is served within six months after the assured receives written notice of the adjustment which the company will make. (c. 407, §§16, 17).

Actions under Art. 6 of Uniform Commercial Code—Bulk Transfers, must be brought within six months after date on which transferee took possession of goods unless transfer has been concealed. (c. 382-A, §6-110).

New Actions.—If plaintiff fails in an action brought within the time limited therefor but the right of action is not barred by the judgment in such action, a new action may be brought within one year after such judgment. (c. 508, §10). But where an action for damages for laying out or altering a highway is discontinued, a new action therefor can be brought within six months thereafter, but not later. (c. 234, §59).

Disabilities.—A person who was an infant or insane when the cause of action accrued may bring an action to recover real estate within five years (c. 508, §§2-3), or a personal action within two years (c. 508, §§4, 8), after disability ceases.

Absence.—The time for bringing a personal action does not run while defendant is absent and residing out of the state. (c. 508, §9).

Revival of Barred Debts.—No statutory provisions.

Contractual limitations are permitted. See supra, subhead Six Months.

See also category Business Regulation and Commerce, topic Sales.

PARTITION:

Jurisdiction and Venue.—Probate Court has exclusive jurisdiction of partition. (c. 498, §1; c. 547-C, §2). Petition may be filed in county in which estate or any part thereof lies. (c. 547-C, §2).

If there is no dispute about the title, a petition for partition may be filed with the judge of probate for the county where the real estate or the greater part thereof lies. (c. 547-C, §19).

Proceedings.—Any person owning present undivided legal estate in land, not subject to redemption, or holder of equity of redemption may institute partition proceedings. (c. 547-C, §1). If such estate is in fee, he shall be entitled to partition in fee; if life estate or term for years he shall be entitled to partition thereof to continue so long as his estate endures. (c. 547-C, §1). Life tenant, remainderman, or tenant for years of whose term at least 20 years remains unexpired may in exercise of court's equitable powers, have partition of fee. (c. 547-C, §1). Existence of lease of whole or part of land to be divided shall not prevent partition, but such partition shall not disturb possession of lessee under lease covering interests of all co-tenants. Petition must particularly describe estate, names of all owners or persons interested, if known, and share of petitioner therein. (c. 547-C, §2). If persons interested in real estate are unknown, property must be described in same manner as is required in case of taxing unimproved lands of nonresidents and share held by each petitioner must be specified, and petition must state that real estate is held with persons unknown. (c. 547-C, §4). Provision is made for notice to all parties and appointment of guardians or agents for all incapacitated parties. (c. 547-C, §§5-8).

Partition in Kind.—Upon the entry of a judgment that partition be made the court appoints a committee, consisting of three suitable persons, residents of the county, to make partition of the estate, to set off the shares of the several petitioners according to their respective titles and to award costs as they deem just. (c. 547-C, §11). After notice and hearing committee makes partition of estate as directed in its commission, by setting off to each petitioner his just share thereof, according to his right, by proper metes and bounds or other distinct description. (c. 547-C, §§11-14). Upon return to court judgment is rendered upon report of committee and partition so made is recorded in registry of deeds for county where real estate lies. (c. 547-C, §15).

Sale.—Where an estate is so situated that it cannot be divided so as to give each owner his share thereof without great prejudice or inconvenience, the whole or any part thereof may be assigned, if the parties consent, to one of them, he paying to the others such sums as the committee shall award. (c. 547-C, §22). If parties will not consent, superior court may order entire land sold and proceeds thereof divided among owners according to their respective titles. (c. 547-C, §25).

PLEADING:

No writ, declaration, etc., will be abated or quashed, for any error or mistake when the person or case may be rightly understood by the court, nor through any defect or want of form or addition only; and courts and justices may, on motion, order amendment in such case. Amendments in matters of substance may be permitted in any action, in any stage of the proceedings, upon such terms as the court shall deem just and reasonable, but the rights of third persons may not be affected thereby. (c. 514, §§8, 9).

No special plea is required in a civil action, except a plea of title to real estate in actions in municipal court; but any defense may be proved under general issue, upon a brief statement thereof being filed in such time as court may order. (c. 515, §3).

If the defendant pleads specially, the plaintiff may file such reply as the case requires. (c 515, §4).

Mutual demands and debts may be set off one against the other. (c. 515, §7). The defendant may plead such set-off, or give notice thereof with the general issue, describing the debt or demand with the same certainty as is required in a declaration. (c. 515, §11).

Frivolous Claims.—In any contract or tort action, any party which brings claim or raises defense which is frivolous or intended to harass prevailing party is subject to penalty of costs and reasonable attorneys' fees incurred by prevailing party. Such conduct shall also be reported to Supreme Court Committee on Professional Conduct. (c. 507, §15; Superior Court Rule 59).

Preparation of Foreign Claims.—No statutory provisions. Those preparing foreign claims for suit in this state bear in mind that common law rules of procedure are here in force, but that great leniency is allowed in matters of form.

Rules of superior court relating to procedure are not in statutes. Citations following are to such rules.

All writs at time of service upon defendant must have attached thereto a specification setting forth particulars of claim or a special declaration, but court, for good cause shown, may waive this requirement on motion of plaintiff, which must be filed at time of entry of writ and accompanied by such specification or special declaration and a statement that copies of same have been mailed or delivered to defendant or his attorney, but court for good cause shown upon motion also filed with writ may extend time for filing specification or special declaration. (Rule 23).

No plaintiff may have leave to amend, unless in matters of form, after a default, until a notice upon the defendant, to show cause why the amendment should not be allowed has been served. (Rule 24).

Amendments in matters of substance may be made on such terms as justice may require. (Rule 26).

All special pleas and brief statements must be filed within 30 days following return day of writ; otherwise cause must be tried upon general issue. (Rule 28). Appearances must be filed within seven days of return date. (Rule 14).

Either party may, by motion, obtain an order on the other to plead.

Pleas in abatement must be filed and a copy delivered to counsel for the adverse party, within 30 days after return day of writ. (Rule 30).

No set-off may be filed after 30 days from entry of action, except by leave of court and upon payment of costs; and when set-off is filed, copy must be given to plaintiff or his attorney. (Rule 33).

Small Claims.—See topic Practice and category Courts and Legislature, topic Courts.

PRACTICE:

The practice is according to the common law, liberalized by statutes and rules of court.

Discovery rules are analogous to Federal Rules of Civil Procedure (Rule 35a), use of interrogatories (Rule 36) and depositions, including video tape depositions (Rules 37, 45, 45-A).

Small Claims.—Special procedure is provided for actions, not involving title to real estate, in which debt or damage, exclusive of interest and costs, does not exceed $2,500. Plaintiff or his attorney files claim with clerk of municipal court in town in which defendant or plaintiff reside, or if no municipal court, then District Court, who records nature of claim and sets date for hearing. (c. 503, §3-a). If attorney appears on behalf of party, shall file appearance and provide copies to all opposing parties at least seven days prior to hearing. (c. 503, §2-a). Representation of business organization by non-attorney must be by duly authorized official. (c. 503, §11, I-V). Action against nonresident defendant may be filed in municipal or District Court where defendant or his agent transacts any business, makes contract with resident of town or district, commits tort, or owns, uses, or possesses any real or personal property. (c. 503, §3-b). Entry fee of $25 plus $5 for each defendant in excess of one must be paid. Notice to defendant is sent by registered mail, directing him to appear at time and place of hearing, which must be not less than 14 days from date of mailing notice. (c. 503, §§1-8). See also category Courts and Legislature, topic Courts.

Direct Actions Against Insurer.—See category Transportation, topic Motor Vehicles, subhead Direct Actions.

See also topics Actions, Appeal and Error, Depositions and Discovery, Injunctions, Judgments, Pleading, Process; category Debtor and Creditor, topics Attachment, Executions, Garnishment.

PROCESS:

Original process in superior court consists of summons and attachment. (c. 509, §4).

Original writs, before service thereof, must be indorsed by the plaintiff or by his agent or attorney, if the plaintiff is an inhabitant of the state, otherwise by some responsible person who is such inhabitant. (c. 509, §8).

See note at head of Digest as to 1998 legislation covered.

See Topical Index in front part of this volume.

PROCESS . . . *continued*

Who May Serve.—Writs of summons returnable to superior or supreme court must be directed to sheriff of any county or his deputy. (c. 509, §3). Writs of attachment returnable to superior court shall be directed to sheriff, plaintiff, or any other person. (id.) Writs issued by justices of municipal and district courts must be directed to sheriff of county or his deputy, or to any constable of any town in county, or to either of said officers; provided, however, that writs of attachment may also be directed to plaintiff, his attorney, or any other person. (c. 509, §11). Where defendant in action before municipal court has personal property liable to attachment in county of which he is not inhabitant, original writ and execution may be directed to sheriff of any county, his deputy or to any constable of any town in which defendant resides or has such property. (c. 509, §13). Constables serve and return writs and other civil precepts to them directed wherein amount demanded in damages does not exceed $75, and no others, and have similar powers and are subject to similar liabilities in relation thereto as sheriffs. (c. 104, §9).

Personal Service.—All writs and other processes are served by giving to defendant or leaving at his abode an attested copy thereof, except in cases otherwise provided for. (c. 510, §2).

Service of writs against corporations may be made upon registered agent (c. 293-A, §5.04), or upon clerk, treasurer, cashier, or one of directors, trustees or managers, if any in state; otherwise upon any principal member or stockholder, or upon any agent, overseer or other person having care of any of property or charge of any of business of corporation (c. 510, §14).

Service of writs or other process against unincorporated associations, joint stock companies, syndicates, orders or any mutual association of persons, other than a partnership having not more than four members (where personal service on all required), within this state, may, except when otherwise provided, be made upon any officer thereof; or, if it have no officer, then upon any two members thereof. (c. 510, §13). Service of process upon foreign partnership made by service on registered agent or Secretary of State if not registered. (c. 305-A, §6).

Service of writs against a railroad corporation may be made upon any person doing business of the corporation as ticket master for the sale of passenger tickets, at any station upon its railroad. (c. 510, §15).

Service of a writ against a manufacturing corporation may be made by leaving an attested copy of the writ at the office or counting-room of the corporation. (c. 510, §16).

Service of writs against counties may be made upon one of the county commissioners and treasurer for county; against cities, upon mayor or one of aldermen and city clerk; against towns, upon one of selectmen and town clerk; against school districts, upon one of school board and clerk of district; and against village districts, upon one of commissioners and clerk of district. (c. 510, §10).

Substituted Service.—Service may be made by registered mail in suits against foreign corporations except insurance companies (c. 293-A, §15.10) or foreign insurance companies and fraternal benefit societies (c. 405, §10; c. 418, §18);

Writs against nonresident administrators of domiciled decedents are served upon resident agents appointed for the purpose. (c. 553, §29).

A writ of scire facias may be served, in case the defendant is not an inhabitant of the state, on the attorney who appeared for him in the original action, or by giving him or leaving at his abode outside the state an attested copy of the writ. (c. 510, §§4, 6).

Service on nonresident individuals may be made by service on Secretary of State where any nonresident in person or through an agent commits a tortious act within state, transacts any business within state or has ownership, use or possession of any real or personal property situated in state. (c. 510, §4).

Service may be made upon foreign corporation as "doing business" in State of New Hampshire. (c. 293-A, §15.10). N. H. has adopted so called "long arm" statute whereby foreign corporation making contract to be performed in whole or in part by either party in New Hampshire or committing tort in whole or in part in New Hampshire is deemed to appoint Secretary of State as its agent for service of process in any actions or proceedings arising out of such contract or tort. (c. 293-A, §121).

Publication.—Where notice by publication in a newspaper is ordered by any court upon any petition, writ or other similar process, the original of which is upon file in such court, it is sufficient to publish a citation containing the title of the case, the name of the court in which it is pending, the time and place of the return and hearing, the fact that such original is on file and may be examined by interested parties and such other facts as the court may order. (c. 510, §9).

Order of Notice.—When the defendant is not an inhabitant of the state, and no mode of serving the writ is prescribed, or service thereof cannot be made in the mode prescribed, the action may be entered in court and such notice ordered as the case requires; and notice of the pendency of the suit, given according to the order, is sufficient service. (c. 510, §8).

Time of Service.—Service must be made at least 14 days before the sitting of the court to which they are returnable. (c. 510, §1).

Continuance for Notice.—If no personal service has been made on a defendant in an action which may be entered without such service the court, on suggestion thereof, may order the action to be continued and notice of the pendency thereof to be given by publication, by mail in a registered letter, by personal service or otherwise, as it thinks proper; and, upon satisfactory evidence that the order has been complied with, the notice is sufficient. (c. 514, §3). Specific provisions are made for procedure in this respect in municipal courts. (c. 514, §§4, 5).

Nonresident Motorist.—See category Transportation, topic Motor Vehicles.

Long Arm Statute.—See subhead Substituted Service, supra.

See also topic Practice.

REPLEVIN:

When goods or chattels are unlawfully taken or detained from the owner or person entitled to the possession thereof, or when goods or chattels attached are claimed by a person other than the defendant in the suit in which they are attached, such owner or other person may maintain replevin therefor. (c. 536-A, §1). This action may be maintained by owner of goods or chattels exempt by law from attachment when attached upon mesne process, or by person from whose possession they were taken at any time before they were taken on execution. (c. 536-A, §2).

Proceedings.—The action is commenced by writ in statutory form, directing sheriff, constable or police officer within whose jurisdiction property is located to replevy goods in question and deliver them to plaintiff. (c. 536-A, §8).

Writ of replevin must describe specific property to be seized, and must specify location or locations where there is probable cause to believe property is located. (c. 536-A, §8).

Hearing is required under replevin statute. (c. 536-A, §3). At hearing defendant must show cause why property should not be taken from him. Upon notice of hearing defendant cannot dispose of, or encumber property, but he may retain property by filing bond. (c. 536-A, §14). Ex parte issuance of writ of replevin is possible upon application to judge if defendant gained possession of property by theft, property consists of negotiable instruments or credit cards, or property is in immediate danger of removal or serious harm. (c. 536-A, §12).

Bond.—The plaintiff, in seeking replevin, before service of writ, must give bond to sheriff with sufficient sureties in sum double value of property replevied and he must pay all damages and charges as may be awarded against him if he does not prevail. (c. 536-A, §7).

Custody of Property.—Levying officer may take property into his custody or, upon good cause shown, install keeper. (c. 536-A, §9). Levying officer may deliver property to party preliminarily determined to be entitled thereto, after expiration of time for filing bond. (c. 536-A, §16). If defendant shall give bond to officer, with sufficient surety, in sum not less than double value of goods, with condition that he will pay all costs and charges of keeping and insuring them and all depreciation thereof, if plaintiff in suit shall prevail against him, officer shall return goods within five days after service of notice of filing said bond. (c. 536-A, §14).

Repossession.—No provision for repossession by defendant while proceedings are pending, except through filing of bond in double value of property. (c. 536-A, §14).

Claims of Third Persons.—Common law rules govern.

Judgment or Order.—If the defendant shall prevail in the suit he shall have judgment for the return of the goods, with such further damages as may be awarded to him. (c. 536-A, §18). If goods have been delivered to plaintiff, defendant, if he prevails, may have judgment of return of such of goods and chattels replevied as may at time of trial or judgment remain in possession of plaintiff, or of any part of same, if he shall so elect. (c. 536-A, §18). Whenever defendant shall have so elected, value of goods to be returned is found by jury or ascertained by court, and upon such return their value is deducted from damages assessed in suit in favor of defendant. (c. 536-A, §18).

SEQUESTRATION:

Voting securities in insurance holding company may be sequestered when they have been acquired in violation of insurance holding company legislation. (c. 401-B, §9, III).

SERVICE:

See topics Process, Replevin; category Debtor and Creditor, topics Attachment, Executions, Garnishment, Receivers.

STAY OF EXECUTION:

See topic Appeal and Error; category Debtor and Creditor, topic Executions.

SUBMISSION OF CONTROVERSY:

Declaratory judgment process is designed to make controversy of legal or equitable right justiciable at earlier stage than it would be if matter were pursued at law or equity. (c. 491, §22). See topic Judgments.

VENUE:

Transitory action should be brought in the county or judicial district thereof in which one of parties resides. If neither resides in state action may be brought in any county or judicial district thereof, provided proper service is made. (c. 507, §9).

Specific provisions for venue in particular actions are: Action for forfeiture of state grant where land is in more than one county, either county (c. 535, §6); action against executors or administrator, county or one of counties in which it might have been brought by or against testator or intestate at time of his decease, but an executor or administrator may sue in county wherein he was appointed (c. 507, §10); trustee process, county or judicial district in which suit would have been brought if no trustee were summoned (c. 512, §2); action for injuries caused by defects in highway, county where injuries were received (c. 231, §110); appeal by creditor from disallowance of claim against insolvent estate, county where either party resides (c. 558, §5); abatement of criminal nuisances, county or judicial district where property is located (c. 544, §4); partition in probate court, county in which real estate or greater part thereof lies (c. 538, §18); suit on recognizance, county or judicial district where taken unless court orders change of venue (c. 597, §34); trial of computer crime, venue proper in town where act took place or where computer equipment is located (c. 638, §19); action for bridge defects, county where injuries received (c. 231, §110); civil action against nonprofit health service corporation for unfair trade practices, Merrimack County Superior Court or any U.S. District Court in which claim arose, defendant resides or does business (c. 420-A, §32). Divorce action may be brought in county where both, or one party resides (c. 458, §9); disposition of unclaimed or abandoned property, Merrimack County Superior Court (c. 471-C, §§28, 30).

Change of Venue.—The superior court may change the venue in any civil proceeding when justice or convenience requires it. No lien obtained by attachment or otherwise is abated or in any way affected thereby. (c. 507, §§11, 12). If criminal offense(s) take place in more than one county, offense may be tried in either county or judicial district thereof. (c. 602, §1).

See note at head of Digest as to 1998 legislation covered.

See Topical Index in front part of this volume.

NH – 9

COURTS AND LEGISLATURE

COURTS:

United States District Court.—Clerk's office: Warren B. Rudman U.S. Courthouse, 55 Pleasant St., Room 110, Concord, NH 03301.

Court sits at Concord.

Deposit of $120 must be made with clerk of court at commencement of all actions at law and proceedings in equity.

U.S. Bankruptcy Court.—Deposit of $160 must accompany Chapter 7 or 13 filing. Deposit of $800 must accompany Chapter 11 filing.

New Hampshire Supreme Court.—

Jurisdiction.—Supreme Court has final jurisdiction of questions of law, and exercises general superintendence over inferior courts including approval of rules of court and administration of canons of ethics. It has exclusive authority to issue writs of error and may issue writs of certiorari, prohibition, habeas corpus, and all other writs and processes to other courts, to corporations and to individuals. (c. 490, §4). It has final authority in making of rules regulating practice in probate courts in insolvency proceedings. (c. 568, §5). It hears appeals from Public Utilities Commission (c. 541, §6) and can remand case to Commission to hear new evidence if justice requires (c. 541, §14), and decides questions arising from transfers of questions of law from Public Utilities Commission (c. 365, §20) and likewise transfers of questions of law from district courts. It may appoint and remove reporter of its decisions (c. 505, §1).

Court sits at Concord.

Superior Court.—

Jurisdiction.—Original jurisdiction of superior court embraces all classes of civil and criminal cases that call for a trial by court or jury, as to either questions of law or fact, including factual issues certified by probate court and certain appeals from district courts, divorce, and proceedings in equity. (c. 491, §7; c. 498, §1).

Place of Sitting.—County and court records are kept at county seats which are designated by a *.

Belknap County: Court sits at Laconia *.

Carroll County: Court sits at Ossipee *.

Cheshire County: Court sits at Keene *.

Coos County: Court sits at Lancaster * and at Berlin. Adjournments from Lancaster or Berlin may be made to Colebrook whenever the presiding justice deems it advisable.

Grafton County: Court sits at North Haverhill.

Hillsborough County: Court Northern District of Court sits at Manchester. Southern District of Court sits at Nashua.

Merrimack County: Court sits at Concord *.

Rockingham County: Court sits at Brentwood *.

Strafford County: Court sits at Dover *.

Sullivan County: Court sits at Newport *.

Probate Court.—Court has jurisdiction of probate of wills and of all matters concerning administration of estates of deceased persons, interpretation and construction of wills and testamentary trusts, appointment and removal of conservators and guardians, guardianship proceedings, adoption of children, assignment of homestead in estates of deceased persons, as to trustees, defined in c. 564-A, §1,I, change of names of persons, termination of parental rights, durable power of attorneys for health care, interpretation of living wills, petition to quiet real estate listed in estate of deceased person, or as guardianship, conservatorship, or trustee asset over which court has jurisdiction, and declaratory judgment action concerning same, durable powers of attorney, waiver for marriage of minors (concurrent with Superior Court), petitions for partition of real estate (c. 547, §§3, 10), and cases of insolvency (c. 568, §1).

Probate Court sits as follows:

Belknap County: at Laconia.

Carroll County: at Ossipee.

Cheshire County: at Keene.

Coos County: at Colebrook, at Lancaster, at Gorham and at Berlin.

Grafton County: at North Haverhill.

Hillsborough County: at Manchester and at Nashua.

Merrimack County: at Concord.

Rockingham County: at Brentwood.

Strafford County: at Dover.

Sullivan County: at Claremont and at Newport.

Municipal Courts.—All municipal courts have been abolished except that by special vote at annual town meeting for year 1964, a town was entitled to vote to continue to maintain its existing municipal court so long as the then judge remains in office. (c. 502-A, §35).

District Court.—A district court system has been established which became effective July 1, 1964. Each county in state is divided into districts, each having a separate district court.

In criminal cases, district courts have original jurisdiction, subject to appeal, of all crimes and offenses committed within confines of district in which such court is located, which are punishable by fine not exceeding $2,000 or imprisonment not exceeding one year or both (c. 502-A, §11), and concurrent jurisdiction, subject to appeal, of prosecution of any violation of local ordinance, code, or regulation punishable by civil penalty, in which case penalty imposed may not exceed court's civil jurisdiction (c. 502-A, §11-a).

In civil matters, district courts have concurrent jurisdiction with superior court in actions in which damages claimed do not exceed $25,000 (in some selected district courts, $50,000) and defendant or plaintiff resides within district where such court is located. (c. 502-A, §14, II). District Courts have original and exclusive jurisdiction where damages claimed do not exceed $1,500, title to real estate is not involved and defendant or plaintiff resides within district. (c. 502-A, §14, I). Defendant may remove civil action filed in district court to superior court upon motion setting forth that there is

pending in superior court cause arising out of same transaction, or that defendant has claim arising out of same transaction in which his claim for damages exceeds $1,500. (c. 502-A, §14, III). In cases where damages claimed exceed $1,500 or title to real estate is involved, defendant may request, within five days of entry of action, trial by jury and have case transferred to superior court. (c. 502-A, §15). Questions of law may be transferred directly to Supreme Court. (c. 502-A, §17-a).

Small Claims Courts.—Simplified, informal procedure is provided for in small claims not involving title to real estate, in which debt or damages, exclusive of interest and costs, does not exceed $2,500. (c. 503, §1). Action commenced by filing statement of claim in district court by plaintiff setting forth nature and amount of claim and residence of each party. Written statement notifying defendant of claim and date of hearing mailed by justice to defendant by registered mail. Plaintiff generally must pay court fee of $25. Technical rules of evidence do not apply. Judgment may be entered payable in installments. Prevailing claimant is entitled to interest and costs on judgment. (c. 503, §7).

See also category Civil Actions and Procedure, topic Practice.

LEGISLATURE:

Regular sessions held annually in Jan. (Const., Part 2, art. 3). Governor may call extra sessions. (Const., Part 2, art. 50).

Lobbyists regulated by c. 15.

REPORTS:

Decisions of Supreme Court are reported in New Hampshire Reports (c. 505, §§1-13) and in Atlantic Reporter. Decisions available on Lexis and Westlaw.

Digests.—The latest state digest now in use is West's New Hampshire Digest which includes cases determined in Supreme Court of New Hampshire from year 1760 to date. Supreme Court decisions beginning with 64 N. H. are digested in Atlantic Digest.

STATUTES:

Latest compilation is Revised Statutes of New Hampshire, Annotated, 1955.

Uniform Acts adopted are: Acknowledgment (1943); Aircraft Financial Responsibility (1955); Anatomical Gift (1969); Attendance of Witnesses from Without a State in Criminal Proceedings (1937); Business Corporations (1981); Business Records as Evidence (1953) (repealed effective Jan. 1, 1995); Child Custody Jurisdiction (1979); Choice of Forum, Model (1969); Civil Liability for Support (1955); Commercial Code (1959); Common Trust Fund (1953); Criminal Extradition (1937); Determination of Death (1987); Divorce Recognition (1949); Enforcement of Foreign Judgments (1994); Estate Tax Apportionment (1959); Facsimile Signatures of Public Officials (1959); Federal Tax Lien Registration, Revised (1967); Foreign Depositions (1998); Fraudulent Transfer (1987); Fresh Pursuit (1937); Interstate Compromise of Death Taxes (1941); Interstate Family Support (1997); Limited Partnership (1937); Management of Institutional Funds (1973); Marriage Recognition (1979); Military Justice (1957); Motor Vehicle Certificate of Title and Anti-Theft (1967); Partnership (1973); Paternity (1971); Photographic Copies as Evidence (1951) (repealed effective Jan. 1, 1995); Principal and Income (1990); Professional Corporations (1981); Reciprocal Enforcement of Support (Am'd to Conform with Revised Act) (1968); Recognition of Acknowledgments (1969); Rendition of Prisoners as Witnesses (1957); Securities (1981); Simultaneous Death (1941); Status of Convicted Persons (1967); Testamentary Additions to Trusts (1961); Trade Secrets (1989); Transfers to Minors (1985); Trustees Powers (1969); Veterans' Guardianship, 1928 (1929).

Uniform Commercial Code in effect. See category Business Regulation and Commerce, topic Commercial Code.

For text of Uniform Acts falling within the scope of the Martindale-Hubbell Law Digests see Uniform and Model Acts section.

UNIFORM LAWS:

For list of Uniform Acts in force in the state see topic Statutes. For text of Uniform Acts within the scope of the Martindale-Hubbell Law Digests see Uniform and Model Acts section.

CRIMINAL LAW

BAIL:

See topic Criminal Law.

CRIMINAL LAW:

Criminal code has been established effective Nov. 1, 1973. (1971, c. 625). Criminal procedure is contained in cc. 592-A to 614.

Indictment or Information.—Criminal proceedings are based on indictment by a grand jury (c. 601) or on complaint in case of lesser offenses. Informations are prescribed (c. 601, §4), but statute does not state clearly when they are to be used or by whom signed.

Bail.—All offenses are bailable, except capital offenses where proof is evident or the presumption great. Cash, bail or a bond with sufficient sureties is acceptable. Bail may be taken on Sunday. (c. 597, §§1-2). Unappealed felony convictions are, before sentencing, bailable only if court finds by clear and convincing evidence that defendant is unlikely to flee or pose danger to anyone. Appealed conviction for capital offenses and for those punishable by life imprisonment without parole are not bailable. Appealed felony convictions are bailable only if defendant establishes clearly and convincingly that he is unlikely to flee or pose danger to anyone and by preponderance of evidence that appeal is neither frivolous nor taken to delay. (c. 597, §§1-a, 1-b).

See note at head of Digest as to 1998 legislation covered.

See Topical Index in front part of this volume.

DEBTOR AND CREDITOR

ASSIGNMENTS:

Common law requirements govern assignment of rights, debts or choses in action except where changed by statute.

Statutory provisions relating to assignments are covered by the Uniform Commercial Code. See category Business Regulation and Commerce, topic Commercial Code.

Assignment of Wages.—No assignment of or order for wages to be earned in the future is valid against a creditor of the person making it until it has been accepted in writing and a copy of it and of the acceptance has been filed with the clerk of the town or city where the party making it resides. The clerks of towns and cities must keep for public inspection an alphabetical list of all such orders and assignments filed with them. (c. 506, §§3, 4).

ATTACHMENT:

Prejudgment attachments may be had in all actions at law, upon notice to defendant, and if defendant objects, a showing by plaintiff that there is a reasonable likelihood that he will recover judgment including interest and costs of an amount equal to or greater than amount of attachment and unless defendant can establish that his assets will be sufficient to satisfy such judgment with interest and costs if plaintiff recovers same. (c. 511-A, §3). Court may order prejudgment attachment without prior hearing if plaintiff shows probable cause of his right to recover and amount thereof, and: (1) There is substantial danger property will be damaged, destroyed, concealed, or removed from state; or (2) attachment is necessary to vest quasi-in-rem jurisdiction; or (3) in cases for specific performance where there is imminent danger of transfer to bona fide third party; or (4) notice period under bulk sale is about to expire and absolute vesting of title is imminent; or (5) attachment is necessary to secure important governmental or general public interest. (c. 511-A, §8). Probate court may not grant attachment. (129 N.H. 4, 523 A.2d 28).

In Whose Favor Writ May Issue.—There is no discrimination against nonresidents or foreign corporations, except that all writs brought by nonresidents, corporate or otherwise, must be indorsed by some responsible resident, who thereby becomes liable for costs. (c. 509, §§8, 9).

Claims on Which Writ May Issue.—There is no requirement that the claim sued on be payable in the state and no provision as to issuance of attachment on unmatured claims.

Grounds.—No special grounds are necessary; mere bringing of the action is sufficient.

Bonds.—Plaintiff is not required to furnish any bond in order to obtain attachment.

Excessive Attachments.—If an excessive or unreasonable attachment of any kind has been made, defendant may apply to superior court to have amount of attachment reduced or to have it discharged. Upon such application party making attachment shall have burden of proof to show that attachment is not excessive or unreasonable. If, upon hearing, court finds that attachment is excessive or unreasonable under all circumstances, it shall order reduction or discharge of attachment as justice may require. (c. 511, §53).

Levy.—Real estate may be attached by any person—generally an officer—leaving attested copy of writ and of his return of attachment thereon at office or dwelling house of register of deeds of county in which real estate is situate. (c. 511, §3). Personal property is taken into possession by officer making attachment. After taking possession of live stock or articles which are incapable of being conveniently taken into actual possession, including motor vehicles, trucks, trailers and tractors, attaching officer, may, within 48 hours thereafter, leave attested copy of writ, and of his return of such taking possession or such attachment thereof, at home or office of town clerk, and such levy is effective although actual possession is not taken. (c. 511, §23). Officer, upon completion of such bulky article attachment, is under no duty to care for or preserve attached property unless requested by attaching creditor, who is responsible for all reasonable costs and expenses incurred by officer, including his reasonable fees, in complying with such request. (c. 511, §23).

Indemnity.—Although there is no statutory authority therefor, attaching officer who fears liability for wrongful levy requires indemnity bond for value of property to be attached plus anticipated costs.

Encumbered Property.—A creditor or officer attaching encumbered personal property must pay or tender to the owner of the encumbrance the amount of his lien. (c. 511, §26). Encumbrance on real estate may be discharged by payment or tender of amount of encumbrance to owner thereof. (c. 511, §§10, 11).

Priority.—Attaching creditors acquire liens in the order in which their attachments are made, and do not share pro rata. (c. 511, §§55, 56).

Release of Property.—A defendant whose real estate has been attached may obtain its release upon application to superior court by giving bond to plaintiff with sufficient sureties, conditioned to pay judgment which plaintiff may recover, with costs, within 60 days after judgment. (c. 511, §48).

Duration of Lien.—Attachment lien continues for six years after judgment on real estate and 60 days after judgment on personal property. Attachment of real estate or of right or interest therein where no judgment is involved expires ten years from filing thereof in Registry of Deeds. (c. 511, §55).

Release on Bond of Defendant.—The debtor can, by giving suitable bond, secure the restoration of the property attached whether it be real (c. 511, §48) or personal (c. 511, §§35-37).

Sale of Attached Property.—Personal property attached must be sold by the officer before judgment, if the parties consent thereto in writing. (c. 511, §30). Appraisers will be appointed and attached property will be sold when it consists of living animals, or goods liable to perish or waste, or to be greatly reduced in value by keeping, or which cannot be kept without great expense. (c. 511, §§31-34).

Retirement Accounts.—Individual retirement accounts and simplified employee pensions are subject to seizure, set off or attachment by means of legal process. (c. 515:13-a).

CREDITORS' SUITS:

When property of a debtor against whom execution has been issued and returned unsatisfied is asserted to be so held that it cannot be reached, or to have been conveyed by the debtor in fraud of his creditors, or held by others for the debtor's use, proceedings in equity may be had for a discovery and full relief, and court shall make proper decrees and orders, and issue process to compel a discovery, to prevent a transfer of the property and to make application as justice requires. (c. 498, §8). Such relief does not apply to property exempt from attachment and certain trusts. (c. 498, §9). Usual practice in equity prevails. (c. 498, §2).

EXECUTIONS:

Executions issue against the property, real and personal, of the defendant, and also against his body. (c. 527, §12). Writs of possession (c. 527, §13) and scire facias writs (c. 510, §6) are also used.

Exemptions.—See topic Exemptions.

Time of Issuance.—No execution shall issue until time for appeal has expired. (c. 527, §1). Writs of possession do not issue until two months after the date of judgment, where the same are issued in proceedings to foreclose mortgages upon real estate. (c. 524, §8). Executions may be issued at any time within two years after judgment rendered. However, when real property is attached, execution against such real property may be issued within six years after judgment. (c. 527, §6). Thereafter execution may issue on scire facias. (c. 527, §7).

Return.—Execution from superior court may be made returnable at any return day within six months from date of issuance and, upon notice to the debtor, may be extended to any subsequent return day as justice may require. (c. 527, §§2, 4). Execution from district court is returnable within 90 days from its date. (c. 527, §5).

Stay.—When a bill of exceptions is allowed the court may stay execution upon such terms and conditions as it deems just. (c. 491, §18).

Superior court, on application and notice to debtor may order return day of execution issued by court to be changed to any subsequent return day as justice may require; which order is recorded upon clerk's record of judgment and execution. (c. 527, §4).

Injunctions will issue to stay executions when equity requires the same to be done. (c. 498, §1; c. 527, §17). In such case, however, the existing lien (as in case of attachment) is continued for 30 days after dissolution of the injunction. (c. 527, §17).

Levy and Sale.—Goods and chattels taken on execution must be safely kept by the officer, at the expense of the debtor, four days at least; advertised for sale, by posting notice of the time and place of sale at two of the most public places in the town where the sale is to be, 48 hours before the expiration of said four days; and sold at auction to the highest bidder. (c. 528, §2). When execution is levied upon the debtor's shares in a corporation, notice in writing of the time and place of sale of such shares or interest must be given by the officer to the debtor, or left at his abode, and must be posted at one or more public places in the town where the sale is to be, and in two adjoining towns, 30 days before the sale. If the debtor does not reside in the county, the posting of such notice and the publishing of such notice in some newspaper, if any, in the county, otherwise in an adjoining county, three weeks previous to the sale, are sufficient, without further notice to the debtor. (c. 528, §§16-17). Special notices are prescribed where execution is levied on pews or seats in meeting houses and on the franchise or a corporation to take tolls. (c. 528, §§11, 12).

In levying against real estate, an amount sufficient to satisfy the judgment may be set off to the creditor (c. 529, §1), or any interest of the debtor in land may be sold for the creditor's benefit (c. 529, §19).

In case of setting off real property the officer levying the execution must cause three appraisers to be appointed, one by the creditor, one by the debtor and one by himself, who must be discreet and disinterested men, resident in the county, and must be sworn by a justice impartially to appraise such real estate as shall be shown them as the estate of the debtor. If the debtor, on due notice, neglects to appoint an appraiser, or does not reside in the county or within 20 miles of the property to be appraised, the officer must appoint an appraiser for him. Notice given to the clerk, treasurer, agent or one of the directors of a corporation to choose an appraiser for the corporation, ten days before the levy, is legal notice to the corporation. The appraisers must set off to the creditor, by metes and bounds or other distinct description, the real estate appraised by them, or so much as may be necessary in payment of the execution and costs of levying. The officer must deliver seizin and possession of the property so set off to the creditor or his attorney, make a full return of his proceedings, and cause the execution and return to be recorded at length in the registry of deeds of the county, and to be returned to the office of the clerk of the court to which it is returnable. (c. 529, §§2, 3, 4, 7, 12).

When the debtor's interest in real estate is sold at auction (c. 529, §19), notice of the time and place of sale must be given to the debtor, or left at his abode if he resides in the state and within 20 miles of the property, and a like notice must be posted at two of the most public places in the town in which the property is situate, 30 days before the sale. If the debtor does not reside in the state a like notice must also be published. If the debtor resides within the state, but not in the county or within 20 miles of the property, the notice may be given in hand to the debtor or left at his abode, or may be published. (c. 529, §§20-21). The sale may be adjourned from time to time, but not exceeding ten days at a time nor 60 days in the whole, notice of the adjournment being posted in the same manner as notices of the sale. (c. 529, §22).

Redemption.—The owner may redeem any goods and chattels before the sale, by satisfying the execution and the officer's fees and charges. (c. 528, §3). Debtor may redeem real estate within one year after sale (c. 529, §26), or within one year after return day of execution where execution has been by set-off (c. 529, §14).

Supplementary Proceedings.—Actions on the original judgment may be brought in which new property may be attached (c. 509, §4; c. 511, §1) or additional funds trusteed (c. 557, §1). Equitable proceedings are provided for to discover assets of the debtor and

See note at head of Digest as to 1998 legislation covered.

See Topical Index in front part of this volume.

NH – 11

EXECUTIONS . . . *continued*
to reach and apply the same to satisfy the judgment where the original execution has been returned unsatisfied. (c. 498, §8).

See also category Civil Actions and Procedure, topic Practice.

EXEMPTIONS:

Goods and property exempt from attachment and execution are as follows: Necessary wearing apparel, beds, bedding, and bedsteads for the debtor and his family; household furniture to the extent of $3,500; cooking stove and one refrigerator and its necessary utensils; one sewing machine; provisions and fuel to value of $400; uniform, arms and equipment of every officer and private in militia; Bibles, school books and libraries to value of $800; tools of his occupation to value of $5,000; one hog, and one pig; and pork of same when slaughtered; six sheep and fleeces of same; one cow, yoke of oxen or horse when required for farming or teaming purposes or other actual use, and hay not exceeding four tons; domestic fowls not exceeding $300 in value; debtor's interest in one pew in any meeting house where he or his family usually worship; his interest in one lot or right of burial in cemetery; one automobile to value of $4,000; jewelry to value of $500; interest in any property not to exceed $1,000 in value, plus up to $7,000 of any unused amount of other specified exemptions; any interest in qualified retirement plan subject to provisions (eff. 1/1/99). (c. 511, §2).

Money, rights and credits of defendant are exempt from trustee process in following instances, and trustee is not chargeable therefor: (1) Wages for labor performed by defendant after service of writ upon trustee; (2) wages of defendant earned before service of writ upon trustee, except in actions founded upon debt on judgment issued by N.H. court, in which case wages earned before service shall be exempt to amount of 50 times minimum hourly wage for each week, and except in actions founded upon loan contract, where wages earned before service are exempt to $50 per week. (c. 512, §21); (3) wages for personal services and earnings of wife and minor children of defendant; (4) any pension or bounty money of defendant, allowed by any law of U.S., before it has come into his actual possession; (5) funds held by trustee in capacity of clerk, cashier or other employee of defendant, which were received in ordinary course of such employment; (6) fees due to defendant for attendance at court as a juror or witness; (7) damages recovered for conversion of property exempt from attachment; (8) moneys, rights and credits of defendant in hands of any insurance company or its agents, whenever same are due on account of loss of, or damage by fire to, any property which by laws of this state was exempt from attachment, or levy on execution; provided, that whenever a building or structure so damaged or destroyed was a part of homestead, only so much of amount due therefor is exempt as, together with value of part of homestead remaining, if any, equals sum of $5,000 (c. 512, §21); (9) wages of defendant earned before service of writ upon trustee if defendant is a married woman and action is founded upon any loan contract subject to provisions of c. 399-A on which her husband is an obligor, jointly or severally, contingently or otherwise.

Waiver of Exemption.—Exemption may be waived in advance of levy on the property, either by agreement or by conduct. (71 N. H. 251, 51 Atl. 908).

Necessity of Claiming Exemption.—In the event exempt property is levied on, exemption must be claimed or it will be lost and consent implied from nonaction. (See 71 N. H. 251, 252, 51 Atl. 908.)

Homestead Exemptions.—See topic Homesteads.

See also topic Garnishment.

FORECLOSURE:

See topic Liens; category Mortgages, topic Mortgages of Real Property.

FRAUDULENT SALES AND CONVEYANCES:

Uniform Commercial Code has been adopted (c. 382-A) (see category Business Regulation and Commerce, topic Commercial Code); also Uniform Fraudulent Transfer Act (c. 545-A).

No conveyance, lease or mortgage of household goods, in use by husband and wife, is valid, unless in writing and executed by the owner and the husband or wife of the owner, but this does not apply in case of conditional sale. (c. 460, §11).

Bulk Sales.—Uniform Commercial Code applies. (c. 382-A).

Bulky Articles.—Constructive notice may be given of the sale of bulky articles by written memorandum signed by the vendor and the vendee describing the property, its location and the consideration of the sale, and containing a statutory affidavit and causing the same to be filed where filing is required to perfect a security interest under the Uniform Commercial Code. (c. 340, §§3-4; 382-A, §9-401).

GARNISHMENT:

Personal actions, except actions of replevin, may be begun by a trustee process. (c. 512, §1). If upon the disclosure of the trustee it appears that the trustee had in his possession at the time of the service of the writ upon him, or to the date of the taking of his disclosure, any money, goods, chattels, rights or credits of the defendants, he may be charged therefor, unless such money, etc., is exempt. (c. 512, §21). Bank or similar corporation served as trustee is chargeable only for any goods, rights, or credit of defendant in hands of trustee at time of service. (c. 512, §9-b). See topic Exemptions.

Property Which May Be Reached.—All money, goods, chattels, rights or credits of the defendant, not exempted from trustee process (c. 512, §20), including encumbered property (c. 512, §29) as to which the court may appoint a receiver if more can be obtained for it than the claims upon it.

Earnings in excess of $50 per week earned before service of the writ upon the trustee, are subject to trustee process. (c. 512, §21). Wages for labor performed by the defendant after service of the writ upon the trustees are not subject to trustee process and the trustee will not be chargeable therefor. (c. 512, §21).

Salary or wages of state official or employee may be trusteed by service of writ on State Treasurer who is chargeable for amount due official or employee at time of service of writ. (c. 512, §9a).

If an excessive or unreasonable attachment has been made by trustee process on mesne process, the defendant may apply to the superior court to have the amount of the attachment reduced or to have it discharged. If, upon hearing, the court shall find that the attachment is excessive or unreasonable under all the circumstances, it shall order the reduction or discharge of the attachment as justice may require. (c. 511, §53).

Jurisdiction to Issue Writ.—Any personal action may be begun by trustee process except actions of replevin (c. 512, §1) and this applies as well in municipal as in Superior Court (c. 512, §48).

Answer of Garnishee.—Disclosure of trustees may be given or taken by any party to the action at any time after the service of the writ upon the trustee, after same notice to the adverse party as is required in taking depositions, and upon payment or tender to the trustee of his fees for travel and attendance, as in the case of witnesses. (c. 512, §12).

Practice.—The trustee writ constitutes an attachment and summons and must be served upon the defendant and trustee like a writ of summons; and the goods and estate of the defendant may be attached thereon. (c. 512, §3). Nonresident trustees may be served and charged by service upon and disclosure of agent within the state. (c. 512, §5). The names of any persons may be inserted in the writ as trustees after service thereof upon any other trustee, but not after service upon the defendant. (c. 512, §6). A partnership may not be charged as trustee unless the persons summoned are described as partners and the partners cannot be charged severally unless severally summoned. (c. 512, §7). No trustee may be charged on default until after refusal to answer upon such notice as the court may order (c. 512, §10), but if trustee then defaults he may be held chargeable for the amount of the judgment which may be recovered of the defendant by the plaintiff (c. 512, §11).

Adverse Claims.—If it appears from the depositions taken that the property for which the trustee is sought to be charged is claimed by a third person, such third person must be, on motion and terms as the court may order, admitted to defend his right and he may offer evidence in support thereof. (c. 512, §26). If such a claimant does not appear in court the court may order notice to be given to him personally or by publication to appear or be forever barred. (c. 512, §27). Upon appearance such claimant must be admitted as a party to maintain his claim and may have trial by jury of an issue or issues between plaintiff and claimant as may be framed therefor under the direction of the court. (c. 512, §28).

Judgment.—If upon depositions or trial by jury and verdict thereof it appears that the trustee had in his possession at the time of the service of the writ upon him or at any time thereafter, any money, goods, chattels, rights or credits of the defendant, not exempted from trustee process, the trustee must be adjudged chargeable therefor. (c. 512, §20).

HOMESTEADS:

Any person is entitled to a homestead in his real estate or his interest therein. Homestead does exist in manufactured housing which is owned and occupied as dwelling by same person, but shall not exist in land upon which manufactured housing is situated if that land is not also owned by owner of manufactured housing. (c. 480, §1).

Limitation of Value.—$30,000. (c. 480, §1).

Limitation of Area.—None.

Debts or Liabilities Against Which Exemption Not Available.—The homestead right is not available in the following cases: (1) in the collection of taxes; (2) in the enforcement of liens of mechanics and others for debts created in the construction, repair or improvement of the homestead; (3) in the enforcement of mortgages, which are made a charge thereon according to law, in levy of executions. (c. 480, §4).

Designation of Homestead.—The superior court, upon petition of the owner of a homestead, or the wife or husband of such owner, or upon petition of a judgment creditor and such notice as it may order, may appoint appraisers and cause the homestead right to be set off, and, a record of the proceedings being made in the registry of deeds, the right is established as against all persons. (c. 480, §8-a).

Levy on Homestead.—The officer required to levy an execution on the debtor's property in which a homestead right may exist may levy the execution or sell said property subject to the homestead right. (c. 480, §7).

Waiver of exemption may be executed by owner and wife or husband, if any, with the formalities required for the execution of a conveyance of land. (c. 480, §5-a).

Alienation or Encumbrance.—Where the homestead owner is married, his or her spouse must join in any conveyance or encumbrance thereof except a purchase money mortgage. (c. 480, §5-a).

Rights of Surviving Spouse.—Owner and spouse are entitled to occupy the homestead during owner's lifetime and after decease of owner, spouse is entitled to occupy it during the lifetime of the survivor. Minor children have no rights. (c. 480, §3-a).

The right of a surviving spouse in the homestead of a deceased spouse may be lost by abandonment of spouse, nonsupport of wife by husband, conduct constituting cause for divorce in consequence of which deceased spouse was justifiably living apart at time of death, waiver or release filed in probate court within one year after death of spouse, or marriage settlement stipulated to be in lieu of homestead right. (c. 560, §§14-16, 18, 19).

JUDGMENT NOTES:

See category Business Regulation and Commerce, topic Bills and Notes.

LEVY:

See topics Attachment, Executions.

LIENS:

Uniform Commercial Code has been adopted. See category Business Regulation and Commerce, topic Commercial Code.

LIENS . . . *continued*

Statutory liens are given to following persons: Boarding house keepers (c. 448, §1); boarders or pasturers of animals (c. 448, §2); owners of stallions, upon colts for service fees, which lien continues until colt is eight months old and may be enforced by an attachment of such colt at any time after it is four months old (c. 448, §3); any person who maintains a public garage, public or private airport or hangar or trailer court for storage and care of motor vehicles or aircraft or house trailers brought to his premises or placed in his care by or with consent of legal or equitable owner (c. 450, §1); any person who by himself or others performs labor, furnishes materials, or expends money in repairing, refitting or equipping a motor vehicle or aircraft (c. 450, §2); every person who maintains an establishment for cleaning, pressing, glazing, laundering or dyeing, who places in storage, who does work on personal property at request of owner or legal possessor of same (c. 449, §1); any person who sells or furnishes monumental work to be placed in a cemetery or at a grave (c. 452, §1); jewelers, watchmakers and silversmiths (c. 451, §1); towns, upon stock and goods of itinerant vendors, for local license fees (c. 321, §14); hospitals and home health care providers, on sum collected or to be collected, whether by judgment or settlement, of claim of patient against third party arising out of accident not covered by Workmen's Compensation Act (c. 448-A §1); cities, towns and counties for support of paupers on property passing by will or intestate succession, property settlement or civil judgment for personal injuries (c. 165, §§22-a, 28-a); state on any items used for drug related offenses and subject to forfeiture (c. 318-B, §17-b); state, for hazardous waste cleanup costs (c. 147-B, §10-b); financier of lumbermen (c. 453, §1); radio and television repair shop owner (c. 451-A, §1); storer of boats and boat motors (c. 450-A, §1).

Foreclosure.—After the debt has run 12 months, an article subject to a jeweler's lien may be sold at public or private sale, and the proceeds, after paying the expense of sale, applied in payment of the debt, the balance, if any, to be paid over to the county treasurer of the county where the sale is held, in trust for the debtor. (c. 451, §2). Before any such sale is held notice in writing of the amount due and the time and place of sale must be given the debtor. If the debtor's residence is known such notice must be mailed to him 14 days before the sale; if his address is unknown the notice must be posted in the county courthouse or the city, village or town hall, where the lienholder resides, 30 days before the sale. (c. 451, §3).

If such lien remains undischarged for period of 60 days after work has been completed, or after expiration of agreed terms of storage if any, or in absence of such agreement after expiration of 90 days from date of storage, lienholder may give such article or articles to a duly organized charitable corporation or sell such article at public or private sale. (c. 449, §2).

Thirty days notice in writing of the intention to enforce the lien of a vendor of monumental work must be given the purchaser, or his legal representative, or be left at his usual place of abode. If the purchaser resides out of the state, or his residence is unknown, notice may be given by publication. Upon the expiration of 30 days from such notice, and within two years, the vendor may pay or tender to the purchaser, or his legal representative, or, if neither resides within the state or their residence is unknown, into the town treasury of the town where the monumental work is located, subject to the purchasers' order, all sums which the purchaser has paid in excess of one-third of the contract price. Thereupon, and within the said two years, he may enter upon the premises where the work has been placed, and remove the same, and it is then his property, free from all claim of the purchaser. The vendor must put the lot or grounds from which such removal is made in as good condition as before the monumental work was erected, and may retain the money paid him, not in excess of said one-third, to pay the expense of removal and repairs. Such retaking constitutes payment in full for all claims against the purchaser under the contract. (c. 452, §§2-7).

Liens for license fees on goods of itinerant vendors may be enforced by suit and judgment within ten days from the time goods were first publicly offered or exposed for sale in the town asserting the lien. (c. 321, §14).

Other liens other than security interests covered by Ch. 382-A, Art. 9, are foreclosed by sale at auction as follows, unless otherwise provided by contract. (c. 444, §§1-2; c. 450, §3). Notice of sale must be given by posting in two or more public places in town where property is situate, at least 14 days before sale, and if value of property exceeds $100, by publishing notice. Notice of sale must be served upon general owner, if resident in county, same number of days before sale, stating in writing time and place of sale, property to be sold and amount of lien thereon. Balance of proceeds of sale, if any, after payment of amount of lien and reasonable expenses incident to sale, must be paid to general owner or person entitled thereto, on demand. Holder of lien must cause a copy of notices and an affidavit of service, with an account of sale and of fees and charges thereon, to be recorded in books of town where sale took place. (c. 444, §§3-6). Lienholder must inquire of Division of Motor Vehicles, Secretary of State or town clerk, as appropriate, to determine whether filings of other liens exist. If there is no response 14 days after such inquiry, sale may proceed as hereinbefore described. If determination is made that other liens exist, notice must be sent to such lienholders of record at least 14 days prior to sale. Any such lienholder has right to redeem. (c. 444, §4-a).

Mechanics' Liens.—A person, who by himself or others, performs labor, or furnishes material toward building, repairing, fitting or furnishing a vessel within this state, payment for which is due, has a lien for four days after it is completed. (c. 447, §1). A person who, by himself or others, performs labor, or furnishes materials to the amount of $15 for the erection, alterating or repairing of a building, or for building any dam, canal, sluiceway, well or bridge, or for consumption or use in the prosecution of such work, other than for a municipality, under a contract with the owner thereof, has a lien on the buildings and on the lot of land on which they stand, for the period of 120 days after labor is performed or materials are furnished. (c. 447, §§2, 9).

A person who performs labor or furnishes materials to the amount of $15 or more for making brick under a contract with the owner thereof has a lien upon the kiln containing such brick for 120 days after burning. (c. 447, §§3, 9).

A person, who by himself or others, or by teams or machinery, performs labor or furnishes supplies to the amount of $15 toward rafting, driving, cutting, hauling, sawing or drawing wood, bark, lumber or logs, or toward cooking or hauling supplies in aid of such labor under a contract with the owner of the wood, bark, lumber or logs, has a lien thereon for 120 days. (c. 447, §§4, 9).

A person who by himself or others makes an advance or series of advances of money to the owner of, or person entitled to the possession of, any logs, lumber, of pulp wood for the purpose of financing the cutting, hauling, yarding, piling, trucking, rafting, booming, driving or towing the same, can obtain a lien thereon for two years by placing his registered mark thereon. (c. 453).

A subcontractor can entitle himself to any of the three preceding liens by giving a notice in writing to the owner or to the person having charge of the property, that he shall claim such lien before performing the labor or furnishing the materials for which it is claimed, and by furnishing every 30 days to such owner an account in writing of the labor performed or materials furnished during the 30 days, and if he gives such notice after the labor has been performed or materials have been furnished, his lien will then be valid to the extent of the amount then due or that may be due from the owner. (c. 447, §§5, 6, 8).

A person who performs labor or furnishes materials to the amount of $15 in the grading, masonry, bridging or track-laying of a railroad under a contract with an agent, contractor or subcontractor, of the proprietors, has a lien upon the railroad and the land upon which it is constructed if he give a notice in writing like that before mentioned to such proprietor, or to the person having charge of the railroad, and if he furnish an account once in 30 days, as required of subcontractors in the three preceding liens. (c. 447, §7).

The foregoing liens take precedence of all prior claims except liens on account of taxes.

Any lien may be secured by attachment of the property upon which it exists at any time while the lien continues, the writ and return thereon distinctly expressing that purpose. (c. 447, §10).

Such attachment has precedence over all lien claims for labor, materials and other things done or furnished after attachment was made, except where same were done or furnished in performance of a contract existing when attachment was made or were necessary for preservation of property attached. (c. 447, §11). Such attachments have precedence and priority over any construction mortgage unless mortgagee can show that proceeds of mortgage alone were disbursed either toward payment of invoices from or claims due subcontractors and suppliers of materials or labor for work on mortgaged premises, or upon receipt by mortgagee from mortgagor or his agent of an affidavit that work on mortgaged premises for which such disbursement is to be made has been completed and that subcontractors and suppliers of materials or labor have been paid for their share of such work. This precedence shall not apply to wage claims of mortgagees working for wages under a mortgagor-mortgagee relationship as defined in R.S.A. 275:42. (c. 447, §12-a). Except as stated above, all such attaching lien creditors share pro rata in accordance with amounts of their respective lien judgments in property attached or in its proceeds. (c. 447, §12).

No lien is defeated by taking a note, unless it was taken in discharge of the amount due and of the lien. (c. 447, §14).

Public Works.—Subcontractors' liens for labor performed and materials furnished attach to any money due or to become due from the state or any subdivision thereof by virtue of any contract for any public work or construction, alteration or repair. (c. 447, §15).

Bond to Discharge Liens.—A bond or other security is compulsory in the case of any public works contract involving an expenditure of $25,000, and optional if it involves less than that, in an amount equal to at least 100% of the contract price, or of the estimated cost of the work if no aggregate price is agreed upon, conditioned upon the payment by the contractors and subcontractors for all labor performed or furnished, and for all equipment hired, including trucks, for all material used and for fuels, lubricants, power, tools, hardware and supplies purchased by the principal and used in carrying out the contract, and for labor and parts furnished upon the order of the contractor for the repair of the equipment used in carrying out the contract. (c. 447, §16). To obtain the benefit of the bond, any person, firm or corporation having a claim must, within 90 days after completion and acceptance of project by contracting party, file in office of Secretary of State, if state is a contracting party, or with Department of Public Works and Highways, if state is a party to said contract by or through said Department, or in office of clerk of superior court for county in which contract is to be principally performed, if any political subdivision of state is a contracting party, a statement of claim, a copy of which must be forthwith sent by mail by office where it is filed to principal and surety. (c. 447, §17). Within one year after filing claim, claimant must institute proceedings in superior court for county within which contract has been principally performed. (c. 447, §18).

Merchandise Liens.—Uniform Commercial Code applies. (c. 382-A).

Revised Uniform Federal Tax Lien Registration Act adopted. (c. 454A).

MECHANICS' LIENS:

See topic Liens.

PLEDGES:

Uniform Commercial Code has been adopted. See category Business Regulation and Commerce, topic Commercial Code.

Trust Receipts.—Covered by Uniform Commercial Code. See category Business Regulation and Commerce, topic Commercial Code.

Other Liens.—Any person having a lien on personal property, other than a security interest covered by the Uniform Commercial Code, where no time is limited for the payment of the debt or redemption of the property, may sell the same or so much thereof as is needful at auction, by posting notices of the sale in town where property is situated 14 days at least before sale, and by serving notice of sale upon general owner, if resident in county, same number of days before sale, stating in writing time and place of sale, property to be sold and amount of lien thereon. (c. 444 §§1, 3, 4). If time is limited for payment of debt or redemption of property, property may be sold at any time after expiration of limited time, upon like notice. (c. 444, §2).

PLEDGES . . . *continued*

The balance of the proceeds of sale, if any, after payment of the amount of the lien and the reasonable expenses incident to the sale, shall be paid to general owner or person entitled thereto, on demand. (c. 444, §5).

Record of Sale.—The holder of the lien shall cause a copy of such notices and an affidavit of service, with an account of the sale and of the fees and charges thereon, to be recorded in the books of the town where the sale takes place. (c. 444, §6).

RECEIVERS:

Receivers are appointed by the superior court, either in term time or in vacation, in accordance with the general principles of equity. (c. 498, §§1, 12).

Receivers must file bond with sufficient sureties, for the faithful discharge of their duties, payable to the clerk and his successor for the benefit of all persons interested. They must file inventories within 30 days after their appointment, and file accounts under oath of all their transactions, receipts and expenditures, on the first days of January and July, and at such other times as the court may order. (Rules of Superior Court, No. 165, 99 N. H. 629).

REDEMPTION:

See topic Executions; categories Mortgages, topic Mortgages of Real Property; Taxation, topic Administration, subhead Redemption.

SUPPLEMENTARY PROCEEDINGS:

See topic Executions.

TRUSTEE PROCESS:

See topic Garnishment.

USURY:

No usury law, but see category Business Regulation and Commerce, topic Interest.

DISPUTE RESOLUTION

ALTERNATIVE DISPUTE RESOLUTION:

Mandatory Dispute Resolution.—All writs of summons from superior court and transfers of actions from district courts, with exception of cases submitted by parties to private dispute resolution, shall be assigned to ADR. If parties elect to submit case to private dispute resolution, mandatory court ADR is not required. Counsel may reach agreement on (i) neutral evaluation; (ii) mediation; (iii) nonbinding arbitration; and (iv) binding arbitration. If counsel cannot agree on ADR procedure, ADR procedure with lowest numerical value selected by counsel shall be procedure utilized. Any ADR other than binding arbitration is nonbinding and shall not impair right to trial. ADR proceedings shall be confidential. Statement made and documents prepared and produced in conjunction with ADR shall not be admissible unless otherwise admissible notwithstanding its use at ADR.

Voluntary Dispute Resolution.—Mandatory ADR in superior court can be avoided by parties voluntarily submitting to private ADR. (Superior Court Rule 170).

See also topic Arbitration and Award.

ARBITRATION AND AWARD:

Arbitration agreements are considered valid and enforceable in this state. (c. 542, §1). However, provisions of statute shall not apply to arbitration agreements between employers and employees unless such agreement specifically references statute. (c. 542, §1). Disputes between employers and employees concerning conditions of employment or wages may be submitted to State Board of Conciliation and Arbitration. (c. 273, §§12-27).

Contracts to Arbitrate Future Disputes.—A written contract may provide for settlement by arbitration of any controversy arising out of such contract (c. 542, §1), and court proceedings in an action brought on a contract containing such a provision must be stayed until arbitration has been had in accordance with the terms of the agreement, unless the applicant for the stay is in default in proceedings with the arbitration (c. 542, §2).

Rescission.—A provision in any written contract to settle by arbitration a controversy thereafter arising out of such contract, or an agreement in writing to submit to arbitration any controversy existing at the time of the agreement to submit is valid and irrevocable, except upon such grounds as exist at law or in equity for the revocation of any contract. (c. 542, §1).

Enforcement of Agreement.—The superior court will, upon petition, order a defaulting party to proceed with arbitration proceedings in accordance with the terms of an arbitration agreement. (c. 542, §3).

Appointment of Arbitrators.—If no method of naming arbitrators is provided, or if for any other reason a lapse occurs in the naming of arbitrators, the superior court will appoint arbitrators to act in the enforcement of an agreement. (c. 542, §4).

Powers of Arbitrators.—Arbitrators are empowered to summon witnesses under penalty of punishment for contempt. (c. 542, §5).

Award and Enforcement Thereof.—Upon petition for cause shown, the superior court will confirm, modify or vacate an award. Where an award is vacated and the time within which the agreement required the award to be made has not expired, the court may in its discretion direct a rehearing by the arbitrators or by new arbitrators appointed by the court. (c. 542, §8).

Judgment on Award.—Upon the granting of an order confirming, modifying or correcting an award, judgment may be entered in conformity therewith in the court wherein the order was granted. (c. 542, §9).

Uniform Arbitration Act not adopted.

DOCUMENTS AND RECORDS

ACKNOWLEDGMENTS:

Uniform Recognition of Acknowledgments Act has been adopted. (c. 456-A, §1). It is specifically provided, however, that any instrument may be acknowledged in manner and form as otherwise provided by laws and customs of this state. (c. 456-A, §7).

Under other statutes acknowledgment may be taken by the following officers:

Within state: Justice, notary public, or commissioner. (c. 455, §3; c. 477, §3).

Without state but within United States: Justice or notary public authorized by law of the locality where he acts, or commissioner. (c. 456-A, §2).

Without United States: See §2 of Uniform Act, United States ambassador, minister, envoy or chargé d'affaires in country to which accredited; any consular officer of United States; notary public; commissioner or other agent of New Hampshire having an official seal and power to take acknowledgments in such places. (c. 477, §4).

Persons Serving in or with U. S. Armed Forces.—See §11 of the Uniform Act.

General Requirements as to Taking.—See §3 of the Uniform Act.

Married Women.—No special form used.

Foreign Acknowledgments.—See §2 of the Uniform Act.

Proof of Witnesses.—If grantor dies, becomes insane, or goes out of State before acknowledgment, due execution of conveyance may be made by oath of two witnesses acquainted with handwriting of grantor. (c. 477, §12). If grantor refuses to acknowledge, proof of execution may be made before any court of record pursuant to c. 447, §12. (c. 477, §13).

Authentication may be as provided in §2 of the Uniform Act. The official character of all officers in this state who administer oaths or take acknowledgments may be certified by the Secretary of State. (c. 5, §4). Clerks of courts of record, which include municipal courts (c. 502, §27), are in the habit of issuing certificates as to official character of justices, notaries and commissioners. Such certificates are probably sufficient (c. 499, §11), although no direct statutory authority for such practice has been found. Fee for authentication by Secretary of State (c. 5, §10) or clerk of court (c. 499, §18) is $1.

Forms set forth in §6 of Uniform Act may be used.

Alternative to Acknowledgment or Proof.—No statutory provision.

AFFIDAVITS:

Within the state, affidavits may be taken before a justice of the peace (c. 501, §20; c. 92, §5); notary public (c. 455, §3); commissioner or other person specially authorized to administer oaths (c. 455, §15).

Without the state, affidavits may be taken before a commissioner, appointed by the Governor of New Hampshire with the advice of the Council, to administer oaths in any foreign state, district or territory of the United States, or in any foreign country to which the United States sends a representative. (c. 455, §§12, 14). Although there is no statute touching upon oaths administered by other officers in foreign states, it is the custom to accept an oath administered by anyone entitled to receive oaths within the jurisdiction where the oath is made. When an oath is administered by a foreign official in a foreign state, it is customary to require that the official state when his commission expires. See topic Acknowledgments.

Evidence.—Affidavits are not admissible in evidence.

Form.—No particular form is prescribed. A form in common use is:

I, ..., of . . . . . ., County of . . . . . ., State of New Hampshire, on oath depose and say that, etc. State of New Hampshire, ... County.—ss.

Personally appeared the above-named . . . . . . and subscribed and made oath to the foregoing affidavit.

Before me, ..., Justice of the Peace.

Alternative to Affidavit.—No statutory provision.

NOTARIES PUBLIC:

Jurisdiction is state wide. Oath or acknowledgment may be taken outside of state, if document is to be used in state. (c. 455, §14). Women are eligible. (c. 455, §2). They have the usual powers of the office and the same powers as a justice of the peace in relation to depositions, the acknowledgment of deeds and other instruments and the administering of oaths. (c. 455, §3). Their official character may be certified by the Secretary of State (c. 5, §5; c. 455, §10), or by the clerks of the Supreme or superior courts, or by the clerk of any court of record having an official seal. Fee, 50¢. Notarial seal or legal imprint of stamp bearing words "notary public, New Hampshire" and name of notary shall be affixed to acknowledgments and jurats. Notary public must state date his commission expires. (c. 456, §9).

Fees.—Notaries public are entitled to the following fees: Up to $5 for each oath, witness, service, or certification (c. 455, §11); for services related to taking of depositions, between $5 and $50 (c. 455, §11; c. 517, §19).

RECORDS:

Uniform Commercial Code has been adopted. See category Business Regulation and Commerce, topic Commercial Code.

Place of Recording.—Uniform Commercial Code contains provisions as to the place of recording of all instruments required by the Code to be recorded. See category Business Regulation and Commerce, topic Commercial Code.

Instruments eligible to record with register of deeds for each county are: Deeds and other conveyances of real estate situated in said county, including leases and mortgages thereof (c. 477, §§3-a, 7); powers of attorney to convey real estate (c. 477, §9); discharges of mortgages and decrees thereof (c. 479, §§7, 16), and returns of foreclosure sales of real estate (c. 479, §26); attachments of real estate and discharges thereof (c. 511, §§3, 8); returns of execution levies against and execution sales of real estate and

See note at head of Digest as to 1998 legislation covered.

See Topical Index in front part of this volume.

RECORDS . . . continued

returns of intermediate steps taken to effect same (c. 529, §§29, 30, 31); notices prior to and returns of sales of real estate for nonpayment of taxes, and redemption therefrom (c. 80, §§22, 27); returns of service of writs of possession (c. 527, §19); any instrument required by law to be recorded in office of town clerk where place of recording is unincorporated or unorganized place having no clerk (c. 53, §7).

For list of Counties and County Seats see first page for this state in Volume containing Practice Profiles Section.

Where executions have been returned unsatisfied, bills for discovery against the defendant may be filed with the clerk of the town where the defendant resides, thereby effecting a lien upon the personal property to which the bill relates. (c. 498, §14). Attachments of live stock and bulky articles may be completed without taking them into actual possession by filing a copy of the writ, with a return thereon, of a taking of possession, at the home or office of the clerk of the town where the property is situated. (c. 511, §23).

Assignments of wages should be recorded by the clerk of the town where the assigning party resides. (c. 506, §3).

The following instruments may be recorded with Secretary of State: Any ancient record, plan document or public paper prior to the year 1825. (c. 41, §§64, 65). Address of Secretary of State is: State House, Concord, NH 03301.

Fees of registers of deeds and other recording and certifying officers are as specified in c. 478, §17-g. See category Property, topic Deeds.

Fees for Town Clerks.—Minimum fee of $2 for recording bill of conditional sale, personal property mortgage, for copy of any public record in his custody except copies of vital statistics or for writs of attachment, discharging mortgage on margin of record or recording assignment thereof, 50¢. Uniform Commercial Code contains provisions establishing fees for recording various instruments with municipal clerks. (c. 41, §25).

Consequences of Failure to Record.—For security interests see Uniform Commercial Code. (c. 382-A, §§9-301, 9-302, 9-312). Returns of execution levies upon real estate are invalid against subsequent purchasers without notice and attaching creditors unless properly recorded. (c. 529, §29). Unrecorded conveyances of real estate (c. 477, §7) are invalid against all except grantor or mortgagor, his heirs and administrators. An unrecorded assignment of wages is invalid against a creditor of assigning party. (c. 506, §3).

Torrens System of registering titles to real estate has not been adopted.

Transfer of Decedent's Title.—The probate records, without more, furnish sufficient record evidence of the transfer of a decedent's title to real estate to his devisees or heirs at law. In case of a will probated outside of this state, proceedings should be taken to have such will and probate thereof admitted to probate records in this state. In case of a nonresident intestate, ancillary administration is necessary. See category Estates and Trusts, topic Wills, subhead Foreign Probated Wills.

Filing under Commercial Code.—Proper place to file for perfection of security interest is as follows: When collateral is equipment used in farming operations, or farm products, or accounts, contract rights for general intangibles arising from or relating to sale of farm products by farmer, or consumer goods, then in office of clerk of town where debtor resides, or if debtor is not resident of state, then in office of clerk of town in which goods are kept. When collateral is goods which at time security interest attaches are or are to become fixtures, then in office where mortgage on real estate concerned would be filed or recorded. In all other cases, in office of Secretary of State and in addition, if debtor has place of business in only one town in state, also in office of clerk of such town, or if debtor has no place of business in state, but resides in state, also in office of clerk of town in which he resides. (c. 382-A, §9-401).

Fees for filing are as follows: Financing statement, $10. (c. 382-A, §9-403); termination statement, $10 (c. 382-A, §9-404); assignment of security interest, $2.50 (c. 382-A, §9-405); release of collateral, $10 (c. 382-A, §9-406). See c. 478, §17-g.

Vital Statistics.—Records of births, marriages and deaths are kept by Registrar of Vital Statistics, Concord, N. H. 03301 (c. 126, §2). Copies may be procured from said officials by persons with direct and tangible interest in such records. (c. 126, §14). Division of Public Health may approve release of data to individuals/institutions for health-related research. (c. 126, §14, VI). Fee, $10. (c. 126, §15). Records of divorces are kept by clerks of several courts and Registrar of Vital Statistics. (c. 458, §15).

The Registrar of Vital Statistics may issue to any person with direct and tangible interest in such information, card containing such information as to date and place of birth of such person as is recorded in Registrar's office. (c. 126, §§13,14).

SEALS:

Uniform Commercial Code has been adopted. See category Business Regulation and Commerce, topic Commercial Code.

TORRENS ACT:

Not adopted.

VITAL STATISTICS:

See topic Records.

EMPLOYMENT

EMPLOYER AND EMPLOYEE:

See topic Labor Relations.

LABOR RELATIONS:

The state official in charge of labor affairs is the Labor Commissioner (c. 273, §1), and there is also a Board of Conciliation and Arbitration, consisting of three members (c. 273, §12), whose jurisdiction extends to businesses employing not less than ten employees (c. 273, §§15, 26). Certain matters may be referred to hearings officer. (c. 273-A, §6).

The Commissioner must visit manufacturing, mechanical and mercantile establishments to ascertain whether laws are being complied with and reasonable sanitary and hygienic conditions maintained, may, when deemed necessary, prosecute offenses against labor laws and must make reports to Governor and Council and to Legislature. (c. 273, §§9-11).

In case of a labor dispute the Commissioner must, on application of the employer or a majority of the employees, visit the locality, make inquiry, advise what should be done to adjust the controversy or difference and make a written decision. (c. 273, §§15-17). If employer and employees fail to agree to a settlement through the Commissioner, he must endeavor to have them consent to submit the matter to the Board of Arbitration (c. 273, §19), and if he cannot secure such a reference he must request from each side a statement of the facts and of the reason for not submitting to arbitration, which statement must be given publicity through such newspapers as care to use it (c. 273, §25).

In case of a strike or lockout or threat thereof, the Commissioner must endeavor to effect an amicable settlement or a submission of the matter to the Board. If the parties do not agree to such submission, he must investigate the controversy and make and publish a report fixing the responsibility. (c. 273, §§26-27).

When a matter is submitted to the Board of Conciliation and Arbitration it may summon witnesses and conduct hearings, and must render its decision within seven days after completion of the hearing. Such decision is final and is binding on the parties for six months or until 60 days after either party has given the other written notice of intention not to be bound. (c. 273, §§20, 22-23).

Apprenticeship.—A state apprenticeship council of eight has been created to establish standards for apprenticeship agreements and promote the development of apprenticeship programs. (c. 278).

Labor Contracts.—No person shall coerce or compel, or attempt to coerce or compel, any person into an agreement, either written or oral, in order to join or become a member of any labor organization, as a condition of securing or continuing in any such employment. (c. 275, §1).

In all contracts relating to labor eight hours actual labor constitutes a day's work unless otherwise agreed by the parties. This does not apply to classes of labor for which the law provides day limits. (c. 275, §30).

No employee may obtain money or property of any kind, or a promise thereof, from, for or in behalf of, any person, in payment for procuring employment for such person in the service of the employer, nor may any such offers or promises be made to any such employer. (c. 275, §§6, 7).

No employee may be required to work in any mill or factory on any legal holiday, except to perform such work as is both absolutely necessary and can lawfully be performed on the Lord's Day. (c. 275, §28).

No employee may be required or requested to work more hours in any one day than is limited by law, in order to make up time lost by reason of a legal holiday. (c. 275, §31).

No employee may be required to pay the cost of a medical examination or the cost of furnishing any records required by the employer as a condition of employment. (c. 275, §3).

Employee may not be required to do usual work of his occupation on Sunday, unless he is allowed during the six days next ensuing 24 consecutive hours without labor. (c. 275, §32).

Every employee in any manufacturing or mercantile establishment (with certain exceptions) must be allowed at least 24 consecutive hours of rest in every seven consecutive days. No employer may operate any such manufacturing or mercantile establishment on Sunday unless he has posted in conspicuous places on the premises a schedule containing list of employees required or allowed to work on Sunday, and designating day of rest for each, and filed a copy of such schedule and every change therein with Commissioner of Labor. No employee may be required or allowed to work on day of rest designated for him. (c. 275, §33).

Wages.—Every person, firm or corporation engaged in operation of a manufacturing, mechanical or mercantile establishment, hotels and restaurants, or in mining, quarrying, stone cutting or granite cutting, or in cutting, harvesting and driving pulpwood and timber, or in a railroad, telegraph, telephone, express or aqueduct business, or in erection, alteration, repair or removal of any building or structure, or in construction or repair of any railroad, road, bridge, sewer, gas, water or electric light works, pipes or lines, and every municipal corporation, must inform new employees, before they begin work, of wages they are to receive, and must inform employees of any proposed change in wages before change is made. If wages are on a piece work basis, employees must be informed of rate paid, and in case of wage incentive plans employees must be informed of approximate minimum rates and methods on which supplementary wages are fixed. (c. 275, §§42, 45). If employee reports to work at employer's request, he shall be paid not less than two hour's pay at his regular rate of pay. (c. 275, §43-a). Employers who are responsible for making contributions into health and welfare or pension fund, and fail to do so, may be pursued by Labor Commissioner. Prime contractor may be pursued only after reasonable efforts are made to secure payments from subcontractor. (c. 275, §43, I-a). Every employer in said industries must pay wages earned by employees who work by day or week within eight days, including Sunday, after expiration of each week and must keep posted, in conspicuous place in his or its office, notice, on form prescribed by Commissioner of Labor, that wages will be so paid. (c. 275, §42). Such weekly payment of wages must be made in cash, by electronic transfer, direct deposit, or by check, and no employee may be compelled by his employer to accept any goods or merchandise in payment of wages. Nothing above mentioned prevents payment of wages by check wherever such form of payment is acceptable to employee to whom payment is made. (c. 275, §43). These provisions do not apply to municipal officers whose services are paid for by day, nor to teachers employed by school districts. (c. 275, §44).

On discharge of employee, his earned wages are due immediately and must be paid within 72 hours after demand therefor, except that if employee worked at a place other than employer's principal place of business his wages are due on next regular pay day. If employee quits, his wages are due on next regular pay day. If work is suspended because of an industrial dispute, wages earned and unpaid at time of suspension are

LABOR RELATIONS . . . *continued*
payable on next regular pay day, together with any deposit or other guarantee held by employer for faithful performance of duties of employment. (c. 275, §48).

See also infra, subhead Children.

Minimum Wages.—No person, firm or corporation shall employ any employees at a rate of less than that required by federal minimum wage law, as am'd (c. 279, §21) except employees engaged in household labor, domestic labor, farm labor, outside salesmen, summer camps for minors, employees engaged as newsboys or golf caddies and hotel, motel, cabin, tourist home and restaurant industry employer may take tips received by employee into account in complying with minimum wage requirements. In addition, such employers may deduct certain prescribed allowances for meals and lodging furnished employee. (c. 279, §21-a). Person with less than six months experience in any occupation or person 16 years of age or under need receive only 75% of applicable minimum wage rate. (c. 279, §21). Lesser rates of pay are permissible to employers who employ high school or post secondary school students working for practical experience in jobs approved by Commissioner. (c. 279, §22-aa).

Labor Commissioner has power to investigate and ascertain wages of employees employed in any occupation in state. (c. 279, §3). Appeal lies from written decision of Commissioner to Superior Court. (c. 279, §16-a). Underpaid employee may recover in civil action difference between wage paid and statutory minimum wage plus costs and attorney's fee. (c. 279, §29).

Assignment of Wages.—See category Debtor and Creditor, topic Assignments.

Children.—No minor under 18 years of age may be employed in any hazardous occupation except in apprenticeship, vocational rehabilitation, or training program approved by Commissioner. No such minor, under 17 years of age or who has not graduated from high school nor obtained a G.E.D., is allowed to work without certificate except at work defined as casual or farm labor, or for his parents, grandparents or guardian. Minor under 16 years of age may not be employed in manufacturing, construction, mining and quarrying occupations or in woods and logging. Minor under 16 years of age may not be employed earlier than 7 A.M. or later than 9 P.M., more then three hours per day on school days and 23 hours per week during school weeks, except that on nonschool days he may be employed eight hours per day and during vacations 48 hours per week. Commissioner upon application may suspend this restriction for a minor under 16 years of age in agricultural work. Minor under 12 years of age may not be employed except for his parents, grandparents or guardian, or at casual work or in delivery of newspapers. Certificates must be obtained by employer within three business days of first day of employment. Certificates are issued by principals of schools which show proof of age and adequate health except that certificates of youths 16 years or older show proof of age only. Minor 16 or 17 years of age may not work more than six consecutive days or more than 30 hours during school calendar week or more than 48 hours during school vacations. (c. 276-A).

Safety Appliances.—All places of employment employing one or more employees must provide specified safety appliances. (c. 277, §1). These include medical chests and reasonable and proper toilet facilities and reasonable sanitary and hygienic conditions for employees. (c. 277, §§6, 10). Whenever nature or condition of any such place of employment, or machinery or other appliances therein, are such as to render work therein or in proximity thereto dangerous to safety or health of employees, employer must provide and maintain such safeguards, safety devices, appliances and lighting facilities, and do such other things as may be reasonably necessary and practicable to lessen dangers of such employment. (c. 277, §11). Commissioner is authorized to promulgate rules to implement c. 277. (c. 277, §16, I).

The Labor Commissioner must cause inspections to be made to see that the foregoing provisions are enforced, and may make specific orders relating thereto. (c. 277, §§13-21). Employee may petition commissioner to have his place of employment inspected for violations of this chapter. (c. 277, §13-a). Provision is made for review of Commissioner's orders on rehearing (c. 277, §§25-28), and for appeal therefrom to Superior Court (c. 277, §§29-32).

Occupational Health Unit.—Director, division of public health services, department of health and human services shall develop and conduct comprehensive policies and programs for evaluation of hazards associated with use of chemical or physical agents and for their amelioration; develop and conduct programs with due regard for compatibility with federal programs for consultation regarding chemical or physical agents; advise, consult, and cooperate with other agencies of state, federal government, other states, and interstate agencies, political subdivisions, industries, and with groups concerned with control of chemical or physical agents; have authority to accept, spend for purpose of this subdivision, and administer loans, grants, other funds or gifts, conditional or otherwise, in furtherance of its function, from federal government and from other sources, public or private; encourage, participate in, or conduct studies in training, research, and demonstrations relating to control of chemical or physical agents, measure of these agents, effects on health of exposure to these agents, and related problems as it may deem necessary or advisable to discharge of its duties hereunder; collect and disseminate health education information relating to protection from chemical or physical agents; and develop schedule of fees by rule, pursuant to RSA 541-A, and assess and collect such fees for services provided under this subdivision. Division is authorized to establish revolving fund into which it shall deposit fees collected under this program. Division, with approval of governor and counsel, shall be authorized to utilize moneys from revolving fund so created for purposes outlined in this subdivision. (c. 140, §4).

Labor Unions.—See subhead Labor Contracts, supra.

Unemployment Compensation.—An unemployed individual who is able to work and available for suitable work is eligible to receive weekly benefits. (c. 282-A, §31).

Workmen's Compensation Act.—(Citations in the following resume refer to Revised Statutes Annotated, c. 281-A.)

Employer means a person, partnership, association or corporation who employs one or more persons. (c. 281-A, §2 [VIII][a]). Executive officers are not considered to be employees unless they exceed three in number. Term employer includes employer's insurance carrier. (c. 281-A, §2 [VIII][c]). Any other employer may accept provisions of Act by purchasing valid workmen's compensation insurance. (c. 281-A, §2 [VIII][b]). Counties, cities, towns, school and other districts may accept provisions of Act for designated or all workmen. (c. 281-A, §2 [IX]). Public employees may purchase self-insurance and legislative body of employer shall appropriate sufficient funds to pay for self-insurance. (c. 281-A, §11). Employer not subject to Act which has accepted Act may revoke his or its acceptance by filing termination notice with Commissioner of Labor which shall be effective 30 days after such filing and by posting notice of such revocation in conspicuous place on his or its premises. (c. 281-A, §10). Self-insured worker's compensation programs administered by private employers are covered under statute. (c. 281-A, §5-a, b, c, d).

Employee, with respect to private employment, means any person in service of employer subject to provisions of this chapter under any contract of hire, express or implied, oral or written, except railroad employees engaged in interstate commerce whose rights are governed by Federal Employers' Liability Act, but including, if they elect to be personally covered by this chapter, persons who regularly operate businesses or practice their trades, professions, or occupations, whether individually, or in partnership or association with other persons, whether or not they hire employees. Any person, with few exceptions, who performs services for pay for employer, is presumed to be employee, subject to rebuttal criteria. (c. 281-A, §2 [VI]). See catchline Special Compensation, infra. Employee of employer subject to act is conclusively presumed to have accepted provisions thereof and to have waived his rights of action at common law, NH statute or laws of any other state, to recover for personal injuries against his employer or, except for intentional torts, against any officer, director, agent, servant or employee acting on behalf of employer or employer's insurance carrier. (c. 281-A, §8 [I]). No other person (including spouse) who might otherwise be entitled to recover damages on account of covered employee's injury or death can maintain direct action against employer, employer's insurance carrier or, except for intentional torts, any officer, director, agent, servant or employee acting on behalf of employer or his carrier. (c. 281-A, §8 [II]).

Average Weekly Wages.—Computed by using whatever statutory method yields result most favorable to injured employee. (c. 281-A, §15).

Personal injury, or injury as used in and covered by this chapter means accidental injury or death arising out of and in course of employment or all occupational diseases arising out of and in course of employment, or death resulting therefrom, including disability due to radioactive properties or substances or exposure to ionizing radiation. Injury or personal injury does not mean accidental injury, disease, or death resulting from participation in athletic/recreational activities, on or off premises, unless employee reasonably expected, based on employer's instruction or policy, that such participation was condition of employment or was required for promotion, increased compensation, or continued employment. (c. 281-A, §2[XI]). For purposes of this chapter, occupational disease is defined as injury arising out of and in course of employee's employment and due to causes and conditions characteristic of, and peculiar to, particular trade, occupation or employment. (c. 281-A, §2[XIII]). For purpose of determining date of injury for occupational disease, date of injury shall be taken to be last date of injurious exposure to hazards of such disease or date on which employee first knew or reasonably should have known of condition and its relationship to his employment, whichever is later. (c. 281-A, §16). It shall not include other diseases or death therefrom unless they are direct result of accidental injury arising out of or in course of employment, nor shall it include disease which existed at commencement of employment, nor disease last injurious exposure to hazards which occurred prior to Aug. 31, 1947. (c. 281-A, §2 [XIII]). Total amount of benefit in case of death shall not exceed balance remaining between amounts paid for disability and total compensation payable under this chapter. (c. 281-A, §27). There is presumption that certain cancer, heart, and lung disease in fire fighter is occupationally related. (c. 281-A, §17).

Posting of Notice.—Every employer subject to the act, or who elects to accept its provisions, must keep posted in a conspicuous place upon his premises a notice that he is working under the provisions of the act. (c. 281-A, §4).

Notice of Claim.—Claims for benefits shall be barred unless notice of injury is given to employer within two years of injury unless nature of injury and its possible relationship to employment is not known. In that case, time for filing notice shall not begin to run until earlier of following: (1) Date employee knew or should have known nature of injury and its possible relationship to employment; or (2) in event of death, date dependent knew or should have known of nature of injury and possible relationship to employment. (c. 281-A, §19). Notice of injury in writing on blanks to be approved by Commissioner of Labor must apprise employer of injury and must state name and address of workman injured, and date of place of accident. Notice must be executed in duplicate, both copies to be signed by employee. Employer must acknowledge receipt of notice by signing on both original and duplicate and employee must retain duplicate. (c. 281-A, §20). It may be served personally, or by sending it by certified mail addressed to employer at his last known residence or place of business. (c. 281-A, §21).

Hearings and Awards.—If there is a dispute as to employer's responsibility for compensation, medical and hospital benefits, or other remedial care, or as to any other provision of this chapter, any party to such dispute may petition for hearing and award in premises to Commissioner of Labor. Commissioner must set a time and place for hearing and give at least 14 days notice to parties. Within 30 days after hearing Commissioner must make his award, and must forthwith notify each of parties thereof. Payment of compensation in accordance with Commissioner's decision must be made within five workdays and cannot be terminated except by terms of decision or by final court determination. (c. 281-A, §43 [II]). Appeals shall be taken to compensation appeals board no later than 30 days from decision. 14 days notice of scheduled hearing shall be given. Board shall make its decision within 30 days of hearing, setting forth its findings of fact and rulings of law. Appeals of board's decision may be taken to Supreme Court pursuant to c. 541. (c. 281-A, §43). In any case appealed employee is entitled to reasonable counsel fees and costs and interest at 10% per annum, if he prevails. (c. 281-A, §44). Any person who was prevented from appealing within specified time through mistake, accident, or misfortune and not his own neglect, may petition appeals board at any time within one year thereafter, to be allowed an appeal, setting forth his interest, his reason for appealing and causes of his delay. (c. 281-A, §50). Notices of hearings shall be given in hand or by certified mail, return receipt requested,

See note at head of Digest as to 1998 legislation covered.

See Topical Index in front part of this volume.

NH – 16

LABOR RELATIONS . . . *continued*
to employee, employer and employer's insurance company and, in superior court hearings, by certified mail to Commissioner of Labor. (c. 281-A, §45).

Modification.—Upon application of any party in interest upon ground of change in conditions, mistake as to nature or extent of injury or disability, fraud, undue influence or coercion, Commissioner of Labor may, not later than four years after date of last payment of compensation, or date of last payment for hospital treatment, charges for which are payable under act, make an order ending, diminishing or increasing compensation previously awarded, subject to maximum or minimum provided in act. He must state his reasons therefor. Such a review shall not affect awards as regards any money previously paid. (c. 281-A, §48).

Enforcement of Awards.—Commissioner may assess penalty of $100 per day for noncompliance with his order and for continued noncompliance may petition superior court for injunction. (c. 281-A, §43[b]II). All rights of compensation have same preference or priority against assets of employer as is allowed by law for a claim by an employee against his employer for unpaid wages. (c. 281-A, §51).

Security for Compensation.—Employers subject to the act must secure compensation to their employees in one of the following ways; (1) by insuring and keeping insured the payment of such compensation with a company licensed to write workmen's compensation insurance in this state, and filing with the Commissioner of Labor, in a form prescribed by him, such evidence of such coverage as he may determine; (2) by insuring and keeping insured payment of compensation to domestic employees with company which provides insurance in accordance with RSA 281-A, §6; (3) by furnishing to Commissioner of Labor satisfactory proof of financial ability to pay direct compensation in amounts and manner and when due as provided by act. (c. 281-A, §5). Employers who fail so to secure compensation to their employees are subject to fine of $2,500 and $100 per day per employee for each day of noncompliance, possible injunction from doing business in New Hampshire, and in addition their property is subject to lien of eight years duration for such amount as Labor Commissioner, upon application of employee or his dependents, shall find to be due. (c. 281-A, §7).

Subrogation.—The employer is subrogated to the rights of an injured employee against a third person injuring the employee, to the extent of compensation, medical, hospital or other remedial care already paid or agreed or awarded to be paid under the provisions of the act. Subrogation is specifically applicable to an action for wrongful death, and employer's lien applies to the remainder after deduction of expenses for which employer is not liable under the compensation statute and after deduction of the distributive share of any person to whom nothing is payable under the act. In any case in which the employee neglects to exercise his right of action by failing to proceed at law against such third person for a period of nine months after the injury the employer may so proceed and shall be subrogated to the rights of the injured employee to recover against such third person, provided, if the employer recovers from such other person damages in excess of the compensation, medical, hospital or other remedial care already paid, or agreed or awarded to be paid to the employee, then any such excess shall be paid to the injured employee, less the employer's expenses and costs of action. Settlements of claims against third parties are not binding until approved by the Commissioner of Labor if no suit has been brought or by the Superior Court if suit is brought and settlement made during actual trial or if the action goes to judgment. When recovery is had against a third person, the Labor Commissioner, or the superior court, as the case may be, must order such division of expenses and costs of action, including attorney's fees, between employer and employee as justice may require. (c. 281-A, §13).

Compensation for Total Disability.—Compensation is payable during period of total disability. If employee's average weekly wage is 30% or less of state's average weekly wage, compensation shall be full amount of average weekly but not to exceed 90% of employee's after tax earnings determined by c. 281-A, §15. (c. 281-A, §28-a, I). If employee's average weekly wage is more than 30% of state's average weekly wage, compensation shall be 60% of employee's average weekly wage or 30% of state's average weekly wage, whichever is greater, but shall not exceed 100% of state's average weekly wage or 100% of employee's after tax earnings determined by c. 281-A, §15. (c. 281-A, §28-a, II).

Compensation for Partial Disability.—60% of difference between employee's average weekly wage before injury and average weekly wage which he is able to earn thereafter. Payments are not to continue after disability ends, nor longer than 350 weeks, and in case partial disability begins after period of total disability, period of total disability shall be deducted from such total period of 262 weeks. (c. 281-A, §§31, 31-a).

Compensation for Death.—If death results from injury, compensation shall be paid to dependents of deceased employee in amount according to schedule of weekly payments for total disability. Widow or widower having dependent children may receive compensation until all dependent children have reached 18 or 25 years of age if enrolled as full time student in accredited educational institution, or are self supporting. (c. 281-A, §26). In all cases where compensation is payable to widow or widower for benefit of herself or himself and dependent child or children, Commissioner of Labor shall have power to determine in his discretion what portion of compensation shall be applied for benefit of such child or children, and may order same paid to guardian. (c. 281-A, §26 [I]). In case of remarriage of widow without dependent children, compensation payments cease. In case of remarriage of widow who has dependent children, unpaid balance of compensation which would otherwise become her due shall be payable to mother, guardian, or such other person as Commissioner of Labor may order, for use and benefit of such children during dependency. (c. 281-A, §26 [III]). Employer shall pay expenses of burial not exceeding $3,000. (c. 281-A, §26 [IV]).

Any dependent except a widow, widower, child, or children who at time of injury of injured is in part only dependent upon his earnings, is entitled to receive such portion of benefits provided for those wholly dependent as amount of wage contributed by deceased to such partial dependents at time of injury bore to total support of dependents. (c. 281-A, §26 [V]). Compensation for a dependent child ceases when child becomes 18 years of age or 25 years of age if enrolled as a full time student in an accredited educational institution, unless child is physically or mentally incompetent, or earlier if child is determined by Labor Commissioner to be self-supporting, or upon marriage or legal adoption of such child. (c. 281-A, §26 [VI]). Dependents are defined to mean employee's widow, widower, children, parents, persons in direct line of ascent or descent, or next of kin, who were wholly or partially dependent in fact upon earnings of employee for support at time of injury. Dependents include common law wife or husband of deceased and posthumous child or children. (c. 281-A, §2 [V]).

Medical and Hospital Care, etc.—Employer must furnish reasonable medical, surgical, hospital services, etc., for such period as nature of injury may require. (c. 281-A, §23 [I]). Injured employee, if he so chooses, shall have right of selection of duly qualified physician or other remedial care upon due notice to employer. Employer must pay cost of artificial limbs, eyes, teeth, orthopedic appliances and physical and surgical aids made necessary by injury and shall pay cost of replacement or repair made necessary by wear and tear or by physical change in person and shall pay compensation for resulting disability based on employee's average wages at time of original injury. (c. 281-A, §23 [II]). If in accident employee has suffered loss of glasses, false teeth, artificial member, or hearing aid, said employee shall be paid amount equal to value of property lost. (c. 281-A, §23 [III]). Employer may satisfy requirements of c. 281-A, §23 by providing managed care program approved by Commissioner in accordance with c. 281-A, §23-a.

Special Compensation.—Persons, trades, professions or occupations, whether or not they hire employees, may voluntarily secure coverage and their rate of compensation is computed on basis of 80% of their average weekly wage but no more than $300 weekly. (c. 281-A, §28 [III])

Compensation for Minors.—Compensation and death benefits are doubled in the case of minors under 18 years of age employed in violation of statutes dealing with child labor and apprenticeship, one-half to be paid by the insurance carrier and one-half by the employer. (c. 281-A, §33).

Lump sum settlements except for medical provisions under this chapter may be permitted when best interests of all concerned will be served thereby. Any such settlement must be approved by labor commissioner after hearing. (c. 281-A, §37).

Agreements as to Compensation.—If an employer or his insurer and an injured employee enter into an agreement in regard to compensation payable under the provisions of the act, a memorandum thereof must be filed with the Commissioner of Labor. (c. 281-A, §40).

Penalties.—Civil penalties up to $500 plus $100 per day may be imposed if payments are not made when ordered under this chapter. (c. 281-A, §§7; 42; 53).

WORKERS' COMPENSATION LAW:

See topic Labor Relations.

ENVIRONMENT

ENVIRONMENTAL REGULATION:

General Supervision.—Numerous statutes and regulations exist. Environmental division of Attorney General's Office enforces statutes and common law. (c. 7, §18-a). Various other state agencies have been created to promulgate regulations and to provide oversight relative to specific statutes.

Air Pollution Control Agency has authority to promulgate rules and regulations and issue cease and abate orders pertaining to all aspects of air pollution. (c. 125, §§81, 82).

Permits, approvals or certificates required for construction and operation of new stationary sources of air pollution or of modifications to existing sources (c. 125, §82), any burner, furnace, machine, equipment or article which, in opinion of air pollution control agency, contributes or may contribute to pollution of air (c. 149, §§91, 92), to dredge, excavate, place fill, mine, transport forest products or undertake construction in or on border of any surface waters or to significantly alter characteristics of terrain, in such manner as to impede natural runoff or create unnatural runoff (c. 149, §8-a), to construct sewerage or waste disposal system not connected to public sewer system (c. 149-E, §3), and to subdivide land, except if purpose of subdivision is to correct or conform boundary lines, to exchange land between abutters and no building is contemplated, or for bona fide gift (c. 149-E, §3). Permits are also required before transport of hazardous waste (c. 147-A §6) and for operation of hazardous waste facilities (c. 147-A, §4).

Cleanup Costs.—Municipalities may authorize issuance of bonds in order to pay costs associated with superfund sites.

Enforcement.—Various commissions, boards, and agencies, acting through Environmental Protection Division of Attorney General's Office, may sue for injunctive relief and bring criminal action against violators.

Penalties.—Any operator, generator, or transporter who causes or suffers treatment, storage, transportation or disposal of hazardous waste in violation of RSA 147-A shall be held strictly liable for costs relating to containment of waste, cleanup and removal. (c. 147-A §9). Hazardous Waste Management Act also imposes criminal penalties as well as civil forfeiture of up to $50,000 for each day of continuing violation. (c. 147-A, §§16, 17). Hazardous waste cleanup fund statute also creates strict liability (c. 147-B, §10), creates lien for all costs expended by State pursuant to cleanup fund (c. 147-B, §10-b) and imposes criminal penalty for violations of Act (c. 147-B, §11).

ESTATES AND TRUSTS

ADMINISTRATION:

See topic Executors and Administrators.

ADVANCEMENTS:

See topic Descent and Distribution.

ALLOWANCES:

See topic Executors and Administrators.

See note at head of Digest as to 1998 legislation covered.

See Topical Index in front part of this volume.

NH – 17

CLAIMS:

See topic Executors and Administrators; category Civil Actions and Procedure, topic Pleading.

DEATH:

An administrator may be appointed by the court on the estate of a person who has left his home and has not been heard of or from, directly or indirectly, for one year and whom the court believes to be dead, upon proof that notice has been published and given as hereinafter stated; but no distribution of his estate may be made until three years after granting of administration. (c. 553, §18).

Notice must give name, age and such other characteristics and descriptions as will identify person, and must call for information concerning him. It must be published in a newspaper printed in Concord, and one printed in county in which person had last lived for one year, and posted for one month in at least three public places in town in which he had so lived; such other notice must be given to relatives and heirs as court may order. (c. 553, §19).

A written finding of presumed death or that a person is missing, missing in action, interned in a neutral county, or beleaguered, besieged or captured by an enemy, or is dead, or is alive, as the case may be, made by an officer or employee of the United States pursuant to the Federal Missing Persons Act, is accepted by New Hampshire courts as prima facie evidence of the truth thereof, and all signatures on and certifications of such findings, reports and records are deemed prima facie valid. (c. 523, §§1-3).

Survivorship.—The Uniform Simultaneous Death Act has been adopted. (c. 563, §§1-9).

Actions for Death.—Executor or administrator may sue for personal injuries to decedent which caused his death, where no action for such injuries was commenced by decedent in his lifetime. Such action must be commenced within three years after death. (c. 556, §11 and c. 508; ... N.H. ..., 688 A.2d 564). Damages are limited to $50,000 unless decedent left widow, widower, child or children, or father or mother, or relative dependent on decedent, in which case there is no limitation. (c. 556, §13). Estate of spouse whose death was occasioned by other spouse's negligence may recover against latter though tortfeasor may be sole surviving distributee. Such recovery is limited to costs to estate. (103 N.H. 110, 165 A.2d 590). Health/accident insurer must pay on these facts. (114 N.H. 110, 316 A.2d 177).

Elements of damage: mental and physical pain suffered by decedent in consequence of the injury, reasonable expenses occasioned to his estate by the injury, probable duration of his life but for the injury and his capacity to earn money during his probable working life. (c. 556, §12). If action was pending prior to death of plaintiff, action shall abate unless administrator appears and assumes prosecution within 12 months after death. If decedent was defendant, plaintiff must procure scire facias to be issued to administrator of decedent within 12 months after administrator appointed by Probate Court. (c. 556, §10; 115 N.H. 15, 332 A.2d 168).

Damages, less expenses of recovery, administration, taxes or other debts as approved by probate court become a part of decedent's estate and is distributed in accordance with applicable provisions of law. (c. 556, §14).

If death results from work-related injury, recovery is had under Workmen's Compensation. (c. 281-A, §26).

Uniform Anatomical Gift Act adopted. (c. 291-A).

Certificates of Death.—See category Documents and Records, topic Records, subhead Vital Statistics.

DECEDENTS' ESTATES:

See topics Descent and Distribution, Executors and Administrators, Wills; category Debtor and Creditor, topic Homesteads.

DESCENT AND DISTRIBUTION:

Real Estate and Personalty.—Real estate and personal estate of every person deceased, not devised or bequeathed, subject to any homestead right, and liable to be sold by license from court of probate in cases provided by law, and personalty remaining in hands of administrator on settlement of his account, shall descend or be distributed by decree of probate court: (1) If deceased is survived by a spouse, spouse shall receive: (a) if there is no surviving issue or parent of decedent, entire intestate estate, (b) if there is no surviving issue but decedent is survived by a parent or parents, first $50,000, plus one-half of balance of intestate estate, (c) if there are surviving issue all of whom are issue of surviving spouse also, first $50,000, plus one-half of balance of intestate estate, (d) if there are surviving issue one or more of whom are not issue or surviving spouse, one-half of intestate estate; (2) part of intestate estate not passing to surviving spouse or entire intestate estate if there is no surviving spouse, passes as follows: (a) to issue of decedent, if they are all of same degree of kinship to decedent they take equally, but if of unequal degree, then those of more remote degree take by representation, (b) if there is no surviving issue, to his parent or parents equally, (c) if there is no surviving issue or parent, to brothers and sisters and issue of each deceased brother or sister by representation; if there is no surviving brother or sister, issue of brothers and sisters take equally if they are all of same degree of kinship to decedent, but if of unequal degree then those of more remote degree take by representation, (d) if there is no surviving issue, parent or issue of a parent, but decedent is survived by one or more grandparents or issue of grandparents, half of estate passes to paternal grandparents if both survive, or to surviving paternal grandparent, or to issue of paternal grandparents if both are deceased, issue taking equally if they are all of same degree of kinship to decedent, but if of unequal degree those of more remote degree take by representation: and other half passes to maternal relatives in same manner; but if there be no surviving grandparent or issue of grandparent on either paternal or maternal side, entire estate passes to relatives on other side in same manner as the half. (c. 561, §1). No representation is allowed among collaterals beyond fourth degree of relationship to decedent. (c. 561, §3). If any person die under age and unmarried, his estate, derived by descent or devise from his father or mother, descends to his brothers and sisters, or their legal representatives, if any, to exclusion of other parent. (c. 561, §2).

Rights of Surviving Spouse.—Upon death of either husband or wife, testate, if surviving spouse has elected to waive homestead right, if any, and provisions of will in his or her favor, if any, such surviving spouse shall be vested with following portion of estate remaining after payment of debts and expenses of administration: (1) If there are children of deceased surviving (whether by surviving spouse or by previous marriage) or issue of any deceased children, one third part of personalty and one third part of real estate; (2) if decedent leaves no children or issue of any deceased children, but does leave mother or father or sister or brother surviving, $10,000 in value thereof a personalty and $10,000 in value of real estate, and also one half of remainder above $10,000 in each, real estate to be assigned to surviving spouse in same manner as dower heretofore has been assigned. Where inventory value of the real estate does not exceed $10,000 surviving spouse is entitled to whole of said remainder and no assignment of same is required unless some party in interest petitions to probate court therefor; (3) if decedent leaves no children or issue of any deceased children, nor mother or father, nor sister or brother surviving, $10,000 of value thereof, plus $2,000 for each full year from date of marriage to decease of spouse, and also one half in value of remainder above said sum computed as above, in personalty, and same in real estate, real estate to be assigned in same manner as dower has heretofore been assigned. Where inventory value of real estate does not exceed $10,000, surviving spouse is entitled to whole of said remainder and no assignment of same is required unless some party in interest petitions probate court therefor. That part of estate not passing to surviving spouse per paragraphs 1 through 3 shall pass via terms of will, provided that surviving spouse shall take nothing under will. (c. 560, §10). Deceased spouse's inter vivos transfer of property to trust defeats rights of surviving spouse even if decedent exercised complete control over property during lifetime, unless transfer was for purpose of depriving survivor of those rights. (123 N.H. 175, 450 A.2d 246).

Bar of Right to Inherit.—Surviving spouse is entitled to nothing, except such as may be given to him or her by the will: (1) where surviving husband willfully abandoned decedent, or willfully neglected to support her, or has not been heard from, in consequence of his own neglect, for three years next preceding her death or (2) where, at time of decedent's death, decedent was justifiably living apart from surviving spouse because the latter was, or had been, guilty of conduct constituting cause for divorce. (c. 560, §§18, 19).

As to election between testamentary provision and statutory rights in estates, see topic Wills.

Illegitimate Children.—Child born of unwed parents shall inherit from or through his mother as if born in lawful wedlock. Estate of person born of unwed parents dying intestate and leaving no issue, nor husband, nor wife shall descend to mother, and, if mother is dead, through line of mother as if person so dying were born in lawful wedlock. However, such child shall inherit from or through his father as if born in lawful wedlock if: (a) Parents intermarry after birth; or (b) father acknowledges paternity or legitimation; or (c) paternity is established after father's death by clear and convincing evidence; or (d) decedent had adopted child. (c. 561, §4).

Adopted Children.—See category Family, topic Adoption.

Posthumous children and pretermitted heirs not otherwise made devisees or legatees are entitled to same portion of estate as they would be if decedent died intestate. (c. 551, §10).

Advancements.—If an heir of a person deceased, or any person through whom the heir claims, has been advanced by the deceased in his lifetime, such advancement is accounted, according to its value, as part or the whole of the share of such heir. Such advancements, or any indebtedness of an heir, the amount having been first determined by the judge, may be taken into consideration in the division of the real estate; or they may be considered and adjusted by the judge in the decree of distribution of the personal estate. No deed of real estate is deemed an advancement unless the same is expressed to be made for love or affection, or unless it is proved to be an advancement by some acknowledgment signed by the party receiving it. No personal property delivered is deemed an advancement unless proved to be such by an acknowledgment in writing, signed by the party receiving it, or by some charge or memorandum thereof in writing, made by the deceased or by his order, or unless delivered expressly as an advancement, in the presence of two witnesses who were requested to take notice thereof. (c. 561, §§13-16).

Escheat.—If there be no heir, legatee, devisee or surviving spouse, the entire estate goes to the state. (c. 561, §8).

Unclaimed Shares.—If on settlement of the fiduciary's account there remains in his hands any sum of money in excess of $50 belonging to a person whose place of residence is unknown and cannot be found, or who refuses to accept or receipt for such sum, the probate court may decree that the same be paid over to the State Treasurer and at the expiration of three years after such payment may decree distribution as though such person had no interest in the estate unless he appears and establishes his rights. State treasurer shall hold any such sums received in accordance with RSA 471-C. (c. 561, §10).

See also topic Executors and Administrators.

ESTATES:

See category Property, topic Real Property.

EXECUTORS AND ADMINISTRATORS:

Jurisdiction.—The judges of probate of the several counties have exclusive jurisdiction of probate of wills, of granting of administration and of all matters and things of probate jurisdiction relating to sale, settlement and final distribution of estates of deceased persons. (c. 547, §3). Special administrators may also be appointed by superior court. (c. 553, §21).

Venue.—Probate of will and granting administration on the estate of a person deceased belongs to the judge of probate for the county in which such person was last an inhabitant; or, if such person was not an inhabitant of this state, for any county in which such person had estate, or in which the personal representative or kin of such person has a cause of action. (c. 547, §8).

See note at head of Digest as to 1998 legislation covered.

See Topical Index in front part of this volume.

NH – 18

EXECUTORS AND ADMINISTRATORS . . . *continued*

Right to administer the estate of a deceased person is in the following order: (1) The executor named in his will; (2) the widow, husband or any of the next of kin, or to such suitable person as they or any of them may nominate; (3) one of the devisees or creditors; (4) such other person as the judge may think proper. (c. 553, §2).

Competency.—Minors and persons deemed by the probate judge to be unsuitable cannot administer estates. (c. 553, §4). Married women are eligible to act as executors and administrators (c. 553, §9), as are nonresidents, if judge deems their appointment proper under circumstances. (c. 553, §5). Trust companies, banks or savings associations organized under N. H. laws and national banks or federally chartered savings associations located within state may be appointed executors or trustees, but not administrators. New Hampshire religious, charitable and eleemosynary corporations can act in all fiduciary capacities. No foreign corporation except national bank duly authorized and located within state can be appointed executor or trustee. (c. 390, §13).

Bond.—Every executor or administrator must furnish a bond to the judge of probate with sufficient sureties or, in lieu of bond, other forms of security acceptable to court, conditioned: (1) To return to judge true and perfect inventory or estate of deceased, upon oath, within three months from date of bond; (2) to administer estate according to law; (3) to render to judge account of administration, upon oath, within one year, and annually thereafter; (4) to pay all taxes for which he may be or become liable; (5) to pay and deliver rest and residue of estate which shall be found remaining upon account of administrator to such person or persons respectively as judge, by his decree, according to law, shall limit and appoint; (6) to deliver letters of administration into court of probate, in case will of deceased shall thereafter be approved and allowed. In discretion of judge of probate requirements for giving of bond and sureties may be waived when estate has gross inventory value of less than $50,000, and administrator is sole heir of deceased. (c. 553, §13). If executor to whom administration is granted is residuary legatee, and there is no widow, or if, there being widow, she informs judge in writing that she accepts provisions of will, bond, with sufficient sureties, may be taken from him, with condition only to pay funeral charges, debts, legacies and all legacy and succession taxes, and to render upon oath account of his proceedings, when required. (c. 553, §14). Executor or trustee under will is exempt from giving bond, except bond for payment of debts and legacy and succession taxes, whenever testator by his will so directs; but judge may at any time, upon petition of heir, devisee or creditor, require further bond, with sufficient sureties, if he is of opinion that it is made requisite by change in situation or circumstances of executor or trustee, or by other sufficient cause. (c. 553, §15).

Removal.—Failure to comply with the statutory requirements is ground for removal of administrators. (c. 553, §28).

Special Kinds of Administration.—If the administration on an estate becomes vacant by death, or extinguishment or revocation of letters, probate court may grant administration on estate not before administered to such person as court may think proper, having due regard to order of right to administer. (c. 553, §7).

A special administrator will be appointed, if the interests of the estate require it, whenever, by reason of an appeal from the probate of a will or the appointment of an administrator, or from any other cause, there is delay in determining the final grant of administration. (c. 553, §§20, 21). He must give bond with sufficient sureties for the faithful discharge of his duties or other forms of security acceptable to court (c. 553, §13), and his duties are, in general, to return inventory of estate of deceased, to take care of and preserve his property, and to do all other acts which he may be directed to perform by probate judge or by superior court. (c. 553, §22).

Ancillary administrators will be appointed in proper cases. (c. 547, §8).

Resident Agent.—A nonresident who is appointed executor or administrator in this state, or a resident who is so appointed and subsequently removes from the state or departs therefrom intending to be absent more than one year, must appoint some person resident in this state as agent to receive notice of claims against their respective estates and service of process against such nonresidents. The appointment must be in writing, must state the full name and postoffice address of the agent, and must be filed in the office of the register of probate. When nonresident is appointed, he must insert in the notice of his appointment the name and postoffice address of his agent. (c. 553, §§25, 26).

Inventory and Appraisal.—Every executor or administrator, within three months after his appointment, must return to the probate office, under oath, a full, true and itemized account of all the estate of the deceased which has come to his knowledge.

Inventory must contain a description of the real estate; a correct schedule of all goods, chattels, stocks, bonds and other effects of the deceased, all notes, with their dates and terms of payment, and the date and amount of each indorsement thereon, all deposits in savings banks, with the name and location of each bank, the number of each book, the date of the last dividend, and the whole amount then due thereon less any withdrawals since that date; and a list and description of the decedent's other written evidences of debt. The inventory, and an appraisal of the real estate, goods, chattels, stocks and bonds mentioned therein, must be made by three suitable persons appointed by the judge and sworn to their fidelity and impartiality. The appraisers must class the property under appropriate heads, and must foot each class. The judge may appoint only one appraiser, if in his opinion the nature of the property or the size of the estate makes it advisable so to do. (c. 554, §§1-3). The wearing apparel, etc., of the widow and minor children and personal possessions and trinkets of the deceased of sentimental rather than intrinsic value must not be inventoried or accounted for. (c. 554, §§4-5).

General Powers and Duties.—As the personal representative of the decedent the executor or administrator is charged with the duty of collecting all debts due to the estate and accounting therefor in money. (c. 554, §11). Debts due from an insolvent person may be compromised and discharged by the administrator and he will be chargeable only for the amount received in his discretion. (c. 554, §12). In the event the estate is insolvent the administrator must receive the rents and profits of the real estate and keep the same in repair, accounting for the net proceeds thereof in his administration account. (c. 554, §15). If there are sufficient assets, the administrator must redeem all property of the deceased under mortgage, pledge or levy of execution for less than its value, or which if unredeemed would diminish the value of the estate, unless he by license sells it subject to the encumbrance. Neglect so to redeem constitutes maladministration and waste. (c. 554, §16). When real estate under mortgage is specifically devised, devisee takes such real estate subject to mortgage, unless testator in his will or by insurance has provided expressly or by necessary implication that such mortgage be otherwise paid; and if note or obligation of testator secured by such mortgage is paid out of other property in his estate after his decease, executor of his will, at request of any person interested, and by leave of probate court must sell such specifically devised real estate for purpose of satisfying estate of testator for amount so paid, together with costs and expenses thereof. (c. 554, §16). Real estate purchased by or set off to an administrator to secure or satisfy a debt due estate vests in heirs in same manner as if decedent had died seized thereof, and may be sold for payment of debts, or divided as part of estate. (c. 554, §18). Prior to rendering final account, notification must be given to city or town of persons coming into ownership of real estate by inheritance or devise. (c. 554, §18-a).

Authorization to Continue Decedent's Business.—The probate court may authorize the executor or administrator to continue any business of the decedent, for the benefit of the estate, for not more than one year from the date of his appointment; and such authority may be extended from time to time, but no single extension may be for more than one year. The decree may provide the extent of the liability of the estate, or of the executor or administrator, for obligations incurred in the continuation of the business and such other conditions, restrictions, regulations and requirements as may be deemed for the benefit of the estate and of creditors thereof. (c. 553, §30).

Sale of Personal Property.—All goods and chattels shall be accounted for at appraised value, unless sold at auction or private sale, and all stocks and bonds at prices which they shall bring at public or private sale; and administrator conducting sale with fidelity and impartiality shall be credited with loss, or charged with gain, upon sale. (c. 554, §§7, 8).

Sale of Real Estate.—The executor or administrator must apply for and procure license for the sale of so much of the real estate as may be necessary to pay debts and legacies, if the personal estate is insufficient; and neglect or refusal to obtain such license, to make such sale, to account for the proceeds thereof, or fraudulent conduct therein, is deemed maladministration and a breach of his bond. (c. 554, §17; c. 559).

Unless will provides otherwise, executor or administrator, with written consent of widow or widower and heirs at law or devisees, or guardians or conservators of such of them as are under disability may sell whole or any part of decedent's real estate conducting sale with fidelity and impartiality. Such sale conveys title, free from claims of decedent's creditors and of persons claiming under decedent or under his will, but claims of such persons are a charge on proceeds of sale. Such proceeds must be accounted for to probate court and, except for such deductions as court may make for payment of debts, legacies, inheritance taxes and expenses of administration, must be paid over, on distribution of estate, to persons who would have been entitled to such estate in proportions to which they would have been entitled had it not been sold. (c. 559, §§18-19).

Mortgage of Real Estate.—An executor or administrator, with assent of the heirs or devisees, may obtain a license to mortgage the real estate of the deceased when the personal property is insufficient to pay the just demands by law chargeable to the estate, or to make necessary or desirable repairs to preserve such real estate, or where it is otherwise necessary to raise money to facilitate settlement of the estate. A foreign executor or administrator may obtain such license with respect to land located in this state. No such license may issue later than two years after date of appointment of the administrator or executor, and no license shall be available to sustain a mortgage made under said license unless made within 90 days from the granting thereof. (c. 554, §§30-35).

Redemption of Property.—If there be sufficient assets, the executor or administrator must redeem all property of the deceased under mortgage, pledge or levy of execution for less than its value, or which, if unredeemed, would diminish the value of the estate, unless, by license, he sells it subject to the encumbrance; and neglect so to redeem is deemed maladministration and waste. When real estate under mortgage is specifically devised, the devisee takes subject to the mortgage unless the testator in his will or by insurance has provided expressly or by necessary implication that the mortgage be otherwise paid. (c. 554, §16).

Notice of Appointment.—Every executor must, within 60 days after date of appointment, notify each legatee specifically named in the will that he appears to be interested therein, and must also notify the surviving spouse and heirs at law, if known, that the will has been proved. (c. 552, §15).

Notice to Creditors.—Every executor or administrator must, within 15 days after his appointment, cause notice thereof to be published for two weeks successively in newspaper circulated in vicinity. (c. 21, §32; c. 553, §16; c. 550, §10).

Presentation of Claims.—Claims against the estate of a decedent must be exhibited to the executor or administrator and payment demanded within the time limited therefor, or else they are forever barred. Time allowed for such exhibition and demand is six months from original grant of letters (excluding any time during which administration may have been suspended). (c. 556, §§1, 3). No exhibition is required if estate has been represented insolvent within said six months. (c. 556, §4). Notice sent to representative or his agent by registered mail, setting forth nature and amount of claim and demanding payment, is sufficient. (c. 556, §2). If representative is nonresident, claim must be exhibited to and demand made on resident agent appointed for that purpose. (c. 553, §25).

There are no distinctions operating either in favor of or to the prejudice of nonresident creditors as distinguished from resident creditors. There are no specific provisions as to presentation of secured claims.

Unmatured and contingent demands may be filed in court of probate, and the judge may require the executor or administrator to retain in his hands such sum as may be necessary to pay them; unless widow, heirs or legatees give bond for payment thereof when they become due or absolute. (c. 556, §6).

See note at head of Digest as to 1998 legislation covered.

See Topical Index in front part of this volume.

NH – 19

EXECUTORS AND ADMINISTRATORS . . . *continued*

Proof of Claims.—If executor or administrator so requires, all claims against an estate must be exhibited under oath as follows:

Form

I do solemnly swear that, according to the best of my knowledge and belief, the above is a true statement of my claim against the estate of . . . . . ., late of . . . . . ., and that I have not on my books or elsewhere any credit, nor have I any knowledge of any credit or offset that should be allowed against my claim, except what is stated in the foregoing account. So help me God. (c. 554, §24).

Payment of Claims.—Allowed claims should be paid within six months from original grant of letters (c. 556, §1); if such a claim is not paid claimant may bring an action at law thereon against representative within one year after original grant of administration, exclusive of time such administration may have been suspended. (c. 556, §5).

The judge may require the executor or administrator to retain in his hands such sum as may be necessary to pay unmatured and contingent claims, unless the widow, heirs or legatees give bond for the payment thereof when they become due or absolute. (c. 556, §6).

Priorities.—The executor or administrator must pay all debts, legacies and taxes due from the estate. (c. 554, §19). Order of payment is: (1) administration expenses; (2) funeral expenses; (3) allowance to widow; (4) debts; (5) support of infant children until they reach age of 18 years, if estate is solvent; (6) total amount paid for old age assistance and/or disability; (7) legacies. (c. 554, §19). Executors or administrators of solvent estates may erect suitable monuments at the graves of testators or intestates, and reasonable expense thereof is allowed them on settlement of their accounts. (c. 554, §21). Executors, administrators and trustees may pay, upon order of judge, to cemetery corporation or to city or town in which decedent has burial place, reasonable sum of money for perpetual care of lot in which decedent is buried and monuments thereon. (c. 554, §22).

Actions by Representative.—At any time within one year after the original grant of letters the executor or administrator may bring suit or defend in any suit brought on a right of action existing and surviving in favor of or against the deceased at the time of his death. (c. 556, §7). He may appear and prosecute any action pending at time of death of deceased before end of second term after said time of death. (c. 556, §10).

Actions Against Representative.—No action may be brought against the executor or administrator on a claim against the estate unless such claim has been exhibited to him and payment demanded within six months after original grant of administration. (c. 556, §§1, 3). Right to sue is suspended for six months from original grant of letters (c. 556, §1) unless estate has been represented insolvent (c. 556, §4), and action must be brought within one year from original grant of letters or claim is barred, unless claim is unmatured, in which case action thereon must be brought at maturity (c. 556, §§5-6). Superior court may, however, grant leave to sue after the one year period if justice and equity so require and claimant is not chargeable with culpable neglect. (c. 556, §28).

If an action is pending at the time of the decease of the defendant, the action abates and is forever barred unless the plaintiff procures a scire facias to be issued to the administrator of the deceased party before the end of the second term after the original grant of administration upon his estate, provided that the administrator forthwith notifies in writing the adverse party or his attorney of record of such death and grant of administration, and such action is not barred until the end of the second term after the giving of such notice. Such notice must be by registered mail, return receipt requested, and such administrator must file an affidavit in the probate court, showing compliance with the provisions thereof, provided further, however, that any justice of the superior court must, for good cause shown, grant relief from any of the foregoing requirements as justice may require. (c. 556, §10).

Widow's Quarantine and Support.—The widow may remain in the house of her husband 40 days next after his death without being chargeable with rent therefor, and in the meantime is entitled to her reasonable sustenance out of the estate; and the same is taken into consideration by the judge in the allowance he may make to her. (c. 560, §2). In addition, the judge may make to the widow of a deceased person, a reasonable allowance out of the personal estate, for her present support; and, in the decree of distribution of the personal estate, the whole, or such part thereof as the judge may deem reasonable, must be accounted as part of her distributive share. (c. 560, §1).

Accounts.—The account of the executor or administrator, or the schedules filed therewith, must contain an itemized account of every sum of money received and paid out by him, with the date thereof and a statement of the source from which it was received or of the consideration for which it was paid. (c. 554, §25). Every executor or administrator must file in the probate office an annual account of administration, unless upon petition he is excused by the judge of probate; but in no event may he be excused for a period longer than three years. Before giving notice to settle his final account, he must file it in the probate office of the county where it is to be settled, and cause the fact of such filing to appear in the notice, and at the same time file a statement of the names and residences of the heirs, legatees and beneficiaries, if known to him. (c. 554, §26). When an executor or administrator files his account in the probate court, he must contemporaneously forward to all persons beneficially named copy of account and notice that account may be approved unless written objection is filed within 30 days. (c. 550, §§11, 12). See topic Trusts, subhead Accounts. Notice required in any proceeding in probate court may be dispensed with if all parties entitled thereto assent in writing to such proceeding or in writing waive notice. (c. 550, §13). Accounts are not usually filed during first six months after original grant of administration because claims of creditors can be presented at any time before end of that period. (c. 556, §3). Probate court requires that notice of filing of final account be published for two weeks.

Distribution of Estate.—No time limit is set within which the estate is to be distributed. Distribution is customarily made as soon as possible after the end of the first year after the original grant of administration. Distribution may be made after the first six months by consent of probate court.

Personal property specifically bequeathed must not be sold, if not needed for the payment of debts; and any property may be reserved at the sale, unless so needed, for the benefit or upon the request of the heirs or legatees, and the executor or administrator is discharged by delivery thereof to the persons entitled thereto. The judge may order the executor or administrator to transfer stocks, bonds and other evidences of debt to the heirs or their guardians, in just proportion, whenever he deems it for the interest of the heirs that the same should not be sold; and such guardians are authorized to receive the same. (c. 554, §§9, 10).

Where a minor's share or legacy is less than $5,000, executor or administrator, on petition to and approval by probate court, may pay said sum to parent or parents, or to person having custody of minor if parents are divorced. (c. 561, §20).

Distribution if Abroad.—When it appears that a legatee, distributee, cestui or beneficiary not residing within the territorial limits of the United States or any territorial possession thereof would not have the benefit or use or control of property due him and that special circumstances make it desirable that delivery to him be deferred, the probate court may order that such property be converted into available funds and paid to the State Treasurer to be handled subject to further order of the court, provided a reasonable fee, as allowed by the court of the attorney for such legatee, etc., shall be considered a lien on such funds and shall be paid by the fiduciary to such attorney prior to the payment to the State Treasurer. (c. 561, §12a).

Compensation of Representatives.—No statutory provisions. As a matter of practice, the executor or administrator presents a claim for compensation when he renders his account to the probate court, and the same, if deemed reasonable, is allowed to be paid out of the estate.

Insolvent Estates.—The estate of a deceased person may, on application of the executor or administrator, be decreed to be administered as insolvent, and one or more persons, not exceeding three, must be appointed commissioners to examine and allow the claims of creditors against the estate. If the application is made more than six months after original grant of administration, it may be granted only upon notice of petition by publication, and at discretion of judge. (c. 557, §§1-2). At a time not less than three nor more than six months from date of commission, commissioner, after giving notice to creditors, claimants and others, must hear and allow claims against estate. (c. 557, §§6-8, 12). This time limit may be extended up to one year by probate court for cause shown. (c. 557, §8). Mutual claims of deceased and creditor may be set off against each other. (c. 557, §14).

If a secured claim exceeds the estimated value of the security, the creditor is allowed the excess only. (c. 557, §15). If dissatisfied, he may surrender the security, which is sold and the proceeds paid to him, and his claim allowed for the full excess over the amount realized on the security. (c. 557, §16).

The expenses of administration, the necessary charges for the burial of the deceased, the allowance made by the judge to the widow out of the personal estate and taxes must be allowed by the judge and first paid, giving preference to them in the order in which they are here placed. Claims for the last sickness of the deceased must be designated as such in the commissioner's report, and must be paid in full, if the balance in the hands of the executor or administrator, after the payments before directed are made, is sufficient; otherwise the balance must be distributed pro rata to such claimants in proportion to their respective claims. If, after payment in full of the claims before mentioned, any balance remains in the hands of the administrator, it must be decreed to be distributed among the other creditors in proportion to their respective claims as allowed, or in full payment thereof, with interest. If anything remains after payment of the preferred claims, the debts due from the estate and for the support of the children, if any under seven years of age, such residue must be distributed among the legatees or heirs according to law. (c. 557, §§22-24, 27). If the laws of any foreign state are reciprocal, the New Hampshire property of an insolvent deceased, domiciled in such foreign state, will be so administered that all creditors, here and elsewhere, shall receive an equal share in proportion to their respective debts. (c. 557, §§28-30).

An appeal may be taken from the finding of the commissioner by either the administrator or creditor. (c. 557, §§2, 6).

When Administration Unnecessary.—Simplified administration procedure provided for small estates not exceeding $5,000. (c. 553, §§31, 31-a).

Administration is not required to collect wages, salaries or commissions of deceased person not exceeding $500 where decedent leaves surviving spouse. (c. 560, §20).

Small Estates.—See subhead When Administration Unnecessary, supra.

Foreign Executors and Administrators.—Whenever an executor, administrator, trustee or guardian, duly appointed and acting as such in another state or country, represents a person who owned or is entitled to personal property in this state, he may make petition to the probate court in the county where the property is situated, or, if it is stock in a corporation, to the court in the county where the corporation has its principal place of business, for license to sell, transfer or receive and dispose of the same, and the judge, after such notice as he may order, if no sufficient objection appears, must license him to sell, transfer and convey, or to receive and dispose of, such property and shares in the same manner as he might do if appointed under the laws of this state. Such license may not be granted until the expiration of six months after the death of the testator or interstate, nor unless it appears: (1) That there is no executor, administrator, trustee or guardian appointed under the laws of this state, entitled to the property; (2) that such foreign executor, administrator, trustee or guardian will be liable for the avails of the property and shares in the state or country where he is appointed; (3) that no creditor or person interested, who is a resident of this state, objects to such license or will be liable to be prejudiced thereby; (4) that all taxes due to the state have been paid or secured; (5) that the foreign fiduciary has filed in the probate court authenticated copies of his petition, bond and appointment in such other state or country. (c. 554, §§28-29).

License to sell New Hampshire realty will be granted a executor or administrator under the same conditions enumerated in the above paragraph relative to the sale of personal property. (cc. 559, §18, 553, §5). He must give bond and with sufficient sureties resident in the state, make oath, and is in all respects entitled to the same rights and subject to the same liabilities as if appointed in this state. (c. 559, §13).

Uniform Fiduciaries Act not adopted.

Uniform Principal and Income Act not adopted.

See note at head of Digest as to 1998 legislation covered.

See Topical Index in front part of this volume.

EXECUTORS AND ADMINISTRATORS . . . *continued*

Uniform Simplification of Fiduciary Security Transfers Act not adopted.

Uniform Anatomical Gift Act adopted. (c. 291-A).

See also topic Wills, subhead Foreign Probated Wills.

INTESTACY:

See topic Descent and Distribution.

PROOF OF CLAIMS:

See topic Executors and Administrators; category Civil Actions and Procedure, topic Pleading.

TRUSTS:

Common law rules apply:

All trusts concerning lands, except implied and resulting trusts, must be created or declared by an instrument signed by the party creating the same or by his attorney. (c. 477, §17). Scope of common law doctrine of cy pres enlarged by statute. (c. 498:4a-4e).

Trustees of testamentary trusts are under jurisdiction of probate court and, except towns and cities, must give bond when appointed trustee. (c. 564, §§1, 2). Bond without sureties may be accepted in estates of $5,000 or less where judge finds such to be in interest of estate. (c. 564, §1).

Trustee may resign (c. 564, §8) or, for cause, be removed by judge of probate following hearing noticed to trustee, all known beneficiaries, and such other persons determined by judge to have interest in trust. (c. 564, §9). If trustee appointed in will, no provision being made therein for perpetuating trust, declines to accept it, dies, resigns or is removed, trustee may be appointed by judge in his stead, after notice to persons interested in trust estate. (c. 564, §10). Executor or administrator of deceased trustee will be licensed by judge of probate to convey any real estate held in trust to cestui qui trust or to such other person as may be designated by judge. (c. 564, §20).

General Powers and Duties of Trustees.—Uniform Trustees' Powers Act has been adopted. (c. 564-A).

Eligibility and Competency.—In addition to individuals the following may be appointed trustee: Any New Hampshire trust company or national bank duly authorized and located within this state and any religious, charitable or eleemosynary corporation incorporated under laws of this state. (c. 390, §13; c. 564, §4). Foreign corporations are not eligible.

Agent for Nonresident Trustees.—Every resident trustee who removes from the state or who goes out of the state with the intention of being absent more than a year, and every resident of another state who is appointed trustee within this state, must forthwith appoint some person residing in this state as his agent, to receive notice of claims against the estate and service of process against him as trustee. The appointment must be in writing and state the full name and post-office address of the agent, and it must be filed in the office of the register of probate. (c. 564, §12).

Fiduciaries in Military Service.—While a fiduciary is in military service, a co-fiduciary may be authorized to exercise, or a substituted fiduciary pro tem may be appointed to exercise, all powers which can be transferred to him. (c. 113, §§2, 4, 8).

Supervision.—The judge of probate, on application of a trustee or of any person interested, may, after notice to all persons interested, authorize and require the trustee to sell any property holden in trust, and to invest the proceeds of the sale in such manner as will be most for the interest of all persons concerned therein; and the judge may, from time to time, make such orders and decrees as he may think just and reasonable, in relation to the sale, management, investment and disposition of the trust property and the settlement of the accounts of the trustee. When the purposes for which any trust was created have been performed the judge may, by license and decree, authorize the trustee to transfer, by suitable deed or conveyance, any property remaining in his hands to such person as may be entitled thereto. Authority to mortgage trust property may be granted. When a trust estate is seized of an undivided fractional part of real estate the judge, upon petition of the trustee, notice and hearing, may authorize the trustee to purchase any other undivided fractional part of such real estate when it will be conducive to the interests of the trust estate to do so; and when the trustee is so authorized he may use the funds of the trust to pay the purchase money. (c. 564, §§14-17).

Reports of Trustees of Public Trusts.—First report of a public trust is to be made to Attorney General not later than four months 15 days following close of first calendar or fiscal year in which any part of income or principal is authorized or required to be applied to a charitable purpose and reports are required annually thereafter.

Copies of accounts filed by trustee in court having jurisdiction of trust may be filed with Attorney General as a report if it substantially complies with Attorney General's rules and regulations.

Trustee must file with Attorney General within six months after any authorization or requirement of expenditure of any part of income or principal a copy of instrument providing for title, duty and powers of trustee.

Investments.—Unless otherwise provided in the instrument creating the trust, a trustee may invest in notes secured by mortgages of real estate at least double in value of the notes, or in notes or bonds secured by mortgages insured by the federal housing administrator and guaranteed by the United States of America, by deposit in a savings bank or its equivalent, in stocks and bonds which are legal investments for savings banks in this state, and in such other bonds or stocks, including the shares of an open-end or closed-end management-type investment company which is registered under the Federal Investment Company Act of 1940, as a prudent man would purchase for his own investment having primarily in view the preservation of principal and the amount and regularity of the income to be derived therefrom. (c. 564, §18).

Securities in Name of Nominee.—Corporate trustees when acting in a fiduciary capacity, either alone or jointly with individual or individuals, may, with consent of individual fiduciary or fiduciaries, cause stock or other securities to be registered and held in name of nominee without mention of fiduciary relationship. (c. 390, §18).

Common Trust Funds.—Uniform Common Trust Fund Act adopted. (c. 391).

Gifts to Minors.—See category Family, topic Infants.

Uniform Simplification of Fiduciary Security Transfers Act not adopted.

Uniform Fiduciaries Act not adopted.

Accounts.—Every trustee must file in the probate office an annual account of administration, unless upon petition he is excused by the judge of probate, but in no event can he be excused for a period longer than three years, except that in cases where such filing may be impractical and may work financial hardship to the trust estate, the judge of probate, upon written approval of the attorney-general, may extend such period not exceeding, in the aggregate, five years. Such annual account of administration provided for herein may be allowed by the judge of probate without publication unless he shall otherwise order. Before giving notice to settle his final account, he must file it in the probate office, and cause the fact of such filing to appear in the notice, and must at the same time file a statement of the names and residences of the beneficiaries in the trust estate. (c. 564, §19). Whenever a trustee files an account in the probate court, he must contemporaneously forward to all persons beneficially interested copy of account and notice that account may be approved unless written objection is filed within 30 days of filing of account. Notice must be sent by registered mail, return receipt requested, to last known address of all such persons, and shall contain (1) statement that account has been filed, and, if account is to be settled, date when such account becomes returnable, and (2) fact that person may obtain copy of account from register of probate upon payment of statutory fee. (c. 550, §§11, 12). Notice required in any proceeding in probate court may be dispensed with if all parties entitled thereto assent in writing to such proceeding or in writing waive notice. (c. 550, §13).

Uniform Principal and Income Act not adopted.

Compensation.—A trustee is allowed his reasonable expenses incurred in the execution of his trust; and unless otherwise expressly provided in the trust instrument, he shall have such reasonable compensation for services as the judge of probate may allow. Unless otherwise expressly provided in the trust instrument, such compensation and expenses for trustee of non-charitable trust may be apportioned between principal and income as judge may determine equitable. (c. 564, §21). Compensation and expenses for trustee of charitable trust shall be payable out of income only, unless otherwise provided in trust instrument or where judge determines that certain unusual and non-recurring services and expenses are involved that should be charged to corpus.

Accumulations.—No statutory provisions.

Perpetuities.—See category Property, topic Perpetuities.

Pour Over Trusts.—See topic Wills, subhead Bequests and Devises to Inter Vivos Trusts.

WILLS:

Every person, including married women, of sane mind, of the age of 18 years or married although under that age, may dispose of all his or her property by will. (c. 551, §1).

Formalities.—A will must be in writing, signed by the testator or by some person in his presence and by his express direction, and attested and subscribed in his presence by two or more credible witnesses. Seal is not necessary. (c. 551, §2). Wills may be self-proving, i.e. acknowledged by testator and sworn to by witnesses before notary public or Justice of Peace. (c. 551, §2-a).

Form

The usual form is: I, ..., of . . . . . . County of . . . . . . State of . . . . . . do make this my last will and testament, hereby revoking all former wills by me made, and do hereby dispose of my estate in manner following: . . . . . .

In witness whereof I have hereunto set my hand and seal this . . . . . . day of . . . . . ., 19. . . . .

Signed, sealed, published and declared by . . . . . ., the above named testator, as and for his last will and testament, in the presence of us and each of us, who, at his request and in his presence and in the presence of each other, have hereunto subscribed our names as attesting witnesses this . . . . . . day of . . . . . ., 19. . . . .

Witnesses.—Any beneficial devise or legacy made or given in a will to a subscribing witness thereto or to the wife or husband of such a witness is void unless there be two other subscribing witnesses. (c. 551, §3).

Holographic wills are not recognized.

Nuncupative will is not valid where the property exceeds in value $100, unless declared in the presence of three witnesses who are requested by the testator to bear witness thereto, in his last sickness and in his usual dwelling; except where he was taken sick from home and died before his return, nor unless a memorandum thereof was reduced to writing within six days, and presented to the probate court within six months after the making. (c. 551, §§15, 16).

Revocation.—No will or clause thereof may be revoked unless by some other valid will or codicil, or by some writing executed in the same manner, or by canceling, tearing, obliterating, or otherwise destroying the same by the testator, or by some person by his consent and in his presence. This provision does not, however, control or affect any revocation implied by law from any change in the circumstances of the testator, or his family, devisees, legatees or estate, occurring between the time of making the will and the death of the testator. (c. 551, §§13-14). Marriage and birth of a child would seem such a change of circumstances as to revoke a will executed before the marriage. (See 63 N. H. 507, 3 Atl. 636.) Divorce or annulment after execution of will revokes any disposition or appointment of property to former spouse. (c. 551, §13).

Probate and Contest.—Wills must be proved and allowed by the court of probate and recorded in the office of the register of probate, in order to be effectual. (c. 552, §1).

If probate of a will is not contested the judge of probate may allow and approve it in common form, upon the testimony of one of the subscribing witnesses. (c. 552, §6). No notice need be given to anyone at the time of this probate. (c. 550, §4). If the attesting

WILLS . . . *continued*
witnesses, after the execution of a will, become incompetent from any cause, or if court determines that testimony of such witnesses is unavailable under circumstances, will may be proved and allowed upon other satisfactory evidence. (c. 552, §12).

Any party interested may have probate of a will which has been proved without notice re-examined, and will proved in solemn form before court of probate at any time within six months of such probate. Any issue related to execution of will, testamentary capacity, or fraud, duress, or undue influence shall be tried to court of probate, and any party interested may request same within six months of such probate. Petition for that purpose may be presented to judge, and notice thereof given to executor, personally if practicable, and published. If, upon hearing and re-examination, probate be not confirmed, will and probate are void. (c. 552, §§7, 8). Minor, insane person or person out of U.S., or their legal representative, who is interested may have probate in common form re-examined at any time within one year after removal of disability. (c. 552, §9). No decree approving and allowing or disallowing a will may be made in solemn form until guardians have been appointed for all minors and others interested therein who are incapacitated to take care of their estates, and until agents have been appointed by judge for all persons interested who reside out of state or are unknown. (c. 552, §11).

The usual procedure for contest is to have the will proved in solemn form. If will is allowed, only avenue of appeal is to supreme court. (c. 567-A, §1). Such appeal must be taken within 30 days after probate court has allowed will. (Rules of Sup. Ct., R7).

Self-proved Wills.—Wills following form required by statute may be proved without testimony of any subscribing witness. (c. 551, §2-a). To qualify as self-proved, signatures of testator and witnesses shall be followed by sworn acknowledgment made before notary public or justice of peace or other official authorized to administer oaths in place of execution. Testator and witnesses acknowledge signing of will, voluntariness of act, role of witnesses, capacity of testator and his or her freedom from constraint or undue influence. (c. 551, §2-a).

Legacies.—General legacies are payable at the end of one year after testator's death (94 N.H. 240) and bear interest thereafter. If not paid, legatees may sue on probate bond.

Unclaimed Legacies.—Probate court, when satisfied that due diligence has been used to find a legatee whose residence is unknown and cannot be found, shall decree that the legacy be paid over to state treasurer and such payment shall be a discharge of the executor. Any person entitled to receive such sum may petition probate court at any time before final disposition thereof, and payment to him shall be decreed, upon notice and hearing. (c. 561, §10).

Bequests and Devises to Inter Vivos Trusts.—New Hampshire court has declared pour over trusts to be valid. (95 N. H. 435, 65 A.2d 282). Trust instrument may be amended subsequently to date of testator's will. (c. 563-A). Uniform Testamentary Additions to Trusts Act adopted. (c. 563-A, §1).

Lapse.—If a devisee or legatee dies before the testator, leaving issue who survive, such issue take as their ancestor would have taken if living. (c. 551, §12).

Child Not Named.—Every child born after the decease of the testator, and every child or issue of a child of the deceased not named or referred to in his will, is entitled to the same portion of the estate, real and personal, as if the deceased were intestate, to be made up, if necessary, in just proportion from the property devised or bequeathed to others. (c. 551, §§10, 11).

Election.—Any devise or bequest to a surviving spouse is held to be in lieu of all his or her rights in estate of deceased spouse unless it appears by will that such was not intention. (c. 560, §17). Surviving spouse may, however, receive distributive share of estate, on filing waiver of testamentary provision in lieu thereof. This waiver must be in writing and must be filed at probate office within six months after appointment of an executor or administrator, and not afterwards unless by permission of probate judge for good cause shown. Where real estate is involved, waiver and release shall be recorded in Registry of Deeds of county where real estate is situated. (c. 560, §§10-14).

Living Wills.—Authorized by c. 137-H, §§1-16.

Foreign Executed Wills.—A will made out the state, if valid according to the laws of the country or state where executed, may be proved and allowed. (c. 551, §5).

Foreign Probated Wills.—Where the will of a nonresident has been proved and allowed by a court of probate jurisdiction in another state or in a foreign country, duly authenticated copies of such will and the probate thereof may, on written application of a party in interest and such citation and notice as the court may order, by decree of the court of probate, be filed and recorded in the probate office, and thereupon such will has the same force and effect as if executed according to the law of this state and duly proved and allowed in this state. (c. 552, §13).

Simultaneous Death.—See topic Death, subhead Survivorship.

Testamentary Trust.—See topic Trusts.

Uniform Anatomical Gift Act adopted. (c. 291-A).

FAMILY

ADOPTION:

Any person age 18 or older, resident or nonresident, may petition to adopt any other individual except his or her spouse. (c. 170-B, §3-4).

Consent, unless excused by court, must be obtained from: (1) Child to be adopted if 12 years of age or older; (2) mother (if unwed and under 18 years of age court may require consent of her parents or guardian); (3) legal father; (4) natural father; (5) legal guardian; (6) director of human services or any licensed child placing agency having custody of child through court action or voluntary relinquishment; (7) spouse of person to be adopted. If parent or child has been adjudicated incompetent or is mentally deficient, court shall appoint guardian to represent person's interest. (c. 170-B, §5). Any parent of adult to be adopted or any parent whose parental rights have been terminated by court order need not consent. Consent executed and acknowledged shall give care, custody and control of child to prospective adoptive parents. (c. 170-B, §9). Payment of expenses of natural parent in adoption of unrelated child is limited to those allowed by c. 170-B, §10-a.

Relinquishment.—Parent may relinquish right to control a child and to withhold consent to an adoption prior to an adoption proceeding by a written instrument executed in presence of and with approval of court or court's designee. Court may require consent of parents of an unwed mother who is under 18. Relinquishment is made to division of human services or licensed child placing agency. (c. 170-B, §8). See topic Infants, subhead Involuntary Termination of Parental Rights.

Jurisdiction of adoption proceedings is in probate courts of several counties if individual to be adopted is present in this state or is in legal custody or guardianship of authorized agency located in state. (c. 170-B, §11).

Venue.—Proceedings must be brought in county in which either petitioner or individual to be adopted resides or in which authorized agency has provided services to individual to be adopted.

Petition must be filed within 30 days after child has been placed in an adoptive home, except a petition to adopt an adult or related child may be filed at any time. (c. 170-B, §12). Chapter 170-B, §12-III states information required in petition.

Proceedings.—Prior to a hearing, in adoption of a related child or an adoption through an agency, division for children and youth services or licensed child placing agency designated by court shall make investigation into conditions of petitioner. In adoption of unrelated child or adoption not through agency, petitioner must request such investigation at least 30 days before child is placed in home. (c. 170-B, §14). Seven days notice of hearing must be given to all interested parties including division for children and youth services. (c. 170-B, §13).

Decree.—Interlocutory decree does not become final until child has lived in adoptive home for at least six months after placement by an agency or division of welfare or six months after division of welfare has been notified of custody of minor by petitioner. Final decree may be made immediately if petitioner or petitioner's spouse is a natural parent of child. (c. 170-B, §15).

Name.—Change of name may be decreed if requested. (c. 170-B, §21).

Effect of Adoption.—Adopted child bears same relation to adopting parents and their kindred in all respects, including right of inheritance, as he would if he were natural child of such parents. All rights and obligations as between adopted child and natural parents are extinguished by adoption. (c. 170-B, §20).

Setting Aside Adoption.—Subject to appeal from probate court decree, upon expiration of one year from final decree, decree cannot be questioned by any person for any reason whatsoever. (c. 170-B, §17).

ALIMONY:

See topic Divorce.

COMMUNITY PROPERTY:

System does not obtain.

DESERTION:

See topics Divorce, Husband and Wife.

DISSOLUTION OF MARRIAGE:

See topic Divorce.

DIVORCE:

This subject is governed by c. 458 et seq.

Grounds for divorce are: Impotency; extreme cruelty; conviction, in any state or federal district, of a crime punishable by imprisonment for more than one year, and actual imprisonment under such conviction; adultery; treatment such as to seriously injure health or seriously endanger reason; absence unheard of for two years; habitual drunkenness for two years; joining any religious sect or society which professes to believe relation of husband and wife unlawful, and refusal to cohabit for six months; abandonment and refusal for two years together to cohabit; willing absence of either party for two years without consent of other; when husband has wilfully absented himself from wife for two years together without making suitable provision for her support and maintenance; when wife of any citizen has gone to reside beyond limits of this state, and remained absent and separate from her husband for two years together without his consent, and without returning to claim her marriage rights; when wife of any alien or citizen of any other state, living separate, has resided in state, for two years together, her husband having left U.S. with intention of becoming a citizen of some foreign country, and not having during that period come into this state to claim his marital rights, and not having made suitable provision for his wife's support and maintenance; irreconcilable differences which have caused irremediable breakdown of marriage. (c. 458, §§7, 7-a).

Grounds for legal separation are identical to those enumerated above for absolute divorce. (c. 458, §26).

Jurisdiction of the courts is limited to those causes for divorce which exist or wholly accrue while the plaintiff is domiciled in this state. (c. 458, §6).

Residence Requirements.—Jurisdiction over the parties exists only in the following cases: (1) Where both parties were domiciled in the state when the action was commenced; (2) where the plaintiff was so domiciled and the defendant was personally served with process within the state; (3) where the plaintiff was domiciled in the state for one year next preceding the time when the action was commenced. Where the domiciled plaintiff has filed a libel, and nondomiciled defendant may have affirmative relief upon filing a cross libel. (c. 458, §5).

Venue.—All libels for divorce must be brought in the county in which the parties, or one of them, live. (c. 458, §9).

See note at head of Digest as to 1998 legislation covered.

See Topical Index in front part of this volume.

DIVORCE . . . *continued*

Proceedings.—Effective May 1, 1998, temporary rules govern domestic proceedings in New Hampshire. See Rules of Superior Court, Appendix A: Rules for Regulating the Practice in Domestic Relations. Action for divorce, annulment, legal separation, custody, support, legitimation, registration of foreign judgments and decrees, and interstate enforcement of support is commenced by filing of petition which shall be captioned "In the matter of ... and ...", stating names of parties, their mail address and county of residence. Every petition shall be signed by party and set forth in separately numbered paragraphs facts necessary to invoke jurisdiction under applicable statute. No documents are to be annexed to petition unless necessary to support prays for ex parte orders or as required by court rule or order. Where parties agreed upon all specified facts in petition, they may file joint petition, signed by both parties under oath before justice of peace or notary public.

Upon filing petition, Court shall issue orders of notice, to which clerk shall attach petition. Orders of notice must name return date. Service of petition shall be made by sheriff, or deputy, when residence of respondent is known. Officers authorized to serve similar process outside State may serve respondent if he or she is nonresident. Proof of service made outside State must be under oath, accompanied by official certificate of server's authority. Service may also be made by publication, or by registered or certified mail, return receipt requested, upon order of Court. Respondent may waive service by filing appearance and waiver, acknowledged before notary public or justice of peace, and attorney licensed to practice in New Hampshire who is appearing for party may accept service of petition from sheriff. All service must be completed by filing party at least 14 days before return date.

All petitions and cross petitions which allege adultery, or answers which allege adultery as affirmative defense shall contain name(s) and address(s) of person(s) with whom party is accused of adultery, if known; and, if not, statement to that effect.

Respondent's appearance must be filed on or before return date, or facts in petition will be deemed admitted. Answer or cross petition shall be filed in cases in which responding party wishes to bring cross petition, assert affirmative defense or seek alimony. In all cases, answer may be filed. Responsive pleadings shall be filed within 30 days of return date. Answer to cross petition shall be filed within ten days after cross petition is filed. Responsive pleadings need not be formally served on opposing party by law enforcement officer, but must contain certificate that copy of pleading has been provided to other party, or counsel, in hand or by U.S. Mail.

Domestic relations forms may be obtained at Judicial Branch web site, located at http:\\www.state.nh.us. Use of forms is not mandatory so long as pleadings conform to temporary rules. For domestic relations cases in Rockingham or Grafton Counties, see Family Division Pilot Program Rules.

Marriage Counseling Referral Service.—Whenever a libel for divorce or a petition for legal separation has been filed, the matter may be referred for marriage counseling, either on a compulsory or voluntary basis, to an approved family service agency within the jurisdiction of the Court. (c. 167-B).

Temporary alimony and restraining orders may be granted ex parte. (c. 458, §16).

Decree of divorce becomes final as matter of course on last day of term in which case is heard, except in Hillsborough County where judgment dates are set for cases heard in the preceding month. In any county, if due cause is shown, final decree will be entered immediately on determination that ground for divorce exists.

Alimony.—Upon decree of nullity or divorce, court may order alimony to be paid for such length of time as parties may agree or court orders. In determining amount of alimony, court shall consider length of marriage, age, health, station, occupation, amount and source of income, vocational skills, employability, estate, liabilities, and needs of each of parties and opportunity of each for future acquisition of capital assets and income. Court may also consider contribution of each of parties in acquisition, preservation, or appreciation in value of their respective estates and noneconomic contribution of each of parties to family unit. Court may award lump-sum or periodic payments or both. Unanticipated consequences of changes in federal tax legislation or regulations may be grounds to modify any alimony order or agreement. (c. 458, §19).

Foreign Divorces.—A superior court has jurisdiction to make such orders or temporary orders of alimony to divorced wife or husband or of support to children of divorced parents if justice requires in cases where decree of divorce was not granted in this jurisdiction, even though said divorce decree makes provision for alimony and support, provided wife and children or husband and children are domiciled in this state and husband or wife is served with process herein. (c. 458, §19a).

Uniform Divorce Recognition Act has been adopted. (c. 459).

Division of Property of Spouses.—Upon a decree of divorce, the court may restore to the wife all or any part of her estate, and may assign to her such part of the estate of her husband as may be deemed just. (c. 458, §19). Property includes both tangible and intangible, real and personal assets, however held. Court may order "equitable" division of property between parties which can be equal or unequal depending upon how court analyzes variety of factors. (c. 458, §16-a). Court has power to issue restraining orders to safeguard property pending final orders. (c. 458, §16-b).

Support and Custody of Children.—During the pendency of the libel, the superior court or any justice thereof may, on the petition of either party, make such order respecting the custody and maintenance of the minor children of the parties as shall be deemed expedient for the benefit of the children. (c. 458, §16).

Upon decree of divorce the court must make such further decree in relation to the support, education and custody of the children as is most conducive to their benefit, and may order a reasonable provision for their support and education. (c. 458, §17). There is presumption in favor of joint legal custody except where abuse (c. 173-B, §1) has occurred, in which case court will make custody and visitation orders that best protect children, abused spouse, or both (c. 458, §17, II). Where custodial parent of stepchild becomes incapacitated, spouse may make emergency treatment decisions. (c. 458, §17-c). Whenever court, acting under foregoing sections, awards custody of child to commissioner of public welfare, court must make further order requiring town in which child resides at time order is made to bear expense for maintenance and care of said child, and town shall have right of action over for such expense against whoever is legally chargeable for child's support, and court may make orders of reimbursement to town of residence as may be reasonable and just. (c. 458, §18). Premiums for ex-spouse in group health insurance plan of which other spouse is member shall be paid by member spouse, ex-spouse, by both as they may agree or as ordered by court. (c. 458, §18-a). Court may provide for trusteeship for benefit of minor children. (c. 458, §20). See also topic Husband and Wife, subhead Resident Wife of a Nonresident. If court finds it is in interest of child, it may award visitation rights to grandparents or stepparents. (c. 458, §17).

Uniform Child Custody Jurisdiction Act adopted. (c. 458-A).

Trusteeship and Security.—Court may set aside portion of property in separate trust fund for benefit of either party or minor, dependent or incompetent child of parties. (c. 458, §20). In all cases where alimony or allowance is decreed for wife or children court may require security to be given for payment thereof. (c. 458, §21).

Change of Name.—In any domestic relations proceeding except action for separation, court may restore former name of spouse, regardless of whether request therefor had been included in initial pleading. (c. 458, §24).

Remarriage after divorce is subject to no statutory restrictions.

Separation Agreements.—Private agreements between parties for separation without legal proceedings are invalid in this state. (74 N. H. 288, 67 Atl. 406). It would seem that this invalidity extends to agreements in praesenti as well as those to operate in futuro.

Annulment of Marriage.—See topic Marriage.

GUARDIAN AND WARD:

Probate court of county where minor resides or in which underlying cause of action arose has jurisdiction to appoint guardian of his person or his estate or both. (c. 547, §4; c. 463, §4).

Selection of Guardian.—Guardians of minors may be nominated by will, by petition or by written consent to petition by another (c. 463, §5) and such person will be appointed guardian except for cause shown (c. 463, §5). Court will ascertain preference of minor and, although not required to appoint such person so preferred as guardian, will give weight to such preference. (c. 463, §8). Minor over age of 14 may nominate any suitable person to be his guardian. (c. 463, §5). This provision does not apply in context of divorce custody proceedings. (129 N.H. 252, 525 A.2d 704).

Eligibility and Competency.—Nonresident may be appointed as guardian provided nonresident appoints some person in State as agent to receive service of process. (c. 464-A, §24). Office of Division for Children and Youth Services, or licensed child-placing agency (c. 170-a) may be appointed guardian of any minor (c. 463, §6-a). Any competent person, who agrees to so serve, may be appointed guardian of person and estate, or person or estate. Bank having trust powers or trust company may be appointed guardian of estate. No institution or agency providing care and custody of incapacitated person may be appointed as guardian. (c. 464-A, §10). Father or mother of minor child may be appointed his guardian. (c. 463, §§5, 15).

Appointment of Guardian.—Petitions for appointment of guardian of minor may be made by parent, adult sibling, grandparent, aunt, uncle, person who has filed for adoption of minor or any person who has had physical custody of minor not less than 30 consecutive days with consent of parent. (135 N.H. 688). Such petition must set forth that minor's parents, or other person having custody, are unfit or that parents are living apart and circumstances require appointment of guardian in best interests of such minor. (c. 463, §6).

Qualification.—Guardian of person or estate must give bond to probate court, with sureties, in such sum as judge shall approve. In discretion of judge, bond without sureties may be given if gross value of ward's estate does not exceed $10,000 or guardianship is only of person of incapacitated person or minor. (c. 464-A, §21).

Inventory.—Guardian of minor must file statement of property of his ward. (c. 463, §23). Guardian of estate must file inventory in same manner as inventories of estates of persons deceased are made. (c. 464-A, §22).

Powers and Duties.—Guardian of person of minor shall have care, custody and tuition of minor. Guardian of property of minor shall have care and management of estate of minor. (c. 463, §18-a). Guardian of incapacitated person may, subject to certain exceptions, establish place of abode of his ward and may give consent for medical care or treatment of his ward. Court, in its discretion, may limit powers of guardian of incapacitated person. (c. 464-A, §25). Guardian of incapacitated person is under duty to provide for care, comfort and maintenance of his ward and, whenever appropriate, to arrange for ward's training, education or rehabilitation. (c. 464-A, §25). Guardian of estate shall have possession and control over his ward's real and personal property and shall, in general, have power to perform every act which persons of prudence, discretion and intelligence and exercising care as in management of their own affairs would perform for purposes of guardianship. Guardian or estate must file annual account with probate court unless court finds that it is not appropriate. (c. 464-A, §26). Such powers include, but are not limited to, powers specified in Uniform Trustee's Powers Act. (c. 564-A, §3; c. 464-A, §26).

Settlements on Behalf of Minor.—See topic Infants.

Investments.—Governed by c. 463, §§20-23a in case of minors.

Securities in Name of Nominee.—See category Estates and Trusts, topic Trusts, subhead Securities in Name of Nominee.

Real Estate.—Upon petition, judge may authorize guardian of minor to purchase with his ward's funds real estate situate in state as home for him. (c. 463, §23-a). Upon petition, court may authorize guardian of estate to sell property, including real estate, of his ward for purpose of providing for care or for paying debts of said ward. (c. 464-A, §27). Before such sale, guardian of estate must give oath that he will act in best interests of ward in form specified by statute. (c. 464-A, §28). Upon petition and subject to certain restrictions, guardian of estate may purchase homestead for ward out of ward's estate. (c. 464-A, §33).

See note at head of Digest as to 1998 legislation covered.

See Topical Index in front part of this volume.

NH – 23

GUARDIAN AND WARD . . . *continued*

Accounts.—Guardian of person of incapacitated person must file report of his ward's condition biennially within 60 days after anniversary of his appointment. (c. 464-A, §35). Subject to provisions of c. 464-a, §26, guardian of estate shall file account annually within 90 days after anniversary of his appointment. (c. 464-A, §36). At time of filing, guardian must forward to ward and all parties of record copy of account and notice indicating that interested party has 30 days in which to object. (c. 464-A, §36). Upon termination of guardianship, or upon resignation, removal or death of guardian, such guardian or his personal representative must render final account. (c. 464-A, §40).

Termination of Guardianship.—Guardian of minor shall continue to hold such office until minor reaches age 18, until discharged or until court's jurisdiction over minor has ended. (c. 463, §18-a). Upon petition of ward or other interested person, court may remove guardian. (c. 464-A, §39). Upon petition, if court finds that ward is no longer incapacitated, it may terminate guardianship. (c. 464-A, §39).

Incapacitated Persons.—Any relative, public official or interested person, or individual himself, may petition for finding of incapacity and appointment of guardian. (c. 464-A, §4). Court will appoint attorney to represent rights of person claimed to be incapacitated. (c. 464-A, §6). Hearing must be held at which ward must be present unless physically unable to attend, but court may waive personal attendance of ward if petitioner or counsel for ward files written statement with court at least 24 hours prior to hearing indicating that proposed ward does not express desire to attend hearing. However, if ward first expressed desire not to attend hearing at such time as to make it unreasonable to require filing of written statement at least 24 hours prior to hearing, then court may waive personal attendance of ward at hearing upon filing of required written statement at any time up to time of hearing. Statement must include physician's affidavit indicating that overall physical, emotional, or psychological condition of ward is such that he is likely to suffer harm or that ward has no ability to understand nature and consequence of proceedings. (c. 464-A, §8).

Temporary guardian may be appointed for period not to exceed 60 days. (c. 464-A, §12).

Foreign Guardians.—Nonresident guardian must appoint agent within state. (c. 464-A, §24). Guardian duly appointed by another state will be appointed in N. H. without further notice or hearing. (c. 464-A, §44).

Gifts to Minors.—See topic Infants.

Uniform Fiduciaries Act not adopted.

Uniform Simplification of Fiduciary Security Transfers Act not adopted.

Uniform Child Custody Jurisdiction Act adopted. (c. 458-A).

HUSBAND AND WIFE:

Separate Property.—A married woman holds to her own use, free from the interference or control of her husband, all property at any time earned, acquired or inherited by, or bequeathed, given or conveyed to her, either before or after marriage, if such earning, acquisition, conveyance, gift or bequest were not occasioned by payment or pledge of the property of the husband. (c. 460, §1).

Contracts.—Every married woman has the same rights and remedies, and is subject to the same liabilities in relation to property held by her in her own right, as if she were unmarried, and may convey, make contracts, and sue and be sued, in all matters in law and equity, and upon any contract by her made, or for any wrong by her done, as if she were unmarried. (c. 460, §2).

Premarital Debts of Wife.—Husband is not liable for debts contracted by the wife prior to marriage. (c. 460, §3).

Actions.—A married woman may sue or be sued for her torts and upon her contracts as though she were unmarried. Either spouse may sue the other. (c. 460, §§2, 2-a; 55 N. H. 279; 78 N. H. 4, 95 Atl. 657).

Conveyance or Encumbrance of Property.—Real estate may be conveyed directly by husband to wife, or wife to husband, in all cases where same thing might lawfully be done through intervention of a third person. (c. 460, §5). With exception of liens reserved on household goods sold conditionally, no lease or mortgage of household goods in use by husband and wife in their household is valid unless made in writing and executed by owner and husband or wife of owner. (c. 460, §11). A married woman of full age may convey her real estate. A married spouse, though not of full age, may join with her (his) husband or wife in release of homestead. (c. 460, §4).

A married man or woman, who is justifiably living apart from his or her spouse because such spouse has been guilty of conduct which constitutes cause for divorce, may apply by petition to the judge of probate for the county in which real estate owned by him or her lies for a license to convey the same in such manner as to bar all rights of homestead therein to which such guilty party may then or thereafter be entitled. (c. 460, §8).

Resident Wife of a Nonresident.—If a woman, the wife of an alien or of a man residing in another state, has resided in this state six months successively, separate from her husband, she may convey all real and personal estate, held by her in this state, the same as if she were sole and unmarried. (c. 460, §12).

If the husband of such woman becomes a citizen of this state, and they cohabit together, the fact of his becoming such citizen, and such cohabitation, has the same effect upon any contract or business of the wife as if the marriage between them had then first been solemnized. (c. 460, §13).

If the husband of such woman obtains a divorce from his wife in a court of tribunal of any other state or country, or if a divorce be decreed upon application of the wife during such separate residence, she retains the exclusive custody and guardianship and receives the earnings of her minor children living with her. (c. 460, §14). No person may take from the custody of such wife any minor child of the marriage residing with her, or remove the child from this state against the consent of the mother. (c. 460, §15). Upon her application, a guardian may be appointed for the child, and the superior court, or a justice thereof, may issue an injunction restraining the father and all other persons from

removing the child from this state against the consent of the mother, and may make such further orders and degrees as shall secure to her or to the guardian the custody of the child. (c. 460, §16).

Resident Husband of a Nonresident.—The rights of a resident husband of a nonresident wife are identical to those of the resident wife of a nonresident husband, as is above set forth. (c. 460, §17).

Abandonment.—If any wife or mother separates herself from her husband without cause, or from her children, she shall be guilty of misdemeanor and subject to fine, to be applied in discretion of court to benefit of deserted husband or children or both. (c. 460, §28).

Uniform Interstate Family Support Act adopted. Jurisdiction vested in Superior Court or Department of Health and Human Services. Support enforcement agency must provide services to extent permitted by Title IV-D of Social Security Act. (c. 546-B:18, I).

Antenuptial Agreements.—Man and woman in contemplation of marriage may enter into written, interspousal contract and courts of this state shall give same effect to such contracts entered in other jurisdictions as would courts of such other jurisdictions. However, no contract otherwise enforceable under this section may contain any terms which attempt to abrogate statutory or common law rights of minor children of contemplated marriage. (c. 460, §2-a).

Separate Maintenance.—Whenever either party is insane, or whenever a cause is in existence which is, or if continued, will be, a cause for divorce, the superior court may, upon petition and such procedure thereon as in divorce cases, restrain either party from interfering with the personal liberty of the other and from entering the tenement wherein the other resides, may grant temporarily or permanently, the custody, care, education and maintenance of their minor children, if any, and may make reasonable allowance for support, all subjects to such limitations as the court shall deem just. (c. 458, §31). Domicile requirements of c. 458, §§4, 5, and 6 do not apply to this section and court may grant relief to a nonresident plaintiff if defendant is a resident. (c. 458, §31).

Community property system does not obtain.

INFANTS:

Age of majority is 18, effective June 3, 1973. However, legal drinking age is 21. (c. 179:5 and 6).

Minors and their sureties are bound by their recognizances. (c. 597, §14). They may hold shares in a building and loan association or a credit union and be held to stockholder's liability thereon. (c. 393, §10; c. 394-B, §25). Savings banks and other institutions for savings may pay minors the deposits to their credit as if they were of age, and their receipts are sufficient discharges for the same. (c. 386, §18).

Minors can join with their spouses in valid release of their respective homestead interests in real estate. (c. 460, §4).

Actions.—Next friend actions are commonly used. No net settlement exceeding $10,000 in any such action is valid unless approved by court in which action is pending or to which writ is returnable. In any suit involving minor which exceeds $10,000, any person or entity who receives money on behalf of minor must be appointed guardian of estate of such minor by probate court. Court may make all necessary orders to protect interests of infant. (c. 464-A, §42).

Parental Responsibility.—Parent not vicariously liable for torts of child, but parent is responsible if parent can be shown to be independently negligent. (100 N.H. 98, 120 A.2d 335). Under certain circumstances when parents or guardian of child committing act of vandalism are found to have failed to exercise reasonable supervision and control, such parents or guardians can be ordered to make restitution to victim. (c. 169-B, §45; c. 507, §8-e).

Involuntary Termination of Parental Rights.—Probate court has exclusive original jurisdiction over petitions to terminate when child is present in state or in legal custody of authorized agency in state. Petition shall be filed in probate court of county in which child or parents reside at time of filing, or in probate court of county where authorized agency has provided services to child. (c. 170-C:3). Petition may be filed by either parent, guardian, foster parents, or authorized agency. (c. 170-C:4). Petition may be granted where court finds that one or more of following conditions exist: Parent has abandoned or neglected child; parent due to mental deficiency or illness is incapable of giving child proper care and protection; parent has knowingly or willfully severely abused or permitted another to severely abuse child. (c. 170-C:5). Court shall appoint guardian to represent interests of child in all termination hearings. (c. 170-C:8).

War Veterans.—The disability or minority of any person otherwise eligible for a loan, or guaranty or insurance of a loan, pursuant to the act of Congress entitled the Servicemen's Readjustment Act of 1944 (58 Stat. 284) as heretofore or hereafter amended (38 U. S. C. 693 et seq.), and of the minor spouse of any eligible veteran, in connection with any transaction entered into pursuant to said Act of Congress, as heretofore or hereafter amended, shall not affect the binding effect of any obligation incurred by such eligible person or spouse as an incident to any such transaction, including incurring of indebtedness and acquiring, encumbering, selling, releasing, or conveying property, or any interest therein, if all or part of any such obligation be guaranteed or insured by the government or the Administrator of Veterans' Affairs pursuant to said act and amendments thereto; or if the Administrator be the creditor, by reason of a loan or a sale pursuant to said act and amendments. The Act does not create, or render enforceable, any other or greater rights or liabilities than would exist if neither such person nor such spouse were a minor. (c. 117, §1).

Uniform Transfers to Minors Act adopted. (c. 463-A). Age of majority under Act, 21.

Uniform Securities Ownership by Minors Act not adopted.

Adoption.—See topic Adoption.

Uniform Child Custody Jurisdiction Act adopted. (c. 458-A).

See note at head of Digest as to 1998 legislation covered.

See Topical Index in front part of this volume.

MARRIAGE:

The "age of consent" is fixed by statute at 18 for both sexes, but if special cause exists rendering marriage of a person under the age of consent (and not below the age of 14 in case of a male or 13 in case of a female) desirable, a judge of the superior court or the probate judge of the county where such party resides may, on due application, grant permission for such marriage. (c. 457, §§4-7).

License.—Persons proposing to marry within the state must complete marriage license application, with all facts required by rules of Department of Health and Human Services (c. 126), to be entered in any town clerk's office. Clerk shall record application in book to be kept for that purpose. (c. 457, §22). (See c. 457, §23—AIDS education and affidavit required for license.) Town clerk shall deliver to parties marriage license embodying facts required in application and specifying time and date when application was entered, which license shall be delivered to minister or magistrate who is to officiate, before marriage is solemnized. License shall be valid for not less than three days and not more than 90 days from date of filing. (c. 457, §26). On application to superior court justice or probate judge within county where proposed marriage is to be solemnized, period of three days may be shortened but not if both parties and their parents are nonresidents. (c. 457, §27).

New Requirements.—In addition to requirements under paragraph 1, no marriage license shall be issued unless it includes affidavit on back which bride and groom shall sign affirming they have received and discussed brochure prepared by Division of Public Health Services, Department of Health and Human Services, under RSA 141-f:3, XIII. (c. 457, §23).

Solemnization.—Marriage may be solemnized by a justice of the peace commissioned in the state; by Art. III federal judges or U.S. magistrate judges appointed pursuant to federal law; by any minister of gospel in state who has been ordained according to usage of his denomination, resides in state and is in regular standing with his denomination; and, within his parish, by minister residing out of state, but having pastoral charge wholly or partly in this state. (c. 457, §31). Secretary of State may issue special license to ordained minister, or Jewish rabbi, who is citizen of U.S., residing out of state, authorizing him in special case to marry couple within state. (c. 457, §§32, 37).

The validity of a marriage solemnized before a person professing to be a justice of the peace or minister of the gospel is not affected by want of jurisdiction or authority in such supposed justice or minister, or on account of any omission or informality in the certificate of intention of marriage. If the marriage is in other respects lawful and has been consummated with the belief on the part of the either of the parties thereto that they were lawfully married. (c. 457, §36).

Friends or Quakers and Jewish rabbis who are citizens of the United States, residing in this state, are allowed to solemnize marriages according to their usual practices. (c. 457, §37).

Reports of Marriages.—Every person who solemnizes a marriage shall make record of it and all facts required by Department of Health and Human Services and, within six days thereafter, shall forward record to town clerk who issued marriage license. Town clerk shall forward record to Bureau of Vital Records and Health Statistics. (c. 126, §8). See also category Documents and Records, topic Records.

Record.—See category Documents and Records, topic Records, subhead Vital Statistics.

Common law marriages are not recognized except to limited extent of c. 457, §39. (134 N.H. 675).

Proxy marriages are not authorized by any statute.

Presumption of Legal Marriage.—Persons cohabiting and acknowledging each other as husband and wife, and generally reputed to be such for three years, and until the decease of one of them, are thereafter deemed to have been legally married. (c. 457, §39).

Prohibited Marriages.—A man may not marry his mother, his daughter, his granddaughter, stepdaughter, sister, aunt, niece, first cousin, mother-in-law or widow of his father, son or grandson or any other man, and there are corresponding prohibitions against marriage of woman. (c. 457, §§1-3). Male below the age of 14 or female below age of 13 may not marry. (c. 457, §4). Permission may be obtained from superior court or probate court if special cause exists where man or woman is below age 18, so long as man is at least 14 and woman is at least 13, but no waiver of age of consent is granted where both parties are nonresidents. (c. 457, §6). One who has former wife or husband known to be alive and undivorced may not marry another person. All such marriages are void. (c. 458, §1).

Foreign Marriages.—Any marriage by nondomiciliaries which is legally contracted in another state will be recognized as valid if parties become permanent residents. (c. 457, §3). Uniform Marriage Recognition Act adopted. (c. 457, §§43 & 44).

Annulment.—Marriages between parties below the age of consent may be annulled at the suit of the party who was married below the age or at the suit of his or her parent or guardian unless the party after arriving at such age has confirmed the marriage. (c. 457, §5). No other statutory grounds of annulment. There is no specific statutory provision limiting the time within which an action for annulment on the ground of nonage must be brought. Superior court has jurisdiction of annulment cases. (c. 491, §7).

In any proceedings for annulment for any cause, whether under the statute or under common law, a New Hampshire court will assume jurisdiction as to a marriage entered into in this state even though neither party has been at any time a resident herein. (c. 458, §3).

MARRIED WOMEN:

See topics Husband and Wife, Marriage; categories Civil Actions and Procedure, topic Evidence, subhead Witnesses; Debtor and Creditor, topic Homesteads; Documents and Records, topic Acknowledgments; Estates and Trusts, topics Executors and Administrators, Wills; Property, topic Dower.

INSURANCE

INSURANCE COMPANIES:

Business of insurance is under supervision of Insurance Commissioner. (c. 400-A; c. 402-C).

Corporations may be formed for practically all kinds of insurance business. (c. 401, §§1, 5).

Insurance holding companies, mergers involving insurance company, and acquisitions of insurance companies are regulated. (c. 401-B). Securities regulation falls under administrative supervision of Insurance Commissioner. (c. 400-A, §39 et seq.).

Special statutes govern employers' mutual associations, and fraternal benefit societies. (c. 418).

Mutual Companies; Members' Liability.—Members of a mutual insurance company are not individually liable for debts of the company, beyond their liability to assessments for losses occurring therein, nor to such assessments beyond the amount of their deposit notes. (c. 402, §1). Any mutual fire or casualty insurance company organized under the laws of this state, which charges a full cash premium, may limit the liability of policyholders to assessment by a stipulation in the policy, which has the same effect as a deposit note signed by the insured; but such contingent liability of a member may not be less than an amount equal to and in addition to the cash premium written in this policy. (c. 402, §2). No person insured in such company, or in any class thereof, in which the amount insured is less than $50,000, may be assessed any greater sum than he would be if that amount were insured; but the officers of the company are individually liable for the indebtedness of the company not provided for by such assessments. (c. 402, §3).

Deposit Requirements.—An insurance company of another state must make such deposit with the Insurance Commissioner as the laws of its home state require of foreign companies doing business therein. (c. 402, §73).

Reports.—Every insurance company doing business in this state must, on or before Mar. 1 of each year, make and transmit to the Commissioner a statement, under oath of its president and secretary, in accordance with The National Association of Insurance Commissioners Annual Statement Blank following The National Association of Insurance Commissioners Annual Statement Instructions and those accounting procedures and practices prescribed by National Association of Insurance Commissioners Accounting Practices and Procedures Manual, showing amount of its capital stock, assets, liabilities, outstanding risks, premium notes, receipts, expenditures, losses, assessments, salaries and emoluments, and any other information calculated fully to disclose condition and method of management of company for year ending preceding Dec. 31, which statement must include whole amount of premiums written during preceding year for insurance on property or risks located or persons resident in this state. Commissioner may require like statement or further information at any other time. (c. 400-A, §36). Commissioner may extend time for filing such statement for not more than 60 days. Life insurance companies are not required to file that part of their annual statement known as gain and loss exhibit until succeeding May 1. (c. 400-A, §36).

Federal Liability Risk Retention Act of 1986.—Formation and regulation of risk retention groups pursuant to "RRA 1986" are governed by state statute. (c. 405-A).

Discrimination is prohibited in cancellation, renewal or issuance of automobile and personal liability and property insurance. (c. 417-A, §3; c. 417-B, §2). Specific grounds for cancellation are laid out. (c. 417-B, §3).

Rates.—Premium rates are subject to the approval of the Commissioner in the following classes of insurance: Fire and certain casualty (c. 414), employers' liability under workmen's compensation law (c. 412, §8), automobile liability (c. 412, §§14-15).

Policies.—Forms of policies are subject to the approval of the Commissioner in the following classes of insurance: fire (c. 407, §1), motor vehicle (c. 264, §14; c. 412, §2), accident and health (c. 415, §1), group life (c. 408, §§15, 16).

Standard nonforfeiture and valuation laws have been adopted. (c. 409; c. 409-A; c. 410).

Investigation of Claims.—The assured must give immediate written notice of loss under fire insurance policy after loss occurs (c. 407, §22), and company must begin adjustment of loss within 15 days after receipt of such notice (c. 407, §12). Under liability policies, investigation must be commenced within 20 days after receipt of written notice of accident. (c. 412, §6).

Reinsurance.—No domestic life insurance company may transfer its risks or any part thereof to, or reinsure its risks, or any part thereof except reinsurance effected in the ordinary course of business in, any insurance corporation, association or society which is not at the time of such transfer or reinsurance authorized to do business in this state. (c. 411, §30). Insurer authorized to do business in this state may not reinsure or assume any risk in this state underwritten by an unadmitted company. (c. 412, §5).

Miscellaneous Prohibitions.—Giving and receiving rebates are criminal (c. 402, §§39-40), as are misrepresentations of the terms of an insurance policy either in one's own company or in another; credit card charges are exempted, however (c. 402, §§46-49). There is special statute covering embezzlement by insurance agents and illegal fees. (c. 402, §§50-53). Insurance company cannot contribute to any political campaign. (c. 402, §43).

Special statute specifically prohibits unfair practices in business of insurance under following classifications: (1) Misrepresentations; (2) misrepresentations in insurance applications or transactions; (3) false information and advertising generally; (4) defamation; (5) boycott, coercion and intimidation; (6) false financial statements; (7) stock operations and advisory board contracts; (8) unfair discrimination; (9) rebates; (10) title insurance commissions, rebates and discounts; (11) political contributions; (12) collecting improper premiums; (13) separate charge for insurance; (14) coverage reduction; (15) unfair claim settlement practices by insurers; (16) requiring as a condition precedent to loaning money upon security of any real or personal property that owner of property to whom money is to be loaned negotiate any policy of insurance covering such property through a particular insurance agent or broker; (17) complaint handling procedures applicable to insurance companies; (18) conflict of interest (c. 417, §4); (19)

See note at head of Digest as to 1998 legislation covered.

See Topical Index in front part of this volume.

NH-25

INSURANCE COMPANIES . . . *continued*

whenever instrument requires that purchaser, mortgagor, or borrower furnish insurance of any kind on real or personal property which is being conveyed or which is collateral security to loan, mortgagee or lender shall refrain from disclosing or using any and all such insurance information to his or its own advantage and to detriment of either borrower, purchaser, mortgagor, insurer, or company or agency complying with requirements relating to insurance; (20) notwithstanding any other law to contrary, creditor or lender of loan secured by interest in real property shall not require borrower to keep mortgaged property insured under property insurance policy in sum in excess of value of buildings on real property (c. 417, §4, XVI [c] and [d]). Insurance Commissioner is empowered, upon hearing, to issue cease and desist orders, to suspend, revoke, or refuse to renew license of person and to impose a penalty of up to $2,500, subject to appeal to Supreme Court. (c. 417, §§5, 10, 11, 12, 13; c. 541). Borrower may not be required to insure mortgaged property for sum greater than value of buildings thereon. (c. 417, §4 XVI[d]). No person who is a director of another insurance company, either foreign or domestic, may be a director of a domestic insurance company if effect thereof is to substantially lessen competition generally in insurance business or tends to create a monopoly therein. (c. 417, §17). No liability insurer shall require that a bodily injury claim be settled or adjudicated as a condition precedent to settlement of a property damage claim arising out of same motor vehicle accident. (c. 264, §18,VII).

Life insurance made payable to a married woman inures to her benefit, or, in case of her death, to her children's benefit, against the claims of creditors or representatives of the person effecting the same. (c. 408, §1). The party to whom a life insurance policy is made payable is entitled to the sum so insured against the claims of the creditors or representatives of the party effecting the same. (c. 408, §2).

Foreign Companies.—No foreign company can do business within the state without first obtaining a license from the Insurance Commissioner. (c. 405, §1; c. 416, §7). The license is revocable if the company violates the law or if the Commissioner deems it no longer safe, reliable, or entitled to confidence. (c. 405, §§12-13).

Licensed resident agents may be authorized by Commissioner to procure insurance policies and contracts of insurance or sureties to be effective in this state in foreign insurance companies not authorized to transact business in this state, but which are duly authorized to do business in some state having an insurance commissioner, in such amounts as the agent cannot place with an admitted company. (c. 405, §24). Policy must contain statement that it is with out of state company and not guaranteed by N.H. in case of company insolvency. (c. 405, §24).

Requirements as to Capital and Assets.—No stock insurance company may be licensed to do business in the state unless it possesses a paid-up capital of $800,000, invested in securities readily convertible into cash, one-half at least of which are not loans secured by real estate; nor unless it possesses, in addition to such capital, assets equal in amount to all its outstanding liabilities, estimating as liabilities 50% of premiums received on unexpired fire risks running one year or less from date of policy, and a pro rata amount of all premiums received on unexpired risks running more than one year from date of policy, and on marine risks 50% of the amount of premiums written on policies on yearly risks, and on risks covering more than one passage not terminated, and the full amount of premiums written on policies of all other marine risks not terminated. (c. 405, §2).

No mutual insurance company may be licensed to do business in the state unless it has $800,000 of cash assets invested as above stated, nor unless its assets equal its outstanding liabilities, including reinsurance. (c. 405, §4).

Qualification.—The company must also file with the Commissioner a certified copy of its charter and by-laws and a full statement, under oath, of its president and secretary, showing the financial standing and condition of the company, in accordance with blanks furnished by the Commissioner, except in cases where the company has already filed such papers, and must otherwise comply with all laws relating to such companies. (c. 405, §11).

Process Agent.—No joint stock or mutual insurance company, nor its agents, may do business in this state until it has filed with the Commissioner a written stipulation, agreeing that legal process affecting the company, served on the Commissioner for the time being, shall have the same effect as if served personally on the company within the state. Service of such process is made by leaving copy of process in hands of Commissioner or in his office and paying fee of $2. (c. 405, §10).

Unauthorized Insurers.—Certain acts by an unauthorized foreign or alien insurer such as issuance of contracts of insurance to residents, solicitation of such insurance, collection of premiums and any other transaction of business constitute an appointment by such insurer of insurance commissioner as its true and lawful attorney upon whom may be served all lawful process in any action or proceedings arising out of contracts of insurance. (c. 406-B).

Filing of Pleadings.—Before any unauthorized foreign or alien insurer shall file or cause to be filed any pleading in any action or proceeding instituted against it, it must procure a certificate of authority to transact business in this state or deposit cash or securities or file a bond with the clerk in an amount to be fixed by the court sufficient to secure the payment of any final judgment unless the court, in its discretion, dispenses with such deposit or bond in certain cases. (c. 406-B:6).

Attorney's fees, not exceeding 12½% of amount recovered, may be included in a judgment against an unauthorized foreign or alien insurer in certain cases. (c. 406-B:7).

Unauthorized Insurers False Advertising Process Act.—Special act confers jurisdiction on insurance commissioner and the courts to prevent insurers not authorized to transact business in this state from placing in or sending into this state any false advertising designed to induce residents to purchase insurance from them. (c. 406-A). So-called "insurance consultants" are licensed and regulated and must pay civil penalty for noncompliance. (c. 405, §44-a et seq.).

Returns.—Each such company must, on or before Mar. 1 of each year, make a return, under oath, to the Commissioner, showing the gross premiums in force on risks in this state on Dec. 31 previous and the unabsorbed portion of such premiums computed at the rate of return actually made on annual policies expiring during the year by said companies. (c. 405, §9).

Resident Agents.—Foreign insurance or surety companies shall only write insurance through agents who are regularly commissioned and licensed to transact business in this state. (c. 405, §17-b). Agents must be residents of this state or residents in any other state granting similar licenses to residents of this state. (c. 405, §16). Commissioner, upon annual payment of fee as provided in c. 400-A:29, may issue licenses to licensed resident agents subject to revocation at any time and expiring annually on Mar. 31, permitting agent named therein to procure insurance policy and contracts of insurance or suretyship to be effective in this state in foreign insurance companies not authorized to do business in some state having insurance commissioner. (c. 405, §24). Such insurance or suretyship placed with unadmitted company shall be for such amount as agent cannot place with admitted company, and shall not be placed until agent has first satisfied Insurance Commissioner that he cannot procure such insurance in admitted company. (c. 405, §24). Every licensee before delivering to insured must stamp on base of binder or policy following: "the company issuing this policy has not been licensed by the State of New Hampshire and the rates charged have not been approved by the Commissioner of Insurance. If the company issuing this policy becomes insolvent, the New Hampshire Insurance Guarantee Fund shall not be liable for any claims made against this policy." (c. 405, §24).

Reinsurance.—Formation and operation of risk retention groups and purchasing groups are regulated pursuant to Federal Liability Risk Retention Act of 1986, 15 U.S.C. §3901 et seq. (c. 405-A, §1 et seq.).

Investments.—See c. 411-A.

Retaliatory Law.—The Commissioner may revoke licenses of companies of any state where New Hampshire companies are unfairly treated or unjustly taxed, fined, etc. (c. 405, §§53-59).

Separate statutes prescribe the law pertaining to fraternal benefit societies, and foreign casualty companies operating upon the assessment plan.

Privilege Tax.—See schedule in c. 400-A, §29.

Premium Tax.—Every insurer (excluding ocean marine) shall pay to insurance commissioner tax of 2% of net premiums. On quarterly basis insurers are required to pay amount equal to ¼ of previous year's tax as partial payment for that year. Minimum annual tax is $200. Penalty for failure to comply is 10% on amount of tax due. Commissioner may suspend or revoke license of insurer for noncompliance. (c. 400-A, §32).

Administrative Fee.—Administrative fee is imposed annually based on premiums charged. Minimum fee payable by each insurer is $100. (c. 400-A, §39).

Direct Actions Against Insurer.—See category Transportation, topic Motor Vehicles, subhead Direct Actions.

No-Fault Insurance.—See category Transportation, topic Motor Vehicles, subhead No-Fault Insurance.

SURETY AND GUARANTY COMPANIES:

Foreign companies may transact business in this state upon complying with the provisions of all laws relating to foreign insurance companies and their agents, and not otherwise. (c. 416, §7). See topic Insurance Companies.

Rights.—The judge, head of department, or other officer authorized to approve the bond of any person required by law to give a bond, may accept as a surety upon the bond any such company which has been licensed to do business in this state, and, if satisfied with the financial ability of the company, he need not require other sureties. A reasonable sum for the expense of procuring such surety may be allowed in the settlement of the account of a person required by law to give a bond. (c. 416, §§2, 3).

Reinsurance.—No surety company, domestic or foreign, may assume any liability as surety on any bond exceeding 10% of its net assets, without reinsuring in some surety company authorized to do business in this state the amount by which such liability may exceed 10%. (c. 416, §5).

INTELLECTUAL PROPERTY

TRADEMARKS AND TRADENAMES:

Model State Trademark Act was adopted in 1969. (c. 350-A).

TRADE SECRETS:

Uniform Trade Secrets Act adopted. (c. 350-B).

LEGAL PROFESSION

ATTORNEYS AND COUNSELORS:

The state bar is integrated.

Jurisdiction over Admission.—The Supreme Court has jurisdiction over the admission of persons to practice as attorneys in all courts of the state (c. 311, §2), and has enacted rules governing the admission of candidates.

Eligibility.—Any citizen of the age of 18 or over, of good moral character and suitable qualifications, may be admitted to practice as an attorney. (c. 311, §2).

Registration as law student not required.

Educational Requirements.—(a) Every applicant must furnish satisfactory proof that before beginning study of law he successfully completed at least three years of work required for a bachelor's degree in accredited college. (b) Every applicant must have graduated from law school approved by American Bar Association having three-year course and requiring students to devote substantially all their working time to study, called full time law school, or from law school approved by American Bar Association having course of not less than four school years equivalent in number of working hours to three year course in full time law school and in which students devote

See note at head of Digest as to 1998 legislation covered.

See Topical Index in front part of this volume.

ATTORNEYS AND COUNSELORS *. . . continued*

only part of their working time to their studies, called part time law school. Combination of study in full time and part time law schools will be accepted only if such law schools meet above requirements, and applicant shall have graduated from one or other. Study in any law school which conducts its courses by correspondence or does not require attendance of its students at its lectures or classes does not constitute compliance with rule. (Sup. Ct. Rules, §42[4][b]).

Petition for Admission.—Person wishing to be examined must file with Committee on character and fitness and with clerk of New Hampshire Supreme Court, Concord, on or before May 1 for July examination or Dec. 1 for Feb. examination, petition and sworn questionnaire upon form to be furnished by clerk; signed by two persons certifying applicant's good moral character. If papers so filed show that he is entitled to be examined he will be allowed to take next scheduled examination. Prior to his original and any subsequent examination, he must pay to clerk examination fee and character and fitness investigation fee, both of which are nonrefundable. (Sup. Ct. Rules, §42[5][I]). Applicant must also furnish evidence of satisfactory completion of Multistate Professional Responsibility Examination. (Sup. Ct. Rules, §42[7][f].

Clerkship.—No requirement that clerkship be served.

Examination.—A committee consisting of members of bar of state will be appointed to examine candidates. Two examinations, consisting of two days each are given annually in Concord in July and Feb. Multi-State Bar Examination given first day. Second day consists of essay questions on broad range of subjects. Multi-State Bar Examination results from other states may not be transferred.

Admission Without Examination.—Procedures allowing admission to bar on motion and without examination have been rescinded; and, until such procedures are readopted, no admission without examination is allowed.

Disabilities.—No person may act as attorney in any cause in which person has acted as judge. (c. 311, §5).

Liens.—Attorney has lien for reasonable fee and expenses on client's cause of action, the judgment decree or other order of court. (c. 311, §13).

Attorney Ethics.—American Bar Association Model Rules of Professional Conduct adopted with modification as New Hampshire Rules of Professional Conduct.

Disbarment.—Supreme Court may suspend or disbar attorney for fraud, malpractice or contempt of court. (c. 311, §8).

Unauthorized practice of law may be restrained by Supreme or Superior Court through action of Attorney General or New Hampshire Bar Association. (c. 311, §7-a).

Professional Corporation.—See category Business Organizations, topic Corporations, subhead Professional Corporations.

MINERAL, WATER AND FISHING RIGHTS

MINES AND MINERALS:

C. 277 refers to safety and health of employees and applies to mines.

C. 219, §19 provides for issuance of license to prospect on unimproved state forest lands and reservations and in beds of great ponds and navigable rivers.

C. 12-E governs mining and reclamation of mined lands. Commissioner of department of resources and economic development has supervision and control under provisions of this chapter.

MORTGAGES

CHATTEL MORTGAGES:

Uniform Commercial Code has been adopted. See category Business Regulation and Commerce, topic Commercial Code. However, secured party has 20 days (rather than ten) to perfect interest. (c. 382-A, §§9-301[2] & 9-312[4]).

Recording Fee.—See category Business Regulation and Commerce, topic Commercial Code.

Improper removal or concealment of mortgaged property with the intent of placing it beyond the control of the mortgagee, by mortgagor or another, is a criminal offense. (c. 360, §24).

Forms.—No official approval of a form of security agreement has been made. Illustrative form for motor vehicle follows (modifications of form would have to be made for other types of financing arrangements) (For UCC-1 and UCC-3 forms, see end of this Digest):

Purchase Money Security Agreement

Name   No. and street   city or town

. . . .

County   State   and zone
(hereinafter called the "Seller") hereby agrees to sell, and

Name   No. and street   city or town

. . . .

County   State   and zone
(hereinafter called the "Buyer") hereby agrees to buy the goods described below (hereinafter called the "Goods") upon the terms hereinafter stated. The Buyer acknowledges receipt of the Goods in satisfactory condition and accepts the same and also acknowledges that they conform to the description and to any sample or model previously examined by the Buyer.

New Used	Description (including make and year)	Model No.	Serial No.	Motor No.

together with all equipment used therewith and accessories therefor, all of which is hereinafter included in the term "Goods." It is agreed by the Buyer that there are no warranties, express or implied, of merchantability or otherwise, which extend the above description of the goods. The Buyer agrees to pay to the Seller the Time Balance, computed as follows:

A. CASH PRICE		$
B. EQUIPMENT AND ACCESSORIES		$
C. SERVICE		$
D. SALES TAX		$. . . .
E. CASH SALE PRICE		$
F. DOWN PAYMENT:		
1. TRADE-IN ALLOWANCE		
. . . .$		
year make model		
LESS 2. ENCUMBRANCE TO	$. . . .	
3. NET TRADE-IN ALLOWANCE	$	
4. OTHER CREDIT ALLOWANCES, IF ANY	$	
5. CASH DOWN PAYMENT	$. . . .	
G. TOTAL DOWN PAYMENT AND ALLOWANCES		$. . . .
H. BALANCE (ITEM E. LESS ITEM G.)		$
I. INSURANCE:		

TYPE OF   COVERAGE
COVERAGE   PERIOD   PREMIUMS
1. COMPREHENSIVE FIRE & THEFT $
2. COLLISION ($ deductible) $
3. BODILY INJURY $
4. PROPERTY DAMAGE $
5. $
6. $
7. LIABILITY INSURANCE COVERAGE FOR BODILY INJURY AND PROPERTY DAMAGE CAUSED TO OTHERS IS NOT INCLUDED (UNLESS PREMIUMS ARE STATED).
J. TOTAL INSURANCE PREMIUMS $. . . .
K. PRINCIPAL BALANCE $
L. FINANCE CHARGE $. . . .
M. TIME BALANCE $

Payable in . . . . monthly installments of $. . . each on the . . day of each month beginning . . . ., 19. ., and a final installment of $. . . on . . . ., 19. ..
N.   RECORDING CHARGES $
O.   TOTAL TIME PRICE $
(Sum of Items E, J, L, and N)

The Buyer agrees to pay, in the event that any installment shall be in default for ten (10) days or more, a delinquency and collection charge on demand which shall be with respect to each such installment the lesser of five per cent (5%) of such installment or the sum of Five Dollars ($5.00). The Buyer agrees to pay interest on unpaid installments from maturity or as soon after maturity as is permitted by State law at the rate of six per cent (6%) per annum.

The Buyer hereby warrants and covenants for the purpose of inducing the Seller to sell to the Buyer the property hereby sold that:

1. The property is bought or to be used primarily for
☐ personal, family or household purposes
☐ farming operations use
☐ business use.

2. The goods shall be kept at:

. . . .
No. and street   city or town   County   State
until such time as written consent to a change of location is obtained from the Seller or its assignee.

3. If the Goods are bought primarily for personal, family or household purposes or for farming operations use, or if the Buyer has no place of business in said State, the Buyer's residence in said State is that shown at the beginning of this agreement.

4. If the Goods are bought primarily for business use, the Buyer's place of business in said State, if any, is that shown at the beginning of this agreement; and all other places of business of the Buyer in said State outside of the city or town mentioned in the previous clause are located as follows: . . . .

. . . .

5. If the Goods are to be attached to real estate, a description of the real estate is as follows: . . . .

. . . .

and the name of the record owner is . . . ., and if the Goods are attached to real estate prior to the perfection of the security interest granted hereby, the Buyer, on demand of the Seller, shall furnish the latter with a disclaimer or disclaimers, signed by all persons having an interest in the real estate, of any interest in the Goods which is prior to the Seller's interest. The Buyer agrees to notify the Seller in writing of any intended sale, mortgage or conveyance of the realty and to give written notice of the terms and conditions of this contract to any prospective purchaser, mortgagee or grantee of said realty and a copy of such notice to the Seller.

See note at head of Digest as to 1998 legislation covered.

See Topical Index in front part of this volume.

CHATTEL MORTGAGES... *continued*

6. If the Goods are of a type normally used in more than one State and the Buyer has a place of business in more than one State, the Buyer's chief place of business is

. . . .

No. and Street City or Town State

or, if left blank, is that shown at the beginning of this agreement, and the Buyer shall immediately notify the Seller in writing of any change in the Buyer's chief place of business. If Certificates of Title are issued or outstanding in respect to any of the Goods, the Buyer shall cause the interest of the Seller to be properly noted thereon.

All rights of the Seller in, to and under this agreement and in and to the Goods shall pass to and may be exercised by any assignee thereof. The Buyer agrees that if the Seller gives notice to the Buyer (a) of an intended assignment of said rights and thereafter such an assignment is made or (b) of such an assignment having been made then, in either event, the liability of the Buyer to the assignee shall be immediate and absolute and the Buyer will not set up any claim against the Seller as a defense, counterclaim or set-off to any action brought by any such assignee for the unpaid balance owed hereunder or for possession of the Goods. The Buyer hereby acknowledges receipt of notice that the Seller intends to assign all said rights to . . . . Bank.

THIS AGREEMENT IS SUBJECT TO THE ADDITIONAL PROVISIONS SET FORTH ON THE REVERSE SIDE HEREOF, THE SAME BEING INCORPORATED HEREIN BY REFERENCE.

IN WITNESS WHEREOF the parties hereto have executed this agreement as a sealed instrument this . . . . day of . . . . . ., 19. . . . .

. . . . }
By . . . . }
. . . . } Signature
By . . . . } of

Further Warranties and Covenants of The Buyer. The Buyer hereby warrants and covenants that:

1. The Buyer shall not sell or offer to sell or otherwise transfer or encumber the Goods or any interest therein without the prior written consent of the Seller.

2. No financing statement covering any of the Goods or any proceeds thereof is on file in any public office. The Buyer shall immediately notify the Seller in writing of any change in address from that or those shown in this agreement and shall also upon demand furnish to the Seller such further information and shall execute and deliver to the Seller such financing statements and other papers and shall do all such acts and things as the Seller may at any time or from time to time reasonably request or as may be necessary or appropriate to establish and maintain a perfected security interest in the Goods, as security for the Obligations, subject to no prior liens or encumbrances.

3. The Buyer shall keep the Goods at all times insured against risks of loss or damage by fire (including so-called extended coverage), theft and such other casualties as the Seller may reasonably require, including collision in the case of any motor vehicle, all in such amounts, under such forms of policies, upon such terms, for such periods and written by such companies or underwriters as the Seller may approve, losses in all cases to be payable to the Seller and the Buyer as their interests may appear. All policies of insurance shall provide for at least ten days' prior written notice of cancellation to the Seller; and the Buyer shall furnish the Seller with certificates of such insurance or other evidence satisfactory to the Seller as to compliance with the provisions of this paragraph. The Seller may act as attorney for the Buyer in making, adjusting and settling claims under and cancelling such insurance and endorsing the Buyer's name on any drafts drawn by insurers of the Goods.

4. The Buyer shall keep the Goods free from any adverse lien, security interest or encumbrance and in good order and repair, shall not waste or destroy the Goods or any part thereof and shall not use the Goods in violation of any applicable statute, ordinance or policy of insurance thereon. The Seller may examine and inspect the Goods at any reasonable time or times wherever located.

5. The Buyer shall pay promptly when due all taxes and assessments upon the Goods or for their use or operation or upon this agreement. Additional Rights of Parties: The Buyer authorizes the Seller, in its discretion, to discharge taxes, liens or security interest or other encumbrances at any time levied or placed on the Goods, to place and pay for insurance thereon, to order and pay for the repair, maintenance and preservation thereof and to pay any necessary filing or recording fees. The Buyer agrees to reimburse the Seller on demand for any payment made or any expense incurred by the Seller pursuant to the foregoing authorization. Until default it shall be lawful for the collateral to remain in the possession of the Buyer, liable however, to be taken and removed by the Seller, as well before as after such default; and for that purpose the Seller may, without judicial process, enter the place where the Goods are at the time located and remove the same at pleasure.

Events of Default—Remedies: Upon the occurrence of any of the following events or conditions, namely: (i) default in the payment or performance of any of the Obligations or of any covenant or liability contained or referred to herein; (ii) any warranty, representation or statement made or furnished to the Seller by or on behalf of the Buyer in connection with this agreement proving to have been false in any material respect when made or furnished; (iii) loss, theft, substantial damage, destruction, sale or encumbrance to or of any of the Goods, or the making of any levy, seizure or attachment thereof or thereon; (iv) death, dissolution, termination of existence, insolvency, business failure, appointment of a receiver of any part of the property of, assignment for the benefit of creditors by, or the commencement of any proceeding under any bankruptcy or insolvency laws by or against the Buyer or any guarantor or surety for the Buyer;—thereupon, or at any time thereafter (such default not having previously been cured) the Seller at its option may declare all of the Obligations to be immediately due and payable and shall then have the remedies of a secured party under the Uniform Commercial Code of New Hampshire (regardless of whether the Code has been enacted in the jurisdiction where rights or remedies are asserted), including without limitation thereto, the right to take possession of the Goods, and for that purpose the Seller may, so far as the Buyer can give authority therefor, enter upon any premises on which the Goods or any part thereof may be situated and remove the same therefrom. The Seller may require the Buyer to make the Goods available to the Seller at a place to be designated by the Seller which is reasonably convenient to both parties. Unless the Goods are perishable or threaten to decline speedily in value or are of a type customarily sold on a recognized market, the Seller shall give the Buyer at least five (5) days' prior written notice of the time and place of any public sale thereof or of the time after which any private sale or any other intended disposition thereof is to be made. The Buyer agrees that the standard of commercial reasonableness in the disposition of the Goods will be met by either a public sale or a private sale. The requirements of reasonable notice shall be met if such notice is mailed, postage prepaid to the address of the Buyer shown at the beginning of this agreement at least five (5) days before the time of the sale or disposition, and in the case of a public sale shall post such notice in two (2) public places in the City or Town in which said public sale is to be held at least five (5) days before said public sale. Expenses of retaking, holding, preparing for sale, selling or the like shall include the Seller's reasonable attorneys' fee and legal expenses. General: This agreement and the security interest in the Goods created hereby shall terminate when the Obligations have been paid in full. No waiver by the Seller of any default shall be effective unless in writing nor operate as a waiver of any other default or of the same default on a future occasion. All rights of the Seller hereunder shall inure to the benefit of its successors and assigns; and all obligations of the Buyer shall bind the heirs, legal representatives, successors and assigns of the Buyer. If there be more than one Buyer, their obligations hereunder shall be joint and several.

If and to the extent that applicable law confers any rights or imposes any duties inconsistent with or in addition to any of the provisions of this agreement, the affected provisions shall be considered amended to conform thereto, but all other provisions hereof shall remain in full force and effect.

COLLATERAL SECURITY:

See category Debtor and Creditor, topic Pledges.

MORTGAGES OF PERSONAL PROPERTY:

See topic Chattel Mortgages.

MORTGAGES OF REAL PROPERTY:

Subject to priority provisions of c. 447, §12-a, recorded mortgage takes priority as of date of its recording as to advances or obligations thereafter made or incurred that do not exceed maximum amount stated in mortgage. (c. 479, §3). Mortgage or deed of trust which purports to be given in whole or in part as security for notes or bonds thereafter to be issued or other expectant future obligations, and which states nature of obligations designed to be secured by it, amount thereof presently to be issued, if any, and limitations, if any, contained in mortgage or deed of trust or in contract referred to in mortgage or deed of trust with respect to total or maximum amount thereof ultimately to be issued, shall become lawful security for same as, when and to extent that they shall actually be issued or come into existence as valid obligations of mortgagor. (c. 479, §5).

Suit upon a mortgage note may be maintained separately without loss of the mortgage security, and a suit upon the note and a suit to foreclose the mortgage may be maintained at the same time. (c. 524, §10).

Title theory of mortgage applies. (1 N.H. 169).

Formal Requisites.—No conveyance in writing of lands may be defeated, nor any estate encumbered, by an agreement, unless it is inserted in the condition of the conveyance and made part thereof, stating the sum of money to be secured, or other thing to be performed. (c. 479, §2).

A deed in substance following the form prescribed by statute, when duly executed and delivered, has the force and effect of a mortgage deed to the use of the mortgagee and his heirs, successors and assigns with the mortgage covenants and upon the statutory conditions and with the statutory power of sale as defined in the following:

(a) In a conveyance of real estate the words "mortgage covenants" shall include in their meaning the same meaning as given to "warranty covenants" in §27 of c. 477.

(b) The words "statutory conditions," except as otherwise specifically stated in the mortgage shall mean: "Provided, nevertheless, that if the mortgagor, his heirs, executors and administrators, successors and assigns shall pay unto the mortgagee or his executors, administrators, successors or assigns the principal and interest secured by the mortgage, shall perform any and each obligation provided in the note or other instrument secured by the mortgage, until such payment and performance shall pay when due and payable all taxes, charges and assessments for which the property mortgaged may become liable, shall keep the buildings on said premises insured against fire in a sum not less than the amount secured by the mortgage, or as otherwise provided therein, for the benefit of the mortgagee and his executors, administrators, successors and assigns in such form as he or they shall approve, deliver the policies therefor to him or them, and shall not commit or suffer any strip or waste of the mortgaged premises, or any breach of any covenant in said mortgage, then this mortgage deed shall be void."

(c) The words "statutory power of sale" shall be understood as giving the mortgagee and his executors, administrators, successors and assigns the right, upon any default of the performance of the statutory condition as above defined, or any other condition contained in the mortgage, to foreclose by sale under c. 479, §§25-27.

Execution and Recording.—A mortgage must show mailing address of grantee and be signed by party granting same, acknowledged by grantor before justice, notary public or commissioner, and recorded at length in registry of deeds in county in which land lies. (c. 477, §3).

Building situated on land not belonging to owners of building is deemed real estate for purposes of transfer, whether voluntary or involuntary, and is conveyed, mortgaged or leased, and is subject to attachment, other liens, foreclosure, and execution, in same manner and with same formality as real estate. (c. 477, §44, I).

Recording Fees.—$10 for first recorded page, $4 for each additional recorded page. (c. 478, §17g). On July 1, 2001 these fees increase to $30 for first page, $8 each additional page.

Timber.—Whenever standing trees have been mortgaged as real estate, or are covered by a mortgage of land on which they stand, mortgagee may indorse upon said

See note at head of Digest as to 1998 legislation covered.

See Topical Index in front part of this volume.

NH – 28

MORTGAGES OF REAL PROPERTY . . . *continued*
mortgage over his signature a consent that trees may be cut, which consent must be recorded on margin of record of said mortgage in registry of deeds. Statute provides that both parties to mortgage may then execute and attach thereto affidavit required by law to be attached to mortgages of personal property; however affidavits are no longer required under Uniform Commercial Code. Mortgage, consent and affidavit may then be recorded with proper town clerk, as mortgages of personal property are required to be recorded; and thereupon lien of mortgage is extended to cover trees after they are cut, and lumber therefrom, as fully as though same had been mortgaged as personal property after cutting. (c. 477, §§37-38).

Redemption.—Mortgaged lands may be redeemed by the mortgagor, after condition broken, by payment of all demands and performance of all things secured by the mortgage, and the payment of all damages and costs sustained and incurred by reason of the nonperformance of its condition, or by a legal tender thereof, before foreclosure. (c. 479, §18).

Discharge.—Upon performance of the condition of the mortgage and the payment of all damages and costs arising from the nonperformance thereof, or upon the legal tender of such performance and payment, the mortgage is void. (c. 479, §6). Within 60 days of satisfaction of mortgage and tendering of reasonable charges to mortgagee, mortgagee must issue and record discharge and provide written confirmation of discharge to payor of final payment. Recording fees may be charged to mortgagor if so provided in prior written disclosure. (c. 479, §7). Upon refusal of mortgagee to execute discharge, mortgagor may, by petition, have superior court decree mortgage discharged. (c. 479, §§10-12).

The mortgagor upon written request is entitled to receive from the mortgagee a just and true account of all of the latter's demands secured by the mortgage, and of all damages and costs incurred by reason of the nonperformance of the condition thereof, and of all rents and profits received by him. (c. 479, §13). Upon the mortgagee's refusal, the mortgagor may within one year thereafter obtain a decree from the superior court of the amount due, and secure a discharge of the mortgage by paying that amount into court. (c. 479, §§14-17).

Validation.—Every duly recorded satisfaction piece or instrument executed prior to Jan. 1, 1980, with intent to cancel and discharge or assign mortgage of real estate, fully identifying mortgage so intended to be canceled and discharged or assigned, but not drawn in formal accordance with statutory requirements shall be held valid discharge or assignment of such mortgage and release or assignment of mortgage interest in such real estate, except as to such satisfaction pieces or instruments, validity of which had been brought in question in any suit pending in any of courts of this state on Jan. 1, 1987. (c. 479, §9).

Ancient Undischarged Mortgages.—All mortgages which have been on record for a period of more than 50 years on or before Jan. 1, 1960, become void on Jan. 1, 1960, unless prior to that date the mortgagee or assignee thereof has recorded an affidavit signed by the mortgagor and the mortgagee or assignee stating that the mortgage is not discharged and is still in full force and effect, and upon the recording of such affidavit such mortgage retains its full legal effect and priority for an additional period of 50 years from the date of such recording. This provision does not apply to mortgages held by banks, trust companies, building and loan associations and federal savings and loan associations, whether as named mortgagee or assignee of record. (c. 479, §§28-9).

Foreclosure.—(a) Mortgages without power of sale may be foreclosed in the following modes: (1) Entry under process; i.e., entry into the mortgaged premises under process of law, and continued actual possession thereof for one year. (2) Entry and publication; i.e., peaceable entry into the mortgaged premises, and continued, actual, peaceable possession thereof for the space of one year, and by publishing in some newspaper printed in the same county, if any there be, otherwise in some newspaper printed in an adjoining county, three weeks successively, a notice stating the time at which the possession for condition broken commenced, the object of such possession, the name of the mortgagor and mortgagee, the date of the mortgage and a description of the premises, the first publication to be at least six months before the right to redeem would be foreclosed. (3) Possession and publication; i.e., by mortgagee in possession of mortgaged premises publishing in some newspaper printed in same county, if any there be, otherwise in some newspaper printed in an adjoining county, three weeks successively, a notice stating that from and after a certain day, specified in notice, not more than four weeks after last day of publication of notice, such possession will be held for condition broken and for purpose of foreclosing right of mortgagor, and of all persons claiming under him, to redeem same, and stating names of mortgagor and of mortgagee, date of mortgage and a description of premises; and by retaining actual, peaceable possession of premises for one year after day specified in notice. (c. 479, §19). Affidavit of party making an entry into real estate, under second method of foreclosure, and of witnesses thereto, as to time, manner and purposes of entry, and a copy of published notice required under second and third methods of foreclosure respectively, verified by affidavit as to time, place and mode of publication, recorded in registry of deeds for county in which lands lie, are evidence of entry, possession and publication. (c. 479, §21).

(b) If suit is brought on a mortgage containing a power of sale and a conditional judgment rendered, the demandant may, instead of a writ of possession, have a decree entered that the property be sold pursuant to such power, and thereupon the demandant must give such notices and do all such acts as are authorized and required by the power or by the court in its decree. (c. 479, §22). The party selling must, within ten days after the sale, make to the court under oath a report of the sale and of his doings, and file the same in the clerk's office, and the same may be confirmed and allowed, or set aside and a new sale ordered. Any person interested may intervene or be summoned and heard on such proceedings, and the order of the court confirming the sale is conclusive evidence as against all persons that the power was duly executed. (c. 479, §§23-24).

Instead of such suit and decree of sale, mortgagee or assignee may, upon breach of condition, give such notices and do all such acts as are authorized or required by power including giving of foreclosure deed upon completion of said foreclosure; but no sale under and by virtue of such power is valid and effectual to foreclose mortgage, unless following conditions are complied with: (1) Notice of sale must be published once a week for three successive weeks in some newspaper of state-wide circulation or of general circulation within town or county in which property is situated. In event that publication must be not less than 20 days before day of sale calculated by excluding date of publication of first notice and date of sale. (2) Copy of notice shall be served on mortgagor or sent by registered or certified mail to his last known address or to such person as may be agreed upon in mortgage at least 25 days before sale. Term "mortgagor" shall include mortgagor or then record owner of premises. Like notice to be sent to any person having lien on premises of record, provided such lien is recorded in registry of deeds for county in which property is situated at least 30 days before date of sale. Notice shall be sent not less than 21 days before sale. Such notice of sale shall be sufficient if it fully sets forth date, time and place of sale; town, county, street or highway and street number, if any, of mortgaged premises, date of mortgage, volume and page of recording of mortgage, location where original mortgage instrument may be examined and terms of sale. Waiver of notice obtained by mortgagee is effective and shall be recorded in appropriate registry of deeds. Notice of sale as served on, or mailed to mortgagor shall include following language: "You are hereby notified that you have a right to petition the superior court for the county in which the mortgaged premises are situated, with service upon the mortgagee, and upon such bond as the court may require, to enjoin the scheduled foreclosure sale." Failure to institute such petition and complete service upon foreclosing party, or his agent, conducting sale prior to sale shall thereafter bar any action or right of action of mortgagor based on validity of foreclosure. (3) Sale must be held on premises unless different place of sale is agreed upon in mortgage. (c. 479, §25). Person selling under power must, within 60 days after sale, cause foreclosure deed, copy of notice of sale, and his affidavit setting forth fully and particularly his acts in premises, to be recorded in registry of deeds in county where property is situated; and such affidavit, or duly certified copy of record thereof, is evidence on question whether power of sale was duly executed. (c. 479, §26). Mortgagee selling under power contained in mortgage may be purchaser at sale, unless mortgage contains provision to contrary. (c. 479, §27).

Where a mortgage is foreclosed under a statutory power of sale the mortgagee may give a deed to the purchaser in the short form prescribed by statute. See Forms, infra. A deed in substance in that form, when duly executed and delivered, has the force and effect of a deed in fee simple to the grantee, his heirs, successors and assigns, to his and their own use, with covenants on the part of the grantor, for himself, that at the time of the delivery of such deed, he was duly authorized to make sale of the premises; that in all of his proceedings in the sale thereof he has complied with the requirements of the statute in such case provided; and that he will warrant and defend the same to the grantee, his heirs, successors and assigns against the lawful claims of all persons claiming by, for or under him. (c. 477, §31).

In actions on mortgages the judgment must be conditional, that if the mortgagor or person having his right pays to the mortgagee or person having his right the sum the court adjudges due, within two months after judgment rendered, with interest, such judgment shall be void; otherwise that a writ of possession shall issue (c. 524, §8), or, in the case of a power of sale mortgage, that a sale be held (c. 479, §22).

Forms

The statutory short form of power of sale mortgage (c. 477, §29) is:

. . . . . ., of . . . . . ., ... County, State of . . . . . ., for consideration paid, grant to . . . . . ., of . . . . street, town (city) of . . . . . ., ... County, State of . . . . . ., with mortgage covenants, to secure the payments of . . . . . . dollars, with . . . . . . per cent interest payable semiannually and also perform all the agreements and conditions as provided in note . . . . . . of even date, the (description of land or interest therein being conveyed; incumbrances, reservations,exceptions, if any). This mortgage is upon the statutory conditions, for any breach of which the mortgagee shall have the statutory power of sale.

. . . . . ., wife (husband) of the said mortgagor, release all rights of homestead and other interests in the mortgaged premises.

(Here add acknowledgment)

The statutory form for foreclosure deed under power of sale (c. 477, §31) is:

. . . . . ., of . . . . . ., ... County, State of . . . . . ., holder of a mortgage from . . . . . . to . . . . . ., dated . . . . . ., recorded in . . . . . . Registry of Deeds, Vol. . . . . . ., Page . . . . . ., by the power conferred by said mortgage and every other power, for . . . . . . dollars paid, grant to . . . . . ., of . . . . street, town, (city) of . . . . . ., ... County, State of . . . . . ., the premises conveyed by said mortgage.

(Here add acknowledgment)

Assignment: For value received, I sell, assign, transfer and set over unto A. B. of . . . . . . all my right, title and interest to the within mortgage and to the debt secured thereby, with full power to collect and discharge the same, or to dispose of the same in my name.

Discharge: For value received, ..., holder of a mortgage from . . . . to . . . ., dated . . . ., and recorded in . . . . County Registry of Deeds at Book . . . ., Page . . . ., hereby discharges said mortgage.

Chattel Mortgages.—See topic Chattel Mortgages.

PROPERTY

ABSENTEES:

Administration will be granted on estate of person who has left home, has not been heard from directly or indirectly for one year, and is believed to be dead. No distribution for three years. (c. 553, §18). See category Estates and Trusts, topic Death.

If an absentee from the state neglects to make provision for his or her minor child, and if guardian has been appointed, said guardian may be authorized to sell such portion of said absentee's property as is necessary for comfortable support, education and maintenance of child. (c. 463, §28).

Absentee Serving in Armed Forces or as Merchant Seaman.—A conservator of the property of an absentee serving in the U. S. Armed Forces or as a merchant seaman,

See note at head of Digest as to 1998 legislation covered.

See Topical Index in front part of this volume.

NH – 29

ABSENTEES . . . *continued*

who has been reported missing, or missing in action, or interned in a neutral country, or beleaguered, besieged or captured by an enemy, may be appointed upon the probate court's own motion or upon that of any person who would have an interest in the property of the absentee if the latter were deceased, upon giving of suitable bond; said conservatorship to terminate at any time upon petition signed by the absentee or by an attorney in fact acting under an adequate power of attorney granted by absentee. In absence of appointment of guardian, spouse or if absentee has no spouse, next of kin, may apply to probate court for authority to act with respect to particular item or portion of property or matter requiring consent of absentee. (c. 464-A, §1 et seq.).

Escheat.—Unclaimed property generally presumed abandoned if unclaimed after seven years, at which time report of abandonment and delivery of property is made to State Treasurer. Within 90 days after close of calendar year in which Treasurer receives abandoned property, petition must be filed with Merrimack Superior Court for declaration of escheat. Publication of notice is required for two weeks prior to hearing. (c. 471-C).

N. H. has adopted Unclaimed and Abandoned Property Act which is similar to Uniform Disposition of Unclaimed Property Act. (c. 471-C).

See categories Business Regulation and Commerce, topic Banks and Banking, subhead Unclaimed Deposits; Estates and Trusts, topics Descent and Distribution, subhead Escheat, and Wills, subhead Unclaimed Legacies.

ADVERSE POSSESSION:

No statutory provisions with respect to character of possession necessary to acquire title adversely.

No person may acquire, by adverse possession: Any right to any land, as against the state or its grantees (c. 539, §6); any right to any part of a highway, as against the public (c. 249, §30); any right to impede or in any way injure navigation, the passage of fish or any other public easement in any waters of the state (c. 477, §33); any part of a townhouse, school-house, church lot or any public ground (c. 477, §34).

No title to real estate or any interest therein shall be acquired by or against a railroad by adverse possession, however exclusive or long continued. (c. 127, §45).

Duration of Possession.—Twenty years possession is necessary. (c. 508, §2).

Disabilities.—If the person first entitled to bring an action against an adverse possessor is an infant, or an insane person, at the time the right accrues, the action may be brought within five years after such disability is removed. (c. 508, §3).

Improvements.—Where the defendant in an action for the recovery of real property, and those under whom he claims, have been in actual peaceable possession, under a supposed legal title, for more than six years before commencement of the action, and have made improvements increasing the value of the property, he is entitled to have a judgment for plaintiff conditioned upon payment of such increased value within one year. (c. 524, §§2-4).

CONVEYANCES:

See topic Deeds.

CURTESY:

Right of curtesy has been abolished. (c. 560, §3).

DEEDS:

Execution.—Deeds must be signed by grantor, and acknowledged and show mailing address of grantee. (c. 477, §3). See also category Documents and Records, topics Acknowledgments, Seals. Deed which is not acknowledged or not recorded is valid only as against grantor and his heirs. (c. 477, §7). Deed must show names of all municipalities in which property is located in first line of description and must have names of all persons signing, printed or typed beneath their signatures. (c. 478, §4-a).

If homestead is to be released, husband or wife should join in conveyance. (c. 480, §§3-a, 5-a; c. 460, §4; c. 462, §21). Acknowledgment is required if homestead right is to be barred. (c. 480, §§3-a, 5-a). See also topic Real Property; categories Debtor and Creditor, topic Homesteads, subhead Alienation or Encumbrance; Family, topic Husband and Wife, subhead Conveyance or Encumbrance of Property.

Notification.—Prior to executing contract for conveyance of building, seller shall disclose possibility of radon gas; lead paint; private water supply condition; sewage disposal condition; and, in case of 1-4 family dwelling, description of insulation. (c. 477, §4-a).

Conveyance by Attorney.—A conveyance of land can be made by an attorney in fact (c. 477, §1), if the power of attorney is signed and acknowledged (c. 477, §9).

Recording.—All deeds must be and powers of attorney may be (c. 477, §§1, 9) recorded in the registry of deeds in the county in which the land lies (c. 477, §§1, 3, 7). See also category Documents and Records, topic Records.

Operation and Effect.—Statutory forms of deeds are authorized, but other forms appropriate for the conveyance of real estate may be used. (c. 477, §23). The word "grant" in a conveyance of real estate is, without more, a sufficient word of conveyance in either a warranty or a quitclaim deed. In a conveyance or reservation of real estate the term "heirs", "assigns" or other technical words of inheritance or succession are not necessary to convey or reserve an estate in fee. A deed or reservation of real estate will be construed to convey or reserve an interest in fee simple unless a different intention clearly appears in the instrument. (c. 477, §24). Statute of uses not to affect trusts: conveyance or devise of real estate vests legal title in grantee or devisee, as trustee. (c. 477, §25). In a conveyance of real estate or any interest therein, all rights, easements, privileges and appurtenances belonging to the granted estate or interest shall be deemed to be included in the conveyance, unless the contrary is stated in the deed, and it is unnecessary in order for their inclusion to enumerate or mention them either generally or specifically. (c. 477, §26).

A deed in substance in the short form of warranty deed prescribed by the statute has the force and effect of a deed in fee simple to the grantee, heirs, successors and assigns,

to his and their own use, with covenant on the part of the grantor, for himself, his heirs, executors and administrators, that, at the time of the delivery of such deed, he was lawfully seized in fee simple of the granted premises, that the said premises were free from all incumbrances, except as stated, that he had good right to sell and convey the same to the grantee, his heirs, successors and assigns, and that he will, and his heirs, executors and administrators shall, warrant and defend the same to the grantee and his heirs, successors and assigns, against the lawful claims and demands of all persons. (c. 477, §27).

A deed in substance in the short form of quitclaim deed prescribed by the statute has the force and effect of a deed in fee simple to the grantee, heirs, successors and assigns, to his and their own use, with covenants on the part of the grantor, for himself, his heirs, executors and administrators, with the grantee, his heirs, successors and assigns, that at the time of the delivery of such deed the premises were free from all incumbrances made by the grantor, except as stated, and that he will, and his heirs, executors and administrators shall, warrant and defend the same to the grantee and his heirs, successors and assigns forever against the lawful claims and demands of all persons claiming by, through or under the grantor, but against none other. (c. 477, §28).

A deed in substance in the short form of fiduciary deed prescribed by the statute has the force and effect of a deed in fee simple to the grantee, his heirs, successors and assigns, to his and their own use, with covenants on the part of the grantor, for himself, that, at the time of the delivery of such deed, he was duly authorized to make the sale of the premises; that in all of his proceedings in the sale thereof, he has complied with the requirements of the statute in such case provided; and that he will warrant and defend the same to the grantee, his heirs, successors and assigns, against the lawful claims of all persons claiming by, from or under him in the capacity aforesaid. (c. 477, §30).

Notice of lease consisting of an instrument in writing executed, witnessed, and acknowledged by all persons who are parties to lease may be recorded in lieu of lease provided that notice contains following information: (1) Names and addresses of each party to lease; (2) date of execution of lease; (3) description of demised premises as it appears in lease; (4) term of such lease; (5) date of commencement of such term and all rights of extension or renewal. (c. 477, §§3, 7-a).

Validation of Ancient Documents.—When any instrument in writing has been recorded in office of register of deeds for a period of ten years, and there is a defect in such instrument because it omitted to state any consideration therefor, or because it was not sealed by grantors or any of them, or because it was not witnessed or because it was not validly acknowledged; it then becomes valid, and imparts to subsequent purchasers, incumbrancers and all other persons whomsoever, notice of such instrument so far as and to same extent that same then is recorded, copied or noted in such books of record notwithstanding such defect. Rights acquired by grantees, assignees or incumbrancers subsequent to filing of such instrument for record and prior to expiration of ten years from filing of such instrument for record are not affected by foregoing provision. (c. 477, §16).

Recording Fees.—$10 for first recorded page plus $4 for each additional recorded page. If more than one grantor or grantee 50¢ for each additional grantor or grantee. (c. 478, §17g). On July 1, 2001 these fees increase to $30 for first page, $8 each additional page.

Taxes.—Tax is imposed on each of purchaser and seller upon sale or transfer of real estate other than by devise at rate of 50¢ per $100 or fractional part thereof except where consideration is less than $4,000. Minimum tax is $21. Tax does not apply to transfer by governmental authority, mortgage, discharge of mortgage, corrective deed or tax collector's deed. (c. 78-B, §1).

Forms

The statutory short form of warranty deed (c. 477, §27) is:

. . . . . ., of . . . . . ., ... County, State of . . . . . ., for consideration paid, grant to . . . . . ., of . . . . street, town(city) of . . . . . ., ... County, State of . . . . . ., with warranty covenants, the (description of land or interest being conveyed; incumbrances, exceptions, reservations, if any).

. . . . . ., wife (husband) of said grantor, release to said grantee all rights of homestead and other interests therein.

(Here add acknowledgment)

The statutory short form of quitclaim deed (c. 477, §28) is:

. . . . . ., of . . . . . ., ... County, State of . . . . . ., for consideration paid, grant to . . . . . ., of . . . . street, town(city) of . . . . . ., ... County, State of . . . . . ., with quitclaim covenants, the (description of land or interest therein being conveyed; incumbrances, exceptions, reservations, if any).

. . . . . ., wife (husband) of said grantor, release to said grantee all rights of homestead and other interests therein.

(Here add acknowledgment)

The statutory short form of fiduciary deed (c. 477, §30) is:

. . . . . ., of . . . . . ., ... County, State of . . . . . ., executor under the will (administrator of the estate) (trustee under the will) (guardian) (conservator) (receiver of the estate) (commissioner) of . . . . . ., of . . . . . ., by the power conferred by . . . . . . and every other power, for . . . . . . dollars paid, grant to . . . . of . . . . street, town(city) of . . . . . ., ... County, State of . . . . . ., the (insert description of land or interest therein being conveyed; incumbrances, reservations, exceptions).

(Here add acknowledgment)

Statutory short form of Manufactured Housing Warranty Deed (c. 477, §44) is:

. . . ., of . . . . County, State of . . . ., for consideration paid, grant to . . . . of . . . . .Street, Town (City) of . . . ., ...County, State of . . . ., with warranty covenants, the . . . . (Description of manufactured housing being conveyed: name of manufacturer, model and serial number and incumbrances, exceptions, reservations, if any) which manufactured housing is situated, or is to be

DEEDS . . . *continued*

situated, at . . . . (state name or park, if any, and street address), Town (City) of . . . . ,. . . . . County, State of New Hampshire. The tract or parcel of land upon which the manufactured housing is situated, or is to be situated, is owned by . . . . by deed dated . . . . and recorded at Book . . . . , Page . . . . , in the . . . . County Registry of Deeds. . . . . (wife) (husband) of said grantor, release to said grantee all rights and other interests therein.

(Here add acknowledgment)

—

. . . ., owner of the tract or parcel of land upon which the aforesaid manufactured housing is situated, or is to be situated, hereby consents to the conveyance of the manufactured housing.

(Here add acknowledgment)

—

DEEDS OF TRUST:

See category Mortgages, topic Mortgages of Real Property.

DOWER:

Right of dower has been abolished. (c. 560, §3).

ESCHEAT:

See topic Absentees, subhead Escheat; categories Business Regulation and Commerce, topic Banks and Banking, subhead Unclaimed Deposits; Estates and Trusts, topics Descent and Distribution, subhead Escheat, and Wills, subhead Unclaimed Legacies.

LANDLORD AND TENANT:

General rights and liabilities of parties are governed by common law. c. 540-A sets forth illegal and unfair practices by landlords and tenants. Actions against tenants are governed by c. 540.

Kinds of Tenancy.—Every tenancy or occupancy is deemed to be at will, and the rent payable upon demand, unless a different contract is shown. (c. 540, §1).

Leases.—No lease for more than seven years is valid against any person except the grantor and his heirs, unless executed, attested, acknowledged and recorded like a deed. (c. 477, §7). See topic Deeds. Lessor must deliver copy of lease to lessee within 30 days after execution by all parties. (c. 477, §7-b).

Security Deposits.—Regulated by c. 540-A, §§5-8.

Agreements Affecting Interest of Landlord.—No specific statutory provision but see c. 382-A, §9-316, §9-401 for filing requirements in general.

Levy on Landlord's Interest.—If a judgment debtor is seized of a rent or of the income of real estate, a levy may be made thereon, and the appraisers may set off the same for such term as they judge sufficient to pay the judgment, interest and costs; and the sheriff must cause the tenant to attorn and become tenant to the creditor, and, upon his refusal, turn him out of possession, and deliver seizin to the creditor to hold for the term of the setoff. (c. 529, §11).

Improper Use of Premises.—If a tenant uses the premises or any part thereof for lewdness, assignation, or prostitution or for the illegal manufacture, sale or keeping for sale of intoxicating liquor, such use annuls and makes void the lease or other title under which he holds and, without any act of the owner, causes the right of possession to revert to him, and he may, without process of law, make immediate entry upon the premises. (c. 544, §§1, 41).

Landlord's Remedies to Recover Possession.—Any tenancy may be terminated by lessor or owner by giving to tenant or occupant notice to quit. (c. 540, §2). Notice period varies with type of tenancy. If nonresidential tenant neglects or refuses to pay rent due and in arrears, upon demand, seven days notice is sufficient; if rent payable more frequently than once in three months, whether rent due or not, notice equal to rent period is sufficient, and three months notice is sufficient in all cases. Residential tenancy may not be terminated except upon giving notice in writing to tenant to quit within period of not less than 30 days; provided that if reasons for termination are nonpayment of rent, substantial damage to premises or behavior adversely affecting health or safety of other tenants, landlord or his representatives, such tenancy may be terminated upon seven days notice (c. 540, §3). Demand is sufficient if made on tenant or occupant at any time after rent becomes due and prior to service of notice to quit. (c. 540, §4). If notice to quit is based on nonpayment of rent, notice shall inform tenant of his right, if any, to avoid eviction by payment of arrearages and $15 in liquidated damages. (c. 540, §3).

Where to constitute forfeiture for violation of written lease, demand for rent is required such demand may be made when rent is due or in arrears, but lessor must not demand greater sum than whole rent in arrears when demand is made. (c. 540, §§7, 8). No tenancy shall be terminated for nonpayment of rent, utility charges or any other lawful charge if tenant, prior to expiration of notice period, tenders all arrearages plus $15 as liquidated damages; provided that tenant may not defeat eviction for nonpayment by use of this section more than three times in one calendar year. (c. 540, §9).

No tenancy in mobile home park may be terminated without giving notice as follows: 30 days for nonpayment; 60 days for violation of applicable law, damage, repeated conduct disturbing peace or violation of park ordinance; 18 months for condemnation or change of use of park. (c. 205-A, §§3, 4). No manufactured housing park owner shall make final unconditional acceptance of any offer for sale of such park without first giving 60 days' notice to each tenant of intent to sell and of terms of acceptable offer. Owner shall consider any offer received from tenants or their association within notice period and shall negotiate with them in good faith. (c. 205-A, §21).

In all instances, a demand for rent and notice to quit may be served by any person by a true and attested copy thereof, return of such service to be shown by true and attested copy of notice accompanied by affidavit of service, sworn or unsworn. Notice of

demand for rent is sufficient if served any time after rent becomes due and before service of notice to quit. (c. 540, §§5, 7).

After a proper notice to quit has been served, owner or lessor may serve on tenant a writ of summons, returnable before a municipal court, setting forth in substance that plaintiff is entitled to possession of demanded premises, and that defendant is in possession thereof without right, after notice in writing to quit same, which writ must be served seven days before return day thereof. (c. 540, §§12-13).

Effective Jan. 1, 1999, landlord may make claim for unpaid rent in writ of summons. If this claim is made, tenant may put forth any defense, claim, or counterclaim which offsets or reduces amount owed to landlord. If court finds landlord is entitled to possession on grounds of nonpayment of rent, landlord will be awarded money judgment for rent. If amount owed by landlord to tenant exceeds or equals amount of rent owed to landlord, judgment for possession shall be granted to tenant, plus any additional amount owed to tenant. Money judgement is limited to $1,500, and shall not preclude either party from making subsequent claims in appropriate court to recover amount in excess of $1,500 judgment. (c. 540, §13).

During pendency of possessory action based on nonpayment of rent, landlord may accept payment of rental arrearage without creating new tenancy, provided landlord informs tenant in writing of landlord's intention to proceed with eviction in spite of acceptance of payment. (c. 540, §13, VII).

Writ shall be accompanied by notice from district court, including all elements set forth in c. 540, §13, II. If defendant makes default, or if on trial it is considered by court that plaintiff has sustained his complaint, judgment must be rendered that plaintiff recover possession of demanded premises and costs, and a writ of possession shall issue. (c. 540, §14). Judgment may be enforced, at sole discretion of plaintiff, either by directing sheriff to serve writ of possession or by seeking judicial relief against defendant for civil contempt. (c. 540, §14). Writ of possession shall authorize sheriff to remove defendant from premises. (c. 540, §14). If tenant proves retaliation, however, damages of up to three months' rent may be awarded to tenant. (c. 540, §14). Records of complaints made by other tenants may be used by landlord in possessory action based on allegations of behavior so long as records are authenticated as genuine and prepared at or near time of complaint and court deems them admissible. (c. 540, §16-a). If defendant pleads plea which may bring in question title to demanded premises he must forthwith recognize plaintiff, with sufficient sureties, in such sum as court shall order, to enter and prosecute action at next return day of superior court for county, and to pay all rent then due or which shall become due pending action, and damages and costs which may be awarded against him. After filing of such plea and entry of such recognizance no further proceedings may be had before municipal court, but action may be entered and prosecuted in superior court in same manner as if it were originally begun there. (c. 540, §§17-18). Party aggrieved by judgment of municipal court upon issue joined in such case may, within seven days after rendition of judgment, appeal therefrom to Supreme Court. (c. 540, §20).

If tenant appeals in case of nonpayment of rent, tenant must pay weekly rent into district court. (c. 540, §§14, 20, 25).

Nothing in the foregoing may be construed to prevent a landlord from pursuing his legal remedy at common law. (c. 540, §26).

Whenever the estate occupied by a tenant at will or sufferance is conveyed by a landlord his grantee has the rights and remedies which the grantor would have had if the estate had not been conveyed. (c. 540, §27). Any lease provision by which tenant waives any rights granted by c. 540 shall be null and void. (c. 540, §28). Any federal law relative to federally subsidized rental units shall supersede contrary or inconsistent provisions of N.H. law. (c. 540, §29).

Guest of public lodging facility may be ejected if he remains in rental unit beyond registered departure date. Facility owner may use law enforcement personnel to effect removal. (c. 353, §3-c).

Termination by Lessee.—A lessee may terminate his lease by notice in writing, in the same manner as the lessor, and the notice has the same effect for all purposes as a notice by the lessor to the lessee. (c. 540, §11).

Conversion of Rental Units.—Governed by c. 356-C.

LEASES:

See topic Landlord and Tenant.

PERPETUITIES:

Trust created by employer as part of a stock bonus, pension, disability, death benefit or profit-sharing plan not invalid as violating rule against perpetuities. (c. 275, §48-a).

PERSONAL PROPERTY:

Tenancy by entirety in personal property not recognized.

POWERS OF ATTORNEY:

Revocation.—Durable power of attorney authorized. (c. 506, §6).

REAL PROPERTY:

All common law estates are recognized except those in coparcenary (20 N. H. 150) and those by entirety (56 N. H. 105). Deed which names grantees to be tenants by entirety creates joint tenancy. (c. 477, §18). Statutory provision is made for homestead right of $30,000. (c. 480, §1).

Conveyances and devises of real estate to two or more persons are construed to create an estate in common and not in joint tenancy unless the contrary is expressly provided. A conveyance to a husband and wife as tenants by the entirety creates a joint tenancy. (c. 477, §18). Joint heirs are deemed tenants in common. (c. 477, §19).

Rule in Shelley's Case.—Abolished. (c. 551, §8).

Foreign Conveyances or Encumbrances.—Must conform to New Hampshire law. (c. 477, §§1, 7).

Condominiums are permitted. (c. 356-B).

—

See note at head of Digest as to 1998 legislation covered.

See Topical Index in front part of this volume.

REAL PROPERTY . . . *continued*

See also topics Curtesy, Deeds, Dower, Landlord and Tenant; categories Business Regulation and Commerce, topic Consumer Protection; Civil Actions and Procedure, topic Partition; Debtor and Creditor, topic Homesteads; Documents and Records, topic Records; Family, topic Husband and Wife; Mortgages, topic Mortgages of Real Property.

TRUST DEEDS:

See category Mortgages, topic Mortgages of Real Property.

TAXATION

ADMINISTRATION:

Actions Against Nonresidents.—The officers responsible for the collection of any tax in any state or commonwealth of the United States or political subdivision thereof, have the right to bring an action or suit in the courts of this state to recover any unpaid tax against a person within this jurisdiction, when the same or a similar right is accorded to the proper officer of this state or any of its political subdivisions by such state or commonwealth either by law or comity. (c. 80, §51).

Discount.—Any town may direct a discount to be made to persons paying taxes (except resident taxes) within such periods as town may limit. (c. 80, §52). If authorized by appropriate legislative body, taxes and fees may be paid by credit card provided service charge for acceptance of card is added to amount due. (c. 80, §52-c).

Abatement.—Selectmen may for good cause shown abate any tax, including any portion of interest accrued on such tax, assessed by them or by their predecessors. Application for abatement must be in writing on proper form within two months after notice of tax. Upon receipt of application, selectmen must review application and grant or deny it within six months after notice of such tax and failure to do so shall constitute denial. (c. 76, §16). If selectmen neglect or refuse to abate, any person aggrieved, having complied with statutory requirements as to filing of inventories upon payment of application fee of $65 may, within eight months, after notice of such tax, and not afterwards, apply in writing to board of tax and land appeals, for abatement. (c. 76, §16-a). Any person so aggrieved, having complied with statutory requirements as to filing of inventories, may, within eight months after notice of tax, or, having first applied to board, within three months after notice in writing of decision of board of tax and land appeals, apply by petition to superior court in county, which must make such order thereon as justice requires. (c. 76, §17). Whenever board of tax and land appeals or superior court grants abatement, selectmen or assessors shall thereafter use correct assessment value. (c. 76, §17-c).

Contractors' Taxes.—Whenever a contractor enters into a contract or agreement with the state or any political subdivision thereof and such contractor brings into this state any property which is or may be subject to being taxed in this state, it shall be a term or condition of such contract that the state or political subdivision shall withhold or retain from the contract price provided for in said contract such sum of sums as will secure the payment of the taxes levied and assessed upon such property until such taxes are paid by such contractor, or are authorized paid by him from the sums so withheld, provided the collector of taxes or other person responsible for the collection of the taxes notifies the treasurer of the state or political subdivision that such taxes have been assessed but are unpaid. If the taxes so assessed are not paid by Dec. 1 of the year of assessment the treasurer, upon notice from the collector of taxes, shall pay over the same to the collector and take his receipt therefor. (c. 80, §7).

Subcontractors' Taxes.—Whenever a person, firm or corporation enters into a contract or agreement with state or any political subdivision thereof and such contractor employs a subcontractor to perform any of work contemplated by such contract or agreement, it must be a stated term or condition of such contract, that said contractor will be liable for payment of any taxes assessed in name of and upon property of subcontractor, used by said subcontractor in performance of said subcontract if assessed while said contract is being performed, to extent of any sum or sums that may be due from contractor to subcontractor at time of or after contractor has been notified by collector of taxes in writing that payment of said taxes has been demanded of said subcontractor but said subcontractor has failed, neglected or refused to pay same. Said contractor may retain from contract price, amount for which he is liable hereunder. Amount of taxes for which said contractor may be liable hereunder may be withheld or retained from contract price under provisions for Contractors' Taxes above. (c. 80, §7-a).

User's Taxes.—Whenever a person, firm or corporation enters into a contract or agreement with state or any political subdivision thereof and such contractor has in his possession and uses any taxable property owned by another upon job to be performed under contract or agreement, it must be a stated term or condition of such contract that contractor having such property in his possession will be liable for amount of taxes assessed against such property in name of owner of such property while same is in possession of such contract to extent of amount of any sum or sums of money that may be due from said contractor to owner of such property for rental or hire thereof at time of or after collector of taxes has notified said contractor in writing that he has made demand upon owner of such property for payment of taxes assessed upon said property but that owner of such property has failed, neglected or refused to pay said taxes. Said contractor may retain from sums to be paid for use of such property amount for which he is liable hereunder. Amount of taxes for which said contractor may be liable hereunder may be withheld or retained from contract price under provisions for Contractors' Taxes above. (c. 80, §7-b).

Exemption from Attachment.—Sums so withheld by treasurer of state or any political subdivision thereof upon notice from collector of taxes under provisions for Contractors', Subcontractors' and Users' Taxes shall be exempt from attachment, garnishment and trustee process by any person except in an action or suit brought by collector of taxes to collect such taxes. (c. 80, §7-c).

Tax liens continue until one year from Oct. 1 following assessment. All such liens shall have priority over all other liens. (c. 80, §19).

Tax Sales—Personal Property.—Collector may distrain the goods, chattels, personal estate, property interest, right or credit of any person or corporation neglecting to pay taxes. (c. 80, §8). Collector must keep personal property distrained for four days at cost of owner. If tax, costs and charges are not then paid, he must post, in two or more public places in town where sale is to be, 24 hours before time of sale, notice of place, day and hour of sale, with particular description of property to be sold; and at time and place appointed, which must be in town where distress is made, between 10 A. M. and 6 P. M. and within 48 hours after expiration of said four days, he must sell same at auction. (c. 80, §10). Owner is entitled to account in writing. (c. 80, §11).

Tax Sales—Real Property.—That portion of common and undivided interest in real estate of any delinquent taxpayer necessary to pay delinquent taxes plus interest and costs may be sold by collector if taxes are not paid on or before Dec. 1 next after their assessment. (c. 80, §§20, 24). Collector must give notice of every sale by posting advertisements thereof in two or more public places in town at least 25 days before sale, exclusive of day of posting and day of sale, in which shall be stated name of owner or of person to whom same was taxed, description of property as recorded by selectmen, amount of tax, interest due thereon, and costs and fees incident to advertising and posting, and place, day and hour of sale. He must also, before posting, but not more than 30 days before posting, send like notice by registered mail to last known post-office address of owner or person against whom tax was assessed (c. 80, §21) and within 15 days thereafter deliver or forward by registered mail to register of deeds for county in which real estate is situated, copy of notice, with affidavit that it was so posted and mailed (c. 80, §22). Sale must be at auction, in some public place in town or place where land is situated, between 10 A. M. and 6 P. M., and must be of so much of property as will pay taxes and incidental charges. Sale may be adjourned from day to day, not exceeding three days, by proclamation made at place of sale within hours aforesaid. (c. 80, §24). When such sale is of less than whole estate, collector shall sell only undivided interest in property and no portion thereof shall be sold in severalty by metes and bounds. (c. 80, §24). Any town or county or state may purchase at such sale. (c. 80, §26). Within 30 days after sale, tax collector must deliver or forward by registered mail to register of deeds for county in which real estate is situated detailed statement of particulars of sale. (c. 80, §27).

Notice of Sale to Mortgagees.—Within 45 days from date of sale, purchaser must notify all persons holding mortgages upon such property as recorded in office of registry of deeds. Such notice must give date of tax sale, name of delinquent taxpayer, total amount for which real estate was sold, and amount of costs for notifying mortgagee. Tax collector shall send similar notice to any mortgagee within 30 days of time of payment of any subsequent tax thereon by purchaser. Copy of notice must be given to each mortgagee in hand, left at his usual place of abode or sent by registered mail to his last known address. Failure to give this notice voids sale of encumbered real estate as against mortgagee not receiving notice. (c. 80, §§28, 29).

Notice to Commissioner of Health and Human Services is required of all tax sales of real estate upon which there is lien for old age assistance recorded in registry of deeds. (c. 80, §31).

Release of Share of Part Owner.—If the share of a part owner of taxable real estate has been definitely determined and recorded in the annual inventory and in warrant book as committed to collector, part owner may pay taxes on his share or interest in property and only residue may be sold. (c. 80, §35).

Tax Deed.—If land is not redeemed (see subhead Redemption, infra) within two years after sale, tax collector must execute a deed to the purchaser except where purchaser is municipality which has notified tax collector it will not accept deed due to potential environmental liability to owner of property. (c. 80, §38). At least 30 days prior to executing deed, tax collector must notify current owner of impending deeding. (c. 80, §38-a). During two-year period, municipality cannot convey to any person tax lien upon real estate acquired by it at tax collector's sale. (c. 80, §42). Authority to transfer or to sell shall continue for one year from date of town meeting or action by city council or, if warrant article or vote specifically provides, may continue indefinitely. (c. 80, §42). Tax collector's deed is incontestable after ten years from date of record. (c. 80, §39).

Redemption.—Any person with legal interest in land sold may redeem same by paying or tendering to collector, or in his absence at his usual place of abode, at any time before deed is given by collector (see subhead Tax Sales—Real Property, catchline Tax Deed, supra), amount for which land was sold and cost of notifying mortgagees, if any, with 18% interest on whole amount from time of sale, together with redemption costs. (c. 80, §32). Partial payments in sum of $5 or multiples thereof may be made. (c. 80, §33-a).

A part owner of an interest in land separately assessed to him may redeem his interest in the land by paying his assessed portion of the taxes, accrued interests and costs incident to advertisement and sale of the real estate. (c. 80, §35).

Optional Tax Lien Procedure.—Municipality may adopt optional tax lien procedure. (c. 80, §§59-87). Such tax lien shall have priority over all other liens. (c. 80, §59).

Collection.—Commissioner of Revenue Administration has general supervision over all tax collectors in performance of their duties. (c. 41, §39). Any town which has a town manager may vote to transfer the office of collector of taxes to that of town manager. (c. 37, §16).

Penalties.—

General Property Taxes.—Interest at 12% per annum is charged upon all taxes except resident taxes not paid on or before Dec. 1 after their assessment or 30 days from mailing of tax bill, whichever is later. (c. 76, §13).

Resident Tax.—Penalty of $1 if tax not paid by Dec. 1 following assessment. (c. 76, §13[a]).

Upon neglect or refusal to pay taxes assessed, tax collector may distrain goods or chattels, personal estate, property interest, right, or credit of taxpayer. (c. 80, §8).

Legacy and Succession Tax (Inheritance Tax).—Interest at rate of 1¼% per month charged from time tax became payable. (c. 86, §56).

Bank Tax.—Repealed, effective July 1, 1993.

See note at head of Digest as to 1998 legislation covered.

See Topical Index in front part of this volume.

ADMINISTRATION . . . *continued*

Business Profits Tax.—Repealed.

Interest and Dividends (Tax on Intangibles).—Filing of fraudulent return or failing to file return within 20 days after receiving notice of such delinquency from Commissioner of Revenue Administration, subjects person to prosecution for misdemeanor if natural person or for felony if any other person. (c. 77, §30).

Gasoline Tax.—See c. 260, §§32 et seq.

Refined Petroleum Products Tax.—Late payment charge of 10% of defaulted payment plus 1% per month or fraction thereof until paid. (c. 78-C, §4).

Timber Tax.—Unpaid tax bears interest at 18% from due date.

BUSINESS TAXES:

Business Profits Tax.—Tax at rate of 8% (reduced to 7.5% for fiscal year 1994 and 7% for fiscal year 1995) is imposed upon taxable business profits of every business organization. (c. 77-A, §2).

Business organizations include any enterprise which is organized for gain or profit and which carries on business activities within state, except such enterprises as are expressly made exempt from income taxation under U.S. Internal Revenue Code (1954) and except such enterprises state taxation of which is limited by U.S. Code c. 12, §548, as am'd.

Taxable business profits mean gross business profits adjusted by additions and deductions provided under law (c. 77-A, §4) and then adjusted by appropriate method of apportionment (c. 77-A, §3).

Gross business profits are defined in relation to type of business enterprise. (c. 77-A, §1, III).

Taxable period is same as that used by taxpayer for U.S. income tax purposes. (c. 77-A, §1, V).

Allocations.—Certain business organizations which derive gross business profits from business activity both within and without state are permitted to apportion their gross business profits, according to formula set forth in detail in statute. (c. 77-A, §3).

Returns must be filed by every business organization having gross business income in excess of $50,000 on or before 15th day of third month following expiration of taxpayer's taxable period in case of corporations and fourth month of noncorporate taxpayers. At same time, declaration of estimated taxable business profits and tax for its subsequent taxable period must be filed. (c. 77-A, §6).

Payments.—25% of estimated business profits tax is due and payable on 15th day of fourth month of subsequent taxable year; 25% is due on 15th day of sixth month; 25% is due on 15th day of ninth month; 25% is due on 15th day of 12th month. (c. 77-A, §7).

If taxpayer is exempted from filing declaration, tax, if any, is due and payable at time return is filed.

Business Enterprise Tax.—Tax rate of 1/4 of 1% is imposed upon taxable enterprise value tax base of every business enterprise. (c. 77-E, §2).

Business enterprise means any profit or nonprofit enterprise or organization engaged in or carrying on any business activity within state, except such enterprises as are exempt from income taxation under §501(c)(3) of the U.S. Internal Revenue Code, to extent such enterprise does not engage in any business activity constituting unrelated business activity as defined in §513 of U.S. Internal Revenue Code. (c. 77-E, §1,III).

Gross business receipts means all income for federal income tax purposes from whatever source derived in conduct of business activity. (c. 77-E, §1,IX).

Taxable enterprise value tax base means sum of all compensation paid or accrued, interest paid or accrued, and dividends paid by business enterprise adjusted by appropriate method of apportionment. (c. 77-E, §§4, I,XV).

Taxable period means calendar or fiscal year, or fractional part of year, which business enterprise uses for federal income tax purposes, or if not required to file federal income tax return, calendar or fiscal year adopted for financial purposes. (c. 77-E, §1,XVI).

Apportionment.—Certain business enterprises which engage in or carry on business activities which are taxable both within and without this state are permitted to apportion their enterprise value tax according to formula set forth in detail in statute.(c. 77-E, §4).

Returns.—Every business enterprise having gross business receipts in excess of $100,000 during taxable period or enterprise tax value base of which is greater than $50,000 shall, on or before 15th day of third month in case of corporations and on or before 15th day of fourth month in case of all other business enterprises following expiration of taxable period, file return with commissioner together with declaration of estimated business enterprise tax for subsequent taxable period unless less than $200. (c. 77-E, §5).

Payment is due with return. (c. 77-E, §6).

Credit Against Business Profits Tax.—Business enterprise liable for taxes under both this statute and Business Profits Tax statute is entitled to credit against business profits tax as set forth in statute. (cc. 77-E, §13; 77-A, §5,X).

Insurance Company Taxes.—See category Insurance, topic Insurance Companies.

ESTATE TAX:

In addition to the inheritance tax, an estate tax is imposed upon the transfer of all estates which are subject to an estate tax under the provisions of the United States Internal Revenue Code and amendments thereto where the decedent at time of his death was domiciled in this state. The amount of the New Hampshire estate tax shall be equal to the extent, if any, of the excess of the credit allowable under said United States internal revenue code over the aggregate amount of all estate, inheritance, transfer, legacy and succession taxes paid to any state or territory or the District of Columbia in respect to any property in the estate of said decedent, provided that such estate tax hereby imposed shall in no case exceed the extent to which its payment will effect a saving or diminution in the amount of the United States estate tax payable by or out of the estate of the decedent had this chapter not been enacted. Furthermore, an estate tax is imposed upon transfer of real property and tangible personal property in this state of every person who at time of his death was a resident of U.S. but not domiciled in this state, and upon transfer of all property, real and personal, within this state, of every person who at time of his death was not a resident of U.S., amount of which shall be a sum equal to such proportion of amount by which credit allowable under applicable U.S. revenue act for estate, transfer, legacy, succession and inheritance taxes actually paid to the several states exceeds amount actually paid for such taxes exclusive of estate taxes based on difference between such credit and other estate, transfer, legacy, succession and inheritance taxes, as value of property in this state bears to value of entire estate, subject to an estate tax under provisions of U.S. Internal Revenue Code. Amount of this tax will automatically be changed with any change in federal estate tax law with respect to credit allowed for inheritance, etc., taxes paid to states and territories. (c. 87, §1).

Apportionment.—Uniform Estate Tax Apportionment Act is in effect. (c. 88-A).

Valuation Date.—Date of death or alternate federal date, whichever is used by estate.

Interstate Co-operation.—The provision for settling taxes in case of disputes as to domicile (see topic Inheritance Tax, subhead Disputes as to Domicile) applies to estate taxes. (c. 86, §71; c. 87, §12).

GASOLINE AND PETROLEUM PRODUCTS TAXES:

Gasoline Tax.—Imposed by c. 260, §32.

Refined Petroleum Products Tax.—1/10 of 1% of fair market value per barrel at refinery site. (c. 78-C).

GIFT TAX:

None; but inheritance tax applies to gifts in contemplation of death or to take effect at or after death of donor.

INCOME TAX:

None. Commuters Income Tax (c. 77B) declared unconstitutional (95 S.Ct. 1191).

INHERITANCE TAX:

Inheritance tax is imposed on all property within jurisdiction of state, real or personal, or any interest therein belonging to domiciliaries of state and on all real estate within state or any interest therein belonging to nonresident, which passes by will, intestate succession, or deed, grant, bargain, sale or gift made in contemplation of death or to take effect at or after death of grantor or donor. (c. 86, §6). The right of the survivor of jointly held property is deemed a taxable transfer in the same manner as though the whole property to which such transfer relates was owned by the joint owners as tenants in common and had been devised or bequeathed to the survivor, unless only property is joint account with less than $10,000 subject to proviso that sums expended by survivor for funeral expenses, expenses of last sickness and medical expenses shall be deducted therefrom. (c. 86, §8).

Exemptions.—Property passing to or for use of husband, wife, or decedent's lineal ascendants and lineal descendants, and spouses of said ascendants and descendants, including adopted children or stepchildren in decedent's line of succession or for care of cemetery lots, or to city or town in this state for public municipal purposes, or to or for use of educational, religious, cemetery, or other institutions, societies or associations of public charity in this state or any other state, territory or country laws of which, at time of death of decedent, either (1) do not impose transfer tax or death tax of any kind; or (2) grant exemption similar to that hereby provided to domiciliaries of such state, territory or country in favor of property passing to charities in this state. Decedents share of homestead which for at least one year preceding death was owned in whole or in part by decedent and occupied as place of residence by brother or sister or both of decedent is exempt if it passes to or for use of said brother or sister or both. (c. 86, §6).

Rate.—Flat rate of 18% on all property. (c. 86, §6).

Returns.—Every administrator must prepare a statement in duplicate, showing, as far as can be ascertained, the names of all the heirs-at-law, and every executor must prepare a like statement showing the names of all legatees named in the will or entitled to take thereunder, and stating whether or not the same were living at the time of the decedent's death, and shall file the same with the register of probate at the time of his appointment. (c. 86, §18). Such statements shall also show the relationship to the decedent of all heirs-at-law or legatees and age at time of death of decedent, of all persons to whom property is bequeathed or devised for a term of years, or subject to a contingency or the exercise of discretion. (c. 86, §19).

Every executor or administrator must, within six months from date of his appointment, file with appropriate register of probate and with Department of Revenue Administration, upon a form provided by that Division, a report of following so far as same shall come to his knowledge; all transfers made by decedent (1) in contemplation of death or to take effect in possession or enjoyment after death; (2) during last two years of decedent's life if property has a value of over $500, except bona fide sales for a reasonable consideration in money or money's worth; (3) a report of all property held in joint tenancy by decedent at time of his death and names and addresses of survivors if known. (c. 86, §22). Every deed, grant or completed gift, except in case of a bona fide transfer for reasonable consideration in money or money's worth, made within two years prior to death of grantor or donor, shall prima facie be deemed to have been made in contemplation of death of grantor or donor. (c. 86, §6a).

Determination of Tax.—Register of probate is then required to send to Department of Revenue Administration a copy of every such statement, except that as to taxable transfers, filed by executors and administrators, a copy of every will containing legacies which are subject to a tax, and a copy of inventory and appraisal of every estate any part of which is subject to a tax, also a copy of every account of an executor or administrator. (c. 86, §25). If an executor or administrator fails to file an inventory and appraisal in probate court or if Department of Revenue Administration is not satisfied with inventory and appraisal which is filed, Department of Revenue Administration may employ a suitable person to appraise property. (c. 86, §27). Executor or administrator computes tax due and prepares required returns for submission to Department of Revenue Administration. (c. 86, §39). Upon application of any party interested in succession, or of executor, administrator or trustee, made at any time within three months after notice of such determination, probate court shall appoint three disinterested appraisers or, with

See note at head of Digest as to 1998 legislation covered.

See Topical Index in front part of this volume.

NH – 33

INHERITANCE TAX . . . *continued*
consent of Department of Revenue Administration, one disinterested appraiser, who shall appraise such property at its actual market value as of date of death of decedent and make return thereof to said court. (c. 86, §41). Such return, when accepted by court, is final, provided, that any party aggrieved thereby may have appeal upon matters of law. (c. 86, §42).

Compromise.—Department of Revenue Administration is authorized to effect a present settlement of tax liability in any case where there is a devise, descent or bequest conditioned upon happening of a contingency or dependent upon exercise of a discretion or where right of Department of Revenue Administration to recover tax is in question or where he deems it advisable (c. 86, §69), also in all cases of a bequest or devise of property for life or for a term of years which gives tenant for life or term of years power of appointing by deed or will or both (c. 86, §70).

Valuation Date.—Date of death of decedent or alternate valuation as determined by §2032 of U.S. Internal Revenue Code (1986). (c. 86, §40).

Time of Payment.—Nine months after date of decedent's death. (c. 86, §54). If probate court has ordered executor or administrator to retain funds to satisfy claim of creditor, payment of tax may be suspended by court to await disposition of such claim. (c. 86, §55). If taxes are not paid when due, interest at rate of 1¼% per month is charged and collected from time same became payable. (c. 86, §56).

To What Officer Payment Made.—Department of Revenue Administration.

Who Liable for Payment.—Administrators, executors, trustees, grantees, and donees under a conveyance made during grantor's life and taxable hereunder are liable for such taxes, with interest, until same have been paid. (c. 86, §57). An executor, administrator, trustee, grantee or donee holding property subject to inheritance tax must deduct tax therefrom, or collect it from legatee or person entitled to said property, and must not deliver property or a specific legacy subject to said tax until he has collected tax thereon. (c. 86, §60). No account of an executor, administrator or trustee shall be allowed by probate court until certificate of Department of Revenue Administration has been filed in said court that all inheritance taxes have been paid or provision made for payment therefor by deposit or by lien on real estate. (c. 86, §31).

Property of Nonresident Decedents.—Personal property within this state of nonresident decedents is subject to a tax of 2% except stock or obligations of a corporation organized under New Hampshire laws and owned by a nonresident, if, at the time of the death of the owner, all the business conducted by the corporation under the authority of its charter is actually carried on outside the state, and except deposits of a nonresident decedent at the time of his death in any bank or trust company within the jurisdiction of this state. (c. 89, §§1, 4). Other intangible personal property in New Hampshire belonging to a nondomiciled decedent is exempt from this tax, if the state of the domicile of the deceased imposes no tax upon intangibles located therein belonging to a foreign decedent, or if the state of the domicile of the decedent allows reciprocal exemption to intangible personal property located therein belonging to nondomiciled decedents. (c. 89, §29).

In case of nonresident decedents, taxability and amount of tax may be determined by Department of Revenue Administration upon application of foreign executor or administrator or of grantee of decedent without ancillary administration. (c. 86, §51).

Reciprocal Protection of Other States.—Executor or administrator of estate of nonresident decedent, before expiration of 15 months after qualification in probate court in this state, must file with such court proof that all legacy and succession taxes, together with interest or penalties thereon which are due in state of domicile of decedent or to any political subdivision thereof, have been paid or secured, or that no such taxes, interest or penalties are due, as the case may be, unless it appears that letters have been issued in state of domicile. Such proof may be in form of certificate issued by official or body charged with administration of legacy and succession tax laws of domiciliary state. If such proof be not filed within time limited, register of probate court must forthwith mail to said official or body of domiciliary state notice that such executor or administrator has not filed the required proof. Said notice must also state, in so far as known to the register, the name, date of death and last domicile of decedent, and value of his property at time of his death, and there must be attached thereto a plain copy of decedent's will, if any, and a list of heirs or legatees. Within 60 days after mailing of such notice, official or body charged with administration of legacy and succession laws of domiciliary state, may file with the probate court in this state a petition for an accounting of such estate, and if this is done the probate court must order an account to be filed, and on such account being allowed, must decree remission to fiduciary appointed by domiciliary probate court of the balance of the intangible property, after payment of creditors and expenses of administration in this state. The foregoing requirements apply to the estate of any nonresident decedent, if laws of his domicile contain a provision whereby this state is given reasonable assurance of collection of its legacy and succession taxes, interest and penalties, from estates of decedents dying domiciled in this state, where such estates are being administered by the probate court of such other state, or if such other state does not grant letters on nonresident estates until after letters have been issued by the state of domicile. Unless such requirements have been complied with, the executor or administrator is not entitled to allowance of his account or decree of distribution in this state. (c. 86, §§84-89).

Disputes as to Domicile.—In case of dispute as to domicile of a decedent, Department of Revenue Administration, may enter into a written agreement with taxing authorities of other state or states claiming that decedent was domiciled therein and with executor or administrator, fixing amount which shall be paid to each state in full of inheritance, legacy and succession taxes thereof. This applies only if all states involved have substantially similar laws. (c. 86, §71; c. 90, §3). A special statute provides procedure for determination of disputed domicile where an agreement cannot be reached (c. 90), which applies only to cases in which each of states involved has in effect a law substantially similar to New Hampshire Act (c. 90, §6).

MEDICAID ENHANCEMENT TAX:

See c. 84-A. Rate set by Legislature each biennium.

NUCLEAR STATION PROPERTY TAX:

See c. 83-D.

PROPERTY TAXES:

General Property Tax.—All nonexempt real estate except growing wood and timber is liable to taxation. (c. 72, §6; c. 79, §2). Manufactured housing (horse trailers, travel trailers and mobile homes) is taxable as real estate. (c. 72, §7-a). Radio antennas, towers, and related structures used exclusively in operation of amateur communications station under F.C.C. amateur radio service rules and regulations are not taxable as real estate. (c. 72, §7-c). Following personal estate is taxable: Certain boats. (c. 72-A).

Taxes in Unincorporated Places.—Commissioners of every county must annually assess real estate in each unincorporated or unorganized place to owner or claimant thereof. (c. 81, §1).

Exemptions which are applicable to real estate include value of improvements made to residential real estate for purpose of assisting physically handicapped person who resides on property (c. 72:37-a), public cemeteries and all property held in trust for benefit of public burial places (c. 72, §22). Following real estate and personal property is exempt from taxation: Lands and buildings thereon and personal property owned by state, cities, towns, school districts and village districts unless used or occupied by other than state or city, town, school district or village district under lease or agreement; lands, buildings and personal properties owned and used by any county for governmental purposes, including hospitals, court houses, registry buildings, and county correctional facilities; however, county farms and their lands, buildings and taxable personal property shall be taxed; houses of public worship, parish houses, church parsonages occupied by their pastors, convents, monasteries, buildings and lands appertaining to them owned, used, and occupied directly for religious training or for other religious purposes by any regularly recognized and constituted denomination, creed or sect, organized or incorporated in this state and personal property used by them for which they are established; buildings and structures of schools, seminaries of learning, colleges, academies and universities organized or incorporated legally doing business in this state and owned, used and occupied directly by them for purposes for which they are established, provided none of income or profits are divided among members or stockholders or used or appropriated for any other purpose than purpose for which they are organized or established; provided further that if value of dormitories, dining rooms and kitchens shall exceed $150,000, value thereof in excess of said sum is taxable. Town at annual town meeting or governing body of city may vote to increase amount of exemption upon dormitories, dining rooms and kitchens. Also exempt are buildings, land and personal property owned by charitable organizations and societies organized, incorporated or legally doing business in this state owned, used, and occupied by them directly for purposes for which they are established. (c. 72, §23). Every charitable organization or society, except those religious and educational organizations and societies whose real estate is exempt shall annually before June 1 file with municipality in which property is located financial statement. (c. 72, §23). Real estate and personal property owned, occupied and used directly by New Hampshire Veterans Association, United Spanish War Veterans, Veterans of Foreign Wars, American Legion, Disabled American Veterans, Sons of Union Veterans of the Civil War, Veterans of World War I Incorporated and any other veterans organization incorporated by Act of Congress or of its departments or local chapters or posts is exempt from taxation. (c. 72, §23-a). Also exempt is real estate and personal property belonging to American National Red Cross (c. 72, §23-b); real estate and personal property owned by New Hampshire Congregational-Christian Conference, or a subsidiary corporation thereof, occupied and used by conference or subsidiary corporation to provide community housing for elderly persons, if none of income of profits of community housing is used for any purpose other than purpose for which housing is established. Elderly person is one who is 62 or more years of age. Age of head of family determines eligibility of family unit in community housing. On or before Dec. 1 of each year, owner of community housing pays to town or city in which property is situated, in lieu of taxes, sum representing 10% of shelter rent received by owner during preceding calendar year. Board of tax and land appeals may abate all or portion of payment in lieu of taxes for cause shown. Owner on or before June 1 of each year files with municipality in which property is located statement of financial condition for preceding year. (c. 72, §23-d). Real estate and personal property of charitable, nonprofit community housing and community health care facilities for elderly and disabled persons, if none of income or profits is used for any purpose other than community health care, is exempt from taxation. Elderly person is one who is 62 or more years of age. Age of head of family determines eligibility of family unit in project. (c. 72, §23-K).

Every resident of New Hampshire who has served not less than 90 days in Armed Forces of U.S. in any of following wars or armed conflicts: Spanish War, Philippine Insurrection, Boxer Rebellion, World War I, World War II (including Merchant Marine Veterans), Korean Conflict, Viet Nam Conflict, or any other war or armed conflict since May 8, 1975 (as defined in c. 72, §28) who has been honorably discharged, or officer honorably separated from service receives credit each year from taxation upon residential real estate in amount of $100 in taxes. Spouse of such resident or surviving spouse of such resident is also entitled to tax credit unless remarried. Status as surviving spouse is regained in event of divorce from, but not in event of death of, new spouse. Every resident or spouse of such resident whose services were terminated, for service-connected disability and surviving spouse of any resident who suffered service-connected death, in consideration of such service also receives credit of $700 or $1,400 (c. 72, §28, et seq.). If any person or persons entitled to credit shall own fractional interest in residential real estate, each such person shall be granted tax credit in proportion to his interest therein with other persons so entitled, but in no case shall total tax credit exceed tax credit allowed under RSA 72:28, II or V except as provided for by exemption for husband and wife below. (c. 72, §30). If any person entitled to service credit as specified above shall be totally and permanently disabled from service connection and satisfactory proof of such service connection is furnished to assessors, or if such person be double amputee or paraplegic as result of service connection, he or his wife or surviving spouse shall receive credit from taxation on real or personal property to amount of $700 or $1,400 of property taxes on residential property. (c. 72, §35).

See note at head of Digest as to 1998 legislation covered.

See Topical Index in front part of this volume.

PROPERTY TAXES... *continued*

Person who is discharged from military service of U.S. under conditions other than dishonorable or officer honorably separated from military service and who is totally and permanently disabled from service connection and satisfactory proof of such service connection is furnished to assessors and who is a double amputee or paraplegic as result of service connection and who owns a specially adapted homestead which has been acquired with assistance of Veterans Administration or which has been acquired using proceeds from sale of any previous homestead which was acquired with assistance of Veterans Administration, person or person's surviving spouse is exempt from all taxation on said homestead. (c. 72, §36-a). Husband and wife, each qualified for exemption, are entitled to exemption of $100 in taxes on their residential real estate. (c. 72, §31).

Every inhabitant who is legally blind is exempt each year on assessed value of his or her residential real estate to value of $15,000 and city or town may exempt any amount it may determine is appropriate to address significant increases in property values. (c. 72, §37).

Town, by vote of a majority of those present and voting at any regular town meeting, acting under an article duly incorporated in warrant for said meeting, and a city, by vote of governing body thereof, may exempt owner of privately owned air navigation facility available for public use without charge, who holds as of Apr. 1 of any year a certificate for such facility from department of transportation, division of aeronautics, that facility is necessary for maintenance of effective airway system, from taxation of such facility for each such year and owners of certain private airports may seek state reimbursement grant for certain property taxes paid. (c. 72, §38).

Residential real estate, as defined by RSA 72:29 II, to assessed value of $5,000 is exempt for property tax purposes if it is: (1) Owned by resident 68 years of age or over; or (2) owned by resident jointly or in common with his spouse, either of whom is 68 years of age or over; or (3) owned by resident 68 years of age or over jointly or in common with person not his spouse; (4) owned by resident whose spouse is 68 years of age or over and who has been living with his spouse as man and wife for at least five years in house for which exemption is requested; or (5) owned by resident whose spouse is 68 years of age or over and who has been living with his spouse as man and wife for at least ten years in this state. (c. 72, §39). City or town by majority vote may expand elderly exemptions as follows: (a) 65-74 years of age: $5,000; (b) 75-79 years of age: $10,000; (c) 80 and older: $20,000; provided property must be: (1) Owned by resident; or (2) owned by resident jointly or in common with his spouse, either of whom meets age requirement for exemption claimed; or (3) owned by resident jointly or in common with person not his spouse, if resident meets applicable age requirement for exemption claimed; or (4) owned by resident, or his spouse, either of whom meets age requirement for exemption claimed, and has been living with his spouse as man and wife at least five years. (c. 72, §43a-b).

No exemption shall be allowed under RSA 72:39 unless person applying therefor: (1) Has resided in this state for at least five years preceding Apr. 1 in year in which exemption is claimed; (2) had in calendar year preceding said Apr. 1 a net income from all sources of less than $5,000, or if married, a combined net income of less than $6,000, such net income to be determined by deducting from all monies received from any source whatsoever amount of any of following or sum thereof: (a) Life insurance paid on death of any insured, (b) expenses and costs incurred in course of conducting a business enterprise, (c) proceeds from sale of assets, (d) social security payments; (3) owns assets of any kind, tangible or intangible, less bona fide encumbrances, not in excess of $35,000. (c. 72, §40). Same requirements apply if city or town adopts expanded exemption and in addition, income, as defined above, cannot exceed $7,000 or if married total of $9,000 and person owns assets of any kind, tangible or intangible, less bona fide encumbrances, not in excess of $50,000. (c. 72, §43-c).

If any entitled person or persons shall own a fractional interest in residential real estate, each such entitled person shall be granted exemption in proportion to his interest therein with other persons so entitled, but in no case shall total exemption to all persons so entitled exceed amount provided in c. 72, §39-b. (c. 72, §41).

In addition to other conditions hereunder no exemption shall be allowed under RSA c. 72, §39-b where resident applying therefor has received transfer of real estate from person under age of 65 related to him by blood or marriage, within preceding five years. (c. 72, §40-a). Applications for exemption or tax credits claimed under c. 72 shall be filed by Mar. 1 following date of notice of tax under RSA 72:1-d. (c. 72, §33).

City or town by majority vote can provide for exemption for solar energy systems, for purpose of heating, cooling or providing electricity, wind-powered energy systems or centralized wood heating systems (c. 72, §§61-72), for totally and permanently disabled persons as defined under federal Social Security Act (c. 72, §37-b), or for elderly (c. 72, §§43-e and 43-f).

No exemptions for members of Armed Forces except as above stated.

Certain ski area equipment is exempt from taxation as real property. (c. 72, §12-c).

Time of Assessment.—Every person is taxed in the town where he resides on Apr. 1, for his resident tax and estate. (c. 73, §1).

Mode of Assessment.—Selectmen of each town, annually in Apr., make a list of all polls and take an inventory of all taxable estate in such town on Apr. 1. (c. 74, §1). Every person or corporation must fill out an inventory of all of his or its taxable property, make oath to same, and mail it to selectmen or assessors on or before Apr. 15 (c. 74, §§4-7) or before June 1 if delay is due to accident, mistake or misfortune (c. 74, §8). Failure to file inventory results in additional tax of 1% of property tax, but not less than $10 nor more than $50. (c. 74, §7-a). On return of inventory, selectmen appraise property at its full and true value in money (c. 75, §1) and assess tax according to such appraisal (c. 74, §11; c. 76). Any person who refuses to consent to selectmen or appraising officials to enter property for purpose of completing inventory or appraising property shall lose right to appeal any matter pertaining to property tax or any exemptions to which person may be entitled. (c. 74, §17). Owner of residence located in industrial or commercial zone may apply for special assessment based upon value at its current use as residence. (c. 75, §11). Open space land, at request of owner, may be taxed according to its current use, provided that if use changes there shall be land use charge tax of 10% of full and true value of land. (c. 78-A). Distinct interests in same real estate may, on request, be appraised and assessed to owners thereof separately (c. 75, §2), except that when one person erects building on land of another, land and building may be taxed together as real estate to owner of land if one of selectmen gives proper statutory notice to said owner (c. 75, §3). List of all property taxes assessed is made by selectmen under their own hands, with warrant under their hands and seal, directed to collector of such town, requiring him to collect same. (c. 76, §10). List of taxes assessed on real estate must contain: Value of property (c. 75, §4); name of owner, if known; number of lot and range, if lotted, otherwise such description as land may be readily known by; number of acres, if known; amount of taxes assessed thereon. (c. 76, §7).

Jeopardy Assessment.—Whenever it appears to the selectmen or assessors that the assessment of taxes against any property be made as soon as possible in order to insure payment of the taxes and to protect the public interest, they may, on or after Apr. 1, make a reasonable jeopardy assessment of the taxes against the owner or person to whom such property is assessed and commit a warrant to the collector for the same, and the collector, after making written demand for such taxes, may immediately use any of the remedies provided by law to collect the taxes assessed to him in such warrant. Provision is made for refunding an overpayment and collecting any under-assessment. (c. 76, §10-a).

Personal Property on Land of Another.—Whenever any person leaves upon the real estate of another person, with such person's consent, any taxable personal property, the tax upon the same may be assessed to the owner of the land if not paid when due by owner of personal property, provided selectman or assessor, before or at time of taking inventory, gives notice in writing to such landowner that such personal property is to be taxed to him. These provisions do not apply to manufactured housing. Owner of land has lien upon such personal property for payment of tax. (c. 73, §16-a).

Payment and Collection.—See topic Administration, subhead Penalties, catchline General Property Taxes, infra. In addition, real estate is liable for all taxes against owner thereof. (c. 80, §19). Homeowner who is 65 years of age or older or who is eligible for benefits for totally or permanently disabled under federal social security act and who has owned his homestead for at least five years may give tax lien in lieu of real estate taxes to city or town for up to 85% of equity value of his real estate; upon death of owner, lien plus interest at 5% shall become due. (c. 72, §38-a).

Environmental Investigation.—Prior to or in connection with tax lien procedure or tax sale, town, county, or state may enter upon property to conduct environmental site assessment or audit, provided 30 days notice is given to owner or consent is obtained. (80, §19-a).

Redemption.—See topic Administration, subhead Redemption.

Exemption from Attachment.—See topic Administration, subhead Exemption from Attachment.

Tax Liens.—See topic Administration, subhead Tax Liens.

REAL ESTATE CONVEYANCE TAX:

See category Property, topic Deeds, subhead Taxes.

RESIDENT TAX:

Resident tax of $10 on every resident over 18 and under 65 except paupers, insane persons, and surviving spouses of certain veterans. (c. 72, §1).

Time of Assessment.—Every person is taxed in town where he resides on Apr. 1, for his resident tax and estate. (c. 73, §1).

REVISED UNIFORM FEDERAL TAX LIEN REGISTRATION ACT:

Revised Uniform Federal Tax Lien Registration Act adopted. (c. 454B).

SALES AND USE TAXES:

Sales Tax.—Tax at rate of 8% on meals and rooms. (c. 78-A).

Use Tax.—None.

STAMP TAX:

None, except on tobacco.

TAX ON INTANGIBLES:

Tax is imposed on income received from intangibles, including dividends (except stock dividends and dividends declared to be return of capital and other exclusions under c. 77, §§4-a, 4-b, 4-c, 4-d), and interest from bonds, notes, money at interest and debts due taxpayer (except interest on deposits in savings banks and similar institutions and on notes or bonds of any political subdivision of this state, interest on notes or bonds of this state, and interest on College Tuition Savings Plans qualifying under c. 195-G). Income up to $1,200 is exempt. Rate: 5%. Not applicable to corporations. (c. 77, §§1-4).

The estates of deceased persons who last dwelt in this state are subject to this tax upon all taxable income received by such persons during their lifetime which has not already been taxed. The income received by such estates during administration is taxable to the estate, except such proportion thereof as equals the proportion of the estate to be distributed to nontaxable persons or organizations. (c. 77, §9).

Annual returns must be made to Commissioner of Revenue Administration on forms prescribed by it. Declaration of estimated taxes must be given if taxes exceed $200. (c. 77, §§18, 18a). Tax is payable to Commissioner of Revenue Administration. (c. 77, §23).

TIMBER TAX:

Yield tax on timber at rate of 10% of stumpage value at time of cutting is assessed against owner of growing wood and timber within 30 days of filing by owner of report of cutting with assessing officials. Tax is payable within 30 days of time bill is mailed. (c. 79, §3). Owner intending to cut any wood or timber shall give written notice of his intention prior to such cutting to assessing officials. (c. 79, §10). Assessing officials or

See note at head of Digest as to 1998 legislation covered.

See Topical Index in front part of this volume.

NH – 35

TIMBER TAX . . . *continued*
Commissioner of Revenue Administration may require an owner to insure payment of tax. (c. 79, §§3, 10-a).

TOBACCO TAX:
See c. 78.

UNEMPLOYMENT COMPENSATION TAX:
Unemployment compensation tax, in the guise of "contributions," is imposed by c. 282-A.

Contributions are exacted from: (1) Every employing unit which, in each of 20 weeks (whether or not consecutive) during the current or preceding calendar year, has or had in employment one or more individuals, irrespective of whether same individuals are or were employed in each day; (2) every other employing unit subject to tax levied by Federal Unemployment Tax Act as amended. (c. 282-A:8).

Rate is not less than 2.7% except for certain merit rates. (c. 282-A, §69). Tax is imposed on wages paid for employment during calendar year, not to exceed $7,000 paid to individual in calendar year. (c. 282-A, §69, I).

Contributions are payable to a special fund in the state treasury known as the unemployment compensation and employment service administration fund, in accordance with such regulations as may be prescribed by Commissioner of department of employment security. (c. 282-A, §138).

UTILITIES TAXES:
Electricity Consumption Tax.—Every consumer is liable for a per kilowatt hour tax on consumption of electricity. Providers shall collect such taxes unless consumer seeks state permission to pay tax directly to state.

Gas and Electric Utilities Tax.—(c. 83-C, §§2, 4). Repealed, 1997.

Communications Services Tax.—See c. 82-A.

TRANSPORTATION
MOTOR VEHICLES:
Department of Safety, Director of Motor Vehicles, Hazen Drive, Concord, N. H. 03301 has general supervision. (c. 260).

Vehicle License.—Generally required. (c. 261, §40). Reregistration required annually (c. 261, §62) or upon transfer of ownership (c. 261, §66).

Driver's License.—Generally required. (c. 263, §1). Expires in four years. (c. 263, §10). Age required for driver's license 18 unless applicant 16 or older has successfully completed driver education course. (c. 263, §19). School bus driver must be 18 or older. (c. 263, §24). Applicant for commercial license must be 18 or older. (c. 263, §27).

Titles.—Certificate of title required. Issued by Division of Motor Vehicles when change in registration required by sale. (c. 261, §1).

Sales.—Transfer of title accomplished by execution and warranty of title to transferee on certificate. Certificate must then be mailed or delivered to transferee or Division of Motor Vehicles. (c. 261, §14). Transferee must make application for new certificate. (c. 261, §1). Regulations generally covering consumer motor vehicle warranties are set forth in c. 357-D, §1. Defects on any new motor vehicle must be disclosed by manufacturer to dealer and by dealer to purchaser prior to delivery. (c. 357-C, §5, III [d]).

Liens.—Security interest perfected at time of creation if certificate of title so indicating is delivered to Division of Motor Vehicles within 20 days thereafter. (c. 261, §24). Garageman's lien available to one who repairs or stores motor vehicle. (c. 450).

Identification Marks.—Willful alteration is misdemeanor. (c. 262, §9).

Operation Prohibited.—Persons without valid driver's license may not operate motor vehicle. (c. 263, §1). No physical defect of applicant for driver's license shall debar him from receiving license unless it can be shown by common experience that such defect incapacitates him from safely driving motor vehicle. (c. 263, §6).

Size and Weight Limits.—Regulated by c. 266, §§9-26.

Emissions Certificate Required.—(c. 261, §72-a). Repealed.

Equipment Required.—Regulated by c. 266, §§27-84.

Lights Required.—Regulated by c. 266, §§31-46.

Seatbelts and Child Restraints.—No person shall carry person under 18 years of age in motor vehicle without seatbelts or child restraints. If child is less than four years of age, child restraint must comply with 49 CFR 571.213. Nonuse shall not be evidence of contributory negligence. (c. 265, §107-a I and II).

Inspection.—Required once a year for all motor vehicles manufactured during six most recent calendar years, and twice a year for all other vehicles, excepting OHRV, snow traveling vehicles and mopeds. Motorcycles and antique cars must be inspected once a year. (c. 266, §1).

Traffic Regulations.—Regulated by c. 265.

Accidents.—Driver of vehicle involved in accident involving death, bodily injury or property damage must stop and give driver of any other vehicle involved, person injured or owner of property damaged, his name, address, number of driver's license, registration number of vehicle and name and address of each occupant of his vehicle. If injury, death or property damage in excess of $1,000 results, driver must report facts to Division of Motor Vehicles within five days thereafter. (c. 264, §25).

Liability of Owner.—Common law rules of agency not extended by statute. Family car doctrine not recognized.

Guests.—No guest statute.

Proof of Financial Responsibility.—Required upon conviction of driving under influence of intoxicating liquor or drugs, failing to stop and report accident, homicide or assault arising from operation of motor vehicle, second speeding offense and second offense reckless operation. (c. 264, §2). Required within 60 days after receipt of report of accident if driver deemed responsible by Division of Motor Vehicles does not have liability insurance policy with limits of $25,000 or more for bodily injury to one person, $50,000 or more for bodily injury to two or more persons or $25,000 for property damage. If no insurance amount of proof up to such amounts is required. (c. 264, §§8, 20). Uninsured driver must maintain proof of financial responsibility in future. Proof of financial responsibility must be furnished to Division of Motor Vehicles by filing certificate of insurance company or surety company, depositing money or securities or, in case of corporation, by satisfying Director of Motor Vehicles of financial ability. (c. 264, §21).

Insurance.—No requirement for compulsory insurance. But see subhead Proof of Financial Responsibility, supra.

No-Fault Insurance.—Not adopted.

Foreign Vehicles.—May be operated by nonresident to extent that state of registration would allow N. H. resident. (c. 261, §44). If state of registration would impose restrictions, taxes, penalties, etc. on N. H. resident, in excess of those imposed by N. H., such shall be imposed on nonresident. (c. 261, §43). Bus registration tax proration and reciprocity agreement is in effect. (c. 261, §§49-51). Nonresident who has his regular place of abode or business in this state for more than six months in any year is deemed resident. (c. 259, §67). Nonresident who becomes resident has 60 days thereafter in which to register motor vehicle (c. 261, §45) and to obtain driver's license (c. 263, §35).

Nonresident Operators.—See subhead Foreign Vehicles, supra.

Action Against Nonresident.—Service of process made on Director of Motor Vehicles (c. 264, §13) or Secretary of State (c. 510, §4).

Direct Actions.—Not allowed against liability insurer by injured person.

Motor Vehicle Carriers.—Common and contract carriers of passengers are governed by the New Hampshire Motor Carrier Act. (c. 376).

All common and contract carriers of passengers, except those expressly exempted (see infra), are subject to jurisdiction of Public Service Commission and must hold certificates issued by the Commission. (c. 376, §§4, 7). The Commission has jurisdiction over rates or fares charged by common carriers (c. 376, §14), minimum charges and contracts of contract carriers (c. 376, §18) and practices which may result in discriminatory or preferential charges or unfair competition.

The Commission has authority to establish requirements and regulations with respect to reasonable and adequate service, transportation of baggage and express, uniform system of accounts, records and reports, preservation of records and safety of operation and equipment. (c. 376, §21).

All carriers holding certificates must annually register each vehicle operated under the provisions of the certificates. (c. 376, §§24, 25). Carriers must file with the Commission annual reports furnishing such information as Commission deems necessary. (c. 376, §20).

Carrier must keep in force an insurance policy or indemnity bond in such amount as Commission requires, providing for payment of any judgments recovered against the carrier for death of or bodily injury to passengers. (c. 376, §13).

The following are exempt from the provisions of the Motor Carrier Act: (1) Motor vehicles while employed solely in transporting school children and teachers to and from school; (2) taxicabs having a manufacturer's rated capacity of not more than seven passengers, unless, after investigation, the commission shall be of the opinion that the service provided is in competition with the schedules of a common carrier by highway or railroad; (3) motor vehicles owned and operated by hotels and used exclusively for transportation of hotel patrons between hotels and local railroad or carrier stations; (4) motor vehicles engaged exclusively in work for any branch of United States government, for any department of the state or for any county, city, town or village; (5) motor vehicles engaged exclusively in delivery of U. S. mail or (6) vans engaged in carpooling not less than eight people and no more than 15 people to/from work on nonprofit basis. (c. 376, §3).

Intrastate common carriers of property for hire on public highways must obtain certificate of public convenience from Public Utilities Commission; must file schedule of rates and charges with Commission, obtain special number plates and are subject to regulation by Commission generally. (c. 375-B).

Contract carrier operating in competition with common carrier must file with Commission rates, rules or regulations applying to such service, unless property is to be transported for common carrier whose rates are filed. (c. 375-B, §4).

With certain exceptions, carriage of passengers for a consideration in motor vehicle designed or constructed exclusively for transportation of goods, materials or commodities is prohibited. (c. 265, §§106, 107).

School buses are regulated by c. 262-A, §53; c. 263, §§27-29.

Taxicabs.—Towns may provide for registration of taxicabs and require insurance or bond for protection of passengers therein. (c. 31, §40).

Motor Vehicle Taxes.—Tax imposed on use of fuel other than gasoline. (c. 260, §52).

Gasoline Tax.—See category Taxation, topic Gasoline and Petroleum Products Taxes.

RAILROADS:
See category Business Regulation and Commerce, topic Carriers.

See note at head of Digest as to 1998 legislation covered.

See Topical Index in front part of this volume.

COMMERCIAL CODE FORMS

See also categories Mortgages, topic Chattel Mortgages and Business Regulation and Commerce, topic Commercial Code. Following forms of a Financing Statement and Statements of Continuation, Partial Release, Assignment, etc. have been approved by the Secretary of State:

Uniform Commercial Code—Financing Statement—Form UCC-1

This FINANCING STATEMENT is presented to a filing officer for filing pursuant to the Uniform Commercial Code:

3 Maturity date (if any):

1 Debtor(s) (Last Name First) and address(es)	2 Secured Party(ies) and address(es)	For Filing Officer (Date, Time, Number, and Filing Office)

4 This financing statement covers the following types (or items) of property:

ASSIGNEE OF SECURED PARTY

Check ☒ if covered: ☐ Proceeds of collateral are also covered ☐ Products of Collateral are also covered
No. of additional Sheets presented:

Filed with . . . .

. . . .

By: . . . .   By: . . . .
          Signature(s) of Debtor(s)   Signature(s) of Secured Party(ies)

Uniform Commercial Code

Statements of Continuation, Partial Release, Assignment, Etc.—Form UCC-3

This STATEMENT is presented to a filing officer for filing pursuant to the Uniform Commercial Code:

3 Maturity date (if any):

1 Debtor(s) (Last Name First) and address(es)	2 Secured Party(ies) and address(es)	For Filing Officer (Date, Time, Number, and Filing Office)

This statement refers to original Financing Statement No. . . . . Dated . . . . , 19. . . .

A. Continuation . . . .☐ The original financing statement between the foregoing Debtor and Secured Party, bearing the file number shown above, is still effective.	B. Partial Release . . . . .☐ From the collateral described in the financing statement bearing the file number shown above, the Secured Party releases the following:	C. Assignment . . . . . .☐ The Secured Party certifies that the Secured Party has assigned to the Assignee whose name and address is shown below, Secured Party's rights under the financing statement bearing the file number shown above in the following property:	D. Other: . . . .☐

. . . .

Dated: . . . . , 19. . .   By: . . . .
                                           Signature(s) of Secured Party(ies)

See note at head of Digest as to 1998 legislation covered.

See Topical Index in front part of this volume.